WEBSTER'S NEW WORLD™

DICTIONARY
— AND —
THESAURUS

Compiled by the Staff of
Webster's New World Dictionary

Michael Agnes
Editor in Chief

With Principal Thesaurus Text by
Charlton Laird

MACMILLAN • USA

Macmillan General Reference
A Simon & Schuster Macmillan Company
1633 Broadway
New York, NY 10019-6785

A Webster's New World™ Book

MACMILLAN is a registered trademark of Macmillan, Inc.
WEBSTER'S NEW WORLD DICTIONARY is a
registered trademark of Simon & Schuster, Inc.

Dictionary Editorial Offices:
New World Dictionaries
850 Euclid Avenue
Cleveland, Ohio 44114

Library of Congress Cataloging-in-Publication Data
Webster's New World dictionary and thesaurus / compiled by the staff
    of Webster's New World Dictionary ; Michael Agnes, editor in chief ;
    with principal thesaurus text by Charlton Laird.
        p.   cm.
    "A Webster's New World book"—T.p. verso.
    ISBN 0-02-861318-X (paperback)
    1. English language—Dictionaries. 2. English language—Synonyms
and antonyms. I. Agnes, Michael. II. Laird, Charlton Grant, 1901-1984

PE1628.W56314 1996
423—dc20   95-17738
                                                     CIP

Database service and principal typesetting
by Lexi-Comp, Inc., Hudson, Ohio.
Manufactured in the United States of America
        5 6 7 8 9 10   98 99

CONTENTS

STAFF

FOREWORD

The publication of *Webster's New World Dictionary and Thesaurus* marks the first time a combination one-volume dictionary and thesaurus has been made available to American readers in this extraordinarily useful format. With its matching entries displayed on every page for ease of use and the maximum display of different types of information, this new work shows clearly Webster's New World's commitment to publishing innovative dictionaries and language books of all types.

The work at hand is derived from *Webster's New World Compact School and Office Dictionary* and from an abridged version of *Webster's New World Thesaurus,* originally compiled by Charlton Laird. Over the years, these two works have each proved extremely effective in their coverage of the language encountered and used by most readers in everyday reading and writing. Although they were not originally conceived of as complementary works, they have nevertheless proved to be ideal reference companions. It should be noted, however, that the present work's specific form is not new; readers in Great Britain and elsewhere outside of the U.S. have had similar works available for some time.

The initial stage of compilation of the present work consisted of a computerized match of headwords in each of the source books' databases. Because of the complexities of English (for example, the phenomenon of words with different meanings having the same spelling), such a match is inevitably unreliable for producing a work of this type. Therefore, staff editors conducted an entry-by-entry check of the matches, correcting errors and tailoring entry-block matches to ensure that the two references dovetail properly.

Each of the original works had a core style and structure designed to meet its own special requirements. These elements had over the years met the test of time, and it was decided to leave the separate formats unchanged. The reader is therefore advised to read the individual sections in the "Guide to the Use of This Book."

The final, reworked format is a remarkably handy solution to a long-felt reference need. The advantage of combining, on the same page, the functions of a dictionary and a thesaurus are, we believe, many and manifest. The special advantage for thesaurus users is the ease with which they can check the meaning of new words suggested by thesaurus synonym entries. The new format solves one of the principal problems associated with thesaurus use—the difficulty in choosing among synonyms when all of their meanings are not well grasped: the meanings needed are immediately available in the dictionary section. We are confident that many readers will find this dictionary and thesaurus the ideal reference work for all language requirements, from business correspondence to everyday reading.

Michael Agnes
Editor in Chief

GUIDE TO THE USE OF
THIS BOOK

THE DICTIONARY

I. The Main Entry Word

A. *Arrangement of Entries*—All main entries, including single words, hyphenated and unhyphenated compounds, proper names, prefixes, suffixes, and abbreviations, are listed in strict alphabetical order and are set in large, boldface type.

a[1] or **A** (ā) *n.* ...
a[2] (ə; *stressed*, ā) *adj.* ...
a-[2] *prefix* ...
a or **a.** 1 about 2 acre(s) ...
aard·vark (ärd′värk′) *n.* ...
Aaron (er′ən) *Bible* ...
ab- ⟦L⟧ *prefix* ...
AB 1 Bachelor of Arts: also **A.B.** ...
aback (ə bak′) *adv.* [Archaic] backward ... —**taken aback** startled ...

Idiomatic phrases listed after a main entry have also been entered alphabetically within each group.

fly[1] (flī) *vi.* ... —**fly into** ... —**let fly (at)** ... —**on the fly** ...

B. *Variant Spellings & Forms*—When variant spellings of a word are some distance apart alphabetically, the definition appears with the spelling most frequently used, and the other spellings are cross-referred to this entry. If two commonly used variant spellings are alphabetically close to each other, they are entered as a joint boldface entry, but the order of entry does not necessarily indicate that the form entered first is "more correct," or is to be given preference.

thea·ter or **thea·tre** (thē′ə tər) *n.* ...

If a less common variant spelling is alphabetically close to the prevailing spelling, it is given at the end of the entry block in small boldface.

par·af·fin ... *n.* ... Also **par′af·fine** ...

C. *Cross-references*—When an entry is cross-referred to another term that has the same meaning but is more frequently used, the entry cross-referred to is in small capitals. All cross-references in the Dictionary portion of the book are to other Dictionary entries. No cross-references are made between the Dictionary and the Thesaurus.

an·aes·thesia ... *n.* ANESTHESIA ...

D. *Homographs*—Main entries that are spelled alike but are different in meaning and origin, as **bat** (a club), **bat** (the animal), and **bat** (to wink), are marked by superscript numbers following the boldface spellings.

bat[1] ... *n.* ...
bat[2] ... *n.* ...
bat[3] ... *vt.* ...

E. *Foreign Terms*—Foreign words and phrases encountered with some frequency in English but not completely naturalized are set in boldface italic type. The user of the Dictionary is thus signaled that such terms are usually printed in italics or underlined in writing.

bon·jour (bōn zhōōr′) *interj., n.* ⟦Fr⟧ ...

F. *Prefixes, Suffixes, & Combining Forms*—Prefixes and initial combining forms are indicated by a hyphen following the entry form.

hemi- ... *prefix* half ...

Suffixes and terminal combining forms are indicated by a hyphen preceding the entry form.

-able ... *suffix* 1 that can ...

The abundance of these forms, whose syllabification and pronunciation can be determined from the words containing them, makes it possible for the reader to understand and pronounce countless complex terms not entered in the Dictionary but formed with affixes and words that are entered.

G. *Word Division*—Word divisions (or syllabifications) are shown where end-of-line word breaks have been traditionally allowed. Users will note that many computer-generated typesetting systems do not adhere to the traditional rules and, in fact, sometimes break words within a syllable rather than between two syllables.

Word divisions are indicated by separating syllables with either a centered dot [·] or with a primary or secondary stress mark.

fun·da·men·tal (fun′də ment′'l) *adj.* ...
coun′ter·rev′o·lu′tion *n.* ...

II. Pronunciation

A. *Introduction*—The pronunciations given in this Dictionary are those used by good speakers of American English across a broad portion of the United States. Very often, more than one pronunciation is prevalent, and such variants have also been given. (A number of British English pronunciations have also been included when thought to be appropriate.) There are, however, regional variations in pronunciation which give speakers in different parts of the country their distinctive "dialects." It is impossible within the compass of this book to indicate all such variation on a word-by-word basis. The explanatory notes following the pronunciation key, below, point out some of the main regional variations.

B. *Key to Pronunciation*

Symbol	Key Words	Symbol	Key Words
ə	a in ago	n	no, pan
	e in agent	ŋ	ring, drink
	i in sanity		
	o in comply	ō	own, go
	u in focus	ô	horn, all
a	at, gas	oo	look, pull
ā	ate, day	ōo	tool, crew
ä	car, father		
		oi	oil, toy
b	bed, tab	ou	out, how
ch	chin, march	p	put, tap
d	dip, wad	r	red, far
		s	sell, toss
e	end, ten	sh	she, wash
ē	eve, be		
f	fit, if	t	top, sat
		th	thin, truth
		th	the, father
g	get, tag		
		u	up, bud
h	he, ahead	ᵤr	urn, fur
i	is, lid		
ī	ice, high	v	vat, have
j	joy, agile	w	will, away
k	kid, take	y	yet, yard
l	lid, sail	z	zebra, haze
		zh	azure, leisure
m	met, aim		

A few explanatory notes on some of the more complex of these symbols follow.

' The apostrophe before an *l, m,* or *n* indicates that the following consonant forms the nucleus of a syllable with no appreciable vowel sound, as in *cattle* (kat′l) or *satin* (sat′n). Some speakers will articulate a vowel sound in such syllables, saying for example (sa′tin).

ə This symbol, called the schwa, represents the indistinct, neutral vowel sound heard in the unstressed syllables of *ago, over,* etc.

ä This symbol represents essentially the sound of *a* in *car* but may also represent the vowel sound sometimes heard in New England for *bath* (bäth). In words like *alms* and *hot,* the usual sound of the letters *a* and *o* is the same as the sound of *a* in *ah.* Many speakers, however, use a sound that approaches or is the same as the sound of the *o* in *horn.*

e This symbol represents the sound of *e* in *ten* and is also used, followed and hence colored by *r,* to represent the vowel sound of *care* (ker).

ē This symbol represents the vowel sound in *meet* and is also used for the vowel in the unstressed final syllable of such words as *happy* (hap′ē), *pretty* (prit′ē), etc.

i This symbol represents the vowel sound in *hit* and is also used for the vowel in the unstressed syllables of such words as *garbage* (gär′bij), *rely* (ri lī′), etc. In such contexts reductions to ə (gär′bəj), (rə lī′), etc. are commonly heard and may be assumed as variants. This symbol is also used, followed and hence colored by *r,* to represent the vowel sound of *dear* (dir).

ô This symbol represents essentially the sound of *a* in *all.* When followed by *r,* as in *more* (môr), vowels ranging to ō (mōr or mō′ər) are often heard and may be assumed as variants.

r This symbol represents the sound of the letter *r* in *red, part,* and *far.* In words like *part* and *far,* however, the spelled *r* is usually not pronounced by speakers in the South and along the eastern seaboard.

ŋ This symbol represents the nasal sound of the *-ng* of *sing* and of the *n* before *k* and *g,* as in *drink* (driŋk) and *finger* (fiŋ′gər).

C. *Foreign Sounds* —In recording the approximate pronunciation of foreign words, it has been necessary to use the following five symbols in addition to those preceding.

ë This symbol represents the sound made by rounding the lips as for (ô) and pronouncing (e).

ö This symbol represents the sound made by rounding the lips as for (ō) and pronouncing (ā).

ü This symbol represents the sound made by rounding the lips as for (ōo) and pronouncing (ē).

kh This symbol represents the sound made by placing the tongue as for (k) but allowing the breath to escape in a continuous stream, as in pronouncing (h).

n This symbol indicates that the vowel immediately preceding it is given a nasal sound, as in Fr. *bonjour* (bōn zhōōr′).

D. *Styling of Pronunciation* —Pronunciations are given inside parentheses, immediately following the boldface entry, using the symbols described above. In addition, stress marks are used to indicate the level of stress, or relative force given to a particular part of a word. A heavy stroke (′) indicates strong, or primary, stress and a lighter stroke (′) indicates weaker, or secondary, stress. The use of qualifying words and the practice of truncating pronunciations are explained in the following sections.

happi coat (hap′ē) . . .
happy (hap′ē) . . .
hap′py-go-luck′y . . .

E. *Variants* —Two or more pronunciations may be given for the same word. If no qualifying note (such as *also, chiefly Brit.,* etc.) is given, then each pronunciation shown is considered equally acceptable, regardless of the order in which it appears.

F. *Truncation* —Variant pronunciations for a headword or a run-in entry are truncated, or shortened, whenever possible. A hyphen after the shortened variant marks it as an initial syllable or syllables; one before the variant, as terminal; and hyphens before and after the variant, as internal.

ab·jure (ab joor′, əb-) ...
domi·cile (däm′ə sīl′, -sil; *also* dō′mə-) ...
fu·tu·rity (fyōō toor′ə tē, -tyoor′-) ...

Variant pronunciations involving different parts of speech in the same entry block usually appear as follows:

abuse (ə byōōz′; *for n.,* ə byōōs′) *vt.* ...

III. Part-of-Speech Labels

Part-of-speech labels are given for run-in derived forms and for headwords (excluding most proper nouns) that are solid or hyphenated forms, but not for prefixes, suffixes, and abbreviations. When an entry word has more than one part of speech in an entry block, long dashes introduce each different part-of-speech label, which appears in boldface italic type.

round ... *adj.* ... *—n.* ... *—vt.* ... *—vi.* ... *—adv.* ... *—prep.* ...

Two or more part-of-speech labels are given jointly for an entry when the definition or definitions, or the cross-reference, will suffice for both or all.

des·patch ... *vt., n.* DISPATCH

IV. Inflected Forms

Inflected forms regarded as irregular or offering difficulty in spelling are entered in small boldface immediately following the part-of-speech labels. They are truncated where possible, and syllabified and pronounced where necessary.

happy ... *adj.* -pier, -pi·est ...
city ... *n., pl.* -ies ...
amoe·ba ... *n., pl.* -bas or -bae (-bē) ...

Forms regarded as regular inflections, and hence not normally indicated, include:

a) plurals formed by adding -*s* to the singular (or -*es* after *s, x, z, ch,* and *sh*), as *bats, boxes*
b) present tenses formed by adding -*s* to the infinitive (or -*es* after *s, x, z, ch,* and *sh*), as *waits, searches*
c) past tenses and past participles formed by simply adding -*ed* to the infinitive, as *waited, searched*
d) present participles formed by simply adding -*ing* to the infinitive, as *waiting, searching*
e) comparatives and superlatives formed by simply adding -*er* and -*est* to the base of an adjective or adverb, as *taller, tallest* or *sooner, soonest*

Where two inflected forms are given for a verb, the first is the form for the past tense and the past participle, and the second is the form for the present participle.

make ... *vt.* made, mak′ing ...

Where three forms are given, the first represents the past tense, the second the past participle, and the third the present participle.

give ... *vt.* gave, giv′en, giv′ing ...

Where there are alternative forms for any of the principal parts, these are given and properly indicated.

bid ... *vt.* bade or bid, bid′den or bid, bid′ding ...

V. Etymology

The etymology, or word derivation, appears inside open double brackets immediately before the definitions proper. The symbols, as < for "derived from," and the abbreviations of language labels, etc. used in the etymologies are dealt with in the section "Abbreviations and Symbols Used in This Book," pp. xiv-xv.

di·shevel ... ⟦ < OFr *des-*, DIS- + *chevel*, hair ⟧ ...

No etymology is shown where one would be superfluous, as where the elements making up the word are immediately apparent.

VI. The Definitions

A. *Order of Senses*—The standard, general senses of a word are given first, and colloquial, slang, etc. senses come next. Technical senses requiring special field labels, as *Astron., Chem.,* etc., follow in order.

B. *Numbering & Grouping of Senses*—Senses are numbered consecutively within any given part of speech in boldface numerals. Where a primary sense of a word can easily be subdivided into several closely related meanings, such meanings are indicated by italicized letters.

time ... *n.* ... **1** every ... **2** a system ... **3** the period ... **11** *Music a)* rhythm ... *b)* tempo—*vt.* ... **1** to arrange ... **2** to adjust ... *—adj.* **1** having to ... **2** set to ... **3** having ... *—in time* **1** eventually **2** before ... **3** keeping ...

C. *Capitalization*—If a headword is capitalized in all its senses, the entry word itself is printed with a capital letter. If a capitalized headword has a sense or senses that are uncapitalized, these are marked with the corresponding small-boldface, lowercase letter followed by a short dash and enclosed in brackets.

Pu·ri·tan ... *n.* ... **1** ... **2** [p-] ...

Conversely, capitalized letters are shown, where pertinent, with lowercase headwords. In some instances these designations are qualified by the self-explanatory "*often,*" "*occas.,*" etc.

left[1] ... *—n.* **1** ... **2** [*often* L-] ...

D. *Plural Forms*—In a singular noun entry, the designation "[*pl.*]" (or "[*often pl.*]," "[*usually pl.*]," etc.) before a definition indicates that it is (or *often, usually,* etc. is) the plural form of the entry word that has the meaning given in the definition.

look ...   *vi.* ... *—n.* **1** ...   **2** ...   **3** [Colloq.] *a)* [*usually pl.*] appearance *b)* [*pl.*] personal appearance ...

If a plural noun entry or sense is construed as singular, the designation [*with sing. v.*] is added.

phys·ics ...   *n.pl.* ...   [*with sing. v.*] ...

E. *Verbs Followed by Prepositions or Objects*—Where certain verbs are, in usage, invariably or usually followed by a specific preposition or prepositions, this has been indicated in either of the following ways: the preposition has been worked into the definition, italicized and usually enclosed in parentheses, or a note has been added after the definition indicating that the preposition is so used.

In definitions of transitive verbs, the specific or generalized object of the verb, where given, is enclosed in parentheses, since such an object is not part of the definition.

VII.   Usage Labels

Usage labels, if they are to be useful, must be conventional words that are clearly understood by the reader. The labels used in this dictionary are given below, with an explanation of each.

Colloquial: The term or sense is in widespread use and is generally characteristic of conversation and informal writing. It is not to be regarded as substandard or illiterate.

Slang: The term or sense is not generally regarded as conventional or standard usage, but is used, even by the best speakers, in highly informal contexts. Usually slang terms either pass into disuse in time or come to have a standard status.

Obsolete: The term or sense is no longer used but occurs in earlier writings.

Archaic: The term or sense is rarely used today except in certain restricted contexts, as in church ritual, but occurs in earlier writings.

Old Poetic: The term or sense was never part of the everyday language, but was used chiefly in earlier poetry, or in prose where a poetic quality was desired.

Dialect: The term or sense is used regularly only in some geographical areas or in a certain designated area (*South, West,* etc.) of the United States.

British: The term or sense is restricted to the British Isles as a whole. The label "Brit., etc." indicates the term or sense is found generally throughout the English-speaking world outside the U.S. The label "Brit., etc. (exc. Cdn.)" indicates the term or sense is in general use throughout the English-speaking world except North America.

Canadian (or *Irish,* etc.): The term or sense is characteristic specifically of Canadian (or Irish, etc.) English.

Historical: The term or sense refers to something that no longer exists and to which no more current term applies.

Old-fashioned: The term or sense is not yet considered archaic but seems out-of-date.

Rare: The term or sense has never been common.

Vulgar: The term or sense is regarded by most people as highly inappropriate in most social contexts. Many such terms are also slang.

In addition to the above usage labels, supplementary information is often given after the definition, indicating whether the term or sense is generally regarded as vulgar, substandard, or derogatory, used with ironic, familiar, or hyperbolic connotations, etc.

pate ...   *n.*   ...   a humorous term

VIII.   Run-in Derived Entries

It is possible in English to form an almost infinite number of derived forms simply by adding certain prefixes or suffixes to the base word. The editors have included as run-in entries in boldface type as many of these common derived words as space permitted, but only when the meaning of such words can be immediately understood from the meanings of the base word and the affix. Thus, **greatness** and **liveliness** are run in at the end of the entries for **great** and **lively**, the suffix **-ness** being found as a separate entry meaning "state, quality, or instance of being." Many words formed with common suffixes, as **-able, -er, -less, -like, -ly, -tion,** etc. are similarly treated as run-in entries with the base word from which they are derived. All such entries are syllabified and either accented to show stress in pronunciation or, where necessary, pronounced in full or in part.

THE THESAURUS

I.   Arrangement of Entries

As in the Dictionary portion of this book, all headwords, including single words, hyphenated and unhyphenated compounds, and phrases, are listed in strict alphabetical order and are set in large, boldface type.

account *n.* ...
accountant *n.* ...
account for *v.* ...
acquaintance *n.* ...
acquainted (with) *a.* ...
acquaint with *v.* ...
acting *a.* ...
acting *n.* ...

Idiomatic phrases listed within an entry have also been alphabetized.

action *n.* ... **—bring action** ... **—see action** ... **—take action** ...

II. Part-of-Speech Labels

Part-of-speech labels are given for all headwords, including single words, hyphenated and open compounds, and phrases. Generally, a word having more than one part of speech is given a separate entry block for each part of speech.

abuse *n.* perversion, misuse, debasement, ...
abuse *v.* insult, injure, hurt, ...

Sometimes, though, its synonyms can be conveniently grouped together in a single entry block.

above *a., prep.* 1 [High in position] over, high, higher, ...

III. The Entry Block

A. *Synonyms*—Every entry block in the Thesaurus lists synonyms (words or phrases that are similar in meaning).

wholly *a.* totally, entirely, fully; see COMPLETELY.
why *a., conj.* for what reason?, how so?, how?, how is it that?, on whose account? ...

Since we do not have space to list every synonym at every entry block, we have chosen certain entry blocks or numbered senses to be the primary location of synonyms belonging to a particular family of meaning. These primary locations are "main entries." Main entries always contain more than three synonyms.

dwell *v.* live, inhabit, stay, lodge, stop, settle, remain, live in, live at, continue, go on living, ...

Entry blocks or numbered senses containing only three synonyms are "brief entries." Brief entries always refer the user to the primary location of synonyms in the Thesaurus and often refer to two or more main entries.

abide *v.* 1 [To lodge] stay, room, reside; see DWELL. ...
locate *v.* ... 2 [To take up residence] settle down, establish oneself, inhabit; see DWELL, SETTLE 5.

When we wish to call the user's attention to another, closely related, family of synonyms, we have placed a cross-reference from one main entry to another.

settle *v.* ... 5 [To establish residence] locate, lodge, become a citizen, reside, ... establish a home, keep house; see also DWELL. ...

All cross-references in the Thesaurus portion of the book are to other Thesaurus entries. No cross-references are made between the Dictionary and the Thesaurus.

B. *Definitions*—Distinct senses located in a single entry block are numbered consecutively in boldface numerals and may be further distinguished by brief definitions or explanatory notes in brackets.

capital *n.* 1 [A seat of government] ... 2 [Money and property] ... 3 [A letter usually used initially] ...

calm *a.* 1 [*Said especially of persons*] ... 2 [*Said often of things*] ...

C. *Lists of Examples*—Often, a writer or speaker is looking not for other words similar to a word at hand, but for a specific thing in a general category. So, in addition to providing synonyms, the Thesaurus also provides lists of concrete examples.

boat *n. Types of small boats include the following:* sailboat, rowboat, shell, scull, kayak, dugout, canoe, scow, raft, ...
verb *n. Verbs include the following:* finite, active, passive, transitive, intransitive, modal, auxiliary, linking, ...
writer *n.* ... *Major writers include the following—British:* Henry Fielding, Sir Walter Scott, Charlotte Brontë, George Eliot, Jane Austen, ... ; *Spanish:* Miguel de Cervantes, Jorge Luis Borges; *Yiddish:* I.B. Singer.

D. *Antonyms*—Antonyms (words that are opposite or nearly opposite in meaning) are listed after the synonyms.

insulted *a.* slandered, libeled, reviled, disgraced, ... shamed; see also HURT.—*Ant.* PRAISED, admired, extolled.
a[2] *a., indefinite article, prep.* 1 ... —*Ant.* THE, this, that.

Antonyms in small capitals are Thesaurus entries that the user is especially advised to consult.

E. *The Asterisk*—A headword, run-on idiomatic phrase, definition in brackets, synonym, or antonym may be marked with an asterisk. An asterisk is intended to alert the user that the word, definition, etc. is slang, informal, dialectal, regional, archaic, etc. The user is thus cautioned to consider whether that term is appropriate for his or her purposes. The Dictionary will usually provide information on a word marked with an asterisk, but remember that not every synonym or antonym in the Thesaurus is entered in the Dictionary.

IV. Superscripts

Superscripts in the Dictionary portion of this book are used to distinguish *homographs*—headwords that are spelled alike but that are different in meaning and origin. In the Thesaurus, however, homographs may be joined together in a single entry, so long as they share the same part of speech.

batter[2,3] *n.* 1 [One who bats] ... 2 [Baking mixture] ...

Superscripts in the Thesaurus are used to link an entry block in the Thesaurus half of a page to an entry block in the Dictionary half of the same page. So, the superscript "1" for the Thesaurus headword **elder**[1] indicates that it is the Dictionary entry **elder**[1] (and not **elder**[2]) that is to be consulted for further information.

Sometimes a Thesaurus entry may be linked to more than one entry block in the Dictionary.

host[2,3] *n.* **1** [A person who entertains] ... **2** [A large group] ... **3** [Organism on which a parasite subsists] ...

The superscripts "2,3" link this Thesaurus entry block to both **host**[2] and **host**[3] in the Dictionary.

V. Suggestions for Using the Thesaurus

For convenience, here is a summary of things you may want to have in mind while you use the Thesaurus:

1. Look up any word you have thought of but do not want to use.
2. Unless you have thought of a rare word, you should find: (a) a main entry, with many alternate terms, some antonyms, and possibly a "see also" cross-reference, or (b) a brief entry, with three synonyms and one or more cross-references.
3. If you have turned to a main entry, check to see whether more than one meaning is recognized, and if so, pick the one you want. The various meanings will be numbered in boldface numerals.
4. Work through the list, looking for an appropriate term. Try the cross-reference at the end if you need it.
5. If you find a word or phrase you may want but do not know very well, look it up in the Dictionary.
6. If you have looked up a brief entry, it will provide a few common synonyms. If you do not want any of them, turn to the main entry or entries cross-referred. The entry to which you are referred may have more than one grammatical use—*fast* can be an adjective, adverb, noun, or verb. Choose the part of speech that corresponds to the use of the word from which you got the cross-reference.

ABBREVIATIONS AND SYMBOLS
USED IN THE DICTIONARY

abbrev.	abbreviated; abbreviation
adj.	adjective
adv.	adverb
Afr	African
Afrik	Afrikaans
alt.	alternative
Am	American
AmInd	American Indian
AmSp	American Spanish
Anat.	Anatomy
Anglo-Fr	Anglo-French
Ar	Arabic
Aram	Aramaic
Archit.	Architecture
Biol.	Biology
Bot.	Botany
Brit	British
C	Celsius
c.	circa
c.	century
cap.	capital city
Cdn	Canadian
Celt	Celtic
cf.	compare
Ch.	Church
Chem.	Chemistry
Chin	Chinese
Colloq.	colloquial
compar.	comparative
Comput.	Computer Science
conj.	conjunction
contr.	contraction (grammar)
Dan	Danish
Dial., dial.	dialectal
dim.	diminutive
Du	Dutch
E	eastern
Eccles.	Ecclesiastical
Educ.	Education
e.g.	for example
Egypt	Egyptian
Elec.	Electricity
Eng	English
Esk	Eskimo
esp.	especially
etc.	and/or the like
Ex.	example

exc.	except
F	Fahrenheit
fem.	feminine
Fl	Flemish
fol.	following entry
Fr	French
ft.	foot, feet
Gael	Gaelic
Geol.	Geology
Geom.	Geometry
Ger	German
Gmc	Germanic
Gr	classical Greek
Gram.	Grammar
Haw	Hawaiian
Heb	Hebrew
Hung	Hungarian
IE	Indo-European
i.e.	that is
in.	inch(es)
indic.	indicative
infl.	influenced
intens.	intensive
interj.	interjection
Ir	Irish
It	Italian
Jpn	Japanese
km	kilometer(s)
L	classical Latin
lb.	pound(s)
lit.	literally
LL	Late Latin
LowG	Low German
m	meter(s)
masc.	masculine
Math.	Mathematics
MDu	Middle Dutch
ME	Middle English
Mech.	Mechanics
Med.	Medicine
Mex	Mexican
MHG	Middle High German
mi.	mile(s)
Mil.	Military
ML	Middle Latin
ModGr	Modern Greek
ModL	modern scientific Latin

Myth	Mythology	Psychol.	Psychology
N	northern	pt.	past tense
n.	noun	R.C.Ch.	Roman Catholic Church
Naut.	nautical usage	Rom.	Roman
NE	northeastern	Russ	Russian
Norm	Norman	S	southern
Norw	Norwegian	Sans	Sanskrit
n.pl.	plural noun	Scand	Scandinavian
n.sing.	singular noun	Scot	Scottish
NW	northwestern	SE	southeastern
Obs., obs.	obsolete	sing.	singular
occas.	occasionally	Sp	Spanish
OE	Old English	sp.	spelling, spelled
OFr	Old French	specif.	specifically
OHG	Old High German	sq.	square
ON	Old Norse	superl.	superlative
orig.	origin; originally	SW	southwestern
OS	Old Saxon	Swed	Swedish
OSlav	Old Church Slavonic	Theol.	Theology
pers.	person (grammar)	transl.	translated, translation
Pers	Persian	Turk	Turkish
Photog.	Photography	ult.	ultimately
pl.	plural	v.	verb
Poet.	poetic	var.	variant
Pol	Polish	v.aux.	auxiliary verb
pop.	population	vi.	intransitive verb
Port	Portuguese	VL	Vulgar Latin
poss.	possessive	vt.	transitive verb
pp.	past participle	W	western
prec.	preceding entry	WInd	West Indian
prep.	preposition	Yidd	Yiddish
pres.	present tense		
prob.	probably		
pron.	pronoun	<	derived from
Prov	Provençal	?	uncertain or unknown
prp.	present participle	+	plus
pseud.	pseudonym	&	and

ABBREVIATIONS AND SYMBOLS
USED IN THE THESAURUS

a. = adjective or adverb
      (i.e., modifier)
n. = noun

v. = verb
* = slang, colloquial, dialectal,
    regional, archaic, etc.

a¹ or **A** (ā) *n., pl.* **a's, A's** (āz) the first letter of the English alphabet

a² (ə; *stressed*, ā) *adj.,* ***indefinite article*** ⟦< AN⟧ **1** one; one sort of **2** each; any one **3** per *[once a day]* Before words beginning with a consonant sound, *a* is used *[a child, a home, a uniform]* See AN

A (ā) *n.* **1** a blood type **2** a grade indicating excellence **3** *Music* the sixth tone in the scale of C major

a-¹ ⟦< OE⟧ *prefix* **1** in, into, on, at, to *[ashore]* **2** in the act or state of *[asleep]*

a-² *prefix* **1** ⟦< OE⟧ up, out *[arise]* **2** ⟦< OE⟧ off, of *[akin]* **3** ⟦< Gr⟧ not, without *[amoral]*

a or **a.** **1** about **2** acre(s) **3** adjective **4** alto **5** answer

A or **A.** **1** alto **2** answer **3** April **4** August

AA or **A.A.** **1** Alcoholics Anonymous **2** Associate in (or of) Arts

aard·vark (ärd′värk′) *n.* ⟦Du, earth pig⟧ a nocturnal, ant-eating S African mammal

Aaron (er′ən) *Bible* the first high priest of the Hebrews

AB *n.* a blood type

ab- ⟦L⟧ *prefix* away, from, from off, down *[abdicate]*

AB **1** Bachelor of Arts: also **A.B.** **2** *Baseball* (times) at bat

aback (ə bak′) *adv.* [Archaic] backward; back —**taken aback** startled and confused; surprised

aba·cus (ab′ə kəs) *n., pl.* **-cuses** or **-ci′** (-sī′) ⟦< Gr *abax*⟧ a frame with sliding beads for doing arithmetic

abaft (ə baft′) *adv.* ⟦< OE *on*, on + *be*, by + *æftan*, aft⟧ aft

aba·lone (ab′ə lō′nē) *n.* ⟦< AmInd⟧ an edible sea mollusk with an oval, somewhat spiral shell

aban·don (ə ban′dən) *vt.* ⟦< OFr *mettre a bandon*, to put under (another's ban)⟧ **1** to give up completely **2** to desert — *n.* unrestrained activity; exuberance —**aban′don·ment** *n.*

aban′doned *adj.* **1** deserted **2** shamefully wicked **3** unrestrained

abase (ə bās′) *vt.* **abased′, abas′ing** ⟦< ML *abassare*, to lower⟧ to humble —**abase′ment** *n.*

abash (ə bash′) *vt.* ⟦< OFr *es-*, intens. + *baer*, gape⟧ to make ashamed and uneasy; disconcert —**abash′edly** *adv.*

abate (ə bāt′) *vt., vi.* **abat′ed, abat′ing** ⟦< OFr *abattre*, beat down⟧ **1** to make or become less **2** *Law* to end —**abate′ment** *n.*

ab·at·toir (ab′ə twär′, ab′ə twär′) *n.* ⟦Fr: see prec.⟧ a slaughterhouse

abbé (a′bā) *n.* ⟦Fr: see ABBOT⟧ a French priest's title

ab·bess (ab′əs) *n.* ⟦see ABBOT⟧ a woman who heads a convent of nuns

ab·bey (ab′ē) *n.* **1** a monastery or convent **2** a church belonging to an abbey

ab·bot (ab′ət) *n.* ⟦< Aram *abbā*, father⟧ a man who heads a monastery

abbr. or **abbrev.** **1** abbreviated **2** abbreviation

ab·bre·vi·ate (ə brē′vē āt′) *vt.* **-at′ed, -at′ing** ⟦< L *ad-*, to + *brevis*, brief⟧ to make shorter; esp., to shorten (a word) by omitting letters

ab·bre·vi·a′tion (-ā′shən) *n.* **1** a shortening **2** a shortened form of a word or phrase, as *Mr.* for *Mister*

ABC (ā′bē′sē′) *n., pl.* **ABC's** **1** [*usually pl.*] the alphabet **2** the basic elements (of a subject); rudiments

A

ab·di·cate (ab′di kāt′) *vt., vi.* **-cat′ed, -cat′ing** ⟦< L *ab-*, off + *dicare*, to proclaim⟧ **1** to give up formally (a throne, etc.) **2** to surrender (a right, responsibility, etc.) —**ab′di·ca′tion** *n.*

ab·do·men (ab′də mən, ab dō′-) *n.* ⟦L⟧ the part of the body between the diaphragm and the pelvis; belly —**ab·dom′i·nal** (-däm′ə nəl) *adj.*

ab·duct (ab dukt′) *vt.* ⟦< L *ab-*, away + *ducere*, to lead⟧ to kidnap —**ab·duc′tion** *n.* —**ab·duc′tor** *n.*

abeam (ə bēm′) *adv.* at right angles to a ship's length or keel

abed (ə bed′) *adv., adj.* in bed

Abel (ā′bəl) *Bible* the second son of Adam and Eve: see CAIN

ab·er·ra·tion (ab′ər ā′shən) *n.* ⟦< L *ab-*, from + *errare*, wander⟧ **1** a deviation from what is right, true, normal, etc. **2** mental derangement or lapse **3** *Optics* the failure of light rays from one point to converge at a single focus —**ab·er′rant** (-er′ənt) *adj.* —**ab·er·ra′tional** *adj.*

abet (ə bet′) *vt.* **abet′ted, abet′ting** ⟦< OFr *a-*, to + *beter*, to bait⟧ to urge on or help, esp. in crime —**abet′tor** or **abet′ter** *n.*

abey·ance (ə bā′əns) *n.* ⟦< OFr *a-*, to, at + *bayer*, wait expectantly⟧ temporary suspension, as of an activity or ruling

ab·hor (ab hôr′) *vt.* **-horred′, -hor′ring** ⟦< L *ab-*, from + *horrere*, to shudder⟧ to shrink from in disgust, hatred, etc. —**ab·hor′rence** *n.*

ab·hor′rent (-ənt) *adj.* causing disgust, hatred, etc.; detestable —**ab·hor′rently** *adv.*

abide (ə bīd′) *vi.* **abode′** or **abid′ed, abid′ing** ⟦< OE *ā-*, intens. + *bīdan*, bide⟧ **1** to remain **2** [Archaic] to reside — *vt.* to put up with —**abide by 1** to live up to (a promise, etc.) **2** to submit to and carry out —**abid′ance** *n.*

abid′ing *adj.* enduring; lasting

abil·ity (ə bil′ə tē) *n., pl.* **-ties** ⟦< L *habilitas*⟧ **1** a being able; power to do **2** talent; skill

-ability (ə bil′ə tē) ⟦L *-abilitas*⟧ *suffix* a (specified) ability, capacity, or tendency

ab·ject (ab′jekt′, ab jekt′) *adj.* ⟦< L *ab-*, from + *jacere*, to throw⟧ **1** miserable; wretched **2** degraded —**ab·ject′ly** *adv.* —**ab·jec′tion** *n.*

ab·jure (ab joor′, əb-) *vt.* **-jured′, -jur′ing** ⟦< L *ab-*, away + *jurare*, swear⟧ to give up (rights, allegiance, etc.) on oath; renounce —**ab·ju·ra′tion** (ab′jə rā′shən) *n.* —**ab·jur·a·to′ry** (-ə tôr′ē) *adj.* —**ab·jur′er** *n.*

ab·late (ab lāt′) *vt.* **-lat′ed, -lat′ing** ⟦see fol.⟧ **1** to remove, as by surgery **2** to wear away, burn away, or vaporize — *vi.* to be ablated, as a rocket shield in reentry —**ab·la′tion** *n.*

ab·la·tive (ab′lə tiv) *n.* ⟦< L *ab-*, away + *ferre*, to bear⟧

▰ THESAURUS ▰

a² *a.,* ***indefinite article, prep.*** **1** [The indefinite article; *before vowels, written "an"*] some, one, any, each, some kind of, some particular, any of, any one of, a certain.—*Ant.* THE, this, that. **2** [An indication of frequency] per, every, at the rate of; see EACH 2.

abandon *n.* unrestraint, spontaneity, freedom, exuberance, spirit, enthusiasm, vigor.

abandon *v.* **1** [To give up] leave, quit, withdraw, discontinue, break off, go off from, cast away, cast aside, let go, cease, cast off, discard, vacate, give away, part with, evacuate, surrender, yield, desist, concede, renounce, abdicate, lose hope of, go back on, secede, waive, forgo, back down from, lay aside, dispose of, have done with, throw in the towel*, break the habit. **2** [To leave someone or something in trouble] desert, forsake, ostracize, back out on, break with, break up with, run away, defect, reject, disown, cast off, maroon, depart from, throw overboard, jettison, leave behind, slip away from, stand up*, leave in the lurch, turn one's back on, run out on*, walk out on*, doublecross*, let down, drop*.

abandoned *a.* deserted, desolate, destitute, desperate, empty, unused, vacated, left, neglected, relinquished, lonely, forsaken, solitary, hopeless, cast off, cast aside, cast away, forgotten, shunned, forlorn, avoided, outcast, rejected, helpless, unfortunate, alone, discarded, scorned, lost, doomed, friendless, wretched, thrown overboard*, out on a limb*, waiting at the church*, left in the lurch, left in the cold, left holding the bag*.—*Ant.* INHABITED, used, in use.

abbreviate *v.* shorten, cut, condense; see DECREASE 2.

abbreviation *n.* contraction, abridgment, sketch, brief, abstract, synopsis, reduction, abstraction, condensation, digest, resumé, outline, summary, short form; see also SUMMARY.

abdicate *v.* relinquish, give up, with-

draw; see ABANDON 1.

abdomen *n.* midsection, belly, gut; see STOMACH.

abduct *v.* capture, seize, carry off; see KIDNAP.

abide *v.* **1** [To lodge] stay, room, reside; see DWELL. **2** [To submit to] put up with, bear, bear with, withstand; see also ENDURE 2. —**abide by** follow, observe, comply with; see FOLLOW 3.

ability *n.* aptitude, intelligence, innate qualities, powers, potency, worth, talent, gift, genius, capability, competence, proficiency, adeptness, qualifications, knowledge, self-sufficiency, tact, finish, technique, craft, skill, artistry, cunning, skillfulness, dexterity, facility, finesse, mastery, cleverness, deftness, experience, ingenuity, strength, understanding, faculty, comprehension, makings, sense, what it takes*, brains, knack, hang, know-how*.—*Ant.* IGNORANCE, incompetence, inexperience.

Gram. the case expressing removal, cause, agency, etc., as in Latin

ablaze (ə blāz′) *adj.* **1** flaming **2** greatly excited

able (ā′bəl) *adj.* **a′bler, a′blest** ⟦< L *habere,* have⟧ **1** having enough power, skill, etc. to do something **2** skilled; talented **3** *Law* competent —**a′bly** *adv.*

-able (ə bəl) ⟦< L⟧ *suffix* **1** that can or will *[perishable]* **2** capable of being ____ed *[manageable]* **3** worthy of being ____ed *[lovable]* **4** having qualities of *[comfortable]* **5** inclined to *[peaceable]*

a′ble-bod′ied *adj.* strong; healthy

able-bodied seaman a trained or skilled seaman Also **able seaman**

abloom (ə bloom′) *adj.* in bloom

ab·lu·tion (ab loo′shən) *n.* ⟦< L *ab-,* off + *luere,* to wash⟧ *[usually pl.]* a washing of the body, esp. as a religious ceremony

-ably (ə blē) *suffix* in a way indicating a (specified) ability, tendency, etc.

ABM *n.* anti-ballistic missile

ab·ne·gate (ab′nə gāt′) *vt.* **-gat′ed, -gat′ing** ⟦< L *ab-,* from + *negare,* deny⟧ to deny and refuse; renounce (a claim, etc.) —**ab′ne·ga′tion** *n.*

ab·nor·mal (ab nôr′məl) *adj.* not normal, average, or typical; irregular —**ab·nor′mal·ly** *adv.*

ab·nor·mal′i·ty (-mal′ə tē) *n.* **1** an abnormal condition **2** *pl.* **-ties** an abnormal thing; malformation

aboard (ə bôrd′) *adv., prep.* on or in (a train, ship, etc.)

abode (ə bōd′) *vi., vt.* alt. *pt. & pp.* of ABIDE —*n.* a home; residence

abol·ish (ə bäl′ish) *vt.* ⟦< L *abolere,* destroy⟧ to do away with; void

abo·li·tion (ab′ə lish′ən) *n.* **1** complete destruction; annulment **2** *[occas.* A-] the abolishing of slavery in the U.S. —**ab′o·li′tion·ist** *n.*

abomi·nable (ə bäm′ə nə bəl) *adj.* [see fol.] **1** disgusting; vile **2** very bad —**abom′i·nably** *adv.*

abom′i·nate′ (-nāt′) *vt.* **-nat′ed, -nat′ing** ⟦< L *abominari,* regard as an ill omen⟧ **1** to hate; loathe **2** to dislike —**abom′i·na′tion** *n.*

ab·orig·i·nal (ab′ə rij′ə nəl) *adj.* **1** existing (in a region) from the beginning; first; indigenous **2** of aborigines —*n.* an aborigine

ab′orig′i·ne′ (-ə nē′) *n., pl.* **-nes′** ⟦< L *ab-,* from + *origine,* origin⟧ any of the first known inhabitants of a region

aborn·ing (ə bôr′niŋ) *adv.* while being born or created *[the plan died aborning]*

abort (ə bôrt′) *vi.* ⟦< L *aboriri,* miscarry⟧ to have a miscarriage —*vt.* **1** to check before fully developed **2** to cut short (a flight, etc.), as because of an equipment failure

abor′tion *n.* any expulsion of a fetus before it is able to survive, esp. if induced on purpose —**abor′tion·ist** *n.*

abor′tive *adj.* **1** unsuccessful; fruitless **2** *Biol.* arrested in development

abound (ə bound′) *vi.* ⟦< L *ab-,* away + *undare,* rise in waves⟧ to be plentiful; teem Often with *in* or *with*

about (ə bout′) *adv.* ⟦< OE *onbūtan,* around⟧ **1** all around **2** near **3** in an opposite direction **4** nearly *[about ready]* —*adj.* astir *[he is up and about]* —*prep.* **1** on all sides of **2** near to **3** with **4** on the point of **5** concerning

about′-face′ (-fās′, -fās′; *for v.,* ə bout′fās′) *n.* a reversal of position or opinion —*vi.* **-faced′, -fac′ing** to turn or face in the opposite direction

above (ə buv′) *adv.* ⟦OE *abūfan*⟧ **1** in a higher place; up **2** earlier (in a book, etc.) **3** higher in rank, etc. —*prep.* **1** over; on top of **2** better or more than *[above the average]* —*adj.* mentioned earlier —**above** all most of all; mainly

above′board′ *adv., adj.* without dishonesty or concealment

abrade (ə brād′) *vt., vi.* **abrad′ed, abrad′ing** ⟦< L *ab-,* away + *radere,* to scrape⟧ to rub off; scrape away

Abra·ham (ā′brə ham′) *Bible* the first patriarch of the Hebrews

abra·sion (ə brā′zhən) *n.* **1** an abrading **2** an abraded spot

abra′sive (-siv) *adj.* **1** causing abrasion **2** aggressively annoying; irritating —*n.* a substance, as sandpaper, used for grinding, polishing, etc.

abreast (ə brest′) *adv., adj.* **1** side by side **2** informed (*of*); aware

abridge (ə brij′) *vt.* **abridged′, abridg′ing** ⟦< LL *abbreviare,* abbreviate⟧ **1** to shorten, lessen, or curtail **2** to shorten (a piece of writing) while keeping the substance —**abridg′ment** or **abridge′ment** *n.*

abroad (ə brôd′) *adv.* **1** far and wide **2** in circulation; current **3** outdoors **4** to or in foreign lands —**from abroad** from a foreign land

ab·ro·gate (ab′rō gāt′, -rə-) *vt.* **-gat′ed, -gat′ing** ⟦< L *ab-,* away + *rogare,* ask⟧ to abolish; repeal; annul —**ab′ro·ga′tion** *n.* —**ab′ro·ga′tor** *n.*

abrupt (ə brupt′) *adj.* ⟦< L *ab-,* off + *rumpere,* to break⟧ **1** sudden; unexpected **2** brusque **3** very steep **4** disconnected, as some writing —**abrupt′ly** *adv.* —**abrupt′ness** *n.*

Ab·sa·lom (ab′sə ləm) *Bible* David's son who rebelled against him

ab·scess (ab′ses′) *n.* ⟦< L *ab(s)-,* from + *cedere,* go⟧ a swollen area in body tissues, containing pus —*vi.* to form an abscess —**ab′scessed′** *adj.*

ab·scissa (ab sis′ə) *n., pl.* **-sas** or **-sae** (-ē) ⟦L < *ab-,* from + *scindere,* to cut⟧ *Math.* the horizontal distance of a point from a vertical axis

ab·scond (ab skänd′, əb-) *vi.* ⟦< L *ab(s)-,* from + *condere,* hide⟧ to leave hastily and secretly, esp. to escape the law —**ab·scond′er** *n.*

ab·sence (ab′səns) *n.* **1** a being absent **2** the time of this **3** a lack

ab·sent (ab′sənt; *for v.,* ab sent′) *adj.* ⟦< L *ab-,* away + *esse,* be⟧ **1** not present **2** not existing; lacking **3** not attentive —*vt.* to keep (oneself) away —*prep.* in the

---

THESAURUS

able *a.* intelligent, ingenious, worthy, talented, gifted, fitted, capable, effective, efficient, qualified, masterful, adequate, competent, expert, experienced, skilled, learned, clever, suitable, smart, crafty, cunning, bright, knowing, dexterous, endowed, deft, apt, agile, adept, alert, adaptable, smooth, ready, versatile, equal to, suited, suited to, well-rounded, mighty, powerful, strong, robust, sturdy, brawny, vigorous, courageous, fit for, sharp*, cut out for*, having an ear for*.—*Ant.* STUPID, bungling, unadaptable.

able-bodied *a.* fit, powerful, sturdy; see STRONG 1.

abnormal *a.* strange, irregular, unnatural; see UNUSUAL 2.

abnormality *n.* peculiarity, singularity, malformation; see IRREGULARITY.

aboard *a.* on board, on ship, shipped, loaded, on board ship, freight on board, being shipped, en route, consigned, in transit, being transported, embarked, afloat, at sea, on deck, traveling.

abolish *v.* suppress, eradicate, terminate, exterminate, obliterate, annul, remove, revoke, end, finish, nullify, set aside, annihilate, repeal, subvert, reverse, rescind, prohibit, extinguish, cancel, erase, root out, pull up, uproot, demolish, invalidate, overturn, overthrow, declare null and void, do away with, stamp out, undo, throw out, put an end to, inhibit, dispense with, cut out, raze, squelch, ravage; see also DESTROY.

abort *v.* miscarry, fall short, miss; see FAIL 1.

about *a., prep.* **1** [Approximately] roughly, nearly, in general; see APPROXIMATELY. **2** [Concerning] regarding, respecting, touching, of, on, in realtion to, relative to, relating to, as regards, in regard to, in which, with respect to, in the matter of, with reference to, referring to, so far as something is concerned, in connection with, concerned with, thereby, wherein, as for, dealing with. **3** [Around] surrounding, round about, on all sides; see AROUND.

above *a., prep.* **1** [High in position] over, high, higher, superior, beyond, raised, above one's head, in a higher place, aloft, overhead, toward the sky; see also HIGHER, OVER 1.—*Ant.*

BELOW, low, beneath. **2** [Referring to something earlier] before, foregoing, earlier; see PRECEDING. —**above all** in the first place, chiefly, especially; see PRINCIPALLY.

aboveboard *a.* candidly, honestly, frankly; see OPENLY 1.

abrasive *a.* **1** grinding, sharpening, cutting; see ROUGH 1. **2** irritating, annoying, caustic; see DISTURBING.

abreast *a.* in line, equal, side by side; see BESIDE.

abroad *a.* away, at large, adrift, wandering, elsewhere, overseas, traveling, touring, outside, distant, far away, gone, out of the country, removed.

abrupt *a.* **1** [Said of things, usually landscape] uneven, rough, jagged; see STEEP. **2** [Said of people or acts of people] blunt, hasty, gruff; see RUDE.

absence *n.* **1** [The state of being elsewhere] truancy, nonattendance, nonappearance, loss, vacancy, cut*, hooky. **2** [The state of lacking something] deficiency, need, inadequacy; see LACK 1.

absent *a.* away, missing, elsewhere, vanished, gone, gone out, not at

ab·sen·tee (ab′sən tē′) *n.* one who is absent, as from work — *adj.* designating, of, or from one who is absent —**ab′ sen·tee′ism′** *n.*

absentee ballot a ballot to be marked and sent to a board of elections by a person (**absentee voter**) unable to be at the polls at election time

ab′sent-mind′ed *adj.* 1 not attentive; preoccupied 2 habitually forgetful —**ab′sent-mind′edly** *adv.* — **ab′sent-mind′edness** *n.*

absent without leave *Mil.* absent from duty without official permission

ab·sinthe or **ab·sinth** (ab′sinth′) *n.* ⟦< Gr⟧ a green, bitter, toxic liqueur

ab·so·lute (ab′sə lōōt′) *adj.* ⟦see ABSOLVE⟧ 1 perfect; complete 2 not mixed; pure 3 not limited *[absolute* power*]* 4 positive 5 not doubted; real *[absolute* truth*]* 6 not relative —**ab′so·lute′ly** *adv.*

absolute value the value of a real number, disregarding its positive or negative sign *[the absolute value* of -4 or +4 is 4*]*

absolute zero the lower limit on physically obtainable temperatures: equal to -273.15°C or -459.67°F

ab·so·lu·tion (ab′sə lōō′shən) *n.* 1 a freeing *(from* guilt); forgiveness 2 remission *(of* sin or penalty for it)

ab·so·lut·ism (ab′sə lōōt′iz′əm) *n.* government by absolute rule; despotism —**ab′so·lut′ist** *n.*, *adj.*

ab·solve (ab zälv′, ab-) *vt.* -solved′, -solv′ing ⟦< L *ab-*, from + *solvere*, loosen⟧ 1 to free from guilt, a duty, etc. 2 to give religious absolution to

ab·sorb (ab sôrb′, -zôrb′; ab-) *vt.* ⟦< L *ab-*, from + *sorbere*, drink in⟧ 1 to suck up 2 to interest greatly; engross 3 to assimilate 4 to pay for (costs, etc.) 5 to take in (a shock, etc.) without recoil 6 to take in and not reflect (light or sound) —**ab·sorb′ing** *adj.*

ab·sorb′ent *adj.* capable of absorbing moisture, etc. — *n.* a thing that absorbs —**ab·sorb′ency** *n.*

ab·sorp·tion (ab sôrp′shən, -zôrp′-; ab-) *n.* 1 an absorbing or being absorbed 2 great interest —**ab·sorp′tive** *adj.*

ab·stain (ab stān′, ab-) *vi.* ⟦< L *ab(s)-*, from + *tenere*, to hold⟧ to voluntarily do without; refrain *(from)* —**ab· stain′er** *n.* —**ab·sten′tion** (-sten′shən) *n.*

ab·ste·mi·ous (ab stē′mē əs, əb-) *adj.* ⟦< L *ab(s)-*, from + *temetum*, strong drink⟧ moderate in eating and drinking; temperate

ab·sti·nence (ab′stə nəns) *n.* an abstaining from some or all food, liquor, etc. —**ab′sti·nent** *adj.*

ab·stract (*for adj.*, ab strakt′, ab′strakt′; *for n. & vt.* 2, ab′ strakt′; *for vt. 1*, ab strakt′) *adj.* ⟦< L *ab(s)-*, from + *trahere*, to draw⟧ 1 thought of apart from material objects 2 expressing a quality so thought of 3 theoretical 4 *Art* not representing things realistically — *n.* a summary — *vt.* 1 to take away 2 to summarize —**ab·stract′ly** *adv.*

ab·stract′ed *adj.* absent-minded

ab·strac·tion (ab strak′shən) *n.* 1 an abstracting; removal 2 an abstract idea, thing, etc. 3 mental withdrawal 4 an abstract painting, etc.

ab·struse (ab strōōs′) *adj.* ⟦< L *ab(s)-*, away + *trudere*, to thrust⟧ hard to understand —**ab·struse′ly** *adv.* —**ab· struse′ness** *n.*

ab·surd (ab surd′, -zurd′; əb-) *adj.* ⟦< L *ab-*, intens. + *surdus*, dull, insensible⟧ so unreasonable as to be ridiculous —**ab·surd′ity** *n.* —**ab·surd′ly** *adv.*

abun·dance (ə bun′dəns) *n.* ⟦see ABOUND⟧ great plenty; more than enough —**abun′dant** *adj.* —**abun′dantly** *adv.*

abuse (ə byōōz′; *for n.*, ə byōōs′) *vt.* abused′, abus′ing ⟦< L *ab-*, away + *uti*, to use⟧ 1 to use wrongly 2 to mistreat 3 to insult; revile — *n.* 1 wrong use 2 mistreatment 3 a corrupt practice 4 insulting language —**abu·sive** (ə byōō′ siv) *adj.* —**abu′sively** *adv.*

abut (ə but′) *vi.*, *vt.* abut′ted, abut′ting ⟦< OFr *a-*, to + *bout*, end⟧ to border (*on* or *upon*)

abut′ment *n.* 1 an abutting 2 a part supporting an arch, bridge, etc.

abys·mal (ə biz′məl) *adj.* 1 of or like an abyss; not measurable 2 very bad; wretched —**abys′mally** *adv.*

abyss (ə bis′) *n.* ⟦< Gr *a-*, without + *byssos*, bottom⟧ 1 a bottomless gulf 2 anything too deep for measurement *[an abyss* of shame*]*

-ac (ak, ək) ⟦< Gr⟧ *suffix* 1 characteristic of *[elegiac]* 2 relating to *[cardiac]* 3 affected by *[maniac]*

Ac *Chem. symbol for* actinium

▰▰▰ THESAURUS ▰▰▰

home, not present, out, wanting, lacking, abroad, lost, astray, nowhere to be found, on vacation, AWOL*, playing hooky.

absent-minded *a.* preoccupied, dreamy, listless, lost, absent, thoughtless, oblivious, inattentive, daydreaming, unconscious, unaware, withdrawn, removed, faraway, distracted, remote, forgetful, in the clouds*.—*Ant.* OBSERVANT, attentive, alert.

absolute *a.* 1 [Without limitation] total, complete, entire, infinite, unqualified, supreme, full, unrestricted, unlimited, unconditional, unbounded, independent, wholehearted, sheer, pure, unmitigated, utter, unabridged, thorough, clean, perfect, full, blanket, all-out, outand-out.—*Ant.* RESTRICTED, limited, qualified. 2 [Without limit in authority] authoritarian, domineering, supreme, arbitrary, official, autocratic, tyrannical, fascist, haughty, overbearing, czarist, nazi, totalitarian, oppressive, antidemocratic, imperative, dogmatic, commanding, controlling, compelling, despotic, intimidating, fanatic, dictatorial, arrogant, with an iron hand, high and mighty*.—*Ant.* LENIENT, tolerant, temperate. 3 [Certain] positive, unquestionable, undeniable; see CERTAIN 2.

absolutely *a.* 1 [Completely] utterly, unconditionally, thoroughly; see COMPLETELY. 2 [Positively] unquestionably, certainly, definitely; see SURELY.

absolve *v.* pardon, set free, clear; see EXCUSE.

absorb *v.* digest, take in, ingest, suck up, assimilate, blot, imbibe, swallow, consume, incorporate, sop up, soak up, sponge up.—*Ant.* EJECT, expel, discharge.

absorbed *a.* assimilated, taken in, swallowed up, consumed, drunk, imbibed, dissolved, incorporated, fused, united, digested.—*Ant.* REMOVED, unassimilated, unconsumed.

absorbent *a.* porous, spongy, permeable, dry, soft, penetrable, receptive, retentive, thirsty.

absorbing *a.* engaging, exciting, enthralling; see INTERESTING.

absorption *n.* assimilation, digestion, osmosis, saturation, penetration, fusion, intake, union, merging, blending, consumption, ingestion, swallowing up, taking in, reception, retention, incorporation, appropriation, drinking in, suction, sopping up, soaking up, sponging up, inhalation.—*Ant.* REMOVAL, ejection, discharge.

abstain *v.* refrain, refrain from, renounce, desist, withhold, avoid, stop, deny oneself, refuse, decline, hold back, shun, evade, cease, dispense with, do without, fast, starve, have nothing to do with, let alone, do nothing, keep from, keep one's hands off, swear off, lay off*, turn over a new leaf, have no hand in, take the pledge.—*Ant.* JOIN, indulge, gorge.

abstinence *n.* abstaining, temperance, denial, self-denial, self-control, self-restraint, continence, fasting, frugality, renunciation, avoidance, sobriety, austerity, refraining, nonindulgence, chastity, moderation, soberness, Puritanism.—*Ant.* INDUL-GENCE, intemperance, overindulgence.

abstract *a.* general, intellectual, ideal; see OBSCURE 1.

absurd *a.* preposterous, ridiculous, ludicrous; see STUPID.

absurdity *n.* improbability, foolishness, senselessness; see NONSENSE 1, 2.

abundance *n.* bounty, more than enough, profusion; see PLENTY.

abundant *a.* sufficient, ample, copious; see PLENTIFUL 2.

abundantly *a.* plentifully, lavishly, richly, handsomely, in large measure, profusely, amply, sufficiently, generously, affluently, inexhaustibly, many times over*, to one's heart's content, off the fat of the land; see also ADEQUATELY.

abuse *n.* perversion, misuse, debasement, degradation, desecration, injury, damage, harm, hurt, wrong, injustice, insult, mistreatment, violation, malevolence, mishandling, mismanagement, pollution, defilement, prostitution.—*Ant.* CARE, respect, veneration.

abuse *v.* insult, injure, hurt, harm, damage, impair, offend, overwork, illtreat, misuse, maltreat, mistreat, wrong, persecute, molest, victimize, oppress, ruin, mar, spoil, do wrong to, mishandle, pervert, profane, prostitute, desecrate, pollute, harass, manhandle, do an injustice to, violate, defile, impose upon, deprave, taint, debase, corrupt.—*Ant.* DEFEND, protect, befriend.

abused *a.* wronged, injured, harmed; see HURT.

AC, A.C., ac, or **a.c. 1** air conditioning **2** alternating current

a·ca·cia (ə kā′shə) *n.* ⟦< Gr *akē*, thorn⟧ **1** a tree or shrub with yellow or white flower clusters **2** the locust tree

aca·dem·ic (ak′ə dem′ik) *adj.* **1** of academies or colleges **2** having to do with liberal arts rather than technical education **3** formal; pedantic **4** merely theoretical —**ac′a·dem′i·cal·ly** *adv.*

acad·emi·cian (ə kad′ə mish′ən, ak′ə də-) *n.* a member of an ACADEMY (sense 3)

acad·emy (ə kad′ə mē) *n., pl.* **-mies** ⟦< Gr *akadēmeia*, place where Plato taught⟧ **1** a private secondary school **2** a school for special instruction **3** an association of scholars, writers, etc., for advancing an art or science

acan·thus (ə kan′thəs) *n., pl.* **-thuses** or **-thi′** (-thī′) ⟦< Gr *akanthos*, a point⟧ **1** a plant with lobed, often spiny leaves **2** *Archit.* a representation of these leaves

a cap·pella (ä′ kə pel′ə) ⟦It, in chapel style⟧ without instrumental accompaniment: said of choral singing

ac·cede (ak sēd′) *vi.* **-ced′ed, -ced′ing** ⟦< L *ad-*, to + *cedere*, go, yield⟧ **1** to enter upon the duties (of an office) **2** to assent; agree (*to*)

ac·cel·er·ate (ak sel′ər āt′, ək-) *vt.* **-at′ed, -at′ing** ⟦< L *ad-*, to + *celerare*, hasten⟧ **1** to increase the speed of **2** to cause to happen sooner — *vi.* to go faster —**ac·cel′era′tion** *n.*

ac·cel′era′tor *n.* a person or thing that accelerates; esp., the foot throttle of a motor vehicle

ac·cent (ak′sent′; *for v. also* ak sent′) *n.* ⟦< L *ad-*, to + *canere*, sing⟧ **1** emphasis given a spoken syllable or word **2** a mark showing such emphasis or indicating pronunciation **3** a distinguishing manner of pronunciation [an Irish *accent*] **4** special emphasis or attention **5** *Music, Prosody* rhythmic stress — *vt.* **1** to mark with an accent **2** to emphasize; stress

ac·cen·tu·ate (ak sen′chōō āt′, ək-) *vt.* **-at′ed, -at′ing** to accent; emphasize —**ac·cen′tua′tion** *n.*

ac·cept (ak sept′, ək-) *vt.* ⟦< L *ad-*, to + *capere*, take⟧ **1** to receive, esp. willingly **2** to approve **3** to agree to **4** to believe in **5** to agree to pay

ac·cept′able *adj.* worth accepting; satisfactory —**ac·cept′abil′ity** or **ac·cept′able·ness** *n.*

ac·cept′ance *n.* **1** an accepting **2** approval **3** belief in; assent **4** a promise to pay

ac·cept′ed *adj.* generally regarded as true, proper, etc.; conventional; approved

ac·cess (ak′ses′) *n.* ⟦see ACCEDE⟧ **1** approach or means of approach **2** the right to enter, use, etc. **3** an outburst; fit [an *access* of anger] — *vt.* to get data from, or add data to, a database

ac·ces′sible *adj.* **1** that can be approached or entered, esp. easily **2** obtainable —**ac·ces′sibil′ity** *n.* —**ac·ces′sibly** *adv.*

ac·ces·sion (ak sesh′ən) *n.* **1** the act of attaining (a throne, power, etc.) **2** assent **3** *a)* increase by addition *b)* an addition, as to a collection

ac·ces·sory (ak ses′ər ē, ək-) *adj.* ⟦see ACCEDE⟧ **1** additional; extra **2** helping in an unlawful act — *n., pl.* **-ries 1** something extra or complementary **2** one who, though absent, helps another to break the law

ac·ci·dent (ak′sə dənt) *n.* ⟦< L *ad-*, to + *cadere*, to fall⟧ **1** an unintended happening **2** a mishap **3** chance

ac′ci·den′tal (-dent′′l) *adj.* happening by chance —**ac′ci·den′tally** *adv.*

ac′cident-prone′ (-prōn′) *adj.* seemingly inclined to become involved in accidents

ac·claim (ə klām′) *vt.* ⟦< L *ad-*, to + *clamare*, to cry out⟧ to greet or announce with loud approval or applause; hail — *n.* loud approval

ac·cla·ma·tion (ak′lə mā′shən) *n.* **1** loud applause or approval **2** an approving vote by voice

ac·cli·mate (ə klī′mət, ak′lə māt′) *vt., vi.* **-mated, -mating** ⟦< L *ad-*, to + Gr *klima*, region⟧ to accustom or become accustomed to a new climate or environment Also **ac·cli′ma·tize′, -tized′, -tiz′ing** —**ac′cli·ma′tion** *n.*

ac·cliv·ity (ə kliv′ə tē) *n., pl.* **-ties** ⟦< L *ad-*, up + *clivus*, hill⟧ an upward slope

ac·co·lade (ak′ə lād′) *n.* ⟦< L *ad*, to + *collum*, neck⟧ an approving mention; award

ac·com·mo·date (ə käm′ə dāt′) *vt.* **-dat′ed, -dat′ing** ⟦< L *ad-*, to + *commodare*, to fit⟧ **1** to adapt **2** to do a favor for **3** to have space for; lodge

ac·com′mo·dat′ing *adj.* obliging

ac·com′mo·da′tion *n.* **1** adjustment **2** willingness to do favors **3** a help; convenience **4** [*pl.*] *a)* lodgings *b)* traveling space, as in a train

ac·com·pa·ni·ment (ə kum′pə nə mənt, -nē-; ə kump′nə-, -nē-) *n.* anything that accompanies something else, as an instrumental part supporting a solo voice, etc.

ac·com·pany (ə kum′pə nē, ə kump′nē) *vt.* **-nied, -ny·ing** ⟦see AD- & COMPANION⟧ **1** to go with **2** to add to **3** to play or sing an accompaniment for or to —**ac·com′pa·nist** *n.*

ac·com·plice (ə käm′plis) *n.* ⟦< ME *a* (the article) + LL *complex*, a confederate⟧ a partner in crime

ac·com·plish (ə käm′plish) *vt.* ⟦< L *ad-*, intens. + *complere*, fill up⟧ to succeed in doing; complete

ac·com′plished *adj.* **1** done; completed **2** skilled; expert

ac·com′plish·ment *n.* **1** completion **2** work completed; an achievement **3** a social art or skill

ac·cord (ə kôrd′) *vt.* ⟦< L *ad-*, to + *cor*, heart⟧ **1** to make

---

THESAURUS

academic *a.* scholastic, erudite, scholarly; see LEARNED.

academy *n.* preparatory school, boarding school, finishing school, secondary school, prep school; see also SCHOOL 1.

accelerate *v.* quicken, speed up, hurry; see HASTEN 2.

acceleration *n.* speeding up, hastening, increase of speed, quickening, hurrying, stepping up, picking up speed; see also SPEED.

accent *n.* stress, beat, stroke, emphasis, pitch, accentuation, inflection, intonation, rhythm, meter, cadence.

accept *v.* receive, get, admit, be resigned, give into, believe, trust, surrender, suffer, endure, grant, allow, tolerate, take in one's stride, consent, acquiesce; see also AGREE.

acceptable *a.* satisfactory, agreeable, pleasing; see PLEASANT 2.

acceptance *n.* recognition, assent, approval; see AGREEMENT 1.

accepted *a.* taken, received, assumed, approved, adopted, recognized, endorsed, verified, acclaimed, welcomed, engaged, hired, claimed, delivered, used, employed, affirmed, upheld, authorized, preferred, acknowledged, accredited, allowed, settled, established, sanctioned, unopposed, customary, authentic, confirmed, chosen, acceptable, popular, formally admitted, stereotyped,

orthodox, standard, conventional, current, taken for granted, credited, OK'd; see also POPULAR 1, 3.—*Ant.* REFUSED, denied, nullified.

access *n.* admittance, entree, introduction; see ENTRANCE 1, 2.

accessible *a.* approachable, obtainable, attainable; see AVAILABLE.

accessories *n.* frills, ornaments, adornments, decorations, additions, attachments, gimmicks*, doodads*.

accessory *n.* **1** [An accomplice] helper, aid, assistant; see ASSOCIATE. **2** [Something added] attachment, consequence, attendant, complement, supplement, addition.

accident *n.* luck, fortune, contingency, occurrence, circumstance, event, occasion; see also CHANCE 1.

accidental *a.* adventitious, chance, coincidental; see AIMLESS, UNFORTUNATE.

accidentally *a.* unintentionally, involuntarily, unwittingly, unexpectedly, inadvertently, casually, by chance, haphazardly, incidentally, randomly, not purposely, by a fluke*.—*Ant.* DELIBERATELY, voluntarily, intentionally.

accommodate *v.* **1** [To render a service] help, aid, comfort, make comfortable, oblige, suit, serve, gratify, please, arrange, settle, provide, benefit, tender, supply, furnish, assist, support, sustain, do a favor,

indulge, humor, pamper, accept, put oneself out for, do a service for. **2** [To suit one thing to another] fit, adapt, correspond; see ADJUST 1. **3** [To provide lodging] house, rent, give lodging to; see ENTERTAIN 2.

accommodations *n.* quarters, rooms, lodging, housing, apartment, hotel, room and board, roof over one's head; see also HOME 1.

accompanied *a.* attended, escorted, tended, shown around, shown about, chaperoned, not alone.

accompaniment *n.* harmony, instrumental music, musical background; see MUSIC 1.

accompany *v.* escort, attend, tend, be with, follow, keep company with, guard, guide, usher, show in, show around, show the way, conduct, go along, go along with, chaperon, associate with, consort with, look after, go hand in hand, go side by side with, hang around with*.

accomplice *n.* confederate, helper, aid; see ASSOCIATE.

accomplish *v.* fulfill, perform, finish; see ACHIEVE, SUCCEED 1.

accomplished *a.* **1** [Done] completed, consummated, concluded; see FINISHED. **2** [Skilled] proficient, expert, skillful; see ABLE.

accomplishment *n.* execution, fulfillment, attainment; see SUCCESS 2.

agree **2** to grant **—vi.** to agree; harmonize (*with*) **—n.** mutual agreement; harmony **—of one's own accord** willingly **—with one accord** all agreeing

ac·cord′ance *n.* agreement; conformity **—ac·cord′ant** *adj.*

ac·cord′ing *adj.* in harmony **—according to 1** in agreement with **2** as stated by

ac·cord′ing·ly *adv.* **1** in a fitting and proper way **2** therefore

ac·cor·dion (ə kôr′dē ən) *n.* ⟦prob. < It *accordare*, to be in tune⟧ a keyed musical instrument with a bellows, which is pressed to force air through reeds

ac·cost (ə kôst′) *vt.* ⟦< L *ad-*, to + *costa*, side⟧ to approach and speak to, esp. in a bold or forward way

ac·count (ə kount′) *vt.* ⟦< OFr *a-*, to + *conter*, tell⟧ to judge to be **—vi. 1** to give a financial reckoning (*to*) **2** to give reasons (*for*) **—n. 1** a counting **2** [*often pl.*] a record of business transactions **3** *a*) BANK ACCOUNT *b*) CHARGE ACCOUNT **4** a credit customer or client **5** worth; importance **6** an explanation **7** a report **—on account** as partial payment **—on account of** because of **—on no account** under no circumstances **—take into account** to consider

ac·count′a·ble *adj.* **1** responsible; liable **2** explainable **—ac·count′a·bil′i·ty** *n.*

ac·count·ant (ə kount′'nt) *n.* one whose work is accounting

ac·count′ing *n.* the figuring and recording of financial accounts

ac·cou·ter (ə kōōt′ər) *vt.* ⟦prob. < L *consuere*, to sew⟧ to outfit; equip

ac·cou·ter·ments or **ac·cou·tre·ments** (ə kōōt′ər mənts, -kōō′trə-) *n.pl.* **1** clothes **2** a soldier's equipment

ac·credit (ə kred′it) *vt.* ⟦see CREDIT⟧ **1** to authorize; certify **2** to believe in **3** to attribute **—ac·cred′i·ta′tion** (-ə tā′shən) *n.*

ac·cre·tion (ə krē′shən) *n.* ⟦< L *ad-*, to + *crescere*, to grow⟧ **1** growth in size, esp. by addition **2** accumulated matter **3** a growing together of parts

ac·crue (ə krōō′) *vi.* **-crued′, -cru′ing** ⟦see prec.⟧ to come as a natural growth or periodic increase, as interest on money **—ac·cru′al** *n.*

acct. account

ac·cul·tur·ate (ə kul′chər āt′) *vi., vt.* **-at′ed, -at′ing** to undergo, or change by, acculturation

ac·cul·tura·tion (ə kul′chər ā′shən) *n.* **1** adaptation to a culture, esp. a new or different one **2** mutual influence of different cultures

ac·cu·mu·late (ə kyōōm′yōō lāt′, -yə-) *vt., vi.* **-lat′ed, -lat′ ing** ⟦< L *ad-*, to + *cumulare*, to heap⟧ to pile up or collect **—ac·cu′mu·la′tion** *n.* **—ac·cu′mu·la′tive** *adj.*

ac·cu·racy (ak′yoor ə sē, -yər-) *n.* the state of being accurate; precision

ac′cu·rate (-it) *adj.* ⟦< L *ad-*, to + *cura*, care⟧ **1** careful and exact **2** free from errors; precise **—ac′cu·rate·ly** *adv.* **—ac′cu·rate·ness** *n.*

ac·cursed (ə kur′sid, -kurst′) *adj.* **1** under a curse **2** damnable Also **ac·curst′ —ac·curs′ed·ness** *n.*

ac·cu·sa·tion (ak′yōō zā′shən, -yə-) *n.* **1** an accusing **2** what one is accused of **—ac·cu·sa·tory** (ə kyōō′zə tôr′ē) *adj.*

ac·cu·sa·tive (ə kyōō′zə tiv) *n.* ⟦see fol.⟧ *Gram.* the case of the direct object of a verb; also, the objective case in English

ac·cuse (ə kyōōz′) *vt.* **-cused′, -cus′ing** ⟦< L *ad-*, to + *causa*, a cause⟧ **1** to blame **2** to bring charges against **—ac·cus′er** *n.*

ac·cus·tom (ə kus′təm) *vt.* to make familiar by custom, habit, or use

ac·cus′tomed *adj.* **1** customary; usual **2** used (*to*); in the habit of

AC/DC or **A.C./D.C.** (ā′sē′dē′sē′) *adj.* ⟦< a(*lternating*) *c*(*urrent or*) *d*(*irect*) *c*(*urrent*)⟧ [Slang] bisexual

ace (ās) *n.* ⟦< L *as*, unit⟧ **1** a playing card, etc. with one spot **2** a point, as in tennis, won by a single stroke **3** *Golf* a hole in one **4** an expert, esp. in combat flying **—adj.** [Colloq.] first-rate **—vt. aced, ac′ing 1** [Slang] to defeat completely: often with *out* **2** [Colloq.] to earn a grade of A in, on, etc.

Ace bandage *trademark for* an elasticized cloth bandage used to provide support, as for a sprain

ace in the hole [Slang] any advantage held in reserve

ac·er·bate (as′ər bāt′) *vt.* **-bat′ed, -bat′ing** ⟦< L *acerbare*⟧ **1** to make sour or bitter **2** to irritate; vex

acer·bity (ə sur′bə tē) *n., pl.* **-ties** ⟦< L *acerbus*, bitter⟧ **1** sourness **2** sharpness of temper, words, etc. **—acer′bic** *adj.*

ac·eta·mino·phen (as′i ə min′ə fən; ə sē′tə-) *n.* a crystalline powder used to lessen fever and pain

ac·et·ani·lide (as′ət an′ə lid′) *n.* ⟦< ACETIC + ANILINE⟧ a drug used to lessen pain and fever

ac·etate (as′i tāt′) *n.* **1** a salt or ester of acetic acid **2** something, esp. a fabric, made with an acetate of cellulose

a·cetic (ə sēt′ik) *adj.* ⟦< L *acetum*, vinegar⟧ of the sharp, sour liquid (**acetic acid**) found in vinegar

ac·etone (as′i tōn′) *n.* ⟦see prec.⟧ a colorless, flammable liquid used as a solvent, esp. in making rayon **—ac′eton′ic** (-tän′ik) *adj.*

acety·lene (ə set′'l ēn′) *n.* a gas used for lighting and, with oxygen, in welding

acetyl·sali·cylic acid (ə set′'l sal′ə sil′ik) ASPIRIN

ache (āk) *vi.* **ached, ach′ing** ⟦< OE *acan*⟧ **1** to have or give dull, steady pain **2** [Colloq.] to yearn **—n.** a dull, continuous pain **—ach′y** *adj.*

achene (ā kēn′, ə-) *n.* ⟦< Gr *a-*, not + *chainein*, to gape⟧ any small, dry fruit with one seed

━━━━━━ THESAURUS ━━━━━━

accordingly *a.* in consequence, consequently, equally, respectively, duly, subsequently, in respect to, thus, hence, therefore, as a result, as a consequence, as the case may be, on the ground, under the circumstances, as things go, to that end, in that event.

according to *prep.* in accordance with, as, to the degree that, conforming to, just as, in keeping with, in line with, in agreement with, consistent with.

account *n.* bulletin, annual, report; see RECORD 1. **—give a good account of oneself** acquit oneself creditably, do well, do oneself proud*, behave courageously. **—on account** charged, in layaway, on layaway, on call; see also UNPAID 1. **—on account of** because of, by virtue of, since; see BECAUSE. **—on no account** for no reason, no way, under no circumstances; see NEVER. **—on someone's account** because of someone, for someone's sake, in someone's behalf; see BECAUSE. **— take account of** judge, evaluate, investigate; see EXAMINE 1. **—take into account** judge, allow for, weigh; see CONSIDER.

accountant *n.* bookkeeper, auditor,

CPA; see CLERK.

account for *v.* clarify, resolve, elucidate; see EXPLAIN.

accumulate *v.* hoard, get together, gather, gather into a mass, collect, heap, store, assemble, concentrate, compile, provide, pile up, accrue, scrape up, stockpile, store up, acquire, gain, load up, rake up, unite, add to, profit, build up, gain control, roll in*, bank*; see also GET 1.

accuracy *n.* efficiency, exactness, precision, correctness, skillfulness, sharpness, incisiveness, mastery, dependability, strictness, certainty, sureness.—*Ant.* ERROR, inaccuracy, mistake.

accurate *a.* **1** [Free from error] exact, correct, perfect; see RIGHT 1. **2** [Characterized by precision] deft, reliable, trustworthy, true, correct, exact, specific, dependable, skillful, methodical, systematic, distinct, particular, realistic, authentic, genuine, careful, close, critical, detailed, factual, severe, rigorous, rigid, strict, meticulous, sharp, faithful, punctual, scientific, objective, matter-of-fact, rational, unmistakable, reasonable, right, explicit, definite, defined, on the button*, on the spot*, on the

nose*, solid.—*Ant.* INCOMPETENT, faulty, slipshod.

accurately *a.* correctly, precisely, exactly; see CAREFULLY 1.

accusation *n.* indictment, allegation, denunciation, slur, complaint, citation, charge, insinuation, beef*, smear*, frame-up*, rap*.

accuse *v.* denounce, charge, prosecute; see BLAME.

accused *a.* arraigned, indicted, incriminated, charged with, under suspicion, alleged to be guilty, apprehended, held for questioning, liable, involved, under attack, under fire, up for.—*Ant.* DISCHARGED, acquitted, cleared.

accuser *n.* prosecutor, plaintiff, adversary; see OPPONENT 1.

accustomed *a.* usual, customary, habitual; see CONVENTIONAL 1. **—accustomed to** in the habit of, used to, inclined to; see ADDICTED (TO).

ace *n.* expert, master, champion; see SPECIALIST.

ace *a.* expert, first-rate, outstanding; see DISTINGUISHED 2, ABLE.

ache *n.* twinge, pang, spasm; see PAIN 2.

ache *v.* pain, throb, be sore; see HURT.

achieve (ə chēv′) *vt.* **achieved′, achiev′ing** [< OFr < a-, to + L *caput*, head] **1** to do successfully **2** to get by effort —**achiev′able** *adj.*

achieve′ment *n.* **1** an achieving **2** a thing achieved; feat

Achil·les (ə kil′ēz′) a Greek hero killed in the Trojan War

Achilles' heel (one's) vulnerable spot

achro·matic (ak′rō mat′ik; -rə-) *adj.* [< Gr a-, without + *chrōma*, color] refracting white light without breaking it up into its component colors

acid (as′id) *adj.* [L *acidus*, sour] **1** sour; sharp; tart **2** of an acid —*n.* **1** a sour substance **2** [Slang] LSD **3** *Chem.* any compound that reacts with a base to form a salt — **acid·ity** (ə sid′ə tē), *pl.* **-ties,** *n.* —**ac′idly** *adv.*

acidi·fy (ə sid′ə fī′) *vt., vi.* **-fied′, -fy′ing 1** to make or become sour **2** to change into an acid

aci·do·sis (as′ə dō′sis) *n.* a condition in which there is an abnormal retention of acid or loss of alkali in the body

acid rain rain with a high concentration of acids produced by the gases from burning fossil fuels

acid test a crucial, final test

acidu·lous (ə sij′ŏŏ ləs) *adj.* **1** somewhat acid or sour **2** sarcastic

-acious (ā′shəs) [< L] *suffix* inclined to, full of [*tenacious*]

-acity (as′ə tē) [< L] *suffix* a (specified) characteristic, quality, or tendency [*tenacity*]

ac·knowl·edge (ak näl′ij, ək-) *vt.* **-edged, -edg·ing** [see KNOWLEDGE] **1** to admit as true **2** to recognize the authority or claims of **3** to respond to **4** to express thanks for **5** to state that one has received (a letter, etc.) —**ac·knowl′edg·ment** or **ac·knowl′edge·ment** *n.*

ACLU American Civil Liberties Union

acme (ak′mē) *n.* [Gr *akmē*, a point, top] the highest point; peak

acne (ak′nē) *n.* [see prec.] a skin disorder usually causing pimples on the face, etc.

aco·lyte (ak′ə līt′) *n.* [< Gr *akolouthos*, follower] **1** an altar boy **2** an attendant; helper

aco·nite (ak′ə nīt′) *n.* [< Gr] a plant with hoodlike flowers

acorn (ā′kôrn′) *n.* [< OE *æcern*, nut] the nut of the oak tree

acorn squash a kind of winter squash, acorn-shaped with dark-green skin and yellow flesh

acous·tic (ə kōōs′tik) *adj.* [< Gr *akouein*, to hear] **1** having to do with hearing or acoustics **2** of or using a musical instrument that is not amplified Also **acous′ti·cal** —**acous′ti·cally** *adv.*

acous′tics (-tiks) *n.pl.* **1** the qualities of a room, etc. that determine how clearly sounds can be heard in it **2** [*with sing. v.*] the branch of physics dealing with sound

ac·quaint (ə kwānt′) *vt.* [< L *ad-*, to + *cognoscere*, know] **1** to inform **2** to make familiar (*with*)

ac·quaint′ance *n.* **1** knowledge got from personal experience **2** a person whom one knows slightly

ac·qui·esce (ak′wē es′) *vi.* **-esced′, -esc′ing** [< L *ad-*, to + *quiescere*, grow quiet] to consent without protest: often with *in* —**ac′qui·es′cence** *n.* —**ac′qui·es′cent** *adj.*

ac·quire (ə kwīr′) *vt.* **-quired′, -quir′ing** [< L *ad-*, to + *quaerere*, to seek] **1** to gain by one's own efforts **2** to get as one's own —**ac·quir′able** *adj.* —**ac·quire′ment** *n.*

ac·qui·si·tion (ak′wə zish′ən) *n.* **1** an acquiring **2** something acquired

ac·quis·i·tive (ə kwiz′ə tiv) *adj.* eager to acquire (money, etc.); grasping —**ac·quis′i·tive·ness** *n.*

ac·quit (ə kwit′) *vt.* **-quit′ted, -quit′ting** [< L *ad-*, to + *quietare*, to quiet] **1** to release from an obligation, etc. **2** to clear (a person) of a charge **3** to conduct (oneself); behave —**ac·quit′tal** *n.*

acre (ā′kər) *n.* [OE *æcer*, field] a measure of land, 43,560 sq. ft.

a′cre·age′ (-ij′) *n.* acres collectively

ac·rid (ak′rid) *adj.* [< L *acris*, sharp] **1** sharp or bitter to the taste or smell **2** sharp in speech, etc. —**acrid·ity** (ə krid′ə tē) *n.* —**ac′ridly** *adv.*

ac·ri·mony (ak′ri mō′nē) *n., pl.* **-nies** [< L *acer*, sharp] bitterness or harshness of manner or speech —**ac′ri·mo′ni·ous** *adj.*

acro·bat (ak′rə bat′) *n.* [< Gr *akrobatos*, walking on tiptoe] a performer on the trapeze, tightrope, etc.; gymnast —**ac′ro·bat′ic** *adj.*

ac′ro·bat′ics (-iks) *n.pl.* [*also with sing v.*] **1** an acrobat's tricks **2** any tricks requiring great skill

acro·nym (ak′rə nim′) *n.* [< Gr *akros*, at the end + *onyma*, name] a word formed from the first (or first few) letters of several words, as *radar*

acro·pho·bia (ak′rō fō′bē ə) *n.* [< Gr *akros*, at the top + PHOBIA] an abnormal fear of being in high places

Acrop·o·lis (ə kräp′ə lis) [< Gr *akros*, at the top + *polis*, city] the fortified hill in Athens on which the Parthenon was built

across (ə krôs′) *adv.* **1** crosswise **2** from one side to the other —*prep.* **1** from one side to the other of **2** on or to

achieve *v.* complete, end, terminate, conclude, finish, finish up, finish off, do, perform, execute, fulfill, carry out, carry through, bring about, settle, effect, bring to a conclusion, close, stop, produce, realize, actualize, discharge, wind up, work out, adjust, resolve, solve, accomplish, make an end of, enact, manage, contrive, negotiate, sign, seal, bring to pass, see it through, get done, close up, put the lid on, carry to completion, follow through, take measures, lose oneself in, deliver, knock off*, fill the bill*, round out*, come through, polish off*, clean up*, mop up*, put across*, pull off*, make short work of, put through, go all the way*, go the limit*, call it a day*, put the finishing touch on*, dispose of.—*Ant.* ABANDON, fail, give up.

achievement *n.* fulfillment, feat, exploit, accomplishment, triumph, hit, success, realization, creation, completion, execution, actualization, masterpiece, performance, deed, act, enactment, victory, conquest, attainment, feather in one's cap.—*Ant.* FAILURE, blunder, collapse.

acid *a.* sharp, tart, biting; see SOUR.

acid *n.* **1** [A sour substance] strong acid, weak acid, corrosive, Lewis acid. **2** [A drug] LSD, DMT, mescaline; see DRUG. *Common acids include the following:* vinegar, verjuice, lemon juice; citric, ascorbic, nicotinic, boric, acetic, sulfuric, hydrochloric, formic, stearic, phosphoric, carbolic, nitric, benzoic, amino, fatty acid.

acidity *n.* sourness, bitterness, tartness, sharpness, pungency, harshness, causticity.

acknowledge *v.* **1** [To admit] concede, confess, declare; see ADMIT 2. **2** [To recognize the authority of] endorse, certify, confirm, uphold, support, recognize, ratify, approve, defend, subscribe to, accede to, attest to, take an oath by, defer to.

acknowledged *a.* admitted, confessed, recognized, unquestioned, accepted, authorized, confirmed, received, sanctioned, accredited, approved, out-and-out.

acknowledgment *n.* greeting, reply, answer, response, nod, confession, statement, apology, guarantee, return, support, signature, receipt, letter, card, contract, applause, vote of thanks, IOU.

acquaintance *n.* **1** [A person one knows] colleague, associate, neighbor; see FRIEND. **2** [Acquired knowledge] familiarity, awareness, experience; see AWARENESS, EXPERIENCE.

acquainted (with) *a.* introduced, on speaking terms, having some connections; see FAMILIAR WITH.

acquaint with *v.* introduce, make acquainted, present; see INTRODUCE 3.

acquire *v.* take, earn, procure; see GET 1.

acquired *a.* reached, inherited, given, accrued, derived, granted, endowed, transmitted, handed down, bequeathed, allowed, awarded, passed on, willed to, attained, accomplished, learned, adopted, earned, collected, gathered, harvested, secured, procured, obtained, captured, regained, realized, gotten by the sweat of one's brow*, dug out*, raked in*, cornered*, netted*, salted away*, grabbed; see also WON.

acquisition *n.* inheritance, gift, donation, grant, wealth, riches, fortune, profit, gain, earnings, wages, salary, income, winnings, return, returns, proceeds, benefit, prize, reward, award, accomplishment, achievement, premium, bonus, fee, commission, pension, annuity, allowance, gain, dividend.

acquit *v.* clear, absolve, vindicate; see EXCUSE.

acquittal *n.* absolution, clearance, exoneration, dismissal, deliverance, amnesty, discharge, pardon, reprieve, exemption, liberation, release, freedom.—*Ant.* PUNISHMENT, sentence, imprisonment.

acre *n.* plot, acreage, bit of land, estate; see also PROPERTY 2.

acrobat *n.* tumbler, clown, trampolinist, aerialist, trapeze artist, contortionist, performer, tightrope walker, stunt man, figure skater, vaudeville performer, ballet dancer, gymnast.

across *a., prep.* crosswise, crossed, to the opposite side of, over, opposite, on the other side, from side to side of, from one side to another, the other side of 3 into contact with by chance /to come **across** an old friend/

across'-the-board' *adj.* 1 combining win, place, and show, as a bet 2 affecting all classes or groups

acros·tic (ə krôs'tik) *n.* ⟦Gr *akrostichos* < *akros*, at the end + *stichos*, line of verse⟧ a poem, etc. in which certain letters in each line, as the first or last, spell out a word, motto, etc.

acryl·ic (ə kril'ik) *adj.* 1 designating any of a group of synthetic fibers used to make fabrics 2 designating any of a group of clear, synthetic resins used to make paints, plastics, etc.

act (akt) *n.* ⟦< L *agere*, to do⟧ 1 a thing done 2 a doing 3 a law 4 a main division of a drama or opera 5 a short performance, as on a variety show 6 something done merely for show — *vt.* to perform in (a play or part) — *vi.* 1 to perform in a play, movie, etc. 2 to behave 3 to function 4 to have an effect (*on*) 5 to appear to be —**act up** [Colloq.] to misbehave

ACTH ⟦*a(dreno)c(ortico)t(ropic) h(ormone)*⟧ a pituitary hormone that acts on the adrenal cortex

act·ing (ak'tiŋ) *adj.* temporarily doing the duties of another — *n.* the art of an actor

ac·ti·nide series (ak'tə nīd') a group of radioactive chemical elements from element 89 (actinium) through element 103 (lawrencium)

ac·tin·i·um (ak tin'ē əm) *n.* ⟦< Gr *aktis*, ray⟧ a white, metallic radioactive chemical element

ac·tion (ak'shən) *n.* 1 the doing of something 2 a thing done 3 [*pl.*] behavior 4 the way of working, as of a machine 5 the moving parts, as of a gun 6 the sequence of events, as in a story 7 a lawsuit 8 military combat 9 [Slang] activity

ac·ti·vate (ak'tə vāt') *vt.* -vat'ed, -vat'ing 1 to make active 2 to put (a military unit) on active status 3 to make radioactive 4 to purify sewage by aeration —**ac'ti·va'tion** *n.* —**ac'ti·va'tor** *n.*

activated carbon a form of highly porous carbon that can adsorb gases, vapors, and colloidal particles

ac·tive (ak'tiv) *adj.* 1 acting; working 2 causing motion or change 3 lively; agile 4 indicating the voice of a verb whose subject performs the action —**ac'tively** *adv.*

ac'tiv·ism' (-tə viz'əm) *n.* the taking of direct action to achieve a political or social end —**ac'tiv·ist** *adj.*, *n.*

ac·tiv·i·ty (ak tiv'ə tē) *n.*, *pl.* -ties 1 a being active 2 liveliness 3 a specific action /student *activities*/

ac·tor (ak'tər) *n.* 1 one who does a thing 2 one who acts in plays, movies, etc. —**ac'tress** *n.fem.*

ac·tual (ak'chōō əl) *adj.* ⟦< L *agere*, to do⟧ 1 existing in reality 2 existing at the time —**ac'tu·ally** *adv.*

ac·tu·al·i·ty (-al'ə tē) *n.* 1 reality 2 *pl.* -ties an actual thing

ac·tu·al·ize' (-əl iz') *vt.* -ized', -iz'ing 1 to make actual or real 2 to make realistic

ac·tu·ar·y (ak'chōō er'ē) *n.*, *pl.* -ies ⟦L *actuarius*, clerk⟧ one who figures insurance risks, premiums, etc. —**ac'tu·ar'ial** *adj.*

ac·tu·ate (ak'chōō āt') *vt.* -at'ed, -at'ing 1 to put into action 2 to impel to action —**ac'tua'tor** *n.*

acu·i·ty (ə kyōō'ə tē) *n.* ⟦< L *acus*, needle⟧ keenness of thought or vision

acu·men (ə kyōō'mən) *n.* ⟦< L *acuere*, sharpen⟧ keenness of mind or insight

acu·punc·ture (ak'yōō puŋk'chər) *n.* ⟦< L *acus*, needle + PUNCTURE⟧ the ancient practice, esp. among the Chinese, of piercing parts of the body with needles to treat disease or relieve pain —**ac'u·punc'tur·ist** *n.*

acute (ə kyōōt') *adj.* ⟦< L *acuere*, sharpen⟧ 1 sharp-pointed 2 keen of mind 3 sensitive /*acute* hearing/ 4 severe, as pain 5 severe but not chronic /an *acute* disease/ 6 very serious 7 less than 90° /*acute* angles/ —**acute'ly** *adv.* —**acute'ness** *n.*

acute accent a mark (ˊ) showing primary stress, the quality of a vowel, etc.

-acy (ə sē) ⟦ult. < Gr⟧ *suffix* quality, condition, etc. /*supremacy*/

acy·clo·vir (ā sī'klō vir') *n.* a synthetic powder used in the treatment of certain viral infections, as herpes

---

THESAURUS

transversely, in front of, opposite to, beyond.

act *n.* 1 [An action] deed, performance, exploit; see ACTION 2. 2 [An official or legal statement] law, proposal, judgment, order, commitment, verdict, amendment, announcement, edict, ordinance, decree, statute, writ, bull, warrant, summons, subpoena, document, bill, code, clause, law of the land*. 3 [A division of a play] scene, prologue, epilogue, introduction; first act, second act, third act, etc. 4 [A pose] falsification, feigning, affectation; see PRETENSE 1.

act *v.* 1 [To perform an action] do, execute, carry out, carry on, operate, transact, accomplish, achieve, consummate, carry into, effect, perpetrate, persist, labor, work, officiate, function, preside, serve, go ahead, step into, take steps, play a part, begin, move in, enforce, maneuver, operate, create, practice, develop, make progress, interfere, interpose, be active, intrude, commit, fight, combat, respond, keep going, answer, pursue, put forth energy, hustle*, get going*. —*Ant.* WAIT, await, rest. 2 [To conduct oneself] behave, seem, appear, carry oneself, give the appearance of, represent oneself, take on, play one's part, impress one as, put on airs*; see also BEHAVE. 3 [To take part in a play] perform, impersonate, represent, act out, simulate, pretend, mimic, burlesque, parody, feign, portray, rehearse, take a part in, dramatize, star, play the part of, debut. —**act up** goof off*, be naughty, create a disturbance; see MISBEHAVE. —**act upon (or on)** 1 [To act in accordance with] adjust, regulate, behave; see ACT 1, 2. 2 [To influence] affect, sway, impress; see

INFLUENCE.

acting *a.* substituting, alternate, assistant; see TEMPORARY.

acting *n.* pretending, feigning, simulating, gesturing, ranting, dramatizing, performing, behaving, playing, showing off, impersonation, depiction, portrayal, pantomime, rendition, dramatics, theatricals, performance, dramatic action, mime.

action *n.* 1 [Any state opposed to rest and quiet] activity, conflict, business, occupation, work, response, reaction, movement, industry, bustle, turmoil, stir, flurry, animation, vivacity, enterprise, energy, liveliness, alertness, agility, vigor, life, commotion, rush, motion, mobility, haste, speed, go*, life, doings*. 2 [An individual deed] feat, exploit, performance, performing, execution, blow, stroke, maneuver, step, stunt, achievement, act, deed, thing, stratagem, something done, accomplishment, commision, effort, enterprise, manipulation, move, movement, doing, effect, transaction, exertion, operation, handiwork, dealings, procedure, manufacture. —**bring action** accuse, start a lawsuit, take to court; see SUE. —**see action** do battle, engage in combat, conflict; see FIGHT. —**take action** become active, do, initiate activity; see ACT 1.

actions *n.* deportment, conduct, manners; see BEHAVIOR.

activate *v.* stimulate, initiate, arouse; see BEGIN 1.

active *a.* busy, eventful, lively, dynamic, energetic, alive, mobile, hasty, going, rapid, progressive, speedy, walking, traveling, movable, bustling, humming, efficient, functioning, working, moving, restless,

swarming, rustling, flowing, in process, in effect, in force, simmering, overflowing, streaming, stirring, effective, at work, operating, operative, agitated, brisk, industrious, enthusiastic, agile, quick, nimble, rapid, dexterous, spry, fresh, sprightly, frisky, wiry, alert, ready, sharp, keen, wide-awake, animated, enlivened, ardent, purposeful, persevering, resolute, aggressive, forceful, intense, determined, diligent, hard-working, assiduous, enterprising, inventive, vigorous, strenuous, eager, zealous, bold, daring, dashing, high-spirited, hopping*, going full blast, in high gear*, snappy*, on the ball*, peppy*, turned on to*.

activity *n.* motion, movement, liveliness; see ACTION 1.

actor *n.* player, performer, character, star, comedian, impersonator, leading man, leading woman, entertainer, artist, television star, villain, motion picture actor, stage player, supporting actor, mimic, mime, clown, ventriloquist, pantomimist, understudy, Thespian, protagonist, leading hit player*, ham*, extra, movie idol; see also CAST 2.

actress *n.* comedienne, starlet, leading lady; see ACTOR, CAST 2.

actual *a.* original, real, exact; see GENUINE 1.

actually *a.* truly, in fact, as a matter of fact; see REALLY 1.

acute *a.* 1 [Crucial] decisive, important, vital; see CRITICAL. 2 [Sharp] severe, keen, cutting; see INTENSE. 3 [Shrewd] clever, bright, perceptive; see INTELLIGENT.

acutely *a.* keenly, sharply, severely; see VERY.

ad (ad) *n.* [Colloq.] an advertisement

ad- [L] *prefix* motion toward, addition to, nearness to: becomes a-, ac-, af-, ag-, al-, an-, etc. before certain consonants

AD or **A.D.** *abbrev.* [L *Anno Domini,* in the year of the Lord] of the Christian era: used with dates

ad·age (ad'ij) *n.* [< L *ad-,* to + *aio,* I say] an old saying; proverb

ada·gio (ə dä'jō, -zhō) *adv.* [It *ad agio,* at ease] *Music* slowly —*adj.* slow —*n., pl.* **-gios** 1 a slow movement in music 2 a slow ballet dance

Adam (ad'əm) [Heb < *adam,* a human being] *Bible* the first man

ada·mant (ad'ə mənt) *n.* [< Gr *a-,* not + *daman,* subdue] a very hard substance —*adj.* inflexible; unyielding

Adam's apple the projection of cartilage in the front of the throat, esp. of a man

adapt (ə dapt') *vt.* [< L *ad-,* to + *aptare,* to fit] 1 to make suitable, esp. by changing 2 to adjust (oneself) to new circumstances —**ad·ap·ta·tion** (ad'əp tā'shən) *n.*

adapt'able *adj.* able to adjust or be adjusted —**adapt'abil'ity** *n.*

add (ad) *vt.* [< L *ad-,* to + *dare,* to give] 1 to join (to) so as to increase 2 to state further 3 to combine (numbers) into a sum —*vi.* 1 to cause an increase (to) 2 to find a sum —**add up** to seem reasonable —**add up to** to mean; signify —**add'able** or **add'ible** *adj.*

ad·dend (ad'end') *n.* [< fol.] *Math.* a number or quantity to be added to another

ad·den·dum (ə den'dəm) *n., pl.* **-da** (-də) [L] a thing added, as an appendix

ad·der (ad'ər) *n.* [< OE *nædre*] 1 a poisonous snake of Europe 2 any of various other snakes, some harmless

ad·dict (ə dikt'; *for n.,* ad'ikt) *vt.* [< L *addicere,* give assent] 1 to give (oneself) up *to* a strong habit 2 to cause to become addicted —*n.* one addicted to a habit, as to using drugs —**ad·dic'tion** *n.* —**ad·dic'tive** *adj.*

ad·di·tion (ə dish'ən) *n.* 1 an adding of numbers to get a sum 2 a joining of one thing to another 3 a part added —**in addition (to)** besides

ad·di'tional (-əl) *adj.* added; more; extra —**ad·di'tion·al·ly** *adv.*

ad·di·tive (ad'ə tiv) *adj.* of addition —*n.* something added

ad·dle (ad''l) *vi., vt.* **-dled, -dling** [< OE *adela,* mud] to make or become confused

add'-on' *n.* an optional item that can be purchased to supplement another consumer item

ad·dress (ə dres'; *for n. esp. 2, 3, & 5, also* a'dres') *vt.* [< L *dirigere,* to direct] 1 to direct (words) *to* 2 to speak or write *to* 3 to write the destination on (a letter, etc.) 4 to apply (oneself) *to* —*n.* 1 a speech 2 the place where one lives or receives mail 3 the destination indicated on an envelope 4 skill; tact 5 a computer code identifying the location of an item of information

ad·dressee (a'dres ē') *n.* the person to whom mail, etc. is addressed

ad·duce (ə dōōs') *vt.* **-duced', -duc'ing** [< L *ad-,* to + *ducere,* to lead] to give as a reason or proof

-ade (ād) [ult. < L] *suffix* 1 the act of _____ing *[blockade]* 2 participant(s) in an action *[brigade]* 3 [after LEMONADE] drink made from *[limeade]*

ad·enine (ad'ə nēn') *n.* a purine base contained in the DNA, RNA, and ADP of all tissue

ad·enoids (ad''n oidz', ad'noidz') *n.pl.* [< Gr *adēn,* gland + -OID] lymphoid growths in the throat behind the nose: they can obstruct nasal breathing

adept (ə dept') *adj.* [< L *ad-,* to + *apisci,* attain] highly skilled —*n.* **ad·ept** (ad'ept') an expert —**adept'ly** *adv.* —**adept'ness** *n.*

ad·equate (ad'i kwət) *adj.* [< L *ad-,* to + *aequus,* equal] enough for what is required; sufficient; suitable —**ad'equa·cy** (-kwə sē) *n.* —**ad'equate·ly** *adv.*

ad·here (ad hir', əd-) *vi.* **-hered', -her'ing** [< L *ad-,* to + *haerere,* to stick] 1 to stick fast; stay attached 2 to give allegiance or support (to) —**ad·her'ence** *n.*

ad·her'ent *n.* a supporter or follower (of a cause, etc.)

ad·he·sion (ad hē'zhən) *n.* 1 an adhering or a being stuck together 2 body tissues abnormally joined

ad·he'sive (-siv) *adj.* 1 sticking 2 sticky —*n.* an adhesive substance

ad hoc (ad häk') [L, to this] for a specific purpose *[an ad hoc committee]*

adieu (ə dyōō', -dōō'; *Fr* ä dyö') *interj., n., pl.* **adieus'** or **Fr. adieux'** (-dyö') [Fr] goodbye

ad in·fi·ni·tum (ad in'fə nit'əm) [L] endlessly; without limit

adi·os (a'dē ōs', ä'-; *Sp* ä dyôs') *interj.* [Sp] goodbye

adi·pose (ad'ə pōs') *adj.* [ult. < Gr *aleipha,* fat] of animal fat; fatty

adj. 1 adjective 2 adjustment

ad·ja·cent (ə jā'sənt) *adj.* [< L *ad-,* to + *jacere,* to lie] near or close (to); adjoining —**ad·ja'cency** *n.* —**ad·ja'cently** *adv.*

ad·jec·tive (aj'ik tiv) *n.* [< L *adjacere,* lie near] a word used to modify a noun or other substantive —**ad'jec·ti'val** (-ti'vəl) *adj.* —**ad'jec·ti'vally** *adv.*

ad·join (ə join', ə-) *vt.* [< L *ad-,* to + *jungere,* to join] to be next to —*vi.* to be in contact —**ad·join'ing** *adj.*

ad·journ (ə jurn') *vt.* [< OFr *a,* at + *jorn,* day] to suspend (a meeting, session, etc.) for a time —*vi.* 1 to close a

---

▪ THESAURUS ▪

ad* *n.* announcement, display, notice; see ADVERTISEMENT.

AD or **A.D.** *abbrev.* of the Christian era, after Christ, post-Christian, year of our Lord.

adage *n.* axiom, saying, maxim; see PROVERB.

adapt *v.* modify, revise, readjust; see ALTER 1.

adaptability *n.* changeability, flexibility, versatility, adjustability, conformability, pliancy, docility, compliancy, pliability, plasticity.

adaptable *a.* adjustable, elastic, pliable; see FLEXIBLE.

add *v.* 1 [To bring together, usually by mathematics] total, sum up, sum, figure, figure up, count up, compute, calculate, add up, count up, tally, reckon, enumerate, hitch on*.—*Ant.* DECREASE, subtract, take away. 2 [To make a further remark] append, say further, continue, write further, annex, supplement, affix, add a postscript, reply, tack on. —**add to** augment, amplify, expand; see INCREASE. —**add up** be plausible, be probable, be reasonable, be logical, stand to reason, hold water; see also MAKE SENSE. —**add up to** indicate, signify, imply; see MEAN 1.

addict *n.* drug abuser, user, cokehead*, head*, dope fiend*, drug fiend*, mainliner*, junkie*, alcoholic, druggie*, freak*.

addicted (to) *a.* disposed to, inclined, in the habit of, prone, accustomed, attached, abandoned, wedded, devoted, predisposed, used to, imbued with, fanatic about, obsessed with, hooked on*.

addiction *n.* fixation, inclination, bent; see HABIT 2, OBSESSION.

addition *n.* 1 [That which has been added] interest, raise, additive, gain, profit, dividend, bonus, supplement, reinforcement, appendage, appendix, accessory, attachment, extension, increase, annex.—*Ant.* LOSS, reduction, shrinkage. 2 [A real estate development] annex, annexation, subdivision, shopping center, development, extension, expansion, branch, construction.

additional *a.* supplementary, new, further; see EXTRA.

address *n.* 1 [A formal speech] oration, lecture, sermon; see SPEECH 3. 2 [Place at which one may be reached] residence, legal residence, home, quarters, living quarters, dwelling, headquarters, place of business, box number; see also HOME 1.

address *v.* 1 [To provide directions for delivery] label, mark, prepare for mailing; see WRITE 2. 2 [To speak formally to an assemblage] lecture, lecture to, discuss, give a talk, give an address, give a speech, take the floor,

harangue, rant, sermonize, spout off*, spiel*.

adept *a.* skillful, proficient, capable; see ABLE.

adequate *a.* sufficient, equal to the need, satisfactory; see ENOUGH 1.

adequately *a.* sufficiently, appropriately, suitably, fittingly, satisfactorily, abundantly, copiously, acceptably, tolerably, decently, modestly, fairly well, well enough, capably, good enough, to an acceptable degree, competently; see also WELL 2, 3.—*Ant.* INADEQUATELY, badly, insufficiently.

adhere (to) *v.* 1 [To serve] follow, be devoted to, practice; see OBEY. 2 [To stick to] attach, cling, hold fast; see STICK 1.

adhesive *a.* gummy, clinging, pasty; see STICKY.

ad infinitum *a.* endlessly, forever, ceaselessly; see REGULARLY.

adjacent *a.* beside, alongside, bordering; see NEAR 1.

adjective *n.* modifier, article, determiner, attribute, attributive, qualifier, descriptive word, limiting word, adjectival construction, identifier, qualifying word, accessory, addition, dependent.

adjourn *v.* leave, postpone, discontinue; see SUSPEND 2.

meeting, etc. for a time **2** [Colloq.] to retire (*to* another room, etc.) —**ad·journ′ment** *n.*

ad·judge (ə juj′) *vt.* **-judged′, -judg′ing** ⟦< L *ad-*, to + *judicare*, to judge⟧ **1** to decide by law **2** to declare, order, or award by law

ad·ju·di·cate (ə jōō′di kāt′) *vt.* **-cat′ed, -cat′ing** to hear and decide (a case) — *vi.* to serve as a judge (*in* or *on*) — **ad·ju′di·ca′tion** *n.* —**ad·ju′di·ca′tor** *n.* —**ad·ju′di·ca·to′ry** (-kə tôr′ē) *adj.*

ad·junct (aj′uŋkt′) *n.* ⟦see ADJOIN⟧ a secondary or nonessential addition

ad·jure (ə joor′, ə-) *vt.* **-jured′, -jur′ing** ⟦< L *ad-*, to + *jurare*, to swear⟧ **1** to charge solemnly under oath **2** to ask earnestly —**ad′ju·ra′tion** *n.*

ad·just (ə just′) *vt.* ⟦< OFr *a-*, to + *joster*, to tilt⟧ **1** to change so as to fit **2** to regulate (a watch, etc.) **3** to settle rightly **4** to decide the amount to be paid in settling (an insurance claim) — *vi.* to adapt oneself —**ad·just′able** *adj.* —**ad·just′er** or **ad·jus′tor** *n.* —**ad·just′ment** *n.*

ad·ju·tant (aj′ə tənt) *n.* ⟦< L *ad-*, to + *juvare*, to help⟧ **1** an assistant **2** a military staff officer who assists the commanding officer

ad-lib (ad′lib′) *vt., vi.* **-libbed′, -lib′bing** ⟦< L *ad libitum*, at pleasure⟧ [Colloq.] to improvise (words, etc. not in a prepared script, etc.) —*n.* [Colloq.] an ad-libbed remark: also **ad lib** —*adj.* [Colloq.] spoken or done extemporaneously —*adv.* [Colloq.] extemporizing freely: also **ad lib**

ad′man′ *n., pl.* **-men′** a man whose work is advertising

ad·min·is·ter (ad min′is tər, əd-) *vt.* ⟦< L *ad-*, to + *ministrare*, to serve⟧ **1** to manage; direct **2** to give out, as punishment **3** to apply (medicine, etc.) **4** to tender (an oath, etc.)

ad·min′is·trate′ (-trāt′) *vt.* **-trat′ed, -trat′ing** to administer; manage

ad·min·is·tra′tion (-trā′shən) *n.* **1** management **2** [*often* A-] the executive officials of a government, etc. and their policies **3** their term of office **4** the administering (*of* punishment, medicine, etc.) —**ad·min′is·tra′tive** *adj.*

ad·min′is·tra′tor *n.* **1** one who administers **2** *Law* one appointed to settle an estate

ad·mi·ra·ble (ad′mə rə bəl) *adj.* deserving admiration; excellent —**ad′mi·ra·bly** *adv.*

ad·mi·ral (ad′mə rəl) *n.* ⟦< Ar *ʔamir*, leader + *ṣāli*, high⟧ **1** the commanding officer of a fleet **2** a naval officer of the highest rank

ad′mi·ral·ty (-tē) *n., pl.* **-ties** [*often* A-] the governmental department in charge of naval affairs, as in England

ad·mi·ra·tion (ad′mə rā′shən) *n.* **1** an admiring **2** pleased approval

ad·mire (ad mīr′, əd-) *vt.* **-mired′, -mir′ing** ⟦< L *ad-*, at + *mirari*, to wonder⟧ **1** to regard with wonder and delight **2** to esteem highly —**ad·mir′er** *n.*

ad·mis·si·ble (ad mis′ə bəl, əd-) *adj.* that can be accepted or admitted —**ad·mis′si·bil′i·ty** *n.*

ad·mis·sion (ad mish′ən, əd-) *n.* **1** an admitting or being admitted **2** an entrance fee **3** a conceding, confessing, etc. **4** a thing conceded, confessed, etc.

ad·mit (ad mit′, əd-) *vt.* **-mit′ted, -mit′ting** ⟦< L *ad-*, to + *mittere*, to send⟧ **1** to permit or entitle to enter or use **2** to allow; leave room for **3** to concede or confess — *vi.* to allow: with *of* —**ad·mit′tance** *n.*

ad·mit′tedly *adv.* by admission or general agreement

ad·mix·ture (ad miks′chər) *n.* ⟦< L *ad-*, to + *miscere*, to mix⟧ **1** a mixture **2** a thing added in mixing

ad·mon·ish (ad män′ish, əd-) *vt.* ⟦< L *ad-*, to + *monere*, to warn⟧ **1** to warn **2** to reprove mildly **3** to exhort —**ad·mo·ni·tion** (ad′mə nish′ən) *n.* —**ad·mon′i·to′ry** (-i tôr′ē) *adj.*

ad nau·seam (ad nô′zē əm′) ⟦L⟧ to the point of disgust

ado (ə dōō′) *n.* fuss; trouble

ado·be (ə dō′bē) *n.* ⟦Sp⟧ **1** unburnt, sun-dried brick **2** clay for making this brick **3** a building of adobe

ado·les·cence (ad′'l es′'ns) *n.* the time of life between puberty and maturity; youth

ad′o·les′cent *adj.* ⟦< L *ad-*, to + *alescere*, grow up⟧ of or in adolescence —*n.* a person during adolescence

Ado·nis (ə dōn′is, -dän′-) *Gr. Myth.* a young man loved by Aphrodite —*n.* a handsome young man

adopt (ə däpt′) *vt.* ⟦< L *ad-*, to + *optare*, to choose⟧ **1** to take legally into one's own family and raise as one's own

---

THESAURUS

adjournment *n.* intermission, pause, break; see RECESS 1.

adjust *v.* **1** [To bring to agreement] settle, arrange, conclude, complete, accord, reconcile, clarify, conform, sort, allocate, grade, tally, regulate, organize, systematize, coordinate, straighten, standardize, clean up. **2** [To place or regulate parts] fix, connect, square, balance, regulate, tighten, fit, repair, focus, fine-tune, readjust, rectify, correct, set, mend, improve, overhaul, grind, sharpen, renovate, polish, bring into line, align, calibrate, put in working order, temper, service.

adjustable *a.* adaptable, stretchable, tractable; see FLEXIBLE.

adjustment *n.* settlement, arrangement, pay, remuneration, reimbursement, compensation, compromise, reconciliation, agreement, making up, improvement, regulation, fixing, adaptation, correction, mutual understanding.

ad-lib* *v.* improvise, make up, devise; see INVENT 1.

administer *v.* **1** [To manage] conduct, direct, control; see MANAGE 1. **2** [To furnish] extend, dispense, give; see OFFER 1.

administration *n.* **1** [The direction of affairs] government, supervision, command; see MANAGEMENT. **2** [Those who direct affairs] directors, administrators, officers, supervisors, superintendents, advisers, command, executives, strategists, officials, committee, board, board of directors, executive, executive branch, legislature, president, presidency, chief executive, cabinet, ministry, commander, chairman, general, admiral, commander in chief, central office, headquarters, the management,

bureau, consulate, embassy, legation, department, Washington, party in power, brass*, front office*, the powers that be, the man*. **3** [The period in which a political administration is operative] term of office, regime, reign; see sense 2.

administrative *a.* executive, controlling, ruling; see GOVERNING.

administrator *n.* manager, director, chairman; see EXECUTIVE.

admirable *a.* worthy, attractive, good; see EXCELLENT.

admiration *n.* praise, deference, approval, regard, fondness, esteem, respect, appreciation, favor, adoration, applause, glorification, idolatry, honor, recognition, valuing, liking, love, high regard, high opinion, reverence, veneration, homage.—*Ant.* OBJECTION, disregard, distrust.

admire *v.* esteem, honor, applaud, praise, extol, respect, approve, revere, venerate, laud, boost, glorify, reverence, hold dear, appreciate, credit, commend, value, treasure, prize, look up to, rate highly, pay homage to, idolize, adore, hail, put a high price on, have a high opinion of, think highly of, show deference to, think well of, take great stock in, put great stock in, put on a pedestal.— *Ant.* BLAME, censure, deride.

admirer *n.* supporter, believer, patron; see FOLLOWER.

admissible *a.* proper, suitable, right; see PERMITTED.

admission *n.* **1** [The act of granting entrance] acceptance, admittance, permission, reception, welcome, recognition, acknowledgment, confirmation, selection, initiation.—*Ant.* REMOVAL, rejection, expulsion. **2**

[The entrance fee] cover charge, fee, price, ticket, charges, toll, tax, minimum, donation, cover*, gate. **3** [Something acknowledged] statement, disclosure, confession, acknowledgment, affirmation, concession, divulgence, declaration, confirmation, assertion, testimony, allegation, deposition, affidavit.— *Ant.* DENIAL, disallowance, repudiation.

admit *v.* **1** [To grant entrance] bring in, give access to, allow entrance to; see RECEIVE 4. **2** [To confess] acknowledge, indicate, disclose, bare, unveil, uncover, expose, proclaim, declare, open up, bring to light, go over, go into details, confide to, tell, relate, narrate, enumerate, divulge, reveal, communicate, make known, tell the whole story, plead guilty, own up to, talk, sing*, cough up*, come clean*, spill the beans*.—*Ant.* HIDE, cover up, obscure.

admonish *v.* reprove, chide, rebuke; see SCOLD.

admonition *n.* advice, notice, exhortation; see WARNING.

adolescence *n.* young adulthood, puberty, teens; see YOUTH 1.

adolescent *a.* pubescent, juvenile, youthful; see YOUNG 1.

adolescent *n.* youngster, minor, teenager; see YOUTH 3.

adopt *v.* **1** [To take as a son or daughter] pick, choose, select, transfer, father, mother, take in, raise, make one's heir, take as one's own, naturalize, foster. **2** [To take as one's own] embrace, appropriate, seize, take up, take over, choose, assume, use, utilize, imitate, borrow, mimic.—*Ant.* DENY, repudiate, reject.

child **2** to take as one's own **3** to choose or accept —**adop′tion** *n.*

adop·tive (ə dǎp′tiv) *adj.* that has become so by adoption

ador·able (ə dôr′ə bəl) *adj.* **1** [Rare] worthy of adoration **2** [Colloq.] delightful; charming —**ador′ably** *adv.*

ado·ra·tion (ad′ə rā′shən) *n.* **1** a worshiping **2** great love or devotion

adore (ə dôr′) *vt.* **-dored′, -dor′ing** [< L *ad-*, to + *orare*, to speak] **1** to worship as divine **2** to love greatly **3** [Colloq.] to like very much

adorn (ə dôrn′) *vt.* [< L *ad-*, to + *ornare*, fit out] **1** to be an ornament to **2** to put decorations on —**adorn′ment** *n.*

ADP (ā′dē′pē′) [*a*(*denosine*) *d*(*i*)*p*(*hosphate*)] a basic unit of nucleic acids vital to the energy processes of all living cells

adre·nal (ə drē′nəl) *adj.* [AD- + RENAL] **1** near the kidneys **2** of two ductless glands (**adrenal glands**), just above the kidneys

Adrena·lin (a dren′ə lin′) *trademark for* a hormone secreted by the adrenal glands or synthesized for use as a drug —*n.* [a-] this hormone, which increases endurance, muscular strength, etc.

adrift (ə drift′) *adv., adj.* floating without mooring or direction

adroit (ə droit′) *adj.* [< Fr *à*, to + L *dirigere*, lay straight] skillful and clever —**adroit′ly** *adv.* —**adroit′ness** *n.*

ad·sorb (ad sôrb′) *vt.* [< AD- + L *sorbere*, drink in] to collect (a gas, etc.) in condensed form on a surface —**ad·sorp′tion** (-sôrp′shən) *n.*

adu·late (a′jōō lāt′, -jə-) *vt.* **-lat′ed, -lat′ing** [< L *adulari*, fawn upon] to flatter servilely —**ad′u·la′tion** *n.*

adult (ə dult′, ad′ult′) *adj.* [see ADOLESCENT] grown up; mature — *n.* a mature person, animal, or plant —**adult′hood** *n.*

adul·ter·ant (ə dul′tər ənt) *n.* a substance that adulterates — *adj.* adulterating

adul·ter·ate (ə dul′tər āt′) *vt.* **-at′ed, -at′ing** [< L *ad-*, to + *alter*, other] to make inferior, impure, etc. by adding an improper substance —**adul′tera′tion** *n.*

adul·tery (ə dul′tər ē) *n., pl.* **-ies** sexual intercourse between a married person and another not the spouse —**adul′terer** *n.* —**adul′ter·ess** *n.fem.* —**adul′ter·ous** *adj.*

ad·um·brate (ad um′brāt′, ad′əm brāt′) *vt.* **-brat′ed, -brat′ing** [< L *ad-*, to + *umbra*, shade] **1** to outline vaguely **2** to foreshadow —**ad′um·bra′tion** *n.*

adv. 1 adverb **2** advertisement

ad va·lo·rem (ad′ və lôr′əm) [L] in proportion to the value: a phrase applied to duties levied on goods, etc. as a percentage of their value: abbrev. **ad val.**

ad·vance (ad vans′, əd-) *vt.* **-vanced′, -vanc′ing** [< L *ab-*, from + *ante*, before] **1** to bring forward **2** to promote **3** to suggest **4** to raise the rate of **5** to lend —*vi.* **1** to go forward **2** to improve; progress **3** to rise in rank, price, etc. —*n.* **1** a moving forward **2** an improvement **3** a rise in value **4** [*pl.*] approaches to get favor **5** a payment before due —*adj.* **1** in front [*advance* guard] **2** beforehand —**in advance 1** in front **2** ahead of time —**ad·vance′ment** *n.*

ad·vanced′ *adj.* **1** in front **2** old **3** ahead or higher in progress, price, etc.

advance man a person hired to travel in advance of a theatrical company, political candidate, etc. to arrange for publicity, appearances, etc.

ad·van·tage (ad vant′ij, əd-) *n.* [< L *ab-* + *ante*: see ADVANCE] **1** superiority **2** a favorable circumstance, event, etc. **3** gain; benefit —*vt.* **-taged, -tag·ing** to be a benefit to —**take advantage of 1** to use for one's own benefit **2** to impose upon —**ad′van·ta′geous** (-van tā′jəs, -vən-) *adj.*

Ad·vent (ad′vent′) *n.* [< L *ad-*, to + *venire*, to come] **1** the period including the four Sundays just before Christmas **2** [a-] a coming

ad·ven·ti·tious (ad′ven tish′əs) *adj.* [see prec.] not inherent; accidental

ad·ven·ture (ad ven′chər, əd-) *n.* [see ADVENT] **1** a daring, hazardous undertaking **2** an unusual, stirring, often romantic experience — *vi.* **-tured, -tur·ing** to engage in adventure —**ad·ven′tur·ous** or **ad·ven′ture·some** *adj.* —**ad·ven′tur·ously** *adv.*

ad·ven′turer *n.* **1** one who has or looks for adventures **2** one who seeks to become rich, etc. by dubious schemes —**ad·ven′tur·ess** *n.fem.*

ad·verb (ad′vurb′) *n.* [< L *ad-*, to + *verbum*, word] a word used to modify a verb, an adjective, or another adverb, by expressing time, place, manner, degree, etc. —**ad·ver′bial** *adj.* —**ad·ver′bi·ally** *adv.*

ad·ver·sar·ial (ad′vər ser′ē əl) *adj.* of or relating to adversaries, as in a lawsuit

ad′ver·sar′y *n., pl.* **-ies** [see ADVERT] an opponent; foe

ad·verse (ad vurs′, ad′vurs′) *adj.* [see ADVERT] **1** opposed **2** unfavorable —**ad·verse′ly** *adv.*

ad·ver·sity (ad vur′sə tē) *n.* **1** misfortune; wretched or troubled state **2** *pl.* **-ties** a calamity; disaster

ad·vert (ad vurt′) *vi.* [< L *ad-*, to + *vertere*, to turn] to call attention (*to*)

ad·ver·tise (ad′vər tīz′) *vt.* **-tised′, -tis′ing** [see prec.] to describe or praise publicly, usually so as to promote sales — *vi.* **1** to call public attention to things for sale **2** to ask (*for*) by public notice Also **advertize** —**ad′ver·tis′er** *n.* —**ad′ver·tis′ing** *n.*

THESAURUS

adoption *n.* choosing, election, choice; see SELECTION 1.
adorable* *a.* delightful, lovable, cute; see CHARMING.
adoration *n.* devotion, homage, veneration; see WORSHIP 1.
adore *v.* **1** [To worship] venerate, revere, glorify; see WORSHIP. **2** [To love] cherish, treasure, prize; see LOVE 1.
adorn *v.* beautify, embellish, ornament; see DECORATE.
adorned *a.* trimmed, decked, garnished; see ORNATE.
adult *a.* of age, grown, developed; see MATURE.
adult *n.* mature person, grown-up, fully developed member of a species; see MAN 2, WOMAN 1.
adulterate *v.* dilute, lessen, taint; see POLLUTE, WEAKEN.
adultery *n.* promiscuity, infidelity, unfaithfulness; see FORNICATION.
advance *n.* **1** [The act of moving forward] impetus, progression, motion; see PROGRESS 1. **2** [Promotion] enrichment, betterment, increase; see IMPROVEMENT 1. —**in advance** ahead of, earlier, in time; see BEFORE.
advance *v.* **1** [To move forward physically] progress, proceed, move on, forge ahead, press on, push ahead, go on, go forth, gain ground, make headway, step forward, come

to the front, conquer territory, march on, move onward, continue ahead, push on, press on.—*Ant.* STOP, halt, stand still. **2** [To propose] set forth, introduce, suggest; see PROPOSE 1. **3** [To promote] further, encourage, urge; see PROMOTE 1. **4** [To lend] loan, provide with, furnish; see LEND. **5** [To improve] develop, make progress, get better; see IMPROVE 2.
advanced *a.* **1** [Superior] precocious, first, exceptional; see EXCELLENT. **2** [Aged] seasoned, venerable, time-honored; see OLD 1, 3. **3** [Progressive] radical, unconventional, ahead of the times; see LIBERAL.
advancement *n.* **1** [Promotion in rank] improvement, elevation, raise; see PROMOTION 1. **2** [Progress] gain, headway, progression; see PROGRESS 1.
advantage *n.* luck, favor, approval, help, aid, sanction, good, patronage, support, preference, odds, protection, start, leg up*, helping hand, upper hand, leverage, hold, opportunity, dominance, superiority, supremacy, lead, influence, power, mastery, authority, prestige, sway, pull*, edge*, ace in the hole*.—*Ant.* WEAKNESS, handicap, disadvantage. —**have the advantage of** be superior, have the opportunity, be privileged; see SUCCEED 1. —**take advantage of** exploit, profit by, utilize; see

DECEIVE, USE 1.
adventure *n.* happening, experience, episode; see EVENT.
adventurer *n.* explorer, pirate, soldier of fortune, daredevil, hero, pioneer, mountain climber, wild game hunter, romantic; see also PIONEER 2, TRAVELER.
adventurous *a.* bold, daring, courageous; see BRAVE.
adverse *a.* untimely, improper, unfortunate; see UNFAVORABLE.
adversely *a.* negatively, resentfully, unsympathetically; see UNFAVORABLY.
adversity *n.* misfortune, distress, trouble; see DIFFICULTY 1, 2.
advertise *v.* publicize, proclaim, herald, announce, declare, notify, warn, display, exhibit, show, reveal, expose, disclose, unmask, divulge, uncover, communicate, publish abroad, issue, broadcast, print, circulate, show off, parade, propagate, disseminate, inform, celebrate, spread, call public attention to, promulgate, give out, plug*, play up*; see also DECLARE.
advertised *a.* announced, posted, noted, publicized, billed, printed, published, made public, broadcast, emphasized, pointed out, displayed, exhibited, shown, offered, presented, put on sale, flaunted, plugged*, boosted, built up, pushed*.

ad·ver·tise·ment (ad′vər tīz′mənt, ad′vər tīz′-, ad vʉr′ tīz-) *n.* a public notice, usually paid for

ad·vice (ad vīs′, əd-) *n.* ⟦< L *ad-*, at + *videre*, to look⟧ opinion given as to what to do; counsel

ad·vis·able (ad vīz′ə bəl, əd-) *adj.* proper to be advised; wise; sensible —**ad·vis′abil′ity** *n.*

ad·vise (ad vīz′, əd-) *vt.* **-vised′, -vis′ing** ⟦< ML *advisum*, advice⟧ **1** to give advice to; counsel **2** to offer as advice **3** to inform —**ad·vi′sor** or **ad·vis′er** *n.*

ad·vis′edly (-id lē) *adv.* deliberately

ad·vise′ment *n.* careful consideration —**take under advisement** to consider carefully

ad·vi·sory (ad vī′zə rē, əd-) *adj.* advising or empowered to advise — *n., pl.* **-ries** a report, esp. about weather conditions

ad·vo·cate (ad′və kit; *for v.,* -kāt′) *n.* ⟦< L *ad-*, to + *vocare*, to call⟧ one who pleads another's cause or in support of something — *vt.* **-cat′ed, -cat′ing** to speak or write in support of —**ad′vo·cacy** (-kə sē) *n.*

advt. advertisement

adz or **adze** (adz) *n.* ⟦< OE *adesa*⟧ an axlike tool for dressing wood, etc.

aegis (ē′jis) *n.* ⟦< Gr *aigis*, shield of Zeus⟧ **1** protection **2** sponsorship

Aene·as (i nē′əs) *Gr. & Rom. Myth.* a Trojan whose adventures are told in a poem (the **Aeneid**) by Virgil

aeon (ē′ən, ē′än′) *n.* EON

aer·ate (er′āt′, ā′ər-) *vt.* **-at′ed, -at′ing** ⟦AER(O)- + -ATE[1]⟧ **1** to expose to air **2** to charge (liquid) with gas, as to make soda water —**aera′tion** *n.* —**aer′a·tor** *n.*

aer·ial (er′ē əl) *adj.* ⟦< Gr *aēr*, air + -AL⟧ **1** of, in, or by air **2** unreal; imaginary **3** of aircraft or flying — *n.* a radio or TV antenna

aeri·al·ist (er′ē əl ist) *n.* an acrobat on a trapeze, high wire, etc.

aerie (ā′ər ē, ē′rē, er′ē, ir′ē) *n.* ⟦prob. < L *ager*, field⟧ **1** the high nest of an eagle or other bird of prey **2** a house or stronghold on a high place Also **aery**

aero- ⟦< Gr *aēr*, air⟧ *combining form* **1** air **2** aircraft or flying **3** gas, gases Also **aer-** or **aeri-**

aero·bat·ics (er′ō bat′iks) *n.pl.* ⟦prec. + (ACRO)BATICS⟧ stunts done while flying an aircraft

aero·bic (er ō′bik) *adj.* ⟦< Gr *aēr*, air + *bios*, life⟧ **1** able to live or grow only where free oxygen is present **2** of exercise, as running, that conditions the heart and lungs by increasing efficient intake of oxygen by the body — *n.* [*pl., with sing. or pl. v.*] aerobic exercises

aero·dy·nam·ics (er′ō dī nam′iks) *n.pl.* **1** [*with sing. v.*] the branch of mechanics dealing with forces exerted by air or other gases in motion **2** the characteristics of a vehicle's body that affect its efficient movement through the air —**aer′o·dy·nam′ic** *adj.*

aer·o·nau·tics (-nôt′iks; er′ə-) *n.pl.* [*with sing. v.*] the science of making and flying aircraft —**aer′o·nau′ti·cal** *adj.*

aero·plane (er′ə plān′) *n.* [Brit., etc. (exc. Cdn.)] *var. of* AIRPLANE

aero·sol (er′ō säl′, -sôl′; er′ə-) *n.* ⟦AERO- + SOL(UTION)⟧ a suspension of insoluble particles in a gas — *adj.* of a container in which gas under pressure dispenses liquid spray through a valve

aer′o·space (-spās′) *n.* the earth's atmosphere and the space outside it — *adj.* of missiles, etc. for flight in aerospace

aes·thete (es′thēt′) *n.* ⟦Gr *aisthētēs*, one who perceives⟧ a person who is or pretends to be highly sensitive to art and beauty

aes·thetic (es thet′ik) *adj.* **1** of aesthetics **2** of beauty **3** sensitive to art and beauty

aes·thet′ics *n.pl.* [*with sing. v.*] the philosophy of art and beauty

afar (ə fär′) *adv.* [Archaic] at or to a distance

af·fable (af′ə bəl) *adj.* ⟦< L *ad-*, to + *fari*, to speak⟧ pleasant; friendly —**af′fabil′ity** *n.* —**af′fably** *adv.*

af·fair (ə fer′) *n.* ⟦< L *ad-*, to + *facere*, to do⟧ **1** a thing to do **2** [*pl.*] matters of business **3** any matter, event, etc. **4** an amorous episode

af·fect (ə fekt′; *for 3 & 4,* a fekt′) *vt.* ⟦< L *ad-*, to + *facere*, to do⟧ **1** to have an effect on; influence **2** to stir the emotions of **3** to like to use, wear, etc. **4** to make a pretense of feeling, feeling, etc.

af·fec·ta·tion (af′ek tā′shən) *n.* **1** a pretending to like, have, etc. **2** artificial behavior

af·fected (ə fekt′id) *adj.* **1** afflicted **2** influenced **3** emotionally moved **4** assumed or assuming for effect **5** full of affectation

af·fect′ing *adj.* emotionally moving

af·fec·tion (ə fek′shən) *n.* **1** fond or tender feeling **2** a disease

af·fec′tion·ate (-it) *adj.* tender and loving —**af·fec′tion·ately** *adv.*

af·fect·less (af′ekt′lis) *adj.* lacking emotion

af·fer·ent (af′ər ənt) *adj.* ⟦< L *ad-*, to + *ferre*, to carry⟧ bringing inward to a central part, as nerves

af·fi·ance (ə fī′əns) *vt.* **-anced, -anc·ing** ⟦< ML *ad-*, to + *fidare*, to trust⟧ to betroth

af·fi·da·vit (af′ə dā′vit) *n.* ⟦ML, he has made oath⟧ a written statement made on oath

af·fil·i·ate (ə fil′ē āt′; *for n., usually,* -it) *vt.* **-at′ed, -at′ing** ⟦< ML *affiliare*, adopt as a son⟧ **1** to take in as a member **2** to associate (oneself) *with* a group, etc. — *vi.* to join — *n.* an affiliated person, club, etc. —**af·fil′ia′tion** *n.*

af·fin·ity (ə fin′ə tē) *n., pl.* **-ties** ⟦< L *affinis*, adjacent⟧ **1** relationship by marriage **2** close relationship **3** a likeness implying common origin **4** a natural liking or sympathy

af·firm (ə fʉrm′) *vt.* ⟦< L *ad-*, to + *firmare*, make firm⟧ **1** to declare positively; assert **2** to confirm; ratify — *vi. Law* to make a formal statement, but not under oath —**af·fir·ma′tion** (af′ər mā′shən) *n.*

af·firma·tive (ə fʉrm′ə tiv) *adj.* affirming; answering "yes" — *n.* **1** an expression of assent **2** the side upholding the proposition being debated

---

■ THESAURUS ■

advertisement *n.* announcement, notice, publicity, exhibit, exhibition, display, publicity, circular, handbill, placard, poster, public notice, broadcast, bill, proclamation, classified advertisement, sample, endorsement, want ad*, buildup*, plug*, ballyhoo, blurb*, spread*, classified*.

advice *n.* guidance, instruction, consultation, suggestion, preaching, information, admonition, forewarning, warning, caution, a word to the wise, injunction, lesson, directions, opinion, counsel, advisement, encouragement, persuasion, prescription, recommendation, proposition, proposal, view, help, aid, judgment.

advise *v.* recommend, prescribe, guide, exhort, direct, admonish, warn, point out, instruct, counsel, advocate, suggest, urge, prompt, show, tell, inform, move, caution, charge, encourage, preach, teach, persuade, offer an opinion to, forewarn, prepare, straighten out.—*Ant.* DECEIVE, misdirect, lead astray.

advisor *n.* counselor, instructor, consultant.—*Ant.* FRIEND, TEACHER.

advisory *a.* consulting, having power to advise, prudential; see HELPING.

advocate *v.* bolster, push, further, advance; see also PROMOTE 1.

aerial *a.* in the air, atmospheric, flying; see HIGH 2.

aesthetic *a.* creative, artistic, inventive; see BEAUTIFUL.

affair *n.* **1** [Business; *often plural*] concern, responsibility, matter, duty, topic, subject, case, circumstance, thing, question, function, private concern, personal business, calling, employment, occupation, profession, pursuit, avocation, obligation, job, province, realm, interest, mission, assignment, task; see also JOB 1. **2** [An illicit love affair] liaison, rendezvous, intimacy, romance, relationship.

affect *v.* impress, sway, induce; see INFLUENCE.

affected *a.* **1** [Being subject to influence] moved, touched, melted, influenced, awakened, sympathetic, stimulated, stirred, grieved, overwhelmed, moved to tears, hurt, injured, excited, struck, impressed, overwrought, devoured by, concerned, reached, compassionate, tender, sorry, troubled, distressed.—

Ant. INDIFFERENT, unmoved, untouched. **2** [Insincere or artificial] pretentious, melodramatic, unnatural, stilted, superficial, theatrical, stiff, strained, overdone, ostentatious, hollow, shallow, showy, fake, stuck-up*, put-on*.—*Ant.* SIMPLE, natural, genuine.

affection *n.* love, friendship, liking, attachment, good will, partiality, passion, ardor, zealous attachment, friendliness, concern, regard, desire, closeness, kindness, devotion, tenderness, fondness.—*Ant.* HATRED, dislike, enmity.

affectionate *a.* kind, tender, friendly; see LOVING.

affidavit *n.* testimony, sworn statement, affirmation; see OATH 1.

affinity *n.* **1** [Attraction based on affection] fondness, liking, closeness; see AFFECTION. **2** [Similarity] likeness, resemblance, kinship; see SIMILARITY.

affirmative *a.* agreeing, consenting, concurring, approving, assenting, supporting.—*Ant.* NEGATIVE, contradictory, noncommittal. —**in the affirmative** favorably, in assent, in

affirmative action a plan to offset past discrimination in employing or educating women, blacks, etc.

af·fix (ə fiks'; *for n.* af'iks') *vt.* [< L *ad-*, to + *figere*, fasten] 1 to fasten; attach 2 to add at the end —*n.* 1 a thing affixed 2 a prefix or suffix

af·fla·tus (ə flāt'əs) *n.* [< L *ad-*, to + *flare*, to blow] inspiration

af·flict (ə flikt') *vt.* [< L *ad-*, to + *fligere*, to strike] to cause pain or suffering to; distress greatly

af·flic·tion (ə flik'shən) *n.* 1 pain; suffering 2 any cause of suffering

af·flu·ence (af'lōō əns) *n.* [< L *ad-*, to + *fluere*, to flow] 1 great plenty; abundance 2 riches; wealth

af'flu·ent *adj.* 1 plentiful 2 wealthy; rich —**af'flu·ently** *adv.*

af·ford (ə fôrd') *vt.* [< OE *geforthian*, to advance] 1 to spare (money, time, etc.) without much inconvenience 2 to give; yield [it *affords* pleasure] —**af·ford'abil'ity** *n.* —**af·ford'able** *adj.*

af·for·est (ə fôr'ist) *vt.* [see AD- & FOREST] to turn (land) into forest —**af·for'est·a'tion** (-əs tā'shən) *n.*

af·fray (ə frā') *n.* [< OFr *esfraer*, frighten] a noisy brawl

af·front (ə frunt') *vt.* [< ML *ad-*, to + *frons*, forehead] to insult openly —*n.* an open insult

af·ghan (af'gan', -gən) *n.* [after *Afghanistan*] a crocheted or knitted blanket or shawl

afi·cio·na·do (ə fish'ə nä'dō) *n.* [Sp] a devotee of some sport, art, etc.

afield (ə fēld') *adv.* 1 in or to the field 2 away (from home); astray

afire (ə fīr') *adv., adj.* on fire

aflame (ə flām') *adv., adj.* 1 in flames 2 glowing

AFL-CIO American Federation of Labor and Congress of Industrial Organizations

afloat (ə flōt') *adv.* 1 floating 2 at sea 3 flooded

aflut·ter (ə flut'ər) *adv., adj.* in a flutter

afoot (ə foot') *adv.* 1 on foot 2 in motion; in progress

afore·men·tioned (ə fôr'men'chənd) *adj.* mentioned before

afore'said' (-sed') *adj.* spoken of before

afore'thought' *adj.* thought out beforehand; premeditated

afoul (ə foul') *adv., adj.* in a collision or a tangle —**run** (or **fall) afoul of** to get into trouble with

afraid (ə frād') *adj.* [see AFFRAY] feeling frightened: followed by *of, that,* or an infinitive Often used colloquially indicating regret [I'm *afraid* I must go]

Af·ri·can (af'ri kən) *adj.* of Africa, its people, etc. —*n.* a native of Africa

African-Amer'ican *n.* a black American of African ancestry —*adj.* of African-Americans, their culture, etc.

African violet a tropical African plant with violet, white,

or pinkish flowers and hairy, dark-green leaves, often grown as a house plant

Af·ri·kaans (af'ri käns', -känz') *n.* [Afrik < *Afrika*, Africa] an official language of South Africa, based on Dutch

Afro (af'rō) *adj.* [see fol.] designating or of a full, bushy hair style, as worn by some blacks —*n., pl.* **-ros'** an Afro hair style

Afro- [< L *Afer*, an African] combining form African, African and

Af'ro-Amer'ican *n., adj.* AFRICAN-AMERICAN

aft (aft) *adv.* [< OE *æftan*] at, near, or toward the stern of a ship or rear of an aircraft

af·ter (af'tər) *adv.* [OE *æfter*] 1 behind 2 later —*prep.* 1 behind 2 later than 3 in search of 4 as a result of 5 in spite of [after all I've said, he's still going] 6 lower in rank or order than 7 in imitation of 8 for [named *after* Lincoln] —*conj.* following the time when —*adj.* 1 next; later 2 nearer the rear

af'ter·birth' *n.* the placenta and membranes expelled after the birth of offspring

af'ter·burn'er (-burn'ər) *n.* a device attached to some engines for burning or utilizing exhaust gases

af'ter·effect' *n.* an effect coming later, or as a secondary result

af'ter·life' *n.* a life after death

af'ter·math' (-math') *n.* [< AFTER + OE *mæth*, cutting of grass] a result, esp. an unpleasant one

after·noon (af'tər nōōn') *n.* the time from noon to evening —*adj.* in the afternoon

af'ter·thought' *n.* 1 an idea, explanation, part, etc. coming or added later 2 a thought coming too late to be apt

af'ter·ward (-wərd) *adv.* later; subsequently Also **af'ter·wards**

Ag [L *argentum*] *Chem. symbol for* silver

again (ə gen') *adv.* [< OE *on-*, up to + *gegn*, direct] 1 back into a former condition 2 once more 3 besides 4 on the other hand —**again and again** often; repeatedly —**as much again** twice as much

against (ə genst') *prep.* [see prec.] 1 in opposition to 2 toward so as to strike [thrown *against* the wall] 3 next to 4 in preparation for 5 as a charge on —**over against** 1 opposite to 2 as compared with

Aga·mem·non (ag'ə mem'nän') *Gr. Myth.* commander of the Greek army in the Trojan War

agape (ə gāp') *adv., adj.* [A-¹ + GAPE] with the mouth wide open

agar (ä'gär) *n.* [Malay] a gelatinous product made from seaweed, used in bacterial cultures Also **a'gar-a'gar'**

ag·ate (ag'it) *n.* [< Gr *achatēs*] a hard, semiprecious stone with striped or clouded coloring

aga·ve (ə gä'vē) *n.* [< proper name in Gr. myth] a desert plant with thick, fleshy leaves

age (āj) *n.* [< L *aetas*] 1 the length of time that a person or thing has existed 2 a stage of life 3 old age 4 a histori-

---

THESAURUS

agreement, with an affirmative answer; see also YES.

afflict *v.* injure, torment, trouble; see HURT.

affliction *n.* trouble, hardship, plight; see DIFFICULTY 1, 2.

affluent *a.* wealthy, well-off, well-to-do; see RICH 1.

afford *v.* have enough for, make both ends meet, bear, manage, be able to, have the means for, be financially able, stand, be in the market for.

afire *a.* flaming, on fire, blazing; see BURNING.

afloat *a.* adrift, at sea, sailing; see FLOATING.

afoot *a.* on foot, hiking, marching; see WALKING.

afraid *a.* hesitant, anxious, apprehensive, disturbed, frightened, fearful, nervous, uneasy, fidgety, alarmed, intimidated, discouraged, disheartened, perplexed, worried, perturbed, upset, panic-stricken, cowardly, scared, terrified, terrorized, shocked, frozen, aghast, alarmed, startled, aroused, horrified, petrified, stunned, rattled, struck dumb, trembling, distressed, jittery*, jumpy*, leery*, shaky*.—*Ant.* CONFIDENT, self-assured, poised.

African *a.* 1 [Concerning a part of

Africa] North African, Moroccan, Egyptian, Libyan, Algerian, Saharan, Sudanese, East African, Kenyan, Tanzanian, Ugandan, Ethiopian, Somalian, West African, Liberian, Ghanaian, Nigerian, Senegalese, Congolese, Angolan, Central African, Zambian, South African. 2 [Concerning the inhabitants of Africa] Negro, negroid, black, Bantu, Zulu, Swazi, Hottentot, Bushman, Pygmy, Afrikaaner, Boer, Colored, Yoruba, Ibo, Hausa, Masai, Kikuyu, Somali, Ethiopian, Egyptian, Arab, Moorish.

aft *a.* rearward, behind, astern; see BACK.

after *a., prep.* 1 [Behind in space] back of, in the rear, behind; see BACK. 2 [Following] next, later, subsequent; see FOLLOWING.

afternoon *n.* P.M., siesta time, early afternoon, late afternoon, mid-afternoon.

afterward *a.* later, after, subsequently, in a while, a while later, afterwards, by and by, eventually, soon, on the next day, ultimately, another time, then, at a later time.

again *a.* anew, afresh, newly, once more, once again, repeatedly, over, from the beginning, on and on, another time, over again, a second

time, recurrently, ditto.—*Ant.* ONCE, once only, at first. —**again and again** repeatedly, once again, continuously; see AGAIN. —**as much again** doubled, twice as much, multiplied; see DOUBLE.

against *a., prep.* 1 [Counter to] in the face of, into, toward, opposite to, facing. 2 [In contact with] on, upon, in collision with, touching; see also NEXT 2. 3 [Contrary to] in opposition to, opposed to, counter to, adverse to, in violation of, versus, over against. 4 [Opposite] facing, fronting, corresponding; see OPPOSITE 3.

age *n.* 1 [The period of one's existence] span, lifetime, duration; see LIFE 4. 2 [A particular point or time in one's life] infancy, childhood, girlhood, boyhood, adolescence, adulthood, youth, middle age, old age, senility. 3 [A period of time] epoch, era, period, time, century, decade, generation, interval, term, in the time of something; see also LIFE 4. —**of age** adult, twenty-one, having attained majority; see MATURE.

age *v.* grow feeble, decline, wane, advance in years, wrinkle, waste away, have one foot in the grave*, become long in the tooth.

cal or geological period **5** [*often pl.*] [Colloq.] a long time
— *vi.*, *vt.* **aged, ag′ing** or **age′ing** to grow or make old, ripe, mature, etc. —**of age** having reached the age when one is qualified for full legal rights
-age (ij) [*< LL -aticum*] *suffix* **1** act, state, or result of [*usage*] **2** amount or number of [*acreage*] **3** cost of [*postage*] **4** place of [*steerage*]
aged (ā′jid; *for 2* ājd) *adj.* **1** old **2** of the age of —**the aged** old people
age·ism (āj′iz′əm) *n.* [AGE + (RAC)ISM] discrimination against older people
age′less *adj.* **1** seemingly not growing older **2** eternal
agen·cy (ā′jən sē) *n.*, *pl.* **-cies** [*< L agere*, to act] **1** action; power **2** means **3** a firm, etc. empowered to act for another **4** an administrative government division **5** an organization that offers assistance [*a social agency*]
agen·da (ə jen′də) *n.*, *pl.* **-das** [*< L agere*, to do] a list of things to be dealt with at a meeting
agent (ā′jənt) *n.* [*< L agere*, to do] **1** an active force or substance producing an effect **2** a person, firm, etc. empowered to act for another **3** a representative of a government agency
Agent Orange [military code name, from *orange*-colored containers] a highly toxic defoliant
age-old (āj′ōld′) *adj.* ancient
ag·era·tum (aj′ər āt′əm) *n.* [*< Gr agēratos*, not growing old] a plant of the composite family with small, thick heads of bluish flowers
ag·glom·er·ate (ə gläm′ər āt′; *for adj. & n.*, -ər it) *vt.*, *vi.* **-at′ed, -at′ing** [*< L ad-*, to + *glomerare*, form into a ball] to gather into a mass or ball — *adj.* gathered into a mass or ball — *n.* a jumbled heap, mass, etc.
ag·glu·ti·nate (ə glōōt′'n it; *for v.*, -āt′) *adj.* [*< L ad-*, to + *gluten*, glue] stuck together — *vt.*, *vi.* **-nat′ed, -nat′ing** to stick together, as with glue —**ag·glu′ti·na′tion** *n.*
ag·gran·dize (ə gran′dīz′; *also*, ag′rən-) *vt.* **-dized′, -diz′ing** [*< Fr a-*, to + *grandir*, to increase] to make greater, more powerful, richer, etc. —**ag·gran·dize·ment** (ə gran′diz mənt, ag′rən diz′-) *n.*
ag·gra·vate (ag′rə vāt′) *vt.* **-vat′ed, -vat′ing** [*< L ad-*, to + *gravis*, heavy] **1** to make worse **2** [Colloq.] to annoy; vex —**ag′gra·va′tion** *n.*
ag′gra·vat′ed *adj.* *Law* designating a grave form of a specified offense
ag·gre·gate (ag′rə git; *for v.*, -gāt′) *adj.* [*< L ad-*, to + *grex*, a herd] total — *n.* a mass of distinct things gathered into a total or whole — *vt.* **-gat′ed, -gat′ing** **1** to gather into a mass **2** to total —**ag′gre·ga′tion** *n.*
ag·gres·sion (ə gresh′ən) *n.* [*< L aggredi*, to attack] **1** an unprovoked attack or warlike act **2** a being aggressive —**ag·gres′sor** *n.*
ag·gres·sive (ə gres′iv) *adj.* **1** boldly hostile; quarrelsome **2** bold and active; enterprising —**ag·gres′sive·ly** *adv.* —**ag·gres′sive·ness** *n.*

ag·grieve (ə grēv′) *vt.* **-grieved′, -griev′ing** [see AGGRAVATE] to cause grief or injury to; offend; slight
aghast (ə gast′) *adj.* [*< OE gast*, ghost] feeling great horror or dismay
ag·ile (aj′əl) *adj.* [*< L agere*, to act] quick and easy of movement —**ag′ile·ly** *adv.* —**agil·ity** (ə jil′ə tē) *n.*
agi·tate (aj′i tāt′) *vt.* **-tat′ed, -tat′ing** [*< L agere*, to act] **1** to stir up or shake up **2** to excite the feelings of — *vi.* to stir up people so as to produce changes —**ag′i·ta′tion** *n.* —**ag′i·ta′tor** *n.*
agleam (ə glēm′) *adv.*, *adj.* gleaming
aglit·ter (ə glit′ər) *adv.*, *adj.* glittering
aglow (ə glō′) *adv.*, *adj.* in a glow (of color or emotion)
ag·nos·tic (ag näs′tik) *n.* [*< Gr a-*, not + base of *gignōskein*, know] one who believes it impossible to know if God exists — *adj.* of an agnostic —**ag·nos′ti·cism** (-ti siz′əm) *n.*
ago (ə gō′) *adj.* [*< OE agan*, pass away] gone by; past [*years ago*] — *adv.* in the past [*long ago*]
agog (ə gäg′) *adv.*, *adj.* [*< OFr en*, in + *gogue*, joke] with eager anticipation or excitement
ago·nize (ag′ə nīz′) *vi.* **-nized′, -niz′ing** **1** to struggle **2** to be in agony — *vt.* to torture
ago·ny (ag′ə nē) *n.*, *pl.* **-nies** [*< Gr agōn*, a contest] **1** great mental or physical pain **2** death pangs **3** a strong outburst (*of* emotion)
agrar·ian (ə grer′ē ən) *adj.* [*< L ager*, field] **1** of land or the ownership of land **2** of agriculture
agree (ə grē′) *vi.* **-greed′, -gree′ing** [*< L ad*, to + *gratus*, pleasing] **1** to consent (*to*) **2** to be in accord **3** to be of the same opinion (*with*) **4** to arrive at an understanding (*about* prices, etc.) **5** to be suitable, healthful, etc.: followed by *with* — *vt.* to grant [*I agree that it's true*]
agree′able *adj.* **1** pleasing or pleasant **2** willing to consent **3** conformable **4** acceptable —**agree′ably** *adv.*
agree·ment (ə grē′mənt) *n.* **1** an agreeing **2** an understanding between people, countries, etc. **3** a contract
agri- *combining form* agriculture: also **agro-**
agri·business (ag′rə biz′niz, -nis) *n.* [see fol. + BUSINESS] farming and associated businesses and industries
agri·cul·ture (ag′ri kul′chər) *n.* [*< L ager*, field + *cultura*, cultivation] the work of producing crops and raising livestock; farming —**ag′ri·cul′tural** *adj.* —**ag′ri·cul′tur·ally** *adv.* —**ag′ri·cul′tur·ist** *n.*
agrono·my (ə grän′ə mē) *n.* [*< Gr agros*, field + *nemein*, govern] the science and economics of crop production —**agron′o·mist** *n.*
aground (ə ground′) *adv.*, *adj.* on or onto the shore, a reef, etc.
ague (ā′gyōō′) *n.* [*< ML (febris) acuta*, violent (fever)] a fever, usually malarial, marked by chills

THESAURUS

aged *a.* gray, elderly, worn; see OLD.
agency *n.* **1** [Place where business is transacted] firm, bureau, company; see OFFICE 3, BUSINESS 4. **2** [That by which something is done] power, auspices, action; see MEANS 1.
agenda *n.* list, plan, schedule; see PROGRAM 2.
agent *n.* broker, promoter, operator, representative, salesman, assistant, emissary, intermediary, appointee, servant, executor, attorney, lawyer, go-between, surrogate, mediary, deputy, minister, envoy, middleman, commissioner, delegate, proxy, substitute, steward, functionary, ambassador, proctor, negotiator, advocate, coagent, press agent, booking agent, bookie*.
aggravate *v.* exasperate, annoy, provoke; see BOTHER 2.
aggravation *n.* **1** [A cause of aggravation] worry, affliction, distress; see DIFFICULTY 1, 2, TROUBLE 1. **2** [Annoyance] irritation, provocation, exasperation; see ANNOYANCE 1.
aggression *n.* offensive, assault, invasion; see ATTACK 1.
aggressive *a.* warlike, attacking, combative, threatening, advancing, offensive, firm, strong, disruptive, disturbing, hostile, intrusive, contentious, destructive, intruding, invad-

ing, assailing, barbaric, up in arms, on the warpath.—*Ant.* SERENE, peace-loving, peaceful.
agile *a.* nimble, quick, spry, deft, vigorous, athletic, sure-footed, light-footed, frisky, spirited, lithe, sprightly, supple, dexterous, easy-moving, rapid, active, ready, alive, buoyant, energetic, stirring, brisk, lively, swift, alert, bustling.—*Ant.* AWKWARD, slow, clumsy.
agility *n.* nimbleness, dexterity, spryness, quickness, briskness, swiftness, deftness, adroitness, fleetness, friskiness, liveliness, alertness.
agitate *v.* stir, move, arouse; see EXCITE.
agitated *a.* disturbed, upset, aroused; see EXCITED.
ago *a.* gone, since, past; see BEFORE.
agony *n.* suffering, torture, anguish; see PAIN 1, 2.
agree *v.* coincide, get along, side with, harmonize with, match up, concur, stand together, parallel, go along with, fit in, suit, say yes to, conform, go hand in hand with, equal, correspond, go together, synchronize, measure up to, square with*, click*, hit it off with, see eye to eye*.—*Ant.* DIFFER, disagree, debate. —**agree about** come to terms, see eye to eye*, settle; see SET-

TLE 1. —**agree on** come to terms, make an arrangement, make a bargain; see SETTLE 1. —**agree to** promise, consent, approve; see ACCEPT. —**agree with** coincide, accord, harmonize; see AGREE.
agreeable *a.* pleasing, satisfactory, acceptable; see PLEASANT 1, 2.
agreeably *a.* kindly, politely, pleasantly, well, wonderfully, satisfactorily, genially, cheerfully, peacefully; see also FAVORABLY.—*Ant.* OPPOSITE, disagreeably, negatively.
agreement *n.* **1** [The state of being in accord] conformity, friendship, accordance, accommodation, correspondence, harmony, concord, unison, concert, common view, understanding, brotherhood, affiliation, alliance, fellowship, companionship, goodwill, cooperation, assent, approval, compromise, treaty, pact, contract, bargain, settlement, satisfaction, affinity, closeness, concurrence, reconciliation, uniformity, balance, kinship, peace, love, unity, union, tie.—*Ant.* DISAGREEMENT, enmity, disunity. **2** [An expression of agreement] approval, treaty, contract; see DEAL 1.
agriculture *n.* tillage, cultivation, horticulture; see FARMING.

ah (ä, ô) *interj.* an exclamation of pain, delight, surprise, etc.

aha (ä hä′) *interj.* an exclamation of satisfaction, triumph, etc.

ahead (ə hed′) *adv., adj.* 1 in or to the front 2 forward; onward 3 in advance 4 winning or profiting —**get ahead** to advance financially, etc.

ahem (ə hem′) *interj.* a cough, etc. made to get someone's attention, etc.

-a·hol·ic (ə häl′ik) *combining form* one preoccupied with (something specified)

ahoy (ə hoi′) *interj.* a call used in hailing [ship ahoy!]

aid (ād) *vt., vi.* [< L ad-, to + juvare, to help] to help; assist — *n.* 1 help or assistance 2 a helper

aide (ād) *n.* [Fr] 1 an assistant 2 an aide-de-camp

aide-de-camp or **aid-de-camp** (ād′də kamp′) *n., pl.* **aides′-** or **aids′-** [Fr] a military officer serving as an assistant to a superior

AIDS (ādz) *n.* [A(cquired) I(mmune) D(eficiency) S(yndrome)] a condition of deficiency of certain leukocytes, resulting in infections, cancer, etc.

aigrette or **aigret** (ā gret′, ā′gret′) *n.* [see EGRET] a bunch of feathers, or long, white, showy plumes of the egret

ail (āl) *vt.* [OE eglian, to trouble] to cause pain and trouble to — *vi.* to be in poor health

aileron (ā′lə rän′) *n.* [Fr < L ala, wing] a pilot-controlled airfoil at the trailing edge of an airplane wing, for controlling rolling

ail·ment (āl′mənt) *n.* a mild illness

aim (ām) *vi., vt.* [< L ad-, to + aestimare, to estimate] 1 to direct (a weapon, blow, etc.) so as to hit 2 to direct (one's efforts) 3 to intend — *n.* 1 an aiming 2 the ability to hit a target 3 intention —**take aim** to aim a weapon, etc.

aim′less *adj.* having no purpose —**aim′lessly** *adv.* —**aim′less·ness** *n.*

ain′t (ānt) [< amn′t, contr. of am not] [Colloq.] am not: also a dialectal or substandard contraction for *is not, are not, has not,* and *have not*

ai·oli or **aï·oli** (ī ō′lē) *n.* [ult. < L allium, garlic + oleum, oil] a mayonnaise containing crushed raw garlic

air (er) *n.* [< Gr aēr] 1 the invisible mixture of gases surrounding the earth 2 a) a breeze; wind b) fresh air 3 an outward appearance [an air of dignity] 4 general mood 5 [pl.] affected, superior manners 6 public expression 7 AIR CONDITIONING 8 a tune — *adj.* of or by aircraft — *vt.* 1 to let air into 2 to publicize 3 to broadcast — *vi.* to be broadcast —**in the air** prevalent —**on** (or **off**) **the air** that is (or is not) broadcasting —**up in the air** not settled

air bag a bag that inflates instantly within an automobile in a collision, to protect riders from being thrown forward

air base a base for military aircraft

air′borne′ *adj.* 1 carried by or through the air 2 aloft or flying

air brake a brake operated by the action of compressed air on a piston

air′brush′ *n.* an atomizer worked by compressed air and used for spraying on paint, etc. Also **air brush**

air′bus′ *n.* an extremely large passenger airplane, esp. for short trips

air conditioning a method of keeping air humidity and temperature at desired levels in buildings, cars, etc. —**air′-condi′tion** *vt.* —**air conditioner**

air′-cooled′ *adj.* cooled by having air passed over, into, or through it

air′craft′ *n., pl.* **-craft′** any machine for traveling through the air

aircraft carrier a warship with a large, flat deck, for carrying aircraft

air′drop′ *n.* the dropping of supplies, troops, etc. from an aircraft in flight —**air′drop′** *vt.*

Aire·dale (er′dāl′) *n.* [after Airedale, valley in England] a large terrier with a wiry coat

air′field′ *n.* a field where aircraft can take off and land

air′foil′ *n.* a wing, rudder, etc. of an aircraft

air force the aviation branch of a country's armed forces

air gun a gun or gunlike device operated by compressed air

air′head′ *n.* [Slang] a frivolous, silly, and ignorant person

air lane a route for travel by air; airway

air′lift′ *n.* a system of transporting troops, supplies, etc. by aircraft — *vt.* to transport by airlift

air′line′ *n.* a system or company for moving freight and passengers by aircraft — *adj.* of or on an airline

air′lin′er *n.* a large airline-operated aircraft for carrying passengers

air lock an airtight compartment, with adjustable air pressure, between places of unequal air pressure

air′mail′ *n.* mail transported by air overseas at a higher than usual postal rate — *adj.* of or for mail sent by air Also **air mail** —**air′mail′** *vt.*

air′man (-mən) *n., pl.* **-men** 1 an aviator 2 an enlisted person in the U.S. Air Force

air mass *Meteorol.* a huge, uniform body of air having the properties of its place of origin

air′plane′ *n.* a motor-driven or jet-propelled aircraft kept aloft by the forces of air upon its wings

air′play′ *n.* the playing of a recording over radio or TV

air pocket an atmospheric condition that causes an aircraft to make a sudden, short drop while in flight

air′port′ *n.* a place where aircraft can land and take off, usually with facilities for repair, etc.

air power the total capacity of a nation for air war

air pressure the pressure of the atmosphere or of compressed air

air raid an attack by aircraft, esp. bombers

air rifle a rifle operated by compressed air

air′ship′ *n.* a self-propelled, steerable aircraft that is lighter than air

air′sick′ *adj.* nauseated because of air travel —**air′sick′ness** *n.*

air′space′ *n.* the space above a nation over which it can claim jurisdiction

air′strike′ *n.* an attack made by aircraft

air′strip′ *n.* a temporary airfield

air′tight′ *adj.* 1 too tight for air or gas to enter or escape 2 having no weaknesses [an airtight alibi]

air′waves′ *n.pl.* the medium through which radio signals are transmitted

---

◼ THESAURUS ◼

ahead *a.* before, earlier, in advance, ahead of, advanced, preceding, foremost, leading, in the lead, at the head of, in the foreground, to the fore, in the van, first, in front of, preliminary.—*Ant.* behind, back, toward the end. —**get ahead** advance, prosper, progress; see SUCCEED.

aid *n.* comfort, benefit, favor; see HELP 1.

ailing *a.* ill, feeble, weak; see SICK.

ailment *n.* sickness, infirmity, disease; see ILLNESS 1, 2.

aim *n.* intention, object, plan; see PURPOSE 1. —**take aim** point, direct, train; see AIM, *v.*

aim *v.* train, steer, level, direct, set up, set the sights, sight, take aim, zero in on, draw a bead on.

aimed *a.* proposed, marked, intended for, directed, designed, calculated, leveled, trained, steered, set, planned, anticipated.

aimless *a.* purposeless, pointless, erratic, thoughtless, careless, heedless, rambling, wandering, blind, random, unsettled, flightly, capricious, wayward, without aim, chance, haphazard, to no purpose, drifting, stray, accidental, undirected, casual, indecisive, irresolute, fitful, fanciful, fickle, eccentric, unplanned, helpless, unpredictable, shiftless.—*Ant.* CAREFUL, purposeful, planned.

air *n.* 1 [The gaseous envelope of the earth] atmosphere, stratosphere, troposphere, wind, breeze, draft, the open air, sky, oxygen, the open, ventilation, the out-of-doors. 2 [The apparent quality] look, mien, demeanor; see LOOKS. —**in the air** prevalent, abroad, current; see FASHIONABLE, POPULAR 1. —**off the air** not being broadcast, closed, signed off; see QUIET. —**on the air** broadcasting, going on, televising, telecasting, in progress, speaking, performing, being telecast, live. —**up in the air** undecided, unsettled, unsure; see UNCERTAIN.

air *v.* ventilate, open, freshen, air out, circulate air, air-condition, expose to air, draw in air, fan, refresh, cool, purify.

aired *a.* 1 [Exposed to the air] ventilated, opened, freshened, purified, hung out, sunned, dried.—*Ant.* CLOSED, stuffy, dark. 2 [Exposed to public attention] exposed, disclosed, discussed, revealed, told, unveiled; see also EXPOSED.—*Ant.* SECRET, undisclosed, concealed.

air force *n.* aviation service, air power, air cover; see ARMY 1.

airline *n.* air carrier, commercial airline, air freight carrier; see BUSINESS 4.

airman *n.* pilot, copilot, navigator; see PILOT.

airplane *n.* aircraft, aeroplane, airliner; see PLANE 3.

airport *n.* airfield, spaceport, flying field, landing field, airstrip, hangar, heliport, installations.

airtight *a.* impermeable to air, closed, shut tight; see TIGHT 2.

air'way' *n.* AIR LANE

airy (er'ē) *adj.* **-i·er, -i·est** **1** of air **2** open to the air; breezy **3** unsubstantial as air **4** light as air; graceful **5** lighthearted **6** affectedly nonchalant —**air'i·ly** *adv.* —**air'i·ness** *n.*

aisle (īl) *n.* ⟦ < L *ala*, wing ⟧ a passageway, as between rows of seats

ajar (ə jär') *adv., adj.* ⟦OE *cier*, a turn ⟧ slightly open, as a door

akim·bo (ə kim'bō) *adv., adj.* ⟦ < ON *keng*, bent + *bogi*, a bow ⟧ with hands on hips and elbows bent outward /with arms *akimbo*/

akin (ə kin') *adj.* **1** of one kin; related **2** similar

Al *Chem. symbol for* aluminum

-al (əl, 'l) ⟦ < L ⟧ *suffix* **1** of, like, or suitable for /theatrical/ **2** the act or process of ___ing /rehearsal/

à la or **a la** (ä'lə, -lä) ⟦Fr⟧ in the manner or style of

ala·bas·ter (al'ə bas'tər) *n.* ⟦ < Gr *alabastros*, perfume vase ⟧ a translucent, whitish variety of gypsum, used for statues, vases, etc.

a la carte (ä'lə kärt') ⟦Fr⟧ with a separate price for each item on the menu

alac·ri·ty (ə lak'rə tē) *n.* ⟦ < L *alacer*, lively ⟧ eager willingness, often with quick, lively action

Alad·din (ə lad''n) a boy in *The Arabian Nights* who finds a magic lamp

à la king (ä'lə kiŋ') in a cream sauce containing mushrooms, pimentos, etc.

a la mode (ä'lə mōd') ⟦Fr⟧ **1** in fashion **2** served in a certain style, as pie with ice cream Also **à la mode**

alar (ā'lər) *adj.* ⟦ < L *ala*, a wing ⟧ **1** of a wing **2** having wings

alarm (ə lärm') *n.* ⟦ < It *all'arme*, to arms ⟧ **1** [Archaic] a sudden call to arms **2** a warning of danger **3** a mechanism that warns of danger, arouses from sleep, etc. **4** fear caused by danger — *vt.* **1** to warn of danger **2** to frighten

alarm'ing *adj.* frightening

alarm'ist *n.* one who spreads alarming rumors, exaggerated reports of danger, etc. — *adj.* of an alarmist

alas (ə las') *interj.* an exclamation of sorrow, pity, etc.

alb (alb) *n.* ⟦ < L *albus*, white ⟧ a white robe worn by a priest at Mass

al·ba·core (al'bə kôr') *n.* ⟦ < Ar *al*, the + *buko*, young camel ⟧ a tuna with unusually long pectoral fins

al·ba·tross (al'bə trôs') *n.* ⟦ < Sp < Ar *al qādūs*, a scoop ⟧ **1** a large, web-footed sea bird **2** a burden

al·beit (ôl bē'it) *conj.* ⟦ME *al be it*, al(though) it be ⟧ although

al·bi·no (al bī'nō) *n., pl.* **-nos** ⟦ < L *albus*, white ⟧ a person, animal, or plant lacking normal coloration: human albinos have white skin, whitish hair, and pink eyes

al·bum (al'bəm) *n.* ⟦ < L *albus*, white ⟧ **1** a book with blank pages for mounting pictures, stamps, etc. **2** a single recording, as of a set of related musical works

al·bu·men (al byōō'mən) *n.* ⟦L < *albus*, white ⟧ **1** the white of an egg **2** the nutritive protein in seeds, etc. **3** ALBUMIN

al·bu·min (al byōō'min) *n.* ⟦see prec.⟧ a water-soluble protein found in milk, egg, blood, vegetable tissues, etc. — **al·bu'mi·nous** *adj.*

al·chemy (al'kə mē) *n.* ⟦ < Ar < Gr *chēmeia*; infl. by Gr *cheein*, pour ⟧ the chemistry of the Middle Ages, the chief aim of which was to change the baser elements into gold —**al'chemist** *n.*

al·co·hol (al'kə hôl') *n.* ⟦ < Ar *alkuḥl*, antimony powder ⟧ **1** a colorless, volatile, pungent liquid, used in various forms

as a fuel, an intoxicating ingredient in fermented liquors, etc. **2** any such intoxicating liquor

al·co·hol·ic *adj.* **1** of alcohol **2** suffering from alcoholism — *n.* one who has chronic alcoholism

al·co·hol·ism' *n.* the habitual excessive drinking of alcoholic liquor, or a resulting diseased condition

al·cove (al'kōv') *n.* ⟦ < Ar *al*, the + *qubba*, an arch ⟧ a recessed section of a room

al·der (ôl'dər) *n.* ⟦OE *alor*⟧ a small tree or shrub of the birch family

al·der·man (ôl'dər mən) *n., pl.* **-men** ⟦ < OE *eald*, old + *man* ⟧ in some U.S. cities, a municipal officer representing a certain district or ward

ale (āl) *n.* ⟦OE *ealu*⟧ a fermented drink of malt and hops, like beer

a·lea·to·ry (ā'lē ə tôr'ē) *adj.* ⟦ < L *aleatorius*, of gambling < *alea*, chance ⟧ depending on chance or luck

alem·bic (ə lem'bik) *n.* ⟦ < Ar *al-anbīq* < Gr *ambix*, a cup ⟧ **1** an apparatus formerly used for distilling **2** anything that purifies

alert (ə lurt') *adj.* ⟦ < L *erigere*, to erect ⟧ **1** watchful; vigilant **2** active; nimble — *n.* a warning signal; alarm — *vt.* to warn to be ready, etc. —**on the alert** vigilant — **alert'ly** *adv.* —**alert'ness** *n.*

ale·wife (āl'wīf') *n., pl.* **-wives'** ⟦ < ? ⟧ a NW Atlantic fish resembling the herring, used for food and in fertilizers

al·falfa (al fal'fə) *n.* ⟦Sp < Ar *al-fiṣfiṣa*, fodder ⟧ a plant of the pea family, used for fodder, pasture, and as a cover crop

al·fresco (al fres'kō, äl-) *adv.* ⟦It < *al*, in the + *fresco*, cool ⟧ outdoors — *adj.* outdoor Also **al fresco**

al·gae (al'jē') *n.pl., sing.* **al'ga** (-gə) ⟦pl. of L *alga*, seaweed ⟧ a group of simple organisms, one-celled or many-celled, containing chlorophyll and found in water or damp places

al·ge·bra (al'jə brə) *n.* ⟦ < Ar *al*, the + *jabara*, to reunite ⟧ a mathematical system using symbols, esp. letters, to generalize certain arithmetical operations and relationships —**al'ge·bra'ic** (-brā'ik) *adj.* —**al'ge·bra'i·cally** *adv.*

-algia (al'jə) ⟦ < Gr *algos*⟧ *combining form* pain /neuralgia/

Al·gon·quian (al gän'kē ən, -kwē-) *adj.* designating or of a widespread family of North American Indian languages — *n.* this family of languages

al·go·rithm (al'gə rith'əm) *n.* ⟦ult. < Ar⟧ any systematic method of solving a certain kind of mathematical problem

ali·as (ā'lē əs) *n., pl.* **-ases** ⟦L < *alius*, other ⟧ an assumed name — *adv.* otherwise named /Bell alias Jones/

Ali Baba (al'ə bab'ə, ä'lē bä'bə) in *The Arabian Nights*, a poor man who finds the treasure of forty thieves

ali·bi (al'ə bī') *n., pl.* **-bis'** ⟦L < *alius ibi*, elsewhere ⟧ **1** *Law* the plea or fact that an accused person was elsewhere than at the scene of the crime **2** [Colloq.] an excuse — *vi., vt.* **-bied', -bi'ing** [Colloq.] to offer an excuse (for)

alien (āl'yən, ā'lē ən) *adj.* ⟦ < L *alius*, other ⟧ **1** foreign **2** not natural; strange **3** of aliens — *n.* **1** a foreigner **2** a foreign-born resident who is not naturalized **3** a hypothetical being from outer space

al'ien·able (-ə bəl) *adj.* capable of being transferred to a new owner

al'ien·ate' (-āt') *vt.* **-at'ed, -at'ing** **1** to transfer the ownership of (property) to another **2** to make unfriendly or withdraw **3** to cause a transference of (affection) — **al'iena'tion** *n.*

THESAURUS

airy *a.* windy, breezy, draughty, exposed, ventilated, open, spacious, lofty, atmospheric, well-ventilated, aerial, out-of-doors, outdoors, in the open.

aisle *n.* passageway, opening, way, walk, path, course, clearing, avenue, corridor, passage, gangway, alley, lane.

alarm *n.* drum, siren, horn, signal, fog horn, fire siren, call, SOS, red light, hoot, blast, shout, warning sound, danger signal, cry, yell, scream, air raid siren.

alarmed *a.* frightened, fearful, aroused; see AFRAID.

alarming *a.* frightening, foreboding, distressing; see DISTURBING.

album *n.* collection, stamp book, register, index, scrapbook, notebook, photograph album, portfolio, commonplace book.

alcohol *n.* spirits, liquor, intoxicant; see DRINK 1.

alcoholic *a.* spirituous, fermented, distilled; see STRONG 4.

alcoholic *n.* addict, heavy drinker, sot; see DRUNKARD.

alcoholism *n.* intoxication, insobriety, dipsomania; see DRUNKENNESS.

alert *a.* wary, on guard, wide-awake; see OBSERVANT. —**on the alert** watchful, vigilant, on guard; see OBSERVANT.

alert *v.* inform, put on guard, signal; see WARN.

alibi *n.* proof of absence, plea, explanation, declaration, defense, statement, case, allegation, avowal, assurance, profession, excuse, assertion, answer, reply, retort, vindication.

alien *a.* exotic, strange, unknown; see FOREIGN.

alien *n.* foreigner, stranger, refugee, displaced person, outsider, migrant, colonist, immigrant, guest, visitor, newcomer, barbarian, Ishmael, settler, stateless person, intruder, squatter, interloper, invader, noncitizen, man without a country.—*Ant.* INHABITANT, native, citizen.

alienate *v.* estrange, turn away, set against, withdraw the affections of, make unfriendly, come between, disunite, separate, divide, part, turn off*.—Ant.* UNITE, reconcile, acclimate.

alight[1] (ə lit′) *vi.* **alight′ed** or **alit′, alight′ing** [ME *alihtan*] 1 to get down or off; dismount 2 to come down after flight

alight[2] (ə lit′) *adj.* lighted up; burning

align (ə lin′) *vt.* [< Fr *a-*, to + *ligne*, LINE[1]] 1 to bring into a straight line 2 to bring (components or parts) into adjustment 3 to bring into agreement, etc. — *vi.* to line up —**align′ment** *n.*

alike (ə lik′) *adj.* [< OE *gelic*] like one another — *adv.* 1 similarly 2 equally

ali·ment (al′ə mənt) *n.* [< L *alere*, nourish] nourishment; food

al′i·men′tary (-men′tə rē) *adj.* 1 of food or nutrition 2 nourishing

alimentary canal (or **tract**) the passage in the body (from the mouth to the anus) that food goes through

ali·mony (al′ə mō′nē) *n.* [< L *alere*, nourish] money a court orders paid to a person by that person's legally separated or divorced spouse

aline (ə lin′) *vt., vi.* **alined′, alin′ing** ALIGN —**aline′ment** *n.*

alit (ə lit′) *vi. alt. pt. & pp. of* ALIGHT[1]

alive (ə liv′) *adj.* [< OE *on*, in + *life*, life] 1 having life; living 2 in existence, operation, etc. 3 lively; alert —**alive to** aware of —**alive with** teeming with

ali·yah or **ali·ya** (ä′lē yä′) *n.* [< Heb, lit., ascent] immigration by Jews to Israel

al·kali (al′kə li′) *n., pl.* **-lies′** or **-lis′** [< Ar *al-qili*, the ashes of a certain plant] 1 any base, as soda, that is soluble in water and gives off ions in solution 2 a mineral salt, etc. that can neutralize acids

al′ka·line (-lin′, -lin′) *adj.* of or like an alkali —**al′ka·lin′ity** (-lin′ə tē) *n.*

al′ka·lin·ize′ (-lin iz′) *vt.* **-ized′, -iz′ing** ALKALIZE

al′ka·lize′ (-liz′) *vt.* **-lized′, -liz′ing** to make alkaline —**al′ka·li·za′tion** *n.*

al′ka·loid (-loid′) *n.* a bitter, alkaline substance, such as caffeine, morphine, etc., containing nitrogen

alky (al′kē) *n., pl.* **-kies** [Slang] an alcoholic

al·kyd (al′kid′) *n.* [ult. < ALKALI + (ACI)D] a synthetic resin used in paints, varnishes, etc. Also **alkyd resin**

all (ôl) *adj.* [OE *eal*] 1 the whole quantity of *[all the gold]* 2 every one of *[all men]* 3 the greatest possible *[in all sincerity]* 4 any *[beyond all doubt]* 5 alone; only *[all work and no play]* — *pron.* 1 *[with pl. v.]* everyone 2 everything 3 every part or bit — *n.* 1 one's whole property, effort, etc. *[gave his all]* 2 a totality; whole — *adv.* 1 wholly; entirely *[all worn out]* 2 apiece *[a score of two all]* —**after all** nevertheless —**all in** [Colloq.] very tired —**all in all** 1 considering everything 2 as a whole —**all out** completely —**all the better** (or **worse**) so much the better (or worse) —**all the same** 1 nevertheless 2 unimportant —**at all** 1 in the least 2 in any way 3 under any considerations —**in all** altogether

all- *combining form* 1 entirely *[all-American]* 2 for every *[all-purpose]* 3 of everything *[all-inclusive]*

Al·lah (al′ə, ä′lə) [< Ar *al*, the + *ilāh*, god] *the Muslim name for* God

all′-Amer′ican *adj.* representative of the U.S. as a whole, or chosen as the best in the U.S. — *n.* 1 a hypothetical football team, etc. made up of U.S. college players voted the best of the year 2 a player on such a team

all′-around′ *adj.* having many abilities, talents, or uses; versatile

al·lay (ə lā′, ə-) *vt.* **-layed′, -lay′ing** [< OE *a-*, down + *lecgan*, lay] 1 to calm; quiet 2 to relieve (pain, etc.)

all′-clear′ *n.* a siren or other signal that an air raid or alert is over

al·le·ga·tion (al′ə gā′shən) *n.* an assertion, esp. one without proof or to be proved

al·lege (ə lej′) *vt.* **-leged′, -leg′ing** [< L *ex-*, out of + *litigare*, to dispute] 1 to declare or assert, esp. without proof 2 to offer as an excuse

al·leged (ə lejd′, ə lej′id) *adj.* 1 declared, but without proof 2 so-called *[alleged* friends] —**al·leg′edly** *adv.*

al·le·giance (ə lē′jəns) *n.* [< OFr *liege*, liege] 1 the duty of being loyal to one's ruler, country, etc. 2 loyalty; devotion, as to a cause

al·le·gory (al′ə gôr′ē) *n., pl.* **-ries** [< Gr *allos*, other + *agoreuein*, speak in assembly] a story in which people, things, and events have a symbolic meaning, often instructive —**al′le·gor′i·cal** *adj.* —**al′le·gor′i·cally** *adv.* —**al′le·go′rist** *n.*

al·le·gretto (al′ə gret′ō) *adj., adv.* [It, dim. of *allegro*] *Musical Direction* moderately fast

al·le·gro (ə le′grō′, -lā′-) *adj., adv.* [It] *Musical Direction* fast

al·lele (ə lēl′) *n.* [< Gr *allēlōn*, of one another] a gene transferring inherited characteristics

al·le·luia (al′ə lōō′yə) *interj., n.* [LL(Eccles.)] HALLELUJAH

Al·len wrench (al′ən) a thin, L-shaped wrench with hexagonal ends for fitting the sockets of certain screws and bolts

al·ler·gen (al′ər jən) *n.* [Ger] a substance inducing an allergic reaction —**al′ler·gen′ic** (-jen′ik) *adj.*

al·ler·gic (ə lur′jik) *adj.* 1 of, caused by, or having an allergy 2 [Colloq.] averse (*to*)

al·ler·gist (al′ər jist) *n.* a doctor who specializes in treating allergies

al·lergy (al′ər jē) *n., pl.* **-gies** [Ger < Gr *allos*, other + *ergon*, work] 1 a hypersensitivity to a specific substance (as a food, pollen, dust, etc.) or condition (as heat or cold) 2 an aversion

al·le·vi·ate (ə lē′vē āt′) *vt.* **-at′ed, -at′ing** [< L *ad-*, to + *levis*, light] 1 to lessen or relieve (pain, etc.) 2 to decrease (poverty, etc.) —**al·le′via′tion** *n.*

al·ley (al′ē) *n., pl.* **-leys** [< OFr *aler*, go] 1 a narrow street between or behind buildings 2 a bowling lane

alley cat a homeless, mongrel cat

al′ley·way′ *n.* an alley between buildings

all-fired (ôl′fird′) *adj., adv.* [< *hell-fired*] [Slang] extreme(ly)

al·li·ance (ə li′əns) *n.* [see ALLY] 1 an allying or close association, as of nations for a common objective, families by marriage, etc. 2 an agreement for this 3 the countries, groups, etc. in such association

al·lied (ə lid′, al′id′) *adj.* 1 united by kinship, treaty, etc. 2 closely related

---

THESAURUS

align *v.* arrange, straighten, regulate; see ADJUST 1, 2.

alike *a.* like, same, equal, identical, matching, selfsame, akin, similar, comparable, parallel, resembling, related, approximate, equivalent, allied, of a kind, twin, one, indistinguishable, facsimile, duplicate, matched, mated, one and the same, all one, in the same boat, on all fours with.

alimony *n.* upkeep, maintenance, provision; see PAYMENT 1.

alive *a.* live, animate, living, breathing, existing, existent, vital, not dead, mortal, organic, extant, viable, growing, having life, conscious, alive and kicking*, above ground*, among the living.—*Ant.* DEAD, lifeless, inanimate.

all *a.* 1 [Completely] totally, wholly, entirely; see COMPLETELY. 2 [Each] every, any, each and every, any and every, every member of, for everybody, for anybody, for anyone, for anything, for everything, barring no

one, bar none, beginning and end, from A to Z.—*Ant.* no, not any, none. 3 [Exclusively] alone, nothing but, solely; see ONLY 1.

all *n.* everything, everyone, every person, sum, collection, group, ensemble, total, totality, quantity, unit, entity, whole kit and caboodle*; lock, stock and barrel*; the works*.—*Ant.* NONE, nobody, nothing. —**after all** nevertheless, in spite of everything, despite; see ALTHOUGH. —**at all** anyhow, ever, in any way, in any case, in any respect, under any condition, under any circumstances, anywise, in the least, in any manner, to any extent, in the least degree, anyways*. —**in all** all told, collectively, on the whole; see ALTOGETHER.

allegedly *a.* assertedly, according to the statement, supposedly; see APPARENTLY.

allegiance *n.* fidelity, homage, fealty; see LOYALTY.

allergic to *a.* sensitive to, affected by, subject to, susceptible to, repelled

by, oversensitive to.—*Ant.* IMMUNE, unaffected by, hardened to.

allergy *n.* hypersensitive bodily reaction, hypersensitivity, antipathy to certain substances; see ILLNESS 2.

alley *n.* back street, lane, rear way; see ROAD 1. —**up** (or **down**) **one's alley*** suited to one's abilities, in keeping with one's tastes, enjoyable, useful, what the doctor ordered*.

alliance *n.* 1 [The state of being allied] connection, membership, affinity, participation, cooperation, support, union, agreement, common understanding, marriage, kinship, relation, collaboration, federation, friendship, partnership, coalition, association, affiliation, confederation, implication, bond, tie. 2 [The act of joining] fusion, combination, coupling; see UNION 1. 3 [A union] league, federation, company; see ORGANIZATION 2.

allied *a.* unified, confederated, associated; see UNITED.

al·li·ga·tor (al'ə gāt'ər) *n.* [< Sp *el*, the + L *lacerta*, lizard] a large reptile of the U.S., similar to the crocodile but having a short, blunt snout

alligator pear AVOCADO

all'-impor'tant *adj.* highly important; necessary; essential

all'-inclu'sive *adj.* including everything; comprehensive

al·lit·era·tion (ə lit'ər ā'shən) *n.* [< L *ad*-, to + *littera*, letter] repetition of an initial sound in two or more words of a phrase —**al·lit'era·tive** *adj.*

all-nighter (ôl'nīt'ər) *n.* [Colloq.] something lasting the night, as a study session

al·lo·cate (al'ō kāt', al'ə-) *vt.* -cat'ed, -cat'ing [< L *ad*-, to + *locus*, a place] 1 to set apart for a specific purpose 2 to distribute or allot —**al'lo·ca'tion** *n.*

al·lot (ə lät') *vt.* -lot'ted, -lot'ting [< OFr *a*-, to + *lot*, lot] 1 to distribute in arbitrary shares; apportion 2 to assign as one's share —**al·lot'ment** *n.*

all'-out' *adj.* complete or wholehearted [an *all-out* effort]

all'o'ver *adj.* over the whole surface

al·low (ə lou') *vt.* [see ALLOCATE] 1 to permit; let [I'm not *allowed* to go] 2 to let have [she *allowed* herself no sweets] 3 to acknowledge as valid 4 to provide (a certain amount), as for shrinkage, waste, etc. —**allow for** to leave room, time, etc. for —**al·low'able** *adj.*

al·low'ance (-əns) *n.* 1 an allowing 2 something allowed 3 an amount of money, food, etc. given regularly to a child, soldier, etc. 4 a reduction in price, as for a trade-in —**make allowance(s) for** to excuse because of mitigating factors

al·loy (al'oi; *also, and for v. usually,* ə loi') *n.* [< L *ad*-, to + *ligare*, to bind] 1 a substance that is a mixture of two or more metals 2 something that debases another thing when mixed with it — *vt.* to make into an alloy

all'-pur'pose *adj.* useful in many ways

all right 1 satisfactory 2 unhurt 3 correct 4 yes; very well

all'-round' *adj., adv. var. of* ALL-ROUND

all·spice (ôl'spīs') *n.* a spice, combining the tastes of several spices, made from the berry of a West Indian tree of the myrtle family

all'-star' *adj.* 1 made up of outstanding or star performers 2 of or characteristic of an all-star event — *n.* a member of an all-star team

all'-time' *adj.* unsurpassed until now

al·lude (ə lōōd') *vi.* -lud'ed, -lud'ing [< L *ad*-, to + *ludere*, to play] to refer indirectly (*to*)

al·lure (ə loor') *vt., vi.* -lured', -lur'ing [< OFr *a*-, to + *loirer*, to lure] to tempt with something desirable; attract

— *n.* fascination; charm —**al·lure'ment** *n.* —**al·lur·ing** (ə loor'iŋ, a-) *adj.*

al·lu·sion (ə lōō'zhən) *n.* 1 an alluding 2 an indirect or casual reference

al·lu·sive (ə lōōs'iv) *adj.* 1 containing an allusion 2 full of allusions —**al·lu'sively** *adv.* —**al·lu'sive·ness** *n.*

al·lu·vium (ə lōō'vē əm) *n., pl.* -vi·ums or -via (-vē ə) [< L *ad*-, to + *luere*, to wash] sand, clay, etc. deposited by moving water —**al·lu'vial** *adj.*

ally (ə lī'; *also, and for n. usually,* al'ī) *vt., vi.* -lied', -ly'ing [< L *ad*-, to + *ligare*, to bind] 1 to unite or join for a specific purpose 2 to relate by similarity of structure, etc. — *n., pl.* -lies a country or person joined with another for a common purpose

alma ma·ter (al'mə mät'ər, äl'mə mät'ər) [L, fostering mother] 1 the college or school that one attended 2 its anthem

al·ma·nac (ôl'mə nak', al'-) *n.* [< *c.* 5th-c. Gr *almenichiaka*, calendar] a calendar with astronomical data, weather forecasts, etc.

al·mighty (ôl mīt'ē) *adj.* all-powerful —**the Almighty** God

al·mond (ä'mənd; *also* am'ənd) *n.* [< Gr *amygdalē*] 1 the edible, nutlike kernel of a peachlike fruit 2 the tree it grows on — *adj.* shaped like an almond; oval and pointed at one or both ends

al·most (ôl'mōst', ôl mōst') *adv.* very nearly; all but

alms (ämz) *n., pl.* alms [< Gr *eleos*, mercy] money, food, etc. given to poor people —**alms'giv'er** *n.*

alms'house' *n.* 1 [Historical] a poorhouse 2 [Brit.] a privately endowed home for the poor

aloe (al'ō') *n., pl.* -oes' [< Gr *aloē*] an African plant of the lily family

aloft (ə lôft') *adv.* [ME < *o*, on + *loft*, loft] 1 high up 2 in the air; flying 3 high above the deck of a ship

alo·ha (ä lō'hə, -hä'; ə lō'ə) *n., interj.* [Haw, love] a word used as a greeting or farewell

alone (ə lōn') *adj., adv.* [ME < *al*, all + *one*, one] 1 apart from anything or anyone else 2 without any other person 3 only 4 without equal —**let alone** 1 to refrain from interfering with 2 not to speak of [we hadn't a dime, *let alone* a dollar]

along (ə lôŋ') *prep.* [< OE *and*-, over against + -*lang*, long] 1 on or beside the length of 2 in conformity with — *adv.* 1 lengthwise 2 progressively onward or advanced 3 together (*with*) 4 with one [take me *along*] —**all along** from the beginning —**be along** [Colloq.] to come or arrive

---

THESAURUS

allot *v.* earmark, allocate, dole; see ASSIGN, DISTRIBUTE.

allotment *n.* portion, lot, part; see SHARE.

all-out *a.* total, entire, complete; see ABSOLUTE 1.

allow *v.* permit, let, sanction, grant, consent to, tolerate, favor, yield, bear, approve of, give leave to, endorse, certify, have no objection to, release, pass, authorize, license, warrant, put up with, give the green light to*, give the go-ahead to. DENY, forbid, prohibit. —**allow for** take into account, take into consideration, provide for; see CONSIDER.

allowable *a.* permissible, proper, legal; see ADMISSIBLE.

allowance *n.* salary, wage, commission, fee, hire, remittance, stipend, gift, grant, pension, alimony, annuity, settled rate, endowment, scholarship, fellowship, prize, subsidy, pay, bequest, legacy, inheritance, contribution, aid, handout, pocket money. —**make allowances for** weigh, excuse, rationalize; see CONSIDER.

alloy *n.* compound, mixture, combination; see METAL. *Common metal alloys include the following:* ferromanganese, ferrosilicon, pewter, chromesteel, nichrome, tungsten steel, stainless steel, nonmagnetic steel, chromium steel, chrome-nickel steel, high tensile steel, tungsten-chromium-cobalt, cobalt steel, finishing steel, structural steel, carbon

steel, brass, bronze, green gold, nickel-silver, zinc-aluminum, aluminum-bronze, boron bronze, copper-aluminum, aluminum-manganese-copper, manganese-copper, tin-manganese, tin-copper, antimony.

all right *a.* 1 [Adequately] tolerably, acceptably, fairly well; see ADEQUATELY. 2 [Yes] agreed, very well, of course; see YES. 3 [Certainly] without a doubt, definitely, positively; see SURELY. 4 [Uninjured] safe, well, unhurt; see WHOLE. 5 [Correct] exact, precise, right; see RIGHT 1.

all-time *a.* unsurpassed, record-breaking, to the greatest extent; see BEST 1.

ally *n.* confederate, partner, collaborator; see ASSOCIATE.

almanac *n.* calendar, yearbook, annual, register, world almanac, chronicle, journal, record, register of the year.

almighty *a.* 1 [Omnipotent] invincible, all-powerful, mighty; see POWERFUL 1. 2 [Omnipresent] infinite, eternal, godlike, all-knowing, all-seeing, deathless, immortal, celestial, divine, godly, pervading.

almost *a.* all but, nearly, approximately, roughly, to all intents, as good as, near to, substantially, essentially, in effect, on the verge of, relatively, for all practical purposes, to that effect, not quite, about to, with

some exceptions, in the vicinity of, bordering on, within sight of, with little tolerance, close upon, in the neighborhood of, about, just about*, not quite, most*, around*, within a hair of, by a narrow squeak*.

aloft *a.* on high, overhead, up; see ABOVE 1, OVER 1.

alone *a.* lone, lonely, solitary, deserted, abandoned, individual, forsaken, desolate, detached, friendless, unaccompanied, isolated, lonesome, apart, by oneself, single, widowed, unattached, unconnected.—*Ant.* ACCOMPANIED, attended, escorted. —**let alone** 1 [Besides] not to mention, also, in addition to; see BESIDES. 2 [Neglect] ignore, isolate, refrain from disturbing; see NEGLECT 2. —**let well enough alone** forget, ignore, let alone; see NEGLECT 2.

along *a.* 1 [Near] by, at, adjacent; see NEAR 1. 2 [Ahead] on, onward, forward; see AHEAD. 3 [Together with] with, accompanying, in addition to, in company with, along with, side by side, coupled with, at the same time, simultaneously. —**all along** all the time, from the beginning, constantly; see REGULARLY. —**get along** 1 [To succeed] prosper, get by, make ends meet; see SUCCEED 1. 2 [To advance] move on, push ahead; see ADVANCE 1. 3 [To agree] accord, stand together, equal; see AGREE.

—get along 1 to advance **2** to manage **3** to succeed **4** to be compatible

along′shore′ *adv.* near or beside the shore

along′side′ *adv.* at or by the side; side by side —*prep.* beside —**alongside of** at the side of

aloof (ə lōōf′) *adv.* [< *a*-, on & Du *loef*, windward side] at a distance but in view —*adj.* cool and reserved [an *aloof* manner] —**aloof′ness** *n.*

aloud (ə loud′) *adv.* **1** loudly **2** with the normal voice

alp (alp) *n.* [after *Alps*, mountains in south central Europe] a high mountain

al·paca (al pak′ə) *n.* [< AmInd] **1** a South American llama **2** its silky wool, or cloth woven from it

al·pha (al′fə) *n.* the first letter of the Greek alphabet (A, α)

al′pha·bet′ (-bet′) *n.* [< Gr *alpha* & *bēta*, first two letters of the Gr alphabet] the letters used in writing a language, esp. as arranged in their usual order —**al′pha·bet′i·cal** *adj.* —**al′pha·bet′i·cal·ly** *adv.*

al·pha·bet·ize (al′fə bə tiz′) *vt.* **-ized′, -iz′ing** to arrange in the usual order of the alphabet —**al′pha·bet′i·za′tion** (-bet′i zā′shən) *n.*

al′pha·nu·mer′ic (-nōō mer′ik) *adj.* having both alphabetical and numerical symbols

alpha particle a positively charged particle given off by certain radioactive substances

alpha ray a stream of alpha particles

alpha wave an electrical brain wave indicating relaxation Also **alpha rhythm**

al·pine (al′pin′) *adj.* of or like alps

al·ready (ôl red′ē) *adv.* **1** by or before the given or implied time **2** even now or even then

al·right (ôl rit′) *adv. var. sp. of* ALL RIGHT: a disputed usage

also (ôl′sō) *adv.* [< OE *eall*, all + *swa*, so] in addition; likewise; too

al′so-ran′ *n.* [Colloq.] a defeated contestant in a race, election, etc.

alt. *abbrev.* **1** alternate **2** altitude **3** alto

al·tar (ôl′tər) *n.* [< L *altus*, high] **1** a platform where sacrifices are made to a god, etc. **2** a table, etc. for sacred purposes in a place of worship

altar boy a boy or man who helps a priest at religious services, esp. at Mass

al·ter (ôl′tər) *vt., vi.* [< L *alter*, other] to change; make or become different —**al′tera′tion** *n.*

al·ter·ca·tion (ôl′tər kā′shən) *n.* [< L *altercari*, to dispute] an angry or heated argument; quarrel

al·ter ego (ôl′tər ē′gō) [L, other I] **1** another aspect of oneself **2** a constant companion

al·ter·nate (ôl′tər nit; *for v.,* -nāt′) *adj.* [< L *alternus*, one after the other] **1** succeeding each other **2** every other — *n.* a substitute —*vt.* **-nat′ed, -nat′ing** to do or use by turns —*vi.* **1** to act, happen, etc. by turns **2** to take turns regularly —**al′ter·nately** *adv.* —**al′ter·na′tion** *n.*

alternating current an electric current reversing direction periodically

al·ter·na·tive (ôl tur′nə tiv) *adj.* **1** providing a choice between things **2** of an institution, etc. appealing to unconventional interests [an *alternative* school] —*n.* **1** a choice between things **2** one of the things to be chosen **3** something left to choose

al·ter·na·tor (ôl′tər nāt′ər) *n.* an electric generator producing alternating current

al·though (ôl thō′) *conj.* [ME < *al*, even + THOUGH] in spite of the fact that; though Also sp. **al·tho**

al·tim·eter (al tim′ət ər) *n.* [< L *altus*, high + -METER] an instrument for measuring altitude

al·ti·tude (al′tə tōōd′) *n.* [< L *altus*, high] **1** the height of a thing, esp. above sea level **2** a high place

alto (al′tō) *n., pl.* **-tos** [It < L *altus*, high] **1** the range of a voice between tenor and mezzo-soprano **2** a singer with this range —*adj.* of, for, or in the alto range

al·togeth·er (ôl′tōō geth′ər) *adv.* **1** completely **2** in all **3** on the whole

al·tru·ism (al′trōō iz′əm) *n.* [< L *alter*, other] unselfish concern for the welfare of others —**al′tru·ist** *n.* —**al′tru·is′tic** (-is′tik) *adj.* —**al′tru·is′ti·cally** *adv.*

alum (al′əm) *n.* [< L *alumen*] any of a group of salts of aluminum, etc., used in manufacturing and medicine

alu·min·ium (al′yōō min′ē əm) *n.* [Brit., etc. (exc. Cdn.)] *var. of* ALUMINUM

alu·mi·num (ə lōō′mə nəm) *n.* [< L *alumen*, alum] a silvery, lightweight metallic chemical element

alum·nus (ə lum′nəs) *n., pl.* **-ni′** (-ni′) [L, foster son] a boy or man who has attended or is a graduate of a particular school, college, etc. —**alum′na** (-nə), *pl.* **-nae** (-nē), *n.fem.*

al·ways (ôl′wāz, -wiz) *adv.* [OE *ealne weg*] **1** at all times **2** continually **3** at any time **4** in every instance

Alz·hei·mer′s disease (älts′hi′mərz) [after A. *Alzheimer*, 20th-c. Ger doctor] a degenerative brain disease

am (am, əm) *vi.* [OE *eom*] *1st pers. sing., pres. indic., of* BE

AM 1 amplitude modulation **2** [L *ante meridiem*] before noon: used to designate the time from midnight to noon: also **A.M., am,** or **a.m. 3** [L *Artium Magister*] master of arts: also **A.M.**

Am. 1 America **2** American

AMA American Medical Association

amal·gam (ə mal′gəm) *n.* [< Gr *malagma*, an emollient] **1** any alloy of mercury with another metal [a dental filling of silver *amalgam*] **2** a mixture; blend

amal′ga·mate′ (-gə māt′) *vt., vi.* **-mat′ed, -mat′ing** to unite; mix; combine —**amal′ga·ma′tion** *n.*

aman·dine (ä′mən dēn′) *adj.* [Fr] prepared with almonds

amanu·en·sis (ə man′yōō en′sis) *n., pl.* **-ses′** (-sēz′) [L < *a-*, from + *manus*, hand + *-ensis*, relating to] a secretary: now a jocular usage

ama·ranth (am′ə ranth′) *n.* [< Gr *amarantos*, unfading] **1** any of a family of plants, some bearing showy flowers **2** [Old Poet.] an imaginary flower that never dies

THESAURUS

alongside *a., prep.* parallel to, close by, close at hand, by the side of, at the side of, along the side, side by side, equal with, on the same plane with, almost touching, neck and neck.—*Ant.* BEYOND, ahead, behind.

aloof *a.* remote, reserved, distant; see INDIFFERENT.

aloud *a.* vociferously, audibly, noisily; see LOUDLY.

alphabet *n.* letters, rune, pictograph, ideograph, characters, symbols, signs, hieroglyphs, cryptograms, phonemes, morphemes, sounds; see also LETTER 1.

alphabetical *a.* systematic, logical, consecutive, progressive, one after another, step by step, graded, planned, ordered, letter by letter, from A to Z, indexed.

alphabetize *v.* arrange alphabetically, index, systematize; see ORDER 3.

alpine *a.* mountainous, high, lofty, snowcapped, rocky, soaring, rangy, snow-clad, elevated, towering; see also HIGH 1, 2.

already *a.* previously, by now, now, even now, by this time, at present,

just now, in the past, up to now, by that time, then.

also *a.* too, likewise, besides, as well, in addition, additionally, along with, more than that, over and above, in conjunction with, thereto, together with, ditto, more, moreover, further, furthermore, including, plus, to boot.—*Ant.* WITHOUT, excluding, otherwise.

alter *v.* **1** [To change for a purpose] vary, turn, diminish, replace, mutate, warp, alternate, remodel, renovate, evolve, translate, disguise, restyle, revolutionize, reduce, substitute, reorganize, increase, intensify, shape, shift, modify, transform, remake, convert, reform, tailor, adjust, adapt, invert, reverse, reconstruct. **2** [To become different] convert, develop, decay; see CHANGE 2.

alteration *n.* exchange, modification, revision; see CHANGE 1.

altered *a.* modified, qualified, revised; see CHANGED 2.

alternate *a.* alternative, substitute, makeshift; see TEMPORARY.

alternate *n.* replacement, equivalent, double; see SUBSTITUTE.

alternate *v.* **1** [To take or do by turns] substitute, follow in turn, happen by turns, follow one another, do by turns, do one then the other, relieve, fill in for, exchange. **2** [To fluctuate] vary, rise and fall, shift; see WAVER.

alternative *n.* option, discretion, opportunity; see CHOICE.

although *conj.* though, even though, despite, still, despite the fact that, in spite of, even if, while, however, for all that.

altitude *n.* elevation, loftiness, eminence; see HEIGHT.

altogether *a.* all told, collectively, on the whole, in the aggregate, in sum total, in a mass, all in all, all things considered, by and large, all, taking all things together, as a whole, for the most part.

always *a.* **1** [Constantly] periodically, continually, ceaselessly; see REGULARLY. **2** [Forever] perpetually, eternally, evermore; see FOREVER.

AM or **A.M.** *abbrev.* after midnight, morning, early hours, before noon, forenoon, dawn, sunup.

ama·retto (am'ə ret'ō) *n.* [It, rather bitter] [*also* A-] a liqueur with an almond flavor

ama·ryl·lis (am'ə ril'is) *n.* [< Gr *Amaryllis*, name for a shepherdess] a bulb plant with white, purple, pink, or red, lilylike flowers

amass (ə mas') *vt.* [< Fr < L *massa*, a lump] to pile up; accumulate

ama·teur (am'ə chər, -choor'; -ə tʉr', -ə tər) *n.* [Fr < L *amare*, to love] 1 one who does something for pleasure, not for money; nonprofessional 2 one who is somewhat unskillful — *adj.* of or done by amateurs —**am'a·teur'ish** (-choor'-) *adj.* —**am'a·teur·ism'** *n.*

am'a·to'ry (-tôr'ē) *adj.* [< L *amare*, to love] of or showing sexual love

amaze (ə māz') *vt.* **amazed'**, **amaz'ing** [OE *āmasian*] to fill with great surprise or wonder; astonish —**amaze'ment** *n.* —**amaz'ing** *adj.* —**amaz'ingly** *adv.*

Ama·zon (am'ə zän') *n.* 1 *Gr. Myth.* any of a race of female warriors 2 [a-] a large, strong, masculine woman

am·bas·sa·dor (am bas'ə dər) *n.* [< Prov *ambaissador*] the highest-ranking diplomatic representative of one country to another —**am·bas'sa·do'ri·al** (-dôr'ē əl) *adj.* —**am·bas'sa·dor·ship'** *n.*

am·ber (am'bər) *n.* [< Ar *'anbar*, ambergris] 1 a brownish-yellow fossil resin used in jewelry, etc. 2 its color — *adj.* amberlike or amber-colored

am'ber·gris' (-grēs', -gris') *n.* [< OFr *ambre gris*, gray amber] a waxy substance secreted by certain whales, used in making perfumes

ambi- [L] *combining form* both [*ambidextrous*]

ambi·dex·trous (am'bə deks'trəs) *adj.* [< earlier *ambidexter* + -OUS] using both hands with equal ease —**am'bi·dex·ter'i·ty** (-deks ter'ə tē) *n.*

am·bi·ence (am'bē əns) *n.* [Fr: see fol.] an environment or its distinct atmosphere Also **am'bi·ance** (-əns)

am'bi·ent (-ənt) *adj.* [< L *ambi-*, around + *ire*, to go] surrounding

am·bi·gu·ity (am'bə gyōō'ə tē) *n.* 1 a being ambiguous 2 *pl.* -ties an ambiguous expression

am·big·u·ous (am big'yōō əs) *adj.* [< L *ambi-*, around + *agere*, to do] 1 having two or more meanings 2 not clear; vague —**am·big'u·ously** *adv.*

am·bi·tion (am bish'ən) *n.* [< L *ambitio*, a going around (to solicit votes)] 1 a strong desire for fame, power, etc. 2 the thing desired

am·bi·tious (-əs) *adj.* 1 full of or showing ambition 2 demanding great effort —**am·bi'tiously** *adv.*

am·biva·lence (am biv'ə ləns) *n.* [AMBI- + VALENCE] simultaneous conflicting feelings —**am·biv'a·lent** *adj.* —**am·biv'a·lently** *adv.*

am·ble (am'bəl) *vi.* **-bled**, **-bling** [< L *ambulare*, to walk] 1 to move at an easy gait, as a horse 2 to walk in a leisurely way — *n.* 1 a horse's ambling gait 2 a leisurely walking pace

am·bro·sia (am brō'zhə) *n.* [< Gr *a-*, not + *brotos*, mortal] 1 *Gr. & Rom. Myth.* the food of the gods 2 anything that tastes or smells delicious —**am·bro'sial** *adj.*

am·bu·lance (am'byə ləns) *n.* [< L *ambulare*, to walk] a vehicle equipped for carrying the sick or wounded

am·bu·late (am'byōō lāt', -byə-) *vi.* **-lat'ed**, **-lat'ing** to move about; walk —**am'bu·lant** (-lənt) *adj.* —**am'bu·la'tion** *n.*

am'bu·la·to'ry (-lə tôr'ē) *adj.* 1 of or for walking 2 able to walk

am·bus·cade (am'bəs kād') *n.*, *vt.*, *vi.* **-cad'ed**, **-cad'ing** AMBUSH

am·bush (am'boosh') *n.* [< ML *in-*, in + *boscus*, woods] 1 a deployment of persons in hiding to make a surprise attack 2 their hiding place — *vt.*, *vi.* to attack from ambush

ameba (ə mē'bə) *n.*, *pl.* **-bas** or **-bae** (-bē) *alt. sp. of* AMOEBA —**ame'bic** (-bik) *adj.*

amelio·rate (ə mēl'yə rāt') *vt.*, *vi.* **-rat'ed**, **-rat'ing** [< Fr < L *melior*, better] to make or become better; improve —**amel'io·ra'tion** *n.*

amen (ā'men', ä'-) *interj.* [< Heb *amen*, truly] may it be so!: used after a prayer or to express approval

ame·nable (ə mē'nə bəl, -men'ə-) *adj.* [< OFr < L *minare*, to drive (animals)] 1 responsible or answerable 2 able to be controlled; submissive —**ame'nabil'ity** *n.* —**ame'nably** *adv.*

amend (ə mend') *vt.* [< L *emendare*] 1 to correct; emend 2 to improve 3 to change or revise (a law, etc.) — *vi.* to improve one's conduct —**amend'able** *adj.*

amend'ment *n.* 1 a correction of errors, faults, etc. 2 improvement 3 a revision or change proposed or made in a bill, law, etc.

amends (ə mendz') *n.pl.* [see AMEND] [*sometimes with sing. v.*] payment made or satisfaction given for injury, loss, etc.

amen·ity (ə men'ə tē, -mēn'-) *n.*, *pl.* **-ties** [< L *amoenus*, pleasant] 1 pleasantness 2 an attractive feature or convenience 3 [*pl.*] courteous acts

am·ent (am'ənt, ā'mənt) *n.* [< L *amentum*, thong] CATKIN

Am·er·asian (am'ər ā'zhən) *n.* [AMER(ICAN) + ASIAN] a person of both American and Asian descent

amerce (ə mʉrs') *vt.* **amerced'**, **amerc'ing** [< OFr *a merci*, at the mercy of] to punish, esp. by imposing a fine —**amerce'ment** *n.*

Ameri·can (ə mer'i kən) *adj.* 1 of or in America 2 of the U.S., its people, etc. — *n.* 1 a native or inhabitant of North or South America 2 a citizen of the U.S.

Ameri·can'a (-kan'ə) *n.pl.* books, papers, objects, etc. having to do with the U.S., its people, and its history

American Indian a member of any of the aboriginal peoples of North or South America or the West Indies

Ameri·can·ism' *n.* 1 a custom or belief of the U.S. 2 a word or idiom originating in American English 3 devotion to the U.S., its customs, etc.

Ameri·can·ize' (-īz') *vt.*, *vi.* **-ized'**, **-iz'ing** to make or become American in character, manners, etc. —**Ameri·cani·za'tion** *n.*

American plan a system of hotel operation in which the price charged covers room, service, and meals

American Revolution the war (1775-83) fought by the American colonies to gain independence from Great Britain

Am·er·in·dian (am'ər in'dē ən) *n.*, *adj.* AMERICAN INDIAN —**Am'er·ind'** *n.*

am·ethyst (am'i thist) *n.* [< Gr *amethystos*, not drunken: the Greeks thought the amethyst prevented intoxication]

■ THESAURUS ■

amass *v.* gather, hoard, store up; see ACCUMULATE.

amateur *n.* beginner, novice, learner, nonprofessional, dabbler, recruit, dilettante, hopeful, neophyte, initiate, apprentice, freshman, tenderfoot, rookie*, greenhorn, cub.—*Ant.* VETERAN, professional, expert.

amaze *v.* astonish, perplex, astound; see SURPRISE.

amazement *n.* astonishment, awe, bewilderment; see WONDER 1.

amazing *a.* astonishing, astounding, marvelous; see UNUSUAL 1.

ambassador *n.* representative, envoy, minister; see DIPLOMAT.

ambiguity *n.* doubtfulness, incertitude, vagueness; see UNCERTAINTY 1.

ambiguous *a.* equivocal, enigmatic, vague; see OBSCURE 1.

ambition *n.* hope, earnestness, aspiration, yearning, eagerness, longing, craving, passion, lust, itch, hunger, thirst, appetite, energy, ardor, zeal, enthusiasm, spirit, vigor, enterprise,

get up and go*, what it takes*.—*Ant.* INDIFFERENCE, apathy, laziness.

ambitious *a.* aspiring, longing, hopeful, zealous, hungry, thirsty, inspired, industrious, goal-oriented, enthusiastic, energetic, avid, sharp, climbing, ardent, designing, earnest, enterprising, aggressive, resourceful, pushy*.

ambush *n.* pitfall, snare, deception; see TRAP 1.

ambush *v.* waylay, ensnare, lay for, set a trap, keep out of sight, decoy, entrap, hook in, lurk, lie in wait for, surround, hem in; see also ATTACK.

amend *v.* correct, mend, revise; see ALTER 1.

amendment *n.* bill, measure, act, clause, motion, revision, supplement, rider.

American *a.* 1 [Related to the Western Hemisphere] continental, North American, Latin American, South American, Central American, Pan-American. *In reference to spe-*

cific countries of the Western Hemisphere, the following are used: Canadian, Mexican, Nicaraguan, Costa Rican, Guatemalan, Honduran, San Salvadorian, Panamanian, Cuban, Haitian, Puerto Rican, Colombian, Venezuelan, Guianan, Brazilian, Peruvian, Ecuadorian, Chilean, Argentinian, Uruguayan, Paraguayan, Bolivian, etc. 2 [Related to the United States of America] republican, constitutional, democratic, patriotic, freedom-loving, all-American.

American *n.* citizen of the United States, United States national, Yankee, Northerner, Southerner, Indian, pioneer.

Americanism *n.* patriotism, nationalism, isolationism, provincialism, flag waving, clean living, fair play, friendly rivalry, free enterprise, America first, the competitive system, spirit of '76*.

1 a purple or violet quartz or corundum, used in jewelry **2** purple or violet

ami·able (ā′mē ə bəl) *adj.* ‖< L *amicus*, friend‖ good-natured; friendly —**a′mi·abil′ity** *n.* —**a′mi·ably** *adv.*

ami·cable (am′i kə bəl) *adj.* ‖see prec.‖ friendly; peaceable —**am′i·cabil′ity** *n.* —**am′i·cably** *adv.*

amid (ə mid′) *prep.* in the middle of; among: also **amidst** (ə midst′)

am·ide (am′īd′) *n.* any of several organic compounds derived from ammonia

amid′ships′ *adv.*, *adj.* in or toward the middle of a ship

ami·go (ə mē′gō) *n.*, *pl.* **-gos′** (-gōz′) ‖Sp‖ a friend

ami·no acid (ə mē′nō, am′i nō′) ‖< AMMONIA‖ any of the nitrogenous organic acids that form proteins necessary for all life

Am·ish (äm′ish, am′-) *n.pl.* ‖after Jacob *Ammann* (or *Amen*), the founder‖ the members of a Christian sect that favors plain living in an agrarian society — *adj.* of this sect

amiss (ə mis′) *adv.* ‖see A-[1] & MISS[1]‖ in a wrong way; astray — *adj.* wrong, faulty, improper, etc. [what is *amiss?*]

am·ity (am′i tē) *n.*, *pl.* **-ties** ‖< L *amicus*, friend‖ peaceful relations

am·meter (am′mēt′ər) *n.* ‖AM(PERE) + -METER‖ an instrument for measuring an electric current in amperes

ammo (am′ō) *n.* [Slang] ammunition

am·mo·nia (ə mōn′yə) *n.* ‖prob. from a salt found near Egyptian shrine of Jupiter *Ammon*‖ **1** a colorless, pungent gas, a compound of nitrogen and hydrogen **2** a 10% water solution of this gas: in full, **ammonia water**

am·mu·ni·tion (am′yoo nish′ən) *n.* ‖< L *munire*, fortify‖ **1** bullets, gunpowder, bombs, grenades, rockets, etc. **2** any means of attack or defense

am·ne·sia (am nē′zhə) *n.* ‖< Gr *a-*, not + *mnasthai*, to remember‖ partial or total loss of memory

am·nesty (am′nəs tē) *n.*, *pl.* **-ties** ‖< Gr *amnēstia*, a forgetting‖ a pardon, esp. for political offenses — *vt.* **-tied, -ty·ing** to pardon

am·nio·cen·tesis (am′nē ō′sen tē′sis) *n.* ‖< fol. + Gr *kentēsis*, a pricking‖ the surgical procedure of extracting amniotic fluid from a pregnant woman to determine the sex of the fetus, detect disease, etc.

am·nion (am′nē ən, -än′) *n.*, *pl.* **-ni·ons** or **-nia** (-ə) ‖Gr, dim. of *amnos*, lamb‖ the membrane enclosing the embryo of a mammal, reptile, or bird: it is filled with a watery fluid (**amniotic fluid**) —**am′ni·ot′ic** (-ät′ik) *adj.*

amoe·ba (ə mē′bə) *n.*, *pl.* **-bas** or **-bae** (-bē) ‖< Gr *ameibein*, to change‖ a one-celled, microscopic organism reproducing by fission —**amoe′bic** (-bik) *adj.*

amok (ə muk′) *n.* ‖< Malay *amuk*, attacking furiously‖ in Indonesia and the Philippines, a state in which a person loses control and kills indiscriminately —**run** (or **go**) **amok 1** to rush about in a frenzy to kill **2** to lose control and behave violently **3** to become undisciplined

among (ə muŋ′) *prep.* ‖< OE *on*, in + *gemang*, a crowd‖ **1** surrounded by [among friends] **2** in the group of [best among books] **3** to or for each or several of [divide it among the crowd] **4** by the joint action of Also **amongst** (ə muŋst′)

Amon-Re (ä′mən rā′) the ancient Egyptian sun god

amon·til·lado (ə män′tə lä′dō) *n.* ‖< Sp, after *Montilla*, town in Spain‖ a pale, relatively dry sherry

amor·al (ā môr′əl) *adj.* **1** neither moral nor immoral **2** without moral sense —**a′mo·ral′ity** *n.* —**amor′ally** *adv.*

amo·rous (am′ə rəs) *adj.* ‖< L *amor*, love‖ **1** fond of making love **2** full of love **3** of sexual love —**am′o·rously** *adv.*

amor·phous (ə môr′fəs) *adj.* ‖< Gr *a-*, without + *morphē*, form‖ **1** without definite form **2** vague or indefinite **3** *Chem.* not crystalline

am·or·tize (am′ər tīz′, ə môr′-) *vt.* **-tized′, -tiz′ing** ‖< ME < L *ad*, to + *mors*, death‖ to put money aside at intervals for gradual payment of (a debt, etc.) —**am′or·ti·za′tion** *n.*

amount (ə mount′) *vi.* ‖< OFr *amont*, upward < L *ad*, to + *mons*, mountain‖ **1** to add up (*to*) **2** to be equal (*to*) in value, etc. — *n.* **1** a sum total **2** the whole value or effect **3** a quantity

amour (ə moor′, ə-) *n.* ‖< L *amor*, love‖ a love affair, esp. an illicit one

amour-propre (ä moor prō′pr′) *n.* ‖Fr‖ self-esteem

amp. *abbrev.* **1** amperage **2** ampere(s)

am·per·age (am′pər ij, am pir′-) *n.* the strength of an electric current in amperes

am·pere (am′pir′) *n.* ‖< A. M. *Ampère*, 19th-c. Fr physicist‖ the standard unit for measuring an electric current, equal to one coulomb per second

am·per·sand (am′pər sand′) *n.* ‖< *and per se and*, (the sign) & by itself (is) *and* ‖ a sign (&), meaning *and*

am·phet·amine (am fet′ə mēn′, -min) *n.* a drug used esp. as a stimulant and to lessen appetite

am·phib·ian (am fib′ē ən) *n.* ‖see fol.‖ **1** any amphibious animal or plant **2** any aircraft that can take off from or land on water or land — *adj.* AMPHIBIOUS

am·phib′i·ous *adj.* ‖Gr *amphibios*, living a double life < *amphi-*, around + *bios*, life‖ that can live or operate on land and in water

amphi·thea·ter or **amphi·thea·tre** (am′fə thē′ət ər) *n.* ‖< Gr *amphi-*, around + *theatron*, theater‖ a round or oval building with rising rows of seats around an open space

am·ple (am′pəl) *adj.* **-pler, -plest** ‖< L *amplus*‖ **1** large in size, scope, etc. **2** more than enough **3** adequate —**am′ply** *adv.*

am·pli·fier (am′plə fī′ər) *n.* one that amplifies; esp., a device for strengthening electrical signals

am′plify′ (-fī′) *vt.* **-fied′, -fy′ing** ‖< L *amplus*, large + *facere*, to make‖ **1** to make stronger; esp., to strengthen (electrical signals) **2** to develop more fully —**am′pli·fi·ca′tion** *n.*

am·pli·tude (am′plə tood′) *n.* ‖see AMPLE‖ **1** scope, extent, breadth, etc. **2** abundance **3** range from mean to extreme, as of an alternating current

amplitude modulation the changing of the amplitude of the transmitting radio wave in accordance with the signal being broadcast

am·pul (am′pool) *n.* ‖< L *ampulla*, bottle‖ a sealed glass container for one dose of a hypodermic medicine Also **am′pule** (-pyool) or **am′poule** (-pool)

am·pu·tate (am′pyoo tāt′) *vt.*, *vi.* **-tat′ed, -tat′ing** ‖< L *am-*, AMBI- + *putare*, to prune‖ to cut off (an arm, etc.), esp. by surgery —**am′pu·ta′tion** *n.*

am′pu·tee′ (-tē′) *n.* one who has had a limb or limbs amputated

amt. amount

Am·trak (am′trak′) ‖*Am(erican) tr(avel) (tr)a(c)k*‖ a national U.S. passenger railroad system

amuck (ə muk′) *n.* AMOK

amu·let (am′yoo lit) *n.* ‖< L‖ something worn to protect against evil

amuse (ə myooz′) *vt.* **amused′, amus′ing** ‖< Fr < à, at + OFr *muser*, to gaze‖ **1** to keep pleasantly occupied; entertain **2** to make laugh, smile, etc. —**a·mus′edly** *adv.*

amuse′ment *n.* **1** a being amused **2** something that amuses

amusement park an outdoor place with devices for entertainment, as a merry-go-round, roller coaster, etc.

amyl·ase (am′ə lās′) *n.* ‖< Gr *amylon*, starch‖ an enzyme that helps change starch into sugar, found in saliva, etc.

an (an; *unstressed*, ən, 'n) *adj.*, *indefinite article* ‖< OE *an*, one‖ **1** one; one sort of **2** each; any one **3** per [two an hour] *An* is used before words beginning with a vowel sound [an eye, an honor] See also A[2]

-an (ən, in, 'n) ‖< L *-anus*‖ *suffix* **1** (one) belonging to

---

THESAURUS

amiable *a.* pleasant, genial, charming; see FRIENDLY.

ammunition *n.* Types of ammunition include the following: projectile, charge, grenade, buckshot, gunpowder, cartridge, bullet, bomb, missile, hand grenade, fuse, shrapnel, torpedo, shell, ball, cannonball, shot, ammo*; see also BOMB, BULLET, EXPLOSIVE, GAS 3, SHOT 1.

among *prep.* between, in, in between, in the midst of, in the middle of, encompassed by, surrounded by, in connection with, amid, amongst,

amidst, in the company of, betwixt*.

amount *n.* **1** [The total of several quantities] sum, product, sum total; see WHOLE. **2** [Price] expense, output, outlay; see PRICE. **3** [Quantity] bulk, mass, number; see QUANTITY.

amount to *v.* reach, extend to, come to, effect, be equal to, approximate, check with, total up to, be in all, be in the whole, total, tally with, add up to, be tantamount to.

ample *a.* sufficient, plentiful, adequate; see ENOUGH 1.

amplify *v.* expand, augment, elaborate; see INCREASE.

amply *a.* enough, sufficiently, copiously; see ADEQUATELY.

amputate *v.* cut off, sever, cut away; see REMOVE.

amuse *v.* divert, cheer, enliven; see ENTERTAIN 1.

amusement *n.* recreation, pastime, play; see ENTERTAINMENT.

amusing *a.* engaging, diverting, enchanting; see ENTERTAINING.

[diocesan] **2** (one) born in or living in *[Mexican]* **3** (one) believing in *[Lutheran]*

anach·ro·nism (ə nak'rə niz'əm) *n.* ⟦ < Gr *ana-*, against + *chronos*, time⟧ **1** anything out of its proper historical time **2** the representation of this —**anach'ro·nis'tic** *adj.*

ana·con·da (an'ə kän'də) *n.* ⟦ < Sinhalese *henacandāya*, a snake of Sri Lanka⟧ a South American boa that crushes its prey in its coils

an·aero·bic (an'ər ō'bik) *adj.* ⟦ < Gr *an-*, without + *āēr*, air + *bios*, life⟧ able to live and grow without air or free oxygen, as certain bacteria

an·aes·the·sia (an'əs thē'zhə) *n.* ANESTHESIA —**an'aes·thet'ic** (-thet'ik) *adj., n.*

ana·gram (an'ə gram') *n.* ⟦ < Gr *anagrammatizein*, transpose letters⟧ **1** a word, etc. made by rearranging letters (Ex.: *now — won*) **2** *[pl., with sing. v.]* a word game based on this

anal (ā'nəl) *adj.* of or near the anus

an·al·gesia (an'l jē'zē ə) *n.* ⟦ < Gr *an-*, without + *algēsia*, pain⟧ a fully conscious state in which pain is not felt

an·al·ge'sic (-zik) *adj.* of or causing analgesia —*n.* a drug that produces analgesia

ana·log (an'ə lôg') *adj.* **1** of an analog computer **2** of electronic devices in which the signal corresponds to a physical change **3** using hands, dials, etc. to show numerical amounts, as on a clock: cf. DIGITAL (sense 2) —*n.* ANALOGUE

analog computer a computer for processing data represented by a continuous physical variable, as electric current: cf. DIGITAL COMPUTER

analo·gize (ə nal'ə jiz') *vi., vt.* **-gized', -giz'ing** to use, or explain by, analogy

anal'o·gous (-gəs) *adj.* ⟦ see ANALOGY⟧ similar in some way —**anal'o·gously** *adv.*

ana·logue (an'ə lôg') *n.* something analogous

anal·ogy (ə nal'ə jē) *n., pl.* **-gies** ⟦ < Gr *ana-*, according to + *logos*, word, reckoning⟧ **1** similarity in some ways **2** the inference that certain resemblances imply further similarity

analy·sand (ə nal'ə sand') *n.* a person undergoing psychoanalysis

anal'y·sis (-sis) *n., pl.* **-ses'** (-sēz') ⟦ < Gr *ana-*, up + *lysis*, a loosing⟧ **1** a breaking up of a whole into its parts to find out their nature, etc. **2** a statement of the results of this **3** PSYCHOANALYSIS **4** *Chem.* an analysis of compounds or mixtures —**ana·lytic** (an'ə lit'ik) or **an'a·lyt'i·cal** *adj.* —**an'a·lyt'i·cally** *adv.*

ana·lyst (an'ə list) *n.* **1** one who analyzes **2** a psychoanalyst

an'a·lyze' (-līz') *vt.* **-lyzed', -lyz'ing 1** to make an analysis of; examine in detail **2** to psychoanalyze —**an'a·lyz'able** *adj.* —**an'a·lyz'er** *n.*

ana·pest (an'ə pest') *n.* ⟦ < Gr *ana-*, back + *paiein*, to strike⟧ a metrical foot of two unaccented syllables followed by an accented one

an·ar·chism (an'ər kiz'əm) *n.* **1** the theory that all forms of government interfere unjustly with individual liberty **2** resistance to all government —**an'ar·chist'** *n.* —**an'ar·chis'tic** *adj.*

an·ar·chy (-kē) *n., pl.* **-chies** ⟦ < Gr *an-*, without + *archos*, leader⟧ **1** the absence of government **2** political disorder and violence **3** disorder; confusion —**an·ar·chic** (an är'kik) *adj.* —**an·ar'chi·cally** *adv.*

anath·ema (ə nath'ə mə) *n., pl.* **-mas** ⟦Gr, thing devoted to evil⟧ **1** a thing or person accursed or damned **2** a thing or person greatly detested **3** a formal curse, as in excommunication

anath'ema·tize' (-tīz') *vt., vi.* **-tized', -tiz'ing** to utter an anathema (against); curse

anato·mize (ə nat'ə mīz') *vt., vi.* **-mized', -miz'ing** ⟦ see ANATOMY⟧ **1** to dissect (an animal or plant) in order to examine the structure **2** to analyze —**anat'o·mist** *n.*

anat'o·my (-mē) *n., pl.* **-mies** ⟦ < Gr *ana-*, up + *temnein*, to cut⟧ **1** dissection of an organism to study its structure **2** the science of the structure of animals or plants **3** the

structure of an organism **4** any analysis —**ana·tomi·cal** (an'ə täm'i kəl) or **an'a·tom'ic** *adj.*

-ance (əns) ⟦ < L⟧ *suffix* **1** the act or process of ___ing *[discontinuance]* **2** the quality or state of being *[forbearance]* **3** a thing that ___s *[hindrance]* **4** a thing that is ___ed *[utterance]*

an·ces·tor (an'ses'tər) *n.* ⟦ < L *ante-*, before + *cedere*, go⟧ **1** a person from whom one is descended; forebear **2** a precursor or forerunner —**an·ces'tral** (an ses'trəl) *adj.* —**an·ces·tress** (an'ses'trəs) *n.fem.*

an'ces'try (-trē) *n., pl.* **-tries 1** family descent **2** ancestors collectively

an·chor (aŋ'kər) *n.* ⟦ < L *ancora*, an anchor, hook⟧ **1** a heavy object, usually an iron weight with flukes, lowered from a vessel, as by cable, to prevent drifting **2** anything giving stability **3** one who anchors a newscast: also **an'chor·man', an'chor·wom'an,** or **an'chor·per'son** —*vt.* **1** to hold secure as by an anchor **2** to be the final contestant on (a relay team, etc.) **3** to serve as coordinator and chief reporter for (a newscast) —*vi.* **1** to lower an anchor **2** to be or become fixed —**at anchor** anchored

an'chor·age (-ij) *n.* **1** an anchoring or being anchored **2** a place to anchor

an·cho·rite (aŋ'kə rīt') *n.* ⟦ < Gr *ana-*, back + *chōrein*, retire⟧ a religious recluse; hermit

an·cho·vy (an'chə vē, an'chō-) *n., pl.* **-vies** ⟦ < Port *anchova*⟧ a herringlike fish, eaten as a relish

an·cient (ān'chənt) *adj.* ⟦ < L *ante*, before⟧ **1** of times long past **2** very old —*n.* an aged person

an·cil·lary (an'sə ler'ē) *adj.* ⟦ < L *ancilla*, maidservant⟧ **1** subordinate: often with *to* **2** auxiliary

-ancy (ən sē) *suffix* -ANCE

and (and; *unstressed*, ənd, ən) *conj.* ⟦OE⟧ **1** also; in addition **2** plus **3** as a result **4** in contrast; but **5** [Colloq.] to *[try and come today]*

an·dante (än dän'tā) *adj., adv.* ⟦It < *andare*, to walk⟧ *Musical Direction* moderate in tempo

and·iron (and'ī'ərn) *n.* ⟦ < OFr *andier*⟧ either of a pair of metal supports for logs in a fireplace

and/or either *and* or or *[personal and/or real property]*

an·dro·gen (an'drō jən) *n.* ⟦ < Gr *andros*, of man + -GEN⟧ a type of steroid that acts as a male sex hormone —**an'dro·gen'ic** (-jen'ik) *adj.*

an·drogy·nous (an drä'jə nəs) *adj.* ⟦ < Gr *andros*, of man + *gynē*, woman⟧ **1** both male and female in one **2** that blends male and female characteristics, etc.

an·droid (an'droid') *n.* ⟦ < Gr *andros*, of man + -OID⟧ in science fiction, an automaton made to resemble a human being

an·ec·dote (an'ik dōt') *n.* ⟦ < Gr *anekdotos*, unpublished⟧ a short, entertaining account of some event —**an'ec·dot'al** *adj.*

anemia (ə nē'mē ə) *n.* ⟦ < Gr *an-*, without + *haima*, blood⟧ a condition in which the blood is low in red cells or in hemoglobin, resulting in paleness, weakness, etc. —**ane'mic** *adj.*

an·emom·eter (an'ə mäm'ət ər) *n.* ⟦ < Gr *anemos*, the wind + -METER⟧ a gauge for determining the force or speed of the wind; wind gauge

anemo·ne (ə nem'ə nē') *n.* ⟦ < Gr *anemos*, the wind⟧ **1** a plant with cup-shaped flowers of white, pink, red, or purple **2** SEA ANEMONE

anent (ə nent') *prep.* ⟦ < OE *on efen*, on even (with)⟧ [Now Rare] concerning; about

aneroid barometer (an'ər oid') ⟦ < Gr *a-*, without + *nēros*, liquid + -OID⟧ a barometer working by the bending of a thin metal disk instead of by the rise or fall of mercury

an·es·thesia (an'es thē'zhə) *n.* ⟦ < Gr *an-*, without + *aisthēsis*, feeling⟧ a partial or total loss of the sense of pain, touch, etc.

THESAURUS

analysis *n.* study, investigation, search; see EXAMINATION 1.

analyze *v.* dissect, examine, investigate, separate, break down, disintegrate, resolve into elements, determine the essential features of, decentralize.

anarchy *n.* turmoil, chaos, mob rule; see DISORDER.

anatomy *n.* physique, form, figure; see BODY 1.

ancestor *n.* progenitor, forebear,

founder of the family; see FOREFATHER.

ancestral *a.* inborn, congenital, inherited; see INHERENT.

ancestry *n.* lineage, heritage, parentage; see FAMILY.

anchor *n.* stay, tie, grapnel, mooring, grappling iron, support, mainstay, ballast, safeguard, security, protection, hold, fastener, grip, defense, protection, foothold.

anchor *v.* make port, tie up, moor,

berth, bring a ship in, drop anchor, cast anchor.

ancient *a.* antique, antiquated, aged; see OLD 1, 2, 3.

and *conj.* in addition to, also, including, plus, together with, as well as, furthermore, moreover.

anecdote *n.* tale, incident, episode; see STORY.

anemic *a.* pallid, weak, sickly; see PALE 1.

an·es·the'si·ol'o·gist (-thē'zē äl'ə jist) *n.* a doctor who specializes in giving anesthetics —**an·es·the'si·ol'ogy** *n.*

an·es·thet'ic (-thet'ik) *adj.* of or producing anesthesia —*n.* a drug, gas, etc. used to produce anesthesia, as before surgery

an·es·thetist (ə nes'thə tist') *n.* one trained to give anesthetics

an·es'the·tize' (-tīz') *vt.* **-tized'**, **-tiz'ing** to cause anesthesia in —**an·es'the·ti·za'tion** *n.*

aneu·rysm or **aneu·rism** (an'yōō riz'əm) *n.* ⟦< Gr *ana-*, up + *eurys*, broad⟧ a sac formed by an enlargement in a weakened wall of an artery, a vein, or the heart

anew (ə nōō') *adv.* **1** once more; again **2** in a new manner or form

an·gel (ān'jəl) *n.* ⟦< Gr *angelos*, messenger⟧ **1** *Theol.* a) a messenger of God b) a supernatural being with greater than human power, etc. **2** an image of a human figure with wings and a halo **3** a person regarded as beautiful, good, innocent, etc. **4** [Colloq.] a financial backer, as for a play —**an·gelic** (an jel'ik) or **an·gel'i·cal** *adj.* —**an·gel'i·cally** *adv.*

angel dust [Slang] a powerful psychedelic drug

An·ge·leno (an'jə lē'nō) *n., pl.* **-nos** ⟦AmSp⟧ an inhabitant of Los Angeles

angel·fish (ān'jəl fish') *n., pl.* **-fish'** or (for different species) **-fish'es** a bright-colored tropical fish with spiny fins

angel (food) cake a light, spongy, white cake made with egg whites

an·ger (aŋ'gər) *n.* ⟦< ON *angr*, distress⟧ hostile feelings because of opposition, a hurt, etc. —*vt., vi.* to make or become angry

an·gina (pec·to·ris) (an ji'nə pek'tər is) ⟦L, lit., squeezing of the breast⟧ a condition marked by chest pain, caused by a decrease of blood to the heart

an·gio·plasty (an'jē ō plas'tē) *n.* any of various surgical techniques for repairing or replacing damaged blood vessels

an·gio·sperm (an'jē ō spurm') *n.* ⟦< Gr *angos*, vessel + *sperma*, seed⟧ a plant having seeds produced within a closed pod or ovary

an·gle[1] (aŋ'gəl) *n.* ⟦< Gr *ankylos*, bent⟧ **1** the shape or space made by two straight lines or plane surfaces that meet **2** this space, measured in degrees, etc. **3** a sharp corner **4** a point of view; aspect **5** [Colloq.] a tricky method for achieving a purpose —*vt., vi.* **-gled**, **-gling 1** to move or bend at an angle **2** [Colloq.] to give a specific aspect to (a story, etc.)

an·gle[2] (aŋ'gəl) *vi.* **-gled**, **-gling** ⟦< OE *angul*, fishhook⟧ **1** to fish with a hook and line **2** to use tricks to get something *[to angle for a promotion]* —**an'gler** *n.*

angle iron a piece of iron or steel bent at a right angle, used for joining or reinforcing two beams, girders, etc.

An·gles (aŋ'gəlz) *n.pl.* a Germanic people that settled in E England in the 5th c. A.D.

an'gle·worm' *n.* an earthworm

An·gli·can (aŋ'gli kən) *adj.* ⟦< ML *Anglicus*, of the Angles⟧ of or connected with the Church of England —*n.* an Anglican church member

An'gli·cism' (-glə siz'əm) *n.* a word or trait peculiar to the English

An'gli·cize' (-sīz') *vt., vi.* **-cized'**, **-ciz'ing** to change to English idiom, pronunciation, customs, etc. —**An'gli·ci·za'tion** (-si zā'shən) *n.*

Anglo- *combining form* **1** English **2** Anglican

An'glo-Amer'ican (aŋ'glō-) *adj.* English and American —*n.* an American of English birth or ancestry

An'glo-French' *adj.* English and French —*n.* the French spoken in England from the Norman Conquest through the Middle Ages

An'glo-Sax'on *n.* **1** a member of the Germanic peoples in England at the time of the Norman Conquest **2** their language, OLD ENGLISH **3** an Englishman —*adj.* of the Anglo-Saxons

An·gora (aŋ gôr'ə) *n.* ⟦former name of Ankara, city in Turkey⟧ **1** a breed of animal; specif., a cat, goat, or rabbit with long, silky fur or hair **2** a) yarn of Angora rabbit hair b) mohair

an·gry (aŋ'grē) *adj.* **-grier**, **-gri·est 1** feeling or showing anger **2** wild and stormy —**an'grily** (-grə lē) *adv.*

ang·strom (unit) (aŋ'strəm) ⟦after A. J. *Angström*, 19th-c. Swed physicist⟧ one hundred-millionth of a centimeter: a unit used in measuring the length of light waves

an·guish (aŋ'gwish) *n.* ⟦< L *angustia*, tightness⟧ great mental or physical pain; agony —*vi., vt.* to feel or cause to feel anguish —**an'guished** *adj.*

an·gu·lar (aŋ'gyōō lər) *adj.* **1** having or forming an angle or angles; having sharp corners **2** lean; gaunt **3** without ease or grace; stiff —**an'gu·lar'ity** (-lar'ə tē), *pl.* **-ties**, *n.*

ani·line (an'ə lin) *n.* ⟦< Ar *an-nil*, the indigo plant⟧ a colorless, poisonous, oily derivative of benzene, used in making dyes, resins, etc.

ani·mad·vert (an'i məd vurt', -mad'-) *vi.* ⟦L *animadvertere*, lit., to turn the mind⟧ to comment adversely (*on* or *upon*) —**an·i·mad·ver'sion** *n.*

ani·mal (an'i məl) *n.* ⟦L < *anima*, breath, soul⟧ **1** any living organism, excluding plants and bacteria, typically able to move about **2** any such organism other than a human being; esp., any four-footed creature **3** a brutish or inhuman person —*adj.* **1** of or like an animal **2** gross, bestial, etc.

ani·mal·cule (an'i mal'kyōōl') *n.* [Obs.] a microscopic animal; protozoan

ani·mate (an'i māt'; *for adj.*, -mit) *vt.* **-mat'ed**, **-mat'ing** ⟦see ANIMAL⟧ **1** to give life or motion to **2** to make merry or spirited **3** to inspire —*adj.* living —**an'i·mat'ed** *adj.* —**an'i·ma'tion** *n.* —**an'i·ma'tor** *n.*

animated cartoon a film made by photographing a series of drawings so that the figures in them seem to move

ani·mism (an'i miz'əm) *n.* ⟦< L *anima*, soul⟧ the belief that all life is produced by a spiritual force, or that all natural phenomena have souls —**an'i·mis'tic** *adj.*

═ THESAURUS ═

anesthetic *n.* hypnosis, gas, opiate; see DRUG.

angel *n.* Angel of Death, good angel, dark angel, archangel, guardian angel, spirit, cherub, celestial spirit, winged being, saint.—*Ant.* DEVIL, demon, Satan.

angelic *a.* saintly, good, humble, heavenly, spiritual, kind, radiant, beautiful, divine, holy, pure, lovely, devout, virtuous, above reproach, righteous, cherubic.—*Ant.* WICKED, demonic, evil.

anger *n.* wrath, rage, fury, passion, temper, bad temper, animosity, indignation, hatred, resentment, ire, hot temper, impatience, vexation, annoyance, provocation, violence, turbulence, excitement, frenzy, tantrum, exasperation, huff, irritation, dander*.—*Ant.* PATIENCE, mildness, calm.

anger *v.* infuriate, annoy, irritate; see ENRAGE.

angle[1] *n.* **1** [Figure or plane formed at an intersection] notch, crotch, elbow, fork, cusp, incline, decline, Y, V, point where two lines meet.—*Ant.*

CURVE, arc, oval. **2** [Point of view] standpoint, outlook, perspective; see VIEWPOINT.

angle for *v.* plot, scheme, maneuver; see PLAN 1.

angler *n.* fisher, fisherwoman, Waltonian; see FISHERMAN.

angrily *a.* heatedly, indignantly, irately, grouchily, crisply, sharply, savagely, hotly, fiercely, tartly, bitterly, furiously, wildly, violently.—*Ant.* CALMLY, softly, quietly.

angry *a.* enraged, fierce, fiery, irate, raging, fuming, infuriated, furious, wrathful, stormy, indignant, cross, vexed, resentful, irritated, bitter, ferocious, offended, sullen, hateful, annoyed, provoked, displeased, riled, affronted, huffy, hostile, rabid, having flown off the handle*, mad, up in the air*, hot under the collar*, boiling, steamed up*, at the boiling point*, with one's back up, all worked up, up in arms.—*Ant.* CALM, quiet, restrained. —**get angry** become enraged, become furious, lose one's temper, get mad, blow up*, blow one's cool*, lose one's cool*, get

hot under the collar*, get steamed up*, fly off the handle*, blow a fuse*.

anguish *n.* wretchedness, pain, agony; see PAIN 1.

angular *a.* sharp-cornered, intersecting, crossing, oblique, divaricate, with corners, Y-shaped, V-shaped, crotched, forked, bent, crooked, pointed, triangular, rectangular, jagged, staggered, zigzag.—*Ant.* ROUND, parallel, side by side.

animal *a.* bestial, beastly, swinish, brutish, wild, beastlike, untamed, mammalian, bovine, canine, feline, reptilian.

animal *n.* living thing, creature, human being, beast, being, fish, crustacean, amphibian, vertebrate, invertebrate, reptile, insect, bird, wild animal, domestic animal, mammal; see also BIRD, FISH, INSECT, MAN 1.

animate *v.* activate, vitalize, inform, make alive, arouse, give life to, energize, put life into, breathe new life into.

animated *a.* spirited, gay, lively; see HAPPY.

ani·mos·ity (an′ə mäs′ə tē) *n.*, *pl.* **-ties** ⟦see fol.⟧ a feeling of strong dislike or hatred; hostility

ani·mus (an′ə məs) *n.* ⟦L, passion⟧ animosity; hostility

an·ion (an′ī′ən) *n.* ⟦< Gr *anion*, thing going up⟧ a negatively charged ion: in electrolysis, anions move toward the anode

an·ise (an′is) *n.* ⟦< Gr *anison*⟧ 1 a dicotyledonous plant related to the umbel 2 its fragrant seed, used for flavoring: also **an′i·seed′** (-i sēd′)

ani·sette (an′i zet′, -set′) *n.* ⟦Fr⟧ a sweet, anise-flavored liqueur

An·jou pear (an′jōō′) a thick, green, oval-shaped pear that ripens during the winter

ankh (aŋk) *n.* ⟦Egypt, life, soul⟧ a cross with a loop at the top, an ancient Egyptian symbol of life

an·kle (aŋ′kəl) *n.* ⟦OE *ancleow*⟧ 1 the joint that connects the foot and the leg 2 the area of the leg between the foot and calf

anklet (aŋk′lit) *n.* 1 an ornament worn around the ankle 2 a short sock

an·nals (an′əlz) *n.pl.* ⟦< L *annus*, year⟧ 1 a written account of events year by year 2 historical records; history —**an′nal·ist** *n.*

an·neal (ə nēl′) *vt.* ⟦< OE *an-*, on + *æl*, fire⟧ to heat (glass, metals, etc.) and cool slowly to prevent brittleness

an·nelid (an′ə lid′) *n.* ⟦< L dim. of *anulus*, a ring⟧ any of various wormlike animals having long, segmented bodies, including leeches

an·nex (ə neks′; *for n.*, an′eks′) *vt.* ⟦< L *ad-*, to + *nectere*, to tie⟧ 1 to attach, esp. to something larger 2 to incorporate into a state the territory of (another state) — *n.* something annexed; esp., an addition to a building —**an·nexa·tion** (an′eks ā′shən) *n.*

an·ni·hi·late (ə nī′ə lāt′) *vt.* **-lat′ed, -lat′ing** ⟦< L *ad*, to + *nihil*, nothing⟧ to destroy completely —**an·ni′hi·la′tion** *n.* —**an·ni′hi·la′tor** *n.*

anni·ver·sary (an′ə vur′sə rē) *n.*, *pl.* **-ries** ⟦< L *annus*, year + *vertere*, to turn⟧ the yearly return of the date of some event — *adj.* of an anniversary

an·no·tate (an′ō tāt′) *vt.*, *vi.* **-tat′ed, -tat′ing** ⟦< L *ad-*, to + *nota*, a sign⟧ to provide explanatory notes for —**an′no·ta′tion** *n.* —**an′no·ta′tor** *n.*

an·nounce (ə nouns′) *vt.* **-nounced′, -nounc′ing** ⟦< L *ad-*, to + *nuntius*, messenger⟧ 1 to declare publicly 2 to make known the arrival of 3 to be an announcer for — *vi.* to serve as announcer —**an·nounce′ment** *n.*

an·nouncer (ə noun′sər) *n.* one who announces; specif., one who introduces radio or television programs

an·noy (ə noi′) *vt.* ⟦< VL *in odio*, in hate⟧ to irritate or bother, as by a repeated action —**an·noy′ance** *n.* —**an·noy′ing** *adj.* —**an·noy′ingly** *adv.*

an·nual (an′yōō əl) *adj.* ⟦< L *annus*, year⟧ 1 of or measured by a year 2 yearly 3 living only one year or season — *n.* 1 a periodical published once a year 2 a plant living only one year or season —**an′nu·ally** *adv.*

an·nu·ity (ə nōō′ə tē) *n.*, *pl.* **-ties** ⟦see prec.⟧ 1 an investment yielding periodic payments, esp. yearly 2 such a payment —**an·nu′i·tant** *n.*

an·nul (ə nul′) *vt.* **-nulled′, -nul′ling** ⟦< L *ad-*, to + *nullum*, nothing⟧ 1 to do away with 2 to deprive of legal force; nullify —**an·nul′ment** *n.*

an·nu·lar (an′yōō lər) *adj.* ⟦< L *anulus*, a ring⟧ like or forming a ring

an·nun·cia·tion (ə nun′sē ā′shən) *n.* an announcing — **the Annunciation** 1 the angel Gabriel's announcement to Mary that she would bear Jesus 2 the church festival commemorating this

an·ode (an′ōd′) *n.* ⟦< Gr *anodos*, a way up⟧ 1 the positive electrode in an electrolytic cell 2 the principal electrode for collecting electrons in an electron tube 3 the negative electrode in a battery

ano·dyne (an′ō din′) *n.* ⟦< Gr *an-*, without + *odynē*, pain⟧ anything that relieves pain or soothes

anoint (ə noint′) *vt.* ⟦< L *in-*, on + *unguere*, to smear⟧ to put oil on, as in consecrating —**anoint′ment** *n.*

anoma·lous (ə näm′ə ləs) *adj.* ⟦< Gr *an-*, not + *homos*, the same⟧ 1 abnormal 2 inconsistent or odd

anom′a·ly (-lē) *n.*, *pl.* **-lies** 1 abnormality 2 anything anomalous

ano·mie or **ano·my** (an′ə mē) *n.* ⟦Fr < Gr *anomia*, lawlessness⟧ lack of purpose, identity, etc.; rootlessness

anon (ə nän′) *adv.* ⟦< OE *on an*, into one⟧ 1 soon 2 at another time

anon. anonymous

anony·mous (ə nän′ə məs) *adj.* ⟦< Gr *an-*, without + *onyma*, name⟧ 1 with no name known 2 given, written, etc. by one whose name is withheld or unknown 3 lacking individuality —**ano·nym·ity** (an′ə nim′ə tē) *n.* —**anon′y·mously** *adv.*

anoph·eles (ə näf′ə lēz′) *n.* ⟦< Gr *anōphelēs*, harmful⟧ the mosquito that can transmit malaria

ano·rex·ia (an′ə reks′ē ə) *n.* ⟦< Gr *an-*, without + *orexis*, desire⟧ an eating disorder characterized by obsession with weight loss In full **anorexia ner·vosa** (nər vō′sə) — **an′o·rex′ic** *adj.*, *n.*

an·other (ə nuth′ər) *adj.* 1 one more; an additional 2 a different — *pron.* 1 one additional 2 a different one 3 one of the same kind

an·swer (an′sər) *n.* ⟦< OE *and-*, against + *swerian*, swear⟧ 1 a reply to a question, letter, etc. 2 any act in

---

THESAURUS

animosity *n.* dislike, enmity, displeasure; see HATRED.

ankle *n.* anklebone, joint, tarsus; see BONE, FOOT 2.

annex *n.* expansion, additional quarters, new wing; see ADDITION 1, 2.

annex *v.* append, attach, affix; see ADD.

annihilate *v.* demolish, exterminate, obliterate; see DESTROY.

anniversary *n.* holiday, saint's day, birth date, birthday, yearly observance of an event, feastday, ceremony, annual meeting, biennial, triennial, quadrennial, quintennial, silver anniversary, golden anniversary, diamond jubilee, jubilee, festival, fiesta, centennial, red-letter day.

announce *v.* proclaim, publish, state; see DECLARE.

announced *a.* reported, given out, told, broadcast, issued, circulated, proclaimed, declared, published, disclosed, divulged, released, made known, disseminated, revealed, publicized, made public.—*Ant.* HIDDEN, unannounced, unrevealed.

announcement *n.* declaration, notification, prediction, proclamation, communication, publication, report, statement, advertisement, decision, news, tidings, returns, brief, bulletin, edict, white paper, message, notice, interim report, survey, advice, item, detail, communiqué, speech, release,

handbill, poster, pamphlet, circular, billboard, brochure, form letter, telegram, cablegram, letter, leaflet; see also ADVERTISEMENT.—*Ant.* SECRET, ban, silence.

announcer *n.* program announcer, broadcaster, television announcer, telecaster, commentator, sportscaster, newscaster, radio announcer, disc jockey.

annoy *v.* pester, irritate, trouble; see BOTHER 2.

annoyance *n.* 1 [A feeling of annoyance] vexation, irritation, pique, uneasiness, disgust, displeasure, provocation, nervousness, exasperation, indignation, touchiness, perturbation, moodiness, mortification, vexation, worry, distress, unhappiness, discontent, heartache, misery, aches and pains, dissatisfaction, impatience, peeve*.—*Ant.* JOY, pleasure, delight. 2 [A source of annoyance] worry, inconvenience, nuisance; see DIFFICULTY 1, 2, TROUBLE 1.

annoying *a.* irritating, bothersome, vexatious; see DISTURBING.

annual *a.* yearly, each year, every year, once a year, lasting a year, anniversary, seasonal.

annually *a.* each year, once a year, periodically; see YEARLY.

annul *v.* invalidate, render void, repeal, revoke; see also CANCEL.

annulment *n.* invalidation, nullification, dissolution; see CANCELLATION.

anonymous *a.* unsigned, nameless, unknown, unnamed, unacknowledged, unclaimed, unidentified, secret, of unknown authorship, without a name, bearing no name, incognito, pseudo.—*Ant.* NAMED, signed, acknowledged.

another *a.* 1 [Additional] one more, a further, added; see EXTRA. 2 [Different] a separate, a distinct, some other; see UNLIKE.

another *n.* someone else, a different person, one more, addition, something else.—*Ant.* ONE, same, each.

answer *n.* 1 [A reply] response, return, statement, retort, echo, repartee, password, rebuttal, approval, acknowledgment, sign, rejoinder, comeback.—*Ant.* QUESTION, query, request. 2 [A solution] discovery, find, disclosure, revelation, explanation, interpretation, clue, resolution, key, the why and the wherefore.

answer *v.* 1 [To reply] reply, respond, rejoin, retort, acknowledge, give answer, say, echo, return, refute, react, rebut, argue, plead, claim, remark, talk back, come back.—*Ant.* QUESTION, inquire, ask. 2 [To provide a solution] solve, elucidate, clarify; see EXPLAIN. —**answer for** be responsible for, take the blame for, accept the responsibility for, response **3** a solution to a problem — *vi.* **1** to reply **2** to be sufficient **3** to be responsible or liable (*to* a person *for*) **4** to conform (*to*) [*he answers to the description*] — *vt.* **1** to reply or respond to **2** to serve [*to answer the purpose*] **3** to defend oneself against (a charge) **4** to conform to [*she answers the description*] —**answer back** [Colloq.] to reply forcefully or insolently —**an'swer·able** *adj.*

ant (ant) *n.* [< OE *æmet(t)e*] any of a family of insects, generally wingless, that live in complex colonies

-ant (ənt) [ult. < L] *suffix* **1** that has, shows, or does [*defiant*] **2** one that [*occupant*]

ant·acid (ant'as'id) *adj.* counteracting acidity — *n.* an antacid substance

an·tag·o·nism (an tag'ə niz'əm) *n.* [see ANTAGONIZE] **1** opposition or hostility **2** an opposing force, principle, etc. —**an·tag·o·nis'tic** *adj.* —**an·tag·o·nis'ti·cal·ly** *adv.*

an·tag·o·nist *n.* an adversary; opponent

an·tag·o·nize (-nīz') *vt.* **-nized', -niz'ing** [< Gr *anti-*, against + *agōn*, a contest] to incur the dislike of

ant·arc·tic (ant ärk'tik, -är'-) *adj.* [see ANTI- & ARCTIC] of or near the South Pole or the region around it

ant bear a large anteater of Central America and tropical South America

ante (an'tē) *n.* [L, before] *Poker* the stake that each player must put into the pot before receiving cards — *vt.*, *vi.* **-ted** or **-teed**, **-te·ing** *Poker* to put in (one's ante): also **ante up**

ante- [see prec.] *prefix* before in time or place

ant'eat·er *n.* a mammal with a long snout, that feeds mainly on ants

ante·bel·lum (an'tē bel'əm) *adj.* [L] before the war; specif., before the American Civil War

ante·ced·ent (an'tə sēd'nt) *adj.* [< L *ante-*, before + *cedere*, go] prior; previous — *n.* **1** any thing prior to another **2** [*pl.*] one's ancestry, past life, etc. **3** *Gram.* the word or phrase to which a pronoun refers

ante·cham·ber (an'tē chăm'bər) *n.* a smaller room leading into a larger or main room

an'te·date' (-dāt') *vt.* **-dat'ed, -dat'ing 1** to put a date on that is earlier than the actual date **2** to come before in time

ante·di·lu·vian (an'tē də lōō'vē ən) *adj.* [< ANTE- + *diluvium*, a flood + -AN] **1** of the time before the Biblical Flood **2** very old or old-fashioned

an·te·lope (an'tə lōp') *n.* [< Gr *antholops*, deer] a swift, cud-chewing, horned animal resembling the deer

ante me·ri·diem (an'tē mə rid'ē əm) [L] before noon

an·tenna (an ten'ə) *n.* [L, sail yard] **1** *pl.* **-nae** (-ē) or **-nas** either of a pair of feelers on the head of an insect, crab, etc. **2** *pl.* **-nas** *Radio, TV* an arrangement of wires, rods, etc. used in sending and receiving electromagnetic waves

an·te·rior (an tir'ē ər) *adj.* [< L *ante*, before] **1** at or toward the front **2** previous; earlier

ante·room (an'tē rōōm') *n.* a room leading to a larger or main room

an·them (an'thəm) *n.* [< Gr *anti-*, over against + *phōnē*, voice] **1** a religious choral song **2** a song of praise or devotion, as to a nation

an·ther (an'thər) *n.* [< Gr *antheros*, blooming] the part of a stamen that contains the pollen

ant·hill (ant'hil') *n.* the soil heaped up by ants around their nest opening

an·tholo·gize (an thăl'ə jīz') *vi.* **-gized', -giz'ing** to make anthologies — *vt.* to include in an anthology —**an·thol'o·gist** (-jist) *n.*

an·thol·ogy (an thăl'ə jē) *n., pl.* **-gies** [< Gr *anthos*, flower + *legein*, gather] a collection of poems, stories, songs, etc.

an·thra·cite (an'thrə sīt') *n.* [< Gr *anthrax*, coal] hard coal, which gives much heat and little smoke

an·thrax (an'thraks') *n.* [< Gr, coal, carbuncle] an infectious disease of cattle, sheep, etc. which can be transmitted to man

anthropo- [< Gr *anthrōpos*, man] *combining form* man, human

an·thropo·cen·tric (an'thrə pō'sen'trik) *adj.* [see ANTHROPO-] centering one's view of everything around man, or humans

an·thro·poid (an'thrə poid') *adj.* [see ANTHROPO- & -OID] **1** resembling a human **2** apelike — *n.* any of certain highly developed primates, as the chimpanzee and gorilla

an·thropol·ogy (an'thrə păl'ə jē) *n.* [ANTHROPO- + -LOGY] the study of the characteristics, customs, etc. of humanity —**an·thropo·log'i·cal** (-pō läj'i kəl) *adj.* —**an·thropol'o·gist** *n.*

an'thropo·mor'phism (-pō'môr'fiz'əm) *n.* the attributing of human characteristics to gods, objects, etc. —**an'thropo·mor'phic** *adj.* —**an'thropo·mor'phi·cal·ly** *adv.*

anti (an'tī, -tē) *n., pl.* **-tis'** [< fol.] [Colloq.] a person opposed to something — *prep.* [Colloq.] opposed to

anti- [< Gr *anti*, against] *prefix* **1** against, hostile to **2** that operates against **3** that prevents, cures, or neutralizes **4** opposite, reverse **5** rivaling Also **ant-**

anti·air·craft (an'tī er'kraft') *adj.* used against hostile aircraft

an'ti·bal·lis'tic missile (-bə lis'tik) a missile intended to destroy an enemy missile in flight

an'ti·bi·ot'ic (-bī ät'ik, -bē-) *n.* [< ANTI- + Gr *bios*, life] any of certain substances, as penicillin or streptomycin, produced by various microorganisms and capable of destroying or weakening bacteria, etc. — *adj.* of antibiotics

anti·body (an'tī bäd'ē) *n., pl.* **-bod'ies** a protein produced in the body to neutralize an antigen

an·tic (an'tik) *adj.* [< L: see ANTIQUE] odd and funny — *n.* a playful or ludicrous act, trick, etc.

Anti·christ (an'ti krist') *Bible* the great opponent of Christ: 1 John 2:18

an·tici·pate (an tis'ə pāt') *vt.* **-pat'ed, -pat'ing** [< L *ante-*, before + *capere*, take] **1** to look forward to **2** to forestall **3** to use or deal with in advance **4** to be ahead of in doing —**an·tic'i·pa'tion** *n.* —**an·tic'i·pa·to'ry** (-pə tôr'ē) *adj.*

anti·cli·max (an'tī klī'maks') *n.* **1** a sudden drop from the important to the trivial **2** a descent which is in disappointing contrast to a preceding rise —**an'ti·cli·mac'tic** (-klī mak'tik) *adj.*

anti·cline (an'tī klīn') *n.* [< ANTI- + Gr *klinein*, to lean] *Geol.* a sharply arched fold of stratified rock

anti·co·agu·lant (an'tī kō ag'yōō lənt) *n.* a drug or substance that delays or prevents the clotting of blood

an'ti·depres'sant (-dē pres'ənt) *adj.* lessening emotional depression — *n.* an antidepressant drug

anti·dote (an'tə dōt') *n.* [< Gr *anti-*, against + *dotos*, given] **1** a remedy to counteract a poison **2** anything that works against an evil

anti·freeze (an'tī frēz') *n.* a substance used, as in the radiator of an automobile, to prevent freezing

anti·gen (an'tə jən) *n.* [ANTI- + -GEN] a substance to which the body reacts by producing antibodies

anti·hero (an'tī hir'ō) *n., pl.* **-roes** the protagonist of a novel, etc. who lacks the stature of a traditional hero

anti·his·ta·mine (an'tī his'tə mēn', -min) *n.* any of several drugs used in treating such allergic conditions as hay fever and hives

anti·knock (an'tī näk') *n.* a substance added to the fuel of internal-combustion engines to reduce noise resulting from too rapid combustion

anti·loga·rithm (an'tī lôg'ə rith'əm) *n.* the resulting number when a base is raised to a power by a logarithm

anti·ma·cas·sar (an'tī mə kas'ər) *n.* [ANTI- + *macassar*, a

---

THESAURUS

take upon oneself, sponsor, do at one's own risk, take the rap for*. — **answer to** be responsible to, be ruled by, respect the authority of; see RESPECT 2.
answerable *a.* responsible, liable, amendable; see RESPONSIBLE 1.
antagonism *n.* enmity, hostility, opposition; see HATRED.
antagonistic *a.* opposing, hostile, inimical; see UNFRIENDLY.
antecedent *a.* preliminary, previous, prior; see PRECEDING.
antenna *n.* aerial, TV antenna, receiving wire; see WIRE.

anthem *n.* hymn, divine song, melody; see SONG.
antibiotic *n.* antitoxin, wonder drug, miracle drug; see MEDICINE 2.
antibody *n.* immunizer, neutralizer, immunoglobulin; see PREVENTION.
anticipate *v.* expect, forecast, prophesy, predict, hope for, look forward to, wait for, count on, plan on, have a hunch, bargain for, hold in view, have in prospect, assume, suppose, divine, conjecture, promise oneself, lean upon, entertain the hope, await, reckon on, count on, have a funny feeling*, look into the

future, feel it in one's bones.—*Ant.* FEAR, be surprised, be caught unawares.
anticipated *a.* foreseen, predictable, prepared for; see EXPECTED, LIKELY 1.
anticipation *n.* expectancy, outlook, trust, promise, prospect, impatience, preoccupation, hope, prevision, presentiment, intuition, foresight, inkling, premonition, apprehension, foreboding, awareness, forethought, hunch*, a feeling in one's bones.— *Ant.* SURPRISE, shock, wonder.
antidote *n.* antitoxin, counteractant, remedy; see MEDICINE 2.

hair oil] a small cover on the back or arms of a chair, sofa, etc. to prevent soiling

anti·mat·ter (an′ti mat′ər) *n.* a form of matter in which the electrical charge or other property of each particle is the reverse of that in the usual matter of our universe

anti·mis·sile (an′ti mis′əl) *adj.* designed as a defense against ballistic missiles

an·ti·mony (an′tə mō′nē) *n.* [< ML] a silvery-white, non-metallic chemical element used in alloys to harden them

anti·pasto (an′ti päs′tō, -pas′-) *n.* [It < *anti-*, before + *pasto*, food] an appetizer of marinated vegetables, meats, cheeses, etc.

an·tip·a·thy (an tip′ə thē) *n., pl.* **-thies** [< Gr *anti-*, against + *pathein*, to suffer] 1 strong dislike; aversion 2 the object of such dislike

anti·per·son·nel (an′ti pur′sə nel′) *adj.* intended to destroy people rather than objects *[antipersonnel mines]*

an′ti·per′spi·rant (-pur′spə rənt) *n.* a substance applied to the skin to reduce perspiration

an·ti·phon (an′tə fən, -fän′) *n.* [see ANTHEM] a hymn, psalm, etc. sung in responsive, alternating parts —**an·tiph·o·nal** (an tif′ə nəl) *adj.*

an·tip·o·des (an tip′ə dēz′) *n.pl.* [< Gr *anti-*, opposite + *pous*, foot] any two places directly opposite each other on the earth —**an·tip′o·dal** *adj.*

an·ti·quar·ian (an′ti kwer′ē ən) *adj.* 1 of antiques or antiquities 2 of antiquaries — *n.* an antiquary

an·ti·quary (an′ti kwer′ē) *n., pl.* **-quar′ies** a collector or student of antiquities

an′ti·quate′ (-kwāt′) *vt.* -quat′ed, -quat′ing [see fol.] to make old, out-of-date, or obsolete —**an′ti·quat′ed** *adj.* —**an′ti·qua′tion** *n.*

an·tique (an tēk′) *adj.* [< L *antiquus*, ancient] 1 of ancient times 2 out-of-date 3 of, or in the style of, a former period 4 dealing in antiques — *n.* 1 any ancient relic 2 a piece of furniture, etc. from a former period — *vt.* -tiqued′, -tiqu′ing to make look antique

an·tiq·ui·ty (an tik′wə tē) *n., pl.* **-ties** [see prec.] 1 the ancient period of history 2 great age 3 [*pl.*] relics, etc. of the distant past

anti·semitic (an′ti sə mit′ik) *adj.* 1 having prejudice against Jews 2 discriminating against or persecuting Jews —**an′ti·sem′ite** (-sem′īt′) *n.* —**an′ti·sem′itism** (-ə tiz′əm) *n.*

anti·sep·sis (an′tə sep′sis) *n.* [ANTI- + SEPSIS] 1 a being antiseptic 2 the use of antiseptics

an′ti·sep′tic (-tik) *adj.* 1 preventing infection, decay, etc.; effective against bacteria, etc. 2 using antiseptics 3 sterile — *n.* any antiseptic substance —**an′ti·sep′ti·cally** *adv.*

anti·serum (an′ti sir′əm) *n., pl.* **-rums** or **-ra** a serum containing antibodies

an′ti·slav′ery (an′ti-) *adj.* against slavery

an′ti·so′cial *adj.* 1 not sociable 2 harmful to the welfare of people

an′ti·tank′ *adj.* for use against tanks in war

an·tith·esis (an tith′ə sis) *n., pl.* **-ses** (-sēz′) [< Gr *anti-*, against + *tithenai*, to place] a contrast or opposition, as of ideas 2 the exact opposite —**anti·thet·i·cal** (an′tə thet′i kəl) *adj.* —**an′ti·thet′i·cally** *adv.*

anti·toxin (an′ti täks′in) *n.* 1 a circulating antibody formed by the body to act against a specific toxin 2 a serum containing an antitoxin, injected into a person to prevent a disease

anti·trust (an′ti trust′) *adj.* opposed to or regulating trusts, or business monopolies

anti·vi·ral (an′ti vī′rəl) *adj.* that can check the growth of a virus

an′ti·viv′i·sec′tion·ist (-viv′ə sek′shən ist) *n.* one opposing vivisection

ant·ler (ant′lər) *n.* [< OFr *antoillier*] the branched, bony growth on the head of any animal of the deer family — **ant′lered** (-lərd) *adj.*

an·to·nym (an′tə nim′) *n.* [< Gr *anti-*, opposite + *onyma*, name] a word meaning the opposite of another

anus (ā′nəs) *n., pl.* **a′nus·es** or **a′ni′** (-nī′) [L] the opening at the lower end of the alimentary canal

an·vil (an′vəl) *n.* [< OE *anfilt*] an iron or steel block on which metal objects are hammered into shape

anx·i·ety (aŋ zī′ə tē) *n., pl.* **-ties** [see fol.] 1 worry or uneasiness about what may happen 2 an eager but uneasy desire *[anxiety to do well]*

anx·ious (aŋk′shəs) *adj.* [< L *angere*, to choke] 1 worried 2 causing anxiety 3 eagerly wishing —**anx′iously** *adv.*

any (ən′ē) *adj.* [OE *ænig*] 1 one, no matter which, of more than two *[any boy may go]* 2 some *[has he any pain?]* 3 without limit *[any number can play]* 4 even one or the least amount of *[I haven't any dimes]* 5 every *[any child can do it]* — *pron.* (*sing. & pl.*) any one or ones — *adv.* to any degree or extent; at all *[is he any better?]*

an′y·bod′y (-bäd′ē, -bud′ē) *pron.* 1 any person 2 an important person

an′y·how′ *adv.* ANYWAY

an′y·more′ *adv.* now; nowadays

an′y·one′ *pron.* any person; anybody

any one any single (person or thing)

an′y·place′ *adv.* [Colloq.] ANYWHERE

an′y·thing′ *pron.* any object, event, fact, etc. — *n.* a thing, no matter of what kind — *adv.* in any way —**anything but** not at all

an′y·way′ *adv.* 1 in any manner 2 nevertheless; anyhow 3 haphazardly

an′y·where′ *adv.* 1 in, at, or to any place 2 [Colloq.] at all —**get anywhere** [Colloq.] to have any success

A/o or **a/o** account of

A-OK (ā′ō kā′) *adj.* [A(LL) OK] [Colloq.] excellent, fine, in working order, etc. Also **A′-Okay′**

A one (ā′ wun′) first-class Also **A 1** or **A number 1**

aorta (ā ôr′tə) *n., pl.* **-tas** or **-tae** (-tē) [< Gr *aeirein*, to raise] the main artery of the body, carrying blood from the heart —**aor′tic** or **aor′tal** *adj.*

AP Associated Press

apace (ə pās′) *adv.* at a fast pace

Apache (ə pach′ē) *n., pl.* **-es** or **-e** [AmSp] a member of a group of SW U.S. Indians

apart (ə pärt′) *adv.* [< L *ad*, to, at + *pars*, part] 1 aside 2 away in place or time 3 in or to pieces — *adj.* separated — **apart from** other than —**tell apart** to distinguish between

apart·heid (ə pärt′āt′, -tīt′) *n.* [Afrik, separateness] strict racial segregation as practiced in South Africa

---

THESAURUS

antique *a.* ancient, archaic, prehistoric; see OLD 3.

antique *n.* relic, artifact, heirloom, survival, rarity, monument, vestige, ruin.

antiseptic *a.* clean, germ-free, sterilized; see PURE 2.

antiseptic *n.* detergent, prophylactic, preservative, preventive, preventative, counterirritant, sterilizer, immunizing agent, germicide, insecticide, disinfectant, deodorant; see also MEDICINE 2.

antitoxin *n.* vaccine, antibody, serum; see MEDICINE 2.

antlers *n.* horns, tusks, prongs; see HORN 2.

anxiety *n.* concern, trouble, misgiving; see FEAR.

anxious *a.* 1 [Disturbed in mind] apprehensive, concerned, dreading; see TROUBLED. 2 [Eager] desirous, eager, fervent; see ZEALOUS.

any *a.* either, whatever, any sort, any kind, any one, in general, each, some, several, each and every, all, one and all; see also EACH 1, SOME.—*Ant.* ONE, only, single.

anybody *pron.* anyone, everyone, everybody, all, the whole world, the public, the rabble, the masses, each and every one, any person, any of.—*Ant.* NOBODY, no one, somebody.

anyhow *a.* in any event, at any rate, nevertheless, at all, in spite of, in any case, regardless, anyway, in any way, in whatever way, under any circumstances, in one way or the other, in any respect, in either way, whatever happens, irregardless*, somehow or other.

anyone *pron.* a person, one, anyone at all; see ANYBODY.

anyplace* *a.* everywhere, wherever, in any place; see ANYWHERE.

anything *pron.* everything, all, any-

thing at all, anyone, any one thing, whatever one wants, you name it*, anything around.—*Ant.* NOTHING, something, one thing.

anyway *a.* in any event, however, in any manner; see ANYHOW.

anywhere *a.* wherever, in any place, all over, everywhere, in whatever place, wherever you go, anyplace*.—*Ant.* NOWHERE, in no place, somewhere. —**get anywhere*** prosper, thrive, advance; see SUCCEED 1.

apart *a.* 1 [Separated] disconnected, distant, disassociated; see SEPARATED. 2 [Distinct] separate, special, isolated; see INDIVIDUAL. 3 [Separately] freely, exclusively, alone; see INDEPENDENTLY. —**take apart** dismember, dissect, reduce; see ANALYZE, DIVIDE. —**tell apart** characterize, discriminate, differentiate; see DISTINGUISH 1.

apart′ment *n.* 〖< It *appartare*, to separate〗 a room or suite of rooms to live in, esp. one of a number in an **apartment building** (or **house**)

apa·thy (ap′ə thē) *n., pl.* **-thies** 〖< Gr *a-*, without + *pathos*, emotion〗 **1** lack of emotion **2** indifference; listlessness —**ap′a·thet′ic** (-thet′ik) *adj.* —**ap′a·thet′i·cally** *adv.*

apa·tite (ap′ə tit′) *n.* 〖< Ger < Gr *apatē*, deceit〗 a mineral incorporating calcium phosphate and found in rocks, bones, and teeth

APB all-points bulletin

ape (āp) *n.* 〖< OE *apa*〗 **1** any gibbon or great ape **2** loosely, any monkey **3** a mimic **4** a person who is gross or clumsy — *vt.* **aped, ap′ing** to mimic —**ape′like′** *adj.*

aperi·tif (ə per′ə tēf′) *n.* 〖Fr〗 an alcoholic drink taken before a meal

ap·er·ture (ap′ər chər) *n.* 〖< L *aperire*, to open〗 an opening; hole

apex (ā′peks′) *n., pl.* **a′pex′es** or **api·ces** (ap′ə sēz′) 〖L〗 **1** the highest point **2** the pointed end; tip **3** the climax

apha·sia (ə fā′zhə) *n.* 〖Gr < *a-*, not + *phanai*, to say〗 loss of the power to use or understand words —**apha′sic** (-zik) *adj., n.*

apheli·on (ə fē′lē ən) *n., pl.* **-li·ons** or **-lia** (-ə) 〖< Gr *apo-*, from + *hēlios*, sun〗 the point farthest from the sun in the orbit of a planet or comet, or of a man-made satellite

aphid (ā′fid, af′id) *n.* 〖< ModL *aphis*〗 an insect that lives on plants by sucking their juices

apho·rism (af′ə riz′əm) *n.* 〖< Gr *apo-*, from + *horizein*, to bound〗 a concise statement of a truth; maxim; adage —**aph′o·ris′tic** *adj.* —**aph′o·ris′ti·cally** *adv.*

aph·ro·disi·ac (af′rə diz′ē ak′) *adj.* 〖ult. after fol.〗 arousing sexual desire — *n.* an aphrodisiac drug, etc.

Aph·ro·dite (af′rə dīt′ē) the Greek goddess of love and beauty

api·ary (ā′pē er′ē) *n., pl.* **-ar′ies** 〖< L *apis*, bee〗 a place where bees are kept —**a′pia·rist** (-ə rist) *n.*

apiece (ə pēs′) *adv.* 〖ME *a pece*〗 for each one; each

aplenty (ə plen′tē) *adj., adv.* [Colloq.] in abundance

aplomb (ə pläm′, -plum′) *n.* 〖Fr: see PLUMB〗 self-possession; poise

apoca·lypse (ə päk′ə lips′) *n.* 〖< Gr *apokalyptein*, disclose〗 any revelation of a violent struggle in which evil will be destroyed —[A-] *Bible* the book of Revelation —**apoc′a·lyp′tic** (-lip′tik) *adj.*

Apoc·ry·pha (ə päk′rə fə) 〖< Gr *apo-*, away + *kryptein*, to hide〗 fourteen books of the Septuagint rejected in Judaism and Protestantism: eleven are in the Roman Catholic Bible

apoc′ry·phal (-fəl) *adj.* **1** of doubtful authenticity **2** not genuine; spurious

apo·gee (ap′ə jē′) *n.* 〖< Gr *apo-*, from + *gē*, earth〗 the point farthest from the earth in the orbit of a satellite

apo·liti·cal (ā′pə lit′i kəl) *adj.* not concerned with political matters —**a′po·lit′i·cally** *adv.*

Apol·lo (ə päl′ō) the Greek and Roman god of music, poetry, prophecy, and medicine —*n., pl.* **-los** any handsome young man

apolo·getic (ə päl′ə jet′ik) *adj.* showing regret; making an apology —**apol′o·get′i·cally** *adv.*

apolo·gist (ə päl′ə jist) *n.* one who defends or attempts to justify a doctrine, faith, action, etc.

apol′o·gize′ (-jīz′) *vi.* **-gized′, -giz′ing** to make an apology

apolo·gy (ə päl′ə jē) *n., pl.* **-gies** 〖< Gr *apo-*, from + *logos*, speech〗 **1** a formal defense of some idea, doctrine, etc.: also **apo·lo·gia** (ap′ə lō′jē ə) **2** an expression of regret for a fault, insult, etc.

apo·plexy (ap′ə plek′sē) *n.* 〖< Gr *apo-*, from + *plēssein*, to strike〗 severe hemorrhage or infarction, esp. in the brain; stroke —**ap′o·plec′tic** *adj.*

apos·tasy (ə päs′tə sē) *n., pl.* **-sies** 〖< Gr *apo-*, away + *stasis*, a standing〗 an abandoning of what one has believed in, as a faith, cause, etc.

apos′tate′ (-tāt′) *n.* a person guilty of apostasy; renegade

apos′ta·tize′ (-tə tiz′) *vt.* **-tized′, -tiz′ing** to become an apostate

a pos·terio·ri (ā′ päs tir′ē ôr′ī) 〖L〗 **1** from effect to cause **2** based on observation or experience

apos·tle (ə päs′əl) *n.* 〖< Gr *apo-*, from + *stellein*, send〗 **1** [*usually* A-] any of the disciples of Jesus, esp. the original twelve **2** the leader of a new movement

ap·os·tolic (ap′əs täl′ik) *adj.* **1** of the Apostles, their teachings, work, etc. **2** [*often* A-] of the pope; papal

apos·tro·phe (ə päs′trə fē) *n.* 〖< Gr *apo-*, from + *strephein*, to turn〗 **1** a mark (′) indicating: *a*) omission of a letter or letters from a word (Ex.: *it′s* for *it is*) *b*) the possessive case (Ex.: *Mary′s* dress) *c*) certain plural forms (Ex.: five *6′s*, dot the *i′s*) **2** an exclamatory address to a person or thing

apoth·ecary (ə päth′ə ker′ē) *n., pl.* **-ies** 〖< Gr *apothēkē*, storehouse〗 a pharmacist or druggist

apo·thegm (ap′ə them′) *n.* 〖< Gr *apo-*, from + *phthengesthai*, to utter〗 a short, pithy saying

apoth·eo·sis (ə päth′ē ō′sis, ap′ə thē′ə sis) *n., pl.* **-ses′** (-sēz′) 〖< Gr *apo-*, from + *theos*, god〗 **1** the deifying of a person **2** the glorification of a person or thing **3** a glorified ideal

ap·pall or **ap·pal** (ə pôl′) *vt.* **-palled′, -pal′ling** 〖ult. < L *ad*, to + *pallere*, to be pale〗 to horrify, dismay, or shock

ap·pa·loosa (ap′ə lōō′sə) *n.* 〖after *Palouse* Indians of NW U.S.〗 a Western saddle horse with black and white spots on the rump and loins

ap·pa·ra·tus (ap′ə rat′əs, -rāt′-) *n., pl.* **-tus** or **-tuses** 〖< L *ad-*, to + *parare*, prepare〗 **1** the materials, tools, etc. for a specific use **2** any complex device, machine, or system

ap·parel (ə per′əl) *n.* 〖ult. < L *ad-*, to + *parere*, prepare〗 clothing; attire — *vt.* **-eled** or **-elled, -el·ing** or **-el·ling** to clothe; dress

ap·par·ent (ə per′ənt) *adj.* 〖see APPEAR〗 **1** readily seen; visible **2** evident; obvious **3** appearing real or true —**ap·par′ently** *adv.*

ap·pa·ri·tion (ap′ə rish′ən) *n.* 〖see APPEAR〗 **1** anything that appears unexpectedly or strangely **2** a ghost; phantom **3** a becoming visible

ap·peal (ə pēl′) *vt.* 〖< L *ad-*, to + *pellere*, to drive〗 to make an appeal of (a case) — *vi.* **1** to appeal a law case to a higher court **2** to make an urgent request (*for* help, etc.) **3** to be attractive or interesting — *n.* **1** a call upon some authority for a decision **2** a request for the transference of a case to a higher court for rehearing **3** a request for help, etc. **4** attraction; interest —**ap·peal′ing** *adj.*

ap·pear (ə pir′) *vi.* 〖< L *ad-*, to + *perere*, be visible〗 **1** to come into sight **2** to become understood or obvious **3** to

---

THESAURUS

apartment *n.* rooms, quarters, flat, suite, penthouse, residence, home, duplex, pad*, walk-up.

apartment house *n.* tenement, hotel, apartment building, condominium, high-rise apartments.

apathetic *a.* unemotional, cold, unconcerned; see INDIFFERENT.

apathy *n.* dullness, insensitivity, unconcern; see INDIFFERENCE.

ape *n.* gorilla, orangutan, chimpanzee, baboon, gibbon; see also MONKEY.

ape *v.* copy, mimic, impersonate; see IMITATE 1.

apiece *a.* respectively, separately, individually; see EACH.

apologetic *a.* regretful, self-incriminating, explanatory, atoning, rueful, contrite, remorseful, sorry, penitent, down on one's knees*.—*Ant.* STUBBORN, obstinate, unregenerate.

apologize *v.* beg pardon, excuse oneself, atone, ask forgiveness, make amends, make apology for, purge,

give satisfaction, clear oneself, make up with, confess, admit one's guilt, retract, withdraw, eat crow*, eat one's words.—*Ant.* INSULT, offend, hurt.

apology *n.* excuse, plea, justification; see EXPLANATION.

apostle *n.* messenger, witness, companion; see FOLLOWER.

appall *v.* amaze, horrify, dismay; see SHOCK 2.

appalling *a.* horrifying, shocking, dreadful; see FRIGHTFUL.

apparatus *n.* appliances, machinery, outfit; see EQUIPMENT.

apparel *n.* clothes, attire, suit; see DRESS 1.

apparent *a.* **1** [Open to view] visible, clear, manifest; see OBVIOUS 1. **2** [Seeming, but not actual] probable, possible, plausible; see LIKELY 1.

apparently *a.* obviously, at first sight, in plain sight, unmistakably, at a glance, indubitably, perceptibly,

plainly, patently, evidently, clearly, openly, supposedly, overtly, conspicuously, palpably, tangibly, presumably, possibly, manifestly, most likely, reasonably, seemingly, reputedly, as if, as though, to all appearances, in almost every way, allegedly, as it were, on the face of it, to the eye.—*Ant.* SURELY, certainly, undoubtedly.

appeal *n.* **1** [A plea] request, bid, claim, suit, petition, question, entreaty, prayer, invocation, supplication, address, demand, call, requisition, application, proposition, proposal.—*Ant.* DENIAL, refusal, renunciation. **2** [Attractiveness] charm, glamour, interest, seductiveness, sex appeal, class*.

appeal *v.* **1** [To ask another seriously] urge, request, petition; see BEG. **2** [To attract] interest, engage, tempt; see FASCINATE.

appear *v.* **1** [To become visible]

ap·pear′ance *n.* **1** an appearing **2** the look or outward
aspect of anything **3** an outward show; pretense —**keep
up appearances** to maintain an outward show of being
proper, etc.

ap·pease (ə pēz′) *vt.* **-peased′, -peas′ing** [ult. < L *ad*, to
+ *pax*, peace] to pacify, quiet, or satisfy, esp. by giving in
to the demands of —**ap·pease′ment** *n.* —**ap·peas′er** *n.*

ap·pel·lant (ə pel′ənt) *n.* a person who appeals to a higher
court

ap·pel′late (-it) *adj. Law* having to do with appeals [an
appellate court]

ap·pel·la·tion (ap′ə lā′shən) *n.* [see APPEAL] **1** a naming
2 a title

ap·pend (ə pend′) *vt.* [< L *ad*-, to + *pendere*, hang] to
attach or affix; add as a supplement or appendix

ap·pend·age *n.* **1** anything appended **2** any external
organ or part, as a tail

ap·pen·dec·to·my (ap′ən dek′tə mē) *n., pl.* **-mies** [see
-ECTOMY] the surgical removal of the appendix

ap·pen·di·ci·tis (ə pen′də sīt′is) *n.* [see AD- & -ITIS] inflammation of the appendix

ap·pen·dix (ə pen′diks) *n., pl.* **-dixes** or **-di·ces′** (-də sēz′)
[L, appendage] **1** additional material at the end of a book
2 a small, saclike appendage of the large intestine

ap·per·tain (ap′ər tān′) *vi.* [< L *ad*-, to + *pertinere*, to
reach] to belong as a function, part, etc.; pertain

ap·pe·ten·cy (ap′ə tən sē) *n., pl.* **-cies** [see fol.] **1** a craving; appetite **2** a propensity **3** a natural attraction

ap·pe·tite (ap′ə tit′) *n.* [< L *ad*-, to + *petere*, to desire] **1**
a desire for food **2** any strong desire or craving

ap′pe·tiz′er (-tī′zər) *n.* a small portion of a tasty food to
stimulate the appetite

ap′pe·tiz′ing *adj.* **1** stimulating the appetite **2** savory;
delicious

ap·plaud (ə plôd′) *vt., vi.* [< L *ad*-, to + *plaudere*, clap
hands] **1** to show approval (of) by clapping the hands,
etc. **2** to praise —**ap·plaud′er** *n.*

ap·plause (ə plôz′) *n.* approval, esp. as shown by clapping
hands

ap·ple (ap′əl) *n.* [< OE *æppel*, fruit, apple] **1** a round,
firm, edible fruit **2** the tree it grows on

apple butter a thick spread made from apples stewed
with spices

ap′ple·jack′ (-jak′) *n.* brandy distilled from fermented
cider

ap′ple·sauce′ (-sôs′) *n.* apples cooked to a pulp in water
and sweetened

ap·pli·ance (ə pli′əns) *n.* a device or machine, esp. one for
household use

ap·pli·cable (ap′li kə bəl) *adj.* that can be applied; appropriate —**ap′pli·ca·bil′ity** (-bil′ə tē) *n.*

ap′pli·cant (-kənt) *n.* one who applies, as for employment, help, etc.

ap·pli·ca·tion (ap′li kā′shən) *n.* **1** an applying **2** anything applied, as a remedy **3** a specific use **4** a request, or
a form filled out in making one [an employment *application*] **5** continued effort; diligence **6** relevance or practicality

ap′pli·ca′tor *n.* any device for applying medicine or paint,
polish, etc.

ap·plied (ə plid′) *adj.* used in actual practice [applied sci-
ence]

ap·pli·qué (ap′li kā′) *n.* [Fr] a decoration made of one
material attached to another — *vt.* **-quéd′, -qué′ing** to
decorate with appliqué

ap·ply (ə pli′) *vt.* **-plied′, -ply′ing** [< L *ad*-, to + *plicare*,
to fold] **1** to put or spread on [apply glue] **2** to put to
practical or specific use [apply your knowledge] **3** to
devote (oneself or one's faculties) diligently — *vi.* **1** to
make a formal request **2** to be suitable or relevant —**ap·
pli′er** *n.*

ap·point (ə point′) *vt.* [< L *ad*, to + *punctum*, a point] **1**
to set (a date, place, etc.) **2** to name for an office, position,
etc. **3** to furnish [well-*appointed*] —**ap·point′ee′** *n.*

ap·point′ive *adj.* of or filled by appointment [an *appoint-
ive* office]

ap·point′ment *n.* **1** an appointing or being appointed **2**
a position filled by appointing **3** an engagement to meet
someone or be somewhere **4** [pl.] furniture; equipment

ap·por·tion (ə pôr′shən) *vt.* [see AD- & PORTION] to distribute in shares according to a plan —**ap·por′tion·ment**
n.

ap·pose (ə pōz′) *vt.* **-posed′, -pos′ing** [< L *ad*-, to +
ponere, put] to put side by side or opposite

ap·po·site (ap′ə zit) *adj.* [see prec.] appropriate; apt —
ap′po·site·ly *adv.* —**ap′po·site·ness** *n.*

ap·po·si·tion (ap′ə zish′ən) *n.* **1** an apposing, or the position resulting from this **2** the placing of a word or phrase
beside another in explanation, as *my cousin* in "Mary, my
cousin, is here" —**ap·pos′i·tive** (ə päz′ə tiv) *adj., n.*

ap·praisal (ə prāz′əl) *n.* **1** an appraising **2** an appraised
value

ap·praise (ə prāz′) *vt.* **-praised′, -prais′ing** [< L *ad*, to
+ *pretium*, price] **1** to set a price for; estimate the value
of **2** to judge the quality or worth of —**ap·prais′er** *n.*

THESAURUS

emerge, rise, come in view, come
forth, come out, come forward, be in
sight, become plain, loom, arrive,
come to light, enter the picture,
recur, materialize, become visible,
loom up, break through, show up,
crop up, burst forth, turn up, stand
out, spring up, bob up, see the light
of day*, meet the eye, break cover.—
Ant. DISAPPEAR, depart, vanish. **2**
[To seem] look, have the appearance,
resemble; see SEEM.

appearance *n.* **1** [Looks] bearing,
mien, features; see LOOKS. **2** [That
which only seems to be real] impression, idea, image, reflection, sound,
mirage, vision, façade, dream, illusion, semblance, seeming.—*Ant.*
FACT, being, substance. —**keep up
appearances** be outwardly proper,
hide one's faults, keep up with the
Joneses*; see DECEIVE. —**make (or
put in) an appearance** appear publicly, be present, come; see ARRIVE.

appease *v.* do, be enough, serve; see
SATISFY 1, 3.

appeasement *n.* amends, settlement, reparation, conciliation, compromise; see also SATISFACTION 2.

appendix *n.* supplement, attachment, index; see ADDITION 1.

appetite *n.* hunger, thirst, craving,
longing, dryness, need for food, need
for liquid, starvation, empty stomach, thirstiness, ravenousness,
desire; see also HUNGER, THIRST.—
Ant. indifference, satiety, surfeit.

appetizing *a.* savory, tasty, delectable; see DELICIOUS.

applaud *v.* cheer, clap, acclaim; see
PRAISE 1.

applause *n.* ovation, cheers, hurrahs;
see PRAISE 1.

appliance *n.* instrument, machine,
apparatus; see DEVICE 1. *Common
household appliances include:*
broiler, deep-fryer, electric can
opener, electric carving knife, coffee
maker, blender, mixer, electric fry-
pan, portable oven, hair dryer,
toaster, dishwasher, disposal, clothes
dryer, clothes washer, stove, oven,
microwave, refrigerator, freezer,
water heater, electric toothbrush,
waffle iron, iron, sewing machine,
vacuum cleaner, air conditioner.

applicable *a.* suitable, appropriate,
usable; see FIT.

applicant *n.* petitioner, claimant,
appellant; see CANDIDATE.

application *n.* **1** [Putting to use]
employment, appliance, utilization;
see USE 1. **2** [The ability to apply
oneself] devotion, zeal, diligence; see
ATTENTION. **3** [A request] petition,
entreaty, demand; see APPEAL 1. **4**
[The instrument by which a request
is made] petition, form, blank, paper,
letter, credentials, certificate, statement, requisition, draft, check, bill.

applied *a.* used, related, enforced,
practiced, utilized, brought to bear,
adapted, devoted, tested, adjusted,

activated.

apply *v.* **1** [To make a request] petition, demand, appeal; see BEG. **2** [To
make use of] utilize, employ, practice, exploit; see also USE 1. **3** [To be
relevant] be pertinent, pertain, bear
on, bear upon, have a bearing on,
relate to, allude to, concern, touch
on, touch upon, involve, affect,
regard, have reference to, connect,
refer, suit, be in relationship, hold
true, come into play*. —**apply oneself** attend to, dedicate oneself,
address oneself, be occupied with,
keep one's mind on, direct oneself to,
concentrate on, persevere, persist in,
be industrious, buckle down*.

appoint *v.* select, designate, elect; see
DELEGATE 1, 2.

appointed *a.* selected, chosen, delegated; see NAMED 2.

appointment *n.* **1** [The act of
appointing] designation, election,
selection, nomination, approval,
choice, promotion, assignment,
authorization, installation, delegation, certification, empowering. **2**
[An engagement] interview, meeting,
rendezvous, assignment, invitation,
errand, something to do, date. —
keep an appointment show up, be
on time, be there; see ARRIVE.

appraisal *n.* examination, evaluation, assessment; see ESTIMATE.

appraise *v.* assess, price, assay; see
PRICE.

ap·pre·ci·able (ə prē'shə bəl, -shē ə-) *adj.* ⟦ see prec. ⟧ enough to be perceived or estimated; noticeable —**ap·pre'ci·ably** *adv.*

ap·pre·ci·ate (ə prē'shē āt') *vt.* **-at'ed, -at'ing** ⟦ see APPRAISE ⟧ **1** to think well of; esteem **2** to recognize gratefully **3** to estimate the quality of **4** to be fully or sensitively aware of — *vi.* to rise in value —**ap·pre'cia·tor** *n.* —**ap·pre'cia·to·ry** (-shə tôr'ē, -shē ə-) *adj.*

ap·pre·ci·a'tion *n.* **1** grateful recognition, as of a favor **2** sensitive awareness, as of art **3** a rise in value or price

ap·pre'ci·a·tive (-shə tiv, -shē ə-) *adj.* feeling or showing appreciation —**ap·pre'cia·tively** *adv.*

ap·pre·hend (ap'rē hend') *vt.* ⟦ < L ad-, to + prehendere, seize ⟧ **1** to capture or arrest **2** to perceive; understand **3** to fear; dread

ap'pre·hen'sion (-hen'shən) *n.* **1** capture or arrest **2** perception or understanding **3** fear; anxiety

ap'pre·hen'sive (-siv) *adj.* anxious; uneasy —**ap'pre·hen'sively** *adv.* —**ap'pre·hen'sive·ness** *n.*

ap·pren·tice (ə pren'tis) *n.* ⟦ see APPREHEND ⟧ **1** a person being taught a craft or trade, now usually as a member of a labor union **2** any beginner — *vt.* **-ticed, -tic·ing** to place or accept as an apprentice —**ap·pren'tice·ship'** *n.*

ap·prise or **ap·prize** (ə prīz') *vt.* **-prised'** or **-prized', -pris'ing** or **-priz'ing** ⟦ see APPREHEND ⟧ to notify

ap·proach (ə prōch') *vi.* ⟦ < L ad-, to + propius, nearer ⟧ to come closer — *vt.* **1** to come nearer to **2** to approximate **3** to make a proposal or request to **4** to begin dealing with — *n.* **1** a coming closer **2** an approximation **3** an overture (*to* someone): *usually used in pl.* **4** a means of reaching a person or place; access **5** a means of attaining a goal —**ap·proach'able** *adj.*

ap·pro·ba·tion (ap'rə bā'shən) *n.* ⟦ see APPROVE ⟧ approval

ap·pro·pri·ate (ə prō'prē āt'; *for adj.,* -it) *vt.* **-at'ed, -at'ing** ⟦ < L ad-, to + proprius, one's own ⟧ **1** to take for one's own use, often improperly **2** to set aside (money, etc.) for a specific use — *adj.* suitable; fit; proper —**ap·pro'pri·ately** *adv.* —**ap·pro'pri·ate·ness** *n.* —**ap·pro'pri·a'tor** *n.*

ap·pro'pri·a'tion *n.* **1** an appropriating or being appropriated **2** money set aside for a specific use

ap·prov·al (ə prōō'vəl) *n.* **1** the act of approving **2** favorable attitude or opinion **3** formal consent —**on approval**

for the customer to examine and decide whether to buy or return

ap·prove (ə prōōv') *vt.* **-proved', -prov'ing** ⟦ < L ad-, to + probus, good ⟧ **1** to give one's consent to **2** to consider to be good, satisfactory, etc. — *vi.* to have a favorable opinion (*of*) —**ap·prov'ingly** *adv.*

ap·prox·i·mate (ə präk'sə mit; *for v.,* -māt') *adj.* ⟦ < L ad-, to + proximus, nearest ⟧ **1** much like; resembling **2** more or less correct or exact — *vt.* **-mat'ed, -mat'ing** to come near to; be almost the same as —**ap·prox'i·mately** *adv.*

ap·prox'i·ma'tion (-mā'shən) *n.* an estimate or guess that is approximately correct

ap·pur·te·nance (ə purt'ʼn əns) *n.* ⟦ see APPERTAIN ⟧ **1** anything added to a more important thing **2** [*pl.*] apparatus or equipment **3** *Law* an incidental right attached to some thing

a·pri·cot (ap'ri kät', ā'pri-) *n.* ⟦ < L praecoquum, early matured (fruit) ⟧ **1** a small, yellowish-orange, peachlike fruit **2** the tree it grows on

April (ā'prəl) *n.* ⟦ < L ⟧ the fourth month of the year, having 30 days: abbrev. **Apr.**

a priori (ā' prī ôr'ī) ⟦ L ⟧ **1** from cause to effect **2** based on theory instead of experience

apron (ā'prən) *n.* ⟦ < L mappa, napkin ⟧ **1** a garment worn over the front part of the body to protect one's clothes **2** any extending or protecting part **3** a paved area, as where a driveway broadens to meet the road **4** the front part of a stage

a·pro·pos (ap'rə pō') *adv.* ⟦ Fr à propos, to the purpose ⟧ at the right time; opportunely — *adj.* relevant; apt —**apropos of** with regard to

apse (aps) *n.* ⟦ L apsis, an arch ⟧ a semicircular or polygonal projection of a church, usually domed or vaulted

apt (apt) *adj.* ⟦ < L aptus ⟧ **1** appropriate; fitting **2** tending or inclined; likely **3** quick to learn —**apt'ly** *adv.* —**apt'ness** *n.*

apt. apartment

ap·ti·tude (ap'tə tōōd', -tyōōd') *n.* ⟦ see APT ⟧ **1** suitability; fitness **2** a natural tendency, ability, or talent **3** quickness to learn

aqua (ak'wə, äk'-) *n., pl.* **-uas** or **-uae** (-wē') ⟦ L ⟧ water — *adj.* ⟦ < AQUAMARINE ⟧ bluish-green

aq'ua·cul'ture (-kul'chər) *n.* ⟦ prec. + CULTURE ⟧ the cultivation of water plants and animals for human use

---

■ THESAURUS ■

appreciable *a.* considerable, sizable, tangible; see LARGE 1.

appreciate *v.* **1** [To be grateful] welcome, enjoy, be obliged, be indebted, acknowledge, never forget, give thanks, overflow with gratitude; see also THANK.—*Ant.* COMPLAIN, find fault with, minimize, object. **2** [To recognize worth] esteem, honor, praise; see ADMIRE.

appreciation *n.* **1** [Sense of gratitude] thankfulness, recognition, gratefulness; see GRATITUDE. **2** [Favorable opinion] esteem, enjoyment, love, affection, sensitivity, attraction, commendation, high regard; see also ADMIRATION.

appreciative *a.* grateful, obliged, satisfied; see THANKFUL.

apprehend *v.* **1** [To understand] perceive, comprehend, grasp; see UNDERSTAND 1. **2** [To arrest] seize, place under arrest, take into custody; see ARREST.

apprehension *n.* **1** [Foreboding] trepidation, dread, misgiving; see FEAR. **2** [Understanding] comprehension, grasp, perspicacity; see JUDGMENT 1. **3** [Arrest] capture, seizure, detention; see ARREST.

apprehensive *a.* fearful, worried, uncertain; see TROUBLED.

apprentice *n.* beginner, student, learner; see AMATEUR.

approach *n.* **1** [A way] path, entrance, gate; see WAY 1, 2. **2** [Plan of action] method, program, procedure; see PLAN 2.

approach *v.* **1** [To approach personally] appeal to, address, speak to, talk to, propose, request, make advances to, make overtures to, take

aside, talk to in private, buttonhole, corner, descend on.—*Ant.* AVOID, shun, turn away. **2** [To come near in space] drift toward, loom up, creep up, drive up, near, go near, draw near, close in, surround, come near to, come up to, bear down on, edge up to, ease up to, head into*; see also APPEAR 1.—*Ant.* LEAVE, recede, depart. **3** [To come near in time] be imminent, threaten, near, draw near, impend, stare one in the face*.—*Ant.* INCREASE, extend, stretch out. **4** [To approximate] come near, take after, come close to; see RESEMBLE.

approaching *a.* nearing, advancing, impending, oncoming, touching, approximating, coming, drawing near, next to come, threatening, rising, moving closer, gaining.

appropriate *a.* proper, suitable, suited, fitting; see also FIT.

appropriate *v.* **1** [To seize] secure, usurp, take possession of; see GET 1. **2** [To provide money] set aside, set apart, allocate, assign to a particular use, reserve, apportion, devote, appoint, allow for, budget, allot.

appropriately *a.* fittingly, suitably, justly, aptly, rightly, properly, agreeably, happily, fortunately.—*Ant.* BADLY, inappropriately, improperly.

appropriation *n.* stipend, grant, fund, allotment, allowance, allocation, contribution, cash, budget, gift, remuneration, donation, support, pay.

approval *n.* **1** [Favorable opinion] regard, esteem, favor; see ADMIRATION. **2** [Sanction] endorsement, support, consent; see PERMISSION.

approve *v.* ratify, affirm, encourage, support, endorse, seal, confirm, license, favor, consent to, agree to, sanction, empower, charter, validate, legalize, recognize, accredit, recommend, authorize, second, subscribe to, allow, go along with, maintain, vote for, advocate, establish, pass, OK, give the green light to*, hold with.—*Ant.* OPPOSE, reject, veto.

approved *a.* certified, authorized, validated, passed, affirmed, legalized, ratified, sanctioned, permitted, endorsed, vouched for, praised, recognized, recommended, backed, supported, upheld, made official, agreed to, allowed, proven, ordered, established, OK'd.—*Ant.* REFUSED, censured, disapproved.

approximate *a.* rough, inexact, uncertain, guessed, imprecise, imperfect, close, surmised, unscientific, by means of trial and error, almost, more or less, not quite, coming close, fair, nearly correct.

approximately *a.* nearly, closely, roughly, close to, near to, almost, around, about, in general, in round numbers, not quite, not far from, more or less, practically, just about, on the edge of, for all practical purposes, bordering on, generally.

apron *n.* cover, smock, bib; see CLOTHES.

apt *a.* **1** [Quick to learn] adept, clever, bright; see INTELLIGENT. **2** [Inclined] prone, tending, liable; see LIKELY 4.

aptitude *n.* capability, competence, capacity; see ABILITY.

aqua·ma·rine (ak′wə mə rēn′, äk′-) *n.* ⟦L *aqua marina,* sea water⟧ bluish green — *adj.* bluish-green

aqua·naut (ak′wə nôt′, äk′-) *n.* ⟦AQUA + (ASTRO)NAUT⟧ one trained to use a watertight underwater chamber as a base for undersea experiments

aq′ua·plane′ (-plān′) *n.* ⟦AQUA + PLANE¹⟧ a board on which one rides standing up as it is pulled by a motorboat — *vi.* **-planed′, -plan′ing** to ride on such a board as a sport

aquar·ium (ə kwer′ē əm) *n., pl.* **-i·ums** or **-ia** (-ə) ⟦< L *aquarius,* of water⟧ 1 a tank, etc. for keeping live water animals and plants 2 a building where such collections are exhibited

Aquar′ius (-əs) ⟦L, water carrier⟧ the 11th sign of the zodiac

aquat·ic (ə kwat′ik, -kwät′-) *adj.* 1 growing or living in water 2 done in or upon the water *[aquatic sports]*

aqua·vit (ak′wə vēt′, äk′-) *n.* ⟦< L *aqua vitae,* water of life⟧ a Scandinavian alcoholic liquor distilled from grain or potatoes and flavored with caraway

aque·duct (ak′wə dukt′) *n.* ⟦< L *aqua,* water + *ductus,* leading⟧ 1 a large pipe or conduit for bringing water from a distant source 2 an elevated structure supporting this

aque·ous (ā′kwē əs, ak′wē-) *adj.* of, like, or formed by water

aqueous humor a watery fluid filling chambers in front of the lens of the eye .

aqui·fer (ak′wə fər, äk′-) *n.* ⟦< L *aqua,* water + *ferre,* carry⟧ an underground layer of porous rock, etc. containing water

aqui·line (ak′wə līn′, -lin) *adj.* ⟦< L *aquila,* eagle⟧ 1 of or like an eagle 2 curved like an eagle's beak *[an aquiline nose]*

Ar *Chem. symbol for* argon

Arab (ar′əb, er′-) *n.* 1 a native of Arabia 2 any of a Semitic people orig. native to Arabia; popularly, a Bedouin —**Ara′bian** (ə rā′bē ən) *adj., n.*

ara·besque (ar′ə besk′, er′-) *n.* ⟦< It *Arabo,* Arab⟧ an elaborate design of intertwined lines suggesting flowers, foliage, etc.

Arabian camel the one-humped camel ranging from N Africa to India

Arabian Nights, The a collection of tales from Arabia, India, Persia, etc.

Ara·bic (ar′ə bik, er′-) *adj.* 1 of Arabia 2 of the Arabs — *n.* the Semitic language of the Arabs, spoken in Arabia, Syria, Jordan, Iraq, N Africa, etc.

Arabic numerals the figures 1, 2, 3, 4, 5, 6, 7, 8, 9, and the 0 (zero)

ar·able (ar′ə bəl) *adj.* ⟦< L *arare,* to plow⟧ suitable for plowing

arach·nid (ə rak′nid) *n.* ⟦< Gr *arachnē,* spider⟧ any of a class of arthropods with four pairs of legs, including spiders and scorpions

Ara·maic (ar′ə mā′ik) *n.* a Semitic language spoken during Biblical times

ar·bi·ter (är′bət ər) *n.* ⟦L, a witness⟧ an arbitrator; judge

ar·bi·tra·ment (är bi′trə mənt) *n.* 1 arbitration 2 an arbitrator's verdict or award

ar·bi·trary (är′bə trer′ē) *adj.* ⟦see ARBITER⟧ 1 left to one's judgment 2 based on one's preference or whim; capricious 3 absolute; despotic —**ar′bi·trar′i·ly** *adv.* —**ar′bi·trar′i·ness** *n.*

ar·bi·trate (är′bə trāt′) *vt., vi.* **-trat′ed, -trat′ing** ⟦see ARBITER⟧ 1 to submit (a dispute) to an arbitrator 2 to decide (a dispute) as an arbitrator —**ar′bi·tra′tion** *n.*

ar′bi·tra′tor *n.* a person selected to judge a dispute

ar·bor (är′bər) *n.* ⟦< L *herba,* herb⟧ a place shaded by trees, shrubs, or vines on a latticework; bower

ar·bo·real (är bôr′ē əl) *adj.* ⟦< L *arbor,* tree⟧ 1 of or like a tree 2 living in trees

ar·bo·retum (är′bə rēt′əm) *n., pl.* **-tums** or **-ta** (-ə) ⟦L⟧ a place where many kinds of trees and shrubs are grown for exhibition or study

ar·bor·vi·tae (är′bər vīt′ē) *n.* ⟦L, tree of life⟧ any of various cypress trees having sprays of scalelike leaves

ar·bu·tus (är byo͞ot′əs) *n.* ⟦L⟧ 1 a tree or shrub with dark-green leaves and strawberrylike fruit 2 a trailing plant with white or pink flower clusters

arc (ärk) *n.* ⟦< L *arcus,* a bow, arch⟧ 1 a bowlike curved line or object 2 the band of incandescent light formed when a current leaps a short gap between electrodes 3 any part of a curve, esp. of a circle — *vi.* **arced** or **arcked, arc′ing** or **arck′ing** to move in a curved course or form an arc

ar·cade (är kād′) *n.* ⟦see prec.⟧ 1 a covered passageway, esp. one lined with shops 2 a line of arches and their supporting columns 3 a penny arcade or similar place with coin-operated games

ar·cane (är kān′) *adj.* ⟦< L *arcanus,* hidden⟧ secret or esoteric

arch¹ (ärch) *n.* ⟦see ARC⟧ 1 a curved structure used as a support over an open space, as in a doorway 2 the form of an arch 3 anything shaped like an arch — *vt.* to span with or as an arch — *vi.* to form an arch

arch² (ärch) *adj.* ⟦< fol.⟧ 1 chief; principal 2 gaily mischievous; pert

arch- ⟦< Gr *archos,* first, ruler⟧ *prefix* chief, principal *[archenemy]*

-arch (ärk) ⟦see prec.⟧ *suffix* ruler *[matriarch]*

arch. 1 archaic 2 architecture

archae·ol·ogy (är′kē äl′ə jē) *n.* ⟦< Gr *archaios,* ancient + -LOGY⟧ the study of the life of ancient peoples, as by excavation of ancient cities, etc. Also sp. **archeology** —**ar′chaeo·log′i·cal** (-ə läj′i kəl) *adj.* —**ar′chaeo·log′i·cally** *adv.* —**ar′chae·ol′o·gist** *n.*

ar·chaic (är kā′ik) *adj.* ⟦< Gr *archaios,* ancient⟧ 1 ancient 2 old-fashioned 3 no longer used except in poetry, church ritual, etc., as the word *thou*

ar·cha·ism (är′kā iz′əm) *n.* an archaic word, usage, style, etc. —**ar′cha·ist** *n.*

arch·angel (ärk′ān′jəl) *n.* an angel of high rank

arch·bishop (ärch′bish′əp) *n.* a bishop of the highest rank —**arch′bish′op·ric** (-rik) *n.*

arch·dea′con (-dē′kən) *n.* a church official ranking just below a bishop

arch·di′o·cese′ *n.* the diocese of an archbishop —**arch′di·oc′esan** (-dī äs′ə sən) *adj.*

arch·duke′ (-do͞ok′) *n.* a prince of the former Austrian imperial family —**arch′duch′ess** *n.fem.*

arch′en′emy *n., pl.* **-mies** a chief enemy —**the archenemy** Satan

archer (är′chər) *n.* ⟦< L *arcus,* bow⟧ one who shoots with bow and arrow

arch′ery *n.* the sport of shooting with bow and arrow

arche·type (är′kə tīp′) *n.* ⟦< Gr *archos,* first + *typos,* mark⟧ an original pattern, or model; prototype —**ar′che·typ′al** (-tīp′əl) or **ar′che·typ′i·cal** (-tīp′i kəl) *adj.*

archi·epis·co·pal (är′kē ē pis′kə pəl) *adj.* of or related to an archbishop

archi·pela·go (är′kə pel′ə gō′) *n., pl.* **-goes′** or **-gos′** ⟦< Gr *archi-,* chief + *pelagos,* sea⟧ 1 a sea with many islands 2 a group of many islands

archi·tect (är′kə tekt′) *n.* ⟦< Gr *archi-,* chief + *tektōn,* carpenter⟧ 1 one who designs buildings and supervises their construction 2 any designer or planner

archi·tec·ton·ics (är′kə tek′niks) *n.pl.* ⟦*usually with sing. v.*⟧ 1 the science of architecture 2 structural design, as of a symphony —**ar′chi·tec·ton′ic** *adj.*

archi·tec·ture (är′kə tek′chər) *n.* 1 the science or profession of designing and constructing buildings 2 a style of construction 3 design and construction —**ar′chi·tec′tural** *adj.* —**ar′chi·tec′tur·ally** *adv.*

archi·trave (är′kə trāv′) *n.* ⟦< L *archi-,* first + *trabs,* a beam⟧ in a classical building, the beam resting directly on the tops of the columns

---

■ THESAURUS ■

Arabian *a.* Arabic, Semitic, from Arabia, Middle Eastern, Near Eastern, Moorish, Levantine.

arbitrary *a.* willful, tyrannical, unsatisfactory, temporary, unpremeditated, irrational, generalized, deceptive, superficial, unscientific, unreasonable, whimsical, fanciful, determined by no principle, optional, uncertain, inconsistent, discretionary, subject to individual will, halfway.

arbitrate *v.* settle, adjust, reconcile; see NEGOTIATE.

arbitrator *n.* arbiter, referee, mediator; see JUDGE.

arc *n.* bend, curve, segment of a circle; see ARCH.

arch¹ *n.* arc, curve, vault, dome, cupola, bend, arching, archway, curvature, cove.

arch¹ *v.* extend, round, stretch, curve, bend, shape, hunch, cover, hump,

hook, arch over.—*Ant.* STRAIGHTEN, unbend, smooth.

archaic *a.* antiquated, old, obsolete; see OLD-FASHIONED.

architect *n.* planner, designer, draftsman, artist, engineer, builder, master builder, designer of buildings.

architecture *n.* construction, planning, designing, building, structure, architectonics, house-building, ship-building, bridge-building.

ar·chive (är′kīv′) *n.* ⟦< Gr *archeion*, town hall⟧ [*usually pl.*] **1** a place for keeping public records, documentary material, etc. **2** the records, material, etc. kept there —**ar·chi·vist** (är′kə vist, -kī′-) *n.*

arch·way (ärch′wā′) *n.* a passage under an arch, or the arch itself

-archy (är kē) ⟦< Gr *archein*, to rule⟧ *combining form* ruling [*monarchy*]

arc·tic (ärk′tik, är′-) *adj.* ⟦< Gr *arktikos*, northern⟧ **1** of near the North Pole **2** very cold

-ard (ərd) ⟦< MHG *hart*, bold⟧ *suffix* one who does something to excess [*drunkard*]

ar·dent (är′d′nt) *adj.* ⟦< L *ardere*, to burn⟧ **1** passionate **2** zealous **3** glowing or burning —**ar′dent·ly** *adv.*

ar·dor (är′dər) *n.* ⟦< L *ardor*, a flame⟧ **1** emotional warmth; passion **2** zeal **3** intense heat Also Brit., etc. sp., **ar′dour** *n.*

ar·du·ous (är′jōō əs) *adj.* ⟦L *arduus*, steep⟧ **1** difficult to do; laborious **2** using much energy; strenuous —**ar′du·ous·ly** *adv.*

are (är) *vi.* ⟦OE *aron*⟧ *pl. & 2d pers. sing., pres. indic.,* of BE

area (er′ē ə) *n.* ⟦L, vacant place⟧ **1** a part of the earth's surface; region **2** the measure, in square units, of a surface **3** a location having a specific use or character [*play area*] **4** scope or extent

area code a three-digit telephone code assigned to a specific area of the U.S., Canada, etc.

arena (ə rē′nə) *n.* ⟦L, sandy place⟧ **1** a place or building for contests, shows, etc. **2** any sphere of struggle [*political arena*]

arena theater a theater having a central stage surrounded by seats

aren't (ärnt) are not

Ares (er′ēz′) *Gr. Myth.* the god of war

ar·gent (är′jənt) *adj.* ⟦L *argentum*, silver⟧ [Old Poet.] silvery

Ar·gen·tine (är′jən tēn′, -tīn′) *n.* a native or inhabitant of Argentina —*adj.* of Argentina, its people, etc. Also **Ar′gen·tin′i·an** (-tin′ē ən)

ar·gon (är′gän′) *n.* ⟦Gr, inert⟧ a chemical element, a nonreactive gas found in the air and used in light bulbs, radio tubes, etc.

Ar·go·naut (är′gə nôt′) *n. Gr. Myth.* any of those who sail with Jason to search for the Golden Fleece

ar·go·sy (är′gə sē) *n., pl.* **-sies** ⟦after *Ragusa*, It name of Dubrovnik in Croatia⟧ [Old Poet.] a large merchant ship or a fleet of such ships

ar·got (är′gō, -gət) *n.* ⟦Fr⟧ the specialized vocabulary of a particular group, as of criminals

ar·gue (är′gyōō) *vi.* **-gued, -gu·ing** ⟦< L *arguere*, prove⟧ **1** to give reasons (*for* or *against*) **2** to quarrel; dispute —*vt.* **1** to discuss; debate **2** to maintain; contend **3** to persuade by giving reasons —**ar′gu·able** *adj.*

ar·gu·ment (är′gyōō mənt) *n.* **1** a reason or reasons offered in arguing **2** an arguing; debate **3** a summary

ar·gu·men·ta·tion (-men tā′shən) *n.* the process of arguing; debate

ar·gu·men·ta·tive (-men′tə tiv) *adj.* **1** controversial **2** apt to argue; contentious Also **ar′gu·men′tive**

ar·gyle (är′gīl′) *adj.* ⟦after *Argyll*, Scotland⟧ knitted or woven in a diamond-shaped pattern, as socks

aria (ä′rē ə) *n.* ⟦It < L *aer*, air⟧ a song, as in an opera, for solo voice

-arian (er′ē ən, ar′-) ⟦< L⟧ *suffix* **1** (one) characterized by [*octogenarian*] **2** (one) believing in or associated with [*Unitarian*]

arid (ar′id, er′-) *adj.* ⟦< L *arere*, be dry⟧ **1** dry and barren **2** uninteresting; dull —**arid·ity** (ə rid′ə tē) *n.*

Ari·es (er′ēz′) ⟦L, the Ram⟧ the first sign of the zodiac

aright (ə rīt′) *adv.* correctly

arise (ə rīz′) *vi.* **arose** (-rōz′), **aris′en** (-riz′ən), **aris′ing** ⟦< OE *a-*, out + *risan*, to rise⟧ **1** to get up, as from sleeping **2** to ascend **3** to come into being **4** to result (*from*)

ar·is·toc·racy (ar′i stä′krə sē) *n., pl.* **-cies** ⟦< Gr *aristos*, best + *kratos*, to rule⟧ **1** government by a privileged minority, usually of inherited wealth **2** a country with such government **3** a privileged ruling class

aris·to·crat (ə ris′tə krat′) *n.* **1** a member of the aristocracy **2** one with the tastes, manners, etc. of the upper class —**aris′to·crat′ic** *adj.*

arith·me·tic (ə rith′mə tik) *n.* ⟦< Gr *arithmos*, number⟧ the science or art of computing by positive, real numbers —**ar·ith·met·i·cal** (ar′ith met′i kəl) or **ar′ith·met′ic** *adj.* —**ar′ith·me·ti·cian** (-mə tish′ən) *n.*

arithmetic mean the average obtained by dividing a sum by the number of its addends

ark (ärk) *n.* ⟦< L *arcere*, enclose⟧ **1** ARK OF THE COVENANT **2** an enclosure in a synagogue for the scrolls of the Torah **3** *Bible* the boat in which Noah, his family, and two of every kind of creature survived the Flood

ark of the covenant the chest containing the two stone tablets inscribed with the Ten Commandments

arm¹ (ärm) *n.* ⟦OE *earm*⟧ **1** an upper limb of the human body **2** anything like this in shape, function, position, etc. —**with open arms** cordially

arm² (ärm) *n.* ⟦< L *arma*, weapons⟧ **1** a weapon: *usually used in pl.* **2** any branch of the military forces —*vt.* to provide with weapons, etc. —*vi.* to prepare for war or any struggle —**under arms** ready for war —**up in arms 1** prepared to fight **2** indignant

ar·ma·da (är mä′də) *n.* ⟦Sp < L *arma*, weapons⟧ **1** a fleet of warships **2** a fleet of military aircraft

ar·ma·dillo (är′mə dil′ō) *n., pl.* **-los** ⟦Sp: see prec.⟧ a burrowing mammal of tropical America, covered with bony plates

Ar·ma·ged·don (är′mə ged′'n) *n.* **1** *Bible* the site of the last, decisive battle between the forces of good and evil **2** any great, decisive battle

ar·ma·ment (är′mə mənt) *n.* ⟦< L *armare*, to arm⟧ **1** [*often pl.*] all the military forces and equipment of a nation **2** all the military equipment of a warship, tank, etc. **3** an arming or being armed for war

ar·ma·ture (är′mə chər) *n.* ⟦< L *armare*, to arm⟧ **1** any protective covering **2** the iron core wound with wire in which electromotive force is produced in a generator or motor

---

THESAURUS

archives *n.* **1** [Place to store documents] repository, vault, treasury; see MUSEUM. **2** [Documents] chronicles, annals, public papers; see RECORDS.

arctic *a.* polar, frozen, icy; see COLD 1.

ardent *a.* fervent, impassioned, warm; see ZEALOUS.

arduous *a.* hard, severe, laborious; see DIFFICULT 1.

area *n.* section, lot, neighborhood, plot, zone, sector, patch, square, quarter, block, precinct, ward, field, territory, district, ghetto, township, region, tract, enclosure, parcel, division, city, parish, diocese, principality, dominion, kingdom, empire, state; see also MEASURE 1.

arena *n.* field, pit, ground, park, coliseum, square, stadium, playing field, amphitheater, bowl, stage, platform, course, gymnasium, gym*.

argue *v.* plead, appeal, explain, justify, show, reason with, dispute, contend, wrangle, oppose, battle,

demonstrate, establish, have it out, put up an argument, bicker, have a brush with.—*Ant.* NEGLECT, ignore, scorn.

argument *n.* **1** [An effort to convince] discussion, exchange, contention; see DISCUSSION. **2** [Verbal disagreement] debate, quarrel, row; see DISPUTE.

argumentative *a.* hostile, contentious, factious; see QUARRELSOME.

arid *a.* parched, barren, dried; see DRY 1.

arise *v.* **1** [To get up] rise, stand up, turn out, get out of bed, get out of a chair, get to one's feet, jump up, roll out, hit the deck*.—*Ant.* FALL, SIT, LIE. **2** [To ascend] mount, go up, climb; see RISE 1.

aristocracy *n.* nobility, privileged class, superior group, ruling class, noblemen, the elite, gentry, high society, upper classes, persons of rank, patricians.

aristocrat *n.* nobleman, peer, lord, noble, baron, earl, prince, patrician,

ruler, gentleman, thoroughbred, duke, viscount, count, emperor, empress, queen, princess, duchess, countess, baroness, knight, lady, marquis; see also KING 1, LADY 2.

aristocratic *a.* noble, refined, well-bred; see NOBLE 1, 2, 3.

arithmetic *n.* addition, subtraction, calculation; see MATHEMATICS.

arm¹ *n.* **1** [The upper human limb] member, appendage, forelimb, forearm, fin*, flapper*, soupbone*. **2** [Anything resembling an arm] bend, crook, projection, cylinder, sofa-end, branch, limb, rod, bough, offshoot, wing, prong, stump, hook, handle, bow. —**at arm's length** at a distance, not friendly, not intimate, aloof. —**with open arms** warmly, affectionately, joyously; see FRIENDLY.

arm² *v.* furnish weapons, load, give firearms, issue weapons, equip with arms, outfit, fit out.—*Ant.* DISARM, demilitarize, deactivate.

arm′chair′ *n.* a chair with supports at the sides for one's arms

armed forces all the military, naval, and air forces of a country

arm·ful (ärm′fool) *n., pl.* **-fuls** as much as the arms or one arm can hold

arm′hole′ *n.* an opening for the arm in a garment

ar·mi·stice (är′mə stis) *n.* ⟦ < L *arma*, weapons + *stare*, to stand ⟧ a truce preliminary to the signing of a peace treaty

Armistice Day VETERANS DAY

arm·let (ärm′lət) *n.* an ornamental band worn around the upper arm

ar·mor (är′mər) *n.* ⟦ < L *armare*, to arm ⟧ any defensive or protective covering — *vt., vi.* to put armor on —**ar′mored** (-mərd) *adj.*

armored car a vehicle covered with armor plate, as a truck for carrying money to or from a bank

ar·mo·rial (är môr′ē əl) *adj.* of coats of arms; heraldic

ar·mory (är′mər ē) *n., pl.* **-mor·ies** ⟦see ARMOR⟧ 1 an arsenal 2 a National Guard unit drill hall

arm′pit′ *n.* the hollow under the arm at the shoulder

arm′rest′ *n.* a support for the arm, as on the inside of an automobile door

army (är′mē) *n., pl.* **-mies** ⟦ult. < L *arma*, weapons⟧ 1 a large, organized body of soldiers for waging war, esp. on land 2 a large number of persons, animals, etc. /an *army* of ants/

aro·ma (ə rō′mə) *n.* ⟦ < Gr *arōma*, spice ⟧ a pleasant odor; fragrance

aro·matic (ar′ə mat′ik) *adj.* of or having an aroma; fragrant or pungent — *n.* an aromatic plant, chemical, etc. — **aro′mat′i·cal·ly** *adv.*

arose (ə rōz′) *vi. pt.* of ARISE

around (ə round′) *adv.* ⟦ME⟧ 1 in a circle 2 in every direction 3 in circumference 4 to the opposite direction 5 [Colloq.] nearby /stay *around*/ — *prep.* 1 so as to encircle or envelop 2 on the border of 3 in various places in or on 4 about /*around* 1890/

arouse (ə rouz′) *vt.* **aroused′, arous′ing** 1 to awaken, as from sleep 2 to stir, as to action 3 to evoke /to *arouse* pity/ —**arous′al** *n.*

ar·peg·gio (är pej′ō) *n., pl.* **-gios** ⟦It < *arpa*, a harp⟧ a chord whose notes are played in quick succession

ar·raign (ə rān′) *vt.* ⟦< L *ad*, to + *ratio*, reason⟧ 1 to bring before a law court to answer charges 2 to call to account; accuse —**ar·raign′ment** *n.*

ar·range (ə rānj′) *vt.* **-ranged′, -rang′ing** ⟦< OFr *a-*, to + *renger*, to range⟧ 1 to put in the correct order 2 to classify 3 to prepare or plan 4 to arrive at an agreement about 5 *Music* to adapt (a composition) to particular instruments or voices — *vi. Music* to write arrangements, esp. as a profession —**ar·rang′er** *n.*

ar·range′ment *n.* 1 an arranging 2 a result or manner of arranging 3 [*usually pl.*] a plan 4 a settlement 5 *Music* a) an arranging of a composition b) the composition as thus arranged

ar·rant (ar′ənt) *adj.* ⟦var. of ERRANT⟧ out-and-out; notorious

ar·ras (ar′əs) *n.* ⟦after Arras, Fr city⟧ a wall hanging, esp. of tapestry

ar·ray (ə rā′) *vt.* ⟦< OFr *areer*⟧ 1 to place in order 2 to dress in finery — *n.* 1 an orderly grouping, esp. of troops 2 an impressive display 3 fine clothes

ar·rears (ə rirz′) *n.pl.* ⟦< L *ad*, to + *retro*, behind⟧ overdue debts —**in arrears** behind in paying a debt, doing one's work, etc.

ar·rest (ə rest′) *vt.* ⟦< L *ad-*, to + *restare*, to stop⟧ 1 to stop or check 2 to seize by authority of the law 3 to catch and keep (one's attention, etc.) — *n.* an arresting or being arrested —**under arrest** in legal custody

ar·rest′ing *adj.* attracting attention; interesting

ar·rhyth·mia (ə rith′mē ə) *n.* ⟦< Gr *a-*, without + *rhythmos*, measure⟧ an irregularity in the heart's rhythm —**ar·rhyth′mic** or **ar·rhyth′mi·cal** (-rith′mi kəl) *adj.*

ar·rival (ə rī′vəl) *n.* 1 an arriving 2 a person or thing that arrives

ar·rive (ə rīv′) *vi.* **-rived′, -riv′ing** ⟦< L *ad-*, to + *ripa*, shore⟧ 1 to reach one's destination 2 to come /the time has *arrived*/ 3 to attain fame, etc. —**arrive at** to reach by thinking, etc.

ar·ri·ve·der·ci (är rē′ve der′chē) *interj.* ⟦It⟧ goodbye

ar·ro·gant (ar′ə gənt) *adj.* ⟦< L *arrogare*, to claim⟧ full of or due to pride; haughty —**ar′ro·gance** *n.* —**ar′ro·gantly** *adv.*

ar′ro·gate′ (-gāt′) *vt.* **-gat′ed, -gat′ing** ⟦< L *ad-*, for +

■■■ THESAURUS ■■■

armchair *n.* easy chair, rocker, recliner; see CHAIR.

armed *a.* equipped, outfitted, in battle formation, loaded, provided with arms, fortified, protected, fitted out, in arms, well-armed, heavily armed.—*Ant.* UNARMED, vulnerable, unprotected.

armistice *n.* treaty of peace, ceasefire, temporary peace; see PEACE.

armor *n.* tanks, tank force, Panzer divisions, armored personnel carriers, armored column, gun carriers, armor divisions.

armory *n.* ordnance headquarters, training center, drilling place, depot, arsenal, gymnasium, drill center, shooting range, National Guard building, reserve corps headquarters.

arms *n.* armament, armor, ammunition, firearms, munitions, guns, small arms, instruments of war, deadly arms, lethal weapons, pistols, rifles, machine guns, submachine guns, equipment, supplies, ordnance, artillery, material, hardware, ammo*; see also WEAPON. —**bear arms** carry weapons, be armed, be militant; see ARM. —**take up arms** go to war, rebel, do battle; see FIGHT. —**up in arms** hostile, indignant, willing to fight; see ANGRY.

army *n.* 1 [Military land forces] armed force, standing army, regulars, soldiery, troops, men, cavalry, infantry, artillery, air corps, reserves. 2 [A unit of an army] division, regiment, armored division, airborne division, infantry division, battalion, company, corps, brigade, flight, wing, amphibious force, task force, detail, detachment, squad, troop, blocking force, patrol, unit, command, formation, point, column, legion, platoon, outfit.

aroma *n.* fragrance, perfume, odor; see SMELL 1, 2.

around *a., prep.* 1 [Surrounding] about, in this area, on all sides, on every side, in circumference, neighboring, in the vicinity of, all around, round about, encompassing, nearby, approximately, in a circle, along a circuit, all about, close to, nearly in a circle, on various sides, round and round, right and left.—*Ant.* DISTANT, remote, far-off. 2 [Approximately] almost, about, close to; see APPROXIMATELY. —**have been around*** worldly, sophisticated, knowledgeable; see EXPERIENCED.

arouse *v.* move, stir up, stimulate; see EXCITE.

arrange *v.* 1 [To put in order] order, regulate, systematize; see ORDER 3. 2 [To make arrangements] determine, plan, devise, contrive, prepare for, get ready, make ready, draft, scheme, design, provide, make preparations, set the stage, prepare, put into shape, make plans for, line up, organize, adjust, manage, direct, establish, decide, resolve.—*Ant.* BOTHER, disorganize, disturb.

arrangement *n.* 1 [The result of arranging] method, system, form; see ORDER 3. 2 [An agreement] settlement, adjustment, compromise; see AGREEMENT 1. 3 [A design] pattern, composition, combination; see DESIGN.

arrest *n.* appropriation, imprisonment, apprehension, commitment, confinement, incarceration, capture, captivity, protective custody, taking by force, taking into custody, constraint, duress, seizure, detention, bust*.—*Ant.* FREEDOM, acquittal, release. —**under arrest** arrested, caught, apprehended, taken into custody, seized, taken in, handcuffed, confined, jailed, imprisoned, detained, shut up, penned up, put in irons, sent to prison, sent to jail, busted*, pinched*, booked, collared*, nabbed*, sent up the river*.

arrest *v.* apprehend, hold, place under arrest, take into custody, capture, imprison, jail, incarcerate, detain, secure, seize, get, catch, take prisoner, nab*, pick up, bust*.—*Ant.* FREE, liberate, parole.

arrival *n.* 1 [The act of arriving] entrance, advent, coming, entry, appearance, landing, homecoming, debarkation, approach, return, meeting.—*Ant.* DEPARTURE, leaving, leave-taking. 2 [That which has arrived] passenger, visitor, tourist, guest, newcomer, delegate, traveler, cargo, freight, mail, shipment, package, parcel.

arrive *v.* enter, land, disembark, alight, dismount, halt, roll up, reach, get in, visit, make shore, drop anchor, reach home, appear, get to, hit*, touch*, blow into*, breeze in*, check in*, pull in, hit town*.—*Ant.* LEAVE, go, depart.

arrogance *n.* insolence, smugness, vanity, audacity, haughtiness; see also PRIDE 2.

arrogant *a.* domineering, autocratic, sneering; see EGOTISTIC.

arrogantly *a.* proudly, haughtily, insolently, loftily, with one's nose in the air*.

rogare, to ask] to claim or seize without right —**ar'ro·ga'·tion** *n.*

ar·row (ar'ō) *n.* [OE *arwe*] 1 a pointed shaft for shooting from a bow 2 a sign (←), used to indicate direction

ar'row·head' *n.* the separable, pointed tip of an arrow

ar'row·root' *n.* [from use as antidote for poisoned arrows] 1 a tropical plant with starchy roots 2 a starch made from its roots

ar·roy·o (ə roi'ō) *n., pl.* **-os** [Sp < L *arrugia*, mine shaft] [Southwest] 1 a dry gully 2 a rivulet or stream

ar·se·nal (är'sə nəl) *n.* [< Ar *dār aṣṣināˁa*, workshop] 1 a place for making or storing weapons 2 a store or collection

ar·se·nic (är'sə nik'; *for adj.* är sen'ik) *n.* [< Gr *arsenikon*] a very poisonous chemical element, compounds of which are used in insecticides, etc. —*adj.* of or containing arsenic: also **ar·sen'i·cal** (-sen'i kəl)

ar·son (är'sən) *n.* [< L *ardere*, to burn] the crime of purposely setting fire to a building or property —**ar'son·ist** *n.*

art¹ (ärt) *n.* [< L *ars*] 1 human creativity 2 skill 3 any specific skill or its application 4 any craft or its principles 5 creative work or its principles 6 any branch of creative work, as painting or sculpture 7 products of this, as paintings or statues 8 *a*) a branch of learning *b*) [*pl.*] LIBERAL ARTS 9 cunning 10 sly trick; wile: *usually used in pl.*

art² (ärt) *vi.* archaic 2d pers. sing., pres. indic., of BE: used with *thou*

art. 1 article 2 artificial

art deco (dek'ō) a decorative style of the late 1920's and the 1930's, derived from cubism

ar·te·ri·al (är tir'ē əl) *adj.* 1 of or in the arteries 2 of a main road

ar·te·ri·ole (är tir'ē ōl') *n.* [see ARTERY] any of the small blood vessels between the arteries and capillaries

ar·te·rio·scle·ro·sis (är tir'ē ō'sklə rō'sis) *n.* [< Gr *artēria*, artery + SCLEROSIS] a thickening and hardening of the arteries, as in old age

ar·ter·y (ärt'ər ē) *n., pl.* **-ter·ies** [< Gr *aeirein*, to lift] 1 any of the blood vessels that carry blood away from the heart 2 a main route

ar·te·sian well (är tē'zhən) [Fr *artésien*, of Artois (in France)] a deep well in which water is forced up by pressure of underground water draining from higher ground

art·ful (ärt'fəl) *adj.* 1 skillful or clever 2 cunning; crafty —**art'ful·ly** *adv.* —**art'ful·ness** *n.*

ar·thri·tis (är thrīt'is) *n.* [Gr < *arthron*, joint + -ITIS] inflammation of a joint or joints —**ar·thrit·ic** (är thrit'ik) *adj.*

arthro- [< Gr *arthron*, joint] *combining form* joint, joints

arthro·pod (är'thrō päd') *n.* [prec. + -POD] any of a phylum of invertebrates with jointed legs and a segmented body

ar'thro·scope' (-skōp') *n.* [ARTHRO- + -SCOPE] an endoscope used inside a joint —**ar'thro·scop'ic** (-skäp'ik) *adj.*

Ar·thur (är'thər) legendary 6th-c. king of Britain —**Ar·thu·ri·an** (är thoor'ē ən) *adj.*

ar·ti·choke (ärt'ə chōk') *n.* [ult. < Ar *al-ḥarshaf*] 1 a thistlelike plant 2 its edible flower head

ar·ti·cle (ärt'i kəl) *n.* [< L *artus*, joint] 1 one of the sections of a document 2 a complete piece of writing, as in a newspaper, magazine, etc. 3 a separate item [an *article* of luggage] 4 *Gram.* any one of the words *a*, *an*, or *the*, used as adjectives

ar·tic·u·late (är tik'yōō lit; *for v.*, -lāt') *adj.* [see prec.] 1 jointed: usually **ar·tic'u·lat'ed** 2 made up of distinct sounds, as speech 3 able to speak 4 expressing oneself clearly — *vt.* **-lat'ed, -lat'ing** 1 to connect by joints 2 to arrange in connected sequence 3 to utter distinctly 4 to express clearly — *vi.* 1 to speak distinctly 2 to be jointed or connected —**ar·tic'u·late·ly** *adv.* —**ar·tic'u·la'tion** *n.*

ar·ti·fact (ärt'ə fakt') *n.* any object made by human work

ar·ti·fice (ärt'ə fis) *n.* [< L *ars*, art + *facere*, make] 1 skill or ingenuity 2 trickery 3 an artful trick

ar·ti·fi·cer (är tif'ə sər) *n.* 1 a skilled craftsman 2 an inventor

ar·ti·fi·cial (ärt'ə fish'əl) *adj.* [see ARTIFICE] 1 made by human work; not natural 2 simulated [artificial teeth] 3 affected [an *artificial* smile] —**ar'ti·fi'ci·al'ity** (-fish'ē al'ə tē), *pl.* **-ties,** *n.* —**ar'ti·fi'cial·ly** *adv.*

artificial intelligence the development of computers capable of reasoning, learning, etc.

artificial respiration the maintenance of breathing by artificial means, as by forcing air into the mouth

ar·til·ler·y (är til'ər ē) *n.* [< OFr *atillier*, equip] 1 mounted guns, as cannon or missile launchers 2 gunnery —**the artillery** the branch of an army using heavy mounted guns —**ar·til'lery·man** (-mən), *pl.* **-men,** *n.*

ar·ti·san (ärt'ə zən) *n.* [ult. < L *ars*, art] a skilled craftsman

art·ist (ärt'ist) *n.* 1 one who is skilled in any of the fine arts 2 one who does anything very well 3 a professional in any of the performing arts

ar·tis·tic (är tis'tik) *adj.* 1 of art or artists 2 done skillfully and tastefully 3 sensitive to beauty —**ar·tis'ti·cally** *adv.*

art·ist·ry (ärt'is trē) *n.* artistic quality, ability, or work

art·less (ärt'lis) *adj.* 1 lacking skill or art 2 simple; natural 3 without guile; ingenuous —**art'less·ly** *adv.*

art·y (ärt'ē) *adj.* **art'i·er, art'i·est** [Colloq.] affectedly artistic —**art'i·ness** *n.*

ar·um (er'əm) *n.* [L] any of a family of plants with flowers enveloped within a hoodlike leaf

Ar·y·an (ar'ē ən, er'-) *n.* [< Sans *āzya-*, noble] 1 [Obs.] the hypothetical parent language of the Indo-European family 2 a person supposed to be a descendant of the prehistoric peoples who spoke this language: *Aryan* is not a valid ethnological term

as (az, əz) *adv.* [< ALSO] 1 equally [just *as* happy at home] 2 for instance [a card game, *as* bridge] 3 when related in a specified way [my view *as* contrasted with yours] — *conj.* 1 to the same amount or degree that [straight *as* an arrow] 2 in the same manner that [do *as* you are told] 3 while [she wept *as* she spoke] 4 because [*as* you object, we won't go] 5 that the consequence is [so obvious *as* to need no reply] 6 though [tall *as* he was, he couldn't reach it] — *pron.* 1 a fact that [we are tired, *as* you can see] 2 that (preceded by *such* or *the same*) [such books *as* I own] —

THESAURUS

arrow *n.* shaft, dart, missile; see WEAPON.

arson *n.* pyromania, firing, deliberate burning of property; see CRIME.

art¹ *n.* representation, illustration, abstraction, imitation, modeling, description, portrayal, design, performance, personification, sketching, molding, shaping, painting, characterization, creating, sculpting, carving; see also ARCHITECTURE, DANCE 1, LITERATURE 1, MUSIC 1, PAINTING, SCULPTURE.

artery *n.* 1 [Main channel of communication or travel] highway, thoroughfare, line, supply route, canal; see also ROAD 1, WAY 2. 2 [Blood vessel] tube, aorta, arterial passageway; see VEIN 3.

artful *a.* clever, adroit, ingenious; see ABLE.

article *n.* 1 [An individual thing] object, substance, commodity; see THING 1. 2 [Nonfiction appearing in a periodical] essay, editorial, commentary; see WRITING 2.

articulate *v.* 1 [To speak clearly] enunciate, pronounce, verbalize; see SPEAK 1. 2 [To join] fit together, combine, connect, link; see also JOIN 1.

artificial *a.* unreal, synthetic, counterfeit; see FALSE 3.

artillery *n.* gunnery, arms, weapons; see ARMS.

artist *n.* master, creator, painter, composer, virtuoso, musician, poet, novelist, dramatist, essayist, actress, actor, playwright, writer, performing artist, cartoonist, opera singer, dancer, ballet performer, ballerina, sculptor, etcher, engraver, designer, architect, photographer.

artistic *a.* inventive, skillful, imaginative, discriminating, creative, graceful, talented, accomplished, well-executed, well-wrought, pleasing, sublime, ideal, cultured, tasteful, exquisite, sensitive, fine, elegant, harmonious, grand, stimulating, elevated, noble, beautiful.

artistry *n.* workmanship, skill, proficiency; see ABILITY.

as *a., conj., prep.* 1 [While] in the process of, in the act of, on the point of; see WHILE 1. 2 [Because] since, inasmuch as, for the reason that; see BECAUSE. 3 [To a degree] in the same way, in the same manner, equally, comparatively, similarly. 4 [For a given purpose, end, use, etc.] just as, just for, serving as, functioning as, acting as, being, in and of itself, by its nature, essentially. —**as a matter of fact** truly, actually, indeed; see REALLY 1. —**as if** just as if, just as though, as it were, in such a way that, as if it were, supposing, quasi, so to speak, as would be if, as might be, just like. —**as is*** as it stands, as usual, just the same, the same way. —**as it were** so to speak, figuratively speaking, in a way, as it seems, as it would seem, in some sort, in a manner, so to say, kind of*, in a manner of speaking, sort of*. —**as though** just as, just as if, just as though; see AS IF.

prep. in the role or function of *[he poses as a friend]* **—as for (or to)** concerning **— as if (or though)** as it (or one) would if **—as is** [Colloq.] just as it is **—as it were** as if it were so

As *Chem.* symbol for arsenic

as·bes·tos (as bes′təs, az-) *n.* [< Gr *a-*, not + *sbennynai*, extinguish] a nonconducting, fireproof mineral used in electrical insulation, roofing, etc.

as·cend (ə send′) *vi.* [< L *ad-*, to + *scandere*, to climb] to move upward; rise — *vt.* **1** to move upward along; mount **2** to succeed to (a throne)

as·cend′ancy or **as·cend′ency** (-ən sē) *n.* a position of control; domination

as·cend′ant or **as·cend′ent** (-ənt) *adj.* **1** rising **2** in control; dominant **—in the ascendant** at or approaching the height of power, fame, etc.

as·cen·sion (ə sen′shən) *n.* **1** an ascending **2** [A-] the 40th day after Easter, celebrating the Ascension **—the Ascension** *Bible* the bodily ascent of Jesus into heaven

as·cent (ə sent′) *n.* **1** an ascending **2** an upward slope

as·cer·tain (as′ər tān′) *vt.* [see AD- & CERTAIN] to find out with certainty

as·cetic (ə set′ik) *adj.* [< Gr *askein*, to train the body] self-denying; austere — *n.* [< Gr *awkētēs*, monk] one who leads a life of strict self-denial, esp. for religious purposes **—as·cet′i·cism′** (-siz′əm) *n.*

ascor·bic acid (ə skôr′bik) [A-² + SCORB(UTIC) + -IC] vitamin C

as·cot (as′kət, -kät′) *n.* a necktie with very broad ends hanging from the knot

as·cribe (ə skrīb′) *vt.* **-cribed′, -crib′ing** [< L *ad-*, to + *scribere*, write] **1** to assign (*to* a supposed cause) **2** to regard as belonging (*to*) or coming from someone **—as·crip·tion** (ə skrip′shən) *n.*

asep·tic (ā sep′tik, ə-) *adj.* free from disease-producing bacteria, etc.

asex·ual (ā sek′shōō əl) *adj.* **1** having no sex or sexual organs **2** without the union of male and female germ cells **3** not asexual *[asexual* clothing] **—asex′u·al·ly** *adv.*

ash¹ (ash) *n.* [< OE *æsce*] **1** the grayish powder left after something has burned **2** fine, volcanic lava **3** the gray color of wood ash See also ASHES

ash² (ash) *n.* [< OE *æsc*] **1** a shade tree of the olive family **2** its wood

ashamed (ə shāmd′) *adj.* **1** feeling shame **2** reluctant because fearing shame beforehand **—asham·edly** (ə shām′id lē) *adv.*

ashen (ash′ən) *adj.* **1** of ashes **2** like ashes, esp. in color; pale

ashes (ash′iz) *n.pl.* **1** the grayish powder and small particles left after a thing has burned **2** human remains, esp. the part left after cremation

ashore (ə shôr′) *adv., adj.* **1** to or on the shore **2** to or on land

ash·ram (äsh′rəm) *n.* [< Sans *ā*, toward + *śrama*, penance] **1** a secluded place for a Hindu religious community **2** such a community

ash′tray′ *n.* a container for smokers' tobacco ashes, etc. Also **ash tray**

Ash Wednesday the first day of Lent: from the putting of ashes on the forehead in penitence

ash′y *adj.* **-i·er, -i·est 1** of or covered with ashes **2** ashen; pale

Asian (ā′zhən) *adj.* of Asia, its people, etc. — *n.* a native or inhabitant of Asia Also **Asi·atic** (ā′zhē at′ik)

aside (ə sīd′) *adv.* **1** on or to one side **2** in reserve *[put one aside for me]* **3** apart; notwithstanding *[joking aside]* — *n.* words spoken by an actor but supposedly heard only by the audience **—aside from 1** with the exception of **2** apart from

asi·nine (as′ə nīn′) *adj.* [< L *asinus*, ass] like an ass; stupid; silly **—as′i·nine′ly** *adv.* **—as′i·nin′ity** (-nin′ə tē) *n.*

ask (ask) *vt.* [OE *āscian*] **1** to use words in seeking the answer to (a question) **2** to inquire of (a person) **3** to request or demand **4** to invite — *vi.* **1** to make a request (*for*) **2** to inquire (*about* or *after*) **—ask′er** *n.*

askance (ə skans′) *adv.* [ME] **1** with a sideways glance **2** with suspicion, disapproval, etc.

askew (ə skyōō′) *adv.* to one side; awry — *adj.* on one side; awry

asking price the price asked by a seller, esp. as a basis for bargaining

aslant (ə slant′) *adv.* on a slant — *prep.* on a slant across — *adj.* slanting

asleep (ə slēp′) *adj.* **1** sleeping **2** inactive; dull **3** numb **4** dead — *adv.* into a sleeping condition

aso·cial (ā sō′shəl) *adj.* **1** avoiding contact with others **2** selfish

asp (asp) *n.* [< Gr *aspis*] a poisonous snake of Africa, Arabia, etc.

as·para·gus (ə spar′ə gəs, -sper′-) *n.* [< Gr *asparagos*] **1** a plant of the lily family, with edible shoots **2** these shoots

as·par·tame (as pär′tām′) *n.* an artificial, low-calorie sweetener, used in soft drinks, candy, etc.

as·pect (as′pekt′) *n.* [< L *ad-*, to + *specere*, to look] **1** the way one appears **2** the appearance of something from a specific position or viewpoint **3** a side facing in a given direction

as·pen (as′pən) *n.* [OE *æspe*] a poplar tree whose leaves flutter in the least breeze

as·per·ity (ə sper′ə tē) *n., pl.* **-ties** [< L *asper*, rough] **1** roughness or harshness **2** sharpness of temper

as·perse (ə spurs′) *vt.* **-persed′, -pers′ing** [< L *ad-*, to + *spargere*, to sprinkle] to slander

as·per·sion (ə spur′zhən) *n.* a damaging or disparaging remark; slander

as·phalt (as′fôlt′) *n.* [< Gr *asphaltos*] a brown or black tarlike substance mixed with sand and gravel and used for paving, roofing, etc. — *vt.* to pave, roof, etc. with asphalt

as·pho·del (as′fə del′) *n.* [< Gr *asphodelos*] a plant of the lily family, having white or yellow flowers

as·phyxi·ate (as fik′sē āt′) *vt., vi.* **-at′ed, -at′ing** [< Gr *a-*, not + *sphyzein*, to throb] **1** to make or become unconscious from lack of oxygen in the blood **2** to suffocate **—as·phyxi·a′tion** *n.*

as·pic (as′pik′) *n.* [< OFr *aspe*, asp] a cold jelly of meat juice, tomato juice, etc., served as a garnish or in a mold

as·pi·rant (as′pə rənt, ə spī′-) *adj.* aspiring **—** *n.* one who aspires

as·pi·rate (as′pə rāt′; *for n.*, -pər it) *vt.* **-rat′ed, -rat′ing 1** to begin (a word) with the sound of English (h) **2** to follow (a consonant) with an audible puff of breath **3** to suck in or draw in — *n.* an aspirated sound

as·pi·ra·tion (as′pə rā′shən) *n.* **1** *a)* strong desire or ambition, as for advancement *b)* the thing desired **2** a drawing in by breathing or suction

as·pi·ra′tor *n.* an apparatus using suction to remove air, fluids, etc.

■■■ THESAURUS ■■■

ascend *v.* go upward, sprout, soar; see RISE 1.

ascent *n.* ascendance, climbing, ascension; see RISE 1.

ashamed *a.* embarrassed, shamed, regretful, meek, repentant, penitent, apologetic, debased, abashed, conscience-stricken, mortified, uncomfortable, hesitant, perplexed, bewildered, shamefaced, bowed down, disconcerted, sputtering, stammering, stuttering, gasping, floundering, rattled, muddled, confused, blushing, flustered, distraught, submissive, feeling like a jackass, off balance, in a hole*, taken down a peg, red in the face*, looking silly, at a loss.

ashes *n.* dust, powder, cinders, slag, embers, charcoal, soot.

Asian *a.* Oriental, Mongolian, Chinese, Hindu, Japanese, Mongoloid.

aside *a.* to the side, to one side, on one side, at rest, out, by oneself, apart, by the side of, at one side, by itself, alone, alongside, out of the way, aloof, away, in safekeeping, beside, sideways, sideways, abreast, at a short distance, by. **—aside from** beside, in addition to, excluding; see BESIDES.

ask *v.* request, query, question, interrogate, examine, cross-examine, demand, raise a question, inquire, frame a question, order, command, put questions to, requisition, bid, charge, petition, call upon, invite, urge to, challenge, pry into, scour, investigate, hunt for, quiz, grill, needle*, sound out*, pump*, put through the third degree*.—*Ant.* ANSWER, refute, rejoin.

asleep *a.* sleeping, dreaming, quiet, resting, snoring, in a sound sleep, fast asleep, sound asleep, slumbering, reposing, taking a siesta, hibernating, dozing, wakeless, napping, unconscious, dead to the world*, in the Land of Nod, snoozing*, conked out*, out like a light*.—*Ant.* AWAKE, waking, alert. **—fall asleep** go to sleep, doze, drop off*; see SLEEP.

aspect *n.* **1** [Looks] countenance, face, features; see LOOKS. **2** [View] perspective, regard, slant; see VIEWPOINT.

aspiration *n.* yearning, eagerness, inclination; see AMBITION.

as·pire (ə spīr′) *vi.* **-pired′, -pir′ing** 〚< L *ad-*, to + *spirare*, breathe〛 to be ambitious (*to* get or do something); seek (*after*)

as·pi·rin (as′pə rin′, -prin′) *n.* 〚Ger〛 **1** a white, crystalline powder used for reducing fever, relieving pain, etc. **2** a tablet of this

asquint (ə skwint′) *adv., adj.* with a squint

ass (as) *n.* 〚< L *asinus*〛 **1** a horselike animal having long ears and a short mane **2** a stupid or silly person

as·sail (ə sāl′) *vt.* 〚< L *ad-*, to + *salire*, to leap〛 **1** to attack physically and violently **2** to attack with arguments, etc. —**as·sail′a·ble** *adj.*

as·sail′ant (-ənt) *n.* an attacker

as·sas·sin (ə sas′ən) *n.* 〚< Ar *ḥashshāshīn*, hashish users〛 **1** a murderer who strikes suddenly **2** the murderer of a politically important person

as·sas′si·nate′ (-āt′) *vt.* **-nat′ed, -nat′ing** to murder as an assassin does —**as·sas′si·na′tion** *n.*

as·sault (ə sôlt′) *n.* 〚< L *ad-*, to + *salire*, to leap〛 **1** a violent attack **2** *euphemism for* RAPE[1] **3** *Law* an unlawful threat or attempt to harm another physically — *vt., vi.* to make an assault (upon)

assault and battery *Law* the carrying out of threatened physical harm

as·say (as′ā, a sā′; *for v.* a sā′) *n.* 〚< OFr *essai*, trial〛 **1** a testing **2** an analysis of the ingredients of an ore, drug, etc. — *vt.* **1** to make an assay of; test **2** to try; attempt — *vi.* to be shown by assay to have a specified proportion of something —**as·say′er** *n.*

as·sem·blage (ə sem′blij) *n.* **1** an assembling **2** a group of persons or things gathered together **3** *Art* things assembled in a sculptured collage

as·sem′ble (-bəl) *vt., vi.* **-bled, -bling** 〚< L *ad-*, to + *simul*, together〛 **1** to gather into a group; collect **2** to fit or put together the parts of —**as·sem′bler** *n.*

as·sem′bly (-blē) *n., pl.* **-blies 1** an assembling **2** a group of persons gathered together **3** *a)* a legislative body *b)* [A-] the lower house of some State legislatures **4** a fitting together of parts to make a whole

assembly line in many factories, a method whereby each worker performs a specific task in assembling the work as it is passed along

as·sem′bly·man (-mən) *n., pl.* **-men** a member of a legislative assembly —**as·sem′bly·wom′an**, *pl.* **-wom′en**, *n.fem.*

as·sent (ə sent′) *vi.* 〚< L *ad-*, to + *sentire*, to feel〛 to express acceptance; agree (*to*) — *n.* consent or agreement

as·sert (ə sʉrt′) *vt.* 〚< L *ad-*, to + *serere*, join〛 **1** to declare; affirm **2** to maintain or defend (rights, etc.) —

assert oneself to insist on one's rights, or on being recognized —**as·sert′er** or **as·ser′tor** *n.*

as·ser·tion (ə sʉr′shən) *n.* **1** an asserting **2** a positive statement

as·ser·tive (ə sʉrt′iv) *adj.* persistently positive or confident —**as·ser′tive·ly** *adv.* —**as·ser′tive·ness** *n.*

as·sess (ə ses′) *vt.* 〚< L *ad-*, to + *sedere*, sit〛 **1** to set an estimated value on (property, etc.) for taxation **2** to set the amount of (a tax, fine, etc.) **3** to impose a tax, etc. on **4** to judge the worth or importance of —**as·sess′ment** *n.* —**as·ses′sor** *n.*

as·set (as′et) *n.* 〚< L *ad*, to + *satis*, enough〛 **1** anything owned that has value **2** a desirable thing [charm is an *asset*] **3** [pl.] the accounting entries showing the resources of a person or business **4** [pl.] *Law* property available to pay debts

as·sev·er·ate (ə sev′ə rāt′) *vt.* **-at′ed, -at′ing** 〚< L *ad-*, to + *severus*, earnest〛 to state positively; assert —**as·sev′er·a′tion** *n.*

as·sid·u·ous (ə sij′o̅o̅ əs) *adj.* 〚< L *assidere*, to assist〛 diligent; persevering; careful —**as·si·du·i·ty** (as′ə dyo̅o̅′ə tē), *pl.* **-ties,** *n.* —**as·sid′u·ous·ly** *adv.* —**as·sid′u·ous·ness** *n.*

as·sign (ə sīn′) *vt.* 〚< L *ad-*, to + *signare*, to sign〛 **1** to set apart or mark for a specific purpose; designate **2** to appoint, as to a duty **3** to give out as a task; allot **4** to ascribe; attribute **5** *Law* to transfer (a right, etc.) —**as·sign′a·ble** *adj.* —**as·sign′er** or *Law* **as·sign·or** (ə sīn′ôr′) *n.*

as·sig·na·tion (as′ig nā′shən) *n.* an appointment to meet, esp. one made secretly by lovers

as·sign′ment *n.* **1** an assigning or being assigned **2** anything assigned

as·simi·late (ə sim′ə lāt′) *vt.* **-lat′ed, -lat′ing** 〚< L *ad-*, to + *similare*, make similar〛 **1** to absorb and incorporate; digest **2** to make like or alike — *vi.* **1** to become like or alike **2** to be absorbed and incorporated —**as·sim′i·la′tion** *n.*

as·sist (ə sist′) *vt., vi.* 〚< L *ad-*, to + *sistere*, make stand〛 to help; aid — *n.* an instance or act of helping —**assist at** to be present at; attend

as·sist·ance (ə sis′təns) *n.* help; aid

as·sist′ant (-tənt) *adj.* assisting; helping — *n.* one who assists; helper; aid

as·siz·es (ə sīz′iz) *n.pl.* [see ASSESS] **1** court sessions held periodically in each county of England **2** the time or place of these

assn. association

assoc. **1** associate(s) **2** association

as·so·ci·ate (ə sō′shē āt′, -sē-; *for n. & adj.,* -it) *vt.* **-at′ed, -at′ing** 〚< L *ad-*, to + *socius*, companion〛 **1** to connect; combine; join **2** to bring into relationship as partner, etc.

<hr>

█████████ **THESAURUS** ▶██████

aspire *v.* strive, struggle, yearn; see TRY 1.

aspiring *a.* ambitious, hopeful, enthusiastic; see ZEALOUS.

ass *n.* **1** [A stupid person] dolt, dunce, blockhead; see FOOL. **2** [A donkey] burro, jackass, jennet; see ANIMAL.

assailant *n.* antagonist, foe, enemy; see OPPONENT.

assassin *n.* murderer, slayer, butcher; see KILLER.

assassinate *v.* slay, slaughter, put to death; see KILL 1.

assassination *n.* killing, shooting, slaying; see MURDER.

assault *n.* **1** [An attack] charge, advance, onslaught; see ATTACK. **2** [A rape] attack, abduction, violation; see RAPE.

assault *v.* **1** [To attack] assail, advance, strike; see ATTACK. **2** [To rape] attack, violate, ravish; see RAPE.

assemble *v.* **1** [To bring together] rally, call, convoke, muster, round up, group, convene, summon, mobilize, call together, accumulate, amass, invite guests, gather, collect, hold a meeting, unite, pack them in, throw a party*, herd together*, rally round, gather around, gang around*.—*Ant.* SCATTER, break up, send away. **2** [To put together] piece together, set up, erect, construct, join, unite, solder,

mold, weld, glue, model.—*Ant.* BREAK, disassemble, break down.

assembly *n.* **1** [A gathering of persons] assemblage, meeting, association; see GATHERING. **2** [The process of bringing parts together] construction, collection, piecing together, fitting in, joining, assembling, modeling, attachment, adjustment, welding, soldering, molding, fixing.—*Ant.* SEPARATION, dismantling, wrecking.

assent *n.* approval, authorization, consent; see PERMISSION.

assert *v.* state, say, affirm; see DECLARE.

assertion *n.* affirmation, statement, report; see DECLARATION.

assess *v.* **1** [To tax] charge, exact tribute, exact from; see TAX 1. **2** [To estimate] judge, reckon, guess; see ESTIMATE.

assets *n.* holdings, possessions, capital; see PROPERTY.

assign *v.* commit, commission, authorize, hand over, earmark, allocate, detail, appoint, allot, prescribe, nominate, name, select, hold responsible, empower, entrust, allow, cast, deputize, attach, charge, accredit, hire, elect, ordain, enroll, relegate, draft.—*Ant.* MAINTAIN, reserve, keep back.

assignment *n.* **1** [An appointment] designation, authorization, nomina-

tion; see APPOINTMENT 1. **2** [Something assigned] job, responsibility, task; see DUTY 2.

assimilate *v.* **1** [To absorb] take up, digest, osmose; see ABSORB. **2** [To understand] grasp, learn, sense; see UNDERSTAND 1.

assist *v.* support, aid, serve; see HELP.

assistance *n.* comfort, support, compensation; see HELP 1.

assistant *n.* aid, aide, deputy, henchman, friend, follower, adherent, auxiliary, lieutenant, associate, companion, colleague, partner, helper, apprentice, fellow-worker, secretary, helping hand, patron, backer, bodyguard, aide-de-camp, ally, accessory, clerk, collaborator, confederate, mate, helpmate, accomplice, copartner, co-worker, flunky, man Friday, right arm*, yes man*, right-hand man, friend in need*.—*Ant.* ENEMY, rival, antagonist.

associate *n.* comrade, brother-in-arms, peer, colleague, partner, copartner, friend, ally, buddy*, accomplice, assistant, aid, attendant, henchman, confederate, auxiliary, coworker, helper, collaborator, fellow-worker, helping hand, right-hand man, man Friday, teammate; see also ASSISTANT.—*Ant.* ENEMY, foe, antagonist.

associate *v.* **1** [To keep company with] work with, join with, get along

3 to connect in the mind — **vi.** to join (*with*) as a partner, friend, etc. — **n.** **1** a friend, partner, co-worker, etc. **2** anything joined with another **3** a degree granted by a junior college — **adj.** **1** joined with others in work, etc. **2** having less than full status

as·so′cia′tion (-ā′shən) **n.** **1** an associating or being associated **2** fellowship; partnership **3** an organization, society, etc. **4** a mental connection between ideas, etc.

association football soccer

as·so′cia′tive (-āt′iv) **adj.** **1** of, by, or causing association **2** *Math.* producing the same result regardless of how the elements are grouped

as·so·nance (as′ə nəns) **n.** [[< L *ad-*, to + *sonare*, to sound]] **1** likeness of sound **2** a partial rhyme made by like vowel sounds —**as′so·nant** *adj.*, *n.*

as·sort (ə sôrt′) **vt.** [[< L *ad-*, to + *sors*, lot]] to sort or classify

as·sort′ed **adj.** **1** various; miscellaneous **2** sorted; classified

as·sort′ment **n.** **1** an assorting **2** a miscellaneous collection; variety

asst. assistant

as·suage (ə swāj′) **vt.** **-suaged′**, **-suag′ing** [[< L *ad-*, to + *suavis*, sweet]] **1** to lessen (pain, distress, etc.) **2** to calm (anger, etc.) **3** to satisfy or slake (thirst, etc.)

as·sume (ə sōōm′) **vt.** **-sumed′**, **-sum′ing** [[< L *ad-*, to + *sumere*, to take]] **1** to take on (the appearance, role, etc. of) **2** to seize; usurp **3** to undertake **4** to take for granted; suppose **5** to pretend to have; feign —**as·sum′able** *adj.*

as·sumed′ **adj.** **1** pretended; fictitious **2** taken for granted

as·sump·tion (ə sump′shən) **n.** **1** [A-] *R.C.Ch.* *a*) the ascent of the Virgin Mary into heaven *b*) a feast on Aug. 15 celebrating this **2** an assuming **3** a supposition —**as·sump′tive** *adj.*

as·sur·ance (ə shoor′əns) **n.** **1** an assuring or being assured **2** a promise, guarantee, etc. **3** self-confidence **4** [Brit., etc.] insurance

as·sure (ə shoor′) **vt.** **-sured′**, **-sur′ing** [[< L *ad-*, to + *securus*, secure]] **1** to make (a person) sure of something **2** to give confidence to; reassure **3** to tell or promise confidently **4** to guarantee **5** [Brit., etc.] to insure against loss

as·sured′ **adj.** **1** made sure; certain **2** confident; sure of oneself —**as·sur·edly** (ə shoor′id lē) *adv.*

as·ter (as′tər) **n.** [[< Gr *astēr*, star]] any of several plants of the composite family with variously colored daisylike flowers

as·ter·isk (as′tər isk′) **n.** [[< Gr dim. of *astēr*, star]] a starlike sign (*) used in printing to mark footnotes, etc.

astern (ə sturn′) **adv.** **1** behind a ship or aircraft **2** AFT **3** backward

as·ter·oid (as′tər oid′) **n.** [[see ASTER & -OID]] any of the small planets circling the sun between Mars and Jupiter

asth·ma (az′mə) **n.** [[Gr]] a chronic disorder characterized by coughing, difficulty in breathing, etc. —**asth·mat′ic** (-mat′ik) *adj.*, *n.*

astig·ma·tism (ə stig′mə tiz′əm) **n.** [[< Gr *a-*, without + *stigma*, a mark + -ISM]] a defect of a lens or the eyes that prevents light rays from meeting in a single focal point — **as·tig·mat·ic** (as′tig mat′ik) *adj.*

astir (ə stur′) *adv.*, *adj.* **1** in motion **2** out of bed

as·ton·ish (ə stän′ish) **vt.** [[< L *ex-*, intens. + *tonare*, to thunder]] to fill with sudden wonder; amaze —**as·ton′ish·ing** *adj.* —**as·ton′ish·ing·ly** *adv.* —**as·ton′ish·ment** *n.*

as·tound (ə stound′) **vt.** [[see prec.]] to astonish greatly — **as·tound′ing** *adj.* —**as·tound′ing·ly** *adv.*

astrad·dle (ə strad′'l) *adv.* in a straddling position

as·tra·khan (as′trə kən) **n.** [[after *Astrakhan*, Russ city]] loosely curled fur from young lamb pelts, or a wool fabric resembling this

as·tral (as′trəl) *adj.* [[< Gr *astron*, star]] of, from, or like the stars

astray (ə strā′) *adv.* [[ME < pp. of OFr *estraier*, stray]] **1** off the right path **2** so as to be in error

astride (ə strīd′) *adv.* with a leg on either side —**prep.** **1** with a leg on either side of **2** extending over or across

as·trin·gent (ə strin′jənt) *adj.* [[< L *ad-*, to + *stringere*, to draw]] **1** that contracts body tissue **2** harsh; biting — **n.** an astringent substance —**as·trin′gen·cy** *n.*

astro- [[< Gr *astron*, star]] *combining form* star or stars [*astrophysics*]

astro·bi·ol·o·gy (as′trō bī äl′ə jē) **n.** the branch of biology that investigates the existence of living organisms on planets other than earth

as′tro·dy·nam′ics *n.pl.* [with sing. v.] the branch of dynamics dealing with the motion and gravitation of objects in space

as·trol·o·gy (ə sträl′ə jē) **n.** [[< Gr *astron*, star + -*logia*, -LOGY]] a pseudoscience claiming that the moon, sun, and stars affect human affairs and can be used to foretell the future —**as·trol′o·ger** *n.* —**as·tro·logi·cal** (as′trə läj′i kəl) *adj.*

as·tro·naut (as′trə nôt′) **n.** [[< Fr < Gr *astron*, star + *nautēs*, sailor]] one trained to make flights in outer space —**as′tro·nau′tics** *n.*

as·tro·nomi·cal (as′trə näm′i kəl) *adj.* **1** of astronomy **2** very large, as numbers Also **as′tro·nom′ic** —**as′tro·nom′i·cally** *adv.*

astronomical unit a unit of length based on the mean distance of the earth from the sun, c. 149.6 million km

as·trono·my (ə strän′ə mē) **n.** [[< Gr *astron*, star + *nomos*, law]] the science that deals with the origin, size, motion, etc. of stars, planets, etc. —**as·tron′o·mer** *n.*

astro·phys·ics (as′trō fiz′iks) *n.pl.* [with sing v.] the branch of astronomy dealing with the physical properties of the universe —**as′tro·phys′i·cist** (-ə sist) *n.*

As′tro·Turf′ (-turf) *trademark for* a grasslike synthetic carpet used in stadiums, etc.

as·tute (ə stōōt′) *adj.* [[< L *astus*, craft]] clever or shrewd; keen —**as·tute′ly** *adv.* —**as·tute′ness** *n.*

asun·der (ə sun′dər) *adv.* [[< OE *on sundran*]] **1** into pieces **2** apart in direction or position

---

THESAURUS

with, be friendly with; see also GO WITH, JOIN 2. **2** [To relate] correlate, link, connect, join; see also COMPARE.

association *n.* **1** [The act of associating] frequenting, fraternization, friendship, acquaintanceship, cooperation, assistance, relationship, affiliation, agreement, participation, companionship, fellowship, familiarity, friendliness, camaraderie, membership, acquaintance, mingling, union, community.—*Ant.* DISAGREEMENT, severance, rupture. **2** [The process of intellectual comparison] connection, relation, mental connection, train of thought, connection of ideas in thought, recollection, impression, remembrance, suggestibility, combination. **3** [An organization] union, federation, corporation; see ORGANIZATION 2.

assorted *a.* varied, miscellaneous, mixed; see VARIOUS.

assortment *n.* variety, combination, group; see COLLECTION.

assume *v.* suppose, presume, posit, understand, gather, find, collect, theorize, presuppose, ascertain, draw the inference, judge at random, divine, get the idea, have an idea that, suspect, postulate, regard, consider, infer, hypothesize, guess, conjecture, suppose as fact, deem, imagine, surmise, opine, judge, estimate, speculate, fancy, take the liberty, be of the opinion, dare say, deduce, conclude, put two and two together, be inclined to think, hold the opinion, think, calculate, hope, feel, be afraid, believe, have faith, take it, expect, allow, reckon*.—*Ant.* DOUBT, be surprised, be unaware that.

assumed *a.* presumed, understood, presupposed, counted on, inferred, given, granted, taken as known, conjectured, accepted, supposed, hypothetical, hypothesized.

assumption *n.* **1** [The act of taking for granted] supposition, presupposition, presumption, conjecture, assuming, suspicion, surmise, theorization, hypothesization.—*Ant.* PROOF, demonstrating, establishing. **2** [Something assumed] hypothesis, theory, postulate; see OPINION 1.

assurance *n.* **1** [A guaranty] insurance, support, pledge; see PROMISE 1. **2** [Confidence] conviction, trust, certainty; see FAITH 1.

assure *v.* **1** [To guarantee] vouch for, aver, attest; see GUARANTEE. **2** [To convince] prove, persuade, induce; see CONVINCE.

assured *a.* **1** [Certain] sure, undoubted, guaranteed; see CERTAIN. **2** [Confident] self-possessed, bold, unhesitating; see CONFIDENT.

astonish *v.* shock, amaze, astound; see SURPRISE.

astonishing *a.* surprising, startling, extraordinary; see UNUSUAL 1.

astonishment *n.* surprise, amazement, bewilderment; see WONDER 1.

astound *v.* amaze, shock, startle; see SURPRISE.

astray *a.* straying, roaming, adrift; see WANDERING 1.

astronaut *n.* space traveler, cosmonaut, spaceman, space pilot, rocket pilot, rocketeer, rocket man, space walker, explorer.

asunder *a.* apart, in two, in half, to shreds, into bits and pieces, dismantled, dissected, in two parts, divided, into separate parts, separated, disjoined, rent, carved, dismembered, torn apart, split; see also BROKEN 1, TORN.—*Ant.* WHOLE, together, sound.

asy·lum (ə sī'ləm) *n.* ‖< Gr *a-*, without + *sylon*, right of seizure ‖ 1 a place of safety; refuge 2 an old name for an institution for the mentally ill, the poor, etc.

asym·me·try (ā sim'ə trē) *n.* lack of symmetry —**asym·met·ri·cal** (ā'sə me'tri kəl) *adj.*

asymp·to·matic (ā'simp tə ma'tik) *adj.* without symptoms

at (at, ət) *prep.* ‖< OE *æt* ‖ 1 on; in; near; by *[at the office]* 2 to or toward *[look at her]* 3 from *[visible at one mile]* 4 attending *[at a party]* 5 busy with *[at work]* 6 in the state or manner of *[at war, at a trot]* 7 because of *[sad at his death]* 8 with reference to *[good at tennis]* 9 in the amount, etc. of *[at five cents each]* 10 on or near the time or age of *[at noon]*

ata·vism (at'ə viz'əm) *n.* ‖< L *at-*, beyond + *avus*, grandfather ‖ resemblance or reversion to remotely ancestral characteristics —**at'a·vis'tic** *adj.*

ataxia (ə tak'sē ə) *n.* ‖< Gr *a-*, not + *tassein*, arrange ‖ an inability to coordinate one's movements, as in walking —**atax'ic** *adj.*, *n.*

ate (āt; *Brit,* or *U.S. dial.*, et) *vt.*, *vi. pt. of* EAT

-ate[1] (āt; *for 2, also* it) *suffix* 1 to become, cause to become, form, provide with *[maturate, ulcerate]* 2 of or characteristic of, characterized by, having *[passionate]*

-ate[2] (āt, it) *suffix* an office, function, agent, or official *[potentate]*

at·elier (at''l yā') *n.* ‖Fr ‖ a studio or workshop, esp. of an artist

Atha·bas·kan or **Atha·bas·can** (ath'ə bas'kən) *n.* a family of North American Indian languages —*adj.* designating or of these languages or their native speakers

athe·ism (ā'thē iz'əm) *n.* ‖< Gr *a-*, without + *theos*, god ‖ the belief that there is no God —**a'the·ist'** *n.* —**a'the·is'tic** *adj.*

Athena (ə thē'nə) the Greek goddess of wisdom, skills, and warfare

ath·ero·sclero·sis (ath'ər ō'sklə rō'sis) *n.* ‖< Gr *atheroma*, grainy tumor + SCLEROSIS ‖ formation of fatty nodules on hardening artery walls

athirst (ə thurst') *adj.* 1 [Archaic] thirsty 2 eager; longing *(for)*

ath·lete (ath'lēt) *n.* ‖< Gr *athlon*, a prize ‖ a person trained in exercises or games requiring strength, skill, stamina, etc.

athlete's foot ringworm of the feet

ath·letic (ath let'ik) *adj.* 1 of or like athletes or athletics 2 physically strong, active, etc. —**ath·let'i·cally** *adv.*

ath·let'ics *n.pl.* [*sometimes with sing. v.*] athletic sports, games, etc.

-a·thon (ə thän') ‖< (MAR)ATHON ‖ *suffix* an event marked by length or endurance *[walkathon]*

athwart (ə thwôrt') *prep.* 1 across 2 against —*adv.* crosswise

atilt (ə tilt') *adj.*, *adv.* tilted

-ation (ā'shən) ‖< Fr or L ‖ *suffix* the act, condition, or result of *[alteration]*

-ative (ə tiv, āt'iv) ‖< Fr or L ‖ *suffix* of or relating to, serving to *[informative]*

At·lan·tis (at lan'tis) ‖< Gr ‖ legendary sunken continent in the Atlantic

At·las (at'ləs) *Gr. Myth.* a giant who supports the heavens on his shoulders —*n.* [a-] a book of maps

ATM (ā'tē em') *n.* ‖a(utomated) t(eller) m(achine)‖ a computer terminal that allows a bank customer to deposit, withdraw, or transfer funds automatically

at·mos·phere (at'məs fir') *n.* ‖< Gr *atmos*, vapor + *sphaira*, sphere ‖ 1 the air surrounding the earth 2 pervading mood or spirit 3 the general tone or effect 4 a unit of pressure equal to 101,325 newtons per sq. m —**at'mos·pher'ic** (-fer'ik) *adj.* —**at'mos·pher'i·cally** *adv.*

at·oll (a'tôl') *n.* ‖< Malayalam *atolu* ‖ a ring-shaped coral island surrounding a lagoon

atom (at'əm) *n.* ‖< Gr *a-*, not + *temnein*, to cut ‖ 1 a tiny particle; jot 2 *Chem.*, *Physics* any of the smallest particles of an element that combine with similar particles of other elements —**the atom** nuclear energy

atom bomb ATOMIC BOMB

atom·ic (ə täm'ik) *adj.* 1 of an atom or atoms 2 of or using atomic energy or atomic bombs 3 tiny —**atom'i·cally** *adv.*

atomic bomb an extremely destructive bomb whose power results from a chain reaction of nuclear fission

atomic energy NUCLEAR ENERGY

atomic number *Chem.* a number indicating the number of protons in the nucleus of an atom of an element

atomic weight *Chem.* the weight of one atom of an element based upon the average weight of the element's isotopes

at·om·izer (at'əm ī zər) *n.* a device used to shoot out a fine spray, as of medicine or perfume

ato·nal·ity (ā'tō nal'ə tē) *n. Music* the organization of tones without relation to a key —**aton·al** (ā tōn'əl) *adj.*

atone (ə tōn') *vi.* atoned', aton'ing ‖< ME *at one*, in accord ‖ to make amends *(for* wrongdoing, etc.)

atone'ment *n.* 1 an atoning 2 amends —**the Atonement** *Theol.* the redeeming of mankind by Jesus' death

atop (ə täp') *adv.* on or at the top —*prep.* on the top of

-atory (ə tôr'ē) ‖< L ‖ *suffix* -ORY

ATP ‖a(denosine) t(ri)p(hosphate) ‖ an organic compound present in, and vital to, all living cells

atri·um (ā'trē əm) *n.*, *pl.* **a'tria** (-ə) or **a'tri·ums** ‖L ‖ 1 the main room of an ancient Roman house 2 an entrance hall 3 either of the heart chambers that receive blood

atro·cious (ə trō'shəs) *adj.* ‖< L *atrox*, fierce ‖ 1 very cruel, evil, etc. 2 very bad; offensive —**atro'ciously** *adv.* —**atro'cious·ness** *n.*

atroc·ity (ə träs'ə tē) *n.*, *pl.* -**ties** 1 atrocious behavior 2 an atrocious act 3 [Colloq.] a very displeasing thing

at·ro·phy (a'trə fē; *for v., also,* -fī) *n.* ‖< Gr *a-*, not + *trephein*, to feed ‖ a wasting away or failure to grow, esp. of body tissue, an organ, etc. —*vi.* -**phied, -phy·ing** to undergo atrophy —*vt.* to cause atrophy in

at·ro·pine (at'rə pēn', -pin') *n.* ‖< Gr *Atropos*, one of the Fates + -INE[3] ‖ an alkaloid obtained from belladonna, used to relieve spasms, etc.

at·tach (ə tach') *vt.* ‖< OFr *estache*, a post ‖ 1 to fasten by tying, etc. 2 to join: often used reflexively 3 to connect by ties of affection, etc. 4 to add (a signature, etc.) 5 to

---

■ THESAURUS ■

at *prep.* 1 [Position] on, by, near to, about, occupying the precise position of, in the vicinity of, placed at, situated at, found in, in front of, appearing in; see also IN 1, NEAR 1. 2 [Direction] toward, in the direction of, through; see TO 1.

atheism *n.* heresy, agnosticism, godlessness, ungodliness, impiety, positivism, denial of God, iconoclasm, disbelief in God, irreverence, rationalism, infidelity, materialism, skepticism, freethinking, disbelief; see also DOUBT.

athlete *n.* acrobat, gymnast, player, contestant, champion, sportsman, amateur, professional, semiprofessional, contender, challenger, letterman, muscle man*, jock*. *Athletes include the following:* baseball player, football player, basketball player, soccer player, boxer, wrestler, swimmer, golfer, tennis player, badminton player, jockey, trackman, javelin thrower, high-jumper, discus thrower, shot putter, skier, ski jumper, slalom racer, runner, relay runner, long jumper, pole vaulter, hurdler, bowler, billiard player, polo player, hockey player, skater, bicyclist, fencer, swordsman, marksman, cricket player, miler.

athletic *a.* muscular, husky, heavy-set, wiry, springy, slim, fast, solid, strapping, hardy, robust, strong, vigorous, powerful, brawny, sinewy, sturdy, well-proportioned, well-built, manly, Herculean, Amazonian, built like an ox*.—*Ant.* SICK, weak, fat.

athletics *n.* gymnastics, acrobatics, games; see SPORT 3.

atlas *n.* book of maps, book of charts, book of tables; see BOOK.

atmosphere *n.* 1 [The air] layer of air, gaseous envelope, air pressure; see AIR 1. 2 [A pervading quality] sense, impression, taste; see CHARACTER 1, CHARACTERISTIC.

atmospheric *a.* climatic, meteorological, aerial; see AIRY.

atom *n.* grain, mite, speck, particle, molecule, iota; see also BIT 1, ELEMENT. *Parts and forms of atoms include the following:* electron, proton, neutron, positron, neutrino, positive electron, neutral electron, cathode ray, alpha ray, beta ray, gamma ray.

atom bomb *n.* atomic bomb, nuclear weapon, nuclear device, thermonuclear device, hydrogen bomb, A-bomb, H-bomb.

atomic *a.* microscopic, tiny, diminutive; see MINUTE 1.

atone for *v.* compensate for, do penance, make amends; see PAY FOR.

atrocity *n.* 1 [Brutality] inhumanity, wickedness, barbarity; see CRUELTY. 2 [A cruel deed] offense, outrage, horror; see CRIME.

attach *v.* 1 [To join] connect, append, add; see JOIN 1. 2 [To attribute] associate, impute, ascribe; see GIVE 1.

at·ta·ché (at′ə shā′; *chiefly Brit* ə tash′ā) *n.* 〖Fr: see prec.〗 a member of an ambassador's diplomatic staff

attaché case a briefcase

at·tach′ment *n.* **1** an attaching or being attached **2** anything that attaches; fastening **3** devotion **4** anything attached **5** an accessory for an electrical appliance, etc. **6** *Law* a taking of property into custody

at·tack (ə tak′) *vt.* 〖< It *attaccare*〗 **1** to use force against in order to harm **2** to speak or write against **3** to undertake vigorously **4** to begin acting upon harmfully — *vi.* to make an assault — *n.* **1** an attacking **2** an onset of a disease **3** a beginning of a task, undertaking, etc. —**at·tack′er** *n.*

at·tain (ə tān′) *vt.* 〖< L *ad-*, to + *tangere*, to touch〗 **1** to gain; accomplish; achieve **2** to reach; arrive at —**at·tain′abil′ity** *n.* —**at·tain′able** *adj.*

at·tain′der (-dər) *n.* 〖see prec.〗 loss of civil rights and property of one sentenced to death or outlawed

at·tar (at′ər) *n.* 〖< Ar *ṣiṭr*, perfume〗 a perfume made from flower petals, esp. of roses (**attar of roses**)

at·tempt (ə tempt′) *vt.* 〖< L *ad-*, to + *temptare*, to try〗 to try to do, get, etc. — *n.* **1** a try; endeavor **2** an attack, as on a person's life

at·tend (ə tend′) *vt.* 〖< L *ad-*, to + *tendere*, to stretch〗 **1** to take care of **2** to go with **3** to accompany as a result **4** to be present at — *vi.* **1** to pay attention **2** to wait (*on* or *upon*) **3** to apply oneself (*to*) **4** to give the required care (*to*)

at·tend′ance *n.* **1** an attending **2** the number of persons attending

at·tend′ant *adj.* **1** attending or serving **2** being present **3** accompanying — *n.* one who attends or serves

at·ten·tion (ə ten′shən) *n.* 〖see ATTEND〗 **1** mental concentration or readiness **2** notice or observation **3** care or consideration **4** an act of courtesy or devotion: *usually used in pl.* **5** the erect posture of soldiers ready for a command

at·ten′tive (-tiv) *adj.* **1** paying attention **2** courteous, devoted, etc. —**at·ten′tively** *adv.*

at·ten·u·ate (ə ten′yo͞o āt′) *vt.* **-at′ed, -at′ing** 〖< L *ad-*, to + *tenuis*, thin〗 **1** to make thin **2** to dilute **3** to lessen or weaken — *vi.* to become thin, weak, etc. —**at·ten′u·a′tion** *n.*

at·test (ə test′) *vt.* 〖< L *ad-*, to + *testari*, to bear witness〗 **1** to declare to be true or genuine **2** to certify, as by oath **3** to serve as proof of — *vi.* to bear witness (*to*) —**at′tes·ta′tion** *n.*

at·tic (at′ik) *n.* 〖< Gr *Attikos*, of Attica (ancient Gr state): with reference to architectural style〗 the room or space just below the roof; garret

at·tire (ə tir′) *vt.* **-tired′, -tir′ing** 〖< OFr *a*, to + *tire*, order〗 to dress; clothe — *n.* clothes

at·ti·tude (at′ə to͞od′) *n.* 〖ult. < L *aptus*, apt〗 **1** a bodily posture showing mood, action, etc. **2** a manner showing one's feelings or thoughts **3** one's disposition, opinion, etc.

at·ti·tu·di·nize (at′ə to͞od′'n iz′) *vi.* **-nized′, -niz′ing** to pose for effect

Attn. or **attn.** attention

at·tor·ney (ə tur′nē) *n., pl.* **-neys** 〖< OFr *a-*, to + *torner*, to turn〗 any person legally empowered to act for another; esp., a lawyer

attorney at law a lawyer

attorney general *pl.* **attorneys general** or **attorney generals** the chief law officer of a government

at·tract (ə trakt′) *vt.* 〖< L *ad-*, to + *trahere*, to draw〗 **1** to draw to itself or oneself **2** to get the admiration, attention, etc. of; allure — *vi.* to be attractive —**at·tract′able** *adj.*

at·trac·tion (ə trak′shən) *n.* **1** an attracting or being attracted **2** power to attract; esp., charm **3** anything that attracts **4** *Physics* the mutual tendency of bodies to draw together

at·trac′tive (-tiv) *adj.* that attracts; esp., pleasing, charming, pretty, etc. —**at·trac′tively** *adv.* —**at·trac′tive·ness** *n.*

at·trib·ute (ə trib′yo͞ot; *for n.* a′trə byo͞ot′) *vt.* **-uted, -ut′ing** 〖< L *ad-*, to + *tribuere*, assign〗 to think of as belonging *to* a certain person or thing — *n.* a characteristic or quality of a person or thing —**at·trib′ut·able** *adj.* —**at·tri·bu·tion** (a′trə byo͞o′shən) *n.*

at·tribu·tive (ə trib′yo͞o tiv) *adj.* **1** attributing **2** preceding the noun it modifies: said of an adjective —**at·trib′u·tively** *adv.*

at·tri·tion (ə trish′ən) *n.* 〖< L *ad-*, to + *terere*, to rub〗 **1** a wearing away by or as by friction **2** a normal loss of personnel, as by retirement

at·tune (ə to͞on′) *vt.* **-tuned′, -tun′ing** **1** to tune **2** to bring into harmony

atty. attorney

ATV (ā′tē′vē′) *n., pl.* **ATVs** 〖*A*(*ll-*)*T*(*errain*) *V*(*ehicle*)〗 a small motor vehicle for traveling over rough ground, snow, and ice, or through shallow water

atwit·ter (ə twit′ər) *adv., adj.* twittering

THESAURUS

attachment *n.* **1** [Affection] fondness, liking, devotion; see AFFECTION. **2** [Something attached] accessory, adjunct, annex; see ADDITION 1.

attack *n.* **1** [Offensive tactical action] assault, raid, onslaught, advance, charge, thrust, offense, drive, aggression, onset, outbreak, skirmish, encounter, volley, shooting, barrage, siege, firing, trespass, blockade, cross-fire, invasion, offensive, intrusion, intervention, onrush, inroad, encroachment, incursion.— *Ant.* WITHDRAWAL, retreat, retirement. **2** [Verbal attack] libel, slander, denunciation; see BLAME. **3** [Illness] seizure, breakdown, relapse; see DISEASE 1. **4** [Rape] assault, violation, defilement; see RAPE.

attack *v.* **1** [To fight offensively; *used of an army*] assault, beset, besiege, invade, storm, advance, infiltrate, raid, assail, march against, shell, board, take by surprise, make a push, bombard, bomb, go over the top, lay siege to, open fire, lay into, launch an attack, ambush, strafe, waylay, engage, tilt against, set upon, torpedo, stone, push, combat, attempt violence against, charge, strike the first blow, bayonet, saber, stab, close with, rake, have at.— *Ant.* RETREAT, fall back, recoil. **2** [To assault; *used of an individual*] molest, beat, overwhelm; see FIGHT, RAPE. **3** [To assail with words] revile, refute, reprove; see BLAME. **4** [To proceed vigorously] take up, deal

with, start on; see ACT 1.

attacked *a.* assaulted, bombed, bombarded, assailed, stoned, torpedoed, fired upon, stormed, under attack, strafed, invaded, besieged; see also RUINED 1.

attacker *n.* aggressor, fighter, assailant, antagonist, invader, foe, enemy, criminal, plunderer, intruder, trespasser, violator, ravager, spoiler, felon.— *Ant.* VICTIM, prey, martyr.

attain *v.* win, achieve, accomplish; see SUCCEED.

attempt *n.* trial, struggle, endeavor; see EFFORT.

attempt *v.* endeavor, strive, venture; see TRY 1.

attend *v.* be present at, frequent, sit in on, be a guest, revisit, haunt, be a member, be an habitué, make an appearance.— *Ant.* LEAVE, be missing, absent oneself.

attendance *n.* **1** [The act of attending] presence, participation, appearance, being present, putting in an appearance, being in evidence, turning up, showing up.— *Ant.* ABSENCE, nonappearance, nonattendance. **2** [The persons attending] audience, spectators, assembly; see GATHERING.

attendant *n.* aid, orderly, valet, nurse, usher, bellhop, servant, domestic, secretary, understudy, disciple, pupil, auditor, steward, stewardess, maid; see also ASSISTANT.

attention *n.* observation, observ-

ance, regard, vigilance, mindfulness, inspection, heed, heedfulness, watching, listening, consideration, intentness, study, alertness, thought, application, diligence, caution, preoccupation, thoroughness, recognition, observance, regard, vigilance, mindfulness, inspection.

attitude *n.* mood, opinion, idea about, belief, air, demeanor, condition of mind, state of feeling, position, reaction, bias, set, leaning, bent, inclination, propensity, cast, emotion, temper, temperament, sensibility, disposition, mental state, notion, philosophy, view, orientation to, nature, make-up, frame of mind, character; see also VIEWPOINT.

attorney *n.* attorney at law, barrister, counsel; see LAWYER.

attract *v.* **1** [To draw] pull, drag, bring; see DRAW 1. **2** [To allure] entice, lure, charm; see FASCINATE.

attraction *n.* **1** [The act of drawing toward] magnetism, drawing power, allurement, fascination, temptation, pull, gravitation, affinity, inclination, tendency, enticement; see also APPEAL 2. **2** [An event] spectacle, display, demonstration; see EVENT.

attractive *a.* good-looking, winning, engaging; see BEAUTIFUL, HANDSOME.

attribute *n.* peculiarity, quality, trait; see CHARACTERISTIC.

attribute *v.* ascribe, impute, connect with; see GIVE 1.

atyp·i·cal (ā tip′i kəl) *adj.* not typical; abnormal —**atyp′i·cally** *adv.*

Au [[L *aurum*]] *Chem. symbol for* gold

au·burn (ô′bərn) *adj., n.* [[< L *albus*, white: infl. by ME *brun*, brown]] reddish brown

auc·tion (ôk′shən) *n.* [[< L *augere*, to increase]] a public sale of items to the highest bidders — *vt.* to sell at auction —**auction off** to sell at auction —**auc′tion·eer′** *n.*

au·da·cious (ô dā′shəs) *adj.* [[< L *audax*, bold]] 1 bold; daring 2 too bold; brazen; insolent —**auda′ciously** *adv.* —**auda′cious·ness** *n.*

au·dac·i·ty (ô das′ə tē) *n.* 1 bold courage 2 insolence; impudence 3 *pl.* -ties an audacious act or remark

au·di·ble (ô′də bəl) *adj.* [[< L *audire*, hear]] loud enough to be heard —**au′di·bil′i·ty** (-bil′ə tē) *n.* —**au′di·bly** *adv.*

au·di·ence (ô′dē əns) *n.* [[< L *audire*, hear]] 1 those assembled to hear and see something 2 all those reached by a TV or radio program, book, etc. 3 a hearing, esp. a formal interview

au·di·o (ô′dē ō′) *adj.* [[< L *audire*, hear]] 1 of frequencies corresponding to audible sound waves 2 of sound reproduction, as of the sound phase of television

au′di·ol′o·gy (-äl′ə jē) *n.* the treatment of persons having hearing defects —**au′di·ol′o·gist** *n.*

au′di·om′eter (-äm′ət ər) *n.* an instrument for measuring the, sharpness and range of hearing —**au′dio·met′ric** (-ō me′trik) *adj.*

au·di·o·phile (ô′dē ō fīl′) *n.* a devotee of high-fidelity sound reproduction, as from recordings

au·di·o·vis·u·al (ô′dē ō vizh′ōō əl) *adj.* involving both hearing and sight

au·dit (ôd′it) *n.* [[< L *auditus*, a hearing]] a formal checking of financial records — *vt., vi.* 1 to check (accounts, etc.) 2 to attend (a college class) as a listener receiving no credits

au·di·tion (ô dish′ən) *n.* [[< L *audire*, hear]] a hearing to try out an actor, singer, etc. — *vt., vi.* to try out in an audition

au·di·tor (ô′dit ər) *n.* 1 a listener 2 one who audits accounts 3 one who audits classes

au·di·to·ri·um (ô′də tôr′ē əm) *n.* 1 a room where an audience sits 2 a building or hall for speeches, concerts, etc.

au·di·to·ry (ô′də tôr′ē) *adj.* of hearing or the sense of hearing

auf Wie·der·se·hen (ouf vē′dər zā′ən) [[Ger]] goodbye

au·ger (ô′gər) *n.* [[< OE *nafu*, hub (of a wheel) + *gar*, a spear]] a tool for boring holes in wood

aught (ôt) *n.* [[< OE *a*, ever + *wiht*, creature]] 1 anything whatever 2 [[< (N)AUGHT]] a zero

aug·ment (ôg ment′) *vt., vi.* [[< L *augere*, to increase]] to make or become greater —**aug′men·ta′tion** *n.* —**aug·ment′er** *n.*

au gra·tin (ō grat′′n, -grät′-) [[Fr]] with a crust of crumbs and grated cheese

au·gur (ô′gər) *n.* [[L, priest at fertility rites]] a prophet; soothsayer —*vt., vi.* 1 to prophesy 2 to be an omen (of) —**augur ill (or well)** to be a bad (or good) omen

au·gu·ry (ô′gyōō rē) *n., pl.* -ries 1 the practice of divination 2 an omen

au·gust (ô gust′) *adj.* [[L *augustus*]] inspiring awe; imposing —**august′ly** *adv.* —**august′ness** *n.*

Au·gust (ô′gəst) *n.* [[< L *Augustus*]] the eighth month of the year, having 31 days: abbrev. **Aug.**

au jus (ō zhōō′, ō jōōs′) [[Fr]] served in its natural juices: said of meat

auk (ôk) *n.* [[< ON *alka*]] a diving bird of northern seas, with webbed feet and short wings used as paddles

auld lang syne (ôld′ laŋ′ zīn′) [[Scot. lit., old long since]] the good old days

aunt (ant, änt) *n.* [[< L *amita*]] 1 a sister of one's mother or father 2 the wife of one's uncle

au poivre (ō pwäv′rə) [[Fr]] with crushed black peppercorns and a sauce

au·ra (ô′rə) *n., pl.* -ras or -rae (-rē) [[< Gr]] 1 an invisible emanation 2 a particular quality surrounding a person or thing

au·ral (ô′rəl) *adj.* [[< L *auris*, ear]] of the ear or the sense of hearing

au·re·ole (ô′rē ōl′) *n.* [[< L *aurum*, gold]] 1 a halo 2 a sun's corona

au re·voir (ō′rə vwär′) [[Fr]] goodbye

au·ri·cle (ô′ri kəl) *n.* [[< L dim. of *auris*, ear]] the outer part of the ear

Au·ro·ra (ô rôr′ə) the Rom. goddess of dawn — *n., pl.* -ras or -rae (-ē) [a-] 1 the dawn 2 either of the luminous bands sometimes seen in the night sky: in the S Hemisphere, called the **aurora aus·tra·lis** (ô strā′lis), in the N Hemisphere, the **aurora bo·re·al·is** (bôr′ē al′is)

aus·cul·ta·tion (ôs′kəl tā′shən) *n.* [[L *auscultare*, to listen]] a listening, often with a stethoscope, to sounds in the chest, abdomen, etc. so as to determine the condition of the heart, lungs, etc. —**aus′cul·tate′** *vt., vi.*

aus·pice (ôs′pis) *n., pl.* -pic·es (-pə siz, -sēz′) [[< L *auspicium*, omen]] 1 an omen 2 a favorable omen or sign 3 [*pl.*] sponsorship; patronage

aus·pi·cious (ôs pish′əs) *adj.* 1 favorable; propitious 2 successful —**aus·pi′ciously** *adv.*

Aus·sie (ôs′ē) *adj., n.* [Colloq.] Australian

aus·tere (ô stir′) *adj.* [[< Gr *austeros*, dry]] 1 stern; harsh 2 morally strict 3 unadorned; plain —**aus·tere′ly** *adv.*

aus·ter·i·ty (ô ster′ə tē) *n., pl.* -ties 1 sternness 2 an austere practice 3 tightened economy

aus·tral (ôs′trəl) *adj.* [[< L *auster*, the south]] southern

Aus·tral·ian (ô strāl′yən) *n.* a native or inhabitant of Australia —*adj.* of Australia

Aus·tri·an (ôs′trē ən) *n.* a native or inhabitant of Austria —*adj.* of Austria

au·then·tic (ô then′tik) *adj.* [[< Gr *authentikos*, genuine]] 1 credible, reliable, etc., as a report 2 genuine; real —**au·then′ti·cally** *adv.* —**au·then·tic·i·ty** (ô′than tis′ə tē) *n.*

au·then′ti·cate′ (-ti kāt′) *vt.* -cat·ed, -cat·ing 1 to make valid 2 to verify 3 to prove to be genuine —**au·then′ti·ca′tion** *n.*

au·thor (ô′thər) *n.* [[< L *augere*, to increase]] 1 one who makes or creates something 2 a writer of books, etc. — *vt.* to be the author of —**au′thor·ship′** *n.*

au·thor·i·tar·i·an (ə thôr′ə ter′ē ən) *adj.* believing in or characterized by absolute obedience to authority — *n.* an advocate or enforcer of such obedience —**author′i·tar′i·an·ism′** *n.*

au·thor′i·ta′tive (-tāt′iv) *adj.* 1 having authority; official 2 based on competent authority; reliable —**author′i·ta′tively** *adv.*

au·thor′i·ty (-tē) *n., pl.* -ties [see AUTHOR] 1 the power or right to command, act, etc. 2 [*pl.*] officials with this power

---

THESAURUS

auction *n.* disposal, bidding, public sale; see SALE.

auction *v.* put on sale, sell at auction, put under the hammer; see SELL.

audible *a.* perceptible, discernible, distinct, actually heard, loud enough to be heard, capable of being heard, within earshot, within hearing distance, hearable, sounding, resounding, loud, deafening, roaring, aloud, clear, plain, emphatic; see also HEARD.

audience *n.* witnesses, spectators, patrons; see GATHERING.

audit *n.* checking, scrutiny, inspection; see EXAMINATION 1.

audit *v.* examine, check, inspect; see EXAMINE 1.

auditorium *n.* hall, lecture room, theater, playhouse, movie house, reception hall, amphitheater, assembly hall, opera house, music hall, concert hall, chapel, assembly room.

Sections of an auditorium include the following: stage, proscenium, orchestra, parquet, stalls, boxes, pit, orchestra circle, dress circle, balcony, gallery, top gallery, tiers, box office.

auger *n.* bit, twist drill, screw auger; see DRILL 2.

augment *v.* enlarge, expand, magnify; see INCREASE.

aunt *n.* mother's sister, father's sister, uncle's wife, grandaunt, great-aunt, auntie*; see also RELATIVE.

auspices *n.* protection, aegis, support, sponsorship, backing.

austere *a.* harsh, hard, ascetic; see SEVERE 1, 2.

austerity *n.* sternness, severity, strictness, harshness, sharpness, hardness, grimness, stiffness, seriousness, rigidity, gravity, rigor, formality; see also DETERMINATION.

authentic *a.* 1 [Reliable] trustworthy, authoritative, factual; see

RELIABLE. 2 [Genuine] real, true, actual; see GENUINE 1.

authenticate *v.* verify, confirm, validate; see PROVE.

author *n.* writer, journalist, columnist, dramatist, playwright, poet, novelist, short story writer, essayist, paperback writer, mystery writer, science fiction writer, contributor, script writer, correspondent, reporter, copywriter, ghost writer, encyclopedist, lexicographer, scholar, publicist, critic, annotator, hack writer, freelance, adman; see also EDITOR, WRITER.

authoritative *a.* 1 [Official] well-supported, authentic, well-documented; see RELIABLE. 2 [Authorized] lawful, legal, mandatory; see APPROVED, AUTHORIZED. 3 [Suggestive of authority] dogmatic, autocratic, domineering; see ABSOLUTE 2.

authority *n.* 1 [Power based on

3 influence resulting from knowledge, prestige, etc. **4** a person, writing, etc. cited to support an opinion **5** an expert

author·ize (ô′thər iz′) *vt.* **-ized′, -iz′ing 1** to give official approval to **2** to give power or authority to **3** to justify — **au′thori·za′tion** *n.*

Authorized Version the revised English translation of the Bible published in England in 1611 with the authorization of King James I

autism (ô′tiz′əm) *n.* ⟦AUT(O)- + -ISM⟧ *Psychol.* a mental state marked by disregard of external reality —**autis′tic** (-tis′tik) *adj.*

auto (ôt′ō) *n., pl.* **-tos** an automobile

auto- ⟦< Gr *autos*, self⟧ *combining form* **1** self **2** by oneself or itself

auto·bi·og·ra·phy (ôt′ə bi ä′grə fē) *n., pl.* **-phies** the story of one's own life written by oneself —**au′to·bi′o·graph′i·cal** (-bi′ə graf′i kəl) *adj.*

autoc·racy (ô tä′krə sē) *n., pl.* **-cies** ⟦see fol.⟧ government in which one person has absolute power

auto·crat (ôt′ə krat′) *n.* ⟦< Gr *autos*, self + *kratos*, power⟧ **1** a ruler with absolute power **2** any domineering person —**au′to·crat′ic** *adj.* —**au′to·crat′i·cally** *adv.*

auto·di·dact (ôt′ō di′dakt′) *n.* ⟦see AUTO- & DIDACTIC⟧ a person who is self-taught

auto·graph (ôt′ə graf′) *n.* ⟦< Gr *autos*, self + *graphein*, write⟧ a person's own signature or handwriting — *vt.* to write one's signature on or in

au′to·mate′ (-māt′) *vt.* **-mat′ed, -mat′ing** ⟦< AUTOMATION⟧ to convert to or use automation

au′to·mat′ic (-mat′ik) *adj.* ⟦Gr *automatos*, self-moving⟧ **1** done unthinkingly, as from habit or by reflex **2** working by itself **3** using automatic equipment **4** capable of firing continuously until the trigger is released — *n.* **1** an automatic firearm **2** a motor vehicle with a transmission that shifts gears automatically —**au′to·mat′i·cally** *adv.*

automatic pilot a gyroscopic instrument that automatically keeps an aircraft, missile, etc. to a predetermined course and position

au′to·ma′tion (-mā′shən) *n.* ⟦AUTOMA(TIC) + -TION⟧ a manufacturing system in which many or all of the processes are automatically performed or controlled, as by electronic devices

automa·tism (ô täm′ə tiz′əm) *n.* automatic quality, condition, or action —**autom′a·tize′** (-tīz′) *vt.*

autom′a·ton′ (-tän′, -tən) *n., pl.* **-tons′** or **-ta** (-tə) ⟦see AUTOMATIC⟧ **1** any automatic device, esp. a robot **2** a person acting like a robot

auto·mo·bile (ôt′ə mə bēl′) *n.* ⟦Fr: see AUTO- & MOBILE⟧ a four-wheeled passenger car with a built-in engine

au′to·mo′tive (-mōt′iv) *adj.* ⟦AUTO- + -MOTIVE⟧ **1** self-moving **2** having to do with automobiles, trucks, etc.

au′to·nom′ic (-näm′ik) *adj.* of or controlled by that part of the nervous system that regulates the motor functions of the heart, lungs, etc.

autono·mous (ô tän′ə məs) *adj.* ⟦< Gr *autos*, self + *nomos*, law⟧ **1** having self-government **2** existing or functioning independently —**auton′o·mously** *adv.* — **auton′o·my** (-mē) *n.*

autop·sy (ô′täp′sē) *n., pl.* **-sies** ⟦< Gr *autos*, self + *opsis*, a sight⟧ examination of a corpse to discover the cause of death

autumn (ôt′əm) *n.* ⟦< L *autumnus*⟧ the season between summer and winter; fall —**autum′nal** (ô tum′nəl) *adj.*

aux·il·ia·ry (ôg zil′yə rē, -ə rē) *adj.* ⟦< L *augere*, to increase⟧ **1** helping **2** subsidiary **3** supplementary — *n., pl.* **-ries** an auxiliary person or thing

auxiliary verb *Gram.* a verb that helps form tenses, moods, voices, etc. of other verbs, as *have* or *be*

auxin (ôk′sin) *n.* ⟦< L *auxein*, to increase⟧ a plant hormone that promotes and controls growth

avail (ə vāl′) *vi., vt.* ⟦< L *ad*, to + *valere*, be strong⟧ to be of use, help, or worth (to) — *n.* use or help; advantage [to no *avail*] —**avail oneself of** to take advantage of; utilize

avail·able (ə vāl′ə bəl) *adj.* **1** that can be used **2** that can be got or had; handy —**avail′abil′ity** *n.*

ava·lanche (av′ə lanch′) *n.* ⟦Fr⟧ **1** a large mass of loosened snow, earth, etc. sliding down a mountain **2** an overwhelming amount

avant-garde (ə vänt′gärd′, ä′-) *n.* ⟦Fr⟧ the leaders in new movements, esp. in the arts — *adj.* of such movements

ava·rice (av′ə ris) *n.* ⟦< L *avere*, to desire⟧ greed for money —**ava·ri·cious** (av′ə rish′əs) *adj.* —**av′a·ri′ciously** *adv.*

avast (ə vast′) *interj.* ⟦< Du *houd vast*, hold fast⟧ *Naut.* stop! cease!

ava·tar (av′ə tär′) *n.* ⟦Sans *avatāra*, descent⟧ **1** *Hinduism* a god's coming to earth in bodily form **2** an embodiment, as of a quality in a person

avaunt (ə vônt′) *interj.* ⟦< L *ab*, from + *ante*, before⟧ [Archaic] go away!

avdp. avoirdupois

Ave Ma·ria (ä′vā mə rē′ə) ⟦L⟧ *R.C.Ch.* **1** "Hail, Mary," the first words of a prayer **2** this prayer

avenge (ə venj′) *vt., vi.* **avenged′, aveng′ing** ⟦< L *ad*, to + *vindicare*, to claim⟧ **1** to get revenge for (an injury, etc.) **2** to take vengeance on behalf of —**aveng′er** *n.*

av·enue (av′ə noo̅′, -nyoo̅′) *n.* ⟦< L *ad-*, to + *venire*, come⟧ **1** a street, drive, etc. when broad **2** a way of approach

---

▬ THESAURUS ▬

right] right, authorization, jurisdiction; see POWER 2. **2** [The appearance of having authority] prestige, political influence, esteem; see INFLUENCE. **3** [One who knows] expert, veteran, professional; see SPECIALIST.

authorization *n.* sanction, signature, support; see PERMISSION.

authorize *v.* **1** [To allow] permit, tolerate, suffer; see ALLOW. **2** [To approve] sanction, ratify, endorse; see APPROVE.

authorized *a.* allowed, official, legal, lawful, mandatory, authoritative, decisive, valid, standard, sanctioned, confirmed; see also APPROVED.

auto *n.* car, vehicle, wheels*; see AUTOMOBILE.

autobiography *n.* memoirs, personal history, self-portrayal, confession, life, experiences, diary, adventures, biography, life story, journal, letters, log.

autocratic *a.* dictatorial, domineering, aggressive; see ABSOLUTE 2.

autograph *n.* name, seal, John Hancock*; see SIGNATURE.

automated *a.* mechanical, mechanized, motorized, computerized, automatic, electronic, programmed, cybernetic; see also AUTOMATIC.

automatic *a.* self-starting, motorized, self-regulating, automated, mechanized, under its own power, electric, cybernetic, computerized,

self-moving, self-propelling, programmed, electronic, self-activating, push-button, involuntary, unthinking, mechanical, instinctive, spontaneous, reflex, intuitive, unintentional, unforced, unconscious, unwilling.

automobile *n.* motor car, car, vehicle, passenger car, machine, auto, wheels*. *Types of automobiles include the following:* subcompact, squad car, hearse, limousine, sedan, hardtop, compact, sports car, convertible, station wagon, taxicab, hatchback, limo*, van, minivan, conversion van, recreational vehicle, RV, stretch limo*, jeep, crate*, buggy*, clunker*, jalopy*. *Principal parts of an automobile include the following:* wheels, tires, fenders, chassis, motor, radiator, engine, fan, cylinders, carburetor, exhaust, muffler, throttle, gear shift, clutch, steering wheel, transmission, universal joint, generator, distributor, alternator, windshield, windshield wipers, catalytic converter, brakes, starter, speedometer, spark plugs, axles, emergency brake, accelerator, shock absorbers, pistons, intake and exhaust valves, fuel pump, gas tank, control panel, steering column, instrument gauges, water pump, air conditioner, heater, radio, belts, hoses, filters, drive shaft, oil pan, computer module, battery,

seats, seat belts, headlights, brake lights, turn signals.

autonomous *a.* self-governing, self-ruling, independent; see FREE 1.

autonomy *n.* liberty, independence, sovereignty; see FREEDOM 1.

autopsy *n.* post-mortem examination, dissection, investigation; see EXAMINATION 1.

autumn *n.* harvest time, Indian summer, fall; see FALL 3.

auxiliary *a.* **1** [Subsidiary] secondary, accessory, subservient; see SUBORDINATE. **2** [Supplementary] spare, supplemental, reserve; see EXTRA.

available *a.* accessible, usable, ready, convenient, serviceable, prepared, handy, on call, ready for use, open to, derivable from, obtainable, attainable, practicable, achievable, feasible, possible, procurable, realizable, reachable, within reach, at one's disposal, at one's beck and call, at hand, at one's elbow, on tap*, on deck*.—*Ant.* OCCUPIED, unavailable, unobtainable.

avalanche *n.* **1** [A mass moving down a slope] mudslide, snowslide, landslide, rockslide, icefall. **2** [Any overwhelming mass] flood, deluge, torrent; see PLENTY.

avenue *n.* street, boulevard, drive; see ROAD 1.

aver (ə vur') *vt.* **averred'**, **aver'ring** ⟦< L *ad-*, to + *verus*, true⟧ to declare to be true; affirm; assert

av·er·age (av'ər ij, av'rij) *n.* ⟦< OFr *avarie*, damage to ship or goods; hence, idea of shared losses⟧ 1 the result of dividing the sum of two or more quantities by the number of quantities 2 the usual kind, amount, etc. — *adj.* 1 constituting an average 2 usual; normal — *vt.* **-aged**, **-ag·ing** 1 to figure out the average of 2 to do, take, etc. on an average /to *average* six sales a day/ 3 to divide proportionally —**average out** to arrive at an average eventually —**on the average** as an average amount, rate, etc.

averse (ə vurs') *adj.* ⟦see AVERT⟧ unwilling; opposed (*to*)

aver·sion (ə vur'zhən) *n.* 1 an intense dislike 2 the object arousing this

avert (ə vurt') *vt.* ⟦< L *a-*, from + *vertere*, to turn⟧ 1 to turn (the eyes, etc.) away 2 to ward off; prevent

avg. average

avi·an (ā'vē ən) *adj.* ⟦< L *avis*, bird + -AN⟧ of or having to do with birds

avi·ary (ā'vē er'ē) *n., pl.* **-ar·ies** ⟦< L *avis*, bird⟧ a large cage or building for keeping many birds

avia·tion (ā'vē ā'shən) *n.* ⟦see prec.⟧ 1 the science of flying airplanes 2 the field of aircraft design, construction, etc.

a'via·tor *n.* ⟦Fr *aviateur*⟧ an airplane pilot —**a'via'trix** (-triks) *n.fem.*

avid (av'id) *adj.* ⟦< L *avere*, to desire⟧ very eager or greedy —**avid'ity** (ə vid'ə tē) *n.* —**av'idly** *adv.*

avi·on·ics (ā'vē än'iks) *n.pl.* ⟦AVI(ATION) + (ELECTR)ONICS⟧ [*with sing. v.*] electronics as applied in aviation and astronautics

avita·mino·sis (ā'vīt'ə mi nō'sis) *n.* ⟦A-² + VITAMIN + -OSIS⟧ any disease caused by a vitamin deficiency

avo·cado (av'ə kä'dō, ä'və-) *n., pl.* **-dos** ⟦< AmInd⟧ 1 a thick-skinned, pear-shaped tropical fruit with yellow, buttery flesh 2 the tree it grows on

avo·ca·tion (av'ə kā'shən) *n.* ⟦< L *a-*, away + *vocare*, to call⟧ something done in addition to one's regular work; hobby —**av'o·ca'tional** *adj.*

avoid (ə void') *vt.* ⟦ME < OFr *esvuidier*, to empty⟧ to keep away from; evade; shun —**avoid'able** *adj.* —**avoid'ably** *adv.* —**avoid'ance** *n.*

avoir·du·pois (av'ər də poiz') *n.* ⟦< OFr *aveir de peis*, goods of weight⟧ 1 a system of weights in which 16 oz. = 1 lb.: also **avoirdupois weight** 2 [Colloq.] weight, esp. of a person

avouch (ə vouch') *vt.* ⟦see ADVOCATE⟧ 1 to vouch for 2 to affirm

avow (ə vou') *vt.* ⟦see ADVOCATE⟧ to declare; acknowledge —**avow'al** *n.* —**avowed'** *adj.* —**avow'edly** *adv.*

avun·cu·lar (ə vuŋ'kyoo lər) *adj.* ⟦< L *avunculus*⟧ of an uncle

aw (ô) *interj.* a sound of protest, etc.

await (ə wāt') *vt.* 1 to wait for 2 to be in store for

awake (ə wāk') *vt., vi.* **awoke'** or **awaked'**, **awaked'** or **awok'en**, **awak'ing** ⟦< OE⟧ 1 to rouse from sleep 2 to rouse from inactivity Also **awak'en** — *adj.* 1 not asleep 2 active or alert

awak'en·ing *n., adj.* 1 (a) waking up 2 (an) arousing or reviving

award (ə wôrd') *vt.* ⟦< ME < Anglo-Fr *eswarder*⟧ 1 to give, as by legal decision 2 to give (a prize, etc.); grant — *n.* 1 a decision, as by a judge 2 a prize

aware (ə wer') *adj.* ⟦< OE *wær*, cautious⟧ knowing; realizing; conscious —**aware'ness** *n.*

awash (ə wôsh') *adv., adj.* 1 at a level where the water washes over the surface 2 flooded 3 afloat

away (ə wā') *adv.* ⟦< OE *on weg*⟧ 1 from a place /run *away*/ 2 in another place or direction /*away* from here/ 3 off; aside /turn *away*/ 4 far /*away* behind/ 5 from one's possession /give it *away*/ 6 at once /fire *away*/ 7 continuously /kept working *away*/ —*adj.* 1 absent 2 at a distance /a mile *away*/ —*interj.* begone! —**away with** go, come, or take away —**do away with** get rid of or kill

awe (ô) *n.* ⟦< ON *agi*⟧ a mixed feeling of reverence, fear, and wonder — *vt.* **awed**, **aw'ing** to fill with awe —**stand (or be) in awe of** to respect and fear

aweigh (ə wā') *adj.* just clear of the bottom: said of an anchor

awe·some (ô'səm) *adj.* inspiring awe —**awe'somely** *adv.* —**awe'some·ness** *n.*

awe-struck (ô'struk') *adj.* filled with awe Also **awe'strick·en** (-strik'ən)

aw·ful (ô'fəl) *adj.* 1 inspiring awe 2 terrifying 3 very bad — *adv.* [Colloq.] very —**aw'ful·ness** *n.*

aw·fully (ô'fə lē, ô'flē) *adv.* 1 in an awful way 2 [Colloq.] very

awhile (ə wil', -hwil') *adv.* for a short time

awk·ward (ôk'wərd) *adj.* ⟦< ON *ǫfugr*, turned backward⟧ 1 clumsy; bungling 2 hard to handle; unwieldy 3 uncom-

---

THESAURUS

average *a.* ordinary, medium, mediocre; see COMMON 1.

average *n.* midpoint, standard, center, median, norm, middle, normal individual, standard performance, typical kind, rule, average person.— *Ant.* EXTREME, highest, lowest.

average *v.* 1 [To compute an average] split the difference, find the mean, find the arithmetic average; see BALANCE 2. 2 [To do, on an average] complete, make, receive; see DO 1, EARN 2, PERFORM 1. —**average out** stabilize, balance, make even; see EQUALIZE. —**on the average** usually, commonly, ordinarily; see REGULARLY.

avert *v.* turn aside, sidetrack, shove aside, shunt, turn away from, look away, look another way, cast one's eyes down.

aviation *n.* flying, flight, aeronautics, theory of flight, aeronautical engineering, piloting, aerodynamics, airmanship.

aviator *n.* flier, airman, copilot; see PILOT 1.

avid *a.* eager, enthusiastic, desirous; see ZEALOUS.

avoid *v.* keep away from, flee from, abstain from, shrink from, escape from, evade, shun, fall back, elude, dodge, give one the slip, draw back, hold off, turn aside, recoil from, keep at arm's length, withdraw, back out of, shirk, let alone, keep out of the way, keep clear of, keep at a respectful distance, let well enough alone, keep in the background, keep one's distance, keep away from, refrain from, steer clear of, lay off*, pass up*, shake off.—*Ant.* FACE, meet, undertake.

avoidance *n.* evasion, delay, elusion, escape, retreat, restraint, abstention, nonparticipation, evasive action, temperance, flight, recoil, recession, escape mechanism, dodge, duck.— *Ant.* MEETING, encounter, participation.

await *v.* wait for, anticipate, expect; see ANTICIPATE.

awake *a.* alert, vigilant, observant; see CONSCIOUS.

awake *v.* open one's eyes, become aware, gain consciousness, see the light, stir, get up, come out of sleep, rub one's eyes, rise up, stretch one's limbs, show signs of life, arise, wake up, rise and shine*.—*Ant.* SLEEP, doze off, slumber.

awaken *v.* awake, call, play reveille, arouse, rouse, wake up, excite, stir up, stimulate.

awakening *n.* rebirth, arousal, renewal; see REVIVAL 1.

award *n.* citation, honor, scholarship; see PRIZE.

award *v.* grant, confer, bestow; see GIVE 1.

aware *a.* knowledgeable, cognizant, informed; see CONSCIOUS.

awareness *n.* sensibility, mindfulness, discernment, cognizance, consciousness, alertness, keenness, attentiveness, recognition, comprehension, perception, apprehension, appreciation, experience.

away *a.* absent, not present, distant, at a distance, not here, far afield, at arm's length, remote, out of, far off, apart, beyond, off.—*Ant.* HERE, present, at hand. —**do away with** 1 [To eliminate] get rid of, cancel, take away; see ELIMINATE, REMOVE 1. 2 [To kill] slay, execute, put to death; see KILL 1.

awe *n.* fright, wonder, admiration; see REVERENCE.

awesome *a.* striking, moving, impressive; see GRAND.

awful *a.* 1 [Frightful] horrible, terrible, dreadful; see FRIGHTFUL. 2 [Shocking] appalling, disgusting, repulsive; see OFFENSIVE 2. 3 [*Very great] gigantic, colossal, stupendous; see BIG 1.

awfully *a.* 1 [Badly] poorly, imperfectly, clumsily; see BADLY 1. 2 [*Very] very much, indeed, truly; see VERY.

awhile *a.* for a moment, briefly, momentarily, for a short time, for some time, not for long, temporarily, for a little while, for a spell*.—*Ant.* FOREVER, permanently, for a long time.

awkward *a.* clumsy, bungling, ungraceful, gawky, floundering, stumbling, ungainly, unwieldy, unable, fumbling, bumbling, lacking dexterity, without skill, unskilled, inept, unfit, inexperienced, shuffling, uncouth, incompetent, rusty, unused to, green, amateurish, butterfingered*, all thumbs, with two left feet*.—*Ant.* ABLE, dexterous, smooth.

fortable [an *awkward* pose] **4** embarrassed or embarrassing —**awk′ward·ly** *adv.* —**awk′ward·ness** *n.*

awl (ôl) *n.* [< OE *æl*] a small, pointed tool for making holes in wood, leather, etc.

awn (ôn) *n.* [< ON *ǫgn*] the bristly fibers on a head of barley, oats, etc.

awn·ing (ôn′iŋ) *n.* [< ? MFr *auvent*, a sloping roof] a structure, as of canvas, extended before a window, door, etc. as a protection from the sun or rain

awoke (ə wōk′) *vt., vi. pt. of* AWAKE

AWOL or **awol** (ā′wôl′) *adj., adv.* absent without leave

awry (ə rī′) *adv., adj.* [see A-¹ & WRY] **1** with a twist to a side; askew **2** wrong; amiss [our plans went *awry*]

ax or **axe** (aks) *n., pl.* **ax′es** [< OE *æx*] a tool with a long handle and bladed head, for chopping wood, etc. — *vt.* **axed**, **ax′ing 1** to trim, split, etc. with an ax **2** to get rid of —**give** (or **get**) **the ax** [Colloq.] to discharge (or be discharged) from a job —**have an ax to grind** [Colloq.] to have an object of one's own to gain or promote

ax·ial (ak′sē əl) *adj.* **1** of, like, or forming an axis **2** around, on, or along an axis —**ax′i·al·ly** *adv.*

axi·om (ak′sē əm) *n.* [< Gr *axios*, worthy] **1** *a*) a statement universally accepted as true; maxim *b*) a self-evident truth **2** an established principle, scientific law, etc. —**ax′io·mat′ic** (-ə mat′ik) *adj.* —**ax′io·mat′i·cally** *adv.*

axis (ak′sis) *n., pl.* **ax′es** (-sēz′) [L] **1** a real or imaginary straight line on which an object rotates **2** a central line around which the parts of a thing, system, etc. are evenly arranged —**the Axis** Germany, Italy, and Japan in World War II

axle (ak′səl) *n.* [< ON *ǫxull*] **1** a rod on or with which a wheel turns **2** *a*) a bar connecting two opposite wheels, as of an automobile *b*) the spindle at either end of such a bar

ax′le·tree′ (-trē′) *n.* [< prec. + ON *tre*, beam] an axle of a wagon, carriage, etc.

Ax·min·ster (aks′min′stər) *n.* [< English town where first made] varicolored, patterned carpet with a cut pile

axo·lotl (ak′sə lät′'l) *n.* [< AmInd] a dark salamander of Mexico and the W U.S.

axon (ak′sän′) *n.* [< Gr *axōn*, axis] that part of a nerve cell through which impulses travel away from the cell body

aya·tol·lah (ī′yə tō′lə, -tō lä′) *n.* [< Ar *āyat*, sign + *Allah*, Allah] a leader of a Muslim sect, serving as teacher, judge, etc.

aye¹ (ā) *adv.* [< ON *ei*] [Old Poet.] always; ever Also **ay**

aye² (ī) *adv.* [prob. < *I*, pers. pron.] yes — *n.* an affirmative vote or voter Also **ay**

aza·lea (ə zāl′yə) *n.* [< Gr *azaleos*, dry: it thrives in dry soil] **1** a shrub of the heath family, with flowers of various colors **2** the flower

azi·muth (az′ə məth) *n.* [< Ar *al*, the + *samt*, way] *Astronomy, Surveying* distance clockwise in degrees from the north point or, in the Southern Hemisphere, south point

AZT (ā′zē′tē′) *n.* an antiviral drug used in the treatment of AIDS

Az·tec (az′tek) *n.* **1** a member of an Amerindian people who had an advanced civilization in Mexico before the Spanish conquest in 1519 **2** their language — *adj.* of the Aztecs, their culture, etc. Also **Az′tecan**

az·ure (azh′ər) *adj.* [< Pers *lāzhuward*, lapis lazuli] sky-blue — *n.* **1** sky blue or any similar blue color **2** [Old Poet.] the blue sky

---

THESAURUS

awkwardly *a.* clumsily, unskillfully, lumberingly, ineptly, ponderously, uncouthly, gracelessly, inelegantly, incompetently, artlessly, amateurishly, ungracefully, stiffly, woodenly, rigidly, with difficulty, with embarrassment.—*Ant.* GRACEFULLY, skillfully, adroitly.

awkwardness *n.* ineptitude, inability, incompetence, ineptness, artlessness, crudeness, ignorance, heavy-handedness, ungainliness, oafishness, ungracefulness, gracelessness.—*Ant.* ABILITY, grace, competence.

awl *n.* bit, drill, pick; see TOOL 1.

awning *n.* canvas covering, canopy, sunshade; see COVER 1.

ax *n.* hatchet, adz, tomahawk, battle-ax, poleax, pickax, mattock, cleaver, broadax, hand ax. —**get the ax*** be fired, be dismissed, be discharged; see GET IT 2. —**have an ax to grind*** want something, have a purpose, complain about something; see WANT 1.

axis *n.* shaft, pivot, axle, pole, stem, support, dividing line, spindle, arbor, line of symmetry, line of rotation, line of revolution.

axle *n.* shaft, spindle, pin; see AXIS.

B

b or **B** (bē) *n.*, *pl.* **b's, B's** the second letter of the English alphabet

B (bē) *n.* **1** a blood type **2** a grade indicating above-average but not outstanding work **3** *Music* the seventh tone in the scale of C major — *adj.* inferior to the best /a class *B* motion picture/

b or **b.** **1** bachelor **2** *Baseball a)* base *b)* baseman **3** *Music* bass **4** born Also, for 1-3, **B** or **B.**

B *Chem. symbol for* boron

Ba *Chem. symbol for* barium

BA or **B.A.** Bachelor of Arts

baa (bä) *n.*, *vi.* ⟦echoic⟧ bleat

Baal (bā'əl) *n.* ⟦< Heb⟧ **1** an ancient fertility god **2** an idol

bab·ble (bab'əl) *vi.* **-bled, -bling** ⟦echoic⟧ **1** to talk like a small child; prattle **2** to talk foolishly or too much **3** to murmur, as a brook — *vt.* to say incoherently or foolishly — *n.* **1** incoherent vocal sounds **2** foolish talk **3** a murmuring sound —**bab'bler** *n.*

babe (bāb) *n.* **1** a baby **2** a naive person: also **babe in the woods 3** [Slang] a girl or young woman

Ba·bel (bā'bəl) *Bible* a city thwarted in building a tower to heaven when God created a confusion of tongues — *n.* [*also* b-] a confusion of voices, sounds, etc. or the scene of this

ba·boon (ba bo̅o̅n', bə-) *n.* ⟦< OFr babuin, ape, fool⟧ a large, fierce, dog-faced, short-tailed monkey of Africa and Arabia

ba·bushka (bə boosh'kə) *n.* ⟦Russ, grandmother⟧ a woman's scarf worn on the head and tied under the chin

baby (bā'bē) *n.*, *pl.* **-bies** ⟦ME babi⟧ **1** a very young child; infant **2** one who acts like an infant **3** a very young animal **4** the youngest or smallest in a group **5** [Slang] darling; honey **6** [Slang] any person or thing — *adj.* **1** of or for an infant **2** very young **3** small of its kind **4** childish — *vt.* **-bied, -by·ing** to pamper; coddle —**ba'by·hood'** *n.* —**ba'by·ish** *adj.*

baby beef meat from a prime heifer or steer that is one to two years old

baby boom·er (bo̅o̅'mər) a person born during the birthrate increase (the **baby boom**) after 1945

baby carriage a light carriage for wheeling a baby about Also **baby buggy**

baby grand a small grand piano

ba·by's breath (bā'bēz) a plant with small, delicate, white or pink flowers

baby sitter a person hired to take care of a child or children, as when the parents are away for the evening — **ba'by-sit', -sat', -sit'ting,** *vi.*

bac·ca·lau·re·ate (bak'ə lôr'ē ət) *n.* ⟦< ML baccalaris, young nobleman seeking knighthood⟧ **1** the degree of bachelor of arts, bachelor of science, etc. **2** a commencement address

bac·cha·nal (bak'ə nal') *n.* **1** a worshiper of Bacchus **2** a drunken carouser **3** a drunken orgy —**bac'cha·na'lian** (-nā'lē ən) *adj.*, *n.*

Bac·chus (bak'əs) the Greek and Roman god of wine and revelry

bach·elor (bach'ə lər) *n.* ⟦< ML baccalaris: see BACCALAUREATE⟧ an unmarried man —**bach'elor·hood'** *n.*

Bachelor of Arts (or **Science**, etc.) **1** a degree given by a college or university to one who has completed a four-year course in the humanities (or in science, etc.): also **bachelor's degree 2** one who holds this degree

bachelor's button a plant with white, pink, or blue flowers, as the cornflower

ba·cil·lus (bə sil'əs) *n.*, *pl.* **-cil'li'** (-ī') ⟦< L bacillum, little stick⟧ **1** any of a genus of rod-shaped bacteria **2** loosely, any of the bacteria —**bac·il·lary** (bas'ə ler'ē, bə sil'ər ē) *adj.*

back (bak) *n.* ⟦< OE baec⟧ **1** the rear part of the body from the nape of the neck to the end of the spine **2** the backbone **3** a part that supports or fits the back **4** the rear part or reverse of anything **5** *Sports* a player or position behind the front line — *adj.* **1** at the rear **2** remote **3** of or for the past /back pay/ **4** backward — *adv.* **1** at, to, or toward the rear **2** to or toward a former condition, time, etc. **3** in reserve or concealment **4** in return or requital /pay him back/ — *vt.* **1** to move backward **2** to support **3** to bet on **4** to provide or be a back for — *vi.* to go backward —**back and forth** backward and forward — **back down** to withdraw from a position or claim —**back off** (or **away,** etc.) to move back (or away, etc.) —**back out** (**of**) **1** to withdraw from an enterprise **2** to evade keeping a promise, etc. —**back up 1** to support **2** to move backward **3** to accumulate because of restricted movement /traffic backed up/ —**go back on** [Colloq.] **1** to be disloyal to; betray **2** to fail to keep (one's word, etc.) —**turn one's back on 1** to turn away from, as in contempt **2** to abandon

back'ache' *n.* an ache or pain in the back

back'beat *n.* in popular music, a primary accent on the second and fourth beats of a four-beat measure

back'bite' (-bīt') *vt.*, *vi.* **-bit', -bit'ten** or **-bit', -bit'ing** to slander (someone absent) —**back'bit'er** *n.*

back'board' *n.* **1** a board at or forming the back of something **2** *Basketball* the board behind the basket

back'bone' *n.* **1** the spine **2** a main support **3** willpower, courage, etc.

back'break'ing *adj.* very tiring

back'drop' *n.* **1** a curtain, often scenic, at the back of a stage **2** background or setting

---

THESAURUS

babble *n.* jabber, chatter, twaddle; see NONSENSE 1.

babble *v.* talk incoherently, talk foolishly, rant, rave, gush, run on, go on*, gossip, murmur, chat, chatter, prattle, tattle, jabber, blurt, run off at the mouth*, talk off the top of one's head*, rattle on, gab*, cackle, blab, sputter, gibber, blabber*, clatter; see also TALK 1.

baby *a.* youthful, babyish, juvenile; see CHILDISH.

baby *n.* suckling, babe, child, toddler, tot, brat, young one, little one, papoose, bambino, chick, kid*, cherub, little shaver*, little newcomer*, bundle of joy*, another mouth to feed*.—*Ant.* MAN, adolescent, grown-up.

baby *v.* pamper, coddle, pet, spoil, fondle, caress, nurse, cherish, foster, cuddle, make much of, humor, indulge; see also PAMPER.

babyhood *n.* infancy, nursery days, diaper days*; see CHILDHOOD.

baby-sit *v.* watch, care for, sit; see GUARD.

bachelor *n.* unmarried man, single man, single, misogynist, woman-hater, lone wolf*.—*Ant.* HUSBAND, married man, benedict.

back *a.* rear, after, backward, hindmost, behind, astern, hind, rearward, aft, to the rear, in the rear, dorsal, caudal, following, posterior, terminal, in the wake, in the background, final.—*Ant.* FRONT, forward, head.

back *n.* **1** [The rear part or side] hind part, posterior, stern, poop, aft, tailpiece, tail, back end.—*Ant.* FRONT, fore part, fore. **2** [The rear of the torso] posterior, backside, spinal area; see SPINE. **3** [One who plays behind the line, especially in football] linebacker, fullback, halfback, quarterback, cornerback, safety, running back, tailback, wingback, slot back, blocking back. —**behind someone's back** in secret, slyly, hidden; see SECRETIVE. —**(flat) on one's back** ill, defeated, helpless; see SICK. —**get off someone's back*** let alone, ignore, stop nagging; see NEGLECT 1. —**get one's back up** become angry, be stubborn, lose one's temper; see RAGE 1. —**go back on** betray, reject, turn against; see DECEIVE. —**in back of** at the rear, behind, coming after; see FOLLOWING. —**turn one's back on** reject, desert, fail; see ABANDON 1. —**with one's back to the wall** desperate,

cornered, stopped; see HOPELESS.

back *v.* **1** [To push backward] drive back, repel, repulse; see PUSH 2. **2** [To further] uphold, stand behind, encourage; see SUPPORT 2. **3** [To equip with a back] stiffen, reinforce, line; see LINE 1, STRENGTHEN. —**back down** withdraw, recoil, back out; see RETREAT. —**back off** fall back, withdraw, retire; see RETREAT. —**back out** withdraw, shrink from, escape; see RETREAT. —**back up 1** [To move backward] fall back, withdraw, reverse; see RETREAT. **2** [To support] aid, assist, help; see SUPPORT 2.

back and forth *a.* zigzag, in and out, from side to side; see TO AND FRO.

backbone *n.* **1** [Line of bones in the back supporting the body] spinal column, vertebrae, chine; see SPINE 2. **2** [Determination] firmness, fortitude, resolution; see DETERMINATION.

backed *a.* **1** [Propelled backward] driven back, shoved, repelled, repulsed, pushed, retracted.—*Ant.* AHEAD, moved forward, impelled. **2** [Supported] upheld, encouraged, approved, heartened, aided, assisted,

back′er *n.* 1 a patron; sponsor 2 one who bets on a contestant

back′field′ *n. Football* the players behind the line; esp., the offensive unit

back′fire′ *n.* 1 the burning out of a small area, as in a forest, to check the spread of a big fire 2 premature explosion in an internal-combustion engine 3 reverse explosion in a gun — *vi.* **-fired′, -fir′ing** 1 to explode as a backfire 2 to go wrong or boomerang, as a plan

back′gam′mon *n.* [BACK + ME *gammen*, game] a game for two, with dice governing moves of pieces on a special board

back′ground′ *n.* 1 the distant part of a scene 2 surroundings, sounds, etc. behind or subordinate to something 3 one's training and experience 4 events leading up to something

back′ground′er *n.* a press briefing at which background information is provided

back′hand′ *n.* 1 handwriting that slants up to the left 2 a backhand catch, stroke, etc. — *adj.* 1 done with the back of the hand turned inward, as for a baseball catch, or forward, as for a tennis stroke, and with the arm across the body 2 written in backhand — *adv.* with a backhand — *vt.* to hit, catch, swing, etc. backhand

back′hand′ed *adj.* 1 BACKHAND 2 not direct and open; devious — *adv.* with a backhand

back′ing *n.* 1 something forming a back for support 2 support given to a person or cause 3 supporters; backers

back′lash′ *n.* sharp reaction; recoil

back′log′ *n.* an accumulation or reserve — *vi., vt.* **-logged′, -log′ging** to accumulate as a backlog

back order an order not yet filled

back′pack′ *n.* a knapsack, often attached to a lightweight frame, worn by campers or hikers — *vi., vt.* to wear, or carry in, a backpack —**back′pack′er** *n.*

back′ped′al *vi.* **-ped′aled** or **-ped′alled, -ped′al·ing** or **-ped′al′ling** 1 to pedal backward, as in braking a bicycle 2 to move backward; retreat; withdraw

back′rest′ *n.* a support for or at the back

back′side′ *n.* 1 the back part 2 the rump

back′slap′per (-slap′ər) *n.* [Colloq.] an effusively friendly person

back′slide′ *vi.* **-slid′, -slid′** or **-slid′den, -slid′ing** to slide backward in morals, etc. —**back′slid′er** *n.*

back′space′ *vi.* **-spaced′, -spac′ing** to move a typewriter carriage, cursor, etc. one or more spaces back along the line

back′spin′ *n.* a backward spin in a ball, etc., making it bound backward upon hitting the ground

back′stage′ *adv., adj.* behind and off the stage, as in the wings or dressing rooms

back′stairs′ *adj.* involving intrigue or scandal; secret Also **back′stair′**

back′stop′ *n.* a fence, screen, etc. to keep balls from going too far, as behind the catcher in baseball

back′stretch′ *n.* the part of a racetrack opposite the homestretch

back′stroke′ *n.* a swimming stroke made while lying face upward

back′swing′ *n.* that part of a swing in which the golf club, tennis racket, etc. is swung backward before swinging it forward

back talk [Colloq.] saucy or insolent retorts

back′-to-back′ *adj.* [Colloq.] one right after another

back′track′ *vi.* 1 to return by the same path 2 to retreat or recant

back′up′ or **back′-up′** *adj.* 1 standing by as an alternate or auxiliary 2 supporting — *n.* a backing up; specif., *a)* an accumulation *b)* a support or help

back′ward *adv.* 1 toward the back 2 with the back foremost 3 in reverse order 4 in a way opposite to usual 5 into the past Also **back′wards** — *adj.* 1 turned toward the rear or in the opposite way 2 shy 3 slow or retarded —**back′ward·ness** *n.*

back′wash′ *n.* 1 water or air moved backward, as by a ship, propeller, etc. 2 a reaction caused by some event

back′wa′ter *n.* 1 water moved or held back by a dam, tide, etc. 2 stagnant water in an inlet, etc. 3 a backward place or condition

back′woods′ *n.pl.* [*occas. with sing. v.*] 1 heavily wooded remote areas 2 any remote, thinly populated area — *adj.* of or like the backwoods —**back′woods′man,** *pl.* **-men** (-mən), *n.*

ba·con (bā′kən) *n.* [< OS *baco*, side of bacon] salted and smoked meat from the back or sides of a hog —**bring home the bacon** [Colloq.] 1 to earn a living 2 to succeed

bac·te·ri·a (bak tir′ē ə) *n.pl., sing.* **-rium** (-əm) [< Gr *baktērion*, small staff] microorganisms which have no chlorophyll and multiply by simple division: some bacteria cause diseases, but others are necessary for fermentation, etc. —**bac·te′ri·al** *adj.*

bac·te′ri·cide′ (-tir′ə sid′) *n.* an agent that destroys bacteria —**bac·te′ri·cid′al** *adj.*

bac·te′ri·ol′o·gy (-tir′ē äl′ə jē) *n.* the science that deals with bacteria —**bac·te·rio·log′i·cal** (-ē ə läj′i kəl) *adj.* — **bac·te′ri·ol′o·gist** *n.*

bad¹ (bad) *adj.* **worse, worst** [ME] 1 not good; not as it should be 2 inadequate or unfit 3 unfavorable [*bad news*] 4 rotten or spoiled 5 incorrect or faulty 6 *a)* wicked; immoral *b)* mischievous 7 harmful 8 severe 9 ill 10 sorry; distressed [he feels *bad* about it] 11 offensive — *adv.* [Colloq.] badly — *n.* anything bad —**in bad** [Colloq.] in trouble or disfavor —**bad′ness** *n.*

bad² (bad) *vt., vi. archaic pt. of* BID

bad blood (mutual) enmity

bade (bad) *vt., vi. alt. pt. of* BID

bad egg [Slang] a mean or dishonest person   Also **bad actor, bad apple, bad hat,** or **bad lot**

bad faith insincerity; dishonesty

badge (baj) *n.* [ME *bage*] 1 an emblem worn to show rank, membership, etc. 2 any distinctive sign, etc.

THESAURUS

advanced, promoted, sustained, fostered, favored, championed, advocated, supplied, maintained, asserted, established, helped, bolstered, propped, furthered, seconded, prompted, served, pushed, boosted, primed.—*Ant.* OPPOSED, discouraged, obstructed. 3 [Supplied with a back, or backing] stiffened, built up, strengthened; see REINFORCED.

backer *n.* benefactor, supporter, follower; see PATRON.

backfire *v.* 1 [To explode] burst, erupt, detonate; see EXPLODE. 2 [To go awry] boomerang, ricochet, have an unwanted result; see FAIL 1.

background *n.* 1 [Setting] backdrop, framework, environment; see SETTING. 2 [The total of one's experiences] education, qualifications, preparation, grounding, rearing, credentials, capacities, accomplishments, achievements, attainments, deeds, actions; see also EXPERIENCE, KNOWLEDGE 1. —**in the background** retiring, unseen, out of sight; see OBSCURE 3, UNNOTICED, WITHDRAWN.

backhanded *a.* obscure, sarcastic, unfavorable; see INDIRECT.

backing *n.* 1 [Assistance] subsidy, encouragement, aid; see HELP 1. 2 [Support] reinforcement, buttress, lining; see SUPPORT 2.

backlash *n.* response, repercussion, resentment; see REACTION.

backlog *n.* reserve, supply, stock; see RESERVE 1.

backslide *v.* revert, break faith, fall from grace; see RELAPSE.

backstop *n.* screen, net, barrier; see FENCE.

backward *a.* 1 [To the rear] rearward, astern, behind, retrograde, regressive.—*Ant.* FORWARD, progressive, onward. 2 [Reversed] turned around, counterclockwise, inverted; see REVERSED. 3 [Behind in development] underdeveloped, slow, slow to develop, retarded, delayed, arrested, checked, late, undeveloped, underprivileged; see also DULL 3. —**bend over backward** try hard to please, conciliate, be fair; see TRY 1.

bacon *n.* flitch, Canadian bacon, salt pork; see MEAT. —**bring home the bacon*** provide for, triumph, achieve; see EARN 2, PROVIDE 1, SUCCEED 1, SUPPORT 3.

bacteria *n.* bacilli, microbes, organisms; see GERM.

bad¹ *a.* 1 [Wicked] evil, sinful, immoral, wrong, corrupt, base, foul, gross, profane, naughty, degenerate, decadent, depraved, heartless, degraded, debauched, indecent, mean, scandalous, nasty, vicious, fiendish, devilish, criminal, murderous, sinister, monstrous, dangerous, vile, rotten*, dirty, crooked.—*Ant.* GOOD, honest, pure. 2 [Spoiled] rancid, decayed, putrid; see ROTTEN 1, 2. 3 [Below standard] defective, inferior, imperfect; see POOR 2. 4 [In poor health] ill, diseased, ailing; see SICK. 5 [Injurious] hurtful, damaging, detrimental; see HARMFUL. 6 [*Very good*] stylish, nice, pretty; see FASHIONABLE, EXCELLENT. —**go bad** degenerate, deteriorate, rot; see SPOIL. —**not bad*** all right, pretty good, passable; see FAIR 2.

badge *n.* 1 [Outward evidence] marker, symbol, identification; see EMBLEM. 2 [A device worn as evidence] pin, emblem, seal, medal, insignia, shield, epaulet, ribbon, medallion, marker, feather, rosette,

badger (baj′ər) *n.* ⟦< ?⟧ 1 a burrowing animal with a broad back and thick, short legs 2 its fur — *vt.* to nag at; torment

badi·nage (bad′n äzh′) *n.* ⟦Fr⟧ playful talk; banter

bad·lands (bad′landz′) *n.pl.* an area of barren land with dry soil and soft rocks eroded into odd shapes

badly (bad′lē) *adv.* **worse, worst** 1 in a bad manner 2 [Colloq.] very much; greatly

bad′man′ *n.*, *pl.* **-men** a cattle thief or desperado of the old West

bad·min·ton (bad′mint′′n) *n.* ⟦after *Badminton,* Eng estate⟧ a game in which a feathered cork is batted back and forth with rackets across a net

bad′-mouth′ *vt.*, *vi.* [Slang] to find fault (with)

bad′-tem′pered *adj.* irritable

Bae·de·ker (bā′də kər) *n.* 1 any of a series of guidebooks to foreign countries, first published in Germany 2 loosely, any guidebook

baf·fle (baf′əl) *vt.* **-fled, -fling** ⟦< ?⟧ 1 to perplex completely; bewilder 2 to impede; check — *n.* a screen to deflect air, sound, etc. —**baf′fle·ment** *n.* —**baf′fler** *n.* — **baf′fling** *adj.*

bag (bag) *n.* ⟦< ON *baggi*⟧ 1 a nonrigid container of paper, plastic, etc., with a top opening that can be closed 2 a satchel; suitcase; etc. 3 a purse 4 game taken in hunting 5 a baglike shape or part 6 [Slang] an unattractive woman 7 [Slang] one's special interest 8 *Baseball* a base — *vt.* **bagged, bag′ging** 1 to make bulge 2 to put into a bag 3 to capture 4 to kill in hunting 5 [Slang] to get — *vi.* 1 to swell 2 to hang loosely —**in the bag** [Slang] certain; assured

baga·telle (bag′ə tel′) *n.* ⟦Fr < L *baca,* berry⟧ a trifle

ba·gel (bā′gəl) *n.* ⟦Yidd⟧ a hard bread roll shaped like a small doughnut

bag′ful′ *n.*, *pl.* **-fuls′** as much as a bag will hold

bag·gage (bag′ij) *n.* ⟦< ML *bagga,* chest, bag⟧ 1 the bags, etc. of a traveler; luggage 2 a lively girl

bag′ger *n.* one whose job is filling bags, as with food bought in a supermarket

Bag·gie (bag′ē) *trademark for* a plastic bag, used for storing food, etc. — *n.* [b-] any plastic bag of this kind

baggy (bag′ē) *adj.* **-gier, -gi·est** puffy or hanging loosely, like a bag —**bag′gily** *adv.* —**bag′gi·ness** *n.*

bag lady [Slang] a homeless, poor woman who wanders city streets carrying her belongings in shopping bags

bag′pipe′ *n.* [*often pl.*] a wind instrument, now chiefly Scottish, played by forcing air from a bag into reed pipes and fingering the stops

bah (bä, ba) *interj.* an exclamation of contempt, scorn, or disgust

bail¹ (bāl) *n.* ⟦< L *bajulare,* bear a burden⟧ 1 money deposited with the court to get a prisoner temporarily released 2 such a release 3 the person giving bail — *vt.* 1 to have (a prisoner) set free by giving bail 2 to help out of financial or other difficulty Often with *out* —**bail′able** *adj.*

bail² (bāl) *n.* ⟦ME *baille,* bucket⟧ a bucket for dipping up water from a boat — *vi.*, *vt.* to dip out (water) from (a boat): usually with *out* —**bail out** to parachute from an aircraft

bail³ (bāl) *n.* ⟦ME *beil*⟧ a hoop-shaped handle for a bucket, etc.

bail·iff (bāl′if) *n.* ⟦ME *bailif*⟧ 1 a deputy sheriff 2 a court officer who guards the jurors, keeps order in the court, etc. 3 in England, *a*) a district official *b*) a steward of an estate

baili·wick (bal′i wik′) *n.* ⟦ME < *baili,* bailiff + *wik,* village⟧ 1 a bailiff's district 2 one's particular area of activity, authority, interest, etc.

bails·man (bālz′mən) *n.*, *pl.* **-men** (-mən) a person who gives bail for another

bairn (bern) *n.* [Scot.] a child

bait (bāt) *vt.* ⟦< ON *beita*⟧ 1 to set dogs on for sport [to *bait* bears] 2 to torment or harass, esp. by verbal attacks 3 to put food on (a hook or trap) as a lure for game 4 to lure; entice; tempt — *n.* 1 food, etc. put on a hook or trap as a lure 2 anything used as a lure; enticement

bait′-and-switch′ *adj.* of, or using an unethical sales technique in which a seller lures customers by advertising an often nonexistent bargain item and then tries to switch their attention to more expensive items

baize (bāz) *n.* ⟦< L *badius,* brown⟧ a coarse, feltlike woolen cloth

bake (bāk) *vt.* **baked, bak′ing** ⟦< OE *bacan*⟧ 1 to cook (food) by dry heat, esp. in an oven 2 to dry and harden (pottery) by heat; fire — *vi.* 1 to bake bread, etc. 2 to become heated — *n.* 1 a baking 2 a social affair at which baked food is served

baked beans navy beans baked with salt pork, seasonings, and molasses

baker (bā′kər) *n.* one whose work or business is baking bread, etc.

baker's dozen thirteen

bak·ery (bā′kər ē) *n.* 1 *pl.* **-er·ies** a place where bread, etc. is baked or sold 2 [Colloq.] baked goods

baking powder a leavening agent containing baking soda and an acid-forming substance

baking soda sodium bicarbonate, used as a leavening agent and as an antacid

bala·laika (bal′ə līk′ə) *n.* ⟦Russ⟧ a Russian stringed instrument somewhat like a guitar

bal·ance (bal′əns) *n.* ⟦< LL *bilanx,* having two scales⟧ 1 an instrument for weighing, esp. one with two matched hanging scales 2 a state of equilibrium in weight, value, etc. 3 bodily or mental stability 4 harmonious proportion of elements in a design, etc. 5 a weight, value, etc. that counteracts another 6 equality of debits and credits, or

---

THESAURUS

clasp, button, signet, crest, star, chevron, stripe.

badger *v.* harass, annoy, pester; see BOTHER 2.

badly *a.* 1 [In an ineffectual or incompetent manner] wrongly, imperfectly, ineffectively, inefficiently, poorly, unsatisfactorily, crudely, boorishly, unskillfully, defectively, weakly, haphazardly, clumsily, carelessly, negligently, incompetently, stupidly, blunderingly, mistakenly, awkwardly, faultily, shiftlessly, abominably, awfully*, terribly*.—*Ant.* CAREFULLY, competently, adequately. 2 [*To a marked degree] severely, seriously, greatly; see VERY.—**go badly** miscarry, fall short, dissatisfy; see DISAPPOINT, FAIL 1.

baffle *v.* perplex, puzzle, bewilder; see CONFUSE.

bag *n.* purse, sack, pouch, grip, handbag, tote bag, knapsack, backpack, carpetbag, kit, satchel, saddlebag, gunny sack, suitcase, briefcase, attaché case, duffel bag, pack, container, feedbag, quiver, packet, pocketbook, holster, vanity bag, valise, case, wallet, haversack, holdall, carryall. —**in the bag** absolute, sure, definite; see CERTAIN 2. —**left holding the bag***

deceived, tricked, deserted; see ABANDONED.

bag *v.* trap, seize, get; see CATCH 1.

baggage *n.* luggage, gear, bags, trunks, valises, suitcases, overnight cases, parcels, paraphernalia, effects, equipment, packs, things.

baggy *a.* slack, unshapely, bulging; see LOOSE 1.

bail¹ *n.* bond, surety, recognizance, pledge, warrant, guaranty, collateral.

bail² *v.* 1 [To dip] scoop, spoon out, dredge; see DIP 2. 2 [To empty] clear, drain, deplete; see EMPTY.

bail out *v.* release, give security for, post bail for, assure, underwrite, guarantee, warrant, insure, deliver, go bail for, spring*.

bait *n.* lure, inducement, bribe; see ATTRACTION.

bait *v.* 1 [To torment] anger, nag, tease; see BOTHER 2. 2 [To lure] entice, attract, draw; see FASCINATE.

bake *v.* roast, toast, warm; see COOK.

baked *a.* parched, scorched, dried, toasted, warmed, heated, cooked, grilled, burned, charred, roasted, incinerated.

baker *n.* pastry cook, chef, confectioner; see COOK.

bakery *n.* bake shop, pastry shop, confectionery, bread store, patisserie, cake shop.

balance *n.* 1 [Whatever remains] excess, surplus, residue; see REMAINDER. 2 [An equilibrium] poise, counterpoise, symmetry, offset, equivalence, counterbalance, tension, equalization, equality of weight, parity.—*Ant.* INCONSISTENCY, topheaviness, imbalance. 3 [An excess of credits over debits] surplus, dividend, credit balance; see PROFIT 2. —**in the balance** undetermined, undecided, critical; see UNCERTAIN.

balance *v.* 1 [To offset] counterbalance, compensate for, allow for; see sense 2. 2 [To place in balance] place in equilibrium, steady, stabilize, neutralize, set, level, equalize, support, poise, oppose, even, weigh, counteract, make equal, compensate, tie, adjust, square, parallel, coordinate, readjust, pair off, equate, match, level off, attune, harmonize, tune, accord, correspond.—*Ant.* UPSET, turn over, topple. 3 [To demonstrate that debits and credits are in balance] estimate, compare, audit; see CHECK 2.

the difference between them **7** a remainder — **vt. -anced, -anc·ing** **1** to weigh in or as in a balance **2** to compare as to relative value, etc. **3** to counteract; offset **4** to bring into proportion, harmony, etc. **5** to make or be equal to in weight, value, etc. **6** to find the difference between, or to equalize, the debits and credits of (an account) — **vi.** **1** to be in equilibrium **2** to be equal in weight, value, etc. **3** to have the credits and debits equal —**in the balance** not yet settled

balance sheet a statement showing the financial status of a business

bal·cony (bal′kə nē) **n., pl. -nies** ⟦< It *balcone*⟧ **1** a platform projecting from an upper story and enclosed by a railing **2** an upper floor of seats in a theater, etc. often projecting over the main floor

bald (bôld) **adj.** ⟦< ME⟧ **1** having a head with white fur, etc. growing on it **2** lacking hair on the head **3** not covered by natural growth **4** plain or blunt *[bald* truth*]* — **bald′ly adv. —bald′ness n.**

bald eagle a large eagle of North America, with a white-feathered head

bal·der·dash (bôl′dər dash′) **n.** ⟦orig. (17th c.), an odd mixture⟧ nonsense

bald·faced (bôld′fāst′) **adj.** brazen; shameless *[a baldfaced* lie*]*

bald′ing adj. becoming bald

bal·dric (bôl′drik′) **n.** ⟦ult. < L *balteus*, belt⟧ a belt worn over one shoulder to support a sword, etc.

bale (bāl) **n.** ⟦< OHG *balla*, ball⟧ a large bundle, esp. a standardized quantity of goods, as raw cotton compressed and bound — **vt. baled, bal′ing** to make into bales — **bal′er n.**

ba·leen (bə lēn′) **n.** ⟦ult. < Gr *phallaina*, whale⟧ WHALE-BONE

bale·ful (bāl′fəl) **adj.** ⟦< OE *bealu*, evil⟧ deadly; harmful; ominous

balk (bôk) **n.** ⟦OE *balca*, ridge⟧ **1** an obstruction, hindrance, etc. **2** [Obs.] a blunder; error **3** *Baseball* an illegal motion by the pitcher entitling base runners to advance one base — **vt.** to obstruct; foil — **vi.** **1** to stop and refuse to move or act **2** to hesitate or recoil (*at*)

Bal·kan (bôl′kən) **adj.** of the Balkans, their people, etc.

balky (bôk′ē) **adj. -i·er, -i·est** stubbornly resisting; balking

ball¹ (bôl) **n.** ⟦ME *bal*⟧ **1** any round object; sphere; globe **2** *a)* a round or egg-shaped object used in various games *b)* any of several such games, esp. baseball **3** a throw or pitch of a ball *[a fast ball]* **4** a missile for a cannon, rifle, etc. **5** a rounded part of the body **6** *Baseball* a pitched ball that is not hit and is not a strike — **vi., vt.** to form into a ball —**ball up** [Slang] to muddle or confuse —**be on the ball** [Slang] to be alert; be efficient

ball² (bôl) **n.** ⟦< Fr < Gr *ballizein*, to dance⟧ **1** a formal social dance **2** [Slang] a good time

bal·lad (bal′əd) **n.** ⟦< OFr *ballade*, dancing song⟧ **1** a sentimental song with the same melody for each stanza **2** a narrative song or poem, usually anonymous, with simple words, short stanzas, and a refrain **3** a slow, sentimental popular song —**bal′lad·eer′ n. —bal′ladry n.**

ball-and-socket joint (bôl′ən säk′it) a joint, as of the hip, formed by a ball in a socket

bal·last (bal′əst) **n.** ⟦< MDu *bal*, bad⟧ **1** anything heavy carried in a ship or vehicle to give stability **2** crushed rock or gravel, used in railroad beds, etc. — **vt.** to furnish with ballast

ball bearing **1** a bearing in which the parts turn on freely rolling metal balls **2** one of these balls

bal·le·ri·na (bal′ə rē′nə) **n.** ⟦It⟧ a girl or woman ballet dancer

bal·let (ba lā′, bal′ā) **n.** ⟦Fr⟧ **1** an artistic dance form of graceful, precise gestures and movements used to tell a story **2** ballet dancers

ball·game (bôl′gām′) **n.** **1** a game played with a ball **2** [Colloq.] a set of circumstances *[a different ballgame]*

ballistic missile a long-range guided missile designed to fall free as it approaches its target

bal·lis·tics (bə lis′tiks) **n.pl.** [*with sing. v.*] the science dealing with the motion and impact of projectiles —**bal·lis′tic adj.**

ball joint a ball-and-socket joint used in automotive vehicles to connect the tie rods to the turning wheels

bal·loon (bə lōōn′) **n.** ⟦< Fr < It *palla*, ball⟧ **1** a large, airtight bag that rises when filled with hot air or a gas lighter than air **2** an airship with such a bag **3** an inflatable rubber bag, used as a toy — **vt.** to inflate — **vi.** to swell; expand — **adj.** like a balloon —**bal·loon′ist n.**

bal·lot (bal′ət) **n.** ⟦< It *palla*, ball⟧ **1** a ticket, paper, etc. by which a vote is registered **2** act or right of voting, as by ballots **3** the total number of votes cast — **vi.** to vote

ball′park′ n. a baseball stadium

ball-peen hammer (bôl′pēn′) a hammer with one end of the head rounded and the other end flat

ball′play′er n. a baseball player

ball′point′ (pen) a fountain pen with a small ball bearing instead of a point Also **ball′-point′ n.**

ball′room′ n. a large hall for dancing

bal·lute (bə lōōt′) **n.** ⟦BALL(OON) + (PARACH)UTE⟧ a heat-resistant, balloonlike device used to slow down a spacecraft reentering the atmosphere

bal·ly·hoo (bal′ē hōō′) **n.** ⟦< ?⟧ noisy talk, sensational advertising, etc. — **vt., vi. -hooed′, -hoo′ing** [Colloq.] to promote with ballyhoo

balm (bäm; *occas.* bälm) **n.** ⟦< Gr *balsamon*⟧ **1** a fragrant, healing ointment or oil **2** anything healing or soothing

balm′y adj. -ier, -iest **1** soothing, mild, etc. **2** [Slang, Chiefly Brit.] crazy

ba·lo·ney (bə lō′nē) **n.** ⟦< *bologna*⟧ **1** bologna **2** [Slang] nonsense

balsa (bôl′sə) **n.** ⟦Sp⟧ **1** the wood, very light in weight, of a tropical American tree **2** the tree

bal·sam (bôl′səm) **n.** ⟦see BALM⟧ **1** an aromatic resin obtained from certain trees **2** any of various aromatic, resinous oils or fluids **3** balm **4** any of various trees yielding balsam

bal·us·ter (bal′əs tər) **n.** ⟦< Gr *balaustion*, wild pomegranate flower: from the shape⟧ any of the small posts of a railing, as on a staircase

bal·us·trade (bal′əs trād′) **n.** a railing held up by balusters

bam·boo (bam bōō′) **n.** ⟦Malay *bambu*⟧ a treelike tropical grass with woody, jointed, often hollow stems used for furniture, canes, etc.

bamboo curtain [*often* B- C-] the ideological differences that separated China from the West

bam·boo·zle (bam bōō′zəl) **vt. -zled, -zling** ⟦< ?⟧ **1** to trick; cheat; dupe **2** to confuse; puzzle

ban (ban) **vt. banned, ban′ning** ⟦< OE *bannan*, summon⟧ to prohibit or forbid, esp. officially — **n.** **1** a con-

---

THESAURUS

balanced *a.* **1** [Made even] equalized, poised, offset, in equilibrium, evened, counterweighted, equivalent, stabilized, symmetrical, counterpoised, counterbalanced, on an even keel.—*Ant.* UNSTABLE, unbalanced, unequal. **2** [Audited] validated, confirmed, certified; see APPROVED.

balance of power *n.* equilibrium, distribution, apportionment; see BALANCE 2.

balcony *n.* gallery, mezzanine, terrace; see UPSTAIRS.

bald *a.* hairless, shaven, shaved, bare, featherless, glabrous, shiny, smooth, like a billiard ball*; see also SMOOTH 3.—*Ant.* HAIRY, covered, bearded.

balderdash *n.* senseless talk, gibberish, bombast; see NONSENSE 1.

bale *n.* bundle, bunch, parcel; see PACKAGE.

balk *v.* turn down, demur, desist; see REFUSE.

balky *a.* contrary, obstinate, perverse; see STUBBORN.

ball¹,² *n.* **1** [A spherical body] marble, globe, spheroid, sphere, balloon, rounded object, orb, globule, globular object, pellet, pill, drop, knot. **2** [A game played with a ball] baseball, football, catch; see SPORT 3. **3** [A dance] grand ball, promenade, reception; see PARTY 1. —**carry the ball*** assume responsibility, take control, bear the burden; see LEAD 1. —**get the ball rolling*** initiate action, commence, start; see BEGIN 1. —**have something on the ball*** be skilled, have ability, be efficient; see ABLE.

ballad *n.* carol, chant, folk song; see SONG.

ballast *n.* sandbags, counterbalance, counterweight; see WEIGHT 2.

ballet *n.* toe dancing, choreography, tap dancing; see DANCE 1.

ballet dancer *n.* ballerina, danseuse, danseur; see DANCER.

balloon *n.* dirigible, aircraft, airship, weather balloon, hot-air balloon, radiosonde, barrage balloon, lighter-than-air craft, toy balloon, zeppelin, observation balloon, blimp*, gasbag.

ballot *n.* tally, ticket, poll; see VOTE 1.

balm *n.* **1** [Anything healing and soothing] solace, consolation, comfort, relief, refreshment, remedy, cure. **2** [An ointment of resin] salve, lotion, dressing; see MEDICINE 2.

bamboozle *v.* swindle, trick, dupe; see DECEIVE.

ban *n.* taboo, prohibition, limitation; see REFUSAL.

ban *v.* outlaw, prevent, declare illegal; see FORBID, PREVENT.

demnation by church authorities **2** a curse **3** an official prohibition **4** strong public condemnation

ba·nal (bā′nəl, bə nal′) *adj.* [Fr: see prec.] trite; hackneyed —**ba·nal′i·ty**, *pl.* **-ties,** *n.* —**ba′nal·ly** *adv.*

ba·nana (bə nan′ə) *n.* [Sp & Port] **1** a treelike tropical plant with large clusters of edible fruit **2** the narrow, somewhat curved fruit, having a creamy flesh and a yellow or red skin

band[1] (band) *n.* [ON] **1** something that binds, ties, or encircles, as a strip or ring of wood, rubber, metal, etc. **2** a strip of color or of material **3** a division of an LP phonograph record **4** a range of wavelengths — *vt.* to put a band on or around

band[2] (band) *n.* [< Gothic *bandwa*, a sign] **1** a group of people united for some purpose **2** a group of musicians playing together, esp. upon wind and percussion instruments — *vi., vt.* to unite for some purpose

band·age (ban′dij) *n.* [Fr < *bande*, a strip] a strip of cloth, etc. used to bind or cover an injury — *vt.* **-aged, -ag·ing** to put a bandage on

Band-Aid (band′ād′) [prec. + AID] *trademark for* a small bandage of gauze and adhesive tape — *n.* [*also* **b- a-**] such a bandage Also **band′aid′**

ban·danna *or* **ban·dana** (ban dan′ə) *n.* [Hindi *bāndhnū*, a method of dyeing] a large, colored handkerchief

band·box (band′bäks′) *n.* a light, round box to hold hats, collars, etc.

ban·deau (ban dō′) *n., pl.* **-deaux** (-dōz′) [Fr] **1** a narrow ribbon **2** a narrow brassiere

ban·dit (ban′dit) *n.* [< It] a robber; highwayman —**ban′ditry** *n.*

ban·do·leer *or* **ban·do·lier** (ban′də lir′) *n.* [< Fr] a broad belt with pockets for bullets, etc., worn over one shoulder and across the chest

band saw an endless toothed steel belt on pulleys, powered for sawing

bands·man (bandz′mən) *n., pl.* **-men** a member of a band of musicians

band·stand′ *n.* a platform for a band, esp. one for outdoor concerts

band′wag·on *n.* a wagon for a band to ride on, as in a parade —**on the bandwagon** [Colloq.] on the popular or apparently winning side

bandy[1] (ban′dē) *vt.* **-died, -dy·ing** [Fr *bander*, bandy at tennis] **1** to toss or hit back and forth **2** to pass (rumors, etc.) freely **3** to exchange (words), esp. angrily

bandy[2] (ban′dē) *adj.* [Fr *bandé*, bent] curved outward; bowed

ban′dy·leg′ged (-leg′id, -legd′) *adj.* having bandy legs; bowlegged

bane (bān) *n.* [OE *bana*] **1** ruin, death, harm, or their cause **2** [Obs.] poison —**bane′ful** *adj.*

bang[1] (baŋ) *vt.* [ON *banga*, to pound] to hit, shut, etc. hard and noisily — *vi.* **1** to make a loud noise **2** to hit noisily or sharply — *n.* **1** a hard, noisy blow or impact **2** a loud, sudden noise **3** [Colloq.] a burst of vigor **4** [Slang] a thrill — *adv.* **1** hard and noisily **2** abruptly —**bang up to** damage

bang[2] (baŋ) *n.* [< prec.: see *adv.*, 2] [*usually pl.*] hair cut to hang straight across the forehead

ban·gle (baŋ′gəl) *n.* [Hindi *baṅgrī*] a decorative bracelet or anklet

bang-up (baŋ′up′) *adj.* [Colloq.] very good; excellent

ban·ish (ban′ish) *vt.* [< OFr *banir*] **1** to exile **2** to drive away; get rid of —**ban′ish·ment** *n.*

ban·is·ter (ban′is tər) *n.* [< BALUSTER] a handrail, specif. one with balusters

banjo (ban′jō′) *n., pl.* **-jos′** *or* **-joes′** [of Afr orig.] a musical instrument with a long neck, circular body, and strings that are plucked —**ban′jo·ist** *n.*

bank[1] (baŋk) *n.* [ult. < OHG *bank*, bench] **1** an establishment for receiving or lending money **2** a reserve supply; pool — *vt., vi.* **1** to put into a bank —**bank on** [Colloq.] to rely on —**bank′a·ble** *adj.*

bank[2] (baŋk) *n.* [< ON *bakki*] **1** a long mound or heap **2** a steep slope **3** a rise of land along a river, etc. **4** a shallow place, as in a sea **5** the lateral, slanting turn of an aircraft — *vt.* **1** to cover (a fire) with ashes and fuel so that it will burn slowly **2** to pile up so as to form a bank **3** to slope (a curve in a road, etc.) **4** to make (an aircraft) slant laterally on a turn **5** to make (a billiard ball) recoil from a cushion

bank[3] (baŋk) *n.* [< OFr *banc*, bench] **1** a row of oars **2** a row or tier, as of keys in a keyboard — *vt.* to arrange in a row or tier

bank account money deposited in a bank and credited to the depositor

bank′book′ *n.* a book recording a bank depositor's deposits; passbook

bank card a plastic card with an encoded strip, issued by a bank as for use at an ATM

bank′er *n.* a person who owns or manages a bank

bank′ing *n.* the business of a bank

bank note a promissory note issued by a bank: a form of paper money

bank′roll′ *n.* a supply of money — *vt.* [Colloq.] to supply with money; finance

bank·rupt (baŋk′rupt′) *n.* [< Fr < It *banca*, bench + *rotta*, broken] a person legally declared unable to pay debts — *adj.* **1** that is a bankrupt; insolvent **2** lacking in some quality [morally *bankrupt*] — *vt.* to make bankrupt —**bank′rupt·cy,** *pl.* **-cies,** *n.*

ban·ner (ban′ər) *n.* [ME *banere* < OFr *baniere*] **1** a flag **2** a headline running across a newspaper page — *adj.* foremost

banns (banz) *n.pl.* [see BAN] the proclamation made in church of an intended marriage

ban·quet (baŋ′kwət) *n.* [ult. < OHG *bank*, bench] **1** a feast **2** a formal dinner — *vt.* to honor with a banquet

ban·shee *or* **ban·shie** (ban′shē) *n.* [< Ir *bean*, woman + *sith*, fairy] *Celt. Folklore* a female spirit whose wailing warns of impending death

ban·tam (ban′təm) *n.* [after *Bantam*, former province in Java] **1** any of various small, domestic fowls **2** a small but aggressive person — *adj.* like a bantam

ban′tam·weight′ *n.* a boxer weighing 113 to 118 lb.

ban·ter (ban′tər) *vt.* [17th-c. slang] to tease playfully — *vi.* to exchange banter (*with* someone) — *n.* playful teasing —**ban′ter·ing·ly** *adv.*

Bantu (ban′tōō′) *n.* [Bantu *ba-ntu*, the men] **1** *pl.* **-tus** or

---

THESAURUS

banal *a.* dull, trite, hackneyed; see COMMON 1.

band[1,2] *n.* **1** [A beltlike strip] circuit, meridian, latitude, circle, ring, orbit, zodiac, circumference, zone, ribbon, belt, line, strip, stripe, tape, sash, twine, scarf, bandage, girdle, thong, wristband, bond, tie, binding, stay, truss, belt, cord, harness, brace, strap, binding, waistband, collar, hatband, cable, rope, link, chain, line, string, guy wire. **2** [A company of people] group, collection, association; see GATHERING. **3** [A group of musicians] orchestra, company, troupe, ensemble, string quartet, group, combo*. *Kinds of bands include the following:* military, brass, marching, concert, parade, jazz, stage, dance, Dixieland, jug, rock, swing.

bandage *n.* compress, cast, gauze; see DRESSING 3.

bandage *v.* tie, fix, bind up; see BIND 1, FASTEN.

bandit *n.* burglar, thief, raider; see ROBBER.

bang[1] *n.* **1** [A loud report] blast, roar, detonation; see NOISE 1. **2** [A blow] hit, cuff, whack; see BLOW. **3** [*A thrill*] enjoyment, pleasant feeling, kick*; see EXCITEMENT.

bang[1] *v.* **1** [To beat] strike, slam, whack; see HIT 1. **2** [To make a noise] crash, clatter, rattle; see SOUND.

banish *v.* exile, deport, cast out, expel, expatriate, ostracize, sequester, excommunicate, transport, outlaw, extradite, isolate, dismiss.—*Ant.* RECEIVE, welcome, accept.

banishment *n.* expatriation, deportation, expulsion; see EXILE 1.

banister *n.* railing, hand rail, guard rail; see RAIL 1.

bank[1,2] *n.* **1** [Ground rising above adjacent water] ledge, embankment, edge; see SHORE. **2** [A financial establishment] national bank, state bank, commercial bank, savings bank, savings and loan association,

thrift, lender, mortgage company, Federal Reserve Bank, private bank, countinghouse, banking house, credit union, trust company, treasury.

bank[1,2] *v.* **1** [To deposit money] save, put in the bank, enter in an account; see DEPOSIT 2. **2** [To tilt on a curve] lean, bend, slope; see LEAN 1. — **bank on*** depend on, believe in, be sure about; see TRUST 1.

banker *n.* treasurer, teller, officer of the bank, broker, financier, capitalist, investment banker, moneylender.

banking *n.* investment, funding, moneylending; see BUSINESS 1.

bankrupt *a.* failed, out of business, broke*; see RUINED 3.

bankruptcy *n.* insolvency, destitution, distress; see FAILURE 1.

banner *n.* colors, pennant, flag; see EMBLEM.

banquet *n.* repast, fete, festivity; see DINNER.

-tu a member of a group of Negroid peoples of equatorial and southern Africa 2 any of the related languages of these people

ban·yan (ban′yən) *n.* ⟦ult. < Sans⟧ a fig tree of India: its branches take root and become trunks

bao·bab (bā′ō bab′, bä′-) *n.* ⟦< ? Ethiopian native name⟧ a thick-trunked tree of Africa, with edible, gourdlike fruit

bap·tism (bap′tiz′əm) *n.* ⟦see BAPTIZE⟧ 1 the sacrament of admitting a person into a Christian church by immersing the individual in water or by sprinkling water on the individual 2 an initiating experience —**bap·tis′mal** (-tiz′məl) *adj.*

Bap′tist (-tist) *n.* a member of a Protestant denomination practicing baptism of believers by immersion

bap·tis·tery (-tis tər ē, -trē) *n., pl.* -**ies** a place, esp. in a church, used for baptizing Also **bap′tis·try,** pl. -**tries**

baptize (bap tiz′, bap′tiz) *vt.* -**tized′, -tiz′ing** ⟦< Gr baptizein, to immerse⟧ 1 to administer baptism to 2 to initiate 3 to christen

bar (bär) *n.* ⟦< ML barra⟧ 1 any long, narrow piece of wood, metal, etc., often used as a barrier, lever, etc. 2 an oblong piece, as of soap 3 anything that obstructs or hinders 4 a band or strip 5 a law court, esp. that part, enclosed by a railing, where the lawyers sit 6 lawyers collectively 7 the legal profession 8 a counter, as for serving alcoholic drinks 9 a place with such a counter 10 *Music* a) a vertical line dividing a staff into measures b) a measure — *vt.* **barred, bar′ring** 1 to fasten with a bar 2 to obstruct; close 3 to oppose 4 to exclude — *prep.* excluding /the best, bar none/ —**cross the bar** to die

barb (bärb) *n.* ⟦< L barba, beard⟧ 1 a beardlike growth 2 a sharp point projecting backward from the main point of a fishhook, etc. 3 a cutting remark — *vt.* to provide with a barb —**barbed** *adj.*

bar·bar·ian (bär ber′ē ən) *n.* ⟦see BARBAROUS⟧ 1 a member of a people considered primitive, savage, etc. 2 a cruel person — *adj.* uncivilized, cruel, etc. —**bar·bar′i·an·ism′** *n.*

bar·bar·ic (-ber′ik) *adj.* 1 uncivilized; primitive 2 wild, crude, etc.

bar·ba·rism (bär′bə riz′əm) *n.* 1 a word or expression that is not standard 2 the state of being primitive or uncivilized 3 a barbarous act or custom

bar·bar·ity (bär ber′ə tē) *n., pl.* -**ties** 1 cruelty; brutality 2 a barbaric taste, manner, etc.

bar·ba·rize (bär′bə riz′) *vt.* -**rized′, -riz′ing** to make or become barbarous —**bar·ba·ri·za′tion** *n.*

bar·ba·rous (bär′bə rəs) *adj.* ⟦< Gr barbaros, foreign⟧ 1 uncivilized; primitive 2 crude, coarse, etc. 3 cruel; brutal —**bar′ba·rously** *adv.*

bar·be·cue (bär′bə kyōō′) *n.* ⟦AmSp barbacoa⟧ 1 a) a hog, steer, etc. roasted whole over an open fire b) any meat broiled over an open fire 2 a party, picnic, or restaurant featuring this — *vt.* -**cued′, -cu′ing** to roast or broil over an open fire, often with a highly seasoned sauce (**barbecue sauce**)

barbed wire wire with barbs at close intervals Also **barb′wire′** *n.*

bar·bel (bär′bəl) *n.* ⟦< L barba, beard⟧ a threadlike growth from the lips or jaws of certain fishes

bar·bell (bär′bel′) *n.* ⟦BAR + (DUMB)BELL⟧ a metal bar with weights attached at each end, used for weight-lifting exercises Also **bar bell**

bar·ber (bär′bər) *n.* ⟦see BARB⟧ one whose work is cutting hair, shaving beards, etc. — *vt., vi.* to cut the hair (of), shave, etc.

bar·berry (bär′ber′ē, -bə rē) *n., pl.* -**ries** ⟦< ML barberis⟧ 1 a spiny shrub with sour, red berries 2 the berry

bar·bi·tu·rate (bär bich′ər it, bär′bə tyoor′it) *n.* ⟦< Ger⟧ a salt or ester of a crystalline acid (**barbituric acid**), used as a sedative

bar·ca·role or **bar·ca·rolle** (bär′kə rōl′) *n.* ⟦< Fr < It⟧ a Venetian gondolier song, or music like this

bar code UNIVERSAL PRODUCT CODE

bard (bärd) *n.* ⟦Gael & Ir⟧ 1 an ancient Celtic poet 2 a poet

bare (ber) *adj.* **bar′er, bar′est** ⟦OE bær⟧ 1 not covered or clothed; naked 2 without furnishings; empty 3 simple; plain 4 mere /bare needs/ — *vt.* **bared, bar′ing** to make bare; uncover —**lay bare** to uncover; expose —**bare′ness** *n.*

bare′back′ *adv., adj.* on a horse with no saddle

bare′-bones′ *adj.* simple; basic

bare′faced′ *adj.* 1 with the face uncovered 2 open; shameless

bare′foot′ *adj., adv.* without shoes and stockings —**bare′foot′ed** *adj.*

bare′hand′ed *adj., adv.* 1 with hands uncovered or unprotected 2 without weapons, etc.

bare′head′ed *adj., adv.* wearing no hat or other covering on the head

bare′leg′ged (-leg′id, -legd′) *adj., adv.* with the legs bare

barely (ber′lē) *adv.* 1 plainly 2 only just; scarcely 3 scantily

bar·gain (bär′gən) *n.* ⟦< OFr bargaignier, haggle⟧ 1 a mutual agreement or contract 2 an agreement with regard to its worth /a bad bargain/ 3 something sold at a price favorable to the buyer — *vi.* 1 to haggle 2 to make a bargain —**bargain for** (or **on**) to expect; count on —**into** (or **in**) **the bargain** besides —**bar′gainer** *n.*

bargain counter a store counter for displaying goods at reduced prices

barge (bärj) *n.* ⟦< ML barga⟧ 1 a large, flat-bottomed boat for freight on rivers, etc. 2 a large pleasure boat — *vi.* **barged, barg′ing** 1 to move slowly and clumsily 2 to come or go (in or into) rudely or abruptly

bar graph a graph in which the lengths of parallel bars are used to compare quantities, etc.

bari·tone (bar′ə tōn′, ber′-) *n.* ⟦< Gr barys, deep + tonos,

━━━━━━━━━━━━━━ THESAURUS ━━━━━━━━━━━━━━

baptism *n.* dedication, christening, initiation; see CEREMONY 2.

baptize *v.* immerse, purify, regenerate, sprinkle, dip, christen, name, administer baptism to.

bar *n.* 1 [A relatively long, narrow object] strip, stake, stick, crossbar, boom, rib, crosspiece, pole, spar, rail, lever, rod, crowbar, shaft, slab. 2 [A counter serving refreshments, especially drinks] barroom, tavern, cocktail lounge, saloon, public house, counter, hotel, inn, canteen, beer parlor, cabaret, restaurant, cafeteria, roadhouse, brass rail, snack bar, beer garden, watering hole*, dive*, pub (British)*, grill. 3 [The legal profession] lawyers, counselors, barristers, solicitors, jurists, attorneys, bar association, advocates, judiciary. 4 [An obstruction] hindrance, obstacle, hurdle; see BARRIER. 5 [A relatively long, narrow area] strip, stripe, ribbon; see BAND 1.

bar *v.* 1 [To raise a physical obstruction] barricade, dam, dike, fence, wall, erect a barrier, brick up, blockade, clog, exclude, shut out, lock out, keep out, bolt, cork, plug, seal, stop, impede, roadblock.—*Ant.* OPEN, free,

clear. 2 [To obstruct by refusal] ban, forbid, deny, refuse, prevent, stop, boycott, ostracize, preclude, shut out, keep out, exclude, exile, reject, outlaw, condemn, discourage, interfere with, restrain, frustrate, circumvent, override, segregate, interdict, freeze out*.—*Ant.* ALLOW, admit, welcome. 3 [To close] shut, lock, seal; see CLOSE 4.

barbarian *n.* savage, brute, cannibal, rascal, ruffian, monster, Yahoo, Philistine, troglodyte, clod; see also BEAST 2.

barbaric *a.* inhuman, brutal, fierce; see CRUEL.

barbarity *n.* savageness, cruelty, brutality; see CRUELTY.

barbecue *n.* 1 [A grill] roaster, grill, broiler; see APPLIANCE. 2 [A picnic] cookout, wiener roast, picnic; see MEAL 2.

barbecue *v.* grill, sear, broil; see COOK.

barbed wire *n.* fence wire, fencing, barb-wire; see FENCE.

bare *a.* 1 [Without covering] uncovered, bald, stripped; see NAKED 1,

OPEN 4. 2 [Plain] unadorned, simple, unornamented; see MODEST 2. 3 [Without content] barren, void, unfurnished; see EMPTY.

barefaced *a.* 1 [Open] unconcealed, clear, apparent; see OBVIOUS 1, 2. 2 [Impudent] shameless, audacious, bold; see RUDE 2.

barefoot *a.* shoeless, barefooted, unshod; see NAKED 1.

barely *a.* almost, scarcely, just; see HARDLY.

bargain *n.* 1 [An agreement] pact, compact, contract; see DEAL 1. 2 [An advantageous purchase] good value, good deal, discount, reduction, marked-down price, buy*, steal*, giveaway*, deal. —**into the bargain** in addition, too, additionally; see ALSO.

bargain *v.* 1 [To trade] barter, do business, merchandise; see BUY, SELL. 2 [To negotiate] make terms, arrange, confer; see NEGOTIATE 1. —**bargain for** expect, plan on, foresee; see ANTICIPATE.

bargaining *n.* trade, transaction, haggling; see BUSINESS 1.

tone] **1** the range of a male voice between tenor and bass **2** a singer or instrument with this range

bar·ium (ber′ē əm) *n.* [< Gr *barys*, heavy] a metallic chemical element

bark[1] (bärk) *n.* [< ON *bǫrkr*] the outside covering of trees and woody plants — *vt.* **1** to remove bark from (a tree, etc.) **2** [Colloq.] to scrape; skin (the knees, etc.)

bark[2] (bärk) *vi.* [OE *beorcan*] **1** to make the sharp, abrupt cry of a dog or a similar sound **2** to speak sharply; snap — *n.* the characteristic cry of a dog, or any noise like this —**bark up the wrong tree** to misdirect one's attack, energies, etc.

bark[3] (bärk) *n.* [< LL *barca*] **1** [Old Poet.] a boat **2** a sailing vessel with two forward square-rigged masts and a rear mast rigged fore-and-aft

bar′keep′er (-kē′pər) *n.* **1** an owner of a barroom **2** a bartender Also **bar′keep′**

barker (bär′kər) *n.* one who talks loud to attract customers to a sideshow, etc.

bar·ley (bär′lē) *n.* [OE *bærlic*] **1** a cereal grass **2** its grain, used in making barley malt, in soups, etc.

bar′maid′ *n.* a waitress who serves alcoholic drinks in a bar

bar mitz·vah (bär mits′və) [< Yidd < Aram *bar*, son of + Heb *mitsva*, commandment] [*also* **B- M-**] **1** a Jewish boy who has arrived at the age of religious responsibility, thirteen years **2** the ceremony celebrating this event —**bat mitzvah** (bät-) or **bas mitzvah** (bäs-) *fem.*

barn (bärn) *n.* [OE *bern*] a farm building for sheltering harvested crops, livestock, machines, etc.

bar·na·cle (bär′nə kəl) *n.* [ME *bernacle*] a saltwater shellfish that attaches itself to rocks, ship bottoms, etc.

barn·storm (bärn′stôrm′) *vi., vt.* to tour (the country, esp. rural areas) giving speeches, plays, etc.

barn′yard′ *n.* the ground near a barn — *adj.* of, like, or fit for a barnyard

ba·rom·eter (bə räm′ət ər) *n.* [< Gr *baros*, weight + -METER] **1** an instrument for measuring atmospheric pressure and thus forecasting weather **2** anything that marks change —**baro·met·ric** (bar′ə me′trik) *adj.*

baron (bar′ən, ber′-) *n.* [ME] **1** a member of the lowest rank of British nobility **2** a magnate —**bar′on·age** (-ij) *n.* —**bar′on·ess** *n.fem.* —**ba·ro·nial** (bə rō′nē əl) *adj.*

bar′onet′ (-ət′, -it) *n.* a man holding the lowest hereditary British title, below a baron —**bar′on·et′cy** *n.*

ba·roque (bə rōk′) *adj.* [Fr < Port *barroco*, imperfect pearl] **1** [*often* **B-**] *a*) very ornate and full of curved lines, as much art and architecture of about 1550-1750 *b*) full of highly embellished melodies, fugues, etc., as much music of that time **2** fantastically ornate

bar·racks (bar′əks, ber′-) *n.pl.* [< Sp *barro*, clay] [*often with sing. v.*] a building or buildings for housing soldiers, etc.

bar·ra·cuda (bar′ə kōō′də, ber′-) *n., pl.* **-da** or **-das** [AmSp] a fierce, pikelike fish of tropical seas

bar·rage (bə räzh′, -räj′) *n.* [Fr < *barrer*, to stop] **1** a curtain of artillery fire **2** any prolonged attack — *vi., vt.* **-raged′, -rag′ing** to subject to a barrage

barred (bärd) *adj.* **1** having bars or stripes **2** closed off with bars **3** not allowed

bar·rel (bar′əl, ber′-) *n.* [< ML *barillus*] **1** *a*) a large, cylindrical container with slightly bulging sides and flat ends *b*) its standard capacity (31½ gal.) **2** any similar container or cylinder **3** the straight tube of a gun — *vt.* **-reled** or **-relled, -rel·ing** or **-rel·ling** to put in barrels — *vi.* [Slang] to move at high speed

barrel organ a mechanical musical instrument played by turning a crank

bar·ren (bar′ən, ber′-) *adj.* [< OFr] **1** that cannot bear offspring; sterile **2** without vegetation **3** unproductive **4** boring; dull **5** devoid (*of*) —**bar′ren·ness** *n.*

bar·rette (bə ret′) *n.* [Fr] a bar or clasp for holding a woman's hair in place

bar·ri·cade (bar′i kād′, ber′-; *also, esp. for v.*, bar′ə kād′) *n.* [Fr < It *barricare*, fortify] a barrier, esp. one put up hastily for defense — *vt.* **-cad′ed, -cad′ing** to block with a barricade

bar·rier (bar′ē ər, ber′-) *n.* [< ML *barra*] **1** an obstruction, as a fence **2** anything that blocks or hinders

bar·ring (bär′iŋ) *prep.* excepting

bar·ris·ter (bar′is tər, ber′-) *n.* [< *bar* (law court)] in England, a lawyer who pleads cases in court

bar′room′ *n.* a room with a bar where alcoholic drinks are sold

bar·row[1] (bar′ō, ber′-) *n.* [< OE *beran*, to bear] a handbarrow or wheelbarrow

bar·row[2] (bar′ō, ber′-) *n.* [< OE *beorg*, hill] a heap of earth or rocks covering a grave

bar′tend′er *n.* one who serves alcoholic drinks at a bar

bar·ter (bärt′ər) *vi., vt.* [< OFr *barater*] to trade by exchanging (goods) without money — *n.* **1** a bartering **2** anything bartered —**bar′terer** *n.*

bary·on (bar′ē än′, ber′-) *n.* [< Gr *barys*, heavy + (ELECTR)ON] any of certain heavy atomic particles

ba·sal (bā′səl) *adj.* **1** of or at the base **2** basic; fundamental

basal metabolism the minimum quantity of energy used by an organism at rest to sustain its life

ba·salt (bə sôlt′, bā′sôlt′) *n.* [L *basaltes*] a hard, dark volcanic rock

base[1] (bās) *n.* [< Gr *basis*] **1** the thing or part on which something rests **2** the most important element or principal ingredient **3** the part of a word to which affixes are attached **4** a basis **5** any of the four markers a baseball player must consecutively touch to score a run **6** a headquarters or a source of supply **7** *Chem.* a substance that forms a salt when it reacts with an acid — *adj.* forming a base — *vt.* **based, bas′ing 1** to make a base for **2** to establish

base[2] (bās) *adj.* **bas′er, bas′est** [< VL *bassus*, low] **1** mean; ignoble **2** menial **3** poor in quality **4** comparatively low worth [*base metal*] —**base′ly** *adv.* —**base′ness** *n.*

base′ball′ *n.* ,**1** a game played with a ball and bat by two opposing teams on a field with four bases forming a diamond **2** the ball used in this game

base′board′ *n.* a board or molding at the base of a wall

base hit *Baseball* a play in which the batter hits a fair ball and gets on base without an error or without forcing out a teammate

---

THESAURUS

bark[1,2] *n.* **1** [An outer covering, especially of trees] peel, cork, husk; see COVER 1, SHELL 1. **2** [A short, explosive sound] yelp, yap, grunt; see NOISE 1.

bark[2] *v.* yelp, yap, bay, howl, cry, growl, snarl, yip, woof, arf. —**bark up the wrong tree** miscalculate, misdirect one's effort, make a mistake; see MISJUDGE 2.

barn *n.* outbuilding, shed, outhouse, shelter, lean-to, coop, hutch, sty, pen, kennel, stable.

barnyard *n.* feedyard, pen, corral, stableyard, lot, feedlot, run.

barred *a.* **1** [Equipped or marked with bars] striped, banded, streaked, pleated, pied, motley, calico, mottled, dappled, crosshatched, veined, ribbed, ridged, marked, piped, lined. **2** [Prohibited] banned, outlawed, unlawful; see ILLEGAL.

barrel *n.* cask, keg, vat, tub, receptacle, container, vessel.

barren *a.* **1** [Incapable of producing young] impotent, infertile, childless; see STERILE 1. **2** [Incapable of producing vegetation] fallow, unproductive, fruitless; see STERILE 2.

barricade *n.* obstacle, bar, obstruction; see BARRIER.

barricade *v.* obstruct, block, fortify; see BAR 1.

barrier *n.* bar, obstruction, difficulty, hindrance, obstacle, hurdle, stumbling block, fence, sound barrier, restriction, restraint, impediment, drawback, check, stop, stay, bulwark, barricade, rampart, wall, earthwork, embankment, blockade, barbed wire, bamboo curtain, iron curtain.—*Ant.* WAY, path, trail.

barroom *n.* tavern, saloon, pub*; see BAR 2.

barter *n.* trade, exchange, traffic; see BUSINESS 1.

barter *v.* trade, bargain, swap*; see BUY, SELL.

base[1] *n.* **1** [A point from which the action is initiated] camp, field, land-ing field, airport, airfield, airstrip, port, headquarters, terminal, base camp, home base, fire base, base of operations, center, depot, supply base, dock, harbor, station. **2** [The bottom, thought of as a support] root, foot, footing; see FOUNDATION 2. **3** [Foundation of a belief or statement] principle, authority, evidence; see BASIS. **4** [A goal, especially in baseball] mark, bound, station, plate, post, goal; first base, second base, third base, home plate. —**off base*** erring, mistaken, incorrect; see WRONG 2.

base[2] *a.* low, foul, sordid; see VULGAR.

baseball *n.* ball, little league, the national pastime; see SPORT 3.

baseball player *n.* pitcher, catcher, infielder, batter, shortstop, left fielder, right fielder, center fielder, first baseman, second baseman, third baseman, hitter, slugger*.

based *a.* confirmed, planted, founded; see ESTABLISHED 2.

base′less *adj.* having no basis in fact; unfounded —**base′·less·ness** *n.*

base line 1 a line serving as a base **2** *Baseball* the lane between any two consecutive bases **3** *Basketball, Tennis* the line at either end of the court Also **base′line′**

base′man (-mən) *n., pl.* **-men** *Baseball* an infielder stationed at first, second, or third base

base′ment *n.* the story below the main floor

base on balls *Baseball* WALK

base pay the basic rate of pay not counting overtime pay, etc.

base runner *Baseball* a player who is on base or is trying to reach a base

bash (bash) *vt.* ⟦echoic⟧ [Colloq.] to hit hard — *n.* [Slang] a party

bash′ful *adj.* ⟦(A)BASH + -FUL⟧ easily embarrassed; shy — **bash′fully** *adv.* —**bash′ful·ness** *n.*

basic (bā′sik) *adj.* **1** fundamental **2** *Chem.* alkaline — *n.* a basic principle, factor, etc. —**bas′i·cally** *adv.*

BASIC (bā′sik) *n.* ⟦*B*(*eginner's*) *A*(*ll-purpose*) *S*(*ymbolic*) *I*(*nstruction*) *C*(*ode*)⟧ a simple computer language that uses common words and algebra

basil (baz′əl, bā′zəl) *n.* ⟦< Gr *basilikon*⟧ a fragrant herb of the mint family, used in cooking

ba·sil′i·ca (bə sil′i kə) *n.* ⟦< Gr *basilikē* (*stoa*), royal (portico)⟧ **1** a church with a broad nave, side aisles, and an apse **2** *R.C.Ch.* a church with certain ceremonial rights

ba·sin (bās′ən) *n.* ⟦< VL *bacca*, water vessel⟧ **1** a wide, shallow container for liquid **2** its contents **3** a sink **4** any shallow, rounded hollow, often containing water **5** RIVER BASIN

ba·sis (bā′sis) *n., pl.* **-ses′** (-sēz′) ⟦< Gr, a base⟧ **1** a base or foundation **2** a principal constituent **3** a fundamental principle or theory

bask (bask) *vi.* ⟦ME *basken*, to wallow⟧ to expose oneself pleasantly to warmth, another's favor, etc.

bas·ket (bas′kit) *n.* ⟦ME⟧ **1** a container made of interwoven cane, wood strips, etc. **2** its contents **3** *Basketball a)* the goal, a round, open, hanging net *b)* a goal made by shooting the ball through this net

bas′ket·ball′ *n.* ⟦invented & named (1891) by James A. Naismith (1861-1939)⟧ **1** a team game played with a bouncy, round, inflated ball on a court having a raised basket at each end **2** this ball

basket weave a weave of fabrics resembling the weave used in making baskets

bas′ket·work′ *n.* work that is woven like a basket; wickerwork

Basque (bask) *n.* **1** a member of a people living in a mountain region between France & Spain **2** their language — *adj.* of the Basques

bas-relief (bä′ri lēf′, bas′-) *n.* ⟦Fr < It: see BASS¹ & RELIEF⟧ sculpture in which figures project slightly from a flat background

bass¹ (bās) *n.* ⟦< VL *bassus*, low⟧ **1** the range of the lowest male voice **2** a singer or instrument with this range; specif., a double bass **3** a low, deep sound — *adj.* of, for, or having the range of a bass

bass² (bas) *n., pl.* **bass** or **bass′es** ⟦OE *baers*⟧ a spiny-finned food and game fish of fresh or salt water

bas·set (bas′it) *n.* ⟦< OFr *bas*, low⟧ a hunting hound with a long body, short forelegs, and long, drooping ears

bas·si·net (bas′ə net′) *n.* ⟦< Fr dim. of *berceau*, a cradle⟧ a basketlike bed for an infant, often hooded and on wheels

basso (bas′ō, bäs′-) *n., pl.* **-sos** or **-si** (-sē) ⟦< VL *bassus*, low⟧ a bass voice or singer

bas·soon (ba sōōn′, bə-) *n.* ⟦< VL *bassus*, low⟧ a double-reed bass woodwind instrument

bast (bast) *n.* ⟦OE *bæst*⟧ plant fiber used in ropes, mats, etc.

bas·tard (bas′tərd) *n.* ⟦< OFr⟧ an illegitimate child — *adj.* **1** of illegitimate birth **2** inferior, sham, etc. —**bas′tardy** (-tər dē) *n.*

bas·tard·ize (bas′tər dīz′) *vt.* **-ized′, -iz′ing 1** to make, declare, or show to be a bastard **2** to make corrupt; debase —**bas′tardi·za′tion** *n.*

baste¹ (bāst) *vt.* **bast′ed, bast′ing** ⟦< Gmc *bastjan*, make with bast⟧ to sew temporarily with long, loose stitches until properly sewed

baste² (bāst) *vt.* **bast′ed, bast′ing** ⟦< OFr *bassin*, basin⟧ to moisten (meat) with melted butter, drippings, etc. while roasting —**bast′er** *n.*

baste³ (bāst) *vt.* **bast′ed, bast′ing** ⟦ON *beysta*⟧ **1** to beat soundly **2** to attack with words

bas·tille or **bas·tile** (bas tēl′) *n.* ⟦< OFr *bastir*, to build⟧ a prison —**the Bastille** a state prison in Paris destroyed (1789) in the French Revolution

bas·tion (bas′chən, -tē ən) *n.* ⟦see BASTILLE⟧ **1** a projection from a fortification **2** any strong defense

bat¹ (bat) *n.* ⟦OE *batt*⟧ **1** a stout club **2** a club to hit the ball in baseball, etc. **3** a turn at batting **4** [Colloq.] a blow — *vt.* **bat′ted, bat′ting** to hit, as with a bat — *vi.* to take a turn at batting

bat² (bat) *n.* ⟦< Scand⟧ a furry, nocturnal flying mammal with membranous wings

bat³ (bat) *vt.* **bat′ted, bat′ting** ⟦< OFr *battre*, to batter⟧ [Colloq.] to wink —**not bat an eye** [Colloq.] not show surprise

batch (bach) *n.* ⟦OE *bacan*, to bake⟧ **1** the amount (of bread, etc.) in one baking **2** one set, lot, group, etc. **3** an amount of work for processing by a computer in a single run

bate (bāt) *vt.* **bat′ed, bat′ing** ⟦< OFr *abattre*, beat down⟧ to abate or lessen —**with bated breath** holding the breath, as in fear

bath (bath) *n., pl.* **baths** (ba*th*z, baths) ⟦OE *bæth*⟧ **1** a washing, esp. of the body, in water **2** water, etc. for bathing or for soaking or treating something **3** a bathtub **4** a bathroom **5** a BATHHOUSE (sense 1)

bathe (bā*th*) *vt.* **bathed, bath′ing** ⟦OE *bæth*⟧ **1** to put into a liquid **2** to give a bath to **3** to cover as with liquid — *vi.* **1** to take a bath **2** to soak oneself in something — **bather** (bā′*th*ər) *n.*

bath′house′ *n.* **1** a public building for taking baths **2** a building used by bathers for changing clothes

bathing suit a swimsuit

bath′mat′ *n.* a mat used in or next to a bathtub

bathos (bā′thäs′, -thôs′) *n.* ⟦< Gr *bathys*, deep⟧ **1** ANTICLIMAX (sense 1) **2** excessive sentimentality **3** triteness —**ba·thet·ic** (bə thet′ik) *adj.*

bath′robe′ *n.* a loose robe worn to and from the bath, etc.

bath′room′ *n.* a room with a bathtub, toilet, etc.

bath′tub′ *n.* a tub to bathe in

bathy·scaph (bath′i skaf′, -ə-) *n.* ⟦< Gr *bathys*, deep + *skaphē*, boat⟧ a deep-sea diving apparatus for reaching

---

■ THESAURUS ■

basement *n.* cellar, excavation, storage room, wine cellar, furnace room, vault, crypt.

bashful *a.* retiring, reserved, timid; see HUMBLE 1, MODEST 2.

basic *a.* essential, central, primary; see FUNDAMENTAL, NECESSARY.

basically *a.* fundamentally, primarily, radically; see ESSENTIALLY.

basin *n.* pan, tub, bowl; see CONTAINER.

basis *n.* support, foundation, justification, reason, explanation, background, source, authority, principle, groundwork, assumption, premise, backing, sanction, proof, evidence, nucleus, center.

bask *v.* relax, enjoy, indulge; see WALLOW.

basket *n.* bushel, crate, bin; see CONTAINER.

basketball *n.* court game, cage meet, roundball*; see SPORT 3.

bastard *a.* illegitimate, natural, false, mongrel, baseborn, misbegotten.— *Ant.* TRUE, legitimate, well-born.

bastard *n.* **1** [An illegitimate child] natural child, whoreson, love child, woods colt*, Sunday's child*. **2** [*A rascal*] scoundrel, cheat, SOB; see RASCAL.

baste¹,² *v.* **1** [To sew temporarily] stitch, catch, tack; see SEW. **2** [To dress cooking meat with fat or sauce] moisten, grease, season; see COOK.

bat¹ *n.* club, racket, stick; see STICK. —**blind as a bat** sightless, unseeing, blinded; see BLIND 1. —**go to bat for*** intervene for, support, back up; see DEFEND 2. —**have bats in one's belfry*** be mad, be eccentric, be peculiar; see INSANE. —**not bat an eye*** not be surprised, not be shocked, not be amazed, ignore,

remain unruffled; see also NEGLECT 1. —**(right) off the bat*** at once, without delay, instantly; see IMMEDIATELY.

bat¹ *v.* strike, whack, sock*; see HIT 1.

batch *n.* stack, group, shipment; see BUNCH.

bath *n.* **1** [The act of cleansing the body] washing, sponge bath, shower, tub, bath, steam bath, sauna, soak*, dip, soaking*. **2** [An enclosure prepared for bathing] bathroom, toilet, shower, washroom, powder room, lavatory, steam bath, sauna, public baths, shower room.

bathe *v.* soap, scour, scrub; see WASH 1.

bathrobe *n.* robe, dressing gown, kimono; see CLOTHES.

bathroom *n.* shower, toilet, lavatory; see BATH 2, TOILET.

great depths without a cable Also **bath'y·scaphe'** (-skaf', -skāf')

ba·tik (bə tēk') *n.* ⟦Malay⟧ cloth with a design made by dyeing only the parts not coated with wax

ba·tiste (bə tēst', ba-) *n.* ⟦Fr: after supposed orig. maker, *Baptiste*⟧ a fine, thin cloth of cotton, rayon, etc.

ba·ton (bə tän', ba-) *n.* ⟦Fr⟧ **1** a staff serving as a symbol of office **2** a slender stick used in directing music **3** a metal rod twirled by a drum major

bat·tal·ion (bə tal'yən) *n.* ⟦< VL *battalia*, battle⟧ a tactical military unit forming part of a division

bat·ten[1] (bat'ʼn) *n.* ⟦var. of *baton*⟧ **1** a sawed strip of wood **2** a strip of wood put over a seam between boards as a fastening or covering — *vt.* to fasten or supply with battens

bat·ten[2] (bat'ʼn) *vi., vt.* ⟦ON *batna*, improve⟧ to fatten; thrive

bat·ten[3] (bat'ʼn) *n.* ⟦< OFr *battre*, to batter⟧ in a loom, the movable frame that presses into place the threads of a woof

bat·ter[1] (bat'ər) *vt.* ⟦< L *battuere*, to beat⟧ **1** to strike with blow after blow **2** to injure by pounding, hard wear, or use — *vi.* to pound noisily

bat·ter[2] (bat'ər) *n. Baseball, Cricket* the player at bat

bat·ter[3] (bat'ər) *n.* ⟦OFr *bature*⟧ a flowing mixture of flour, milk, etc. for making cakes, pancakes, etc.

battering ram a heavy beam, etc. for battering down gates, etc.

bat·tery (bat'ər ē) *n., pl.* **-ies** ⟦< OFr *battre*, to batter⟧ **1** a battering **2** a set of things used together **3** *Baseball* the pitcher and the catcher **4** *Elec.* a cell or group of cells storing an electrical charge and able to furnish a current **5** *Law* any illegal beating of another person: see ASSAULT AND BATTERY **6** *Mil.* a set of heavy guns, rockets, etc.

bat·ting (bat'ʼn, -iŋ) *n.* ⟦OE *batt*, BAT[1]⟧ cotton, wool, or synthetic fiber wadded into sheets

bat·tle (bat'ʼl) *n.* ⟦< L *battuere*, to beat⟧ **1** a large-scale fight between armed forces **2** armed fighting **3** any fight or conflict — *vt., vi.* **-tled, -tling** to fight — **give** (or **do**) **battle** to fight

bat'tle-ax' or **bat'tle-axe'** *n.* **1** a heavy ax formerly used as a weapon **2** [Slang] a harsh, domineering woman

bat'tle·dore' (-dôr') *n.* ⟦< OFr *battre*, to batter⟧ a racket used to hit a shuttlecock in a game like badminton

bat'tle·field' *n.* the site of a battle Also **bat'tle·ground'**

bat'tle·ment (-mənt) *n.* ⟦< OFr *batailler*, fortify⟧ a parapet with spaces for shooting, built atop a tower, etc.

battle royal *pl.* **battles royal** **1** a free-for-all **2** a heated dispute

bat'tle·ship' *n.* a large warship with big guns and very heavy armor

batty (bat'ē) *adj.* **-tier, -ti·est** ⟦< BAT[2]⟧ [Slang] crazy or eccentric

bau·ble (bô'bəl) *n.* ⟦< L *bellus*, pretty⟧ a showy trifle; trinket

baud (bôd) *n.* ⟦after J. M. E. *Baudot* (1845-1903), Fr inventor⟧ the number of bits per second transmitted in a computer system

baux·ite (bôks'īt') *n.* ⟦Fr, after (*Les*) *Baux*, town in S France⟧ a claylike ore, the source of aluminum

bawd (bôd) *n.* ⟦< ? OFr *baud*, licentious⟧ [Literary] a person, esp. a woman, who keeps a brothel

bawdy (bô'dē) *adj.* **-i·er, -i·est** indecent; lewd —**bawd'i·ness** *n.*

bawl (bôl) *vi., vt.* ⟦< ML *baulare*, to bark⟧ **1** to shout **2** to weep loudly — *n.* **1** an outcry **2** a noisy weeping — **bawl out** [Slang] to scold angrily

bay[1] (bā) *n.* ⟦< ML *baia*⟧ a wide inlet of a sea or lake, along the shoreline

bay[2] (bā) *n.* ⟦< VL *batare*, to gape⟧ **1** an alcove or recess **2** BAY WINDOW

bay[3] (bā) *vi.* ⟦< OFr *baiier*⟧ to bark or howl in long, deep tones — *n.* **1** the sound of baying **2** the situation of a hunted animal forced to turn and fight —**at bay** **1** cornered **2** held off —**bring to bay** to corner

bay[4] (bā) *n.* ⟦< L *baca*, berry⟧ **1** LAUREL (*n.* 1) **2** [*pl.*] a laurel wreath

bay[5] (bā) *adj.* ⟦< L *badius*⟧ reddish-brown — *n.* **1** a reddish-brown horse, etc. **2** reddish brown

bay'ber'ry *n., pl.* **-ries** **1** a shrub with small, wax-coated, berrylike fruit **2** the fruit

bay leaf the dried, aromatic leaf of certain plants, as the laurel, used as a spice

bay·o·net (bā'ə net', bā'ə nət) *n.* ⟦< Fr: after *Bayonne*, city in France⟧ a detachable blade put on a rifle muzzle, for stabbing — *vt., vi.* **-net'ed** or **-net'ted, -net'ing** or **-net'ting** to stab with a bayonet

bay·ou (bī'ō̄o') *n.* ⟦< AmInd *bayuk*, small stream⟧ in S U.S., a marshy inlet or outlet of a lake, river, etc.

bay window **1** a window or set of windows jutting out from a wall **2** [Slang] a large protruding belly

ba·zaar (bə zär') *n.* ⟦Pers *bāzār*⟧ **1** a marketplace, esp. in the Middle East **2** a benefit sale for a church, etc.

ba·zoo·ka (bə zōō'kə) *n.* ⟦< name of a comic horn⟧ a portable weapon for launching armor-piercing rockets

BB (shot) ⟦designation of size⟧ a size of shot (diameter, .18 in.) for an air rifle (**BB gun**) or shotgun

BC or **B.C.** *abbrev.* before Christ

B cell any of the lymphatic leukocytes not derived from the thymus, that build antibodies: cf. T CELL

be (bē, bi) *vi.* **was** or **were, been, being** ⟦OE *beon*⟧ **1** to exist; live **2** to happen; occur **3** to remain or continue *Note:* be is used to link its subject to a predicate complement *[she is nice]* or as an auxiliary: (1) with a past participle: *a)* to form the passive voice *[he will be sued] b)* to form the perfect tense *[Christ is risen]* (2) with a present participle to express continuation *[he is running]* (3) with a present participle or infinitive to express futurity, possibility, obligation, intention, etc. *[she is going soon, is to cut it] Be* is conjugated in the present indicative: (I) *am*, (he, she, it) *is*, (we, you, they) *are*; in the past indicative: (I, he, she, it) *was*, (we, you, they) *were*

be- ⟦< OE *bi-, be-*, at⟧ *prefix* **1** around *[beset]* **2** completely *[bedeck]* **3** away *[betake]* **4** about *[bemoan]* **5** to make *[besot]* **6** to furnish with, affect by *[becloud]*

Be *Chem. symbol for* beryllium

beach (bēch) *n.* ⟦E dial., pebbles⟧ a sandy shore — *vt., vi.* to ground (a boat) on a beach

beach'comb'er (-kom'ər) *n.* **1** COMBER (sense 2) **2** one who lives on items found on beaches —**beach'comb'ing** *n.*

beach'head' *n.* a position gained, specif. by invading an enemy shore

bea·con (bē'kən) *n.* ⟦< OE *beacen*, a signal⟧ **1** a light for warning or guiding **2** a radio transmitter sending guiding signals for aircraft

bead (bēd) *n.* ⟦< OE *bed*, prayer bead⟧ **1** a small ball of glass, etc., pierced for stringing **2** [*pl.*] a rosary **3** [*pl.*] a

---

■■■ THESAURUS ■■■

battalion *n.* unit, force, corps; see ARMY 2.

batter[2,3] *n.* **1** [One who bats] hitter, pinch-hitter, switch-hitter; see BASEBALL PLAYER. **2** [Baking mixture] dough, mix, paste, recipe, concoction, mush; see also MIXTURE 1.

battery *n.* **1** [Cells which generate or store electricity] dry cell, storage cells, storage battery, energy unit, flashlight battery, solar battery, atomic battery, electric cell. **2** [The act of beating] assault, attack, thumping, beating, physical violence, mugging.

battle *n.* strife, contention, struggle, combat, bombing, fighting, bloodshed, clash, onslaught, onset, barrage, conflict, warfare, fray, assault, crusade, military campaign, hostilities, havoc, carnage; see also FIGHT.

—give (or **do**) **battle** fight back, struggle, engage in a battle; see ATTACK, FIGHT.

battlefield *n.* field of battle, battleground, front, theater of war, disputed territory, no man's land.

battleship *n.* man of war, floating fortress, battlewagon*; see SHIP.

bawl *v.* weep, shed tears, sob; see CRY 1. —**bawl out*** chide, berate, admonish; see SCOLD.

bay[1] *n.* inlet, gulf, bayou, loch, bight, sound, fiord, firth, estuary, strait, narrows, road, arm of the sea, mouth, lagoon, cove, harbor.

bayonet *n.* spike, lance, pike; see KNIFE.

BC or **B.C.** *abbrev.* before Christ, ante-Christian, pre-Christian; see OLD 3.

be *v.* **1** [To have being] live, stay, be alive, exist, remain, endure, go on, stand, subsist, breathe, last, prevail, abide, survive, move, act, do, hold, have place.—*Ant.* DIE, disappear, stop. **2** [To mean] signify, denote, imply; see MEAN 1.

beach *n.* seaside, sand, the coast; see SHORE.

beached *a.* stranded, marooned, aground; see ABANDONED.

beacon *n.* flare, lantern, guide, signal fire, lighthouse, lamp, beam, radar, sonar, airline beacon, radio beacon, air control beacon.

bead *n.* drop, droplet, pellet, grain, particle, speck, dot, dab, pea, shot, pill, driblet.

beads *n.* necklace, pendant, string of jewels; see NECKLACE.

string of beads **4** any small, round object, as the front sight of a rifle **5** a drop or bubble **6** the rim edge of a rubber tire — *vt.* to decorate with beads —**draw a bead on** to take careful aim at —**say one's beads** to pray with a rosary —**bead'y, -i·er, -i·est,** *adj.*

bea·dle (bēd″l) *n.* ⟦ME *bidel*⟧ a minor officer in the Church of England, who kept order in church

bea·gle (bē′gəl) *n.* ⟦ < ? Fr *bee gueule,* wide throat⟧ a small hound with short legs and drooping ears

beak (bēk) *n.* ⟦ < L *beccus*⟧ **1** a bird's bill **2** a beaklike part, as the snout of various insects

beaker (bēk′ər) *n.* ⟦ < ? Gr *bikos,* vessel with handles⟧ **1** a goblet **2** *Chem.* a glass or metal container with a beaklike lip for pouring

beam (bēm) *n.* ⟦ME⟧ **1** a long, thick piece of wood, metal, etc. **2** the crossbar of a balance **3** a ship's breadth at its widest point **4** a shaft of light, etc. **5** a radiant look, smile, etc. **6** a steady radio or radar signal for guiding aircraft or ships — *vt.* **1** to give out (shafts of light) **2** to direct (a radio signal, etc.) — *vi.* **1** to shine brightly **2** to smile warmly

bean (bēn) *n.* ⟦OE *bean*⟧ **1** a plant of the pea family, bearing kidney-shaped seeds **2** the edible, smooth seed of this plant **3** any beanlike seed /*coffee bean*/ **4** [Slang] the head or brain — *vt.* [Slang] to hit on the head —**full of beans** [Slang] lively —**spill the beans** [Colloq.] to tell a secret

bear[1] (ber) *vt.* **bore, borne** or **born, bear'ing** ⟦OE *beran*⟧ **1** to carry **2** to have or show **3** to give birth to **4** to produce or yield **5** to support or sustain **6** to withstand or endure **7** to need /*this bears watching*/ **8** to carry or conduct (oneself) **9** to give /*to bear witness*/ — *vi.* **1** to be productive **2** to lie, point, or move in a given direction **3** to have bearing (on) **4** to tolerate —**bear down (on)** **1** to exert pressure or effort (on) **2** to approach —**bear out** to confirm —**bear up** to endure —**bear'able** *adj.* —**bear'er** *n.*

bear[2] (ber) *n.* ⟦OE *bera*⟧ **1** a large, heavy mammal with shaggy fur and a short tail **2** [B-] either of two constellations in the Northern Hemisphere (**Great Bear** and **Little Bear**) **3** one who is clumsy, rude, etc. **4** one who sells stocks, etc. hoping to buy them back later at a lower price — *adj.* falling in price —**bear'like**′ *adj.*

beard (bird) *n.* ⟦OE⟧ **1** the hair on the chin and cheeks of a man **2** any beardlike part **3** an awn — *vt.* **1** to defy **2** to provide with a beard —**beard'ed** *adj.* —**beard'less** *adj.*

bear·ing (ber′iŋ) *n.* **1** way of carrying and conducting oneself **2** a supporting part **3** a producing or ability to produce **4** endurance **5** [*often pl.*] relative direction or position **6** [*pl.*] awareness of one's situation **7** relevance; relation **8** a part of a machine on which another part revolves, slides, etc.

bear'ish *adj.* **1** bearlike; rude, rough, etc. **2** falling, or causing, expecting, etc. a fall, in prices on the stock exchange —**bear'ishly** *adv.*

bé·ar·naise sauce (bā′är nāz′) a creamy sauce, esp. for meat or fish

bear'skin′ *n.* **1** the fur or hide of a bear **2** a rug, coat, etc. made from this

beast (bēst) *n.* ⟦ < L *bestia*⟧ **1** any large, four-footed animal **2** one who is gross, brutal, etc.

beast'ly *adj.* **-lier, -li·est** **1** of or like a beast; brutal, etc. **2** [Colloq.] disagreeable; unpleasant —**beast'li·ness** *n.*

beast of burden any animal used for carrying things

beast of prey any animal that hunts and kills other animals for food

beat (bēt) *vt.* **beat, beat'en, beat'ing** ⟦OE *beatan*⟧ **1** to hit repeatedly; pound **2** to punish by so hitting; whip, spank, etc. **3** to dash repeatedly against **4** *a)* to form (a path, etc.) by repeated treading or riding *b)* to keep walking on /*to beat the pavements*/ **5** to mix (eggs, etc.) by hard stirring **6** to move (esp. wings) up and down **7** to search through (a forest, etc.) **8** to defeat or outdo **9** to mark (time or rhythm) by tapping, etc. **10** [Colloq.] to baffle **11** [Colloq.] to cheat **12** [Slang] to escape the penalties of — *vi.* **1** to hit or dash repeatedly **2** to throb — *n.* **1** a beating, as of the heart **2** any of a series of strokes **3** a throb **4** a habitual route **5** the unit of musical rhythm **6** BEATNIK — *adj.* **1** [Colloq.] tired out **2** of a group of young persons, esp. of the 1950's, expressing social disillusionment by unconventional dress, actions, etc. —**beat down** to put or force down —**beat it!** [Slang] go away! —**beat**

THESAURUS

beak *n.* nose, prow, bill, mandible, projection, proboscis, snout, nozzle.

beam *n.* **1** [A relatively long, stout bar] timber, brace, scantling, rafter, stringer, stud, two-by-four, strut, joist, bolster, axle, girder, sleeper, stay, crosspiece, prop, support, trestle, spar, pole, crossbar, T-beam, I-beam, steel beam, boom, post, column, pillar, sill, jamb, cantilever, shaft, scaffolding; see also BAR 1. **2** [Radio waves intended as a guide] direction finder, unidirectional radio signal, radar; see BEACON. —**off the beam*** faulty, incorrect, inaccurate; see WRONG 2. —**on the beam*** alert, keen, efficient; see ABLE.

beam *v.* **1** [To emit] transmit, broadcast, give out; see SEND 1. **2** [To shine] radiate, glitter, glare; see SHINE 1. **3** [To smile] grin, laugh, smirk; see SMILE.

beaming *a.* **1** [Giving forth beams] radiant, glowing, gleaming; see BRIGHT 1. **2** [In very genial humor] grinning, animated, sunny; see HAPPY.

bean *n.* Varieties include the following: kidney, navy, lima, soy, castor, black, pinto, string, black-eyed, black-eye, green, wax; see also VEGETABLE. —**full of beans*** **1** lively, vital, energetic; see ACTIVE. **2** mistaken, erring, incorrect; see WRONG 2. —**spill the beans*** divulge information, tell secrets, talk; see TELL 1.

bear[1] *v.* **1** [To suffer] tolerate, support, undergo; see ENDURE 2. **2** [To support weight] sustain, hold up, shoulder; see SUPPORT 1. **3** [To give birth to] be delivered of, bring to birth, bring forth; see PRODUCE 1. —**bear down on** (or **upon**) **1** [To press] squeeze, compress, push; see

PRESS 1. **2** [To try] endeavor, strive, attempt; see TRY 1. —**bear out** confirm, substantiate, support; see PROVE. —**bear up** persist, persevere, carry on; see ENDURE 2. —**bear upon** pertain to, refer to, relate to, regard; see also CONCERN 1. —**bear with** tolerate, be patient with, suffer, put up with; see also ENDURE 2.

bear[2] *n.* grizzly, polar bear, brown bear, black bear; see also ANIMAL.

bearable *a.* endurable, tolerable, passable, admissible, supportable, sufferable.

beard *n.* whiskers, brush, Van Dyke, chin whiskers, imperial, muttonchops, goatee, spade beard, forked beard, side whiskers.

bearded *a.* bewhiskered, bushy, unshaven; see HAIRY.

bearing *n.* **1** [A point of support] frame, ball bearing, roller bearing; see SUPPORT 2. **2** [Manner of carriage] mien, deportment, manner; see BEHAVIOR, POSTURE 1.

beast *n.* **1** [A large animal] brute, creature, lower animal; see ANIMAL. **2** [A person of brutish nature] monster, brute, degenerate, animal, fiend, swine, pervert, lout, savage, barbarian, pig, satyr, goat, hog, monstrosity, glutton, gargoyle, Bluebeard; see also PERVERT.

beastly *a.* brutal, savage, coarse, repulsive, gluttonous, obscene, unclean, piggish, hoggish, irrational, boorish, brutish, depraved, abominable, loathsome, vile, low, degraded, sensual, foul, base, disgusting, inhuman, gross, vulgar.—*Ant.* REFINED, sweet, nice.

beat* *a.* weary, fatigued, worn-out; see TIRED.

beat *n.* **1** [A throb] thump, pound, quake, flutter, pulse, pulsation, cadence, flow, vibration, turn, ripple, pressure, impulse, quiver, shake, surge, swell, palpitation, undulation, rhythm. **2** [A unit of music] accent, vibration, division, stress, measure, rhythm.

beat *v.* **1** [To thrash] hit, punish, whip, pistol-whip, flog, trounce, spank, scourge, switch, lash, slap, cuff, box, strap, birch, cane, horsewhip, buffet, pommel, tap, rap, strike, bump, pat, knock, pound, club, punch, bat, flail, batter, maul, whack, hammer, clout, smack, bang, swat*, slug*, beat black and blue*, whale*, belt*, whack*, beat the tar out of*, beat the daylights out of*, beat the hell out of*, knock the stuffing out of*, wallop*, lick*, paste*, bash*, work over*, thwack. **2** [To pulsate] pound, thump, pulse; see THROB. **3** [To worst] overcome, surpass, conquer; see DEFEAT 2, 3. **4** [To mix] stir, whip, knead; see MIX 1.

beaten *a.* **1** [Defeated] worsted, humbled, thwarted, bested, disappointed, frustrated, baffled, conquered, overthrown, subjugated, ruined, mastered, trounced, undone, vanquished, crushed, overwhelmed, overpowered, licked*, done in*, done for*, kayoed*, mugged, skinned*, trimmed*, had it*, washed up*, sunk*.—*Ant.* SUCCESSFUL, victorious, triumphant. **2** [Made firm and hard] hammered, tramped, stamped, rolled, milled, forged, trod, pounded, tramped down, tamped.—*Ant.* SOFT, spongy, loose. **3** [Made light by beating] whipped, frothy, foamy, mixed, churned, creamy, bubbly, meringued.

off to drive back —**beat up (on)** [Slang] to give a beating to —**beat′er** *n.*

be·a·tif·ic (bē′ə tif′ik) *adj.* 1 making blessed 2 showing happiness or delight

be·at·i·fy (bē at′ə fī′) *vt.* **-fied′, -fy′ing** [< L *beatus*, happy + *facere*, to make] 1 to make blissfully happy 2 *R.C.Ch.* to declare (a deceased person) to be in heaven —**be·at′i·fi·ca′tion** *n.*

beat′ing *n.* 1 the act of one that beats 2 a whipping 3 a throbbing 4 a defeat

be·at·i·tude (bē at′ə tōōd′) *n.* [< L *beatus*, happy] perfect blessedness or happiness —**the Beatitudes** the pronouncements in the Sermon on the Mount

beat·nik (bēt′nik) *n.* a member of the beat group

beat′-up′ *adj.* [Slang] worn-out, dilapidated, etc.

beau (bō) *n., pl.* **beaus** or **beaux** (bōz) [Fr < L *bellus*, pretty] [Old-fashioned] a woman's sweetheart

beau·te·ous (byōōt′ē əs) *adj.* [ME] beautiful —**beau′te·ous·ly** *adv.*

beau·ti·cian (byōō tish′ən) *n.* one who works in a beauty shop

beau·ti·ful (byōōt′ə fəl) *adj.* having beauty —**beau′ti·ful·ly** *adv.*

beau·ti·fy (-fī′) *vt., vi.* **-fied′, -fy′ing** to make or become beautiful —**beau′ti·fi·ca′tion** (-fi kā′shən) *n.* —**beau′ti·fi′er** *n.*

beau·ty (byōōt′ē) *n., pl.* **-ties** [< L *bellus*, pretty] 1 the quality of being very pleasing, as in form, color, etc. 2 a thing with this quality 3 good looks 4 a very attractive person, feature, etc.

beauty salon (or **shop, parlor,** etc.) a place where esp. women go for hair styling, manicuring, etc.

bea·ver (bē′vər) *n.* [< OE *beofor*] 1 *a)* a large amphibious rodent with soft, brown fur, webbed hind feet, and a flat, broad tail *b)* its fur 2 a man's high silk hat

be·calm (bē käm′, bi-) *vt.* 1 to make calm 2 to make (a ship) motionless from lack of wind

be·cause (bē kôz′, -kuz′; bi-) *conj.* [ME *bi*, by + *cause*] for the reason or cause that —**because of** by reason of

beck (bek) *n.* a beckoning gesture —**at the beck and call of** at the service of

beck·on (bek′n) *vi., vt.* [OE *beacnian*] 1 to summon by a gesture 2 to lure; entice

be·cloud (bē kloud′, bi-) *vt.* 1 to cloud over 2 to confuse; muddle

be·come (bē kum′, bi-) *vi.* **-came′, -come′, -com′ing** [OE *becuman*] to come or grow to be — *vt.* to befit; suit —**become of** to happen to

be·com′ing *adj.* 1 appropriate; fit 2 suitable to the wearer

bed (bed) *n.* [OE] 1 a piece of furniture for sleeping on 2 a plot of soil where plants are raised 3 the bottom of a river, lake, etc. 4 any flat surface used as a foundation 5 a stratum — *vt.* **bed′ded, bed′ding** 1 to put to bed 2 to embed 3 to plant in a bed of earth 4 to arrange in layers — *vi.* 1 to go to bed; rest; sleep 2 to stratify

be·daz·zle (bē daz′əl, bi-) *vt.* **-zled, -zling** to dazzle thoroughly; bewilder

bed′bug′ *n.* a small, wingless, biting insect that infests beds, etc.

bed′clothes′ (-klōz′, -klōthz′) *n.pl.* sheets, blankets, etc. used on a bed

bed′cov′er *n.* a bedspread; coverlet

bed′ding (-iŋ) *n.* 1 mattresses and bedclothes 2 a bottom layer; base

be·deck (bē dek′, bi-) *vt.* to adorn

be·dev·il (bē dev′əl, bi-) *vt.* **-iled** or **-illed, -il·ing** or **-il·ling** to plague or bewilder —**be·dev′il·ment** *n.*

bed′fel′low *n.* 1 a person who shares one's bed 2 an associate, ally, etc.

be·dim (bē dim′, bi-) *vt.* **-dimmed′, -dim′ming** to make (the eyes or the vision) dim

bed·lam (bed′ləm) *n.* [after (the old London mental hospital of St. Mary of) *Bethlehem*] any place or condition of noise and confusion

bed of roses [Colloq.] a situation or position of ease and luxury

Bed·ouin (bed′ōō in′) *n., pl.* **-ins** or **-in** [< Ar *badāwin*, desert dwellers] [*also* **b-**] 1 an Arab of the desert tribes of Arabia, Syria, or N Africa 2 any wanderer

bed′pan′ *n.* a shallow pan for use as a toilet by one confined to bed

be·drag·gle (bē drag′əl, bi-) *vt.* **-gled, -gling** to make wet, limp, and dirty, as by dragging through mire

bed′rid′den (-rid′'n) *adj.* confined to bed by illness, infirmity, etc.

bed′rock′ *n.* 1 solid rock beneath the soil, etc. 2 a foundation or bottom

bed′roll′ *n.* a portable roll of bedding, as for sleeping outdoors

bed′room′ *n.* a room for sleeping

bed′side′ *n.* the space beside a bed — *adj.* near a bed

bed′sore′ *n.* a sore on the body of a bedridden person, caused by chafing

bed′spread′ *n.* an ornamental spread covering the blanket on a bed

bed′stead′ (-sted′) *n.* a framework for the spring and mattress of a bed

bed′time′ *n.* one's usual time for going to bed

bee¹ (bē) *n.* [OE *beo*] a broad-bodied, four-winged, hairy insect that gathers pollen and nectar and that can sting

bee² (bē) *n.* [OE *ben*, compulsory service] a meeting of people to work together or compete

THESAURUS

beater *n.* whipper, mixer, egg-beater; see APPLIANCE.

beating *n.* thrashing, whipping, drubbing; see DEFEAT.

beatnik *n.* Bohemian, hippie-type, nonconformist; see RADICAL.

beautiful *a.* lovely, attractive, appealing, comely, pleasing, pretty, fair, fine, nice, dainty, good-looking, delightful, charming, enticing, fascinating, admirable, rich, graceful, ideal, delicate, refined, elegant, symmetrical, well-formed, shapely, well-made, splendid, gorgeous, brilliant, radiant, exquisite, dazzling, resplendent, magnificent, superb, marvelous, wonderful, grand, awe-inspiring, imposing, majestic, excellent, impressive, handsome, divine, blooming, rosy, beauteous, statuesque, well-favored, bewitching, personable, taking, alluring, slender, svelte, lissome, lithe, bright-eyed, classy*, easy on the eyes*, long on looks*, built*.—*Ant.* UGLY, deformed, hideous.

beautifully *a.* gracefully, exquisitely, charmingly, attractively, prettily, delightfully, appealingly, seductively, alluringly, elegantly, gorgeously, splendidly, magnificently, ideally, tastefully, sublimely, handsomely, superbly, divinely.

beauty *n.* 1 [A pleasing physical quality] grace, comeliness, fairness, pulchritude, charm, delicacy, elegance, attraction, fascination, allurement, shapeliness, majesty, attractiveness, good looks, glamour, loveliness, bloom, class*.—*Ant.* UGLINESS, homeliness, deformity. 2 [A beautiful woman] goddess, belle, attraction, siren, enchantress, seductress, Venus, *femme fatale* (French), looker*, charmer*.—*Ant.* WITCH, blemish, fright.

because *conj.* on account of, in consequence of, in view of, by reason of, for the reason that, for the sake of, in behalf of, on the grounds that, in the interest of, as a result of, as things go, by virtue of, in that, since, by the agency of, due to*, being as how*, owing to.

beckon *v.* signal, motion, sign; see SUMMON.

become *v.* develop into, change into, turn into, grow into, eventually be, emerge as, turn out to be, come to be, shift, assume the form of, be reformed, be converted to, convert, mature, shift toward, incline to, melt into; see also GROW 2.

becoming *a.* attractive, beautiful, neat, agreeable, handsome, seemly, comely, tasteful, well-chosen, fair, trim, graceful, flattering, effective, excellent, acceptable, welcome, nice.

bed *n.* 1 [A place of rest] mattress, cot, couch, bedstead, berth, bunk, hay*, sack*, rack*, feathers*, roost. *Beds include the following:* single bed, double bed, davenport, cot, four-poster, trundle bed, twin bed, foldaway bed, Murphy bed, hammock, feather bed, double-deck bed, stretcher, folding bed, bunk bed, litter, cradle, crib, bassinet, king-size bed, queen-size bed, water bed, hospital bed, circular bed, day bed. 2 [A foundation] base, bottom, groundwork; see FOUNDATION 2. 3 [A seed plot] patch, row, planting; see GARDEN.

bedding *n.* bedclothes, bed linen, thermal blankets, covers, bedcovers, pillows, coverlets, sheets, quilts, spreads, comforters.

bed down *v.* turn in, retire, hit the hay*; see SLEEP.

bedlam *n.* confusion, pandemonium, clamor; see CONFUSION, NOISE 2.

bedridden *a.* incapacitated, confined to bed, laid up; see DISABLED.

bedroom *n.* sleeping room, guest room, master bedroom; see ROOM 2.

bedspread *n.* spread, quilt, comforter; see BEDDING.

bedtime *n.* slumbertime, time to hit the hay*, sack time*; see NIGHT.

beech (bēch) *n.* ⟦OE *bece*⟧ 1 a tree with smooth, gray bark, hard wood, and edible nuts 2 its wood

beech′nut′ *n.* the small, three-cornered, edible nut of the beech tree

beef (bēf) *n., pl.* **beeves** or **beefs** ⟦< L *bos*, ox⟧ 1 a full-grown ox, cow, bull, or steer, esp. one bred for meat 2 such animals collectively 3 their meat 4 [Colloq.] *a)* human flesh *b)* strength 5 [Slang] a complaint — *vi.* [Slang] to complain —**beef up** [Colloq.] to reinforce

beef′cake′ *n.* ⟦BEEF (*n.* 4a) + (CHEESE)CAKE⟧ [Colloq.] display of the figure of a nude or partly nude, muscular man, as in a photograph

beef′steak′ *n.* a thick slice of beef for broiling or frying

beef′y *adj.* **-i·er, -i·est** brawny —**beef′i·ness** *n.*

bee′hive′ *n.* 1 a shelter for a colony of bees 2 a place of great activity

bee′keep′er *n.* one who keeps bees for producing honey —**bee′keep′ing** *n.*

bee′line′ *n.* a straight line or direct route

Be·el′ze·bub (bē el′zə bub′) *Bible* the chief devil; Satan

been (bin, ben; *Brit* bēn) *vi. pp. of* BE

beep (bēp) *n.* ⟦echoic⟧ the brief, high-pitched sound of a horn or electronic signal — *vi., vt.* to make or cause to make this sound

beep′er *n.* any beeping electronic device, esp. a small, portable receiver used to contact people for messages

beer (bir) *n.* ⟦OE *beor*⟧ 1 an alcoholic, fermented drink made from malt and hops 2 a soft drink made from extracts of roots, etc. *[ginger beer]*

bees′wax′ *n.* wax secreted by honeybees, used to make their honeycombs

beet (bēt) *n.* ⟦< L *beta*⟧ 1 a plant with edible leaves and a thick, fleshy, white or red root 2 the edible root, also a source of sugar

bee·tle¹ (bēt′'l) *n.* ⟦OE *bitan*, to bite⟧ an insect with hard front wings that cover the membranous hind wings when these are folded

bee·tle² (bēt′'l) *vi.* **-tled, -tling** ⟦prob. < fol.⟧ to overhang — *adj.* overhanging: also **bee′tling**

bee′tle-browed′ (-broud′) *adj.* ⟦< ME < ? *bitel*, sharp + *brouwe*, brow⟧ 1 having bushy eyebrows 2 frowning

be·fall (bē fôl′, bi-) *vi., vt.* **-fell′, -fall′en, -fall′ing** ⟦< OE *be-*, BE- + *feallan*, to fall⟧ to happen or occur (to)

be·fit (bē fit′, bi-) *vt.* **-fit′ted, -fit′ting** to be suitable or proper for; be suited to —**be·fit′ting** *adj.*

be·fog (bē fôg′, -fäg′; bi-) *vt.* **-fogged′, -fog′ging** 1 to envelop in fog; make foggy 2 to obscure; confuse

be·fore (bē fôr′, bi-) *adv.* ⟦OE *be-*, *foran*, fore⟧ 1 ahead; in front 2 previously 3 earlier; sooner — *prep.* 1 ahead of 2 in front of 3 in or to the sight, presence, etc. of 4 earlier than 5 in preference to — *conj.* 1 earlier than

the time that *[call before you go]* 2 rather than *[I'd die before I'd tell]*

before′hand′ *adv., adj.* ahead of time; in anticipation

be·foul (bē foul′, bi-) *vt.* 1 to make filthy 2 to slander

be·friend (bē frend′, bi-) *vt.* to act as a friend to; help

be·fud·dle (bē fud′'l, bi-) *vt.* **-dled, -dling** to confuse or stupefy

beg (beg) *vt., vi.* **begged, beg′ging** ⟦< Du *beggaert*, religious mendicant⟧ 1 to ask for (alms) 2 to ask earnestly; entreat —**beg off** to ask to be released from —**go begging** to be available but unwanted

be·gan (bē gan′, bi-) *vi., vt. pt. of* BEGIN

be·get (bē get′, bi-) *vt.* **-got′** or *[Archaic]* **-gat′** (-gat′), **-got′ten** or **-got′, -get′ting** ⟦< OE *begietan*, acquire⟧ 1 to be the father of 2 to produce; cause

beg′gar (beg′ər) *n.* 1 one who begs 2 a pauper — *vt.* 1 to make poor 2 to make (a description, etc.) seem inadequate —**beg′gary**, *pl.* **-ies,** *n.*

beg′gar·ly *adj.* very poor, worthless, inadequate, etc.

be·gin (bē gin′, bi-) *vi., vt.* **-gan′, -gun′, -gin′ning** ⟦< OE *beginnan*⟧ 1 to start doing, acting, etc. 2 to originate

be·gin′ner *n.* one just beginning to do or learn something; novice

be·gin′ning *n.* 1 a starting 2 the time or place of starting; origin 3 the first part 4 *[usually pl.]* an early stage

be·gone (bē gôn′, bi-) *interj., vi.* (to) be gone; go away; get out

be·go·nia (bi gōn′yə) *n.* ⟦after M. *Bégon* (1638-1710), Fr patron of science⟧ a tropical plant with showy flowers and ornamental leaves

be·got (bē gät′, bi-) *vt. pt. & alt. pp. of* BEGET

be·got′ten (-'n) *vt. alt. pp. of* BEGET

be·grime (bē grīm′, bi-) *vt.* **-grimed′, -grim′ing** to cover with grime; soil

be·grudge (bē gruj′, bi-) *vt.* **-grudged′, -grudg′ing** 1 to resent another's possession of (something) 2 to give with reluctance —**be·grudg′ing·ly** *adv.*

be·guile (bē gīl′, bi-) *vt.* **-guiled′, -guil′ing** 1 to mislead or deprive (*of*) by guile; deceive 2 to pass (time) pleasantly 3 to charm or delight —**be·guile′ment** *n.* —**be·guil′er** *n.*

be·gun (bē gun′, bi-) *vi., vt. pp. of* BEGIN

be·half (bē haf′, bi-) *n.* ⟦OE *be*, by + *healf*, side⟧ support —**in** (or **on**) **behalf of** in the interest of; for

be·have (bē hāv′, bi-) *vt., vi.* **-haved′, -hav′ing** ⟦see BE- & HAVE⟧ 1 to conduct (oneself) in a specified way 2 to conduct (oneself) properly

be·hav′ior (-yər) *n.* way of behaving; conduct or action —**be·hav′ioral** *adj.*

THESAURUS

beef *n.* 1 [Bovine flesh used as food] cow's flesh, steer beef, red meat; see MEAT. 2 [A grown animal of the genus *Bos*] bovine, bull, steer; see COW. 3 [*A complaint] dispute, protestation, gripe*; see OBJECTION.

beef up* *v.* intensify, augment, increase; see STRENGTHEN.

beer *n.* malt beverage, malt liquor, brew, suds*. *Varieties include the following:* lager, bock beer, ale, stout, porter, pale beer, light beer, dark beer, black beer.

beetle¹ *n.* bug, scarab, crawling thing; see INSECT.

before *a.* previously, earlier, in the past, since, gone by, in old days, heretofore, former, formerly, back, sooner, up to now, ahead, in front, in advance, facing.—*Ant.* AFTERWARD, in the future, to come.

before *prep.* prior to, previous to, in front of, ahead of, under jurisdiction of, antecedent to.—*Ant.* BEHIND, following, at the rear.

beforehand *a.* previously, already, in anticipation; see BEFORE.

befriend *v.* encourage, advise, stand by; see HELP.

beg *v.* entreat, implore, beseech, supplicate, crave, solicit, pray for, urge, plead, sue, importune, petition, apply to, request, press, appeal to, requisition, conjure, adjure, apostrophize, canvass; see also ASK.—*Ant.* ADMIT,

concede, accede.

beggar *n.* pauper, poor man, hobo, tramp, indigent, vagrant, poverty-stricken person, destitute person, dependent, ghetto-dweller, bankrupt, panhandler*, moocher*, bum*.

begging *a.* anxious, in need, imploring, supplicating; see also WANTING 1.

begin *v.* 1 [To initiate] start, cause, inaugurate, make, occasion, impel, produce, effect, set in motion, launch, mount, start in, start on, start up, start off, induce, do, create, bring about, get going, set about, institute, lead up to, undertake, enter upon, open, animate, motivate, go ahead, lead the way, bring on, bring to pass, act on, generate, drive, actualize, introduce, originate, found, establish, set up, trigger, give birth to, take the lead, plunge into, lay the foundation for, break ground.—*Ant.* END, finish, terminate. 2 [To come into being, or start functioning] commence, get under way, set out, start in, start out, come out, arise, rise, dawn, sprout, originate, crop up, come to birth, come into the world, be born, emanate, come into existence, occur, burst forth, issue forth, come forth, bud, grow, flower, blossom, break out, set to work, kick off, jump off*, go to it*, dig in*, take off*, see the light of day*.—*Ant.* STOP, cease, subside.

beginner *n.* novice, freshman, apprentice; see AMATEUR.

beginning *n.* 1 [The origin in point of time or place] source, outset, root; see ORIGIN 2. 2 [The origin, thought of as the cause] germ, heart, antecedent; see ORIGIN 3.

begun *a.* started, initiated, instituted, under way, in motion, in progress, on foot, inaugurated, happening, proceeding, going, active, existing, operative, working, in force.

behalf *n.* interest, benefit, sake; see WELFARE.

behave *v.* act with decorum, observe the golden rule, do unto others as you would have others do unto you, be nice, be good, be civil, mind one's p's and q's, be orderly, play one's part, live up to, observe the law, reform, mind one's manners, comport oneself, deport oneself, behave oneself, be on one's best behavior, act one's age, avoid offense, toe the mark, play fair.

behavior *n.* bearing, deportment, comportment, demeanor, air, presence, carriage, conduct, manners, actions, attitudes, way of life, speech, talk, tone, morals, habits, tact, social graces, correctness, decorum, form, convention, propriety, taste, management, routine, practice, what's done, style, expression, performance,

behavioral science any of the sciences, as sociology, psychology, etc., that study human behavior

be·head (bē hed′, bi-) *vt.* to cut off the head of

be·held (bē held′, bi-) *vt. pt. & pp. of* BEHOLD

be·he·moth (bi hē′məth) *n.* [< Heb *behema*, beast] 1 *Bible* some huge animal 2 any huge or powerful animal or thing

be·hest (bē hest′, bi-) *n.* [< OE *behæs*, a vow] a command or earnest request

be·hind (bē hind′, bi-) *adv.* [< OE *behindan*] 1 in or to the rear 2 in a former time, place, etc. 3 in or into arrears 4 slow; late — *prep.* 1 remaining after 2 in or to the rear of 3 inferior to 4 later than *[behind* schedule] 5 beyond 6 advocating *[*he is *behind* the plan] 7 hidden by *[*what's *behind* this news] — *n.* [Colloq.] the buttocks

be·hold (bē hōld′, bi-) *vt.* **-held′, -hold′ing** [< OE *bihealdan*] to look at; see — *interj.* look! see! — **be·hold′er** *n.*

be·hold′en (-ən) *adj.* indebted

be·hoove (bē hōōv′, bi-) *vt.* **-hooved′, -hoov′ing** [< OE *behofian*, to need] to be incumbent upon or proper for *[*it *behooves* you to go]

beige (bāzh) *n.* [Fr] grayish tan — *adj.* grayish-tan

be·ing (bē′iŋ) *n.* [see BE] 1 existence; life 2 fundamental nature 3 one that lives or exists — **being as** (or **that**) [Colloq. or Dial.] since; because — **for the time being** for now

be·jewel (bē jōō′əl, bi-) *vt.* **-eled** or **-elled, -el·ing** or **-el·ling** to decorate with or as with jewels

be·la·bor (bē lā′bər, bi-) *vt.* 1 to beat severely 2 to scold 3 to spend too much time on

be·lated (bē lāt′id, bi-) *adj.* tardy —**be·lat′edly** *adv.*

be·lay (bi lā′) *vt., vi.* **-layed′, -lay′ing** [< OE *belecgan*, make fast] 1 to make (a rope) secure by winding around a cleat, etc. 2 [Colloq.] *Naut.* to hold; stop 3 to secure by a rope

bel canto (bel′kän′tō) [It] a style of singing with brilliant vocal display and purity of tone

belch (belch) *vi., vt.* [OE *bealcian*] 1 to expel (gas) through the mouth from the stomach 2 to throw forth (its contents) violently — *n.* a belching

be·lea·guer (bē lē′gər, bi-) *vt.* [< Du < *be-*, around + *leger*, a camp] 1 to besiege by encircling 2 to beset or harass

bel·fry (bel′frē) *n., pl.* **-fries** [ult. < OHG] 1 a bell tower 2 the part of a tower that holds the bells

Belg. Belgium

Bel·gian (bel′jen) *n.* a native or inhabitant of Belgium — *adj.* of Belgium

be·lie (bē lī′, bi-) *vt.* **-lied′, -ly′ing** 1 to disguise or misrepresent 2 to leave unfulfilled 3 to prove false

be·lief (bə lēf′, bē-) *n.* [< OE *geleafa*] 1 conviction that certain things are true 2 religious faith 3 trust or confidence 4 creed or doctrine 5 an opinion; expectation; judgment

be·lieve (bə lēv′, bē-) *vt.* **-lieved′, -liev′ing** [< OE *geliefan*] 1 to take as true, real, etc. 2 to trust a state-

ment or promise of (a person) 3 to suppose or think — *vi.* to have faith (*in*) —**be·liev′able** —**be·liev′er** *n.*

be·lit·tle (bē lit′'l, bi-) *vt.* **-tled, -tling** to make seem little, less important, etc. —**be·lit′tle·ment** *n.*

bell (bel) *n.* [OE *belle*] 1 a hollow, cuplike object, as of metal, which rings when struck 2 the sound of a bell 3 anything shaped like a bell 4 *Naut.* a bell rung to mark the periods of the watch — *vt.* to attach a bell to — *vi.* to flare out like a bell

bella·donna (bel′ə dän′ə) *n.* [< It, beautiful lady] 1 a poisonous plant with purplish flowers and black berries 2 ATROPINE

bell′-bot′tom *adj.* flared at the ankles, as trousers or slacks Also **bell′-bot′tomed** — *n.* [*pl.*] bell-bottom trousers

bell′boy′ *n.* BELLHOP

belle (bel) *n.* [Fr, fem. of *beau*] a pretty woman or girl

belles-lettres (bel le′tr′, -trə) *n.pl.* [Fr] literature as distinguished from technical writings

bell′hop′ *n.* one employed by a hotel, club, etc. to carry luggage and do errands

bel·li·cose (bel′i kōs′) *adj.* [< L *bellicus*, of war] quarrelsome; warlike —**bel′li·cos′ity** (-käs′ə tē) *n.*

bel·lig·er·ent (bə lij′ər ənt) *adj.* [< L *bellum*, war + *gerere*, carry on] 1 at war 2 of war 3 warlike 4 ready to fight or quarrel — *n.* a belligerent person, group, or nation —**bel·lig′er·ence** *n.* —**bel·lig′er·ency** *n.* —**bel·lig′er·ently** *adv.*

bell jar a bell-shaped container made of glass, used to keep air, moisture, etc. in or out Also **bell glass**

bel·low (bel′ō) *vi.* [< OE *bylgan*] 1 to roar with a reverberating sound, as a bull 2 to cry out loudly, as in anger — *vt.* to utter loudly or powerfully — *n.* a bellowing sound

bel·lows (bel′ōz′) *n.sing., n.pl.* [< OE *beli*, belly] 1 a device that forces air out when its sides are pressed together: used in pipe organs, for blowing fires, etc. 2 anything collapsible like a bellows

bell pepper a large, sweet red pepper

Bell's palsy [after C. *Bell* (1774-1842), Scot anatomist] a usually temporary, sudden paralysis of the muscles on one side of the face

bell·wether (bel′weth′ər) *n.* [ME] 1 a male sheep, usually wearing a bell, that leads the flock 2 a leader

belly (bel′ē) *n., pl.* **-lies** [< OE *belg*, leather bag] 1 the part of the body between the chest and thighs; abdomen 2 the underside of an animal's body 3 the stomach 4 the deep interior, as of a ship — *vt., vi.* **-lied, -ly·ing** to swell out

bel′ly·ache′ *n.* pain in the abdomen — *vi.* **-ached′, -ach′ing** [Slang] to complain

bel′ly·but′ton *n.* [Colloq.] the navel

bel′ly·ful′ *n.* 1 more than enough to eat 2 [Slang] all that one can bear

belly laugh [Colloq.] a hearty laugh

be·long (bē lôŋ′, bi-) *vi.* [< ME] 1 to have a proper place *[*it *belongs* here] 2 to be related (*to*) 3 to be a member: with *to* 4 to be owned: with *to*

THESAURUS

code, role, observance, course, guise, act, deed, ethics, way, front.

behind *a., prep.* 1 [To the rear in space] back of, following, after; see BACK. 2 [Late in time] tardy, dilatory, behind time; see LATE 1, SLOW 2. 3 [Slow in progress] sluggish, slow-moving, delayed, backward, underdeveloped, retarded, behind schedule, belated; see also SLOW 2.—*Ant.* FAST, rapid, on time.

being *n.* 1 [Existence] presence, actuality, animation; see LIFE 1. 2 [The essential part] nature, core, marrow; see ESSENCE 1. 3 [A living thing] creature, conscious agent, beast; see ANIMAL. —**for the time being** temporarily, tentatively, for now, for the present; see also BRIEFLY, NOW.

belated *a.* remiss, tardy, overdue; see LATE 1, SLOW 3.

belief *n.* idea, opinion, faith, feeling, hope, intuition, view, expectation, acceptance, trust, notion, persuasion, position, understanding, conviction, confidence, suspicion, knowledge,

conclusion, presumption, surmise, hypothesis, thinking, judgment, certainty, impression, assumption, conjecture, fancy, theory, guess, conception, inference.

believable *a.* trustworthy, creditable, acceptable; see CONVINCING.

believe *v.* accept, hold, think, understand, consider, swear by, conceive, affirm, conclude, be of the opinion, have faith, have no doubt, take at one's word, take someone's word for, be convinced, be certain of, give credence to, rest assured.—*Ant.* DENY, doubt, suspect. —**believe in** swear by, look to, have faith in; see TRUST 1.

believer *n.* convert, devotee, adherent, apostle, disciple, prophet, confirmed believer; see also FOLLOWER.

believing *a.* maintaining, trusting, presuming, assuming, holding, accepting, under the impression.

belittle *v.* lower, disparage, decry; see ABUSE.

bell *n.* chimes, siren, signal, gong, buzzer; see also ALARM.

belligerent *a.* warlike, pugnacious, hostile; see AGGRESSIVE.

bellow *n.* howl, cry, roar; see CRY 1.

bellow *v.* howl, call, shout; see CRY 2, YELL.

belly *n.* paunch, abdomen, gut; see STOMACH.

bellyache* *v.* whine, grumble, protest; see COMPLAIN.

belong *v.* 1 [To be properly placed] fit in, have a place, see FIT 1. 2 [To be acceptable in a group; *said of persons*] fit in, have a place, have its place, be born so, be a member, take one's place with, be one of, be counted among, be included in, owe allegiance to, be a part of, be one of the family.—*Ant.* DIFFER, fight, not fit in. —**belong to** pertain to, relate to, be occupied by, be enjoyed by, be owned by, be in the possession of, be at the disposal of, be the property of, concern, come with, go with, fall under.—*Ant.* ESCAPE, be free, have no owner.

be·long'ings *n.pl.* possessions
be·loved (bi luv'id, -luvd') *adj.* [ME *biloven*] dearly loved — *n.* a dearly loved person
be·low (bi lō') *adv., adj.* [see BE- & LOW¹] 1 in or to a lower place; beneath 2 later (in a book, etc.) 3 in or to hell 4 on earth 5 under in rank, amount, etc. — *prep.* 1 lower than 2 unworthy of
Bel·shaz'zar (bel shaz'ər) *Bible* the last king of Babylon
belt (belt) *n.* [ult. < L *balteus*] 1 a band of leather, etc. worn around the waist 2 any encircling thing like this 3 an endless band for transferring motion, as with pulleys, or conveying 4 a distinctive area [the corn *belt*] 5 [Colloq.] a hard blow; punch 6 [Slang] *a)* a gulp, esp. of liquor *b)* a thrill — *vt.* 1 to encircle or fasten with a belt 2 to hit hard, as with a belt 3 [Colloq.] to sing loudly: usually with *out* 4 [Slang] to gulp (liquor) —**below the belt** unfair(ly) —**tighten one's belt** to live more thriftily
belt'way' *n.* an expressway passing around an urban area
be·mire (bē mir', bi-) *vt.* -mired', -mir'ing 1 to make dirty as with mire or mud 2 to cause to bog down in mud
be·moan (bē mōn', bi-) *vt., vi.* to lament
be·muse (bē myōōz', bi-) *vt.* -mused', -mus'ing [BE- + MUSE] 1 to muddle 2 to preoccupy
bench (bench) *n.* [OE *benc*] 1 a long, hard seat 2 the place where judges sit in a court [*sometimes* B-] *a)* the status of a judge *b)* judges collectively *c)* a law court 4 WORKBENCH — *vt. Sports* to take (a player) out of a game —**on the bench** 1 serving as a judge 2 *Sports* not taking part in the game
bench mark a standard in measuring, judging quality, etc. Also **bench'mark'** *n.*
bench press a weight-lifting exercise, done while one is lying on a bench with the feet on the floor, in which a barbell is pushed upward from the chest —**bench'-press'** *vt.*
bench warrant an order issued by a judge or court for the arrest of a person
bend¹ (bend) *vt.* bent, bend'ing [< OE *bendan*, confine with a string] 1 to make curved or crooked 2 to turn, esp. from a straight line 3 to make submit — *vi.* 1 to turn, esp. from a straight line 2 to yield by curving, as from pressure 3 to curve the body; stoop (*over* or *down*) 4 to give in; yield — *n.* 1 a bending or being bent 2 a bent part —**bend'able** *adj.*
bend² (bend) *n.* [ME < prec.] any of various knots for tying rope
be·neath (bē nēth', bi-) *adv., adj.* [OE *beneothan*] in a lower place; underneath — *prep.* 1 below 2 underneath 3 unworthy of [it is *beneath* him to cheat]
ben·e·dic·tion (ben'ə dik'shən) *n.* [< L *bene*, well + *dicere*, speak] 1 a blessing 2 an invocation of blessing, esp. at the end of a religious service
ben·e·fac·tion (ben'ə fak'shən) *n.* [< L *bene*, well + *facere*, do] 1 the act of helping, esp. by charitable gifts 2 the money or help given
ben·e·fac·tor (ben'ə fak'tər) *n.* one who has given help, esp. financially; patron —**ben'efac'tress** *n.fem.*
ben·e·fice (ben'ə fis) *n.* [< L *beneficium*, kindness] an endowed church office providing a living for a vicar, etc.

be·nef·i·cence (bə nef'ə səns) *n.* [see BENEFACTION] 1 a being kind 2 a charitable act or gift
be·nef'i·cent (-sənt) *adj.* showing beneficence; doing or resulting in good —**be·nef'i·cently** *adv.*
ben·e·fi·cial (ben'ə fish'əl) *adj.* producing benefits; advantageous; favorable —**ben'efi'cially** *adv.*
ben·e·fi·ci·ar'y (-fish'ē er'ē, -fish'ər ē) *n., pl.* -ar'ies anyone receiving or to receive benefit, as funds from a will, an insurance policy, etc.
ben·e·fit (ben'ə fit, -fət) *n.* [see BENEFACTION] 1 anything contributing to improvement; advantage 2 [*often pl.*] payments made by an insurance company, public agency, etc. as during sickness, retirement, etc. or for death 3 a public performance, bazaar, etc. the proceeds of which are to help some person or cause — *vt.* -fited, -fit·ing to help; aid — *vi.* to receive advantage; profit
be·nev·o·lence (bə nev'ə ləns) *n.* [< L *bene*, well + *volens*, to wish] 1 an inclination to do good; kindliness 2 a kindly, charitable act —**be·nev'o·lent** *adj.* —**be·nev'o·lently** *adv.*
be·night·ed (bē nit'id, bi-) *adj.* 1 surrounded by darkness 2 ignorant
be·nign (bi nin') *adj.* [< L *benignus*, well-born] 1 good-natured; kindly 2 favorable; beneficial 3 *Med.* not malignant —**be·nign'ly** *adv.*
be·nig·nant (bi nig'nənt) *adj.* [< prec.] 1 kindly or gracious 2 BENIGN (senses 2 & 3)
be·nig·nity (-nə tē) *n., pl.* -ties 1 kindliness 2 a kind act
bent¹ (bent) *vt., vi. pt. & pp. of* BEND¹ — *adj.* 1 curved or crooked 2 strongly determined: with *on* 3 [Slang] *a)* dishonest *b)* eccentric; odd — *n.* 1 a tendency 2 a natural leaning; propensity
bent² (bent) *n.* [OE *beonot*] a dense, low-growing bent that spreads by runners, used for lawns
bent'wood' *adj.* of furniture made of wood permanently bent
be·numb (bē num', bi-) *vt.* 1 to make numb 2 to deaden the mind, will, etc. of
ben·zene (ben'zēn, ben zēn') *n.* [< Ar *lubān jāwi*, incense of Java] a clear, flammable, poisonous liquid used as a solvent, in plastics, etc.
ben·zo·caine (ben'zō kān', -zə-) *n.* [BENZ(ENE) + (C)OCAINE] a white, odorless powder used in ointments as a local anesthetic and to protect against sunburn
be·queath (bē kwēth', -kwēth'; bi-) *vt.* [< OE *be-*, BE- + *cwethan*, say] 1 to leave (property) to another by one's will 2 to hand down; pass on
be·quest (-kwest') *n.* 1 a bequeathing 2 anything bequeathed
be·rate (bē rāt', bi-) *vt.* -rat'ed, -rat'ing [BE- + RATE²] to scold severely
Ber·ber (bur'bər) *n.* 1 a member of a people of N Africa 2 their language — *adj.* of the Berbers
be·reave (bē rēv', bi-) *vt.* -reaved' or -reft' (-reft'), -reav'ing [< OE *be-*, BE- + *reafian*, rob] 1 to deprive: now usually in the pp. *bereft [bereft* of hope] 2 to leave in a sad or lonely state, as by death —**be·reave'ment** *n.*

■■■■■■ THESAURUS ■■■■■■

belongings *n.* possessions, goods, things*; see PROPERTY 1.
beloved *a.* loved, adored, worshiped, cherished, dear, favorite, idolized, precious, prized, dearest, yearned for, revered, treasured, favored, doted on, nearest to someone's heart, dearly beloved, after someone's own heart, darling, admired, popular, well-liked, cared for, respected, pleasing.—*Ant.* HATED, abhorred, disliked.
beloved *n.* fiancé, sweetheart, object of someone's affection; see LOVER 1.
below *a., prep.* 1 [Lower in position] beneath, underneath, down from; see UNDER 1. 2 [Lower in rank or importance] inferior, subject, under; see SUBORDINATE. 3 [Farther along in written material] later, on a following page, in a statement to be made, hereafter, subsequently.—*Ant.* ABOVE, earlier, on a former page. 4 [On earth] existing, in this world, here below, under the sun, on the face of the earth, in this our life, here. 5 [In hell] in the underworld, damned, condemned; see DAMNED 1.

belt *n.* girdle, ribbon, string; see BAND 1. —**below the belt** unjust, foul, unsporting; see UNFAIR. —**tighten one's belt** endure hunger, suffer, bear misfortune; see ENDURE 2. — **under one's belt** past, finished, completed; see DONE 1.
bench *n.* 1 [A long seat] pew, seat, stall; see CHAIR 1. 2 [A long table] workbench, desk, counter; see TABLE 1.
bend¹ *n.* crook, bow, arch; see CURVE.
bend¹ *v.* twist, contort, deform, round, crimp, flex, spiral, coil, crinkle, detour, curl, buckle, crook, bow, incline, deflect, double, loop, twine, curve, arch, wind, stoop, lean, waver, zigzag, reel, crumple, meander, circle, swerve, diverge, droop.—*Ant.* STRAIGHTEN, extend, stretch.
bending *a.* twisting, veering, curving, buckling, twining, spiraling, looping, doubling, drooping, leaning, inclining, bowing, arching, curling, winding, stooping, crumpling, waving, wavering.

beneath *a., prep.* 1 [Under] below, underneath, in a lower place; see UNDER 1. 2 [Lower in rank or importance] subject to, inferior to, under; see SUBORDINATE.
benefactor *n.* helper, protector, angel*; see PATRON.
beneficiary *n.* recipient, receiver, inheritor; see HEIR.
benefit *n.* gain, profit, good; see ADVANTAGE.
benefit *v.* serve, profit, avail; see HELP.
bent¹ *a.* curved, warped, hooked, beaked, looped, sinuous, twined, crooked, bowed, contorted, stooped, doubled over, limp, wilted, drooping, humped, slumped, hunched, humpbacked, bowlegged, inclined; see also TWISTED 1.—*Ant.* STRAIGHT, rigid, erect.
bent¹ *n.* leaning, tendency, propensity; see INCLINATION 1.
bequeath *v.* grant, hand down, pass on; see GIVE 1.

be·ret (bə rā′) *n.* ⟦< Fr < L *birrus*, a hood⟧ a flat, round, soft cap

berg (burg) *n.* ICEBERG

beri·beri (ber′ē ber′ē) *n.* ⟦Sinhalese, intens. of *beri*, weakness⟧ a disease caused by lack of vitamin B₁ and characterized by nerve disorders, etc.

berm (burm) *n.* ⟦< MDu *baerm*⟧ a ledge or shoulder, as along the edge of a paved road

Bermuda shorts (bər myōō′də) knee-length pants Also **ber·mu′das** *n.pl.*

berry (ber′ē) *n., pl.* **-ries** ⟦OE *berie*⟧ 1 any small, juicy, fleshy fruit, as a strawberry 2 the dry seed of various plants, as a coffee bean — *vi.* **-ried, -ry·ing** 1 to bear berries 2 to pick berries —**ber′ry·like′** *adj.*

ber·serk (bər surk′, -zurk′) *adj., adv.* ⟦ON *berserkr*, warrior⟧ in or into a violent rage or frenzy

berth (burth) *n.* ⟦< BEAR¹ + -TH¹⟧ 1 a place where a ship anchors or moors 2 a position, job, etc. 3 a built-in bed, as on a ship or train — *vt.* to put into or furnish with a berth — *vi.* to occupy a berth —**give (a) wide berth to** to keep well clear of

beryl (ber′əl) *n.* ⟦< Gr *bēryllos*⟧ a very hard mineral of which emerald and aquamarine are two varieties

be·ryl·lium (bə ril′ē əm) *n.* ⟦< L *beryllus*, beryl⟧ a hard, rare, metallic chemical element used in forming alloys

be·seech (bē sēch′, bi-) *vt.* **-sought′** or **-seeched′, -seech′ing** ⟦< OE *be-* + *secan*, seek⟧ to ask (for) earnestly; entreat —**be·seech′ing·ly** *adv.*

be·seem (bē sēm′, bi-) *vi.* [Archaic] to be suitable or appropriate (to)

be·set (bē set′, bi-) *vt.* **-set′, -set′ting** ⟦< OE *be-* + *settan*, set⟧ 1 to attack from all sides; harass 2 to surround or hem in

be·set′ting *adj.* constantly harassing

be·side (bē sīd′, bi-) *prep.* ⟦OE *bi sidan*⟧ 1 at the side of; near 2 in comparison with [*beside* yours my share seems small] 3 in addition to 4 other than —**beside oneself** wild or upset, as with fear, rage, etc.

be·sides′ (-sīdz′) *adv.* 1 in addition 2 except for that mentioned 3 moreover — *prep.* 1 in addition to 2 other than

be·siege (bē sēj′, bi-) *vt.* **-sieged′, -sieg′ing** 1 to hem in with armed forces 2 to close in on 3 to overwhelm, harass, etc. [*besieged* with queries]

be·smear (bē smir′, bi-) *vt.* ⟦OE *bismerian*⟧ to smear over

be·smirch (bē smurch′, bi-) *vt.* to soil

be·som (bē′zəm) *n.* ⟦OE *besma*⟧ a broom, esp. one made of twigs tied to a handle

be·sot (bē sät′, bi-) *vt.* **-sot′ted, -sot′ting** to make a sot of; stupefy, as with liquor —**be·sot′ted** *adj.*

be·sought (bē sôt′, bi-) *vt. alt. pt. & alt. pp. of* BESEECH

be·span·gle (bē span′gəl, bi-) *vt.* **-gled, -gling** to cover with or as with spangles

be·spat·ter (bē spat′ər, bi-) *vt.* to spatter, as with mud or slander

be·speak (bē spēk′, bi-) *vt.* **-spoke′, -spo′ken** or **-spoke′, -speak′ing** 1 to speak for in advance; reserve 2 to be indicative of; show

best (best) *adj.* ⟦OE *betst*⟧ 1 *superl. of* GOOD 2 most excellent 3 most suitable, desirable, etc. 4 largest [the *best* part of a day] — *adv.* 1 *superl. of* WELL² 2 in the most excellent manner 3 in the highest degree — *n.* 1 the most excellent person, thing, etc. 2 the utmost — *vt.* to defeat or outdo —**all for the best** turning out to be good —**at best** under the most favorable conditions —**get** (or **have) the best of** 1 to defeat 2 to outwit —**make the best of** to do as well as one can with

bes·tial (bes′chəl, -tyəl; *often* bēs′-) *adj.* ⟦< L *bestia*, beast⟧ like a beast; savage; brutal, etc. —**bes·ti·al·ity** (bes′ chē al′ə tē, -tē-; *often* bēs′-), *pl.* **-ties,** *n.*

bes·tial·ize (bes′chəl īz′, -tyəl-; *often* bēs′-) *vt.* **-ized′, -iz′ing** to make bestial

bes·ti·ary (bes′tē er′ē) *n., pl.* **-ies** ⟦< L *bestia*, beast⟧ a medieval book with fables about real or mythical animals

be·stir (bē stur′, bi-) *vt.* **-stirred′, -stir′ring** to stir to action; busy (oneself)

best man the principal attendant of the bridegroom at a wedding

be·stow (bē stō′, bi-) *vt.* ⟦see BE- & STOW⟧ to present as a gift: with *on* or *upon* —**be·stow′al** *n.*

be·strew (bē strōō′, bi-) *vt.* **-strewed′, -strewed′** or **-strewn′, -strew′ing** to strew or scatter about

be·stride (bē strīd′, bi-) *vt.* **-strode′, -strid′den, -strid′ing** to sit on, mount, or stand astride

bet (bet) *n.* ⟦prob. < ABET⟧ 1 an agreement in which the one proved wrong about the outcome of something will do or pay what is stipulated 2 the thing or sum thus staked 3 a person or thing likely to bring about a desired result — *vt., vi.* **bet** or **bet′ted, bet′ting** 1 to declare as in a bet 2 to stake (money, etc.) in a bet with someone

beta (bāt′ə) *n.* the second letter of the Greek alphabet (Β, β)

beta blocker a drug used to control heartbeat, treat hypertension, etc.

beta caro·tene (kar′ə tēn′) a hydrocarbon found in certain foods, as butter and carrots, and converted by the liver into vitamin A

be·take (bē tāk′, bi-) *vt.* **-took′, -tak′en, -tak′ing** ⟦ME *bitaken*⟧ to go (used reflexively)

beta particle an electron or positron ejected from the nucleus of an atom during radioactive disintegration

beta ray a stream of beta particles

beta wave an electrical brain wave indicating mental activity and alertness Also **beta rhythm**

betel nut (bēt′l) ⟦Port < Malayalam *veṭṭilai*⟧ the fruit of a palm (**betel palm**), chewed together with a lime and leaves of a pepper plant (**betel pepper**) by some Asians as a mild stimulant

be·think (bē thiŋk′, bi-) *vt.* **-thought′, -think′ing** [Archaic] to bring (oneself) to think of, recollect, etc.

be·tide (bē tīd′, bi-) *vi., vt.* **-tid′ed, -tid′ing** ⟦< ME *be-*, BE- + *tiden*, happen⟧ to happen (to); befall

be·times (bē tīmz′, bi-) *adv.* [Archaic] 1 early or early enough 2 promptly

be·to·ken (bē tō′kən, bi-) *vt.* ⟦ME *betocnen*⟧ 1 to be a token or sign of 2 to presage

be·tray (bē trā′, bi-) *vt.* ⟦< L *tradere*, hand over⟧ 1 to help the enemy of (one's country, etc.) 2 to expose treacherously 3 to fail to uphold [to *betray* a trust] 4 to deceive;

THESAURUS

berry *n. Common berries include the following:* raspberry, blackberry, blueberry, loganberry, boysenberry, cranberry, huckleberry, gooseberry, currant, strawberry, mulberry.

berth *n.* place, situation, employment; see JOB 1, PROFESSION 1. — **give a wide berth** keep clear of, evade, stay away from; see AVOID.

beside *a., prep.* at the side of, at the edge of, adjacent to, next to, adjoining, alongside, near, close at hand, by, with, abreast, side by side, bordering on, neighboring, overlooking, next door to, to one side, nearby, connected with.

besides *a.* in addition to, additionally, moreover, over and above, added to, likewise, further, furthermore, beyond, exceeding, secondly, more than, apart from, extra, in excess of, plus, also, in other respects, exclusive of, with the exception of, as well as, not counting, other than, too, to boot, on top of that, aside from, else.

best *a.* 1 [Generally excellent] first, greatest, finest, highest, transcendent, prime, premium, supreme, incomparable, crowning, paramount, matchless, unrivaled, unparalleled, second to none, unequaled, inimitable, beyond compare, superlative, foremost, peerless, boss*, tough*, cool*, first-rate; see also EXCELLENT.—*Ant.* WORST, poorest, lowest. 2 [Applied especially to actions and persons] noblest, sincerest, most praiseworthy; see NOBLE.

best *n.* first, favorite, choice, finest, top, pick, prime, flower, cream, cream of the crop*. —**all for the best** favorable, fortunate, advantageous; see HELPFUL 1, HOPEFUL 2. — **as best one can** skillfully, ably, capably; see ABLE. —**at best** good, highest, most favorable; see BEST. — **at one's best** well, in one's prime, capable; see ABLE, STRONG 1. —**get** (or **have) the best of** outdo, surpass, defeat; see EXCEED. —**make the best of** suffer, tolerate, get by; see

ENDURE 2. —**with the best** excellently, well, ably; see ABLE.

best *v.* worst, get the better of, overcome; see DEFEAT 3.

bestow *v.* bequeath, present, offer; see GIVE 1.

bet *n.* gamble, wager, venture, pot, hazard, tossup, stake, speculation, betting, raffle, uncertainty, chance, lottery, game of chance, sweepstakes, risk, ante, long shot*, shot in the dark*.

bet *v.* wager, gamble, stake, bet on, bet against, venture, hazard, trust, play against, speculate, play for, put money down, put money on, risk, chance, make a bet, take a chance, lay down*, buy in on*, lay odds, lay even money*. —**you bet** certainly, by all means, yes indeed; see SURELY, YES.

betray *v.* 1 [To deliver into the hands of an enemy] delude, trick, double-cross; see DECEIVE. 2 [To reveal] divulge, disclose, make specif., to seduce and then desert **5** to reveal unknowingly —be·tray′al *n.* —be·tray′er *n.*

be·troth (bē trôth′, -trŏth′; bi-) *vt.* ⟦< ME: see BE- & TRUTH⟧ to promise in marriage —be·troth′al *n.*

be·trothed′ (-trôtht′, -trŏthd′) *adj.* engaged to be married — *n.* one engaged to be married

betta (bet′ə) *n.* ⟦ModL⟧ a brightly colored, tropical, freshwater gourami of SE Asia

bet·ter (bet′ər) *adj.* ⟦OE betera⟧ **1** *compar. of* GOOD **2** more excellent **3** more suitable, desirable, etc. **4** larger *[the better part of a day]* **5** improved in health — *adv.* **1** *compar. of* WELL² **2** in a more excellent manner **3** in a higher degree **4** more — *n.* **1** a person superior in authority, etc. **2** a more excellent thing, condition, etc. — *vt.* **1** to outdo; surpass **2** to improve —**better off** in a better situation —**get** (or **have**) **the better of 1** to outdo **2** to outwit

bet′ter·ment *n.* a bettering; improvement

bet′tor *n.* one who bets Also **bet′ter**

be·tween (bē twēn′, bi-) *prep.* ⟦OE betweonum⟧ **1** in the space, time, etc. that separates (two things) **2** connecting *[a bond between friends]* **3** by the joint action of **4** in the combined possession of **5** from one or the other of *[choose between us]* **6** involving *[a struggle between powers]* — *adv.* in an intermediate space, time, etc. — **between ourselves** as a secret: also **between you and me**

be·twixt (bē twikst′, bi-) *prep., adv.* ⟦< OE be, by + twegen, twain⟧ between: archaic except in **betwixt and between,** in an intermediate position

BeV or **Bev** (bev) *n., pl.* **BeV** or **Bev** ⟦b(illion) e(lectron-)v(olts)⟧ a unit of energy in the U.S., equal to one billion (10^9) electron-volts

bevel (bev′əl) *n.* ⟦< ?⟧ **1** a tool for measuring or marking angles, etc. **2** an angle other than a right angle **3** angled part or surface — *adj.* beveled — *vt.* **-eled** or **-elled, -el′ing** or **-el′ling** to cut to an angle other than a right angle — *vi.* to slope at an angle

bevel gear a gearwheel meshed with another at an angle

bev·er·age (bev′ər ij′) *n.* ⟦< L bibere, to drink⟧ any liquid for drinking, esp. one other than water

bevy (bev′ē) *n., pl.* **-ies** ⟦ME bevey⟧ **1** a group, esp. of girls or women **2** a flock: now chiefly of quail

be·wail (bē wāl′) *vt.* to wail over; lament; mourn

be·ware (bē wer′) *vi., vt.* **-wared′, -war′ing** ⟦prob. < OE bewarian, keep watch⟧ to be wary or careful (of)

be·wigged (bē wigd′) *adj.* wearing a wig

be·wil·der (bē wil′dər) *vt.* ⟦ult. < OE wilde, wild⟧ to confuse hopelessly; befuddle —be·wil′der·ment *n.*

be·witch (bē wich′) *vt.* ⟦< OE wicca, sorcerer⟧ **1** to cast a spell over **2** to attract and delight greatly

be·yond (bē änd′) *prep.* ⟦< OE be, by + geond, yonder⟧ **1** farther on than; past **2** later than **3** outside the reach of *[beyond help]* **4** more than — *adv.* farther away —**the** (**great**) **beyond** whatever follows death

bezel (bez′əl) *n.* ⟦< ?⟧ **1** a sloping surface, as the cutting edge of a chisel **2** the slanting faces of a cut gem **3** the groove and flange holding a gem, watch crystal, etc. in place

Bi *Chem. symbol for* bismuth

bi- ⟦L⟧ *prefix* **1** having two **2** doubly **3** happening every two (specified periods) **4** happening twice during every

(specified period) **5** using two or both **6** joining or involving two

bi·an·nual (bī an′yoo əl) *adj.* coming twice a year; semiannual

bias (bī′əs) *n., pl.* **-ases** ⟦Fr biais, a slant⟧ **1** a slanting or diagonal line, cut or sewn in cloth **2** partiality; prejudice — *adj.* slanting; diagonal — *adv.* diagonally — *vt.* **-ased** or **-assed, -as′ing** or **-as′sing** to prejudice —**on the bias** diagonally

bi·ath·lon (bī ath′lən) *n.* ⟦BI- + Gr athlon, contest⟧ a winter sports event combining cross-country skiing and rifle marksmanship

bib (bib) *n.* ⟦< L bibere, to drink⟧ **1** a cloth or plastic cover tied around a child's chin at meals **2** the upper front part of an apron

Bib. 1 Bible **2** Biblical

bibb lettuce (bib) ⟦after J. Bibb (1789-1884), who developed it⟧ a type of lettuce with loose heads of crisp, darkgreen leaves

Bi·ble (bī′b'l) ⟦< Gr biblos, papyrus < Byblos, Phoenician city that exported papyrus⟧ **1** the sacred book of Christianity; Old Testament and New Testament **2** the Holy Scriptures of Judaism; Old Testament — *n.* [b-] any book regarded as authoritative or official —**bib·li·cal** or **Bib·li·cal** (bib′li kəl) *adj.*

biblio- ⟦< Gr biblion, book⟧ *combining form* book, books *[bibliophile]*

bib·li·og·ra·phy (bib′lē äg′rə fē) *n., pl.* **-phies** a list of writings on a given subject or by a given author, or of those used by the author of a given work —**bib′li·og′ra·pher** *n.* —**bib′lio·graph′ic** (-ə graf′ik) *adj.*

bib′lio·phile′ (-ə fīl′) *n.* a person who loves or collects books

bib·u·lous (bib′yoo ləs) *adj.* ⟦< L bibere, to drink⟧ addicted to or fond of alcoholic beverages

bi·cam·eral (bī kam′ər əl) *adj.* ⟦< BI- + L camera, chamber⟧ having two legislative chambers

bicarbonate of soda (bī kär′bən it) SODIUM BICARBONATE

bi·cen·ten·nial (bī′sen ten′ē əl) *adj.* happening once in every 200 years — *n.* a 200th anniversary

bi·ceps (bī′seps′) *n., pl.* **-ceps** or **-cepses′** ⟦< L < bis, two + caput, head⟧ a muscle with two points of origin; esp., the large muscle in the front of the upper arm

bicker (bik′ər) *vi., n.* ⟦ME bikeren⟧ squabble; quarrel — **bick′erer** *n.*

bi·con·cave (bī kän′kāv′) *adj.* concave on both surfaces *[a biconcave lens]*

bi·con′vex′ (-veks′) *adj.* convex on both surfaces *[a biconvex lens]*

bi·cus·pid (bī kus′pid) *adj.* ⟦< BI- + L cuspis, pointed end⟧ having two points — *n.* any of eight adult teeth with two-pointed crowns

bi·cy·cle (bī′sik′əl) *n.* ⟦Fr: see BI- & CYCLE⟧ a vehicle consisting of a metal frame on two wheels, with handlebars and a seat — *vi.* **-cled, -cling** to ride or travel on a bicycle — *vt.* **1** to carry as on a bicycle **2** to travel over by bicycle —bi′cy′clist *n.*

bid (bid) *vt.* **bade** or **bid, bid′den** or **bid, bid′ding** ⟦< OE biddan, to urge & beodan, to command⟧ **1** to command or

---

THESAURUS

known; see REVEAL.

betrayal *n.* treason, treachery, disloyalty; see DECEPTION, DISHONESTY.

betrayer *n.* renegade, deceiver, conspirator; see TRAITOR.

better *a.* **1** [Superior] greater, finer, preferred, bigger, stronger, higher; see also BEST. **2** [Recovering health] convalescent, improved in health, improving, on the road to recovery, on the mend.—*Ant.* SICK, failing, wasting away. —**for the better** favorable, fortunate, helpful; see HOPEFUL 2. —**get** (or **have**) **the better of** outdo, overcome, defeat; see EXCEED.

better *v.* ameliorate, revamp, refine; see IMPROVE 1.

between *prep.* separating, within, bounded by, amidst, amid, among, in, in between, mid, intervening, in the midst of, in the middle, centrally located, surrounded by, midway, halfway, in the thick; see also AMONG. —**between you and me** confiden-

tially, privately, personally; see SECRETLY.

beverage *n.* liquor, refreshment, draft; see DRINK 2.

bewilder *v.* confound, disconcert, puzzle; see CONFUSE.

bewildered *a.* confused, amazed, misguided, lost, astonished, thunderstruck, shocked, muddled, upset, dazed, giddy, dizzy, reeling, puzzled, misled, uncertain, surprised, baffled, disconcerted, appalled, aghast, adrift, at sea, off the track, awed, stupefied, astounded, struck speechless, breathless, befuddled, startled, struck dumb, dumbfounded, dazzled, stunned, electrified, confounded, staggered, petrified, awe-struck, flabbergasted, flustered, all balled up*, rattled, up in the air*, stumped*, goofy*.

beyond *a., prep.* on the other side, on the far side, over there, in advance of, away, out of range, a long way off, yonder, past, free of, clear of, farther

off, ahead, behind, more remote.—*Ant.* HERE, on this side, nearer.

bias *n.* bent, preference, leaning; see INCLINATION 1.

bias *v.* influence, prejudice, sway; see INFLUENCE.

Bible *n.* the Good Book, God's word, the Word, the Scriptures, the Canon, the Testaments, Sacred History, the Writings of the Apostles and Prophets, Holy Writ, the Holy Bible, the Word of God, Testament.

bibliography *n.* catalog, compilation, list of books; see LIST.

bicker *v.* wrangle, squabble, dispute; see QUARREL.

bicycle *n.* cycle, bike*, two-wheeler*; see VEHICLE.

bid *n.* proposal, proposition, declaration; see SUGGESTION 1.

bid *v.* **1** [To propose a price for purchase] venture, bid for, submit a bid; see OFFER 1. **2** [To order] tell, charge, direct; see COMMAND 1.

ask **2** to offer (an amount) as the price one will pay or accept **3** to express [to bid farewell] **4** Card Games to state (a number of tricks) and declare (trump) — *vi.* to make a bid — *n.* **1** a bidding **2** an amount bid **3** a chance to bid **4** an attempt or try (*for*) **5** [Colloq.] an invitation —**bid fair** to seem likely —**bid′der** *n.*

biddy (bid′ē) *n., pl.* **-dies** [< ?] **1** a hen **2** [Colloq.] an elderly woman regarded as annoying, gossipy, etc.: usually **old biddy**

bide (bīd) *vi.* **bode** or **bid′ed, bid′ed, bid′ing** [OE *bidan*] [Now Chiefly Dial.] **1** to stay; continue **2** to dwell **3** to wait — *vt.* [Now Chiefly Dial.] to endure —**bide one's time** to wait patiently for an opportunity [she *bided* her time]

bi·det (bē dā′) *n.* [Fr] a low, bowl-shaped bathroom fixture, with running water, for bathing the crotch

bi·en·nial (bī en′ē əl) *adj.* [< L *bi-,* BI- + *annus,* year] **1** happening every two years **2** lasting for two years — *n.* **1** a biennial event **2** Bot. a plant that lasts two years —**bi·en′ni·al·ly** *adv.*

bier (bir) *n.* [OE *bær*] a portable framework on which a coffin is placed

bi·fo·cals (bī′fō′kəlz) *n.pl.* eyeglasses with lenses having one part ground for close focus and the other for distant focus

bi·fur·cate (bī′fər kāt′) *vt., vi.* **-cat′ed, -cat′ing** [< L *bi-,* BI- + *furca,* a fork] to divide into two parts or branches —**bi′fur·ca′tion** *n.*

big (big) *adj.* **big′ger, big′gest** [ME] **1** of great size; large **2** great in amount or force **3** full-grown **4** elder [his *big* sister] **5** noticeably pregnant (*with*) **6** loud **7** important **8** extravagant **9** noble [a *big* heart] — *adv.* [Colloq.] **1** boastfully **2** impressively —**big′ness** *n.*

biga·my (big′ə mē) *n.* [< L *bi-,* BI- + Gr *gamos,* marriage] the crime of marrying a second time when one is already legally married —**big′a·mist** *n.* —**big′a·mous** *adj.*

big′-bang′ theory a theory that the expansion of the universe began with a gigantic explosion between 12 and 20 billion years ago

big game 1 large wild animals hunted for sport, as lions, tigers, moose, etc. **2** the object of any important or dangerous undertaking

big′heart′ed (-här′tid) *adj.* quick to give or forgive; generous

big′horn′ *n.* a Rocky Mountain wild sheep with large horns

bight (bīt) *n.* [OE *byht*] **1** orig., a bend or angle **2** a slack part in a rope **3** a curve in a coastline **4** a bay

big′mouth′ *n.* [Slang] a person who talks too much, esp. in an opinionated way

bigot (big′ət) *n.* [Fr < ?] one who holds blindly and intolerantly to a particular creed, opinion, etc. —**big′oted** *adj.* —**big′otry** (-ə trē) *n.*

big shot [Slang] an important or influential person Also **big wheel**

bike (bīk) *n.* [Colloq.] **1** a bicycle **2** a motorcycle —**bik′er** *n.*

bi·kini (bi kē′nē) *n.* [Fr after *Bikini,* Pacific atoll] **1** a very brief two-piece swimsuit for women **2** very brief legless underpants or swimming trunks

bi·lat·eral (bī lat′ər əl) *adj.* **1** of, having, or involving two sides, factions, etc. **2** affecting both sides equally; reciprocal —**bi·lat′er·al·ly** *adv.*

bile (bīl) *n.* [Fr < L *bilis*] **1** the bitter, greenish fluid secreted by the liver: it aids digestion **2** bad temper; anger

bilge (bilj) *n.* [var. of BULGE] **1** the rounded, lower part of

a ship's hold **2** stagnant water that collects there: also **bilge water 3** [Slang] nonsense

bi·lin·gual (bī liŋ′gwəl) *adj.* [< L *bi-,* BI- + *lingua,* tongue] of, in, or using two languages —**bi·lin′gual·ism′** *n.*

bil·ious (bil′yəs) *adj.* [< L *bilis,* bile] **1** having or appearing to have some ailment of the bile or liver **2** bad-tempered

bilk (bilk) *vt.* [? < BALK] to cheat or swindle; defraud —**bilk′er** *n.*

bill¹ (bil) *n.* [< L *bulla,* sealed document] **1** a statement of charges for goods or services; invoice **2** a list, as a menu or theater program **3** a poster or handbill **4** a draft of a proposed law **5** a bill of exchange **6** a piece of paper money **7** Law a written declaration of charges or complaints filed — *vt.* **1** to make out a bill of (items) **2** to present a statement of charges to **3** *a*) to advertise by bills *b*) to book (a performer) —**fill the bill** [Colloq.] to meet the requirements —**bill′able** *adj.*

bill² (bil) *n.* [OE *bile*] **1** the projecting jaws of a bird, usually pointed; beak **2** a beaklike mouth part, as of a turtle — *vi.* to touch bills together —**bill and coo** to kiss, talk softly, etc. in a loving way

bill′board′ *n.* a signboard, usually outdoors, for advertising posters

bil·let (bil′it) *n.* [see BILL¹] **1** *a*) a written order to provide lodging for military personnel *b*) the lodging **2** a position, job, or situation — *vt.* to assign to lodging by billet

billet-doux (bil′ā dōō′) *n., pl.* **billets-doux** (bē′yā dōō′) [Fr, sweet letter] a love letter

bill·fold (bil′fōld′) *n.* a wallet

bil·liard (bil′yərd) *adj.* of or for billiards

bil′liards (-yərdz) *n.* [< Fr *billard,* orig. a cue] a game played with hard balls moved by a cue on a table with raised, cushioned edges

bill·ing (bil′iŋ) *n.* **1** the listing of actors' names on a theater marquee, etc. **2** the order in which the names are listed

bil·lings·gate (bil′iŋz gāt′) *n.* [< a London fish market] foul, vulgar, abusive talk

bil·lion (bil′yən) *n.* [Fr < *bi-,* BI- + (*mi*)*llion*] **1** a thousand millions (1,000,000,000) **2** *old Brit. term for* TRILLION (a million millions) —**bil′lionth** *adj., n.*

bil′lion·aire′ (-yə ner′) *n.* a person whose wealth comes to at least a billion dollars, pounds, francs, etc.

bill of exchange a written order to pay a certain sum of money to the person named

bill of fare a menu

bill of lading a receipt issued to a shipper by a carrier, describing the goods to be shipped

Bill of Rights the first ten amendments to the U.S. Constitution, which guarantee civil liberties

bill of sale a written statement transferring ownership of something by sale

bil·low (bil′ō) *n.* [ON *bylgja*] **1** a large wave **2** any large swelling mass or surge, as of smoke — *vi.* to surge or swell in a billow —**bil′lowy** *adj.*

billy (bil′ē) *n., pl.* **-lies** [ult. < OFr *bille,* tree trunk] a club, esp. a policeman's heavy stick

billy goat a male goat

bi·metal·lic (bī′mə tal′ik) *adj.* [< Fr *bi-,* BI- + *métallique,* metallic] **1** of, containing, or using two metals **2** of or based on bimetallism

bi·metal·lism (bī met′'l iz′əm) *n.* the use of two metals, esp. gold and silver, as the monetary standard, with fixed values in relation to each other

bi·monthly (bī munth′lē) *adj., adv.* **1** once every two months **2** [Now Rare] twice a month

---

THESAURUS

big *a.* **1** [Of great size] huge, great, swollen, fat, obese, bloated, overgrown, gross, mammoth, wide, grand, vast, immense, considerable, substantial, massive, extensive, spacious, colossal, gigantic, titanic, monstrous, towering, mighty, magnificent, enormous, giant, tremendous, whopping*.—*Ant.* LITTLE, tiny, small. **2** [Grown, or partially grown] grown-up, full-grown, adult; see MATURE. **3** [Important] prominent, significant, influential; see IMPORTANT 1, 2. **4** [Pompous] presumptuous, pretentious, imperious; see EGOTISTIC. **5** [Generous] magnanimous, liberal, unselfish; see GENER-

OUS, KIND.

bigot *n.* dogmatist, fanatic, opinionated person, partisan, enthusiast, extremist, diehard, crank*, redneck*; see also RADICAL.

bigoted *a.* biased, dogmatic, opinionated; see PREJUDICED.

bigotry *n.* intolerance, narrowmindedness, injustice; see FANATICISM, PREJUDICE.

big shot* *n.* big wheel*, bigwig*, big man on campus; see EXECUTIVE.

bill¹ *v.* dun, solicit, render account of indebtedness, draw upon.

bill¹,² *n.* **1** [A statement of account] itemized account, statement of

indebtedness, request for payment; see STATEMENT 2. **2** [A piece of paper money] Federal Reserve note, bank note, greenback; see MONEY 1. **3** [A statement prepared for enactment into law] measure, proposal, piece of legislation; see LAW 3. **4** [A beak] nib, mandible, projection; see BEAK. — **fill the bill** meet requirements, be satisfactory, serve the purpose; see SATISFY 3.

billboard *n.* bulletin board, display panel, poster board; see ADVERTISEMENT, ANNOUNCEMENT.

billfold *n.* card case, pocketbook, purse; see WALLET.

bin (bin) *n.* ⟦OE, crib⟧ a box, crib, etc. for storing grain, coal, etc.

bi·nary (bī'nə rē) *adj.* ⟦< L *bis*, double⟧ **1** made up of two parts; double **2** designating or of a number system in which the base used is two, each number being expressed by using only two digits, specif. 0 and 1 — *n., pl.* **-ries** a set of two

bi·na·tional (bī nash'ə nəl) *adj.* involving two nations or two nationalities

bind (bīnd) *vt.* **bound, bind'ing** ⟦< OE *bindan*⟧ **1** to tie together, as with rope **2** to hold or restrain **3** to encircle with a belt, etc. **4** to bandage: often with *up* **5** to constipate **6** to reinforce or ornament the edges of by a band, as of tape **7** to fasten together the pages of (a book) and protect with a cover **8** to obligate by duty, love, etc. **9** to compel, as by oath, legal restraint, or contract — *vi.* **1** to do the act of binding **2** to be or become tight or stiff **3** to stick together **4** to be obligatory or binding in force — *n.* **1** anything that binds **2** [Colloq.] a difficult or restrictive situation — **bound** *adj.* — **bind'ing** *adj.*

bind'er *n.* **1** one that binds **2** a substance that binds, as tar **3** a cover for holding sheets of paper together

bind'er·y *n., pl.* **-er·ies** a place where books are bound

bind'ing *n.* a thing that binds, as a band, a tape, the covers and backing of a book, a cohesive substance, etc. — *adj.* that binds, obligates, etc.

binge (binj) *n.* [Colloq.] a spree — *vi.* **binged, binge'ing** [Colloq.] to indulge without restraint: with *on*

bingo (biŋ'gō) *n.* a gambling game resembling lotto

bin·na·cle (bin'ə kəl) *n.* ⟦ult. < L *habitaculum*, dwelling place⟧ the case holding a ship's compass

binocu·lar (bī näk'yə lər) *adj.* ⟦< L *bini*, double + *oculus*, eye⟧ using, or for, both eyes — *n.* [*usually pl.*] a binocular instrument, as field glasses

bi·no·mial (bī nō'mē əl) *n.* ⟦< L *bi-*, BI- + Gr *nomos*, law⟧ **1** *Math.* an expression consisting of two terms connected by a plus or minus sign **2** a two-word scientific name of a plant or animal, indicating the genus and species

bio- ⟦Gr < *bios*, life⟧ *combining form* life, of living things

bi·o·chem'is·try *n.* the study of the chemistry of life processes in plants and animals — **bi·o·chem'ist** *n.*

bi·o·degrad'a·ble (-di grā'də bəl) *adj.* ⟦BIO- + *degrad(e)*, decompose + -ABLE⟧ capable of being readily decomposed by the action of microbes

bi·o·di·ver'si·ty *n.* variety in the living things of a particular area

bi·o·feed'back *n.* a technique of seeking to control certain emotional states by training oneself, using electronic devices, to modify autonomic body functions, such as heartbeat

biog. **1** biographical **2** biography

bi·og'ra·phy (bī äg'rə fē) *n., pl.* **-phies** ⟦< Gr: see BIO- & -GRAPHY⟧ an account of a person's life written by another — **bi·og'ra·pher** *n.* — **bi·o·graph'i·cal** (bī'ə grafi kəl) *adj.*

biol. **1** biological **2** biology

biological warfare the use of toxic microorganisms, etc. in war

bi·ology (bī äl'ə jē) *n.* ⟦see BIO- & -LOGY⟧ the science that deals with the origin, history, characteristics, habits, etc. of plants and animals — **bi·o·log'i·cal** (bī'ə läj'i kəl) *adj.* — **bi·o·log'i·cally** *adv.* — **bi·ol'o·gist** *n.*

bi·onic (bī än'ik) *adj.* ⟦see fol.⟧ **1** of bionics **2** having an artificial bodily part or parts, as in science fiction, so as to enhance strength, abilities, etc.

bi·on'ics (-än'iks) *n.pl.* ⟦BI(O)- + (ELECTR)ONICS⟧ [with sing. *v.*] the science of designing instruments or systems modeled after living organisms

bio·phys·ics (bī'ō fiz'iks) *n.pl.* [with sing. *v.*] the study of biological phenomena in relation to physics — **bi'o·phys'i·cal** *adj.* — **bi'o·phys'i·cist** *n.*

bi·opsy (bī'äp'sē) *n., pl.* **-sies** ⟦< BI(O)- + Gr *opsis*, a sight⟧ *Med.* the removal of bits of living tissue for diagnosis

bio·rhythm (bī'ō rith'əm) *n.* any biological cycle that involves periodic changes in blood pressure, body temperature, etc.

bio·tin (bī'ə tin) *n.* ⟦< Gr *bios*, life⟧ a factor of the vitamin B group

bi·par·ti·san (bī pär'tə zən) *adj.* of, representing, or supported by two parties — **bi·par'ti·san·ship'** *n.*

bi·par·tite (bī pär'tīt') *adj.* ⟦< L *bi-*, BI- + *partire*, to divide⟧ **1** having two parts **2** involving two

bi·ped (bī'ped') *n.* ⟦< L *bi-*, BI- + *pes*, foot⟧ any two-footed animal

bi·plane (bī'plān') *n.* an airplane with two sets of wings, one above the other

bi·ra·cial (bī rā'shəl) *adj.* consisting of or involving two races

birch (bʉrch) *n.* ⟦OE *beorc*⟧ **1** a tree having smooth bark in thin layers, and hard, closegrained wood **2** its wood **3** a bunch of birch twigs used for whipping

bird (bʉrd) *n.* ⟦< OE *bridd*, young bird⟧ any of a class of warmblooded vertebrates with feathers and wings — *vi.* to observe wild birds in their habitat — **birds of a feather** people with the same traits or tastes — **for the birds** [Slang] ridiculous, worthless, etc.

birder (bʉrd'ər) *n.* one who engages in birding

birdie (bʉrd'ē) *n. Golf* a score of one stroke under par for a hole

bird·ing (bʉrd'iŋ) *n.* a hobby involving observation of wild birds in their habitat

bird's-eye (bʉrdz'ī') *adj.* having marks resembling birds' eyes [*bird's-eye* maple]

bird's-eye view **1** a view from high above **2** an overall, but cursory, view

bi·retta (bə ret'ə) *n.* ⟦< LL *birrettum*, small cloak⟧ a square ceremonial hat with three or four vertical projections, worn by Roman Catholic clergy

birth (bʉrth) *n.* ⟦< ON *byrth*⟧ **1** the act of bringing forth offspring **2** a being born **3** origin or descent **4** the beginning of anything **5** natural inclination [an actress by *birth*] — *vi., vt.* to give birth (to) — **give birth to 1** to bring forth (offspring) **2** to create

birth'day' *n.* the anniversary of the day of a person's birth — **in one's birthday suit** [Colloq.] naked

birth'mark' *n.* a skin blemish or mark present at birth

birth'place' *n.* the place of one's birth or of a thing's origin

birth'rate' *n.* the number of births per year per thousand people in a given area, group, etc. Also **birth rate**

birth'right' *n.* any right that a person has by birth

birth'stone' *n.* a gem symbolizing the month of a person's birth

bis·cuit (bis'kit) *n., pl.* **-cuits** or **-cuit** ⟦< L *bis*, twice + *coquere*, to cook⟧ **1** [Chiefly Brit.] a cracker or cookie **2** *a)* a quick bread baked in small pieces *b)* any of these pieces

---

THESAURUS

bin *n.* storeroom, granary, silo; see CONTAINER.

binary *a.* double, twofold, paired; see DOUBLE.

bind* *n.* dilemma, tight situation, quandary; see PREDICAMENT.

bind *v.* **1** [To constrain with bonds] truss up, tie up, shackle, fetter, cinch, clamp, chain, leash, constrict, manacle, enchain, lace, pin, restrict, hamper, handcuff, muzzle, hitch, secure, yoke, pin down, fix, strap, tether, bind up, lash down, clamp down on*, hogtie*. **2** [To hold together or in place] secure, attach, adhere; see FASTEN. **3** [To obligate] oblige, necessitate, compel; see FORCE. **4** [To dress] treat, dress, bandage; see HEAL. **5** [To join] unite, put together, connect; see JOIN 1.

binding *a.* obligatory, requisite, required; see NECESSARY.

binding *n.* **1** [The act of joining] merging, coupling, junction; see UNION 1. **2** [Anything used to bind] tie, adhesive, binder; see FASTENER. **3** [A cover] wrapper, jacket, book cover; see COVER 1.

biography *n.* life story, saga, memoir, journal, experiences, autobiography, life, adventures, life history, confessions, personal anecdote, profile, sketch, biographical account; see also RECORD 1, STORY.

biological *a.* organic, life, living, zoological, botanical, concerning life.

biology *n.* science of organisms, ecology, natural science, natural history, nature study, life science; see also SCIENCE 1.

bird *n. Common birds include the following:* sparrow, starling, robin, blue jay, hawk, meadowlark, owl, vulture, buzzard, turkey buzzard, woodpecker, cardinal, kingfisher, canary, chickadee, swallow, skylark, nightingale, nuthatch, whippoorwill, thrush, bluebird, cuckoo, bobolink, wren, gull, eagle, osprey, blackbird, dove, duck, goose, pheasant, chicken, parakeet, crane, heron, mockingbird, auk. — **eat like a bird** fast, starve, restrain one's appetite; see DIET. — **for the birds*** ridiculous, absurd, useless; see STUPID, WORTHLESS.

birth *n.* delivery, parturition, nativity, beginning, blessed event*, visit from the stork*. — *Ant.* DEATH, decease, demise. — **give birth to** bring forth, have a child, reproduce; see PRODUCE 1.

birthday *n.* natal day, name day, celebration; see ANNIVERSARY.

biscuit *n.* cracker, wafer, roll; see BREAD.

bi·sect (bī sekt′) *vt.* ⟦< L *bi-*, BI- + *secare*, to cut⟧ 1 to cut in two 2 *Geom.* to divide into two equal parts — *vi.* to divide; fork —**bi·sec′tor** (-sekt′ər) *n.*

bi·sex·ual (bī sek′shoo əl) *adj.* of, or sexually attracted by, both sexes — *n.* one who is bisexual

bishop (bish′əp) *n.* ⟦< Gr *episkopos*, overseer⟧ 1 a high-ranking member of the Christian clergy, governing a diocese or church district 2 a chess piece that can move in a diagonal direction

bish·op·ric (bish′əp rik) *n.* the district, office, or rank of a bishop

bis·muth (biz′məth) *n.* ⟦< Ger *wismut*⟧ a brittle, grayish-white metallic chemical element used in alloys of low melting point

bi·son (bī′sən) *n., pl.* **bi′son** ⟦< L, wild ox⟧ a bovine ruminant having a shaggy mane and a humped back, as the American buffalo

bisque (bisk) *n.* ⟦Fr⟧ a thick, creamy soup made as from shellfish or vegetables

bis·tro (bēs′trō′) *n.* ⟦Fr⟧ a small cafe

bit[1] (bit) *n.* ⟦< OE *bite*, a bite⟧ 1 the part of a bridle in the horse's mouth, used as a control 2 anything that curbs or controls 3 a drilling or boring tool for use in a brace, drill press, etc.

bit[2] (bit) *n.* ⟦< OE *bita*, a piece⟧ 1 *a*) a small piece or quantity *b*) small extent *[a bit bored]* *c*) a short time 2 [Colloq.] 12½ cents: now usually in *two bits* — *adj.* very small *[a bit role]* —**bit by bit** gradually —**do one's bit** to do one's share

bit[3] (bit) *n.* ⟦*b(inary)* (*dig*)*it*⟧ a single digit in a binary number system

bitch (bich) *n.* ⟦OE *bicce*⟧ the female of the dog, fox, etc. — *vi.* [Slang] to complain —**bitch′y** *adj.*

bite (bīt) *vt.* **bit** (bit), **bit·ten** (bit′'n) or **bit, bit′ing** ⟦OE *bitan*⟧ 1 to seize or pierce with or as with the teeth 2 to cut into, as with a sharp weapon 3 to sting, as an insect 4 to cause to smart 5 to eat into; corrode — *vi.* 1 to press or snap the teeth (*into, at*, etc.) 2 to cause a biting sensation 3 to grip 4 to seize a bait 5 to be caught, as by a trick — *n.* 1 a biting 2 biting quality; sting 3 a wound or sting from biting 4 a mouthful 5 a snack 6 [Colloq.] a sum deducted, as by a tax —**bite the bullet** to confront a painful situation bravely: from the patient's biting a bullet during battlefield surgery without an anesthetic

bit·ing (bīt′iŋ) *adj.* 1 cutting; sharp 2 sarcastic —**bit′ingly** *adv.*

bit·ter (bit′ər) *adj.* ⟦OE *biter*, akin to *bitan*, to bite⟧ 1 having a sharp, often unpleasant taste 2 causing or showing sorrow, pain, etc. 3 sharp and disagreeable; harsh *[a bitter wind]* 4 resentful; cynical —**bit′terly** *adv.* —**bit′ter·ness** *n.*

bit·tern (bit′ərn) *n.* ⟦< OFr *butor*⟧ a wading bird with a thumping cry

bit′ters *n.pl.* a liquor containing bitter herbs, etc. and usually alcohol, used as in some cocktails

bit′ter·sweet′ *n.* 1 a woody vine bearing small orange fruits with bright-red fleshy seeds 2 a poisonous vine with purple flowers and red berries 3 pleasure mixed with sadness — *adj.* 1 both bitter and sweet 2 pleasant and sad

bi·tu·men (bi too′mən) *n.* ⟦L < Celt⟧ any of several materials obtained as residue in the distillation of petroleum, coal tar, etc., or occurring as natural asphalt —**bi·tu′mi·nous** (-mə nəs) *adj.*

bituminous coal coal that yields pitch or tar when it burns; soft coal

bi·va·lent (bī vā′lənt) *adj. Chem.* DIVALENT

bi·valve (bī′valv′) *n.* any mollusk having a shell made of two valves hinged together, as a clam

biv·ouac (biv′wak′) *n.* ⟦Fr < OHG *bi-*, by + *wahta*, watchman⟧ a temporary encampment (esp. of soldiers) in the open — *vi.* **-acked**, **-ack′ing** to encamp in the open

bi·weekly (bī wēk′lē) *adj., adv.* 1 once every two weeks 2 [Now Rare] semiweekly

bi·zarre (bi zär′) *adj.* ⟦Fr < Basque *bizar*, beard⟧ 1 odd; grotesque 2 unexpected; fantastic

bk. 1 bank 2 book

bl. 1 bale(s) 2 barrel(s)

B/L or **b/l** bill of lading

blab (blab) *vt., vi.* **blabbed, blab′bing** ⟦ME *blabben*⟧ 1 to reveal (a secret) 2 to chatter; prattle — *n.* gossip

black (blak) *adj.* ⟦OE *blæc*⟧ 1 opposite to white; of the color of coal 2 *[sometimes* B-*]* of or for the dark-skinned peoples of Africa, etc. or their descendants elsewhere, specif. Afro-Americans in the U.S. *[black studies]* 3 without light; dark 4 dirty 5 evil; wicked 6 sad; dismal 7 sullen — *n.* 1 black color or pigment 2 black clothes, esp. when worn in mourning 3 *[sometimes* B-*]* a member of a black people 4 darkness — *vt., vi.* to blacken —**black out** to lose consciousness —**in the black** operating at a profit —**black′ish** *adj.* —**black′ly** *adv.* —**black′ness** *n.*

black′-and-blue′ *adj.* discolored, as by a bruise

black′ball′ (-bôl′) *n.* a vote against — *vt.* 1 to vote against 2 to ostracize

black belt a black belt or sash awarded to an expert of the highest skill in judo or karate

black′ber′ry *n., pl.* **-ries** 1 the fleshy, purple or black, edible fruit of various brambles of the rose family 2 a bush or vine bearing this fruit

black′bird′ *n.* any of various birds the male of which is almost entirely black

black′board′ *n.* a smooth, usually dark surface on which to write with chalk

black′en (-ən) *vi.* to become black or dark — *vt.* 1 to make black; darken 2 to slander; defame

black eye a discoloration of the skin around an eye, resulting from a blow or contusion

black′-eyed′ Su′san (-īd′ soo′zən) a yellow, daisylike wildflower with a dark center

black·guard (blag′ərd) *n.* a scoundrel; villain

black·head (blak′hed′) *n.* a dark plug of dried fatty matter in a pore of the skin

black hole a hypothetical object in space, perhaps the

THESAURUS

bishop *n.* father, archbishop, primate; see MINISTER 1, PRIEST.

bit[2] *n.* 1 [A small quantity] piece, fragment, crumb, dot, particle, jot, trifle, mite, iota, whit, splinter, parcel, portion, droplet, trickle, driblet, morsel, pinch, snip, shred, atom, speck, molecule, shard, chip, fraction, sliver, segment, section, lump, slice, shaving, sample, specimen, scale, flake, excerpt, scrap, part, division, share, trace, item, chunk, paring, taste, mouthful, stub, butt, stump, a drop in the bucket*, peanuts*, chicken feed*, gob*, hunk*. 2 [A small degree] jot, minimum, inch, hairbreadth, trifle, iota, mite, fraction, tolerance, margin, whisker*, hair*, skin of one's teeth. —**do one's bit** participate, share, do one's share; see JOIN 2. —**every bit** wholly, altogether, entirely; see COMPLETELY.

bite *n.* 1 [What one takes in the mouth at one time] mouthful, chew, taste, spoonful, forkful, morsel, nibble. 2 [The result of being bitten] wound, sting, laceration; see INJURY. 3 [A quick meal] snack, nibble, brunch; see FOOD. —**put the bite**

on* pressure, ask for a loan, touch*; see BORROW.

bite *v.* 1 [To seize or sever with the teeth] snap, gnaw, sink one's teeth in, nip, nibble, chew, mouth, gulp, worry, taste, masticate, clamp, champ, munch, bite into, crunch, mangle, chaw*; see also EAT 1, TASTE 1. 2 [To be given to biting] snap, be vicious, attack; see HURT. 3 [To cut or corrode] rot, decay, decompose; see RUST.

biting *a.* 1 [Acidulous] sharp, keen, tangy; see SOUR. 2 [Sarcastic] caustic, acrimonious, bitter; see SARCASTIC.

bitten *a.* chewed, torn, lacerated, slashed, gulped, gnawed, nibbled, tasted, devoured, eaten, stung, pierced, mangled, punctured, cut, ripped.

bitter *a.* 1 [Acrid] astringent, acid, tart; see SOUR. 2 [Intense] sharp, harsh, severe; see INTENSE. 3 [Sarcastic] acrimonious, caustic, biting; see SARCASTIC.

bitterness *n.* tartness, piquancy, pungency, acidity, sourness, acridity,

brackishness, brininess.

bizarre *a.* odd, fantastic, grotesque; see UNUSUAL 2.

blab *v.* disclose, tell, divulge; see REVEAL.

black *a.* 1 [Opposite to white] dark, blackish, raven, coal-black, dusky, dingy, murky, inklike, somber, swarthy, swart, jet, inky, ebony, pitch-black, black as coal, sooty, gunmetal, flat black, jet black, black as the ace of spades*, black as night*.— *Ant.* WHITE, colored, colorful. 2 [Without light] gloomy, shadowy, clouded; see DARK 1. 3 [Negroid] colored, African, black-skinned; see BLACK *n.* 2.

black *n.* 1 [A chromatic color least resembling white] carbon, darkest gray, jet, sable, ebony, blackness.— *Ant.* WHITE, blond, brightness. 2 [A Negro] colored person, negro, African, Afro-American, African-American. —**in the black** successful, lucratively, gainfully; see PROFITABLY.

blacken *v.* darken, deepen, make black; see SHADE 2.

invisible remains of a collapsed star, with intense gravitation from which light and matter cannot escape

black'jack' (-jak') *n.* **1** a small, leather-covered bludgeon with a flexible handle **2** a gambling card game in which the winner gets cards totaling 21 points or less — *vt.* to hit with a blackjack

black light ultraviolet or infrared radiation used for fluorescent effects

black'list' *n.* a list of those who are censured, refused employment, etc. — *vt.* to put on a blacklist

black lung (disease) a disease of the lungs caused by the inhalation of coal dust

black magic sorcery

black'mail' (-māl') *n.* [lit., black rent < ME *male*, rent] payment extorted to prevent disclosure of information that could bring disgrace — *vt.* to get or try to get blackmail from —**black'mail'er** *n.*

black mark an unfavorable item in one's record

black market a system for selling goods illegally —**black marketeer** (or **marketer**)

black'out' (-out') *n.* **1** an extinguishing of stage lights to end a scene **2** a concealing of lights that might be visible to enemy aircraft at night **3** lack of lights due to a power failure **4** temporary unconsciousness **5** suppression, as of news by censorship

black power political and economic power as sought by black Americans in the struggle for civil rights

black sheep a family or group member regarded as not so respectable or successful as the others

black'smith' *n.* a smith who works in iron and makes and fits horseshoes

black'thorn' *n.* a thorny shrub with purple or black, plumlike fruit; sloe

black'top' *n.* a bituminous mixture, usually asphalt, used as a surface for roads, etc. — *vt.* **-topped'**, **-top'ping** to cover with blacktop

black widow a black spider with a red mark underneath: the female is poisonous and sometimes eats its mate

blad·der (blad'ər) *n.* [OE *blæddre*] **1** a sac that fills with fluid or gas, esp. one that holds urine flowing from the kidneys **2** a thing resembling this [a football *bladder*]

blade (blād) *n.* [OE *blæd*, leaf] **1** *a*) the leaf of a plant, esp. grass *b*) the flat part of a leaf **2** a broad, flat surface, as of an oar **3** the cutting part of a tool, knife, etc. **4** a sword or swordsman

blam·able or **blame·able** (blām'ə bəl) *adj.* that deserves blame —**blam'ably** *adv.*

blame (blām) *vt.* **blamed**, **blam'ing** [see BLASPHEME] **1** to accuse of being at fault; condemn (*for*) **2** to put the responsibility of (an error, etc.) *on* — *n.* **1** a blaming **2** responsibility for a fault —**be to blame** to be at fault —**blame'less** *adj.* —**blame'lessly** *adv.* —**blame'less·ness** *n.*

blame'wor'thy (-wur'thē) *adj.* deserving to be blamed

blanch (blanch) *vt.* [< OFr *blanc*, white] **1** to whiten or bleach **2** to make pale **3** to process (vegetables, almonds, etc.) by scalding — *vi.* to turn pale

bland (bland) *adj.* [L *blandus*, mild] **1** gently agreeable **2** mild and soothing **3** insipid —**bland'ly** *adv.* —**bland'ness** *n.*

blan·dish (blan'dish) *vt.*, *vi.* [< L *blandiri*, to flatter] to flatter; coax; cajole —**blan'dish·ment** *n.*

blank (blaŋk) *adj.* [< OFr *blanc*, white] **1** not written on **2** empty; vacant **3** empty of thought [a *blank* mind] **4** utter; complete [a *blank* denial] — *n.* **1** an empty space, esp. one to be filled out in a printed form **2** such a printed form **3** an empty place or time **4** a powder-filled cartridge without a bullet — *vt.* to hold (an opponent) scoreless —**blank out** to conceal by covering over —**draw a blank** [Colloq.] **1** to be unsuccessful **2** to be unable to remember a particular thing —**blank'ly** *adv.* —**blank'ness** *n.*

blank check **1** a bank check form not yet filled in **2** a signed check with no amount filled in **3** permission to use an unlimited amount of money, authority, etc.

blan·ket (blaŋk'it) *n.* [< OFr dim. of *blanc*, white] **1** a large, soft piece of cloth used for warmth, esp. as a bed cover **2** anything like this [a *blanket* of leaves] — *adj.* including many or all items [*blanket* insurance] — *vt.* **1** to cover; overlie **2** to obscure

blank verse unrhymed verse having five iambic feet per line

blan·quette (blän ket') *n.* [Fr] a stew, as of chicken or veal, in cream sauce

blare (bler) *vt.*, *vi.* **blared**, **blar'ing** [ME *bleren*, to wail] to sound or exclaim loudly — *n.* a loud, harsh sound

blar·ney (blär'nē) *n.* [< *Blarney* stone in Ireland, traditionally kissed to gain skill in flattery] flattery — *vt.*, *vi.* **-neyed**, **-ney·ing** to flatter; coax

blasé (blä zā') *adj.* [Fr] satiated and bored

blas·pheme (blas fēm') *vt.* **-phemed'**, **-phem'ing** [< Gr *blasphēmein*, to speak evil of] **1** to speak profanely of or to (God or sacred things) **2** to curse — *vi.* to utter blasphemy —**blas·phem'er** *n.*

blas'phemy (-fə mē) *n.*, *pl.* **-mies** profane speech, writing, or action toward God or sacred things —**blas'phe·mous** *adj.*

blast (blast) *n.* [OE *blæst*, puff of wind] **1** a strong rush of air **2** the sound of a sudden rush of air, as through a horn **3** a blight **4** an explosion, as of dynamite **5** an outburst, as of criticism — *vi.* **1** to make a loud, harsh sound **2** to set off explosives, etc. — *vt.* **1** to wither; ruin **2** to blow up; explode **3** to criticize sharply —**blast off** to take off; said of a rocket —**(at) full blast** at full speed

blast furnace a smelting furnace in which a blast of air forced in from below produces the intense heat

blast'off' or **blast'-off'** *n.* the launching of a rocket, spacecraft, etc.

bla·tant (blāt'nt) *adj.* [prob. < L *blaterare*, to babble] **1** disagreeably loud; noisy **2** boldly conspicuous or obtrusive —**bla'tancy** *n.*

blaze¹ (blāz) *n.* [OE *blæse*] **1** a bright burst of flame; fire **2** a very bright light **3** a spectacular outburst or display — *vi.* **blazed**, **blaz'ing** **1** to burn rapidly or shine brightly **2** to be excited, as with anger

blaze² (blāz) *n.* [< ON *blesi*] **1** a light-colored spot on an animal's face **2** a mark made on a tree by cutting off bark — *vt.* **blazed**, **blaz'ing** to mark (a tree or trail) with blazes

blaze³ (blāz) *vt.* **blazed**, **blaz'ing** [ME *blasen*, to blow < OE or ON] to proclaim

---

THESAURUS

black magic *n.* sorcery, witchcraft, necromancy; see MAGIC 1, 2.

blackmail *n.* hush money, tribute, protection*; see BRIBE.

blackmail *v.* extort, exact, coerce; see BRIBE, FORCE.

blackness *n.* gloom, duskiness, murkiness; see DARKNESS 1.

black out *v.* **1** [To delete] rub out, eradicate, blot out; see CANCEL, ERASE. **2** [To faint] pass out, lose consciousness, swoon; see FAINT. **3** [To darken] put out the lights, make dark, cause a blackout in; see SHADE 2.

blade *n.* **1** [A cutting instrument] edge, brand, sword; see KNIFE. **2** [A relatively long leaf] frond, spear, flag; see LEAF.

blame *n.* disapproval, condemnation, denunciation, disparagement, depreciation, opposition, abuse, disfavor, objection, reproach, criticism, repudiation, reprimand, invective, slur, accusation, reproof, attack, chiding, rebuke, impeachment, complaint,

diatribe, tirade, charge, indictment, recrimination, arraignment, implication, calumny, frowning upon.—*Ant.* PRAISE, commendation, appreciation.

blame *v.* charge, condemn, criticize, arraign, challenge, involve, attack, brand, implicate, arrest, sue, prosecute, slander, impeach, bring to trial, connect with, indict, impute, put the finger on*, smear*, point the finger at*, bring home to. —**be to blame** guilty, at fault, culpable; see WRONG 2.

blameless *a.* faultless, not guilty, inculpable; see INNOCENT 1.

bland *a.* flat, dull, insipid; see TASTELESS 1.

blank *a.* white, clear, virgin, fresh, plain, empty, untouched, pale, new, spotless, vacant, hollow, meaningless.

blank *n.* **1** [An empty space] void, hollow, hole, cavity, vacancy, womb, gulf, nothingness, hollowness, abyss, opening, vacuum, gap, interval; see also EMPTINESS. **2** [A form] question-

naire, data sheet, information blank; see FORM 5. —**draw a blank** be unable to remember, lose one's memory, disremember*; see FORGET.

blanket *n.* quilt, robe, comforter, featherbed, throw, electric blanket, thermal blanket, rug, mat, cloak.

blanket *v.* envelop, conceal, bury; see COVER 1.

blank out *v.* delete, black out, cross out; see CANCEL, ERASE.

blast *n.* **1** [An explosion] burst, eruption, detonation; see EXPLOSION. **2** [A loud sound] roar, din, bang; see NOISE 1. **3** [An explosive charge] gunpowder, TNT, dynamite; see EXPLOSIVE. —**(at) full blast** at full speed, rapidly, quickly; see FAST 1.

blast *v.* blow up, dynamite, detonate; see EXPLODE. —**blast off** rocket, climb, soar up; see RISE 1.

blaze¹ *n.* conflagration, combustion, burning; see FIRE.

blaze¹ *v.* flame, flash, flare up; see BURN.

blazer (blā′zər) *n.* a light sports jacket usually in a solid color and with metal buttons

bla·zon (blā′zən) *n.* 〖OFr *blason,* a shield〗 **1** a coat of arms **2** showy display — *vt.* **1** to proclaim **2** to adorn

bldg. building

bleach (blēch) *vt., vi.* 〖OE *blæcan*〗 to make or become white or colorless — *n.* a substance for bleaching

bleach′ers *n.pl.* seats, usually roofless, for spectators at sporting events

bleak (blēk) *adj.* 〖ON *bleikr,* pale〗 **1** exposed to wind and cold; bare **2** cold; harsh **3** gloomy **4** not hopeful — **bleak′ly** *adv.* —**bleak′ness** *n.*

bleary (blir′ē) *adj.* **-i·er, -i·est** 〖< ME *blere*〗 dim or blurred, as the eyes by tears, fatigue, etc.; also **blear**

bleat (blēt) *vi.* 〖OE *blætan*〗 to make the cry of a sheep, goat, or calf — *n.* a bleating cry or sound

bleed (blēd) *vi.* **bled** (bled), **bleed′ing** 〖< OE *blod,* blood〗 **1** to emit or lose blood **2** to feel pain, grief, or sympathy **3** to ooze sap, juice, etc. — *vt.* **1** to draw blood from **2** to ooze (sap, juice, etc.) **3** [Colloq.] to extort money from — **bleed′er** *n.*

bleep (blēp) *n., vi.* 〖echoic〗 beep — *vt.* to censor (something said), as in a telecast, with a beep

blem·ish (blem′ish) *vt.* 〖< OFr *blesmir,* injure〗 to mar; spoil — *n.* a flaw, defect, etc., as a spot or scar

blench[1] (blench) *vt., vi.* to blanch

blench[2] (blench) *vi.* 〖< OE *blencan,* deceive〗 to shrink back; flinch

blend (blend) *vt.* **blend′ed** or **blent, blend′ing** 〖OE *blendan*〗 **1** to mix or mingle (varieties of tea, etc.) **2** to mix thoroughly — *vi.* **1** to mix; merge **2** to pass gradually into each other, as colors **3** to harmonize — *n.* **1** a blending **2** a mixture of varieties

blend′er *n.* **1** a person or thing that blends **2** an electrical appliance that can chop, whip, mix, or liquefy foods

bless (bles) *vt.* **blessed** or **blest, bless′ing** 〖< OE *bletsian,* consecrate with blood〗 **1** to make holy **2** to ask divine favor for **3** to endow (*with*) **4** to make happy **5** to praise **6** to make the sign of the cross over

blessed (bles′id, blest) *adj.* **1** holy; sacred **2** fortunate; blissful **3** beatified —**bless′edly** *adv.* —**bless′ed·ness** *n.*

bless′ing *n.* **1** invocation or benediction **2** a grace said before or after eating **3** good wishes or approval **4** anything that gives happiness

blew (blōō) *vi., vt. pt. of* BLOW[1] & BLOW[3]

blight (blīt) *n.* 〖? < ON *blikja,* turn pale〗 **1** any insect, disease, etc. that destroys plants **2** anything that destroys, frustrates, etc. — *vt.* **1** to wither **2** to destroy

blimp (blimp) *n.* [Colloq.] a nonrigid or semirigid airship

blind (blīnd) *adj.* 〖OE〗 **1** without the power of sight **2** of or for sightless persons **3** lacking insight **4** hard to see; hidden **5** closed at one end *[a blind* alley*]* **6** not controlled by intelligence *[blind* destiny*]* **7** guided only by instruments *[blind* flying*]* — *vt.* **1** to make sightless **2** to dazzle **3** to deprive of insight — *n.* **1** anything that obscures sight or keeps out light, as a window shade **2** a place of concealment **3** a decoy —**blind′ly** *adv.* —**blind′ness** *n.*

blind date [Colloq.] **1** a date with a stranger, arranged by a third person **2** either person involved

blind′fold′ (-fōld′) *vt.* 〖< ME *blindfeld,* struck blind〗 to cover the eyes of, as with a cloth — *n.* a cloth used to cover the eyes — *adj.* **1** with the eyes covered **2** reckless

blind′side′ (-sīd′) *vt.* **-sid′ed, -sid′ing** to attack (someone) from an unexpected direction

blink (bliŋk) *vi.* 〖ME *blenken*〗 **1** to wink one or more times **2** to flash on and off **3** to ignore (with *at*) — *vt.* **1** to cause (eyes, light, etc.) to blink **2** to evade or avoid — *n.* **1** a blinking **2** a glimmer —**on the blink** [Slang] out of order

blink′er *n.* a flashing warning light

blintz (blints) *n.* 〖Yidd *blintze* < Russ *blin,* pancake〗 a thin pancake rolled with a filling of cottage cheese, fruit, etc.

blip (blip) *n.* 〖echoic of a brief sound〗 a luminous image on an oscilloscope

bliss (blis) *n.* 〖< OE *blithe,* blithe〗 **1** great happiness **2** spiritual joy —**bliss′ful** *adj.* —**bliss′fully** *adv.* —**bliss′ful·ness** *n.*

blis·ter (blis′tər) *n.* 〖< ?〗 **1** a raised patch of skin, filled with watery matter and caused as by a burn **2** anything like a blister — *vt.* **1** to raise blisters on **2** to lash with words — *vi.* to form blisters

blithe (blīth, blith) *adj.* 〖OE〗 cheerful; carefree: also **blithe′some** (-səm) —**blithe′ly** *adv.* —**blithe′ness** *n.*

blitz (blits) *n.* 〖< Ger *blitz,* lightning〗 a sudden destructive or overwhelming attack — *vt.* to subject to a blitz

bliz·zard (bliz′ərd) *n.* 〖? < dial. *bliz,* violent blow〗 a violent snowstorm with very cold winds

bloat (blōt) *vt., vi.* 〖< ON *blautr,* soft〗 **1** to swell, as with water or air **2** to puff up, as with pride

blob (bläb) *n.* 〖echoic〗 a drop or a small lump or spot — *vt.* **blobbed, blob′bing** to splash, as with blobs

bloc (bläk) *n.* 〖Fr < MDu *block,* log〗 a group of persons, nations, etc. combined for a common purpose

---

THESAURUS

bleach *v.* blanch, wash out, whiten; see FADE.

bleak *a.* dreary, desolate, bare, cheerless, wild, exposed, barren, blank, disheartening, weary, melancholy, lonely, flat, somber, distressing, depressing, comfortless, joyless, uninviting, dull, sad, mournful, monotonous, waste, gloomy, dismal, unsheltered, unpopulated, desert, deserted, scorched, stony, burned over, bulldozed, cleared, frozen.— *Ant.* GREEN, verdant, fruitful.

bleed *v.* lose blood, shed blood, be bleeding, hemorrhage, gush, spurt, be bled, open a vein, draw blood; see also FLOW.

blemish *n.* flaw, defect, stain, spot, smudge, imperfection, disfigurement, defacement, blot, blur, chip, taint, tarnish, smirch, stigma, brand, deformity, dent, discoloration, mole, pock, blister, birthmark, wart, scar, impurity, speckle, bruise, freckle, pimple, patch, lump.—*Ant.* PERFECTION, flawlessness, purity.

blench[2] *v.* flinch, quail, shrink back, wince.

blend *n.* combination, compound, amalgam; see MIXTURE 1.

blend *v.* combine, mingle, compound; see MIX 1.

bless *v.* baptize, canonize, glorify, honor, dedicate, make holy, pronounce holy, exalt, give benediction to, absolve, anoint, ordain, hallow,

consecrate, beatify, sanctify, enshrine, offer, render acceptable to, sacrifice, commend.

blessed *a.* **1** [Marked by God's favor, especially in heaven] saved, redeemed, glorified, translated, exalted, rewarded, resurrected, sanctified, glorious, beatified, holy, spiritual, religious.—*Ant.* DOOMED, lost, accursed. **2** [Consecrated] sacred, dedicated, sanctified; see DIVINE.

blessing *n.* **1** [Benediction] commendation, sanctification, laying on of hands, absolution, baptism, unction, consecration, Eucharist.—*Ant.* CURSE, damnation, anathema. **2** [Anything that is very welcome] boon, benefit, good, advantage, help, asset, good fortune, stroke of luck, godsend, windfall, miracle, manna from heaven.—*Ant.* NUISANCE, obstacle, disadvantage.

blight *n.* disease, withering, mildew; see DECAY.

blight *v.* decay, spoil, ruin; see SPOIL.

blind *a.* **1** [Without sight] sightless, unseeing, eyeless, blinded, visionless, in darkness, dim-sighted, groping, deprived of sight, sun-blind, undiscerning, stone-blind, moon-blind, blind as a bat.—*Ant.* OBSERVANT, perceptive, discerning. **2** [Without looking] obtuse, unseeing, by guesswork, by calculation, with instruments; see also BLINDLY, UNAWARE. **3** [Without passage] obstructed, blocked, with-

out egress; see TIGHT 2, 3. **4** [Random] chance, accidental, unplanned; see AIMLESS.

blind *v.* darken, shadow, dim; see SHADE 2.

blindly *a.* at random, wildly, in all directions, frantically, heedlessly, carelessly, recklessly, passionately, thoughtlessly, impulsively, inconsiderately, willfully, unreasonably, without rhyme or reason, senselessly, instinctively, madly, pell-mell, purposelessly, aimlessly, indiscriminately.—*Ant.* CAREFULLY, directly, considerately.

blindness *n.* sightlessness, stone blindness, purblindness, myopia, astigmatism, night blindness, snow blindness, color blindness.—*Ant.* SIGHT, vision, seeing.

blink *v.* **1** [To wink rapidly] flicker, bat one's eyes, flutter one's eyelids; see WINK. **2** [To twinkle] glimmer, flash on and off, shimmer; see SHINE 1.

bliss *n.* joy, rapture, ecstasy; see HAPPINESS.

blister *n.* vesicle, sac, weal, welt, blood blister, water blister, second-degree burn; see also SORE.

blister *v.* scald, irritate, mark; see HURT.

blizzard *n.* snowstorm, tempest, blast; see STORM.

bloc *n.* cabal, group, ring; see FACTION.

block (bläk) *n.* ⟦< OFr *bloc* & MDu *block*⟧ 1 a large, solid piece of wood, stone, metal, etc. 2 a heavy stand on which chopping, etc. is done 3 an auctioneer's platform 4 an obstruction or hindrance 5 a pulley in a frame 6 [Now Brit.] a group or row of buildings 7 an area with streets or buildings on four sides 8 a number of things regarded as a unit 9 *Printing* a piece of wood, etc. engraved with a design — *vt.* 1 to obstruct; hinder 2 to mount or mold on a block 3 to sketch roughly (often with *out*) —**block'er** *n.*

block·ade (blä kād') *n.* ⟦prec. + -ADE⟧ 1 a shutting off of a place by troops or ships to prevent passage 2 any strategic barrier — *vt.* -**ad'ed**, -**ad'ing** to subject to a blockade

block and tackle pulley blocks and ropes, used for lifting heavy objects

block'bust'ing *n.* [Colloq.] the inducing of owners to sell their homes out of fear that a minority group may move into the neighborhood —**block'bust'er** *n.*

block grant a grant of Federal funds to a State or local government to fund a block of programs

block'head' *n.* a stupid person

block'house' *n.* 1 [Historical] a wooden fort 2 a reinforced structure for observers, as of missile launchings

blond (bländ) *adj.* ⟦OFr < ? Gmc⟧ 1 having light-colored hair and skin 2 light in color Also **blonde** — *n.* a blond person —**blonde** *n.fem.* —**blond'ness** *n.*

blood (blud) *n.* ⟦OE *blod*⟧ 1 the red fluid circulating in the arteries and veins of animals 2 bloodshed 3 the essence of life; life 4 the sap of a plant 5 passion, temperament, etc. 6 parental heritage; lineage 7 kinship 8 people, esp. youthful people *[new blood* in a group*]* —**bad blood** anger; hatred —**in cold blood** 1 with cruelty 2 deliberately

blood bank a supply of blood stored for future use in transfusion

blood count the number of red or white cells in a given volume of blood

blood'cur'dling (-kʉrd'liŋ) *adj.* frightening; terrifying

blood'ed (-id) *adj.* 1 having (a specified kind of) blood *[hot-blooded]* 2 of fine breed

blood'hound' *n.* any of a breed of large tracking dogs with a keen sense of smell

blood'less (-lis) *adj.* 1 without bloodshed 2 anemic or pale 3 having little energy —**blood'lessly** *adv.* —**blood'less·ness** *n.*

blood'mobile' (-mō bēl') *n.* a traveling unit for collecting blood from donors for blood banks

blood poisoning nontechnical term for SEPTICEMIA

blood pressure the pressure of the blood against the blood-vessel walls

blood relation (or **relative**) a person related by birth

blood'shed' *n.* the shedding of blood; killing

blood'shot' *adj.* tinged with red because small blood vessels are broken: said of eyes

blood'suck'er *n.* an animal that sucks blood, esp. a leech

blood'thirst'y *adj.* murderous; very cruel —**blood'thirst'i·ness** *n.*

blood vessel an artery, vein, or capillary

blood'y *adj.* -**i·er**, -**i·est** 1 of, like, containing, or covered with blood 2 involving bloodshed 3 bloodthirsty 4 [Brit. Slang] cursed; damned — *adv.* [Brit. Slang] very — *vt.* -**ied**, -**y·ing** to stain with blood —**blood'i·ly** *adv.* —**blood'i·ness** *n.*

bloom (blōōm) *n.* ⟦< ON *blomi*, flowers⟧ 1 a flower; blossom 2 the state or time of flowering 3 a period of greatest health, vigor, etc. 4 a youthful, healthy glow 5 the powdery coating on some fruits and leaves — *vi.* 1 to blossom 2 to be in one's prime 3 to glow with health, etc.

bloomers (blōōm'ərz) *n.* ⟦after Amelia *Bloomer* (1818-94), U.S. feminist⟧ baggy trousers gathered at the knee, once worn by women for athletics

bloom'ing *adj.* 1 blossoming 2 flourishing 3 [Colloq.] complete

blooper (blōōp'ər) *n.* ⟦*bloop*, echoic + -ER⟧ 1 a stupid mistake 2 *Baseball* a fly that falls just beyond the infield for a hit

blos·som (bläs'əm) *n.* ⟦OE *blostma*⟧ 1 a flower, esp. of a fruit-bearing plant 2 a state or time of flowering — *vi.* 1 to have or open into blossoms 2 to begin to flourish — **blos'somy** *adj.*

blot (blät) *n.* ⟦ME < ?⟧ 1 a spot or stain, esp. of ink 2 anything that spoils or mars 3 a moral stain — *vt.* **blot'ted**, **blot'ting** 1 to spot; stain 2 to disgrace 3 to erase, obscure, or get rid of: with *out* 4 to dry, as with blotting paper — *vi.* 1 to make blots 2 to become blotted 3 to be absorbent

blotch (bläch) *n.* ⟦? < prec.⟧ 1 a discoloration on the skin 2 any large blot or stain — *vt.* to mark with blotches — **blotch'y**, -**i·er**, -**i·est** *adj.*

blot·ter (blät'ər) *n.* 1 a piece of blotting paper 2 a book for recording events as they occur *[a police blotter]*

blotting paper a thick, soft, absorbent paper used to dry a surface freshly written on in ink

blouse (blous) *n.* ⟦Fr, workman's smock⟧ 1 a garment like a shirt, worn by women and children 2 a uniform coat worn by soldiers, etc. — *vi.*, *vt.* **bloused**, **blous'ing** to gather in and drape over loosely

blow[1] (blō) *vi.* **blew**, **blown**, **blow'ing** ⟦OE *blawan*⟧ 1 to move with some force, as the wind 2 to send forth air, as with the mouth 3 to pant 4 to give sound by blowing or

---

block *n.* 1 [A mass, usually with flat surfaces] slab, chunk, piece, square, cake, cube, slice, segment, loaf, clod, bar, hunk. 2 [The area between streets] vicinity, square, lots; see NEIGHBORHOOD. 3 [The distance of the side of a city block] street, city block, intersection; see DISTANCE 3. 4 [An obstruction] hindrance, bar, obstacle; see BARRIER. —**knock someone's block off*** thrash, hit, beat up*; see BEAT 1.

block *v.* 1 [To impede] interfere with, prevent, close off; see HINDER. 2 [In sports, to impede a play] throw a block, tackle, check; see STOP 1. — **block out** 1 [To obscure] conceal, screen, cover; see HIDE 1. 2 [To plan] outline, sketch, chart; see PLAN 2.

blockade *n.* barricade, encirclement, bar; see BARRIER.

blockhead *n.* nitwit, fool, imbecile; see FOOL.

blond *a.* fair, fair-skinned, pale, light, lily-white, white-skinned, creamy, whitish, milky, albino, pearly, platinum, gray-white, towheaded, snowy, light-haired, golden-haired, fair-haired, yellow-haired, sandy-haired, ash-blond, bleached, strawberry-blond, peroxide-blond*.

blood *n.* life's blood, heart's blood, vital fluid, vital juices, gore, sanguine fluid. —**bad blood** malice, rancor, feud; see ANGER, HATRED. —**in cold blood** 1 heartlessly, ruthlessly,

unmercifully; see BRUTALLY. 2 cruelly, intentionally, indifferently; see DELIBERATELY. —**make someone's blood boil** disturb, infuriate, agitate; see ENRAGE. —**make someone's blood run cold** terrify, horrify, scare; see FRIGHTEN.

bloodless *a.* pallid, wan, anemic; see PALE 1.

bloodshed *n.* slaughter, butchery, gore; see BATTLE, MURDER.

bloodshot *a.* inflamed, streaked, red; see BLOODY 1.

bloody *a.* 1 [Showing blood] bleeding, bloodstained, blood-spattered, gaping, unstaunched, grisly, crimson, open, wounded, dripping blood, raw, blood-soaked.—*Ant.* WHOLE, unhurt, uninjured. 2 [Fiercely fought] savage, heavy, murderous; see CRUEL.

bloom *n.* blossom, floweret, efflorescence; see FLOWER.

bloom *v.* flower, burst into bloom, open, bud, prosper, grow, wax, bear fruit, thrive, germinate, flourish, be in health, blossom, come out in flower, be in flower.

blooming *a.* flowering, blossoming, in flower; see BUDDING, GROWING.

blossom *n.* bloom, floweret, bud; see FLOWER.

blossom *v.* flower, blow, burst into blossom; see BLOOM.

blossoming *n.* blooming, flowering,

budding; see BUDDING, GROWING.

blot *n.* spot, stain, smudge; see BLEMISH.

blot *v.* smudge, blotch, soil; see DIRTY. —**blot out** 1 [To mark out] deface, cross out, scratch out, delete; see also CANCEL. 2 [To obscure] darken, blur, shroud; see SHADE 2.

blouse *n.* pullover, overblouse, slipover; see CLOTHES, SHIRT.

blow[1] *v.* 1 [To send forth air rapidly] puff, blast, pant, fan, whiff, whisk, whisper, puff away, exhale, waft, breathe, whistle. 2 [To carry on the wind] waft, flutter, bear, whisk, drive, fling, whirl, flap, flip, wave, buffet, sweep. 3 [To play a wind instrument] pipe, toot, mouth; see PLAY 3. 4 [To sound when blown] trumpet, vibrate, blare; see SOUND. 5 [To give form by inflation] inflate, swell, puff up, pump up; see also FILL 1. 6 [*To fail] miss, flounder, miscarry; see FAIL 1. 7 [*To spend] lay out, pay out, waste, squander; see also SPEND. —**blow up** 1 [To fill] pump up, puff up, swell, inflate; see also FILL 1. 2 [To explode] erupt, rupture, go off; see EXPLODE. 3 [To destroy with explosives] bomb, dynamite, detonate; see ATTACK, DESTROY. 4 [*To lose one's temper] become enraged, rave, lose self-control; see RAGE 1.

being blown **5** to spout water and air, as whales do **6** to be carried by the wind **7** to be stormy **8** to burst suddenly: often with *out* **9** [Colloq.] to brag **10** [Slang] to leave — *vt.* **1** to force air from, into, onto, or through **2** to drive by blowing **3** to sound by blowing **4** to form by blown air or gas **5** to burst by an explosion: often with *up* **6** to melt (a fuse, etc.) **7** [Colloq.] to spend (money) freely **8** [Slang] to leave **9** [Slang] to bungle — *n.* **1** a blowing **2** a blast of air or gale —**blow off** [Colloq.] to release emotions, as by shouting —**blow over** to pass over or by — **blow up** [Colloq.] to lose one's temper —**blow′er** *n.*

blow² (blō) *n.* [ME *blowe*] **1** a hard hit, as with the fist **2** a sudden attack **3** a sudden calamity; shock —**come to blows** to begin fighting one another

blow³ (blō) *vi.* **blew, blown, blow′ing** [OE *blowan*] [Archaic] to bloom

blow′-by-blow′ *adj.* detailed; full

blow′-dry′ *vt.* -**dried′, -dry′ing** to dry (wet hair) with hot air blown from an electric device (**blow′-dry′er**)

blow′fly′ *n., pl.* -**flies′** a fly that lays its eggs on meat, in wounds, etc.

blow′gun′ *n.* a long tube through which darts, etc. are blown

blow′out′ *n.* **1** the bursting of a tire **2** [Slang] a party, banquet, etc.

blow′torch′ *n.* a small liquid-fuel torch that shoots out a hot flame

blow′up′ *n.* **1** an explosion **2** an enlarged photograph **3** [Colloq.] an angry outburst

blow′y *adj.* -**i·er, -i·est** windy

blowzy (blou′zē) *adj.* -**i·er, -i·est** [< obs. *blouze*, wench] slovenly Also **blows′y**

BLT bacon, lettuce, and tomato (sandwich)

blub·ber¹ (blub′ər) *n.* [ME *blober*, a bubble] the fat of the whale —**blub′bery** *adj.*

blub·ber² (blub′ər) *vi.* [ME *bloberen*, to bubble] to weep loudly, like a child

bludgeon (bluj′ən) *n.* [? < earlier Fr *bouge*, club] a short club with a heavy end — *vt., vi.* **1** to strike with a bludgeon **2** to bully or coerce

blue (blōō) *adj.* [< ?] **1** of the color of the clear sky **2** livid: said of the skin **3** gloomy **4** puritanical **5** [Colloq.] indecent; risqué — *n.* **1** the color of the clear sky **2** any blue pigment **3** [*pl.*] [Colloq.] a depressed feeling: with *the* **4** [*pl.*] black folk music having, usually, slow tempo, melancholy words, etc.: often with *the* —**out of the blue** unexpectedly —**the blue 1** the sky **2** the sea

blue baby a baby born with bluish skin, esp. because of a heart defect

blue′bell′ *n.* any of various plants with blue, bell-shaped flowers

blue′ber′ry *n., pl.* -**ries** **1** a shrub bearing small, edible, blue-black berries **2** any of the berries

blue′bird′ *n.* a small North American songbird with a bluish back

blue blood an aristocrat Also **blue′blood′** *n.* —**blue′-blood′ed** *adj.*

blue cheese any strong cheese containing bluish mold

blue′-chip′ *adj.* [< high-value *blue chips* of poker] **1** of any high-priced stock with good earnings and a stable price **2** [Colloq.] valuable

blue′-col′lar *adj.* [< color of work shirts] designating or of industrial workers

blue flu [< *blue* police uniforms] a sickout, esp. by police officers

blue′gill′ *n.* a freshwater sunfish of a bluish color

blue′grass′ *n.* a type of grass with bluish-green horizontal stems

blue′jack′et *n.* an enlisted person in the navy

blue jay a common crested bird with a blue upper body and head Also **blue′jay′** *n.*

blue′jeans′ (-jēnz′) *n.* jeans made of blue denim Also **blue jeans**

blue law a puritanical law, esp. one prohibiting certain activities on Sunday

blue′nose′ *n.* [Colloq.] a puritanical person

blue′-pen′cil *vt.* -**ciled** or **-cilled, -ciling** or **-cilling** to edit or correct with or as with a blue pencil

blue′-plate′ special an inexpensive restaurant meal served at a fixed price

blue′point′ *n.* [after *Blue Point*, Long Island, New York] a small oyster, usually eaten raw

blue′print′ *n.* **1** a photographic reproduction in white on a blue background, as of architectural plans **2** any detailed plan or outline — *vt.* to make a blueprint of

blue′stock′ing *n.* a learned, bookish, or pedantic woman

bluesy (blōōz′ē) *adj.* -**i·er, -i·est** of or characteristic of the blues: see BLUE (sense 4)

bluet (blōō′it) *n.* [< Fr dim. of *bleu*, blue] a small plant having little pale-blue flowers

blue whale a whalebone whale with a blue-gray back

bluff¹ (bluf) *vt., vi.* [prob. < Du *bluffen*, to brag, or *verbluffen*, to baffle] to mislead or frighten (a person) by a false, bold front — *n.* **1** a bluffing **2** one who bluffs: also **bluff′er**

bluff² (bluf) *adj.* [? < Du *blaf*, flat] **1** ascending steeply with a flat front **2** having a rough, frank manner — *n.* a high, steep bank or cliff

blu·ing (blōō′iŋ) *n.* a blue rinse used on white fabrics to prevent yellowing

blu′ish (-ish) *adj.* somewhat blue Also **blue′ish**

blun·der (blun′dər) *vi.* [< ON *blunda*, shut the eyes] **1** to move clumsily **2** to make a foolish mistake — *vt.* to do poorly — *n.* a foolish mistake —**blun′derer** *n.*

blun′der·buss′ (-bus′) *n.* [< Du *donderbus*, thunder box] [Historical] a short gun with a broad muzzle

blunt (blunt) *adj.* [< ?] **1** having a dull edge, etc. **2** plain-spoken — *vt., vi.* to make or become dull —**blunt′ly** *adv.* —**blunt′ness** *n.*

blur (blur) *vt., vi.* **blurred, blur′ring** [< ?] **1** to smear; blot **2** to make or become indistinct in shape, etc. **3** to dim — *n.* **1** an obscuring stain **2** anything indistinct — **blur′ry** *adj.* —**blur′ri·ness** *n.*

blurb (blurb) *n.* [a coinage] an advertisement, as on a book jacket, esp. one that is highly laudatory

blurt (blurt) *vt.* [prob. echoic] to say impulsively: with *out*

blush (blush) *vi.* [< OE *blyscan*, to shine] **1** to become red in the face, as from embarrassment **2** to be ashamed (*at* or *for*) **3** to become rosy — *n.* **1** a reddening of the face, as from shame **2** a rosy color — *adj.* rosy —**at first blush** at first sight

blush′er *n.* **1** one who blushes readily **2** a red or reddish cosmetic powder, cream, etc. for the cheeks

blush wine a dry, pale-pink wine

■■■ THESAURUS ■■■

blow² *n.* hit, strike, swing, bump, wallop, rap, bang, whack, thwack, cuff, box, uppercut, knock, clout, slam, bruise, swipe, kick, stroke, punch, jab, gouge, lunge, thrust, swat, poke, prod, slap, the old one-two*, belt*, lick*, crack*, kayo*, K.O.*.

blowing *a.* blasting, puffing, fanning, panting, whisking, breathing, gasping, fluttering, flapping, waving, streaming, whipping, drifting, tumbling, gliding, straining; see also FLYING.—*Ant.* FALLING, standing still, hovering.

blown *a.* buffeted, fluttered, fanned; see BLOWING.

blowout *n.* eruption, blast, detonation, tear, break, puncture, rupture, leak, gap, seam, flat tire, flat.

blue *a., n.* **1** [One of the primary colors] *Tints and shades of blue include the following:* indigo, sapphire, turquoise, lapis lazuli, aquamarine, blue-black, azure, sky-blue, blue-green; royal, Prussian, navy, powder, baby, cobalt, Chinese, robin's egg, pale, light, dark, deep, livid, electric, etc., blue; see also COLOR. **2** [Despondent] depressed, moody, melancholy; see SAD 1. —**once in a blue moon** rarely, infrequently, once in a while; see SELDOM. —**out of the blue** without warning, unpredicted, unforeseen; see UNEXPECTED.

blues *n.* **1** [A state of despondency; *often with "the"*] depressed spirits, melancholy, dejection; see GLOOM. **2** [Rhythmic lamentation in a minor key] dirge, lament, torch song; see MUSIC 1.

bluff¹ *v.* fool, mislead, trick; see DECEIVE.

bluff¹,² *n.* **1** [A bank] cliff, precipice, steep; see HILL, MOUNTAIN 1. **2** [A

trick] ruse, deception, delusion; see TRICK 1.

blunder *n.* mistake, lapse, oversight; see ERROR.

blunt *a.* **1** [Dull] unsharpened, unpointed, round; see DULL 1. **2** [Abrupt] brusque, curt, bluff; see RUDE 2.

blur *v.* obscure, blur, blear; see SHADE 2.

blurt out *v.* speak unthinkingly, jabber, utter; see TALK 1.

blush *v.* change color, flush, redden, turn red, glow, have rosy cheeks, have heightened color.

blushing *a.* coloring, dyeing, staining, reddening, turning red, flushing, glowing, changing color, burning, red as a rose, rosy-red, with burning cheeks*.

blus·ter (blus'tər) *vi.* 〚? < LowG *blüstern*〛 1 to blow stormily: said of wind 2 to speak in a noisy, swaggering manner — *n.* 1 noisy commotion 2 noisy or swaggering talk —**blus'terer** *n.* —**blus'tery** *adj.*

Blvd. Boulevard

BM [Colloq.] bowel movement

BO body odor

boa (bō'ə) *n.* 〚L〛 1 a tropical snake that crushes its prey in its coils, as the anaconda 2 a woman's long scarf, as of fur or feathers

boar (bôr) *n.* 〚OE *bar*〛 1 an uncastrated male pig 2 a wild hog

board (bôrd) *n.* 〚OE *bord*, plank〛 1 a long, flat piece of sawed wood 2 a flat piece of wood, etc. for some special use /bulletin *board/* 3 pasteboard 4 *a*) a table for meals *b*) meals, esp. as provided regularly for pay 5 a group of administrators; council 6 the side of a ship [*overboard*] — *vt.* 1 to cover (*up*) with boards 2 to provide with meals, or room and meals, regularly for pay 3 to come onto the deck of (a ship) 4 to get on (a train, bus, etc.) — *vi.* to receive meals, or room and meals, regularly for pay —**on board** on a ship, aircraft, etc. —**the boards** the stage (of a theater) —**board'er** *n.*

board'ing·house' *n.* a house where meals, or room and meals, can be had for pay Also **boarding house**

board'walk' *n.* a walk made of thick boards, esp. one along a beach

boast (bōst) *vi.* 〚< Anglo-Fr〛 to talk, esp. about oneself, with too much pride; brag — *vt.* to brag about; glory in — *n.* 1 a boasting 2 anything boasted of —**boast'er** *n.* — **boast'ful** *adj.* —**boast'fully** *adv.*

boat (bōt) *n.* 〚OE *bat*〛 1 a small, open vehicle for traveling on water 2 loosely, a ship 3 a boat-shaped dish —**in the same boat** in the same unfavorable situation —**rock the boat** [Colloq.] to disturb the status quo —**boat'man** (-mən), *pl.* -**men**, *n.*

boatel (bō tel') *n.* 〚prec. + (HOT)EL〛 1 a moored ship used as a hotel 2 a hotel on a waterfront, with docks for boats

boat'er *n.* a stiff straw hat with a flat crown and brim

boat'ing *n.* rowing, sailing, etc.

boat·swain (bō'sən) *n.* a ship's petty officer in charge of the deck crew, the rigging, anchors, boats, etc.

bob (bäb) *n.* 〚ME *bobbe*, hanging cluster; 3 & 4 < the *v.*〛 1 any knoblike hanging weight 2 a woman's or child's short haircut 3 a quick, jerky motion 4 a float on a fishing line — *vt.* **bobbed, bob'bing** 〚ME *bobben*, knock against〛 1 to make move with a jerky motion 2 to cut (hair, etc.) short — *vi.* to move with a jerky motion —**bob up** to appear suddenly

bob·bin (bäb'in) *n.* 〚Fr *bobine* < ?〛 a spool for thread or yarn, used in spinning, machine sewing, etc.

bob·ble (bäb'əl) *n.* [Colloq.] *Sports* an awkward juggling of the ball — *vt.* -**bled, -bling** [Colloq.] to make a bobble with (a ball)

bobby (bäb'ē) *n., pl.* -**bies** 〚after Sir Robert (*Bobby*) Peel (1788-1850), who reorganized the London police force〛 [Brit. Colloq.] a policeman

bobby pin 〚from use with *bobbed* hair〛 a small metal hairpin with the sides pressing close together

bobby socks (or **sox**) 〚< BOB (*vt.* 2)〛 [Colloq.] esp. in the 1940's and 1950's, girls' ankle-length socks

bob'by-sox'er or **bob'by·sox'er** (-säks'ər) *n.* [Colloq.] esp. in the 1940's, a girl in her early teens

bob'cat' *n.* a small North American lynx

bob'sled' *n.* a long racing sled — *vi.* -**sled'ded, -sled'ding** to ride or race on a bobsled

boc·cie, bocce, or **bocci** (bäch'ē) *n.* 〚It *bocce*, (wooden) balls〛 an Italian game similar to bowls

bode[1] (bōd) *vt.* **bod'ed, bod'ing** 〚< OE *boda*, messenger〛 to be an omen of —**bode ill (or well)** to be a bad (or good) omen

bode[2] (bōd) *vi. alt. pt. of* BIDE

bod·ice (bäd'is) *n.* 〚altered < *bodies*, pl. of *body*〛 the upper part of a dress

bodi·ly (bäd''l ē) *adj.* 1 physical 2 of, in, by, or to the body — *adv.* 1 in person 2 as a single group

bod·kin (bäd'kin) *n.* 〚ME *bodekin* < ?〛 1 [Obs.] a dagger 2 a pointed instrument for making holes in cloth 3 a thick, blunt needle

body (bäd'ē) *n., pl.* -**ies** 〚OE *bodig*, cask〛 1 the whole physical substance of a human being, animal, or plant 2 the trunk of a human being 3 a corpse 4 [Colloq.] a person 5 a distinct group of people or things 6 the main part 7 a distinct mass /a *body* of water/ 8 substance or consistency, as of liquid 9 richness of flavor

body bag a rubberized bag sealed with a zipper, used for transporting a dead body

bod'y·build'ing *n.* the practice of lifting weights and performing calisthenics to develop a strong body —**bod'y·build'er** *n.*

bod'y·guard' *n.* a person or persons assigned to guard someone

body language gestures, unconscious bodily movements, etc. which function as a means of communication

body stocking a tightfitting garment, usually of one piece, that covers the torso and, sometimes, the legs

bod'y·suit' *n.* a one-piece, tightfitting garment that covers the torso, usually worn with slacks, a skirt, etc. Also **body shirt**

Boer (boor, bôr) *n.* 〚Du *boer*, peasant〛 a South African of Dutch descent

bog (bäg, bôg) *n.* 〚< Gael & Ir *bog*, soft, moist〛 wet, spongy ground; a small marsh — *vt., vi.* **bogged, bog'ging** to sink in or as in a bog: often with *down* —**bog'gy** *adj.*

bo·gey (bō'gē) *n.* 1 BOGY 2 〚after an imaginary Col. *Bogey*〛 *Golf* one stroke more than par on a hole: also **bo'gie**

bog·gle (bäg'əl) *vi.* -**gled, -gling** 〚< Scot *bogle*, specter〛 1 to be startled (*at*) 2 to hesitate (*at*) — *vt.* to confuse (the mind, imagination, etc.)

bo·gus (bō'gəs) *adj.* 〚< ?〛 not genuine; spurious

bogy (bō'gē, boog'ē) *n., pl.* -**gies** 〚< Scot *bogle*, specter〛 an imaginary evil spirit; goblin Also **bo'gie**

bogy·man or **bogey·man** (boog'ē man', bō'gē-) *n., pl.* -**men'** an imaginary, frightful being

Bo·he·mian (bō hē'mē ən) *n.* 1 CZECH (*n.* 2) a native or inhabitant of Bohemia 3 [*usually* b-] one who lives unconventionally — *adj.* 1 of Bohemia, its people, etc. 2 [*usually* b-] like a bohemian —**Bo·he'mi·an·ism'** *n.*

THESAURUS

bluster *v.* brag, swagger, strut; see BOAST.

board *n.* 1 [A piece of thin lumber] plank, lath, strip; see LUMBER. 2 [Meals] food, fare, provisions; see FOOD, MEAL 2. 3 [A body of persons having specific responsibilities] jury, council, cabinet; see COMMITTEE. —**across the board** general, universal, common; see UNIVERSAL 2. —**go by the board** be lost, go, vanish; see FAIL 1. —**on board** present, in transit, en route; see ABOARD.

board *v.* 1 [Cover] plank, tile, paper; see COVER 1. 2 [Go aboard] embark, cast off, go on board ship; see LEAVE 1. 3 [Take care of] lodge, room, accommodate; see FEED.

boast *n.* brag, vaunt, source of pride, pretension, self-satisfaction, bravado.

boast *v.* gloat, triumph, swagger, bully, exult, show off, vaunt, swell, brag, strut, bluff, flaunt, bluster, flourish, blow*, sound off*, crow, pat oneself on the back*, blow one's own trumpet*, attract attention.—*Ant.* APOLOGIZE, humble oneself, admit defeat.

boastful *a.* bragging, pretentious, bombastic; see EGOTISTIC.

boat *n. Types of small boats include the following:* sailboat, rowboat, shell, scull, kayak, dugout, canoe, scow, raft, launch, motorboat, dory, catboat, tartan, hydrofoil, speedboat, yawl, sloop, cutter, ketch, schooner, lifeboat, barge, punt, outrigger, dinghy, racer, hydroplane, catamaran, skiff, gondola, longboat, war canoe, flatboat, riverboat, canal boat. —**in the same boat** in the same situation, in a similar situation, in the same condition, concurrently; see also TOGETHER 2. —**miss the boat** miss, fall short, neglect; see FAIL 1. —**rock the boat** upset, disturb, distort; see CONFUSE.

bobsled *n.* sleigh, coaster, toboggan; see SLED.

bodily *a.* carnal, fleshly, gross, somatic, solid, physical, unspiritual, tangible, material, substantial, human, natural, normal, organic; see also BIOLOGICAL, PHYSICAL 1.

body *n.* 1 [The human organism] frame, physique, form, figure, shape, make, carcass*, build, make-up. 2 [A corpse] cadaver, *corpus delecti* (Latin), dust, clay, carcass*, dead body, relics, the dead, the deceased, mummy, skeleton, ashes, carrion, bones, remains, cold meat*, stiff*, goner*. 3 [The central portion of an object] chassis, basis, groundwork, frame, fuselage, assembly, trunk, hull, bed, box, skeleton, scaffold, anatomy, bones*, guts*. 4 [Individuals having an organization] society, group, party; see ORGANIZATION 2. 5 [A unified or organized mass] reservoir, supply, variety; see COLLECTION. —**keep body and soul together** stay alive, endure, earn a living; see SURVIVE 1.

boil[1] (boil) *vi.* ⟦< L *bulla*, a bubble⟧ 1 to bubble up and vaporize by being heated 2 to seethe like a boiling liquid 3 to be agitated, as with rage 4 to cook in boiling liquid — *vt.* 1 to heat to the boiling point 2 to cook in boiling liquid — *n.* the act or state of boiling —**boil down** 1 to lessen in quantity by boiling 2 to condense

boil[2] (boil) *n.* ⟦OE *byle*⟧ an inflamed, painful, pus-filled swelling on the skin

boil′er *n.* 1 a container in which to boil things 2 a tank in which water is turned to steam 3 a tank for heating water and storing it

boiling point the point at which one loses one's temper

bois·ter·ous (bois′tər əs) *adj.* ⟦ME *boistreous*, crude⟧ 1 rough and stormy; turbulent 2 loud and exuberant; rowdy —**bois′ter·ous·ly** *adv.*

bok choy (bäk′ choi′) ⟦Chin⟧ a variety of Chinese cabbage

bola (bō′lə) *n.* ⟦< Sp, a ball⟧ a long cord with heavy balls at the ends, thrown to entangle cattle, etc.

bold (bōld) *adj.* ⟦OE *beald*⟧ 1 daring; fearless 2 too free in manner; impudent 3 steep 4 prominent and clear — **bold′ly** *adv.* —**bold′ness** *n.*

bold′faced′ (-fāst′) *adj.* impudent

bole (bōl) *n.* ⟦ON *bolr*⟧ a tree trunk

bo·lero (bō ler′ō) *n., pl.* **-ros** ⟦Sp < L *bulla*, a bubble⟧ 1 a lively Spanish dance, or music for it 2 a short, open vest

boll (bōl) *n.* ⟦ME *bolle*, BOWL[1]⟧ the roundish seed pod of a plant, esp. of cotton or flax

boll weevil a small weevil whose larvae destroy cotton bolls

bo·logna (bə lō′nē) *n.* ⟦after *Bologna*, It city⟧ a large smoked sausage of beef, pork, or veal

Bol·she·vik (bōl′shə vik′) *n., pl.* **-viks** or **-vi′ki** (-vē′kē) ⟦Russ < *ból′she*, larger⟧ [*also* b-] 1 orig., a member of a majority faction that came into power in Russia in 1917 2 a Communist, esp. of the Soviet Union —**Bol′she·vism** *n.* —**Bol′she·vist** *n., adj.*

bol·ster (bōl′stər) *n.* ⟦OE⟧ 1 a long, narrow pillow 2 any bolsterlike object or support — *vt.* to prop up as with a bolster: often with *up*

bolt[1] (bōlt) *n.* ⟦OE⟧ 1 a short, blunt arrow shot from a crossbow 2 a flash of lightning 3 a sudden dash 4 a sliding bar for locking a door, etc. 5 a threaded metal rod used with a nut for joining parts 6 a roll (of cloth, paper, etc.) — *vt.* 1 to say suddenly; blurt (*out*) 2 to swallow (food) hurriedly 3 to fasten as with a bolt 4 to abandon (a party, group, etc.) — *vi.* 1 to start suddenly; spring away 2 to withdraw support from one's party, etc. —**bolt upright** straight up; erect or erectly

bolt[2] (bōlt) *vt.* ⟦< OFr *buleter*⟧ to sift (flour, grain, etc.)

bo·lus (bō′ləs) *n.* ⟦< Gr *bōlos*⟧ 1 a small, round lump 2 a mass injected into a blood vessel, as radioactive tracer 3 a large pill

bomb (bäm) *n.* ⟦prob. < Gr *bombos*, hollow sound⟧ 1 a container filled as with an explosive or incendiary chemical, for dropping, hurling, etc. 2 a small container with compressed gas in it [an aerosol *bomb*] 3 [Colloq.] a complete failure — *vt.* to attack with bombs — *vi.* [Colloq.] to be a complete failure

bom·bard (bäm bärd′) *vt.* ⟦Fr *bombarde*, mortar⟧ 1 to attack with artillery or bombs 2 to attack with questions, etc. 3 to direct particles at (atomic nuclei) —**bom·bard′ment** *n.*

bom′bar·dier′ (-bər dir′) *n.* one who releases the bombs in a bomber

bom·bast (bäm′bast′) *n.* ⟦< Pers *pambak*, cotton⟧ high-sounding, pompous language —**bom·bas′tic** *adj.* —**bom·bas′ti·cally** *adv.*

bomber (bäm′ər) *n.* 1 an airplane for dropping bombs 2 one who bombs

bomb′shell′ *n.* 1 a bomb 2 any sudden, shocking surprise

bona fide (bō′nə fīd′, fī′dē) ⟦L⟧ in good faith; without fraud

bo·nanza (bə nan′zə) *n.* ⟦Sp, prosperity⟧ 1 a rich vein of ore 2 any source of wealth

bon·bon (bän′bän′; Fr bōn bōn′) *n.* ⟦< Fr *bon*, good⟧ a small piece of candy

bond (bänd) *n.* ⟦ult. < Gothic *bindan*, bind⟧ 1 anything that binds, fastens, or unites 2 [*pl.*] shackles 3 a binding agreement 4 an obligation imposed by a contract, promise, etc. 5 the status of goods kept in a warehouse until taxes or duties are paid 6 an interest-bearing certificate issued by a government or business, redeemable on a specified date 7 a) surety against theft, absconding, etc. b) an amount paid as surety or bail — *vt.* 1 to join; bind 2 to furnish a BOND (*n.* 7a) for 3 to place or hold (goods) in bond

bond·age (bän′dij) *n.* ⟦ult. < ON *bua*, inhabit⟧ serfdom or slavery

bond′ing (-diŋ) *n.* the development of a close relationship, as between family members

bond′man *n., pl.* **-men** 1 a serf 2 a slave —**bond′woman**, *pl.* **-wom′en**, *n.fem.*

bonds·man (bändz′mən) *n., pl.* **-men** 1 BONDMAN 2 one who furnishes a BOND (*n.* 7)

bone (bōn) *n.* ⟦< OE *ban*⟧ 1 any of the parts of hard tissue forming the skeleton of most vertebrates 2 this hard tissue 3 a bonelike substance or thing — *vt.* **boned**, **bon′ing** to remove the bones from — *vi.* [Slang] to study hard: usually with *up* —**have a bone to pick** [Colloq.] to have cause to quarrel —**make no bones about** [Colloq.] admit freely —**boneless** *adj.*

bone china translucent china made of white clay to which the ash of burned bones has been added

bone′-dry′ *adj.* [Colloq.] very dry

bone meal crushed or ground bones, used as feed or fertilizer

boner (bōn′ər) *n.* [Slang] a blunder

bon·fire (bän′fīr′) *n.* ⟦ME *banefyre*, bone fire, pyre⟧ an outdoor fire

bong (bôŋ, bäŋ) *n.* ⟦echoic⟧ a deep ringing sound, as of a large bell — *vi.* to make this sound

bongo (bäŋ′gō) *n., pl.* **-gos** ⟦AmSp < ?⟧ either of a pair of small drums of different pitch struck with the fingers In full **bongo drum**

THESAURUS

boil[1] *v.* steep, seethe, stew, bubble, simmer, steam, parboil, boil over, evaporate; see also COOK. —**boil down** condense, summarize, sum up; see DECREASE 2, SUMMARIZE.

boiling *a.* stewing, steeping, percolating, steaming, bubbling, seething, simmering, evaporating, boiling over; see also COOKING.

boisterous *a.* tumultuous, uproarious, noisy; see LOUD 2, RUDE 2.

bold *a.* 1 [Courageous] intrepid, fearless, daring; see BRAVE. 2 [Impertinent] presumptuous, audacious, brazen; see RUDE 2. 3 [Prominent] strong, clear, plain; see DEFINITE 2.

boldly *a.* 1 [*Said of animate beings*] impetuously, headlong, intrepidly, fearlessly, recklessly, courageously, dauntlessly, daringly, valiantly, stoutly, resolutely, brazenly, firmly.—*Ant.* COWARDLY, fearfully, cravenly. 2 [*Said of inanimate objects*] prominently, conspicuously, saliently, sharply, clearly, plainly, openly, abruptly, steeply, eminently, vividly, strongly, palpably, commandingly, compellingly, showily.—*Ant.* VAGUELY, inconspicuously, unobtrusively.

boldness *n.* audacity, self-reliance, hardihood; see COURAGE.

bolster *v.* prop, hold up, reinforce, sustain; see also SUPPORT 1, 2.

bolt[1] *n.* staple, brad, nut, skewer, peg, rivet, pin, spike, stud, coupling, key, pin, pipe; see also NAIL, SCREW.

bomb *n.* weapon, high explosive, charge; see EXPLOSIVE. *Types of bombs include the following:* incendiary, multiple warhead, high explosive, demolition glider, time, smoke, delayed action, antipersonnel bomb; atom bomb, atomic bomb, A-bomb, cobalt bomb, hydrogen bomb, H-bomb, torpedo, depth charge, cherry bomb, hand grenade, Molotov cocktail*, stink bomb.

bomb *v.* shell, bombard, torpedo, napalm, blow up, wipe out, blast, attack from the air, zero in on, raid, dive-bomb.

bombing *n.* bombardment, shelling, an attack; see ATTACK.

bond *n.* 1 [A link] attachment, union, obligation, connection, relation, affinity, affiliation, bond of union, restraint; see also FRIENDSHIP, MARRIAGE, RELATIONSHIP. 2 [A secured debenture] security, warranty, debenture, certificate, registered bond, government bond, municipal bond, long-term bond, short-term bond. 3 [Bail] surety, guaranty, warrant; see BAIL.

bondage *n.* servitude, thralldom, subjugation; see SLAVERY 1.

bone *n.* Bones of the human body include the following: cranium, skull, frontal bone, temporal bone, parietal bone, occipital bone, cheekbone, mandible, jawbone, spinal column, vertebrae, backbone, rib cage, clavicle, collarbone, shoulder blade, humerus, radius, ulna, carpal, metacarpal, phalanges, pelvis, illium, hipbone, femur, thighbone, patella, kneecap, tibia, shinbone, fibula, tarsal, metatarsal. —**feel in one's bones** be convinced, expect, be sure; see TRUST 1. —**have a bone to pick*** have a complaint, be angry, express an objection; see COMPLAIN. —**make no bones*** confess, reveal, expose; see ADMIT 2.

bo·ni·to (bō nēt′ō, bə-) *n., pl.* **-tos** or **-toes** ⟦Sp⟧ any of several saltwater food fishes related to the tuna

bon·jour (bōn zhŏŏr′) *interj., n.* ⟦Fr⟧ good day; hello

bonk·ers (bäŋ′kərz) *adj.* [Slang] crazy

bon mot (bōn′ mō′) *pl.* **bons mots** (bōn′ mōz′) ⟦Fr, lit., good word⟧ a clever or witty remark

bon·net (bän′it) *n.* ⟦< OFr *bonet*⟧ a hat with a chin ribbon, worn by children and women

bonny or **bon·nie** (bän′ē) *adj.* **-nier, -ni·est** ⟦< L *bonus*, good⟧ [Now Chiefly Brit.] 1 handsome or pretty, with a healthy glow 2 pleasant

bon·sai (bän sī′) *n., pl.* **-sai′** ⟦Jpn⟧ a tree or shrub grown in a pot and dwarfed by pruning, etc.

bo·nus (bō′nəs) *n., pl.* **-nuses** ⟦L, good⟧ anything given in addition to the customary or required amount

bon voy·age (bän′ vɔi äzh′) ⟦Fr⟧ pleasant journey

bony (bō′nē) *adj.* **-i·er, -i·est** 1 of, like, or having bones 2 thin; emaciated

bony fish any fish having an air bladder, covered gills, and a bony skeleton

boo (bō) *interj.; n., pl.* **boos** a sound made to express disapproval, etc., or to startle — *vi., vt.* **booed, boo′ing** to shout "boo" at

boo-boo or **boo·boo** (bō′bō′) *n., pl.* **-boos′** [Slang] a stupid mistake

boob tube [Slang] TV or a TV set

booby (bō′bē) *n., pl.* **-bies** ⟦prob. < Sp *bobo*⟧ a fool; nitwit Also **boob** (bōb)

booby trap any scheme or device for tricking a person unawares

boodle (bōd′'l) *n.* ⟦< Du *boedel*, property⟧ [Old Slang] 1 something given as a bribe; graft 2 loot

book (book) *n.* ⟦OE *boc*⟧ 1 a printed work on sheets of paper bound together, usually between protective covers 2 a main division of a literary work 3 a record or account 4 *a)* a libretto *b)* the script of a play 5 a booklike package, as of matches — *vt.* 1 to record in a book; list 2 to engage (rooms, etc.) ahead of time 3 to record charges against on a police record — **by the book** according to the rules — **the (Good) Book** the Bible

book′bind′ing *n.* the art or work of binding books — **book′bind′er** *n.* — **book′bind′ery**, *pl.* **-ies**, *n.*

book′case′ (-kās′) *n.* a set of shelves or a cabinet for holding books

book′end′ (-end′) *n.* a weight or bracket that keeps a row of books upright

book·ie (-ē) *n.* [Slang] a bookmaker

book′ing *n.* an engagement, as for a lecture, performance, etc.

book′ish (-ish) *adj.* 1 inclined to read and study 2 pedantic

book′keep′ing *n.* the work of keeping a systematic record of business transactions — **book′keep′er** *n.*

book′let (-lit) *n.* a small book

book′mak′er *n.* a person in the business of taking bets, as on horses

book′mark′ *n.* a thing put between the pages of a book to mark a place

book matches safety matches of paper fastened in a cardboard holder

book′mobile′ (-mō bēl′) *n.* a lending library traveling in a truck, etc.

book′shelf *n., pl.* **-shelves′** a shelf on which books are kept

book′store′ (-stôr′) *n.* a store where books are sold Also [Brit.] **book′shop′**

book′worm′ *n.* 1 an insect larva that feeds on the binding, paste, etc. of books 2 one who reads much

boom[1] (bōōm) *vi., vt.* ⟦echoic⟧ to make, or say with, a deep, hollow, resonant sound — *n.* this sound

boom[2] (bōōm) *n.* ⟦Du, a beam⟧ 1 a spar extending from a mast to hold the bottom of a sail outstretched 2 a long beam extending as from an upright for supporting and guiding anything lifted 3 a barrier, as of logs, to prevent floating logs from dispersing — *vi.* to go rapidly along

boom[3] (bōōm) *vi.* ⟦< ? prec. *vi.*⟧ to increase or grow rapidly — *vt.* to cause to flourish; support — *n.* 1 swift growth 2 a period of prosperity

boom′box′ *n.* [Slang] a large portable radio and tape player

boom·er·ang (bōōm′ər aŋ′) *n.* ⟦< Australian native name⟧ 1 a flat, curved stick that can be thrown so that it returns to the thrower 2 a scheme gone awry, to the schemer's harm — *vi.* to act as a boomerang

boon[1] (bōōn) *n.* ⟦ON *bon*, a petition⟧ a welcome benefit; blessing

boon[2] (bōōn) *adj.* ⟦< L *bonus*, good⟧ merry; convivial: now only in **boon companion**, a close friend

boon·docks (bōōn′däks′) *n.pl.* ⟦< native Philippine name⟧ [Colloq.] 1 a jungle or wilderness 2 any remote rural region Used with *the*

boon·dog·gle (bōōn′dôg′əl, -däg′-) *n.* trifling, pointless work — *vi.* **-gled, -gling** to engage in boondoggle — **boon′dog′gler** *n.*

boor (boor) *n.* ⟦Du *boer*, a peasant⟧ a rude, awkward, or ill-mannered person — **boor′ish** *adj.* — **boor′ishly** *adv.*

boost (bōōst) *vt.* ⟦< ?⟧ 1 to raise as by a push from below 2 to urge others to support 3 to increase — *n.* 1 a push upward or forward 2 an increase — **boost′er** *n.*

booster shot a later injection of a vaccine, for maintaining immunity

boot[1] (bōōt) *n.* ⟦OFr *bote*⟧ 1 a covering of leather, rubber, etc. for the foot and part of the leg 2 a patch for the inside of a tire casing 3 a kick — *vt.* 1 to put boots on 2 to kick 3 [Slang] to dismiss 4 to load, as from a disk (a program, etc.) into the memory of (a computer) — **the boot** [Slang] dismissal

boot[2] (bōōt) *n., vt., vi.* ⟦OE *bot*, advantage⟧ [Archaic] profit — **to boot** besides; in addition

boot′black′ *n.* one whose work is shining shoes or boots

bootee or **bootie** (bōō tē′; *for 2* bōōt′ē) *n.* 1 a short boot for women or children 2 a baby's knitted shoe

booth (bōōth) *n., pl.* **booths** (bōōthz) ⟦< ON *bua*, dwell⟧ 1 a stall for selling goods 2 a small enclosure for voting at elections 3 a small structure to house a public telephone, etc.

THESAURUS

bonus *n.* gratuity, reward, additional compensation; see GIFT 1, TIP 2.

bony *a.* emaciated, skinny, scrawny; see THIN 2.

book *n.* publication, work, volume, booklet, pamphlet, reprint, preprint, offprint, hardcover, text, edition, brochure, folio, copy, monograph, writing, scroll, periodical, magazine, paperback. *Kinds of books include the following:* manual, handbook, reference book, children's book, atlas, cookbook, guidebook, story book, song book, trade book, textbook, workbook, hymnbook, Bible, treatise, tract. **—by the book** strictly, according to rule, rigidly; see LEGALLY, OFFICIALLY 1. **—in one's book** in one's opinion, for oneself, to one's mind; see PERSONALLY 2. **—in the book** practiced, done, established, prevalent; see also KNOWN 2. **—know like a book** understand, comprehend, be aware of; see KNOW 1. **—one for the books*** source of amazement, shock, novelty; see SUR-PRISE 2. **—on the books** listed, noted, set down; see RECORDED. **—throw the book at*** accuse, charge with every possible offense, be overzealous with; see BLAME.

bookkeeper *n.* controller, comptroller, accountant, auditor; see also CLERK.

boom[1,3] *n.* 1 [A loud noise] roar, blast, blare; see NOISE 1. 2 [Sudden increase, especially sudden prosperity] rush, growth, inflation; see INCREASE.

boom[1,3] *v.* 1 [To make a loud sound] roar, reverberate, thunder; see SOUND. 2 [To increase rapidly] prosper, expand, swell; see GROW 1. **—lower the boom on*** take action against, move against, beat, overcome; see also ATTACK.

boon[1] *n.* benefit, good fortune, help; see BLESSING 2.

boor *n.* peasant, yokel, rustic, lout, clown, bumpkin, churl, oaf, lubber, bear, plowman, lumpkin, gaffer, hick*, rube*, hayseed*, clod, clodhopper.

boorish *a.* awkward, clumsy, churlish; see RUDE 1.

boost *n.* 1 [Aid] assistance, aid, helping hand; see HELP 1. 2 [An increase] addition, advance, hike*; see INCREASE.

boost *v.* 1 [To raise] shove, hoist, advance; see RAISE 1. 2 [To promote] encourage, support, advertise; see PROMOTE 1, 2. 3 [To increase] raise, heighten, expand; see INCREASE.

boot[1] *n.* hip-boot, bootie, wader, galosh, laced boot, high shoe, hiking boot, ski boot, cowboy boot, climbing boot, riding boot. **—bet your boots*** be certain, rely on it, trust in it; see DEPEND ON.

booth *n.* stall, counter, nook, corner, pew, berth, compartment, shed, manger, cubbyhole, coop, pen, hut, enclosure, stand, cubicle, box.

boot′leg′ *vt.*, *vi.* **-legged′**, **-leg′ging** 〚< hiding liquor in a boot〛 to make or sell (esp. liquor) illegally — *adj.* bootlegged; illegal — *n.* bootlegged liquor —**boot′leg′ger** *n.*

boot′less *adj.* 〚BOOT² + -LESS〛 useless

booty (bōōt′ē) *n.*, *pl.* **-ties** 〚LowG *bute*〛 1 spoils of war 2 plunder

booze (bōōz) *vi.* **boozed**, **booz′ing** 〚< MDu *busen*〛 [Colloq.] to drink too much liquor — *n.* [Colloq.] liquor

bop¹ (bäp) *vt.* **bopped**, **bop′ping** [Colloq.] to hit; punch

bop² (bäp) *n.* a style of jazz (c. 1945-55) marked by complex rhythms, harmonic experimentation, etc. — *vi.* **bopped**, **bop′ping** [Slang] to walk, esp. in an easy, strutting way

bo·rax (bôr′aks′) *n.* 〚< Pers *būrah*〛 a white crystalline salt used in the manufacture of glass, soaps, etc.

Bor·deaux (bôr dō′) *n.* 〚after *Bordeaux*, city and region in SW France〛 1 a red or white wine from the Bordeaux region 2 a similar wine made elsewhere

bor·der (bôr′dər) *n.* 〚< OFr *border*, to border〛 1 an edge or part near an edge; margin 2 a dividing line between two countries, etc. 3 a narrow strip along an edge — *vt.* 1 to provide with a border 2 to extend along the edge of — *adj.* of or near a border —**border on** (or **upon**) to be next to **bor′der·land′** *n.* 1 land near a border 2 a vague condition

bor′der·line′ (-līn′) *n.* a boundary — *adj.* 1 on a boundary 2 indefinite

bore¹ (bôr) *vt.* **bored**, **bor′ing** 〚< OE *bor*, auger〛 1 to make a hole in with a drill, etc. 2 to make (a well, etc.) as by drilling 3 to weary by being dull — *vi.* to bore a hole or passage — *n.* 1 a hole made as by boring 2 *a)* the hollow part of a tube or gun barrel *b)* its inside diameter 3 a tiresome, dull person or thing

bore² (bôr) *vt.*, *vi. pt. of* BEAR¹

bore·dom (bôr′dəm) *n.* the condition of being bored or uninterested

boric acid a white crystalline compound, used as an antiseptic

born (bôrn) *vt.*, *vi. alt. pp. of* BEAR¹ — *adj.* 1 brought into life 2 natural, as if from birth /a *born* athlete/

born-again (bôrn′ə gen′) *adj.* professing a new or renewed faith or enthusiasm /a *born-again* Christian/

borne (bôrn) *vt.*, *vi. alt. pp. of* BEAR¹

bo·ron (bôr′än′) *n.* 〚< BORAX〛 a nonmetallic chemical element

bor·ough (bʉr′ō) *n.* 〚OE *burg*, town〛 1 a self-governing, incorporated town 2 any of the five administrative units of New York City

bor·row (bär′ō, bôr′-) *vt.*, *vi.* 〚OE *borgian*〛 1 to take or receive (something) intending to return it 2 to adopt (an idea, etc.) as one's own —**bor′rower** *n.*

borscht or **borsch** (bôrsh) *n.* 〚Russ *borshch*〛 a beet soup, served usually with sour cream

bor·zoi (bôr′zoi′) *n.* 〚Russ *borzój*, swift〛 a large dog with a narrow head, long legs, and silky coat

bosh (bäsh) *n.*, *interj.* 〚Turk, empty〛 [Colloq.] nonsense

bosom (booz′əm, bōō′zəm) *n.* 〚OE *bosm*〛 1 the human breast 2 the breast regarded as the source of feelings 3 the inside; midst /in the *bosom* of one's family/ 4 the part of a garment that covers the breast — *adj.* close; intimate /a *bosom* friend/

bos′omy (-əm ē) *adj.* having large breasts

boson (bōs′än′) *n.* 〚after S. N. *Bose* (1894-1974), Indian physicist + -ON〛 any of certain subatomic particles, including photons and mesons

boss¹ (bôs, bäs) *n.* 〚Du *baas*, a master〛 1 an employer or manager 2 one who controls a political organization — *vt.* 1 to act as boss of 2 [Colloq.] to order (a person) about — *adj.* [Slang] excellent

boss² (bôs, bäs) *n.* 〚OFr *boce*, a swelling〛 a protruding ornament or projecting knob — *vt.* to stud

boss′ism′ *n.* control by bosses, esp. of a political machine or party

boss′y *adj.* **-i·er**, **-i·est** [Colloq.] domineering —**boss′i·ness** *n.*

bo·sun (bōs′ən) *n. alt. sp. of* BOATSWAIN

bot·any (bät′'n ē) *n.* 〚< Gr *botanē*, a plant〛 the science that deals with plants and plant life —**bo·tani·cal** (bō tan′i kəl) or **bo·tan′ic** *adj.* —**bot′a·nist** *n.*

botch (bäch) *vt.* 〚ME *bocchen*, to repair < ?〛 1 to patch clumsily 2 to bungle — *n.* a bungled or unskilled piece of work —**botch′er** *n.*

bot·fly (bät′flī′) *n.*, *pl.* **-flies′** a fly resembling a small bumblebee

both (bōth) *adj.*, *pron.* 〚OE *ba tha*, both these〛 the two /both birds sang loudly/ — *conj.*, *adv.* together; equally /both hungry and hungry/

bother (bäth′ər) *vt.*, *vi.* 〚prob. < *pother*〛 1 to worry; harass 2 to concern (oneself) — *n.* 1 worry; trouble 2 one who gives trouble —**bother·some** (-səm) *adj.*

bot·tle (bät′'l) *n.* 〚< LL *buttis*, a cask〛 1 a narrow-necked container for liquids, usually of glass 2 its contents — *vt.* **-tled**, **-tling** to put into a bottle —**bottle up** to restrain — **hit the bottle** [Slang] to drink much alcoholic liquor — **bot′tler** *n.*

bot′tle·neck′ *n.* 1 a narrow passage or road where progress, as of traffic, is slowed 2 any hindrance to movement or progress

▬ THESAURUS ▬

bootleg *a.* illegal, unlawful, contraband; see ILLEGAL.

booty *n.* plunder, spoils, winnings, stolen goods, pickings, ill-gotten gains, seizure, prize, haul, pickings, loot, take*.

booze* *n.* liquor, alcohol, whiskey; see DRINK 2.

border *n.* 1 [Edge] hem, end, trim; see DECORATION 2, FRINGE. 2 [Boundary] frontier, outpost, perimeter; see BOUNDARY, EDGE 1.

border *v.* be adjacent to, adjoin, abut on; see JOIN 3. —**border on** lie next to, abut, touch; see JOIN 3.

bordering *a.* rimming, bounding, neighboring, fringing, edging, lining, verging, connecting, on the edge of; see also NEAR 1.

bore¹ *n.* nuisance, pest, tiresome person; see TROUBLE.

bore¹ *v.* 1 [To pierce by rotary motion] drill, ream, perforate; see PENETRATE. 2 [To weary] fatigue, tire, put to sleep; see TIRE 2.

bored *a.* wearied, fatigued, jaded, dull, irked, annoyed, bored to death*, in a rut, sick and tired, bored stiff*, bored silly*, fed up*; see also TIRED.—*Ant.* EXCITED, thrilled, exhilarated.

boredom *n.* lack of interest, tiresomeness, apathy, doldrums, listlessness, monotony, indifference, tedium.

boring *a.* tedious, stupid, monoto-nous; see DULL 3, 4.

born *a.* intrinsic, innate, inherent; see NATURAL 1.

borrow *v.* accept the loan of, obtain the use of, take a loan, go into debt, get temporary use of, use, rent, hire, obtain, give a note for, sponge*, hit up for*, bum*, beg, chisel*, mooch*.—*Ant.* LEND, loan, give back.

borrowed *a.* appropriated, taken, acquired, assumed, adopted, hired, plagiarized, imported, cultivated, imitated.—*Ant.* owned, possessed, titular.

boss¹ *n.* supervisor, manager, administrator; see EXECUTIVE.

botanical *a.* concerning plants, vegetable, floral, arboreal, herbaceous, morphological, cytological, agricultural; see also BIOLOGICAL.

botany *n.* phytology, natural history, study of plant life; see BIOLOGY, SCIENCE.

botch *v.* bungle, spoil, mar, ruin, wreck, mutilate, fumble, distort, blunder, mishandle, do clumsily, muddle, make a mess of, trip, flounder, err, fall down, be mistaken, misjudge, mismanage, miscalculate, misconstrue, misestimate, execute clumsily, do unskillfully, stumble, put one's foot in it*, goof up*, butcher, screw up*, mess up*, put out of whack*; see also FAIL 1.—*Ant.* SUCCEED, fix, do well.

both *a.* the two, both together, the one and the other, the pair, the couple, one as well as the other.

bother *n.* 1 [Worry] vexation, distress, anxiety; see CARE 2. 2 [A cause of worry] problem, concern, care; see DIFFICULTY 1, 2, TROUBLE.

bother *v.* 1 [To take trouble] put oneself out, fret, go out of one's way, make a fuss about, fuss over, take pains, make an effort, exert oneself, concern oneself, be concerned about, worry about. 2 [To give trouble] plague, vex, annoy, perplex, pester, molest, irritate, irk, provoke, insult, harass, heckle, aggravate, badger, discommode, discompose, mortify, goad, intrude upon, disquiet, pursue, hinder, impede, carp at, scare, exasperate, bore, afflict, taunt, torment, torture, bedevil, browbeat, tease, tantalize, ride, rub the wrong way, pick on, nag, needle*, bug*, get under someone's skin*.—*Ant.* HELP, please, delight.

bothered *a.* annoyed, agitated, disturbed; see TROUBLED.

bothersome *a.* vexatious, vexing, troublesome; see DISTURBING.

bottle *n.* flask, flagon, decanter, cruet, jug, urn, canteen, cruse, jar, gourd, carafe, hip flask, vial, vacuum bottle, glass. —**hit the bottle*** get drunk, imbibe, become an alcoholic; see DRINK 2.

bot·tom (bät′əm) *n.* ⟦OE *botm*, ground⟧ 1 the lowest part or place 2 the part on which something rests 3 the side underneath 4 the seat of a chair 5 the ground beneath a body of water 6 basis; cause; source 7 [Colloq.] the buttocks —*adj.* lowest; last; basic —**at bottom** fundamentally —**bot′tom·less** *adj.*

bottom line 1 [Colloq.] profits or losses, as of a business 2 [Slang] *a)* the basic factor, etc. *b)* the final statement, decision, etc.

botu·lism (bäch′ə liz′əm) *n.* ⟦< L *botulus*, sausage⟧ poisoning from the toxin produced by a bacillus sometimes found in foods improperly canned or preserved

bou·doir (bo͞o dwär′, bo͞o′dwär′) *n.* ⟦< Fr, lit., pouting room⟧ a woman's private room

bouf·fant (bo͞o fänt′) *adj.* ⟦< Fr *bouffer*, puff out⟧ puffed out; full

bou·gain·vil·lea or **bou·gain·vil·laea** (bo͞o′gən vil′ē ə, -vil′yə, -vē′yə) *n.* ⟦ModL⟧ a woody tropical vine having large, showy, purple or red bracts

bough (bou) *n.* ⟦OE *bog*, shoulder⟧ a main branch of a tree

bought (bôt) *vt., vi. pt. & pp. of* BUY

bouil·lon (bo͞ol′yän′, -yən) *n.* ⟦< Fr *bouillir*, to boil⟧ a clear broth

boul·der (bōl′dər) *n.* ⟦< ME *bulderston*, noisy stone⟧ a large rock worn by weather and water

boule·vard (bo͞ol′ə värd′) *n.* ⟦Fr < MDu *bolwerc*, bulwark⟧ a broad street, often lined with trees, etc.

bounce (bouns) *vi.* **bounced, bounc′ing** ⟦ME *bounsen*, to thump⟧ 1 to spring back, as upon impact; rebound 2 to spring; leap 3 [Slang] to be returned: said of a worthless check — *vt.* 1 to cause (a ball, etc.) to bounce 2 [Slang] to put (a person) out by force 3 [Slang] to fire from a job — *n.* 1 *a)* a bouncing; rebound *b)* a leap or jump 2 capacity for bouncing 3 [Colloq.] energy, zest, etc. —**the bounce** [Slang] dismissal —**bounc′y** *adj.*

bouncer (boun′sər) *n.* [Slang] a person hired to remove disorderly people from a nightclub, restaurant, etc.

bounc′ing (-siŋ) *adj.* big, healthy, etc.

bound¹ (bound) *vi.* ⟦< OFr *bondir*, to leap⟧ 1 to move with a leap or leaps 2 to bounce; rebound — *vt.* to cause to bound or bounce — *n.* 1 a jump; leap 2 a bounce; rebound

bound² (bound) *vt., vi. pt. & pp. of* BIND —*adj.* 1 tied 2 closely connected 3 certain *[bound to lose]* 4 obliged 5 having a binding, as a book 6 [Colloq.] determined; resolved

bound³ (bound) *adj.* ⟦< ON *bua*, prepare⟧ going; headed *[bound east]*

bound⁴ (bound) *n.* ⟦< ML *butina*, boundary⟧ 1 a boundary 2 [*pl.*] an area near a boundary — *vt.* 1 to limit 2 to be a limit or boundary to 3 to name the boundaries of —**out of bounds** 1 beyond the boundary 2 forbidden

bounda·ry (boun′də rē, -drē) *n., pl.* **-ries** anything marking a limit; bound

bound′en (-dən) *adj.* ⟦old pp. of BIND⟧ 1 [Archaic] obligated; indebted 2 obligatory *[one's bounden duty]*

bound′er (-dər) *n.* ⟦< BOUND¹⟧ [Colloq., Chiefly Brit.] a cad

boun·te·ous (boun′tē əs) *adj.* ⟦see fol.⟧ 1 generous 2 plentiful —**boun′ti·ful** (-tə fəl) *adj.*

boun·ty (-tē) *n., pl.* **-ties** ⟦< L *bonus*, good⟧ 1 generosity 2 a generous gift 3 a reward or premium

bou·quet (bo͞o kā′; *often* bō-) *n.* ⟦Fr⟧ 1 a bunch of flowers 2 aroma, as of wine

bour·bon (bʉr′bən, boor′-) *n.* ⟦after *Bourbon* County, Ky.⟧ [*sometimes* B-] a whiskey distilled from corn mash

bour·geois (boor zhwä′, boor′zhwä) *n., pl.* **-geois** ⟦Fr < OFr *borc*, town⟧ a member of the bourgeoisie — *adj.* of the bourgeoisie: used variously to mean conventional, smug, respectable, etc.

bour·geoi·sie (boor′zhwä zē′) *n.* [*with sing. or pl. v.*] the social class between the very wealthy and the working class; middle class

bour·geoi·si·fy (-zə fī′) *vt.* **-fied′, -fy′ing** to make bourgeois in characteristics, attitudes, etc. —**bour·geoi·si·fi·ca′tion** *n.*

bout (bout) *n.* ⟦ME *bught*⟧ 1 a struggle or contest 2 a period spent in some activity; spell

bou·tique (bo͞o tēk′; *often*, bō-) *n.* ⟦Fr < L *apotheca*, storehouse⟧ a small shop where fashionable articles are sold

bou·ton·niere or **bou·ton·nière** (bo͞o′tə nir′, -tən yer′) *n.* ⟦Fr, buttonhole⟧ a flower worn in a buttonhole

bo·vine (bō′vīn′, -vēn′) *adj.* ⟦< L *bos*, ox⟧ 1 of an ox or cow 2 slow, dull, stupid, etc.

bow¹ (bou) *vi.* ⟦< OE *bugan*, to bend⟧ 1 to bend the head or body in respect, agreement, etc. 2 to yield; submit — *vt.* 1 to bend (the head or body) in respect, etc. 2 to weigh (*down*) — *n.* a bending of the head or body, as in respect, greeting, etc. —**take a bow** to acknowledge applause, etc.

bow² (bō) *n.* ⟦OE *boga*⟧ 1 anything curved *[a rainbow]* 2 a curve; bend 3 a flexible, curved strip of wood with a cord connecting the two ends, for shooting arrows 4 a slender stick strung with horsehairs, for playing a violin, etc. 5 BOWKNOT —*adj.* curved —*vt., vi.* 1 to bend; curve 2 to play (a violin, etc.) with a bow

bow³ (bou) *n.* ⟦< LowG *bûg*⟧ the front part of a ship, etc.

bowd·ler·ize (boud′lər iz′) *vt.* **-ized′, -iz′ing** ⟦after T. *Bowdler* (1754-1825), Eng editor⟧ to expurgate —**bowd′ler·izm′** *n.* —**bowd′ler·i·za′tion** *n.*

bowel (bou′əl) *n.* ⟦< L *botulus*, sausage⟧ 1 an intestine, esp. of a human being 2 [*pl.*] the inner part —**move one's bowels** to defecate

bower (bou′ər) *n.* ⟦< OE *bur*, dwelling⟧ a place enclosed by boughs or vines; arbor

bowie knife (bo͞o′ē, bō′-) ⟦after Col. J. *Bowie* (c. 1799-1836)⟧ a long single-edged hunting knife

bow·knot (bō′nät′) *n.* a decorative knot, usually with two loops and two ends

---

■ THESAURUS ■

bottom *n.* underside, base, nadir, foot, depths, bed, floor, lowest part, deepest part, sole, ground.—*Ant.* TOP, peak, pinnacle. —**at bottom** fundamentally, basically, actually; see REALLY 1. —**be at the bottom of** originate, be the reason for, activate; see CAUSE. —**bet one's bottom dollar*** bet, risk, wager; see GAMBLE.

bottomless *a.* deep, unfathomable, boundless; see INFINITE.

bottom line* *n.* 1 [Profits or losses] net income, net loss, net profits; see INCOME, PROFIT 2, LOSS 3. 2 [Final decision] conclusion, determination, last word; see END 2.

bottoms *n.* low land, marsh, bottomland; see SWAMP.

bough *n.* limb, arm, fork; see BRANCH 2.

bought *a.* purchased, procured, budgeted for, requisitioned, paid for, on order, to be delivered, contracted for, included in the purchase; see also ORDERED 1.—*Ant.* STOLEN, sold, given away.

boulder *n.* stone, slab, crag; see ROCK 2.

boulevard *n.* street, avenue, highway; see ROAD 1.

bounce *v.* ricochet, recoil, glance off,

spring back, leap, hop, bolt, vault, skip, bob, buck, jump, bound, jerk up and down, snap back, boomerang, backlash.

bound¹,⁴ *v.* 1 [To move in leaps] leap, spring, vault; see JUMP 1. 2 [To rebound] bounce, ricochet, recoil; see BOUNCE. 3 [To set limits] restrict, confine, circumscribe; see DEFINE 1. —**out of bounds** off limits, not permitted, restricted; see ILLEGAL.

bound² *a.* 1 [Literally confined in bonds] fettered, shackled, trussed up, manacled, enchained, handcuffed, hobbled, captive, pinioned, muzzled, in leash, tied up, harnessed, bound hand and foot, lashed fast, pinned down, tethered, picketed, secured, roped, gagged.—*Ant.* FREE, unrestrained, loose. 2 [Figuratively constrained] impelled, compelled, obliged, obligated, restrained, under compulsion, constrained, forced, coerced, driven, pressed, urged, necessitated, under necessity, made, having no alternative, required. —**bound to** certain to, sure to, destined to; see INEVITABLE.

boundary *n.* outline, border, verge, rim, beginning, end, confine, bounds,

radius, terminus, landmark, march, extremity, fence, compass, side, hem, frame, skirt, termination, margin, line, barrier, frontier, outpost, perimeter, parameter, extent, circumference, horizon, periphery, fringe, mark, confines, limit, borderland.

bounded *a.* limited, enclosed, bordered; see SURROUNDED.

bounty *n.* prize, premium, bonus; see PAY 1, 2.

bouquet *n.* nosegay, bunch of flowers, garland, vase of flowers, flower arrangement, wreath, spray.

bow¹ *v.* 1 [To bend] curtsey, stoop, dip; see BEND. 2 [To submit] surrender, acquiesce, capitulate; see YIELD 1.

bow¹,³ *n.* 1 [Front of a boat] forepart, bowsprit, prow, head, stem, fore; see also FRONT 1. 2 [A bend from the waist] nod, curtsey, bowing and scraping; see ACKNOWLEDGMENT. —**take a bow** accept praise, be congratulated, feel honored; see BEND.

bow² *n.* longbow, crossbow, single-piece bow; see WEAPON.

bowels *n.* viscera, entrails, guts; see INSIDES.

bowl¹ (bōl) *n.* ⟦OE *bolla*⟧ 1 a deep, rounded dish 2 the contents of a bowl 3 a bowllike thing or part 4 an amphitheater or stadium —**bowl′like′** *adj.*

bowl² (bōl) *n.* ⟦< L *bulla*, bubble⟧ 1 the wooden ball used in the game of bowls 2 a roll of the ball in bowling —*vi.* 1 to roll (a ball) or participate in bowling 2 to move swiftly and smoothly —**bowl over** 1 to knock over 2 [Colloq.] to astonish —**bowl′er** *n.*

bowl·der (bōl′dər) *n. alt. sp. of* BOULDER

bow·leg (bō′leg′) *n.* a leg with outward curvature —**bow′legged** (-leg′id, -legd′) *adj.*

bowl·ing (bōl′iŋ) *n.* 1 a game in which a heavy ball is bowled along a wooden lane (**bowling alley**) at ten wooden pins 2 BOWLS

bowls (bōlz) *n.* a bowling game played on a smooth lawn (**bowling green**)

bow·man (bō′mən) *n., pl.* -**men** an archer

bow·sprit (bou′sprit′, bō′-) *n.* ⟦prob. < Du⟧ a tapered spar extending forward from the bow of a sailing ship

bow tie (bō) a necktie tied in a bow

box¹ (bäks) *n.* ⟦< Gr *pyxos*, BOX³⟧ 1 a container, usually rectangular and lidded; case 2 the contents of a box 3 a boxlike thing or space [a jury *box*] 4 a small, enclosed group of seats, as in a theater 5 a booth 6 *Baseball* an area designated for the batter, catcher, etc. —*vt.* to put into a box —**box in** (or **up**) to shut in or keep in; surround or confine —**in a box** [Colloq.] in difficulty —**box′like′** *adj.*

box² (bäks) *n.* ⟦< ?⟧ a blow struck with the hand —*vt.* 1 to strike with such a blow 2 to fight by boxing with —*vi.* to fight with the fists

box³ (bäks) *n.* ⟦< Gr *pyxos*⟧ an evergreen shrub with small leathery leaves Also **box′wood′**

box′car′ *n.* a fully enclosed railroad freight car

box′er *n.* 1 one who boxes; prizefighter 2 a medium-sized dog with a sturdy body and a smooth coat

box′ing *n.* the skill or sport of fighting with the fists, esp. in padded leather mittens (**boxing gloves**)

box office 1 a place where admission tickets are sold, as in a theater 2 [Colloq.] the power, as of a performer, to attract a paying audience

boy (boi) *n.* ⟦ME *boie*⟧ 1 a male child 2 any man: familiar term 3 a male servant: a patronizing term —*interj.* [Slang] an exclamation of pleasure, surprise, etc.: often **oh, boy!** —**boy′hood′** *n.* —**boy′ish** *adj.*

boy·cott (boi′kät′) *vt.* ⟦after Capt. *Boycott*, Irish land agent so treated⟧ to join together in refusing to deal with, buy, etc. so as to punish or coerce —*n.* a boycotting

boy′friend′ *n.* 1 [Colloq.] a sweetheart or escort of a girl or woman 2 a boy who is one's friend

Boy Scout a member of the **Boy Scouts**, a boys' organization that stresses outdoor life and service to others

boysen·berry (boi′zən ber′ē) *n., pl.* -**ries** ⟦after R. *Boysen*, U.S. horticulturist⟧ a berry that is a cross of the raspberry, loganberry, and blackberry

Br *Chem. symbol for* bromine

Br. 1 Britain 2 British 3 Brother

bra (brä) *n.* ⟦< BRASSIERE⟧ a brassiere

brace (brās) *vt.* **braced, brac′ing** ⟦< Gr *brachiōn*, arm⟧ 1 to bind 2 to strengthen by supporting the weight of, etc. 3 to make ready for an impact, shock, etc. 4 to stimulate —*n.* 1 a couple; pair 2 a thing that clasps or connects 3 [*pl.*] [Brit.] suspenders 4 a device for setting up or main-

taining tension 5 either of the signs { }, used to connect words, lines, etc. 6 any propping device 7 *a*) a device for supporting a weak part of the body *b*) [*often pl.*] a device worn for straightening the teeth 8 a tool for holding a drilling bit —**brace up** to call forth one's courage, etc.

brace and bit a tool for boring, consisting of a removable drill (*bit*) in a rotating handle (*brace*)

brace·let (brās′lit) *n.* ⟦< Gr *brachiōn*, arm⟧ an ornamental band or chain worn about the wrist or arm

bracken (brak′ən) *n.* ⟦ME *braken*⟧ a large, coarse, weedy fern found in meadows, woods, and wastelands

bracket (brak′it) *n.* ⟦< Fr *brague*, knee pants⟧ 1 a support projecting from a wall, etc. 2 any angle-shaped support 3 either of the signs [ ], used to enclose a word, etc. 4 a classification [high income *bracket*] —*vt.* 1 to support with brackets 2 to enclose within brackets 3 to classify together

brack·ish (brak′ish) *adj.* ⟦< MDu *brak*⟧ 1 salty 2 nauseating

bract (brakt) *n.* ⟦L *bractea*, thin metal plate⟧ a modified leaf growing at the base of a flower or on its stalk

brad (brad) *n.* ⟦ON *broddr*, arrow⟧ a thin wire nail with a small head

brae (brā, brē) *n.* ⟦ON *bra*, brow⟧ [Scot.] a sloping bank; hillside

brag (brag) *vt., vi.* **bragged, brag′ging** ⟦ME *braggen* < ?⟧ to boast —*n.* boastful talk —**brag′ger** *n.*

brag′gart (-ərt) *n.* an offensively boastful person —*adj.* boastful

Brahma (brä′mə) the chief member of the Hindu trinity (Brahma, Vishnu, and Siva), regarded as the creator of the universe

Brah·man (brä′mən) *n., pl.* -**mans** ⟦Hindi < Sans. worship⟧ 1 a member of the priestly Hindu caste 2 a breed of domestic cattle developed from the zebu of India and having a large hump

braid (brād) *vt.* ⟦< OE *bregdan*, to move quickly⟧ 1 to interweave three or more strands of (hair, straw, etc.) 2 to make by such interweaving —*n.* 1 a strip, as of hair, formed by braiding 2 a woven band of cloth, etc., used to bind or decorate clothing

Braille (brāl) *n.* ⟦after L. *Braille* (1809-52), its Fr inventor⟧ [*also* b-] a system of printing for the blind, using raised dots felt with the fingers

brain (brān) *n.* ⟦OE *brægen*⟧ 1 the mass of nerve tissue in the cranium of vertebrates 2 [*often pl.*] intelligence —*vt.* to dash out the brains of

brain′child′ *n.* [Colloq.] an idea, plan, etc. produced by one's mental labor

brain drain [Colloq.] an exhausting of the intellectual or professional resources of a country, region, etc., esp. through emigration

brain′less *adj.* foolish or stupid

brain′storm′ *n.* [Colloq.] a sudden inspiration, idea, or plan —*vi.* to engage in brainstorming

brain′storm′ing *n.* the unrestrained offering of ideas by all members of a group to seek solutions to problems

brain′wash′ *vt.* [Colloq.] to indoctrinate so thoroughly as to effect a radical change of beliefs

brain wave 1 rhythmic electric impulses from the nerve centers in the brain 2 [Colloq.] a brainstorm

brain′y *adj.* -**i·er**, -**i·est** [Colloq.] having a good mind; intelligent

braise (brāz) *vt.* **braised, brais′ing** ⟦< Fr *braise*, live coals⟧ to brown (meat, etc.) and then simmer slowly

THESAURUS

bowl¹ *n.* vessel, tureen, pot, saucer, crock, jar, urn, pitcher, basin, casserole, boat; see also CONTAINER, DISH.

bowling *n.* ninepins, tenpins, boccie; see SPORT 3.

box¹ *n.* receptacle, crate, carton; see CONTAINER.

box¹,² *v.* 1 [To enclose in a box] confine, package, crate; see PACK 2. 2 [To fight for sport] spar, punch, slug; see FIGHT.

boxer *n.* pugilist, fighter, prizefighter; see FIGHTER 1.

boxing *n.* pugilism, prizefighting, the fights*; see SPORT 3.

boy *n.* lad, youth, stripling, fellow, schoolboy, youngster, whippersnapper, male child, junior, little gentleman; see also CHILD.

boycott *v.* withhold patronage, hold aloof from, ostracize; see AVOID,

STRIKE 2.

boyfriend *n.* young man, beau*, companion, steady*, lover, sweetheart, suitor, paramour, main man*, old man*.

boyhood *n.* schoolboy days, formative period, adolescence; see CHILDHOOD, YOUTH 1.

boyish *a.* puerile, boylike, adolescent; see CHILDISH, YOUNG 1.

boy scout *n.* cub scout, explorer scout, troop member; see SCOUT 2.

brace *n.* prop, bolster, stay, support, lever, beam, girder, block, rib, buttress, reinforcement, bearing, upholder, bracket, strengthener, band, bracer, stirrup, arm, splint, boom, bar, staff, rafter, jack, crutch.

brace *v.* prop, bolster, hold up; see SUPPORT 1.

bracelet *n.* arm band, ornament,

bangle; see JEWELRY.

brag *v.* swagger, exult, gloat; see BOAST.

braggart *n.* boaster, blowhard*, windbag*, trumpeter, swaggerer, strutter, peacock, blusterer, bragger, know-it-all*.

brain *n.* 1 [The organ of intelligence] cerebrum, gray matter, brain cells; see HEAD 1. 2 [The intelligence] intellect, genius, mentality; see MIND 1. 3 [*A very intelligent person*] academician, scholar, egghead*; see INTELLECTUAL. —**have on the brain** be obsessed with, be involved with, fuss over, stew about; see also BOTHER 2.

brainwash* *v.* indoctrinate, instill, catechize; see CONVINCE, INFLUENCE, TEACH.

brake (brāk) *n.* 〖< Ger *breken*, to break〗 any device for slowing or stopping a vehicle or machine, as by causing a block or band to press against a moving part — *vt., vi.* braked, brak'ing to slow down or stop as with a brake — brake'less *adj.*

brake'man (-mən) *n., pl.* -men a railroad worker who operated the brakes on a train, but is now chiefly an assistant to the conductor

bram·ble (bram'bəl) *n.* 〖< OE *brom*, broom〗 a prickly shrub of the rose family, as the raspberry, blackberry, etc. —bram'bly *adj.*

bran (bran) *n.* 〖OFr *bren*〗 the husk of grains of wheat, rye, etc. separated from the flour, as by sifting

branch (branch) *n.* 〖< LL *branca*, a claw〗 1 any woody extension from a tree or shrub; limb 2 a tributary stream 3 any part or extension of a main body or system, as a division of a family or a separately located unit of a business — *vi.* 1 to put forth branches 2 to come out (*from* the main part) as a branch —branch off 1 to separate into branches 2 to diverge —branch out to extend one's interests, activities, etc. —branched (brancht) *adj.* —branch'like' *adj.*

brand (brand) *n.* 〖OE < *biernan*, to burn〗 1 a burning or partially burned stick 2 a mark burned on the skin, formerly used to punish criminals, now used on cattle to show ownership 3 the iron used in branding 4 a stigma 5 *a*) an identifying mark or label *b*) the make of a commodity *[a brand* of coffee*] c*) a special kind — *vt.* 1 to mark with a brand 2 to put a stigma on —brand'er *n.*

bran·dish (bran'dish) *vt.* 〖< OFr *brandir*〗 to wave menacingly or as a challenge; flourish

brand name the name by which a certain brand or make of commodity is known —brand'-name' *adj.*

brand'-new' *adj.* 〖orig., fresh from the fire: see BRAND〗 entirely new

brandy (bran'dē) *n., pl.* -dies 〖< Du *brandewijn*, distilled wine〗 an alcoholic liquor distilled from wine or from fermented fruit juice — *vt.* -died, -dy·ing to flavor or preserve with brandy

brant (brant) *n.* 〖< ?〗 a wild goose of Europe and North America

brash (brash) *adj.* 〖orig. Brit dial.; < ?〗 1 hasty and reckless 2 insolent; impudent —brash'ness *n.*

brass (bras) *n., pl.* brass'es 〖OE *bræs*〗 1 a yellowish metal, an alloy of copper and zinc 2 *[often with pl. v.]* brass instruments 3 [Colloq.] bold impudence 4 *[often with pl. v.]* [Slang] officers or officials of high rank — *adj.* of brass —brass'y, -i·er, -i·est, *adj.*

bras·siere or bras·sière (brə zir') *n.* 〖Fr < *bras*, an arm〗 an undergarment worn by women to support the breasts

brass tacks [Colloq.] basic facts

brat (brat) *n.* 〖< Gael *bratt*, cloth, rag〗 a child, esp. an impudent, unruly child: scornful or playful term

brat·wurst (brät'voorst') *n.* 〖Ger < OHG, *brato*, lean meat + *wurst*, sausage〗 highly seasoned, fresh sausage of veal and pork

71 **brake / break**

braun·schwei·ger (broun'shwī'gər) *n.* 〖after *Braunschweig*, Germany, where orig. made〗 smoked liver sausage

bra·vado (brə vä'dō) *n.* 〖< Sp < *bravo*, brave〗 pretended courage or feigned confidence

brave (brāv) *adj.* brav'er, brav'est 〖Fr < It *bravo*〗 1 not afraid; having courage 2 having a fine appearance — *n.* 1 any brave man 2 a North American Indian warrior — *vt.* braved, brav'ing 1 to face with courage 2 to defy; dare —brave'ly *adv.* —brave'ness *n.*

brav·ery (brāv'ər ē) *n.* courage; valor

bravo (brä'vō) *interj.* 〖It〗 Well done! excellent! — *n., pl.* -vos a shout of "bravo!"

bra·vura (brə vyoor'ə) *n.* 〖It < *bravo*, brave〗 1 bold daring; dash 2 a brilliant musical passage or technique

brawl (brôl) *vi.* 〖< Du *brallen*, to boast〗 to quarrel or fight noisily — *n.* a noisy quarrel or fight

brawn (brôn) *n.* 〖< OFr *braon*, muscle〗 1 strong, well-developed muscles 2 muscular strength —brawn'y, -i·er, -i·est, *adj.* —brawn'i·ness *n.*

bray (brā) *vi.* 〖< OFr *braire*〗 to make the loud, harsh cry of a donkey — *n.* the harsh cry of a donkey, or a sound like this

braze (brāz) *vt.* brazed, braz'ing 〖Fr *braser*〗 to solder with a metal having a high melting point

bra·zen (brā'zən) *adj.* 〖< OE *bræsen*, brass〗 1 of brass 2 like brass in color, etc. 3 shameless; bold 4 harsh and piercing —brazen it out to act in a bold, unashamed way —bra'zenly *adv.* —bra'zen·ness *n.*

bra·zier[1] (brā'zhər) *n.* 〖see BRAISE〗 a metal container to hold burning coals

bra·zier[2] (brā'zhər) *n.* 〖see BRASS〗 a person who works in brass

Bra·zil·ian (brə zil'yən) *n.* a native or inhabitant of Brazil — *adj.* of Brazil

Brazil nut the edible, three-sided seed of a tree of South America

breach (brēch) *n.* 〖< OE *brecan*, to break〗 1 a failure to observe a law, promise, etc. 2 an opening made by a breakthrough 3 a break in friendly relations — *vt.* to make a breach in —breach of promise a breaking of a promise to marry

bread (bred) *n.* 〖OE, crumb〗 1 a baked food made of flour or meal mixed with water, etc. 2 livelihood *[to earn one's bread]* — *vt.* to coat with bread crumbs before cooking —break bread to eat

breadth (bredth) *n.* 〖< OE *brad*, broad〗 1 width 2 scope; extent

bread·winner (bred'win'ər) *n.* one who supports dependents by his or her earnings

break (brāk) *vt.* broke, bro'ken, break'ing 〖OE *brecan*〗 1 to split or crack into pieces; smash 2 to cut open the surface of (soil, the skin, etc.) 3 to make unusable by cracking, disrupting, etc. 4 to tame as with force 5 to get

THESAURUS

brake *n.* check, hamper, curb, deterrent, obstacle, damper, hindrance, retarding device, governor.

bramble *n.* brier, thorn, burr, stinging nettle, prickly shrub, goose grass, thistle, shrub, bramble bush, hedge.

branch *n.* 1 [A part, usually of secondary importance] member, office, bureau; see DIVISION 2. 2 [A secondary shoot] bough, limb, offshoot, sprig, twig, bud, arm, fork, growth.

branch off *v.* diverge, separate, part; see DIVIDE.

branch out *v.* expand, extend, add to; see GROW 1, INCREASE.

brand *n.* stigma, scar, sear, welt, range brand, earmark, owner's mark.

brand *v.* blaze, stamp, imprint; see MARK 1.

brandish *v.* flourish, gesture, warn; see THREATEN.

brass *n.* 1 [An alloy of copper and zinc] copper alloy, pinchbeck, brassware, yellow metal. 2 [*High-ranking officials] officers, front office*, brass hats; see OFFICER 3. 3 [*Impudence] effrontery, impertinence, audacity; see RUDENESS.

brat *n.* impudent child, unruly child, youngster, kid*; see also CHILD.

brave *a.* fearless, daring, dauntless, valiant, intrepid, undaunted, undismayed, confident, unabashed, chivalrous, valorous, heroic, bold, imprudent, adventurous, reckless, foolhardy, dashing, venturesome, forward, audacious, gallant, resolute, militant, defiant, hardy, unafraid, stout, stout-hearted, lion-hearted, manly, firm, plucky, high-spirited, unshrinking, strong, stalwart, unflinching, unyielding, indomitable, game, unconquerable, spunky*, nervy*, gutsy*.—*Ant.* COWARDLY, timid, craven.

bravely *a.* courageously, fearlessly, valiantly, boldly, daringly, dauntlessly, intrepidly, heroically, gallantly, hardily, stoutly, manfully, staunchly, with courage, with fortitude, resolutely, valorously, spiritedly, audaciously, chivalrously, firmly, indomitably, with guts*, like a man*.—*Ant.* COWARDLY, fearfully, timidly.

bravery *n.* valor, intrepidity, fearlessness; see COURAGE, STRENGTH.

brawl *n.* fuss, squabble, riot; see FIGHT 1.

breach *n.* violation, infringement,

transgression; see CRIME, VIOLATION.

bread *n.* loaf, baked goods, the staff of life. *Types of bread include the following:* whole wheat, rye, salt-rising, leavened, unleavened, corn, sourdough, raisin, pumpernickel, French, white, black, dark brown, Boston brown, potato, hardtack. *Breadline foods include the following:* spoon bread, cake, dumpling, turnover, bun, cookie, English muffin, corn bread, scone, shortbread, Indian bread. —break bread partake, have a meal, indulge; see EAT 1. —know which side one's bread is buttered on be prudent, save, look out for number one*; see UNDERSTAND 1.

breadth *n.* largeness, extent, vastness, compass, magnitude, greatness, extensiveness, scope, broadness, width, comprehensiveness, amplitude; see also SIZE 2.

break *n.* 1 [The act of breaking] fracture, rift, split, schism, cleavage, breach, rupture, eruption, bursting, failure, division, parting, collapse.—*Ant.* REPAIR, mending, maintenance. 2 [A pause] intermission, interim, lapse; see PAUSE. 3 [*Fortunate change or event; often plural]* good rid of (a habit) **6** to demote **7** to make poor, ill, bankrupt, etc. **8** to surpass (a record) **9** to violate (a law, promise, etc.) **10** to disrupt the order of *[break* ranks*]* **11** to interrupt (a journey, electric circuit, etc.) **12** to reduce the force of by interrupting (a fall, etc.) **13** to bring to an end suddenly or by force **14** to penetrate (silence, darkness, etc.) **15** to disclose **16** to decipher or solve *[break* a code*]* — *vi.* **1** to split into pieces; come apart **2** to force one's way (*through* obstacles, etc.) **3** to stop associating (*with*) **4** to become unusable **5** to change suddenly *[his* voice *broke]* **6** to begin suddenly *[to break* into song*]* **7** to come suddenly into being, notice, etc. *[the* story *broke]* **8** to stop activity temporarily **9** to suffer a collapse of spirit — *n.* **1 a** breaking **2 a** beginning or appearance *[the break* of day*]* **4** an interruption of regularity **5** a gap, interval, or rest **6** a sudden change **7** an escape **8** a chance piece of luck —**break down 1** to go out of working order **2** to have a physical or nervous collapse **3** to analyze —**break in 1** to enter forcibly **2** to interrupt **3** to train (a beginner) **4** to prepare (something new) by use or wear —**break off** to stop abruptly — **break out 1** to become covered with pimples, etc. **2** to escape suddenly —**break up 1** to separate; disperse **2** to stop **3** [Colloq.] to laugh or make laugh —**give (someone) a break** [Colloq.] to stop treating harshly, critically, etc. —**break·able** *adj., n.*

break′age′ (-ij′) *n.* **1** a breaking **2** things broken **3** loss due to breaking **4** the sum allowed for such loss

break′down′ *n.* **1** a breaking down **2** a failure of health **3** an analysis

break′er *n.* **1** a thing that breaks **2** a wave that breaks into foam

break′fast (brek′fəst) *n.* the first meal of the day — *vi.* to eat breakfast

break·front (brāk′frunt′) *adj.* having a projecting center section in front — *n.* a breakfront cabinet

break′-in′ *n.* the act of forcibly entering a building, esp. in order to rob

break·neck (brāk′nek′) *adj.* highly dangerous *[breakneck* speed*]*

break′through′ *n.* **1** the act of forcing a way through against resistance, as in warfare **2** a very important advance or discovery

break′up′ *n.* **1** a dispersion **2** a disintegration **3** a collapse

break′wa′ter *n.* a barrier to break the impact of waves, as before a harbor

breast (brest) *n.* ⟦OE *breost*⟧ **1** either of two milk-secreting glands on a woman's body **2** the upper, front part of the body **3** the part of a garment, etc. over the breast **4** the breast regarded as the center of emotions — *vt.* to face firmly; oppose

breast′bone′ *n.* STERNUM

breast′-feed′ *vt.* -fed′, -feed′ing to feed (a baby) milk from the breast

breast′plate′ *n.* a piece of armor for the breast

breast stroke a swimming stroke in which both arms are brought out sideways from the chest

breast′work′ *n.* a low wall put up quickly as a defense in battle

breath (breth) *n.* ⟦OE *bræth*, odor⟧ **1** air taken into the lungs and then let out **2** respiration **3** the power to breathe easily **4** life; spirit **5** a fragrant odor **6** a slight breeze **7** a whisper; murmur —**catch one's breath 1** to gasp **2** [Colloq.] to rest or pause —**out of breath** breathless, as from exertion —**take one's breath away** to thrill —**under** (or **below**) **one's breath** in a whisper

breathe (brēth) *vi., vt.* **breathed, breath′ing 1** to take (air) into the lungs and let it out again; inhale and exhale **2** to live **3** to rest —**breathe again** to have a feeling of relief —**breath′a·ble** *adj.*

breather (brē′thər) *n.* **1** one who breathes **2** [Colloq.] a pause for rest

breath·less (breth′lis) *adj.* **1** without breath **2** panting; gasping **3** unable to breathe easily because of emotion — **breath′lessly** *adv.*

breath′tak′ing (-tāk′iŋ) *adj.* very exciting

breath′y (-ē) *adj.* -i·er, -i·est marked by an audible emission of breath

bred (bred) *vt., vi. pt. & pp. of* BREED

breech (brēch) *n.* ⟦OE *brec*⟧ **1** the buttocks **2** the part of a gun behind the barrel

breech′cloth′ *n.* LOINCLOTH

breeches (brich′iz) *n.pl.* ⟦see BREECH⟧ **1** trousers reaching to the knees **2** [Colloq.] any trousers

breed (brēd) *vt.* **bred, breed′ing** ⟦< OE *brod*, fetus⟧ **1** to bring forth (offspring) **2** to be the source of; produce **3** to raise (animals) **4** to rear; train — *vi.* **1** to be produced; originate **2** to reproduce — *n.* **1** a stock; strain **2** a sort; type —**breed′er** *n.*

breed′ing *n.* **1** the producing of young **2** good upbringing **3** the producing of plants and animals, esp. for improving the stock

breeze (brēz) *n.* ⟦16th-c. nautical term *brise*, prob. < Du⟧ **1** a gentle wind **2** [Colloq.] a thing easy to do — *vi.* [Colloq.] to move or go quickly

---

■ THESAURUS ■

luck, advantage, favorable circumstances; see LUCK 1.

break *v.* **1** [To start a rupture] burst, split, crack, rend, sunder, sever, fracture, tear, cleave, break into, break through, force open, puncture, split, snap, slash, gash, dissect, slice, disjoin, separate; see also CUT. **2** [To shatter] smash, shiver, crash, break up, crush, splinter, pull to pieces, burst, break into pieces, break into smithereens*, fall apart, fall to pieces, collapse, break down, come apart, come unglued, go to wrack and ruin, get wrecked, bust*, split up; see also DISINTEGRATE and sense 1. **3** [To bring to ruin or to an end] demolish, annihilate, eradicate; see DESTROY. **4** [To happen] come to pass, occur, develop; see HAPPEN 2. —**break down 1** [To analyze] examine, investigate, dissect; see ANALYZE. **2** [To malfunction] fail, stop, falter, misfire, give out, go down, crack up*, cease, backfire, conk out*, peter out*, fizzle out*, collapse, go kaput*, come unglued*, run out of gas*. —**break in 1** [Train] educate, instruct, prepare; see TEACH. **2** [Intrude] rob, burglarize, trespass; see MEDDLE 2, STEAL. —**break off** end, cease, discontinue; see STOP 2. —**break out 1** [To start] begin, commence, occur; see BEGIN 2. **2** [To escape] burst out, flee, depart; see LEAVE 1. **3** [To erupt] get blemishes, have acne, get a rash, get hives, get pimples. —**break through** pen-

etrate, force a way, intrude; see PENETRATE. —**break up 1** [To scatter] disperse, disband, separate; see DISINTEGRATE, DIVIDE. **2** [To stop] put an end to, halt, terminate; see STOP 2. **3** [*To distress] hurt, sadden, wound; see HURT. **4** [*To end relations] discontinue, break off, stop; see END 1.

breakable *a.* fragile, delicate, frail; see WEAK 1.

breakage *n.* harm, wreckage, ruined goods; see DAMAGE 2.

breakdown *n.* collapse, stoppage, disruption; see FAILURE 1.

breakfast *n.* morning meal, first meal of the day, early meal, brunch, breaking the fast; see also MEAL 2.

breaking *a.* bursting, splitting, cracking, rending, sundering, parting, severing, exploding, erupting, shattering, splintering, fracturing, tearing, cleaving, snapping, breaking up, dispersing, separating, smashing, shivering, crashing, splintering, disintegrating, collapsing, caving in, falling, busting*, going to pot*.—*Ant.* STRONG, stable, enduring.

breakthrough *n.* discovery, finding, invention; see DISCOVERY.

breakwater *n.* pier, wharf, jetty; see DOCK.

breast *n.* **1** [The forepart of the body above the abdomen] thorax, heart, bosom; see CHEST 2. **2** [An enlarged mammary gland or glands] bosom, chest, teat, tit*, nipple, bust, udder, boob*, jug*, knocker*. —**beat**

one's breast repent, humble oneself, be sorry; see APOLOGIZE, REGRET 1. —**make a clean breast of** confess, reveal, expose; see ADMIT 2.

breath *n.* inspiration, expiration, inhalation, exhalation, breathing, gasp, sigh, pant, wheeze. —**catch one's breath** rest, stop, slow down; see PAUSE. —**in the same breath** simultaneously, concurrently, at the same time; see TOGETHER 2. —**out of breath** gasping, choking, out of wind; see BREATHLESS. —**save one's breath*** be quiet, stop talking, never mind; see SHUT UP 1. —**take someone's breath away** thrill, stimulate, invigorate; see EXCITE. —**under one's breath** quietly, in a whisper, murmuring; see WHISPERING.

breathe *v.* respire, use one's lungs, inhale, exhale, draw in, breathe in, breathe out, gasp, pant, wheeze, snort, sigh, take air into one's nostrils, scent, sniff.

breathless *a.* out of breath, winded, spent, exhausted, used up, gasping, choking, windless, wheezing, short-winded, puffing, panting, asthmatic, short of breath, out of wind*.

breed *n.* strain, variety, kind; see RACE 1.

breed *v.* **1** [To produce] give birth to, deliver, bring forth; see PRODUCE 1. **2** [To cause] bring about, effect, produce; see BEGIN 1.

breeze *n.* draft, gust, blast; see WIND. —**in a breeze*** effortlessly, readily,

breeze'way' *n.* a covered passageway, as between a house and garage

breez'y (-ē) *adj.* **-i·er, -i·est 1** slightly windy **2** light and lively —**breez'i·ly** *adv.* —**breez'i·ness** *n.*

breth·ren (breth'rən) *n.pl.* ⟦ME *bretheren*⟧ brothers: chiefly religious

bre·vet (brə vet') *n.* ⟦< L *brevis*, brief⟧ [Historical] *Mil.* a commission giving higher honorary rank without extra pay —*vt.* **-vet'ted** or **-vet'ed, -vet'ting** or **-vet'ing** to give a brevet to

bre·vi·ary (brē'vē er'ē) *n., pl.* **-ar·ies** ⟦< L *brevis*, brief⟧ a book of Psalms, prayers, etc. to be recited daily by priests, nuns, etc.

brev·i·ty (brev'ə tē) *n.* ⟦< L *brevis*, brief⟧ briefness

brew (brōō) *vt.* ⟦OE *breowan*⟧ **1** to make (beer, ale, etc.) from malt and hops by boiling and fermenting **2** to steep (tea, etc.) **3** to plot; scheme —*vi.* to begin to form —*n.* a beverage brewed —**brew'er** *n.*

brew·ery (brōō'ər ē) *n., pl.* **-er·ies** a place where beer, etc. is brewed

briar (brī'ər) *n.* BRIER[1] or BRIER[2]

bribe (brīb) *n.* ⟦< OFr *briber*, to beg⟧ anything given or promised as an inducement, esp. to do something illegal or wrong —*vt.* **bribed, brib'ing** to offer or give a bribe to —**brib'ery** *n.*

bric-a-brac (brik'ə brak') *n.* ⟦< Fr *de bric et de brac*, by hook or by crook⟧ **1** small artistic objects used to ornament a room **2** knickknacks

brick (brik) *n.* ⟦MDu < *breken*, piece of baked clay⟧ **1** an oblong shaped block of baked clay, used in building, etc. **2** anything shaped like a brick —*adj.* built or paved with brick —*vt.* to build or cover with brick

brick'bat' *n.* **1** a piece of brick used as a missile **2** an unfavorable remark

brick'lay'er *n.* one whose work is building with bricks —**brick'lay'ing** *n.*

bridal (brīd''l) *adj.* ⟦< OE *bryd ealu*, marriage feast⟧ **1** of a bride **2** of a wedding

bride (brīd) *n.* ⟦OE *bryd*⟧ a woman just married or about to be married

bride'groom' *n.* ⟦< OE *bryd*, bride + *guma*, man⟧ a man just married or about to be married

brides·maid (brīdz'mād') *n.* one of the women who attend the bride at a wedding

bridge[1] (brij) *n.* ⟦OE *brycge*⟧ **1** a structure built over a river, etc. to provide a way across **2** a thing that provides connection, contact, etc. **3** the bony part of the nose **4** a raised platform on a ship **5** a mounting for false teeth —*vt.* **bridged, bridg'ing** to build or be a bridge over —**burn one's bridges (behind one)** to follow a course from which there is no retreat —**bridge'able** *adj.*

bridge[2] (brij) *n.* ⟦< ? Russ⟧ a card game, for two pairs of players, in which they bid for the right to name the trump suit or declare no-trump

bridge'head' *n.* a fortified position established by an attacking force in enemy territory

bridge'work' *n.* a dental bridge or bridges

bri·dle (brīd''l) *n.* ⟦OE *bregdan*, move quickly⟧ **1** a head harness for guiding a horse **2** anything that controls or restrains —*vt.* **bri'dled, bri'dling 1** to put a bridle on **2** to curb or control —*vi.* to pull one's head back as an expression of anger, scorn, etc.

bridle path a path for horseback riding

brief (brēf) *adj.* ⟦< L *brevis*⟧ **1** short **2** concise —*n.* **1** a summary, specif. of the main points of a law case **2** [*pl.*] legless undershorts —*vt.* **1** to summarize **2** to supply with all pertinent information —**brief'ing** *n.* —**brief'ly** *adv.* —**brief'ness** *n.*

brief'case' *n.* a flat, flexible case for carrying papers, books, etc.

brier[1] (brī'ər) *n.* ⟦OE *brer*⟧ any thorny bush, as a bramble

brier[2] (brī'ər) *n.* ⟦Fr *bruyère*⟧ a variety of heath, whose root is used for making tobacco pipes

brig (brig) *n.* **1** ⟦< brigantine⟧ a two-masted ship with square sails **2** ⟦< ?⟧ a prison, as on a warship

bri·gade (bri gād') *n.* ⟦< It *briga*, strife⟧ **1** a military unit composed of two or more battalions with service and administrative units **2** a group of people organized to function as a unit in some work [a fire *brigade*]

brigadier general *pl.* **brigadier generals** a military officer ranking just above a colonel

brig·and (brig'ənd) *n.* ⟦see BRIGADE⟧ a bandit, esp. one of a roving band

brig'and·age (-ənd ij') *n.* plundering by brigands

brig·an·tine (brig'ən tēn') *n.* ⟦< It *brigantino*, pirate vessel⟧ a ship with a square-rigged foremast and a square-rigged topsail on the mainmast

bright (brīt) *adj.* ⟦OE *bryht*⟧ **1** shining with light **2** brilliant in color or sound; vivid **3** lively; cheerful **4** mentally quick; clever **5** favorable or hopeful **6** illustrious —**bright'ly** *adv.* —**bright'ness** *n.*

bright'en (-'n) *vt., vi.* to make or become bright or brighter

bril·liant (bril'yənt) *adj.* ⟦< Fr < It *brillare*, to sparkle⟧ **1** shining brightly **2** vivid **3** very splendid **4** very intelligent, talented, etc. —**bril'liance** or **bril'liancy** *n.* —**bril'liantly** *adv.*

brillian·tine (bril'yən tēn') *n.* ⟦< Fr⟧ an oily dressing for the hair

brim (brim) *n.* ⟦ME *brimme*⟧ **1** the topmost edge of a cup, glass, etc. **2** a projecting rim, as of a hat —*vt., vi.*

THESAURUS

simply; see EASILY. —**shoot the breeze*** converse, chat, chatter; see TALK 1.

brew *n.* concoction, preparation, distillation, compound, broth, liquor, blend, beer, ale; see also DRINK 1, 2.

brew *v.* concoct, ferment, mull; see COOK.

bribe *n.* fee, reward, hush money, lure, gift, graft, compensation, remuneration, protection, bait, tip, blackmail, price, present, gratuity.

bribe *v.* corrupt, get to, reward, tip, coax, hire, entice, tempt, pervert, lure, buy, influence, buy off, fix*.

brick *n.* cube, chunk, section, block, slab, cinder block, glass block, adobe brick, building brick, paving stone, floor tile; see also STONE.

bridal *a.* nuptial, marriage, wedding, matrimonial, marital, conjugal, wedded.

bride *n.* spouse, mate, partner; see WIFE.

bridegroom *n.* groom, mate, spouse; see HUSBAND.

bridge[1] *v.* connect, span, link; see JOIN 1.

bridge[1,2] *n.* **1** [An elevated structure] viaduct, platform, catwalk, gangplank, drawbridge, trestle, aqueduct, scaffold. *Types of bridges include the following:* arch, pier, girder, concrete arch, suspension, cantilever, bascule,

pontoon, swing, floating, covered, cable-stayed, steel arch, lift, truss. **2** [A game at cards] contract bridge, auction bridge, duplicate bridge; see GAME 1. **3** [A link] connection, bond, tie; see JOINT 1, LINK.

brief *a.* **1** [Abrupt] hasty, curt, blunt; see RUDE 2. **2** [Short in time] short-term, fleeting, concise; see SHORT 2. —**in brief** concisely, to the point, cut short, abbreviated; see also BRIEFLY.

briefing *n.* instruction, training session, orientation; see INTRODUCTION 4, PREPARATION 1.

briefly *a.* shortly, curtly, abruptly, quickly, hastily, hurriedly, momentarily, fleetingly, suddenly, temporarily, in passing, casually, lightly, briskly, in brief, in outline, in a few words, in a capsule, in a nutshell.

bright *a.* **1** [Shining or vivid] gleaming, shiny, glittering, luminous, lustrous, burnished, polished, sparkling, mirrorlike, glowing, flashing, scintillating, shimmering, incandescent, twinkling, illumined, light, golden, silvery, illuminated, shining, irradiated, glistening, radiant, burning, glaring, beaming, glimmering, splendid, resplendent, brilliant, dazzling, alight, aglow, lighted up, full of light, ablaze, flamelike, moonlit, sunlit, on fire, phosphorescent, blazing, glossy,

colored, colorful, tinted, intense, deep, sharp, rich, tinged, hued, touched with color, fresh, clear, ruddy, psychedelic. —*Ant.* DULL, clouded, dark. **2** [Intelligent] clever, quick, alert; see INTELLIGENT. **3** [Not rainy] clear, sunny, mild; see FAIR 3. **4** [Cheerful] lively, vivacious, joyful; see HAPPY.

brighten *v.* **1** [To become brighter] clear up, lighten, grow calm, improve, grow sunny, glow. **2** [To make brighter] polish, intensify, lighten; see SHINE 3.

brightly *a.* lustrously, radiantly, splendidly, brilliantly, dazzlingly, sparklingly, glowingly, shinily, gaily, freshly, vividly, colorfully, cleverly, sunnily.—*Ant.* dully, dingily, darkly.

brightness *n.* shine, luster, illumination; see LIGHT 1.

brilliant *a.* **1** [Shining] dazzling, gleaming, sparkling; see BRIGHT 1. **2** [Showing remarkable ability] ingenious, profound, smart; see INTELLIGENT.

brilliantly *a.* **1** [Very brightly] shiningly, radiantly, blazingly; see BRIGHTLY. **2** [With superior intelligence] cleverly, shrewdly, knowledgeably; see INTELLIGENTLY.

brim *n.* margin, rim, border; see EDGE 1.

brimmed, brim′ming to fill or be full to the brim —**brim′less** *adj.*
brim′ful′ *adj.* full to the brim
brim′stone′ *n.* [< OE *bærnan,* to kindle + *stan,* stone] sulfur
brin·dle (brin′dəl) *adj.* BRINDLED —*n.* a brindled color
brin′dled (-dəld) *adj.* [prob. < ME *brennen,* to burn] having a gray or tawny coat streaked or spotted with a darker color
brine (brīn) *n.* [OE] 1 water full of salt 2 the ocean —**brin′y** *adj.*
bring (briŋ) *vt.* **brought, bring′ing** [OE *bringan*] 1 to carry or lead "here" or to the place where the speaker will be 2 to cause to happen 3 to lead to an action or belief 4 to sell for —**bring about** to cause —**bring forth** to give birth to; produce —**bring off** to accomplish —**bring out** 1 to reveal 2 to offer (a play, book, etc.) to the public —**bring up** 1 to rear (children) 2 to introduce, as into discussion 3 to cough or vomit up
brink (briŋk) *n.* [< Ger or Dan, shore] the edge, esp. at the top of a steep place; verge
brink′man·ship′ (-mən ship′) *n.* the policy of pursuing a risky course of action to the brink of disaster Also **brinks′man·ship′**
bri·oche (brē ōsh′) *n.* [Fr] a light, rich roll made with flour, eggs, etc.
bri·quette or **bri·quet** (bri ket′) *n.* [Fr < *brique,* brick] a small block of compressed coal dust, etc.
brisk (brisk) *adj.* [< ? Fr *brusque,* brusque] 1 quick in manner; energetic 2 keen, bracing, etc. —**brisk′ly** *adv.* —**brisk′ness** *n.*
bris·ket (bris′kit) *n.* [ME *brusket*] meat cut from the breast of an animal
bris·tle (bris′əl) *n.* [OE *byrst*] any short, stiff hair —*vi.* **-tled, -tling** 1 to be stiff and erect 2 to have the bristles become erect 3 to become tense with fear, anger, etc. 4 to be thickly covered (*with*) —**bris′tly** (-lē), **-tlier, -tli·est,** *adj.*
bris′tle·cone pine (-kōn) a Rocky Mountain pine tree of the SW U.S.
Brit. British
britches (brich′iz) *n.pl.* [Colloq.] BREECHES (sense 2)
Briti·cism (brit′ə siz′əm) *n.* a word or idiom peculiar to British English
Brit·ish (brit′ish) *adj.* of Great Britain or its people —**the British** the people of Great Britain
British thermal unit a unit of heat equal to about 252 calories
Briton (brit′′n) *n.* 1 a member of an early Celtic people of S Britain 2 a native or inhabitant of Great Britain, esp. of England

brit·tle (brit′l) *adj.* [OE *breotan,* to break] easily broken or shattered —*n.* a brittle, crunchy candy with nuts in it —**brit′tle·ness** *n.*
broach (brōch) *n.* [< ML *brocca,* a spike] a tapering bit for boring holes —*vt.* 1 to make a hole in so as to let out liquid 2 to ream with a broach 3 to start a discussion of
broad (brôd) *adj.* [OE *brad*] 1 of large extent from side to side; wide 2 extending about; full [broad daylight] 3 obvious [a broad hint] 4 tolerant; liberal [a broad view] 5 wide in range [a broad variety] 6 not detailed; general [in broad outline] —**broad′ly** *adv.* —**broad′ness** *n.*
broad′cast′ (-kast′) *vt., vi.* **-cast′** or **-cast′ed, -cast′ing** 1 to scatter or spread widely 2 to transmit by radio or TV —*adj.* 1 widely scattered 2 of or for radio or TV broadcasting —*n.* 1 a sowing by broadcasting 2 a radio or TV program —*adv.* far and wide —**broad′cast′er** *n.*
broad′cloth′ *n.* a fine, smooth woolen, cotton, or silk cloth
broad′en (-′n) *vt., vi.* to widen
broad jump old name of LONG JUMP
broad′loom′ *adj.* woven on a wide loom
broad′-mind′ed *adj.* tolerant of unconventional behavior, etc.; liberal —**broad′-mind′edly** *adv.* —**broad′-mind′edness** *n.*
broad′side′ *n.* 1 the side of a ship above the waterline 2 the firing of all guns on one side of a warship 3 a vigorous critical attack —*adv.* 1 with the side facing 2 in the side [hit broadside] 3 indiscriminately
broad′-spec′trum *adj.* effective against a wide range of germs
broad′sword′ *n.* a broad-bladed sword for slashing
bro·cade (brō kād′) *n.* [< Sp < It *broccare,* embroider] a rich cloth with a raised design woven into it —*vt.* **-cad′ed, -cad′ing** to weave a raised design into (cloth)
broc·coli (bräk′ə lē) *n.* [It < ML *brocca,* a spike] a plant related to the cauliflower but bearing tender shoots with greenish buds
bro·chette (brō shet′) *n.* [Fr] a skewer for broiling chunks of meat, etc.
bro·chure (brō shoor′) *n.* [Fr < *brocher,* to stitch] a pamphlet
bro·gan (brō′gən) *n.* [Ir] a heavy work shoe, fitting high on the ankle
brogue[1] (brōg) *n.* [< ?] a dialectal pronunciation, esp. that of English by the Irish
brogue[2] (brōg) *n.* [< Ir *brōg,* a shoe] a man's heavy oxford shoe
broil (broil) *vt., vi.* [< OFr *bruillir*] to cook by exposure to direct heat —*n.* a broiling
broil′er *n.* 1 a pan, grill, etc. for broiling 2 a chicken fit for broiling
broke (brōk) *vt., vi. pt. of* BREAK —*adj.* [Colloq.] without money; bankrupt
bro·ken (brō′kən) *vt., vi. pp. of* BREAK —*adj.* 1 splintered, fractured, etc. 2 not in working order 3 violated [a

THESAURUS

bring *v.* 1 [To transport] convey, take along, bear; see CARRY 1, PICK UP 6. 2 [To be worth in sale] sell for, earn, bring in; see PAY 2. 3 [To cause] produce, effect, make; see BEGIN 1. —**bring about** 1 [To achieve] do, accomplish, realize; see ACHIEVE, SUCCEED 1. 2 [To cause] produce, effect, do; see BEGIN 1, MANAGE 1. —**bring forth** deliver, bear, yield; see PRODUCE 1, 2. —**bring off** accomplish, realize, execute; see ACHIEVE, SUCCEED 1. —**bring out** 1 [To excite] elicit, arouse, evoke; see EXCITE. 2 [To publish] print, issue, put out; see PUBLISH 1. 3 [To produce a play] present, put on the stage, exhibit; see PERFORM 2. 4 [To intensify] heighten, sharpen, magnify; see EMPHASIZE, INCREASE. —**bring up** 1 [To rear] educate, teach, train; see RAISE 2, SUPPORT 3. 2 [To discuss] tender, submit, advance; see DISCUSS, PROPOSE 1.
bringing *n.* fetching, carrying, transporting, accompanying, introducing, shipping, bearing, hauling, bringing in, getting, providing, procuring.
brink *n.* limit, brim, rim; see EDGE 1.
brisk *a.* lively, refreshing, invigorating; see STIMULATING.
briskly *a.* energetically, quickly, brusquely, rapidly, impulsively, nim-

bly, agilely, dexterously, decisively, firmly, actively, promptly, readily, vigorously, in a lively manner; see also EMPHATICALLY.—*Ant.* SLOWLY, listlessly, sluggishly.
bristle *n.* hair, fiber, quill; see POINT 2.
British *a.* Anglo-Saxon, Celtic, Brit*; see ENGLISH.
brittle *a.* fragile, crisp, inelastic; see WEAK 2.
broad *a.* 1 [Physically wide] deep, extended, large, extensive, ample, spacious, expansive, immense, wide, roomy, outstretched, thick, widespread, full, stocky.—*Ant.* NARROW, thin, slender. 2 [Wide in range] cultivated, experienced, cosmopolitan; see CULTURED. 3 [Tolerant] progressive, open-minded, unbiased; see LIBERAL.
broadcast *n.* radio program, newscast, telecast; see PERFORMANCE.
broadcast *v.* announce, relay, telephone, send out, telegraph, radio, transmit, televise, telecast, air, put on the air, go on the air, be on the air; see also SEND 2.
broadcasting *n.* radio transmission, announcing, television, airing, putting on a radio program, telecasting, newscasting, transmitting, reporting.

broaden *v.* widen, expand, increase; see GROW 1, INCREASE.
broad-minded *a.* tolerant, progressive, unprejudiced; see LIBERAL.
brochure *n.* handout, circular, pamphlet; see ADVERTISEMENT.
broil *v.* sear, bake, roast; see COOK.
broiler *n.* oven, grill, barbecue; see APPLIANCE.
broke *a.* bankrupt, out of money, indebted; see RUINED 3. —**go for broke** gamble, wager, risk everything; see RISK. —**go broke** become bankrupt, lose everything; be reduced to poverty; see FAIL 4, LOSE 2.
broken *a.* 1 [Fractured] shattered, hurt, ruptured, burst, splintered, smashed, in pieces, collapsed, destroyed, pulverized, crumbled, mutilated, bruised, injured, damaged, rent, split, cracked, mangled, dismembered, fragmentary, disintegrated, crippled, shredded, crushed, gashed, defective.—*Ant.* WHOLE, intact, sound. 2 [Not functioning properly] defective, inoperable, in need of repair, in disrepair, out of order, busted*, gone to pot*, screwed up*, shot*, gone haywire*, on the fritz*, on the blink*, gone to pieces, out of whack*, out of commission;

imperfectly spoken 7 tamed —**bro′kenly** *adv.* —**bro′ken·ness** *n.*

bro′ken-down′ *adj.* 1 sick or worn out 2 out of order; useless

bro′ken·heart′ed *adj.* crushed by sorrow, grief, etc.

bro·ker (brō′kər) *n.* [< OFr *brokier*, to tap; orig. sense "wine dealer"] a person hired as an agent in negotiating contracts, buying and selling, etc.

bro′ker·age (-ij′) *n.* 1 the business of a broker 2 a broker's fee

bro·mide (brō′mīd′) *n.* 1 a compound of bromine with another element or a radical 2 potassium bromide, used as a sedative 3 a trite saying

bro·mid′ic (-mid′ik) *adj.* trite or dull

bro·mine (brō′mēn′) *n.* [< Gr *brōmos*, stench] a chemical element, a reddish-brown, corrosive liquid

bron·chi (brän′kī) *n.pl., sing.* **-chus** (-kəs) [< Gr *bronchos*, windpipe] the two main branches of the windpipe — **bron′chial** (-kē əl) *adj.*

bron·chi′tis (-kīt′is) *n.* an inflammation of the bronchial tubes

bron·co (bräŋ′kō) *n., pl.* **-cos** [Sp, rough] a wild or only partly tamed horse or pony of the western U.S. Also **bron′cho** *n., pl.* **-chos**

bron·co·bust′er *n.* [Colloq.] a tamer of broncos — **bron′co·bust′ing** *n.*

bron·to·saur (brän′tō sôr′, -tə-) *n.* [< Gr *brontē*, thunder + *sauros*, lizard] a very large, plant-eating dinosaur Also **bron′to·saur′us**

bronze (bränz) *n.* [Fr, prob. ult. < Pers *birinǧ*, copper] 1 an alloy of copper and tin 2 a reddish-brown color —*adj.* of or like bronze — *vt.* **bronzed, bronz′ing** [Fr *bronzer* < the *n.*] to make bronze in color

brooch (brōch) *n.* [see BROACH] a large ornamental pin with a clasp

brood (brood) *n.* [OE *brod*] 1 a group of birds hatched at one time 2 the children in a family — *vi.* 1 to sit on and hatch eggs 2 to worry: often with *on, over,* or *about*

brood′er *n.* 1 one that broods 2 a heated shelter for raising fowl

brood′mare′ *n.* a mare kept for breeding

brook¹ (brook) *n.* [< OE *broc*] a small stream

brook² (brook) *vt.* [OE *brucan,* to use] to put up with; endure

broom (broom, broom) *n.* [OE *brom,* brushwood] 1 a flowering shrub of the pea family 2 a bundle of fibers or straws fastened to a long handle (**broom′stick′**) used for sweeping

Bros. or **bros.** brothers

broth (brôth) *n.* [OE] a thin soup made by boiling meat, etc. in water

brothel (brôth′əl) *n.* [< OE *broethan,* go to ruin] a house of prostitution

brother (bruth′ər) *n., pl.* **-ers** or **breth′ren** [OE *brothor*] 1 a male related to one by having the same parents 2 a friend who is like a brother 3 a fellow member of the same race, church, profession, etc. 4 [*often* B-] a lay member of a men's religious order

broth′er·hood′ *n.* 1 the bond between brothers 2 an association of men united in some interest, work, etc.

broth′er-in-law′ *n., pl.* **broth′ers-in-law′** 1 the brother of one's spouse 2 the husband of one's sister 3 the husband of the sister of one's spouse

broth′erly *adj.* 1 of or like a brother 2 friendly, kind, loyal, etc.

brought (brôt) *vt. pt. & pp. of* BRING

brou·ha·ha (broo′hä hä′) *n.* [Fr] an uproar or commotion

brow (brou) *n.* [OE *bru*] 1 the eyebrow 2 the forehead 3 the edge of a cliff

brow′beat′ (-bēt′) *vt.* **-beat′, -beat′en, -beat′ing** to intimidate with harsh, stern looks and talk; bully

brown (broun) *adj.* [OE *brun*] 1 having the color of chocolate, a mixture of red, black, and yellow 2 tanned; dark-skinned — *n.* brown color — *vt., vi.* to make or become brown —**brown′ish** *adj.*

brown′-bag′ *vt., vi.* **-bagged′, -bag′ging** to carry (one's lunch) to work or school, as in a brown paper bag

brownie (broun′ē) *n.* 1 a small, helpful elf 2 a small bar cut from a flat chocolate cake

brown′out′ *n.* a turning off of some lights in a city, as during an electric power shortage

brown rice unpolished rice

brown′stone′ *n.* a reddish-brown sandstone, used for building

brown study deep thought; reverie

brown sugar sugar whose crystals retain a brown coating of syrup

browse (brouz) *n.* [< OS *brustian,* to sprout] leaves, shoots, etc. which animals feed on — *vt., vi.* **browsed, brows′ing** 1 to nibble at (leaves, shoots, etc.) 2 to examine (a book, articles for sale, etc.) in a casual way — **brows′er** *n.*

bruin (broo′in) [Du, brown] a bear

bruise (brooz) *vt.* **bruised, bruis′ing** [< OE *brysan,* crush] 1 to injure and discolor (body tissue) without breaking the skin 2 to injure the surface of, causing spoilage, denting, etc. 3 to hurt (the feelings, spirit, etc.) — *vi.* 1 to bruise tissue, etc. 2 to be or become bruised — *n.* a bruised area, as of tissue

bruis′er *n.* [Colloq.] a strong, pugnacious man

bruit (broot) *vt.* [< OFr, noise, rumor] to spread (*about*) by rumor

brunch (brunch) *n.* [Colloq.] a combined breakfast and lunch

bru·net (broo net′) *adj.* [< OFr, dim. of *brun,* brown] having dark or dark-brown hair, often with dark eyes and complexion — *n.* a brunet person

bru·nette (-net′) *adj.* BRUNET — *n.* a brunette woman or girl

brunt (brunt) *n.* [ME *bront*] 1 the shock (of an attack) or impact (of a blow) 2 the hardest part

brush¹ (brush) *n.* [< OFr *broce,* bush] 1 BRUSHWOOD 2 sparsely settled country 3 a device for cleaning, painting, etc., having bristles, wires, etc. fastened into a back 4 a

---

■■■ THESAURUS ■■■

see also FAULTY. 3 [Discontinuous] spasmodic, erratic, intermittent; see IRREGULAR 1, 4. 4 [Incoherent; *said of speech*] muttered, unintelligible, mumbled; see INCOHERENT.

broken-down *a.* shattered, dilapidated, battered; see OLD 2.

brokenhearted *a.* despondent, crushed, grieved; see SAD 1.

brood *n.* flock, offspring, young; see FAMILY, HERD.

brood *v.* 1 [To hatch] set, cover, incubate, warm, sit; see also PRODUCE 1. 2 [To nurse one's troubles] think, meditate, grieve, fret, sulk, mope, ponder, consider, muse, deliberate, dwell upon, speculate, daydream, reflect, dream, chafe inwardly, give oneself over to reflections, mull over, eat one's heart out; see also WORRY 2.

brook¹ *n.* creek, stream, streamlet; see RIVER.

broom *n.* sweeper, carpet sweeper, whisk broom, mop, feather duster.

broth *n.* brew, concoction, soup, consommé, purée, bouillon, stock, chowder, gumbo, porridge, hodge-podge, potpourri; see also FOOD, SOUP.

brotherhood *n.* fellowship, equality, kinship, intimacy, relationship, affiliation, association, society, fraternity, family, race, comradeship, camaraderie, friendship, amity.

brotherly *a.* kindly, humane, sympathetic; see FRIENDLY, KIND, LOVING.

browbeat *v.* bully, intimidate, frighten; see THREATEN.

brown *n.* *Shades and tints of brown include the following:* tan, bay, chestnut, nutbrown, copper-colored, mahogany, bronze, russet, chocolate, cinnamon, hazel, reddish-brown, sorrel, sepia, tawny, ochre, rust-colored, rust, brownish, puce, fawn, liver-colored, beige, dust, drab, coffee, khaki, maroon, cocoa, umber, brick, ginger, light brown, dark brown, auburn, buff; see also COLOR.

brown *v.* toast, scorch, sauté; see COOK, FRY.

browse *v.* skim, peruse, scan, glance at, look through, run through, flip through, look over, survey, inspect loosely, examine cursorily, glance over, check over, run over, go

through carelessly, dip into, wander here and there*.

bruise *n.* abrasion, wound, swelling; see BLEMISH.

bruise *v.* beat, injure, wound; see DAMAGE, HURT.

brunet *a.* dark, tawny, dusky, brown, tanned, swarthy, dark-complexioned, dark-haired, dark-skinned.—*Ant.* FAIR, light-skinned, light-complexioned.

brush¹ *n.* 1 [A brushing instrument] *Varieties include the following:* bristle, fiber, nail, clothes, camel's hair, rotary, paint, tooth, scrubbing, floor, hair, wire, scrub. 2 [A touch] rub, tap, stroke; see TOUCH 2. 3 [Underbrush] bush, thicket, undergrowth, second growth, chaparral, cover, brushwood, shrubbery, canebrake, hedge, fern, underwood, scrub, brake.

brush¹ *v.* 1 [To cleanse by brushing] sweep, whisk, wipe; see CLEAN. 2 [To touch lightly] stroke, smooth, graze; see TOUCH 1.

brush up on *v.* reread, look over again, review; see STUDY.

brushing **5** a light, grazing stroke **6** a bushy tail, as of a fox — *vt.* **1** to clean, paint, etc. with a brush **2** to apply, remove, etc. as with a brush **3** to touch or graze in passing — *vi.* to graze past something —**brush up** to refresh one's memory

brush² (brush) *vi.* ⟦ME *bruschen*⟧ to rush; hurry — *n.* a short, quick fight

brush'off' *n.* [Slang] curt dismissal, esp. in the phrase **give (or get) the brushoff**

brush'wood' *n.* **1** chopped-off tree branches **2** underbrush

brusque (brusk) *adj.* ⟦< Fr < ML *bruscus*, brushwood⟧ rough and abrupt in manner or speech; curt Also **brusk** —**brusque'ly** *adv.* —**brusque'ness** *n.*

Brus·sels sprouts (brus''lz) **1** a plant that bears small cabbagelike heads on an erect stem **2** its edible heads

bru·tal (brōōt''l) *adj.* **1** like a brute; very savage, cruel, etc. **2** very harsh —**bru'tally** *adv.*

bru·tal·i·ty (brōō tal'ə tē) *n.* **1** a being brutal **2** *pl.* **-ties** a brutal act

bru·tal·ize (brōōt''l īz') *vt.* **-ized'**, **-iz'ing 1** to make brutal **2** to treat brutally —**bru'tali·za'tion** *n.*

brute (brōōt) *adj.* ⟦< L *brutus*, irrational⟧ **1** lacking the ability to reason *[a brute beast]* **2** of or like an animal; specif., savage, stupid, etc. — *n.* **1** an animal **2** a brutal person —**brut'ish** *adj.* —**brut'ishly** *adv.*

bs or **b.s.** bill of sale

BS or **B.S.** Bachelor of Science

Btu British thermal unit(s) Also **BTU** or **btu**

bub·ble (bub'əl) *n.* ⟦echoic⟧ **1** a film of liquid forming a ball around air or gas **2** a tiny ball of air or gas in a liquid or solid **3** a transparent dome **4** a plausible scheme that proves worthless — *vi.* **-bled, -bling 1** to rise in bubbles; boil **2** to make a gurgling sound —**bub'bly** *adv.*

bubble gum a kind of chewing gum that can be blown into large bubbles

bubo (byōō'bō') *n., pl.* **-boes'** ⟦< Gr *boubōn*, groin⟧ an inflamed swelling of a lymph node, esp. in the groin

bu·bon'ic plague (-bän'ik) a contagious disease characterized by buboes, fever, and delirium

buc·ca·neer (buk'ə nir') *n.* ⟦< Fr *boucanier*⟧ a pirate

buck¹ (buk) *n.* ⟦OE *bucca*, male goat⟧ **1** a male deer, goat, etc.: see DOE **2** the act of bucking **3** BUCKSKIN **4** [Colloq.] a bold, vigorous young man — *vi.* **1** to rear upward quickly, as to throw off a rider: said of a horse **2** [Colloq.] to resist something as if plunging against it — *vt.* **1** to dislodge or throw by bucking **2** [Colloq.] to resist stubbornly —**buck for** [Slang] to work eagerly for (a promotion, etc.) —**buck up** [Colloq.] to cheer up

buck² (buk) *n.* ⟦< ?⟧ [Slang] a dollar —**pass the buck** [Colloq.] to throw the responsibility on another

buck'board' *n.* ⟦BUCK¹, *vi.* + BOARD⟧ an open carriage whose floorboards rest directly on the axles

bucket (buk'it) *n.* ⟦< OE *buc*, pitcher⟧ **1** a cylindrical container with a curved handle, for carrying water, etc.; pail **2** the amount held by a bucket: also **buck'et·ful'**, *pl.* **-fuls' 3** a thing like a bucket, as a scoop on a steam shovel —**kick the bucket** [Slang] to die

bucket seat a single contoured seat with a movable back, as in sports cars

buck'eye' (buk'ī') *n.* ⟦BUCK¹ + EYE < the appearance of the seed⟧ **1** a horse chestnut with large burs enclosing shiny brown seeds **2** the seed

buckle¹ (buk'əl) *n.* ⟦< L *buccula*, cheek strap of a helmet⟧ a clasp for fastening a strap, belt, etc. — *vt., vi.* **-led, -ling** to fasten with a buckle —**buckle down** to apply oneself

buckle² (buk'əl) *vt., vi.* **-led, -ling** ⟦prob. infl. by OFr *bocler*, to bulge: see prec.⟧ to bend or crumple — *n.* a bend, bulge, etc.

buck·ler (buk'lər) *n.* ⟦< OFr *bocler*⟧ a small, round shield

buck'-pass'er *n.* [Colloq.] one who regularly shifts blame or responsibility to someone else —**buck'-pass'ing** *n.*

buck·ram (buk'rəm) *n.* ⟦? < *Bukhara*, city in central Asia⟧ a coarse, stiff cloth used in bookbinding, etc.

buck·saw' *n.* a wood-cutting saw set in a frame

buck'shot' *n.* a large lead shot for shooting deer and other large game

buck'skin' *n.* **1** a soft leather made from the skins of deer or sheep **2** [*pl.*] clothes made of buckskin

buck'tooth' *n., pl.* **-teeth'** a projecting front tooth —**buck'toothed'** *adj.*

buck·wheat (buk'hwēt', -wēt') *n.* ⟦< OE *boc-*, beech + WHEAT⟧ **1** a plant with beechnut-shaped seeds **2** a dark flour made from the seeds

bu·col·ic (byōō käl'ik) *adj.* ⟦< Gr *boukolos*, herdsman⟧ **1** of shepherds; pastoral **2** rural; rustic — *n.* a pastoral poem —**bu·col'i·cally** *adv.*

bud (bud) *n.* ⟦ME *budde*⟧ **1** a small swelling on a plant, from which a shoot, leaf, or flower develops **2** an early stage of development — *vi.* **bud'ded, bud'ding 1** to put forth buds **2** to begin to develop —**in (the) bud 1** in a budding condition **2** in an early stage —**bud'like'** *adj.*

Bud·dhism (bood'iz'əm) *n.* ⟦after *Buddha*, Indian founder in 6th c. B.C.⟧ a religion of Asia teaching that by right thinking and self-denial one achieves Nirvana — **Bud'dhist** *n., adj.*

buddy (bud'ē) *n., pl.* **-dies** ⟦< ?⟧ [Colloq.] a comrade

budge (buj) *vt., vi.* **budged, budg'ing** ⟦< OFr *bouger*, to move⟧ to move even a little

budg·er·i·gar (buj'ər i gär') *n.* ⟦native name⟧ a greenish-yellow Australian parakeet: also [Colloq.] **budg'ie**

budget (buj'it) *n.* ⟦< L *bulga*, bag⟧ **1** a stock of items **2** a plan adjusting expenses to income **3** estimated cost of living, operating, etc. — *vt.* **1** to put on a budget **2** to plan *[budget your time]* —**budg'et·ar'y** *adj.*

buff (buf) *n.* ⟦< Fr < It *bufalo*, buffalo⟧ **1** a heavy, soft, brownish-yellow leather **2** a military coat made of this **3** a dull brownish yellow **4** [Colloq.] a devotee; fan — *adj.* **1** made of buff **2** of the color buff — *vt.* to clean or shine with leather or a leather-covered wheel —**in the buff** naked

buf·falo (buf'ə lō') *n., pl.* **-loes'** or **-lo'** ⟦< It < Gr *bous*, ox⟧ **1** any of various wild oxen, as the water buffalo of India **2** popularly, the American bison — *vt.* **-loed', -lo'ing** [Slang] to baffle, bluff, etc.

buffer¹ (buf'ər) *n.* ⟦BUFF, *v.* + -ER⟧ **1** one who buffs **2** a buffing wheel, stick, block, or cloth

buffer² (buf'ər) *n.* ⟦< OFr. *buffe*, a blow⟧ **1** anything that lessens shock, as of collision **2** a temporary storage area in a computer, for data being transferred to another device

buf·fet¹ (buf'it) *n.* ⟦OFr <. *buffe*, a blow⟧ a blow or shock — *vt.* **1** to punch; fight **2** to thrust about

buf·fet² (bə fā', boo-) *n.* ⟦Fr⟧ **1** a sideboard **2** a counter or table at which guests, etc. serve themselves food **3** a meal served on such a table, etc.

buf·foon (bə fōōn') *n.* ⟦< Fr < It *buffare*, to jest⟧ one who is always clowning and trying to be funny; clown —**buf·foon'ery** *n.* —**buf·foon'ish** *adj.*

bug (bug) *n.* ⟦prob. < ME *bugge*⟧ **1** an insect with sucking mouthparts **2** any small arthropod, as a cockroach **3**

■■■■■■ THESAURUS ■■■■■■

brutal *a.* pitiless, harsh, unmerciful; see CRUEL.

brutality *n.* savageness, grossness, unfeelingness; see CRUELTY.

brutally *a.* ruthlessly, cruelly, callously, relentlessly, mercilessly, heartlessly, grimly, viciously, meanly, inhumanly, inhumanely, savagely, pitilessly, barbarously, remorselessly, unkindly, wildly, fiercely, hardheartedly, murderously, ferociously, animalistically, demoniacally, diabolically, barbarically, in cold blood.—*Ant.* NICELY, kindly, gently.

bubble *n.* sac, air bubble, balloon, foam, froth, spume, effervescence, lather.

bubble *v.* froth, gurgle, gush, well, trickle, effervesce, boil, percolate,

simmer, seep, eddy, ferment, erupt, issue, fester.

bucket *n.* pail, canister, can; see CONTAINER, POT 1. —**kick the bucket*** expire, lose one's life, pass away; see DIE 1.

buckle¹ *n.* clasp, harness, fastening; see FASTENER.

buckle down *v.* apply oneself, attend to, keep one's mind on; see CONCENTRATE 2.

buck up* *v.* cheer, comfort, hearten; see ENCOURAGE.

bud *n.* shoot, embryo, germ; see FLOWER. —**nip in the bud** check, halt, stop; see PREVENT.

budding *a.* maturing, developing, opening, blossoming, bursting forth, putting forth shoots, vegetating,

flowering, fresh, pubescent, blooming, promising, young, sprouting, germinating, immature, latent, embryonic, in bud; see also GROWING.

buddy* *n.* peer, companion, pal*; see ASSOCIATE, FRIEND.

budge *v.* stir, change position, shift; see MOVE 1.

budget *n.* estimates, estimated expenses, allocations, accounts, financial statement, financial plan, cost of operation, funds; see also ESTIMATE.

budget *v.* allocate expenditures, balance income and expenses, forecast, allow for, figure in, estimate necessary expenditures; see also ESTIMATE.

bug *n.* **1** [An insect] beetle, pest, gnat; see INSECT. **2** [*A microbe]

[Colloq.] a germ or virus 4 [Slang] a hidden microphone 5 [Slang] a defect, as in a machine — *vt.* **bugged, bug′ging** [Slang] 1 to hide a microphone in (a room, etc.) 2 to annoy, anger, etc.

bug′bear′ *n.* [ME *bugge*, a bug + BEAR²] 1 a bogy 2 a cause of needless fear Also **bug′a·boo′** (-ə bōō′) *n., pl.* **-boos′**

bug′-eyed′ *adj.* [Slang] with bulging eyes

buggy (bug′ē) *n., pl.* **-gies** [< ?] 1 a light, one-horse carriage with one seat 2 BABY CARRIAGE

bu·gle (byōō′gəl) *n.* [< L *buculus*, young ox] a brass instrument like a small trumpet, usually without valves — *vi., vt.* **-gled, -gling** to signal by blowing a bugle —**bu′gler** *n.*

build (bild) *vt.* **built, build′ing** [< OE *bold*, house] 1 to make by putting together materials, parts, etc.; construct 2 to establish; base *[build* a theory on facts*]* 3 to create or develop: often with *up* — *vi.* 1 to put up buildings 2 to grow or intensify: often with *up* — *n.* the way a thing is built or shaped *[a* stocky *build]* —**build up** to make more attractive, healthy, etc. —**build′er** *n.*

build′ing *n.* 1 anything that is built; structure 2 the work or business of making houses, etc.

build′up′ or **build′-up′** *n.* [Colloq.] 1 praise or favorable publicity 2 a gradual increase or expansion

built (bilt) *vt., vi. pt. & pp. of* BUILD

built′-in′ *adj.* 1 made as part of the structure 2 inherent

built′-up′ *adj.* 1 made higher, stronger, etc. with added parts *[built-up* heels*]* 2 having many buildings on it

bulb (bulb) *n.* [< Gr *bolbos*] 1 an underground bud with roots and a short, scaly stem, as in a lily or onion 2 a tuber or tuberous root resembling a bulb, as in a crocus 3 anything shaped like a bulb *[an electric light bulb]* —**bul′bous** *adj.*

bulge (bulj) *n.* [< L *bulga*, leather bag] an outward swelling; protuberance — *vi., vt.* **bulged, bulg′ing** to swell or bend outward —**bulg′y** *adj.*

bu·li·ma·rex·i·a (byōō′li mə rek′sē ə) *n.* a disorder characterized by eating large quantities of food followed by self-induced vomiting, etc. Also **bulimia ner·vosa** (nər vō′sə)

bu·limia (byōō lē′mē ə, -lim′ē ə) *n.* [< Gr *bous*, ox + *limos*, hunger] 1 *Med.* a continuous, abnormal hunger 2 BULI-MAREXIA —**bu·lim′ic** *adj.*

bulk (bulk) *n.* [< ON *bulki*, a heap] 1 size, mass, or volume, esp. if great 2 the main mass; largest part — *vi.* to have, or to increase in, size or importance — *adj.* 1 total; aggregate 2 not put up in individual packages —**bulk′y**, **-i·er, -i·est,** *adj.*

bulk·head (bulk′hed′) *n.* [< ON *balkr*, partition + HEAD] 1 an upright partition, as in a ship, that is watertight, fireproof, etc. 2 a retaining wall 3 a boxlike structure over an opening

bull¹ (bool) *n.* [< OE *bula*, a steer] 1 the adult male of any bovine animal, as the ox, or of certain other large animals, as the elephant, whale, etc. 2 a speculator who buys stocks expecting their prices to rise, or seeks to bring about such a rise 3 [Slang] insincere talk; nonsense — *adj.* 1 male 2 rising in price

bull² (bool) *n.* [< LL *bulla*, a seal] an official document from the pope

bull′dog′ *n.* a short-haired, square-jawed, heavily built dog noted for its strong, stubborn grip — *adj.* like a bulldog; stubborn — *vt.* **-dogged′, -dog′ging** to throw (a steer) by holding its horns and twisting its neck

bull′doze′ (-dōz′) *vt.* **-dozed′, -doz′ing** [< *bull*, a flogging + DOSE] 1 [Colloq.] to force or frighten by threatening; bully 2 to move, make level, etc. with a bulldozer

bull′doz′er *n.* a tractor with a large, shovel-like blade in front, for pushing earth, debris, etc.

bul·let (bool′it) *n.* [< L *bulla*, a knob] a small, shaped piece of lead, steel, etc., to be shot from a firearm

bul·le·tin (bool′ət'n) *n.* [< L *bulla*, a seal] 1 a brief statement of late news 2 a regular publication, as of an organization, etc.

bulletin board a board or wall area on which bulletins, notices, etc. are put up

bul′let·proof′ *adj.* that bullets cannot pierce — *vt.* to make bulletproof

bull′fight′ (-fīt′) *n.* a spectacle in which a bull is provoked in various ways and then killed with a sword by the matador —**bull′fight′er** *n.*

bull′frog′ *n.* a large North American frog with a deep, loud croak

bull′head′ed (-hed′id) *adj.* stubborn; headstrong

bull′horn′ (-hôrn′) *n.* a portable electronic voice amplifier

bul·lion (bool′yən) *n.* [< OFr *billon*, small coin] ingots, bars, etc. of gold or silver

bull′ish′ *adj.* 1 of or like a bull 2 rising, or causing a rise, as in prices on the stock exchange 3 optimistic

bull′ock (-ək) *n.* [< OE dim. of *bula*, steer] a castrated bull; steer

bull′pen′ (-pen′) *n.* 1 [Colloq.] a temporary detention room in a jail 2 *Baseball a)* a practice area for relief pitchers *b)* the relief pitchers of one team

bull′s-eye (boolz′ī′) *n.* 1 the central mark of a target 2 a direct hit

bully (bool′ē) *n., pl.* **-lies** [< MHG *buole*, lover; later infl. by BULL¹] a person who hurts or browbeats those who are weaker — *vt.* **-lied, -ly·ing** to act the bully (toward) — *adj., interj.* [Colloq.] fine; good

bul·rush (bool′rush′) *n.* [< ME *bol*, stem + *rusche*, a rush] a tall plant of the sedge family, found in wet places

bul·wark (bool′wərk) *n.* [MDu *bolwerc*] 1 a defensive wall; rampart 2 a defense; protection 3 [usually pl.] a ship's side above the deck

bum (bum) *n.* [prob. < Ger *bummeln*, go slowly] [Colloq.] 1 a vagrant 2 a loafer 3 a devotee, as of golf or skiing — *vi.* **bummed, bum′ming** to live as a bum or by begging — *vt.* [Slang] to get by begging *[to* bum a cigar*]* — *adj.* **bum′mer, bum′mest** [Slang] 1 poor in quality 2 false 3 lame —**bum (someone) out** [Slang] to annoy, depress, bore, etc. —**on the bum** [Colloq.] 1 living as a vagrant 2 out of repair

bum·ble (bum′bəl) *vi.* **-bled, -bling** 1 to blunder 2 to stumble — *vt.* to bungle or botch —**bum′bler** *n.*

bumble·bee (bum′bəl bē′) *n.* [< ME *bomben*, buzz] a large, hairy, yellow-and-black bee

bum·mer (bum′ər) *n.* [Slang] an unpleasant experience

THESAURUS

bacillus, disease germ, virus; see GERM. 3 [*A defect] flaw, fault, imperfection; see BLEMISH, DEFECT. 4 [*An enthusiast] devotee, zealot, fanatic; see FOLLOWER.

bug* *v.* 1 [To annoy] irritate, plague, pester; see BOTHER 2, DISTURB. 2 [To install hidden microphones] spy, overhear, listen in on, wiretap, tap; see also EAVESDROP.

build *v.* create, form, erect, frame, raise, make, manufacture, put together, fit together, fabricate, contrive, assemble, put up, model, hammer together, set up, reconstruct, pile stone on stone, sculpture, fashion, compose, evolve, compile, cast, produce, forge, bring about, devise, carve, weave. —*Ant.* DESTROY, demolish, wreck. —**build up** 1 [To increase] strengthen, add to, expand; see INCREASE. 2 [To construct] make, erect, establish; see BUILD.

building *n.* edifice, erection, construction, fabrication, house, frame-

work, superstructure, frame, structure, apartment house, barn, castle, church, factory, home, hotel, motel, skyscraper, mall, store, school; see also ARCHITECTURE.

built *a.* constructed, fabricated, manufactured, made, put together, produced, assembled, contrived, remodeled, completed, joined, perfected, finished, realized, created; see also FORMED.

bulb *n.* globe, globule, ball, knob, corn, tuber, protuberance, head, bunch, swelling, tumor, nodule.

bulge *n.* swelling, bunch, lump, protuberance, hump, bump, bulb, outgrowth, protrusion, nodule, sagging, growth, prominence, excess, bagginess, appendage, projection, tumor, egg, sac, knob, horn, ridge, wart, promontory.

bulge *v.* puff out, distend, protrude; see SWELL.

bulk *n.* greater part, main part, predominant part, better part, most, majority, plurality, biggest share, greater number, nearly all, body, more than half, best, gross, lion's share.—*Ant.* BIT, remnant, fraction.

bulky *a.* massive, big, huge; see HIGH 1, LARGE 1, LONG 1.

bull¹ *n.* 1 [The male of various cattle] steer, ox, service bull; see COW. 2 [*Nonsense] balderdash, rubbish, trash; see NONSENSE 1.

bullet *n.* shell, cartridge, ball, projectile, missile, piece of ammunition, slug, ammo*; see also SHOT 1.

bulletin *n.* release, notice, communiqué; see ANNOUNCEMENT.

bully *n.* ruffian, rowdy, tough; see RASCAL.

bully *v.* tease, domineer, harass; see THREATEN.

bum *n.* hobo, tramp, vagrant; see BEGGAR.

bump (bump) *vt.*, *vi.* 〖echoic〗 1 to collide (with); hit against 2 to move with jolts — *n.* 1 a knock; light jolt 2 a swelling, esp. one caused by a blow —**bump into** [Colloq.] to meet unexpectedly —**bump off** [Slang] to murder — **bump'y** *adj.*

bump'er[1] *n.* a device to absorb the shock of a collision; esp., a bar at the front and rear of a motor vehicle

bump'er[2] *adj.* 〖prob. < *bombard*, liquor jug〗 unusually abundant *[a bumper crop]*

bumper sticker a gummed paper with a printed slogan, etc., for sticking on a vehicle's bumper

bump·kin (bump'kin) *n.* 〖prob. < MDu *bommekijn*, small cask〗 an awkward or simple person from the country

bump'tious (-shəs) *adj.* 〖prob. < BUMP〗 disagreeably conceited or forward —**bump'tiously** *adv.*

bun (bun) *n.* 〖prob. < OFr *buigne*, a swelling〗 1 a small roll made of bread dough, sometimes sweetened 2 hair worn in a roll or knot

bunch (bunch) *n.* 〖< Fl *boudje*, little bundle〗 1 a cluster of similar things growing or grouped together 2 [Colloq.] a group of people — *vt.*, *vi.* to collect into a bunch — **bunch'y** *adj.*

bun·combe (buŋ'kəm) *n.* 〖after *Buncombe* county, N.C.〗 [Colloq.] empty, insincere talk   Also **bun'kum**

bun·dle (bun'dəl) *n.* 〖MDu *bondel*〗 1 a number of things bound together 2 a package 3 a bunch; collection — *vt.* **-dled, -dling** 1 to make into a bundle 2 to hustle (*away*, *off*, *out*, or *into*) —**bundle up** to dress warmly

Bundt (bunt, boont) *trademark for* a deep, round, grooved pan with a hollow tube in the center

bung (buŋ) *n.* 〖< MDu *bonge*〗 a stopper for a bunghole

bun·ga·low (buŋ'gə lō') *n.* 〖< Hindi *bāngla*, thatched house〗 a small, one-storied house or cottage

bun·gee cord (bun'jē) elasticized cord used to hold objects in place or secure persons jumping for sport from great heights

bung·hole (buŋ'hōl') *n.* a hole in a barrel or keg for pouring in or drawing out liquid

bun·gle (buŋ'gəl) *vt.*, *vi.* **-gled, -gling** 〖< ?〗 to do clumsily; spoil; botch — *n.* 1 a bungling 2 a bungled piece of work —**bun'gler** *n.*

bun·ion (bun'yən) *n.* 〖< OFr: see BUN〗 an inflamed swelling at the base of the big toe

bunk[1] (buŋk) *n.* 〖prob. < Scand cognate of BENCH〗 1 a shelflike bed built against a wall, as in a ship 2 [Colloq.] any sleeping place — *vi.* to sleep in a bunk — *vt.* to provide a sleeping place for

bunk[2] (buŋk) *n.* [Slang] buncombe

bunker (buŋ'kər) *n.* 〖Scot < ?〗 1 a large bin, as for a ship's fuel 2 an underground fortification 3 an area serving as a hazard on a golf course

bunk'house' *n.* a barracks for ranch hands, etc.

bunny (bun'ē) *n.*, *pl.* **-nies** 〖dim. of dial. *bun*〗 a rabbit: a child's term

buns (bunz) *n.pl.* [Slang] the human buttocks

Bun·sen burner (bun'sən) 〖after R. W. *Bunsen*, 19th-c. Ger. chemist〗 a small tubular gas burner that produces a hot, blue flame

bunt (bunt) *vt.*, *vi.* 〖< ? ME *bounten*, to return〗 *Baseball* to bat (a pitch) lightly without swinging so that it rolls within the infield — *n.* a bunted ball

bun·ting[1] (bun'tiŋ) *n.* 〖< ? ME *bonten*, sift〗 1 a thin cloth for making flags, etc. 2 decorative flags

bun·ting[2] (bun'tiŋ) *n.* 〖ME〗 a small, brightly colored, short-billed bird

buoy (boi; *also*, bōō'ē) *n.* 〖< L *boia*, fetter〗 1 a floating object anchored in water to warn of a hazard, etc. 2 LIFE PRESERVER — *vt.* 〖< Sp *boyar*, to float〗 1 to mark with a buoy 2 to keep afloat 3 to lift up in spirits

buoy·ant (boi'yənt, bōō'yənt) *adj.* 〖< ? Sp *boyar*, to float〗 1 having the ability or tendency to float 2 cheerful — **buoy'ancy** *n.*

bur (bur) *n.* 〖< Scand〗 1 a rough, prickly seed capsule of certain plants 2 a plant with burs 3 BURR[1] & BURR[2]

Bur Bureau

burbs (burbz) *n.pl.* [Colloq.] *short for* suburbs: see SUBURB

bur·den[1] (burd'n) *n.* 〖< OE *byrthen*〗 1 anything that is carried; load 2 heavy load, as of work, care, etc. 3 the carrying capacity of a ship — *vt.* to put a burden on; oppress —**bur'den·some** *adj.*

bur'den[2] *n.* 〖< OFr *bourdon*, a humming〗 1 a chorus or refrain of a song 2 a repeated, central idea; theme

bur·dock (bur'däk') *n.* 〖BUR + DOCK[3]〗 a plant with large leaves and purple-flowered heads with prickles

bu·reau (byoor'ō) *n.*, *pl.* **-reaus** or **-reaux'** (-ōz') 〖Fr, desk〗 1 a chest of drawers, as for clothing 2 an agency 3 a government department

bu·reauc·ra·cy (byoo rä'krə sē) *n.*, *pl.* **-cies** 1 government by departmental officials following an inflexible routine 2 the officials collectively 3 governmental officialism 4 the concentration of authority in administrative bureaus —**bu'reau·crat** (byoor'ə krat') *n.* —**bu'reau·crat'ic** *adj.* —**bu'reau·crat'i·cally** *adv.*

bu·reauc'ra·tize' (-tiz') *vt.*, *vi.* **-tized', -tiz'ing** to develop into a bureaucracy —**bu·reauc'ra·ti·za'tion** *n.*

burg (burg) *n.* [Colloq.] a quiet or dull town

bur·geon (bur'jən) *vi.* 〖< OFr *burjon*, a bud〗 1 to put forth buds, etc. 2 to grow or develop rapidly

bur·ger (bur'gər) *n.* [Colloq.] a hamburger or cheeseburger

burgh (burg; *Scot* bu'rə) *n.* 〖Scot var. of BOROUGH〗 1 [Brit.] a borough 2 in Scotland, a chartered town

burgh'er *n.* a citizen of a town

bur·glar (bur'glər) *n.* 〖< OFr *burgeor*〗 one who commits burglary

bur'glar·ize' *vt.* **-ized', -iz'ing** to commit burglary in

bur'glary *n.*, *pl.* **-ries** the act of breaking into a building to commit a felony, as theft, or a misdemeanor

bur·gle (bur'gəl) *vt.*, *vi.* **-gled, -gling** [Colloq.] to burglarize or commit burglary

burgo·mas·ter (bur'gō mas'tər, -gə-) *n.* 〖< MDu *burg*, town + *meester*, master〗 the mayor of a town in the Netherlands, Flanders, Austria, or Germany

Bur·gun·dy (bur'gən dē) *n.*, *pl.* **-dies** 〖*often* b-〗 a red or white wine, typically dry, orig. made in Burgundy, a region in SE France —**Bur·gun'di·an** *adj.*, *n.*

buri·al (ber'ē əl) *n.* the burying of a dead body in a grave, tomb, etc.

burl (burl) *n.* 〖< OFr *bourle*, ends of threads〗 1 a knot in thread or yarn that makes cloth look nubby 2 a knot on

---

◼ THESAURUS ◼

bump *n.* 1 [A jarring collision] knock, bang, bounce, jar, box, smash, pat, crack, jolt, crash, sideswipe, punch, hit, clap, push, shove, thrust, boost, shock, clash, impact, stroke, rap, tap, slap, clout, jab, jerk, crash, prod, jolt, slam, nudge, buffet, swat*, bash*, wallop*, belt*, bat*, swipe*, thump*, whack*, poke*, clump*, clunk*, sock*, whop*, lick*, smack*, cuff, slug*. 2 [A swelling] projection, protuberance, knob; see BULGE, LUMP.

bump *v.* 1 [To collide with] collide, run against, strike; see CRASH 4, HIT 1. 2 [To make a bumping sound] thud, whack, smack; see SOUND.

bumper[1] *n.* cover, guard, protector; see DEFENSE 2, FENDER.

bun *n.* muffin, biscuit, roll; see BREAD, ROLL 4, PASTRY.

bunch *n.* clump, group, batch, spray, sheaf, tuft, shock, stack, thicket, group, gathering, host, galaxy, bundle, knot, accumulation, collection, mess*, slug*, oodles*.

bundle *n.* packet, parcel, pack; see PACKAGE.

bungle *v.* blunder, fumble, mishandle; see BOTCH, FAIL 1.

bungler *n.* fumbler, lout, blunderer, flounderer, muddler, numskull, featherbrain, dolt, scatterbrain, dunce, clod, ignoramus, idiot, duffer, addlebrain, butterfingers, bonehead*, blockhead*, blunderhead*, goof-off*, clumsy oaf, bull in a china shop*, harebrain*, klutz*.

bungling *a.* clumsy, unskillful, inept; see AWKWARD, INCOMPETENT.

bunk[1,2] *n.* 1 [A bed] berth, cot, mattress; see BED 1. 2 [*Anything untrue, silly, or unreliable] rubbish, rot, hogwash; see NONSENSE 1.

buoy *n.* float, drift, floating marker; see FLOAT.

burden[1] *n.* 1 [Something carried] cargo, freight, pack; see LOAD 1. 2 [Anything hard to support or endure] encumbrance, punishment, misery; see DIFFICULTY 2, MISFORTUNE.

burden[1] *v.* weigh down, force, hinder, encumber, overwhelm, hamper, strain, load with, saddle with, handicap, obligate, tax, afflict, vex, try, trouble, pile, bog down, crush, depress, impede, overload, oppress, make heavy, press down.—*Ant.* LIGHTEN, relieve, unload.

burdensome *a.* heavy, oppressive, troublesome; see DIFFICULT 1, 2, DISTURBING.

bureau *n.* 1 [Committee] commission, authority, board; see COMMITTEE. 2 [Chest of drawers] highboy, dresser, cabinet; see CHEST 1, FURNITURE.

bureaucracy *n.* the Establishment, the authorities, the system; see GOVERNMENT 1, 2.

burglar *n.* thief, housebreaker, robber; see CRIMINAL.

burglary *n.* housebreaking, stealing, robbery; see CRIME, THEFT.

burial *n.* last rites, interment,

bur·lap (bʉr'lap') *n.* ⟦< ? ME *borel*⟧ a coarse cloth of jute or hemp

bur·lesque (bər lesk') *n.* ⟦Fr < It *burla*, a jest⟧ 1 any broadly comic or satirical imitation; parody 2 a sort of vaudeville with low comedy, striptease acts, etc. — *vt., vi.* **-lesqued', -lesqu'ing** to imitate comically

bur·ley (bʉr'lē) *n.* ⟦< ? ⟧ [*also* B-] a thin-leaved, light-colored tobacco grown in Kentucky, etc.

burly (bʉr'lē) *adj.* **-lier, -li·est** ⟦ME *borlich*, excellent⟧ 1 big and strong 2 hearty in manner

burn (bʉrn) *vt.* **burned** or **burnt, burn'ing** ⟦< OE *beornan*, to be on fire⟧ 1 to set on fire, as in order to produce heat, light, or power 2 to destroy by fire 3 to injure or damage by fire, acid, etc. 4 to consume as fuel 5 to sunburn 6 to cause (a hole, etc.) as by fire 7 to cause a sensation of heat in — *vi.* 1 to be on fire 2 to give out light or heat 3 to be destroyed or injured by fire or heat 4 to feel hot 5 to be excited — *n.* 1 an injury or damage caused by fire, heat, etc. 2 the process or result of burning —**burn down** to burn to the ground —**burn out** to exhaust or become exhausted from overwork, etc. —**burn up** [Slang] to make or become angry —**burn'able** *adj., n.*

burn'er *n.* the part of a stove, furnace, etc. from which the flame comes

bur·nish (bʉr'nish) *vt., vi.* ⟦< OFr *brunir*, make brown⟧ to make or become shiny by rubbing — *n.* a gloss or polish —**bur'nisher** *n.*

bur·noose (bər nōōs') *n.* ⟦< Ar *burnus*⟧ a hooded cloak worn by Arabs

burn·out (bʉrn'out') *n.* 1 the point at which a rocket's fuel is burned up and the rocket enters free flight or is jettisoned 2 emotional exhaustion from mental stress

burnt (bʉrnt) *vt., vi. alt. pt. & pp. of* BURN

burp (bʉrp) *n., vi.* ⟦echoic⟧ [Colloq.] belch — *vt.* to cause (a baby) to belch

burr¹ (bʉr) *n.* ⟦var. of BUR⟧ 1 a bur 2 a rough edge left on metal, etc. by cutting or drilling — *vt.* to form a rough edge on

burr² (bʉr) *n.* ⟦prob. echoic⟧ 1 the trilling of *r*, as in Scottish speech 2 a whir

burro (bʉr'ō) *n., pl.* **-ros** ⟦Sp < LL *burricus*, small horse⟧ a donkey

bur·row (bʉr'ō) *n.* ⟦see BOROUGH⟧ 1 a hole dug in the ground by an animal 2 any similar hole — *vi.* 1 to make a burrow 2 to live or hide in a burrow 3 to search, as if by digging — *vt.* 1 to make burrows in 2 to make by burrowing

bursa (bʉr'sə) *n., pl.* **-sae** (-sē) or **-sas** ⟦< Gr. *byrsa*, a hide⟧ *Anat.* a sac or cavity with a lubricating fluid, as between a tendon and bone

bur·sar (bʉr'sər) *n.* ⟦< ML *bursa*, a purse⟧ a treasurer, as of a college

bur·si·tis (bər sīt'is) *n.* ⟦< BURSA + -ITIS⟧ inflammation of a bursa

burst (bʉrst) *vi.* **burst, burst'ing** ⟦OE *berstan*⟧ 1 to come apart suddenly and violently; explode 2 to give sudden vent; break (*into* tears, etc.) 3 to appear, start, etc. suddenly 4 to be as full or crowded as possible — *vt.* to cause to burst — *n.* 1 a bursting 2 a break or rupture 3 a sudden action or effort; spurt 4 a volley of shots

bury (ber'ē) *vt.* **-ied, -y·ing** ⟦OE *byrgan*⟧ 1 to put (a dead body) into the earth, a tomb, etc. 2 to hide or cover 3 to put away 4 to immerse

bus (bus) *n., pl.* **bus'es** or **bus'ses** ⟦< (OMNI)BUS⟧ a large motor coach for many passengers, usually following a regular route — *vt.* **bused** or **bussed, bus'ing** or **bus·sing** to transport by bus — *vi.* 1 to go by bus 2 to do the work of a busboy

bus'boy' *n.* a waiter's assistant who clears tables, brings water, etc.

busby (buz'bē) *n., pl.* **-bies** ⟦prob. < name *Busby*⟧ a tall fur hat worn with a full-dress uniform, as by guardsmen

bush (boosh) *n.* ⟦OE *busc*⟧ 1 a low woody plant with spreading branches; shrub 2 anything like a bush 3 uncleared land — *vi.* to grow thickly —**beat around the bush** to talk around a subject without getting to the point —**bush'y, -ier, -iest,** *adj.*

bushed (boosht) *adj.* [Colloq.] very tired; exhausted

bushel (boosh'əl) *n.* ⟦< OFr *boisse*, grain measure⟧ a dry measure equal to 4 pecks or 32 quarts

bush·ing (boosh'iŋ) *n.* ⟦< MDu *busse*, box⟧ a removable metal lining for reducing friction on moving parts

bush league [Slang] a small or second-rate minor league, etc. —**bush'-league'** *adj.* —**bush leaguer**

bush'man (-mən) *n., pl.* **-men** one who lives in the Australian bush

bush'mas'ter (-mas'tər) *n.* a large poisonous snake of Central and South America

bush'whack' (-hwak') *vt.* ⟦prob. < BUSH + WHACK⟧ to ambush —**bush'whack'er** *n.*

busi·ly (biz'ə lē) *adv.* in a busy manner

business (biz'niz, -nis) *n.* ⟦OE *bisignes*: see BUSY⟧ 1 one's work; occupation 2 a special task, duty, etc. 3 rightful concern 4 a matter or affair 5 commerce; trade 6 a commercial or industrial establishment — *adj.* of or for business —**mean business** [Colloq.] to be in earnest

business agent a representative of a labor union local

business college (or **school**) a school of typing, bookkeeping, etc.

THESAURUS

entombment; see FUNERAL.

burn *n.* scorch, wound, impairment; see BLISTER.

burn *v.* ignite, kindle, incinerate, burn up, burn down, blaze, flame, flare, burst into flame, rage, consume, enkindle, cremate, consume with flames, set a match to, set on fire, set ablaze, set afire, sear, singe, scorch, brand, fire, light, torch, char, roast, toast, heat, bake; see also COOK.—*Ant.* EXTINGUISH, put out, quench.

burned *a.* scorched, charred, seared, burnt, singed, branded, cauterized, marked, blistered, scalded. — **burned up*** angered, enraged, infuriated; see ANGRY.

burning *a.* fiery, blazing, glowing, ablaze, afire, on fire, smoking, in flames, aflame, inflamed, kindled, enkindled, ignited, scorching, turning to ashes, searing, in a blaze, blistering, red-hot, white-hot; see also PASSIONATE 2.—*Ant.* COLD, frozen, out.

burnt *a.* scorched, singed, charred; see BURNED.

burst *n.* 1 [An explosion] blowout, blast, blowup; see EXPLOSION. 2 [A sudden spurt] rush, outburst, torrent; see FIT 2.

burst *v.* 1 [To explode] blow up, erupt, rupture; see BREAK 2, DISINTEGRATE, EXPLODE. 2 [To break] crack,

split, fracture; see BREAK 1, DESTROY. —**burst into tears** weep, start crying, sob; see CRY 1.

bury *v.* 1 [To inter] lay in the grave, entomb, enshrine, deposit in the earth, to give burial to, embalm, hold funeral services for, lay out. 2 [To cover] conceal, mask, stow away; see HIDE 1. 3 [To defeat] overcome, win over, conquer; see DEFEAT 2, 3.

bus *n.* autobus, passenger bus, limousine, sightseeing bus, motor coach, common carrier, public conveyance, Greyhound (trademark).

bus *v.* transport, ship, redistrict; see CARRY.

bush *n.* bramble, thicket, hedge, shrubbery, briar bush, rose bush; see also PLANT. —**beat around the bush** speak evasively, avoid the subject, be deceptive; see EVADE.

bushy *a.* fuzzy, disordered, thick, shaggy, rough, full, tufted, fringed, woolly, nappy, fluffy, furry, crinkly, stiff, wiry, rumpled, prickly, feathery, leafy, bristly, heavy.—*Ant.* THIN, sleek, smooth.

busily *a.* diligently, actively, energetically, strenuously, eagerly, earnestly, seriously, intently, rapidly, dexterously, industriously, carefully, intently, studiously, hurriedly, briskly, purposefully, ardently, ardu-

ously, fervently, nimbly, zealously, vigorously, restlessly, enthusiastically, speedily, hastily, persistently, like hell*.—*Ant.* SLOWLY, listlessly, idly.

business *n.* 1 [Industry and trade] commerce, exchange, trade, traffic, barter, commercial enterprise, gainful occupation, buying and selling, negotiation, production and distribution, dealings, affairs, sales, contracts, transaction, bargaining, trading, banking, marketing, undertaking, speculation, market, mercantilism, wholesale and retail, capital and labor, free enterprise, game*, racket*. 2 [Occupation] trade, profession, vocation; see JOB 1. 3 [A person's proper concerns] affair, concern, interest; see AFFAIR 1. 4 [A commercial enterprise] firm, factory, mill, store, company, shop, corporation, concern, combine, conglomerate, cooperative, establishment, enterprise, partnership, institution, house, market, syndicate, cartel, trust, monopoly, holding company. —**do business with** deal with, trade with, patronize; see BUY, SELL, TREAT 1. —**get the business*** be mistreated, be abused, endure; see SUFFER 1. —**give the business*** mistreat, bother, victimize; see ABUSE. —**mean business*** be serious, stress, impress; see EMPHASIZE.

busi'ness·like' *adj.* efficient, methodical, systematic, etc.
busi'ness·man' *n., pl.* **-men'** a man in business, esp. as an owner —**busi'ness·wom'an,** *pl.* **-wom'en,** *n.fem.*
bus·ing or **bus·sing** (bus'iŋ) *n.* the transporting of children by bus to a school outside of their neighborhood, esp. so as to desegregate the school
bus·kin *n.* [? < MDu *brosekin,* small boot] 1 a high, laced boot worn in ancient tragedy 2 tragic drama
buss (bus) *n., vt., vi.* [prob. of echoic orig.] [Now Chiefly Dial.] kiss
bust[1] (bust) *n.* [< It *busto*] 1 a sculpture of a person's head and shoulders 2 a woman's bosom
bust[2] (bust) *vt., vi.* [< BURST] [Colloq.] 1 to burst or break 2 to make or become bankrupt or demoted 3 to hit 4 to arrest — *n.* [Colloq.] 1 a failure 2 financial collapse 3 a punch 4 a spree 5 an arrest —**bust'ed** *adj.*
bus·tle[1] (bus'əl) *vi., vt.* **-tled, -tling** [< ME *busken,* prepare] to hurry busily — *n.* busy and noisy activity
bus·tle[2] (bus'əl) *n.* [< ?] a padding formerly worn to fill out the upper back of a woman's skirt
busy (biz'ē) *adj.* **-i·er, -i·est** [OE *bisig*] 1 active; at work 2 full of activity 3 in use, as a telephone 4 too detailed — *vt.* **bus'ied, bus'y·ing** to make or keep busy —**bus'y·ness** *n.*
bus'y·bod'y (-bäd'ē) *n., pl.* **-ies** a meddler in the affairs of others
but (but; *unstressed* bət) *prep.* [OE *butan,* without] except; save [*nobody* went *but* me] — *conj.* 1 yet; still [it's good, *but* not great] 2 on the contrary [I am old, *but* you are young] 3 unless [it never rains *but* it pours] 4 that [I don't doubt *but* you're right] 5 that . . . not [I never gamble *but* I lose] — *adv.* 1 only [if I had *but* known] 2 merely [he is *but* a child] 3 just [I heard it *but* now] — *pron.* who . . . not; which . . . not [not a man *but* felt it] — **but for** if it were not for
bu·tane (byōō'tān) *n.* [ult. < L *butyrum,* butter] a hydrocarbon used as a fuel, etc.
butch (booch) *adj.* [< ? fol.] 1 [Colloq.] designating a man's closely cropped haircut 2 [Slang] masculine: said of a lesbian
butcher (booch'ər) *n.* [< OFr *bouc,* he-goat] 1 one whose work is killing and dressing animals for meat 2 one who cuts meat for sale 3 a brutal killer — *vt.* 1 to kill or dress (animals) for meat 2 to kill brutally or senselessly 3 to botch —**butch'er·y,** *pl.* **-ies,** *n.*
but·ler (but'lər) *n.* [< OFr *bouteille,* bottle] a manservant, usually the head servant of a household
butt[1] (but) *n.* [< ?] 1 the thick end of anything 2 a stub or stump, as of a cigar 3 a target 4 an object of ridicule 5 [Slang] a cigarette — *vt., vi.* to join end to end
butt[2] (but) *vt., vi.* [< OFr *buter,* thrust against] 1 to ram with the head 2 to project — *n.* a butting —**butt in** (or **into**) [Colloq.] to mix into (another's business, etc.)
butt[3] (but) *n.* [< LL *buttis,* cask] a large cask for wine or beer

butte (byōōt) *n.* [Fr, mound] a steep hill standing alone in a plain
but·ter (but'ər) *n.* [< Gr *bous,* cow + *tyros,* cheese] 1 the solid, yellowish, edible fat that results from churning cream 2 any substance somewhat like butter — *vt.* 1 to spread with butter 2 [Colloq.] to flatter: often with *up* — **but'tery** *adj.*
butter bean a light-colored bean, as a lima bean or wax bean
but'ter·cup' *n.* a plant with yellow, cup-shaped flowers
but'ter·fat' *n.* the fatty part of milk, from which butter is made
but'ter·fin'gers *n.* [Colloq.] one who often fumbles and drops things
but'ter·fly' (-flī') *n., pl.* **-flies'** [OE *buttorfleoge*] an insect with a slender body and four broad, usually brightly colored wings
but'ter·milk' *n.* the liquid left after churning butter from milk
but'ter·nut' *n.* 1 a walnut tree of E North America 2 its edible, oily nut
but'ter·scotch' *n.* 1 a hard, sticky candy made with brown sugar, butter, etc. 2 the flavor of this candy 3 a syrup with this flavor
but·tock (but'ək) *n.* [< OE *buttuc,* end] 1 either of the fleshy, rounded parts of the hips 2 [pl.] the rump
but·ton (but''n) *n.* [< OFr *boton*] 1 any small disk or knob used as a fastening, ornament, etc., as on a garment 2 anything small and shaped like a button — *vt., vi.* to fasten with a button or buttons
but'ton-down' *adj.* 1 designating a collar, as on a shirt, fastened down by small buttons 2 conservative, unimaginative, etc. [a *button-down* mind]
but'ton·hole' *n.* a slit or loop through which a button is inserted — *vt.* **-holed', -hol'ing** 1 to make buttonholes in 2 to detain and talk to
but·tress (bu'tris) *n.* [see BUTT[2]] 1 a structure built against a wall to support or reinforce it 2 a support or prop — *vt.* to prop up; bolster
buxom (buk'səm) *adj.* [ME, humble] having a shapely, full-bosomed figure: said of a woman or girl
buy (bī) *vt.* **bought, buy'ing** [OE *bycgan*] 1 to get by paying money; purchase 2 to get by an exchange [*buy* victory with human lives] 3 to bribe 4 [Slang] to accept as true [I can't *buy* this excuse] — *n.* 1 anything bought 2 [Colloq.] something worth its price —**buy off** to bribe —**buy out** to buy all the stock, rights, etc. of —**buy up** to buy all that is available of
buy'back' (-bak') *n. Finance* the buying by a corporation of its own stock to reduce the outstanding shares
buy'er *n.* 1 one who buys; consumer 2 one whose work is to buy merchandise for a retail store
buy'out' *n.* the outright purchase of a business, as by the employees or management
buzz (buz) *vi.* [echoic] 1 to hum like a bee 2 to gossip 3 to be filled with noisy activity or talk — *vt.* to fly an airplane low over — *n.* a sound like a bee's hum
buz·zard (buz'ərd) *n.* [< L *buteo,* kind of hawk] 1 a kind

THESAURUS

businesslike *a.* purposeful, systematic, methodical; see PRACTICAL.
businessman *n.* industrialist, capitalist, employer, tycoon, broker, retailer, stockbroker, manager, buyer, operator, backer, financier, systems expert, company man, comptroller, accountant, investor, speculator, entrepreneur, purchasing agent, storekeeper, tradesman; see also EXECUTIVE.
busy *a.* 1 [Engaged] occupied, diligent, employed, working, in conference, in a meeting, in the field, in the laboratory, on an assignment, on duty, on the job, at work, busy with, on the run, on the road, hard-working, busy as a bee*, hustling*, up to one's ears*, hard at it*, having other fish to fry.—*Ant.* IDLE, unemployed, unoccupied. 2 [In use] employed, occupied, taken; see RENTED.
busybody *n.* meddler, tattletale, troublemaker; see GOSSIP 2.
but *conj., prep.* 1 [Indicating contrast] however, on the other hand, in contrast, nevertheless, still, yet, though, on the contrary, but then, but as you see; see also ALTHOUGH. 2

[Indicating an exception] save, disregarding, without, not including, not taking into account, let alone, aside from, with the exception of, not to mention, passing over, barring, setting aside, forgetting; see also EXCEPT. 3 [Indicating a limitation] only, merely, simply, barely, solely, purely, just, no more, exactly, no other than, without; see also ONLY 1.
butcher *v.* 1 [To slaughter for human consumption] stick, pack, dress, clean, cure, smoke, salt, cut, put up. 2 [To kill inhumanly] slaughter, slay, massacre; see KILL 1. 3 [To ruin] mess up, spoil, wreck; see BOTCH, DESTROY.
butt[1] *n.* base, tail end, bottom, hilt, extremity, tail, tip, fundament, stump, tub, bottom, seat, posterior; see also BOTTOM.
butt[2] *v.* hit, ram, push headfirst, bump, batter, knock, collide with, run into, smack, strike, gore, buck, toss, crash into.
butter *n. Varieties of butter include the following:* creamery, sweet, dairy, cube, country, tub, vegetable, soy.
button *n.* knob, catch, disk; see FAS-

TENER. —**on the button*** correctly, precisely, accurately; see RIGHT 1.
button *v.* close, clasp, make firm; see FASTEN.
buy* *n.* value, good deal, steal*; see BARGAIN 2.
buy *v.* purchase, get, bargain for, procure, gain, contract for, sign for, get in exchange, go marketing, buy and sell, order, invest in, make an investment, shop for, acquire ownership of, procure title to, pay for, redeem, pay a price for, buy into, score*. —**buy off** corrupt, influence, fix*; see BRIBE.
buyer *n.* purchasing agent, purchaser, customer, client, prospect, consumer, representative, patron, user, shopper.—*Ant.* SELLER, vendor, dealer.
buying *n.* purchasing, getting, obtaining, acquiring, paying, investing, exchange, bartering, bargaining, procuring, trafficking.—*Ant.* SELLING, vending, auctioning.
buzz *n.* murmur, buzzing, hum; see NOISE 1.
buzz *v.* drone, hum, whir; see SOUND.

of hawk that is slow and heavy in flight **2** TURKEY VULTURE

buzz′er *n.* an electrical device that makes a buzzing sound as a signal

buzz saw a saw with teeth around the edge of a large disk fixed on a motor-driven shaft

bx box

by (bī) *prep.* ⟦OE *be, bi*⟧ **1** near; at /sit *by* the fire/ **2** *a*) in or during /to travel *by* day/ *b*) for a fixed time /to work *by* the hour/ *c*) not later than /be back *by* noon/ **3** *a*) through; via /to Boston *by* Route 6/ *b*) past; beyond /he walked right *by* me/ **4** in behalf of /she did well *by* me/ **5** through the agency of /gained *by* fraud/ **6** *a*) according to /to go *by* the book/ *b*) in /to die *by* degrees/ *c*) following in series /marching two *by* two/ **7** *a*) in or to the amount of /apples *by* the peck/ *b*) and in another dimension /two *by* four/ *c*) using (the given number) as multiplier or divisor —*adv.* **1** close at hand /stand *by*/ **2** away; aside /to put money *by*/ **3** past /she sped *by*/ **4** at the place specified /stop *by* on your way/ —**by and by** soon or eventually —**by and large** considering everything —**by the by** incidentally

by- *prefix* **1** near **2** secondary /byproduct/

by-and-by (bī′′n bī′) *n.* a future time

bye (bī) *n.* ⟦var. of BY⟧ the privilege, with an uneven number of participants, of not being paired with another contestant in the first round

bye-bye (bī′bī′) *n., interj.* goodbye

by·gone (bī′gôn′) *adj.* past; former —*n.* anything gone or past

by·law (bī′lô′) *n.* ⟦< ME *bi,* village + *laue,* law⟧ any of a set of rules adopted by an organization or assembly for its own meetings or affairs

by′line′ *n.* a line identifying the writer of a newspaper or magazine article

by′pass′ *n.* **1** a way, pipe, channel, etc. between two points that avoids or is auxiliary to the main way **2** a surgical operation to allow fluid to pass around a diseased or blocked part or organ — *vt.* **1** to detour **2** to furnish with a bypass **3** to ignore

by′path′ or **by′-path′** *n.* a secluded, little-used path; byway

by′play′ *n.* action, gestures, etc. going on aside from the main action or conversation

by′prod′uct or **by′-prod′uct** *n.* anything produced in the course of making another thing

by′road′ *n.* a road that is not a main road

by′stand′er *n.* a person who stands near but does not participate

byte (bīt) *n.* ⟦arbitrary formation⟧ a string of binary digits (*bits*), usually eight, operated on as a basic unit by a digital computer

by′way′ *n.* a side road or path

by′word′ *n.* **1** a proverb **2** one well-known for some quality **3** an object of scorn or ridicule

---

THESAURUS

buzzer *n.* siren, signal, bell; see ALARM, WARNING, WHISTLE 1.

by *prep.* **1** [Near] close to, next to, nigh; see NEAR 1, NEXT 2. **2** [By stated means] over, with, through, by means of, in the name of, at the hand of, along with, through the medium of, with the assistance of, with the aid of, on, supported by.

bylaw *n.* ordinance, local law, regulation; see LAW 3.

bypass *n.* detour, temporary route, side road; see ROAD 1.

bypass *v.* miss, evade, detour around; see AVOID.

bystander *n.* onlooker, watcher, spectator; see OBSERVER.

C

c or **C** (sē) *n.*, *pl.* **c's, C's** the third letter of the English alphabet

C (sē) *n.* **1** a Roman numeral for 100 **2** *Educ.* a grade for average work **3** *Music* the first tone in the scale of C major

C *symbol for* **1** *Chem.* carbon **2** Celsius (or centigrade)

C or **C. 1** carat(s) **2** catcher **3** Catholic **4** cent(s) **5** center **6** centimeter(s) **7** century; centuries **8** chapter(s) **9** circa **10** college **11** copyright **12** cup(s) **13** cycle(s) Also, except 3, **c** or **c.**

Ca *Chem. symbol for* calcium

cab (kab) *n.* [< Fr *cabriole*, a leap] **1** a carriage, esp. one for public hire **2** TAXICAB **3** the place in a truck, crane, etc. where the operator sits — *vi.* **cabbed, cab'bing** [Colloq.] to take or drive a taxicab

ca·bal (kə bal') *n.* [Fr, intrigue] **1** a small group joined in a secret intrigue **2** the intrigue itself

caba·la (kab'ə lə, kə bä'lə) *n.* [< Heb *kabala*, tradition] **1** a medieval occult Jewish philosophy **2** occultism

ca·bal·lero (kab'ə ler'ō, -əl yer'ō) *n.*, *pl.* **-ros** [Sp] **1** a Spanish gentleman **2** [Southwest] *a*) a horseman *b*) a lady's escort

ca·bana (kə ban'ə, -bä'nə) *n.* [Sp < LL *capanna*] **1** a cabin or hut **2** a small shelter used as a bathhouse

caba·ret (kab'ə rā') *n.* [Fr, tavern] a cafe with musical entertainment

cab·bage (kab'ij) *n.* [OFr *caboche* < ?] a vegetable with thick leaves formed into a round, compact head

cabby or **cab·bie** (kab'ē) *n.*, *pl.* **-bies** [Colloq.] one who drives a cab

caber·net (kab'ər nā') *n.* [*also* C-] a dry red wine; esp., CABERNET SAUVIGNON

cabernet sau·vi·gnon (sō vē nyon') [*also* C- S-] a fragrant, dry red wine

cabin (kab'in) *n.* [< LL *capanna*, hut] **1** a small, crudely or simply built house; hut **2** a room on a ship or boat **3** the space for passengers, crew, or cargo in an aircraft

cabi·net (kab'ə nit) *n.* [Fr, prob. ult. < L *cavea*, cage] **1** a case with drawers or shelves **2** a case holding a TV, radio, etc. **3** [*often* C-] a body of official advisors to a chief executive

cab'i·net·mak'er *n.* a maker of fine furniture

cab'i·net·work' *n.* articles made by a cabinetmaker Also **cab'i·netry** (-ni trē)

cabin fever a condition of increased anxiety caused by being confined or isolated

ca·ble (kā'bəl) *n.* [< L *capere*, to take hold] **1** a thick, heavy rope, often of wire strands **2** a bundle of insulated wires to carry an electric current **3** a cablegram **4** CABLE TV — *vt.* **-bled, -bling 1** to fasten with a cable **2** to send a cablegram to — *vi.* to send a cablegram

cable car a car drawn by a moving cable, as up a steep incline

ca'ble·cast' (-kast') *vt.* **-cast', -cast'ing** to transmit to receivers by coaxial cable — *n.* a program that is cablecast

ca'ble·gram' (-gram') *n.* a message sent by undersea cable

cable TV a TV system in which various antennas receive local and distant signals and transmit them by cable to subscribers' receivers

cabo·chon (kab'ə shän') *n.* [Fr < *caboche*, head] any precious stone cut in convex shape

ca·boodle (kə bōōd'əl) *n.* [< BOODLE] [Colloq.] lot; group [the whole *caboodle*]

ca·boose (kə bōōs') *n.* [MDu *kambuis*, cabin house] the trainmen's car at the rear of a freight train

ca·cao (kə kā'ō, -kä'-) *n.*, *pl.* **-os'** [Sp < AmInd (Mexico)] **1** the seed of a tropical American tree from which cocoa and chocolate are made: also **cacao bean 2** this tree

cache (kash) *n.* [Fr < L *cogere*, to collect] **1** a place in which stores of food, supplies, etc. are hidden **2** anything so hidden — *vt.* **cached, cach'ing** to place in a cache

cache·pot (kash'pät, -pō') *n.* [Fr < *cacher*, to hide] a decorative jar for holding potted plants Also **cache pot**

ca·chet (ka shā') *n.* [Fr] **1** a stamp or official seal, as on a document **2** any sign of official approval, or of quality, prestige, etc. **3** a design on an envelope that marks some event

cackle (kak'əl) *vi.* **-led, -ling** [echoic] **1** to make the shrill, broken vocal sounds of a hen **2** to laugh or chatter with similar sounds — *n.* a cackling

ca·coph·o·ny (kə käf'ə nē) *n.*, *pl.* **-nies** [< Gr *kakos*, bad + *phōnē*, voice] harsh, jarring sound; discord —**ca·coph'o·nous** *adj.*

cac·tus (kak'təs) *n.*, *pl.* **-tuses** or **-ti** (-tī') [< Gr *kaktos*, kind of thistle] any of a family of desert plants with fleshy stems and spinelike leaves

cad (kad) *n.* [< CADET] a man whose behavior is not gentlemanly —**cad'dish** *adj.* —**cad'dishly** *adv.* —**cad' dish·ness** *n.*

ca·daver (kə dav'ər) *n.* [L, prob. < *cadere*, to fall] a corpse, as for dissection

ca·dav'er·ous (-əs) *adj.* [< L] of or like a cadaver; esp., pale, ghastly, etc.

CAD/CAM (kad'kam') *n.* [C(omputer-)A(ided) D(esign)/- C(omputer-)A(ided) M(anufacturing)] a computer system combining design techniques and manufacturing principles

cad·die (kad'ē) *n.* [Scot form of Fr *cadet*: see CADET] one who attends a golfer, carrying the clubs — *vi.* **-died, -dy·ing** to act as a caddie

caddy[1] (kad'ē) *n.*, *pl.* **-dies** [< Malay *kātī*, unit of weight] a small container, specif., one used for tea

caddy[2] (kad'ē) *n.*, *vi.* CADDIE

-cade (kād) [< (CAVAL)CADE] *suffix* procession, parade [motorcade]

ca·dence (kād'ns) *n.* [< L *cadere*, to fall] **1** fall of the voice in speaking **2** flow of rhythm **3** measured movement, as in marching

ca·denza (kə den'zə) *n.* [It: see prec.] an elaborate passage for the solo instrument in a concerto

ca·det (kə det') *n.* [Fr < L dim. of *caput*, head] **1** a student in training at an armed forces academy **2** any trainee, as a practice teacher

cadge (kaj) *vt.*, *vi.* **cadged, cadg'ing** [< ?] to beg or get by begging; sponge —**cadg'er** *n.*

cad·mium (kad'mē əm) *n.* [< L *cadmia*, zinc ore (with which it occurs)] a metallic chemical element used in alloys, pigments, etc.

ca·dre (ka'drē', -drā'; *also*, kä'-) *n.* [< Fr < L *quadrum*, a square] a nucleus around which an expanded organization, as a military unit, can be built

ca·du·ceus (kə dōō'sē əs) *n.*, *pl.* **-cei'** (-sē ī') [L] the winged staff of Mercury: now a symbol of the medical profession

Cae·sar (sē'zər) *n.* [after Julius *Caesar* (c. 100-44 B.C.), Rom. dictator] **1** the title of the Roman emperors from 27 B.C. to A.D. 138 **2** [*often* c-] any emperor or dictator

Cae·sar·ean section (sə zer'ē ən) [from the ancient story that Julius *Caesar* was born this way: see prec.] [*also* c- s-] the delivery of a baby by cutting through the mother's abdominal and uterine walls

cae·sura (si zyoor'ə, -zhoor'ə) *n.*, *pl.* **-ras** or **-rae** (-ē) [L < *caedere*, to cut down] a break or pause in a line of verse, usually in the middle

cafe or **café** (kə fā', ka-) *n.* [Fr, coffeehouse] a small restaurant or a barroom, nightclub, etc.

caf·eteria (kaf'ə tir'ē ə) *n.* [AmSp, coffee store] a self-service restaurant

caf·feine or **caf·fein** (kaf'ēn') *n.* [Ger *kaffein*] the alkaloid present in coffee, tea, and kola: it is a stimulant

caf·tan (kaf'tan) *n.* [Turk *qaftān*] a long-sleeved robe, worn in eastern Mediterranean countries

cage (kāj) *n.* [< L *cavea*, hollow place] **1** a structure of wires, bars, etc., for confining animals **2** any openwork

---

THESAURUS

cab *n.* taxi, taxicab, hack*; see AUTOMOBILE, VEHICLE.

cabin *n.* log house, cottage, hut; see HOME 1, SHELTER.

cabinet *n.* council, advisory council, authority, bureaucracy, committee, bureau, governing body, administrators, assembly, assistants, department heads, advisors, United States Cabinet, ministry, backstairs cabinet, brain trust; see also GOVERNMENT 2.

cable *n.* cord, preformed cable, wire twist; see CHAIN, WIRE 1.

cackle *v.* chuckle, snicker, giggle; see LAUGH.

cactus *n. Cactuses include the following:* giant, saguaro, barrel, choya, hedgehog, cochineal, nipple, night-blooming cereus, century plant, prickly pear, mescal; see also PLANT.

cad *n.* rogue, scoundrel, rake; see RASCAL.

cadence *n.* rhythm, meter, flow; see BEAT 2, MEASURE 3.

cafe *n.* cafeteria, lunchroom, coffee shop; see RESTAURANT.

cage *n.* coop, jail, crate; see ENCLOSURE 1, PEN 1.

cag·er (kā′jər) *n.* [Slang] a basketball player
ca·gey or **cag·y** (kā′jē) *adj.* **-gier, -gi·est** [< ?] [Colloq.] 1 sly; tricky; cunning 2 cautious —**ca′gi·ly** *adv.* —**ca′gi·ness** *n.*
ca·hoots (kə hōōts′) *n.pl.* [< ?] [Slang] partnership: chiefly in phr. **in cahoots (with)** implying scheming
Cain (kān) *Bible* oldest son of Adam and Eve: he killed his brother Abel —**raise Cain** [Slang] to create a great commotion
cairn (kern) *n.* [Scot] a conical heap of stones built as a monument
cais·son (kā′sən) *n.* [Fr < L *capsa*, box] 1 a two-wheeled wagon with a chest for ammunition 2 a watertight box for underwater construction work
cai·tiff (kāt′if) *n.* [< L *captivus*, CAPTIVE] a mean, evil, or cowardly person — *adj.* evil, mean, or cowardly
ca·jole (kə jōl′) *vt., vi.* **-joled′, -jol′ing** [< Fr] to coax with flattery and insincere talk —**ca·jol′er** *n.* —**ca·jol′ery** *n.*
Ca·jun or **Ca·jan** (kā′jən) *n.* 1 a native of Louisiana of Canadian French ancestry 2 the dialect of Cajuns
cake (kāk) *n.* [< ON] 1 a small, flat mass of baked or fried dough, batter, hashed food, etc. 2 a mixture of flour, eggs, sugar, etc. baked as in a loaf and often covered with icing 3 a shaped, solid mass, as of soap — *vt., vi.* **caked, cak′ing** to form into a hard mass or crust —**piece of cake** [Slang] something easy or pleasurable to do —**take the cake** [Slang] to win the prize —**cak′y** or **cak′ey** *adj.*
cal. 1 caliber 2 calorie(s)
cala·bash (kal′ə bash′) *n.* [< Sp *calabaza*] 1 the gourdlike fruit of a tropical American tree 2 *a)* the bottle-shaped, gourdlike fruit of a tropical vine *b)* a large smoking pipe made from it 3 a gourd
cala·boose (kal′ə bōōs′) *n.* [Sp *calabozo*] [Slang] a prison; jail
ca·la·mari (kä′lə mä′rē) *n.* squid cooked as food, esp. as an Italian dish
cala·mine (kal′ə mīn′) *n.* [Fr < L *cadmia*, zinc ore] a zinc oxide powder used in skin lotions
ca·lam·ity (kə lam′ə tē) *n., pl.* **-ties** [< L *calamitas*] a great misfortune; disaster —**ca·lam′i·tous** *adj.* —**ca·lam′i·tously** *adv.*
cal·car·eous (kal ker′ē əs) *adj.* [< L *calx*, lime] of or like limestone, calcium, or lime
cal·cif·er·ous (kal sif′ər əs) *adj.* [< L *calx*, lime + -FEROUS] containing calcite
cal·ci·fy (kal′sə fī′) *vt., vi.* **-fied′, -fy′ing** [< L *calx*, lime + -FY] to change into a hard, stony substance by the deposit of lime or calcium salts —**cal′ci·fi·ca′tion** *n.*
cal′ci·mine′ (-mīn′) *n.* [< L *calx*, lime] a white or tinted liquid, used as a wash for plastered surfaces — *vt.* **-mined′, -min′ing** to coat with calcimine
cal·cine (kal′sīn′) *vt., vi.* **-cined′, -cin′ing** [< L *calx*, lime] to change to an ashy powder by heat
cal·cite (kal′sīt′) *n.* calcium carbonate, a mineral found as limestone, chalk, and marble
cal·cium (kal′sē əm) *n.* [< L *calx*, lime] a soft, silver-white, metallic chemical element found combined in limestone, chalk, etc.
calcium carbonate a white powder or crystalline compound found in limestone, chalk, bones, shells, etc.

cal·cu·late (kal′kyōō lāt′, -kyə-) *vt.* **-lat′ed, -lat′ing** [< L *calculare*, reckon] 1 to determine by using mathematics; compute 2 to determine by reasoning; estimate 3 to plan or intend for a purpose — *vi.* 1 to reckon 2 to rely (*on*) — **cal′cu·lable** (-lə bəl) *adj.*
cal′cu·lat′ed *adj.* deliberately planned or carefully considered
cal′cu·lat′ing *adj.* shrewd or cunning; scheming
cal′cu·la′tion *n.* 1 a calculating 2 something deduced by calculating 3 careful planning or forethought —**cal′cu·la′tive** *adj.*
cal′cu·la′tor *n.* 1 one who calculates 2 a device for the rapid performance of mathematical operations
cal·cu·lus (kal′kyōō ləs, -kyə-) *n., pl.* **-li′** (-lī′) or **-luses** [L, pebble used in counting] 1 an abnormal stony mass in the body 2 a method of calculation or analysis in higher mathematics
cal·dera (kal der′ə) *n.* [Sp < L *caldarium*, room for hot baths] a broad, craterlike basin of a volcano
cal·dron (kôl′drən) *n.* [< L *calidus*, warm] 1 a large kettle or boiler 2 a state of violent agitation
cal·en·dar (kal′ən dər) *n.* [< L *kalendarium*, account book] 1 a system of determining the length and divisions of a year 2 a table that shows the days, weeks, and months of a given year 3 a schedule, as of pending court cases
cal·en·der (kal′ən dər) *n.* [< Gr *kylindros*, cylinder] a machine with rollers for giving paper, cloth, etc. a smooth or glossy finish — *vt.* to process (paper, etc.) in a calender
calf¹ (kaf) *n., pl.* **calves** (kavz) or **calfs** [< OE *cealf*] 1 a young cow or bull 2 the young of some other large animals, as the elephant, seal, etc. 3 leather from a calf's hide
calf² (kaf) *n., pl.* **calves** [ON *kalfi*] the fleshy back part of the leg below the knee
calf′skin′ *n.* 1 the skin of a calf 2 a soft leather made from this
cali·ber (kal′ə bər) *n.* [Fr & Sp, ult. < Gr *kalopodion*, shoemaker's last] 1 the diameter of a cylindrical body, esp. of a bullet or shell 2 the diameter of the bore of a gun 3 quality or ability Also, esp. Brit., **cal′i·bre**
cali·brate (kal′ə brāt′) *vt.* **-brat′ed, -brat′ing** 1 to determine the caliber of 2 to fix or correct the graduations of (a measuring instrument) —**cal′i·bra′tion** *n.* —**cal′i·bra′tor** *n.*
cali·co (kal′i kō′) *n., pl.* **-coes** or **-cos** [after *Calicut*, city in India] a printed cotton fabric — *adj.* spotted like calico [a *calico* cat]
cali·per (kal′ə pər) *n.* [var. of CALIBER] 1 [*usually pl.*] an instrument consisting of a pair of hinged legs, for measuring thickness or diameter 2 a part of a braking system on a bicycle or motor vehicle — *vt., vi.* to measure with calipers
ca·liph (kā′lif; *also*, kal′if) *n.* [Ar *khalifa*] supreme ruler: the title taken by Mohammed's successors as heads of Islam —**ca′liph·ate** *n.*
cal·is·then·ics (kal′is then′iks) *n.pl.* [< Gr *kallos*, beauty + *sthenos*, strength] athletic exercises —**cal′is·then′ic** *adj.*
calk (kôk) *vt.* CAULK —**calk′er** *n.*
call (kôl) *vt.* [< ON *kalla*] 1 to say in a loud tone; shout 2 to summon 3 to give or apply a name to 4 to describe as

---

THESAURUS

cake *n.* 1 [A flattish, compact mass] cube, bar, loaf; see BLOCK 1. 2 [Sweet baked goods] *Kinds of cake include the following:* wedding, birthday, angel food, devil's-food, corn, sponge, fruit, burnt-sugar, caramel, German chocolate, upside-down, pound, Martha Washington, maple, orange, white lemon, citron, walnut, almond, layer, white mountain, spice, marble, Lady Baltimore, coffeecake, jellyroll, gingerbread, shortbread; see also BREAD, PASTRY. —**take the cake*** excel, outdo, win the prize; see EXCEED.
cake *v.* crust, solidify, pack; see FREEZE 1, HARDEN, THICKEN.
calamity *n.* cataclysm, distress, trial; see CATASTROPHE, DISASTER, MISFORTUNE, TRAGEDY 1.
calculate *v.* count, measure, reckon, enumerate, determine, rate, forecast, weigh, gauge, number, figure, figure up, account, compute, sum up,

divide, multiply, subtract, add, work out, cipher, tally, dope out*; see also ESTIMATE.
calculation *n.* 1 [The act of calculating] adding, totaling, count; see ESTIMATE. 2 [A forecast] prediction, divination, prognostication; see FORECAST.
calendar *n.* list, program, record, timetable, schedule, annals, journal, diary, daybook, chronology, log, logbook, table, register, almanac, agenda, docket; see also ALMANAC.
calf¹ *n.* young cow, young bull, yearling; see COW.
calisthenics *n.* exercises, workout, aerobics; see EXERCISE 1, GYMNASTICS.
call *n.* 1 [A shout] yell, whoop, hail; see ALARM, CRY 1. 2 [Characteristic sound] twitter, tweet, shriek; see CRY 2. 3 [A visit] visiting, a few words, afternoon call; see VISIT. 4 [Word of

command] summons, battle cry, reveille; see ALARM, COMMAND, CRY 1. 5 [An invitation] bidding, solicitation, proposal; see INVITATION, REQUEST. —**on call** usable, ready, prepared; see AVAILABLE. —**within call** close by, approximate, not far away; see NEAR 1.
call *v.* 1 [To raise the voice] shout, call out, exclaim; see YELL. 2 [To bring a body of people together] collect, convene, muster; see ASSEMBLE 2. 3 [To address] denominate, designate, term; see NAME 1. 4 [To invite] summon, request, ask; see INVITE. —**call down*** rebuke, chide, admonish; see SCOLD. —**call for** 1 [To ask] ask for, request, make inquiry about; see ASK. 2 [To need] require, want, lack; see NEED. 3 [To come to get] come for, collect, fetch; see GET 1, PICK UP 6. —**call in** [To collect] collect, remove, receive; see WITHDRAW.

specified **5** to awaken **6** to telephone **7** to give orders for **8** to stop (a game, etc.) **9** to demand payment of (a loan, etc.) **10** *Poker* to equal (the preceding bet) or to equal the bet of (the last previous bettor) — *vi.* **1** to shout **2** to visit for a short while: often with *on* **3** to telephone — *n.* **1 a** calling **2** a loud utterance **3** the distinctive cry of an animal or bird **4 a** summons; invitation **5** an economic demand, as for a product **6** need *[no call for tears]* **7 a** demand for payment **8 a** brief visit **9** an option to buy a stock, commodity, etc. at a specified price and time —**call down** [Colloq.] to scold —**call for 1** to demand **2** to come and get —**call off** to cancel (a scheduled event) —**call up 1** to recall **2** to summon for duty **3** to telephone —**on call** available when summoned —**call'er** *n.*

cal·la (kal'ə) *n.* ⟦< L, a plant (of uncertain kind)⟧ a plant with a large, white leaf surrounding a yellow flower spike Also **Calla lily**

call girl a prostitute who is called by telephone to assignations

cal·lig·ra·phy (kə lig'rə fē) *n.* ⟦< Gr *kallos*, beauty + *graphein*, write⟧ handwriting, esp. when attractive —**cal·lig'ra·pher** *n.* —**cal·li·graphic** (kal'ə graf'ik) *adj.*

call'ing *n.* **1** the act of one that calls **2** one's work or profession **3** an inner urging toward some vocation

cal·li·o·pe (kə lī'ə pē', kal'ē ōp') *n.* ⟦< Gr *kallos*, beauty + *ops*, voice⟧ a keyboard instrument like an organ, having a series of steam whistles

call letters the letters, and sometimes numbers, that identify a radio or TV station

cal·lous (kal'əs) *adj.* ⟦< L *callum*, hard skin⟧ **1** hardened: usually **calloused 2** unfeeling —**cal·los·ity** (kə läs'ə tē) *n.* —**cal'lously** *adv.* —**cal'lous·ness** *n.*

cal·low (kal'ō) *adj.* ⟦OE *calu*, bare, bald⟧ immature; inexperienced —**cal'low·ness** *n.*

cal·lus (kal'əs) *n., pl.* **-luses** ⟦L, var. of *callum*, hard skin⟧ a hardened, thickened place on the skin

calm (käm) *n.* ⟦< Gr *kauma*, heat⟧ stillness; tranquillity —*adj.* still; quiet; tranquil —*vt., vi.* to make or become calm: often with *down* —**calm'ly** *adv.* —**calm'ness** *n.*

ca·lor·ic (kə lôr'ik) *adj.* **1** of heat **2** of calories

calo·rie (kal'ə rē) *n.* ⟦Fr < L *calor*, heat⟧ a unit for measuring heat, esp. for measuring the energy produced by food when oxidized in the body

calo·rific (kal'ə rif'ik) *adj.* ⟦< L *calor*, heat + *facere*, make⟧ producing heat

calu·met (kal'yə met') *n.* ⟦CdnFr < L *calamus*, reed⟧ a long-stemmed ceremonial pipe, smoked by North American Indians, as a token of peace

ca·lum·ni·ate (kə lum'nē āt') *vt., vi.* **-at'ed, -at'ing** ⟦see fol.⟧ to slander —**ca·lum'nia'tion** *n.* —**ca·lum'nia'tor** *n.*

cal·umny (kal'əm nē) *n., pl.* **-nies** ⟦< L *calumnia*, slander⟧ a false and malicious statement; slander

Cal·vary (kal'və rē) *Bible* the place where Jesus was crucified

calve (kav) *vi., vt.* **calved, calv'ing** to give birth to (a calf)

calves (kavz) *n. pl. of* CALF[1] & CALF[2]

Cal·vin·ism (kal'vin iz'əm) *n.* the Christian doctrines of John Calvin, 16th-c. Fr. protestant, and his followers, esp. predestination —**Cal'vin·ist** *n., adj.* —**Cal'vin·is'tic** *adj.*

cal·vi·ties (kal vish'i ēz') *n.* ⟦L⟧ a loss of hair, esp. on top of the head

ca·lyp·so (kə lip'sō) *n.* ⟦< ?⟧ a lively, topical folk song, orig. of Trinidad

ca·lyx (kā'liks', kal'iks') *n., pl.* **-lyx'es** or **-ly·ces'** (-lə sēz') ⟦L, pod⟧ the outer whorl of protective leaves, or sepals, of a flower

cam (kam) *n.* ⟦Du *cam*, orig., a comb⟧ a wheel, projection on a wheel, etc. that gives irregular motion, as to a wheel or shaft, or receives such motion from it

ca·ma·ra·derie (kam'ə räd'ə rē, käm'-) *n.* ⟦Fr⟧ loyalty and warm, friendly feeling among comrades

cam·ber (kam'bər) *n.* ⟦OFr < L *camur*, arched⟧ a slight convex curve of a surface, as of a road — *vt., vi.* to arch slightly

cam·bium (kam'bē əm) *n.* ⟦< LL *cambiare*, change⟧ a layer of cells between the wood and bark in woody plants, which will eventually become wood and bark —**cam'bial** *adj.*

cam·bric (kām'brik) *n.* ⟦after *Cambrai*, Fr city⟧ a fine linen or cotton cloth

cam·cord·er (kam'kôrd'ər) *n.* a small, portable videotape recorder and TV camera

came (kām) *vi. pt. of* COME

camel (kam'əl) *n.* ⟦ult. < Heb *gāmāl*⟧ a large, domesticated mammal with a humped back and long neck: because it can store water in its body, it is used in Asian and African deserts

ca·mel·lia (kə mēl'yə, -mē'lē ə) *n.* ⟦after G. J. *Kamel* (1661-1706), missionary to the Far East⟧ **1** an Asiatic evergreen tree or shrub with glossy leaves and roselike flowers **2** the flower

Cam·em·bert (cheese) (kam'əm ber', -bərt) ⟦after *Camembert*, Fr village⟧ a soft, creamy, rich cheese

cameo (kam'ē ō') *n., pl.* **-os'** ⟦< It < ML *camaeus*⟧ **1 a** gem carved with a figure raised in relief **2 a)** an outstanding bit role *b)* a bit of fine writing

cam·era (kam'ər ə) *n.* ⟦L, vault⟧ **1** the private office of a judge **2** a device for taking photographs: a closed box containing a sensitized plate or film on which an image is formed when light enters through a lens **3** *TV* the device that receives the image and transforms it into a flow of electrical impulses for transmission —**in camera** in privacy or secrecy

cam'era·man' *n., pl.* **-men'** **1** an operator of a film or TV camera **2** a cinematographer

cami·sole (kam'i sōl') *n.* ⟦Fr < LL *camisia*, shirt⟧ a woman's sleeveless undergarment for the upper body

camo·mile (kam'ə mil', -mēl') *n. alt. sp. of* CHAMOMILE

cam·ou·flage (kam'ə fläzh', -fläj') *n.* ⟦Fr < *camoufler*, to disguise⟧ **1 a** disguising, as of ships or guns, to conceal them from the enemy **2 a** disguise; deception — *vt., vi.* **-flaged', -flag'ing** to disguise in order to conceal —**cam'ou·flag'er** *n.*

▰▰▰ THESAURUS ▰▰▰

—**call off** cancel, postpone, cease; see HALT, STOP 2. —**call on (or upon)** stop in, have an appointment with, go to see; see VISIT. —**call up 1** [To remember] recollect, recall, summon up; see REMEMBER 1, SUMMON. **2** [To summon] send for bid, order; see INVITE. **3** [To telephone] phone, call, ring; see TELEPHONE.

called *a.* christened, termed, labeled; see NAMED 1.

calling *n.* occupation, vocation, work; see JOB 1, PROFESSION 1, TRADE 2.

callous *a.* unfeeling, hardened, insensitive; see INDIFFERENT.

calm *a.* **1** [Said especially of persons] dignified, reserved, cool, composed, collected, unmoved, levelheaded, coolheaded, impassive, detached, aloof, unconcerned, disinterested, unhurried, neutral, gentle, sedate, serene, unanxious, unexcited, contented, meek, satisfied, pleased, amiable, temperate, placid, civil, kind, moderate, confident, poised, tranquil, self-possessed, restful, relaxed, dispassionate, mild, still, patient, self-controlled, untroubled, cool as a

cucumber, unflappable*; see also RESERVED 3, PATIENT 1.—*Ant.* VIOLENT, excited, furious. **2** [Said often *of things*] quiet, undisturbed, unruffled, comfortable, moderate, in order, soothing, at peace, placid, smooth, still, restful, harmonious, peaceful, pacific, balmy, waveless, windless, serene, motionless, slow; see also QUIET.—*Ant.* ROUGH, agitated, aroused. —**keep calm** take one's time, keep cool, be patient; see CALM DOWN, RELAX.

calm *n.* **1** [Peace] stillness, peacefulness, quiet; see PEACE 2, REST 1, SILENCE 1. **2** [Composure] serenity, tranquillity, peace of mind; see COMPOSURE, PATIENCE 1, RESTRAINT 1.

calm *v.* tranquilize, soothe, pacify; see QUIET 1. —**calm down** compose oneself, control oneself, calm oneself, keep oneself under control, keep cool, take it easy, get organized, rest, get hold of oneself, cool it*, cool off, cool down, simmer down, keep one's shirt on*; see also RELAX.

calmly *a.* quietly, unexcitedly, tranquilly, unconcernedly, serenely, confidently, sedately, collectedly,

composedly, placidly, smoothly, restfully, motionlessly, peacefully, naturally, comfortably, unhurried, without anxiety, without fuss, dully; see also EASILY, EVENLY.—*Ant.* EXCITEDLY, agitatedly, disturbedly.

calmness *n.* quietness, tranquillity, calm; see COMPOSURE, PATIENCE 1, PEACE 2.

calumny *n.* slander, defamation, detraction; see LIE.

camera *n. Kinds of cameras include the following:* cinecamera, X-ray machine, microcamera, photomicroscope, photostat, spectrograph, motion-picture, television, TV, video, camcorder, press, movie, film, flash, still, electron-diffraction, box, stereo, zoom-lens, Polaroid (trademark), single-lens reflex, double-lens reflex, spectroscopic, telescopic.

camouflage *n.* dissimulation, masquerade, simulation, cloak, shade, shroud, veil, blackout, masking, paint, netting, deceit; see also DISGUISE, SCREEN 1.

camouflage *v.* cover, conceal, veil; see DECEIVE, DISGUISE, HIDE 1.

camp (kamp) *n.* 〖< L *campus*, field〗 **1** *a*) a place where temporary tents, huts, etc. are put up, as for soldiers *b*) a group of such tents, etc. **2** the supporters of a particular cause **3** a recreational place in the country for vacationers, esp. children **4** the people living in a camp **5** [Slang] banality, artifice, etc. so extreme as to amuse or have a perversely sophisticated appeal — *vi.* **1** to set up a camp **2** to live or stay in a camp: often with *out* —**break camp** to dismantle a camp and depart

cam·paign (kam pān′) *n.* 〖Fr < L *campus*, field〗 **1** a series of military operations with a particular objective **2** a series of planned actions, as for electing a candidate — *vi.* to participate in a campaign —**cam·paign′er** *n.*

cam·pa·nile (kam′pə nē′lē) *n., pl.* **-les** or **-li** (-lē) 〖It < LL *campana*, a bell〗 a bell tower

camper (kam′pər) *n.* **1** a vacationer at a camp **2** a motor vehicle or trailer equipped for camping out

camp′fire′ *n.* **1** an outdoor fire at a camp **2** a social gathering around such a fire

cam·phor (kam′fər) *n.* 〖< Sans *karpuraḥ*, camphor tree〗 a crystalline substance with a strong odor, derived from the wood of an Oriental evergreen tree (**camphor tree**): used to repel moths, in medicine as a stimulant, etc. — **cam′phor·at′ed** *adj.*

camp meeting a religious meeting held outdoors or in a tent, etc.

camp′site′ *n.* **1** any site for a camp **2** an area in a park set aside for camping

cam·pus (kam′pəs) *n., pl.* **-puses** 〖L, a field〗 the grounds, and sometimes buildings, of a school or college — *adj.* of a school or college 〖*campus* politics〗

camp′y *adj.* **-i·er, -i·est** [Slang] characterized by CAMP (*n.* 5)

cam′shaft′ *n.* a shaft having a cam, or to which a cam is fastened

can[1] (kan, kən) *v.aux., vi. pt.* **could** 〖< OE *cunnan*, to know〗 **1** know(s) how to **2** am, are, or is able to **3** am, are, or is likely to 〖*can* that be true?〗 **4** have or has the right to **5** [Colloq.] am, are, is permitted to; may —**can but** can only

can[2] (kan) *n.* 〖OE *canne*, a cup〗 **1** a container, usually metal, with a separate cover 〖a garbage *can*〗 **2** a tinned metal container in which foods, etc. are sealed for preservation **3** the amount a can holds — *vt.* **canned, can′ning 1** to put up in cans or jars for preservation **2** [Slang] to dismiss

Ca·naan (kā′nən) *Bible* the Promised Land of the Israelites

Ca·na·dian (kə nā′dē ən) *n.* a native or inhabitant of Canada — *adj.* of Canada

Canadian bacon cured, smoked pork taken from the loin

Canadian English English as spoken and written in Canada

Ca·na′di·an·ism′ *n.* **1** a custom or belief of Canada **2** a word or phrase originating in Canadian English

ca·nal (kə nal′) *n.* 〖< L *canalis*, channel〗 **1** an artificial waterway for transportation or irrigation **2** *Anat.* a tubular passage or duct

ca·na·pé (kan′ə pā′, kan′ə pē) *n.* 〖Fr〗 a small piece of bread or a cracker, spread with spiced meat, cheese, etc., served as an appetizer

ca·nard (kə närd′) *n.* 〖Fr, a duck〗 a false, esp. malicious, report

ca·nary (kə ner′ē) *n., pl.* **-ies** 〖after *Canary* Islands〗 **1** a small, yellow finch **2** a light yellow

ca·nasta (kə nas′tə) *n.* 〖Sp, basket〗 a card game using a double deck

can·can (kan′kan′) *n.* 〖Fr〗 a lively dance with much high kicking

can·cel (kan′səl) *vt.* **-celed** or **-celled, -cel·ing** or **-cel·ling** 〖< L *cancellus*, lattice〗 **1** to mark over with lines, etc., as in deleting written matter or marking a postage stamp, check, etc. as used **2** to make invalid **3** to do away with; abolish **4** to neutralize or balance: often with *out* **5** *Math.* to remove (a common factor, equivalents, etc.) — **can′cel·la′tion** *n.*

can·cer (kan′sər) *n.* 〖< L, a crab〗 [C-] the fourth sign of the zodiac — *n.* **1** a malignant tumor that can spread **2** any spreading evil —**can′cer·ous** *adj.*

can·de·la·brum (kan′də lä′brəm, -lä′-, -la′-) *n., pl.* **-bra** (-brə) or **-brums** 〖L: see CHANDELIER〗 a large branched candlestick Also **can′de·la′bra,** *pl.* **-bras**

can·did (kan′did) *adj.* 〖L *candidus*, white, sincere〗 **1** very honest or frank **2** unposed and informal 〖a *candid* photo〗 —**can′did·ly** *adv.* —**can′did·ness** *n.*

can·di·date (kan′də dāt′, -dət) *n.* 〖L *candidatus*, white-robed, as office seekers〗 one seeking an office, award, etc. —**can′di·dacy** (-də sē), *pl.* **-cies,** *n.*

can·died (kan′dēd) *adj.* **1** cooked in sugar **2** sugary in expression

can·dle (kan′dəl) *n.* 〖< L *candela*〗 a cylinder of tallow or wax with a wick through it, which gives light when burned — *vt.* **-dled, -dling** to examine (eggs) for freshness by placing in front of a light —**can′dler** *n.*

can′dle·stick′ *n.* a cupped or spiked holder for a candle or candles

can′-do′ *adj.* [Colloq.] confident of one's ability

can·dor (kan′dər) *n.* 〖L, openness〗 honesty or frankness in expressing oneself Brit. sp. **can′dour**

candy (kan′dē) *n., pl.* **-dies** 〖< Pers *qand*, cane sugar〗 a solid confection of sugar or syrup with flavoring, fruit, nuts, etc. — *vt.* **-died, -dy·ing 1** to cook in sugar, esp. to preserve **2** to crystallize into sugar

cane (kān) *n.* 〖< Gr *kanna*〗 **1** the slender, jointed stem of certain plants, as bamboo **2** a plant with such a stem, as

---

THESAURUS

camp *n.* **1** [A temporary living place] camping ground, campground, campsite, encampment, tents, tent city, wigwams, tepees, wickiups. **2** [Temporary living quarters] tent, lean-to, cottage, tilt, shack, hut, lodge, cabin, chalet, shed, log house, summer home, cottage. —**break camp** dismantle, depart, pack up; see LEAVE 1.

camp *v.* bivouac, stop over, make camp, encamp, dwell, nest, locate, pitch camp, pitch a tent, tent, quarter, lodge, sleep out, station, put up for the night, camp out, rough it, sleep under the stars.

campaign *n.* operations, crusade, warfare; see ATTACK, FIGHT.

campaign *v.* crusade, electioneer, run, agitate, contend for, contest, canvass for, solicit votes, lobby, barnstorm, mend fences, go to the grass roots*, stump, beat the bushes*, whistle-stop; see also COMPETE.

campus *n.* seat of learning, buildings and grounds, physical plant, alma mater, quad; see also COLLEGE, UNIVERSITY.

can[1,2] *v.* **1** [To preserve] bottle, put up, keep; see PRESERVE 3. **2** [To be able] could, may, be capable of, be equal to, be up to*, lie in one's power, be within one's control, manage, can

do, take care of, make it*, make the grade, make out, cut the mustard*, have it made*.

can[2] *n.* **1** [A container] tin can, tin (British), canister, receptacle, package, jar, bottle, quart can, bucket, gallon can, vessel; see also CONTAINER. **2** [*Jail] prison, penitentiary, stir*; see JAIL. **3** [*A toilet] lavatory, restroom, washroom; see TOILET.

canal *n.* waterway, trench, ditch; see CHANNEL, WATER 2.

cancel *v.* repudiate, nullify, ignore, invalidate, suppress, countermand, call off, set aside, rule out, refute, rescind, remove, repeal, counteract, recall, retract, abrogate, discharge, void, make void, put an end to, abort, offset, revoke, overthrow, scratch, drop; see also ABOLISH.—*Ant.* SUSTAIN, approve, uphold.

cancellation *n.* cancelling, annulment, nullification, abrogation, dissolution, invalidation, revocation, repudiation, repeal, abolition, retraction, reversal, voiding, recall, overruling, withdrawing, abandoning, undoing; see also REMOVAL.

cancer *n.* growth, tumor, malignancy; see GROWTH 3, ILLNESS 2.

cancerous *a.* carcinogenic, virulent,

mortal; see HARMFUL.

candid *a.* straightforward, sincere, open; see FRANK, HONEST 1.

candidate *n.* aspirant, possible choice, nominee, applicant, political contestant, office-seeker, successor, competitor, bidder, solicitor, petitioner; see also CONTESTANT.

candle *n.* taper, rush, torch; see LIGHT 3. —**burn the candle at both ends** dissipate, squander, use up; see WASTE 1, 2. —**not hold a candle to** be unequal to, be subordinate to, be inferior to; see FAIL 1.

candlestick *n.* candelabrum, candelabra, taper holder, flat candlestick, menorah, candleholder.

candy *n.* confection, confectionery, sweetmeat, bonbon. *Varieties of candy include the following:* caramel, taffy, fudge, cream, lemon drop, cotton candy, nougat, peanut brittle, praline, fruit roll, marshmallow, crystallized fruit, coconut bar, Turkish delight, lollipop, halvah, marchpane, gum drop, divinity, toffee, after-dinner mint, Life Saver (trademark), stick, hard, spun-sugar, all-day sucker.

cane *n.* walking stick, staff, pole; see STICK.

sugar cane **3** WALKING STICK **4** split rattan —*vt.* **caned, can'ing 1** to flog with a cane **2** to make (chair seats, etc.) with cane —**can'er** *n.*

cane·brake (kān'brāk') *n.* a dense growth of cane plants

ca·nine (kā'nīn') *adj.* ⟦< L *canis*, dog⟧ **1** of or like a dog **2** of the family of carnivores that includes dogs, wolves, and foxes — *n.* **1** a dog or other canine animal **2** any of the sharp-pointed teeth next to the incisors: in full **canine tooth**

can·is·ter (kan'is tər) *n.* ⟦< Gr *kanastron*, wicker basket⟧ a small box or can for coffee, tea, etc.

can·ker (kaŋ'kər) *n.* ⟦< L *cancer*, a crab⟧ an ulcerlike sore, esp. in the mouth —**can'ker·ous** *adj.*

can·na·bis (kan'ə bis') *n.* ⟦L, hemp⟧ **1** HEMP **2** the female flowering tops of the hemp

canned (kand) *adj.* **1** preserved, as in cans **2** [Slang] recorded for reproduction, as on radio or TV

can·nery (kan'ər ē) *n., pl.* **-ies** a factory where foods are canned

can·ni·bal (kan'ə bəl) *n.* ⟦Sp *canibal*⟧ **1** a person who eats human flesh **2** an animal that eats its own kind — *adj.* of or like cannibals —**can'ni·bal·ism'** *n.* —**can'ni·bal·is'tic** *adj.*

can·ni·bal·ize' (-īz') *vt., vi.* **-ized', -iz'ing** to strip (old or worn equipment) of parts for use in other units

can·non (kan'ən) *n., pl.* **-nons** or **-non** ⟦< L *canna*, cane⟧ **1** a large, mounted piece of artillery **2** an automatic gun on an aircraft

can·non·ade' (-ād') *n.* a continuous firing of artillery — *vt., vi.* **-ad'ed, -ad'ing** to fire artillery at

can·not (kan'nät', kə nät') can not — **cannot but** have no choice but to

canny (kan'ē) *adj.* **-nier, -ni·est** ⟦< CAN¹⟧ cautious and shrewd —**can'ni·ly** *adv.* —**can'ni·ness** *n.*

ca·noe (kə nōo') *n.* ⟦< Sp *canoa* < WInd⟧ a narrow, light boat moved by paddles — *vi.* **-noed', -noe'ing** to paddle, or go in, a canoe —**ca·noe'ist** *n.*

ca·nola oil (kə nō'lə) an oil from the seed of the rape, used in cooking

canon (kan'ən) *n.* ⟦OE, a rule < L⟧ **1** a law or body of laws of a church **2** *a*) a basic rule or principle *b*) a criterion **3** an official list, as of books of the Bible **4** the complete works, as of an author **5** *Music* a round **6** a clergyman serving in a cathedral

ca·ñon (kan'yən) *n. alt. sp. of* CANYON

ca·non·i·cal (kə nän'i kəl) *adj.* **1** of or according to church law **2** of or belonging to a canon

can·on·ize (kan'ən īz') *vt.* **-ized', -iz'ing 1** to declare (a person) a saint **2** to glorify —**can'oni·za'tion** *n.*

can·o·py (kan'ə pē) *n., pl.* **-pies** ⟦< Gr *kōnōpeion*, couch with mosquito nets⟧ **1** a drapery, etc. fastened above a bed, throne, etc., or held over a person **2** a rooflike projection — *vt.* **-pied, -py·ing** to place or form a canopy over; cover

cant¹ (kant) *n.* ⟦< L *cantus*, song⟧ **1** the secret slang of beggars, thieves, etc.; argot **2** the special vocabulary of those in a certain occupation; jargon **3** insincere talk, esp. when pious — *vi.* to use cant

cant² (kant) *n.* ⟦L *cantus*, tire of a wheel⟧ **1** an outside angle **2** a beveled edge **3** a tilt, turn, slant, etc. — *vt., vi.* to slant; tilt

can't (kant, känt) cannot

can·ta·loupe or **can·ta·loup** (kant'ə lōp') *n.* ⟦Fr < It *Cantalupo*, estate near Rome, where first grown in Europe⟧ a muskmelon, esp. one with a rough rind and juicy, orange flesh

can·tan·ker·ous (kan taŋ'kər əs) *adj.* ⟦prob. < ME *contakour*, troublemaker⟧ bad-tempered; quarrelsome —**can·tan'ker·ous·ly** *adv.* —**can·tan'ker·ous·ness** *n.*

can·tata (kän tät'ə, kən-) *n.* ⟦It < *cantare*, to sing⟧ a choral composition for a story to be sung but not acted

can·teen (kan tēn') *n.* ⟦< Fr < It *cantina*, wine cellar⟧ **1** a recreation center for servicemen, teenagers, etc. **2** a place where food is dispensed, as in a disaster area **3** a small flask for carrying water

can·ter (kant'ər) *n.* ⟦< *Canterbury gallop*, a riding pace⟧ a moderate gallop — *vi., vt.* to ride at a canter

can·ti·cle (kan'ti kəl) *n.* ⟦< L *cantus*, song⟧ a song or chant, esp. a hymn with words from the Bible

can·ti·lever (kant''l ē'vər, -ev'ər) *n.* ⟦< ?⟧ a bracket or block projecting as a support; esp., a projecting structure anchored to a pier or wall — *vt.* to support by means of cantilevers —**can'ti·le'vered** *adj.*

canto (kan'tō) *n., pl.* **-tos** ⟦It < L *cantus*, song⟧ any of the main divisions of certain long poems

can·ton (kan'tən, kan tän') *n.* ⟦Fr < LL *cantus*, corner⟧ any of the states in the Swiss Republic

Can·ton·ese (kan'tə nēz') *n.* **1** *pl.* **-ese'** a native or inhabitant of Canton, China **2** their Chinese dialect — *adj.* of Canton

can·ton·ment (kan tän'mənt, -tōn'-) *n.* ⟦Fr: see CANTON⟧ temporary quarters for troops

can·tor (kan'tər) *n.* ⟦L, singer⟧ a singer of liturgical solos in a synagogue

can·vas (kan'vəs) *n.* ⟦< L *cannabis*, hemp⟧ **1** a coarse cloth of hemp, cotton, etc., used for tents, sails, etc. **2** a sail, tent, etc. **3** an oil painting on canvas

can'vas·back' *n.* a North American wild duck with a grayish back

can·vass (kan'vəs) *vt., vi.* ⟦< *canvas* < ?⟧ use of canvas for sifting⟧ to go through (places) or among (people) asking for votes, opinions, orders, etc. — *n.* a canvassing —**can'vasser** *n.*

can·yon (kan'yən) *n.* ⟦Sp *cañón*, tube < L *canna*, a reed⟧ a long, narrow valley between high cliffs

cap (kap) *n.* ⟦< LL *cappa*, hooded cloak⟧ **1** any closefitting head covering, visored or brimless **2** a caplike part or thing; cover or top — *vt.* **capped, cap'ping 1** to put a cap on **2** to cover (the end of) **3** to equal or excel

cap. **1** capacity **2** capital

ca·pable (kā'pə bəl) *adj.* ⟦< L *capere*, to take⟧ having ability; skilled; competent —**capable of 1** having the qualities necessary for **2** able or ready to —**ca'pabil'ity** (-bil'ə tē), *pl.* **-ties,** *n.* —**ca'pably** *adv.*

ca·pa·cious (kə pā'shəs) *adj.* ⟦< L *capere*, to take⟧ roomy; spacious —**ca·pa'ciously** *adv.* —**ca·pa'cious·ness** *n.*

ca·paci·tor (kə pas'ə tər) *n.* a device for storing an electric charge

ca·pac·ity (-tē) *n., pl.* **-ties** ⟦< L *capere*, take⟧ **1** the ability to contain, absorb, or receive **2** all that can be contained; volume **3** ability **4** maximum output **5** position; function

ca·pari·son (kə par'i sən, -zən) *n.* ⟦< LL *cappa*, cloak⟧ trappings for a horse — *vt.* to cover (a horse) with trappings

cape¹ (kāp) *n.* ⟦see prec.⟧ a sleeveless garment fastened at the neck and hanging over the back and shoulders

cape² (kāp) *n.* ⟦< L *caput*, head⟧ a piece of land projecting into water

ca·per¹ (kā'pər) *vi.* ⟦? < Fr *capriole*, a leap⟧ to skip about in a playful manner — *n.* **1** a playful leap **2** a prank —**cut a caper** (or **capers**) **1** to caper **2** to play silly tricks

ca·per² (kā'pər) *n.* ⟦< Gr *kapparis*⟧ the green flower bud of a Mediterranean bush, pickled and used as a seasoning

---

THESAURUS

canned *a.* bottled, conserved, kept; see PRESERVED 2.

cannon *n.* Types of cannon include the following: self-propelled, muzzle-loading, breech-loading, tank destroyer, turret, mountain, siege, coast defense, field, antiaircraft, railway, antitank gun, knee mortar, recoilless rifle, howitzer.

canoe *n.* kayak, dugout, outrigger; see BOAT.

canon *n.* decree, rule, order; see COMMAND, DECLARATION, LAW 3.

canonize *v.* saint, sanctify, beatify; see BLESS, LOVE 1, WORSHIP.

canopy *n.* awning, sunshade, umbrella; see COVER 1.

canteen *n.* jug, flask, water supply; see BOTTLE, CONTAINER.

canvas *n.* **1** [A coarse cloth] tenting, awning cloth, sailcloth, duck, coarse cloth; see also CLOTH. **2** [Anything made of canvas] sail, awning, tarpaulin; see COVER 1, TENT. **3** [A painting on canvas] portrait, still life, oil; see ART, PAINTING 1.

canyon *n.* gulch, gorge, gully; see RAVINE, VALLEY.

cap *n.* beret, mortarboard, bonnet; see HAT.

capability *n.* capacity, skill, aptitude; see ABILITY, INCLINATION 1.

capable *a.* proficient, competent, fitted; see ABLE, INTELLIGENT.

capacity *n.* contents, limit, space, room, size, volume, holding power,

extent, compass, magnitude, spread, expanse, scope, latitude, bulk, dimensions, measure, range, quantity, size, reach, holding ability, sweep, proportions, mass, sufficiency.

cape¹,² *n.* **1** [Land jutting into the water] headland, peninsula, foreland, point, promontory, jetty, head, tongue, neck of land, ness, mole, finger, arm. **2** [An overgarment] cloak, wrapper, mantilla, mantle, shawl, wrap, overdress, poncho; see also COAT 1.

caper¹ *n.* prank, trick, escapade; see JOKE.

caper¹ *v.* frolic, gambol, cavort; see PLAY 1, 2.

cape′skin′ *n.* [orig. made from the skin of goats from the *Cape of Good Hope*] fine leather made from sheepskin

cap·il·lary (kap′ə ler′ē) *adj.* [< L *capillus*, hair] very slender — *n., pl.* **-ies** 1 a tube with a very small bore: also **capillary tube** 2 any of the tiny blood vessels connecting the arteries with veins

capillary attraction the action by which liquids in contact with solids, as in a capillary tube, rise or fall Also **capillary action**

cap·i·tal (kap′ət 'l) *adj.* [< L *caput*, head] 1 punishable by death 2 principal; chief 3 of, or being, the seat of government 4 of capital, or wealth 5 excellent — *n.* 1 CAPITAL LETTER 2 a city that is the seat of government of a state or nation 3 money or property owned or used in business 4 [*often* C-] capitalists collectively 5 the top part of a column

capital gain profit resulting from the sale of capital investments, as stocks

cap·i·tal·ism (kap′ət 'l iz′əm) *n.* the economic system in which the means of production and distribution are privately owned and operated for profit

cap′i·tal·ist (-ist) *n.* 1 an owner of wealth used in business 2 an upholder of capitalism 3 a wealthy person —**cap′i·tal·is′tic** (-is′tik) *adj.*

cap′i·tal·ize′ (-īz′) *vt.* **-ized′, -iz′ing** 1 to use as or convert into capital 2 to use to one's advantage: used with *on* 3 to supply capital to or for 4 to begin (a word) with a capital letter —**cap′i·tali·za′tion** *n.*

capital letter the form of an alphabetical letter used to begin a sentence or proper name, as A, B, C, etc.

cap′i·tally *adv.* very well

capital punishment penalty of death for a crime

Capi·tol (kap′ət 'l) [< L *Capitolium*, temple of Jupiter in Rome] the building in which the U.S. Congress meets in Washington, D.C. — *n.* [*usually* c-] the building in which a State legislature meets

ca·pitu·late (kə pich′yoo lāt′, -pich′ə lāt′) *vi.* **-lat′ed, -lat′ing** [< LL *capitulare*, arrange conditions] 1 to give up (*to* an enemy) on prearranged conditions 2 to stop resisting —**ca·pit′u·la′tion** *n.*

cap′let (kap′lit) *n.* a pharmaceutical tablet with a tamper-resistant, capsulelike coating

ca·pon (kā′pän′, -pən) *n.* [< L *capo*] a castrated rooster fattened for eating

cap·puc·cino (kä′pə chē′nō, kap′ə-) *n.* [It] espresso coffee mixed with steamed milk and topped with cinnamon, etc.

ca·price (kə prēs′) *n.* [Fr < It] 1 a sudden, impulsive change in thinking or acting 2 a capricious quality

ca·pri·cious (kə prish′əs) *adj.* subject to caprices; erratic —**ca·pri′ciously** *adv.* —**ca·pri′cious·ness** *n.*

Cap·ri·corn (kap′ri kôrn′) [< L *caper*, goat + *cornu*, horn] the tenth sign of the zodiac

cap·size (kap′sīz′, kap sīz′) *vt., vi.* **-sized′, -siz′ing** [< ?] to overturn or upset: said esp. of a boat

cap·stan (kap′stən) *n.* [< L *capere*, to take] an upright drum, as on ships, around which cables are wound so as to haul them in

cap·stone (kap′stōn′) *n.* 1 the top stone of a structure 2 the pinnacle, as of achievement

cap·sule (kap′səl, -syōōl′) *n.* [Fr < L *capsa*, box] 1 a soluble gelatin container enclosing a dose of medicine 2 a detachable compartment to hold men, instruments, etc. in a rocket: in full **space capsule** 3 *Bot.* a seedcase — *adj.* in a concise form —**cap′su·lar** *adj.*

cap′sul·ize′ (-īz′) *vt.* **-ized′, -iz′ing** 1 to enclose in a capsule 2 to condense

Capt. Captain

cap·tain (kap′tən) *n.* [< L *caput*, head] 1 a chief; leader 2 *U.S. Mil.* an officer ranking just above first lieutenant 3 *U.S. Navy* an officer ranking just above commander 4 *a*) the master of a ship *b*) the pilot of an airplane 5 the leader of a team, as in sports — *vt.* to be captain of —**cap′taincy**, *pl.* **-cies,** *n.*

cap·tion (kap′shən) *n.* [< L *capere*, take] 1 a heading or title, as of a newspaper article or illustration 2 *Film, TV* a subtitle — *vt.* to supply a caption for

cap′tious (-shəs) *adj.* [see prec.] 1 made for the sake of argument, as a remark 2 quick to find fault —**cap′tiously** *adv.* —**cap′tious·ness** *n.*

cap·ti·vate (kap′tə vāt′) *vt.* **-vat′ed, -vat′ing** to capture the attention or affection of —**cap′ti·va′tion** *n.* —**cap′ti·va′tor** *n.*

cap·tive (kap′tiv) *n.* [< L *capere*, to take] a prisoner — *adj.* 1 taken or held prisoner 2 obliged to listen —**cap·tiv′ity**, *pl.* **-ties,** *n.*

cap′tor (-tər) *n.* one who captures

cap′ture (-chər) *vt.* **-tured, -tur·ing** [< L *capere*, to take] 1 to take or seize by force, surprise, etc. 2 to represent in a more permanent form [to *capture* her charm on canvas] — *n.* a capturing or being captured

car (kär) *n.* [< L *carrus*, chariot] 1 any vehicle on wheels 2 a vehicle that moves on rails, as a streetcar 3 an automobile 4 an elevator cage

cara·cul (kar′ə kul′, -kəl) *n.* KARAKUL (esp. sense 2)

ca·rafe (kə raf′, -räf′) *n.* [Fr] a glass bottle for wine, water, or coffee

cara·mel (kär′məl, kar′ə məl) *n.* [Fr] 1 burnt sugar used to color or flavor food 2 a chewy candy made from sugar, milk, etc.

car′a·mel·ize′ (-mə līz′) *vt., vi.* **-ized′, -iz′ing** to turn into caramel

cara·pace (kar′ə pās′) *n.* [Fr < Sp] an upper shell, as of the turtle

carat (kar′ət) *n.* [Fr < Gr *keration*, little horn] 1 a unit of weight for precious stones, equal to 200 milligrams 2 KARAT

cara·van (kar′ə van′) *n.* [< Pers *kārwān*] 1 a company of people traveling together for safety, as through a desert 2 VAN[2]

cara·van·sary (kar′ə van′sə rē) *n., pl.* **-ries** [< Pers *kārwān*, caravan + *sarāī*, palace] in the Orient, an inn for caravans

cara·way (kar′ə wā′) *n.* [< Ar *al-karawiyā′*] the spicy seeds of a plant, used to flavor bread, etc.

car·bide (kär′bīd′) *n.* a solid compound of carbon with a metal; esp., calcium carbide

car·bine (kär′bīn′, -bēn′) *n.* [< Fr *scarabée*, beetle] 1 a short-barreled rifle 2 a light, semiautomatic or automatic rifle of relatively limited range

carbo- *combining form* carbon Also **carb-**

carbo·hy′drate (kär′bō hi′drāt, -bə-) *n.* [prec. + HYDRATE] an organic compound composed of carbon, hydrogen, and oxygen, as a sugar or starch

car·bolic acid (kär bäl′ik) PHENOL

car·bon (kär′bən) *n.* [< L *carbo*, coal] 1 a nonmetallic chemical element found esp. in all organic compounds: diamond and graphite are pure carbon: a radioactive isotope of carbon (**carbon-14**) is used in dating fossils, etc.

THESAURUS

capital *n.* 1 [A seat of government] metropolis, principal city, capitol; see CENTER 2, CITY. 2 [Money and property] cash, assets, interests; see ESTATE, PROPERTY 1, WEALTH. 3 [A letter usually used initially] initial, upper case, majuscule; see LETTER 1.

capitalism *n.* capitalistic system, free enterprise, private ownership; see DEMOCRACY, ECONOMICS, GOVERNMENT 2.

capitalist *n.* entrepreneur, investor, landowner; see BANKER, BUSINESSMAN, FINANCIER.

capitol *n.* statehouse, state capitol, seat of government; see CENTER 2.

capitulate *v.* surrender, submit, give up; see YIELD 1.

capsize *v.* overturn, invert, tip over; see UPSET 1.

caption *n.* inscription, title, subtitle; see HEADING.

captive *a.* restrained, incarcerated, jailed; see BOUND 1, 2, RESTRICTED.

captive *n.* hostage, convict, con*; see PRISONER.

captivity *n.* imprisonment, jail, restraint, slavery, bondage, subjection, servitude, duress, detention, incarceration, enslavement, constraint, the guardhouse, custody; see also CONFINEMENT.—*Ant.* FREEDOM, liberty, independence.

capture *n.* capturing, arrest, recovery, seizing, taking, seizure, acquisition, obtaining, securing, gaining, winning, occupation, appropriation, ensnaring, abduction, laying hold of, grasping, catching, trapping, commandeering, apprehending, confiscation, apprehension, taking into custody, fall.—*Ant.* RESCUE, liberation, setting free.

capture *v.* seize, take, apprehend; see ARREST, SEIZE 2.

captured *a.* taken, seized, arrested, apprehended, detained, grasped, overtaken, grabbed, snatched, kidnapped, abducted, netted, hooked, secured, collared*, nabbed*, bagged; see also UNDER ARREST.—*Ant.* RELEASED, unbound, loosed.

car *n.* auto, motorcar, automotive vehicle; see AUTOMOBILE, VEHICLE. *Types of cars include the following:* passenger car, limousine, sedan, hardtop, compact, subcompact, sports car, convertible, town car, ranch wagon, station wagon, taxicab, squad car, prowl car, staff car, bus, truck, jeep, dune buggy.

2 CARBON PAPER **3** a copy made with carbon paper: in full **carbon copy** —*adj.* of or like carbon

car·bo·na·ceous (kär′bə nā′shəs) *adj.* of or containing carbon

car′bon·ate (-bə nit; *also, and for v. always,* -nāt′) *n.* a salt or ester of carbonic acid —*vt.* **-at′ed, -at′ing** to charge with carbon dioxide —**car′bona′tion** *n.*

carbon black finely divided carbon produced by the incomplete burning of oil or gas

car′bon-date′ *vt.* **-dat′ed, -dat′ing** to establish the approximate age of (fossils, etc.) by measuring the amount of carbon-14 in them

carbon di·ox·ide (dī äks′īd) a heavy, colorless, odorless gas: it passes out of the lungs in respiration

car′bonic acid (kär bän′ik) a weak acid formed by carbon dioxide in water

car·bon·if·er·ous (kär′bə nif′ər əs) *adj.* containing carbon or coal

car′bon·ize′ (-nīz′) *vt., vi.* **-ized′, -iz′ing** to change into carbon, as by partial burning —**car′boni·za′tion** *n.*

carbon mon·ox·ide (mə näks′īd) a colorless, odorless, highly poisonous gas

carbon paper thin paper coated on one side, as with a carbon preparation, used to make copies of letters, etc.

carbon tetra·chlo·ride (te′trə klôr′īd) a nonflammable liquid, used as a solvent for fats and oils, etc.

Car·bo·run·dum (kär′bə run′dəm) [CARB(ON) + (c)*orundum*] *trademark* for a hard abrasive, esp. of carbon and silicon — *n.* [c-] such a substance

car′boy (kär′boi′) *n.* [< Pers *qarābah*] a large bottle to hold corrosive liquids, enclosed in a protective container

car·bun·cle (kär′buŋ′kəl) *n.* [< L dim. of *carbo*, coal] a painful, pus-bearing inflammation of the tissue beneath the skin —**car·bun′cu·lar** (-kyōō lər) *adj.*

car·bu·retor (kär′bə rāt′ər) *n.* a device for mixing air with gasoline spray to make an explosive mixture in an internal-combustion engine

car·cass (kär′kəs) *n.* [< Fr *carcasse*] **1** the dead body of an animal **2** a framework or shell

car·cino·gen (kär sin′ə jən) *n.* [< fol. + -GEN] any substance that produces cancer —**car·ci·no·genic** (kär′sə nō jen′ik) *adj.*

car·ci·noma (kär′sə nō′mə) *n., pl.* **-mas** or **-mata** (-mə tə) [L < Gr *karkinos*, crab] any of several kinds of epithelial cancer

car coat a short overcoat

card¹ (kärd) *n.* [< Gr *chartēs*, layer of papyrus] **1** a flat, stiff piece of paper or pasteboard; specif., *a)* any of a pack of playing cards *b)* a card identifying a person, esp. as a member, agent, etc. *c)* a post card *d)* a card bearing a greeting *e)* any of a series of cards on which information

is recorded **2** an attraction *[drawing card]* **3** [Colloq.] a witty or clowning person —**put (or lay) one′s cards on the table** to reveal something frankly

card² (kärd) *n.* [< L *carrere*, to card] a metal comb or a machine with wire teeth for combing fibers of wool, cotton, etc. — *vt.* to use a card on

card′board′ *n.* stiff, thick paper or pasteboard, for cards, boxes, etc.

car·diac (kär′dē ak′) *adj.* [< Gr *kardia*, heart] of or near the heart

cardiac arrest the complete failure of the heart to pump blood

car·di·gan (kär′di gən) *n.* [after 7th Earl of *Cardigan*] a sweater or jacket that opens down the front

car·di·nal (kärd′n əl) *adj.* [< L *cardo*, pivot] **1** principal; chief **2** bright-red — *n.* **1** an official appointed by the pope to his council **2** bright red **3** a bright-red American songbird **4** CARDINAL NUMBER

cardinal number any number used in counting or in showing how many (e.g., two, forty, 627, etc.)

cardio- [< Gr *kardia*, heart] *combining form* of the heart

cardio·gram (kär′dē ō gram′, -dē ə-) *n.* ELECTROCARDIOGRAM —**car′dio·graph′** (-graf′) *n.*

car′di·ol′o·gy (-äl′ə jē) *n.* the branch of medicine dealing with the heart —**car′di·ol′o·gist** *n.*

cardio·pul·mo·nary (kär′dē ō pool′ mə ner′ē) *adj.* of or involving the heart and lungs

car′dio·vas′cu·lar (-vas′kyōō lər) *adj.* of the heart and the blood vessels as a unified body system

cards (kärds) *n.pl.* any game played with a deck of playing cards, as poker

card′sharp′ *n.* [Colloq.] a professional cheater at cards Also **card shark**

care (ker) *n.* [< OE *caru*, sorrow] **1** *a)* a troubled state of mind; worry *b)* a cause of such a mental state **2** close attention; heed **3** a liking or regard (*for*) **4** charge; protection **5** a responsibility — *vi.* **cared, car′ing 1** to feel concern **2** to feel love or a liking (*for*) **3** to look after; provide (*for*) **4** to wish (*for*); want — *vt.* **1** to feel concern about or interest in **2** to wish —**care of** at the address of —**take care of 1** to attend to **2** to provide for

ca·reen (kə rēn′) *vt., vi.* [< L *carina*, keel] to lean or cause to lean sideways; tip; tilt; lurch

ca·reer (kə rir′) *n.* [< L *carrus*, car] **1** a swift course **2** one′s progress through life **3** a profession or occupation — *vi.* to rush wildly

ca·reer′ist *n.* one interested exclusively or excessively in one′s professional ambitions

care′free′ *adj.* without care

care′ful *adj.* **1** cautious; wary **2** accurate; thorough; painstaking —**care′fully** *adv.* —**care′ful·ness** *n.*

care′less *adj.* **1** carefree; untroubled **2** not paying enough heed; neglectful **3** done or made without enough atten-

---

▌ THESAURUS ▐

carcass *n.* corpse, cadaver, remains; see BODY 2.

card¹ *n.* cardboard, ticket, sheet, square, Bristol board, fiberboard. *Varieties of cards include the following:* poster, window card, show card, ticket, fortunetelling cards, tarot cards, label, badge, tally, check, billet, voucher, pass; calling card, playing card, address card, visiting card, credit card, bank card, greeting card, registration card, filing card, index card, check-cashing card, police card, social security card, identification card, I.D. card; see also PAPER 1. —**in the cards** probable, predicted, possible; see LIKELY 1. —**put one′s cards on the table** reveal, tell the truth, expose; see ADMIT 2.

care *n.* **1** [Careful conduct] heed, concern, caution, consideration, regard, thoughtfulness, forethought, attention, precaution, wariness, vigilance, watchfulness, watching, diligence, nicety, pains, application, conscientiousness, thought, discrimination, exactness, exactitude, watch, concentration; see also ATTENTION, PRUDENCE.—*Ant.* CARELESSNESS, neglect, negligence. **2** [Worry] concern, anxiety, distress; see WORRY 2. **3** [Custody] supervision, administration, keeping; see CUSTODY. **4** [A cause of worry] problem, care, con-

cern; see DISASTER, MISFORTUNE. —**take care** be careful, be cautious, beware, heed; see also MIND 3, WATCH OUT. —**take care of** protect, attend to, be responsible for; see GUARD.

care *v.* **1** [To be concerned] attend, take pains, regard; see CONSIDER. **2** [To be careful] look out for, be on guard, watch out; see MIND 3. —**care about** cherish, be fond of, hold dear; see LIKE 2, LOVE 1. —**care for 1** [To look after] provide for, attend to, nurse; see RAISE 2, SUPPORT 3. **2** [To like] be fond of, hold dear, prize; see LIKE 2, LOVE 1. —**care to** prefer, desire, wish; see LIKE 1, WANT 1.

career *n.* occupation, vocation, work; see JOB 1, PROFESSION 1.

carefree *a.* lighthearted, cheerful, jovial; see HAPPY, CALM 1.

careful *a.* thorough, concerned, deliberate, conservative, prudent, meticulous, particular, rigorous, fussy, finicky, prim, exacting, wary, sober, vigilant, watchful, suspicious, alert, wide-awake, scrupulous, religious, hard to please, discriminating, sure-footed, precise, painstaking, exact, on one′s guard, on the alert, conscientious, attentive, calculating, mindful, cautious, guarded, considerate, shy, circumspect, discreet, noncommittal, self-possessed, cool, calm,

self-disciplined, solid, farsighted, frugal, thrifty, stealthy, observant, on guard, apprehensive, leery, choosy, picky*, feeling one′s way, seeing how the land lies, going to great lengths.—*Ant.* CARELESS, heedless, haphazard.

carefully *a.* **1** [Scrupulously] conscientiously, exactly, rigidly, correctly, strictly, precisely, minutely, painstakingly, faithfully, honorably, attentively, rigorously, providently, deliberately, reliable, particularly, solicitously, concernedly, meticulously, laboriously, thoroughly, dependably, in detail.—*Ant.* haphazardly, neglectfully, indifferently. **2** [Cautiously] prudently, discreetly, watchfully; see CAUTIOUSLY.

careless *a.* loose, lax, remiss, unguarded, incautious, forgetful, unthinking, unobservant, reckless, unheeding, indiscreet, inadvertent, unconcerned, wasteful, regardless, imprudent, unconsidered, hasty, inconsiderate, heedless, mindless, untroubled, negligent, neglectful, thoughtless, indifferent, casual, oblivious, absent-minded, listless, abstracted, nonchalant, undiscerning, offhand, slack, blundering; see also RASH.—*Ant.* THOUGHTFUL, attentive, careful.

ca·ress (kə res′) *vt.* ⟦ult. < L *carus,* dear⟧ to touch lovingly or gently — *n.* an affectionate touch, kiss, etc.

caret (kar′it, ker′-) *n.* ⟦L, there is lacking⟧ a mark (∧) used to show where something is to be inserted in a written or printed line

care′tak′er *n.* **1** a person hired to take care of something or someone **2** one acting as temporary replacement

care′worn′ *adj.* worn out by troubles and worry; haggard

car′fare (kär′fer′) *n.* the price of a ride on a subway, bus, etc.

cargo (kär′gō) *n., pl.* **-goes** or **-gos** ⟦< Sp *cargar,* to load⟧ the load carried by a ship, truck, etc.; freight

car′hop′ *n.* ⟦CAR + (BELL)HOP⟧ one who serves food at a drive-in restaurant

cari·bou (kar′ə bōō′) *n.* ⟦CdnFr⟧ a large North American reindeer

cari·ca·ture (kar′i kə chər) *n.* ⟦Fr < It *caricare,* exaggerate⟧ **1** the exaggerated imitation of a person, literary style, etc. for satirical effect **2** a picture, etc. in which this is done — *vt.* **-tured, -tur·ing** to depict as in a caricature —**car′i·ca·tur·ist** *n.*

car·ies (ker′ēz′) *n.* ⟦L, decay⟧ decay of bones or, esp., of teeth

car·il·lon (kar′ə län′) *n.* ⟦Fr, chime of four bells < L *quattuor,* four⟧ a set of bells tuned to the chromatic scale

ca·ri·tas (kär′ē täs′) *n.* love for all people

car′load′ *n.* a load that fills a car, esp. a car of a freight train

car·mine (kär′min, -mīn′) *n.* ⟦ult. < Ar *qirmiz,* crimson⟧ a red or purplish-red color — *adj.* red or purplish-red

car·nage (kär′nij) *n.* ⟦Fr < L *caro,* flesh⟧ extensive slaughter; massacre

car′nal (-nəl) *adj.* ⟦< L *caro,* flesh⟧ **1** of the flesh; material; worldly **2** sensual or sexual —**car·nal′i·ty** (-nal′i tē)*, pl.* **-ties,** *n.* —**car′nal·ly** *adv.*

car·na·tion (kär nä′shən) *n.* ⟦< L *caro,* flesh⟧ **1** a plant of the pink family, widely cultivated for its white, pink, or red flowers **2** its flower

car·nel·ian (kär nēl′yən) *n.* ⟦< L *carnis,* of flesh (color)⟧ a red variety of chalcedony, used in jewelry

car·ni·val (kär′nə vəl) *n.* ⟦< Fr *carnaval* (or It *carnevale*)⟧ **1** the period of feasting and revelry just before Lent **2** a reveling; festivity **3** an entertainment with sideshows, rides, etc.

car·ni·vore (kär′nə vôr′) *n.* a carnivorous animal or plant

car·niv·o·rous (kär niv′ə rəs) *adj.* ⟦< L *caro,* flesh + *vorare,* to devour⟧ **1** flesh-eating **2** of the carnivores — **car·niv′o·rous·ness** *n.*

carol (kar′əl) *n.* ⟦< OFr *carole,* kind of dance⟧ a song of joy or praise; esp., a Christmas song — *vi., vt.* **-oled** or **-olled, -ol·ing** or **-ol·ling** to sing; warble —**car′ol·er** or **car′ol·ler** *n.*

carom (kar′əm) *n.* ⟦< Sp *carambola*⟧ **1** Billiards a shot in which the cue ball successively hits two balls **2** a hitting and rebounding — *vi.* **1** to make a carom **2** to hit and rebound

ca·rotid (kə rät′id) *adj.* ⟦Gr *karōtis*⟧ designating or of either of the two main arteries, one on each side of the neck, which convey blood to the head — *n.* a carotid artery

ca·rousal (kə rou′zəl) *n.* a carouse

ca·rouse (kə rouz′) *vi.* **-roused′, -rous′ing** ⟦< Ger *gar austrinken,* to drink⟧ to engage in a noisy drinking party — *n.* a noisy drinking party

carou·sel (kar′ə sel′, -zel′) *n.* ⟦Fr < It dial. (Naples) *carusiello,* kind of tournament⟧ a merry-go-round

carp[1] (kärp) *n., pl.* **carp** or **carps** ⟦< VL *carpa*⟧ an edible freshwater fish widely cultivated for food

carp[2] (kärp) *vi.* ⟦ON *karpa,* to brag⟧ to find fault in a petty or nagging way —**carp′er** *n.*

car·pal (kär′pəl) *adj.* of the carpus — *n.* a bone of the carpus

carpal tunnel syndrome a condition of pinched nerves in the wrist, often caused by repetitive movement

car·pel (kär′pəl) *n.* ⟦< Gr *karpos,* fruit⟧ a simple pistil, regarded as a modified leaflike structure

car·pen·ter (kär′pən tər) *n.* ⟦< L *carpentum,* a cart⟧ one who builds and repairs wooden things — *vi.* to do a carpenter's work —**car′pen·try** (-trē) *n.*

carpenter ant a large ant that gnaws holes in trees, wood buildings, etc. for its nest

car·pet (kär′pət) *n.* ⟦< L *carpere,* to card⟧ **1** a heavy fabric for covering a floor **2** anything that covers like a carpet — *vt.* to cover as with a carpet —**on the carpet** being reprimanded

car′pet·bag′ *n.* an old-fashioned traveling bag, made of carpeting

car′pet·bag′ger *n.* a Northerner who went South to profit from unsettled conditions after the Civil War

car′pet-bomb′ *vt.* to drop many bombs on in advance of ground forces —**car′pet-bomb′ing** *n.*

car′pet·ing *n.* carpets or carpet fabric

car pool a plan by a group to rotate the use of their cars, as for going to work

car·port (kär′pôrt′) *n.* an automobile shelter built as a roof at the side of a building

car·pus (kär′pəs) *n., pl.* **-pi′** (-pī′) ⟦< Gr *karpos,* wrist⟧ *Anat.* the wrist, or the wrist bones

car·rel or **car′rell** (kar′əl) *n.* ⟦< ML *carula*⟧ a small enclosure in a library, for privacy in studying or reading

car·riage (kar′ij; *for 2, usually* kar′ē ij′) *n.* ⟦ult. < L *carrus,* chariot⟧ **1** a carrying; transportation **2** the manner of carrying oneself; bearing **3** *a)* a four-wheeled, horse-drawn passenger vehicle *b)* a baby carriage **4** a moving part, as on a typewriter, that supports and shifts something

car·rier (kar′ē ər) *n.* **1** one that carries **2** one in the business of transporting **3** one that transmits disease germs **4** AIRCRAFT CARRIER

carrier pigeon *old name of* HOMING PIGEON

car·rion (kar′ē ən) *n.* ⟦< L *caro,* flesh⟧ the decaying flesh of a dead body

car·rot (kar′ət) *n.* ⟦< Gr *karōton*⟧ **1** a plant with an edible, fleshy, orange-red root **2** the root

car·rou·sel (kar′ə sel′, -zel′) *n. alt. sp. of* CAROUSEL

carry (kar′ē) *vt.* **-ried, -ry·ing** ⟦< L *carrus,* chariot⟧ **1** to hold or support **2** to take from one place to another **3** to lead or impel **4** to transmit [air *carries* sounds] **5** to

---

THESAURUS

carelessly *a.* heedlessly, negligently, neglectfully, thoughtlessly, nonchalantly, offhandedly, rashly, unconcernedly, at random, happen what may, incautiously, improvidently, wastefully, without caution, without care, without concern, with no attention, like crazy*.

carelessness *n.* unconcern, nonchalance, heedlessness, rashness, omission, slackness, delinquency, indolence, procrastination, dereliction, neglect, negligence, disregard, imprudence, haphazardness; see also INDIFFERENCE.—*Ant.* CARE, consideration, caution.

caress *n.* embrace, stroke, feel*; see HUG, KISS, TOUCH 2.

caress *v.* embrace, cuddle, pat; see LOVE 2, TOUCH 1.

caretaker *n.* porter, keeper, janitor; see CUSTODIAN, WATCHMAN.

cargo *n.* shipload, baggage, lading; see FREIGHT, LOAD 1.

carnal *a.* fleshly, bodily, sensuous; see LEWD 2, SENSUAL 2.

carnival *n.* side show, circus, fair; see ENTERTAINMENT, SHOW 1.

carol *n.* hymn, Christmas song, ballad; see SONG.

carpenter *n.* mason, craftsman, builder; see LABORER, WORKMAN.

carpet *n.* wall-to-wall carpet, carpeting, linoleum, floor covering, matting; see also RUG. —**(called) on the carpet** reprimanded, censured, interrogated; see IN TROUBLE.

carriage *n.* **1** [The manner of carrying the body] walk, pace, step, attitude, aspect, presence, look, cast, gait, bearing, posture, pose, demeanor, poise, air; see also BEHAVIOR. **2** [A horse-drawn passenger vehicle] buggy, surrey, coach, coach-and-four, buckboard, cart, dogcart, two-wheeler, trap, gig, sulky, hansom, coupe, four-wheeler, stagecoach, chariot, hack, hackney coach; see also WAGON.

carrier *n.* aircraft carrier, escort carrier, flattop*; see SHIP.

carry *v.* **1** [To transport] convey, move, transplant, transfer, cart, import, transmit, freight, remove, conduct, bear, take, bring, shift, haul, change, convoy, relocate, relay, lug, tote, fetch; see also SEND 1. **2** [To transmit] pass on, transfer, relay; see SEND 1. **3** [To support weight] bear, sustain, shoulder; see SUPPORT 1. **4** [To give support] corroborate, back up, confirm; see APPROVE, SUPPORT 2, STRENGTHEN. —**be (or get) carried away** zealous, aroused, exuberant; see EXCITED. —**carry on** **1** [To continue] keep going, proceed, persist; see ACHIEVE, CONTINUE 1, 2, ENDURE 1. **2** [To manage] conduct, engage in, administer; see MANAGE 1. **3** [To behave badly] blunder, be indecorous, raise Cain*; see MISBEHAVE. —**carry out** complete, accomplish, fulfill; see ACHIEVE, COMPLETE, SUCCEED 1. —**carry over** continue, persist, survive; see ENDURE 1.

carry (oneself) *v.* appear, seem, behave; see ACT 2, WALK 1.

transfer or extend **6** to involve; imply /to carry a guarantee/ **7** to bear (oneself) in a specified way **8** a) to gain support for b) to win (an election, argument, etc.) **9** a) to keep in stock b) to keep on one's account books, etc. — *vi.* **1** to act as a bearer, conductor, etc. **2** to cover a range, as a voice — *n., pl.* **car'ries 1** the distance covered by a gun, ball, etc. **2** a portage —**be** (**or get**) **carried away** to become very emotional or enthusiastic —**carry on 1** to engage in **2** to go on (*with*) **3** [Colloq.] to behave wildly or childishly —**carry out** (**or through**) **1** to put (plans, etc.) into practice **2** to accomplish —**carry over** to postpone; continue

carrying charge interest paid on the balance owed in installment buying

car'ry-on' *adj.* small enough to fit under an airplane seat or in an overhead compartment — *n.* a piece of carry-on luggage

car'ry-out' *adj.* designating or of prepared food sold as by a restaurant to be consumed elsewhere

car'ry-o'ver *n.* something carried over, as a remainder of crops or goods

car seat a seat in an automobile; specif., a portable automobile seat used for securing a small child

car'sick' *adj.* nauseated from riding in an automobile, bus, etc.

cart (kärt) *n.* ⟦< ON *kartr*⟧ a small wagon — *vt., vi.* to carry in a cart, truck, etc.; transport

cart·age (kärt'ij) *n.* **1** the work of carting **2** the charge for this

carte blanche (kärt' blänsh') ⟦Fr, lit., white card⟧ full authority

car·tel (kär tel') *n.* ⟦< Ger < Fr⟧ an association of businesses in an international monopoly; trust

car·ti·lage (kärt'l ij) *n.* ⟦< L *cartilago*⟧ a tough, elastic tissue forming parts of the skeleton; gristle —**car'ti·lag'i·nous** (-aj'ə nəs) *adj.*

car·tog·ra·phy (kär täg'rə fē') *n.* ⟦see CARD[1] & -GRAPHY⟧ the art of making maps or charts —**car·tog'ra·pher** *n.*

car·ton (kärt'n) *n.* ⟦Fr < It *carta*, card⟧ a cardboard box or container

car·toon (kär tōōn') *n.* ⟦< Fr: see prec.⟧ **1** a drawing caricaturing a person or event **2** a) COMIC STRIP b) ANIMATED CARTOON — *vt., vi.* to draw a cartoon (of) —**car·toon'ist** *n.*

car·tridge (kär'trij) *n.* ⟦< Fr < It *carta*, card⟧ **1** a cylindrical case of cardboard, metal, etc. containing the charge and primer, and usually the projectile, for a firearm **2** a small container, as for camera film, a phonograph needle, etc.

cart'wheel' *n.* **1** a handspring performed sideways **2** [Slang] a large coin

carve (kärv) *vt.* **carved, carv'ing** ⟦OE *ceorfan*⟧ **1** to make or shape by or as by cutting **2** to decorate the surface of with cut designs **3** to divide by cutting; slice — *vi.* **1** to carve statues or designs **2** to carve meat —**carv'er** *n.* —**carv'ing** *n.*

car'wash' *n.* an establishment at which automobiles are washed

car·y·at·id (kar·ē at'id) *n., pl.* **-ids** (-idz) **or -i·des'** (-ə dəz') ⟦< Gr *karyatides*, priestesses at Karyai, in ancient Greece⟧ a supporting column having the form of a draped female figure

ca·saba (kə sä'bə) *n.* ⟦after *Kasaba*, town in Asia Minor⟧ a kind of cultivated melon with a hard, yellow rind

Casa·nova (kaz'ə nō'və, kas'ə-) *n.* ⟦after G. *Casanova* (1725-98), It adventurer⟧ a man who has many love affairs

cas·cade (kas kād') *n.* ⟦Fr < L *cadere*, to fall⟧ **1** a small, steep waterfall **2** a shower, as of sparks, etc. — *vt., vi.* **-cad'ed, -cad'ing** to fall or drop in a cascade

cas·cara (kas ker'ə) *n.* ⟦Sp *cáscara*, bark⟧ a thorny tree growing on the Pacific coast of the U.S.

case[1] (kās) *n.* ⟦< L *casus*, a chance < *cadere*, to fall⟧ **1** an example or instance /a *case* of flu/ **2** a person being helped, as by a doctor **3** any matter requiring study **4** a statement of the facts, as in a law court **5** convincing arguments /he has no *case*/ **6** a lawsuit **7** a) a relation shown, as in Latin, by inflection of nouns, etc. b) the form a word takes to show this c) loosely, as in English, such a relation, with or without inflection — *vt.* **cased, cas'ing** [Slang] to look over carefully —**in any case** anyhow —**in case** in the event that; if —**in case of** in the event of —**in no case** by no means

case[2] (kās) *n.* ⟦< L *capsa*, box⟧ **1** a container, as a box **2** a protective cover /a watch *case*/ **3** a full box or its contents /a *case* of beer/ **4** a frame, as for a window — *vt.* **cased, cas'ing 1** to put in a container **2** to enclose

case'hard'en (-härd'n) *vt. Metallurgy* to form a hard surface on (an iron alloy)

ca·sein (kā'sē in, -sēn') *n.* ⟦< L *caseus*, cheese⟧ a protein that is one of the chief constituents of milk

case'load' *n.* the number of cases handled by a court, social agency, etc.

case·ment (kās'mənt) *n.* ⟦ult. < OFr *enchassement*⟧ a window frame that opens on hinges along the side

case'work' *n.* social work in which guidance is given in cases of personal or family maladjustment —**case'work·er** *n.*

cash (kash) *n.* ⟦< L *capsa*, box⟧ **1** money that a person actually has; esp., ready money **2** money, a check, etc. paid at the time of purchase — *vt.* to give or get cash for — *adj.* of or for cash —**cash in** to exchange for cash

cashew (kash'ōō; *also*, kə shōō') *n.* ⟦< AmInd (Brazil) *acajú*⟧ **1** a tropical tree bearing kidney-shaped nuts **2** the nut

cash·ier[1] (ka shir') *n.* ⟦Fr⟧ a person in charge of the cash transactions of a bank or store

cash·ier[2] (ka shir') *vt.* ⟦< LL *cassare*, destroy⟧ to dismiss in dishonor

cash·mere (kash'mir', kazh'-) *n.* ⟦after *Kashmir*, region in India⟧ **1** a fine carded wool from goats of N India and Tibet **2** a soft, twilled cloth as of this wool

cash register a device, usually with a money drawer, used for registering visibly the amount of a sale

cas·ing (kās'iŋ) *n.* **1** skin of a sausage **2** the outer covering of a pneumatic tire **3** a frame, as for a door

ca·sino (kə sē'nō) *n., pl.* **-nos** ⟦It < *casa*, house⟧ **1** a room or building for dancing, gambling, etc. **2** a card game for two to four players

cask (kask) *n.* ⟦ult. < L *quassare*, shatter⟧ **1** a barrel of any size, esp. one for liquids **2** its contents

cas·ket (kas'kit) *n.* ⟦< NormFr *casse*, box⟧ **1** a small box or chest, as for valuables **2** a coffin

Cas·san·dra (kə san'drə) *Gr. Myth.* a Trojan prophetess of doom whose prophecies are not heeded

cas·sava (kə sä'və) *n.* ⟦< Fr < WInd *casávi*⟧ **1** a tropical American plant with starchy roots **2** a starch made from these roots, used in tapioca

cas·se·role (kas'ə rōl') *n.* ⟦Fr < Gr *kyathos*, a bowl⟧ **1** a baking dish in which food can be cooked and served **2** food baked in such a dish

cas·sette (kə set'; *also*, ka-) *n.* ⟦< NormFr *casse*, box⟧ a

---

◼◼◼ THESAURUS ◼◼◼

carry-over *n.* holdover, vestige, remains; see REMAINDER.

cart *n.* truck, wheelbarrow, little wagon, tip cart, handcart, gig, dray, two-wheeler, pushcart, gocart, two-wheeled cart; see also CARRIAGE 2, WAGON. —**put the cart before the horse** reverse, be illogical, err; see MISTAKE.

cartoon *n.* caricature, parody, joke; see RIDICULE.

carve *v.* create, form, hew, chisel, engrave, etch, sculpture, incise, mold, fashion, cut, shape, model, tool, block out, scrape, pattern, trim; see also CUT 1, ENGRAVE.

carved *a.* incised, graven, cut, chiseled, chased, furrowed, formed, hewn, hewed, etched, sculptured, scratched, slashed, done in relief,

scrolled, grooved, sliced, scissored; see also ENGRAVED.—*Ant.* PLAIN, cast, molded.

case[1,2] *n.* **1** [An example] instance, illustration, sample; see EXAMPLE 1. **2** [Actual conditions] incident, occurrence, fact; see CIRCUMSTANCE 1, EVENT, FACT 2, STATE. **3** [A legal action] suit, litigation, lawsuit; see TRIAL 2. **4** [An organized argument] argument, petition, evidence; see CLAIM, PROOF 1. **5** [A container or its contents] carton, canister, crate, crating, box, baggage, trunk, casing, chest, drawer, holder, tray, receptacle, coffer, crib, chamber, bin, bag, grip, cabinet, sheath, scabbard, wallet, safe, basket, casket; see also CONTAINER. —**in any case** in any event, anyway, however; see ANYHOW. —**in**

case in the event that, provided, if it should happen that; see IF. —**in case of** in the event of, in order to be prepared for, as a provision against; see IF.

cash *n.* money in hand, ready money, liquid assets, currency, legal tender, principal, available means, working assets, funds, payment, capital, finances, stock, resources, wherewithal, investments, savings, riches, reserve, treasure, moneys, security; see also MONEY 1, WEALTH.

cash *v.* cash in, change, draw; see PAY 1. —**cash in** realize, change, exchange, turn into money, discharge, draw, pay.

cashier[1] *n.* purser, treasurer, receiver; see CLERK.

case with magnetic tape or film in it, for loading a tape recorder, VCR, camera, etc. quickly

cas·sia (kash′ə, kas′ē ə) *n.* ⟦ult. < Heb *qeṣī'āh*, lit., something scraped off⟧ **1** *a)* the bark of a tree of SE Asia: used as the source of cinnamon *b)* the tree **2** any of various tropical plants whose leaves yield senna

cas·sino (kə sē′nō) *n.* CASINO

cas·sock (kas′ək) *n.* ⟦prob. < Turk *qazaq*, nomad⟧ a long, closefitting vestment worn by clergymen, etc.

cast (kast) *vt.* **cast, cast′ing** ⟦< ON *kasta*⟧ **1** to throw with force; hurl **2** to deposit (a ballot or vote) **3** to direct *[to cast one's eyes]* **4** to project *[to cast light]* **5** to throw off or shed (a skin) **6** to shape (molten metal, etc.) by pouring into a mold **7** to select (an actor) for (a role or play) — *vi.* to throw — *n.* **1** a casting; throw **2** something formed in a mold **3** a plaster form for immobilizing a limb **4** the set of actors in a play or movie **5** an appearance, as of features **6** a kind; quality **7** a tinge; shade —**cast about** to look (*for*) —**cast aside** (or **away**) to discard —**cast off 1** to discard **2** to free a ship from a dock, etc. —**cast up 1** to turn upward **2** to add up

cas·ta·nets (kas′tə nets′) *n.pl.* ⟦< Sp < L *castanea*, chestnut: from the shape⟧ a pair of small, hollowed pieces of hard wood or ivory, clicked together in the hand in time to music

cast′a·way′ *n.* **1** a person or thing cast off **2** a shipwrecked person — *adj.* **1** discarded **2** shipwrecked

caste (kast) *n.* ⟦Fr < L *castus*, pure⟧ **1** any of the hereditary Hindu social classes of a formerly segregated system of India **2** any exclusive group **3** rigid class distinction based on birth, wealth, etc. —**lose caste** to lose social status

cast′er *n.* **1** a container for vinegar, oil, etc. at the table **2** any of a set of small wheels for supporting and moving furniture

cas·ti·gate (kas′ti gāt′) *vt.* **-gat′ed, -gat′ing** ⟦< L *castigare*⟧ to rebuke severely, esp. by public criticism —**cas′ti·ga′tion** *n.* —**cas′ti·ga′tor** *n.*

cast′ing *n.* a thing, esp. of metal, cast in a mold

cast iron a hard, brittle alloy of iron made by casting —**cast′-i′ron** *adj.*

cas·tle (kas′əl) *n.* ⟦< L *castrum*, fort⟧ **1** a large, fortified building or group of buildings **2** any massive dwelling like this **3** *Chess* ROOK²

cast′off′ *adj.* discarded; abandoned — *n.* a person or thing cast off

castor-oil plant (kas′tər oil′) a tropical plant with large seeds which yield an oil (**castor oil**) used as a cathartic

cas·trate (kas′trāt′) *vt.* **-trat′ed, -trat′ing** ⟦< L *castrare*⟧ to remove the testicles of; emasculate —**cas·tra′tion** *n.*

cas·ual (kazh′ōō əl) *adj.* ⟦< L *casus*, chance⟧ **1** happening by chance; not planned; incidental **2** occasional **3** careless or cursory **4** nonchalant **5** for informal use —**cas′u·al·ly** *adv.* —**cas′u·al·ness** *n.*

cas·u·al·ty (kazh′ōō al tē) *n.*, *pl.* **-ties 1** an accident, esp. a fatal one **2** a member of the armed forces killed, wounded, captured, etc. **3** anyone hurt or killed in an accident

cas·u·ist·ry (kazh′ōō is trē) *n.*, *pl.* **-ries** ⟦< L *casus*, CASE¹⟧ subtle but false reasoning, esp. about moral issues; sophistry —**cas′u·ist** *n.*

cat (kat) *n.* ⟦OE⟧ **1** a small, soft-furred animal, often kept as a pet or for killing mice **2** any flesh-eating mammal related to this, as the lion, tiger, leopard, etc. **3** a spiteful woman —**let the cat out of the bag** to let a secret be found out —**cat′like′** *adj.*

cata·clysm (kat′ə kliz′əm) *n.* ⟦< Gr *kata-*, down + *klyzein*, to wash⟧ any sudden, violent change, as in war —**cat′a·clys′mic** (-kliz′mik) *adj.*

cata·comb (kat′ə kōm′) *n.* ⟦< ? L *cata*, by + *tumba*, tomb⟧ a gallery in an underground burial place

cat′a·falque′ (-falk′, -fôlk′) *n.* ⟦Fr < It *catafalco*, funeral canopy⟧ a wooden framework on which a body in a coffin lies in state

cat′a·lep′sy (-lep′sē) *n.* ⟦< Gr *katalēpsis*, a seizing⟧ a condition of muscle rigidity and sudden, temporary loss of consciousness and feeling, as in epilepsy —**cat′a·lep′tic** *adj.*, *n.*

cata·log or **cata·logue** (kat′ə lôg′) *n.* ⟦< Gr *kata-*, down + *legein*, to count⟧ a complete list, as an alphabetical card file of the books in a library, a list of articles for sale, etc. — *vt.*, *vi.* **-loged′** or **-logued′**, **-log′ing** or **-logu′ing** to arrange in a catalog —**cat′a·log′er** or **cat′a·logu′er** *n.*

ca·tal·pa (kə tal′pə) *n.* ⟦< AmInd⟧ a tree with large, heart-shaped leaves and slender pods

ca·tal·y·sis (kə tal′ə sis) *n.*, *pl.* **-ses′** (-sēz′) ⟦< Gr *katalysis*, dissolution⟧ the speeding up or, sometimes, slowing down of a chemical reaction by adding a substance which itself is not changed thereby

cata·lyst (kat′ə list′) *n.* a substance serving as the agent in catalysis —**cat′a·lyt′ic** (-lit′ik) *adj.*

catalytic converter a chemical filter connected to the exhaust system of an automotive vehicle, so as to reduce air pollution

cata·ma·ran (kat′ə mə ran′) *n.* ⟦Tamil *kaṭṭumaram*⟧ **1** a narrow log raft propelled by sails or paddles **2** a boat like this with two parallel hulls

cat′-and-mouse′ *adj.* [Colloq.] of behavior like that of a cat toying with a mouse; specif., of a strategy of teasing an opponent before striking

cata·pult (kat′ə pult′) *n.* ⟦< Gr *kata-*, down + *pallein*, to hurl⟧ **1** an ancient military contrivance for throwing stones, etc. **2** a device for launching an airplane, missile, etc. as from a deck or ramp — *vt.* to shoot as from a catapult — *vi.* to leap

cata·ract (kat′ə rakt′) *n.* ⟦< Gr *kata-*, down + *rhassein*, to strike or ? *arassein*, to smite⟧ **1** a large waterfall **2** an eye disease in which the lens becomes opaque, causing partial or total blindness

ca·tas·tro·phe (kə tas′trə fē) *n.* ⟦< Gr *kata-*, down + *strephein*, to turn⟧ any great and sudden disaster —**cata·strophic** (kat′ə sträf′ik) *adj.* —**cat′a·stroph′i·cally** *adv.*

cata·to·nia (kat′ə tō′nē ə) *n.* ⟦< Gr *kata-*, down + *tonos*, tension⟧ a syndrome, esp. of schizophrenia, marked by stupor or catalepsy —**cat′a·ton′ic** (-tän′ik) *adj.*, *n.*

cat′bird′ *n.* a slate-gray North American songbird with a call like a cat's

cat′boat′ *n.* a sailboat with a single sail and mast set well forward

---

THESAURUS

cast *n.* **1** [A plaster reproduction] facsimile, duplicate, replica; see COPY, SCULPTURE. **2** [Those in a play] persons in the play, list of characters, players, roles, parts, dramatis personae, company, troupe, producers, dramatic artists. **3** [Aspect] complexion, face, appearance; see LOOKS. **4** [A surgical dressing] plaster-of-Paris dressing, plaster cast, arm, cast, leg cast, knee cast, body cast, splints; see also DRESSING 3. **5** [A tinge] hue, shade, tint; see COLOR.

cast *v.* **1** [To throw] pitch, fling, hurl; see THROW 1. **2** [To form in a mold] shape, roughcast, wetcast; see FORM 1. **3** [To select actors for a play] appoint, designate, decide upon, determine, pick, give parts, detail, name; see also ASSIGN, CHOOSE. — **cast away** dispose of, reject, throw out; see ABANDON 1. —**cast off** reject, jettison, throw away; see ABANDON 1.

castle *n.* stronghold, manor, seat, villa, fortress, château, citadel, keep,

fort, hold, safehold; see also FORTIFICATION.

castrate *v.* emasculate, sterilize, asexualize, mutilate, cut, spay, geld, unman, steer, caponize, effeminize, deprive of manhood; see also MAIM.

casual *a.* **1** [Accidental] chance, unexpected, unplanned; see SPONTANEOUS. **2** [Nonchalant] blasé, apathetic, unconcerned; see CARELESS, INDIFFERENT.

casually *a.* **1** [Accidentally] unintentionally, by chance, inadvertently; see ACCIDENTALLY. **2** [Nonchalantly] indifferently, coolly, unemotionally; see CARELESSLY, EASILY.

casualty *n.* fatalities, losses, death toll; see LOSS 3.

cat *n.* **1** [A domestic animal] tomcat, kitten, kit, tabby, puss, pussy, mouser, kitty. *House cats include the following:* Maltese, Persian, Siamese, Angora, tortoise shell, alley, tiger, calico; see also ANIMAL. **2** [A member of the cat family] lion, tiger, leopard,

puma, wildcat, cheetah, lynx, bobcat, mountain lion, ocelot, cougar, jaguar; see also ANIMAL. —**let the cat out of the bag** expose, tell a secret, let slip; see REVEAL.

catalog *n.* register, file, directory, schedule, inventory, index, bulletin, syllabus, brief, slate, table, calendar, list, docket, classification, record, draft, roll, timetable, table of contents, prospectus, program, rent roll; see also LIST.

catalog *v.* classify, record, index; see LIST 1.

catastrophe *n.* calamity, mishap, mischance, misadventure, misery, accident, trouble, casualty, infliction, affliction, stroke, havoc, ravage, wreck, fatality, grief, crash, devastation, desolation, hardship, blow, ruin, reverse, emergency, scourge, convulsion, tragedy, adversity, bad luck, upheaval, down; see also DISASTER.

cat′call′ *n.* a shrill shout or whistle expressing derision, etc. — *vt., vi.* to make catcalls (at)

catch (kach; *often,* kech) *vt.* **caught, catch′ing** ⟦< L *capere,* to take hold⟧ 1 to seize and hold; capture 2 to take by a trap 3 to deceive 4 to surprise 5 to get to in time /to *catch* a train/ 6 to lay hold of; grab /to *catch* a ball/ 7 to become infected with /he *caught* a cold/ 8 to understand 9 to get entangled 10 [Colloq.] to see, hear, etc. — *vi.* 1 to become held, fastened, etc. 2 to take hold, as fire 3 to keep hold, as a lock — *n.* 1 a catching 2 a thing that catches 3 something caught 4 one worth catching as a spouse 5 a snatch or fragment 6 a break in the voice 7 [Colloq.] a tricky qualification or condition — **catch at** to seize desperately —**catch on** 1 to understand 2 to become popular —**catch up** 1 to seize; snatch 2 to overtake

catch′all′ (-ôl′) *n.* a container or place for holding all sorts of things

catch′er *n. Baseball* the player behind home plate, who catches pitched balls

catch′ing *adj.* 1 contagious; infectious 2 attractive

catch′word′ *n.* a word or phrase that comes to represent a group, etc. through frequent repetition

catch′y *adj.* **-i·er, -i·est** 1 easily caught up and remembered 2 tricky

cat·echism (kat′ə kiz′əm) *n.* ⟦< Gr *kata-,* thoroughly + *ēchein,* to sound⟧ 1 a handbook of questions and answers for teaching the principles of a religion 2 a close questioning

cat′echize′ (-kiz′) *vt.* **-chized′, -chiz′ing** ⟦see prec.⟧ to question searchingly Also sp. **cat′echise′**

cat·egor·i·cal (kat′ə gôr′i kəl) *adj.* 1 positive; explicit: said of a statement, etc. 2 of, as, or in a category —**cat′egor′i·cally** *adv.*

cat·ego·rize (kat′ə gə riz′) *vt.* **-rized′, -riz′ing** to place in a category; classify

cat′ego·ry (-gôr′ē) *n., pl.* **-ries** ⟦< Gr *katēgorein,* to assert⟧ a division in a scheme of classification

ca·ter (kāt′ər) *vi.* ⟦< L *ad-,* to + *capere,* take hold⟧ 1 to provide food and service, as for parties 2 to seek to gratify another's desires: with *to* —**ca′terer** *n.*

cater-cornered (kat′ə kôr′nərd, kat′ē-) *adj.* ⟦< OFr *catre,* four + CORNERED⟧ diagonal — *adv.* diagonally Also **cat′er-cor′ner**

cat·er·pil·lar (kat′ər pil′ər, kat′ə-) *n.* ⟦< L *catta pilosus,* hairy cat⟧ the wormlike larva of a butterfly, moth, etc.

cat·er·waul (kat′ər wôl′) *vi.* ⟦prob. echoic⟧ to make a shrill sound like that of a cat; wail — *n.* such a sound

cat′fish′ *n., pl.* **-fish′** or (for different species) **-fish′es** a scaleless fish with long, whiskerlike feelers about the mouth

cat′gut′ *n.* a tough thread made from dried intestines, as of sheep, and used for surgical sutures, etc.

ca·thar·sis (kə thär′sis) *n.* ⟦< Gr *katharos,* pure⟧ 1 a purging, esp. of the bowels 2 a relieving of the emotions, as through the arts or psychotherapy

ca·thar′tic *adj.* of catharsis; purging — *n.* a medicine for purging the bowels; purgative

ca·thedral (kə thē′drəl) *n.* ⟦< Gr *kata-,* down + *hedra,* a seat⟧ 1 the main church of a bishop's see 2 any large, imposing church

cath·eter (kath′ət ər) *n.* ⟦< Gr *kata-,* down + *hienai,* to send⟧ a slender tube inserted into a body passage, as into the bladder for drawing off urine —**cath′eter·ize′** (-iz′), **-ized′, -iz′ing,** *vt.*

cath·ode (kath′ōd′) *n.* ⟦< Gr < *kata-,* down + -ODE⟧ 1 the negative electrode in an electrolytic cell 2 the electron emitter in a vacuum tube 3 the positive terminal of a battery

cathode rays streams of electrons projected from a cathode: they produce X-rays when they strike solids

cath′ode-ray′ tube (-rā′) a vacuum tube in which a stream of electrons can be focused on a fluorescent screen: such tubes are used as picture tubes, etc.

catho·lic (kath′ ə lik, kath′lik) *adj.* ⟦< Gr *kata-,* completely + *holos,* whole⟧ 1 all-inclusive; universal 2 broad in sympathies, tastes, etc. 3 [C-] ROMAN CATHOLIC — *n.* [C-] ROMAN CATHOLIC —**Ca·tholi·cism** (kə thäl′ə siz′əm) *n.* —**catho·lic·ity** (kath′ə lis′i tē) *n.*

cat·ion (kat′i′ən) *n.* ⟦< Gr *kata,* down + *ienai,* to go⟧ a positively charged ion: in electrolysis, cations move toward the cathode

cat·kin (kat′kin) *n.* ⟦< Du *katte,* cat⟧ a drooping, scaly spike of small flowers without petals, as on poplars, walnuts, etc.

cat′nap′ *n.* a short nap; doze — *vi.* **-napped′, -nap′ping** to doze briefly

cat′nip′ *n.* ⟦CAT + dial. *nep,* catnip⟧ an herb of the mint family: cats like its odor

cat-o′-nine-tails (kat′ə nin′tālz′) *n., pl.* **-tails′** a whip made of nine knotted cords attached to a handle

CAT scan (kat) ⟦*c*(omputerized) *a*(xial) *t*(omography)⟧ 1 a diagnostic X-raying of soft tissues, using many single-plane X-rays (*tomograms*) to form the image 2 such an image —**CAT scanner** —**CAT scanning**

cat′s cradle a game in which a string looped over the fingers is transferred back and forth on the hands of the players so as to form different designs

cat′s-paw (kats′pô′) *n.* a person used to do distasteful or unlawful work

cat·sup (kat′səp) *n.* KETCHUP

cat·tail (kat′tāl′) *n.* a tall marsh plant with long, brown, fuzzy spikes

cat·tle (kat′'l) *n.pl.* ⟦ult. < L *caput,* head⟧ 1 [Now Chiefly Dial.] livestock 2 cows, bulls, steers, or oxen —**cat′tle·man** (-mən), *pl.* **-men,** *n.*

catty (kat′ē) *adj.* **-tier, -ti·est** 1 of or like a cat 2 spiteful, mean, malicious, etc. —**cat′tily** *adv.* —**cat′ti·ness** *n.*

cat′ty-cor′nered *adj., adv.* CATER-CORNERED Also **cat′ty-cor′ner**

cat′walk′ *n.* a narrow, elevated walk

Cau·ca·sian (kô kā′zhən) *adj.* 1 of the Caucasus, region between SE Europe & W Asia 2 CAUCASOID — *n.* 1 a native of the Caucasus 2 CAUCASOID

Cau·ca·soid (kô′kə soid′) *adj.* designating or of one of the major geographical varieties of human beings, loosely called the *white race* — *n.* a member of the Caucasoid population

cau·cus (kô′kəs) *n.* ⟦< ?⟧ 1 a meeting of a party or faction to decide on policy, pick candidates, etc. 2 the group attending such a meeting 3 a faction of politicians — *vi.* **-cused** or **-cussed, -cus·ing** or **-cus·sing** to hold a caucus

cau·dal (kôd′'l) *adj.* ⟦< L *cauda,* tail + -AL⟧ of, like, at, or near the tail

caught (kôt) *vt., vi. pt. & pp.* of CATCH

caul·dron (kôl′drən) *n. alt. sp.* of CALDRON

cau·li·flower (kô′lə flou′ər) *n.* ⟦< It *cavolo,* cabbage + *fiore,* flower⟧ 1 a variety of cabbage with a dense white head of fleshy flower stalks 2 the head, eaten as a vegetable

caulk (kôk) *vt.* ⟦< L *calx,* a heel⟧ to stop up (cracks, etc.)

THESAURUS

catch *n.* 1 [A likely mate] boyfriend, sweetheart, fiancé; see LOVER 1. 2 [Something stolen] capture, grab, haul*; see BOOTY. 3 [*A trick] puzzle, trick, trap; see JOKE. 4 [A hook] clasp, clamp, snap; see FASTENER.

catch *v.* 1 [To seize hold of] snatch, take, take hold of, snag, grab, pick, pounce on, fasten upon, snare, pluck, hook, claw, clench, clasp, grasp, clutch, grip, nab, net, bag*; see also SEIZE. 2 [To bring into captivity] trap, apprehend, capture; see ARREST, SEIZE 2. 3 [To come to from behind] overtake, reach, come upon; see PASS 1. 4 [To contract a disease] get, fall ill with, become infected with, incur, become subject to, be liable to, fall victim to, take, succumb to, break out with, receive, come down with.—

Ant. ESCAPE, ward off, get over. —

catch on 1 [To understand] grasp, comprehend, perceive; see UNDERSTAND 1. 2 [To become popular] become fashionable, become prevalent, become common, become widespread, become acceptable, grow in popularity, find favor; see also SUCCEED 1. —**catch up** catch, join, equal; see REACH 1.

catching *a.* contagious, communicable, transmittable, infectious, epidemic, endemic, pestilential, noxious, dangerous, pandemic; see also CONTAGIOUS.

category *n.* level, section, classification; see CLASS 1, DIVISION 2, KIND.

cathedral *n.* temple, house of God, house of prayer, Holy place, basilica,

minster; see also CHURCH 1. *Parts of a cathedral include the following:* altar, sanctuary, holy of holies, sacristy, sacrarium, holy table, baptistery, chancel, apse, choir, nave, aisle, transept, crypt, pew, seat, pulpit, confessional. *Famous cathedrals include the following:* St. Peter's, Rome; St. Paul's, London; Notre Dame, Paris; St. John the Divine, New York; St. Patrick's, New York.

cattle *n.* stock, cows, steers, calves, herd, beef cattle, dairy cattle; see also COW.

caucus *n.* assembly, meeting, council; see GATHERING.

caught *a.* taken, seized, arrested; see CAPTURED, UNDER ARREST.

of (a boat, etc.) as with a puttylike sealant or oakum —*n.* a soft, puttylike compound used in caulking —**caulk'er** *n.*

causal (kôz'əl) *adj.* 1 of, being, or expressing a cause 2 relating to cause and effect —**cau·sal·i·ty** (kô zal'i tē), *pl.* -ties, *n.* —**caus'ally** *adv.*

cau·sa·tion (kô zā'shən) *n.* 1 a causing 2 a causal agency; anything producing an effect

cause (kôz) *n.* [< L *causa*] 1 anything producing an effect or result 2 a reason or motive for producing an effect 3 any objective or movement that people are interested in and support 4 *Law* a case to be resolved by a court —*vt.* **caused, caus'ing** to be the cause of; bring about —**caus'a·tive** *adj.* —**cause'less** *adj.* —**caus'er** *n.*

cau·serie (kō'zə rē') *n.* [Fr] 1 a chat 2 a short, chatty composition

cause·way (kôz'wā') *n.* [ult. < L *calx*, lime + WAY] a raised path or road, as across wet ground

caus·tic (kôs'tik) *adj.* [< Gr *kaiein*, to burn] 1 that can burn tissue by chemical action; corrosive 2 sarcastic; biting —*n.* a caustic substance —**caus'ti·cally** *adv.* —**caus·tic'i·ty** (-tis'i tē) *n.*

cau·ter·ize (kôt'ər īz') *vt.* **-ized', -iz'ing** [see prec.] to burn with a hot needle, a laser, a caustic substance, etc. so as to destroy dead tissue, etc. —**cau'ter·i·za'tion** *n.*

cau·tion (kô'shən) *n.* [< L *cautio*] 1 a warning 2 wariness; prudence —*vt.* to warn —**cau'tion·ar'y** *adj.*

cau·tious (kô'shəs) *adj.* full of caution; careful to avoid danger —**cau'tiously** *adv.* —**cau'tious·ness** *n.*

cav·al·cade (kav'əl kād', kav'əl kād') *n.* [Fr < L *caballus*, horse] a procession, as of horsemen, carriages, etc.

cava·lier (kav'ə lir') *n.* [Fr: see prec.] 1 an armed horseman; knight 2 a gallant gentleman, esp. a lady's escort —*adj.* 1 casual 2 arrogant —**cava·lier'ly** *adv.*

cav·al·ry (kav'əl rē) *n., pl.* **-ries** [< Fr: see CAVALCADE] combat troops mounted originally on horses but now often riding in motorized armored vehicles —**cav'al·ry·man** (-mən), *pl.* **-men,** *n.*

cave (kāv) *n.* [< L *cavus*, hollow] a hollow place inside the earth; cavern —*vt., vi.* **caved, cav'ing** to collapse or make collapse: with *in*

ca·veat emp·tor (kā'vē at' emp'tôr') [L] let the buyer beware

cave'-in' *n.* 1 a caving in 2 a place where the ground, etc. has caved in

cave man a prehistoric human being of the Stone Age who lived in caves

cav·ern (kav'ərn) *n.* a cave, esp. a large cave —**cav'ern·ous** *adj.*

cavi·ar or **cavi·are** (kav'ē är') *n.* [Fr < Pers *khāya*, egg + -*dār*, bearing] the salted eggs of sturgeon, etc. eaten as an appetizer

cavil (kav'əl) *vi.* **-iled** or **-illed, -il·ing** or **-il·ling** [< L *cavilla*, jeering] to object unnecessarily; quibble —*n.* a trivial objection; quibble —**cav'iler** or **cav'il·ler** *n.*

cav·i·ty (kav'i tē) *n., pl.* **-ties** [see CAVE] a hollow place, as in a tooth

ca·vort (kə vôrt') *vi.* [< ?] 1 to prance or caper 2 to romp; frolic

caw (kô) *n.* [echoic] the harsh cry of a crow —*vi.* to make this sound

cay·enne (pepper) (kī en', kā-) [< AmInd (Brazil) *kynnha*] very hot red pepper made from the dried fruit of a pepper plant

cay·use (kī'yōōs', -ōōs'; kī yōōs', -ōōs') *n., pl.* **-us'es** [< AmInd tribal name] a small Western horse used by cowboys

CB (sē'bē') *adj.* [c(*itizens'*) b(*and*)] designating or of shortwave radio frequencies set aside by the FCC for local use by private persons or businesses

cc 1 carbon copy 2 cubic centimeter(s)

CD (sē'dē') *n.* compact disc

Cd *Chem. symbol for* cadmium

CDC Centers for Disease Control

Cdn. Canadian

CD-ROM (sē'dē'räm') *n.* a compact disc on which stored computer data can be accessed

cease (sēs) *vt., vi.* **ceased, ceas'ing** [see CEDE] to end; stop

cease'-fire' *n.* a temporary cessation of warfare; truce

cease'less (-lis) *adj.* unceasing; continual —**cease'lessly** *adv.*

ce·cum (sē'kəm) *n., pl.* **-ca** (-kə) [< L *caecus*, blind] the pouch at the beginning of the large intestine

ce·dar (sē'dər) *n.* [< Gr *kedros*] a pine tree having fragrant, durable wood 2 its wood —*adj.* of cedar

cede (sēd) *vt.* **ced'ed, ced'ing** [< L *cedere*, to yield] 1 to surrender formally 2 to transfer the title of

ce·dilla (sə dil'ə) *n.* [Sp dim. of *zeda*, a zeta or *z*] a hooklike mark put under *c*, as in some French words (Ex.: *façade*) to show that it has an *s* sound

ceil·ing (sēl'iŋ) *n.* [< L *caelum*, heaven] 1 the inside top part of a room, opposite the floor 2 an upper limit [a price *ceiling*] 3 *Aeronautics* the upper limit of visibility —**hit the ceiling** [Slang] to lose one's temper

cel·an·dine (sel'ən dīn', -dēn') *n.* [< Gr *chelidōn*, a swallow] 1 a variety of poppy with yellow flowers 2 a variety of buttercup

cel·ebrate (sel'ə brāt') *vt.* **-brat'ed, -brat'ing** [< L *celebrare*, to honor] 1 to perform (a ritual, etc.) 2 to commemorate (an anniversary, holiday, etc.) with festivity 3 to honor publicly —*vi.* [Colloq.] to have a good time —**cel'ebrant** (-brənt) *n.* —**cel'ebra'tion** *n.*

cel'ebrat'ed *adj.* famous; renowned

ce·leb·ri·ty (sə leb'rə tē) *n.* 1 fame 2 *pl.* **-ties** a famous person

ce·ler·i·ty (sə ler'i tē) *n.* [< L *celer*, swift] swiftness; speed

cel·ery (sel'ər ē, sel'rē) *n.* [< Gr *selinon*, parsley] a plant whose crisp leafstalks are eaten as a vegetable

ce·les·tial (sə les'chəl) *adj.* [< L *caelum*, heaven] 1 of or in the sky or universe 2 of heaven; divine 3 perfect

celi·bacy (sel'ə bə sē) *n.* 1 the state of being unmarried 2 complete sexual abstinence

celi·bate (sel'ə bət) *n.* [< L *caelebs*] 1 an unmarried person 2 one who abstains from sexual intercourse —*adj.* of or in a state of celibacy

cell (sel) *n.* [< L *cella*] 1 a small room, as in a prison 2 a small hollow, as in a honeycomb 3 a small unit of proto-

---

════ THESAURUS ════

cause *n.* 1 [Purpose] motive, causation, object, purpose, explanation, inducement, incitement, prime mover, motive power, mainspring, ultimate cause, ground, matter, element, stimulation, instigation, foundation, the why and wherefore; see also BASIS, REASON 3.—*Ant.* RESULT, effect, outcome. 2 [Moving force] agent, case, condition; see CIRCUMSTANCES. 3 [A belief] principles, conviction, creed; see BELIEF, FAITH 2.

cause *v.* originate, provoke, generate, occasion, let, kindle, give rise to, lie at the root of, be at the bottom of, bring to pass, bring to effect, sow the seeds of; see also BEGIN.

caution *n.* care, heed, discretion; see ATTENTION, PRUDENCE.

caution *v.* forewarn, alert, advise; see WARN.

cautious *a.* circumspect, watchful, wary; see CAREFUL.

cautiously *a.* tentatively, prudently, discreetly, watchfully, wisely, sparingly, thoughtfully, heedfully, delicately, mindfully, anxiously, with care, with caution, gingerly, with forethought, slowly.

cave *n.* rock shelter, cavern, grotto; see HOLE.

cavern *n.* cave, hollow, grotto; see HOLE.

cavity *n.* 1 [Sunken area] pit, depression, basin; see HOLE. 2 [Hollow place in a tooth] dental caries, distal pit, gingival pit; see DECAY.

cease *v.* desist, terminate, discontinue; see HALT, STOP 1, 2.

ceaseless *a.* continual, endless, unending; see CONSTANT, ETERNAL.

celebrate *v.* 1 [To recognize an occasion] keep, observe, consecrate, hallow, dedicate, commemorate, honor, proclaim, ritualize.—*Ant.* FORGET, overlook, neglect. 2 [To indulge in celebration] feast, give a party, carouse, rejoice, kill the fatted calf, revel, go on a spree, make whoopee*, blow off steam*, let off steam, have a party, have a ball, kick up one's heels*, let loose*, let go, live it up, whoop it up, make merry, kick up a row*, beat the drum*.

celebrated *a.* renowned, well-known, noted; see FAMOUS, IMPORTANT 2.

celebration *n.* commemoration, holiday, anniversary, jubilee, inauguration, installation, coronation, presentation, carnival, revelry, spree, festivity, festival, feast, merry-making, gaiety, frolic, hilarity, joviality, merriment, remembrance, ceremonial, keeping observance, fete, Mardi Gras, birthday.

celebrity *n.* famous man, famous woman, hero, heroine, leader, notable, magnate, dignitary, worthy, figure, personage, famous person, man of note, someone, somebody, VIP*, luminary, lion, lioness, star, bigwig*, big gun*, big shot*, ace.

cell *n.* 1 [A unit of living organism] corpuscle, cellule, microorganism, vacuole, spore, plastid, organism, egg, ectoplasm, embryo, germ, follicle. 2 [A room] vault, hold, pen, cage, tower, hole, coop, keep, bastille, chamber, den, recess, retreat, alcove, manger, crypt, crib, nook, burrow, plasm: all plants and animals are made up of one or more cells **4** a receptacle for generating electricity by chemical reactions **5** a small unit of an organization —**celled** (seld) *adj.*

cel·lar (sel′ər) *n.* ⟦see prec.⟧ a room or rooms below ground and usually under a building

cello (chel′ō) *n., pl.* **-los** or **-li** (-ē) ⟦< VIOLONCELLO⟧ an instrument of the violin family, between the viola and double bass in pitch —**cel′list** *n.*

cel·lo·phane (sel′ə fān′) *n.* a thin, transparent material made from cellulose, used as a wrapping

cel·lu·lar (sel′yōō lər) *adj.* of, like, or containing a cell or cells

cellular phone system a computer-controlled system connecting a telephone system to a network of mobile radiotelephones

cel·lu·lite (sel′yōō līt′, -lēt′; sel′yōō lēt′) *n.* ⟦Fr⟧ fatty deposits on the hips and thighs: a nonmedical term

cel·lu·loid (sel′yōō loid′) *n.* ⟦fol. + -OID⟧ a tough, flammable plastic substance made from nitrocellulose and camphor

cel·lu·lose (sel′yōō lōs′) *n.* ⟦Fr < L cella, cell + -OSE[1]⟧ the chief substance in the cell walls of plants, used in making paper, textiles, etc.

cellulose acetate any of several acetic esters of cellulose, used in making plastics, lacquers, etc.

Cel·sius (sel′sē əs) *adj.* ⟦after A. *Celsius* (1701-44), Swed astronomer, the inventor⟧ designating of or a thermometer on which 0° is the freezing point and 100° is the boiling point of water

Celt (selt, kelt) *n.* ⟦< L⟧ a Celtic-speaking person

Celtic (sel′tik, kel′-) *adj.* of the Celts, their languages, etc. —*n.* a subfamily of languages including Gaelic and Welsh

ce·ment (sə ment′) *n.* ⟦< L *caementum*, rough stone⟧ **1** a powdered substance of lime and clay, mixed with water and sand to make mortar or with water, sand, and gravel to make concrete: it hardens upon drying **2** anything that bonds —*vt.* **1** to unite as with cement **2** to cover with cement —*vi.* to become cemented —**ce·ment′er** *n.*

cem·etery (sem′ə ter′ē) *n., pl.* **-ies** ⟦< Gr < *koiman*, to put to sleep⟧ a place for the burial of the dead

ceno·bite (sen′ə bīt′) *n.* ⟦< Gr < *koinos*, common + *bios*, life⟧ a member of a religious order living in a monastery or convent

ceno·taph (sen′ə taf′) *n.* ⟦< Gr *kenos*, empty + *taphos*, tomb⟧ a monument honoring a dead person whose remains are elsewhere

Ce·no·zoic (sē′nə zō′ik, sen′ə-) *adj.* ⟦*ceno-* (< Gr *kainos*, recent) + ZO(O)- + -IC⟧ designating the geologic era that includes the present, during which the various mammals have developed

cen·ser (sen′sər) *n.* a container in which incense is burned

cen·sor (sen′sər) *n.* ⟦L < *censere*, to judge⟧ an official with the power to examine literature, mail, etc. and remove or prohibit anything considered obscene, objectionable, etc.

—*vt.* to subject (a book, etc.) to censorship —**cen′sor·ship′** *n.*

cen·so·ri·ous (sen sôr′ē əs) *adj.* inclined to find fault; harshly critical

cen·sure (sen′shər) *n.* ⟦< L *censor*, censor⟧ strong disapproval; condemnation —*vt.* **-sured, -sur·ing** to condemn as wrong —**cen′sur·able** *adj.*

cen·sus (sen′səs) *n.* ⟦L < *censere*, enroll⟧ an official count of population and recording of age, sex, economic status, etc.

cent (sent) *n.* ⟦< L *centum*, hundred⟧ a 100th part of a dollar, or a coin of this value; penny

cent. century; centuries

cen·taur (sen′tôr′) *n.* ⟦< Gr *Kentauros*⟧ *Gr. Myth.* a monster with a man's head and trunk and a horse's body

cen·ta·vo (sen tä′vō) *n., pl.* **-vos** ⟦Sp, a hundredth < L *centum*, hundred⟧ the 100th part of the monetary unit of Mexico, the Philippines, and some South American countries

cen·te·nar·ian (sen′tə ner′ē ən) *n.* ⟦< fol.⟧ a person at least 100 years old

cen·te·nary (sen′tə ner′ē, sen ten′ər ē) *adj.* ⟦< L < *centum*, hundred⟧ **1** of a century **2** of a centennial —*n., pl.* **-ies** CENTENNIAL

cen·ten·nial (sen ten′ē əl) *adj.* ⟦< L *centum*, hundred + *annus*, year + -AL⟧ of or lasting 100 years —*n.* a 100th anniversary or its commemoration

cen·ter (sen′tər) *n.* ⟦< Gr *kentron*, sharp point⟧ **1** a point equally distant from all points on the circumference of a circle or surface of a sphere **2** a pivot **3** the approximate middle point or part of anything **4** a focal point of activity **5** [*often* C-] a group or position between the left (liberals) and right (conservatives) **6** *Sports* a player at the center of a line, floor, etc. —*vt.* **1** to place in or near the center **2** to gather to one place —*vi.* to be centered

cen′ter·board′ *n.* a movable board or plate, like a keel, lowered through a slot in the floor of a shallow sailboat

cen′ter·fold′ *n.* the center facing pages of a magazine, often with an extra fold, showing a photograph, as of a nude woman or man

center of gravity that point in a body or system around which its weight is evenly balanced

cen′ter·piece′ *n.* an ornament for the center of a table

centi- ⟦L⟧ *combining form* **1** one hundred **2** a 100th part of

cen·ti·grade (sen′tə grād′) *adj.* ⟦Fr: see prec. & GRADE⟧ CELSIUS

cen·time (sän′tēm′) *n.* ⟦Fr⟧ the 100th part of a franc

cen·ti·meter (sen′tə mēt′ər) *n.* ⟦Fr: see CENTI- & METER[1]⟧ a unit of measure, 1⁄100 meter Brit. **cen′ti·me′tre**

cen·ti·pede (sen′tə pēd′) *n.* ⟦Fr < L *centi-*, CENTI- + *pes*, FOOT⟧ an elongated arthropod with a pair of legs for each body segment

cen·tral (sen′trəl) *adj.* ⟦L *centralis*⟧ **1** in, near, or of the center **2** equally accessible from various points **3** main; basic **4** of a controlling source in a system —**cen′trally** *adv.*

THESAURUS

stall, closet, booth, cloister, compartment, lockup; see also ROOM 2.

cellar *n.* half basement, underground room, basement apartment; see BASEMENT.

cement *n.* glue, putty, tar, gum, mortar, paste, adhesive, rubber cement, epoxy resin, bond.

cement *v.* mortar, plaster, connect; see FASTEN, JOIN 1.

cemetery *n.* burial ground, memorial park, funerary grounds, churchyard, necropolis, potter's field, catacomb, city of the dead, tomb, vault, crypt, charnel house, sepulcher, graveyard, mortuary, last resting place, Golgotha, boneyard*.

censor *n.* inspector, judge, expurgator, guardian of morals; see also EXAMINER.

censor *v.* control, restrict, strike out, forbid, suppress, ban, withhold, enforce censorship, control the flow of news, inspect, oversee, abridge, expurgate, review, criticize, exert pressure, conceal, prevent publication, blacklist, blue pencil, cut, black out; see also RESTRICT.

censorship *n.* licensing, restriction,

forbidding, controlling the press, infringing the right of freedom of speech, governmental control, security blackout, news blackout, thought control; see also RESTRAINT.

censure *n.* criticism, reproof, admonition; see BLAME, OBJECTION.

censure *v.* **1** [To blame] criticize, judge, disapprove; see BLAME. **2** [To scold] rebuke, reprove, attack; see SCOLD.

census *n.* statistics, enumeration, valuation, account, registration, listing, evaluation, demography, figures, statement, numbering, registering, roll call, tabulation, tally, poll, count, counting, nose count; see also COUNT.

cent *n.* penny, a copper, 100th part of a dollar; see MONEY 1.

center *a.* mid, middle, inmost, inner, midway, medial, deepest, at the inmost, innermost, internal, interior, at the halfway point; see also MIDDLE.—*Ant.* OUTSIDE, outer, exterior.

center *n.* **1** [A central point] point, middle, focus, nucleus, core, place, heart, hub, navel, point of convergence, point of concentration, focal

point, midst, middle point, centrality, marrow, kernel, bull's eye, pivot, axis, pith, dead center; see also MIDDLE. **2** [A point that attracts people] city, town, metropolis, plaza, capital, shopping center, trading center, station, hub, mart, market, crossroads, mall, social center, meeting place, club, market place. **3** [Essence] core, gist, kernel; see CHARACTER 1.

center *v.* concentrate, centralize, focus, intensify, unify, unite, combine, converge upon, join, meet, gather, close on, consolidate, bring to a focus, center round, center in, gather together, flock together, collect, draw together, bring together, focus attention, attract; see also MEET 1.—*Ant.* SPREAD, decentralize, branch off.

central *a.* middle, midway, equidistant, medial, focal, nuclear, midmost, mean, inner, median, inmost, middlemost, intermediate, interior, in the center of; see also MIDDLE.—*Ant.* OUTER, peripheral, verging on.

centrally *a.* in the middle, focal, middlemost, in the center, in the

central city the crowded, industrial, central area of a large city

cen'tral·ize' (-īz') *vt.* **-ized', -iz'ing 1** to make central; bring to a center **2** to organize under one control — *vi.* to become centralized **—cen'trali·za'tion** *n.* **—cen'tral·iz'er** *n.*

cen·tre (sent'ər) *n., vt., vi.* **-tred, -tring** chiefly Brit. sp. of CENTER

centri- combining form CENTRO-

cen·trifu·gal (sen trif'yōō gəl, -yə gəl) *adj.* [< prec. + L *fugere,* to flee + -AL] using or acted on by a force (**centrifugal force**) that tends to make rotating bodies move away from the center of rotation

cen·tri·fuge (sen'trə fyōōj') *n.* a machine using centrifugal force to separate particles of varying density

cen·trip·etal (sen trip'ət'l) *adj.* [< CENTRI- + L *petere,* rush at] using or acted on by a force (**centripetal force**) that tends to make rotating bodies move toward the center of rotation

cen·trist (sen'trist) *n.* a person with moderate political opinions

centro- [< L *centrum,* center] combining form center

cen·tu·rion (sen toor'ē ən, -tyoor'-) *n.* [see fol.] the commanding officer of an ancient Roman military unit, originally of 100 men

cen·tury (sen'chə rē) *n., pl.* **-ries** [L < *centum,* hundred] a period of 100 years, esp. as reckoned from 1 A.D.

CEO chief executive officer

ce·phalic (sə fal'ik) *adj.* [< Gr < *kephalē,* head] **1** of the head or skull **2** in, on, near, or toward the head

cephalo- [see prec.] combining form the head, skull, or brain

ce·ramic (sə ram'ik) *adj.* [Gr < *keramos,* potter's clay] **1** of pottery, porcelain, etc. **2** of ceramics — *n.* **1** [*pl., with sing v.*] the art or work of making pottery, etc. **2** an object made of baked clay

ce·ram·ist (ser'ə mist, sə ram'ist) *n.* one who works in ceramics; ceramic artist Also **ce·ram·i·cist** (sə ram'ə sist)

ce·real (sir'ē əl) *adj.* [< L *Cerealis,* of Ceres, Rom goddess of agriculture] of grain — *n.* **1** any grain used for food, as wheat, oats, rice, etc. **2** any grass producing such grain **3** food made from grain

cer·ebel·lum (ser'ə bel'əm) *n., pl.* **-lums** or **-la** [L, dim. of *cerebrum*] the section of the brain behind and below the cerebrum

cer·ebral (ser'ə brəl, sə rē'-) *adj.* **1** of the brain or cerebrum **2** intellectual

cerebral palsy spastic paralysis due to brain damage

cer·ebrate (ser'ə brāt') *vi.* **-brat'ed, -brat'ing** [< L *cerebrum,* the brain + -ATE¹] to think **—cer'ebra'tion** *n.*

cer·ebrum (ser'ə brəm, sə rē'brəm) *n., pl.* **-brums** or **-bra** [L] the upper, main part of the brain of vertebrates

cer·ement (ser'ə mənt, sir'mənt) *n.* [< Gr *kēros,* wax] [*usually pl.*] a shroud for a dead person

cer·emo·nial (ser'ə mō'nē əl) *adj.* of or consisting of ceremony; formal — *n.* **1** a system of rites; ritual **2** a rite or ceremony **—cer'emo'ni·ally** *adv.*

cer·emo'ni·ous (-nē əs) *adj.* **1** full of ceremony **2** very polite or formal **—cer'emo'ni·ously** *adv.*

cer·emony (ser'ə mō'nē) *n., pl.* **-nies** [< L *caerimonia*] **1** a set of formal acts proper to a special occasion, as a religious rite **2** behavior that follows rigid etiquette **3** *a)* formality *b)* empty or meaningless formality **—stand on ceremony** to insist on formality

ce·rise (sə rēz', -rēs') *n., adj.* [< OFr *cerise,* cherry] bright red; cherry red

cer·met (sur'met') *n.* [CER(AMIC) + MET(AL)] a bonded mixture of ceramic material and a metal

cer·tain (surt'n) *adj.* [< L *certus,* determined] **1** fixed; settled **2** inevitable **3** reliable; dependable **4** sure; positive **5** definite, but unnamed [a *certain* person] **6** some [to a *certain* extent] **—for certain** without doubt

cer'tainly *adv.* undoubtedly; surely

cer'tainty (-tē) *n.* **1** the state or fact of being certain **2** *pl.* **-ties** anything certain

cer·tifi·cate (sər tif'i kit; *for v.,* -kāt') *n.* [see CERTIFY] a document attesting to a fact, qualification, etc. — *vt.* **-cat'ed, -cat'ing** to issue a certificate to

certificate of deposit a bank certificate issued for a specified large deposit of money drawing interest and requiring written notice for withdrawal

certified public accountant a public accountant certified as passing a state examination

cer·tify (surt'ə fī') *vt.* **-fied', -fy'ing** [< L *certus,* certain + -FY] **1** to declare (a thing) true, accurate, etc. by formal statement **2** to declare officially insane **3** to guarantee (a check, document, etc.) **4** to issue a certificate or license to **—cer'ti·fi'able** *adj.* **—cer'ti·fi·ca'tion** *n.*

cer·ti·tude (surt'ə tōōd', -tyōōd') *n.* sureness; inevitability

ce·ru·lean (sə rōō'lē ən) *adj.* [< L < *caelum,* heaven] sky-blue; azure

cer·vix (sur'viks') *n., pl.* **cer·vi·ces** (sər vī'sēz', sur'və-) or **-vixes** [L, neck] a necklike part, as of the uterus **—cer'vi·cal** (-vi kəl) *adj.*

ce·sium (sē'zē əm) *n.* [ult. < L *caesius,* bluish-gray] a metallic chemical element, used in photoelectric cells, radiation therapy, etc.

ces·sa·tion (se sā'shən) *n.* [< L *cessare,* cease] a ceasing or stopping

ces·sion (sesh'ən) *n.* [< L *cedere,* to yield] a ceding or giving up (of rights, property, etc.) to another

cess·pool (ses'pōōl') *n.* [< ? It *cesso,* privy] a deep hole in the ground to receive drainage or sewage from the sinks, toilets, etc. of a house

ce·ta·cean (sə tā'shən) *n.* [< L *cetus,* whale] a fishlike water mammal, including the whale, porpoise, and dolphin — *adj.* of the cetaceans

cf. [L *confer*] compare

cg centigram(s)

Ch. or **ch.** **1** chapter **2** church

Cha·blis (sha blē') *n.* [occas. **c-**] a dry, white Burgundy wine, orig. from Chablis, France

chafe (chāf) *vt.* **chafed, chaf'ing** [< L *calefacere,* make warm] **1** to rub so as to make warm **2** to wear away or make sore by rubbing **3** to annoy; irritate — *vi.* **1** to rub (on or against) **2** to be vexed

chaff (chaf) *n.* [OE *ceaf*] **1** threshed or winnowed husks of grain **2** anything worthless **3** teasing; banter — *vt., vi.* to tease in a good-natured way

chaf·ing dish (chāf'iŋ) a pan with a heating apparatus beneath it, to cook food at the table or to keep food hot

cha·grin (shə grin') *n.* [Fr] embarrassment and annoyance due to failure, disappointment, etc. — *vt.* **-grined', -grin'ing** to cause to feel chagrin

chain (chān) *n.* [< L *catena*] **1** a flexible series of joined links **2** [*pl.*] *a)* bonds; shackles *b)* captivity **3** a chainlike

---

THESAURUS

heart of; see also CENTRAL.

century *n.* 100 years, centenary, era; see AGE 3, TIME 1.

ceramics *n.* earthenware, crockery, porcelain; see POTTERY, SCULPTURE.

cereal *n.* corn, breakfast food, seed; see GRAIN 1.

ceremonial *a.* ritual, formal, stately; see CONVENTIONAL 3.

ceremony *n.* **1** [A public event] function, commemoration, services; see CELEBRATION. **2** [A rite] observance, ritual, rite, service, solemnity, formality, custom, tradition, liturgy, ordinance, sacrament, liturgical practice, conformity, etiquette, politeness, propriety, preciseness, decorum, strictness, nicety, formalism, conventionality.

certain *a.* **1** [Confident] calm, assured, sure, positive, satisfied, self-confident, undoubting, believing,

secure, untroubled, unconcerned, undisturbed, unperturbed, fully convinced, assertive, cocksure; see CONFIDENT. **2** [Beyond doubt] indisputable, unquestionable, assured, positive, real, true, genuine, plain, clear, undoubted, guaranteed, unmistakable, sure, incontrovertible, supreme, undeniable, definite, unqualified, infallible, undisputed, unerring, sound, reliable, trustworthy, evident, conclusive, authoritative, irrefutable, unconditional, incontestable, unquestioned, absolute, unequivocal, inescapable, conclusive, in the bag*, on ice*, done up*, salted away*; see also TRUE 1, 3. **3** [Fixed] settled, concluded, set; see DEFINITE 1, DETERMINED 1. **4** [Specific but not named] special, definite, individual, marked, specified, defined, one, some, a few, a couple,

several, upwards of, regular, particular, singular, precise, specific, express; see also SOME. **—for certain** without doubt, absolutely, certainly; see SURELY.

certainly *a.* positively, absolutely, unquestionably; see SURELY.

certificate *n.* declaration, warrant, voucher, testimonial, credentials, license, testament, endorsement, affidavit, certification, coupon, document, pass, ticket, warranty, guarantee, testimony, receipt, affirmation, docket, record; see also RECORD 1.

certify *v.* swear, attest, state; see DECLARE, TESTIFY 2.

chain *n.* **1** [A series of links] series, train, set, string, connection, cable, link, charm bracelet, ring series, shackle, manacle; see also SERIES. **2**

measuring instrument, as for surveying **4** a series of things connected causally, logically, physically, etc. **5** a number of stores, etc. owned by one company — *vt.* **1** to fasten with chains **2** to restrain, etc.

chain gang a gang of prisoners chained together, as when working

chain'-link' *adj.* designating a fence made of galvanized steel links that are continuously interwoven

chain reaction **1** a self-sustaining series of chemical or nuclear reactions in which the reaction products keep the process going **2** a series of events, each of which results in the following one

chain saw a portable power saw with an endless chain that carries the cutting teeth

chair (cher) *n.* [< L *cathedra:* see CATHEDRAL] **1** a piece of furniture with a back, for one person to sit on **2** an important or official position **3** a chairman — *vt.* **1** to seat **2** to preside over as chairman

chair'lift' *n.* seats suspended from a power-driven endless cable, used to carry skiers up a slope

chair'man (-mən) *n., pl.* **-men** a person in charge of a meeting, committee, etc. Also **chair'per·son** —**chair'-man·ship'** *n.* —**chair'wom'an,** *pl.* **-wom'en,** *n.fem.*

chaise (shāz) *n.* [Fr] a lightweight carriage, having two or four wheels

chaise longue (shāz' lôŋ'; *often also* lounj') *pl.* **chaise longues** (lôŋz') [Fr, lit., long chair] a couchlike chair with a long seat Also **chaise lounge** (lounj')

cha·let (shal ā', shal'ā) *n.* [Swiss-Fr] **1** a Swiss house with overhanging eaves **2** any similar building

chal·ice (chal'is) *n.* [< L *calix,* cup] **1** a cup **2** the cup for Communion wine

chalk (chôk) *n.* [< L *calx,* limestone] **1** a soft, whitish limestone **2** a piece of chalk or chalklike substance used for writing on a blackboard — *adj.* made with chalk — *vt.* to mark or rub with chalk —**chalk up** **1** to score, get, or achieve **2** to charge or credit —**chalk'i·ness** *n.* —**chalk'y, -i·er, -i·est,** *adj.*

chalk'board' *n.* BLACKBOARD

chal·lenge (chal'ənj) *n.* [< L *calumnia,* calumny] **1** a demand for identification **2** a calling into question **3** a call to a duel, contest, etc. **4** anything that calls for special effort — *vt.* **-lenged, -leng·ing** to subject to a challenge — *vi.* to make a challenge —**chal'lenger** *n.*

chal·lis or **chal·lie** (shal'ē) *n.* [< ?] a soft, lightweight fabric of wool, etc.

cham·ber (chām'bər) *n.* [< LL *camera,* a chamber, room] **1** a room, esp. a bedroom **2** [*pl.*] a judge's office near the courtroom **3** an assembly hall **4** a legislative or judicial body **5** a council [*chamber* of commerce] **6** an enclosed space **7** the part of a gun holding the charge or of a revolver holding the cartridge —**cham'bered** *adj.*

cham'ber·lain (-lin) *n.* [< OHG *chamarlinc*] **1** an officer in charge of the household of a ruler or lord; steward **2** a high official in certain royal courts **3** [Brit.] a treasurer

cham'ber·maid' *n.* a woman whose work is taking care of bedrooms

chamber music music for performance by a small group, as a string quartet

chamber of commerce an association established to further the business interests of its community

cham·bray (sham'brā') *n.* [var. of *cambric*] a smooth cotton fabric of white threads woven across a colored warp

cha·meleon (kə mēl'ē ən, -mēl'yən) *n.* [< Gr *chamai,* on the ground + *leōn,* LION] any of various lizards that can change the color of their skin

cham·ois (sham'ē) *n., pl.* **cham'ois** [Fr] **1** a small, goat-like antelope of the mountains of Europe and the Caucasus **2** a soft leather made from the skin of chamois, sheep, deer, etc.: also **chammy** (sham'ē), *pl.* **cham'mies**

chamo·mile (kam'ə mil', -mēl') *n.* [< Gr *chamaimēlon,* earth apple] a plant whose dried, daisylike flower heads are used in a medicinal tea

champ¹ (champ) *vt.* [prob. echoic] to chew hard and noisily; munch

champ² (champ) *n.* [Colloq.] CHAMPION (sense 2)

cham·pagne (sham pān') *n.* an effervescent white wine, orig. from Champagne, region in NE France

cham·paign (sham pān') *n.* [< L *campus,* field] flat, open country

cham·pion (cham'pē ən) *n.* [< LL *campio,* gladiator] **1** one who fights for another or for a cause; defender **2** a winner of first place in a competition — *adj.* excelling all others — *vt.* to fight for; defend; support —**cham'pi·on·ship'** *n.*

chance (chans) *n.* [< L *cadere,* to fall] **1** the happening of events without apparent cause; luck **2** an unpredictable event **3** a risk or gamble **4** a ticket in a lottery **5** an opportunity **6** [*often pl.*] a possibility or probability — *adj.* accidental — *vi.* **chanced, chanc'ing** to have the fortune, good or bad (*to*) — *vt.* to risk —**by chance** accidentally —**chance on** (or **upon**) to find or meet by chance —**(the) chances are** the likelihood is —**on the (off) chance** relying on the (remote) possibility

chan·cel (chan'səl) *n.* [< L *cancelli,* lattices] the part of a church around the altar, for the clergy and the choir

chan'cel·ler·y (-ər ē) *n., pl.* **-ies** [< ML *cancellaria*] the rank or position of a chancellor

chan·cel·lor (chan'sə lər) *n.* [< LL *cancellarius,* secretary] **1** a high government official, as, in certain countries, a prime minister **2** in some universities, the president or other executive officer

chance'-med'ley *n.* **1** accidental homicide **2** haphazard action

chan·cery (chan'sər ē) *n., pl.* **-ies** [< ML *cancellaria*] **1** a court of equity **2** an office of public archives **3** *R.C.Ch.* the diocesan office performing secretarial services for the bishop

chan·cre (shaŋ'kər) *n.* [Fr: see CANCER] a sore or ulcer of syphilis

chancy (chan'sē) *adj.* **-i·er, -i·est** risky; uncertain — **chanc'i·ness** *n.*

chan·de·lier (shan'də lir') *n.* [Fr < L *candela,* candle] a lighting fixture hung from a ceiling, with branches for candles, light bulbs, etc.

chandler (chand'lər) *n.* [< L *candela,* candle] **1** a maker of candles **2** a retailer of supplies, as for ships

change (chānj) *vt.* **changed, chang'ing** [< L *cambire,* to barter] **1** to put or take (a thing) in place of something else [*change* jobs] **2** to exchange [*change* seats] **3** to

---

THESAURUS

[A sequence] succession, progression, continuity; see SERIES.

chain *v.* connect, attach, secure; see FASTEN, HOLD 1.

chair *n.* **1** [A single seat] seat, place, room, space, cathedra; see also FURNITURE. *Chairs include the following:* stool, throne, footstool, rocker, wing chair, armchair, easy chair, wheelchair, highchair, occasional chair, dining-room chair, desk chair, kitchen chair, deck chair, lawn chair, swivel chair, folding chair. **2** [A position of authority] throne, professorship, fellowship; see INFLUENCE.

chairman *n.* chairperson, chairwoman, president, administrator, director, toastmaster, speaker, moderator, monitor, leader, principal, captain, master of ceremonies, MC, emcee; see also LEADER 2.

chalk up *v.* credit, enter, register; see ADD 1, RECORD 1, SCORE 1.

challenge *n.* dare, provocation, threat; see OBJECTION.

challenge *v.* **1** [To invite to a con-

test] defy, denounce, invite competition; see DARE 2, THREATEN. **2** [To question] dispute, inquire, search out; see ASK, DOUBT, QUESTION.

champion *n.* vanquisher, conqueror, victor; see HERO 1, WINNER.

chance *a.* accidental, unplanned, unintentional; see AIMLESS, INCIDENTAL.

chance *n.* **1** [The powers of uncertainty] fate, fortune, hazard, casualty, lot, accident, luck, good luck, bad luck, destiny, outcome, cast, lottery, gamble, adventure, contingency, happening, future, doom, destination, occurrence, Lady Luck*, turn of the cards, heads or tails*. —*Ant.* PURPOSE, aim, design. **2** [A possibility] opening, occasion, prospect; see OPPORTUNITY 1, POSSIBILITY 2. **3** [Probability; *often plural*] likelihood, feasibility, indications; see ODDS. — **by chance** by accident, as it happens, unexpectedly; see ACCIDENTALLY. —**on the off chance** in case, in the event that, supposing; see IF.

chance *v.* venture, stake, hazard, wager, jeopardize, speculate, tempt fate, tempt fortune, play with fire, take a shot, take a leap in the dark, buy a pig in a poke, go out on a limb*, chance it, take a fling at, put all one's eggs in one basket, skate on thin ice, run the risk; see also RISK.

change *n.* **1** [An alteration] modification, correction, remodeling, switch, reformation, reconstruction, shift, reform, conversion, transformation, revolution, rearrangement, adjustment, readjustment, reorganization, reshaping, renovation, realignment, redirection, reprogramming, variation, addition, refinement, advance, development, diversification, turn, turnover, enlargement, revision, qualification, distortion, compression, contraction, widening, narrowing, lengthening, flattening, shortening, fitting, setting, adjusting, rounding, gone every which way, ups and downs. **2** [Substitution] switch, replacement, make different; alter — *vi.* **1** to alter; vary **2** to leave one train, plane, etc. and board another **3** to put on other clothes **4** to make an exchange — *n.* **1** a substitution, alteration, or variation **2** variety **3** another set of clothes **4** *a*) money returned as the difference between the price and the greater sum presented *b*) coins or bills that together equal a single larger coin or bill *c*) small coins — **change off** to take turns — **ring the changes** to ring a set of bells with all possible variations —**change′a·ble** *adj.* —**change′less** *adj.*

change′ling (-liŋ) *n.* a child secretly put in the place of another, as by fairies

change of life MENOPAUSE

change′o′ver *n.* a complete change, as in goods produced

chan·nel (chan′əl) *n.* ⟦see CANAL⟧ **1** the bed or deeper part of a river, harbor, etc. **2** a body of water joining two larger ones **3** any means of passage **4** [*pl.*] the official course of transmission of communications **5** a groove or furrow **6** a frequency band assigned to a radio or television station — *vt.* **-neled** or **-nelled, -nel·ing** or **-nel·ling 1** to make a channel in **2** to send through a channel

chan′nel·ize′ (-īz′) *vt.* **-ized′, -iz′ing** to provide a channel for

chan·son (shän sōn′) *n., pl.* **-sons** (-sōn′) ⟦Fr⟧ a song

chant (chant) *n.* ⟦< L *cantare,* to sing⟧ **1** a song; esp., a liturgical song with a series of syllables or words sung to each tone **2** a singsong way of speaking — *vi., vt.* to sing or say in a chant —**chant′er** *n.*

chan·teuse (shan tœz′) *n.* ⟦Fr⟧ a woman singer, esp. of popular ballads

chan·tey (shan′tē, chan′tē) *n., pl.* **-teys** a song formerly sung by sailors in rhythm with their motions while working Also **chan′ty,** *pl.* **-ties**

chan·ti·cleer (chan′ti klir′) *n.* ⟦< OFr *chante-cler,* lit., sing loud⟧ a rooster

Cha·nu·kah (khä′noo kä′) HANUKA

chaos (kā′äs′) *n.* ⟦< Gr, space⟧ extreme confusion or disorder —**cha·ot·ic** (kā ät′ik) *adj.*

chap¹ (chäp, chap) *n.* ⟦< ?⟧ CHOP²

chap² (chap) *n.* ⟦< Brit *chapman,* peddler⟧ [Colloq.] a man; fellow

chap³ (chap) *vt., vi.* **chapped** or **chapt, chap′ping** ⟦ME *chappen,* cut⟧ to crack open; split; roughen, as skin — *n.* a chapped place in the skin

chap. 1 chaplain **2** chapter

chap·ar·ral (chap′ə ral′, shap′-) *n.* ⟦Sp < *chaparro,* evergreen oak⟧ [Southwest] a thicket of shrubs, etc.

cha·peau (sha pō′) *n., pl.* **-peaus′** or **-peaux′** (-pōz′) ⟦Fr⟧ a hat

chapel (chap′əl) *n.* ⟦< ML *cappella,* dim. of *cappa,* cape⟧ **1** a small church **2** a private place of worship, as in a hospital

chap·er·on or **chap·er·one** (shap′ər ōn′, shap′ər ōn′) *n.* ⟦< OFr, hood⟧ a person, esp. an older woman, who accompanies young unmarried people to supervise their behavior — *vt., vi.* **-oned′, -on′ing** to act as chaperon (to) —**chap′er·on·age** *n.*

chap·lain (chap′lən) *n.* ⟦see CHAPEL⟧ **1** a clergyman attached to a chapel **2** a clergyman serving in a religious capacity with the armed forces, or in a prison, hospital, etc.

chap·let (chap′lit) *n.* ⟦< LL *cappa,* cape⟧ **1** a garland for the head **2** a string of beads, esp. prayer beads

chaps (chaps, shaps) *n.pl.* ⟦< MexSp *chaparreras*⟧ leather trousers without a seat, worn over ordinary trousers by cowboys to protect their legs

chap·ter (chap′tər) *n.* ⟦< L *caput,* head⟧ **1** a main division, as of a book **2** a local branch of an organization

char (chär) *vt., vi.* **charred, char′ring** ⟦< CHARCOAL⟧ **1** to reduce to charcoal by burning **2** to burn slightly; scorch

char·ac·ter (kar′ək tər, kar′ik-) *n.* ⟦< Gr *charassein,* engrave⟧ **1** any letter, figure, or symbol used in writing and printing **2** a distinctive trait **3** kind or sort **4** behavior typical of a person or group **5** moral strength **6** reputation **7** status; position **8** a person in a play, novel, etc. **9** [Colloq.] an eccentric person

char′ac·ter·is′tic (-is′tik) *adj.* typical; distinctive — *n.* a distinguishing trait or quality —**char′ac·ter·is′ti·cal·ly** *adv.*

char′ac·ter·ize′ (-īz′) *vt.* **-ized′, -iz′ing 1** to describe the particular traits of **2** to be a characteristic of —**char′ac·ter·i·za′tion** *n.*

cha·rade (shə rād′) *n.* ⟦Fr < Prov *charrar,* to gossip⟧ **1** [*pl.*] a game in which words to be guessed are pantomimed, often syllable by syllable **2** a pretense or fiction

char·broil or **char-broil** (chär′broil′) *vt.* to broil over a charcoal fire

char·coal (chär′kōl′) *n.* ⟦ME *char cole*⟧ a dark, porous form of carbon made by partially burning wood or other organic matter in an airless kiln or retort: used for fuel, etc.

THESAURUS

exchange; see SHIFT 1. **3** [Variety] diversity, novelty, variance; see DIFFERENCE 1, VARIETY 1. **4** [Small coins] silver, coins, chicken feed*; see MONEY 1.
change *v.* **1** [To make different] vary, turn, alternate; see ALTER 1. **2** [To become different] alter, vary, modify, evolve, be converted, turn into, resolve into, grow, ripen, mellow, mature, transform, reform, moderate, adapt, adjust; see also BECOME. **3** [To put in place of another] displace, supplant, transpose; see EXCHANGE 1, REPLACE 1, SUBSTITUTE. **4** [To change clothing] undress, disrobe, make one's toilet; see DRESS 1.
changeable *a.* **1** [Said of persons] fickle, flighty, unreliable; see UNSTABLE 2. **2** [Said of conditions] variable, unsteady, unsettled; see UNCERTAIN.
changed *a.* **1** [Exchanged] substituted, replaced, traded; see RETURNED. **2** [Altered] qualified, reconditioned, modified, limited, reformed, shifted, moved, mutated, deteriorated, aged, run down, rewritten, conditioned, modernized, remodeled, reprogrammed, rescheduled, redone, done over, brought up to date, edited, moderated, innovated, deviated, diverted, fluctuated, chopped, warped, passed to, recreated, converted, transfigured, metamorphosed, transmuted.—*Ant.* UNCHANGED, PERMANENT, final.
changing *a.* changeful, changeable,

mobile, dynamic, alternative, unstable, inconstant, uncertain, mutable, fluid, mercurial, declining, deteriorating, degenerating, unsteady, irresolute, wavering; see also UNCERTAIN.—*Ant.* FIXED, stable, unchanging.
channel *n.* conduit, tube, canal, duct, course, gutter, furrow, trough, runway, tunnel, strait, sound, race, sewer, main, artery, vein, ditch, aqueduct, canyon; see also WAY 2.
channel *v.* route, send, direct; see SEND 1.
chant *n.* religious song, chorus, incantation; see SONG.
chant *v.* intone, chorus, carol; see SING.
chaos *n.* turmoil, anarchy, discord; see CONFUSION, DISORDER.
chaotic *a.* disorganized, disordered, uncontrolled; see CONFUSED 2.
chapel *n.* place of worship, tabernacle, God's house; see CHURCH 1.
chapter *n.* part, section, book; see DIVISION 2.
character *n.* **1** [The dominant quality] temper, temperament, attitude, nature, sense, complex, mood, streak, attribute, badge, tone, style, aspect, complexion, spirit, genius, humor, frame, grain, vein; see also CHARACTERISTIC. **2** [The sum of a person's characteristics] personality, reputation, constitution, repute, individuality, estimation, record, caliber, standing, type, shape, quality, habit, appearance; see also KIND 2. **3** [A

symbol, especially in writing] sign, figure, emblem; see LETTER 1, MARK 1. **4** [A queer or striking person] personality, figure, personage, original, eccentric, crank*, nut*, oddball*, weirdo*, freak*, psycho*. —**in character** consistent, usual, predictable; see CONVENTIONAL 1. —**out of character** inconsistent, unpredictable, unusual; see UNEXPECTED.
characteristic *a.* innate, fixed, essential, distinctive, distinguishing, marked, discriminative, symbolic, individualizing, representative, specific, personal, original, peculiar, individualistic, individual, idiosyncratic, unique, special, particular, symptomatic, private, exclusive, inherent, inborn, inbred, ingrained, native, indicative, inseparable, in the blood; see also NATURAL 2, TYPICAL.—*Ant.* IRREGULAR, erratic, aberrant.
characteristic *n.* flavor, attribute, quality, faculty, peculiarity, individuality, style, aspect, tone, tinge, feature, distinction, manner, bearing, inclination, nature, personality, temperament, frame, originality, singularity, qualification, virtue, mark, essence, caliber, complexion, particularity, idiosyncrasy, trick, earmark, mannerism, trademark, badge, symptom, disposition, specialty, mood, character, bent, tendency, component, thing, bag*.
characterize *v.* delineate, designate, portray; see DEFINE 2, DESCRIBE.

chard (chärd) *n.* [< L *carduus*, thistle] a kind of beet with large, edible leaves and stalks

char·don·nay (shär'də nā') *n.* [also C-] a dry white wine

charge (chärj) *vt.* **charged, charg'ing** [ult. < L *carrus*, wagon] 1 to load or fill (*with* something) 2 to add an electrical charge to (a battery, etc.) 3 to give as a duty, command, etc. to 4 to accuse 5 to make liable for (an error, etc.) 6 to ask as a price 7 to record as a debt 8 to attack vigorously — *vi.* 1 to ask payment (*for*) 2 to attack vigorously — *n.* 1 a load or burden 2 the necessary quantity, as of fuel, for a container or device 3 the amount of chemical energy stored in a battery 4 a cartridge or shell, or the amount of gunpowder needed to fire a gun, etc. 5 responsibility or care (*of*) 6 a person or thing entrusted to one's care 7 instruction; command 8 accusation; indictment 9 cost 10 a debt, debit, or expense 11 an onslaught —**in charge** (**of**) having the responsibility, control, or supervision (of) —**charge'able** *adj.*

charge account an arrangement by which a customer may pay for purchases within a specified future period

charge card (or **plate**) a thin, flat, plastic card embossed with the owner's name, account number, etc., used as a stamp on bills when charging purchases

charg'er *n.* 1 a person or thing that charges 2 a horse ridden in battle

chari·ot (char'ē ət) *n.* [see CAR] a horse-drawn, two-wheeled cart used in ancient times for war, racing, etc. — **char'i·oteer'** (-ə tir') *n.*

cha·risma (kə riz'mə) *n., pl.* **-mata** (-mə tə) [< Gr, favor, grace] a special charm or allure that inspires allegiance or devotion

char·is·matic (kar'iz mat'ik) *adj.* 1 of or having charisma 2 designating or of a religious group that stresses direct divine inspiration, manifested as in glossolalia, etc. — *n.* a member of a charismatic group

chari·table (char'i tə bəl) *adj.* 1 generous to the needy 2 of or for charity 3 kind and forgiving —**char'i·tably** *adv.*

char·ity (char'i tē) *n., pl.* **-ties** [< L *caritas*, affection] 1 *Christian Theol.* love for one's fellow men 2 leniency in judging others 3 *a*) generosity toward the needy *b*) help so given 4 a welfare institution, fund, etc.

char·la·tan (shär'lə tən) *n.* [ult. < VL *cerretanus*, seller of papal indulgences] a fraud; quack; impostor —**char'la·tan·ism** or **char'la·tanry** *n.*

Charles·ton (chärls'tən) *n.* [after *Charleston*, seaport in S.C.] a lively dance of the 1920's, in 4/4 time

char'ley horse (chär'lē) [Colloq.] a cramp in a muscle, esp. a thigh muscle

charm (chärm) *n.* [< L *carmen*] 1 an action, object, or words assumed to have magic power 2 a trinket worn on a bracelet, etc. 3 a quality that attracts or delights — *vt., vi.*

1 to act on as if by magic 2 to fascinate; delight — **charm'er** *n.* —**charm'ing** *adj.* —**charm'ingly** *adv.*

char·nel (**house**) (chär'nəl) [< LL *carnale*, graveyard] a building or place where corpses or bones are deposited

Cha·ron (ker'ən) *Gr. Myth.* the ferryman on the river Styx

chart (chärt) *n.* [< Gr *chartēs*, layer of papyrus] 1 a map, esp. for use in navigation 2 an information sheet with tables, graphs, etc. 3 a table, graph, etc. — *vt.* 1 to make a chart of 2 to plan (a course of action)

char·ter (chärt'ər) *n.* [see prec.] 1 a franchise granted by a government 2 a written statement of basic laws or principles; constitution 3 written permission to form a local chapter or lodge of a society — *vt.* 1 to grant a charter to 2 to hire for exclusive use

charter member a founder or original member

char·treuse (shär trōōz', -trōōs') *n.* [Fr] pale, yellowish green

char·woman (chär'woom'ən) *n., pl.* **-wom'en** [see CHORE] a cleaning woman

chary (cher'ē, char'-) *adj.* **-i·er, -i·est** [< OE *cearig*, sorrowful] 1 not taking chances; cautious 2 sparing — **char'i·ly** *adv.* —**char'i·ness** *n.*

chase[1] (chās) *vt.* **chased, chas'ing** [ult. < L *capere*, take] 1 to follow so as to catch 2 to run after 3 to drive away 4 to hunt — *vi.* 1 to go in pursuit 2 [Colloq.] to rush — *n.* 1 a chasing; pursuit 2 the hunting of game — **give chase** to pursue

chase[2] (chās) *vt.* **chased, chas'ing** [< OFr *enchasser*] to ornament (metal) as by engraving

chas'er *n.* [Colloq.] a mild drink, as water, taken after whiskey, etc.

chasm (kaz'əm) *n.* [< Gr *chasma*] 1 a deep crack in the earth's surface; abyss 2 any break or gap; rift

chas·sis (chas'ē, shas'-) *n., pl.* **-sis'** (-ēz') [Fr] 1 the frame, wheels, etc. of a motor vehicle, but not the body or engine 2 *a*) a frame, as for the parts of a TV set *b*) the assembled frame and parts

chaste (chāst) *adj.* [< L *castus*, pure] 1 not indulging in unlawful sexual activity 2 decent; modest 3 simple in style; not ornate —**chaste'ly** *adv.*

chas·ten (chās'ən) *vt.* [< L *castigare*, punish] 1 to punish so as to correct 2 to restrain or subdue

chas·tise (chas tiz') *vt.* **-tised', -tis'ing** [see prec.] 1 to punish, esp. by beating 2 to scold sharply —**chas·tise'ment** *n.* —**chas·tis'er** *n.*

chas·tity (chas'tə tē) *n.* a being chaste; specif., *a*) virtuousness *b*) sexual abstinence; celibacy *c*) decency or modesty

chasu·ble (chaz'ə bəl, chas'-) *n.* [< ML *casula*] a sleeveless outer vestment worn by priests at Mass

chat (chat) *vi.* **chat'ted, chat'ting** [< CHATTER] to talk in a light, informal manner — *n.* light, informal talk

châ·teau (sha tō') *n., pl.* **-teaux'** or **-teaus'** (-tōz', -tō') [Fr < L *castellum*, castle] 1 a French feudal castle 2 a

---

◼ THESAURUS ◼

charge *n.* 1 [A charged sale] entry, debit, credit; see PRICE. 2 [An attack] assault, invasion, outbreak; see ATTACK. —**in charge** responsible, controlling, managing; see RESPONSIBLE 1.

charge *v.* 1 [To ask a price] require, sell for, fix the price at; see PRICE. 2 [To enter on a charge account] debit, put to account, charge to, run up an account, take on account, put on one's account, incur a debt, put down, credit, encumber, sell on credit, buy on credit, chalk up, put on the books, carry, put on the cuff; see also BUY, SELL. 3 [To attack] assail, assault, invade; see ATTACK. 4 [To accuse] indict, censure, impute; see BLAME.

charged *a.* 1 [Bought but not paid for] debited, placed on the account of, unpaid, on credit, on time, owing, owed, on the cuff*, on the tab*; see also BOUGHT, DUE. 2 [Accused] taxed, confronted with, arraigned; see ACCUSED.

charitable *a.* open-handed, liberal, philanthropic; see GENEROUS, KIND.

charity *n.* 1 [Kindness] benevolence, magnanimity, compassion; see KINDNESS 1, TOLERANCE 1. 2 [An organization to aid the needy] charitable institution, welfare organization, eleemosynary foundation; see

FOUNDATION 3.

charm *n.* 1 [An object thought to possess power] amulet, talisman, fetish, mascot, good-luck piece, lucky piece, rabbit's foot. 2 [The quality of being charming] grace, attractiveness, attraction; see BEAUTY 1.

charm *v.* enchant, captivate, voodoo, possess, enrapture, enthrall, transport, delight, please, entrance, bewitch, mesmerize; see also FASCINATE.

charmed *a.* enchanted, bewitched, enraptured, entranced, captivated, attracted, lured, tempted, enticed, bedazzled, hypnotized, mesmerized, under a spell, in a trance, spellbound, moonstruck, possessed, obsessed, psyched*, out of it*; see also FASCINATED.

charming *a.* enchanting, bewitching, entrancing, captivating, cute, fascinating, delightful, lovable, sweet, winning, irresistible, attractive, amiable, appealing, alluring, charismatic, pleasing, nice, graceful, winsome, seducing, seductive, desirable, enticing, tempting, inviting, ravishing, enrapturing, glamorous, elegant, infatuating, dainty, delicate, absorbing, tantalizing, engrossing, titillating, engaging, enthralling, rapturous, electrifying, lovely, intriguing, thrilling, fair, exquisite, likable, diverting,

fetching, provocative, delectable, sexy*, sharp*, smooth*.—*Ant.* OFFENSIVE, disgusting, unpleasant.

chart *n.* graph, outline, diagram; see MAP, PLAN 1.

chart *v.* map, outline, draft; see PLAN 2.

charter *n.* contract, settlement, pact; see AGREEMENT 2, TREATY.

chase[1] *v.* trail, track, seek; see HUNT 1, PURSUE 1.

chaste *a.* immaculate, unstained, clean, innocent, virginal, unblemished, unsullied, moral, modest, proper, decent, uncontaminated, virgin, celibate, platonic, controlled, unmarried, unwed, spotless, infallible, strong; see also INNOCENT 2.—*Ant.* WEAK, corruptible, frail.

chastise *v.* scold, discipline, spank; see PUNISH.

chastity *n.* innocence, purity, virtue, uprightness, honor, celibacy, integrity, decency, delicacy, cleanness, goodness, bachelorhood, unmarried state, demureness, abstinence, morality, chasteness, modesty, sinlessness, continence, coldness, restraint, virginity, spotlessness.— *Ant.* LEWDNESS, adultery, licentiousness.

chat *v.* converse, prattle, chatter; see TALK 1.

chat·elaine (shat″l ān′) *n.* ⟦Fr⟧ **1** the mistress of a château **2** a woman's ornamental chain or clasp

chat·tel (chat″l) *n.* ⟦see CATTLE⟧ a movable item of personal property

chat·ter (chat′ər) *vi.* ⟦echoic⟧ **1** to make short, rapid,
indistinct sounds, as apes do **2** to talk much and foolishly
3 to click together rapidly, as teeth do from cold — *n.* **1** a
chattering **2** foolish talk —**chat′terer** *n.*

chat′ter·box′ *n.* an incessant talker

chat·ty (chat′ē) *adj.* **-tier, -ti·est** fond of chatting —**chat′-
tily** (-′lē) *adv.* —**chat′ti·ness** *n.*

chauf·feur (shō′fər, shō fur′) *n.* ⟦Fr, lit., stoker⟧ one
hired to drive a private automobile for someone else — *vt.*
to act as chauffeur to

chau·vin·ism (shō′vin iz′əm) *n.* ⟦after N. *Chauvin*,
fanatical Fr patriot⟧ **1** militant and fanatic patriotism;
jingoism **2** unreasoning devotion to one's race, sex, etc. —
chau·vin·ist *n., adj.* —**chau·vin·is′tic** *adj.* —**chau′vin·**
is′ti·cally *adv.*

cheap (chēp) *adj.* ⟦ult. < L *caupo*, tradesman⟧ **1** low in
price **2** worth more than the price **3** easily got **4** of little
value **5** contemptible **6** [Colloq.] stingy — *adv.* at a low
cost —**cheap′ly** *adv.* —**cheap′ness** *n.*

cheap′en *vt., vi.* to make or become cheap or cheaper

cheap shot [Slang] an unnecessarily rough or mean action
or remark

cheap′skate′ *n.* [Slang] a stingy person

cheat (chēt) *n.* ⟦< L *ex-*, out + *cadere*, to fall⟧ **1** a fraud;
swindle **2** a swindler — *vt.* **1** to defraud; swindle **2** to foil
or elude ⟦to *cheat* death⟧ — *vi.* **1** to be dishonest or deceitful **2** [Slang] to be sexually unfaithful: often with *on* —
cheat′er *n.*

check (chek) *n.* ⟦< OFr *eschec*, a check in chess⟧ **1** a
sudden stop **2** any restraint **3** one that restrains **4** a
supervision or test of accuracy, etc. **5** a mark (✓) to show
verification **6** an identification ticket, token, etc. ⟦a hat
check⟧ **7** one's bill at a restaurant or bar **8** a written order
to a bank to pay a sum of money **9** a pattern of squares, or
one of the squares **10** *Chess* the state of a king that is in
danger — *interj.* [Colloq.] agreed! right! — *vt.* **1** to stop
suddenly **2** to restrain; curb; block **3** to test, verify, etc.
by examination or comparison: often with *out* **4** to mark
with a check (✓): often with *off* **5** to mark with a pattern
of squares **6** to deposit temporarily **7** to clear (esp. luggage) for shipment **8** *Chess* to place (the opponent's king)
in check — *vi.* **1** to agree with one another, item for item:
often with *out* **2** to investigate or verify: often with *on, up
on* —**check in 1** to register at a hotel, etc. **2** [Colloq.] to
present oneself, as at work —**check out 1** to pay and
leave a hotel, etc. **2** to add up the prices of (items

selected) for payment **3** to prove to be accurate, etc. —**in
check** under control —**check′er** *n.*

check′book′ *n.* a book of detachable forms for writing
bank checks

checked (chekt) *adj.* having a pattern of squares

check′er·board′ *n.* a square board with 64 squares of two
alternating colors, used in checkers and chess

check·ered (chek′ərd) *adj.* **1** having a pattern of squares
2 varied

check′ers (-ərz) *n.pl.* **1** [*with sing. v.*] a game for two
played with flat disks on a checkerboard **2** the disks

checking account a bank account against which the
depositor can draw checks

check′list′ *n.* a list of things, names, etc. to be referred to
Also **check list**

check′mate′ (-māt′) *n.* ⟦ult. < Pers *šāh māt*, the king is
dead⟧ **1** *Chess a*) the move that wins the game by checking the opponent's king so that it cannot be protected *b*)
the condition of the king after this move **2** total defeat,
frustration, etc. — *vt.* **-mat′ed, -mat′ing 1** to place in
checkmate **2** to defeat; thwart

check′off′ *n.* the withholding of members' dues for the
union by the employer

check′out′ *n.* **1** the act or place of checking out purchases
2 the time by which one must check out of a hotel, etc.

check′point′ *n.* a place on a road, etc. where traffic is
inspected

check′room′ *n.* a room in which hats, coats, etc. may be
left until called for

check′up′ *n.* a medical examination

Ched·dar (cheese) (ched′ər) ⟦after *Cheddar*, England⟧
⟦*often* **c-**⟧ a hard, smooth cheese

cheek (chēk) *n.* ⟦OE *ceoke*, jaw⟧ **1** either side of the face
below the eye **2** [Colloq.] sauciness; impudence —**tongue
in cheek** jestingly; mockingly

cheek′bone′ *n.* the bone across the upper cheek, just
below the eye

cheek′y *adj.* **-i·er, -i·est** [Colloq.] saucy; impudent —
cheek′i·ness *n.*

cheep (chēp) *n.* ⟦echoic⟧ the short, shrill sound made by a
young bird — *vt., vi.* to make, or utter with, this sound —
cheep′er *n.*

cheer (chir) *n.* ⟦< Gr *kara*, the head⟧ **1** state of mind or
of feeling; spirit ⟦be of good *cheer*⟧ **2** gladness; joy **3** festive entertainment **4** encouragement **5** *a*) a glad, excited
shout to urge on, greet, etc. *b*) a rallying cry — *vt.* **1** to
gladden; comfort: often with *up* **2** to urge on, greet, or
applaud with cheers — *vi.* **1** to become cheerful: usually
with *up* **2** to shout cheers

THESAURUS

chatter *v.* gossip, chat, prattle; see
BABBLE.

cheap *a.* **1** [Low in relative price]
inexpensive, low-priced, moderate,
family-size, economy-size, budget,
depreciated, slashed, cut-rate, on
sale, competitive, lowered, thrifty,
bargain, irregular, reduced, cut-
priced, low-cost, at a bargain, reasonable, marked down, half-priced,
popular-priced, worth the money,
dime-a-dozen*, dirt-cheap*, for peanuts*, for a song, second, bargain-
basement*; see also ECONOMICAL.—
Ant. EXPENSIVE, dear, costly. **2** [Low
in quality] inferior, ordinary, shoddy;
see COMMON 1, POOR 2. **3** [Dishonest
or base] dirty, tawdry, low; see DIS-
HONEST, MEAN 3, VULGAR.

cheapen *v.* spoil, depreciate,
demean; see CORRUPT, DAMAGE.

cheaply *a.* economically, inexpensively, advantageously, at a bargain
price, at a good price, on sale, at cost,
below cost, discounted, at a discount,
reduced, at a reduced price, sacrificed, dirt cheap*, given away*,
stolen*.

cheat *n.* rogue, cheater, confidence
man, quack, charlatan, conniver,
fraud, swindler, chiseler, beguiler,
fake, bluff, deceiver, inveigler, hypocrite, trickster, pretender, dodger,

humbug, crook, wolf in sheep's clothing, con man*, shark*, fourflusher*,
shill*; see also CRIMINAL.

cheat *v.* defraud, swindle, beguile; see
DECEIVE.

cheated *a.* defrauded, swindled,
deprived of, tricked, imposed upon,
victimized, beguiled, trapped, foiled,
lured, taken in*, bamboozled, hoodwinked; see also DECEIVED.

cheating *n.* lying, defrauding,
deceiving; see DECEPTION, DISHON-
ESTY.

check *n.* **1** [An order on a bank]
money order, letter of credit, traveler's check, bank check, cashier's
check, note, remittance; see also
MONEY 1. **2** [A control] poll, roll call,
rein; see RESTRAINT 2. **3** [An exami-
nation] investigation, analysis,
inquiry; see EXAMINATION 1, 3. **4**
[The symbol ✓] cross, ex, sign, line,
stroke, score, dot; see also MARK 1. **5**
[A pattern in squares] patchwork,
checkered design, checkerboard; see
DESIGN. —**in check** controlled,
under control, checked; see HELD.

check *v.* **1** [To bring under control]
bridle, repress, inhibit, control,
checkmate, counteract, discourage,
repulse, neutralize, squelch; see also
RESTRAIN.—*Ant.* FREE, liberate, loose.

2 [To determine accuracy] review,
monitor, balance accounts, balance
the books, keep account of, correct,
compare, find out, investigate, vet*,
count, tell, call the roll, take account
of, take stock, go through, go over
with a fine-toothed comb*, keep tabs
on*, keep track of; see also EXAMINE.
3 [To halt] hold, terminate, cut
short; see HALT, STOP 1. —**check in**
appear, sign in, come; see ARRIVE,
REGISTER 4. —**check off** mark off,
notice, correct; see MARK 2. —**check
out** depart, pay one's bill, settle up;
see LEAVE 1, PAY 1. —**check up on***
watch, investigate, control; see EXAM-
INE.

cheek *n.* jowl, gill, chop; see FACE 1.

cheer *n.* **1** [An agreeable mental
state] delight, mirth, glee; see JOY. **2**
[An encouraging shout] roar,
applause, hurrah, hurray, college yell;
approval; see also YELL.

cheer *v.* **1** [To hearten] console,
inspirit, brighten; see COMFORT 1,
ENCOURAGE, HELP. **2** [To support
with cheers] applaud, shout, salute;
see SUPPORT 2, YELL. —**cheer up**
enliven, inspirit, exhilarate, inspire,
brighten, rally, restore, perk up,
boost, buck up*, pat on the back; see
also IMPROVE 1.

cheer'ful *adj.* 1 full of cheer; gay 2 bright and attractive 3 willing *[a cheerful helper]* —**cheer'fully** *adv.* —**cheer'ful·ness** *n.*

cheer'io' (-ē ō') *interj., n., pl.* -**os'** [Brit. Colloq.] 1 goodbye 2 good health: used as a toast

cheer'lead'er (-lē'dər) *n.* a leader of cheers, as at football games

cheer'less *adj.* not cheerful; dismal; dreary —**cheer'lessly** *adv.* —**cheer'less·ness** *n.*

cheers (chirz) *interj.* [Chiefly Brit.] good health: used as a toast

cheer'y *adj.* -**i·er**, -**i·est** cheerful; lively; bright —**cheer'i·ly** *adv.* —**cheer'i·ness** *n.*

cheese (chēz) *n.* ⟦OE *cyse*⟧ a solid food made from milk curds

cheese'burg'er (-bʉr'gər) *n.* a hamburger topped with melted cheese

cheese'cake' *n.* 1 a cake made with cottage cheese or cream cheese 2 [Colloq.] photographic display of the figure, esp. the legs, of a pretty woman

cheese'cloth' *n.* ⟦from its use for wrapping cheese⟧ a thin cotton cloth with a very loose weave

chees'y (-ē) *adj.* -**i·er**, -**i·est** 1 like cheese 2 [Slang] inferior; poor

chee·tah (chēt'ə) *n.* ⟦Hindi < Sans *chitraka*, spotted⟧ a swift cat of Africa and S Asia, with long legs and a spotted coat

chef (shef) *n.* ⟦Fr, head, chief⟧ 1 a head cook 2 any cook

chem. 1 chemical(s) 2 chemistry

chemi·cal (kem'i kəl) *adj.* 1 of, made by, or used in chemistry 2 made with or operated by chemicals 3 [Slang] of or involving a drug, alcohol, etc. *[chemical dependency]* — *n.* any substance used in or obtained by a chemical process —**chem'i·cally** *adv.*

chemical abuse the habitual use of a mood-altering drug, alcohol, etc. —**chemical abuser**

chemical engineering the science or profession of applying chemistry to industrial uses

chemical warfare warfare by means of poisonous gases, etc.

che·mise (shə mēz') *n.* ⟦< LL *camisia*, tunic⟧ 1 a woman's loose, short slip 2 a straight, loose dress

chem·ist (kem'ist) *n.* ⟦ult. < Ar < ? Gr *cheein*, to pour⟧ 1 a specialist in chemistry 2 [Brit.] a pharmacist, or druggist

chem·is·try (kem'is trē) *n.* ⟦< prec.⟧ 1 the science dealing with the composition and properties of substances, and with the reactions by which substances are produced from or converted into other substances 2 [Colloq.] rapport

chemo- *combining form* of, with, or by chemicals Also, before a vowel, **chem-**

che'mo·ther'a·py *n.* the use of chemical drugs in medicine

chem·urgy (kem'ər jē) *n.* chemistry dealing with the use of organic, esp. farm, products in industrial manufacture

che·nille (shə nēl') *n.* ⟦Fr, lit., caterpillar⟧ 1 a tufted, velvety yarn 2 a fabric filled or woven with this

cheque (chek) *n. Brit. sp. of* CHECK (*n.* 8)

cher·ish (cher'ish) *vt.* ⟦< L *carus*, dear⟧ 1 to hold dear 2 to cling to the idea or feeling of

Chero·kee (cher'ə kē') *n., pl.* -**kees'** or -**kee'** a member of a North American Indian people now chiefly of SW U.S.

che·root (shə rōōt') *n.* ⟦< Tamil⟧ a cigar with both ends cut square

cherry (cher'ē) *n., pl.* -**ries** ⟦< Gr *kerasion*⟧ 1 a small, fleshy fruit with a smooth, hard pit 2 the tree that bears this fruit 3 the wood of this tree 4 a bright red

chert (chʉrt) *n.* a fine-grained rock composed mainly of silica

cher·ub (cher'əb) *n., pl.* -**ubs**, -**u·bim'** (-yōō bim', -ə bim'), or -**u·bims** ⟦< Heb *kerūbh*⟧ 1 any of a kind of angel, often represented as a chubby, rosy-faced child with wings 2 a child with a sweet, innocent face —**che·ru·bic** (chə rōō'bik) *adj.* —**che·ru'bi·cally** *adv.*

cher·vil (chʉr'vəl) *n.* ⟦< Gr *chairephyllon*⟧ a plant like parsley, with leaves used to flavor salads, soups, etc.

chess (ches) *n.* ⟦< OFr *eschec*, a check in chess⟧ a game played on a chessboard by two players, using a variety of pieces (**chess'men**)

chess'board' *n.* a checkerboard used for playing chess

chest (chest) *n.* ⟦< Gr *kistē*, a box⟧ 1 a box with a lid 2 a cabinet with drawers, as for clothes 3 a cabinet with shelves, as for medicines 4 the part of the body enclosed by the ribs, breastbone, and diaphragm

ches·ter·field (ches'tər feld') *n.* ⟦after a 19th-c. Earl of *Chesterfield*⟧ a single-breasted topcoat, usually with a velvet collar

chest'nut (ches'nut', -nət) *n.* ⟦< Gr *kastaneia*⟧ 1 the edible nut of a tree of the beech family 2 this tree, or its wood 3 reddish brown 4 [Colloq.] an old, stale joke, story, etc.

chevi·ot (chev'ē ət, shev'ē ət) *n.* ⟦after Cheviot Hills, on the Scottish-English border⟧ a rough, twilled wool fabric

chevre (shev'rə) *n.* a soft cheese made from goat's milk

chev·ron (shev'rən) *n.* ⟦Fr, rafter⟧ a V-shaped bar on the sleeve of a uniform, showing rank

chew (chōō) *vt., vi.* ⟦OE *ceowan*⟧ to bite and crush with the teeth —*n.* 1 a chewing 2 something chewed or for chewing —**chew'er** *n.* —**chew'y**, -**i·er**, -**i·est**, *adj.*

chew'ing gum a gummy substance, as chicle, flavored for chewing

chg. charge

chi (kī, kē) *n.* the 22d letter of the Greek alphabet (Χ, χ)

Chi·anti (kē än'tē, -an'-) *n.* ⟦It⟧ a dry red wine

chia·ro·scuro (kē ä'rō skōō'rō) *n., pl.* -**ros** ⟦It < L *clarus*, clear + *obscurus*, dark⟧ 1 treatment of light and shade in a painting, etc., esp. when emphasized 2 a painting, drawing, etc. notable for this

chic (shēk) *n.* ⟦Fr < Medieval LowG *schick*, skill⟧ smart elegance —*adj.* smartly stylish

chi·can·ery (shi kān'ər ē) *n., pl.* -**ies** ⟦< Fr⟧ 1 trickery 2 a trick

Chi·cano (chi kä'nō) *n., pl.* -**nos** ⟦< AmSp⟧ [*also* c-] a U.S. citizen or inhabitant of Mexican descent

chi-chi or **chi-chi** (shē'shē) *adj.* ⟦Fr⟧ extremely chic, specif. in an affected or showy way

chick (chik) *n.* ⟦ME *chike*⟧ 1 a young chicken or bird 2 [Slang] a young woman

chicka·dee (chik'ə dē') *n.* ⟦echoic⟧ a kind of titmouse

chicken (chik'ən) *n.* ⟦< OE *cycen*⟧ 1 a common farm bird raised for its edible eggs or flesh; hen or rooster, esp. a young one 2 its flesh —*adj.* [Slang] cowardly —*vi.* [Slang] to quit from fear: usually with *out*

chicken feed [Slang] a paltry sum

THESAURUS

cheerful *a.* 1 [*Said especially of persons*] gay, merry, joyful; see HAPPY. 2 [*Said especially of things*] bright, sunny, sparkling; see COMFORTABLE 2, PLEASANT 2.

cheerfully *a.* cheerily, gladly, willingly, happily, merrily, joyfully, lightheartedly, blithely, brightly, vivaciously, airily, genially, jovially, sportively, elatedly, winsomely, pleasantly, gleefully, gaily, mirthfully, hopefully, breezily, briskly, with good cheer.—*Ant.* SADLY, unwillingly, reluctantly.

cheers *interj.* here's to you, to your health, *skoal* (Scandinavian); see TOAST 1.

cheese *n.* *Varieties of cheese include the following:* mild, American, Cheddar, Monterey Jack, Philadelphia cream, creamed cottage, Edam, Roquefort, Brie, mozzarella, provolone, Gorgonzola, Swiss, Camembert,

Liederkranz, Neufchâtel, Gruyère, Parmesan, Stilton, Gouda, Limburger, Muenster, Port du Salut, pot, ricotta, feta, Romano; see also FOOD.

chemical *a.* synthetic, artificial, ersatz; see FALSE 3.

chemical *n.* substance, synthetic, compound; see DRUG, MEDICINE 2.

chemistry *n.* *Branches of chemistry include the following:* pure, quantitative, qualitative, organic, inorganic, theoretical, physical, physiological, pathological, metallurgical, mineralogical, geological, applied, agricultural, pharmaceutical, sanitary, industrial, technical, engineering chemistry; biochemistry, electrochemistry, zoochemistry; see also MEDICINE 3, SCIENCE 1.

cherish *v.* treasure, value, adore; see LOVE 1, 2.

cherry *a.* ruddy, reddish, rosy; see

RED, PINK.

chest *n.* 1 [A boxlike container] case, box, coffer, cabinet, strongbox, receptacle, crate, locker, bureau, coffin, casket, treasury; see also CONTAINER. 2 [The ribbed portion of the body] breast, thorax, bosom, rib cage, heart, upper trunk, pulmonary cavity, peritoneum, ribs.

chew *v.* bite, champ, munch, crunch, masticate, nibble, feast upon, gnaw, gulp, grind, rend, scrunch, ruminate; see also EAT 1.

chicken *n.* 1 [A barnyard fowl] chick, hen, rooster; see FOWL. 2 [Flesh of the chicken] giblets, dark meat, white meat; see MEAT. 3 [*A coward*] recreant, dastard, craven; see COWARD. —**count one's chickens before they are hatched** rely on, depend on, put trust in; see ANTICIPATE.

chick'en·fried' *adj.* coated with seasoned flour or batter and fried

chick'en-heart'ed *adj.* cowardly; timid Also **chick'en·liv'ered**

chick'en·pox' *n.* an acute, contagious viral disease, esp. of children, characterized by skin eruptions

chicken wire light, pliable wire fencing

chick'pea' *n.* **1** a bushy annual plant with short, hairy pods **2** its edible seed

chick'weed' *n.* a low-growing plant often found as a lawn weed

chicle (chik'əl) *n.* ⟦AmSp⟧ a gumlike substance from a tropical American tree, used in chewing gum

chico·ry (chik'ə rē) *n., pl.* **-ries** ⟦< Gr *kichora*⟧ **1** a plant with blue flowers and with leaves used for salad **2** its root, ground for mixing with coffee or as a coffee substitute

chide (chīd) *vt., vi.* **chid'ed** or **chid** (chid), **chid'ed** or **chid** or **chid·den** (chid''n), **chid'ing** ⟦OE *cidan*⟧ to reprove mildly —**chid'ing·ly** *adv.*

chief (chēf) *n.* ⟦< L *caput*, head⟧ a leader; head —*adj.* main; principal

chief'ly *adv.* **1** most of all **2** mainly —*adj.* of or like a chief

chief'tain (-tən) *n.* ⟦< L *caput*, head⟧ a chief, esp. of a clan or tribe

chif·fon (shi fän') *n.* ⟦Fr⟧ a sheer, silky fabric —*adj.* **1** of chiffon **2** made fluffy as with beaten egg whites

chig·ger (chig'ər) *n.* ⟦of Afr orig.⟧ the tiny, red larva of certain mites, whose bite causes severe itching

chi·gnon (shēn'yän') *n.* ⟦Fr < L *catena*, chain⟧ a coil of hair worn at the back of the neck

Chi·hua·hua (chi wä'wä) *n.* ⟦after *Chihuahua*, a Mex. state⟧ a breed of very small dog with large, pointed ears

chil·blain (chil'blān') *n.* ⟦CHIL(L) + *blain* < OE *blegen*, a sore⟧ a painful swelling or sore, esp. on the fingers or toes, caused by exposure to cold

child (chīld) *n., pl.* **chil'dren** ⟦OE *cild*⟧ **1** an infant **2** a boy or girl before puberty **3** a son or daughter —**with child** pregnant —**child'hood'** *n.* —**child'less** *adj.*

child'birth' *n.* the act of giving birth to a child

child'ish *adj.* of or like a child; specif., immature, silly, etc. —**child'ish·ly** *adv.* —**child'ish·ness** *n.*

child'like' *adj.* of or like a child; specif., innocent, trusting etc.

chil·dren (chil'drən) *n. pl. of* CHILD

child's play any very simple task

chili (chil'ē) *n., pl.* **-ies** ⟦MexSp⟧ **1** the very hot, dried pod of red pepper, often ground as a seasoning (**chili powder**) **2** any of certain other peppers used in Mexican cooking **3** a highly spiced dish of beef, chilies or chili powder, and often beans and tomatoes: in full **chili con carne** (kən kär'nē) Also **chil'e**

chili dog a hot dog served with chili con carne

chili sauce a spiced sauce of chopped tomatoes, sweet peppers, onions, etc.

chill (chil) *n.* ⟦< OE *ciele*⟧ **1** coldness or coolness causing shivers **2** a moderate coldness **3** a sudden fear, etc. **4** unfriendliness —*adj.* CHILLY —*vi., vt.* **1** to make or become cold **2** to cause a chill (in) —**chill'ing·ly** *adv.*

chill factor the combined effect of low temperatures and high winds on exposed skin

chill'y *adj.* **-i·er, -i·est** **1** moderately cold **2** unfriendly —**chill'i·ness** *n.*

chime (chīm) *n.* ⟦< Gr *kymbalon*, cymbal⟧ **1** [*usually pl.*] *a*) a set of tuned bells or metal tubes *b*) the musical sounds made by these **2** a single bell, as in a clock —*vi.* **chimed, chim'ing** **1** to sound as a chime or bells **2** to agree —*vt.* to give (the time) by chiming —**chime in** **1** to join in **2** to agree —**chim'er** *n.*

Chi·mera (kī mir'ə, ki-) ⟦< Gr *chimaira*, orig., she-goat⟧ *Gr. Myth.* a monster, with a lion's head, goat's body, and serpent's tail —*n.* [**c-**] an impossible fancy

chi·mer'i·cal (-mer'i kəl) *adj.* **1** imaginary; unreal **2** fanciful

chim·ney (chim'nē) *n., pl.* **-neys** ⟦ult. < Gr *kaminos*, oven⟧ **1** the passage or structure through which smoke escapes from a fire, often extending above the roof **2** a glass tube around the flame of a lamp

chim·pan·zee (chim'pan zē', chim pan'zē) *n.* ⟦< Bantu⟧ a medium-sized great ape of Africa Also [Colloq.] **chimp** (chimp)

chin (chin) *n.* ⟦OE *cin*⟧ the part of the face below the lower lip —*vt.* **chinned, chin'ning** to pull (oneself) up, while hanging by the hands from a bar, until the chin is just above the bar

Chin. Chinese

china (chī'nə) *n.* ⟦orig. made in China⟧ **1** porcelain or any ceramic ware like porcelain **2** dishes, etc. made of china **3** any earthenware Also **chi'na·ware'**

chin·chilla (chin chil'ə) *n.* ⟦prob. dim. of Sp. *chinche*, a small bug⟧ **1** *a*) a small rodent of South America *b*) its soft, gray fur **2** a heavy wool cloth

chine (chīn) *n.* ⟦< OFr *eschine*, spine⟧ a cut of meat from the backbone

Chi·nese (chī nēz', -nēs') *n.* **1** *pl.* **-nese** a native or inhabitant of China **2** a language of the Chinese —*adj.* of China, its people, language, etc.

Chinese checkers a game in which marbles are moved as checkers, on a board with holes in a star-shaped pattern

Chinese lantern a paper lantern that can be folded up

chink¹ (chiŋk) *n.* ⟦OE *chine*⟧ a crack —*vt.* to close up the chinks in

chink² (chiŋk) *n.* ⟦echoic⟧ a sharp, clinking sound —*vi., vt.* to make or cause to make this sound

chino (chē'nō, shē'-) *n., pl.* **-nos** ⟦< ?⟧ **1** a strong, twilled cotton, khaki cloth **2** [*pl.*] pants of chino for casual wear

Chi·nook (shə nook', -nōōk'; chə-) *n., pl.* **-nooks'** or **-nook'** ⟦< AmInd name⟧ a member of a North American Indian people of Wash. and Oreg.

chintz (chints) *n.* ⟦< Hindi *chhint*⟧ a cotton cloth printed in colored designs and usually glazed

chintz'y (-ē) *adj.* **-i·er, -i·est** ⟦prec. + -y³⟧ **1** like chintz **2** [Colloq.] cheap, stingy, etc.

chip (chip) *vt.* **chipped, chip'ping** ⟦< OE⟧ to break or cut off small pieces from —*vi.* to break off in small pieces —*n.* **1** a small piece of wood, etc. cut or broken off **2** a place

---

THESAURUS

chief *a.* leading, first, foremost; see MAIN, PRINCIPAL.

chief *n.* principal, manager, overseer, governor, president, foreman, proprietor, supervisor, director, chairman, ringleader, general, master, dictator, superintendent, head, prince, emperor, duke, majesty, monarch, overlord, lord, potentate, sovereign, chieftain, ruler, captain, commander, bigwig*, prima donna*, boss, it*; see also LEADER.

chiefly *a.* mainly, particularly, in the first place; see PRINCIPALLY.

child *n.* newborn, infant, youth, adolescent, youngster, daughter, son, grandchild, stepchild, offspring, innocent, minor, juvenile, tot, cherub, papoose, moppet*, kid*, kiddie*, whelp*, brat*, imp, small fry; see also BOY, GIRL.—*Ant.* PARENT, forefather, adult. —**with child** carrying a child, going to have a baby, fertile; see PREGNANT.

childbirth *n.* delivery, childbearing, parturition, childbed, labor, nativity, delivering, accouchement, lying in,

confinement, procreation, reproduction, propagation, giving birth, blessed event*; see also BIRTH.

childhood *n.* infancy, youth, minority, school days, adolescence, nursery days, babyhood, boyhood, girlhood, teens, puberty, immaturity, tender age.—*Ant.* AGE, maturity, senility.

childish *a.* childlike, foolish, stupid, baby, infantile, juvenile, youthful, babyish, boyish, girlish, adolescent, green, soft, immature; see also NAIVE, SIMPLE 1, YOUNG 2.—*Ant.* MATURE, adult, grown.

chill *n.* crispness, coolness, coldness; see COLD 1.

chill *v.* **1** [To reduce temperature] frost, refrigerate, make cold; see COOL, FREEZE 1. **2** [To check] dispirit, dishearten, dampen; see DEPRESS 2, DISCOURAGE.

chilly *a.* brisk, fresh, crisp; see COLD 1, COOL 1.

chime *v.* tinkle, clang, toll; see RING 2, SOUND.

chimney *n.* smokestack, fireplace, furnace, hearth, flue, vent, pipe, funnel, smokeshaft, stack.

chin *n.* mentum, mandible, jawbone; see JAW.

china *n.* earthenware, pottery, crockery; see DISH.

Chinese *a.* Sinaic, Asian, Asiatic; see ORIENTAL.

chip *n.* **1** [A fragment] fragment, slice, wedge; see BIT 1, FLAKE, PART 1. **2** [A microcircuit] integrated circuit, semiconductor, microprocessor, computer on a chip. —**having a chip on one's shoulder** ready to fight, disturbed, agitated; see ANGRY. —**when the chips are down** in a crisis, having trouble, in a difficult position; see IN TROUBLE.

chip *v.* slash, hew, hack, crumble, snip, fragment, incise, whittle, crack off, splinter, notch, sliver, cut off, chop, split, slice, chisel, clip, break, crack, flake, cut away, nick, shiver, reduce, shear; see also BREAK.

where a small piece has been chipped off **3** a small disk used in gambling games as a counter **4** a thin slice of food [a potato *chip*] **5** INTEGRATED CIRCUIT —**chip in** [Colloq.] to contribute (money, etc.) —**chip on one's shoulder** [Colloq.] an inclination to fight

chip·munk′ (-muŋk′) *n.* ⟦< AmInd⟧ a small, striped North American squirrel

chipped beef dried or smoked beef sliced into shavings

chip·per (chip′ər) *adj.* ⟦< N Brit Dial.⟧ [Colloq.] sprightly; in good spirits

chiro- ⟦< Gr *cheir*, hand⟧ *combining form* hand

chi·rog·ra·phy (kī räg′rə fē) *n.* ⟦prec. + -GRAPHY⟧ handwriting

chi·ropo·dy (kī räp′ə dē) *n.* ⟦CHIRO- + -POD + -Y⁴⟧ PODIATRY —**chi·rop′o·dist** *n.*

chi·ro·prac·tic (kī′rō prak′tik) *n.* ⟦< CHIRO- + Gr *praktikos*, practical⟧ a method of treating disease by manipulation of the body joints, esp. of the spine —**chi′ro·prac′tor** *n.*

chirp (churp) *vi., vt.* ⟦echoic⟧ to make, or utter in, short, shrill tones, as some birds do — *n.* this sound

chir·rup (chir′əp) *vi.* ⟦< prec.⟧ to chirp repeatedly — *n.* a chirruping sound

chisel (chiz′əl) *n.* ⟦< L *caedere*, to cut⟧ a sharp-edged hand tool for cutting or shaping wood, stone, etc. — *vi., vt.* -**eled** or -**elled**, -**el·ing** or -**el·ling** **1** to cut or shape with a chisel **2** [Colloq.] to swindle or get by swindling —**chis′eler** or **chis′el·ler** *n.*

chit (chit) *n.* ⟦< Hindi⟧ a voucher of a small sum owed for drink, food, etc.

chit·chat (chit′chat′) *n.* ⟦< CHAT⟧ **1** light, informal talk **2** gossip

chi·tin (kī′tin) *n.* ⟦< Gr *chitōn*, tunic⟧ the tough, horny outer covering of insects, crustaceans, etc.

chi·ton (kī′tən) *n.* ⟦Gr *chitōn*, tunic⟧ a small marine mollusk with a dorsal shell of eight plates

chit·ter·lings, chit·lins, or **chit·lings** (chit′linz) *n.pl.* ⟦< Gmc base⟧ small intestines of pigs, used for food

chiv·al·rous (shiv′əl rəs) *adj.* **1** gallant, courteous, etc. like an ideal knight **2** of chivalry Also **chi·val′ric** (-rik′, shi val′rik) —**chiv′al·rous·ly** *adv.* —**chiv′al·rous·ness** *n.*

chiv′al·ry (-rē) *n.* ⟦< OFr *chevaler*, knight < *cheval*, horse⟧ **1** medieval knighthood **2** the qualities of an ideal knight, as courage, honor, etc.

chives (chīvz) *n.pl.* ⟦< L *cepa*, onion⟧ [*sometimes with sing. v.*] an herb with slender, hollow leaves and a mild onion odor, used for flavoring

chla·my·dia (klə mid′ē ə) *n.* a widespread venereal disease

chloral (hydrate) (klôr′əl) a colorless, crystalline compound used as a sedative

chlo′ride′ (-īd′) *n.* a compound of chlorine with another element or radical

chlo·ri·nate′ (-ə nāt′) *vt.* -**nat′ed,** -**nat′ing** to combine (a substance) with chlorine; esp., to treat (water or sewage) with chlorine for purification —**chlo′ri·na′tion** *n.*

chlo′rine′ (-ēn′) *n.* ⟦< Gr *chlōros*, pale green⟧ a greenish-yellow, poisonous, gaseous chemical element with a disagreeable odor, used in bleaching, water purification, etc.

chloro- ⟦< Gr *chlōros*, pale green⟧ *combining form* **1** green **2** having chlorine in the molecule

chloro·form′ (klôr′ə fôrm′) *n.* ⟦< Fr: see prec. & FORMIC⟧ a colorless, volatile liquid used as a solvent and, formerly, as an anesthetic — *vt.* to anesthetize or kill with chloroform

chlo′ro·phyll′ or **chlo′ro·phyl′** (-fil′) *n.* ⟦< Fr, ult. < Gr *chlōros*, green + *phyllon*, leaf⟧ the green pigment found in plant cells, essential to photosynthesis

chock (chäk) *n.* ⟦NormFr *choque*, a block⟧ a block or wedge placed under a wheel, etc. to prevent motion — *vt.* to wedge fast as with a chock — *adv.* as close or tight as can be

chock′-full′ *adj.* as full as possible

choco·late (chôk′ə lət, chäk′ə-; chôk′lət, chäk′-) *n.* ⟦ult. < AmInd (Mexico)⟧ **1** a substance made from roasted and ground cacao seeds **2** a drink or candy made with chocolate **3** reddish brown — *adj.* **1** made of or flavored with chocolate **2** reddish-brown —**choc′o·laty** or **choc′o·latey** *adj.*

choice (chois) *n.* ⟦< OFr < Gothic *kausjan*, to test⟧ **1** a choosing; selection **2** the right or power to choose **3** a person or thing chosen **4** the best part **5** a variety from which to choose **6** an alternative — *adj.* **choic′er, choic′est 1** of special excellence **2** carefully chosen

choir (kwir) *n.* ⟦< L < Gr *choros*⟧ **1** a group of singers, esp. in a church **2** the part of a church they occupy

choke (chōk) *vt.* **choked, chok′ing** ⟦< OE *aceocian*⟧ **1** to prevent from breathing by blocking the windpipe; strangle; suffocate **2** to obstruct by clogging **3** to hinder the growth or action of **4** to cut off some air from the carburetor of a gasoline engine) so as to make a richer gasoline mixture — *vi.* **1** to be suffocated **2** to be obstructed — *n.* **1** a choking **2** a sound of choking **3** the valve that chokes a carburetor —**choke back** to hold back (feelings, sobs, etc.) —**choke down** to swallow with difficulty —**choke off** to bring to an end —**choke up** [Colloq.] to be unable to perform because of fear, tension, etc.

choke collar a training collar for a dog, that tightens when the dog strains at the leash

chok′er *n.* a closefitting necklace

choler (käl′ər) *n.* ⟦< L *cholera*: see fol.⟧ [Now Rare] anger or ill humor

chol·era (käl′ər ə) *n.* ⟦< Gr *cholē*, bile⟧ any of several severe intestinal diseases

chol′eric *adj.* easily angered

cho·les·terol (kə les′tər ôl′, -ōl′) *n.* ⟦< Gr *cholē*, bile + *stereos*, solid⟧ a crystalline alcohol found esp. in animal fats, blood, nerve tissue, and bile

chomp (chämp) *vt., vi.* **1** CHAMP¹ **2** to bite down (*on*) repeatedly

choose (chōoz) *vt., vi.* **chose, cho′sen, choos′ing** ⟦OE *ceosan*⟧ **1** to take as a choice; select **2** to decide or prefer [*to choose to go*] —**cannot choose but** cannot do otherwise than —**choos′er** *n.*

choos′y or **choos′ey** *adj.* -**i·er,** -**i·est** [Colloq.] careful or fussy in choosing

chop¹ (chäp) *vt.* **chopped, chop′ping** ⟦ME *choppen*⟧ **1** to cut by blows with a sharp tool **2** to cut into small bits; mince — *vi.* to make quick, cutting strokes — *n.* **1** a short, sharp stroke **2** a cut of meat and bone from the rib, loin, or shoulder **3** a short, broken movement of waves

chop² (chäp) *n.* ⟦var. of CHAP¹⟧ **1** a jaw **2** [*pl.*] the mouth and lower cheeks

chop′house′ *n.* a restaurant that specializes in chops and steaks

chop·per (chäp′ər) *n.* **1** one that chops **2** [*pl.*] [Slang] teeth **3** [Colloq.] a helicopter

chop′py *adj.* -**pi′er,** -**pi·est 1** rough with short, broken waves, as the sea **2** making abrupt starts and stops — **chop′pi·ness** *n.*

chop′sticks′ *n.pl.* ⟦Pidgin English⟧ two small sticks held together in one hand and used, mainly in parts of Asia, to lift food to the mouth

chop suey (chäp′ sōo′ē) ⟦< Chin *tsa-sui*, various pieces⟧

━━ THESAURUS ━━

chip in* *v.* contribute, pay, pitch in*; see SHARE 1.

chirp *v.* twitter, warble, cheep; see SOUND.

chisel *n.* gouge, blade, edge; see KNIFE, TOOL 1.

chisel *v.* **1** [To work with a chisel] carve, hew, incise; see CUT 1. **2** [*To get by imposition*] impose upon, defraud, gyp*; see DECEIVE, STEAL.

chivalrous *a.* courteous, heroic, valiant; see BRAVE, NOBLE 1, 2, POLITE.

chivalry *n.* valor, gallantry, fairness; see COURTESY 1.

chock-full *a.* packed, crammed, stuffed; see FULL 1.

choice *a.* superior, fine, exceptional; see BEST 1.

choice *n.* selection, preference, alternative, election, substitute, favorite, pick, a good bet; see also JUDGMENT 2.

choke *v.* asphyxiate, strangle, strangulate, stifle, throttle, garrote, drown, noose, smother, grab by the throat, wring the neck of, stop the breath of, gag, gasp, suffocate, choke off, be choked, die out, die by asphyxiation; see also DIE. —**choke up*** give way to one's feelings, weep, break down; see CRY 1.

choose *v.* decide, take, pick out, draw lots, cull, prefer, make a choice of, accept, weigh, judge, sort, appoint, embrace, will, call for, fancy, take up, separate, favor, determine, resolve, discriminate, make a decision, adopt, collect, mark out for, cut out, arrange, keep, take up, make one's choice, pick and choose, settle on, use one's discretion, determine upon, fix on, place one's trust in, glean, single out, espouse, exercise one's option, make up one's mind, set aside, set apart, commit oneself, separate the wheat from the chaff, incline toward, opt for, burn one's bridges; see also DECIDE.—*Ant.* DISCARD, reject, refuse.

choosing *n.* selecting, picking, judging; see CHOICE.

chop¹ *v.* fell, cut with an ax, whack; see CUT 1.

Chinese-American dish of meat, bean sprouts, etc., served with rice

cho·ral (kôr′əl) *adj.* of, for, or sung by a choir or chorus — **cho′rally** *adv.*

cho·rale or **cho·ral** (kə ral′, -räl′) *n.* 1 a hymn tune 2 a choir or chorus

chord[1] (kôrd) *n.* ⟦altered (infl. by L *chorda*) < CORD⟧ 1 [Archaic] the string of a musical instrument 2 a straight line joining any two points on an arc

chord[2] (kôrd) *n.* ⟦< ME *accord*, accord⟧ *Music* a combination of three or more tones sounded together in harmony

chor·date (kôr′dāt′) *n.* ⟦L *chorda*, CORD + -ATE[1]⟧ any of a phylum of animal having a dorsal nerve cord, including the vertebrates

chore (chôr) *n.* ⟦< OE *cierr*, job⟧ 1 a routine task 2 a hard task

chor·eo·graph (kôr′ē ə graf′) *vt., vi.* ⟦< fol.⟧ to design or plan the movements of (a dance) —**chor′eog′ra·pher** (-äg′rə fər)

chor·eog·ra·phy (kôr′ē äg′rə fē) *n.* ⟦Gr *choreia*, dance + -GRAPHY⟧ 1 dancing, esp. ballet dancing 2 the art of devising dances, esp. ballets —**chor′eo·graph′ic** (-ə graf′ik) *adj.*

chor·is·ter (kôr′is tər) *n.* ⟦see CHORUS⟧ a member of a choir

cho·roid (kôr′oid) *n.* ⟦Gr < *chorion*, fetal membrane + -*eidēs*, -OID⟧ the dark, middle membrane of the eye

chor·tle (chôrt′′l) *vi., vt.* -**tled**, -**tling** ⟦prob.< CHUCKLE + SNORT⟧ to make, or utter with, a gleeful chuckling or snorting sound — *n.* such a sound —**chor′tler** *n.*

cho·rus (kôr′əs) *n.* ⟦< Gr *choros*⟧ 1 a group of dancers and singers performing together 2 the part of a drama, song, etc. performed by a chorus 3 a group singing or speaking something together 4 music written for group singing 5 the refrain of a song — *vt., vi.* to sing, speak, or say in unison —**in chorus** in unison

chose (chōz) *vt., vi. pt. & obs. pp. of* CHOOSE

cho·sen (chō′zən) *vt., vi. pp. of* CHOOSE — *adj.* selected; choice

chow (chou) *n.* ⟦< Chin⟧ 1 any of a breed of medium-sized dog, originally from China 2 [Slang] food

chow·der (chou′dər) *n.* ⟦Fr *chaudière*, a pot⟧ a thick soup usually of onions and potatoes and, often, clams and milk

chow mein (chou′ mān′) ⟦Chin *ch′ao*, fry + *mien*, flour⟧ a Chinese-American dish of meat, bean sprouts, etc., served with fried noodles

chrism (kriz′əm) *n.* ⟦< Gr *chrisma*, oil⟧ holy oil used as in baptism

Christ (krīst) ⟦< Gr *christos*, the anointed⟧ Jesus of Nazareth, regarded by Christians as the prophesied Messiah

chris·ten (kris′ən) *vt.* 1 to take into a Christian church by baptism; baptize 2 to give a name to, esp. at baptism —**chris′ten·ing** *n.*

Chris′ten·dom (-dəm) *n.* 1 Christians collectively 2 those parts of the world where most of the inhabitants profess Christianity

Chris·tian (kris′chən) *n.* a believer in Jesus as the Messiah prophesied in the Old Testament, or in the religion based on the teachings of Jesus — *adj.* 1 of Jesus Christ 2 of or professing the religion based on his teachings 3 having the qualities taught by Jesus Christ, as love, kindness, humility, etc. 4 of Christians or Christianity

Chris·ti·an·ity (kris′chē an′ə tē) *n.* 1 Christians collectively 2 the Christian religion 3 the state of being a Christian

Chris·tian·ize (kris′chən īz′) *vt.* -**ized′**, -**iz′ing** 1 to convert to Christianity 2 to make Christian in character

Christian name the baptismal name or given name, as distinguished from the surname or family name

Christian Science a religion and system of healing: official name **Church of Christ, Scientist**

Chris·tie (kris′tē) *n., pl.* -**ties** ⟦after *Christiania*, former name of Oslo, Norway⟧ *Skiing* a high-speed turn with the skis parallel

Christ·mas (kris′məs) *n.* ⟦see CHRIST & MASS⟧ a holiday on Dec. 25 celebrating the birth of Jesus Christ

chro·matic (krō mat′ik) *adj.* ⟦< Gr *chrōma*, color⟧ 1 of or having color or colors 2 *Music* progressing by half tones —**chro·mat′i·cally** *adv.*

chro·ma·tin (krō′mə tin′) *n.* ⟦< Gr *chrōma*, color⟧ a substance in cell nuclei that readily absorbs a coloring agent, as for observation under a microscope

chrome (krōm) *n.* ⟦Fr: see CHROMIUM⟧ chromium or chromium alloy — *adj.* designating any of various pigments (**chrome red, chrome yellow**) made from chromium compounds — *vt.* **chromed, chrom′ing** to plate with chromium

-chrome (krōm) ⟦< Gr *chrōma*, color⟧ *combining form* 1 color or coloring agent 2 chromium

chro·mium (krō′mē əm) *n.* ⟦< Gr *chrōma*, color⟧ a hard, metallic chemical element resistant to corrosion

chromo- ⟦< Gr *chrōma*, color⟧ *combining form* color or pigment *[chromosome]* Also **chrom-**

chromo·some (krō′mə sōm′) *n.* ⟦< prec.⟧ any of the microscopic rod-shaped bodies carrying genes

chronic (krän′ik) *adj.* ⟦< Gr *chronos*, time⟧ 1 lasting a long time or recurring: said of a disease 2 having had an ailment for a long time 3 habitual —**chron′i·cally** *adv.*

chroni·cle (krän′i kəl) *n.* ⟦< Gr *chronika*, annals⟧ a historical record of events in the order in which they happened — *vt.* -**cled, -cling** to tell the history of; recount; record —**chron′i·cler** *n.*

chrono- ⟦< Gr *chronos*, time⟧ *combining form* time Also **chron-**

chro·nol·ogy (krō näl′ə jē) *n., pl.* -**gies** ⟦prec. + -LOGY⟧ 1 the science of measuring time and of dating events 2 the arrangement of events in the order of occurrence — **chrono·log·i·cal** (krän′ō läj′i kəl) *adj.* —**chron′o·log′i·cally** *adv.*

chro·nom′eter (-näm′ət ər) *n.* ⟦CHRONO- + -METER⟧ a highly accurate kind of clock or watch

chrysa·lis (kris′ə lis) *n.* ⟦< Gr *chrysallis*⟧ 1 the pupa of a butterfly, encased in a cocoon 2 the cocoon

chrys·an·themum (kri san′thə məm) *n.* ⟦< Gr *chrysos*, gold + *anthemon*, flower⟧ 1 a late-blooming plant of the composite family, with showy flowers 2 the flower

chub (chub) *n.* ⟦ME *chubbe*⟧ a small, freshwater fish related to the minnow and carp

---

▬▬ THESAURUS ▬▬

chord[2] *n.* harmonizing tones, triad, octave; second; third, fourth, fifth, etc. chord; diminished chord, augmented chord, inverted chord, broken chord; primary, secondary, tertiary chord; tetrachord, perfect fourth, arpeggio, common chord; see also HARMONY 1, MUSIC 1.

chore *n.* task, routine, errand; see JOB 2.

chorus *n.* 1 [A body of singers] choir, singing group, choristers, voices, glee club, singing society, church singers, male chorus, female chorus, mixed chorus, operatic group; see also MUSIC 1. 2 [A refrain] melody, strain, tune; see SONG.

chosen *a.* picked, elected, preferred; see NAMED 2.

Christ *n.* the Saviour, Jesus, Jesus of Nazareth, the Redeemer, Messiah, Immanuel, the Word, the Son, the Son of Man, the Son of God, God the Son, the Son of David, the Son of Mary, the Risen, the King of Glory, the Prince of Peace, the Good Shep-

herd, the King of the Jews, the Lamb of God, the Only Begotten, King of Kings, Lord of Lords, Christ Our Lord, the Way, the Door, the Truth, the Life, the Light of the World, the Incarnate Word, the Word made Flesh, Rose of Sharon; see also GOD 2.

christen *v.* immerse, sprinkle, take into a Christian church; see BAPTIZE, BLESS, NAME 1.

Christian *a.* pious, reverent, devoted; see HUMBLE 1, RELIGIOUS 1, 2.

Christian *n.* Protestant, Catholic, gentile; see CHURCH 3, SAINT.

Christianity *n.* 1 [A religion based upon the divinity of Christ] teachings of Christ, the Gospel, the Faith; see FAITH 2, RELIGION 2. 2 [The body of Christian people] Christendom, Christians, followers of Christ; see CHURCH 3. 3 [An attitude associated with Christianity] Christian spirit, forgiving disposition, loving-kind-

ness; see KINDNESS 1, TOLERANCE 1.

Christmas *n.* Xmas*, Noel, Yule; see HOLIDAY, WINTER.

chronic *a.* inveterate, confirmed, settled, rooted, deep-seated, continuing, persistent, stubborn, incurable, lasting, lingering, deep-rooted, perennial, fixed, continual, incessant, longstanding, recurring, continuous, of long duration, long-lived, protracted, ceaseless, sustained, lifelong, prolonged, recurrent, obstinate, inborn, inbred, ingrained, ever-present; see also CONSTANT, HABITUAL, PERMANENT.—*Ant.* TEMPORARY, acute, casual.

chronicle *n.* narrative, annals, account; see HISTORY, RECORD 1.

chronological *a.* temporal, historical, tabulated, classified, according to chronology, in the order of time, sequential, consecutive, properly dated, measured in time, in sequence, progressive in time, ordered, in order, in due course.

chubby (chub′ē) *adj.* **-bier, -bi·est** round and plump — **chub′bi·ness** *n.*

chuck[1] (chuk) *vt.* 〖< ? Fr *choquer*, strike against〗 1 to tap playfully, esp. under the chin 2 to throw; toss 3 [Slang] to get rid of — *n.* a chucking

chuck[2] (chuk) *n.* 〖prob. var. of CHOCK〗 1 a cut of beef from around the neck and shoulder blade 2 a clamplike holding device, as on a lathe

chuck′-full′ *adj. var. of* CHOCK-FULL

chuck′hole′ *n.* 〖see CHOCK & HOLE〗 a rough hole in pavement

chuckle (chuk′əl) *vi.* **-led, -ling** 〖? < var. of CLUCK〗 to laugh softly in a low tone — *n.* a soft, low-toned laugh

chuck wagon a wagon equipped as a kitchen for feeding cowboys, etc.

chuck·walla (chuk′wäl′ə) *n.* 〖< AmInd (Mexico)〗 a large, edible iguana of Mexico and SW U.S.

chug (chug) *n.* 〖echoic〗 a puffing or explosive sound, as of a locomotive — *vi.* **chugged, chug′ging** to make, or move with, such sounds

chukka (boot) (chuk′ə) an ankle-high bootlike shoe

chum (chum) *n.* 〖< *chamber (mate)*〗 [Colloq.] a close friend — *vi.* **chummed, chum′ming** [Colloq.] to be close friends —**chum′mi·ness** *n.* —**chum′my, -mier, -mi·est,** *adj.*

chump (chump) *n.* 〖akin to MHG *kumpf,* dull〗 [Colloq.] a stupid person; fool

chunk (chuŋk) *n.* 〖< ? CHUCK[2]〗 a short, thick piece

chunky (chuŋ′kē) *adj.* **-i·er, -i·est** 1 short and thick 2 stocky —**chunk′i·ness** *n.*

church (church) *n.* 〖< Gr *kyriakē* (*oikia*), Lord's (house)〗 1 a building for public worship, esp. Christian worship 2 religious service 3 [*usually* C-] *a*) all Christians *b*) a particular Christian denomination 4 ecclesiastical, as opposed to secular, government

church′go′er (-gō′ər) *n.* a person who attends church, esp. regularly

church′man (-mən) *n., pl.* **-men** 1 a clergyman 2 a church member

Church of England the episcopal church of England; Anglican Church: it is an established church headed by the sovereign

church′war′den (-wôrd′'n) *n.* a lay officer handling certain secular matters in a church

church′yard′ *n.* the ground adjoining a church, often used as a cemetery

churl (churl) *n.* 〖OE *ceorl,* peasant〗 1 a peasant 2 a surly, ill-bred person; boor —**churl′ish** *adj.* —**churl′ish·ness** *n.*

churn (churn) *n.* 〖OE *cyrne*〗 a container in which milk or cream is stirred and shaken to form butter — *vt., vi.* 1 to stir and shake (milk or cream) in a churn 2 to make (butter) thus 3 to stir up or move vigorously

chute[1] (shōōt) *n.* 〖Fr, a fall〗 an inclined or vertical trough or passage down which things slide or drop

chute[2] (shōōt) *n. short for* PARACHUTE

chut·ney (chut′nē) *n., pl.* **-neys** 〖Hindi *chatnī*〗 a relish of fruits, spices, herbs, and vinegar Also **chut′nee**

chutz·pah or **chutzpa** (hoots′pə) *n.* 〖Yidd > Heb〗 [Colloq.] impudence; brass

chyme (kīm) *n.* 〖< Gr *chymos,* juice〗 the semifluid mass formed as the stomach digests food: it passes into the small intestine

CIA Central Intelligence Agency

ci·cada (si kā′də) *n., pl.* **-das** or **-dae** (-dē) 〖L〗 a large, flylike insect with transparent wings: the male makes a loud, shrill sound

cica·trix (sik′ə triks′) *n., pl.* **cica·tri·ces** (sik′ə trī′sēz′) or **cica·trixes** 〖L〗 a scar

-cide (sīd) 〖< L *caedere,* to kill〗 *suffix* 1 a killer 2 a killing

ci·der (sī′dər) *n.* 〖< Gr *sikera,* an intoxicant〗 juice pressed from apples, used as a drink or for making vinegar

ci·gar (si gär′) *n.* 〖Sp *cigarro*〗 a cylindrical roll of cured tobacco wrapped in another leaf for smoking

ciga·rette or **ciga·ret** (sig′ə ret′) *n.* 〖Fr〗 a small roll of finely cut tobacco wrapped in thin paper for smoking

ciga·rillo (sig′ə ril′ō) *n., pl.* **-los** 〖Sp, dim. of *cigarro, cigar*〗 a small, thin cigar

cil·ia (sil′ē ə) *n.pl., sing.* **-ium** (-ē əm) 〖< L〗 *Bot.* small hairlike projections extending from certain plant cells and forming a fringe

ci·meti·dine (sə met′ə dēn′) *n.* a drug that blocks histamine receptors, reducing gastric secretion: used to treat peptic ulcers

cinch (sinch) *n.* 〖< Sp < L *cingulum,* girdle〗 1 a saddle or pack girth 2 [Slang] a thing easy to do or sure to happen — *vt.* 1 to fasten (a saddle) on 2 [Slang] to make sure of

cin·chona (sin kō′nə) *n.* 〖after 17th-c. Peruvian Countess del *Chinchón*〗 1 a tropical tree with a bitter bark from which quinine is made 2 this bark

cinc·ture (siŋk′chər) *n.* 〖L *cinctura*〗 a belt or girdle

cin·der (sin′dər) *n.* 〖OE *sinder,* slag〗 1 a tiny piece of partly burned wood, etc. 2 [*pl.*] ashes from coal or wood

Cin·der·ella (sin′dər el′ə) in a fairy tale, a household drudge who eventually marries a prince

cin·ema (sin′ə mə) *n.* 〖< Gr *kinēma,* motion〗 [Chiefly Brit.] a film theater —**the cinema** 1 the making of films 2 films collectively —**cin′emat′ic** *adj.*

cin·ema·tog·ra·phy (sin′ə mə täg′rə fē) *n.* the art, science, and work of photography in making films —**cin′ema·tog′ra·pher** *n.* —**cin′emat′o·graph′ic** (-mat′ə graf′ik) *adj.*

cin·na·bar (sin′ə bär′) *n.* 〖< Gr *kinnabari*〗 mercuric sulfide, a heavy, bright-red mineral

cin·na·mon (sin′ə mən) *n.* 〖< Heb *qinnāmōn*〗 1 the light-brown spice made from the dried inner bark of a laurel tree 2 this bark 3 this bark

ci·pher (sī′fər) *n.* 〖< Ar *ṣifr*〗 1 the symbol 0; zero 2 a nonentity 3 secret writing based on a key; code 4 the key to such a code — *vi.* [Now Rare] to solve arithmetic problems

circa (sur′kə) *prep.* 〖L〗 about: used before an approximate date or figure

cir·ca·dian (sər kā′dē ən) *adj.* 〖coined < L *circa,* about + *dies,* day〗 of the behavioral or physiological rhythms associated with the 24-hour cycle of the earth's rotation

Circe (sur′sē) in the *Odyssey,* an enchantress who turns men into swine

cir·cle (sur′kəl) *n.* 〖< Gr *kirkos*〗 1 a plane figure bounded by a single curved line every point of which is equally distant from the center 2 this curved line 3 anything like a circle, as a ring 4 a complete or recurring series; cycle 5 a group of people with common interests 6 extent, as of influence; scope — *vt.* **-cled, -cling** 1 to form a circle

---

THESAURUS

chubby *a.* plump, round, pudgy; see FAT.

chuckle *n.* giggle, smile, grin; see LAUGH.

chuckle *v.* giggle, smile, snigger; see LAUGH.

chummy* *a.* affectionate, intimate, constant; see FRIENDLY.

chunk *n.* piece, mass, lump; see PART 1.

chunky *a.* stocky, thickset, stout; see FAT.

church *n.* 1 [A building consecrated to worship] cathedral, house of God, Lord's house, temple, synagogue, mosque, house of worship, meeting house, chapel, basilica, tabernacle, abbey, sanctuary, house of prayer, mission, shrine, pagoda. 2 [A divine service] rite, prayers, prayer meeting, Sunday school, worhsip, Mass, Lord's Supper, sacrament, the holy sacrament, rosary, ritual, religious rite, morning service, evening service, congregational worship, fellowship, devotion, office, revival meeting, chapel service, sermon, communion; see also CEREMONY. 3 [An organized religious body] congregation, gathering, denomination, sect, chapter, body, order, communion, faith, religion, religious order, affiliation, persuasion, belief, faction, doctrine, creed, cult. *Christian churches include the following:* Methodist, Presbyterian, Unitarian, Episcopalian, Baptist, Christian Science, Mormon, Congregational, Lutheran, Roman Catholic, Eastern Orthodox, Greek, Russian, Pentecostal, Church of England, Church of the Nazarene, Society of Friends.

churn *v.* stir, beat, agitate; see MIX 1.

cigarette *n.* fag*, smoke*, coffin nail*, weed*.

cinema *n.* film, motion pictures, the movies; see MOVIE.

circle *n.* 1 [A round closed plane figure] ring, loop, wheel, sphere, globe, orb, orbit, zodiac, bowl, vortex, hoop, horizon, perimeter, periphery, circumference, full turn, circuit, disk, meridian, equator, ecliptic, cycle, bracelet, belt, wreath. 2 [An endless sequence of events] cycle, course, succession; see PROGRESS 1, SERIES, SEQUENCE 1. —**come full circle** go through a cycle, come back, revert; see RETURN 1.

circle *v.* round, encircle, loop, tour, circumnavigate, ring, belt, embrace, encompass, wind about, revolve around, circumscribe, curve around, circuit, enclose, spiral, coil, circulate, detour, wind, roll, wheel, swing past, go round about, evade; see also SURROUND 1.—*Ant.* DIVIDE, bisect, cut across.

cir′clet (-klit) *n.* 1 a small circle 2 a circular ornament, as for the head

cir·cuit (sur′kit) *n.* ⟦ < L *circum*, around + *ire*, go ⟧ 1 a boundary line or its length 2 a going around something 3 the regular journey through a district of a person at work, as a preacher 4 a chain or association, as of theaters or resorts 5 the path or line of an electric current — *vi.* to go in a circuit — *vt.* to make a circuit about —**cir′cuital** *adj.*

circuit breaker a device that automatically interrupts the flow of an electric current

circuit court a court that holds sessions in various places within its district

cir·cui·tous (sər kyōō′ət əs) *adj.* roundabout; indirect — **cir·cu′i·tously** *adv.* —**cir·cu′i·tous·ness** *n.*

cir·cuitry (sur′kə trē) *n.* the system or the elements of an electric circuit

cir·cu·lar (sur′kyə lər) *adj.* 1 in the shape of a circle; round 2 moving in a circle 3 circuitous — *n.* an advertisement, etc., intended for many readers —**cir′cu·lar′i·ty** (-ler′ə tē) *n.*

cir·cu·lar·ize (′-lər iz′) *vt.* **-ized′, -iz′ing** 1 to make circular 2 to send circulars to 3 to canvass —**cir′cu·lar·i·za′tion** *n.* —**cir′cu·lar·iz′er** *n.*

cir·cu·late (sur′kyōō lāt′) *vi.* **-lat′ed, -lat′ing** ⟦ < L *circulari*, form a circle ⟧ 1 to move in a circle or circuit and return, as the blood 2 to go from person to person or from place to place — *vt.* to make circulate —**cir′cu·lat′or** *n.* —**cir′cu·la·to′ry** (-lə tôr′ē) *adj.*

cir·cu·la·tion (sur′kyōō lā′shən) *n.* 1 a circulating 2 the movement of blood through the arteries and veins 3 distribution of newspapers, magazines, etc.

circum- ⟦ < L *circum* ⟧ *prefix* around, about, surrounding

cir·cum·cise (sur′kəm siz′) *vt.* **-cised′, -cis′ing** ⟦ < L < *circum*, around + *caedere*, to cut ⟧ to cut off all or part of the foreskin of —**cir′cum·ci′sion** (-sizh′ən) *n.*

cir·cum·fer·ence (sər kum′fər əns) *n.* ⟦ < L *circum*, around + *ferre*, to carry ⟧ 1 the line bounding a circle, ball, etc. 2 the length of this line

cir·cum·flex (sur′kəm fleks′) *n.* ⟦ < L *circum*, around + *flectere*, to bend ⟧ a mark (^, ˋ, ˜) used over a vowel letter or symbol to indicate pronunciation

cir·cum·lo·cu′tion (-lō kyōō′shən) *n.* ⟦ < L: see CIRCUM- & LOCUTION ⟧ a roundabout way of saying something

cir′cum·nav′i·gate′ (-nav′ə gāt′) *vt.* **-gat′ed, -gat′ing** ⟦ < L: see CIRCUM- & NAVIGATE ⟧ to sail or fly around (the earth, etc.) —**cir′cum·nav′i·ga′tion** *n.*

cir′cum·scribe′ (-skrib′) *vt.* **-scribed′, -scrib′ing** ⟦ < L: see CIRCUM- & SCRIBE ⟧ 1 to trace a line around; encircle 2 to limit; confine —**cir′cum·scrip′tion** (-skrip′shən) *n.*

cir′cum·spect′ (-spekt′) *adj.* ⟦ < L *circumspicere*, look about ⟧ cautious —**cir′cum·spec′tion** *n.*

cir′cum·stance′ (-stans′) *n.* ⟦ < L *circum*, around + *stare*, to stand ⟧ 1 a fact or event accompanying another 2 [*pl.*] conditions affecting a person, esp. financial conditions 3

chance; luck 4 ceremony; show — *vt.* **-stanced′, -stanc′ing** to place in certain circumstances —**under no circumstances** never —**cir′cum·stanced′** *adj.*

cir′cum·stan′tial (-stan′shəl) *adj.* 1 having to do with, or depending on, circumstances 2 incidental 3 complete in detail —**cir′cum·stan′tially** *adv.*

circumstantial evidence *Law* indirect evidence of a fact at issue, based on attendant circumstances

cir′cum·stan′ti·ate′ (-stan′shē āt′) *vt.* **-at′ed, -at′ing** to give detailed proof or support of —**cir′cum·stan′tia′tion** *n.*

cir′cum·vent′ (-vent′) *vt.* ⟦ < L *circum*, around + *venire*, come ⟧ to get the better of or prevent by craft or ingenuity —**cir′cum·ven′tion** *n.*

cir·cus (sur′kəs) *n.* ⟦ L, a circle ⟧ 1 in ancient Rome, an amphitheater 2 a traveling show of acrobats, trained animals, clowns, etc. 3 [Colloq.] a source of great fun

ciré (sē rā′) *adj.* ⟦ < Fr *cire*, wax ⟧ having a smooth, glossy finish

cir·rho·sis (sə rō′sis) *n.* ⟦ < Gr *kirrhos*, tawny + -OSIS ⟧ a degenerative disease, esp. of the liver, marked by excess formation of connective tissue —**cir·rhotic** (-rät′ik) *adj.*

cir·rus (sir′əs) *n.* ⟦ L, a curl ⟧ the type of cloud resembling a wispy filament and found at high altitudes

cis- ⟦ < L *cis*, on this side ⟧ *prefix* on this side of

cis·tern (sis′tərn) *n.* ⟦ < L *cista*, chest ⟧ a large tank for storing water

cita·del (sit′ə del′) *n.* ⟦ < L *civitas*, city ⟧ a fortress

cite (sit) *vt.* **cit′ed, cit′ing** ⟦ < L *citare*, summon ⟧ 1 to summon before a court of law 2 to quote 3 to mention by way of example, proof, etc. 4 to mention in an official report as meritorious —**ci·ta′tion** *n.*

citi·fied (sit′i fid′) *adj.* having the manners, dress, etc. of city people

citi·zen (sit′ə zən) *n.* ⟦ < L *civis*, townsman ⟧ a member of a state or nation who owes allegiance to it by birth or naturalization and is entitled to certain rights, as the right to vote, etc. —**cit′i·zen·ship′** *n.*

cit′i·zenry (-rē) *n.* all citizens as a group

cit·ric (si′trik) *adj.* designating or of an acid obtained from citrus fruits

cit′ron (-trən) *n.* ⟦ < Fr, lemon ⟧ 1 a yellow, thick-skinned, lemonlike fruit 2 its candied rind

cit·ron·ella (si′trə nel′ə) *n.* ⟦ see prec. ⟧ a sharp-smelling oil used in perfume, insect repellents, etc.

cit′rus (-trəs) *n.* ⟦ L ⟧ 1 any of the trees that bear oranges, lemons, limes, etc. 2 any such fruit — *adj.* of these trees: also **cit′rous**

city (sit′ē) *n., pl.* **-ies** ⟦ < L *civis*, townsman ⟧ 1 a population center larger or more important than a town 2 in the U.S., an incorporated municipality with boundaries and powers defined by State charter 3 the people of a city — *adj.* of, in, or for a city

---

THESAURUS

circuit *n.* circumference, course, circle; see ORBIT 1, REVOLUTION 1.

circular *a.* spherical, cyclical, globular; see ROUND 1.

circular *n.* handbill, broadside, leaflet; see ADVERTISEMENT, PAMPHLET.

circulate *v.* 1 [To go about] move around, go about, wander; see TRAVEL, WALK 1. 2 [To send about] diffuse, report, broadcast; see DISTRIBUTE.

circulation *n.* 1 [Motion in a circle] rotation, current, flowing; see FLOW, REVOLUTION 1. 2 [Number of copies distributed] transmission, apportionment, dissemination; see DISTRIBUTION.

circumference *n.* perimeter, periphery, border; see CIRCLE 1.

circumscribe *v.* encircle, encompass, girdle; see SURROUND 1.

circumstance *n.* 1 [An attendant condition] situation, condition, contingency, phase, factor, detail, item, fact, case, place, time, cause, status, element, feature, point, incident, article, stipulation, concern, matter, event, occurrence, crisis, coincidence, happenstance*. 2 [An occurrence] episode, happening, incident; see EVENT.

circumstances *n.* 1 [Condition in life] worldly goods, outlook, prospects, chances, means, assets, prosperity, financial condition, resources, standing, property, net worth, financial standing, credit rating, terms, way of life, rank, class, degree, capital, position, financial responsibility, footing, income, sphere, substance, stock in trade, lot, prestige, what one is worth, place on the ladder; see also STATE 2, WEALTH. 2 [Attendant conditions] situation, environment, surroundings, facts, particulars, factors, features, motives, controlling factors, governing factors, the times, occasion, basis, grounds, setting, background, needs, requirements, necessities, course of events, legal status, change, life, fluctuation, phase, case, condition, state of affairs, surrounding facts, the score*, the scene*, the story*, where it's at*, how the land lies, the lay of the land, current regime, ups and downs. —**under no circumstances** under no conditions, by no means, absolutely not; see NEVER. —**under the circumstances** conditions being what they are, for this reason, because of; see BECAUSE.

circumstantial *a.* presumptive, inferential, inconclusive; see UNCERTAIN.

circumvent *v.* 1 [To go around] encircle, encompass, entrap; see SURROUND 1. 2 [To avoid] dodge, elude, shun; see AVOID, EVADE.

circus *n.* hippodrome, spectacle, fair; see ENTERTAINMENT.

citation *n.* bidding, charge, summons; see COMMAND.

citizen *n.* inhabitant, denizen, national, subject, cosmopolite, commoner, civilian, urbanite, taxpayer, member of the community, householder, native, occupant, settler, voter, dweller, immigrant, naturalized person, townsman, the man on the street, villager, John Q. Public; see also RESIDENT.

city *a.* metropolitan, civil, civic; see MUNICIPAL.

city *n.* town, place, municipality, capital, megalopolis, metropolis, suburb, county seat, trading center, inner city, downtown, shopping center, shopping district, business district, financial district, incorporated town, village, metropolitan area, township; see also CENTER 2.

city hall a building which houses a municipal government

civet (siv'it) *n.* 〚< Ar *zabād*〛 **1** the musky secretion of a catlike carnivore (**civet cat**) of Africa and S Asia: used in some perfumes **2** the animal, or its fur

civic (siv'ik) *adj.* 〚< L *civis*, townsman〛 of a city, citizens, or citizenship

civ'ics (-iks) *n.pl.* [*with sing. v.*] the study of civic affairs and the duties and rights of citizenship

civil (siv'əl) *adj.* 〚see CIVIC〛 **1** of a citizen or citizens **2** civilized **3** polite **4** of citizens in matters not military or religious —**civ'illy** *adv.*

civil disobedience nonviolent opposition to a law through refusal to comply with it, on grounds of conscience

civil engineering engineering dealing with the construction of highways, bridges, harbors, etc. —**civil engineer**

ci·vil·ian (sə vil'yən) *n.* 〚see CIVIC〛 a person not in military or naval service —*adj.* of or for civilians; nonmilitary

ci·vil'i·ty (-ə tē) *n., pl.* -**ties 1** politeness **2** a civil, or polite, act

civi·li·za·tion (siv'ə lə zā'shən) *n.* **1** a civilizing or being civilized **2** the total culture of a people, period, etc. **3** the peoples considered to have attained a high social development

civ'i·lize' (-līz') *vt., vi.* -**lized', -liz'ing** 〚see CIVIC〛 **1** to bring or come out of a primitive or savage condition to a higher level of social organization and of cultural and scientific development **2** to refine —**civ'i·lized'** *adj.*

civil law the body of law having to do with private rights

civil liberties liberties guaranteed to all individuals by law, custom, court decisions, etc.; rights, as of speaking or acting as one likes, without hindrance except in the interests of the public welfare

civil rights those rights guaranteed to all individuals by the 13th, 14th, 15th, and 19th Amendments to the U.S. Constitution, as the right to vote and the right to equal treatment under the law

civil servant a civil service employee

civil service all those employed in government service, esp. through competitive public examination

civil war war between different factions of the same nation —**the Civil War** the war between the North and the South in the U.S. (1861-65)

civ·vies (siv'ēz) *n.pl.* [Colloq.] civilian clothes Also **civ'ies**

ck. check

Cl *Chem. symbol for* chlorine

cl centiliter(s)

clack (klak) *vi., vt.* 〚prob. echoic < ON〛 to make or cause to make a sudden, sharp sound — *n.* this sound

clad (klad) *vt. alt. pt. & pp. of* CLOTHE —*adj.* clothed; dressed

claim (klām) *vt.* 〚< L *clamare*, cry out〛 **1** to demand as rightfully belonging to one **2** to require; deserve [to *claim* attention] **3** to assert — *n.* **1** a claiming **2** a right to something **3** something claimed **4** an assertion —**claim'able** *adj.* —**claim'ant** or **claim'er** *n.*

clair·voy·ance (kler voi'əns) *n.* 〚Fr < *clair*, clear + *voyant*, seeing〛 the supposed ability to perceive things that are not in sight —**clair·voy'ant** *n., adj.*

clam (klam) *n.* 〚< obs. *clam*, a clamp〛 any of various hard-shelled, usually edible, bivalve mollusks — *vi.* **clammed, clam'ming** to dig for clams —**clam up** [Colloq.] to keep silent —**clam'mer** *n.*

clam'bake' *n.* **1** a picnic at which steamed or baked clams are served **2** [Colloq.] any large, noisy party

clam·ber (klam'bər) *vi., vt.* 〚ME *clambren*〛 to climb clumsily, esp. by using both the hands and the feet

clammy (klam'ē) *adj.* -**mier, -mi·est** 〚ME, prob. < OE *clam*, mud〛 moist, cold, and sticky —**clam'mi·ness** *n.*

clamor (klam'ər) *n.* 〚< L *clamare*, cry out〛 **1** a loud outcry; uproar **2** a loud demand or complaint — *vi.* to make a clamor —**clam'or·ous** *adj.*

clamp (klamp) *n.* 〚< MDu *klampe*〛 a device for clasping or fastening things together — *vt.* to fasten or brace, as with a clamp —**clamp down (on)** to become more strict (with)

clan (klan) *n.* 〚< Gael < L *planta*, offshoot〛 **1** a group of families claiming descent from a common ancestor **2** a group of people with interests in common —**clans·man** (klanz'mən), *pl.* -**men**, *n.*

clan·des·tine (klan des'tin) *adj.* 〚< L *clam*, secret〛 secret or hidden; furtive —**clan·des'tine·ly** *adv.*

clang (klaŋ) *vi., vt.* 〚echoic〛 to make or cause to make a loud, ringing sound, as by striking metal — *n.* this sound

clang'or (-ər) *n.* 〚L < *clangere*, to sound〛 a continuous clanging sound —**clang'or·ous** *adj.* —**clang'or·ously** *adv.*

clank (klaŋk) *n.* 〚echoic〛 a sharp, metallic sound — *vi., vt.* to make or cause to make this sound

clan·nish (klan'ish) *adj.* **1** of a clan **2** tending to associate closely with one's own group only —**clan'nishly** *adv.* —**clan'nish·ness** *n.*

clap (klap) *vi.* **clapped, clap'ping** 〚OE *clæppan*, to beat〛 **1** to make a sudden, explosive sound, as of two flat surfaces struck together **2** to strike the hands together, as in applauding — *vt.* **1** to strike together briskly **2** to strike with an open hand **3** to put, move, etc. abruptly [*clapped* into jail] — *n.* **1** the sound or act of clapping **2** a sharp slap

clap·board (klab'ərd) *n.* 〚transl. of MDu *klapholt* < *klappen*, to fit + *holt*, wood〛 a thin board with one thicker edge, used as siding — *vt.* to cover with clapboards

clap'per *n.* a thing that makes a clapping sound, as the tongue of a bell

clap'trap' *n.* 〚CLAP + TRAP¹〛 insincere, empty talk intended to get applause

claque (klak) *n.* 〚Fr < *claquer*, to clap〛 a group of people paid to applaud at a play, opera, etc.

claret (klar'it) *n.* 〚< OFr (*vin*) *claret*, clear (wine)〛 a dry red wine

clari·fy (klar'ə fī') *vt., vi.* -**fied', -fy'ing** 〚< L *clarus*, clear + *facere*, to make〛 to make or become clear —**clar'i·fi·ca'tion** *n.*

clari·net (klar'ə net') *n.* 〚< Fr < L *clarus*, clear〛 a single-reed woodwind instrument played by means of holes and keys —**clar'i·net'ist** or **clar'i·net'tist** *n.*

clari·on (klar'ē ən) *adj.* 〚< L *clarus*, clear〛 clear, sharp, and ringing [a *clarion* call]

clar·ity (klar'ə tē) *n.* 〚< L *clarus*, clear〛 clear quality; clearness

---

THESAURUS

civic *a.* civil, urban, municipal; see PUBLIC 1, 2.

civil *a.* **1** [Civic] local, civic, public; see MUNICIPAL. **2** [Polite] formal, courteous, refined; see POLITE.

civilian *n.* private citizen, noncombatant, person not in the armed forces; see CITIZEN.

civilization *n.* cultivation, polish, enlightenment, refinement, civility, illumination, advancement of knowledge, elevation, edification, culture, advancement, social well-being, degree of cultivation, material well-being, education, breeding; see also CULTURE 1, PROGRESS 1.—*Ant.* barbarism, savagery, degeneration.

civilize *v.* enlighten, cultivate, enrich, reclaim, refine, acculturate, spiritualize, humanize, edify, uplift, tame, foster, instruct, promote, indoctrinate, idealize, elevate, educate, advance, ennoble; see also DEVELOP 1, TEACH.

civilized *a.* enlightened, refined, humanized; see CULTURED, EDUCATED.

civil rights *n.* civil liberties, equality, four freedoms; see CHOICE, FREEDOM 1.

claim *n.* demand, declaration, profession, entreaty, petition, suit, ultimatum, call, request, requirement, application, case, assertion, plea, right, interest, title, part; see also APPEAL 1. —**lay claim to** demand, challenge, stake out a claim to; see OWN 1.

claim *v.* **1** [To assert a claim to] demand, attach, lay claim to; see OWN 1. **2** [To assert] insist, pronounce, pretend; see BELIEVE, DECLARE.

clam *n.* bivalve, mollusk, shellfish; see FISH.

clammy *a.* moist, damp, soggy; see COLD 1, WET 1.

clamor *n.* din, outcry, discord; see NOISE 2, UPROAR.

clamp *n.* snap, clasp, catch; see FASTENER, LOCK 1.

clan *n.* group, clique, moiety; see ORGANIZATION 2, RACE 2.

clang *n.* ring, clatter, jangle; see NOISE 1.

clank *n.* chink, bang, clink; see NOISE 1.

clap *v.* **1** [To applaud] cheer, acclaim, approve; see PRAISE 1. **2** [To strike] bang, slap, slam; see HIT 1.

clarification *n.* exposition, elucidation, description; see DEFINITION, EXPLANATION, INTERPRETATION.

clarify *v.* interpret, define, elucidate; see EXPLAIN.

clarity *n.* limpidity, clearness, purity, brightness, precision, explicitness, exactness, distinctness, plain speech, openness, directness, evidence, prominence, salience, transparency, conspicuousness, certainty, lucid-

clash (klash) *vi.* [echoic] **1** to collide with a loud, harsh, metallic noise **2** to conflict; disagree — *vt.* to strike with a clashing noise — *n.* **1** the sound of clashing **2** conflict

clasp (klasp) *n.* [ME *claspe*] **1** a fastening, as a hook, to hold things together **2** a grasping; embrace **3** a grip of the hand — *vt.* **1** to fasten with a clasp **2** to hold or embrace tightly **3** to grip with the hand

class (klas) *n.* [< L *classis*] **1** a number of people or things grouped together because of certain likenesses; kind; sort **2** social or economic rank /the working *class]* **3** *a)* a group of students taught together *b)* a meeting of such a group *c)* a group graduating together **4** grade or quality **5** [Slang] excellence, as of style — *vt.* to classify — **class′less** *adj.*

class action (suit) a legal action brought by one or more persons on behalf of themselves and a much larger group

clas·sic (klas′ik) *adj.* [< L *classis*, class] **1** being an excellent model of its kind **2** CLASSICAL (senses 2 & 3) **3** balanced, formal, regular, simple, etc. **4** famous as traditional or typical — *n.* **1** a literary or artistic work of the highest excellence **2** a creator of such a work **3** [*pl.*] *a)* the works of outstanding ancient Greek and Roman authors (usually with *the*) *b)* [*with sing. v.*] the study of these works and of ancient Greek and Latin **4** a famous traditional or typical event

clas·si·cal (-i kəl) *adj.* **1** CLASSIC (senses 1 & 3) **2** of the art, literature, etc. of the ancient Greeks and Romans **3** typical of or derived from the artistic standards of the ancient Greeks and Romans **4** versed in Greek and Roman culture **5** standard and traditional *[classical economics]* **6** designating, of, or like music conforming to certain standards of form, complexity, etc. — **clas′si·cally** *adv.*

clas·si·cism′ (-ə siz′əm) *n.* **1** the aesthetic principles of ancient Greece and Rome **2** adherence to these principles **3** knowledge of classical literature and art — **clas′si·cist** *n.*

classified advertising advertising arranged according to subject, usually under such listings as *help wanted*

clas·si·fy (klas′ə fī′) *vt.* **-fied′, -fy′ing 1** to arrange in classes according to a system **2** to designate (government documents) to be secret or restricted — **clas′si·fi·ca′tion** *n.* — **clas′si·fi′er** *n.*

class′mate′ *n.* a member of the same class at a school or college

class′room′ *n.* a room in a school or college in which classes are taught

classy (klas′ē) *adj.* **-i·er, -i·est** [Slang] first-class, esp. in style; elegant — **class′i·ness** *n.*

clat·ter (klat′ər) *vi., vt.* [ME *clateren*] to make or cause to make a clatter — *n.* **1** a rapid succession of loud, sharp noises **2** a tumult; hubbub

clause (klôz) *n.* [< L *claudere*, to close] **1** a group of words containing a subject and a finite verb: see DEPENDENT CLAUSE, INDEPENDENT CLAUSE **2** a particular article or provision in a document — **claus′al** *adj.*

claustro·pho·bia (klôs′trə fō′bē ə) *n.* [< L *claustrum*, enclosed place + -PHOBIA] abnormal fear of enclosed places — **claus′tro·pho′bic** *adj.*

clavi·chord (klav′i kôrd′) *n.* [< L *clavis*, key + *chorda*, string] a stringed musical instrument with a keyboard, predecessor of the piano

clavi·cle (klav′i kəl) *n.* [< L *clavis*, key] a bone connecting the breastbone with the shoulder blade

cla·vier (klə vir′; *for 1, also* klă′vē ər) *n.* [Fr < L *clavis*, key] **1** the keyboard of an organ, piano, etc. **2** any stringed keyboard instrument

claw (klô) *n.* [OE *clawu*] **1** a sharp, hooked nail on an animal's or bird's foot **2** the pincers of a lobster, etc. — *vt., vi.* to scratch, clutch, tear, etc. with or as with claws

clay (klā) *n.* [OE *clæg*] **1** firm, plastic earth, used in making bricks, etc. **2** *a)* earth *b)* the human body — **clay′ey, clay′i·er, clay′i·est,** *adj.*

clean (klēn) *adj.* [OE *clæne*] **1** free from dirt and impurities; unsoiled **2** morally pure **3** fair; sportsmanlike **4** neat and tidy **5** well-formed **6** free from flaws **7** clear **8** thorough — *adv.* completely — *vt., vi.* to make or be made clean — **clean up** **1** to make neat **2** [Colloq.] to finish **3** [Slang] to make much profit — **come clean** [Slang] to confess — **clean′ly** *adv.* — **clean′ness** *n.*

clean′-cut′ *adj.* **1** clearly outlined **2** well-formed **3** trim, neat, etc.

clean′er *n.* a person or thing that cleans; specif., one who dry-cleans

══ THESAURUS ══

ity.—*Ant.* DARKNESS, haze, obscurity.

clash *n.* **1** [Collision] crash, encounter, impact; see COLLISION. **2** [Disagreement] opposition, conflict, argument; see DISAGREEMENT ·1, DISPUTE.

clash *v.* be dissimilar, mismatch, not go with; see CONTRAST, DIFFER 1.

clasp *n.* buckle, pin, clamp; see FASTENER.

clasp *v.* clamp, pin, buckle; see FASTEN.

class *n.* **1** [A classification] degree, order, rank, grade, standing, genus, division, distinction, breed, type, kingdom, subdivision, phylum, subphylum, superorder, family, sect, category, rate, collection, denomination, department, sort, species, variety, branch, group, genre, range, brand, set, kind, section, domain, nature, color, origin, character, frame, temperament, school, designation, sphere, spirit, vein, persuasion, province, make, grain, source, name, mood, habit, form, selection, stamp, status, range, property, aspect, disposition, tone; see also CLASSIFICATION. **2** [A group organized for study] lecture, seminar, study session; see SCHOOL 1. **3** [A division of society] set, caste, social level; see FAMILY. **—in a class by itself** unusual, different, one of a kind; see UNIQUE.

class *v.* identify, rank, grade; see CLASSIFY, MARK 2.

classic *n.* opus, masterwork, exemplar; see MASTERPIECE.

classical *a.* **1** [Of recognized importance] standard, first-rate, established, ideal, flawless, distinguished, paramount, aesthetic, superior, artistic, well-known; see also EXCEL-

LENT.—*Ant.* POPULAR, modern, transitory. **2** [Concerning ancient Greece or Rome] humanistic, academic, classic; see OLD 3.

classification *n.* arrangement, assortment, grouping, ordering, allotment, organization, gradation, coordination, disposition, categorizing, apportionment, analysis, division, assignment, designation, assorting, distribution, allocation, categorization; see also CLASS 1, ORDER 3.

classified *a.* assorted, grouped, classed, indexed, filed, orderly, recorded, listed, registered, detailed, arranged, regulated, compiled, coordinated, ranked, distributed, cataloged, separated, labeled, numbered, systematized, tabulated, alphabetized, typed, on file, rated.—*Ant.* MIXED, confused, jumbled.

classify *v.* arrange, order, pigeonhole, tabulate, organize, distribute, categorize, systematize, coordinate, correlate, incorporate, label, alphabetize, place in a category, range, form into classes, divide, allocate, number, rate, class, rank, catalog, segregate, distinguish, allot, analyze, regiment, name, group, tag, type, put in order, break down, assort, sort, index, grade, match, size, reduce to order; see also FILE 1, LIST 1.—*Ant.* DISORGANIZE, disorder, disarrange.

clatter *v.* rattle, clash, crash; see SOUND.

clause *n.* **1** [A provision] condition, codicil, ultimatum; see LIMITATION 2, REQUIREMENT 1. **2** [A grammatical structure] limiters, sentence modifiers, transformations; see GRAMMAR.

claw *n.* talon, hook, spur, paw, grappling iron, grappling hook, forked end, clutching hand, grapnel, crook,

barb, pincers, fingernail.

claw *v.* tear, scratch, rip open; see BREAK 1, HURT, RIP.

clay *n.* loam, earth, till, marl, kaolin, potter's clay, clayware, green pottery, terra cotta, green brick, china clay, porcelain clay, adobe; see also MUD.

clean *a.* **1** [Not soiled] spotless, washed, stainless, laundered, untarnished, unstained, neat, tidy, clear, blank, white, unblemished, unspotted, snowy, well-kept, dustless, cleansed, immaculate, unsoiled, unpolluted, spic and span*, clean as a whistle*.—*Ant.* DIRTY, soiled, stained. **2** [Not contaminated] unadulterated, wholesome, sanitary; see PURE 2. **3** [Having sharp outlines] clear-cut, sharp, distinct; see DEFINITE 2. **4** [Thorough] complete, entire, total; see ABSOLUTE 1, WHOLE 1. **5** [Fair] reliable, decent, lawful; see FAIR 1, HONEST 1. **—come clean*** confess, reveal, expose; see ADMIT 2.

clean *v.* cleanse, clean up, clear up, clear out, purify, soak, shake out, wash down, scrub off, disinfect, tidy up, deodorize, swab, polish, sterilize, scrape, sweep out, scour, launder, vacuum, scald, dust, mop, cauterize, rinse, sponge, brush, dress, comb, whisk, scrub, sweep, wipe up, clarify, rake, clean away, make clear, bathe, soap, erase, neaten, shampoo, refine, flush, blot, dry up*, spruce up, slick up*; see also WASH 1, 2.—*Ant.* DIRTY, soil, smear.

cleaner *n.* detergent, disinfectant, cleaning agent; see CLEANSER, SOAP.

cleaning *a.* cleansing, purgative, detergent, washing, delousing, dusting, sweeping, scouring, soaking, sterilizing, laundering, vacuuming,

cleanly (klen′lē) *adj.* **-lier, -li·est** 1 keeping oneself or one's surroundings clean 2 always kept clean —**clean′li·ness** *n.*

clean room a room, as in a computer center, designed to be nearly 100% free of dust, pollen, etc.

cleanse (klenz) *vt.* **cleansed, cleans′ing** [OE *clænsian*] to make clean, pure, etc. —**cleans′er** *n.*

clean′up′ *n.* 1 a cleaning up 2 elimination of crime 3 [Slang] profit; gain

clear (klir) *adj.* [< L *clarus*] 1 free from clouds; bright 2 transparent 3 easily seen or heard; distinct 4 keen or logical *[a clear mind]* 5 not obscure; obvious 6 certain; positive 7 free from guilt 8 free from deductions; net 9 free from debt 10 free from obstruction; open — *adv.* 1 in a clear manner 2 all the way; completely — *vt.* 1 to make clear 2 to free from impurities, blemishes, etc. 3 to make lucid; clarify 4 to open *[to clear a path]* 5 to get rid of 6 to prove the innocence of 7 to pass or leap over, by, etc., esp. without touching 8 to be passed or approved by 9 to make as profit 10 *Banking* to pass (a check, etc.) through a clearinghouse — *vi.* to become clear —**clear away** 1 to remove so as to leave a cleared space 2 to go away —**clear off** to clear away —**clear out** [Colloq.] to depart —**clear up** to make or become clear —**in the clear** 1 free from obstructions 2 [Colloq.] guiltless —**clear′ly** *adv.* —**clear′ness** *n.*

clear′ance (-əns) *n.* the clear space between a moving object and that which it is passing

clear′-cut′ *adj.* 1 clearly outlined 2 distinct; definite

clear′ing *n.* an area of land cleared of trees

clear′ing·house′ *n.* 1 an office maintained by several banks for exchanging checks, balancing accounts, etc. 2 a central office, as for exchanging information

cleat (klēt) *n.* [ME *clete*] a piece of wood or metal fastened to something to strengthen it or give secure footing

cleav·age (klēv′ij′) *n.* 1 a cleaving; dividing 2 a cleft; fissure; division

cleave[1] (klēv) *vt., vi.* **cleaved** or **cleft** or **clove, cleaved** or **cleft** or **clo′ven, cleav′ing** [OE *cleofan*] to divide by a blow; split; sever —**cleav′able** *adj.*

cleave[2] (klēv) *vi.* **cleaved, cleav′ing** [OE *cleofian*] 1 to adhere; cling (*to*) 2 to be faithful (*to*)

cleaver (klēv′ər) *n.* a heavy cutting tool with a broad blade, used by butchers

clef (klef) *n.* [Fr < L *clavis*, key] a symbol used at the beginning of a musical staff to indicate the pitch of the notes

cleft[1] (kleft) *n.* [< OE *cleofan*: see CLEAVE[1]] an opening made by cleaving; crack; crevice

cleft[2] (kleft) *vt., vi.* alt. *pt. & pp.* of CLEAVE[1] — *adj.* split; divided

cleft palate a cleft from front to back along the middle of the roof of the mouth, from incomplete prenatal development

clema·tis (klem′ə tis) *n.* [< Gr *klēma*, vine] a vine of the buttercup family, with bright-colored flowers

clem·ent (klem′ənt) *adj.* [L *clemens*] 1 lenient; merciful 2 mild, as weather —**clem′ency** (-ən sē) *n.*

clench (klench) *vt.* [< OE (*be*)*clencan*, to make cling] 1 to close (the teeth or fist) firmly 2 to grip tightly — *n.* a firm grip

clere·story (klir′stôr′ē) *n., pl.* **-ries** [< ME *cler*, clear + *storie*, story (of a building)] the upper part of a wall, as of a church, with windows for lighting the central space

clergy (klur′jē) *n., pl.* **-gies** [see CLERK] ministers, priests, rabbis, etc., collectively

cler′gy·man (-mən) *n., pl.* **-men** a member of the clergy; minister, priest, rabbi, etc. —**cler′gy·wom′an,** *pl.* **-wom′en,** *n.fem.*

cleric (kler′ik) *n.* a member of the clergy

cler′i·cal (-i kəl) *adj.* 1 of the clergy or one of its members 2 of office clerks or their work

cler′i·cal·ism′ (-iz′əm) *n.* political power of the clergy —**cler′i·cal·ist** *n.*

clerk (klurk) *n.* [< Gr *klērikos*, a cleric] 1 a lay member of a church with minor duties 2 an office worker who types, files, etc. 3 an official who keeps the records of a court, town, etc. 4 a salesclerk — *vi.* to work as a salesclerk

---

THESAURUS

scalding, purifying.

cleaning *n.* cleansing, purge, scrubbing, scouring, purification, scrub, sweeping, brush, prophylaxis, sterilizing, washing, brushing, purifying, deodorizing, catharsis.

cleanliness *n.* cleanness, neatness, pureness, tidiness, trimness, spruceness, immaculateness, spotlessness, dapperness, orderliness, whiteness, disinfection, sanitation.—*Ant.* FILTH, dirtiness, griminess.

cleanse *v.* 1 [To remove dirt from the surface] launder, wash, scrub; see CLEAN. 2 [To remove impurities from within] refine, disinfect, purge; see CLEAN, PURIFY.

cleanser *n.* cleansing agent, cleaning agent, abrasive, lather, solvent, purgative, deodorant, fumigant, soap flakes, polish, disinfectant, antiseptic, purifier, scouring powder, spray cleaner, cleaner, detergent, soap powder, cleaning fluid, dry cleaner, suds; see also SOAP. *Cleansers include the following:* water, soap and water, soap, washing powder, oven cleaner, naphtha, furniture polish, borax, lye, household ammonia, solvent, bluing, carbon tetrachloride, toilet-bowl cleanser, baking soda, chlorine compound, silver-polish, kerosene, gasoline, vinegar, rug shampoo.

clear *a.* 1 [Open to the sight or understanding] explicit, plain, manifest; see OBVIOUS 1, 2. 2 [Offering little impediment to the vision] lucid, pure, transparent, apparent, limpid, translucent, crystal, crystalline, thin, crystal clear.—*Ant.* OPAQUE, dark, muddy. 3 [Unclouded] sunny, bright, rainless; see FAIR 3. 4 [Freed from legal charges] free, guiltless, cleared, exonerated, blameless, inno-

cent, sinless, dismissed, discharged, absolved; see also INNOCENT 1.—*Ant.* GUILTY, accused, blamed. 5 [Audible] loud enough to be heard, distinct, definite; see AUDIBLE. —**in the clear** guiltless, not suspected, cleared; see FREE 2, INNOCENT 1.

clear *v.* 1 [To free from uncertainty] clear up, relieve, clarify; see EXPLAIN. 2 [To free from obstacles] disentangle, rid, unloose; see FREE, REMOVE 1. 3 [To profit] realize, net, make; see RECEIVE 1. —**clear out** 1 [To remove] clean out, dispose of, get rid of; see ELIMINATE, EXCRETE. 2 [*To leave] depart, go, remove oneself; see LEAVE 1. —**clear up** 1 [To become clear; *said especially of weather]* improve, blow over, stop raining, stop snowing, run its course, die away, pass away, die down, show improvement, pick up, lift, become fair, have fair weather. 2 [To make clear] explicate, clarify, make plausible, make explicable, make reasonable; see also EXPLAIN.

clear-cut *a.* precise, plain, evident; see OBVIOUS 1, 2.

cleared *a.* 1 [Emptied] cleaned, unloaded, cleared away; see EMPTY. 2 [Freed of charges] vindicated, absolved, set right; see DISCHARGED, FREE 2.

clearing *n.* 1 [The act of clearing] clearance, freeing, removing; see REMOVAL. 2 [A cleared space] open space, opening, clearance; see AREA, COURT, EXPANSE, YARD 1.

clearly *a.* 1 [Distinctly; *said of sight]* plainly, precisely, lucidly, purely, brightly, perceptibly, unmistakably, in full view, in focus, discernibly, decidedly, incontestably, undoubtedly, noticeably, admittedly,

before one's eyes, beyond doubt, prominently, obviously, openly, overtly, observably, certainly, apparently, manifestly, recognizably, conspicuously, in plain sight, definitely, markedly, surely, visibly, positively, seemingly, evidently, at first sight, to all appearances, on the face of.—*Ant.* HAZY, dully, cloudily. 2 [Distinctly; *said of sounds]* sharply, acutely, ringingly, penetratingly, audibly, bell-like.—*Ant.* indistinct, mutteringly, unclearly.

clearness *n.* brightness, distinctness, lucidity; see CLARITY.

clench *v.* grip, grasp, double up; see HOLD 1.

clergy *n.* priesthood, prelacy, pastorate; see MINISTRY 2.

clergyman *n.* pastor, rabbi, preacher; see MINISTER 1, PRIEST.

clerical *a.* 1 [Concerning clerks] stenographic, accounting, bookkeeping, secretarial, typing, written, assistant, subordinate. 2 [Concerning the clergy] ministerial, priestly, apostolic, monastic, monkish, churchly, cleric, papal, episcopal, canonical, pontifical, ecclesiastic, sacred, holy, ecclesiastical, in God's service, devoted to the Lord, in the Lord's work.

clerk *n.* salesgirl, saleswoman, saleslady, shopgirl, shop assistant, salesclerk, salesman, salesperson, counterman, seller, auditor, bookkeeper, recorder, registrar, stenographer, office girl, office boy, timekeeper, cashier, teller, office worker, notary, controller, copyist, law clerk, switchboard, operator; see also SECRETARY 2.

clever (klev′ər) *adj.* ⟦? < Norw *klöver*⟧ 1 skillful; adroit 2 intelligent; ingenious; smart —**clev′erly** *adv.* —**clev′er·ness** *n.*

clevis (klev′is) *n.* ⟦see CLEAVE[2]⟧ a U-shaped piece of iron with holes for a pin, for attaching one thing to another

clew (kl$\overline{oo}$) *n.* ⟦OE *cliwen*⟧ 1 a ball of thread or yarn 2 CLUE

cli·ché (klē shā′) *n.* ⟦Fr < *clicher*, to stereotype⟧ a trite expression or idea

click (klik) *n.* ⟦echoic⟧ a slight, sharp sound like that of a door latch snapping into place — *vi.*, *vt.* to make or cause to make a click

cli·ent (klī′ənt) *n.* ⟦< L *cliens*, follower⟧ 1 a person or company for whom a lawyer, accountant, etc. is acting 2 a customer

cli·en·tele (klī′ən tel′) *n.* ⟦< Fr < L *clientela*, patronage⟧ all one's clients or customers, collectively

cliff (klif) *n.* ⟦OE *clif*⟧ a high, steep face of rock, esp. one on a coast

cliff′hang′er or **cliff′-hang′er** (-haŋ′ər) *n.* a suspenseful movie, story, situation, etc.

cli·mac·teric (klī mak′tər ik, klī′mak ter′ik) *n.* ⟦< Gr *klimax*, ladder⟧ a crucial period in life, esp. the menopause — *adj.* crucial

cli·mate (klī′mət) *n.* ⟦< Gr *klima*, region⟧ 1 the prevailing weather conditions of a place 2 a region with reference to its prevailing weather —**cli·mat′ic** (-mat′ik) *adj.*

cli·max (klī′maks) *n.* ⟦L < Gr *klimax*, ladder⟧ 1 the final, culminating element in a series; highest point of interest, excitement, etc. 2 the turning point of action in a drama, etc. — *vi.*, *vt.* to reach, or bring to, a climax —**cli·mac′tic** (-mak′tik) *adj.*

climb (klīm) *vi.*, *vt.* **climbed, climb′ing** ⟦OE *climban*⟧ 1 to move up by using the feet and often the hands 2 to ascend gradually 3 to move (*down, over, along*, etc.) using the hands and feet 4 to grow upward — *n.* 1 a climbing 2 a place to be climbed —**climb′able** *adj.* —**climb′er** *n.*

clime (klīm) *n.* ⟦see CLIMATE⟧ [Old Poet.] a region, esp. with regard to climate

clinch (klinch) *vt.* ⟦var. of CLENCH⟧ 1 to fasten (a driven nail, etc.) by bending the projecting end 2 to settle (an argument, bargain, etc.) definitely — *vi.* 1 *Boxing* to grip the opponent with the arms so as to hinder his punching 2 [Slang] to embrace — *n.* a clinching

clinch′er *n.* 1 one that clinches 2 a decisive point, argument, act, etc.

cling (kliŋ) *vi.* **clung, cling′ing** ⟦OE *clingan*⟧ 1 to adhere; hold fast, as by embracing 2 to be or stay near 3 to be emotionally attached —**cling′er** *n.*

clinic (klin′ik) *n.* ⟦< Gr *klinē*, bed⟧ 1 the teaching of medicine by treatment of patients in the presence of students 2 a place where medical specialists practice as a group 3 an outpatient department, as in a hospital 4 an intensive session of group instruction, as in a certain skill

clin′i·cal (-i kəl) *adj.* 1 of or connected with a clinic or sickbed 2 having to do with the treatment and observation of patients, as distinguished from theoretical study 3 purely scientific; impersonal —**clin′i·cally** *adv.*

cli·ni·cian (kli nish′ən) *n.* one who practices clinical medicine, psychology, etc.

clink (kliŋk) *vi.*, *vt.* ⟦echoic⟧ to make or cause to make a

slight, sharp sound, as of glasses striking together — *n.* 1 such a sound 2 [Colloq.] a jail

clink′er (-ər) *n.* ⟦Du *klinker*⟧ 1 [Archaic] a hard brick 2 a hard mass of fused stony matter, formed as from burned coal 3 [Slang] a mistake

clio·met·rics (klī′ō me′triks′) *n.pl.* ⟦< *Clio*, Gr Muse of history + Gr *metron*, measure⟧ [*with sing. v.*] use of mathematics and statistics in the analysis of historical data —**cli′o·met′ric** *adj.* —**cli′o·metri′cian** (-mə trish′ən) *n.*

clip[1] (klip) *vt.* **clipped, clip′ping** ⟦< ON *klippa*⟧ 1 to cut, as with shears 2 to cut short 3 to cut the hair of 4 [Colloq.] to hit sharply 5 [Slang] to swindle — *vi.* 1 to clip something 2 to move rapidly — *n.* 1 a clipping 2 a thing clipped 3 a rapid pace 4 [Colloq.] a quick, sharp blow

clip[2] (klip) *vi.*, *vt.* **clipped, clip′ping** ⟦OE *clyppan*, to embrace⟧ to grip tightly; fasten — *n.* any of various devices that clip, fasten, hold, etc.

clip′board′ *n.* a writing board with a hinged clip at the top to hold papers

clip joint [Slang] a nightclub, store, etc. that charges excessive prices

clipped form a shortened form of a word, as *pike* (for *turnpike*) or *fan* (for *fanatic*)

clip·per (klip′ər) *n.* 1 [*usually pl.*] a tool for cutting or trimming 2 a sailing ship built for great speed

clip′ping *n.* a piece cut out or off, as an item clipped from a newspaper

clique (klēk) *n.* ⟦Fr < OFr *cliquer*, make a noise⟧ a small, exclusive circle of people; coterie —**cliqu′ish** *adj.* —**cliqu′ishly** *adv.*

clito·ris (klīt′ər is) *n.*, *pl.* **clit′o·rises** (-is iz) or **cli·tori·des** (kli tôr′i dēz′) ⟦< Gr⟧ a small, sensitive, erectile organ of the vulva

cloa·ca (klō ā′kə) *n.*, *pl.* **-cae** (-sē′, -kē′) or **-cas** ⟦L < *cluere*, to cleanse⟧ a cavity, as in reptiles and birds, into which both the intestinal and the genitourinary tracts empty

cloak (klōk) *n.* ⟦< ML *clocca*, bell: from its shape⟧ 1 a loose, usually sleeveless outer garment 2 something that covers or conceals; disguise — *vt.* 1 to cover with a cloak 2 to conceal

clob·ber (kläb′ər) *vt.* ⟦< ?⟧ [Slang] 1 to beat or hit repeatedly 2 to defeat decisively

cloche (klōsh) *n.* ⟦Fr, a bell⟧ a woman's closefitting, bell-shaped hat

clock[1] (kläk) *n.* ⟦ME *clokke*, orig., clock with bells < ML *clocca*, bell⟧ a device for measuring and indicating time, usually by means of pointers moving over a dial — *vt.* to record the time of (a race, etc.) with a stopwatch

clock[2] (kläk) *n.* ⟦< ? prec., because of orig. bell shape⟧ a woven or embroidered ornament on a sock, going up from the ankle

clock radio a radio with a built-in clock that can turn it on or off

clock′wise′ *adv.*, *adj.* in the direction that the hands of a clock rotate

---

THESAURUS

clever *a.* 1 [Apt, particularly with one's hands] skillful, expert, adroit; see ABLE. 2 [Mentally quick] smart, bright, shrewd; see INTELLIGENT, SLY.

cleverly *a.* neatly, skillfully, tactfully, dexterously, ingeniously, resourcefully, deftly, nimbly, agilely, adroitly, proficiently, expertly, smoothly, quickly, speedily, readily; see also EASILY.—*Ant.* AWKWARDLY, clumsily, unskillfully.

cleverness *n.* skill, adroitness, ingenuity; see ABILITY.

cliché *n.* commonplace, platitude, stereotype, proverb, saying, slogan, trite phrase, stereotyped saying, vapid expression, triteness, banality, triviality, staleness, hackneyed phrase, trite idea; see also MOTTO.

click *n.* tick, snap, bang; see NOISE 1.

click *v.* 1 [To make a clicking sound] tick, snap, bang; see SOUND. 2 [*To be successful] match, go off well, meet with approval; see SUCCEED 1.

client *n.* customer, patient, patron; see BUYER.

cliff *n.* bluff, crag, steep rock; see HILL, MOUNTAIN 1, WALL 1.

climate *n.* characteristic weather, atmospheric conditions, meteorologic conditions, aridity, humidity, weather conditions; see also COLD 1, HEAT 1, WEATHER.

climax *n.* peak, apex, highest point, culmination, acme, pinnacle, crest, zenith, summit, apogee, extremity, limit, pitch, utmost extent, highest degree, turning point, crowning point; see also MAXIMUM, TOP 1.— *Ant.* DEPRESSION, anticlimax, nadir.

climax *v.* culminate, tower, end, top, conclude, reach a peak, come to a head, reach the zenith, break the record; see also ACHIEVE.

climb *n.* 1 [The act of climbing] climbing, clamber, mounting; see RISE. 2 [An ascending place] slope, incline, dune; see GRADE 1, HILL.

climb *v.* scale, work one's way up, ascend gradually, scramble up, clamber up, swarm up, start up, go up,

ascend, struggle up, get on, climb on, progress upward, rise, lift, rise hand over hand, come up, creep up, escalate, surmount, shinny up, shoot up. —**climb down** step off, come down, dismount; see DESCEND.

cling *v.* adhere, clasp, hold fast; see STICK 1.

clip[1] *v.* snip, crop, clip off; see CUT 1, DECREASE 2.

clippers *n.* shears, cutting instruments, barber's tools; see SCISSORS.

clique *n.* coterie, clan, club; see FACTION, ORGANIZATION 2.

clock[1] *n.* timekeeper, timepiece, time-marker, timer, ticker*. *Kinds of clocks include the following:* alarm, cuckoo, electric, grandfather, pendulum clock; hourglass, stopwatch, sundial, wristwatch; see also WATCH 1. —**around the clock** continuously, continually, twenty-four hours a day; see REGULARLY.

clock[1] *v.* time, measure time, register speed; see MEASURE 1.

clock'work' (-wurk') *n.* **1** the mechanism of a clock **2** any similar mechanism, with springs and gears —**like clockwork** very regularly

clod (kläd) *n.* [OE] **1** a lump, esp. of earth or clay **2** a dull, stupid person —**clod'dish** *adj.* —**clod'dy** *adj.*

clod'hop'per *n.* [prec. + HOPPER] **1** a plowman **2** a clumsy, stupid person **3** a coarse, heavy shoe

clog (kläg) *n.* [ME *clogge*, lump of wood] **1** anything that hinders or obstructs **2** a shoe with a thick, usually wooden, sole — *vt.* **clogged, clog'ging 1** to hinder **2** to obstruct (a passage); stop up; jam — *vi.* to become stopped up —**clog'gy** *adj.*

cloi·sonné (kloi'zə nā') *adj.* [Fr, lit., partitioned] designating enamel work in which the surface decoration is set in hollows formed by thin strips of wire

clois·ter (klois'tər) *n.* [< L *claudere*, to close] **1** a monastery or convent **2** monastic life **3** a covered walk along a courtyard wall with an open colonnade — *vt.* to confine as in a cloister

clomp (klämp) *vi.* to walk heavily or noisily

clone (klōn) *n.* [< Gr *klōn*, a twig] **1** all the descendants derived asexually from a single organism **2** a genetically identical duplicate of an organism, produced by replacing the nucleus of an unfertilized ovum with the nucleus of a body cell from the organism **3** [Colloq.] a person or thing very much like another — *vt.* **cloned, clon'ing** to produce as a clone

clop (kläp) *n.* [echoic] a clattering sound, like hoofbeats — *vi.* **clopped, clop'ping** to make, or move with, such sounds

close[1] (klōs) *adj.* **clos'er, clos'est** [see fol.] **1** confined or confining **2** hidden; secluded **3** secretive; reserved **4** miserly; stingy **5** warm and stuffy, as stale air **6** with little space between; near together **7** compact; dense [*close* weave] **8** near to the surface [a *close* shave] **9** intimate; familiar [a *close* friend] **10** strict; careful [a *close* search] **11** nearly alike [a *close* resemblance] **12** nearly equal or even [a *close* contest] **13** hard to get [credit is *close*] —*adv.* in a close manner —**close'ly** *adv.* —**close'ness** *n.*

close[2] (klōz) *vt.* **closed, clos'ing** [< L *claudere*, to close] **1** to shut **2** to fill up or stop (an opening) **3** to finish — *vi.* **1** to undergo shutting **2** to come to an end **3** to come close or together — *n.* an end or conclusion —**close down** (or **up**) to shut or stop entirely —**close in** to draw near

from all directions; surround —**close out** to dispose of (goods) by sale

close call (klōs) [Colloq.] a narrow escape from danger Also **close shave**

closed circuit a system for telecasting by cable only to receivers connected in the circuit —**closed'-cir'cuit** *adj.*

close·fisted (klōs'fis'tid) *adj.* stingy

close'fit'ting *adj.* fitting tightly

close'-knit' *adj.* closely united

close'mouthed' (-mouthd', -moutht') *adj.* not talking much; taciturn

closet (kläz'it) *n.* [< L *claudere*, to close] **1** a small room or cupboard for clothes, supplies, etc. **2** a small, private room — *vt.* to shut up in a private room for confidential talk

close-up (klōs'up') *n.* a photograph, etc. taken at very close range

clo·sure (klō'zhər) *n.* [< L *claudere*, to close] **1** a closing or being closed **2** a finish; end **3** anything that closes **4** CLOTURE

clot (klät) *n.* [OE] a soft lump or thickened mass [a blood *clot*] — *vi.* **clot'ted, clot'ting** to form into a clot or clots; coagulate

cloth (klôth) *n., pl.* **cloths** (klôthz, klôths) [OE *clath*] **1** a woven, knitted, or pressed fabric of fibrous material, as cotton, wool, silk, synthetic fibers, etc. **2** a tablecloth, washcloth, etc. — *adj.* made of cloth —**the cloth** the clergy

clothe (klōth) *vt.* **clothed** or **clad, cloth'ing** [see prec.] **1** to provide with or dress in clothes **2** to cover

clothes (klōthz, klōz) *n.pl.* [OE *clathas*] articles, usually of cloth, for covering, adorning, etc. the body

clothes'pin' *n.* a small clip for fastening clothes on a line

cloth·ier (klōth'yər) *n.* a dealer in clothes or cloth

cloth·ing (klō'thin) *n.* **1** clothes; garments **2** a covering

clo·ture (klō'chər) *n.* [see CLOSURE] the ending of legislative debate by having the bill put to immediate vote

cloud (kloud) *n.* [OE *clud*, mass of rock] **1** a visible mass of condensed water droplets or ice crystals in the sky **2** a mass of smoke, dust, steam, etc. **3** a crowd; swarm [a *cloud* of locusts] **4** anything that darkens, obscures, etc. — *vt.* **1** to darken or obscure as with clouds **2** to make gloomy **3** to sully — *vi.* to become cloudy, gloomy, etc. — **in the clouds 1** impractical **2** in a daydream —**under a cloud** under suspicion —**cloud'less** *adj.* —**cloudy** (kloud'ē), -i·er, -i·est, *adj.*

cloud'burst' *n.* a sudden, heavy rain

■ THESAURUS ■

clog *v.* stop up, seal, obstruct; see CLOSE 2, HINDER.

close[1] *a.* **1** [Nearby] neighboring, across the street, around the corner; see NEAR 1. **2** [Intimate] confidential, intimate, familiar; see PRIVATE. **3** [Compact] dense, solid, compressed; see THICK 1. **4** [Stingy] narrow, parsimonious, niggardly; see STINGY. **5** [Stifling] sticky, stuffy, unventilated, moldy, heavy, motionless, uncomfortable, choky, stale-smelling, musty, stagnant, confined, suffocating, sweltering, tight, stale, oppressive, breathless; see also UNCOMFORTABLE 2.—*Ant.* FRESH, refreshing, brisk. **6** [Similar] resembling, having common qualities, much the same; see ALIKE, LIKE.

close[2] *n.* termination, adjournment, ending; see END 2.

close[2] *v.* **1** [To put a stop to] conclude, finish, terminate; see END 1. **2** [To put a stopper into] shut, stop down, choke off, stuff, clog, prevent passage, shut off, turn off, lock, block, bar, dam, cork, seal, button; see also CLOSE 2.—*Ant.* OPEN, uncork, unseal. **3** [To come together] meet, unite, agree; see JOIN 1. **4** [To shut] slam, close down, shut down, shut up, seal, fasten, bolt, clench, bar, shutter, clap, lock, bring to.

closed *a.* **1** [Terminated] ended, concluded, final; see FINISHED 1. **2** [Not in operation] shut down, out of order, out of service, bankrupt, closed up, padlocked, folded up*; see also BROKEN 2. **3** [Not open] shut, fastened, sealed; see TIGHT 2.

closely *a.* approximately, similarly, exactly, nearly, strictly, firmly, intimately, jointly, in conjunction with; see also ALMOST.—*Ant.* INDIVIDUALLY, separately, one by one.

closet *n.* cabinet, recess, cupboard, buffet, locker, wardrobe, receptacle, safe, bin, drawer, chest of drawers, vault, cold storage, clothes room.

clot *n.* lump, bulk, clotting, curdling, coagulation, mass, clump, coagulum, thickness, coalescence, curd.

clot *v.* coagulate, set, lump; see THICKEN.

cloth *n.* fabric, material, stuff; see GOODS.

clothe *v.* attire, dress up, costume; see DRESS 1.

clothed *a.* clad, invested, costumed, robed, shod, dressed, attired, decked, disguised, covered, draped, veiled.— *Ant.* NAKED, exposed, stripped.

clothes *n.* wearing apparel, raiment, clothing, garments, garb, vesture, vestments, attire, array, casual wear, informal wear, evening clothes, work clothes, suit of clothes, costume, wardrobe, trappings, gear, underclothes, outfit, get-up*, rags, toggery*, togs*, duds*, threads*, things; see also COAT 1, DRESS 1, 2, HAT, PANTS 1, SHIRT. *Men's clothes include the following:* business suit, jacket and slacks, trousers, shorts, breeches, knickers*, tuxedo, tux*, dress suit, dinner jacket, uniform, shirt, body shirt, hiphugger pants, continental suit, socks; long underwear, long johns*. *Women's clothes include the*

following: housecoat, negligee, morning dress, evening gown, kimono, shorts, frock, blouse, jumper, slip, shirtwaist, robe, underwear, slacks, panties, brassiere, bra, pantyhose, girdle; nightgown, nightie*, pajamas, pj's*, dress, street dress, suit, cardigan, sweater, pullover, slipover sweater, house dress, dickey, nylon stockings, nylons, miniskirt, shift, muumuu, hiphugger slacks, smock, skirt, coat, petticoat, hat, bonnet. *Clothes worn by both men and women include the following:* blue jeans, levis, turtleneck, sweat shirt, tank top, kimono, raincoat, tights, bell-bottom pants, cutoffs*. *Children's clothes include the following:* rompers, playsuit, coveralls, snowsuit, leggings. *Work clothes include the following:* overalls, windbreaker, blue jeans, coveralls, jumper, cords*.

clothing *n.* attire, raiment, garb; see CLOTHES, DRESS 1.

cloud *n.* haze, mist, fogginess, haziness, film, puff, billow, frost, smoke, veil, cloud cover, overcast. *Types of clouds include the following:* cirrus, cumulus, stratus, nimbus, cirrocumulus, cirro-stratus. —**in the clouds** fanciful, fantastic, romantic; see IMPRACTICAL. —**under a cloud** suspect, dubious, uncertain; see SUSPICIOUS 2.

cloudy *a.* **1** [Hazy] overcast, foggy, sunless; see DARK 1. **2** [Not clear] dense, nontransparent, nontranslucent; see OPAQUE 1.

clout (klout) *n.* ⟦< OE *clut*, a patch⟧ **1** a blow, as with the hand **2** [Colloq.] power, esp. political power —*vt.* **1** [Colloq.] to strike, as with the hand **2** to hit (a ball) hard
clove[1] (klōv) *n.* ⟦< L *clavus*, nail: from its shape⟧ **1** the dried flower bud of a tropical evergreen tree, used as a spice **2** the tree
clove[2] (klōv) *n.* ⟦OE *clufu*⟧ a segment of a bulb, as of garlic
clove[3] (klōv) *vt., vi. alt. pt. of* CLEAVE[1]
clo·ven (klō′vən) *vt., vi. alt. pp. of* CLEAVE[1] —*adj.* divided; split
clo·ver (klō′vər) *n.* ⟦OE *clafre*⟧ any of various low-growing plants of the pea family, with leaves of three leaflets and small flowers in dense heads
clo′ver·leaf′ (-lēf′) *n., pl.* -leafs′ a highway interchange with an overpass and curving ramps, allowing traffic to move unhindered in any of four directions
clown (kloun) *n.* ⟦< ? Scand⟧ **1** a clumsy or boorish person **2** one who entertains, as in a circus, by antics, jokes, etc. —*vi.* to act as a clown does —**clown′ish** *adj.*
cloy (kloi) *vt., vi.* ⟦< OFr *encloyer*, nail up < L *clavus*, nail⟧ to surfeit by too much that is sweet, rich, etc.
club (klub) *n.* ⟦< ON *klubba*, cudgel⟧ **1** a heavy stick used as a weapon **2** any stick used in a game, as golf **3** *a*) a group of people associated for a common purpose *b*) its meeting place **4** *a*) any of a suit of playing cards marked with a black trefoil (♣) *b*) [*pl.*] this suit —*vt.* clubbed, club′bing to strike as with a club —*vi.* to unite for a common purpose
club′foot′ *n., pl.* -feet′ a congenitally misshapen, often clublike, foot
club′house′ (-hous′) *n.* **1** a building used by a club **2** a locker room used by an athletic team
club soda SODA WATER
cluck (kluk) *vi.* ⟦echoic⟧ to make a low, clicking sound, as of a hen calling her chicks —*n.* this sound
clue (klōō) *n.* a fact, object, etc. that helps to solve a mystery or problem —*vt.* clued, clu′ing to provide with clues or needed facts
clump (klump) *n.* ⟦< LowG *klump*⟧ **1** a lump; mass **2** a cluster, as of trees **3** the sound of heavy footsteps —*vi.* **1** to walk heavily **2** to form clumps —**clump′y, -i·er, -i·est,** *adj.*
clumsy (klum′zē) *adj.* -si·er, -si·est ⟦ME *clumsid*, numb with cold⟧ **1** lacking grace or skill; awkward **2** awkwardly shaped or made —**clum′si·ly** *adv.* —**clum′si·ness** *n.*
clung (kluŋ) *vi. pt. & pp. of* CLING
clunk (kluŋk) *n.* ⟦echoic⟧ a dull, heavy, hollow sound
clunker (kluŋk′ər) *n.* [Slang] an old machine or automobile in poor repair
clus·ter (klus′tər) *n.* ⟦OE *clyster*⟧ a number of persons or things grouped together —*vi., vt.* to gather or grow in a cluster
clutch[1] (kluch) *vt.* ⟦OE *clyccan*, clench⟧ to grasp or hold eagerly or tightly —*vi.* to snatch or seize (*at*) —*n.* **1** [*usually pl.*] power; control **2** a grasp; grip **3** a device for engaging and disengaging a motor or engine
clutch[2] (kluch) *n.* ⟦< ON *klekja*, to hatch⟧ **1** a nest of eggs **2** a brood of chicks **3** a cluster
clut·ter (klut′ər) *n.* ⟦< CLOT⟧ **1** a number of things scattered in disorder; jumble **2** the interfering traces on a radarscope caused by hills —*vt.* to put into disorder; jumble: often with *up*

cm centimeter(s)
cni·dar·ian (ni der′ē ən) *n.* any of a phylum of invertebrates, as jellyfishes, having stinging cells and a saclike body with only one opening
co- ⟦var. of COM-⟧ *prefix* **1** together **2** equally [*coextensive*] **3** joint or jointly [*copilot*]
Co *Chem. symbol for* cobalt
CO Commanding Officer
C/O care of
Co. or **co. 1** company **2** county
coach (kōch) *n.* ⟦after *Kócs*, village in Hungary⟧ **1** a large, covered, four-wheeled carriage **2** a railroad passenger car **3** the lowest-priced class of airline accommodations **4** a bus **5** an instructor or trainer, as of athletes, actors, or singers —*vt., vi.* to instruct and train (students, etc.)
coach′man (-mən) *n., pl.* -men the driver of a coach, or carriage
co·ad·ju·tor (kō aj′ə tər, kō′ə jōōt′ər) *n.* ⟦< L co-, together + *adjuvare*, to help⟧ an assistant, esp. to a bishop
co·ag·u·late (kō ag′yōō lāt′) *vt.* -lat′ed, -lat′ing ⟦< L co-, together + *agere*, to drive⟧ to cause (a liquid) to become semisolid; clot —*vi.* to become coagulated —**co·ag′u·lant** (-lənt) *n.* —**co·ag′u·la′tion** *n.* —**co·ag′u·la′tive** *adj.* —**co·ag′u·la′tor** *n.*
coal (kōl) *n.* ⟦OE *col*⟧ **1** a black, combustible mineral solid used as fuel **2** a piece (or pieces) of this **3** an ember —*vt., vi.* to supply or be supplied with coal —**haul** (or **rake, drag,** or **call**) **over the coals** to criticize sharply
coa·lesce (kō′ə les′) *vi.* -lesced′, -lesc′ing ⟦< L co-, together + *alescere*, grow up⟧ to unite into a single body or group —**co′a·les′cence** *n.*
co′a·li′tion (-lish′ən) *n.* ⟦see prec.⟧ a combination or alliance, as of factions, esp. a temporary one
coal tar a thick black liquid obtained from the distillation of bituminous coal: used in dyes, medicines, etc.
coarse (kôrs) *adj.* coars′er, coars′est ⟦< COURSE in sense of "usual"⟧ **1** of poor quality; common **2** consisting of rather large particles [*coarse* sand] **3** rough; harsh **4** unrefined; vulgar; crude —**coarse′ly** *adv.* —**coarse′ness** *n.*
coars′en *vt., vi.* to make or become coarse
coast (kōst) *n.* ⟦< L *costa*, rib, side⟧ **1** land alongside the sea; seashore **2** a slide down an incline, as on a sled —*vi.* **1** to sail near or along a coast **2** to go down an incline, as on a sled **3** to continue in motion on momentum —**coastal** (kōs′təl) *adj.*
coast′er *n.* **1** a person or thing that coasts **2** a small mat, etc. placed under a glass to protect a table
coaster brake a brake on a bicycle operated by reverse pressure on the pedals
coast guard 1 a governmental force employed to defend a nation's coasts, aid vessels in distress, etc. **2** [C- G-] such a branch of the U.S. armed forces
coast′line′ *n.* the outline of a coast
coat (kōt) *n.* ⟦OFr *cote*, a coat⟧ **1** a sleeved outer garment opening down the front **2** the natural covering of a plant or animal **3** a layer of some substance, as paint, over a surface —*vt.* to cover with a coat or layer
coat′ing *n.* a surface coat or layer

clown *n.* buffoon, fool, joker, harlequin, punch, funnyman, humorist, jester, comedian, cut-up*; see also ACTOR.
clown (around) *v.* fool around, kid around, cut up*; see JOKE.
club *n.* **1** [A social organization] association, order, society; see FACTION, ORGANIZATION 2. **2** [A cudgel] bat, hammer, mallet; see STICK.
club *v.* batter, whack, pound; see BEAT 1, HIT 1.
clue *n.* evidence, trace, mark; see PROOF 1, SIGN 1.
clump *n.* cluster, bundle, knot; see BUNCH.
clumsily *a.* crudely, gawkily, stumblingly; see AWKWARDLY.
clumsiness *n.* crudity, ineptitude, boorishness; see AWKWARDNESS.
clumsy *a.* ungainly, gawky, inexpert; see AWKWARD.
cluster *n.* group, batch, clump; see BUNCH.
clutch[1] *v.* grab, grasp, grip; see HOLD

1, SEIZE 1.
clutches *n.* control, grasp, keeping; see POWER 2.
clutter *n.* disarray, jumble, disorder; see CONFUSION.
coach *n.* **1** [A carriage] fourwheeler, chaise, victoria; see CARRIAGE 2, VEHICLE. **2** [An instructor] physical education instructor, drillmaster, mentor; see TEACHER, TRAINER.
coach *v.* train, drill, instruct; see TEACH.
coagulate *v.* curdle, clot, congeal; see THICKEN.
coal *n.* sea coal, stone coal, mineral coal; see FUEL. —**haul** (or **rake** or **drag**) **over the coals*** reprimand, criticize, castigate; see BLAME.
coalition *n.* compact, conspiracy, association; see FACTION.
coarse *a.* **1** [Not fine] rough, rude, unrefined; see CRUDE. **2** [Vulgar] low, common, base; see RUDE 1, VULGAR.
coast *n.* shoreline, beach, seaboard; see SHORE.

coast *v.* glide, float, ride on the current; see DRIFT, RIDE 1.
coat *n.* **1** [An outer garment] topcoat, overcoat, cloak, suit coat, tuxedo, dinner jacket, sport coat, dress coat, mink coat, fur coat, ski jacket, mackintosh, raincoat, jacket, windbreaker, peacoat, three-quarter length coat, wrap, leather jacket, southwester, slicker; see also CLOTHES. **2** [The covering of an animal] protective covering, husk, shell, crust, scale, fleece, epidermis, rind, ectoderm, pelt, membrane; see also FUR, HIDE, SKIN. **3** [An applied covering] coating, layer, set, wash, primer, finish, glaze, crust, painting, overlay, whitewashing, varnish, lacquer, gloss, tinge, prime coat, plaster; see also FINISH 2.
coat *v.* surface, glaze, enamel; see PAINT 2, VARNISH.
coating *n.* crust, covering, layer; see COAT 3.

coat of arms a shield with heraldic emblems, as the insignia of some group

coat'tail' (-tāl') *n.* either half of the divided lower back part of a coat

co·author (kō'ô'thər) *n.* a joint author; collaborator

coax (kōks) *vt., vi.* ⟦< obs. slang *cokes*, a fool⟧ to urge or get with soft words, flattery, etc. —**coax'er** *n.* —**coax'ingly** *adv.*

co·ax·ial (kō ak'sē əl) *adj.* 1 having a common axis 2 designating a double-conductor high-frequency transmission line, as for television

cob (käb) *n.* ⟦prob. < LowG⟧ 1 a corncob 2 a short, thickset horse

co·balt (kō'bôlt') *n.* ⟦< Ger *kobold*, lit., goblin⟧ a hard, steel-gray metallic chemical element

cob·ble (käb'əl) *vt.* **-bled, -bling** ⟦ME < *cobelere*, cobbler⟧ 1 to mend (shoes, etc.) 2 to put together clumsily

cob·bler[1] (käb'lər) *n.* ⟦< ?⟧ a kind of deep-dish fruit pie

cob·bler[2] (käb'lər) *n.* ⟦ME *cobelere* < ?⟧ one who makes or mends shoes

cob'ble·stone' *n.* a rounded stone formerly much used for paving streets

COBOL (kō'bôl') *n.* ⟦*co(mmon) b(usiness) o(riented) l(anguage)*⟧ a computer language using English words, for business applications

co·bra (kō'brə) *n.* ⟦< Port⟧ a very poisonous snake of Asia and Africa

cob·web (käb'web') *n.* ⟦ME *coppe*, spider + WEB⟧ 1 a web spun by a spider 2 anything flimsy, gauzy, or ensnaring like this —**cob'web'by** *adj.*

co·caine or **co·cain** (kō kān') *n.* ⟦< *coca*, tropical shrub from whose leaves it is extracted⟧ an alkaloid drug used as a local anesthetic and, illegally, as a stimulant

coc·cus (käk'əs) *n., pl.* **coc'ci** (-sī') ⟦< Gr *kokkos*, kernel⟧ a bacterium of a spherical shape

coc·cyx (käk'siks) *n., pl.* **coc·cy·ges** (käk sī'jēz') ⟦< Gr *kokkyx*, cuckoo: it is shaped like a cuckoo's beak⟧ a small, triangular bone at the base of the spine

coch·lea (käk'lē ə) *n., pl.* **-ae** (-ē') or **-as** ⟦< Gr *kochlias*, snail⟧ the spiral-shaped part of the inner ear

cock[1] (käk) *n.* ⟦OE *coc*⟧ 1 a rooster or other male bird 2 a faucet or valve 3 *a)* the hammer of a gun *b)* its firing position 4 a jaunty tilt, as of a hat — *vt.* 1 to tilt jauntily 2 to raise or turn alertly 3 to set (a gun's hammer) in firing position

cock[2] (käk) *n.* ⟦ME *cokke*⟧ a small, cone-shaped pile, as of hay

cock·ade (käk ād') *n.* ⟦< OFr *coq*, COCK[1] (*n.* 1)⟧ a rosette, knot of ribbon, etc. worn on the hat as a badge

cocka·ma·mie (käk'ə mā'mē) *adj.* ⟦< *decalcomania*: see DECAL⟧ [Slang] 1 poor; inferior 2 silly; ridiculous

cock-and-bull story (käk'ən bool') an absurd, improbable story

cocka·too (käk'ə tōō') *n., pl.* **-toos'** ⟦< Malay *kakatua*⟧ a crested parrot of Australia and the East Indies

cocka·trice (käk'ə tris') *n.* ⟦< L *calcare*, to tread⟧ a fabulous serpent supposedly able to kill by a look

cocked hat a three-cornered hat

cock·erel (käk'ər əl) *n.* a young rooster, less than a year old

cocker (spaniel) ⟦< use in hunting woodcock⟧ a small spaniel with long, silky hair and drooping ears

cock·eyed (käk'īd') *adj.* ⟦< COCK[1], *v.* + EYE⟧ 1 cross-eyed 2 [Slang] *a)* crooked; awry *b)* silly; foolish *c)* drunk

cock'fight' *n.* a fight between gamecocks, usually wearing metal spurs —**cock'fight'ing** *n.*

cockle (käk'əl) *n.* ⟦< Gr *konchē*, mussel⟧ a mollusk, often edible, that has two heart-shaped shells —**cockles of one's heart** one's deepest emotions

cock·ney (käk'nē) *n., pl.* **-neys** ⟦ME *cokenei*, spoiled child, milksop⟧ [*often* C-] 1 a native of the East End of London, England, speaking a characteristic dialect 2 this dialect

cock'pit' *n.* 1 a pit for cockfighting 2 the space in a small airplane for the pilot and passengers, or in a large airplane for the pilot, copilot, etc.

cock'roach' (-rōch') *n.* ⟦Sp *cucaracha*⟧ an insect with long feelers and a flat, soft body: a common household pest

cocks'comb' (käks'kōm') *n.* 1 the red, fleshy growth on a rooster's head 2 a plant with flowers like this

cock·sure (käk'shoor') *adj.* ⟦COCK[1] + SURE⟧ absolutely sure or self-confident, esp. in an arrogant way

cock·tail (käk'tāl') *n.* ⟦< ?⟧ 1 a mixed alcoholic drink, usually iced 2 an appetizer, as of shrimp or juice

cocky (käk'ē) *adj.* **-i·er, -i·est** ⟦< COCK[1] + -Y[2]⟧ [Colloq.] jauntily conceited; aggressively self-confident —**cock'i·ly** *adv.* —**cock'i·ness** *n.*

coco (kō'kō') *n., pl.* **-cos'** ⟦Sp < Gr *kokkos*, berry⟧ 1 the coconut palm tree 2 its fruit; coconut

co·coa (kō'kō') *n.* ⟦var. of CACAO⟧ 1 powder made from roasted cacao seeds 2 a drink made of this and sugar, hot milk, etc. 3 a reddish-yellow brown

cocoa butter a yellowish-white fat prepared from cacao seeds

coco·nut or **cocoa·nut** (kō'kō nut', -kə-) *n.* the fruit of a tropical tree (**coconut palm**), a thick, brown, oval husk with edible white meat and a sweet, milky fluid (**coconut milk**) inside

co·coon (kə kōōn') *n.* ⟦< Fr < ML *coco*, shell⟧ the silky case which the larva of certain insects spins about itself for shelter during the pupa stage

cod (käd) *n., pl.* **cod** or **cods** ⟦ME⟧ a food fish of northern seas

COD or **c.o.d.** cash, or collect, on delivery

coda (kō'də) *n.* ⟦It < L *cauda*, tail⟧ *Music* an added concluding passage

cod·dle (käd'l) *vt.* **-dled, -dling** ⟦< ?⟧ 1 to cook (esp. eggs in shells) in water not quite boiling 2 to pamper

code (kōd) *n.* ⟦< L *codex*, wooden tablet⟧ 1 a systematized body of laws 2 a set of principles, as of ethics 3 a set of signals for sending messages 4 a system of symbols for secret writing, etc. — *vt.* **cod'ed, cod'ing** to put into code —**cod'er** *n.*

co·deine (kō'dēn') *n.* ⟦< Gr *kōdeia*, poppy head⟧ an alkaloid derived from opium: used for pain relief and in cough medicines Also **co'dein'**

co'de·pend'ent or **co'-depend'ent** *adj.* psychologically influenced by or needing another who is addicted to alcohol, etc. — *n.* one who is codependent —**co'de·pend'ency** or **co'-depend'ency, pl. -cies,** *n.*

co·dex (kō'deks') *n., pl.* **-di·ces** (-də sēz') ⟦L: see CODE⟧ a manuscript volume, esp. of the Scriptures or of a classic text

cod'fish' (käd'-) *n., pl.* **-fish'** or (for different species) **-fish'es** a cod

codger (käj'ər) *n.* ⟦< ?⟧ [Colloq.] an elderly fellow, sometimes one who is eccentric

codi·cil (käd'i səl) *n.* ⟦see CODE⟧ an addition to a will

codi·fy (käd'ə fī') *vt.* **-fied', -fy'ing** to arrange (laws, rules, etc.) systematically —**cod'i·fi·ca'tion** *n.* —**cod'i·fi'er** *n.*

cod'-liv'er oil oil from the liver of the cod: it is rich in vitamins A & D

coed or **co-ed** (kō'ed') *n.* [Colloq.] a young woman attending a coeducational college — *adj.* [Colloq.] 1 coeducational 2 of a coed

co·edu·ca·tion (kō'ej'ə kā'shən) *n.* an educational system in which students of both sexes attend classes together —**co'edu·ca'tional** *adj.*

co·ef·fi·cient (kō'ə fish'ənt) *n.* ⟦CO- + EFFICIENT⟧ 1 a factor that contributes to a result 2 a multiplier of a variable or unknown quantity (as *6* in *6ab*) 3 a number used as a multiplier in measuring some property

coe·len·ter·ate (si len'tər it) *n.* ⟦< Gr *koilos*, hollow + *enteron*, intestine⟧ CNIDARIAN

co·equal (kō ē'kwəl) *adj., n.* equal —**co'equal'ity** (-ē kwäl'ə tē) *n.* —**co·e'qually** *adv.*

co·erce (kō urs') *vt.* **-erced', -erc'ing** ⟦< L *co-*, together + *arcere*, confine⟧ 1 to restrain by force 2 to compel 3 to enforce —**co·er'cion** (-ur'shən) *n.* —**co·er'cive** (-siv) *adj.*

co·eval (kō ē'vəl) *adj., n.* ⟦< L *co-*, together + *aevum*, age⟧ contemporary

---

THESAURUS

coax *v.* persuade, cajole, inveigle; see INFLUENCE, URGE 2.

cocktail *n.* mixed drink, aperitif, highball. *Cocktails include the following:* Manhattan, martini, old-fashioned, champagne, Margarita, pink lady, whisky sour, screwdriver, Bloody Mary, black Russian, Daiquiri, Bacardi, Alexander; see also DRINK 2.

code *n.* codex, method, digest; see LAW 2, SYSTEM.

coerce *v.* impel, compel, constrain; see FORCE.

coercion *n.* compulsion, persuasion, constraint; see PRESSURE 2, RESTRAINT 2.

co′ex·ist′ (-ig zist′) **vi.** **1** to exist together, at the same time, or in the same place **2** to live together peacefully, despite differences —**co′ex·ist′ence** **n.**

co′ex·ten′sive (-ik sten′siv) **adj.** extending equally in time or space

cof·fee (kôf′ē) **n.** ⟦< Ar *qahwa*⟧ **1** a drink made from the roasted, ground, beanlike seeds of a tall tropical shrub of the madder family **2** the seeds, whole or ground, or the shrub **3** light brown

coffee break a brief respite from work when coffee, etc. is taken

cof′fee·cake′ **n.** a kind of cake or roll to be eaten as with coffee

cof′fee·house′ **n.** a place where coffee is served and people gather for talk, entertainment, etc.

cof′fee·pot′ **n.** a container with a spout, for making or serving coffee

coffee shop a small restaurant serving coffee and light refreshments or meals

coffee table a low table, usually in front of a sofa

cof·fer (kôf′ər) **n.** ⟦see fol.⟧ **1** a chest for holding money or valuables **2** [*pl.*] a treasury; funds

cof·fin (kôf′in) **n.** ⟦< Gr *kophinos*, basket⟧ the case or box in which a dead body is buried

cog (käg) **n.** ⟦ME⟧ **1** one of the teeth on the rim of a cogwheel **2** a cogwheel

co·gent (kō′jənt) **adj.** ⟦< L *co-*, together + *agere*, to drive⟧ convincingly to the point —**co′gency** **n.**

cogi·tate (käj′ə tāt′) **vi.,** **vt.** **-tat′ed, -tat′ing** ⟦< L⟧ to think deeply (about); ponder —**cog′i·ta′tion** **n.** —**cog′i·ta′tive** **adj.** —**cog′i·ta′tor** **n.**

co·gnac (kän′yak′, kōn′-) **n.** ⟦Fr⟧ **1** a brandy from Cognac, France **2** loosely, brandy

cog·nate (käg′nāt′) **adj.** ⟦< L *co-*, together + *gnasci*, to be born⟧ **1** related by family **2** from a common original form, as two words **3** related; similar — **n.** a cognate person or thing

cog·ni·tion (käg nish′ən) **n.** ⟦< L *co-*, together + *gnoscere*, know⟧ **1** the process of knowing, perceiving, etc. **2** an idea, perception, etc. —**cog′ni·tive** (-nə tiv) **adj.**

cog′ni·zable (käg′nə bəl) **adj.** **1** that can be known or perceived **2** *Law* within the jurisdiction of a court

cog′ni·zance (käg′nə zəns) **n.** **1** perception or knowledge **2** notice; heed —**cog′ni·zant** **adj.**

cog·no·men (käg nō′mən) **n.,** **pl.** **-no′mens** ⟦< L *co-*, with + *nomen*, name⟧ **1** surname **2** any name; esp., a nickname

cog·wheel (käg′hwēl′, -wēl′) **n.** a wheel rimmed with teeth that mesh with those of another wheel, etc., to transmit or receive motion

co·habit (kō hab′it) **vi.** ⟦< L *co-*, together + *habitare*, dwell⟧ to live together as husband and wife, esp. when not legally married —**co·hab′i·ta′tion** **n.**

co·heir (kō′er′, kō er′) **n.** one who inherits jointly with another or others

co·here (kō hir′) **vi.** **-hered′, -her′ing** ⟦< L *co-*, together + *haerere*, to stick⟧ **1** to stick together **2** to be connected naturally or logically

co·her′ent (-ənt) **adj.** **1** sticking together; cohering **2** logically connected and intelligible —**co·her′ence** **n.** — **co·her′ently** **adv.**

co·he·sion (kō hē′zhən) **n.** a cohering; tendency to stick together —**co·he′sive** (-hēs′iv) **adj.**

co·hort (kō′hôrt′) **n.** ⟦< L *cohors*, enclosure⟧ **1** a band of soldiers **2** any group or band **3** an associate

coif (koif; *for 2 usually* kwäf) **n.** **1** ⟦< LL *cofea*, a cap⟧ a closefitting cap **2** ⟦< fol.⟧ a hairstyle

coif·fure (kwä fyoor′) **n.** ⟦Fr⟧ **1** a headdress **2** a hairstyle

coil (koil) **vt.,** **vi.** ⟦< L *com-*, together + *legere*, gather⟧ to wind into circular or spiral form — **n.** **1** a series of rings or a spiral, or anything in this form **2** a single turn of a coil **3** *Elec.* a spiral of wire

coin (koin) **n.** ⟦< L *cuneus*, a wedge⟧ **1** a piece of stamped metal, issued by a government as money **2** such pieces collectively — **vt.** **1** to stamp (metal) into coins **2** to invent (a new word, phrase, etc.) —**coin′age** **n.**

co·incide (kō′in sid′) **vi.** **-cid′ed, -cid′ing** ⟦< L *co-*, together + *incidere*, fall upon⟧ **1** to take up the same place in space **2** to occur at the same time **3** to agree exactly

co·inci·dence (kō in′sə dəns) **n.** **1** a coinciding **2** an accidental, but seemingly planned, occurrence of events, ideas, etc. at the same time —**co·in′ci·dent** or **co·in′ci·den′tal** **adj.** —**co·in′ci·den′tally** **adv.**

co·itus (kō′it əs) **n.** ⟦< L *co-*, together + *ire*, go⟧ sexual intercourse Also **co·ition** (kō ish′ən)

coke (kōk) **n.** ⟦< ME *colke*, core⟧ coal from which most of the gases have been removed by heating: used as an industrial fuel

col- *prefix* COM- Used before *l*

col. column

COL **1** Colonel: also **Col.** **2** cost of living

cola (kō′lə) **n.** ⟦< Afr name⟧ **1** an African tree with nuts that yield an extract used in soft drinks and medicine **2** a carbonated soft drink flavored with this extract

col·an·der (kul′ən dər, käl′-) **n.** ⟦prob. ult. < L *colum*, strainer⟧ a perforated pan for draining off liquids

cold (kōld) **adj.** ⟦OE *cald*⟧ **1** of a temperature much lower than that of the human body **2** too cool; chilly **3** unfriendly, indifferent, or depressing **4** devoid of feeling; emotionless **5** *a*) not fresh (said of a hunting scent) *b*) off the track **6** [Colloq.] unprepared /to enter a game *cold]* **7** [Slang] perfectly memorized **8** [Slang] unconscious /knocked *cold]* —**adv.** [Colloq.] completely /she was

---

THESAURUS

coexist *v.* exist together, synchronize, be contemporary; see ACCOMPANY.

coexistence *n.* order, conformity, accord; see PEACE 1, 2.

coffee *n.* beverage, decoction, java*; see DRINK 2. *Prepared coffee includes the following:* Turkish, Armenian, drip, percolated, vacuum, instant, French roast, coffee with cream, demitasse.

coffin *n.* box, casket, sarcophagus, lead coffin, burial urn, funerary urn, funerary box, mummy case; see also CONTAINER.

cohabit *v.* shack up with*, play house with*, be roommates; see ACCOMPANY.

coherence *n.* stickiness, viscosity, gumminess, cementation, soldering, adhesiveness, sticking together, coagulation, viscidity, adherence, set, fusion, sticking, union, adhesion, cohesiveness, consistency.

coherent *a.* comprehensible, sound, intelligible; see LOGICAL, UNDERSTANDABLE.

coil *n.* curl, turn, ring, wind, convolution, twine, twist, twirl, lap, loop, curlicue, corkscrew, roll, spiral, helix, scroll; see also CIRCLE 1.

coil *v.* scroll, wind, loop, twist, fold, twine, intertwine, entwine, convolute, lap, twirl, spire, wreathe; see also CURL.—*Ant.* UNFOLD, unwind, ravel.

coin *n.* legal tender, silver, copper; see MONEY 1.

coin *v.* **1** [To mint money] mint, strike, stamp; see MANUFACTURE. **2** [To invent a word, etc.] create, originate, make up; see INVENT 1.

coincide *v.* **1** [Correspond] accord, harmonize, match; see AGREE. **2** [Happen] occur, come about, take place; see HAPPEN 2.

coincidence *n.* luck, fortune, circumstance; see ACCIDENT, CHANCE 1.

coincidental *a.* **1** [Occurring simultaneously] concurrent, concomitant, contemporaneous; see SIMULTANEOUS. **2** [Apparently accidental] chance, unpredictable, unplanned; see RANDOM.

cold *a.* **1** [Said of the weather] crisp, cool, icy, freezing, frosty, frigid, wintry, bleak, nippy, brisk, keen, penetrating, snowy, frozen, cutting, snappy, piercing, chill, bitter, numbing, severe, stinging, glacial, intense, Siberian, chilly, sharp, raw, nipping, arctic, polar, below zero, biting.— *Ant.* HOT, warm, heated. **2** [Said of persons, animals, etc.] coldblooded, frozen, clammy, stiff, chilled, frostbitten, shivering, blue from cold.—

Ant. HOT, perspiring, thawed. **3** [Said of temperament] unconcerned, apathetic, distant; see INDIFFERENT, RESERVED 3.

cold *n.* **1** [Conditions having a cold temperature] coldness, frozenness, chilliness, frostiness, draft, frostbite, absence of warmth, want of heat, chill, shivers, coolness, shivering, goose flesh, numbness, iciness, frigidity, freeze, glaciation, refrigeration; see also WEATHER.—*Ant.* HEAT, warmth, heat wave. **2** [Head or respiratory congestion] cough, hack, sore throat, sickness, cold in the head, sinus trouble, cold in one's chest, bronchial irritation, common cold, laryngitis, hay fever, whooping cough, influenza, flu, asthma, bronchitis, strep throat*, strep*, sniffles*, frog in one's throat; see also ILLNESS 2. —**catch cold** come down with a cold, become ill, get a cold; see SICKEN 1. —**have** (or **get**) **cold feet** go back on one's word, hold back, back down; see FEAR, STOP 2. — **leave out in the cold** ignore, slight, neglect; see ABANDON 1. —**(out) in the cold** forgotten, ignored, rejected; see NEGLECTED. —**throw cold water on** dishearten, squelch, dampen; see DISCOURAGE.

stopped *cold]* — *n.* **1** lack of heat or warmth **2** cold weather **3** a viral infection of the respiratory tract, causing sneezing, coughing, etc. —**catch** (or **take**) **cold** to become ill with a cold —**have** (or **get**) **cold feet** [Colloq.] to be (or become) timid —**in the cold** neglected —**cold′ly** *adv.* —**cold′ness** *n.*

cold′blood′ed *adj.* **1** having a body temperature that varies with the surrounding air, water, etc., as fish and reptiles **2** cruel or callous

cold cream a creamy preparation for softening and cleansing the skin

cold cuts sliced cold meats and, usually, cheeses

cold duck a drink made from sparkling burgundy and champagne

cold front the forward edge of a cold air mass advancing under a warmer mass

cold shoulder [Colloq.] a slight; rebuff; snub —**cold′-shoul′der** *vt.*

cold sore a viral infection characterized by little blisters in or around the mouth during a cold or fever; herpes simplex **2** any of these blisters

cold turkey [Slang] **1** the abrupt and total withdrawal from drugs or tobacco by an addict or user **2** without preparation

cold war hostility and conflict without actual warfare

cole (kōl) *n.* [< L *caulis*, cabbage] any of various plants related to the cabbage; esp., rape

cole′slaw′ (-slô′) *n.* [< Du: see prec. & SLAW] a salad of shredded raw cabbage   Also **cole slaw**

co·leus (kō′lē əs) *n.* [< Gr *koleos*, a sheath] any of various plants of the mint family with bright-colored leaves

colic (käl′ik) *n.* [< Gr *kōlon*, colon] acute abdominal pain —**col′icky** *adj.*

coli·seum (käl′ə sē′əm) *n.* [< L *colosseum*] a large stadium

co·li·tis (kō līt′is) *n.* [< COLON² + -ITIS] inflammation of the colon

coll. 1 collect **2** college

col·labo·rate (kə lab′ə rāt′) *vi.* **-rat′ed, -rat′ing** [< L *com-*, with + *laborare*, to work] **1** to work together, esp. in some literary or scientific undertaking **2** to cooperate with the enemy —**col·lab′o·ra′tion** *n.* —**col·lab′o·ra′tor** *n.*

col·lage (kə läzh′) *n.* [Fr, a pasting] an art form in which bits of objects are pasted together on a surface

col·lapse (kə laps′) *vi.* **-lapsed′, -laps′ing** [< L *com-*, together + *labi*, to fall] **1** to fall down or cave in **2** to break down suddenly **3** to fail suddenly in health **4** to fold together compactly — *vt.* to make collapse — *n.* a collapsing —**col·laps′ible** *adj.*

col·lar (käl′ər) *n.* [< L *collum*, neck] **1** the part of a garment that encircles the neck **2** a band of leather, etc. for an animal's neck **3** anything like a collar — *vt.* **1** to put a collar on **2** to seize, as by the collar

-collar *combining form* designating any of various categories of employed persons [pink-*collar* workers]

col′lar·bone′ *n.* CLAVICLE

col·lard (käl′ərd) *n.* [< ME] a kind of kale with coarse leaves

col·late (kə lāt′, käl′āt′) *vt.* **-lat′ed, -lat′ing** [< L *com-*, together + *latus*, brought] **1** to compare (texts, etc.) carefully **2** to put (pages) in proper order —**col·la′tor** *n.*

col·lat·eral (kə lat′ər əl) *adj.* [< L *com-*, together + *lateralis*, lateral] **1** parallel or corresponding **2** accompanying or supporting [*collateral* evidence] **3** having the same ancestors but in a different line **4** designating or of security given as a pledge for the repayment of a loan, etc. — *n.* **1** a collateral relative **2** collateral security

col·la·tion (kə lā′shən) *n.* **1** the act or result of collating **2** a light meal

col·league (käl′ēg′) *n.* [< Fr < L *com-*, with + *legare*, appoint as deputy] a fellow worker; associate in office

col·lect (kə lekt′) *vt.* [< L *com-*, together + *legere*, gather] **1** to gather together **2** to gather (stamps, etc.) as a hobby **3** to call for and receive (money) for (bills, etc.) **4** to regain control of (oneself) — *vi.* to assemble or accumulate — *adj., adv.* with payment to be made by the receiver [to telephone *collect*] —**col·lect′ible** or **col·lect′able** *adj., n.* —**col·lec′tor** *n.*

col·lect′ed *adj.* **1** gathered together **2** in control of oneself; calm

col·lec′tion *n.* **1** a collecting **2** things collected **3** a mass or pile; accumulation **4** money collected

col·lec′tive *adj.* **1** formed by collecting **2** of or as a group [*collective* effort] **3** designating a singular noun, as *tribe*, denoting a collection of individuals — *n.* **1** any collective enterprise; specif., a collective farm **2** the people who work together in it **3** a collective noun —**col·lec′tively** *adv.*

collective bargaining negotiation between organized workers and their employer concerning wages, hours, etc.

col·lec′tiv·ism′ *n.* collective ownership and control, esp. under socialism —**col·lec′tiv·ist** *n., adj.* —**col·lec′tiv·ize′, -ized′, -iz′ing,** *vt.*

col·leen (käl′ēn′, kä lēn′) *n.* [< Ir *caile*, girl] [Irish] a girl

col·lege (käl′ij) *n.* [see COLLEAGUE] **1** a group of individuals with certain powers and duties [the electoral *college*] **2** an institution of higher education that grants degrees **3** any of the schools of a university **4** a school offering specialized instruction [a business *college*] **5** the building or buildings of a college

col·legian (kə lē′jən) *n.* a college student

col·le′giate (-jit, -jē it) *adj.* of or like a college or college students

col·lide (kə līd′) *vi.* **-lid′ed, -lid′ing** [< L *com-*, together + *laedere*, to strike] **1** to come into violent contact; crash **2** to conflict; clash

col·lie (käl′ē) *n.* [< ?] a large, long-haired dog, orig. bred in Scotland

col·lier (käl′yər) *n.* [< ME: see COAL & -IER] [Chiefly Brit.] **1** a coal miner **2** a coal freighter

col′liery *n., pl.* **-ies** [Chiefly Brit.] a coal mine and its buildings, etc.

col·li·sion (kə lizh′ən) *n.* **1** a colliding **2** a clash or conflict

col·lo·cate (käl′ə kāt′) *vt.* **-cat′ed, -cat′ing** [< L *com-*, together + *locare*, to place] to arrange; esp., to set side by side —**col′lo·ca′tion** *n.*

col·loid (käl′oid′) *n.* [< Gr *kolla*, glue + -OID] a substance made up of tiny, insoluble, nondiffusible particles that remain suspended in a medium of different matter —**col·loi′dal** *adj.*

colloq. colloquial

col·lo·quial (kə lō′kwē əl) *adj.* [see COLLOQUY] designating or of the words, phrases, etc. characteristic of informal speech and writing; informal —**col·lo′qui·al·ism′** *n.* —**col·lo′qui·al·ly** *adv.*

THESAURUS

coldblooded *a.* relentless, callous, unfeeling; see CRUEL.

collaborate *v.* work together, conspire, work with; see COOPERATE.

collapse *n.* breakdown, downfall, destruction; see FAILURE 1, WRECK.

collapse *v.* drop, deflate, give way; see FAIL 1, FALL 1, 2.

collar *n.* neckband, neckpiece, dickey; see CLOTHES.

collateral *n.* security, guarantee, pledge; see INSURANCE, MONEY 1, WEALTH.

colleague *n.* partner, collaborator, teammate; see ASSOCIATE.

collect *v.* **1** [To bring into one place] amass, consolidate, convoke; see ACCUMULATE, ASSEMBLE 2, CONCENTRATE 1. **2** [To come together] congregate, assemble, flock; see GATHER. **3** [To obtain funds] solicit, raise,

secure; see GET 1.

collected *a.* **1** [Composed] self-possessed, poised, cool; see CALM 1. **2** [Assembled] accumulated, amassed, compiled; see GATHERED.

collection *n.* specimens, samples, examples, extracts, gems, models, assortment, medley, accumulation, pile, stack, group, assemblage, compilation, mass, quantity, selection, treasury, anthology, miscellany, aggregation, combination, number, store, stock, digest, arrangement, concentration, discoveries, finds, batch, mess, lot, heap, bunch; see also ORDER 3.

collector *n.* authority, hobbyist, fancier, serious amateur, gatherer, discoverer, curator, compiler, finder, assembler, hoarder, librarian; see

also SCIENTIST, SPECIALIST.

college *n.* institute, institution, community college, liberal arts college, teachers college, junior college, state college, denominational college, nondenominational college, private college, business school, technical school, higher education, graduate school, medical school, law school, seminary; see also UNIVERSITY.

collide *v.* **1** [To come into violent contact] hit, strike, smash; see CRASH 4. **2** [To come into conflict] clash, conflict, disagree; see OPPOSE 1.

collision *n.* impact, contact, shock, accident, encounter, crash, colliding, bump, jar, jolt, sideswipe, strike, hit, slam, blow, thud, thump, knock, smash, butt, rap, head-on crash, fender-bender*; see also DISASTER.

col·lo′quium *n., pl.* **-quia** or **-qui·ums** 〚L: see fol.〛 an organized conference or seminar on some subject

col′lo·quy (käl′ə kwē) *n., pl.* **-quies** 〚< L *com-*, together + *loqui*, speak〛 a conversation or conference

col·lu′sion (kə lōō′zhən) *n.* 〚< L *com-*, with + *ludere*, to play〛 a secret agreement for fraudulent or illegal purpose; conspiracy —**col·lu′sive** (-siv) *adj.* —**col·lu′sively** *adv.*

co·logne (kə lōn′) *n.* 〚< Fr *eau de cologne*, lit., water of Cologne, city in Germany〛 a perfumed toilet water made of alcohol and aromatic oils

co·lon¹ (kō′lən) *n.* 〚< Gr *kōlon*, verse part〛 a mark of punctuation (:) used before a long quotation, explanation, example, series, etc. and after the salutation of a formal letter

co·lon² (kō′lən) *n., pl.* **-lons** or **-la** (-lə) 〚< Gr *kolon*〛 that part of the large intestine extending from the cecum to the rectum

colonel (kur′nəl) *n.* 〚< It *colonna*, (military) column〛 a military officer ranking just above a lieutenant colonel — **colo′nel·cy,** *pl.* **-cies,** *n.*

co·lo·nial (kə lō′nē əl) *adj.* 1 of, in, or having a colony 2 [*often* C-] of the thirteen British colonies that became the U.S. — *n.* an inhabitant of a colony —**co·lo′ni·ally** *adv.*

co·lo′ni·al·ism′ (-iz′əm) *n.* the system by which a country maintains foreign colonies, esp. for economic exploitation —**co·lo′ni·al·ist** *n., adj.*

colo·nist (käl′ə nist) *n.* a settler or inhabitant of a colony

col′o·nize′ (-nīz′) *vt., vi.* **-nized′, -niz′ing** 1 to found a colony (in) 2 to settle in a colony —**col′o·ni·za′tion** *n.* — **col′o·niz′er** *n.*

col·on·nade (käl′ə nād′) *n.* 〚< L *columna*, column〛 *Archit.* a row of columns, as along the side of a building

colo·ny (käl′ə nē) *n., pl.* **-nies** 〚< L *colere*, cultivate〛 **1** *a)* a group of settlers in a distant land, under the jurisdiction of their native land *b)* the region settled **2** any territory ruled over by a distant state **3** a community of the same nationality or pursuits, as within a city **4** *Biol.* a group living or growing together

colo·phon (käl′ə fən, -fän′) *n.* 〚LL < Gr *kolophōn*, top〛 a publisher's emblem

color (kul′ər) *n.* 〚L〛 **1** the property of reflecting light of a particular visible wavelength: the *colors* of the spectrum are red, orange, yellow, green, blue, indigo, and violet **2** any coloring matter; dye; pigment **3** color of the face or skin **4** [*pl.*] a colored badge, etc. to identify the wearer **5** [*pl.*] a flag **6** outward appearance **7** vivid quality — *vt.* **1** to give color to; paint, dye, etc. **2** to change the color of **3** to alter, as by distorting [*to color* a story] — *vi.* **1** to become colored **2** to change color **3** to blush or flush — **show one's (true) colors** to reveal one's true self

col′or·ant (kul′ər ənt) *n.* a dye or other coloring agent

col′ora′tion (-ər ā′shən) *n.* a coloring

colo·ra·tura (kul′ə rə toor′ə, -tyoor′-) *n.* 〚It〛 **1** brilliant runs, trills, etc., used to display a singer's skill **2** a soprano capable of singing such music: also **coloratura soprano**

col′or·blind′ *adj.* **1** unable to distinguish certain colors or any colors **2** not influenced by considerations of race — **col′or·blind′ness** *n.*

col′ored (-ərd) *adj.* **1** having color **2** non-Caucasoid; specif., black

col′or·fast′ (-fast′) *adj.* with color not subject to fading or running

col′or·ful *adj.* **1** full of color **2** picturesque, vivid, etc. — **col′or·fully** *adv.* —**col′or·ful·ness** *n.*

col′or·ing *n.* **1** anything applied to impart color; pigment, etc. **2** the way a thing is colored **3** false appearance

col′or·less *adj.* **1** without color **2** lacking variety or interest; dull —**col′or·lessly** *adv.* —**col′or·less·ness** *n.*

color line the barrier of social, political, and economic restrictions imposed on blacks or other nonwhites Also **color bar**

co·los·sal (kə läs′əl) *adj.* enormous in size, degree, etc.; astonishingly great —**co·los′sally** *adv.*

co·los·sus (kə läs′əs) *n., pl.* **-si′** (-ī′) or **-suses** 〚< Gr〛 **1** a gigantic statue **2** anything huge or important

co·los·tomy (kə läs′tə mē) *n., pl.* **-mies** surgical construction of an artificial anal opening from the colon

co·los·trum (kə läs′trəm) *n.* 〚L〛 the first fluid secreted by the mammary glands just after a birth

col·our (kul′ər) *n., vt., vi. Brit. sp. of* COLOR

colt (kōlt) *n.* 〚OE〛 a young male horse, donkey, etc.

colt′ish *adj.* of or like a colt; esp., frisky, frolicsome, etc. — **colt′ishly** *adv.*

col·um·bine (käl′əm bīn′) *n.* 〚< L *columbinus*, dovelike〛 a plant of the buttercup family, having dainty flowers of various colors with petals forming backward spurs

col·umn (käl′əm) *n.* 〚< L *columna*〛 **1** a slender upright structure, usually a supporting member in a building **2** anything like a column [*the spinal column*] **3** a file formation of troops, etc. **4** any of the vertical sections of printed matter on a page **5** a feature article appearing regularly in a newspaper, etc. —**co·lum·nar** (kə lum′nər) *adj.*

col·um·nist (käl′əm nist′) *n.* a writer of a COLUMN (sense 5)

com- 〚< L *com-*, with〛 *prefix* with, together Also used as an intensive

Com. **1** Commissioner **2** Committee

coma (kō′mə) *n.* 〚< Gr *kōma*, deep sleep〛 deep, prolonged unconsciousness caused by injury or disease

co·make (kō′māk′) *vt.* **-made′, -mak′ing** COSIGN —**co′mak′er** *n.*

co·ma·tose (kō′mə tōs′, käm′ə-) *adj.* **1** of, like, or in a coma **2** lethargic

comb (kōm) *n.* 〚< OE *camb*〛 **1** a thin strip of hard rubber, plastic, etc., with teeth, used to arrange or clean the hair **2** any similar tool, as for cleaning and straightening wool, flax, etc. **3** a red, fleshy outgrowth on the head, as of a rooster **4** a honeycomb — *vt.* **1** to arrange, etc. with a comb **2** to search thoroughly

com·bat (*for v.* kəm bat′, käm′bat′; *for n.* käm′bat′) *vt.* **-bat′ed** or **-bat′ted, -bat′ing** or **-bat′ting** 〚< Fr < L *com-*, with + *battuere*, to fight〛 to fight, contend, or struggle — *vt.* to fight or actively oppose — *n.* **1** armed fighting;

THESAURUS

colonial *a.* **1** [Concerning a colony] pioneer, isolated, dependent, settled, provincial, frontier, Pilgrim, emigrant, immigrant, territorial, outland, distant, overseas, remote, early American, overseas, protectoral, dominion, established. **2** [Having qualities suggestive of colonial life] hard, raw, crude, harsh, wild, unsettled, limited, uncultured, new, unsophisticated.

colonization *n.* immigration, settlement, expansion; see FOUNDATION 2.

colonize *v.* found, people, pioneer; see ESTABLISH 2, SETTLE 5.

colony *n.* settlement, dependency, subject state, colonial state, dominion, offshoot, political possession, province, group, new land, protectorate, hive, daughter country, satellite state, community, group migration; see also NATION 1.

color *n.* hue, tone, tint, shade, tinge, dye, taint, dash, touch, complexion, brilliance, undertone, value, iridescence, intensity, coloration, discoloration, pigmentation, coloring, cast, glow, blush, wash, tincture. *Colors*

include the following—colors in the solar spectrum: red, orange, yellow, green, blue, violet; *physiological primary colors:* red, green, blue; *psychological primary colors:* red, yellow, green, blue, black, white; *primary colors in painting:* red, blue, yellow; see also BLACK 1, BLUE 1, PURPLE, BROWN, GREEN 1, ORANGE 1, PINK, RED, YELLOW. —**change color** flush, redden, become red in the face; see BLUSH. —**lose color** become pale, blanch, faint; see WHITEN 1.

color *v.* gloss, chalk, daub, gild, enamel, lacquer, suffuse, stipple, pigment, glaze, tinge, tint, stain, tone, shade, dye, wash, crayon, chrome, enliven, embellish, give color to, adorn, imbue, emblazon, illuminate, rouge; see also DECORATE, PAINT 1, 2.

colored *a.* **1** [Treated with color] hued, tinted, tinged, shaded, flushed, reddened, glowing, stained, dyed, washed, rouged; see also PAINTED 2. **2** [Belonging to a dark-skinned race] brown, black, red; see NEGRO.

colorful *a.* vivid, glossy, realistic; see BRIGHT 1.

colorless *a.* drab, pale, neutral; see DULL 2, TRANSPARENT 1.

colossal *a.* huge, enormous, immense; see LARGE 1.

colt *n.* foal, filly, yearling; see HORSE.

column *n.* **1** [A pillar] support, prop, shaft, monument, totem, pylon, obelisk, tower, minaret, cylinder, mast, monolith, upright, pedestal; see also POST. **2** [Journalistic commentary] comment, article, editorial; see NEWS 1.

columnist *n.* newspaperman, journalist, correspondent; see REPORTER, WRITER.

coma *n.* unconsciousness, trance, stupor; see SLEEP.

comb *n.* pocket comb, pick, currycomb; see BRUSH 1.

comb *v.* untangle, disentangle, cleanse, scrape, arrange, straighten, lay smooth, smooth.

combat *n.* struggle, warfare, conflict; see BATTLE, FIGHT.

combat *v.* battle, oppose, resist; see FIGHT.

battle **2** any struggle or conflict —**com·bat·ant** (kəm bat′ 'nt, käm′bə tənt) *adj., n.*

combat fatigue a psychoneurosis with anxiety, depression, etc., as after prolonged combat in warfare

com·bat·ive (kəm bat′iv, käm′bə tiv′) *adj.* ready or eager to fight

comber (kōm′ər) *n.* **1** one that combs **2** a wave, curling at the top

com·bi·na·tion (käm′bə nā′shən) *n.* **1** a combining or being combined **2** a thing formed by combining **3** an association of persons, firms, etc. for a common purpose **4** the series of numbers to which a dial is turned on a lock (**combination lock**) to open it

com·bine (kəm bīn′; *for n.* käm′bīn′) *vt., vi.* **-bined′, -bin′ ing** ⟦< L *com-*, together + *bini*, two by two⟧ to join into one, as by blending; unite — *n.* **1** a machine for harvesting and threshing grain **2** an association of persons, corporations, etc. for commercial or political, often unethical, purposes —**com·bin′er** *n.*

comb·ings (kō′miŋz) *n.pl.* loose hair, wool, etc. removed in combing

combining form a word form occurring only in compounds and derivatives (Ex.: *cardio-* in *cardiograph*)

combo (käm′bō′) *n., pl.* **-bos′** a combination; specif., a small jazz ensemble

com·bus·ti·ble (kəm bus′tə bəl) *adj.* that can burn; flammable —**com·bus′tibil′ity** *n.* —**com·bus′tibly** *adv.*

com·bus·tion (-chən) *n.* ⟦< L *com-*, intens. + *urere*, to burn⟧ the act or process of burning

come (kum) *vi.* **came, come, com′ing** ⟦< OE *cuman*⟧ **1** to move from "there" to "here" **2** to arrive or appear **3** to extend; reach **4** to happen **5** to occur in a certain order *[after 8 comes 9]* **6** to be derived or descended **7** to be caused; result **8** to become *[to come loose]* **9** to be available *[it comes in four sizes]* **10** to amount (*to*) — *interj.* an expression of irritation, impatience, etc. —**come about 1** to happen **2** to turn about —**come across** (or **upon**) to meet or find by chance —**come along 1** to appear or

arrive **2** to proceed or succeed —**come around** (or **round**) **1** to recover **2** to yield —**come by** to get; gain —**come into 1** to enter into **2** to inherit —**come off 1** to become detached **2** to end up **3** [Colloq.] to prove effective, etc. —**come out 1** to be disclosed **2** to make a debut **3** to end up —**come out for** to announce endorsement of —**come through 1** to complete something successfully **2** [Colloq.] to do or give what is wanted —**come to to** recover consciousness —**come up** to arise, as a point in a discussion —**how come?** [Colloq.] why?

come′back′ *n.* **1** a return to a previous state or position, as of power **2** a witty answer; retort

co·me·di·an (kə mē′dē ən) *n.* an actor who plays comic parts —**co·me′di·enne′** (-en′) *n.fem.*

co·me′dic (-dik) *adj.* of or having to do with comedy

come′down′ *n.* a loss of status

com·e·dy (käm′ə dē) *n., pl.* **-dies** ⟦< Gr *kōmos*, revel + *aeidein*, sing⟧ **1** a humorous play, etc. with a nontragic ending **2** an amusing event

comely (kum′lē) *adj.* **-li·er, -li·est** ⟦< OE *cymlic*⟧ attractive; fair —**come′li·ness** *n.*

come′-on′ *n.* [Slang] an inducement

co·mes·ti·ble (kə mes′tə bəl) *n.* ⟦< L *com-*, intens. + *edere*, to eat⟧ *[usually pl.]* food

comet (käm′it) *n.* ⟦< Gr *komē*, hair⟧ a small, frozen mass of dust and gas revolving around the sun: as it nears the sun it vaporizes, usually forming a long, luminous tail

come′·up·pance (kum′up′əns) *n.* [Colloq.] deserved punishment

com·fit (kum′fit, käm′-) *n.* ⟦< L *com-*, with + *facere*, do⟧ a candy or sweetmeat

com·fort (kum′fərt) *vt.* ⟦< L *com-*, intens. + *fortis*, strong⟧ to soothe in distress or sorrow; console — *n.* **1** relief from distress, etc. **2** one that comforts **3** a state of, or thing that provides, ease and quiet enjoyment —**com′ fort·ing** *adj.* —**com′fort·less** *adj.*

com·fort·able (kum′fərt ə bəl, kumf′tər bəl) *adj.* **1** providing comfort **2** at ease in body or mind **3** [Colloq.] sufficient to satisfy *[a comfortable salary]* —**com′fort·ably** *adv.*

THESAURUS

combination *n.* **1** [The act of combining] uniting, joining, unification; see UNION 1. **2** [An association] union, alliance, federation; see ORGANIZATION 2. **3** [Something formed by combining] compound, aggregate, blend; see MIXTURE 1.

combine *v.* **1** [To bring together] connect, couple, link; see JOIN 1. **2** [To become one] fuse, merge, blend; see MIX 1, UNITE.

combined *a.* linked, mingled, connected; see JOINED.

combustion *n.* flaming, kindling, oxidization; see FIRE 1.

come *v.* **1** [To move toward] close in, advance, draw near; see APPROACH 2. **2** [To arrive] appear at, reach, attain; see ARRIVE. **3** [To be available] appear, be at one's disposal, be ready, be obtainable, be handy, be accessible, be able to be reached, show up, turn up; see also APPEAR 1. **4** [*To have an orgasm*] to reach sexual fulfillment, ejaculate, climax; see ACHIEVE, COPULATE. —**as good as they come** excellent, superior, fine; see BEST. —**come about** occur, take place, result; see HAPPEN 2. —**come across 1** [To find] uncover, stumble upon, notice; see DISCOVER, FIND. **2** [*To give*] deliver, pay, hand over; see GIVE 1. —**come along 1** [To accompany] accompany, go with, attend; see ARRIVE, ADVANCE 1. **2** [To progress] show improvement, do well, prosper; see IMPROVE 2. —**come around 1** [To recover] improve, recuperate, rally; see RECOVER 3, REVIVE 2. **2** [*To visit*] call on, stop by, drop in on; see VISIT. —**come by 1** [To pass] go by, overtake, move past; see PASS 1. **2** [To acquire] get, win, procure; see GET 1. —**come into 1** [To inherit] fall heir to, succeed to, acquire; see INHERIT, RECEIVE 1. **2** [To join] enter

into, associate with, align; see JOIN 2. —**come off 1** [To become separated] be disconnected, be disengaged, be severed, be parted, be disjoined, be detached, be disunited; see also DIVIDE. **2** [To happen] occur, turn out, come about; see HAPPEN 2. —**come out 1** [To be made public] be published, be made known, be announced, be issued, be brought out, be reported, be revealed, be divulged, be disclosed, be exposed; see also APPEAR 1. **2** [To result] end, conclude, terminate; see SUCCEED 1. —**come out for** announce, state, affirm; see DECLARE, SUPPORT 1. — **come through 1** [To be successful] accomplish, score, triumph; see ACHIEVE, SUCCEED 1. **2** [To survive] live through, persist, withstand; see ENDURE 2. **3** [To do] accomplish, achieve, carry out; see PERFORM 1. — **come to 1** [To recover] rally, come around, recuperate; see RECOVER 3, REVIVE 2. **2** [To result in] end in, terminate by, conclude; see HAPPEN 2, RESULT. —**come up** appear, arise, move to a higher place; see RISE 1. — **how come?*** for what reason?, how so?, what is the cause of that?; see WHY.

comeback* *n.* **1** [Improvement] revival, progress, betterment; see IMPROVEMENT 1, RECOVERY 1, 2. **2** [Witty answer] retort, reply, rejoinder; see ANSWER 1.

comedian *n.* comic, jester, entertainer; see ACTOR, CLOWN.

comedown *n.* reversal, blow, defeat; see FAILURE 1.

comedy *n.* comic drama, tragicomedy, stand-up comedy, situation comedy, sitcom, musical comedy, farce, satire, burlesque, slapstick, light entertainment; see also DRAMA.

comfort *n.* rest, quiet, relaxation, repose, relief, poise, well-being,

cheer, abundance, sufficiency, gratification, luxury, warmth, plenty, pleasure, happiness, contentment, restfulness, peacefulness, cheerfulness, coziness, exhilaration, complacency, bed of roses*; see also EASE 1, ENJOYMENT, SATISFACTION 2.—*Ant.* WEAKNESS, discomfort, uneasiness.

comfort *v.* **1** [To console] share with, commiserate, solace, grieve with, cheer, gladden, uphold, hearten, pat on the back, put someone in a good humor, sustain, support, help, aid, confirm, reassure, refresh; see also ENCOURAGE, PITY 1.—*Ant.* DISCOURAGE, be indifferent, depress. **2** [To make easy physically] alleviate, relieve, make comfortable, assuage, soothe, mitigate, gladden, quiet one's fears, help one in need, lighten one's burden, encourage, calm, revive, sustain, aid, assist, nourish, support, compose, delight, divert, bolster up, invigorate, refresh, put at ease, reassure, warm, lighten, soften, remedy, release, restore, free, make well, revitalize; see also EASE 1, HELP, STRENGTHEN.—*Ant.* WEAKEN, make uneasy, worsen.

comfortable *a.* **1** [In physical ease] contented, cheerful, easy, at rest, relaxed, at ease, untroubled, healthy, rested, pleased, complacent, soothed, relieved, strengthened, restored, in comfort, at home with, without care, snug as a bug in a rug*; see also HAPPY, SATISFIED.—*Ant.* UNEASY, ill, disturbed. **2** [Conducive to physical ease] satisfactory, snug, cozy, warm, sheltered, convenient, protected, cared for, appropriate, useful, roomy, spacious, luxurious, rich, satisfying, restful, in comfort, well-off, well-to-do; see also PLEASANT 2.—*Ant.* SHABBY, run-down, uncomfortable.

comfortably *a.* luxuriously, in comfort, restfully, snugly, cozily, pleas-

com·fort·er (kum'fər tər) *n.* 1 one that comforts 2 a quilted bed covering

comfort station a public toilet or restroom

comfy (kum'fē) *adj.* -fier, -fi·est [Colloq.] comfortable

comic (käm'ik) *adj.* 1 of comedy 2 amusing; funny —*n.* 1 a comedian 2 the humorous element in art or life 3 *a)* COMIC STRIP *b)* [*pl.*] a section of comic strips

com'i·cal (-i kəl) *adj.* causing amusement; humorous; funny —**com'i·cal'i·ty** (-kal'ə tē) *n.* —**com'i·cally** *adv.*

comic strip a series of cartoons telling a humorous or adventurous story, as in a newspaper or in a booklet (comic book)

com·ing (kum'iŋ) *adj.* 1 approaching; next 2 showing promise of being successful, etc. —*n.* arrival; approach

com·ity (käm'ə tē) *n.*, *pl.* -ties [< L *comis*, polite] courtesy

comm. 1 commission 2 committee

comma (käm'ə) *n.* [< Gr *komma*, clause] a mark of punctuation (,) used to indicate a slight separation of sentence elements

com·mand (kə mand') *vt.* [< L *com-*, intens. + *mandare*, entrust] 1 to give an order to; direct 2 to have authority over; control 3 to have for use [to *command* a fortune] 4 to deserve and get [to *command* respect] 5 to control (a position); overlook —*vi.* to have authority —*n.* 1 an order; direction 2 controlling power or position 3 mastery 4 military or naval force, or district, under a specified authority

com·man·dant (käm'ən dant') *n.* a commanding officer, as of a fort

com'man·deer' (-dir') *vt.* [see COMMAND] to seize (property) for military or government use

com·mand'er *n.* 1 one who commands 2 *U.S. Navy* an officer ranking just above a lieutenant commander

commander in chief *pl.* **commanders in chief** the supreme commander of the armed forces of a nation

com·mand'ment *n.* a command; specif., any of the TEN COMMANDMENTS

com·mando (kə man'dō) *n.*, *pl.* -dos or -does [Afrik < Port] a member of a small force trained to raid enemy territory

command post the field headquarters of a military unit, from which operations are directed

com·memo·rate (kə mem'ə rāt') *vt.* -rat'ed, -rat'ing [< L *com-*, intens. + *memorare*, remind] 1 to honor the memory of, as by a ceremony 2 to serve as a memorial to

—**com·mem'o·ra'tion** *n.* —**com·mem'o·ra'tive** *adj.* —**com·mem'o·ra'tor** *n.*

com·mence (kə mens') *vi.*, *vt.* -menced', -menc'ing [< L *com-*, together + *initiare*, begin] to begin

com·mence'ment *n.* 1 a beginning; start 2 the ceremony of conferring degrees or diplomas at a school

com·mend (kə mend') *vt.* [see COMMAND] 1 to put in the care of another; entrust 2 to recommend 3 to praise — **com·mend'able** *adj.* —**com·mend'ably** *adv.* —**com·men·da·tion** (käm'ən dā'shən) *n.*

com·menda·tory (kə men'də tôr'ē) *adj.* praising or recommending

com·men·su·rable (kə men'shoor ə bəl, -sər-) *adj.* [< L *com-*, together + *mensura*, measurement] measurable by the same standard or measure

com·men'su·rate (-shoor it, -sər-) *adj.* [see prec.] 1 equal in measure or size; coextensive 2 proportionate 3 commensurable

com·ment (käm'ent') *n.* [< L *com-*, intens. + *meminisse*, remember] 1 an explanatory or critical note 2 a remark or observation 3 talk; gossip —*vi.* to make a comment or comments

com·men·tary (käm'ən ter'ē) *n.*, *pl.* -ies a series of explanatory notes or remarks

com'men·tate' (-tāt') *vi.* -tat'ed, -tat'ing to perform as a commentator

com'men·ta'tor (-tāt'ər) *n.* one who reports and analyzes events, trends, etc., as on television

com·merce (käm'ərs) *n.* [< L *com-*, together + *merx*, merchandise] trade on a large scale, as between countries

com·mer·cial (kə mur'shəl) *adj.* 1 of commerce or business 2 made or done for profit —*n. Radio, TV* a paid advertisement —**com·mer'cial·ism'** *n.* —**com·mer'cially** *adv.*

com·mer'cial·ize' (-īz') *vt.* -ized', -iz'ing to put on a business basis, esp. so as to make a profit —**com·mer' ciali·za'tion** *n.*

com·min·gle (kəm miŋ'gəl, kə-) *vt.*, *vi.* -gled, -gling to mingle together

com·mis·er·ate (kə miz'ər āt') *vt.* -at'ed, -at'ing [< L *com-*, intens. + *miserari*, to pity] to feel or show sorrow or pity for —*vi.* to condole or sympathize (*with*) —**com·mis' era'tion** *n.* —**com·mis'era'tive** *adj.*

com·mis·sar (käm'ə sär') *n.* [Russ *komissar*] the head of

THESAURUS

antly, warmly, conveniently, adequately, with ease, competently, amply; see also EASILY.—*Ant.* INADEQUATELY, insufficiently, poorly.

comforting *a.* sympathetic, cheering, encouraging, invigorating, health-giving, warming, consoling, sustaining, reassuring, inspiring, refreshing, upholding, relieving, soothing, lightening, mitigating, alleviating, softening, curing, restoring, releasing, freeing, revitalizing, tranquilizing.—*Ant.* DISTURBING, distressing, upsetting.

comic *a.* ridiculous, humorous, ironic; see FUNNY 1.

comical *a.* witty, amusing, humorous; see FUNNY 1.

coming *a.* 1 [Approaching] advancing, drawing near, progressing, nearing, in the offing, arriving, gaining upon, pursuing, getting near, converging, subsequent, coming in, close at hand, coming on, near at hand, almost upon, immediate, future, in view, preparing, to come, eventual, fated, written, hereafter, at hand, in store, due, about to happen, hoped for, deserving, close, imminent, prospective, anticipated, forthcoming, certain, ordained, impending, to be, expected, near, pending, foreseen, in the cards, in the wind; see also EXPECTED, LIKELY 1.—*Ant.* DISTANT, going, leaving. 2 [Having a promising future] promising, advancing, probable; see ABLE, AMBITIOUS. 3 [Future] lying ahead, pending, impending; see EXPECTED, FUTURE.

coming *n.* approach, landing, homecoming; see ARRIVAL 1.

command *n.* order, injunction, direction, dictation, demand, decree, prohibition, interdiction, canon, rule, call, summons, imposition, precept, mandate, charge, behest, edict, proclamation, instruction, proscription, ban, requirement, dictate, subpoena, commandment, dictum, word of command, writ, citation, notification, will, regulation, ordinance, act, fiat, bidding, word, requisition, ultimatum, exaction, enactment, caveat, prescript, warrant; see also LAW 3, POWER 2, REQUEST.

command *v.* 1 [To issue an order] charge, tell, demand; see ORDER 1. 2 [To have control] rule, dominate, master; see CONTROL.

commandeer *v.* appropriate, take, confiscate; see SEIZE 2.

commander *n.* commandant, officer, head; see ADMINISTRATION 2, ADMINISTRATOR, CHIEF, LEADER 2.

commanding *n.* 1 [Ruling] leading, directing, determining, ordering, instructing, dictating, dominating, compelling, managing, checking, curbing, forcing, coercing, requiring, restraining, in command, in authority, in charge, regulating. 2 [Important] decisive, impressive, significant; see IMPORTANT 1.

commemorate *v.* solemnize, honor, memorialize; see ADMIRE, CELEBRATE 1.

commemoration *n.* recognition, remembrance, observance; see CELEBRATION, CEREMONY, CUSTOM.

commemorative *a.* dedicated to the memory of, in remembrance of,

in honor of; see MEMORABLE 1.

commence *v.* start, initiate, set in motion; see BEGIN 2.

commend *v.* laud, support, acclaim; see APPROVE, PRAISE 1.

commendable *a.* praiseworthy, laudable, deserving; see EXCELLENT.

commendation *n.* tribute, approval, approbation; see HONOR, PRAISE 1.

comment *n.* report, commentary, editorial; see DISCUSSION, EXPLANATION, REMARK.

comment *v.* observe, remark, criticize, notice, state, express, pronounce, assert, say, note, touch upon, disclose, bring out, point out, conclude; see also MENTION, TALK 1.

commentary *n.* criticism, analysis, description; see EXPLANATION, INTERPRETATION.

commerce *n.* buying and selling, trading, marketing; see BUSINESS 1, ECONOMICS.

commercial *a.* trading, business, financial, economic, materialistic, practical, profitable, mercantile, merchandising, bartering, exchange, fiscal, monetary, trade, market, retail, wholesale, marketable, in the market, for sale, profit-making, money-making, across the counter; see also INDUSTRIAL, PROFITABLE.

commercial *n.* message from the sponsor, commercial announcement, plug*; see ADVERTISEMENT.

commercialize *v.* lessen, degrade, cheapen; see ABUSE.

any former U.S.S.R. COMMISSARIAT (sense 2): now called *minister*

com·mis·sar′i·at (-ser′ē ət) *n.* [Fr < L: see COMMIT] 1 an army branch providing food and supplies 2 a government department in the U.S.S.R.: now called *ministry*

com·mis·sary (käm′ə ser′ē) *n., pl.* **-ies** [see COMMIT] 1 [Obs.] an army officer in charge of supplies 2 a store, as in an army camp, where food and supplies are sold 3 a restaurant in a movie or TV studio

com·mis·sion (kə mish′ən) *n.* [see COMMIT] 1 *a)* an authorization to perform certain duties or tasks *b)* a document giving such authorization *c)* the authority so granted 2 that which one is authorized to do 3 a group of people appointed to perform specified duties 4 a committing; doing 5 a percentage of money from sales, allotted to an agent, etc. 6 *Mil. a)* an official certificate conferring rank *b)* the rank conferred — *vt.* 1 to give a commission to 2 to authorize 3 to put (a vessel) into service —**in** (or **out of**) **commission** in (or not in) working order

commissioned officer an officer in the armed forces holding a commission

com·mis′sioner *n.* 1 a person authorized to do certain things by a commission or warrant 2 a member of a COMMISSION (*n.* 3) 3 an official in charge of a government bureau, etc. 4 a person selected to regulate and control a professional sport

com·mit (kə mit′) *vt.* **-mit′ted, -mit′ting** [< L *com-,* together + *mittere,* send] 1 to give in charge; consign 2 to put in custody or confinement *[committed* to prison*]* 3 to do or perpetrate (a crime) 4 to bind, as by a promise; pledge —**com·mit′ment** *n.* —**com·mit′table** *adj.* —**com·mit′tal** *n.*

com·mit·tee (kə mit′ē) *n.* [see prec.] a group of people chosen to report or act upon a certain matter —**com·mit′tee·man** (-mən), *pl.* **-men,** *n.* —**commit′tee·wom′an,** *pl.* **-wom′en,** *n.fem.*

com·mode (kə mōd′) *n.* [Fr < L: see COM- & MODE] 1 a chest of drawers 2 a movable washstand 3 a toilet

com·mo·di·ous (kə mō′dē əs) *adj.* [see prec.] spacious; roomy

com·mod·ity (kə mäd′ə tē) *n., pl.* **-ties** [see COMMODE] 1 any useful thing 2 anything bought and sold 3 [*pl.*] staple products, as of agriculture

com·mo·dore (käm′ə dôr′) *n.* [see COMMAND] *U.S. Navy* [Historical] an officer ranking just above a captain

com·mon (käm′ən) *adj.* [< L *communis*] 1 belonging to or shared by each or all 2 of an entire community; public 3 general; widespread 4 familiar; usual 5 below ordinary;

inferior 6 vulgar; coarse 7 designating a noun (as *book*) that refers to any of a group — *n.* [*sometimes pl.*] land owned or used by all the inhabitants of a place —**in common** shared by each or all —**com′monly** *adv.*

com′mon·alty (-əl tē) *n., pl.* **-ties** the common people; public

common carrier a person or company in the business of transporting people or goods for a fee

common denominator 1 a common multiple of the denominators of two or more fractions 2 a characteristic, etc. held in common

common divisor (or **factor**) a factor common to two or more numbers

com′moner *n.* a person not of the nobility; one of the common people

common law the law based on custom, usage, and judicial decisions

com′mon-law′ marriage *Law* a marriage not solemnized by religious or civil ceremony

common market an association of countries for closer economic union

common multiple *Math.* a multiple of each of two or more quantities

com′mon·place′ *n.* 1 a trite remark; platitude 2 anything common or ordinary — *adj.* trite or ordinary

common pleas *Law* in some States, a court having jurisdiction over civil and criminal trials

com·mons (käm′ənz) *n.pl.* 1 the common people 2 [C-] HOUSE OF COMMONS 3 [*often with sing. v.*] a dining room, as at a college

common sense good sense or practical judgment — **com′mon-sense′** *adj.*

common stock stock in a company without the privileges of preferred stock, but usually giving its owner a vote

com′mon·weal′ (-wēl′) *n.* the public good; general welfare

com′mon·wealth′ (-welth′) *n.* 1 the people of a nation or state 2 a democracy or republic 3 a federation of states

com·mo·tion (kə mō′shən) *n.* [< L *com-,* together + *movere,* to move] 1 violent motion 2 confusion; bustle

com·mu·nal (käm′yōō nəl, kə myōō′nəl) *adj.* 1 of a commune 2 of the community; public 3 marked by common ownership of property —**com′mu·nal·ize′, -ized′, -iz′ing,** *vt.* —**com′mu·nally** *adv.*

com·mune¹ (kə myōōn′) *vi.* **-muned′, -mun′ing** [< OFr *comuner,* to share] to talk together intimately

com·mune² (käm′yōōn′) *n.* [< L *communis,* common] 1 the smallest administrative district of local government in some European countries 2 a small group of people living communally

com·mu·ni·cable (kə myōō′ni kə bəl) *adj.* that can be

THESAURUS

commission *n.* 1 [An authorization] order, license, command; see PERMISSION. 2 [A committee] commissioners, representatives, board; see COMMITTEE. 3 [A payment] royalty, fee, rake-off*; see PAY 2, PAYMENT 1. —**out of commission** damaged, not working, out of order; see BROKEN 2.

commission *v.* send, delegate, appoint, authorize, charge, empower, constitute, ordain, commit, entrust, send out, dispatch, deputize, assign, engage, employ, inaugurate, invest, name, nominate, hire, enable, license, command, elect, select; see also DELEGATE 1.

commissioner *n.* spokesman, magistrate, government official; see EXECUTIVE.

commit *v.* 1 [To perpetrate] do something wrong, be guilty of, execute; see PERFORM 1. 2 [To entrust] confide, delegate, relegate to, leave to, give to do, promise, assign, turn over to, put in the hands of, charge, invest, rely upon, depend upon, confer a trust, bind over, make responsible for, put an obligation upon, empower, employ, dispatch, send, vest in, invest with power, authorize, deputize, grant authority to, engage, commission; see also ASSIGN.—*Ant.* DISMISS, relieve of, discharge.

commitment *n.* pledge, responsibility, agreement; see DUTY 1, PROMISE

1, GUARANTY.

committee *n.* consultants, board, bureau, council, cabinet, investigators, trustees, appointed group, board of inquiry, representatives, investigating committee, executive committee, standing committee, planning board, ad hoc committee, special committee, grand jury, referees, task force, study group, court, subcommittee; see also REPRESENTATIVE 2.

commodity *n.* goods, articles, stocks, merchandise, wares, materials, possessions, property, assets, belongings, things, stock in trade, consumers' goods, line, what one handles, what one is showing.

common *a.* 1 [Ordinary] universal, familiar, natural, normal, everyday, accepted, commonplace, characteristic, customary, bourgeois, conventional, passable, general, informal, wearisome, unassuming, pedestrian, lower-level, habitual, prevalent, probable, typical, prosaic, simple, current, prevailing, trite, household, second-rate, banal, unvaried, homely, colloquial, trivial, stock, oft repeated, indiscriminate, tedious, worn-out, hackneyed, monotonous, stale, casual, undistinguished, uneducated, artless, workaday, provincial, unsophisticated, unrefined, untutored, plain, uncultured, vulgar, unadorned, ugly, obvious, average, orthodox, mediocre, humdrum, well-known,

insipid, stereotyped, patent, moderate, middling, abiding, indifferent, tolerable, temperate, innocuous, undistinguished, run-of-the-mill*, not too bad*, garden variety, fair-to-middling*, so-so, nothing to write home about*; see also CONVENTIONAL 1, DULL 4, POPULAR 1, 3, TRADITIONAL.—*Ant.* UNIQUE, extraordinary, unnatural. 2 [Of frequent occurrence] customary, constant, usual; see FREQUENT 1, HABITUAL, REGULAR 3. 3 [Generally known] general, prevalent, well-known; see FAMILIAR, TRADITIONAL. 4 [Low] cheap, inferior, shoddy; see POOR 2, SUBORDINATE. 5 [Held or enjoyed in common] shared, joint, mutual; see COOPERATIVE, PUBLIC 2. —**in common** shared, communal, mutually held; see PUBLIC 2.

commonly *a.* usually, ordinarily, generally; see REGULARLY.

commonplace *a.* usual, hackneyed, mundane; see COMMON 1, CONVENTIONAL 1, 3.

common sense *n.* good sense, judgment, horse sense*; see SENSE 2, WISDOM.

commotion *n.* violence, tumult, uproar; see DISTURBANCE 2, FIGHT.

communal *a.* shared, cooperative, mutual; see PUBLIC 2.

commune² *n.* community, collective, co-op*; see COOPERATIVE.

communicated, as an idea, or transmitted, as a disease — **com·mu'ni·cabil'i·ty** *n.*

com·mu'ni·cant (-kənt) *n.* one who receives Holy Communion

com·mu·ni·cate (kə myōō'ni kāt') *vt.* **-cat'ed, -cat'ing** 〚< L *communicare*〛 1 to impart; transmit 2 to give (information, etc.) — *vi.* 1 to receive Holy Communion 2 to give or exchange information 3 to have a meaningful relationship 4 to be connected, as rooms —**com·mu'ni·ca'tor** *n.*

com·mu·ni·ca'tion *n.* 1 a transmitting 2 *a)* a giving or exchanging of information, messages, etc. *b)* a message, letter, etc. 3 a means of communicating —**com·mu'ni·ca'tive** *adj.*

com·mun·ion (kə myōōn'yən) *n.* 〚see COMMON〛 1 possession in common 2 a communing 3 a Christian denomination 4 [C-] HOLY COMMUNION

com·mu·ni·qué (kə myōō'ni kā', kə myōō'ni kā') *n.* 〚Fr〛 an official communication

com·mu·nism (käm'yōō niz'əm, -yə-) *n.* 〚see COMMON〛 1 any theory or system of common ownership of property 2 [*often* C-] *a)* socialism as formulated by Marx, Lenin, etc. *b)* any government or political movement supporting this

com'mu·nist (-nist) *n.* 1 an advocate or supporter of communism 2 [C-] a member of a Communist Party — *adj.* of, like, or supporting communism or communists — **com'mu·nis'tic** *adj.*

com·mu·ni·ty (kə myōō'nə tē) *n.,* pl. **-ties** 〚see COMMON〛 1 *a)* any group living in the same area or having interests, work, etc. in common *b)* such an area 2 the general public 3 a sharing in common

community college a junior college serving a certain community

com·mu·ta·tive (kə myōōt'ə tiv, käm'yə tāt'iv) *adj.* 1 involving exchange 2 *Math.* of an operation in which the order of the elements does not affect the result, as, in addition, $3 + 2 = 2 + 3$

com·mute (kə myōōt') *vt.* **-mut'ed, -mut'ing** 〚< L com-, intens. + *mutare*, to change〛 1 to exchange; substitute 2 to change (an obligation, punishment, etc.) to a less severe one — *vi.* to travel as a commuter — *n.* [Colloq.] the trip of a commuter —**com·mu·ta'tion** (käm'yə tā'shən) *n.*

com·mut'er *n.* a person who travels regularly, esp. by train, bus, etc., between two points at some distance

comp. 1 comparative 2 compound

com·pact (kəm pakt', käm'pakt; *for n.* käm'pakt) *adj.* 〚< L com-, with, together + *pangere*, to fix〛 1 closely and firmly packed 2 taking little space 3 terse — *vt.* 1 to pack or join firmly together 2 to make by putting together — *n.* 1 a small cosmetic case, usually containing face powder and a mirror 2 a relatively small car 3 an agreement; covenant —**com·pact'ly** *adv.* —**com·pact'ness** *n.*

compact disc (or **disk**) a digital disc on which music, etc. has been encoded for playing on a device using a laser beam to read the encoded matter

com·pac·tor (kəm pak'tər, käm'pak'tər) *n.* a device that compresses trash into small bundles

com·pan·ion (kəm pan'yən) *n.* 〚< L com-, with + *panis*, bread〛 1 an associate; comrade 2 a person paid to live or travel with another 3 one of a pair or set —**com·pan'ion·able** *adj.* —**com·pan'ion·ship'** *n.*

com·pan'ion·way' *n.* a stairway from a ship's deck to the space below

com·pany (kum'pə nē) *n.,* pl. **-nies** 〚see COMPANION〛 1 companionship; society 2 a group of people gathered or associated for some purpose 3 a guest or guests 4 an associate or associates 5 a body of troops 6 a ship's crew —**keep company** 1 to associate (*with*) 2 to go together, as a couple intending to marry —**part company** to stop associating (*with*)

com·pa·ra·ble (käm'pə rə bəl) *adj.* 1 that can be compared 2 worthy of comparison —**com'pa·rably** *adv.*

com·para·tive (kəm par'ə tiv) *adj.* 1 involving comparison 2 not absolute; relative 3 *Gram.* designating the second degree of comparison of adjectives and adverbs — *n.* *Gram.* the comparative degree 〔"finer" is the *comparative* of "fine"〕 —**com·par'a·tively** *adv.*

com·pare (kəm per') *vt.* **-pared', -par'ing** 〚< L com-, with + *parare*, make equal〛 1 to liken (*to*) 2 to examine for similarities or differences 3 *Gram.* to form the degrees of comparison of — *vi.* 1 to be worth comparing (*with*) 2 to make comparisons —**beyond** (or **past** or **without**) **compare** incomparably good, bad, great, etc.

com·pari·son (kəm par'ə sən) *n.* 1 a comparing or being compared 2 likeness; similarity 3 *Gram.* change in an adjective or adverb to show the positive, comparative, and

▀ THESAURUS ▀

communicate *v.* 1 [To impart information] convey, inform, advise; see TEACH, TELL 1. 2 [To be in communication] correspond, be in touch, have access to, contact, reach, hear from, be within reach, be in correspondence with, be near, be close to, have the confidence of, associate with, establish contact with, be in agreement with, be in agreement about, confer, talk, converse, chat, speak together, deal with, write to, telephone, wire, cable, fax*, network, reply, answer, have a meeting of minds, find a common denominator; see also AGREE.—*Ant.* AVOID, withdraw, elude.

communication *n.* talk, utterance, announcing, extrasensory perception, telepathy, ESP, publication, writing, drawing, painting, broadcasting, televising, correspondence, disclosure, speaking, disclosing, conference, faxing*, telephoning, wiring, cabling, networking, description, mention, announcement, presentation, interchange, expression, narration, relation, declaration, assertion, elucidation, transmission, reception, reading, translating, interpreting, news, ideas, statement, speech, language, warning, communiqué, briefing, bulletin, summary, information, report, account, publicity, translation, printed work, advice, tidings, conversation. *Means of communication include the following:* book, letter, newspaper, magazine, radio, proclamation, broadcast, dispatch, fax, wire, printout, telecast, telephone call, telegram, cable, broadside, circular, notes, memorandum, post card, poster, billboard; see also

MAIL, NEWS 1, 2, RADIO 2, TELEPHONE, TELEVISION.

communications *n.* mail, mass media, telephone; see COMMUNICATION.

communism *n.* state socialism, Marxism, dictatorship of the proletariat, collectivism, state ownership of production; see also GOVERNMENT 2.

communist *n.* Marxist, commie*, red*; see RADICAL.

community *n.* 1 [A town] village, colony, hamlet; see CITY, TOWN 1. 2 [Society] the public, the people, the nation; see SOCIETY 2.

commute *v.* 1 [To exchange for something less severe] reduce, lessen, mitigate; see DECREASE 1. 2 [Travel] go back and forth, drive, take the train; see TRAVEL.

commuter *n.* suburbanite, city worker, daily traveler; see DRIVER, TRAVELER.

companion *n.* attendant, comrade, escort, chaperon, protector, guide, friend, bodyguard.

companionship *n.* fraternity, rapport, association; see BROTHERHOOD, FELLOWSHIP 1, FRIENDSHIP.

company *n.* 1 [A group of people] assembly, throng, band; see GATHERING. 2 [People organized for business] partnership, firm, corporation; see BUSINESS 4. 3 [A guest or guests] visitors, callers, overnight guests; see GUEST. —**keep (a person) company** stay with, visit, amuse; see ENTERTAIN 1. —**keep company (with)** fraternize, accompany, associate, go together, date, go with*, take up with*, hang around

with*, pal around with*. —**part company** separate, part, stop associating with; see LEAVE 1.

comparable *a.* 1 [Worthy of comparison] as good as, equivalent, tantamount; see EQUAL. 2 [Capable of comparison] similar, akin, relative; see ALIKE, LIKE.

comparatively *a.* relatively, similarly, analogously; see APPROXIMATELY.

compare *v.* 1 [To liken] relate, connect, make like, notice the similarities, associate, link, distinguish between, bring near, put alongside, reduce to a common denominator, declare similar, equate, match, express by metaphor, correlate, parallel, show to be analogous, identify with, bring into meaningful relation with, collate, balance, parallel, bring into comparison, estimate relatively, set over against, compare notes, exchange observations, weigh one thing against another, set side by side, correlate, measure, place in juxtaposition, note the similarities and differences of, juxtapose, draw a parallel between, tie up, come up to, stack up with; see also DISTINGUISH 1. 2 [To examine on a comparative basis] contrast, set against, weigh; see ANALYZE, EXAMINE. 3 [To stand in relationship to another] match, vie, rival; see EQUAL, MATCH 3. — **beyond** (or **past** or **without**) **compare** incomparable, without equal, distinctive; see UNIQUE. —**compare to** (or **with**) put side by side, relate to, equate; see COMPARE 1.

comparison *n.* likening, metaphor, resemblance, analogy, illustration, superlative degrees —**in comparison with** compared with

com·part·ment (kəm pärt′mənt) *n.* 〖< L *com-*, intens. + *partire,* divide〗 **1** any of the divisions into which a space is partitioned off **2** a separate section or category —**com·part·men·tal·ize** (käm′pärt ment″'l iz′), -**ized**′, -**iz′ing**, *vt.*

com·pass (kum′pəs, käm′-) *vt.* 〖< L *com-*, together + *passus,* a step〗 **1** [Archaic] to go around **2** to surround **3** to understand **4** to achieve or contrive — *n.* **1** [*often pl.*] an instrument with two pivoted legs, for drawing circles, for measuring, etc. **2** a boundary **3** an enclosed area **4** range; scope **5** an instrument for showing direction, esp. one with a swinging magnetic needle pointing north

com·pas·sion (kəm pash′ən) *n.* 〖< L *com-*, together + *pati,* suffer〗 deep sympathy; pity —**com·pas′sion·ate** *adj.* —**com·pas′sion·ate·ly** *adv.*

com·pat·i·ble (kəm pat′ə bəl) *adj.* 〖see prec.〗 **1** getting along or going well together **2** *Bot.* that can be cross-fertilized or grafted readily —**com·pat·i·bil′i·ty** *n.* —**com·pat′i·bly** *adv.*

com·pa·triot (kəm pā′trē ət) *n.* 〖see COM- & PATRIOT〗 a countryman — *adj.* of the same country

com·peer (käm′pir′, käm pir′) *n.* 〖see COM- & PAR〗 **1** an equal; peer **2** a comrade

com·pel (kəm pel′) *vt.* -**pelled**′, -**pel′ling** 〖< L *com-*, together + *pellere,* to drive〗 to force or get by force —**com·pel′lingly** *adv.*

com·pen·dium (kəm pen′dē əm) *n., pl.* -**ums** *or* -**a** (-ə) 〖< L *com-*, together + *pendere,* weigh〗 a concise but comprehensive summary

com·pen·sate (käm′pən sāt′) *vt.* -**sat′ed**, -**sat′ing** 〖< L *com-*, with + *pendere,* weigh〗 **1** to make up for; counterbalance **2** to pay — *vi.* to make amends (*for*) —**com·pen·sa′tion** *n.* —**com·pen·sa·to·ry** (kəm pen′sə tôr′ē) *adj.*

com·pete (kəm pēt′) *vi.* -**pet′ed**, -**pet′ing** 〖< L *com-*, together + *petere,* to desire〗 to be in rivalry; contend; vie (*in* a contest, etc.)

com·pe·tence (käm′pə təns) *n.* **1** sufficient means for one's needs **2** ability; fitness **3** legal power, jurisdiction, etc. Also **com′pe·ten·cy** (-tən sē)

com′pe·tent (-tənt) *adj.* 〖see COMPETE〗 **1** capable; fit **2** sufficient; adequate **3** having legal competence —**com′pe·tent·ly** *adv.*

com·pe·ti·tion (käm′pə tish′ən) *n.* 〖L *competitio*〗 **1** a competing; rivalry, esp. in business **2** a contest; match — **com·peti·tive** (kəm pet′ə tiv) *adj.*

com·peti·tor (kəm pet′ət ər) *n.* 〖L〗 one who competes, as a business rival

com·pile (kəm pīl′) *vt.* -**piled**′, -**pil′ing** 〖< L *com-*, together + *pilare,* to compress〗 **1** to collect and assemble (data, writings, etc.) **2** to compose (a book, etc.) of materials from various sources —**com·pi·la·tion** (käm′pə lā′shən) *n.*

com·pla·cency (kəm plā′sən sē) *n.* 〖< L *com-*, intens. + *placere,* to please〗 contentment; often, specif., self-satisfaction, or smugness Also **com·pla′cence** —**com·pla′cent** *adj.*

com·plain (kəm plān′) *vi.* 〖< L *com-*, intens. + *plangere,* to strike〗 **1** to express pain, displeasure, etc. **2** to find fault **3** to make an accusation —**com·plain′er** *n.*

com·plain′ant (-ənt) *n.* a plaintiff

com·plaint′ (-plānt′) *n.* **1** a complaining **2** a cause for complaining **3** an ailment **4** *Law* a formal charge

com·plai·sant (kəm plā′zənt, -sənt) *adj.* 〖see COMPLACENCY〗 willing to please; obliging —**com·plai′santly** *adv.* —**com·plai′sance** *n.*

com·plect′ed (-plek′tid) *adj.* COMPLEXIONED

com·ple·ment (käm′plə mənt; *for v.,* -ment′) *n.* 〖see fol.〗 **1** that which completes or perfects **2** the amount needed to fill or complete **3** an entirety **4** *Math.* the number of degrees that must be added to a given angle to make it equal 90 degrees — *vt.* to make complete —**com′ple·men′tary** (-men′tə rē) *adj.*

com·plete (kəm plēt′) *adj.* 〖< L *com-*, intens. + *plere,* fill〗 **1** whole; entire **2** finished **3** thorough — *vt.* -**plet′ed**, -**plet′ing** **1** to finish **2** to make whole or perfect —**com·plete′ly** *adv.* —**com·plete′ness** *n.* —**com·ple′tion** (-plē′shən) *n.*

com·plex (käm pleks′, käm′pleks′; kəm pleks′; *for n.* käm′pleks′) *adj.* 〖< L *com-*, with + *plectere,* to weave〗 **1** consisting of two or more related parts **2** complicated — *n.* **1** a complex whole **2** an assemblage of units, as build-

---

══ THESAURUS ══

correspondence, relation, correlation, parable, allegory, similarity, likening, identification, equation, measurement, example, contrast, association, parallel, connection, paralleling; see also ASSOCIATION 2.

compartment *n.* section, portion, subdivision; see PART 1.

compassion *n.* sympathy, consideration, clemency; see KINDNESS 1, PITY.

compassionate *a.* merciful, humane, sympathetic; see MERCIFUL.

compatible *a.* agreeable, congruous, cooperative; see HARMONIOUS 2.

compel *v.* enforce, constrain, coerce; see FORCE.

compensate *v.* recompense, remunerate, requite; see PAY 1, REPAY 1.

compensation *n.* remuneration, recompense, indemnity, satisfaction, remittal, return for services, commission, gratuity, reimbursement, allowance, deserts, remittance, salary, stipend, wages, hire, earnings, settlement, honorarium, coverage, consideration, damages, repayment, fee, reckoning, bonus, premium, amends, reward, advantage, profit, benefit, gain, kickback*; see also PAY 2, PAYMENT 1.—*Ant.* LOSS, deprivation, confiscation.

compete *v.* enter competition, take part, strive, struggle, vie with, be in the running, become a competitor, enter the lists, run for, participate in, engage in a contest, oppose, wrestle, be rivals, battle, bid, spar, fence, collide, face, clash, encounter, match wits, play, grapple, take on all comers, go in for*, lock horns, go out for; see also FIGHT.

competence *n.* capability, skill, fitness; see ABILITY.

competent *a.* fit, qualified, skilled;

see ABLE.

competition *n.* race, match, contest, meet, fight, bout, boxing match, game of skill, trial, sport, athletic event, wrestling; see also GAME 1, SPORT 1, 3. —**in competition with** opposed to, competing against, over; see AGAINST 3.

competitive *a.* competing, antagonistic, opposing; see RIVAL.

competitor *n.* foe, rival, antagonist; see CONTESTANT, OPPONENT 1.

compile *v.* collect, arrange, assemble; see ACCUMULATE, EDIT.

complacent *a.* self-satisfied, contented, self-righteous; see EGOTISTIC, HAPPY, SATISFIED, SMUG.

complain *v.* disapprove, accuse, deplore, criticize, denounce, differ, disagree, dissent, charge, report adversely, reproach, oppose, grumble, whine, whimper, remonstrate, fret, protest, fuss, moan, make a fuss, take exception to, object to, deprecate, enter a demurrer, demur, defy, carp, impute, indict, attack, refute, grouse*, kick*, bitch*, grouch, gripe*, grunt*, beef*, bellyache*, kick up a fuss*.—*Ant.* APPROVE, sanction, countenance.

complaining *a.* objecting, lamenting, murmuring, mourning, regretting, bewailing, deploring, weeping, moaning, protesting, charging, accusing, disapproving, grumbling, fretting, whining, imputing, resenting, dissenting, registering a protest, filing a complaint, making an adverse report, kicking.—*Ant.* enjoying, appreciating, praising.

complaint *n.* **1** [An objection] charge, criticism, reproach; see ACCUSATION, OBJECTION. **2** [An illness] ailment, disease, infirmity; see ILLNESS 1.

complementary *a.* paired, mated, corresponding; see ALIKE, MATCHED.

complete *a.* **1** [Not lacking in any part] total, replete, entire; see FULL 1, WHOLE 1. **2** [Finished] concluded, terminated, ended; see FINISHED 1. **3** [Perfect] flawless, unblemished, impeccable; see PERFECT, WHOLE 2.

complete *v.* execute, consummate, perfect, accomplish, realize, perform, achieve, fill out, fulfill, equip, actualize, furnish, make up, elaborate, make good, make complete, develop, fill in, refine, effect, carry out, crown, get through, round out; see also CREATE.—*Ant.* BEGIN, start, commence.

completed *a.* achieved, ended, concluded; see BUILT, DONE 2, FINISHED 1.

completely *a.* entirely, fully, totally, utterly, wholly, perfectly, exclusively, simply, effectively, competently, solidly, bodily, absolutely, unanimously, thoroughly, en masse, exhaustively, minutely, painstakingly, extensively, conclusively, unconditionally, finally, to the utmost, ultimately, altogether, comprehensively, to the end, from beginning to end, on all counts, in all, in full measure, to the limit, to the nth degree, to a frazzle*, downright, through thick and thin, down to the ground, through and through, in no way or shine, in one lump, from A to Z, from head to foot; hook, line, and sinker*.—*Ant.* PARTLY, somewhat, partially.

completion *n.* finish, conclusion, fulfillment; see END 2.

complex *a.* **1** [Composed of several parts] composite, heterogeneous, conglomerate, multiple, mosaic, manifold, multiform, compound, complicated, aggregated, involved, combined, compact, compounded, ings **3** *Psychoanalysis a)* a group of mainly unconscious impulses, etc. strongly influencing behavior *b)* popularly, an obsession —**com·plex′i·ty** *n.*

com·plex·ion (kəm plek′shən) *n.* ⟦see prec.⟧ **1** the color, texture, etc. of the skin, esp. of the face **2** nature; character; aspect —**com·plex′ion·al** *adj.*

com·plex′ioned *adj.* having a (specified) complexion ⟦*light-complexioned*⟧

complex sentence a sentence consisting of an independent clause and one or more dependent clauses

com·pli·ance (kəm plī′əns) *n.* **1** a complying; acquiescence **2** a tendency to give in readily to others Also **com·pli′an·cy** —**com·pli′ant** *adj.*

com·pli·cate (käm′pli kāt′) *vt., vi.* **-cat′ed, -cat′ing** ⟦< L *com-*, together + *plicare*, to fold⟧ to make or become intricate, difficult, or involved —**com′pli·ca′tion** *n.*

com′pli·cat′ed *adj.* intricately involved; hard to solve, analyze, etc.

com·plic·i·ty (kəm plis′ə tē) *n., pl.* **-ties** ⟦see COMPLICATE⟧ partnership in wrongdoing

com·pli·ment (käm′plə mənt; *for v.,* -ment′) *n.* ⟦Fr < L: see COMPLETE⟧ **1** a formal act of courtesy; esp., something said in praise **2** [*pl.*] respects — *vt.* to pay a compliment to

com′pli·men′ta·ry (-men′tə rē) *adj.* **1** paying or containing a compliment **2** given free as a courtesy

com·ply (kəm plī′) *vt.* **-plied′, -ply′ing** ⟦see COMPLETE⟧ to act in accordance (*with* a request, order, etc.)

com·po·nent (kəm pō′nənt) *adj.* ⟦see COMPOSITE⟧ serving as one of the parts of a whole — *n.* a part, element, or ingredient

com·port (kəm pôrt′) *vt.* ⟦< L *com-*, together + *portare*, carry⟧ to behave (oneself) in a specified manner — *vi.* to accord (*with*) —**com·port′ment** *n.*

com·pose (kəm pōz′) *vt.* **-posed′, -pos′ing** ⟦< OFr *com-*, with + *poser*, to place⟧ **1** to make up; constitute **2** to put in proper form **3** to create (a musical or literary work) **4** to make calm **5** *a)* to set (type) *b)* to produce (printed matter) as by composing, etc. — *vi.* to create musical works, etc.

com·posed′ *adj.* calm; self-possessed

com·pos·er (-pō′zər) *n.* one who composes, esp. one who composes music

com·pos·ite (kəm päz′it) *adj.* ⟦< L *com-*, together + *ponere*, to place⟧ **1** compound **2** *Bot.* designating a large family of plants with flower heads composed of dense clusters of small flowers, including the daisy and the chrysanthemum — *n.* a composite thing —**com·pos′ite·ly** *adv.*

com·po·si·tion (käm′pə zish′ən) *n.* **1** a composing, esp. of literary or musical works **2** the makeup of a person or thing **3** something composed

com·pos·i·tor (kəm päz′ət ər) *n.* one who sets matter for printing, esp. a typesetter

com·post (käm′pōst′) *n.* ⟦see COMPOSITE⟧ a mixture of decomposing vegetable refuse for fertilizing soil

com·po·sure (kəm pō′zhər) *n.* ⟦see COMPOSE⟧ calmness; self-possession

com·pote (käm′pōt′) *n.* ⟦Fr: see COMPOSITE⟧ **1** a dish of stewed fruits **2** a long-stemmed dish, as for candy

com·pound¹ (käm pound′, käm′pound′; kəm pound′; *for adj. usually & for n. always,* käm′pound′) *vt.* ⟦see COMPOSITE⟧ **1** to mix or combine **2** to make by combining parts **3** to compute (compound interest) **4** to intensify by adding new elements — *adj.* made up of two or more parts — *n.* **1** a thing formed by combining parts **2** a substance containing two or more elements chemically combined — **compound a felony** (or **crime**) to agree, for payment, not to prosecute a felony (or crime)

com·pound² (käm′pound′) *n.* ⟦Malay *kampong*⟧ an area enclosing a building or buildings

compound eye an eye made up of numerous simple eyes functioning collectively, as in insects

compound fracture a fracture in which the broken bone pierces the skin

compound interest interest paid on both the principal and the accumulated unpaid interest

compound sentence a sentence consisting of two or more independent, coordinate clauses

com·pre·hend (käm′prē hend′, -pri-) *vt.* ⟦< L *com-*, with + *prehendere*, seize⟧ **1** to grasp mentally; understand **2** to include; take in; comprise —**com′pre·hen′si·ble** (-hen′sə bəl) *adj.* —**com′pre·hen′sion** *n.*

com′pre·hen′sive *adj.* wide in scope; inclusive —**com′pre·hen′sive·ly** *adv.* —**com′pre·hen′sive·ness** *n.*

THESAURUS

miscellaneous, multiplex, multifarious, variegated; see also MIXED 1. **2** [Difficult to understand] entangled, tangled, circuitous, convoluted, puzzling, mixed, mingled, muddled, jumbled, impenetrable, inscrutable, unfathomable, undecipherable, bewildering, intricate, perplexing, complicated, involved, enigmatic, hidden, knotted, meandering, winding, tortuous, snarled, rambling, twisted, disordered, devious, discursive, cryptic, inextricable, knotty, roundabout; see also CONFUSED 2, DIFFICULT 2.—*Ant.* UNDERSTANDABLE, plain, apparent.

complex *n.* **1** [An obsession] phobia, mania, repressed emotions, repressed desires; see also FEAR, INSANITY. **2** [A composite] conglomerate, syndrome, ecosystem, aggregation, association, totality; see also COLLECTION.

complexion *n.* tone, glow, color, coloration, general coloring, tinge, cast, flush, skin texture, tint, hue, pigmentation; see also SKIN. *Descriptions of complexions include the following:* blond, fair, pale, sallow, sickly, dark, brunet, olive, bronze, sandy, rosy, red, ruddy, brown, yellow, black, peaches-and-cream*.

compliant *a.* obedient, pliant, acquiescent; see DOCILE.

complicate *v.* combine, fold, multiply, twist, snarl up, associate with, involve, obscure, confound, muddle, clog, jumble, interrelate, elaborate, embarrass, implicate, tangle, conceal, mix up, impede, perplex, hinder, hamper, handicap, tie up with, ball up*; see also CONFUSE, ENTANGLE.—*Ant.* SIMPLIFY, clear up, unfold.

complicated *a.* intricate, various, mixed; see COMPLEX 2, CONFUSED 2,

DIFFICULT 2.

complication *n.* complexity, dilemma, development; see CONFUSION, DIFFICULTY 1, 2.

compliment *n.* felicitation, tribute, approval, commendation, endorsement, confirmation, sanction, applause, flattery, acclaim, adulation, notice, puff, regards, honor, appreciation, respects, blessing, ovation, veneration, admiration, congratulation, homage, good word, sentiment; see also PRAISE 2.—*Ant.* ABUSE, censure, disapproval.

compliment *v.* wish joy to, remember, commemorate, pay one's respects, honor, cheer, salute, hail, toast, applaud, extol, celebrate, felicitate, pay tribute to, be in favor of, commend, endorse, sanction, confirm, acclaim, please, satisfy, pay a compliment to, sing the praises of, speak highly of, exalt, applaud, worship, eulogize, glorify, magnify, fawn upon, butter up*, puff, hand it to*; see also PRAISE 1.—*Ant.* DENOUNCE, disapprove of, censure.

complimentary *a.* flattering, laudatory, approving, celebrating, honoring, respectful, congratulatory, well-wishing, highly favorable, praising, singing the praises of, with highest recommendations, with high praise; see also POLITE.

compose *v.* **1** [To be the parts or the ingredients] constitute, comprise*, go into the making of, make up, merge into, be a component, be an element of, belong to, consist of, be made of; see also COMPRISE, INCLUDE 1. **2** [To create] fabricate, produce, write music, score, orchestrate, forge, discover, design, conceive, imagine, make up, turn out, draw up; see also

CREATE, INVENT 1.

composed *a.* **1** [Made] created, made up, fashioned; see FORMED. **2** [Calm] poised, confident, cool*; see CALM 1, CONFIDENT 1.

composer *n.* arranger, song-writer, musical author; see AUTHOR, MUSICIAN, POET, WRITER.

composition *n.* creation, making, fashioning, formation, conception, presentation, invention, fiction, novel, tale, essay, play, drama, poem, stanza, symphony, concerto, quartet, song, rhapsody, melody; see also BIOGRAPHY, LITERATURE 2, MUSIC 1, POETRY, WRITING 2.

composure *n.* serenity, peace of mind, calm, calmness, self-possession, nonchalance, cool-headedness, control, self-control, balance, contentment, tranquility, stability, harmony, assurance, self-assurance, poise, composed state of mind, even temper, equanimity, coolness, level-headedness, fortitude, moderation, gravity, sobriety, a cool head, presence of mind, equilibrium, aplomb, self-restraint, ease, evenness, complacence, tolerance, content, quiet, command of one's faculties, forbearance, cool*; see also PATIENCE 1, PEACE.—*Ant.* EXUBERANCE, passion, wildness.

compound¹ *n.* composite, union, aggregate; see MIXTURE 1.

comprehend *v.* grasp, discern, perceive; see KNOW 1, UNDERSTAND 1.

comprehension *n.* understanding, perception, cognizance; see AWARENESS, KNOWLEDGE 1.

comprehensive *a.* extensive, sweeping, complete; see ABSOLUTE 1, GENERAL 1, INFINITE, LARGE 1.

com·press (kəm pres′; *for n.* käm′pres′) *vt.* ⟦< L *com-*, together + *premere*, to press⟧ to press together and make more compact —*n.* a pad of folded cloth, often wet or medicated, applied to the skin —**com·pressed′** *adj.* —**com·pres′sion** *n.*

com·pres′sor (-pres′ər) *n.* a machine, esp. a pump, for compressing air, gas, etc.

com·prise′ (-prīz′) *vt.* **-prised′, -pris′ing** ⟦see COMPREHEND⟧ 1 to include; contain 2 to consist of 3 to make up; form: a loose usage

com·pro·mise (käm′prə mīz′) *n.* ⟦< L *com-*, together + *promittere*, to promise⟧ 1 a settlement in which each side makes concessions 2 something midway — *vt., vi.* **-mised′, -mis′ing** 1 to adjust by compromise 2 to lay open to suspicion, disrepute, etc.

comp·trol·ler (kən trō′lər) *n.* ⟦altered (infl. by Fr *compte*, an account) < CONTROLLER⟧ CONTROLLER (sense 1, esp. in government usage)

com·pul·sion (kəm pul′shən) *n.* a compelling or being compelled; force —**com·pul′sive** (-siv) *adj.* —**com·pul′sively** *adv.* —**com·pul′sive·ness** *n.*

com·pul·sory (-sə rē) *adj.* 1 obligatory; required 2 compelling

com·punc·tion (kəm puŋk′shən) *n.* ⟦< L *com-*, intens. + *pungere*, to prick⟧ an uneasy feeling prompted by guilt

com·pute (kəm pyōōt′) *vt., vi.* **-put′ed, -put′ing** ⟦< L *com-*, with + *putare*, reckon⟧ to determine (an amount, etc.) by arithmetic —**com·pu·ta·tion** (käm′pyōō tā′shən) *n.*

com·put′er *n.* an electronic machine that performs rapid, complex calculations or compiles and correlates data —**com·put′er·ize′, -ized′, -iz′ing** *vt.*

com·rade (käm′rad′, -rəd) *n.* ⟦< Sp *camarada*, chamber mate < L *camera*, room⟧ 1 a friend; close companion 2 an associate —**com′rade·ship′** *n.*

Com·sat (käm′sat′) *n.* ⟦< COM(MUNICATION) + SAT(ELLITE)⟧ *trademark for* any of various communications satellites for relaying microwave transmissions, as of television

con¹ (kän) *adv.* ⟦< L *contra*⟧ against —*n.* an opposing reason, vote, etc.

con² (kän) *vt.* **conned, con′ning** ⟦< OE *cunnan*, know⟧ to study carefully

con³ (kän) *adj.* [Slang] CONFIDENCE *[a con man]* — *vt.* **conned, con′ning** [Slang] to swindle or trick

con⁴ (kän) *n.* [Slang] *short for* CONVICT

con- *prefix* COM- Used before *c, d, g, j, n, q, s, t, v,* and sometimes *f*

con·cat·e·na·tion (kən kat″n ā′shən, kän-) *n.* ⟦< L *com-*, together + *catena*, a chain⟧ a connected series, as of events

con·cave (kän kāv′, kän′kāv′) *adj.* ⟦< L *com-*, intens. + *cavus*, hollow⟧ hollow and curved like the inside half of a hollow ball —**con·cav′ity** (-kav′ə tē), *pl.* **-ties,** *n.*

con·ceal (kən sēl′) *vt.* ⟦< L *com-*, together + *celare*, to hide⟧ 1 to hide 2 to keep secret —**con·ceal′ment** *n.*

con·cede (kən sēd′) *vt.* **-ced′ed, -ced′ing** ⟦< L *com-*, with + *cedere*, cede⟧ 1 to admit as true, valid, certain, etc. 2 to grant as a right

con·ceit (kən sēt′) *n.* ⟦see CONCEIVE⟧ 1 an exaggerated opinion of oneself, one's merits, etc.; vanity 2 a fanciful expression or notion

con·ceit′ed *adj.* vain

con·ceiv·able (kən sēv′ə bəl) *adj.* that can be understood or believed —**con·ceiv′abil′ity** *n.* —**con·ceiv′ably** *adv.*

con·ceive (kən sēv′) *vt.* **-ceived′, -ceiv′ing** ⟦< L *com-*, together + *capere*, take⟧ 1 to become pregnant with 2 to form in the mind; imagine 3 to understand —*vi.* 1 to become pregnant 2 to form an idea (*of*)

con·cel·ebrate (kän sel′ə brāt′, kən-) *vt.* **-brat′ed, -brat′ing** ⟦< L *com-*, together + *celebrare*, to honor⟧ to celebrate (the Eucharistic liturgy) jointly, two or more priests officiating —**con′cel·ebra′tion** *n.*

con·cen·trate (kän′sən trāt′) *vt.* **-trat·ed, -trat′ing** ⟦< L *com-*, together + *centrum*, center + -ATE¹⟧ 1 to focus (one's thoughts, efforts, etc.) 2 to increase the strength, density, etc. of —*vi.* to fix one's attention (*on* or *upon*) —*n.* a concentrated substance —**con′cen·tra′tion** *n.*

concentration camp a prison camp for political dissidents, members of minority ethnic groups, etc.

con·cen·tric (kən sen′trik) *adj.* ⟦< L *com-*, together + *centrum*, center⟧ having a center in common, as circles —**con·cen′tri·cally** *adv.*

con·cept (kän′sept′) *n.* ⟦see CONCEIVE⟧ an idea or thought; abstract notion

---

THESAURUS

compress *v.* condense, compact, press together, consolidate, squeeze together, tighten, cramp, contract, crowd, constrict, abbreviate, shrivel, make brief, reduce, dehydrate, pack, shorten, shrink, narrow, abridge, bind tightly, wrap closely, wedge, boil down, cram; see also PRESS 1, TIGHTEN 1.—*Ant.* SPREAD, stretch, expand.

comprise *v.* comprehend, contain, embrace, include, involve, enclose, embody, encircle, encompass, sum up, cover, consist of, be composed of, be made up of, constitute, incorporate, span, hold, engross, take into account, be contained in, add up to, amount to, take in; see also COMPOSE 1, INCLUDE 1.—*Ant.* BAR, lack, exclude.

compromise *n.* covenant, bargain, give-and-take; see AGREEMENT.

compromise *v.* agree, conciliate, find a middle ground; see NEGOTIATE 1.

compulsion *n.* 1 [Force] drive, necessity, need; see REQUIREMENT 2. 2 [An obsession] preoccupation, obsession, engrossment; see REQUIREMENT 2.

compulsive *a.* driving, impelling, besetting; see PASSIONATE 2.

compulsory *a.* obligatory, required, requisite; see NECESSARY.

compute *v.* count, figure, measure; see CALCULATE.

computer *n.* electronic brain, thinking machine, calculator, data processor, electronic circuit, cybernetic device, analog computer, digital computer, programmer; see also MACHINE.

computer language *n.* macroinstruction system, machine language, programming language, computer-processed instructions. *Some computer languages include the following:* Ada, ALGOL, BASIC, COBOL, FORTRAN, Pascal, PL/I; see also LANGUAGE 1.

comrade *n.* confidant, confidante, intimate; see ASSOCIATE, FRIEND.

con¹ *a.* conversely, opposed to, in opposition; see AGAINST 1.

con³* *n.* deception, swindle, fraud; see TRICK 1.

con³* *v.* cheat, dupe, mislead; see DECEIVE.

concave *a.* curved, sunken, cupped; see ROUND 2.

conceal *v.* screen, secrete, cover; see HIDE 1.

concealed *a.* covered, obscured, unseen; see HIDDEN.

concealment *n.* hiding, covering, camouflage; see DISGUISE.

concede *v.* yield, grant, acknowledge; see ADMIT 2, ALLOW.

conceit *n.* arrogance, self-admiration, narcissism; see VANITY.

conceited *a.* vain, arrogant, stuck-up*; see EGOTISTIC.

conceivable *a.* understandable, credible, believable; see CONVINCING, IMAGINABLE, LIKELY 1.

conceive *v.* 1 [To form a concept or image of] consider, formulate, speculate; see IMAGINE, THINK 1. 2 [To become pregnant] be with child, get pregnant, be impregnated, be in the family way*.

concentrate *v.* 1 [To bring or come together] amass, mass, assemble, combine, consolidate, compact, condense, reduce, hoard, garner, centralize, store, bring into a small compass, bring toward a central point, embody, localize, strengthen, direct toward one object, constrict, cramp, focus, reduce, intensify, crowd together, flock together, contract, muster, bunch, heap up, swarm, conglomerate, stow away, congest, narrow, compress, converge, center, collect, cluster, congregate, huddle; see also ACCUMULATE, GATHER 2, PACK 2. 2 [To employ all one's mental powers] think intensely, give attention to, meditate upon, ponder, focus attention on, direct attention to one object, weigh, consider closely, scrutinize, regard carefully, contemplate, study deeply, examine closely, brood over, put one's mind to, be engrossed in, be absorbed in, attend, give exclusive attention to, occupy the thoughts with, fix one's attention, apply the mind, give heed to, one's thought, give the mind to, direct the mind upon, center, think hard, rack one's brains, be on the beam*, keep one's eye on the ball*, knuckle down, buckle down; see also ANALYZE, EXAMINE, THINK 1.—*Ant.* DRIFT, be inattentive, ignore.

concentrated *a.* 1 [Undiluted] rich, unmixed, unadulterated, straight; see also STRONG 4, THICK 1. 2 [Intense] intensive, deep, hard; see INTENSE.

concentration *n.* 1 [Attention] close attention, concern, application; see THOUGHT 1. 2 [Density] solidity, consistency, frequency; see CONGESTION, DENSITY.

concept *n.* idea, theory, notion; see THOUGHT 2.

con·cep·tion (kən sep'shən) *n.* **1** a conceiving or being conceived in the womb **2** the beginning, as of a process **3** the formulation of ideas **4** a concept **5** an original idea or design

con·cep'tual (-chōō əl) *adj.* of conception or concepts —**con·cep'tu·al·ly** *adv.*

con·cep'tu·al·ize' (-chōō əl īz') *vt.* **-ized', -iz'ing** to form a concept of —**con·cep'tu·al·i·za'tion** *n.*

con·cern (kən surn') *vt.* ⟦ < L *com-*, with + *cernere*, sift ⟧ **1** to have a relation to **2** to engage or involve — *n.* **1** a matter; affair **2** interest in or regard for a person or thing **3** reference **4** worry **5** a business firm —**as concerns** in regard to —**concern oneself 1** to busy oneself **2** to be worried

con·cerned' *adj.* **1** involved or interested (*in*) **2** uneasy or anxious

con·cern'ing *prep.* relating to

con·cert (kän'sərt) *n.* ⟦ < L *com-*, with + *certare*, strive ⟧ **1** mutual agreement; concord **2** a performance of music —**in concert** in unison

con·cert·ed (kən surt'id) *adj.* mutually arranged or agreed upon; combined —**con·cert'ed·ly** *adv.*

con·cer·ti·na (kän'sər tē'nə) *n.* ⟦ < CONCERT ⟧ a small accordion

con·cert·ize (kän'sər tīz') *vi.* **-ized', -iz'ing** to perform as a soloist in concerts, esp. on a tour

con'cert·mas'ter *n.* the leader of the first violin section of a symphony orchestra, and often the assistant to the conductor

con·cer·to (kən cher'tō) *n.*, *pl.* **-tos** or **-ti** (-tē) ⟦It⟧ a musical composition for one or more solo instruments and an orchestra

con·ces·sion (kən sesh'ən) *n.* **1** a conceding **2** a thing conceded; acknowledgment **3** a privilege granted by a government, company, etc., as the right to sell food at a park

con·ces'sion·aire' (-ə ner') *n.* ⟦ < Fr ⟧ the holder of a CONCESSION (sense 3)

conch (käŋk, känch) *n.*, *pl.* **conchs** (käŋks) or **conches** (kän'chiz) ⟦ < Gr *konchē* ⟧ **1** the spiral, one-piece shell of various sea mollusks **2** the mollusk

con·ci·erge (kän'sē erzh'; Fr kōn syerzh') *n.* ⟦Fr < L *conservus*, fellow slave ⟧ a custodian or head porter, as of an apartment house or hotel

con·cil·i·ar (kən sil'ē ər) *adj.* of, from, or by means of a council

con·cil'i·ate' (-āt') *vt.* **-at'ed, -at'ing** ⟦see COUNCIL⟧ to win over; make friendly; placate —**con·cil'i·a'tion** *n.* —**con·cil'i·a·tor** *n.* —**con·cil'i·a·to'ry** (-ə tôr'ē) *adj.*

con·cise (kən sīs') *adj.* ⟦ < L *com-*, intens. + *caedere*, to cut ⟧ brief and to the point; terse —**con·cise'ly** *adv.* —**con·cise'ness** *n.* —**con·ci'sion** (-sizh'ən) *n.*

con·clave (kän'klāv') *n.* ⟦ < L *com-*, with + *clavis*, a key ⟧ **1** a private meeting; specif., one held by cardinals to elect a pope **2** any large convention

con·clude (kən klōōd') *vt.*, *vi.* **-clud'ed, -clud'ing** ⟦ < L *com-*, together + *claudere*, to shut ⟧ **1** to end; finish **2** to deduce **3** to decide; determine **4** to arrange (a treaty, etc.)

con·clu·sion (-klōō'zhən) *n.* **1** the end **2** a judgment or opinion formed after thought **3** an outcome **4** a concluding (*of* a treaty, etc.) —**in conclusion** lastly; in closing

con·clu'sive (-siv) *adj.* final; decisive —**con·clu'sive·ly** *adv.* —**con·clu'sive·ness** *n.*

con·coct (kän käkt') *vt.* ⟦ < L *com-*, together + *coquere*, to cook ⟧ **1** to make by combining ingredients **2** to devise; plan —**con·coc'tion** *n.*

con·com'i·tant (-käm'ə tənt) *adj.* ⟦ < L *com-*, together + *comes*, companion ⟧ accompanying; attendant — *n.* a concomitant thing —**con·com'i·tant·ly** *adv.*

con·cord (kän'kôrd', käŋ'-) *n.* ⟦ < L *com-*, together + *cor*, heart ⟧ **1** agreement; harmony **2** peaceful relations, as between nations

con·cord·ance (kən kôr'd'ns) *n.* **1** agreement **2** an alphabetical list of the words in a book, with references to the passages in which they occur

con·cord'ant *adj.* agreeing

con·cor·dat (kən kôr'dat') *n.* ⟦Fr < L: see CONCORD ⟧ a formal agreement

Con·cord (grape) (käŋ'kərd) ⟦after *Concord*, a town in E Mass.⟧ a large, dark-blue grape used esp. for juice and jelly

con·course (kän'kôrs') *n.* ⟦see CONCUR ⟧ **1** a crowd; throng **2** an open space for crowds, as in a park **3** a broad thoroughfare

con·crete (kän krēt'; *also, and for n. & vt. 2 usually,* kän' krēt') *adj.* ⟦ < L *com-*, together + *crescere*, grow ⟧ **1** having a material existence; real; actual **2** specific, not general **3** made of concrete — *n.* **1** anything concrete **2** a hard building material made of sand and gravel, bonded together with cement — *vt.*, *vi.* **-cret'ed, -cret'ing** **1** to solidify **2** to cover with concrete —**con·crete'ly** *adv.* —**con·crete'ness** *n.*

con·cre·tion (kən krē'shən) *n.* **1** a solidifying **2** a solidified mass

con·cu·bine (käŋ'kyoo bīn', kän'-) *n.* ⟦ < L *com-*, with + *cubare*, lie down ⟧ in some societies, a secondary wife having inferior status

con·cu·pis·cence (kən kyoo'pə səns) *n.* ⟦ < L *com-*, intens. + *cupiscere*, to desire ⟧ strong desire, esp. sexual desire; lust —**con·cu'pis·cent** *adj.*

con·cur (kən kur') *vi.* **-curred', -cur'ring** ⟦ < L *com-*, together + *currere*, to run ⟧ **1** to occur at the same time **2** to act together **3** to agree (*with*) —**con·cur'rence** *n.*

con·cur'rent *adj.* **1** occurring at the same time **2** acting together **3** *Law* having equal authority —**con·cur'rently** *adv.*

con·cus·sion (kən kush'ən) *n.* ⟦ < L *com-*, together + *quatere*, to shake ⟧ **1** a violent shaking; shock, as from impact **2** impaired functioning, esp. of the brain, caused by a violent blow

con·demn (kən dem') *vt.* ⟦ < L *com-*, intens. + *damnare*, to harm ⟧ **1** to disapprove of strongly **2** to declare guilty **3** to inflict a penalty upon **4** to doom **5** to appropriate (property) for public use **6** to declare unfit for use —**con·dem·na·tion** (kän'dem nā'shən, -dəm-) *n.* —**con·dem·na·tory** (kən dem'nə tôr'ē) *adj.* —**con·demn'er** *n.*

con·dense (kən dens') *vt.* **-densed', -dens'ing** ⟦ < L *com-*, intens. + *densus*, dense ⟧ **1** to make more dense or compact **2** to express in fewer words **3** to change to a denser

---

THESAURUS

conception *n.* **1** [The act of conceiving mentally] perception, apprehension, comprehension, imagining, speculating, meditation, dreaming, cogitating, deliberating, concentrating, meditating, realization, consideration, speculation, understanding, cognition, mental grasp, apperception, forming an idea, formulation of a principle; see also THOUGHT 1. **2** [The act of conceiving physically] inception, impregnation, insemination; see FERTILIZATION 2.

concern *n.* **1** [Affair] business, matter, interest; see AFFAIR 1. **2** [Regard] care, interest, solicitude; see ATTENTION.

concern *v.* **1** [To have reference to] refer to, pertain to, relate to, be related to, have significance for, bear on, regard, be connected with, be about, have to do with, be a matter of concern to, have a bearing on, have connections with, be applicable to, depend upon, be dependent upon, answer to, deal with, belong to, touch upon, figure in; see also INFLUENCE,

TREAT 1. **2** [Concern oneself] be concerned, become involved, take pains; see BOTHER 1, CARE, WORRY 2.

concerning *a.* respecting, touching, regarding; see ABOUT 2.

concert *n.* musical selections, musicale, recital; see PERFORMANCE.

concise *a.* succinct, brief, condensed; see SHORT 1.

conclude *v.* **1** [To finish] terminate, bring to an end, complete; see ACHIEVE. **2** [To deduce] presume, reason, gather; see ASSUME.

conclusion *n.* **1** [An end] finish, termination, completion; see END 2. **2** [A decision] determination, resolve, resolution; see JUDGMENT 3. —**in conclusion** lastly, in closing, in the end; see FINALLY 1.

conclusive *a.* final, decisive, absolute; see CERTAIN 2.

concord *n.* harmony, consensus, accord; see AGREEMENT, UNITY 1.

concrete *a.* **1** [Specific] particular, solid, precise; see DEFINITE 1, DETAILED, REAL 2. **2** [Made of con-

crete] cement, poured, prefabricated, precast, concrete and steel, compact, unyielding; see also FIRM 2.

concrete *n.* concretion, ferroconcrete, reinforced concrete; see CEMENT, PAVEMENT.

concur *v.* accord with, be consonant with, be in harmony with; see AGREE, APPROVE, EQUAL.

concurrent *a.* synchronal, parallel, coexisting; see SIMULTANEOUS.

concussion *n.* rupture, gash, crack; see FRACTURE, INJURY.

condemn *v.* doom, sentence, damn, pass sentence on, find guilty, seal the doom of, pronounce judgment, prescribe punishment; see also CONVICT, PUNISH.—*Ant.* EXCUSE, acquit, exonerate.

condemnation *n.* denunciation, disapprobation, reproach; see ACCUSATION, BLAME, OBJECTION.

condense *v.* **1** [To compress] press together, constrict, consolidate; see COMPRESS, CONTRACT 1, DECREASE 1, 2. **2** [To abridge] abbreviate, sumform, as from gas to liquid — *vi.* to become condensed — **con·den·sa·tion** (kän′dən sā′shən) *n.*

condensed milk a thick milk made by evaporating part of the water from cow's milk and adding sugar

con·dens′er *n.* one that condenses; specif., *a*) an apparatus for liquefying gases *b*) a lens for concentrating light rays *c*) *Elec.* CAPACITOR

con·de·scend (kän′di send′) *vi.* [< L *com-*, together + *descendere*, descend] 1 to be gracious about doing a thing regarded as beneath one's dignity 2 to deal with others patronizingly —**con′de·scend′ing·ly** *adv.* —**con′de·scen′sion** *n.*

con·dign (kən dīn′, kän′dīn′) *adj.* [< L *com-*, intens. + *dignus*, worthy] deserved; suitable: said esp. of punishment

con·di·ment (kän′də mənt) *n.* [< L *condire*, to pickle] a seasoning or relish, as pepper, mustard, sauces, etc.

con·di·tion (kən dish′ən) *n.* [< L *com-*, together + *dicere*, to speak] 1 anything required for the performance, completion, or existence of something else; provision or prerequisite 2 *a*) state of being *b*) [Colloq.] an illness *c*) a healthy state 3 social position; rank —*vt.* 1 to stipulate 2 to impose a condition on 3 to bring into fit condition 4 to make accustomed (*to*) —**on condition that** provided that; if —**con·di′tioner** *n.*

con·di′tion·al *adj.* containing, expressing, or dependent on a condition; qualified —*n. Gram.* a word, clause, tense, etc. expressing a condition —**con·di′tion·al·ly** *adv.*

con·di′tioned (-ənd) *adj.* 1 subject to conditions 2 in a desired condition 3 affected by conditioning 4 accustomed (*to*)

con·do (kän′dō′) *n., pl.* **-dos** or **-does** *short for* CONDOMINIUM (sense 3)

con·dole (kən dōl′) *vi.* **-doled′, -dol′ing** [< L *com-*, with + *dolere*, grieve] to express sympathy; commiserate — **con·do′lence** *n.*

con·dom (kän′dəm, kun′-) *n.* [< It *guanto*, a glove] a thin, elastic sheath for the penis, used as a prophylactic or contraceptive

con·do·min·ium (kän′də min′ē əm) *n.* [ult. < L *com-*, with + *dominium*, ownership] 1 joint rule by two or more states 2 the territory ruled 3 one of the units in a multiunit dwelling, each separately owned

con·done (kən dōn′) *vt.* **-doned′, -don′ing** [< L *com-*, intens. + *donare*, give] to forgive or overlook (an offense) —**con·don′able** *adj.*

con·dor (kän′dər) *n.* [< Sp < AmInd (Peru)] 1 a large vulture of the South American Andes, with a bare head 2 a similar vulture of S Calif.

con·duce (kən dōōs′) *vi.* **-duced′, -duc′ing** [< L *com-*, together + *ducere*, to lead] to tend or lead (*to* an effect) — **con·du′cive** *adj.*

con·duct (kän′dukt′; *for v.* kən dukt′) *n.* [< L *com-*, together + *ducere*, to lead] 1 management 2 behavior — *vt.* 1 to lead 2 to manage 3 to direct (an orchestra, etc.) 4 to behave (oneself) 5 to transmit or convey —**con·duc′tion** *n.* —**con·duc′tive** *adj.* —**con′duc·tiv′i·ty** (-tiv′ə tē) *n.*

con·duct·ance (kən dukt′əns) *n.* the ability to conduct electricity

con·duc′tor *n.* 1 the leader of an orchestra, etc. 2 one in charge of the passengers on a train 3 a thing that conducts electricity, heat, etc.

con·duit (kän′dōo it) *n.* [see CONDUCE] 1 a channel for conveying fluids 2 a tube for electric wires

cone (kōn) *n.* [< Gr *kōnos*] 1 a solid with a circle for its base and a curved surface tapering to a point 2 any cone-shaped object 3 the scaly fruit of evergreen trees 4 a light-sensitive cell in the retina

con·fab (kän′fab′) *n.* [ult. < L *com-*, together + *fabulari*, to converse] [Colloq.] a chat

con·fec·tion (kən fek′shən) *n.* [< L *com-*, with + *facere*, make] a candy or other sweet, as ice cream

con·fec′tion·er *n.* one who makes or sells candy and other confections

con·fec′tion·er·y (-er′ē) *n., pl.* **-ies** a confectioner's shop; candy store

con·fed·er·a·cy (kən fed′ər ə sē) *n., pl.* **-cies** a league or alliance —**the Confederacy** the 11 Southern States that seceded from the U.S. in 1860 & 1861

con·fed·er·ate (kən fed′ər it; *for v.* -āt′) *adj.* [< L *com-*, together + *foedus*, a league] 1 united in an alliance 2 [C-] of the Confederacy —*n.* 1 an ally; associate 2 an accomplice 3 [C-] a Southern supporter of the Confederacy —*vt., vi.* **-at′ed, -at′ing** to unite in a confederacy; ally

con·fed·er·a′tion *n.* a league or federation

con·fer (kən fur′) *vt.* **-ferred′, -fer′ring** [< L *com-*, together + *ferre*, bring] to give or bestow —*vi.* to have a conference —**con·fer·ee** (kän′fər ē′) *n.* —**con·fer′ment** or **con·fer′ral** *n.* —**con·fer′rer** *n.*

con·fer·ence (kän′fər əns) *n.* 1 a formal meeting for discussion 2 an association of schools, churches, etc.

con·fess (kən fes′) *vt., vi.* [< L *com-*, together + *fateri*, acknowledge] 1 to admit or acknowledge (a fault, crime, belief, etc.) 2 *a*) to tell (one's sins) to a priest *b*) to hear the confession of (a person) —**confess to** to acknowledge

con·fess′ed·ly (-id lē) *adv.* admittedly

con·fes·sion (kən fesh′ən) *n.* 1 a confessing 2 something confessed 3 *a*) a creed *b*) a church having a creed

con·fes′sional *n.* an enclosure in a church, where a priest hears confessions

con·fes′sor *n.* 1 one who confesses 2 a priest who hears confessions

con·fet·ti (kən fet′ē) *n.pl.* [It, sweetmeats] [*with sing. v.*] bits of colored paper scattered about at celebrations

---

THESAURUS

marize, digest; see DECREASE 2.

condensed *a.* 1 [Shortened] concise, brief, succinct; see SHORT 2. 2 [Concentrated] undiluted, rich, evaporated; see THICK 3.

condescend *v.* stoop, lower oneself, agree, humble oneself, demean oneself, submit with good grace, assume a patronizing air, lower one's tone, descend, comply, oblige, favor, concede, grant, accord, accommodate to, come down a peg*, come down off one's high horse*; see also PATRONIZE 2.

condescending *a.* patronizing, complaisant, superior; see EGOTISTIC.

condition *n.* 1 [A state] situation, position, status; see STATE 2. 2 [A requisite] stipulation, contingency, provision; see REQUIREMENT 1. 3 [A limitation] restriction, qualification, prohibition; see LIMITATION 2, RESTRAINT 2. 4 [State of health] fitness, tone, trim, shape*; see also HEALTH. 5 [*Illness] ailment, infirmity, temper; see ILLNESS 1, 2. —**in condition** physically fit, conditioned, in the pink*; see HEALTHY, STRONG 1.

condition *v.* adapt, modify, work out; see PRACTICE 1, TRAIN 1.

conditional *a.* provisional, subject,

contingent, limited, restricted, relying on, subject to, restrictive, guarded, not absolute, granted on certain terms; see also DEPENDENT 3.

conditionally *a.* hypothetically, subject to a condition, with reservations, with limitations, tentatively, possible; see also TEMPORARILY.

conditioned *a.* altered, disciplined, modified; see TRAINED.

condominium *n.* cooperative apartment dwelling, condo, commonly owned apartment house, jointly owned dwelling, co-op*; see also APARTMENT, HOME 1.

condone *v.* pardon, excuse, overlook; see APPROVE.

conduct *n.* 1 [Behavior] deportment, demeanor, manner; see BEHAVIOR. 2 [Management] supervision, plan, organization; see MANAGEMENT.

conduct *v.* 1 [To guide] escort, convoy, attend; see ACCOMPANY, LEAD 1. 2 [To manage] administer, handle, carry on; see MANAGE 1. —**conduct oneself** comport oneself, act properly, acquit oneself well; see BEHAVE.

conductor *n.* 1 [That which conducts] conduit, conveyor, transmitter; see CHANNEL, WIRE 1, WIRING. 2

[One who conducts] orchestra leader, pilot, head; see ADMINISTRATOR, GUIDE, LEADER 2. 3 [One in charge of a car or train] trainman, railroad man, ticket taker, brakeman, streetcar conductor, motorman, bus driver; see also DRIVER.

Confederacy *n.* Confederate States of America, rebel states, Confederacy, the South, Dixie; see also SOUTH.

confer *v.* converse, deliberate, parley; see DISCUSS.

conference *n.* conversation, discussion, interchange; see GATHERING.

conferring *a.* discussing, conversing, in conference; see TALKING.

confess *v.* acknowledge, own, concede; see ADMIT 2.

confession *n.* 1 [The act of confessing] concession, allowance, owning to, owning up, revelation, disclosure, publication, affirmation, assertion, declaration, telling, exposure, narration, exposé, proclamation, making public; see also ACKNOWLEDGMENT.— *Ant.* DENIAL, concealment, disclaimer. 2 [A sacrament] absolution, contrition, repentance; see SACRAMENT.

con·fi·dant (kän'fə dant') *n.* a close, trusted friend —**con'·fi·dante'** *n.fem.*

con·fide (kən fīd') *vi.* **-fid'ed, -fid'ing** [< L *com-*, intens. + *fidere*, to trust] to trust (*in* someone), esp. by sharing secrets —*vt.* 1 to tell about as a secret 2 to entrust

con·fi·dence (kän'fə dəns) *n.* 1 trust; reliance 2 assurance 3 belief in one's own abilities 4 the belief that another will keep a secret 5 something told as a secret —*adj.* swindling or used to swindle

confidence game a swindle effected by one (**confidence man**) who first gains the confidence of the victim

con'fi·dent (-dənt) *adj.* full of confidence; specif., *a*) certain *b*) sure of oneself —**con'fi·dent·ly** *adv.*

con'fi·den'tial (-den'shəl) *adj.* 1 secret 2 of or showing trust 3 entrusted with private matters —**con'fi·den'ti·al'·ity** (-shē al'ə tē) *n.* —**con'fi·den'tial·ly** *adv.*

con·fig·u·ra·tion (kən fig'yōō rā'shən) *n.* [< L *com-*, together + *figurare*, to form] contour; outline

con·fine (kän'fīn'; *for v.* kən fīn') *n.* [< L *com-*, with + *finis*, an end] [*usually pl.*] a boundary or bounded region —*vt.* **-fined', -fin'ing** 1 to keep within limits; restrict 2 to keep shut up, as in prison, a sickbed, etc. —**con·fine'ment** *n.*

con·firm (kən fʉrm') *vt.* [< L *com-*, intens. + *firmare*, strengthen] 1 to make firm 2 to give formal approval to 3 to prove the truth of 4 to admit to church membership by confirmation

con·fir·ma·tion (kän'fər mā'shən) *n.* 1 a confirming 2 something that confirms 3 a ceremony admitting a person to full church membership

con·firmed' *adj.* 1 firmly established; habitual 2 corroborated

con·fis·cate (kän'fis kāt') *vt.* **-cat'ed, -cat'ing** [< L *com-*, together + *fiscus*, treasury] 1 to seize (private property) for the public treasury 2 to seize as by authority; appropriate —**con'fis·ca'tion** *n.*

con·fis·ca·tory (kən fis'kə tôr'ē) *adj.* of or effecting confiscation

con·fla·gra·tion (kän'flə grā'shən) *n.* [< L *com-*, intens. + *flagrare*, to burn] a big, destructive fire

con·flict (kən flikt'; *for n.* kän'flikt') *vi.* [< L *com-*, together + *fligere*, to strike] to be antagonistic; incompatible, etc. —*n.* 1 a fight or war 2 sharp disagreement, as of interests or ideas 3 emotional disturbance

con·flict'ed *adj.* emotionally disturbed

conflict of interest a conflict between one's obligation to the public and one's self-interest, as in the case of a public officeholder

con·flu·ence (kän'flōō əns) *n.* [< L *com-*, together + *fluere*, to flow] 1 a flowing together, esp. of streams 2 the place of this 3 a crowd —**con'flu·ent** *adj.*

con·form (kən fôrm') *vt.* [< L *com-*, together + *formare*, to form] 1 to make similar 2 to bring into agreement —*vi.* 1 to be or become similar 2 to be in agreement 3 to act in accordance with rules, customs, etc. —**con·form'ism** *n.* —**con·form'ist** *n.*

con·for·ma·tion (kän'fôr mā'shən) *n.* 1 a symmetrical arrangement of the parts of a thing 2 the shape or outline, as of an animal

con·form·ity (kən fôrm'ə tē) *n., pl.* **-ties** 1 agreement; correspondence; similarity 2 conventional behavior

con·found (kən found'; *for 2* kän'-) *vt.* [< L *com-*, together + *fundere*, pour] 1 to confuse or bewilder 2 to damn: a mild oath —**con·found'ed** *adj.*

con·fra·ter·ni·ty (kän'frə tʉr'nə tē) *n., pl.* **-ties** [see CON- & FRATERNAL] 1 brotherhood 2 a religious society, usually of laymen

con·frere (kän'frer') *n.* [OFr] a colleague or associate

con·front (kən frunt') *vt.* [< L *com-*, together + *frons*, forehead] 1 to face, esp. boldly or defiantly 2 to bring face to face (*with*) —**con·fron·ta·tion** (kän'frən tā'shən) *n.* —**con'fron·ta'tional** *adj.*

con·fuse (kən fyōōz') *vt.* **-fused', -fus'ing** [see CON-FOUND] 1 to mix up; put into disorder 2 to bewilder or

---

THESAURUS

confidant *n.* adherent, intimate associate, companion; see FRIEND.

confide *v.* disclose, admit, divulge; see REVEAL, TELL 1.

confidence *n.* self-confidence, self-reliance, morale, fearlessness, boldness, resolution, firmness, sureness, faith in oneself, tenacity, fortitude, certainty, daring, spirit, reliance, grit, cool*, heart, backbone, nerve, spunk*; see also COURAGE, DETERMINATION.

confident *a.* 1 [Self-assured] self-confident, assured, being certain, fearless, self-reliant, sure of oneself, dauntless, self-sufficient, bold; see also CERTAIN 1. 2 [Trusting] presumptuous, hopeful, depending on, counting on, relying on, expectant.

confidential *a.* classified, intimate, privy; see PRIVATE, SECRET 1, 3.

confidentially *a.* privately, personally, in confidence; see SECRETLY.

confidently *a.* in an assured way, with conviction, assuredly; see BOLDLY 1, POSITIVELY 1.

confine *v.* 1 [To restrain] repress, hold back, keep within limits; see HINDER, RESTRAIN. 2 [To imprison] cage, incarcerate, shut up; see ENSLAVE, IMPRISON.

confined *a.* 1 [Restricted] limited, hampered, compassed; see BOUND 1, 2, RESTRICTED. 2 [Bedridden] on one's back, ill, laid up; see SICK. 3 [In prison] behind bars, locked up, in bonds, in irons, in chains, in jail, imprisoned, jailed, immured, incarcerated, detained, under lock and key.—*Ant.* FREE, released, at liberty.

confinement *n.* restriction, limitation, constraint, repression, control, coercion, keeping, safekeeping, custody, curb, bounds, check, bonds, detention, imprisonment, incarceration; see also JAIL.—*Ant.* FREEDOM, release, independence.

confines *n.* bounds, limits, periphery; see BOUNDARY.

confining *a.* limiting, restricting, bounding, prescribing, restraining, hampering, repressing, checking, enclosing, imprisoning, incarcerating, detaining, keeping locked up, keeping behind bars.

confirm *v.* 1 [To ratify] sanction, affirm, settle; see APPROVE, ENDORSE 2. 2 [To prove] verify, authenticate, validate; see EXPLAIN, PROVE.

confirmation *n.* 1 [The act of confirming] ratification, proving, authentication, corroboration, support, endorsement, sanction, authorization, verification, affirmation, acceptance, passage, validation, approval, attestation, assent, admission, recognition, witness, consent, testimony, agreement, evidence; see also AGREEMENT, PROOF 1.—*Ant.* CANCELLATION, annulment, disapproval. 2 [A sacrament] rite, consecration, liturgy; see CEREMONY, SACRAMENT.

confirmed *a.* 1 [Firmly established] proved, valid, accepted; see CERTAIN 2, ESTABLISHED 2, GUARANTEED. 2 [Inveterate] ingrained, seasoned, regular; see CHRONIC, HABITUAL.

confiscate *v.* appropriate, impound, usurp; see SEIZE 2, STEAL.

conflict *n.* struggle, strife, engagement; see BATTLE, FIGHT.

conflict *v.* clash, contrast, contend; see DIFFER 1, FIGHT, OPPOSE 1, 2.

conform *v.* comply, accord, submit, accommodate, live up to, fit, suit, acclimate, accustom, be regular, harmonize, adapt, be guided by, fit the pattern, be in fashion, reconcile, obey, grow used to, do as others do, get in line, fall in with, go by, adhere to, adjust to, keep to, keep up, get one's bearings, keep up with the Joneses*, chime in with, join the parade, play the game, go according to Hoyle, follow the beaten path, toe the line, follow suit, run with the pack, follow the crowd, when in Rome do as the Romans do; see also AGREE, FOLLOW 2, OBEY.—*Ant.* DIFFER, CONFLICT, disagree. —**conform to** correspond, parallel, fit; see AGREE, COMPARE 1.

conforming *a.* agreeing, in line with, in agreement; see HARMONIOUS 2.

conformist *n.* conformer, philistine, advocate; see FOLLOWER.

conformity *n.* 1 [Similarity] congruity, correspondence, resemblance; see SIMILARITY. 2 [Obedience] willingness, submission, compliance; see AGREEMENT.

confound *v.* puzzle, perplex, bewilder; see CONFUSE.

confounded *a.* confused, bewildered, disconcerted; see DOUBTFUL.

confront *v.* brave, defy, repel; see DARE 2, FACE 1.

confrontation *n.* meeting, battle, strife; see DISPUTE, FIGHT 1.

confuse *v.* upset, befuddle, mislead, misinform, puzzle, perplex, confound, fluster, bewilder, embarrass, daze, astonish, disarrange, disorder, jumble, blend, mix, mingle, cloud, fog, stir up, disconcert, abash, agitate, amaze, worry, trouble, snarl, unsettle, muddle, clutter, complicate, involve, rattle, derange, baffle, frustrate, perturb, dismay, distract, entangle, encumber, befog, obscure, mystify, make a mess of, throw off the scent, cross up, foul up, mix up, ball up*, lead astray, stump, rattle, make one's head swim; see also DISTURB, TANGLE.—*Ant.* CLEAR UP, clarify, untangle.

confused *a.* 1 [Puzzled in mind] disconcerted, abashed, perplexed; see DOUBTFUL. 2 [Not properly distinguished] mistaken, jumbled, snarled, deranged, bewildered, out of order, disarrayed, confounded, mixed, mixed up, chaotic, disordered, muddled, fuddled, befuddled, slovenly, untidy, messy, involved, misunderembarrass **3** to mistake the identity of —**con·fus′edly** *adv.*

con·fu′sion (-fyōō′zhən) *n.* a confusing or being confused; specif., disorder, bewilderment, etc.

con·fute (kən fyōōt′) *vt.* **-fut′ed, -fut′ing** 〚L *confutare*〛 to prove to be in error or false —**con·fu·ta′tion** (kän′fyōō tā′shən) *n.*

Cong. 1 Congregational **2** Congress

con·geal (kən jēl′) *vt., vi.* 〚< L *com-*, together + *gelare*, freeze〛 **1** to freeze **2** to thicken; coagulate; jell —**con·geal′ment** *n.*

con·genial (kən jēn′yəl) *adj.* 〚see CON- & GENIAL〛 **1** kindred; compatible **2** like-minded; friendly **3** suited to one's needs; agreeable —**con·ge′ni·al′i·ty** (-jē′nē al′ə tē) *n.* — **con·ge′nially** *adv.*

con·gen·i·tal (kən jen′ə təl) *adj.* 〚< L *congenitus*, born with〛 existing as such at birth —**con·gen′i·tally** *adv.*

con·ger (eel) (käŋ′gər) 〚< Gr *gongros*〛 a large, edible saltwater eel

con·ge·ries (kän′jə rēz′) *n., pl.* **-ries′** 〚L: see fol.〛 a heap or pile of things

con·gest (kən jest′) *vt.* 〚< L *com-*, together + *gerere*, carry〛 **1** to cause too much blood, mucus, etc. to accumulate in (a part of the body) **2** to fill to excess; overcrowd — **con·ges′tion** *n.* —**con·ges′tive** *adj.*

con·glom·er·ate (kən gläm′ər āt′; *for adj. & n.,* -ər it) *vt., vi.* **-at′ed, -at′ing** 〚< L *com-*, together + *glomus*, ball〛 to form into a rounded mass — *adj.* **1** formed into a rounded mass **2** formed of substances collected into a single mass, esp. of rock fragments or pebbles cemented together by clay, silica, etc. — *n.* **1** a conglomerate mass **2** a large corporation formed by merging many diverse companies **3** a conglomerate rock —**con·glom′er·a′tion** *n.*

con·gratu·late (kən grach′ə lāt′) *vt.* **-lat′ed, -lat′ing** 〚< L *com-*, together + *gratulari*, wish joy〛 to express to (another) one's pleasure at that person's good fortune, etc.; felicitate *[congratulate the winner]* —**con·grat′u·la·to′ry** (-lə tôr′ē) *adj.*

con·grat′u·la′tion *n.* **1** a congratulating **2** *[pl.]* expressions of pleasure over another's good fortune, etc.

con·gre·gate (käŋ′grə gāt′) *vt., vi.* **-gat′ed, -gat′ing** 〚< L *com-*, together + *grex*, a flock〛 to gather into a crowd; assemble

con·gre·ga′tion *n.* **1** a gathering; assemblage **2** an assembly of people for religious worship

con·gre·ga′tional *adj.* **1** of or like a congregation **2** [C-] of a Protestant denomination in which each member church is self-governing

con·gress (käŋ′grəs) *n.* 〚< L *com-*, together + *gradi*, to walk〛 **1** an association or society **2** an assembly or conference **3** a legislature, esp. of a republic **4** [C-] the legislature of the U.S.; the Senate and the House of Representatives —**con·gres′sional** (kən gresh′ə nəl) *adj.* —**con·gres′sion·ally** *adv.*

con′gress·man (-mən) *n., pl.* **-men** a member of Congress, esp. of the House of Representatives Also **con′gress·per′son**

con·gru·ent (käŋ′grōō ənt) *adj.* 〚< L *congruere*, agree〛 corresponding; harmonious —**con′gru·ence** *n.*

con·gru·ous (käŋ′grōō əs) *adj.* **1** congruent **2** fitting; suitable; appropriate —**con·gru′i·ty** (kän grōō′ə tē, kən-), *pl.* **-ties,** *n.* —**con′gru·ously** *adv.*

coni·cal (kän′i kəl) *adj.* **1** of a cone **2** resembling or shaped like a cone Also **con′ic** —**con′i·cally** *adv.*

coni·fer (kän′ə fər, kō′nə-) *n.* 〚< L *conus*, cone + *ferre*, to bear〛 any of a class of cone-bearing trees and shrubs, mostly evergreens —**co·nif·er·ous** (kō nif′ər əs, kə-) *adj.*

conj. 1 conjugation **2** conjunction

con·jec·ture (kən jek′chər) *n.* 〚< L *com-*, together + *jacere*, to throw〛 **1** an inferring, theorizing, or predicting from incomplete evidence; guesswork **2** a guess — *vt., vi.* **-tured, -tur·ing** to guess —**con·jec′tural** *adj.*

con·join (kən join′) *vt., vi.* 〚< L *com-*, together + *jungere*, join〛 to join together; unite —**con·joint′** *adj.* —**con·joint′ly** *adv.*

con·ju·gal (kän′jə gəl) *adj.* 〚< L *conjunx*, spouse〛 of marriage or the relation between husband and wife —**con′ju·gally** *adv.*

con·ju·gate (kän′jə gət; *also, and for v. always,* -gāt′) *adj.* 〚< L *com-*, together + *jugare*, join〛 joined together, esp. in a pair — *vt.* **-gat′ed, -gat′ing 1** [Archaic] to join together **2** *Gram.* to give in order the inflectional forms of (a verb) —**con′ju·ga′tion** *n.*

con·junc·tion (kən juŋk′shən) *n.* 〚see CONJOIN〛 **1** a joining together; union; combination **2** coincidence **3** a word used to connect words, phrases, or clauses (Ex.: *and, but, if,* etc.) —**con·junc′tive** *adj.*

con·junc·ti·va (kän′jəŋk tī′və) *n., pl.* **-vas** or **-vae** (-vē) 〚see CONJOIN〛 the mucous membrane covering the inner eyelid and the front of the eyeball

con·junc·ti·vi·tis (kən juŋk′tə vīt′is) *n.* inflammation of the conjunctiva

con·junc·ture (kən juŋk′chər) *n.* 〚see CONJOIN〛 a combination of events creating a crisis

con·jure (kun′jər, kän′-; *for vt.* kən joor′) *vi.* **-jured, -jur·ing** 〚< L *com-*, together + *jurare*, swear〛 **1** to summon a demon or spirit by magic **2** to practice magic — *vt.* to entreat solemnly —**conjure up** to cause to appear as by magic —**con′ju·ra′tion** *n.* —**con′jurer** or **con′ju·ror** *n.*

conk (kôŋk) *n.* 〚< CONCH〛 [Slang] hit on the head — **conk out** [Slang] **1** to fail suddenly, as a motor **2** to fall asleep from fatigue

con man [Slang] a confidence man; swindler

conn (kän) *vt.* **conned, conn′ing** 〚see CONDUCE〛 *Naut.* to direct the course of (a vessel)

con·nect (kə nekt′) *vt.* 〚< L *com-*, together + *nectere*, fasten〛 **1** to join (two things together, or one thing *with* or *to* another) **2** to show or think of as related — *vi.* to join —**con·nec′tor** or **con·nect′er** *n.*

THESAURUS

stood, blurred, obscured, topsy-turvy, balled up*, fouled up*, screwed up*, in a mess, haywire*, snafu*; see also OBSCURE 1, TANGLED.—*Ant.* DISTINGUISHED, discriminated, ordered.

confusing *a.* disconcerting, confounding, baffling, puzzling, disturbing, unsettling, upsetting, embarrassing, obscuring, blurring, befuddling, tangling, snarling, cluttering, muddling, disarranging; see also DIFFICULT 2, OBSCURE 1.—*Ant.* ORDERLY, reassuring, clear.

confusion *n.* complication, intricacy, muss, untidiness, complexity, difficulty, mistake, bewilderment, turmoil, tumult, pandemonium, commotion, stir, ferment, disarray, jumble, convulsion, bustle, trouble, row, riot, uproar, fracas, distraction, agitation, emotional upset, daze, astonishment, surprise, fog, haze, consternation, racket, excitement, chaos, turbulence, dismay, uncertainty, irregularity, maze, interruption, stoppage, clutter, entanglement, backlash, clog, break, breakdown, knot, obstruction, trauma, congestion, interference, nervousness, disorganization, muddle, mass, lump, snarl, to-do*, hubbub, tie-up, botch,

rumpus, scramble, shuffle, mess, hodgepodge, stew, going round and round*, jam*, fix*, bull in a china shop; see also DISORDER.—*Ant.* ORDER, quiet, calm.

confute *v.* confound, dismay, invalidate; see DENY, OPPOSE 1.

congenial *a.* kindred, agreeable, genial; see FRIENDLY, HARMONIOUS 2.

congestion *n.* profusion, crowdedness, overpopulation, press, traffic jam, overcrowding, overdevelopment, too many, too much, concentration, surplus; see also EXCESS 1.

congratulate *v.* felicitate, wish joy to, toast; see COMPLIMENT, PRAISE 1.

congratulations *interj.* best wishes, compliments, bless you; see COMPLIMENT.

congregate *v.* convene, meet, converge; see GATHER 1.

congregation *n.* meeting, group, assemblage; see GATHERING.

congress *n.* *[often capital C]* parliament, assembly, legislative body; see COMMITTEE, GOVERNMENT, LEGISLATURE.

congruent *a.* in agreement, harmonious, corresponding; see HARMONIOUS 2.

congruous *a.* suitable, appropriate, fitting; see HARMONIOUS 2.

conjunction *n.* **1** [Act of joining together] combination, connection, association; see UNION 1. **2** [A syntactic connecting word] *Conjunctions include the following:* and, but, if, for, or, nor, so, yet, only, else, than, before, since, then, though, when, where, why, both, either, while, as, neither, although, because, unless, until.

conjure up *v.* call, invoke, materialize; see SUMMON, URGE 2.

connect *v.* **1** [To join] combine, unite, attach; see JOIN 1. **2** [To associate] relate, equate, correlate; see COMPARE 1.

connected *a.* **1** [Joined together] united, combined, coupled; see JOINED. **2** [Related] associated, applicable, pertinent; see RELATED 2, RELEVANT.

connecting *a.* joining, linking, combining, uniting, associating, relating, tying, cementing, knitting, fusing, hooking, bringing together, clinching, fastening, mixing, mingling, intertwining, welding, pairing, coupling; see also JOINED.

con·nec·tion (kə nek'shən) *n.* **1** a connecting or being connected **2** a thing that connects **3** a relationship; association **4** *a*) a relative, as by marriage *b*) an influential associate, etc.: *usually used in pl.* **5** a transferring from one bus, plane, etc. to another

con·nec·tive (kə nekt'iv) *adj.* connecting — *n.* that which connects, esp. a connecting word, as a conjunction

connective tissue body tissue, as cartilage, serving to connect and support other tissues

con·nip·tion (fit) (kə nip'shən) [pseudo-L] [Colloq.] a fit of anger, hysteria, etc.; tantrum Also **con·nip'tions** *n.pl.*

con·nive (kə nīv') *vi.* **-nived'**, **-niv'ing** [< L *conivere*, to wink, connive] **1** to pretend not to look (*at* crime, etc.), thus giving tacit consent **2** to cooperate secretly (*with* someone), esp. in wrongdoing; scheme — **con·niv'ance** *n.* — **con·niv'er** *n.*

con·nois·seur (kän'ə sur') *n.* [< Fr < L *cognoscere*, know] one who has expert knowledge and keen discrimination, esp. in the fine arts

con·note (kə nōt') *vt.* **-not'ed**, **-not'ing** [< L *com-*, together + *notare*, to mark] to suggest or convey (associations, etc.) in addition to the explicit, or denoted, meaning — **con·no·ta·tion** (kän'ə tā'shən) *n.* — **con'no·ta'tive** or **con'no·ta'tional** *adj.*

con·nu·bial (kə noo'bē əl) *adj.* [< L *com-*, together + *nubere*, marry] of marriage; conjugal

con·quer (käŋ'kər) *vt.* [< L *com-*, intens. + *quaerere*, seek] **1** to get control of as by winning a war **2** to overcome; defeat — **con'quer·or** *n.*

con·quest (käŋ'kwest', kän'-) *n.* **1** a conquering **2** something conquered **3** a winning of someone's affection

con·quis·ta·dor (kän kwis'tə dôr', -kēs'-) or **con·quis·ta·do·res** (-dôr'ēz', -dôr'ās') [Sp, conqueror] any of the 16th-c. Spanish conquerors of Mexico, Peru, etc.

con·san·guin·e·ous (kän'saŋ gwin'ē əs) *adj.* [see CON- & SANGUINE] having the same ancestor — **con'san·guin'ity** *n.*

con·science (kän'shəns) *n.* [< L *com-*, with + *scire*, know] a sense of right and wrong, with an urge to do right — **con'science·less** *adj.*

con·sci·en·tious (kän'shē en'shəs) *adj.* [see prec. & -OUS] **1** governed by one's conscience; scrupulous **2** painstaking — **con'sci·en'tiously** *adv.* — **con'sci·en'tious·ness** *n.*

conscientious objector one who for reasons of conscience refuses to take part in warfare

con·scious (kän'shəs) *adj.* [< L: see CONSCIENCE] **1** having an awareness (*of* or *that*) **2** able to feel and think;

awake **3** aware of oneself as a thinking being **4** intentional [*conscious* humor] — **con'sciously** *adv.*

con'scious·ness *n.* **1** the state of being conscious; awareness **2** the totality of one's thoughts and feelings

con·script (kən skript'; *for adj. & n.* kän'skript') *vt.* [< L *com-*, with + *scribere*, write] to enroll for compulsory service in the armed forces; draft — *n.* a draftee — **con·scrip'tion** *n.*

con·se·crate (kän'si krāt') *vt.* **-crat'ed**, **-crat'ing** [< L *com-*, together + *sacrare*, make holy] to set apart as holy; devote to sacred or serious use — **con'se·cra'tion** *n.*

con·secu·tive (kən sek'yoō tiv) *adj.* [see CONSEQUENCE] following in order, without interruption; successive — **con·sec'u·tively** *adv.*

con·sen·sus (kən sen'səs) *n.* [see fol.] **1** an opinion held by all or most **2** general agreement, esp. in opinion

con·sent (kən sent') *vi.* [< L *com-*, with + *sentire*, feel] to agree, permit, or assent — *n.* **1** permission; approval **2** agreement *[by common consent]*

con·se·quence (kän'si kwens') *n.* [< L *com-*, with + *sequi*, follow] **1** a result; effect **2** importance — **take the consequences** to accept the results of one's actions

con'se·quent' (-kwent', -kwənt) *adj.* following as a result; resulting — **con'se·quent'ly** *adv.*

con'se·quen'tial (-kwen'shəl) *adj.* **1** consequent **2** important

con·ser·va·tion (kän'sər vā'shən) *n.* **1** a conserving **2** the official care or management of natural resources — **con'ser·va'tion·ist** *n.*

con·serv·a·tive (kən sur'və tiv) *adj.* **1** tending to conserve **2** tending to preserve established institutions, etc.; opposed to change **3** moderate; cautious — *n.* a conservative person — **con·serv'a·tism'** *n.* — **con·serv'a·tively** *adv.*

con·serv·a·to·ry (kən sur'və tôr'ē) *n., pl.* **-ries** **1** a greenhouse **2** a music school

con·serve (kən surv'; *for n.*, *usually* kän'surv') *vt.* **-served'**, **-serv'ing** [< L *com-*, with + *servare*, keep] to keep from being damaged, lost, or wasted; save — *n.* [*often pl.*] a jam made of two or more fruits

con·sider (kən sid'ər) *vt.* [< L *considerare*, observe] **1** to think about in order to understand or decide **2** to keep in mind **3** to be thoughtful of (others) **4** to regard as

con·sid'er·able *adj.* **1** worth considering; important **2** much or large — **con·sid'er·ably** *adv.*

THESAURUS

connection *n.* **1** [Relationship] kinship, association, reciprocity; see ASSOCIATION 2, RELATIONSHIP. **2** [A junction] combination, juncture, consolidation; see UNION 1. **3** [A link] attachment, fastening, bond; see LINK. —**in connection with** in conjunction with, associated with, together with; see WITH.

connotation *n.* implication, intention, essence; see MEANING.

conquer *v.* subdue, overcome, crush; see DEFEAT 2.

conqueror *n.* vanquisher, master, champion; see HERO 1, WINNER.

conquest *n.* triumph, success, conquering; see VICTORY.

conscience *n.* moral sense, inner voice, the still small voice; see DUTY 1, MORALS, SHAME 2. —**have on one's conscience** be culpable for, be blamable for, be responsible for; see GUILTY. —**in (all) conscience** rightly, fairly, properly; see JUSTLY 1.

conscientious *a.* fastidious, meticulous, complete; see CAREFUL, RELIABLE.

conscientiousness *n.* exactness, care, honor; see CARE 1, DUTY 1, HONESTY, RESPONSIBILITY 1.

conscious *a.* cognizant, informed, sure, certain, assured, discerning, knowing, sensible, sensitive, acquainted, attentive, watchful, mindful, vigilant, understanding, keen, alert, alert to, alive to, sensitive to, conscious of, mindful of, cognizant of, hip to*, on to*, with it*; see

also INTELLIGENT.—*Ant.* UNAWARE, insensitive, inattentive.

consciousness *n.* alertness, cognizance, mindfulness; see AWARENESS, KNOWLEDGE 1.

consecrate *v.* hallow, sanctify, anoint; see BLESS.

consecrated *a.* blessed, sanctified, hallowed; see DIVINE.

consecration *n.* making holy, sanctification, exalting; see CELEBRATION.

consecutive *a.* continuous, chronological, serial, in turn, progressive, connected, in order, in sequence, sequential, going on, continuing, one after another, one after the other, serialized, numerical; see also CONSTANT, REGULAR 3.

consecutively *a.* following, successively, continuously; see GRADUALLY.

consensus *n.* consent, unison, accord; see AGREEMENT.

consent *n.* assent, approval, acquiescence; see PERMISSION.

consent *v.* accede, assent, acquiesce; see AGREE, ALLOW, APPROVE.

consequence *n.* **1** [Effect] outgrowth, end, outcome; see RESULT. **2** [Importance] moment, value, weight; see IMPORTANCE. —**in consequence of** because of, owing to, consequently; see BECAUSE. —**take the consequences** accept the results of one's actions, suffer, bear the burden of; see ENDURE 2.

conservation *n.* maintenance, keeping, preservation, preserving, con-

serving, guarding, protecting, saving, safekeeping, storage, upkeep, economy, keeping in trust; see also PRESERVATION.—*Ant.* WASTE, misuse, destruction.

conservative *a.* conserving, preserving, unchanging, unchangeable, stable, constant, steady, traditional, reactionary, conventional, moderate, unprogressive, firm, obstinate, inflexible, opposed to change, cautious, sober, Tory, taking no chances, timid, fearful, unimaginative, rightwing, in a rut*, in a groove*; see also CAREFUL, MODERATE 3.—*Ant.* RADICAL, risky, changing.

conservative *n.* reactionary, rightwinger, die-hard, Tory, Whig, Federalist, champion of the status quo, opponent of change, classicist, traditionalist, unprogressive, conventionalist, John Bircher, mossback*, old fogy, fossil*.—*Ant.* RADICAL, progressive, liberal.

consider *v.* allow for, provide for, grant, take up, concede, acknowledge, recognize, favor, value, take under advisement, deal with, regard, make allowance for, take into consideration, keep in mind, reckon with, play around with*, toss around, see about; see also RECONSIDER, THINK 1.—*Ant.* REFUSE, deny, reject.

considerable *a.* **1** [Important] noteworthy, significant, essential; see IMPORTANT 1. **2** [Much] abundant, lavish, bountiful; see MUCH 2, PLENTI-

con·sid·er·ate (-it) *adj.* having regard for others and their feelings —**con·sid´er·ate·ly** *adv.*

con·sid·er·a´tion (-ər ā´shən) *n.* **1** the act of considering; deliberation **2** thoughtful regard for others **3** something considered in making a decision **4** a recompense; fee **5** something given, as to make a binding contract —**take into consideration** to keep in mind —**under consideration** being thought over

con·sid·ered (-ərd) *adj.* arrived at after careful thought

con·sid´er·ing *prep.* in view of; taking into account

con·sign (kən sīn´) *vt.* [< L *consignare*, to seal] **1** to hand over; deliver **2** to entrust **3** to assign to an inferior place **4** to send (goods)

con·sign´ment (-mənt) *n.* **1** a consigning or being consigned **2** a shipment of goods sent to a dealer for sale —**on consignment** with payment due after sale of the consignment

con·sist (kən sist´) *vi.* [< L *com-*, together + *sistere*, stand] **1** to be formed or composed (*of*) **2** to be contained or inherent (*in*)

con·sis´ten·cy (-sis´tən sē) *n., pl.* **-cies 1** firmness or thickness, as of a liquid **2** agreement; harmony **3** conformity with previous practice

con·sis´tent *adj.* **1** in agreement or harmony; compatible **2** holding to the same principles or practice —**con·sis´tent·ly** *adv.*

con·sis·to·ry (kən sis´tə rē) *n., pl.* **-ries** [see CONSIST] **1** a church council or court, as the papal senate **2** a session of such a body

con·so·la·tion (kän´sə lā´shən) *n.* **1** comfort; solace **2** one that consoles

con·sole[1] (kən sōl´) *vt.* **-soled´, -sol´ing** [< L *com-*, with + *solari*, to comfort] to make feel less sad or disappointed; comfort —**con·sol´ing·ly** *adv.*

con·sole[2] (kän´sōl´) *n.* [Fr] **1** the desklike frame containing the keys, stops, etc. of an organ **2** a radio, television, or phonograph cabinet designed to stand on the floor **3** a control panel for operating aircraft, computers, electronic systems, etc. **4** a raised portion between automobile bucket seats

con·sol·i·date (kən säl´ə dāt´) *vt., vi.* **-dat´ed, -dat´ing** [< L *com-*, together + *solidus*, solid] **1** to combine into one; unite **2** to make or become strong or stable —**con·sol´i·da´tion** *n.* —**con·sol´i·da´tor** *n.*

con·som·mé (kän´sə mā´) *n.* [Fr] a clear, strained meat soup

con·so·nance (kän´sə nəns) *n.* [< L *com-*, with + *sonus*, sound] harmony, esp. of musical sounds

con·so·nant (-nənt) *adj.* in harmony or accord —*n.* **1** a speech sound made by obstructing the air stream **2** a letter representing such a sound, as *p, t, l, f, etc.*

con·sort (kän´sôrt´; *for v.* kən sôrt´) *n.* [< L *com-*, with + *sors*, a share] a wife or husband, esp. of a reigning king or queen —*vt., vi.* to associate

con·sor·tium (kən sôrt´ē əm, -sôr´shē əm) *n., pl.* **-tia** (-ə) [see prec.] an international alliance, as of business firms or banks

con·spec·tus (kən spek´təs) *n.* [L: see fol.] **1** a general view **2** a summary; digest

con·spic·u·ous (kən spik´yoo əs) *adj.* [< L *com-*, intens. + *specere*, see] **1** easy to see **2** outstanding; striking —**con·spic´u·ous·ly** *adv.*

con·spir·a·cy (kən spir´ə sē) *n., pl.* **-cies 1** a conspiring **2** an unlawful plot **3** a conspiring group

con·spire (kən spir´) *vi.* **-spired´, -spir´ing** [< L *com-*, together + *spirare*, breathe] **1** to plan together secretly, esp. to commit a crime **2** to work together toward a single end —**con·spir´a·tor** (-spir´ət ər) *n.* —**con·spir´a·to´ri·al** (-spir´ə tôr´ē əl) *adj.*

con·sta·ble (kän´stə bəl) *n.* [< LL *comes stabuli*, lit., count of the stable] **1** a peace officer in a small town **2** [Chiefly Brit.] a police officer

con·stab·u·lar·y (kən stab´yoo ler´ē) *n., pl.* **-ies 1** constables, collectively **2** a militarized police force

con·stant (kän´stənt) *adj.* [< L *com-*, together + *stare*, to stand] **1** not changing; faithful, regular, etc. **2** continual; persistent —*n.* anything that does not change or vary —**con´stan·cy** *n.* —**con´stant·ly** *adv.*

con·stel·la·tion (kän´stə lā´shən) *n.* [< L *com-*, with + *stella*, star] a group of stars thought to resemble some object, animal, etc. in outline

con·ster·na·tion (kän´stər nā´shən) *n.* [< L *consternare*, terrify] great fear or shock

con·sti·pate (kän´stə pāt´) *vt.* **-pat´ed, -pat´ing** [< L *com-*, together + *stipare*, cram] to cause constipation in

con·sti·pa´tion (-pā´shən) *n.* infrequent and difficult movement of the bowels

con·stit·u·en·cy (kən stich´oo ən sē) *n., pl.* **-cies** the voters in a district

con·stit·u·ent (-ənt) *adj.* [see fol.] **1** necessary to the whole; component [a *constituent* part] **2** that elects **3** authorized to make or revise a constitution —*n.* **1** a voter in a district **2** a component

con·sti·tute (kän´stə toot´) *vt.* **-tut´ed, -tut´ing** [< L *com-*, together + *statuere*, to set] **1** to establish (a law, government, etc.) **2** to set up (an assembly, etc.) in a legal form **3** to appoint **4** to form; compose —**con´sti·tu´tive** *adj.*

con´sti·tu´tion (-too´shən) *n.* **1** a constituting **2** structure; organization **3** *a*) the system of basic laws and prin-

---

THESAURUS

FUL 1.

considerate *a.* charitable, kind, solicitous; see POLITE, THOUGHTFUL 2.

consideration *n.* **1** [The state of being considerate] kindliness, thoughtfulness, attentiveness; see COURTESY 1, KINDNESS 1, TOLERANCE 1. **2** [Payment] remuneration, salary, wage; see PAYMENT 1. **3** [Something to be considered] situation, problem, judgment, notion, fancy, puzzle, proposal, difficulty, incident, evidence, new development, occurrence, taste, pass, occasion, emergency, idea, thought, trouble, plan, particulars, items, scope, extent, magnitude; see also IDEA 1, PLAN 2. —**in consideration of** because of, on account of, for; see CONSIDERING. —**take into consideration** take into account, weigh, keep in mind; see CONSIDER. —**under consideration** thought over, discussed, evaluated; see CONSIDERED.

considered *a.* carefully thought about, treated, gone into, contemplated, weighed, meditated, examined, investigated; see also DETERMINED 1.

considering *prep., conj.* in light of, in view of, in consideration of, pending, taking into account, everything being equal, inasmuch as, insomuch as, with something in view.

consign *v.* convey, dispatch, transfer; see GIVE 1, SEND 1.

consistency *n.* **1** [Harmony] union, compatibility, accord; see AGREEMENT, SYMMETRY. **2** [The degree of firmness or thickness] hardness, softness, firmness; see DENSITY, TEXTURE 1.

consistent *a.* compatible, equable, expected; see LOGICAL, RATIONAL 1, REGULAR 3.

consist of *v.* embody, contain, involve; see COMPRISE, INCLUDE 1.

consolation *n.* sympathy, compassion, support; see PITY, RELIEF 1, 4.

console[1] *v.* solace, sympathize with, hearten; see COMFORT 1, ENCOURAGE.

consolidate *v.* connect, mix, unify; see COMPRESS, PACK 2.

consolidation *n.* alliance, association, federation; see UNION 1.

consonant *n. Linguistic terms referring to consonant sounds include the following:* voiceless, voiced; stop, fricative, resonant, sibilant, implosive, plosive, nasal, click, glide, continuant, trill. *In spelling, English consonants are as follows:* b,c,d,f, g,h,j,k,l,m,n,p,q,r,s,t,v,w,x,y,z; see also LETTER, SOUND 2, VOWEL.

conspicuous *a.* outstanding, eminent, distinguished, celebrated, noted, renowned, famed, notorious, important, influential, notable, illustrious, striking, prominent, well-known, arresting, remarkable, noticeable, flagrant, glaring, standing out like a sore thumb*; see also PROMINENT 1.—*Ant.* UNKNOWN, inconspicuous, unsung.

conspiracy *n.* intrigue, collusion, connivance; see TRICK 1.

conspirator *n.* betrayer, schemer, cabalist; see TRAITOR.

conspire *v.* plot, scheme, contrive; see PLAN 1.

constant *a.* steady, uniform, perpetual, unchanging, continual, uninterrupted, unvarying, connected, even, incessant, unbroken, nonstop, monotonous, standardized, regularized; see also REGULAR 3.

constantly *a.* uniformly, steadily, invariably; see REGULARLY.

constituency *n.* the voters, electorate, body politic, electors, voting public, balloters, the people; see also VOTER.

constituent *n.* component, element, ingredient; see PART 1.

constitute *v.* **1** [To found] establish, develop, create; see ESTABLISH 2. **2** [To make up] frame, compound, aggregate; see COMPOSE 1.

constitution *n.* **1** [Health] vitality, physique, build; see HEALTH. **2** [A basic political document] code, written law, doctrines; see LAW 2.

ciples of a government, society, etc. *b*) a document stating these *c*) [**C-**] such a document of the U.S.

con·sti·tu′tion·al *adj.* **1** of or in one's constitution or structure; basic **2** of or in accordance with the constitution of a government, society, etc. —*n.* a walk taken for one's health —**con′sti·tu′tion·al′i·ty** (-shə nal′ə tē) *n.* —**con′sti·tu′tion·al·ly** *adv.*

con·strain (kən strān′) *vt.* ⟦< L *com-*, together + *stringere*, draw tight⟧ **1** to confine **2** to restrain **3** to compel

con·straint′ *n.* **1** confinement or restriction **2** force; compulsion **3** forced, unnatural manner

con·strict (kən strikt′) *vt.* ⟦see CONSTRAIN⟧ to make smaller or narrower by squeezing, etc. —**con·stric′tion** *n.*

con·stric′tor (-strik′tər) *n.* a snake that kills its prey by squeezing

con·struct (kən strukt′) *vt.* ⟦< L *com-*, together + *struere*, pile up⟧ to build, devise, etc. —**con·struc′tor** *n.*

con·struc′tion (-struk′shən) *n.* **1** a constructing or manner of being constructed **2** a structure **3** an interpretation, as of a statement **4** the arrangement of words in a sentence

con·struc′tion·ist *n.* a person who interprets a law, document, etc. in a specified way

con·struc′tive *adj.* helping to construct; leading to improvement —**con·struc′tive·ly** *adv.*

con·strue (kən strōō′) *vt., vi.* **-strued′, -stru′ing** ⟦see CONSTRUCT⟧ **1** to analyze the construction of (a sentence) **2** to translate **3** to explain; interpret

con·sul (kän′səl) *n.* ⟦< L *consulere*, to deliberate⟧ **1** a chief magistrate of ancient Rome **2** a government official appointed to live in a foreign city and look after his or her country's citizens and business there —**con′sular** (-ər) *adj.*

con′sul·ate (-it) *n.* **1** the position, powers, etc. of a consul **2** the office or residence of a consul

con·sult (kən sult′) *vi.* ⟦< L *consulere*, consider⟧ to talk things over; confer —*vt.* **1** to seek advice or information from **2** to consider —**con·sul·ta·tion** (kän′səl tā′shən) *n.*

con·sult′ant *n.* **1** a person who consults another **2** an expert who gives professional or technical advice

con·sume′ (-sōōm′) *vt.* **-sumed′, -sum′ing** ⟦< L *com-*, together + *sumere*, to take⟧ **1** to destroy, as by fire **2** to use up or waste (time, money, etc.) **3** to eat or drink up; devour

con·sum′er *n.* one that consumes; specif., one who buys goods or services for personal needs only rather than to produce other goods

con·sum′er·ism′ *n.* a movement for protecting the consumer against defective products, misleading business practices, etc.

con·sum·mate (kən sum′it, kän′sə mit; *for v.* kän′sə māt′) *adj.* ⟦< L *com-*, together + *summa*, a sum⟧ perfect; supreme —*vt.* **-mat′ed, -mat′ing 1** to complete **2** to complete (a marriage) by sexual intercourse —**con·sum′mate·ly** *adv.* —**con·sum·ma′tion** (kän′sə mā′shən) *n.*

con·sump·tion (kən sump′shən) *n.* **1** a consuming or being consumed **2** the using up of goods or services **3** the amount consumed **4** a wasting disease; esp., tuberculosis of the lungs

cont. or **contd.** continued

con·tact (kän′takt′) *n.* ⟦< L *com-*, together + *tangere*, to touch⟧ **1** a touching or meeting **2** the state of being in association (*with*) **3** a connection —*vt.* **1** to come into contact with **2** to get in touch with —*vi.* to come into contact

contact flying piloting an airplane by observing objects on the ground

contact lens a tiny, thin correctional lens worn directly over the cornea of the eye

con·ta·gion (kən tā′jən) *n.* ⟦see CONTACT⟧ **1** the spreading of disease by contact **2** a contagious disease **3** the spreading of an emotion, idea, etc.

con·ta′gious (-jəs) *adj.* **1** spread by contact: said of diseases **2** carrying the causative agent of a contagious disease **3** spreading from person to person —**con·ta′gious·ness** *n.*

con·tain (kən tān′) *vt.* ⟦< L *com-*, together + *tenere*, to hold⟧ **1** to have in it; hold **2** to have the capacity for holding **3** to hold back or restrain within fixed limits —**con·tain′ment** *n.*

con·tain′er *n.* a thing for containing something; box, can, etc.

con·tain′er·ize *vt.* **-ized′, -iz′ing** to pack (cargo) into huge, standardized containers for shipment

con·tam·i·nant (kən tam′ə nənt) *n.* a contaminating substance

con·tam′i·nate (-nāt′) *vt.* **-nat′ed, -nat′ing** ⟦< L *com-*, together + *tangere*, to touch⟧ to make impure, corrupt, etc. by contact; pollute; taint —**con·tam′i·na′tion** *n.*

con·temn (kən tem′) *vt.* ⟦< L *com-*, intens. + *temnere*, to scorn⟧ to treat with contempt; scorn

con·tem·plate (kän′təm plāt′) *vt.* **-plat′ed, -plat′ing** ⟦< L *contemplari*, observe⟧ **1** to look at or think about intently **2** to expect or intend —*vi.* to muse —**con′tem·pla′tion** *n.* —**con·tem·pla·tive** (kən tem′plə tiv′, kän′təm plāt′iv) *adj.*

con·tem·po·ra·neous (kən tem′pə rā′nē əs) *adj.* ⟦see fol.⟧ happening in the same period —**con·tem′po·ra·ne′i·ty** (-pə rə nē′ə tē; -nā′-) *n.* —**con·tem′po·ra′neous·ly** *adv.*

con·tem′po·rar′y (-rer′ē) *adj.* ⟦< L *com-*, with + *tempus*, time⟧ **1** living or happening in the same period **2** of about the same age **3** modern —*n., pl.* **-ies** one living in the same period as another or others

con·tempt (kən tempt′) *n.* ⟦see CONTEMN⟧ **1** the feeling one has toward somebody or something one considers low, worthless, etc. **2** the condition of being despised **3** a

---

THESAURUS

constitutional *a.* lawful, safeguarding liberty, democratic; see LEGAL, DEMOCRATIC.

constrain *v.* necessitate, compel, stifle; see FORCE, URGE 2.

constraint *n.* **1** [The use of force] coercion, force, compulsion; see PRESSURE 2. **2** [Shyness] bashfulness, restraint, humility; see RESERVE 2. **3** [Confinement] captivity, detention, restriction; see ARREST, CONFINEMENT.

constrict *v.* contract, cramp, choke up; see TIGHTEN 1.

construct *v.* make, erect, fabricate; see BUILD, CREATE.

construction *n.* **1** [The act of constructing] formation, manufacture, building; see ARCHITECTURE, BUILDING, PRODUCTION 1. **2** [A method of constructing] structure, arrangement, organization, system, plan, development, steel and concrete, contour, format, mold, cast, outline, type, shape, build, cut, fabric, formation, turn, framework, configuration, brick and mortar, prefab. —**under construction** in production, in preparation, being built, going up.

constructive *a.* useful, valuable, effective; see HELPFUL 1.

construe *v.* infer, deduce, interpret;

see EXPLAIN.

consult *v.* take counsel, deliberate, confer, parley, conspire with, be closeted with, compare notes about, put heads together, commune, treat, negotiate, debate, argue, talk over, call in, ask advice of, turn to, seek advice; see also ASK, DISCUSS.

consultation *n.* interview, conference, deliberation; see DISCUSSION.

consume *v.* **1** [To use] use, use up, wear out; see SPEND, USE 1. **2** [To eat or drink] absorb, feed, devour; see EAT 1.

consumer *n.* user, customer, shopper; see BUYER.

consumption *n.* using, spending, expense; see DESTRUCTION 1, USE 1, WASTE 1.

contact *n.* touch, junction, connection; see MEETING 1. —**in contact with 1** [Contiguous] meeting, joining, connecting, bordering, adjacent, close; see also NEAR 1.—*Ant.* DISTANT, out of contact, far. **2** [Communicating with] in touch with, writing to, corresponding with, in communication.

contact *v.* speak to, reach, make contact with; see COMMUNICATE 2, TALK

1, MEET.

contagion *n.* poison, virus, illness; see ILLNESS 1.

contagious *a.* communicable, infectious, transmittable, spreading, poisonous, epidemic, deadly, endemic, tending to spread; see also CATCHING.

contain *v.* **1** [Include] comprehend, embrace, be composed of; see INCLUDE 1. **2** [Restrict] hold, keep back, stop; see RESTRAIN.

container *n.* receptacle, basket, bin, bowl, dish, tub, holder, cauldron, vessel, capsule, package, packet, chest, purse, pod, pouch, cask, sack, pot, pottery, jug, bucket, canteen, pit, box, carton, canister, crate, pail, kettle; see also BAG, CAN 1, CASE 5, JAR 1, VASE.

contaminate *v.* pollute, infect, defile; see CORRUPT, DIRTY.

contamination *n.* disease, contagion, taint; see POLLUTION.

contemplate *v.* ponder, muse, speculate on; see STUDY, THINK 1.

contemporary *a.* present, fashionable, current; see MODERN 1, 3.

contempt *n.* scorn, derision, slight; see HATRED.

showing disrespect for the dignity of a court (or legislature)

con·tempt′ible *adj.* deserving of contempt or scorn; despicable —**con·tempt′ibly** *adv.*

con·temp·tu·ous (kən temp′choo əs) *adj.* full of contempt; scornful —**con·temp′tu·ously** *adv.* —**con·temp′tu·ous·ness** *n.*

con·tend (kən tend′) *vi.* ⟦< L *com-*, together + *tendere*, to stretch⟧ 1 to fight or argue 2 to compete — *vt.* to assert —**con·tend′er** *n.*

con·tent[1] (kən tent′) *adj.* ⟦see CONTAIN⟧ happy with one's lot; satisfied — *vt.* to satisfy — *n.* contentment

con·tent[2] (kän′tent′) *n.* ⟦see CONTAIN⟧ 1 [*usually pl.*] *a)* what is in a container *b)* what is dealt with in a book, speech, etc. 2 substance or meaning 3 amount contained

con·tent′ed *adj.* satisfied —**con·tent′edly** *adv.* —**con·tent′ed·ness** *n.*

con·ten·tion (kən ten′shən) *n.* ⟦see CONTEND⟧ 1 strife, dispute, etc. 2 a point argued for —**con·ten′tious** *adj.* —**con·ten′tiously** *adv.* —**con·ten′tious·ness** *n.*

con·tent′ment *n.* the state or fact of being contented

con·ter·mi·nous (kən turm′ə nəs) *adj.* ⟦< L *com-*, together + *terminus*, an end⟧ 1 having a common boundary 2 contained within the same boundaries —**con·ter′mi·nously** *adv.*

con·test (kən test′; *for n.* kän′test′) *vt.* ⟦< L *com-*, together + *testis*, a witness⟧ 1 to dispute (a point, etc.) 2 to fight for (a position, etc.) — *vi.* to struggle (*with* or *against*) — *n.* 1 a fight; struggle 2 a competitive game, race, etc. — **con·test′able** *adj.*

con·test′ant *n.* ⟦Fr⟧ a competitor in a game, etc.

con·text (kän′tekst′) *n.* ⟦< L *com-*, together + *texere*, to weave⟧ the parts just before and after a passage, that determine its meaning —**con·tex·tual** (kən teks′choo əl) *adj.*

con·tig·u·ous (kən tig′yoo əs) *adj.* ⟦see CONTACT⟧ 1 in contact; touching 2 near or next —**con·ti·gu·ity** (kän′tə gyoo′ə tē) *n.*

con·ti·nence (kän′tə nəns) *n.* ⟦see CONTAIN⟧ 1 self-restraint 2 self-restraint in sexual activity, esp. total abstinence

con·ti·nent (-nənt) *adj.* ⟦see CONTAIN⟧ characterized by self-restraint, esp. in sexual activity — *n.* any of the main large land areas of the earth

con·ti·nen·tal (-nent′'l) *adj.* 1 of a continent 2 [*sometimes* C-] European 3 [C-] of the American colonies at the time of the American Revolution

continental drift the theory that continents slowly shift position

continental shelf submerged land sloping out gradually from the edge of a continent

con·tin·gen·cy (kən tin′jən sē) *n., pl.* **-cies** 1 dependence on chance 2 a possible or chance event

con·tin·gent *adj.* ⟦see CONTACT⟧ 1 possible 2 accidental 3 dependent (*on* or *upon* an uncertainty) — *n.* 1 a chance happening 2 a quota, as of troops 3 a part of a larger group

con·tin·u·al (kən tin′yoo əl) *adj.* 1 repeated often 2 continuous —**con·tin′u·ally** *adv.*

con·tin′u·ance *n.* 1 a continuing 2 duration 3 *Law* postponement or adjournment

con·tin′u·a′tion (-ā′shən) *n.* 1 a continuing 2 a beginning again; resumption 3 a part added; sequel

con·tin·ue (kən tin′yoo) *vi.* **-ued, -u·ing** ⟦< L *continuare*, join⟧ 1 to last; endure 2 to go on in a specified action or condition 3 to extend 4 to stay 5 to go on again after an interruption — *vt.* 1 to go on with 2 to extend 3 to cause to remain, as in office 4 *Law* to postpone

con·ti·nu·ity (kän′tə noo′ə tē, -nyoo′-) *n., pl.* **-ties** ⟦OFr < L *continuitas*⟧ 1 a continuous state or quality 2 an unbroken, coherent whole 3 the script for a film, radio or TV program, etc.

con·tin·u·ous (kən tin′yoo əs) *adj.* going on without interruption; unbroken —**con·tin′u·ously** *adv.*

con·tin′uum (-yoo əm) *n., pl.* **-ua** (-yoo ə) or **-u·ums** ⟦L⟧ a continuous whole, quantity, or series

con·tort (kən tôrt′) *vt., vi.* ⟦< L *com-*, together + *torquere*, to twist⟧ to twist or wrench out of shape; distort —**con·tor′tion** *n.*

con·tor′tion·ist *n.* one who can contort his or her body into unnatural positions

con·tour (kän′toor′) *n.* ⟦Fr < L *com-*, intens. + *tornare*, to turn⟧ the outline of a figure, land, etc. — *vt.* to shape to the contour of something — *adj.* conforming to the shape or contour of something

con·tra (kän′trə, kōn′-) *n.* ⟦AmSp⟧ any member of those groups seeking to overthrow the Nicaraguan government established in 1979

contra- ⟦< L *contra*⟧ *prefix* against, opposite, opposed to

con·tra·band (kän′trə band′) *n.* ⟦< Sp < It⟧ smuggled goods — *adj.* illegal to import or export

con·tra·cep·tion (kän′trə sep′shən) *n.* ⟦CONTRA- + (CON)CEPTION⟧ prevention of the fertilization of an ovum —**con′tra·cep′tive** *adj., n.*

con·tract (kän′trakt′ *for n. & usually for vt.* 1 *& vi.* 1; kən trakt′ *for v. generally*) *n.* ⟦< L *com-*, together + *trahere*, draw⟧ an agreement between two or more people, esp. a

---

THESAURUS

contend *v.* contest, battle, dispute; see FIGHT.

content[1] *a.* appeased, gratified, comfortable; see HAPPY, SATISFIED.

contented *a.* happy, pleased, thankful; see HAPPY, SATISFIED.

contention *n.* 1 [A quarrel] struggle, belligerency, combat; see COMPETITION, DISPUTE, FIGHT. 2 [An assertion supported by argument] explanation, stand, charge; see ATTITUDE, DECLARATION.

contentment *n.* peace, pleasure, happiness; see COMFORT, EASE 1, SATISFACTION 2.

contents *n.* gist, essence, meaning, significance, intent, implication, connotation, text, subject matter, sum, substance, sum and substance, details; see also INGREDIENTS, MATTER 1.

contest *n.* trial, match, challenge; see GAME 1, SPORT 1.

contest *v.* oppose, battle, quarrel; see DARE, FIGHT.

contestant *n.* competitor, opponent, participant, rival, challenger, contester, disputant, antagonist, adversary, combatant, player, team member; see also PLAYER 1.

context *n.* connection, text, substance; see MEANING.

continent *n.* mainland, continental land mass, body of land.

continual *a.* uninterrupted, unbroken, connected; see CONSECUTIVE, REGULAR 3.

continually *a.* steadily, continuously, constantly; see FREQUENTLY, REGULARLY.

continuation *n.* succession, line, extension, increase, endurance, sustaining, preservation, perseverance, correction, translation, revision, supplement, complement, new version; see also ADDITION 1, SEQUENCE 1.—*Ant.* END, pause, delay.

continue *interj.* keep on, carry on; keep going, keep talking, keep reading, etc.; keep it up.

continue *v.* 1 [To persist] persevere, carry forward, maintain, carry on, keep on, go on, run on, live on, never stop, sustain, promote, progress, uphold, forge ahead, remain, press onward, make headway, move ahead, keep the ball rolling, leave no stone unturned*, chip away at*; see also ADVANCE 1, ENDURE 1.—*Ant.* END, cease, give up. 2 [To resume] begin again, renew, begin over, return to, take up again, begin where one left off, be reestablished, be restored; see also RESUME.—*Ant.* HALT, discontinue, postpone.

continuing *a.* persevering, carrying on, progressing; see CONSTANT, REGULAR 3.

continuity *n.* continuousness, constancy, continuance, flow, succession, unity, sequence, chain, linking, train, progression, dovetailing, extension; see also CONTINUATION.—*Ant.* INTERRUPTION, stop, break.

continuous *a.* unfaltering, repeated, perpetual; see CONSECUTIVE, CONSTANT, REGULAR 3.

contort *v.* deform, misshape, twist; see DISTORT 2.

contortion *n.* deformity, distortion, grimace, twist, ugliness, pout, crookedness.

contour *n.* profile, silhouette, shape; see FORM 1.

contraband *n.* plunder, smuggling, illegal goods; see BOOTY.

contraceptive *n.* prophylactic, birth-control device, preventative. *Contraceptives include the following:* birth-control pill, the Pill*, condom, rubber*, diaphragm, IUD, loop, coil*, foam.

contract *n.* agreement, compact, stipulation, contractual statement, contractual obligation, understanding, promise, pledge, covenant, obligation, guarantee, settlement, gentlemen's agreement, commitment, bargain, pact, arrangement, the papers, deal; see also AGREEMENT, TREATY.

contract *v.* 1 [To diminish] draw in, draw back, shrivel, weaken, shrink, become smaller, decline, fall away, subside, grow less, ebb, wane, lessen, lose, dwindle, recede, fall off, wither, waste, condense, constrict, deflate, evaporate; see also DECREASE 1.—*Ant.* STRETCH, expand, strengthen. 2 [To cause to diminish] abbreviate, written one enforceable by law —*vt.* **1** to undertake by contract **2** to get or incur (a disease, debt, etc.) **3** to reduce in size; shrink —*vi.* **1** to make a contract **2** to become smaller

con·trac·tile (kən trak′til) *adj.* having the power of contracting

con·trac·tion (kən trak′shən) *n.* **1** a contracting or being contracted **2** the shortening of a muscle of the uterus during labor **3** the shortened form of a word or phrase (Ex.: *aren't* for *are not*)

con·trac·tor (kän′trak′tər) *n.* a builder, etc. who contracts to supply materials or do work

con·trac·tual (kən trak′chōō əl) *adj.* of, or having the nature of, a contract —**con·trac′tu·ally** *adv.*

con·tra·dict (kän′trə dikt′) *vt.* [< L *contra-*, against + *dicere*, speak] **1** to assert the opposite of **2** to deny the statement of (a person) **3** to be contrary to —**con′tra·dic′tion** *n.* —**con′tra·dic′tory** *adj.*

con·tra·dis·tinc′tion (-dis tiŋk′shən) *n.* distinction by contrast

con·trail (kän′trāl′) *n.* [CON(DENSATION) + TRAIL] a white trail of water vapor in an airplane's wake

contra·in·di·cate (kän′trə in′di kāt′) *vt.* **-cat′ed, -cat′ing** to make (as an indicated medical treatment) inadvisable

con·tralto (kən tral′tō) *n., pl.* **-tos** [It: see CONTRA- & ALTO] **1** the range of the lowest female voice **2** a voice or singer with this range

con·trap·tion (kən trap′shən) *n.* [< ?] a contrivance or gadget

con·tra·pun·tal (kän′trə punt′'l) *adj.* [< It *contrappunto*, counterpoint] of or characterized by counterpoint

con·trari·wise (kän′trer′ē wiz′) *adv.* **1** on the contrary **2** in the opposite way, order, etc.

con·trary (kän′trer′ē; *for adj.* 4, *often* kən trer′ē) *adj.* [< L *contra*, against] **1** opposed **2** opposite in nature, order, etc.; altogether different **3** unfavorable **4** always resisting; perverse —*n., pl.* **-ies** the opposite —**on the contrary** as opposed to what has been said —**to the contrary** to the opposite effect —**con′tra·ri′ety** (-trə ri′ə tē) *n.* —**con′trar·i·ly** *adv.* —**con′trar·i·ness** *n.*

con·trast (kən trast′; *for n.* kän′trast′) *vt.* [< L *contra*, against + *stare*, to stand] to compare so as to point out the differences —*vi.* to show differences when compared —*n.* **1** a contrasting or being contrasted **2** a striking difference between things being compared **3** a person or thing showing differences when compared with another —**con·trast′able** *adj.*

con·tra·vene (kän′trə vēn′) *vt.* **-vened′, -ven′ing** [< L *contra*, against + *venire*, come] **1** to go against; violate **2** to contradict

contre·temps (kän′trə tän′) *n., pl.* **-temps′** (-tän′) [Fr] a confusing, embarrassing, or awkward occurrence

con·trib·ute (kən trib′yōōt) *vt., vi.* **-uted, -ut·ing** [< L: see CON- & TRIBUTE] **1** to give jointly with others **2** to write (an article, etc.) as for a magazine **3** to furnish (ideas, etc.) —**contribute to** to share in bringing about — **con·trib′u·tor** *n.* —**con·trib′u·to′ry** *adj.*

con·tri·bu·tion (kän′trə byōō′shən) *n.* **1** a contributing **2** something contributed, as money

con·trite (kən trit′) *adj.* [< L *com-*, together + *terere*, to rub] deeply sorry for having done wrong; repentant — **con·trite′ly** *adv.* —**con·trite′ness** *n.* —**con·tri′tion** (-trish′ən) *n.*

con·triv·ance (kən tri′vəns) *n.* **1** the act, way, or power of contriving **2** something contrived; device, etc.

con·trive (kən triv′) *vt.* **-trived′, -triv′ing** [ult. < VL *contropare*, compare] **1** to think up; devise **2** to make inventively **3** to bring about; manage —**con·triv′er** *n.*

con·trol (kən trōl′) *vt.* **-trolled′, -trol′ling** [< ML *contrarotulus*, a register] **1** to regulate or direct **2** to verify (an experiment) by comparison **3** to exercise authority over; direct **4** to restrain —*n.* **1** power to direct or regulate **2** a means of controlling; check **3** an apparatus to regulate a mechanism: *usually used in pl.* —**con·trol′lable** *adj.*

controlled substance a drug whose sale is regulated by law

con·trol′ler *n.* **1** the person in charge of finances, as in a business **2** a person or device that controls

con·tro·ver·sial (kän′trə vur′shəl) *adj.* subject to controversy; debatable

con′tro·ver′sy (-sē) *n., pl.* **-sies** [< L *contra*, against + *vertere*, to turn] a conflict of opinion; dispute

con·tro·vert (kän′trə vurt′, kän′trə vurt′) *vt.* **1** to argue against; dispute **2** to argue about; debate —**con′tro·vert′ible** *adj.*

con·tu·macy (kän′tyōō mə sē) *n., pl.* **-cies** [< L *com-*, intens. + *tumere*, swell up] stubborn resistance to authority —**con′tu·ma′cious** (-mā′shəs) *adj.*

con·tu·mely (kän′tyōō mēl′ē, kən tyōōm′ə lē) *n., pl.* **-lies** [< L *contumelia*, abuse] **1** humiliating treatment **2** a scornful insult —**con′tu·me′li·ous** (-mē′lē əs) *adj.*

con·tu·sion (kən tyōō′zhən, -tōō′-) *n.* [< L *com-*, intens. + *tundere*, to beat] a bruise

co·nun·drum (kə nun′drəm) *n.* [pseudo-L] **1** a riddle whose answer contains a pun **2** any puzzling problem

con·ur·ba·tion (kän′ər bā′shən) *n.* [< CON- & L *urbs*, city

---

THESAURUS

narrow, condense; see COMPRESS, DECREASE 2. **3** [To enter into an agreement by contract] pledge, undertake, come to terms, make terms, adjust, dicker, make a bargain, agree on, limit, bound, establish by agreement, engage, stipulate, consent, enter into a contractual obligation, sign the papers, negotiate a contract, accept an offer, obligate oneself, put something in writing, swear to, sign for, give one's word, shake hands on it, initial, close; see also AGREE. **4** [To catch; *said of diseases*] get, incur, become infected with; see CATCH 4.

contraction *n.* shrinkage, shrinking, recession, reduction, withdrawal, consumption, condensation, omission, deflation, evaporation, constriction, shortening, compression, decrease, confinement, curtailment, omitting, abridgment, cutting down, consolidating, consolidation, lowering; see also ABBREVIATION, REDUCTION 1, SHRINKAGE.—*Ant.* INCREASE, expansion, extension.

contractor *n.* builder, jobber, constructor; see ARCHITECT.

contradict *v.* differ, call in question, confront; see DARE 2, OPPOSE 1.

contradiction *n.* incongruity, inconsistency, opposition; see DIFFERENCE 1, OPPOSITE.

contrary *a.* **1** [Opposed] antagonistic to, hostile, counter; see AGAINST 3, OPPOSED. **2** [Unfavorable] untimely,

bad, unpropitious; see UNFAVORABLE. **3** [Obstinate] willful, contradictory, headstrong; see STUBBORN. **—on the contrary** conversely, antithetically, inversely, contrasting, on the other hand, at the opposite pole, on the other side; see also NOT. **—to the contrary** in disagreement with, in opposition to, in contradiction to; see AGAINST 1, ON THE CONTRARY.

contrast *n.* divergence, incompatibility, variation, variance, dissimilarity, inequality, distinction, oppositeness, contradiction, diversity, disagreement, opposition; see also DIFFERENCE 1.—*Ant.* AGREEMENT, similarity, uniformity. **—in contrast to (or with)** as against, opposed to, contrasting; see AGAINST 1, OPPOSED.

contrast *v.* contradict, disagree, conflict, set off, be contrary to, diverge from, depart from, deviate from, differ from, vary, show difference, stand out; see also DIFFER 1, OPPOSE 1.— *Ant.* AGREE, concur, be identical.

contribute *v.* add, share, endow, supply, furnish, bestow, present, confer, bequest, commit, dispense, settle upon, grant, afford, donate, dispense, assign, give away, subscribe, devote, will, bequeath, subsidize, hand out, ante up*, chip in*, kick in*, have a hand in, get in the act*, go Dutch*; see also GIVE 1, OFFER 1, PROVIDE 1.— *Ant.* RECEIVE, accept, take.

contributing *a.* aiding, helpful, sup-

porting, secondary, subordinate, valuable, sharing, causative, forming a part of, not to be overlooked, to be considered, coming into the picture*; see also HELPFUL.

contribution *n.* donation, present, bestowal; see GIFT 1, GRANT.

contributor *n.* subscriber, giver, grantor; see DONATION, PATRON.

contrive *v.* make, improvise, devise; see CREATE, INVENT 1.

control *n.* **1** [The power to direct] dominion, reign, direction; see POWER 2. **2** [The document executed to bind a contract] deposition, paper, evidence; see PROOF 1, RECORD 1.

control *v.* **1** [To hold in check] constrain, master, repress; see CHECK 1, RESTRAIN. **2** [To direct] lead, rule, dominate, direct, determine, master, conquer, conduct, administer, supervise, run, coach, head, dictate, manage, influence, prevail, domineer, constrain, charge, subdue, push, coerce, oblige, train, limit, officiate, drive, move, regulate, take over, rule the roost*, crack the whip*, call the shots*; see also GOVERN.

controlling *a.* ruling, supervising, regulating; see GOVERNING.

controversial *a.* disputable, debatable, suspect; see UNCERTAIN.

controversy *n.* contention, debate, quarrel; see DIFFERENCE 1, DISCUSSION.

+ -ATION] a vast urban area around and including a large city

con·va·lesce (kän′və les′) *vi.* **-lesced′, -lesc′ing** [< L *com-,* intens. + *valere,* be strong] to regain strength and health —**con′va·les′cence** *n.* —**con′va·les′cent** *adj., n.*

con·vec·tion (kən vek′shən) *n.* [< L *com-,* together + *vehere,* carry] **1** a transmitting **2** *a)* movement of parts of a fluid within the fluid because of differences in heat, etc. *b)* heat transference by such movement —**con·vec′tional** *adj.* —**con·vec′tive** *adj.*

con·vene (kən vēn′) *vi., vt.* **-vened′, -ven′ing** [< L *com-,* together + *venire,* come] to assemble for a meeting —**con·ven′er** *n.*

con·ven·ience (kən vēn′ yəns) *n.* [see prec.] **1** the quality of being convenient **2** comfort **3** anything that adds to one's comfort or saves work —**at one's convenience** at a time or place suitable to one

con·ven′ient *adj.* easy to do, use, or get to; handy —**con·ven′iently** *adv.*

con·vent (kän′vənt, -vent′) *n.* [see CONVENE] **1** the residence of a religious community, esp. of women **2** the community itself

con·ven·ti·cle (kən ven′ti kəl) *n.* [see CONVENE] a religious assembly held illegally and secretly

con·ven·tion (kən ven′shən) *n.* [see CONVENE] **1** an assembly, often periodical, or its members **2** an agreement, as between nations **3** custom; usage

con·ven′tional (-shə nəl) *adj.* **1** having to do with a convention **2** sanctioned by or following custom or usage; customary **3** formal **4** nonnuclear [*conventional* weapons] —**con·ven′tion·al′ity** (-nal′ə tē), *pl.* **-ties,** *n.* —**con·ven′tion·al·ly** *adv.*

con·ven′tion·al·ize′ (-īz′) *vt.* **-ized′, -iz′ing** to make conventional

con·verge (kən vʉrj′) *vi.* **-verged′, -verg′ing** [< L *com-,* together + *vergere,* to bend] to come together at a point —**con·ver′gence** *n.* —**con·ver′gent** *adj.*

con·ver·sant (kən vʉr′sənt, kän′vər-) *adj.* familiar or acquainted (*with*)

con·ver·sa·tion (kän′vər sā′shən) *n.* a conversing; informal talk —**con′ver·sa′tional** *adj.* —**con′ver·sa′tion·al·ist** *n.* —**con′ver·sa′tion·al·ly** *adv.*

conversation piece something, as an unusual article of furniture, that attracts attention or invites comment

con·verse¹ (kən vʉrs′; *for n.* kän′vʉrs′) *vi.* **-versed′,**

-vers′ing [< L *conversari,* live with] to hold a conversation; talk — *n.* conversation

con·verse² (kän′vʉrs; *also, for adj.,* kən vʉrs′) *adj.* [see CONVERT] reversed in position, order, etc.; opposite; contrary — *n.* a converse thing; the opposite —**con·verse′ly** *adv.*

con·ver·sion (kən vʉr′zhən) *n.* a converting or being converted

con·vert (kən vʉrt′; *for n.* kän′vʉrt′) *vt.* [< L *com-,* together + *vertere,* to turn] **1** to change; transform **2** to change from one religion, doctrine, etc. to another **3** to exchange for something equal in value **4** to misappropriate — *vi.* to be converted — *n.* a person converted, as to a religion —**con·vert′er** *n.*

con·vert·ible (kən vʉrt′ə bəl) *adj.* that can be converted — *n.* an automobile with a folding top

con·vex (kän veks′, kän′veks′) *adj.* [< L *com-,* together + *vehere,* bring] curving outward like the surface of a sphere —**con·vex′i·ty** *n.*

con·vey (kən vā′) *vt.* [< L *com-,* together + *via,* way] **1** to take from one place to another; transport **2** to transmit —**con·vey′able** *adj.* —**con·vey′or** or **con·vey′er** *n.*

con·vey′ance *n.* **1** a conveying **2** a means of conveying; esp., a vehicle

con·vict (kən vikt′; *for n.* kän′vikt′) *vt.* [see CONVINCE] to prove or find (a person) guilty — *n.* a convicted person serving a prison sentence

con·vic·tion (kən vik′shən) *n.* **1** a convicting or being convicted **2** a being convinced; strong belief

con·vince (kən vins′) *vt.* **-vinced′, -vinc′ing** [< L *com-,* intens. + *vincere,* conquer] to persuade by argument or evidence; make feel sure —**con·vinc′ing** *adj.* —**con·vinc′ingly** *adv.*

con·viv·i·al (kən viv′ē əl) *adj.* [< L *com-,* together + *vivere,* to live] **1** festive **2** fond of eating, drinking, and good company; sociable —**con·viv′i·al′ity** (-al′ə tē) *n.*

con·vo·ca·tion (kän′vō kā′shən) *n.* **1** a convoking **2** an assembly

con·voke (kən vōk′) *vt.* **-voked′, -vok′ing** [< L *com-,* together + *vocare,* to call] to call together; convene

con·vo·lut·ed (kän′və lōōt′id) *adj.* **1** having convolutions; coiled **2** involved; complicated

con·vo·lu·tion (-lōō′shən) *n.* [< L *com-,* together + *volvere,* to roll] **1** a twisting, coiling, or winding together **2** a fold, twist, or coil

con·voy (kän′voi′) *vt.* [see CONVEY] to escort in order to

THESAURUS

convene *v.* unite, congregate, collect; see ASSEMBLE 2, GATHER 1.

convenience *n.* **1** [The quality of being convenient] fitness, availability, accessibility, suitability, appropriateness, decency, acceptability, receptiveness, openness, accord, consonance, adaptability, usefulness. **2** [An aid to ease or comfort] ease, comfort, accommodation, help, aid, assistance, means, support, luxury, personal service, relief, cooperation, promotion, advancement, satisfaction, service, benefit, contribution, advantage, utility, labor saver, time saver, lift; see also ADVANTAGE, APPLI-ANCE. —**at one's convenience** suitable, conveniently, when convenient; see APPROPRIATELY.

convenient *a.* **1** [Serving one's convenience] ready, favorable, suitable, adapted, available, fitted, suited, adaptable, roomy, well-arranged, appropriate, well-planned, decent, agreeable, acceptable, useful, serviceable, assisting, aiding, beneficial, accommodating, advantageous, conducive, comfortable, opportune, timesaving, labor-saving; see also HELPFUL.—*Ant.* DISTURBING, disadvantageous, unserviceable. **2** [Near] handy, close by, easy to reach; see NEAR 1.

convention *n.* **1** [An occasion for which delegates assemble] assembly, convocation, meeting; see GATHER-ING. **2** [Custom] practice, habit, fashion; see CUSTOM.

conventional *a.* **1** [Established by convention] accustomed, prevailing,

accepted, customary, regular, standard, orthodox, normal, typical, expected, usual, routine, general, everyday, commonplace, ordinary, plain, current, popular, prevalent, predominant, expected, in established usage, well-known, stereotyped; see also COMMON 1, FAMILIAR, HABITUAL.—*Ant.* UNUSUAL, atypical, unpopular. **2** [In accordance with convention] established, sanctioned, correct; see POPULAR 3. **3** [Devoted to or bound by convention] formal, stereotyped, orthodox, narrow, narrow-minded, dogmatic, parochial, strict, rigid, puritanical, inflexible, hidebound, conservative, conforming, believing, not heretical, literal, bigoted, obstinate, straight*, straight-laced; see also PREJU-DICED.—*Ant.* LIBERAL, broad-minded, unconventional.

conversation *n.* talk, discussion, communion, consultation, hearing, conference, gossip, chat, rap*, dialogue, discourse, expression of views, mutual exchange, questions and answers, traffic in ideas, getting to know one another, general conversation, question, talking it out, heart-to-heart talk, powwow, bull session*, chitchat; see also COMMUNICATION, SPEECH 3.

converse² *n.* inverse, antithesis, reverse; see OPPOSITE.

conversion *n.* turn, spiritual change, regeneration, rebirth, being baptized, seeing the light, new birth.

convert *n.* proselyte, neophyte, disciple; see FOLLOWER.

convert *v.* **1** [To alter the form or use] turn, transform, alter; see CHANGE 2. **2** [To alter convictions] regenerate, save, baptize; see REFORM 1.

convertible *n.* open car, sports car, ragtop*; see AUTOMOBILE.

convey *v.* pass on, communicate, conduct; see SEND 1, 2.

convict *n.* captive, malefactor, felon; see CRIMINAL, PRISONER.

convict *v.* find guilty, sentence, pass sentence on, doom, declare guilty of an offense, bring to justice, send up; see also CONDEMN.—*Ant.* FREE, acquit, find not guilty.

conviction *n.* persuasion, confidence, reliance; see BELIEF, FAITH 2.

convince *v.* prove to, persuade, establish, refute, satisfy, assure, demonstrate, argue into, change, effect, overcome, turn, win over, bring around, put across, bring to one's senses, bring to reason, gain the confidence of, cram into one's head, sell a bill of goods; see also PROVE, TEACH. —**convince oneself** be convinced, be converted, persuade oneself, make up one's mind; see also BELIEVE, PROVE.

convinced *a.* converted, indoctrinated, talked into something; see CHANGED 2.

convincing *a.* trustworthy, credible, acceptable, reasonable, creditable, plausible, probable, likely, presumable, possible, dependable, hopeful, worthy of confidence, to be depended on; see also RELIABLE.

con·vulse (kən vuls′) *vt.* **-vulsed′, -vuls′ing** ⟦ < L *com-*, together + *vellere*, to pluck ⟧ 1 to shake violently; agitate 2 to cause to shake with laughter, rage, etc.

con·vul′sion (-vul′shən) *n.* 1 a violent, involuntary spasm of the muscles: *often in pl.* 2 a fit of laughter 3 a violent disturbance —**con·vul′sive** *adj.* —**con·vul′sively** *adv.*

coo (ko͞o) *vi.* ⟦echoic⟧ to make the soft, murmuring sound of pigeons or doves — *n.* this sound

cook (ko͝ok) *n.* ⟦ < L *coquere*, to cook ⟧ one who prepares food — *vt.* to prepare (food) by boiling, baking, frying, etc. — *vi.* 1 to be a cook 2 to undergo cooking —**cook up** [Colloq.] to devise; invent —**cook′er** *n.*

cook′book′ *n.* a book containing recipes and other food-preparation information

cook′ery *n.* [Chiefly Brit.] the art or practice of cooking

cook′ie (-ē) *n.* ⟦prob. < Du *koek*, cake ⟧ a small, sweet, flat cake, often crisp Also **cook′y**, pl. **-ies**

cook′-off′ *n.* a cooking contest in which participants prepare their own recipes, held as a public event

cook′out′ *n.* a meal cooked and eaten outdoors

cool (ko͞ol) *adj.* ⟦OE *col* ⟧ 1 moderately cold 2 tending to reduce the effects of heat *[cool clothes]* 3 not excited; composed 4 showing dislike or indifference 5 calmly bold 6 [Colloq.] without exaggeration *[a cool $1,000]* 7 [Slang] very good — *n.* 1 a cool place, time, etc. *[the cool of the evening]* 2 [Slang] cool, dispassionate manner — *vt., vi.* to make or become cool —**cool′ly** *adv.* —**cool′ness** *n.*

cool′ant *n.* a fluid or other substance for cooling engines, etc.

cool′er *n.* 1 a container or room for keeping things cool 2 a cold, refreshing drink 3 [Slang] jail

coo·lie (ko͞o′lē) *n.* ⟦Hindi *quli*, servant⟧ an unskilled native laborer, esp. formerly, in India, China, etc.

coon (ko͞on) *n. short for* RACCOON

coon′skin′ *n.* the skin of a raccoon, used as a fur

coop (ko͞op) *n.* ⟦ < L *cupa*, cask ⟧ a small pen as for poultry — *vt.* to confine as in a coop

co-op (kō′äp′) *n.* [Colloq.] a cooperative

cooper (ko͞op′ər) *n.* ⟦see COOP⟧ one whose work is making or repairing barrels and casks —**coop′er·age** (-ij′) *n.*

co·op·er·ate or **co-operate** (kō äp′ər āt′) *vi.* **-at′ed, -at′ing** ⟦ < L *co-*, with + *opus*, work ⟧ to act or work together with another or others —**co·op′era′tion** or **co-op′era′tion** *n.*

co·op′era·tive or **co-op′erative** (-ər ə tiv, -ər āt′iv) *adj.* 1 cooperating 2 owned collectively by members who share in its benefits — *n.* a cooperative store, etc.

co-opt (kō äpt′, kō′äpt′) *vt.* ⟦ < L *co-*, with + *optare*, choose⟧ 1 to appoint as an associate 2 to get (an opponent) to join one's side

co·ordi·nate or **co-ordinate** (kō ôr′də nit; *also, and for v. always,* -də nāt′) *adj.* ⟦ < L *co-*, with + *ordo*, order ⟧ 1 of the same order or importance *[coordinate* clauses in a sentence*]* 2 of coordination or coordinates — *n.* a coordinate person or thing — *vt.* **-nat′ed, -nat′ing** 1 to make coordinate 2 to bring into proper order or relation; adjust —**co·or′di·na′tor** or **co-or′dina′tor** *n.*

coordinating conjunction a conjunction connecting coordinate words, clauses, etc. (Ex.: *and, but, nor*)

co·or′di·na′tion or **co-or′dina′tion** *n.* 1 a coordinating or being coordinated 2 harmonious action, as of muscles

coot (ko͞ot) *n.* ⟦ME *cote* ⟧ 1 a ducklike water bird 2 [Colloq.] an eccentric

cootie (ko͞ot′ē) *n.* [Slang] a louse

cop (käp) *vt.* **copped, cop′ping** ⟦prob. < L *capere*, take⟧ [Slang] to seize, steal, etc. — *n.* [Slang] a policeman —**cop out** [Slang] 1 to renege 2 to give up; quit

co·part·ner (kō pärt′nər, kō′pärt′-) *n.* a partner

cope[1] (kōp) *vi.* **coped, cop′ing** ⟦ < OFr *coper*, to strike⟧ 1 to fight or contend (*with*) successfully 2 to deal with problems, etc.

cope[2] (kōp) *n.* ⟦ < LL *cappa*⟧ 1 a large, capelike vestment worn by priests 2 any cover like this

copi·er (käp′ē ər) *n.* 1 one who copies 2 a duplicating machine

co·pilot (kō′pil′ət) *n.* the assistant pilot of an airplane

cop·ing (kō′piŋ) *n.* ⟦ < COPE[2]⟧ the top layer of a masonry wall

co·pi·ous (kō′pē əs) *adj.* ⟦ < L *copia*, abundance⟧ plentiful; abundant —**co′pi·ously** *adv.* —**co′pi·ous·ness** *n.*

cop′-out′ *n.* [Slang] a copping out, as by reneging or quitting

cop·per (käp′ər) *n.* ⟦ < LL *cuprum*⟧ 1 a reddish-brown, ductile, metallic chemical element 2 a reddish brown — *adj.* 1 of copper 2 reddish-brown —**cop′pery** *adj.*

cop′per·head′ *n.* a poisonous North American snake

co·pra (kä′prə, kō′-) *n.* ⟦ Port < Hindi *khoprā*⟧ dried coconut meat, the source of coconut oil

copse (käps) *n.* ⟦ < OFr *coper*, to strike⟧ a thicket of small trees or shrubs Also **cop·pice** (käp′is)

cop·ter (käp′tər) *n. short for* HELICOPTER

copu·la (käp′yo͞o lə) *n., pl.* **-las** ⟦L, a link⟧ a verb form, as of *be, seem, appear,* etc., that links a subject with a predicate —**cop′u·la′tive** (-lāt′iv) *adj.*

THESAURUS

convulsion *n.* paroxysm, epilepsy, attack; see FIT 1.

cook *n.* short-order cook, chef, head cook; see SERVANT.

cook *v.* prepare, fix, warm up, warm over, stew, simmer, sear, braise, scald, broil, parch, scorch, poach, dry, chafe, fricasee, percolate, steam, bake, griddle, brew, boil down, seethe, barbecue, grill, roast, pan fry, pan broil, deep fry, French fry, brown; see also FRY, HEAT 1. —**cook up*** make up, concoct, falsify; see ARRANGE 2, PLAN 1, 2.

cookie *n.* small cake, sweet wafer, bun; see BREAD, CAKE 2, PASTRY. *Common varieties of cookies include the following:* cream, lemon, icebox, oatmeal, vanilla, chocolate, sugar, molasses, ginger, etc., cookie; gingersnap, fig bar, raisin bar, Scotch shortbread, doughnut, macaroon, tart, fruit bar, brownie, wafer.

cooking *a.* simmering, heating, scalding, brewing, stewing, steeping, frying, broiling, griddling, grilling, browning, roasting, baking; see also BOILING.

cooking *n.* cookery, dish, dainty; see FOOD.

cool *a.* 1 [Having a low temperature] cooling, frigid, frosty, wintry, some-what cold, chilly, shivery, chill, chilling, refrigerated, air-conditioned, snappy, nippy, biting; see also COLD 1.—*Ant.* WARM, tepid, heated. 2 [Calm] unruffled, imperturbable, composed; see CALM 1. 3 [Somewhat angry or disapproving] disapproving, annoyed, offended; see ANGRY, INDIFFERENT. 4 [*Excellent] neat*, keen*, groovy*; see EXCELLENT. —**play it cool** hold back, underplay, exercise restraint; see RESTRAIN.

cool *v.* lose heat, lessen, freeze, reduce, calm, chill, cool off, become cold, be chilled to the bone, become chilly, moderate, refrigerate, air-cool, air-condition, pre-cool, frost, freeze, quick-freeze; see also FREEZE 1.—*Ant.* BURN, warm, defrost.

cool it* *v.* quiet down, hold back, be sensible; see CALM DOWN.

cooperate *v.* unite, combine, concur, conspire, pool, join forces, act in concert, hold together, stick together, comply with, join in, go along with, make common cause, unite efforts, share in, second, take part, work in unison, participate, work side by side with, side with, take sides with, join hands with, play along with, play fair, throw in with, fall in with, be in cahoots*, chip in*, stand shoulder to shoulder, pull together; see also AGREE.—*Ant.* DIFFER, act independently, diverge.

cooperation *n.* collaboration, participation, combination, concert, union, confederacy, confederation, conspiracy, alliance, society, company, partnership, coalition, federation, clanship, unanimity, concord, harmony; see also AGREEMENT, UNITY 2.—*Ant.* DISAGREEMENT, discord, separation.

cooperative *a.* cooperating, agreeing, joining, combining, collaborating, coactive, uniting, concurring, participating, in joint operation; see also HELPFUL, UNITED.

cooperative *n.* marketing cooperative, consumer's cooperative, communal society, kibbutz, commune, collective, co-op*; see also UNITY 2.

coordinate *v.* harmonize, regulate, organize; see ADJUST 1, AGREE.

coordinator *n.* superintendent, supervisor, organizer; see EXECUTIVE.

cope with *v.* encounter, suffer, confront; see ENDURE 2, FACE 1.

copper *n.* biological trace element, major element of the alloys bronze and brass; see ELEMENT 2, METAL.

copu·late (käp'yōō lāt') vi. -lat'ed, -lat'ing 〚< L co-, together + apere, to join〛 to have sexual intercourse — **cop'u·la'tion** n.

copy (käp'ē) n., pl. **-ies** 〚< L copia, plenty〛 1 a thing made just like another 2 any of a number of books, magazines, etc. having the same contents 3 matter to be set in type 4 the words of an advertisement — vt., vi. **cop'ied, cop'y·ing** 1 to make a copy of 2 to imitate —**cop'y·ist** n.

cop'y·cat' (-kat') n. an imitator

cop'y·right' n. the exclusive right to the publication, sale, etc. of a literary or artistic work — vt. to protect (a book, etc.) by copyright

cop'y·writ'er n. a writer of copy, esp. for advertisements

co·quette (kō ket') n. 〚Fr〛 a girl or woman flirt — vi. **-quet'ted, -quet'ting** to flirt —**co·quet'tish** adj.

cor- prefix COM- Used before r

coral (kôr'əl) n. 〚< Gr korallion〛 1 the hard skeleton secreted by certain marine polyps: reefs and atolls of coral occur in tropical seas 2 a piece of coral 3 a yellowish red — adj. of coral

coral snake a small, poisonous snake marked with coral, yellow, and black bands

cor·bel (kôr'bəl) n. 〚< L corvus, raven〛 a piece of stone, wood, etc. projecting from a wall and supporting a cornice, arch, etc.

cord (kôrd) n. 〚< Gr chordē〛 1 a thick string 2 a measure of wood cut for fuel (128 cubic feet) 3 a rib on the surface of a fabric 4 ribbed cloth 5 [pl.] corduroy trousers 6 Anat. any part like a cord 7 Elec. a slender cable — vt. to provide with cords

cord'age (-ij') n. cords and ropes

cor·dial (kôr'jəl) adj. 〚< L cor, heart〛 warm; hearty; sincere — n. a liqueur —**cor'di·al'ity** (-jē al'ə tē) n. —**cor'dially** adv.

cor·dil·lera (kôr'dil yer'ə, -də ler'ə) n. 〚Sp < L chorda, a cord〛 a system or chain of mountains

cord·ite (kôrd'īt') n. 〚< CORD: it is stringy〛 a smokeless explosive made of nitroglycerin, etc.

cord·less (kôrd'lis) adj. operated by batteries, as an electric shaver

cor·don (kôr'dən) n. 〚see CORD〛 1 a line or circle of police, troops, etc. guarding an area 2 a cord or braid worn as a decoration — vt. to encircle with a cordon

cor·do·van (kôr'də vən) n. 〚after Córdoba, Spain〛 a soft, colored leather

cor·du·roy (kôr'də roi') n. 〚prob. < CORD + obs. duroy, a coarse fabric〛 a heavy, ribbed cotton fabric

core (kôr) n. 〚prob. < L cor, heart〛 1 the central part of an apple, pear, etc. 2 the central part of anything 3 the most important part — vt. **cored, cor'ing** to remove the core of

co·respond·ent (kō'ri spän'dənt) n. 〚CO- + RESPONDENT〛 Law a person charged with having committed adultery with the wife or husband from whom a divorce is being sought

co·ri·an·der (kôr'ē an'dər) n. 〚< Gr koriandron〛 an annual herb with strong-smelling, seedlike fruit used as a flavoring

cork (kôrk) n. 〚ult. < L quercus, oak〛 1 the light, thick, elastic outer bark of an oak tree (**cork oak**) 2 a piece of cork; esp., a stopper for a bottle, etc. 3 any stopper — adj. of cork — vt. to stop with a cork

cork'screw' n. a spiral-shaped device for pulling corks out of bottles — adj. spiral — vi., vt. to twist

corm (kôrm) n. 〚< Gr kormos, a log〛 a fleshy, underground stem of certain plants, as the gladiolus

cor·mo·rant (kôr'mə rənt) n. 〚< L corvus, raven + marinus, marine〛 a large, voracious sea bird

corn¹ (kôrn) n. 〚OE〛 1 a small, hard seed, esp. of a cereal grass 2 a) an American cereal plant with kernels growing in rows along a woody, husk-enclosed core (**corncob**); maize b) the kernels 3 [Brit.] grain, esp. wheat 4 the leading cereal crop in a place 5 [Colloq.] ideas, humor, etc. regarded as old-fashioned, trite, etc. — vt. to pickle (meat, etc.) in brine

corn² (kôrn) n. 〚< L cornu, horn〛 a hard, thick, painful growth of skin, esp. on a toe

corn'ball' (-bôl') adj. 〚CORN¹, n. 5 + (SCREW)BALL〛 [Slang] corny

corn bread bread made with cornmeal

cor·nea (kôr'nē ə) n. 〚< L cornu, horn〛 the transparent outer coat of the eyeball —**cor'neal** adj.

cor·ner (kôr'nər) n. 〚< L cornu, horn〛 1 the point or place where lines or surfaces join and form an angle 2 the angle formed 3 any of the angles formed at a street intersection 4 a remote, secluded place 5 a region; quarter 6 a position hard to escape from 7 a monopoly acquired on a stock or commodity so as to raise the price — vt. 1 to force into a CORNER (n.6) 2 to get a monopoly on (a stock, etc.) — adj. at, on, or for a corner —**cut corners** to cut down expenses, time, etc. —**cor'nered** adj.

cor'ner·back' n. Football either of two defensive backs positioned between the line of scrimmage and the safety men

cor'ner·stone' n. 1 a stone at the corner of a building, often laid at a ceremony 2 the basic or main part; foundation

cor·net (kôr net') n. 〚< L cornu, horn〛 a brass instrument similar to the trumpet but more compact

corn'flow'er n. an annual plant of the composite family, with white, pink, or blue flowers

cor·nice (kôr'nis) n. 〚< Gr korōnis, wreath〛 a horizontal molding projecting along the top of a wall, etc.

corn'meal' n. meal made from corn (maize)

corn'starch' n. a starch made from corn, used in cooking

corn syrup a syrup made from cornstarch

cor·nu·co·pia (kôr'nyōō kō'pē ə, -nōō-, -nə-) n. 〚L cornu copiae, horn of plenty〛 1 a horn-shaped container overflowing with fruits, flowers, etc. 2 an abundance

corny (kôrn'ē) adj. **-i·er, -i·est** [Colloq.] trite, sentimental, etc.

co·rolla (kə rōl'ə, -räl'ə) n. 〚< L, dim. of corona, crown〛 the petals of a flower

cor·ol·lary (kôr'ə ler'ē) n., pl. **-ies** 〚see prec.〛 1 a proposition that follows from one already proved 2 a normal result

co·rona (kə rō'nə) n., pl. **-nas** or **-nae** (-nē) 〚L〛 1 the layer of ionized gas surrounding the sun 2 a ring of colored light seen around a luminous body, as the sun or moon

coro·nary (kôr'ə ner'ē) adj. 1 of or like a crown 2 of the

THESAURUS

copulate v. sleep with, make love, go to bed, unite, couple, cover, lie with, know, have relations, have sexual relations, have marital relations, have extramarital relations, be carnal, unite sexually, have sexual intercourse, have intercourse, breed, cohabit, fornicate, lay*, fool around*, screw*, do it*, make it*, get it on*, ball*.—Ant. ABSTAIN, be continent, be celibate.

copulation n. coitus, intercourse, sex, sex act, sexual union, sexual congress, coupling, mating, coition, carnal knowledge, love, screwing*; see also SEX 1, 4.

copy n. imitation, facsimile, photostat, likeness, print, similarity, mimeograph sheet, simulation, mirror, impersonation, offprint, xerox, semblance, imitation of an original, forgery, counterfeit, reprint, rubbings, transcript, carbon, replica, typescript, cast, tracing, counterpart, likeness, portrait, model, reflection, representation, study, photograph, carbon copy, certified copy, office copy, typed copy, pencil copy, fair copy, ditto; see also DUPLICATE, REPRODUCTION 2.

copy v. 1 [To imitate] follow, mimic, ape; see IMITATE 1. 2 [To reproduce] represent, duplicate, counterfeit, forge, cartoon, depict, portray, picture, draw, sketch, paint, sculpture, mold, engrave; see also REPRODUCE 2.

cord n. string, cordage, fiber; see ROPE.

cordial a. genial, hearty, warmhearted; see FRIENDLY.

core n. 1 [Essence] gist, kernel, heart; see ESSENCE 1. 2 [Center] hub, focus, pivot; see CENTER 1.

cork n. stopper, tap, spike; see PLUG 1.

corn¹ n. oats, millet, maize; see FOOD,

GRAIN 1.

corn bread n. corn pone, hoe cakes, corndodgers, corncakes, hot bread, johnnycake, hush puppies, spoon bread; see also BREAD, CAKE 2.

corner n. 1 [A projecting edge] ridge, sharp edge, projection; see EDGE 1, RIM. 2 [A recess] niche, nook, indentation; see HOLE 1. 3 [A sharp turn] bend, veer, shift; see CURVE, TURN 2. 4 [The angle made where ways intersect] V, Y, intersection; see ANGLE 1. 5 [*Difficulty] impediment, distress, knot; see DIFFICULTY 2. —**around the corner** immediate, imminent, next; see NEAR 1, SOON. —**cut corners** cut down, shorten, reduce; see DECREASE 2.

corner v. trap, trick, fool; see CATCH 1, DECEIVE.

corny* a. stale, trite, stereotyped; see DULL 4, STUPID.

arteries supplying blood to the heart muscle — *n., pl.* **-ies** a thrombosis in a coronary artery: in full **coronary thrombosis**

coro·na·tion (kôr′ə nā′shən) *n.* the crowning of a sovereign

coro·ner (kôr′ə nər) *n.* ⟦ME, officer of the crown⟧ a public officer who must determine the cause of any death not obviously due to natural causes

coro·net (kôr′ə net′, kôr′ə net′) *n.* ⟦< OFr *corone,* crown⟧ 1 a small crown worn by nobility 2 a band of jewels, flowers, etc. for the head

Corp. or **corp.** corporation

cor·po·ral[1] (kôr′pə rəl) *n.* ⟦< L *caput,* head⟧ the lowest-ranking noncommissioned officer, just below a sergeant

cor·po·ral[2] (kôr′pə rəl) *adj.* ⟦< L *corpus,* body⟧ of the body; bodily

corporal punishment bodily punishment, as flogging

cor·po·rate (kôr′pə rit) *adj.* ⟦< L *corpus,* body⟧ 1 of, like, or being a corporation 2 shared; joint

cor·po·ra·tion (-pə rā′shən) *n.* a legal entity, usually a group of people, that has a charter granting it certain legal powers generally given to individuals, as to buy and sell property or to enter into contracts

cor·po·real (kôr pôr′ē əl) *adj.* ⟦< L *corpus,* body⟧ 1 of or for the body; physical 2 of a material nature; tangible

corps (kôr) *n., pl.* **corps** (kôrz) ⟦< L *corpus,* body⟧ 1 a body of people associated under common direction 2 *Mil. a)* a specialized branch of the armed forces *b)* a tactical subdivision of an army

corpse (kôrps) *n.* ⟦var. of prec.⟧ a dead body, esp. of a person

cor·pu·lence (kôr′pyoo ləns, -pyə-) *n.* ⟦< L *corpus,* body⟧ fatness; obesity —**cor′pu·lent** *adj.*

cor·pus (kôr′pəs) *n., pl.* **cor′pora** (-pə rə) ⟦L⟧ 1 a body, esp. a dead one 2 a complete collection, as of laws

cor′pus·cle (-pus′əl , -pə səl) *n.* ⟦< L dim. of *corpus,* body⟧ 1 a very small particle 2 a cell in the blood, lymph, etc. of vertebrates

corpus de·licti (də lik′tī′) ⟦ModL, lit., body of the crime⟧ 1 the facts constituting a crime 2 loosely, the body of a murder victim

cor·ral (kə ral′) *n.* ⟦Sp < L *currere,* to run⟧ an enclosure for horses, cattle, etc.; pen — *vt.* **-ralled′, -ral′ling** 1 to drive into or confine in a corral 2 to surround or capture

cor·rect (kə rekt′) *vt.* ⟦< L *com-,* together + *regere,* to rule⟧ 1 to make right 2 to mark the errors of 3 to scold or punish 4 to cure or remove (a fault, etc.) — *adj.* 1 conforming to an established standard 2 true; accurate; right —**cor·rect′able** *adj.* —**cor·rec′tive** *adj., n.* —**cor·rect′ly** *adv.* —**cor·rect′ness** *n.*

cor·rec·tion (-rek′shən) *n.* 1 a correcting or being corrected 2 a change that corrects a mistake 3 punishment to correct faults —**cor·rec′tional** *adj.*

cor·re·late (kôr′ə lāt′) *vi., vt.* **-lat′ed, -lat′ing** ⟦see COM- & RELATE⟧ to be in or bring into mutual relation —**cor′re·la′tion** *n.*

cor·rela·tive (kə rel′ə tiv′) *adj.* 1 having a mutual relationship 2 *Gram.* expressing mutual relation and used in

135

pairs, as the conjunctions *neither* and *nor* — *n.* a correlative word, etc.

cor·re·spond (kôr′ə spänd′) *vi.* ⟦< L *com-,* together + *respondere,* respond⟧ 1 to be in agreement (*with* something) 2 to be similar or equal (*to* something) 3 to communicate by letters —**cor′re·spond′ingly** *adv.*

cor′re·spond′ence *n.* 1 agreement 2 similarity 3 *a)* communication by letters *b)* the letters

cor′re·spond′ent *adj.* corresponding — *n.* 1 a thing that corresponds 2 one who exchanges letters with another 3 one hired by a newspaper, radio network, etc. to furnish news, etc. from a distant place

cor·ri·dor (kôr′ə dər, -dôr) *n.* ⟦Fr < L *currere,* to run⟧ a long hall

cor·robo·rate (kə räb′ə rāt′) *vt.* **-rat′ed, -rat′ing** ⟦< L *com-,* intens. + *robur,* strength⟧ to confirm; support —**cor·rob′o·ra′tion** *n.* —**cor·rob′o·ra′tive** *adj.* —**cor·rob′o·ra′tor** *n.*

cor·rode (kə rōd′) *vt., vi.* **-rod′ed, -rod′ing** ⟦< L *com-,* intens. + *rodere,* gnaw⟧ to eat into or wear away gradually, as by chemical action —**cor·ro′sion** (-rō′zhən) *n.* —**cor·ro′sive** (-rōs′iv) *adj., n.* —**cor·ro′sively** *adv.*

cor·ru·gate (kôr′ə gāt′) *vt., vi.* **-gat′ed, -gat′ing** ⟦< L *com-,* intens. + *rugare,* to wrinkle⟧ to shape into parallel grooves and ridges —**cor′ru·ga′tion** *n.*

cor·rupt (kə rupt′) *adj.* ⟦< L *com-,* together + *rumpere,* to break⟧ 1 evil; depraved 2 taking bribes — *vt., vi.* to make or become corrupt —**cor·rupt′ible** *adj.* —**cor·rup′tion** *n.* —**cor·rupt′ly** *adv.*

cor·sage (kôr säzh′) *n.* ⟦see CORPS & -AGE⟧ a small bouquet for a woman to wear, as at the waist or shoulder

cor·sair (kôr′ser′) *n.* ⟦< Fr < L *cursus,* course⟧ a pirate or pirate ship

cor·set (kôr′sit) *n.* ⟦see CORPS⟧ a closefitting undergarment worn, chiefly by women, to give support or a desired figure to the body

cor·tege or **cor·tège** (kôr tezh′, -tāzh′) *n.* ⟦Fr < L *cohors*⟧ 1 a retinue 2 a ceremonial procession

cor·tex (kôr′teks′) *n., pl.* **-ti·ces** (-tə sēz′) ⟦L, bark of a tree⟧ 1 the outer part of an internal organ; esp., the outer layer of gray matter over most of the brain 2 an outer layer of plant tissue —**cor′ti·cal** (-ti kəl) *adj.*

cor·ti·sone (kôrt′ə sōn′, -zōn′) *n.* ⟦so named by E. C. Kendall (1886-1972), U.S. physician⟧ a hormone used in adrenal insufficiency and for inflammatory diseases, etc.

co·run·dum (kə run′dəm) *n.* ⟦< Sans *kuruwinda,* ruby⟧ a very hard mineral used for grinding and polishing

cor·us·cate (kôr′ə skāt′) *vi.* **-cat′ed, -cat′ing** ⟦< L *coruscus,* vibrating⟧ to glitter; sparkle —**cor′us·ca′tion** *n.*

cor·vette (kôr vet′) *n.* ⟦Fr⟧ a fast warship smaller than a destroyer and used chiefly for convoy duty

co·sign (kō′sīn′, kō′sīn′) *vt., vi.* 1 to sign (a promissory note) in addition to the maker, thus becoming responsible if the maker defaults 2 to sign jointly —**co′sign′er** *n.*

co·sig·na·to·ry (-sig′nə tôr′ē) *n., pl.* **-ries** one of two or more joint signers, as of a treaty

---

■■ THESAURUS ■■

corporation *n.* partnership, enterprise, company; see BUSINESS 4.

corps *n.* troops, brigade, regiment; see ARMY 2, ORGANIZATION 2.

corpse *n.* carcass, remains, cadaver; see BODY 2.

correct *a.* 1 [Accurate] exact, true, right; see ACCURATE 2. 2 [Proper] suitable, becoming, fitting; see FIT.

correct *v.* better, help, remove the errors of, remove the faults of, remedy, alter, rectify, accommodate for, make right, mend, amend, fix up, do over, reform, remodel, review, reconstruct, reorganize, edit, revise, make corrections, put to rights, put in order, doctor, touch up, polish; see also REPAIR.

corrected *a.* rectified, amended, reformed; see CHANGED 2.

correction *n.* revisal, reexamination, rereading, remodeling, rectification, editing, righting, reparation, mending, fixing, amending, changing; see also REPAIR.

corrective *a.* restorative, curative, healing; see MEDICAL.

correctly *a.* rightly, precisely, per-

fectly; see RIGHT 1.

correctness *n.* 1 [Accuracy] precision, exactness, rightness; see ACCURACY, TRUTH. 2 [Propriety] decency, decorum, fitness; see PROPRIETY.

correlate *v.* connect, equate, associate; see COMPARE 1.

correlation *n.* interdependence, alternation, equivalence; see RELATIONSHIP.

correspond *v.* 1 [To be alike] compare, match, be identical; see RESEMBLE. 2 [To communicate with, usually by letter] write to, reply to, drop a line to; see ANSWER 1, COMMUNICATE 2. —**correspond** to accord, concur, harmonize; see AGREE.

correspondence *n.* 1 [The quality of being alike] conformity, equivalence, accord; see AGREEMENT, SIMILARITY. 2 [Communication, usually by letter] messages, reports, exchange of letters; see COMMUNICATION.

corresponding *a.* identical, similar, coterminous; see LIKE.

corrode *v.* rot, degenerate, deterio-

rate; see RUST.

corrupt *a.* exploiting, underhanded, mercenary, fraudulent, crooked, nefarious, profiteering, unscrupulous, shady*, fixed*, padded*, on the take*; see also DISHONEST.

corrupt *v.* pervert, degrade, demean, lower, pull down, reduce, adulterate, depreciate, deprave, debauch, defile, demoralize, pollute, taint, contaminate, infect, stain, spoil, blight, blemish, undermine, impair, mar, injure, harm, hurt, damage, deface, disfigure, deform, abuse, maltreat, illtreat, outrage, mistreat, misuse, dishonor, disgrace, violate, waste, ravage, cause to degenerate; see also RAPE, WEAKEN 2.—*Ant.* CLEAN, purify, restore.

corrupted *a.* debased, perverted, depraved; see WICKED.

corruption *n.* 1 [Vice] baseness, depravity, degradation; see CRIME, EVIL 1. 2 [Conduct involving graft] extortion, exploitation, fraudulence, misrepresentation, dishonesty, bribery, racket; see also CRIME.

cos·metic (käz met′ik) *adj.* ⟦< Gr *kosmos*, order⟧ beautifying, or correcting faults in, the face, hair, etc. —*n.* a cosmetic preparation, as lipstick —**cos·met′i·cally** *adv.*

cos′me·tol′ogy (-mə täl′ə jē) *n.* the work of a beautician —**cos′me·tol′o·gist** *n.*

cos·mic (käz′mik) *adj.* ⟦< Gr *kosmos*, universe⟧ 1 of the cosmos 2 vast

cosmic rays streams of high-energy charged particles from outer space

cos·mogo·ny (käz mäg′ə nē) *n.* ⟦< Gr *kosmos*, universe + *-gonos*, generation⟧ 1 the study of the origin of the universe 2 *pl.* **-nies** a theory of this

cos·mol′ogy (-mäl′ə jē) *n.* ⟦< ML⟧ the study of the form, evolution, etc. of the universe —**cos′mo·log′i·cal** (-mə läj′ə k'l) *adj.*

cos·mo·naut (käz′mə nôt′) *n.* ⟦Russ *kosmonaut*⟧ a Soviet or Russian astronaut

cos·mo·poli·tan (käz′mə päl′ə tən) *adj.* ⟦< Gr *kosmos*, universe + *polis*, city-state⟧ 1 common to or representative of all or many parts of the world 2 not bound by local or national habits or prejudices; at home in all places —*n.* a cosmopolitan person or thing: also **cos·mop′o·lite′** (-mäp′ə lit′)

cos·mos (käz′məs, -mōs′) *n.* ⟦< Gr *kosmos*, universe⟧ 1 the universe considered as an orderly system 2 any complete and orderly system

co·spon·sor (kō′spän′sər) *n.* a joint sponsor, as of a proposed piece of legislation —*vt.* to be a cosponsor of —**co′spon′sor·ship** *n.*

Cos·sack (käs′ak′, -ək) *n.* a member of any of several groups of peasants that lived in autonomous communal settlements, esp. in the Ukraine, until the late 19th c.

cost (kôst) *vt.* **cost**, **cost′ing** ⟦< L *com-*, together + *stare*, to stand⟧ 1 to be obtained for (a certain price) 2 to require the expenditure, loss, etc. of —*n.* 1 the amount of money, etc. asked or paid for a thing; price 2 loss; sacrifice —**at all costs** by any means required

co·star (kō′stär′; *for v., usually* kō′stär′) *n.* any featured actor or actress given equal billing with another in a movie, play, etc. —*vt., vi.* **-starred′, -star′ring** to present as or be a costar

cost-effective (kôst′ə fek′tiv) *adj.* producing good results for the amount of money spent; efficient —**cost′-effec′tiveness** *n.*

cost′ly *adj.* **-lier, -li·est** ⟦ME⟧ 1 costing much; expensive 2 magnificent —**cost′li·ness** *n.*

cost of living the average cost of the necessities of life, as food, shelter, and clothes

cos·tume (käs′tōōm′, -tyōōm′) *n.* ⟦< L *consuetudo*, custom⟧ 1 *a*) the style of dress typical of a certain country, period, profession, etc. *b*) a set of such clothes 2 a set of outer clothes —*vt.* **-tumed′, -tum′ing** to provide with a costume

cosy (kō′zē) *adj.* **-sier, -si·est** *chiefly Brit. sp. of* COZY —*n.*, *pl.* **-sies** COZY —**co′sily** *adv.* —**co′si·ness** *n.*

cot[1] (kät) *n.* ⟦< Sans *khátvā*⟧ a narrow, collapsible bed, as one made of canvas on a folding frame

cot[2] (kät) *n.* ⟦OE⟧ 1 a small shelter 2 a sheath, as for a hurt finger

cote (kōt) *n.* ⟦ME⟧ a small shelter for fowl, sheep, etc.

co·terie (kōt′ər ē) *n.* ⟦Fr⟧ a close circle of friends; clique

co·ter·mi·nous (kō tʉr′mə nəs) *adj.* CONTERMINOUS

co·til·lion (kō til′yən) *n.* ⟦< OFr *cote*, coat⟧ 1 an intricate, formal group dance 2 a formal ball Also **co·til′lon**

cot·tage (kät′ij) *n.* ⟦ME⟧ 1 a small house 2 a house used for vacations —**cot′tager** *n.*

cottage cheese a soft, white cheese made from the curds of sour milk

cot·ter (kät′ər) *n.* [Scot.] a tenant farmer Also **cot′tar**

cotter pin a split pin fastened in place by spreading both its ends after it is inserted

cot·ton (kät′'n) *n.* ⟦< Ar *qutun*⟧ 1 the soft, white hairs around the seeds of certain mallow plants 2 such a plant or plants 3 thread or cloth made of cotton —**cotton to** [Colloq.] to take a liking to —**cot′tony** *adj.*

cotton gin ⟦see GIN[2]⟧ a machine for separating cotton from the seeds

cot′ton·mouth′ *n.* WATER MOCCASIN

cot′ton·seed′ *n.* the seed of the cotton plant, yielding an oil (**cottonseed oil**) used in margarine, cooking oil, soap, etc.

cot′ton·tail′ *n.* a common American rabbit with a short, fluffy tail

cot′ton·wood′ *n.* a poplar that has seeds thickly covered with cottony or silky hairs

coty·ledon (kät′ə lēd′'n) *n.* ⟦< Gr *kotylē*, cavity⟧ the first leaf or one of the first pair of leaves produced by the embryo of a flowering plant

couch (kouch) *n.* ⟦< OFr *coucher*, lie down⟧ an article of furniture on which one may sit or lie down; sofa —*vt., vi.* 1 to recline as on a couch 2 to put in words; express

couch potato [Slang] a habitual television viewer

cou·gar (kōō′gər) *n.* ⟦< AmInd (Brazil)⟧ a large, powerful, tawny wild cat

cough (kôf) *vi.* ⟦ME *coughen*⟧ to expel air suddenly and noisily from the lungs —*vt.* to expel by coughing —*n.* 1 the act of coughing 2 a condition causing frequent coughing —**cough up** [Slang] to hand over (money, etc.)

cough drop a small medicated tablet for the relief of coughs, etc.

could (kood) *v.aux.* 1 *pt. of* CAN[1] 2 an auxiliary verb generally equivalent to CAN[1], expressing esp. a shade of doubt [it could be so]

cou·lomb (kōō läm′) *n.* ⟦after C. A. de *Coulomb* (1736-1806), Fr physicist⟧ a unit of electric charge equal to the charge of 6.28×10^{18} electrons

coun·cil (koun′səl) *n.* ⟦< L *com-*, together + *calere*, to call⟧ 1 a group of people called together for discussion, advice, etc. 2 an administrative, advisory, or legislative body —**coun′cil·man** (-mən), *pl.* **-men**, *n.* —**coun′cil·wom′an**, *pl.* **-wom′en**, *n.fem.*

coun·ci·lor (-sə lər) *n.* a member of a council

coun·sel (koun′səl) *n.* ⟦< L *consilium*⟧ 1 a mutual exchange of ideas, etc.; discussion 2 advice 3 a lawyer or group of lawyers 4 a consultant —*vt.* **-seled** or **-selled**, **-sel·ing** or **-sel·ling** 1 to give advice to 2 to recommend (an action, etc.) —*vi.* to give or take advice

coun′se·lor or **coun′sel·lor** (-sə lər) *n.* 1 an advisor 2 a lawyer

---

THESAURUS

cosmetic *n.* beautifier, beauty preparation, get-up, face*; see also MAKEUP 1. *Cosmetics include the following:* hair, body, sun tan, etc., oil; hair, eye, cold, cleansing, hormone, complexion, skin, hand, etc., cream; aftershave, hand, sun tan, etc., lotion; talcum, face, bath, tooth, etc., powder; eyebrow pencil, mascara, eye shadow, eye liner, lipstick, nail polish, moisturizer, foundation, powder, perfume, toilet water, cologne, hair tonic, hair dye, hair bleach, mouthwash, toothpaste, shampoo, shaving soap, shaving cream, shaving foam, depilatory, deodorant, antiperspirant; see also LOTION, PERFUME, SOAP.

cosmic *a.* vast, empyrean, grandiose; see UNIVERSAL 1.

cosmopolitan *a.* metropolitan, gregarious, catholic; see INTERNATIONAL, PUBLIC 2.

cosmos *n.* solar system, galaxy, star system; see UNIVERSE.

cost *n.* payment, value, charge; see PRICE, VALUE 1.

cost *v.* require, take, be priced at, be marked at, be valued at, be worth, amount to, be for sale at, command a price of, mount up to, bring in, sell for, set one back, go for.

costing *a.* as much as, to the amount of, priced at, no less than, estimated at, selling for, on sale at, reduced to, a bargain at, a steal at.

costly *a.* high-priced, dear, precious; see EXPENSIVE.

costs *n.* price, outgo, living costs; see EXPENSES. —**at all costs** by any means, in spite of difficulties, without fail; see REGARDLESS 2.

costume *n.* attire, apparel, garb; see CLOTHES, DRESS 1.

cottage *n.* cot, cabin, small house; see HOME 1.

cotton *n.* *Cotton cloth includes the following:* chintz, organdy, dotted swiss, voile, cambric, calico, flannel, denim, ticking, net, muslin, crinoline, flannelette, gingham, jersey, lace, monk's cloth, poplin, velveteen, gabardine, crepe, twill, canvas, percale, terry cloth, sailcloth, cheesecloth, theatrical gauze.

couch *n.* sofa, lounge, davenport; see CHAIR 1, FURNITURE.

cough *n.* hem, hack, frog in one's throat; see COLD 2, ILLNESS 2.

cough *v.* hack, convulse, bark*; see CHOKE.

council *n.* advisory board, cabinet, directorate; see COMMITTEE.

counsel *n.* 1 [Advice] guidance, instruction, information; see ADVICE, SUGGESTION 1. 2 [A lawyer] attorney, legal adviser, barrister; see LAWYER. —**keep one's own counsel** be secretive, conceal oneself, keep quiet; see HIDE 1.

counsel *v.* admonish, direct, inform; see ADVISE, TEACH.

counselor *n.* guide, instructor, mentor; see TEACHER.

count¹ (kount) *vt.* ⟦< L *computare*, compute⟧ **1** to name or add up, unit by unit, to get a total **2** to take account of; include **3** to believe to be; consider — *vi.* **1** to name numbers or add up items in order **2** to be taken into account; have importance **3** to have a specified value: often with *for* **4** to rely or depend (*on* or *upon*) — *n.* **1** a counting **2** the total number **3** a reckoning **4** *Law* any of the charges in an indictment

count² (kount) *n.* ⟦< L *comes*, companion⟧ a European nobleman with a rank equal to that of an English earl

count'down' *n.* **1** the schedule of operations just before the firing of a rocket, etc. **2** the counting off, in reverse order, of time units in this schedule

coun·te·nance (koun'tə nəns, kount"n əns) *n.* ⟦< L *continentia*, bearing⟧ **1** facial expression **2** the face **3** approval; support — *vt.* **-nanced, -nanc·ing** to approve or tolerate

counter¹ (kount'ər) *n.* **1** a person, device, etc. that counts something **2** a small disk for keeping count in games **3** an imitation coin or token **4** a long table, cabinet top, etc. for the displaying of goods, serving of food, etc. **—over the counter** direct trading Said of stock sales not conducted through a stock exchange **—under the counter** in a secret manner Said of sales, etc. made illegally

coun·ter² (kount'ər) *adv.* ⟦< L *contra*, against⟧ in opposition; opposite — *adj.* contrary; opposed — *n.* the opposite; contrary — *vt., vi.* to act, do, etc. counter to; oppose

counter- ⟦< L *contra-*, against⟧ *combining form* **1** contrary to *[counterclockwise]* **2** in retaliation *[counterattack]* **3** complementary *[counterpart]*

coun'ter·act' *vt.* to act against; neutralize **—coun'ter·ac'tion** *n.*

coun'ter·at·tack' *n.* an attack made in opposition to another attack — *vt., vi.* to attack to offset the enemy's attack

coun'ter·bal'ance *n.* a weight, force, etc. that balances another — *vt.* **-anced, -anc·ing** to be a counterbalance to; offset

counter·claim (kount'ər klām'; *for v.*, *also* kount'ər klām') *n.* an opposing claim — *vt., vi.* to present as a counterclaim

coun'ter·clock'wise' (-wīz') *adj., adv.* in a direction opposite to that in which the hands of a clock move

coun'ter·cul'ture *n.* a culture with a lifestyle that is opposed to the prevailing culture

coun·ter·es'pio·nage' *n.* actions to prevent or thwart enemy espionage

counter·feit (kount'ər fit') *adj.* ⟦< OFr *contre-*, counter- + *faire*, make⟧ **1** made in imitation of something genuine so as to deceive; forged **2** sham; pretended — *n.* an imitation made to deceive — *vt., vi.* **1** to make an imitation of (money, etc.), usually to deceive **2** to pretend **—coun'ter·feit'er** *n.*

count'er·man' *n., pl.* **-men'** a man who serves customers at a counter, as of a lunchroom

coun'ter·mand' (-mand') *vt.* ⟦< L *contra*, against + *mandare*, to command⟧ to cancel or revoke by a contrary order

coun'ter·pane' (-pān') *n.* ⟦ult. < L *culcita puncta*, embroidered quilt⟧ a bedspread

coun'ter·part' *n.* **1** a person or thing that closely resembles another **2** a copy or duplicate

coun'ter·point' *n.* ⟦< It: see COUNTER- & POINT⟧ **1** the technique of combining two or more distinct lines of music that sound simultaneously **2** any melody played or sung against a basic melody **3** a thing set up in contrast with another

coun'ter·poise' *n.* ⟦see COUNTER² & POISE⟧ **1** a counterbalance **2** equilibrium — *vt.* **-poised', -pois'ing** to counterbalance

coun'ter·pro·duc'tive *adj.* having results contrary to those intended

coun'ter·rev'o·lu'tion *n.* a political movement against a government set up by a previous revolution **—coun'ter·rev'o·lu'tion·ar'y**, *pl.* **-ies**, *n., adj.*

coun'ter·sign' *n.* **1** a signature added to a previously signed document, as for confirmation **2** a secret signal to another, as a password — *vt.* to confirm with one's own signature

coun'ter·sink' *vt.* **-sunk', -sink'ing 1** to enlarge the top part of (a hole) so that the head of a bolt, etc. will fit flush with the surface **2** to sink (a bolt, etc.) into such a hole

coun'ter·ten'or *n.* **1** the range of the highest male voice, above tenor **2** a singer or voice with such a range

coun'ter·weight' *n.* a counterbalance

count·ess (kount'is) *n.* **1** the wife or widow of a count or earl **2** a woman of nobility with a rank equal to that of a count or earl

count·less (kount'lis) *adj.* too many to count; innumerable; myriad

coun·try (kun'trē) *n., pl.* **-tries** ⟦< L *contra*, against⟧ **1** an area of land; region **2** the whole land, or the people, of a nation **3** the land of one's birth or citizenship **4** land with farms and small towns

country club a social club with a clubhouse, golf course, etc.

coun'try·man (-mən) *n., pl.* **-men** a man of one's own country

country music popular music that derives from the rural folk music of the S U.S.

coun'try·side' *n.* a rural region

county (kount'ē) *n., pl.* **-ties** ⟦< ML *comitatus*, jurisdiction of a count⟧ a small administrative district of a country, State, etc.

coup (ko͞o) *n., pl.* **coups** (ko͞oz) ⟦Fr < L *colaphus*, a blow⟧ **1** a sudden, successful action **2** COUP D'ÉTAT

coup de grâce (ko͞o' də gräs') ⟦Fr, stroke of mercy⟧ **1** the blow, shot, etc. that brings death to a sufferer **2** a finishing stroke

coup d'état (ko͞o' dā tä') ⟦Fr, stroke of state⟧ the sudden, forcible overthrow as of a ruler

coupe (ko͞op) *n.* ⟦< Fr *couper*, to cut⟧ a closed, two-door automobile

cou·ple (kup'əl) *n.* ⟦< L *copula*⟧ **1** a link **2** a pair of things or persons, as a man and woman who are engaged, etc. **3** [Colloq.] a few — *vt., vi.* **-pled, -pling** to link or unite

cou'plet (-lit) *n.* two successive lines of poetry, esp. two that rhyme

cou'pling (-liŋ) *n.* **1** a joining together **2** a mechanical device for joining parts together

cou·pon (ko͞o'pän', kyo͞o'-) *n.* ⟦Fr < *couper*, to cut⟧ **1** a detachable printed statement on a bond, specifying the interest due at a given time **2** a certificate entitling one to a specified right, as a discount, gift, etc.

cour·age (kur'ij) *n.* ⟦< L *cor*, heart⟧ the quality of being brave; valor

---

THESAURUS

count¹ *n.* number, enumeration, account, listing, statistics, returns, figures, tabulation, tally, poll, sum, outcome; see also RESULT, WHOLE.

count¹ *v.* compute, reckon, enumerate, number, add up, figure, count off, count up, foot up, count noses; see also ADD, TOTAL. **—count on** rely on, depend on, depend upon, lean upon, expect from, take for granted, believe in, swear by; see also TRUST 1.

counter¹ *n.* board, shelf, ledge; see BENCH 2, TABLE 1. **—under the counter** unofficial, black-market, underhanded; see ILLEGAL.

counteract *v.* frustrate, check, invalidate; see HALT, HINDER, PREVENT.

counterfeit *a.* sham, spurious, fictitious; see FALSE 3.

counterfeit *v.* copy money, make counterfeit money, circulate bad money; see FORGE.

countless *a.* innumerable, incalculable, numberless; see INFINITE, MANY.

country *a.* **1** [*Said of people*] rural, homey, unpolished; see IGNORANT 2, RUDE 1. **2** [*Said of areas*] rustic, agrarian, provincial; see RURAL.

country *n.* **1** [Rural areas] farms, farmland, farming district, rural region, rural area, range, country district, back country, bush, forests, woodlands, backwoods, sparsely settled areas, sticks*, the boondocks*, boonies*; see also FARM, FOREST.— *Ant.* CITY, borough, municipality. **2** [A nation] government, a people, a sovereign state; see NATION 1. **3** [Land and all that is associated with it] homeland, native land, fatherland; see LAND 2.

countryside *n.* rural district, farmland, woods; see COUNTRY 1.

county *n.* province, constituency, shire; see AREA, REGION 1.

couple *n.* **1** [A pair] two, set, brace; see PAIR. **2** [*A few*] two, several, a handful; see FEW.

couple *v.* unite, come together, link; see COPULATE, JOIN 1.

coupon *n.* token, box top, order blank, detachable portion, premium certificate, ticket; see also CARD, TICKET 1.

courage *n.* bravery, valor, boldness, fearlessness, spirit, audacity, audaciousness, temerity, manliness, pluck, mettle, enterprise, stoutheartedness, firmness, self-reliance, hardihood, heroism, gallantry, daring, prowess, power, resolution, dash, recklessness, defiance, the courage of one's convictions, spunk*, grit, backbone, guts*, what it takes*, nerve; see

cou·ra·geous (kə rā'jəs) *adj.* having or showing courage; brave —**cou·ra'geous·ly** *adv.*

cou·ri·er (koor'ē ər, kur'-) *n.* 〚< L *currere*, to run 〛 1 a messenger 2 a person hired to take care of hotel accommodations, etc. for a traveler

course (kôrs) *n.* 〚< L *currere*, to run 〛 1 an onward movement; progress 2 a way, path, or channel 3 the direction taken 4 a regular manner of procedure or conduct /our wisest *course*/ 5 a series of like things in order 6 a part of a meal served at one time 7 *Educ. a)* a complete series of studies, as for a degree *b)* any of the separate units of such a series — *vi.* **coursed, cours'ing** to run or race —**in due course** in the usual sequence (of events) —**in the course of** during —**of course** 1 naturally 2 certainly

cours·er (kôr'sər) *n.* a graceful, spirited, or swift horse

court (kôrt) *n.* 〚< L *cohors*, enclosure 〛 1 a courtyard 2 a short street 3 a space for playing a game, as basketball 4 *a)* the palace, or the family, etc., of a sovereign *b)* a sovereign and councilors, etc. as a governing body *c)* a formal gathering held by a sovereign 5 courtship; wooing 6 *a)* a judge or judges *b)* a place where trials are held *c)* a judicial assembly — *vt.* 1 to pay attention to (a person) so as to get something 2 to seek as a mate; woo 3 to try to get /to *court* favor/ — *vi.* to carry on a courtship —**court'er** *n.*

cour·teous (kurt'ē əs) *adj.* 〚see prec. & -EOUS 〛 polite and gracious —**cour'teous·ly** *adv.*

cour·te·san (kôrt'ə zən) *n.* 〚see COURT 〛 a prostitute Also **cour'te·zan**

cour·tesy (kurt'ə sē) *n., pl.* **-sies** 1 courteous behavior 2 a polite or considerate act or remark

court'house' *n.* 1 a building housing law courts 2 a building housing offices of a county government

cour·tier (kôrt'ē ər, -yər) *n.* an attendant at a royal court

court'ly *adj.* **-lier, -li·est** suitable for a king's court; dignified; elegant —**court'li·ness** *n.*

court'-mar'tial *n., pl.* **courts'-mar'tial;** for 2, now often **court'-mar'tials** 1 a court in the armed forces for the trial of persons accused of breaking military law 2 a trial by a court-martial 3 a conviction by a court-martial — *vt.* **-tialed** or **-tialled, -tialing** or **-tialling** to try by a court-martial

court'room' *n.* a room in which a law court is held

court'ship' *n.* the act, process, or period of wooing

court'yard' *n.* a space enclosed by walls, adjoining or in a large building

cous·cous (koos'koos') *n.* 〚Fr < Ar *kaskasa*, to grind 〛 a N African dish made with crushed grain, served as with lamb in a spicy sauce

cousin (kuz'ən) *n.* 〚ult. < L *com-*, with + *soror*, sister 〛 1 the son or daughter of one's uncle or aunt 2 loosely, any relative by blood or marriage

cou·tu·ri·er (koo tü ryā'; *Eng* koo'toor ē ā') *n.* 〚Fr 〛 a designer of women's fashions —**cou·tu·ri·ère'** (-ryer'; *Eng*, -ē er') *n.fem.*

cove (kōv) *n.* 〚OE *cofa*, cave 〛 a small bay or inlet

coven (kuv'ən) *n.* 〚see CONVENE 〛 a gathering or meeting, esp. of witches

cov·enant (kuv'ə nənt) *n.* 〚see CONVENE 〛 an agreement; compact — *vt.* to promise by a covenant — *vi.* to make a covenant

cover (kuv'ər) *vt.* 〚< L *co-*, intens. + *operire*, to hide 〛 1 to place something on or over 2 to extend over 3 to clothe 4 to conceal; hide 5 to shield, protect, or watch (someone or something) 6 to include; deal with /to *cover* a subject/ 7 to protect financially /to *cover* a loss/ 8 to accept (a bet) 9 to travel over 10 to point a firearm at 11 *Journalism* to gather the details of (a news story) — *vi.* 1 to spread over a surface, as a liquid does 2 to provide an alibi (*for*) — *n.* 1 anything that covers, as a lid, top, etc. 2 a shelter for protection 3 a tablecloth and setting 4 COVER CHARGE 5 something used to hide one's real actions, etc. —**cover up** to keep blunders, crimes, etc. from being known —**take cover** to seek shelter —**under cover** in secrecy or concealment

cov'er·age' (-ij') *n.* the amount, extent, etc. covered by something

cov'er·all' *n.* [*usually pl.*] a one-piece outer garment, often worn over regular clothing while working, etc.

cover charge a fixed charge added to the cost of food and drink at a nightclub, etc.

cover crop a crop, as clover, grown to keep soil fertile and uneroded

covered wagon a large wagon with an arched cover of canvas

cov'er·ing *n.* anything that covers

■ THESAURUS ■

also STRENGTH.—*Ant.* FEAR, cowardice, timidity.

courageous *a.* daring, gallant, intrepid; see BRAVE.

course *n.* 1 [A route] passage, path, way; see ROUTE 1. 2 [A prepared way, especially for racing] lap, cinder path, cinder track; see ROAD 1. 3 [A plan of study] subject, studies, curriculum; see EDUCATION 1. 4 [A series of lessons] classes, lectures, seminar; see EDUCATION 1. —**in due course** in due time, properly, conveniently; see APPROPRIATELY. —**in the course of** during, in the process of, when; see WHILE 1. —**of course** certainly, by all means, indeed; see SURELY. — **off course** misdirected, erratic, going the wrong way; see WRONG 2. —**on course** on target, correct, going in the right direction; see ACCURATE 2.

court *n.* 1 [An enclosed, roofless area] square, courtyard, patio; see YARD 1. 2 [An instrument for administering justice] tribunal, bench, magistrate, bar, session. *Types of courts include the following:* the Supreme Court of the United States, appellate court of the United States, Federal court, State supreme court, district court, county court, justice's court, magistrate's court, mayor's court, police court. 3 [A ruler and his surroundings] lords and ladies, attendants, royal household; see GOVERNMENT 2, ROYALTY, RULER 1. 4 [An area for playing certain games] arena, rink, ring; see FIELD 2.

court *v.* attract, allure, solicit, beseech, entice, pursue, accompany, follow, plead, make love, pay court, pay attentions to, pay court to, make

overtures, go courting, propose, ask in marriage, set one's cap for*, pop the question*, go steady, go together*, go with*, make a play for*; see also DATE 2.

courteous *a.* courtly, affiable, cultivated; see POLITE.

courteously *a.* civilly, affably, obligingly; see POLITELY.

courtesy *n.* 1 [Courteous conduct] kindness, friendliness, affability, courteousness, gentleness, consideration, thoughtfulness, sympathy, geniality, cordiality, graciousness, tact, good manners, politeness, refinement, chivalry, gallantry, respect, deference, polished manners, good breeding; see also GENEROSITY, KINDNESS 1. 2 [Courteous act] compassion, generosity, charity; see KINDNESS 2.

cousin *n.* kin, an aunt's child, an uncle's child; see RELATIVE.

cove *n.* inlet, sound, lagoon; see BAY.

cover *n.* 1 [A covering object] covering, ceiling, canopy, hood, sheath, sheet, awning, tent, umbrella, dome, stopper, lid, canvas, tarpaulin, book cover, folder, wrapper, wrapping paper, jacket, case, spread, tarp*; see also BLANKET, ENVELOPE, FOLDER, ROOF. 2 [A covering substance] paint, varnish, polish; see COAT 3, SHEET 2. 3 [Shelter] harbor, asylum, refuge; see RETREAT 2, SHELTER. — **take cover** conceal oneself, take shelter, go indoors; see HIDE 1. — **under cover** secretive, hiding, concealed; see HIDDEN.

cover *v.* 1 [To place as a covering] carpet, put on, overlay, surface,

board up, superimpose, black in, black out; see also SPREAD 3. 2 [To wrap] envelop, enshroud, encase; see WRAP. 3 [To protect] shield, screen, house; see DEFEND 1, 2, SHELTER. 4 [To hide] screen, camouflage, mask; see DISGUISE, HIDE 1. 5 [To include] embrace, comprise, incorporate; see INCLUDE 1. 6 [To travel] traverse, journey over, cross; see TRAVEL. 7 [To send down in plenty] drench, engulf, overcome; see FLOOD. 8 [To report upon, especially for a newspaper] recount, narrate, relate; see BROADCAST, RECORD 3. —**cover up for** lie for, take the rap for*, be the goat*; see DEFEND 1, 2, SHELTER.

covered *a.* 1 [Provided with cover] topped, lidded, roofed, wrapped, enveloped, bound, painted, varnished, coated, camouflaged, sheltered, shielded, separated, disguised, masked, secreted, protected, concealed; see also HIDDEN.—*Ant.* OBVIOUS, revealed, exposed. 2 [Plentifully bestrewn] scattered with, sprinkled over, spattered, spangled, dotted, strewn with, starred, starry with, flowered, spotted with, sown, dusted over, powdered, spread with.—*Ant.* EMPTY, bare, unfurnished. 3 [Attended to] noted, taken note of, reported, recorded, written, included, marked, explored, regarded, scrutinized, examined, surveyed, investigated, observed, looked to, hurdled, cared for; see also DONE 1, RECOGNIZED.—*Ant.* unheeded, unnoticed, passed over.

covering *n.* concealment, top, spread; see COVER 1.

cov·er·let (kuv′ər lit) *n.* 〚< OFr *covrir*, to cover + *lit*, bed〛 any covering, esp. a bedspread

cover story the article in a magazine that deals with the subject depicted on the cover

cov·ert (kuv′ərt, kō′vərt) *adj.* 〚see COVER〛 hidden or disguised — *n.* a protected shelter, as for game —**cov′ertly** *adv.*

cov′er·up′ *n.* something used for hiding one's real activities, etc.

covet (kuv′it) *vt., vi.* 〚< L *cupiditas*, cupidity〛 to want ardently (esp., something that another person has)

cov′et·ous (-ət əs) *adj.* tending to covet; greedy —**cov′et·ously** *adv.* —**cov′et·ous·ness** *n.*

covey (kuv′ē) *n., pl.* **-eys** 〚< OFr *cover*, to hatch〛 a small flock of birds, esp. partridges or quail

cow[1] (kou) *n.* 〚OE *cu*〛 1 the mature female of domestic cattle, valued for its milk 2 the mature female of certain other mammals, as the whale

cow[2] (kou) *vt.* 〚< ON *kūga*, subdue〛 to make timid; intimidate

cow·ard (kou′ərd) *n.* 〚ult. < L *cauda*, tail〛 one who lacks courage, esp. one who is shamefully afraid — *adj.* cowardly

cow′ard·ice (-ər dis′) *n.* lack of courage

cow′ardly *adj.* of or like a coward — *adv.* in the manner of a coward —**cow′ard·li·ness** *n.*

cow′boy′ *n.* a ranch worker who herds cattle Also **cow′hand′** —**cow′girl′** *n.fem.*

cower (kou′ər) *vi.* 〚ME *couren*〛 to crouch or huddle up, as from fear or cold; shrink; cringe

cow′hide′ *n.* 1 the hide of a cow 2 leather from it 3 a whip made of this

cowl (koul) *n.* 〚< L *cucullus*, hood〛 a monk's hood or a monk's cloak with a hood

cow·lick (kou′lik′) *n.* 〚< its looking as if licked by a cow〛 a tuft of hair that cannot easily be combed flat

cowl·ing (koul′iŋ) *n.* 〚see COWL〛 a metal covering for an airplane engine, etc.

co′-work′er *n.* a fellow worker

cow′poke′ *n.* [Colloq.] COWBOY

cow pony a horse for herding cattle

cow′pox′ *n.* a disease of cows: people vaccinated with its virus have temporary immunity to smallpox

cow′slip′ *n.* a European primrose

cox·comb (käks′kōm′) *n.* 〚for *cock's comb*〛 a silly, vain fellow; dandy

cox·swain (käk′sən, -swān′) *n.* 〚< *cock*, small boat + SWAIN〛 one who steers a boat or racing shell

coy (koi) *adj.* 〚ME, quiet〛 1 bashful; shy 2 pretending to be shy —**coy′ly** *adv.* —**coy′ness** *n.*

coyo·te (kī ōt′ē, kī′ōt′) *n.* 〚< AmInd (Mex)〛 a small, wolflike animal of North America

cozen (kuz′ən) *vt., vi.* 〚< ME *cosin*, fraud〛 to cheat; deceive —**coz′en·age** *n.*

cozy (kō′zē) *adj.* **-zier, -zi·est** 〚Scot〛 warm and comfortable; snug — *n., pl.* **-zies** a padded cover for a teapot, to keep the tea hot —**cozy up to** [Colloq.] to try to ingratiate oneself with —**co′zily** *adv.* —**co′zi·ness** *n.*

CPA Certified Public Accountant

CPO Chief Petty Officer

CPR cardiopulmonary resuscitation

CPU (sē′pē′yōō′) *n.* central processing unit Also **cpu**

Cr *Chem. symbol for* chromium

crab (krab) *n.* 〚OE *crabba*〛 1 a crustacean with four pairs of legs and a pair of pincers 2 a peevish person — *vi.* **crabbed, crab′bing** [Colloq.] to complain

crab apple 1 a small, very sour apple 2 a tree bearing crab apples

crab·bed (krab′id) *adj.* 〚< CRAB (APPLE)〛 1 peevish 2 hard to read or understand, as writing —**crab′bed·ness** *n.*

crab′by *adj.* **-bier, -bi·est** 〚see prec.〛 cross and complaining —**crab′bily** *adv.* —**crab′bi·ness** *n.*

crab grass a weedy grass, with freely rooting stems, that spreads rapidly

crack (krak) *vi.* 〚< OE *cracian*, resound〛 1 to make a sudden, sharp noise, as in breaking 2 to break or split, usually without separation of parts 3 to rasp or shift erratically in vocal tone 4 [Colloq.] to break down, as from strain — *vt.* 1 to cause to make a sharp, sudden noise 2 to cause to break or split 3 to break down (petroleum hydrocarbons) into the lighter hydrocarbons of gasoline, etc. 4 [Colloq.] to hit hard 5 to solve 6 [Colloq.] to break into or force open 7 [Slang] to make (a joke) — *n.* 1 a sudden, sharp noise 2 a partial break; fracture 3 a chink; crevice 4 a cracking of the voice 5 [Colloq.] a sudden, sharp blow 6 [Colloq.] an attempt or try 7 [Slang] a joke — *adj.* [Colloq.] excellent; first-rate —**crack down (on)** to become strict (with) —**cracked up to be** [Colloq.] believed to be —**crack up** 1 to crash 2 [Colloq.] *a*) to break down physically or mentally *b*) to laugh or cry

crack′down′ *n.* a resorting to strict or stricter discipline or punishment

cracked (krakt) *adj.* 1 having a crack or cracks 2 sounding harsh or strident 3 [Colloq.] crazy

crack′er *n.* 1 a firecracker 2 a thin, crisp wafer

crack′er·jack′ *adj.* [Slang] outstanding; excellent — *n.* [Slang] an excellent person or thing

crackle (krak′əl) *vi.* **-led, -ling** 〚ME *crakelen*, to crack〛 to make a series of slight, sharp, popping sounds — *n.* 1 a series of such sounds 2 the fine, irregular surface cracks on some pottery, etc.

crack′pot′ *n.* [Colloq.] an eccentric person — *adj.* [Colloq.] eccentric

crack′up′ *n.* 1 a crash 2 [Colloq.] a physical or mental breakdown

-cracy (krə sē) 〚< Gr *kratos*, rule〛 *combining form* a (specified) type of government; rule by [*autocracy*]

cra·dle (krād′l) *n.* 〚OE *cradol*〛 1 a baby's small bed, usually on rockers 2 infancy 3 the place of a thing's beginning 4 anything like a cradle — *vt.* **-dled, -dling** 1 to place, rock, or hold in or as in a cradle 2 to take care of in infancy

cra′dle·song′ *n.* a lullaby

THESAURUS

covet *v.* desire, envy, wish for; see WANT 1.

cow[1] *n.* heifer, milk cow, dairy cow, critter, bossy; see also CATTLE.

coward *n.* sneak, milksop, shirker, deserter, weakling, alarmist, slacker*, quitter*, chicken*, lily-liver*, scaredy-cat*, chicken-heart*, fraidy-cat*, yellow-belly*.

cowardice *n.* cowardliness, timidity, faint-heartedness, fear, weakness, quailing, lack of courage, apprehension, shyness, dread, fearfulness, yellow streak*, cold feet*; see also FEAR.—*Ant.* bravery, valor, fearlessness.

cowardly *a.* timid, frightened, afraid, fearful, shy, backward, cowering, apprehensive, nervous, anxious, dismayed, faint-hearted, panicky, scared, scary, jittery*, craven, mean-spirited, weak, soft, chicken-livered*, lily-livered*, yellow*, skulking, sneaking, cringing, trembling, shaken, crouching, running, quaking, shaking like a leaf, shaking in one's boots*; see also AFRAID, WEAK 3.—*Ant.* BRAVE, fearless, open.

cowboy *n.* cowhand, hand, wrangler, rider, herder, cattle-herder, drover, gaucho, cowpuncher*, cowpoke*, buckaroo; see also RANCHER.

cower *v.* cringe, shrink, fear, run, quake, shiver, tremble, shake, snivel, flinch, quail; see also GROVEL.

coy *a.* bashful, shy, demure; see HUMBLE 1.

cozy *a.* secure, sheltered, snug; see COMFORTABLE 2, SAFE 1.

crab *n.* crayfish, crustacean, seafood; see SHELLFISH.

crack* *a.* first-rate, first-class, skilled; see ABLE, EXCELLENT.

crack *n.* 1 [An incomplete break] chink, split, cut; see HOLE 1. 2 [A crevice] cleft, fissure, rift; see HOLE 1. 3 [A blow] hit, thwack, stroke; see BLOW. 4 [*A witty or brazen comment*] return, witticism, jest; see JOKE, REMARK.

crack *v.* 1 [To become cracked] cleave, burst, split; see BREAK. 2 [To cause to crack] cleave, split, sever; see BREAK. 3 [To damage] injure, hurt, impair; see DAMAGE. 4 [*To become mentally deranged*] become insane, go crazy, blow one's mind*; see CRACK UP 2. 5 [To solve] figure out, answer, decode; see SOLVE. — **crack a joke** quip, jest, jape; see JOKE. —**crack up** 1 [*To crash a vehicle*] collide, be in an accident, smash up; see CRASH 4. 2 [*To fail suddenly in health, mind, or strength*] go to pieces, fail, deteriorate, sicken, go insane, go crazy, become demented, freak out*, blow one's mind*, go out of one's mind, go off one's rocker*, blow a fuse*, go off the deep end*; see also WEAKEN 1. 3 [*To laugh*] roar, howl, roll in the aisles*; see LAUGH. —**get cracking*** get going, go, start; see BEGIN 2, MOVE 1.

cracked *a.* shattered, split, fractured; see BROKEN 1.

cracker *n.* wafer, cookie, soda cracker, oyster cracker, biscuit, saltine, hardtack, sea biscuit, wheat biscuit; see also BREAD.

cradle *n.* trundle bed, crib, bassinet; see BED 1, FURNITURE.

craft (kraft) *n.* ⟦OE *cræft*, power⟧ **1** a special skill or art **2** an occupation requiring special skill **3** the members of a skilled trade **4** guile; slyness **5** *pl.* **craft** a boat, ship, or aircraft

crafts·man (krafts′mən) *n., pl.* **-men** a skilled worker; artisan —**crafts′man·ship′** *n.*

craft′y *adj.* **-i·er, -i·est** ⟦ME *crafti*, sly⟧ subtly deceitful; sly; cunning —**craft′i·ly** *adv.* —**craft′i·ness** *n.*

crag (krag) *n.* ⟦< Celt⟧ a steep, rugged rock rising from a rock mass —**crag′gy, -gi·er, -gi·est,** *adj.*

cram (kram) *vt.* **crammed, cram′ming** ⟦OE *crammian*⟧ **1** to pack full or too full **2** to stuff; force **3** to feed to excess — *vi.* **1** to eat too much or too quickly **2** to study a subject in a hurried, intensive way, as for an examination

cramp (kramp) *n.* ⟦< OFr *crampe*, bent⟧ **1** a sudden, painful, involuntary contraction of muscles from chill, strain, etc. **2** [*usually pl.*] abdominal or uterine spasms and pain — *vt.* **1** to cause a cramp or cramps in **2** ⟦< MDu *krampe*, bent in⟧ to hamper; restrain

cramped (krampt) *adj.* **1** confined or restricted **2** irregular and crowded, as some handwriting

cran·berry (kran′ber′ē, -bər ē) *n., pl.* **-ries** ⟦< Du *kranebere*⟧ **1** a firm, sour, edible, red berry, the fruit of an evergreen shrub **2** the shrub

crane (krān) *n.* ⟦OE *cran*⟧ **1** a large wading bird with very long legs and neck **2** a machine for lifting or moving heavy weights, using a movable projecting arm or a horizontal traveling beam — *vt., vi.* **craned, cran′ing** to stretch (the neck)

cra·nium (krā′nē əm) *n., pl.* **-ni·ums** or **-nia** (-ə) ⟦< Gr *kranion*⟧ the skull, esp. the part containing the brain — **cra′nial** *adj.*

crank (kraŋk) *n.* ⟦OE *cranc-*, something twisted⟧ **1** a handle or arm bent at right angles and connected to a machine shaft to transmit motion **2** [Colloq.] an eccentric or irritable person — *vt.* to start or operate by a crank

crank′case′ *n.* the metal casing that encloses the crankshaft of an internal-combustion engine

crank′shaft′ *n.* a shaft with one or more cranks for transmitting motion

crank′y *adj.* **-i·er, -i·est 1** apt to operate poorly **2** irritable **3** eccentric —**crank′i·ly** *adv.*

cranny (kran′ē) *n., pl.* **-nies** ⟦< VL *crena*, a notch⟧ a crevice; crack

crap (krap) *n.* ⟦< ML *crappa*, chaff⟧ [Vulgar] **1** nonsense **2** junk; trash —**crap′py, -pi·er, -pi·est,** *adj.*

crape (krāp) *n.* **1** CREPE (sense 1) **2** a piece of black crepe as a sign of mourning

crap·pie (krap′ē) *n.* a small North American sunfish

craps (kraps) *n.pl.* ⟦Fr *crabs*⟧ a gambling game played with two dice

crap·shooter (krap′shoot′ər) *n.* a gambler at craps

crash (krash) *vi.* ⟦ME⟧ **1** to fall, collide, or break with a loud noise **2** to collapse; fail — *vt.* **1** to cause (a car, airplane, etc.) to crash **2** to force with or as with a crashing noise: with *in, out, through,* etc. **3** [Colloq.] to get into (a party, etc.) without an invitation, etc. — *n.* **1** a loud, sudden noise **2** a crashing **3** a sudden collapse, as of business — *adj.* [Colloq.] using all possible resources, effort, and speed *[a crash* program to build roads*]*

crash′-land′ *vt., vi.* to bring (an airplane) down in a forced landing, esp. without use of the landing gear — **crash landing**

crash pad [Slang] a place to live or sleep temporarily

crass (kras) *adj.* ⟦L *crassus*, thick⟧ tasteless, insensitive, materialistic —**crass′ly** *adv.*

-crat (krat) ⟦< Gr *kratos*, rule⟧ *combining form* member or supporter of (a specified kind of) government

crate (krāt) *n.* ⟦L *cratis*, wickerwork⟧ a packing case made of slats of wood — *vt.* **crat′ed, crat′ing** to pack in a crate

cra·ter (krāt′ər) *n.* ⟦< Gr *kratēr*, mixing bowl⟧ **1** a bowl-shaped cavity, as at the mouth of a volcano **2** a pit made by an exploding bomb, etc.

cra·vat (krə vat′) *n.* ⟦< Fr⟧ a necktie

crave (krāv) *vt.* **craved, crav′ing** ⟦OE *crafian*⟧ **1** to ask for earnestly; beg **2** to long for eagerly

cra·ven (krā′vən) *adj.* ⟦< L *crepare*, to rattle⟧ cowardly — *n.* a coward —**cra′venly** *adv.* —**cra′ven·ness** *n.*

crav·ing (krā′viŋ) *n.* an intense and prolonged desire, as for affection or for a food or drug

craw (krô) *n.* ⟦ME *craue*⟧ **1** the crop of a bird **2** the stomach

craw·fish (krô′fish′) *n., pl.* **-fish′** or (for different species) **-fish′es** crayfish

crawl (krôl) *vi.* ⟦< ON *krafla*⟧ **1** to move slowly by dragging the body along the ground **2** to go on hands and knees; creep **3** to move slowly **4** to move or act in a servile manner **5** to swarm (*with* crawling things) — *n.* **1** a slow movement **2** an overarm swimming stroke

crawl space an unfinished space, as under a floor, allowing access to wiring, plumbing, etc.

crawl′y *adj.* **-i·er, -i·est** CREEPY

cray·fish (krā′fish′) *n., pl.* **-fish′** or (for different species) **-fish′es** ⟦< OHG *krebiz*⟧ a freshwater crustacean somewhat like a little lobster

crayon (krā′ən, -än′) *n.* ⟦Fr, pencil < L *creta*, chalk⟧ **1** a small stick of chalk, charcoal, or colored wax, used for drawing, coloring, or writing **2** a drawing made with crayons — *vt.* to draw or color with crayons

craze (krāz) *vt., vi.* **crazed, craz′ing** ⟦ME *crasen*, to crack⟧ to make or become insane — *n.* a fad

crazy (krā′zē) *adj.* **-zier, -zi·est** ⟦< CRAZE⟧ **1** unsound of mind; insane **2** [Colloq.] foolish; not sensible **3** [Colloq.] very enthusiastic or eager — *interj.* [Slang] an exclamation of pleasure, etc. — *n., pl.* **-zies** [Slang] a crazy person —**cra′zily** *adv.* —**cra′zi·ness** *n.*

crazy bone FUNNY BONE

crazy quilt a patchwork quilt with no regular design

creak (krēk) *vi., vt.* ⟦echoic⟧ to make, cause to make, or move with a harsh, squeaking sound — *n.* such a sound — **creak′y, -i·er, -i·est,** *adj.* —**creak′i·ly** *adv.* —**creak′i·ness** *n.*

THESAURUS

craft *n.* **1** [Skill] proficiency, competence, aptitude; see ABILITY. **2** [Trade] occupation, career, work; see JOB 1, PROFESSION 1. **3** [Ship] vessel, aircraft, spacecraft; see BOAT, SHIP.

craftsman *n.* artisan, skilled worker, journeyman, maker, technician, manufacturer, machinist, handcraftsman, mechanic; see also ARTIST, LABORER, SPECIALIST.

crafty *a.* clever, sharp, shrewd; see INTELLIGENT.

cram *v.* **1** [To stuff] crush, jam, press; see COMPRESS, PACK. **2** [To study hurriedly] read, teach, review; see STUDY.

cramp *n.* spasm, crick, pang; see PAIN 2.

cramped *a.* narrow, confined, restraining; see RESTRICTED, UNCOMFORTABLE 1.

cranium *n.* brain, cerebrum, cerebellum, brain encasing, brainpan, skull; see also HEAD 1.

crank *n.* **1** [A device for revolving a shaft] bracket, turning device, bend; see ARM 2, HANDLE 1. **2** [A person with an obsession] eccentric, fanatic, monomaniac; see CHARACTER 4. **3** [*An ill-natured person] eccentric, misanthrope, complainer; see GROUCH.

cranky *a.* disagreeable, cross, perverse; see IRRITABLE.

crash *n.* **1** [A crashing sound] clatter, clash, din; see NOISE 1, SOUND 2. **2** [A collision] wreck, accident, shock; see COLLISION.

crash *v.* **1** [To fall with a crash] overturn, upset, break down, plunge, be hurled, pitch, smash, dive, hurtle, lurch, sprawl, tumble, fall headlong, fall flat, drop, slip, collape; see also FALL 1. **2** [To break into pieces] shatter, shiver, splinter; see BREAK, SMASH. **3** [To make a crashing sound] clatter, bang, smash; see SOUND. **4** [To have a collision] collide, run together, run into, smash into, bang into, meet, jostle, bump, butt, knock, punch, jar, jolt, crack up; see also HIT 3. **5** [*To collapse] fall asleep, pass out, become unconscious; see FAINT, SLEEP. **6** [*To go uninvited] disturb, gate-crash, intrude; see INTERRUPT, MEDDLE 1.

crash program *n.* crash project, immediate undertaking, intensive program, around-the-clock endeavor, revised plan, speed-up; see also EMERGENCY.

crass *a.* gross, tasteless, coarse; see IGNORANT 1, 2, VULGAR.

crate *n.* carton, box, cage; see CONTAINER, PACKAGE.

crater *n.* hollow, opening, abyss; see HOLE 1.

craving *n.* need, longing, yearning; see DESIRE 1.

crawl *v.* creep, worm along, wriggle, squirm, slither, move on hands and knees, writhe, go on all fours, worm one's way, go on one's belly; see also GROVEL, SNEAK.

crayon *n.* chalk, pastel, colored wax; see PENCIL.

craze *n.* fad, rage, fashion; see FAD.

crazily *a.* furiously, irrationally, hastily, madly, rashly, insanely, psychotically, maniacally; see also VIOLENTLY, WILDLY.

crazy *a.* crazed, demented, mad; see INSANE 1. —**go crazy** become insane, lose one's wits, get angry; see RAGE 1.

cream (krēm) *n.* ⟦< OFr⟧ 1 the oily, yellowish part of milk 2 a cosmetic, emulsion, or food with a creamy consistency 3 the best part 4 yellowish white —*adj.* made of or with cream —*vt.* 1 to add cream to 2 to beat into a creamy consistency 3 [Slang] *a)* to beat or defeat soundly *b)* to hurt, etc., as by striking with great force —**cream of** creamed purée of —**cream'y, -i·er, -i·est,** *adj.* —**cream'·i·ness** *n.*

cream cheese a soft, white cheese made of cream or of milk and cream

cream'er *n.* 1 a pitcher for cream 2 a nondairy substance used in place of cream

cream'ery (-ər ē) *n., pl.* **-ies** a place where dairy products are processed or sold

cream of tartar a white substance used in baking powder, medicine, etc.

crease (krēs) *n.* ⟦< ME *creste,* crest⟧ 1 a line made by folding and pressing 2 a fold or wrinkle —*vt.* **creased, creas'ing** 1 to make a crease in 2 to wrinkle —*vi.* to become creased

cre·ate (krē āt') *vt.* **-at'ed, -at'ing** ⟦< L *creare*⟧ 1 to cause to come into existence; make; originate 2 to bring about; give rise to; cause

crea'tion (-ā'shən) *n.* 1 a creating or being created 2 the universe 3 anything created —**the Creation** God's creating of the world

creation science a theory of the origin of the universe stating that the biblical account of creation can be verified scientifically

crea'tive (-āt'iv) *adj.* 1 creating or able to create 2 inventive 3 stimulating the imagination —**crea'tively** *adv.* —**cre'a·tiv'ity** (-ā tiv'ə tē) *n.*

crea'tor (-āt'ər) *n.* ⟦L⟧ one who creates —[C-] God

crea·ture (krē'chər) *n.* ⟦< L *creatura*⟧ a living being, animal or human

crèche (kresh, krāsh) *n.* ⟦Fr⟧ a display of the stable scene of Jesus' birth

cre·dence (krēd'ns) *n.* ⟦< L *credere,* believe⟧ belief, esp. in the reports or testimony of another

cre·den·tial (kri den'shəl) *n.* ⟦see prec.⟧ [usually pl.] a letter or certificate showing one's right to a certain position or authority

cre·denza (kri den'zə) *n.* ⟦It⟧ a type of buffet or sideboard

credibility gap 1 a disparity between what is said and the facts 2 the inability to have one's truthfulness or honesty accepted

cred·ible (kred'ə bəl) *adj.* ⟦< L *credere,* believe⟧ that can be believed; reliable —**cred·ibil'ity** *n.* —**cred'ibly** *adv.*

credit (kred'it) *n.* ⟦< L *credere,* believe⟧ 1 belief; confidence 2 favorable reputation 3 praise or approval 4 a person or thing bringing approval or honor 5 *a)* acknowledgment of work done *b)* [pl.] a list of such acknowledgments in a movie, book, etc. 6 a sum available to one, as in a bank account 7 the entry, in an account, of payment on a debt 8 trust in one's ability to meet payments when due 9 the time allowed for payment 10 a completed unit of study in a school —*vt.* 1 to believe; trust 2 to give credit to or commendation for 3 to give credit in a bank account, etc. —**do credit to** to bring honor to —**on credit** agreeing to pay later

cred'it·able *adj.* deserving some credit or praise —**cred'it·ably** *adv.*

credit card a card entitling one to charge purchases, etc. at certain businesses

cred'i·tor (-it ər) *n.* one to whom money is owed

credit union a cooperative association for pooling savings of members and making low-interest loans to them

credo (krē'dō, krā'-) *n., pl.* **-dos'** ⟦L, I believe⟧ a creed

credu·lous (krej'oo ləs, -ə ləs) *adj.* ⟦< L *credere,* believe⟧ tending to believe too readily —**cre·du·lity** (krə dōō'lə tē, -dyoo-) *n.* —**cred'u·lously** *adv.*

creed (krēd) *n.* ⟦< L *credo,* I believe⟧ 1 a brief statement of religious belief, esp. one accepted as authoritative by a church 2 any statement of belief, principles, etc.

creek (krēk, krik) *n.* ⟦< ON *kriki,* a bend, winding⟧ a small stream —**up the creek** [Slang] in trouble

creel (krēl) *n.* ⟦< L *cratis,* wickerwork⟧ a wicker basket for holding fish

creep (krēp) *vi.* **crept, creep'ing** ⟦OE *creopan*⟧ 1 to move with the body close to the ground, as on hands and knees 2 to move slowly or stealthily 3 to grow along the ground or a wall, as ivy —*n.* 1 the act of creeping 2 [Slang] an annoying or disgusting person —**make one's flesh creep** to give one a feeling of fear, disgust, etc. —**the creeps** [Colloq.] a feeling of fear, disgust, etc. —**creep'er** *n.*

creep'y *adj.* **-i·er, -i·est** having or causing a feeling of fear or disgust —**creep'i·ly** *adv.* —**creep'i·ness** *n.*

cre·mains (krē mānz') *n.pl.* the ashes remaining after cremation

cre·mate (krē'māt', kri māt') *vt.* **-mat'ed, -mat'ing** ⟦< L *cremare*⟧ to burn (a dead body) to ashes —**cre·ma'tion** *n.*

cre·ma·tory (krē'mə tôr'ē, krem'ə-) *n., pl.* **-ries** a furnace for cremating Also **cre'ma·to'rium** (-ē əm), *pl.* **-ri·ums, -ria** (-ə), or **-ries** —*adj.* of or for cremation

crème de menthe (krem' də mänt', krem'; krēm') ⟦Fr, cream of mint⟧ a sweet, mint-flavored liqueur

crème fraîche (krem' fresh') ⟦Fr, fresh cream⟧ slightly fermented high-fat cream, served with fresh fruit, etc. and used in sauces

cren·el·ate or **cren·el·late** (kren'əl āt') *vt.* **-el·at'ed, -el·lat'ed, -el·at'ing** or **-el·lat'ing** ⟦< VL *crena,* a notch⟧ to furnish with battlements or with squared notches —**cren'ela'tion** or **cren'el·la'tion** *n.*

Cre·ole or **cre·ole** (krē'ōl') *n.* ⟦< Fr < Port *crioulo,* native⟧ 1 a person descended from the original French settlers of Louisiana 2 a person of mixed Creole and black descent 3 [c-] a language that develops when different languages remain in contact with each other —*adj.* [usually c-] prepared with sautéed tomatoes, green peppers, onions, spices, etc.

creo·sote (krē'ə sōt') *n.* ⟦< Gr *kreas,* flesh + *sōzein,* to save⟧ an oily liquid with a pungent odor, distilled from wood tar or coal tar: used as an antiseptic and as a wood preservative

---

THESAURUS

cream *n.* 1 [The fatty portion of milk] rich milk, creamy milk, crème, coffee cream, whipping cream, ice cream, half-and-half, butterfat; see also MILK. 2 [A creamy substance] emulsion, salve, jelly; see COSMETIC, LOTION.

creamy *a.* smooth, buttery, creamed; see RICH 2, SOFT 1.

crease *n.* tuck, overlap, pleat; see FOLD, WRINKLE.

crease *v.* double, rumple, plait; see FOLD 1, WRINKLE.

create *v.* make, produce, form, perform, cause to exist, bring into being, bring into existence, build, fashion, constitute, originate, generate, construct, discover, shape, forge, design, plan, fabricate, cause to be, conceive, give birth to; see also COMPOSE 2, INVENT 1, PRODUCE 2.

creation *n.* 1 [The process of creating] imagination, production, formulation; see CONCEPTION 1, MAKING. 2 [All that has been created] cosmos, nature, totality; see EARTH 1, UNIVERSE. 3 [A work of art] labor of love, masterpiece, brainchild*; see PRODUCTION 1.

creative *a.* formative, inventive, productive; see ARTISTIC, ORIGINAL 2.

Creator *n.* First Cause, Deity, Maker; see GOD.

creature *n.* creation, being, beast; see ANIMAL.

credential *n.* declaration, warrant, voucher; see CERTIFICATE, RECORD 1.

credibility *n.* likelihood, probability, chance; see POSSIBILITY 2.

credible *a.* trustworthy, dependable, sincere; see RELIABLE.

credit *n.* 1 [Belief] credence, reliance, confidence; see FAITH 1. 2 [Unencumbered funds] assets, stocks, bonds, paper credit, bank account, mortgages, liens, securities, debentures, cash; see also WEALTH. 3 [Permission to defer payment] extension, respite, continuance, trust; see also LOAN. —**do credit to** bring approval to, please, do honor to; see SATISFY 1. —**give credit to** believe in, rely on, have confidence in; see TRUST 1. —**give one credit for** believe in, rely on, have confidence in; see TRUST 1. —**on credit** on loan, delayed, postponed; see UNPAID 1. —**to one's credit** good, honorable, beneficial; see WORTHWHILE.

credit card *n.* charge card, smart card, plastic*, charge plate.

creditor *n.* realtor, lender, mortgager; see BANKER.

creed *n.* belief, doctrine, dogma; see FAITH 2.

creek *n.* stream, spring, brook; see RIVER. —**up the creek** * in difficulty, desperate, lost; see in TROUBLE.

creep *v.* slither, writhe, worm along; see CRAWL.

creeping *a.* crawling, worming, squirming, writhing, wriggling, crouching, cowering, slinking, skulking, inching, dragging, lagging, limping, faltering, shuffling, hobbling, sneaking, moving slowly, barely moving, going at a snail's place, worming along.

crepe or **crêpe** (krāp; *for 5, also* krep) *n.* ⟦< Fr < L *crispus,* curly⟧ 1 a thin, crinkled cloth of silk, rayon, wool, etc. 2 CRAPE (sense 2) 3 wrinkled soft rubber: also **crepe rubber** 4 thin paper like crepe: also **crepe paper** 5 a thin pancake, rolled and filled

crêpes su·zette (krāp′ sōō zet′) ⟦Fr⟧ crêpes rolled in a hot, orange-flavored sauce and served in flaming brandy

crept (krept) *vi. pt. & pp. of* CREEP

cre·scen·do (kri shen′dō′) *adj., adv.* ⟦It < L *crescere,* grow⟧ *Music* gradually increasing in loudness — *n., pl.* **-dos′** a gradual increase in loudness, force, etc.

cres·cent (kres′ənt) *n.* ⟦< L *crescere,* grow⟧ 1 a phase of a planet or a moon, when it appears to have one concave edge and one convex edge 2 anything shaped like this — *adj.* shaped like a crescent

cress (kres) *n.* ⟦OE *cressa*⟧ a plant, as watercress, whose leaves are used in salads

crest (krest) *n.* ⟦< L *crista*⟧ 1 any growth on the head of an animal, as a comb or tuft 2 a heraldic device placed on seals, silverware, etc. 3 the top line or surface; summit 4 the highest point, level, degree, etc. — *vi.* to form or reach a crest —**crested** (kres′tid) *adj.*

crest′fall′en *adj.* dejected, disheartened, or humbled

Cre·ta·ceous (kri tā′shəs, krē-) *adj.* ⟦< L *creta,* chalk⟧ of the latest period of the Mesozoic Era, marked by the dying out of dinosaurs, the rise of mammals and flowering plants, and the depositing of chalk beds

cre·tonne (krē tän′, krē′tän′) *n.* ⟦Fr, after *Creton,* village in Normandy⟧ a heavy, printed cotton or linen cloth, used for curtains, slipcovers, etc.

cre·vasse (krə vas′) *n.* ⟦Fr⟧ a deep crack, esp. in a glacier

crev·ice (krev′is) *n.* ⟦< L *crepare,* to rattle⟧ a narrow opening caused by a crack or split; fissure

crew[1] (krōō) *n.* ⟦< L *crescere,* grow⟧ a group of people working together ⟦a road *crew*⟧ —**crew′man,** *pl.* **-men,** *n.*

crew[2] (krōō) *vi.* [Chiefly Brit.] *alt. pt. of* CROW[2] (sense 1)

crew cut a man's haircut in which the hair is cropped close to the head

crewel (krōō′əl) *n.* ⟦ME *crule*⟧ a loosely twisted, worsted yarn used in embroidery —**crew′el·work′** *n.*

crib (krib) *n.* ⟦OE, ox stall⟧ 1 a rack or box for fodder 2 a small bed with high sides, for a baby 3 an enclosure for storing grain 4 an underwater structure serving as a pier, water intake, etc. 5 [Colloq.] a translation or other aid used dishonestly in doing schoolwork — *vt.* **cribbed, crib′bing** 1 to confine 2 to furnish with a crib 3 [Colloq.] to plagiarize — *vt.* [Colloq.] to do schoolwork dishonestly

crib·bage (krib′ij′) *n.* a card game in which the object is to form combinations for points

crib death SUDDEN INFANT DEATH SYNDROME

crick (krik) *n.* ⟦< ON *kriki,* bend⟧ a painful cramp in the neck, back, etc.

cricket[1] (krik′it) *n.* ⟦< OFr *criquer,* to creak⟧ a leaping insect similar to a grasshopper

cricket[2] (krik′it) *n.* ⟦OFr *criquet,* a bat⟧ an outdoor game played by two teams of eleven players each, using a ball, bats, and wickets

cried (krīd) *vi., vt. pt. & pp. of* CRY

crier (krī′ər) *n.* 1 one who cries 2 one who shouts out announcements, news, etc.

crime (krīm) *n.* ⟦< L *crimen,* offense⟧ 1 an act committed or omitted in violation of a law 2 a sin

crimi·nal (krim′ə nəl) *adj.* 1 having the nature of crime 2 relating to or guilty of crime — *n.* a person guilty of a crime —**crim′i·nal′ity** (-nal′ə tə) *n.* —**crim′i·nally** *adv.*

crim′i·nol′ogy (-näl′ə jē) *n.* the scientific study of crime and criminals —**crim′i·nol′o·gist** *n.*

crimp (krimp) *vt.* ⟦< MDu *crimpen,* to wrinkle⟧ 1 to press into narrow folds; pleat 2 to curl (hair) — *n.* 1 a crimping 2 anything crimped —**put a crimp in** [Colloq.] to hinder

crim·son (krim′zən, -sən) *n.* ⟦< Ar *qirmiz*⟧ deep red — *adj.* deep-red — *vt., vi.* to make or become crimson

cringe (krinj) *vi.* **cringed, cring′ing** ⟦< OE *cringan,* to fall (in battle)⟧ 1 to draw back, crouch, etc., as when afraid; cower 2 to fawn

crin·kle (kriŋ′kəl) *vi., vt.* **-kled, -kling** ⟦see prec.⟧ 1 to wrinkle 2 to rustle, as crushed paper —**crin′kly, -klier, -kli·est,** *adj.*

crino·line (krin′ə lin′) *n.* ⟦Fr < It < *crino,* horsehair + *lino,* linen⟧ 1 a coarse, stiff cloth used as a lining in garments 2 HOOP SKIRT

crip·ple (krip′əl) *n.* ⟦< OE *creopan,* to creep⟧ one who is lame or otherwise disabled — *vt.* **-pled, -pling** 1 to lame 2 to disable; impair

cri·sis (krī′sis) *n., pl.* **-ses′** (-sēz′) ⟦L < Gr *krinein,* to separate⟧ 1 the turning point of a disease for better or worse 2 a decisive or crucial time, stage, or event

crisp (krisp) *adj.* ⟦< L *crispus,* curly⟧ 1 brittle; easily crumbled 2 fresh and firm 3 sharp and clear 4 fresh and invigorating 5 curled and wiry Also **crisp′y** —**crisp′ly** *adv.* —**crisp′ness** *n.*

criss·cross (kris′krôs′) *n.* ⟦ME *Christcros,* Christ's cross⟧ a mark or pattern made of crossed lines — *adj.* marked by crossing lines — *vt.* to mark with crossing lines — *vi.* to move crosswise — *adv.* 1 crosswise 2 awry

cri·teri·on (krī tir′ē ən) *n., pl.* **-ria** (-ē ə) *or* **-ri·ons** ⟦< Gr *kritēs,* judge⟧ a standard, rule, or test by which something can be judged

critic (krit′ik) *n.* ⟦< Gr *krinein,* discern⟧ 1 one who judges books, music, plays, etc., as for a newspaper 2 one who finds fault

crit′i·cal (-i kəl) *adj.* 1 tending to find fault 2 of critics or criticism 3 of or forming a crisis; decisive —**crit′i·cally** *adv.*

THESAURUS

crevice *n.* chasm, cleft, slit; see GAP 3.

crew[1] *n.* 1 [Company of seamen] seafarers, sailors, hands, able seamen, ship's company, mariners, sea dogs, gobs*. 2 [A group of men organized to do a particular job] company, troupe, squad; see ORGANIZATION 2, TEAM 1.

crime *n.* transgression, misdemeanor, vice, outrage, wickedness, immorality, infringement, depravity, evil behavior, wrongdoing, misconduct, corruption, delinquency, wrong, trespass, malefaction, dereliction, lawlessness, atrocity, felony, capital crime, offense, white-collar crime*, scandal, infraction, violation, cold-blooded crime, mortal sin, homicide, voluntary manslaughter, involuntary manslaughter, simple assault, aggravated assault, battery, larceny, robbery, burglary, holdup, kidnapping, swindling, fraud, defrauding, embezzlement, smuggling, extortion, bribery, mugging, rape, statutory rape, attack, sexual molestation, breach of promise, malicious mischief, breach of the peace, libel, perjury, fornication, sodomy, conspiracy, counterfeiting, inciting to revolt, sedition; see also CORRUPTION, EVIL 2, MURDER, RAPE, SIN, THEFT, TREASON.

criminal *a.* unlawful, felonious, illegal; see BAD 1.

criminal *n.* lawbreaker, felon, crook. *Criminals include the following:* murderer, killer, desperado, thug, gangster, gang leader, burglar, safecracker, swindler, clip artist*, confidence man, con man*, thief, bandit, second-story man*, cattle thief, cattle rustler, horse thief, automobile thief, pickpocket, counterfeiter, forger, smuggler, extortionist, kidnapper, gunman, trigger man*, accomplice, informer, stool pigeon*, stoolie*, squealer*, convict, con*, dope peddler, pusher*.

crimson *a.* blood-red, bright red, scarlet; see COLOR *n.,* RED *n.*

cringe *v.* flinch, quail, wince; see COWER, CRAWL.

crinkle *v.* coil, wind, crease; see WRINKLE.

cripple *v.* stifle, mangle, injure; see HURT.

crippled *a.* maimed, mutilated, mangled; see DEFORMED, DISABLED.

crisis *n.* straits, urgency, necessity, dilemma, puzzle, pressure, embarrassment, pinch, juncture, pass, change, contingency, situation, condition, plight, impasse, deadlock, predicament, corner, trauma, quandary, extremity, trial, crux, moment of truth, turning point, critical situation, pickle*, stew*, fix*, mess, big trouble*, hot water*. —*Ant.* STABILITY, normality, regularity.

crisp *a.* 1 [Fresh and firm] green, plump, firm; see FRESH 1, RIPE 1. 2 [Brisk] fresh, invigorating, bracing; see STIMULATING.

criterion *n.* basis, foundation, test, standard, rule, proof, scale, prototype, pattern, example, standard of judgment, standard of criticism, archetype, norm, original, precedent, fact, law, principle; see also MEASURE 2, MODEL 2.

critic *n.* 1 [One who makes adverse comments] faultfinder, censor, quibbler, detractor, slanderer, complainer, doubter, nagger, fretter, scolder, worrier, mud-slinger*.—*Ant.* BELIEVER, praiser, supporter. 2 [One who endeavors to interpret and judge] commentator, reviewer, analyst, connoisseur, writer of reviews, cartoonist, caricaturist, expert; see also EXAMINER, WRITER.

critical *a.* 1 [Disapproving] faultfinding, trenchant, derogatory, disapproving, hypercritical, demanding, satirical, cynical, nagging, scolding, condemning, censuring, reproachful,

crit'i·cism' (-ə siz'əm) *n.* **1** the act of making judgments, esp. of literary or artistic work **2** a review, article, etc. expressing such judgment **3** censure **4** the art, principles, or methods of critics

crit'i·cize' (-ə sīz') *vi.*, *vt.* **-cized'**, **-ciz'ing 1** to analyze and judge as a critic **2** to find fault (with) —**crit'i·ciz'able** *adj.* —**crit'i·ciz'er** *n.*

cri·tique (kri tēk') *n.* ⟦Fr⟧ a critical analysis or review — *vt.*, *vi.* **-tiqued'**, **-tiqu'ing** to criticize (a subject, art work, etc.)

crit·ter (krit'ər) *n.* dial. var. of CREATURE

croak (krōk) *vi.* ⟦echoic⟧ **1** to make a deep, hoarse sound, as a frog does **2** [Slang] to die — *vt.* to utter in deep, hoarse tones — *n.* a croaking sound

cro·chet (krō shā') *n.* ⟦Fr, small hook⟧ needlework done with one hooked needle — *vi.*, *vt.* **-cheted'** (-shād'), **-chet'ing** to do, or make by, crochet —**cro·chet'er** (-shā'ər) *n.*

crock (kräk) *n.* ⟦OE crocca⟧ an earthenware pot or jar — **crock'ery** *n.*

crocked (kräkt) *adj.* ⟦< crock, to disable⟧ [Slang] drunk

croco·dile (kräk'ə dīl') *n.* ⟦< Gr krokodilos, lizard⟧ a large, lizardlike reptile of tropical streams, having a long, narrow head with massive jaws

cro·cus (krō'kəs) *n.*, *pl.* **-cuses** or **-ci'** (-sī') ⟦< Gr krokos, saffron⟧ a spring-blooming plant of the iris family, with fleshy underground stems and a yellow, purple, or white flower

Croe·sus (krē'səs) *n.* ⟦after Croesus, a wealthy king of ancient times⟧ a very rich man

crois·sant (krōō sänt', krə sänt') *n.* ⟦Fr, crescent⟧ a crescent-shaped, flaky bread roll

Cro-Magnon (krō mag'nən) *adj.* ⟦after Cro-Magnon cave in France⟧ of a Stone Age type of tall human of the European continent

crone (krōn) *n.* ⟦< MDu kronje, old ewe⟧ an ugly, withered old woman

crony (krō'nē) *n.*, *pl.* **-nies** ⟦< Gr chronos, time⟧ a close friend

crook (krook) *n.* ⟦< ON krōkr, hook⟧ **1** a hooked or curved staff, etc.; hook **2** a bend or curve **3** [Colloq.] a swindler — *vt.*, *vi.* **crooked** (krookt), **crook'ing** to bend or curve

crooked (krookt; for 2 & 3 krook'id) *adj.* **1** having a crook **2** not straight; bent **3** dishonest —**crook'edly** *adv.* — **crook'ed·ness** *n.*

crook'neck' *n.* a squash with a long, curved neck

croon (krōōn) *vi.*, *vt.* ⟦ME cronen⟧ to sing or hum in a low, gentle tone — *n.* a low, gentle singing or humming — **croon'er** *n.*

crop (kräp) *n.* ⟦OE croppa, a cluster⟧ **1** a saclike part of a bird's gullet, in which food is stored before digestion **2** any agricultural product, growing or harvested **3** the yield of any product in one season or place **4** a group **5** the handle of a whip **6** a riding whip **7** hair cut close to the head — *vt.* **cropped**, **crop'ping 1** to cut or bite off the tops or ends of **2** to reap **3** to cut short —**crop out** (or **up**) to appear unexpectedly

crop'-dust'ing *n.* the spraying of crops with pesticides from an airplane —**crop'-dust'** *vi.*, *vt.*

crop'per *n.* **1** one that crops **2** a sharecropper —**come a cropper** [Colloq.] to come to ruin; fail

cro·quet (krō kā') *n.* ⟦Fr, dial. form of crochet, small hook⟧ an outdoor game in which the players use mallets to drive a ball through hoops in the ground

cro·quette (krō ket') *n.* ⟦Fr < croquer, to crunch⟧ a small mass of meat, fish, etc. fried in deep fat

cro·sier (krō'zhər) *n.* ⟦< OFr croce⟧ the staff carried by a bishop or abbot

cross (krôs) *n.* ⟦< L crux⟧ **1** an upright post with a bar across it, on which the ancient Romans executed people **2** a representation of this as a symbol of the crucifixion of Jesus, hence of Christianity **3** any trouble or affliction **4** any design or mark made by two intersecting lines, bars, etc. **5** a crossing of varieties or breeds — *vt.* **1** to make the sign of the cross (upon) **2** to place or lie across or crosswise **3** to intersect **4** to draw a line or lines across **5** to go or extend across **6** to meet and pass (each other) **7** to oppose **8** to interbreed (animals or plants) — *adj.* **1** lying or passing across **2** contrary; opposed **3** cranky; irritable **4** of mixed variety or breed —**cross off** (or **out**) to cancel as by drawing lines across —**cross one's mind** to come suddenly to one's mind —**cross one's path** to meet one —**cross'ly** *adv.*

cross'bar' *n.* a bar, line, or stripe placed crosswise

cross'beam' *n.* any transverse beam in a structure

cross'bones' *n.* a representation of two bones placed across each other, under a skull, used to symbolize death

cross'bow' (-bō') *n.* a weapon consisting of a bow set transversely on a wooden stock —**cross'bow'man**, *pl.* **-men**, *n.*

cross'breed' *vt.*, *vi.* **-bred'** (-bred'), **-breed'ing** HYBRIDIZE — *n.* HYBRID (sense 1)

cross'-coun'try *adj.*, *adv.* across open country or fields, as a race

cross'cut' **saw** a saw designed to cut across the grain of wood

cross'-exam'ine (-ig zam'in) *vt.*, *vi.* **-ined'**, **-in'ing** Law to question (a witness called by the opposing side) to challenge the witness's previous testimony —**cross'-exam'ina'tion** *n.*

cross'-eye' *n.* an abnormal condition in which the eyes are turned toward each other —**cross'-eyed'** (-īd') *adj.*

cross'hatch' (-hach') *vt.*, *vi.* to shade (a drawing) with two sets of parallel lines that cross each other

cross'ing *n.* **1** the act of passing across, interbreeding, etc. **2** an intersection, as of streets **3** a place where a street, etc. may be crossed

cross'piece' *n.* a piece lying across another

cross'-pol'linate' *vt.*, *vi.* **-nat'ed**, **-nat'ing** to transfer pollen from the anther of (a flower) to the stigma of (a genetically different flower) —**cross'-pol'lina'tion** *n.*

cross'-pur'pose *n.* a contrary purpose —**at cross-purposes** having a misunderstanding as to each other's purposes

cross'-ref'erence *n.* a reference from one part of a book, etc. to another — *vt.* **-enced**, **-encing** to provide (an index, etc.) with cross-references —**cross'-refer'** *vt.*, *vi.*

cross'road' *n.* **1** a road that crosses another **2** [usually pl., often with sing. v.] a) the place where roads intersect b) any center of activity, etc. c) a time of important changes or major decisions

cross section 1 a) a cutting through something b) a piece so cut off c) a representation of this **2** a representative part of a whole —**cross'-sec'tion** *n.*

cross'-town' *adj.* going across a city [a cross-town bus]

cross'walk' *n.* a lane marked off for pedestrians to use in crossing a street

cross'wise' (-wīz') *adv.* so as to cross; across Also **cross'ways'** (-wāz')

THESAURUS

disapproving, disparaging, exacting, sharp, cutting, biting; see also SARCASTIC. **2** [Capable of observing and judging] penetrating, perceptive, discerning; see DISCREET, OBSERVANT. **3** [Crucial] decisive, significant, deciding; see IMPORTANT 1.

criticism *n.* **1** [A serious estimate or interpretation] study, analysis, critique; see JUDGMENT 2, REVIEW 1. **2** [An adverse comment] caviling, carping, faultfinding; see OBJECTION.

criticize *v.* **1** [To make a considered criticism] study, probe, scrutinize; see ANALYZE, EXAMINE. **2** [To make adverse comments] chastise, reprove, reprimand; see BLAME.

crook* *n.* **1** [Criminal] swindler, thief, rogue; see CRIMINAL. **2** [A bend] fork, V, notch; see ANGLE 1.

crooked *a.* **1** [Having a crook]

curved, curving, hooked, devious, winding, bowed, spiral, serpentine, not straight, zigzag, twisted, meandering, tortuous, sinuous; see also ANGULAR, BENT, OBLIQUE.—*Ant.* STRAIGHT, unbent, direct. **2** [Dishonest] iniquitous, corrupt, nefarious; see DISHONEST.

crop *n.* harvest, yield, product, crops, reaping, hay, fodder, grains, vintage, fruits; see also PRODUCE.

cross *a.* jumpy, easily annoyed, pettish; see CRITICAL, IRRITABLE.

cross *n.* **1** [Religious symbol, especially of Christianity] crucifix, Greek cross, swastika, papal cross, Maltese cross, Latin cross. **2** [A tribulation] affliction, trial, misfortune; see DIFFICULTY 2. **3** [A mixed offspring] mongrel, crossbreed, half-breed; see HYBRID, MIXTURE 1.

cross *v.* **1** [To pass over] traverse, go across, go over, pass, ford, cut across, span. **2** [To lie across] intersect, lean on, rest across; see DIVIDE. **3** [To mix breeds] mingle, interbreed, cross-pollinate; see MIX 1.

cross-examine *v.* investigate, check, interrogate; see EXAMINE, QUESTION.

crossing *n.* **1** [A place to cross] intersection, overpass, crosswalk; see BRIDGE 1. **2** [A mixing of breeds] hybridization, interbreeding, cross-pollination; see MIXTURE 1.

crossroad *n.* intersecting road, service road, junction; see ROAD 1.

crosswise *a.* across, cross, perpendicular, transversely, vertically, horizontally, at right angles, awry, over, sideways, crisscross, askew, cross-

cross′word′ puzzle an arrangement of numbered squares to be filled in with the letters of words whose synonyms and definitions are given as clues

crotch (kräch) *n.* ⟦ME *crucche*, crutch⟧ 1 a forked place, as on a tree 2 the place where the legs fork from the human body

crotchet (kräch′it) *n.* ⟦< OFr *croc*, a hook⟧ a peculiar whim or stubborn notion —**crotch′ety** (-ē) *adj.*

crouch (krouch) *vi.* ⟦< OFr *croc*, a hook⟧ 1 to stoop or bend low 2 to cringe — *n.* a crouching position

croup (kro͞op) *n.* ⟦< obs. *croup*, speak hoarsely⟧ an inflammation of the respiratory passages, with labored breathing, hoarse coughing, etc.

crou·pier (kro͞o′pē ā′, -ər) *n.* ⟦Fr⟧ one in charge of a gambling table

crou·ton (kro͞o′tän′, kro͞o tän′) *n.* ⟦Fr < *croûte*, a crust⟧ a small, piece of toasted bread put in soup or a salad

crow[1] (krō) *n.* ⟦OE *crawa*⟧ a large, glossy-black bird with a harsh call —**as the crow flies** in a straight, direct line —**eat crow** [Colloq.] to admit an error

crow[2] (krō) *vi.* **crowed** or, for 1, [Chiefly Brit.] **crew** (kro͞o), **crowed**, **crow′ing** ⟦OE *crawan*⟧ 1 to make the shrill cry of a rooster 2 to boast in triumph 3 to make a sound of pleasure — *n.* a crowing sound

crow′bar′ *n.* a long metal bar used as a lever for prying, etc.

crowd (kroud) *vi.* ⟦OE *crudan*⟧ 1 to push one's way (*into*) 2 to throng — *vt.* 1 to press or push 2 to fill too full; cram — *n.* 1 a large number of people or things grouped closely 2 the common people; the masses 3 [Colloq.] a set; clique —**crowd′ed** *adj.*

crow′foot′ (krō′-) *n., pl.* **-foots′** or **-feet′** a plant of the buttercup family, with leaves resembling a crow's foot

crown (kroun) *n.* ⟦< Gr *korōnē*, wreath⟧ 1 a wreath worn on the head in victory 2 a reward; honor 3 a monarch's headdress 4 [*often* C-] *a*) the power of a monarch *b*) the monarch 5 a British coin equal to 25 (new) pence: no longer minted 6 the top part, as of the head 7 the highest quality, state, etc. of anything 8 *a*) the part of a tooth outside the gum *b*) an artificial substitute for this — *vt.* 1 to put a crown on 2 to make (a person) a monarch 3 to honor 4 to be the highest part of 5 to complete successfully

crown prince the male heir apparent to a throne — **crown princess**

crow's-foot (krōz′fo͞ot′) *n., pl.* **-feet′** any of the wrinkles that often develop at the outer corners of the eyes of adults

crow′s′-nest′ (-nest′) *n.* a lookout's platform high on a ship's mast

cro·zier (krō′zhər) *n.* CROSIER

CRT (sē′är′tē′) *n.* cathode-ray tube

cru·cial (kro͞o′shəl) *adj.* ⟦< L *crux*, a cross⟧ 1 decisive; critical 2 severe; difficult —**cru′cially** *adv.*

cru·ci·ble (kro͞o′sə bəl) *n.* ⟦ML *crucibulum*, lamp⟧ 1 a heat-resistant container for melting ores, metals, etc. 2 a severe trial

cru·ci·fix (kro͞o′sə fiks′) *n.* ⟦< L *crux*, a cross + *figere*, fasten⟧ a cross with the figure of the crucified Jesus Christ on it

cru′ci·fix′ion (-fik′shən) *n.* 1 a crucifying 2 [C-] the crucifying of Jesus, or a representation of this

cru′ci·form′ *adj.* formed in a cross

cru′ci·fy′ (-fī′) *vt.* **-fied′**, **-fy′ing** ⟦see CRUCIFIX⟧ 1 to execute by nailing to a cross and leaving to die 2 to be very cruel to; torment

crude (kro͞od) *adj.* **crud′er**, **crud′est** ⟦< L *crudus*, raw⟧ 1 in a raw or natural condition 2 lacking grace, taste, etc. 3 roughly made —**crude′ly** *adv.* —**crude′ness** *n.* —**cru·dity** (kro͞o′də tē) *n.*

cru·di·tés (kro͞o′də tā′) *n.pl.* ⟦Fr, raw things⟧ raw vegetables cut up and served as hors d'oeuvres, usually with a dip

cruel (kro͞o′əl) *adj.* ⟦see CRUDE⟧ causing pain and suffering; pitiless —**cru′elly** *adv.* —**cru′elty,** *pl.* **-ties,** *n.*

cruet (kro͞o′it) *n.* ⟦< OFr *crue*, earthen pot⟧ a small glass bottle to hold vinegar, oil, etc. for the table

cruise (kro͞oz) *vi.* **cruised, cruis′ing** ⟦< Du *kruisen*, to cross⟧ 1 to sail or ride about from place to place, as for pleasure or in search of something 2 to move at the most efficient speed for sustained travel 3 to operate at a predetermined speed by use of a regulating mechanism (**cruise control**) — *vt.* to sail or journey over or about — *n.* a cruising voyage

cruise missile a long-range, jet-propelled winged missile that can be launched from an airplane, submarine, ship, etc. and guided by remote control

cruis′er *n.* 1 anything that cruises, as a police car 2 a fast warship smaller than a battleship

crul·ler (krul′ər) *n.* ⟦Du < *krullen*, to curl⟧ a kind of twisted doughnut

crumb (krum) *n.* ⟦< OE *cruma*, scraping from bread crust⟧ 1 a small piece broken off, as of bread 2 any bit or scrap *[crumbs of knowledge]* — *vt. Cooking* to cover with crumbs —**crumby** (krum′ē), **-i·er, -i·est,** *adj.*

crum·ble (krum′bəl) *vt.* **-bled, -bling** ⟦< prec.⟧ to break into crumbs — *vi.* to fall to pieces —**crum′bly** (-blē), **-blier, -bli·est,** *adj.*

crummy (krum′ē) *adj.* **-mier, -mi·est** [Slang] shabby, mean, etc.

crum·pet (krum′pit) *n.* ⟦< OE *crump*, twisted⟧ a batter cake baked on a griddle

crum·ple (krum′pəl) *vt.* **-pled, -pling** ⟦< MDu *crimpen*, to wrinkle⟧ to crush together into wrinkles

crunch (krunch) *vi., vt.* ⟦echoic⟧ to chew, press, grind, etc. with a noisy, crackling sound — *n.* 1 the act or sound of crunching 2 [Slang] a showdown or tight situation —**crunch′y, -i·er, -i·est,** *adj.*

THESAURUS

ways; see also ANGULAR.

crotch *n.* 1 [Angle] fork, corner, elbow; see ANGLE 1, CURVE. 2 [Loins] pubic area, groin, pelvic girdle; see BODY 1.

crouch *v.* 1 [To stoop] dip, duck, bow; see BEND. 2 [To cower] cringe, flinch, quail; see COWER, CRAWL.

crowd *n.* host, horde, flock, mob, company, swarm, press, crush, surge, legion, rout, group, body, pack, army, drove, party, flood, throng, troupe, deluge, multitude, congregation, cluster, assembly, crew, herd, bunch, gang, batch; see also GATHERING.

crowd *v.* stuff, jam, squeeze; see PACK 2, PUSH 1.

crowded *a.* packed, huddled, crushed; see FULL 1.

crown *n.* diadem, headdress, tiara, coronet, circlet.

crown *v.* commission, authorize, invest, enable, sanction, inaugurate, fix, exalt, raise, heighten, set up, ennoble, establish; see also DELEGATE 1.

crucial *a.* 1 [Critical] decisive, climactic, deciding; see IMPORTANT 1. 2 [Severe] trying, taxing, hard; see DIFFICULT 1.

crude *a.* rude, rough, unpolished, in a raw state, homemade, thick, coarse,

harsh, rudimentary, homespun, rough-hewn, unfashioned, undeveloped, in the rough, raw, immature, sketchy; see also UNFINISHED 1.—*Ant.* FINISHED, polished, refined.

crudely *a.* clumsily, coarsely, impudently; see RUDELY.

cruel *a.* malevolent, spiteful, depraved, wicked, vengeful, evil, sinful, degenerate, brutish, demonic, rampant, outrageous, tyrannical, gross, demoralized, evil-minded, vicious, brutal, rough, wild, bestial, ferocious, monstrous, demoniac, debased, destructive, harmful, mischievous, callous, unnatural, merciless, sadistic, unpitying, unmerciful, unyielding, remorseless, pitiless, unfeeling, inflexible, bloodthirsty, unrelenting, relentless, grim, inhuman, atrocious, harsh, heartless, stony, unconcerned, knowing no mercy*, turning a deaf ear*, hard as nails*.—*Ant.* MERCIFUL, kindly, compassionate.

cruelly *a.* savagely, inhumanly, viciously; see BRUTALLY.

cruelty *n.* brutality, barbarity, sadism, inhumanity, barbarism, mercilessness, wickedness, coarseness, ruthlessness, severity, malice, rancor,

venom, coldness, unfeelingness, insensibility, indifference, fierceness, bestiality, ferocity, savagery, grimness, monstrousness, inflexibility, fiendishness, hardness of heart, bloodthirstiness, torture, relentlessness, persecution, harshness, heartlessness, atrocity; see also EVIL 1, 2, TYRANNY.—*Ant.* KINDNESS, benevolence, humanity.

cruise *n.* voyage, sail, jaunt; see JOURNEY.

cruise *v.* voyage, navigate, coast; see SAIL 1, TRAVEL.

cruiser *n.* cabin cruiser, boat, privateer; see SHIP.

crumb *n.* particle, scrap, pinch; see BIT 1.

crumble *v.* fall apart, decay, break up; see DISINTEGRATE.

crumbly *a.* breaking up, breaking down, falling to pieces, decayed, degenerated, perishing, deteriorating, soft, corroded, rusted, rotted, worn away, fragile, brittle, frail, rotten, breakable, eroded, disintegrated, tumbling down; see also DECAYING, GRITTY.—*Ant.* FIRM, sound, undecayed.

crumple *v.* rumple, crush, crease; see WRINKLE.

crup·per (krup′ər, kroop′-) *n.* 〚< OFr *crope*, rump〛 a leather strap attached to a saddle or harness and passed under a horse's tail

cru·sade (krōō sād′) *n.* 〚ult. < L *crux*, a cross〛 **1** [*sometimes* C-] any of the Christian military expeditions (11th-13th c.) to recover the Holy Land from the Muslims **2** vigorous, concerted action for some cause, or against some abuse — *vi.* **-sad′ed**, **-sad′ing** to engage in a crusade — **cru·sad′er** *n.*

cruse (krōōs, krōōz) *n.* 〚OE〛 a small container for water, oil, etc.

crush (krush) *vt.* 〚< OFr *croisir*, to crash, break〛 **1** to press with force so as to break or put out of shape **2** to grind or pound into small bits **3** to subdue; overwhelm **4** to extract by squeezing — *vi.* to become crushed — *n.* **1** a crushing; severe pressure **2** a crowded mass of people **3** [Colloq.] an infatuation —**crush′er** *n.*

crust (krust) *n.* 〚< L *crusta*〛 **1** the hard, outer part of bread **2** any dry, hard piece of bread **3** the pastry shell of a pie **4** any hard surface layer, as of snow **5** [Slang] insolence **6** *Geol.* the solid, outer layer of the earth — *vt., vi.* to cover or become covered with a crust —**crust′y**, **-i·er**, **-i·est**, *adj.*

crus·ta·cean (krus tā′shən) *n.* 〚see prec.〛 any of a class of arthropods, including shrimps, crabs, lobsters, etc. that have a hard outer shell

crutch (kruch) *n.* 〚OE *crycce*, staff〛 **1** a staff with a top crosspiece that fits under the armpit, used to aid the lame in walking **2** any prop or support

crux (kruks) *n.* 〚L, a cross〛 **1** a difficult problem **2** the essential or deciding point

cry (krī) *vi.* **cried**, **cry′ing** 〚< L *quiritare*, to wail〛 **1** to utter a loud sound, as in pain, fright, etc. **2** to sob and shed tears; weep **3** to plead or clamor (*for*) **4** to utter its characteristic call: said of an animal — *vt.* **1** to utter loudly; shout **2** to call out (wares for sale, etc.) — *n., pl.* **cries 1** a loud vocal sound; call; shout **2** a plea; appeal **3** a fit of weeping **4** the characteristic call of an animal —**a far cry** a great distance or difference

cry′ba·by *n., pl.* **-bies** one who complains constantly, in a childish way

cryo·gen·ics (krī′ō jen′iks, -ə-) *n.pl.* 〚< Gr *kryos*, cold + -GEN + -ICS〛 the science that deals with the production of very low temperatures and their effect on the properties of matter

cry′o·sur′gery *n.* 〚< Gr *kryos*, cold + SURGERY〛 surgery that destroys tissues by freezing

crypt (kript) *n.* 〚< Gr *kryptein*, to hide〛 an underground vault, esp. one under a church, used for burial

cryp·tic (krip′tik) *adj.* **1** hidden or mysterious; baffling **2** obscure and curt —**cryp′ti·cally** *adv.*

crypto- 〚see CRYPT〛 *combining form* **1** secret or hidden [*cryptogram*] **2** being secretly and not publicly [a *crypto*-Fascist]

crypto·gram (krip′tō gram′, -tə-) *n.* 〚prec. + -GRAM〛 a message in code or cipher

cryp·tog·ra·phy (krip tä′grə fē) *n.* 〚CRYPTO- + -GRAPHY〛 the art of writing or deciphering messages in code —**cryp·tog′ra·pher** *n.*

crys·tal (kris′təl) *n.* 〚< Gr *kryos*, frost〛 **1** a clear, transparent quartz **2** *a*) a very clear, brilliant glass *b*) articles of such glass, as goblets **3** anything clear like crystal, as the covering over a watch face **4** a solidified form of a substance having plane faces arranged in a symmetrical, three-dimensional pattern — *adj.* **1** of crystal **2** like crystal; clear

crys′tal·line (-in) *adj.* **1** made of crystals **2** like crystal in clearness, structure, etc.

crys′tal·lize′ (-īz′) *vi., vt.* **-lized′**, **-liz′ing 1** to become or cause to become crystalline **2** to take on or cause to take on a definite form —**crys′tal·li·za′tion** *n.*

cs. case(s)

Cs *Chem. symbol for* cesium

C′-sec′tion *n.* [Colloq.] CAESAREAN SECTION

CST Central Standard Time

ct. 1 cent **2** court

cu. cubic

Cu 〚L *cuprum*〛 *Chem. symbol for* copper

cub (kub) *n.* 〚< ? Ir *cuib*, whelp〛 **1** a young fox, bear, lion, whale, etc. **2** a youth or novice

cubby·hole (kub′ē hōl′) *n.* 〚< Brit dial. *cub*, little shed + HOLE〛 a small, enclosed space Also **cub′by**

cube (kyōōb) *n.* 〚< Gr *kybos*〛 **1** a solid with six equal, square sides **2** the product obtained by multiplying a given number by its square [the *cube* of 3 is 27] — *vt.* **cubed**, **cub′ing 1** to obtain the cube of (a number) **2** to cut or shape into cubes —**cub′er** *n.*

cube root the quantity of which a given quantity is the cube [the *cube root* of 8 is 2]

cu·bic (kyōō′bik) *adj.* **1** having the shape of a cube: also **cu′bi·cal 2** having three dimensions: a cubic foot is the volume of a cube one foot in length, width, and height

cu·bi·cle (kyōō′bi kəl) *n.* 〚< L *cubare*, lie down〛 a small compartment

cub·ism (kyōōb′iz′əm) *n.* a school of modern art characterized by the use of cubes and other geometric forms —**cub′ist** *n., adj.* —**cu·bis′tic** *adj.*

cu·bit (kyōō′bit) *n.* 〚< L *cubitum*〛 an ancient measure of length, about 18 to 22 inches

cuck·old (kuk′əld) *n.* 〚see fol.〛 a man whose wife has committed adultery — *vt.* to make a cuckold of —**cuck′oldry** (-rē) *n.*

cuck·oo (kōō′kōō′, kook′ōō) *n.* 〚< OFr *cucu*, echoic〛 **1** a gray-brown bird with a long, slender body: many species lay eggs in the nests of other birds **2** its call — *adj.* [Slang] crazy

cu·cum·ber (kyōō′kum′bər) *n.* 〚< L *cucumis*〛 a long, green-skinned fruit with firm, white flesh, used in salads or preserved as pickles

cud (kud) *n.* 〚OE *cudu*〛 a mouthful of swallowed food regurgitated from the first stomach of cattle and other ruminants and chewed again

cud·dle (kud′'l) *vt.* **-dled**, **-dling** 〚< ?〛 to embrace and fondle — *vi.* to lie close and snug

cud·dly (-lē) *adj.* **-dlier**, **-dli·est** that invites cuddling; lovable Also **cud′dle·some** (-'l səm)

cudg·el (kuj′əl) *n.* 〚< OE *cycgel*〛 a short, thick stick or club — *vt.* **-eled** or **-elled**, **-el·ing** or **-el·ling** to beat with a cudgel

cue¹ (kyōō) *n.* 〚< *q* (? for L *quando*, when) found in 16th-c. plays〛 **1** a signal in dialogue, etc. for an actor's entrance or speech **2** any signal to do something **3** a hint — *vt.* **cued**, **cu′ing** or **cue′ing** to give a cue to

cue² (kyōō) *n.* 〚var. of QUEUE〛 a long, tapering rod used in billiards and pool to strike the ball (**cue ball**)

cuff (kuf) *n.* 〚< ME *cuffe*, glove〛 **1** a band at the wrist end of a sleeve **2** a turned-up fold at the bottom of a trouser leg **3** a slap — *vt.* to slap —**off the cuff** [Slang] in an

---

THESAURUS

crush *v.* **1** [To break into small pieces] smash, pulverize, powder; see GRIND. **2** [To bruise severely] press, mash, bruise; see BEAT 1, BREAK 1. **3** [To defeat utterly] overwhelm, force down, annihilate; see DEFEAT 2.

crust *n.* **1** [A crisp covering] hull, rind, pie crust; see SHELL 1. **2** [The edge] verge, border, band; see EDGE 1.

cry *n.* **1** [A loud utterance] outcry, exclamation, clamor, shout, call, battle cry, halloo, hurrah, cheer, scream, shriek, yell, whoop, squall, groan, bellow, howl, bawl, holler, uproar, acclamation, roar; see also sense 2 and NOISE 2.—*Ant.* WHISPER, murmur, silence. **2** [A characteristic call] howl, hoot, wail, bawl, screech, bark, squawk, squeak, yelp, meow, whinny, moo, chatter, bay, cluck, crow, whine, pipe, trill, quack, clack,

cackle, caw, bellow, coo, whistle, gobble, hiss, growl; see also YELL. **3** [A fit of weeping] sobbing, wailing, shedding tears, sorrowing, mourning, whimpering; see also TEARS. —**a far cry (from)** unlike, dissimilar, opposed to; see DIFFERENT.

cry *v.* **1** [To weep] weep, sob, wail, shed tears, snivel, squall, lament, bewail, bemoan, moan, howl, keen, whimper, whine, weep over, complain, deplore, sorrow, grieve, fret, groan, burst into tears, choke up, cry one's eyes out, break down*, break up*, blubber, bawl.—*Ant.* LAUGH, rejoice, exult. **2** [To call; *said of other than human creatures*] howl, bark, hoot, scream, screech, squawk, squeak, yelp, grunt, roar, shriek, meow, whinny, moo, bawl, snarl, chatter, bay, cluck, crow, whine, pipe,

trill, coo, whistle, caw, bellow, quack, gabble, hiss, growl, croak, cackle, twitter, tweet; see also YELL.

crying *n.* shrieking, sorrow, sobbing; see TEARS. —**for crying out loud*** for God's sake; for heaven's sake; oh, no; see CURSE, NO.

crystallize *v.* become definite, take shape, be outlined; see FORM 4.

cub *n.* young, offspring, whelp; see ANIMAL.

cube *n.* six-sided solid, hexahedron, die; see SOLID.

cuddle *v.* snuggle, huddle, curl up; see NESTLE.

cue¹ *n.* prompt, warning signal, opening bars; see SIGN 1.

cuff *n.* **1** [Edge of a sleeve or pants leg] French cuff, armband, wristband; see BAND 1. **2** [A blow] slap, offhand manner; extemporaneously **—on the cuff** [Slang] on credit

cuff link a pair of linked buttons, or any similar small device for fastening a shirt cuff

cui·sine (kwē zēn', kwi-) *n.* ⟦Fr < L *coquere*, to cook⟧ **1** a style of cooking or preparing food **2** the food prepared, as at a restaurant

cul-de-sac (kul'də sak') *n., pl.* **-sacs'** ⟦Fr, bottom of a sack⟧ a blind alley

cu·li·nary (kyōō'lə ner'ē, kul'ə-) *adj.* ⟦< L *culina*, kitchen⟧ of cooking

cull (kul) *vt.* ⟦< L *colligere*, collect⟧ to pick out; select and gather **—** *n.* something picked out for rejection as not being up to standard

cul·mi·nate (kul'mə nāt') *vi.* **-nat'ed, -nat'ing** ⟦< L *culmen*, peak⟧ to reach its highest point or climax **—cul'mi·na'tion** *n.*

cu·lotte (kyōō lät', kōō-) *n.* ⟦Fr < L *culus*, posterior⟧ [*often pl.*] a woman's garment consisting of pants, usually knee-length, made to resemble a skirt

cul·pa·ble (kul'pə bəl) *adj.* ⟦< L *culpa*, fault⟧ deserving blame **—cul'pa·bil'i·ty** (-bil'ə tē) *n.* **—cul'pa·bly** *adv.*

cul·prit (kul'prit) *n.* ⟦< Anglo-Fr *culpable*, guilty + *prit*, ready (to prove)⟧ a person accused, or found guilty, of a crime

cult (kult) *n.* ⟦< L *cultus*, care, cultivation⟧ **1** a system of religious worship or ritual **2** devoted attachment to a person, principle, etc. **3** a sect **—cult'ism'** *n.* **—cult'ist** *n.*

cul·ti·vate (kul'tə vāt') *vt.* **-vat'ed, -vat'ing** ⟦< L *colere*, to till⟧ **1** to prepare (land) for growing crops; till **2** to loosen the soil and kill weeds around (plants) **3** to grow (plants) **4** to develop or improve [*cultivate* your mind] **5** to seek to become familiar with **—cul'ti·va·ble** (-və bəl) or **cul'ti·vat'a·ble** *adj.* **—cul'ti·va'tor** *n.*

cul·ti·va·tion *n.* **1** the act of cultivating **2** refinement, or culture

cul·ture (kul'chər) *n.* ⟦see CULT⟧ **1** cultivation of the soil **2** a growth of bacteria, etc. in a prepared substance **3** improvement of the mind, manners, etc. **4** development by special training or care **5** the skills, arts, etc. of a given people in a given period; civilization **—** *vt.* **-tured, -tur·ing** to cultivate **—cul'tural** *adj.* **—cul'tur·al·ly** *adv.*

culture shock the alienation, confusion, etc. that may be experienced by someone encountering new surroundings, a different culture, etc.

cul·vert (kul'vərt) *n.* ⟦< ?⟧ a drain or conduit under a road or embankment

cum·ber (kum'bər) *vt.* ⟦< OFr *combre*, barrier⟧ to hinder; hamper

cum'ber·some (-səm) *adj.* burdensome; unwieldy Also **cum'brous** (-brəs)

cumin (kum'in) *n.* ⟦< Gr *kyminon*⟧ a plant related to parsley and celery **2** its aromatic fruits, used for flavoring

cum·mer·bund (kum'ər bund') *n.* ⟦< Ar-Pers *kamar*, loins + Pers *band*, band⟧ a wide sash worn as a waistband, esp. with men's formal dress

cu·mu·la·tive (kyōō'myōō lāt'iv, -myə-; -lə tiv') *adj.* ⟦< L *cumulus*, a heap⟧ increasing in effect, size, etc. by successive additions **—cu'mu·la'tively** *adv.*

cu·mu·lus (kyōō'myōō ləs, -myə-) *n., pl.* **-li'** (-lī') ⟦L, a heap⟧ a white, billowy cloud type with a dark, flat base

cu·nei·form (kyōō nē'ə fôrm') *adj.* ⟦< L *cuneus*, a wedge + -FORM⟧ wedge-shaped, as the characters in ancient Assyrian and Babylonian inscriptions **—** *n.* cuneiform writing

cun·ning (kun'iŋ) *adj.* ⟦< ME *cunnen*, know⟧ **1** sly; crafty **2** made with skill **3** pretty; cute **—** *n.* slyness; craftiness **—cun'ningly** *adv.*

cup (kup) *n.* ⟦< L *cupa*, tub⟧ **1** a small, bowl-shaped container for beverages, usually with a handle **2** a cup and its contents **3** a cupful **4** anything shaped like a cup **—** *vt.* **cupped, cup'ping** to shape like a cup

cup·board (kub'ərd) *n.* a closet or cabinet with shelves for cups, plates, food, etc.

cup'cake' *n.* a small cake

cup'ful' *n., pl.* **-fuls'** as much as a cup will hold; specif., eight ounces

Cu·pid (kyōō'pid) *Rom. Myth.* the god of love **—** *n.* [c-] a representation of Cupid as a winged boy with bow and arrow

cu·pid·i·ty (kyōō pid'ə tē) *n.* ⟦< L *cupere*, to desire⟧ strong desire for wealth; avarice

cu·po·la (kyōō'pə lə) *n.* ⟦It < L *cupa*, a tub⟧ a small dome, etc. on a roof **—cu'po·laed** (-ləd) *adj.*

cur (kur) *n.* ⟦prob. < ON *kurra*, to growl⟧ **1** a dog of mixed breed; mongrel **2** a contemptible person

cu·rate (kyoor'it) *n.* ⟦< L *cura*, care⟧ a member of the clergy who assists a vicar or rector **—cu'racy** (-ə sē), *pl.* **-cies,** *n.*

cu·ra·tive (kyoor'ət iv) *adj.* having the power to cure **—** *n.* a remedy

cu·ra·tor (kyōō rāt'ər, kyoor'āt'ər) *n.* ⟦< L *curare*, take care of⟧ a person in charge of a museum, library, etc. **—cu·ra·to·rial** (kyoor'ə tôr'ē əl) *adj.*

curb (kurb) *n.* ⟦< L *curvus*, bent⟧ **1** a chain or strap attached to a horse's bit, used to check the horse **2** anything that checks or restrains **3** a stone or concrete edging along a street **—** *vt.* to restrain; control

curb service service offered to customers in parked cars, as at some restaurants

curb'stone' *n.* the stone or stones making up a curb

curd (kurd) *n.* ⟦< ME *crud*, coagulated substance⟧ [*often pl.*] the coagulated part of soured milk, from which cheese is made

cur·dle (kurd'l) *vt., vi.* **-dled, -dling** to form into curd; coagulate

cure (kyoor) *n.* ⟦< L *cura*, care⟧ **1** a healing or being healed **2** a remedy **3** a method of medical treatment **—** *vt.* **cured, cur'ing 1** to restore to health **2** to get rid of (an ailment, evil, etc.) **3** *a)* to preserve (meat), as by salting or smoking *b)* to process (tobacco, leather, etc.), as by drying or aging **—cur'able** *adj.* **—cur'er** *n.*

THESAURUS

punch, hit; see BLOW. **—off the cuff*** extemporaneous, unofficial, offhand; see INFORMAL. **—on the cuff*** on credit, charged, delayed; see UNPAID 1.

culminate *v.* finish, close, end up*; see END 1.

culprit *n.* offender, felon, fugitive; see CRIMINAL.

cult *n.* clique, clan, band; see FACTION, RELIGION 2.

cultivate *v.* **1** [Plant] till, garden, seed; see HARVEST, PLANT. **2** [Educate] nurture, refine, improve; see TEACH.

cultivation *n.* horticulture, agriculture, gardening; see FARMING.

cultural *a.* educational, socializing, refining, refined, constructive, influential, nurturing, disciplining, enlightening, civilizing, instructive, humanizing, beneficial, learned, educative, polishing, enriching, promoting, elevating, uplifting, ennobling, raising, broadening, expanding, widening, developmental.—*Ant.* PRIMITIVE, barbaric, crude.

culture *n.* **1** [Civilizing tradition] folklore, folkways, instruction, education, study, law, society, family, convention, habit, inheritance, learning, arts, sciences, custom, mores, knowledge, letters, literature, poetry, painting, music, lore, architecture, history, religion, humanism, the arts and sciences; see also CIVILIZATION.—*Ant.* DISORDER, barbarism, chaos. **2** [Refinement and education] breeding, gentility, enlightenment, learning, capacity, ability, skill, science, lore, education, training, art, perception, discrimination, finish, taste, grace, dignity, politeness, savoir-faire, manners, urbanity, dress, fashion, address, tact, nobility, kindness, polish; see also COURTESY 1, ELEGANCE, EXPERIENCE.—*Ant.* IGNORANCE, crudeness, vulgarity.

cultured *a.* cultivated, educated, informed, advanced, accomplished, enlightened, polished, well-bred, genteel, elegant, courteous, intellectual, sophisticated, sensitive, intelligent, *au courant* (French), able, well-read, up-to-date, well-informed, traveled, experienced, tolerant, understanding, appreciative, civilized, literary, urbane, mannerly, gently bred, chivalrous, erudite, gallant, lettered, high-brow*, high-class*; see also LIBERAL, POLITE, REFINED 2.—*Ant.* PREJUDICED, narrow, backward.

cunning *a.* clever, skillful, ingenious; see INTELLIGENT.

cup *n.* vessel, bowl, goblet, mug, tumbler, beaker, stein, bumper, teacup, coffee cup, measuring cup, chalice; see also CAN 1, CONTAINER.

cupboard *n.* closet, locker, storeroom; see FURNITURE.

curable *a.* improvable, subject to cure, not hopeless, correctable, capable of improvement, healable, restorable, mendable.

curb *n.* **1** [Restraint] hindrance, chain, check; see BARRIER, RESTRAINT 2. **2** [Edge] border, ledge, lip; see EDGE 1, RIM.

curb *v.* retard, impede, subdue; see HINDER, RESTRAIN, RESTRICT.

curdle *v.* coagulate, condense, clot; see THICKEN.

cure *n.* restorative, healing agent, antidote; see MEDICINE 2.

cure *v.* make healthy, restore, make whole; see HEAL.

curé (kyōō rā′) *n.* [Fr < L *cura*, care] in France, a parish priest

cure′-all *n.* something supposed to cure all ailments or evils

cu·ret·tage (kyōō ret′ij, kyōō′rə tăzh′) *n.* [Fr] the process of cleaning or scraping the walls of a body cavity with a spoonlike instrument

cur·few (kur′fyōō′) *n.* [< OFr *covrefeu*, lit., cover fire: orig. a nightly signal to cover fires and retire] a time in the evening beyond which children, etc. may not appear on the streets

Cu·ri·a (kyōō′rē ə, kyoor′ē ə) *n., pl.* **-riae** (-ē′) [L] the official body governing the Roman Catholic Church under the authority of the pope

cu·ri·o (kyoor′ē ō′) *n., pl.* **-os′** [contr. of fol.] an unusual or rare article

cu·ri·os·i·ty (kyoor′ē äs′ə tē) *n., pl.* **-ties** 1 a desire to learn 2 inquisitiveness 3 anything curious or rare

cu·ri·ous (kyoor′ē əs) *adj.* [< L *curiosus*, careful] 1 eager to learn or know 2 prying or inquisitive 3 unusual; strange —**cu′ri·ous·ly** *adv.*

curl (kurl) *vt.* [< ME *crul*, curly] 1 to twist (esp. hair) into ringlets 2 to cause to bend around — *vi.* to become curled — *n.* 1 a ringlet of hair 2 anything with a curled shape —**curl′er** *n.* —**curl′y, -i·er, -i·est,** *adj.*

cur·lew (kur′lōō′, kurl′yōō′) *n.* [echoic] a large, brownish wading bird with long legs

curli·cue (kurl′i kyōō′) *n.* [< CURLY + CUE²] a fancy curve, flourish, etc.

curl·ing (kurl′iŋ) *n.* a game for two teams, played on ice by sliding a flat stone toward a mark

cur·mudg·eon (kər muj′ən) *n.* [< ?] a surly, cantankerous person —**cur·mudg′eonly** *adj.*

cur·rant (kur′ənt) *n.* [ult. < *Corinth*, ancient Gr city] 1 a small, seedless raisin from the Mediterranean region 2 *a)* the sour berry of several species of hardy shrubs *b)* any such shrub

cur·ren·cy (kur′ən sē) *n., pl.* **-cies** [see fol.] 1 circulation 2 the money in circulation in any country 3 general use or acceptance

cur·rent (kur′ənt) *adj.* [< L *currere*, to run] 1 now going on; of the present time 2 circulating 3 commonly accepted; prevalent — *n.* 1 a flow of water or air in a definite direction 2 a general tendency 3 the flow or rate of flow of electricity in a conductor —**cur′rently** *adv.*

cur·ric·u·lum (kə rik′yōō ləm, -yə-) *n., pl.* **-la** (-lə) or **-lums** [L, course for racing] a course of study in a school —**cur·ric′u·lar** (-lər) *adj.*

curry¹ (kur′ē) *vt.* **-ried, -ry·ing** [< OFr *correier*, to put in order] 1 to rub down and clean the coat of (a horse, etc.) with a comb or brush 2 to prepare (tanned leather) 3 to try to win (favor) by flattery, etc.

curry² (kur′ē) *n., pl.* **-ries** [Tamil *kari*, sauce] 1 a powder prepared from various spices, or a sauce made with this 2 a stew made with curry — *vt.* **-ried, -ry·ing** to prepare with curry

cur′ry·comb′ *n.* a comb with teeth or ridges, for currying a horse — *vt.* to use a currycomb on

curse (kurs) *n.* [OE *curs*] 1 a calling on God or the gods to bring evil on some person or thing 2 a profane or obscene oath 3 evil coming as if in answer to a curse — *vt.* **cursed** or **curst, curs′ing** 1 to call evil down on 2 to swear at 3 to afflict — *vi.* to swear; blaspheme —**be cursed with** to suffer from

cursed (kur′sid, kurst) *adj.* 1 under a curse 2 deserving to be cursed; evil; hateful

cur·sive (kur′siv) *adj.* [ult. < L *currere*, to run] designating writing in which the letters are joined

cur·sor (kur′sər) *n.* [L, runner] a movable indicator light on a computer video screen marking the current position at which a character may be entered

cur·sory (kur′sə rē) *adj.* [ult. < L *currere*, to run] hastily, often superficially, done —**cur′so·ri·ly** *adv.*

curt (kurt) *adj.* [L *curtus*, short] brief, esp. to the point of rudeness —**curt′ly** *adv.* —**curt′ness** *n.*

cur·tail (kər tāl′) *vt.* [< L *curtus*, short] to cut short; reduce —**cur·tail′ment** *n.*

cur·tain (kurt′n) *n.* [< LL *cortina*] a piece of cloth, etc. hung at a window, in front of a stage, etc. to decorate or conceal — *vt.* to provide with or shut off as with a curtain

curtain call 1 a call, usually by applause, for performers to return to the stage 2 such a return

curtsy (kurt′sē) *n., pl.* **-sies** [var. of COURTESY] a woman's bow of greeting, respect, etc. made by bending the knees and lowering the body slightly — *vi.* **-sied, -sy·ing** to make a curtsy Also **curt′sey**

cur·va·ceous (kər vā′shəs) *adj.* [< CURVE] having a full, shapely figure: said of a woman

cur·va·ture (kur′və chər) *n.* 1 a curving or being curved 2 a curve

curve (kurv) *n.* [< L *curvus*, bent] 1 a line having no straight end; bend with no angles 2 something shaped like, or moving in, a curve — *vt., vi.* **curved, curv′ing** 1 to form a curve by bending 2 to move in a curve —**curv′y, -i·er, -i·est,** *adj.*

cur·vi·lin·ear (kur′və lin′ē ər) *adj.* consisting of or enclosed by curved lines

cush·ion (koosh′ən) *n.* [< ML *coxinum*] 1 a pillow or pad 2 a thing like this in shape or use 3 anything that absorbs shock — *vt.* to provide with a cushion

cushy (koosh′ē) *adj.* **-i·er, -i·est** [< Pers *khūsh*, pleasant] [Slang] easy; comfortable

cusp (kusp) *n.* [L *cuspis*] a point or pointed end, as on the chewing surface of a tooth

cus·pid (kus′pid) *n.* [see prec.] a tooth with one cusp; canine

cus·pi·dor (kus′pə dôr′) *n.* [< Port *cuspir*, to spit] a spittoon

cuss (kus) *n., vt., vi.* [Colloq.] CURSE

cus·tard (kus′tərd) *n.* [< L *crusta*, crust] a mixture of eggs, milk, sugar, etc., boiled or baked

cus·to·di·an (kus tō′dē ən, kəs-) *n.* [< fol.] 1 one who has something in one's custody or care; caretaker 2 a person

---

THESAURUS

curfew *n.* late hour, time limit, check-in time; see LIMITATION 2.

curiosity *n.* 1 [Interest] concern, regard, inquiring mind, inquisitiveness, thirst for knowledge, a questing mind, questioning, interest, desire to know, interest in learning, scientific interest, healthy curiosity. 2 [An unusual object] exoticism, rarity, marvel; see WONDER 2.

curious *a.* 1 [Strange or odd] rare, queer, unique; see UNUSUAL 2. 2 [Interested] inquiring, inquisitive, questioning; see INTERESTED 1.

curl *n.* coil, spiral, wave; see HAIR 1.

curl *v.* curve, coil, bend, spiral, crinkle, wind, twine, loop, crimp, scallop, lap, fold, roll, contort, form into a spiral, form into a curved shape, meander, ripple, buckle, zigzag, wrinkle, twirl.—*Ant.* STRAIGHTEN, uncurl, unbend.

curly *a.* curled, kinky, wavy, waving, coiled, crinkly, looped, winding, wound; see also ROLLED 1.

currency *n.* coin, bank notes, cash; see MONEY 1.

current *a.* prevailing, contemporary, in fashion; see FASHIONABLE, MODERN

1, POPULAR 3.

current *n.* drift, tidal motion, ebb and flow; see FLOW, TIDE.

curse *n.* 1 [Profanity] oath, blasphemy, obscenity, sacrilege, anathema, ban, cursing, profanity, denunciation, damning, cuss word, cussing, swearword*, four-letter word*. *Common exclamations and curses include the following (many of which are old-fashioned):* Lord, oh God, the Devil, bless my soul, bless me, mercy, gracious, goodness, in Heaven's name, gee*, sakes alive*, good night*, darn*, hang it all*, dang*, blast*, damn it*, damn*, by golly*, for crying out loud*, Judas Priest*, Jesus H. Christ*, hell's bells*, geez*. 2 [*Menstruation]* menses, period, red letter days*; see FLOW.

curse *v.* blaspheme, profane, swear, use foul language, be foul-mouthed, be obscene, take the Lord's name in vain, damn, turn the air blue*, abuse, revile, swear at, insult, call down curses on the head of, blast, doom, fulminate, denounce, call names, cuss*, cuss out*.

cursed *a.* blighted, doomed, confounded; see DAMNED 1.

curt *a.* brief, concise, terse; see SHORT 2.

curtain *n.* hanging, screen, shade, drape, drapery, window covering, blind. *Kinds of curtains include the following:* draw curtain, roller shade, shutter, portiere, cafe curtains, vertical blinds, Venetian blinds.

curve *n.* sweep, bow, arch, circuit, curvature, crook. *Types of curves include the following:* bell curve, bell-shaped curve, hairpin curve, S-curve, sine curve, extrapolated curve, hyperbolic curve, parabolic curve, normal curve, logarithmic curve, French curve, circle, ellipse, arc.

curve *v.* bow, crook, twist; see BEND.

curved *a.* bowed, arched, rounded; see BENT.

cushion *n.* mat, seat, rest; see PILLOW.

custodian *n.* superintendent, janitor, porter, cleaner, cleaning man, cleaning woman, attendant, caretaker, building superintendent, keeper, gatekeeper, night watchman;

responsible for the maintenance of a building —**cus·to′di·an·ship′** *n.*

cus·to·dy (kus′tə dē) *n., pl.* **-dies** ⟦< L *custos*, a guard⟧ a guarding or keeping safe; care —**in custody** under arrest —**cus·to′di·al** (-tō′dē əl) *adj.*

cus·tom (kus′təm) *n.* ⟦< L *com-*, intens. + *suere*, be accustomed⟧ **1** a usual practice; habit **2** social conventions carried on by tradition **3** [*pl.*] duties or taxes imposed on imported goods **4** the regular patronage of a business — *adj.* **1** made to order **2** making things to order

cus′tom·ar′y (-tə mer′ē) *adj.* in keeping with custom; usual; habitual —**cus′tom·ar′i·ly** *adv.*

cus′tom-built′ *adj.* built to order, to the customer′s specifications

cus′tomer *n.* a person who buys, esp. one who buys regularly

cus′tom·house′ *n.* an office where customs or duties are paid

cus′tom·ize′ (-īz′) *vt.* **-ized′, -iz′ing** to make according to individual specifications

cus′tom-made′ *adj.* made to order, to the customer′s specifications

cut (kut) *vt.* **cut, cut′ting** ⟦ME *cutten*⟧ **1** to make an opening in with a sharp-edged instrument; gash **2** to pierce sharply so as to hurt **3** to have (a new tooth) grow through the gum **4** to divide into parts with a sharp-edged instrument; sever **5** to hew **6** to reap **7** to reduce; curtail **8** to trim; pare **9** to divide (a pack of cards) **10** to make or do as by cutting **11** to hit (a ball) so that it spins **12** [Colloq.] to pretend not to recognize (a person) **13** [Colloq.] to be absent from (a school class, etc.) **14** [Slang] to stop — *vi.* **1** to pierce, sever, gash, etc. **2** to take cutting [*pine cuts easily*] **3** to go (*across* or *through*) **4** to swing a bat, etc. (*at* a ball) **5** to change direction suddenly — *adj.* **1** that has been cut **2** made or formed by cutting — *n.* **1** a cutting or being cut **2** a stroke or opening made by a sharp-edged instrument **3** a piece cut off, as of meat **4** a reduction **5** a passage or channel cut out **6** the style in which a thing is cut **7** an act, remark, etc. that hurts one′s feelings **8** a block or plate engraved for printing, or the impression from this **9** [Colloq.] an unauthorized absence from school, etc. **10** [Colloq.] a share, as of profits —**cut and dried 1** arranged beforehand **2** lifeless; dull —**cut down (on)** to reduce; lessen —**cut it out** [Colloq.] to stop doing what one is doing —**cut off 1** to sever **2** to stop abruptly; shut off —**cut out for** [Colloq.] suited for —**cut up 1** to cut into pieces **2** [Slang] to clown, joke, etc.

cu·ta·neous (kyoo tā′nē əs) *adj.* ⟦< L *cutis*, skin⟧ of or on the skin

cut′away′ *n.* a man′s formal coat cut so as to curve back to the tails

cut′back′ *n.* a reduction or discontinuance, as of production

cute (kyoot) *adj.* **cut′er, cut′est** ⟦< ACUTE⟧ [Colloq.] **1** clever; shrewd **2** pretty or attractive, esp. in a dainty way —**cute′ly** *adv.* —**cute′ness** *n.*

cutesy or **cute·sie** (kyoot′sē) *adj.* **-sier, -si·est** [Colloq.] cute in an affected way

cuti·cle (kyoot′i kəl) *n.* ⟦< L *cutis*, skin⟧ **1** the outer layer of the skin **2** hardened skin, as at the base and sides of a fingernail

cut·lass or **cut·las** (kut′ləs) *n.* ⟦< L *culter*, plowshare⟧ a short, thick, curved sword

cut·lery (kut′lər ē) *n.* ⟦< L *culter*, plowshare⟧ cutting implements, as knives; often, specif., eating implements

cut·let (kut′lit) *n.* ⟦< L *costa*, rib⟧ **1** a small slice of meat from the ribs or leg **2** a small, flat croquette of chopped meat or fish

cut′off′ *n.* a road, etc. that is a shortcut

cut′-rate′ *adj.* selling or on sale at a lower price

cut·ter (kut′ər) *n.* **1** a person or thing that cuts **2** a small, swift vessel

cut′throat′ *n.* a murderer — *adj.* **1** murderous **2** merciless; ruthless

cut·ting (kut′iŋ) *n.* a shoot cut away from a plant for rooting or grafting — *adj.* **1** that cuts; sharp **2** chilling or piercing **3** sarcastic; wounding —**cut′tingly** *adv.*

cuttle·fish (kut′′l fish′) *n., pl.* **-fish′** or (for different species) **-fish′es** ⟦OE *cudele*⟧ a sea mollusk with eight sucker-bearing arms and two tentacles and a hard internal shell (**cut′tle·bone′**)

cwt. hundredweight

-cy (sē) ⟦< L *-kia*⟧ *suffix* **1** quality, condition, or fact of being [*hesitancy*] **2** position, rank, or office of [*captaincy*]

cya·nide (sī′ə nīd′) *n.* a highly poisonous, white, crystalline compound

cy·ber·net·ics (sī′bər net′iks) *n.pl.* ⟦< Gr *kybernan*, to steer + -ICS⟧ [*with sing. v.*] the comparative study of human control systems, as the brain, and complex electronic systems —**cy′ber·net′ic** *adj.*

cy·ber·punk (sī′bər puŋk′) *n.* ⟦*cyber-* (see prec.) + PUNK[2]⟧ science fiction describing a future characterized by violence, computers, and drugs

cy·cla·men (sī′klə mən) *n.* ⟦< Gr *kyklaminos*⟧ a plant of the primrose family with heart-shaped leaves

cy·cle (sī′kəl) *n.* ⟦< Gr *kyklos*, a circle⟧ **1** *a*) a period of time within which a round of regularly recurring events is completed *b*) a complete set of such events **2** a series of poems or songs on one theme **3** a bicycle, motorcycle, etc. **4** *Elec.* one complete period of the reversal of an alternating current from positive to negative and back again — *vi.* **-cled, -cling** to ride a bicycle, etc. —**cy·clic** (sīk′lik) or **cy·cli·cal** (sīk′li kəl, sīk′-) *adj.*

cy·clist (sīk′list) *n.* a cycle rider

cyclo- ⟦< Gr *kyklos*, a circle⟧ *combining form* of a circle or wheel

cy·clom·eter (sī kläm′ət ər) *n.* ⟦prec. + -METER⟧ an instrument that records the revolutions of a wheel for measuring distance traveled

cy·clone (sī′klōn′) *n.* ⟦< Gr *kyklōma*, wheel⟧ a storm with strong winds rotating about a center of low pressure

---

■ THESAURUS ■

see also WATCHMAN.

custody *n.* care, guardianship, supervision, keeping, safekeeping, watch, superintendence, safeguard; see also MANAGEMENT. —**take into custody** capture, apprehend, seize; see ARREST.

custom *n.* habit, practice, usage, wont, fashion, routine, precedent, use, form, addiction, rule, procedure, observance, characteristic, second nature, matter of course, beaten path*, rut*, manner, way, mode, method, system, style, vogue, convention, habit, rule, practice, formality, form, mold, pattern, design, type, taste, character, ritual, rite, attitude, mores, dictate of society, unwritten law, etiquette, conventionality.— *Ant.* DEPARTURE, deviation, shift.

customarily *a.* usually, commonly, generally; see REGULARLY.

customary *a.* usual, wonted, habitual; see COMMON 1, CONVENTIONAL 1, 2.

customer *n.* clientele, patron, consumer; see BUYER.

cut *a.* **1** [Formed] shaped, modeled, arranged; see FORMED. **2** [Reduced] lowered, debased, marked down; see REDUCED 1, 2. **3** [Severed] split, divided, sliced through; see CARVED.

cut *n.* **1** [The using of a sharp instrument] slash, thrust, dig, prick, gouge, penetrating, dividing, separation, severance, slitting, hack, slice, carve, chop, stroke, incision, cleavage, penetration, gash, cleft, mark, nick, notch, opening, passage, groove, furrow, slit, wound, fissure; see also HOLE 1, INJURY. **2** [A reduction] decrease, diminution, lessening; see REDUCTION 1. **3** [The shape] fashion, figure, construction; see FORM 1. **4** [A section] segment, slice, portion; see PART 1, PIECE 1. **5** [A piece of butchered meat] piece, slice, chunk; see MEAT. **6** [*An insult] indignity, offense, abuse; see INSULT. —**a cut above** superior, higher, more capable or competent or efficient, etc.; see BETTER 1.

cut *v.* **1** [To sever] separate, slice through, slice, cut into, cleave, mow, prune, reap, shear, dice, chop down, chop, slit, split, cut apart, hew, fell, rip, saw through, chisel, cut away, snip, chip, quarter, clip, behead, scissor, bite, shave, dissect, bisect, amputate, gash, lance, truncate, lacerate, slash, notch, nick, indent, score, mark, scratch, rake, furrow, wound, gouge; see also CARVE. **2** [To cross] intersect, pass, move across; see CROSS 1. **3** [To shorten] curtail, delete, lessen; see DECREASE 2. **4** [To divide] split, break apart, separate; see DIVIDE. **5** [*To absent oneself] shirk, avoid, stay away; see EVADE. **6** [To record electronically] make a record, film, tape; see RECORD 3. — **cut back** reduce, curtail, shorten; see DECREASE 2. —**cut off 1** [To remove] eliminate, turn off, cut out; see REMOVE 1. **2** [To interrupt] intrude on, break in on, cut in; see INTERRUPT. —**cut out for** suitable, adequate, good for; see FIT. —**cut up 1** [To chop] chop up, slice, dice; see CUT 1. **2** [To cavort] show off, play jokes, fool around*; see JOKE, PLAY 2.

cute *a.* dainty, attractive, delightful; see CHARMING, PLEASANT 1, 2.

cycle *n.* revolution of time, period, recurrence; see AGE 3, SEQUENCE 1, SERIES.

cyclone fence a heavy-duty fence of interwoven steel links

Cy·clops (sī′kläps′) *n.*, *pl.* **Cy·clo·pes** (sī klō′pēz′) *Gr. Myth.* any of a race of one-eyed giants

cy·clo·tron (sī′klō trän′, -klə-) *n.* ⟦CYCLO- + (ELEC)TRON⟧ a circular apparatus for giving high energy to positive ions, as protons, etc., used in atomic research

cyg·net (sig′net, -nit) *n.* ⟦< Gr *kyknos*, swan⟧ a young swan

cyl·in·der (sil′ən dər) *n.* ⟦< Gr *kylindein*, to roll⟧ 1 a solid figure described by a line having end points in common with two equal, parallel, circular bases and moving parallel to a perpendicular axis 2 anything with this shape; specif., *a*) the turning part of a revolver *b*) the piston chamber of an engine —**cy·lin·dri·cal** (sə lin′dri kəl) *adj.*

cym·bal (sim′bəl) *n.* ⟦< Gr *kymbē*, hollow of a vessel⟧ *Music* a circular brass plate that makes a sharp, ringing sound when hit —**cym′bal·ist** *n.*

cynic (sin′ik) *n.* ⟦< Gr *kynikos*, doglike⟧ a cynical person

cyn′i·cal (-i kəl) *adj.* 1 denying the sincerity of people's motives and actions 2 sarcastic, sneering, etc. —**cyn′i·cally** *adv.*

cyn′i·cism′ (-ə siz′əm) *n.* 1 the attitude or beliefs of a cynic 2 a cynical remark, idea, etc.

cy·no·sure (sī′nə shoor′, sin′ə-) *n.* ⟦< Gr *kynosoura*, dog's tail⟧ a center of attention or interest

cy·press (sī′prəs) *n.* ⟦< Gr *kyparissos*⟧ 1 an evergreen tree with cones and dark foliage 2 its wood

cyst (sist) *n.* ⟦< Gr *kystis*, sac⟧ a saclike structure in plants or animals, esp. one filled with diseased matter —**cystic** (sis′tik) *adj.*

cystic fibrosis a children's disease marked by fibrosis of the pancreas and frequent respiratory infections

cy·tol·ogy (sī täl′ə jē) *n.* ⟦< Gr *kytos*, a hollow + -LOGY⟧ the branch of biology dealing with cells

cyto·plasm (sīt′ō plaz′əm) *n.* ⟦< Gr *kytos*, a hollow + *plasma*, something molded⟧ the protoplasm of a cell that is outside the nucleus

cy·to·sine (sīt′ō sēn′) *n.* ⟦Ger *zytosin*⟧ one of the four bases that combine to form DNA

czar (zär) *n.* ⟦Russ < L *Caesar*⟧ 1 the title of any of the former emperors of Russia 2 an autocrat —**cza·rina** (zä rē′nə) *n.fem.*

Czech (chek) *n.* 1 a member of a Slavic people of central Europe 2 the West Slavic language of the Czechs 3 a native or inhabitant of Czech Republic or, loosely, Czechoslovakia —*adj.* of the Czechs, their language, etc.

THESAURUS

cylinder *n.* 1 [An automobile part] compression chamber, combustion chamber, cylinder block; see AUTOMOBILE. 2 [A geometric form] circular cylinder, right cylinder, barrel; see CIRCLE 1.

cynic *n.* misanthrope, misogynist, mocker, satirist, scoffer, pessimist, sarcastic person, caviler, carper, sneerer, unbeliever, egotist, man-hater, skeptic, doubter, questioner, detractor, doubting Thomas; see also CRITIC 1.—*Ant.* BELIEVER, optimist, idealist.

cynical *a.* scornful, disrespectful, sneering; see SARCASTIC.

cynicism *n.* criticism, ridicule, contempt; see SARCASM.

czar *n.* emperor, autocrat, despot; see DICTATOR, KING, LEADER 2.

D

d or **D** (dē) *n.*, *pl.* **d's, D's** the fourth letter of the English alphabet

D (dē) *n.* **1** a Roman numeral for 500 **2** a grade for below-average work **3** *Music* the second tone in the scale of C major

'd 1 had or would: a shortened form used in contractions [*I'd* seen; *they'd* see] **2** old sp. of -ED [*foster'd*]

d or **d.** **1** day(s) **2** degree **3** diameter **4** died **5** [L *denarii*] penny; pence

D or **D.** **1** December **2** Democrat

DA or **D.A.** District Attorney

dab (dab) *vt.*, *vi.* **dabbed, dab'bing** [ME *dabben*, to strike] **1** to touch lightly and quickly; pat **2** to put on (paint, etc.) with light, quick strokes — *n.* **1** a tap; pat **2** a soft or moist bit of something

dab·ble (dab'əl) *vi.* **-bled, -bling** [Du *dabbelen*, freq. of MDu *dabben*, to strike, dab] **1** to play in water, as with the hands **2** to do something superficially: with *in* or *at* — **dab'bler** *n.*

dachs·hund (däks'hoont') *n.* [Ger < *dachs*, badger + *hund*, dog] a small dog with a long body, short legs, and drooping ears

Da·cron (dā'krän', dak'rän') *trademark* for a synthetic wrinkle-resistant fabric — *n.* [*also* d-] this fabric

dac·tyl (dak'til) *n.* [< Gr *daktylos*, finger] a metrical foot of three syllables, one accented and two unaccented — **dac·tyl'ic** (-til'ik) *adj.*

dad (dad) *n.* [< child's cry *dada*] [Colloq.] father: also **daddy** (dad'ē), *pl.* **-dies**

daddy long'legs' an arachnid with long legs

dado (dā'dō) *n.*, *pl.* **-does** [< L *datum*, a die] **1** the part of a pedestal between the cap and the base **2** the lower part of a wall if decorated differently from the upper part

dae·mon (dē'mən) *n.* [< Gr *daimōn*] **1** *Gr. Myth.* a secondary deity **2** a guardian spirit **3** DEMON (sense 1) — **dae·monic** (di män'ik) *adj.*

daf·fo·dil (daf'ə dil') *n.* [< Gr *asphodelos*] a narcissus with long leaves and yellow flowers

daffy (daf'ē) *adj.* **-fier, -fi·est** [< ME *dafte*, daft] [Colloq.] crazy; silly —**daf'fi·ness** *n.*

daft (daft) *adj.* [< OE (ge)*dæfte*, mild] **1** silly **2** insane

dag·ger (dag'ər) *n.* [< Prov *daga*] **1** a weapon with a short, pointed blade, used for stabbing **2** *Printing* a reference mark (†)

da·guerreo·type (də ger'ō tīp') *n.* [after L. J. M.

Daguerre, 19th-c. Fr inventor] an early kind of photograph made on a chemically treated plate — *vt.* **-typed', -typ'ing** to photograph by this method

dahlia (dal'yə, dal'-) *n.* [after A. *Dahl*, 18th-c. Swed botanist] a perennial plant with large, showy flowers

dai·li·ness (dā'lē nəs) *n.* the ordinary, routine aspects of a way of life

daily (dā'lē) *adj.* done, happening, or published every (week)day — *n.*, *pl.* **-lies** a daily newspaper — *adv.* every day

daily double a bet or betting procedure in which winning depends on choosing both winners in two specified races

dainty (dān'tē) *n.*, *pl.* **-ties** [< OFr *deinté*] a delicacy — *adj.* **-tier, -ti·est 1** delicious and choice **2** delicately pretty **3** *a*) of refined taste; fastidious *b*) squeamish — **dain'tily** *adv.* —**dain'ti·ness** *n.*

dai·quiri (dak'ər ē) *n.* [after *Daiquirí*, Cuban village] a cocktail made of rum, sugar, and lime or lemon juice

dairy (der'ē) *n.*, *pl.* **-ies** [ME *daie*, dairymaid] **1** a building or room where milk and cream are made into butter and cheese, etc. **2** a farm that produces, or a store that sells, milk and milk products —**dair'y·man** (-mən), *pl.* **-men,** *n.*

dair'y·ing *n.* the business of producing or selling dairy products

dais (dā'is) *n.*, *pl.* **da·ises** [< ML *discus*, table] a raised platform

daisy (dā'zē) *n.*, *pl.* **-sies** [< OE *dæges eage*, day's eye] a plant of the composite family, bearing flowers with white rays around a yellow disk

dale (dāl) *n.* [OE *dæl*] a valley

dally (dal'ē) *vi.* **-lied, -ly·ing** [< OFr *dalier*, to trifle] **1** to flirt **2** to deal carelessly (*with*); trifle **3** to waste time; loiter —**dal·li·ance** (dal'yəns, -ē əns) *n.*

Dal·ma·tian (dal mā'shən) *n.* a large, short-haired dog with dark spots on a white coat

dam¹ (dam) *n.* [ME] a barrier built to hold back flowing water — *vt.* **dammed, dam'ming 1** to build a dam in **2** to keep back or confine

dam² (dam) *n.* [see DAME] the female parent of any four-legged animal

dam·age (dam'ij) *n.* [< L *damnum*] **1** injury or harm resulting in a loss **2** [*pl.*] *Law* money compensating for injury, loss, etc. — *vt.* **-aged, -ag·ing** to do damage to — **dam'age·able** *adj.*

dam·ask (dam'əsk) *n.* [< It after *Damascus*, Syria] **1** a reversible fabric in figured weave, used for table linen, etc. **2** steel decorated with wavy lines **3** deep pink or rose — *adj.* **1** of or like damask **2** deep-pink or rose

dame (dām) *n.* [< L *domina*, lady] **1** [D-] in Great Britain, a woman's title of honor **2** [Slang] any woman

damn (dam) *vt.* **damned, damn'ing** [< L *damnare*, condemn] **1** to condemn to an unhappy fate **2** *Theol.* to condemn to hell **3** to condemn as bad, inferior, etc. **4** to

THESAURUS

dab *n.* small quantity, fragment, lump; see BIT 1.

dab *v.* tap, pat, nudge; see TOUCH 1.

dabble *v.* trifle, trifle, engage in superficially, amuse oneself with, dally, be an amateur, have sport with, fiddle with, flirt with, toy with, putter, idle away time, work superficially, putter around, fool with*, fool around*, dip into*.—*Ant.* STUDY, work at, become an expert.

dad* *n.* daddy*, male parent, pop*; see FATHER, PARENT.

dagger *n.* stiletto, point, blade; see KNIFE. —**look daggers at** glower, look at with anger, scowl at; see DISLIKE.

daily *a.* diurnal, per diem, every day, occurring every day, issued every day, periodic, cyclic, day after day, once daily, by day, once a day, during the day, day by day, from day to day; see also REGULAR 3.

dainty *a.* delicate, fragile, petite, frail, thin, light, pretty, beautiful, lovely, attractive, trim, graceful, fine, neat, elegant, exquisite, precious, rare, soft, tender, airy, lacy, nice, darling*, cute*, sweet; see also CHARMING, WEAK.—*Ant.* ROUGH, coarse, gross.

dairy *n.* creamery, dairy farm, ice-cream plant, cheese factory, buttery,

milk station, pasteurizing plant, cooperative; see also FARM.

dally with *v.* flirt with, trifle with, toy with; see DABBLE.

dam¹ *n.* dike, ditch, wall, bank, embankment, gate, levee, irrigation dam, beaver dam, cofferdam; see also BARRIER.

dam¹ *v.* hold back, check, obstruct, bar, slow, retard, restrict, stop up, close, clog, choke, block up, impede, hold, stop, block, confine; see also HINDER, RESTRAIN.—*Ant.* FREE, release, open up.

damage *n.* **1** [Injury] harm, hurt, wound, bruise, wrong, casualty, suffering, illness, stroke, affliction, accident, catastrophe, adversity, outrage, hardship, disturbance, mutilation, impairment, mishap, evil, blow, devastation, mischief, reverse; see also DISASTER, INJURY, MISFORTUNE.—*Ant.* BLESSING, benefit, boon. **2** [Loss occasioned by injury] ruin, breakage, ruined goods, wreckage, deprivation, waste, shrinkage, depreciation, pollution, corruption, blemish, contamination, defacement, degeneration, deterioration, ravage, havoc, erosion, disrepair, debasement, corrosion, wear and tear*, foul play; see also DESTRUCTION 2, LOSS 1.—*Ant.* IMPROVEMENT, betterment, growth.

damage *v.* ruin, wreck, tarnish, burn, scorch, dirty, rot, smash, bleach, drench, batter, discolor, mutilate, scratch, smudge, crack, bang up, abuse, maltreat, mar, deface, disfigure, mangle, contaminate, crumple, dismantle, cheapen, blight, disintegrate, pollute, ravage, sap, stain, tear, undermine, gnaw, corrode, break, split, stab, crack, pierce, lacerate, cripple, rust, warp, maim, mutilate, wound, taint, despoil, incapacitate, pervert, bruise, spoil, wear away, abuse, defile, wrong, corrupt, infect; see also BREAK, DESTROY.

damaged *a.* **1** [Less valuable than formerly] injured, in need of repair, in poor condition; see BROKEN 1, 2. **2** [Reduced in value because of damage] secondhand, used, leftover; see CHEAP 1.

damages *n.* reparations, costs, reimbursement; see EXPENSE, EXPENSES.

damn *v.* curse, ban, doom, banish, excommunicate, sentence, convict, excoriate, cast into hell, torment, condemn to hell, condemn to eternal punishment, call down curses on; see also CONDEMN.—*Ant.* FORGIVE, bless, elevate. —**not give a damn*** not care, be indifferent, reject; see NEGLECT 1. —**not worth a damn*** useless, unproductive, valueless; see swear at by saying "damn" — *n.* the saying of "damn" as a curse — *adj., adv.* [Colloq.] *short for* DAMNED — *interj.* an expression of anger, etc.

dam·na·ble (dam′nə bəl) *adj.* 1 deserving damnation 2 deserving to be sworn at —**dam′na·bly** *adv.*

dam·na·tion (-nā′shən) *n.* a damning or being damned — *interj.* an expression of anger, etc.

damned (damd) *adj.* 1 condemned, as to hell 2 [Colloq.] deserving cursing; outrageous — *adv.* [Colloq.] very

Dam·o·cles (dam′ə klēz′) *Classical Legend* a man whose king seated him under a sword hanging by a hair to show him the perils of a ruler's life

damp (damp) *n.* [MDu, vapor] a slight wetness — *adj.* somewhat moist or wet; humid — *vt.* 1 to bank (a fire) 2 to check or reduce —**damp′ness** *n.*

damp′-dry′ *vt.* **-dried′, -dry′ing** to dry (laundry) so that some moisture is retained — *adj.* designating of or laundry so treated

dampen (dam′pən) *vt.* 1 to make damp; moisten 2 to deaden, depress, or reduce — *vi.* to become damp —**damp′ener** *n.*

damp′er (-pər) *n.* [see DAMP] 1 anything that deadens or depresses 2 a valve in a flue to control the draft 3 a device to check vibration in piano strings

dam·sel (dam′zəl) *n.* [see DAME] [Old-fashioned] a girl; maiden

dam′sel·fly′ *n., pl.* **-flies′** a slow-flying, brightly colored dragonfly

dam·son (dam′zən) *n.* [ult. < L *Damascenus,* of Damascus, city in Syria] a small, purple plum

Dan. Danish

dance (dans) *vi.* **danced, danc′ing** [< OFr *danser*] 1 to move the body and feet in rhythm, ordinarily to music 2 to move lightly, rapidly, gaily, etc. — *vt.* 1 to perform (a dance) 2 to cause to dance — *n.* 1 rhythmic movement, ordinarily to music 2 a particular kind of dance 3 the art of dancing 4 a party for dancing 5 a piece of music for dancing 6 rapid movement —**danc′er** *n.*

D and C dilatation (of the cervix) and curettage (of the uterus)

dan·de·lion (dan′də lī′ən) *n.* [< OFr *dent,* tooth + *de,* of + *lion,* lion] a common weed with yellow flowers

dan·der (dan′dər) *n.* [< ?] [Colloq.] anger or temper

dan·dle (dan′dəl) *vt.* **-dled, -dling** [< ?] to dance (a child) up and down on the knee or in the arms

dan·druff (dan′drəf) *n.* [< earlier *dandro* + dial. *hurf,* scab] little scales of dead skin on the scalp

dandy (dan′dē) *n., pl.* **-dies** [< ?] 1 a man overly attentive to his clothes and appearance 2 [Colloq.] something very good — *adj.* **-dier, -di·est** [Colloq.] very good; fine

Dane (dān) *n.* a native or inhabitant of Denmark

dan·ger (dān′jər) *n.* [ult. < L *dominus,* a master] 1 liability to injury, damage, loss, etc.; peril 2 a thing that may cause injury, pain, etc.

dan′ger·ous *adj.* full of danger; unsafe —**dan′ger·ously** *adv.*

dan·gle (daŋ′gəl) *vi.* **-gled, -gling** [< Scand] to hang swinging loosely — *vt.* to cause to dangle —**dan′gler** *n.*

Dan·iel (dan′yəl) *Bible* a Hebrew prophet whose faith saved him in the lions' den

Dan·ish (dān′ish) *adj.* of Denmark, the Danes, or their language — *n.* 1 the language of the Danes 2 [*also* **d-**] (a) rich, flaky pastry filled with fruit, cheese, etc.: in full **Danish pastry**

D'An·jou pear (dan′jōō) ANJOU PEAR

dank (daŋk) *adj.* [ME] disagreeably damp —**dank′ly** *adv.* —**dank′ness** *n.*

dan·seuse (dän sooz′) *n.* [Fr] a female ballet dancer

dap·per (dap′ər) *adj.* [MDu, nimble] 1 small and active 2 trim; neat

dap·ple (dap′əl) *adj.* [< ON *depill,* a spot] marked with spots; mottled: also **dap′pled** — *vt.* **-pled, -pling** to cover with spots

dare (der) *vt., vi.* **dared** or [Now Chiefly Dial.] **durst, dared, dar′ing** [OE *durran*] 1 to have enough courage for (some act) 2 to face (something) bravely 3 to challenge (someone) to do something — *n.* a challenge —**dare** *say* to think probable —**dar′er** *n.*

dare′dev′il (-dev′əl) *adj.* bold and reckless — *n.* a bold, reckless person

dar′ing *adj.* fearless; bold — *n.* bold courage —**dar′ingly** *adv.*

dark (därk) *adj.* [< OE *deorc*] 1 entirely or partly without light 2 *a)* almost black *b)* not light in color 3 hidden 4 gloomy 5 evil 6 ignorant — *n.* 1 the state of being dark 2 night —**dark′ly** *adv.* —**dark′ness** *n.*

Dark Ages [< prec., *adj.* 6] the Middle Ages, esp. the earlier part

dark′en *vt., vi.* to make or become dark or darker —**dark′ener** *n.*

dark horse [Colloq.] a little-known contestant thought unlikely to win

---

THESAURUS

WORTHLESS.

damnation *n.* damning, condemnation, doom; see BLAME, CURSE.

damned *a.* 1 [Consigned to hell] cursed, condemned, accursed, lost, infernal, gone to blazes*; see also UNFORTUNATE.—*Ant.* BLESSED, saved, holy. 2 [*Disapproved of*] bad, unwelcome, blankety-blank*, blasted*, bloody*, danged*, darned*, doggone*, lousy*; see also BAD 1, UNDESIRABLE.—*Ant.* WELCOMED, desirable, favorite. —**do** (or **try**) **one's damnedest*** endeavor, do one's best, give one's all; see TRY 1.

damp *a.* moist, soaked, soggy; see WET 1.

dampen *v.* sprinkle, water, rinse; see MOISTEN.

dance *n.* 1 [Rhythmic movement] hop, jig, shuffle, fling, hoedown. *Dances include the following—social:* fox trot, polka, rhumba, tango, cha-cha, disco, mambo, samba, twist, jitterbug, two-step, box-step, Charleston, bunny hop, hokey-pokey; *theatrical:* ballet, modern dance, tap dance, soft-shoe; *traditional:* cotillion, polonaise, waltz, quadrille, pavane, mazurka, bolero, fandango, square dance, minuet, Virginia reel; *folkloristic and primitive:* sun dance, ghost dance, rain dance, sword dance, snake dance, fertility dance, Highland fling, flamenco, Irish jig, tarantella, hornpipe, clog, hora, hula. 2 [A dancing party] grand ball, dress ball, reception, ball, sock hop*, hoedown, shindig*, prom; see also PARTY 1.

dance *v.* waltz, shimmy, samba, jitterbug, twist, disco, fox-trot, cha-cha, mambo, tango, polka, hop, skip, jump, leap, bob, scamper, bounce, sway, swirl, sweep, swing, cut a rug*, rock*; see also MOVE 1.

dancer *n.* ballerina, chorus girl, showgirl, stripper*, hoofer*; ballet, tap, toe, hula, belly, go-go, folk, square, modern, flamenco, geisha, break, etc. dancer.

dandy* *n.* very good, fine, first-rate; see EXCELLENT.

danger *n.* uncertainty, risk, peril, jeopardy, threat, hazard, insecurity, instability, exposure, venture, menace, vulnerability; see also CHANCE 1.—*Ant.* SAFETY, security, certainty.

dangerous *a.* perilous, critical, serious, pressing, vital, vulnerable, exposed, full of risk, threatening, alarming, urgent, hazardous, risky, menacing, serious, ugly, nasty, formidable, terrible, deadly, insecure, precarious, ticklish, delicate, unstable, touchy, treacherous, bad, thorny, breakneck, shaky*, on a collision course*, hairy*, under fire*, unhealthy, hot*; see also ENDANGERED, UNCERTAIN, UNSAFE.—*Ant.* CERTAIN, sure, secure.

dangerously *a.* desperately, precariously, severely; see SERIOUSLY 1.

dangle *v.* hover, swing, suspend; see HANG 1, 2.

dare *v.* 1 [To be courageous] take a chance, venture, adventure, undertake, try, attempt, endeavor, try one's hand, hazard, take the bull by the horns*, go ahead, go for it*; see also CHANCE, RISK, TRY 1.—*Ant.* AVOID, dread, fear. 2 [To defy] meet, confront, oppose, disregard, brave, scorn, insult, resist, threaten, spurn, denounce, bully, mock, laugh at, challenge, have the nerve, have the courage of one's convictions, face the music*, face up to, call someone's bluff; see also FACE 1.—*Ant.* AVOID, shun, evade.

daredevil *n.* stunt man, madman, gambler; see ADVENTURER.

daring *a.* bold, courageous, fearless; see BRAVE.

dark *a.* 1 [Lacking illumination] unlighted, unlit, dim, shadowy, somber, cloudy, foggy, sunless, lightless, indistinct, dull, faint, vague, dusky, murky, gloomy, misty, obscure, nebulous, shady, shaded, clouded, darkened, overcast, opaque, without light, inky; see also BLACK 1, HAZY.—*Ant.* BRIGHT, lighted, illuminated. 2 [Dark in complexion] tan, swarthy, dark-complexioned; see BLACK 1. 3 [Evil] wicked, immoral, corrupt; see BAD 1.

dark *n.* gloom, evening, dusk; see DARKNESS 1. —**in the dark** uninformed, unaware, naive; see IGNORANT 1.

darken *v.* 1 [To grow darker] cloud up, cloud over, become dark; see SHADE 3. 2 [To make darker] cloud, shadow, blacken; see SHADE 2.

darkness *n.* 1 [Gloom] dark, dusk, murkiness, dimness, shade, blackness, pitch darkness, twilight,

dark′room′ *n.* a darkened room for developing photographs

dar·ling (där′liŋ) *n.* ⟦OE *deorling*⟧ a person much loved by another — *adj.* 1 very dear; beloved 2 [Colloq.] cute

darn[1] (därn) *vt., vi.* ⟦< Fr dial. *darner*⟧ to mend (cloth) by sewing a network of stitches across the gap — *n.* a darned place in fabric

darn[2] (därn) *vt., n., adj., adv., interj.* [Colloq.] damn: a euphemism —**darned** *adj., adv.*

dart (därt) *n.* ⟦< OFr⟧ 1 a small, pointed missile for throwing or shooting 2 a sudden movement 3 a short, tapered seam 4 [*pl., with sing. v.*] a game in which darts (see sense 1) are thrown at a target (**dartboard**) — *vt., vi.* to send out or move suddenly and fast

Dar·von (där′vän′) *trademark for* an analgesic drug containing a narcotic painkiller

Dar·win·ian (där win′ē ən) *adj.* ⟦after C. *Darwin*, 19th-c. Eng naturalist⟧ of Charles Darwin or his theory of evolution — *n.* a believer in this theory —**Dar′win·ism′** *n.*

dash (dash) *vt.* ⟦< Scand⟧ 1 to smash; destroy 2 to strike violently (*against*) 3 to throw or thrust (*away, down,* etc.) 4 to splash — *vi.* 1 to strike violently (*against*) 2 to rush — *n.* 1 a splash 2 a bit of something added 3 a rush 4 a short, fast race 5 spirit; vigor 6 the mark of punctuation (—) used to indicate a break, omission, etc. —**dash off** to do, write, etc. hastily —**dash′er** *n.*

dash′board′ *n.* a panel with controls and gauges, as in an automobile

da·shiki (dä shē′kē) *n.* a loosefitting, brightly colored robe modeled after an African tribal garment

dash′ing *adj.* 1 full of dash or spirit; lively 2 showy; striking —**dash′ingly** *adv.*

das·tard (das′tərd) *n.* ⟦ME, a craven⟧ a sneaky, cowardly evildoer

das′tardly *adj.* mean, cowardly, etc.

dat. dative

data (dāt′ə, dat′ə) *n.pl.* [*now usually with sing. v.*] facts or figures from which conclusions can be drawn

da·ta·base′ *n.* a mass of data in a computer, arranged for rapid expansion, updating, and retrieval: also **data base**

data processing the handling of large amounts of information, esp. by a computer —**data processor**

date[1] (dāt) *n.* ⟦< L *dare*, give⟧ 1 the time at which a thing happens, was made, etc. 2 the day of the month 3 *a*) an appointment *b*) a social engagement with a person of the opposite sex *c*) this person — *vt.* **dat′ed, dat′ing** 1 to mark (a letter, etc.) with a date 2 to find out or give the date of 3 to make seem old-fashioned 4 to have social engagements with — *vi.* 1 to belong to a definite period in the past 2 to date persons of the opposite sex —**dat′er** *n.*

date[2] (dāt) *n.* ⟦< Gr *daktylos*, a date⟧ the sweet, fleshy fruit of a desert palm tree (**date palm**)

date′line′ *n.* the date and place of writing or issue, as given in a line in a newspaper story, etc.

da·tive (dāt′iv) *n.* ⟦< L *dativus*, relating to giving⟧ *Gram.* the case of the indirect object of a verb

da·tum (dāt′əm, dat′-) *n.* ⟦L, what is given⟧ *sing. of* DATA

daub (dôb) *vt., vi.* ⟦< L *de-*, intens. + *albus*, white⟧ 1 to cover or smear with sticky, soft matter 2 to paint badly — *n.* 1 anything daubed on 2 a daubing stroke 3 a poorly painted picture —**daub′er** *n.*

daugh·ter (dôt′ər) *n.* ⟦< OE *dohtor*⟧ 1 a girl or woman as she is related to either or both parents 2 a female descendant —**daugh′terly** *adj.*

daugh′ter-in-law′ *n., pl.* **daugh′ters-in-law′** the wife of one's son

daunt (dônt) *vt.* ⟦< L *domare*, to tame⟧ to frighten or dishearten

daunt′less *adj.* that cannot be daunted or intimidated; fearless —**daunt′lessly** *adv.* —**daunt′less·ness** *n.*

dau·phin (dô′fin) *n.* ⟦Fr, dolphin⟧ the eldest son of the king of France: a title used from 1349 to 1830

dav·en·port (dav′ən pôrt′) *n.* ⟦< ?⟧ a large couch or sofa

Da·vid (dā′vid) *Bible* the second king of Israel and Judah

da·vit (dā′vit, dav′it) *n.* ⟦OFr dim. of *David*⟧ either of a pair of uprights on a ship for lowering or raising a small boat

daw·dle (dôd′'l) *vi., vt.* **-dled, -dling** ⟦< ?⟧ to waste (time) in trifling; loiter —**daw′dler** *n.*

dawn (dôn) *vi.* ⟦< OE *dagian*⟧ 1 to begin to be day 2 to begin to appear, develop, etc. 3 to begin to be understood or felt — *n.* 1 daybreak 2 the beginning (*of* something)

day (dā) *n.* ⟦OE *dæg*⟧ 1 the period of light between sunrise and sunset 2 the time (24 hours) that it takes the earth to rotate once on its axis 3 [*also pl.*] a period; era 4 a time of power, glory, etc. 5 daily work period [an 8-hour day] —**day after day** every day: also **day in, day out**

day′bed′ *n.* a couch that can also be used as a bed

day′break′ *n.* the time in the morning when light first appears

day care daytime care given to children, as at a day nursery, or to the elderly, as at a social agency —**day′-care′** *adj.*

day′dream′ *n.* 1 a pleasant, dreamy series of thoughts 2 a visionary scheme — *vi.* to have daydreams —**day′dream′er** *n.*

day′light′ *n.* 1 the light of day 2 dawn 3 understanding

daylight saving time [*often* D- S- T-] time that is one hour later than standard time

day nursery a place for daytime care of preschool children, as of working parents

Day of Atonement Yom Kippur

day′time′ *n.* the time between dawn and sunset

THESAURUS

eclipse, nightfall, obscurity, cloudiness; see also NIGHT 1. 2 [Evil] wickedness, sin, corruption; see EVIL 1. 3 [Secrecy] concealment, isolation, seclusion; see PRIVACY, SECRECY.

darling *n.* lover, sweetheart, dear one, beloved, dear heart, heart's desire, dearest, pet*, angel*, love, sweetie-pie*, sugar*, honey*, precious*, sweetie*, hon*, light of my life*, baby*, one and only*.

darn[1] *v.* mend, knit, embroider; see REPAIR, SEW.

dart *n.* missile, barb, arrow; see WEAPON.

dart *v.* shoot, shoot out, speed, plunge, launch, thrust, hurtle, fling, heave, pitch, dash, spurt, spring, spring up, fly, fire off*, scoot*; see also MOVE 1.—*Ant.* STOP, amble, loiter.

dash *n.* 1 [A short, swift movement] spurt, charge, rush; see RUN 1. 2 [Punctuation marking a break in thought] em, em dash, en dash, hyphen; see also MARK 1, PUNCTUATION. 3 [A little of something] a few drops, hint, sprinkle, scattering, seasoning, touch, grain, trace, suspicion, suggestion, squirt, taste; see also BIT 1, PART 1.—*Ant.* TOO MUCH, quantity, excess.

dash *v.* 1 [To discourage] dampen, dismay, dispirit; see DISCOURAGE. 2

[To sprint] race, speed, hurry; see RUN 1.

data *n.* evidence, reports, details, results, notes, documents, abstracts, testimony, facts, raw data, memorandums, statistics, figures, measurements, conclusions, information, circumstances, experiments, info*, dope*; see also DECLARATION, KNOWLEDGE 1, PROOF 1.

date[1] *n.* 1 [A specified time or period of time] epoch, period, era, generation, day, term, course, spell, duration, span, moment, year, reign, hour, century; see also AGE 3, TIME 2, YEAR. 2 [An appointment] meeting, rendezvous, engagement, interview, call, visit; see also APPOINTMENT 2. 3 [Person with whom one has a date] partner, companion, associate; see FRIEND, LOVER 1. —**out of date** obsolete, passé, antiquated; see OLD-FASHIONED. —**to date** until now, as yet, so far; see NOW 1. —**up to date** modern, contemporary, current; see FASHIONABLE.

date[1] *v.* 1 [To indicate historical time] ascertain the time of, determine, assign a time to, measure, mark with a date, fix the date of, chronicle, isolate, measure, carbon-date; see also DEFINE 1, MEASURE 1, RECORD 1. 2 [To court or be courted] escort, associate with, take out, keep

company with, go out with*, go together*, make a date with*, go steady*; see also ACCOMPANY.

daughter *n.* female child, girl, offspring, descendant, stepdaughter, infant; see also CHILD, GIRL.

dawn *n.* dawning, sunrise, daybreak; see MORNING 1.

day *n.* 1 [The time of light or work] daylight, daytime, full day, working day, daylight hours, eight-hour day, sizzler*, scorcher*; good, bad, hot, damp, etc. day. 2 [A special day] feast day, celebration, festival; see HOLIDAY. 3 [A period of time] era, age, time; see also AGE 3. —**call it a day** finish, quit working, end; see STOP 1. —**day after day** continually, monotonously, steadily; see REGULARLY. —**day in and day out** consistently, steadily, every day; see DAILY, REGULARLY. —**from day to day** without thought for the future, sporadically, as well as one can; see IRREGULARLY.

daydream *n.* trance, vision, fantasy; see DREAM.

daylight *n.* daytime, daylight hours, broad daylight; see DAY 1. —**scare (or beat or knock) the daylights out of*** frighten, scare, beat; see THREATEN.

day'-to-day' *adj.* daily; routine
daze (dāz) *vt.* **dazed, daz'ing** ⟦< ON *dasi,* tired⟧ to stun or bewilder —*n.* a dazed condition —**daz'edly** *adv.*
daz·zle (daz'əl) *vt., vi.* **-zled, -zling** ⟦freq. of DAZE⟧ **1** to overpower or be overpowered by bright light **2** to surprise or arouse admiration with brilliant qualities, display, etc. — *n.* a dazzling —**daz'zler** *n.*
db or **dB** decibel(s)
DC direct current Also **D.C., dc,** or **d.c.**
DD or **D.D.** Doctor of Divinity
DDS or **D.D.S.** Doctor of Dental Surgery
DDT (dē'dē'tē') *n.* ⟦< its chemical name⟧ a powerful insecticide
de- ⟦< Fr *dé-* or L *de*⟧ *prefix* **1** away from, off *[derail]* **2** down *[decline]* **3** entirely *[defunct]* **4** reverse the action of *[decode]*
DEA Drug Enforcement Administration
dea·con (dē'kən) *n.* ⟦< Gr *diakonos,* servant⟧ **1** a cleric ranking just below a priest **2** a church officer who helps the minister —**dea'con·ess** *n.fem.*
de·ac·ti·vate (dē ak'tə vāt') *vt.* **-vat'ed, -vat'ing 1** to make (an explosive, chemical, etc.) inactive **2** *Mil.* to demobilize —**de·ac'ti·va'tion** *n.*
dead (ded) *adj.* ⟦OE⟧ **1** no longer living **2** without life **3** deathlike **4** lacking warmth, interest, brightness, etc. **5** without feeling, motion, or power **6** extinguished; extinct **7** no longer used; obsolete **8** unerring *[a dead shot]* **9** complete *[a dead stop]* **10** [Colloq.] very tired —*n.* the time of most cold, most darkness, etc. *[the dead of night]* —*adv.* **1** completely **2** directly —**the dead** those who have died
dead'beat' *n.* [Slang] one who tries to evade paying debts
dead'bolt' *n.* a lock for a door, with a bolt that can be moved only by turning the key
deaden (ded''n) *vt.* **1** to lessen the vigor or intensity of; dull **2** to numb **3** to make soundproof
dead end 1 a street, alley, etc. closed at one end **2** an impasse —**dead'-end'** *adj.*
dead heat a race in which two or more contestants finish even
dead letter 1 a rule, law, etc. no longer enforced **2** an unclaimed letter
dead'line' *n.* the latest time by which something must be done
dead'lock' *n.* a standstill resulting from the action of equal and opposed forces —*vt., vi.* to bring or come to a deadlock
dead'ly *adj.* **-lier, -li·est 1** causing or likely to cause death **2** implacable **3** typical of death *[deadly pallor]* **4** extreme **5** very boring **6** very accurate — *adv.* extremely —**dead'li·ness** *n.*
dead'pan' *adj., adv.* without expression; blank(ly)
dead'wood' (-wood') *n.* anything useless or burdensome
deaf (def) *adj.* ⟦OE⟧ **1** unable to hear **2** unwilling to respond, as to a plea —**deaf'ness** *n.*
deaf'en (-ən) *vt.* **1** to make deaf **2** to overwhelm with noise —**deaf'en·ing** *adj.*

deaf'-mute' *n.* a person who is deaf and has not learned to speak
deal[1] (dēl) *vt.* **dealt** (delt), **deal'ing** ⟦< OE *dǽlan*⟧ **1** to portion out or distribute **2** to give; administer (a blow, etc.) **3** [Slang] to sell (illegal drugs) — *vi.* **1** to have to do *(with)* *[science deals with facts]* **2** to conduct oneself *[deal fairly with others]* **3** to do business; trade *(with* or *in)* — *n.* **1** the distributing of playing cards **2** a business transaction **3** a bargain or agreement, esp. when secret **4** [Colloq.] treatment *[a fair deal]* —**deal'er** *n.*
deal[2] (dēl) *n.* ⟦OE *dǽl,* a part⟧ an indefinite amount —**a good** (or **great**) **deal 1** a large amount **2** very much
deal'er·ship' *n.* a franchise to sell a product in a specified area
deal'ing *n.* **1** way of acting **2** [usually *pl.*] transactions or relations
dean (dēn) *n.* ⟦< LL *decanus,* chief of ten (monks, etc.)⟧ **1** the presiding official of a cathedral **2** a college official in charge of students or faculty **3** the senior member of a group
dean's list a list of students at a college who have earned high grades
dear (dir) *adj.* ⟦OE *deore*⟧ **1** much loved **2** esteemed: a polite form of address *[Dear Sir]* **3** high-priced; costly **4** earnest *[our dearest wish]* — *n.* a loved one; darling —**dear'ly** *adv.* —**dear'ness** *n.*
Dear John (**letter**) [Colloq.] a letter, as to a fiancé, breaking off a close relationship
dearth (durth) *n.* ⟦ME *derth*⟧ scarcity or lack
death (deth) *n.* ⟦OE⟧ **1** the act or fact of dying **2** the state of being dead **3** end or destruction **4** the cause of death —**death'like'** *adj.*
death'bed' *n.* **1** the bed on which a person dies **2** a person's last hours
death'blow' *n.* **1** a blow that kills **2** a thing fatal *(to* something)
death'less *adj.* that cannot die; immortal —**death'lessly** *adv.*
death'ly *adj.* **1** causing death; deadly **2** like or characteristic of death — *adv.* extremely *[deathly ill]*
death'trap' *n.* any unsafe structure
deb (deb) *n.* [Colloq.] a debutante
de·ba·cle (di bä'kəl) *n.* ⟦Fr *débâcler,* break up⟧ **1** a crushing defeat **2** a ruinous collapse
de·bar (dē bär') *vt.* **-barred', -bar'ring** ⟦< Anglo-Fr: see DE- & BAR⟧ **1** to keep (a person) *from* some right, etc. **2** to prevent or prohibit —**de·bar'ment** *n.*
de·bark (dē bärk') *vt., vi.* ⟦< Fr: see DE- & BARK[3]⟧ to unload from or leave a ship or aircraft —**de·bar·ka·tion** (dē'bär kā'shən) *n.*
de·base (dē bās') *vt.* **-based', -bas'ing** ⟦DE- + BASE[2]⟧ to make lower in value, dignity, etc. —**de·base'ment** *n.*

═══ THESAURUS ═══

daze *n.* stupor, trance, bewilderment; see CONFUSION.
dazed *a.* confused, bewildered, perplexed; see DOUBTFUL.
dead *a.* **1** [Without life] not existing, expired, deceased, perished, lifeless, inanimate, late, defunct, breathless, no longer living, devoid of life, departed, brain dead, clinically dead, gone, no more*, done for*, gone the way of all flesh*, gone to one's reward*, gone to meet one's Maker*, at rest with God*, out of one's misery*, snuffed out*, pushing up daisies*, rubbed out*, wasted*, liquidated*, erased*, gone by the board*, resting in peace*.—*Ant.* ALIVE, animate, enduring. **2** [Without the appearance of life] inert, still, stagnant; see DULL 2. **3** [Numb] insensible, deadened, anesthetized; see NUMB 1, UNCONSCIOUS. **4** [*Exhausted] wearied, worn, spent; see TIRED.
deaden *v.* blunt, impair, dull, repress, slow, paralyze, freeze, anesthetize, put to sleep, numb, knock out, incapacitate, depress, stifle, benumb, smother, retard, destroy, KO*; see also HURT, WEAKEN 2.—*Ant.* EXCITE,

revitalize, invigorate.
deadlock *n.* standstill, stalemate, cessation; see PAUSE.
deadly *a.* fatal, lethal, murderous, mortal, homicidal, virulent, poisonous, bloody, destructive, venomous, malignant, injurious, carcinogenic, suicidal, bloodthirsty, cannibalistic, harmful, violent; see also DANGEROUS.
deaf *a.* stone-deaf, unable to hear, without hearing, deaf and dumb, deafened, stunned, hard of hearing.
deafening *a.* thunderous, overpowering, shrieking; see LOUD 1, 2.
deal[1] *v.* trade, bargain, barter; see BUY, SELL. —**deal with** handle, manage, have to do with; see TREAT 1.
deal[1,2] *n.* **1** [An agreement] pledge, compromise, pact; see AGREEMENT, CONTRACT. **2** [A secret or dishonest agreement] swindle, robbery, graft; see CRIME, THEFT. **3** [A lot] much, abundance, superabundance; see PLENTY. —**a good** (or **great**) **deal** a lot, quite a bit, a considerable amount; see MUCH. —**make a big deal out of** expand, magnify, blow up; see EXAGGERATE.
dealer *n.* retailer, trader, vendor; see

BUSINESSMAN, MERCHANT.
dealings *n.* business, trade, transactions; see BUSINESS 1, 4.
dear *a.* precious, respected, cherished; see BELOVED.
dear *n.* loved one, sweetheart, love; see DARLING, LOVER 1.
dearly *a.* **1** [In an affectionate manner] fondly, affectionately, yearningly; see LOVINGLY. **2** [To a great extent] greatly, extremely, profoundly; see VERY.
death *n.* decease, dying, demise, passing, loss of life, departure, release, parting, end of life, afterlife, other world, grave, tomb, paradise, heaven, hell, extinction, mortality, exit*, end, finish*, the way of all flesh*, the Grim Reaper*, eternal rest, last rest*; see also DESTRUCTION 1.—*Ant.* LIFE, birth, beginning. —**at death's door** failing, wasting away, nearly dead; see DYING 1, 2. —**to death** very much, extremely, to the extreme; see MUCH 1. —**to the death** to the end, constantly, faithfully; see LOYALTY.
debatable *a.* disputable, unsettled, up for discussion; see CONTROVERSIAL, QUESTIONABLE 1.

de·bate (dē bāt′) *vi.*, *vt.* **-bat′ed, -bat′ing** ⟦< OFr: see DE- & BATTER¹⟧ 1 to discuss reasons for and against (something) 2 to take part in a debate with (a person) or about (a question) — *n.* 1 a discussion of opposing reasons 2 a formal contest of skill in reasoned argument —**de·bat′able** *adj.* —**de·bat′er** *n.*

de·bauch (dē bôch′) *vt.* ⟦< OFr *desbaucher*, seduce⟧ to lead astray morally; corrupt — *n.* an orgy —**de·bauch′ery**, *pl.* **-ies,** *n.*

deb·au·chee (deb′ô shē′, di bôch′ē′) *n.* a dissipated person

de·ben·ture (di ben′chər) *n.* ⟦< L: see DEBT⟧ 1 a voucher acknowledging a debt 2 an interest-bearing bond, often issued without security

de·bili·tate (dē bil′ə tāt′) *vt.* **-tat′ed, -tat′ing** ⟦< L *debilis*, weak⟧ to make weak; enervate —**de·bil′i·ta′tion** *n.*

de·bil·ity (də bil′ə tē) *n.*, *pl.* **-ties** ⟦see prec.⟧ weakness; feebleness

debit (deb′it) *n.* ⟦< L *debere*, owe⟧ 1 an entry in an account of money owed 2 the total of such entries — *vt.* to enter as a debit

debo·nair (deb′ə ner′) *adj.* ⟦< OFr *de bon aire*, lit., of good breed⟧ 1 carefree; jaunty 2 urbane —**deb′o·nair′ly** *adv.*

de·brief (dē brēf′) *vt.* ⟦DE- + BRIEF⟧ to receive information from (a pilot, etc.) about a recent mission

de·bris or **dé·bris** (da brē′) *n.* ⟦Fr < OFr *desbrisier*, break apart⟧ bits and pieces of stone, rubbish, etc.

debt (det) *n.* ⟦< L *debere*, owe⟧ 1 something owed to another 2 the condition of owing *[to be in debt]*

debt′or (-ər) *n.* one who owes a debt

de·bug (dē bug′) *vt.* **-bugged′, -bug′ging** ⟦DE- + BUG⟧ 1 to correct defects in 2 [Colloq.] to find and remove hidden electronic listening devices from

de·bunk (dē buŋk′) *vt.* ⟦DE- + BUNK²⟧ to expose the exaggerated or false claims, etc. of

de·but or **dé·but** (dā byo͞o′, də-; dā′byo͞o′) *n.* ⟦Fr *débuter*, to lead off⟧ 1 a first public appearance 2 the formal introduction of a girl into society — *vi.* to make a debut

debu·tante (deb′yo͞o tänt′) *n.* ⟦Fr⟧ a girl making a debut into society

Dec. December

deca- ⟦< Gr *deka*, ten⟧ *combining form* ten Also **dec-**

dec·ade (dek′ād′) *n.* ⟦< Gr *deka*, ten⟧ a period of ten years

deca·dence (dek′ə dəns, di kād′ns) *n.* ⟦< L *de-*, from + *cadere*, to fall⟧ a decline, as in morals, art, etc.; deterioration —**dec′a·dent** *adj., n.*

de·caf·fein·ated (dē kaf′ə nāt′id) *adj.* with caffeine removed

de·cal (dē′kal′, dē kal′) *n.* ⟦< *decalcomania* < Fr < L *calcare*, to tread + Gr *mania*, madness⟧ a picture or design transferred from prepared paper to glass, wood, etc.

Deca·logue or **Deca·log** (dek′ə lôg′) *n.* ⟦see DECA- & -LOGUE⟧ *[sometimes d-]* TEN COMMANDMENTS

de·camp (dē kamp′) *vi.* ⟦< Fr: see DE- & CAMP⟧ 1 to break camp 2 to go away suddenly and secretly

de·cant (dē kant′) *vt.* ⟦< Fr < L *de-*, from + *canthus*, tire of a wheel⟧ to pour gently from one container into another

de·cant·er *n.* a decorative glass bottle for serving wine, etc.

de·capi·tate (dē kap′ə tāt′) *vt.* **-tat′ed, -tat′ing** ⟦< L *de-*, off + *caput*, head⟧ to behead —**de·cap′i·ta′tion** *n.*

decath·lon (di kath′län′) *n.* ⟦DEC(A)- + Gr *athlon*, a prize⟧ an athletic contest in which each contestant takes part in ten TRACK (sense 6*b*) events

de·cay (dē kā′) *vi.* ⟦see DECADENCE⟧ 1 to lose strength, prosperity, etc. gradually; deteriorate 2 to rot 3 to undergo radioactive disintegration — *vt.* to cause to decay — *n.* 1 deterioration 2 a rotting or rottenness

de·cease (dē sēs′) *n.* ⟦< L *de-*, from + *cedere*, go⟧ death — *vi.* **-ceased′, -ceas′ing** to die

de·ceased′ (-sēst′) *adj.* dead —**the deceased** the dead person or persons

de·cedent (dē sēd′nt) *n.* ⟦see DECEASE⟧ *Law* a deceased person

de·ceit (dē sēt′) *n.* 1 a deceiving or lying 2 a lie 3 deceitful quality

de·ceit′ful *adj.* 1 apt to lie or cheat 2 deceptive —**de·ceit′fully** *adv.*

de·ceive (dē sēv′) *vt.*, *vi.* **-ceived′, -ceiv′ing** ⟦< L *de-*, from + *capere*, take⟧ to make (a person) believe what is not true; mislead —**de·ceiv′er** *n.* —**de·ceiv′ingly** *adv.*

de·cel·er·ate (dē sel′ər āt′) *vt.*, *vi.* **-at′ed, -at′ing** ⟦DE- + (AC)CELERATE⟧ to reduce the speed (of); slow down —**de·cel′era′tion** *n.*

De·cem·ber (dē sem′bər) *n.* ⟦< L *decem*, ten: tenth month in Roman calendar⟧ the twelfth and last month of the year, having 31 days

de·cency (dē′sən sē) *n.*, *pl.* **-cies** a being decent; propriety, courtesy, etc.

de·cen·nial (dē sen′ē əl) *adj.* ⟦< L *decem*, ten + *annus*, year⟧ 1 happening every ten years 2 lasting ten years

de·cent (dē′sənt) *adj.* ⟦< L *decere*, befit⟧ 1 proper and fitting 2 not obscene 3 respectable 4 adequate *[decent wages]* 5 fair and kind —**de′cently** *adv.*

de·cen·tral·ize (dē sen′trə līz′) *vt.* **-ized′, -iz′ing** to break up a concentration of (governmental authority, industry, etc.) and distribute more widely —**de·cen′trali·za′tion** *n.*

THESAURUS

debate *n.* contest, match, dispute; see DISCUSSION.

debate *v.* refute, oppose, question, contend, contest, reason with, wrangle, answer, ponder, weigh, differ, dispute, quarrel, bandy words with, argue the pros and cons of; see also ARGUE, DISCUSS.—*Ant.* AGREE, concur, concede.

debauched *a.* corrupted, debased, depraved; see WICKED.

debit *n.* deficit, obligation, liability; see DEBT.

debris *n.* rubbish, litter, wreckage; see TRASH 1.

debt *n.* liability, obligation, mortgage, duty, arrears, deficit, note, bill, account payable, indebtedness; see also OBLIGATION.—*Ant.* CASH, asset, capital.

debtor *n.* one that owes, borrower, mortgagor; see BUYER.

debunk *v.* expose, uncover, disclose; see EXPOSE 1.

decadence *n.* deterioration, decline, degeneration; see DECAY, EVIL 1.

decadent *a.* immoral, wicked, degenerate; see BAD 1.

decay *n.* decline, decrease, consumption, decomposition, collapse, downfall, decadence, depreciation, corruption, spoilage, wasting away, degeneration, dry rot, putrefaction,

corruption, dissolution, rottenness, spoiling, breakup, breakdown, mold, rust, atrophy, emaciation, blight, mildew, deterioration, ruination, extinction, disintegration, ruin, crumbling, waste, corrosion, wear and tear, crack-up*.

decay *v.* corrode, rot, wither; see SPOIL 1.

decayed *a.* decomposed, putrid, spoiled; see ROTTEN 1.

decaying *a.* rotting, crumbling, spoiling, breaking down, breaking up, wasting away, falling, deteriorating, wearing away, disintegrating, worsening, tumbling down; see also ROTTEN 1.

deceased *a.* late, lifeless, departed; see DEAD 1.

deceit *n.* fraud, trickery, duplicity; see DECEPTION, DISHONESTY.

deceitful *a.* tricky, cunning, insincere; see DISHONEST.

deceive *v.* mislead, swindle, outwit, fool, delude, rob, defraud, not play fair, play a practical joke on, victimize, betray, beguile, take advantage of, entrap, ensnare, hoodwink, dupe, fleece, con*, skin*, sucker*, string along*, screw out of*, do in*, lead astray*, bamboozle*, cross up*, bilk*, gouge*, clip*, fake, gyp*, put on*, burn*, sell out*, chisel*, double-

cross*, shake down*, make a sucker out of*, take to the cleaners*, take for a ride*, snow*, put one over on*, take in*, pull the wool over someone's eyes*, flimflam*, give someone the runaround*, do a snow job on*, play upon*, make a monkey of*, stack the cards*; see also TRICK.

deceived *a.* duped, fooled, humbugged, hoaxed, snared, trapped, decoyed, baited, deluded, defrauded, hoodwinked, betrayed, bamboozled*, sucked in*, conned*; see also CHEATED.—*Ant.* TRUSTED, dealt with openly, informed.

deceiver *n.* conniver, swindler, impostor; see CHEAT.

decency *n.* propriety, righteousness, respectability; see HONESTY, VIRTUE 1.

decent *a.* 1 [In accordance with common standards] accepted, standard, approved; see CONVENTIONAL 3. 2 [In accordance with the moral code] nice, proper, moral, honest, honorable, chaste, modest, pure, ethical, reserved, spotless, respectable, prudent, mannerly, virtuous, immaculate, delicate, stainless, clean, trustworthy, upright, worthy, untarnished, unblemished, straight; see also GOOD 1.

de·cep·tion (dē sep′shən) *n.* 1 a deceiving or being deceived 2 an illusion or fraud —**de·cep′tive** *adj.*

deci- 〚< L *decem*, ten〛 *combining form* one tenth part of

deci·bel (des′ə bəl) *n.* 〚prec. + *bel*, after A. G. *Bell* (1847-1922), U.S. inventor〛 a unit for measuring relative loudness of a sound

de·cide (dē sīd′) *vt.* -**cid′ed**, -**cid′ing** 〚< L *de-*, off + *caedere*, to cut〛 1 to end (a contest, dispute, etc.) by giving one side the victory 2 to reach a decision about; resolve — *vi.* to reach a decision —**de·cid′able** *adj.*

de·cid′ed *adj.* 1 definite; clear-cut 2 determined —**de·cid′edly** *adv.*

de·cid·u·ous (dē sij′ōō əs) *adj.* 〚< L *de-*, off, down + *cadere*, to fall〛 1 falling off at a certain season, as some leaves or antlers 2 shedding leaves annually

deci·mal (des′ə məl) *adj.* 〚< L *decem*, ten〛 of or based on the number 10 —*n.* a fraction with a denominator of 10 or some power of 10, shown by a point (**decimal point**) before the numerator (Ex.: .5 = $\frac{5}{10}$)

deci·mate (des′ə māt′) *vt.* -**mat·ed**, -**mat′ing** 〚< L *decem*, ten〛 to destroy or kill a large part of (lit., a tenth part of) —**dec′i·ma′tion** *n.*

de·ci·pher (dē sī′fər) *vt.* 〚DE- + CIPHER〛 1 DECODE 2 to make out the meaning of (a scrawl, etc.)

de·ci·sion (dē sizh′ən) *n.* 1 the act of deciding or settling a dispute or question 2 the act of making up one's mind 3 a judgment or conclusion 4 determination; firmness of mind

de·ci′sive (-sī′siv) *adj.* 1 that settles a dispute, question, etc. 2 showing decision —**de·ci′sively** *adv.*

deck[1] (dek) *n.* 〚prob. < earlier LowG *verdeck*〛 1 a floor of a ship 2 a pack of playing cards 3 TAPE DECK

deck[2] (dek) *vt.* 〚MDu *decken*, to cover〛 to array or adorn: often with *out*

deck′hand′ *n.* a common sailor

de·claim (dē klām′) *vi., vt.* 〚< L *de-*, intens. + *clamare*, to cry〛 to recite or speak in a studied, dramatic, or impassioned way —**dec·la·ma·tion** (dek′lə mā′shən) *n.* —**de·clama·tory** (dē klam′ə tôr′ē) *adj.*

dec·la·ra·tion (dek′lə rā′shən) *n.* 1 a declaring; announcement 2 a formal statement

de·clara·tive (dē kler′ə tiv) *adj.* making a statement or assertion

de·clare (dē kler′) *vt.* -**clared′**, -**clar′ing** 〚< L *de-*, intens. + *clarus*, clear〛 1 to announce openly or formally 2 to show or reveal 3 to say emphatically

de·clar′er *n.* 1 one who declares 2 *Bridge* the member of the partnership which made the winning bid who plays both his own and the dummy's hand

de·clas·si·fy (dē klas′ə fī′) *vt.* -**fied′**, -**fy′ing** to make (secret documents, etc.) available to the public

de·clen·sion (dē klen′shən) *n.* 〚see fol.〛 1 a descent 2 a decline 3 *Gram.* the inflection of nouns, pronouns, or adjectives

de·cline (dē klīn′) *vi.* -**clined′**, -**clin′ing** 〚< L *de-*, from + *clinare*, to bend〛 1 to bend or slope downward 2 to deteriorate 3 to refuse something — *vt.* 1 to cause to bend or slope downward 2 to refuse politely 3 *Gram.* to give the inflected forms of (a noun, pronoun, or adjective) — *n.* 1 a declining; dropping, failing, decay, etc. 2 a period of decline 3 a downward slope —**dec·li·na·tion** (dek′lə nā′shən) *n.* —**de·clin′er** *n.*

de·cliv·i·ty (dē kliv′ə tē) *n., pl.* -**ties** 〚< L *de-*, down + *clivus*, a slope〛 a downward slope

de·code (dē kōd′) *vt.* -**cod′ed**, -**cod′ing** to decipher (a coded message)

dé·col·le·té (dā käl′ə tā′) *adj.* 〚Fr < L *de*, from + *collum*, neck〛 cut low so as to bare the neck and shoulders

de·colo·ni·za·tion (dē käl′ə nə zā′shən) *n.* a freeing or being freed from colonial status —**de·col′o·nize′** (-ə nīz′), -**nized′**, -**niz′ing**, *vt., vi.*

de·com·pose (dē′kəm pōz′) *vt., vi.* -**posed′**, -**pos′ing** 〚< Fr: see DE- & COMPOSE〛 1 to break up into basic parts 2 to rot —**de′com·po·si′tion** (-käm pə zish′ən) *n.*

de·com·press (dē′kəm pres′) *vt.* to free from pressure, esp. from air pressure —**de′com·pres′sion** *n.*

de·con·gest·ant (dē′kən jes′tənt) *n.* a medication that relieves congestion, as in the nose

de′con·tam′i·nate′ (-tam′ə nāt′) *vt.* -**nat′ed**, -**nat′ing** to rid of a harmful substance, as radioactive products

dé·cor or **de·cor** (dā kôr′) *n.* 〚Fr〛 a decorative scheme, as of a room

deco·rate (dek′ə rāt′) *vt.* -**rat′ed**, -**rat′ing** 〚< L *decus*, an ornament〛 1 to adorn; ornament 2 to paint or wallpaper 3 to give a medal or similar honor to —**deco·ra·tive** (dek′rə tiv, -ə rāt′iv) *adj.* —**dec′o·ra′tor** *n.*

dec′o·ra′tion *n.* 1 a decorating 2 an ornament 3 a medal, etc.

Decoration Day MEMORIAL DAY

deco·rous (dek′ə rəs, di kôr′əs) *adj.* having or showing decorum, good taste, etc. —**dec′o·rously** *adv.*

de·co·rum (di kôr′əm, -kôr′əm) *n.* 〚< L *decorus*, proper〛 propriety and good taste in behavior, speech, etc.

de·cou·page or **dé·cou·page** (dā′kōō päzh′) *n.* 〚< Fr *dé-*,

---

THESAURUS

deception *n.* trickery, double-dealing, untruth, insincerity, craftiness, juggling, treachery, treason, betrayal, mendacity, disinformation, falsehood, trickiness, lying, deceitfulness, deceit, duplicity, cunning, fast one*, snow job*, hokum*; see also DISHONESTY.—*Ant.* HONESTY, frankness, sincerity.

deceptive *a.* misleading, ambiguous, deceitful; see FALSE 2, 3.

decide *v.* settle, determine, judge, conclude, compromise, choose, terminate, vote, poll, make a decision, come to a conclusion, form an opinion, form a judgment, make up one's mind, make a selection, select, pick, make one's choice, commit oneself, come to an agreement, have the final word*; see also AGREE, RESOLVE.—*Ant.* DELAY, hesitate, hedge.

decided *a.* 1 [Determined] settled, decided upon, arranged for; see DETERMINED 1. 2 [Certain] clear, emphatic, determined; see DEFINITE 1.

deciding *a.* determining, crucial, conclusive; see IMPORTANT 1, NECESSARY.

decipher *v.* interpret, translate, explain; see SOLVE.

decision *n.* resolution, result, declaration; see JUDGMENT 3, OPINION 1.

decisive *a.* final, definitive, absolute; see DEFINITE 1, DETERMINED 1.

deck[1] *n.* 1 [The floor of a ship] level, flight, story, layer, tier, topside; see also FLOOR 1, 2. 2 [Cards sufficient for a game] pack, set, pinochle deck, playing cards, the cards; see also CARD. —**on deck*** prepared, available, on hand; see READY 2.

declaration *n.* statement, assertion, utterance, information, affirmation, profession, manifesto, announcement, document, bulletin, denunciation, proclamation, confirmation, ultimatum, notice, notification, resolution, affidavit, testimony, charge, indictment, allegation, canon, bill of rights, constitution, creed, article of faith, presentation, exposition, communication, disclosure, explanation, revelation, publication, answer, advertisement, saying, report, oath, admission, acknowledgment; see also ACKNOWLEDGMENT, ANNOUNCEMENT.

declare *v.* assert oneself, announce, pronounce, claim, tell, state, point out, affirm, maintain, attest to, testify to, confess, reveal, swear, disclose, impart, represent, indicate, notify, repeat, insist, contend, advance, allege, argue, demonstrate, propound, bring forward, put forward, set forth, stress, cite, advocate, pass, proclaim, acknowledge, profess, give out, certify, swear; see also REPORT 1, SAY.—*Ant.* HIDE, equivocate, withhold.

decline *n.* deterioration, dissolution, lessening; see DECAY.

decline *v.* 1 [To refuse] desist, beg to be excused, send regrets; see REFUSE. 2 [To decrease] degenerate, deteriorate, backslide; see DECREASE 1.

decompose *v.* rot, crumble, break up; see DISINTEGRATE.

decomposition *n.* dissolution, breakdown, disintegration; see DECAY.

decontaminate *v.* disinfect, purify, sterilize; see CLEAN.

decor *n.* decoration, ornamentation, adornment; see DECORATION 1.

decorate *v.* adorn, beautify, ornament, deck, paint, color, renovate, enrich, brighten, enhance, festoon, embellish, illuminate, spangle, elaborate, enamel, bead, polish, varnish, grace, garnish, finish, tile, redecorate, add the finishing touches, perfect, dress up, fix up, deck out*, pretty up*.

decorated *a.* adorned, ornamented, embellished; see ORNATE.

decoration *n.* 1 [The act of decorating] adornment, ornamentation, embellishment; see DESIGN, IMPROVEMENT 1. 2 [Something used for decorating] tinsel, thread work, lace, ribbon, braid, gilt, color, appliqué, scroll, wreath, glass, flourish, tooling, inlay, figure work, spangle, finery, filigree, design, ornament, extravagance; see also JEWELRY, PAINT 1. 3 [An insignia of honor] citation, medal, ribbon; see EMBLEM.

decorative *a.* embellishing, beautifying, florid; see ORNATE.

DE- + *couper*, to cut ⟧ the art of decorating a surface with paper cutouts

de·coy (dē koi'; *for n., also* dē'koi') *n.* ⟦ < Du *de kooi*, the cage ⟧ 1 an artificial or trained bird, etc. used to lure game within gun range 2 a thing or person used to lure into danger — *vt.* to lure into danger

de·crease (dē krēs'; *for n. also* dē'krēs') *vi., vt.* **-creased', -creas'ing** ⟦ < L *de-*, from + *crescere*, grow ⟧ to become or make less, smaller, etc.; diminish — *n.* 1 a decreasing 2 amount of decreasing

de·cree (dē krē') *n.* ⟦ < L *de-*, from + *cernere*, to judge ⟧ an official order or decision — *vt.* **-creed', -cree'ing** to order or decide by decree

de·crep·it (dē krep'it) *adj.* ⟦ < L *de-*, intens. + *crepare*, to creak ⟧ broken down or worn out by old age or long use — **de·crep'i·tude'** (-ə tōod') *n.*

de·crim·i·nal·ize (dē krim'ə nəl īz') *vt.* **-ized', -iz'ing** to eliminate or reduce the penalties for (a crime)

de·cry (dē krī') *vt.* **-cried', -cry'ing** ⟦ < Fr: see DE- & CRY ⟧ to speak out against openly; denounce

ded·i·cate (ded'i kāt') *vt.* **-cat'ed, -cat'ing** ⟦ < L *de-*, intens. + *dicare*, proclaim ⟧ 1 to set apart for, or devote to, a special purpose 2 to address (a book, etc.) to someone as a sign of honor — **ded'i·ca'tion** *n.*

ded'i·cat·ed *adj.* devoted

de·duce (dē dōōs', -dyōōs') *vt.* **-duced', -duc'ing** ⟦ < L *de-*, down + *ducere*, to lead ⟧ to infer or decide by reasoning — **de·duc'ible** *adj.*

de·duct (dē dukt') *vt.* ⟦ see prec. ⟧ to take away or subtract (a quantity)

de·duct'ible (-ə bəl) *adj.* that can be deducted — *n.* an amount stipulated in an insurance policy to be paid by the person insured in the event of a loss, etc., with the insurer paying the remainder

de·duc'tion (-duk'shən) *n.* 1 a deducting 2 an amount deducted 3 *a)* reasoning from the general to the specific *b)* a conclusion reached by such reasoning — **de·duc'tive** *adj.*

deed (dēd) *n.* ⟦ < OE *ded* ⟧ 1 a thing done; act 2 a feat of courage, skill, etc. 3 a legal document which transfers a property — *vt.* to transfer (property) by deed

deem (dēm) *vt., vi.* ⟦ < OE *deman*, to judge ⟧ to think, believe, or judge

de-emphasize (dē em'fə sīz') *vt.* **-sized', -siz'ing** to lessen the importance of — **de-em'phasis** (-sis) *n.*

deep (dēp) *adj.* ⟦ OE *deop* ⟧ 1 extending far downward, inward, or backward 2 hard to understand; abstruse 3 serious; profound 4 dark and rich *[a deep red]* 5 absorbed by: with *in [deep in thought]* 6 great in degree; intense 7 of low pitch *[a deep voice]* 8 large; big — *n.* a deep place — *adv.* far down, far back, etc. —**the deep** [Old Poet.] the ocean —**deep'ly** *adv.* —**deep'ness** *n.*

deepen (dē'pən) *vt., vi.* to make or become deep or deeper

deep'freeze' *n.* a condition of suspended activity, etc. — *vt.* **-froze', -fro'zen, -freez'ing** to subject (foods) to sudden freezing so as to preserve and store

deep'-fry' *vt.* **-fried', -fry'ing** to fry in a deep pan of boiling fat or oil

deep'-root'ed *adj.* 1 having deep roots 2 firmly fixed

deep'-seat'ed *adj.* 1 buried deep 2 firmly fixed

deep'-six' *vt.* ⟦ < six fathoms ⟧ [Slang] to get rid of, as by throwing overboard

deep space OUTER SPACE

deer (dir) *n., pl.* **deer** *or* **deers** ⟦ OE *deor*, wild animal ⟧ a kind of ruminant, the male of which grows and sheds antlers annually

de-escalate (dē es'kə lāt') *vi., vt.* **-lat'ed, -lat'ing** to reduce in scope, magnitude, etc. —**de-es'cala'tion** *n.*

de·face (dē fās') *vt.* **-faced', -fac'ing** ⟦ see DE- & FACE ⟧ to spoil the look of; mar —**de·face'ment** *n.*

de facto (dē fak'tō) ⟦ L ⟧ actually existing but not officially approved

de·fal·cate (dē fal'kāt') *vi.* **-cat'ed, -cat'ing** ⟦ < L *de-*, from + *falx*, a sickle ⟧ to steal or misuse funds entrusted to one's care; embezzle —**de·fal·ca'tion** *n.*

de·fame (dē fām') *vt.* **-famed', -fam'ing** ⟦ < L *dis-*, from + *fama*, fame ⟧ to attack the reputation of; slander or libel —**defa·ma·tion** (def'ə mā'shən) *n.* —**de·fama·tory** (dē fam'ə tôr'ē) *adj.* —**de·fam'er** *n.*

de·fault (dē fôlt') *n.* ⟦ < L *de-*, away + *fallere*, fail ⟧ failure to do or appear as required; specif., failure to pay money due — *vi., vt.* 1 to fail to do or pay when required 2 to lose (a contest) by default —**de·fault'er** *n.*

de·feat (dē fēt') *vt.* ⟦ < L *dis-*, from + *facere*, do ⟧ 1 to win victory over 2 to bring to nothing; frustrate — *n.* a defeating or being defeated

de·feat'ist *n.* one who too readily accepts defeat —**de·feat'ism'** *n.*

▬ THESAURUS ▬

decoy *n.* imitation, bait, fake; see CAMOUFLAGE, TRICK 1.

decrease *n.* shrinkage, lessening, contraction; see DISCOUNT, REDUCTION 1.

decrease *v.* 1 [To grow less] lessen, diminish, decline, wane, deteriorate, degenerate, dwindle, sink, settle, lighten, slacken, ebb, melt, lower, moderate, subside, shrink, shrivel up, depreciate, soften, quiet, narrow down, waste, fade away, run low, weaken, crumble, let up, dry up, slow down, calm down, burn away, burn down, die away, die down, decay, evaporate, slack off, wear off, wear away, wear out, wear down, slump; see also CONTRACT 1.—*Ant.* GROW, increase, multiply. 2 [To make less] cut, reduce, check, curb, restrain, quell, tame, compose, hush, still, sober, pacify, blunt, curtail, lessen, lower, subtract, abridge, abbreviate, condense, shorten, minimize, diminish, slash, dilute, shave, pare, prune, modify, digest, limit, level, deflate, compress, strip, thin, make smaller, curtail, clip, lighten, trim, level off, take from, take off, roll back, hold down, step down, scale down, boil down, let up, cut off, cut down, cut short, cut back, chisel*, wind down*, knock off*; see also COMPRESS.—*Ant.* INCREASE, expand, augment.

decree *n.* edict, pronouncement, proclamation; see DECLARATION, JUDGMENT 3.

dedicate *v.* devote, apply, give, appropriate, set aside, surrender, apportion, assign, give over to, donate; see also GIVE 1.

dedication *n.* sanctification, devo-

tion, glorification; see CELEBRATION.

deduct *v.* take away, diminish by, subtract; see DECREASE 2.

deduction *n.* 1 [The act of deducing] inferring, concluding, reasoning; see THOUGHT 1. 2 [A conclusion] result, answer, inference; see JUDGMENT 3, OPINION 1. 3 [A reduction] subtraction, abatement, decrease; see DISCOUNT, REDUCTION 1.

deed *n.* 1 [An action] act, commission, accomplishment; see ACTION 2. 2 [Legal title to real property] document, release, agreement, charter, title deed, record, certificate, voucher, indenture, warranty, lease; see also PROOF 1, RECORD 1, SECURITY 2. —**in deed** in fact, actually, really; see SURELY.

deep *a.* 1 [Situated or extending far down] low, below, beneath, bottomless, submerged, subterranean, submarine, inmost, deep-seated, immersed, dark, dim, impenetrable, buried, inward, underground, downreaching, of great depth, depthless, immeasurable, yawning; see also UNDER 1.—*Ant.* SHALLOW, near the surface, surface. 2 [Extending laterally or vertically] extensive, far, wide, yawning, penetrating, distant, thick, fat, spread out, to the bone*, up to the hilt*; see also BROAD, LONG 1.—*Ant.* NARROW, thin, shallow. 3 [Showing evidence of thought and understanding] penetrating, acute, incisive; see PROFOUND. —**go off the deep end*** 1 [To act rashly] go to extremes, go too far, rant; see EXAGGERATE, RAGE 1. 2 [To break down] collapse, lose control of oneself, become insane; see CRACK UP 2.

deepen *v.* intensify, expand, extend; see DEVELOP 1, GROW 1, INCREASE.

deeply *a.* surely, profoundly, genuinely; see SINCERELY, TRULY.

deer *n.* doe, buck, fawn, roe, stag, venison, member of the deer family, cervine animal, cervid animal. *Creatures popularly called deer include the following:* spotted, white-tailed, mule, red, musk; antelope, American elk, wapiti, moose, caribou, reindeer, roebuck.

deface *v.* disfigure, scratch, mutilate; see DESTROY.

default *n.* failure, lack, error, offense, failure to act, wrongdoing, transgression, imperfection, oversight, neglect, shortcoming, inadequacy, insufficiency, failure to appear, failure to pay, lapse, weakness, vice, blunder; see also FAILURE 1. —**in default of** lacking, absent, in the absence of; see WANTING.

defeat *n.* repulse, reverse, rebuff, conquest, rout, overthrow, subjugation, destruction, breakdown, collapse, extermination, annihilation, check, trap, ambush, breakthrough, withdrawal, setback, stalemate, ruin, blow, loss, butchery, massacre, Waterloo, beating, whipping, thrashing, fall, comedown, upset, battering*, pasting*, walloping*, whaling*, slaughter*, massacre*, KO*, the old one-two*; see also LOSS 1.—*Ant.* VICTORY, triumph, conquest.

defeat *v.* 1 [To get the better of another] master, subjugate, overwhelm; see OVERCOME. 2 [To worst in war] overcome, vanquish, conquer, rout, entrap, subdue, overrun, best,

def·e·cate (def′i kāt′) *vi.* **-cat′ed, -cat′ing** ⟦< L *de-*, from + *faex*, dregs⟧ to excrete waste matter from the bowels — **def′e·ca′tion** *n.*

de·fect (dē′fekt′; *also, and for v. always,* dē fekt′) *n.* ⟦< L *de-*, from + *facere*, do⟧ **1** lack of something necessary for completeness **2** an imperfection; fault — *vi.* to forsake a party, cause, etc., esp. so as to join the opposition —**de·fec′tion** *n.* —**de·fec′tor** *n.*

de·fec·tive (dē fek′tiv) *adj.* having defects; imperfect; faulty

de·fend (dē fend′) *vt.* ⟦< L *de-*, away + *fendere*, to strike⟧ **1** to guard from attack; protect **2** to support or justify **3** *Law a*) to oppose (an action) *b*) to act as lawyer for (an accused) —**de·fend′er** *n.*

de·fec·tant (dē fen′dənt) *n. Law* the person sued or accused

de·fense (dē fens′, dē′fens′) *n.* **1** a defending against attack **2** something that defends **3** justification by speech or writing **4** *a*) the arguments of a defendant *b*) the defendant and his counsel   Brit., etc. sp. **defence** —**de·fense′less** *adj.* —**de·fen′sible** *adj.*

defense mechanism any thought process used unconsciously to protect oneself against painful feelings

de·fen·sive *adj.* **1** defending **2** of or for defense — *n.* a position of defense —**de·fen′sive·ly** *adv.*

de·fer[1] (dē fur′) *vt., vi.* **-ferred′, -fer′ring** ⟦see DIFFER⟧ **1** to postpone; delay **2** to postpone the induction of (a person) into compulsory military service —**de·fer′ment** or **de·fer′ral** *n.*

de·fer[2] (dē fur′) *vi.* **-ferred′, -fer′ring** ⟦< L *de-*, down + *ferre*, to BEAR[1]⟧ to yield with courtesy (*to*)

def·er·ence (def′ər əns) *n.* **1** a yielding in opinion, judgment, etc. **2** courteous respect

def·er·en·tial (-en′shəl) *adj.* showing deference; very respectful

de·fi·ance (dē fī′əns) *n.* a defying; open, bold resistance to authority —**de·fi′ant** *adj.* —**de·fi′antly** *adv.*

de·fi·ciency (dē fish′ən sē) *n.* ⟦< L *de-*, from + *facere*, do⟧ **1** a being deficient **2** *pl.* **-cies** a shortage

deficiency disease a disease caused by a lack of vitamins, minerals, etc. in the diet

de·fi·cient (-ənt) *adj.* ⟦see DEFICIENCY⟧ **1** lacking in some essential; incomplete **2** inadequate in amount

def·i·cit (def′ə sit) *n.* ⟦L < *deficere*, to lack⟧ the amount by which a sum of money is less than the required amount

de·file[1] (dē fīl′) *vt.* **-filed′, -fil′ing** ⟦< OFr *defouler*, tread underfoot⟧ **1** to make filthy **2** to profane; sully —**de·file′ment** *n.* —**de·fil′er** *n.*

de·file[2] (dē fīl′, dē′fīl′) *vi.* **-filed′, -fil′ing** ⟦< Fr *dé-*, from + *fil*, thread⟧ to march in single file — *n.* a narrow passage, valley, etc.

de·fine (dē fīn′) *vt.* **-fined′, -fin′ing** ⟦< L *de-*, from + *finis*, boundary⟧ **1** to determine the limits or nature of; describe exactly **2** to state the meaning of (a word, etc.) — **de·fin′er** *n.*

def·i·nite (def′ə nit) *adj.* ⟦see prec.⟧ **1** having exact limits **2** precise in meaning; explicit **3** certain; positive **4** *Gram.* limiting or specifying /*"the"*is the *definite* article/ —**def′i·nitely** *adv.* —**def′i·nite·ness** *n.*

def·i·ni·tion (-nish′ən) *n.* **1** a defining or being defined **2** a statement of the meaning of a word **3** clarity of outline, sound, etc.

de·fin·i·tive (dē fin′ə tiv) *adj.* **1** conclusive; final **2** most nearly complete **3** serving to define

---

■ THESAURUS ■

overthrow, crush, smash, drive off, annihilate, overwhelm, scatter, repulse, halt, reduce, outflank, finish off, encircle, slaughter, butcher, outmaneuver, ambush, demolish, sack, torpedo, sink, swamp, wipe out*, decimate, obliterate, roll back, mop up*, chew up*, mow down*; see also DESTROY, RAVAGE.—*Ant.* YIELD, give up, relinquish. **3** [To worst in sport or in personal combat] beat, overpower, outplay, trounce, knock out, throw, floor, pommel, pound, flog, outhit, outrun, outjump, thrash, edge*, shade*, lay low*, skin*, lick*, wallop*, clean up on*, beat up*, take*, KO*, put down*, beat the pants off of*, pulverize*, steamroll*, plow under*, smear*, cream*; see also BEAT 1.—*Ant.* FAIL, suffer, be defeated.

defeated *a.* crushed, overcome, conquered; see BEATEN 1.

defect *n.* imperfection, flaw, drawback; see FAULT 1.

defect *v.* fall away from, run away, forsake; see ABANDON 2, DESERT, LEAVE 1.

defective *a.* imperfect, incomplete, inadequate; see FAULTY, POOR 2, UNFINISHED 1.

defend *v.* **1** [To keep off an enemy; *often used figuratively*] shield, shelter, screen; see PROTECT. **2** [To support an accused person or thing] plead for, justify, uphold, second, exonerate, back, vindicate, aid, espouse the cause of, befriend, say in defense of, guarantee, endorse, warrant, maintain, recommend, rationalize, plead someone's cause, say a good word for, speak for, stand up for, put in a good word for, apologize for, go to bat for*, cover for*, back up*, stick up for*; see also SUPPORT 2.—*Ant.* CONVICT, accuse, charge.

defendant *n.* the accused, defense, offender; see PRISONER.

defended *a.* protected, guarded, safeguarded; see SAFE 1.

defender *n.* champion, patron, sponsor; see GUARDIAN 1, PROTECTOR.

defense *n.* **1** [The act of defending] resistance, protection, safeguard,

preservation, security, custody, stand, front, backing, guardianship, the defensive, precaution, inoculation, excusing, apologizing, explaining, justifying, exoneration, explanation.—*Ant.* OFFENSE, retaliation, aggression. **2** [A means or system for defending] trench, bulwark, dike, stockade, machine-gun nest, bastion, fortification, fort, chemical and biological warfare, barricade, garrison, rampart, fence, wall, embankment, citadel, fortress, armor, antiaircraft, camouflage, gas mask, shield, screen, stronghold, parapet, buttress, guard; see also FORTIFICATION, TRENCH.—*Ant.* ATTACK, siege, blitzkrieg. **3** [In law, the reply of the accused] denial, plea, answer; see DECLARATION, PROOF 1, STATEMENT 1.

defensible *a.* justfiable, proper, permissible; see FIT 1, 2, LOGICAL.

defensive *a.* protecting, guarding, watchful, protective, vigilant; see also CAREFUL.

defensively *a.* protectively, guardedly, suspiciously; see CAREFULLY 1.

defer[1,2] *v.* **1** [To postpone] put off, postpone, shelve; see DELAY, SUSPEND 2. **2** [To yield] submit, accede, concede; see AGREE.

deference *n.* veneration, acclaim, homage; see REVERENCE.

deferred *a.* delayed, prolonged, held up; see POSTPONED.

defiance *n.* insubordination, rebellion, insurgence; see DISOBEDIENCE.

defiant *a.* resistant, obstinate, disobedient; see REBELLIOUS.

deficiency *n.* want, need, absence; see LACK 2.

deficient *a.* insufficient, skimpy, meager; see INADEQUATE.

deficit *n.* shortage, paucity, deficiency; see LACK 2.

defile[1] *v.* ravish, violate, molest; see HURT 1, RAPE.

define *v.* **1** [To set limits] bound, confine, limit, outline, fix, settle, circumscribe, mark, set, distinguish, establish, encompass, mark the lim-

its of, determine the boundaries of, fix the limits of, curb, edge, border, enclose, set bounds to, fence in, rim, encircle, hedge in, wall in, envelop, flank, stake out; see also LIMIT.—*Ant.* CONFUSE, distort, mix. **2** [To provide a name or description] determine, entitle, label, designate, characterize, elucidate, interpret, illustrate, represent, individuate, find out, popularize, spell out, translate, exemplify, specify, prescribe, nickname, dub; see also DESCRIBE, EXPLAIN, NAME 1.—*Ant.* MISUNDERSTAND, misconceive, mistile.

definite *a.* **1** [Determined with exactness] fixed, exact, precise, positive, accurate, correct, decisive, absolute, clearly defined, well-defined, limited, strict, explicit, specific, settled, decided, prescribed, restricted, assigned, unequivocal, special, conclusive, categorical, particular, unerring, to the point, beyond doubt; see also CERTAIN 2, DETERMINED.—*Ant.* OBSCURE, indefinite, inexact. **2** [Clear in detail] sharp, visible, audible, tangible, distinct, vivid, unmistakable in meaning, straightforward, obvious, marked, plain, not vague, well-drawn, clearly defined, well-marked, well-defined, clear-cut, explicit, unmistakable, distinguishable, undistorted, crisp, bold, graphic, downright, undisguised, in plain sight, clear as day, standing out like a sore thumb*.—*Ant.* CONFUSED, vague, hazy. **3** [Positive] sure, beyond doubt, convinced; see CERTAIN 1.

definitely *a.* clearly, unmistakably, unquestionably; see SURELY.

definition *n.* meaning, terminology, signification, diagnosis, synonym, exposition, interpretation, explication, clue, key, translation, comment, rationale, commentary, explanation, representation, characterization, solution, answer; see also DESCRIPTION, EXPLANATION.

definitive *a.* final, ultimate, conclusive; see ABSOLUTE 1.

de·flate (dē flāt′) *vt.*, *vi.* **-flat′ed, -flat′ing** ⟦DE- + (IN)FLATE⟧ **1** to collapse by letting out air or gas **2** to lessen in size, importance, etc. **3** to cause deflation of (currency, etc.)

de·fla′tion *n.* **1** a deflating **2** a lessening of the amount of money in circulation, making it rise in value

de·flect (dē flekt′) *vt.*, *vi.* ⟦< L *de-*, from + *flectere*, to bend⟧ to turn or make go to one side —**de·flec′tion** *n.* — **de·flec′tive** *adj.* —**de·flec′tor** *n.*

de·flower (dē flou′ər) *vt.* **1** to make (a woman) no longer a virgin **2** to ravage or spoil

de·fog·ger (dē fôg′ər) *n.* an apparatus for clearing condensed moisture, as from a car window

de·fo·li·ant (dē fō′lē ənt) *n.* a chemical substance that causes leaves to fall from growing plants

de·fo′li·ate′ (-āt′) *vt.* **-at′ed, -at′ing** ⟦< L *de-*, from + *folium*, leaf⟧ to strip (trees, etc.) of leaves —**de·fo′li·a′tion** *n.*

de·for·est (dē fôr′ist) *vt.* to clear (land) of forests or trees —**de·for′est·a′tion** *n.*

de·form (dē fôrm′) *vt.* ⟦< L *de-*, from + *forma*, form⟧ **1** to impair the form of **2** to make ugly —**de·for·ma·tion** (dē′fôr mā′shən, def′ər-) *n.*

de·formed′ *adj.* misshapen

de·form·i·ty (dē fôr′mə tē) *n.*, *pl.* **-ties 1** a deformed part, as of the body **2** ugliness or depravity

de·fraud (dē frôd′) *vt.* to take property, rights, etc. from by fraud; cheat —**de·fraud′er** *n.*

de·fray (dē frā′) *vt.* ⟦Fr *défrayer*⟧ to pay (the cost or expenses) —**de·fray′able** *adj.* —**de·fray′al** *n.*

de·frost (dē frôst′) *vt.*, *vi.* to rid or get rid of frost or ice — **de·frost′er** *n.*

deft (deft) *adj.* ⟦see DAFT⟧ skillful; dexterous —**deft′ly** *adv.*

de·funct (dē funkt′) *adj.* ⟦< L *defungi*, to finish⟧ no longer existing; dead or extinct

de·fuse (dē fyōoz′) *vt.* **-fused′, -fus′ing 1** to remove the fuse from (a bomb, etc.) **2** to make harmless, less tense, etc.

de·fy (dē fī′) *vt.* **-fied′, -fy′ing** ⟦< LL *dis-*, from + *fidus*, faithful⟧ **1** to resist or oppose boldly or openly **2** to dare to do or prove something

de·gen·er·ate (dē jen′ər it; *for v.*, -ər āt′) *adj.* ⟦< L *de-*, from + *genus*, race⟧ **1** having sunk below a former or normal condition, etc.; deteriorated **2** depraved — *n.* a degenerate person — *vi.* **-at′ed, -at′ing** to lose former normal or higher qualities —**de·gen′era·cy** (-ə sē) *n.* —**de·gen′er·a′tion** *n.* —**de·gen′er·ative** *adj.*

de·grade (dē grād′) *vt.* **-grad′ed, -grad′ing** ⟦< L *de-*, down + *gradus*, a step⟧ **1** to demote **2** to lower in quality,

moral character, dignity, etc.; debase, dishonor, etc. — **deg·ra·da·tion** (deg′rə dā′shən) *n.*

de·gree (di grē′) *n.* ⟦see prec.⟧ **1** any of the successive steps in a process **2** social or official rank **3** extent, amount, or intensity **4** a rank given by a college or university to one who has completed a course of study, or to a distinguished person as an honor **5** a grade of comparison of adjectives and adverbs /the superlative *degree*/ **6** *Law* the seriousness of a crime /murder in the first *degree*/ **7** *Math.* a unit of measure for angles or arcs, one 360th of the circumference of a circle **8** *Physics* a unit of measure for temperature —**to a degree** somewhat

de·hu·man·ize (dē hyōo′mə nīz′) *vt.* **-ized′, -iz′ing** to deprive of human qualities; make machinelike —**de·hu′mani·za′tion** *n.*

de·hu·midi·fy (dē′hyōo mid′ə fī′) *vt.* **-fied′, -fy′ing** to remove moisture from (air, etc.) —**de·hu·mid′i·fi′er** *n.*

de·hy·drate (dē hī′drāt′) *vt.* **-drat′ed, -drat′ing** to remove water from; dry — *vi.* to lose water —**de·hy·dra′tion** *n.* —**de·hy′dra′tor** *n.*

de-ice (dē īs′) *vt.* **-iced′, -ic′ing** to melt ice from —**de-ic′er** *n.*

dei·fy (dē′ə fī′) *vt.* **-fied′, -fy′ing** ⟦< L *deus*, god + *facere*, make⟧ **1** to make a god of **2** to look upon as a god —**de′i·fi·ca′tion** (-fi kā′shən) *n.*

deign (dān) *vi.*, *vt.* ⟦< L *dignus*, worthy⟧ to condescend (to do or give)

de·in·sti·tu·tion·al·ize (dē′in′stə tōo′shən ə liz′) *vt.* **-ized′, -iz′ing** to discharge (a patient) as from a mental institution

de·ism (dē′iz′əm) *n.* ⟦< L *deus*, god⟧ the belief that God exists and created the world but takes no part in its functioning —**de′ist** *n.*

de·ity (dē′ə tē) *n.* ⟦< L *deus*, god⟧ **1** the state of being a god **2** *pl.* **-ties** a god or goddess —**the Deity** God

déjà vu (dā zhä vü′) ⟦Fr, already seen⟧ a feeling of having been in a place or experienced something before

de·ject (dē jekt′) *vt.* ⟦< L *de-*, down + *jacere*, throw⟧ to dishearten; depress —**de·ject′ed** *adj.* —**de·jec′tion** *n.*

de·lay (dē lā′) *vt.* ⟦< OFr *de-*, intens. + *laier*, to leave⟧ **1** to put off; postpone **2** to make late; detain — *vi.* to linger — *n.* a delaying or being delayed

de·lec·ta·ble (dē lek′tə bəl) *adj.* ⟦see DELIGHT⟧ delightful or delicious

de·lec·ta·tion (dē′lek tā′shən) *n.* ⟦see DELIGHT⟧ delight; enjoyment

del·egate (del′ə gət; *also*, -gāt′; *for v.*, -gāt′) *n.* ⟦< L *de-*, from + *legare*, send⟧ a person authorized to act for others; representative — *vt.* **-gat′ed, -gat′ing 1** to appoint as a delegate **2** to entrust (authority, etc.) to another

del·ega′tion *n.* **1** a delegating or being delegated **2** a body of delegates

---

THESAURUS

deflate *v.* exhaust, flatten, void; see EMPTY 1, 2.

deflect *v.* swerve, diverge, curve; see TURN 3, 6.

deform *v.* disfigure, deface, injure; see DAMAGE.

deformed *a.* damaged, distorted, misshapen, disfigured, crippled, misproportioned, malformed, cramped, badly made, disjointed, unseemly, illfavored, dwarfed, hunchbacked, clubfooted, unshapely, mangled, crushed, warped, curved, contorted, gnarled, crooked, grotesque, lame, irregular; see also TWISTED 1, UGLY 1.—*Ant.* REGULAR, shapely, well-formed.

deformity *n.* malformation, ugliness, unsightliness; see CONTORTION, DAMAGE 1.

defraud *v.* hoax, dupe, cheat; see DECEIVE.

defy *v.* insult, resist, confront; see DARE 2, OPPOSE 1, 2.

degenerate *a.* depraved, immoral, corrupt; see BAD.

degradation *n.* depravity, corruption, degeneration; see EVIL 1.

degrade *v.* demote, discredit, diminish; see HUMBLE.

degraded *a.* disgraced, debased, depraved; see BAD.

degree *n.* **1** [One in a series used for measurement] measure, grade, step, mark, interval, space, measurement,

gradation, size, dimension, shade, point, line, plane, step in a series, gauge, rung, term, tier, stair, ratio, period, level; see also DIVISION 2. **2** [An expression of relative excellence, attainment, or the like] extent, station, order, quality, development, height, expanse, length, potency, range, proportion, compass, quantity, standing, strength, reach, intensity, scope, caliber, pitch, stage, sort, status, rate; see also RANK 3. **3** [Recognition of academic achievement] distinction, testimonial, honor, qualification, dignity, eminence, credit, credentials, baccalaureate, doctorate, sheepskin*; see also DIPLOMA, GRADUATION. —**by degrees** step by step, slowly but surely, inch by inch; see GRADUALLY. —**to a degree** somewhat, partially, to an extent; see PARTLY.

dehydrate *v.* dessicate, parch, drain; see DRY 1.

dejected *a.* depressed, dispirited, cast down; see SAD 1.

delay *n.* deferment, adjournment, putting off, procrastination, suspension, moratorium, reprieve, setback, stay, stop, discontinuation, cooling-off period*, holdup*; see also PAUSE.

delay *v.* postpone, defer, retard, hold up, deter, clog, choke, slacken, keep, hold, keep back, impede, discourage,

interfere with, detain, stay, stop, withhold, arrest, check, prevent, repress, curb, obstruct, inhibit, restrict, prolong, encumber, procrastinate, adjourn, block, bar, suspend, table, slow, put aside, hold back, hold off, hold everything, bide one's time, slow up, stall, put off, restrain, put on ice*, shelve*, pigeonhole; see also HINDER, INTERRUPT.—*Ant.* SPEED, accelerate, encourage.

delayed *a.* held up, slowed, put off; see LATE 1, POSTPONED.

delegate *n.* legate, emissary, proxy, deputy, substitute, consul, appointee, minister, alternate, nominee, ambassador, congressman, senator, stand-in*, sub*, pinch hitter*; see also AGENT, REPRESENTATIVE 2.

delegate *v.* **1** [To give authority to another] authorize, commission, appoint, name, nominate, select, choose, assign, license, empower, deputize, swear in, ordain, invest, elect, give someone the green light*, give someone the go-ahead*; see also APPROVE.—*Ant.* DISMISS, repudiate, reject. **2** [To give duties to another] entrust, parcel out, hold responsible for; see ASSIGN.

delegation *n.* **1** [The act of assigning to another] assignment, giving over, nomination, trust, commissioning, ordination, authoriza-

de·lete (dē lēt′) *vt.* **-let′ed, -let′ing** [< L *delere*, destroy] to take out (a word, etc.); cross out —**de·le′tion** *n.*

del·e·teri·ous (del′ə tir′ē əs) *adj.* [< Gr *dēleisthai*, injure] harmful to health or well-being; injurious

delft·ware (delft′wer′) *n.* [after *Delft*, city in Holland] glazed earthenware, usually blue and white Also **delft**

deli (del′ē) *n. short for* DELICATESSEN

de·lib·er·ate (di lib′ər it; *for v.,* -āt′) *adj.* [< L *de-*, intens. + *librare*, weigh] **1** carefully thought out; premeditated **2** not rash or hasty **3** unhurried — *vi.,* *vt.* **-at′ed, -at′ing** to consider carefully —**de·lib′er·ately** *adv.* —**de·lib′er·a′tive** *adj.*

de·lib′er·a′tion *n.* **1** a deliberating **2** [*often pl.*] consideration of alternatives **3** carefulness; slowness

deli·cacy (del′i kə sē) *n., pl.* **-cies** **1** the quality of being delicate; fineness, weakness, sensitivity, etc. **2** a choice food

del′i·cate (-kit) *adj.* [< L *delicatus*, delightful] **1** pleasing in its lightness, mildness, etc. **2** beautifully fine in texture, workmanship, etc. **3** slight and subtle **4** easily damaged **5** frail in health **6** *a)* needing careful handling *b)* showing tact, consideration, etc. **7** finely sensitive —**del′i·cately** *adv.* —**del′i·cate·ness** *n.*

deli·ca·tes·sen (del′i kə tes′ən) *n.* [< Ger *pl.* < Fr *délicatesse*, delicacy] **1** prepared cooked meats, fish, cheeses, salads, etc., collectively **2** a shop where such foods are sold

de·li·cious (di lish′əs) *adj.* [see fol.] **1** delightful **2** very pleasing to taste or smell —**de·li′ciously** *adv.* —**de·li′cious·ness** *n.*

de·light (di līt′) *vt.* [< L *de-*, from + *lacere*, entice] to give great pleasure to — *vi.* **1** to give great pleasure **2** to be highly pleased; rejoice — *n.* **1** great pleasure **2** something giving great pleasure —**de·light′ed** *adj.*

de·light′ful *adj.* giving delight; very pleasing —**de·light′fully** *adv.*

De·li·lah (di lī′lə) *Bible* the mistress and betrayer of Samson

de·limit (dē lim′it) *vt.* to fix the limits of —**de·lim′i·ta′tion** *n.*

de·lin·eate (di lin′ē āt′) *vt.* **-at′ed, -at′ing** [< L *de-*, from + *linea*, a line] **1** to draw; sketch **2** to depict in words —**de·lin·ea′tion** *n.*

de·lin·quent (di lin′kwənt) *adj.* [< L *de-*, from + *linquere*, leave] **1** failing to do what duty or law requires **2** overdue, as taxes — *n.* a delinquent person; esp., a juvenile delinquent —**de·lin′quency,** *pl.* **-cies,** *n.* —**de·lin′quently** *adv.*

deli·quesce (del′i kwes′) *vi.* **-quesced′, -quesc′ing** [< L < *de-*, from + *liquere*, be liquid] to become liquid by absorbing moisture from the air —**del′i·ques′cent** *adj.*

de·liri·ous (di lir′ē əs) *adj.* **1** in a state of delirium **2** of or caused by delirium **3** wildly excited —**de·lir′i·ously** *adv.* —**de·lir′i·ous·ness** *n.*

de·lir·ium (-əm) *n.* [< L *de-*, from + *lira*, a line] **1** a temporary mental disturbance, as during a fever, marked by confused speech and hallucinations **2** uncontrollably wild excitement

de·liver (di liv′ər) *vt.* [< L *de-*, intens. + *liber*, free] **1** to set free or rescue **2** to assist at the birth of **3** to make (a speech, etc.) **4** to hand over **5** to distribute (mail, etc.) **6** to strike (a blow) **7** to throw (a ball, etc.)

de·liv′er·ance *n.* a freeing or being freed; rescue

de·liv′ery *n., pl.* **-er·ies** **1** a handing over **2** a distributing, as of mail **3** a giving birth **4** any giving forth **5** the act or manner of delivering a speech, ball, etc. **6** something delivered

dell (del) *n.* [OE *del*] a small, secluded valley or glen, usually wooded

del·phin·ium (del fin′ē əm) *n.* [< Gr *delphin*, dolphin] a tall plant bearing spikes of flowers, usually blue

delta (del′tə) *n.* **1** the fourth letter of the Greek alphabet (Δ, δ) **2** a deposit of soil, usually triangular, formed at the mouth of some rivers

delta wave an electrical brain wave indicating, in adults, deep sleep or brain disease Also **delta rhythm**

de·lude (di lo̅o̅d′) *vt.* **-lud′ed, -lud′ing** [< L *de-*, from + *ludere*, to play] to mislead; deceive

del·uge (del′yo̅o̅j′) *n.* [< L *dis*, off + *luere*, to wash] **1** a great flood **2** a heavy rainfall — *vt.* **-uged′, -ug′ing** **1** to flood **2** to overwhelm

de·lu·sion (di lo̅o̅′zhən) *n.* **1** a deluding or being deluded **2** a false belief, specif. one that persists psychotically —**de·lu′sive** *adj.*

THESAURUS

tion, charge, deputation, referring, transferring; see also APPOINTMENT 1. **2** [A group with a specific mission] representatives, deputation, commission; see COMMITTEE, GATHERING, ORGANIZATION 2.

deliberate *a.* thought out, predetermined, conscious, advised, prearranged, fixed, with forethought, well-considered, cautious, studied, intentional, planned in advance, done on purpose, willful, considered, thoughtful, purposed, planned, reasoned, calculated, intended, purposeful, premeditated, voluntary, designed, coldblooded, resolved, cut-and-dried; see also CAREFUL.

deliberately *a.* resolutely, determinedly, emphatically, knowingly, meaningfully, voluntarily, consciously, on purpose, willfully, premeditatedly, in cold blood, with malice aforethought, advisedly, freely, independently, without any qualms, by design, intentionally, purposely, all things considered, pointedly, to that end, with eyes wide open*; see also CAREFULLY 1.

delicacy *n.* **1** [Fineness of texture] airiness, daintiness, transparency, flimsiness, softness, smoothness, subtlety, tenderness; see also LIGHTNESS 2. **2** [A rare commodity, especially for the table] tidbit, luxury, gourmet dish, gourmet food, dessert, sweet, delight, party dish, imported food, delicatessen, chef's special*; see also FOOD.

delicate *a.* **1** [Sickly] susceptible, in delicate health, feeble; see SICK, WEAK 1. **2** [Dainty] fragile, frail, fine; see DAINTY.

delicately *a.* deftly, skillfully, cau-

tiously; see CAREFULLY 1.

delicatessen *n.* **1** [Ready-to-serve-foods] *Varieties of delicatessen include the following:* cold meats, luncheon meats, salad, dairy products, salami, pastrami, bologna, wurst, sausage, frankfurters, olives, sauerkraut, pickled peppers, pickled fish, dill pickles, sweet pickles, kosher pickles, gherkins, caviar, anchovies, pâté; see also BREAD, CHEESE, DESSERT, FISH, FRUIT, MEAT, WINE. **2** [A place that sells delicatessen] food store, butcher store, grocery; see MARKET 1.

delicious *a.* tasty, savory, good, appetizing, choice, well-seasoned, well-done, spicy, sweet, rich, delectable, exquisite, dainty, luscious, tempting, yummy*, fit for a king*; see also EXCELLENT, RICH 4.—*Ant.* ROTTEN, flat, stale.

delight *n.* enjoyment, joy, pleasure; see HAPPINESS.

delight *v.* fascinate, amuse, please; see ENTERTAIN 1.

delighted *a.* **1** [Greatly pleased] entranced, excited, pleasantly surprised; see HAPPY. **2** [An expression of acceptance or pleasure] thank you, by all means, to be sure, splendid, excellent, overwhelmed, charmed, so glad.

delightful *a.* charming, amusing, clever; see PLEASANT 1.

delinquent *a.* **1** [Lax in duty] slack, behindhand, tardy, procrastinating, criminal, neglectful, faulty, blamable, negligent, derelict, remiss; see also CARELESS.—*Ant.* PUNCTUAL, punctilious, scrupulous. **2** [Not paid on time; *said especially of taxes*] owed,

back, overdue; see DUE, UNPAID 1.

delinquent *n.* defaulter, tax evader, offender, dropout, reprobate, loafer, derelict, bad debtor, poor risk, felon, law breaker, wrongdoer, sinner, juvenile offender, juvenile delinquent, JD*, punk*, outlaw, black sheep*; see also CRIMINAL.

delirious *a.* demented, crazy, irrational; see INSANE.

deliver *v.* **1** [To free] set free, liberate, save; see FREE. **2** [To transfer] pass, remit, hand over; see GIVE 1. **3** [To speak formally] present, read, give; see ADDRESS 2. **4** [To bring to birth] bring forth, be delivered of, provide obstetrical attention; see PRODUCE 2. **5** [To distribute] allot, dispense, give out; see DISTRIBUTE.

delivered *a.* brought, deposited, transported, checked in, forwarded, expressed, hand-delivered, mailed, dispatched, at the door, sent out by truck, trucked; see also MAILED.

delivery *n.* **1** [Bringing goods into another's possession] consignment, carting, shipment, transfer, portage, freighting, dispatch, conveyance, mailing, special delivery, parcel post, giving over, handing over, cash on delivery, COD, free on board, FOB; see also TRANSPORTATION. **2** [Delivery of a child] birth, parturition, confinement, childbirth, labor, bringing forth, midwifery, obstetrics, Caesarean section; see also BIRTH. **3** [The manner of a speaker] articulation, enunciation, accent, utterance, pronunciation, emphasis, elocution; see also ELOQUENCE.

delusion *n.* **1** phantasm, hallucination, fancy; see ILLUSION.

de·luxe (di luks′, -looks′) *adj.* ⟦Fr, of luxury⟧ of extra fine quality — *adv.* in a deluxe manner

delve (delv) *vi.* **delved, delv′ing** ⟦OE *delfan*⟧ 1 [Now Dial., Chiefly Brit.] to dig 2 to search (*into*) —**delv′er** *n.*

Dem. 1 Democrat 2 Democratic

de·mag·net·ize (dē mag′nə tīz′) *vt.* **-ized′, -iz′ing** to remove magnetism or magnetic properties from —**de·mag′net·i·za′tion** *n.*

dem·a·gogue or **dem·a·gog** (dem′ə gäg′) *n.* ⟦< Gr *dēmos*, the people + *agōgos*, leader⟧ one who tries to stir up people's emotions in order to win them over and so gain power —**dem′a·gog′y** (-gä′jē, -gäg′ē) or **dem′a·gogu′ery** (-gäg′ər ē) *n.*

de·mand (di mand′) *vt.* ⟦< L *de-*, from + *mandare*, entrust⟧ 1 to ask for boldly or urgently 2 to ask for as a right 3 to require; need — *vi.* to make a demand — *n.* 1 a demanding 2 a thing demanded 3 a strong request 4 an urgent requirement 5 *Economics* the desire for a commodity together with ability to pay for it; also, the amount people are ready to buy —**in demand** wanted or sought —**on demand** when presented for payment

de·mand′ing *adj.* making difficult demands on one's patience, energy, etc.

de·mar·ca·tion (dē′mär kā′shən) *n.* ⟦< Sp *de-*, from + *marcar*, to mark⟧ 1 the act of setting and marking limits or boundaries 2 a limit or boundary

de·mean[1] (dē mēn′) *vt.* ⟦DE- + MEAN[2]⟧ to degrade; humble

de·mean[2] (dē mēn′) *vt.* ⟦see fol.⟧ to behave or conduct (oneself)

de·mean·or (di mēn′ər) *n.* ⟦< OFr *demener*, to lead⟧ outward behavior; conduct; deportment Brit. sp. **demean·our**

de·ment·ed (dē ment′id) *adj.* ⟦see fol.⟧ mentally deranged; insane

de·men·tia (di men′shə) *n.* ⟦< L *de-*, out from + *mens*, the mind⟧ severe mental deficiency or impairment

de·merit (dē mer′it) *n.* ⟦< L *de-*, intens. + *merere*, to deserve, with *de-* taken as negative⟧ 1 a fault; defect 2 a mark recorded against a student, etc. for poor conduct or work

de·mesne (di mān′; *also*, -mēn′) *n.* ⟦see DOMAIN⟧ a region or domain

De·me·ter (di mēt′ər) *Gr. Myth.* the goddess of agriculture

demi- ⟦< L *dimidius*, half⟧ *prefix* 1 half 2 less than usual in size, power, etc. *[demigod]*

demi·god (dem′i gäd′) *n.* 1 a minor deity 2 a godlike person

dem′i·john (-jän′) *n.* ⟦Fr *dame-jeanne*⟧ a large bottle of glass or earthenware in a wicker casing

de·mili·ta·rize (dē mil′ə tə rīz′) *vt.* **-rized′, -riz′ing** to free from organized military control

demi·monde (dem′i mänd′) *n.* ⟦Fr < *demi-* + *monde*, world⟧ the class of women who have lost social standing because of sexual promiscuity

de·mise (dē miz′) *n.* ⟦< L *de-*, down + *mittere*, send⟧ 1 *Law* a transfer of an estate by lease 2 death — *vt.* **-mised′, -mis′ing** to transfer (an estate) by lease

demi·tasse (dem′i täs′, -tas′) *n.* ⟦Fr < *demi-* + *tasse*, cup⟧ a small cup of or for after-dinner coffee

demo (dem′ō) *n.* a recording made to demonstrate a song, the talent of a performer, etc.

de·mo·bi·lize (dē mō′bə liz′) *vt.* **-lized′, -liz′ing** to disband (troops) —**de·mo′bi·li·za′tion** *n.*

de·moc·ra·cy (di mäk′rə sē) *n., pl.* **-cies** ⟦< Gr *dēmos*, the people + *kratein*, to rule⟧ 1 government by the people, directly or through representatives 2 a country, etc. with such government 3 equality of rights, opportunity, and treatment

dem·o·crat (dem′ə krat′) *n.* 1 one who supports or practices democracy 2 [D-] a Democratic Party member

dem′o·crat′ic *adj.* 1 of or for democracy 2 of or for all the people 3 not snobbish 4 [D-] of the Democratic Party —**dem′o·crat′i·cally** *adv.*

Democratic Party one of the two major political parties in the U.S.

de·modu·la·tion (dē mä′jōō lā′shən) *n. Radio* the recovery, at the receiver, of a signal that has been modulated on a carrier wave

dem·o·graph·ics (dem′ə graf′iks) *n.pl.* demographic characteristics of a population, as age, sex, income, etc., for analysis

de·mog·ra·phy (di mä′grə fē) *n.* ⟦< Gr *dēmos*, the people + -GRAPHY⟧ the statistical study of human populations —**de·mog′ra·pher** *n.* —**dem·o·graphic** (dem′ə graf′ik) *adj.* —**dem′o·graph′i·cally** *adv.*

de·mol·ish (di mäl′ish) *vt.* ⟦< L *de-*, down + *moliri*, build⟧ to wreck —**demo·li·tion** (dem′ə lish′ən) *n.*

de·mon (dē′mən) *n.* ⟦< L *daemon*⟧ 1 a devil; evil spirit 2 a person or thing regarded as evil, cruel, etc. —**de·monic** (di män′ik) *adj.*

de·mon·etize (dē män′ə tīz′) *vt.* **-tized′, -tiz′ing** to deprive (esp. currency) of its standard value

de·mo·niac (dē mō′nē ak′) *adj.* of or like a demon; fiendish; frenzied Also **de·mo·nia·cal** (dē′mə nī′ə kəl)

de·mon·stra·ble (di män′strə bəl) *adj.* that can be demonstrated, or proved —**de·mon′strably** *adv.*

dem·on·strate (dem′ən strāt′) *vt.* **-strat′ed, -strat′ing** ⟦< L *de-*, from + *monstrare*, to show⟧ 1 to show by reasoning; prove 2 to explain by using examples, etc. 3 to show how something works — *vi.* to show feelings or views publicly by meetings, etc. —**dem′on·stra′tion** *n.* —**dem′on·stra′tor** *n.*

de·mon·stra·tive (di män′strə tiv) *adj.* 1 illustrative 2 giving proof (*of*) 3 showing feelings openly 4 *Gram.* pointing out ["this" is a *demonstrative* pronoun] — *n. Gram.* a demonstrative pronoun or adjective

de·mor·al·ize (dē môr′ə liz′) *vt.* **-ized′, -iz′ing** 1 to lower the morale of 2 to throw into confusion —**de·mor′ali·za′tion** *n.*

de·mote (dē mōt′) *vt.* **-mot′ed, -mot′ing** ⟦DE- + (PRO)MOTE⟧ to reduce to a lower rank —**de·mo′tion** *n.*

de·mul·cent (dē mul′sənt) *adj.* ⟦< L *de-*, down + *mulcere*, to stroke⟧ soothing — *n.* a soothing ointment

de·mur (dē mʉr′, di-) *vi.* **-murred′, -mur′ring** ⟦< L *de-*, from + *mora*, a delay⟧ to hesitate, as because of doubts; have scruples; object — *n.* a demurring: also **de·mur′ral**

de·mure (di myoor′) *adj.* ⟦< ME *de-* (prob. intens.) + OFr *mʉr*, mature⟧ 1 decorous; modest 2 affectedly modest; coy —**de·mure′ly** *adv.*

de·mur·rage (di mʉr′ij) *n.* 1 the compensation payable

THESAURUS

deluxe *a.* elegant, luxurious, grand; see LUXURIOUS.

demand *n.* 1 [A peremptory communication] order, call, charge; see COMMAND. 2 [Willingness to purchase] trade, request, sale, bid, need, requirement, interest, call, rush, search, inquiry, desire to buy; see also DESIRE 1.—*Ant.* INDIFFERENCE, lack of interest, sales resistance. — **in demand** sought, needed, requested; see WANTED. —**on demand** ready, prepared, usable; see AVAILABLE.

demand *v.* charge, direct, command; see ASK.

demanding *a.* fussy, imperious, exacting; see CRITICAL.

demented *a.* crazy, bemused, unbalanced; see INSANE.

demerit *n.* bad mark, loss of points, poor grade; see FAULT 1, PUNISHMENT.

demobilize *v.* disband, disperse, withdraw; see DISARM.

democracy *n.* justice, the greatest good for the greatest number, equality, popular suffrage, individual enterprise, capitalism, laissez faire, rugged individualism, freedom of religion, freedom of speech, freedom of the press, the right to work, private ownership, emancipation, political equality, democratic spirit, the American Way*; see also EQUALITY, FREEDOM 2.—*Ant.* dictatorship, feudalism, tyranny.

democrat *n.* republican, Social Democrat, state socialist, advocate of democracy, constitutionalist, individualist.—*Ant.* DICTATOR, Nazi, autocrat.

Democrat *n.* Southern Democrat, constitutional Democrat, Jeffersonian Democrat, Dixiecrat*, Fair Dealer*, Great Society Democrat*, New Dealer*; see also REPUBLICAN.— *Ant.* REPUBLICAN, Tory, Socialist.

democratic *a.* popular, constitutional, representative, free, equal, common, bourgeois, individualistic, communal, laissez-faire.

demolish *v.* wreck, devastate, obliterate; see DESTROY.

demolition *n.* extermination, annihilation, wrecking; see DESTRUCTION 1, EXPLOSION.

demon *n.* imp, vampire, incubus; see DEVIL.

demonstrate *v.* 1 [To prove] show, make evident, confirm; see PROVE. 2 [To present for effect] exhibit, manifest, parade; see DISPLAY.

demonstration *n.* 1 [An exhibition] showing, presentation, exhibit; see DISPLAY, SHOW 1. 2 [A mass rally] picket line, march, sit-in; see PROTEST.

demoralize *v.* weaken, unman, enfeeble; see DISCOURAGE.

demoralized *a.* unnerved, weakened, depressed; see SAD 1.

demote *v.* downgrade, lower, bust*; see DECREASE 2, DISMISS.

for delaying a vehicle or vessel carrying freight, as by failure to load or unload **2** the delay itself

de·mur·rer (di mur′ər) *n.* ⟦see DEMUR⟧ **1** a plea for dismissal of a lawsuit because statements supporting a claim are defective **2** an objection

den (den) *n.* ⟦OE *denn*⟧ **1** the lair of a wild animal **2** a haunt, as of thieves **3** a small, cozy room where one can be alone to read, work, etc.

de·na·ture (dē nā′chər) *vt.* **-tured, -tur·ing 1** to change the nature of **2** to make (alcohol) unfit to drink

den·drite (den′drīt) *n.* ⟦< Gr *dendron*, tree⟧ the part of a nerve cell that carries impulses toward the cell body

de·nial (dē nī′əl) *n.* **1** a denying; saying "no" (to a request, etc.) **2** a contradiction **3** a refusal to believe or accept (a doctrine, etc.) **4** SELF-DENIAL

de·nier[1] (den′yər) *n.* ⟦< L *deni*, by tens⟧ a unit of weight for measuring the fineness of threads of silk, nylon, etc.

de·nier[2] (dē nī′ər) *n.* one who denies

deni·grate (den′ə grāt′) *vt.* **-grat′ed, -grat′ing** ⟦< L < *de-*, entirely + *nigrare*, blacken⟧ to belittle the character of; defame —**den′i·gra′tion** *n.* —**den′i·gra′tor** *n.*

denim (den′im) *n.* ⟦< Fr (serge) de *Nîmes*, (serge) of Nîmes, town in France⟧ a coarse, twilled, cotton cloth

deni·zen (den′ə zən) *n.* ⟦< L *de intus*, from within⟧ an inhabitant or frequenter of a particular place

de·nomi·nate (dē näm′ə nāt′) *vt.* **-nat′ed, -nat′ing** ⟦< L *de-*, intens. + *nominare*, to name⟧ to name; call

de·nom·i·na·tion (-nā′shən) *n.* **1** the act of naming **2** a name **3** a class or kind, as of coins, having a specific name or value **4** a particular religious body —**de·nom′i·na′tional** *adj.* of, or under the control of, a religious denomination

de·nom′i·na′tor (-nāt′ər) *n.* **1** a shared characteristic **2** *Math.* the term below the line in a fraction

de·note (dē nōt′) *vt.* **-not′ed, -not′ing** ⟦< L *de-*, down + *notare*, to mark⟧ **1** to indicate **2** to signify; mean —**de·no·ta·tion** (dē′nō tā′shən) *n.*

de·noue·ment or **dé·noue·ment** (dā′nōō män′) *n.* ⟦Fr⟧ the outcome or unraveling of a plot in a drama, etc.

de·nounce (dē nouns′) *vt.* **-nounced′, -nounc′ing** ⟦see DENUNCIATION⟧ **1** to accuse publicly; inform against **2** to condemn strongly —**de·nounce′ment** *n.*

dense (dens) *adj.* **dens′er, dens′est** ⟦< L *densus*, compact⟧ **1** packed tightly together **2** difficult to get through **3** stupid —**dense′ly** *adv.* —**dense′ness** *n.*

den·sity (den′sə tē) *n., pl.* **-ties 1** a dense condition **2** stupidity **3** number per unit, as of area **4** ratio of the mass of an object to its volume

dent (dent) *n.* ⟦ME, var. of DINT⟧ **1** a slight hollow made in a surface by a blow **2** a slight effect — *vt., vi.* to make or receive a dent (in)

den·tal (dent′'l) *adj.* ⟦< L *dens*, tooth⟧ of or for the teeth or dentistry

dental floss thread for removing food particles between the teeth

den·ti·frice (den′tə fris) *n.* ⟦< L *dens*, tooth + *fricare*, rub⟧ any preparation for cleaning teeth

den·tin (den′tin) *n.* ⟦see DENTAL⟧ the hard tissue under the enamel of a tooth Also **den′tine′** (-tēn′, -tin)

den·tist (den′tist) *n.* one whose profession is the care and repair of teeth —**den′tistry** *n.*

den·ture (den′chər) *n.* ⟦see DENTAL⟧ a set of teeth

de·nu·clear·ize (dē nōō′klē ər īz′) *vt.* **-ized′, -iz′ing** to prohibit the possession of nuclear weapons in

de·nude (dē nōōd′) *vt.* **-nud′ed, -nud′ing** ⟦< L *de-*, off + *nudare*, to strip⟧ to make bare or naked; strip

de·nun·ci·a·tion (dē nun′sē ā′shən) *n.* ⟦< L *de-*, intens. + *nuntiare*, announce⟧ the act of denouncing

deny (dē nī′) *vt.* **-nied′, -ny′ing** ⟦< L *de-*, intens. + *negare*, to deny⟧ **1** to declare (a statement) untrue **2** to refuse to accept as true or right **3** to repudiate **4** to refuse to grant or give **5** to refuse the request of —**deny oneself** to do without desired things

de·odor·ant (dē ō′dər ənt) *adj.* that can counteract undesired odors — *n.* any deodorant preparation

de·o′dor·ize′ (-dər īz′) *vt.* **-ized′, -iz′ing** to counteract the odor of —**de·o′dor·iz′er** *n.*

de·part (dē pärt′) *vi.* ⟦< L *dis-*, apart + *partire*, divide⟧ **1** to go away; leave **2** to die **3** to deviate (from) — *vt.* to leave

de·part′ed *adj.* **1** gone away **2** dead —**the departed** the dead

de·part·ee (dē′pär tē′) *n.* one who has departed, as from a job, country, etc.

de·part·ment (dē pärt′mənt) *n.* **1** a separate part or division, as of a business **2** a field of activity —**de′part·men′tal** (-ment′'l) *adj.*

de·part·men·tal·ize′ (-ment′'l īz′) *vt.* **-ized′, -iz′ing** to organize into departments —**de′part·men′tali·za′tion** *n.*

department store a large retail store for the sale of many kinds of goods arranged in departments

de·par·ture (dē pär′chər) *n.* **1** a departing **2** a starting out, as on a trip **3** a deviation (from)

de·pend (dē pend′) *vi.* ⟦< L *de-*, down + *pendere*, to hang⟧ **1** to be determined by something else; be contingent (on) **2** to have trust; rely (on) **3** to rely (on) for support or aid

de·pend′able *adj.* trustworthy; reliable —**de·pend′abil′ity** *n.*

de·pend′ence *n.* **1** a being dependent **2** reliance (on) for support or aid **3** reliance; trust **4** DEPENDENCY (sense 4)

de·pend′ency *n., pl.* **-cies 1** dependence **2** something

---

THESAURUS

den *n.* **1** [The home of an animal] cavern, lair, cave; see HOLE 1. **2** [A private or secluded room] study, recreation room, rec room*; see RETREAT 2, ROOM 2.

denial *n.* repudiation, disclaimer, rejection, refutation, rejecting, retraction, dismissal, renunciation, refusal to recognize, the cold shoulder*, the brush-off*; see also OPPOSITION 2.—*Ant.* ACKNOWLEDGMENT, avowal, confession.

denomination *n.* **1** [A class] category, classification, group; see CLASS 1. **2** [A religious group] belief, creed, sect; see CHURCH 3.

denounce *v.* condemn, threaten, charge, blame, accuse, indict, arraign, implicate, incriminate, upbraid, impugn, prosecute, revile, stigmatize, ostracize, reproach, castigate, brand, boycott, rebuke, dress down, take to task, damn, impeach, scold, reprimand, reprove, condemn openly, charge with, blacklist, propose, knock*, rip into*, blackball*; see also DENY.—*Ant.* PRAISE, laud, commend.

dense *a.* **1** [Close together] solid, compact, impenetrable; see THICK 1. **2** [Slow-witted] stupid, dumb*, imbecilic; see DULL 3, IGNORANT 2.

density *n.* solidity, thickness, impenetrability, consistency, quantity, bulk, heaviness, body, compactness,

denseness; see also MASS 1, WEIGHT 1.—*Ant.* LIGHTNESS, rarity, thinness.

dent *n.* indentation, depression, impression, dimple, nick, notch, dip, cavity, cut, incision, sinkhole, pit, trough, furrow, scratch; see also HOLE 1.

dent *v.* hollow, depress, indent, gouge, sink, dig, imprint, mark, dimple, pit, notch, scratch, nick, make a dent in, perforate, ridge, furrow.—*Ant.* STRAIGHTEN, bulge, make protrude.

dentist *n.* DDS, dental practitioner, specialist; see DOCTOR.

deny *v.* contradict, disagree with, disprove, disallow, gainsay, disavow, disclaim, negate, repudiate, controvert, revoke, rebuff, reject, renounce, discard, not admit, take exception to, disbelieve, spurn, doubt, veto, discredit, nullify, say "no" to; see also DENOUNCE, REFUSE.—*Ant.* ADMIT, accept, affirm.

deodorant *n.* disinfectant, deodorizer, fumigator; see CLEANSER, COSMETIC.

depart *v.* go, quit, withdraw; see LEAVE 1.

departed *a.* **1** [Dead] defunct, expired, deceased; see DEAD 1. **2** [Gone away] left, disappeared, moved; see GONE 1.

department *n.* **1** [The field of one's

activity] jurisdiction, activity, interest, occupation, province, bureau, business, capacity, dominion, administration, station, function, office, walk of life, vocation, specialty, field, duty, assignment, bailiwick; see also JOB 1. **2** [An organized subdivision] section, office, bureau, precinct, tract, range, quarter, area, arena, corps, agency, board, administration, circuit, territory, ward, state office, district office, force, staff, beat; see also DIVISION 2.

department store *n.* variety store, supermarket, shopping center, shopper's square, mall, drygoods store, mail-order house, bazaar, fair, bargain store; see also MARKET 1.

departure *n.* going, departing, separation, embarkation, taking leave, sailing, withdrawal, hegira, evacuation, passage, setting out, setting forth, parting, takeoff, taking off, becoming airborne, starting, leaving, flight, exodus, exit, walkout, getaway; see also RETREAT 1.—*Ant.* ARRIVAL, landing, invasion.

dependable *a.* trustworthy, steady, sure; see RELIABLE.

dependence *n.* reliance, servility, inability to act independently, subordination to the direction of another, subjection to control, subservience;

dependent 3 a territory, as a possession, subordinate to its governing country 4 addiction to alcohol or drugs

de·pend'ent *adj.* 1 hanging down 2 determined by something else 3 relying (*on*) for support, etc. 4 subordinate 5 addicted — *n.* one relying on another for support, etc. Also **de·pend'ant** —**de·pend'ently** *adv.*

dependent clause *Gram.* a clause that cannot function as a complete sentence by itself

de·pict (dē pikt') *vt.* ⟦< L *de-*, intens. + *pingere*, to paint ⟧ 1 to represent by drawing, painting, etc. 2 to describe — **de·pic'tion** *n.*

de·pila·tory (di pil'ə tôr'ē) *adj.* ⟦< L *de-*, from + *pilus*, hair⟧ serving to remove unwanted hair — *n.*, *pl.* **-ries** a depilatory substance or device

de·plane (dē plān') *vi.* **-planed'**, **-plan'ing** to leave an airplane after it lands

de·plete (dē plēt') *vt.* **-plet'ed**, **-plet'ing** ⟦< L *de-*, from + *plere*, fill⟧ 1 to use up (funds, etc.) 2 to use up the resources, etc. of —**de·ple'tion** *n.*

de·plor·able (dē plôr'ə bəl) *adj.* regrettable, very bad, wretched, etc. —**de·plor'ably** *adv.*

de·plore (dē plôr') *vt.* **-plored'**, **-plor'ing** ⟦< L *de-*, intens. + *plorare*, weep⟧ 1 to regret deeply 2 to disapprove of

de·ploy (dē ploi') *vt.*, *vi.* ⟦< L *dis-*, apart + *plicare*, to fold⟧ to spread out or place (military troops, etc.), as by a plan —**de·ploy'ment** *n.*

de·po·lar·ize (dē pō'lər iz') *vt.* **-ized'**, **-iz'ing** to destroy or counteract the polarization of —**de·po'lari·za'tion** *n.*

de·po·liti·cize (dē pə lit'ə siz') *vt.* **-cized'**, **-ciz'ing** to remove from political influence

de·pon·ent (dē pōn'ənt) *n.* ⟦< L *de-*, down + *ponere*, put⟧ *Law* one who gives written testimony under oath

de·popu·late (dē päp'yə lāt') *vt.* **-lat'ed**, **-lat'ing** to reduce the population of —**de·pop'u·la'tion** *n.*

de·port (dē pôrt') *vt.* ⟦< L *de-*, from + *portare*, carry⟧ 1 to behave (oneself) 2 to expel (an alien) —**de'por·ta'tion** *n.*

de·port'ment *n.* conduct; behavior

de·pose (dē pōz') *vt.* **-posed'**, **-pos'ing** ⟦< OFr *de-*, from + *poser*, cease⟧ 1 to remove from office 2 *a*) to testify *b*) to take the deposition of

de·posit (dē päz'it) *vt.* ⟦< L *de-*, down + *ponere*, put⟧ 1 to place (money, etc.) for safekeeping, as in a bank 2 to give as a pledge or partial payment 3 to set down 4 to cause (sediment, etc.) to settle — *n.* 1 something placed for safekeeping, as money in a bank 2 a pledge or part payment 3 something deposited or left lying —**de·pos'i·tor** *n.*

depo·si·tion (dep'ə zish'ən) *n.* 1 a deposing or being deposed 2 testimony 3 something deposited

de·posi·tory (dē päz'ə tôr'ē) *n.*, *pl.* **-ries** a place where things are put for safekeeping

de·pot (dē'pō; *military & Brit* dep'ō) *n.* ⟦< Fr: see DEPOSIT⟧ 1 a warehouse 2 a railroad or bus station 3 a storage place for military supplies

de·prave (dē prāv') *vt.* **-praved'**, **-prav'ing** ⟦< L *de-*, intens. + *pravus*, crooked⟧ to make morally bad; corrupt —**de·praved'** *adj.* —**de·prav'ity** (-prav'ə tē), *pl.* **-ties**, *n.*

dep·re·cate (dep'rə kāt') *vt.* **-cat'ed**, **-cat'ing** ⟦< L *de-*, off + *precari*, pray⟧ 1 to express disapproval of 2 to belittle —**dep're·ca'tion** *n.* —**dep're·ca'to·ry** (-kə tôr'ē) *adj.*

de·pre·ci·ate (dē prē'shē āt') *vt.*, *vi.* **-at'ed**, **-at'ing** ⟦< L *de-*, from + *pretium*, price⟧ 1 to lessen in value or price 2 to belittle —**de·pre'cia'tion** *n.*

dep·re·da·tion (dep'rə dā'shən) *n.* ⟦< L *de-*, intens. + *praedari*, to plunder⟧ a robbing or plundering

de·press (dē pres') *vt.* ⟦< L *de-*, down + *premere*, to press⟧ 1 to press down 2 to sadden; deject 3 to make less active 4 to lower in value, price, etc. —**de·pressed'** *adj.*

de·pres'sant *n.* a medicine, drug, etc. that lessens nervous activity

de·pres·sion (dē presh'ən) *n.* 1 a depressing or being depressed 2 a hollow or low place 3 low spirits; dejection 4 a decrease in force, activity, etc. 5 a period of reduced business, much unemployment, etc.

de·pres·sive (dē pres'iv) *adj.* 1 tending to depress 2 characterized by psychological depression — *n.* one suffering from psychological depression

de·prive (dē priv') *vt.* **-prived'**, **-priv'ing** ⟦< L *de-*, intens. + *privare*, to separate⟧ 1 to take away from forcibly 2 to keep from having, etc. —**dep·ri·va·tion** (dep'rə vā'shən) *n.*

de·pro·gram (dē prō'gram', -grəm) *vt.* **-grammed'** or **-gramed'**, **-gram'ming** or **-gram'ing** to cause to abandon rigidly held beliefs, etc. by undoing the effects of indoctrination

dept. 1 department 2 deputy

depth (depth) *n.* ⟦< ME *dep*, deep + -TH[1]⟧ 1 the distance from the top downward, or from front to back 2 deepness 3 intensity 4 [*usually pl.*] the deepest or inmost part —**in depth** comprehensively

---

THESAURUS

see also NECESSITY 3.

dependent *a.* 1 [Subordinate] inferior, secondary, lesser; see SUBORDINATE. 2 [Needing outside support] helpless, poor, immature, clinging, not able to sustain itself, on a string*; see also WEAK 5. 3 [Contingent] liable to, subject to, incidental to, conditioned, sustained by, unable to exist without, subordinate, accessory to, subservient, controlled by, regulated by, determined by; see also CONDITIONAL.

dependent *n.* retired person, old man, old woman, foster child, charge, orphan, minor, delinquent, protegé, hanger-on.

depending (on) *a.* contingent upon, regulated by, controlled by, determined by, in the event of, on the condition that, subject to, providing, provided, secondary to, growing from; see also CONDITIONAL.

depend on *v.* 1 [To be contingent] be determined by, rest with, rest on, be subordinate to, be dependent on, be based on, be subject to, hinge on, turn on, turn upon, be in the power of, be conditioned by, revolve on, trust to, be at the mercy of. 2 [To rely on] put faith in, confide in, believe in; see TRUST 1.

depleted *a.* emptied, exhausted, spent; see WASTED.

depletion *n.* exhaustion, consumption, deficiency; see EMPTINESS.

deport *v.* exile, ship out, ship away, expel from a given place; see also BANISH, DISMISS.

deposit *v.* 1 [To lay down] drop, place, put; see INSTALL. 2 [To present money for safekeeping] invest, amass, store, keep, stock up, bank, hoard, collect, treasure, lay away, put in the bank, entrust, transfer, put for safekeeping, put aside for a rainy day*, salt away*; see also ACCUMULATE, SAVE 2.—*Ant.* SPEND, withdraw, put out. —**on deposit** hoarded, stored, saved; see KEPT 2.

depot *n.* station, base, lot, freight depot, passenger depot, railway depot, railroad depot, terminal, railway station, railroad yards, stockyards, sidetrack, loading track, ammunition dump, ticket office, waiting room, junction, central station, airport, harbor, station house, stopping-place, destination.

deprave *v.* pervert, debase, degrade; see CORRUPT.

depraved *a.* low, mean, base; see BAD.

depreciate *v.* deteriorate, lessen, worsen; see DECREASE 1.

depreciation *n.* harm, reduction, shrinkage; see LOSS 3.

depress *v.* 1 [To bring to a lower level] press down, squash, settle; see FLATTEN, PRESS 1. 2 [To bring to a lower state] reduce, dampen, dishearten, debase, degrade, abase, dismay, sadden, mock, darken, scorn, reduce to tears, deject, weigh down, keep down, cast down, beat down, chill, dull, oppress, lower in spirits, throw cold water on*; see also DISCOURAGE, DISGRACE, HUMBLE, HUMILIATE.—*Ant.* URGE, animate, stimulate.

depressed *a.* discouraged, pessimistic, cast down; see SAD 1.

depressing *a.* discouraging, disheartening, saddening; see DISMAL, SAD 1.

depression *n.* 1 [Something lower than its surroundings] cavity, dip, sinkhole; see HOLE 1. 2 [Low spirits] despair, despondency, sorrow, unhappiness, gloom, dejection, melancholy, misery, trouble, worry, discouragement, hopelessness, distress, desperation, desolation, dreariness, dullness, cheerlessness, darkness, bleakness, oppression, gloominess, dumps, bleaks*, doldrums; see also GRIEF, SADNESS.—*Ant.* JOY, cheer, satisfaction. 3 [Period of commercial stress] decline, unemployment, slack times, hard times, bad times, inflation, crisis, economic decline, over-production, economic stagnation, recession, panic, crash, slump; see also FAILURE 1.

deprive *v.* strip, despoil, divest; see SEIZE 2.

depth *n.* 1 [Vertical or lateral distance] lowness, pitch, extent down from a given point, downward measure, perpendicular measurement from the bottom; see also EXPANSE.—*Ant.* HEIGHT, shallowness, flatness. 2 [Deepness] profundity, intensity, abyss, pit, base, bottom of the sea; see also BOTTOM. 3 [Intellectual power] profundity, weightiness, acumen; see WISDOM. —**in depth** extensively, broadly, comprehensively, thoroughly.

depu·ta·tion (dep′yoo tā′shən) *n.* 1 a deputing 2 a delegation

de·pute (dē pyoot′) *vt.* **-put′ed, -put′ing** ⟦< L *de-*, from + *putare*, cleanse⟧ 1 to give (authority, etc.) to a deputy 2 to appoint as one's substitute, etc.

depu·tize (dep′yoo tīz′) *vt.* **-tized′, -tiz′ing** to appoint as deputy

depu·ty (dep′yoo tē) *n., pl.* **-ties** a person appointed to act for another

de·rail (dē rāl′) *vt., vi.* to run off the rails, as a train —**de·rail′ment** *n.*

de·rail·leur (də rāl′ər) *n.* ⟦Fr⟧ a gear-shifting mechanism on a bicycle for shifting the sprocket chain from one size of sprocket wheel to another

de·range (dē rānj′) *vt.* **-ranged′, -rang′ing** ⟦< OFr *des-*, apart + *rengier*, to range⟧ 1 to upset the arrangement or working of 2 to make insane —**de·range′ment** *n.*

Der·by (dur′bē; *Brit* där′-) *n., pl.* **-bies** 1 ⟦after an Earl of *Derby*, who founded the race (1780)⟧ any of various horse races, as ones held annually in England, Kentucky, etc. 2 any of various contests or races, open to anyone 3 [d-] a stiff felt hat with a round crown

de·regu·late (dē reg′yə lāt′) *vt.* **-lat′ed, -lat′ing** to remove regulations governing —**de·reg·u·la′tion** *n.*

der·elict (der′ə likt′) *adj.* ⟦< L *de-*, intens. + *relinquere*: see RELINQUISH⟧ 1 deserted by the owner; abandoned 2 negligent — *n.* 1 an abandoned ship on the open sea 2 a destitute and rejected person

der′elic′tion (-lik′shən) *n.* 1 a forsaking or being forsaken 2 a neglect of, or failure in, duty

de·ride (di rīd′) *vt.* **-rid′ed, -rid′ing** ⟦< L *de-*, down + *ridere*, to laugh⟧ to laugh at in scorn; ridicule —**de·ri′sion** (-rizh′ən) *n.* —**de·ri′sive** (-rī′siv) *adj.* —**de·ri′sively** *adv.*

deri·va·tion (der′ə vā′shən) *n.* 1 a deriving or being derived 2 the source or origin of something 3 the origin and development of a word

de·riva·tive (də riv′ə tiv) *adj.* derived — *n.* something derived

de·rive (di rīv′) *vt.* **-rived′, -riv′ing** ⟦< L *de-*, from + *rivus*, a stream⟧ 1 to get or receive (something) *from* a source 2 to deduce or infer 3 to trace from or to a source — *vi.* to be derived

der·ma·ti·tis (dur′mə tīt′is) *n.* ⟦< Gr *derma*, skin + -ITIS⟧ inflammation of the skin

der·ma·tol·ogy (dur′mə täl′ə jē) *n.* ⟦< Gr *derma*, skin + -LOGY⟧ the branch of medicine dealing with the skin —**der′ma·tol′o·gist** *n.*

der·mis (dur′mis) *n.* ⟦see EPIDERMIS⟧ the layer of skin just below the epidermis

dero·gate (der′ə gāt′) *vi., vt.* **-gat′ed, -gat′ing** ⟦< L *de-*, from + *rogare*, ask⟧ to detract or disparage —**der′o·ga′tion** *n.*

de·roga·tory (di räg′ə tôr′ē) *adj.* ⟦see prec.⟧ 1 detracting 2 disparaging; belittling

der·rick (der′ik) *n.* ⟦after Thos. *Derrick*, London hangman of the early 17th c.: orig. applied to a gallows⟧ 1 a pivoted beam for lifting and moving heavy objects 2 a tall framework, as over an oil well, to support drilling machinery, etc.

der·rière (der′yer′, der′ē er′) *n.* ⟦Fr, back part⟧ the buttocks

der·rin·ger (der′in jər) *n.* ⟦after H. *Deringer*, 19th-c. U.S. gunsmith⟧ a small, short-barreled pistol

der·vish (dur′vish) *n.* ⟦< Pers *darvēsh*, beggar⟧ a member of a Muslim ascetic religious group

de·sali·na·tion (dē′sal′ə nā′shən) *n.* ⟦DE- + SALIN(E) + -ATION⟧ the removal of salt, esp. from sea water to make it drinkable —**de·sal′i·nate′** *vt.*

des·cant (des′kant′, des kant′) *vi.* ⟦< L *dis-*, apart + *cantus*, song⟧ 1 to discourse (*on* or *upon*) 2 to sing

de·scend (dē send′) *vi.* ⟦< L *de-*, down + *scandere*, climb⟧ 1 to move down to a lower place 2 to pass from an earlier to a later time, from greater to less, etc. 3 to stoop downward 4 to come down (*from* a source) 5 to stoop (*to*) 6 to make a sudden attack or visit (*on*) — *vt.* to move down along

de·scend′ant *n.* an offspring of a certain ancestor, family, group, etc.

de·scent (dē sent′) *n.* 1 a coming down or going down 2 ancestry 3 a downward slope 4 a way down 5 a sudden attack 6 a decline

de·scribe (di skrīb′) *vt.* **-scribed′, -scrib′ing** ⟦< L *de-*, from + *scribere*, write⟧ 1 to tell or write about 2 to trace the outline of —**de·scrib′er** *n.*

de·scrip·tion (di skrip′shən) *n.* 1 the act or technique of describing 2 a statement or passage that describes 3 sort; kind 4 a tracing or outlining —**de·scrip′tive** (-tiv) *adj.*

de·scry (di skrī′) *vt.* **-scried′, -scry′ing** ⟦< OFr *descrier*, proclaim⟧ 1 to catch sight of; discern 2 to detect

des·ecrate (des′i krāt′) *vt.* **-crat′ed, -crat′ing** ⟦DE- (sense 4) + (CON)SECRATE⟧ to violate the sacredness of; profane —**des′ecra′tion** *n.*

de·seg·re·gate (dē seg′rə gāt′) *vt., vi.* **-gat′ed, -gat′ing** to abolish racial segregation in (public schools, etc.) —**de·seg′re·ga′tion** *n.*

de·sen·si·tize (dē sen′sə tīz′) *vt.* **-tized′, -tiz′ing** to make less sensitive, as to an allergen

de·sert¹ (di zurt′) *vt., vi.* ⟦< L *de-*, from + *serere*, join⟧ 1 to abandon; forsake 2 to leave (one's military post, etc.) without permission and with no intent to return —**de·sert′er** *n.* —**de·ser′tion** (-zur′shən) *n.*

des·ert² (dez′ərt) *n.* ⟦see prec.⟧ 1 an uninhabited region; wilderness 2 a dry, barren, sandy region

de·sert³ (di zurt′) *n.* ⟦see DESERVE⟧ [*often pl.*] deserved reward or punishment

■■■ **THESAURUS** ■■■

deputy *n.* lieutenant, appointee, aide; see ASSISTANT, DELEGATE.

derail *v.* run off the rails, be wrecked, fall off; see CRASH 1, WRECK.

derange *v.* madden, craze, unbalance; see CONFUSE, DISTURB.

deranged *a.* demented, crazy, mad; see INSANE.

deride *v.* scorn, jeer, mock; see RIDICULE.

derision *n.* scorn, mockery, disdain; see RIDICULE.

derivation *n.* root, source, beginning; see ORIGIN 3.

derive *v.* draw a conclusion, work out, conclude; see ASSUME.

derogatory *a.* belittling, faultfinding, detracting; see CRITICAL, SARCASTIC.

descend *v.* slide, settle, gravitate, slip, dismount, topple, plunge, sink, dip, pass downward, pitch, light, deplane, tumble, move downward, come down upon, slump, trip, stumble, flutter down, plummet, submerge, step down, climb down, go down, swoop down, get off; see also DIVE, DROP 1, FALL 1.—*Ant.* CLIMB, ascend, mount.

descendants *n.* offspring, kin, children; see FAMILY.

descent *n.* 1 [A downward incline] declivity, fall, slide; see HILL, INCLINATION 2. 2 [The act of descending] slump, downfall, drop, lapse, subsiding, falling, coming down, sinking, reduction, landslide, tumble, decline; see also FALL 1.—*Ant.* RISE, mounting, growth. 3 [Lineal relationship] extraction, origin, lineage; see FAMILY, RELATIONSHIP.

describe *v.* delineate, characterize, portray, depict, picture, illuminate, make clear, make apparent, make vivid, give the details of, specify, give meaning to, elucidate, report, draw, paint, illustrate, detail, make sense of, relate, express, narrate, label, name, call, term, write up, give the dope on*, spell out*; see also DEFINE, EXPLAIN.

description *n.* narration, story, portrayal, word picture, account, report, delineation, sketch, specifications, characterization, declaration, rehearsal, information, definition, record, brief, summary, depiction, explanation, write-up; see also RECORD 1.

descriptive *a.* designating, identifying, definitive, photographic, describing, expository, interpretive, narrative, characterizing, expressive, clear, true to life, illustrative, lifelike, vivid, picturesque, circumstantial, eloquent, detailed, pictorial, indicative, revealing; see also CHARACTERISTIC, EXPLANATORY, GRAPHIC 1, 2.—*Ant.* DULL, analytical, expository.

desert¹ *v.* defect, be absent without leave, abandon one's post, sneak off, run away from duty, violate one's oath, leave unlawfully, go AWOL*, go over the hill*; see also ABANDON 2.—*Ant.* OBEY, stay, do one's duty.

desert² *n.* waste, sand, wastelands, barren plains, arid region, deserted region, sand dunes, lava beds, infertile region, salt flats, abandoned land; see also WILDERNESS.

deserted *a.* left, forsaken, relinquished; see ABANDONED, EMPTY.

deserter *n.* runaway, fugitive, refugee, truant, defector, derelict, delinquent, lawbreaker, betrayer, traitor, backslider, slacker; see also CRIMINAL, TRAITOR.

desertion *n.* abandonment, flight, escape, departure, leaving, defection, defecting, renunciation, withdrawal, avoidance, evasion, elusion, truancy, retirement, resignation, divorce, backsliding, running out on*, going back on*; see also ESCAPE.—*Ant.* LOYALTY, cooperation, union.

de·serve (di zurv′) *vt., vi.* **-served′, -serv′ing** ⟦ < L *de-*, intens. + *servire*, serve ⟧ to be worthy (of); merit —**de·serv′edly** (-zur′vid lē) *adv.*

des·ic·cate (des′i kāt′) *vt., vi.* **-cat′ed, -cat′ing** ⟦ < L *de-*, intens. + *siccus*, dry ⟧ to dry out completely

de·sid·er·atum (di zid′ər āt′əm) *n., pl.* **-ta** (-ə) ⟦see DESIRE ⟧ something needed and wanted

de·sign (di zin′) *vt.* ⟦ < L *de-*, out + *signum*, a mark ⟧ 1 to sketch an outline for; plan 2 to contrive 3 to plan to do; intend —*vi.* to make original plans, etc. —*n.* 1 a plan; scheme 2 purpose; aim 3 a working plan; pattern 4 arrangement of parts, form, color, etc.; artistic invention —**by design** purposely —**de·sign′er** *n.*

des·ig·nate (dez′ig nāt′) *vt.* **-nat′ed, -nat′ing** ⟦see prec.⟧ 1 to point out; specify 2 to name 3 to appoint —**des′ig·na′tion** *n.*

designated driver the person in a group who abstains from drinking alcoholic beverages so that he or she may safely transport the others by car

de·sign′ing *adj.* scheming; artful —*n.* the art of creating designs, etc.

de·sir·able (di zir′ə bəl) *adj.* 1 worth having 2 pleasing —**de·sir′abil′ity** *n.* —**de·sir′ably** *adv.*

de·sire (di zir′) *vt.* **-sired′, -sir′ing** ⟦ < L *desiderare* ⟧ 1 to long for; crave 2 to ask for —*vi.* to have a desire —*n.* 1 a wish; craving 2 sexual appetite 3 a request 4 a thing desired

de·sir′ous *adj.* desiring

de·sist (di zist′) *vi.* ⟦ < L *de-*, from + *stare*, to stand ⟧ to cease; stop

desk (desk) *n.* ⟦ < ML *desca*, table ⟧ a table for writing, drawing, or reading —*adj.* of, for, or at a desk [a *desk* job]

desk′top′ publishing the production of printed matter by means of a microcomputer and special software for laying out text and illustrations

des·o·late (des′ə lit; *for v.*, -lāt′) *adj.* ⟦ < L *de-*, intens. + *solus*, alone ⟧ 1 lonely; solitary 2 uninhabited 3 laid waste 4 forlorn —*vt.* **-lat′ed, -lat′ing** 1 to rid of inhabitants 2 to lay waste 3 to make forlorn

des′o·la′tion *n.* 1 a making desolate 2 a desolate condition or place 3 misery 4 loneliness

de·spair (di sper′) *vi.* ⟦ < L *de-*, without + *sperare*, to hope ⟧ to lose hope —*n.* 1 loss of hope 2 a person or thing causing despair

des·patch (di spach′) *vt., n.* DISPATCH

des·per·ado (des′pər ä′dō, -ā′-) *n., pl.* **-does** or **-dos** ⟦ 17th-c. Sp < L *desperare:* see DESPAIR ⟧ a dangerous criminal; bold outlaw

des·per·ate (des′pər it) *adj.* 1 rash or violent because of despair 2 having a very great need 3 very serious 4 drastic —**des′per·ately** *adv.*

des·pe·ra·tion (des′pər ā′shən) *n.* 1 the state of being desperate 2 recklessness resulting from despair

des·pi·ca·ble (des′pi kə bəl, di spik′ə-) *adj.* deserving scorn; contemptible —**des′pi·cably** *adv.*

de·spise (di spiz′) *vt.* **-spised′, -spis′ing** ⟦ < L *de*, down + *specere*, look at⟧ 1 to scorn 2 to loathe

de·spite (di spit′) *prep.* ⟦see prec.⟧ in spite of; notwithstanding

de·spoil (dē spoil′) *vt.* ⟦ < L *de-*, intens. + *spoliare*, to strip ⟧ to rob; plunder —**de·spoil′ment** *n.*

de·spond·ency (di spän′dən sē) *n.* ⟦ < L *de-*, from + *spondere*, to promise ⟧ loss of hope; dejection Also **de·spond′ence** —**de·spond′ent** *adj.*

des·pot (des′pət) *n.* ⟦ < Gr *despotēs*, a master ⟧ 1 an absolute ruler 2 a tyrant —**des·pot′ic** (-pät′ik) *adj.* —**des′pot·ism′** (-pət iz′əm) *n.*

des·sert (di zurt′) *n.* ⟦ < L *de*, from + *servire*, serve ⟧ the final course of a meal, typically cake, pie, etc.

des·ti·na·tion (des′tə nā′shən) *n.* 1 the purpose for which something or someone is destined 2 the place toward which one is going or sent

des·tine (des′tin) *vt.* **-tined, -tin·ing** ⟦ < L *de-*, intens. + *stare*, to stand ⟧ 1 to predetermine, as by fate 2 to intend —**destined for** 1 bound for 2 intended for

des·ti·ny (des′tə nē) *n., pl.* **-nies** 1 the seemingly inevitable succession of events 2 (one's) fate

des·ti·tute (des′tə tōōt′) *adj.* ⟦ < L *de-*, down + *statuere*, to set ⟧ 1 lacking: with *of* 2 totally impoverished —**des′ti·tu′tion** *n.*

de·stroy (di stroi′) *vt.* ⟦ < L *de-*, down + *struere*, to build ⟧ 1 to tear down; demolish 2 to wreck; ruin 3 to do away with 4 to kill

THESAURUS

deserve *v.* merit, be worthy of, earn, be deserving, lay claim to, have the right to, be given one's due, be entitled to, warrant, rate*, have it coming*.—*Ant.* FAIL, be unworthy, usurp.

deserved *a.* merited, earned, justified, appropriate, suitable, equitable, right, rightful, proper, fitting, just, due, well-deserved; see also FIT.

deserving *a.* needy, rightful, fitting; see WORTHY.

design *n.* pattern, layout, conception, diagram, drawing, preliminary sketch, draft, blueprint, picture, tracing, outline, depiction, chart, map, plan, perspective, treatment, idea, study; see also COMPOSITION, FORM 1, PURPOSE 1.—*Ant.* CONFUSION, jumble, mess. —**by design** on purpose, with intent, purposely; see DELIBERATELY.

design *v.* block out, outline, sketch; see PLAN 2.

designate *v.* indicate, point out, name; see CHOOSE.

designation *n.* classification, key word, appellation; see CLASS 1, NAME 1.

designer *n.* planner, draftsman, modeler; see ARCHITECT, ARTIST, SCULPTOR.

desirable *a.* 1 [Stimulating erotic desires] seductive, fascinating, alluring; see CHARMING. 2 [Having many good qualities] good, welcome, acceptable; see EXCELLENT.

desire *n.* 1 [The wish to enjoy] aspiration, wish, motive, will, urge, eagerness, propensity, fancy, frenzy, craze, mania, hunger, thirst, attraction, longing, yearning, fondness, liking, inclination, proclivity, craving, relish, hankering*, itch*, yen*; see also AMBITION, GREED.—*Ant.* INDIFFERENCE, unconcern, apathy. 2 [Erotic wish to possess] lust, passion, hunger, appetite, fascination, infatuation, fervor, excitement, sexual love, nymphomania, libido, sensual appetite, carnal passion, eroticism, biological urge, rut*, heat*.—*Ant.* ABSTINENCE, coldness, frigidity.

desire *v.* 1 [To wish for] covet, crave, wish for; see NEED, WANT 1. 2 [To request] ask for, seek, solicit; see BEG. 3 [To want sexually] lust after, hunger for, have the hots for*, be turned on by*; see also WANT 1.

desk *n.* 1 [A piece of furniture] secretary, bureau, box, lectern, frame, case, pulpit; see also FURNITURE, TABLE 1. 2 [A department of an editorial office] jurisdiction, occupation, bureau; see DEPARTMENT.

desolate *a.* deserted, forsaken, uninhabited; see ABANDONED, ISOLATED, ALONE.

desolation *n.* bareness, barrenness, devastation, havoc, ruin, dissolution, wreck, demolition, annihilation, extinction; see also DESERT.

despair *n.* hopelessness, depression, discouragement; see DESPERATION, GLOOM.

despair *v.* lose hope, lose faith, lose heart, give up hope, abandon hope, have no hope, have a heavy heart, abandon oneself to fate; see also ABANDON 1.

despairing *a.* hopeless, despondent, miserable; see SAD 1.

desperado *n.* outlaw, bandit, ruffian; see CRIMINAL.

desperate *a.* 1 [Hopeless] despairing, despondent, downcast; see HOPELESS, SAD 1. 2 [Reckless] incautious, frenzied, wild; see CARELESS, RASH.

desperately *a.* severely, harmfully, perilously; see CARELESSLY, SERIOUSLY 1.

desperation *n.* despondency, despair, depression, discomfort, dejection, distraction, distress, desolation, anxiety, anguish, agony, melancholy, grief, sorrow, worry, trouble, pain, hopelessness, torture, pang, heartache, concern, misery, unhappiness; see also FEAR, FUTILITY, GLOOM.—*Ant.* HOPE, hopefulness, confidence.

despicable *a.* contemptible, abject, base; see MEAN 3.

despise *v.* scorn, disdain, condemn; see HATE 1.

despite *prep.* in spite of, in defiance of, regardless of, even with.

despondent *a.* dejected, discouraged, depressed; see SAD 1.

dessert *n.* sweet, tart, cobbler, jelly, custard, ice, sundae, compote, fruit salad, pudding, ice cream; see also CAKE 2, CANDY, CHEESE, DELICACY 2, FRUIT, PASTRY, PIE.

destination *n.* objective, goal, aim; see PURPOSE 1.

destined *a.* fated, compulsory, foreordained, menacing, near, forthcoming, threatening, in prospect, predestined, predetermined, compelled, condemned, at hand, impending, inexorable, that is to be, in store, to come, directed, ordained, settled, sealed, closed, predesigned, in the wind, in the cards; see also DOOMED, INEVITABLE.—*Ant.* INVOLUNTARY, at will, by chance.

destiny *n.* fate, future, fortune; see DOOM.

destitute *a.* impoverished, poverty-stricken, penniless; see POOR 1.

destroy *v.* ruin, demolish, exterminate, raze, tear down, plunder, ran-

de·stroy′er *n.* 1 one that destroys 2 a small, fast warship

de·struct (di strukt′, dē′strukt′) *vi.* ⟦< fol.⟧ to be automatically destroyed

de·struc·tion (di struk′shən) *n.* 1 a destroying or being destroyed 2 a cause or means of destroying —**de·struc′tive** *adj.* —**de·struc′tively** *adv.*

desue·tude (des′wi tōōd′) *n.* ⟦< L *de-*, from + *suescere*, be accustomed⟧ disuse

des·ul·tory (des′əl tôr′ē) *adj.* ⟦< L *de-*, from + *salire*, to leap⟧ 1 aimless; disconnected 2 random

de·tach (dē tach′) *vt.* ⟦< Fr: see DE- & ATTACH⟧ 1 to unfasten and remove; disconnect 2 to send (troops) on a special mission —**de·tach′able** *adj.*

de·tached′ *adj.* 1 not connected 2 aloof; disinterested; impartial

de·tach′ment *n.* 1 a detaching 2 a unit of troops, etc. on a special mission 3 impartiality or aloofness

de·tail (dē tāl′, dē′tāl) *n.* ⟦< Fr < *dé-*, from + *tailler*, to cut⟧ 1 a dealing with things item by item 2 a minute account 3 a small part; item 4 *a)* one or more soldiers, etc. on special duty *b)* the duty — *vt.* 1 to tell, item by item 2 to assign to special duty —**in detail** with particulars

de·tain (dē tān′) *vt.* ⟦< L *de-*, off + *tenere*, to hold⟧ 1 to keep in custody; confine 2 to keep from going on —**de·tain′ment** *n.*

de·tect (dē tekt′) *vt.* ⟦< L *de-*, from + *tegere*, to cover⟧ to discover (something hidden, not clear, etc.) —**de·tect′able** or **de·tect′ible** *adj.* —**de·tec′tion** *n.* —**de·tec′tor** *n.*

de·tec′tive *n.* one whose work is to investigate crimes, uncover evidence, etc.

dé·tente or **de·tente** (dā tänt′) *n.* ⟦Fr⟧ a lessening of tension, esp. between nations

de·ten·tion (dē ten′shən) *n.* 1 a detaining or being detained 2 the punishment of having to stay after school

detention home a place where juvenile offenders are held in custody

de·ter (dē tur′) *vt.* **-terred′, -ter′ring** ⟦< L *de-*, from + *terrere*, frighten⟧ to keep or discourage (a person) from doing something through fear, doubt, etc. —**de·ter′ment** *n.*

de·ter·gent (dē tur′jənt) *adj.* ⟦< L *de-*, off + *tergere*, wipe⟧ cleansing — *n.* a soaplike cleansing substance

de·te·rio·rate (dē tir′ē ə rāt′) *vt., vi.* **-rat′ed, -rat′ing** ⟦< L *deterior*, worse⟧ to make or become worse —**de·te′rio·ra′tion** *n.*

de·ter·mi·nant (dē tur′mi nənt) *n.* a thing or factor that determines

de·ter′mi·nate (-nit) *adj.* clearly determined; fixed; settled

de·ter·mi·na·tion (dē tur′mi nā′shən) *n.* 1 a determining or being determined 2 a firm intention 3 firmness of purpose

de·ter·mine (dē tur′mən) *vt.* **-mined, -min·ing** ⟦< L *de-*, from + *terminus*, a limit⟧ 1 to set limits to 2 to settle conclusively 3 to decide or decide upon 4 to be the deciding factor in; direct 5 to find out exactly — *vi.* to decide — **de·ter′mi·nable** *adj.*

de·ter′mined (-mənd) *adj.* 1 having one's mind made up 2 resolute; firm

THESAURUS

sack, eradicate, overthrow, root up, root out, devastate, butcher, consume, liquidate, break up, dissolve, blot out, quash, quell, level, abort, stamp out, suppress, squelch, scuttle, undo, annihilate, lay waste, overturn, impair, damage, ravish, deface, shatter, split up, crush, obliterate, knock to pieces, abolish, crash, extinguish, wreck, dismantle, upset, bomb, mutilate, smash, trample, overturn, maim, mar, end, nullify, blast, neutralize, gut, snuff out, erase, sabotage, repeal, pull down, terminate, conclude, finish, bring to ruin, stop, put a stop to, wipe out, do in*, do away with, finish off, make short work of, total*, cream*, destruct, self-destruct, put an end to; see also DEFEAT, RAVAGE, STOP 1.—*Ant.* BUILD, construct, establish.

destroyed *a.* wrecked, annihilated, killed, lost, devastated, wasted, demolished, overturned, overwhelmed, upset, nullified, undone, put to an end, shattered, smashed, scuttled, ravished, engulfed, submerged, overrun, extinguished, eradicated, devoured, consumed, burned up, burned down, gone to pieces, razed, lying in ruins, sacked; see also BROKEN 1, DEAD 1, RUINED 1.—*Ant.* SAVED, protected, restored.

destroyer *n.* 1 [A destructive agent] assassin, executioner, slayer; see CRIMINAL, KILLER, WEAPON. 2 [A swift armed surface vessel] warship, battleship, fighting vessel; see SHIP, WARSHIP.

destruction *n.* 1 [The act of destroying] demolition, annihilation, eradication, slaughter, liquidation, overthrow, extermination, elimination, abolition, killing, murder, assassination, killing, disintegration, bombardment, disruption, extinction, annihilating, wreckage, dissolution, butchery, sabotage, sacking, extinguishing, eliminating, crashing, falling, felling, tearing down; see also DAMAGE 1, DISASTER.—*Ant.* PRODUCTION, formation, erection. 2 [The condition after destruction] waste, ashes, wreck, annihilation, remnants, devastation, vestiges, desolation, ruins, overthrow, decay, loss,

remains, havoc, prostration, injury, downfall, end, starvation, plague, shipwreck, dissolution, disorganization; see also DAMAGE 2, WRECK.

destructive *a.* 1 [Harmful] hurtful, injurious, troublesome; see HARMFUL. 2 [Deadly] fatal, ruinous, devastating; see DEADLY, VICIOUS.

detach *v.* separate, withdraw, disengage; see DIVIDE.

detached *a.* 1 [Cut off or removed] loosened, divided, disjoined; see SEPARATED. 2 [Indifferent] apathetic, uninvolved, unconcerned; see INDIFFERENT.

detail *n.* item, portion, particular, trait, specialty, feature, aspect, article, peculiarity, fraction, specification, article, technicality; see also CIRCUMSTANCE, PART 1.—*Ant.* WHOLE, entirety, synthesis. —**in detail** minutely, item by item, part by part, step by step, inch by inch, systematically, intimately.—*Ant.* VAGUELY, generally, indefinitely.

detail *v.* itemize, exhibit, show, report, relate, narrate, tell, designate, catalogue, recite, specialize, depict, enumerate, mention, uncover, reveal, recount, recapitulate, analyze, set forth, produce, go into the particulars, get down to cases*; see also DESCRIBE.—*Ant.* DABBLE, summarize, epitomize.

detailed *a.* enumerated, specified, explicit, specific, particularized, individual, individualized, developed, itemized, definite, minute, described, precise, full, narrow, complete, exact, fussy, particular, meticulous, point by point, circumstantial, accurate, unfolded, disclosed, elaborated, complicated, comprehensive, at length, gone into; see also ELABORATE 2.—*Ant.* GENERAL, brief, hazy.

details *n.* analysis, trivia, minutiae, particulars, bill, itemized account, trivialities, fine points, items; see also DETAIL.

detain *v.* hold, keep, inhibit; see DELAY, RESTRAIN.

detect *v.* distinguish, recognize, identify; see DISCOVER.

detection *n.* apprehension, exposure, disclosure; see DISCOVERY, EXPOSURE.

detective *n.* policeman, agent, plainclothesman, private eye*, narcotics agent, police sergeant, police officer, FBI agent, wiretapper, investigator, criminologist, prosecutor, patrolman, sleuth, shadow, eavesdropper, spy, shamus*, flatfoot*, dick*, G-man*, copper*, cop*, fed*, narc*; see also POLICEMAN.

detention *n.* custody, impediment, quarantine; see ARREST, CONFINEMENT, RESTRAINT 2.

deter *v.* caution, stop, dissuade; see PREVENT, WARN.

detergent *n.* cleansing agent, disinfectant, washing substance; see CLEANSER, SOAP.

deteriorate *v.* depreciate, lessen, degenerate; see DECREASE 1.

deterioration *n.* decadence, rotting, degeneration; see DECAY.

determinable *a.* definable, discoverable, capable of being determined; see DEFINITE 2.

determination *n.* resolution, certainty, persistence, stubbornness, obstinacy, resolve, certitude, decision, assurance, conviction, boldness, fixity of purpose, hardihood, tenacity, courage, independence, self-confidence, purposefulness, fortitude, self-assurance, firmness, self-reliance, nerve, heart, bravery, fearlessness, will, energy, vigor, stamina, perseverance, strength of will, a brave front, a bold front, a stout heart, enterprise, guts*, spunk*, a stiff upper lip*; see also CONFIDENCE, FAITH 1, PURPOSE 1.

determine *v.* 1 [To define] limit, circumscribe, delimit; see DEFINE 1, RESTRICT. 2 [To find out the facts] ascertain, find out, learn; see DISCOVER. 3 [To resolve] fix upon, settle, conclude; see DECIDE, RESOLVE.

determined *a.* 1 [Already fixed or settled] decided, agreed, acted upon, agreed upon, concluded, contracted, set, ended, resolved, closed, terminated, achieved, finished, over, at an end, checked, measured, tested, budgeted, passed, given approval, given the green light*, given the go-ahead, over and done with; see also APPROVED.—*Ant.* UNFINISHED, sus-

de·ter·rence (dē tur′əns) *n.* 1 a deterring 2 the stockpiling of nuclear weapons to deter nuclear attack

de·ter′rent *adj.* deterring — *n.* something that deters

de·test (dē test′) *vt.* 〚< L *detestari*, to curse by the gods〛 to dislike intensely; hate —**de·test′a·ble** *adj.* —**de·test′a·bly** *adv.* —**de·tes·ta′tion** (-tes tā′shən) *n.*

de·throne (dē thrōn′) *vt.* **-throned′, -thron′ing** to depose (a monarch)

det·o·nate (det′'n āt′) *vi., vt.* **-nat′ed, -nat′ing** 〚< L *de-*, intens. + *tonare*, to thunder〛 to explode violently —**det′o·na′tion** *n.* —**det′o·na′tor** *n.*

de·tour (dē′toor) *n.* 〚< Fr: see DE- & TURN〛 1 a roundabout way 2 a substitute route — *vi., vt.* to go or route on a detour

de·tox (dē tāks′, dē′tāks′) *vt.* [Colloq.] short for DETOXIFY — *n.* [Colloq.] short for DETOXIFICATION

de·tox·i·fy (dē tāk′si fī′) *vt.* **-fied′, -fy′ing** 〚DE- + TOXI(N) + -FY〛 to remove a poison or poisonous effect from —**de·tox′i·fi·ca′tion** *n.*

de·tract (dē trakt′) *vt.* 〚< L *de-*, from + *trahere*, to draw〛 to take away — *vi.* to take something desirable (*from*) —**de·trac′tion** *n.* —**de·trac′tor** *n.*

det·ri·ment (de′trə mənt) *n.* 〚< L *de-*, off + *terere*, to rub〛 1 damage; injury 2 anything that causes this —**det′ri·men′tal** *adj.*

de·tri·tus (dē trīt′əs) *n.* 〚L, a rubbing away: see prec.〛 rock fragments, etc. from disintegration

deuce (doos) *n.* 〚< L *duo*, two〛 1 a playing card or side of a die with two spots 2 *Tennis, Badminton, etc.* a tie score after which one side must score twice in a row to win

deu·te·ri·um (doo tir′ē əm) *n.* 〚< Gr *deuteros*, second〛 a hydrogen isotope used in nuclear reactors, etc.

Deu·ter·on·o·my (doot′ər än′ə mē) 〚< Gr *deuteros*, second + *nomos*, law〛 the fifth book of the Pentateuch

deut·sche mark (doi′chə märk′) *pl.* **mark** or **marks** the monetary unit of Germany

de·value (dē val′yoo) *vt.* **-ued, -u·ing** 1 to lessen the value of 2 to lower the exchange value of (a currency) —**de·val′u·a′tion** *n.*

dev·as·tate (dev′əs tāt′) *vt.* **-tat′ed, -tat′ing** 〚< L *de-*, intens. + *vastus*, empty〛 1 to lay waste; ravage; destroy 2 to overwhelm —**dev′as·ta′tion** *n.* —**dev′as·ta′tor** *n.*

de·velop (di vel′əp) *vt.* 〚< OFr *des-*, apart + *voloper*, to wrap〛 1 to make fuller, bigger, better, etc. 2 to show or work out by degrees 3 to enlarge upon 4 *Photog.* to put (a film, etc.) into chemicals to make the pictures visible — *vi.*

1 to come into being or activity; occur 2 to become developed —**de·vel′op·er** *n.* —**de·vel′op·ment** *n.*

de·vi·ant (dē′vē ənt) *adj.* deviating, esp. from what is considered normal — *n.* one whose behavior is deviant

de·vi·ate (dē′vē āt′; *for adj. & n. usually,* -it) *vi.* **-at′ed, -at′ing** 〚< L *de-*, from + *via*, road〛 to turn aside (*from* a course, standard, etc.); diverge — *adj.* DEVIANT — *n.* a deviant, esp. in sexual behavior —**de′vi·a′tion** *n.* —**de′vi·a′tor** *n.*

de·vice (di vīs′) *n.* 〚see DEVISE〛 1 a thing devised; plan, scheme, or trick 2 a mechanical contrivance 3 an ornamental design, esp. on a coat of arms —**leave to one's own devices** to allow to do as one wishes

devil (dev′əl) *n.* 〚ult. < Gr *diabolos*, slanderous〛 1 *Theol.* a) [often **D**-] the chief evil spirit; Satan (with *the*) b) any evil spirit; demon 2 a very wicked person 3 a person who is mischievous, reckless, unlucky, etc. 4 anything hard to operate, control, etc. — *vt.* **-iled** or **-illed, -il·ing** or **-il·ling** 1 to prepare (food) with hot seasoning 2 to annoy; tease —**dev′il·ish** *adj.*

dev′il-may-care′ *adj.* reckless

dev′il·ment *n.* mischievous action

devil's advocate a person upholding the wrong side for argument's sake

dev′il's-food′ cake a rich chocolate cake

dev′il·try (-trē) *n., pl.* **-tries** reckless mischief, fun, etc. Also **dev′il·ry** (-rē)

de·vi·ous (dē′vē əs) *adj.* 〚< L *de-*, off + *via*, road〛 1 not direct; roundabout or deviating 2 not straightforward — **de′vi·ous·ness** *n.*

de·vise (di vīz′) *vt., vi.* **-vised′, -vis′ing** 〚< L *dividere*, to divide〛 1 to work out or create (a plan, device, etc.) 2 to bequeath (real property) by will — *n.* a bequest of property

de·vi·tal·ize (dē vīt′'l īz′) *vt.* **-ized′, -iz′ing** to deprive of vitality

de·void (di void′) *adj.* 〚see DE- & VOID〛 completely without; empty (*of*)

de·volve (di välv′) *vt., vi.* **-volved′, -volv′ing** 〚< L *de-*, down + *volvere*, to roll〛 to pass (*on*) to another: said of duties, responsibilities, etc.

de·vote (di vōt′) *vt.* **-vot′ed, -vot′ing** 〚< L *de-*, from + *vovere*, to vow〛 to set apart for or give up to some purpose, activity, or person; dedicate

de·vot′ed (-id) *adj.* very loving, loyal, or faithful —**de·vot′edly** *adv.*

devo·tee (dev′ə tē′, -tā′) *n.* one strongly devoted to something

de·vo·tion (di vō′shən) *n.* 1 a devoting or being devoted 2 piety 3 religious worship 4 [*often pl.*] one or more

■ THESAURUS ■

pended, argued. 2 [Having a fixed attitude] resolute, firm, strongminded; see STUBBORN.

deterrent *n.* hindrance, impediment, obstacle; see RESTRAINT.

detest *v.* abhor, loathe, despise; see HATE.

detonate *v.* touch off, discharge, blast; see EXPLODE, SHOOT 1.

detour *n.* temporary route, alternate route, byway, back road, service road, alternate highway, secondary highway, bypass, circuit, roundabout course.

detract *v.* decrease, take away a part, subtract, draw away, diminish, lessen, withdraw, derogate, depreciate, discredit; see also SLANDER.

devalue *v.* revalue, depreciate, mark down; see DECREASE 2.

devastate *v.* ravage, sack, pillage; see DESTROY.

devastation *n.* destruction, defoliation, waste; see DESOLATION.

develop *v.* 1 [To improve] enlarge, expand, extend, promote, advance, magnify, build up, refine, enrich, cultivate, elaborate, polish, finish, perfect, deepen, lengthen, heighten, widen, intensify, fix up, shape up*; see also GROW 1, IMPROVE 1, 2, STRENGTHEN.—*Ant.* DAMAGE, disfigure, spoil. 2 [To grow] mature, evolve, advance; see GROW 1. 3 [To reveal slowly] unfold, disclose, exhibit, unravel, disentangle, uncover, make known, explain, unroll, explicate, produce, detail, tell,

state, recount, account for, give an account of; see also REVEAL.—*Ant.* HIDE, conceal, blurt out. 4 [To work out] enlarge upon, elaborate upon, go into detail; see EXPLAIN, INCREASE.

developed *a.* grown, refined, advanced; see MATURED, PERFECTED.

development *n.* growth, unfolding, elaboration, maturing, progress, ripening, maturation, enlargement, addition, spread, gradual evolution, evolving, advancement, improvement, growing, increasing, spreading, adding to, making progress, advancing; see also IMPROVEMENT 1, INCREASE, PROGRESS 1.—*Ant.* REDUCTION, decrease, lessening.

deviate *v.* deflect, digress, swerve, vary, wander, stray, turn aside, keep aside, stay aside, go out of control, shy away, depart, break the pattern, not conform, go out of the way, veer, go off on a tangent, go haywire*, swim against the stream*; see also DIFFER 1.—*Ant.* CONFORM, keep on, keep in line.

deviation *n.* change, deflection, alteration; see DIFFERENCE 1, VARIATION 2.

device *n.* 1 [An instrument] invention, contrivance, mechanism, gear, equipment, appliance, contraption, means, agent, material, implement, utensil, construction, apparatus, outfit, article, accessory, gadget, thing, whatnot*, whatsit*, whatchamacallit*; see also MACHINE, TOOL 1. 2 [A shrewd method] artifice, scheme,

design, trap, dodge, trick, pattern, loophole, wile, craft, ruse, expedient, subterfuge, plan, project, plot, racket*, game, finesse, catch*; see also DISCOVERY, METHOD, TRICK 1.

devil *n.* Satan, fiend, adversary, error, sin, imp, mischiefmaker, Beelzebub, fallen angel, hellhound, Mammon, Molloch, Hades, Lucifer, Mephistopheles, diabolical force, the Tempter, Prince of Darkness, Evil One; see also EVIL 1.—*Ant.* GOD, angel, Christ. —**give the devil his due** give one credit, give credit where credit is due, recognize; see ACKNOWLEDGE 2. —**go to the devil** 1 [To decay] degenerate, fall into bad habits, go to pot*; see FAIL 1. 2 [A curse] go to hell, damn you, be damned; see CURSE. —**raise the devil** cause trouble, riot, be unruly; see DISTURB, FIGHT.

devious *a.* foxy, insidious, shrewd; see DISHONEST, SLY.

devote *v.* apply, consecrate, give; see BLESS, DEDICATE.

devoted *a.* dutiful, loyal, constant; see FAITHFUL.

devotion *n.* allegiance, service, consecration, devotedness, adoration, piety, zeal, ardor, earnestness, faithfulness, fidelity, deference, sincerity, adherence, observance; see also LOYALTY, WORSHIP 1.—*Ant.* INDIFFERENCE, apathy, carelessness.

devotions *n.* religious worship, church services, prayers; see CHURCH

de·vour (di vour') *vt.* ⟦< L *de-*, intens. + *vorare*, swallow whole⟧ 1 to eat hungrily 2 to swallow up 3 to take in greedily, as with the eyes

de·vout (di vout') *adj.* ⟦see DEVOTE⟧ 1 very religious; pious 2 earnest; sincere —**de·vout'ly** *adv.*

dew (dōō) *n.* ⟦OE *deaw*⟧ 1 atmospheric moisture condensed in drops on cool surfaces at night 2 anything refreshing, pure, etc., like dew —**dew'y, -i·er, -i·est,** *adj.*

dew'ber'ry *n., pl.* **-ries** 1 a trailing blackberry plant 2 its berry

dew'drop' *n.* a drop of dew

dew'lap' *n.* ⟦see DEW & LAP¹⟧ loose skin under the throat of cattle, etc.

dew point the temperature at which water vapor in the air starts to condense into liquid

dex·ter·i·ty (deks ter'ə tē) *n.* ⟦see fol.⟧ skill in using one's hands, body, or mind

dex·ter·ous (deks'tər əs, -trəs) *adj.* ⟦< L *dexter*, right⟧ having or showing dexterity Also **dex'trous**

dex·trose (deks'trōs) *n.* a glucose found in plants and animals

dhoti (dō'tē) *n.* ⟦Hindi *dhoti*⟧ a loincloth worn by Hindu men

dhur·rie or **dur·rie** (dur'ē, dur'-) *n.* a coarse rug woven in India

di-¹ ⟦Gr *di-* < *dis-*, twice⟧ *prefix* twice, double, twofold

di-² *prefix* DIS-

di·a·betes (dī'ə bēt'ēz', -is) *n.* ⟦< Gr *diabainein*, to pass through⟧ a disease caused by an insulin deficiency and characterized by excess sugar in the blood and urine Also **sugar diabetes** —**di'a·bet'ic** (-bet'ik) *adj., n.*

di·a·bolic (dī'ə bäl'ik) *adj.* ⟦see DEVIL⟧ very wicked or cruel; fiendish Also **di'a·bol'i·cal** —**di'a·bol'i·cal·ly** *adv.*

di·a·crit·ic (dī'ə krit'ik) *adj.* ⟦< Gr *dia-*, across + *krinein*, to separate⟧ distinguishing Also **di'a·crit'i·cal** — *n.* a mark, as a macron, added to a letter or symbol to show pronunciation, etc.: in full **diacritical mark**

di·a·dem (dī'ə dem') *n.* ⟦< Gr *diadēma*, a band, fillet⟧ 1 a crown 2 an ornamental headband

di·ag·nose (dī'əg nōs') *vt., vi.* **-nosed', -nos'ing** to make a diagnosis (of)

di·ag·no·sis (-nō'sis) *n., pl.* **-ses'** (-sēz') ⟦< Gr *dia-*, through + *gignoskein*, to know⟧ 1 the act of deciding the nature of a disease, situation, problem, etc. by examination and analysis 2 the resulting decision —**di'ag·nos'tic** (-näs'tik) *adj.* —**di'ag·nos·ti'cian** (-tish'ən) *n.*

di·ag·o·nal (dī ag'ə nəl) *adj.* ⟦< Gr *dia-*, through + *gōnia*, an angle⟧ 1 extending slantingly between opposite corners 2 slanting; oblique — *n.* a diagonal line, plane, course, part, etc. —**di·ag'o·nal·ly** *adv.*

di·a·gram (dī'ə gram') *n.* ⟦< Gr *dia-*, across + *graphein*, write⟧ a sketch, plan, graph, etc. that explains something, as by outlining its parts — *vt.* **-gramed'** or **-grammed'**, **-gram'ing** or **-gram'ming** to make a diagram of

di·al (dī'əl) *n.* ⟦< L *dies*, day⟧ 1 the face of a clock, etc. 2 the face of a meter, etc. for indicating, as by a pointer, an amount, direction, etc. 3 a graduated disk, strip, knob, etc., as on a radio or TV for tuning in stations, etc. 4 a rotating disk, or set of numbered push buttons, on a telephone, used to make automatic connections — *vt., vi.* **-aled** or **-alled, -al·ing** or **-al·ling** 1 to show on or measure with a dial 2 to tune in (a radio station, etc.) 3 to call by using a telephone dial

dial. 1 dialect(al) 2 dialectic(al)

di·a·lect (dī'ə lekt') *n.* ⟦< Gr *dia*, between + *legein*, to talk⟧ the form of a spoken language peculiar to a region, social group, etc. —**di'a·lec'tal** *adj.*

di·a·lec·tic (dī'ə lek'tik) *n.* 1 [*often pl.*] a logical test of ideas for validity 2 logical debate — *adj.* DIALECTICAL

di·a·lec·ti·cal (-ti kəl) *adj.* 1 of or using dialectics 2 of a dialect

di·a·logue or **di·a·log** (dī'ə lôg', -läg') *n.* ⟦see DIALECT⟧ 1 interchange of ideas by open discussion 2 the passages of talk in a play, story, etc.

di·al·y·sis (dī al'ə sis) *n., pl.* **-ses'** (-sēz') ⟦< Gr *dia-*, apart + *lyein*, loose⟧ the separation of dissolved substances from colloids in a solution by diffusion through a membrane: used in purifying the blood during kidney failure

di·am·e·ter (dī am'ət ər) *n.* ⟦< Gr *dia-*, through + *metron*, a measure⟧ 1 a line segment passing through the center of a circle, sphere, etc. from one side to the other 2 its length

di·a·met·ri·cal (dī'ə me'tri kəl) *adj.* designating an opposite, difference, etc. that is wholly so; complete —**di'a·met'ri·cally** *adv.*

di·a·mond (dīm'ənd, dī'ə mənd) *n.* ⟦< Gr *adamas*⟧ 1 a nearly pure, brilliant, crystalline carbon, the hardest mineral known 2 a gem, etc. cut from it 3 *a*) the plane figure (◇) *b*) a playing card so marked 4 *Baseball* the infield or the whole field — *adj.* 1 of a diamond 2 marking the 60th, or sometimes 75th, year

di'amond·back' *n.* a large, poisonous rattlesnake of the S U.S.

Di·ana (dī an'ə) *Rom. Myth.* the goddess of the moon and of hunting

di·a·pa·son (dī'ə pā'zən) *n.* ⟦< Gr *dia*, through + *pas*, all⟧ an organ stop covering the instrument's entire range

di·a·per (dī'pər, dī'ə pər) *n.* ⟦< ML *diasprum*, flowered cloth⟧ a soft, absorbent cloth folded and arranged between the legs and around the waist of a baby — *vt.* to put a diaper on (a baby)

di·aph·a·nous (dī af'ə nəs) *adj.* ⟦< Gr *dia-*, through + *phainein*, to show⟧ letting much light through

di·a·phragm (dī'ə fram') *n.* ⟦< Gr *dia-*, through + *phragma*, fence⟧ 1 the muscular partition between the chest and abdominal cavities 2 a vibrating disk producing sound waves 3 a vaginal contraceptive device —**di'a·phrag·mat'ic** (-frag mat'ik) *adj.*

di·ar·rhea or **di·ar·rhoea** (dī'ə rē'ə) *n.* ⟦< Gr *dia-*, through + *rhein*, to flow⟧ too frequent and loose bowel movements

di·a·ry (dī'ə rē) *n., pl.* **-ries** ⟦< L *dies*, day⟧ a daily written record of one's experiences, etc. —**di'a·rist** *n.*

di·a·stase (dī'ə stās') *n.* ⟦< Gr *dia*, apart + *histanai*, stand⟧ an enzyme in the seed of grains and malt capable of changing starches into dextrose

di·as·tole (dī as'tə lē') *n.* ⟦< Gr *dia-*, apart + *stellein*, put⟧ the usual rhythmic expansion of the heart —**dia·stolic** (dī'ə stäl'ik) *adj.*

di·a·thermy (dī'ə thur'mē) *n.* ⟦< Gr *dia-*, through + *thermē*, heat⟧ medical treatment in which heat is produced in tissues beneath the skin by a high-frequency electric current

di·a·tom (dī'ə täm', -ə təm) *n.* ⟦< Gr *diatomos*, cut in two⟧ any of various microscopic algae that are an important source of food for marine life

di·a·tom·ic (dī'ə täm'ik) *adj.* ⟦DI-¹ + ATOMIC⟧ having two atoms or radicals in the molecule

di·a·tonic (dī'ə tän'ik) *adj.* ⟦< Gr *dia-*, through + *teinein*, to stretch⟧ *Music* designating or of a scale of eight tones that is either a MAJOR SCALE or a MINOR SCALE

di·a·tribe (dī'ə trīb') *n.* ⟦< Gr *dia-*, through + *tribein*, to rub⟧ a bitter, abusive denunciation

dib·ble (dib'əl) *n.* ⟦ME *dibbel*⟧ a pointed tool used for making holes in the soil for seeds, bulbs, etc.

dice (dīs) *n.pl., sing.* **die** or **dice** ⟦see DIE²⟧ small cubes marked on each side with a different number of spots (from one to six), used in games of chance — *vi.* **diced, dic'ing** to play or gamble with dice — *vt.* to cut (vegetables, etc.) into small cubes —**no dice** [Colloq.] 1 no: used in refusing a request 2 no luck

---

THESAURUS

2, WORSHIP 1.

devour *v.* gulp, swallow, gorge; see EAT 1.

devout *a.* devoted, pious, reverent; see FAITHFUL, HOLY, RELIGIOUS 2.

diagnosis *n.* analysis, determination, investigation; see SUMMARY.

diagonal *a.* slanting, inclining, askew; see OBLIQUE.

diagram *n.* sketch, layout, picture; see DESCRIPTION, DESIGN, PLAN 1.

dial *n.* face, control, gauge, indicator, meter, register, measuring device,

compass; see also INDEX.

dialect *n.* idiom, accent, local speech, regional speech, broken English, pidgin English, brogue, lingo, trade language, lingua franca, usage level, pig Latin, jargon, cant, vernacular, patois; see also LANGUAGE 1.

dialogue *n.* talk, exchange, remarks; see CONVERSATION.

diameter *n.* breadth, measurement across, broadness; see WIDTH.

diametrical *a.* contrary, adverse,

facing; see OPPOSITE 3.

diamond *n.* 1 [A crystalline jewel] precious stone, solitaire, engagement ring, brilliant, crystal, ring, stone*, rock*, sparkler*, glass*, ice*; see also JEWEL. 2 [Shape or figure] lozenge, solid, rhombus; see FORM 1. 3 [A baseball playing field, particularly the infield] lot, ball park, sandlot; see FIELD 2, PARK 1.

diary *n.* chronicle, journal, log; see RECORD 1.

di·choto·my (dī kät′ə mē) *n., pl.* **-mies** 〖< Gr *dicha*, in two + *temnein*, to cut〗 division into two parts

dick (dik) *n.* [Slang] a detective

dicker (dik′ər) *vi.* 〖ult. < L *decem*, ten〗 to bargain or haggle

dickey (dik′ē) *n., pl.* **-eys** 〖< nickname *Dick*〗 1 a detachable shirt front 2 a small bird: also **dickey bird** Also **dick′y**, *pl.* **-ies**

di·coty·ledon (dī′kät′ə lēd′′n) *n.* a plant with two seed leaves (cotyledons) —**di′cot′y·le′don·ous** *adj.*

Dic·ta·phone (dik′tə fōn′) 〖fol. + -PHONE〗 *trademark* for a machine that records and plays back speech for typed transcripts, etc. — *n.* this machine

dic·tate (dik′tāt′; *also, for v.* dik tāt′) *vt., vi.* **-tat′ed, -tat′ing** 〖< L *dicere*, to speak〗 1 to speak (something) aloud for someone else to write down 2 to command forcefully 3 to give (orders) with authority — *n.* an authoritative order —**dic·ta′tion** *n.*

dic′ta·tor *n.* one who dictates; esp., a ruler or tyrant with absolute power —**dic·ta·to′rial** (-tə tôr′ē əl) *adj.* —**dic·ta′tor·ship′** *n.*

dic·tion (dik′shən) *n.* 〖< L *dicere*, say〗 1 manner of expression in words; choice of words 2 enunciation

dic·tion·ary (dik′shə ner′ē) *n., pl.* **-ar′ies** 〖see prec.〗 a book of alphabetically listed words in a language, with definitions, pronunciations, etc.

dic·tum (dik′təm) *n., pl.* **-tums** or **-ta** (-tə) 〖< L *dicere*, say〗 a formal statement of opinion; pronouncement

did (did) *pt. of* DO[1]

di·dac·tic (dī dak′tik) *adj.* 〖< Gr *didaskein*, teach〗 1 intended for instruction 2 morally instructive

did·dle (did′′l) *vt., vi.* **-dled, -dling** 〖< ?〗 [Colloq.] 1 to cheat 2 to waste (time) in trifling

dido (dī′dō) *n., pl.* **-does** or **-dos** 〖< ?〗 [Colloq.] a mischievous trick; prank

die[1] (dī) *vi.* **died, dy′ing** 〖< ON *deyja*〗 1 to stop living 2 to stop functioning; end 3 to lose force or activity 4 [Colloq.] to wish very much [I'm *dying* to go] —**die away** (or **down**) to cease gradually —**die off** to die one by one until all are gone —**die out** to stop existing

die[2] (dī) *n., pl.* for 2, **dies** (dīz) 〖< L *dare*, give〗 1 *sing. of* DICE 2 a tool for shaping, punching, etc. metal or other material

die′-hard′ or **die′hard′** *n.* a person stubbornly resistant to new ideas, reform, etc.

di·elec·tric (dī′i lek′trik) *n.* 〖< *dia-*, across + ELECTRIC〗 a material that does not conduct electricity

di·er·esis (dī er′ə sis) *n., pl.* **-ses′** (-sēz′) 〖< Gr *dia-*, apart + *hairein*, to take〗 a mark (¨) placed over the second of two consecutive vowels to show that it is pronounced separately

die·sel (dē′zəl, -səl) *n.* 〖after R. *Diesel* (1858-1913), Ger inventor〗 [*often* D-] an internal-combustion engine that burns oil ignited by heat from air compression: also **diesel engine** (or **motor**) — *vi.* to continue to run after the ignition is turned off: said of an internal-combustion engine

diet[1] (dī′ət) *n.* 〖< Gr *diaita*, way of life〗 1 what a person or animal usually eats or drinks 2 a special or limited selection of food and drink, chosen or prescribed as to bring about weight loss — *vi., vt.* to adhere to or place on a diet —**di′et·er** *n.* —**di′etar′y** (-ə ter′ē) *adj.*

diet[2] (dī′ət) *n.* 〖< ML *dieta*〗 a formal assembly

di·etet′ic (-ə tet′ik) *adj.* of or for a particular diet of food and drink

di·etet′ics (-iks) *n.pl.* [*with sing. v.*] the study of the kinds and quantities of food needed for health

di·eti·tian (dī′ə tish′ən) *n.* an expert in dietetics

dif- *prefix* DIS-: used before *f*

dif·fer (dif′ər) *vi.* 〖< L *dis-*, apart + *ferre*, to bring〗 1 to be different 2 to be of a different opinion; disagree

dif·fer·ence (dif′ər əns, dif′rəns) *n.* 1 a being different 2 the way in which people or things are different 3 a differing in opinion; disagreement 4 a dispute 5 the amount by which one quantity is less than another

dif′fer·ent *adj.* 1 not alike 2 not the same 3 various 4 unusual —**dif′fer·ently** *adv.*

dif·fer·en·tial (dif′ər en′shəl) *adj.* of, showing, or constituting a difference — *n.* 1 a differentiating amount, degree, etc. 2 a differential gear

differential gear (or **gearing**) a gear arrangement allowing one axle to turn faster than the other

dif′fer·en′ti·ate′ (-shē āt′) *vt.* **-at′ed, -at′ing** 1 to constitute a difference in or between 2 to make unlike 3 to distinguish between — *vi.* 1 to become different or differentiated 2 to note a difference —**dif′fer·en′tia′tion** *n.*

dif·fi·cult (dif′i kult′, -kəlt) *adj.* 1 hard to do, understand, etc. 2 hard to satisfy, deal with, etc.

THESAURUS

dicker *v.* trade, barter, bargain; see ARGUE, BUY, SELL.

dictate *v.* speak, deliver, give forth, interview, compose, formulate, verbalize, record, orate, give an account; see also TALK 1.

dictator *n.* autocrat, despot, tyrant, czar, fascist, absolute ruler, oppressor, terrorist, master, leader, ringleader, magnate, lord, commander, chief, advisor, overlord, taskmaster, disciplinarian, headman, cock of the walk*, man at the wheel*, slave driver*; see also LEADER 2, RULER 1.

dictatorial *a.* despotic, authoritarian, arbitrary; see ABSOLUTE 2.

dictatorship *n.* despotism, unlimited rule, coercion; see GOVERNMENT 2, TYRANNY.

diction *n.* style, enunciation, expression, wording, usage, choice of words, command of language, locution, rhetoric, fluency, oratory, articulation, vocabulary, language, line*; gift of gab*; see also ELOQUENCE, SPEECH 2.

dictionary *n.* word book, word list, lexicon, thesaurus, reference work, glossary, encyclopedia, Webster, dictionary of synonyms.

die[1] *v.* 1 [To cease living] expire, pass away, pass on, depart, perish, succumb, go, commit suicide, suffocate, lose one's life, cease to exist, drown, hang, fall, meet one's death, be no more, drop dead, be done for*, rest in peace*, go to one's final resting place*, pass over to the great beyond*, give up the ghost*, go the way of all flesh*, return to dust*, cash in one's chips*, push up daisies*, buy the farm*, kick the bucket*, bite the dust*, lay down one's life*, breathe one's last*, croak*, check out*, kick off*, go by the board*.—*Ant.* LIVE, thrive, exist. 2 [To cease existing] disappear, vanish, become extinct; see STOP 2. 3 [To decline as though death were inevitable] fade, ebb, wither; see DECAY, WEAKEN 2. —**die away** decline, go away, sink; see STOP 2. **die down** decline, disappear, recede; see DIE 2, 3, DECREASE 1. —**die off** (or **out**) go, cease to exist, disappear; see VANISH.

die-hard *n.* zealot, reactionary, extremist; see CONSERVATIVE.

diet[1] *n.* 1 [What one eats] menu, fare, daily bread*; see FOOD. 2 [Restricted intake of food] weight-reduction plan, fast, abstinence from food, starvation diet, bread and water*.

diet[1] *v.* lose weight, go without, starve oneself, slim down, go on a diet, reduce, tighten one's belt*.

differ *v.* 1 [To be unlike] vary, modify, not conform, digress, take exception, turn, reverse, qualify, alter, change, diverge from, contrast with, bear no resemblance, not look like, jar with, clash with, conflict with, be distinguished from, diversify, stand apart, depart from, go off on a tangent*; see also CONTRAST.—*Ant.* RESEMBLE, parallel, take after. 2 [To oppose] disagree, object, fight; see OPPOSE 1.

difference *n.* 1 [The quality of being different] disagreement, divergence, non-conformity, contrariness, deviation, opposition, antithesis, dissimilarity, inequality, diversity, departure, variance, discrepancy, separation, differentiation, distinctness, separateness, asymmetry; see also CONTRAST, VARIETY 1.—*Ant.* AGREEMENT, similarity, resemblance. 2 [That which is unlike in comparable things] deviation, departure, exception; see VARIATION 2. 3 [Personal dissension] discord, estrangement, dissent; see DISPUTE. —**make a difference** change, have an effect, affect; see MATTER. —**split the difference** compromise, go half way, come to an agreement; see AGREE. — **what's the difference?*** what does it matter?, what difference does it make?, so what?*; see WHY.

different *a.* 1 [Unlike in nature] distinct, separate, not the same; see UNLIKE. 2 [Composed of unlike things] diverse, miscellaneous, assorted; see VARIOUS. 3 [Unusual] unconventional, strange, startling; see UNUSUAL 1, 2.

differentiate *v.* contrast, set apart, separate; see DISTINGUISH 1.

differently *a.* variously, divergently, individually, distinctively, creatively, uniquely, separately, each in his own way, severally, diversely, incongruously, abnormally, not normally, nonconformably, asymmetrically, in a different manner, with a difference, otherwise.—*Ant.* EVENLY, uniformly, invariably.

difficult *a.* 1 [Hard to achieve] laborious, hard, unyielding, strenuous, exacting, stiff, heavy, arduous, painful, labored, trying, bothersome, troublesome, demanding, burdensome, backbreaking, not easy, wearisome, onerous, rigid, crucial, uphill,

dif·fi·cul·ty *n., pl.* **-ties** ⟦< L *dis*-, not + *facilis*, easy⟧ **1 a** being difficult **2** something difficult, as a problem, obstacle, or objection **3** trouble

dif·fi·dent (-dənt) *adj.* ⟦< L *dis*-, not + *fidere*, to trust⟧ lacking self-confidence; shy —**dif′fi·dence** *n.*

dif·frac·tion (di frak′shən) *n.* ⟦< L *dis*-, apart + *frangere*, to break⟧ the spreading of a wave motion, as light, as it passes an obstacle and expands into the region that is behind the obstacle

dif·fuse (di fyo͞os′; *for v.,* -fyo͞oz′) *adj.* ⟦< L *dis*-, apart + *fundere*, to pour⟧ **1** spread out; not concentrated **2** using more words than are needed — *vt., vi.* **-fused′, -fus′ing** to pour in every direction; spread widely —**dif·fuse′ly** *adv.* —**dif·fuse′ness** *n.* —**dif·fu′sion** *n.* —**dif·fu′sive** *adj.*

dig (dig) *vt.* **dug, dig′ging** ⟦< OFr < Du *dijk*, dike⟧ **1** to turn up or remove (ground, etc.) as with a spade, the hands, etc. **2** to make (a hole, etc.) by digging **3** to get out by digging **4** to find out, as by careful study **5** to jab **6** [Slang] *a)* to understand *b)* to like — *vi.* to excavate — *n.* **1** [Colloq.] *a)* a poke, nudge, etc. *b)* a taunt **2** an archaeological excavation —**dig′ger** *n.*

di·gest (di′jest′; *for v.* di jest′, dī-) *n.* ⟦< L *di*-, apart + *gerere*, to bear⟧ a collection of condensed, systematic information; summary — *vt.* **1** to summarize **2** to change (food taken into the body) into an absorbable form **3** to absorb mentally — *vi.* to undergo digestion —**di·gest′ible** *adj.*

di·ges′tion *n.* **1** a digesting or being digested **2** the ability to digest —**di·ges′tive** *adj.*

digit (dij′it) *n.* ⟦< L *digitus*, a finger⟧ **1** a finger or toe **2** any number from 0 to 9

dig·i·tal (dij′i tal, -it′l) *adj.* **1** of or like a digit **2** using a row of digits, rather than numbers on a dial *[a digital watch]* **3** designating a recording technique in which sounds or images are converted into electronic bits: the bits are read electronically, as by a laser beam, for reproduction

digital computer a computer for processing data represented by physical signals, as the presence or absence of an electric current

dig·i·tal·is (dij′i tal′is) *n.* ⟦ModL, foxglove: see DIGIT⟧ **1** a plant with long spikes of thimblelike flowers; foxglove **2** a medicine made from the leaves of the purple foxglove, used as a heart stimulant

dig·ni·fied (dig′nə fīd′) *adj.* having or showing dignity

dig·ni·fy (dig′nə fī′) *vt.* **-fied′, -fy′ing** ⟦< L *dignus*, worthy + *facere*, to make⟧ to give dignity to; exalt

dig·ni·tar·y (-ter′ē) *n., pl.* **-tar′ies** ⟦< L *dignitas*, dignity⟧ a person holding a high position or office

dig′ni·ty (-tē) *n., pl.* **-ties** ⟦< L *dignus*, worthy⟧ **1** honorable quality; worthiness **2** high repute or honor, or the degree of this **3** a high position, rank, or title **4** stately appearance or manner **5** self-respect

di·graph (dī′graf′) *n.* a combination of two letters to represent one sound (Ex.: *read*, *graphic*)

di·gress (di gres′, dī-) *vi.* ⟦< L *dis*-, apart + *gradi*, to go⟧ to turn aside, esp. from the main subject, in talking or writing —**di·gres′sion** (-gresh′ən) *n.* —**di·gres′sive** *adj.*

Di·jon mustard (dē zhōn′) ⟦after *Dijon*, city in France⟧ a mild mustard paste blended with white wine

dike (dīk) *n.* ⟦OE *dic*, ditch⟧ an embankment or dam made to prevent flooding as by the sea

di·lap·i·dated (də lap′ə dāt′id) *adj.* ⟦< L *dis*-, apart + *lapidare*, throw stones at⟧ falling to pieces; broken down —**di·lap′i·da′tion** *n.*

di·late (dī′lāt′, dī lāt′) *vt., vi.* **-lat′ed, -lat′ing** ⟦< L *dis*-, apart + *latus*, wide⟧ **1** to make or become wider or larger **2** to speak or write in detail (*on* or *upon* a subject) —**di·la′tion** or **dila·ta′tion** (dil′ə tā′shən) *n.* —**di′la′tor** *n.*

dila·to·ry (dil′ə tôr′ē) *adj.* ⟦see prec.⟧ **1** causing delay **2** inclined to delay; slow; tardy

di·lem·ma (di lem′ə; *also* dī-) *n.* ⟦< LGr *di*-, two + *lēmma*, proposition⟧ **1** any situation requiring a choice between unpleasant alternatives **2** any serious problem

dil·et·tante (dil′ə tant′, -tän′tē; dil′ə tänt′, -tän′tē; dil′ə tänt′) *n., pl.* **-tantes′** or **-tan′ti′** (-tē′, -tē) ⟦It < L *delectare*, to delight⟧ one who dabbles in art, literature, etc. in a superficial way —**dil′et·tant′ish** *adj.* —**dil′et·tant′ism′** *n.*

dili·gent (dil′ə jənt) *adj.* ⟦< L *di*-, apart + *legere*, choose⟧ **1** persevering and careful in work; hard-working **2** done carefully —**dil′i·gence** *n.* —**dil′i·gently** *adv.*

dill (dil) *n.* ⟦OE *dile*⟧ a plant related to the parsley, with aromatic seeds and leaves, used to flavor pickles, etc.

dilly (dil′ē) *n., pl.* **-lies** ⟦? < DEL(IGHTFUL) + -Y²⟧ [Slang] a remarkable person or thing

dilly-dally (dil′ē dal′ē) *vi.* **-lied, -ly·ing** ⟦< DALLY⟧ to waste time by hesitating; loiter or dawdle

di·lute (di lo͞ot′, dī-) *vt.* **-lut′ed, -lut′ing** ⟦< L *dis*-, off + *lavare*, to wash⟧ to thin down or weaken as by mixing with water — *adj.* diluted —**di·lu′tion** *n.*

■■■ THESAURUS ■■■

challenging, exacting, formidable, ambitious, immense, tough*, heavy*, no picnic*, stiff*; see also SEVERE 1.— *Ant.* EASY, wieldy, light. **2** [Hard to understand] intricate, involved, perplexing, abstruse, abstract, delicate, hard, knotty, thorny, troublesome, ticklish, obstinate, puzzling, mysterious, mystifying, subtle, confusing, bewildering, confounding, esoteric, unclear, mystical, tangled, hard to explain, hard to solve, profound, rambling, loose, meandering, inexplicable, awkward, complex, complicated, deep, stubborn, hidden, formidable, enigmatic, paradoxical, incomprehensible, unintelligible, inscrutable, inexplicable, unanswerable, not understandable, unsolvable, unfathomable, concealed, unaccountable, ambiguous, equivocal, metaphysical, inconceivable, unknown, deep*, over one's head*, too deep for*, not making sense*, Greek to*; see also OBSCURE 1, 3.—*Ant.* CLEAR, obvious, simple.

difficulty *n.* **1** [Something in one's way] obstacle, obstruction, stumbling block, impediment, complication, hardship, adversity, misfortune, distress, deadlock, dilemma, hard job, maze, stone wall, barricade, impasse, knot, opposition, quandary, struggle, crisis, trouble, embarrassment, entanglement, thwart, mess, paradox, muddle, emergency, matter, standstill, hindrance, perplexity, bar, trial, check, predicament, hot water*, pickle*, fix*, stew*, scrape*, hard nut to crack*, hitch*, dead end*, snag*,

monkey wrench in the works*, pinch, deep water*, jam*, the devil to pay*, hangup*; see sense 2 and BARRIER.—*Ant.* HELP, aid, assistance. **2** [Something mentally disturbing] trouble, annoyance, to-do, ado, worry, weight, complication, distress, oppression, depression, aggravation, anxiety, discouragement, touchy situation, embarrassment, burden, grievance, irritation, strife, puzzle, responsibility, frustration, harassment, misery, predicament, setback, pressure, stress, strain, charge, struggle, maze, jam*, hangup*, mess*, pickle*, pinch*, scrape*; see also sense 1 and CRISIS, EMERGENCY.— *Ant.* EASE, comfort, happiness.

dig* *n.* **1** [Insult] slur, innuendo, cut; see INSULT. **2** [Excavation] digging, archaeological expedition, exploration; see EXPEDITION.

dig *v.* **1** [To stir the earth] delve, spade, mine, excavate, channel, deepen, till, drive a shaft, clean, undermine, burrow, dig out, gouge, dredge, scoop out, tunnel out, hollow out, clean out, stope, grub, bulldoze; see also SHOVEL.—*Ant.* BURY, embed, fill. **2** [To remove by digging] dig up, uncover, turn up; see HARVEST. **3** [*To like] enjoy, love, appreciate; see LIKE 1, 2. **4** [*To understand] comprehend, recognize, follow; see UNDERSTAND 1. —**dig into** investigate, research, probe; see EXAMINE. —**dig up** find, uncover, excavate; see DIG 2, DISCOVER.

digest *n.* epitome, précis, condensa-

tion; see SUMMARY.

digest *v.* transform food, consume, absorb; see EAT 1.

digestible *a.* eatable, absorbable, good to eat; see EDIBLE.

digit *n.* symbol, arabic notation, numeral; see NUMBER.

dignified *a.* stately, somber, solemn, courtly, reserved, ornate, elegant, classic, lordly, aristocratic, majestic, formal, noble, regal, superior, magnificent, grand, eminent, sublime, august, grave, distinguished, magisterial, imposing, portly, haughty, honorable, decorous, lofty, proud, classy*, snazzy*, sober as a judge*, high-brow*; see also CULTURED, REFINED 2.—*Ant.* RUDE, undignified, boorish.

dignify *v.* exalt, elevate, prefer; see PRAISE 1.

dignity *n.* nobility, self-respect, lofty bearing, grand air, quality, culture, distinction, stateliness, elevation, worth, worthiness, character, importance, renown, splendor, majesty, class*; see also HONOR, PRIDE 1.— *Ant.* HUMILITY, lowness, meekness.

dilemma *n.* quandary, perplexity, predicament; see DIFFICULTY 1.

diligence *n.* alertness, earnestness, quickness, perseverance, industry, vigor, carefulness, heed, intent, intensity, assiduity; see also ATTENTION, CARE 1.—*Ant.* CARELESSNESS, sloth, laziness.

dilute *v.* mix, reduce, thin; see WEAKEN 2.

dim (dim) *adj.* **dim′mer, dim′mest** ⟦OE⟧ **1** not bright, clear, or distinct; dull, obscure, etc. **2** not clearly seeing, hearing, or understanding **3** [Colloq.] stupid — *vt.*, *vi.* **dimmed, dim′ming** to make or grow dim —**dim′ly** *adv.* —**dim′ness** *n.*

dim. diminutive

dime (dim) *n.* ⟦< L *decem*, ten⟧ a U.S. and Canadian 10-cent coin

di·men·sion (də men′shən) *n.* ⟦< L *dis-*, off, from + *metiri*, to measure⟧ **1** any measurable extent, as length, width, etc. **2** [*pl.*] measurements in length, width, and often depth **3** [*often pl.*] extent; scope —**di·men′sional** *adj.*

dime store FIVE-AND-TEN-CENT STORE

di·min·ish (də min′ish) *vt.*, *vi.* ⟦< L *diminuere*, reduce⟧ to make or become smaller in size, degree, importance, etc.; lessen —**dimi·nu′tion** (dim′ə noo͞o′shən, -nyoo͞o′-) *n.*

di·minu·endo (də min′yoo͞o en′dō) *adj.*, *adv.* ⟦It: see prec.⟧ *Music* with gradually diminishing volume

di·minu·tive (də min′yoo͞o tiv) *adj.* ⟦see DIMINISH⟧ very small; tiny — *n.* a word having a suffix that expresses smallness, endearment, etc.

dimity (dim′ə tē) *n.*, *pl.* **-ties** ⟦< Gr *dis-*, two + *mitos*, a thread⟧ a thin, corded or patterned cotton cloth

dim′mer *n.* a device, as a rheostat, for dimming electric lights

dim·ple (dim′pəl) *n.* ⟦ME *dimpel*⟧ a small, natural hollow, as on the cheek or chin — *vi.*, *vt.* **-pled, -pling** to form dimples (in) —**dim′ply** (-plē) *adj.*

dim sum (dim′ tsoom′) ⟦Chin⟧ small dumplings filled with meat, vegetables, etc.

dim′wit′ *n.* [Slang] a stupid person; simpleton —**dim′wit′ted** *adj.*

din (din) *n.* ⟦OE *dyne*⟧ a loud, continuous noise; confused uproar — *vt.* **dinned, din′ning 1** to beset with a din **2** to repeat insistently or noisily

din-din (din′din′) *n.* [Colloq.] dinner

dine (din) *vi.* **dined, din′ing** ⟦ult. < L *dis-*, away + *jejunus*, hungry⟧ to eat dinner — *vt.* to provide a dinner for

diner (din′ər) *n.* **1** a person eating dinner **2** a railroad car equipped to serve meals **3** a small restaurant built to look like such a car

di·nette (di net′) *n.* an alcove or small space used as a dining room

ding (diŋ) *n.* ⟦< Scand⟧ the sound of a bell Also **ding′-dong′** (-dôŋ′)

din·ghy (diŋ′gē, diŋ′ē) *n.*, *pl.* **-ghies** ⟦Hindi *ḍiṅgi*⟧ any of various small boats, as one carried on a ship

din·gle (diŋ′gəl) *n.* ⟦ME *dingel*, abyss⟧ a small, deep, wooded valley

dingo (diŋ′gō) *n.*, *pl.* **-goes** ⟦native name⟧ the Australian wild dog, usually tawny in color

dingus (diŋ′əs) *n.* ⟦< Du *ding*, thing⟧ [Colloq.] any device; gadget

dingy (din′jē) *adj.* **-gier, -gi·est** ⟦orig. dial. var. < DUNG⟧ **1** not bright or clean; grimy **2** dismal; shabby —**din′gi·ness** *n.*

dining room a room where meals are eaten

dinky (diŋ′kē) *adj.* **-ier, -i·est** ⟦< Scot *dink*, trim⟧ [Colloq.] small

din·ner (din′ər) *n.* ⟦see DINE⟧ **1** the chief meal of the day **2** a banquet in honor of a person or event

din′ner·ware′ (-wer′) *n.* **1** plates, cups, saucers, etc., collectively **2** a set of such dishes

di·no·saur (di′nə sôr′) *n.* ⟦< Gr *deinos*, terrible + *sauros*, lizard⟧ a prehistoric, extinct reptile, often huge

dint (dint) *n.* ⟦OE *dynt*⟧ **1** force; exertion: now chiefly in **by dint of 2** a dent

di·o·cese (di′ə sis, -sēs′, -sēz′) *n.* ⟦< Gr *dioikein*, to keep house⟧ the district under a bishop's jurisdiction —**di·oc′esan** (-äs′ə sən, -zən) *adj.*

di·ode (di′ōd′) *n.* ⟦DI-¹ + -ODE⟧ an electron tube used esp. as a rectifier

Di·o·ny·sus or **Di·o·ny·sos** (di′ə ni′səs) *Gr. Myth.* the god of wine

di·o·rama (di′ə ram′ə) *n.* ⟦< Gr *dia-*, through + *horama*, a view⟧ a scenic display, as of three-dimensional figures against a painted background

di·oxin (di äks′in) *n.* a highly toxic chemical contaminant

dip (dip) *vt.* **dipped, dip′ping** ⟦OE *dyppan*⟧ **1** to immerse briefly **2** to scoop (liquid) up or out **3** to lower (a flag, etc.) and immediately raise again — *vi.* **1** to plunge into a liquid and quickly come out **2** to sink suddenly **3** to decline slightly **4** to slope down **5** to lower a container, the hand, etc. as into water **6** to read or inquire superficially: with *into* — *n.* **1** a dipping or being dipped **2** a brief plunge into water, etc. **3** a liquid, sauce, etc. into which something is dipped **4** whatever is removed by dipping **5** a downward slope or plunge

diph·theria (dif thir′ē ə; *widely* dip-) *n.* ⟦< Gr *diphthera*, leather⟧ an acute infectious disease marked by high fever and difficult breathing

diph·thong (dif′thôŋ; *often* dip′-) *n.* ⟦< Gr *di-*, two + *phthongos*, sound⟧ a sound made by gliding from one vowel to another in one syllable, as in *oil*

di·ploma (də plō′mə) *n.* ⟦< Gr *diplōma*, folded letter⟧ a certificate issued by a school, college, etc. indicating graduation or the conferring of a degree

di·plo′macy (-sē) *n.* ⟦see fol.⟧ **1** the conducting of relations between nations **2** tact

dip·lo·mat (dip′lə mat′) *n.* **1** a representative of a government who conducts relations with another government **2** a tactful person

dip′lo·mat′ic *adj.* **1** of diplomacy **2** tactful —**dip′lo·mat′i·cally** *adv.*

di·pole (di′pōl′) *n.* a kind of radio or TV antenna with a single line separated at the center for connection to the receiver

dip·per (dip′ər) *n.* a long-handled cup, etc. for dipping — **[D-]** either of two groups of stars in the shape of a dipper **(Big Dipper, Little Dipper)**

dipso·ma·nia (dip′sə mā′nē ə) *n.* ⟦< Gr *dipsa*, thirst + *mania*, madness⟧ an abnormal craving for alcoholic drink —**dip′so·ma′niac′** (-ak′) *n.*

dip′stick′ *n.* a graduated rod for measuring quantity or depth

Dir. Director

dire (dir) *adj.* **dir′er, dir′est** ⟦L *dirus*⟧ **1** dreadful; terrible: also **dire′ful 2** urgent *[a dire need]*

■ THESAURUS ■

dim *a.* faint, dusky, shadowy; see DARK 1.

dime *n.* ten cents, thin dime, ten-cent piece; see MONEY 1.

dimensions *n.* size, measurements, extent; see HEIGHT, LENGTH 1, 2, WIDTH.

diminish *v.* lessen, depreciate, abbreviate; see DECREASE.

din *n.* clamor, commotion, hubbub; see CONFUSION, NOISE 2.

dine *v.* lunch, feast, sup; see EAT 1.

dingy *a.* grimy, muddy, soiled; see DIRTY 1.

dining room *n.* *Varieties include the following:* dining hall, breakfast nook, dinette, tea shop, lunch counter, lunch room, cafeteria, café, ice-cream parlor, drug store, grill, coffee shop, fast-food outlet, soda fountain, steak house, sandwich shop, diner, mess hall, galley, automat, greasy spoon*; see also RESTAURANT.

dinner *n.* feast, banquet, main meal, supper, repast; see also MEAL 2.

dip *n.* **1** [The action of dipping] plunge, immersion, soaking, ducking, drenching, sinking; see also BATH 1. **2** [Material into which something is dipped] preparation, solution, suspension, dilution, concoction, saturation, mixture; see also LIQUID. **3** [A low place] depression, slope, inclination; see HOLE 1. **4** [A swim] plunge, bath, dive; see SWIM.

dip *v.* **1** [To put into a liquid] plunge, lower, wet, slosh, submerge, irrigate, steep, drench, douse, souse, moisten, splash, slop, water, duck, bathe, rinse, baptize, dunk; see also IMMERSE, SOAK 1, WASH 2. **2** [To transfer by means of a vessel] scoop, shovel, ladle, bale, spoon, dredge, lift, draw, dish, dip up, dip out, offer; see also SERVE.—*Ant.* EMPTY, pour, let stand. **3** [To fall] slope, decline, recede, tilt, swoop, slip, spiral, sink, plunge, bend, verge, veer, slant, settle, slump, slide, go down; see also DIVE, DROP 2, FALL 1.

diploma *n.* degree, graduation certificate, credentials, honor, award, recognition, commission, warrant, voucher, confirmation, sheepskin*; see also GRADUATION.

diplomacy *n.* artfulness, skill, discretion; see TACT.

diplomat *n.* ambassador, consul, minister, legate, emissary, envoy, agent; see also REPRESENTATIVE 2, STATESMAN.

diplomatic *a.* tactful, suave, gracious, calculating, shrewd, opportunistic, smooth, capable, conciliatory, conniving, sly, artful, wily, subtle, crafty, sharp, cunning, contriving, scheming, discreet, deft, intriguing, politic, strategic, astute, clever; see also POLITE.

dipped *a.* immersed, plunged, bathed, ducked, doused, drenched, soused, covered, dunked; see also SOAKED, WET 1.

dire *a.* dreadful, terrible, horrible; see

di·rect (də rekt′, dī-) *adj.* ⟦< L *di-*, apart + *regere*, to rule⟧ **1** not roundabout or interrupted; straight **2** honest; frank *[a direct answer]* **3** with nothing between; immediate **4** in an unbroken line of descent; lineal **5** exact; complete *[the direct opposite]* **6** in the exact words *[a direct quote]* — *vt.* **1** to manage; guide **2** to order; command **3** to turn or point; aim; head **4** to tell (a person) the way to a place **5** to address (a letter, etc.) **6** to supervise the action and effects of (a play, etc.) — *adv.* directly —**di·rect′ness** *n.*

direct current an electric current flowing in one direction

di·rec·tion (də rek′shən; *also* dī-) *n.* **1** a directing **2** *[usually pl.]* instructions for doing, using, etc. **3** a command **4** the point toward which something faces or the line along which it moves or lies —**di·rec′tional** *adj.*

di·rec′tive (-rek′tiv) *adj.* directing — *n.* a general order issued authoritatively

di·rect′ly *adv.* **1** in a direct way or line; straight **2** with nothing or no one between **3** exactly *[directly opposite]* **4** instantly; right away

direct object *Gram.* the word or words denoting the receiver of the action of a verb (Ex.: *me* in "he hit me")

di·rec′tor *n.* one who directs a school, corporation, etc. or a play, choir, etc. —**di·rec′tor·ship′** *n.*

di·rec′tor·ate (-it) *n.* **1** the position of director **2** a board of directors

di·rec′tory (-tə rē) *n.*, *pl.* **-ries** a book listing the names, addresses, etc. of a specific group of persons

dirge (dʉrj) *n.* ⟦< L *dirige* (direct), first word of a prayer⟧ a song, poem, etc. of grief or mourning

diri·gible (dir′ə jə bəl, də rij′ə-) *n.* ⟦see DIRECT & -IBLE⟧ AIRSHIP

dirk (dʉrk) *n.* ⟦< ?⟧ a long dagger

dirndl (dʉrn′dəl) *n.* ⟦< Ger *dirne*, girl⟧ a full skirt gathered at the waist

dirt (dʉrt) *n.* ⟦< ON *drita*, excrement⟧ **1** any unclean matter, as mud, trash, etc.; filth **2** earth; soil **3** dirtiness, corruption, etc. **4** obscenity **5** malicious gossip

dirt bike a light, off-road motorcycle with special tires, large fenders, etc.

dirt′-cheap′ *adj.*, *adv.* [Colloq.] very inexpensive(ly)

dirt′y *adj.* **-i·er, -i·est** **1** not clean **2** obscene **3** contemptible or nasty **4** unfair; dishonest **5** rough, as weather — *vt.*, *vi.* **dirt′ied, dirt′y·ing** to make or become dirty — **dirt′i·ness** *n.*

dis- ⟦< L⟧ *prefix* separation, negation, reversal *[disbar, disable, disintegrate]*

dis·abil·ity (dis′ə bil′ə tē) *n.*, *pl.* **-ties** **1** a disabled condition **2** that which disables or disqualifies

dis·a′ble (-ā′bəl) *vt.* **-bled, -bling** to make unable, unfit, or disqualified

dis·abuse (dis′ə byōōz′) *vt.* **-bused′, -bus′ing** to rid of false ideas

dis·ad·van·tage (dis′əd vant′ij) *n.* **1** an unfavorable situation or circumstance **2** detriment —**dis′ad′van′ta′geous** (-ad′vən tā′jəs) *adj.*

dis′ad·van′taged *adj.* underprivileged

dis·af·fect (dis′ə fekt′) *vt.* to make unfriendly, discontented, or disloyal —**dis·af·fec′tion** *n.*

dis·af·fil′i·ate′ (-ə fil′ē āt′) *vt.*, *vi.* **-at′ed, -at′ing** to end an affiliation (with) —**dis·af·fil′i·a′tion** *n.*

dis·agree′ (-ə grē′) *vi.* **-greed′, -gree′ing** **1** to fail to agree; differ **2** to differ in opinion; quarrel **3** to give distress: with *with* —**dis·agree′ment** *n.*

dis·agree′able *adj.* **1** unpleasant; offensive **2** quarrelsome —**dis·agree′ably** *adv.*

dis·al·low (dis′ə lou′) *vt.* to refuse to allow (a claim, etc.); reject

dis·ap·pear′ (-ə pir′) *vi.* **1** to cease to be seen; vanish **2** to cease existing —**dis·ap·pear′ance** *n.*

■ THESAURUS ■

FRIGHTFUL 1.

direct *a.* **1** [Without divergence] in a straight line, straight ahead, undeviating, uninterrupted, unswerving, shortest, nonstop, as the crow flies*, straight as an arrow*, in a beeline*, point-blank; see also STRAIGHT 1.— *Ant.* ZIGZAG, roundabout, circuitous. **2** [Frank] straightforward, outspoken, candid; see FRANK, HONEST. **3** [Immediate] prompt, succeeding, resultant; see IMMEDIATE.

direct *v.* **1** [To show the way] conduct, show, guide; see LEAD 1. **2** [To decide the course of affairs] regulate, govern, influence; see MANAGE 1. **3** [To aim a weapon] sight, train, level; see AIM. **4** [To command] command, bid, charge; see ORDER 1.

directed *a.* supervised, controlled, conducted, sponsored, under supervision, assisted, counseled, guided, serviced, managed, organized, orderly, modern, purposeful, functioning; see also AIMED, ORGANIZED.

direction *n.* **1** [A position] point of the compass, objective, bearing, region, area, place, spot; see also WAY 2. *Points of the compass include the following:* north (N), south (S), east (E), west (W), NE, NW, SE, SW, NNE, NNW, SSE, SSW, ENE, ESE, WNW, WSW. **2** [Supervision] management, superintendence, control; see ADMINISTRATION 2. **3** [A tendency] bias, bent, proclivity; see INCLINATION 1.

directions *n.* instructions, advice, notification, specification, indication, orders, assignment, recommendations, summons, directive, regulation, prescription, plans.

directly *a.* instantly, at once, quickly; see IMMEDIATELY.

director *n.* manager, supervisor,

executive; see LEADER 2.

directory *n.* list, syllabus, notice, register, record, almanac, roster, dictionary, gazetteer, telephone book, Yellow Pages, city directory, Social Register, Who's Who, blue book; see also CATALOG, INDEX.

dirt *n.* **1** [Earth] soil, loam, clay; see EARTH 2. **2** [Filth] rottenness, filthiness, smut; see FILTH.

dirty *a.* **1** [Containing dirt] soiled, unclean, unsanitary, unhygienic, filthy, polluted, nasty, slovenly, dusty, messy, squalid, sloppy, disheveled, uncombed, unsightly, untidy, straggly, unwashed, stained, tarnished, spotted, smudged, foul, fouled, grimy, greasy, muddy, mucky, sooty, smoked, slimy, rusty, unlaundered, unswept, crummy*, grubby, scuzzy*, scummy.—*Ant.* PURE, unspotted, sanitary. **2** [Obscene] pornographic, smutty, lewd; see LEWD 1, 2, SENSUAL. **3** [Nasty] mean, contemptible, disagreeable; see MEAN 3, RUTHLESS.

dirty *v.* soil, sully, defile, pollute, foul, tarnish, spot, smear, blot, blur, smudge, smoke, spoil, sweat up, blotch, spatter, splash, stain, debase, corrupt, taint, contaminate.—*Ant.* CLEAN, cleanse, rinse.

disability *n.* feebleness, inability, incapacity; see INJURY, WEAKNESS 1.

disable *v.* cripple, impair, put out of action; see DAMAGE, WEAKEN 2.

disabled *a.* crippled, helpless, useless, wrecked, stalled, maimed, wounded, mangled, lame, mutilated, run-down, worn-out, weakened, impotent, castrated, paralyzed, handicapped, senile, decrepit, laid up*, done for*, done in*, cracked up*, out of action*; see also HURT, USELESS 1, WEAK 1.—*Ant.* HEALTHY, strong,

capable.

disadvantage *n.* **1** [Loss] damage, harm, deprivation; see LOSS 3. **2** [A position involving difficulties] bar, obstacle, handicap; see RESTRAINT 2. **3** [Unfavorable details or prospects: *often plural*] inconvenience, obstacle, drawbacks; see WEAKNESS 1.

disagree *v.* **1** [To differ] dissent, object, oppose; see DIFFER 1. **2** [To have uncomfortable effect] nauseate, make ill, be hard on one's stomach*; see BOTHER 2.

disagreeable *a.* **1** [Having an unpleasant disposition] difficult, obnoxious, offensive; see IRRITABLE, RUDE 2. **2** [Irritating: *said of things and conditions*] bothersome, unpleasant, upsetting; see DISTURBING, OFFENSIVE 2.

disagreement *n.* **1** [Discord] contention, strife, conflict, controversy, wrangle, dissension, animosity, ill feeling, ill will, misunderstanding, division, opposition, hostility, breach, discord, feud, clashing, antagonism, bickering, squabble, tension, split, quarreling, falling-out, break, rupture, quarrel, clash, opposition, contest, friction; see also BATTLE, COMPETITION, FIGHT. **2** [Inconsistency] discrepancy, dissimilarity, disparity; see DIFFERENCE 1. **3** [A quarrel] fight, argument, feud; see DISPUTE.

disappear *v.* cease, fade, die; see ESCAPE, EVAPORATE, VANISH.

disappearance *n.* vanishing, fading, departure, ebbing away, removal, dissipation, ceasing to exist, ceasing to appear, desertion, flight, retirement, escape, exodus, vanishing point, going, disintegration, exit, withdrawal, decline and fall, eclipse; see also ESCAPE, EVAPORATION.

dis·ap·point' (-ə point') *vt.* to fail to satisfy the hopes or expectations of —**dis'ap·point'ment** *n.*

dis·ap·pro·ba·tion (dis'ap'rə bā'shən) *n.* a disapproving; disapproval

dis·ap·prove (dis'ə prōōv') *vt., vi.* -proved', -prov'ing 1 to have or express an unfavorable opinion (of) 2 to refuse to approve —**dis'ap·prov'al** *n.* —**dis'ap·prov'ingly** *adv.*

dis·arm (dis ärm', dis'-) *vt.* 1 to take away weapons from 2 to make harmless 3 to make friendly — *vi.* to reduce armed forces and armaments law —**dis·ar'ma·ment** (-är'mə mənt) *n.*

dis·ar·range (dis'ə rānj') *vt.* -ranged', -rang'ing to undo the order of —**dis'ar·range'ment** *n.*

dis·ar·ray' (-ə rā') *vt.* to throw into disorder — *n.* disorder

dis·as·sem·ble (-ə sem'bəl) *vt.* -bled, -bling to take apart

dis·as·so·ci·ate (-ə sō'shē āt', -sē-) *vt.* -at'ed, -at'ing to sever association with; dissociate

dis·as·ter (di zas'tər) *n.* [< L *dis-*, away + *astrum*, a star] any happening that causes great harm or damage; calamity —**dis·as'trous** (-trəs) *adj.*

dis·avow (dis'ə vou') *vt.* to deny any knowledge of or responsibility for; disclaim —**dis·avow'al** *n.*

dis·band (dis band') *vt., vi.* to break up, as an organization

dis·bar' (-bär') *vt.* -barred', -bar'ring to deprive (a lawyer) of the right to practice law —**dis·bar'ment** *n.*

dis·be·lieve (dis'bə lēv') *vt., vi.* -lieved', -liev'ing to refuse to believe —**dis·be·lief'** (-lēf') *n.*

dis·burse (dis burs') *vt.* -bursed', -burs'ing [< OFr *desbourser*] to pay out; expend —**dis·burse'ment** *n.*

disc (disk) *n.* 1 DISK 2 a phonograph record

dis·card (dis kärd'; *for n.* dis'kärd') *vt.* [< OFr: see DIS- & CARD[1]] 1 *Card Games* to remove (a card or cards) from

one's hand 2 to get rid of as no longer useful — *n.* 1 a discarding or being discarded 2 something discarded

disc brake a brake, as on a car, with two friction pads that press on a disc rotating along with the wheel

dis·cern (di zurn', -surn') *vt.* [< L *dis-*, apart + *cernere*, to separate] to perceive or recognize clearly —**dis·cern'ible** *adj.* —**dis·cern'ment** *n.*

dis·cern·ing *adj.* having good judgment; astute —**dis·cern'ingly** *adv.*

dis·charge (dis chärj'; *for n., usually* dis'chärj') *vt.* -charged', -charg'ing [< L *dis-*, from + *carrus*, wagon] 1 to release or dismiss 2 to unload (a cargo) 3 to shoot (a gun or projectile) 4 to emit *[to discharge pus]* 5 to pay (a debt) or perform (a duty) 6 *Elec.* to remove stored energy from (a battery, etc.) — *vi.* 1 to get rid of a load, etc. 2 to go off, as a gun — *n.* 1 a discharging or being discharged 2 that which discharges or is discharged

dis·ci·ple (di sī'pəl) *n.* [< L *dis-*, apart + *capere*, to hold] 1 a pupil or follower of any teacher or school 2 an early follower of Jesus, esp. one of the Apostles —**dis·ci'ple·ship'** *n.*

dis·ci·pli·nar·ian (dis'ə pli ner'ē ən) *n.* a person who believes in or enforces strict discipline

dis·ci·pline (dis'ə plin', -plən) *n.* [see DISCIPLE] 1 training that develops self-control, efficiency, etc. 2 strict control to enforce obedience 3 orderly conduct 4 a system of rules, as for a monastic order 5 treatment that corrects or punishes —*vt.* -plined', -plin'ing 1 to train; control 2 to punish —**dis'ci·pli·nar'y** (-pli ner'ē) *adj.*

disc jockey one who conducts a radio program of recorded music

dis·claim (dis klām') *vt.* 1 to give up any claim to 2 to repudiate

dis·claim'er *n.* a denial or renunciation, as of responsibility

---

THESAURUS

disappoint *v.* fail, delude, deceive, dissatisfy, disillusion, harass, embitter, chagrin, dumbfound, fall short of, cast down, frustrate, torment, tease, miscarry, abort, thwart, foil, baffle, balk, mislead, bungle, let down, leave in the lurch*, fizzle out*.

disappointed *a.* dissatisfied, discouraged, unsatisfied, despondent, depressed, objecting, complaining, distressed, hopeless, balked, disconcerted, aghast, disgruntled, disillusioned; see also SAD.—*Ant.* SATISFIED, pleased, content.

disappointing *a.* unsatisfactory, ineffective, uninteresting, discouraging, unpleasant, inferior, lame, insufficient, failing, at fault, limited, second-rate, mediocre, ordinary, unexpected, unhappy, depressing, disconcerting, disagreeable, irritating, annoying, troublesome, disheartening, unlucky, uncomfortable, bitter, distasteful, disgusting, deplorable, short of expectations; see also INADEQUATE.

disappointment *n.* 1 [The state of being disappointed] dissatisfaction, frustration, chagrin, lack of success, despondency, displeasure, distress, discouragement, disillusionment, check, disillusion, setback, adversity, hard fortune; see also DEFEAT, FAILURE 1, REGRET 1.—*Ant.* SUCCESS, fulfillment, realization. 2 [A person or thing that disappoints] miscarriage, misfortune, calamity, blunder, bad luck, setback, downfall, slip, defeat, mishap, error, mistake, discouragement, obstacle, miscalculation, fiasco, no go*, blind alley*, washout*, lemon*, dud*, letdown, bust*, false alarm*; see also sense 1 and FAILURE 2.—*Ant.* ACHIEVEMENT, successful venture, success.

disapproval *n.* criticism, censure, disparagement; see OBJECTION ät.

disapprove *v.* blame, chastise, reprove; see DENOUNCE. —**disapprove of** object to, dislike, deplore; see COMPLAIN, OPPOSE 1.

disarm *v.* demobilize, disable, unarm, weaken, debilitate, incapacitate, muzzle, deprive of weapons, deprive of means of defense, subdue, strip, tie the hands of*, clip the wings of*; see also DEFEAT 2, 3.—*Ant.* ARM, outfit, equip.

disarmament *n.* arms reduction, cease-fire, de-escalation; see PEACE 1.

disaster *n.* accident, calamity, mishap, debacle, casualty, emergency, adversity, harm, misadventure, collapse, slip, fall, collision, crash, hazard, setback, defeat, failure, woe, trouble, scourge, grief, undoing, cure, rainy day, bankruptcy, upset, blast, blow, wreck, bad luck, comedown*, crack-up, pileup*, smashup, washout*, flop*, bust*; see also CATASTROPHE, MISFORTUNE.

disastrous *a.* calamitous, ruinous, unfortunate; see HARMFUL, UNFAVORABLE.

disband *v.* scatter, disperse, dismiss; see LEAVE 1.

disbelief *n.* unbelief, skepticism, mistrust; see DOUBT.

disbeliever *n.* doubter, skeptic, agnostic; see CRITIC 1.

disburse *v.* expend, use, contribute; see PAY 1, SPEND.

discard *v.* reject, expel, repudiate, protest, cast aside, cast away, cast out, cast off, throw away, throw aside, throw overboard, throw out, get rid of, give up, renounce, have done with, dump, make away with, dismantle, discharge, write off, banish, eject, divorce, dispossess, dispense with, shake off, pass up, free oneself from, free of, give away, part with, dispose of, do away with, dispense with, shed, relinquish, thrust aside, cast aside, sweep away, cancel, abandon, forsake, desert, cut, have nothing to do with, brush away, scotch*, chuck*, drop, wash one's bands of*, junk*; see also ABANDON 1, DISMISS.—*Ant.* SAVE, retain, preserve.

discarded *a.* rejected, repudiated, cast off, thrown away, dismantled, dismissed, useless, damaged, outworn, worn out, done with, run down, not worth saving, abandoned, obsolete, shelved, neglected, deserted, forsaken, outmoded, out of date, out of style, out of fashion, old-fashioned, old hat*.—*Ant.* KEPT, worthwhile, modern.

discern *v.* find out, determine, discriminate; see DISCOVER.

discerning *a.* discriminating, perceptive, penetrating; see DISCREET.

discharge *v.* 1 [To unload] unpack, release, remove cargo; see EMPTY, UNLOAD. 2 [To remove] take off, send, carry away; see REMOVE 1. 3 [To cause to fire] blast, shoot off, fire; see SHOOT 1. 4 [To release] emancipate, liberate, let go; see FREE.

discharged *a.* mustered out, sent home, recalled, freed, liberated, released, let go, sent away, emancipated, expelled, ejected, dismissed, fired, ousted, canned*, axed*; see also FREE 2, 3.

disciple *n.* 1 [A follower] adherent, pupil, believer; see FOLLOWER. 2 [A follower of Christ] apostle, witness, revealer. *Christ's disciples mentioned in the New Testament include:* Matthew, John, Peter, Bartholomew, James, Philip, Andrew, Thaddeus, Thomas, James the son of Alphaeus, Judas Iscariot, Simon the Canaanite.

discipline *n.* 1 [Mental self-training] preparation, development, exercise, drilling, training, regulation, self-disciplining; see also DRILL 3, EDUCATION 1. 2 [A system of obedience] conduct, regulation, drill, orderliness, restraint, limitation, curb, indoctrination, brainwashing; see also TRAINING.

discipline *v.* chastise, correct, limit; see PUNISH.

disc jockey *n.* radio announcer, commentator, DJ*; see ANNOUNCER, REPORTER.

dis·close (dis klōz′) *vt.* **-closed′, -clos′ing** to uncover; reveal —**dis·clo′sure** (-klō′zhər) *n.*

disco (dis′kō) *n.* **1** *pl.* **-cos** *short for* DISCOTHÈQUE **2** a kind of popular dance music with a strong beat

dis·col′or, *vi.* to change in color as by fading, streaking, or staining Brit. sp. **dis·col′our** —**dis·color·a′tion** *n.*

dis·com·fit (dis kum′fit) *vt.* ⟦< L *dis-*, away + *conficere*, prepare⟧ **1** to frustrate the plans of **2** to disconcert —**dis·com′fi·ture** (-fi chər) *n.*

dis·com′fort *n.* **1** lack of comfort; uneasiness **2** anything causing this — *vt.* to cause discomfort to

dis·com·mode (dis′kə mōd′) *vt.* **-mod′ed, -mod′ing** ⟦< DIS- + L *commodare*, to make suitable⟧ to cause bother to; inconvenience

dis·com·pose (-kəm pōz′) *vt.* **-posed′, -pos′ing** to disturb; fluster —**dis·com·po′sure** (-pō′zhər) *n.*

dis·con·cert (-kən surt′) *vt.* to upset; embarrass; confuse

dis′con·nect′ (-kə nekt′) *vt.* to break the connection of; separate —**dis′con·nec′tion** *n.*

dis′con·nect′ed *adj.* **1** separated **2** incoherent —**dis′con·nect′ed·ly** *adv.*

dis·con·so·late (dis kän′sə lit) *adj.* ⟦see DIS- & CONSOLE[1]⟧ inconsolable; dejected —**dis·con′so·late·ly** *adv.*

dis·con·tent (dis′kən tent′) *adj.* ⟦ME⟧ DISCONTENTED — *n.* dissatisfaction with one's situation Also **dis′con·tent′ment** — *vt.* to make discontented

dis′con·tent′ed *adj.* not contented; wanting something more or different —**dis′con·tent′ed·ly** *adv.*

dis·con·tinue (dis′kən tin′yōō) *vt., vi.* **-ued, -u·ing** to stop; cease; give up —**dis′con·tin′u·ance** *n.* —**dis′con·tin′u·a′tion** *n.*

dis·con·tin′u·ous *adj.* not continuous; having interruptions or gaps

dis·cord (dis′kôrd′) *n.* ⟦< L *dis-*, apart + *cor*, heart⟧ **1** disagreement **2** a harsh noise **3** a lack of musical harmony —**dis·cord′ant** *adj.*

dis·co·thèque (dis′kə tek′) *n.* ⟦Fr⟧ a place for dancing to recorded music

dis·count (dis′kount′; *for v., also* dis kount′) *n.* ⟦see DIS- & COMPUTE⟧ **1** a reduction from a usual or list price **2** the rate of interest charged on a discounted bill, note, etc.: also called **discount rate** — *vt.* **1** to pay or receive the

value of (a bill, promissory note, etc.), minus a deduction for interest **2** to deduct an amount from (a bill, price, etc.) **3** to sell at less than the regular price **4** *a)* to allow for exaggeration, bias, etc. in (a story, etc.) *b)* to disregard **5** to lessen the effect of by anticipating

dis·coun·tenance (dis kount′′n əns) *vt.* **-nanced, -nanc·ing** **1** to make ashamed or embarrassed **2** to refuse approval or support

discount house (or **store**) a retail store that sells goods for less than regular price

dis·cour·age (di skur′ij) *vt.* **-aged, -ag·ing** **1** to deprive of courage or confidence **2** to persuade (a person) to refrain **3** to try to prevent by disapproving —**dis·cour′age·ment** *n.*

dis·course (dis′kôrs′; *for v., usually* dis kôrs′) *n.* ⟦< L *dis-*, from + *currere*, to run⟧ **1** talk; conversation **2** a formal treatment of a subject, in speech or writing — *vi.* **-coursed′, -cours′ing** to talk

dis·cour·teous (dis kur′tē əs) *adj.* impolite; rude; ill-mannered

dis·cour′tesy (-kurt′ə sē) *n.* **1** lack of courtesy; rudeness **2** *pl.* **-sies** a rude or impolite act or remark

dis·cover (di skuv′ər) *vt.* ⟦see DIS- & COVER⟧ **1** to be the first to find out, see, etc. **2** to learn of the existence of —**dis·cov′er·er** *n.*

dis·cov·ery (di skuv′ər ē) *n., pl.* **-er·ies** **1** a discovering **2** anything discovered

dis·credit (dis kred′it) *vt.* **1** to disbelieve **2** to cast doubt on **3** to disgrace — *n.* **1** loss of belief; doubt **2** disgrace —**dis·cred′it·able** *adj.*

dis·creet (di skrēt′) *adj.* ⟦see DISCERN⟧ careful about what one says or does; prudent —**dis·creet′ly** *adv.*

dis·crep·ancy (di skrep′ən sē) *n., pl.* **-cies** ⟦< L *dis-*, from + *crepare*, to rattle⟧ disagreement; inconsistency

dis·crete (di skrēt′) *adj.* ⟦see DISCERN⟧ separate and distinct; unrelated —**dis·crete′ly** *adv.*

dis·cre·tion (di skresh′ən) *n.* **1** the freedom to make decisions **2** the quality of being discreet; prudence —**dis·cre′tion·ar′y** (-er′ē) *adj.*

◼ THESAURUS ◼

disclose *v.* make known, confess, publish; see REVEAL.

disclosure *n.* exposé, acknowledgment, confession; see ADMISSION 3, DECLARATION.

discolor *v.* stain, rust, tarnish; see COLOR, DIRTY.

discoloration *n.* blot, blotch, splotch; see BLEMISH, STAIN.

discomfort *n.* trouble, displeasure, uneasiness; see ANNOYANCE, EMBARRASSMENT.

disconnect *v.* separate, detach, disengage; see CUT 1, DIVIDE.

disconnected *a.* broken off, detached, switched off; see SEPARATED.

discontent *n.* envy, uneasiness, depression; see REGRET 1.

discontented *a.* unhappy, disgruntled, malcontented; see SAD 1.

discontinue *v.* finish, close, cease; see END 1, STOP 2.

discontinued *a.* ended, terminated, given up; see ABANDONED.

discord *n.* **1** [Conflict] strife, contention, dissension; see DISAGREEMENT 1. **2** [Noise] din, tumult, racket; see NOISE 2.

discount *n.* deduction, allowance, rebate, decrease, markdown, concession, percentage, premium, subtraction, commission, exemption, modification, qualification, drawback, depreciation, cut rate; see also REDUCTION 1.—*Ant.* INCREASE, markup, surcharge. —**at a discount** discounted, cheap, below face value; see REDUCED 2.

discount *v.* reduce, remove, redeem, diminish, depreciate, deduct from, lower, make allowance for, allow, take off, charge off, rebate, mark down, anticipate, discredit, rake off*;

see also DECREASE 2.—*Ant.* RAISE, mark up, advance.

discourage *v.* repress, appall, intimidate, break one's heart, deject, unnerve, scare, confuse, dampen, dismay, daunt, bully, demoralize, throw a wet blanket on*, throw cold water on*, dampen the spirits, dash one's hopes; see also DEPRESS 2, FRIGHTEN.—*Ant.* ENCOURAGE, cheer, inspire.

discouraged *a.* downcast, pessimistic, depressed; see SAD 1.

discouragement *n.* **1** [Dejection] melancholy, despair, the blues*; see DEPRESSION 2, SADNESS. **2** [A restriction] constraint, hindrance, deterrent; see IMPEDIMENT 1.

discouraging *a.* **1** [Acting to discourage one] depressing, disheartening, repressing; see DISMAL. **2** [Suggesting an unwelcome future] inopportune, disadvantageous, dissuading; see UNFAVORABLE.

discourteous *a.* boorish, crude, impolite; see RUDE 2.

discourtesy *n.* impudence, impoliteness, vulgarity; see RUDENESS.

discover *v.* invent, find out, ascertain, detect, discern, recognize, distinguish, determine, observe, explore, hear of, hear about, awake to, bring to light, uncover, ferret out, root out, trace out, unearth, look up, stumble on, stumble upon, come on, come upon, run across, fall upon, strike upon, think of, perceive, glimpse, identify, devise, catch, spot, create, make out, sense, feel, sight, smell, hear, spy, bring out, find a clue, put one's finger on, get wise to*, dig out*, dig up*, turn up*, sniff out, come up with, happen upon, get wind of, hit upon, lay one's hands on; see also

FIND, LEARN.—*Ant.* MISS, pass by, omit.

discovered *a.* found, searched out, come on, happened on, happened upon, unearthed, ascertained, detected, revealed, disclosed, unveiled, observed, sighted, shown, exposed, traced out, made out, met with, come across, recognized, identified, laid bare, opened, presented, spotted, perceived, learned; see also REAL 2.—*Ant.* HIDDEN, unfound, lost.

discovery *n.* invention, detection, exploration, identification, discernment, distinction, determination, calculation, experimentation, feeling, hearing, sighting, strike, results, findings, formula, device, find, contrivance, design, machine, invention, process, breakthrough, data, principle, law, theorem, innovation, conclusion, method, way; see also RESULT.

discredit *v.* question, disbelieve, distrust; see DOUBT.

discreet *a.* cautious, prudent, discerning, discriminating, not rash, strategic, noncommittal, heedful, vigilant, civil, sensible, reserved, alert, awake, wary, watchful, wise, circumspect, attentive, considerate, intelligent, guarded, politic, diplomatic, tight-lipped, cagey*; see also CAREFUL, THOUGHTFUL 2.—*Ant.* RASH, indiscreet, imprudent.

discretion *n.* caution, foresight, carefulness, wariness, sound judgment, thoughtfulness, attention, heed, concern, consideration, observation, watchfulness, precaution, good sense, providence, maturity, discernment, forethought, calculation, deliberation, vigilance, discrimination, responsibility, presence of

dis·crim·i·nate (di skrim′i nāt′) *vi.* -nat′ed, -nat′ing [see DISCERN] 1 to distinguish 2 to make distinctions in treatment; show partiality or prejudice —**dis·crim′i·nat′ing** *adj.* —**dis·crim′i·na′tion** *n.*

dis·crim′i·na·to′ry (-nə tôr′ē) *adj.* showing discrimination or bias

dis·cur·sive (dis kur′siv) *adj.* [see DISCOURSE] wandering from one topic to another; rambling —**dis·cur′sive·ness** *n.*

dis·cus (dis′kəs) *n.* [< Gr *diskos*] a disk, as of metal and wood, thrown in a contest of strength and skill

dis·cuss (di skus′) *vt.* [< L *dis-*, apart + *quatere*, to shake] to talk or write about; consider the pros and cons of —**dis·cus′sion** (-skush′ən) *n.*

dis·cuss′ant (-ənt) *n.* a participant in an organized discussion

dis·dain (dis dān′) *vt.* [< L *dis-*, DIS- + *dignari*, deign] to regard as beneath one's dignity; scorn — *n.* aloof contempt —**dis·dain′ful** *adj.*

dis·ease (di zēz′) *n.* [< OFr *des-*, DIS- + *aise*, ease] 1 illness in general 2 a particular destructive process in an organism; specif., an illness —**dis·eased′** *adj.*

dis·em·bark (dis′im bärk′) *vi.*, *vt.* to leave, or unload from, a ship, aircraft, etc. —**dis′em·bar·ka′tion** *n.*

dis′em·bod′y (-im bäd′ē) *vt.* -bod′ied, -bod′y·ing to free from bodily existence —**dis′em·bod′i·ment** *n.*

dis′em·bow′el (-im bou′əl) *vt.* -eled or -elled, -el·ing or -el·ling to take out the entrails of

dis′en·chant′ (-in chant′) *vt.* 1 to free from an enchantment or illusion 2 DISILLUSION (sense 2) —**dis′en·chant′ment** *n.*

dis′en·cum′ber (-in kum′bər) *vt.* to relieve of a burden

dis′en·gage′ *vt.*, *vi.* -gaged′, -gag′ing to release or get loose from something that engages, holds, entangles, etc.; unfasten —**dis′en·gage′ment** *n.*

dis′en·tan′gle *vt.* -gled, -gling to free from something that entangles, confuses, etc.; extricate; untangle

dis′es·teem′ *n.* lack of esteem

dis·fa·vor (dis fā′vər) *n.* 1 an unfavorable opinion; dislike; disapproval 2 the state of being disliked, etc.

dis·fig·ure (-fig′yər) *vt.* -ured, -ur·ing to hurt the appearance of; mar —**dis·fig′ure·ment** *n.*

dis·fran·chise (dis fran′chīz′) *vt.* -chised′, -chis′ing to deprive of a right, privilege, etc., esp. the right to vote Also **dis′en·fran′chise′**

dis·gorge′ (-gôrj′) *vt.*, *vi.* -gorged′, -gorg′ing [< OFr: see DIS- & GORGE] 1 to vomit 2 to pour forth (its contents); empty (itself)

dis·grace′ (-grās′) *n.* [< It *dis-*, not + *grazia*, favor] 1 loss of favor or respect; shame; disrepute 2 a person or thing bringing shame — *vt.* -graced′, -grac′ing to bring shame or dishonor upon —**dis·grace′ful** *adj.*

dis·grun′tle (-grunt′'l) *vt.* -tled, -tling [ult. < DIS- + GRUNT] to make peevishly discontented; make sulky

dis·guise′ (-gīz′) *vt.* -guised′, -guis′ing [< OFr: see DIS- & GUISE] 1 to make appear, sound, etc. so different as to be unrecognizable 2 to hide the real nature of — *n.* 1 anything that disguises 2 a being disguised

dis·gust′ (-gust′) *n.* [< DIS- + L *gustus*, a taste] a sickening dislike — *vt.* to cause to feel disgust —**dis·gust′ed** *adj.* —**dis·gust′ing** *adj.*

dish (dish) *n.* [see DISCUS] 1 a container, generally shallow and concave, for holding food 2 as much as a dish holds 3 a particular kind of food — *vt.* to serve in a dish: with *up* or *out*

dis·ha·bille (dis′ə bēl′) *n.* [< Fr *dés-*, DIS- + *habiller*, to dress] the state of being dressed only partially or in night clothes

dish antenna a radio antenna consisting of a dish-shaped reflector

dis·har·mony (dis här′mə nē) *n.* absence of harmony; discord —**dis′har·mo′ni·ous** (-mō′nē əs) *adj.*

dish′cloth′ *n.* a cloth for washing dishes

dis·hearten (dis härt′'n) *vt.* to discourage; depress

di·shevel (di shev′əl) *vt.* -eled or -elled, -el·ing or -el·ling [< OFr *des-*, DIS- + *chevel*, hair] to cause (hair,

---

THESAURUS

mind; see also CARE 1, PRUDENCE, TACT.—*Ant.* CARELESSNESS, thoughtlessness, rashness. —**at one's discretion** as one wishes, whenever appropriate, discreetly; see APPROPRIATELY.

discriminate *v.* 1 [To differentiate] specify, separate, tell apart; see DISTINGUISH 1. 2 [To be (racially) prejudiced] be a bigot, show prejudice, set apart, segregate; see also HATE, SEPARATE 1.

discrimination *n.* 1 [The power to make distinctions] perception, acuteness, understanding; see INTELLIGENCE 1. 2 [The act of drawing a distinction] separation, differentiation, difference; see JUDGMENT 2. 3 [Partiality] unfairness, bias, bigotry; see HATRED, PREJUDICE.

discuss *v.* argue, debate, dispute, talk of, talk about, explain, contest, confer, deal with, reason with, take up, look over, consider, talk over, talk out, take up in conference, engage in conversation, go into, think over, telephone about, have a conference on, discourse about, argue for and against, canvass, consider, handle, present, review, recite, treat of, speak of, converse, discourse, take under advisement, comment upon, have out, speak on, kick around*, toss around*, chew the fat*, jaw*, air out*, knock around*, compare notes*, chew the rag*; see also TALK 1.—*Ant.* DELAY, table, postpone.

discussed *a.* talked over, debated, argued; see CONSIDERED.

discussion *n.* exchange, conversation, consultation, interview, deliberation, argumentation, contention, dialogue, talk, conference, argument, debate, panel discussion, summit meeting, dealing with the agenda, controversy, altercation, review, reasons, dispute, symposium, quarrel, powwow*, bull session*; see also CON-VERSATION, DISPUTE.—*Ant.* AGREEMENT, decision, conclusion.

disease *n.* 1 [A bodily infirmity] sickness, malady, ailment; see ILLNESS 1. 2 [Loosely used term for any ailment] condition, defect, infirmity; see ILLNESS 2.

diseased *a.* unhealthy, unsound, ailing; see SICK.

disengage *v.* loose, undo, disentangle; see FREE.

disengaged *a.* detached, unattached, disjoined; see SEPARATED.

disentangle *v.* disengage, untangle, untwist; see FREE.

disfavor *n.* displeasure, disapproval, disrespect; see DISAPPOINTMENT 1.

disfigure *v.* deface, mar, mutilate; see DAMAGE, HURT.

disgrace *n.* scandal, shame, stain, slur, slight, stigma, brand, spot, slander, dishonor, infamy, reproach, disrepute, humiliation, degradation, taint, tarnish, mark of Cain*, scarlet letter; see also INSULT.—*Ant.* PRIDE, praise, credit.

disgrace *v.* debase, shame, degrade, abase, dishonor, disparage, discredit, deride, disregard, strip of honors, dismiss from favor, disrespect, mock, humble, reduce, put to shame, tarnish, stain, blot, sully, taint, defile, stigmatize, brand, tar and feather, put down*, snub, derogate, belittle, take down a peg*; see also HUMILIATE, RIDICULE, SLANDER.—*Ant.* PRAISE, honor, exalt.

disgraced *a.* discredited, in disgrace, dishonored; see ASHAMED.

disgraceful *a.* dishonorable, disreputable, shocking; see OFFENSIVE, SHAMEFUL 1, 2.

disguise *n.* mask, deceptive covering, make-up, faking, false front, deception, smoke screen, blind, concealment, counterfeit, pseudonym, costume, masquerade, veil, cover, façade, put-on*; see also CAMOUFLAGE.

disguise *v.* mask, conceal, camouflage, pretend, screen, cloak, shroud, cover, veil, alter, obscure, feign, counterfeit, varnish, age, redo, make up, simulate, muffle, dress up, touch up, doctor up; see also CHANGE 2, DECEIVE, HIDE.—*Ant.* REVEAL, open, strip.

disguised *a.* cloaked, masked, camouflaged; see CHANGED 2, COVERED 1, HIDDEN.

disgust *n.* loathing, abhorrence, aversion; see HATRED, OBJECTION.

disgust *v.* repel, revolt, offend, displease, nauseate, sicken, make one sick, fill with loathing, cause aversion, be repulsive, irk, scandalize, shock, upset, turn one's stomach*; see also DISTURB, INSULT.

disgusted *a.* overwrought, offended, sickened, displeased, repelled, unhappy, revolted, appalled, outraged, having had a bellyful*, fed up*, having had it*, having had enough*; see also INSULTED, SHOCKED. —**disgusted** with repelled by, sick of*, fed up with*; see INSULTED, SHOCKED.

disgusting *a.* repugnant, revolting, sickening; see OFFENSIVE 2.

dish *n.* 1 [Plate] vessel, pottery, ceramic; see PLATE 3. *Table dishes include the following:* dinner plate, luncheon plate, salad plate, bread and butter plate, platter, casserole, cake plate, coffee cup, coffee mug, espresso cup, demitasse, teacup, egg cup, saucer, beer mug, cereal bowl, soup bowl, gravy boat, relish tray, cruet, teapot, coffeepot, cream pitcher, water pitcher, lemonade pitcher, sugar bowl, butter dish, salt cellar; see also CONTAINER, CUP, POTTERY. 2 [Meal] course, serving, helping; see MEAL 2.

clothing, etc.) to become disarranged; rumple —di·shev′ el·ment *n.*

dis·hon′est *adj.* not honest; lying, cheating, etc. —**dis· hon′estly** *adv.*

dis·hon′esty *n.* **1** a being dishonest **2** *pl.* **-ties** a dishonest act

dis·hon′or *n.* **1** loss of honor or respect; shame; disgrace **2** a cause of dishonor — *vt.* **1** to insult or disgrace **2** to refuse to pay (a check, etc.) —**dis·hon′or·able** *adj.* —**dis· hon′or·ably** *adv.*

dish′pan′ *n.* a pan in which dishes, cups, etc. are washed

dish′rag′ *n.* DISHCLOTH

dish′wash′er *n.* a person or machine that washes dishes, cups, etc.

dis·il′lu·sion *vt.* **1** to free from illusion **2** to take away the idealism of and make bitter, etc. —**dis·il·lu′sion·ment** *n.*

dis·in·cline (dis′in klīn′) *vt.* **-clined′, -clin′ing** to make unwilling

dis·in·fect (dis′in fekt′) *vt.* to destroy the harmful bacteria, viruses, etc. in; sterilize —**dis·in·fect′ant** *n.*

dis·in·for·ma′tion *n.* deliberately false information leaked so as to confuse another nation's intelligence operations

dis·in·gen·u·ous (dis′in jen′yōō əs) *adj.* not candid or frank

dis·in·her·it (dis′in her′it) *vt.* to deprive of an inheritance

dis·in·te·grate (dis in′tə grāt′) *vt., vi.* **-grat′ed, -grat′ing** to separate into parts or fragments; break up —**dis′in·te· gra′tion** *n.*

dis·in·ter (dis′in tur′) *vt.* **-terred′, -ter′ring** to remove from a grave, etc.

dis·in·ter·ested (dis in′tris tid, -tər is-) *adj.* **1** impartial; unbiased **2** uninterested; indifferent

dis′in′ter·me′di·a′tion (-in′tər mē′dē ā′shən) *n.* the withdrawal of funds from banks to invest them at higher rates of interest, as in government securities

dis·joint′ *vt.* **1** to put out of joint; dislocate **2** to dismember **3** to destroy the unity, connections, etc. of —**dis· joint′ed** *adj.*

disk (disk) *n.* 〚 L *discus*: see DISCUS 〛 **1** any thin, flat, circular thing **2** DISC **3** a thin, flat, circular plate coated with magnetic particles, for storing computer data

disk·ette (di sket′) *n.* FLOPPY DISK

dis·like′ *vt.* **-liked′, -lik′ing** to have a feeling of not liking — *n.* a feeling of not liking; distaste

dis·lo·cate (dis′lō kāt′) *vt.* **-cat′ed, -cat′ing** **1** to displace (a bone) from its proper position **2** to disarrange; disrupt —**dis′lo·ca′tion** *n.*

dis·lodge′ *vt., vi.* **-lodged′, -lodg′ing** to force from or leave a place where lodged, hiding, etc.

dis·loy′al *adj.* not loyal or faithful —**dis·loy′alty** *n.*

dis·mal (diz′məl) *adj.* 〚 < ML *dies mali*, evil days 〛 **1** causing gloom or misery **2** dark and gloomy; dreary —**dis′ mally** *adv.*

dis·man·tle (dis mant′'l) *vt.* **-tled, -tling** 〚 see DIS- & MANTLE 〛 **1** to strip (a house, etc.), as of furniture **2** to take apart —**dis·man′tle·ment** *n.*

dis·may′ (-mā′) *vt.* 〚 < Anglo-Fr 〛 to make afraid at the prospect of trouble; daunt — *n.* consternation

dis·mem′ber (-mem′bər) *vt.* 〚 see DIS- & MEMBER 〛 **1** to cut or tear the limbs from **2** to pull or cut to pieces —**dis· mem′ber·ment** *n.*

dis·miss′ (-mis′) *vt.* 〚 < L *dis-*, from + *mittere*, send 〛 **1** to cause or allow to leave **2** to discharge from an office, employment, etc. **3** to put aside mentally **4** *Law* to reject (a claim, etc.) —**dis·miss′al** *n.*

dis·mount′ *vi.* to get off, as from a horse — *vt.* **1** to remove (a thing) from its mounting **2** to take apart

dis·obe′di·ence (dis′ō bē′dē əns, -ə bē′-) *n.* refusal to obey; insubordination —**dis′obe′di·ent** *adj.*

dis′obey′ *vt., vi.* to refuse to obey

■■■■■ THESAURUS ■■■■■

dishonest *a.* deceiving, fraudulent, double-dealing, backbiting, treacherous, deceitful, cunning, sneaky, tricky, wily, crooked, deceptive, misleading, elusive, slippery, shady, swindling, cheating, sneaking, traitorous, villainous, sinister, lying, underhanded, two-timing*, two-faced, double-crossing*, unprincipled, shiftless, unscrupulous, undependable, disreputable, questionable, dishonorable, counterfeit, infamous, corrupt, immoral, discredited, unworthy, shabby, mean, low, venial, self-serving, contemptible, rotten*, fishy*, crooked; see also FALSE 1, LYING 1.—*Ant.* HONEST, irreproachable, scrupulous.

dishonesty *n.* infidelity, faithlessness, falsity, falsehood, deceit, trickery, duplicity, insidiousness, cunning, guile, slyness, double-dealing, trickiness, treachery, crookedness, corruption, cheating, stealing, lying, swindle, fraud, fraudulence, forgery, perjury, treason, flim-flam, hocus-pocus*, hanky-panky*; see also DECEPTION, HYPOCRISY, LIE.—*Ant.* HONESTY, virtue, integrity.

dishonor *n.* shame, ignominy, abasement; see DISGRACE.

dish towel *n.* tea towel, kitchen towel, drying towel; see TOWEL.

disillusion *v.* disenchant, strip of ideals, embitter; see DISAPPOINT.

disinfect *v.* purify, fumigate, use disinfectant upon; see CLEAN.

disinherit *v.* disown, evict, dispossess; see DISMISS, NEGLECT 2.

disintegrate *v.* break down, separate, divide, dismantle, break into pieces, disunite, disperse, crumble, disband, take apart, disorganize, detach, break apart, come apart, fall apart, sever, disconnect, fall to pieces, fade away, reduce to ashes; see also DISSOLVE.—*Ant.* UNITE, put together, combine.

disinterested *a.* impartial, not involved, unconcerned; see INDIFFER-

ENT, UNMOVED 2.

disjoint *v.* dismember, cut up, carve; see CUT 1, DIVIDE, SEPARATE 1.

disjointed *a.* disconnected, divided, unattached; see SEPARATED.

dislike *n.* opposition, offense, distaste; see HATE, HATRED, OBJECTION.

dislike *v.* detest, condemn, deplore, regret, lose interest in, speak down to, have hard feelings toward, not take kindly to, not be able to say much for, not speak well of, not have any part of, not care for, bear a grudge, have nothing to do with, keep one's distance from, care nothing for, resent, not appreciate, not endure, be averse to, abhor, hate, abominate, disapprove, loathe, despise, object to, shun, shrink from, mind, shudder at, scorn, avoid, be displeased by, turn up the nose at, look on with aversion, not be able to stomach, regard with displeasure, not like, take a dim view of*, have it in for*, be down on*, look down one's nose at*, have a bone to pick with*; see also HATE.

dislocate *v.* disjoint, disunite, disengage; see BREAK 1, DIVIDE, SEPARATE 1.

dislocation *n.* displacement, discontinuity, luxation; see BREAK 1, DIVISION 1.

dislodge *v.* eject, evict, uproot; see OUST, REMOVE 1.

disloyalty *n.* treason, betrayal, bad faith; see DISHONESTY, TREASON.

dismal *a.* gloomy, monotonous, dim, melancholy, desolate, dreary, sorrowful, morbid, troublesome, horrid, shadowy, overcast, cloudy, unhappy, discouraging, hopeless, black, unfortunate, ghastly, horrible, boring, gruesome, tedious, mournful, dull, disheartening, regrettable, cheerless, dusky, dingy, sepulchral, joyless, funereal, comfortless, murky, wan, bleak, somber, disagreeable, creepy, spooky*, blue; see also DARK 1.—*Ant.* HAPPY, joyful, cheerful.

dismantle *v.* take apart, disassemble, break down, take down, tear down, knock down, undo, demolish, level, ruin, unrig, subvert, raze, take to pieces, fell, take apart; see also DESTROY.

dismay *n.* terror, dread, anxiety; see FEAR.

dismember *v.* dissect, disjoint, amputate; see CUT 1, DIVIDE.

dismiss *v.* discard, reject, decline, repel, let out, repudiate, disband, detach, lay off, pack off, cast off, cast out, relinquish, dispense with, disperse, remove, expel, abolish, relegate, push aside, shed, do without, have done with, dispose of, sweep away, clear, rid, chase, dispossess, boycott, exile, expatriate, banish, outlaw, deport, excommunicate, get rid of, send packing*, drop, brush off*, kick out*, blackball, write off; see also OUST, REFUSE.—*Ant.* MAINTAIN, retain, keep.

dismissal *n.* deposition, displacement, expulsion; see REMOVAL.

dismissed *a.* sent away, ousted, removed; see DISCHARGED, FREE 2, 3.

disobedience *n.* insubordination, defiance, insurgence, disregard, violation, neglect, mutiny, revolt, nonobservance, strike, stubbornness, noncompliance, infraction of the rules, unruliness, sedition, rebellion, sabotage, riot; see also REVOLUTION 2.

disobedient *a.* insubordinate, refractory, defiant; see REBELLIOUS, UNRULY.

disobey *v.* balk, decline, neglect, desert, be remiss, ignore the commands of, refuse submission to, disagree, differ, evade, disregard the authority of, break rules, object, defy, resist, revolt, strike, violate, infringe, transgress, shirk, misbehave, withstand, counteract, take the law into one's own hands, not mind, pay no attention to, go counter to, not listen to; see also DARE 2, OPPOSE 1,

dis·o·blige' *vt.* -bliged', -blig'ing 1 to refuse to oblige 2 to offend

dis·or'der *n.* 1 a lack of order; confusion 2 a breach of public peace; riot 3 an upset of normal function; ailment — *vt.* 1 to throw into disorder 2 to upset the normal functions of

dis·or'der·ly *adj.* 1 untidy 2 violating public peace, safety, etc. —**dis·or'der·li·ness** *n.*

dis·or·gan·ize (dis ôr'gə nīz') *vt.* -ized', -iz'ing to break up the order or system of; throw into confusion —**dis·or'gani·za'tion** *n.*

dis·o'ri·ent' (-ôr'ē ent') *vt.* ⟦see DIS- & ORIENT, *v.*⟧ 1 to cause to lose one's bearings 2 to confuse mentally —**dis·o'ri·en·ta'tion** *n.*

dis·own' *vt.* to refuse to acknowledge as one's own; repudiate

dis·par·age (di spar'ij) *vt.* -aged', -ag·ing ⟦< OFr *des-* (see DIS-) + *parage*, rank⟧ 1 to discredit 2 to belittle — **dis·par'age·ment** *n.*

dis·pa·rate (dis'pə rət) *adj.* ⟦< L *dis-*, not + *par*, equal⟧ distinct or different in kind; unequal —**dis·par·i·ty** (di spar'ə tē), *pl.* -ties, *n.*

dis·pas'sion·ate *adj.* free from passion or bias; calm; impartial —**dis·pas'sion·ate·ly** *adv.*

dis·patch (di spach') *vt.* ⟦< L *dis-*, away + *pes*, foot⟧ 1 to send promptly, as on an errand 2 to kill 3 to finish quickly — *n.* 1 a sending off 2 a killing 3 speed; promptness 4 a message 5 a news story sent by a reporter —**dis·patch'er** *n.*

dis·pel' (di spel') *vt.* -pelled', -pel'ling ⟦< L *dis-*, apart + *pellere*, to drive⟧ to scatter and drive away

dis·pen·sa·ble (di spen'sə bəl) *adj.* 1 that can be dealt out 2 that can be dispensed with; not important

dis·pen'sa·ry (-sə rē) *n., pl.* -ries a room or place where medicines and first-aid treatment are available

dis·pen·sa·tion (dis'pən sā'shən) *n.* 1 a dispensing 2 anything distributed 3 an administrative system 4 a release from an obligation 5 *Theol.* a) the ordering of events under divine authority b) any religious system

dis·pense (di spens') *vt.* -pensed', -pens'ing ⟦< L *dis-*, out + *pendere*, weigh⟧ 1 to give out; distribute 2 to prepare and give out (medicines) 3 to administer (the law or justice) —**dispense with** 1 to get rid of 2 to do without —**dis·pens'er** *n.*

dis·perse' (-spurs') *vt.* -persed', -pers'ing ⟦< L *dis-*, out + *spargere*, scatter⟧ 1 to break up and scatter 2 to dispel (mist, etc.) — *vi.* to scatter —**dis·per'sal** *n.* —**dis·per'sion** *n.*

dis·pir·it (di spir'it) *vt.* to depress; discourage —**dispir'ited** *adj.*

dis·place' *vt.* -placed', -plac'ing 1 to move from its usual place 2 to remove from office 3 to replace

displaced person one forced from one's country, esp. as a result of war

dis·place'ment *n.* 1 a displacing or being displaced 2 the weight or volume of air, water, or other fluid displaced by a floating object

dis·play (di splā') *vt.* ⟦< L *dis-*, apart + *plicare*, to fold⟧ 1 [Obs.] to spread out 2 to exhibit — *n.* 1 an exhibition 2 anything displayed

dis·please' *vt., vi.* -pleased', -pleas'ing to fail to please; offend

dis·pleas'ure (-plezh'ər) *n.* a being displeased; dissatisfaction

dis·port (di spôrt') *vi.* ⟦< OFr *des-* (see DIS-) + *porter*, carry⟧ to play; frolic — *vt.* to amuse (oneself)

dis·pos·al (di spō'zəl) *n.* 1 a disposing 2 a device in the drain of a kitchen sink to grind up garbage

dis·pose' (-spōz') *vt.* -posed', -pos'ing ⟦see DIS- & POSITION⟧ 1 to arrange 2 to settle (affairs) 3 to make willing —**dispose of** 1 to settle 2 to give away or sell 3 to get rid of —**dis·pos'able** *adj.*

dis·po·si·tion (dis'pə zish'ən) *n.* 1 arrangement 2 management of affairs 3 a selling or giving away 4 the authority to settle, etc.; control 5 a tendency 6 one's temperament

dis·pos·sess' *vt.* to deprive of the possession of land, a house, etc.; oust

dis·praise (dis prāz') *vt.* -praised', -prais'ing ⟦< OFr *despreisier*⟧ to blame; censure — *n.* blame

dis·pro·por'tion *n.* a lack of proportion —**dis·pro·por'tion·ate** *adj.*

dis·prove' *vt.* -proved', -proved' or -prov'en, -prov'ing to prove to be false —**dis·proof'** *n.*

dis·pu·ta·tion (dis'pyōō tā'shən) *n.* 1 a disputing 2 debate

---

THESAURUS

REBEL.—*Ant.* OBEY, follow, fulfill.

disorder *n.* tumult, discord, turmoil, complication, chaos, mayhem, terrorism, rioting, mob rule, anarchy, anarchism, lawlessness, entanglement, commotion, agitation, insurrection, revolution, rebellion, strike, disorganization, riot, reign of terror, uproar, dither, static*; see also DISTURBANCE 2, TROUBLE 1.—*Ant.* ORDER, peace, tranquillity.

disorder *v.* disarrange, clutter, scatter; see CONFUSE, DISORGANIZE.

disordered *a.* displaced, misplaced, dislocated, mislaid, out of place, deranged, in disorder, out of kilter, out of hand, in confusion, in a mess, all over the place, in a mess, in a jumble, upset, unsettled, disorganized, disarranged, moved, removed, shifted, tampered with, tumbled, ruffled, rumpled, jumbled, jarred, tossed, stirred up, rolled, jolted, muddled; see also CONFUSED 2, TANGLED.—*Ant.* ORDERED, arranged, settled.

disorderly *a.* 1 [Lacking orderly arrangement] confused, jumbled, undisciplined, unrestrained, scattered, dislocated, unsystematic, messy, slovenly, untidy, cluttered, unkempt, scrambled, badly managed, in confusion, untrained, disorganized, out of control, topsy-turvy, all over the place*, mixed-up; see also DISORDERED.—*Ant.* REGULAR, neat, trim. 2 [Creating a disturbance] intemperate, drunk, rowdy; see UNRULY.

disorganization *n.* disunion, dissolution, derangement; see CONFUSION.

disorganize *v.* break up, disperse, destroy, scatter, litter, clutter, break down, put out of order, disarrange, disorder, upset, disrupt, derange, dislocate, disband, jumble, muddle, unsettle, disturb, perturb, shuffle, toss, turn topsy-turvy, complicate, confound, overthrow, overturn, scramble; see also CONFUSE.—*Ant.* SYSTEMATIZE, order, distribute.

disown *v.* repudiate, deny, retract; see DISCARD.

dispatch *v.* 1 [To send something on its way] transmit, express, forward; see SEND 1. 2 [To make an end] finish, conclude, perform; see ACHIEVE.

dispel *v.* disperse, deploy, dissipate; see DISTRIBUTE, SCATTER.

dispensable *a.* removable, excessive, unnecessary; see TRIVIAL, USELESS 1.

dispense *v.* apportion, assign, allocate; see DISTRIBUTE, GIVE 1. —**dispense with** ignore, pass over, brush aside; see DISREGARD, NEGLECT 2.

dispenser *n.* vendor, tap, vending machine, spray can, spray gun, cigarette machine, Coke machine (trademark), automat, squeeze bottle.

disperse *v.* break up, separate, disband; see SCATTER.

displace *v.* 1 [To remove] replace, transpose, dislodge; see REMOVE 1. 2 [To put in the wrong place] mislay, misplace, disarrange; see LOSE 2.

display *n.* exhibition, exhibit, presentation, representation, exposition, arrangement, demonstration, performance, revelation, procession, parade, pageant, example, appearance, waxworks, fireworks, tinsel, carnival, fair, pomp, splendor, unfolding; see also SHOW 1.

display *v.* show, show off, exhibit, uncover, open up, unfold, spread, parade, unmask, present, represent, perform, flaunt, lay out, put out, set out, disclose, unveil, arrange, make known; see also EXPOSE.—*Ant.* HIDE, conceal, veil.

displayed *a.* presented, visible, on display; see ADVERTISED, SHOWN 1.

displease *v.* vex, provoke, enrage; see ANGER.

displeasure *n.* disapproval, annoyance, resentment; see ANGER.

disposal *n.* action, provision, determination, disposition, distribution, arrangement, conclusion, assortment, settlement, control, winding up; see also RESULT. —**at someone's disposal** ready, prepared, usable; see AVAILABLE.

dispose *v.* settle, adapt, condition; see ADJUST 1, PREPARE 1. —**dispose of** relinquish, throw away, part with; see DISCARD, SELL.

disposed *a.* inclined, prone, apt; see LIKELY 4.

disposition *n.* 1 [Arrangement] decision, method, distribution; see ORGANIZATION 1, PLAN 2. 2 [Temperament] character, nature, temper; see MOOD, TEMPERAMENT.

disproportionate *a.* unsymmetrical, incommensurate, excessive; see IRREGULAR 4.

disprove *v.* prove false, throw out, set aside, find fault in, invalidate, weaken, overthrow, tear down, confound, expose, cut the ground from under, poke holes in*; see also DENY.

disputable *a.* debatable, doubtful, dubious; see QUESTIONABLE 1, UNCERTAIN.

dis·pu·ta·tious (-pyōō tā′shəs) *adj.* inclined to dispute; contentious —**dis·pu·ta′tiously** *adv.*

dis·pute (di spyōōt′) *vi.* -**put′ed,** -**put′ing** 〖< L *dis*-, apart + *putare,* to think〗 1 to argue; debate 2 to quarrel — *vt.* 1 to argue (a question) 2 to doubt 3 to oppose in any way — *n.* 1 a disputing; debate 2 a quarrel —**in dispute** not settled —**dis·pu′tant** *adj., n.*

dis·qual′i·fy′ *vt.* -**fied′,** -**fy′ing** to make or declare unqualified, unfit, or ineligible —**dis·qual′i·fi·ca′tion** *n.*

dis·quiet (dis kwī′ət) *vt.* to make uneasy; disturb — *n.* restlessness: also **dis·qui′etude′** (-ə tōōd′)

dis·qui·si·tion (dis′kwi zish′ən) *n.* 〖< L *dis*-, apart + *quaerere,* to seek〗 a formal discussion; treatise

dis·re·gard (dis′ri gärd′) *vt.* 1 to pay little or no attention to 2 to treat without due respect — *n.* 1 lack of attention 2 lack of due regard or respect —**dis′re·gard′ful** *adj.*

dis·re·pair′ *n.* the condition of needing repairs; state of neglect

dis·rep′u·table *adj.* 1 not reputable 2 not fit to be seen

dis·re·pute′ *n.* lack or loss of repute; bad reputation; disgrace

dis·re·spect′ *n.* lack of respect; discourtesy —**dis′re·spect′ful** *adj.*

dis·robe (dis rōb′) *vt., vi.* -**robed′,** -**rob′ing** to undress

dis·rupt (dis rupt′) *vt., vi.* 〖< L *dis*-, apart + *rumpere,* to break〗 1 to break apart 2 to disturb or interrupt —**dis·rup′tion** *n.* —**dis·rup′tive** *adj.*

dis·sat′isfy′ *vt.* -**fied′,** -**fy′ing** to fail to satisfy; displease —**dis·sat′is·fac′tion** *n.*

dis·sect (di sekt′) *vt.* 〖< L *dis*-, apart + *secare,* to cut〗 1 to cut apart piece by piece, as a body for purposes of study 2 to analyze closely —**dis·sec′tion** *n.* —**dis·sec′tor** *n.*

dis·sem·ble (di sem′bəl) *vt., vi.* -**bled,** -**bling** 〖< OFr *dessembler*〗 to conceal (the truth, one's feelings, etc.) under a false appearance —**dis·sem′blance** *n.* —**dis·sem′bler** *n.*

dis·sem·i·nate (di sem′ə nāt′) *vt.* -**nat′ed,** -**nat′ing** 〖< L *dis*-, apart + *seminare,* to sow〗 to scatter about; spread widely —**dis·sem′i·na′tion** *n.* —**dis·sem′i·na′tor** *n.*

dis·sen·sion (di sen′shən) *n.* a dissenting; disagreement or quarreling

dis·sent (di sent′) *vi.* 〖< L *dis*-, apart + *sentire,* feel〗 1 to disagree 2 to reject the doctrines of an established church — *n.* a dissenting —**dis·sent′er** *n.*

dis·ser·ta·tion (dis′ər tā′shən) *n.* 〖< L *dis*-, apart + *serere,* join〗 a formal discourse or treatise, esp. one written to fulfill the requirements for a doctorate from a university

dis·serv·ice (dis sur′vis) *n.* harm

dis·sever (di sev′ər) *vt.* 1 to sever 2 to divide into parts — *vi.* to separate; disunite

dis·si·dence (dis′ə dəns) *n.* 〖< L *dis*-, apart + *sidere,* sit〗 disagreement —**dis′si·dent** (-dənt) *adj., n.*

dis·sim·i·lar (dis′ə lər) *adj.* not similar; different — **dis·sim′i·lar′ity** (-lar′ə tē), *pl.* -**ties,** *n.*

dis·si·mil·i·tude (dis′si mil′ə tōōd′) *n.* dissimilarity; difference

dis·sim·u·late (di sim′yōō lāt′) *vt., vi.* -**lat′ed,** -**lat′ing** 〖see DIS- & SIMULATE〗 to dissemble —**dis·sim′u·la′tion** *n.* —**dis·sim′u·la′tor** *n.*

dis·si·pate (dis′ə pāt′) *vt.* -**pat′ed,** -**pat′ing** 〖< L *dis*-, apart + *supare,* to throw〗 1 to scatter; disperse 2 to make disappear 3 to waste or squander — *vi.* 1 to vanish 2 to indulge in pleasure to the point of harming oneself — **dis′si·pa′tion** *n.*

dis·so·ci·ate (di sō′shē āt′) *vt.* -**at′ed,** -**at′ing** 〖< L *dis*-, apart + *sociare,* join〗 1 to break the connection between; disunite —**dis·so′cia′tion** *n.*

dis·so·lute (dis′ə lōōt′) *adj.* 〖see DISSOLVE〗 dissipated and immoral —**dis′so·lute′ly** *adv.* —**dis′so·lute′ness** *n.*

dis·so·lu·tion (dis′ə lōō′shən) *n.* a dissolving or being dissolved; specif., *a*) a breaking up or into parts *b*) a termination *c*) death

dis·solve (di zälv′, -zôlv′) *vt., vi.* -**solved′,** -**solv′ing** 〖< L *dis*-, apart + *solvere,* loosen〗 1 to make or become liquid; melt 2 to pass or make pass into solution 3 to break up 4 to end as by breaking up 5 to disappear or make disappear

dis·so·nance (dis′ə nəns) *n.* 〖< L *dis*-, apart + *sonus,* a sound〗 1 an inharmonious combination of sounds; discord 2 any lack of harmony or agreement —**dis′so·nant** *adj.*

dis·suade (di swād′) *vt.* -**suad′ed,** -**suad′ing** 〖< L *dis*-, away + *suadere,* to persuade〗 to turn (a person) aside (*from* a course, etc.) by persuasion or advice —**dis·sua′sion** *n.*

dis·taff (dis′taf′) *n.* 〖< OE *dis*-, flax + *stæf,* staff〗 a staff on which flax, wool, etc. is wound for use in spinning — *adj.* female

dis·tal (dis′təl) *adj.* 〖DIST(ANT) + -AL〗 *Anat.* farthest from the point of attachment or origin —**dis′tally** *adv.*

dis·tance (dis′təns) *n.* 〖< L *dis*-, apart + *stare,* to stand〗 1 a being separated in space or time; remoteness 2 an interval between two points in space or time 3 a remoteness in behavior; reserve 4 a faraway place

dis′tant (-tənt) *adj.* 1 far away in space or time 2 away [*100 miles distant*] 3 far apart in relationship 4 aloof; reserved 5 from or at a distance —**dis′tantly** *adv.*

dis·taste (dis tāst′) *n.* dislike —**dis·taste′ful** *adj.*

THESAURUS

dispute *n.* argument, quarrel, debate, misunderstanding, conflict, strife, discussion, polemic, bickering, squabble, disturbance, feud, commotion, tiff, fracas, controversy, altercation, dissension, squall, difference of opinion, rumpus*, row, flare-up, fuss, fire-works*; see also DISAGREEMENT 1.

dispute *v.* debate, contradict, quarrel; see ARGUE, DISCUSS.

disqualify *v.* preclude, disentitle, disbar; see BAR 2.

disquieting *a.* disturbing, troubling, disconcerting; see DISTURBING.

disregard *v.* ignore, pass over, let pass, make light of, have no use for, laugh off, take no account of, brush aside, turn a deaf ear to, be blind to, shut one's eyes to; see also NEGLECT 1.

disrepair *n.* decrepitude, deterioration, dilapidation; see DECAY.

disreputable *a.* low, objectionable, discreditable; see OFFENSIVE 2, SHAMEFUL 1, 2.

disrespect *n.* discourtesy, coarseness, irreverence; see RUDENESS.

disrespectful *a.* ill-bred, discourteous, impolite; see RUDE 2.

disrobe *v.* strip, divest, unclothe; see UNDRESS.

disrupt *v.* fracture, intrude, obstruct; see BREAK 1, INTERRUPT.

disruption *n.* debacle, disturbance, agitation; see CONFUSION.

dissatisfaction *n.* dislike, displeasure, disapproval; see OBJECTION.

dissatisfied *a.* displeased, unsatisfied, fed up*; see DISAPPOINTED.

dissect *v.* dismember, quarter, operate; see CUT 1, DIVIDE.

disseminate *v.* sow, propagate, broadcast; see DISTRIBUTE.

dissension *n.* difference, quarrel, trouble; see DISAGREEMENT 1, DISPUTE.

dissent *n.* nonconformity, difference, heresy; see DISAGREEMENT 1, OBJECTION, PROTEST.

dissent *v.* disagree, refuse, contradict; see DIFFER 1, OPPOSE 1.

dissenter *n.* disputant, dissentient, demonstrator; see NONCONFORMIST, RADICAL, REBEL.

disservice *n.* wrong, injury, outrage; see DAMAGE 1, INJUSTICE, INSULT.

dissipate *v.* 1 [To dispel] spread, diffuse, disseminate; see SCATTER 2. 2 [To squander] use up, consume, misuse; see SPEND, WASTE 2.

dissipated *a.* 1 [Scattered] dispersed, strewn, disseminated; see SCATTERED. 2 [Wasted] squandered, spent, consumed; see EMPTY, WASTED.

dissipation *n.* 1 [Dispersion] scattering, dispersal, spread; see DISTRIBUTION. 2 [Debauchery] indulgence, intemperance, dissolution; see EVIL 1.

dissolve *v.* liquefy, melt, thaw, soften, run, defrost, waste away, cause to become liquid; see also EVAPORATE, MELT 1.—*Ant.* HARDEN, freeze, solidify.

distance *n.* 1 [A degree or quantity of space] reach, span, range; see EXPANSE, EXTENT, LENGTH 1, 2. 2 [A place or places far away] background, horizon, as far as the eye can reach, sky, heavens, outskirts, foreign countries, different worlds, strange places, distant terrain, objective, the country, beyond the horizon.—*Ant.* NEIGHBORHOOD, surroundings, neighbors. 3 [A measure of space] statute mile, rod, yard, foot, kilometer, meter, centimeter, millimeter, league, fathom, span, hand, cubit, furlong, a stone's throw. —**go the distance** finish, bring to an end, see through; see COMPLETE. —**keep at a distance** ignore, reject, shun; see AVOID. —**keep one's distance** be aloof, ignore, shun; see AVOID.

distant *a.* afar, far off, abroad, far-away, yonder, backwoods, removed, abstracted, inaccessible, unapproachable, out-of-the-way, at arm's length, stretching to, out of range, out of reach, out of earshot, out of sight, in the background, in the distance, separate, farther, further, far away, at a distance, abroad, different; see also SEPARATED.—*Ant.* CLOSE, near, next.

distaste *n.* aversion, dislike, abhorrence; see HATRED.

distasteful *a.* disagreeable, repugnant, undesirable; see OFFENSIVE 2.

dis·tem·per (dis tem'pər) *n.* ⟦< ML *distemperare*, to disorder⟧ an infectious viral disease of young dogs

dis·tend (di stend') *vt., vi.* ⟦< L *dis-*, apart + *tendere*, to stretch⟧ 1 to stretch out 2 to make or become swollen — **dis·ten'tion** or **dis·ten'sion** *n.*

dis·till or **dis·til** (di stil') *vi., vt.* **-tilled', -till'ing** ⟦< L *de-*, down + *stillare*, to drop⟧ 1 to fall or let fall in drops 2 to undergo, subject to, or produce by distillation —**dis·till'er** *n.*

dis·til·late (dis'tə lāt', -lit) *n.* a liquid obtained by distilling

dis·til·la·tion (dis'tə lā'shən) *n.* 1 the process of heating a mixture and condensing the resulting vapor to produce a more nearly pure substance 2 anything distilled

dis·till'ery *n., pl.* **-ies** a place where alcoholic liquors are distilled

dis·tinct (di stiŋkt') *adj.* ⟦see DISTINGUISH⟧ 1 not alike 2 separate 3 clearly marked off; plain 4 unmistakable — **dis·tinct'ly** *adv.*

dis·tinc'tion (-stiŋk'shən) *n.* 1 the act of making or keeping distinct 2 difference 3 a quality or feature that differentiates 4 fame; eminence 5 the quality that makes one seem superior 6 a mark of honor

dis·tinc'tive *adj.* making distinct; characteristic —**dis·tinc'tive·ly** *adv.* —**dis·tinc'tive·ness** *n.*

dis·tin·guish (di stiŋ'gwish) *vt.* ⟦< L *dis-*, apart + *-stinguere*, to prick⟧ 1 to perceive or show the difference in 2 to characterize 3 to perceive clearly 4 to classify 5 to make famous — *vi.* to make a distinction (*between* or *among*) —**dis·tin'guish·able** *adj.*

dis·tin'guished *adj.* celebrated; famous

dis·tort (di stôrt') *vt.* ⟦< L *dis-*, intens. + *torquere*, to twist⟧ 1 to twist out of shape 2 to misrepresent (facts, etc.) —**dis·tor'tion** *n.*

dis·tract (di strakt') *vt.* ⟦< L *dis-*, apart + *trahere*, draw⟧ 1 to draw (the mind, etc.) away in another direction; divert 2 to confuse; bewilder —**dis·tract'ed** *adj.* —**dis·tract'ing** *adj.*

dis·trac'tion *n.* 1 a distracting or being distracted 2 anything that distracts confusingly or amusingly; diversion 3 great mental distress

dis·trait (di strā') *adj.* ⟦see DISTRACT⟧ absent-minded; inattentive

dis·traught' (-strôt') *adj.* ⟦var. of prec.⟧ 1 mentally confused; distracted 2 driven mad; crazed

dis·tress (di stres') *vt.* ⟦ult. < L *dis-*, apart + *stringere*, to stretch⟧ to cause misery or suffering to — *n.* 1 pain, suffering, etc. 2 an affliction 3 a state of danger or trouble

dis·trib·ute (di strib'yσt) *vt.* **-uted, -ut·ing** ⟦< L *dis-*, apart + *tribuere*, allot⟧ 1 to give out in shares 2 to spread out 3 to classify 4 to put (things) in various distinct places —**dis·tri·bu'tion** *n.*

dis·trib'u·tor *n.* one that distributes; specif., a) a dealer who distributes goods to consumers b) a device for distributing electric current to the spark plugs of a gasoline engine

dis·trict (dis'trikt) *n.* ⟦< L *dis-*, apart + *stringere*, to stretch⟧ 1 a division of a state, city, etc. made for a specific purpose 2 any region

district attorney the prosecuting attorney for the State or the Federal government in a specified district

dis·trust' *n.* a lack of trust; doubt — *vt.* to have no trust in; doubt —**dis·trust'ful** *adj.*

dis·turb (di sturb') *vt.* ⟦< L *dis-*, intens. + *turbare*, to disorder⟧ 1 to break up the quiet or settled order of 2 to make uneasy; upset 3 to interrupt —**dis·turb'er** *n.*

■ THESAURUS ■

distend *v.* enlarge, widen, inflate; see DISTORT, INCREASE, STRETCH 1, 2.

distill *v.* vaporize and condense, steam, precipitate; see CONCENTRATE 1, EVAPORATE.

distinct *a.* 1 [Having sharp outlines] lucid, plain, obvious; see CLEAR 2, DEFINITE 2. 2 [Not connected with another] discrete, separate, disunited; see SEPARATED. 3 [Clearly heard] clear, sharp, enunciated; see AUDIBLE.

distinction *n.* 1 [The act or quality of noticing differences] separation, difference, refinement; see DEFINITION. 2 [That which makes a thing distinct] distinctive feature, particular, qualification; see CHARACTERISTIC, DETAIL. 3 [A mark of personal achievement] repute, renown, prominence; see FAME.

distinctive *a.* peculiar, unique, distinguishing; see CHARACTERISTIC.

distinctly *a.* precisely, sharply, plainly; see CLEARLY 1, 2, SURELY.

distinguish *v.* 1 [To make distinctions] discriminate, differentiate, classify, specify, identify, individualize, characterize, separate, divide, collate, sort out, sort into, set apart, mark off, criticize, select, draw the line, tell from, pick and choose, separate the wheat from the chaff, separate the sheep from the goats; see also DEFINE 2. 2 [To discern] detect, discriminate, notice; see DISCOVER, SEE 1. 3 [To bestow honor upon] pay tribute to, honor, celebrate; see ACKNOWLEDGE 2, ADMIRE, PRAISE 1.

distinguishable *a.* separable, perceptible, discernible; see AUDIBLE, OBVIOUS, TANGIBLE.

distinguished *a.* 1 [Made recognizable by markings] characterized, labeled, marked, stamped, signed, signified, identified, made certain, obvious, set apart, branded, earmarked, separate, unique, differentiated, observed, distinct, conspicuous; see also SEPARATED.—*Ant.*

TYPICAL, unidentified, indistinct. 2 [Notable for excellence] eminent, illustrious, venerable, renowned, honored, memorable, celebrated, well-known, noted, noteworthy, highly regarded, well-thought-of, esteemed, prominent, reputable, superior, outstanding, brilliant, glorious, extraordinary, singular, great, special, striking, unforgettable, shining, foremost, dignified, famed, talked of, first-rate, big-name*, headline*; see also FAMOUS.—*Ant.* OBSCURE, insignificant, unimportant.

distort *v.* 1 [To alter the meaning] pervert, misinterpret, misconstrue; see DECEIVE. 2 [To change shape] contort, sag, twist, slump, knot, get out of shape, buckle, writhe, melt, warp, deform, collapse; see also CHANGE 2.

distortion *n.* 1 [Deformity] twist, malformation, mutilation; see CONTORTION. 2 [Misrepresentation] perversion, misinterpretation, misuse; see LIE.

distract *v.* detract, occupy, amuse, entertain, draw away, call away, draw one's attention from, lead astray, attract from; see also MISLEAD.

distracted *a.* distraught, panicked, frenzied; see TROUBLED.

distraction *n.* 1 [Confusion] perplexity, abstraction, complication; see CONFUSION. 2 [Diversion] amusement, pastime, preoccupation; see ENTERTAINMENT, GAME 1.

distress *n.* worry, anxiety, misery, sorrow, wretchedness, pain, dejection, irritation, suffering, ache, heartache, ordeal, desolation, anguish, affliction, woe, torment, shame, embarrassment, disappointment, tribulation, pang; see also GRIEF, TROUBLE 1.—*Ant.* JOY, happiness, jollity.

distress *v.* irritate, disturb, upset; see BOTHER 1, 2.

distribute *v.* dispense, divide, share, deal, bestow, issue, dispose, disperse,

mete out, pass out, parcel out, dole out, hand out, give away, assign, allocate, ration, appropriate, pay dividends, dish out, divvy up*; see also GIVE 1.—*Ant.* HOLD, keep, preserve.

distributed *a.* delivered, scattered, shared, dealt, divided, apportioned, assigned, awarded, peddled from door to door, sowed, dispensed, dispersed, appropriated, budgeted, made individually available, equally divided, spread evenly, returned, rationed, given away, handed out, parceled out, spread.

distribution *n.* dispersal, allotment, partitioning, partition, dividing up, deal, circulation, disposal, apportioning, prorating, arrangement, scattering, dissemination, sorting, spreading, parceling out, handing out, peddling, assorting, frequency, occurrence, ordering, pattern, combination, relationship, appearance, configuration, scarcity, number, plenty, saturation, population, spread, concentration; see also DIVISION 1, 2, ORDER 3.—*Ant.* COLLECTION, retention, storage.

distributor *n.* wholesaler, jobber, merchant; see BUSINESSMAN.

district *a.* community, provincial, territorial; see LOCAL 1.

district *n.* neighborhood, community, vicinity; see AREA.

distrust *v.* mistrust, suspect, disbelieve; see DOUBT.

distrustful *a.* distrusting, doubting, fearful; see SUSPICIOUS 1.

disturb *v.* trouble, worry, agitate, perplex, rattle, startle, shake, amaze, astound, alarm, excite, arouse, badger, plague, fuss, perturb, vex, upset, outrage, molest, grieve, depress, distress, irk, ail, tire, provoke, afflict, irritate, pain, make uneasy, harass, exasperate, pique, gall, displease, complicate, involve, astonish, fluster, ruffle, burn up*; see also BOTHER 2, CONFUSE.—*Ant.* QUIET, calm, soothe.

dis·turb′ance *n.* **1** a disturbing or being disturbed **2** anything that disturbs **3** commotion; disorder

dis·unite (dis′yoo nit′) *vt., vi.* **-nit′ed, -nit′ing** to divide or separate into parts, factions, etc. —**dis·u′ni·ty** *n.*

dis·use′ (-yoos′) *n.* lack of use

ditch (dich) *n.* 〚OE *dic*〛 a long, narrow channel dug into the earth, as for drainage —*vt.* **1** to make a ditch in **2** [Slang] to get rid of

dith·er (di*th*′ər) *vi.* 〚ME *dideren*〛 to be nervously excited or confused — *n.* a nervously excited or confused state

dit·to (dit′ō) *n., pl.* **-tos** 〚It < L *dicere*, to say〛 **1** the same (as above or before) **2** DITTO MARK

ditto mark a mark (″) used in lists or tables to show that the item above is to be repeated

dit·ty (dit′ē) *n., pl.* **-ties** 〚< L *dicere*, to say〛 a short, simple song

di·uret·ic (di′yoo ret′ik) *adj.* 〚< Gr *dia-*, through + *ourein*, urinate〛 increasing the flow of urine — *n.* a diuretic drug or substance

di·ur·nal (di ur′nəl) *adj.* 〚< L *dies*, day〛 **1** daily **2** of the daytime —**di·ur′nally** *adv.*

div. **1** dividend **2** division

di·va (dē′və) *n., pl.* **-vas** or **-ve** (-ve) 〚It < L, goddess〛 PRIMA DONNA

di·va·lent (di′vā′lənt, di vā′-) *adj. Chem.* having two valences or a valence of two

di·van (di′van′, di van′) *n.* 〚< Pers *diwān*〛 a large, low couch or sofa

dive (div) *vi.* **dived** or **dove**, **dived**, **div′ing** 〚OE *dyfan*〛 **1** to plunge headfirst into water **2** to submerge **3** to plunge suddenly into something **4** to make a steep descent, as an airplane — *n.* **1** a diving **2** any sudden plunge **3** a sharp descent **4** [Colloq.] a cheap, disreputable saloon, etc. —**div′er** *n.*

di·verge (di vurj′, di-) *vi.* **-verged′, -verg′ing** 〚< L *dis-*, apart + *vergere*, to turn〛 **1** to go or move in different directions; branch off **2** to differ, as in opinion —**di·ver′gence** *n.* —**di·ver′gent** *adj.*

di·vers (di′vərz) *adj.* 〚see fol.〛 various

di·verse (də vurs′, di-) *adj.* 〚< L *dis-*, apart + *vertere*, to turn〛 **1** different **2** varied —**di·verse′ly** *adv.*

di·ver·sify (də vur′sə fi′) *vt.* **-fied′, -fy′ing** to make diverse; vary —**di·ver′si·fi·ca′tion** *n.*

di·ver·sion (də vur′zhən, di-) *n.* **1** a diverting or turning aside **2** distraction of attention **3** a pastime

di·ver′sion·ar′y *adj.* serving to divert or distract [*diversionary* tactics]

di·ver·si·ty (də vur′sə tē, di-) *n., pl.* **-ties** **1** difference **2** variety

di·vert (də vurt′, di-) *vt.* 〚see DIVERSE〛 **1** to turn (a person or thing) aside **2** to amuse

di·ver·tic·u·li·tis (di′vər tik′yoo lit′is) *n.* 〚< L *de-*, from + *vertere*, to turn + *-ITIS*〛 inflammation of a sac (**di′ver·tic′u·lum**) opening out from a tubular organ or main cavity

di·vest (də vest′, di-) *vt.* 〚< L *dis-*, from + *vestire*, to dress〛 **1** to strip (*of* clothing, etc.) **2** to deprive (*of* rank, rights, etc.) **3** to rid (*of* something unwanted)

di·vide (də vid′) *vt.* **-vid′ed, -vid′ing** 〚< L *dividere*〛 **1** to separate into parts; sever **2** to classify **3** to make or keep separate **4** to apportion **5** to cause to disagree **6** *Math.* to separate into equal parts by a divisor — *vi.* **1** to be or become separate **2** to disagree **3** to share **4** *Math.* to do division — *n.* a ridge that divides two drainage areas —**di·vid′er** *n.*

divi·dend (div′ə dend′) *n.* **1** the number or quantity to be divided **2** *a)* a sum to be divided among stockholders, etc. *b)* a single share of this **3** a bonus

divi·na·tion (div′ə nā′shən) *n.* 〚see fol.〛 **1** the practice of trying to foretell the future **2** a prophecy

di·vine (də vin′) *adj.* 〚< L *divus*, god〛 **1** of, like, or from God or a god; holy **2** devoted to God; religious **3** supremely great, good, etc. — *n.* a clergyman — *vt.* **-vined′, -vin′ing** **1** to prophesy **2** to guess **3** to find out by intuition —**di·vine′ly** *adv.*

divining rod a forked stick alleged to dip downward when held over an underground supply of water, etc.

di·vin·ity (də vin′ə tē) *n., pl.* **-ties** **1** a being divine **2** a god **3** theology —**the Divinity** God

di·vis·ible (də viz′ə bəl) *adj.* that can be divided, esp. without leaving a remainder —**di·vis′ibil′ity** *n.*

di·vi·sion (də vizh′ən) *n.* **1** a dividing or being divided **2** an apportioning **3** a difference of opinion **4** anything that divides **5** a segment, section, department, class, etc. **6** the

---

■ THESAURUS ■

disturbance *n.* **1** [Interpersonal disruption] quarrel, brawl, fisticuffs; see FIGHT 1. **2** [Physical disruption] turmoil, rampage, tumult, clamor, violence, restlessness, uproar, riot, disruption, agitation, turbulence, change, bother, stir, racket, ferment, spasm, convulsion, tremor, shock, explosion, eruption, earthquake, flood, shock wave, storm, whirl; see also TROUBLE. **3** [A political or social uprising] revolt, insurrection, riot; see REVOLUTION 2.

disturbed *a.* **1** [Disturbed physically] upset, disorganized, confused; see DISORDERED. **2** [Disturbed mentally] agitated, disquieted, upset; see TROUBLED.

disturbing *a.* disquieting, upsetting, tiresome, perturbing, bothersome, unpleasant, provoking, annoying, alarming, painful, discomforting, inauspicious, foreboding, aggravating, disagreeable, troublesome, worrisome, burdensome, trying, distressing, perplexing, frightening, startling, threatening, galling, difficult, severe, hard, inconvenient, discouraging, pessimistic, gloomy, depressing, irritating, harassing, unpropitious, unlikely, embarrassing, ruffling, agitating; see also OMINOUS.

disunite *v.* dissociate, disjoin, separate; see DIVIDE.

ditch *n.* canal, moat, furrow; see CHANNEL, TRENCH.

ditch* *v.* desert, forsake, leave; see ABANDON 2, DISCARD.

ditto *n.* ditto mark (″), the very same, as is; see ALIKE.

dive *n.* **1** [A sudden motion downward] plunge, leap, spring, nosedive, headlong leap, pitch, ducking, swim, swoop, dip; see also FALL 1, JUMP 1. **2**

[*An establishment offering accommodation] saloon, tavern, cafe; see BAR 2, RESTAURANT.

dive *v.* plunge, spring, jump, vault, leap, go headfirst, plummet, sink, dip, duck, submerge, nose-dive; see also FALL 1, JUMP 1.

diver *n.* high diver, fancy diver, submarine diver, deep-sea diver, aquanaut, pearl diver, skin diver, scuba diver, swimmer, athlete, frogman; see also ATHLETE.

diverge *v.* radiate, veer, swerve; see DEVIATE.

diverse *a.* different, assorted, distinct; see VARIOUS.

diversify *v.* vary, expand, alter; see CHANGE 2, INCREASE.

diversion *n.* **1** [The act of changing a course] detour, alteration, deviation; see CHANGE 1. **2** [Entertainment] amusement, recreation, play; see ENTERTAINMENT, SPORT 1.

divert *v.* **1** [To deflect] turn aside, redirect, avert; see TURN 3. **2** [To distract] attract the attention of, lead away from, disturb; see DISTRACT.

diverted *a.* deflected, turned aside, redirected, perverted, averted, turned into other channels, rechanneled, taken, adopted, used, made use of, taken over; see also CHANGED 2.— *Ant.* UNTOUCHED, undiverted, left.

divide *v.* part, cut up, fence off, detach, disengage, dissolve, sever, rupture, dismember, sunder, split, unravel, carve, cleave, intersect, cross, bisect, rend, tear, segment, halve, quarter, third, break down, divorce, dissociate, isolate, count off, pull away, chop, slash, gash, carve, splinter, pull to pieces, tear apart,

break apart, segregate, fork, branch, tear limb from limb*, split off, split up; see also BREAK 1, CUT 1, SEPARATE 1.—*Ant.* UNITE, combine, connect.

dividend *n.* pay, check, coupon, proceeds, returns, quarterly dividend, annual dividend, share, allotment, appropriation, remittance, allowance, cut*, rakeoff*; see also PROFIT 2.

divine *a.* sacred, hallowed, spiritual, sacramental, ceremonial, ritualistic, consecrated, dedicated, devoted, venerable, pious, religious, anointed, sanctified, ordained, sanctioned, set apart, sacrosanct, scriptural, blessed, worshiped, revered, venerated, mystical, adored, solemn, faithful; see also HOLY.

divine *v.* predict, prophesy, prognosticate; see FORETELL.

divinity *n.* deity, godhead, higher power; see GOD.

divisible *a.* separable, distinguishable, distinct, divided, fractional, fragmentary, detachable; see also SEPARATED.—*Ant.* INSEPARABLE, indivisible, fast.

division *n.* **1** [The act or result of dividing] separation, detachment, apportionment, partition, parting, distribution, severance, cutting, subdivision, dismemberment, distinction, distinguishing, selection, analysis, diagnosis, reduction, splitting, breakdown, fracture, disjuncture.—*Ant.* UNION, joining, glueing. **2** [A part produced by dividing] section, kind, sort, portion, compartment, share, split, member, subdivision, parcel, segment, fragment, department, category, branch, fraction, dividend, degree, piece, process of finding how many times a number (the *divisor*) is contained in another (the *dividend*) **7** a major military unit

di·vi·sive (də vī′siv) *adj.* causing disagreement or dissension —**di·vi′sive·ly** *adv.* —**di·vi′sive·ness** *n.*

di·vi·sor (də vī′zər) *n.* the number by which the dividend is divided

di·vorce (də vôrs′) *n.* ⟦ < L *dis-*, apart + *vertere*, to turn ⟧ **1** legal dissolution of a marriage **2** complete separation — *vt.* **-vorced′, -vorc′ing 1** to dissolve legally a marriage between **2** to dissolve the marriage with (one's spouse) **3** to separate —**di·vorce′ment** *n.*

di·vor·cée or **di·vor·cee** (div′ôr sā′, -sē′) *n.* ⟦Fr⟧ a divorced woman

divot (div′ət) *n.* ⟦Scot⟧ *Golf* a lump of turf dislodged in making a stroke

di·vulge (də vulj′) *vt.* **-vulged′, -vulg′ing** ⟦ < L *dis-*, apart + *vulgare*, make public ⟧ to make known; reveal

divvy (div′ē) *vt., vi.* **-vied, -vy·ing** [Slang] to share; divide (*up*)

Dixie (dik′sē) ⟦ < *Dixie*, the minstrel song ⟧ the Southern States of the U.S.

Dix′ie·land′ *adj.* in, of, or like a style of jazz with a rag-time tempo

dizzy (diz′ē) *adj.* **-zier, -zi·est** ⟦OE *dysig*, foolish ⟧ **1** feeling giddy or unsteady **2** causing giddiness **3** confused **4** [Colloq.] silly; harebrained —**diz′zily** *adv.* —**diz′zi·ness** *n.*

DJ (dē′jā′) *n.* DISC JOCKEY

djel·laba or **djel·la·bah** (jə lä′bə) *n.* ⟦ < Ar ⟧ a long, loose outer garment, worn in Arabic countries

DNA ⟦ < *d(eoxyribo)n(ucleic) a(cid)* ⟧ the basic chromosomal material, containing and transmitting the hereditary pattern

do[1] (dōō) *vt.* **did, done, do′ing** ⟦OE *don* ⟧ **1** to perform (an action, etc.) **2** to complete; finish **3** to cause [it *does* no harm] **4** to exert [*do* your best] **5** to deal with as is required [*do* the ironing] **6** to have as one's occupation; work at **7** [Colloq.] to cheat **8** [Colloq.] to serve (a jail term) — *vi.* **1** to behave [*do* as you please] **2** to be active [up and *doing*] **3** to get along; fare [he is *doing* well] **4** to be adequate [the black hat will *do*] **5** to take place [anything *doing* tonight?] **6** auxiliary uses of *do*: *a*) to give emphasis [*do* stay a while] *b*) to ask a question [*did* you go?] *c*) to serve as a substitute verb [act as I *do* (act)] — **do in 1** [Slang] to kill **2** [Colloq.] to tire out —**do over** [Colloq.] to redecorate —**do up** to wrap up —**do with** to make use of —**do without** to get along without —**have to do with** to be related to

do·able (dōō′ə bəl) *adj.* that can be done

Do·ber·man pin·scher (dō′bər mən pin′chər) ⟦< Ger after L. *Dobermann*, 19th-c. breeder + *pinscher*, terrier⟧ a large dog with a short, dark coat

doc (däk) *n.* [Slang] DOCTOR

do·cent (dō′sənt) *n.* ⟦ < L *docere*, to teach ⟧ a lecturer or tour guide, as at a museum

doc·ile (däs′əl) *adj.* ⟦see prec.⟧ easy to discipline; submissive —**do·cil·ity** (dō sil′ə tē, dä-) *n.*

dock[1] (däk) *n.* ⟦ < It *doccia*, canal ⟧ **1** an excavated basin for receiving ships **2** a wharf; pier **3** the water between two piers **4** a platform for loading and unloading trucks, etc. — *vt.* to pilot (a ship) to a dock — *vi.* to come to a dock

dock[2] (däk) *n.* ⟦ < Fl *dok*, a cage ⟧ the place where the accused stands or sits in court

dock[3] (däk) *n.* ⟦OE *docce*⟧ a tall, coarse weed of the buckwheat family

dock[4] (däk) *vt.* [ME *dok*, tail] **1** to cut off the end of (a tail, etc.); bob **2** to deduct from (wages, etc.)

docket (däk′it) *n.* ⟦ < ? ⟧ **1** a list of cases to be tried by a law court **2** an agenda — *vt.* to enter in a docket

dock′yard′ *n.* SHIPYARD

doc·tor (däk′tər) *n.* ⟦ < L, teacher ⟧ **1** one who holds a doctorate **2** a physician or surgeon **3** one licensed to practice any of the healing arts — *vt.* [Colloq.] **1** to try to heal **2** to mend **3** to tamper with —**doc′toral** *adj.*

doc′tor·ate (-it) *n.* **1** the highest degree awarded by universities **2** the status of doctor

Doctor of Philosophy the highest doctorate awarded for original research

doc·tri·naire (däk′tri ner′) *adj.* ⟦Fr⟧ adhering to a doctrine dogmatically —**doc′tri·nair′ism′** *n.*

doc·trine (däk′trin) *n.* ⟦see DOCTOR⟧ something taught, esp. as the principles of a religion, political party, etc.; tenet or tenets; dogma —**doc′tri·nal** (-tri nəl) *adj.*

docu·ment (däk′yōō mənt, -yə-; *for v.,* -ment′) *n.* ⟦ < L *documentum*, proof⟧ anything printed, written, etc. that is relied upon to record or prove something — *vt.* to provide with or support by documents

doc′u·men′tary (-ment′ə rē) *adj.* **1** of or supported by documents **2** depicting news events, social conditions, etc. in nonfictional but dramatic form — *n., pl.* **-ries** a documentary film, TV show, etc.

doc′u·men·ta′tion (-mən tā′shən, -men-) *n.* **1** the supplying of documents **2** the documents thus supplied **3** instructions for using computer hardware or software

dod·der (däd′ər) *vi.* ⟦ME *daderen*⟧ **1** to shake or tremble, as from old age **2** to totter —**dod′der·ing** *adj.*

◼ THESAURUS ◼

slice, lump, wedge, cut, book, chapter, verse, class, race, clan, tribe, caste; see also PART 1. **3** [Discord or disunion] trouble, words, difficulty; see DISAGREEMENT 1, DISPUTE. **4** [A military unit] armored division, airborne division, infantry division; see ARMY 2. **5** [An organized area] state, government, range; see NATION.

divorce *n.* separation, partition, divorcement, bill of divorcement, annulment, separate maintenance, parting of the ways, dissolution, split-up*.—*Ant.* MARRIAGE, betrothal, wedding.

divorce *v.* separate, annul, nullify, put away, split up*; see also CANCEL.

divorced *a.* dissolved, parted, disunited, divided, split*, washed-up*; see also SEPARATED.—*Ant.* MARRIED, joined, mated.

divulge *v.* disclose, impart, confess; see ADMIT 2, EXPOSE 1.

dizzy *a.* confused, lightheaded, giddy, bemused, staggering, upset, dazzled, dazed, dumb, faint, with spots before one's eyes, out of control, weak-kneed, wobbly; see also UNSTABLE 1.

DNA *n.* genetic alphabet, double helix, hereditary information, deoxyribonucleic acid, genetic code.

do[1] *v.* **1** [To discharge one's responsibilities] effect, execute, achieve, act, perform, finish, complete, work, labor, produce, create, effect, accomplish; see also ACHIEVE, PERFORM 1, SUCCEED 1. **2** [To execute commands or instructions] carry out, complete, fulfill; see OBEY. **3** [To suffice] serve, be sufficient, give satisfaction; see SATISFY 3. **4** [To solve] figure out, work out, puzzle, decode; see also SOLVE. **5** [To present a play, etc.] give, put on, produce; see PERFORM 2. **6** [To act] perform, portray, render the role of; see ACT 3. **7** [To conduct oneself] behave oneself, comport oneself, acquit oneself, seem, appear; see also BEHAVE. —**do in*** eliminate, slay, murder; see DESTROY, KILL 1. —**do without** dispense with, get along without, forgo; see ENDURE 1, 2, NEED. —**have to do with** be related to, be connected with, bear on; see CONCERN 1. —**make do** get by, get along, manage, survive; see also ENDURE 2.

docile *a.* meek, mild, tractable, pliant, submissive, accommodating, adaptable, resigned, agreeable, willing, obliging, well-behaved, manageable, tame, yielding, teachable, easily influenced, easygoing, usable, soft, childlike; see also GENTLE 3, HUMBLE 1, OBEDIENT 1.

docility *n.* obedience, gentleness, adaptability; see HUMILITY, SHYNESS.

dock[1] *n.* landing pier, wharf, lock, boat landing, marina, dry dock, embarcadero, waterfront.

dock[4] *v.* lessen, withhold, deduct; see DECREASE 2.

doctor *n.* Doctor of Medicine (M.D.), physician, general practitioner (G.P.), surgeon, medical attendant, consultant, specialist, intern, house physician, resident, veterinarian, chiropractor, homeopath, osteopath, acupuncturist, faith healer, witch doctor, shaman, medicine man, quack, doc*, sawbones*. *Types of doctors include the following:* heart specialist; eye, ear, nose, and throat specialist; inhalation therapist, anesthetist, dentist, pediatrician, gynecologist, oculist, obstetrician, psychiatrist, psychoanalyst, orthopedist, neurologist, cardiologist, pathologist, dermatologist, endocrinologist, ophthalmologist, urologist, hematologist; see also MEDICINE 3.

doctor* *v.* tamper with, change, alter; see ALTER 1.

doctrine *n.* principle, proposition, precept, article, concept, conviction, opinion, convention, attitude, tradition, unwritten law, natural law, common law, teachings, accepted belief, article of faith, canon, regulation, rule, pronouncement, declaration; see also LAW 2, 4.

document *n.* paper, diary, report; see RECORD 1.

dodge (däj) *vi., vt.* **dodged, dodg'ing** 〚< ?〛 **1** to move quickly aside, or avoid by so moving **2** to use tricks or evasions, or evade by so doing — *n.* **1** a dodging **2** a trick used in evading or cheating —**dodg'er** *n.*
dodo (dō'dō) *n., pl.* **-dos** or **-does** 〚Port *doudo*, lit., stupid〛 a large, flightless bird, now extinct
doe (dō) *n.* 〚OE *da*〛 the female deer, antelope, etc.
doer (dōō'ər) *n.* **1** one who does something **2** one who gets things done
does (duz) *vt., vi.* 3d pers. sing., pres. indic., of DO¹
doe'skin' *n.* **1** leather from the skin of a female deer **2** a soft wool cloth
doff (däf, dôf) *vt.* 〚see DO¹ & OFF〛 to take off (one's hat, clothes, etc.)
dog (dôg) *n.* 〚OE *docga*〛 **1** any of various canines, esp. one of a domesticated breed kept as a pet, for hunting, etc. **2** a mean, contemptible fellow **3** [*pl.*] [Slang] feet **4** [Slang] an unattractive person or unsatisfactory thing **5** *Mech.* a device for holding or grappling — *vt.* **dogged, dog'ging** to follow or hunt like a dog —**go to the dogs** [Colloq.] to deteriorate
dog'ear' *n.* a turned-down corner of the leaf of a book — **dog'eared'** *adj.*
dog'fish' *n., pl.* **-fish'** or (for different species) **-fish'es** any of various small sharks
dog·ged (dôg'id) *adj.* persistent; stubborn —**dog'gedly** *adv.*
dog·gerel (dôg'ər əl) *n.* 〚ME *dogerel*〛 trivial, awkward verse, usually having a monotonous rhythm
dog·gie bag (dôg'ē) a bag supplied by a restaurant for carrying leftovers, as for one's dog
dog'gone' *interj.* damn! darn! — *vt.* **-goned', -gon'ing** [Colloq.] to damn
dog'house' *n.* a dog's shelter —**in the doghouse** [Slang] in disfavor
do·gie (dō'gē) *n.* 〚< ?〛 in the W U.S., a stray calf
dogma (dôg'mə) *n.* 〚< Gr, opinion〛 a doctrine; tenet; belief; esp., a body of theological doctrines strictly adhered to
dog·mat·ic (-mat'ik) *adj.* **1** of or like dogma **2** asserted without proof **3** stating opinion positively or arrogantly —**dog·mat'i·cally** *adv.*
dog'ma·tism' (-mə tiz'əm) *n.* dogmatic assertion of opinion —**dog'ma·tist** *n.*
do'-good'er *n.* [Colloq.] an idealistic, but impractical person who seeks to correct social ills
dog'trot' *n.* a slow, easy trot
dog'wood' *n.* a small, flowering tree of the E U.S.
doily (doi'lē) *n., pl.* **-lies** 〚after a 17th-c. London draper〛 a small decorative mat, as of lace
do·ing (dōō'iŋ) *n.* something done; action, etc.: *usually used in pl.*
do'-it-yourself' *n.* the practice of making or repairing things oneself, instead of hiring another —**do'-it-your-self'er** *n.*
Dolby (dōl'bē) 〚after R. *Dolby*, U.S. recording engineer〛

trademark *for* an electronic system used to reduce unwanted noise in a tape recording
dol·drums (dōl'drəmz, däl'-) *n.pl.* 〚< ? DULL〛 **1** *a*) low spirits *b*) sluggishness **2** equatorial ocean regions having little or no wind
dole (dōl) *n.* 〚OE *dal*, a share〛 **1** money or food given in charity **2** money paid by a government to the unemployed — *vt.* **doled, dol'ing** to give sparingly or as a dole
dole'ful (-fəl) *adj.* 〚< L *dolere*, suffer〛 sad; mournful —**dole'fully** *adv.*
doll (däl) *n.* 〚< nickname for *Dorothy*〛 **1** a child's toy made to resemble a human being **2** [Slang] any attractive or lovable person — *vt., vi.* [Colloq.] to dress stylishly or showily: with *up*
dol·lar (däl'ər) *n.* 〚< Ger *thaler*, a coin〛 **1** the monetary unit of the U.S., equal to 100 cents **2** the monetary unit of various other countries, as of Canada **3** a piece of money worth one dollar
dol·lop (däl'əp) *n.* 〚< ?〛 **1** a soft mass **2** a quantity, often a small one
dolly (däl'ē) *n., pl.* **-lies 1** a doll: child's word **2** a low, flat, wheeled frame for moving heavy objects
dol·men (dōl'mən, däl'-) *n.* 〚Fr〛 a prehistoric monument consisting of a large, flat stone laid across upright stones
do·lo·mite (dō'lə mit', däl'ə-) *n.* 〚after D. *Dolomieu*, 18th-c. Fr geologist〛 a mineral which forms vast layers of rock
do·lor·ous (dō'lər əs, däl'ər-) *adj.* 〚< L *dolere*, suffer〛 sorrowful; sad —**do'lor·ously** *adv.*
dol·phin (däl'fin, dôl'-) *n.* 〚< Gr *delphis*〛 a highly intelligent toothed whale with a beaklike snout
dolt (dōlt) *n.* 〚prob. < ME *dolte*〛 a stupid person —**dolt'ish** *adj.*
-dom (dəm) 〚OE *dom*, state〛 *suffix* **1** rank or domain of [*kingdom*] **2** fact or state of being [*martyrdom*] **3** all who are [*officialdom*]
do·main (dō mān') *n.* 〚< L *dominus*, a lord〛 **1** territory under one government **2** field of activity
dome (dōm) *n.* 〚< Gr *dōma*, housetop〛 **1** a rounded roof or ceiling **2** any dome-shaped object
do·mes·tic (dō mes'tik, də-) *adj.* 〚< L *domus*, house〛 **1** of the home or family **2** of or made in one's country **3** tame: said of animals **4** home-loving — *n.* a maid, cook, etc. in the home —**do·mes'ti·cally** *adv.*
do·mes'ti·cate' (-ti kāt') *vt.* **-cat'ed, -cat'ing 1** to accustom to home life **2** to tame for human use —**do·mes'ti·ca'tion** *n.*
do·mes·tic·ity (dō'mes tis'ə tē) *n.* home life or devotion to it
domi·cile (däm'ə sil', -sil; *also* dō'mə-) *n.* 〚< L *domus*, home〛 a home; residence — *vt.* **-ciled', -cil'ing** to establish in a domicile
domi·nant (däm'ə nənt) *adj.* dominating; ruling; prevailing —**dom'i·nance** *n.* —**dom'i·nantly** *adv.*

THESAURUS

dodge *n.* trick, strategy, scheme; see METHOD, PLAN 1.
dodge *v.* duck, elude, evade; see AVOID.
doer *n.* actor, performer, instrument; see MEANS 1.
dog *n.* hound, bitch, puppy, pup, mongrel, stray, canine, cur, pooch*, mutt*. *Types and breeds of dogs include the following:* hunting dog, field dog, racing dog, boxer, shepherd dog, bloodhound, wolfhound, greyhound, whippet, St. Bernard, Great Dane, German shepherd, Doberman pinscher, Afghan hound, Irish wolfhound, Labrador retriever, Chesapeake Bay retriever, malamute, husky, collie, Old English sheep dog, Irish setter, pointer, spaniel, cocker spaniel, basset, beagle, dachshund, Dalmatian, poodle, French poodle, Pekingese, Chihuahua, Airedale, schnauzer, fox terrier, wirehaired terrier, Scottie, bull terrier, Boston terrier. —**a dog's life*** wretched existence, bad luck, trouble; see POVERTY 1. —**go to the dogs*** deteriorate, degenerate, weaken; see WEAKEN 1, 2. —**let sleeping dogs lie*** ignore, leave well enough alone, pass over; see NEGLECT 1. —**put on the**

dog* show off, entertain lavishly, exhibit; see DISPLAY. —**teach an old dog new tricks*** influence, convince, change; see PERSUADE.
dogged *a.* stubborn, tenacious, firm; see STUBBORN.
dogmatic *a.* **1** [Based on an assumption of absolute truth] authoritarian, on faith, by nature; see ABSOLUTE 1. **2** [Acting as though possessed of absolute truth] dictatorial, stubborn, egotistical, bigoted, fanatical, intolerant, opinionated, overbearing, magisterial, arrogant, domineering, tyrannical, obstinate, confident, downright, arbitrary, unequivocal, definite, formal, stubborn, determined, emphatic, narrow-minded, one-sided, hidebound, high and mighty*, pigheaded, bullheaded, stubborn as a mule*; see also ABSOLUTE 2.—*Ant.* LIBERAL, tolerant, dubious.
doing *n.* performing, accomplishing, achieving; see PERFORMANCE.
doings *n.* activities, conduct, dealings; see ACTION 1.
dole out *v.* share, assign, parcel out; see DISTRIBUTE.
doll *n.* baby, figurine, manikin, model,

dolly, doll baby*; see also TOY 1.
dollar *n.* coin, legal tender, dollar bill, silver dollar, currency, bank note, greenback, folding money*, buck*; see also MONEY 1.
dollop *n.* bit, touch, dash; see DASH 3, BIT 1.
doll up *v.* fix up, put on one's best clothes, primp; see DRESS 1.
dolt *n.* simpleton, nitwit, blockhead; see FOOL.
domain *n.* dominion, field, specialty; see AREA.
dome *n.* ceiling, top, vault; see ROOF.
domestic *a.* **1** [Home-loving] houseloving, domesticated, stay-at-home, household, family, quiet, sedentary, indoor, tame; see also CALM 1, 2, TRANQUIL.—*Ant.* UNRULY, roving, restless. **2** [Home-grown] indigenous, handcrafted, native; see HOMEMADE.
domesticate *v.* tame, breed, housebreak; see TEACH, TRAIN 2.
domesticated *a.* tamed, trained, housebroken; see TAME 1.
dominant *a.* commanding, authoritative, assertive; see AGGRESSIVE, POWERFUL 1.

dom'i·nate' (-nāt') *vt., vi.* **-nat'ed, -nat'ing** [< L *dominus*, a master] 1 to rule or control by superior power 2 to rise above (the surroundings) —**dom'i·na'tion** *n.*

domi·neer (däm'ə nir') *vi., vt.* [< Du: see prec.] to rule (*over*) in a harsh or arrogant way; tyrannize

dom'i·neer'ing *adj.* overbearing

do·min·ion (də min'yən) *n.* [see DOMINATE] 1 rule or power to rule 2 a governed territory or country

domi·no (däm'ə nō') *n., pl.* **-noes** or **-nos** [Fr & It] 1 a hooded cloak and a mask, worn at masquerades 2 a mask for the eyes 3 a small, oblong tile marked with dots 4 [*pl.,* with *sing. v.*] a game played with such tiles

domino theory the theory that if one nation falls to Communism, nearby nations will also, like a row of dominoes falling down

don¹ (dän) *n.* [Sp < L *dominus*, master] 1 [D-] Sir; Mr.: a Spanish title of respect 2 a Spanish gentleman 3 [Colloq.] a teacher at a British university 4 a Mafia leader

don² (dän) *vt.* **donned, don'ning** [contr. of *do on*] to put on (clothes)

Doña (dō'nyä) *n.* [Sp] Lady; Madam: a Spanish title of respect

do·nate (dō'nāt') *vt., vi.* **-nat'ed, -nat'ing** [< L *donum*, gift] to give or contribute —**do·na'tion** *n.*

done (dun) *vt., vi. pp. of* DO¹ — *adj.* 1 completed 2 cooked —**done (for)** [Colloq.] dead, ruined, etc.

Don Juan (dän' wän') Sp. *Legend* a dissolute nobleman and seducer of women

don·key (dän'kē, dôŋ'-, duŋ'-) *n., pl.* **-keys** [< ?] 1 a domesticated ass 2 a stupid or foolish person

donny·brook (dän'ē brook') *n.* [after a fair formerly held near Dublin] [Colloq.] a rowdy fight or free-for-all

do·nor (dō'nər) *n.* one who donates

Don Qui·xote (dän' kē hōt'ē, -ā) 1 a 17th-c. Spanish satirical novel 2 its chivalrous but unrealistic hero

don't (dōnt) do not

do·nut (dō'nut') *n. colloq. sp. of* DOUGHNUT

doo·dle (dōōd''l) *vi.* **-dled, -dling** [Ger *dudeln*, to trifle] to scribble aimlessly —*n.* a mark made in doodling —**doo'dler** *n.*

doom (dōōm) *n.* [OE *dom*] 1 a judgment; sentence 2 fate 3 ruin or death — *vt.* 1 to pass judgment on; condemn 2 to destine to a tragic fate

dooms'day' *n.* Judgment Day

door (dôr) *n.* [OE *duru*] 1 a movable structure for opening or closing an entrance 2 a doorway 3 a means of access —**out of doors** outdoors

door'bell' *n.* a bell, etc. at the entrance of a building or room, sounded to alert the occupants of a visitor

door'man' (-man', -mən) *n., pl.* **-men'** (-men', -mən) one whose work is opening the door of a building, hailing taxicabs, etc.

door'mat' *n.* a mat to wipe the shoes on before entering a house, etc.

door'step' *n.* a step that leads from an outer door to a path, lawn, etc.

door'way' *n.* 1 an opening in a wall that can be closed by a door 2 any means of access

door'yard' *n.* a yard onto which a door of a house opens

dopa (dō'pə) *n.* [< chemical name] an amino acid that is converted by an enzyme in the bloodstream into certain biological chemicals: one isomer (*L-dopa*) is used in treating Parkinson's disease

dope (dōp) *n.* [Du *doop*, sauce] 1 any thick liquid used as a lubricant, varnish, filler, etc. 2 [Colloq.] a drug or narcotic 3 [Colloq.] a stupid person 4 [Slang] information — *vt.* **doped, dop'ing** to drug —**dope out** [Slang] to solve — **dop'er** *n.*

dopey or **dopy** (dō'pē) *adj.* **-i·er, -i·est** [Colloq.] lethargic or stupid —**dop'i·ness** *n.*

Doric (dôr'ik) *adj.* designating or of a classical style of architecture marked by fluted columns with plain capitals

dorm (dôrm) *n.* [Colloq.] DORMITORY

dor·mant (dôr'mənt) *adj.* [< L *dormire*, to sleep] 1 inactive 2 *Biol.* in a resting or torpid state —**dor'man·cy** *n.*

dor·mer (dôr'mər) *n.* [see prec.] 1 a window set upright in a structure projecting from a sloping roof: also **dormer window** 2 such a structure

dor·mi·tory (dôr'mə tôr'ē) *n., pl.* **-ries** [see DORMANT] 1 a room with beds for a number of people 2 a building with rooms for sleeping and living in, as by students at a college

dor·mouse (dôr'mous') *n., pl.* **-mice'** (-mīs') [ME *dormous*] a small, furry-tailed European rodent

dor·sal (dôr'səl) *adj.* [< L *dorsum*, the back] of, on, or near the back

dory (dôr'ē) *n., pl.* **-ries** [AmInd (Central America) *dori*, dugout] a small, flat-bottomed fishing boat with high sides

DOS *Comput.* disk operating system

dose (dōs) *n.* [< Gr *dosis*, a giving] an amount of a medicine to be taken at one time — *vt.* **dosed, dos'ing** to give doses to —**dos'age** *n.*

do·sim·eter (dō sim'ət ər) *n.* a device for measuring exposure to ionizing radiation

dos·sier (dä'sē ā') *n.* [Fr] a collection of documents about some person or matter

dost (dust) *vt., vi. archaic 2d pers. sing., pres. indic., of* DO¹: used with *thou*

dot (dät) *n.* [OE *dott*, head of boil] 1 a tiny speck or mark 2 a small, round spot — *vt.* **dot'ted, dot'ting** to mark with or as with a dot or dots —**on the dot** [Colloq.] at the exact time

dot·age (dōt'ij) *n.* [ME < *doten*, DOTE] childish state due to old age

dot'ard (-ərd) *n.* one in one's dotage

dote (dōt) *vi.* **dot'ed, dot'ing** [ME *doten*] 1 to be weak-minded, esp. because of old age 2 to be excessively fond: with *on* or *upon*

doth (duth) *vt., vi. archaic 3d pers. sing., pres. indic., of* DO¹

dot·ing (dōt'iŋ) *adj.* foolishly or excessively fond —**dot'ingly** *adv.*

dot'-ma'trix *adj.* of or by printing in which characters are formed of closely spaced dots

Douay Bible (dōō ā') an English version of the Bible for Roman Catholics: after Douai, France, where the Old Testament was published

dou·ble (dub'əl) *adj.* [< L *duplus*] 1 twofold 2 having two layers 3 having two of one kind 4 being of two kinds

---

THESAURUS

dominate *v.* rule, manage, control, dictate to, subject, subjugate, tyrannize, have one's own way, have influence over, domineer, lead by the nose, boss*, keep under one's thumb; see also GOVERN.

domination *n.* rule, control, mastery; see COMMAND, POWER 2.

domineering *a.* despotic, imperious, oppressive; see EGOTISTIC.

dominion *n.* region, district, state; see AREA, NATION 1.

donate *v.* grant, bestow, bequeath; see DISTRIBUTE, GIVE 1, PROVIDE 1.

donation *n.* contribution, offering, present; see GIFT 1.

done *a.* 1 [Accomplished] over, through, completed, realized, effected, executed, performed, fulfilled, brought to pass, brought about, perfected; see also FINISHED 1.—*Ant.* UNFINISHED, unrealized, failed. 2 [Cooked] brewed, stewed, broiled, boiled, crisped, crusted, fried, browned, done to a turn; see also BAKED.—*Ant.* RAW, burned,

uncooked. —**done for*** defeated, conquered, vanquished; see BEATEN 1.

Don Juan *n.* Lothario, pursuer, Romeo, libertine, philanderer, rake, seducer, lecher, wolf*.

donkey *n.* burro, ass, jackass; see HORSE.

donor *n.* benefactor, contributor, patron, philanthropist, giver, subscriber, altruist, Good Samaritan, fairy godmother*; see also PATRON.

doom *n.* fate, lot, destination, predestination, future, fortune, ruin, goal.

doomed *a.* ruined, cursed, sentenced, lost, condemned, unfortunate, ill-fated, foreordained, predestined, threatened, menaced, suppressed, wrecked; see also DESTROYED, FATED.

door *n.* entry, portal, hatchway, doorway, gateway, opening; see also ENTRANCE 2, GATE. —**out of doors** outside, in the air, out; see OUTDOORS. —**show someone the door** show out, ask to leave, eject; see OUST.

dope *n.* 1 [*A drug] narcotic, stimu-

lant, opiate; see DRUG. 2 [*Pertinent information] details, account, developments; see INFORMATION 1, KNOWLEDGE 1, NEWS 1. 3 [*A dull-witted person] dunce, dolt, simpleton; see FOOL.

dope *v.* anesthetize, drug, put to sleep; see DEADEN.

dormitory *n.* barracks, residence hall, dorm*; see HOTEL.

dose *n.* prescription, dosage, treatment, spoonful, portion, doctor's orders*; see also QUANTITY, SHARE.

dot *n.* point, spot, speck; see MARK 1. —**on the dot*** precisely, accurately, punctually; see PUNCTUAL.

dote *v.* adore, pet, admire; see LOVE 1.

double *a.* twofold, two times, paired, coupled, binary, doubled, redoubled, duplex, renewed, dual, both one and the other, repeated, second, increased, as much again, duplicated; see also TWICE, TWIN.—*Ant.* ALONE, single, apart. —**on the double*** hastily, rapidly, hurriedly; see QUICKLY.

[a *double* standard] **5** twice as much, as many, etc. **6** made for two — *adv.* **1** twofold or twice **2** two together — *n.* **1** anything twice as much, as many, etc. as normal **2** a duplicate; counterpart **3** a fold **4** [*pl.*] a game of tennis, etc. with two players on each side **5** *Baseball* a hit on which the batter reaches second base **6** *Bridge* the doubling of an opponent's bid — *vt.* **-bled, -bling 1** to make twice as much or as many **2** to fold **3** to repeat or duplicate **4** *Bridge* to increase the point value or penalty of (an opponent's bid) — *vi.* **1** to become double **2** to turn sharply backward [to *double* on one's tracks] **3** to serve as a double **4** to serve an additional purpose **5** *Baseball* to hit a double —**double up 1** to clench (one's fist) **2** to bend over, as in pain **3** to share a room, etc. with someone

double agent a spy employed by two rival espionage organizations

dou'ble-bar'reled *adj.* **1** having two barrels, as a kind of shotgun **2** having a double purpose or meaning

double bass (bās) the largest, deepest-toned instrument of the violin family

dou'ble-blind' *adj.* designating or of a test of the effects of a drug in which neither the subjects nor the researchers know who is receiving the drug

double boiler a cooking utensil in which one pan, for food, fits over another, for boiling water

dou'ble-breast'ed *adj.* overlapping across the breast, as a coat

dou'ble-cross' *vt.* [Colloq.] to betray —**dou'ble-cross'er** *n.*

double date [Colloq.] a social engagement shared by two couples —**dou'ble-date', -dat'ed, -dat'ing,** *vi., vt.*

dou'ble-deal'ing *n.* duplicity

dou'ble-deck'er *n.* **1** any structure or vehicle with an upper deck **2** [Colloq.] a two-layer sandwich made with three slices of bread

double dipping an unethical receiving of pay from two or more sources

dou'ble-edged' *adj.* **1** having two cutting edges **2** applicable both ways, as an argument

double-entendre (dub'əl än tän'drə, dōō'blôn tôn'-) *n.* [< Fr] a term with two meanings, esp. when one is risqué

dou'ble-head'er *n.* two games played in succession on the same day

dou'ble-joint'ed *adj.* having joints that permit limbs, fingers, etc. to bend at other than the usual angles

dou'ble-knit' *adj.* knit with a double stitch that makes the fabric extra thick

dou'ble-park' *vt., vi.* to park (a vehicle) parallel to another parked alongside a curb

double play *Baseball* a play in which two players are put out

dou'ble-reed' *adj.* designating or of a woodwind instrument, as the oboe, having two reeds separated by a narrow opening

dou'ble-speak' *n.* ambiguous language, esp. if meant to deceive

double standard a system, code, etc. applied unequally; specif., a moral code stricter for women than for men

dou'blet (dub'lit) *n.* [< OFr *double*, orig., something folded] **1** a man's closefitting jacket of the 14th-16th c. **2** a pair, or one of a pair

double take a delayed reaction following unthinking acceptance

double talk 1 ambiguous and deceptive talk **2** meaningless syllables made to sound like talk

dou·bloon' (dub lōōn') *n.* [< Fr < L *duplus*, double] an obsolete Spanish gold coin

dou·bly (dub'lē) *adv.* **1** twice **2** two at a time

doubt (dout) *vi.* [< L *dubius*, uncertain] to be uncertain or undecided — *vt.* **1** to be uncertain about **2** to tend to disbelieve — *n.* **1** *a*) a wavering of opinion or belief *b*) lack of trust **2** a condition of uncertainty **3** an unsettled point or matter —**beyond (or without) doubt** certainly —**no doubt 1** certainly **2** probably —**doubt'er** *n.* —**doubt'ingly** *adv.*

doubt'ful *adj.* **1** uncertain **2** causing doubt or suspicion **3** feeling doubt —**doubt'fully** *adv.*

doubt'less *adv.* **1** certainly **2** probably —**doubt'lessly** *adv.*

douche (dōōsh) *n.* [Fr < It *doccia*] **1** a jet of liquid applied externally or internally to the body **2** a device for douching — *vt., vi.* **douched, douch'ing** to apply a douche (to)

dough (dō) *n.* [OE *dag*] **1** a mixture of flour, liquid, etc. worked into a soft mass for baking **2** [Slang] money

dough'nut' *n.* a small, usually ring-shaped cake, fried in deep fat

doughty (dout'ē) *adj.* **-tier, -ti·est** [OE *dohtig*] [Now Rare] valiant; brave

doughy (dō'ē) *adj.* **-i·er, -i·est** of or like dough; soft, pasty, etc. —**dough'i·ness** *n.*

Doug·las fir (dug'ləs) [after D. *Douglas*, 19th-c. Scot botanist in U.S.] a giant North American evergreen tree valued for its wood

dour (door, dour) *adj.* [< L *durus*, hard] **1** [Scot.] stern; severe **2** sullen; gloomy —**dour'ness** *n.*

douse (dous) *vt.* **doused, dous'ing** [< ?] **1** to thrust suddenly into liquid **2** to drench **3** [Colloq.] to put out (a light, etc.)

dove¹ (duv) *n.* [ME *douve*] **1** any of the smaller species of pigeon: often used as a symbol of peace **2** an advocate of measures which avoid or end wars

dove² (dōv) *vi. alt. pt. of* DIVE

dove·cote (duv'kōt') *n.* a box with compartments for nesting pigeons

dove·tail (duv'tāl') *n.* a projecting part that fits into a corresponding cut-out space to form a joint — *vt.* to fasten or piece together, as by means of dovetails — *vi.* to fit together closely or logically

dowa·ger (dou'ə jər) *n.* [< L *dotare*, endow] **1** a widow with a title or property derived from her dead husband **2** an elderly, wealthy woman

dowdy (dou'dē) *adj.* **-dier, -di·est** [< ME *doude*, plain woman] not neat or smart in dress —**dow'di·ness** *n.*

dowel (dou'əl) *n.* [ME *doule*] a peg of wood, etc., usually fitted into corresponding holes in two pieces to fasten them together — *vt.* **-eled** or **-elled, -el·ing** or **-el·ling** to fasten with dowels

dower (dou'ər) *n.* [< L *dare*, give] **1** that part of a man's

---

THESAURUS

double *v.* **1** [To make or become double] make twice as much, duplicate, multiply; see GROW 1, INCREASE. **2** [To replace] substitute, stand in, fill in; see SUBSTITUTE. —**double back** backtrack, reverse, circle; see RETURN 1, TURN 2, 6. —**double up** combine, join, share; see JOIN 1, 2, UNITE.

double-cross *v.* cheat, defraud, trick; see DECEIVE.

double-dealing *n.* deceit, cheating, trickery; see DISHONESTY, HYPOCRISY.

doubly *a.* twofold, redoubled, increased; see AGAIN, DOUBLE, TWICE.

doubt *n.* distrust, mistrust, disbelief, suspicion, misgiving, skepticism, apprehension, agnosticism, incredulity, lack of faith, lack of confidence, jealousy, rejection, scruple, misgiving, indecision, lack of conviction, ambiguity, dilemma, reluctance, quandary, feeling of inferiority; see also UNCERTAINTY 1, 2.—*Ant.* BELIEF, conviction, certainty. —**beyond (or without) doubt** doubtless, certainly,

without doubt; see SURELY. —**no doubt** doubtless, in all likelihood, certainly; see PROBABLY, SURELY.

doubt *v.* wonder, question, query, ponder, dispute, be dubious, be uncertain, be doubtful, refuse to believe, demur, have doubts about, have one's doubts, stop to consider, have qualms, call in question, give no credit to, throw doubt upon, have no conception, not know which way to turn, not know what to make of, close one's mind, not admit, not believe, refuse to believe, not buy*; see also ASK, DENY, QUESTION 1.— *Ant.* TRUST, believe, confide.

doubter *n.* questioner, unbeliever, agnostic; see CYNIC.

doubtful *a.* **1** [Uncertain in mind] dubious, doubting, questioning, undecided, unsure, wavering, hesitating, undetermined, uncertain, unsettled, confused, disturbed, lost, puzzled, perplexed, flustered, baffled, distracted, unresolved, in a quandary, of two minds, unable to make

up one's mind, troubled with doubt, having little faith, of little faith, in question, not knowing what's what, not following, up a tree*, not able to make head or tail of, going around in circles*, out of focus, up in the air, wishy-washy*, iffy; see also SUSPICIOUS 1. **2** [Improbable] probably wrong, questionable, unconvincing; see OBSCURE 1, UNCERTAIN.

doubtless *a.* positively, certainly, unquestionably; see SURELY.

dough *n.* **1** [A soft mixture] paste (especially of flour), pulp, mash; see BATTER 2, MIXTURE 1. **2** [*Money] dollars, change, silver; see MONEY 1, WEALTH.

doughnut *n.* friedcake, cruller, sinker*; see CAKE 2, PASTRY.

douse *v.* submerge, splash, drench; see IMMERSE, SOAK 1.

dove¹ *n.* peacemaker, activist, pacifier; see PACIFIST.

dowdy *a.* untidy, slovenly, plain; see SHABBY.

property which his widow inherits for life 2 a dowry — *vt.* to endow (*with*)

down[1] (doun) *adv.* ⟦OE *adune*, from the hill⟧ 1 to, in, or on a lower place or level 2 in or to a low or lower condition, amount, etc. 3 from an earlier to a later period 4 out of one's hands *[put it down]* 5 in a serious manner *[get down to work]* 6 completely *[loaded down]* 7 in cash *[$5 down and $5 a week]* 8 in writing *[take down notes]* — *adj.* 1 descending 2 in a lower place 3 gone, brought, etc. down 4 dejected; discouraged 5 ill 6 finished *[four down, six to go]* 7 in cash *[a down payment]* 8 inoperative *[the computer is down]* — *prep.* down toward, along, through, into, or upon — *vt.* to put or throw down — *n.* 1 a misfortune *[ups and downs]* 2 *Football* one of a series of plays in which a team tries to advance the ball —**down and out** penniless, ill, etc. —**down on** [Colloq.] angry or annoyed with —**down with!** do away with!

down[2] (doun) *n.* ⟦< ON *dūnn*⟧ 1 soft, fine feathers 2 soft, fine hair

down[3] (doun) *n.* ⟦OE *dun*, hill⟧ open, high, grassy land: *usually used in pl.*

down'beat' *n. Music* the downward stroke of the conductor's hand indicating the first beat of each measure

down'cast' *adj.* 1 directed downward 2 unhappy; dejected

Down East [*also* d- e-] [Colloq.] New England, esp. Maine

down'er *n.* [Slang] any depressant or sedative

down'fall' *n.* 1 *a)* a sudden fall, as from power *b)* the cause of this 2 a heavy fall, as of snow

down'fall'en *adj.* fallen; ruined

down'grade' *n.* a downward slope — *adj., adv.* downward — *vt.* **-grad'ed, -grad'ing** 1 to demote 2 to belittle

down'heart'ed *adj.* discouraged

down'hill' *adv.* toward the bottom of a hill — *adj.* 1 going downward 2 without difficulty

down'play' *vt.* to play down; minimize

down'pour' *n.* a heavy rain

down'right' *adv.* utterly — *adj.* 1 absolute; utter 2 plain; frank

down'scale' *adj.* of or for people who are unstylish, not affluent, etc.

down'stage' *adj., adv.* of or toward the front of the stage

down'stairs' *adv.* 1 down the stairs 2 on or to a lower floor — *adj.* on a lower floor — *n.* a lower floor

down'state' *adj., adv.* in, to, or from the southerly part of a State

down'stream' *adv., adj.* in the direction of the current of a stream

down'swing' *n.* 1 a downward swing, as of a golf club 2 a downward trend: also **down'turn'**

Down (or **Down's**) **syndrome** ⟦after J. *Down*, 19th-c.

Brit physician⟧ a congenital condition characterized by mental deficiency, a broad face, etc.

down'-to-earth' *adj.* realistic or practical

down'town' *adj., adv.* in or toward the main business section of a city — *n.* the downtown section of a city

down'trod'den *adj.* oppressed

down'ward (-wərd) *adv., adj.* toward a lower place, position, etc.: also **down'wards** *adv.*

down'y *adj.* **-i·er, -i·est** 1 covered with soft, fine feathers or hair 2 soft and fluffy, like down

dowry (dou'rē) *n., pl.* **-ries** ⟦see DOWER⟧ the property that a woman brings to her husband at marriage

dowse (douz) *vi.* **dowsed, dows'ing** ⟦< ?⟧ to use a divining rod

dox·ol·o·gy (däks äl'ə jē) *n., pl.* **-gies** ⟦< Gr *doxa*, praise + *-logia*, -LOGY⟧ a hymn of praise to God

doz. dozen(s)

doze (dōz) *vi.* **dozed, doz'ing** ⟦prob. < Scand⟧ to sleep lightly; nap — *n.* a light sleep —**doz'er** *n.*

dozen (duz'ən) *n., pl.* **-ens** *or* **-en** ⟦< L *duo*, two + *decem*, ten⟧ a set of twelve —**doz'enth** *adj.*

DP 1 displaced person 2 *Baseball* double play

dpt. 1 department 2 deponent

Dr *or* **Dr.** 1 Doctor 2 Drive

drab (drab) *n.* ⟦< VL *drappus*, cloth⟧ a dull yellowish brown — *adj.* **drab'ber, drab'best** 1 dull yellowish-brown 2 dull; dreary —**drab'ness** *n.*

drachma (drak'mə) *n.* ⟦< Gr *drachmē*⟧ 1 an ancient Greek coin 2 the monetary unit of modern Greece

draft (draft) *n.* ⟦OE *dragan*, to draw⟧ 1 a drawing or pulling, as of a vehicle or load 2 *a)* a drawing in of a fish net *b)* the amount of fish caught in one draw 3 *a)* a drinking or the amount taken at one drink *b)* [Colloq.] a portion of beer, etc. drawn from a cask 4 an inhalation 5 a preliminary or tentative piece of writing 6 a plan or drawing of a work to be done 7 a current of air 8 a device for regulating the current of air in a heating system 9 a written order for payment of money; check 10 *a)* the choosing or taking of persons, esp. for compulsory military service *b)* those so taken 11 the depth of water that a ship needs in order to float — *vt.* 1 to take, as for military service, by drawing from a group 2 to make a sketch of or plans for — *adj.* 1 used for pulling loads 2 drawn from a cask *[draft beer]* —**draft'er** *n.*

draftee (draft ē') *n.* a person drafted, esp. for military service

drafts·man (drafts'mən) *n., pl.* **-men** 1 one who draws plans, as of machinery 2 an artist skillful in drawing — **drafts'man·ship'** *n.*

draft'y *adj.* **-i·er, -i·est** full of or exposed to drafts of air —**draft'i·ly** *adv.* —**draft'i·ness** *n.*

drag (drag) *vt., vi.* **dragged, drag'ging** ⟦see DRAW⟧ 1 to pull or be pulled with effort, esp. along the ground 2 to search (a lake bottom, etc.) with a dragnet or the like 3 to draw (something) out over a period of time; move or pass too slowly: often with *on* or *out* — *n.* 1 a dragging 2 a

---

THESAURUS

down[1] *a., prep.* forward, headlong, bottomward, downhill, on a downward course, from higher to lower, to the bottom, to a lower position, declining, falling, descending, gravitating, slipping, sliding, sagging, slumping, dropping, sinking, earthward, groundward, downward; see also BACKWARD 1.—*Ant.* UP, upward, rising. —**down and out** ruined, defeated, finished; see BEATEN. — **down on*** against, disillusioned about, furious with; see OPPOSED.

down[1] *v.* put down, throw down, knock down, throw, fell, subdue, tackle, trip, overthrow, overpower, upset, overturn; see also DEFEAT 3, HIT 1.—*Ant.* RAISE, lift, elevate.

down[2] *n.* feathers, fluff, fur; see HAIR 1.

downcast *a.* discouraged, dejected, unhappy; see SAD 1.

downfall *n.* drop, comedown, ruin; see DESTRUCTION 2.

downgrade *v.* minimize, deprecate, lower; see DECREASE 2.

downhearted *a.* dejected, despondent, downcast; see SAD 1.

downpour *n.* rain, deluge, flood, monsoon; see also STORM.

downright *a.* total, complete, utter;

see ABSOLUTE 1, WHOLE 1.

downstairs *a.* underneath, below decks, on the floor below; see BELOW 4, UNDER 1.

downstairs *n.* first floor, ground floor, cellar; see BASEMENT.

down-to-earth *a.* sensible, mundane, practicable; see COMMON 1, PRACTICAL, RATIONAL 1.

downtown *a.* city, central, inner-city, main, midtown, in the business district, on the main street, metropolitan, business, shopping; see also URBAN.—*Ant.* RURAL, suburban, residential.

downtown *n.* hub, crossroads, inner city; see CENTER 2, CITY.

downtrodden *a.* tyrannized, subjugated, overcome; see OPPRESSED.

downward *a.* earthward, descending, downwards; see DOWN.

downy *a.* woolly, fuzzy, fluffy; see LIGHT 5, SOFT 2.

doze *v.* nap, drowse, slumber; see SLEEP.

dozen *a.* twelve, baker's dozen, long dozen, handful, pocketful.

drab *a.* 1 [Dismal] dingy, colorless, dreary; see DULL 2, 4. 2 [Dun-colored] yellowish-brown, dull brown,

dull gray; see BROWN, GRAY.

draft *n.* 1 [A preliminary sketch] plans, blueprint, sketch; see DESIGN. 2 [A breeze] current of air, gust, puff; see WIND. 3 [An order for payment] cashier's check, bank draft, money order; see CHECK 1. 4 [The selection of troops] conscription, induction, recruiting; see SELECTION 1.

draft *v.* 1 [Make a rough plan] outline, delineate, sketch; see PLAN 1, 2. 2 [Select for military service] select, conscript, choose; see RECRUIT 1.

draftsman *n.* sketcher, designer, drawer; see ARCHITECT, ARTIST.

drag *n.* 1 [A restraint] hindrance, burden, impediment; see BARRIER. 2 [*An annoying person, thing, or situation] bother, annoyance, hang-up*; see NUISANCE 2.

drag *v.* 1 [To go slowly; *said of animate beings]* lag, straggle, dawdle; see LOITER, PAUSE. 2 [To go slowly; *said of an activity]* slow down, be delayed, fail to show progress, crawl*; see also DELAY.—*Ant.* IMPROVE, progress, pick up. 3 [To pull an object] haul, move, transport; see DRAW 1. —**drag on** go on slowly, keep going, persist; see CONTINUE 1, ENDURE 1.

dragnet, grapnel, etc. **3** anything that hinders **4** [Slang] influence **5** [Slang] clothing of the opposite sex, esp. as worn by a male homosexual **6** [Slang] a puff of a cigarette, etc. **7** [Slang] street /the main *drag*/ **8** [Slang] a dull person, situation, etc.

drag'gy (-ē) *adj.* **-gier, -gi·est** dragging; slow-moving, dull, etc.

drag'net' *n.* **1** a net dragged along a lake bottom, etc., as for catching fish **2** an organized system or network for catching criminals, etc.

dragon (drag'ən) *n.* 〚< Gr *drakōn* 〛 a mythical monster, usually shown as a large, winged reptile breathing out fire

drag'on·fly' *n., pl.* **-flies'** a large, long-bodied insect with transparent, net-veined wings

dra·goon (drə gōōn') *n.* 〚< Fr *dragon*, DRAGON 〛 a heavily armed cavalryman — *vt.* to force *into* doing something; coerce

drag race a race between cars accelerating from a standstill on a short, straight course (**drag strip**) —**drag'-race', -raced', -rac'ing,** *vi.*

drain (drān) *vt.* 〚OE *dryge*, dry〛 **1** to draw off (liquid) gradually **2** to draw liquid from gradually **3** to exhaust (strength, resources, etc.) gradually — *vi.* **1** to flow off or trickle through gradually **2** to become dry by draining — *n.* **1** a channel or pipe for draining **2** a draining — **drain'er** *n.*

drain'age (-ij) *n.* **1** a draining **2** a system of drains **3** that which is drained off **4** an area drained

drain'pipe' *n.* a large pipe used to carry off water, sewage, etc.

drake (drāk) *n.* 〚ME〛 a male duck

dram (dram) *n.* 〚< Gr *drachmē*, handful〛 **1** a unit of apothecaries' weight equal to 3.89 grams **2** a unit of avoirdupois weight equal to 1.77 grams **3** a small drink of alcoholic liquor

drama (drä'mə, dram'ə) *n.* 〚< Gr〛 **1** a literary composition to be performed by actors; play, esp. one that is not a comedy **2** the art of writing, acting, or producing plays **3** a series of events suggestive of those of a play **4** dramatic quality

Drama·mine (dram'ə mēn') *trademark for* a drug to relieve motion sickness — *n.* [**d-**] a tablet of this drug

dra·matic (drə mat'ik) *adj.* **1** of drama **2** like a play **3** vivid, striking, etc. —**dra·mat'i·cally** *adv.*

dra·mat·ics *n.pl.* **1** [*usually with sing. v.*] the performing or producing of plays **2** exaggerated emotionalism

drama·tist (dram'ə tist, drä'mə-) *n.* a playwright

dram'a·tize' (-tīz') *vt.* **-tized', -tiz'ing 1** to make into a drama **2** to regard or show in a dramatic manner — **dram'a·ti·za'tion** *n.*

drank (draŋk) *vt., vi. pt. of* DRINK

drape (drāp) *vt.* **draped, drap'ing** 〚< VL *drappus*, cloth〛 **1** to cover or hang as with cloth in loose folds **2** to arrange (a garment, etc.) in folds or hangings — *n.* cloth hanging in loose folds; esp., a heavy curtain: *usually used in pl.*

draper (drā'pər) *n.* [Brit.] a dealer in cloth and dry goods

drap'ery *n., pl.* **-er·ies 1** [Brit.] DRY GOODS **2** hangings or clothing arranged in loose folds **3** [*pl.*] curtains of heavy material

dras·tic (dras'tik) *adj.* 〚Gr *drastikos*, active〛 having a violent effect; severe; harsh —**dras'ti·cally** *adv.*

draught (draft) *n., vt., adj. now chiefly Brit. sp. of* DRAFT

draughts (drafts) *n.pl.* [Brit.] the game of checkers

draw (drô) *vt.* **drew, drawn, draw'ing** 〚OE *dragan* 〛 **1** to make move toward one; pull **2** to pull up, down, back, in, or out **3** to need (a specified depth of water) to float in: said of a ship **4** to attract **5** to breathe in **6** to elicit (a reply, etc.) **7** to bring on; provoke **8** to receive /to *draw* a salary/ **9** to withdraw (money) held in an account **10** to write (a check or draft) **11** to deduce **12** to take or get (cards, etc.) **13** to stretch **14** to make (lines, pictures, etc.), as with a pencil **15** to make (comparisons, etc.) — *vi.* **1** to draw something **2** to be drawn **3** to come; move **4** to shrink **5** to allow a draft of air, smoke, etc. to move through **6** to make a demand (*on*) — *n.* **1** a drawing or being drawn **2** the result of drawing **3** a thing drawn **4** a tie; stalemate **5** a thing that attracts —**draw out 1** to extend **2** to take out **3** to get (a person) to talk —**draw up 1** to arrange in order **2** to draft (a document) **3** to stop

draw'back' *n.* anything that prevents or lessens satisfaction; shortcoming

draw'bridge' *n.* a bridge that can be raised or drawn aside, as to permit passage of ships

drawer (drô'ər; *for 2* drôr) *n.* **1** a person or thing that draws **2** a sliding box in a table, chest, etc.

drawers (drôrz) *n.pl.* an undergarment for the lower part of the body

draw'ing *n.* **1** the act of one that draws; specif., the art of making pictures, etc., as with a pencil **2** a picture, etc. thus made **3** a lottery

drawing card an entertainer, show, etc. that draws a large audience

drawing room 〚< *withdrawing room*: guests withdrew there after dinner〛 a room where guests are received or entertained

drawl (drôl) *vt., vi.* 〚prob. < DRAW, *v.*〛 to speak slowly, prolonging the vowels — *n.* a manner of speaking thus

drawn (drôn) *vt., vi. pp. of* DRAW —*adj.* **1** disemboweled **2** tense; haggard

drawn butter melted butter

draw'string' *n.* a string drawn through a hem, as to tighten a garment

dray (drā) *n.* 〚OE *dragan*, to draw〛 a low cart for carrying heavy loads

dread (dred) *vt.* 〚OE *ondrædan*〛 to anticipate with fear or distaste — *n.* **1** intense fear **2** fear mixed with awe — *adj.* inspiring dread

dread'ful *adj.* **1** inspiring dread; awesome; terrible **2** [Colloq.] very bad, offensive, etc. —**dread'fully** *adv.*

■ THESAURUS ■

dragon *n.* mythical beast, serpent, hydra; see MONSTER 1, SNAKE.

drain *n.* duct, channel, sewer; see CHANNEL, PIPE 1. —**down the drain*** wasted, ruined, gone; see LOST 1.

drain *v.* **1** [To withdraw fluid] tap, draw off, remove; see EMPTY 2. **2** [To withdraw strength] exhaust, weary, tire out; see SPEND, WEAKEN 2. **3** [To seep away] run off, run out, flow away, seep out, exude, trickle out, filter off, ooze, find an opening, decline, diminish, leave dry; see also FLOW.

drama *n.* play, theatrical piece, theatrical production, dramatization, stage show, theatre. *Types of drama include the following:* melodrama, tragicomedy, comedy of manners, burlesque, pantomime, mime, grand opera, operetta, light opera, musical comedy, musical, mystery, murder mystery, farce, classical drama, historical drama, theatre of the absurd, epic, pageant, miracle play, revival; see also ACTING, COMEDY, PERFORMANCE.

dramatic *a.* tense, climactic, moving; see EXCITING.

dramatist *n.* playwright, script writer, scenario writer, scripter*; see also AUTHOR, WRITER. *Major dramatists include the following—Great Britain:* Christopher Marlowe, Ben Jonson, William Shakespeare, Oscar Wilde, George Bernard Shaw, Sean O'Casey, Harold Pinter; *United States:* Thornton Wilder, Eugene O'Neill, William Inge, Tennessee Williams, Arthur Miller, Edward Albee; *Greece:* Aeschylus, Sophocles, Euripides; *France:* Moliere, Pierre Corneille, Jean Racine, Jean Anouilh, Eugene Ionesco, Jean Genet, Jean Cocteau; *Germany:* Wolfgang von Goethe, Friedrich Schiller, Bertolt Brecht; *other:* Maxim Gorky, Anton Chekov, Henrik Ibsen, August Strindberg, Samuel Beckett, Karel Capek.

dramatize *v.* enact, produce, execute; see PERFORM 2.

drape *v.* clothe, wrap, model; see DRESS.

drapes *n.* window covering, drapery, hanging; see CURTAIN.

drastic *a.* extravagant, exorbitant, radical; see EXTREME.

draw *v.* **1** [To move an object] pull, drag, attract, move, bring, tug, lug, tow, carry, jerk, wrench, yank, haul, extract.—*Ant.* REPEL, repulse, reject. **2** [To make a likeness by drawing] sketch, describe, etch, pencil, outline, tract, make a picture of, depict, model, portray, engrave, chart, map; see also PAINT 1. —**beat to the draw*** be quicker than another, forestall, stop; see ANTICIPATE, PREVENT. —**draw away** pull away from, gain on, increase a lead; see ADVANCE 1, DEFEAT 1, LEAVE 1. —**draw back** withdraw, recede, draw in; see RETREAT. —**draw on** take from, extract from, employ; see USE 1. — **draw out 1** [To induce to talk] make talk, lead on, interrogate; see INTERVIEW. **2** [To pull] drag, tug, attract; see DRAW 1. —**draw up** draft, prepare, prepare; see WRITE 1.

drawback *n.* detriment, hindrance, check; see LACK 1.

drawing *n.* sketching, designing, illustrating, tracing, etching, design, illustration, commercial designing; see also PICTURE 3, REPRESENTATION.

dread *n.* awe, horror, terror; see FEAR.

dreadful *a.* hideous, fearful, shameful; see FRIGHTFUL 1.

dread′locks′ (-läks′) *n.pl.* hair worn in long, thin braids or uncombed, twisted locks

dread′nought′ or **dread′naught′** (-nôt′) *n.* a large, heavily armored battleship

dream (drēm) *n.* ⟦OE, joy, music⟧ **1** a sequence of images, etc. passing through a sleeping person's mind **2** a daydream; reverie **3** a fond hope **4** anything dreamlike — *vi., vt.* **dreamed** or **dreamt** (dremt), **dream′ing** to have a dream or remote idea (*of*) —**dream up** [Colloq.] to devise (a fanciful plan, etc.) —**dream′er** *n.* —**dream′less** *adj.* —**dream′like′** *adj.*

dream′land′ *n.* **1** any lovely but imaginary place **2** sleep

dream world 1 DREAMLAND **2** the realm of fantasy

dream′y *adj.* **-i·er, -i·est 1** filled with dreams **2** fond of daydreaming **3** like something in a dream **4** soothing **5** [Slang] wonderful —**dream′i·ly** *adv.*

dreary (drir′ē) *adj.* **-i·er, -i·est** ⟦OE *dreorig*, sad⟧ dismal: also [Old Poet.] **drear** —**drear′i·ly** *adv.* —**drear′i·ness** *n.*

dredge[1] (drej) *n.* ⟦prob. < MDu⟧ an apparatus for scooping up mud, etc., as in deepening channels — *vt., vi.* **dredged, dredg′ing 1** to search (*for*) or gather (*up*) as with a dredge **2** to enlarge or clean out with a dredge

dredge[2] (drej) *vt.* **dredged, dredg′ing** ⟦ME *dragge*, sweetmeat⟧ to coat (food) with flour or the like

dregs (dregz) *n.pl.* ⟦< ON *dregg*⟧ **1** particles settling at the bottom in a liquid **2** the most worthless part

drench (drench) *vt.* ⟦OE *drincan*, to drink⟧ to make wet all over; soak

dress (dres) *vt.* **dressed** or **drest, dress′ing** ⟦< L *dirigere*, lay straight⟧ **1** to put clothes on; clothe **2** to trim; adorn **3** to arrange (the hair) in a certain way **4** to align (troops) **5** to apply medicines and bandages to (a wound, etc.) **6** to prepare for use, esp. for cooking [*to dress a fowl*] **7** to smooth or finish (stone, wood, etc.) — *vi.* **1** to put on clothes **2** to dress formally **3** to line up in rank — *n.* **1** clothing **2** the usual outer garment of women, generally of one piece with a skirt — *adj.* **1** of or for dresses **2** for formal wear —**dress down** to scold — **dress up** to dress formally, elegantly, etc.

dres·sage (dre säzh′) *n.* ⟦Fr, training⟧ horsemanship using slight movements to control the horse

dress circle a semicircle of seats in a theater, etc., usually behind and above the orchestra seats

dress′er *n.* **1** one who dresses (in various senses) **2** a chest of drawers for clothes, usually with a mirror

dress′ing *n.* **1** the act of one that dresses **2** bandages, etc. applied to wounds **3** a sauce for salads, etc. **4** a stuffing for roast fowl, etc.

dress′ing-down′ *n.* a sound scolding

dressing gown a loose robe for one not fully clothed, as when lounging

dress′mak′er *n.* one who makes dresses, etc. —**dress′mak′ing** *n.*

dress rehearsal a final rehearsal, as of a play, with costumes, etc.

dress′y *adj.* **-i·er, -i·est 1** showy or elaborate in dress or appearance **2** elegant; smart —**dress′i·ness** *n.*

drew (drōō) *vt., vi. pt. of* DRAW

drib·ble (drib′əl) *vi., vt.* **-bled, -bling** ⟦< DRIP⟧ **1** to flow, or let flow, in drops **2** to drool **3** *Sports* to move (a ball or puck) along by repeated bouncing, kicking, or tapping — *n.* **1** a dribbling **2** a tiny amount: also **drib′let** (-lit) — **drib′bler** *n.*

dried (drīd) *vt., vi. pt. & pp. of* DRY

drier (drī′ər) *n.* **1** a substance added to paint, etc. to make it dry fast **2** DRYER — *adj. compar. of* DRY

dri′est (-ist) *adj. superl. of* DRY

drift (drift) *n.* ⟦OE *drifan*, to drive⟧ **1** *a*) a being carried along, as by a current *b*) the course of this **2** a trend; tendency **3** general meaning **4** a heap of snow, sand, etc. piled up by wind — *vi.* **1** to be carried along, as by a current **2** to go along aimlessly **3** to pile up in drifts — *vt.* to make drift —**drift′er** *n.*

drift′wood′ *n.* wood drifting in the water or washed ashore

drill[1] (dril) *n.* ⟦< Du *drillen*, to bore⟧ **1** a tool for boring holes **2** *a*) systematic military or physical training *b*) the method or practice of teaching by repeated exercises — *vt., vi.* **1** to bore with a drill (the tool) **2** to train in, or teach by means of, a drill —**drill′er** *n.*

drill[2] (dril) *n.* ⟦< ?⟧ a planting machine for making holes or furrows and dropping seeds into them

drill[3] (dril) *n.* ⟦< L *trilix*, three-threaded⟧ a coarse, twilled cotton cloth, used for uniforms, etc.

▰▰▰ THESAURUS ▰▰▰

dream *n.* nightmare, apparition, hallucination, image, trance, idea, impression, emotion, reverie, daydream, castle in the air, castle in Spain, chimera; see also FANTASY, ILLUSION, THOUGHT 2, VISION 3, 4.— *Ant.* REALITY, verity, truth.

dream *v.* **1** [To have visions, usually during sleep or fever] hallucinate, fancy, visualize; see IMAGINE. **2** [To entertain or delude oneself with imagined things] fancy, imagine, conceive, have notions, conjure up, create, picture, idealize, daydream, fantasize, be in the clouds, pipedream*; see also INVENT 1. —**dream up*** devise, contrive, concoct; see IMAGINE.

dreamer *n.* visionary, utopist, theorizer; see RADICAL.

dreaming *a.* thinking, daydreaming, in a reverie; see THOUGHTFUL 1.

dreamy *a.* whimsical, fanciful, daydreaming, visionary, given to reverie, illusory, introspective, otherworldly, idealistic, mythical, utopian, romantic; see also IMAGINARY, IMPRACTICAL.—*Ant.* PRACTICAL, ACTIVE, REAL.

dreary *a.* damp, raw, windy; see COLD 1, DISMAL.

dregs *n.* scum, grounds, remains; see RESIDUE.

drench *v.* wet, saturate, flood; see IMMERSE, SOAK 1.

dress *n.* **1** [Clothing] ensemble, attire, garments, outfit, garb, apparel, array, costume, wardrobe, uniform, habit, livery, formal dress, evening clothes, trappings, things, get-up*, threads*, rags*, duds*; see also CLOTHES, COAT 1, PANTS 1, SHIRT, SUIT 3, UNDERWEAR. **2** [A woman's outer garment] frock, gown, wedding dress, evening gown, formal, cocktail dress, suit, skirt, robe, shift, sundress, wraparound, housedress, smock; see also CLOTHES.

dress *v.* **1** [To put on clothes] don, wear, garb, clothe, robe, attire, drape, array, cover, spruce up, dress up, bundle up, get into*, doll up*, put on the dog*, dress to the nines*; see also WEAR 1. **2** [To provide with clothes] costume, outfit, clothe; see SUPPORT 3. **3** [To give medical treatment] treat, bandage, give first aid; see HEAL. —**dressed up** dressed formally, in full dress, dolled up*; see FANCY, FASHIONABLE, ORNATE. — **dress up** primp, deck out, put on the dog*; see DRESS 1.

dresser *n.* dressing table, chest of drawers, bureau; see FURNITURE, TABLE 1.

dressing *n.* **1** [A food mixture] stuffing, filling, forcemeat. *Dressings include the following:* bread, giblet, oyster, chestnut, potato, prune, plum, apple, duck, turkey, chicken, fish, clam, wild rice. **2** [A flavoring sauce] *Salad dressings include the following:* ranch, French, Russian, Thousand Island, blue cheese, Roquefort, Italian, Caesar, oil and vinegar; see also SAUCE. **3** [An external medical application] bandage, plaster cast, adhesive tape, Band-Aid (trademark), compress, gauze, tourniquet, pack; see also CAST 4.

dressmaker *n.* seamstress, designer, dress fitter; see TAILOR.

dressy *a.* dressed up, elegant, elaborate; see FANCY, FASHIONABLE, ORNATE.

dribble *v.* trickle, spout, squirt; see DROP 1.

dried *a.* drained, dehydrated, desiccated; see DRY 1, PRESERVED 2.

drift *n.* **1** [The tendency in movement] bent, trend, tendency, end, inclination, impulse, propulsion, aim, scope, goal, push, bias, set, leaning, progress, disposition, bearing, line, set; see also DIRECTION 1, WAY 2.— *Ant.* INDIFFERENCE, aimlessness, inertia. **2** [The measure or character of movement] current, diversion, sweep; see FLOW.

drift *v.* float, ride, sail, wander, sweep, move with the current, gravitate, tend, be carried along by the current, move toward, go with the tide, be caught in the current, move without effort, move slowly; see also FLOW, MOVE 1.—*Ant.* LEAD, steer, pull.

drill[1] *v.* **1** [To bore] pierce, sink in, puncture; see DIG 1, PENETRATE. **2** [To train] practice, rehearse, discipline; see TEACH.

drill[1,2] *n.* **1** [Practice] preparation, repetition, learning by doing; see PRACTICE 3. **2** [A tool for boring holes] borer, wood bit, steel drill, steam drill, diamond drill, compressed-air drill, boring tool, tapborer, auger, corkscrew, awl, riveter, jackhammer; see also TOOL 1. **3** [Exercise, especially in military formation] training, maneuvers, marching, close-order drill, open-order drill, conditioning, survival training, guerrilla training; see also PARADE 1. **4** [Device for planting seed in holes] planter, seeder, implement; see TOOL 1.

drill′mas′ter *n.* **1** an instructor in military drill **2** one who teaches by drilling

drill press a power-driven machine for drilling holes in metal, etc.

drily (drī′lē) *adv.* DRYLY

drink (driŋk) *vt.* **drank, drunk, drink′ing** ⟦OE *drincan*⟧ **1** to swallow (liquid) **2** to absorb (liquid) **3** to swallow the contents of —*vi.* **1** to swallow liquid **2** to drink alcoholic liquor, esp. to excess —*n.* **1** any liquid for drinking **2** alcoholic liquor —**drink in** to take in eagerly with the senses or mind —**drink to** to drink a toast to —**drink′able** —**drink′er** *n.*

drip (drip) *vi., vt.* **dripped** or **dript, drip′ping** ⟦OE *dryppan*⟧ to fall, or let fall, in drops —*n.* **1** a dripping **2** [Slang] an insipid person —**drip′per** *n.*

drip′-dry′ *adj.* designating garments that dry quickly when hung wet and require little or no ironing

drip′pings *n.* the juices that drip from roasting meat

drive (drīv) *vt.* **drove, driven** (driv′ən), **driv′ing** ⟦OE *drifan*⟧ **1** to force to go **2** to force into or from a state or act **3** to force to work, esp. to excess **4** to hit (a ball, etc.) hard **5** to make penetrate **6** *a*) to control the movement of; operate (a car, bus, etc.) *b*) to transport in a car, etc. **7** to push (a bargain, etc.) through —*vi.* **1** to advance violently **2** to try hard, as to reach a goal **3** to drive a blow, ball, etc. **4** to be driven: said of a car, bus, etc. **5** to operate, or go in, a car, etc. —*n.* **1** a driving **2** a trip in a car, etc. **3** *a*) a road for cars, etc. *b*) a driveway **4** a rounding up of animals **5** a campaign **6** energy and initiative **7** a strong impulse or urge **8** the propelling mechanism of a machine, etc. —**drive at** to mean; intend —**drive in 1** to force in, as by a blow **2** *Baseball* to cause (a runner) to score or (a run) to be scored

drive′-in′ *n.* a restaurant, movie theater, bank, etc. designed to serve people seated in their cars

drivel (driv′əl) *vi., vt.* **-eled** or **-elled, -el·ing** or **-el·ling** ⟦OE *dreflian*⟧ **1** to let (saliva) drool **2** to speak or say in a silly, stupid way —*n.* silly, stupid talk —**driv′eler** or **driv′el·ler** *n.*

driv′er *n.* a person or thing that drives, as *a*) one who drives a car, etc. *b*) one who herds cattle *c*) a golf club for hitting the ball from the tee

drive shaft a shaft that transmits motion, as to the rear axle of a car

drive′train′ *n.* the system that transmits an engine's power to wheels, propeller, etc.

drive′way′ *n.* a path for cars, from a street to a garage, house, etc.

driz·zle (driz′əl) *vi., vt.* **-zled, -zling** ⟦prob. < ME⟧ to rain in fine, misty drops —*n.* a fine, misty rain —**driz′zly** *adj.*

drogue (drōg) *n.* ⟦prob. < Scot *drug*, drag⟧ a funnel-shaped device towed behind an aircraft or spacecraft, as for its drag effect, or as a target, etc.

droll (drōl) *adj.* ⟦< Fr < MDu *drol*, stout fellow⟧ amusing in an odd way —**droll′ery** (-ər ē), *pl.* **-ies,** *n.* —**droll′ness** *n.* —**drol′ly** *adv.*

drom·edary (dräm′ə der′ē) *n., pl.* **-ies** ⟦< LL *dromedarius* (*camelus*), running (camel)⟧ the one-humped camel

drone¹ (drōn) *n.* ⟦OE *dran*⟧ **1** a male bee that does no work **2** an idler; loafer

drone² (drōn) *vi.* **droned, dron′ing** ⟦< prec.⟧ **1** to make a continuous humming sound **2** to talk in a monotonous way —*vt.* to utter in a monotonous tone —*n.* a droning sound

drool (drool) *vi.* ⟦< DRIVEL⟧ **1** to let saliva flow from one's mouth **2** to flow from the mouth, as saliva

droop (droop) *vi.* ⟦< ON *drūpa*⟧ **1** to sink, hang, or bend down **2** to lose vitality **3** to become dejected —*vt.* to let sink or hang down —*n.* a drooping —**droop′y, -i·er, -i·est,** *adj.* —**droop′i·ness** *n.*

drop (dräp) *n.* ⟦OE *dropa*⟧ **1** a bit of liquid rounded in shape by falling, etc. **2** anything like this in shape, etc. **3** a very small quantity **4** a sudden fall, descent, slump, etc. **5** something that drops, as a curtain or trapdoor **6** the distance between a higher and lower level —*vi.* **dropped, drop′ping 1** to fall in drops **2** to fall **3** to fall exhausted, wounded, or dead **4** to pass into a specified state [to *drop* off to sleep] **5** to come to an end [let the matter *drop*] —*vt.* **1** to let or make fall **2** to utter (a hint, etc.) casually **3** to send (a letter) **4** to stop, end, or dismiss **5** to lower **6** [Colloq.] to leave at a specified place —**drop in** (or **over** or **by**) to pay a casual visit —**drop out** to stop participating —**drop′let** *n.*

drop kick *Football* a kick of a dropped ball just as it hits the ground —**drop′-kick′** *vt., vi.* —**drop′-kick′er** *n.*

THESAURUS

drink *n.* **1** [A draft] gulp, sip, potion, drop, bottle, glass, refreshment, tall drink, shot*, stiff one*, slug*, belt*, nip*, swig*, spot*, short one*, nightcap*, hair of the dog*, one for the road*. **2** [Something drunk] rye, bourbon, Scotch, Irish whiskey, ale, stout, rum, liqueur, tequila, vodka, distilled water, mineral water, carbonated water, mixer, tonic, seltzer, cocoa, hot chocolate, chocolate milk, milkshake, frappé, lemonade, punch, soft drink, soda water, ginger ale, ice-cream soda; orange juice, tomato juice, grapefruit juice, etc.; pop, soda, soda pop; see also BEER, COFFEE, MILK, WATER 1, WHISKEY, WINE.

drink *v.* **1** [To swallow liquid] gulp down, take in, sip, suck in, guzzle, imbibe, wash down, gargle; see also SWALLOW. **2** [To consume alcoholic liquor] tipple, swill, swig, guzzle, belt*, take a drop*, take a nip, wet one's whistle*, down*, booze*, hit the bottle*, go on a binge*.

drinker *n.* tippler, alcoholic, lush*; see DRUNKARD.

drip *v.* dribble, trickle, plop; see DROP 1.

drive *n.* **1** [A ride in a vehicle] ride, trip, outing, airing, tour, excursion, jaunt, spin, Sunday drive*; see also JOURNEY. **2** [A road] approach, avenue, boulevard, entrance, street, roadway, parkway, lane, track, path, pavement; see also ROAD 1. **3** [Impelling force] energy, effort, impulse; see FORCE 2.

drive *v.* **1** [To urge on] impel, propel, instigate, incite, animate, hasten, egg on, urge on, compel, coerce, induce, force, press, stimulate, hurry, provoke, arouse, make, put up to, inspire, prompt, rouse, work on, act upon; see also sense 2 and ENCOURAGE, PUSH 2.—*Ant.* STOP, hinder, drag. **2** [To manage a propelled vehicle] direct, manage, handle, run, wheel, bicycle, bike*, cycle, transport, float, drift, dash, put in motion, start, set going, speed, roll, coast, get under way, keep going, back up, burn up the road*, go like hell*, step on it*, floor it*, gun it*, burn rubber*, give it the gas*; see also RIDE 1.—*Ant.* WALK, crawl, stay. —**drive a bargain** deal, close a deal, bargain; see BUY, SELL. —**drive at** allude to, indicate, signify; see MEAN 1. —**drive away** drive off, disperse, banish; see SCATTER 2.

driven *a.* blown, drifted, herded, pushed, pounded, washed, guided, steered, directed, urged on, forced, shoved, sent, hard pressed, impelled, unable to help oneself, with one's back to the wall.

driver *n.* chauffeur, motorist, licensed operator, bus driver, truck driver, cab driver, person in the driver's seat, cabbie*, hack*.

driveway *n.* drive, entrance, approach; see DRIVE 2, ROAD 1.

drizzle *v.* spray, shower, sprinkle; see DROP 1, RAIN.

drone¹,² *n.* **1** [A continuous sound] hum, buzz, vibration; see NOISE 1. **2** [An idle person] idler, loafer, parasite; see LOAFER.

drone² *v.* hum, buzz, vibrate; see SOUND.

drool *v.* drivel, drip, salivate, spit, dribble, trickle, ooze, run; see also DROP 1.

droop *v.* settle, sink, hang down; see LEAN 1.

drop *n.* **1** [Enough fluid to fall] drip, trickle, droplet, bead, teardrop, dewdrop, raindrop; see also TEAR. **2** [A lowering or falling] fall, tumble, reduction, decrease, slide, descent, slump, lapse, slip, decline, downfall, upset; see also FALL 1. **3** [A small quantity] speck, dash, dab; see BIT 1. —**at the drop of a hat*** without warning, at the slightest provocation, quickly; see IMMEDIATELY.

drop *v.* **1** [To fall in drops] drip, fall, dribble, trickle, descend, leak, ooze, seep, drain, filter, sink, bleed, bead, splash, hail; see also RAIN.—*Ant.* RISE, spurt, squirt. **2** [To cause or to permit to fall] let go, give up, release, shed, relinquish, abandon, loosen, lower, floor, ground, shoot, knock down, fell, topple; see also DUMP.—*Ant.* RAISE, elevate, send up. **3** [To discontinue] give up, quit, leave; see STOP 2. **4** [To break off an acquaintance] break with, part from, cast off; see ABANDON 1. —**drop a hint** suggest, intimate, imply; see HINT, PROPOSE 1. —**drop a line** write to, post, communicate with; see COMMUNICATE, WRITE 1. —**drop behind** slow down, worsen, decline; see FAIL 1, LOSE 3. —**drop dead*** expire, collapse, succumb; see DIE. —**drop in** call, stop, look in on; see VISIT. —**drop off 1** [*To sleep] fall asleep, doze, drowse; see SLEEP. **2** [*To deliver] leave, hand over, present; see GIVE 1. —**drop out** withdraw, cease, quit; see ABANDON 1, RETREAT.

drop′-off′ *n.* **1** a very steep drop **2** a decline, as in sales, prices, etc.

drop′out′ *n.* one who withdraws from school before graduating

drop′per *n.* a small tube with a hollow rubber bulb at one end, used to measure out a liquid in drops

drop·sy (dräp′sē) *n.* [< Gr *hydrōps* < *hydōr*, water] *old term for* EDEMA —**drop′si·cal** (-si kəl) *adj.*

dross (drôs) *n.* [OE *dros*] **1** scum on molten metal **2** refuse; rubbish

drought (drout) *n.* [< OE *drugoth*, dryness] prolonged dry weather

drove[1] (drōv) *n.* [OE *draf*] **1** a number of cattle, sheep, etc. driven or moving along as a group; flock; herd **2** a moving crowd of people: *usually used in pl.*

drove[2] (drōv) *vt., vi. pt. of* DRIVE

dro·ver (drō′vər) *n.* one who herds droves of animals, esp. to market

drown (droun) *vi.* [ME *drounen*] to die by suffocation in water — *vt.* **1** to kill by such suffocation **2** to flood **3** to be so loud as to overcome (another sound): usually with *out*

drowse (drouz) *vi.* drowsed, drows′ing [< OE *drusian*, become sluggish] to be half asleep; doze — *n.* a doze

drow·sy (drou′zē) *adj.* -i·er, -i·est being or making sleepy or half asleep —**drows′i·ly** *adv.* —**drows′i·ness** *n.*

drub (drub) *vt.* drubbed, drub′bing [< Ar *daraba*, to cudgel] **1** to beat as with a stick **2** to defeat soundly — **drub′ber** *n.* —**drub′bing** *n.*

drudge (druj) *n.* [ME *druggen*] one who does hard, menial, or tedious work — *vi.* drudged, drudg′ing to do such work —**drudg′ery,** *pl.* -ies, *n.*

drug (drug) *n.* [< OFr *drogue*] **1** any substance used as or in a medicine **2** a narcotic, hallucinogen, etc. — *vt.* drugged, drug′ging **1** to put a harmful drug in (a drink, etc.) **2** to stupefy as with a drug —**drug on the market** a thing in plentiful supply for which there is little or no demand

drug′gie (-ē) *n.* [Slang] a habitual user of drugs Also **drug′gy,** *pl.* -gies

drug′gist (-ist) *n.* **1** a dealer in drugs, medical supplies, etc. **2** a pharmacist **3** a drugstore owner or manager

drug′store′ *n.* a store where drugs, medical supplies, and various items are sold and prescriptions are filled

druid (drōō′id) *n.* [< Celt] [*often* D-] a member of a Celtic religious order in ancient Britain, Ireland, and France —**dru′id·ism′** *n.*

drum (drum) *n.* [< Du *trom*] **1** a percussion instrument consisting of a hollow cylinder with a membrane stretched over the end or ends **2** the sound produced by beating a drum **3** any drumlike cylindrical object **4** the eardrum — *vi.* drummed, drum′ming **1** to beat a drum **2** to tap

continually — *vt.* **1** to play (a rhythm, etc.) as on a drum **2** to instill (ideas, facts, etc. *into*) by continued repetition —**drum out of** to expel from in disgrace —**drum up** to get (business, etc.) by soliciting

drum·lin (drum′lin) *n.* [< Ir] a long ridge formed of gravel, etc. deposited by a glacier

drum major one who leads a marching band, keeping time with a baton —**drum ma′jor·ette′** (-et′) *fem.*

drum′mer *n.* **1** a drum player **2** [Colloq.] a traveling salesman

drum′stick′ *n.* **1** a stick for beating a drum **2** the lower half of the leg of a cooked fowl

drunk (druŋk) *vt., vi. pp. of* DRINK — *adj.* **1** overcome by alcoholic liquor; intoxicated **2** [Colloq.] DRUNKEN (sense 2) Usually used in the predicate — *n.* **1** [Colloq.] a drunken person **2** [Slang] a drinking spree

drunk′ard (-ərd) *n.* a person who often gets drunk

drunk′en (-ən) *adj.* **1** intoxicated **2** caused by or occurring during intoxication Used before a noun —**drunk′enly** *adv.* —**drunk′en·ness** *n.*

drupe (drōōp) *n.* [< Gr *druppa* (*elaa*), olive] any fleshy fruit with an inner stone, as a peach

dry (drī) *adj.* dri′er, dri′est [OE *dryge*] **1** not under water *[dry land]* **2** not wet or damp **3** lacking rain or water; arid **4** thirsty **5** not yielding milk **6** solid; not liquid **7** not sweet *[dry wine]* **8** prohibiting alcoholic beverages *[a dry town]* **9** funny in a quiet but sharp way *[dry wit]* **10** unproductive **11** boring; dull — *n., pl.* drys [Colloq.] a prohibitionist — *vt., vi.* dried, dry′ing to make or become dry —**dry up 1** to make or become thoroughly dry **2** to make or become unproductive **3** [Slang] to stop talking —**dry′ly** *adv.* —**dry′ness** *n.*

dry·ad (drī′ad′) *n.* [< Gr *drys*, tree] [*also* D-] *Gr. & Rom. Myth.* a tree nymph

dry cell a voltaic cell containing a dry electrolyte which cannot spill

dry′-clean′ *vt.* to clean (garments, etc.) with a solvent other than water, as naphtha —**dry cleaner** —**dry cleaning**

dry dock a dock from which the water can be emptied, used for building and repairing ships

dry′er *n.* **1** a person or thing that dries; specif., an appliance for drying clothes with heat **2** DRIER

dry farming farming without irrigation, by conserving the soil's moisture

dry goods cloth, cloth products, etc.

dry ice carbon dioxide solidified for use as a refrigerant

dry rot a fungous decay causing seasoned timber to crumble to powder

dry run [Colloq.] a simulated or practice performance; rehearsal

dry′wall′ *n.* PLASTERBOARD

DST daylight saving time

Du. Dutch

THESAURUS

dropout *n.* failing student, truant, quitter; see FAILURE 1.

drought *n.* dry season, dehydration, dry spell; see WEATHER.

drove[1] *n.* flock, pack, rout; see CROWD, HERD.

drown *v.* **1** [To cover with liquid] swamp, inundate, overflow; see FLOOD. **2** [To lower into a liquid] dip, plunge, submerge; see IMMERSE, SINK 2. **3** [To kill or die by drowning] go down three times, suffocate, asphyxiate; see DIE, KILL 1. — **drown out** silence, hush, muffle; see QUIET 2.

drowned *a.* suffocated, sunk, foundered; see DEAD 1, GONE 2.

drowsy *a.* sleepy, languid, indolent; see LAZY 1.

drudge *n.* slave, menial, hard worker; see LABORER, WORKMAN.

drug *n.* sedative, potion, essence, smelling salts, powder, tonic, opiate, pills, uppers*, downers*. *Kinds of drugs include the following—general:* caffeine, alcohol, adrenalin, amphetamine, nicotine, dope*; *hallucinogens:* marijuana, pot*, grass*, weed*; peyote, mescaline, psilocybin; D-lysergic acid diethylamide, LSD, acid*; *stimulants:* cocaine, coke*, snow*, crack*; benzedrine, bennies*,

pep pills*; dexedrine, dexies*; methedrine, meth*, speed*; amyl nitrate, poppers*; *narcotics:* opium; morphine; heroin, H*, horse*, junk*, smack*; codeine; see also MEDICINE 2.

drug *v.* anesthetize, desensitize, dope*; see DEADEN.

drugged *a.* comatose, doped, stupefied; see UNCONSCIOUS.

druggist *n.* apothecary, chemist, registered pharmacist, licensed pharmacist, manufacturing pharmacist, proprietor, drugstore owner, merchant; see also DOCTOR.

drum *n.* snare drum, skins*, traps*; see MUSICAL INSTRUMENT.

drum up *v.* attract, provide, succeed in finding; see DISCOVER, FIND.

drunk *a.* intoxicated, inebriated, befuddled, tipsy, overcome, sottish, drunken, stoned*, feeling no pain*, out of it*, seeing double*, smashed*, blotto*, gassed*, plowed*, under the table*, tanked*, wiped out*, soused*, high*, pickled*, stewed*, boozed up*, tight*, higher than a kite*; see also DIZZY.—*Ant.* SOBER, steady, temperate.

drunkard *n.* sot, inebriate, heavy drinker, tippler, alcoholic, drunken sot, drunk*, sponge*, boozer*, barfly*, pub-crawler*, wino*, lush*,

alky*; see also ADDICT.

drunkenness *n.* inebriety, intoxication, intemperance, insobriety, alcoholism, jag*.—*Ant.* ABSTINENCE, sobriety, temperance.

dry *a.* **1** [Having little or no moisture] arid, parched, waterless, hard, dried up, evaporated, desiccated, barren, dehydrated, drained, rainless, not irrigated, bare, thirsty, waterproof, rainproof, baked, shriveled, desert, dusty, depleted, dry as a bone*; see also STERILE 2.—*Ant.* WET, moist, damp. **2** [Thirsty] parched, dehydrated, athirst; see THIRSTY. **3** [Lacking in interest] boring, uninteresting, tedious; see DULL 4. **4** [Possessed of intellectual humor] sarcastic, cynical, biting; see FUNNY 1.

dry *v.* **1** [To become dry] dry up, shrivel, wilt; see EVAPORATE, WITHER. **2** [To cause to become dry] air-dry, condense, concentrate, dehydrate, freeze-dry, blot, sponge, parch, scorch, dry up, exhaust; see also DRAIN 1, EMPTY 2. —**dry out** (or **up**) drain, dehydrate, undergo evaporation; see DRY 1, 2.

dry goods *n.* cloth, yard goods, yardage; see COTTON, LINEN, WOOL.

dryness *n.* aridity, lack of moisture, drought; see THIRST.

dual (dōō′əl) *adj.* 〖< L *duo,* two〗 **1** of two **2** double; two-fold —**du′al·ism′** *n.* —**du·al′i·ty** (-al′ə tē) *n.*

dub[1] (dub) *vt.* **dubbed, dub′bing** 〖< OE *dubbian,* to strike〗 **1** *a)* to confer a title or rank upon *b)* to name or nickname **2** to smooth by hammering, scraping, etc. **3** [Slang] to bungle (a golf stroke, etc.) —**dub′ber** *n.*

dub[2] (dub) *vt.* **dubbed, dub′bing** 〖< DOUBLE〗 to provide with a soundtrack, esp. one with dialogue in another language —**dub in** to insert (dialogue, music, etc.) in the soundtrack —**dub′ber** *n.*

dub·bin (dub′in) *n.* 〖< DUB[1]〗 a greasy preparation for waterproofing leather

du·bi·e·ty (dōō bī′ə tē) *n.* **1** a being dubious **2** *pl.* **-ties** a doubtful thing

du·bi·ous (dōō′bē əs) *adj.* 〖< L *dubius,* uncertain〗 **1** causing doubt **2** feeling doubt; skeptical **3** questionable —**du′bi·ous·ly** *adv.*

du·cal (dōō′kəl) *adj.* 〖< LL *ducalis,* of a leader〗 of a duke or dukedom

duc·at (duk′ət) *n.* 〖see DUCHY〗 any of several former European coins

duch·ess (duch′is) *n.* **1** a duke's wife or widow **2** a woman ruling a duchy

duch·y (-ē) *n., pl.* **-ies** 〖< L *dux,* leader〗 the territory ruled by a duke or duchess

duck[1] (duk) *n.* 〖< OE *duce,* diver〗 **1** a small waterfowl with a flat bill, a short neck, and webbed feet **2** the flesh of a duck as food

duck[2] (duk) *vt., vi.* 〖ME *douken*〗 **1** to plunge or dip under water for a moment **2** to lower or bend (the head, body, etc.) suddenly, as to avoid a blow **3** [Colloq.] to avoid (a task, person, etc.) —*n.* a ducking

duck[3] (duk) *n.* 〖Du *doek*〗 a cotton or linen cloth like canvas but finer and lighter in weight

duck′bill′ *n.* PLATYPUS

duck′ling *n.* a young duck

duck′pins′ *n.pl.* [*with sing. v.*] a game like bowling, played with smaller pins and balls

duck′y *adj.* **-i·er, -i·est** [Slang] pleasing, delightful, etc.

duct (dukt) *n.* 〖< L *ducere,* to lead〗 a tube, channel, or pipe, as for passage of a liquid —**duct′less** *adj.*

duc·tile (duk′til) *adj.* 〖see prec.〗 **1** that can be drawn or hammered thin without breaking: said of metals **2** easily led —**duc·til′i·ty** (-til′ə tē) *n.*

ductless gland an endocrine gland

dud (dud) *n.* 〖prob. < Du *dood,* dead〗 [Colloq.] **1** a bomb or shell that fails to explode **2** a failure

dude (dōōd) *n.* 〖< ?〗 **1** a dandy; fop **2** [Slang] any man or boy —*vt., vi.* **dud′ed, dud′ing** [Slang] to dress up, esp. in showy clothes: usually with *up*

dude ranch a vacation resort on a ranch

dudg·eon (duj′ən) *n.* 〖prob. < Anglo-Fr *en digeon,* at the dagger hilt〗 anger or resentment: now chiefly in **in high dudgeon,** very angry or resentful

duds (dudz) *n.pl.* 〖ME *dudde,* cloth, cloak < ?〗 [Colloq.] **1** clothes **2** belongings

due (dōō, dyōō) *adj.* 〖< L *debere,* owe〗 **1** owed or owing as a debt; payable **2** suitable; proper **3** enough [*due care*] **4** expected or scheduled to arrive —*adv.* exactly; directly [*due west*] —*n.* **1** deserved recognition **2** [*pl.*] fees or other charges [union *dues*] —**due to 1** caused by **2** [Colloq.] because of —**pay one's dues** [Slang] to earn a right, etc., as by having suffered in struggle

due bill a receipt for money paid, exchangeable for goods or services only

duel (dōō′əl) *n.* 〖< medieval L *duellum*〗 **1** a prearranged fight between two persons armed with deadly weapons **2** any contest like this —*vi.,* *vt.* **-eled** or **-elled, -el·ing** or **-el·ling** to fight a duel with —**du′el·ist** or **du′el·list, du′el·er** or **du′el·ler** *n.*

du·en·na (dōō en′ə) *n.* 〖< Sp < L *domina,* mistress〗 a chaperon or governess

due process (of law) legal proceedings established to protect individual rights and liberties

du·et (dōō et′) *n.* 〖< L *duo,* two〗 **1** a composition for two voices or instruments **2** the two performers of this

duf·fel (or **duf·fle**) **bag** (duf′əl) 〖after *Duffel,* town in Belgium〗 a large cloth bag for carrying clothing, etc.

duf·fer (duf′ər) *n.* 〖< thieves' slang *duff,* to fake〗 [Colloq.] **1** a slow-witted or dawdling elderly person **2** a relatively unskilled golfer

dug (dug) *vt., vi. pt. & pp. of* DIG

dug′out′ *n.* **1** a boat hollowed out of a log **2** a shelter, as in warfare, dug in the ground **3** *Baseball* a covered shelter for the players

DUI *n.* a citation for driving while under the influence of alcohol, drugs, etc.

du jour (dōō zhōōr′) offered on this day [soup *du jour*]

duke (dōōk) *n.* 〖< L *dux,* leader〗 **1** a prince ruling an independent duchy **2** a nobleman next in rank to a prince —**duke′dom** *n.*

dul·cet (dul′sit) *adj.* 〖< L *dulcis,* sweet〗 soothing or pleasant to hear

dul·ci·mer (dul′sə mər) *n.* 〖< L *dulce,* sweet + *melos,* song〗 a musical instrument with metal strings, which are struck with two small hammers or plucked with a plectrum or quill

dull (dul) *adj.* 〖OE *dol*〗 **1** mentally slow; stupid **2** physically slow; sluggish **3** boring; tedious **4** not sharp; blunt **5** not feeling or felt keenly **6** not vivid or bright [a *dull* color] —*vt., vi.* to make or become dull —**dull′ness** *n.* —**dul′ly** *adv.*

dull′ard (-ərd) *n.* a stupid person

du·ly (dōō′lē) *adv.* in due manner; in the proper way, at the right time, etc.

dumb (dum) *adj.* 〖OE〗 **1** lacking the power of speech; mute **2** silent **3** 〖Ger *dumm*〗 [Colloq.] stupid —**dumb′ly** *adv.* —**dumb′ness** *n.*

THESAURUS

dual *a.* binary, twofold, coupled; see DOUBLE, TWIN.

dubious *a.* **1** [Doubtful] indecisive, perplexed, hesitant; see DOUBTFUL, UNCERTAIN. **2** [Vague] ambiguous, indefinite, unclear; see OBSCURE 1.

dubiously *a.* doubtfully, doubtingly, indecisively; see SUSPICIOUSLY.

duck[1] *n.* teal, mallard, fresh water duck, sea duck; see also BIRD. —**like water off a duck's back*** ineffective, ineffectual, weak; see USELESS 1.

duck[2] *v.* **1** [To immerse quickly] plunge, submerge, drop; see DIP 1, IMMERSE. **2** [*To avoid] dodge, escape, elude; see AVOID, EVADE.

duct *n.* tube, canal, channel; see PIPE 1.

dud* *n.* failure, flop, debacle; see FAILURE 1.

duds* *n.* garb, garments, gear; see CLOTHES.

due *a.* payable, owed, owing, overdue, collectible, unsatisfied, unsettled, not met, receivable, to be paid, chargeable, outstanding, in arrears; see also UNPAID 1, 2. —**become (or fall) due** be owed, payable, remain unsatisfied, mature. —**due to** because of, resulting from, accordingly; see BECAUSE.

duel *n.* combat, engagement, contest;

see FIGHT 1.

dues *n.* contribution, obligation, toll, duty, levy, collection, fee, annual assessment, tax, rates; see also PAY 1, TAX 1.

dull *a.* **1** [Without point or edge] blunt, blunted, unsharpened, pointless, unpointed, round, square, flat, nicked, broken, toothless.—*Ant.* SHARP, sharpened, keen. **2** [Lacking brightness or color] gloomy, sober, somber, drab, dismal, dark, dingy, dim, dusky, colorless, plain, obscure, tarnished, opaque, leaden, grave, grimy, pitchy, sooty, inky, dead, black, coal-black, unlighted, sordid, dirty, muddy, gray, lifeless, rusty, flat.—*Ant.* BRIGHT, colorful, gleaming. **3** [Lacking intelligence: *said usually of living beings*] slow, retarded, witless; see STUPID. **4** [Lacking interest: *said usually of writing, speaking, or inanimate things*] heavy, prosaic, trite, hackneyed, monotonous, humdrum, tedious, dreary, dismal, dry, arid, colorless, insipid, boring, vapid, flat, senseless, long-winded, stupid, commonplace, ordinary, common, usual, old, ancient, stale, moth-eaten, out-of-date, archaic, worn-out, tiring,

banal, tired, uninteresting, driveling, pointless, uninspiring, piddling, senile, proverbial, tame, routine, familiar, known, well-known, conventional, depressing, sluggish, repetitious, repetitive, soporific, tiresome, lifeless, wearying, unexciting, flat, stereotyped, stock, the usual thing, the same old thing, the same thing day after day, slow, dry as a bone*, cut and dried, dead as a doornail*.—*Ant.* EXCITING, fascinating, exhilarating. **5** [Not loud or distinct] low, soft, softened; see FAINT 3. **6** [Showing little activity] still, routine, regular; see SLOW 1. **7** [Gloomy] cloudy, dim, unlit; see DARK 1.

dullness *n.* **1** [Quality of being boring] flatness, sameness, routine, evenness, aridity, depression, dimness, commonplaceness, mediocrity, tedium, tameness, familiarity; see also BOREDOM, MONOTONY.—*Ant.* ACTION, liveliness, interest. **2** [Stupidity] stupidness, insensibility, slow-wittedness; see STUPIDITY 1.

duly *a.* rightfully, properly, decorously; see JUSTLY 1.

dumb *a.* **1** [Unable to speak] silent, inarticulate, deaf and dumb, voice-

dumb·bell (dum′bel′) *n.* **1** a device consisting of round weights joined by a short bar, used for muscular exercise **2** [Slang] a stupid person

dumb·found or **dum·found** (dum′found′) *vt.* ⟦DUMB + (CON)FOUND⟧ to make speechless by shocking; amaze

dumb′wait′er *n.* a small elevator for sending food, etc. between floors

dum·dum (bullet) (dum′dum′) ⟦after *Dumdum*, arsenal in India⟧ a soft-nosed bullet that expands when it hits

dummy (dum′ē) *n., pl.* **-mies 1** a figure made in human form, as for displaying clothing **2** an imitation; sham **3** [Slang] a stupid person **4** *Bridge* the declarer's partner, whose hand is exposed on the table and played by the declarer — *adj.* sham

dump (dump) *vt.* ⟦prob. < ON⟧ **1** to unload in a heap or mass **2** to throw away (rubbish, etc.) **3** to sell (a commodity) in a large quantity at a low price **4** *Comput. a)* to transfer (data) to another section of storage *b)* to make a printout of (data) — *n.* **1** a place for dumping rubbish, etc. **2** *Mil.* a temporary storage center in the field **3** an ugly, run-down place —**(down) in the dumps** in low spirits — **dump on** [Slang] to treat with contempt

dump·ling (dump′liŋ) *n.* ⟦< ?⟧ **1** a small piece of steamed or boiled dough served with meat or soup **2** a crust of baked dough filled with fruit

Dump′ster (dump′stər) *trademark for* a large, metal trash bin, often one emptied by a special truck — *n.* [d-] such a trash bin

dump′y *adj.* **-i·er, -i·est 1** short and thick; squat **2** [Colloq.] ugly, run-down, etc.

dun¹ (dun) *adj., n.* ⟦OE⟧ dull grayish-brown

dun² (dun) *vt., vi.* **dunned, dun′ning** ⟦? dial. var. of DIN⟧ to ask (a debtor) repeatedly for payment — *n.* an insistent demand, for payment

dunce (duns) *n.* ⟦after John *Duns* Scotus, 13th-c. Scot scholar⟧ a dull, ignorant person

dun·der·head (dun′dər hed′) *n.* ⟦< Du *donder*, thunder⟧ a stupid person; dunce

dune (do͞on) *n.* ⟦Fr < MDu⟧ a rounded hill or ridge of drifted sand

dung (duŋ) *n.* ⟦OE⟧ animal excrement; manure

dun·ga·ree (duŋ′gə rē′) *n.* ⟦Hindi *dungrī*⟧ **1** a coarse cotton cloth **2** [*pl.*] work trousers or overalls of this

dun·geon (dun′jən) *n.* ⟦< OFr *donjon*⟧ a dark underground cell or prison

dung′hill′ *n.* a heap of dung

dunk (duŋk) *vt.* ⟦Ger *tunken*⟧ **1** to dip (bread, etc.) into coffee, etc. before eating it **2** to immerse briefly

duo (do͞o′ō) *n., pl.* **du′os** ⟦It⟧ **1** DUET (esp. sense 2) **2** a pair; couple

duo·de·num (do͞o′ō dē′nəm, do͞o äd′'n əm) *n., pl.* **-na** (-nə) or **-nums** ⟦< L *duodeni*, twelve each: its length is about twelve fingers' breadth⟧ the first section of the small intestine, below the stomach —**du′o·de′nal** *adj.*

dup. duplicate

dupe (do͞op) *n.* ⟦< L *upupa*, stupid bird⟧ a person easily tricked — *vt.* **duped, dup′ing** to deceive; fool; trick — **dup′er** *n.*

du·plex (do͞o′pleks′) *adj.* ⟦L < *duo*, TWO + *-plex*, -fold⟧

double — *n.* **1** an apartment with rooms on two floors **2** a house consisting of two separate family units

du·pli·cate (do͞o′pli kit; *for v.*, -kāt′) *adj.* ⟦< L *duplicare*, to double⟧ **1** double **2** corresponding exactly — *n.* an exact copy — *vt.* **-cat′ed, -cat′ing 1** to make an exact copy of **2** to make or do again —**du′pli·ca′tion** *n.*

duplicating machine a machine for making copies of a letter, drawing, etc.

du·plic·i·ty (do͞o plis′ə tē) *n., pl.* **-ties** ⟦< LL *duplicitas*⟧ hypocritical cunning or deception

du·ra·ble (door′ə bəl) *adj.* ⟦< L *durare*, to last⟧ **1** lasting in spite of hard wear or frequent use **2** stable —**du′ra·bil′i·ty** *n.* —**du′ra·bly** *adv.*

dura ma·ter (do͞o′rə māt′ər) ⟦< ML, lit., hard mother, transl. of Ar term⟧ the tough, outermost membrane covering the brain and spinal cord

dur·ance (door′əns) *n.* ⟦see DURABLE⟧ imprisonment: esp. in **in durance vile**

du·ra·tion (do͞o rā′shən) *n.* ⟦see DURABLE⟧ the time that a thing continues or lasts

du·ress (do͞o′res′, do͞o res′) *n.* ⟦< L *durus*, hard⟧ **1** imprisonment **2** coercion

dur·ing (door′iŋ, dyoor′-) *prep.* ⟦see DURABLE⟧ **1** throughout the entire time of **2** in the course of

durst (durst) *now chiefly dial. pt. of* DARE

du·rum (do͞o′rəm) *n.* ⟦< L *durus*, hard⟧ a hard wheat that yields flour for macaroni, spaghetti, etc.

dusk (dusk) *n.* ⟦< OE *dox*, dark-colored⟧ **1** the dim part of twilight **2** gloom —**dusk′y, -i·er, -i·est,** *adj.*

dust (dust) *n.* ⟦OE⟧ **1** powdery earth or any finely powdered matter **2** earth **3** disintegrated mortal remains **4** anything worthless — *vt.* **1** to sprinkle with dust, powder, etc. **2** to rid of dust, as by wiping — *vi.* to remove dust, as from furniture —**bite the dust** [Colloq.] to die, esp. in battle —**dust′less** *adj.*

dust bowl an arid region with eroded topsoil easily blown off by winds

dust′er *n.* **1** a person or thing that dusts **2** a lightweight housecoat

dust′pan′ *n.* a shovel-like receptacle into which floor dust is swept

dust′y *adj.* **-i·er, -i·est 1** covered with or full of dust **2** powdery **3** dust-colored —**dust′i·ness** *n.*

Dutch (duch) *n.* the language of the Netherlands — *adj.* **1** of the Netherlands or its people, language, or culture **2** [Obs. or Slang] German —**go Dutch** [Colloq.] to have each pay his own expenses —**in Dutch** [Colloq.] in trouble or disfavor —**the Dutch** Dutch people

Dutch door a door with upper and lower halves opening separately

Dutch oven a heavy pot with an arched lid, for pot roasts, etc.

Dutch treat [Colloq.] any date, etc. on which each pays his own expenses

Dutch uncle [Colloq.] one who bluntly and sternly lectures another, often with benevolent intent

du·teous (do͞ot′ē əs) *adj.* dutiful; obedient —**du′teous·ly** *adv.*

du·ti·able (do͞ot′ē ə bəl) *adj.* necessitating payment of a duty or tax

---

THESAURUS

less, speechless, having a speech impediment; see also MUTE 1, QUIET. **2** [Slow of wit] simple-minded, feebleminded, moronic; see DULL 3, STUPID.

dumbbell* *n.* blockhead, fool, dunce; see FOOL.

dummy *n.* **1** [*Fool] dolt, blockhead, oaf; see FOOL. **2** [Imitation] sham, counterfeit, duplicate; see COPY, IMITATION 2.

dump *n.* refuse heap, junk pile, garbage dump, city dump, dumping ground, swamp, garbage lot.

dump *v.* empty, unload, deposit, unpack, discharge, evacuate, drain, eject, exude, expel, throw out, throw over, throw overboard; see also DISCARD.—*Ant.* LOAD, fill, pack.

dumps *n.* despondency, dejection, despair; see DESPERATION, GLOOM.

dunce *n.* dolt, lout, moron; see FOOL.

dune *n.* rise, knoll, ridge; see HILL.

dung *n.* offal, defecation, compost, manure, guano, fertilizer, excreta;

horse dung, cow dung, etc.; chips, pellets, leavings, muck, feces, filth, garbage, sludge, slop, sewage; see also EXCREMENT, FERTILIZER.

duo *n.* couple, two, twosome; see PAIR.

duplicate *n.* double, second, mate, facsimile, replica, carbon copy, likeness, counterpart, analogue, parallel, correlate, repetition, duplication, recurrence, match, twin, Xerox (trademark), chip off the old block; see also COPY, IMITATION. —**in duplicate** duplicated, doubled, copied; see REPRODUCED.

duplicate *v.* **1** [To copy] reproduce, counterfeit, make a replica of; see COPY. **2** [To double] make twofold, multiply, make twice as much; see INCREASE. **3** [To repeat] redo, remake, rework; see REPEAT 1.

durability *n.* durableness, stamina, persistence; see ENDURANCE.

durable *a.* strong, firm, enduring; see PERMANENT.

duration *n.* span, continuation, con-

tinuance; see TERM 2.

duress *n.* compulsion, discipline, control; see PRESSURE 2, RESTRAINT 2.

during *a., prep.* as, at the time, at the same time as, the whole time, the time between, in the course of, in the middle of, when, all along, pending, throughout, in the meanwhile, in the interim, all the while, for the time being; see also MEANWHILE, WHILE 1.

dusk *n.* gloom, twilight, dawn; see NIGHT 1.

dust *n.* dirt, lint, soil, sand, flakes, ashes, cinders, grime, soot, grit, filings, sawdust; see also EARTH 2, FILTH. —**bite the dust*** be killed, fall in battle, succumb; see DIE. — **make the dust fly** move swiftly, work hard, be active; see ACT 1, MOVE 1.

dust *v.* sprinkle, sift, powder; see SCATTER 2.

dusty *a.* undusted, untouched, unused; see DIRTY 1.

du·ti·ful (dōōt′i fəl) *adj.* showing, or resulting from, a sense of duty; obedient —**du′ti·fully** *adv.*

duty (dōōt′ē) *n., pl.* **-ties** ⟦see DUE & -TY⟧ **1** obedience or respect to be shown to one's parents, elders, etc. **2** any action required by one's position or by moral or legal considerations, etc. **3** service, esp. military service *[overseas duty]* **4** a tax, as on imports —**on** (or **off**) **duty** at (or temporarily relieved from) one's work

du·vet (dōō vā′, dyōō-) *n.* a comforter, often filled with down

dwarf (dwôrf) *n., pl.* **dwarfs** or **dwarves** (dwôrvz) ⟦< OE *dweorg*⟧ **1** any abnormally small person, animal, or plant **2** *Folklore* a little being in human form, with magic powers — *vt.* **1** to stunt the growth of **2** to make seem small in comparison — *vi.* to become dwarfed — *adj.* undersized — **dwarf′ish** *adj.* —**dwarf′ism′** *n.*

dweeb (dwēb) *n.* [Slang] a person regarded as dull, awkward, unsophisticated, etc.

dwell (dwel) *vi.* **dwelt** or **dwelled, dwell′ing** ⟦< OE *dwellan*, to hinder⟧ to make one's home; reside —**dwell on** (or **upon**) to linger over —**dwell′er** *n.*

dwell′ing (place) ⟦ME: see prec.⟧ a residence; abode

DWI *n.* a citation for driving while intoxicated

dwin·dle (dwin′dəl) *vi., vt.* **-dled, -dling** ⟦< OE *dwīnan*, waste away⟧ to keep on becoming or making smaller or less; diminish; shrink

dyb·buk (dib′ək) *n.* ⟦Heb *dibbūq*⟧ *Jewish Folklore* the spirit of a dead person, that enters someone living

dye (dī) *n.* ⟦< OE *deag*⟧ a substance or solution for coloring fabric, hair, etc.; also, the color produced — *vt.* **dyed, dye′ing** to color with dye —**dy′er** *n.*

dye′stuff′ *n.* a dye or a substance yielding a dye

dy·ing (dī′iŋ) *vi. prp. of* DIE[1] — *adj.* **1** about to die or end **2** at death — *n.* death

dy·namic (dī nam′ik) *adj.* ⟦< Gr *dynasthai*, be able⟧ **1** of energy or physical force in motion **2** energetic; vigorous —**dy·nam′i·cally** *adv.*

dy·nam′ics *n.pl.* [*with sing. v. for 1*] **1** the science dealing with motions produced by given forces **2** the forces operative in any field

dy·na·mite (dī′nə mīt′) *n.* ⟦see DYNAMIC⟧ a powerful explosive made with nitroglycerin — *vt.* **-mit′ed, -mit′ing** to blow up with dynamite

dy·namo (dī′nə mō′) *n., pl.* **-mos′** ⟦see DYNAMIC⟧ **1** *early term for* GENERATOR **2** a dynamic person

dy·nasty (dī′nəs tē) *n., pl.* **-ties** ⟦< Gr *dynasteia*, rule⟧ a succession of rulers who are members of the same family —**dy·nas′tic** (-nas′tik) *adj.*

dys- ⟦Gr⟧ *prefix* bad, ill, difficult, etc.

dys·en·tery (dis′ən ter′ē) *n.* ⟦< Gr *dys-*, bad + *entera*, bowels⟧ an intestinal inflammation characterized by abdominal pain and bloody diarrhea

dys·func·tion (dis fuŋk′shən) *n.* abnormal or impaired functioning

dys·lexia (dis lek′sē ə) *n.* ⟦< DYS- + L *lexis*, speech⟧ impairment of the ability to read —**dys·lex′ic** or **dys·lec′tic** *adj., n.*

dys·pep·sia (dis pep′sē ə, -shə) *n.* ⟦< Gr *dys-*, bad + *pepsis*, digestion⟧ indigestion —**dys·pep′tic** *adj., n.*

dz. dozen(s)

■ THESAURUS ■

dutiful *a.* devoted, respectful, conscientious; see FAITHFUL, OBEDIENT 1.

duty *n.* **1** [A personal sense of what one should do] moral obligation, conscience, liability, charge, accountability, faithfulness, pledge, burden, good faith, honesty, integrity, sense of duty, call of duty; see also RESPONSIBILITY 1, 2.—*Ant.* DISHONESTY, irresponsibility, disloyalty. **2** [Whatever one has to do] work, task, occupation, function, business, province, part, calling, charge, office, service, mission, obligation, contract, station, trust, burden, undertaking, commission, engagement, assignment, routine, chore, pains, responsibility; see also JOB 2.—*Ant.* ENTERTAINMENT, amusement, sport. **3** [A levy, especially on goods] charge, revenue, custom; see TAX 1. —**off duty** not engaged, free, inactive; see UNEMPLOYED. —**on duty** employed, engaged, at work; see BUSY 1.

dwarf *a.* dwarfed, low, diminutive; see LITTLE 1.

dwarf *v.* minimize, overshadow, dominate, predominate over, tower over, detract from, belittle, rise over, rise above, look down upon.—*Ant.* INCREASE, magnify, enhance.

dwell *v.* live, inhabit, stay, lodge, stop, settle, remain, live in, live at, continue, go on living, rent, tenant, have a lease on, make one's home at, have one's address at, keep house, be at home, room, bunk*; see also OCCUPY 2. —**dwell on** involve oneself in, think about, be engrossed in; see CONSIDER, EMPHASIZE.

dweller *n.* tenant, inhabitant, occupant; see RESIDENT.

dwelling *n.* house, establishment, lodging; see HOME 1.

dye *n.* tinge, stain, tint; see COLOR.

dye *v.* tint, stain, impregnate with color; see COLOR.

dying *a.* **1** [Losing life] sinking, passing away, fated, going, perishing, failing, expiring, moribund, withering away, at death's door*, done for*, cashing in one's chips*, with one foot in the grave; see also WEAK 2. **2** [Becoming worse or less] declining, going down, receding, retarding, decreasing, disappearing, dissolving, disintegrating, vanishing, failing, fading, ebbing, decaying, overripe, decadent, passé, doomed, neglected; see also SICK, WEAK 2.

dynamic *a.* energetic, potent, compelling, forceful, changing, progressive, productive, vigorous, magnetic, electric, effective, influential, charismatic, high-powered, peppy*, hopped up*; see also ACTIVE, POWERFUL 1.

dynamite *n.* trinitrotoluene, TNT, detonator; see EXPLOSIVE.

dynasty *n.* sovereignty, empire, absolutism; see NATION 1.

E

e or **E** (ē) *n., pl.* **e's, E's** the fifth letter of the English alphabet

E (ē) *n.* **1** *Educ.* a grade for below-average work or, sometimes, excellence **2** *Music* the third tone in the scale of C major

e- *prefix* EX-

E *Physics symbol for* energy

E or **E.** **1** east **2** easterly **3** eastern

each (ēch) *adj., pron.* ⟦OE *ælc*⟧ every one of two or more considered separately —*adv.* apiece Abbrev. **ea.**

eager (ē'gər) *adj.* ⟦< L *acer*⟧ keenly desiring; impatient or anxious —**ea'ger·ly** *adv.* —**ea'ger·ness** *n.*

eagle (ē'gəl) *n.* ⟦< L *aquila*⟧ **1** a large bird of prey, with sharp vision and powerful wings **2** a representation of the eagle, as the U.S. emblem **3** a former U.S. $10 gold coin **4** *Golf* a score of two under par on a hole

ea'gle-eyed' *adj.* having keen vision

eaglet (ē'glit) *n.* a young eagle

ear[1] (ir) *n.* ⟦OE *ēare*⟧ **1** the part of the body that perceives sound **2** the visible, external part of the ear **3** one's sense of hearing or hearing ability **4** anything like an ear —**be all ears** to listen attentively —**give** (or **lend**) **ear** to give attention; heed —**play by ear** to play (music) without using notation —**play it by ear** [Colloq.] to improvise

ear[2] (ir) *n.* ⟦< OE *ēar*⟧ the grain-bearing spike of a cereal plant, esp. of corn —*vi.* to sprout ears

ear'ache' *n.* an ache in the ear

ear'drum' *n.* TYMPANIC MEMBRANE

earl (url) *n.* ⟦< OE *eorl*, warrior⟧ a British nobleman ranking above a viscount —**earl'dom** *n.*

early (ur'lē) *adv., adj.* **-lier, -li·est** ⟦< OE *ær*, before + *-lice*, -ly⟧ **1** near the beginning **2** before the expected or usual time **3** in the distant past **4** in the near future —**early on** at an early stage —**ear'li·ness** *n.*

ear'mark' *n.* **1** a brand put on the ear of livestock **2** an identifying mark or feature — *vt.* **1** to set such a brand or mark on **2** to reserve for a special purpose

ear'muffs' (-mufs') *n.pl.* coverings worn over the ears in cold weather

earn (urn) *vt.* ⟦OE *earnian*⟧ **1** to receive (wages, etc.) for one's work **2** to get as deserved **3** to gain (interest, etc.) as profit —**earn'er** *n.*

ear·nest[1] (ur'nist) *adj.* ⟦OE *eornoste*⟧ **1** serious and intense; not joking **2** important —**in earnest** **1** serious **2** in a determined manner —**ear'nestly** *adv.* —**ear'nest·ness** *n.*

ear·nest[2] (ur'nist) *n.* ⟦ult. < Heb *eravon*⟧ money, etc. given as a pledge in binding a bargain

earn'ings *n.pl.* **1** wages or other recompense **2** profits, interest, etc.

ear'phone' *n.* a receiver for radio, etc., held to, or put into, the ear

ear'ring' *n.* a ring or other small ornament for the lobe of the ear

ear'shot' (-shät') *n.* the distance within which a sound can be heard

ear'split'ting *adj.* so loud as to hurt the ears; deafening

earth (urth) *n.* ⟦OE *eorthe*⟧ **1** [*often* E-] the planet we live on, the third planet from the sun: see PLANET **2** this world, as distinguished from heaven and hell **3** land, as distinguished from sea or sky **4** soil; ground —**down to earth** **1** practical; realistic **2** sincere; without affectation

earth'en *adj.* made of earth or clay

earth'en·ware' *n.* clay pottery

earth'ling *n.* a person who lives on the earth; human being

earth'ly *adj.* **1** *a*) terrestrial *b*) worldly **2** conceivable

earth'quake' *n.* a trembling of the earth's crust, caused by underground volcanic forces or shifting of rock

earth station a device for sending or receiving signals to or from communications satellites

earth'ward (-wərd) *adv., adj.* toward the earth Also **earth'wards** *adv.*

earth'work' *n.* an embankment or fortification made by piling up earth

earth'worm' *n.* a round, segmented worm that burrows in the soil

earthy (urth'ē) *adj.* **-i·er, -i·est** **1** of or like earth **2** coarse; unrefined —**earth'i·ness** *n.*

◼◼◼ THESAURUS ◼◼◼

each *a.* **1** [Every] all, any, one by one, separate, particular, specific, private, several, respective, various, piece by piece, individual, personal, without exception. **2** [For each time, person, or the like] individually, proportionally, respectively, for one, per unit, singly, per capita, apiece, separately, every, without exception, by the, per, a whack*, a throw*, a shot*.

each *pron.* each one, one, each for himself, each in his own way, every last one, one another, each other.

eager *a.* anxious, keen, fervent; see ZEALOUS.

eagerly *a.* zealously, intently, anxiously, sincerely, vigorously, readily, earnestly, willingly, heartily, strenuously, fiercely, rapidly, hungrily, thirstily, fervently, actively, with enthusiasm, gladly, lovingly, with all the heart, from the bottom of one's heart, with delight.—*Ant.* SLOWLY, unwillingly, grudgingly.

eagerness *n.* zest, anticipation, excitement; see ZEAL.

eagle *n.* hawk, falcon, bird of prey; see BIRD.

eagle-eyed *a.* discerning, keen-sighted, clear-sighted; see OBSERVANT.

ear[1] *n.* outer ear, middle ear, inner ear, eardrum, labyrinth, acoustic organ, auditory apparatus. —**all ears** attentive, hearing, paying attention; see LISTENING. —**bend someone's ear*** jabber, chatter, gossip; see TALK 1. —**fall on deaf ears** be ignored, fail to attract notice, be received with indifference; see FAIL 1,

WAIT 1. —**have** (or **keep**) **an ear to the ground*** be aware of, observe, keep one's eyes open; see LISTEN, MIND 3. —**in one ear and out the other** ignored, forgotten, received with indifference; see NEGLECTED. — **play it by ear*** improvise, concoct, go along; see INVENT 1. —**set on its ear*** stir up, agitate, arouse; see EXCITE. —**turn a deaf ear (to)** disregard, ignore, shun; see NEGLECT 1.

earlier *a.* former, previous, prior; see PRECEDING.

early *a.* **1** [Near the beginning] recent, primitive, prime, new, brand-new, fresh, budding.—*Ant.* LATE, old, superannuated. **2** [Sooner than might have been expected] quick, premature, in advance, far ahead, in the bud, preceding, advanced, immediate, unexpected, speedy, ahead of time, direct, prompt, punctual, briefly, shortly, presently, beforehand, on short notice, on the dot*, with time to spare.—*Ant.* SLOW, late, tardy.

earmark *n.* characteristic, attribute, quality; see CHARACTERISTIC.

earmark *v.* reserve, set aside, keep back; see MAINTAIN 3.

earn *v.* **1** [To deserve as reward] win, merit, gain; see DESERVE. **2** [To receive in payment] obtain, attain, get, procure, realize, obtain a return, make money by, acquire, profit, net, clear, score, draw, gather, secure, derive, make money, bring home, bring in, collect, pick up, scrape together*.—*Ant.* SPEND, consume, exhaust.

earnest[1] *a.* ardent, zealous, warm; see ENTHUSIASTIC.

earnestly *a.* solemnly, soberly, thoughtfully; see SERIOUSLY 2.

earnings *n.* net proceeds, balance, receipts; see PAY 2.

earring *n.* pendant, ornament, jewel; see JEWELRY.

earth *n.* **1** [The world] globe, sphere, planet, *terra*, mundane world, creation, terrestrial sphere, orb, cosmos, universe, star. **2** [The earthly crust] dirt, clean dirt, loam, humus, clay, gravel, sand, land, dry land, terrain, mud, muck, soil, ground, fill, compost, topsoil, alluvium, terrane, surface, shore, coast, deposit. —**come back** (or **down**) **to earth** be practical, be sensible, return to one's senses, quit dreaming; see also CALM DOWN, WORK 1. —**down to earth** earthly, realistic, mundane; see PRACTICAL. —**on earth** of all things, of everything, what; see WHATEVER.

earthen *a.* clay, stone, mud, dirt, rock, fictile, made of earth, made of baked clay.

earthenware *n.* crockery, ceramics, china; see POTTERY.

earthly *a.* human, mortal, global, mundane, worldly, under the sun, in all creation.—*Ant.* UNNATURAL, unearthly, superhuman.

earthquake *n.* tremor, temblor, trembler, earthquake shock, shock, quake, fault, slip, movement of the earth's crust, earth tremor, earth shock, volcanic quake.

earthy *a.* **1** [Characteristic of earth] dusty, made of earth, muddy; see EARTHEN. **2** [Unrefined] coarse, dull, unrefined; see CRUDE.

ease (ēz) *n.* ⟦< L *adjacens*, lying nearby⟧ 1 freedom from pain or trouble; comfort 2 natural manner; poise 3 freedom from difficulty; facility 4 affluence — *vt.* **eased, eas′ing** 1 to free from pain or trouble; comfort 2 to lessen (pain, anxiety, etc.) 3 to facilitate 4 to reduce the strain or pressure of 5 to move by careful shifting, etc. — *vi.* to become less tense, severe, etc.

easel (ē′zəl) *n.* ⟦ult. < L *asinus*, ass⟧ an upright frame or tripod to hold an artist's canvas, etc.

ease·ment (ēz′mənt) *n.* 1 an easing or being eased 2 *Law* a right that one may have in another's land

easi·ly (ē′zə lē) *adv.* 1 with ease 2 without a doubt 3 very likely

east (ēst) *n.* ⟦OE⟧ 1 the direction in which sunrise occurs; 90° on a compass, opposite west 2 a region in or toward this direction — *adj.* 1 in, of, toward, or facing the east 2 from the east ⟦an *east* wind⟧ — *adv.* in or toward the east

Eas·ter (ēs′tər) *n.* ⟦< OE *Eastre*, dawn goddess⟧ an annual Christian festival in the spring, celebrating the resurrection of Jesus

east′erly *adj., adv.* 1 in or toward the east 2 from the east

east′ern *adj.* 1 in, of, or toward the east 2 from the east

east′erner *n.* a native or inhabitant of the east

east′ward (-wərd) *adv., adj.* toward the east Also **east′wards** *adv.*

easy (ē′zē) *adj.* **-i·er, -i·est** ⟦see EASE⟧ 1 not difficult 2 free from anxiety, pain, etc. 3 comfortable; restful 4 free from constraint; not stiff 5 not strict or severe 6 *a*) unhurried *b*) gradual — *adv.* ⟦Colloq.⟧ easily —**take it easy** ⟦Colloq.⟧ 1 to refrain from anger, haste, etc. 2 to relax; rest —**eas′i·ness** *n.*

easy chair a stuffed armchair

eas′y·go′ing *adj.* dealing with things in a relaxed or lenient way

eat (ēt) *vt.* **ate, eat′en, eat′ing** ⟦OE *etan*⟧ 1 to chew and swallow (food) 2 to consume or ravage: with *away* or *up* 3 to destroy, as acid does; corrode 4 to make by or as by eating ⟦acid *eats* holes in cloth⟧ 5 [Slang] to worry or bother — *vi.* to eat food; have a meal —**eat′able** *adj.* —**eat′er** *n.*

eat·ery (ēt′ər ē) *n., pl.* **-ies** [Colloq.] a restaurant

eats (ēts) *n.pl.* [Colloq.] food

eau de Co·logne (ō′də kə lōn′) COLOGNE

eaves (ēvz) *n.pl., sing.* **eave** ⟦< OE *efes*, edge⟧ the projecting lower edge or edges of a roof

eaves′drop′ (-dräp′) *vi.* **-dropped′, -drop′ping** ⟦prob. < *eavesdropper*, one who stands under eaves to listen⟧ to listen secretly to a private conversation —**eaves′drop′per** *n.*

ebb (eb) *n.* ⟦OE *ebba*⟧ 1 the flow of the tide back toward the sea 2 a lessening; decline — *vi.* 1 to recede, as the tide 2 to lessen; decline

eb·ony (eb′ə nē) *n., pl.* **-ies** ⟦< Gr *ebenos*⟧ the hard, heavy, dark wood of certain tropical trees — *adj.* 1 of ebony 2 like ebony; dark or black

ebul·lient (i bool′yənt, -bul′-) *adj.* ⟦< L *e-*, out + *bullire*, to boil⟧ 1 bubbling; boiling 2 enthusiastic; exuberant —**ebul′lience** *n.*

ebul·li·tion (eb′ə lish′ən) *n.* ⟦see prec.⟧ 1 a boiling or bubbling up 2 a sudden outburst, as of emotion

EC European Community

ec·cen·tric (ək sen′trik) *adj.* ⟦< Gr *ek-*, out of + *kentron*, center⟧ 1 not having the same center, as two circles 2 off-center 3 not exactly circular 4 odd, as in conduct; unconventional — *n.* 1 a disk set off center on a shaft, for converting circular motion into back-and-forth motion 2 an eccentric person —**ec·cen·tric·i·ty** (ek′sen tris′ə tē), *pl.* **-ties,** *n.*

THESAURUS

ease *n.* 1 [Freedom from pain] comfort, rest, quietness, peace, prosperity, leisure, repose, satisfaction, calm, calmness, restfulness, tranquility, solace, consolation.—*Ant.* PAIN, discomfort, unrest. 2 [Freedom from difficulty] expertness, facility, efficiency, knack, readiness, quickness, skillfulness, dexterity, cleverness, smoothness; child's play, clear sailing*, snap*, breeze*, cinch*, pushover*.—*Ant.* DIFFICULTY, trouble, clumsiness. —**at ease** relaxed, collected, resting; see CALM 1.

ease *v.* 1 [To relieve of pain] alleviate, allay, drug, keep under sedation, tranquilize, sedate, anesthetize, give relief, comfort, relieve pressure, cure, attend to, doctor, nurse, relieve, soothe, set at ease, cheer.—*Ant.* HURT, injure, pain. 2 [To lessen pressure or tension] prop up, lift, bear, hold up, make comfortable, raise, unburden, release, soften, relieve one's mind, lighten, let up on, give rest to, relax, quiet, calm, pacify. 3 [To move carefully] induce, remove, extricate, set right, right, insert, join, slide, maneuver, handle.—*Ant.* HURRY, rush, blunder.

easily *a.* readily, with ease, in an easy manner, effortlessly, simply, with no effort, without trouble, evenly, regularly, steadily, efficiently, smoothly, plainly, comfortably, calmly, coolly, surely, just like that*, with one hand tied behind one's back*.

easiness *n.* carelessness, nonchalance, facility; see ABILITY.

east *a.* 1 [Situated to the east] eastward, in the east, on the east side of, toward the sunrise, east side, eastern, easterly, easternmost. 2 [Going toward the east] eastbound, eastward, to the east, headed east, in an easterly direction. 3 [Coming from the east] westbound, headed west, out of the east, westward, westerly, tending to the west.

East *n.* 1 [The eastern part of the United States] the eastern states, the Atlantic seaboard, the Eastern seaboard, land east of the Alleghenies, east of the Appalachians, land east of the Mississippi. *Areas in the East include the following:* East Coast, Atlantic Coast, Appalachia, Middle Atlantic States, New England, down East, the Thirteen Colonies. 2 [The eastern part of Eurasia] Asia, Asia Minor, Near East, Far East, Middle East, Siberia, Mongolia, southeast Asia, Arabia, Orient, Levant.

eastern *a.* 1 [Concerning the direction to the east] easterly, eastward, on the east side of; see EAST 1. 2 [Concerning the eastern part of the United States] East, Atlantic, Atlantic Seaboard, east of the Appalachian Mountains, Allegheny, Appalachian, New England, Middle Atlantic, South Atlantic. 3 [Concerning the Near East or Middle East] Southwest Asian, Egyptian, of the Holy Land, Arab, Arabic, Israeli, Hellenic, Hebraic, in Asia Minor. 4 [Concerning the Orient] Far Eastern, East Asian, Asian; see ORIENTAL.

easy *a.* 1 [Free from constraint] secure, at ease, prosperous, leisurely, unembarrassed, spontaneous, calm, peaceful, tranquil, careless, carefree, untroubled, moderate, hospitable, soft*.—*Ant.* DIFFICULT, impoverished, hard. 2 [Providing no difficulty] simple, facile, obvious, apparent, yielding, easily done, smooth, manageable, accessible, wieldy, slight, little, paltry, inconsiderable, nothing to it*, simple as ABC*, pushover*, easy as pie*, like taking candy from a baby*.—*Ant.* HARD, difficult, complicated. 3 [Lax] lenient, indulgent, easygoing; see KIND. —**take it easy** relax, rest, slow down; see CALM DOWN.

easygoing *a.* tranquil, carefree, patient; see CALM 1.

eat *v.* 1 [To take as food] consume, bite, chew, devour, swallow, feast on, dine out, get away with, peck at, gorge, gobble up, eat up, digest, masticate, feed on, breakfast, dine, eat out, sup, lunch, feed, feast, banquet, fall to, live on, feed on, take in, enjoy a meal, have a bite*, put away*, make a pig of oneself*, eat out of house and home*.—*Ant.* FAST, starve, vomit. 2 [To reduce gradually] eat up, eat away, liquefy, melt, disappear, vanish, waste, rust away, spill, dissipate, squander, drain, spill, fool away, run through.—*Ant.* INCREASE, swell, build. 3 [To bother] worry, vex, disturb; see BOTHER 2.

eatable *a.* digestible, nutritious, delicious; see EDIBLE.

eating *n.* consuming, consumption, devouring, feasting on, gorging on, feeding on, biting, chewing, dining, breakfasting, lunching, eating out, dining out, eating up, having a coffee break, having a lunch break, having a bite, having a snack, breaking bread, making a pig of oneself, bolting, swallowing, gulping down, gobbling up, gobbling down, putting on the feed bag*, eating out of house and home*.

eats* *n.* food, victuals, meal; see FOOD.

eavesdrop *v.* overhear, wiretap, listen, listen in on, try to overhear, bend an ear*, bug*, tap.

ebb *n.* recession, decline, outward flow, outward sweep, shrinkage, wane, waste, depreciation, reduction, lessening, ebb tide, regression, withdrawal, decrease, depreciation.—*Ant.* INCREASE, flow, rise.

ebb *v.* recede, subside, retire, flow back, sink, decline, decrease, drop off, melt, fall away, peter out, wane, fall off, decay.—*Ant.* INCREASE, flow, rise.

eccentric *a.* odd, queer, strange; see UNUSUAL 2.

eccentricity *n.* peculiarity, abnormality, idiosyncrasy; see CHARACTERISTIC.

Ec·cle·si·as·tes (e klē̆'zē as'tēz') 〚< Gr *ek-*, out + *kalein*, to call〛 a book of the Old Testament

ec·cle'si·as'tic (-tik) *adj.* 〚see prec.〛 ECCLESIASTICAL — *n.* a Christian clergyman

ec·cle'si·as'ti·cal (-ti kəl) *adj.* of the church or the clergy

ech·elon (esh'ə län') *n.* 〚< Fr < L *scala*, ladder〛 1 a steplike formation of ships, troops, or aircraft 2 a subdivision of a military force 3 any of the levels of responsibility in an organization

echi·no·derm (ē ki'nō dʉrm') *n.* 〚< ModL〛 a marine animal with a hard, spiny skeleton and radial body, as the starfish

echo (ek'ō) *n., pl.* **-oes** 〚< Gr *ēchō*〛 1 the repetition of a sound by reflection of sound waves from a surface 2 a sound so produced 3 any repetition or imitation of the words, ideas, etc. of another — *vi.* **-oed, -o·ing** 1 to reverberate 2 to make an echo — *vt.* to repeat (another's words, ideas, etc.)

echo·ic (e kō'ik) *adj.* imitative in sound, as the word *tinkle*

éclair (ā kler', i-, ē-) *n.* 〚Fr, lit., lightning〛 an oblong, frosted pastry shell filled with custard, etc.

éclat (ā klä', i-, ē-) *n.* 〚Fr < *éclater*, burst (out)〛 1 brilliant success 2 striking effect 3 acclaim; fame

ec·lec·tic (ek lek'tik) *adj.* 〚< Gr *ek-*, out + *legein*, choose〛 selecting or selected from various sources — *n.* one who uses eclectic methods —**ec·lec'ti·cally** *adv.* —**ec·lec'ti·cism'** *n.*

eclipse (i klips') *n.* 〚< Gr *ek-*, out + *leipein*, leave〛 1 the obscuring of the sun when the moon comes between it and the earth (**solar eclipse**), or of the moon when the earth's shadow is cast upon it (**lunar eclipse**) 2 any obscuring of light, or of fame, glory, etc. — *vt.* **eclipsed', eclips'ing** 1 to cause an eclipse of 2 to surpass

eclip·tic (i klip'tik) *n.* the great circle of the celestial sphere; the sun's apparent annual path, as seen from the orbiting earth

ec·logue (ek'lôg') *n.* 〚see ECLECTIC〛 a short pastoral poem

eco- 〚< Gr *oikos*, house〛 *combining form* environment or habitat

eco·cide (ek'ō sīd') *n.* 〚prec. + -CIDE〛 the destruction of the environment, as by pollutants

ecol·ogy (ē käl'ə jē) *n.* 〚< Gr *oikos*, house + *-logia*, -LOGY〛 the branch of biology that deals with the relations between living organisms and their environment —**ec'o·log'i·cal** *adj.* —**ecol'o·gist** *n.*

econ. 1 economic(s) 2 economy

eco·nomic (ek'ə näm'ik, ē'kə-) *adj.* 1 of the management of income, expenditures, etc. 2 of economics 3 of the satisfaction of the material needs of people

ec'o·nom'i·cal *adj.* 1 not wasting money, time, etc.; thrifty 2 of economics —**ec'o·nom'i·cally** *adv.*

ec'o·nom'ics *n.pl.* [*with sing. v.*] 1 the science that deals with the production, distribution, and consumption of wealth 2 economic factors

econo·mist (i kän'ə mist, ē-) *n.* a specialist in economics

econ'o·mize' (-mīz') *vi.* **-mized', -miz'ing** to avoid waste or reduce expenses — *vt.* to manage or use with thrift — **econ'o·miz'er** *n.*

econ'o·my (-mē) *n., pl.* **-mies** 〚< Gr *oikos*, house + *nomos*, law〛 1 the management of the income, expenditures, etc. of a household, government, etc. 2 careful management of wealth, etc.; thrift 3 an instance of thrift 4 a system of producing and distributing wealth

eco·sys·tem (ek'ō sis'təm, ē'kō-) *n.* 〚< Gr *oikos*, house + SYSTEM〛 a community of animals and plants, together with its environment

ecru (ek'rōō') *adj., n.* 〚< OFr *escru*, unbleached〛 light tan; beige

ec·stasy (ek'stə sē) *n., pl.* **-sies** 〚< Gr *ek-*, out + *histanai*, to set〛 a state or feeling of overpowering joy; rapture — **ec·static** (ek stat'ik) *adj.*

-ectomy (ek'tə mē) 〚< Gr *ek-*, out + *temnein*, to cut〛 *combining form* a surgical excision of

ECU (ā'kōō, ē'sē'yōō') *n.* European Currency Unit (a European Community monetary unit)

ecu·meni·cal (ek'yōō men'i kəl) *adj.* 〚< Gr *oikoumenē* (*gē*), the inhabited (world)〛 1 general, or universal; esp., of the Christian church as a whole 2 furthering religious unity, esp. among Christian churches —**ec'u·men'i·cally** *adv.*

ecu·men·ism (ek'yōō mə niz'əm, e kyōō'-) *n.* the ecumenical movement, esp. among Christian churches Also **ec'u·men'i·cism'** —**ec'u·men·ist** *n.*

ec·zema (ek'zə mə, eg'zə-; ig zē'-) *n.* 〚< Gr *ek-*, out + *zein*, to boil〛 a skin disorder characterized by inflammation, itching, and scaliness

-ed 〚OE〛 *suffix* 1 forming the past tense or past participle of certain verbs 2 forming adjectives from nouns or verbs [*cultured, bearded*]

ed. 1 edited (by) 2 *a*) edition *b*) editor 3 education

Edam (cheese) (ē'dəm) 〚after *Edam*, Netherlands〛 a mild, yellow cheese

eddy (ed'ē) *n., pl.* **-dies** 〚prob. < ON *itha*〛 a little whirlpool or whirlwind — *vi.* **-died, -dy·ing** to whirl

edel·weiss (ā'dəl vīs') *n.* 〚Ger < *edel*, noble + *weiss*, white〛 a small, flowering plant, esp. of the Alps, with white and woolly leaves

ede·ma (ē dē'mə) *n., pl.* **-mas** or **-mata** (-mə tə) 〚< Gr *oidēma*, swelling〛 an abnormal accumulation of fluid in body tissues or cavities

Eden (ēd''n) *Bible* the garden where Adam and Eve first lived; Paradise — *n.* any delightful place —**Eden·ic** (ē den'ik) *adj.*

edge (ej) *n.* 〚OE *ecg*〛 1 the sharp, cutting part of a blade 2 sharpness; keenness 3 the projecting ledge of a cliff, etc.; brink 4 the part farthest from the middle; border; margin 5 [Colloq.] advantage [he has the *edge* on me] — *vt., vi.* **edged, edg'ing** 1 to form an edge (on) 2 to make (one's way) sideways 3 to move gradually —**on edge** 1 very tense; irritable 2 impatient —**edg'er** *n.*

edge'ways' (-wāz') *adv.* with the edge foremost Also **edge'wise'** (-wīz')

edg'ing *n.* trimming along an edge

THESAURUS

echo *n.* repetition, imitation, reply; see ANSWER 1.

echo *v.* repeat, mimic, impersonate; see IMITATE 1.

eclipse *n.* solar eclipse, lunar eclipse, total eclipse; see DARKNESS 1.

ecologist *n.* environmentalist, conservationist, naturalist, ecological engineer, oceanographer, biologist, botanist; see also SCIENTIST.

ecology *n.* ecological engineering, human environment, anti-pollution projects, pollution control, survival studies, study of ecosystems, conservation of natural resources; see also SCIENCE 1, ZOOLOGY.

economic *a.* industrial, business, financial; see COMMERCIAL.

economical *a.* 1 [Careful of expenditures] saving, sparing, careful, economizing, thrifty, prudent, frugal, miserly, stingy, mean, close, watchful, tight*, closefisted, penny-pinching*; see also STINGY.—*Ant.* GENEROUS, liberal, wasteful. 2 [Advantageously priced] cheap, sound, low, reasonable, fair, moderate, inexpensive, marked down, on

sale. 3 [Making good use of materials] practical, efficient, methodical; see EFFICIENT 1.

economics *n.* commerce, finance, public economy, political economy, science of wealth, economic theory, commerical theory, theory of business, theory of finance, principles of business, principles of finance, study of industry, study of production and distribution, theory of trade, economic principles; see also LAW 4, SCIENCE 1.

economist *n.* statistician, business analyst, efficiency expert; see SCIENTIST.

economize *v.* husband, manage, stint, conserve, scrimp, skimp, be frugal, be prudent, pinch, cut costs, cut corners, meet expenses, keep within one's means, cut down, meet a budget, make both ends meet, tighten one's belt*, save for a rainy day*, pinch pennies; see also ACCUMULATE, MAINTAIN 3, SAVE 3.—*Ant.* SPEND, waste, splurge.

economy *n.* curtailment, cutback, business recession, retrenchment,

rollback, reduction, layoff, wage decrease, cut in wages.—*Ant.* INCREASE, outlay, raise.

ecstasy *n.* joy, rapture, delight; see HAPPINESS.

edge *n.* 1 [The outer portion] border, frontier, extremity, threshold, brink, boundary, end, limit, brim, rim, margin, ring, frame, side, corner, point, bend, peak, turn, crust, verge, bound, ledge, skirt, outskirt, lip, limb, hem, seam, fringe, frill, mouth, shore, strand, bank, beach, curb, periphery, circumference.—*Ant.* CENTER, surface, interior. 2 [Anything linear and sharp] blade, cutting edge, razor edge; see KNIFE. 3 [*Advantage] upper hand, handicap, head start; see ADVANTAGE. —**on edge** nervous, tense, uptight*; see IRRITABLE. —**set one's teeth on edge** irritate, annoy, provoke; see also BOTHER 2. —**take the edge off** weaken, subdue, dull; see SOFTEN.

edge *v.* 1 [To trim] border, fringe, bind; see TRIM 2, DECORATE. 2 [*To defeat narrowly] nose out, slip past, squeeze by; see DEFEAT 3.

ed·ible (ed′ə bəl) *adj.* ‖ < L *edere*, eat ‖ fit to be eaten — *n.* food: *usually used in pl.* —**ed·ibil′i·ty** (-bil′ə tē) *n.*

edict (ē′dikt′) *n.* ‖ < L *e-*, out + *dicere*, speak ‖ a public order; decree

edi·fice (ed′i fis) *n.* ‖see fol.‖ a building, esp. a large, imposing one

edi·fy (ed′i fī′) *vt.* **-fied′, -fy′ing** ‖ < L *aedificare*, build ‖ to instruct so as to improve or uplift morally —**ed′i·fi·ca′tion** *n.* —**ed′i·fi′er** *n.*

edit (ed′it) *vt.* ‖ < EDITOR ‖ 1 to prepare (a manuscript) for publication by arranging, revising, etc. 2 to control the policy and publication of (a newspaper, etc.) 3 to prepare (a film, tape, etc.) for presentation by cutting, dubbing, etc. 4 to make changes in (a computer file)

edit. 1 edited (by) 2 edition 3 editor

edi·tion (ē dish′ən, i-) *n.* ‖see fol.‖ 1 the size or form in which a book is published 2 the total number of copies of a book, etc. published at one time 3 any particular issue of a newspaper

edi·tor (ed′it ər) *n.* ‖ L < *e-*, out + *dare*, give ‖ 1 one that edits 2 a department head of a newspaper, etc.

edi·to·rial (ed′i tôr′ē əl) *adj.* of or by an editor — *n.* a statement of opinion in a newspaper, etc., as by an editor, publisher, or owner —**ed′i·to′ri·al·ly** *adv.*

ed′i·to′ri·al·ize′ (-īz′) *vt., vi.* **-ized′, -iz′ing** to express editorial opinions about (something)

editor in chief *pl.* **editors in chief** the editor who heads the editorial staff of a publication

educ. 1 education 2 educational

edu·cable (ej′ōō kə bəl, ej′ə-) *adj.* that can be educated or trained —**ed′u·cabil′i·ty** *n.*

edu·cate (ej′ōō kāt, ej′ə-) *vt.* **-cat′ed, -cat′ing** ‖ < L *e-*, out + *ducere*, to lead ‖ 1 to develop the knowledge, skill, or character of, esp. by formal schooling; teach 2 to pay for the schooling of —**ed′u·ca′tor** *n.*

ed′u·ca′tion *n.* 1 the process of educating; teaching 2 knowledge, etc. thus developed 3 formal schooling —**ed′u·ca′tional** *adj.*

educe (ē dōōs′) *vt.* **educed′, educ′ing** ‖see EDUCATE ‖ 1 to draw out; elicit 2 to deduce

-ee (ē) ‖ < Anglo-Fr pp. ending ‖ *suffix* 1 the recipient of an action *[appointee]* 2 one in a (specified) condition *[absentee]*

EEG electroencephalogram

eel (ēl) *n.* ‖OE *æl*‖ a long, slippery, snakelike fish

EEOC Equal Employment Opportunity Commission

e′er (er, ar) *adv. old poet. contr.* of EVER

-eer (ir) ‖ < L *-arius*‖ *suffix* 1 *a*) one having to do with *[auctioneer]* *b*) one who writes, makes, etc. *[profiteer]* 2 to have to do with *[electioneer]*

ee·rie or **eery** (ir′ē) *adj.* **-rier, -ri·est** ‖ < OE *earg*, timid ‖ mysterious, uncanny, or weird —**ee′ri·ly** *adv.* —**ee′ri·ness** *n.*

ef- *prefix* EX- Used before *f*

ef·face (ə fās′, i-) *vt.* **-faced′, -fac′ing** ‖ < L *ex-*, out + *facies*, face ‖ 1 to rub out; erase 2 to make (oneself) inconspicuous —**ef·face′ment** *n.*

ef·fect (e fekt′, i-) *n.* ‖ < L *ex-*, out + *facere*, do ‖ 1 anything brought about by a cause; result 2 the power to cause results 3 influence 4 meaning *[spoke to this effect]* 5 an impression made on the mind, or its cause 6 a being operative or in force 7 *[pl.]* belongings; property — *vt.* to bring about; accomplish —**in effect** 1 actually 2 virtually 3 in operation —**take effect** to become operative

ef·fec′tive *adj.* 1 producing a desired effect; efficient 2 in effect; operative 3 impressive —**ef·fec′tively** *adv.* —**ef·fec′tive·ness** *n.*

ef·fec′tual (e fek′chōō əl, i-) *adj.* 1 producing, or able to produce, the desired effect 2 having legal force; valid —**ef·fec′tu·ally** *adv.*

ef·fec′tu·ate′ (-āt′) *vt.* **-at′ed, -at′ing** to bring about; effect

ef·femi·nate (e fem′ə nit, i-) *adj.* ‖ < L *ex-*, out + *femina*, woman ‖ having qualities attributed to women, as weakness, delicacy, etc.; unmanly —**ef·fem′i·nacy** *n.*

ef·fer·ent (ef′ər ənt) *adj.* ‖ < L *ex-*, out + *ferre*, to bear ‖ carrying away from a central part, as nerves

ef·fer·vesce (ef′ər ves′) *vi.* **-vesced′, -vesc′ing** ‖ < L *ex-*, out + *fervere*, to boil ‖ 1 to give off gas bubbles; bubble 2 to be lively —**ef·fer·ves′cence** *n.* —**ef·fer·ves′cent** *adj.*

ef·fete (e fēt′, i-) *adj.* ‖ < L *ex-*, out + *fetus*, productive ‖ 1 no longer able to produce; sterile 2 decadent, soft, too refined, etc. —**ef·fete′ly** *adv.* —**ef·fete′ness** *n.*

ef·fi·ca·cious (ef′i kā′shəs) *adj.* ‖see EFFECT ‖ that produces the desired effect —**ef·fi·ca′ciously** *adv.* —**ef′fi·cacy** (-kə sē) *n.*

ef·fi·cient (e fish′ənt, i-) *adj.* ‖see EFFECT ‖ producing the desired result with a minimum of effort, expense, or waste —**ef·fi′ciency** *n.* —**ef·fi′ciently** *adv.*

ef·figy (ef′i jē) *n., pl.* **-gies** ‖ < L *ex-*, out + *fingere*, to form ‖ a statue or other image; often, a crude representation (for hanging or burning) of a despised person

ef·flu·ent (ef′lōō ənt) *adj.* ‖ < L *effluere*, flow out ‖ flowing out — *n.* the outflow of a sewer, septic tank, etc. —**ef′flu·ence** *n.*

■ THESAURUS ■

edgy *a.* irritable, touchy, excitable; see NERVOUS.

edible *a.* palatable, good, delicious, satisfying, fit to eat, savory, tasty, culinary, yummy*, nutritious, digestible; see also DELICIOUS.

edifice *n.* structure, architectural monument, pile; see BUILDING.

edit *v.* revise, alter, rewrite, arrange materials for publication, prepare for the press, compose, compile, select, arrange, set up, censor, polish, finish, analyze, revise and correct, delete, condense, discard, strike out, write, proofread, cut, trim, blue-pencil, doctor up*.

edition *n.* printing, reprint, revision; see BOOK.

editor *n.* reviser, copyreader, supervisor, director, manager, editor-in-chief, proofreader, reader, editorial writer, desk man, newspaperman; see also AUTHOR, WRITER.

editorial *n.* essay, article, column; see COMPOSITION.

educate *v.* tutor, instruct, train; see TEACH.

educated *a.* trained, accomplished, skilled, well-taught, scientific, scholarly, intelligent, learned, well-informed, well-read, well-versed, well-grounded, disciplined, prepared, instructed, developed, civilized, fitted, versed in, informed in, acquainted with, professional, expert, polished, cultured, finished, initiated, enlightened, literate, lettered, tutored, schooled.—*Ant.* IGNORANT, illiterate, unlettered.

education *n.* 1 [The process of directing learning] schooling, study, training, direction, instruction, guidance, apprenticeship, teaching, tutelage, learning, reading, discipline, preparation, adult education, book learning, information, indoctrination, brainwashing, cultivation, background, rearing. 2 [Knowledge acquired through education] learning, wisdom, scholarship; see KNOWLEDGE 1. 3 [The teaching profession] teaching, tutoring, pedagogy, instruction, training, the field of education, the educational profession, progressive education, lecturing.

educational *a.* enlightening, instructive, enriching; see CULTURAL.

educator *n.* pedagogue, instructor, tutor; see TEACHER.

eerie *a.* strange, ghostly, weird; see FRIGHTFUL 1.

effect *n.* conclusion, consequence, outcome; see RESULT. —**for effect** artificially, hypocritically, ostentatiously; see DELIBERATELY. —**in effect** as a result, in fact, actually; see REALLY 1. —**take effect** work, produce results, become operative; see ACT 1. —**to the effect (that)** as a result, so that, therefore; see FOR.

effect *v.* produce, cause, make; see BEGIN 1, CAUSE.

effective *a.* efficient, serviceable, useful, operative, effectual, sufficient, adequate, productive, capable, competent, yielding, practical, valid, resultant.—*Ant.* USELESS, inoperative, inefficient.

effectively *a.* efficiently, completely, finally, expertly, conclusively, definitely, persuasively, adequately, capably, productively; see also WELL 2, 3.

effects *n.* personal property, baggage, possessions; see PROPERTY 1.

effectual *a.* adequate, efficient, qualified; see EFFECTIVE.

efficiency *n.* productivity, capability, capableness; see ABILITY.

efficient *a.* 1 [Said of persons] competent, businesslike, good at, apt, adequate, fitted, able, capable, qualified, skillful, clever, talented, energetic, skilled, adapted, familiar with, deft, adept, expert, experienced, equal to, practiced, practical, proficient, accomplished, active, productive, dynamic, decisive, tough, shrewd.—*Ant.* INCOMPETENT, inefficient, incapable. 2 [Said of things] economical, fitting, suitable, suited, effectual, effective, adequate, serviceable, useful, saving, profitable, valuable, expedient, handy, conducive, well-designed, streamlined, good for.—*Ant.* INADEQUATE, unsuitable, ineffectual.

effluent *a.* emanating, issuing forth, seeping; see FLOWING.

ef·flu·vium (e floo'vē əm) *n., pl.* **-via** (-ə) or **-vi·ums** ⟦see prec.⟧ a disagreeable vapor or odor

ef·fort (ef'ərt) *n.* ⟦< L *ex-*, intens. + *fortis*, strong⟧ **1** the use of energy to do something **2** a try; attempt **3** a result of working or trying —**ef'fort·less** *adj.* —**ef'fort·lessly** *adv.*

ef·fron·tery (e frunt'ər ē, i-) *n.* ⟦< L *ex-*, from + *frons*, forehead⟧ impudence; audacity

ef·ful·gence (e ful'jəns, i-) *n.* ⟦< L *ex-*, forth + *fulgere*, shine⟧ radiance; brilliance —**ef·ful'gent** *adj.*

ef·fuse (e fyooz', i-) *vt., vi.* **-fused', -fus'ing** ⟦< L *ex-*, out + *fundere*, pour⟧ **1** to pour out or forth **2** to spread out; diffuse

ef·fu'sion (-fyoo'zhən) *n.* **1** a pouring forth **2** unrestrained expression in speaking or writing —**ef·fu'sive** *adj.* —**ef·fu'sively** *adv.* —**ef·fu'sive·ness** *n.*

e.g. ⟦L *exempli gratia*⟧ for example

e·gad (ē gad') *interj.* ⟦prob. < *oh God*⟧ [Archaic] a softened oath

egali·tar·ian (ē gal'ə ter'ē ən) *adj.* ⟦< Fr *égalité*, equality⟧ advocating full political and social equality for all people —*n.* one advocating this

egg[1] (eg) *n.* ⟦ON⟧ **1** the oval body laid by a female bird, fish, etc., containing the germ of a new individual **2** a female reproductive cell; ovum **3** a hen's egg, raw or cooked

egg[2] (eg) *vt.* ⟦< ON *eggja*, give edge to⟧ to urge or incite: with *on*

egg'beat'er *n.* a kitchen utensil for beating eggs, cream, etc.

egg foo yong (or **young**) (eg' foo yuŋ') a Chinese-American dish of eggs beaten and cooked with bean sprouts, onions, minced pork or shrimp, etc.

egg'head' *n.* [Slang] an intellectual

egg'nog' *n.* ⟦EGG[1] + *nog*, strong ale⟧ a drink made of beaten eggs, milk, sugar, and, often, whiskey or rum

egg'plant' *n.* **1** a plant with a large, ovoid, purple-skinned fruit eaten as a vegetable **2** the fruit

egg roll a Chinese-American dish, a roll of egg dough wrapped around minced vegetables, meat, etc. and deep-fried

egis (ē'jis) *n. alt. sp. of* AEGIS

eg·lan·tine (eg'lan tīn', -tēn') *n.* ⟦< L *aculeus*, a sting⟧ a European rose with sweet-scented leaves and pink flowers

ego (ē'gō) *n., pl.* **-gos** ⟦L, I⟧ **1** the self; the individual as self-aware **2** egotism **3** *Psychoanalysis* that part of the psyche which governs action rationally

e'go·cen'tric (-sen'trik) *adj.* viewing everything in relation to oneself —**e'go·cen'tri·cally** *adv.*

e'go·ism' *n.* **1** selfishness; self-interest **2** egotism; conceit —**e'go·ist** *n.* —**e'go·is'tic** or **e'go·is'ti·cal** *adj.*

ego·tism (ē'gō tiz'əm, ē'gə-) *n.* **1** excessive reference to oneself in speaking or writing **2** self-conceit —**e'go·tist** *n.*

—e'go·tis'tic or **e'go·tis'ti·cal** *adj.* —**e'go·tis'ti·cally** *adv.*

ego trip [Slang] an experience that gratifies or indulges the ego

egre·gious (ē grē'jəs, i-) *adj.* ⟦< L *e-*, out + *grex*, a herd⟧ remarkably bad; flagrant —**egre'giously** *adv.*

egress (ē'gres) *n.* ⟦< L *e-*, out + *gradi*, go⟧ a way out; exit

egret (ē'gret', -grit) *n.* ⟦< OFr *aigrette*⟧ **1** a kind of heron with long, white plumes **2** AIGRETTE

Egyp·tian (ē jip'shən, i-) *n.* **1** the language of the ancient Egyptians **2** a native or inhabitant of Egypt —*adj.* of Egypt, its people, etc.

eh (ā, e) *interj.* **1** an exclamation of surprise **2** an expression of doubt or inquiry

eider (ī'dər) *n.* ⟦ult. < ON *æthr*⟧ **1** a large sea duck of northern regions **2** EIDERDOWN

ei'der·down' *n.* the soft, fine down of the eider duck, used as a stuffing for quilts, pillows, etc.

eight (āt) *adj., n.* ⟦< OE *eahta*⟧ one more than seven; 8; VIII —**eighth** (ātth) *adj., n.*

eight ball a black ball with the number eight on it, used in playing pool —**behind the eight ball** [Slang] in a very unfavorable position

eight·een (ā'tēn') *adj., n.* eight more than ten; 18; XVIII —**eight'eenth'** (-tēnth') *adj., n.*

eighty (āt'ē) *adj., n., pl.* **-ies** eight times ten; 80; LXXX — **the eighties** the numbers or years, as of a century, from 80 through 89 —**eight'i·eth** *adj., n.*

either (ē'thər, ī'-) *adj.* ⟦OE *æghwæther*⟧ **1** one or the other (of two) **2** each (of two) —*pron.* one or the other —*conj.* a correlative used with *or* to imply a choice of alternatives *[either* go *or* stay] —*adv.* any more than the other; also *[if* you don't go, I won't *either]*

ejacu·late (ē jak'yoo lāt', i-) *vt., vi.* **-lat'ed, -lat'ing** ⟦see fol.⟧ **1** to eject (esp. semen) **2** to utter suddenly; exclaim —**ejac'u·la'tion** *n.*

eject (ē jekt', i-) *vt.* ⟦< L *e-*, out + *jacere*, to throw⟧ to throw or force out; expel; discharge —**ejec'tion** *n.*

eke (ēk) *vt.* **eked, ek'ing** ⟦< OE *eacan*, to increase⟧ to manage to make (a living) with difficulty: with *out*

EKG electrocardiogram

elabo·rate (ē lab'ə rit, i-; *for v.,* -ə rāt') *adj.* ⟦< L *e-*, out + *labor*, work⟧ developed in great detail; complicated —*vt.* **-rat'ed, -rat'ing** to work out in great detail —*vi.* to add more details: usually with *on* or *upon* —**elab'o·rate'ly** *adv.* —**elab'o·rate'ness** *n.* —**elab'o·ra'tion** *n.*

élan (ā län') *n.* ⟦Fr < *élancer*, to dart⟧ spirited self-assurance; dash

elapse (ē laps', i-) *vi.* **elapsed', elaps'ing** ⟦< L *e-*, out + *labi*, to glide⟧ to slip by; pass: said of time

elas·tic (ē las'tik, i-) *adj.* ⟦< Gr *elaunein*, set in motion⟧ **1** able to spring back to its original size, shape, etc. after being stretched, squeezed, etc.; flexible **2** able to recover easily, as from dejection; buoyant **3** adaptable —*n.* an elastic band or fabric —**e'las·tic'ity** (-tis'ə tē) *n.*

elas'ti·cize' (-tə sīz') *vt.* **-cized', -ciz'ing** to make (fabric) elastic

---

THESAURUS

effort *n.* attempt, enterprise, undertaking, struggle, battle, try, trial, work, venture, aim, aspiration, purpose, intention, resolution, exercise, discipline, drill training, crack*, go*, whirl*; see also ACTION 1, 2.

effortless *a.* simple, offhand, smooth; see EASY 2.

egg[1] *n.* ovum, seed, germ, spawn, bud, embryo, nucleus, cell. *Prepared eggs include the following:* fried, scrambled, poached, deviled, hard boiled, soft boiled, soufflé, raw, buttered, on toast, egg salad, ham or bacon and eggs, over easy, sunnyside up. —**lay an egg*** be unsuccessful, err, make a mistake; see FAIL 1. —**put (or have) all one's eggs in one basket** chance, gamble, bet; see RISK.

egg on *v.* encourage, goad, incite; see DRIVE 1, 2, URGE 2, 3.

ego *n.* personality, individuality, self; see CHARACTER 1, 2.

egotism *n.* egoism, conceit, vanity, pride, assurance, self-love, self-confidence, self-glorification, self-worship, arrogance, insolence, overconfidence, haughtiness.—*Ant.* MODESTY, humility, meekness.

egotist *n.* conceited person, boaster,

egoist; see BRAGGART.

egotistic *a.* conceited, vain, boastful, inflated, pompous, arrogant, insolent, puffed up, affected, self-centered, self-glorifying, presumptuous, blustering, showy, boisterous, haughty, snobbish, contemptuous, proud, bullying, sneering, aloof, pretentious, assuming, cocky*, brazen, impertinent, selfish, bragging, insulting, theatrical, garish, gaudy, spectacular, reckless, impudent, inflated, stiff, overbearing, domineering, bold, rash, overconfident, self-satisfied, stuck up*, looking down one's nose*, snooty*, uppity, wrapped up in oneself*, on one's high horse*, high and mighty*, too big for one's breeches*, big as you please*.—*Ant.* HUMBLE, meek, modest.

egotistically *a.* vainly, boastfully, arrogantly, haughtily, pretentiously, loftily.

either *a., conj.* on the one hand, whether or not, unless, it could be that, it might be that.

either *pron.* one, one or the other, this one, either/or, each of two, as soon one as the other, one of two.

eject *v.* dislodge, discard, reject, run

out, kick out, throw out, put out, force out, spit out, turn out, squeeze out, oust, do away with, evict, banish, throw off, vomit, excrete, dump, get rid of, send packing, give the boot*, ditch*, bounce*.

ejection *n.* eviction, expulsion, dismissal; see REMOVAL.

elaborate *a.* **1** [Ornamented] gaudy, decorated, garnished, showy, fussy, dressy, refined, flowery, flashy; see also ORNATE.—*Ant.* COMMON, ordinary, unpolished. **2** [Detailed] complicated, extensive, laborious, minute, intricate, involved, many-faceted, complex, a great many, painstaking, studied.—*Ant.* GENERAL, usual, unified.

elaborate *v.* embellish, bedeck, deck; see DECORATE. —**elaborate upon** expand, discuss, comment upon; see EXPLAIN.

elapse *v.* transpire, pass away, slip by; see PASS 2.

elastic *a.* plastic, tempered, pliant; see FLEXIBLE.

elasticity *n.* resiliency, buoyancy, pliability; see FLEXIBILITY.

elate (ē lāt′, i-) *vt.* **-lat′ed, -lat′ing** [< L *ex-*, out + *ferre*, to bear] to raise the spirits of; make very proud, happy, etc. —**ela′tion** *n.*

el·bow (el′bō′) *n.* [see ELL² & BOW²] 1 the joint between the upper and lower arm; esp., the outer angle made by a bent arm 2 anything bent like an elbow — *vt., vi.* to shove as with the elbows

elbow grease [Colloq.] vigorous physical effort

el′bow·room′ *n.* ample space or room

elder¹ (el′dər) *adj.* [< OE *eald*, old] 1 older 2 of superior rank, position, etc. 3 earlier; former — *n.* 1 an older or aged person 2 an older person with some authority, as in a tribe 3 any of certain church officers

el·der² (el′dər) *n.* [OE *ellern*] a shrub or tree of the honeysuckle family, with red or purple berries

el′der·ber′ry (-ber′ē) *n., pl.* **-ries** 1 ELDER² 2 its berry, used for making wines, jelly, etc.

eld′er·ly *adj.* 1 somewhat old 2 in old age; aged

eld·est (el′dist) *adj.* oldest; esp., firstborn

El Do·ra·do or **El·do·ra·do** (el′də rä′dō) *n., pl.* **-dos** [Sp, the gilded] any place supposed to be rich in gold, opportunity, etc.

elect (ē lekt′, i-) *adj.* [< L *e-*, out + *legere*, choose] 1 chosen 2 elected but not yet installed in office *[mayor-elect]* — *vt., vi.* 1 to select for an office by voting 2 to choose; select —**elect′able** *adj.* —**elect′abil′ity** *n.*

elec·tion (ē lek′shən, i-) *n.* 1 a choosing or choice 2 a choosing or being chosen by vote

elec′tioneer′ (-shə nir′) *vi.* to canvass votes in an election

elec′tive (-tiv) *adj.* 1 *a)* filled by election *[an elective office] b)* chosen by election 2 having the power to choose 3 optional — *n.* an optional course or subject in a school curriculum

elec′tor (-tər) *n.* 1 one who elects; specif., a qualified voter 2 a member of the electoral college —**elec′toral** *adj.*

electoral college an assembly elected by the voters to perform the formal duty of electing the president and vice president of the U.S.

elec′tor·ate (-it) *n.* all those qualified to vote in an election

Elec·tra (ē lek′trə, i-) *Gr. Myth.* a daughter of Agamemnon: she plots the death of her mother

elec·tric (ē lek′trik, i-) *adj.* [< Gr *ēlektron*, amber: from the effect of friction upon amber] 1 of or charged with electricity 2 producing, or produced by, electricity 3 operated by electricity 4 using electronic amplification *[electric guitar]* 5 very tense or exciting Also **elec′tri·cal** —**elec′tri·cally** *adv.*

electric chair a chair used in electrocuting those sentenced to death

elec·tri·cian (ē′lek trish′ən, ē lek′-) *n.* one whose work is the construction and repair of electric apparatus

e′lec·tric′i·ty (-tris′i tē) *n.* 1 a property of certain fundamental particles of all matter, as electrons (negative charges) and protons or positrons (positive charges): electrical charge is generated by friction, induction, or chemical change 2 an electric current 3 electric current as a public utility for lighting, heating, etc.

elec·trify (ē lek′trə fī′, i-) *vt.* **-fied′, -fy′ing** 1 to charge with electricity 2 to excite; thrill 3 to equip for the use of electricity —**elec′tri·fi·ca′tion** *n.* —**elec′tri·fi′er** *n.*

electro- *combining form* electric, electricity

electro·car·dio·gram (ē lek′trō kär′dē ə gram′, i-) *n.* a tracing showing the variations in electric force which trigger heart contractions

elec′tro·car′dio·graph′ (-graf′) *n.* an instrument for making electrocardiograms

elec′tro·cute′ (-trə kyōōt′) *vt.* **-cut′ed, -cut′ing** [ELECTRO- + (EXE)CUTE] to kill or execute with electricity — **elec′tro·cu′tion** *n.*

elec′trode′ (-trōd′) *n.* [ELECTR(O)- + -ODE] any terminal by which electricity enters or leaves a battery, etc.

elec′tro·en·ceph′a·lo·gram′ (-trō en sef′ə lō gram′) *n.* [see ENCEPHALITIS & -GRAM] a tracing of the variations in electric force in the brain

elec′tro·en·ceph′a·lo·graph′ (-graf′) *n.* an instrument for making electroencephalograms

elec·trolo·gist (ē′lek träl′ə jist, i-) *n.* a practitioner of ELECTROLYSIS (sense 2)

e′lec·trol′y·sis (-i sis) *n.* [ELECTRO- + -LYSIS] 1 the decomposition of an electrolyte by the action of an electric current passing through it 2 the eradication of unwanted hair with an electrified needle

electro·lyte (ē lek′trō līt′, i-) *n.* [ELECTRO- + -LYTE] any substance which in solution is capable of conducting an electric current by the movement of its dissociated ions — **elec′tro·lyt′ic** (-līt′ik) *adj.*

elec′tro·mag′net (-mag′nit) *n.* a soft iron core that becomes a magnet when an electric current flows through a surrounding coil —**elec′tro·mag·net′ic** (-net′ik) *adj.*

electromagnetic wave a wave generated by an oscillating electric charge

elec′tro·mo′tive (-mōt′iv) *adj.* producing an electric current through differences in potential

elec·tron (ē lek′trän′, i-) *n.* [see ELECTRIC] a stable, negatively charged elementary particle that forms a part of all atoms

elec·tronic (ē′lek trän′ik, i-) *adj.* 1 of electrons 2 operating, produced, or done by the action of electrons —**elec′tron′i·cally** *adv.*

electronic music music in which the sounds are originated or altered by electronic devices

e′lec·tron′ics *n.pl.* [*with sing. v.*] the science dealing with the action of electrons, and with the use of electron tubes, transistors, etc.

electron microscope a device that focuses a beam of electrons on a fluorescent screen, etc. to form a greatly enlarged image of an object

electron tube a sealed glass or metal tube with gas or a vacuum inside, used to control the flow of electrons

electro·plate (ē lek′trō plāt′, i-) *vt.* **-plat′ed, -plat′ing** to deposit a coating of metal on by electrolysis

elec′tro·scope′ (-skōp′) *n.* a device for detecting very small charges of electricity or radiation —**elec′tro·scop′ic** (-skäp′ik) *adj.*

elec′tro·shock′ therapy (-shäk′) shock therapy using electricity

elec′tro·type′ (-tīp′) *n. Printing* a plate made by electroplating a wax or plastic impression of the surface to be reproduced

el·eemosy·nary (el′i mäs′ə ner′ē, el′ē ə-) *adj.* [< Gr *eleēmosynē*, pity] of, for, or supported by charity

el·egant (el′ə gənt) *adj.* [< L *e-*, out + *legere*, choose] 1 having dignified richness and grace, as of manner, design,

---

═══ THESAURUS ═══

elbow *n.* joint, angle, funny bone; see BONE. —**rub elbows with** mingle with, associate with, be friends with; see JOIN 2. —**up to the elbows (in)** engaged, employed, working at; see BUSY 1.

elbowroom *n.* sweep, range, margin; see SPACE 1.

elder¹ *n.* veteran, old lady, old man, old woman, superior, old timer, senior, one of the old folks, one of the older generation, patriarch, chief, tribal head, dignitary, counselor, father, uncle, grandfather, ancestor.

elderly *a.* declining, retired, venerable; see OLD 1.

elect *v.* choose, name, select; see CHOOSE.

elected *a.* chosen, duly elected, picked; see NAMED 2.

election *n.* poll, polls, ballot, balloting, ticket, bote, voting, vote-casting, primaries, suffrage, referendum, franchise, constitutional right.

elective *a.* voluntary, selective, not compulsory; see OPTIONAL.

electric *a.* electrical, magnetic, galvanic, electronic, power driven, vibrating, telegraphic, electrified, pulsing, dynamic, energetic.—*Ant.* OLD-FASHIONED, manual, steam.

electricity *n.* power, current, service, heat, light, ignition, spark, utilities, alternating current (AC), direct current (DC), 110 volts, 220 volts, high voltage, high tension, kilowatts, kilowatt hours, kilocycles, megacycles.

electrify *v.* wire, charge, power, heat, light, equip, lay cables, provide service, magnetize, galvanize, energize, subject to electricity, pass an electric current through, give an electric shock to, charge with electricity.

electrocute *v.* execute, put to death, kill by electric shock, put in the electric chair, send to the hot seat*, fry*, burn*.

electron *n.* negative particle, negatron, electrically charged element; see ATOM.

electronic *a.* photoelectric, cathodic, anodic, voltaic, photoelectronic, autoelectronic, computerized, automatic, automated; see also ELECTRIC.

electronics *n.* radionics, electron physics, radar, physics, photoelectronics, automatics, cybernetics, computer electronics; see also SCIENCE 1.

elegance *n.* culture, tastefulness, taste, cultivation, politeness, polish, grace, delicacy, splendor, beauty, balance, purity, grace, gracefulness, delicacy, magnificence, courtliness, nobility, charm, sophistication, propriety, style.

elegant *a.* ornate, polished, perfected, elaborate, finished, ornadress, etc.; tastefully luxurious **2** cleverly apt and simple *[an elegant* solution*]* **3** [Colloq.] excellent —**el′egance** *n.* —**el′egant·ly** *adv.*

el·egi·ac (el ē′jē ak′, el′ə ji′ak′) *adj.* **1** of, like, or fit for an elegy **2** sad; mournful

el·egy (el′ə jē) *n.,* pl. **-gies** ⟦< Gr *elegos,* a lament⟧ a mournful poem, esp. of lament and praise for the dead

el·ement (el′ə mənt) *n.* ⟦< L *elementum*⟧ **1** the natural or suitable environment for a person or thing **2** a component part or quality, often one that is basic or essential **3** *Chem.* any substance that cannot be separated into different substances except by radioactive decay or by nuclear reactions: all matter is composed of such substances —**the elements 1** the first principles; rudiments **2** wind, rain, etc.; forces of the atmosphere

el·emen·tal (el′ə ment′'l) *adj.* **1** of or like basic, natural forces; primal **2** ELEMENTARY (sense *2a*) **3** being an essential part or parts

el′emen′tary (-ə rē) *adj.* **1** ELEMENTAL **2** *a)* of first principles or fundamentals; basic; simple *b)* of the formal instruction of children in basic subjects

elementary particle a subatomic particle, as a neutron, electron, etc.

elementary school a school of the first six (sometimes eight) grades, where basic subjects are taught

el·ephant (el′ə fənt) *n.* ⟦< Gr *elephas*⟧ a huge, thick-skinned mammal with a long, flexible snout, or trunk, and, usually, two ivory tusks

el·ephan·tia·sis (el′ə fan tī′ə sis) *n.* a chronic disease causing the enlargement of certain body parts and hardening of the surrounding skin

el·ephan·tine (el′ə fan′tin, -tin′) *adj.* like an elephant; huge, clumsy, etc.

el·evate (el′ə vāt′) *vt.* **-vat′ed, -vat′ing** ⟦< L *e-,* out + *levare,* to lift⟧ **1** to lift up; raise **2** to raise in rank **3** to raise to a higher intellectual or moral level **4** to elate; exhilarate

el′eva′tion *n.* **1** an elevating or being elevated **2** a high place or position **3** height above the surface of the earth or above sea level

el′eva′tor *n.* **1** one that elevates, or lifts up **2** a suspended cage for hoisting or lowering people or things **3** a warehouse for storing and discharging grain: in full **grain elevator**

elev·en (ē lev′ən, i-) *adj., n.* ⟦OE *endleofan*⟧ one more than ten; 11; XI —**elev′enth** (-ənth) *adj., n.*

elf (elf) *n.,* pl. **elves** (elvz) ⟦OE *ælf*⟧ *Folklore* a tiny, often mischievous fairy —**elf′in** or **elf′ish** *adj.*

elic·it (ē lis′it, i-) *vt.* ⟦< L *e-,* out + *lacere,* entice⟧ to draw forth; evoke (a response, etc.) —**elic′i·ta′tion** *n.*

elide (ē līd′, i-) *vt.* **elid′ed, elid′ing** ⟦< L *e-,* out + *laedere,* to hurt⟧ to leave out; esp., to slur over (a vowel, etc.) in pronunciation —**eli′sion** (-lizh′ən) *n.*

eli·gible (el′i jə bəl) *adj.* ⟦see ELECT⟧ fit to be chosen; qualified —**el′i·gibil′i·ty** *n.*

Eli·jah (ē lī′jə, i-) *Bible* a prophet of Israel in the 9th c. B.C.

elimi·nate (ē lim′ə nāt′, i-) *vt.* **-nat′ed, -nat′ing** ⟦< L *e-,* out + *limen,* threshold⟧ **1** to remove; get rid of **2** to leave out of consideration; omit **3** to excrete —**elim′i·na′tion** *n.*

elite (ā lēt′, i-) *n.* ⟦Fr < L: see ELECT⟧ *[also with pl. v.]* the group or part of a group regarded as the best, most powerful, etc.

elit′ism′ (-iz′əm) *n.* government or control by an elite — **elit′ist** *adj., n.*

elix·ir (ē liks′ir, i-) *n.* ⟦< Ar *al-iksīr*⟧ **1** a hypothetical substance sought by medieval alchemists to change base metals into gold or (in full **elixir of life**) to prolong life indefinitely **2** *Pharmacy* a sweetened solution used for medicine, etc.

Eliza·bethan (ē liz′ə bē′thən, -beth′ən) *adj.* of or characteristic of the time of Elizabeth I's reign (1558-1603) — *n.* an English person, esp. a writer, of that time

elk (elk) *n.* ⟦< OE *eolh*⟧ **1** MOOSE: the common term in Europe **2** WAPITI

ell¹ (el) *n.* **1** an extension or wing at right angles to the main structure **2** an L-shaped pipe, etc.

ell² (el) *n.* ⟦< OE *eln*⟧ a former English unit of measure, equal to 45 inches

el·lipse (e lips′, i-) *n.,* pl. **-lip′ses′** (-sēz′) ⟦< Gr *elleipein,* fall short⟧ *Geom.* a closed curve in the form of a symmetrical oval

el·lip·sis (-lip′sis) *n.,* pl. **-ses′** (-sēz′) ⟦see prec.⟧ **1** *Gram.* the omission of a word or words understood in the context (Ex.: "if (it is) possible") **2** a mark (. . .) indicating an omission of words

el·lip·ti·cal (-ti kəl) *adj.* **1** of, or having the form of, an ellipse **2** of or characterized by ellipsis Also **el·lip′tic** — **el·lip′ti·cally** *adv.*

■■■ THESAURUS

mented, adorned, embellished, embroidered, flowing, artistic, fancy, rich, pure, fluent, neat.—*Ant.* DULL, ill-chosen, inarticulate.

element *n.* **1** [A constitution] portion, particle, detail, component, constituent, ingredient, factor; see also PART 1. **2** [A form of matter] *The older sciences determined the following elements:* earth, air, fire, water; *modern chemistry and physics identify the following elements:* actinium (Ac), aluminum (Al), americium (Am), antimony (Sb), argon (A), arsenic (As), astatine (At), barium (Ba), berkelium (Bk), beryllium (Be), bismuth (Bi), boron (B), bromine (Br), cadmium (Cd), calcium (Ca), californium (Cf) carbon (C), cerium (Ce), cesium (Cs), chlorine (Cl), chromium (Cr), cobalt (Co), copper (Cu), curium (Cm), dysprosium (Dy), einsteinium (E), erbium (Er), europium (Eu), fermium (Fm), fluorine (F), francium (Fr), gadolinium (Gd), gallium (Ga), germanium (Ge), gold (Au), hafnium (Hf), hahnium (Ha), helium (He), holmium (Ho), hydrogen (H), indium (In), iodine (I), iridium (Ir), iron (Fe), krypton (Kr), lanthanum (La), lawrencium (Lr), lead (Pb), lithium (Li), lutetium (Lu), magnesium (Mg), manganese (Mn), mendelevium (Mv), mercury (Hg), molybdenum (Mo), neodymium (Nd), neon (Ne), neptunium (Np), nickel (Ni), niobium *or* columbium (Nb), nitrogen (N), nobelium (No), osmium (Os), oxygen (O), palladium (Pd), phosphorus (P), platinum (Pt), plutonium (Pu), polonium (Po), potassium (K), praseodymium (Pr), promethium (Pm), protactinium (Pa), radium (Ra), radon (Rn), rhenium (Re), rhodium (Rh), rubidium (Rb), ruthenium (Ru), rutherfordium (Rf), samarium (Sm), scandium (Sc), selenium (Se), silicon (Si), silver (Ag), sodium (Na), strontium (Sr), sulfur (S), tantalum (Ta), technetium (Tc), tellurium (Te), terbium (Tb), thallium (Ti), thorium (Th), thulium (Tm), tin (Sn), titanium (Ti), tungsten (W), uranium (U), vanadium (V), xenon (Xe), ytterbium (Yb), yttrium (Y), zinc (Zn), zirconium (Zr).

elementary *a.* **1** [Suited to beginners] primary, rudimentary, introductory; see EASY 2. **2** [Fundamental] foundational, essential, basic; see FUNDAMENTAL.

elements *n.* basic material, fundamentals, grammar, ABC's, initial stage, basis, beginning, first step, principles, rudiments, groundwork.

elevate *v.* **1** [To lift bodily] hoist, heave, tilt; see RAISE 1. **2** [To promote] advance, appoint, further; see PROMOTE 1.

elevated *a.* aerial, towering, tall; see HIGH 2, RAISED 1.

elevation *n.* top, roof, platform; see HEIGHT.

elevator *n.* **1** [Machine for lifting] lift, escalator, conveyor, elevator shaft, chair lift, passenger elevator, freight elevator, automatic elevator, hoist, chute. **2** [A building handling

grain] bin, storage plant, silo; see BARN.

elf *n.* brownie, sprite, leprechaun; see FAIRY.

eligibility *n.* fitness, acceptability, capability; see ABILITY.

eligible *a.* qualified, fit, suitable, suited, equal to, worthy of being chosen, capable of, fitted for, satisfactory, trained, employable, usable, becoming, likely, in the running, in line for, up to*.—Ant.* UNFIT, ineligible, disqualified.

eliminate *v.* take out, wipe out, clean out, throw out, stamp out, blot out, cut out, phase out, drive out, dispose of, get rid of, do away with, put aside, set aside, exclude, eject, cast off, disqualify, oust, depose, evict, cancel, eradicate, erase, expel, discharge, dislodge, reduce, invalidate, abolish, repeal, exterminate, annihilate, kill, murder, throw overboard, be done with, discard, dismiss, obliterate, discount, exile, banish, deport, expatriate, maroon, blackball, ostracize, fire, dump*, can*, ditch*, scrap, bounce*, sack*, drop.—*Ant.* INCLUDE, accept, welcome.

elimination *n.* **1** [The act of removing] dismissal, expulsion, exclusion; see REMOVAL. **2** [The act of declining to consider] rejection, repudiation, denial, disqualification, avoidance.

elite *n.* society, nobility, celebrities; see ARISTOCRACY.

ellipse *n.* oval, conic section, curve; see CIRCLE 1.

elm (elm) *n.* 〖OE〗 **1** a tall, hardy, deciduous shade tree **2** its hard, heavy wood

elo·cu·tion (el'ə kyōō'shən) *n.* 〖see ELOQUENT〗 the art of public speaking —**el'o·cu'tion·ist** *n.*

elo·dea (ē lō'dē ə, el'ə dē'ə) *n.* 〖< Gr *helōdēs*, swampy〗 a submerged water plant with whorls of short, grasslike leaves

elon·gate (ē lôn'gāt, i-) *vt., vi.* **-gat'ed, -gat'ing** 〖< L *e-*, out + *longus*, long〗 to make or become longer; stretch — **e'lon·ga'tion** *n.*

elope (ē lōp', i-) *vi.* **eloped', elop'ing** 〖prob. < OE *a-*, away + *hleapan*, to run〗 to run away secretly, esp. in order to get married —**elope'ment** *n.*

elo·quent (el'ə kwənt) *adj.* 〖< L *e-*, out + *loqui*, speak〗 vivid, forceful, fluent, etc. in speech or writing —**el'o·quence** *n.* —**el'o·quent·ly** *adv.*

else (els) *adj.* 〖OE *elles*〗 **1** different; other 〔somebody *else*〕 **2** in addition 〔is there anything *else*?〕 —*adv.* **1** differently; otherwise 〔where *else* can I go?〕 **2** if not 〔study, (or) *else* you will fail〕

else·where' (-hwer', -wer') *adv.* in or to some other place; somewhere else

elu·ci·date (ə lōō'sə dāt') *vt., vi.* **-dat'ed, -dat'ing** 〖< L *e-*, out + *lucidus*, clear〗 to make (something) clear; explain —**elu·ci·da'tion** *n.*

elude (ē lōōd', i-) *vt.* **elud'ed, elud'ing** 〖< L *e-*, out + *ludere*, to play〗 **1** to avoid or escape from by quickness, cunning, etc.; evade **2** to escape the mental grasp of 〔his name *eludes* me〕

elu·sive (-lōō'siv) *adj.* tending to elude —**elu·sive·ness** *n.*

elves (elvz) *n.* pl. of ELF

Ely·sium (ē lizh'əm, -liz'ē əm; i-) *Gr. Myth.* the dwelling place of virtuous people after death —*n.* any state of ideal bliss —**Ely·sian** (-lizh'ən, -liz'ē ən) *adj.*

em (em) *n.* 〖< the letter *M*〗 *Printing* a unit of measure, as of column width

'em (əm) *pron.* [Colloq.] them

em- *prefix* EN- Used before *b, m,* or *p*

ema·ci·ate (ē mā'shē āt', -sē-; i-) *vt.* **-at'ed, -at'ing** 〖< L *e-*, out + *macies*, leanness〗 to cause to become abnormally lean —**ema'cia'tion** *n.*

e-mail (ē'māl') *n.* [*also* E-] messages sent from one computer terminal to another, as by telephone line

ema·nate (em'ə nāt') *vi.* **-nat'ed, -nat'ing** 〖< L *e-*, out + *manare*, to flow〗 to come forth; issue, as from a source — **em'a·na'tion** *n.*

eman·ci·pate (ē man'sə pāt', i-) *vt.* **-pat'ed, -pat'ing** 〖< L *e-*, out + *manus*, the hand + *capere*, to take〗 **1** to set free (a slave, etc.) **2** to free from restraint —**eman'ci·pa'tion** *n.* —**eman'ci·pa'tor** *n.*

emas·cu·late (ē mas'kyōō lāt') *vt.* **-lat'ed, -lat'ing** 〖< L *e-*, out + *masculus*, male〗 **1** to castrate **2** to weaken — **emas'cu·la'tion** *n.*

em·balm (em bäm') *vt.* 〖see EN- & BALM〗 to preserve (a dead body) with various chemicals —**em·balm'er** *n.*

em·bank (em baŋk', im-) *vt.* to protect, support, or enclose with a bank of earth, etc. —**em·bank'ment** *n.*

em·bargo (em bär'gō, im-) *n., pl.* **-goes** 〖Sp < L *in-*, in + ML *barra*, a bar〗 **1** a government order prohibiting the entry or departure of commercial ships at its ports **2** any legal restriction of commerce — *vt.* **-goed, -go·ing** to put an embargo upon

em·bark (em bärk', im-) *vt.* 〖ult. < L *in-*, in + *barca*, small boat〗 to put or take (goods, etc.) aboard a ship, aircraft, etc. — *vi.* **1** to go aboard a ship, aircraft, etc. **2** to begin a journey **3** to engage in an enterprise —**em'bar·ka'tion** *n.*

em·bar·rass (em bar'əs, im-) *vt.* 〖< It *in-*, in + *barra*, a bar〗 **1** to cause to feel self-conscious **2** to hinder **3** to cause to be in debt —**em·bar'rass·ing** *adj.* —**em·bar'rass·ment** *n.*

em·bassy (em'bə sē) *n., pl.* **-sies** 〖see AMBASSADOR〗 **1** the residence or offices of an ambassador **2** an ambassador and his or her staff **3** a group sent on an official mission

em·bat·tled (em bat''ld) *adj.* 〖< OFr〗 engaged in battle or conflict

em·bed (em bed', im-) *vt.* **-bed'ded, -bed'ding** to set or fix firmly in a surrounding mass —**em·bed'ment** *n.*

em·bel·lish (em bel'ish, im-) *vt.* 〖< OFr *em-*, in + *bel*, beautiful〗 **1** to decorate; adorn **2** to improve (a story, etc.) by adding details, often fictitious —**em·bel'lish·ment** *n.*

em·ber (em'bər) *n.* 〖OE *æmerge*〗 **1** a glowing piece of coal, wood, etc. **2** [*pl.*] the smoldering remains of a fire

em·bez·zle (em bez'əl, im-) *vt.* **-zled, -zling** 〖< OFr *en-*, in + *besillier*, destroy〗 to steal (money, etc. entrusted to one) —**em·bez'zle·ment** *n.* —**em·bez'zler** *n.*

em·bit·ter (-bit'ər) *vt.* to make bitter

em·bla·zon (-blā'zən) *vt.* 〖EM- (see EN-) + BLAZON〗 **1** to decorate (*with* coats of arms, etc.) **2** to display brilliantly **3** to extol —**em·bla'zon·ment** *n.*

em·blem (em'bləm) *n.* 〖< Gr *en-*, in + *ballein*, throw〗 a visible symbol of a thing, idea, etc.; sign; badge —**em'blem·at'ic** (-blə mat'ik) *adj.*

em·body (em bäd'ē, im-) *vt.* **-ied, -y·ing 1** to give bodily form to **2** to give definite form to **3** to bring together into an organized whole; incorporate —**em·bod'i·ment** *n.*

em·bold·en (-bōl'dən) *vt.* to give courage to; cause to be bold

em·bo·lism (em'bə liz'əm) *n.* 〖< Gr *en-*, in + *ballein*, to throw〗 the obstruction of a blood vessel as by a blood clot or air bubble

THESAURUS

elongate *v.* prolong, lengthen, extend; see STRETCH.

eloquence *n.* fluency, wit, wittiness, expression, expressiveness, appeal, ability, diction, articulation, delivery, power, force, vigor, facility, style, poise, expressiveness, flow, command of language, gift of gab*.

eloquent *a.* vocal, articulate, outspoken; see FLUENT.

elsewhere *a.* gone, somewhere else, not here, in another place, in some other place, to some other place, away, absent, abroad, hence, removed, remote, outside, formerly, subsequently.—*Ant.* HERE, at this point, in this spot.

elude *v.* dodge, shun, escape; see AVOID.

elusive *a.* slippery, fleeting, fugitive; see TEMPORARY.

emaciated *a.* gaunt, famished, wasted; see THIN 2.

emanate *v.* exude, radiate, exhale; see EMIT.

emancipate *v.* release, liberate, deliver; see FREE.

emancipation *n.* liberty, release, liberation; see FREEDOM.

emasculate *v.* geld, unman, mutilate; see CASTRATE.

embalm *v.* preserve, process, freeze, anoint, wrap, mummify, prepare for burial, lay out.

embankment *n.* dike, breakwater, pier; see DAM.

embargo *n.* restriction, prohibition, impediment; see RESTRAINT 2.

embark *v.* set out, leave port, set sail; see LEAVE 1.

embarrass *v.* perplex, annoy, puzzle, vex, distress, disconcert, agitate, bewilder, confuse, chagrin, confound, upset, bother, plague, tease, worry, trouble, distract, discomfort, disturb, let down, perturb, fluster, irk, shame, stun, rattle, put on the spot*, make a monkey out of*.—*Ant.* ENCOURAGE, cheer, please.

embarrassed *a.* abashed, perplexed, disconcerted; see ASHAMED.

embarrassing *a.* difficult, disturbing, confusing, distracting, bewildering, puzzling, rattling, perplexing, delicate, unbearable, distressing, disconcerting, upsetting, discomforting, ticklish, flustering, troublesome, worrisome, uncomfortable, awkward, disagreeable, helpless, unseemly, impossible, uneasy, mortifying, shameful, annoying, irksome, exasperating, inconvenient, unmanageable, sticky*.—*Ant.* COMFORTABLE, easy, agreeable.

embarrassment *n.* confusion, chagrin, mortification, discomfiture, shame, humiliation, shyness, timidity, inhibition, dilemma, puzzle, perplexity, tangle, strait, pinch, quandary, mistake, blunder, clumsiness, indebtedness, uncertainty, hindrance, poverty, destitution, distress, difficulties, involvement, obligation, indiscretion, awkward situation, predicament, plight, pinch*, fix*, snag*, hitch*, hot seat*, hot water*, pickle*, stew.

embassy *n.* commission, mission, delegation; see COMMITTEE, DIPLOMAT.

embed *v.* plant, implant, secure; see FASTEN.

embezzle *v.* thieve, forge, pilfer; see STEAL.

embezzlement *n.* fraud, misappropriation, stealing; see THEFT.

embezzler *n.* thief, robber, defaulter; see CRIMINAL.

embitter *v.* irritate, aggravate, annoy; see BOTHER 2.

emblem *n.* symbol, figure, image, design, token, sign, insignia, banner, seal, colors, crest, coat of arms, representation, effigy, reminder, mark, badge, souvenir, keepsake, medal, character, motto, hallmark, flag, pennant, banner, standard.

embodiment *n.* incarnation, matter, structure; see CHARACTERISTIC, ESSENCE 1, IMAGE 2.

em·boss (em bôs′, -bäs′; im-) *vt.* ⟦see EN- & BOSS²⟧ 1 to decorate with raised designs, patterns, etc. 2 to raise (a design, etc.) in relief —**em·boss′er** *n.*

em·bou·chure (äm′bōō shoor′) *n.* ⟦Fr < L *in*, in + *bucca*, cheek⟧ the method of applying the lips to the mouthpiece of a wind instrument

em·brace (em brās′, im-) *vt.* **-braced′, -brac′ing** ⟦< L *im*-, in + *brachium*, an arm⟧ 1 to clasp in the arms lovingly; hug 2 to accept readily 3 to take up or adopt 4 to encircle 5 to include — *vi.* to clasp each other in the arms — *n.* an embracing; hug —**em·brace′able** *adj.*

em·bra·sure (em brā′zhər, im-) *n.* ⟦Fr < *embraser*, widen an opening⟧ 1 an opening (for a door, window, etc.) wider on the inside than on the outside 2 an opening in a wall for a gun, with the sides slanting outward

em·broi·der (em broi′dər, im-) *vt.*, *vi.* ⟦< OFr *en*-, on + *brosder*, embroider⟧ 1 to make (a design, etc.) on (fabric) with needlework 2 to embellish (a story); exaggerate

em·broi′dery *n.*, *pl.* **-ies** 1 the art of embroidering 2 embroidered work or fabric 3 embellishment

em·broil (em broil′, im-) *vt.* ⟦< OFr *en*-, in + *brouillier*, to dirty⟧ 1 to confuse; muddle 2 to involve in conflict or trouble —**em·broil′ment** *n.*

em·bryo (em′brē ō′) *n.*, *pl.* **-os′** ⟦< Gr *en*-, in + *bryein*, to swell⟧ 1 an animal in the earliest stages of its development in the uterus 2 the rudimentary plant contained in a seed 3 an early stage of something —**em′bry·on′ic** (-än′ik) *adj.*

em·bry·ol·o·gy (-äl′ə jē) *n.* ⟦prec. + -LOGY⟧ the branch of biology dealing with the formation and development of embryos —**em′bry·ol′o·gist** *n.*

em·cee (em′sē′) *vt.*, *vi.* **-ceed′, -cee′ing** ⟦< MC, sense 1⟧ [Colloq.] to act as master of ceremonies (for) — *n.* [Colloq.] a master of ceremonies

emend (ē mend′, i-) *vt.* ⟦< L *emendare*, to correct⟧ to make scholarly corrections in (a text) —**emen·da·tion** (ē′men dā′shən, em′ən-) *n.*

em·er·ald (em′ər əld) *n.* ⟦< Gr *smaragdos*⟧ 1 a bright-green, transparent precious stone 2 bright green

emerge (ē murj′, i-) *vi.* **emerged′, emerg′ing** ⟦< L *e*-, out + *mergere*, to dip⟧ 1 to rise as from a fluid 2 to become visible or apparent 3 to evolve —**emer′gence** *n.* —**emer′gent** *adj.*

emer·gency (ē mur′jən sē, i-) *n.*, *pl.* **-cies** ⟦orig. sense, emergence⟧ a sudden, generally unexpected occurrence demanding immediate action

emer·i·tus (ē mer′i təs, i-) *adj.* ⟦< L *e*-, out + *mereri*, to serve⟧ retired from active service, usually for age, but retaining one's title [professor *emeritus*]

em·ery (em′ər ē) *n.* ⟦< Gr *smyris*⟧ a dark, coarse variety of corundum used for grinding, polishing, etc.

emet·ic (ē met′ik, i-) *adj.* ⟦< Gr *emein*, to vomit⟧ causing vomiting — *n.* an emetic substance

-emia (ē′mē ə) ⟦< Gr *haima*, blood⟧ combining form a (specified) condition of the blood [leukemia]

emi·grate (em′i grāt′) *vt.* **-grat′ed, -grat′ing** ⟦< L *e*-, out + *migrare*, to move⟧ to leave one country or region to settle in another —**em′i·grant** (-grənt) *adj.*, *n.* —**em′i·gra′tion** *n.*

émi·gré or **emi·gré** (em′i grā, em′i grā′) *n.* ⟦Fr⟧ one forced to flee his country for political reasons

emi·nence (em′i nəns) *n.* ⟦< L *eminere*, stand out⟧ 1 a high place, thing, etc. 2 superiority in rank, position, etc. 3 [E-] a title of honor of a cardinal: preceded by *Your* or *His*

em′i·nent *adj.* ⟦< L *eminens*⟧ 1 high; lofty 2 projecting; prominent 3 renowned; distinguished 4 outstanding —**em′i·nently** *adv.*

eminent domain the right of a government to take or purchase private property for public use

emir (e mir′, ə-) *n.* ⟦< Ar *amara*, to command⟧ in Muslim countries, a ruler or prince

em·is·sary (em′i ser′ē) *n.*, *pl.* **-ies** ⟦see EMIT⟧ one, esp. a secret agent, sent on a specific mission

emis·sion (ē mish′ən, i-) *n.* 1 an emitting 2 something emitted; discharge

emit (ē mit′, i-) *vt.* **emit′ted, emit′ting** ⟦< L *e*-, out + *mittere*, send⟧ 1 to send out; give forth; discharge 2 to utter (words, etc.) —**emit′ter** *n.*

emol·lient (ē mäl′yənt, i-) *adj.* ⟦< L *e*-, out + *mollire*, soften⟧ softening; soothing — *n.* something that softens or soothes, as a medicine

emol′u·ment (-yōō mənt) *n.* ⟦< L *e*-, out + *molere*, grind⟧ gain from employment or position; salary, fees, etc.

emote (ē mōt′, i-) *vi.* **emot′ed, emot′ing** [Colloq.] to act in a theatrical manner

emo·tion (ē mō′shən, i-) *n.* ⟦< L *e*-, out + *movere*, move⟧ 1 strong feeling 2 any specific feeling, as love, hate, fear, anger, etc.

emo′tional *adj.* 1 of or showing emotion 2 easily aroused to emotion 3 appealing to the emotions —**emo′tion·al·ism′** *n.* —**emo′tion·ally** *adv.*

emo′tion·al·ize′ *vt.* **-ized′, -iz′ing** to treat in an emotional way

em·pa·thet·ic (em′pə thet′ik) *adj.* of or showing empathy

em·pa·thize (em′pə thīz′) *vt.* **-thized′, -thiz′ing** to feel empathy (*with*)

em·pa·thy (-thē) *n.* ⟦< Gr *en*-, in + *pathos*, feeling⟧ ability to share in another's emotions, thoughts, or feelings

em·per·or (em′pər ər) *n.* ⟦< L *in*-, in + *parare*, to set in order⟧ the supreme ruler of an empire

em·pha·sis (em′fə sis) *n.*, *pl.* **-ses′** (-sēz′) ⟦< Gr *en*-, in + *phainein*, to show⟧ 1 force of expression, action, etc. 2 special stress given to a word or phrase in speaking 3 importance; stress

---

THESAURUS

emboss *v.* raise, design, enchase; see DECORATE.

embrace *v.* enfold, squeeze, grip; see HUG.

embroider *v.* stitch, knit, quilt; see SEW.

embryo *n.* fetus, incipient organism, nucleus; see EGG.

embryonic *a.* incipient, immature, undeveloped; see EARLY 1.

emerald *n.* green beryl, valuable gem, precious stone; see JEWEL.

emerge *v.* rise, arrive, come out; see APPEAR 1.

emergence *n.* rise, evolution, visibility; see VIEW.

emergency *n.* accident, unforeseen occurrence, misadventure, strait, urgency, necessity, pressure, tension, distress, turn of events, obligation, pass, crisis, predicament, turning point, impasse, dilemma, quandary, pinch, fix*, hole*; see also DIFFICULTY 1, 2.

emigrant *n.* exile, expatriate, colonist, migrant, displaced person, D.P., traveler, foreigner, pilgrim, refugee, fugitive, wayfarer, wanderer, immigrant, alien, outcast, man without a country.

emigrate *v.* migrate, immigrate, quit; see LEAVE 1.

emigration *n.* reestablishing, departure, removal, leaving, expatriation, displacement, moving away, crossing, migrating, exodus, exile, trek, journey, movement, trend, march, travel, voyage, wayfaring, wandering, migration, shift, settling, homesteading.— *Ant.* immigration, arriving, remaining.

émigré *n.* exile, emigrant, refugee; see REFUGEE.

eminence *n.* standing, prominence, distinction; see FAME.

eminent *a.* renowned, celebrated, prominent; see DIGNIFIED, DISTINGUISHED 2.

emissary *n.* intermediary, ambassador, consul; see AGENT.

emission *n.* ejection, effusion, eruption; see RADIATION 1.

emit *v.* give off, let off, give out, let out, send forth, send out, throw up, throw out, spill out, pour out, give forth, eject, blow, hurl, gush, secrete, spurt, shoot, erupt, squirt, shed, expel, expend, vomit, belch, excrete, issue, perspire, spew, spit, ooze, exhale, emanate; see also EMPTY 2.

emotion *n.* agitation, tremor, commotion, excitement, disturbance, sentiment, feeling, tumult, turmoil, sensation. *Emotions include the following:* love, passion, ecstasy, warmth, glow, fervor, ardor, zeal, thrill, elation, joy, satisfaction, happiness, sympathy, tenderness, concern, grief, remorse, sorrow, sadness, melancholy, despondency, despair, depression, worry, disquiet, uneasiness, dread, fear, apprehension, hate, resentment, conflict, jealousy, greed, anger, rage, ire, shame, pride, sensuality, lust, desire.

emotional *a.* hysterical, demonstrative, fiery, warm, zealous, sensuous, fervent, ardent, enthusiastic, passionate, excitable, impulsive, spontaneous, ecstatic, impetuous, nervous, wrought-up, overwrought, temperamental, irrational, sensitive, oversensitive, hypersensitive, sentimental, maudlin, overflowing, affectionate, loving, neurotic, fickle, wearing one's heart on one's sleeve, high-strung, mushy*.—*Ant.* COLD, rational, hard.

emotionalism *n.* hysteria, sentimentality, excitement; see EMOTION.

empathy *n.* vicarious emotion, insight, understanding; see PITY.

emperor *n.* monarch, sovereign, dictator; see RULER 1.

emphasis *n.* stress, accent, weight; see IMPORTANCE.

em·pha·size (-sīz′) *vt.* **-sized′, -siz′ing** to give emphasis to; stress

em·phat·ic (em fat′ik, im-) *adj.* **1** felt or done with emphasis **2** using emphasis in speaking, etc. **3** forcible; striking **—em·phat′i·cally** *adv.*

em·phy·se·ma (em′fə sē′mə, -zē′-) *n.* ⟦< Gr *en*-, in + *physaein*, to blow⟧ a condition of the lungs in which the air sacs become distended and lose elasticity

em·pire (em′pīr′) *n.* ⟦see EMPEROR⟧ **1** supreme rule **2** government by an emperor or empress **3** a group of states or territories under one ruler **4** an extensive organization under the control of a single person, corporation, etc.

em·pir·i·cal (em pir′i kəl) *adj.* ⟦< Gr *en*-, in + *peira*, trial⟧ relying or based on experiment or experience **—em·pir′i·cally** *adv.* **—em·pir′i·cism′** (-siz′əm) *n.*

em·place·ment (em plās′ mənt, im-) *n.* the prepared position from which a heavy gun or guns are fired

em·ploy (em ploi′, im-) *vt.* ⟦< L *in*-, in + *plicare*, to fold⟧ **1** to use **2** to keep busy or occupied **3** to engage the services of; hire **—** *n.* employment

em·ploy′a·ble *adj.* that can be employed; specif., physically or mentally fit to be hired for work

em·ploy·ee or **em·ploye** (em ploi′ē, im-) *n.* one hired by another for wages or salary

em·ploy′er *n.* one who employs others for wages or salary

em·ploy′ment *n.* **1** an employing or being employed **2** work; occupation **3** the number or percentage of persons gainfully employed

em·po·ri·um (em pôr′ē əm) *n.*, *pl.* **-ri·ums** or **-ria** (-ə) ⟦< Gr *en*-, in + *poros*, way⟧ a large store with a wide variety of things for sale

em·power (em pou′ər, im-) *vt.* **1** to give power to; authorize **2** to enable

em·press (em′pris) *n.* **1** an emperor's wife **2** a woman ruler of an empire

empty (emp′tē) *adj.* **-tier, -ti·est** ⟦OE *æmettig*⟧ **1** having nothing or no one in it; unoccupied **2** worthless *[empty pleasure]* **3** insincere *[empty promises]* **—** *vt.* **-tied, -ty·ing 1** to make empty **2** to remove (the contents) of something **—** *vi.* **1** to become empty **2** to pour out; discharge **—** *n.*, *pl.* **-ties** an empty truck, bottle, etc. **—emp′tily** *adv.* **—emp′ti·ness** *n.*

emp′ty-hand′ed *adj.* bringing or carrying away nothing

em·py·re·an (em pir′ē ən, em′pī rē′ən) *n.* ⟦< Gr *en*-, in + *pyr*, fire⟧ **1** the highest heaven **2** the sky; firmament

emu (ē′myōō) *n.* ⟦< Port *ema*, a crane⟧ a large, flightless Australian bird, like the ostrich but smaller

em·u·late (em′yōō lāt′, -yə-) *vt.* **-lat′ed, -lat′ing** ⟦< L *aemulus*, trying to equal or excel⟧ **1** to try to equal or surpass **2** to imitate (a person or thing admired) **3** to rival successfully **—em′u·la′tion** *n.* **—em′u·la′tive** *adj.* **—em′u·la′tor** *n.*

emul·si·fy (ē mul′sə fī′, i-) *vt.*, *vi.* **-fied′, -fy′ing** to form into an emulsion **—emul′si·fi·ca′tion** *n.*

emul·sion (ē mul′shən, i-) *n.* ⟦< L *e*-, out + *mulgere*, to milk⟧ a fluid formed by the suspension of one liquid in another, as some medications, etc.

en- ⟦< L *in*-, in⟧ *prefix* **1** to put or get into or on *[enthrone]* **2** to make, cause to be *[endanger]* **3** in or into *[encase]*

-en (ən, 'n) ⟦OE⟧ *suffix* **1** *a)* to become or cause to be *[darken]* *b)* to cause to have *[heighten]* **2** made of *[wooden]* **3** forming plurals *[children]* **4** forming diminutives *[chicken]*

en·able (en ā′bəl, in-) *vt.* **-bled, -bling** to make able; provide with means, power, etc. (*to* do something)

en·act (en akt′, in-) *vt.* **1** to pass (a bill, law, etc.) **2** to represent as in a play **—en·act′ment** *n.*

en·amel (e nam′əl, i-) *n.* ⟦< OFr *esmail*⟧ **1** a glassy, opaque substance fused to metal, pottery, etc. as an ornamental or protective coating **2** the hard, white coating of teeth **3** paint that dries to a smooth, glossy surface **—** *vt.* **-eled** or **-elled, -el·ing** or **-el·ling** to coat with enamel **— en·am′eler** or **en·am′el·ler** *n.*

en·amor (en am′ər, in-) *vt.* ⟦ult. < L *in*-, in + *amor*, love⟧ to fill with love; charm: now mainly in the passive voice, with *of [enamored* of her*]*

en bloc (en bläk′) ⟦Fr, lit., in a block⟧ in a mass; all together

en bro·chette (än brō shet′) ⟦Fr⟧ broiled on small skewers

en·camp (en kamp′, in-) *vi.*, *vt.* to set up, or put in, a camp **—en·camp′ment** *n.*

en·cap·su·late (en kap′sə lāt′) *vt.* **-lat′ed, -lat′ing 1** to enclose in a capsule **2** to make concise; condense Also **en·cap′sule** (-səl, -syool′), **-suled, -sul·ing —en·cap′su·la′tion** *n.*

en·case (en kās′, in-) *vt.* **-cased′, -cas′ing** to enclose, as in a case

en cas·se·role (en kas′ə rōl′) ⟦Fr⟧ (baked and served) in a casserole

-ence (əns, 'ns) ⟦< L⟧ *suffix* act, state, or result *[conference]*

en·cepha·li·tis (en sef′ə līt′is) *n.* ⟦< Gr *en*-, in + *kephalē*, the head + -ITIS⟧ inflammation of the brain

en·chain (en chān′) *vt.* to bind with chains; fetter

en·chant (en chant′, in-) *vt.* ⟦< L *in*-, intens. + *cantare*, sing⟧ **1** to cast a spell over **2** to charm greatly; delight **— en·chant′er** *n.* **—en·chant′ing** *adj.* **—en·chant′ment** *n.*

THESAURUS

emphasize *v.* make clear, make emphatic, underline, underscore, highlight, dramatize, pronounce, enunciate, articulate, accentuate, accent, stress, point up, point out, strike, call to the attention of, reiterate, repeat, insist, maintain, impress, affirm, indicate, rub in*, pound into one's head*, drum into one's head*, labor the point, make a fuss about.

emphatic *a.* assured, strong, determined, forceful, forcible, earnest, positive, energetic, potent, powerful, dynamic, stressed, pointed, flat, definitive, categorical, dogmatic, explicit.

emphatically *a.* definitely, certainly, of course, undoubtedly, decidedly, decisively, absolutely, entirely, flatly, distinctly.—*Ant.* SLOWLY, hesitantly, indistinctly.

empire *n.* union, people, federation; see NATION 1.

employ *v.* **1** [To make use of] operate, manipulate, apply; see USE 1. **2** [To obtain services for pay] engage, contract, procure; see HIRE.

employed *a.* working, occupied, busy, laboring, gainfully employed, not out of work, in one's employ, on the job, hired, operating, active, engaged, on duty, on the payroll.—*Ant.* UNEMPLOYED, out of work, jobless.

employee *n.* worker, laborer, serv-

ant, domestic, agent, representative, hired hand, salesman, salesperson, assistant, associate, attendant, apprentice, operator, workman, laboring man, workingman, breadwinner, craftsman, wage earner, hireling, lackey, underling, flunky.

employer *n.* owner, manager, proprietor, management, head, director, executive, superintendent, supervisor, president, chief, businessman, manufacturer, corporation, company, boss, front office, big shot*.

employment *n.* job, profession, vocation; see BUSINESS 1, TRADE 2, WORK 2.

emptiness *n.* void, vacuum, vacancy, gap, chasm, blankness, blank, exhaustion, hollowness.

empty *a.* hollow, bare, clear, blank, unfilled, unfurnished, unoccupied, vacated, vacant, void, vacuous, void of, devoid, lacking, wanting, barren, emptied, abandoned, exhausted, depleted, deserted, stark, deprived of, dry, destitute, negative, deflated, evacuated.—*Ant.* FULL, filled, occupied.

empty *v.* **1** [To become empty] discharge, leave, pour, flow out, ebb, run out, open into, be discharged, void, release, exhaust, leak, drain off, drain, rush out, escape.—*Ant.* ABSORB, flow in, enter. **2** [To cause to become empty] dump, dip, ladle,

tap, void, pour, spill out, let out, deplete, exhaust, deflate, drain, bail out, clean out, clear out, evacuate, eject, expel, draw off, draw out, disgorge, suck dry, drink.—*Ant.* FILL, pack, stuff.

emulate *v.* challenge, contend, imitate; see COMPETE, FOLLOW 2.

enable *v.* make possible, sanction, give power to, give authority to, invest, endow, authorize, allow, let, permit, license; see also APPROVE.

enact *v.* decree, sanction, ordain, order, dictate, make into law, legislate, pass, establish, ratify, vote in, proclaim, vote favorably, determine, authorize, appoint, institute, railroad through*, get the floor, put in force, make laws, put through, constitute, fix, set, formulate.

enactment *n.* edict, decree, statute; see LAW 3.

enamel *n.* lacquer, coating, finish, polish, gloss, top coat, varnish, glaze, veneer.

enamel *v.* lacquer, glaze, gloss, paint, veneer, coat, varnish, finish, paint.

encampment *n.* village, campsite, bivouac; see CAMP 1.

enchant *v.* entrance, entice, allure; see FASCINATE.

enchanted *a.* enraptured, entranced, captivated; see FASCINATED.

en·chi·lada (en'chi lä'də) *n.* ⟦AmSp⟧ a tortilla rolled with meat inside, served with a chili-flavored sauce

en·cir·cle (en sʉr'kəl, in-) *vt.* **-cled, -cling 1** to surround **2** to move in a circle around —**en·cir'cle·ment** *n.*

en·clave (en'klāv', än'-) *n.* ⟦< L *in*, in + *clavis*, a key⟧ a territory surrounded by another country's territory

en·close (en klōz', in-) *vt.* **-closed', -clos'ing 1** to shut in all around; surround **2** to insert in an envelope, etc., often along with a letter, etc.

en·clo'sure (-klō'zhər, in-) *n.* **1** an enclosing or being enclosed **2** something that encloses **3** something enclosed, as in an envelope or by a wall

en·code (en kōd', in-) *vt.* **-cod'ed, -cod'ing** to put (a message, etc.) into code

en·co·mium (en kō'mē əm) *n., pl.* **-ums** or **-a** (-ə) ⟦< Gr *en*-, in + *kōmos*, a revel⟧ high praise; eulogy

en·com·pass (en kum'pəs, in-) *vt.* **1** to surround **2** to contain; include

en·core (än'kôr') *interj.* ⟦Fr⟧ again; once more — *n.* a further performance, etc. in answer to an audience's applause

en·coun·ter (en koun'tər, in-) *vt.* ⟦< L *in*, in + *contra*, against⟧ **1** to meet unexpectedly **2** to meet in conflict — *n.* **1** a direct meeting, as in battle **2** a meeting, esp. when unexpected

en·cour·age (en kʉr'ij, in-) *vt.* **-aged, -ag·ing 1** to give courage, hope, or confidence to **2** to give support to; help —**en·cour'age·ment** *n.*

en·croach (en krōch', in-) *vi.* ⟦< OFr *en*-, in + *croc*, a hook⟧ to trespass or intrude (*on* or *upon*) —**en·croach'ment** *n.*

en croûte (än krōōt') ⟦Fr⟧ wrapped in pastry and baked: said esp. of meats

en·crust (en krust') *vt.* to cover as with a crust — *vi.* to form a crust —**en·crus·ta'tion** *n.*

en·cum·ber (en kum'bər, in-) *vt.* ⟦see EN- & CUMBER⟧ **1** to hold back the motion or action of; hinder **2** to burden —**en·cum'brance** *n.*

-ency (ən sē) ⟦L *-entia*⟧ *suffix* -ENCE [*dependency*]

en·cyc·li·cal (en sik'li kəl, in-) *n.* ⟦< Gr *en*-, in + *kyklos*, a circle⟧ a papal document addressed to the bishops

en·cy·clo·pedia or **en·cy·clo·pae·dia** (en si'klō pē'dē ə, -klə-; in-) *n.* ⟦< Gr *enkyklios*, general + *paideia*, education⟧ a book or set of books with alphabetically arranged articles on all branches, or on one field, of knowledge —**en·cy'clo·pe'dic** or **en·cy'clo·pae'dic** *adj.*

en·cyst (en sist') *vt., vi.* to enclose or become enclosed in a cyst, capsule, or sac —**en·cyst'ment** *n.*

end (end) *n.* ⟦OE *ende*⟧ **1** a limit; boundary **2** the last part of anything; finish; conclusion **3** a ceasing to exist; death or destruction **4** the part at or near an extremity; tip **5** an object; purpose **6** an outcome; result **7** *Football* a player at either end of the line — *vt., vi.* to bring or come to an end; finish; stop — *adj.* at the end; final —**make (both) ends meet** to manage to keep one's expenses within one's income —**put an end to 1** to stop **2** to do away with

en·dan·ger (en dān'jər, in-) *vt.* to expose to danger, harm, etc.; imperil

endangered species a species of animal or plant in danger of becoming extinct

en·dear (en dir', in-) *vt.* to make dear or beloved —**en·dear'ing** *adj.*

en·dear'ment *n.* **1** an endearing **2** a word or act expressing affection

en·deavor (en dev'ər, in-) *vi.* ⟦< EN- + OFr *deveir*, duty⟧ to make an earnest attempt; try Usually with an infinitive — *n.* an earnest attempt or effort Brit. sp. **en·deav'our**

en·demic (en dem'ik) *adj.* ⟦< Gr *en*-, in + *dēmos*, people⟧ prevalent in or restricted to a particular locality, as a disease or plant —**en·dem'i·cally** *adv.*

end·ing (en'diŋ) *n.* **1** the last part; finish **2** death

en·dive (en'dīv', än'dēv') *n.* ⟦< Gr *entybon*⟧ a cultivated plant with curled, narrow leaves used in salads

end'less *adj.* **1** having no end; eternal; infinite **2** lasting too long [*an endless speech*] **3** continual [*endless problems*] **4** with the ends joined to form a closed unit [*an endless chain*] —**end'lessly** *adv.* —**end'less·ness** *n.*

end'most' *adj.* at the end; farthest

THESAURUS

encircle *v.* encompass, circle, throw a cordon about; see SURROUND 1.

enclose *v.* insert, jail, corral, impound, confine, blockade, imprison, block off, fence off, set apart, lock up, lock in, keep in, box in, close in, shut in, wall in, box off, box up.—*Ant.* FREE, liberate, open.

enclosed *a.* locked in, penned in, jailed, packed up, wrapped up, shut up, buried, encased, imprisoned.

enclosure *n.* **1** [A space enclosed] pen, sty, yard, jail, garden, corral, cage, asylum, pound, park, zone, precinct, plot, court, patch, coop, den, cell, dungeon, vault, paddock, stockade, concentration camp, prison; see also BUILDING, PLACE 2, ROOM 2. **2** [Something inserted] information, check, money, circular, copy, questionnaire, forms, documents, printed matter.

encompass *v.* encircle, compass, gird; see SURROUND 1.

encounter *n.* **1** [A coming together] interview, rendezvous, appointment; see MEETING 1. **2** [Physical violence] conflict, clash, collision; see FIGHT 1.

encounter *v.* **1** [To meet unexpectedly] meet, confront, come across; see FIND. **2** [To meet in conflict] battle, attack, struggle; see FIGHT.

encourage *v.* cheer, refresh, enliven, exhilarate, inspire, cheer up, praise, restore, revitalize, gladden, fortify, console, ease, relieve, help, aid, comfort, approve, reassure, assist, befriend, uphold, reinforce, back, bolster, brace, further, favor, strengthen, side with, cheer on, back up, egg on, root for*, pat on the back.—*Ant.* RESTRAIN, discourage, caution.

encouraged *a.* inspired, enlivened, renewed, aided, supported, hopeful, confident, enthusiastic, roused, cheered; see also HELPED.—*Ant.* SAD, discouraged, disheartened.

encouragement *n.* aid, faith, help, assistance, support, cheer, confidence, trust, advance, promotion, reward, reassurance, incentive, backing, optimism, comfort, consolation, hope, relief, pat on the back, lift, shot in the arm.

encouraging *a.* bright, good, promising; see HOPEFUL 1, 2.

encyclopedia *n.* book of facts, book of knowledge, compilation, general reference work, encyclopedic reference work, cyclopedia.

encyclopedic *a.* exhaustive, broad, all-encompassing; see COMPREHENSIVE, GENERAL 1, WIDESPREAD.

end *n.* **1** [Purpose] aim, object, intention; see PURPOSE 1. **2** [The close of an action] expiration, completion, target date, termination, adjournment, final event, ending, close, finish, conclusion, finis, finale, retirement, accomplishment, attainment, determination, achievement, fulfillment, pay-off, realization, period, consummation, culmination, execution, performance, last line, curtain, terminus, last word*, wrap-up*, windup, cutoff, end of the line*.—*Ant.* ORIGIN, beginning, opening. **3** [A result] conclusion, effect, outcome; see RESULT. **4** [The extremity] terminal, termination, terminus, boundary, limit, borderline, point, stub, stump, tail end, edge, tip, top, head, butt end.—*Ant.* CENTER, middle, hub. **5** [The close of life] demise, passing, doom; see DEATH. —**in the end** at length, in conclusion, as a result; see FINALLY 2. —**keep one's end up*** do one's share, join, participate; see SHARE 1. —**make ends meet** manage, get by,

survive; see ENDURE 2. —**no end*** very much, extremely, greatly; see MUCH, VERY. —**on end 1** [Endless] ceaseless, without interruption, constant; see ENDLESS. **2** [Upright] erect, vertical, standing up; see STRAIGHT 1. —**put an end to** stop, finish, cease; see END 1.

end *v.* **1** [To bring to a halt] stop, finish, quit, close, halt, shut down, settle, bring to an end, make an end of, break off, break up, put an end to, discontinue, postpone, delay, conclude, interrupt, dispose of, drop, call it a day*, cut short, wind up, get done, call off, give up, wrap up*.—*Ant.* BEGIN, initiate, start. **2** [To bring to a conclusion] settle, conclude, terminate; see ACHIEVE. **3** [To come to an end] desist, cease, die; see STOP 2. **4** [To die] expire, depart, pass away; see DIE.

endanger *v.* imperil, jeopardize, expose to danger, expose to hazard, expose to peril, be careless with, lay open, put on the spot*, leave in the middle.—*Ant.* SAVE, protect, preserve.

endangered *a.* exposed, imperiled, in a dilemma, in a predicament, jeopardized, in danger, in jeopardy, in a bad way*, on thin ice*, hanging by a thread*.

endeavor *n.* effort, try, attempt; see EFFORT.

endeavor *v.* attempt, aim, essay; see TRY 1.

ending *n.* finish, closing, terminus; see END 2.

endless *a.* infinite, interminable, untold, without end, unbounded, unlimited, immeasurable, limitless, boundless, incalculable, unfathomable.

endo- ⟦< Gr *endon* ⟧ *combining form* within, inner

endo·crine (en′dō krin′, -krīn′; -də-) *adj.* ⟦prec. + Gr *krinein*, to separate⟧ designating or of any gland producing a hormone

en·dorse (en dôrs′, in-) *vt.* **-dorsed′, -dors′ing** ⟦< L *in*, on + *dorsum*, the back⟧ **1** to write on the back of (a title, check, etc.) to transfer ownership, make a deposit, etc. **2** to sanction, approve, or support **3** to recommend (an advertised product) for a fee —**en·dorse′ment** *n.* —**en·dors′er** *n.*

endo·scope (en′dō skōp′, -də-) *n.* an instrument for examining visually the inside of a hollow organ, as the rectum

en·dow (en dou′, in-) *vt.* ⟦< OFr *en-*, in + *dotare*, to endow⟧ **1** to provide with some talent, quality, etc. [*endowed* with courage] **2** to give money to (a college, etc.) —**en·dow′ment** *n.*

end product the final result of a series of changes, processes, etc.

end table a small table placed at the end of a sofa, etc.

en·due (en dōō′, in-) *vt.* **-dued′, -du′ing** ⟦< L *in-*, in + *ducere*, to lead⟧ to provide (*with* qualities)

en·dur·ance (en door′əns, in-) *n.* the ability to last, stand pain, etc.

en·dure (en door′, in-) *vt.* **-dured′, -dur′ing** ⟦< L *durus*, hard⟧ **1** to hold up under (pain, fatigue, etc.) **2** to tolerate — *vi.* **1** to continue; last **2** to bear pain, etc. without flinching —**en·dur′able** *adj.*

en·dur·ing *adj.* lasting; permanent

end′ways′ (′-wāz′) *adv.* **1** on end; upright **2** with the end foremost **3** lengthwise Also **end′wise′** (′-wīz′)

-ene (ēn) ⟦after Gr *-enos*, adj. suffix⟧ *Chem. suffix* a certain type of hydrocarbon [*benzene*]

en·ema (en′ə mə) *n., pl.* **-mas** or **-ma·ta** (-mə tə) ⟦< Gr *en-*, in + *hienai*, send⟧ the forcing of a liquid, as a purgative, medicine, etc., into the colon through the anus

en·emy (en′ə mē) *n., pl.* **-mies** ⟦< L *in-*, not + *amicus*, friend⟧ **1** one who hates and wishes to injure another **2** *a)* a nation or force hostile to another *b)* troops, ship, etc. of a hostile nation **3** one hostile to an idea, cause, etc. **4** anything injurious

en·er·get·ic (en′ər jet′ik) *adj.* having or showing energy; vigorous —**en′er·get′i·cally** *adv.*

en·er·gize (en′ər jīz′) *vt.* **-gized′, -giz′ing** to give energy to; activate —**en′er·giz′er** *n.*

en·er·gy (en′ər jē) *n., pl.* **-gies** ⟦< Gr *en-*, in + *ergon*, work⟧ **1** force of expression **2** *a)* inherent power; capacity for action *b)* [*often pl.*] such power, esp. in action **3** a resource, as oil, gas, etc., from which usable energy can be produced **4** *Physics* the capacity for doing work

en·er·vate (en′ər vāt′) *vt.* **-vat′ed, -vat′ing** ⟦< L e-, out + *nervus*, nerve⟧ to deprive of strength, force, vigor, etc.; devitalize —**en′er·va′tion** *n.*

en·fee·ble (en fē′bəl, in-) *vt.* **-bled, -bling** to make feeble

en·fi·lade (en′fə lād′, en′fə lād′) *n.* ⟦Fr⟧ gunfire directed along a line of troops

en·fold (en fōld′, in-) *vt.* **1** to wrap in folds; wrap up **2** to embrace

en·force (en fôrs′, in-) *vt.* **-forced′, -forc′ing** **1** to impose by force [*to enforce* one's will] **2** to compel observance of (a law, etc.) —**en·force′able** *adj.* —**en·force′ment** *n.* —**en·forc′er** *n.*

en·fran·chise (en fran′chīz′, in-) *vt.* **-chised′, -chis′ing 1** to free from slavery **2** to give the right to vote —**en·fran′chise·ment** (-chiz mənt) *n.*

Eng. 1 England **2** English

en·gage (en gāj′, in-) *vt.* **-gaged′, -gag′ing** ⟦see EN- & GAGE[1]⟧ **1** to pledge (oneself) **2** to bind by a promise of marriage **3** to hire **4** to involve or occupy **5** to attract and hold (the attention, etc.) **6** to enter into conflict with (the enemy) **7** to mesh (gears, etc.) — *vi.* **1** to pledge oneself **2** to occupy or involve oneself [*to engage* in dramatics] **3** to enter into conflict **4** to mesh

en·gaged′ *adj.* **1** betrothed **2** occupied; employed **3** involved in combat, as troops **4** meshed

en·gage′ment *n.* an engaging or being engaged; specif., *a)* a betrothal *b)* an appointment *c)* employment *d)* a conflict; battle

en·gag′ing *adj.* attractive; charming —**en·gag′ingly** *adv.*

en·gen·der (en jen′dər, in-) *vt.* ⟦< L *in-*, in + *generare*, beget⟧ to bring into being; cause; produce

en·gine (en′jən) *n.* ⟦< L *in-*, in + base of *gignere*, beget⟧ **1** any machine that uses energy to develop mechanical power **2** a railroad locomotive **3** any machine

---

■■■ THESAURUS ■■■

endorse *v.* **1** [To inscribe one's name] sign, put one's signature to, put one's signature on, countersign, underwrite, sign one's name on, subscribe, notarize, add one's name to, put one's John Hancock on*, sign on the dotted line*. **2** [To indicate one's active support of] approve, confirm, sanction, ratify, guarantee, underwrite, support, stand up for, stand behind, be behind, vouch for, uphold, recommend, praise, give one's word for, OK, back up, go to bat for*.— *Ant.* BLAME, censure, condemn.

endorsed *a.* signed, notarized, legalized, ratified, sealed, settled, approved, upheld, supported, recommended, sanctioned, advocated, backed*, OK'd.

endorsement *n.* support, sanction, permission; see SIGNATURE.

endow *v.* enrich, provide, supply; see GIVE 1.

endowment *n.* benefit, provision, bequest, gratuity, grant, pension, stipend, legacy, inheritance, subsidy, revenue, trust, nest egg.

endurable *a.* sustainable, tolerable, supportable; see BEARABLE.

endurance *n.* sufferance, fortitude, capacity to endure, long-suffering, resignation, patience, tolerance, courage, perseverance, stamina, restraint, resistance, will, backbone, guts*, spunk*.—*Ant.* WEAKNESS, feebleness, infirmity.

endure *v.* **1** [To continue] persist, remain, last, continue, exist, be, stay, prevail, wear, sustain, survive, outlast, carry on, live on, go on, hold on, hang on, keep on, linger, outlive, hold out, never say die*, stick to*, ride out.—*Ant.* DIE, cease, end. **2** [To sustain adversity] suffer, tolerate,

bear with, bear up, allow, permit, support, undergo, sit through, take, withstand, bear up under, stand, accustom oneself to, submit to, sustain, go through, get through, encounter, be patient with, keep up, resign oneself, weather, brave, face, put up with, live through, stand for*, swallow, stomach, never say die*, grin and bear it, take it*, brace oneself, like it or lump it*, hang on, keep one's chin up.—*Ant.* AVOID, resist, refuse.

enduring *a.* lasting, abiding, surviving; see PERMANENT.

enemy *n.* foe, rival, assailant, competitor, attacker, antagonist, opponent, adversary, public enemy, criminal, opposition, guerrillas, guerrilla force, fifth column, saboteur, spy, foreign agent, assassin, murderer, betrayer, traitor, terrorist, revolutionary, rebel, invader.—*Ant.* FRIEND, ally, supporter.

energetic *a.* industrious, vigorous, forcible; see ACTIVE.

energy *n.* **1** [One's internal powers] force, power, virtility; see STRENGTH. **2** [Power developed or released by a device] horsepower, power, pressure, potential energy, kinetic energy, atomic energy, solar energy, high pressure, foot-pounds, magnetism, friction, voltage, kilowatt-hours, current, electricity, gravity, heat, suction, radioactivity, potential, fuel consumption.

enfold *v.* envelope, encase, enclose; see SURROUND 1, WRAP.

enforce *v.* urge, compel, incite, exert, drive, demand, carry out vigorously, put in force, dictate, exact, require, execute, coerce, oblige, insist upon, emphasize, necessitate, press, impel,

make, sanction, force upon, goad, stress, spur, hound, crack down.— *Ant.* ABANDON, neglect, evade.

enforced *a.* compelled, established, exacted, required, executed, pressed, sanctioned, forced upon, kept, dictated, admonished, advocated, charged, meted out, cracked down.

enforcement *n.* requirement, enforcing, prescription, compulsion, constraint, coercion, pressure, duress, obligation, necessity, insistence, carrying out, fulfilling.

engage *v.* **1** [To hire] employ, contract, retain; see HIRE. **2** [To engross] absorb, captivate, bewitch; see FASCINATE. **3** [To enmesh, especially gears] interlock, mesh, interlace; see FASTEN. —**engage in** take part in, attack, undertake; see PERFORM 1.

engaged *a.* **1** [Promised in marriage] bound, pledged, betrothed, matched, hooked*.—*Ant.* FREE, unpledged, unbetrothed. **2** [Not at liberty] working, occupied, employed; see BUSY 1. **3** [In a profession, business, or the like] employed, practicing, performing, dealing in, doing, interested, absorbed in, pursuing, at work, working at, involved with, involved in, engaged with, engaged in, connected with; see also EMPLOYED.—*Ant.* UNEMPLOYED, out of a job, without connection.

engagement *n.* **1** [A predetermined action] meeting, rendezvous, errand; see APPOINTMENT 2. **2** [The state of being betrothed] contract, match, betrothal, espousal, betrothing.

engine *n.* motor, power plant, dynamo, generator, turbine, diesel engine, traction engine, source of

en·gi·neer (en'jə nir') *n.* **1** one skilled in some branch of engineering **2** one who operates or supervises the operation of engines or technical equipment *[a locomotive engineer]* — *vt.* **1** to plan, construct, etc. as an engineer **2** to manage skillfully

en·gi·neer·ing *n.* **1** the science concerned with putting scientific knowledge to practical uses **2** the planning, designing, construction, etc. of machinery, roads, bridges, etc.

Eng·lish (iŋ'glish) *adj.* **1** of England, its people, etc. **2** of their language — *n.* **1** the language of the people of England, the official language of the Commonwealth of Nations, the U.S., etc. **2** *[sometimes* **e-]** a spinning motion given to a ball —**the English** the people of England

English horn a double-reed woodwind instrument

Eng·lish·man (-mən) *n., pl.* **-men** a native or inhabitant of England —**Eng'lish·wom'an,** *pl.* **-wom'en,** *n.fem.*

en·gorge (en gôrj', in-) *vt.* **-gorged', -gorg'ing** [< OFr *en-,* in + *gorge,* gorge] **1** to devour greedily **2** *Med.* to congest (tissue, etc.) with fluid, as blood

en·grave (en grāv', in-) *vt.* **-graved', -grav'ing** [< Fr *en-,* in + *graver,* to incise] **1** to cut or etch letters, designs, etc. in or on (a metal plate, etc.) **2** to print with such a plate **3** to impress deeply —**en·grav'er** *n.*

en·grav·ing *n.* **1** the act or art of one who engraves **2** an engraved plate, drawing, etc. **3** a print made from an engraved surface

en·gross (en grōs', in-) *vt.* [< OFr *engroissier,* become thick] to take the entire attention of; occupy wholly —**en·gross'ing** *adj.*

en·gulf (en gulf', in-) *vt.* to swallow up

en·hance (en hans', in-) *vt.* **-hanced', -hanc'ing** [< L *in-,* in + *altus,* high] to make greater, better, etc.; heighten —**en·hance'ment** *n.*

enig·ma (i nig'mə, e-) *n.* [< Gr *ainos,* story] **1** a riddle **2** a perplexing or baffling matter, person, etc. —**en·ig·mat·ic** (en'ig mat'ik, ē'nig-) *adj.*

en·jamb·ment or **en·jambe·ment** (en jam'mənt) *n.* [< Fr *enjamber,* to encroach] the running on of a sentence from one line to the next of a poem

en·join (en join', in-) *vt.* [< L *in-,* in + *jungere,* join] **1** to command; order **2** to prohibit, esp. by legal injunction

en·joy (en joi', in-) *vt.* [< OFr *en-,* in + *joir,* rejoice] **1** to get pleasure from; relish **2** to have the use or benefit of —**enjoy oneself** to have a good time —**en·joy'able** *adj.* —**en·joy'ment** *n.*

en·large (en lärj', in-) *vt.* **-larged', -larg'ing** to make larger; expand — *vi.* **1** to become larger; expand **2** to speak or write at greater length: with *on* or *upon* —**en·large'ment** *n.*

en·lighten (en līt'’n, in-) *vt.* **1** to free from ignorance, prejudice, etc. **2** to inform —**en·light'en·ment** *n.*

en·list (en list', in-) *vt., vi.* **1** to enroll in some branch of the armed forces **2** to engage in support of a cause or movement —**enlist'ee** (-ē) *n.* —**en·list'ment** *n.*

enlisted man any person in the armed forces who is not a commissioned officer or warrant officer

en·liven (en lī'vən, in-) *vt.* to make active, cheerful, etc.; liven up

en masse (en mas') [Fr, lit., in mass] in a group; as a whole

en·mesh (en mesh', in-) *vt.* to catch as in the meshes of a net; entangle

en·mity (en'mə tē) *n., pl.* **-ties** [see ENEMY] the attitude or feelings of an enemy or enemies; hostility

en·no·ble (en nō'bəl, i-) *vt.* **-bled, -bling** to give a noble quality to; dignify —**en·no'ble·ment** *n.*

en·nui (än'wē) *n.* [Fr] a feeling of weariness and boredom

enor·mity (ē nôr'mə tē, i-) *n., pl.* **-ties** [< L *enormis,* immense] **1** great wickedness **2** an outrageous act **3** enormous size or extent

enor·mous (ē nôr'məs, i-) *adj.* [see prec.] of great size, number, etc.; huge; vast —**enor'mously** *adv.*

enough (ē nuf', i-) *adj.* [OE *genoh*] as much or as many as necessary; sufficient — *n.* the amount needed — *adv.* **1** sufficiently **2** fully; quite *[oddly enough]* **3** tolerably

enow (ē nou', i-) *adj., n., adv.* [Archaic] enough

en·plane (en plān', in-) *vi.* **-planed', -plan'ing** to board an airplane

en·quire (en kwir', in-) *vt., vi.* **-quired', -quir'ing** INQUIRE —**en·quir'y** (-ē), *pl.* **-ies,** *n.*

en·rage (en rāj', in-) *vt.* **-raged', -rag'ing** to put into a rage; infuriate

en·rap·ture (en rap'chər, in-) *vt.* **-tured, -tur·ing** to fill with delight

en·rich (en rich', in-) *vt.* to make rich or richer; give greater value, better quality, etc. to —**en·rich'ment** *n.*

■■■ THESAURUS ■■■

power, diesel.

engineer *n.* **1** [A professional engineer] surveyor, designer, planner, builder. *Types of engineers include the following:* mining, civil, metallurgical, geological, electrical, architectural, chemical, construction, military, naval, flight, industrial. **2** [The operator of a locomotive] motorman, brakeman, stoker; see DRIVER.

engineering *n.* design, planning, blueprinting, structure, structures, surveying, metallurgy, architecture, shipbuilding, installations, stresses, communications.

English *a.* British, Britannic, Anglian, Anglican, Anglo-, England's, His Majesty's, Her Majesty's, Commonwealth, anglicized, English-speaking, Norman.

engrave *v.* etch, bite, stipple, lithograph, cut, burn, incise, grave, chisel, crosshatch.

engraved *a.* carved, decorated, etched, scratched, bitten into, embossed, furrowed, incised, deepened, marked deeply, lithographed.

engraving *n.* print, wood engraving, etching, aquatint, graphotype, rotogravure, lithograph, cut, woodcut, illustration, impression, copy, proof.

engross *v.* absorb, busy, fill; see OCCUPY 3.

engulf *v.* swallow up, submerge, inundate; see SINK 2.

enhance *v.* heighten, magnify, amplify; see INCREASE.

enigma *n.* problem, riddle, parable; see PUZZLE 3.

enjoy *v.* **1** [To get pleasure from] relish, luxuriate in, delight in; see LIKE

1. 2 [To have the use or benefit of] experience, partake of, share, undergo, make use of, use. —**enjoy oneself** take pleasure, celebrate, have a good time, revel in, delight in, luxuriate in, be pleased with; see also PLAY 1.

enjoyable *a.* agreeable, welcome, genial; see PLEASANT 1, 2.

enjoyment *n.* satisfaction, gratification, triumph, loving, enjoying, rejoicing, having, using, occupation, use, diversion, entertainment, luxury, sensuality, indulgence, self-indulgence, hedonism.—*Ant.* ABUSE, dislike, displeasure.

enlarge *v.* **1** [To increase] expand, spread, swell; see GROW 1. **2** [To cause to increase] extend, augment, expand; see INCREASE.

enlarged *a.* increased, augmented, expanded, developed, exaggerated, extended, amplified, spread, added to, lengthened, broadened, widened, thickened, magnified, filled-out, inflated, stretched, heightened, intensified, blown up*.

enlargement *n.* **1** [Growth or extension] augmentation, amplification, expansion; see INCREASE. **2** [An enlarged photograph] view, enlarged print, blowup; see PHOTOGRAPH, PICTURE 2.

enlighten *v.* inform, divulge, acquaint; see TEACH, TELL 1.

enlightened *a.* instructed, learned, informed; see EDUCATED.

enlightenment *n.* wisdom, culture, education; see KNOWLEDGE 1.

enlist *v.* **1** [To enroll others] sign up, press into service, hire, retain, call up, recruit, mobilize, induct, register,

list, initiate, employ, place, admit, draft, conscribe, muster, call to arms.—*Ant.* REFUSE, neglect, turn away. **2** [To enroll oneself] enter, sign up, serve; see JOIN 2, REGISTER 4.

enlisted *a.* recruited, commissioned, registered; see ENROLLED.

enlistment *n.* conscription, levy, recruitment; see ENROLLMENT 1, INDUCTION 3.

en masse *a.* bodily, ensemble, together; see TOGETHER 2, UNIFIED.

enmity *n.* animosity, malice, rancor; see HATRED.

enormous *a.* monstrous, immense, huge; see LARGE 1.

enough *a.* **1** [Sufficient] plenty, abundant, adequate, acceptable, ample, satisfactory, complete, copious, plentiful, satisfying, unlimited, suitable.—*Ant.* INADEQUATE, deficient, insufficient. **2** [Sufficiently] satisfactorily, amply, abundantly; see ADEQUATELY. **3** [Fully] quite, rather, just; see VERY. **4** [Just adequately] tolerably, fairly, barely; see ADEQUATELY.

enough *n.* abundance, sufficiency, adequacy; see PLENTY.

enrage *v.* anger, incite, provoke, irk, bother, annoy, tease, pester, agitate, arouse, stir, goad, bait, inflame, incense, infuriate, madden; see also INCITE.

enrich *v.* adorn, better, decorate; see IMPROVE 1.

enriched *a.* improved, bettered, embellished; see IMPROVED.

enrichment *n.* advancement, promotion, endowment; see IMPROVEMENT 1.

en·roll or **en·rol** (en rōl′, in-) *vt.*, *vi.* **-rolled′, -roll′ing** **1** to record or be recorded in a roll or list **2** to enlist **3** to make or become a member —**en·roll′ment** or **en·rol′ment** *n.*

en route (en rōōt′, än-) ⟦Fr⟧ on the way

en·sconce (en skäns′, in-) *vt.* **-sconced′, -sconc′ing** ⟦< Du *schans*, small fort⟧ to place or settle snugly or securely

en·sem·ble (än säm′bəl) *n.* ⟦Fr < L *in-*, in + *simul*, at the same time⟧ **1** total effect **2** a whole costume of matching parts **3** *a*) a small group of musicians, actors, etc. *b*) the performance of such a group

en·shrine (en shrīn′, in-) *vt.* **-shrined′, -shrin′ing** **1** to enclose in a shrine **2** to hold as sacred; cherish —**en·shrine′ment** *n.*

en·shroud (en shroud′, in-) *vt.* to cover as if with a shroud; hide; obscure

en·sign (en′sin′; *also, & for 2 always,* -sən) *n.* ⟦see INSIGNIA⟧ **1** *a* flag or banner **2** *U.S. Navy* a commissioned officer of the lowest rank

en·si·lage (en′sə lij′) *n.* ⟦Fr < *ensiler*, preserve in an underground granary⟧ SILAGE

en·slave (en slāv′, in-) *vt.* **-slaved′, -slav′ing** **1** to make a slave of **2** to subjugate —**en·slave′ment** *n.*

en·snare′ *vt.* **-snared′, -snar′ing** to catch as in a snare

en·sue (en sōō′, in-) *vi.* **-sued′, -su′ing** ⟦< L *in-*, in + *sequi*, follow⟧ **1** to come afterward **2** to result

en·sure′ (-shoor′, -sher′) *vt.* **-sured′, -sur′ing** **1** to make sure **2** to protect

-ent (ənt) ⟦< OFr *-ent*, L *-ens*, prp. ending⟧ *suffix* **1** that has, shows, or does *[insistent]* **2** a person or thing that *[superintendent, solvent]*

en·tail (en tāl′, in-) *vt.* ⟦< OFr *taillier*, to cut⟧ **1** *Law* to limit the inheritance of (real property) to a specific line of heirs **2** to make necessary; require

en·tan·gle *vt.* **-gled, -gling** **1** to involve in a tangle **2** to involve in difficulty **3** to confuse **4** to complicate —**en·tan′gle·ment** *n.*

en·tente (än tänt′) *n.* ⟦Fr < OFr *entendre*, understand⟧ **1** an understanding or agreement, as between nations **2** the parties to this

en·ter (ent′ər) *vt.* ⟦< L *intra*, within⟧ **1** to come or go into **2** to penetrate **3** to insert **4** to write down in a list, etc. **5** to become a member of or participant in **6** to get (a person, etc.) admitted **7** to begin **8** to put on record, formally or before a law court —*vi.* **1** to come or go into some place **2** to penetrate —**enter into** **1** to take part in **2** to form a part of —**enter on** (or **upon**) to begin; start

en·ter·i·tis (ent′ər īt′is) *n.* ⟦< Gr *enteron*, intestine + *-ITIS*⟧ inflammation of the intestine

en·ter·prise (ent′ər priz′) *n.* ⟦ult. < L *inter*, in + *prehendere*, take⟧ **1** an undertaking, esp. a big, bold, or difficult one **2** energy and initiative

en·ter·pris′ing *adj.* showing enterprise; full of energy and initiative

en·ter·tain (ent′ər tān′) *vt.* ⟦ult. < L *inter*, between + *tenere*, to hold⟧ **1** to amuse; divert **2** to have as a guest **3** to have in mind; consider —*vi.* to give hospitality to guests

en·ter·tain′er *n.* one who entertains; esp., a popular singer, comedian, etc.

en·ter·tain′ing *adj.* interesting and pleasurable; amusing —**en·ter·tain′ing·ly** *adv.*

en·ter·tain′ment *n.* **1** an entertaining or being entertained **2** something that entertains; esp., a show

en·thrall or **en·thral** (en thrôl′, in-) *vt.* **-thralled′, -thrall′ing** ⟦see EN- & THRALL⟧ to captivate; fascinate

en·throne′ *vt.* **-throned′, -thron′ing** **1** to place on a throne **2** to exalt

en·thuse (en thōōz′, in-) *vi.* **-thused′, -thus′ing** [Colloq.] to express enthusiasm —*vt.* [Colloq.] to make enthusiastic

en·thu·si·asm (en thōō′zē az′əm, in-) *n.* ⟦< Gr *en-*, in + *theos*, god⟧ intense or eager interest; zeal —**en·thu′si·ast′** (-ast′) *n.* —**en·thu′si·as′tic** *adj.* —**en·thu′si·as′ti·cally** *adv.*

en·tice (en tis′, in-) *vt.* **-ticed′, -tic′ing** ⟦< L *in*, in + *titio*, a burning brand⟧ to tempt with hope of reward or pleasure —**en·tice′ment** *n.*

en·tire (en tir′, in-) *adj.* ⟦< L *integer*, whole⟧ not lacking any parts; whole; complete; intact —**en·tire′ly** *adv.*

═══ **THESAURUS** ═══

enroll *v.* **1** [To obtain for service] recruit, obtain, employ; see HIRE. **2** [To register oneself] enter, sign up, enlist; see JOIN 3, REGISTER 4.

enrolled *a.* joined, inducted, registered, installed, settled, pledged, enlisted, commissioned, employed, recruited, signed up.—*Ant.* SEPARATED, mustered out, discharged.

enrollment *n.* **1** [The act of enrolling] registering, listing, inducting, recording, enlistment, matriculation, induction, entry, enlisting, selecting, registration. **2** [The persons enrolled] group, students, student body, conscript, volunteers, number enrolled, response, registration, entrance, subscription.

en route *a.* on the way, in transit, flying, driving, traveling, midway, in passage, on the road, making headway toward, bound, heading toward.—*Ant.* MOTIONLESS, delayed, stalled.

enslave *v.* bind, imprison, incarcerate, shut in, enclose, confine, hold under, hold, subjugate, restrain, oppress, restrict, fetter, coerce, check, subdue, capture, suppress, make a slave of, hold in bondage, compel, chain, jail, deprive, tie, shackle.

enslavement *n.* oppression, subjection, servitude; see SLAVERY 1.

ensnare *v.* entrap, trap, snare; see CATCH 1.

ensure *v.* secure, assure, warrant; see GUARANTEE.

entail *v.* require, necessitate, evoke; see NEED.

entangle *v.* ensnare, entrap, trap, implicate, complicate, involve, snarl, corner, catch, embroil, tangle, ravel, unsettle, foul up*, mess up*, goof up*.—*Ant.* FREE, liberate, disentangle.

entanglement *n.* complexity, intricacy, complication; see DIFFICULTY 1, 2.

enter *v.* invade, set foot in, pass into, come in, drive in, burst in, rush in, go in, break into, get in, barge in, penetrate, intrude, reenter, slip, sneak, infiltrate, insert, move in, fall into*, crowd in, worm oneself into.—*Ant.* LEAVE, depart, exit. —**enter into** engage in, take part in, become part of; see JOIN 2. —**enter on** (or **upon**) start, take up, make a beginning; see BEGIN 2.

entered *a.* filed, listed, posted; see RECORDED.

enterprise *n.* undertaking, endeavor, affair; see BUSINESS.

entertain *v.* **1** [To keep others amused] amuse, cheer, please, interest, enliven, delight, divert, beguile, charm, captivate, inspire, stimulate, satisfy, humor, enthrall, elate, tickle, distract, indulge, flatter, relax, make merry, comfort.—*Ant.* TIRE, bore, weary. **2** [To act as host or hostess] receive, host, invite, treat, charm, feed, dine, wine, give a party, do the honors, welcome, give a warm reception to, receive with open arms.—*Ant.* NEGLECT, ignore, bore.

entertained *a.* amused, diverted, pleased, occupied, charmed, cheered, interested, relaxed, delighted, engrossed, enjoying oneself, happy, in good humor, in good company.—*Ant.* BORED, depressed, irritated.

entertainer *n.* performer, player, artist; see ACTOR.

entertaining *a.* diverting, amusing, engaging, enchanting, sprightly, lively, witty, clever, interesting, gay, charming, enjoyable, delightful, funny, pleasing, edifying, engrossing, compelling, rousing, cheerful, relaxing, moving, inspiring, captivating, thrilling, entrancing, stirring, poignant, impressive, soul-stirring, stimulating, absorbing, exciting, provocative, fascinating, ravishing, satisfying, seductive; see also FUNNY 1.—*Ant.* BORING, irritating, dull.

entertainment *n.* amusement, enjoyment, merriment, fun, pleasure, sport, recreation, pastime, diversion, relaxation, distraction, play, feast, banquet, picnic, show, television, the movies, treat, game, party, reception, spree.

enthused * *a.* excited, approving, eager; see ENTHUSIASTIC.

enthusiasm *n.* fervor, ardor, eagerness; see ZEAL.

enthusiast *n.* **1** [A zealous person] zealot, fanatic, partisan; see BELIEVER. **2** [One who has strong interest in something] hobbyist, supporter, participant; see FOLLOWER.

enthusiastic *a.* interested, fascinated, willing, thrilled, feverish, concerned, passionate, raging, pleased, excited, attracted, exhilarated, anxious, eager, yearning, dying to*, inflamed, absorbed, devoted, diligent, ardent, fiery, longing, desiring, spirited, zestful, fervent, ecstatic, impatient, delighted, enraptured, avid, wild about*, crazy about*, mad about*, hot for*, gung-ho, aching to*.—*Ant.* OPPOSED, reluctant, apathetic.

entice *v.* lure, allure, attract; see FASCINATE.

enticement *n.* lure, bait, promise; see ATTRACTION.

entire *a.* complete, untouched, undamaged; see WHOLE 1, 2.

entirely *a.* **1** [Completely] totally, fully, wholly; see COMPLETELY. **2** [Exclusively] uniquely, solely, undividedly; see ONLY 1.

en·tire·ty (-tē) *n., pl.* **-ties** **1** the state or fact of being entire; wholeness **2** an entire thing; whole

en·ti·tle (en tīt′'l, in-) *vt.* **-tled, -tling** **1** to give a title or name to **2** to give a right or claim to

en·ti·tle·ment *n.* something to which one is entitled, esp. a benefit, as Medicare, provided by certain government programs

en·ti·ty (en′tə tē) *n., pl.* **-ties** 〖ult. < L *esse*, to be〗 **1** existence **2** a thing that has definite existence

en·tomb (en tōōm′, in-) *vt.* to place in a tomb; bury —**en·tomb′ment** *n.*

en·to·mol·o·gy (en′tə mäl′ə jē) *n.* 〖< Gr *entomon*, insect + -LOGY〗 the branch of zoology that deals with insects —**en·to·mo·log′i·cal** (-mə läj′i kəl) *adj.* —**en′to·mol′o·gist** *n.*

en·tou·rage (än′tōō räzh′) *n.* 〖Fr < *entourer*, surround〗 a group of accompanying attendants, etc.; retinue

en·trails (en′trālz, -trəlz) *n.pl.* 〖< L *interaneus*, internal〗 the inner organs; specif., the intestines; viscera

en·trance¹ (en′trəns) *n.* **1** the act of entering **2** a place for entering; door, etc. **3** permission or right to enter; admission

en·trance² (en trans′, in-) *vt.* **-tranced′, -tranc′ing** 〖see EN- & TRANCE 〗 to fill with delight; enchant

en·trant (en′trənt) *n.* one who enters

en·trap (en trap′, in-) *vt.* **-trapped′, -trap′ping** to catch as in a trap

en·treat (en trēt′, in-) *vt., vi.* 〖< OFr *en-*, in + *traiter*, to treat〗 to ask earnestly; beseech; implore

en·treat′y *n., pl.* **-ies** an earnest request; prayer

en·tree or **en·trée** (än′trā′) *n.* 〖Fr < OFr *entrer*, enter〗 **1** right to enter **2** the main course of a meal

en·trench (en trench′, in-) *vt.* **1** to surround with trenches **2** to establish securely —**en·trench′ment** *n.*

en·tre·pre·neur (än′trə prə nur′) *n.* 〖Fr: see ENTERPRISE 〗 one who organizes a business undertaking, assuming the risk for the sake of the profit

en·tro·py (en′trə pē) *n.* 〖< Gr *entropē*, a turning toward〗 **1** a thermodynamic measure of the energy unavailable for useful work in a system **2** the tendency of an energy system to run down

en·trust (en trust′, in-) *vt.* **1** to charge with a trust or duty **2** to turn over for safekeeping

en·try (en′trē) *n., pl.* **-tries** 〖< OFr: see ENTER 〗 **1** an entering; entrance **2** a way by which to enter **3** an item or note in a list, journal, etc. **4** one entered in a race, etc.

en·twine (en twīn′, in-) *vt., vi.* **-twined′, -twin′ing** to twine together or around

enu·mer·ate (ē nōō′mər āt′, i-) *vt.* **-at′ed, -at′ing** 〖< L *e-*, out + *numerare*, to count〗 **1** to count **2** to name one by one —**enu′mera′tion** *n.*

enun·ci·ate (ē nun′sē āt′, i-) *vt., vi.* **-at′ed, -at′ing** 〖< L *e-*, out + *nuntiare*, announce〗 **1** to state definitely **2** to announce **3** to pronounce (words) —**enun′ci·a′tion** *n.*

en·velop (en vel′əp, in-) *vt.* 〖< OFr: see EN- & DEVELOP〗 **1** to wrap up; cover completely **2** to surround **3** to conceal; hide —**en·vel′op·ment** *n.*

en·velope (än′və lōp′, en′-) *n.* **1** a thing that envelops; covering **2** a folded paper container for a letter, etc., usually with a gummed flap

en·venom (en ven′əm, in-) *vt.* **1** to put venom into **2** to fill with hate

en·vi·able (en′vē ə bəl) *adj.* good enough to be envied or desired —**en′vi·ably** *adv.*

en·vi·ous (en′vē əs) *adj.* feeling or showing envy —**en′vi·ously** *adv.*

en·vi·ron·ment (en vī′rən mənt, in-) *n.* 〖see ENVIRONS 〗 **1** surroundings **2** all the conditions, etc. surrounding, and affecting the development of, an organism —**en·vi′ron·men′tal** *adj.*

en·vi·ron·men·tal·ist *n.* one working to solve environmental problems, as air and water pollution

en·vi·rons (en vī′rənz, in-) *n.pl.* 〖< OFr *en-*, in + *viron*, a circuit〗 **1** the districts surrounding a city; suburbs **2** surrounding area; vicinity

en·vis·age (en viz′ij, in-) *vt.* **-aged, -ag·ing** 〖see EN- & VISAGE 〗 to form an image of in the mind; visualize

en·vi·sion (en vizh′ən, in-) *vt.* 〖EN- + VISION 〗 to imagine (something not yet in existence)

en·voy (än′voi, en′-) *n.* 〖< Fr < L *in*, in + *via*, way〗 **1** a messenger **2** a diplomatic agent just below an ambassador

envy (en′vē) *n., pl.* **-vies** 〖< L *in-*, in + *videre*, to look〗 **1** discontent and ill will over another's advantages, possessions, etc. **2** desire for something that another has **3** an object of such feeling — *vt.* **-vied, -vy·ing** to feel envy toward or because of —**en′vy·ingly** *adv.*

en·zyme (en′zīm′) *n.* 〖< Gr *en-*, in + *zymē*, leaven〗 a protein, formed in plant and animal cells or made synthetically, acting as a catalyst in chemical reactions

eon (ē′ən, ē′än′) *n.* 〖< Gr *aiōn*, an age〗 an extremely long, indefinite period of time

-eous (ē əs) 〖< L *-eus* + -OUS 〗 *suffix var. of* -OUS *[gaseous]*

EPA Environmental Protection Agency

ep·au·let or **ep·au·lette** (ep′ə let′, ep′ə let′) *n.* 〖< Fr dim. of *épaule*, shoulder〗 a shoulder ornament, esp. on military uniforms

epee or **épée** (ā pā′) *n.* 〖Fr〗 a fencing sword like a foil, but heavier and more rigid

ephed·rine (e fe′drin) *n.* 〖< L *ephedra*, the plant horsetail〗 an alkaloid used to relieve nasal congestion and asthma

ephem·er·al (e fem′ər əl, i-) *adj.* 〖< Gr *epi-*, upon + *hēmera*, day〗 **1** lasting one day **2** short-lived; transitory

epi- 〖< Gr *epi*, at, on〗 *prefix* on, upon, over, among *[epiglottis]*

epic (ep′ik) *n.* 〖< Gr *epos*, a word, song, epic〗 a long narrative poem in a lofty style about the deeds of a hero or heroes — *adj.* of or like an epic; heroic; grand

epi·cen·ter (ep′i sent′ər) *n.* **1** the area of the earth's surface directly above the place of origin of an earthquake **2** a focal or central point

epi·cure (ep′i kyoor′) *n.* 〖after *Epicurus*, ancient Gr philosopher〗 one who enjoys and has a discriminating taste for fine foods and drinks

epi·cu·rean (ep′i kyōō rē′ən) *adj.* fond of sensuous pleasure, esp. that of eating and drinking — *n.* an epicure

---

THESAURUS

entirety *n.* total, aggregate, sum; see WHOLE.

entitle *v.* authorize, empower, qualify; see ALLOW.

entity *n.* item, article, something; see THING 1.

entourage *n.* retinue, associates, followers; see FOLLOWING.

entrails *n.* viscera, guts, insides; see INTESTINES.

entrance¹ *n.* **1** [The act of coming in] arrival, entry, passage, approach, induction, initiation, admission, admittance, appearance, introduction, penetration, trespass, debut, enrollment, baptism, invasion, immigration.—*Ant.* ESCAPE, exit, issue. **2** [The opening that permits entry] gate, door, doorway, vestibule, entry, gateway, portal, port, inlet, opening, passage, staircase, porch, hall, hallway, path, way, entrance, passageway, threshold, lobby, corridor, approach.

entrance² *v.* charm, captivate, hypnotize; see FASCINATE.

entrap *v.* catch, ensnare, decoy; see CATCH 1.

entrapment *n.* snare, ambush, ruse; see TRAP 1.

entree *n.* main course, main dish, meat dish; see MEAL.

entrepreneur *n.* owner, capitalist, employer; see BUSINESSMAN.

entrust *v.* deposit with, trust to, leave with; see TRUST 4.

entry *n.* approach, hall, lobby, foyer, door, gate; see also ENTRANCE 2.

enumerate *v.* list, mention, identify; see RECORD 1.

enumeration *n.* inventory, catalog, register; see RECORD 1.

envelop *v.* encompass, contain, hide; see SURROUND 1, WRAP.

envelope *n.* receptacle, pouch, pocket, bag, container, box, covering, case, wrapper, enclosure, cover, sheath, casing.

enviable *a.* welcome, good, superior; see EXCELLENT.

envious *a.* covetous, desirous, resentful, desiring, wishful, longing for, aspiring, greedy, grasping, craving, begrudging, green-eyed, hankering, green with envy; see also JEALOUS.—*Ant.* GENEROUS, trustful, charitable.

environment *n.* conditions, living conditions, circumstances, surroundings, scene, external conditons, background, milieu, setting, habitat, situation.

envoy *n.* emissary, ambassador, intermediary; see AGENT.

envy *n.* jealousy, ill-will, spite, rivalry, opposition, grudge, malice, prejudice, malevolence, covetousness, enviousness, backbiting, maliciousness, the green-eyed monster*.

envy *v.* begrudge, covet, lust after, crave, be envious of, feel ill toward, have hard feelings toward, feel resentful toward, have a grudge against, object to.

eon *n.* eternity, cycle, time; see AGE 3.

epic *a.* heroic, classic, grand; see IMPORTANT 1.

epic *n.* narrative poem, saga, legend; see POEM, STORY.

epi·dem·ic (ep′ə dem′ik) *adj.* ⟦< Fr < Gr *epi-*, among + *dēmos*, people⟧ spreading rapidly among many people in a community, as a disease — *n.* **1** an epidemic disease **2** the spreading of such a disease **3** a rapid, widespread growth —**ep′i·dem′i·cal·ly** *adv.*

epi·dem·i·ol·o·gy (ep′ə dē′mē äl′ə jē) *n.* ⟦prec. + -LOGY⟧ the branch of medicine that studies epidemics

epi·der·mis (ep′ə dur′mis) *n.* ⟦< Gr *epi-*, upon + *derma*, the skin⟧ the outermost layer of the skin —**ep′i·der′mal** or **ep′i·der′mic** *adj.*

epi·glot·tis (ep′ə glät′is) *n.* ⟦see EPI- & GLOTTIS⟧ the thin cartilage lid that covers the windpipe during swallowing

epi·gram (ep′ə gram′) *n.* ⟦< Gr *epi-*, upon + *graphein*, write⟧ a terse, witty, pointed statement —**ep′i·gram·mat′ic** (-grə mat′ik) *adj.*

epig·ra·phy (ē pig′rə fē, i-) *n.* the study of inscriptions, esp. ancient ones

epi·lep·sy (ep′ə lep′sē) *n.* ⟦< Gr *epi-*, upon + *lambanein*, seize⟧ a recurrent disorder of the nervous system, characterized by seizures causing convulsions, unconsciousness, etc.

ep′i·lep′tic (-tik) *adj.* of or having epilepsy — *n.* one who has epilepsy

epi·logue or **epi·log** (ep′ə lôg′) *n.* ⟦< Gr *epi-*, upon + *legein*, speak⟧ a closing section added to a novel, play, etc., providing further comment, as a speech by an actor to the audience

Epiph·a·ny (ē pif′ə nē, i-) *n., pl.* **-nies** ⟦< Gr *epiphainein*, show forth⟧ a Christian feast day (Jan. 6) commemorating the revealing of Jesus as the Christ to the Gentiles

epis·co·pacy (ē pis′kə pə sē, i-) *n., pl.* **-cies** ⟦< Gr *epi-*, upon + *skopein*, to look⟧ **1** church government by bishops **2** EPISCOPATE

epis′co·pal (-pəl) *adj.* **1** of or governed by bishops **2** [E-] designating or of any of various churches governed by bishops

Epis·co·pa′lian (-pāl′yən) *adj.* Episcopal — *n.* a member of the Protestant Episcopal Church

epis′co·pate (-pit, -pāt′) *n.* **1** the position, rank, etc. of a bishop **2** bishops collectively

epi·sode (ep′ə sōd′) *n.* ⟦< Gr *epi-*, upon + *eisodos*, entrance⟧ **1** any part of a novel, poem, etc. that is complete in itself **2** an event or series of events complete in itself —**ep′i·sod′ic** (-säd′ik) *adj.* —**ep′i·sod′i·cally** *adv.*

epis·tle (ē pis′əl) *n.* ⟦< Gr *epi-*, to + *stellein*, send⟧ **1** a letter **2** [E-] any of the letters in the New Testament — **epis′to·lar′y** (-tə ler′ē) *adj.*

epi·taph (ep′ə taf′) *n.* ⟦< Gr *epi-*, upon + *taphos*, tomb⟧ an inscription on a tomb, etc. in memory of a dead person

epi·the·li·um (ep′i thē′lē əm) *n., pl.* **-li·ums** or **-lia** (-ə) ⟦< Gr *epi-*, upon + *thēlē*, nipple⟧ cellular tissue covering external body surfaces or lining internal surfaces —**ep′i·the′li·al** (-əl) *adj.*

epi·thet (ep′ə thet′) *n.* ⟦< Gr *epi-*, on + *tithenai*, put⟧ a word or phrase characterizing some person or thing

epit·o·me (ē pit′ə mē′, i-) *n., pl.* **-mes′** (-mēz′) ⟦< Gr *epi-*, upon + *temnein*, to cut⟧ **1** an abstract; summary **2** a person or thing that typifies a whole class

epit′o·mize′ (-mīz′) *vt.* **-mized′, -miz′ing** to make or be an epitome of

e plu·ri·bus unum (ē′ ploor′ē boos′ ōō′noom) ⟦L⟧ out of many, one: a motto of the U.S.

ep·och (ep′ək) *n.* ⟦< Gr *epi-*, upon + *echein*, to hold⟧ **1** the start of a new period in the history of anything **2** a period of time in terms of noteworthy events, persons, etc. —**ep′och·al** *adj.*

ep·oxy (ē päk′sē, i-) *adj.* ⟦EP(I)- + OXY(GEN)⟧ designating a resin used in strong, resistant glues, enamels, etc. — *n., pl.* **-ies** an epoxy resin

ep·si·lon (ep′sə län′) *n.* ⟦Gr *e psilon*⟧ the fifth letter of the Greek alphabet (E, ε)

Ep·som salts (or **salt**) (ep′sem) ⟦after *Epsom*, town in England⟧ a white, crystalline salt, magnesium sulfate, used as a cathartic

Epstein-Barr virus (ep′stēn bär′) a herpes-like virus that causes infectious mononucleosis and may cause various forms of cancer

eq·ua·ble (ek′wə bəl) *adj.* ⟦see fol.⟧ steady; uniform; even; tranquil —**eq′ua·bil′i·ty** *n.* —**eq′ua·bly** *adv.*

equal (ē′kwəl) *adj.* ⟦< L *aequus*, even⟧ **1** of the same quantity, size, value, etc. **2** having the same rights, ability, rank, etc. **3** evenly proportioned **4** having the necessary ability, strength, etc.: with *to* — *n.* any person or thing that is equal — *vt.* **e′qualed** or **e′qualled, e′qual·ing** or **e′qual·ling 1** to be equal to **2** to do or make something equal to —**equal′i·ty** (ē kwôl′ə tē, -kwäl′-), *pl.* **-ties,** *n.* — **e′qual·ly** *adv.*

equal·ize (ē′kwəl īz′) *vt.* **-ized′, -iz′ing** to make equal or uniform —**e′quali·za′tion** *n.* —**e′qual·iz′er** *n.*

equal sign (or **mark**) the sign (=), indicating that the terms on either side of it are equal or equivalent

equa·nim·i·ty (ek′wə nim′ə tē, ē′kwə-) *n.* ⟦< L *aequus*, even + *animus*, mind⟧ evenness of mind; composure

equate (ē kwāt′, i-) *vt.* **equat′ed, equat′ing 1** to make equal **2** to treat, regard, or express as equal —**equat′able** *adj.*

equa·tion (ē kwā′zhən, i-) *n.* **1** an equating or being equated **2** a statement of equality between two quantities, as shown by the equal sign (=)

equa·tor (ē kwāt′ər, i-) *n.* an imaginary circle around the earth, equally distant from both the North Pole and the South Pole —**equa·to·ri·al** (ē′kwə tôr′ē əl, ek′wə-) *adj.*

equer·ry (ek′wər ē, ē kwer′ē) *n., pl.* **-ries** ⟦< Fr⟧ **1** an officer in charge of royal horses **2** an officer who attends a person of royalty

eques·tri·an (ē kwes′trē ən, i-) *adj.* ⟦< L *equus*, horse⟧ **1** of horses or horsemanship **2** on horseback — *n.* a rider or circus performer on horseback —**eques′tri·enne′** (-trē en′) *n.fem.*

equi- *combining form* equal, equally *[equidistant]*

equi·dis·tant (ē′kwi dis′tənt) *adj.* equally distant

e′qui·lat′er·al (-lat′ər əl) *adj.* ⟦< L *aequus*, even + *latus*, side⟧ having all sides equal

e′qui·lib′ri·um (-lib′rē əm) *n., pl.* **-ri·ums** or **-ria** (-ə) ⟦< L *aequus*, even + *libra*, a balance⟧ a state of balance between opposing forces

equine (ē′kwin′) *adj.* ⟦< L *equus*, horse⟧ of or like a horse

equi·nox (ē′kwi näks′, ek′wə näks′) *n.* ⟦< L *aequus*, even + *nox*, night⟧ the time when the sun crosses the equator, making night and day of equal length in all parts of the earth —**e′qui·noc′tial** (-näk′shəl) *adj.*

═══════════════ **THESAURUS** ═══════════════

epidemic *n.* plague, scourge, pestilence; see ILLNESS 1.

epidermis *n.* cuticle, dermis, hide; see SKIN.

episode *n.* happening, occurrence, incident; see EVENT.

epoch *n.* era, period, time; see AGE 3.

equal *a.* even, regular, like, same, identical, similar, uniform, invariable, fair, unvarying, commensurate, just, impartial, unbiased, to the same degree, on a footing with, without distinction, equitable, one and the same, level, parallel, corresponding, equivalent, proportionate, comparable, tantamount.—*Ant.* IRREGULAR, unequal, uneven. —**equal to** adequate, capable, qualified; see ABLE.

equal *n.* parallel, match, counterpart, complement, peer, fellow, twin, double, likeness, companion, copy, duplicate, rival, competitor, opposite

number.

equal *v.* match, equalize, rank with, be the same, rival, equate, approach, live up to, come up to, amount to, consist of, comprise, be composed of, be made of, measure up to, even off, break even, come to, compare, square with, tally with, agree, correspond, be tantamount to, be identical, keep pace with, be commensurate, meet, rise to.

equality *n.* balance, parity, uniformity, sameness, likeness, identity, evenness, equalization, equilibrium, impartiality, fairness, civil rights, equivalence, tolerance, all for one and one for all*, six of one and half a dozen of the other*, even-steven*, fair shake.—*Ant.* INJUSTICE, inequality, unfairness.

equalize *v.* make even, make equal, balance, equate, match, level, adjust, establish equilibrium, even up.

equally *a.* evenly, symmetrically, proportionally, coordinately, equivalently, on a level, both, either ... or, impartially, justly, fairly, across the board, on even terms, as well as, the same for one as for another.

equate *v.* **1** [To equalize] make equal, average, balance; see EQUALIZE. **2** [To compare] match, link, relate; see COMPARE 1.

equation *n.* mathematical statement, formal statement of equivalence, chemical statement. *Kinds of equations include the following:* linear, quadratic, conic, cubic, balanced, unbalanced.

equator *n.* middle, circumference of the earth, tropics; see JUNGLE.

equatorial *a.* tropical, mediterranean, central; see HOT 1.

equilibrium *n.* stability, center of gravity, steadiness; see BALANCE 2.

equip (ē kwip′, i-) *vt.* **equipped′, equip′ping** ⟦< OFr *esquiper,* embark⟧ to provide with what is needed

equi page (ek′wi pij′) *n.* a carriage with horses and liveried servants

equip ment (ē kwip′mənt, i-) *n.* **1** an equipping or being equipped **2** whatever one is equipped with; supplies, furnishings, etc.

equi poise (ek′wi poiz′, ē′kwi-) *n.* ⟦EQUI- + POISE⟧ **1** state of equilibrium **2** counterbalance

eq′ui table (-wit ə bəl) *adj.* ⟦see EQUITY⟧ fair; just — **eq′ui tably** *adv.*

equi ta tion (ek′wi tā′shən) *n.* ⟦< L *equitare,* to ride⟧ horsemanship

equi ty (ek′wit ē) *n., pl.* **-ties** ⟦< L *aequus,* even⟧ **1** fairness; impartiality; justice **2** the value of property beyond the amount owed on it **3** *Finance a)* assets minus liabilities; net worth *b)* [*pl.*] shares of stock **4** *Law* a system of doctrines supplementing common and statute law

equiva lent (ē kwiv′ə lənt, i-) *adj.* ⟦< L *aequus,* equal + *valere,* be strong⟧ equal in quantity, value, force, meaning, etc. — *n.* an equivalent thing —**equiv′a lence** *n.*

equivo cal (ē kwiv′ə kəl, i-) *adj.* ⟦< L *aequus,* even + *vox,* voice⟧ **1** having two or more meanings; purposely ambiguous **2** uncertain; doubtful **3** suspicious —**equiv′o cally** *adv.* —**equiv′o cal ness** *n.*

equiv′o cate′ (-kāt′, i-) *vi.* **-cat′ed, -cat′ing** to use equivocal terms in order to deceive or mislead —**equiv′o ca′tion** *n.* —**equiv′o ca′tor** *n.*

-er (ər) ⟦ME⟧ *suffix* **1** *a)* a person or thing having to do with *[hatter] b)* a person living in *[New Yorker] c)* one that ——s *[roller] d)* repeatedly *[flicker]* **2** forming the comparative degree *[later]*

era (ir′ə, er′ə) *n.* ⟦LL *aera*⟧ **1** a period of time measured from some important event **2** a period of time having some special characteristic

ERA **1** *Baseball* earned run average: also **era** **2** Equal Rights Amendment

eradi cate (ē rad′i kāt′, i-) *vt.* **-cat′ed, -cat′ing** ⟦< L *e-,* out + *radix,* root⟧ to uproot; wipe out; destroy —**erad′i ca′tion** *n.* —**erad′i ca′tor** *n.*

erase (ē rās′, i-) *vt.* **erased′, eras′ing** ⟦< L *e-,* out + *radere,* scrape⟧ **1** to rub, scrape, or wipe out (esp. writing) **2** to remove (something recorded) from (magnetic tape) **3** to obliterate, as from the mind —**eras′able** *adj.*

eras′er *n.* a thing that erases; specif., a rubber device for erasing ink or pencil marks, or a pad for removing chalk marks from a blackboard

era sure (ē rā′shər, i-) *n.* **1** an erasing **2** an erased word, mark, etc.

ere (er) *prep.* ⟦OE ær⟧ [Archaic] before (in time) — *conj.* [Old Poet.] before **2** rather than

erect (ē rekt′, i-) *adj.* ⟦< L *e-,* up + *regere,* make straight⟧ upright — *vt.* **1** to construct (a building, etc.) **2** to set in an upright position **3** to set up; assemble —**erec′tion** *n.* —**erect′ly** *adv.* —**erect′ness** *n.* —**erec′tor** *n.*

erec tile (ē rek′til, i-) *adj.* that can become erect, as tissue that becomes rigid when filled with blood

ere long (er′lôŋ′) *adv.* [Archaic] before long; soon

erg (ʉrg) *n.* ⟦< Gr *ergon,* work⟧ *Physics* a unit of work or energy

ergo (er′gō) *conj., adv.* ⟦L⟧ therefore

er gos terol (ʉr gäs′tə ôl′, -ōl′) *n.* a steroid alcohol prepared from yeast, that produces vitamin D when exposed to ultraviolet rays

Erin (er′in) ⟦Ir *Erinn*⟧ *old poet. name for* Ireland

er mine (ʉr′min) *n.* ⟦prob. < OHG *harmo,* weasel⟧ **1** a weasel whose fur is white in winter **2** its white fur

erode (ē rōd′, i-) *vt.* **erod′ed, erod′ing** ⟦< L *e-,* out + *rodere,* gnaw⟧ **1** to wear away **2** to form by wearing away gradually *[the stream eroded a gully]* — *vi.* to become eroded

erog enous (ē räj′ə nəs, i-) *adj.* ⟦< Gr *erōs,* love + -GEN + -OUS⟧ sensitive to sexual stimulation Also **ero to genic** (er′ə tō′jen′ik)

Eros (er′äs′, ir′-) *Gr. Myth.* the god of love — *n.* [e-] sexual love or desire

ero sion (ē rō′zhən, i-) *n.* an eroding or being eroded — **ero′sive** (-siv) *adj.*

erot ic (ē rät′ik, i-) *adj.* ⟦< Gr *erōs,* love⟧ of or arousing sexual feelings or desires; amatory —**erot′i cally** *adv.*

erot′i ca (-i kə) *n.pl.* [*often with sing. v.*] erotic books, pictures, etc.

err (ʉr, er) *vi.* ⟦< L *errare,* wander⟧ **1** to be wrong or mistaken **2** to deviate from the established moral code

er rand (er′ənd) *n.* ⟦OE *ærende,* mission⟧ **1** a trip to do a thing, as for someone else **2** the thing to be done

er rant (er′ənt) *adj.* [see ERR] **1** roving or wandering, esp. in search of adventure **2** erring **3** shifting about

er ratic (er rat′ik; e rat′-, i-) *adj.* ⟦< L *errare,* wander⟧ **1** irregular; random **2** eccentric; queer —**er rat′i cally** *adv.*

er ra tum (er rāt′əm, -rät′-) *n., pl.* **-ta** (-ə) ⟦see ERR⟧ an error in a work already printed

er ro neous (ər rō′nē əs; e rō′-, i-) *adj.* containing error; mistaken; wrong —**er ro′neous ly** *adv.*

er ror (er′ər) *n.* ⟦see ERR⟧ **1** the state of believing what is untrue **2** a wrong belief **3** something incorrectly done; mistake **4** a transgression **5** *Baseball* any misplay in fielding

er satz (er′zäts, er zäts′) *n., adj.* ⟦Ger⟧ substitute or synthetic and inferior

Erse (ʉrs) *n., adj.* ⟦ME *Erish,* var. of *Irisc,* Irish⟧ GAELIC

erst (ʉrst) *adv.* ⟦< OE ær, ere⟧ [Archaic] formerly

erst′while′ (-hwīl′) *adv.* [Archaic] formerly — *adj.* former

eruct (ē rukt′) *vt., vi.* ⟦< L *e-,* out + *ructare,* belch⟧ to belch —**e′ruc ta′tion** *n.*

eru dite (er′yōō dīt′, -ōō-) *adj.* ⟦< L *e-,* out + *rudis,* rude⟧ learned; scholarly —**er′u dite′ly** *adv.*

eru di tion (er′yōō dish′ən) *n.* learning acquired by reading and study

erupt (ē rupt′, i-) *vi.* ⟦< L *e-,* out + *rumpere,* to break⟧ **1** to burst forth or out *[erupting lava]* **2** to throw forth lava, water, etc. **3** to break out in a rash — *vt.* to cause to burst forth

erup tion (ē rup′shən, i-) *n.* **1** a bursting forth or out **2** *a)* a breaking out in a rash *b)* a rash

-ery (ər ē) ⟦< LL *-aria*⟧ *suffix* **1** a place to *[tannery]* **2** a

---

═══ THESAURUS ═══

equip *v.* furnish, outfit, supply; see PROVIDE 1.

equipment *n.* material, materiel, tools, facilities, implements, utensils, apparatus, furnishings, appliances, paraphernalia, belongings, devices, outfit, accessories, attachments, extras, conveniences, articles, tackle, rig, machinery, fittings, trappings, fixtures, contraptions, supplies, accompaniments, gear, fixings, stuff, gadgets, things; see also MACHINE, PART 3.

equipped *a.* outfitted, furnished, supplied, rigged up, fitted out, arrayed, dressed, accoutered, assembled, readied, provided, implemented, decked, bedecked, appareled, completed, supplemented, set up.

equitable *a.* impartial, just, moral; see FAIR 1.

equity *n.* investment, money, capital; see PROPERTY 1.

equivalent *a.* commensurate, comparable, similar; see EQUAL.

era *n.* epoch, period, date; see AGE 3, TIME 2.

eradicate *v.* eliminate, exterminate, annihilate; see DESTROY.

eradication *n.* extermination, annihilation, elimination; see DESTRUCTION 1.

erase *v.* delete, expunge, omit, obliterate, cut, clean, nullify, eradicate; see also CANCEL.

erect *a.* upright, vertical, perpendicular; see STRAIGHT 1.

erect *v.* construct, raise, fabricate; see BUILD.

erected *a.* constructed, completed, raised; see BUILT.

erection *n.* building, erecting, constructing; see CONSTRUCTION 2.

erode *v.* decay, corrode, consume; see DISINTEGRATE.

erosion *n.* wearing away, decrease, carrying away; see DESTRUCTION 1, 2.

erotic *a.* amorous, stimulating, carnal; see SENSUAL 1, 2.

err *v.* misjudge, blunder, be mistaken; see FAIL 1.

errand *n.* mission, task, commission; see DUTY 2.

erratic *a.* **1** [Wandering] nomadic, rambling, roving; see WANDERING 1. **2** [Strange] eccentric, queer, irregular; see UNUSUAL 2. **3** [Variable] inconsistent, unpredictable, variable; see IRREGULAR 1.

erring *a.* mistaken, faulty, blundering; see WRONG 1.

erroneous *a.* untrue, inaccurate, incorrect; see FALSE 2.

error *n.* blunder, mistake, fault, oversight, inaccuracy, omission, deviation, misdoing, faux pas, fall, slip, wrong, lapse, miss, failure, slight, misunderstanding, flaw, boner*, bad job, blooper*, muff, booboo*, botch. —**in error** mistakenly, inaccurately, by mistake; see BADLY 1, WRONG 2, WRONGLY.

ersatz *a.* artificial, synthetic, imitation; see FALSE 3.

erupt *v.* go off, eject, emit; see EXPLODE.

eruption *n.* burst, outburst, flow; see EXPLOSION.

place for *[nunnery]* **3** the practice or act of *[surgery]* **4** the product of *[pottery]* **5** a collection of *[greenery]* **6** the condition of *[drudgery]*

ery·sip·e·las (er'i sip'ə ləs) *n.* ⟦< Gr *erythros*, red + *-pelas*, skin⟧ an acute infectious disease of the skin causing inflammation and fever

eryth·ro·cyte (e rith'rō sīt') *n.* ⟦< Gr *erythros*, red + *kytos*, a hollow⟧ a mature red blood cell that contains hemoglobin, which carries oxygen to the body tissues

-es (iz, əz, z) ⟦< OE⟧ *suffix* **1** forming plurals *[glasses]* **2** forming the 3d person sing., pres. indic., of verbs *[he kisses]*

Esau (ē'sô') *Bible* Isaac's son who sold his birthright to his brother, Jacob

es·ca·late (es'kə lāt') *vi.* **-lat'ed, -lat'ing 1** to rise as on an escalator **2** to expand step by step **3** to increase rapidly **—es·ca·la'tion** *n.*

es·ca·la·tor (-ər) *n.* ⟦ult. < L *scala*, ladder⟧ a moving stairway on an endless belt

es·cal·lop or **es·ca·lop** (e skäl'əp, -skal'-) *n., vt.* SCALLOP

es·ca·pade (es'kə pād', es'kə pād') *n.* ⟦Fr: see fol.⟧ a reckless adventure or prank

es·cape (e skāp', i-) *vi.* **-caped', -cap'ing** ⟦< L *ex-*, out of + *cappa*, cloak⟧ **1** to get free **2** to avoid an illness, accident, etc. **3** to leak away *— vt.* **1** to get away from **2** to avoid *[to escape death]* **3** to come from involuntarily **4** to be missed or forgotten by *— n.* **1** an escaping **2** a means of escape **3** a leakage **4** a temporary mental release from reality *— adj.* providing an escape

es·cap·ee (e skāp'ē', -skāp'ē'; i-) *n.* one who has escaped, as from prison

es·cape·ment *n.* a notched wheel with a detaining catch that controls the action of a mechanical clock or watch

escape velocity the minimum speed required for a particle, satellite, etc. to escape permanently from the gravitational field of a planet, star, etc.

es·cap·ism *n.* a tendency to escape from reality, responsibilities, etc. through the imagination **—es·cap'ist** *adj., n.*

es·car·got (es kär gō') *n.* ⟦Fr⟧ an edible snail

es·ca·role (es'kə rōl') *n.* ⟦Fr⟧ ENDIVE

es·carp·ment (e skärp'mənt) *n.* ⟦< Fr⟧ a steep slope or cliff

-escence (es'əns) ⟦see fol.⟧ *suffix* the process of becoming *[obsolescence]*

-escent (es'ənt) ⟦L *-escens*⟧ *suffix* **1** starting to be, being, or becoming *[obsolescent]* **2** giving off light *[phosphorescent]*

es·chew (es chōō') *vt.* ⟦< OHG *sciuhan*, to fear⟧ to shun; avoid

es·cort (es'kôrt'; *for v.* es kôrt', is-) *n.* ⟦< L *ex-*, out + *corrigere*, set right⟧ **1** one or more persons, cars, etc. accompanying another to protect it or show honor **2** a man accompanying a woman *— vt.* to go with as an escort

es·cri·toire (es'kri twär') *n.* ⟦< L *scribere*, write⟧ a writing desk

es·crow (es'krō') *n.* ⟦see SCROLL⟧ the state of a deed, etc. put in the care of a third party until certain conditions are fulfilled

es·cutch·eon (e skuch'ən, i-) *n.* ⟦< L *scutum*, shield⟧ a shield on which a coat of arms is displayed

-ese (ēz, ēs) ⟦< L *-ensis*⟧ *suffix* **1** of a country or place *[Javanese]* **2** in the language of *[Cantonese]*

Es·ki·mo (es'kə mō') *n.* ⟦< Fr < AmInd⟧ **1** *pl.* **-mos'** or **-mo'** a member of a people from Greenland, N Canada, or Alaska **2** any of the languages of the Eskimos *— adj.* of the Eskimos, their language, etc.

Eskimo dog a strong breed of dog used by the Eskimos to pull sleds

esoph·a·gus (i säf'ə gəs, ē-) *n., pl.* **-gi'** (-jī') ⟦< Gr *oisophagos*⟧ the passage for food from the pharynx to the stomach

es·o·ter·ic (es'ə ter'ik) *adj.* ⟦< Gr *esōteros*, inner⟧ meant for or understood by only a chosen few **—es·o·ter'i·cally** *adv.*

esp. especially

ESP extrasensory perception

es·pa·drille (es'pə dril') *n.* ⟦Fr < Sp *esparto*, coarse grass⟧ a casual shoe with a canvas upper and a sole of twisted rope

es·pal·ier (es pal'yər) *n.* ⟦Fr < It *spalla*, shoulder⟧ **1** a lattice on which trees or shrubs are trained to grow flat **2** such a plant

es·pe·cial (e spesh'əl, i-) *adj.* special; particular **—es·pe'cially** *adv.*

Es·pe·ran·to (es'pə rän'tō, -ran'-) *n.* an invented international language based on the European word roots

es·pi·o·nage (es'pē ə näzh') *n.* ⟦< Fr < It *spia*, spy⟧ the act or practice of spying

es·pla·nade (es'plə näd', -näd') *n.* ⟦< Fr < It < L *explanare*, to level⟧ a level stretch of ground, as a public walk

es·pous·al (e spou'zəl, i-) *n.* **1** *[often pl.]* a wedding **2** an espousing of some cause, idea, etc.); advocacy

es·pouse (e spouz', i-) *vt.* **-poused', -pous'ing** ⟦see SPOUSE⟧ **1** to marry **2** to advocate (some cause, idea, etc.)

es·pres·so (es spres'ō) *n., pl.* **-sos** ⟦It⟧ coffee made by forcing steam through finely ground coffee beans

es·prit de corps (e sprē' də kôr') ⟦Fr⟧ group spirit; pride, etc. shared by those in the same group

es·py (e spī', i-) *vt.* **-pied', -py'ing** ⟦see SPY⟧ to catch sight of; spy

-esque (esk) ⟦< Fr < It *-esco*⟧ *suffix* **1** in the manner or style of *[Romanesque]* **2** like *[statuesque]*

es·quire (es'kwir') *n.* ⟦< L *scutum*, a shield⟧ **1** [Historical] a candidate for knighthood; squire **2** in England, a member of the gentry ranking just below a knight **3** [E-] a title of courtesy: in the U.S., now specif. used for lawyers: usually abbrev. **Esq.** or **Esqr.**

-ess (es, is, əs) ⟦< LL *-issa*⟧ *suffix* female *[lioness]*

es·say (e sā'; *for n.* 1 *usually, & for n.* 2 *always,* es'ā) *vt.* ⟦< LL *ex-*, out of + *agere*, to do⟧ to try; attempt *— n.* **1** a trying or testing **2** a short, personal literary composition dealing with a single subject **—es·say'er** *n.* **—es·say·ist** (es'ā ist) *n.*

es·sence (es'əns) *n.* ⟦< L *esse*, to be⟧ **1** the basic nature (of something) **2** *a*) a concentrated substance that keeps the flavor, etc. of that from which it is extracted *b*) perfume

Es·sene (es'ēn', e sēn') *n.* a member of an ancient Jewish ascetic sect (2d c. B.C. to the 2d c. A.D.)

es·sen·tial (e sen'shəl, i-, ə-) *adj.* **1** of or constituting the essence of something; basic **2** absolutely necessary; indis-

---

THESAURUS

escalate *v.* heighten, intensify, make worse; see INCREASE.

escalation *n.* intensification, growth, acceleration; see INCREASE, RISE 2.

escapade *n.* caper, adventure, prank; see JOKE.

escape *n.* flight, retreat, disappearance, evasion, avoidance, leave, departure, withdrawal, liberation, deliverance, desertion, abdication, break, rescue, freedom, release.— *Ant.* IMPRISONMENT, retention, bondage.

escape *v.* flee, fly, leave, depart, elude, avoid, evade, shun, run off, run away, make off, disappear, vanish, steal off, steal away, flow out, get away, break out, break away, wriggle out, desert, slip away, run out*, go scot-free, take flight, elope, duck out*, get clear of, break loose, cut and run, worm out of, clear out*, bail out*, crawl out of, save one's neck,

scram*, make a break*.—*Ant.* RETURN, come back, remain.

escaped *a.* out, at liberty, liberated; see FREE 2.

escort *n.* guide, attend, guard; see COMPANION.

escort *v.* go with, attend, take out*; see ACCOMPANY, DATE 2.

esophagus *n.* gullet, food tube, neck; see THROAT.

especially *a.* **1** [To an unusual degree] particularly, unusually, abnormally, extraordinarily, uncommonly, peculiarly, unexpectedly, preeminently, eminently, supremely, remarkably, strangely, curiously, notably, uniquely, singularly, to a marked degree, above all. **2** [For one more than for others] chiefly, mainly, primarily; see PRINCIPALLY.

espionage *n.* undercover work, reconnaissance, spying; see INFORMATION 1.

espouse *v.* advocate, adopt, uphold; see SUPPORT 2.

essay *n.* dissertation, treatise, article; see WRITING 2.

essence *n.* **1** [Basic material] pith, core, kernel, spirit, gist, root, nature, basis, being, essential quality, reality, constitution, substance, nucleus, vital part, base, quintessence, primary element, germ, heart, marrow, backbone, soul, bottom, life, grain, structure, principle, character, fundamentals. **2** [Distinctive quality] principle, nature, essential quality; see CHARACTERISTIC. **—in essence** ultimately, fundamentally, basically; see ESSENTIALLY.

essential *a.* **1** [Necessary] imperative, required, indispensable; see NECESSARY. **2** [Rooted in the basis or essence] basic, primary, quintessential; see FUNDAMENTAL.

pensable — *n.* something necessary or fundamental —**es·sen′tially** *adv.*

essen′tialize′ (-iz′) *vt.* **-ized′, -iz′ing** to concentrate on the essential meanings or aspects of

-est (est, ist, əst) 〖OE〗 *suffix* forming the superlative degree *[greatest]*

est. **1** established **2** estimate **3** estimated

EST Eastern Standard Time

es·tab·lish (e stab′lish, i-) *vt.* 〚 < L *stabilis*, stable 〛 **1** to order, ordain, or enact (a law, etc.) permanently **2** to set up (a nation, business, etc.) **3** to cause to be; bring about **4** to set up in a business, etc. **5** to cause to be accepted **6** to prove; demonstrate

es·tab′lish·ment *n.* **1** an establishing or being established **2** a thing established, as a business —**the Establishment** an inner circle thought of as holding decisive power in a nation, institution, etc.

es·tate (e stāt′, i-) *n.* 〚 < OFr *estat* 〛 **1** a condition or stage of life **2** property; possessions **3** a large, individually owned piece of land containing a residence

es·teem (e stēm′, i-) *vt.* 〚 < L *aestimare*, to value 〛 **1** to value highly; respect **2** to consider — *n.* favorable opinion

es·ter (es′tər) *n.* 〚Ger < *essig*, vinegar + *äther*, ether 〛 an organic compound formed by the reaction of an acid and an alcohol

Es·ther (es′tər) *Bible* the Jewish wife of a Persian king: she saved her people from slaughter

es′thete′ *n.* AESTHETE —**es·thet′ic** *adj.* —**es·thet′ics** *n.pl.*

es·ti·mable (es′tə mə bəl) *adj.* worthy of esteem

es·ti·mate (es′tə māt′; *for n.,* -mit) *vt.* **-mat′ed, -mat′ing** 〚see ESTEEM 〛 **1** to form an opinion about **2** to calculate approximately (size, cost, etc.) — *n.* **1** a general calculation; esp., an approximate computation of probable cost **2** an opinion or judgment —**es′ti·ma′tor** *n.*

es·ti·ma′tion *n.* **1** an estimate or judgment **2** esteem; regard

es·trange (e strānj′, i-) *vt.* **-tranged′, -trang′ing** 〚 < L *extraneus*, strange 〛 to turn (a person) from an affectionate attitude to an indifferent or unfriendly one —**es·trange′ment** *n.*

es·tro·gen (es′trə jən) *n.* 〚 < Gr *oistros*, frenzy + -GEN 〛 any of several female sex hormones or synthetic compounds

es·trous cycle (es′trəs) the regular female reproductive cycle of most placental mammals

es·tuary (es′tyoo er′ē, -choo-) *n., pl.* **-ies** 〚 < L *aestus*, the tide 〛 the wide mouth of a river into which the tide flows from the sea

-et (et, it, ət) 〚 < LL *-itus* 〛 *suffix* little *[islet]*

eta (āt′ə, ēt′ə) *n.* the seventh letter of the Greek alphabet (H, η)

é·ta·gère (ā tä zher′) *n.* 〚Fr 〛 a stand with open shelves, for displaying art objects, ornaments, etc.

et al. 〚 L *et alii* 〛 and others

et cet·era (et set′ər ə, se′trə) 〚L 〛 and others; and the like: abbrev. **etc.**

etch (ech) *vt.* 〚 < MHG *ezzen*, eat 〛 to make (a drawing, design, etc.) on metal, glass, etc. by the action of an acid —**etch′er** *n.*

etch′ing *n.* **1** the art of an etcher **2** a print made from an etched plate

eter·nal (ē tur′nəl, i-) *adj.* 〚 < L *aeturnus* 〛 **1** without beginning or end; everlasting **2** always the same; unchanging **3** seeming never to stop —**eter′nally** *adv.* —**eter′nal·ness** *n.*

eter·nity (ē tur′nə tē, i-) *n., pl.* **-ties 1** the state or fact of being eternal **2** infinite or endless time **3** a long period of time that seems endless **4** the endless time after death

eth·ane (eth′ān′) *n.* 〚 < fol. 〛 an odorless, colorless, gaseous hydrocarbon, found in natural gas and used as a fuel

ether (ē′thər) *n.* 〚 < Gr *aithein*, to burn 〛 **1** an imaginary substance once thought to pervade space **2** the upper regions of space **3** a volatile, colorless, highly flammable liquid used as an anesthetic and solvent

ethe·real (ē thir′ē əl, i-) *adj.* **1** very light; airy; delicate **2** not earthly; heavenly —**ethe′real·ly** *adv.*

ethic (eth′ik) *n.* 〚see fol. 〛 a system of moral standards

ethi·cal (eth′i kəl) *adj.* 〚 < Gr *ēthos*, character 〛 **1** having to do with ethics; of or conforming to moral standards **2** conforming to professional standards of conduct —**eth′i·cally** *adv.*

eth·ics (eth′iks) *n.pl.* **1** [*with sing. v.*] the study of standards of conduct and moral judgment **2** the system of morals of a particular person, religion, group, etc.

Ethio·pian (ē′thē ō′pē ən) *n.* a native or inhabitant of Ethiopia —*adj.* of Ethiopia

eth·nic (eth′nik) *adj.* 〚 < Gr *ethnos*, nation 〛 designating or of a group of people having common customs, characteristics, language, etc. — *n.* a member of an ethnic group, esp. a minority or nationality group —**eth′ni·cally** *adv.*

eth·nic·ity (eth nis′ə tē) *n.* ethnic classification or affiliation

eth·nol·ogy (eth näl′ə jē) *n.* 〚 < Gr *ethnos*, nation + -LOGY 〛 the branch of anthropology that studies comparatively the cultures of contemporary, or recent, societies or

■■■■■ THESAURUS ■■■■■

essentially *a.* basically, fundamentally, radically, at bottom, at heart, centrally, originally, intimately, chiefly, naturally, inherently, permanently, necessarily, primarily, significantly, importantly, at the heart of, in effect, in essence, materially, in the main, at first, characteristically, intrinsically, substantially, typically, approximately, precisely, exactly, actually, truly, really; see also PRINCIPALLY.

establish *v.* **1** [To set up in a formal manner] institute, found, authorize; see ORGANIZE 2. **2** [To work or settle in a permanent place] build up, set up, install, build, erect, plant, root, place, settle, practice, live, stay, start.—*Ant.* LEAVE, break up, depart. **3** [To prove] verify, authenticate, confirm; see PROVE. **4** [To make secure] fix, secure, stabilize; see FASTEN.

established *a.* **1** [Set up to endure] endowed, founded, organized, instituted, set up, originated, chartered, incorporated, settled, begun, initiated, realized, codified, produced, completed, finished; see also FINISHED 1, CERTAIN.—*Ant.* TEMPORARY, unsound, insolvent. **2** [Conclusively proved] approved, verified, guaranteed, endorsed, demonstrated, determined, confirmed, substantiated, assured, concluded, authenticated, ascertained, achieved, upheld, certain, validated, identified, proved, undeniable.—*Ant.* FALSE, invali-

dated, untrue.

establishment *n.* **1** [A business, organization, or the like] company, corporation, enterprise; see BUSINESS 4. **2** [The act of proving] verification, substantiation, demonstration; see PROOF 1.

estate *n.* property, bequest, inheritance, fortune, endowment, wealth, legacy, heritage, belongings, effects, earthly possessions, personal property, private property.

esteem *n.* regard, respect, appreciation; see ADMIRATION.

esteem *v.* prize, respect, appreciate; see ADMIRE.

esthetic *a.* creative, appreciative, sensitive; see ARTISTIC, BEAUTIFUL.

estimate *n.* evaluation, assessment, valuation, guess, appraisal, estimation, calculation, gauging, rating, survey, measure, reckoning; see also JUDGMENT 2.

estimate *v.* rate, value, measure, calculate, appraise, assess, account, compute, evaluate, count, number, reckon, guess, expect, judge, figure, plan, outline, run over, rank, furnish an estimate, set a value on, see a figure, appraise, assay, consider, predict, suppose, suspect, reason, think through, surmise, determine, decide, budget.

estimated *a.* supposed, approximated, guessed at; see LIKELY 1.

estimation *n.* opinion, appraisal,

valuation; see JUDGMENT 2.

et cetera (etc.) *a.* and so forth, and so on, and others; see AND.

etching *n.* print, cut, work of art; see ENGRAVING.

eternal *a.* endless, interminable, continual, unbroken, continuous, continued, unceasing, ceaseless, constant, unending, incessant, relentless, undying, enduring, persistent, always, uninterrupted, everlasting, perpetual, indestructible, unconquerable, never-ending, indefinite, permanent, ageless, boundless, timeless, immortal, forever, indeterminable, immeasurable, having no limit, imperishable, to one's dying day, for ever and ever*.—*Ant.* TEMPORARY, finite, ending.

eternally *a.* endlessly, continually, perpetually; see REGULARLY.

eternity *n.* endlessness, forever, infinite, duration, timelessness, world without end, the future, infinity, all eternity, other world, after life, life after death, for ever and ever*.—*Ant.* INSTANT, moment, second.

ethical *a.* humane, moral, respectable; see DECENT 2, HONEST, NOBLE 1, 2.

ethics *n.* conduct, morality, mores, decency, integrity, moral conduct, social values, moral code, principles, right and wrong, natural law, honesty, goodness, honor, social laws, human nature, the Golden Rule.

language groups —**eth·no·log·i·cal** (-nō läj′i kəl, -nə-) *adj.*
—**eth·nol′o·gist** *n.*

ethos (ē′thäs′) *n.* ⟦Gr *ēthos*, character⟧ the characteristic attitudes, habits, etc. of an individual or group

ethyl (eth′əl) *n.* ⟦< ETHER⟧ the hydrocarbon radical which forms the base of ethyl alcohol, ether, etc.

ethyl alcohol ALCOHOL (sense 1)

ethyl·ene (eth′əl ēn′) *n.* ⟦ETHYL + -ENE⟧ a colorless, flammable, gaseous hydrocarbon used to synthesize organic chemicals, esp. polyethylene

ethylene gly·col (glī′kôl′) a colorless, viscous liquid used as an antifreeze, solvent, etc.

eti·ol·ogy (ēt′ē äl′ə jē) *n., pl.* **-gies** ⟦< Gr *aitia*, cause + *logia*, description⟧ **1** the cause assigned, as for a disease **2** the science of causes or origins —**e′tio·log′ic** (-ə läj′ik) *adj.*

eti·quette (et′i kit, -ket′) *n.* ⟦Fr *étiquette*, lit., ticket⟧ the forms, manners, etc. conventionally acceptable or required in society, a profession, etc.

Etrus·can (ē trus′kən, i-) *adj.* of an ancient country (*Etruria*) in what is now central Italy

et seq. ⟦L *et sequens*⟧ and the following

-ette (et) ⟦Fr: see -ET⟧ *suffix* **1** little *[statuette]* **2** female *[majorette]*

étude (ā′tōōd′) *n.* ⟦Fr, study⟧ a musical composition for a solo instrument, designed to give practice in some point of technique

ety·mol·ogy (et′ə mäl′ə jē) *n., pl.* **-gies** ⟦< Gr *etymos*, true + *logos*, word⟧ **1** the origin and development of a word **2** the scientific study of word origins —**et′y·mo·log′i·cal** (-mə läj′i kəl) *adj.* —**et′y·mol′o·gist** *n.*

eu- ⟦Fr < Gr⟧ *prefix* good, well *[eulogy, euphony]*

euca·lyp·tus (yōō′kə lip′təs) *n., pl.* **-tuses** or **-ti′** (-tī′) ⟦< Gr *eu-*, well + *kalyptos*, covered⟧ a tall, aromatic, chiefly Australian evergreen tree of the myrtle family

Eucha·rist (yōō′kə rist) *n.* ⟦< Gr *eucharistia*, gratitude⟧ **1** HOLY COMMUNION **2** the consecrated bread and wine used in this —**Eu′cha·ris′tic** *adj.*

euchre (yōō′kər) *n.* ⟦< ?⟧ a card game played with thirty-two cards

eugen·ics (yōō jen′iks) *n.pl.* ⟦see EU- & GENESIS⟧ *[with sing. v.]* the movement devoted to improving the human species by controlling heredity —**eugen′ic** *adj.* —**eugen′i·cally** *adv.* —**eugen′i·cist** (-ə sist) *n.*

eulo·gize (yōō′lə jiz′) *vt.* **-gized′, -giz′ing** ⟦see fol.⟧ to praise highly —**eu′lo·gist** or **eu′lo·giz′er** *n.*

eu·logy (-jē) *n., pl.* **-gies** ⟦< Gr *eulegein*, speak well of⟧ **1** speech or writing praising a person or thing; esp., a funeral oration **2** high praise —**eu′lo·gis′tic** (-jis′tik) *adj.*

eunuch (yōō′nək, -nuk′) *n.* ⟦< Gr *eunē*, bed + *echein*, have⟧ a castrated man

euphemism (yōō′fə miz′əm) *n.* ⟦< Gr *eu-*, good + *phēmē*, voice⟧ **1** the use of a less direct word or phrase for one considered offensive **2** a word or phrase so substituted —**eu′phemis′tic** *adj.* —**eu′phemis′ti·cally** *adv.*

eupho·ni·ous (yōō fō′nē əs) *adj.* having a pleasant sound; harmonious —**eupho′ni·ously** *adv.*

eupho·ny (yōō′fə nē) *n., pl.* **-nies** ⟦< Gr *eu-*, well + *phōnē*, voice⟧ a pleasant combination of agreeable sounds, as in speech

eu·pho·ria (yōō fôr′ē ə) *n.* ⟦< Gr *eu-*, well + *pherein*, to bear⟧ a feeling of well-being —**euphor′ic** *adj.*

Eur·asian (yoo rā′zhən) *adj.* of mixed European and Asian descent — *n.* a Eurasian person

eureka (yōō rē′kə) *interj.* ⟦< Gr *heurēka*, I have found (it)⟧ an exclamation of triumphant achievement

Euro·pean (yoor′ə pē′ən) *adj.* of Europe, its people, etc. — *n.* a native or inhabitant of Europe

European Community an organization of European countries to bring about the political and economic unification of western Europe

European plan a system of hotel operation in which guests are charged for rooms, and pay for meals separately

eu·ryth·mics (yōō rith′miks) *n.pl.* ⟦< Gr *eu-*, well + *rhythmos*, rhythm⟧ *[with sing. v.]* the art of performing bodily movements in rhythm, usually to music

eusta·chian tube (yōō stā′kē ən, -stā′shən) ⟦after B. *Eustachio*, 16th-c. It anatomist⟧ *[also* E- t-*]* a slender tube between the middle ear and the pharynx

eutha·na·sia (yōō′thə nā′zhə) *n.* ⟦< Gr *eu-*, well + *thanatos*, death⟧ act of causing death painlessly, so as to end suffering

euthanize (yōō′thə nīz′) *vt.* **-ized′, -iz′ing** to put to death by euthanasia

euthen·ics (yōō then′iks) *n.pl.* ⟦< Gr *euthēnein*, to flourish⟧ *[with sing. v.]* the science of improving the human species by controlling the environment

evacu·ate (ē vak′yōō āt′) *vt.* **-at′ed, -at′ing** ⟦< L *e-*, out + *vacuus*, empty⟧ **1** to make empty **2** to discharge (bodily waste, esp. feces) **3** to withdraw from; remove — *vi.* to withdraw —**evac′u·a′tion** *n.* —**evac′u·ee′** (-ē′) *n.*

evade (ē vād′) *vi., vt.* **evad′ed, evad′ing** ⟦< L *e-*, out, from + *vadere*, go⟧ **1** to avoid or escape (from) by deceit or cleverness **2** to avoid doing or answering directly —**evad′er** *n.*

evalu·ate (ē val′yōō āt′) *vt.* **-at′ed, -at′ing** ⟦ult. < L *ex-*, out + *valere*, be worth⟧ **1** to find the value or amount of **2** to judge the worth of —**eval′u·a′tion** *n.*

eva·nes·cent (ev′ə nes′ənt) *adj.* ⟦< L *e-*, out + *vanescere*, vanish⟧ tending to fade from sight; fleeting; ephemeral —**ev′a·nes′cence** *n.*

evan·geli·cal (ē′van jel′i kəl, ev′ən-) *adj.* ⟦< Gr *euangelos*, bringing good news⟧ **1** of or according to the Gospels or the New Testament **2** of those Protestant churches that emphasize salvation by faith in Jesus

evan·gelist (ē van′jə list) *n.* **1** *[E-]* any of the four writers of the Gospels **2** a revivalist or a preacher who holds large public services in various cities, now often televised —**evan′gelism′** *n.*

THESAURUS

etiquette *n.* conduct, manners, social graces; see BEHAVIOR.

Eucharist *n.* sacrament, host, communion; see SACRAMENT.

eulogize *v.* laud, extol, applaud; see PRAISE 1.

eulogy *n.* tribute, glorification, commendation; see PRAISE 2.

euphoria *n.* joy, delight, glee; see HAPPINESS.

European *a.* Continental, Old Country, Old World, Eurasian, Indo-European, West European, East European. *Terms associated with particular areas include the following:* Anglo-Saxon, British, English, Irish, Scottish, Scots, Welsh, Cornish, French, Norman, Gallic, German, Germanic, Dutch, Belgian, Flemish, Low German, Saxon, Bavarian, Prussian, Gothic, Teutonic, Nordic, Scandinavian, Danish, Swedish, Norwegian, Icelandic, Swiss, Greek, Hellenic, Athenian, Corinthian, Spartan, Peloponnesian, Mycenean, Cretan, Thracian, Ionian, Slovak, Romanian, Bulgarian, Slavic, Slav, Aegean, Balkan, Adriatic, Yugoslavian, Serbian, Croatian, Austrian, Hungarian, Czechoslovakian, Czech, Bohemian, Turk, Turkish,

Russian, Polish, Baltic, Latvian, Lithuanian, Ukrainian, Finnish, Lap, Italian, Latin, Corsican, Roman, Venetian, Florentine, Neapolitan, Sicilian, Maltese, Sardinian, Tyrolese, Apennine, Spanish, Hispanic, Iberian, Portuguese, Catalan, Basque, Majorcan, Castilian, Andalusian, Jewish, Yiddish; see also ENGLISH, GERMAN, GREEK, ITALIAN, ROMAN, SPANISH.

European *n. Terms associated with Europeans from particular areas include the following:* Englishman, Briton, Scotsman, Scot, Highlander, Welshman, Irishman, Celt, Anglo-Saxon, Frenchman, Norman, Basque, German, Teuton, Prussian, Bavarian, Saxon, Swiss, Dutchman, Hollander, Belgian, Scandinavian, Dane, Norwegian, Swede, Norseman, Icelander, Finn, Lapp, Italian, Roman, Sicilian, Venetian, Florentine, Spaniard, Castilian, Andalusian, Portuguese, Austrian, Hungarian, Czechoslovakian, Czech, Bohemian, Slovak, Slav, Russian, Pole, Lithuanian, Latvian, Estonian, Ukrainian, White Russian, Yugoslavian, Bulgarian, Romanian, Balkan,

Greek, Turk, Jew, Gypsy; see also EUROPEAN, *a.,* FRENCH, GERMAN, GREEK.

evacuate *v.* **1** [To empty] void, exhaust, deplete; see REMOVE 1. **2** [To abandon] vacate, desert, leave; see ABANDON 1.

evacuation *n.* **1** [Removal] draining, depletion, exhaustion; see REMOVAL. **2** [Withdrawal] abandonment, removal, retreat; see DEPARTURE.

evade *v.* lie, prevaricate, dodge, shun, put off, avoid, elude, trick, baffle, quibble, shift, mystify, cloak, cover, conceal, deceive, screen, veil, hide, drop the subject, pretend, confuse, dodge the issue, beat around the bush, give someone the run-around*, throw off the scent*, lead on a merry chase, pass up, put off, get around, lie out of; see also AVOID.—*Ant.* EXPLAIN, make clear, elucidate.

evaluate *v.* appraise, judge, assess; see DECIDE, ESTIMATE.

evangelical *a.* pious, fervent, spiritual; see RELIGIOUS 2.

evangelist *n.* preacher, missionary, revivalist; see MINISTER 1.

evan'gelize' (-līz') *vt.* **-lized'**, **-liz'ing** to convert to Christianity — *vi.* to preach the gospel

evapo·rate (ē vap'ə rāt') *vt.* **-rat'ed**, **-rat'ing** ⟦ < L *e-*, out, from + *vaporare*, emit vapor ⟧ 1 to change (a liquid or solid) into vapor 2 to remove moisture from (milk, etc.), as by heating, so as to get a concentrated product — *vi.* 1 to become vapor 2 to give off vapor 3 to vanish — **evap'o·ra'tion** *n.* — **evap'o·ra'tor** *n.*

eva·sion (ē vā'zhən) *n.* 1 an evading; specif., an avoiding of a duty, question, etc. by deceit or cleverness 2 a way of doing this; subterfuge

eva·sive (-siv) *adj.* 1 tending or seeking to evade; tricky 2 elusive — **eva'sively** *adv.* — **eva'sive·ness** *n.*

eve (ēv) *n.* ⟦ < OE *æfen*, evening ⟧ 1 [Old Poet.] evening 2 [*often* **E-**] the evening or day before a holiday 3 the period just prior to some event

Eve (ēv) *Bible* the first woman, Adam's wife

even (ē'vən) *adj.* ⟦OE *efne*⟧ 1 flat; level; smooth 2 not varying; constant [an *even* tempo] 3 calm; tranquil [an *even* temper] 4 in the same plane or line [*even* with the rim] 5 owing and being owed nothing 6 equal in number, quantity, etc. 7 exactly divisible by two 8 exact [an *even* mile] — *adv.* 1 however improbable; indeed 2 exactly; just [it happened *even* as I expected] 3 still; yet [he's *even* better] — *vt.*, *vi.* to make or become even — **even if** though — **e'ven·ly** *adv.* — **e'ven·ness** *n.*

e'ven·hand'ed *adj.* impartial; fair

eve·ning (ēv'niŋ) *n.* ⟦ < OE *æfnung* ⟧ 1 the last part of the day and early part of night 2 [Dial.] afternoon

even money equal stakes in betting, with no odds

event (ē vent') *n.* ⟦ < L *e-*, out + *venire*, come ⟧ 1 an occurrence, esp. when important 2 [Archaic] an outcome 3 a particular contest in a program of sports — **in any event** anyhow — **in the event of** in case of — **in the event that** if it should happen that

e'ven-tem'pered *adj.* not quickly angered; calm

event'ful *adj.* 1 full of outstanding events 2 having an important outcome — **event'fully** *adv.* — **event'ful·ness** *n.*

even·tide (ē'vən tīd') *n.* [Archaic] evening

even·tual (ē ven'chōō əl) *adj.* ultimate; final — **even'tual·ly** *adv.*

even'tual'ity (-al'ə tē) *n.*, *pl.* **-ties** a possible event or outcome

even'tu·ate' (-āt') *vi.* **-at'ed**, **-at'ing** to happen in the end; result

ever (ev'ər) *adv.* ⟦ < OE *æfre* ⟧ 1 always [*ever* the same] 2 at any time [do you *ever* see her?] 3 at all; by any chance [how can I *ever* repay you?] — **ever so** [Colloq.] very

ev'er·glade' (-glād') *n.* marshy land

ev'er·green' *adj.* having green leaves all year long, as most conifers — *n.* an evergreen plant or tree

ev'er·last'ing *adj.* lasting forever; eternal — *n.* eternity

ev'er·more' *adv.* [Archaic] forever; constantly

ev'ery (ev'rē) *adj.* ⟦OE *æfre ælc*, lit., ever each ⟧ 1 each, individually and separately 2 the greatest possible [to make *every* effort] 3 each interval [take a pill *every* three hours] — **every now and then** occasionally; also [Colloq.] **every so often** — **every other** each alternate, as the first, third, fifth, etc. — **every which way** [Colloq.] in complete disorder

ev'ery·bod'y (-bäd'ē, -bud'ē) *pron.* every person; everyone

ev'ery·day' *adj.* 1 daily 2 suitable for ordinary days [*everyday* shoes] 3 usual; common

ev'ery·one' *pron.* every person

every one every person or thing of those named [*every one* of the boys]

ev'ery·thing' *pron.* every thing; all

ev'ery·where' *adv.* in or to every place

evict (ē vikt') *vt.* ⟦ < L *e-*, intens. + *vincere*, conquer ⟧ to remove (a tenant) by legal procedure — **evic'tion** *n.*

evi·dence (ev'ə dəns; *also, esp. for v.*, -dens') *n.* 1 something that makes another thing evident; sign 2 a statement of a witness, an object, etc. bearing on or establishing the point in question in a court of law — *vt.* **-denced**, **-denc·ing** to make evident — **in evidence** plainly seen

evi·dent (ev'ə dənt) *adj.* ⟦ < L *e-*, from + *videre*, see ⟧ easy to see or perceive; clear — **ev'i·dently** *adv.*

evil (ē'vəl) *adj.* ⟦OE *yfel*⟧ 1 morally bad or wrong; wicked 2 harmful; injurious 3 unlucky; disastrous — *n.* 1 wicked-

---

THESAURUS

evangelize *v.* proselytize, instruct, convert; see PREACH.

evaporate *v.* diffuse, vanish, fade, dissolve, dissipate, steam, steam away, boil away, fume, distill, turn to steam, rise in a mist.

evaporation *n.* drying, dehydration, vanishing, steaming away, boiling away, vaporization, distillation, dissipation, disappearance, vanishing into thin air.

evasion *n.* quibble, subterfuge, equivocation; see LIE, TRICK 1.

evasive *a.* elusory, fugitive, shifty; see SLY.

eve *n.* evening before, night preceding, evening; see NIGHT 1.

even *a.* 1 [Lying in a smooth plane] smooth, level, surfaced; see FLAT 1. 2 [Similar] uniform, unbroken, homogeneous; see ALIKE, REGULAR 3. 3 [Equal] commensurate, coterminous, equivalent; see EQUAL. 4 [In addition] also, too, as well; see AND. — **break even** make nothing, tie, neither win nor lose; see BALANCE 2.

evening *n.* twilight, dusk, late afternoon; see NIGHT 1.

evenly *a.* 1 [On an even plane] smoothly, regularly, without bumps, without lumps, uniformly, placidly, unvaryingly, steadily, constantly, fluently, on an even keel, without variation, neither up nor down. 2 [Equally proportioned or distributed] exactly, justly, fairly, precisely, equally, impartially, identically, equitably, symmetrically, proportionately, synonymously, analogously, correspondingly, tied, alike, fifty-fifty*, squarely*. — *Ant.* WRONGLY, unfairly.

evenness *n.* smoothness, similarity, likeness; see REGULARITY.

event *n.* occurrence, happening, episode, incident, circumstance, affair, phenomenon, development, function, transaction, experience, appearance, turn, tide, shift, phase, accident, chance, pass, situation, story, case, matter, occasion, catastrophe, mishap, mistake, experience, parade, triumph, coincidence, miracle, adventure, holiday, wonder, marvel, celebration, crisis, predicament, misfortune, situation, calamity, emergency, something to write home about*; see also DISASTER, HOLIDAY, WONDER 2. — **in any event** anyway, no matter what happens, however; see ANYHOW. — **in the event of** (or **that**) in case of, if it should happen that, if there should happen to be; see IF.

eventful *a.* momentous, memorable, signal; see IMPORTANT 1.

eventual *a.* inevitable, ultimate, consequent; see LAST 1.

eventually *a.* in the end, at last, ultimately; see FINALLY 2.

ever *a.* eternally, always, at all times; see REGULARLY. — **for ever and a day** * always, for ever and ever, perpetually; see FOREVER.

evergreen *n.* coniferous tree, ornamental shrub, fir; see PINE, TREE.

everlasting *a.* permanent, unending, perpetual; see ETERNAL.

every *a.* each one, all, without exception; see EACH 1. — **every now and then** * sometimes, occasionally, once in a while; see FREQUENTLY: also **every so often**.

everybody *n.* each one, every one, all, the public, old and young; men, women, and children; the people, the populace, the voters; the buying public, the voting public; generality, anybody, all sorts, the masses, the man in the street*, you and I; see also MAN

1. — *Ant.* NOBODY, no one, not a one.

everyday *a.* commonplace, normal, plain; see COMMON 1.

everyone *pron.* all, each person, whoever; see EVERYBODY.

everything *pron.* all, all things, the universe, the whole complex, the whole, many things, all that, every little thing, the whole kit and kaboodle*; lock, stock, and barrel; the works, the lot.

everywhere *a.* everyplace, here and there, at all points, wherever one turns, at each point, without exception, universally, at all times and places; here, there and everywhere; in every direction, on all hands, all over the place, throughout, to the four winds*, in all creation*, to hell and back*, inside and out*, from beginning to end*, high and low, all around, the world over.

evict *v.* remove, expel, oust; see DISMISS.

eviction *n.* ouster, ejection, dispossession; see REMOVAL.

evidence *n.* testimony, data, confirmation; see PROOF 1. — **in evidence** evident, visible, manifest; see OBVIOUS 1, 2.

evident *a.* apparent, visible, manifest; see OBVIOUS 1.

evidently *a.* seemingly, obviously, so far as one can see; see APPARENTLY.

evil *a.* immoral, sinful, corrupt; see BAD.

evil *n.* 1 [The quality of being evil] sin, wickedness, depravity, crime, sinfulness, corruption, vice, immorality, iniquity, perversity, badness, vileness, baseness, meanness, malevolence, indecency, hatred, viciousness, wrong, debauchery, lewdness, wantonness, grossness,

ness; sin **2** anything that causes harm, pain, etc. —**e′vil·ly** *adv.*

e′vil·do′er (-dōō′ər) *n.* one who does evil —**e′vil·do′ing** *n.*

evince (ē vins′) *vt.* **evinced′, evinc′ing** ‖ < L *e-*, intens. + *vincere*, conquer ‖ to show plainly; make clear

evis·cer·ate (ē vis′ər āt′) *vt.* **-at′ed, -at′ing** ‖ < L *e-*, out + *viscera*, viscera ‖ **1** to remove the entrails from **2** to deprive of an essential part —**evis′cera′tion** *n.*

evoke (ē vōk′) *vt.* **evoked′, evok′ing** ‖ < L *e-*, out, from + *vox*, voice ‖ **1** to call forth **2** to elicit (a reaction, etc.) — **evoca·tive** (ē väk′ə tiv) *adj.* —**evo·ca·tion** (ev′ə kā′shən, ē′vō-) *n.*

evo·lu·tion (ev′ə lōō′shən) *n.* ‖ see fol. ‖ **1** an unfolding; process of development or change **2** a thing evolved **3** a movement that is part of a series **4** *Biol. a)* the development of a species, organism, etc. from its original to its present state *b)* the theory that all species developed from earlier forms —**ev′o·lu′tion·ar′y** *adj.* —**ev′o·lu′tion·ist** *n.*

evolve (ē välv′, -vôlv′) *vt., vi.* **evolved′, evolv′ing** ‖ < L *e-*, out + *volvere*, to roll ‖ **1** to develop gradually; unfold **2** to develop by evolution

ewe (yōō) *n.* ‖ OE *eowu* ‖ a female sheep

ewer (yōō′ər) *n.* ‖ < L *aqua*, water ‖ a large, wide-mouthed water pitcher

ex- ‖ < OFr or L ‖ *prefix* **1** *a)* from, out [*expel*] *b)* beyond *c)* thoroughly *d)* upward **2** former, previous [*ex-*president*]*

ex. **1** example **2** exchange

ex·ac·er·bate (eg zas′ər bāt′) *vt.* **-bat′ed, -bat′ing** ‖ < L *ex-*, intens. + *acerbus*, bitter ‖ **1** to aggravate (pain, annoyance, etc.) **2** to exasperate; irritate —**ex·ac′er·ba′tion** *n.*

ex·act (eg zakt′) *adj.* ‖ < L *ex-*, out + *agere*, to do ‖ **1** characterized by or requiring accuracy; methodical; correct **2** without variation; precise — *vt.* **1** to extort **2** to demand; require —**ex·act′ly** *adv.* —**ex·act′ness** *n.*

ex·act′ing *adj.* **1** making severe demands; strict **2** demanding great care, effort, etc.; arduous —**ex·act′ingly** *adv.*

ex·ac·tion (eg zak′shən) *n.* **1** an exacting **2** an extortion **3** an exacted fee, tax, etc.

ex·ac′ti·tude′ (-tə tōōd′) *n.* ‖ Fr ‖ the quality of being exact; accuracy

ex·ag·ger·ate (eg zaj′ər āt′) *vt., vi.* **-at′ed, -at′ing** ‖ < L *ex-*, out + *agger*, a heap ‖ to think or tell of (something) as greater than it is; overstate —**ex·ag′gera′tion** *n.* —**ex·ag′gera′tive** *adj.* —**ex·ag′gera′tor** *n.*

ex·alt (eg zôlt′) *vt.* ‖ < L *ex-*, up + *altus*, high ‖ **1** to raise in status, dignity, etc. **2** to praise; glorify **3** to fill with joy, pride, etc.; elate —**ex·al·ta·tion** (eg′zôl tā′shən) *n.*

ex·ami·na·tion (eg zam′ə nā′shən) *n.* **1** an examining or being examined **2** a set of questions asked in testing: also [Colloq.] **ex·am′**

ex·am·ine (eg zam′ən) *vt.* **-ined, -in·ing** ‖ < L *examinare*, weigh ‖ **1** to look at critically or methodically; investigate; inspect **2** to test by questioning —**ex·am′in·er** *n.*

ex·am·ple (eg zam′pəl) *n.* ‖ < L *eximere*, take out ‖ **1** something selected to show the character of the rest; sample **2** a case that serves as a warning **3** a model; pattern **4** an instance that illustrates a principle

ex·as·per·ate (eg zas′pər āt′) *vt.* **-at′ed, -at′ing** ‖ < L *ex-*, out + *asper*, rough ‖ to irritate; anger; vex —**ex·as′pera′tion** *n.*

ex·ca·vate (eks′kə vāt′) *vt.* **-vat′ed, -vat′ing** ‖ < L *ex-*, out + *cavus*, hollow ‖ **1** to make a hole or cavity in **2** to form (a tunnel, etc.) by hollowing out **3** to unearth **4** to dig out (earth, soil, etc.) —**ex′ca·va′tion** *n.* —**ex′ca·va′tor** *n.*

ex·ceed (ek sēd′) *vt.* ‖ < L *ex-*, out + *cedere*, to go ‖ **1** to go or be beyond (a limit, etc.) **2** to surpass

ex·ceed′ing (-iŋ) *adj.* surpassing; extreme —**ex·ceed′ingly** *adv.*

ex·cel (ek sel′) *vi., vt.* **-celled′, -cel′ling** ‖ < L *ex-*, out of + *-cellere*, to rise ‖ to be better or greater than (another or others)

ex·cel·lence (ek′sə ləns) *n.* **1** the fact or state of excelling; superiority **2** a particular virtue

ex′cel·lency (-lən sē) *n., pl.* **-cies 1** [E-] a title of honor for certain dignitaries **2** EXCELLENCE

THESAURUS

foulness, degradation, obscenity.— *Ant.* VIRTUE, good, goodness. **2** [A harmful or malicious action] ill, harm, mischief, misfortune, scandal, calamity, pollution, contamination, catastrophe, blow, disaster, plague, outrage, foul play, ill wind*, crying shame*, double cross*, raw deal*.

evildoer *n.* malefactor, sinner, wrongdoer; see CRIMINAL.

evoke *v.* summon forth, call out, invoke; see SUMMON.

evolution *n.* growth, unfolding, natural process; see DEVELOPMENT.

evolve *v.* result, unfold, emerge; see DEVELOP 3, GROW 2.

exact *a.* **1** [Accurate] precise, correct, perfect; see ACCURATE 2, DEFINITE 1. **2** [Clear] sharp, distinct, clear-cut; see DEFINITE 2.

exacting *a.* precise, careful, critical; see DIFFICULT 1, 2.

exactly *a.* precisely, specifically, correctly; see DETAILED.

exactness *n.* precision, nicety, scrupulousness; see ACCURACY.

exaggerate *v.* overestimate, overstate, misrepresent, falsify, magnify, expand, amplify, pile up, heighten, intensify, distort, enlarge on, stretch, overdo, misquote, go to extremes, give color to, misjudge, elaborate, romance, embroider, color, make too much of, lie, fabricate, corrupt, paint in glowing colors*, carry too far*, lay it on thick*, make a mountain out of a molehill, cook up*, build up, make much of, make the most of.—*Ant.* UNDERESTIMATE, tell the truth, minimize.

exaggerated *a.* colored, magnified, overwrought, extravagant, preposterous, impossible, fabulous, sensational, spectacular, melodramatic, out of proportion, fantastic, highflown, far-fetched, false, distorted,

fabricated, strained, artificial, glaring, pronounced, unrealistic, whopping*, too much.—*Ant.* ACCURATE, exact, precise.

exaggeration *n.* overestimation, misrepresentation, extravagance, elaboration, coloring, flight of fancy, fantasy, fancy, stretch of the imagination, figure of speech, yarn, making a mountain out of a molehill, tall story*, whopper*.—*Ant.* TRUTH, accuracy, understatement.

exalt *v.* commend, glorify, laud; see PRAISE 1.

exaltation *n.* rapture, elation, rhapsody; see HAPPINESS.

examination *n.* **1** [The act of seeking evidence] search, research, survey, scrutiny, investigation, inquiry into, inspection, observation, checking, exploration, analysis, audit, study, questioning, test, trial, cross-examination, third degree*. **2** [A formal test] experiment, review, questionnaire, battery, quiz, exam, make-up*, midterm*, final, blue book, orals, written tens*; see also TEST. **3** [A medical checkup] checkup, physical examination, physical; see TEST.

examine *v.* **1** [To inspect with care] inspect, analyze, criticize, scrutinize, investigate, go into, inquire into, scan, probe, sift, explore, reconnoiter, audit, take stock of, take note of, make an inventory of, consider, canvass, find out, search out, review, assay, check, check out, check up on, re-examine, go back over, concentrate on, give one's attention to, look at, look into, look over, conduct research on, run checks on, put to the test, sound out, feel out, subject to scrutiny, peer into, look into, pry into, hold up to the light, finger, pick over, sample, experiment with, give

the once-over*, size up*, smell around, see about, see into, poke into, nose around, look up and down, go over with a fine-toothed comb*, dig into*. **2** [To test] question, interrogate, cross-examine; see TEST.

examined *a.* checked, tested, inspected; see INVESTIGATED.

examiner *n.* tester, questioner, observer; see INSPECTOR.

example *n.* **1** [A representative] illustration, representation, warning, sample, citation, case in point, concrete example, case, prototype, archetype, stereotype, original, copy, instance, quotation. **2** [Something to be imitated] standard, pattern, sample; see MODEL 2. —**for example** for instance, as a model, as an example, to illustrate, to cite an instance, to give an illustration, a case in point, like. —**set an example** instruct, behave as a model, set a pattern; see TEACH.

excavate *v.* shovel, empty, hollow out; see DIG 1.

excavation *n.* cavity, hollow, pit; see HOLE 1, TUNNEL.

exceed *v.* excel, outdo, overdo, outdistance, pass, outrun, beat, get the better of, go beyond, surpass, transcend, eclipse, rise above, pass over, run circles around*, get the edge on*, excel in, have it all over someone*, get the drop on*, beat to the draw*, break the record*, have the best of, have the jump on*, be ahead of the game, have the advantage, gain the upper hand.

exceedingly *a.* greatly, remarkably, in a marked degree; see VERY.

excel *v.* surpass, transcend, improve upon; see EXCEED.

excellence *n.* superiority, worth, distinction; see PERFECTION.

ex·cel·lent (ek′sə lənt) *adj.* 〖see EXCEL〗 outstandingly good of its kind; of exceptional merit —**ex′cel·lently** *adv.*

ex·cel·sior (ek sel′sē ôr′; *for n.* ek sel′sē ər) *interj.* 〖see EXCEL〗 always upward! —*n.* long, thin wood shavings used for packing

ex·cept (ek sept′) *vt.* 〖< L *ex-*, out + *capere*, to take〗 to leave out or take out; exclude —*prep.* leaving out; but —*conj.* [Colloq.] were it not that; only —**except for** if it were not for

ex·cept′ing *prep., conj.* EXCEPT

ex·cep′tion *n.* **1** an excepting **2** *a*) a case to which a rule does not apply *b*) a person or thing different from others of the same class **3** an objection —**take exception to** object

ex·cep′tion·able *adj.* liable to exception; open to objection

ex·cep′tion·al *adj.* **1** unusual; esp., unusually good **2** needing special education, as because mentally handicapped —**ex·cep′tion·ally** *adv.*

ex·cerpt (ek sʉrpt′; *for n.* ek′sʉrpt′) *vt.* 〖< L *ex-*, out + *carpere*, to pick〗 to select or quote (passages from a book, etc.); extract —*n.* a passage selected or quoted; extract

ex·cess (ek ses′; *also, esp. for adj.*, ek′ses′) *n.* 〖see EXCEED〗 **1** action that goes beyond a reasonable limit **2** an amount greater than is necessary **3** the amount by which one thing exceeds another; surplus —*adj.* extra; surplus —**in excess of** more than

ex·ces′sive *adj.* being too much; immoderate —**ex·ces′sively** *adv.*

ex·change (eks chānj′) *vt., vi.* **-changed′, -chang′ing** 〖see EX- & CHANGE〗 **1** to give or receive (something) for another thing; barter; trade **2** to interchange (similar things) —*n.* **1** an exchanging; interchange **2** a thing exchanged **3** a place for exchanging [a stock *exchange*] **4** a central office providing telephone service **5** the value of one currency in terms of another —**ex·change′able** *adj.*

exchange rate the rate at which one currency can be exchanged for another

ex·chequer (eks chek′ər, eks′chek′-) *n.* 〖ME *escheker*, lit., chessboard < OFr *eschekier*: accounts of revenue were kept on a squared board〗 **1** a national treasury **2** funds; finances

ex·cise¹ (ek′sīz, -sīs′) *n.* 〖ult. < L *assidere*, assist (in office)〗 a tax on various commodities, as liquor, etc., within a country Also **excise tax**

ex·cise² (ek sīz′) *vt.* **-cised′, -cis′ing** 〖< L *ex-*, out + *caedere*, to cut〗 to remove by cutting out —**ex·ci′sion** (-sizh′ən) *n.*

ex·cit·able (ek sīt′ə bəl) *adj.* easily excited —**ex·cit′a·bil′ity** *n.*

ex·cite (ek sīt′) *vt.* **-cit′ed, -cit′ing** 〖< L *ex-*, out + *ciere*, to call〗 **1** to make active; stir up **2** to arouse; provoke **3** to arouse the feelings of —**ex·ci·ta·tion** (ek′sī tā′shən) *n.* —**ex·cit′ed·ly** *adv.* —**ex·cit′er** *n.*

ex·cite′ment *n.* **1** an exciting or being excited; agitation **2** that which excites

ex·cit′ing *adj.* causing excitement; stirring, thrilling, etc.

ex·claim (ek sklām′) *vi., vt.* 〖< L *ex-*, out + *clamare*, to shout〗 to cry out; say suddenly and vehemently

ex·cla·ma·tion (ek′sklə mā′shən) *n.* **1** an exclaiming **2** something exclaimed; interjection —**ex·clam·a·tory** (ek sklam′ə tôr′ē) *adj.*

exclamation point (or **mark**) a mark (!) used in punctuating to show surprise, strong emotion, etc.

ex·clude (eks klōōd′) *vt.* **-clud′ed, -clud′ing** 〖< L *ex-*, out + *claudere*, to close〗 **1** to refuse to admit, consider, etc.; reject **2** to put or force out —**ex·clu′sion** (-klōō′zhən) *n.*

ex·clu·sive (-klōō′siv) *adj.* **1** excluding all others **2** not shared or divided; sole *[an exclusive right]* **3** excluding certain people, as for social or economic reasons —**exclu-**

▬ THESAURUS ▬

excellent *a.* first-class, premium, choice, first, choicest, prime, high, picked, the best obtainable, select, exquisite, high-grade, very fine, finest, good, desirable, admirable, distinctive, attractive, great, highest, superior, exceptional, superb, striking, supreme, unique, custom-made, incomparable, surprising, transcendent, priceless, rare, invaluable, highest priced, magnificent, wonderful, skillfull, above par, superlative, worthy, refined, well-done, cultivated, to be desired, competent, skilled, notable, first-rate, terrific*, sensational*, sharp*, groovy*, all right, A-1*, grade A*, classy*, topnotch*, cream*, tops*.—*Ant.* POOR, inferior, imperfect.

excellently *a.* perfectly, exquisitely, splendidly; see WELL 2.

except *prep.* excepting, excluding, rejecting, omitting, barring, save, but, with the exception of, other than, if not, not for, without, outside of, aside from, leaving out, exempting, minus.

except *v.* exclude, reject, leave out; see BAR 1.

exception *n.* exclusion, omission, making an exception of, rejection, barring, reservation, leaving out, segregation, limitation, exemption, elimination, expulsion, excusing.—**take exception (to)** **1** [To differ] object, disagree, demur; see DIFFER 1. **2** [To dislike] resent, be offended, take offense; see DISLIKE.

exceptional *a.* uncommon, extraordinary, rare; see UNUSUAL 1, 2.

exceptionally *a.* unusually, particularly, abnormally; see ESPECIALLY 1.

excerpt *n.* selection, extract, citation; see QUOTATION.

excess *n.* **1** [More than is needed] profusion, abundance, surplus, remainder, too much, too many, exorbitance, waste, wastefulness, luxuriance, lavishness, over-supply, plenty, bellyful*, too much of a good thing*.—*Ant.* LACK, dearth, deficiency. **2** [Conduct that is not temperate] prodigality, dissipation, intemperance; see GREED, WASTE 1. —**in excess of** additional, surplus, more than; see EXTRA. —**to excess** too much, excessively, extravagantly; see EXTREME.

excessive *a.* immoderate, extravagant, exorbitant; see EXTREME.

excessively *a.* extravagantly, extremely, unreasonably; see VERY.

exchange *n.* **1** [The act of replacing one thing with another] transfer, substitute, replacement, change, rearrangement, shift, revision, sleight-of-hand, reciprocity, barter, correspondence, interdependence, buying and selling, negotiation, transaction, commerce, trade, give and take. **2** [A substitution] change, shift, swap*, trade, interchange, replacing, shuffle, reciprocation, replacement, switch.

exchange *v.* **1** [To replace one thing with another] substitute, transfer, replace, go over to, give in exchange, remove, pass to, reverse, provide a replacement, shuffle, shift, revise, rearrange, change, interchange, transact, reset, change hands, borrow from Peter to pay Paul, swap*. **2** [To give and receive reciprocally] reciprocate, barter, trade with, buy and sell, deal with, do business with, correspond, swap*.

exchanged *a.* restored, traded, brought back; see RETURNED.

excitable *a.* sensitive, high-strung, impatient; see NERVOUS.

excite *v.* stimulate, inflame, arouse, anger, delight, move, tease, worry, infuriate, madden, stir up, fire up, work up, goad, taunt, mock, provoke, incite, astound, amaze, annoy, jolt, fan the flames, carry away, warm, irritate, offend, bother.

excited *a.* aroused, stimulated, inflamed, agitated, hot, annoyed, seething, wrought up, frantic, flushed, overwrought, restless, feverish, apprehensive, roused, disturbed, perturbed, flustered, upset, angry, tense, discomposed, embarrassed, hurt, angered, distracted, distraught, edgy, furious, beside oneself, delighted, eager, enthusiastic, frenzied, troubled, ruffled, moved, avid, hysterical, passionate, provoked, quickened, inspired, wild, nervous, animated, ill at ease, jumpy, jittery*, turned on*, hyped up*, hopped up*, worked up*, in a tizzy*, up tight*, all nerves*, blue in the face*, on fire*.—*Ant.* CALM, reserved, self-confident.

excitedly *a.* tensely, apprehensively, hysterically; see EXCITED.

excitement *n.* confusion, disturbance, tumult, enthusiasm, rage, turmoil, stir, excitation, agitation, movement, feeling, exhilaration, emotion, stimulation, drama, melodrama, activity, commotion, fuss*, hullabaloo, bother, dither, hubbub, bustle, to-do*.—*Ant.* PEACE, calm, quiet.

exciting *a.* stimulating, moving, animating, provocative, arousing, arresting, stirring, thrilling, dangerous, breathtaking, overwhelming, interesting, new, mysterious, overpowering, inspiring, impressive, soul-stirring, sensational, astonishing, bracing, appealing, bloodcurdling, racy, hair-raising*, mindblowing*.—*Ant.* DULL, pacifying, tranquilizing.

exclaim *v.* cry out, call out, burst out, assert, shout, call aloud, say loudly; see also YELL.

exclamation *n.* yell, clamor, vociferation; see CRY 1.

exclude *v.* shut out, reject, ban; see BAR 1, 2.

exclusion *n.* keeping out, rejection, elimination, prohibition, nonadmission, omission, segregation, isolation, blockade, repudiation, separation, eviction, dismissal, suspension, refusal, expulsion, barring.—*Ant.* WELCOME, invitation, inclusion.

exclusive *a.* restricted, restrictive, fashionable, aristocratic, preferential, privileged, particular, licensed, sive of not including —ex·clu'sive·ly *adv.* —ex·clu'sive·ness *n.*

ex·com·mu·ni·cate (eks'kə myōō'ni kāt') *vt.* -cat'ed, -cat'ing to exclude from communion with a church —ex'com·mu·ni·ca'tion *n.*

ex·co·ri·ate (eks kôr'ē āt') *vt.* -at'ed, -at'ing ⟦< L *ex-*, off + *corium*, the skin⟧ to denounce harshly —ex·co'ria'tion *n.*

ex·cre·ment (eks'krə mənt) *n.* waste matter excreted from the bowels

ex·cres·cence (eks kres'əns) *n.* ⟦< L *ex-*, out + *crescere*, grow⟧ an abnormal outgrowth or addition

ex·cre·ta (eks krēt'ə) *n.pl.* waste matter excreted from the body

ex·crete (eks krēt') *vt., vi.* -cret'ed, -cret'ing ⟦< L *ex-*, out of + *cernere*, sift⟧ to eliminate (waste matter) from the body —ex·cre'tion *n.* —ex·cre·tory (eks'krə tôr'ē) *adj.*

ex·cru·ci·at·ing (eks krōō'shē āt'iŋ) *adj.* 1 intensely painful; agonizing 2 intense or extreme

ex·cul·pate (eks'kul'pāt') *vt.* -pat'ed, -pat'ing ⟦< L *ex*, out + *culpa*, fault⟧ to free from blame; prove guiltless —ex'cul·pa'tion *n.*

ex·cur·sion (eks kur'zhən) *n.* ⟦< L *ex-*, out + *currere*, to run⟧ 1 a short trip, as for pleasure 2 a round trip at reduced rates 3 a digression —*adj.* for an excursion —ex·cur'sion·ist (-ist) *n.*

ex·cur·sive (eks kur'siv) *adj.* rambling; digressive —ex·cur'sive·ly *adv.* —ex·cur'sive·ness *n.*

ex·cuse (eks skyōōz'; *for n.*, -skyōōs') *vt.* -cused', -cus'ing ⟦< L *ex-*, from + *causa*, a charge⟧ 1 to apologize or give reasons for 2 to overlook (an offense or fault) 3 to release from an obligation, etc. 4 to permit to leave 5 to justify —*n.* 1 a defense of some action; apology 2 something that excuses 3 a pretext —excuse oneself 1 to apologize 2 to ask for permission to leave —ex·cus'able *adj.*

ex·ecrable (ek'si krə bəl) *adj.* ⟦see fol.⟧ 1 detestable 2 very inferior

ex'ecrate' (-krāt') *vt.* -crat'ed, -crat'ing ⟦< L *execrare*, to curse⟧ 1 to denounce scathingly 2 to loathe; abhor —ex'ecra'tion *n.*

ex·ecute (ek'si kyōōt') *vt.* -cut'ed, -cut'ing ⟦see EXECUTOR⟧ 1 to carry out; do 2 to administer (laws, etc.) 3 to put to death by a legal sentence 4 to create in accordance with a plan, etc. 5 to make valid (a deed, will, etc.)

ex'ecu'tion *n.* 1 an executing; specif., *a*) a carrying out, performing, etc. *b*) a putting to death by a legal sentence 2 the manner of performing

ex'ecu'tioner *n.* one who carries out a court-imposed death penalty

ex·ecu·tive (eg zek'yōō tiv) *adj.* ⟦see fol.⟧ 1 of or capable of carrying out duties, functions, etc. 2 empowered to administer (laws, government affairs, etc.) —*n.* 1 the branch of government administering the laws and affairs of a nation 2 one who administers or manages affairs

ex·ecu·tor (eg zek'yōō tər) *n.* ⟦< L *ex-*, intens. + *sequi*, to follow⟧ a person appointed to carry out the provisions of a will

ex·egesis (ek'sə jē'sis) *n., pl.* -ge'ses' (-sēz') ⟦< Gr *ex-*, out + *hēgeisthai*, to lead⟧ interpretation of a word, passage, etc., esp. in the Bible

ex·em·plar (eg zem'plər, -plär') *n.* ⟦< L *exemplum*, a pattern⟧ 1 a model; pattern 2 a typical specimen

ex·em·plary (eg zem'plə rē) *adj.* ⟦< L *exemplum*, a pattern⟧ serving as a model or example *[an exemplary life]*

ex·em·plify (eg zem'plə fī') *vt.* -fied', -fy'ing ⟦< L *exemplum*, example + *facere*, to make⟧ to show by example —ex·em'pli·fi·ca'tion *n.*

ex·empt (eg zempt') *vt.* ⟦< L *ex-*, out + *emere*, to buy⟧ to free from a rule or obligation which applies to others —*adj.* freed from a usual rule, duty, etc. —ex·emp'tion *n.*

ex·er·cise (ek'sər sīz') *n.* ⟦< L *exercere*, put to work⟧ 1 active use or operation 2 performance (of duties, etc.) 3 activity for developing the body or mind 4 a task to be practiced for developing some skill 5 *[pl.]* a program of speeches, etc. —*vt.* -cised', -cis'ing 1 to put into action; use 2 to put into use so as to develop or train 3 to exert (influence, etc.) 4 to worry; disturb —*vi.* to do exercises

ex·ert (eg zurt') *vt.* ⟦< L *exserere*, stretch out⟧ 1 to put into action 2 to apply (oneself) with great effort

ex·er'tion *n.* 1 the act, fact, or process of exerting 2 effort

ex·hale (eks hāl') *vt., vi.* -haled', -hal'ing ⟦< L *ex-*, out +

▬▬▬ THESAURUS ▬▬▬

select, private, segregated, prohibitive, clannish, independent, swank*.—*Ant.* FREE, inclusive, unrestricted.

exclusively *a.* particularly, solely, completely; see ONLY 1.

excommunicate *v.* expel, curse, oust; see DISMISS.

excommunication *n.* expulsion, dismissal, suspension; see REMOVAL.

excrement *n.* excretion, stool, fecal matter, offal, droppings, discharge, dung, manure, urine, effluvium, feces, sweat, perspiration, excreta, poop*.

excrete *v.* remove, eliminate, eject, defecate, urinate, discharge, secrete, go to the bathroom, go to the toilet, answer a call of nature, pass, expel, exude, perspire, sweat, squeeze out, give off, dump*, poop*.

excretion *n.* eliminating, elimination, urinating, discharging, secreting, secretion, defecation, ejecting, ejection, passing off.

excruciating *a.* torturing, intense, agonizing; see PAINFUL 1.

excursion *n.* jaunt, ramble, tour; see JOURNEY.

excusable *a.* pardonable, forgivable, understandable, justifiable, reasonable, defensible, permissible, trivial, passable, slight, plausible, allowable, explainable, not excessive, not fatal, not too bad, not inexcusable, not injurious, moderate, temperate, all right, fair, within limits, OK.

excuse *n.* apology, reason, defense; see EXPLANATION. —a poor excuse for inferior, poor, unsatisfactory; see INADEQUATE. —make one's excuses regret, apologize, offer an explanation; see APOLOGIZE, EXPLAIN.

excuse *v.* pardon, forgive, justify,

discharge, vindicate, apologize for, release from, dispense with, free, set free, overlook, purge, exempt from, rationalize, acquit, condone, appease, reprieve, absolve, exonerate, clear of, give absolution to, pass over, give as an excuse, make excuses for, make allowances for, make apologies for, grant amnesty to, provide with an alibi for, plead ignorance of, whitewash, let off easy, let go scot-free, wink at*, wipe the slate clean, shrug off, take the rap for*. —excuse me pardon me, forgive me, begging your pardon, I'm sorry.

excused *a.* forgiven, freed, permitted; see PARDONED.

execute *v.* 1 [To carry out instructions] act, do, effect; see PERFORM 1. 2 [To put to death] electrocute, hang, behead; see KILL 1.

executed *a.* 1 [Performed] completed, done, carried out; see FINISHED 1. 2 [Formally put to death] killed, hanged, electrocuted, gassed, shot at sunrise, sent before a firing squad, beheaded, guillotined, crucified, sent to the chair*, fried*, cooked*.

execution *n.* punishment, capital punishment, killing, electrocution, hanging, gassing, beheading, decapitation, guillotining, crucifixion, martyrdom.

executive *a.* administrative, governing, ruling; see MANAGING.

executive *n.* businessman, president, vice-president, secretary, treasurer, supervisor, chairman, dean, head, chief, superintendent, bureaucrat, leader, governor, controller, organizer, commander, director, boss, big shot, official, manager; see

also BUSINESSMAN, LEADER 2.

exemplify *v.* illustrate, give an example, represent; see EXPLAIN.

exempt *a.* freed, cleared, liberated, privileged, excused, absolved, not subject to, released from, not responsible for, not responsible for, set apart, excluded, released, not liable, unrestrained, unbound, uncontrolled, unrestricted, freed from, not restricted to, not restricted to, outside.—*Ant.* RESPONSIBLE, liable, subject.

exempt *v.* free, liberate, pass by; see EXCUSE.

exemption *n.* exception, immunity, privilege; see FREEDOM.

exercise *n.* 1 [Action undertaken for training] practice, exertion, drill, drilling, gymnastics, sports, calisthenics, workout. 2 [The means by which training is promoted] performance, action, activity; see ACTION. 3 [Use] application, employment, operation; see USE 1.

exercise *v.* 1 [To move the body] stretch, bend, pull, tug, hike, work, promote muscle tone, labor, strain, loosen up, discipline, drill, execute, perform exercises, practice, take a walk, work out, limber up, warm up; see also TRAIN 1. 2 [To use] employ, practice, exert, apply, operate, execute, sharpen, handle, utilize, devote, put in practice; see also USE 1. 3 [To train] drill, discipline, give training to; see TEACH, TRAIN 1.

exert *v.* put forth, bring to bear, exercise; see USE 1. —exert oneself strive, attempt, endeavor; see TRY 1.

exertion *n.* struggle, attempt, endeavor; see EFFORT.

halare, breathe ‖ **1** to breathe forth (air) **2** to give off (vapor, etc.) —**ex·ha·la·tion** (eks'hə lā'shən) *n.*

ex·haust (eg zôst') *vt.* ‖ < L *ex-,* out + *haurire,* to draw ‖ **1** to use up **2** to empty completely; drain **3** to tire out **4** to deal with thoroughly — *n.* **1** the discharge of used steam, gas, etc. from an engine **2** the pipes through which it is released **3** fumes, etc. given off —**ex·haust'i·ble** *adj.*

ex·haus·tion (eg zôs'chən) *n.* **1** an exhausting **2** great fatigue

ex·haus'tive *adj.* leaving nothing out

ex·hib·it (eg zib'it) *vt.* ‖ < L *ex-,* out + *habere,* to hold ‖ **1** to show; display **2** to present to public view — *vi.* to put art objects, etc. on public display — *n.* **1** a display **2** a thing exhibited **3** *Law* an object produced as evidence in a court —**ex·hib'i·tor** *n.*

ex·hi·bi·tion (ek'sə bish'ən) *n.* **1** an exhibiting **2** that which is exhibited **3** a public showing, as of art

ex'hi·bi'tion·ism' *n.* **1** a tendency to call attention to oneself or show off **2** a tendency to expose oneself sexually —**ex'hi·bi'tion·ist** *n.*

ex·hil·a·rate (eg zil'ə rāt') *vt.* **-rat'ed, -rat'ing** ‖ < L *ex-,* intens. + *hilaris,* glad ‖ **1** to make cheerful or lively **2** to stimulate —**ex·hil'a·ra'tion** *n.* —**ex·hil'a·ra'tive** *adj.*

ex·hort (eg zôrt') *vt., vi.* ‖ < L *ex-,* out + *hortari,* to urge ‖ to urge earnestly; advise strongly —**ex·hor·ta·tion** (eg'zôr tā'shən, ek'sər-) *n.*

ex·hume (eks hyōōm', eg zyōōm') *vt.* **-humed', -hum'ing** ‖ < L *ex-,* out + *humus,* the ground ‖ to dig out of the earth; disinter —**ex·hu·ma·tion** (eks'hyōō mā'shən) *n.*

ex·i·gen·cy (eks'ə jən sē) *n., pl.* **-cies** ‖ < L *exigere,* drive out ‖ **1** urgency **2** a situation calling for immediate attention **3** [*pl.*] pressing needs —**ex'i·gent** *adj.*

ex·ig·u·ous (eg zig'yōō əs) *adj.* ‖ see prec. ‖ scanty; meager

ex·ile (eks'īl', egz'īl') *n.* ‖ < L *exul,* an exile ‖ **1** a prolonged living away from one's country, usually enforced **2** a person in exile — *vt.* **-iled', -il'ing** to force (a person) into exile; banish

ex·ist (eg zist') *vi.* ‖ < L *ex-,* out + *sistere,* to set, place ‖ **1** to have reality or being; be **2** to occur or be present **3** to continue being; live

ex·ist'ence *n.* **1** the act or fact of being **2** life; living **3** occurrence —**ex·ist'ent** *adj.*

ex·is·ten·tial (eg'zis ten'shəl) *adj.* **1** of existence **2** of existentialism

ex'is·ten'tial·ism' *n.* a philosophical movement stressing individual existence and holding that human beings are totally free and responsible for their acts —**ex·is·ten'tial·ist** *adj., n.*

exit (eks'it, egz'it) *n.* ‖ < L *ex-,* out + *ire,* to go ‖ **1** an actor's departure from the stage **2** a going out; departure **3** a way out — *vi.* to leave a place

exo- ‖ < Gr *exō* ‖ *prefix* outside, outer, outer part

exo·bi·ol·o·gy (eks'ō bī äl'ə jē) *n.* the branch of biology investigating the possibility of extraterrestrial life

exo·dus (eks'ə dəs) *n.* ‖ < Gr *ex-,* out + *hodos,* way ‖ a going out or forth —**[E-] 1** the departure of the Israelites from Egypt: with *the* **2** the second book of the Bible, describing this

ex of·fi·cio (eks' ə fish'ō', -ē ō') ‖ L, lit., from office ‖ by virtue of one's position

ex·on·er·ate (eg zän'ər āt') *vt.* **-at'ed, -at'ing** ‖ < L *ex-,* out + *onerare,* to load ‖ to declare or prove blameless —**ex·on'era'tion** *n.*

ex·or·bi·tant (eg zôr'bi tənt) *adj.* ‖ < L *ex-,* out + *orbita,* a track ‖ going beyond what is reasonable, just, etc.; excessive —**ex·or'bi·tance** *n.* —**ex·or'bi·tantly** *adv.*

ex·or·cise or **ex·or·cize** (eks'ôr sīz') *vt.* **-cised'** or **-cized', -cis'ing** or **-ciz'ing** ‖ < Gr *ex-,* out + *horkos,* an oath ‖ **1** to drive (an evil spirit) out or away by ritual prayers, etc. **2** to free from such a spirit —**ex'or·cism'** (-siz'əm) *n.* —**ex'or·cist** *n.*

exo·skel·eton (eks'ō skel'ə tən) *n.* any hard, external supporting structure, as the shell of an oyster

ex'o·ther'mic (-thur'mik) *adj.* of a chemical change in which there is a liberation of heat

ex·ot·ic (eg zät'ik) *adj.* ‖ < Gr *exō,* outside ‖ **1** foreign **2** strangely beautiful, enticing, etc. —**ex·ot'i·cally** *adv.* —**ex·ot'i·cism'** (-ə siz'əm) *n.*

exp. experience(d)

ex·pand (ek spand') *vt., vi.* ‖ < L *ex-,* out + *pandere,* to spread ‖ **1** to spread out; unfold **2** to increase in size, scope, etc.; enlarge; develop

ex·panse (ek spans') *n.* a large area or unbroken surface; wide extent

ex·pan'si·ble *adj.* that can be expanded Also **ex·pand'able**

ex·pan'sion *n.* **1** an expanding or being expanded; enlargement **2** an expanded thing or part **3** the degree or extent of expansion

expansion bolt a bolt with an attachment that expands in use to act as a wedge

ex·pan'sive *adj.* **1** that can expand **2** broad; extensive **3** effusive; demonstrative —**ex·pan'sively** *adv.*

ex·pa·ti·ate (eks pā'shē āt') *vi.* **-at'ed, -at'ing** ‖ < L *ex(s)patiari,* wander ‖ to speak or write at length (*on* or *upon*) —**ex·pa'tia'tion** *n.*

ex·pa·tri·ate (eks pā'trē āt'; *for n.,* -it) *vt., vi.* **-at'ed, -at'ing** ‖ < L *ex,* out of + *patria,* fatherland ‖ to exile (a person or oneself) — *n.* an expatriated person —**ex·pa'tria'tion** *n.*

ex·pect (ek spekt') *vt.* ‖ < L *ex-,* out + *spectare,* to look ‖ **1** to look for as likely to occur or appear **2** to look for as proper or necessary **3** [Colloq.] to suppose; guess —**be expecting** [Colloq.] to be pregnant

ex·pect'an·cy *n., pl.* **-cies 1** EXPECTATION **2** that which is expected, esp. on a statistical basis

ex·pect'ant *adj.* that expects; expecting —**ex·pect'antly** *adv.*

ex·pec·ta·tion (ek'spek tā'shən) *n.* **1** an expecting; anticipation **2** a thing looked forward to **3** [*also pl.*] a reason for expecting something

---

THESAURUS

exhalation *n.* emanation, vapor, air; see BREATH.

exhaust *v.* **1** [To consume strength] debilitate, tire, wear out, wear down; see also WEAKEN 1, 2, WEARY 1, 2. **2** [To use entirely] use up, take the last of, deplete; see WEAR 3.

exhausted *a.* **1** [Without further physical resources] debilitated, wearied, worn; see TIRED, WEAK 1. **2** [Having nothing remaining] all gone, consumed, used; see EMPTY.

exhaustion *n.* weariness, fatigue, depletion; see FATIGUE.

exhibit *n.* show, performance, presentation; see DISPLAY.

exhibit *v.* show, present, manifest; see DISPLAY.

exhibited *a.* shown, presented, advertised; see SHOWN 1.

exhibition *n.* exposition, fair, carnival; see SHOW 1.

exile *n.* **1** [Banishment] expulsion, deportation, expatriation, ostracism, displacement, separation. **2** [An outcast] fugitive, outlaw, man without a country; see REFUGEE.

exile *v.* ostracize, outlaw, cast out; see BANISH.

exist *v.* **1** [To have being] breathe,

live, survive; see BE 1. **2** [To carry on life] be alive, endure, go on; see SURVIVE 1.

existence *n.* **1** [The carrying on of life] being, actuality, reality; see LIFE 1. **2** [The state of being] presence, actuality, permanence; see REALITY.

existing *a.* for the time being, temporary, just now; see PRESENT 1.

exit *n.* **1** [A means of egress] way out, outlet, opening; see DOOR. **2** [The act of leaving] going, farewell, exodus; see DEPARTURE.

exorbitant *a.* excessive, extravagant, too much; see WASTEFUL.

exotic *a.* **1** [Foreign] imported, not native, extrinsic; see FOREIGN. **2** [Peculiar] strange, fascinating, different; see FOREIGN, UNUSUAL 2.

expand *v.* extend, augment, dilate; see GROW 1.

expanse *n.* breadth, width, length, extent, reach, stretch, distance, area, belt, space, field, territory, span, spread, room, scope, range, compass, sphere, margin, sweep, radius, wilderness, region, immensity.

expansion *n.* enlargement, augmentation, extension; see INCREASE.

expatriate *n.* exile, emigrant, out-

cast; see REFUGEE.

expatriate *v.* exile, ostracize, deport; see BANISH.

expect *v.* **1** [To anticipate] await, look for, look forward to, count on, plan on, assume, suppose, lean on, feel it in one's bones*, wait for, hope for; see also ANTICIPATE. **2** [To require] demand, insist upon, exact; see REQUIRE 2. **3** [To assume] presume, suppose, suspect; see ASSUME.

expectancy *n.* hope, prospect, likelihood; see ANTICIPATION.

expectant *a.* **1** [Characterized by anticipation] expecting, hoping, hopeful, waiting, awaiting, in anticipation, watchful, vigilant, eager, ready, prepared, in suspense, gaping, wide-eyed, on edge, itching.—*Ant.* INDIFFERENT, UNPREPARED, nonchalant. **2** [Anticipating birth] pregnant, parturient, expecting; see PREGNANT.

expectation *n.* hope, belief, prospect; see ANTICIPATION.

expected *a.* looked for, counted upon, contemplated, looked forward to, hoped for, relied upon, foreseen, predictable, predetermined, foretold, prophesied, planned for, prepared

ex·pec·to·rant (ek spek′tə rənt) *n.* ⟦see fol.⟧ a medicine that helps to bring up phlegm

ex·pec·to·rate (-tə rāt′) *vt., vi.* **-rat′ed, -rat′ing** ⟦< L *ex-*, out + *pectus*, breast⟧ to spit —**ex·pec′to·ra′tion** *n.*

ex·pe·di·ency (ek spē′dē ən sē) *n., pl.* **-cies** **1** a being expedient; suitability for a given purpose **2** the doing of what is selfish rather than of what is right or just; self-interest **3** an expedient Also **ex·pe′di·ence**

ex·pe·di·ent *adj.* ⟦see fol.⟧ **1** useful for effecting a desired result; convenient **2** based on or guided by self-interest — *n.* an expedient thing; means to an end

ex·pe·dite (eks′pə dīt′) *vt.* **-dit′ed, -dit′ing** ⟦< L *expedire*, lit., to free the foot⟧ **1** to speed up the progress of; facilitate **2** to do quickly

ex′pe·dit′er *n.* one employed to expedite urgent or involved projects

ex·pe·di·tion (eks′pə dish′ən) *n.* ⟦see EXPEDITE⟧ **1** *a*) a voyage, march, etc., as for exploration or battle *b*) those on such a journey **2** efficient speed —**ex′pe·di′tion·ar′y** *adj.*

ex′pe·di′tious (-dish′əs) *adj.* efficient and speedy; prompt —**ex′pe·di′tiously** *adv.*

ex·pel (ek spel′) *vt.* **-pelled′, -pel′ling** ⟦< L *ex-*, out + *pellere*, to thrust⟧ **1** to drive out by force **2** to dismiss by authority *[expelled* from college*]* —**ex·pel′la·ble** *adj.* — **ex·pel′ler** *n.*

ex·pend (ek spend′) *vt.* ⟦< L *ex-*, out + *pendere*, to weigh⟧ **1** to spend **2** to use up

ex·pend′a·ble *adj.* **1** that can be expended **2** *Mil.* designating equipment (or men) expected to be used up (or sacrificed) in service

ex·pend′i·ture (-spen′di chər) *n.* **1** an expending of money, time, etc. **2** the amount of money, time, etc. expended

ex·pense (ek spens′) *n.* ⟦see EXPEND⟧ **1** financial cost; charge **2** any cost or sacrifice **3** *[pl.]* charges met with in doing one's work, etc.

ex·pen′sive *adj.* costly; high-priced

ex·pe·ri·ence (ek spir′ē əns) *n.* ⟦< L *experiri*, to try⟧ **1** the act of living through an event **2** anything or everything observed or lived through **3** *a*) training and personal participation *b*) knowledge, skill, etc. resulting from this — *vt.* **-enced, -enc·ing** to have experience of; undergo

ex·pe′ri·enced *adj.* having had or having learned from experience

ex·per·i·ment (ek sper′ə mənt; *for v.,* *usually,* -ment′) *n.* ⟦< L *experimentum*, a trial⟧ a test or trial undertaken to discover or demonstrate something — *vi.* to make an experiment —**ex·per′i·men·ta′tion** (-mən tā′shən) *n.* — **ex·per′i·ment′er** *n.*

ex·per·i·men·tal *adj.* **1** based on or used for experiments **2** testing; trial —**ex·per′i·men′tally** *adv.*

ex·pert (eks′pərt) *adj.* ⟦see EXPERIENCE⟧ very skillful — *n.* one who is very skillful or well-informed in some special field —**ex′pertly** *adv.* —**ex′pert·ness** *n.*

ex·per·tise (ek′spər tēz′) *n.* ⟦Fr⟧ the skill or knowledge of an expert

ex·pi·ate (eks′pē āt′) *vt.* **-at′ed, -at′ing** ⟦< L *ex-*, out + *piare*, to appease⟧ to make amends for (wrongdoing or guilt); atone for —**ex′pia′tion** *n.* —**ex′pia·to′ry** (-ə tôr′ē) *adj.*

ex·pire (ek spīr′) *vi.* **-pired′, -pir′ing** ⟦< L *ex-*, out + *spirare*, breathe⟧ **1** to exhale **2** to die **3** to come to an end —**ex·pi·ra·tion** (ek′spə rā′shən) *n.*

ex·plain (ek splān′) *vt.* ⟦< L *ex-*, out + *planus*, level⟧ **1** to make plain or understandable **2** to give the meaning of; expound **3** to account for — *vi.* to give an explanation — **ex·plain′a·ble** *adj.*

ex·pla·na·tion (eks′plə nā′shən) *n.* **1** an explaining **2** something that explains; interpretation, meaning, etc.

ex·plan·a·to·ry (ek splan′ə tôr′ē) *adj.* explaining or intended to explain

ex·ple·tive (eks′plə tiv) *n.* ⟦< L *ex-*, out, up + *plere*, to fill⟧ an oath or exclamation

ex·pli·ca·ble (eks′pli kə bəl) *adj.* ⟦see fol.⟧ that can be explained

ex′pli·cate′ (-kāt′) *vt.* **-cat′ed, -cat′ing** ⟦< L *ex-*, out + *plicare*, to fold⟧ to make clear; explain fully

ex·plic·it (eks plis′it) *adj.* ⟦see prec.⟧ **1** clearly stated or shown; definite **2** outspoken —**ex·plic′itly** *adv.*

━━━━━━━━━━━━━━━━ **THESAURUS** ━━━━━━━━━━━━━━━━

for, budgeted, within normal expectations, in the works, in the cards, coming up, in the bag*; see also LIKELY.

expecting *a.* expectant, due, about to become a mother; see PREGNANT.

expediency *n.* advantageousness, efficiency, profitableness; see USEFULNESS.

expedient *a.* profitable, useful, convenient; see PRACTICAL.

expedition *n.* **1** [Travel undertaken] excursion, voyage, campaign; see JOURNEY. **2** [That which undertakes travel] party, hunters, explorers, pioneers, traders, soldiers, scouts, archaeologist, tourists, sightseers, caravan, posse; see also CROWD.

expel *v.* **1** [To eject] get rid of, cast out, dislodge; see EJECT. **2** [To dismiss] suspend, discharge, oust; see DISMISS.

expend *v.* pay out, write checks for, lay out; see SPEND.

expenditure *n.* outgo, investment, payment; see EXPENSE.

expense *n.* expenditure, responsibility, obligation, loan, mortgage, lien, debt, liability, investment, insurance, upkeep, alimony, debit, account, cost, price, outlay, charge, payment, outgo, value, worth, sum, amount, risk, capital, rate, tax, carrying charges, budgeted items, cost of materials, overhead, time, payroll, investment.—*Ant.* PROFIT, income, receipts. —**at the expense of** paid by, at the cost of, charged to; see OWED.

expenses *n.* expenses, living expenses, costs, lodging, room and board, incidentals, carrying charge.

expensive *a.* dear, precious, valuable, invaluable, rare, high-priced, costly, prized, choice, rich, priceless, high, too high, unreasonable, exorbitant, extravagant, at a premium, out of sight*, at great cost, sky-high, steep*, stiff*.—*Ant.* CHEAP, inexpensive, low.

experience *n.* background, skill, knowledge, wisdom, practice, maturity, judgment, practical knowledge, sense, patience, caution, know-how*; see also BACKGROUND 2.

experience *v.* undergo, feel, live through; see ENDURE 2, FEEL 2.

experienced *a.* skilled, practiced, instructed, accomplished, versed, qualified, able, skillful, knowing, trained, wise, expert, veteran, mature, with a good background, rounded, knowing the score*, knowing the ropes*, having all the answers, having been around*, having been through the mill*, broken in*.—*Ant.* NEW, apprentice, beginning.

experiment *n.* analysis, essay, examination, trial, inspection, search, organized observation, research, scrutiny, speculation, check, proof, operation, test, exercise, quiz, investigation.

experiment *v.* analyze, investigate, probe, search, venture, explore, test, rehearse, try out, sample, subject to discipline, prove, conduct an experiment, research, study, examine, scrutinize, weigh, play around with, fool with*.

experimental *a.* tentative, trial, temporary, test, provisional, preliminary, preparatory, under probation, on approval, on trial, pending verification, momentary, primary, beginning, laboratory, in its first stage.—*Ant.* PERMANENT, tried, tested.

expert *a.* skillful, practiced, proficient; see ABLE.

expert *n.* graduate, master, trained personnel; see SPECIALIST.

expiration *n.* close, closing, finish; see END 2.

expire *v.* stop, finish, quit; see END 1.

explain *v.* interpret, explicate, account for, elucidate, illustrate, clarify, illuminate, make clear, describe, expound, teach, reveal, point out, demonstrate, tell, read, translate, paraphrase, put in other words, define, justify, untangle, unravel, make plain, come to the point, put across, throw light upon, comment on, remark upon, remark on, offer an explanation of, resolve, clear up, get right, set right, put someone on the right track, spell out, go into detail, get to the bottom of, figure out, cast light upon, get across, get through, bring out, work out, solve, put in plain English*.—*Ant.* CONFUSE, puzzle, confound.

explainable *a.* explicable, accountable, intelligible; see UNDERSTANDABLE.

explained *a.* made clear, interpreted, elucidated; see KNOWN 2, OBVIOUS 2.

explanation *n.* information, answer, account, reason, illustration, description, comment, justification, narrative, story, tale, footnote, anecdote, example, analysis, criticism, exegesis, key, commentary, note, summary, report, brief, the details, budget, breakdown; see also PROOF 1.

explanatory *a.* expository, illustrative, informative, allegorical, interpretative, instructive, guiding, descriptive, analytical, graphic, critical.

explicit *a.* express, sure, plain; see DEFINITE 1, UNDERSTANDABLE.

ex·plode (ek splōd′) *vt.* **-plod′ed, -plod′ing** ⟦orig., to drive off the stage < L *ex-*, off + *plaudere*, applaud⟧ **1** to expose as false **2** to make burst with a loud noise **3** to cause to change suddenly and violently, as from a solid to an expanding gas — *vi.* to burst forth noisily —**ex·plod′able** *adj.*

ex·ploit (eks′ploit′; *for v.*, *usually* ik sploit′) *n.* ⟦see EXPLICATE⟧ a daring act; bold deed —*vt.* **1** to make use of **2** to make unethical use of for one's own profit —**ex′ploi·ta′tion** *n.* —**ex·ploit′a·tive** *adj.* —**ex·ploit′er** *n.*

ex·plore (ek splôr′) *vt.*, *vi.* **-plored′, -plor′ing** ⟦< L *ex-*, out + *plorare*, cry out⟧ **1** to examine (something) carefully; investigate **2** to travel in (a little-known region) for discovery —**ex·plo·ra·tion** (eks′plə rā′shən) *n.* —**ex·plor′a·to′ry** (-ə tôr′ē) *adj.* —**ex·plor′er** *n.*

ex·plo·sion (ek splō′zhən) *n.* **1** an exploding **2** the noise made by exploding **3** a noisy outburst **4** a sudden, widespread increase

ex·plo·sive (-siv) *adj.* **1** of, causing, or like an explosion **2** tending to explode — *n.* a substance that can explode, as gunpowder —**ex·plo′sive·ly** *adv.* —**ex·plo′sive·ness** *n.*

ex·po·nent (eks pōn′ənt; *for n.* **3**, eks′pōn′-) *n.* ⟦see EXPOUND⟧ **1** one who expounds or promotes (principles, etc.) **2** a person or thing that is an example or symbol (*of* something) **3** *Algebra* a symbol placed at the upper right of another to show how many times the latter is to be multiplied by itself (Ex.: $b^2 = b \times b$) —**ex·po·nen·tial** (eks′pō nen′shəl) *adj.*

ex·port (eks pôrt′; *also, and for n.* *always*, eks′pôrt′) *vt.* ⟦< L *ex-*, out + *portare*, to carry⟧ to send (goods) to another country, esp. for sale — *n.* **1** something exported **2** an exporting —**ex′por·ta′tion** *n.* —**ex·port′er** *n.*

ex·pose (eks pōz′) *vt.* **-posed′, -pos′ing** ⟦see EXPOUND⟧ **1** to lay open (*to* danger, attack, etc.) **2** to reveal; exhibit **3** to make (a crime, etc.) known **4** *Photog.* to subject (a sensitized film or plate) to actinic rays, etc.

ex·po·sé (eks′pō zā′) *n.* ⟦Fr⟧ a public disclosure of a scandal, crime, etc.

ex·po·si·tion (eks′pə zish′ən) *n.* ⟦see EXPOUND⟧ **1** a detailed explanation **2** writing or speaking that explains **3** a large public exhibition or show

ex·pos·i·tor (eks päz′ət ər) *n.* one who expounds or explains

ex·pos′i·to′ry (-ə tôr′ē) *adj.* of or containing exposition; explanatory

ex post facto (eks′ pōst fak′tō) ⟦L, from (the thing) done afterward⟧ done afterward, but retroactive

ex·pos·tu·late (eks päs′chə lāt′) *vi.* **-lat′ed, -lat′ing** ⟦< L *ex-*, intens. + *postulare*, to demand⟧ to reason with a person earnestly, objecting to that person's actions —**ex·pos′tu·la′tion** *n.*

ex·po·sure (eks pō′zhər) *n.* **1** an exposing or being exposed **2** a location, as of a house, in relation to the sun, etc. *[an eastern exposure]* **3** frequent appearance before the public **4** *Photog.* *a*) the subjection of a sensitized film or plate to actinic rays, etc. *b*) a section of a film for one picture *c*) the time during which such film is exposed

ex·pound (eks pound′) *vt.* ⟦< L *ex-*, out + *ponere*, to put⟧ **1** to set forth; state in detail **2** to explain

ex·press (eks pres′) *vt.* ⟦< L *ex-*, out + *premere*, to press⟧ **1** to squeeze out (juice, etc.) **2** to put into words; state **3** to reveal; show **4** to symbolize; signify **5** to send by express —*adj.* **1** expressed; stated; explicit **2** exact **3** specific **4** fast and direct *[an express bus]* **5** marked by speed **6** having to do with an express train, bus, service, etc. — *adv.* by express — *n.* **1** an express train, bus, etc. **2** *a*) a service for transporting things rapidly *b*) the things sent by express

ex·pres·sion (eks presh′ən) *n.* **1** a putting into words; stating **2** a manner of expressing, esp. with eloquence **3** a particular word or phrase **4** a showing of feeling, character, etc. **5** a look, intonation, etc. that conveys meaning **6** a mathematical symbol or set of symbols —**ex·pres′sion·less** *adj.*

ex·pres′sion·ism′ *n.* a 20th-c. movement in art, literature, etc. seeking to give symbolic, objective expression to inner experience —**ex·pres′sion·ist** *adj.*, *n.* —**ex·pres′sion·is′tic** *adj.*

ex·pres·sive (eks pres′iv) *adj.* **1** that expresses **2** full of meaning or feeling —**ex·pres′sive·ly** *adv.* —**ex·pres′sive·ness** *n.*

ex·press·ly (eks pres′lē) *adv.* **1** plainly; definitely **2** especially; particularly

express′way′ *n.* a divided highway for high-speed, through traffic, with grade separations at intersections

ex·pro·pri·ate (eks prō′prē āt′) *vt.* **-at′ed, -at′ing** ⟦< L *ex-*, out + *proprius*, one's own⟧ to take (land, etc.) from its owner, esp. for public use —**ex·pro′pria′tion** *n.*

ex·pul·sion (eks pul′shən) *n.* an expelling or being expelled

ex·punge (ek spunj′) *vt.* **-punged′, -pung′ing** ⟦< L *ex-*, out + *pungere*, to prick⟧ to blot or strike out; erase

ex·pur·gate (eks′pər gāt′) *vt.* **-gat′ed, -gat′ing** ⟦< L *ex-*, out + *purgare*, cleanse⟧ to remove passages considered obscene, etc. from (a book, etc.) —**ex′pur·ga′tion** *n.*

ex·qui·site (eks′kwi zit, ik skwiz′it) *adj.* ⟦< L *ex-*, out + *quaerere*, to ask⟧ **1** carefully or elaborately done **2** very beautiful, delicate, etc. **3** of highest quality **4** very intense; keen —**ex′qui·site·ly** *adv.*

THESAURUS

explode *v.* blow up, blow out, blow a fuse, break out, erupt, go off, detonate, discharge, backfire, shatter, fracture, split, collapse, blow off, blast, blow to smithereens*.

exploit *n.* deed, venture, escapade; see ACHIEVEMENT.

exploit *v.* utilize, take advantage of, employ; see USE 1.

exploited *a.* taken advantage of, utilized, worked; see USED.

exploration *n.* investigation, research, search; see EXAMINATION 1.

explore *v.* search, investigate, seek; see EXAMINE.

explorer *n.* adventurer, traveler, pioneer, wayfarer, pilgrim, voyager, space traveler, astronaut, cosmonaut, deep-sea diver, seafarer, mountaineer, mountain climber, scientist, navigator, colonist.

explosion *n.* detonation, blast, burst, discharge, blowout, blowup, eruption, combustion, outburst, firing, ignition, backfire.

explosive *a.* stormy, fiery, forceful, raging, wild, violent, uncontrollable, vehement, sharp, hysterical, frenzied, savage.—*Ant.* MILD, gentle, uneventful.

explosive *n.* mine, gunpowder, ammunition, TNT, plastic, dynamite, nitroglycerine, bomb, missile, grenade, charge, shell, Molotov cocktail; see also AMMUNITION, WEAPON.

export *n.* shipping, trading, overseas shipment, commodity, international trade, foreign trade.

export *v.* send out, sell abroad, trade abroad, ship, transport, consign, dump*.

expose *v.* **1** [To uncover] disclose, smoke out, show up, present, prove, reveal, air, exhibit, unmask, lay open, lay bare, bring to light, open, dig up, give away, bring into view, unfold, let the cat out of the bag, drag through the mud, put the finger on*. **2** [To endeavor to attract attention] show, show off, bare; see DISPLAY. **3** [To open to danger] lay open to, subject to, imperil; see ENDANGER.

exposed *a.* disclosed, defined, revealed, divulged, made public, laid bare, dug up, brought to light, solved, resolved, discovered, found out, see through.—*Ant.* HIDDEN, concealed, disguised.

exposition *n.* **1** [The process of making clear] elucidation, delineation, explication; see EXPLANATION. **2** [A popular exhibition] exhibit, showing, performance; see DISPLAY.

ex post facto *a.* subsequently, retroactively, retrospectively; see FINALLY 2.

exposure *n.* disclosure, betrayal, display, exhibition, publication, showing, revelation, confession, unveiling, acknowledgment, exposé, giveaway*, bombshell, stink*.—*Ant.* SECRECY, protection, concealment.

express *a.* **1** [Explicit] definite, specific, exact; see DEFINITE 1. **2** [Nonstop] fast, direct, high-speed; see FAST 1.

express *v.* declare, tell, signify; see UTTER.

expression *n.* **1** [Significant appearance] look, cast, character; see LOOKS. **2** [Putting into understandable form] representation, art product, interpretation, invention, narration, creation, utterance, declaration, commentary, diagnosis, definition, explanation, illustration; see also COMPOSITION, WRITING 1. **3** [A traditional form of speech] locution, idiom, speech pattern; see PHRASE, WORD 1. **4** [Facial cast] grimace, smile, smirk, mug, sneer, pout, grin; see also SMILE.

expressionless *a.* wooden, dull, vacuous; see BLANK.

expressive *a.* eloquent, demonstrative, revealing, indicative, representative, dramatic, stirring, sympathetic, articulate, touching, significant, meaningful, pathetic, spirited, emphatic, strong, forcible, energetic, lively, tender, passionate, warm, colorful, vivid, picturesque, brilliant, stimulating.—*Ant.* INDIFFERENT, impassive, dead.

expulsion *n.* ejection, suspension, purge; see REMOVAL.

exquisite *a.* fine, scrupulous, precise; see DAINTY.

ex·tant (eks'tənt, ek stant') *adj.* ‖ < L *ex-*, out + *stare*, to stand ‖ still existing; not extinct

ex·tem·po·ra·neous (eks'tem'pə rā'nē əs) *adj.* ‖ see fol. ‖ done or spoken with little preparation; offhand —**ex'tem'po·ra'neous·ly** *adv.*

ex·tem·pore (eks tem'pə rē) *adv., adj.* ‖ < L *ex-*, out of + *tempus*, time ‖ with little preparation; offhand

ex·tem·po·rize (-rīz') *vi., vt.* **-rized', -riz'ing** to speak, perform, etc. extempore; improvise

ex·tend (ek stend') *vt.* ‖ < L *ex-*, out + *tendere*, to stretch ‖ **1** to make longer; stretch out; prolong **2** to enlarge in area, scope, etc.; expand **3** to stretch forth **4** to offer; grant **5** to make (oneself) work very hard — *vi.* to be extended — **ex·tend'ed** *adj.* —**ex·tend'er** *n.* —**ex·ten'sible** (-sten'sə bəl) or **ex·tend'ible** *adj.*

extended care nursing care in a facility for convalescents, the disabled, etc.

extended family a group of parents, their children, and other relatives living in close proximity or together, esp. if three generations are involved

ex·ten·sion (-sten'shən) *n.* **1** an extending or being extended **2** range; extent **3** a part forming a continuation or addition

ex·ten·sive (-siv) *adj.* having great extent; vast; far-reaching; comprehensive —**ex·ten'sive·ly** *adv.* —**ex·ten'sive·ness** *n.*

ex·tent (ek stent') *n.* **1** the space, amount, or degree to which a thing extends; size **2** scope; limits **3** an extended space; vast area

ex·ten·u·ate (ek sten'yo̅o̅ āt') *vt.* **-at'ed, -at'ing** ‖ < L *ex-*, out + *tenuis*, thin ‖ to make (an offense, etc.) seem less serious —**ex·ten'u·a'tion** *n.*

ex·te·ri·or (ek stir'ē ər) *adj.* ‖ see EXTERNAL ‖ **1** *a*) on the outside; outer *b*) to be used on the outside *[exterior paint]* **2** coming from without — *n.* an outside or outside surface —**ex·te'ri·or·ly** *adv.*

ex·ter·mi·nate (ek stur'mə nāt') *vt.* **-nat'ed, -nat'ing** ‖ < L *ex-*, out + *terminus*, boundary ‖ to destroy entirely; wipe out —**ex·ter'mi·na'tion** *n.* —**ex·ter'mi·na'tor** *n.*

ex·ter·nal (eks tur'nəl) *adj.* ‖ < L *externus* ‖ **1** on or of the outside **2** existing apart from the mind; material **3** coming from without **4** superficial **5** foreign — *n.* an outside surface or part —**ex·ter'nal·ly** *adv.*

ex·tinct (ek stiŋkt') *adj.* ‖ see EXTINGUISH ‖ **1** having died down; extinguished **2** no longer in existence

ex·tinc·tion *n.* **1** an extinguishing **2** a destroying or being destroyed **3** a dying out, as a species

ex·tin·guish (ek stiŋ'gwish) *vt.* ‖ < L *ex-*, out + *stinguere*, extinguish ‖ **1** to put out (a fire, etc.) **2** to destroy —**ex·tin'guisher** *n.*

ex·tir·pate (ek'stər pāt') *vt.* **-pat'ed, -pat'ing** ‖ < L *ex-*, out + *stirps*, root ‖ **1** to pull up by the roots **2** to destroy completely —**ex'tir·pa'tion** *n.*

ex·tol or **ex·toll** (eks tōl') *vt.* **-tolled', -tol'ling** ‖ < L *ex-*, up + *tollere*, to raise ‖ to praise highly; laud

ex·tort (eks tôrt') *vt.* ‖ < L *ex-*, out + *torquere*, to twist ‖ to get (money, etc.) from someone by force or threats

ex·tor·tion (eks tôr'shən) *n.* **1** an extorting **2** something extorted —**ex·tor'tion·ate** *adj.* —**ex·tor'tioner** *n.* —**ex·tor'tion·ist** *n.*

ex·tra (eks'trə) *adj.* ‖ < L *extra*, more than ‖ more or better than normal, expected, etc.; additional — *n.* an extra person or thing; specif., *a*) a special edition of a newspaper *b*) an extra benefit *c*) an actor hired by the day to play a minor part — *adv.* more than usually; esp., exceptionally

extra- ‖ see EXTERNAL ‖ *prefix* outside, beyond, besides

ex·tract (eks trakt'; *for n.* eks'trakt') *vt.* ‖ < L *ex-*, out + *trahere*, to draw ‖ **1** to draw out by effort **2** to obtain by pressing, distilling, etc. **3** to deduce; derive **4** to select or quote (a passage, etc.) — *n.* something extracted; specif., *a*) a concentrate *[beef extract]* *b*) an excerpt

ex·trac'tion *n.* **1** the act or process of extracting **2** origin; descent

extra·cur·ric·u·lar (eks'trə kə rik'yo̅o̅ lər) *adj.* not part of the required curriculum

extra·dite (eks'trə dīt') *vt.* **-dit'ed, -dit'ing** ‖ < L *ex*, out + *traditio*, a surrender ‖ to turn over (an alleged criminal, etc.) to the jurisdiction of another country, State, etc. — **ex'tra·di'tion** (-dish'ən) *n.*

ex'tra·le'gal *adj.* outside of legal control

extra·neous (eks trā'nē əs) *adj.* ‖ L *extraneus*, foreign ‖ **1** coming from outside; foreign **2** not pertinent; irrelevant —**extra'neous·ly** *adv.*

extraor·di·nary (ek strôrd'n er'ē) *adj.* ‖ < L *extra ordinem*, out of order ‖ **1** not ordinary **2** going far beyond the ordinary; unusual; remarkable —**extraor'di·nar'i·ly** *adv.*

ex·trap·o·late (ek strap'ə lāt') *vt., vi.* **-lat'ed, -lat'ing** ‖ see EXTRA- & INTERPOLATE ‖ to estimate (something unknown) on the basis of known facts —**ex·trap'o·la'tion** *n.*

extra·sen·sory (eks'trə sen'sə rē) *adj.* apart from, or in addition to, normal sense perception

ex'tra·ter·res'trial *adj.* being, of, or from outside the earth's limits — *n.* an extraterrestrial being, as in science fiction

ex·trav·a·gant (ek strav'ə gənt) *adj.* ‖ < L *extra*, beyond + *vagari*, to wander ‖ **1** going beyond reasonable limits; excessive **2** costing or spending too much; wasteful —**ex·trav'a·gance** *n.*

ex·trav·a·gan·za (ek strav'ə gan'zə) *n.* ‖ < It *estravaganza*, extravagance ‖ a spectacular theatrical production

extra·ve·hic·u·lar (eks'trə vē hik'yo̅o̅ lər) *adj.* designating activity by an astronaut outside a vehicle in space

ex·treme (ek strēm') *adj.* ‖ < L *exterus*, outer ‖ **1** farthest away; utmost **2** very great; excessive **3** unconventional or radical, as in politics **4** harsh; drastic — *n.* **1** either of two

---

THESAURUS

extemporaneous *a.* spontaneous, impromptu, unprepared; see AUTOMATIC, IMMEDIATE, IMMEDIATELY.

extend *v.* **1** [To make larger] lengthen, enlarge, prolong; see INCREASE. **2** [To occupy space to a given point] continue, go as far as, spread; see REACH 1.

extended *a.* **1** [Outspread] spread, widespread, expansive; see WIDESPREAD. **2** [Very long] elongated, drawn-out, lengthened; see LONG 1.

extending *a.* reaching, continuing, continual, perpetual, ranging, stretching, spreading, spanning, going on, running to, drawn out to, lengthening; see also ENDLESS.

extension *n.* section, branch, additional telephone; see ADDITION 2.

extensive *a.* wide, broad, long; see LARGE 1.

extensively *a.* widely, broadly, greatly; see WIDELY.

extent *n.* degree, limit, span, space, area, measure, size, bulk, length, compass, scope, reach, weep, wideness, width, range, amount, expanse, magnitude, intensity; see also EXPANSE.

exterior *a.* outer, outlying, outermost; see OUTSIDE.

exterior *n.* surface, covering, visible portion; see OUTSIDE 1.

exterminate *v.* annihilate, eradicate, abolish; see DESTROY.

external *a.* surface, visible, open to the air; see OBVIOUS 1.

extinct *a.* dead, ended, terminated, exterminated, deceased, lost, unknown, no longer known.

extinction *n.* abolition, extermination, extirpation; see DESTRUCTION 1, MURDER.

extinguish *v.* smother, choke, quench, douse, put out, snuff out, drown out, blow out, stifle, suffocate.

extort *v.* extract, wrench, force; see STEAL.

extortion *n.* fraud, stealing, blackmail; see THEFT.

extortionist *n.* thief, blackmailer, oppressor; see CRIMINAL.

extra *a.* additional, in addition, other, one more, spare, reserve, supplemental, increased, another, new, auxiliary, added, adjunct, besides, also, further, more, beyond, over and above, plus, supplementary, accessory, unused.—*Ant.* LESS, short, subtracted.

extract *n.* distillation, infusion, concentration; see ESSENCE 1.

extract *v.* evoke, derive, secure; see OBTAIN 1.

extradite *v.* obtain, apprehend, bring to justice; see ARREST.

extraordinarily *a.* remarkably, notably, peculiarly; see VERY.

extraordinary *a.* remarkable, curious, amazing; see UNUSUAL 1.

extravagance *n.* lavishness, expenditures, improvidence; see WASTE 1.

extravagant *a.* lavish, prodigal, immoderate; see WASTEFUL.

extravagantly *a.* expensively, beyond one's means, without restraint; see RASHLY, WASTEFULLY.

extreme *a.* radical, intemperate, immoderate, imprudent, excessive, inordinate, extravagant, flagrant, outrageous, unreasonable, irrational, improper, preposterous, thorough, far, fanatical, desperate, severe, intense, drastic, sheer, total, advanced, violent, sharp, acute, unseemly, beyond control, fantastic, to the extreme, exaggerated, monstrous, absurd, foolish.—*Ant.* RESTRAINED, cautious, moderate.

extreme *n.* height, apogee, apex; see END 4, LIMIT 2. —**go to extremes** be excessive, overreact, act rashly; see EXCEED. —**in the extreme**

things that are as different or far as possible from each other 2 an extreme act, state, etc. 3 *Math.* the first or last term of a proportion —**ex·treme′ly** *adv.* —**ex·treme′ ness** *n.*

ex·trem′ism′ (-iz′əm) *n.* a going to extremes, esp. in politics —**ex·trem′ist** *adj., n.*

ex·trem·ity (ek strem′ə tē) *n., pl.* **-ties** 1 the outermost part; end 2 the greatest degree 3 great need, danger, etc. 4 an extreme measure 5 [*pl.*] the hands and feet

ex·tri·cate (eks′tri kāt′) *vt.* **-cat′ed, -cat′ing** [< L *ex-*, out + *tricae*, vexations] to set free (*from* a net, difficulty, etc.) —**ex′tri·ca′tion** *n.*

ex·trin·sic (eks trin′sik) *adj.* [< L *exter*, without + *secus*, otherwise] not essential —**ex·trin′si·cally** *adv.*

extro·vert (eks′trə vurt′) *n.* [< L *extra-*, outside + *vertere*, to turn] one whose interest is more in his environment and in other people than in himself —**ex′tro·ver′sion** (-vur′zhən) *n.* —**ex′tro·vert′ed** *adj.*

ex·trude (eks trōōd′) *vt.* **-trud′ed, -trud′ing** [< L *ex-*, out + *trudere*, to thrust] to force out, as through a small opening —*vi.* to be extruded; esp., to protrude —**ex·tru′ sion** *n.* —**ex·tru′sive** *adj.*

exu·ber·ant (eg zōō′bər ənt) *adj.* [< L *ex-*, intens. + *uberare*, bear abundantly] 1 growing profusely; luxuriant 2 characterized by good health and high spirits —**exu′ ber·ance** *n.* —**exu′ber·antly** *adv.*

ex·ude (eg zōōd′) *vt., vi.* **-ud′ed, -ud′ing** [< L *ex-*, out + *sudare*, to sweat] 1 to ooze 2 to seem to radiate [*to exude* joy] —**exu·da′tion** (eks′yōō dā′shən) *n.*

ex·ult (eg zult′) *vi.* [< L *ex-*, intens. + *saltare*, to leap] to rejoice greatly; glory —**ex·ult′ant** *adj.* —**ex·ul·ta·tion** (eg′zul tā′shən, eks′ul-) *n.*

ex·ur·bia (eks ur′bē ə) *n.* [EX- + (SUB)URBIA] the semi-rural communities beyond the suburbs, lived in by upper-income families —**ex·ur′ban** *adj.* —**ex·ur·ban·ite′** *adj., n.*

eye (ī) *n.* [OE *ēage*] 1 the organ of sight in humans and animals 2 *a*) the eyeball *b*) the iris [brown *eyes*] 3 the area around the eye [a black *eye*] 4 [*often pl.*] sight; vision 5 a look; glance 6 attention; observation 7 the power of judging, etc. by eyesight [an *eye* for distances] 8 [*often pl.*] judgment; opinion [in the *eyes* of the law] 9 a thing like an eye in appearance or function — *vt.* **eyed, eye′ing** or **ey′ing** to look at; observe —**have an eye for** to have a keen appreciation of —**keep an eye on** to look after —**lay** (or **set** or **clap**) **eyes on** to look at —**make eyes at** to look at amorously —**see eye to eye** to agree completely —**with an eye to** paying attention to; considering

eye′ball′ *n.* the ball-shaped part of the eye

eye′brow′ *n.* the bony arch over each eye, or the hair growing on this

eye′-catch′er *n.* something that especially attracts one's attention —**eye′-catch′ing** *adj.*

eye′ful′ (-fool′) *n.* [Slang] a person or thing that looks striking or unusual

eye′glass′ *n.* 1 a lens to help faulty vision 2 [*pl.*] a pair of such lenses in a frame; glasses

eye′lash′ *n.* any of the hairs on the edge of the eyelid

eye′let (-lit) *n.* 1 a small hole for receiving a cord, hook, etc. 2 a metal ring for reinforcing such a hole 3 a small hole edged by stitching in embroidery

eye′lid′ *n.* either of the two folds of flesh that cover and uncover the eyeball

eye′lin′er *n.* a cosmetic applied in a thin line on the eyelid at the base of the eyelashes

eye′-o′pener (-ō′pə nər) *n.* a surprising piece of news, sudden realization, etc.

eye′piece′ *n.* in a telescope, microscope, etc., the lens or lenses nearest the viewer's eye

eye shadow a cosmetic applied to the upper eyelids

eye′sight′ *n.* 1 the power of seeing; sight 2 the range of vision

eye′sore′ *n.* an unpleasant sight

eye′strain′ *n.* a tired or strained condition of the eye muscles

eye′tooth′ *n., pl.* **-teeth′** a canine tooth of the upper jaw

eye′wash′ *n.* 1 a medicated solution for the eyes 2 [Slang] *a*) nonsense *b*) flattery

eye′wit′ness *n.* one who sees or has seen something happen, as an accident, etc.

ey·rie or **eyry** (er′ē, ir′ē) *n., pl.* **-ries** AERIE

THESAURUS

extremely, to the highest degree, inordinately; see MUCH.
extremely *a.* greatly, remarkably, notably; see MUCH.
extremist *n.* zealot, fanatic, die-hard; see RADICAL.
exuberance *n.* fervor, eagerness, exhilaration; see ZEAL.
exuberant *a.* ardent, vivacious, passionate; see ZEALOUS.
eye *n.* 1 [The organ of sight] instrument of vision, compound eye, simple eye, naked eye, optic, orb, peeper*, lamp*. *Parts of the eye include the following:* eyeball, pupil, retina, iris, cornea, eye muscles, optic nerve, white, lens. 2 [Appreciation] perception, taste, discrimination; see TASTE 1, 3. 3 [A center] focus, core, heart; see CENTER 1. —**private eye*** detective, investigator, gumshoe*; see POLICEMAN. —**all eyes*** attentive, aware, perceptive; see OBSERVANT. —**an eye for an eye** punishment, retaliation, vengeance; see REVENGE 1. —**catch one's eye** attract one's attention, cause notice, stand out; see FASCINATE. —**easy on the eyes*** attractive, appealing, pleasant to look at; see BEAUTIFUL. —**give a person the eye*** attract, charm, invite; see SEDUCE. —**have an eye for** appreciate, be interested in, desire; see WANT 1. —**have an eye to** watch out for, be mindful of, attend to; see WATCH OUT. —**have eyes for*** appreciate, be interested in, desire; see WANT 1. —**in a pig's eye*** under no circumstances, impossible, no way; see NEVER. —**in the public eye** well-known, renowned, celebrated; see FAMOUS. —**keep an eye on** look after, watch over, protect; see GUARD. —**keep an eye out for** watch for, be mindful of, attend to; see WATCH OUT. —**keep one's eyes open** (or **peeled**) be aware, be watchful, look out; see WATCH. —**lay eyes on** look at, stare, survey; see SEE 1. —**make eyes at** attract, charm, invite; see SEDUCE. —**open one's eyes** make aware, inform, apprise; see TELL 1. —**shut one's eyes to** refuse, reject, ignore; see REFUSE. —**with an eye to** considering, mindful of, aware of; see OBSERVANT.
eyesight *n.* vision, sense of seeing, visual perception; see SIGHT 1.
eyesore *n.* ugly thing, distortion, deformity; see UGLINESS.
eyewitness *n.* onlooker, passerby, observer; see WITNESS.

f or **F** (ef) *n.*, *pl.* **f's, F's** the sixth letter of the English alphabet

F (ef) *n.* **1** *Educ.* a grade for failing work or, sometimes, fair or average work **2** *Music* the fourth tone in the scale of C major

f or **f.** **1** feminine **2** folio **3** following **4** franc(s)

F *symbol for* **1** Fahrenheit **2** *Chem.* fluorine

F or **F.** **1** female **2** franc(s) **3** Friday

fa (fä) *n.* ⟦< ML⟧ *Music* the fourth tone of the diatonic scale

FAA Federal Aviation Administration

fa·ble (fā′bəl) *n.* ⟦< L *fabula*, a story⟧ **1** a fictitious story, usually about animals, meant to teach a moral lesson **2** a myth or legend **3** a falsehood

fa′bled *adj.* **1** mythical; legendary **2** unreal; fictitious

fab·ric (fab′rik) *n.* ⟦< L *fabrica*, workshop⟧ **1** a framework; structure **2** a material made from fibers, etc. by weaving, knitting, etc.; as cloth

fab·ri·cate (fab′ri kāt′) *vt.* **-cat′ed, -cat′ing** ⟦see prec.⟧ **1** to make, construct, etc.; manufacture **2** to make up (a story, lie, etc.); invent **—fab′ri·ca′tion** *n.* **—fab′ri·ca′tor** *n.*

fabu·lous (fab′yŏŏ ləs) *adj.* ⟦see FABLE⟧ **1** of or like a fable; fictitious **2** incredible; astounding **3** [Colloq.] wonderful **—fab′u·lous·ly** *adv.*

fa·çade or **fa·cade** (fə säd′) *n.* ⟦Fr: see fol.⟧ **1** the front or main face of a building **2** an imposing appearance concealing something inferior

face (fās) *n.* ⟦< L *facies*⟧ **1** the front of the head **2** the expression of the countenance **3** the main or front surface **4** the surface that is marked, as of a clock, etc., or that is finished, as of fabric, etc. **5** appearance; outward aspect **6** dignity; self-respect: usually in **lose** (or **save**) **face** **—** *vt.* **faced, fac′ing 1** to turn, or have the face turned, toward **2** to confront with boldness, etc. **3** to cover with a new surface **—** *vi.* to turn, or have the face turned, in a specified direction **—face to face 1** confronting each other **2** very near: with *with* **—face up to** to face with courage **— in the face of 1** in the presence of **2** in spite of **—make a face** to grimace **—on the face of it** apparently

-faced (fāst) *combining form* having a specified kind of face [round-*faced*]

face′less *adj.* lacking a distinct character; anonymous

face lifting 1 plastic surgery to remove wrinkles, etc. from the face **2** an altering, repairing, etc., as of a building's exterior Also **face lift —face-lift** (fās′lift′) *vt.*

face′-off′ *n. Hockey* the start or resumption of play when the referee drops the puck between two opposing players

face′-sav′ing *adj.* preserving one's dignity or self-respect

facet (fas′it) *n.* ⟦see FACE⟧ **1** any of the polished plane surfaces of a cut gem **2** any of a number of sides or aspects, as of a personality **—** *vt.* **-eted** or **-et·ted, -et·ing** or **-et·ting** to cut or make facets on

fa·cetious (fə sē′shəs) *adj.* ⟦< L *facetus*, witty⟧ joking, esp. at an inappropriate time **—fa·ce′tious·ly** *adv.*

face value 1 the value written on a bill, bond, etc. **2** the seeming value

fa·cial (fā′shəl) *adj.* of or for the face **—** *n.* a cosmetic treatment, massage, etc. for the skin of the face

facial tissue a sheet of soft tissue paper used as a handkerchief, etc.

fac·ile (fas′il) *adj.* ⟦Fr < L *facere*, do⟧ **1** not hard to do **2** working or done easily; fluent **3** superficial

fa·cili·tate (fə sil′ə tāt′) *vt.* **-tat′ed, -tat′ing** ⟦see prec.⟧ to make easy or easier **—fa·cil′i·ta′tion** *n.*

fa·cil′ity (-tē) *n.*, *pl.* **-ties 1** absence of difficulty **2** skill; dexterity **3** [*usually pl.*] the means by which something can be done **4** a building, etc. that facilitates some activity

fac·ing (fās′iŋ) *n.* **1** a lining on the edge of a garment **2** a covering of contrasting material on a building

fac·sim·i·le (fak sim′ə lē) *n.* ⟦< L *facere*, make + *simile*, like⟧ an exact reproduction or copy

fact (fakt) *n.* ⟦< L *facere*, do⟧ **1** a deed, esp. a criminal deed [an accessory before (or after) the *fact*] **2** a thing that has actually happened or is really true **3** reality; truth **4** something stated to be true **—as a matter of fact** in reality: also **in fact**

fac·tion (fak′shən) *n.* ⟦see prec.⟧ **1** a group of people in an organization working in a common cause against the main body **2** dissension **—fac′tional** *adj.* **—fac′tion·al·ism′** *n.*

fac′tious (-shəs) *adj.* producing or tending to produce faction

fac·ti·tious (fak tish′əs) *adj.* ⟦see FACT⟧ forced or artificial

fac·toid (fak′toid) *n.* ⟦FACT + -OID⟧ a trivial or useless fact or statistic

fac·tor (fak′tər) *n.* ⟦< L *facere*, do⟧ **1** one who transacts business for another **2** any of the conditions, etc. that bring about a result **3** *Math.* any of the quantities which form a product when multiplied together **—** *vt. Math.* to resolve into factors **—factor in** (or **into**) to include as a factor

fac·tory (fak′tə rē) *n.*, *pl.* **-ries** ⟦see prec.⟧ a building or buildings in which things are manufactured

fac·to·tum (fak tōt′əm) *n.* ⟦< L *facere*, do + *totum*, all⟧ a handyman

F

═ THESAURUS ═

fable *n.* allegory, tale, parable; see STORY.

fabled *a.* mythical, legendary, unreal; see LEGENDARY.

fabric *n.* textile, stuff, material; see GOODS.

fabricate *v.* **1** [To construct] erect, make, form; see BUILD, MANUFACTURE. **2** [To misrepresent] make up, contrive, prevaricate; see LIE 1.

fabulous *a.* remarkable, amazing, immense; see UNUSUAL 1.

façade *n.* face, appearance, look; see FRONT 3.

face *n.* **1** [The front of the head] visage, countenance, appearance, features, silhouette, profile, front, mug*. **2** [A plane surface] facet, front, surface, finish; see PLANE 1. **3** [Prestige] status, standing, social position; see REPUTATION 2. **—face to face** eye to eye, cheek by jowl, facing; see OPPOSITE 3. **—make a face** distort one's face, grimace, scowl; see FROWN. **—on the face of it** to all appearances, seemingly, according to the evidence; see APPARENTLY. **—pull (or wear) a long face*** look sad, scowl, pout; see FROWN. **—show one's face** be seen, show up, come; see APPEAR 1. **—to one's face** candidly, openly, frankly; see BOLDLY 1.

face *v.* **1** [To confront conflict or trouble] confront, oppose, defy, meet, dare, brave, challenge, withstand, encounter, risk, tolerate, endure, sustain, suffer, bear, tell to one's face, make a stand, meet face to face, cope with, allow, stand, submit, abide, go up against, swallow, stomach, take, take it.—*Ant.* EVADE, elude, shun. **2** [To put a face on a building] refinish, front, redecorate; see COVER 1, PAINT 2. **3** [To look out on] front, border, be turned toward; see LIE 2.

facet *n.* aspect, face, side; see PLANE 1.

facetious *a.* humorous, whimsical, ridiculous; see FUNNY 1.

facile *a.* simple, obvious, apparent; see EASY 2.

facilitate *v.* promote, aid, make easy; see HELP.

facility *n.* **1** [Material means; *usually plural*] tools, plant, buildings; see EQUIPMENT. **2** [Administrative agency] department, bureau, company; see OFFICE 3.

facsimile *n.* duplicate, reproduction, mirror; see COPY.

fact *n.* **1** [A reliable generality] certainty, truth, appearance, evidence, matter, the very thing, not an illusion, what has really happened, something concrete, what is the case, matter of fact, hard evidence, actuality, naked truth, gospel, reality, law, basis, state of being, hard facts*.— *Ant.* FANCY, fiction, imagination. **2** [An individual reality] circumstance, detail, factor, case, evidence, event, action, deed, happening, occurrence, creation, conception, manifestation, being, entity, experience, affair, episode, performance, proceeding, phenomenon, incident, thing done, act, plain fact, accomplishment, accomplished fact, *fait accompli* (French).—*Ant.* error, illusion, untruth. **—in** (or **as a matter of**) **fact** in reality, in fact, actually; see REALLY 1.

faction *n.* cabal, combine, party, conspiracy, plot, gang, crew, wing, block, junta, clique, splinter group, set, clan, club, lobby, camp, inner circle, sect, coterie, partnership, cell, unit, mob, side, machine, band, team, knot, circle, concern, guild, schism, outfit, crowd*, bunch*.

factor *n.* portion, constituent, determinant; see PART 1, 3.

factory *n.* manufactory, plant, shop, industry, workshop, machine shop, mill, laboratory, assembly plant, foundry, forge, loom, mint, carpenter shop, brewery, sawmill, supply house, warehouse, processing plant, works, workroom, firm, packing plant.

fac·tual (fak′chōō əl) *adj.* of or containing facts; real; actual

fac·ul·ty (fak′əl tē) *n., pl.* **-ties** [see FACILE] 1 any natural or specialized power of a living organism 2 special aptitude or skill 3 all the teachers of a school or of one of its departments

fad (fad) *n.* [< Brit dial.] a style, etc. that interests many people for a short time; passing fashion —**fad′dish** *adj.*

fade (fād) *vi.* **fad′ed, fad′ing** [< OFr *fade,* pale] 1 to lose color, brilliance, etc. 2 to lose freshness or strength 3 to disappear slowly; die out — *vt.* to cause to fade —**fade in** (or **out**) *Film, Radio, TV* to appear (or disappear) gradually

fa·erie or **fa·ery** (fā′ər ē, fer′ē) *n.* [Archaic] 1 fairyland 2 *pl.* -ies a fairy

fag (fag) *vi.* **fagged, fag′ging** [< ?] to make or become very tired by hard work

fagot or **fag·got** (fag′ət) *n.* [ult. < Gr *phakelos,* a bundle] a bundle of sticks or twigs, esp. for use as fuel

fag·ot·ing or **fag·got·ing** (fag′ət iŋ) *n.* 1 a hemstitch with wide spaces 2 openwork with crisscross or barlike stitches across the open seam

Fahr·en·heit (fer′ən hīt′) *adj.* [after G. D. *Fahrenheit* (1686-1736), Ger physicist] designating or of a thermometer on which 32° is the freezing point and 212° is the boiling point of water

fail (fāl) *vi.* [< L *fallere,* deceive] 1 to be insufficient; fall short 2 to weaken; die away 3 to stop operating 4 to be negligent in a duty, expectation, etc. 5 to be unsuccessful 6 to become bankrupt 7 *Educ.* to get a grade of failure — *vt.* 1 to be of no help to; disappoint 2 to leave; abandon 3 to neglect [to *fail* to go] 4 *Educ.* to give a grade of failure

to or get such a grade in —**without fail** without failing (to occur, do, etc.)

fail′ing *n.* 1 a failure 2 a fault — *prep.* without; lacking

faille (fīl, fāl) *n.* [Fr] a ribbed, soft fabric of silk or rayon

fail′-safe′ *adj.* of an intricate procedure for preventing accidental operation, as of nuclear weapons

fail·ure (fāl′yər) *n.* 1 *a)* a falling short *b)* a weakening *c)* a breakdown in operation *d)* neglect *e)* a not succeeding *f)* a becoming bankrupt 2 one that does not succeed 3 *Educ.* a failing to pass, or a grade showing this

fain (fān) *adj., adv.* [< OE *fægen,* glad] [Archaic] glad(ly); willing(ly)

faint (fānt) *adj.* [see FEIGN] 1 weak; feeble 2 timid 3 feeling weak and dizzy 4 dim; indistinct — *n.* a state of temporary unconsciousness — *vi.* to fall into a faint — **faint′ly** *adv.* —**faint′ness** *n.*

fair¹ (fer) *adj.* [< OE *fæger*] 1 attractive; beautiful 2 unblemished; clean 3 blond *[fair* hair] 4 clear and sunny 5 easy to read *[a fair* hand] 6 just and honest 7 according to the rules 8 moderately large 9 average *[in fair* condition] 10 that may be hunted *[fair* game] 11 *Baseball* that is not foul — *adv.* 1 in a fair manner 2 squarely —**fair′ness** *n.*

fair² (fer) *n.* [< L *feriae,* festivals] 1 a regular gathering for barter and sale of goods 2 a carnival or bazaar, often for charity 3 a competitive exhibition of farm, household, and manufactured products, with various amusements and educational displays

fair′-haired′ *adj.* 1 having blond hair 2 [Colloq.] favorite

fair′ly *adv.* 1 justly; honestly 2 somewhat; moderately 3 completely or really

fair shake [Colloq.] fair or just treatment

THESAURUS

factual *a.* exact, specific, descriptive; see ACCURATE 1.

faculty *n.* 1 [A peculiar aptitude] peculiarity, strength, forte; see ABILITY. 2 [A group of specialists, usually engaged in instruction or research] staff, teachers, research workers, personnel, instructors, university, college, institute, teaching staff, research staff, teaching assistants, professorate, society, body, organization, mentors, professors, assistant professors, associate professors, docents, tutors, foundation, department, pedagogues, lecturers, advisors, masters, scholars, fellows, profs*.

fad *n.* fancy, style, craze, fashion, humor, fit, prank, quirk, kink, eccentricity, popular innovation, vogue, fantasy, whimsy, passing fancy, latest word, all the rage, the latest thing, the last word*; see also FASHION 2.—*Ant.* CUSTOM, convention, practice.

fade *v.* 1 [To lose color or light] bleach, tone down, wash out, blanch, tarnish, dim, discolor, pale, grow dim, neutralize, become dull, lose brightness, lose luster, lose color.— *Ant.* COLOR, brighten, glow. 2 [To diminish in sound] hush, quiet, sink; see DECREASE 1.

faded *a.* used, bleached, shopworn; see DULL 2.

fail *v.* 1 [To be unsuccessful] fall short, miss, back out, abandon, desert, neglect, slip, lose ground, come to naught, come to nothing, falter, flounder, blunder, break down, get into trouble, abort, fault, come down, fall flat, go amiss, go astray, fall down, get left, be found lacking, go down, go under, not hold a candle to, fold up, go on the rocks, not have it in one, miss the boat*, not measure up, lose out, give out, fall short of, not make the grade*, miss the mark, lose control, fall down on the job, go wrong, be out of it, blow it*, fizzle out*, hit rock bottom, go up in smoke, bomb*, not get to first base*, get hung up*, get bogged down*,

flunk out*, flop*, conk out*, peter out*.—*Ant.* WIN, succeed, triumph. 2 [To prove unsatisfactory] lose out, come short of, displease; see DISAPPOINT. 3 [To grow less] lessen, worsen, sink; see DECREASE 1. 4 [To become insolvent] go bankrupt, go out of business, go broke*; see sense 1. —**without fail** constantly, dependably, reliably; see REGULARLY.

failing *a.* declining, feeble, faint; see WEAK 1.

failure *n.* 1 [An unsuccessful attempt] fiasco, misadventure, abortion, bankruptcy, miscarriage, frustration, misstep, faux pas, breakdown, checkmate, stoppage, collapse, defeat, overthrow, downfall, total loss, stalemate, flop*, bust*, dud*, washout*, sinking ship*, mess.—*Ant.* SUCCESS, accomplishment, triumph. 2 [An unsuccessful person] incompetent, underachiever, bankrupt, derelict, dropout, loser*, lemon*, bum*, dud*.—*Ant.* SUCCESS, winner, star.

faint *a.* 1 [Having little physical strength] shaky, faltering, dizzy; see WEAK 1. 2 [Having little light or color] vague, thin, hazy; see DULL 2. 3 [Having little volume of sound] whispered, breathless, murmuring, inaudible, indistinct, low, stifled, dull, hoarse, soft, heard in the distance, quiet, low-pitched, muffled, hushed, distant, subdued, gentle, softened, from afar, deep, rumbling, far-off, out of earshot.—*Ant.* LOUD, audible, raucous.

faint *v.* lose consciousness, become unconscious, fall, go into a coma, drop, collapse, succumb, pass out, go out like a light*, keel over*, black out.—*Ant.* RECOVER, awaken, come to.

fair¹ *a.* 1 [Just] forthright, impartial, plain, scrupulous, upright, candid, generous, frank, open, sincere, straightforward, honest, lawful, clean, legitimate, decent, honorable, virtuous, righteous, temperate, unbiased, reasonable, civil, courteous, blameless, uncorrupted, square, equi-

table, fair-minded, dispassionate, uncolored, objective, unprejudiced, evenhanded, good, principled, moderate, praiseworthy, aboveboard, trustworthy, due, fit, appropriate, on the level*, on the up-and-up*, fair and square*, straight*.—*Ant.* UNFAIR, unjust, biased. 2 [Moderately satisfactory] average, pretty good, not bad, up to standard, ordinary, mediocre, usual, common, all right, commonplace, fair to middling*, so-so, OK; see also COMMON 1.—*Ant.* POOR, bad, unsatisfactory. 3 [Not stormy or likely to storm] clear, pleasant, sunny, bright, calm, placid, tranquil, favorable, balmy, mild.— *Ant.* STORMY, threatening, overcast. 4 [Of light complexion] blond, light-colored, light-complexioned, pale, white, bleached, white-skinned, flaxen, fair-haired, snow-white, snowy, whitish, light, lily-white, faded, neutral, platinum blond, peroxide blond, bleached blond*, pale-faced, white as a sheet, white as a ghost.—*Ant.* DARK, brunet, black.

fair² *n.* exposition, county fair, state fair, world's fair, carnival, bazaar, exhibition, display, festival, market, exchange, centennial, observance, celebration.

fairly *a.* 1 [In a just manner] honestly, reasonably, honorably; see JUSTLY 1. 2 [A qualifying word] somewhat, moderately, reasonably; see ADEQUATELY.

fairness *n.* decency, honesty, uprightness, truth, integrity, charity, impartiality, justice, tolerance, honor, moderation, consideration, good faith, decorum, propriety, courtesy, reasonableness, rationality, humanity, equity, justness, goodness, measure for measure, give-and-take, fair-mindedness, open-mindedness, just dealing, good sense, fair treatment, even-handed justice, due, accuracy, scrupulousness, correctness, virtue, duty, dutifulness, legality, rightfulness, lawfulness, square deal*, fair play, fair shake*.—*Ant.* INJUSTICE, unfairness, partiality.

fair′way′ (-wā′) *n.* the mowed part of a golf course between a tee and a green

fair′-weath′er *adj.* helpful, dependable, etc. only in easy circumstances *[a fair-weather friend]*

fairy (fer′ē) *n., pl.* **-ies** ⟦ < OFr *fée* ⟧ a tiny, graceful imaginary being in human form, with magic powers — *adj.* 1 of fairies 2 graceful; delicate

fair′y·land′ *n.* 1 the imaginary land where the fairies live 2 a lovely, enchanting place

fairy tale 1 a story about fairies, magic deeds, etc. 2 an unbelievable story; lie

fait ac·com·pli (fe tä kôn plē′) ⟦ Fr ⟧ something done that cannot be changed

faith (fāth) *n.* ⟦ < L *fidere*, to trust ⟧ 1 unquestioning belief, specif. in God, religion, etc. 2 a particular religion 3 complete trust or confidence 4 loyalty

faith′ful (-fəl) *adj.* 1 loyal 2 conscientious 3 accurate; reliable —**faith′ful·ly** *adv.* —**faith′ful·ness** *n.*

faith′less (-lis) *adj.* 1 dishonest or disloyal 2 unreliable —**faith′less·ly** *adv.* —**faith′less·ness** *n.*

fake (fāk) *vt., vi.* **faked**, **fak′ing** to make (something) seem real, etc. by deception — *n.* a fraud; counterfeit — *adj.* 1 sham; false 2 artificial —**fak′er** *n.*

fa·kir (fə kir′) *n.* ⟦Ar *faqīr*, lit., poor⟧ 1 one of a Muslim holy sect of beggars 2 a Hindu ascetic

fa·la·fel (fə läf′əl) *n.* ⟦ < Ar ⟧ a deep-fried patty of ground chickpeas

fal·con (fôl′kən, fô′kən; fal′-) *n.* ⟦ ult. < L *falx*, sickle ⟧ any of certain birds of prey trained to hunt small game —**fal′coner** *n.* —**fal′conry** *n.*

fall (fôl) *vi.* **fell**, **fall′en**, **fall′ing** ⟦OE *feallan*⟧ 1 to come down by gravity; drop; descend 2 to come down suddenly from an upright position; tumble or collapse 3 to be wounded or killed in battle 4 to take a downward direction 5 to become lower, less, weaker, etc. 6 to lose power, status, etc. 7 to do wrong; sin 8 to be captured 9 to take on a sad look *[my face fell]* 10 to take place; occur 11 to come by lot, inheritance, etc. 12 to pass into a specified condition *[to fall ill]* 13 to be directed by chance 14 to be divided (*into*) — *n.* 1 a dropping; descending 2 a coming down suddenly from an upright position 3 a downward direction or slope 4 a becoming lower or less 5 a capture 6 a loss of status, reputation, etc. 7 a yielding to temptation 8 autumn 9 the amount of what has fallen *[a six-inch fall of snow]* 10 the distance that something falls 11 *[pl., often with sing. v.]* water falling over a cliff, etc. 12 a long tress of hair, added to a woman's hairdo — *adj.* of, in, for, or like the fall season —**fall back** to withdraw; retreat —**fall for** [Colloq.] 1 to fall in love with 2 to be tricked by —**fall in** to line up in formation —**fall off** to become smaller, worse, etc. —**fall on** (or **upon**) to attack —**fall out** 1 to quarrel 2 to leave one's place in a formation —**fall short** to fail to reach, suffice, etc. —**fall through** to fail —**fall to** 1 to begin 2 to start eating

fal·la·cious (fə lā′shəs) *adj.* ⟦see fol.⟧ 1 erroneous 2 misleading or deceptive —**fal·la′cious·ly** *adv.*

fal·lacy (fal′ə sē) *n., pl.* **-cies** ⟦ < L *fallere*, deceive ⟧ 1 a mistaken idea; error 2 a flaw in reasoning

fallen (fôl′ən) *adj.* that fell; dropped, prostrate, ruined, dead, etc.

fal·lible (fal′ə bəl) *adj.* ⟦ < L *fallere*, deceive ⟧ liable to be mistaken, deceived, or erroneous —**fal′li·bil′ity** or **fal′lible·ness** *n.* —**fal′libly** *adv.*

fall′ing-out′ *n.* a quarrel

falling star METEOR (sense 1)

fall′off′ *n.* a decline

fal·lo·pian tube (fə lō′pē ən) ⟦after G. *Fallopius*, 16th-c. It anatomist⟧ either of two tubes that carry ova to the uterus Also **Fallopian tube**

fall′out′ *n.* 1 the descent to earth of radioactive particles, as after a nuclear explosion 2 these particles

fal·low (fal′ō) *adj.* ⟦ < OE *fealh* ⟧ 1 left unplanted 2 inactive

false (fôls) *adj.* **fals′er**, **fals′est** ⟦ < L *fallere*, deceive ⟧ 1 not true; incorrect; wrong 2 untruthful; lying 3 unfaithful 4 misleading 5 not real; artificial — *adv.* in a false manner —**false′ly** *adv.* —**false′ness** *n.*

THESAURUS

fairy *n.* spirit, sprite, good fairy, elf, goblin, hobgoblin, nymph, pixy, mermaid, siren, bogie, genie, imp, enchantress, witch, warlock, banshee, werewolf, ogre, demon, succubus, devil, ghoul, harpy, poltergeist, troll, gnome, leprechaun, satyr, fiend, Fate, Weird Sister.

fairy tale *n.* folk tale, children's story, romance; see STORY.

faith *n.* 1 [Complete trust] confidence, trust, credence, credit, assurance, acceptance, troth, dependence, conviction, sureness, fidelity, loyalty, certainty, allegiance, reliance.—*Ant.* DOUBT, suspicion, distrust. 2 [A formal system of beliefs] creed, doctrine, dogma, tenet, revelation, credo, gospel, profession, conviction, canon, principle, church, worship, teaching, theology, denomination, cult, sect. —**bad faith** insincerity, duplicity, infidelity; see DISHONESTY. —**break faith** be disloyal, abandon, fail; see DECEIVE. —**good faith** sincerity, honor, trustworthiness; see HONESTY. —**in faith** indeed, in fact, in reality; see REALLY 1. —**keep faith** be loyal, adhere, follow; see SUPPORT 2.

faithful *a.* reliable, genuine, dependable, incorruptible, straight, honest, upright, honorable, scrupulous, firm, sure, unswerving, conscientious, enduring, unchanging, steady, staunch, attached, obedient, steadfast, sincere, resolute, on the level*, devoted, true, dutiful; see also LOYAL.—*Ant.* FALSE, fickle, faithless.

faithfully *a.* trustingly, conscientiously, truly; see LOYALLY.

faithfulness *n.* trustworthiness, care, duty; see DEVOTION.

fake *a.* pretended, fraudulent, bogus; see FALSE 3.

fake *n.* deception, counterfeit, sham, copy, cheat, imitation, charlatan, fraud, make-believe, pretense, fabri- cation, forgery, cheat, humbug, trick, swindle, phony*, gyp*, put-on*, flimflam.—*Ant.* FACT, original, reality.

fake *v.* feign, simulate, disguise; see PRETEND 1.

fall *n.* 1 [The act of falling] drop, decline, lapse, collapse, breakdown, tumble, spill, downfall, overthrow, defeat, degradation, humiliation, descent, plunge, slump, recession, ebb.—*Ant.* RISE, elevation, ascent. 2 [That which falls] rainfall, snowfall, precipitation; see RAIN 1, SNOW. 3 [The season after summer] autumn, the fall of the year, harvest, September, October, November, harvest time. —**ride for a fall** endanger oneself, take chances, act indiscreetly; see RISK.

fall *v.* 1 [To pass quickly downward] sink, topple, drop, settle, droop, stumble, trip, plunge, tumble, descend, totter, break down, cave in, make a forced landing, decline, subside, collapse, drop down, pitch, be precipitated, fall down, fall flat, fall in, fold up, keel over, tip over, slip, recede, ebb, diminish, flop.—*Ant.* RISE, ascend, climb. 2 [To be overthrown] submit, yield, surrender, succumb, be destroyed, be taken, bend, defer to, obey, resign, capitulate, back down, fall to pieces, break up.—*Ant.* ENDURE, prevail, resist. —**fall for*** become infatuated with, desire, flip over*; see FALL IN LOVE (WITH). —**fall in** get into line, form ranks, take a place; see LINE UP. —**fall off** decline, lessen, wane; see DECREASE 1. —**fall out** argue, disagree, fight; see QUARREL. —**fall short** fail, be deficient, be lacking; see NEED.

fallacy *n.* inconsistency, quibbling, evasion, fallacious reasoning, illogical reasoning, mistake, deceit, deception, subterfuge, inexactness, perversion, bias, prejudice, preconception, ambiguity, paradox, miscalculation, quirk, flaw, irrelevancy, erratum, heresy; see also ERROR.—*Ant.* LAW, theory, reason.

fallible *a.* deceptive, frail, imperfect, ignorant, uncertain, erring, unpredictable, unreliable, in question, prone to error, untrustworthy, questionable; see also WRONG 2.

falling *a.* dropping, sinking, descending, plunging, slipping, sliding, declining, settling, toppling, tumbling, tottering, diminishing, weakening, decreasing, ebbing, subsiding, collapsing, crumbling, dying.—*Ant.* INCREASING, improving, mounting.

fallow *a.* unplowed, unplanted, unproductive; see VACANT 2.

false *a.* 1 [Said of persons] faithless, treacherous, unfaithful, disloyal, dishonest, lying, foul, hypocritical, double-dealing, malevolent, mean, malicious, deceitful, underhanded, corrupt, wicked, unscrupulous, untrustworthy, dishonorable, two-faced.—*Ant.* FAITHFUL, true, honorable. 2 [Said of statements or supposed facts] untrue, spurious, fanciful, lying, untruthful, fictitious, deceptive, fallacious, incorrect, misleading, delusive, imaginary, illusive, erroneous, invalid, inaccurate, deceiving, misrepresentative, fraudulent, trumped up.—*Ant.* ACCURATE, correct, established. 3 [Said of things] sham, counterfeit, fabricated, manufactured, synthetic, bogus, spurious, make-believe, assumed, unreal, copied, forged, pretended, faked, made-up, simulated, pseudo, hollow, mock, feigned, bastard, alloyed, artificial, contrived, colored, disguised, deceptive, adulterated, so-called, fake, phony*, shoddy, not what it's cracked up to be*.—*Ant.* REAL, genuine, authentic.

false'hood' *n.* 1 falsity 2 a lie

fal·setto (fôl set'ō) *n., pl.* **-tos** [It., dim. of *falso*, false] an artificial way of singing in which the voice is much higher pitched than normal

fal·sify (fôl'sə fī') *vt.* **-fied'**, **-fy'ing** 1 to misrepresent 2 to alter (a record, etc.) fraudulently —**fal'si·fi·ca'tion** *n.* —**fal'si·fi'er** *n.*

fal'sity (-tē) *n.* 1 the quality of being false 2 *pl.* **-ties** a lie

Fal·staff (fôl'staf'), Sir **John** in Shakespeare's plays, a fat, witty, boastful knight

fal·ter (fôl'tər) *vi.* 1 to move unsteadily; stumble 2 to stammer 3 to act hesitantly; waver —**fal'ter·ingly** *adv.*

fame (fām) *n.* [< L *fama*] 1 reputation, esp. for good 2 the state of being well known —**famed** *adj.*

fa·mil·ial (fə mil'yəl) *adj.* of or common to a family

fa·mil·iar (fə mil'yər) *adj.* [see FAMILY] 1 friendly or intimate 2 too friendly; unduly intimate 3 closely acquainted (*with*) 4 common; ordinary —**fa·mil'iarly** *adv.*

fa·mil·i·ar·ity (-ē er'ə tē) *n., pl.* **-ties** 1 intimacy 2 free and intimate behavior 3 undue intimacy 4 close acquaintance (*with* something)

fa·mil·iar·ize (-yər īz') *vt.* **-ized'**, **-iz'ing** 1 to make commonly known 2 to make (another or oneself) fully acquainted —**fa·mil·iari·za'tion** *n.*

fam·i·ly (fam'ə lē, fam'lē) *n., pl.* **-lies** [< L *familia*] 1 [Obs.] household 2 parents and their children 3 relatives 4 all those descended from a common ancestor; lineage 5 a group of similar or related things

family planning the regulation, as by birth control methods, of the size, etc. of the family

family room a room in a home set apart for relaxation and recreation

fam·ine (fam'in) *n.* [< L *fames*, hunger] 1 an acute and general shortage of food 2 any acute shortage

fam·ish (-ish) *vt., vi.* [see prec.] to make or be very hungry

fa·mous (fā'məs) *adj.* 1 having fame; renowned 2 [Colloq.] excellent; very good —**fa'mously** *adv.*

fan¹ (fan) *n.* [< L *vannus*, basket for winnowing grain] any device used to set up a current of air for ventilating or cooling — *vt., vi.* **fanned**, **fan'ning** 1 to move (air) as with a fan 2 to direct air toward as with a fan 3 to stir up; excite 4 *Baseball* to strike out —**fan out** to spread out

fan² (fan) *n.* [< FAN(ATIC)] a person enthusiastic about a specified sport, performer, etc.

fa·natic (fə nat'ik) *adj.* [< L *fanum*, temple] unreasonably enthusiastic; overly zealous Also **fa·nat'i·cal** —*n.* a fanatic person —**fa·nat'i·cally** *adv.* —**fa·nat'i·cism'** *n.*

fan·cier (fan'sē ər) *n.* a person with a special interest in something, esp. plant or animal breeding

fan·ci·ful (fan'sə fəl) *adj.* 1 full of fancy; imaginative 2 imaginary; not real —**fan'ci·fully** *adv.*

fancy (fan'sē) *n., pl.* **-cies** [contr. < ME *fantasie*, fantasy] 1 imagination when light, playful, etc. 2 a mental image 3 a notion; caprice; whim 4 an inclination or fondness — *adj.* **-cier**, **-ci·est** 1 capricious; whimsical 2 extravagant [a *fancy* price] 3 ornamental; elaborate [a *fancy* necktie] 4 of superior skill or quality — *vt.* **-cied**, **-cy·ing** 1 to imagine 2 to be fond of 3 to suppose —**fan'cily** *adv.* —**fan'ci·ness** *n.*

fan'cy-free' *adj.* 1 not married, engaged, etc. 2 carefree

fan'cy·work' *n.* embroidery, crocheting, and other ornamental needlework

fan·dom (fan'dəm) *n.* fans, collectively, as of a sport or entertainer

fan·fare (fan'fer') [Fr., prob. < *fanfaron*, braggart] *n.* 1 a loud flourish of trumpets 2 noisy or showy display

fang (faŋ) *n.* [OE < *fon*, seize] 1 one of the long, pointed teeth of meat-eating mammals 2 one of the long, hollow teeth through which poisonous snakes inject venom

fan·ta·size (fant'ə siz') *vt., vi.* **-sized'**, **-siz'ing** to indulge in fantasies or have daydreams (about)

fan·tas·tic (fan tas'tik) *adj.* [see fol.] 1 imaginary; unreal 2 grotesque; odd 3 extravagant 4 incredible —**fan·tas'ti·cally** *adv.* —**fan·tas'ti·cal·ness** *n.*

fan·tasy (fant'ə sē) *n., pl.* **-sies** [< Gr *phainein*, to show] 1 imagination or fancy 2 an illusion or reverie 3 fiction portraying highly IMAGINATIVE (sense 2) characters or settings

fan·zine (fan'zēn') *n.* [FAN² + (MAGA)ZINE] a special-interest magazine usually produced by amateurs for fans of science fiction, comic books, etc.

THESAURUS

falsehood *n.* deception, prevarication, story; see LIE.

falsely *a.* traitorously, treacherously, deceitfully, foully, faithlessly, behind one's back, disloyally, underhandedly, maliciously, malevolently, unfaithfully, dishonestly, unscrupulously, dishonorably.—*Ant.* TRULY, justly, honorably.

falsify *v.* adulterate, counterfeit, misrepresent; see DECEIVE.

falter *v.* waver, fluctuate, be undecided; see HESITATE.

fame *n.* renown, glory, distinction, eminence, honor, celebrity, esteem, name, estimation, public esteem, credit, note, greatness, dignity, rank, splendor, position, standing, preeminence, superiority, regard, character, station, place, degree, popularity.

familiar *a.* everyday, well-known, customary, frequent, homely, humble, usual, intimate, habitual, accustomed, common, ordinary, informal, unceremonious, plain, simple, matter-of-fact, workaday, prosaic, commonplace, homespun, natural, native, unsophisticated, old hat*, garden-variety.—*Ant.* UNUSUAL, exotic, strange. —**familiar with** well-acquainted with, acquainted with, aware of, informed of, on speaking terms with, having some connections with, cognizant of, attuned to.—*Ant.* UNAWARE, UNKNOWN, unacquainted.

familiarity *n.* 1 [Acquaintance with people] friendliness, acquaintanceship, fellowship; see FRIENDSHIP. 2 [Acquaintance with things] the feel of, being at home with, comprehension; see AWARENESS, EXPERIENCE.

familiarize (oneself with) *v.*

acquaint, accustom, habituate, make the acquaintance of, get acquainted with, gain the friendship of, make friends with, awaken to, come to know, become aware of.

family *n.* kin, folk, clan, relationship, relations, tribe, dynasty, breed, house, kith and kin, blood, blood tie, progeny, offspring, descendants, forebears, heirs, race, ancestry, pedigree, genealogy, descent, parentage, extraction, paternity, inheritance, kinship, lineage, line, one's own flesh and blood, strain, siblings, in-laws, people.

famine *n.* starvation, want, misery; see HUNGER.

famished *a.* starving, hungering, starved; see HUNGRY.

famous *a.* eminent, foremost, famed, preeminent, acclaimed, illustrious, celebrated, noted, conspicuous, far-famed, prominent, honored, reputable, renowned, recognized, notable, important, well-known, of note, notorious, exalted, remarkable, extraordinary, great, powerful, noble, grand, mighty, imposing, towering, influential, leading, noteworthy, talked of, outstanding, distinguished, excellent, memorable, elevated, in the spotlight, in the limelight.—*Ant.* UNKNOWN, obscure, humble.

fan¹,² *n.* 1 [An instrument for creating currents of air] ventilator, agitator, blower, forced draft, vane, air conditioner, propeller, electric fan, Japanese fan, windmill. 2 [*Supporter] follower, enthusiast, devotee; see FOLLOWER.

fanatic *n.* devotee, bigot, enthusiast; see ZEALOT.

fanatical *a.* obsessed, passionate,

devoted; see ZEALOUS.

fanaticism *n.* bigotry, intolerance, obsession, prejudice, hatred, superstition, narrow-mindedness, injustice, obstinacy, stubbornness, bias, unfairness, partiality, devotion, violence, immoderation, zeal, willfulness, single-mindedness, infatuation, dogma, arbitrariness, unruliness, enthusiasm, frenzy, passion, rage.—*Ant.* INDIFFERENCE, tolerance, moderation.

fanciful *a.* unreal, incredible, whimsical; see FANTASTIC.

fancy *a.* elegant, embellished, rich, adorned, ostentatious, gaudy, showy, intricate, baroque, lavish; see also ELABORATE, ORNATE.

fancy *n.* 1 [The mind at play] whimsy, frolic, caprice, banter, sport, diversion, whim, notion, quip, prank, wit, buffoonery, fooling, facetiousness, merriment, levity, humor. 2 [The product of a playful mind] whim, notion, impulse; see IDEA. 3 [Inclination] wishes, will, preference; see DESIRE 1.

fang *n.* tusk, prong, venom, duct; see also TOOTH.

fantastic *a.* whimsical, capricious, extravagant, freakish, strange, odd, queer, quaint, peculiar, outlandish, far-fetched, wonderful, comical, humorous, foreign, exotic, extreme, ludicrous, ridiculous, preposterous, grotesque, frenzied, absurd, vague, hallucinatory, high-flown, affected, artificial, out of sight*.—*Ant.* COMMON, conventional, routine.

fantasy *n.* vision, appearance, illusion, flight, figment, fiction, romance, mirage, nightmare, fairyland.

far (fär) *adj.* **far'ther, far'thest** ⟦OE *feorr*⟧ **1** distant in space or time **2** more distant *[the far side]* — *adv.* **1** very distant in space, time, or degree **2** to or from a distance in time or position **3** very much *[far better]* — **as far as** to the distance or degree that — **by far** very much; considerably Also **far and away** — **(in) so far as** to the extent that — **so far** up to this place, time, or degree

far'away' *adj.* **1** distant in time or place **2** dreamy

farce (färs) *n.* ⟦Fr < L *farcire*, to stuff⟧ **1** (an) exaggerated comedy based on broadly humorous situations **2** an absurd or ridiculous action, pretense, etc. — **far'ci·cal** (fär'si kəl) *adj.*

fare (fer) *vi.* **fared, far'ing** ⟦< OE *faran*, go⟧ **1** to happen; result **2** to be in a specified condition *[to fare well]* — *n.* **1** money paid for transportation **2** a passenger who pays a fare **3** food

fare·well (fer wel'; *for adj.* fer'wel') *interj.* goodbye — *n.* good wishes at parting — *adj.* parting; final *[a farewell gesture]*

far-fetched (fär'fecht') *adj.* forced; strained; unlikely

far'-flung' (-fluŋ') *adj.* extending over a wide area

fa·ri·na (fə rē'nə) *n.* ⟦< L, meal⟧ flour or meal made from cereal grains, potatoes, etc. and eaten as a cooked cereal

far·i·na·ceous (far'ə nā'shəs) *adj.* ⟦see prec.⟧ **1** consisting of or made from flour or meal **2** like meal

farm (färm) *n.* ⟦< ML *firma*, fixed payment⟧ a piece of land (with house, barns, etc.) on which crops or animals are raised: orig., such land let out to tenants — *vt.* **1** to cultivate (land) **2** to turn over to another for a fee — *vi.* to work on or operate a farm

farm'er *n.* a person who manages or operates a farm

farm'hand' *n.* a hired farm worker

farm'house' *n.* a house on a farm

farm'ing *n.* the business of operating a farm; agriculture

farm'yard' *n.* the yard surrounding or enclosed by farm buildings

faro (fer'ō) *n.* ⟦Fr *pharaon*, pharaoh: from the picture of a Pharaoh on early French faro cards⟧ a gambling game played with cards

far-off (fär'ôf') *adj.* distant; remote

far'-out' *adj.* [Colloq.] nonconformist; esp., avant-garde

far·ra·go (fə rä'gō, -rä'-) *n., pl.* **-goes** ⟦< L *far*, kind of grain⟧ a jumble

far'-reach'ing *adj.* having a wide range, extent, influence, or effect

far·ri·er (far'ē ər) *n.* ⟦< L *ferrum*, iron⟧ [Brit.] a blacksmith

far·row (far'ō) *n.* ⟦< OE *fearh*, young pig⟧ a litter of pigs — *vt., vi.* to give birth to (a litter of pigs)

far'sight'ed *adj.* **1** planning ahead; provident: also **far'see'ing 2** seeing distant objects more clearly than near ones — **far'sight'ed·ness** *n.*

far·ther (fär'thər) *adj.* **1** *compar. of* FAR **2** more distant **3** additional; more — *adv.* **1** *compar. of* FAR **2** at or to a greater distance **3** to a greater degree Cf. FURTHER

far·thest (fär'thist) *adj.* **1** *superl. of* FAR **2** most distant — *adv.* **1** *superl. of* FAR **2** at or to the greatest distance or degree

far·thing (fär'thiŋ) *n.* ⟦OE *feorthing*⟧ a former British coin worth ¼ penny

fas·ci·nate (fas'ə nāt') *vt.* **-nat'ed, -nat'ing** ⟦< L *fascinum*, a bewitching⟧ **1** to hold motionless, as by inspiring terror **2** to charm; captivate — **fas'ci·na'tion** *n.*

fas·cism (fash'iz'əm) *n.* ⟦< It < L *fasces*, rods bound about an ax, ancient Roman symbol of authority⟧ [*sometimes* F-] a system of government characterized by dictatorship, belligerent nationalism and racism, militarism, etc.: first instituted in Italy (1922-43) — **fas'cist** *n., adj.*

fash·ion (fash'ən) *n.* ⟦< L *factio*, a making⟧ **1** the form or shape of a thing **2** way; manner **3** the current style of dress, conduct, etc. — *vt.* **1** to make; form **2** to fit; accommodate (*to*) — **after** (or **in**) **a fashion** to some extent — **fash'ion·er** *n.*

fash'ion·a·ble *adj.* **1** stylish **2** of or used by people who follow fashion — **fash'ion·a·bly** *adv.*

fast¹ (fast) *adj.* ⟦OE *fæst*⟧ **1** firm; firmly fastened **2** loyal; devoted **3** nonfading *[fast colors]* **4** swift; quick **5** ahead of time *[a fast watch]* **6** wild, promiscuous, or dissipated **7** [Colloq.] glib **8** *Photog.* allowing very short exposure time — *adv.* **1** firmly; fixedly **2** thoroughly *[fast asleep]* **3** rapidly

---

THESAURUS

far *a.* **1** [Distant from the speaker] removed, faraway, remote; see DISTANT. **2** [To a considerable degree] extremely, incomparably, notably; see VERY. —**as far as** to the extent that, to the degree that, up to the time that, insofar as. —**by far** very much, considerably, to a great degree; see MUCH 1, VERY. —**few and far between** scarce, sparse, in short supply; see RARE 2. —**(in) so far as** to the extent that, in spite of, within limits; see CONSIDERING. —**so far** thus far, until now, up to this point; see NOW 1. —**so far, so good** all right, favorable, going well; see SUCCESSFUL.

farce *n.* travesty, burlesque, horseplay; see FUN.

fare *n.* **1** [A fee paid, usually for transportation] ticket, charge, passage, passage money, toll, tariff, expenses, transportation, check, token. **2** [Served food] menu, rations, meals; see FOOD.

fare *v.* prosper, prove, turn out; see HAPPEN 2.

farewell *n.* goodbye, valediction, parting; see DEPARTURE.

far-fetched *a.* forced, strained, unbelievable; see FANTASTIC.

farm *n.* plantation, ranch, homestead, claim, holding, field, kibbutz, pasture, meadow, grassland, truck farm, estate, land, acres, freehold, cropland, soil, acreage, garden, patch, vegetable garden, orchard, nursery, vineyard.

farm *v.* cultivate land, produce crops, cultivate, till, garden, work, run, ranch, crop, graze, homestead, produce, pasture, till the soil. —**farm out** lease, rent, allot; see DISTRIBUTE, RENT 1.

farmer *n.* planter, grower, livestock

breeder, stockman, feeder, agriculturist, rancher, dirt farmer, lessee, homesteader, producer, tiller of the soil, peasant, peon, herdsman, plowman, sharecropper, hired man, cropper, grazer, cattleman, sheepman, harvester, truck gardener, gardener, nurseryman, horticulturist, settler, sodbuster*, farm hand, hired hand, help.

farming *n.* agriculture, tillage, cultivation, husbandry, farm management, soil culture, ranching, sharecropping, homesteading, plantation, horticulture, agronomy, grazing, livestock raising, taking up a claim, hydroponics, growing, cropraising.

farmyard *n.* barnyard, yard, farmstead; see FARM.

far-off *a.* far, remote, strange; see DISTANT.

farsighted *a.* aware, perceptive, sagacious; see INTELLIGENT.

farther *a.* at a greater distance, more distant, beyond, further, more remote, remoter, longer.

farthest *a.* remotest, ultimate, last; see FURTHEST.

fascinate *v.* charm, entrance, captivate, enchant, bewitch, ravish, enrapture, delight, overpower, please, attract, compel, lure, seduce, entice, tempt, draw, engage, excite, stimulate, overwhelm, provoke, arouse, intoxicate, thrill, stir, kindle, absorb, tantalize, win, interest, enthrall, influence, capture, coax, tease, lead on, knock dead*, cast a spell over*, catch one's eye, carry away, invite attention.—*Ant.* DISGUST, repel, horrify.

fascinated *a.* enchanted, bewitched, dazzled, captivated, attracted, seduced, enraptured, charmed, hyp-

notized, delighted, infatuated, thrilled, spellbound; see also CHARMED.—*Ant.* DISGUSTED, repelled, disenchanted.

fascinating *a.* engaging, attractive, delightful; see CHARMING.

fascination *n.* charm, power, enchantment; see ATTRACTION.

fascism *n.* dictatorship, totalitarianism, Nazism; see GOVERNMENT 2.—*Ant.* DEMOCRACY, self-government, socialism.

fascist *n.* reactionary, Nazi, rightist; see RADICAL.

fashion *n.* **1** [The manner of behavior] way, custom, convention, style, vogue, mode, tendency, trend, formality, formula, procedure, practice, device, usage, observance, new look. **2** [Whatever is temporarily in vogue] craze, sport, caprice, whim, hobby, innovation, custom, amusement, eccentricity, rage, cry. —**after** (or **in**) **a fashion** somewhat, to some extent, in a way; see MODERATELY. —**in fashion** stylish, modish, à la mode; see FASHIONABLE, POPULAR 1.

fashion *v.* model, shape, form; see CREATE.

fashionable *a.* in fashion, in style, in vogue, being done, well-liked, favored, smart, stylish, chic, hot*, in*, trendy*, up to the minute.

fashioned *a.* molded, shaped, intended; see FORMED.

fast¹ *a.* **1** [Rapid] swift, fleet, quick, speedy, brisk, accelerated, hasty, nimble, active, electric, agile, ready, quick as lightning, like a flash, racing, like a bat out of hell*, like a house afire*.—*Ant.* SLOW, sluggish, tardy. **2** [Firmly fixed] adherent, attached, immovable; see FIRM 1.

fast² (fast) *vi.* ⟦OE *fæstan*⟧ to abstain from all or certain foods — *n.* 1 a fasting 2 a period of fasting

fast'back' (-bak') *n.* an automobile body which slopes from the roof to the rear bumper

fas·ten (fas'ən) *vt.* ⟦see FAST¹⟧ 1 to attach; connect 2 to make secure, as by locking, buttoning, etc. 3 to fix (the attention, etc.) *on* something — *vi.* to become fastened — **fas'ten·er** *n.*

fas'ten·ing *n.* anything used to fasten; bolt, clasp, hook, etc.

fast'-food' *adj.* designating a business that offers food, as hamburgers, prepared and served quickly

fas·tid·i·ous (fas tid'ē əs) *adj.* ⟦< L *fastus*, disdain⟧ 1 not easy to please 2 daintily refined; oversensitive — **fas·tid'i·ously** *adv.* — **fas·tid'i·ous·ness** *n.*

fast'ness *n.* 1 a being fast 2 a stronghold

fast'-talk' *vt.* [Colloq.] to persuade with smooth, but often deceitful talk

fat (fat) *adj.* **fat'ter, fat'test** ⟦< OE *fætt*⟧ 1 containing fat; oily 2 *a)* fleshy; plump *b)* too plump 3 thick; broad 4 fertile *[fat* land*]* 5 profitable *[a fat* job*]* 6 plentiful — *n.* 1 an oily or greasy material found in animal tissue and plant seeds 2 the richest part of anything 3 superfluous part — **chew the fat** [Slang] to chat — **fat'ly** *adv.* — **fat'ness** *n.*

fa·tal (fāt''l) *adj.* 1 fateful; decisive 2 resulting in death 3 destructive; disastrous — **fa'tally** *adv.*

fa'tal·ism *n.* the belief that all events are determined by fate and are hence inevitable — **fa'tal·ist** *n.* — **fa'tal·is'tic** *adj.* — **fa'tal·is'ti·cally** *adv.*

fa·tal·ity (fā tal'ə tē, fə-) *n., pl.* **-ties** 1 a deadly effect; deadliness 2 a death caused by a disaster or accident

fat'back' *n.* fat from a hog's back, usually dried and salted in strips

fat cat [Slang] a wealthy, influential donor, esp. to a political campaign

fate (fāt) *n.* ⟦< L *fatum*, oracle⟧ 1 the power supposed to determine the outcome of events; destiny 2 one's lot or fortune 3 final outcome 4 death; destruction

fated (fāt'id) *adj.* 1 destined 2 doomed

fate'ful (-fəl) *adj.* 1 prophetic 2 significant; decisive 3 controlled as if by fate 4 bringing death or destruction — **fate'fully** *adv.*

Fates (fāts) *Gr. & Rom. Myth.* the three goddesses who control human destiny and life

fa·ther (fä'thər) *n.* ⟦OE *fæder*⟧ 1 a male parent 2 an ancestor 3 an originator, founder, or inventor 4 [*often*

F-] a Christian priest: used esp. as a title — *vt.* to be the father of — [**F-**] God — **fa'ther·hood'** *n.* — **fa'ther·less** *adj.*

fa'ther-in-law' *n., pl.* **fa'thers-in-law'** the father of one's spouse

fa'ther·land' *n.* one's native land

fa'ther·ly *adj.* of or like a father; kind — **fa'ther·li·ness** *n.*

fathom (fath'əm) *n.* ⟦< OE *fæthm*, the two arms outstretched⟧ a length of 6 feet, used as a nautical unit of depth or length — *vt.* 1 to measure the depth of 2 to understand thoroughly — **fath'om·able** *adj.* — **fath'om·less** *adj.*

fa·tigue (fə tēg') *n.* ⟦Fr < L *fatigare*, to weary⟧ 1 exhaustion; weariness 2 [*pl.*] soldiers' work clothing — *vt., vi.* **-tigued', -tigu'ing** to tire out

fat·ten (fat''n) *vt., vi.* to make or become fat (in various senses)

fat'ty *adj.* **-tier, -ti·est** 1 of or containing fat 2 like fat; greasy

fatty acid any of a group of organic acids in animal or vegetable fats and oils

fatu·ous (fach'ōō əs) *adj.* ⟦L *fatuus*⟧ complacently stupid; foolish — **fa·tu·ity** (fə tōō'ə tē) *n.* — **fat'u·ously** *adv.* — **fat'u·ous·ness** *n.*

fau·cet (fô'sit) *n.* ⟦prob. < OFr *faulser*, to breach⟧ a device with a valve for regulating the flow of a liquid from a pipe, etc.; tap

fault (fôlt) *n.* ⟦< L *fallere*, deceive⟧ 1 something that mars; defect or failing 2 a misdeed or mistake 3 blame for something wrong 4 a fracture in rock strata — **at fault** deserving blame — **find fault (with)** to criticize — **to a fault** excessively

fault'find'ing *n., adj.* criticizing

fault'less *adj.* perfect — **fault'lessly** *adv.*

fault'y *adj.* **fault'i·er, fault'i·est** having a fault or faults; defective — **fault'i·ly** *adv.* — **fault'i·ness** *n.*

faun (fôn) *n.* ⟦< L *faunus*⟧ any of a class of minor Roman deities, half man and half goat

fauna (fô'nə) *n.* ⟦< LL *Fauna*, Rom. goddess⟧ the animals of a specified region or time

Faust (foust) a man in legend and literature who sells his soul to the devil for knowledge and power

faux-naif (fō nä ēf') *adj.* ⟦Fr⟧ 1 artificially naive 2 of a literary or artistic style pretending to be simple, childlike, etc. — *n.* a faux-naif person, style, etc.

faux pas (fō pä') *pl.* **faux pas** (fō päz') ⟦Fr, lit., false step⟧ a social blunder

fa·vor (fā'vər) *n.* ⟦< L *favere*, to favor⟧ 1 friendly regard; approval 2 partiality 3 a kind or obliging act 4 a small

---

THESAURUS

fast² *n.* abstinence, day of fasting, Lent; see ABSTINENCE.

fast² *v.* not eat, go hungry, observe a fast; see ABSTAIN.

fasten *v.* lock, fix, tie, lace, close, bind, tighten, make firm, attach, secure, anchor, grip, zip up, hold, screw up, screw down, clasp, clamp, pin, nail, tack, bolt, rivet, set, weld, cement, glue, hold fast, make secure, make fast, cinch, catch, buckle, bolt, bar, seal up.—*Ant.* RELEASE, loosen, unfasten.

fastened *a.* locked, fixed, tied; see TIGHT 2.

fastener *n.* buckle, hook, hasp, lock, clamp, tie, stud, vise, grip, grappling iron, clasp, snap, bolt, bar, lace, cinch, grip, pin, safety pin, nail, rivet, tack, thumbtack, screw, dowel, hook, brake, binder, binding, button, padlock, catch, bond, band, mooring, rope, cable, anchor, chain, harness, strap, thong, girdle, latch, staple, zipper.

fastening *n.* catch, clasp, hook; see FASTENER.

fat *a.* portly, stout, obese, corpulent, fleshy, potbellied, beefy, brawny, solid, plumpish, plump, burly, bulky, unwieldy, heavy, husky, puffy, on the heavy side, in need of reducing, swollen, inflated, ponderous, lumpish, fat as a pig, tubby*.—*Ant.* THIN, lean, skinny. —**chew the fat*** chat, gossip, confer; see TALK 1.

fat *n.* blubber, lard, oil; see GREASE.

fatal *a.* inevitable, mortal, lethal; see

DEADLY.

fatality *n.* casualty, dying, accident; see DEATH.

fate *n.* fortune, destination, luck; see DOOM.

fated *a.* lost, destined, elected; see DOOMED.

fateful *a.* 1 [Momentous] portentous, critical, decisive; see CRUCIAL 1. 2 [Fatal] destructive, ruinous, lethal; see DEADLY.

father *n.* 1 [A male parent] sire, progenitor, procreator, forebear, ancestor, head of the household, papa, dad*, daddy*, pa*, the old man*, pappy*, pop*. 2 [An originator] founder, inventor, promoter; see AUTHOR. 3 [A priest, especially a Catholic priest] pastor, ecclesiastic, parson; see PRIEST.

Father *n.* Supreme Being, Creator, Author; see GOD 1.

father-in-law *n.* spouse's father, parent, in-law*; see RELATIVE.

fatherland *n.* mother country, homeland, native land; see NATION 1.

fatherly *a.* paternal, patriarchal, benevolent; see KIND.

fatigue *n.* weariness, lassitude, exhaustion, weakness, feebleness, faintness, battle fatigue, nervous exhaustion, dullness, heaviness, listlessness, tiredness.

fatness *n.* plumpness, obesity, weight, flesh, heaviness, grossness, corpulence, bulkiness, girth, breadth, largeness, protuberance, inflation,

fleshiness, stoutness, heftiness*.

fatten *v.* feed, stuff, prepare for market, plump, cram, fill, round out.—*Ant.* STARVE, reduce, constrict.

fatty *a.* greasy, blubbery, containing fat; see OILY 1.

faucet *n.* tap, fixture, petcock, drain, spigot, plumbing, hot-water faucet, cold-water faucet.

fault *n.* 1 [A moral delinquency] misdemeanor, weakness, offense, wrongdoing, transgression, crime, sin, impropriety, juvenile delinquency, misconduct, malpractice, failing; see also MISTAKE. 2 [An error] blunder, mistake, misdeed; see ERROR. 3 [Responsibility] liability, accountability, blame; see RESPONSIBILITY 2. —**at fault** culpable, blamable, in the wrong; see GUILTY. —**find fault (with)** complain about, carp at, criticize; see BLAME.

faulty *a.* imperfect, flawed, blemished, deficient, distorted, weak, tainted, leaky, defective, damaged, unsound, spotted, cracked, warped, injured, broken, wounded, hurt, impaired, worn, battered, frail, crude, botched, insufficient, inadequate, incomplete, out of order, below par, incorrect, unfit; see also UNSATISFACTORY.—*Ant.* WHOLE, perfect, complete.

favor *n.* 1 [Preference] help, support, encouragement; see ENCOURAGEMENT. 2 [Kindness] service, courtesy, boon; see KINDNESS 2.

gift or token — **vt.** 1 to approve or like 2 to be partial to 3 to support; advocate 4 to help 5 to do a kindness for 6 to resemble [to *favor* one's mother] Brit. sp. **fa'vour** — **in favor of** 1 approving 2 to the advantage of —**fa'vorer** *n.*

fa'vor·able *adj.* 1 approving 2 helpful 3 pleasing —**fa'vor·ably** *adv.*

fa·vor·ite (fā'vər it) *n.* 1 a person or thing regarded with special liking 2 a contestant regarded as most likely to win — *adj.* highly regarded; preferred

fa'vor·it·ism' *n.* partiality; bias

fawn[1] (fôn) *vi.* [< OE *fægen,* glad] 1 to show friendliness by licking hands, etc.: said of a dog 2 to cringe and flatter —**fawn'er** *n.*

fawn[2] (fôn) *n.* [< L *fetus,* progeny] 1 a deer less than one year old 2 a pale, yellowish brown — *adj.* of this color

fay (fā) *n.* [see FATE] a fairy

faze (fāz) *vt.* **fazed, faz'ing** [< OE *fesian,* to drive] to disturb

FBI Federal Bureau of Investigation

FCC Federal Communications Commission

FDA Food and Drug Administration

FDIC Federal Deposit Insurance Corporation

Fe [L *ferrum*] *Chem. symbol for* iron

fe·alty (fē'əl tē) *n., pl.* **-ties** [< L *fidelitas,* fidelity] loyalty, esp. as owed to a feudal lord

fear (fir) *n.* [< OE *fær,* sudden attack] 1 anxiety caused by real or possible danger, pain, etc.; fright 2 awe; reverence 3 apprehension; concern 4 a cause for fear — *vt., vi.* 1 to be afraid (of) 2 to be in awe (of) 3 to expect with misgiving —**fear'less** *adj.* —**fear'less·ly** *adv.*

fear'ful (-fəl) *adj.* 1 causing, feeling, or showing fear 2 [Colloq.] very bad, great, etc. —**fear'fully** *adv.* —**fear'ful·ness** *n.*

fear'some *adj.* 1 causing fear; frightful 2 frightened; timid

fea·sible (fē'zə bəl) *adj.* [< OFr *faire,* to do] 1 capable of being done; possible 2 likely; probable 3 suitable —**fea'sibil'ity** *n.* —**fea'sibly** *adv.*

feast (fēst) *n.* [< L *festus,* festal] 1 a religious festival 2 a rich and elaborate meal — *vi.* to have a feast — *vt.* 1 to entertain at a feast 2 to delight [to *feast* one's eyes on a sight]

feat (fēt) *n.* [< L *factum,* a deed] a deed of unusual daring or skill

feather (feth'ər) *n.* [OE *fether*] any of the soft, light growths covering the body of a bird — *vt.* 1 to provide or

adorn with feathers 2 to turn (an oar or propeller blade) so that the edge is foremost —**feather in one's cap** a distinctive achievement —**feath'ery** *adj.*

feath'er·bed'ding (-bed'iŋ) *n.* the practice of limiting output or requiring extra, standby workers

feath'er·weight' *n.* a boxer with a maximum weight of 126 pounds

fea·ture (fē'chər) *n.* [< L *facere,* to make] 1 *a)* [*pl.*] facial form or appearance *b)* any of the parts of the face 2 a distinct or outstanding part or quality of something 3 a special attraction, sale item, newspaper article, etc. 4 a film running more than 34 minutes — *vt., vi.* **-tured, -turing** to make or be a feature of (something)

fe·brile (fē'bril, feb'ril) *adj.* [< L *febris,* FEVER] feverish

Feb·ru·ary (feb'rōō er'ē, feb'yōō-) *n., pl.* **-ies** [< L *Februarius* (*mensis*), orig. month of expiation] the second month of the year, having 28 days (or 29 days in leap years): abbrev. **Feb.**

fe·ces (fē'sēz') *n.pl.* [< L *faeces,* dregs] excrement —**fe'cal** (-kəl) *adj.*

feck·less (fek'lis) *adj.* [Scot < *feck,* effect + -LESS] 1 weak; ineffective 2 irresponsible —**feck'lessly** *adv.*

fe·cund (fē'kənd, fek'ənd) *adj.* [< L *fecundus*] fertile; productive —**fe·cun·dity** (fē kun'də tē) *n.*

fe·cun·date (fē'kən dāt', fek'ən-) *vt.* **-dat'ed, -dat'ing** 1 to make fecund 2 to fertilize

fed (fed) *vt., vi. pt. & pp. of* FEED —**fed up** [Colloq.] having had enough to become disgusted, bored, etc.

Fed. 1 Federal 2 Federation

feda·yeen (fed'ä yēn') *n.pl.* [Ar *fidā°īyīn,* sacrificers] Arab guerrillas

fed·eral (fed'ər əl) *adj.* [< L *foedus,* a league] 1 designating or of a union of states, etc. in which each member subordinates its power to a central authority 2 *a)* designating or of a central government in such a union *b)* [*usually* F-] designating or of the central government of the U.S. 3 [F-] of or supporting a former U.S. political party (**Federalist Party**) which favored a strong centralized government 4 [F-] of or supporting the Union in the Civil War — *n.* [F-] a supporter or soldier of the Union in the Civil War —**fed'er·al·ism'** *n.* —**fed'er·al·ist** *adj., n.* —**fed'er·ally** *adv.*

fed'er·al·ize' (-īz') *vt.* **-ized', -iz'ing** 1 to unite (states, etc.) in a federal union 2 to put under federal authority —**fed'er·ali·za'tion** *n.*

THESAURUS

find favor please, suit, become welcome; see SATISFY 1. —**in favor** liked, esteemed, wanted; see FAVORITE. —**in favor of** approving, endorsing, condoning; see FOR. —**in one's favor** to one's advantage, on one's side, creditable; see FAVORABLE 3.

favor *v.* prefer, like, approve, sanction, praise, regard favorably, be in favor of, pick, choose, lean toward, incline toward, value, prize, esteem, think well of, set great store by, look up to, think the world of*, be partial to, grant favors to, promote, play favorites, show consideration for, spare, make an exception for, pull strings for; see also PROMOTE 1.—*Ant.* HATE, dislike, disesteem.

favorable *a.* 1 [Friendly] well-disposed, kind, well-intentioned; see FRIENDLY. 2 [Displaying suitable or promising qualities] propitious, convenient, beneficial; see HOPEFUL 2. 3 [Commendatory] approving, commending, assenting, complimentary, well-disposed toward, in favor of, agreeable, in one's favor.

favorably *a.* approvingly, agreeably, kindly, helpfully, fairly, willingly, heartily, cordially, genially, graciously, courteously, receptively, in an approving manner, positively, without prejudice.—*Ant.* UNFAVORABLY, adversely, discouragingly.

favorite *a.* liked, beloved, personal, favored, intimate, to one's taste, to one's liking, choice, pet, desired, wished-for, preferred, adored.—*Ant.* UNPOPULAR, unwanted, unwelcome.

favorite *n.* darling, pet, idol, ideal, favored one, mistress, love, favorite son, favorite child, fair-haired boy*, teacher's pet, odds-on favorite, apple of one's eye.

favoritism *n.* bias, partiality, inequity; see INCLINATION 1.

fawn[2] *n.* baby deer, baby doe, baby buck; see DEER.

faze *v.* bother, intimidate, worry; see DISTURB.

fear *n.* fright, terror, horror, panic, dread, dismay, awe, scare, revulsion, aversion, tremor, mortal terror, cowardice, dread, timidity, misgiving, trembling, anxiety, phobia, foreboding, despair, agitation, hesitation, worry, concern, suspicion, doubt, qualm, funk*, cold feet*, cold sweat.—*Ant.* COURAGE, intrepidity, dash. —**for fear of** avoiding, lest, in order to prevent, out of apprehension concerning.

fear *v.* be afraid, shun, avoid, falter, lose courage, be alarmed, be frightened, be scared, live in terror, dare not, have qualms about, cower, flinch, shrink, quail, cringe, turn pale, tremble, break out in a sweat*.—*Ant.* DARE, outface, withstand.

fearful *a.* timid, shy, apprehensive; see COWARDLY.

fearfully *a.* apprehensively, shyly, with fear and trembling, for fear of, in fear.

fearless *a.* bold, daring, courageous; see BRAVE.

feasible *a.* 1 [Suitable] fit, expedi-

ent, worthwhile; see CONVENIENT 1. 2 [Likely] probable, practicable, attainable; see LIKELY 1.

feast *n.* banquet, entertainment, festival, treat, merrymaking, fiesta, barbecue, picnic; see also DINNER.

feat *n.* act, effort, deed; see ACHIEVEMENT.

feather *n.* quill, plume, plumage, down, wing, tuft, crest, fringe. —**in fine** (or **high** or **good**) **feather** well, in good humor, in good health; see HAPPY.

feature *n.* 1 [Anything calculated to attract interest] innovation, highlight, prominent part, drawing card, main bout, specialty, special attraction, featured attraction. 2 [Matter other than news published in a newspaper] article, editorial, feature story; see STORY. 3 [A salient quality] point, peculiarity, notability; see CHARACTERISTIC.

features *n.* lineaments, looks, appearance; see FACE 1.

featuring *a.* presenting, showing, recommending, calling attention to, giving prominence to, emphasizing, making much of, pointing up, drawing attention to, turning the spotlight on, centering attention on, starring.

February *n.* winter month, second month of the year, shortest month of the year; see MONTH, WINTER.

feces *n.* excretion, waste, dung; see EXCREMENT.

federal *a.* general, central, governmental; see NATIONAL 1.

fed·er·ate (fed′ər āt′) *vt.*, *vi.* **-at′ed**, **-at′ing** to unite in a federation

fed·er·a·tion (fed′ər ā′shən) *n.* ⟦see FEDERAL⟧ 1 a union of states, groups, etc. in which each subordinates its power to that of the central authority 2 a federated organization

fe·do·ra (fə dôr′ə) *n.* ⟦Fr⟧ a soft felt hat worn by men

fee (fē) *n.* ⟦ult. < Gmc⟧ a charge for professional services, licenses, etc.

fee·ble (fē′bəl) *adj.* **-bler**, **-blest** ⟦< L *flere*, weep⟧ 1 weak; infirm [a *feeble* old man] 2 without force or effectiveness [a *feeble* attempt] —**fee′ble·ness** *n.* —**fee′bly** *adv.*

feed (fēd) *vt.* **fed**, **feed′ing** ⟦< OE *foda*, food⟧ 1 to give food to 2 to provide something necessary for the growth, operation, etc. of 3 to gratify [to *feed* one's vanity] — *vi.* to eat: said esp. of animals — *n.* 1 food for animals; fodder 2 *a*) the material fed into a machine *b*) the part of the machine supplying this material —**feed′er** *n.*

feed′back′ *n.* 1 the transfer of part of the output back to the input, as of electricity or information 2 a response

feed′lot′ *n.* an enclosed area where livestock are fed and fattened before slaughter

feed′stock′ *n.* raw material for industrial processing

feel (fēl) *vt.* **felt**, **feel′ing** ⟦OE *felan*⟧ 1 to touch; examine by handling 2 to be aware of through physical sensation 3 to experience (an emotion or condition); be affected by 4 to be aware of 5 to think or believe — *vi.* 1 to have physical sensation 2 to appear to be to the senses [it *feels* warm] 3 to grope 4 to be aware of being [I *feel* sad] 5 to be moved to sympathy, pity, etc. (*for*) — *n.* 1 the act of feeling 2 the sense of touch 3 the nature of a thing as perceived through touch —**feel like** [Colloq.] to have a desire for —**feel one's way** to advance cautiously —**feel someone out** to ̇find out the opinions of someone cautiously —**feel up to** [Colloq.] to feel capable of

feel′er *n.* 1 a specialized organ of touch in an animal or insect, as an antenna 2 a remark, offer, etc. made to feel another out

feel′ing *n.* 1 the sense of touch 2 the ability to experience physical sensation 3 an awareness; sensation 4 an emotion 5 [*pl.*] sensibilities [hurt *feelings*] 6 sympathy; pity 7 an opinion or sentiment

fee simple absolute and unrestricted ownership of real property

feet (fēt) *n.* pl. of FOOT

feign (fān) *vt.*, *vi.* ⟦< L *fingere*, to shape⟧ 1 to make up (an excuse, etc.) 2 to pretend; dissemble

feint (fānt) *n.* ⟦see prec.⟧ a pretended attack intended to take the opponent off his guard, as in boxing — *vi.*, *vt.* to deliver (such an attack)

feisty (fīs′tē) *adj.* **-i·er**, **-i·est** ⟦ult. < ME *fisten*, to break⟧ [Colloq.] 1 exuberant 2 pugnacious

feld·spar (feld′spär′) *n.* ⟦< Ger *feld*, field + *spath*, a mineral⟧ any of several hard, crystalline minerals

fe·lic·i·tate (fə lis′i tāt′) *vt.* **-tat′ed**, **-tat′ing** ⟦< L *felix*, happy⟧ to wish happiness to; congratulate —**fe·lic′i·ta′tion** *n.* —**fe·lic′i·ta′tor** *n.*

fe·lic′i·tous (-təs) *adj.* ⟦< fol.⟧ used or expressed in a way suitable to the occasion; appropriate

fe·lic′i·ty *n.*, *pl.* **-ties** ⟦< L *felix*, happy⟧ 1 happiness; bliss 2 anything producing happiness 3 apt and pleasing expression in writing, etc.

fe·line (fē′līn) *adj.* ⟦< L *feles*, cat⟧ 1 of a cat or the cat family 2 catlike; sly — *n.* any animal of the cat family

fell[1] (fel) *vi.*, *vt. pt. of* FALL

fell[2] (fel) *vt.* ⟦OE *fellan*⟧ 1 to knock down 2 to cut down (a tree)

fell[3] (fel) *adj.* ⟦< ML *fello*⟧ fierce; cruel

fel·low (fel′ō, -ə) *n.* ⟦Late OE *feolaga*, partner⟧ 1 an associate 2 one of the same rank; equal 3 one of a pair; mate 4 one holding a fellowship in a college, etc. 5 a member of a learned society 6 [Colloq.] a man or boy — *adj.* 1 having the same position, work, etc. 2 associated [*fellow* workers]

fel′low·ship′ *n.* 1 companionship 2 a mutual sharing 3 a group of people with the same interests 4 an endowment for the support of a student or scholar doing advanced work

fellow traveler a nonmember who supports the cause of a party

fel·on[1] (fel′ən) *n.* ⟦< ML *felo*, villain⟧ a person guilty of a felony; criminal

fel·on[2] (fel′ən) *n.* ⟦ME⟧ a painful infection at the end of a finger or toe

fel·o·ny (fel′ə nē) *n.*, *pl.* **-nies** ⟦< ML *felonia*, treachery⟧ a major crime, as murder, arson, etc. —**fe·lo·ni·ous** (fə lō′nē əs) *adj.*

felt[1] (felt) *n.* ⟦< OE⟧ a fabric of wool, often mixed with fur, hair, cotton, etc., worked together by pressure, etc. — *adj.* made of felt — *vt.* to make into felt

felt[2] (felt) *vt.*, *vi. pt. and pp. of* FEEL

fe·male (fē′māl′) *adj.* ⟦< L *femina*, woman⟧ 1 designating or of the sex that bears offspring 2 of, like, or suitable to women or girls; feminine 3 consisting of women or girls 4 having a hollow part for receiving an inserted part (called *male*): said of electric sockets, etc. — *n.* a female person, animal, or plant

fem·i·nine (fem′ə nin) *adj.* ⟦< L *femina*, woman⟧ 1 of women or girls 2 having qualities characteristic of or suitable to women; gentle, delicate, etc. 3 *Gram.* designating or of the gender of words referring to females or other words with no distinction of sex —**fem′i·nin′i·ty** *n.*

THESAURUS

federation *n.* confederacy, alliance, combination; see ORGANIZATION 2.

fee *n.* remuneration, salary, charge; see PAY 2.

feeble *a.* fragile, puny, strengthless; see WEAK 1.

feed *n.* provisions, supplies, fodder, food for animals, pasture, forage, roughage. *Common feeds include the following:* grain, small grain, corn, oats, barley, rye, wheat, peanuts, hay, clover, sweet clover, alfalfa, sorghum, kale, soybeans, beets, straw.

feed *v.* feast, give food to, satisfy the hunger of, nourish, supply, support, satisfy, fill, stuff, cram, gorge, banquet, dine, nurse, maintain, fatten, provide food for, cater to, stock, furnish, nurture, sustain, encourage, serve.—*Ant.* STARVE, deprive, quench.

feel *n.* touch, quality, air; see FEELING 2.

feel *v.* 1 [To examine by touch] finger, explore, stroke, palm, caress, handle, manipulate, press, squeeze, fondle, tickle, paw, feel for, fumble, grope, grasp, grapple, grip, clutch, clasp, run the fingers over, pinch, poke, contact. 2 [To experience] sense, perceive, receive, be aware of, observe, be moved by, respond, know, acknowledge, appreciate, accept, be affected, be impressed, be excited by, have the sense of,

take to heart.—*Ant.* IGNORE, be insensitive to, be unaware of. 3 [To believe] consider, hold, know; see THINK 1. 4 [To give an impression through touch] appear, exhibit, suggest; see SEEM.

feeler *n.* hint, tentative proposal, trial balloon; see TEST.

feeling *n.* 1 [The sense of touch] tactile sensation, tactility, power of perceiving by touch, tangibility. 2 [State of the body, or of a part of it] sense, sensation, sensibility, feel, sensitiveness, sensory response, perception, perceptivity, susceptibility, activity, consciousness, receptivity, responsiveness, excitability, excitement, awareness, enjoyment, sensuality, pain, pleasure, reaction, motor response, reflex, excitation.—*Ant.* INDIFFERENCE, apathy, numbness. 3 [A personal reaction] opinion, thought, outlook; see ATTITUDE. 4 [Sensitivity] taste, emotion, passion, tenderness, discrimination, delicacy, discernment, sentiment, sentimentality, refinement, culture, cultivation, capacity, faculty, judgment, affection, sympathy, imagination, intelligence, intuition, spirit, soul, appreciation, response.—*Ant.* RUDENESS, crudeness, coldness.

feign *v.* simulate, imagine, fabricate; see PRETEND 1.

feigned *a.* imagined, fictitious, simulated; see IMAGINARY.

fell[2] *v.* pull down, knock down, cause to fall; see CUT 1.

fellow *n.* 1 [A young man] youth, lad, boy, person, teenager, stripling, novice, cadet, apprentice, adolescent, juvenile, youngster, guy*, kid*, squirt*. 2 [An associate] peer, associate, colleague; see FRIEND.

fellowship *n.* 1 [Congenial social feeling] comradeship, conviviality, sociality, sociability, intimacy, acquaintance, friendliness, familiarity, good-fellowship, amity, affability, camaraderie, togetherness.—*Ant.* RUDENESS, unsociability, surliness. 2 [Subsistence payment to encourage study] stipend, scholarship, honorarium, subsidy, teaching fellowship, assistantship.

felon[1] *n.* outlaw, delinquent, convict; see CRIMINAL.

felony *n.* misconduct, offense, transgression; see CRIME.

female *a.* reproductive, fertile, childbearing, of the female gender.—*Ant.* MALE, masculine, virile.

feminine *a.* soft, womanly, delicate, gentle, ladylike, female, matronly, maidenly, tender, womanish, fair; see also WOMANLY.—*Ant.* MALE, masculine, virile.

fem'i·nism' *n.* the movement to win political, economic, and social equality for women —**fem'i·nist** *n.*, *adj.*

fe·mur (fē'mər) *n.*, *pl.* **fe'murs** or **femo·ra** (fem'ə rə) ⟦< L, thigh⟧ the bone extending from the hip to the knee — **fem'o·ral** *adj.*

fen (fen) *n.* ⟦OE⟧ an area of low, flat, marshy land; swamp; bog

fence (fens) *n.* ⟦< ME *defens*, defense⟧ 1 a protective or confining barrier of posts, wire mesh, etc. 2 one who deals in stolen goods — *vt.* **fenced, fenc'ing** 1 to enclose, as with a fence: with *in*, *off*, etc. 2 to keep (*out*) as by a fence 3 to sell (stolen property) to a fence — *vi.* 1 to practice the art of fencing 2 to avoid giving a direct reply — **fenc'er** *n.*

fenc'ing *n.* 1 the art of fighting with a foil or other sword 2 material for making fences 3 a system of fences

fend (fend) *vi.* ⟦ME *fenden*, defend⟧ to resist —**fend for oneself** to manage by oneself —**fend off** to ward off

fend'er *n.* anything that fends off or protects something else, as the part of an automobile body over the wheel

fen·nel (fen'əl) *n.* ⟦< L *fenum*, hay⟧ a tall herb with aromatic seeds used to flavor foods

fe·ral (fir'əl) *adj.* ⟦< L *ferus*, wild⟧ 1 untamed; wild 2 savage

fer·ment (fʉr'ment'; *for v.* fər ment') *n.* ⟦< L *fervere*, to boil⟧ 1 a substance causing fermentation, as yeast 2 excitement or agitation — *vt.* 1 to cause fermentation in 2 to excite; agitate — *vi.* 1 to be in the process of fermentation 2 to be excited or agitated; seethe

fer·men·ta·tion (fʉr'mən tā'shən) *n.* 1 the breakdown of complex molecules in organic compounds, caused by the influence of a ferment /bacteria cause milk to curdle by *fermentation*/ 2 excitement; agitation

fer·mion (fer'mē än', fʉr'-) *n.* ⟦after E. *Fermi*, 20th-c. U.S. nuclear physicist⟧ any of certain subatomic particles, including leptons and baryons

fern (fʉrn) *n.* ⟦< OE *fearn*⟧ any of a large group of non-flowering plants having roots, stems, and fronds, and reproducing by spores

fe·ro·cious (fə rō'shəs) *adj.* ⟦< L *ferus*, wild⟧ 1 fierce; savage; violently cruel 2 [Colloq.] very great /a *ferocious* appetite/ —**fe·ro'cious·ly** *adv.* —**fe·roc·i·ty** (fə räs'ə tē) *n.*

-ferous (fər əs) ⟦< L *ferre*, to bear⟧ *suffix forming adjectives* bearing, yielding

fer·ret (fer'ət) *n.* ⟦< L *fur*, thief⟧ a small European polecat, easily tamed for hunting rats, etc. — *vt.* 1 to force out of hiding with a ferret 2 to find out by investigation: with *out*

fer·ric (fer'ik) *adj.* ⟦< L *ferrum*, iron⟧ of, containing, or derived from iron

Fer·ris wheel (fer'is) ⟦after G. *Ferris* (1859-96), U.S. engineer⟧ a large, upright wheel revolving on a fixed axle and having suspended seats: used as an amusement ride

ferro- ⟦< L *ferrum*, iron⟧ *combining form* 1 iron 2 iron and

fer·rous (fer'əs) *adj.* ⟦< L *ferrum*, iron⟧ of, containing, or derived from iron

fer·rule (fer'əl, -ool') *n.* ⟦< L *viriae*, bracelets⟧ a metal

ring or cap put around the end of a cane, tool handle, etc. to give added strength

ferry (fer'ē) *vt.* **-ried, -ry·ing** ⟦OE *ferian*⟧ 1 to take (people, cars, etc.) across a river, etc. 2 to deliver (airplanes) by flying them 3 to transport by airplane — *n.*, *pl.* **-ries** 1 a system for carrying people, goods, etc. across a river, etc. by boat 2 a boat used for this: also **fer'ry·boat'**

fer·tile (furt'l) *adj.* ⟦< L *ferre*, to bear⟧ 1 producing abundantly; fruitful 2 able to produce young, seeds, fruit, pollen, spores, etc. 3 fertilized —**fer·til·ity** (fər til'ə tē) *n.*

fer'til·ize' (-iz') *vt.* **-ized', -iz'ing** 1 to make fertile 2 to spread fertilizer on 3 to make (the female cell or female) fruitful by pollinating, or impregnating, with the male gamete —**fer'til·iz'able** *adj.* —**fer'tili·za'tion** *n.*

fer'til·iz'er *n.* manure, chemicals, etc., used to enrich the soil

fer·ule (fer'əl, -ool') *n.* ⟦< L *ferula*, a whip, rod⟧ a flat stick or ruler used for punishing children

fer·vent (fʉr'vənt) *adj.* ⟦< L *fervere*, to glow⟧ showing great warmth of feeling; intensely devoted or earnest — **fer'vency** *n.* —**fer'vently** *adv.*

fer·vid (fʉr'vid) *adj.* [see prec.] impassioned; fervent — **fer'vidly** *adv.*

fer·vor (fʉr'vər) *n.* ⟦see FERVENT⟧ great warmth of emotion; ardor; zeal

-fest (fest) ⟦< Ger *fest*, a feast⟧ *combining form* an occasion of much or many [*songfest*]

fes·tal (fes'tal) *adj.* ⟦< L *festum*, feast⟧ of or like a joyous celebration; festive

fes·ter (fes'tər) *n.* ⟦< L *fistula*, ulcer⟧ a small sore filled with pus — *vi.* 1 to form pus 2 to rankle

fes·ti·val (fes'tə val) *n.* ⟦see fol.⟧ 1 a time or day of feasting or celebration 2 a celebration or series of performances 3 merrymaking

fes·tive (fes'tiv) *adj.* ⟦< L *festum*, feast⟧ 1 of or for a feast or festival 2 merry; joyous —**fes'tively** *adv.* —**fes'tive·ness** *n.*

fes·tiv·ity (fes tiv'ə tē) *n.*, *pl.* **-ties** 1 merrymaking; gaiety 2 a festival 3 [*pl.*] things done in celebration

fes·toon (fes toon') *n.* ⟦< It *festa*, feast⟧ a curved garland of flowers, etc. — *vt.* to adorn with festoons

feta (cheese) (fet'ə) ⟦< ModGr < It *fetta*, a slice⟧ a white, soft cheese, orig. made in Greece

fe·tal (fēt'l) *adj.* of a fetus

fetch (fech) *vt.* ⟦OE *feccan*⟧ 1 to go after and bring back; get 2 to cause to come 3 to sell for

fetch'ing *adj.* attractive; charming

fete or **fête** (fāt, fet) *n.* ⟦Fr *fête*: see FEAST⟧ a festival; entertainment, esp. outdoors — *vt.* **fet'ed** or **fêt'ed, fet' ing** or **fêt'ing** to honor with a fete

fetid (fet'id) *adj.* ⟦< L *foetere*, to stink⟧ having a bad smell; stinking; putrid —**fet'id·ness** *n.*

fet·ish (fet'ish) *n.* ⟦< Port *feitiço*⟧ 1 any object believed to have magical power 2 anything to which one is irrationally devoted 3 any nonsexual object that abnormally

---

■■■ THESAURUS ■■■

fence *n.* 1 [That which surrounds an enclosure] picket fence, wire fence, board fence, barbed-wire fence, rail fence, chain fence, iron fence, hedge, backstop, rail, railing, barricade, net, barrier, wall, dike. 2 [A receiver of stolen goods] accomplice, front*, uncle*; see CRIMINAL. —**mend one's fences** renew contacts, look after one's political interests, solicit votes; see CAMPAIGN. —**on the fence** undecided, uncommitted, indifferent; see UNCERTAIN.

fender *n.* guard, mudguard, shield, apron, buffer, mask, cover, frame, cushion, protector, bumper.

fend for oneself *v.* take care of oneself, stay alive, eke out an existence; see SURVIVE 1.

fend off *v.* keep off, ward off, repel; see DEFEND 1.

ferment *v.* effervesce, sour, foam, froth, bubble, seethe, fizz, sparkle, boil, work, ripen, dissolve, evaporate, rise.

fermentation *n.* souring, foaming, seething; see DECAY.

fern *n.* greenery, bracken, lacy plant;

see PLANT.

ferocious *a.* fierce, savage, wild; see FIERCE.—*Ant.* GENTLE, meek, mild.

ferocity *n.* fierceness, brutality, barbarity; see CRUELTY.

ferry *n.* passage boat, barge, packet; see BOAT.

fertile *a.* fruitful, rich, productive, fat, teeming, yielding, arable, flowering.—*Ant.* STERILE, barren, desert.

fertility *n.* fecundity, richness, fruitfulness, potency, virility, pregnancy, productiveness, productivity, generative capacity.

fertilization *n.* 1 [The enrichment of land] manuring, dressing, mulching; see PREPARATION 1. 2 [Impregnation of the ovum] insemination, impregnation, pollination, implantation, breeding, propagation, generation, procreation.

fertilize *v.* 1 [To enrich land] manure, dress, lime, mulch, cover, treat. 2 [To impregnate] breed, make pregnant, generate, germinate, pollinate, inseminate, propagate, procreate, get with child, beget, knock up*.

fertilizer *n.* manure, chemical fertilizer, plant food, compost, humus, mulch. *Common fertilizers include the following:* barnyard manure, guano, sphagnum, peat moss, phosphate, dung, litter, crushed limestone, bone dust, kelp, bone meal, nitrogen, ammonium sulphate, potash.

fervent *a.* zealous, eager, ardent; see ENTHUSIASTIC.

fervor *n.* fervency, ardor, enthusiasm; see ZEAL.

fester *v.* rankle, putrefy, rot; see SPOIL.

festival *n.* festivity, feast, competition; see CELEBRATION.

festive *a.* merry, gay, joyful; see HAPPY.

festivity *n.* revelry, pleasure, amusement; see ENTERTAINMENT.

fetch *v.* bring, get, retrieve; see CARRY 1.

fete *n.* festival, entertainment, ball; see CELEBRATION, PARTY 1.

fetish *n.* fixation, craze, mania; see OBSESSION.

excites erotic feelings Also **fet'ich** —**fet'ish·ism'** *n.* —**fet'ish·ist** *n.*

fet·lock (fet'läk') *n.* ⟦< ME *fet*, feet⟧ 1 a tuft of hair on the back of a horse's leg above the hoof 2 the joint bearing this tuft

feto·scope (fē'tə skōp') *n.* 1 an endoscope used to examine a fetus in the womb 2 a special stethoscope used to listen to the fetal heartbeat

fet·ter (fet'ər) *n.* ⟦< OE *fot*, foot⟧ 1 a shackle or chain for the feet 2 any check or restraint — *vt.* 1 to bind with fetters 2 to restrain

fet·tle (fet''l) *n.* ⟦ME *fetlen*, make ready⟧ condition; state *[in fine fettle]*

fe·tus (fēt'əs) *n.*, *pl.* **-tuses** ⟦L, a bringing forth⟧ the unborn young of an animal, esp. in its later stages and specif., in humans, from about the eighth week after conception until birth

feud (fyo͞od) *n.* ⟦< OFr *faide*⟧ a deadly quarrel, esp. between clans or families — *vi.* to carry on a feud; quarrel

feu·dal (fyo͞od''l) *adj.* ⟦ML *feudalis*⟧ of or like feudalism

feu'dal·ism' *n.* the economic and social system in medieval Europe, in which land, worked by serfs, was held by vassals in exchange for military and other services to overlords

fe·ver (fē'vər) *n.* ⟦< L *febris*⟧ 1 an abnormally increased body temperature 2 any disease marked by a high fever 3 a restless excitement —**fe'ver·ish** *adj.* —**fe'ver·ishly** *adv.*

fever blister (or **sore**) COLD SORE

few (fyo͞o) *adj.* ⟦OE *feawe*⟧ not many — *pron.* not many; a small number —**the few** the minority

fey (fā) *adj.* ⟦OE *fæge*, fated⟧ strange or unusual; specif., eccentric, whimsical, etc. —**fey'ness** *n.*

fez (fez) *n.*, *pl.* **fez'zes** ⟦after *Fez*, city in Morocco⟧ a red, tapering felt hat, worn formerly by Turkish men

ff. 1 folios 2 following (pages, etc.)

fi·ancé (fē'än sā') *n.* ⟦Fr < OFr *fiance*, a promise⟧ a man who is engaged to be married

fi·an·cée (fē'än sā') *n.* ⟦Fr: see prec.⟧ a woman who is engaged to be married

fias·co (fē as'kō) *n.*, *pl.* **-coes** or **-cos** ⟦Fr < It⟧ a complete, ridiculous failure

fiat (fī'at', -ət) *n.* ⟦L, let it be done⟧ 1 a decree; order 2 a sanction

fib (fib) *n.* ⟦< ? FABLE⟧ a small or trivial lie — *vi.* **fibbed**, **fib'bing** to tell such a lie —**fib'ber** *n.*

fi·ber (fī'bər) *n.* ⟦< L *fibra*⟧ 1 a threadlike structure that combines with others to form animal or vegetable tissue 2 any substance that can be separated into threadlike parts for weaving, etc. 3 texture 4 character or nature 5 ROUGHAGE —**fi'brous** (-brəs) *adj.*

fi'ber·board' *n.* a building material consisting of fibers of wood, etc. pressed into stiff sheets

Fi'ber·glas' (-glas') trademark for finespun filaments of glass made into textiles or insulating material — *n.* [f-] this substance: also **fiberglass**

fiber optics 1 the science of transmitting light and images, as around curves, through transparent fibers 2 such fibers —**fi'ber-op'tic** *adj.*

fi·bril·la·tion (fib'ri lā'shən) *n.* ⟦< L *fibra*, fiber + -ATION⟧ a rapid series of contractions of the heart, causing irregular heartbeats

fi·brin (fī'brin) *n.* a fibrous, insoluble blood protein formed in blood clots

fi·brino·gen (fī brin'ə jən) *n.* ⟦prec. + -GEN⟧ a protein in the blood from which fibrin is formed

fi·broid (fī'broid') *adj.* like or composed of fibrous tissue, as a tumor

fi·bro·sis (fī brō'sis) *n.* an excessive growth of fibrous connective tissue in an organ, part, etc.

fibu·la (fib'yo͞o lə) *n.*, *pl.* **-lae** (-lē') or **-las** ⟦L, a clasp⟧ the long, thin outer bone of the lower leg —**fib'u·lar** *adj.*

-fic (fik) ⟦< L *facere*, make⟧ *suffix* making *[terrific]*

FICA Federal Insurance Contributions Act

-fication (fi kā'shən) ⟦see -FIC⟧ *suffix* a making *[glorification]*

fichu (fish'o͞o) *n.* ⟦Fr⟧ a triangular lace or muslin cape for women, worn with the ends fastened in front

fickle (fik'əl) *adj.* ⟦< OE *ficol*, tricky⟧ changeable or unstable; capricious

fic·tion (fik'shən) *n.* ⟦< L *fingere*, to form⟧ 1 an imaginary statement, story, etc. 2 *a)* literary works, collectively, with imaginary characters or events, as novels *b)* a work of this kind —**fic'tional** *adj.*

fic'tion·al·ize' (-shə nəl īz') *vt.* **-ized'**, **-iz'ing** to deal with (historical events) in fictional form

fic·ti·tious (fik tish'əs) *adj.* 1 of or like fiction; imaginary 2 false 3 assumed for disguise *[a fictitious name]*

fic·tive (fik'tiv) *adj.* 1 of fiction 2 imaginary —**fic'tively** *adv.*

fi·cus (fī'kəs) *n.*, *pl.* **fi'cus** ⟦< L, fig tree⟧ any of a genus of tropical shrubs, trees, etc. with glossy, leathery leaves

fid·dle (fid''l) *n.* ⟦OE *fithele*⟧ [Colloq.] a violin — *vi.* **-dled**, **-dling** 1 [Colloq.] to play a fiddle 2 to tinker (*with*) nervously —**fid'dler** *n.*

fid'dle·sticks' *interj.* nonsense!

fi·del·i·ty (fə del'ə tē) *n.*, *pl.* **-ties** ⟦< L *fides*, faith⟧ 1 faithful devotion to duty; loyalty 2 accuracy of description, sound reproduction, etc.

fidget (fij'it) *n.* ⟦< ME < ?⟧ a restless or nervous state: esp. in phrase **the fidgets** — *vi.* to move about restlessly or nervously —**fidg'ety** *adj.*

fi·du·ci·ary (fī do͞o'shē er'ē) *adj.* ⟦< L *fiducia*, trust⟧ holding or held in trust — *n.*, *pl.* **-ies** TRUSTEE (sense 1)

fie (fī) *interj.* for shame!

fief (fēf) *n.* ⟦Fr: see FEE⟧ in feudalism, heritable land held by a vassal

fief'dom (-dəm) *n.* 1 FIEF 2 anything under one's complete control

field (fēld) *n.* ⟦OE *feld*⟧ 1 a stretch of open land 2 a piece of cleared land for crops or pasture 3 a piece of land used for a particular purpose *[a landing field]* 4 any wide, unbroken expanse *[a field of ice]* 5 *a)* a battlefield *b)* a battle 6 a realm of knowledge or work 7 the background, as on a flag 8 all the entrants in a contest 9 *Physics* a physical quantity specified at points throughout a region of space — *vt.* 1 to stop or catch and throw (a baseball, etc.) 2 to put (a player or team) into active play 3

THESAURUS

fetus *n.* organism, embryo, the young of an animal in the womb; see CHILD.

feud *n.* quarrel, strife, bickering; see FIGHT.

fever *n.* abnormal temperature and pulse, febrile disease, high body temperature; see ILLNESS 1.

feverish *a.* burning, above normal, running a temperature; see HOT 1.

few *a.* not many, scarcely any, less, sparse, scanty, thin, widely spaced, inconsiderable, negligible, infrequent, not too many, some, any, scarce, rare, seldom, few and far between.—*Ant.* MANY, numerous, innumerable.

few *pron.* not many, a small number, a handful, scarcely any, not too many, several, a scattering, three or four, a sprinkling.—*Ant.* MANY, a multitude, a great many. —**quite a few** several, some, a large number; see MANY.

fiancé *n.* intended, betrothed, person engaged to be married; see LOVER.

fib *n.* prevarication, fabrication, mis-representation; see LIE.

fiber *n.* thread, cord, string, strand, tissue, filament, vein, hair, strip, shred. *Some common fibers include the following:* vegetable fiber, animal fiber, synthetic fiber, silk, linen, hemp, cotton, wool, jute, rayon, nylon, orlon, polyester, acetate.

fibrous *a.* veined, hairy, coarse; see STRINGY.

fickle *a.* capricious, whimsical, mer-curial; see CHANGING.

fiction *n.* novel, tale, romance; see STORY.

fictitious *a.* made-up, untrue, counterfeit; see FALSE 1, 2.

fiddle* *n.* violin, stringed instrument, cornstalk fiddle; see MUSICAL INSTRU-MENT. —**fit as a fiddle** healthy, strong, sound; see WELL 1. —**play second fiddle (to)** defer to, be inferior to, be less successful than; see FAIL 1.

fidelity *n.* fealty, loyalty, devotion; see LOYALTY.

fidget *v.* stir, twitch, worry; see WIGGLE.

fidgety *a.* nervous, uneasy, apprehensive; see RESTLESS.

field *n.* 1 [Open land] grainfield, hay-field, meadow, pasture, range, acreage, plot, patch, garden, cultivated ground, grassland, green, ranchland, arable land, plowed land, cleared land, cropland, tract, vineyard. 2 [An area devoted to sport] diamond, gridiron, track, rink, court, course, racecourse, golf course, racetrack, arena, stadium, theater, amphitheater, playground, park, turf, green, fairground. 3 [An area devoted to a specialized activity] airfield, airport, flying field, terminal, battlefield, battleground, sector, field of fire, terrain, no man's land, theater of war, field of battle, field of honor, parade ground, range, parking lot. —**play the field** experiment, explore, look elsewhere; see DISCOVER, EXAMINE, TRY 1.

[Colloq.] to answer (a question) extemporaneously —**play the field** to not confine one's activities to one object — **field′er** *n.*

field glasses a small, portable, binocular telescope

field goal 1 *Basketball* a shot made from play, scoring two points or, if from a certain distance, three points **2** *Football* a goal kicked from the field, scoring three points

field hand a hired farm laborer

field hockey HOCKEY (sense 2)

field marshal in some armies, an officer of the highest rank

field′-test′ *vt.* to test (a device, method, etc.) under operating conditions

fiend (fēnd) *n.* ⟦OE *feond*⟧ **1** an evil spirit; devil **2** an inhumanly wicked person **3** [Colloq.] an addict *[a dope fiend, fresh-air fiend]* —**fiend′ish** *adj.*

fierce (firs) *adj.* **fierc′er, fierc′est** ⟦< L *ferus*, wild⟧ **1** savage **2** violent **3** intense *[a fierce embrace]* —**fierce′ly** *adv.* —**fierce′ness** *n.*

fi·er·y (fī′ər ē) *adj.* **-eri·er, -eri·est 1** like fire; glaring, hot, etc. **2** ardent; spirited **3** excitable **4** inflamed

fi·esta (fē es′tə) *n.* ⟦Sp < L *festus*, festal⟧ **1** a religious festival **2** any gala celebration; holiday

fife (fīf) *n.* ⟦Ger *pfeife*⟧ a small flute used mainly with drums in playing marches

fif·teen (fif′tēn′) *adj., n., pl.* ⟦OE *fiftene*⟧ five more than ten; 15; XV —**fif′teenth′** (-tēnth′) *adj., n., adv.*

fifth (fifth) *adj.* ⟦< OE *fif*, five⟧ preceded by four others in a series; 5th — *n.* **1** the one following the fourth **2** any of the five equal parts of something; ⅕ **3** a fifth of a gallon — *adv.* in the fifth place, rank, etc.

Fifth Amendment an amendment to the U.S. Constitution mainly guaranteeing certain protections in criminal cases; specif., the clause protecting persons from being compelled to testify against themselves

fifty (fif′tē) *adj., n., pl.* **-ties** ⟦OE *fiftig*⟧ five times ten; 50; L —**the fifties** the numbers or years, as of a century, from 50 through 59 —**fif′ti·eth** (-ith) *adj., n.*

fif′ty-fif′ty *adj.* [Colloq.] equal; even — *adv.* [Colloq.] equally

fig (fig) *n.* ⟦< L *ficus*⟧ **1** *a*) a small, sweet, pear-shaped fruit that grows on a tree related to the mulberry *b*) the tree **2** a trifle *[not worth a fig]*

fig. 1 figurative(ly) **2** figure(s)

fight (fīt) *vi.* **fought, fight′ing** ⟦OE *feohtan*⟧ to take part in a struggle, contest, etc., esp. against a foe or for a cause — *vt.* **1** to oppose physically or in battle **2** to struggle against **3** to engage in (a war, etc.) **4** to gain (one's way) by struggle — *n.* **1** any struggle, contest, or quarrel **2** power or readiness to fight

fight′er *n.* **1** one that fights; esp., a prizefighter **2** a fast, highly maneuverable combat airplane

fig·ment (fig′mənt) *n.* ⟦< L *fingere*, to form⟧ something merely imagined

fig·ura·tive (fig′yoor ə tiv′) *adj.* **1** representing by means of a figure or symbol **2** not in its usual or exact sense; metaphorical **3** using figures of speech —**fig′ura·tive′ly** *adv.*

fig·ure (fig′yər) *n.* ⟦< L *fingere*, to form⟧ **1** an outline or shape; form **2** the human form **3** a person thought of in a specified way *[a historical figure]* **4** a likeness of a person or thing **5** an illustration; diagram **6** a design; pattern **7** the symbol for a number **8** [*pl.*] arithmetic **9** a sum of money **10** *Geom.* a surface or space bounded by lines or planes — *vt.* **-ured, -ur·ing 1** to represent in definite form **2** to imagine **3** to ornament with a design **4** to compute with figures **5** [Colloq.] to believe; consider — *vi.* **1** to appear prominently **2** to do arithmetic —**figure in** to include —**figure on** to rely on —**figure out 1** to solve **2** to understand —**figure up** to add; total

fig′ure·head′ *n.* **1** a carved figure on the bow of a ship **2** one put in a position of leadership, but having no real power or authority

figure of speech an expression, as a metaphor or simile, using words in a nonliteral or unusual sense

figu·rine (fig′yōō rēn′) *n.* ⟦Fr⟧ a small sculptured or molded figure

fila·ment (fil′ə mənt) *n.* ⟦< L *filum*, thread⟧ a very slender thread or threadlike part; specif., the fine wire in a light bulb or electron tube

fil·bert (fil′bərt) *n.* ⟦ME *filberde*⟧ HAZELNUT

filch (filch) *vt.* ⟦ME *filchen*⟧ to steal (usually something small or petty)

file[1] (fīl) *vt.* **filed, fil′ing** ⟦< L *filum*, thread⟧ **1** to put (papers, etc.) in order for future reference **2** to dispatch or register (a news story, application, etc.) **3** to put on public

---

◼ THESAURUS ◼

fielder *n.* infielder, outfielder, gardener*; see BASEBALL PLAYER.

fiend *n.* **1** [A wicked or cruel person] monster, barbarian, brute; see BEAST. **2** [*An addict] fan, aficionado, monomaniac; see ADDICT.

fiendish *a.* diabolical, demonic, infernal; see BAD.

fierce *a.* ferocious, wild, furious, enraged, raging, impetuous, untamed, angry, passionate, savage, primitive, brutish, animal, raving, outrageous, terrible, vehement, frightening, awful, horrible, venomous, bold, malevolent, malign, brutal, monstrous, severe, rough, rude, vicious, dangerous, frenzied, mad, insane, desperate, ravening, frantic, wrathful, irate, fanatical, bestial, boisterous, violent, threatening, stormy, thunderous, howling, tumultuous, turbulent, uncontrolled, raging, storming, blustering, cyclonic, torrential, frightful, fearful, devastating, hellish, rip-roaring*.—*Ant.* MILD, moderate, calm.

fiercely *a.* ferociously, violently, wildly, terribly, vehemently, angrily, threateningly, frighteningly, awfully, horribly, mightily, passionately, impetuously, boldly, irresistibly, furiously, riotously, brutally, monstrously, forcibly, forcefully, convulsively, hysterically, severely, roughly, rudely, viciously, dangerously, madly, insanely, desperately, outrageously, savagely, frantically, wrathfully, irately, virulently, relentlessly, turbulently, overpoweringly, strongly, deliriously, fanatically, with rage, in a frenzy, tooth and nail.—*Ant.* PEACEFULLY, mildly, reasonably.

fiesta *n.* festival, holiday, feast; see

CELEBRATION.

fifty *a.* half a hundred, half a century, two score and ten, many, five times ten, a considerable number.

fight *n.* **1** [A violent physical struggle] strife, contention, feud, quarrel, contest, encounter, row, dispute, disagreement, battle, confrontation, controversy, brawl, bout, match, fisticuffs, round, fracas, difficulty, altercation, bickering, wrangling, riot, argument, debate, competition, rivalry, conflict, skirmish, clash, scuffle, collision, brush, action, engagement, combat, blow, exchange of blows, wrestling match, squabble, game, discord, estrangement, fuss, tussle, scrap*, free-for-all, ruckus*, run-in*, tiff, flare-up, go*, row, set-to*, difference of opinion. **2** [Willingness or eagerness to fight] mettle, hardihood, boldness; see COURAGE.

fight *v.* strive, war, struggle, resist, assert oneself, challenge, meet, contend, attack, carry on war, withstand, give blow for blow, do battle, war against, persevere, force, go to war, exchange blows, encounter, oppose, tussle, grapple, flare up, engage with, combat, wrestle, box, spar, skirmish, quarrel, bicker, dispute, have it out, squabble, come to grips with, row, light into*, tear into*, mix it up with*.—*Ant.* RETREAT, submit, yield. —**fight back** defend oneself, resist, retaliate; see OPPOSE 2. —**fight off** defend from, hold back, resist; see DEFEND 1.

fighter *n.* **1** [One who fights] contestant, disputant, contender, party to a quarrel, warrior, soldier, combatant, belligerent, assailant, aggressor, antagonist, rival, opponent, cham-

pion, bully, competitor, controversialist, scrapper*. **2** [A professional pugilist] boxer, prize fighter, pug*, bruiser*.

fighting *a.* combative, battling, brawling, unbeatable, resolute, argumentative, angry, ferocious, quarrelsome, ready to fight, belligerent, boxing, wrestling, warlike, contending, up in arms.

fighting *n.* combat, struggle, strife; see FIGHT.

figurative *a.* not literal, metaphorical, allegorical; see ILLUSTRATIVE.

figure *n.* **1** [A form] shape, mass, structure; see FORM 1. **2** [The human torso] body, frame, torso, shape, form, development, configuration, build, appearance, outline, posture, attitude, pose, carriage. **3** [A representation of quantity] sum, total, symbol; see NUMBER. **4** [Price] value, worth, terms; see PRICE.

figure *v.* **1** [To compute] reckon, number, count; see CALCULATE. **2** [To estimate] set a figure, guess, fix a price; see ESTIMATE. **3** [*To come to a conclusion] suppose, think, opine; see DECIDE. **4** [To figure out] comprehend, master, reason; see DISCOVER.

figure of speech *n.* *Varieties include the following:* image, comparison, metaphor, simile, metonymy, synecdoche, trope, personification, hyperbole, litotes, allegory, parable, allusion, euphemism, analogue, parallel, irony, satire, understatement, paradox.

file[1,2] *n.* **1** [An orderly collection of papers] card index, card file, portfolio, record, classified index, list, regisrecord — *vi.* **1** to move in a line **2** to make application (*for* divorce, etc.) — *n.* **1** a container for keeping papers in order **2** an orderly arrangement of papers, etc. **3** a line of persons or things **4** *Comput.* a collection of data stored as a single unit —**file′a·ble** *adj.* —**fil′er** *n.*

file² (fīl) *n.* ⟦OE *feol*⟧ a steel tool with a rough, ridged surface for smoothing or grinding — *vt.* **filed, fil′ing** to smooth or grind, as with a file

fi·let mi·gnon (fi lā′ min yōn′) ⟦Fr, lit., tiny fillet⟧ a thick, round cut of lean beef tenderloin

fil·ial (fil′ē əl, fil′yəl) *adj.* ⟦< L *filius*, son⟧ of, suitable to, or due from a son or daughter

fili·bus·ter (fil′i bus′tər) *n.* ⟦< Sp < MDu *vrijbuiter*, free-booter⟧ **1** the making of long speeches, etc. to obstruct a bill's passage in the Senate **2** a Senator who does this — *vt., vi.* to obstruct (a bill) by a filibuster

fili·gree (fil′i grē′) *n.* ⟦< L *filum*, thread + *granum*, grain⟧ lacelike ornamental work of intertwined wire of gold, silver, etc. — *vt.* **-greed′, -gree′ing** to ornament with filigree

fil·ing (fīl′iŋ) *n.* a small piece scraped off with a file: *usually used in pl.*

Fili·pino (fil′i pē′nō) *n., pl.* **-nos** ⟦Sp⟧ a native of the Philippines — *adj.* Philippine

fill (fil) *vt.* ⟦OE *fyllan*⟧ **1** to put as much as possible into **2** to occupy wholly **3** to put a person into or to occupy (a position, etc.) **4** to supply the things called for in (an order, etc.) **5** to close or plug (holes, etc.) — *vi.* to become full — *n.* **1** enough to make full or to satisfy **2** anything that fills —**fill in 1** to complete by supplying something **2** to supply for completion **3** to be a substitute —**fill out 1** to make or become larger, etc. **2** to make (a document, etc.) complete with data —**fill up** to make or become completely full —**fill′er** *n.*

fil·let (fil′it; *for n. 2 & vt., usually* fi lā′, fil′ā′) *n.* ⟦< L *filum*, thread⟧ **1** a thin strip or band **2** a boneless, lean piece of meat or fish — *vt.* to bone and slice (meat or fish)

fill′-in′ *n.* one that fills a vacancy or gap, often temporarily

fill′ing *n.* a substance used to fill something, as gold in a tooth cavity

filling station SERVICE STATION

fil·lip (fil′ip) *n.* ⟦< FLIP¹⟧ **1** an outward snap of a finger from the thumb **2** something stimulating — *vt.* to strike or toss with a fillip

filly (fil′ē) *n., pl.* **-lies** ⟦< ON *fylja*⟧ a young female horse

film (film) *n.* ⟦OE *filmen*⟧ **1** a fine, thin skin, coating, etc. **2** a flexible cellulose material coated with an emulsion sen-

sitive to light and used in photography **3** a haze or blur **4** a series of still pictures projected on a screen in such rapid succession as to create the illusion of moving persons and objects **5** a play, story, etc. in this form — *vt., vi.* **1** to cover or be covered as with a film **2** to photograph or make a film (of)

film′strip′ *n.* a length of film with still photographs, often of illustrations, charts, etc., for projection separately

film′y *adj.* **-i·er, -i·est 1** gauzy; sheer; thin **2** blurred; hazy

fil·ter (fil′tər) *n.* ⟦< ML *filtrum*, FELT¹⟧ **1** a device for straining out solid particles, impurities, etc. from a liquid or gas **2** a device or substance for screening out electric oscillations, light waves, etc. of certain frequencies — *vt., vi.* **1** to pass through or as through a filter **2** to remove with a filter —**fil′ter·able** or **fil′trable** (-trə bəl) *adj.*

filter tip 1 a cigarette with a tip of cellulose, cotton, etc. for filtering the smoke **2** such a tip

filth (filth) *n.* ⟦OE *fylthe*⟧ **1** foul dirt **2** obscenity —**filth′i·ness** *n.* —**filth′y, -i·er, -i·est,** *adj.*

fil·trate (fil′trāt) *vt.* **-trat′ed, -trat′ing** to filter — *n.* a filtered liquid —**fil·tra′tion** *n.*

fin (fin) *n.* ⟦OE *finn*⟧ **1** any of several winglike organs on the body of a fish, dolphin, etc., used in swimming **2** anything like a fin in shape or use

fi·na·gle (fə nā′gəl) *vt., vi.* **-gled, -gling** ⟦< ?⟧ [Colloq.] to use, or get by, craftiness or trickery —**fi·na′gler** *n.*

fi·nal (fīn′əl) *adj.* ⟦< L *finis*, end⟧ **1** of or coming at the end; last **2** deciding; conclusive — *n.* **1** anything final **2** [*pl.*] the last of a series of contests **3** a final examination —**fi·nal′ity** (-nal′ə tē) *n.* —**fi′nally** *adv.*

fi·nale (fə nal′ē) *n.* ⟦It⟧ the concluding part of a musical work, etc.

fi·nal·ist *n.* a contestant in the final, deciding contest of a series

fi·nal·ize′ *vt.* **-ized′, -iz′ing** ⟦FINAL + -IZE⟧ to make final; complete —**fi′nali·za′tion** *n.*

fi·nance (fi′nans′; *also* fə nans′) *n.* ⟦< L *finis*, end⟧ **1** [*pl.*] money resources, income, etc. **2** the science of managing money — *vt.* **-nanced′, -nanc′ing** to supply or get money for —**fi·nan′cial** (-nan′shəl) *adj.* —**fi·nan′cially** *adv.*

fin·an·cier (fin′ən sir′; *also* fī′nan-) *n.* ⟦Fr⟧ one skilled in finance

finch (finch) *n.* ⟦OE *finc*⟧ any of various small, seed-eating birds, including canaries, goldfinches, etc.

find (fīnd) *vt.* **found, find′ing** ⟦OE *findan*⟧ **1** to discover by chance; come upon **2** to get by searching **3** to perceive; learn **4** to recover (something lost) **5** to reach; attain **6** to

━━━━━ THESAURUS ━━━━━

ter, dossier, notebook. **2** [Steel abrasive] rasp, steel, sharpener. *Types of files include the following:* flat, rat-tail, ignition, triangular, fingernail, wood. **3** [A line] rank, row, column; see LINE 1. —**on file** filed, cataloged, registered; see RECORDED.

file¹,² *v.* **1** [To arrange in order] classify, index, deposit, categorize, catalog, record, register, list, arrange. **2** [To use an abrasive] abrade, rasp, scrape, smooth, rub down, level off, finish, sharpen.

fill *n.* enough, capacity, satiety; see PLENTY.

fill *v.* **1** [To pour to the capacity of the container] pack, stuff, replenish, furnish, supply, satisfy, blow up, fill up, pump up, fill to capacity, fill to overflowing, brim over, swell, charge, inflate.—*Ant.* EMPTY, exhaust, drain. **2** [To occupy available space] take up, pervade, overflow, stretch, bulge out, distend, brim over, stretch, swell, blow up, run over at the top, permeate, take over. —**fill in 1** [To insert] write in, answer, sign; see ANSWER. **2** [To substitute] replace, act for, represent; see SUBSTITUTE. —**fill out 1** [To enlarge] swell out, expand, overgrow; see GROW 1. **2** [To insert] fill in, sign, apply; see ANSWER. —**fill up** saturate, pack, stuff; see FILL 1.

filled *a.* finished, completed, done; see FULL 1.

filling *n.* stuffing, dressing, contents, mixture, center, layer, filler, fill,

sauce, insides, lining, wadding, padding, cement, innards*, guts*.

film *n.* **1** [Thin, membranous matter] gauze, tissue, fabric, sheet, membrane, layer, transparency, foil, fold, skin, coat, coating, scum, veil, cobweb, web, mist, cloud. **2** [A preparation containing a light-sensitive emulsion] negative, positive, microfilm, color film. **3** [A moving picture film] motion picture, cinema, photoplay; see MOVIE.

film *v.* record, take, shoot; see PHOTOGRAPH.

filter *v.* **1** [To soak slowly] seep, penetrate, percolate; see SOAK 1. **2** [To clean by filtering] strain, purify, sift, sieve, refine, clarify, clean, separate.

filth *n.* dirt, dung, feces, contamination, corruption, pollution, foul matter, sewage, muck, manure, slop, squalor, trash, grime, mud, smudge, silt, garbage, carrion, slush, slime, sludge, foulness, filthiness, excrement, dregs, lees, sediment, rottenness, impurity.—*Ant.* CLEANLINESS, purity, spotlessness.

filthy *a.* foul, squalid, nasty; see DIRTY 1.

fin *n.* membrane, paddle, propeller, balance, guide, blade, ridge, organ, spine, pectoral fin, ventral fin, dorsal fin, caudal fin, flipper, fishtail.

final *a.* terminal, concluding, ultimate; see LAST 1.

finalized *a.* concluded, decided, completed; see FINISHED 1.

finally *a.* **1** [As though a matter

were settled] with finality, with conviction, settled, in a final manner, certainly, officially, irrevocably, decisively, definitely, beyond recall, permanently, for all time, conclusively, assuredly, done with, once and for all, for good, beyond the shadow of a doubt.—*Ant.* TEMPORARILY, momentarily, for the time being. **2** [After a long period] at length, at last, in the end, subsequently, in conclusion, lastly, after all, after a while, eventually, ultimately, at long last, at the final point, at the last moment, at the end, tardily, belatedly, when all is said and done, in spite of all.

finance *n.* business, commerce, financial affairs; see ECONOMICS.

finance *v.* fund, pay for, provide funds for; see PAY FOR.

finances *n.* revenue, capital, funds; see WEALTH.

financial *a.* economic, business, monetary; see COMMERCIAL.

financier *n.* capitalist, banker, merchant; see EXECUTIVE.

find *n.* fortunate discovery, findings, acquisition; see DISCOVERY.

find *v.* discover, detect, notice, observe, perceive, arrive at, discern, hit upon, encounter, uncover, recover, expose, stumble on, happen upon, come across, track down, dig up, turn up, scare up*, run across, run into, lay one's hands on, bring to light, spot; see also SEE 1.—*Ant.* LOSE, mislay, miss. —**find out** recognize, learn, identify; see DISCOVER.

decide and declare to be — *vi.* to reach a decision *[the jury found* for the accused*] — n.* 1 a finding 2 something found —**find out** to discover; learn —**find′er** *n.*

find′ing *n.* 1 discovery 2 something found 3 *[often pl.]* the verdict of a judge, scholar, etc.

fine[1] (fīn) *adj.* **fin′er, fin′est** 〚 < L *finis,* end 〛 1 very good; excellent 2 with no impurities; refined 3 clear and bright *[fine* weather*]* 4 not heavy or coarse *[fine* sand*]* 5 very thin or small *[fine* print*]* 6 sharp *[a fine* edge*]* 7 subtle; delicate *[a fine* distinction*]* 8 elegant — *adv.* in a fine manner —**fine′ly** *adv.* —**fine′ness** *n.*

fine[2] (fīn) *n.* 〚 see prec. 〛 a sum of money paid as a penalty — *vt.* **fined, fin′ing** to order to pay a fine

fine art any of the art forms that include drawing, painting, sculpture, etc.: *usually used in pl.*

fin·er·y (fīn′ər ē) *n., pl.* **-ies** elaborate clothes, jewelry, etc.

fines herbes (fēn zerb′) 〚 Fr 〛 a seasoning of chopped herbs, esp. parsley, chives, tarragon, and chervil

fi·nesse (fə nes′) *n.* 〚 see FINE[1] 〛 1 adroitness; skill 2 the ability to handle difficult situations diplomatically 3 cunning; artfulness — *vt.* **-nessed′, -ness′ing** 1 to manage or bring about by finesse 2 to evade (a problem, etc.)

fin·ger (fiŋ′gər) *n.* 〚 OE 〛 1 any of the five jointed parts extending from the palm of the hand, esp. one other than the thumb 2 anything like a finger in shape or use — *vt.* 1 to touch with the fingers; handle 2 *Music* to use the fingers in a certain way in playing —**have** (or **keep**) **one′s fingers crossed** to hope for something —**put one′s finger on** to ascertain exactly

fin′ger·board′ *n.* the part of a stringed instrument against which the strings are pressed to produce the desired tones

fin′ger·ling (-liŋ) *n.* a small fish

fin′ger·nail′ *n.* the horny substance at the upper end of a finger

finger painting a painting done by using the fingers, hand, or arm to spread, on wet paper, paints (**finger paints**) made of starch, glycerin, and pigments —**fin′ger·paint′** *vi., vt.*

fin′ger·print′ *n.* an impression of the lines and whorls on a finger tip, used to identify a person — *vt.* to take the fingerprints of

fin′ger·tip′ *n.* the tip of a finger —**have at one′s fingertips** to have available for instant use

fin·ial (fin′ē əl) *n.* 〚 ult. < L *finis,* end 〛 a decorative, terminal part at the tip of a spire, lamp, etc.

fin·icky (fin′ik ē) *adj.* 〚 < FINE[1] 〛 too particular; fussy Also **fin′i·cal** (-i kəl) or **fin′ick·ing**

finis (fin′is, fē nē′) *n., pl.* **-nises** the end; finish

fin·ish (fin′ish) *vt.* 〚 < L *finis,* end 〛 1 *a)* to bring to an end *b)* to come to the end of 2 to consume all of 3 to give final touches to; perfect 4 to give (wood, etc.) a desired surface effect — *vi.* to come to an end — *n.* 1 the last part; end 2 *a)* anything used to finish a surface *b)* the finished effect 3 means or manner of completing or perfecting 4 polished manners, speech, etc. —**finish off** 1 to end 2 to kill or ruin —**finish with** to bring to an end —**fin′ished** *adj.* — **fin′isher** *n.*

fi·nite (fī′nīt′) *adj.* 〚 < L *finis,* end 〛 having definable limits; not infinite

fink (fiŋk) *n.* 〚 Ger 〛 [Slang] 1 an informer 2 a strikebreaker — *vi.* [Slang] to inform (on)

Finn (fin) *n.* a native or inhabitant of Finland

fin·nan had·die (fin′ən had′ē) 〚 prob. < *Findhorn* (Scotland) *haddock* 〛 smoked haddock

Finn·ish (fin′ish) *n.* the language spoken in Finland — *adj.* of Finland or the Finns, their language, etc.

finny (fin′ē) *adj.* 1 having fins 2 like a fin 3 of, full of, or being fish

fiord (fyôrd) *n.* 〚 Norw < ON *fjörthr* 〛 a narrow inlet of the sea bordered by steep cliffs

fir (fur) *n.* 〚 OE *fyrh* 〛 1 a cone-bearing evergreen tree of the pine family 2 its wood

fire (fīr) *n.* 〚 OE *fyr* 〛 1 the flame, heat, and light of combustion 2 something burning 3 a destructive burning *[a* forest *fire]* 4 strong feeling 5 a discharge of firearms — *vt., vi.* **fired, fir′ing** 1 to start burning; ignite 2 to supply with fuel 3 to bake (bricks, etc.) in a kiln 4 to excite or become excited 5 to shoot (a gun, bullet, etc.) 6 to hurl or direct with force 7 to dismiss from a position; discharge —**catch (on) fire** to ignite —**on fire** 1 burning 2 greatly excited —**under fire** under attack —**fir′er** *n.*

fire′arm′ *n.* any hand weapon from which a shot is fired by explosive force, as a rifle or pistol

fire′base′ *n.* a military base in a combat zone, from which artillery, rockets, etc. are fired

fire′bomb′ *n.* an incendiary bomb — *vt.* to attack or damage with a firebomb

fire′brand′ *n.* 1 a piece of burning wood 2 one who stirs up others to revolt or strife

fire′break′ *n.* a strip of forest or prairie land cleared or plowed to stop the spread of fire

fire·brick (fīr′brik′) *n.* a highly heat-resistant brick for lining fireplaces, furnaces, etc.

THESAURUS

finder *n.* acquirer, discoverer, search party; see OWNER.—*Ant.* LOSER, seeker, failure.

finding *n.* verdict, decision, sentence; see JUDGMENT 3.

findings *n.* data, discoveries, conclusions; see SUMMARY.

fine[1] *a.* 1 [Not coarse] light, powdery, granular; see LITTLE 1. 2 [Of superior quality] well-made, supreme, fashionable; see EXCELLENT. 3 [Exact] precise, distinct, strict; see ACCURATE 2, DEFINITE 2.

fine[2] *n.* penalty, damage, forfeit; see PUNISHMENT.

fine[2] *v.* penalize, exact, tax, confiscate, levy, seize, extort, alienate, make pay; see also PUNISH.

finger *n.* digit, organ of touch, tactile member, forefinger, thumb, index finger, extremity, pointer, feeler, tentacle, pinky*. —**have** (or **keep**) **one′s fingers crossed*** wish, aspire to, pray for; see HOPE. —**lift a finger** make an effort, attempt, endeavor; see TRY 1. —**put one′s finger on** indicate, ascertain, detect; see DISCOVER. —**put the finger on*** inform on, turn in, fink on*; see TELL 1.

finger *v.* 1 [To feel] handle, touch, manipulate; see FEEL 1. 2 [*To choose or specify] appoint, point out, name; see CHOOSE.

fingernail *n.* nail, talon, matrix; see CLAW.

finish *n.* 1 [The end] close, termination, ending; see END 2. 2 [An applied surface] shine, polish, glaze, surface. *Finishes include the following:* shellac, oil, plastic, turpentine, lacquer, stain, varnish, polish, wallpaper, wash, whitewash, paint, casein paint, enamel, gold leaf, wax, veneer, cement, stucco, luster.

finish *v.* 1 [To bring to an end] complete, end, perfect; see ACHIEVE. 2 [To develop a surface] polish, wax, stain; see COVER 1, PAINT 2. 3 [To come to an end] cease, close, end; see STOP.

finished *a.* 1 [Completed] done, accomplished, perfected, achieved, ended, performed, executed, dispatched, concluded, complete, through, fulfilled, closed, over, decided, brought about, ceased, stopped, resolved, settled, made, worked out, rounded out, discharged, satisfied, disposed of, realized, finalized, effected, put into effect, all over with, attained, done with, made an end of, brought to a close, said and done, sewed up*, wound up.—*Ant.* UNFINISHED, imperfect, incomplete. 2 [Given a finish] polished, coated, varnished; see PAINTED 2.

fire *n.* 1 [Burning] flame, conflagration, blaze, campfire, coals, flame and smoke, blazing fire, hearth, burning coals, tinder, bonfire, bed of coals, embers, source of heat, sparks, heat, glow, warmth, luminosity, combustion. 2 [The discharge of ordinance] artillery attack, bombardment, rounds, barrage, explosions, bombings, curtain of fire, volley, sniping, mortar attack, salvos, shells, pattern of fire, fire superiority, cross-fire, machine-gun fire, rifle fire, small-arms fire, antiaircraft fire; see also ATTACK. —**catch (on) fire** begin burning, ignite, flare up; see BURN. —**on fire** 1 [Burning] flaming, fiery, hot; see BURNING. 2 [Excited] full of ardor, enthusiastic, zealous; see EXCITED. —**open fire** start shooting, shoot, attack; see SHOOT 1. —**play with fire** gamble, endanger one′s interests, do something dangerous; see RISK. —**set fire to** ignite, oxidize, make burn; see BURN. —**set the world on fire** achieve, become famous, excel; see SUCCEED 1. — **under fire** criticized, censured, under attack; see QUESTIONABLE 1, 2.

fire *v.* 1 [To set on fire] kindle, enkindle, ignite, inflame, light, burn, set fire to, put a match to, start a fire, set burning, touch off, rekindle, relight.—*Ant.* EXTINGUISH, smother, quench. 2 [To shoot] discharge, shoot off, hurl; see SHOOT 1. 3 [To dismiss] discharge, let go, eject; see DISMISS.

fired *a.* 1 [Subjected to fire] set on fire, burned, baked, ablaze, afire, on fire, aflame, burning, incandescent, scorched, glowing, kindled, enkindled, smoking, smoldering, heated. 2 [Discharged] dropped, let go, given one′s walking papers*; see DISCHARGED.

fire'bug' *n.* [Colloq.] one who compulsively starts destructive fires

fire'crack'er *n.* a roll of paper containing an explosive, set off as a noisemaker at celebrations, etc.

fire'damp' *n.* an explosive gas, largely methane, formed in coal mines

fire engine a motor truck with equipment for fighting fires

fire escape an outside stairway for escape from a burning building

fire'fight' *n.* a short exchange of gunfire between small units of soldiers

fire'fight'er *n.* a person whose work is fighting fires — **fire'fight'ing** *n.*

fire'fly' *n., pl.* **-flies'** a winged beetle whose abdomen glows with a luminescent light

fire'man (-mən) *n., pl.* **-men** 1 FIREFIGHTER 2 a person who tends a fire in a furnace, etc.

fire'place' *n.* a place for a fire, esp. an open place built in a wall

fire'plug' *n.* a street hydrant supplying water for fighting fires

fire'proof' *adj.* not easily destroyed by fire — *vt.* to make fireproof

fire'side' *n.* 1 the space around a fireplace 2 home or home life

fire'storm' *n.* 1 an intense fire over a large area, as one caused by an atomic explosion with its high winds 2 a strong, often violent, outburst or upheaval

fire tower a tower used as a lookout for forest fires

fire'trap' *n.* a building easily set on fire or hard to get out of if on fire

fire'truck' *n.* FIRE ENGINE

fire'wa'ter *n.* alcoholic liquor: now humorous

fire'wood' *n.* wood used as fuel

fire'works' *n.pl.* 1 firecrackers, rockets, etc., for noisy effects or brilliant displays: *sometimes used in sing.* 2 a noisy quarrel or display of anger

firing line 1 the line from which gunfire is directed at the enemy 2 any vulnerable front position

firm[1] (furm) *adj.* ⟦< L *firmus* ⟧ 1 solid; hard 2 not moved easily; fixed 3 unchanging; steady 4 resolute; constant 5 showing determination; strong 6 definite *[a firm contract]* — *vt., vi.* to make or become firm — **firm'ly** *adv.* — **firm'ness** *n.*

firm[2] (furm) *n.* ⟦< It < L *firmus*: see prec.⟧ a business company

fir'ma'ment (furm'ə mənt) *n.* ⟦< L *firmare*, strengthen⟧ the sky, viewed poetically as a solid arch or vault

first (furst) *adj.* ⟦OE *fyrst*⟧ 1 before all others in a series; 1st 2 earliest 3 foremost, as in rank, quality, etc. — *adv.*

1 before any other person or thing 2 for the first time 3 sooner; preferably — *n.* 1 any person or thing that is first 2 the beginning 3 the winning place, as in a race 4 the slowest forward gear ratio of a motor vehicle transmission

first aid emergency treatment for injury, etc., before regular medical care is available — **first'-aid'** *adj.*

first'born' *adj.* born first in a family; oldest — *n.* the firstborn child

first'-class' *adj.* 1 of the highest class, quality, etc. 2 designating the most expensive accommodations 3 of the most expensive class of ordinary mail — *adv.* 1 with first-class accommodations 2 by first-class mail

first family [*often* F- F-] the family of the U.S. president

first'hand' *adj., adv.* from the original producer or source; direct

first lady [*often* F- L-] the wife of the U.S. president

first lieutenant a military officer ranking just above a second lieutenant

first'ly *adv.* in the first place; first

first person the form of a pronoun or verb that refers to the speaker

first'-rate' *adj.* highest in rank, quality, etc. — *adv.* [Colloq.] very well

first'-string' *adj.* [Colloq.] *Sports* that is the first choice for regular play at a specified position

firth (furth) *n.* ⟦< ON *fjörthr*⟧ a narrow inlet or arm of the sea

fis·cal (fis'kəl) *adj.* ⟦< L *fiscus*, public chest⟧ 1 relating to the public treasury or revenues 2 financial — **fis'cally** *adv.*

fish (fish) *n., pl.* **fish** or (for different species) **fish'es** ⟦OE *fisc*⟧ 1 any of a large group of coldblooded vertebrate animals living in water and having gills for breathing, fins, and, usually, scales 2 the flesh of a fish used as food — *vi.* 1 to catch or try to catch fish 2 to try to get something indirectly: often with *for* — *vt.* to grope for, find, and bring to view: often with *out*

fish'er (-ər) *n.* 1 the largest marten, having very dark fur 2 this fur

fish'er·man (-ər mən) *n., pl.* **-men** 1 a person who fishes for sport or for a living 2 a commercial fishing vessel

fish'ery *n., pl.* **-ies** 1 the business of catching fish 2 a place where fish, etc. are caught or bred

fish'hook' *n.* a hook, usually barbed, for catching fish

fish'ing *n.* the catching of fish for sport or for a living

fish meal ground, dried fish, used as fertilizer or fodder

fish'wife' *n., pl.* **-wives'** a coarse, scolding woman

fish'y *adj.* **-i·er, -i·est** 1 like a fish in odor, taste, etc. 2 dull or expressionless *[fishy eyes]* 3 [Colloq.] questionable; odd — **fish'i·ness** *n.*

fis·sion (fish'ən) *n.* ⟦< L *findere*, to split⟧ 1 a splitting apart; cleavage 2 NUCLEAR FISSION — **fis'sion·a·ble** *adj.*

fis·sure (fish'ər) *n.* ⟦see prec.⟧ a cleft or crack

THESAURUS

fireman *n.* 1 [One who extinguishes fires] firefighter, engineman, ladderman, fire chief. 2 [One who fuels engines or furnaces] stoker, engineer's helper, railroad man, trainman, attendant, oil feeder, cinder monkey*, hellholer*.

fireplace *n.* hearth, chimney, hearthside, stove, furnace, blaze, bed of coals, grate.

fireproof *a.* noninflammable, noncombustible, nonflammable, fire-resistant, incombustible, concrete and steel, asbestos.

fireworks *n.* rockets, Roman candles, sparklers; see EXPLOSIVE.

firm[1] *a.* 1 [Stable] fixed, solid, rooted, immovable, fastened, motionless, secured, steady, substantial, durable, rigid, bolted, welded, riveted, soldered, imbedded, nailed, tightened, fast, secure, sound, immobile, unmovable, mounted, stationary, set, settled.—*Ant.* LOOSE, movable, mobile. 2 [Firm in texture] solid, dense, compact, hard, stiff, impenetrable, impervious, rigid, hardened, inflexible, unyielding, thick, compressed, substantial, heavy, close, condensed, impermeable.—*Ant.* SOFT, porous, flabby. 3 [Settled in purpose] determined, steadfast, resolute; see CONSTANT. —

stand (or **hold**) **firm** be steadfast, endure, maintain one's resolution; see FIGHT, RESOLVE.

firmly *a.* 1 [Not easily moved] immovably, solidly, rigidly, stably, durably, enduringly, substantially, securely, heavily, stiffly, inflexibly, soundly, strongly, thoroughly.—*Ant.* LIGHTLY, tenuously, insecurely. 2 [Showing determination] resolutely, steadfastly, doggedly, stolidly, tenaciously, determinedly, staunchly, constantly, intently, purposefully, persistently, obstinately, stubbornly, unwaveringly, unchangeably, through thick and thin.

firmness *n.* stiffness, hardness, toughness, solidity, impenetrability, durability, imperviousness, temper, impermeability, inflexibility.

first *a.* beginning, original, primary, prime, primal, antecedent, initial, virgin, earliest, opening, introductory, primeval, leading, in the beginning, front, head, rudimentary.—*Ant.* LAST, ultimate, final. —**in the first place** firstly, initially, to begin with; see FIRST.

first aid *n.* emergency medical aid, emergency relief, field dressing; see MEDICINE 2, TREATMENT 2.

first-class *a.* superior, supreme, choice; see EXCELLENT.

first-rate *a.* prime, very good, choice; see EXCELLENT.

fiscal *a.* monetary, economic, financial; see COMMERCIAL.

fish *n.* seafood, panfish, denizen of the deep. *Types of fish include the following:* catfish, pickerel, pike, perch, trout, flounder, sucker, sunfish, bass, crappy, mackerel, cod, salmon, carp, minnow, eel, bullhead, herring, shad, barracuda, swordfish, goldfish, gar, octopus, dogfish, flying fish, whitefish, tuna, pompano, haddock, hake, halibut, mullet, loach, muskellunge, sardine, smelt; see also SHELLFISH. —**drink like a fish** drink heavily, get drunk, become inebriated; see DRINK 2. —**like a fish out of water** out of place, alien, displaced; see UNFAMILIAR 1.

fish *v.* go fishing, troll for, net, bob, shrimp, bait the hook, trawl, angle, cast one's net. —**fish for** hint at, elicit, try to evoke; see HINT.

fisherman *n.* angler, fisher, harpooner, sailor, seaman, whaler, fish catcher.

fishing *n.* angling, casting, trawling; see SPORT 1.

fishy* *a.* improbable, dubious, implausible; see UNLIKELY.

fist (fist) *n.* ⟦OE *fyst*⟧ a hand with the fingers closed tightly into the palm

fisti·cuffs (fis′ti kufs′) *n.pl.* [Old-fashioned] a fight with the fists

fis·tula (fis′tyo͞o lə) *n., pl.* **-las** or **-lae′** (-lē′) ⟦L, a pipe, ulcer⟧ an abnormal passage, as from an abscess to the skin

fit[1] (fit) *vt.* **fit′ted** or **fit, fit′ted, fit′ting** ⟦ME *fitten*⟧ 1 to be suitable to 2 to be the proper size, shape, etc. for 3 to adjust so as to fit 4 to equip; outfit — *vi.* 1 [Archaic] to be suitable or proper 2 to have the proper size or shape — *adj.* **fit′ter, fit′test** 1 suited to some purpose, function, etc. 2 proper; right 3 healthy 4 [Colloq.] inclined /she was *fit* to scream/ — *n.* the manner of fitting /a tight *fit*/ —**fit′ly** *adv.* —**fit′ness** *n.* —**fit′ter** *n.*

fit[2] (fit) *n.* ⟦OE *fitt*, conflict⟧ 1 any sudden, uncontrollable attack, as of coughing 2 an outburst, as of anger 3 a seizure involving convulsions, loss of consciousness, etc. —**by fits (and starts)** in an irregular way —**have** (or **throw**) **a fit** [Colloq.] to become very angry or upset

fit′ful (-fəl) *adj.* characterized by intermittent activity; spasmodic —**fit′fully** *adv.* —**fit′ful·ness** *n.*

fit′ting *adj.* suitable; proper — *n.* 1 an adjustment or trying on of clothes, etc. 2 a small part used to join or adapt other parts 3 [*pl.*] fixtures —**fit′tingly** *adv.*

five (fiv) *adj., n.* ⟦OE *fif*⟧ one more than four; 5; V

five′-and-ten′-cent′ store a store that sells a wide variety of inexpensive merchandise   Also **five′-and-ten′** *n.*

fix (fiks) *vt.* **fixed, fix′ing** ⟦< L *figere*, fasten⟧ 1 to fasten firmly 2 to set firmly in the mind 3 to direct (one's eyes) steadily at something 4 to make rigid 5 to make permanent 6 to establish (a date, etc.) definitely 7 to set in order; adjust 8 to repair 9 to prepare (food or meals) 10 [Colloq.] to influence the result or action of (a race, jury, etc.), as by bribery 11 to punish — *vi.* 1 to become fixed 2 [Colloq. or Dial.] to prepare or intend — *n.* 1 the position of a ship, etc. determined from the bearings of two known positions 2 [Colloq.] a predicament 3 [Slang] a contest, etc. that has been fixed 4 [Slang] an injection of a narcotic by an addict —**fix up** [Colloq.] 1 to repair 2 to arrange; set in order —**fix′able** *adj.* —**fix′er** *n.*

fixa·tion (fiks ā′shən) *n.* 1 a fixing or being fixed 2 an obsession 3 a remaining at an early stage of psychosexual development

fixa·tive (fiks′ə tiv) *adj.* that is able or tends to make permanent, prevent fading, etc. — *n.* a fixative substance

fixed (fikst) *adj.* 1 firmly in place 2 established; settled 3 resolute; unchanging 4 persistent /a *fixed* idea/ —**fix·edly** (fiks′id lē) *adv.*

fix·ings (fiks′iŋz′) *n.pl.* [Colloq.] accessories or trimmings

fix·ity (fiks′i tē) *n.* the quality or state of being fixed or steady

fix·ture (fiks′chər) *n.* [see FIX] 1 anything firmly in place 2 any attached piece of equipment in a house, etc. 3 a person long established in a job, etc.

fizz (fiz) *n.* ⟦? akin to fol.⟧ 1 a hissing, sputtering sound 2 an effervescent drink — *vi.* 1 to make a hissing sound 2 to effervesce

fiz·zle (fiz′əl) *vi.* **-zled, -zling** ⟦< ME⟧ 1 FIZZ (*vi.* 1) 2 [Colloq.] to fail, esp. after a good start — *n.* 1 a hissing sound 2 [Colloq.] a failure

fl. 1 floor 2 ⟦L *floruit*⟧ (he or she) flourished 3 fluid

flab (flab) *n.* ⟦< FLABBY⟧ [Colloq.] sagging flesh

flab·ber·gast (flab′ər gast′) *vt.* ⟦18th-c. slang < ?⟧ to dumbfound

flabby (flab′ē) *adj.* **-bier, -bi·est** ⟦< FLAP⟧ 1 limp and soft 2 weak —**flab′bily** *adv.* —**flab′bi·ness** *n.*

flac·cid (flak′sid, flas′id) *adj.* ⟦< L *flaccus*⟧ soft and limp; flabby

flack (flak) *n.* ⟦< ?⟧ [Slang] PRESS AGENT —**flack′ery** *n.*

fla·con (flä kôn′) *n.* ⟦Fr⟧ a small flask with a stopper, as for perfume

flag[1] (flag) *n.* ⟦< FLAG[4], to flutter⟧ a cloth with colors, patterns, etc. used as a symbol of a nation, etc., or as a signal — *vt.* **flagged, flag′ging** to signal with or as with a flag; esp., to signal to stop: often with *down*

flag[2] (flag) *n.* ⟦< ON *flaga*, slab of stone⟧ FLAGSTONE

flag[3] (flag) *n.* ⟦ME *flagge*⟧ any of various irises, or a flower or leaf of one

flag[4] (flag) *vi.* **flagged, flag′ging** ⟦prob. < ON *flǫgra*, to flutter⟧ 1 to become limp; droop 2 to grow weak or tired

flag·el·late (flaj′ə lāt′) *vt.* **-lat′ed, -lat′ing** ⟦< L *flagellum*, a whip⟧ to whip; flog —**flag′el·la′tion** *n.*

fla·gel·lum (flə jel′əm) *n., pl.* **-la** (-ə) or **-lums** ⟦L, a whip⟧ a whiplike part of some cells, as of bacteria or protozoans, used as for moving about

flagon (flag′ən) *n.* ⟦< LL *flasco*⟧ a container for liquids, with a handle, narrow neck, spout, and, often, a lid

flag′pole′ *n.* a pole on which a flag is raised and flown Also **flag′staff′**

fla·grant (flā′grənt) *adj.* ⟦< L *flagrare*, to blaze⟧ glaringly bad; outrageous —**fla′grancy** (-grən sē) or **fla′grance** *n.* —**fla′grantly** *adv.*

flag′ship′ *n.* 1 the ship that carries the commander of a fleet or other large unit 2 the largest or most important member or part, as of a group

flag′stone′ *n.* a flat paving stone

flail (flāl) *n.* ⟦< L *flagellum*, a whip⟧ a farm tool for threshing grain by hand — *vt., vi.* 1 to thresh with a flail 2 to beat 3 to move (one's arms) like flails

flair (fler) *n.* ⟦< L *fragrare*, to smell⟧ 1 a natural talent; aptitude 2 [Colloq.] a sense of style; dash

flak (flak) *n.* ⟦Ger acronym⟧ 1 the fire of antiaircraft guns 2 [Colloq.] strong criticism   Also **flack**

flake (flāk) *n.* ⟦< Scand⟧ 1 a small, thin mass 2 a piece split off; chip — *vt., vi.* **flaked, flak′ing** 1 to form into

---

◼ THESAURUS ◼

fist *n.* clenched hand, clenched fist, hand, clutch, clasp, grasp, grip, hold.

fit[1] *a.* **1** [Appropriate by nature] suitable, proper, fitting, fit, likely, expedient, appropriate, convenient, timely, opportune, feasible, practicable, wise, advantageous, favorable, preferable, beneficial, desirable, adequate, tasteful, becoming, agreeable, seasonable, due, rightful, decent, equitable, legitimate, harmonious, pertinent, according, relevant, in keeping, consistent, applicable, compatible, admissible, concurrent, to the point, adapted to, fitted, suited, calculated, prepared, qualified, competent, matched, ready-made, accommodated, right, happy, lucky, cut out for*.—*Ant.* unfit, unseemly, inappropriate. **2** [In good physical condition] trim, competent, robust; see HEALTHY.

fit[1] *v.* **1** [To be suitable in character] agree, suit, accord, harmonize, apply, belong, conform, consist, fit right in, be in keeping, parallel, relate, concur, match, correspond, be comfortable, respond, have its place, answer the purpose, meet, click*.—*Ant.* OPPOSE, disagree, clash. **2** [To make suitable] arrange, alter, adapt; see ADJUST 1.

fit[2] *n.* **1** [Sudden attack of disease] muscular convulsion, rage, spasm, seizure, stroke, epileptic attack, paroxysm, spell*; see also ILLNESS 1. **2** [Transitory spell of action or feeling] impulsive action, burst, rush, outbreak, torrent, tantrum, mood, outburst, whimsy, huff, rage, spell. — **have** (or **throw**) **a fit*** become angry, lose one's temper, give vent to emotion; see RAGE 1.

fitness *n.* appropriateness, suitability, propriety, expediency, convenience, adequacy, correspondence, decency, decorum, harmony, keeping, consistency, applicability, compatibility, rightness, timeliness, adaptation, qualification, accommodation, competence.

fix *v.* **1** [To make firm] plant, implant, secure; see FASTEN. **2** [To prepare a meal] prepare, heat, get ready; see COOK. **3** [To put in order] correct, improve, settle, put into shape, reform, patch, rejuvenate, touch up, revive, refresh, renew, renovate, rebuild, make compatible, clean, align, adapt, mend, adjust. — **fix up** fix, mend, rehabilitate; see REPAIR.

fixed *a.* **1** [Firm] solid, rigid, immovable; see FIRM 1. **2** [Repaired] rebuilt, in order, timed, synchro-

nized, adjusted, settled, mended, rearranged, adapted, corrected, restored, renewed, improved, patched up, put together, in working order. **3** [*Prearranged] predesigned, put-up*, set-up*; see PLANNED.

fixings *n.* parts, components, constituents; see INGREDIENTS.

fixture *n.* convenience, gas appliance, electric appliance; see APPLIANCE.

fizz *n.* hissing, sputtering, bubbling; see NOISE 1.

fizzle* *n.* disappointment, fiasco, defeat; see FAILURE 1.

flabby *a.* limp, tender, soft; see FAT.

flag[1] *n.* banner, standard, colors; see EMBLEM.

flag[1] *v.* signal, wave, give a sign to; see SIGNAL.

flagrant *a.* notorious, disgraceful, infamous; see OUTRAGEOUS.

flair *n.* talent, aptitude, gift; see ABILITY.

flake *n.* scale, cell, sheet, wafer, peel, skin, slice, sliver, leaf, shaving, plate, section, scab.

flake *v.* scale, peel, sliver, shed, drop, chip, scab, slice, pare, trim, wear away.

flakes 2 to peel off in flakes —**flak′y, -i·er, -i·est,** *adj.* — **flak′i·ness** *n.*

flam·bé (fläm bā′) *adj.* ⟦Fr⟧ served with a sauce of flaming brandy, rum, etc. — *n.* a dessert so served

flam·boy·ant (flam boi′ənt) *adj.* ⟦Fr < L *flamma,* a flame⟧ 1 flamelike or brilliant 2 too showy or ornate — **flam·boy′ance** *n.* —**flam·boy′ant·ly** *adv.*

flame (flām) *n.* ⟦< L *flamma*⟧ 1 the burning gas of a fire, appearing as a tongue of light 2 the state of burning with a blaze 3 a thing like a flame 4 an intense emotion 5 a sweetheart — *vi.* **flamed, flam′ing** 1 to burst into flame 2 to grow red or hot 3 to become excited

fla·menco (flə meŋ′kō) *n.* ⟦Sp⟧ a Spanish gypsy style of dance or music

flame′out′ *n.* a failure of combustion in a jet engine during flight

flame′throw′er *n.* a weapon that shoots flaming oil, napalm, etc.

fla·min·go (flə miŋ′gō′) *n., pl.* **-gos′** or **-goes′** ⟦Port⟧ a tropical wading bird with long legs and pink or red feathers

flam·mable (flam′ə bəl) *adj.* easily set on fire; that will burn readily or quickly —**flam′mabil′i·ty** *n.*

flange (flanj) *n.* ⟦< ? ME⟧ a projecting rim on a wheel, etc., as to hold it in place or give it strength

flank (flaŋk) *n.* ⟦< OFr *flanc*⟧ 1 the side of an animal between the ribs and the hip 2 the side of anything 3 *Mil.* the right or left side of a formation — *vt.* 1 to be at the side of 2 *Mil.* to attack, or pass around, the side of (enemy troops)

flan·nel (flan′əl) *n.* ⟦prob. < Welsh *gwlan,* wool⟧ 1 a loosely woven cloth of wool or cotton 2 *[pl.]* trousers, etc. made of this

flan·nel·ette or **flan·nel·et** (flan′əl et′) *n.* a soft, napped cotton cloth

flap (flap) *n.* ⟦ME *flappe*⟧ 1 anything flat and broad hanging loose at one end 2 the motion or sound of a swinging flap 3 [Archaic] a slap 4 [Colloq.] a commotion; stir — *vt.* **flapped, flap′ping** 1 to slap 2 to move back and forth or up and down, as wings

flap′jack′ *n.* a pancake

flap′per *n.* 1 one that flaps 2 [Colloq.] in the 1920′s, a bold, unconventional young woman

flare (fler) *vi.* **flared, flar′ing** ⟦ME *fleare* < ?⟧ 1 a) to blaze brightly b) to burn unsteadily 2 to burst out suddenly, as in anger: often with *up* or *out* 3 to curve outward, as a bell′s rim — *n.* 1 a bright, unsteady blaze 2 a brightly flaming light for signaling, etc. 3 an outburst, as of emotion 4 a curving outward

flare′-up′ *n.* a sudden outburst of flame or of anger, trouble, etc.

flash (flash) *vi.* ⟦ME *flashen,* to splash⟧ 1 to send out a sudden, brief light 2 to sparkle 3 to come or pass suddenly — *vt.* 1 to cause to flash 2 to send (news, etc.) swiftly — *n.* 1 a sudden, brief light 2 a brief moment 3 a sudden, brief display 4 a brief news report sent by radio, etc. 5 a gaudy display — *adj.* happening swiftly or suddenly —**flash′er** *n.*

flash′back′ *n.* an interruption in the continuity of a story, etc. by telling or showing an earlier episode

flash′bulb′ *n.* an electric light bulb giving a brief, dazzling light, for taking photographs

flash′cube′ *n.* a small, rotating cube with a flashbulb in each of its four sides

flash′-for′ward *n.* an interruption in the continuity of a story, etc. by telling or showing a future episode

flash′ing *n.* sheets of metal used to weatherproof roof joints or edges

flash′light′ *n.* a portable electric light

flash point the lowest temperature at which vapor, as of an oil, will ignite with a flash

flash′y *adj.* **-i·er, -i·est** 1 dazzling 2 gaudy; showy — **flash′i·ness** *n.*

flask (flask) *n.* ⟦< L *flasca,* bottle⟧ 1 any bottle-shaped container used in laboratories, etc. 2 a small, flat pocket container for liquor, etc.

flat¹ (flat) *adj.* **flat′ter, flat′test** ⟦< ON *flatr*⟧ 1 having a smooth, level surface 2 lying spread out 3 broad, even, and thin 4 absolute *[a flat denial]* 5 not fluctuating *[a flat rate]* 6 tasteless; insipid 7 not interesting 8 emptied of air *[a flat tire]* 9 without gloss *[flat paint]* 10 *Music* a) lower in pitch by a half step b) below true pitch — *adv.* 1 in a flat manner or position 2 exactly 3 *Music* below true pitch — *n.* 1 anything flat, esp. a surface, part, or expanse 2 a deflated tire 3 *Music* a) a note one half step below another b) the symbol (♭) for this — *vt.* **flat′ted, flat′ting** *Music* to make flat — *vi.* to sing or play below true pitch —**fall flat** to fail in the desired effect —**flat′ly** *adv.* — **flat′ness** *n.* —**flat′tish** *adj.*

flat² (flat) *n.* ⟦< Scot dial. *flet,* floor⟧ [Chiefly Brit.] an apartment or suite of rooms

flat′bed′ *n.* a truck, trailer, etc. having a bed or platform without sides or stakes

flat′boat′ *n.* a flat-bottomed boat for carrying freight on rivers, etc.

flat′car′ *n.* a railroad freight car without sides or a roof

flat′fish′ *n., pl.* **-fish′** or (for different species) **-fish′es** a fish having both eyes on the same side of a very flat body

flat′foot′ *n.* 1 a condition of the foot in which the instep arch is flattened 2 *pl.* **-foots′** or **-feet′** a policeman — **flat′-foot′ed** *adj.*

flat′i′ron *n.* an iron for clothes

flat′-out′ (-out′) *adj.* [Colloq.] 1 at full speed, with maximum effort, etc. 2 absolute; thorough

flat·ten (flat′′n) *vt., vi.* to make or become flat or flatter

flat·ter (flat′ər) *vt.* ⟦< OFr *flater,* to smooth⟧ 1 to praise insincerely 2 to try to please, as by praise 3 to make seem more attractive than is so 4 to gratify the vanity of —**flat′-terer** *n.* —**flat′ter·ing·ly** *adv.* —**flat′tery** *n.*

flat′top′ *n.* [Slang] an aircraft carrier

flatu·lent (flach′ə lənt) *adj.* ⟦see fol.⟧ 1 having or producing gas in the stomach or intestines 2 pompous —**flat′u·lence** *n.*

fla·tus (flāt′əs) *n.* ⟦L < *flare,* to blow⟧ gas in, or expelled from, the stomach or intestines

flat′ware′ *n.* knives, forks, and spoons

flat′worm′ *n.* any of various worms with flat bodies, as the tapeworm

---

◼ THESAURUS ◼

flamboyant *a.* baroque, bombastic, ostentatious; see ORNATE.

flame *n.* blaze, flare, flash; see FIRE 1.

flame *v.* blaze, oxidize, flare up; see BURN.

flaming *a.* blazing, ablaze, fiery; see BURNING.

flannel *n.* woolen, cotton flannel, flannelette; see WOOL.

flap *n.* fold, tab, lapel, fly, cover, pendant, drop, tail, appendage, tag, accessory, apron, skirt, strip, wing.

flap *v.* flutter, flash, swing; see WAVE 1.

flare *n.* glare, brief blaze, spark; see FLASH.

flare *v.* blaze, glow, burn; see FLASH. —**flare up** 1 [*Said of persons*] lose one′s temper, rant, seethe; see RAGE 1. 2 [*Said of fire*] glow, burst into flame, blaze; see BURN.

flash *n.* glimmer, sparkle, glitter, glisten, gleam, beam, blaze, flicker, flame, glare, burst, impulse, vision, dazzle, shimmer, shine, glow, twin-

kle, twinkling, phosphorescence, reflection, radiation, ray, luster, spark, streak, stream, illumination, incandescence.

flash *v.* glimmer, sparkle, glitter, glisten, gleam, beam, blaze, flame, glare, dazzle, shimmer, shine, glow, twinkle, reflect, radiate, shoot out beams, flicker; see also SHINE 1, 2.

flashlight *n.* flash lamp, spotlight, torch; see LIGHT 1.

flashy *a.* gaudy, showy, ostentatious; see ORNATE.

flask *n.* decanter, jug, canteen; see BOTTLE.

flat¹ *a.* 1 [Lying in a smooth plane] level, even, smooth, spread out, extended, prostrate, horizontal, low, on a level, fallen, level with the ground, prone.—*Ant.* ROUGH, raised, uneven. 2 [Lacking savor] unseasoned, insipid, flavorless; see TASTELESS 1.

flatten *v.* level off, even out, smooth,

spread out, depress, squash, smash, level, even, knock down, wear down, beat down, fell, floor, ground, smooth, roll out, straighten, deflate.—*Ant.* RAISE, elevate, inflate.

flattened *a.* leveled, depressed, smoothed; see FLAT 1.

flatter *v.* overpraise, adulate, glorify; see PRAISE 1.

flatterer *n.* parasite, toady, sycophant, flunky, slave, puppet, groveler, sniveler, yes man*, bootlicker*, apple polisher*, doormat*.

flattering *a.* pleasing, favorable, unduly favorable; see COMPLIMENTARY.

flattery *n.* adulation, compliments, blandishment, sycophancy, applause, false praise, commendation, tribute, gratification, pretty speeches, soft words, fawning, blarney, soft soap*, hokum*, mush*.—*Ant.* HATRED, criticism, censure.

flaunt (flônt) *vi.* ⟦? < dial. *flant*, to strut⟧ to make a gaudy or defiant display — *vt.* **1** to show off proudly or defiantly **2** FLOUT: usage objected to by many —**flaunt′ing·ly** *adv.*

flau·tist (flôt′ist, flout′-) *n.* ⟦< It⟧ *var. of* FLUTIST

fla·vor (flā′vər) *n.* ⟦ult. < L *flare*, to blow⟧ **1** that quality of a substance that is a mixing of its characteristic taste and smell **2** flavoring **3** characteristic quality — *vt.* to give flavor to Brit. sp. **fla′vour** —**fla′vor·ful** *adj.* —**fla′vor·less** *adj.*

fla·vor·ing *n.* an essence, extract, etc. that adds flavor to food or drink

flaw (flô) *n.* ⟦ME, a flake, splinter⟧ **1** a crack, as in a gem **2** a defect; fault —**flaw′less** *adj.* —**flaw′lessly** *adv.* —**flaw′less·ness** *n.*

flax (flaks) *n.* ⟦< OE *fleax*⟧ **1** a slender, erect plant with delicate blue flowers: its seed (**flax′seed**) is used to make linseed oil **2** the fibers of this plant, which are spun into linen thread

flaxen (flak′sən) *adj.* **1** of or made of flax **2** pale-yellow

flay (flā) *vt.* ⟦OE *flean*⟧ **1** to strip off the skin of, as by whipping **2** to criticize harshly

flea (flē) *n.* ⟦OE *fleah*⟧ a small, wingless jumping insect that is a bloodsucking parasite as an adult

flea market an outdoor bazaar dealing mainly in cheap, secondhand goods

fleck (flek) *n.* ⟦ON *flekkr*⟧ a spot, speck, or flake — *vt.* to spot; speckle

fled (fled) *vi., vt. pt. & pp. of* FLEE

fledg·ling (flej′liŋ) *n.* ⟦< ME *flegge*, ready to fly⟧ **1** a young bird just able to fly **2** a young, inexperienced person Also, chiefly Brit., **fledge′ling**

flee (flē) *vi.* **fled, flee′ing** ⟦OE *fleon*⟧ **1** to go swiftly or escape, as from danger **2** to vanish — *vt.* to run away or try to escape from

fleece (flēs) *n.* ⟦OE *fleos*⟧ **1** the wool covering a sheep or similar animal **2** a soft, warm, napped fabric — *vt.* **fleeced, fleec′ing 1** to shear the fleece from **2** to swindle —**fleec′er** *n.*

fleecy (flēs′ē) *adj.* -i·er, -i·est of or like fleece; soft and light —**fleec′i·ness** *n.*

fleet¹ (flēt) *n.* ⟦OE *fleot*⟧ **1** a number of warships under one command **2** any group of ships, trucks, etc. under one control

fleet² (flēt) *adj.* ⟦< OE *fleotan*, to float⟧ swift; rapid — **fleet′ness** *n.*

fleet′ing *adj.* passing swiftly —**fleet′ingly** *adv.* —**fleet′ing·ness** *n.*

Flem·ish (flem′ish) *n.* the West Germanic language of Flanders (N Belgium) — *adj.* of Flanders, its people, or their language

flesh (flesh) *n.* ⟦OE *flæsc*⟧ **1** the soft substance of the body; esp., the muscular tissue **2** meat **3** the pulpy part of fruits and vegetables **4** the body as distinct from the soul **5** all humankind **6** yellowish pink —**in the flesh 1** alive **2** in person —**one's (own) flesh and blood** one's close relatives —**flesh′y, -i·er, -i·est,** *adj.*

flesh′ly *adj.* -lier, -li·est **1** of the body; corporeal **2** sensual

flesh′pot′ *n.* a place where luxuries and sensual pleasures are provided: usually used in pl.

fleur-de-lis (flur′də lē′) *n., pl.* **fleurs-de-lis** (flur′də lēz′) ⟦< OFr *flor de lis*, lit., flower of the lily⟧ a lilylike emblem: the coat of arms of the former French royal family

flew (flōō) *vi., vt. pt. of* FLY¹

flex (fleks) *vt., vi.* ⟦< L *flectere*, to bend⟧ **1** to bend (an arm, knee, etc.) **2** to shorten and thicken (a muscle) in action

flex·ible (flek′sə bəl) *adj.* **1** able to bend without breaking; pliant **2** easily influenced **3** adjustable to change —**flex′ibil′ity** *n.*

flex·time (fleks′tīm′) *n.* a system allowing individual employees some flexibility in choosing when they work

flib·ber·ti·gib·bet (flib′ər ti jib′it) *n.* ⟦< ?⟧ a frivolous, flighty person

flick¹ (flik) *n.* ⟦echoic⟧ a light, quick stroke — *vt.* to strike, remove, etc. with a light, quick stroke

flick² (flik) *n.* ⟦< fol.⟧ [Slang] a movie —**the flicks** [Slang] a showing of a movie

flicker (flik′ər) *vi.* ⟦OE *flicorian*⟧ **1** to move with a quick, light, wavering motion **2** to burn or shine unsteadily — *n.* **1** a flickering **2** a dart of flame or light

flier (flī′ər) *n.* **1** a thing that flies **2** an aviator **3** a bus, train, etc. with a fast schedule **4** a widely distributed handbill **5** [Colloq.] a reckless gamble

flight¹ (flīt) *n.* ⟦OE *flyht*⟧ **1** the act, manner, or power of flying **2** the distance flown **3** a group of things flying together **4** an airplane scheduled to fly a certain trip **5** a trip by airplane **6** a soaring above the ordinary [a *flight* of fancy] **7** a set of stairs, as between landings

flight² (flīt) *n.* ⟦< OE *fleon*, flee⟧ a fleeing from or as from danger

flight attendant an airplane attendant who sees to passengers' comfort and safety

flight′less *adj.* not able to fly

flight′y *adj.* -i·er, -i·est **1** given to sudden whims; frivolous **2** easily excited, upset, etc. —**flight′i·ness** *n.*

flimsy (flim′zē) *adj.* -sier, -si·est ⟦< ?⟧ **1** easily broken or damaged; frail **2** ineffectual [a *flimsy* excuse] —**flim′sily** *adv.* —**flim′si·ness** *n.*

flinch (flinch) *vi.* ⟦< OFr *flenchir*⟧ to draw back from a blow or anything difficult or painful — *n.* a flinching

fling (fliŋ) *vt.* **flung, fling′ing** ⟦< ON *flengja*, to whip⟧ **1** to throw, esp. with force; hurl **2** to put abruptly or violently **3** to move (one's arms, legs, etc.) suddenly — *n.* **1** a flinging **2** a brief time of wild pleasures **3** a spirited dance **4** [Colloq.] a try

flint (flint) *n.* ⟦OE⟧ a very hard, siliceous rock, usually gray, that produces sparks when struck against steel — **flint′y, -i·er, -i·est,** *adj.*

flip¹ (flip) *vt.* **flipped, flip′ping** ⟦echoic⟧ **1** to toss with a quick jerk; flick **2** to snap (a coin) into the air with the thumb **3** to turn or turn over — *vi.* **1** to move jerkily **2** [Slang] to lose self-control — *n.* a flipping —**flip one's lid (or wig)** [Slang] to go berserk

flip² (flip) *adj.* **flip′per, flip′pest** [Colloq.] flippant

flip′-flop′ (-fläp′) *n.* **1** an acrobatic spring backward from feet to hands to feet **2** an abrupt reversal, as of opinion

flaunt *v.* vaunt, display, brandish; see BOAST.

flaunting *a.* gaudy, ostentatious, pretentious; see ORNATE.

flavor *n.* taste, savor, tang, relish, smack, twang, gusto. *Individual flavors include the following:* tartness, sweetness, acidity, saltiness, spiciness, pungency, piquancy, astringency, bitterness, sourness, pepperiness, hotness, gaminess, greasiness, fishy taste.

flavor *v.* season, salt, pepper, spice, give a tang to, make tasty, bring out a flavor in, put in flavoring.

flavoring *n.* essence, extract, seasoning, spice, additive, condiment, sauce, relish; see also HERB, SPICE.

flavorless *a.* insipid, vapid, mawkish; see TASTELESS 1.

flaw *n.* defect, imperfection, stain; see BLEMISH.

flawless *a.* faultless, sound, impeccable; see PERFECT.

flea *n.* dog flea, sand flea, flea louse; see INSECT.

fleck *n.* mite, speck, dot; see BIT 1.

flee *v.* desert, escape, run; see RETREAT.

fleet¹ *n.* armada, naval force, task force; see NAVY.

flesh *n.* meat, fat, muscle, brawn, tissue, cells, flesh and blood, protoplasm, plasm, plasma, body parts, heart, insides*. —**one's (own) flesh and blood** family, kindred, kin; see RELATIVE.

fleshy *a.* obese, plump, corpulent; see FAT.

flexibility *n.* pliancy, plasticity, flexibleness, pliableness, suppleness, elasticity, extensibility, limberness, litheness.

flexible *a.* limber, lithe, supple, plastic, elastic, bending, malleable, pliable, soft, extensible, spongy, tractable, moldable, yielding, formable, bendable, formative, impressionable, like putty, like wax, adjustable, stretchable.—*Ant.* STIFF, hard, rigid.

flicker *v.* sparkle, twinkle, glitter; see FLASH, SHINE 1.

flight¹,² *n.* **1** [Act of remaining aloft] soaring, winging, flying, journey by air, avigation. **2** [Travel by air] aerial navigation, aeronautics, flying, gliding, space flight, air transport, aviation. **3** [Act of fleeing] fleeing, running away, retreating; see RETREAT 1. **4** [Stairs] steps, staircase, stairway; see STAIRS.

flighty *a.* capricious, fickle, whimsical; see CHANGING.

flimsy *a.* slight, infirm, frail, weak, unsubstantial, inadequate, defective, wobbly, fragile, makeshift, decrepit; see also POOR 2.

flinch *v.* start, shrink back, blench; see COWER.

fling *n.* indulgence, party, good time; see CELEBRATION.

fling *v.* toss, sling, dump; see THROW 1.

flippancy *n.* impertinence, impudence, sauciness; see RUDENESS.

flip'pant (-ənt) *adj.* ⟦prob. < FLIP¹⟧ frivolous and disrespectful; saucy —**flip'pancy,** *pl.* **-cies,** *n.* —**flip'pantly** *adv.*

flip'per (-ər) *n.* ⟦< FLIP¹⟧ 1 a broad, flat limb adapted for swimming, as in seals 2 a paddlelike rubber device worn on each foot by skin divers, etc.

flirt (flʉrt) *vt.* ⟦< ?⟧ to move jerkily /the bird *flirted* its tail/ — *vi.* 1 to pay amorous attention to someone, without serious intentions 2 to trifle or toy /to *flirt* with an idea/ — *n.* 1 a quick, jerky movement 2 one who flirts with others

flir·tation (flər tā'shən) *n.* a frivolous love affair —**flir·ta'tious** *adj.*

flit (flit) *vi.* **flit'ted, flit'ting** ⟦< ON *flytja*⟧ to move lightly and rapidly

float (flōt) *n.* ⟦< OE *flota*, a ship⟧ 1 anything that stays on the surface of a liquid, as a raft, a cork on a fishing line, etc. 2 a floating ball, etc. that regulates a valve, as in a water tank 3 a low, flat vehicle decorated for exhibit in a parade — *vi.* 1 to stay on the surface of a liquid 2 to drift easily on water, in air, etc. 3 to move about aimlessly — *vt.* 1 to cause to float 2 to put into circulation /to *float* a bond issue/ 3 to arrange for (a loan) —**float'er** *n.*

flock (fläk) *n.* ⟦OE *flocc*⟧ 1 a group of certain animals, as sheep, birds, etc., living or feeding together 2 any group, esp. a large one — *vi.* to assemble or travel in a flock or crowd

flock·ing (fläk'iŋ) *n.* ⟦< L *floccus*, tuft of wool⟧ 1 tiny fibers of wool, rayon, etc. applied to a fabric, wallpaper, etc. as a velvetlike surface: also **flock** 2 such a fabric, etc.

floe (flō) *n.* ⟦? < Norw *flo*, layer⟧ ICE FLOE

flog (fläg, flôg) *vt.* **flogged, flog'ging** ⟦? < L *flagellare*, to whip⟧ to beat with a stick, whip, etc. —**flog'ger** *n.*

flood (flud) *n.* ⟦OE *flod*⟧ 1 an overflowing of water on an area normally dry 2 the rising of the tide 3 a great outpouring, as of words — *vt.* 1 to cover or fill, as with a flood 2 to put too much water, fuel, etc. on or in — *vi.* 1 to gush out in a flood 2 to become flooded —**the Flood** *Bible* the great flood in Noah's time

flood'light' *n.* 1 a lamp that casts a broad beam of bright light 2 such a beam of light — *vt.* **-light'ed** or **-lit', -light'ing** to illuminate by a floodlight

flood tide the rising tide

floor (flôr) *n.* ⟦OE *flor*⟧ 1 the inside bottom surface of a room 2 the bottom surface of anything /the ocean *floor*/ 3 a story in a building 4 the right to speak in an assembly — *vt.* 1 to furnish with a floor 2 to knock down 3 [Colloq.] a) to defeat b) to flabbergast; astound

floor'board' *n.* 1 a board in a floor 2 the floor of an automobile, etc.

floor exercise any gymnastic exercise done without apparatus

floor'ing *n.* 1 a floor or floors 2 material for making a floor

floor show a show presenting singers, dancers, etc., as in a nightclub

flop (fläp) *vt.* **flopped, flop'ping** ⟦var. of FLAP⟧ to flap or throw noisily and clumsily — *vi.* 1 to move, drop, or flap

around loosely or clumsily 2 [Colloq.] to fail — *n.* 1 the act or sound of flopping 2 [Colloq.] a failure —**flop'py, -pier, -pi·est,** *adj.*

flop'house' *n.* [Colloq.] a cheap hotel

floppy disk a small, flexible computer disk for storing data

flora (flôr'ə) *n.* ⟦L < *flos*, a flower⟧ the plants of a specified region or time

flo'ral (-əl) *adj.* of or like flowers

flo·res·cence (flō res'əns) *n.* ⟦< L *flos*, a flower⟧ a blooming or flowering —**flo·res'cent** *adj.*

florid (flôr'id) *adj.* ⟦< L *flos*, a flower⟧ 1 ruddy: said of the complexion 2 gaudy; showy; ornate

florin (flôr'in) *n.* ⟦< L *flos*, a flower⟧ any of various European or South African silver or gold coins

flo·rist (flôr'ist) *n.* ⟦< L *flos*, a flower⟧ one who grows or sells flowers

floss (flôs, fläs) *n.* ⟦ult. < L *floccus*, tuft of wool⟧ 1 the short, downy waste fibers of silk 2 a soft, loosely twisted thread or yarn, as of silk, for embroidery 3 a substance like this 4 DENTAL FLOSS — *vt.,* *vi.* to clean (the teeth) with dental floss —**floss'y, -i·er, -i·est,** *adj.*

flo·tation (flō tā'shən) *n.* the act or condition of floating

flo·tilla (flō til'ə) *n.* ⟦Sp, dim. of *flota*, a fleet⟧ 1 a small fleet 2 a fleet of boats or small ships

flot·sam (flät'səm) *n.* ⟦< MDu *vloten*, to float⟧ the wreckage of a ship or its cargo floating at sea: chiefly in **flotsam and jetsam**

flounce¹ (flouns) *vi.* **flounced, flounc'ing** ⟦< ? Scand⟧ to move with quick, flinging motions of the body, as in anger — *n.* a flouncing

flounce² (flouns) *n.* ⟦< OFr *froncir*, to wrinkle⟧ a wide ruffle sewn to a skirt, sleeve, etc. —**flounc'y, -i·er, -i·est,** *adj.*

floun·der¹ (floun'dər) *vi.* ⟦< ? FOUNDER⟧ 1 to struggle awkwardly, as in deep mud 2 to speak or act in an awkward, confused manner

floun·der² (floun'dər) *n.* ⟦< Scand⟧ any of various flatfishes caught for food, as the halibut

flour (flour) *n.* ⟦orig., flower (i.e., best) of meal⟧ 1 a fine, powdery substance produced by grinding and sifting grain, esp. wheat 2 any finely powdered substance —**flour'y** *adj.*

flour·ish (flʉr'ish) *vi.* ⟦< L *flos*, a flower⟧ 1 to grow vigorously; thrive 2 to be at the peak of development, etc. — *vt.* to brandish (a sword, etc.) — *n.* 1 anything done in a showy way 2 a brandishing 3 decorative lines in writing 4 a musical fanfare

flout (flout) *vt.,* *vi.* ⟦< ? ME *flouten*, play the flute⟧ to mock or scoff — *n.* a scornful act or remark —**flout'er** *n.*

flow (flō) *vi.* ⟦OE *flowan*⟧ 1 to move as a liquid does 2 to move gently and smoothly 3 to pour out 4 to issue; proceed 5 to hang loose /*flowing* hair/ 6 to be plentiful — *n.* 1 a flowing 2 the rate of flow 3 anything that flows 4 the rising of the tide

flow'chart' *n.* a diagram showing steps in a sequence of operations, as in manufacturing

flower (flou'ər) *n.* ⟦< L *flos*⟧ 1 the seed-producing structure of a flowering plant; blossom 2 a plant cultivated for its blossoms 3 the best or finest part — *vi.* 1 to produce blossoms 2 to reach the best stage —**in flower** flowering

---

THESAURUS

flippant *a.* impudent, saucy, smart; see RUDE 2.

flirt *n.* coquette, tease, siren; see LOVER.

flirt *v.* coquet, make advances, make eyes at; see SEDUCE.

float *n.* buoy, air cell, air cushion, lifesaver, bobber, cork, raft, diving platform, life preserver.

float *v.* waft, stay afloat, swim; see DRIFT.

floating *a.* buoyant, hollow, unsinkable, lighter-than-water, light, swimming, inflated, sailing, soaring, volatile, loose, free.—*Ant.* HEAVY, submerged, sunk.

flock *n.* group, pack, litter; see HERD.

flock *v.* throng, congregate, crowd; see GATHER 1.

flood *n.* deluge, surge, tide, high tide, overflow, torrent, wave, flood tide, tidal flood, tidal flow, inundation.

flood *v.* inundate, swamp, overflow, deluge, submerge, immerse, brim over.

floor *n.* 1 [The lower limit of a room]

floorboards, deck, flagstones, tiles, planking, ground, carpet, rug, linoleum. 2 [The space in a building between two floors] story, stage, landing, level, flat, basement, cellar, ground floor, ground story, lower story, first floor, mezzanine, upper story, downstairs, upstairs, loft, attic, garret, penthouse.

flooring *n.* floors, woodwork, oak flooring, hardwood flooring, tile, flagstones, boards, cement, floor covering, linoleum.

flop *v.* 1 [To move with little control] wobble, teeter, stagger, flounder, wriggle, squirm, stumble, tumble, totter, flounce, quiver, flap, wiggle, spin, jerk. 2 [To fall without restraint] tumble, slump, drop; see FALL 1. 3 [*To be a complete failure] founder, fall short, bomb*; see FAIL 1.

flounder¹ *v.* struggle, wallow, blunder; see FLOP 1, TOSS 2.

flour *n.* meal, pulp, powder, grit, bran, starch, wheat germ, white flour, wheat flour, rye flour, potato flour,

barley meal, corn meal, oatmeal, rolled oats, cake flour, pancake flour, soybean flour, soyabean flour, soyflour.

flourish *v.* thrive, increase, wax; see SUCCEED 1.

flourishing *a.* thriving, doing well, growing; see RICH 1, SUCCESSFUL.

flow *n.* current, movement, progress, stream, tide, run, river, flood, ebb, gush, spurt, spout, leakage, dribble, oozing, flux, overflow, issue, discharge, drift, course, draft, downdraft, up-current, wind, breeze.

flow *v.* stream, course, slide, slip, glide, move, progress, run, pass, float, sweep, rush, whirl, surge, roll, swell, ebb, pour out, spurt, squirt, flood, jet, spout, rush, gush, well up, drop, drip, seep, trickle, overflow, spill, run, spew, stream, brim, surge, leak, run out, ooze, splash, pour forth, bubble.

flower *n.* blossom, bud, spray, cluster, shoot, posy, herb, vine, annual, perennial, flowering shrub, potted

flow′er·pot′ *n.* a container in which to grow plants
flow′er·y *adj.* **-i·er, -i·est 1** covered or decorated with flowers **2** full of ornate expressions and fine words — **flow′er·i·ness** *n.*
flown (flōn) *vi., vt. pp. of* FLY¹
flu (flōō) *n.* **1** *short for* INFLUENZA **2** a respiratory or intestinal infection caused by a virus
flub (flub) *vt., vi.* **flubbed, flub′bing** [< ? FL(OP) + (D)UB¹] [Colloq.] to bungle (a job, stroke, etc.) — *n.* [Colloq.] a blunder
fluc·tu·ate (fluk′chōō āt′) *vi.* **-at·ed, -at·ing** [< L *fluctus*, a wave] to be continually varying in an irregular way — **fluc′tua′tion** *n.*
flue (flōō) *n.* [< ? OFr *fluie*, a flowing] a shaft for the passage of smoke, hot air, etc., esp. in a chimney
flu·ent (flōō′ənt) *adj.* [< L *fluere*, to flow] **1** flowing smoothly **2** able to write or speak easily, expressively, etc. — **flu′ency** *n.* — **flu′ently** *adv.*
fluff (fluf) *n.* [? blend of *flue*, soft mass + PUFF] **1** soft, light down **2** a loose, soft mass, as of hair — *vt.* **1** to shake or pat until loose or fluffy **2** to bungle (one's lines), as in acting
fluff′y *adj.* **-i·er, -i·est** soft and light like fluff; feathery
fluid (flōō′id) *adj.* [< L *fluere*, to flow] **1** that can flow as a liquid or gas does **2** that can change rapidly or easily **3** available for investment or as cash — *n.* a liquid or gas — **flu·id′i·ty** *n.* — **flu′id·ly** *adv.*
fluke¹ (flōōk) *n.* [OE *floc*, a flatfish] TREMATODE
fluke² (flōōk) *n.* [< ?] **1** a pointed end of an anchor, which catches in the ground **2** a barb of a harpoon, etc. **3** a lobe of a whale's tail **4** [Colloq.] a stroke of luck
flung (fluŋ) *vt. pt. & pp. of* FLING
flunk (fluŋk) *vt., vi.* [< ?] [Colloq.] to fail, as in a school assignment
flunky (fluŋ′kē) *n., pl.* **-ies** [orig. Scot] **1** orig., a liveried manservant **2** a toady **3** a person with menial tasks   Also **flunk′ey**
fluo·resce (flōō′ə res′, flōō res′) *vi.* **-resced′, -resc′ing** to produce, show, or undergo fluorescence
fluo·res·cence (flōō′ə res′əns, flōō res′-) *n.* [ult. < L *fluor*, flux] **1** the property of producing light when acted upon by radiant energy **2** the production of such light **3** light so produced — **flu′o·res′cent** *adj.*
fluorescent lamp (or **tube**) a glass tube coated on the inside with a fluorescent substance that gives off light (**fluorescent light**) when mercury vapor in the tube is acted upon by a stream of electrons
fluori·date (flôr′ə dāt′, floor′-) *vt.* **-dat·ed, -dat·ing** to add fluorides to (a supply of drinking water) in order to reduce tooth decay — **flu′ori·da′tion** *n.*
fluo·ride (flôr′īd′, floor′īd′) *n.* any of various compounds of fluorine
fluo·rine (flôr′ēn′, -in; floor′-) *n.* [< L *fluor*, flux] a greenish-yellow gaseous chemical element
fluo·rite (flôr′īt′) *n.* [< L *fluor*, flux] calcium fluoride, a transparent, crystalline mineral: the principal source of fluorine
fluoro·car·bon (flôr′ə kär′bən) *n.* any of certain compounds containing carbon, fluorine, and, sometimes, hydrogen
fluoro·scope (flôr′ə skōp′) *n.* a machine for examining

internal structures by viewing the shadows cast on a fluorescent screen by objects through which X-rays are directed
flurry (flur′ē) *n., pl.* **-ries** [< ?] **1** a sudden gust of wind, rain, or snow **2** a sudden commotion — *vt.* **-ried, -ry·ing** to confuse; agitate
flush¹ (flush) *vi.* [blend of FLASH & ME *flusshen*, fly up suddenly] **1** to flow rapidly **2** to blush or glow **3** to be washed out with a sudden flow of water **4** to start up from cover: said of birds — *vi.* **1** to wash out with a sudden flow of water **2** to make blush or glow **3** to excite **4** to drive (birds) from cover — *n.* **1** a rapid flow, as of water **2** a sudden, vigorous growth **3** sudden excitement **4** a blush; glow **5** a sudden feeling of heat, as in a fever — *adj.* **1** well supplied, esp. with money **2** abundant **3** level or even (*with*) **4** direct; full — *adv.* **1** so as to be level **2** directly
flush² (flush) *n.* [< L *fluere*, to flow] a hand of cards all in the same suit
flus·ter (flus′tər) *vt., vi.* [prob. < Scand] to make or become confused — *n.* a being flustered
flute (flōōt) *n.* [< Prov *fläut*] **1** a high-pitched wind instrument consisting of a long, slender tube with finger holes and keys **2** a groove in the shaft of a column, etc. — **flut′ed** *adj.* — **flut′ing** *n.* — **flut′ist** *n.*
flut·ter (flut′ər) *vi.* [< OE *fleotan*, to float] **1** to flap the wings rapidly, without flying **2** to wave, move, or beat rapidly and irregularly — *vt.* to cause to flutter — *n.* **1** a fluttering movement **2** an excited or confused state — **flut′tery** *adj.*
flux (fluks) *n.* [< L *fluere*, to flow] **1** a flowing **2** a continual change **3** a substance used to help metals fuse together, as in soldering
fly¹ (flī) *vi.* **flew, flown, fly′ing** [OE *fleogan*] **1** to move through the air in an aircraft or by using wings, as a bird **2** to wave or float in the air **3** to move or pass swiftly **4** to flee **5** flied, fly′ing *Baseball* to hit a fly — *vt.* **1** to cause to float in the air **2** to operate (an aircraft) **3** to flee from — *n., pl.* **flies 1** a flap that conceals the zipper, etc. in a garment **2** a flap serving as the door of a tent **3** *Baseball* a ball batted high in the air **4** [*pl.*] *Theater* the space above a stage — **fly into** to have a violent outburst of — **let fly (at) 1** to throw (at) **2** to direct a verbal attack (at) — **on the fly** [Colloq.] while in a hurry
fly² (flī) *n., pl.* **flies** [OE *fleoge*] **1** any of a large group of insects with two transparent wings **2** an artificial fly used as a fish lure
fly′able *adj.* suitable for flying
fly′by′ or **fly′-by′** *n., pl.* **-bys′** a flight past a designated point or place by an aircraft or spacecraft
fly′-by-night′ *adj.* financially irresponsible — *n.* an absconding debtor
fly′-by-wire′ *adj.* of a system for controlling an airplane or spacecraft electronically, as by computer
fly′-cast′ *vt.* **-cast′, -cast′ing** to fish by casting artificial flies
fly′er FLIER (esp. senses 1, 2, & 5)
flying buttress a buttress connected with a wall by an arch, serving to resist outward pressure
flying colors notable success

THESAURUS

plant; see also FRUIT. *Common flowers include the following:* daisy, violet, cowslip, jack-in-the-pulpit, goldenrod, orchid, primrose, bluebell, salvia, geranium, begonia, pansy, calendula, forsythia, daffodil, jonquil, crocus, dahlia, zinnia, tulip, iris, lily, petunia, gladiolus, aster, rose, peony, nasturtium, chrysanthemum, poppy, morning-glory, lily of the valley, clematis, buttercup, bougainvillea, dandelion, fuchsia, bridal wreath, lilac, stock, sweet william, bachelor's button, tuberose, bleeding heart, phlox.
flower *v.* open, blossom, bud; see BLOOM.
flowery *a.* elaborate, ornamented, rococo; see ORNATE.
flowing *a.* sweeping, sinuous, spouting, running, gushing, pouring out, rippling, issuing, fluid, tidal, liquid.
fluctuate *v.* vacillate, waver, falter; see HESITATE.
fluctuation *n.* vacillation, variation, inconstancy; see CHANGE 1.

fluency *n.* facility of speech, volubility, command of language; see ELOQUENCE.
fluent *a.* eloquent, voluble, glib, wordy, smooth, talkative, smooth-spoken, garrulous, verbose, chatty, argumentative, articulate, vocal, cogent, persuasive, silver-tongued*, having the gift of gab*.—*Ant.* DUMB, tongue-tied, stammering.
fluffy *a.* fleecy, fuzzy, lacy; see SOFT 1.
fluid *a.* liquid, fluent, flowing, running, watery, molten, liquefied, juicy.—*Ant.* STIFF, solid, frozen.
fluid *n.* liquor, vapor, solution; see LIQUID.
flunk *v.* miss, drop, have to repeat; see FAIL 1.
flute *n.* pipe, piccolo, wind instrument, fife, panpipe, recorder; see also MUSICAL INSTRUMENT.
flutter *v.* flap, ripple, wiggle; see WAVE 1, 3.
fly¹ *v.* **1** [To pass through the air] wing, soar, float, glide, remain aloft,

take flight, take wing, hover, sail, swoop, dart, drift, flutter, circle. **2** [To move swiftly] rush, dart, flee; see SPEED. **3** [To flee from danger] retreat, hide, withdraw; see ESCAPE. **4** [To manage a plane in the air] pilot, navigate, control, jet, take off, operate, glide, climb, dive, manipulate, maneuver.
fly¹·² *n.* **1** [An insect] housefly, bluebottle, bug, winged insect, gnat, horsefly, fruit fly, tsetse fly. **2** [A ball batted into the air] infield fly, high fly, fly ball, fungo, pop fly*. **3** [A hook baited artificially] lure, fish lure, dry fly, wet fly, spinner, trout fly, bass fly, minnow.
flyer *n.* aviator, navigator, airman; see PILOT 1.
flying *a.* floating, making flight, passing through the air, on the wing, soaring, gliding, winging, swooping, darting, plummeting, drifting, rising, airborne, in midair.

flying fish a fish with winglike fins used in gliding through the air

flying saucer a UFO

fly′leaf′ *n., pl.* **-leaves′** a blank leaf at the beginning or end of a book

fly′pa′per *n.* a sticky or poisonous paper set out to catch flies

fly′speck′ *n.* **1** a speck of fly excrement **2** any tiny spot or petty flaw

fly′way′ *n.* a route taken regularly by birds migrating to and from breeding grounds

fly′weight′ *n.* a boxer who weighs 112 pounds or less

fly′wheel′ *n.* a heavy wheel on a machine, for regulating its speed

FM frequency modulation

f-number (ef′num′bər) *n. Photog.* a number indicating the relative aperture of a lens: a higher number means a smaller opening

foal (fōl) *n.* ⟦OE *fola*⟧ a young horse, mule, etc.; colt or filly — *vt., vi.* to give birth to (a foal)

foam (fōm) *n.* ⟦OE *fam*⟧ **1** the whitish mass of bubbles formed on or in liquids by shaking, etc. **2** something like foam, as frothy saliva **3** a rigid or spongy cellular mass, made from liquid rubber, plastic, etc. — *vi.* to produce foam —**foam′y, -i·er, -i·est,** *adj.*

fob (fäb) *n.* ⟦prob. < dial. Ger *fuppe,* a pocket⟧ **1** a short ribbon or chain attached to a pocket watch **2** any ornament worn on such a chain, etc.

fo·cal (fō′kəl) *adj.* of or at a focus

focal length the distance from the optical center of a lens to the point where the light rays converge

fo′c′sle or **fo′c′s′le** (fōk′s′l) *n. phonetic sp. of* FORECASTLE

fo·cus (fō′kəs) *n., pl.* **-cuses** or **-ci** (-sī′) ⟦L, hearth⟧ **1** the point where rays of light, heat, etc. come together; specif., the point where rays of reflected or refracted light meet **2** FOCAL LENGTH **3** an adjustment of this to make a clear image /move the lens into *focus*/ **4** any center of activity, attention, etc. — *vt.* **-cused** or **-cussed, -cus·ing** or **-cus·sing 1** to bring into focus **2** to adjust the focal length of (the eye, a lens, etc.) so as to produce a clear image **3** to concentrate —**in focus** clear —**out of focus** blurred

fod·der (fäd′ər) *n.* ⟦OE *fodor*⟧ coarse food for cattle, horses, etc., as hay

foe (fō) *n.* ⟦OE *fah,* hostile⟧ an enemy

foetus (fēt′əs) *n. alt. sp. of* FETUS

fog (fôg, fäg) *n.* ⟦prob. < Scand⟧ **1** a large mass of water vapor condensed to fine particles, at or just above the earth's surface **2** a state of mental confusion — *vt., vi.* **fogged, fog′ging** to make or become foggy

fog′gy *adj.* **-gier, -gi·est 1** full of fog **2** dim; blurred **3** confused

fog′horn′ *n.* a horn blown to warn ships in a fog

fogy (fō′gē) *n., pl.* **-gies** ⟦< ?⟧ one who is old-fashioned in ideas and actions Also **fo′gey,** *pl.* **-geys**

foi·ble (foi′bəl) *n.* ⟦< Fr *faible,* feeble⟧ a small weakness in character

foil¹ (foil) *vt.* ⟦< OFr *fuler,* trample⟧ to keep from being successful; thwart

foil² (foil) *n.* ⟦< L *folium,* leaf⟧ **1** a very thin sheet of metal **2** a person or thing that sets off another by contrast **3** ⟦< ?⟧ a long, thin, blunted fencing sword

foist (foist) *vt.* ⟦prob. < dial. Du *vuisten,* to hide in the hand⟧ to get (a thing) accepted, sold, etc. by fraud, deception, etc.; palm off: with *on* or *upon*

fol. 1 folio(s) **2** following

fold¹ (fōld) *vt.* ⟦OE *faldan*⟧ **1** to double (material) up on itself **2** to draw together and intertwine /*fold* your arms/ **3** to embrace **4** to wrap up; envelop — *vi.* **1** to be or become folded **2** [Colloq.] *a)* to fail, as a business, play, etc. *b)* to collapse — *n.* a folded part

fold² (fōld) *n.* ⟦OE *fald*⟧ **1** a pen for sheep **2** a flock of sheep **3** a group of people, as in a church

-fold (fōld) ⟦< OE *-feald*⟧ *suffix* **1** having (a specified number of) parts **2** (a specified number of) times as many or as much /to profit *tenfold*/

fold′away′ *adj.* that can be folded together for easy storage

fold′er *n.* **1** a sheet of heavy paper folded for holding loose papers **2** a pamphlet or circular of one or more folded, unstitched sheets

fo·li·age (fō′lē ij′) *n.* ⟦< L *folia*⟧ leaves, as of a plant or tree

fo·lic acid (fō′lik) ⟦< L *folium,* leaf⟧ a substance belonging to the vitamin B complex, used in treating anemia

fo·lio (fō′lē ō′) *n., pl.* **-os′** ⟦< L *folium,* leaf⟧ **1** a large sheet of paper folded once **2** a large size of book, about 12 by 15 inches, made of sheets so folded **3** the number of a page in a book

folk (fōk) *n., pl.* **folk** or **folks** ⟦OE *folc*⟧ **1** *a)* a people; nation *b)* the common people of a nation **2** [*pl.*] people; persons — *adj.* of or originating among the common people —**one's** (or **the**) **folks** one's family, esp. one's parents

folk′lore′ *n.* ⟦prec. + LORE⟧ the traditional beliefs, legends, etc. of a culture

folk song 1 a song made and handed down among the common people **2** a song composed in imitation of this — **folk singer**

folk′sy (-sē) *adj.* **-sier, -si·est** [Colloq.] friendly or sociable

fol·li·cle (fäl′i kəl) *n.* ⟦< L *follis,* bellows⟧ any small sac, cavity, or gland /a hair *follicle*/

fol·low (fäl′ō) *vt.* ⟦< OE *folgian*⟧ **1** to come or go after **2** to pursue **3** to go along /*follow* the road/ **4** to take up (a trade, etc.) **5** to result from **6** to take as a model; imitate **7** to obey **8** to watch or listen to closely **9** to understand — *vi.* **1** to come or go after something else in place, time, etc. **2** to result —**follow out** (or **up**) to carry out fully — **follow through** to continue and complete a stroke or action

fol′lower *n.* one that follows; specif., *a)* one who follows another's teachings; disciple *b)* an attendant

fol′low·ing *adj.* that follows; next after — *n.* a group of followers — *prep.* after /*following* dinner he left/

fol′low-up′ *n.* a letter, visit, etc. that follows as a review, addition, etc.

THESAURUS

foam *n.* fluff, bubbles, lather; see FROTH.

focus *n.* focal point, locus, point of convergence; see CENTER 1. —**in focus** distinct, obvious, sharply defined; see CLEAR 2. —**out of focus** indistinct, unclear, blurred; see OBSCURE 1.

focus *v.* **1** [To draw toward a center] attract, converge, convene; see CENTER. **2** [To make an image clear] adjust, bring out, get detail; see SHARPEN 2.

foe *n.* opponent, antagonist, adversary; see ENEMY.

fog *n.* mist, haze, cloud, film, steam, wisp, smoke, smog, soup*, pea soup*.

foggy *a.* dull, misty, gray; see HAZY.

fold¹ *n.* lap, pleat, lapel, tuck, folded portion, part turned over, part turned back, doubled material, crease, turn, folded edge, crimp, wrinkle.

fold¹ *v.* **1** [To place together, or lay in folds] double, crease, curl, crimp, wrinkle, ruffle, pucker, gather, double over, lap, overlap, overlay.—*Ant.* UNFOLD, straighten, expand. **2** [*To

fail] become insolvent, declare oneself bankrupt, close; see FAIL 4.

folder *n.* **1** [A folded sheet of printed matter] circular, pamphlet, paper, bulletin, advertisement, enclosure, brochure, throwaway, insert. **2** [A light, flexible case] envelope, binder, portfolio, Manila folder.

folk *n.* race, nation, community, tribe, society, nationality, population, state, settlement, culture, ethnic group, clan, confederation.

folklore *n.* traditions, folk tales, oral tradition, folk wisdom, oral literature, ballad lore, customs, superstitions, legends, folkways, folk wisdom, traditional lore; see also MYTH.

folks *n.* relatives, relations, kin; see FAMILY.

follow *v.* **1** [To be later in time] come next, ensue, postdate; see SUCCEED 2. **2** [To regulate one's action] conform, observe, imitate, copy, take after, match, mirror, reflect, follow the example of, do as, mimic, follow suit, do like, tag along, obey, abide by, adhere to, comply, be in keeping, be consistent with.—*Ant.* NEGLECT,

disregard, depart from. **3** [To observe] heed, regard, keep an eye on; see WATCH. **4** [To understand] comprehend, catch, realize; see UNDERSTAND 1. **5** [To result] proceed from, happen, ensue; see BEGIN 2. — **as follows** the following, next, succeeding; see FOLLOWING.

follower *n.* henchman, attendant, hanger-on, companion, lackey, helper, partisan, recruit, disciple, pupil, protegé, imitator, apostle, adherent, supporter, zealot, backer, participant, sponsor, witness, devotee, believer, advocate, member, admirer, patron, promoter, upholder, copycat*, yes man*.—*Ant.* OPPONENT, deserter, heretic.

following *a.* succeeding, next, ensuing, subsequent, later, after a while, by and by, when, later on, a while later, then, henceforth, afterwards, presently, afterward, coming after, directly after, in the wake of, pursuing, in pursuit of, in search of, resulting, latter, rear, back.—*Ant.* PRECEDING, former, earlier.

following *n.* group, clientele, public,

folly (fäl′ē) *n., pl.* **-lies** ⟦see FOOL⟧ **1** a lack of sense; foolishness **2** a foolish action or belief

fo·ment (fō ment′) *vt.* ⟦< L *fovere*, keep warm⟧ to stir up (trouble); incite —**fo′men·ta′tion** *n.*

fond (fänd) *adj.* ⟦< ME *fonnen*, be foolish⟧ **1** tender and affectionate; loving or doting **2** cherished [a *fond* hope] —**fond of** having a liking for —**fond′ly** *adv.* —**fond′ness** *n.*

fon·dant (fän′dənt) *n.* ⟦Fr < *fondre*, melt⟧ a soft, creamy candy made of sugar

fon·dle (fän′dəl) *vt.* **-dled, -dling** ⟦< FOND⟧ to caress or handle lovingly

fon·due or **fondu** (fän dōō′, fän′dōō) *n.* ⟦Fr < *fondre*, melt⟧ melted cheese, etc. used as a dip for cubes of bread

font¹ (fänt) *n.* ⟦< L *fons*, spring⟧ **1** a basin to hold baptismal water **2** a container for holy water **3** a source

font² (fänt) *n.* ⟦see FOUND²⟧ *Printing* a complete assortment of type in one size and style

fon·ta·nel or **fon·ta·nelle** (fän′tə nel′) *n.* ⟦ME *fontinel*, a hollow⟧ a soft, boneless area in a baby's skull that later closes up

food (fōōd) *n.* ⟦OE *foda*⟧ **1** any substance, esp. a solid, taken in by a plant or animal to enable it to live and grow **2** anything that nourishes

food chain *Ecology* a sequence (as grass, rabbit, fox) of organisms in a community in which each member feeds on the one below it

food poisoning sickness caused by contaminants, as bacteria, in food, or by naturally poisonous foods

food processor an electrical appliance that can blend, purée, slice, grate, chop, etc. foods rapidly

food stamp any of the Federal coupons given to qualifying low-income persons for use in buying food

food′stuff′ *n.* any substance used as food

fool (fōōl) *n.* ⟦< L *follis*, windbag⟧ **1** a silly person; simpleton **2** a jester **3** a dupe —*vi.* **1** to act like a fool **2** to joke **3** [Colloq.] to meddle (*with*) —*vt.* to trick; deceive —**fool around** [Colloq.] to trifle —**fool′ery** *n.*

fool′har′dy *adj.* **-dier, -di·est** foolishly daring; reckless —**fool′har′di·ly** *adv.* —**fool′har′di·ness** *n.*

fool′ish *adj.* silly; unwise; absurd —**fool′ishly** *adv.* —**fool′ish·ness** *n.*

fool′proof′ *adj.* so simple, well-designed, etc. as not to be mishandled, damaged, etc. even by a fool

fools·cap (fōōlz′kap′) *n.* ⟦from a watermark of a jester's cap⟧ a size of writing paper, 13 by 16 in. in the U.S.

foot (foot) *n., pl.* **feet** ⟦OE *fot*⟧ **1** the end part of the leg, on which one stands **2** the base or bottom [the *foot* of a page] **3** the muscular part of a mollusk used in burrowing, moving, etc. **4** a measure of length equal to 12 inches: symbol ′ **5** [Brit.] infantry **6** a group of syllables serving

as a unit of meter in verse —*vt.* **1** to add (a column of figures): often with *up* **2** [Colloq.] to pay (costs, etc.) —**foot it** [Colloq.] to dance or walk —**on foot** walking —**under foot** in the way

foot′age (-ij) *n.* measurement in feet

foot′-and-mouth′ disease a contagious disease of cloven-footed animals, causing blisters in the mouth and around the hoofs

foot′ball′ *n.* **1** a field game played with an inflated leather ball by two teams **2** the ball used

foot′bridge′ *n.* a bridge for pedestrians

foot′-can′dle *n.* a unit for measuring illumination

foot′ed *adj.* having feet of a specified number or kind [four-*footed*]

foot′fall′ *n.* the sound of a footstep

foot′hill′ *n.* a low hill at or near the foot of a mountain or mountain range

foot′hold′ *n.* **1** a secure place for a foot, as in climbing **2** a secure position

foot′ing *n.* **1** a secure placing of the feet **2** a foothold **3** a secure position **4** a basis for relationship

foot′less *adj.* **1** without feet **2** without basis **3** [Colloq.] clumsy; inept

foot′lights′ *n.pl.* a row of lights along the front of a stage floor —**the footlights** the theater or acting

foot′lock′er *n.* a small trunk, usually kept at the foot of a bed

foot′loose′ *adj.* free to go about

foot′man (-mən) *n., pl.* **-men** a male servant who assists the butler

foot′note′ *n.* **1** a note of comment or reference at the bottom of a page **2** such a note at the end of a chapter or a book **3** an additional comment —*vt.* **-not′ed, -not′ing** to add a footnote or footnotes to

foot′path′ *n.* a narrow path for use by pedestrians only

foot′-pound′ *n.* a unit of energy, the amount required to raise one pound a distance of one foot

foot′print′ *n.* **1** a mark made by a foot **2** an area, or its shape, which something affects, occupies, etc.

foot′sore′ *adj.* having sore or tender feet, as from much walking

foot′step′ *n.* **1** the distance covered in a step **2** the sound of a step **3** FOOTPRINT (sense 1)

foot′stool′ *n.* a low stool for supporting the feet of a seated person

foot′wear′ *n.* shoes, boots, etc.

foot′work′ *n.* the manner of using the feet, as in boxing or dancing

THESAURUS

audience, train, adherents, supporters, hangers-on, patrons.

fond *a.* enamored, attached, affectionate; see LOVING.

fondness *n.* partiality, attachment, kindness; see AFFECTION.

food *n.* victuals, foodstuffs, meat and drink, meat, nutriment, refreshment, edibles, table, comestibles, provisions, stores, sustenance, subsistence, rations, board, cooking, cookery, cuisine, nourishment, fare, grub*, vittles*, eats*, chow*; see also MEAL 2. For food in the menu, see also BREAD, BUTTER, CAKE 2, CANDY, CHEESE, DELICATESSEN 1, DESSERT, DRINK 2, EGG, FISH, FLAVORING, FOWL, FRUIT, JAM 1, JELLY, MEAT, MILK, NUT 1, PASTRY, SALAD, SOUP, SPICE, STEW, VEGETABLE.

fool *n.* nitwit, simpleton, dunce, oaf, ninny, cretin, nincompoop, dolt, idiot, jackass, ass, buffoon, blockhead, numskull, boob*, goose, ignoramus, imbecile, moron, clown, loon, dullard, fathead*, half-wit, bonehead*, dope*, sap*, birdbrain*, jerk*, dum-dum*.—*Ant.* PHILOSOPHER, sage, scholar. —**no (or nobody's) fool** shrewd, calculating, capable; see ABLE, INTELLIGENT. —**play the fool** be silly, show off, clown; see JOKE.

fool *v.* trick, dupe, mislead; see DECEIVE. —**fool around** waste time, idle, dawdle; see PLAY 1, 2, WASTE 1, 2.

fooled *a.* tricked, duped, deluded; see DECEIVED.

fooling *a.* joking, jesting, humorous, deceitful, gay, witty, smart, frivolous, flippant, laughable, insincere, misleading, absurd, clever, playful, merry, kidding*, spoofing*.—*Ant.* SERIOUS, grave, earnest.

foolish *a.* silly, simple, half-witted; see STUPID.

foolishly *a.* stupidly, irrationally, idiotically, insanely, imprudently, ineptly, mistakenly, illogically, unwisely, ill-advisedly, crazily, thoughtlessly, carelessly, senselessly, irresponsibly, absurdly, preposterously, ridiculously, with bad judgment, without good sense.

foolishness *n.* folly, weakness, silliness; see STUPIDITY 1.

foot *n.* **1** [A unit of measurement] twelve inches, running foot, front foot, board foot, square foot, cubic foot. **2** [End of the leg] pedal extremity, hoof, paw, pad, dog*, tootsy*. **3** [A foundation] footing, base, pier; see FOUNDATION 2. **4** [A metrical unit in verse] measure, accent, interval, meter, duple meter, triple meter. *Metrical feet include the following:* iamb, dactyl, spondee, trochee, anapest. —**on foot** running, hiking, moving; see WALKING. —**on one's feet** **1** [Upright] standing, erect, vertical; see STRAIGHT. **2**

[Established] sound, settled, secure; see ESTABLISHED 1. —**on the wrong foot** unfavorably, ineptly, incapably; see WRONGLY. —**put one's best foot forward*** do one's best, appear at one's best, try hard; see DISPLAY. —**put one's foot down*** be firm, act decisively, determine; see RESOLVE. —**under foot** on the ground, at one's feet, in the way; see UNDER 1.

football *n.* **1** [A sport] American football, Canadian football, association football, soccer, gridiron pastime*, the pigskin sport*. **2** [The ball used in football] leather oval, pigskin*, sphere; see BALL 1.

football player *n. In the United States, football players include the following:* right end, left end, right tackle, left tackle, right guard, left guard, center, quarterback, left halfback, right halfback, fullback; safety, linebacker, tight end, wide end, cornerback, flanker, nose guard.

foothold *n.* ledge, footing, niche; see STEP 2.

footing *n.* basis, resting place, foot; see STEP 2.

footprint *n.* trace, trail, footstep; see TRACK 2.

footstep *n.* trace, trail, evidence; see TRACK 2. —**follow in someone's footsteps** emulate, succeed, resemble a predecessor; see IMITATE 1.

fop (fäp) *n.* ⟦ME *foppe*, a fool⟧ DANDY (*n.* 1) —**fop′pery,** *pl.* **-ies,** *n.* —**fop′pish** *adj.* —**fop′pishly** *adv.*

for (fôr, fər) *prep.* ⟦OE⟧ **1** in place of /use a rope *for* a belt/ **2** in the interest of /to act *for* another/ **3** in favor of /vote *for* the levy/ **4** in honor of /a party *for* her/ **5** in order to be, get, have, keep, find, etc. /walk *for* exercise, start *for* home/ **6** meant to be received by /flowers *for* a friend/ **7** suitable to /a room *for* sleeping/ **8** with regard to; concerning /an ear *for* music/ **9** as being /to know *for* a fact/ **10** considering the nature of /cool *for* July/ **11** because of /a cry *for* pain/ **12** at the price of /sold *for* $20,000/ **13** to the length, amount, or duration of — *conj.* because

for- ⟦OE⟧ *prefix* away, apart, off /forbid, forgo/

for·age (fôr′ij, fär′-) *n.* ⟦< OFr *forre,* fodder⟧ **1** food for domestic animals **2** a search for food — *vi.* **-aged, -ag·ing 1** to search for food **2** to search for something one wants — *vt.* to take food from; raid —**for′ager** *n.*

foray (fôr′ā) *vt., vi.* ⟦< OFr *forrer,* to forage⟧ to plunder — *n.* a raid in order to seize things

for·bear¹ (fôr ber′) *vt.* **-bore′, -borne′, -bear′ing** ⟦see FOR- & BEAR¹⟧ to refrain from (doing, saying, etc.) — *vi.* **1** to refrain **2** to control oneself

for′bear′² *n. alt. sp. of* FOREBEAR

for·bear′ance (-əns) *n.* **1** the act of forbearing **2** self-restraint

for·bid (fər bid′, fôr-) *vt.* **-bade′** (-bad′) or **-bad′, -bid′den, -bid′ding** ⟦see FOR- & BID⟧ **1** to order (a person) not to do (something); prohibit **2** to prevent

for·bid′ding *adj.* looking dangerous or disagreeable; repellent —**for·bid′dingly** *adv.*

force (fôrs) *n.* ⟦< L *fortis,* strong⟧ **1** strength; power **2** physical coercion against a person or thing **3** the power to control, persuade, etc.; effectiveness **4** military power **5** any group of people organized for some activity /a sales force/ **6** energy that causes or alters motion — *vt.* **forced, forc′ing 1** to make do something by force; compel **2** to break open, into, or through by force **3** to take by force; extort **4** to impose by force: with *on* or *upon* **5** to produce as by force /to force a smile/ **6** to cause (plants, etc.) to develop faster by artificial means —**in force 1** in full strength **2** valid —**force′less** *adj.*

forced (fôrst) *adj.* **1** compulsory /forced labor/ **2** not natural; strained /a forced smile/ —**forc·ed·ly** (fôrs′id lē) *adv.*

force′-feed′ *vt.* **-fed′, -feed′ing** to feed as by a tube through the throat to the stomach

force′ful (-fəl) *adj.* full of force; powerful, vigorous, effective, etc. —**force′fully** *adv.* —**force′ful·ness** *n.*

for·ceps (fôr′seps′) *n., pl.* **-ceps′** ⟦L < *formus,* warm + *capere,* to take⟧ small pincers for grasping, pulling, etc.

for·cible (fôr′sə bəl) *adj.* **1** done by force **2** having force —**for′cibly** *adv.*

ford (fôrd) *n.* ⟦OE⟧ a shallow place in a stream, etc. where one can cross by wading — *vt.* to cross at a ford

fore (fôr) *adv., adj.* ⟦OE⟧ at, in, or toward the front part, as of a ship — *n.* the front — *interj.* Golf a shout warning that one is about to hit the ball

fore- ⟦OE⟧ *prefix* **1** before in time, place, etc. /forenoon/ **2** the front part of /forehead/

fore-and-aft (fôr′n aft′) *adj.* Naut. from the bow to the stern; set lengthwise, as sails

fore′arm′¹ *n.* the part of the arm between the elbow and the wrist

fore·arm′² *vt.* to arm in advance

fore′bear′ (-ber′) *n.* ⟦< FORE + BE + -ER⟧ an ancestor

fore·bode′ (-bōd′) *vt., vi.* **-bod′ed, -bod′ing** ⟦< OE⟧ **1** to foretell; predict **2** to have a presentiment of (something bad) —**fore·bod′ing** *n.*

fore′cast′ *vt.* **-cast′** or **-cast′ed, -cast′ing 1** to predict **2** to serve as a prediction of — *n.* a prediction —**fore′cast′er** *n.*

fore·cas·tle (fōk′s'l) *n.* **1** the upper deck of a ship in front of the foremast **2** the front part of a merchant ship, where the crew's quarters are located

fore·close (fôr klōz′) *vt., vi.* **-closed′, -clos′ing** ⟦< OFr *fors,* outside + *clore,* CLOSE²⟧ to take away the right to redeem (a mortgage, etc.) —**fore·clo′sure** (-klō′zhər) *n.*

fore·doom′ *vt.* to doom in advance

fore′fa′ther *n.* an ancestor

fore′fin′ger *n.* the finger nearest the thumb

fore′foot′ *n., pl.* **-feet′** either of the front feet of an animal

fore′front′ *n.* **1** the extreme front **2** the position of most importance

fore·go′¹ *vt., vi.* **-went′, -gone′, -go′ing** to precede

fore·go′² *vt. alt. sp. of* FORGO

fore′go′ing *adj.* previously said, written, etc.; preceding

fore·gone′ *adj.* **1** previous **2** previously determined; inevitable

fore′ground′ *n.* **1** the part of a scene, etc. nearest to the viewer **2** the most noticeable position — *vt.* to place in the foreground; emphasize

fore′hand′ *n.* a stroke, as in tennis, made with the palm of the hand turned forward — *adj.* done as with a forehand

fore·head (fôr′ed′, -hed′; fär′-) *n.* the part of the face between the eyebrows and the line where the hair normally begins

for·eign (fôr′in, fär′-) *adj.* ⟦< L *foras,* out-of-doors⟧ **1** situated outside one's own country, locality, etc. **2** of, from, or having to do with other countries **3** not belonging; not characteristic

for′eign-born′ *adj.* born in some other country; not native

for′eigner *n.* a person from another country; alien

foreign minister a member of a governmental cabinet in charge of foreign affairs for the country

---

■■■■ THESAURUS ■■■■

for *conj.* as, since, in consequence of the fact that; see BECAUSE.

for *prep.* toward, to, in favor of, intended to be given to, in order to get, under the authority of, in the interest of, during, in order to, in the direction of, to go to, to the amount of, in place of, in exchange for, as, in spite of, supposing, concerning, with respect to, with regard to, notwithstanding, with a view to, for the sake of, in consideration of, in the name of, on the part of.

forbid *v.* prohibit, debar, embargo, restrain, inhibit, preclude, oppose, cancel, hinder, obstruct, bar, prevent, censor, outlaw, declare illegal, withhold, restrict, deny, block, check, disallow, deprive, exclude, ban, taboo, say no to, put under an injunction.— *Ant.* APPROVE, recommend, authorize.

forbidden *a.* denied, taboo, kept back; see REFUSED.

forbidding *a.* unpleasant, offensive, repulsive; see GRIM 1.

force *n.* **1** [Force conceived as a physical property] power, might, energy; see STRENGTH. **2** [Force conceived as part of one's personality] forcefulness, dominance, competence, energy, persistence, willpower, drive, determination, effectiveness,

efficiency, authority, impressiveness, ability, capability, potency, sapience, guts*.—*Ant.* INDIFFERENCE, impotence, incompetence. **3** [An organization] group, band, unit; see ORGANIZATION 2, POLICE. —**in force 1** [Powerfully] in full strength, totally, all together; see ALL 2. **2** [In operation] operative, valid, in effect; see WORKING.

force *v.* compel, coerce, press, drive, make, impel, constrain, oblige, obligate, necessitate, require, enforce, demand, order, command, inflict, burden, impose, insist, exact, put under obligation, contract, charge, restrict, limit, pin down, bring pressure to bear upon, bear down, ram down someone's throat*, high-pressure*, strong-arm*, put the squeeze on*.

forced *a.* compelled, coerced, constrained; see BOUND 2.

forceful *a.* commanding, dominant, electric; see POWERFUL 1.

forcefully *a.* forcibly, stubbornly, willfully; see VIGOROUSLY.

foreboding *n.* premonition, dread, presentiment; see ANTICIPATION.

forecast *n.* prediction, guess, estimate, prognosis, divination, forethought, foresight, prescience,

foreknowledge, conjecture, prophecy, calculation, foreseeing.

forecast *v.* predetermine, predict, guess; see FORETELL.

forefather *n.* ancestor, progenitor, forebear, father, parent, sire, forerunner, author, predecessor, originator, precursor, grandfather, procreator, patriarch, relative, begetter, founder, kinsman.

foregoing *a.* prior, former, previous; see PRECEDING.

foreground *n.* face, forefront, frontage, façade, neighborhood, proximity, nearness, adjacency, range, reach, view.—*Ant.* BACKGROUND, shadow, perspective.

forehead *n.* brow, countenance, temples; see FACE 1.

foreign *a.* remote, exotic, strange, far, distant, inaccessible, unaccustomed, different, unknown, alien, imported, borrowed, immigrant, outside, expatriate, exiled, from abroad, coming from another land, not native, not domestic, nonresident, alienated, faraway, far-off, outlandish.—*Ant.* LOCAL, national, indigenous.

foreigner *n.* stranger, immigrant, newcomer; see ALIEN.

fore·know′ *vt.* **-knew′, -known′, -know′ing** to know beforehand **—fore′knowl′edge** (-näl′ij) *n.*

fore′leg′ *n.* either of the front legs of an animal

fore′lock′ *n.* a lock of hair growing just above the forehead

fore′man (-mən) *n., pl.* **-men 1** the chairman of a jury **2** the head of a group of workers **—fore′wom′an,** *pl.* **-wom′en,** *n.fem.*

fore′mast′ *n.* the mast nearest the bow of a ship

fore′most′ (-mōst′) *adj.* first in place, time, etc. *— adv.* first

fore′noon′ *n.* the time from sunrise to noon; morning

fo·ren·sic (fə ren′sik) *adj.* ⟦ L *forum,* marketplace ⟧ **1** of or suitable for public debate **2** involving the application of scientific, esp. medical, knowledge to legal matters **—fo·ren′si·cal·ly** *adv.*

forensic medicine MEDICAL JURISPRUDENCE

fore′ordain′ *vt.* to ordain beforehand; predestine **—fore′or′di·na′tion** (-ôrd ′n ā′shən) *n.*

fore′run′ner *n.* **1** a herald **2** a sign that tells or warns of something to follow **3** a predecessor; ancestor

fore′sail′ (-sāl′, -səl) *n.* the main sail on the foremast of a schooner

fore·see′ *vt.* **-saw′, -seen′, -see′ing** to see or know beforehand **—fore·see′able** *adj.* **—fore·se′er** *n.*

fore·shad′ow *vt.* to indicate or suggest beforehand; presage

fore·short′en *vt.* in drawing, etc., to shorten some lines of (an object) to give the illusion of proper relative size

fore′sight′ *n.* **1** *a*) a foreseeing *b*) the power to foresee **2** prudent regard or provision for the future

fore′skin′ *n.* the fold of skin that covers the end of the penis

for·est (fôr′ist) *n.* ⟦ < L *foris,* out-of-doors ⟧ a thick growth of trees, etc. covering a large tract of land *— vt.* to plant with trees

fore·stall (fôr stôl′) *vt.* ⟦ < OE *foresteall,* ambush ⟧ **1** to prevent by doing something ahead of time **2** to act in advance of; anticipate

foresta·tion (fôr′is tā′shən) *n.* the planting or care of forests

for′ester *n.* one trained in forestry

for′estry *n.* the science of planting and taking care of forests

fore′taste′ *n.* a taste or sample of what can be expected

fore·tell′ *vt.* **-told′, -tell′ing** to tell or indicate beforehand; predict

fore′thought′ *n.* **1** a thinking or planning beforehand **2** foresight

for·ev·er (fôr ev′ər, fər-) *adv.* **1** for always; endlessly **2** at all times; always Also **for·ev′er·more′**

fore·warn′ *vt.* to warn beforehand

fore′word′ *n.* an introductory statement in a book

for·feit (fôr′fit) *n.* ⟦ < OFr *forfaire,* transgress ⟧ **1** a fine or penalty for some crime, fault, or neglect **2** the act of forfeiting *— adj.* lost or taken away as a forfeit *— vt.* to lose or be deprived of as a forfeit

for′fei·ture (-fə chər) *n.* **1** the act of forfeiting **2** anything forfeited

for·gather (fôr gath′ər) *vi.* to come together; meet; assemble

for·gave (fər gāv′, fôr-) *vt., vi. pt. of* FORGIVE

forge¹ (fôrj) *n.* ⟦ < L *faber,* workman ⟧ **1** a furnace for heating metal to be wrought **2** a place where metal is heated and wrought; smithy *— vt.* **forged, forg′ing 1** to form or shape (metal) by heating and hammering **2** to form; shape **3** to imitate (a signature) fraudulently; counterfeit (a check) *— vi.* **1** to work at a forge **2** to commit forgery **—forg′er** *n.*

forge² (fôrj) *vi.* **forged, forg′ing** ⟦prob. < FORCE⟧ to move forward steadily: often with *ahead*

for′gery *n., pl.* **-ies 1** the act or crime of imitating or counterfeiting documents, signatures, etc. to deceive **2** anything forged

for·get (fər get′, fôr-) *vt., vi.* **-got′, -got′ten** or **-got′, -get′ting** ⟦OE *forgietan*⟧ **1** to be unable to remember **2** to overlook or neglect (something) **—forget oneself** to act in an improper manner **—for·get′table** *adj.*

for·get′ful *adj.* **1** apt to forget **2** heedless or negligent **—for·get′fully** *adv.* **—for·get′ful·ness** *n.*

forget′-me-not′ *n.* a marsh plant with small blue, white, or pink flowers

for·give (fər giv′, fôr-) *vt., vi.* **-gave′, -giv′en, -giv′ing** ⟦OE *forgiefan*⟧ to give up resentment against or the desire to punish; pardon (an offense or offender) **—for·giv′able** *adj.* **—for·give′ness** *n.* **—for·giv′er** *n.*

for·giv′ing *adj.* inclined to forgive **—for·giv′ingly** *adv.*

for·go′ (fôr gō′) *vt.* **-went′, -gone′, -go′ing** ⟦OE *forgan*⟧ to do without; abstain from; give up **—for·go′er** *n.*

for·got (fər gät′) *vt., vi. pt. & alt. pp. of* FORGET

for·got′ten (-′n) *vt., vi. alt. pp. of* FORGET

fork (fôrk) *n.* ⟦ < L *furca* ⟧ **1** an instrument of varying size with prongs at one end, as for eating food, pitching hay,

---

THESAURUS

foreknowledge *n.* foresight, prescience, premonition; see FEELING 4, FORECAST.

foreman *n.* overseer, manager, supervisor, superintendent, head, head man, shop foreman, boss, slave driver.

foremost *a.* fore, original, primary; see FIRST.

forerunner *n.* herald, harbinger, precursor; see FOREFATHER, MESSENGER.

foresee *v.* prophesy, understand, predict; see FORETELL.

foreseen *a.* anticipated, predictable, prepared for; see EXPECTED, LIKELY 1.

foreshadow *v.* imply, presage, suggest; see FORETELL.

foresight *n.* economy, carefulness, husbandry; see PRUDENCE.

forest *n.* wood, jungle, timber, growth, stand of trees, grove, woodland, park, greenwood, cover, clump, forested area, shelter, brake, backwoods, tall timber; see also TREE.

forestall *v.* thwart, prevent, preclude; see HINDER.

forestry *n.* forest management, horticulture, dendrology, woodcraft, forestation, reclamation, woodmanship; see also CONSERVATION.

foretell *v.* predict, prophesy, divine, foresee, announce in advance, prognosticate, augur, portend, foreshadow.—*Ant.* RECORD, confirm, recount.

forethought *n.* judgment, planning, foresight; see PRUDENCE.

forever *a.* everlastingly, permanently, immortally, on and on, ever, perpetually, always, in perpetuity, world without end, eternally, interminably, infinitely, enduringly, unchangingly, durably, ever and again, indestructibly, endlessly, forevermore, for good, till hell freezes over*, for keeps*, for always, now and forever, for life, till death do us part.—*Ant.* TEMPORARILY, for a time, at present.

forewarn *v.* alert, advise, caution; see WARN.

forfeit *v.* sacrifice, give up, relinquish; see ABANDON 1.

forge¹ *v.* falsify, counterfeit, fabricate, trump up, invent, feign, make, fashion, design, imitate, copy, duplicate, reproduce, trace.

forger *n.* falsifier, counterfeiter, con man*; see CRIMINAL.

forgery *n.* imitation, copy, counterfeit, fake, fabrication, sham, phony*.—*Ant.* ORIGINAL, real thing, real article.

forget *v.* lose consciousness of, put out of one's head, fail to remember, be forgetful, have a short memory, overlook, ignore, omit, neglect, slight, disregard, lose sight of, pass over, skip, think no more of, close one's eyes to, not give another thought, draw a blank*, dismiss from the mind, kiss off*, laugh off*.—*Ant.* REMEMBER, recall, recollect. **—forget about** omit, let slip one's memory, miss; see FORGET, NEGLECT

2. —forget oneself offend, go astray, lose control; see MISBEHAVE.

forgetful *a.* inattentive, neglectful, heedless; see CARELESS.

forgetfulness *n.* negligence, neglect, inattention; see CARELESSNESS.

forgivable *a.* venial, trivial, pardonable; see EXCUSABLE.

forgive *v.* pardon, forgive and forget, let pass, excuse, condone, remit, forget, relent, bear no malice, exonerate, exculpate, let bygones be bygones, laugh it off, let up on, let it go, kiss and make up, bury the hatchet, turn the other cheek, make allowance, write off.—*Ant.* HATE, resent, retaliate.

forgiven *a.* reinstated, taken back, welcomed home; see PARDONED.

forgiveness *n.* absolution, pardon, acquittal, exoneration, remission, dispensation, reprieve, justification, amnesty, respite.

forgiving *a.* charitable, openhearted, generous; see KIND.

forgo *v.* quit, relinquish, waive; see ABANDON 1.

forgotten *a.* not remembered, not recalled, not recollected, lost, out of one's mind, erased from one's consciousness, beyond recollection, past recall, not recoverable, blanked out, lapsed; see also ABANDONED.

fork *n.* **1** [A forked implement] table fork, hay fork, pitchfork, salad fork, cooking fork, trident, prong. **2** [A branch of a road or river] bend, turn, etc. **2** something like a fork in shape, etc. **3** the place where a road, etc. divides into branches **4** any of these branches — *vi.* to divide into branches — *vt.* to pick up or pitch with a fork —**fork over** (or **out** or **up**) [Colloq.] to pay out; hand over —**fork′ful′**, *pl.* **-fuls′,** *n.*

fork′lift′ *n.* a device for lifting heavy objects by means of projecting prongs that are slid under the load

for·lorn (fôr lôrn′) *adj.* [< OE *forleosan,* lose utterly] **1** abandoned **2** wretched; miserable **3** without hope —**for·lorn′ly** *adv.*

form (fôrm) *n.* [< L *forma*] **1** shape; general structure **2** the figure of a person or animal **3** a mold **4** a particular mode, kind, type, etc. [ice is a *form* of water, the *forms* of poetry] **5** arrangement; style **6** a way of doing something requiring skill **7** a customary or conventional way of acting; ceremony; ritual **8** a printed document with blanks to be filled in **9** condition of mind or body **10** a chart with information on horses in a race **11** a changed appearance of a word to show inflection, etc. **12** type, etc. locked in a frame for printing — *vt.* **1** to shape; fashion **2** to train; instruct **3** to develop (habits) **4** to make up; constitute — *vi.* to be formed

-form (fôrm) [< L] *combining form* having the form of *[cuneiform]*

for·mal (fôr′məl) *adj.* [< L *formalis*] **1** according to fixed customs, rules, etc. **2** stiff in manner **3** *a)* designed for wear at ceremonies, etc. *b)* requiring clothes of this kind **4** done or made in explicit, definite form [a *formal* contract] **5** designating language usage characterized by expanded vocabulary, complex syntax, etc. — *n.* **1** a formal dance **2** a woman's evening dress —**for′mally** *adv.*

form·al·de·hyde (fôr mal′də hīd′) *n.* [FORM(IC) + *aldehyde*] a pungent gas used in solution as a disinfectant and preservative

for′mal·ism′ *n.* strict attention to outward forms and traditions

for·mal·ity (fôr mal′ə tē) *n., pl.* **-ties** **1** *a)* an observing of customs, rules, etc.; propriety *b)* excessive attention to convention; stiffness **2** a formal act; ceremony

for·mal·ize (fôr′mə līz′) *vt.* **-ized′, -iz′ing** **1** to shape **2** to make formal —**for′mali·za′tion** *n.*

for·mat (fôr′mat′) *n.* [< L *formatus,* formed] **1** the shape, size, and arrangement of a book, etc. **2** the arrangement or plan, as of a TV program

for·ma·tion (fôr mā′shən) *n.* **1** a forming or being formed **2** a thing formed **3** the way in which something is formed; structure **4** an arrangement or positioning, as of troops

forma·tive (fôrm′ə tiv) *adj.* helping or involving formation or development

for·mer (fôr′mər) *adj.* [ME *formere*] **1** earlier; past [in *former* times] **2** being the first mentioned of two

for′merly *adv.* in the past

for·mic (fôr′mik) *adj.* [< L *formica,* ant] designating a colorless acid found in ants, spiders, etc.

For·mica (fôr mī′kə) *trademark for* a laminated, heat-resistant plastic used for counter tops, etc.

for·mi·da·ble (fôr′mə də bəl) *adj.* [< L *formidare,* to dread] **1** causing fear, dread, or awe **2** hard to handle

form·less (fôrm′lis) *adj.* shapeless; amorphous

form letter a standardized letter, usually one of many, with the date, address, etc. added separately

for·mu·la (fôr′myo͞o lə, -myə-) *n., pl.* **-las** or **-lae** (-lē′, -lī′) [L < *forma,* form] **1** a fixed form of words, esp. a conventional expression **2** a conventional rule for doing something **3** a prescription or recipe **4** fortified milk for a baby **5** a set of symbols expressing a mathematical rule **6** *Chem.* an expression of the composition, as of a compound, using symbols and figures

for′mu·late′ (-lāt′) *vt.* **-lat′ed, -lat′ing** **1** to express in a formula **2** to express in a definite way —**for′mu·la′tion** *n.* —**for′mu·la′tor** *n.*

for·ni·cate (fôr′ni kāt′) *vi.* **-cat′ed, -cat′ing** [< L *fornix,* a brothel] to commit fornication —**for′ni·ca′tor** *n.*

for·ni·ca′tion *n.* sexual intercourse between unmarried persons

for·sake (fôr sāk′) *vt.* **-sook′** (-so͝ok′), **-sak′en, -sak′ing** [< OE *for-,* FOR- + *sacan,* to strive] **1** to give up (a habit, etc.) **2** to leave; abandon

for·sooth (fôr so͞oth′) *adv.* [ME *forsoth*] [Archaic] indeed

for·swear (fôr swer′) *vt.* **-swore′, -sworn′, -swear′ing** to deny or renounce on oath — *vi.* to commit perjury

for·sythia (fôr sith′ē ə, fər-) *n.* [after W. Forsyth (1737-1804), Eng botanist] a shrub with yellow, bell-shaped flowers in early spring

fort (fôrt) *n.* [< L *fortis,* strong] **1** a fortified place for military defense **2** a permanent army post

forte¹ (fôrt) *n.* [< OFr: see prec.] that which one does particularly well

forte² (fôr′tā′) *adj., adv.* [It < L *fortis,* strong] *Musical Direction* loud

forth (fôrth) *adv.* [OE] **1** forward; onward **2** out into view

forth′com′ing *adj.* **1** about to appear; approaching **2** ready when needed

forth′right′ *adj.* direct and frank

forth′with′ *adv.* at once

THESAURUS

crossroad, tributary, byway, junction, branch, stream, creek, confluence.

form *n.* **1** [Shape] figure, appearance, plan, arrangement, design, outline, configuration, formation, structure, style, construction, fashion, mode, scheme, framework, contour, stance, profile, silhouette, skeleton, anatomy. **2** [The human form] body, frame, torso; see FIGURE 2. **3** [The approved procedure] manner, mode, custom; see METHOD. **4** [Anything intended to give form] pattern, model, die; see MOLD 1. **5** [A standard letter or blank] mimeographed letter, duplicate, form letter, data sheet, information blank, chart, card, reference form, order form, questionnaire, application; see also COPY.

form *v.* **1** [To give shape to a thing] mold, pattern, model, arrange, make, block out, fashion, construct, devise, plan, design, contrive, produce, invent, frame, scheme, plot, compose, erect, build, cast, cut, carve, chisel, hammer out, put together, whittle, assemble, conceive, create, outline, trace, develop, cultivate, work, complete, finish, perfect, fix, regulate, establish, sculpture, bend, twist, knead, set, determine, arrive at, reach.—*Ant.* DESTROY, demolish, shatter. **2** [To give character to a person] instruct, rear, breed; see TEACH. **3** [To comprise] constitute, figure in, act as; see COMPOSE 1. **4** [To take form] accumulate, con-

dense, harden, set, settle, rise, appear, take shape, grow, develop, unfold, mature, materialize, become a reality, take on character, become visible, shape up*, fall into place*, get into shape*.—*Ant.* DISAPPEAR, dissolve, waste away.

formal *a.* **1** [Notable for arrangement] orderly, precise, set; see REGULAR 3. **2** [Concerned with etiquette and behavior] reserved, distant, stiff; see CONVENTIONAL 3, POLITE. **3** [Official] confirmed, directed, lawful; see APPROVED, LEGAL. **4** [In evening clothes] full dress, black-tie, dressed up; see SOCIAL.

formation *n.* arrangement, composition, constitution, crystallization, deposit, accumulation, development, fabrication, generation, production, creation, genesis.—*Ant.* DESTRUCTION, dissolution, annihilation.

formed *a.* shaped, molded, patterned, modeled, carved, outlined, developed, cultivated, completed, finished, built, forged, created, invented, concocted, designed, accomplished, manufactured, produced, born, perfected, fixed, established, arrived at, solidified, hardened, set, determined.—*Ant.* SHAPELESS, formless, nebulous.

former *a.* earlier, previous, past; see PRECEDING.

formerly *a.* before now, some time ago, once, once upon a time, already, in former times, previously, earlier,

in the early days, eons ago, centuries ago, in the past, in the olden days, used to be, long ago, before this, in time past, heretofore, a while back*.—*Ant.* RECENTLY, subsequently, immediately.

formula *n.* specifications, description, recipe; see METHOD.

formulate *v.* express, give form to, set down; see FORM 1.

fornication *n.* adultery, incontinence, carnality, lechery, illicit intercourse, lewdness, licentiousness, unfaithfulness, fooling around*, promiscuousness, coitus, debauchery, libertinism, copulation, sex, prostitution.

forsake *v.* desert, leave, quit; see ABANDON 2.

forsaken *a.* destitute, deserted, rejected; see ABANDONED.

fort *n.* fortress, citadel, stockade; see FORTIFICATION.

forth *a.* first, out, into; see AHEAD. — **and so forth** and so on, similarly, and the like; see OTHER.

forthcoming *a.* expected, inevitable, anticipated, future, impending, pending, resulting, awaited, destined, fated, predestined, approaching, in store, at hand, inescapable, imminent, in prospect, prospective, in the wind, in preparation, in the cards.

forthright *a.* at once, straight away, directly; see IMMEDIATELY.

fortification *n.* fort, fortress,

for·ti·fy (fôr′tə fī′) *vt.* **-fied′, -fy′ing** [< L *fortis*, strong + *facere*, to make] **1** to strengthen physically, emotionally, etc. **2** to strengthen against attack, as with forts **3** to support **4** to add alcohol to (wine, etc.) **5** to add vitamins, etc. to (milk, etc.) —**for′ti·fi·ca′tion** *n.* —**for′ti·fi′er** *n.*

for·tis·si·mo (fôr tis′ə mō′) *adj., adv.* [It., superl. of *forte*, strong] *Musical Direction* very loud

for·ti·tude (fôr′tə tōōd′) *n.* [< L *fortis*, strong] patient endurance of trouble, pain, etc.; courage

fort·night (fôrt′nīt′) *n.* [ME *fourte(n) niht*] [Chiefly Brit.] a period of two weeks —**fort′night·ly** *adj., adv.*

for·tress (fôr′tris) *n.* [< L *fortis*, strong] a fortified place; fort

for·tui·tous (fôr tōō′ə təs) *adj.* [< L *fors*, luck] **1** happening by chance **2** lucky —**for·tu′i·tously** *adv.*

for·tu·nate (fôr′chə nət) *adj.* **1** having good luck **2** coming by good luck; favorable —**for′tu·nately** *adv.*

for·tune (fôr′chən) *n.* [< L *fors*, luck] **1** luck; chance; fate **2** one's future lot, good or bad **3** good luck; success **4** wealth; riches

for′tune·tell′er *n.* one who professes to foretell the future of others —**for′tune·tell′ing** *n., adj.*

for·ty (fôr′tē) *adj., n., pl.* **-ties** [OE *feowertig*] four times ten; 40; XL —**the forties** the numbers or years, as of a century, from 40 through 49 —**for′ti·eth** (-ith) *adj.*

fo·rum (fôr′əm) *n.* [L] **1** the public square of an ancient Roman city **2** an assembly, program, etc. for the discussion of public matters

for·ward (fôr′wərd) *adj.* [OE *foreweard*] **1** at, toward, or of the front **2** advanced **3** onward **4** prompt; ready **5** bold; presumptuous **6** of or for the future — *adv.* toward the front; ahead — *n. Basketball, Hockey, etc.* a player in a front position — *vt.* **1** to promote **2** to send on

for′wards *adv.* FORWARD

fos·sil (fäs′əl, fôs′-) *n.* [< L *fossilis*, dug up] **1** any hardened remains of a plant or animal of a previous geologic period, preserved in the earth's crust **2** a person with outmoded ideas or ways — *adj.* **1** of or like a fossil **2** dug from the earth [coal is a fossil fuel] **3** antiquated

fos·sil·ize (-īz′) *vt., vi.* **-ized′, -iz′ing** **1** to change into a fossil **2** to make or become out of date, rigid, etc. —**fos′sil·i·za′tion** *n.*

fos·ter (fôs′tər) *vt.* [OE *fostrian*, to nourish] **1** to bring up; rear **2** to help to develop; promote — *adj.* having a specified standing in a family but not by birth [a *foster* brother]

fought (fôt) *vi., vt. pt. & pp.* of FIGHT

foul (foul) *adj.* [OE *ful*] **1** stinking; loathsome **2** extremely dirty **3** indecent; profane **4** wicked; abominable **5** stormy [*foul* weather] **6** tangled [a *foul* rope] **7** not within the limits or rules set **8** designating lines setting limits on a playing area **9** dishonest **10** [Colloq.] unpleasant, disagreeable, etc. — *adv.* in a foul manner — *n. Sports* a hit, blow, move, etc. that is FOUL (*adj.* 7) — *vt.*

1 to make filthy **2** to dishonor **3** to obstruct [grease *fouls* drains] **4** to entangle (a rope, etc.) **5** to make a foul against, as in a game **6** *Baseball* to bat (the ball) foul — *vi.* to be or become fouled —**foul up** [Colloq.] to bungle —**foul′ly** *adv.* —**foul′ness** *n.*

fou·lard (fōō lärd′) *n.* [Fr] a lightweight printed fabric of silk, etc.

foul′-up′ *n.* a mix-up; botch

found[1] (found) [OE *funden*] *vt., vi. pp. & pt.* of FIND

found[2] (found) *vt.* [< L *fundus*, bottom] **1** to set for support; base **2** to bring into being; set up; establish —**found′er** *n.*

found[3] (found) *vt.* [< L *fundere*, pour] **1** to melt and pour (metal) into a mold **2** to make by founding metal

foun·da·tion (foun dā′shən) *n.* **1** a founding or being founded; establishment **2** *a)* an endowment for an institution *b)* such an institution **3** basis **4** the base of a wall, house, etc.

foun·der (foun′dər) *vi.* [< L *fundus*, bottom] **1** to stumble, fall, or go lame **2** to fill with water and sink: said of a ship **3** to break down

found·ling (found′liŋ) *n.* an infant of unknown parents, found abandoned

foundry (foun′drē) *n., pl.* **-ries** a place where metal is cast

fount (fount) *n.* [< L *fons*] **1** [Old Poet.] a fountain or spring **2** a source

foun·tain (fount′'n) *n.* [< L *fons*] **1** a natural spring of water **2** a source **3** *a)* an artificial jet or flow of water [a drinking *fountain*] *b)* the basin where this flows **4** a reservoir, as for ink

foun′tain·head′ *n.* the source, as of a stream

fountain pen a pen which is fed ink from its own reservoir

four (fôr) *adj., n.* [OE *feower*] one more than three; 4; IV

four′-flush′er (-flush′ər) *n.* [< FLUSH[2]] [Colloq.] one who bluffs in an effort to deceive

four′-in-hand′ *n.* a necktie tied in a slipknot with the ends left hanging

four′score′ *adj., n.* four times twenty; eighty

four′some (-səm) *n.* four people

four′square′ *adj.* **1** square **2** unyielding; firm **3** frank; forthright — *adv.* in a square form or manner

four·teen (fôr′tēn′) *adj., n.* [OE *feowertyne*] four more than ten; 14; XIV —**four′teenth′** *adj., n.*

fourth (fôrth) *adj.* [OE *feortha*] preceded by three others in a series; 4th — *n.* **1** the one following the third **2** any of the four equal parts of something; ¼ **3** the fourth forward gear

fourth′-class′ *adj., adv.* of or in a class of mail consisting of merchandise, printed matter, etc. not included in first-class, second-class, or third-class; parcel post

---

THESAURUS

defense, dugout, trench, entrenchment, gun emplacement, barricade, battlement, stockade, outpost, citadel, support, wall, barrier, earthwork, castle, pillbox, bastion, bulwark, breastwork, blockhouse.

fortified *a.* defended, guarded, safeguarded, protected, manned, garrisoned, barricaded, armed, barbed, secured, entrenched, strong, covered, strengthened, supported, surrounded, fortressed, walled, enclosed, stockaded, armored, dug in, hidden, camouflaged.—*Ant.* OPEN, unprotected, unguarded.

fortify *v.* **1** [To strengthen against attack] barricade, entrench, buttress; see DEFEND 1. **2** [To strengthen physically or emotionally] sustain, invigorate, toughen; see STRENGTHEN.

fortitude *n.* firmness, resolution, persistence; see DETERMINATION.

fortunate *a.* lucky, blessed, prosperous, successful, having a charmed life, in luck, favored, well-to-do, happy, triumphant, victorious, overcoming, affluent, thriving, flourishing, healthy, wealthy, well-fixed*, well-heeled*, born with a silver spoon in one's mouth*.—*Ant.* UNFORTUNATE, unlucky, cursed.

fortunately *a.* luckily, happily, in good time, auspiciously, favorably,

prosperously, in the nick of time.—*Ant.* UNFORTUNATELY, unluckily, unhappily.

fortune *n.* **1** [Chance] luck, fate, uncertainty; see CHANCE 1. **2** [Great riches] possessions, inheritance, estate; see WEALTH. —**a small fortune** a high price, a great expense, a large amount of money; see PRICE.

forward *a.* **1** [Going forward] advancing, progressing, ahead, leading, progressive, onward, propulsive, in advance.—*Ant.* BACKWARD, retreating, regressive. **2** [Bold] presumptuous, impertinent, fresh; see RUDE 2.

forwarded *a.* shipped, expressed, dispatched; see DELIVERED.

fossil *n.* remains, reconstruction, specimen, skeleton, relic, find, impression, trace, petrified deposit; see also RELIC.

foster *v.* cherish, nurse, nourish; see RAISE 2.

foul *a.* **1** [Disgusting] nasty, vulgar, coarse; see OFFENSIVE 2. **2** [Unfair] vicious, inequitable, unjust; see DISHONEST.

foul *v.* **1** [To make dirty] defile, pollute, sully; see DIRTY. **2** [To become dirty] soil, spot, stain; see DIRTY.

found[1] *a.* unearthed, revealed, detected; see DISCOVERED.

found[2] *v.* establish, endow, set up; see ESTABLISH 2.

foundation *n.* **1** [An intellectual basis] reason, justification, authority; see BASIS. **2** [A physical basis] footing, base, foot, basement, pier, groundwork, bed, ground, bottom, substructure, wall, underpinning, solid rock, infrastructure, pile, roadbed, support, prop, stand, shore, post, pillar, skeleton, column, shaft, pedestal, buttress, framework, scaffold, beam. **3** [That which has been founded] institution, organization, endowment, institute, society, establishment, company, guild, corporation, association, charity, scholarship fund, trust.

founded *a.* organized, endowed, set up; see ESTABLISHED 1.

founder *n.* originator, sponsor, prime mover; see AUTHOR, FOREFATHER.

fountain *n.* **1** [A jet of water] jet, stream, gush, spout, geyser, spurt, spring, pond, basin, pool; see also WATER 1, 2. **2** [A soda-water dispensary] soda fountain, ice-cream parlor, drugstore fountain; see BAR 2.

fourth dimension in the theory of relativity, time added as a dimension to those of length, width, and depth
fourth estate [*often* F- E-] journalism or journalists
Fourth of July *see* INDEPENDENCE DAY
4WD four-wheel-drive (vehicle)
four'-wheel' *adj.* **1** having four wheels **2** affecting four wheels [*a four-wheel drive*]
fowl (foul) *n.* [OE *fugol*] **1** any bird **2** any of the domestic birds used as food, as the chicken, duck, etc. **3** the flesh of these birds used for food
fox (fäks) *n.* [OE] **1** a small, wild animal of the dog family, considered sly and crafty **2** its fur **3** a sly, crafty person — *vt.* to trick by slyness
fox'glove' *n.* DIGITALIS
fox'hole' *n.* a hole dug in the ground as a protection against enemy gunfire
fox'hound' *n.* a hound with a keen scent, bred and trained to hunt foxes
fox terrier a small, active terrier with a smooth or wiry coat, formerly trained to drive foxes out of hiding
fox trot a dance for couples in 4/4 time, or music for it — **fox'-trot'**, **-trot'ted**, **-trot'ting**, *vi.*
foxy (fäk'sē) *adj.* **-i·er**, **-i·est** **1** foxlike; crafty; sly **2** [Slang] attractive or sexy: used esp. of women
foyer (foi'ər, foi yā') *n.* [< L *focus*, hearth] an entrance hall or lobby, as in a theater or hotel
Fr. **1** Father **2** French
frab·jous (frab'jəs) *adj.* [coined by Lewis Carroll] [Colloq.] splendid; fine
fra·cas (frā'kəs) *n.* [Fr < It *fracassare*, to smash] a noisy fight; brawl
frac·tion (frak'shən) *n.* [< L *frangere*, to break] **1** a small part, amount, etc. **2** *Math.* a) a quantity less than a whole, expressed as a decimal b) any quantity expressed in terms of a numerator and denominator — **frac'tional** *adj.*
frac·tious (frak'shəs) *adj.* [< ?] **1** unruly; rebellious **2** irritable; cross
frac·ture (frak'chər) *n.* [< L *frangere*, to break] a breaking or break, esp. of a bone — *vt.*, *vi.* **-tured**, **-tur·ing** to break, crack, or split
frag·ile (fraj'əl) *adj.* [< L *frangere*, to break] easily broken or damaged; delicate — **fra·gil·i·ty** (frə jil'ə tē) *n.*
frag·ment (frag'mənt) *n.* [< L *frangere*, to break] **1** a part broken away **2** an incomplete part, as of a novel — *vt.*, *vi.* to break up — **frag'men·ta'tion** (-mən tā'shən) *n.*
frag'men·tar'y (-mən ter'ē) *adj.* consisting of fragments; not complete
fra·grant (frā'grənt) *adj.* [< L *fragrare*, to emit a (sweet) smell] having a pleasant odor — **fra'grance** *n.*
frail (frāl) *adj.* [see FRAGILE] **1** easily broken **2** not robust; weak **3** easily tempted; morally weak — **frail'ly** *adv.*
frail'ty (-tē) *n.* **1** a being frail; esp., moral weakness **2** *pl.* **-ties** a fault arising from such weakness

frame (frām) *vt.* **framed**, **fram'ing** [prob. < ON *frami*, profit] **1** to form according to a pattern; design [*to frame laws*] **2** to construct **3** to put into words [*to frame an excuse*] **4** to enclose (a picture, etc.) in a border **5** [Colloq.] to falsify evidence in order to make appear guilty — *n.* **1** body structure **2** the framework, as of a house **3** the structural case enclosing a window, door, etc. **4** an ornamental border, as around a picture **5** the way anything is put together; form **6** mood; temper [*good frame of mind*] **7** one exposure in a filmstrip or movie film **8** *Bowling*, etc. a division of a game — *adj.* having a wooden framework [*a frame house*] — **fram'er** *n.*
frame'-up' *n.* [Colloq.] a secret, deceitful scheme, as a falsifying of evidence to make a person seem guilty
frame'work' *n.* **1** a structure to hold together or support something **2** a basic structure, system, etc.
franc (fraŋk) *n.* [Fr < L *Francorum rex*, king of the French, on the coin in 1360] the monetary unit of Belgium, France, Switzerland, Chad, etc.
fran·chise (fran'chīz') *n.* [< OFr *franc*, free] **1** any special right or privilege granted by a government **2** the right to vote; suffrage **3** the right to sell a product or service — *vt.* **-chised'**, **-chis'ing** to grant a franchise to
Franco- *combining form* French, French and
fran·gible (fran'jə bəl) *adj.* [< L *frangere*, to break] breakable; fragile
frank (fraŋk) *adj.* [< OFr *franc*, free] free in expressing oneself; candid — *vt.* to send (mail) free of postage — *n.* **1** the right to send mail free **2** a mark indicating this right — **frank'ly** *adv.* — **frank'ness** *n.*
Frank (fraŋk) *n.* a member of the Germanic tribes whose 9th-c. empire extended over what is now France, Germany, and Italy
Frank·en·stein (fraŋk'ən stīn') the title character in a novel (1818), creator of a monster that destroys him — *n.* popularly, the monster
frank·furter (fraŋk'fʉrt'ər) *n.* [Ger: after *Frankfurt*, city in Germany] a smoked sausage of beef, beef and pork, etc.; wiener Also [Colloq.] **frank**
frank·in·cense (fraŋk'in sens') *n.* [see FRANK & INCENSE] a gum resin burned as incense
Frank·ish (fraŋk'ish) *n.* the West Germanic language of the Franks — *adj.* of the Franks or their language or culture
fran·tic (frant'ik) *adj.* [< Gr *phrenitis*, delirium] wild with anger, pain, worry, etc. — **fran'ti·cally** *adv.*
frappé (fra pā') *n.* [Fr < *frapper*, to strike] **1** a dessert made of partly frozen fruit juices, etc. **2** a beverage poured over shaved ice **3** [New England] a milkshake Also **frappe** (frap)
fra·ter·nal (frə tʉrn'əl) *adj.* [< L *frater*, brother] **1** of brothers; brotherly **2** designating or of a society organized for fellowship **3** designating twins developed from separate ova and thus not identical
fra·ter·nity (frə tʉr'nət ē) *n.*, *pl.* **-ties** **1** brotherliness **2** a group of men joined together for fellowship, etc., as in college **3** a group of people with the same beliefs, work, etc.

THESAURUS

fowl *n.* barnyard fowl, wild fowl, poultry, chicken, duck, goose, turkey, cock, hen, Cornish hen, pheasant, partridge, prairie chicken, grouse, capon, ptarmigan, swan; see also BIRD.
fox *n.* **1** [A clever person] cheat, trickster, con man*; see RASCAL. **2** [An animal] red fox, gray fox, silver fox; see DOG.
fraction *n.* section, portion, part; see DIVISION 2.
fractional *a.* partial, sectional, fragmentary; see UNFINISHED 1.
fracture *n.* rupture, wound, crack, cleaving, shattering, breach, fragmentation, displacement, dislocation, broken bone, shearing, severing, separating, dismembering.
fragile *a.* brittle, frail, delicate; see DAINTY, WEAK 1, 2.
fragment *n.* piece, scrap, remnant; see BIT 1.
fragrance *n.* perfume, aroma, odor; see SMELL 1.
fragrant *a.* aromatic, sweet, perfumed; see SWEET 3.
frail *a.* feeble, breakable, tender; see DAINTY.

frailty *n.* brittleness, delicacy, feebleness; see WEAKNESS 1.
frame *n.* **1** [The structural portion] skeleton, scaffold, framework, scaffolding, casing, framing, support, substructure, infrastructure, stage, groundwork, organization, anatomy, fabric, architecture, enclosure, span, block, window frame, doorjamb. **2** [A border intended as an ornament] margin, fringe, hem, flounce, trim, trimming, outline, mounting, molding.
frame *v.* **1** [To make] construct, erect, raise; see BUILD. **2** [To enclose in a frame] mount, border, enclose; see SUPPORT 1. **3** [To act as a frame] encircle, confine, enclose; see SURROUND 1. **4** [*To cause a miscarriage of justice] conspire against, double-cross, fix; see DECEIVE.
framed *a.* **1** [Surrounded by a frame] mounted, enclosed, bordered, encircled, fringed, enveloped, outlined, confined, enclosed, wrapped, clasped. **2** [*Arranged beforehand] faked, fixed*, planted*; see FALSE 3.
frame-up* *n.* deception, fraud, con-

spiracy; see TRICK 1.
framework *n.* skeleton, structure, core; see FRAME.
frank *a.* candid, sincere, free, easy, familiar, open, direct, unreserved, uninhibited, downright, ingenuous, unsophisticated, unaffected, plain, aboveboard, forthright, outspoken, tactless, guileless, straightforward, plain-spoken, natural, blunt, matter-of-fact.—*Ant.* DISHONEST, insincere, secretive.
frankfurter *n.* wiener, wiener sausage, weenie*, hot dog*, frank*, dog*, link.
frankly *a.* freely, honestly, candidly; see OPENLY 1.
frankness *n.* openness, sincerity, candidness; see HONESTY.
frantic *a.* distracted, mad, wild, frenetic, furious, raging, raving, frenzied, violent, agitated, deranged, crazy, delirious, insane, angry; see also EXCITED.—*Ant.* CALM, composed, subdued.
fraternity *n.* brotherhood, club, fellowship; see ORGANIZATION 2.

frat·er·nize (frat′ər nīz′) *vi.* **-nized′, -niz′ing** to associate in a friendly way —**frat′er·ni·za′tion** *n.*

frat·ri·cide (fra′trə sīd′) *n.* ⟦< L *frater*, brother + *caedere*, to kill⟧ **1** the killing of one's own brother or sister **2** one who commits fratricide

Frau (frou) *n., pl.* **Frau′en** (-ən) ⟦Ger⟧ a wife: a title corresponding to *Mrs.*

fraud (frôd) *n.* ⟦< L *fraus*⟧ **1** deceit; trickery **2** *Law* intentional deception **3** a trick **4** an impostor

fraudu·lent (frô′jə lənt) *adj.* **1** based on or using fraud **2** done or obtained by fraud —**fraud′u·lence** *n.* —**fraud′u·lently** *adv.*

fraught (frôt) *adj.* ⟦< MDu *vracht*, a load⟧ **1** filled or loaded (*with*) [a life *fraught* with hardship] **2** tense, anxious, etc.

Fräu·lein (froi′līn′) *n., pl.* **-lein** or Eng. **-leins′** ⟦Ger⟧ an unmarried woman: a title corresponding to *Miss*

fray[1] (frā) *n.* ⟦< AFFRAY⟧ a noisy quarrel or fight; brawl

fray[2] (frā) *vt., vi.* ⟦< L *fricare*, to rub⟧ **1** to make or become worn or ragged **2** to make or become weak

fraz·zle (fraz′əl) *vt., vi.* **-zled, -zling** ⟦< dial. *fazle*⟧ [Colloq.] **1** to wear to tatters; fray **2** to tire out —*n.* [Colloq.] a being frazzled

freak (frēk) *n.* ⟦< ?⟧ **1** an odd notion; whim **2** an unusual happening **3** any abnormal animal, person, or plant **4** [Slang] *a*) a drug user *b*) a devotee; buff [a chess *freak*] —*adj.* oddly different; abnormal —**freak out** [Slang] **1** to have hallucinations, etc., as from a psychedelic drug **2** to lose one's composure, control, etc. —**freak′ish** *adj.*

freak′out′ *n.* [Slang] the act or an instance of freaking out

freckle (frek′əl) *n.* ⟦< Scand⟧ a small, brownish spot on the skin — *vt., vi.* **-led, -ling** to make or become spotted with freckles

free (frē) *adj.* **fre′er, fre′est** ⟦< OE *freo*⟧ **1** not under the control or power of another; having liberty; independent **2** having civil and political liberty **3** able to move in any direction; loose **4** not burdened by obligations, debts, discomforts, etc. **5** not confined to the usual rules [*free* verse] **6** not exact [a *free* translation] **7** generous; profuse [a *free* spender] **8** frank **9** with no cost or charge **10** exempt from taxes, duties, etc. **11** clear of obstructions [a *free* road] **12** not fastened [a rope's *free* end] — *adv.* **1** without cost **2** in a free manner — *vt.* **freed, free′ing** to make free; specif., *a*) to release from bondage or arbitrary power, obligation, etc. *b*) to clear of obstruction, etc. — **free from** (or **of**) without —**make free with** to use freely —**free′ly** *adv.* —**free′ness** *n.*

-free (frē) *combining form* free of or from, exempt from

free·base (frē′bās′) *n.* a concentrated form of cocaine for smoking — *vt., vi.* **-based′, -bas′ing** to prepare or use such a form of (cocaine)

free·bie or **free′bee** (frē′bē) *n.* [Slang] something given or gotten free of charge, as a theater ticket

free′boot′er (-bo͞ot′ər) *n.* ⟦< Du *vrij*, free + *buit*, plunder⟧ a pirate

freed·man (frēd′mən) *n., pl.* **-men** a man legally freed from slavery

free·dom (frē′dəm) *n.* **1** a being free; esp., *a*) independence *b*) civil or political liberty *c*) exemption from an obligation, discomfort, etc. *d*) a being able to act, use, etc. freely *e*) ease of movement *f*) frankness **2** a right or privilege

free fall unchecked fall, as of a parachutist before the parachute opens

free flight any flight or part of a flight, as of a rocket, occurring without propulsion —**free′-flight′** *adj.*

free′-for-all′ *n.* a disorganized, general fight; brawl — *adj.* open to anyone

free′hand′ *adj.* drawn by hand without the use of instruments, etc.

free′hold′ *n.* an estate in land held for life or with the right to pass it on through inheritance —**free′hold′er** *n.*

free·lance or **free-lance** (frē′lans′) *n.* a writer, artist, etc. who sells his services to individual buyers Also **free′lanc′er** or **free′-lanc′er** — *adj.* of or working as a freelance — *vi.* **-lanced′, -lanc′ing** to work as a freelance

free′load′er (-lōd′ər) *n.* [Colloq.] a person who habitually imposes on others for free food, etc. —**free′load′** *vi.*

free·man (frē′mən) *n., pl.* **-men** **1** a person not in slavery **2** a citizen

Free·mason (frē′mā′sən) *n.* a member of an international secret society based on brotherliness and mutual aid — **Free′ma′sonry** *n.*

free on board delivered (by the seller) aboard the train, ship, etc. at no extra charge to the buyer

free′stone′ *n.* a peach, etc. in which the pit does not cling to the pulp

free′think′er *n.* one who forms his opinions about religion independently

free trade trade carried on without protective tariffs, quotas, etc.

free university a loosely organized forum for studying subjects not normally offered at universities

free verse poetry without regular meter, rhyme, etc.

free′way′ *n.* a multiple-lane divided highway with fully controlled access

free′will′ *adj.* voluntary

freeze (frēz) *vi.* **froze, fro′zen, freez′ing** ⟦OE *freosan*⟧ **1** to be formed into, or become covered with, ice **2** to become very cold **3** to be damaged or killed by cold **4** to become motionless **5** to be made speechless by strong emotion **6** to become formal or unfriendly — *vt.* **1** to form into, or cover with, ice **2** to make very cold **3** to preserve (food) by rapid refrigeration **4** to kill or damage by cold **5** to make motionless **6** to make formal or unfriendly **7** *a*) to fix (prices, etc.) at a given level by authority *b*) to make (funds, etc.) unavailable to the owners — *n.* **1** a freezing or being frozen **2** a period of freezing weather —**freeze out** **1** to die out through freezing,

THESAURUS

fraud *n.* **1** [Deceit] trickery, duplicity, guile; see DECEPTION. **2** [An imposter] pretender, charlatan, fake; see CHEAT.

fraudulent *a.* deceitful, tricky, swindling; see DISHONEST.

freak *n.* monstrosity, monster, rarity, malformation, freak of nature, oddity, aberration, curiosity, hybrid, anomaly, mutation; see also MONSTER.

freckle *n.* mole, patch, blotch; see BLEMISH.

free *a.* **1** [Not restricted politically] sovereign, independent, autonomous, democratic, self-ruling, self-governing, released, unconstrained, liberated, at liberty, freed.—*Ant.* RESTRICTED, enslaved, subject. **2** [Not restricted in space; *said of persons*] unconfined, at large, cast loose, escaped, let out, scot-free, free as air, free to come and go, unfettered, footloose and fancy-free, freewheeling*, on the loose*.—*Ant.* CONFINED, imprisoned, restrained. **3** [Not restricted in space; *said of things*] unimpeded, unobstructed, unhampered, unattached, loose, not attached, clear from, unentangled, unengaged, disengaged, unfas-

tened.—*Ant.* FIXED, fastened, rooted. **4** [Given without charge] gratuitous, gratis, for nothing, without charge, free of cost, complimentary, for free*, on the house.—*Ant.* PAID, charged, costly. —**for free*** without cost, gratis, for nothing; see FREE 4. —**set free** release, liberate, emancipate; see FREE.

free *v.* release, discharge, deliver, save, emancipate, rescue, extricate, loosen, unbind, disengage, undo, set free, let out, let loose, bail out, cut loose, relieve, absolve, acquit, dismiss, pardon, clear, ransom, redeem, unbind, unchain, disentangle, untie, let go, unlock, unhand, let out of prison, open the cage, turn loose, unfetter, unshackle.—*Ant.* SEIZE, capture, incarcerate.

freedom *n.* **1** [Political liberty] independence, sovereignty, self-government, autonomy, democracy, citizenship, representative government, self-determination; see also LIBERTY 4.—*Ant.* SLAVERY, bondage, regimentation. **2** [Exemption from necessity] privilege, immunity, license, indulgence, facility, range, latitude, scope, play, own accord, free rein, leeway, plenty of rope*.—*Ant.*

RESTRAINT, constraint, hindrance. **3** [Natural ease and facility] readiness, forthrightness, spontaneity; see EASE 2.

freeing *n.* emancipation, releasing, salvation; see RESCUE.

freely *a.* **1** [Without physical restriction] loosely, without encumbrance, unhindered, without restraint, as one pleases, easily, smoothly.—*Ant.* with difficulty, uneasily, stressfully. **2** [Without mental restriction] voluntarily, willingly, fancy-free, of one's own accord, at will, at pleasure, of one's own free will, purposely, deliberately, intentionally, advisedly, spontaneously, frankly, openly.—*Ant.* UNWILLINGLY, under compulsion, hesitantly.

freeway *n.* turnpike, superhighway, toll road; see HIGHWAY, ROAD 1.

freeze *v.* **1** [To change to a solid state] congeal, harden, solidify, ice, quick-freeze, glaciate, chill, benumb, cool, ice up*.—*Ant.* MELT, thaw, liquefy. **2** [To control] seal, terminate, immobilize; see CONTROL.

freezing *a.* frosty, wintry, frigid; see COLD 1.

as plants **2** [Colloq.] to keep out by a cold manner, competition, etc. —**freeze over** to become covered with ice —**freez'able** *adj.*

freeze'-dry' *vt.* **-dried'**, **-dry'ing** to quick-freeze (food, etc.) and then dry under high vacuum

freez'er *n.* **1** a refrigerator, compartment, etc. for freezing and storing perishable foods **2** a machine for making ice cream

freezing point the temperature at which a liquid freezes: the freezing point of water is 32°F or 0°C

freight (frāt) *n.* ⟦< MDu *vracht*, a load⟧ **1** the transporting of goods by water, land, or air **2** the cost for this **3** the goods transported **4** a railroad train for transporting goods: in full **freight train** — *vt.* **1** to load with freight **2** to send by freight

freight'er *n.* a ship for freight

French (french) *adj.* of France, its people, language, etc. — *n.* the language of France —**the French** the people of France —**French'man** (-mən), *pl.* **-men**, *n.*

French bread bread with a crisp crust made with white flour in a long, slender loaf

French cuff a shirt-sleeve cuff turned back and fastened with a cuff link

French doors a pair of doors hinged at the sides to open in the middle

French dressing 1 a salad dressing made of vinegar, oil, etc. **2** an orange-colored, creamy salad dressing

French fries [*often* f- f-] strips of potato that have been French fried

French fry [*often* f- f-] to fry in hot deep fat

French horn a mellow-toned brass instrument with a long spiral tube and a flaring bell: now usually *horn*

French leave an unauthorized departure

French toast sliced bread dipped in a batter of egg and milk and fried

fre·net·ic (frə net'ik) *adj.* ⟦see PHRENETIC⟧ frantic; frenzied —**fre·net'i·cal·ly** *adv.*

frenzy (fren'zē) *n.*, *pl.* **-zies** ⟦< Gr *phrenitis*, madness⟧ wild excitement; delirium —**fren'zied** *adj.* —**fren'ziedly** *adv.*

Freon (frē'än') *trademark* for any of a series of gaseous compounds of fluorine, carbon, etc.: used as refrigerants, aerosol propellants, etc.

fre·quency (frē'kwən sē) *n.*, *pl.* **-cies 1** frequent occurrence **2** the number of times any event recurs in a given period **3** *Physics* the number of oscillations or cycles per unit of time

frequency modulation the variation of the frequency of a carrier wave in accordance with the signal to be transmitted

fre·quent (frē'kwənt; *for v.* frē kwent') *adj.* ⟦< L *frequens*, crowded⟧ **1** occurring often **2** constant; habitual — *vt.* to go to or be at often —**fre'quently** *adv.*

fresco (fres'kō) *n.*, *pl.* **-coes** or **-cos** ⟦It, fresh⟧ a painting with watercolors on wet plaster

fresh[1] (fresh) *adj.* ⟦OE *fersc*⟧ **1** recently made, grown, etc. *[fresh* coffee*]* **2** not salted, pickled, etc. **3** not spoiled **4** not tired; lively **5** not worn, soiled, faded, etc. **6** new; recent **7** inexperienced **8** cool and refreshing *[a fresh* spring day*]* **9** brisk: said of wind **10** not salt: said of water —**fresh'ly** *adv.* —**fresh'ness** *n.*

fresh[2] (fresh) *adj.* ⟦< Ger *frech*, bold⟧ [Slang] bold; saucy; impertinent

fresh'en (-ən) *vt.*, *vi.* to make or become fresh —**freshen up** to bathe, change into fresh clothes, etc. —**fresh'ener** *n.*

fresh'man (-mən) *n.*, *pl.* **-men** ⟦FRESH[1] + MAN⟧ **1** a beginner **2** a person in his or her first year in college, Congress, etc.

fresh'wa'ter *adj.* **1** of or living in water that is not salty **2** sailing only on inland waters

fret[1] (fret) *vt.*, *vi.* **fret'ted, fret'ting** ⟦OE *fretan*, to devour⟧ **1** to gnaw, wear away, rub, etc. **2** to ripple or ruffle **3** to irritate or be irritated; worry — *n.* irritation; worry —**fret'ter** *n.*

fret[2] (fret) *n.* ⟦ME *frette*⟧ a running design of interlacing small bars

fret[3] (fret) *n.* ⟦< OFr *frette*, a band⟧ any of the ridges on the fingerboard of a banjo, guitar, etc.

fret'ful *adj.* irritable; peevish —**fret'fully** *adv.* —**fret'·ful·ness** *n.*

fret'work' *n.* decorative carving or openwork, as of interlacing lines

Freud·ian (froid'ē ən) *adj.* of or according to Sigmund Freud (1856-1939), Austrian founder of psychoanalysis, or his theories — *n.* a follower of Freud

Freudian slip a mistake made in speaking that inadvertently reveals unconscious motives, etc.

fri·able (frī'ə bəl) *adj.* ⟦Fr < L *friare*, to rub⟧ easily crumbled

friar (frī'ər) *n.* ⟦< L *frater*, brother⟧ *R.C.Ch.* a member of certain religious orders

fric·as·see (frik'ə sē', frik'ə sē') *n.* ⟦< Fr *fricasser*, cut up and fry⟧ meat cut into pieces, stewed or fried, and served in a sauce of its own gravy — *vt.* **-seed', -see'ing** to prepare in this way

fric·tion (frik'shən) *n.* ⟦< L *fricare*, to rub⟧ **1** a rubbing of one object against another **2** conflict, as because of differing opinions **3** *Mech.* the resistance to motion of surfaces that touch —**fric'tional** *adj.*

Fri·day (frī'dā, -dē) *n.* ⟦< *Frig*, Germanic goddess⟧ **1** the sixth day of the week: abbrev. **Fri. 2** ⟦< the devoted servant of ROBINSON CRUSOE⟧ a faithful helper: usually **man (or girl) Friday**

fried (frīd) *vt.*, *vi. pt. & pp. of* FRY[1]

fried'cake' *n.* a small cake fried in deep fat; doughnut or cruller

friend (frend) *n.* ⟦OE *freond*⟧ **1** a person whom one knows well and is fond of **2** an ally, supporter, or sympa-

---

THESAURUS

freight *n.* burden, load, contents, weight, bulk, encumbrance, bales, shipment, cargo, shipping, consignment, goods, tonnage, packages, ware.

freighter *n.* tanker, transport, cargo ship; see SHIP.

French *a.* **1** [Referring to the French culture or people] Gallic, Latin, Frenchified, Parisian. **2** [Referring to the French language] Romance, Romantic, Parisian, Gallic.

French *n.* **1** [The French people] Gallic nation, Parisians, Frenchmen, Latins, Basques, Gauls, Normans, Provençals, French provincials. **2** [The French tongue] Romance language, modern French, Middle French, Old French, Norman, Parisian French, Anglo-Norman.

frenzy *n.* rage, craze, furor; see EXCITEMENT, INSANITY.

frequency *n.* recurrence, number, reiteration; see REGULARITY.

frequent *a.* **1** [Happening often] many, repeated, numerous, common, habitual, monotonous, profuse, incessant, continual, customary, intermittent, familiar, commonplace, expected, various, a good many.—

Ant. RARE, infrequent, occasional. **2** [Happening regularly] recurrent, usual, periodic; see REGULAR 3.

frequent *v.* visit often, go to, be seen at daily, attend regularly, be at home in, be often in, be accustomed to, hang around*, hang out*; see also VISIT.

frequently *a.* often, regularly, usually, commonly, successively, many times, in many instances, all the time, notably, repeatedly, intermittently, generally, every now and then, at times, not infrequently, often enough, not seldom, periodically, at regular intervals; see also REGULARLY.—*Ant.* SELDOM, infrequently, rarely.

fresh[1] *a.* **1** [Newly produced] new, green, crisp, raw, recent, current, late, this season's, factory-fresh, garden-fresh, farm-fresh, brand-new, newborn, immature, young, beginning, hot off the press*, just out, newfangled.—*Ant.* OLD, stale, musty. **2** [Not preserved] unsalted, uncured, unsmoked; see sense **1**. **3** [Unspoiled] uncontaminated, green, not stale, good, undecayed, well-preserved, odor-free, in good condition, unblemished, unspotted, preserved,

new, virgin, unimpaired.—*Ant.* DECAYED, spoiled, contaminated. **4** [Not faded] colorful, vivid, sharp; see BRIGHT 1, DEFINITE 2. **5** [Not salt; *said of water*] potable, drinkable, cool, clear, pure, clean, sweet, fit to drink, safe.—*Ant.* DIRTY, brackish, briny. **6** [Refreshed] restored, rested, rehabilitated, like new, unused, new, relaxed, stimulated, relieved, freshened, revived.—*Ant.* TIRED, exhausted, worn-out. **7** [Inexperienced] untrained, untried, unskilled; see INEXPERIENCED.

freshman *n.* beginner, novice, frosh*; see AMATEUR.

fret[1] *v.* disturb, agitate, vex; see BOTHER 2.

friar *n.* brother, padre, father; see MONK.

friction *n.* **1** [The rubbing of two bodies] attrition, abrasion, erosion; see GRINDING. **2** [Trouble between individuals or groups] animosity, quarrel, discontent; see HATRED.

fried *a.* grilled, cooked, browned; see DONE 2.

friend *n.* familiar, schoolmate, playmate, best friend, roommate, companion, intimate, confidant, thizer **3** [F-] a member of the Society of Friends; Quaker —**make** (or **be**) **friends with** to become (or be) a friend of —**friend′less** *adj.*

friend′ly *adj.* **-lier, -li·est 1** of or like a friend; kindly **2** not hostile; amicable **3** supporting; helping —**friend′li·ly** *adv.* —**friend′li·ness** *n.*

friend′ship′ *n.* **1** the state of being friends **2** friendly feeling

frieze (frēz) *n.* ⟦< ML *frisium*⟧ a horizontal band with designs or carvings along a wall or around a room

frig·ate (frig′it) *n.* ⟦< It *fregata*⟧ a fast, medium-sized sailing warship of the 18th and early 19th c.

fright (frīt) *n.* ⟦OE *fyrhto*⟧ **1** sudden fear; alarm **2** something unsightly

fright′en *vt.* **1** to make suddenly afraid; scare **2** to force (*away, off,* etc.) by scaring —**fright′en·ing·ly** *adv.*

fright′ful *adj.* **1** causing fright; alarming **2** shocking; terrible **3** [Colloq.] *a*) unpleasant *b*) great —**fright′fully** *adv.*

frigid (frij′id) *adj.* ⟦< L *frigus*, coldness⟧ **1** extremely cold **2** not warm or friendly **3** sexually unresponsive: said of a woman —**fri·gid′i·ty** *n.* —**frig′id·ly** *adv.*

Frigid Zone either of two zones (**North Frigid Zone** or **South Frigid Zone**) between the polar circles and the poles

frill (fril) *n.* ⟦< ?⟧ **1** any unnecessary ornament **2** a ruffle —**frill′y, -i·er, -i·est,** *adj.*

fringe (frinj) *n.* ⟦< L *fimbria*⟧ **1** a border of threads, etc. hanging loose or tied in bunches **2** an outer edge; border **3** a marginal or minor part — *vt.* **fringed, fring′ing** to be or make a fringe for — *adj.* **1** at the outer edge **2** additional **3** minor

fringe benefit an employee's benefit other than wages, as a pension or insurance

frip·pery (frip′ər ē) *n., pl.* **-ies** ⟦< OFr *frepe*, a rag⟧ **1** cheap, gaudy clothes **2** showy display in dress, etc.

Fris·bee (friz′bē) ⟦< "Mother Frisbie's" pie tins⟧ *trademark* for a plastic, saucer-shaped disk sailed back and forth in a simple game — *n.* [*also* **f-**] such a disk

frisé (frē zā′, fri-) *n.* ⟦Fr < *friser*, to curl⟧ an upholstery fabric with a thick pile of loops

Fri·sian (frizh′ən) *n.* the West Germanic language of an island chain, the Frisian Islands, along the coast of N Netherlands, Germany, & Denmark

frisk (frisk) *vi.* ⟦< OHG *frisc*, lively⟧ to frolic — *vt.* [Slang] to search (a person) for weapons, etc. by passing the hands quickly over his clothing

frisky (fris′kē) *adj.* **-i·er, -i·est** lively; frolicsome — **frisk′i·ly** *adv.* —**frisk′i·ness** *n.*

frit·ter¹ (frit′ər) *vt.* ⟦< L *frangere*, to break⟧ to waste (money, time, etc.) bit by bit: usually with *away*

frit·ter² (frit′ər) *n.* ⟦< L *frigere*, to fry⟧ a small cake of fried batter, usually containing corn, fruit, etc.

frivo·lous (friv′ə ləs) *adj.* ⟦< L *frivolus*⟧ **1** of little value; trivial **2** silly and light-minded; giddy —**fri·vol·ity** (fri val′ə tē), *pl.* **-ties,** *n.* —**friv′o·lously** *adv.*

frizz or **friz** (friz) *vt., vi.* **frizzed, friz′zing** ⟦Fr *friser*⟧

to form into small, tight curls — *n.* hair, etc. that is frizzed —**friz′zly** or **friz′zy** *adj.*

friz·zle¹ (friz′əl) *vt., vi.* **-zled, -zling** ⟦< FRY¹⟧ to sizzle, as in frying

friz·zle² (friz′əl) *n., vt., vi.* **-zled, -zling** FRIZZ

fro (frō) *adv.* ⟦< ON *frā*⟧ backward; back: now only in TO AND FRO (at TO)

frock (fräk) *n.* ⟦< OFr *froc*⟧ **1** a robe worn by friars, monks, etc. **2** a dress

frog (frôg, fräg) *n.* ⟦OE *frogga*⟧ **1** a tailless, leaping amphibian with long hind legs and webbed feet **2** a fancy braided loop used to fasten clothing —**frog in the throat** hoarseness

frog′man′ *n., pl.* **-men′** one trained and equipped for underwater demolition, exploration, etc.

frolic (fräl′ik) *n.* ⟦< MDu *vrō*, merry⟧ **1** a lively party or game **2** merriment; fun — *vi.* **-icked, -ick·ing 1** to make merry; have fun **2** to romp about; gambol —**frol′icker** *n.*

frol′ic·some (-səm) *adj.* playful; merry

from (frum, främ) *prep.* ⟦OE⟧ **1** beginning at; starting with [*from* noon to midnight] **2** out of [*from* her purse] **3** originating with [a letter *from* me] **4** out of the possibility of or use of [kept *from* going] **5** as not being like [to know good *from* evil] **6** because of [to tremble *from* fear]

frond (fränd) *n.* ⟦< L *frons*, leafy branch⟧ the leaf of a fern or palm

front (frunt) *n.* ⟦< L *frons*, forehead⟧ **1** *a*) outward behavior [a bold *front*] *b*) [Colloq.] an appearance of social standing, wealth, etc. **2** the part facing forward **3** the first part; beginning **4** a forward or leading position **5** the land bordering a lake, street, etc. **6** the advanced battle area in warfare **7** an area of activity [the home *front*] **8** a person or group used to hide another's activity **9** *Meteorol.* the boundary between two differing air masses — *adj.* at, to, in, on, or of the front — *vt., vi.* **1** to face **2** to serve as a front (*for*) —**in front of** before —**fron′tal** *adj.*

front·age (frunt′ij) *n.* **1** the front part of a building **2** the front boundary line of a lot or the length of this line **3** land bordering a street, lake, etc.

fron·tier (frun tir′) *n.* ⟦see FRONT⟧ **1** the border between two countries **2** the part of a country which borders an unexplored region **3** any new field of learning, etc. — *adj.* of, on, or near a frontier —**frontiers′man** (-tirz′mən), *pl.* **-men,** *n.*

frontis·piece (frunt′is pēs′) *n.* ⟦< L *frons*, front + *specere*, to look⟧ an illustration facing the title page of a book

front office the management or administration, as of a company

front′-run′ner *n.* a leading contestant

front-wheel drive an automotive design in which only the front wheels receive driving power

---

■ THESAURUS ■

comrade, mate, amigo, fellow, pal*, chum*, crony*, buddy*, side-kick*.— *Ant.* ENEMY, foe, stranger. —**make** or **be friends with** befriend, stand by, become familiar with; see ASSOCIATE 1.

friendless *a.* deserted, alone, forlorn; see ABANDONED.

friendliness *n.* kindness, amiability, geniality; see FRIENDSHIP.

friendly *a.* kind, kindly, helpful, sympathetic, well-disposed, neighborly, well-intentioned, sociable, civil, peaceful, loving, affectionate, fond, warm-hearted, attentive, brotherly, agreeable, genial, amiable, affable, benevolent, accommodating, unoffensive, pleasant, tender, companionable, with open arms, cordial, familiar, intimate, close, devoted, dear, attached, loyal, faithful, steadfast, true, responsive, understanding, congenial, approachable, cheerful, convivial, good-humored, good-natured, generous, gracious, cooperative, whole-hearted, big-hearted*, chummy*, folksy*, thick*, arm in arm.—*Ant.* UNFRIENDLY, antagonistic, spiteful.

friendship *n.* harmony, friendliness,

brotherly love; see FELLOWSHIP 1.

fright *n.* panic, dread, horror; see FEAR.

frighten *v.* scare, scare away, scare off, dismay, terrify, cow, shock, intimidate, threaten, badger, petrify, panic, demoralize, disrupt, give cause for alarm, terrorize, horrify, astound, awe, perturb, disturb, startle, frighten out of one's wits, take someone's breath away, chill to the bone, make someone's hair stand on end, make someone's blood run cold, make someone's flesh creep*, scare one stiff*, curdle the blood.

frightened *a.* terrorized, scared, startled; see AFRAID.

frightful *a.* **1** [Causing fright] fearful, awful, dreadful; see TERRIBLE 1, 2. **2** [Very unpleasant] calamitous, shocking, terrible; see OFFENSIVE 2.

frigid *a.* **1** [Thermally cold] freezing, frosty, refrigerated; see COLD 1. **2** [Unresponsive] unloving, distant, chilly; see COLD 2, INDIFFERENT.

fringe *n.* hem, trimming, border; see EDGE 1.

frisky *a.* spirited, dashing, playful; see ACTIVE.

frivolity *n.* silliness, levity, folly; see FUN.

frivolous *a.* superficial, petty, trifling; see TRIVIAL.

frog *n.* amphibian, tree frog, toad, bullfrog, horned frog, horned toad, polliwog.

from *prep.* in distinction to, out of possession of, outside of; see OF.

front *a.* fore, forward, frontal, foremost, head, headmost, leading, in the foreground.—*Ant.* BACK, rear, hindmost.

front *n.* **1** [The forward part or surface] exterior, forepart, anterior, bow, foreground, face, head, breast, frontal area.—*Ant.* REAR, posterior, back. **2** [The fighting line] front line, no man's land, advance position, line of battle, vanguard, outpost, field of fire, advance guard. **3** [The appearance one presents before others] mien, demeanor, aspect, countenance, face, presence, expression, figure, exterior. —**in front of** before, preceding, leading; see AHEAD.

frontier *n.* hinterland, remote districts, outskirts; see COUNTRY 1.

frost (frôst, fräst) *n.* ⟦OE < *freosan*, freeze⟧ **1** a temperature low enough to cause freezing **2** frozen dew or vapor; rime — *vt.* **1** to cover with frost **2** to cover with frosting **3** to give a frostlike, opaque surface to (glass) —**frost′y,** **-i·er, -i·est,** *adj.*

frost′bite′ *vt.* **-bit′, -bit′ten, -bit′ing** to injure the tissues of (a body part) by exposing to intense cold — *n.* injury caused by such exposure

frost′ing *n.* **1** a mixture of sugar, butter, etc. for covering a cake; icing **2** a dull finish on glass, metal, etc.

frost line the limit of penetration of soil by frost

froth (frôth, fräth) *n.* ⟦< ON *frotha*⟧ **1** foam **2** foaming saliva **3** light, trifling talk, ideas, etc. — *vi.* to foam — **froth′y, -i·er, -i·est,** *adj.*

frou·frou (frōō′frōō′) *n.* ⟦Fr⟧ [Colloq.] excessive ornateness

fro·ward (frō′wərd, -ərd) *adj.* ⟦see FRO & -WARD⟧ not easily controlled; willful; contrary —**fro′ward·ness** *n.*

frown (froun) *vi.* ⟦< OFr *froigne*, sullen face⟧ **1** to contract the brows, as in displeasure **2** to show disapproval: with *on* or *upon* — *n.* a frowning

frowzy (frou′zē) *adj.* **-zier, -zi·est** ⟦< ?⟧ dirty and untidy; slovenly —**frow′zily** *adv.* —**frow′zi·ness** *n.*

froze (frōz) *vi., vt. pt. of* FREEZE

fro·zen (frō′zən) *vi., vt. pp. of* FREEZE — *adj.* **1** turned into or covered with ice **2** damaged or killed by freezing **3** preserved by freezing, as food **4** made motionless **5** kept at a fixed level **6** not readily convertible into cash

frozen custard a food resembling ice cream, but with a lower butterfat content

fruc·ti·fy (fruk′tə fī′) *vi., vt.* **-fied′, -fy′ing** ⟦< L *fructificare*⟧ to bear or cause to bear fruit

fruc·tose (fruk′tōs, frook′-) *n.* ⟦< L *fructus*, fruit + -OSE[1]⟧ a sugar found in sweet fruits and in honey

fru·gal (frōō′gəl) *adj.* ⟦< L *frugi*, fit for food⟧ **1** not wasteful; thrifty **2** inexpensive or meager —**fru·gal′ity** (-gal′ə tē), *pl.* **-ties,** *n.* —**fru′gally** *adv.*

fruit (frōōt) *n.* ⟦< L *fructus*⟧ **1** any plant product, as grain, vegetables, etc.: *usually used in pl.* **2** *a*) a usually sweet, edible plant structure, containing the seeds inside a juicy pulp *b*) *Bot.* the mature, seed-bearing part of a flowering plant **3** the result or product of any action

fruit′cake′ *n.* a rich cake containing nuts, preserved fruit, citron, etc.

fruit fly any of various small flies whose larvae feed on fruits and vegetables

fruit′ful *adj.* **1** bearing much fruit **2** productive; prolific **3** profitable —**fruit′fully** *adv.*

frui·tion (frōō ish′ən) *n.* **1** the bearing of fruit **2** a coming to fulfillment; realization

fruit′less *adj.* **1** without results; unsuccessful **2** bearing no fruit; sterile; barren —**fruit′lessly** *adv.*

fruit′y *adj.* **-i·er, -i·est** **1** like fruit in taste or smell **2** rich or mellow in tone

frump (frump) *n.* ⟦prob. < Du *rompelen*, rumple⟧ a dowdy woman —**frump′ish** or **frump′y** *adj.*

frus·trate (frus′trāt) *vt.* **-trat′ed, -trat′ing** ⟦< L *frustra*, in vain⟧ **1** to cause to have no effect **2** to prevent from achieving a goal or gratifying a desire —**frus·tra′tion** *n.*

fry[1] (frī) *vt., vi.* **fried, fry′ing** ⟦< L *frigere*, to fry⟧ to cook in a pan over direct heat, usually in hot fat — *n., pl.* **fries 1** [*pl.*] fried potatoes **2** a social gathering at which food is fried and eaten

fry[2] (frī) *n., pl.* **fry** ⟦< OFr *freier*, to spawn⟧ young fish — **small fry 1** children **2** insignificant people

fry′er (-ər) *n.* **1** a utensil for deep-frying **2** a chicken for frying

FSLIC or **F.S.L.I.C.** Federal Savings and Loan Insurance Corporation

ft. foot; feet

FTC Federal Trade Commission

fuch·sia (fyōō′shə) *n.* ⟦after L. *Fuchs* (1501-66), Ger botanist⟧ **1** a shrubby plant with pink, red, or purple flowers **2** purplish red

fud·dle (fud′'l) *vt.* **-dled, -dling** ⟦< ?⟧ to confuse or stupefy as with alcoholic liquor — *n.* a fuddled state

fuddy-duddy (fud′ē dud′ē) *n., pl.* **-dies** [Colloq.] a fussy, critical, or old-fashioned person

fudge (fuj) *n.* ⟦< ?⟧ a soft candy made of butter, milk, sugar, flavoring, etc. — *vi.* **fudged, fudg′ing 1** to refuse to commit oneself; hedge **2** to be dishonest; cheat

fuel (fyōō′əl) *n.* ⟦ult. < L *focus*, fireplace⟧ **1** coal, oil, gas, wood, etc., burned to supply heat or power **2** material from which atomic energy can be obtained **3** anything that intensifies strong feeling — *vt., vi.* **fu′eled** or **fu′elled, fu′el·ing** or **fu′el·ling** to supply with or get fuel

fuel injection a system for forcing fuel into combustion chambers of a diesel, gasoline, jet, or rocket engine

fu·gi·tive (fyōō′ji tiv) *adj.* ⟦< L *fugere*, to flee⟧ **1** fleeing, as from danger or justice **2** fleeting — *n.* one who is fleeing from justice, etc.

fugue (fyōōg) *n.* ⟦< L *fugere*, to flee⟧ a musical work in which a theme is taken up successively and developed by the various parts in counterpoint

-ful (fəl; *for* 2, *usually* fool) ⟦< FULL[1]⟧ *suffix* **1** *a*) full of, having [*joyful*] *b*) having the qualities of or tendency to [*helpful*] **2** the quantity that will fill [*handful*]

ful·crum (ful′krem, fool′-) *n., pl.* **-crums** or **-cra** (-krə) ⟦L, a support⟧ the support on which a lever turns in raising something

ful·fill or **ful·fil** (fool fil′) *vt.* **-filled′, -fill′ing** ⟦OE *fullfyllan*⟧ **1** to carry out (a promise, etc.) **2** to do (a duty, etc.); obey **3** to satisfy (a condition) **4** to bring to an end; complete —**ful·fill′ment** or **ful·fil′ment** *n.*

full[1] (fool) *adj.* ⟦OE⟧ **1** having in it all there is space for; filled **2** having eaten all that one wants **3** having a great deal or number (*of*) **4** complete [a *full* dozen] **5** having

---

THESAURUS

frost *n.* frozen dew, permafrost, rime; see ICE.

frosting *n.* icing, topping, finish, covering, coating.

frosty *a.* frigid, freezing, chilly; see COLD 1.

froth *n.* bubbles, scum, fizz, effervescence, foam, ferment, head, lather, suds, spray.

frothy *a.* fizzing, bubbling, foaming, soapy, sudsy, bubbly, fizzy, foamy, with a head on.

frown *n.* scowl, grimace, wry face, gloomy countenance, forbidding aspect, dirty look.

frown *v.* scowl, grimace, pout, glare, sulk, glower, gloom, look stern.— *Ant.* SMILE, laugh, grin.

frozen *a.* chilled, frosted, iced; see COLD 1, 2.

frugal *a.* thrifty, prudent, parsimonious; see CAREFUL.

frugality *n.* carefulness, conservation, management; see ECONOMY.

fruit *n.* berry, grain, nut, root; see also VEGETABLE. *Common fruits include the following:* apple, pear, peach, plum, nectarine, orange, grapefruit, banana, pineapple, watermelon, cantaloupe, honeydew melon, papaya, mango, guava, grape, lime, lemon, persimmon, pomegranate, raspberry, blackberry, blueberry, huckleberry, date, fig, apricot, cherry, raisin, avocado, gooseberry, strawberry.

fruitful *a.* prolific, productive, fecund; see FERTILE.

fruitless *a.* vain, unprofitable, empty; see FUTILE.

frustrate *v.* defeat, foil, balk; see PREVENT.

frustration *n.* disappointment, impediment, failure; see DEFEAT.

fry[1,2] *v.* sauté, sear, singe, brown, grill, pan-fry, deep-fry, French fry, sizzle; see also COOK. —**small fry** children, infants, toddlers; see BABY, CHILD.

fudge *n.* penuche, chocolate fudge, divinity fudge; see CANDY.

fuel *n.* propellant, combustibles, firing material. *Fuels include the following:* coal, gas, oil, coke, charcoal, anthracite, propane, bituminous coal, peat, slack, stoker coal, lignite, carbon, turf, cordwood, firewood, log, kindling, timber, diesel oil, crude oil, fuel oil, natural gas, gasoline, kerosene, wax.

fuel *v.* fill up, tank up*, gas up*; see FILL 1.

fugitive *n.* outlaw, refugee, truant, runaway, exile, vagabond, waif, stray, derelict, outcast, recluse, hermit.

fulfill *v.* accomplish, effect, complete; see ACHIEVE.

fulfilled *a.* accomplished, completed, achieved, realized, effected, finished, obtained, perfected, attained, reached, actualized, executed, concluded, brought about, performed, carried out, put into effect, made good, brought to a close.— *Ant.* DISAPPOINTED, unfulfilled, unrealized.

fulfillment *n.* attainment, accomplishment, realization; see ACHIEVEMENT.

full[1] *a.* **1** [Filled] running over, abundant, weighted, satisfied, saturated, crammed, packed, stuffed, jammed, glutted, gorged, loaded, chock-full, stocked, satiated, crowded, stuffed to the gills*, jam-packed, crawling with*, up to the brim, packed like sardines*.—*Ant.* EMPTY, exhausted, void. **2** [Well supplied] abundant, complete, copious, ample, plentiful, sufficient, adequate, competent, lavish, extravagant, profuse.—*Ant.* INADEQUATE, scanty, insufficient. **3** [Not limited] broad, unlimited, extensive; see ABSOLUTE 1, 2. —**in full 1** for the entire amount, fully, thoroughly; see COMPLETELY. **2** complete, entire, inclusive; see WHOLE 1.

reached the greatest size, extent, etc. **6** plump; round **7** with wide folds; flowing [a *full* skirt] — *n.* the greatest amount, extent, etc. — *adv.* **1** to the greatest degree; completely **2** directly; exactly —**full'ness** or **ful'ness** *n.*

full² (fool) *vt., vi.* [< L *fullo*, cloth fuller] to shrink and thicken (wool cloth) —**full'er** *n.*

full'back' *n. Football* an offensive back stationed behind the quarterback

full'-blood'ed *adj.* **1** of unmixed breed or race **2** vigorous

full'-blown' *adj.* **1** in full bloom **2** fully developed; matured

full'-fledged' *adj.* completely developed or trained; of full status

full moon the moon when it reflects light as a full disk

full'-scale' *adj.* **1** according to the original or standard scale **2** to the utmost degree; all-out

full'-time' *adj.* of or engaged in work, study, etc. that takes all of one's regular working hours

full'y *adv.* **1** completely; thoroughly **2** at least

ful·mi·nate (ful'mə nāt') *vi., vt.* **-nat'ed, -nat'ing** [< L *fulmen*, lightning] **1** to explode **2** to shout forth —**ful'mi·na'tion** *n.*

ful·some (fool'səm) *adj.* [see FULL¹ & -SOME¹, but infl. by ME *ful*, foul] disgusting, esp. because excessive

fum·ble (fum'bəl) *vi., vt.* **-bled, -bling** [prob. < ON *famla*] **1** to grope (*for*) or handle (a thing) clumsily **2** to lose one's grasp on (a football, etc.) — *n.* a fumbling — **fum'bler** *n.*

fume (fyoom) *n.* [< L *fumus*] [*often pl.*] a gas, smoke, or vapor, esp. if offensive or suffocating — *vi.* **fumed, fum'ing 1** to give off fumes **2** to show anger

fu·mi·gate (fyoo'mə gāt') *vt.* **-gat'ed, -gat'ing** [< L *fumus*, smoke + *agere*, do] to expose to fumes, esp. so as to disinfect or kill the vermin in —**fu'mi·ga'tion** *n.* —**fu'mi·ga'tor** *n.*

fumy (fyoom'ē) *adj.* **-i·er, -i·est** full of or producing fumes; vaporous

fun (fun) *n.* [< ME *fonne*, foolish] **1** *a*) lively, joyous play or playfulness *b*) pleasure **2** a source of amusement — **make fun of** to ridicule

func·tion (fuŋk'shən) *n.* [< L *fungi*, to perform] **1** the normal or characteristic action of anything **2** a special duty required in work **3** a formal ceremony or social occasion **4** a thing that depends on and varies with something else — *vi.* to act in a required manner; work; be used — **func'tion·less** *adj.*

func'tional *adj.* **1** of a function **2** performing a function **3** *Med.* affecting a function of some organ without apparent organic changes —**func'tion·al·ly** *adv.*

functional illiterate a person who cannot read well enough to function properly in a complex society

func'tion·ar'y (-shə ner'ē) *n., pl.* **-ies** an official performing some function

function word a word, as an article or conjunction, serving mainly to show grammatical relationship

fund (fund) *n.* [L *fundus*, bottom] **1** a supply that can be drawn upon; stock **2** *a*) a sum of money set aside for a purpose *b*) [*pl.*] ready money — *vt.* **1** to put or convert

into a long-term debt that bears interest **2** to provide funds for (a project, etc.)

fun·da·men·tal (fun'də ment''l) *adj.* [see prec.] of or forming a foundation or basis; basic; essential — *n.* a principle, theory, law, etc. serving as a basis —**fun'da·men'tally** *adv.*

fun'da·men'tal·ism' *n.* [*sometimes* F-] religious beliefs based on a literal interpretation of the Bible —**fun'da·men'tal·ist** *n., adj.*

fu·neral (fyoo'nər əl) *n.* [< L *funus*] the ceremonies connected with burial or cremation of the dead

funeral director one who manages a funeral home

funeral home (or **parlor**) an establishment where the bodies of the dead are prepared for burial or cremation and where funeral services can be held

fu·nereal (fyoo nir'ē əl) *adj.* suitable for a funeral; sad and solemn; dismal —**fu·ne'real·ly** *adv.*

fungi·cide (fun'ji sīd') *n.* [see -CIDE] any substance that kills fungi

fun·gus (fuŋ'gəs) *n., pl.* **fungi** (fun'jī') or **fun'guses** [< L] any of various plants, as molds, mildews, mushrooms, etc., that lack chlorophyll, stems, and leaves and reproduce by spores —**fun'gous** *adj.*

fu·nicu·lar (fyoo nik'yoo lər) *adj.* [< L *funiculus*, little rope] worked by a rope or cable — *n.* a mountain railway with counterbalanced cable cars on parallel sets of rails

funk (fuŋk) *n.* [< ? Fl *fonck*, dismay] [Colloq.] **1** a state of great fear; panic **2** a depressed mood

funky (fuŋ'kē) *adj.* **-i·er, -i·est** [orig., earthy] **1** *Jazz* having an earthy style derived from early blues **2** [Slang] unconventional, eccentric, offbeat, etc.

fun·nel (fun'əl) *n.* [ult. < L *fundere*, to pour] **1** a tapering tube with a cone-shaped mouth, for pouring things into small-mouthed containers **2** the smokestack of a steamship — *vi., vt.* **-neled** or **-nelled, -nel·ing** or **-nel·ling** to move or pour as through a funnel

fun·nies (fun'ēz) *n.pl.* [Colloq.] comic strips

fun·ny (fun'ē) *adj.* **-ni·er, -ni·est 1** causing laughter; humorous **2** [Colloq.] *a*) strange; queer *b*) tricky —**fun'nily** *adv.* —**fun'ni·ness** *n.*

funny bone a place on the elbow where a sharp impact on a nerve causes a strange, tingling sensation

funny farm [Slang] an institution for the mentally ill

fur (fur) *n.* [< OFr *fuerre*, sheath] **1** the soft, thick hair covering certain animals **2** a processed skin bearing such hair —*adj.* of fur —**furred** *adj.*

fur·below (fur'bə lō') *n.* [ult. < Fr *falbala*] **1** a flounce or ruffle **2** a showy, useless decorative addition

fur·bish (fur'bish) *vt.* [< OFr *forbir*] **1** to polish; burnish **2** to renovate

Fu·ries (fyoor'ēz) *Gr. & Rom. Myth.* the three terrible female spirits who punish unavenged crimes

fu·ri·ous (fyoor'ē əs) *adj.* **1** full of fury; very angry **2** very great, intense, wild, etc. —**fu'ri·ously** *adv.*

THESAURUS

fully *a.* entirely, thoroughly, wholly; see COMPLETELY.

fumble *n.* mistake, blunder, dropped ball; see ERROR.

fumble *v.* mishandle, bungle, mismanage; see BOTCH.

fun *n.* play, game, sport, jest, amusement, relaxation, pastime, diversion, frolic, mirth, entertainment, solace, merriment, pleasure, caper, foolery, romping, joke, absurdity, playfulness, laughter, festivity, carnival, tomfoolery, ball*, escapade, antic, romp, prank, comedy, teasing, celebration, holiday, rejoicing, good humor, joking, enjoyment, gladness, good cheer, delight, glee, treat, lark, recreation, joy, time of one's life, blast*, big time*, picnic*, riot*.—*Ant.* UNHAPPINESS, tedium, sorrow. —**for** (or **in**) **fun** for amusement, not seriously, playfully; see HAPPILY. —**make fun of** mock, satirize, poke fun at; see RIDICULE.

function *n.* employment, capacity, faculty; see USE 1.

function *v.* perform, run, work; see OPERATE 2.

functional *a.* occupational, utilitar-

ian, anatomic; see PRACTICAL.

fund *n.* endowment, trust fund, capital; see GIFT 1.

fundamental *a.* basic, underlying, primary, first, rudimentary, elemental, supporting, elementary, cardinal, organic, theoretical, structural, sustaining, central, original.—*Ant.* SUPERFICIAL, incidental, consequent.

fundamentally *a.* basically, radically, centrally; see ESSENTIALLY.

funds *n.* capital, wealth, cash, collateral, money, assets, currency, savings, revenue, wherewithal, proceeds, hard cash, stocks and bonds, money on hand, money in the bank, accounts receivable, means, affluence, belongings, resources, securities, stakes, earnings, winnings, possessions, profits, stocks, nest egg; see also MONEY.

funeral *n.* interment, last rites, burial, burial ceremony, entombment, requiem, cremation.

fungus *n.* mushroom, mold, rust; see DECAY, PARASITE 1.

funnel *n.* duct, shaft, conduit; see

PIPE 1.

funny *a.* **1** [Stirring to laughter] laughable, comic, comical, whimsical, amusing, entertaining, diverting, humorous, witty, jesting, jocular, waggish, droll, facetious, clever, mirthful, ludicrous, jolly, absurd, ridiculous, sly, sportive, playful, merry, joyful, joyous, good-humored, glad, gleeful, hilarious, jovial, farcical, joking, side-splitting.—*Ant.* SAD, serious, melancholy. **2** [*Likely to arouse suspicion] curious, unusual, odd; see SUSPICIOUS 2.

fur *n.* pelt, hide, hair, coat, brush. *Types of fur include the following:* sable, mink, chinchilla, karakul, seal, muskrat, ermine, monkey, beaver, skunk, otter, marten, stone marten, weasel, squirrel, leopard, raccoon, wolverine; white fox, blue fox, red fox, etc.; sheepskin, bearskin, calfskin, rabbit, coney. —**make the fur fly*** fight, bicker, stir up trouble; see EXCITE.

furious *a.* enraged, raging, fierce; see ANGRY.

furl (furl) *vt.* 〖< L *firmus*, FIRM[1] + *ligare*, to tie〗 to roll up (a sail, flag, etc.) tightly and make secure

fur·long (fur′lôŋ) *n.* 〖< OE *furh*, a furrow + *lang*, LONG[1]〗 a measure of distance equal to ⅛ of a mile

fur·lough (fur′lō) *n.* 〖< Du *verlof*〗 a leave of absence, esp. for military personnel — *vt.* to grant a furlough to

fur·nace (fur′nəs) *n.* 〖< L *fornax*, furnace〗 an enclosed structure in which heat is produced, as by burning fuel

fur·nish (fur′nish) *vt.* 〖< OFr *furnir*〗 1 to supply with furniture, etc.; equip 2 to supply; provide

fur·nish·ings *n.pl.* 1 the furniture, carpets, etc. as for a house 2 things to wear /men's *furnishings*/

fur·ni·ture (fur′ni chər) *n.* 〖Fr *fourniture*〗 1 the things in a room, etc. which equip it for living, as chairs, beds, etc. 2 necessary equipment

fu·ror (fyoor′ôr′) *n.* 〖< L〗 1 fury; frenzy 2 *a*) a widespread enthusiasm; craze *b*) a commotion or uproar Also [Chiefly Brit.] **fu·rore** (fyoo·rôr′ē)

fur·ri·er (fur′ē ər) *n.* one who processes furs or deals in fur garments

fur·ring (fur′iŋ) *n.* thin strips of wood fixed on a wall, floor, etc. before adding boards or plaster

fur·row (fur′ō) *n.* 〖< OE *furh*〗 1 a narrow groove made in the ground by a plow 2 anything like this, as a deep wrinkle — *vt.* to make furrows in — *vi.* to become wrinkled

furry (fur′ē) *adj.* **-ri·er, -ri·est** 1 of or like fur 2 covered with fur — **fur′ri·ness** *n.*

fur·ther (fur′thər) *adj.* 〖OE *furthor*〗 1 *alt. compar. of* FAR 2 additional 3 more distant; farther — *adv.* 1 *alt. compar. of* FAR 2 to a greater degree or extent 3 in addition 4 at or to a greater distance; farther — *vt.* to give aid to; promote In sense 3 of the *adj.* and sense 4 of the *adv.*, FARTHER is more commonly used — **fur′ther·ance** *n.*

fur·ther·more′ *adv.* in addition; besides; moreover

fur·thest (fur′thist) *adj.* 1 *alt. superl. of* FAR 2 most distant; farthest: also **fur′ther·most′** — *adv.* 1 *alt. superl. of* FAR 2 at or to the greatest distance or degree

fur·tive (fur′tiv) *adj.* 〖< L *fur*, a thief〗 done or acting in a stealthy manner; sneaky — **fur′tive·ly** *adv.* — **fur′tive·ness** *n.*

fury (fyoor′ē) *n., pl.* **-ries** 〖< L *furere*, to rage〗 1 violent anger; wild rage 2 violence; vehemence

furze (furz) *n.* 〖OE *fyrs*〗 a prickly evergreen shrub native to Europe

fuse[1] (fyōōz) *vt., vi.* **fused, fus′ing** 〖< L *fundere*, to shed〗 1 to melt 2 to unite as if by melting together

fuse[2] (fyōōz) *n.* 〖< L *fusus*, spindle〗 1 a tube or wick filled with combustible material, for setting off an explosive charge 2 *Elec.* a strip of easily melted metal placed in a circuit: it melts and breaks the circuit if the current becomes too strong

fu·see (fyōō zē′) *n.* 〖Fr *fusée*, a rocket〗 a colored flare used as a signal by trainmen, truck drivers, etc.

fu·selage (fyōō′sə lij′, -läzh′) *n.* 〖Fr〗 the body of an airplane, exclusive of the wings, tail assembly, and engines

fu·sible (fyōō′zə bəl) *adj.* that can be fused or easily melted

fu·si·lier or **fu·sil·eer** (fyōō′zi lir′) *n.* 〖Fr〗 [Historical] a soldier armed with a flintlock musket

fu·sil·lade (fyōō′sə läd′) *n.* 〖Fr < *fusiller*, to shoot〗 a simultaneous or rapid discharge of many firearms

fu·sion (fyōō′zhən) *n.* 〖L *fusio*〗 1 a fusing or melting together 2 a blending; coalition 3 NUCLEAR FUSION 4 a style of popular music blending elements of jazz, rock, etc.

fuss (fus) *n.* 〖prob. echoic〗 1 nervous, excited activity; bustle 2 a nervous state 3 a quarrel 4 a showy display of approval, etc. — *vi.* 1 to bustle about or worry over trifles 2 to whine, as a baby

fuss′budg′et (-buj′it) *n.* 〖prec. + BUDGET〗 [Colloq.] a fussy person Also [Colloq., Chiefly Brit.] **fuss′pot′** (-pät′)

fuss′y *adj.* **-i·er, -i·est** 1 *a*) worrying over trifles *b*) hard to please *c*) whining, as a baby 2 full of unnecessary details — **fuss′i·ly** *adv.* — **fuss′i·ness** *n.*

fus·tian (fus′chən) *n.* 〖< L *fustis*, wooden stick〗 pompous, pretentious talk or writing; bombast

fusty (fus′tē) *adj.* **-tier, -ti·est** 〖< OFr *fust*, a cask〗 1 musty; moldy 2 old-fashioned — **fus′ti·ness** *n.*

fut. future

fu·tile (fyōōt′'l) *adj.* 〖< L *futilis*, lit., that easily pours out〗 useless; vain — **fu′tilely** *adv.* — **fu·til·ity** (fyōō til′ə tē), *pl.* **-ties,** *n.*

fu·ton (fōō′tän′) *n.* 〖Sino-Jpn〗 a thin mattress like a quilt, placed on the floor for use as a bed

fu·ture (fyōō′chər) *adj.* 〖< L *futurus*, about to be〗 1 that is to be or come 2 indicating time to come /the *future* tense/ — *n.* 1 the time that is to come 2 what is going to be 3 the chance to succeed, etc. 4 [*usually pl.*] a contract for a commodity bought or sold for delivery at a later date — **fu′tur·is′tic** *adj.*

fu·tu·ri·ty (fyōō toor′ə tē, -tyoor′-) *n., pl.* **-ties** 1 the future 2 a future condition or event 3 a race for two-year-old horses in which the entries are selected before birth: in full **futurity race**

fu·tur·ol·ogy (fyōō′chər äl′ə jē) *n.* 〖FUTUR(E) + -OLOGY〗 the study of probable or presumed future conditions, as by making assumptions based on known facts — **fu′tur·ol′o·gist** *n.*

futz (futs) *vi.* 〖? < Yidd〗 [Slang] to trifle or fool (*around*)

fuzz (fuz) *n.* 〖< ?〗 1 loose, light particles of down, wool, etc.; fine hairs or fibers — **the fuzz** [Slang] a policeman or the police — **fuzz′y, -i·er, -i·est,** *adj.* — **fuzz′i·ly** *adv.* — **fuzz′i·ness** *n.*

fuzzy logic 〖< *fuzzy* (set), coined (1965) by L. A. Zadeh, U.S. scientist〗 a type of logic used in computers for processing imprecise or variable data

-fy (fī) 〖< L *facere*, do〗 *suffix* 1 to make /liquefy/ 2 to cause to have /glorify/ 3 to become /putrefy/

FYI for your information

THESAURUS

furnace *n.* heater, heating system, boiler, hot-air furnace, steam furnace, hot-water furnace, oil burner, gas furnace, electric furnace, kiln, blast furnace, open-hearth furnace, stove, forge.

furnish *v.* fit out, equip, stock; see PROVIDE 1.

furnished *a.* supplied, provided, fitted out; see EQUIPPED.

furniture *n.* movables, household goods, home furnishings. *Furniture includes the following—home:* table, chair, rug, carpeting, drapes, sofa, davenport, couch, cabinet, picture, chest, bureau, buffet, cupboard, stove, washing machine, washer, clothes dryer, dishwasher, refrigerator, bed, dresser, mirror, commode, chiffonier, tapestry, footstool, secretary, sideboard, clock, bookcase; *office:* desk, filing cabinet, stool, chair, table, counter, typewriter table.

furor *n.* tumult, excitement, stir; see DISTURBANCE 2.

further *a.* more, at a greater distance, in addition; see DISTANT.

furthermore *a.* moreover, too, in addition; see BESIDES.

furthest *a.* most remote, most distant, remotest, farthest, uttermost, outermost, ultimate, extreme, outmost.

fury *n.* wrath, fire, rage; see ANGER.

fuse[2] *n.* wick, tinder, kindling; see FUEL. **—blow a fuse*** become angry, lose one's temper, rant; see RAGE 1.

fuss *n.* trouble, complaint, bother; see DISTURBANCE 2.

fuss *v.* whine, whimper, object; see COMPLAIN.

fussy *a.* fastidious, particular, meticulous; see CAREFUL.

futile *a.* vain, useless, in vain, fruitless, hopeless, impractical, worthless, unprofitable, to no effect, not successful, to no purpose, unneeded, unsatisfactory, unsatisfying, ineffective, ineffectual, unproductive, idle, empty, hollow, unreal.—*Ant.* HOPEFUL, practical, effective.

futility *n.* uselessness, falseness, hollowness, frivolity, idleness, emptiness, fruitlessness, hopelessness,

worthlessness, illusion, folly, unimportance, carrying water in a sieve*, wild-goose chase*, running around in circles*, carrying coals to Newcastle*.—*Ant.* IMPORTANCE, fruitfulness, significance.

future *a.* coming, impending, imminent, destined, fated, prospective, to come, in the course of time, expected, inevitable, approaching, eventual, ultimate, planned, scheduled, budgeted, booked, looked toward, likely, coming up, in the cards.—*Ant.* PAST, completed, recorded.

future *n.* infinity, eternity, world to come, subsequent time, coming time, events to come, prospect, tomorrow, the hereafter, by and by.—*Ant.* PAST, historic ages, recorded time. **—in the future** eventually, sometime, in due time; see FINALLY 2, SOMEDAY.

fuzz *n.* nap, fluff, fur; see HAIR 1.

fuzzy *a.* 1 [Like or covered with fuzz] hairy, woolly, furry; see HAIRY. 2 [Not clear] blurred, indistinct, out of focus, hazy, foggy; see also OBSCURE 1, HAZY.

g or **G** (jē) *n., pl.* **g's, G's** the seventh letter of the English alphabet

G (jē) *n. Music* the fifth tone in the scale of C major

g gram

G *trademark for* a film rating indicating content suitable for persons of all ages

G or **G.** 1 game(s) 2 gauge 3 German 4 guard 5 Gulf Also, for 1, 2, & 4, **g** or **g.**

Ga *Chem. symbol for* gallium

gab (gab) *n., vt.* **gabbed, gab′bing** [ON *gabba*, to mock] [Colloq.] chatter

gab·ar·dine (gab′ər dēn′) *n.* [< OFr *gaverdine*, kind of cloak] a twilled cloth of wool, cotton, etc., with a fine, diagonal weave Brit. sp. **gab′er·dine**

gab·ble (gab′əl) *vi., vt.* **-bled, -bling** [< GAB] to talk or utter rapidly or incoherently — *n.* such talk

gab·by (gab′ē) *adj.* **-bier, -bi·est** [Colloq.] talkative —**gab′ bi·ness** *n.*

gab′fest′ (-fest′) *n.* [Colloq.] an informal gathering to talk or gab

ga·ble (gā′bəl) *n.* [< Gmc] the triangular wall enclosed by the sloping ends of a ridged roof —**ga′bled** *adj.*

Ga·bri·el (gā′brē əl) *Bible* one of the archangels, the herald of good news

gad (gad) *vi.* **gad′ded, gad′ding** [ME *gadden*, to hurry] to wander about idly or restlessly —**gad′der** *n.*

gad′about′ *n.* one who gads about, looking for fun, etc.

gad′fly′ *n., pl.* **-flies′** [see GOAD & FLY²] 1 a large fly that bites livestock 2 one who annoys others

gadg·et (gaj′it) *n.* [< ?] any small mechanical contrivance or device —**gadg′et·ry** *n.*

Gael·ic (gāl′ik) *adj.* of the Celtic people of Ireland, Scotland, or the Isle of Man — *n.* the Celtic language of Scotland

gaff (gaf) *n.* [< OProv *gaf* or Sp *gafa*] 1 a large hook on a pole for landing fish 2 a spar supporting a fore-and-aft sail —**stand the gaff** [Slang] to bear up well under punishment, ridicule, etc.

gaffe (gaf) *n.* [Fr] a blunder

gag (gag) *vt.* **gagged, gag′ging** [echoic] 1 to cause to retch 2 to keep from speaking, as by stopping up the mouth of — *vi.* to retch — *n.* 1 something put into or over the mouth to prevent talking, etc. 2 any restraint of free speech 3 a joke

gage¹ (gāj) *n.* [< OFr, a pledge] 1 something pledged; security 2 a glove, etc. thrown down as a challenge to fight 3 a challenge

gage² (gāj) *n., vt.* **gaged, gag′ing** *alt. sp. of* GAUGE

gag·gle (gag′əl) *n.* [echoic] 1 a flock of geese 2 any group or cluster

gai·e·ty (gā′ə tē) *n., pl.* **-ties** 1 the quality of being gay; cheerfulness 2 merrymaking 3 showy brightness

gai·ly (gā′lē) *adv.* in a gay manner; specif., *a)* merrily *b)* brightly

gain (gān) *n.* [< OFr *gaaigne*] 1 an increase; specif., *a)* [often *pl.*] profit *b)* an increase in advantage 2 acquisition — *vt.* 1 to earn 2 to win 3 to attract 4 to get as an addition, profit, or advantage 5 to make an increase in 6 to get to; reach — *vi.* 1 to make progress 2 to increase in weight —**gain on** to draw nearer to (an opponent in a race, etc.)

gain′er *n.* 1 a person or thing that gains 2 a fancy dive forward, but with a backward somersault

gain′ful *adj.* producing gain; profitable —**gain′fully** *adv.*

gain·say (gān′sā′) *vt.* **-said′** (-sed′), **-say′ing** [< OE *gegn*, against + *secgan*, to say] 1 to deny 2 to contradict —**gain′say′er** *n.*

G

gait (gāt) *n.* [< ON *gata*, path] 1 manner of walking or running 2 any of the various foot movements of a horse, as a trot, pace, canter, etc.

gai·ter (gāt′ər) *n.* [< Fr *guêtre*] a cloth or leather covering for the instep, ankle, and lower leg

gal (gal) *n.* a girl

gal. gallon(s)

ga·la (gā′lə, gal′ə) *n.* [ult. < It *gala*] a celebration — *adj.* festive

gala·bia or **gala·biya** (gal′ə bē′ə) *n.* [< Ar] *var. of* DJELLABA

Gal·a·had (gal′ə had′) *Arthurian Legend* the knight who, because of his purity, finds the Holy Grail

gal·axy (gal′ək sē) *n.* [< Gr *gala*, milk] [often G-] MILKY WAY — *n., pl.* **-ies** 1 a large, independent system of stars 2 a group of illustrious people —**ga·lac·tic** (gə lak′tik) *adj.*

gale (gāl) *n.* [< ?] 1 a strong wind 2 an outburst [a gale of laughter]

ga·le·na (gə lē′nə) *n.* [L, lead ore] native lead sulfide, a lead-gray mineral with metallic luster

gall¹ (gôl) *n.* [OE *galla*] 1 BILE (sense 1) 2 something bitter or distasteful 3 bitter feeling 4 [Colloq.] impudence

gall² (gôl) *n.* [see fol.] a sore on the skin caused by chafing — *vt.* 1 to make sore by rubbing 2 to annoy

gall³ (gôl) *n.* [< L *galla*] a tumor on plant tissue caused by stimulation by fungi, insects, or bacteria

gal·lant (gal′ənt; *for adj.* 3 & *n., usually* gə lant′, -länt′) *adj.* [< OFr *galer*, to make merry] 1 stately; imposing 2 brave and noble 3 polite and attentive to women — *n.* 1 [Now Rare] a high-spirited, stylish man 2 a man attentive and polite to women

gal·lant·ry (gal′ən trē) *n., pl.* **-ries** 1 heroic courage 2 the behavior of a gallant 3 a courteous act or remark

gall·blad·der (gôl′blad′ər) *n.* a membranous sac closely attached to the liver, in which excess gall, or bile, is stored

gal·le·on (gal′ē ən) *n.* [ult. < Gr *galeos*, shark] a large sailing ship of the 15th and 16th c.

gal·le·ria (gal′ə rē′ə) *n.* a large arcade or court, sometimes with a glass roof

gal·lery (gal′ər ē) *n., pl.* **-ies** [< ML *galeria*] 1 a covered walk or porch open at one side 2 a long, narrow, outside balcony 3 *a)* a balcony in a theater, etc.; esp., the highest balcony with the cheapest seats *b)* the people in these seats 4 the spectators at a sports event, etc. 5 an establishment for exhibitions, etc.

gal·ley (gal′ē) *n., pl.* **-leys** [< Gr *galeos*, shark] 1 a long, low ship of ancient times, propelled by oars and sails 2 a ship's kitchen 3 *Printing a)* a shallow tray for holding composed type *b)* proof printed from such type (in full, **galley proof**)

Gal·lic (gal′ik) *adj.* 1 of ancient Gaul or its people 2 French

Gal·li·cism (gal′i siz′əm) *n.* [< prec.] [also **g-**] a French idiom, custom, etc.

gal·li·um (gal′ē əm) *n.* [named after L *Gallia*, France] a bluish-white, metallic chemical element, often a super-cooled liquid at room temperature, used in semiconductors, lasers, etc.

■ THESAURUS ■

gab* *n.* gossip, idle talk, prattle; see NONSENSE 1. —**gift of (the) gab*** loquacity, volubility, verbal ability; see ELOQUENCE.

gab* *v.* gossip, jabber, chatter; see BABBLE.

gadget *n.* mechanical contrivance, object, contraption; see DEVICE 1.

gag *v.* 1 [To stop the mouth] choke, muzzle, muffle, obstruct, stifle, throttle, tape up, deaden. 2 [To retch] be nauseated, sicken, choke; see VOMIT.

gaiety *n.* jollity, mirth, exhilaration; see HAPPINESS.

gaily *a.* showily, brightly, vivaciously, spiritedly, brilliantly, splendidly, gaudily, expensively, colorfully, extravagantly, garishly, in a sprightly manner.—*Ant.* PEACEFULLY, quietly,

modestly.

gain *n.* increase, accrual, accumulation; see ADDITION 1.

gain *v.* 1 [To increase] augment, expand, enlarge; see GROW 1, INCREASE. 2 [To advance] progress, overtake, move forward; see ADVANCE 1. 3 [To achieve] attain, realize, reach; see SUCCEED 1.

gainful *a.* lucrative, productive, useful; see PROFITABLE.

gainfully *a.* productively, profitably, usefully; see PROFITABLY.

gait *n.* walk, run, motion, step, tread, stride, pace, tramp, march, carriage, movements.

galaxy *n.* cosmic system, star cluster, nebula; see STAR.

gale *n.* hurricane, blow, typhoon; see STORM, WIND.

gall¹* *n.* effrontery, insolence, impertinence; see RUDENESS.

gall² *v.* annoy, irk, irritate; see BOTHER 2.

gallant *a.* bold, courageous, intrepid; see BRAVE.

gallantry *n.* heroism, valor, bravery; see COURAGE.

gallery *n.* 1 [An elevated section of seats] arcade, upstairs, balcony; see UPSTAIRS. 2 [Onlookers, especially from the gallery] spectators, audience, public; see LISTENER. 3 [A room for showing works of art] salon, museum, exhibition room, studio, hall, exhibit, showroom.

gal·li·vant (gal′ə vant′) *vi.* ⟦arbitrary elaboration of GAL-LANT⟧ to go about in search of amusement

gal·lon (gal′ən) *n.* ⟦< OFr *jalon*⟧ a liquid measure equal to 4 quarts

gal·lop (gal′əp) *vi., vt.* ⟦< OFr *galoper*⟧ to go, or cause to go, at a gallop —*n.* the fastest gait of a horse, etc., a succession of leaping strides

gal·lows (gal′ōz) *n., pl.* **-lows** or **-lowses** ⟦OE *galga*⟧ an upright frame with a crossbeam and a rope, for hanging condemned persons

gall·stone (gôl′stōn′) *n.* a small, solid mass sometimes formed in the gallbladder or bile duct

ga·lore (gə lôr′) *adj.* ⟦Ir *go leōr*, enough⟧ in abundance; plentifully

ga·losh or **ga·loshe** (gə läsh′) *n.* ⟦< OFr *galoche*⟧ a high, warmly lined overshoe of rubber and fabric

gal·van·ic (gal van′ik) *adj.* ⟦after L. *Galvani* (1737-98), It physicist⟧ 1 of or producing an electric current, esp. from a battery 2 startling

gal·va·nism (-və niz′əm) *n.* electricity produced by chemical action

gal·va·nize (gal′və niz′) *vt.* **-nized**′, **-niz**′**ing** 1 to stimulate as if by electric shock; rouse; stir 2 to plate (metal) with zinc

gal·va·nom′e·ter (-näm′ət ər) *n.* an instrument for detecting and measuring a small electric current

gam·bit (gam′bit) *n.* ⟦< Sp *gambito*, a tripping⟧ 1 *Chess* an opening in which a pawn, etc. is sacrificed to get an advantage in position 2 an action intended to gain an advantage

gam·ble (gam′bəl) *vi.* **-bled**, **-bling** ⟦ME *gamen*, to play⟧ 1 to play games of chance for money, etc. 2 to take a risk for some advantage —*vt.* to risk in gambling; bet —*n.* an undertaking involving risk —**gam′bler** *n.*

gam·bol (gam′bəl) *n.* ⟦< It *gamba*, leg⟧ a gamboling; frolic —*vi.* **-boled** or **-bolled**, **-bol**′**ing** or **-bol**′**ling** to jump and skip about in play; frolic

gam·brel (roof) (gam′brəl) a roof with two slopes on each side

game[1] (gām) *n.* ⟦OE *gamen*⟧ 1 any form of play; amusement 2 *a)* amusement or sport involving competition under rules *b)* a single contest in such a competition 3 the number of points required for winning 4 a scheme; plan 5 wild birds or animals hunted for sport or food 6 [Colloq.] a business or job, esp. one involving risk —*vi.* **gamed, gam′ing** to play cards, etc. for stakes; gamble —*adj.* 1 designating or of wild birds or animals hunted for sport or food 2 *a)* plucky; courageous *b)* enthusiastic; ready (*for*) —**the game is up** failure is certain —**game′ly** *adv.* —**game′ness** *n.*

game[2] (gām) *adj.* ⟦< ?⟧ lame or injured *[a game leg]*

game′cock′ *n.* a specially bred rooster trained for cockfighting

game′keep′er *n.* a person who takes care of game birds and animals, as on an estate

game plan 1 the strategy planned before a game 2 any long-range strategy

game point 1 the situation when the next point scored could win a game 2 the winning point

games′man·ship′ (gāmz′mən ship′) *n.* skill in using ploys to gain an advantage

game·ster (gām′stər) *n.* a gambler

gam·ete (gam′ēt, gə mēt′) *n.* ⟦< Gr *gamos*, marriage⟧ a reproductive cell that unites with another to form the cell that develops into a new individual

gamin (gam′in) *n.* ⟦Fr⟧ 1 a neglected child who roams the streets 2 a girl with saucy charm: also **ga·mine**′ (ga mēn′)

gamma (gam′ə) *n.* the third letter of the Greek alphabet (Γ, γ)

gamma globu·lin (gläb′yōō lin) that fraction of blood serum which contains most antibodies

gamma ray an electromagnetic radiation with a very short wavelength, produced as by the reactions of nuclei

gam·ut (gam′ət) *n.* ⟦< Gr letter *gamma*, for the lowest note of the medieval scale⟧ 1 any complete musical scale 2 the entire range or extent

gamy (gām′ē) *adj.* **-i·er, -i·est** 1 having the strong flavor of cooked game 2 slightly tainted 3 risqué 4 coarse or crude —**gam′i·ness** *n.*

gan·der (gan′dər) *n.* ⟦OE *gan(d)ra*⟧ 1 a male goose 2 [Slang] a look

gang (gaŋ) *n.* ⟦< OE *gangan*, to go⟧ a group of people working or acting together; specif., a group of criminals or juvenile delinquents —**gang up on** [Colloq.] to attack as a group

gan·gling (gaŋ′gliŋ) *adj.* ⟦< ?⟧ thin, tall, and awkward Also **gan′gly**

gan·glion (gaŋ′glē ən) *n., pl.* **-glia** (-ə) or **-gli·ons** ⟦ult. < Gr, tumor⟧ a mass of nerve cells from which nerve impulses are transmitted —**gan′gli·on′ic** (-än′ik) *adj.*

gang′plank′ *n.* a movable ramp by which to board or leave a ship

gan·grene (gaŋ′grēn, gaŋ grēn′) *n.* ⟦< Gr *gran*, gnaw⟧ decay of body tissue when the blood supply is obstructed —**gan′grenous** (-grə nəs) *adj.*

gang·ster (gaŋ′stər) *n.* a member of a gang of criminals —**gang′ster·ism**′ *n.*

gang′way′ *n.* ⟦OE *gangweg*⟧ 1 a passageway 2 *a)* an opening in a ship's bulwarks for loading, etc. *b)* GANGPLANK —*interj.* clear the way!

gan·net (gan′it) *n.* ⟦OE *ganot*⟧ a large, web-footed sea bird

gant·let (gônt′lit, gänt′-, gant′-) *n.* ⟦< Swed *gata*, lane + *lopp*, a run⟧ 1 a former punishment in which the offender ran between two rows of men who struck him 2 a series of troubles Now sp. equally *gauntlet*

gan·try (gan′trē) *n., pl.* **-tries** ⟦< L *canterius*, beast of burden⟧ 1 a framework, often on wheels, for a traveling crane 2 a wheeled framework with a crane, platforms, etc., for readying a rocket to be launched

GAO General Accounting Office

gaol (jāl) *n. Brit. sp. of* JAIL

gap (gap) *n.* ⟦< ON *gapa*, to gape⟧ 1 an opening made by breaking or parting 2 a mountain pass or ravine 3 a blank space 4 a lag or disparity

gape (gāp) *vi.* **gaped, gap′ing** ⟦< ON *gapa*⟧ 1 to open the mouth wide, as in yawning 2 to stare with the mouth open 3 to open wide —*n.* 1 a gaping 2 a wide opening

gar (gär) *n., pl.* **gar** or **gars** ⟦< OE *gar*, a spear⟧ a freshwater fish with a beaklike snout Also **gar′fish**′

ga·rage (gə räzh′, -räj′) *n.* ⟦Fr < *garer*, to protect⟧ 1 a shelter for motor vehicles 2 a business place where such vehicles are stored, repaired, etc.

garage sale a sale of used or unwanted household articles, etc.

THESAURUS

gallon *n.* 231 cubic inches, 3.7853 liters, liquid measure, four quarts, eight pints.

gallop *v.* run, spring, leap, jump, go at a gallop, bound, hurdle, swing, stride, lope, amble, trot.

galoshes *n.* overshoes, rubbers, boots; see SHOE.

gamble *n.* chance, lot, hazard; see CHANCE 1.

gamble *v.* game, wager, bet, play, plunge, play at dice, cut the cards, bet against, speculate, back, lay money on, lay odds on, try one's luck, go for broke*, shoot craps; see also RISK.

gambler *n.* backer, sharper, card-sharp, speculator, confidence man, bettor, bookmaker, croupier, banker, player, sport*, highroller*, shark*, shill*, bookie*, con man*.

gambling *n.* betting, staking, venturing, gaming, laying money on, specu-

lating.

game[1] *a.* spirited, hardy, resolute; see BRAVE.

game[1] *n.* 1 [Entertainment] *Card games include the following:* poker, bridge, contract bridge, duplicate bridge, five hundred, casino, war, seven-up, cribbage, solitaire, hearts, twenty-one, blackjack, baccarat. *Children's games include:* hide-and-go-seek, tag, hopscotch, jacks, ball, fox and geese, marbles, crack the whip, statues, London Bridge, ring around the roses, drop the handkerchief, blindman's buff, follow the leader, Simon says, catch, post office, favors, musical chairs, streets and alleys, cops and robbers, soldier, cowboys and Indians, mother-may-I. *Board games include:* chess, checkers, Chinese checkers, backgammon, go, Monopoly, Sorry, Clue, Parcheesie, mahjongg. 2 [Sport]

play, recreation, merrymaking; see SPORT 1. 3 [Wild meat, fish, or fowl] quarry, prey, wildlife; see FISH, FOWL, MEAT. —**ahead of the game*** winning, doing well, thriving; see SUCCESSFUL. —**play the game*** behave properly, act according to custom, do what is expected; see BEHAVE.

gang *n.* horde, band, troop; see ORGANIZATION 2.

gangster *n.* gunman, underworld leader, racketeer; see CRIMINAL.

gang up on* *v.* combat, overwhelm, fight with; see ATTACK.

gap *n.* 1 [A breach] cleft, break, rift; see HOLE 1. 2 [A break in continuity] hiatus, recess, lull; see PAUSE. 3 [A mountain pass] way, chasm, hollow, cleft, ravine, gorge, arroyo, canyon, passageway, notch, gully, gulch.

garage *n.* car stall, parking space, parking garage, parking, parking lot,

garb (gärb) *n.* ‖< It *garbo*, elegance‖ clothing; style of dress *[*clerical *garb]* — *vt.* to clothe

gar·bage (gär′bij) *n.* ‖ME, entrails of fowls‖ spoiled or waste food

gar·ban·zo (gär bän′zō) *n.*, *pl.* **-zos** ‖Sp‖ CHICKPEA

gar·ble (gär′bəl) *vt.* **-bled, -bling** ‖< Ar *gharbāl*, a sieve‖ to distort or confuse (a story, etc.)

gar·con (gär sōn′) *n.* ‖Fr‖ a waiter

gar·den (gärd′'n) *n.* ‖< Frankish‖ 1 a piece of ground for growing vegetables, flowers, etc. 2 an area of fertile land: also **garden spot** 3 *[often pl.]* a public, parklike place, sometimes having displays of animals or plants — *vi.* to take care of a garden — *adj.* of, for, or grown in a garden —**gar′den·er** *n.*

gar·de·nia (gär dēn′yə) *n.* ‖after A. *Garden* (1730-91), Am botanist‖ a plant with fragrant, waxy flowers

gar′den-vari′e·ty *adj.* ordinary; commonplace

Gar·gan·tua (gär gan′chōō ə) a giant king in a satire by Rabelais (16th-c. Fr. writer) —**Gar·gan′tu·an** or **gar·gan′tu·an** *adj.*

gar·gle (gär′gəl) *vt.*, *vi.* **-gled, -gling** ‖< Fr *gargouille*, throat‖ to rinse (the throat) with a liquid kept in motion by the expulsion of air from the lungs — *n.* a liquid for gargling

gar·goyle (gär′goil′) *n.* ‖see prec.‖ a waterspout formed like a fantastic creature, projecting from a building

gar·ish (gar′ish, ger′-) *adj.* ‖prob. < ME *gauren*, to stare‖ too gaudy; showy —**gar′ish·ly** *adv.* —**gar′ish·ness** *n.*

gar·land (gär′lənd) *n.* ‖< OFr *garlande*‖ a wreath of flowers, leaves, etc. —*vt.* to decorate with garlands

gar·lic (gär′lik) *n.* ‖< OE *gar*, a spear + *leac*, leek‖ 1 an herb of the lily family 2 its strong-smelling bulb, used as seasoning —**gar′licky** *adj.*

gar·ment (gär′mənt) *n.* ‖see GARNISH‖ any article of clothing

gar·ner (gär′nər) *vt.* ‖< L *granum*, grain‖ to gather up and store

gar·net (gär′nit) *n.* ‖< ML *granatum*‖ a hard, glasslike mineral: red varieties are often used as gems

gar·nish (gär′nish) *vt.* ‖< OFr *garnir*, furnish‖ 1 to decorate or to decorate (food) with something that adds color or flavor 3 to garnishee — *n.* 1 a decoration 2 something used to garnish food, as parsley

gar·nishee (gär′ni shē′) *vt.* **-eed′, -ee′ing** ‖< prec.‖ *Law* to attach (a debtor's property, wages, etc.) so that it can be used to pay the debt

gar′nish·ment *n. Law* a notice ordering a person in possession of a defendant's property or money not to dispose of it

gar·ret (gar′it) *n.* ‖< OFr *garite*, watchtower‖ an attic

gar·ri·son (gar′ə sən) *n.* ‖< OFr *garir*, to watch‖ 1 troops stationed in a fort or fortified place 2 a military post or station — *vt.* to station (troops) in (a fortified place) for its defense

gar·rote (gə rōt′, ge rät′) *n.* ‖Sp‖ 1 a cord, thong, etc. used in strangling a person in a surprise attack 2 a strangling in this way — *vt.* **-rot′ed** or **-rot′ted, -rot′ing** or **-rot′ting** to execute or attack by such strangling Also **ga·rotte′** or **gar·rotte′** (-rät′, -rōt′) —**gar·rot′er** *n.*

gar·ru·lous (gar′ə ləs, gar′yōō-) *adj.* ‖< L *garrire*, to chatter‖ talking much, esp. about unimportant things —**gar·ru·li·ty** (gə rōō′lə tē) or **gar′ru·lous·ness** *n.* —**gar′ru·lous·ly** *adv.*

gar·ter (gärt′ər) *n.* ‖< OFr *garet*, the back of the knee‖ an elastic band or strap for holding a stocking in place

garter snake a small, harmless snake common in North America

gas (gas) *n.*, *pl.* **gas′es** or **gas′ses** ‖coined < Gr *chaos*, space‖ 1 the fluid form of a substance in which it can expand indefinitely; vapor 2 any mixture of flammable gases used for lighting or heating 3 any gas used as an anesthetic 4 any poisonous substance dispersed in the air, as in war 5 [Colloq.] *a)* GASOLINE *b)* the accelerator in an automobile — *vt.* **gassed, gas′sing** to injure or kill by gas —**gas′eous** (-ē əs) *adj.*

gas chamber a room in which people are put to death with poison gas

gash (gash) *vt.* ‖< Gr *charassein*, to cut‖ to make a long, deep cut in; slash — *n.* a long, deep cut

gas·ket (gas′kit) *n.* ‖prob. < OFr *garcete*, small cord‖ a piece or ring of rubber, metal, etc. used to make a joint leakproof

gas mask a filtering mask to protect against breathing in poisonous gases

gaso·hol (gas′ə hôl′) *n.* a motor fuel mixture of gasoline and alcohol

gaso·line (gas′ə lēn′, gas′ə lēn′) *n.* ‖< *gas* + L *oleum*, oil‖ a volatile, flammable liquid distilled from petroleum, used chiefly as a fuel in internal-combustion engines Also **gas′o·lene′**

gasp (gasp) *vi.* ‖< ON *geispa*, to yawn‖ to inhale suddenly, as in surprise, or to breathe with effort — *vt.* to say with gasps — *n.* a gasping

gas station SERVICE STATION

gas′sy *adj.* **-si·er, -si·est** 1 full of gas; esp., flatulent 2 like gas

gas·tric (gas′trik) *adj.* ‖GASTR(O)- + -IC‖ of, in, or near the stomach

gastric juice the clear, acid digestive fluid produced by glands in the stomach lining

gas·tri·tis (gas trīt′is) *n.* ‖fol. + -ITIS‖ inflammation of the stomach

gastro- ‖< Gr *gastēr*‖ combining form stomach (and)

gas·tron·o·my (gas trän′ə mē) *n.* ‖< Gr *gastēr*, stomach + *nomos*, a rule‖ the art of good eating —**gas′tro·nom′ic** (-trə näm′ik) or **gas′tro·nom′i·cal** *adj.*

gas·tro·pod (gas′trō päd′) *n.* ‖GASTRO- + -POD‖ a mollusk of the class including snails, slugs, etc.

gate (gāt) *n.* ‖OE‖ 1 a movable structure controlling passage through an opening in a fence or wall 2 a gateway 3 a movable barrier 4 a structure controlling the flow of water, as in a canal 5 the total amount or number of paid admissions to a performance —**give (or get) the gate** [Slang] to subject (or be subjected) to dismissal

-gate (gāt) ‖< (*Water*)*gate*, political scandal, after the *Watergate*, building in Washington, D.C., site of 1972 burglary‖ combining form a scandal marked by charges of corruption against public officials, etc.

gate′-crash′er *n.* [Colloq.] one who attends a social affair without an invitation or a performance without paying

gate′fold′ *n.* an oversize page, as in a magazine, bound so it can be unfolded

gate′way′ *n.* 1 an entrance as in a wall, fitted with a gate 2 a means of access

gather (gath′ər) *vt.* ‖OE *gad(e)rian*‖ 1 to bring together in one place or group 2 to get gradually; accumulate 3 to collect by picking; harvest 4 to infer; conclude 5 to draw

---

THESAURUS

carport.

garbage *n.* refuse, waste, table scrapings; see TRASH 1.

garden *n.* vegetable patch, melon patch, cultivated area, truck garden, enclosure, field, plot, bed, herb garden, rock garden, rose garden, formal garden, kitchen garden, hotbed, greenhouse, patio, terrace, back yard, nursery, flower garden, garden spot, oasis.

gardener *n.* vegetable grower, caretaker, landscaper; see FARMER.

gardening *n.* truck farming, vegetable raising, tillage; see FARMING.

gargantuan *a.* enormous, huge, immense; see LARGE 1.

gargle *v.* swash, rinse the mouth, use a mouthwash; see CLEAN.

garish *a.* showy, gaudy, ostentatious; see ORNATE.

garment *n.* dress, attire, apparel; see CLOTHES.

garnish *v.* embellish, beautify, deck; see DECORATE.

gas *n.* 1 [A state of matter] vapor, volatile substance, fumes, aeriform fluid, gaseous mixture. 2 [Gasoline] propellant, petrol, motor fuel; see GASOLINE. 3 [Poisonous gas] systemic poison, mustard gas, tear gas; see POISON. 4 [An anesthetic] ether, general anesthetic, chloroform, nitrous oxide, laughing gas. 5 [A fuel] natural gas, propane, bottled gas, acetylene, coal gas; see also FUEL. —**step on the gas*** rush, hasten, move fast; see HURRY 1.

gaseous *a.* vaporous, effervescent, in the form of gas; see LIGHT 5.

gash *n.* slash, slice, wound; see CUT.

gasoline *n.* petrol, motor fuel, propellant, gas, juice, low octane gasoline, high octane gasoline, ethyl gasoline, gasohol.

gasp *v.* labor for breath, gulp, have difficulty in breathing, pant, puff, wheeze, blow, snort.

gate *n.* entrance, ingress, passage, way, bar, turnstile, revolving door, barrier; see also DOOR.

gather *v.* 1 [To come together] assemble, meet, gather around, congregate, flock in, pour in, rally, crowd, throng, come together, convene, collect, unite, reunite, associate, hold a meeting, hold a reunion, swarm, huddle, draw in, group, converge, concentrate.—*Ant.* SCATTER, disperse, part. 2 [To bring together] collect, aggregate, amass; see ACCUMULATE, ASSEMBLE. 3 [To conclude] infer, deduce, find; see ASSUME.

gathered *a.* assembled, met, congregated, joined, rallied, crowded into folds or puckers — *vi.* **1** to assemble **2** to increase — *n.* a pucker or fold

gath′er·ing *n.* **1** a meeting; crowd **2** a gather in cloth

ga·tor or **'ga·tor** (gā′tər) *n. short for* ALLIGATOR

gauche (gōsh) *adj.* ⟦Fr < MFr *gauchir*, become warped⟧ lacking social grace; awkward; tactless

gau·che·rie (gō′shə rē) *n.* gauche behavior or a gauche act

gau·cho (gou′chō) *n., pl.* **-chos** ⟦AmSp⟧ a South American cowboy

gaudy (gôd′ē) *adj.* **-i·er, -i·est** ⟦< ME *gaude*, trinket⟧ bright and showy, but lacking in good taste —**gaud′i·ly** *adv.* —**gaud′i·ness** *n.*

gauge (gāj) *n.* ⟦Norm Fr⟧ **1** a standard measure or criterion **2** any device for measuring **3** the distance between the rails of a railroad **4** the size of the bore of a shotgun **5** the thickness of sheet metal, wire, etc. — *vt.* **gauged, gaug′ing 1** to measure the size, amount, etc. of **2** to judge

Gaul (gôl) ancient division of the Roman Empire, in W Europe — *n.* any of the people of Gaul

Gaul′ish *n.* the Celtic language of ancient Gaul

gaunt (gônt) *adj.* ⟦ME *gawnte*⟧ **1** thin and bony; haggard, as from great hunger **2** looking grim or forbidding — **gaunt′ness** *n.*

gaunt·let[1] (gônt′lit, gänt′-) *n.* ⟦< OFr *gant*, glove⟧ **1** a knight's armored glove **2** a long glove with a flaring cuff —**throw down the gauntlet** to challenge, as to combat

gaunt·let[2] (gônt′lit, gänt′-) *n. see* GANTLET

gauze (gôz) *n.* ⟦< Fr *gaze* < Ar *kazz*, silk⟧ any very thin, transparent material, as of cotton or silk —**gauz′y, -i·er, -i·est,** *adj.*

gave (gāv) *vt., vi. pt. of* GIVE

gavel (gav′əl) *n.* ⟦< Scot *gable*, fork⟧ a small mallet used, as by a presiding officer, to call for attention, etc.

ga·votte (gə vät′) *n.* ⟦Fr⟧ a 17th-c. dance like the minuet, but livelier

gawk (gôk) *vi.* ⟦prob. < *gowk*, stupid person⟧ to stare stupidly

gawky (gô′kē) *adj.* **-i·er,· -i·est** ⟦see prec.⟧ clumsy; ungainly —**gawk′i·ly** *adv.* —**gawk′i·ness** *n.*

gay (gā) *adj.* ⟦OFr *gai*⟧ **1** joyous and lively; merry **2** bright; brilliant *[gay* colors*]* **3** homosexual — *n.* a homosexual, esp. a male homosexual —**gay′ness** *n.*

gay·ety (gā′ə tē) *n. alt. sp. of* GAIETY

gayly (gā′lē) *adv. alt. sp. of* GAILY

gaze (gāz) *vi.* **gazed, gaz′ing** ⟦< Scand⟧ to look steadily; stare — *n.* a steady look —**gaz′er** *n.*

ga·zebo (gə zē′bō, -zā′-) *n., pl.* **-bos** or **-boes** ⟦< prec.⟧ a summerhouse, windowed balcony, etc. for gazing at scenery

ga·zelle (gə zel′) *n.* ⟦< Ar *ghazāl*⟧ a small, swift antelope of Africa and Asia, with large, lustrous eyes

ga·zette (gə zet′) *n.* ⟦< It dial. *gazeta*, a small coin, price of the newspaper⟧ **1** a newspaper: now mainly in newspaper titles **2** in England, an official publication — *vt.* **-zet′ted, -zet′ting** [Brit.] to publish in a gazette

gaz·et·teer (gaz′ə tir′) *n.* a dictionary or index of geographical names

gaz·pa·cho (gäs pä′chō, gäz-) *n.* ⟦Sp⟧ a cold Spanish soup of tomatoes, chopped cucumbers, onions, peppers, oil, vinegar, etc.

G.B. or **GB** Great Britain

Ge *Chem. symbol for* germanium

gear (gir) *n.* ⟦< ON *gervi*, preparation⟧ **1** clothing **2** equipment, esp. for some task **3** *a)* a toothed wheel designed to mesh with another *b)* [*often pl.*] a system of such gears meshed together to pass motion along *c)* a specific adjustment of such a system *d)* a part of a mechanism with a specific function *[the steering gear]* — *vt.* **1** to connect by or furnish with gears **2** to adapt (one thing) to conform with another *[to gear* supply to demand*]* —**in** (or **out of**) **gear 1** (not) connected to the motor **2** (not) in proper working order

gear′shift′ *n.* the lever for engaging or disengaging any of several sets of transmission gears to a motor, etc.

gear′wheel′ *n.* a toothed wheel in a system of gears; cogwheel

gecko (gek′ō) *n., pl.* **-os** or **-oes** ⟦prob. < Malay⟧ a tropical lizard with suction pads on its feet

gee (jē) *interj.* ⟦< JE(SUS)⟧ [Slang] an exclamation of surprise, etc.

gee·gaw (gē′gô) *n. var. of* GEWGAW

geese (gēs) *n. pl. of* GOOSE

gee·zer (gē′zər) *n.* ⟦< GUISE⟧ [Slang] an eccentric old man

ge·filte fish (gə fil′tə fish) ⟦Yidd⟧ chopped, seasoned fish, boiled and served in balls or cakes

Gei·ger counter (gī′gər) ⟦after H. *Geiger* (1882-1945), Ger physicist⟧ an instrument for detecting and counting ionizing particles, as from radioactive ores

gei·sha (gā′shə) *n., pl.* **-sha** or **-shas** ⟦Sino-Jpn *gei*, art + *sha*, person⟧ a Japanese girl trained as an entertainer to serve as a hired companion to men

gel (jel) *n.* ⟦< fol.⟧ a jellylike substance formed from a colloidal solution — *vi.* **gelled, gel′ling** to form a gel

gela·tin (jel′ə tin) *n.* ⟦< L *gelare*, freeze⟧ a tasteless, odorless substance extracted by boiling bones, horns, etc., or a similar vegetable substance: dissolved and cooled, it forms a jellylike substance used in foods, photographic film, etc. Also **gel′a·tine** —**ge·lati·nous** (jə lat′'n əs) *adj.*

geld (geld) *vt.* **geld′ed** or **gelt, geld′ing** ⟦< ON *geldr*, barren⟧ to castrate (esp. a horse)

geld′ing *n.* a castrated horse

gelid (jel′id) *adj.* ⟦< L *gelu*, frost⟧ extremely cold; frozen

gem (jem) *n.* ⟦< L *gemma*⟧ **1** a cut and polished gemstone or a pearl **2** something very precious or valuable

Gemi·ni. (jem′ə nī′, -nē′) ⟦L, twins⟧ the third sign of the zodiac

gem′stone′ *n.* any mineral that can be used in a piece of jewelry when cut and polished

ge·müt·lich (gə müt′likh) *adj.* ⟦Ger⟧ agreeable, cheerful, cozy, etc.

-gen (jən, jen) ⟦< Gr *-genēs*, born⟧ *suffix* **1** something that produces *[hydrogen]* **2** something produced (in a specified way)

Gen. 1 General **2** *Bible* Genesis

gen·darme (zhän′därm′) *n.* ⟦Fr < *gens d'armes*, men-at-arms⟧ a French police officer

gen·der (jen′dər) *n.* ⟦< L *genus*, origin⟧ **1** *Gram.* the classification by which words are grouped as masculine, feminine, or neuter **2** [Colloq.] a person's sex

gene (jēn) *n.* ⟦see -GEN⟧ any of the units in the chromosomes by which hereditary characters are transmitted

---

THESAURUS

together, thronged, collected, united, associated, swarmed, huddled, grouped, massed, amassed, accumulated, picked, garnered, harvested, stored, combined, brought together, convened, convoked, summoned, compiled, mobilized, lumped together, raked up, concentrated, heaped, stacked, piled, stowed away.—*Ant.* SCATTERED, dispersed, separated.

gathering *n.* assembly, meeeting, conclave, caucus, parley, council, conference, band, congregation, company, rally, crowd, throng, bunch, collection, union, association, society, committee, legislature, house, senate, parliament, swarm, huddle, group, body, mass, herd, turnout, flock, combination, convention, discussion, panel, reunion, meet, congress, attendance, multitude, audience, horde, mob, crush, party, social gathering, crew, gang, school,

bevy, troop, drove, concentration, convocation, gettogether, bull session*.

gaudy *a.* showy, flashy, tawdry; see ORNATE.

gauge *n.* scale, criterion, standard; see MEASURE 2.

gauge *v.* check, weigh, calibrate, calculate; see also MEASURE 1.

gaunt *a.* emaciated, scraggy, skinny; see THIN 2.

gauze *n.* veil, bandage, dressings; see DRESSING 3.

gawk *v.* stare, ogle, gaze; see LOOK 2.

gay *a.* **1** [Happy] cheerful, merry, vivacious; see HAPPY. **2** [Homosexual] homophile, homoerotic, lesbian; see HOMOSEXUAL.

gaze *v.* stare, watch, gape; see LOOK 2.

gear *n.* **1** [Equipment] material, tackle, things; see EQUIPMENT. **2** [A geared wheel] cog, cogwheel, pinion, toothed wheel, sprocket. *Driving*

gears include: first, low, second, intermediate, third, high, fourth, reverse, overdrive. **—in gear** usable, efficient, productive; see WORKING 1. **—out of gear** inefficient, not working, broken; see USELESS 1.

gem *n.* **1** [A jewel] precious stone, bauble, ornament; see JEWEL. *Types of gems include the following:* diamond, emerald, ruby, pearl, brilliant, aquamarine, amethyst, topaz, turquoise, jade, opal, sapphire, garnet, carnelian, jacinth, beryl, cat's eye, chrysoprase, chalcedony, agate, bloodstone, moonstone, onyx, sard, lapis lazuli, chrysolite, carbuncle, coral. **2** [Anything excellent, especially if small and beautiful] jewel, pearl of great price, paragon, ace, nonpareil, perfection, ideal.

gender *n.* sexuality, sort, variety; see KIND 2, SEX 3.

ge·neal·ogy (jē'nē al'ə jē; *often*, -äl'-) *n., pl.* **-gies** ‖< Gr *genea*, race + *-logia*, -LOGY‖ **1** a recorded history of a person's ancestry **2** the study of family descent **3** lineage —**ge'nea·log'i·cal** (-ə läj'i kəl) *adj.* —**ge'neal'o·gist** *n.*

gen·era (jen'ər ə) *n. pl. of* GENUS

gen·eral (jen'ər əl) *adj.* ‖< L *genus*, class‖ **1** of, for, or from all; not local, special, or specialized **2** of or for a whole genus, kind, etc. **3** widespread *[general unrest]* **4** most common; usual **5** not specific or precise *[in general terms]* **6** highest in rank *[attorney general]* — *n.* a military officer ranking above a colonel, specif. one ranking above a lieutenant general —**in general 1** usually **2** without specific details —**gen'er·al·ship'** *n.*

general assembly *[often* G- A-*]* **1** the legislative assembly in some States **2** the deliberative assembly of the United Nations

general delivery delivery of mail at the post office to addressees who call for it

gen·er·al·is·simo (jen'ər ə lis'i mō') *n., pl.* **-mos'** ‖It‖ in some countries, the commander in chief of the armed forces

gen·er·al·ity (jen'ər al'ə tē) *n., pl.* **-ties 1** the quality of being general **2** a general or vague statement, idea, etc. **3** the main body

gen·er·al·ize (jen'ər əl īz') *vt.* **-ized', -iz'ing 1** to state in terms of a general law **2** to infer or derive (a general law) from (particular instances) — *vi.* **1** to formulate general principles **2** to talk in generalities —**gen'er·ali·za'tion** *n.*

gen'er·ally *adv.* **1** widely; popularly **2** usually **3** not specifically

general practitioner a practicing physician who does not specialize in a particular field of medicine

gen·er·ate (jen'ər āt') *vt.* **-at'ed, -at'ing** ‖< L *genus*, race‖ **1** to produce (offspring); beget **2** to bring into being —**gen'era'tive** *adj.*

gen'era'tion *n.* **1** the producing of offspring **2** production **3** a single stage in the succession of descent **4** the average period (*c.* 30 years) between human generations **5** all the people born and living at about the same time —**gen'era'tional** *adj.*

gen'era'tor *n.* a machine for changing mechanical energy into electrical energy; dynamo

ge·neric (jə ner'ik) *adj.* ‖< L *genus*, race, kind‖ **1** of a whole kind, class, or group; inclusive **2** without a trademark — *n.* a product without a brand name: *often used in pl.* —**ge·ner'i·cally** *adv.*

gen·er·ous (jen'ər əs) *adj.* ‖< L *generosus*, noble‖ **1** noble-minded; magnanimous **2** willing to give or share; unselfish **3** large; ample —**gen·er·os·ity** (jen'ər äs'ə tē) *n.* —**gen'er·ously** *adv.*

gen·esis (jen'ə sis) *n.* ‖Gr‖ the beginning; origin —**[G-]** the first book of the Bible

genetic code the order in which four chemical constituents are arranged in huge molecules of DNA

ge·net·ics (jə net'iks) *n.pl.* ‖ult. < GENESIS‖ *[with sing. v.]* the branch of biology dealing with heredity and variation in animal and plant species —**ge·net'ic** *adj.* —**ge·net'i·cally** *adv.* —**ge·net'i·cist** (-ə sist) *n.*

gen·ial (jēn'yəl) *adj.* ‖see GENIUS‖ **1** good for life and growth *[a genial climate]* **2** cheerful and friendly; amiable —**ge·ni·al·ity** (jē·nē al'ə tē) *n.* —**gen'i·ally** *adv.*

ge·nie (jē'nē) *n.* ‖< Fr < Ar *jinnī*‖ JINNI

geni·tal (jen'i təl) *adj.* ‖< L *genere*, beget‖ of reproduction or the sexual organs

gen'i·tals *n.pl.* ‖see prec.‖ the reproductive organs; esp., the external sex organs Also **geni·ta'lia** (-tā'lē ə)

geni·tive (jen'i tiv) *n.* ‖< Gr *genesis*, genus‖ *Gram.* a case expressing possession, source, etc., or referring to a part of a whole

geni·to·uri·nary (jen'i tō yoor'ə ner'ē) *adj.* of the genital and urinary organs

gen·ius (jēn'yəs) *n.* ‖L, guardian spirit‖ **1** particular spirit of a nation, place, age, etc. **2** natural ability; strong inclination (*for*) **3** great mental capacity and inventive ability **4** one having such capacity or ability

geno·cide (jen'ə sīd') *n.* ‖< Gr *genos*, race + -CIDE‖ the systematic killing of a whole people or nation

genre (zhän'rə) *n.* ‖Fr < L *genus*, a kind‖ **1** a distinct kind, or type, as of works of literature, art, or popular fiction **2** painting in which everyday subjects are treated realistically

gent (jent) *n.* [Colloq.] a gentleman

gen·teel (jen tēl') *adj.* ‖< Fr *gentil*‖ polite or well-bred; now, esp., affectedly refined, polite, etc.

gen·tian (jen'shən) *n.* ‖< L *gentiana*‖ a plant typically with blue, fringed flowers

gen·tile (jen'til') *n.* ‖< L *gentilis*, of the same clan‖ *[also* G-*]* any person not a Jew — *adj.* not Jewish

gen·til·ity (jen til'i tē) *n.* ‖see fol.‖ the quality of being genteel

gen·tle (jent''l) *adj.* **-tler, -tlest** ‖< L *gentilis*, of the same clan‖ **1** of the upper classes **2** refined, courteous, etc. **3** generous; kind **4** tame *[a gentle dog]* **5** kindly; patient **6** not harsh or rough *[a gentle tap]* **7** gradual *[a gentle slope]* —**gen'tle·ness** *n.* —**gen'tly** *adv.*

gen'tle·folk' *n.pl.* people of good social standing Also **gen'tle·folks'**

gen'tle·man (-mən) *n., pl.* **-men 1** a man of good family and social standing **2** a courteous, gracious, and honorable man **3** any man: a polite term, esp. as (in pl.) a form

═══ THESAURUS ═══

genealogy *n.* derivation, lineage, extraction; see FAMILY.

general *a.* **1** [Having wide application] comprehensive, comprehending, widespread, universal, limitless, unlimited, extensive, ecumenical, all-embracing, ubiquitous, unconfined, broad, taken as a whole, not particular, not specific, blanket, inclusive, wide, infinite, worldwide, endless.—*Ant.* SPECIAL, particular, limited. **2** [Of common occurrence] usual, customary, prevailing; see COMMON 1. **3** [Not specific] indefinite, uncertain, imprecise; see VAGUE 2. —**in general** generally, usually, ordinarily; see REGULARLY.

generality *n.* abstraction, universality, principle; see LAW 4.

generalize *v.* theorize, speculate, postulate; see UNDERSTAND.

generally *a.* usually, commonly, ordinarily; see REGULARLY.

generate *v.* form, make, beget, create; see also PRODUCE 1.

generation *n.* **1** [The act of producing offspring] procreation, reproduction, breeding; see BIRTH. **2** [One cycle in the succession of parents and children] age, stage, crop, rank, age group. **3** [The time required for a generation] span, 20 to 30 years, period; see AGE 3.

generic *a.* universal, general, nonex-

clusive; see UNIVERSAL 3, GENERAL 1.

generosity *n.* hospitality, benevolence, charity, liberality, philanthropy, altruism, unselfishness; see also KINDNESS 2.—*Ant.* GREED, miserliness, stinginess.

generous *a.* **1** [Open-handed] bountiful, liberal, charitable, altruistic, free-handed, beneficient, unselfish, hospitable, philanthropic, prodigal, lavish, profuse, unsparing, unstinting.—*Ant.* STINGY, close, tight-fisted. **2** [Considerate] kindly, magnanimous, reasonable; see KIND.

generously *a.* **1** [With a free hand] bountifully, liberally, lavishly, unsparingly, unstintingly, in full measure, handsomely, freely, profusely, abundantly, munificently, charitably, copiously, with open hands.—*Ant.* SELFISHLY, grudgingly, sparingly. **2** [With an open heart] charitably, liberally, magnanimously, wholeheartedly, unreservedly, nobly, majestically, royally, honestly, candidly, enthusiastically, unselfishly, disinterestedly, chivalrously, benevolently, genially, warmly.—*Ant.* SELFISHLY, coldly, heartlessly.

genetic *a.* sporogenous, hereditary, genic, patrimonial; see also HISTORICAL.

genetics *n.* heredity, inheritance, eugenics; see HEREDITY.

genial *a.* cordial, kind, warmhearted; see FRIENDLY.

genitals *n.* organs, sexual organs, genitalia, private parts, reproductive organs, pudenda, gonads, testicles, testes, privates.

genius *n.* **1** [The highest degree of intellectual capacity] ability, talent, intellect, brains, intelligence, inspiration, imagination, gift, aptitude, wisdom, astuteness, penetration, grasp, discernment, acumen, acuteness, power, capability, accomplishment, sagacity, understanding, reach, enthusiasm, creative gift, knack, bent, turn. **2** [One having genius] gifted person, prodigy, adept; see ARTIST, AUTHOR, DOCTOR, PHILOSOPHER, POET, WRITER.

gentility *n.* decorum, propriety, refinement; see BEHAVIOR.

gentle *a.* **1** [Soft] tender, smooth, sensitive; see FAINT 3, SOFT 2, 3. **2** [Kind] tender, considerate, benign; see KIND. **3** [Tamed] domesticated, housebroken, disciplined, educated, trained, civilized, tractable, pliable, taught, cultivated, tame.—*Ant.* WILD, savage, untamed.

gentleman *n.* man of honor, man of his word, sir, gentleman and a scholar.

of address —**gen'tle·man·ly** *adv.* —**gen'tle·wom'an,** *pl.*
-**wom'en,** *n.fem.*

gen·tri·fy (jen'tri fī') *vt.* -**fied'**, -**fy'ing** ‖< fol. + -FY ‖ 1 to
convert (an aging neighborhood) into a more affluent one,
as by remodeling homes 2 to raise to a higher status —
gen'tri·fi·ca'tion *n.*

gen·try (jen'trē) *n.* ‖see GENTLE ‖ 1 people of high social
standing 2 people of a particular class or group

genu·flect (jen'yōō flekt') *vi.* ‖< L *genu*, knee + *flectere*,
bend ‖ to bend the knee, as in worship —**gen'u·flec'tion**
n.

genu·ine (jen'yōō in) *adj.* ‖L *genuinus*, inborn ‖ 1 not
counterfeit or artificial; real; true 2 sincere —**gen'u·inely**
adv. —**gen'u·ine·ness** *n.*

ge·nus (jē'nəs) *n., pl.* **gen·era** (jen'ər ə) or **ge'nuses** ‖L,
race, kind ‖ 1 a class; kind; sort 2 a classification of
related plants or animals

geo- ‖< Gr *gē* ‖ *combining form* earth, of the earth

geo·cen·tric (jē'ō sen'trik) *adj.* 1 viewed as from the center of the earth 2 having the earth as a center —**ge'o·cen'**
tri·cally *adv.*

ge·ode (jē'ōd') *n.* ‖< Gr *geoidēs*, earthlike ‖ a stone with a
cavity lined with crystals or silica

geo·desic (jē'ō des'ik) *adj.* 1 GEODETIC (sense 1) 2 *a*) designating the shortest line between two points on a curved
surface *b*) of the geometry of such lines 3 having a surface formed of straight bars in a grid of polygons *[geodesic
dome]*

geo·detic (jē'ō det'ik) *adj.* 1 of or concerned with the
measurement of the earth and its surface 2 GEODESIC
(sense 2)

ge·og·ra·phy (jē äg'rə fē) *n.* ‖< Gr *gē*, earth + *graphein*,
write ‖ 1 the science dealing with the earth's surface, continents, climates, plants, animals, resources, etc. 2 the
physical features of a region —**ge·og'ra·pher** *n.* —**ge'o·**
graph'i·cal (-ə graf'i kəl) or **ge'o·graph'ic** *adj.* —**ge'o·**
graph'i·cally *adv.*

ge·ol·ogy (jē äl'ə jē) *n.* ‖see GEO- & -LOGY‖ the science
dealing with the development of the earth's crust, its rocks
and fossils, etc. —**ge'o·log'ic** (-ə läj'ik) or **ge'o·log'i·cal**
adj. —**ge'o·log'i·cally** *adv.* —**ge·ol'o·gist** *n.*

geo·mag·netic (jē'ō mag net'ik) *adj.* of the magnetic
properties of the earth —**ge'o·mag'ne·tism'** *n.*

ge·om·etry (jē äm'ə trē) *n.* ‖< Gr *gē*, earth + *metrein*, to
measure ‖ the branch of mathematics dealing with the
properties, measurement, and relationships of points,
lines, planes, and solids —**ge'o·met'ric** (-ə me'trik) or
ge'o·met'ri·cal *adj.* —**ge'o·met'ri·cally** *adv.*

geo·phys·ics (jē'ō fiz'iks) *n.pl.* [with sing. v.] the science
dealing with the effects of weather, winds, tides, etc. on
the earth —**ge'o·phys'i·cal** *adj.*

geo·poli·tics (jē'ō päl'ə tiks) *n.pl.* ‖< Ger *geopolitik* ‖
[with sing. v.] the interrelationship of politics and geography —**ge'o·po·lit'i·cal** (-pə lit'i kəl) *adj.*

geo·sta·tion·ary (jē'ō stā'shə ner'ē) *adj.* designating or of
a satellite orbiting the earth at a speed which keeps it
above the same point on the earth's surface Also **ge'o·**
syn'chro·nous (-sin'krə nəs)

ge'o·syn'cline' (-sin'klīn') *n.* a very large depression in
the earth's surface

ge·o·ther'mic (-thər'mik) *adj.* ‖GEO- + Gr *thermē*, heat ‖
of the heat inside the earth Also **ge'o·ther'mal**

Ger. 1 German 2 Germany

ge·ra·nium (jə rā'nē əm) *n.* ‖< Gr *geranos*, a crane ‖ 1 a
common garden plant with showy red, pink, or white flowers 2 a related wildflower

ger·bil (jur'bil) *n.* ‖ult. < Ar ‖ a small rodent with long
hind legs

geri·at·rics (jer'ē a'triks) *n.pl.* ‖< Gr *gēras*, old age +
-IATRICS ‖ [with sing. v.] the branch of medicine dealing
with the diseases of old age —**ger'i·at'ric** *adj.*

germ (jurm) *n.* ‖< L *germen* ‖ 1 the rudimentary form
from which a new organism is developed; seed; bud 2 any
microscopic, disease-bearing organism, esp. one of the
bacteria 3 an origin *[the germ of an idea]*

Ger·man (jur'mən) *n.* 1 a native or inhabitant of Germany 2 the language of Germany, Austria, etc. —*adj.* of
Germany, its people, language, etc.

ger·mane (jər mān') *adj.* ‖see GERM ‖ truly relevant; pertinent

Ger·manic (jər man'ik) *adj.* 1 [Now Rare] German 2
designating or of the original language of the German
peoples or the languages descended from it —*n.* the Germanic branch of languages, including English, Dutch,
Danish, etc.

ger·ma·nium (jər mā'nē əm) *n.* ‖< L *Germania*, Germany ‖ a nonmetallic chemical element used in semiconductors

German measles RUBELLA

germ cell an ovum or sperm cell

ger·mi·cide (jur'mə sīd') *n.* ‖< GERM + -CIDE ‖ any antiseptic, etc. used to destroy germs —**ger'mi·ci'dal** *adj.*

ger·mi·nal (jur'mə nəl) *adj.* 1 of or like germ cells 2 in
the first stage of growth or development

ger'mi·nate' (-nāt') *vi., vt.* -**nat'ed**, -**nat'ing** ‖< L *germen*, a sprout ‖ 1 to sprout, as from a seed 2 to start
developing —**ger'mi·na'tion** *n.*

ger·on·tol·ogy (jer'ən täl'ə jē) *n.* ‖< Gr *gerōn*, old man +
-LOGY ‖ the study of aging and the problems of the aged —
ger'on·tol'o·gist *n.*

ger·ry·man·der (jer'i man'dər; *also* ger'-) *vt., vi.* ‖after
Elbridge *Gerry*, governor of Mass. (1812) + (SALA)MANDER
(from the shape of the county redistricted then) ‖ to divide
(a voting area) unfairly, as to give one political party an
advantage

ger·und (jer'ənd) *n.* ‖< L *gerere*, carry out ‖ *Gram.* a verbal noun ending in -*ing*

Ge·stapo (gə stä'pō) *n.* ‖< Ger *Ge(heime) Sta(ats)-
po(lizei)*, secret state police ‖ the terrorist secret police
force of Nazi Germany

ges·ta·tion (jes tā'shən) *n.* ‖< L *gerere*, to bear ‖ the act
or period of carrying young in the uterus; pregnancy —
ges'tate, -**tat·ed**, -**tat·ing**, *vt.*

ges·ticu·late (jes tik'yōō lāt') *vi.* -**lat'ed**, -**lat'ing** ‖see
fol. ‖ to make gestures —**ges·tic'u·la'tion** *n.*

ges·ture (jes'chər) *n.* ‖< L *gerere*, to bear ‖ 1 a movement
of part of the body to express or emphasize ideas, emotions, etc. 2 any act or remark conveying a state of mind,
intention, etc., often made merely for effect —*vi.* -**tured**,
-**tur·ing** to make gestures

get (get) *vt.* **got**, **got'ten** or **got**, **get'ting** ‖< ON *geta* ‖ 1
to come into the state of having; receive, obtain, acquire,

THESAURUS

gentlemanly *a.* polite, polished, gallant; see REFINED 2.

gentleness *n.* tenderness, softness,
delicacy, smoothness, fragility,
sweetness.—*Ant.* ROUGHNESS, hardness, imperviousness.

gently *a.* considerately, tenderly,
benevolently; see GENEROUSLY 2.

genuine *a.* 1 [Authentic; *said of
things*] real, true, actual, original,
veritable, unadulterated, official,
whole, accurate, proved, tested, good,
natural, unimpeachable, pure,
unquestionable, authenticated, existent, essential, substantial, factual,
palpable, exact, precise, positive,
valid, literal, sound, plain, certain,
legitimate, legit*, for real*, honest-
to-goodness*, in the flesh*.—*Ant.*
VULGAR, spurious, sham. 2 [Sincere]
real, actual, unaffected, unquestionable, certain, absolute, unimpeachable, definite, incontrovertible, well-
established, known, reliable, bona
fide, staunch, trustworthy, certain,

valid, positive, frank.

geographical *a.* terrestrial, geo-
graphic, earthly; see PHYSICAL 1,
WORLDLY.

geography *n.* earth science, geology,
topography, economic geography,
political geography, geopolitics, geo-
political study, physiography, cartog-
raphy; see also SCIENCE 1.

geology *n.* applied geology, mining
geology, paleontology; see GEOGRA-
PHY, SCIENCE 1.

geometrical *a.* square, many-sided,
multilateral, bilateral, triangular, trilateral, quadrilateral.

germ *n.* microbe, antibody, bacteria,
disease germ, microorganism, virus,
parasite, bug*.

German *a.* Germanic, Teutonic,
Prussian, Saxon, Bavarian.

German *n.* 1 [The German Lan-
guage] Teutonic language, Proto-
Germanic, High German, Low German, Old High German, Middle High

German, Modern German, New High
German; see also LANGUAGE. 2 [A
German person] East German, West
German, Teuton, Berliner, East Ber-
liner, West Berliner, Bavarian,
Hanoverian, Prussian, Franconian,
Rhinelander, Saxon, Swabian, Hit-
lerite, Nazi, Aryan.

germinate *v.* generate, live, develop;
see GROW 1.

gestation *n.* reproduction, gravidity,
fecundation; see PREGNANCY.

gesture *n.* gesticulation, indication,
intimation; see SIGN 1.

gesture *v.* make a sign, motion, signal, pantomime, act out, use sign language, use one's hands, indicate,
signalize, point, nod; see also MOVE 1.

get *v.* 1 [To obtain] gain, procure,
occupy, reach, capture, recover, take,
grab, accomplish, attain, gain, win,
secure, achieve, collect, purchase,
earn, receive, realize, possess, get
possession of, take title to, acquire. 2

etc. **2** to arrive at [get home early] **3** to go and bring [get your books] **4** to catch **5** to persuade [get him to leave] **6** to cause to be [get the jar open] **7** to prepare [to get lunch] **8** to manage or contrive [to get to do something] **9** [Colloq.] *a)* to be obliged to (with *have* or *has*) [he's *got* to pass] *b)* to possess (with *have* or *has*) [he's *got* red hair] *c)* to strike, kill, baffle, defeat, etc. *d)* to understand **10** [Slang] to cause an emotional response in [her singing *gets* me] —*vi.* **1** to come, go, or arrive **2** to come to be [to *get* caught] *Get* is used as an auxiliary for emphasis in passive construction [to *get* praised] —*n.* the young of an animal —**get around 1** to move from place to place; circulate: also **get about 2** to circumvent **3** to influence as by flattery —**get away 1** to go away **2** to escape —**get away with** [Slang] to do something without being discovered or punished —**get by** [Colloq.] to survive; manage —**get it** [Colloq.] **1** to understand **2** to be punished —**get off 1** to come off, down, or out of **2** to leave or start **3** to escape or help to escape —**get on 1** to go on or into **2** to put on **3** to proceed **4** to grow older **5** to succeed —**get out 1** to go out or away **2** to take out **3** to be disclosed **4** to publish —**get over 1** to recover from **2** to forget —**get through 1** to finish **2** to manage to survive —**get together 1** to assemble **2** [Colloq.] to reach an agreement —**get up 1** to rise (from sleep, etc.) **2** to organize
get′away′ *n.* **1** the act of starting, as in a race **2** the act of escaping
get′-togeth′er *n.* an informal social gathering or meeting
get′-up′ *n.* [Colloq.] costume; dress
GeV *n.* giga-electron-volt; one billion electron-volts
gew·gaw (gyōō′gô′) *n.* [ME] a trinket
gey·ser (gī′zər) *n.* [< ON *gjosa*, to gush] a spring from which columns of boiling water and steam gush into the air at intervals
ghastly (gast′lē) *adj.* **-lier, -li·est** [< OE *gast*, spirit] **1** horrible; frightful **2** ghostlike; pale **3** [Colloq.] very bad —**ghast′li·ness** *n.*
gher·kin (gur′kin) *n.* [< Pers *angārah*, watermelon] a small pickled cucumber
ghetto (get′ō) *n., pl.* **-tos** or **-toes** [It] **1** a section of some European cities in which Jews were restricted **2** any section of a city in which many members of a minority group live
ghet′to·ize′ (-īz′) *vt.* **-ized′, -iz′ing 1** to restrict to a ghetto **2** to make into a ghetto
ghost (gōst) *n.* [< OE *gast*] **1** the supposed disembodied spirit of a dead person, appearing as a pale, shadowy apparition **2** a slight trace; shadow [not a *ghost* of a chance] —**give up the ghost** to die —**ghost′ly** *adj.* —**ghost′li·ness** *n.*
ghost′writ′er *n.* one who writes books, articles, etc. for another who professes to be the author —**ghost′write′** *vt., vi.*

ghoul (gōōl) *n.* [< Ar *ghāla*, to seize] *Muslim Folklore* an evil spirit that robs graves and feeds on the dead —**ghoul′ish** *adj.* —**ghoul′ishly** *adv.*
GHQ General Headquarters
GI (jē′ī′) *adj.* **1** government issue: designating clothing, etc. issued to military personnel **2** [Colloq.] of or characteristic of the U.S. armed forces [a *GI* haircut] —*n., pl.* **GI's** or **GIs** [Colloq.] a U.S. enlisted soldier
gi·ant (jī′ənt) *n.* [< Gr *gigas*] **1** any imaginary being of superhuman size **2** a person or thing of great size, strength, intellect, etc. —*adj.* like a giant —**gi′ant·ess** *n.fem.*
gib·ber (jib′ər) *vi., vt.* [echoic] to speak rapidly and incoherently
gib′ber·ish *n.* unintelligible chatter
gib·bet (jib′it) *n.* [< OFr *gibet*] **1** a gallows **2** a structure from which bodies of executed criminals were hung and exposed to public scorn —*vt.* to hang on a gibbet
gib·bon (gib′ən) *n.* [Fr] a small, slender, long-armed ape of India, S China, and the East Indies
gibe (jīb) *vi., vt.* **gibed, gib′ing** [< ?] to jeer or taunt —*n.* a jeer or taunt
gib·let (jib′lit) *n.* [< OFr *gibelet*, stew made of game] any of the edible internal parts of a fowl, as the gizzard
giddy (gid′ē) *adj.* **-dier, -di·est** [< OE *gydig*, insane] **1** having or causing a whirling, unsteady sensation; dizzy **2** frivolous —**gid′di·ness** *n.*
Gid·eon (gid′ē ən) *Bible* a judge of Israel and victorious leader in battle
gift (gift) *n.* [< OE *giefan*, give] **1** something given; present **2** the act of giving **3** a natural ability —*vt.* to present with or as a gift
gift′ed *adj.* **1** having a natural ability; talented **2** of superior intelligence
gig[1] (gig) *n.* [ME *gigge*, whirligig] **1** a light, two-wheeled, open carriage **2** a long, light ship's boat
gig[2] (gig) *n.* [< ?] [Slang] a job, esp. one performing jazz or rock
gi·gan·tic (jī gan′tik) *adj.* [see GIANT] huge; enormous; immense —**gi·gan′ti·cally** *adv.*
gig·gle (gig′əl) *vi.* **-gled, -gling** [< Du *giggelen*] to laugh with high, quick sounds in a silly or nervous way —*n.* such a sound —**gig′gler** *n.* —**gig′gly** *adj.*
gigo·lo (jig′ə lō′) *n., pl.* **-los** [Fr] a man paid to be a woman's escort
Gila monster (hē′lə) [after the *Gila* River, Ariz.] a stout, poisonous lizard of the SW U.S. deserts
gild (gild) *vt.* **gild′ed** or **gilt, gild′ing** [< OE *gyldan*] **1** to coat with gold leaf or a gold color **2** to make seem more attractive or valuable than it is —**gild′er** *n.* —**gild′ing** *n.*

■■■ THESAURUS ■■■

[To become] grow, develop into, go; see BECOME. **3** [To receive] be given, take, accept; see RECEIVE 1. **4** [To induce] persuade, talk into, compel; see URGE 2. **5** [*To overcome] beat, vanquish, overpower; see DEFEAT 2, 3. **6** [To prepare] make, arrange, dress; see PREPARE 1. **7** [To contract; *said of bodily disorders*] fall victim to, succumb to, get sick; see CATCH 4. **8** [To learn] acquire, gain, receive; see LEARN. **9** [*To understand] comprehend, perceive, know; see UNDERSTAND 1. **10** [*To irritate] annoy, provoke, vex; see BOTHER 2. **11** [To arrive] come to, reach, land; see ARRIVE. —**get away** flee, run away, elude; see ESCAPE. —**get away with*** escape notice, manage, succeed in; see ACHIEVE, SATISFY 3. — **get by*** manage, get along, do well enough; see SURVIVE 1. —**get it*** **1** [To understand] comprehend, perceive, know; see UNDERSTAND 1. **2** [To be punished] suffer, get what is coming to one, be reprimanded, suffer for, catch it*, get in trouble. — **get off 1** [To go away] depart, escape, go; see LEAVE 1. **2** [To dismount] alight, light, disembark; see DESCEND. —**get on 1** [To mount] go up, mount, scale; see CLIMB. **2** [To succeed] manage, do well enough, get along; see SUCCEED 1. **3** [To age]

grow older, advance in years, approach retirement; see AGE. —**get out 1** [To leave] go, depart, take one's departure; see LEAVE 1. **2** [To escape] break out, run away, flee; see ESCAPE. —**get over** recover, recuperate, survive; see RECOVER 3. — **get through 1** [To complete] discharge, enact, finish; see ACHIEVE. **2** [To endure] live through, survive, subsist; see ENDURE 1, 2. —**get together 1** [To gather] collect, accumulate, congregate; see ASSEMBLE 2. **2** [To reach an agreement] come to terms, settle, make a bargain; see AGREE. —**get up 1** [To climb] ascend, mount, go up; see CLIMB. **2** [To arise] get out of bed, rise, turn out; see ARISE 1.
getting *n.* taking, obtaining, gaining, catching, earning, winning, seizing, securing, capturing, mastering, confiscating, appropriating.
ghastly *a.* **1** [Terrifying] hideous, horrible, frightening; see FRIGHTFUL. **2** [*Unpleasant] repulsive, disgusting, abhorrent; see OFFENSIVE 2.
ghost *n.* vision, specter, apparition, spirit, demon, shade, phantom, appearance, spook; see also DEVIL.
giant *a.* monstrous, colossal, enormous; see LARGE 1.

giant *n.* ogre, Cyclops, Titan, colossus, Goliath, Hercules, Atlas, mammoth, behemoth, monster, whale, elephant, leviathan, mountain, hulk, lump, bulk; see also MONSTER 1.
gibberish *n.* jargon, chatter, claptrap; see NONSENSE 1.
giddy *a.* high, towering, lofty; see STEEP.
gift *n.* **1** [A present] presentation, donation, grant, gratuity, alms, endowment, bequest, bounty, charity, favor, legacy, award, reward, offering, souvenir, token, remembrance, courtesy, bonus, subsidy, tribute, subvention, contribution, subscription, relief, ration, benefit, tip, allowance, handout, hand-medown. **2** [An aptitude] faculty, capacity, capability; see ABILITY. — **look a gift horse in the mouth** carp, criticize, be ungrateful; see JUDGE.
gifted *a.* smart, skilled, talented; see ABLE.
gigantic *a.* massive, huge, immense; see LARGE 1.
giggle *n.* titter, chuckle, snicker; see LAUGH.
gild *v.* varnish, whitewash, paint in rosy colors; see PAINT 2.

gill[1] (gil) *n.* ⟦ME *gile*⟧ the breathing organ of most water animals, as fish

gill[2] (jil) *n.* ⟦< LL *gillo*, cooling vessel⟧ a unit of liquid measure, equal to ¼ pint

gilt (gilt) *vt. alt. pt. & pp. of* GILD — *n.* gold leaf or color — *adj.* coated with gilt

gilt'-edged' *adj.* of the highest quality *[gilt-edged securities]* Also **gilt'-edge'**

gim·bals (gim'bəlz, jim'-) *n.pl.* ⟦< L *gemellus*, twin⟧ *[with sing. v.]* a pair of rings so pivoted that one swings freely within the other: used to keep a ship's compass level

gim·crack (jim'krak') *adj.* ⟦< ME *gibbecrak*, an ornament⟧ showy but cheap and useless — *n.* a gimcrack thing — **gim'crack'er·y** *n.*

gim·let (gim'lit) *n.* ⟦< MDu *wimmel*⟧ a small boring tool with a spiral cutting edge

gim·mick (gim'ik) *n.* ⟦< ?⟧ [Colloq.] 1 a tricky device 2 an attention-getting device or feature, as for promoting a product, etc.

gimpy (gim'pē) *adj.* ⟦prob. < Norw dial. *gimpa*, to rock⟧ [Colloq.] lame; limping

gin[1] (jin) *n.* ⟦< L *juniperus*, juniper⟧ a distilled alcoholic liquor typically flavored with juniper berries

gin[2] (jin) *n.* ⟦< OFr *engin*, engine⟧ 1 a snare, as for game 2 COTTON GIN — *vt.* **ginned, gin'ning** to remove seeds from (cotton) with a gin

gin·ger (jin'jər) *n.* ⟦< Gr *zingiberi*⟧ 1 a tropical herb with rhizomes used esp. as a spice 2 this spice 3 [Colloq.] vigor; spirit — **gin'gery** *adj.*

ginger ale a ginger-flavored, carbonated soft drink

gin'ger·bread' *n.* 1 a cake flavored with ginger 2 showy ornamentation

gin'gerly *adv.* very carefully — *adj.* very careful; cautious

gin'ger·snap' *n.* a crisp cookie flavored with ginger and molasses

ging·ham (giŋ'əm) *n.* ⟦< Malay *ginggang*⟧ a cotton cloth, usually woven in stripes, checks, or plaids

gin·gi·vi·tis (jin'jə vit'is) *n.* ⟦< L *gingiva*, the gum + -ITIS⟧ inflammation of the gums

gink·go (giŋ'kō) *n., pl.* **-goes** ⟦Jpn *ginkyo*⟧ an Asian tree with fan-shaped leaves Also **ging'ko**

gin rummy (jin) a variety of the card game rummy Also **gin**

gip (jip) *n., vt., vi. alt. sp. of* GYP

Gipsy (jip'sē) *n.* GYPSY

gi·raffe (jə raf') *n.* ⟦< Ar *zarāfa*⟧ a large African ruminant with a very long neck and legs

gird (gurd) *vt.* **gird'ed** or **girt, gird'ing** ⟦OE *gyrdan*⟧ 1 to encircle or fasten with a belt 2 to surround 3 to prepare (oneself) for action

girder (gur'dər) *n.* a large wooden or steel beam for supporting joists, the framework of a building, etc.

gir·dle (gur'l) *n.* ⟦OE *gyrdel*⟧ 1 a belt for the waist 2 anything that encircles 3 a woman's elasticized undergarment for supporting the waist and hips — *vt.* **-dled, -dling** to encircle or bind, as with a girdle

girl (gurl) *n.* ⟦ME *girle*, youngster⟧ 1 a female child 2 a young, unmarried woman 3 a female servant 4 [Colloq.] a woman of any age 5 [Colloq.] a sweetheart — **girl'hood'** *n.* — **girl'ish** *adj.*

girl'friend' *n.* [Colloq.] 1 a sweetheart of a boy or man 2 a girl who is someone's friend 3 a woman friend of a woman

Girl Scout a member of the **Girl Scouts of the United States of America**, a girls' organization providing healthful, character-building activities

girt[1] (gurt) *vt. alt. pt. & pp. of* GIRD

girt[2] (gurt) *vt.* to fasten with a girth

girth (gurth) *n.* ⟦< ON *gyrtha*, encircle⟧ 1 a band put around the belly of a horse, etc. to hold a saddle or pack 2 the circumference, as of a tree trunk

gist (jist) *n.* ⟦< OFr *giste*, point at issue⟧ the essence or main point, as of an article or argument

give (giv) *vt.* **gave, giv'ing** ⟦OE *giefan*⟧ 1 to make a gift of 2 to hand over *[to give* the porter a bag*]* 3 to hand over in or for payment 4 to pass (regards, etc.) along 5 to cause to have *[to give* pleasure*]* 6 to act as host or sponsor of 7 to produce; supply *[cows give* milk*]* 8 to devote or sacrifice 9 to concede; yield 10 to offer *[to give* advice*]* 11 to perform *[to give* a concert*]* 12 to utter *[to give* a reply*]* 13 to inflict (punishment, etc.) — *vi.* to bend, move, yield, etc. from force or pressure — *n.* a bending, moving, etc. under pressure — **give away** 1 to make a gift of 2 to present (the bride) to the bridegroom 3 [Colloq.] to reveal or betray — **give forth** (or **off**) to emit — **give in** to yield — **give it to** [Colloq.] to beat or scold — **give or take** plus or minus — **give out** 1 to emit 2 to make public 3 to distribute 4 to become worn out, etc. — **give up** 1 to hand over 2 to cease 3 to stop trying 4 to despair of — **giv'er** *n.*

give'-and-take' *n.* 1 mutual concession 2 repartee or banter

give'away' *n.* 1 an unintentional revelation 2 something given free or sold cheap 3 a radio or television program giving prizes

give'back' *n.* a previously negotiated workers' benefit relinquished to management, as for some concession

given (giv'ən) *vt., vi. pp. of* GIVE — *adj.* 1 accustomed (*to*) by habit, etc. 2 specified 3 assumed; granted — *n.* something assumed or accepted as fact

given name a person's first name

gizmo (giz'mō) *n., pl.* **-mos** ⟦< ?⟧ [Slang] a gadget Also sp. **gis'mo**

giz·zard (giz'ərd) *n.* ⟦< L *gigeria*, cooked entrails of poultry⟧ the muscular second stomach of a bird

Gk. Greek

glacé (gla sā') *adj.* ⟦< L *glacies*, ice⟧ 1 glossy, as silk 2 candied, as fruits — *vt.* **-céed', -cé'ing** to glaze (fruits, etc.)

gla·cial (glā'shəl) *adj.* of or like ice or glaciers — **gla'cially** *adv.*

gla·ci·ate (glā'shē āt') *vt.* **-at'ed, -at'ing** 1 to cover over with ice or a glacier 2 to expose to or change by glacial action

gla·cier (glā'shər) *n.* ⟦< L *glacies*, ice⟧ a large mass of ice and snow moving slowly down a mountain or valley

---

■ THESAURUS ■

gimmick* *n.* catch, secret device, method; see TRICK.

girder *n.* truss, rafter, mainstay; see BEAM 1.

girdle *n.* belt, cincher, sash; see UNDERWEAR.

girdle *v.* encircle, enclose, clasp; see SURROUND 1.

girl *n.* schoolgirl, miss, lass, young woman, coed, lassie, damsel, maid, maiden, tomboy, chick*, skirt*, dame*, babe*.

girlish *a.* juvenile, naive, unsophisticated, fresh, unaffected; see also YOUNG 1.—*Ant.* MATURE, matronly, sophisticated.

girth *n.* circumference, distance around, bigness; see SIZE 2.

gist *n.* substance, essence, significance; see BASIS, SUMMARY.

give *v.* 1 [To transfer] grant, bestow, confer, impart, present, endow, bequeath, award, dispense, subsidize, contribute, hand out, dole out, hand in, hand over, deliver, let have, tip, pass down, convey, deed, sell, will, make over to, put into the hands of,

contribute to, consign, relinquish, cede, lease, invest, dispose of, part with, lay upon, turn over, come through with*, come across with*, shell out*, fork over*, kick in*, palm off*.—*Ant.* MAINTAIN, withhold, take. 2 [To yield under pressure] give way, retreat, collapse, fall, contract, shrink, recede, open, relax, sag, bend, flex, crumble, yield.—*Ant.* RESIST, remain rigid, stand firm. 3 [To allot] assign, dispense, deal; see DISTRIBUTE. 4 [To pass on] communicate, transmit, transfer; see SEND 1. 5 [To administer] minister, provide with, dispense; see PROVIDE 1. —**give away** 1 [*To reveal] betray, divulge, disclose; see REVEAL. 2 [To give] bestow, award, present; see GIVE 1. —**give back** return, refund, reimburse; see REPAY 1. —**give in** capitulate, submit, surrender; see ADMIT 2, YIELD 1. —**give out** 1 [To emit] emanate, expend, exude; see EMIT, SMELL 1. 2 [To deliver] dole out, hand out, pass out; see DISTRIBUTE. 3 [To publish] proclaim, make known,

announce; see ADVERTISE, DECLARE. 4 [To weaken] faint, fail, break down; see TIRE 1, WEAKEN 1. —**give up** 1 [To surrender] stop fighting, cede, hand over; see YIELD 1. 2 [To stop] quit, halt, cease; see END 1.

given *a.* granted, supplied, donated, bestowed, presented, awarded, bequeathed, dispensed, handed out, contributed, offered.—*Ant.* KEPT, taken, withheld.

giver *n.* provider, supplier, donator; see DONOR.

giving *n.* donating, granting, supplying, awarding, presenting, dispensing, passing out, handing out, contributing, conferring, distributing, remitting, transferring, consigning, yielding, giving up, furnishing, allowing, expending, offering, tipping, parting with, pouring forth, discharging, emitting.—*Ant.* GETTING, taking, appropriating.

glacial *a.* icy, frozen, polar; see COLD 1.

glacier *n.* ice floe, floe, iceberg, berg,

glad (glad) *adj.* **glad′der, glad′dest** ‖OE *glæd*‖ 1 happy 2 causing joy 3 very willing 4 bright —**glad′ly** *adv.* —**glad′ness** *n.*

glad·den (glad′n) *vt.* to make glad

glade (glād) *n.* ‖ME‖ an open space in a forest

glad hand [Slang] a cordial or effusive welcome —**glad′-hand′er** *n.*

gladi·ator (glad′ē āt′ər) *n.* ‖L < *gladius*, sword‖ 1 in ancient Rome, a man, often a slave, who fought in an arena as a public show 2 any person taking part in a fight —**glad′i·ato′rial** (-ə tôr′ē əl) *adj.*

gladio·lus (glad′ē ō′ləs) *n., pl.* **-luses** or **-li′** (-lī′) ‖L, small sword‖ a plant of the iris family with swordlike leaves and tall spikes of funnel-shaped flowers Also **glad′io′la** (-lə)

glad·some (glad′səm) *adj.* joyful or cheerful —**glad′somely** *adv.*

glam·or·ize (glam′ər īz′) *vt.* **-ized′, -iz′ing** to make glamorous —**glam′ori·za′tion** *n.*

glam·our or **glamor** (glam′ər) *n.* ‖Scot var. of *grammar*, magic‖ seemingly mysterious allure; bewitching charm —**glam′or·ous** or **glam′our·ous** *adj.*

glance (glans) *vi.* **glanced, glanc′ing** ‖ME *glansen*‖ 1 to strike a surface obliquely and go off at an angle 2 to flash 3 to look quickly —*n.* 1 a glancing off 2 a flash 3 a quick look

gland (gland) *n.* ‖< L *glans*, acorn‖ any organ that separates certain elements from the blood and secretes them for the body to use or throw off —**glan·du·lar** (glan′jə lər) *adj.*

glans (glanz) *n.* ‖L, lit., acorn‖ 1 the head of the penis 2 the tip of the clitoris

glare (gler) *vi.* **glared, glar′ing** ‖ME *glaren*‖ 1 to shine with a steady, dazzling light 2 to stare fiercely —*n.* 1 a steady, dazzling light 2 a fierce stare 3 a bright, glassy surface, as of ice

glar′ing *adj.* 1 dazzlingly bright 2 too showy 3 staring fiercely 4 flagrant *[a glaring error]* —**glar′ingly** *adv.*

glas·nost (glas′nōst′) *n.* ‖Russ, lit., openness‖ Soviet official policy after 1985 of publicizing internal problems and weaknesses

glass (glas) *n.* ‖OE *glæs*‖ 1 a hard, brittle substance, usually transparent, made by fusing silicates with soda, lime, etc. 2 GLASSWARE 3 *a)* a glass article, as a drinking container *b)* [*pl.*] eyeglasses or binoculars 4 the amount held by a drinking glass —*vt.* to equip with glass panes —*adj.* of or made of glass —**glass′ful′** *n.*

glass′ware′ *n.* articles made of glass

glass′y *adj.* **-i·er, -i·est** 1 like glass, as in smoothness 2 expressionless *[a glassy stare]* —**glass′i·ly** *adv.* —**glass′i·ness** *n.*

glau·coma (glô kō′mə) *n.* ‖< Gr *glaukos*, gleaming‖ an eye disorder marked by increased pressure within the eye

glaze (glāz) *vt.* **glazed, glaz′ing** ‖ME *glasen*‖ 1 to fit (windows, etc.) with glass 2 to give a hard, glossy finish to (pottery, etc.) 3 to cover (foods) with a coating of sugar syrup, etc. —*vi.* to become glassy or glossy —*n.* a glassy finish or coating

gla·zier (glā′zhər) *n.* one whose work is fitting glass in windows, etc.

gleam (glēm) *n.* ‖OE *glæm*‖ 1 a flash or beam of light 2 a faint light 3 a reflected brightness, as from a polished surface 4 a faint manifestation, as of hope, understanding, etc. —*vi.* 1 to shine with a gleam 2 to appear suddenly —**gleam′y** *adj.*

glean (glēn) *vt., vi.* ‖< Celt‖ 1 to collect (grain left by reapers) 2 to collect (facts, etc.) gradually

glee (glē) *n.* ‖OE *gleo*‖ lively joy; merriment —**glee′ful** *adj.* —**glee′fully** *adv.*

glee club a group that sings part songs

glen (glen) *n.* ‖Medieval Scot‖ a narrow, secluded valley

glen plaid [*also* G- p-] a plaid pattern with thin cross-barred stripes

glib (glib) *adj.* **glib′ber, glib′best** ‖< or akin to Du *glib-berig*, slippery‖ speaking or spoken smoothly, often too smoothly to be convincing —**glib′ly** *adv.* —**glib′ness** *n.*

glide (glīd) *vi.* **glid′ed, glid′ing** ‖OE *glidan*‖ 1 to move smoothly and easily 2 *Aeronautics* to descend with little or no engine power —*vt.* to cause to glide —*n.* 1 a gliding 2 a disk or ball, as of nylon, under a furniture leg to allow easy sliding

glider (glīd′ər) *n.* 1 an engineless aircraft carried along by air currents 2 a porch swing suspended in a frame

glim·mer (glim′ər) *vi.* ‖< OE *glæm*, gleam‖ 1 to give a faint, flickering light 2 to appear faintly —*n.* 1 a faint, flickering light 2 a faint manifestation —**glim′mer·ing** *n.*

glimpse (glimps) *vt.* **glimpsed, glimps′ing** ‖< OE *glæm*, gleam‖ to catch a brief, quick view of —*vi.* to look quickly —*n.* a brief, quick view

glint (glint) *vi.* ‖ME *glenten*‖ to gleam or glitter —*n.* a glinting

glis·sando (gli sän′dō) *n., pl.* **-di** (-dē) or **-dos** ‖as if It < Fr *glisser*, to slide‖ *Music* a sliding effect achieved by a rapid sounding of tones

glis·ten (glis′ən) *vi.* ‖OE *glisnian*‖ to shine with reflected light, as a wet surface

glitch (glich) *n.* ‖< Ger *glitsche*, a slip‖ [Slang] a mishap, error, etc.

glit·ter (glit′ər) *vi.* ‖prob. < ON *glitra*‖ 1 to shine brightly; sparkle 2 to be brilliant or showy —*n.* 1 a

---

THESAURUS

glacial mass, snow slide, icecap, ice field, ice stream, glacial table.

glad *a.* exhilarated, animated, jovial; see HAPPY.

gladly *a.* joyously, happily, gaily, blithely, cheerfully, ecstatically, blissfully, contendedly, readily, gratefully, enthusiastically, merrily, heartily, willingly, zealously, pleasantly, pleasurably, zestfully, complacently, delightfully, gleefully, cheerily, warmly, passionately, ardently, lovingly, cordially, genially, sweetly, joyfully, with relish, with satisfaction, with full agreement, with full approval, with delight.—*Ant.* SADLY, unwillingly, gloomily.

gladness *n.* cheer, mirth, delight; see HAPPINESS.

glamorous *a.* fascinating, alluring, captivating, bewitching, dazzling; see also CHARMING.

glamour *n.* allurement, charm, attraction; see BEAUTY 1.

glance *n.* glimpse, sight, fleeting impression; see LOOK 3.

glance *v.* 1 [To look] see, peep, glimpse; see LOOK 2. 2 [To ricochet] skip, slide, rebound; see BOUNCE.

gland *n.* endocrine organ, pancreas, kidney, liver, testicle, spleen, epithelial cell. *Kinds of glands include the following:* simple, compound, tubular, sacular, ductless, adrenal, carotid, endocrine, lymphatic, para-

thyroid, parotid, pineal, pituitary, thyroid, thymus, sweat, lacrimal, salivary, mammary, seminal, prostate, urethral, vaginal.

glare *v.* 1 [To shine fiercely] beam, glow, radiate; see SHINE 1, 2. 2 [To stare fiercely] pierce, glower, scowl; see FROWN, LOOK 2.

glaring *a.* 1 [Shining] blinding, dazzling, blazing; see BRIGHT 1. 2 [Obvious] evident, conspicuous, obtrusive; see OBVIOUS 2.

glass *n. Objects referred to as* glass *include the following:* tumbler, goblet, beaker, chalice, cup, looking glass, mirror, barometer, thermometer, hourglass, windowpane, watch crystal, monocle, telescope, microscope, spyglass, burning glass, eyeglass, lens, optical glass.

glasses *n.* spectacles, eyeglasses, bifocals, trifocals, goggles, field glasses, opera glasses, contact lenses, specs*.

glassware *n.* crystal, glasswork, glass; see GLASS. *Types of common* glassware *include the following:* tumbler, jug, decanter, bottle, fruit jar, tableware, glass ovenware, vase, flower bowl, goblet, sherbet glass, wine glass, liqueur glass, champagne glass, cocktail glass, highball glass, old-fashioned glass, brandy snifter, shot glass, cake tray, parfait glass, beer mug.

glassy *a.* vitreous, lustrous, polished; see SMOOTH 1.

glaze *n.* enamel, polish, varnish; see FINISH 2.

glaze *v.* coat, enamel, gloss over; see SHINE 3.

glazed *a.* glassy, translucent, transparent, enameled, varnished, filmed over, shiny, encrusted, burnished, lustrous, smooth.—*Ant.* ROUGH, fresh, unglazed.

glee *n.* joviality, merriment, mirth; see HAPPINESS.

gleeful *a.* joyous, jolly, merry; see HAPPY.

glide *n.* floating, continuous motion, smooth movement, flowing, slide, drift, swoop, skimming, flight, soaring, slither.

glide *v.* float, slide, drift, waft, skim, skip, trip, fly, coast, flit, wing, soar, coast along, slide along, skim along.—*Ant.* HIT, rattle, lurch.

glimmer *n.* beam, flash, flicker; see LIGHT 1.

glimpse *n.* flash, impression, sight; see LOOK 3.

glisten *v.* sparkle, shimmer, flicker; see SHINE 1.

glitter *n.* sparkle, shimmer, gleam; see LIGHT 1.

glitter *v.* glare, shimmer, sparkle; see SHINE 1.

bright, sparkling light **2** striking or showy brilliance **3** bits of glittering material —**glit′tery** *adj.*

glitz (glits) *n.* ⟦< ?⟧ [Colloq.] gaudy or glittery showiness —**glitz′y, -i·er, -i·est,** *adj.*

gloam·ing (glōm′iŋ) *n.* ⟦< OE *glom*⟧ evening dusk; twilight

gloat (glōt) *vi.* ⟦prob. < ON *glotta*, grin scornfully⟧ to gaze or think with malicious pleasure

glob (gläb) *n.* ⟦prob. < GLOBULE⟧ a rounded mass or lump, as of jelly

global (glō′bəl) *adj.* worldwide —**glob′ally** *adv.*

glob′al·ism′ (-iz′əm) *n.* a policy, outlook, etc. that is worldwide in scope

globe (glōb) *n.* ⟦< L *globus*, a ball⟧ **1** anything spherical or somewhat spherical **2** the earth, or a model of the earth

globe′-trot′ter *n.* one who travels widely about the world

globu·lar (gläb′yoo lər) *adj.* **1** spherical **2** made up of globules

glob′ule′ (-yōōl′) *n.* ⟦< L *globulus*⟧ a tiny ball; very small drop

glock·en·spiel (gläk′ən spēl′) *n.* ⟦Ger *glocke*, bell + *spiel*, to play⟧ a percussion instrument with tuned metal bars in a frame, played with hammers

gloom (glōōm) *n.* ⟦prob. < Scand⟧ **1** darkness; dimness **2** deep sadness; dejection —**gloom′y, -i·er, -i·est,** *adj.*

glop (gläp) *n.* ⟦< ? GL(UE) + (SL)OP⟧ [Colloq.] any soft, gluey substance —**glop′py** *adj.*

glo·rify (glôr′ə fī′) *vt.* **-fied′, -fy′ing** ⟦< L *gloria*, glory + *facere*, to make⟧ **1** to give glory to **2** to exalt (God), as in worship **3** to honor; extol **4** to make seem better, greater, etc. than is so —**glo′ri·fi·ca′tion** *n.*

glo′ri·ous (-ē əs) *adj.* **1** having, giving, or deserving glory **2** splendid —**glo′ri·ously** *adv.*

glory (glôr′ē) *n., pl.* **-ries** ⟦< L *gloria*⟧ **1** great honor or fame, or its source **2** adoration **3** great splendor, prosperity, etc. **4** heavenly bliss — *vi.* **-ried, -ry·ing** to exult (*in*)

gloss[1] (glôs, gläs) *n.* ⟦< ? Scand⟧ **1** the shine of a polished surface **2** a deceptive outward show — *vt.* **1** to give a shiny surface to **2** to hide (an error, etc.) or make seem right or trivial —**gloss′y, -i·er, -i·est,** *adj.*

gloss[2] (glôs, gläs) *n.* ⟦< Gr *glōssa*, tongue⟧ a note of comment or explanation, as in a footnote — *vt.* to provide glosses for

glos·sary (glôs′ə rē, gläs′-) *n., pl.* **-ries** ⟦see prec.⟧ a list of difficult terms with explanations, as for a book

glos·so·la·lia (gläs′ō lā′lē ə, glôs′-) *n.* ⟦< Gr *glōssa*, tongue + *lalein*, to speak⟧ an uttering of unintelligible sounds, as in a religious ecstasy

glot·tis (glät′is) *n.* ⟦< Gr *glōssa*, tongue⟧ the opening between the vocal cords in the larynx —**glot′tal** *adj.*

glove (gluv) *n.* ⟦OE *glof*⟧ **1** a covering for the hand, with separate sheaths for the fingers and thumb **2** a baseball player's mitt **3** a padded mitten worn by boxers — *vt.* **gloved, glov′ing** to cover with a glove

glow (glō) *vi.* ⟦OE *glowan*⟧ **1** to give off a bright light as a result of great heat **2** to give out a steady light **3** to give

out heat **4** to be elated **5** to be bright with color — *n.* **1** a light given off, as a result of great heat **2** steady, even light **3** brightness, warmth, etc. —**glow′ing** *adj.* —**glow′ingly** *adv.*

glower (glou′ər) *vi.* ⟦prob. < ON⟧ to stare with sullen anger; scowl

glow′worm′ (glō′-) *n.* a wingless, luminescent female or larva of the firefly

glu·cose (glōō′kōs′) *n.* ⟦Fr < Gr *gleúkos*, sweetness⟧ **1** a crystalline sugar occurring naturally in fruits, honey, etc. **2** a sweet syrup prepared by the hydrolysis of starch

glue (glōō) *n.* ⟦< LL *glus*⟧ **1** a sticky, viscous liquid made from animal gelatin, used as an adhesive **2** any similar substance — *vt.* **glued, glu′ing** to make stick as with glue —**glu′ey, -i·er, -i·est,** *adj.*

glum (glum) *adj.* **glum′mer, glum′mest** ⟦prob. < ME *glomen*, look morose⟧ gloomy; sullen —**glum′ly** *adv.* —**glum′ness** *n.*

glut (glut) *vi.* **glut′ted, glut′ting** ⟦< L *gluttire*, to swallow⟧ to eat to excess — *vt.* **1** to feed, fill, etc. to excess **2** to supply (the market) beyond demand — *n.* **1** a glutting or being glutted **2** a supply greater than the demand

glu·ten (glōōt′n) *n.* ⟦L, glue⟧ a gray, sticky, nutritious mixture of proteins found in wheat, etc. —**glu′ten·ous** *adj.*

glu′ti·nous (-əs) *adj.* ⟦see prec.⟧ gluey; sticky —**glu′ti·nously** *adv.*

glut·ton (glut′'n) *n.* ⟦see GLUT⟧ **1** one who eats to excess **2** one with a great capacity for something —**glut′ton·ous** *adj.* —**glut′ton·ously** *adv.*

glut′tony *n., pl.* **-ies** the habit or act of eating too much

glyc·erin (glis′ər in) *n.* ⟦< Gr *glykeros*, sweet⟧ *nontechnical term for* GLYCEROL   Also **glyc′er·ine** (-in, -ēn′)

glyc·erol (glis′ər ôl′, -ōl′) *n.* ⟦< prec.⟧ a colorless, syrupy liquid made from fats and oils: used in skin lotions, in making explosives, etc.

gly·co·gen (glī′kə jən) *n.* ⟦< Gr *glykys*, sweet + -GEN⟧ a substance in animal tissues that is changed into glucose as the body needs it

GM General Manager

Gmc. Germanic

gnarl (närl) *n.* ⟦< ME *knorre*⟧ a knot on a tree trunk or branch — *vt.* to make knotted; twist —**gnarled** *adj.*

gnash (nash) *vt., vi.* ⟦prob. < ON⟧ to grind (the teeth) together, as in anger — *n.* a gnashing

gnat (nat) *n.* ⟦OE *gnæt*⟧ any of various small, two-winged insects, which often bite

gnaw (nô) *vt.* ⟦OE *gnagen*⟧ **1** to bite away bit by bit; consume **2** to harass or vex — *vi.* to bite repeatedly

gneiss (nīs) *n.* ⟦< OHG *gneisto*, a spark⟧ a granitelike rock formed of layers of quartz, mica, etc.

gnome (nōm) *n.* ⟦< Gr *gnōmē*, thought⟧ *Folklore* a dwarf who dwells in the earth and guards its treasures —**gnom′ish** *adj.*

GNP gross national product

gnu (nōō) *n.* ⟦< the native name⟧ a large African antelope with an oxlike head and a horselike tail; wildebeest

go (gō) *vi.* **went, gone, go′ing** ⟦< OE *gan*⟧ **1** to move along; travel; proceed **2** to work properly; operate /the

---

THESAURUS

globe *n.* balloon, orb, spheroid; see BALL 1.

gloom *n.* woe, sadness, depression, dejection, melancholy, melancholia, dullness, despondency, misery, sorrow, morbidity, pessimism, foreboding, low spirits, cheerlessness, heaviness of mind, weariness, apprehension, misgiving, distress, affliction, despair, anguish, grief, horror, mourning, bitterness, chagrin, discouragement, the blues, the dumps.—*Ant.* HAPPINESS, optimism, gaiety.

gloomy *a.* dreary, depressing, discouraging; see DISMAL.

glorify *v.* laud, commend, acclaim; see PRAISE 1.

glorious *a.* famous, renowned, famed, well-known, distinguished, splendid, excellent, noble, exalted, grand, illustrious, notable, celebrated, esteemed, honored, eminent, remarkable, brilliant, great, heroic, memorable, immortal, time-honored, admirable, praiseworthy, remarkable; see also FAMOUS.—*Ant.* UNIMPORTANT, inglorious, ignominious.

glory *n.* **1** [Renown] honor, distinction, reputation; see FAME. **2** [Splendor] grandeur, radiance, majesty, brilliance, richness, beauty, fineness.—*Ant.* tawdriness, meanness, baseness.

glossy *a.* shining, reflecting, lustrous; see BRIGHT 1.

glove *n.* mitten, mitt, finger mitten; see CLOTHES.

glow *n.* warmth, shine, ray; see HEAT 1, LIGHT 1.

glow *v.* gleam, redden, radiate; see BURN, SHINE 1.

glowing *a.* gleaming, lustrous, phosphorescent; see BRIGHT 1.

glue *n.* paste, mucilage, cement; see ADHESIVE.

glue *v.* paste, gum, cement; see REPAIR.

glum *a.* moody, morose, sullen; see SAD 1.

glut *n.* oversupply, overabundance, excess; see EXCESS 1.

glut *v.* **1** [To oversupply] overwhelm, overstock, fill; see FLOOD. **2** [To overeat] stuff, cram, gorge, eat one's

fill, gobble up, eat out of house and home, fill, feast, wolf, bolt, devour, eat like a horse*.—*Ant.* DIET, starve, fast.

glutton *n.* greedy person, hog, pig; see BEAST 2.

gluttony *n.* voracity, piggishness, intemperance; see GREED.

gnarled *a.* knotted, twisted, contorted; see BENT.

gnaw *v.* crunch, chomp, masticate; see BITE, CHEW.

go *v.* **1** [To leave] quit, withdraw, take leave, depart, move, set out, go away, take off, start, leave, vanish, retire, vacate, flee, get out, fly, run along, say goodby, escape, run away, clear out*, pull out, push off*, scram*, split*, blow*, beat it*, take a powder*, get along*, fade away*; see also LEAVE 1. **2** [To proceed] travel, progress, proceed; see ADVANCE 1, MOVE 1. **3** [To function] work, run, perform; see OPERATE 2. **4** [To fit or suit] conform, accord, harmonize; see AGREE, FIT 1. **5** [To extend] stretch, cover, spread; see REACH 1. **6** [To clock is *going*] **3** to act, sound, etc. as specified /the balloon *went* "pop"/ **4** to turn out; result /the war *went* badly/ **5** to pass: said of time **6** to become /to *go* mad/ **7** to be expressed, sung, etc. /as the saying *goes*/ **8** to harmonize; agree /blue *goes* with gold/ **9** to be accepted, valid, etc. **10** to leave; depart **11** to come to an end; fail /his eyesight is *going*/ **12** to be allotted (*to*) or sold (*for*) **13** to extend, reach, etc. **14** to be able to pass (*through*), fit (*into*), etc. **15** to be capable of being divided (*into*) /5 *goes* into 10 twice/ **16** to belong /socks *go* in that drawer/ —*vt.* **1** to travel along /to *go* the wrong way/ **2** [Colloq.] *a*) to put up with *b*) to furnish (bail) for an arrested person —*n.*, *pl.* **goes 1** a success /to make a *go* of marriage/ **2** [Colloq.] animation; energy **3** [Colloq.] a try; attempt —**go back on** [Colloq.] **1** to betray **2** to break (a promise, etc.) —**go for 1** to try to get **2** [Colloq.] to attack **3** [Colloq.] to be attracted by —**go in for** [Colloq.] to engage or indulge in —**go off 1** to depart **2** to explode —**go on 1** to proceed; continue **2** to happen **3** [Colloq.] to chatter —**go out 1** to be extinguished, become outdated, etc. **2** to attend social affairs, etc. —**go over 1** to examine thoroughly **2** to do again **3** [Colloq.] to be successful —**go through 1** to endure; experience **2** to look through —**go through with** to pursue to the end —**go together 1** to match; harmonize **2** [Colloq.] to date only each other —**go under** to fail, as in business —**let go 1** to let escape **2** to release one's hold —**let oneself go** to be unrestrained —**on the go** [Colloq.] in constant motion or action —**to go** [Colloq.] **1** to be taken out: said of food in a restaurant **2** still to be done, etc.

goad (gōd) *n.* ⟦OE *gad*⟧ **1** a sharp-pointed stick used in driving oxen **2** any driving impulse; spur —*vt.* to drive as with a goad; urge on

go′-ahead′ *n.* permission or a signal to proceed: usually with *the*

goal (gōl) *n.* ⟦ME *gol*, boundary⟧ **1** the place at which a race, trip, etc. is ended **2** an end that one strives to attain

3 in some games, *a*) the line or net over or into which the ball or puck must go to score *b*) the score made

goal′keep′er *n.* in some games, a player stationed at a goal to prevent the ball or puck from entering it Also **goal′ie** (-ē) or **goal′tend′er**

goat (gōt) *n.* ⟦OE *gat*⟧ **1** a cud-chewing mammal with hollow horns, related to the sheep **2** a lecherous man **3** [Colloq.] a scapegoat —**get someone's goat** [Colloq.] to annoy someone

goatee (gō′tē′) *n.* a small, pointed beard on a man's chin

goat′herd′ *n.* one who herds goats

goat′skin′ *n.* the skin of a goat, or leather made from this skin

gob[1] (gäb) *n.* ⟦< OFr *gobe*, mouthful⟧ **1** a soft lump or mass **2** [*pl.*] [Colloq.] a large quantity

gob[2] (gäb) *n.* ⟦< ?⟧ [Slang] a sailor in the U.S. Navy

gob′ble[1] (gäb′əl) *n.* ⟦echoic⟧ the throaty sound made by a male turkey —*vi.* **-bled, -bling** to make this sound

gob′ble[2] (gäb′əl) *vt., vi.* **-bled, -bling** ⟦< OFr *gobet*, mouthful⟧ **1** to eat quickly and greedily **2** to seize eagerly; snatch (*up*)

gob′ble·dy·gook′ (-dē gook′) *n.* ⟦? echoic of turkey cries⟧ [Slang] pompous, wordy talk or writing

gob′bler (gäb′lər) *n.* a male turkey

go-between (gō′bē twēn′) *n.* one who makes arrangements between each of two sides; intermediary

gob′let (gäb′lit) *n.* ⟦< OFr *gobel*⟧ a drinking glass with a base and stem

gob·lin (gäb′lin) *n.* ⟦< ML *gobelinus*⟧ *Folklore* an evil or mischievous spirit

go-by (gō′bī′) *n.* [Colloq.] an intentional disregard or slight

god (gäd, gôd) *n.* ⟦OE⟧ **1** any of various beings conceived of as supernatural and immortal; esp., a male deity **2** an idol **3** a person or thing deified —[G-] in monotheistic

---

THESAURUS

elapse] be spent, waste away, transpire; see PASS 2. **7** [To fail] miss, flunk, fall short; see FAIL 1. **8** [To continue] maintain, carry on, persist; see CONTINUE 1. **9** [To die] pass on, depart, succumb; see DIE. **10** [To end] terminate, finish, conclude; see STOP 2. **11** [To endure] persevere, go on, persist; see ENDURE 1. —**as people (or things) go** in comparison with others, by all standards, according to certain criteria; see ACCORDING TO. —**from the word "go"** from the outset, at the start, beginning with; see FIRST. —**go after 1** [To chase] seek, try to catch, hunt; see PURSUE 1. **2** [To follow in time] come after, supersede, supplant; see SUCCEED 2. —**go against** be opposed to, contradict, counteract; see OPPOSE 1, 2. —**go ahead** move on, proceed, progress; see ADVANCE 1. —**go back on** desert, be unfaithful, forsake; see ABANDON 1. —**go by** move onward, make one's way, proceed; see PASS 1. —**go down 1** [To sink] descend, decline, submerge; see SINK 1. **2** [To lose] be defeated, submit, succumb; see FAIL 1, LOSE 3. **3** [To decrease] fall, decline, lessen; see DECREASE 1. —**go for 1** [To reach for] try to get, aim at, clutch at; see REACH 2. **2** [*To attack] rush upon, run at, spring at; see ATTACK. **3** [*To like] be fond of, fancy, care for; see LIKE 2. —**go in for* 1** [To advocate] endorse, favor, back; see PROMOTE 1. **2** [To like] care for, be fond of, fancy; see LIKE 1. —**go off 1** [To leave] quit, depart, part; see LEAVE 1. **2** [To explode] blow up, detonate, discharge; see EXPLODE. —**go on 1** [To act] execute, behave, conduct; see ACT 1, 2. **2** [To happen] occur, come about, take place; see HAPPEN 2. **3** [To persevere] persist, continue, bear; see ENDURE 1. **4** [*To talk] chatter, converse, speak; see TALK 1. —**go out** cease, die, darken, flicker out, flash out, become dark, become

black, burn out, stop shining. —**go over 1** [To rehearse] repeat, say something repeatedly, practice; see REHEARSE 3. **2** [To examine] look at, investigate, analyze; see EXAMINE, STUDY. —**go through 1** [To inspect] search, audit, investigate; see EXAMINE. **2** [To undergo] withstand, survive, suffer; see ENDURE 2. **3** [To spend] consume, deplete, expend; see SPEND. —**go through with** fulfill, finish, follow through with; see ACHIEVE, COMPLETE. —**go together 1** [To harmonize] be suitable, match, fit; see AGREE. **2** [To keep company] go steady*, escort, go with; see DATE 2, KEEP COMPANY (WITH). —**go under 1** [Drown] sink, drown, suffocate; see DIE. **2** [To become bankrupt] go broke, go bankrupt; see LOSE 2. —**go with 1** [*To keep company with] escort, attend, be with; see ACCOMPANY, DATE 2, KEEP COMPANY (WITH). *2** [To be appropriate to] match, correspond, not clash, go well with, harmonize, complement, fit; see also AGREE. —**have a go at*** attempt, endeavor, try one's hand at; see TRY 1. —**let go** let free, give up, release; see ABANDON 1. —**let oneself go** be unrestrained, free oneself, have fun; see RELAX. —**no go*** impossible, worthless, without value; see USELESS 1. —**on the go*** in constant motion, moving, busy; see ACTIVE.

goad *v.* prod, urge, prick, prompt, spur, drive, whip, press, push, impel, force, stimulate, provoke, tease, excite, needle*, instigate, arouse, animate, encourage, bully, coerce; see also URGE 2.—*Ant.* RESTRAIN, curb, rein in.

goal *n.* object, aim, intent; see END 2, PURPOSE 1.

goat *n.* nanny goat, buck, kid; see ANIMAL. —**get one's goat*** annoy, irritate, anger; see BOTHER 2.

gobble[2] *v.* bolt, cram, stuff; see EAT 1.

go-between *n.* middleman, referee, mediator; see AGENT, MESSENGER.

god *n.* deity, divinity, divine being, spirit, numen, power, demigod, oversoul, prime mover, godhead, omnipotence, world soul, universal life force, infinite spirit. *Greek gods and their Roman counterparts include:* Zeus or Jupiter or Jove, Phoebus or Apollo, Ares or Mars, Hermes or Mercury, Poseidon or Neptune, Hephaestus or Vulcan, Dionysius or Bacchus, Hades or Pluto, Kronos or Saturn, Eros or Cupid. *Norse gods include:* Balder, Frey, Loki, Odin or Woden or Wotan, Thor. For specific female deities see GODDESS.

God *n.* **1** [The Judeo-Christian deity] Lord, Jehovah, Yahweh, the Almighty, the King of Kings, the Godhead, the Creator, the Maker, the Supreme Being, the Ruler of Heaven, Our Father in Heaven, Almighty God, God Almighty, the Deity, the Divinity, Providence, the All-knowing, the Infinite Spirit, the First Cause, the Lord of Lords, the Supreme Soul, the All-wise, the All-merciful, the All-powerful; the Trinity, the Holy Trinity, Threefold Unity; Father, Son, and the Holy Ghost; God the Son, Jesus Christ, Christ, Jesus, Jesus of Nazareth, the Nazarene, the Messiah, the Savior, the Redeemer, the Son of God, the Son of Man, the Son of Mary, the Lamb of God, Immanuel, Emmanuel, the King of the Jews, the Prince of Peace, the Good Shepherd, the Way, the Door, the Truth, the Life, the Light, the Christ Child, the Holy Spirit, the Spirit of God. **2** [The supreme deity of other religions] Allah (Islam); Brahma (Hinduism); Buddha (Buddhism); Mazda or Ormazd (Zoroastrianism).

religions, the creator and ruler of the universe; Supreme Being —**god′like′** *adj.*

god′child′ *n., pl.* **-chil′dren** the person a godparent sponsors

god′daugh′ter *n.* a female godchild

god·dess (gäd′is) *n.* **1** a female god **2** a woman of great beauty, charm, etc.

god′fa′ther *n.* a male godparent

god′head′ *n.* godhood —[G-] God: usually with *the*

god′hood′ *n.* the state of being a god; divinity

Go·di·va (gə di′və) *Eng. Legend* an 11th-c. noblewoman who rides naked through the streets on condition that her husband will abolish a heavy tax

god′less *adj.* **1** irreligious; atheistic **2** wicked —**god′less·ness** *n.*

god′ly *adj.* **-lier, -li·est** devoted to God; devout —**god′li·ness** *n.*

god′moth′er *n.* a female godparent

god′par′ent *n.* a person who sponsors a child, as at baptism, taking responsibility for its faith

god′send′ *n.* anything unexpected and needed or desired that comes at the opportune moment, as if sent by God

god′son′ *n.* a male godchild

go·fer or **go-fer** (gō′fər) *n.* [from being asked to *go for* something] [Slang] an employee who performs menial tasks, as running errands

go-getter (gō′get′ər) *n.* [Colloq.] an enterprising and aggressive person who usually achieves ambitions, goals, etc.

gog·gle (gäg′əl) *vi.* **-gled, -gling** [ME *gogelen*] to stare with bulging eyes —*n.* [*pl.*] large spectacles to protect the eyes against dust, wind, sparks, etc. —*adj.* bulging or rolling: said of the eyes

go-go (gō′gō′) *adj.* [short for *à gogo* < Fr, in plenty] **1** of dancing to rock music, as in discothèques **2** of a dancer performing erotic movements to rock music, as in a bar

go·ing (gō′iŋ) *n.* **1** a departure **2** the condition of the ground or land as it affects traveling, walking, etc. —*adj.* **1** moving; working **2** commonly accepted; current —**be going to** will or shall

go′ing-ov′er *n.* [Colloq.] **1** a thorough inspection **2** a severe scolding or beating

go′ings-on′ *n.pl.* [Colloq.] actions or events, esp. when disapproved of

goi·ter or **goi·tre** (goit′ər) *n.* [< L *guttur*, throat] an enlargement of the thyroid gland, often visible as a swelling in the front of the neck

gold (gōld) *n.* [OE] **1** a heavy, yellow, metallic, highly malleable chemical element: it is a precious metal **2** money; wealth **3** bright yellow

gold′brick′ *n.* [Mil. Slang] one who avoids work: also **gold′brick′er** —*vi.* [Mil. Slang] to shirk a duty or avoid work

gold′en *adj.* **1** made of or containing gold **2** bright-yellow

3 very valuable; excellent **4** flourishing **5** marking the 50th year [*golden* anniversary]

golden ager (ā′jər) [*also* G- A-] [Colloq.] an elderly person, specif. one 65 or older and retired

Golden Fleece *Gr. Myth.* the fleece of gold captured by Jason

gold′en·rod′ *n.* a North American plant with long, branching stalks bearing clusters of small, yellow flowers

golden rule the precept that one should act toward others as one would want them to act toward oneself

gold′-filled′ *adj.* made of a base metal overlaid with gold

gold′finch′ *n.* [OE *goldfinc*] any of various yellow-and-black finches

gold′fish′ *n., pl.* **-fish′** a small, golden-yellow or orange fish, often kept in ponds or aquariums

gold leaf gold beaten into very thin sheets, used for gilding

gold′smith′ *n.* an artisan who makes and repairs articles of gold

gold standard a monetary standard in which the basic currency unit equals a specified quantity of gold

golf (gôlf, gälf) *n.* [? < Du *kolf*, a club] an outdoor game played with a small, hard ball and a set of clubs, the object being to hit the ball into each of a series of 9 or 18 holes with the fewest possible strokes —*vi.* to play golf —**golf′er** *n.*

golf course (or links) a tract of land for playing golf

Go·li·ath (gə li′əth) *Bible* the Philistine giant killed by David

golly (gäl′ē) *interj.* an exclamation of surprise, etc.: a euphemism for *God*

-gon (gän, gən) [< Gr *gōnia*, an angle] combining form a figure having (a specified number of) angles

go·nad (gō′nad) *n.* [< Gr *gonē*, a seed] an animal organ or gland that produces reproductive cells; esp., an ovary or testis

gon·do·la (gän′dō lə, -də-) *n.* [It] **1** a narrow boat used on the canals of Venice **2** a railroad freight car with no top and, often, with low sides **3** a cabin suspended under an airship or balloon

gon′do·lier′ (-lir′) *n.* a man who propels a gondola

gone (gôn, gän) *vi., vt. pp. of* GO —*adj.* [ME *gon* < OE *gan*] **1** departed **2** ruined **3** lost **4** dead **5** used up; consumed **6** ago; past

goner (gôn′ər) *n.* a person or thing certain to die, be ruined, etc.

gong (gôŋ, gäŋ) *n.* [Malay *guṅ*] a slightly convex metallic disk that gives a loud, resonant tone when struck

gon·or·rhea or **gon·or·rhoea** (gän′ə rē′ə) *n.* [< Gr *gonos*, semen + *rheein*, to flow] a venereal disease with inflammation of the genital organs

goo (gōō) *n.* [Slang] **1** anything sticky, or sticky and sweet **2** sentimentality —**goo′ey, -i·er, -i·est,** *adj.*

goo·ber (gōō′bər) *n.* [< Afr *nguba*] [Chiefly South] a peanut

good (good) *adj.* **bet′ter, best** [OE *gōd*] **1** having the proper qualities **2** beneficial **3** valid; real [*good* money] **4** healthy or sound [*good* eyesight] **5** honorable [one's *good*

THESAURUS

goddess *n.* female deity, she-god, beauty; see GOD. *Greek goddesses and their Roman counterparts include the following:* Hera or Juno, Ceres or Demeter, Proserpina or Persephone, Artemis or Diana, Minerva or Athena, Aphrodite or Venus. *Hindu and Brahmanic goddesses include:* Devi, Kali, Parvati, Sarasvati.

godly *a.* righteous, devout, pious; see HOLY 1.

going *a.* flourishing, thriving, profitable; see SUCCESSFUL. —**be going to** shall, be intending to, be prepared to; see WILL 3. —**get one going*** annoy, excite, enrage; see BOTHER 2. —**have (something) going for one*** have an advantage, be talented, have opportunity; see SUCCEED 1. —**keep going** progress, promote, proceed; see ADVANCE 1, IMPROVE 2. —**going strong*** flourishing, surviving, thriving; see SUCCESSFUL.

gold *a.* yellow, gold-colored, red-gold, greenish gold, flaxen, wheat-colored, deep tan, tawny.

gold *n.* **1** [A color] dark yellow, bright yellow, tawny; see COLOR, GOLD *a.* **2** [A precious metal] green gold, white gold, red gold, gold foil,

gold leaf, gold plate, filled gold, commercial gold, gold alloy, cloth of gold, gold thread, gold wire; see also METAL. —**as good as gold*** very good, well-behaved, obedient; see EXCELLENT.

golf *n.* match play, medal play, nine holes, eighteen holes, front nine, back nine, game; see also SPORT 1.

gone *a.* **1** [Having left] gone out, gone away, moved, removed, traveling, transferred, displaced, shifted, withdrawn, retired, left, taken leave, departed, deserted, abandoned, quit, disappeared, not here, no more, flown, run off, decamped.—*Ant.* HERE, returned, remained. **2** [Being no longer in existence] dead, vanished, dissipated, disappeared, dissolved, burned up, disintegrated, decayed, rooted away, extinct. —**far gone 1** advanced, deeply involved, absorbed; see INTERESTED 2. **2** crazy, mad, eccentric; see INSANE.

good *a.* **1** [Moral] upright, just, honest, worthy, respectable, noble, ethical, fair, guiltless, blameless, pure, truthful, decent, kind, conscientious, honorable, charitable. **2** [Kind] considerate, tolerant, generous; see KIND.

3 [Proper] suitable, becoming, desirable; see FIT 1. **4** [Reliable] trustworthy, dependable, loyal; see RELIABLE. **5** [Sound] safe, solid, stable; see RELIABLE. **6** [Pleasant] agreeable, satisfying, enjoyable; see PLEASANT 1, 2. **7** [Qualified] suited, competent, suitable; see ABLE. **8** [Of approved quality] choice, select, high-grade; see EXCELLENT. **9** [Healthy] sound, normal, vigorous; see HEALTHY. **10** [Obedient] dutiful, tractable, well-behaved; see OBEDIENT 1. **11** [Genuine] valid, real, sound; see GENUINE 1. **12** [Delicious] tasty, flavorful, tasteful; see DELICIOUS. **13** [Considerable] great, big, immeasurable; see LARGE 1, MUCH. **14** [Favorable] approving, commendatory, commending; see FAVORABLE 3. —**as good as** in effect, virtually, nearly; see ALMOST. —**for good** permanently, for all time, henceforth; see FOREVER. —**good for 1** [Helpful] useful, beneficial, salubrious; see HELPFUL 1. **2** [Financially sound] safe, competent, worth it; see VALID 2. —**make good 1** [To repay] compensate, adjust, reimburse; see PAY 1, REPAY 1. **2** [To justify] maintain, name/ **6** enjoyable, pleasant, etc. **7** thorough **8** virtuous, devout, kind, dutiful, etc. **9** skilled **10** considerable *[a good* many/ *—n.* something good; worth, benefit, etc. — *adv.* [Colloq. or Dial.] well; fully —**as good as** virtually; nearly —**for good (and all)** permanently —**good and** [Colloq.] very or altogether —**good for 1** able to endure or be used for (a period of time) **2** worth **3** able to pay or give —**make good 1** to repay or replace **2** to fulfill **3** to succeed —**no good** useless; worthless

good'bye' or **good'-bye'** (-bī') *interj., n., pl.* **-byes'** ‖contr. of *God be with ye*‖ farewell Also sp. **good'by'**, **good'-by'**

good faith good intentions; sincerity

Good Friday the Friday before Easter, commemorating the Crucifixion

good'-heart'ed *adj.* kind and generous —**good'-heart'edly** *adv.* —**good'-heart'edness** *n.*

good humor a cheerful, agreeable mood —**good'-hu'mored** *adj.* —**good'-hu'moredly** *adv.*

good'-look'ing *adj.* handsome

good'ly *adj.* **-lier, -li·est 1** of good appearance or quality **2** ample

good'-na'tured *adj.* agreeable; affable —**good'-na'turedly** *adv.*

good'ness *n.* the state or quality of being good; virtue, kindness, etc. —*interj.* an exclamation of surprise

goods (goodz) *n.pl.* **1** movable personal property **2** merchandise; wares **3** fabric; cloth —**get (or have) the goods on** [Slang] to discover (or know) something incriminating about

good Sa·mari·tan (sə mer'ət 'n) one who helps another or others unselfishly: see Luke 10:30-37

good'-sized' *adj.* ample; fairly big

good'-tem'pered *adj.* amiable

good turn a friendly, helpful act

good'will' *n.* **1** benevolence **2** willingness **3** the value of a business as a result of patronage, reputation, etc., beyond its tangible assets Also, exc. for sense 3, **good will**

good'y (good'ē) *n., pl.* **-ies** [Colloq.] something good to eat, as a piece of candy — *interj.* a child's exclamation of delight

good'y-good'y *adj.* [Colloq.] affectedly moral or pious — *n.* [Colloq.] a goody-goody person

goof (goof) *n.* [Slang] **1** a stupid or silly person **2** a mistake; blunder — *vi.* [Slang] **1** to err or blunder **2** to waste time, shirk duties, etc.: with *off* or *around* —**goof'y, -i·er, -i·est,** *adj.* —**goof'i·ness** *n.*

gook (gook, gook) *n.* ‖GOO + (GUN)K‖ [Slang] any sticky or slimy substance

goon (goon) *n.* [Slang] **1** a ruffian or thug **2** a grotesque or stupid person

goop (goop) *n.* ‖GOO + (SOU)P‖ [Slang] any sticky, semiliquid substance

goose (goos) *n., pl.* **geese** ‖< OE *gos*‖ **1** a long-necked, web-footed waterfowl like a duck but larger **2** its flesh as food **3** a silly person —**cook one's goose** [Colloq.] to spoil one's chances

goose'ber'ry *n., pl.* **-ries 1** a small, sour berry **2** the shrub it grows on

goose flesh (or bumps or pimples) a momentary roughened condition of the skin, induced by cold, fear, etc.

goose'neck' *n.* any of various mechanical devices shaped like a goose's neck, as a flexible support for a desk lamp

GOP Grand Old Party (Republican Party)

go·pher (gō'fər) *n.* ‖< ? Fr *gaufre,* honeycomb: from its burrowing‖ **1 a** a burrowing rodent with wide cheek pouches **2** a striped ground squirrel of the prairies of North America

gore[1] (gôr) *n.* ‖OE *gor,* filth‖ blood from a wound, esp. when clotted

gore[2] (gôr) *vt.* **gored, gor'ing** ‖< OE *gar,* a spear‖ **1** to pierce as with a horn or tusk **2** to insert gores in — *n.* a tapering piece of cloth inserted in a skirt, sail, etc. to give it fullness

gorge (gôrj) *n.* ‖< L *gurges,* whirlpool‖ **1** the gullet **2** what has been swallowed **3** resentment, disgust, etc. **4** a deep, narrow pass between steep heights — *vi., vt.* **gorged, gorg'ing** to eat greedily or glut (oneself)

gor·geous (gôr'jəs) *adj.* ‖< OFr *gorgias*‖ **1** brilliantly showy; magnificent **2** [Colloq.] beautiful, delightful, etc. —**gor'geously** *adv.*

go·rilla (gə ril'ə) *n.* ‖< W Afr‖ the largest, and most powerful, of the great apes, native to Africa

gor·mand·ize (gôr'mən diz') *vi., vt.* **-ized', -iz'ing** ‖< Fr *gourmandise,* gluttony‖ to eat like a glutton

gorp (gôrp) *n.* a mix of raisins, nuts, etc. eaten for quick energy

gorse (gôrs) *n.* ‖OE *gorst*‖ FURZE

gory (gôr'ē) *adj.* **-i·er, -i·est 1** covered with gore; bloody **2** with much bloodshed —**gor'i·ness** *n.*

gosh (gäsh, gôsh) *interj.* an exclamation of surprise, etc.: a euphemism for *God*

gos·ling (gäz'lin) *n.* a young goose

gos·pel (gäs'pəl) *n.* ‖< OE *gōdspel,* good news‖ **1** [*often* G-] the teachings of Jesus and the Apostles **2** [G-] any of the first four books of the New Testament **3** anything proclaimed or accepted as the absolute truth: also **gospel truth**

gos·sa·mer (gäs'ə mər) *n.* ‖ME *gosesomer,* lit., goose summer‖ **1** a filmy cobweb **2** a very thin, filmy cloth — *adj.* light, thin, and filmy

gos·sip (gäs'əp) *n.* ‖< Late OE *godsibbe,* godparent‖ **1** one who chatters idly about others **2** such talk — *vi.* to be a gossip —**gos'sipy** *adj.*

got (gät) *vt., vi. pt. & alt. pp.* of GET

Goth (gäth, gôth) *n.* any member of a Germanic people that conquered most of the Roman Empire in the 3d, 4th, and 5th c. A.D.

Gothic (gäth'ik) *adj.* **1** of the Goths or their language **2** designating or of a style of architecture developed in W Europe between the 12th and 16th c., with pointed arches, steep roofs, etc. **3** [*sometimes* g-] uncivilized **4** of a type of fiction that uses remote, gloomy settings and a sinister atmosphere to suggest mystery — *n.* **1** the East Germanic language of the Goths **2** Gothic architecture

got·ten (gät'n) *vt., vi. alt. pp.* of GET

Gouda (cheese) (gou'də, goo'-) ‖after *Gouda,* Netherlands‖ a mild cheese sometimes coated with red wax

gouge (gouj) *n.* ‖< LL *gulbia*‖ **1** a chisel for cutting grooves or holes in wood **2** such a groove or hole — *vt.* **gouged, goug'ing 1** to make a groove, etc. in (some-

---

THESAURUS

support, uphold; see SUPPORT 2. **3** [To succeed] arrive, pay off, prove oneself; see PAY 2, SUCCEED 1.

good *n.* **1** [A benefit] welfare, gain, asset; see ADVANTAGE. **2** [That which is morally approved] ethic, merit, ideal; see VIRTUE 1. —**come to no good** come to a bad end, get into trouble, have difficulty; see FAIL 1. —**no good** useless, valueless, unserviceable; see WORTHLESS. —**to the good** favorable, advantageous, beneficial; see PROFITABLE.

goodbye *interj.* farewell, fare you well, God bless you and keep you, God with you, adieu, adios, so long, bye, bye-bye, see you later, take it easy, have a nice day.

good humor *n.* cordiality, levity, geniality; see HAPPINESS.

good-looking *a.* clean-cut, attractive, impressive; see BEAUTIFUL, HANDSOME.

good-natured *a.* cordial, kindly,

amiable; see FRIENDLY.

goodness *n.* decency, morality, honesty; see VIRTUE 1, 2.

goods *n.* **1** [Effects] equipment, personal property, possessions; see PROPERTY 1. **2** [Commodities] merchandise, materials, wares; see COMMODITY.

goodwill *n.* benevolence, charity, kindness, cordiality, sympathy, tolerance, helpfulness, altruism.—*Ant.* HATRED, malevolence, animosity.

goof* *v.* err, make a mistake, flub; see FAIL 1.

goose *n.* gray goose, snow goose, Canada goose; see BIRD.

gorge *n.* chasm, abyss, crevasse; see RAVINE.

gorge *v.* glut, devour, stuff oneself; see EAT 1, FILL 1.

gorgeous *a.* superb, sumptuous, impressive; see BEAUTIFUL, GRAND.

gory *a.* blood-soaked, bloodstained,

bloody; see OFFENSIVE 2.

gospel *n.* **1** [A record of Christ] New Testament, Christian Scripture, Evangelist; see BIBLE. **2** [Belief or statement supposedly infallible] creed, certainty, dogma; see DOCTRINE, FAITH 2, TRUTH.

gossip *n.* **1** [Local, petty talk] babble, chatter, meddling, small talk, malicious talk, hearsay, rumor, scandal, news, slander, defamation, injury, blackening, skinny*, the grapevine*. **2** [One who indulges in gossip] snoop, busybody, meddler, tattler, newsmonger, scandalmonger, muckraker, backbiter, chatterbox, talkative person, babbler.

gossip *v.* tattle, prattle, tell tales, talk idly, chat, chatter, rumor, report, tell secrets, blab, babble, repeat.

gouge *v.* scoop, chisel, channel; see DIG 1.

thing) as with a gouge **2** to scoop out **3** [Colloq.] to cheat out of money —**goug′er** *n.*

gou·lash (gōō′läsh′, -lash′) *n.* ⟦< Hung *gulyás*⟧ a beef or veal stew seasoned with paprika

gou·rami (gōōr′ə mē, goor′ə-) *n., pl.* **-mies** or **-mi** ⟦Malay *gurami*⟧ any of various tropical, freshwater fishes; esp., a food fish of SE Asia

gourd (gôrd, goord) *n.* ⟦< L *cucurbita*⟧ **1** any trailing or climbing plant of a family that includes the squash, melon, etc. **2** the fruit of one species or its dried, hollowed-out shell, used as a cup, dipper, etc.

gour·mand (goor môn′, -mänd′; goor′môn′, -mänd′) *n.* ⟦OFr⟧ one who likes good food and drink and tends to indulge in them to excess

gour·met (goor′mā; Fr goor me′) *n.* ⟦Fr < OFr, wine taster⟧ one who likes and is an excellent judge of fine foods and drinks

gout (gout) *n.* ⟦< L *gutta*, a drop⟧ a form of arthritis characterized by painful swelling of the joints, esp. in the big toe —**gout′y, -i·er, -i·est,** *adj.*

gov. or **Gov.** **1** government **2** governor

gov·ern (guv′ərn) *vt., vi.* ⟦< Gr *kybernan*, to steer⟧ **1** to exercise authority over; rule, control, etc. **2** to influence the action of; guide **3** to determine —**gov′ern·able** *adj.*

gov′ern·ance (-ər nəns) *n.* the action, function, or power of government

gov′ern·ess (-ər nis) *n.* a woman employed in a private home to train and teach the children

gov·ern·ment (guv′ərn mənt, -ər mənt) *n.* **1** the exercise of authority over a state, organization, etc.; control; rule **2** a system of ruling, political administration, etc. **3** those who direct the affairs of a state, etc.; administration —**gov′ern·men′tal** *adj.*

gov·er·nor (guv′ər nər, -ə nər) *n.* **1** one who governs; esp., *a*) one appointed to govern a province, etc. *b*) the elected head of any State of the U.S. **2** a mechanical device for automatically controlling the speed of an engine —**gov′er·nor·ship′** *n.*

governor general *pl.* **governors general** or **governor generals** a governor who has subordinate or deputy governors

govt. or **Govt.** government

gown (goun) *n.* ⟦< LL *gunna*⟧ a long, loose outer garment; specif., *a*) a woman's formal dress *b*) a nightgown *c*) a long, flowing robe worn by judges, clergymen, scholars, etc.

GP or **G.P.** general practitioner

gr. **1** grain(s) **2** gross

Gr. **1** Greece **2** Greek

grab (grab) *vt.* **grabbed, grab′bing** ⟦prob. < MDu *grabben*⟧ **1** to snatch suddenly **2** to get by unscrupulous methods **3** [Slang] to impress greatly —*n.* a grabbing —**grab′ber** *n.*

grace (grās) *n.* ⟦< L *gratus*, pleasing⟧ **1** beauty or charm of form, movement, or expression **2** goodwill; favor **3** a delay granted for payment of an obligation **4** a short prayer of thanks for a meal **5** [G-] a title of an archbishop, duke, or duchess **6** the love and favor of God toward man —*vt.* **graced, grac′ing** **1** to decorate **2** to dignify —**in the good** (or **bad**) **graces of** in favor (or disfavor) with

grace′ful *adj.* having beauty of form, movement, or expression —**grace′fully** *adv.* —**grace′ful·ness** *n.*

grace′less *adj.* **1** lacking any sense of what is proper **2** clumsy —**grace′lessly** *adv.* —**grace′less·ness** *n.*

gra·cious (grā′shəs) *adj.* ⟦see GRACE⟧ **1** having or showing kindness, courtesy, charm, etc. **2** compassionate **3** polite to supposed inferiors **4** marked by luxury, ease, etc. [*gracious* living] —**gra′ciously** *adv.* —**gra′cious·ness** *n.*

grackle (grak′əl) *n.* ⟦L *graculus*, jackdaw⟧ any of several blackbirds somewhat smaller than a crow

grad (grad) *n.* [Colloq.] a graduate

gra·da·tion (grā dā′shən) *n.* **1** an arranging in grades, or stages **2** a gradual change by stages **3** a step or degree in a graded series

grade (grād) *n.* ⟦< L *gradus*⟧ **1** a stage or step in a progression **2** *a*) a degree in a scale of quality, rank, etc. *b*) a group of people of the same rank, merit, etc. **3** *a*) the degree of slope *b*) a sloping part **4** any of the divisions of a school curriculum, by years **5** a mark or rating in an examination, etc. —*vt.* **grad′ed, grad′ing** **1** to classify by grades; sort **2** to give a GRADE (sense 5) to **3** to make (ground) level or evenly sloped, as for a road —**make the grade** to succeed

▬▬ THESAURUS ▬▬

govern *v.* command, administer, reign, rule, legislate, oversee, assume command, hold office, administer the laws, exercise authority, be in power, supervise, direct, dictate, tyrannize.

governed *a.* commanded, administered, under authority, supervised, directed, dictated to, conducted, guided, piloted, mastered, led, driven, subjugated, subordinate, determined, guided, influenced, swayed, inclined, regulated, directed, ordered, dependent, obedient, under one's jurisdiction.—*Ant.* UNRULY, self-determined, capricious.

governing *a.* commanding, administrative, executive, authoritative, supervisory, regulatory, controlling, directing, overseeing, dictatorial, conducting, guiding, mastering, dominating, dominant, determining, supreme, influential, presidential, absolute, ruling, checking, curbing, inhibiting, limiting.—*Ant.* SUBORDINATE, powerless, tributary.

government *n.* **1** [The process of governing] rule, control, command, regulation, bureaucracy, direction, dominion, sway, authority, jurisdiction, sovereignty, direction, power, management, authorization, mastery, supervision, superintendence, supremacy, domination, influence, politics, state, political practice; see also ADMINISTRATION 2. **2** [The instrument of governing] administration, assembly, legislature, congress, cabinet, executive power, authority, party, council, parliament, senate, department of justice, soviet, synod, convocation, convention, court, house. *Types of government include the following:* absolute monarchy, dictatorship, empire, tyranny, fas-

cism, imperialism, colonialism, despotism, limited monarchy, constitutional monarchy, oligarchy, aristocracy, democracy, popular government, representative government, democratic socialism, communism, socialism, party government. *Divisions of government include:* state, province, kingdom, territory, colony, dominion, commonwealth, soviet, republic, shire, city, county, town, village, township, municipality, borough, commune, ward, district, department, parish.

governmental *a.* political, administrative, executive, regulatory, bureaucratic, legal, supervisory, sovereign, presidential, official, gubernatorial, national.

governor *n.* director, leader, head, presiding officer, ruler; see also LEADER 2.

gown *n.* garb, garment, clothes; see DRESS 2.

grab *v.* clutch, grasp, take; see SEIZE 1, 2.

grace *n.* **1** [The quality of being graceful] suppleness, ease of movement, nimbleness, agility, pliancy, smoothness, form, poise, dexterity, symmetry, balance, style, harmony.—*Ant.* AWKWARDNESS, stiffness, maladroitness. **2** [Mercy] forgiveness, love, charity; see MERCY. —**in the bad graces of** in disfavor, rejected, disapproved; see HATED. — **in the good graces of** favored, accepted, admired; see APPROVED.

graceful *a.* **1** [Said of movement] supple, agile, lithe, pliant, nimble, elastic, springy, easy, dexterous, adroit, smooth, controlled, light-footed, willowy, poised, practiced,

skilled, rhythmic, sprightly, elegant.—*Ant.* AWKWARD, fumbling, stiff. **2** [Said of objects] elegant, neat, well-proportioned, trim, balanced, symmetrical, dainty, pretty, harmonious, beautiful, comely, seemly, handsome, fair, delicate, tasteful, slender, decorative, artistic, exquisite, statuesque.—*Ant.* UGLY, shapeless, cumbersome. **3** [Said of conduct] cultured, seemly, becoming; see POLITE.

gracefully *a.* lithely, agilely, harmoniously, daintily, nimbly, elegantly, trimly, symmetrically, beautifully, delicately, tastefully, artistically, easily, dexterously, smoothly, skillfully, fairly, adroitly, handsomely, rhythmically, exquisitely, neatly, delightfully, charmingly, imaginatively, becomingly, suitably, pleasingly, appropriately, happily, decoratively, prettily.—*Ant.* AWKWARDLY, insipidly, grotesquely.

gracious *a.* **1** [Genial] amiable, courteous, condescending; see POLITE. **2** [Merciful] tender, loving, charitable; see KIND.

grade *n.* **1** [An incline] slope, inclined plane, gradient, slant, inclination, pitch, ascent, descent, ramp, upgrade, downgrade, climb, elevation, height; see also HILL. **2** [An embankment] fill, causeway, dike; see DAM. **3** [Rank or degree] class, category, classification; see DEGREE 2. **4** [A division of a school] standard, form, rank; see GATHERING. —**make the grade** win, prosper, achieve; see SUCCEED 1.

grade *v.* rate, give a grade to, assort; see RANK 3.

grade crossing the place where a railroad intersects another railroad or a roadway on the same level

grade school ELEMENTARY SCHOOL

grade separation a crossing with an overpass or underpass

gra·di·ent (grād′ē ənt) *n.* [< L *gradi*, to step] 1 a slope, as of a road 2 the degree of such slope

gradu·al (gra′jōō əl, -jōō wəl) *adj.* [< L *gradus*, a step] taking place by degrees; developing little by little — **grad′u·ally** *adv.*

grad′u·al·ism′ *n.* the principle of promoting gradual rather than rapid change

gradu·ate (gra′jōō it, -jōō wit; *for v.*, -āt′, -wāt′) *n.* [< L *gradus*, a step] one who has completed a course of study at a school or college — *vt.* **-at′ed, -at′ing** 1 to give a degree or diploma to upon completion of a course of study 2 [Colloq.] to become a graduate of [*to graduate college*] 3 to mark with degrees for measuring 4 to classify into grades according to amount, size, etc. — *vi.* to become a graduate of a school, etc. — *adj.* 1 being a graduate of a school, etc. 2 of or for graduates — **grad′u·a′tor** *n.*

grad′u·a′tion *n.* 1 a graduating from a school or college 2 the ceremony connected with this

graf·fi·to (grə fēt′ō) *n., pl.* **-ti** (-ē) [It < L: see fol.] an inscription or drawing on a wall or other public surface: the plural often takes a sing. verb

graft (graft) *n.* [< Gr *grapheion*, stylus] 1 *a*) a shoot or bud of one plant or tree inserted into another, where it grows permanently *b*) the inserting of such a shoot 2 the transplanting of skin, bone, etc. 3 *a*) the dishonest use of one's position to gain money, etc., as in politics *b*) anything so gained — *vt., vi.* 1 to insert (a graft) 2 to obtain (money, etc.) by graft — **graft′er** *n.*

gra·ham (grā′əm) *adj.* [after S. *Graham*, 19th-c. U.S. dietary reformer] designating or made of whole-wheat flour [*graham* crackers]

Grail (grāl) [< ML *gradalis*, cup] *Medieval Legend* the cup used by Jesus at the Last Supper Also **Holy Grail**

grain (grān) *n.* [< L *granum*] 1 the small, hard seed of any cereal plant, as wheat, corn, etc. 2 cereal plants 3 a tiny, solid particle, as of salt or sand 4 a tiny bit 5 the smallest unit in the system of weights used in the U.S. 6 *a*) the arrangement or direction of fibers, layers, etc. of wood, leather, etc. *b*) the markings or texture due to this 7 disposition; nature

grain′y *adj.* **-i·er, -i·est** 1 having a clearly defined grain, as wood 2 coarsely textured; granular — **grain′i·ness** *n.*

gram (gram) *n.* [< Gr *gramma*, small weight] the basic unit of mass in the metric system, equal to about ⅟₂₈ ounce

-gram (gram) [< Gr *gramma*, writing] *combining form* something written [*telegram*]

gram·mar (gram′ər) *n.* [< Gr *gramma*, writing] 1 language study dealing with the forms of words and with their arrangement in sentences 2 a system of rules for speaking and writing a given language 3 one's manner of speaking or writing as judged by such rules — **gram·mar·ian** (grə mer′ē ən) *n.* — **gram·mat′i·cal** (-mat′i kəl) *adj.* — **gram·mat′i·cally** *adv.*

grammar school [Now Rare] ELEMENTARY SCHOOL

grana·ry (gran′ə rē, grān′-) *n., pl.* **-ries** [< L *granum*, grain] a building for storing threshed grain

grand (grand) *adj.* [< L *grandis*, large] 1 higher in rank than others [a *grand* duke] 2 most important; main [the *grand* ballroom] 3 imposing in size, beauty, and extent 4 distinguished; illustrious 5 complete; overall [the *grand* total] 6 [Colloq.] excellent; delightful — *n., pl.* **grand** [Slang] a thousand dollars — **grand′ly** *adv.*

grand- *combining form* of the generation older (or younger) than [*grandmother, grandson*]

gran·dam (gran′dam′, -dəm) *n.* [see prec. & DAME] [Now Rare] 1 a grandmother 2 an old woman

grand′child′ *n., pl.* **-chil′dren** a child of one's son or daughter

grand′daugh′ter *n.* a daughter of one's son or daughter

grande dame (gränd däm; *Fr* gränd däm′) [Fr] a woman, esp. an older one, of great dignity

gran·dee (gran dē′) *n.* [Sp & Port *grande*: see GRAND] a man of high rank

gran·deur (gran′jər, -joor′; -dyoor′) *n.* [see GRAND] 1 splendor; magnificence 2 nobility; dignity

grand′fa′ther *n.* 1 the father of one's father or mother 2 a forefather — *vt.* [Colloq.] to exempt (a practice, person, etc.) from a new law or regulation

grandfather (or **grandfather's**) **clock** a large clock with a pendulum, in a tall, narrow case

gran·dil·o·quent (gran dil′ə kwənt) *adj.* [< L *grandis*, grand + *loqui*, speak] using pompous, bombastic words — **gran·dil′o·quence** *n.*

gran·di·ose (gran′dē ōs′) *adj.* [< L *grandis*, great] 1 having grandeur; imposing 2 pompous and showy — **gran′di·os′ity** (-äs′ə tē) *n.*

grand jury a jury that investigates accusations and indicts persons for trial if there is sufficient evidence

grandma (gran′mə) *n.* [Colloq.] GRANDMOTHER

grand′mas′ter *n.* any exceptionally skilled chess player

grand′moth′er *n.* the mother of one's father or mother

grand opera opera in which the whole text is set to music

grandpa (gran′pə) *n.* [Colloq.] GRANDFATHER

grand′par′ent *n.* a grandfather or grandmother

THESAURUS

gradual *a.* creeping, regular, continuous; see REGULATED.

gradually *a.* step by step, by degrees, steadily, increasingly, slowly, regularly, a little at a time, little by little, bit by bit, inch by inch, by installments, in small doses, continuously, progressively, successively, sequentially, constantly, unceasingly, imperceptibly, deliberately.—*Ant.* QUICKLY, haphazardly, by leaps and bounds.

graduate *n.* recipient of a degree, recipient of a certificate, recipient of a diploma, alumnus, alumna, former student, holder of a degree, bearer of a degree, holder of a certificate, bearer of a certificate, baccalaureate, grad*, alum*.

graduate *v.* receive a degree, receive a certificate, receive a diploma, be awarded a degree, be awarded a certificate, be awarded a diploma, earn a degree, earn a certificate, earn a diploma, become an alumna, become an alumnus, get out, finish up; get a B.A., M.A., Ph.D., M.D., etc.; get a sheepskin*.

graduated *a.* 1 [Granted a degree] certified, ordained, passed; see OFFICIAL 1. 2 [Arranged or marked according to a scale] graded, sequential, progressive; see ORGANIZED.

graduation *n.* commencement, convocation, granting of diplomas, promotion, bestowal of honors, commissioning.

grain *n.* 1 [Seeds of domesticated grasses] cereals, corn, small grain, seed. *Varieties of grain include the following:* rice, wheat, oats, barley, maize, corn, rye, millet, Indian corn, hybrid corn, popcorn. 2 [Character imparted by fiber] texture, warp and woof, warp and weft, tendency, fabric, tissue, current, direction, tooth, nap. —**against the grain** disturbing, irritating, bothersome; see OFFENSIVE 2.

grammar *n.* syntax, morphology, structure, syntactic structure, sentence structure, language pattern, sentence pattern, linguistic science, generative grammar, stratificational grammar, transformational grammar, universal grammar, tagmemics, synthetic grammar, inflectional grammar, analytic grammar, distributive grammar, traditional grammar, the new grammar; see also LANGUAGE. *Terms in grammar include the following:* tense, mood, aspect, case, modification, incorporation, inflection, concord, agreement, sentence, nexus, coordination, subordination, structure, phrase structure, structural linguistics, phoneme, phonemics, string, head word, morpheme, transform.

grammatical *a.* 1 [Having to do with grammar] linguistic, syntactic, morphological, logical, philological, analytic, analytical. 2 [Conforming to rules of grammar] grammatically correct, conventional, accepted; see CONVENTIONAL 1.

grand *a.* lofty, stately, dignified, elevated, high, regal, noble, illustrious, sublime, great, ambitious, august, majestic, solemn, grave, preeminent, extraordinary, monumental, stupendous, huge, chief, commanding, towering, overwhelming, impressive, imposing, awe-inspiring, mighty, terrific*.—*Ant.* POOR, low, mediocre.

grandeur *n.* splendor, magnificence, pomp, circumstance, impressiveness, eminence, distinction, fame, glory, brilliancy, richness, luxury, stateliness, beauty, ceremony, importance, celebrity, solemnity, fineness, majesty, nobility, scope, dignity, elevation, preeminence, height, greatness, might, breadth, immensity, amplitude, vastness.

grandfather *n.* elder, forefather, ancestor, patriarch, grandpa*, granddaddy*, grandpappy*.

grandmother *n.* matriarch, dowager, ancestor, grandma*, gram*, granny*.

grand piano a large piano with strings set horizontally in a wing-shaped case

grand slam 1 *Baseball* a home run hit when there is a runner on each base 2 *Bridge* the winning of all the tricks in a deal

grand'son' *n.* a son of one's son or daughter

grand'stand' *n.* the main seating structure for spectators at a sporting event

grange (grānj) *n.* ⟦< L *granum*, grain⟧ a farm —[G-] an association of farmers or a local lodge of this

gran·ite (gran'it) *n.* ⟦< L *granum*, grain⟧ a hard, plutonic rock consisting chiefly of feldspar and quartz —**gra·nitic** (grə nit'ik) *adj.*

granny or **gran·nie** (gran'ē) *n., pl.* **-nies** [Colloq.] 1 a grandmother 2 an old woman — *adj.* of a style like that formerly worn by elderly women *[granny glasses]*

gran·ola (grə nō'lə) *n.* ⟦< ? L *granum*, grain⟧ a breakfast cereal of rolled oats, wheat germ, sesame seeds, brown sugar or honey, dried fruit or nuts, etc.

grant (grant) *vt.* ⟦< L *credere*, believe⟧ 1 to give (what is requested, as permission, etc.) 2 to give or transfer by legal procedure 3 to admit as true; concede — *n.* 1 a granting 2 something granted, as property, a right, etc. — **take for granted** to consider as true, already settled, etc.

grant'-in-aid' *n., pl.* **grants'-in-aid'** a grant of funds, as by the Federal government, or by a foundation to a scientist, artist, etc., to support a specific project

grants'man·ship' *n.* skill in acquiring grants-in-aid

granu·lar (gran'yo͞o lər) *adj.* 1 containing or consisting of grains 2 like grains or granules —**gran'u·lar'i·ty** (-ler'ə tē) *n.*

gran'u·late' (-lāt') *vt., vi.* **-lat'ed, -lat'ing** to form into grains or granules —**gran'u·la'tion** *n.*

gran·ule (gran'yo͞ol) *n.* ⟦< L *granum*, grain⟧ a small grain or particle

grape (grāp) *n.* ⟦< OFr *graper*, to gather with a hook⟧ 1 a small, round, juicy berry, growing in clusters on a woody vine 2 a grapevine 3 a dark purplish red

grape'fruit' *n.* a large, round, sour citrus fruit with a yellow rind

grape hyacinth a small plant of the lily family, with spikes of small, blue or white, bell-shaped flowers

grape'shot' *n.* a cluster of small iron balls, formerly fired from a cannon

grape'vine' *n.* 1 a woody vine bearing grapes 2 a secret means of spreading information 3 a rumor

graph (graf) *n.* ⟦short for *graphic formula*⟧ a diagram representing the successive changes in a variable quantity or quantities — *vt.* to represent by a graph

-graph (graf) ⟦< Gr *graphein*, to write⟧ *combining form* 1 something that writes or records *[telegraph]* 2 something written *[monograph]*

graphic (graf'ik) *adj.* ⟦< Gr *graphein*, to write⟧ 1 described in realistic detail; vivid 2 of those arts (**graphic arts**) that include any form of visual artistic representation, esp. painting, drawing, etching, etc. Also **graph'i·cal** —**graph'i·cally** *adv.*

graph'ics *n.pl.* [*with sing. v.*] 1 the graphic arts 2 design as employed in the graphic arts

graph·ite (graf'it') *n.* ⟦< Gr *graphein*, to write⟧ a soft, black form of carbon used in pencils, for lubricants, etc.

graph·ol·ogy (graf äl'ə jē) *n.* ⟦< Fr: see GRAPHIC & -LOGY⟧ the study of handwriting, esp. as a clue to character — **graph·ol'o·gist** *n.*

-graphy (grə fē) ⟦< Gr *graphein*, to write⟧ *combining form* 1 a process or method of writing, or graphically representing *[calligraphy]* 2 a descriptive science *[geography]*

grap·nel (grap'nəl) *n.* ⟦< Prov *grapa*, a hook⟧ 1 a small anchor with several curved, pointed arms 2 an iron bar with claws at one end for grasping things

grap·ple (grap'əl) *n.* ⟦OFr *grapil*⟧ 1 GRAPNEL (sense 2) 2 a hand-to-hand fight — *vt.* **-pled, -pling** to grip and hold — *vi.* 1 to use a GRAPNEL (sense 2) 2 to wrestle 3 to try to cope (*with*)

grappling iron (or **hook**) GRAPNEL (sense 2)

grasp (grasp) *vt.* ⟦ME *graspen*⟧ 1 to grip, as with the hand 2 to take hold of eagerly; seize 3 to comprehend — *vi.* 1 to try to seize: with *at* 2 to accept eagerly: with *at* — *n.* 1 a grasping; grip 2 control; possession 3 the power to hold or seize 4 comprehension —**grasp'able** *adj.*

grasp'ing *adj.* avaricious; greedy

grass (gras, gräs) *n.* ⟦OE *græs*⟧ 1 a plant with long, narrow leaves, jointed stems, and seedlike fruit, as wheat, rye, etc. 2 any of various green plants with narrow leaves, growing densely in meadows, lawns, etc. 3 pasture or lawn 4 [Slang] marijuana —**grass'y, -i·er, -i·est,** *adj.*

grass'hop'per *n.* any of various winged, plant-eating insects with powerful hind legs for jumping

grass roots [Colloq.] 1 the common people 2 the basic source or support, as of a movement —**grass'-roots'** *adj.*

grass widow a woman divorced or separated from her husband

grate¹ (grāt) *vt.* **grat'ed, grat'ing** ⟦< OFr *grater*⟧ 1 to grind into particles by scraping 2 to rub against (an object) or grind (the teeth) together with a harsh sound 3 to irritate; annoy; fret — *vi.* 1 to rub with or make a rasping sound 2 to be irritating —**grat'er** *n.*

grate² (grāt) *n.* ⟦< L *cratis*, a hurdle⟧ 1 GRATING¹ 2 a frame of metal bars for holding fuel in a fireplace, etc. 3 a fireplace

grate·ful (grāt'fəl) *adj.* ⟦obs. *grate* (< L *gratus*), pleasing⟧ 1 thankful 2 welcome —**grate'fully** *adv.* —**grate'ful·ness** *n.*

grati·fy (grat'i fi') *vt.* **-fied', -fy'ing** ⟦< L *gratus*, pleasing + *-ficare*, -FY⟧ 1 to please or satisfy 2 to indulge; humor —**grat'i·fi·ca'tion** *n.*

grat·ing¹ (grāt'iŋ) *n.* a framework of bars set in a window, door, etc.

grat'ing² *adj.* 1 rasping 2 irritating

gra·tis (grāt'is, grat'-) *adv., adj.* ⟦L < *gratia*, a favor⟧ free of charge

grati·tude (grat'i to͞od') *n.* ⟦< L *gratus*, pleasing⟧ thankful appreciation for favors received

gra·tui·tous (grə to͞o'i təs, -tyo͞o'-) *adj.* ⟦< L *gratus*, pleasing⟧ 1 given free of charge 2 uncalled-for —**gra·tu'i·tously** *adv.*

gra·tu'i·ty (-tē) *n., pl.* **-ties** a gift of money, esp. for a service; tip

gra·va·men (grə vā'mən) *n., pl.* **-mens** or **gra·vam'i·na**

■ THESAURUS ■

grant *n.* gift, boon, reward, present, allowance, stipend, donation, matching grant, benefaction, gratuity, endowment, concession, bequest, privilege, federal grant.—*Ant.* DISCOUNT, deprivation, deduction.

grant *v.* 1 [To permit] yield, cede, impart; see ALLOW. 2 [To accept as true] concede, accede, acquiesce; see ACKNOWLEDGE 2.

granted *a.* 1 [Awarded] conferred, bestowed, awarded; see GIVEN. 2 [Allowed] accepted, admitted, acknowledged; see ASSUMED. —**take for granted** accept, presume, consider settled; see ASSUME.

grape *n.* wine grapes, raisin grapes, Concord grapes; see FRUIT.

graph *n.* diagram, chart, linear representation; see DESIGN, PLAN 1.

graphic *a.* 1 [Pictorial] visible, illustrated, descriptive, photographic, visual, depicted, seen, drawn, portrayed, traced, sketched, outlined, pictured, painted, engraved, etched,

chiseled, penciled, printed.—*Ant.* UNREAL, imagined, chimerical. 2 [Vivid] forcible, telling, picturesque, intelligible, comprehensible, clear, explicit, striking, definite, distinct, precise, expressive, eloquent, moving, stirring, concrete, energetic, colorful, strong, figurative, poetic.—*Ant.* OBSCURE, ambiguous, abstract.

grasp *v.* 1 [To clutch] grip, enclose, clasp; see SEIZE 1, 2. 2 [To comprehend] perceive, apprehend, follow; see UNDERSTAND 1.

grasp *n.* hold, clutch, cinch; see GRIP 2.

grass *n.* 1 [Plant for food, grazing, etc.] *Wild grasses include the following:* Johnson grass, salt grass, bluegrass, foxtail, buffalo grass, sandbur, crab grass, deer grass, bunch grass, meadow grass, fescue, orchard grass, pampas grass, June grass, redtop, river grass, ribbon grass, sweet grass, cattail, wild rice. 2 [Grassed area]

grassland, meadow, lawn, turf, pasture, prairie, hayfield; see also FIELD 1, YARD 1. 3 [*A drug*] marijuana, cannabis, pot*; see DRUG.

grassy *a.* grass-grown, verdant, green, reedy, lush, matted, tangled, carpeted, sowed, luxurious, deep.

grate¹ *v.* rasp, grind, abrade; see RUB 1.

grateful *a.* appreciative, pleased, obliged; see THANKFUL.

gratefully *a.* appreciatively, thankfully, with a sense of obligation, delightedly, responsively, admiringly.—*Ant.* RUDELY, ungratefully, thanklessly.

gratitude *n.* thankfulness, appreciation, acknowledgment, response, sense of indebtedness, feeling of obligation, responsiveness, thanks, praise, recognition, honor, thanksgiving, grace.—*Ant.* INDIFFERENCE, ingratitude, thanklessness.

(-vam′i nə) ‖LL, a burden‖ *Law* the essential part of a complaint or accusation

grave[1] (grāv) *adj.* **grav′er, grav′est** ‖< L *gravis,* heavy‖ 1 important 2 serious *[a grave illness]* 3 solemn 4 somber; dull —**grave′ly** *adv.* —**grave′ness** *n.*

grave[2] (grāv) *n.* ‖< OE *grafan,* to dig‖ 1 *a)* a hole in the ground in which to bury a dead body *b)* any burial place; tomb 2 death —*vt.* **graved, grav′en** or **graved, grav′ing** 1 [Archaic] to sculpture or engrave 2 to impress sharply

grave accent a mark (`) showing the quality of a vowel, stress, etc.

gravel (grav′əl) *n.* ‖< OFr *grave,* coarse sand‖ a loose mixture of pebbles and rock fragments coarser than sand

grav′elly (-ē) *adj.* 1 full of or like gravel 2 harsh or rasping

graven (grāv′ən) *vt. alt. pp. of* GRAVE[2]

grave′stone′ *n.* a tombstone

grave′yard′ *n.* a cemetery

graveyard shift [Colloq.] a night work shift, esp. one starting at midnight

gravid (grav′id) *adj.* ‖< L *gravis,* heavy‖ pregnant

gra·vim·eter (grə vim′ət ər) *n.* ‖< L *gravis,* heavy + Fr *-mètre,* -METER‖ 1 a device for determining specific gravity 2 an instrument for measuring the earth's gravitational pull

gravi·tate (grav′i tāt′) *vi.* **-tat′ed, -tat′ing** 1 to move or tend to move in accordance with the force of gravity 2 to be attracted (*toward*)

grav′i·ta′tion *n.* 1 a gravitating 2 *Physics* the force by which every mass attracts and is attracted by every other mass —**grav′i·ta′tional** *adj.*

grav·ity (grav′i tē) *n., pl.* **-ties** ‖< L *gravis,* heavy‖ 1 graveness; seriousness 2 weight *[specific gravity]* 3 *Physics* gravitation; esp., the pull on all bodies in the earth's sphere toward the earth's center

gravy (grā′vē) *n., pl.* **-vies** ‖< ?‖ 1 the juice given off by meat in cooking 2 a sauce made from this juice 3 [Slang] any benefit beyond that expected

gray (grā) *n.* ‖< OE *græg*‖ a color that is a blend of black and white —*adj.* 1 of this color 2 having hair this color 3 *a)* darkish *b)* dreary 4 designating a vague, intermediate area —*vt., vi.* to make or become gray —**gray′ish** *adj.* —**gray′ness** *n.*

gray′beard′ *n.* an old man

gray matter 1 grayish nerve tissue of the brain and spinal cord 2 [Colloq.] intellectual capacity; brains

graze[1] (grāz) *vt.* **grazed, graz′ing** ‖< OE *græs,* grass‖ 1 to put livestock to feed on (growing grass, etc.) 2 to tend (feeding livestock) —*vi.* to feed on growing grass, etc.

graze[2] (grāz) *vt., vi.* **grazed, graz′ing** ‖prob. < prec.‖ to scrape or rub lightly in passing —*n.* a grazing

Gr. Brit. or **Gr. Br.** Great Britain

grease (grēs; *for v., also* grēz) *n.* ‖< L *crassus,* fat‖ 1 melted animal fat 2 any thick, oily substance or lubricant —*vt.* **greased, greas′ing** to smear or lubricate with grease

grease′paint′ *n.* greasy coloring matter used in making up for the stage

greasy (grē′sē, -zē) *adj.* **-i·er, -i·est** 1 soiled with grease 2 containing or like grease; oily —**greas′i·ness** *n.*

great (grāt) *adj.* ‖OE‖ 1 of much more than ordinary size, extent, etc. *[the Great Lakes]* 2 much above the average; esp., *a)* intense *[great pain]* *b)* eminent *[a great writer]* 3 most important; main 4 designating a relationship one generation removed *[great-grandparent]* 5 [Colloq.] skillful: often with *at* 6 [Colloq.] excellent; fine —*n.* a distinguished person —**great′ly** *adv.* —**great′ness** *n.*

great ape any of a family of primates consisting of the gorilla, chimpanzee, and orangutan

Great Dane a very large, muscular dog with a short, smooth coat

great′-grand′child′ *n.* a child of any of one's grandchildren

great′-grand′par′ent *n.* a parent of any of one's grandparents

great′heart′ed *adj.* 1 brave; fearless 2 generous; unselfish

grebe (grēb) *n.* ‖Fr *grèbe*‖ a diving and swimming bird with broadly lobed webbed feet

Gre·cian (grē′shən) *adj., n.* GREEK

Greco- ‖< L *Graecus*‖ *combining form* Greek, Greek and *[Greco-Roman]*

greed (grēd) *n.* ‖< fol.‖ excessive desire, esp. for wealth; avarice

greedy (grēd′ē) *adj.* **-i·er, -i·est** ‖OE *grædig*‖ 1 desiring more than one needs or deserves 2 having too strong a desire for food and drink; gluttonous —**greed′i·ly** *adv.* —**greed′i·ness** *n.*

Greek (grēk) *n.* 1 a native or inhabitant of Greece 2 the language, ancient or modern, of the Greeks —*adj.* of Greece

green (grēn) *adj.* ‖OE *grene*‖ 1 of the color of growing grass 2 overspread with green plants or foliage 3 sickly or bilious 4 unripe 5 inexperienced or naive 6 not dried or seasoned 7 [Colloq.] jealous —*n.* 1 the color of growing grass 2 *[pl.]* green leafy vegetables, as spinach, etc. 3 an

▬ THESAURUS ▬

grave[1] *a.* 1 [Important] momentous, weighty, consequential; see IMPORTANT 1. 2 [Dangerous] critical, serious, ominous; see DANGEROUS. 3 [Solemn] serious, sober, earnest; see SOLEMN.

grave[2] *n.* vault, sepulcher, tomb, pit, crypt, mausoleum, catacomb, long home, six feet of earth, final resting place, place of interment, mound, burial place, charnel house, last home*. —**make one turn (over) in one's grave** do something shocking, sin, err; see MISBEHAVE. —**one foot in the grave** old, infirm, near death; see DYING 2.

gravel *n.* sand, pebbles, shale, macadam, screenings, crushed rock, washings, alluvium, tailings.

graveyard *n.* burial ground, necropolis, God's acre; see CEMETERY.

gravity *n.* 1 [Weight] heaviness, pressure, force; see PRESSURE 1. 2 [Importance] seriousness, concern, significance; see IMPORTANCE.

gravy *n.* sauce, dressing, brown gravy, white gravy, milk gravy, pan gravy, chicken gravy, meat gravy.

gray *a.* neutral, dusky, silvery, dingy, somber, shaded, drab, leaden, grayish, ashen, grizzled. *Shades of gray include the following:* blue-gray, silver-gray, smoke-gray, slate, bat, mouse-colored, iron-gray, lead, ash-gray, pepper-and-salt, dusty, smoky.

gray *n.* shade, drabness, dusk; see COLOR.

graze[1,2] *v.* 1 [To touch or score lightly] brush, scrape, rub; see TOUCH 1. 2 [To pasture] browse, feed, crop, gnaw, nibble, bite, uproot, pull grass, forage, eat, munch, ruminate.

grazing *a.* cropping, feeding, gnawing, nibbling, biting, uprooting, pasturing, pulling grass, foraging, eating, munching, ruminating.

grease *n.* oil, wax, fat, lubricant, salve, petrolatum, petroleum jelly, vaseline, olive oil, cottonseed oil, peanut oil, axle grease; see also OIL 1.

grease *v.* oil, lubricate, smear, salve, coat with oil, cream, pomade, grease the wheels, anoint, swab, give a grease job*.

greasy *a.* creamy, oleaginous, fatty; see OILY 1.

great *a.* 1 [Eminent] noble, grand, majestic, dignified, exalted, commanding, famous, renowned, widely acclaimed, famed, celebrated, distinguished, noted, conspicuous, elevated, prominent, high, stately, honorable, magnificent, glorious, regal, royal, kingly, imposing, preeminent, unrivaled, fabulous, fabled, storied.—*Ant.* OBSCURE, retired, anonymous. 2 [Large] numerous, big, vast; see LARGE 1. 3 [*Excellent] exceptional, surpassing, transcendent; see EXCELLENT.

greatly *a.* exceedingly, considerably, hugely; see VERY.

greatness *n.* 1 [Eminence] prominence, renown, importance; see FAME. 2 [Size] bulk, extent, largeness; see SIZE 2.

greed *n.* greediness, selfishness, eagerness, voracity, excess, gluttony, piggishness, indulgence, hoggishness, niggardliness, acquisitiveness, intemperance, covetousness, desire, grabbiness, an itching palm*.—*Ant.* GENEROSITY, liberality, kindness.

greedy *a.* avid, grasping, rapacious, selfish, miserly, parsimonious, close, closefisted, tight, tight-fisted, niggardly, exploitative, grudging, devouring, ravenous, omnivorous, carnivorous, intemperate, gobbling, indulging one's appetites, mercenary, stingy, covetous, pennypinching.—*Ant.* GENEROUS, munificent, bountiful.

Greek *a.* Grecian, Hellenic, Hellenistic, Minoan, Dorian, Attic, Athenian, Spartan, Peloponnesian, Ionian, Corinthian, Thessalian, ancient, classic; see also CLASSICAL 2.

Greek *n.* 1 [A citizen of Greece] Hellene, Athenian, Spartan; see EUROPEAN. 2 [The Greek language] Hellenic, Ionic, New Ionic; see LANGUAGE 1.

Greeks *n.* Greek culture, Hellenes, the Ancients, Hellenism, classical times, Athens, the glory that was Greece, the Golden Age.

green *a.* 1 [Of the color green] *Tints and shades of green include the following:* emerald, blue-green, sage, aquamarine, chartreuse, lime, kelly, area of smooth turf [a putting *green*] —**green′ish** *adj.* — **green′ness** *n.*

green′back′ *n.* any piece of U.S. paper money printed in green ink on the back

green bean the edible, immature green pod of the kidney bean

green′belt′ *n.* a beltlike area around a city, reserved for park land or farms

green′ery *n., pl.* **-er·ies** green vegetation; verdure

green′-eyed′ *adj.* very jealous

green′gro′cer (-grō′sər) *n.* [Brit.] a retail dealer in fresh vegetables and fruit

green′horn′ *n.* 1 an inexperienced person 2 a person easily deceived

green′house′ *n.* a heated building, mainly of glass, for growing plants

greenhouse effect the warming of the earth and its lower atmosphere, caused by trapped solar radiation

green′mail′ *n.* the buying of a large amount of a company's stock so that the management, fearing a takeover, will buy it back at a premium —**green′mail′er** *n.*

green manure a crop, as of clover, plowed under to fertilize the soil

green onion an immature onion with green leaves, often eaten raw; scallion

green pepper the green, immature fruit of a red pepper, esp. the bell pepper

green power money, as the source of economic power

green′sward′ (-swôrd′) *n.* green, grassy turf

green thumb a talent for growing plants

green′wood′ *n.* a forest in leaf

greet (grēt) *vt.* [OE *gretan*] 1 to address with friendliness 2 to meet or receive (a person, event, etc.) in a specified way 3 to come or appear to —**greet′er** *n.*

greet′ing *n.* 1 the act or words of one who greets 2 [*often pl.*] a message of regards

gre·gari·ous (grə ger′ē əs) *adj.* [< L *grex*, herd] 1 living in herds 2 fond of the company of others; sociable

Gregorian calendar (grə gôr′ē ən) the calendar now widely used, introduced by Pope Gregory XIII in 1582

grem·lin (grem′lin) *n.* [prob. < Dan *gram*, a devil] a small imaginary creature humorously blamed for the disruption of any procedure

gre·nade (grə nād′) *n.* [Fr < OFr, pomegranate] a small bomb detonated by a fuse and usually thrown by hand

grena·dier (gren′ə dir′) *n.* 1 orig., a soldier who threw grenades 2 a member of a special regiment

grena·dine (gren′ə dēn′) *n.* [Fr] a red syrup made from pomegranate juice

grew (grōō) *vi., vt. pt. of* GROW

grey (grā) *adj., n., vt., vi.* Brit. sp: of GRAY

grey′hound′ *n.* a tall, slender, swift dog with a narrow head

grid (grid) *n.* [short for GRIDIRON] 1 a gridiron or grating 2 a metallic plate in a storage battery 3 an electrode, as of wire mesh, for controlling the flow of electrons in an electron tube

grid·dle (grid′l) *n.* [< L *craticula*, gridiron] a heavy, flat, metal pan for cooking pancakes, etc.

grid′dle·cake′ *n.* a pancake

grid·iron (grid′ī′ərn) *n.* [see GRIDDLE] 1 a framework of metal bars or wires for broiling 2 anything resembling this, as a football field

grid′lock′ *n.* a traffic jam in which no vehicle can move in any direction

grief (grēf) *n.* [see GRIEVE] 1 intense emotional suffering caused as by a loss 2 a cause of such suffering —**come to grief** to fail or be ruined

griev·ance (grēv′əns) *n.* 1 a circumstance thought to be unjust and ground for complaint 2 complaint against a real or imagined wrong

grieve (grēv) *vi., vt.* grieved, griev′ing [< L *gravis*, heavy] to feel or cause to feel grief

griev·ous (grēv′əs) *adj.* 1 causing grief 2 showing or full of grief 3 severe 4 deplorable; atrocious —**griev′ously** *adv.*

grif·fin (grif′in) *n.* [< Gr] a mythical monster, part lion and part eagle

grill (gril) *n.* [see GRIDDLE] 1 a griddle 2 grilled food 3 a restaurant that specializes in grilled foods — *vt.* 1 to broil 2 to question relentlessly

grille (gril) *n.* [see GRIDDLE] an open grating forming a screen

grim (grim) *adj.* grim′mer, grim′mest [OE *grimm*] 1 hard and unyielding; stern 2 appearing forbidding, harsh, etc. 3 repellent; ghastly —**grim′ly** *adv.* —**grim′ness** *n.*

gri·mace (gri mās′, grim′is) *n.* [Fr] a distortion of the face, as in expressing pain, disgust, etc. — *vi.* -maced′, -mac′ing to make grimaces

grime (grīm) *n.* [prob. < Fl *grijm*] dirt rubbed into a surface, as of the skin —**grim′y, -i·er, -i·est,** *adj.*

grin (grin) *vi.* grinned, grin′ning [< OE *grennian*, bare the teeth] 1 to smile broadly as in amusement 2 to show the teeth in pain, scorn, etc. — *n.* the act or look of grinning

grind (grīnd) *vt.* ground, grind′ing [OE *grindan*] 1 to crush into fine particles; pulverize 2 to oppress 3 to sharpen or smooth by friction 4 to rub (the teeth, etc.) together gratingly 5 to operate by turning the crank of — *n.* 1 a grinding 2 long, difficult work or study 3 [Colloq.] a student who studies hard —**grind out** to produce by steady or laborious effort

grinder (grīn′dər) *n.* 1 a person or thing that grinds 2 [*pl.*] [Colloq.] the teeth 3 HERO SANDWICH

grind′stone′ *n.* a revolving stone disk for sharpening tools or polishing things —**keep one's nose to the grindstone** to work hard and steadily

grip (grip) *n.* [< OE *gripan*, seize] 1 a secure grasp; firm hold 2 the manner of holding a club, bat, etc. 3 the power

---

THESAURUS

bronze-green, yellow-green, bottle-green, pea-green, sea-green, apple-green, grass-green, forest-green, moss-green, spinach-green, pine-green, olive-green, jade. 2 [Verdant] growing, leafy, sprounting, grassy, grass-grown, flourishing, lush. 3 [Immature] young, growing, unripe, maturing, developing, half-formed, fresh.—*Ant.* MATURE, ripe, gone to seed. 4 [Inexperienced] youthful, callow, raw; see INEXPERIENCED.

green *n.* greenness, verdure, virescence; see COLOR.

greet *v.* welcome, speak to, salute, address, hail, recognize, embrace, shake hands, nod, receive, call to, stop, acknowledge, bow to, approach, give one's love, hold out one's hand, herald, bid good day, bid hello, bid welcome, exchange greetings, usher in, attend, pay one's respects.—*Ant.* IGNORE, slight, slight.

greeting *n.* welcome, address, notice, speaking to, ushering in, acknowledgment, one's compliments, regards. *Common greetings include the following:* hello, how do you do, how are you, good morning, good day, good afternoon, good evening, hi*, hey*, yo*.

grey *a.* dun, drab, grayish; see GRAY.

grief *n.* sorrow, sadness, regret, melancholy, mourning, misery, trouble, anguish, despondency, pain, worry, harassment, anxiety, woe, heartache, malaise, disquiet, discomfort, affliction, gloom, unhappiness, desolation, despair, agony, torture, purgatory.—*Ant.* HAPPINESS, exhilaration, pleasure.

grievance *n.* complaint, injury, case; see OBJECTION.

grieve *v.* lament, bewail, sorrow for; see MOURN.

grill *v.* roast, sauté, barbecue; see COOK.

grim *a.* 1 [Sullen] sour, crusty, gloomy, sulky, morose, churlish, forbidding, glum, grumpy, scowling, grouchy, crabby, glowering, stubborn, cantankerous.—*Ant.* HAPPY, cheerful, gay. 2 [Stern] austere, strict, harsh; see SEVERE 1. 3 [Relentless] unrelenting, implacable, inexorable; see SEVERE 2.

grimace *n.* smirk, smile, sneer; see EXPRESSION 4.

grime *n.* soil, smudge, dirt; see FILTH.

grimy *a.* begrimed, dingy, soiled; see DIRTY 1.

grin *n.* smirk, simper, delighted look; see SMILE.

grin *v.* smirk, simper, beam; see SMILE.

grind *v.* crush, powder, mill, grate, granulate, disintegrate, rasp, scrape, file, abrade, pound, reduce to fine particles, crunch, roll out, pound out, chop up, crumble.—*Ant.* ORGANIZE, mold, solidify.

grinding *a.* abrasive, crushing, pulverizing, grating, rasping, rubbing, milling, powdering, cracking, bone-crushing, crunching, splintering, shivering, smashing, crumbling, scraping, chopping, wearing away, eroding.

grip *n.* 1 [The power and the application of the power to grip] grasp, hold, manual strength, clutch, clasp, catch, cinch, vise, clench, clinch, embrace, handhold, fist, handshake, anchor, squeeze, wrench, grab, enclosure, fixing, fastening, crushing, clamp, hoops of steel, vicelike grip, jaws. 2 [Something suited to grasping] knocker, knob, ear; see HANDLE 1. 3 [A traveling bag] valise, suitcase, satchel; see BAG.

grip *v.* clutch, grasp, clasp; see SEIZE

of grasping firmly **4** mental grasp **5** firm control; mastery **6** a handle **7** a small traveling bag — *vt.* **gripped** or **gript, grip′ping 1** to take firmly and hold fast **2** to get and hold the attention of — *vi.* **1** to get a grip —**come to grips** to struggle (*with*) —**grip′per** *n.*

gripe (grīp) *vt.* **griped, grip′ing** ⟦OE *grīpan*, seize⟧ **1** [Archaic] to distress **2** to cause sharp pain in the bowels of **3** [Slang] to annoy — *vi.* [Slang] to complain — *n.* **1** a sharp pain in the bowels: *usually used in pl.* **2** [Slang] a complaint —**grip′er** *n.*

grippe (grip) *n.* ⟦Fr⟧ INFLUENZA

gris-gris (grē′grē′) *n., pl.* **gris′-gris′** ⟦of Afr orig.⟧ an amulet, charm, or spell associated with voodoo

grisly (griz′lē) *adj.* **-lier, -li·est** ⟦OE *grislic*⟧ terrifying; ghastly —**gris′li·ness** *n.*

grist (grist) *n.* ⟦OE⟧ grain that is to be or has been ground

gristle (gris′əl) *n.* ⟦OE⟧ cartilage, esp. as found in meat — **gris′tly** (-lē) *adj.*

grist′mill′ *n.* a mill for grinding grain

grit (grit) *n.* ⟦< OE *greot*⟧ **1** rough particles, as of sand **2** coarse sandstone **3** stubborn courage; pluck — *vt.* **grit′ ted, grit′ting** to grind (the teeth) as in determination — *vi.* to make a grating sound —**grit′ty, -tier, -ti·est,** *adj.* —**grit′ti·ness** *n.*

grits (grits) *n.pl.* ⟦OE *grytte*⟧ [*often with sing. v.*] coarsely ground grain

griz·zled (griz′əld) *adj.* ⟦< OFr *gris*, gray⟧ **1** gray or streaked with gray **2** having gray hair

griz′zly (-lē) *adj.* **-zlier, -zli·est** grayish; grizzled

grizzly (bear) a large, ferocious, brown or grayish bear of W North America

groan (grōn) *vi., vt.* ⟦< OE *granian*⟧ to utter (with) a deep sound expressing pain, distress, etc. — *n.* such a sound

gro·cer (grō′sər) *n.* ⟦< OFr *grossier*⟧ a dealer in food and household supplies

gro′cery *n., pl.* **-ies 1** a grocer's store **2** [*pl.*] the food and supplies sold by a grocer

grog (gräg) *n.* ⟦after Old *Grog*, nickname of an 18th-c. Brit admiral⟧ **1** rum diluted with water **2** any alcoholic liquor

grog′gy *adj.* **-gier, -gi·est** ⟦< prec. + -Y²⟧ **1** orig., intoxicated **2** dizzy **3** sluggish or dull —**grog′gi·ness** *n.*

groin (groin) *n.* ⟦prob. < OE *grynde*, abyss⟧ **1** the fold where the abdomen joins either thigh **2** *Archit.* the sharp, curved edge at the junction of two vaults

grom·met (gräm′it) *n.* ⟦< obs. Fr *gromette*, a curb⟧ **1** a ring of rope **2** a metal eyelet in cloth, etc.

groom (grōōm, groom) *n.* ⟦ME *grom*, boy⟧ **1** one whose work is tending horses **2** a bridegroom — *vt.* **1** to clean and curry (a horse, etc.) **2** to make neat and tidy **3** to train for a particular purpose

groove (grōōv) *n.* ⟦< ON *grof*, a pit⟧ **1** a long, narrow furrow cut with a tool **2** any channel or rut **3** a settled routine — *vt.* **grooved, groov′ing** to make a groove in

groov′y *adj.* **-i·er, -i·est** [Slang] very pleasing or attractive

grope (grōp) *vi.* **groped, grop′ing** ⟦< OE *grapian*, to touch⟧ to feel or search about blindly or uncertainly — *vt.* to seek or find (one's way) by groping —**grop′er** *n.* — **grop′ingly** *adv.*

gros·beak (grōs′bēk′) *n.* ⟦Fr: see GROSS & BEAK⟧ a songbird with a thick, strong, conical bill

gros·grain (grō′grān′) *n.* ⟦Fr, lit., coarse grain⟧ a ribbed silk or rayon fabric for ribbons, etc.

gross (grōs) *adj.* ⟦< LL *grossus*, thick⟧ **1** fat and coarselooking; burly **2** flagrant; very bad **3** dense; thick **4** lacking in refinement **5** vulgar; coarse **6** with no deductions; total — *n.* **1** *pl.* **gross′es** overall total **2** *pl.* **gross** twelve dozen — *vt., vi.* to earn (a specified total amount) before expenses are deducted —**gross′ly** *adv.* —**gross′ness** *n.*

gross national product the total value of a nation's annual output of goods and services

gro·tesque (grō tesk′) *adj.* ⟦< It *grotta*, grotto: from designs found in caves⟧ **1** distorted or fantastic in appearance, shape, etc. **2** ridiculous; absurd —**gro·tes·que′ly** *adv.*

grotto (grät′ō) *n., pl.* **-toes** or **-tos** ⟦< It < L *crypta*, crypt⟧ **1** a cave **2** a cavelike summerhouse, shrine, etc.

grouch (grouch) *vi.* ⟦< ME *grucchen*⟧ to grumble or complain sulkily — *n.* **1** one who grouches **2** a sulky mood — **grouch′y,** *-i·er, -i·est, adj.*

ground¹ (ground) *n.* ⟦OE *grund*, bottom⟧ **1** the solid surface of the earth **2** soil; earth **3** [*often pl.*] a tract of land [*grounds* of an estate] **4** area, as of discussion **5** [*often pl.*] *a*) basis; foundation *b*) valid reason or motive **6** the background, as in a design **7** [*pl.*] sediment [*coffee grounds*] **8** the connection of an electrical conductor with the ground — *adj.* of, on, or near the ground — *vt.* **1** to set on the ground **2** to cause to run aground **3** to base; found; establish **4** to instruct in the first principles of **5** *a*) to keep (an aircraft or pilot) from flying *b*) [Colloq.] to punish (a teenager) by not permitting him or her to leave home for dates, etc. **6** *Elec.* to connect (a conductor) with the ground — *vi.* **1** to run ashore **2** *Baseball* to be put out on a grounder: usually with *out* —**break ground 1** to dig; excavate **2** to plow **3** to start building —**gain (or lose) ground** to gain (or lose) in achievement, popularity, etc. —**give ground** to retreat; yield — **hold (or stand) one's ground** to remain firm, not yielding

ground² (ground) *vt., vi. pt. & pp. of* GRIND

ground′break′ing *adj.* **1** designating the ceremony of breaking ground, as for a new building **2** pioneering — *n.* a groundbreaking ceremony

ground control personnel and equipment on the ground, for guiding airplanes and spacecraft in takeoff, landing, etc.

ground cover low, dense-growing plants used for covering bare ground

ground crew a group of workers who maintain and repair aircraft

THESAURUS

1. —**come to grips** engage, encounter, cope with; see FIGHT, TRY 1.

gripe* *n.* complaint, grievance, beef*; see OBJECTION.

gripe* *v.* grumble, mutter, fuss; see COMPLAIN.

gristle *n.* ossein, cartilage, bony matter; see BONE.

grit *n.* sand, dust, crushed rock; see GRAVEL.

gritty *a.* rough, abrasive, sandy, rasping, lumpy, gravelly, muddy, dusty, powdery, granular, crumbly, loose, scratchy.

groan *n.* moan, sob, grunt; see CRY 1.

groan *v.* moan, murmur, keen; see CRY 1.

groceries *n.* food, edibles, produce, comestibles, foodstuffs, perishables, vegetables, staples, green groceries, fruits, dairy products, processed foods, frozen foods, freeze-dried foods, dried foods, packaged foods, canned foods.

grocery *n.* food store, vegetable market, corner store; see MARKET 1.

groggy *a.* sleepy, dizzy, reeling; see TIRED.

groom *n.* bridegroom, married man, successful suitor; see HUSBAND.

groom *v.* rub down, comb, brush; see PREPARE 1.

groove *n.* channel, trench, gouge, depression, scratch, canal, valley, notch, furrow, rut, incision, slit, gutter, ditch, crease. —**in the groove** efficient, skillful, operative; see WORKING 1.

grope *v.* fumble, touch, feel blindly; see FEEL 1.

gross *a.* **1** [Fat] corpulent, obese, huge; see FAT. **2** [Obscene] foul, swinish, indecent; see LEWD 1, 2. **3** [Without deduction] in sum, total, entire; see WHOLE 1.

gross *n.* total, aggregate, total amount; see WHOLE.

gross *v.* earn, bring in, take in; see EARN 2.

grotesque *a.* malformed, ugly, distorted; see DEFORMED.

grouch *n.* complainer, grumbler, growler, bear*, sourpuss*, sorehead*, crab*, crank*, bellyacher*.

grouch *v.* mutter, grumble, gripe*; see COMPLAIN.

grouchy *a.* surly, ill-tempered, crusty; see IRRITABLE.

ground¹ *n.* **1** [Soil] sand, dirt, clay;

see EARTH 2. **2** [An area] spot, terrain, territory; see AREA. —**break ground** start, initiate, commence; see BEGIN 1. —**cover ground** move, go on, progress; see ADVANCE 1. — **from the ground up** thoroughly, wholly, entirely; see COMPLETELY. — **gain ground** move, go on, progress; see ADVANCE 1. —**get off the ground** start, commence, come into being; see BEGIN 2. —**hold (or stand) one's ground** maintain one's position, defend, sustain; see ENDURE 2. —**lose ground** withdraw, fall behind, drop back; see LAG. —**run into the ground*** exaggerate, do too much, press; see OVERDO 1.

ground¹ *v.* **1** [To bring to the ground] floor, bring down, prostrate; see TRIP 2. **2** [To restrict] cause to remain on the ground, confine, prevent from driving; see RESTRICT. **3** [To instruct in essentials] train, indoctrinate, educate; see TEACH.

grounds *n.* **1** [Real estate] lot, environs, territory; see PROPERTY 2. **2** [Basis] reasons, arguments, proof; see BASIS. **3** [Sediment] dregs, lees, leavings; see RESIDUE.

ground′er *n. Baseball* a batted ball that travels along the ground

ground floor that floor of a building approximately level with the ground; first floor —**in on the ground floor** [Colloq.] in at the start (of a business, etc.)

ground glass nontransparent glass, whose surface has been ground to diffuse light

ground′hog′ *n.* WOODCHUCK

ground′less *adj.* without reason or cause

ground rule 1 *Baseball* a rule adapted to playing conditions in a specific ballpark **2** any basic rule

ground swell 1 a violent rolling of the ocean **2** a wave of popular feeling: usually **ground′swell′**

ground′work′ *n.* a foundation; basis

group (grōōp) *n.* ⟦< It *gruppo*⟧ a number of persons or things gathered or classified together —*vt., vi.* to form into a group or groups

grou·per (grōō′pər) *n.* ⟦Port *garupa*⟧ a large sea bass found in warm seas

groupie (grōō′pē) *n.* [Colloq.] a female fan of rock groups or other popular personalities, who follows them about

group therapy (or **psychotherapy**) a form of treatment for a group of patients with similar emotional problems, as by mutual criticism

grouse[1] (grous) *n., pl.* **grouse** ⟦< ?⟧ a game bird with a round, plump body, feathered legs, and mottled feathers

grouse[2] (grous) *vi.* **groused, grous′ing** ⟦< ?⟧ [Colloq.] to complain —**grous′er** *n.*

grout (grout) *n.* ⟦ME⟧ a thin mortar used as between tiles

grove (grōv) *n.* ⟦< OE *graf*⟧ a group of trees, without undergrowth

grovel (gruv′əl, gräv′-) *vi.* **-eled** or **-elled, -el·ing** or **-el·ling** ⟦< ME *grufelinge*, down on one's face⟧ **1** to lie or crawl in a prostrate position, esp. abjectly **2** to behave abjectly —**grov′eler** or **grov′el·ler** *n.*

grow (grō) *vi.* **grew, grown, grow′ing** ⟦< OE *growan*⟧ **1** to come into being or be produced naturally **2** to develop or thrive, as a living thing **3** to increase in size, quantity, etc. **4** to become [to grow weary] —*vt.* to cause to or let grow; raise; cultivate —**grow on** [Colloq.] to have an increasing effect on —**grow up** to mature —**grow′er** *n.*

growl (groul) *n.* ⟦ME *groulen*⟧ a rumbling, menacing sound such as an angry dog makes —*vi., vt.* to make, or express by, such a sound

grown (grōn) *vi., vt. pp.* of GROW —*adj.* having completed its growth; mature

grown′-up′ *adj., n.* adult Also, for *n.*, **grown′up′**

growth (grōth) *n.* **1** a growing or developing **2** *a)* increase in size, etc. *b)* the full extent of this **3** something that

grows or has grown **4** a tumor or other abnormal mass of tissue

grub (grub) *vi.* **grubbed, grub′bing** ⟦ME *grubben*⟧ **1** to dig in the ground **2** to work hard —*vt.* **1** to clear (ground) of roots **2** to uproot —*n.* **1** a wormlike larva, esp. of a beetle **2** a drudge **3** [Slang] food

grub′by *adj.* **-bier, -bi·est** dirty; untidy —**grub′bi·ness** *n.*

grub′stake′ (-stāk′) *n.* ⟦GRUB, *n.* 3 + STAKE⟧ [Colloq.] money or supplies advanced, as to a prospector

grudge (gruj) *vt.* **grudged, grudg′ing** ⟦< OFr *grouchier*⟧ **1** BEGRUDGE **2** to give with reluctance —*n.* resentment or ill will over some grievance —**grudg′ingly** *adv.*

gruel (grōō′əl) *n.* ⟦< ML *grutum*, meal⟧ thin porridge made by cooking meal in water or milk

gru·el·ing or **gru·el·ling** *adj.* ⟦prp. of obs. v. *gruel*, punish⟧ extremely trying; exhausting

grue·some (grōō′səm) *adj.* ⟦< dial. *grue*, to shudder + -SOME[1]⟧ causing horror or disgust; grisly

gruff (gruf) *adj.* ⟦< Du *grof*⟧ **1** rough or surly **2** harsh and throaty; hoarse —**gruff′ly** *adv.* —**gruff′ness** *n.*

grum·ble (grum′bəl) *vi.* **-bled, -bling** ⟦prob. < Du *grommelen*⟧ **1** to growl **2** to mutter in discontent **3** to rumble —*vt.* to express by grumbling —*n.* a grumbling —**grum′bler** *n.*

grumpy (grum′pē) *adj.* **-i·er, -i·est** ⟦prob. echoic⟧ grouchy; peevish —**grump′i·ness** *n.*

grungy (grun′jē) *adj.* **-gier, -gi·est** [Slang] dirty, messy, etc.

grun·ion (grōōn′yən) *n.* ⟦prob. < Sp *gruñón*, grumbler⟧ a fish of the California coast: it spawns on sandy beaches

grunt (grunt) *vi., vt.* ⟦< OE *grunian*⟧ to utter (with) the deep, hoarse sound of a hog —*n.* this sound

Gru·yère (cheese) (grōō yer′, grē-) ⟦after *Gruyère*, Switzerland⟧ [*often* **g- c-**] a light-yellow Swiss cheese, rich in butterfat

G-string (jē′striŋ′) *n.* ⟦< ?⟧ **1** a narrow loincloth **2** a similar band worn by striptease dancers

gua·nine (gwä′nēn) *n.* ⟦< fol. + -INE[3]⟧ a crystalline base contained in the nucleic acids of all tissue

guano (gwä′nō) *n., pl.* **-nos** ⟦Sp < AmInd (Peru)⟧ manure of sea birds, used as fertilizer

guar·an·tee (gar′ən tē′) *n.* **1** GUARANTY (sense 1) **2** *a)* a pledge to replace something if it is not as represented *b)* an assurance that something will be done as specified **3** a guarantor —*vt.* **-teed′, -tee′ing 1** to give a guarantee for **2** to promise

guar·an·tor (gar′ən tôr′) *n.* one who gives a guaranty or guarantee

guar·an·ty (-tē) *n., pl.* **-ties** ⟦< OFr *garant*, a warrant⟧ **1** a pledge or security for another's debt or obligation **2** an

---

▬▬▬▬ THESAURUS ▬▬▬▬

groundwork *n.* background, base, origin; see BASIS, FOUNDATION 2.

group *n.* **1** [A gathering of persons] assembly, assemblage, crowd; see GATHERING. **2** [Collected things] accumulation, assortment, combination; see COLLECTION. **3** [An organized body of people] association, club, society; see ORGANIZATION 2.

group *v.* file, assort, arrange; see CLASSIFY.

grovel *v.* crawl, beg, sneak, stoop, kneel, crouch before, kowtow to, sponge, cower, snivel, beseech, wheedle, flatter, cater to, humor, pamper, curry favor with, court, act up to, play up to, beg for mercy, prostrate oneself, soft-soap, butter up*, make up to, kiss one's feet*, lick another's boots*, knuckle under, polish the apple*, eat dirt*, brown-nose*.—*Ant.* HATE, spurn, scorn.

grow *v.* **1** [To become larger] increase, expand in size, swell, wax, thrive, gain, enlarge, advance, dilate, stretch, mount, build, burst forth, spread, multiply, develop, mature, flourish, grow up, rise, sprout, shoot up, jump up, start up, spring up, spread like wildfire.—*Ant.* WITHER, lessen, shrink. **2** [To change slowly] become, develop, alter, tend, pass, evolve, flower, shift, flow, progress, advance; get bigger, larger, etc.; wax, turn into, improve, mellow, age, bet-

ter, ripen into, blossom, open out, resolve itself into, mature. **3** [To cultivate] raise, nurture, tend, nurse, foster, produce, plant, breed.—*Ant.* HARM, impede, neglect.

growing *a.* increasing, ever-widening, expanding, budding, germinating, maturing, waxing, enlarging, amplifying, swelling, developing, mushrooming, spreading, thriving, flourishing, stretching, living, sprouting, viable, organic, animate, spreading like wildfire.—*Ant.* CONTRACTION, withering, shrinking.

growl *n.* snarl, gnarl, moan, bark, bellow, rumble, roar, howl, grumble, grunt.

growl *v.* snarl, bark, gnarl; see CRY 2.

grown *a.* of age, adult, grown up; see MATURE.

grown-up *n.* adult, grown person, big person, grown man, grown woman.

growth *n.* **1** [The process of growing] extension, organic development, germination; see INCREASE. **2** [The result of growing] completion, adulthood, fullness; see MAJORITY 2. **3** [A swelling] tumor, cancer, mole, fungus, parasite, outgrowth, thickening.

grubby *a.* dirty, sloppy, grimy; see DIRTY 1.

grudge *n.* spite, rancor, animosity; see HATRED.

grudge *v.* begrudge, covet, be reluctant; see ENVY.

grueling *a.* exhausting, tiring, fatiguing; see DIFFICULT 1, 2.

gruesome *a.* grim, grisly, fearful; see FRIGHTFUL, OFFENSIVE 2.

gruff *a.* harsh, grating, rough; see HOARSE.

grumble *v.* whine, protest, fuss; see COMPLAIN.

grumpy *a.* sullen, grouchy, cantankerous; see IRRITABLE.

grunt *v.* snort, squawk, squeak; see CRY 2.

guarantee *v.* attest, testify, vouch for, declare, assure, answer for, be responsible for, pledge, give bond, go bail, wager, stake, give a guarantee, stand good for, back, sign for, become surety for, endorse, secure, make certain, warrant, insure, witness, prove, reassure, support, affirm, confirm, cross one's heart.

guaranteed *a.* warranted, certified, bonded, secured, endorsed, insured, pledged, confirmed, assured, approved, attested, sealed, certificated, protected, affirmed, surefire*.—*Ant.* ANONYMOUS, unsupported, unendorsed.

guaranty *n.* warrant, warranty, bond, contract, certificate, charter, testament, security.

agreement that secures the existence or maintenance of something

guard (gärd) *vt.* ‖< OFr *garder* ‖ **1** to watch over and protect; defend **2** to keep from escape or trouble — *vi.* **1** to keep watch (*against*) **2** to act as a guard — *n.* **1** defense; protection **2** a posture of readiness for defense **3** any device to protect against injury or loss **4** a person or group that guards **5** *Basketball* either of two players who are the main ball handlers **6** *Football* either of the two players next to the center —**on (one's) guard** vigilant
guard'ed *adj.* **1** kept safe **2** cautious *[a guarded reply]* — **guard'edly** *adv.*
guard'house' *n. Mil.* **1** a building used by a guard when not walking a post **2** a jail for temporary confinement
guard'ian (-ē ən) *n.* **1** one who guards or protects; custodian **2** a person legally in charge of the affairs of a minor or of a person of unsound mind — *adj.* protecting — **guard'i·an·ship'** *n.*
guard'rail' *n.* a protective railing, as on a staircase
guava (gwä'və) *n.* ‖< native name ‖ a yellow, pear-shaped, tropical American fruit
gu·ber·na·to·ri·al (gōō'bər nə tôr'ē əl) *adj.* ‖L *gubernator*, governor ‖ of a governor or the office of governor
Guern·sey (gurn'zē) *n., pl.* **-seys** ‖after *Guernsey*, one of the Channel Islands ‖ a breed of dairy cattle, usually fawn-colored with white markings
guer·ril·la or **gue·ril·la** (gə ril'ə) *n.* ‖Sp, dim. of *guerra*, war ‖ a member of a small defensive force of irregular soldiers, making surprise raids
guess (ges) *vt., vi.* ‖ME *gessen* ‖ **1** to form a judgment or estimate of (something) without actual knowledge; surmise **2** to judge correctly by doing this **3** to think or suppose — *n.* **1** a guessing **2** something guessed; conjecture
guess'work' *n.* **1** a guessing **2** a judgment, result, etc. arrived at by guessing
guest (gest) *n.* ‖< ON *gestr* ‖ **1** a person entertained at the home, club, etc. of another **2** any paying customer of a hotel, restaurant, etc. — *adj.* **1** for guests **2** performing by special invitation *[a guest artist]*
guff (guf) *n.* ‖echoic ‖ [Slang] **1** nonsense **2** brash or insolent talk
guf·faw (gu fô') *n.* ‖echoic ‖ a loud, coarse burst of laughter — *vi.* to laugh in this way
guid·ance (gīd'ns) *n.* **1** a guiding; leadership **2** advice or assistance
guide (gīd) *vt.* **guid'ed, guid'ing** ‖< OFr *guider* ‖ **1** to point out the way for; lead **2** to direct the course of; control — *n.* **1** one whose work is conducting tours, etc. **2** a controlling device **3** a book of basic instruction
guide'book' *n.* a book containing directions and information for tourists
guided missile a military missile whose course is controlled by radar, etc.
guide'line' *n.* a principle by which to determine a course of action

guild (gild) *n.* ‖< OE *gieldan*, to pay ‖ an association for mutual aid and the promotion of common interests
guil·der (gil'dər) *n.* ‖< MDu *gulden*, golden ‖ the monetary unit of the Netherlands
guile (gīl) *n.* ‖< OFr ‖ slyness and cunning in dealing with others —**guile'ful** *adj.* —**guile'less** *adj.*
guil·lo·tine (gil'ə tēn'; *for v., usually* gil'ə tēn') *n.* ‖Fr: after J. *Guillotin* (1738-1814), Fr physician who advocated its use‖ an instrument for beheading, having a heavy blade dropped between two grooved uprights — *vt.* **-tined', -tin'ing** to behead with a guillotine
guilt (gilt) *n.* ‖OE *gylt*, a sin ‖ **1** the state of having done a wrong or committed an offense **2** a feeling of self-reproach from believing that one has done a wrong — **guilt'less** *adj.*
guilt'y *adj.* **-i·er, -i·est 1** having guilt **2** legally judged an offender **3** of or showing guilt *[a guilty look]* —**guilt'i·ly** *adv.* —**guilt'i·ness** *n.*
guinea (gin'ē) *n.* ‖first coined of gold from *Guinea* ‖ a former English gold coin equal to 21 shillings
guinea fowl (or **hen**) *n.* ‖orig. imported from *Guinea* ‖ a domestic fowl with a rounded body and speckled feathers
guinea pig ‖prob. orig. brought to England by ships plying between England, *Guinea*, and South America ‖ **1** a small, fat rodent used in biological experiments **2** any subject used in an experiment
guise (gīz) *n.* ‖< OHG *wisa*, manner ‖ **1** manner of dress; garb **2** semblance **3** a false appearance; pretense
gui·tar (gi tär') *n.* ‖ult. < Gr *kithara*, lyre ‖ a musical instrument with usually six strings plucked with the fingers or a plectrum —**gui·tar'ist** *n.*
gulch (gulch) *n.* ‖prob. < dial., to swallow greedily ‖ a deep, narrow ravine
gulf (gulf) *n.* ‖ult. < Gr *kolpos*, bosom ‖ **1** a large area of ocean reaching into land **2** a wide, deep chasm **3** a wide gap or separation
gull[1] (gul) *n.* ‖< Celt ‖ a white and gray water bird with webbed feet
gull[2] (gul) *n.* ‖ME, lit., unfledged bird ‖ a person easily tricked; dupe — *vt.* to cheat or trick
gul·let (gul'ət) *n.* ‖< L *gula*, throat ‖ **1** the esophagus **2** the throat
gul·li·ble (gul'ə bəl) *adj.* easily gulled; credulous —**gul'libil'ity** *n.*
gul·ly (gul'ē) *n., pl.* **-lies** ‖see GULLET ‖ a small, narrow ravine
gulp (gulp) *vt., vi.* ‖prob. < Du *gulpen* ‖ **1** to swallow hastily or greedily **2** to choke back as if swallowing — *n.* a gulping or swallowing
gum[1] (gum) *n.* ‖< LL *gumma* ‖ **1** a sticky substance found in certain trees and plants **2** an adhesive **3** CHEWING GUM — *vt.* **gummed, gum'ming** to coat or unite with gum —

━━━ THESAURUS ━━━

guard *n.* sentry, sentinel, protector; see WATCHMAN. —**off one's guard** unaware, unprotected, defenseless; see UNPREPARED. —**on one's guard** alert, mindful, vigilant; see READY 2.
guard *v.* watch, observe, superintend, patrol, picket, police, look out, look after, see after, supervise, tend, keep in view, keep an eye on, attend, overlook, hold in custody, stand over, babysit, care for, see to, chaperone, oversee, ride herd on*, keep tabs on*.—*Ant.* NEGLECT, disregard, forsake.
guarded *a.* **1** [Protected] safeguarded, secured, defended; see SAFE 1. **2** [Cautious] circumspect, attentive, overcautious; see CAREFUL.
guardian *n.* **1** [One who regulates or protects] overseer, safeguard, curator, guard, protector, preserver, trustee, custodian, keeper, patrol, warden, defender, supervisor, babysitter, sponsor, superintendent, sentinel. **2** [A foster parent] adoptive parent, foster mother, foster father; see FATHER 1, MOTHER 1.
guerrilla *a.* auxiliary, independent, predatory; see FIGHTING.
guerrilla *n.* irregular soldier, saboteur, independent; see SOLDIER.
guess *n.* conjecture, surmise, supposi-

tion, theory, hypothesis, presumption, opinion, postulate, estimate, suspicion, guesswork, view, belief, assumption, speculation, fancy, inference, conclusion, deduction, induction, shot in the dark.
guess *v.* conjecture, presume, infer, suspect, speculate, imagine, surmise, theorize, hazard a guess, suggest, figure, venture, suppose, presume, imagine, think likely, reckon, calculate. —**guess at** reckon, calculate, survey; see ESTIMATE.
guessing *n.* guesswork, supposition, imagination, fancy, inference, deduction, presupposition, reckoning, surmise, theorizing, taking for granted, postulating, assuming, presuming, jumping to conclusions.
guest *n.* visitor, caller, house guest, dinner guest, luncheon guest, visitant, confidant, confidante, friend.
guidance *n.* direction, leadership, supervision; see ADMINISTRATION 2.
guide *n.* pilot, captain, pathfinder, scout, escort, courier, director, explorer, lead, guru, conductor, pioneer, leader, superintendent.
guide *v.* conduct, escort, show the way; see LEAD 1.
guilt *n.* culpability, blame, error, fault, crime, sin, offense, liability,

criminality, sinfulness, misconduct, misbehavior, malpractice, delinquency, transgression, indiscretion, weakness, failing, felonious conduct.—*Ant.* INNOCENCE, blamelessness, honor.
guilty *a.* found guilty, guilty as charged, condemned, sentenced, criminal, censured, impeached, incriminated, indicted, liable, condemned, convictable, judged, damned, doomed, at fault, sinful, to blame, in the wrong, in error, wrong, blameable, reproachable, chargeable.—*Ant.* INNOCENT, blameless, right.
gulch *n.* gully, ditch, gorge; see RAVINE.
gulf *n.* **1** [Chasm] abyss, gap, depth; see RAVINE. **2** [An arm of the sea] inlet, sound, cove; see BAY.
gullible *a.* innocent, trustful, simple; see NAIVE.
gully *n.* ditch, chasm, crevasse; see RAVINE.
gulp *v.* swig, choke down, toss off; see SWALLOW.
gum[1] *n.* resin, glue, pitch, tar, pine tar, amber, wax. *Commercial gums include the following:* chewing gum, sealing wax, rosin, mucilage, chicle, latex, gum arabic.

vi. to become sticky or clogged —**gum up** [Slang] to cause to go awry —**gum′my, -mier, -mi·est,** *adj.*

gum² (gum) *n.* [OE *goma*] [*often pl.*] the firm flesh surrounding the base of the teeth — *vt.* **gummed, gum′ming** to chew with toothless gums

gum arabic a gum from certain acacias, used in medicine, candy, etc.

gumbo (gum′bō) *n.* [< Bantu name for okra] a soup thickened with okra

gum′drop′ *n.* a small, firm candy of sweetened gelatin, etc.

gump·tion (gump′shən) *n.* [< Scot] [Colloq.] initiative; enterprise

gun (gun) *n.* [< ME *gonnilde,* cannon < ON] 1 a weapon with a metal tube from which a projectile is discharged by the force of an explosive 2 any similar device not discharged by an explosive [an air *gun*] 3 anything like a gun — *vi.* **gunned, gun′ning** to shoot or hunt with a gun — *vt.* 1 [Colloq.] to shoot (a person) 2 [Slang] to advance the throttle of (an engine) —**gun for** [Slang] to try to get — **jump the gun** [Colloq.] to begin before the proper time — **stick to one's guns** [Colloq.] to stand fast; be firm — **under the gun** [Colloq.] in a tense situation, often one involving a deadline

gun′boat′ *n.* a small armed ship

gun′fight′ *n.* a fight between persons using pistols or revolvers

gun′fire′ *n.* the firing of guns

gung-ho (gun′hō′) *adj.* [Chin *kung-ho,* lit., work together] [Colloq.] enthusiastic

gunk (gunk) *n.* [< ?] [Slang] a viscous or thick, messy substance

gun′man *n., pl.* **-men** an armed gangster or hired killer

gun′met′al *n.* 1 a bronze with a dark tarnish 2 its dark-gray color

gun′ner *n.* 1 a soldier, etc. who helps fire artillery 2 a naval warrant officer in charge of guns, missiles, etc.

gun′nery *n.* the science of making and using heavy guns and projectiles

gunny (gun′ē) *n., pl.* **-nies** [< Sans *gōnī,* a sack] a coarse fabric of jute or hemp

gun′ny·sack′ *n.* a sack made of gunny

gun′play′ *n.* an exchange of gunshots, as between gunmen and police

gun′pow′der *n.* an explosive powder used in guns, for blasting, etc.

gun′run′ning *n.* the smuggling of guns and ammunition —**gun′run′ner** *n.*

gun′ship′ *n.* a heavily armed helicopter used to assault enemy ground forces

gun′shot′ *n.* shot fired from a gun

gun′-shy′ *adj.* easily frightened at the firing of a gun [a *gun-shy* dog]

gun′smith′ *n.* one who makes or repairs small guns

gun·wale (gun′əl) *n.* [< bulwarks supporting a ship's guns] the upper edge of the side of a ship or boat

guppy (gup′ē) *n., pl.* **-pies** [after R. J. L. *Guppy,* of Trinidad] a tiny freshwater fish of the West Indies, etc.

gur·gle (gur′gəl) *vi.* **-gled, -gling** [< L *gurgulio,* gullet] to make a bubbling sound — *n.* such a sound

guru (gōō′rōō′, goo rōō′) *n.* [< Sans *guruḥ,* venerable] in Hinduism, one's personal spiritual advisor or teacher

gush (gush) *vi.* [ME *guschen*] 1 to flow out plentifully 2 to have a sudden flow 3 to talk or write effusively — *vt.* to cause to gush — *n.* a gushing —**gush′y, -i·er, -i·est,** *adj.*

gush′er *n.* 1 one who gushes 2 an oil well from which oil spouts forth

gus·set (gus′it) *n.* [< OFr *gousset*] a triangular piece inserted in a garment, etc. to make it stronger or roomier

gussy or **gus·sie** (gus′ē) *vt., vi.* **-sied, -sy·ing** [Slang] to dress (*up*) in a fine or showy way

gust (gust) *n.* [< ON *gjosa,* to gush] 1 a sudden, strong rush of air 2 a sudden outburst of rain, laughter, etc. — **gust′y, -i·er, -i·est,** *adj.*

gus·ta·tory (gus′tə tôr′ē) *adj.* [< L *gustus,* taste] of the sense of taste

gusto (gus′tō) *n.* [see prec.] 1 zest; relish 2 great vigor or liveliness

gut (gut) *n.* [< OE *geotan,* to pour] 1 [*pl.*] the bowels or the stomach 2 the intestine 3 tough cord made from animal intestines 4 [*pl.*] [Colloq.] daring; courage — *vt.* **gut′ted, gut′ting** 1 to remove the intestines from 2 to destroy the interior of — *adj.* [Slang] 1 basic 2 easy; simple

gut′less *adj.* [Colloq.] lacking courage

gutsy (gut′sē) *adj.* **-i·er, -i·est** [Colloq.] courageous, forceful, etc.

gutta-percha (gut′ə pur′chə) *n.* [< Malay < *getah,* tree sap + ? *perca,* clothstrip] a rubberlike gum from the latex of certain Asian trees

gut·ter (gut′ər) *n.* [< L *gutta,* a drop] a channel to carry off water, as along the eaves of a roof or the side of a street — *vi.* to flow in a stream

gut·tural (gut′ər əl) *adj.* [L *guttur,* throat] 1 of the throat 2 produced in the throat; rasping

guy¹ (gī) *n.* [< OFr *guier,* to guide] a rope, chain, etc. used to steady or guide something — *vt.* to guide or steady with a guy

guy² (gī) *n.* [after *Guy* Fawkes, Eng conspirator] [Slang] 1 a man or boy 2 any person — *vt.* to tease

guz·zle (guz′əl) *vi., vt.* **-zled, -zling** [< ? OFr *gosier,* throat] to drink greedily or immoderately —**guz′zler** *n.*

gym (jim) *n.* [Colloq.] 1 *short for* GYMNASIUM 2 PHYSICAL EDUCATION

gym·na·sium (jim nā′zē əm) *n., pl.* **-si·ums** or **-sia** (-ə) [< Gr *gymnos,* naked] a room or building equipped for physical training and sports

gym·nas·tics (jim nas′tiks) *n.pl.* a sport combining tumbling and acrobatic feats —**gym′nast′** *n.* —**gym·nas′tic** *adj.* —**gym·nas′ti·cal·ly** *adv.*

gym·no·sperm (jim′nō spurm′, -nə-) *n.* [< Gr *gymnos,* naked + *sperma,* seed] any of a large division of seed plants having the ovules not enclosed within an ovary, as seed ferns, conifers, etc.

gy·ne·col·o·gy (gī′ni käl′ə jē; jin′i-, jī′ni-) *n.* [< Gr *gynē,* woman + -LOGY] the branch of medicine dealing with women's diseases, etc. —**gy′necol′o·gist** *n.*

gyp (jip) *n.* [prob. < GYPSY] [Colloq.] 1 a swindle 2 a swindler: also **gyp′per** or **gyp′ster** — *vt., vi.* **gypped, gyp′ping** [Colloq.] to swindle; cheat

gyp·sum (jip′səm) *n.* [< Gr *gypsos*] a sulfate of calcium used for making plaster of Paris, in treating soil, etc.

Gypsy (jip′sē) *n., pl.* **-sies** [< *Egipcien,* Egyptian: orig. thought to be from Egypt] 1 [*also* g-] a member of a

---

═══ THESAURUS ═══

gummy *a.* sticky, cohesive, viscid; see STICKY.

gun *n. Types include the following:* rifle, automatic rifle, repeating rifle, repeater, recoilless rifle, air rifle, shotgun, sawed-off shotgun, musket, hand gun, automatic, semiautomatic pistol, squirrel gun, carbine, long rifle, laser gun, revolver, pistol, rod*; see also MACHINE GUN. —**jump the gun*** start too soon, act inappropriately, give oneself away; see BEGIN 1, HURRY 1.

gunfire *n.* bombardment, fire to pin down someone, artillery support, air support, air strike, mortar fire, heavy arms attack, explosion, shooting, shot, report, artillery, volley, discharge, detonation, blast, firing, burst, barrage, cannonade, fire superiority, salvo, fire power.

gunman *n.* killer, thug, gangster; see CRIMINAL.

gunner *n.* machine gunner, rocketeer, missile launcher, bazooka launcher, sniper, sharpshooter, aerial gunner, artilleryman, cannoneer.

gurgle *v.* ripple, murmur, pour; see FLOW.

gush *v.* pour, well, spew; see FLOW.

gusto *n.* zeal, fervor, ardor; see ZEAL.

gut *n.* small intestine, large intestine, duodenum; see INTESTINES.

guts *n.* 1 [Bowels] viscera, insides, belly; see INTESTINES. 2 [*Fortitude] pluck, hardihood, effrontery; see COURAGE. —**hate someone's guts*** detest, dislike, despise; see HATE.

gutter *n.* canal, gully, sewer, watercourse, channel, dike, drain, moat, trough; see also TRENCH.

guttural *a.* throaty, gruff, deep; see HOARSE.

guy² *n.* chap, lad, person; see FELLOW

1, MAN 2, PERSON 1.

guzzle *v.* swill, quaff, swig; see DRINK 1.

gymnasium *n.* health center, recreation center, playing floor, exercise room, sports center, field house, court, athletic club, arena, coliseum, theater, circus, stadium, ring, rink, pit, gym*.

gymnast *n.* acrobat, tumbler, jumper; see ATHLETE.

gymnastics *n.* trapeze performance, health exercises, acrobatics, aerobatics, therapeutics, body-building exercises, tumbling, vaulting, work on the rings, bars, balance beam, horizontal bars, horse.

gyp* *n.* cheat, fraud, trick; see FAKE, TRICK 1.

gypsy *n.* tramp, Bohemian, vagrant; see TRAVELER.

wandering Caucasoid people, perhaps orig. from India, with dark skin and black hair **2** their language **3** [g-] one who looks or lives like a Gypsy

gypsy moth a moth in E U.S.: its larvae feed on leaves, damaging trees

gy·rate (jī′rāt′) *vi.* **-rat′ed, -rat′ing** ‖ < Gr *gyros*, a circle ‖ to move in a circular or spiral path; whirl —**gy·ra′tion** *n.* —**gy′ra·tor** *n.*

gyro (yir′ō, jī′rō′) *n., pl.* **-ros** ‖ see prec. ‖ **1** layers of lamb and beef roasted and sliced **2** a sandwich of this Also **gyros** (yir′ôs)

gyro- ‖ see GYRATE ‖ *combining form* gyrating [*gyroscope*]

gyro·scope (jī′rō skōp′, -rə-) *n.* ‖ prec. + -SCOPE ‖ a wheel mounted in a set of rings so that its axis is free to turn in any direction: when the wheel is spun rapidly, it will keep its original plane of rotation

gyve (jīv) *n., vt.* **gyved, gyv′ing** ‖ ME *give* ‖ [Archaic] fetter; shackle

h or **H** (āch) *n., pl.* **h's, H's** the eighth letter of the English alphabet

H *Chem. symbol for* hydrogen

H, H., h, or **h.** **1** height **2** high **3** *Baseball* hit(s) **4** hour(s) **5** hundred(s) **6** husband

ha (hä) *interj.* [echoic] an exclamation of wonder, surprise, anger, triumph, etc.

ha·be·as cor·pus (hā′bē əs kôr′pəs) [L, (that) you have the body] *Law* a writ requiring that a detained person be brought before a court to decide the legality of the detention

hab·er·dasher (hab′ər dash′ər) *n.* [< ME] a dealer in men's hats, shirts, neckties, etc. —**hab′er·dash′ery** *n.*

ha·bil·i·ment (hə bil′ə mənt) *n.* [< MFr *habiller*, to clothe] **1** [*usually pl.*] clothing; attire **2** [*pl.*] trappings

habit (hab′it) *n.* [< L *habere*, to have] **1** a distinctive costume, as of a nun, etc. **2** a thing done often and, hence, easily **3** a usual way of doing **4** an addiction, esp. to narcotics

hab′it·able *adj.* fit to be lived in

hab·i·tat (hab′i tat′) *n.* [L, it inhabits] **1** the region where a plant or animal naturally lives **2** the place where a person is ordinarily found

hab·i·ta′tion *n.* **1** an inhabiting **2** a dwelling; home

hab′it-form′ing *adj.* resulting in the formation of a habit or in addiction

ha·bit·u·al (hə bich′ōō əl) *adj.* **1** done or acquired by habit **2** steady; inveterate [a *habitual* smoker] **3** much seen, done, or used; usual —**ha·bit′u·ally** *adv.* —**ha·bit′u·al·ness** *n.*

ha·bit′u·ate′ (-āt′) *vt.* **-at′ed, -at′ing** to accustom (*to*) —**ha·bit′ua′tion** *n.*

ha·bitué (hə bich′ōō ā′) *n.* [Fr] one who frequents a certain place

ha·ci·en·da (hä′sē en′də) *n.* [Sp < L *facere*, do] in Spanish America, a large estate or ranch, or its main house

hack¹ (hak) *vt.* [OE *haccian*] to chop or cut crudely, roughly, etc. — *vi.* **1** to make rough cuts **2** to give harsh, dry coughs — *n.* **1** a tool for hacking **2** a gash or notch **3** a harsh, dry cough —**hack′er** *n.*

hack² (hak) *n.* [< HACKNEY] **1** a horse for hire **2** an old, worn-out horse **3** a literary drudge **4** a coach for hire **5** [Colloq.] a taxicab — *adj.* **1** employed as, or done by, a hack [*hack* writer] **2** trite; hackneyed

hack′er (-ər) *n.* a talented amateur user of computers

hackle (hak′əl) *n.* [ME *hechele*] **1** the neck feathers of a rooster, pigeon, etc., collectively **2** [*pl.*] the hairs on a dog's neck and back that bristle

hack·ney (hak′nē) *n., pl.* **-neys** [after *Hackney,* England] **1** a horse for driving or riding **2** a carriage for hire

hack′neyed′ (-nēd′) *adj.* made trite by overuse

hack′saw′ *n.* a fine-toothed saw for cutting metal Also **hack saw**

had (had) *vt. pt. & pp. of* HAVE

had·dock (had′ək) *n., pl.* **-dock** or **-docks** [ME *hadok*] an Atlantic food fish, related to the cod

Ha·des (hā′dēz′) [Gr *Haidēs*] *Gr. Myth.* the home of the dead — *n.* [*often* h-] hell

haft (haft, häft) *n.* [OE *hæft*] the handle or hilt of a knife, ax, etc.

hag (hag) *n.* [< OE *hægtes*] **1** a witch **2** an ugly, often vicious old woman —**hag′gish** *adj.*

hag·gard (hag′ərd) *adj.* [MFr *hagard,* untamed (hawk)] having a wild, wasted, worn look; gaunt

hag·gle (hag′əl) *vi.* **-gled, -gling** [< Scot *hag,* to hack] to argue about terms, price, etc. — *n.* a haggling —**hag′gler** *n.*

hah (hä) *interj., n.* HA

haiku (hī′kōō′) *n.* [Jpn] **1** a Japanese verse form of three unrhymed lines of 5, 7, and 5 syllables, respectively **2** *pl.* **-ku** a poem in this form

hail¹ (hāl) *vt.* [< ON *heill,* whole, sound] **1** to greet with cheers; acclaim **2** to call out to — *n.* a greeting — *interj.* an exclamation of tribute, greeting, etc. —**hail from** to be from

hail² (hāl) *n.* [OE *hægel*] **1** frozen raindrops falling during thunderstorms **2** a shower of or like hail — *vt., vi.* to pour down like hail

hail′stone′ *n.* a pellet of hail

hail′storm′ *n.* a storm with hail

hair (her, har) *n.* [OE *hær*] **1** any of the threadlike outgrowths from the skin **2** a growth of these, as on the human head **3** a very small space, degree, etc. **4** a threadlike growth on a plant —**get in one's hair** [Slang] to annoy one —**split hairs** to quibble —**hair′less** *adj.* —**hair′like′** *adj.*

hair′ball′ *n.* a ball of hair often found in the stomach of a cow, cat, or other animal that licks its coat

hair′breadth′ (-bredth′) *n.* a very small space or amount — *adj.* very narrow; close Also **hairs′breadth′**

hair′cut′ *n.* the act of, or a style of, cutting the hair

hair′do′ *n., pl.* **-dos′** the style in which hair is arranged; coiffure

hair′dress′er *n.* one whose work is dressing hair

-haired (herd) having (a specified kind of) hair [*short-haired*]

hair′line′ *n.* **1** a very thin line **2** the outline of the hair on the head

hair′piece′ *n.* a toupee or wig

hair′pin′ *n.* a small, bent piece of wire, etc., for keeping the hair in place — *adj.* U-shaped [a *hairpin* turn]

hair′-rais′ing *adj.* terrifying or shocking

hair′split′ting *adj., n.* making petty distinctions; quibbling

hair′spring′ *n.* a slender, hairlike coil spring, as in a watch

hair′y *adj.* **-i·er, -i·est** covered with hair —**hair′i·ness** *n.*

hake (hāk) *n., pl.* **hake** or **hakes** [prob. < ON] a marine food fish related to the cod

hal·berd (hal′bərd) *n.* [< MHG *helmbarte*] a combination spear and battle-ax of the 15th and 16th c.

THESAURUS

habit *n.* **1** [A customary action] mode, wont, routine, rule, characteristic, practice, disposition, way, fashion, manner, propensity, bent, turn, proclivity, addiction, predisposition, susceptibility, weakness, bias, persuasion, second nature; see also CUSTOM. **2** [An obsession] addiction, fixation, hang-up; see OBSESSION.

habitat *n.* locality, territory, natural surroundings; see ENVIRONMENT, HOME 1, POSITION 1.

habitual *a.* ingrained, confirmed, frequent, periodic, continual, routine, mechanical, automatic, seasoned, permanent, perpetual, fixed, rooted, systematic, recurrent, periodical, methodical, repeated, disciplined, practiced, accustomed, established, set, repetitious, cyclic, reiterated, settled, trite, stereotyped, in a groove, in a rut.—*Ant.* DIFFERENT, exceptional, departing.

hack¹ *v.* chop, whack, mangle; see CUT 1.

hack¹,² *n.* **1** [A literary drudge] pulp-story writer, ghost writer, propagandist, commercial writer, popular novelist; see also WRITER. **2** [A cut] notch, nick, cleavage; see CUT 1. **3** [*Commercial driver, especially of a taxicab*] cab driver, chauffeur, cabbie*; see DRIVER.

hag *n.* crone, virago, withered old woman, shrew, ogress, hellcat, fishwife, harridan, old witch, battle-ax*; see also WITCH.

haggle *v.* deal, wrangle, argue; see BUY, SELL.

hail¹ *v.* cheer, welcome, honor; see GREET. —**hail from** come from, be born in, be a native of; see BEGIN 2.

hail² *n.* hailstorm, sleet, icy particles, ice; see also RAIN 1.

hair *n.* **1** [Threadlike growth] locks, wig, moustache, whiskers, eyebrow, eyelash, sideburn, mane, fluff; see also BEARD, FUR. **2** [Anything suggesting the thickness of a hair] a hairbreadth, a narrow margin, hair trigger, hairspring, splinter, shaving, sliver; see also BIT 1. —**get in one's**

hair* irritate, annoy, disturb; see BOTHER 2. —**let one's hair down*** be informal, have fun, let oneself go; see RELAX. —**make one's hair stand on end** terrify, scare, horrify; see FRIGHTEN.

haircut *n.* trim, trimming, bob, crew cut, flattop*, Beatle, page boy, pigtails, French roll, bun, ponytail, braid, feathercut, bangs, butch*, DA*, ducktail*.

hairdo *n.* coiffure, hairdressing, hair style; see HAIRCUT.

hairless *n.* clean-shaven, beardless, smooth-faced; see BALD, SMOOTH 3.

hairpin *n.* bobby pin, hair clip, barrette; see FASTENER.

hairsplitting *a.* unimportant, minute, subtle; see TRIVIAL, IRRELEVANT, UNIMPORTANT.

hairy *a.* bristly, shaggy, woolly, unshorn, downy, fleecy, whiskered, tufted, unshaven, bearded, bewhiskered, furry, fuzzy, hirsute, fluffy.—*Ant.* BALD, hairless, smooth.

hal·cyon (hal′sē ən) *adj.* ⟦< Gr *alkyōn*, kingfisher (fabled calmer of the sea)⟧ tranquil, happy, idyllic, etc.

hale[1] (hāl) *adj.* hal′er, hal′est ⟦OE *hal*⟧ vigorous and healthy

hale[2] (hāl) *vt.* **haled, hal′ing** ⟦< OFr *haler*⟧ to force (a person) to go

half (haf, häf) *n., pl.* **halves** ⟦OE *healf*⟧ **1** either of the two equal parts of something **2** either of the two equal parts of some games —*adj.* **1** being a half **2** incomplete; partial —*adv.* **1** to the extent of a half **2** partly *[half done]* **3** at all: used with *not [not half bad]*

half- *combining form* **1** one half *[half-life]* **2** partly *[half-baked]*

half′-and-half′ *n.* something that is half of one thing and half of another, as a mixture of milk and cream —*adj.* combining two things equally —*adv.* in two equal parts

half′back′ *n.* *Football* an offensive back stationed behind the quarterback and typically smaller and faster than a fullback

half′-baked′ *adj.* **1** only partly baked **2** not completely thought out

half′-breed′ *n.* one whose parents are of different ethnic types: now offensive

half brother a brother through one parent only

half′-cocked′ *adj.* with the hammer cocked halfway — **go off half-cocked** to speak or act thoughtlessly

half dollar a coin of the U.S. and Canada, worth 50 cents

half′heart′ed *adj.* with little enthusiasm, determination, interest, etc. —**half′heart′ed·ly** *adv.*

half′-life′ (-līf′) *n.* the constant time period required for the disintegration of half of the atoms in a sample of a radioactive substance Also **half life**

half′-mast′ *n.* the position of a flag halfway down its staff, esp. as a sign of mourning

half note *Music* a note having one half the duration of a whole note

half′pen·ny (hāp′nē, hā′pən ē) *n., pl.* **-pence** (hā′pəns) or **-pennies** a former British coin equal to half a penny

half sister a sister through one parent only

half sole a sole (of a shoe or boot) from the arch to the toe

half′track′ *n.* an army truck, armored vehicle, etc. with tractor treads instead of rear wheels

half′way′ *adj.* **1** midway between two points, etc. **2** partial *[halfway measures]* —*adv.* **1** to the midway point **2** partially —**meet halfway** to be willing to compromise with

halfway house a place for helping people adjust to society after being imprisoned, hospitalized, etc.

half′-wit′ *n.* a stupid or silly person; fool —**half′-wit′ted** *adj.*

hal·i·but (hal′ə bət) *n., pl.* **-but** or **-buts** ⟦ME *hali,* holy + *butt,* a flounder (so called because eaten on holidays)⟧ a large, edible flatfish found in northern seas

hal·ite (hal′īt′, hā′līt′) *n.* rock salt

hal·i·to·sis (hal′i tō′sis) *n.* ⟦< L *halitus,* breath⟧ bad-smelling breath

hall (hôl) *n.* ⟦OE *heall*⟧ **1** the main dwelling of an estate **2** a public building with offices, etc. **3** a large room for gath-

erings, exhibits, etc. **4** a college building **5** a vestibule at the entrance of a building **6** a hallway

hal·le·lu·jah or **hal·le·lu·iah** (hal′ə lōō′yə) *interj.* ⟦< Heb < *hallelū,* praise + *yāh,* Jehovah⟧ praise (ye) the Lord! —*n.* a hymn of praise to God

hall·mark (hôl′märk′) *n.* ⟦< the mark stamped on gold and silver articles at Goldsmith's Hall in London⟧ a mark or symbol of genuineness or high quality

hal·loo (hə lōō′) *interj., n.* a shout to attract attention — *vi., vt.* **-looed′, -loo′ing** to shout or call

hal·low (hal′ō) *vt.* ⟦OE *halgian*⟧ to make or regard as holy

hal·lowed (hal′ōd, -ō ed′, -ō id) *adj.* holy or sacred

Hal·low·een or **Hal·low·e′en** (hal′ō ēn′, hal′ə wēn′) *n.* ⟦contr. < *all hallow even*⟧ the evening of Oct. 31, followed by All Saints' Day

hal·lu·ci·nate (hə lōō′si nāt′) *vi., vt.* **-nat′ed, -nat′ing** ⟦see fol.⟧ to have or cause to have hallucinations

hal·lu·ci·na·tion (hə lōō′si nā′shən) *n.* ⟦< L *hallucinari,* to wander mentally⟧ the apparent perception of sights, sounds, etc. that are not actually present —**hal·lu′ci·na·to′ry** (-ə tôr′ē) *adj.* a passageway; corridor

hal·lu·ci·no·gen (-nə jen, hal′yōō sin′ə-) *n.* a drug or other substance that produces hallucinations

hall′way′ *n.* a passageway; corridor

ha·lo (hā′lō) *n., pl.* **-los** or **-loes** ⟦< Gr *halōs,* circular threshing floor⟧ **1** a ring of light, as around the sun **2** a symbolic ring of light around the head of a saint, etc., as in pictures

hal·o·gen (hal′ō jən, -jen′; hal′ə-) *n.* ⟦< Gr *hals,* salt⟧ any of the five nonmetallic chemical elements fluorine, chlorine, bromine, astatine, and iodine

halt[1] (hôlt) *n., vi., vt.* ⟦< Ger *halt machen*⟧ stop

halt[2] (hôlt) *vi.* ⟦< OE *healt*⟧ **1** [Archaic] to limp **2** to hesitate —*the halt* those who are lame

hal·ter (hôl′tər) *n.* ⟦OE *hælftre*⟧ **1** a rope or strap for tying or leading an animal **2** a hangman's noose **3** a woman's upper garment, held up by a loop around the neck

halt′ing *adj.* **1** awkward or unsteady *[a halting gait]* **2** hesitant or uncertain; disconnected, etc. *[halting speech]* —**halt′ing·ly** *adv.*

halve (hav, häv) *vt.* **halved, halv′ing 1** to divide into two equal parts **2** to reduce to half

halves (havz, hävz) *n. pl. of* HALF —**by halves** halfway; imperfectly —**go halves** to share expenses equally

hal·yard (hal′yərd) *n.* ⟦< ME *halier:* see HALE[2]⟧ a rope or tackle for raising or lowering a flag, sail, etc.

ham (ham) *n.* ⟦OE *hamm*⟧ **1** the back of the thigh **2** the upper part of a hog's hind leg, salted, smoked, etc. **3** [Colloq.] an amateur radio operator **4** [Slang] an actor who overacts —*adj.* **-mier, -mi·est, -miest** *adj.*

ham·burg·er (ham′bʉrg′ər) *n.* ⟦after *Hamburg,* Germany⟧ **1** ground beef **2** a cooked patty of such meat, often in a sandwich Also **ham′burg**

ham·let (ham′lit) *n.* ⟦< OFr *hamelete* < Old LowG *hamm,* enclosed area⟧ a very small village

---

THESAURUS

half *a.* partial, divided by two, equally distributed in halves, mixed, divided, halved, bisected; see also HALFWAY.— *Ant.* FULL, all, whole. —**by half** considerably, many, very much; see MUCH. —**in half** into halves, split, divided; see HALF. —**not the half of it** not all of it, partial, incomplete; see UNFINISHED.

halfback *n.* right halfback, left halfback, back; see FOOTBALL PLAYER.

half-baked *a.* senseless, brainless, indiscreet; see STUPID.

half-breed *a.* half-caste, crossbreed, half-blood; see HYBRID.

half dollar *n.* fifty cents, fifty-cent piece, four bits*; see MONEY 1.

halfhearted *a.* lukewarm, indecisive, irresolute; see INDIFFERENT.

halfway *a.* midway, half the distance, in the middle, incomplete, unsatisfactory, partially, fairly, imperfectly, in part, partly, nearly, insufficiently, to a degree, to some extent, comparatively, moderately, at half the distance, in some measure, middling*; see also HALF.—*Ant.* COMPLETELY, wholly, entirely.

halfway house *n.* addiction facility, referral center, rest home; see HOSPITAL.

hall *n.* **1** [A large public or semi-public building or room] legislative chamber, assembly room, meeting place, banquet hall, town hall, concert hall, dance hall, music hall, arena, ballroom, clubroom, church, salon, lounge, chamber, stateroom, gymnasium, dining hall, armory, amphitheater, council chamber, reception room, waiting room, lecture room, gallery, gym*, mess hall. **2** [An entrance way] foyer, corridor, hallway; see ENTRANCE 2, ROOM 2.

hallelujah *interj.* praise God, praise the Lord, glory be; see YELL.

hallmark *n.* endorsement, seal, mark of acceptance; see EMBLEM.

hallowed *a.* sacred, sacrosanct, consecrated; see DIVINE.

hallway *n.* foyer, entrance way, corridor; see ENTRANCE 2.

halt[1] *v.* pull up, check, terminate, suspend, put an end to, interrupt, break into, block, cut short, adjourn, hold off, cause to halt, stem, deter, bring

to a standstill, stall, bring to an end, curb, stop, restrict, arrest, hold in check, defeat, thwart, hamper, frustrate, suppress, clog, intercept, extinguish, blockade, obstruct, repress, inhibit, hinder, barricade, impede, overthrow, vanquish, override, dam, upset, stand in the way of, baffle, contravene, overturn, reduce, counteract, quell, prohibit, outdo, put down, finish, forbid, oppose, crush, nip in the bud*, break it up, put on the brakes*, hold on*, throw a wet blanket on*, throw a monkey wrench in the works*, clip one's wings*, tie one's hands*, take the wind out of one's sails, squelch*.— *Ant.* BEGIN, start, instigate.

halter *n.* leash, bridle, rein; see ROPE.

halve *v.* split, bisect, cut in two; see DIVIDE.

ham *n.* **1** [Smoked pork thigh] sugar-cured ham, Virginia ham, picnic ham; see MEAT. **2** [An incompetent actor] inferior player, nonprofessional, ham actor*; see AMATEUR.

hamburger *n.* ground round, ground beef, burger; see MEAT.

Ham·let (ham′lit) the title hero of a tragedy by Shakespeare

ham·mer (ham′ər) *n.* ⟦OE *hamor*⟧ 1 a tool for pounding, having a metal head and a handle 2 a thing like this in shape or use, as the part of a gun that strikes the firing pin —*vt., vi.* 1 to strike repeatedly, as with a hammer 2 to drive, force, or shape, as with hammer blows —**hammer (away) at** to keep emphasizing —**ham′merer** *n.*

hammer and sickle the emblem of Communist parties in some countries

ham′mer·head′ *n.* 1 the head of a hammer 2 a shark with a mallet-shaped head having an eye at each end

ham′mer·toe′ *n.* a toe that is deformed, with its first joint bent downward

ham·mock (ham′ək) *n.* ⟦Sp *hamaca*, of WInd orig.⟧ a bed of canvas, etc. swung from ropes at both ends

ham·per[1] (ham′pər) *vt.* ⟦ME *hampren*⟧ to hinder; impede; encumber

ham·per[2] (ham′pər) *n.* ⟦< OFr *hanap*, a cup⟧ a large basket, usually covered

ham·ster (ham′stər) *n.* ⟦< OHG *hamustro*⟧ a ratlike animal of Europe and Asia, used in scientific experiments

ham·string (ham′striŋ′) *n.* a tendon at the back of the knee —*vt.* **-strung′**, **-string′ing** to disable, as by cutting a hamstring

hand (hand) *n.* ⟦OE⟧ 1 the part of the arm below the wrist, used for grasping 2 a side or direction *[at my right hand]* 3 possession or care *[the land is in my hands]* 4 control *[to strengthen one's hand]* 5 an active part *[take a hand in the work]* 6 a promise to marry 7 skill 8 one having a special skill 9 manner of doing something 10 handwriting 11 applause 12 help *[to lend a hand]* 13 a hired worker *[a farm hand]* 14 a source *[to get news at first hand]* 15 anything like a hand, as a pointer on a clock 16 the breadth of a hand 17 *Card Games a)* the cards held by a player at one time *b)* a round of play —*adj.* of, for, or controlled by the hand —*vt.* 1 to give as with the hand 2 to help or conduct with the hand —**at hand** near —**hand in hand** together —**hand it to** [Slang] to give credit to —**hand over fist** [Colloq.] easily and in large amounts —**hands down** easily —**on hand** 1 near 2 available 3 present —**on the one** (or **other**) **hand** from one (or the opposed) point of view

hand′bag′ *n.* a woman's purse

hand′ball′ *n.* a game in which players bat a small rubber ball against a wall or walls with the hand

hand′bar′row *n.* a frame carried by two people holding handles at the ends

hand′bill′ *n.* a small printed notice to be passed out by hand

hand′book′ *n.* a compact reference book; manual

hand′breadth′ *n.* the breadth of the human palm, about 4 inches

hand′car′ *n.* a small, open car, orig. hand-powered, used on railroads

hand′cart′ *n.* a small cart pulled or pushed by hand

hand′clasp′ (-klasp′) *n.* HANDSHAKE

hand′craft′ *n.* HANDICRAFT —*vt.* to make skillfully by hand

hand′cuff′ *n.* either of a pair of connected rings for shackling the wrists of a prisoner: *usually used in pl.* —*vt.* to put handcuffs on; manacle

-handed (han′did) *combining form* having or involving (a specified kind or number of) hands *[right-handed, two-handed]*

hand′ful′ *n., pl.* **-fuls′** 1 as much or as many as the hand will hold 2 a few; not many 3 [Colloq.] someone or something hard to manage

hand′gun′ *n.* any firearm that is held and fired with one hand, as a pistol

handi·cap (han′di kap′, -dē-) *n.* ⟦< *hand in cap*, former kind of lottery⟧ 1 a competition in which difficulties are imposed on, or advantages given to, the various contestants to equalize their chances 2 such a difficulty or advantage 3 *a)* any hindrance *b)* a physical disability —*vt.* **-capped′**, **-cap′ping** 1 to give a handicap to 2 to hinder —**the handicapped** those who are physically disabled or mentally retarded

hand′i·cap′per *n.* a person, as a sportswriter, who tries to predict the winners in horse races

handi·craft (han′di kraft′, -dē-) *n.* skill with the hands, or work calling for it

hand′i·work′ *n.* 1 HANDWORK 2 work done by a particular person

hand·ker·chief (haŋ′kər chif′) *n.* ⟦HAND + KERCHIEF⟧ a small cloth for wiping the nose, face, etc.

han·dle (han′dəl) *n.* ⟦OE < *hand*⟧ that part of a tool, etc. by which it is held or lifted —*vt.* **-dled**, **-dling** 1 to touch, lift, operate, etc. with the hand 2 to manage; control 3 to deal with; treat 4 to sell or deal in —*vi.* to respond to control *[the car handles well]* —**han′dler** *n.*

han′dle·bar′ *n.* *[often pl.]* a curved metal bar with handles on the ends, for steering a bicycle, etc.

hand′made′ *adj.* made by hand, not by machine

■ THESAURUS ■

hammer *n.* maul, mallet, mace, club, gavel, steam hammer, triphammer, jackhammer, sledge; see also STICK, TOOL 1.

hammer *v.* strike, bang, pound away at; see BEAT 1, HIT.

hammock *n.* porch swing, hanging bed, bunk; see BED 1.

hamper[1] *v.* impede, thwart, embarrass; see HINDER.

hand *n.* 1 [The termination of the arm] fingers, palm, grip, grasp, hold, knuckles; see also FIST. 2 [A workman] helper, worker, hired hand; see LABORER. 3 [Handwriting] chirography, script, penmanship; see HANDWRITING. 4 [Aid] help, guidance, instruction; see HELP 1. 5 [Applause] standing ovation, thunderous reception, handclapping; see PRAISE 2. 6 [Round of cards] single hand, deal, round; see GAME 1. —**at hand** immediate, approximate, close by; see NEAR 1. —**by hand** handcrafted, homemade, manual; see HOMEMADE. —**change hands** transfer, pass on, shift; see GIVE 1. —**from hand to hand** shifted, given over, changed; see TRANSFERRED. —**from hand to mouth** from day to day, by necessity, in poverty; see POOR 1. —**hand in hand** closely associated, working together, related; see TOGETHER 2, UNITED. —**hold hands** touch, press, squeeze; see HOLD 1. —**in hand** under control, in order, all right; see MANAGED 2. —**join hands** unite, associate, agree; see JOIN 1. —**keep one's hand in** carry on, continue, make a practice of; see PRACTICE 1. —**lay hands on** get, acquire, grasp; see SEIZE 1, 2. —**lend a hand** assist, aid, succor; see HELP. —**not lift a hand** do nothing, be lazy, not try; see NEGLECT 1, 2. —**off one's hands** out of one's responsibility, no longer one's concern, not accountable for; see IRRESPONSIBLE. —**on hand** ready, close by, usable; see AVAILABLE. —**on one's hands** in one's care or responsibility, chargeable to one, accountable to; see RESPONSIBLE 1. —**on the other hand** otherwise, conversely, from the opposite position; see OTHERWISE 1, 2. —**out of hand** out of control, wild, unmanageable; see UNRULY. —**take in hand** take responsibility for, take over, handle; see TRY 1. —**throw up one's hands** give up, resign, quit; see YIELD 1. —**wash one's hands of** deny, reject, refuse; see DENOUNCE.

hand *v.* deliver, give to, return; see GIVE 1. —**hand around** hand out, pass around, allot; see DISTRIBUTE, GIVE 1. —**hand in** deliver, submit, return; see GIVE 1, OFFER 1. —**hand out** give to, deliver, distribute; see GIVE 1, PROVIDE 1. —**hand over** deliver, surrender, give up; see GIVE 1, YIELD 1.

handbag *n.* lady's pocketbook, bag, clutch purse; see PURSE.

handbook *n.* textbook, directory, guidebook; see BOOK.

handed *a.* given to, conveyed, bestowed; see GIVEN.

handful *n.* a small quantity, some, a sprinkling; see FEW.

handicap *n.* 1 [A disadvantage] hindrance, obstacle, block; see BARRIER. 2 [A physical injury] impairment, affliction, chronic disorder; see IMPEDIMENT 2, INJURY.

handicapped *a.* thwarted, crippled, impeded, burdened, hampered, obstructed, encumbered, put at a disadvantage, checked, blocked, limited, restrained, wounded, curbed, put behind; see also DISABLED, RESTRICTED.—*Ant.* HELPED, aided, supported.

handily *a.* skillfully, intelligently, smoothly; see CLEVERLY, EASILY.

handiwork *n.* handicraft, creation, handwork; see WORKMANSHIP.

handkerchief *n.* kerchief, rag*, hanky*; see TOWEL.

handle *n.* 1 [A holder] handhold, hilt, grasp, crank, knob, stem, grip, arm; see also HOLDER. 2 [*A title] nickname, designation, moniker*; see NAME 1, TITLE 3. —**fly off the handle** become angry, lose one's temper, blow off steam*; see RAGE 1.

handle *v.* 1 [To deal in] retail, market, offer for sale; see SELL. 2 [To touch] finger, check, examine; see FEEL 1, TOUCH 1. 3 [To do whatever is necessary] manipulate, operate, work; see MANAGE 1.

handling *n.* treatment, approach, styling; see MANAGEMENT.

handmade *a.* made by hand, handicraft, handcrafted; see HOMEMADE.

hand'maid'en *n.* [Archaic] a woman or girl servant Also **hand'maid'**

hand'-me-down' *n.* [Colloq.] a used garment, etc. passed on to one

hand'out' *n.* **1** a gift of food, clothing, etc., as to a beggar **2** a leaflet handed out **3** an official news release

hand'pick' *vt.* **1** to pick by hand **2** to choose with care or for a purpose

hand'rail' *n.* a rail serving as a guard or support, as along a staircase

hand'set' *n.* a telephone mouthpiece and receiver in a single unit

hand'shake' *n.* a gripping of each other's hand in greeting, agreement, etc.

hands'-off' *adj.* designating or of a policy, etc. of not interfering

hand·some (han'səm, hand'-) *adj.* [orig., easily handled] **1** considerable **2** generous; gracious **3** good-looking, esp. in a manly or impressive way

hand'spring' *n.* a spring in which one turns over in mid-air with one or both hands touching the ground

hand'-to-hand' *adj.* at close quarters: said of fighting

hand'-to-mouth' *adj.* consuming all that is obtained

hand'work' *n.* work done by hand

hand'writ'ing *n.* **1** writing done by hand, as with a pen **2** a style of such writing —**hand'writ'ten** *adj.*

hand'y *adj.* **-i·er, -i·est** **1** close at hand; easily reached **2** easily used; convenient **3** clever with the hands —**hand'i·ly** *adv.* —**hand'i·ness** *n.*

hand'y·man *n., pl.* **-men'** a man who does odd jobs

hang (haŋ) *vt.* **hung, hang'ing;** for vt. 3 & vi. 5, **hanged** is preferred pt. & pp. [OE *hangian*] **1** to attach from above with no support from below; suspend **2** to attach (a door, etc.) so as to permit free motion at the point of attachment **3** to kill by suspending from a rope about the neck **4** to attach (wallpaper, etc.) to walls **5** to let (one's head) droop downward **6** to deadlock (a jury) —*vi.* **1** to be attached above with no support from below **2** to hover in the air **3** to swing freely **4** to fall or drape, as cloth **5** to die by hanging **6** to droop; bend —*n.* the way a thing hangs —**get (or have) the hang of 1** to learn (or have) the knack of **2** to understand the meaning or idea of —**hang around (or about)** [Colloq.] to loiter around —**hang back (or off)** to be reluctant, as from shyness —**hang in (there)** [Colloq.] to persevere —**hang loose** [Slang] to be relaxed, easygoing, etc. —**hang on 1** to go on; persevere **2** to depend on **3** to listen attentively to —**hang out** [Slang] to spend much time —**hang up 1** to put on a hanger, hook, etc. **2** to end a telephone call by replacing the receiver **3** to delay

hangar (haŋ'ər) *n.* [Fr] a repair shed or shelter for aircraft

hang'dog' *adj.* abject or ashamed

hang'er *n.* **1** one who hangs things **2** that on which something is hung

hang gliding the sport of gliding through the air while hanging suspended by a harness from a large type of kite (**hang glider**)

hang'ing *adj.* that hangs —*n.* **1** a killing by hanging **2** something hung on a wall, etc., as a drapery

hang'man (-mən) *n., pl.* **-men** one who hangs convicted criminals

hang'nail' *n.* [OE *angnægl*, a corn (on the toe)] a bit of torn skin hanging next to a fingernail

hang'o'ver *n.* **1** a survival **2** headache, nausea, etc. as an aftereffect of drinking much alcoholic liquor

hang'-up' *n.* [Slang] an emotional or psychological problem, difficulty, etc.

hank (haŋk) *n.* [prob. < Scand] a skein of yarn or thread

han·ker (haŋ'kər) *vi.* [prob. < Du] to long or yearn (*for*) —**han'ker·ing** *n.*

hanky-panky (haŋ'kē paŋ'kē) *n.* [altered < HOCUS-POCUS] [Colloq.] trickery or deception

han·som (cab) (han'səm) [after J. A. *Hansom* (1803-82), Eng inventor] a two-wheeled covered carriage pulled by one horse, with the driver's seat above and behind

Ha·nuka (khä'noo kä', -kə; hä'-) *n.* [< Heb *chanuka*, lit., dedication] an 8-day Jewish festival commemorating the rededication of the Temple Also **Ha'nuk·kah'**

hap (hap) *n.* [< ON *happ*] luck

hap·haz·ard (hap'haz'ərd) *adj.* not planned; random —*adv.* by chance

hap·less (hap'lis) *adj.* unlucky

hap·loid (hap'loid') *adj. Biol.* having the full number of chromosomes normally occurring in the mature germ cell or half the number of the usual somatic cell —*n.* a haploid cell or gamete

hap'ly *adv.* [Archaic] by chance

hap·pen (hap'ən) *vi.* [ME *happenen*] **1** to take place; occur **2** to be, occur, or come by chance **3** to have the luck or occasion [I *happened* to see it] —**happen on (or upon)** to meet or find by chance

hap'pen·ing *n.* occurrence; event

hap'pen·stance' (-stans') *n.* [Colloq.] chance or accidental happening

happi coat (hap'ē) [< Jpn + COAT] a short, light Japanese coat worn with a sash

hand-me-down *n.* secondhand article, discard; old clothes, etc.; see SECONDHAND.

handout *n.* contribution, donation, free meal; see GIFT 1, GRANT.

handsome *a.* smart, impressive, stately, good-looking, attractive, athletic, personable, strong, muscular, robust, well-dressed, slick*; see also BEAUTIFUL.—*Ant.* UGLY, homely, unsightly.

hand-to-hand *a.* face-to-face, facing, close; see NEAR 1.

handwriting *n.* penmanship, hand, writing, cursive, script, longhand, scrawl, scribble, manuscript, a style of writing, calligraphy, scratching*, chicken scratch*.

handwritten *a.* in writing, in long hand, not typed; see REPRODUCED, WRITTEN 2.

handy *a.* **1** [Near] nearby, at hand, close by; see NEAR 1. **2** [Useful] beneficial, advantageous, gainful; see HELPFUL 1, PROFITABLE, USABLE.

hang *v.* **1** [To suspend] dangle, attach, drape, hook up, hang up, nail on the wall, put on a clothesline, fix, pin up, tack up, drape on the wall, fasten up; see also FASTEN.—*Ant.* DROP, throw down, let fall. **2** [To be suspended] overhang, wave, flap, be loose, droop, flop, be in midair, swing, dangle, be fastened, hover, stay up.—*Ant.* FALL, come down, drop. **3** [To kill by hanging] execute,

lynch, hand by the neck until dead; see KILL 1. —**hang around*** associate with, get along with, have relations with; see KEEP COMPANY (WITH). —**hang on** persist, remain, continue; see ENDURE 1, 2. —**hang out*** loiter, spend time, haunt; see VISIT. —**hang up** finish a telephone call, ring off, hang up the phone; see END 1.

hanged *a.* lynched, strung up, brought to the gallows; see EXECUTED 2.

hanger *n.* coat hook, nail, peg, coat hanger, clothes hanger, holder, clothes rod, wire hanger, collapsible hanger; see also HOLDER.

hanging *a.* dangling, swaying, swinging, overhanging, projecting, suspended, fastened to, pendulous, drooping.

hangover *n.* nausea, sickness, headache; see DRUNKENNESS, ILLNESS 1.

hang-up* *n.* problem, predicament, disturbance; see DIFFICULTY 1, 2.

haphazard *a.* offhand, casual, random, careless, slipshod, incidental, unthinking, unconscious, uncoordinated, reckless, unconcerned, unpremeditated, loose, indiscriminate, unrestricted, irregular, blind, purposeless, unplanned, hit-or-miss, willy-nilly; see also AIMLESS.—*Ant.* CAREFUL, studied, planned.

happen *v.* **1** [To be by chance] come up, come about, turn up, crop up,

chance, occur unexpectedly, come face to face with, befall, hit one like a ton of bricks*, be just one's luck. **2** [To occur] take place, come to pass, arrive, ensue, befall, come after, arise, take effect, come into existence, recur, come into being, spring, proceed, follow, come about, fall, repeat, appear, go on, become a fact, turn out, become known, be found, come to mind, transpire, come off; see also RESULT.

happening *n.* incident, affair, accident; see EVENT.

happily *a.* joyously, gladly, joyfully, cheerily, gaily, laughingly, smilingly, jovially, merrily, brightly, vivaciously, hilariously, with pleasure, peacefully, blissfully, cheerfully, gleefully, playfully, heartily, lightheartedly, lightly, to one's delight, optimistically, with all one's heart, with relish, with good will, in a happy manner, with zeal, with good grace, zestfully, with open arms, sincerely, willingly, freely, graciously, tactfully, lovingly, agreeably.—*Ant.* SADLY, morosely, dejectedly.

happiness *n.* mirth, merrymaking, cheer, merriment, joyousness, vivacity, laughter, delight, gladness, good spirits, hilarity, playfulness, exuberance, gaiety, cheefulness, good will, rejoicing, exhilaration, glee, geniality, good cheer, lightheartedness, joy; see also JOY.

happy (hap′ē) *adj.* **-pier, -pi·est** ⟦< HAP⟧ **1** lucky; fortunate **2** having, showing, or causing great pleasure or joy **3** suitable and clever; apt —**hap′pily** *adv.* —**hap′pi·ness** *n.*

hap′py-go-luck′y *adj.* easygoing

happy hour a time, as in the late afternoon, when a bar features drinks at reduced prices

hara-kiri (här′ə kir′ē) *n.* ⟦Jpn < *hara*, belly + *kiri*, a cutting⟧ ritual suicide by cutting the abdomen

ha·rangue (hə raŋ′) *n.* ⟦< OIt *aringo*, site for public assemblies⟧ a long, blustering speech; tirade — *vi., vt.* **-rangued′, -rangu′ing** to speak or address in a harangue

har·ass (hə ras′, har′əs) *vt.* ⟦< OFr *harer*, to set a dog on⟧ **1** to worry or torment **2** to trouble by repeated raids or attacks —**har·ass′ment** *n.*

har·bin·ger (här′bin jər) *n.* ⟦< OFr *herberge*, a shelter⟧ a forerunner; herald

har·bor (här′bər) *n.* ⟦< OE *here*, army + *beorg*, shelter⟧ **1** a shelter **2** a protected inlet for anchoring ships; port — *vt.* **1** to shelter or house **2** to hold in the mind /to *harbor* envy/ — *vi.* to take shelter Brit. sp. **har′bour**

hard (härd) *adj.* ⟦OE *heard*⟧ **1** firm and unyielding to the touch; solid and compact **2** powerful /a *hard* blow/ **3** difficult to do, understand, or deal with **4** *a)* unfeeling /a *hard* heart/ *b)* unfriendly /*hard* feelings/ **5** harsh; severe **6** having mineral salts that interfere with lathering **7** energetic /a *hard* worker/ **8** containing much alcohol /*hard* liquor/ **9** addictive and harmful /heroin is a *hard* drug/ **10** *a)* of currency, not credit (said of money) *b)* readily accepted as foreign exchange /a *hard* currency/ — *adv.* **1** energetically /work *hard*/ **2** with strength /hit *hard*/ **3** with difficulty /*hard*-earned/ **4** close; near /we live *hard* by/ **5** so as to be solid /frozen *hard*/ **6** sharply /turn *hard* right/ —**hard and fast** invariable; strict — **hard of hearing** partially deaf —**hard up** [Colloq.] in great need of money —**hard′ness** *n.*

hard′back′ *n.* a hardcover book

hard′ball′ *n.* BASEBALL

hard′-bit′ten *adj.* tough; dogged

hard′-boiled′ *adj.* **1** boiled until solid: said of eggs **2** [Colloq.] unfeeling; tough; callous

hard copy a computer printout, often supplied along with or instead of a video screen display

hard′-core′ *adj.* absolute; unqualified

hard′cov′er *adj.* designating any book bound in a stiff cover

harden (härd′n) *vt., vi.* to make or become hard —**hard′ener** *n.*

hard hat **1** a protective helmet worn by construction workers, miners, etc. **2** [Slang] such a worker

hard′head′ed *adj.* **1** shrewd and unsentimental; practical **2** stubborn

hard′heart′ed *adj.* unfeeling; cruel

har·di·hood (här′dē hood′) *n.* boldness

hard′-line′ *adj.* aggressive; unyielding, as in politics, etc.

hard′-lin′er (-ər) *n.* one who takes a hard-line position

hardly (härd′lē) *adv.* **1** only just; scarcely **2** probably not; not likely

hard′-nosed′ *adj.* [Colloq.] tough and stubborn or shrewd

hard·scrab·ble (härd′skrab′əl) *adj.* producing or earning only a very small amount; barren /a *hardscrabble* farm, life, etc./

hard sell high-pressure salesmanship

hard′ship′ *n.* a thing hard to bear, as poverty, pain, etc.

hard′stand′ *n.* a paved area for parking aircraft or other vehicles

hard′tack′ (-tak′) *n.* unleavened bread made in hard, large wafers

hard′top′ *n.* an automobile like a sedan but having no post between the front and rear windows

hard′ware′ (-wer′) *n.* **1** articles made of metals, as tools, nails, fittings, etc. **2** the mechanical, magnetic, and electronic devices of a computer

hard′wood′ *n.* **1** any tough, heavy timber with a compact texture **2** the wood of any tree with broad, flat leaves, as the oak, maple, etc.

hardy (här′dē) *adj.* **-dier, -di·est** ⟦< OFr *hardir*, to make bold⟧ **1** bold and resolute **2** robust; vigorous —**har′dily** *adv.* —**har′di·ness** *n.*

hare (her) *n.* ⟦OE *hara*⟧ a mammal related to and resembling the rabbit

hare′brained′ *adj.* giddy, rash, etc.

Hare Krishna (hä′rē) ⟦< Hindi⟧ **1** a cult, founded in the U.S. in 1966, involving devotion to Krishna **2** a member of this cult

hare′lip′ *n.* a congenital deformity consisting of a cleft of the upper lip

ha·rem (her′əm, har′-) *n.* ⟦Ar *harim*, lit., prohibited (place)⟧ **1** that part of a Muslim household in which the women live **2** the women in a harem

hark (härk) *vi.* ⟦ME *herkien*⟧ to listen carefully: usually in the imperative —**hark back** to go back in thought or speech

harken (här′kən) *vi.* HEARKEN

▰▰▰ THESAURUS ▰▰▰

happy *a.* joyous, joyful, merry, mirthful, glad, gleeful, delighted, cheerful, gay, laughing, contented, genial, satisfied, enraptured, congenial, cherry, jolly, hilarious, sparkling, enchanted, transported, rejoicing, blissful, jovial, delightful, delirious, exhilarated, pleased, gratified, peaceful, comfortable, intoxicated, debonair, light, bright, ecstatic, charmed, pleasant, hearty, overjoyed, lighthearted, radiant, vivacious, sunny, smiling, content, animated, lively, spirited, exuberant, good-humored, elated, jubilant, rollicking, playful, thrilled, fun-loving, carefree, at peace, in good spirits, in high spirits, happy as a lark, in ecstasy, beside oneself, bubbling over, tickled pink, tickled to death, tickled silly, happy-go-lucky, in seventh heaven*.—Ant.* SAD, sorrowful, melancholy.

happy-go-lucky *a.* cheerful, easygoing, unconcerned; see IRRESPONSIBLE.

harass *v.* tease, vex, irritate; see BOTHER 2.

harbinger *n.* indication, sign, signal; see MESSENGER, SIGNAL.

harbor *n.* port, pier, inlet; see DOCK.

harbor *v.* **1** [To protect] shelter, provide refuge, secure; see DEFEND 2. **2** [To consider] entertain, cherish, regard; see CONSIDER.

hard *a.* **1** [Compact] unyielding, thick, solid, heavy, strong, impermeable, tough, tempered, hardened, dense; see also FIRM 2. **2** [Difficult] arduous, tricky, impossible, trying,

tedious, complex, abstract, puzzling, troublesome, laborious; see also DIFFICULT 1, 2. **3** [Cruel] perverse, unrelenting, vengeful; see CRUEL. **4** [Severe] harsh, exacting, grim; see SEVERE 1, 2. **5** [Alcoholic] intoxicating, inebriating, stimulating; see STRONG 4. **6** [With difficulty] strenuously, laboriously, with great effort; see CAREFULLY 1, VIGOROUSLY. —**be hard on** treat severely, be harsh toward, be painful to; see ABUSE. —**hard of hearing** almost deaf, having a hearing problem, in need of a hearing aid; see DEAF. —**hard up** in trouble, poverty-stricken, in the lower income brackets; see POOR 1.

hard-core *a.* dedicated, steadfast, unwavering; see FAITHFUL.

harden *v.* steel, temper, solidify, precipitate, crystallize, freeze, coagulate, clot, granulate, make firm, make compact, make tight, make hard, petrify, starch, cure, bake, dry, flatten, cement, compact, concentrate, sun, fire, fossilize, vulcanize, toughen, concrete, encrust; see also STIFFEN.—*Ant.* SOFTEN, unloose, melt.

hardened *a.* **1** [Made hard] compacted, stiffened, stiff; see FIRM 2. **2** [Inured to labor or hardship] accustomed, conditioned, tough; see HABITUAL.

hardening *n.* thickening, crystallization, setting; see SOLIDIFICATION.

hardheaded *a.* willful, stubborn, headstrong; see STUBBORN.

hardhearted *a.* cold, unfeeling,

heartless; see CRUEL.

hardly *a.* scarcely, barely, just, merely, imperceptibly, not noticeably, gradually, not markedly, no more than, not likely, not a bit, almost not, only just, with difficulty, with trouble, by a narrow margin, not by a great deal, seldom, almost not at all, but just, in no manner, by no means, little, infrequently, somewhat, not quite, here and there, simply, not much, rarely, slightly, sparsely, not often, once in a blue moon*, by the skin of one's teeth*; see also ONLY.—*Ant.* EASILY, without difficulty, readily.

hard-nosed *a.* stubborn, unyielding, hardheaded; see OBSTINATE, RESOLUTE.

hardship *n.* trial, sorrow, worry; see DIFFICULTY 2, GRIEF.

hardware *n.* domestic appliances, fixtures, metal manufactures, casting, plumbing, metalware, implements, tools, housewares, fittings, aluminum ware, cutlery, house furnishings, kitchenware, household utensils, equipment.

hardy *a.* tough, toughened, in good shape, in good condition, hardened, resistant, solid, staunch, seasoned, capable of endurance, able-bodied, physically fit, well-equipped, acclimatized, rugged, mighty, well, fit, robust, hearty, sound, fresh, hale, brawny, able, vigorous, powerful, firm, sturdy, solid, substantial; see also STRONG.—*Ant.* WEAK, unaccustomed, unhabituated.

Har·le·quin (här′li kwin, -kin) a comic character in panto-mime, who wears a mask and diamond-patterned tights of many colors — *n.* [h-] a clown

har·lot (här′lət) *n.* [< OFr, rogue] PROSTITUTE —**har′lotry** (-lə trē) *n.*

harm (härm) *n.* [OE *hearm*] hurt; injury; damage — *vt.* to do harm to

harm′ful *adj.* causing harm; hurtful —**harm′fully** *adv.*

harm′less *adj.* causing no harm —**harm′lessly** *adv.*

har·mon·ic (här män′ik) *adj.* of or in harmony — *n. Music* a pure tone making up a composite tone —**har·mon′i·cally** *adv.*

har·mon′i·ca (-i kə) *n.* a small wind instrument with a series of metal reeds that produce tones when air is blown or sucked across them

har·mo·ni·ous (här mō′nē əs) *adj.* **1** having parts arranged in an orderly or pleasing way **2** having similar ideas, interests, etc. **3** having musical tones combined to give a pleasing effect —**har·mo′ni·ously** *adv.*

har·mo·nize (här′mə nīz′) *vi.* **-nized′, -niz′ing 1** to be in harmony **2** to sing in harmony — *vt.* to make harmonious —**har′mo·ni·za′tion** *n.* —**har′mo·niz′er** *n.*

har·mo·ny (här′mə nē) *n., pl.* **-nies** [< Gr *harmos*, a fit-ting] **1** pleasing arrangement of parts in color, size, etc. **2** agreement in action, ideas, etc.; friendly relations **3** the pleasing combination of tones in a chord

har·ness (här′nis) *n.* [< OFr *harneis*, armor] **1** the leather straps and metal pieces by which a horse, etc. is fastened to a vehicle, etc. **2** something like a harness — *vt.* **1** to put a harness on **2** to control so as to use the power of

harp (härp) *n.* [OE *hearpe*] a musical instrument with strings stretched vertically in an open, triangular frame and played by plucking — *vi.* **1** to play a harp **2** to persist in talking or writing tediously (*on* or *upon* something) —**harp′ist** *n.*

har·poon (här pōōn′) *n.* [< ON *harpa*, to squeeze] a barbed spear with a line attached to it, used for spearing whales, etc. — *vt.* to strike with a harpoon

harp·si·chord (härp′si kôrd′) *n.* [< It *arpa*, harp + *corda*, CORD] a pianolike keyboard instrument whose strings are plucked rather than struck

Harpy (här′pē) *n., pl.* **-pies** [< Gr *harpazein*, to snatch] **1** *Gr. Myth.* any of several monsters, part woman and part bird **2** [h-] *a)* a greedy person *b)* a shrewish woman

har·ri·dan (har′i dən) *n.* [< Fr *haridelle*, worn-out horse] a nasty, bad-tempered old woman

har·ri·er (har′ē ər) *n.* [< HARE + -IER] **1** a small hound used for hunting hares **2** a cross-country runner

har·row (har′ō) *n.* [prob. < ON] a heavy frame with spikes or disks, used for breaking up and leveling plowed ground, etc. — *vt.* **1** to draw a harrow over (land) **2** to cause mental distress to —**har′row·ing** *adj.*

harry (har′ē) *vt.* **-ried, -ry·ing** [< OE *here*, army] **1** to raid and ravage or rob **2** to torment or worry

harsh (härsh) *adj.* [ME *harsk*] **1** unpleasantly rough to the eye, ear, taste, or touch **2** offensive to the mind or feelings **3** cruel or severe —**harsh′ly** *adv.* —**harsh′ness** *n.*

hart (härt) *n.* [OE *heorot*] a full-grown, male European red deer

har·te·beest (här′tə bēst′, härt′bēst′) *n.* [obs. Afrik < *harte*, hart + *beest*, beast] a large African antelope with long horns curved backward

harum-scarum (her′əm sker′əm) *adj.* [< ?] reckless or irresponsible — *adv.* in a harum-scarum way

har·vest (här′vist) *n.* [OE *hærfest*] **1** the time of the year when grain, fruit, etc. are gathered in **2** a season's crop **3** the gathering in of a crop **4** the outcome of any effort — *vt., vi.* to gather in (a crop, etc.) —**har′vester** *n.*

has (haz; *before* "to" has) *vt.* 3d *pers. sing., pres. indic., of* HAVE

has′-been′ *n.* [Colloq.] a person or thing whose popularity is past

hash (hash) *vt.* [< Fr *hacher*, to chop] to chop up (meat or vegetables) for cooking — *n.* **1** a chopped mixture of cooked meat and vegetables, usually baked **2** a mixture **3** a muddle; mess **4** [Slang] hashish —**hash out** [Colloq.] to settle by long discussion —**hash over** [Colloq.] to discuss at length

hash·ish (hash′ēsh′, -ish) *n.* [Ar *hashīsh*, dried hemp] a narcotic and intoxicant made from hemp

hasp (hasp, häsp) *n.* [OE *hæsp*] a hinged fastening for a door, etc.; esp., a metal piece fitted over a staple and fastened as by a bolt or padlock

has·sle (has′əl) *n.* [< ?] [Colloq.] **1** a heated argument; squabble **2** a troublesome situation — *vi.* **-sled, -sling** [Colloq.] to have a hassle — *vt.* [Slang] to annoy, harass, etc.

has·sock (has′ək) *n.* [OE *hassuc*, (clump of) coarse grass] a firm cushion used as a footstool or seat

hast (hast) *vt.* archaic 2d *pers. sing., pres. indic., of* HAVE: used with *thou*

haste (hāst) *n.* [OFr] quickness of motion; rapidity — *vt., vi.* **hast′ed, hast′ing** [Rare] HASTEN —**make haste** to hurry

---

THESAURUS

harm *n.* **1** [Injury] hurt, infliction, impairment; see INJURY. **2** [Evil] wickedness, outrage, foul play; see ABUSE, EVIL 1, WRONG.

harm *v.* injure, wreck, cripple; see HURT.

harmed *a.* damaged, injured, wounded; see HURT.

harmful *a.* injurious, detrimental, hurtful, noxious, evil, mischievous, ruinous, adverse, sinister, subversive, incendiary, virulent, cataclysmic, corroding, toxic, baleful, painful, wounding, crippling, bad, malicious, malignant, sinful, pernicious, unwholesome, corrupting, menacing, dire, prejudicial, damaging, corrupt, vicious, insidious, treacherous, cata-strophic, disastrous, wild, murder-ous, destructive, unhealthy, killing, fatal, mortal, serious, dangerous, fraught with evil, doing harm, doing evil, painful, sore, distressing, dia-bolic, brutal, unhealthful, satanic, grievous, lethal, venomous, cruel, unfortunate, disadvantageous, feloni-ous, objectionable, fiendish, unlucky, malign, devilish, corrosive.

harmless *a.* pure, innocent, painless, powerless, controllable, manageable, safe, sure, reliable, trustworthy, sani-tary, germproof, sound, sterile, dis-armed.—*Ant.* HARMFUL, injurious, poisonous.

harmonica *n.* mouth organ, har-monicon, mouth harp; see MUSICAL INSTRUMENT.

harmonious *a.* **1** [Harmonic] melo-dious, tuneful, musical, rhythmical, melodic, symphonic, in tune, in uni-son. **2** [Congruous] agreeable to, cor-responding, suitable, adapted, similar, like, peaceful, cooperative, in step, in accordance with, in concord with, in favor with, in harmony with, on a footing with, friendly, conform-ing, well-matched, evenly balanced, symmetrical, congruent; see also FIT.—*Ant.* OPPOSED, incongruous, incompatible.

harmonize *v.* blend, arrange, put to harmony, adapt, set, orchestrate, tune, sing a duet, sing in harmony.

harmony *n.* **1** [Musical concord] chord, consonance, accord, sym-phony, harmonics, counterpoint, concert, music, chorus, blending, unity, accordance, chime, unison, overtone, musical pattern, musical blend. **2** [Social concord] compat-ibility, equanimity, unanimity; see AGREEMENT 1, PEACE 2. **3** [Musical composition] melody, piece, arrange-ment; see COMPOSITION, MUSIC 1.

harness *n.* tackle, gear, yoke, appa-ratus, bridle, rigging, fittings; see also EQUIPMENT.

harness *v.* fetter, saddle, yoke, outfit, bridle, hold in leash, hitch up, con-trol, limit, cinch, strap, collar, put in harness, rig up, rig out, tie, secure, rein in, curb, check, constrain.

harp *n.* lyre, multi-stringed instru-ment, claviharp; see MUSICAL INSTRU-MENT.

harp on *v.* repeat, pester, nag; see COMPLAIN, TALK 1.

harsh *a.* discordant, jangling, cacophonous, grating, rusty, disso-nant, assonant, strident, creaking, clashing, sharp, jarring, jangled, clamorous, cracked, hoarse, out of tune, unmelodious, rasping, screech-ing, earsplitting, disturbing, noisy, flat, sour, out of key, tuneless, unmu-sical, off-key; see also SHRILL.

harshly *a.* sternly, powerfully, grimly; see BRUTALLY, FIRMLY 2, LOUDLY, SERIOUSLY 1, 2.

harshness *n.* crudity, brutality, roughness; see ANGER, CRUELTY, TYR-ANNY.

harvest *n.* reaping, yield, crop; see CROP, FRUIT, GRAIN 1, PRODUCE, VEG-ETABLE.

harvest *v.* gather, accumulate, pile up, collect, garner, crop, cut, pluck, pick, cull, take in, draw in, glean, gather in the harvest, hoard, mow.—*Ant.* SOW, plant, seed.

hash *n.* ground meat and vegetables, leftovers, casserole; see MEAT, STEW.

hash over* *v.* debate, argue about, review; see DISCUSS.

hassle* *n.* quarrel, squabble, row; see DISPUTE.

hassle* *v.* bother, annoy, harass; see BOTHER 2.

haste *n.* hurry, scramble, bustle, scurry, precipitation, flurry, hurly-burly, impetuosity, rashness, dis-patch, impetuousness, foolhardiness, want of caution, hustling, press,

has·ten (hās'ən) *vt.* to cause to be or come faster; speed up — *vi.* to move or act swiftly; hurry

hasty (hās'tē) *adj.* **-i·er, -i·est** **1** done with haste; hurried **2** done, made, or acting too quickly or rashly —**hast'i·ly** *adv.* —**hast'i·ness** *n.*

hat (hat) *n.* [OE *hætt*] a head covering, usually with a brim and a crown —**pass the hat** to take up a collection —**talk through one's hat** [Colloq.] to talk nonsense — **throw one's hat into the ring** to enter a contest, esp. one for political office —**under one's hat** [Colloq.] strictly confidential

hatch¹ (hach) *vt.* [ME *hacchen*] **1** to bring forth (young) from (an egg or eggs) **2** to contrive (a plan, plot, etc.) — *vi.* **1** to bring forth young: said of eggs **2** to emerge from the egg

hatch² (hach) *n.* [OE *hæcc*, grating] **1** HATCHWAY **2** a lid for a hatchway

hatch³ (hach) *vt.* [< OFr *hache*, an ax] to mark or engrave with fine, crossed or parallel lines —**hatch'ing** *n.*

hatch'back' *n.* [HATCH² + BACK] an automobile with a rear that swings up, giving wide entry to a storage area

hat'check' *adj.* of or working in a checkroom for hats, coats, etc.

hatch'er·y *n., pl.* **-ies** a place for hatching eggs, esp. of fish or poultry

hatchet (hach'it) *n.* [< OFr *hache*, an ax] a small ax with a short handle —**bury the hatchet** to make peace

hatchet job [Colloq.] a biased, malicious attack on another's character

hatch'way' *n.* an opening in a ship's deck, or in a floor or roof

hate (hāt) *vt.* **hat'ed, hat'ing** [OE *hatian*] **1** to have strong dislike or ill will for **2** to wish to avoid [to hate fights] — *vi.* to feel hatred — *n.* **1** a strong feeling of dislike or ill will **2** a person or thing hated —**hat'er** *n.*

hate'ful *adj.* deserving hate —**hate'fully** *adv.* —**hate'ful·ness** *n.*

hath (hath) *vt.* archaic 3d pers. sing., pres. indic., of HAVE

ha·tred (hā'trid) *n.* strong dislike or ill will; hate

hat·ter (hat'ər) *n.* one who makes, sells, or cleans men's hats

hau·berk (hô'bərk) *n.* [< Frankish *hals*, neck + *bergan*, to protect] a medieval coat of armor, usually of chain mail

haughty (hôt'ē) *adj.* **-tier, -ti·est** [< OFr *haut*, high] having or showing great pride in oneself and contempt for others; arrogant —**haugh'tily** *adv.* —**haugh'ti·ness** *n.*

haul (hôl) *vt.* [< OFr *haler*] **1** to move by pulling; drag **2** to transport by wagon, truck, etc. — *n.* **1** the act of hauling; pull **2** the amount gained, caught, etc. at one time **3** the distance over which something is transported —**haul off** [Colloq.] to draw the arm back before hitting —**in (or over) the long haul** over a long period of time

haunch (hônch, hänch) *n.* [< OFr *hanche* < Gmc] **1** the hip, buttock, and upper thigh together **2** an animal's loin and leg together

haunt (hônt) *vt.* [< OFr *hanter*, to frequent] **1** to visit often or continually **2** to recur repeatedly to [haunted by memories] — *n.* a place often visited

haunt'ed *adj.* supposedly frequented by ghosts [a haunted house]

haunt'ing *adj.* often recurring to the mind; not easily forgotten

hau·teur (hō tur'; *Fr* ō tër') *n.* [Fr < *haut*, high] disdainful pride; haughtiness

have (hav; *before "to"* haf) *vt.* **had, hav'ing** [OE *habban*] **1** to hold; own; possess [to have money, a week has 7 days] **2** to experience [have a good time] **3** to hold mentally [to have an idea] **4** to state [so rumor has it] **5** to get, take, consume, etc. [have a drink] **6** to bear or beget (offspring) **7** to engage in [to have a fight] **8** to cause to; cause to be [have her leave] **9** to permit; tolerate [I won't have this noise!] **10** [Colloq.] *a)* to hold at a disadvantage *b)* to deceive; cheat *Have* is used as an auxiliary to express completed action (Ex.: I *had* left) and with infinitives to express obligation or necessity (Ex.: we *have* to go). *Have got* often replaces *have. Have* is conjugated in the present indicative: (I) *have,* (he, she, it) *has,* (we, you, they) *have* — *n.* a wealthy person or nation —**have it out** to settle an issue by fighting or discussion —**have on** to be wearing

---

■■■ THESAURUS ■■■

recklessness, rush, hastiness, carelessness, irrationality, rashness, giddiness, impatience, heedlessness, plunge, testiness, excitation, outburst, abruptness, anticipation.— *Ant.* PRUDENCE, caution, attention. —**in haste** hastening, in a hurry, moving fast; see FAST. —**make haste** hurry, act quickly, speed up; see HURRY 1.

hasten *v.* **1** [To make haste] rush, fly, sprint; see HURRY 1. **2** [To expedite] accelerate, speed up, advance, move up, quicken, stimulate, hurry up, push, make short work of, urge, goad, press, agitate, push ahead, put into action, get started, give a start, drive on, set in motion, take in hand, blast off, gear up; see also SPEED.—*Ant.* DELAY, defer, put off.

hastily *a.* **1** [Rapidly] hurriedly, speedily, nimbly; see QUICKLY. **2** [Carelessly] thoughtlessly, recklessly, rashly; see CARELESSLY.

hasty *a.* **1** [Hurried] quick, speedy, swift; see FAST 1. **2** [Careless] illadvised, precipitate, foolhardy; see CARELESS, RASH.

hat *n.* headgear, millinery, headpiece, helmet, chapeau, bonnet. *Hatlike coverings include the following—for men:* cap, yarmulke, derby, straw hat, felt hat, sombrero, cowboy hat, top hat, bowler, panama, fedora, beret, turban; *for women:* hood, snood, cowl, kerchief, beret, bandanna, cloche, boater, bonnet, turban, pillbox, scarf, babushka. — **take one's hat off to** salute, cheer, congratulate; see PRAISE 1. —**talk through one's hat*** chatter, talk nonsense, make foolish statements; see BABBLE. —**throw one's hat into the ring** enter a contest, run for office, enter politics; see CAMPAIGN.

—**under one's hat*** confidential, private, hidden; see SECRET 1.

hatch¹ *v.* bear, lay eggs, give birth; see PRODUCE 1.

hate *n.* ill will, animosity, enmity; see HATRED.

hate *v.* **1** [To detest] abhor, abominate, loathe, scorn, despise, have an aversion toward, look at with loathing, spit upon, curse, dislike intensely, shudder at, not care for, have enough of, be repelled by, feel repulsion for, have no use for, dislike to, bear a grudge against, shun, denounce, resent, curse, be sick of, be tired of, reject, revolt against, deride, have no stomach for, disfavor, look down upon, hold in contempt, be disgusted with, view with horror, be down on*, have it in for*.—*Ant.* LOVE, adore, worship. **2** [To dislike; *often used with infinitive or participle*] object to, shudder at, not like; see DISLIKE.

hated *a.* despised, loathed, abhorred, detested, disliked, cursed, unpopular, avoided, shunned, out of favor, condemned; see also UNDESIRABLE.

hateful *a.* odious, detestable, repugnant; see OFFENSIVE 2, UNDESIRABLE.

hater *n.* enemy of, racist, antagonist; see BIGOT, ENEMY.

hatred *n.* abhorrence, loathing, rancor, detestation, antipathy, repugnance, repulsion, disgust, contempt, intense dislike, scorn, abomination, distaste, disapproval, horror, hard feelings, displeasure, ill will, bitterness, antagonism, animosity, pique, grudge, malice, malevolence, revulsion, prejudice, spite, revenge, hate, venom, envy, spleen, coldness, distaste, contempt, hostility, alienation, bad blood, chip on one's shoulder*,

grudge; see also ANGER.—*Ant.* DEVOTION, friendship, affection.

haughty *a.* arrogant, disdainful, proud; see EGOTISTIC.

haul *n.* **1** [A pull] tug, lift, wrench; see PULL 1. **2** [The distance something is hauled] trip, voyage, yards; see DISTANCE 3. **3** [*Something obtained, especially loot*] find, spoils, take; see BOOTY.

haul *v.* pull, drag, bring; see DRAW 1.

haunt *v.* **1** [To frequent persistently] habituate, visit often, hang around; see LOITER. **2** [To prey upon] recur in one's mind, obsess, torment, beset, possess, trouble, weigh on one's mind, craze, madden, hound, terrify, plague, vex, harass, prey on, pester, worry, tease, terrorize, frighten, annoy, cause regret, cause sorrow, molest, appall, agitate, drive one nuts*; see also BOTHER 2, DISTURB.

haunted *a.* frequented, visited by, preyed upon; see TROUBLED.

haunting *a.* eerie, unforgettable, seductive; see FRIGHTFUL, REMEMBERED.

have *v.* **1** [To be in possession of] own, possess, keep, retain, guard, use, maintain, control, treasure, keep title to, hold; see also OWN 1. **2** [To be obliged; *used with infinitive*] be compelled to, be forced to, should, ought to, be one's duty to, fall on, be up to, have got to; see also MUST. **3** [To bear] beget, give birth to, bring forth; see PRODUCE 1. **4** [To have sexual intercourse with] seduce, sleep with, deflower; see COPULATE. —**have on** be clothed in, be wearing, try on; see WEAR 1. —**have something on someone** be able to expose, have special knowledge of, be able to control; see CONVICT, KNOW 1.

ha·ven (hā′vən) *n.* [OE *hæfen*] 1 a port 2 any sheltered place; refuge

have-not (hav′nät′) *n.* a person or nation with little or no wealth

hav·er·sack (hav′ər sak′) *n.* [< Ger *habersack*, lit., sack of oats] a canvas bag for rations, etc., worn over one shoulder, as by soldiers or hikers

havoc (hav′ək) *n.* [< OFr *havot*] great destruction and devastation —**play havoc with** to devastate; ruin

haw[1] (hô) *n.* [OE *haga*] 1 the berry of the hawthorn 2 HAWTHORN

haw[2] (hô) *vi.* [echoic] to grope for words Usually in **hem and haw** (see HEM[2])

Ha·wai·ian (hə wī′ən, -yən) *n.* 1 a native or inhabitant of Hawaii 2 the Polynesian language of the Hawaiians —*adj.* of Hawaii, its people, etc.

hawk[1] (hôk) *n.* [OE *hafoc*] 1 a bird of prey with short, rounded wings, a long tail, and a hooked beak and claws 2 an advocate of war

hawk[2] (hôk) *vt.* [< HAWKER] to advertise or peddle (goods) in the streets by shouting

hawk[3] (hôk) *vi., vt.* [echoic] to clear the throat (of) audibly

hawk·er (hôk′ər) *n.* [< Old LowG *hoker*] a peddler or huckster

hawk′-eyed′ (-īd′) *adj.* keen-sighted

haw·ser (hô′zər) *n.* [< OFr *haucier* < L *altus*, high] a large rope used for towing or mooring a ship

haw·thorn (hô′thôrn′) *n.* [< OE *haga*, hedge + THORN] a thorny shrub or small tree of the rose family, with flowers and small, red fruits

hay (hā) *n.* [< OE *hieg*] grass, clover, etc. cut and dried for fodder —*vi.* to mow and dry grass, etc. for hay —**hit the hay** [Slang] to go to bed to sleep

hay′cock′ *n.* a small, conical heap of hay drying in a field

hay fever an acute inflammation of the eyes and respiratory tract: an allergic reaction to some kinds of pollen

hay′loft′ *n.* a loft, or upper story, in a barn or stable, for storing hay

hay′mow′ (-mou′) *n.* 1 a pile of hay in a barn 2 HAYLOFT

hay′stack′ *n.* a large heap of hay piled up outdoors

hay′wire′ *adj.* [Colloq.] 1 out of order; disorganized 2 crazy —**go haywire** [Colloq.] 1 to behave erratically 2 to become crazy

haz·ard (haz′ərd) *n.* [< OFr *hasard*, game of dice] 1 risk; danger 2 an obstacle on a golf course —*vt.* to risk

haz′ard·ous *adj.* risky; dangerous

haze[1] (hāz) *n.* [prob. < HAZY] 1 a thin vapor of fog, smoke, etc. in the air 2 slight vagueness of mind —*vi., vt.* **hazed, haz′ing** to make or become hazy: often with *over*

haze[2] (hāz) *vt.* **hazed, haz′ing** [< ?] to force to do ridiculous or painful things, as in initiation

ha·zel (hā′zəl) *n.* [OE *hæsel*] 1 a shrub or tree of the birch family, with edible nuts 2 a reddish brown —*adj.* light reddish-brown

ha′zel·nut *n.* FILBERT

hazy (hā′zē) *adj.* **-zier, -zi·est** [prob. < OE *hasu*, dusky] 1 somewhat foggy or smoky 2 somewhat vague —**ha′zily** *adv.* —**ha′zi·ness** *n.*

H-bomb (āch′bäm′) *n.* HYDROGEN BOMB

he (hē) *pron., pl. see* THEY [OE] 1 the man, boy, or male animal previously mentioned 2 anyone *[he* who laughs last laughs best] —*n.* a male

He *Chem. symbol for* helium

head (hed) *n.* [OE *heafod*] 1 the part of the body containing the brain, and the jaws, eyes, ears, nose, and mouth 2 the mind; intelligence 3 *pl.* **head** a unit of counting *[ten head of cattle]* 4 the main side of a coin 5 the uppermost part or thing; top 6 the topic or title of a section, chapter, etc. 7 the foremost or projecting part; front 8 the part designed for holding, striking, etc. *[the head of a nail]* 9 the part of a tape recorder that records or plays back the magnetic signals on the tape 10 the membrane across the end of a drum, etc. 11 the source of a river, etc. 12 froth, as on beer 13 a position of leadership or honor 14 a leader, ruler, etc. —*adj.* 1 most important; principal 2 at the top or front 3 striking against the front *[head current]* —*vt.* 1 to be the chief of; command 2 to lead; precede 3 to cause to go in a specified direction —*vi.* to set out; travel *[to head eastward]* —**come to a head** 1 to be about to suppurate, as a boil 2 to culminate, or reach a crisis —**go to one's head** 1 to confuse or intoxicate one 2 to make one vain —**head off** to get ahead of and intercept —**head over heels** deeply; completely —**heads up!** [Colloq.] look out! —**keep (or lose) one's head** to keep (or lose) one's poise, self-control, etc. —**on (or upon) one's head** as one's responsibility or misfortune —**over one's head** 1 too difficult for one to understand 2 to a higher authority —**turn one's head** to make one vain —**head′less** *adj.*

head′ache′ (-āk′) *n.* 1 a continuous pain in the head 2 [Colloq.] a cause of worry, annoyance, or trouble

head′board′ (-bôrd′) *n.* a board that forms the head of a bed, etc.

head cold a common cold with congestion of the nasal passages

head′dress′ *n.* 1 a decorative covering for the head 2 a hairdo; coiffure

-headed (-id) *combining form* having a head or heads *[clear-headed, two-headed]*

head′first′ *adv.* 1 with the head in front; headlong 2 recklessly; rashly

head′gear′ *n.* a hat, cap, etc.

head′hunt′er *n.* 1 a member of any of certain primitive tribes who remove and preserve the heads of slain enemies 2 [Slang] an agent who recruits executives for corporations

▬ THESAURUS ▬

haven *n.* port, harbor, roadstead; see REFUGE 1, SHELTER.

having *a.* owning, possessing, enjoying, commanding, holding, controlling; see also COMMANDING.

havoc *n.* devastation, plunder, ruin; see DESTRUCTION 2.

hawk[1] *n.* 1 [A member of the Accipitridae] bird of prey, osprey, falcon; see BIRD. 2 [A warlike person] militarist, chauvinist, warmonger; see CONSERVATIVE, RADICAL.

hay *n.* fodder, roughage, forage, feed; see also GRASS 1. *Hay includes the following:* red clover, wild hay, timothy, alsike, sweet clover, soybeans, swamp hay, alfalfa, oat hay, millet. —**hit the hay*** go to bed, rest, recline; see SLEEP.

hazard *n.* risk, peril, jeopardy; see DANGER.

hazard *v.* stake, try, guess; see CHANCE, GAMBLE, RISK.

hazardous *a.* perilous, uncertain, precarious; see DANGEROUS.

haze[1] *n.* mist, smog, cloudiness; see FOG.

hazy *a.* cloudy, foggy, murky, misty, unclear, overcast, steaming, screened, filmy, gauzy, vaporous, smoky, dim, dull, indistinct, nebu-

lous, shadowy, dusky, obscure, thick, opaque, frosty, veiled, blurred, semitransparent, blurry, faint; see also DARK 1.—*Ant.* CLEAR, bright, cloudless.

he *pron.* this one, the male, the above-named, the man, the boy, third person, masculine singular.

head *n.* 1 [The skull] brainpan, scalp, crown, headpiece, bean*, noggin*, noodle*. 2 [A leader or supervisor] commander, commanding officer, ruler; see LEADER 2. 3 [The top] summit, peak, crest; see TOP 1. 4 [The beginning] front, start, source; see ORIGIN 2. 5 [An attachment] cap, bottle top, cork; see COVER 1. 6 [*Intelligence] brains, foresight, ingenuity; see JUDGMENT 1. 7 [Drug addict] habitual user of drugs, acidhead*, pothead*; see ADDICT. —**come to a head** culminate, reach a crisis, come to a climax; see CLIMAX. —**get it through one's head** learn, comprehend, see; see UNDERSTAND 1. —**go to one's head** stir mentally, stimulate, intoxicate; see EXCITE. —**hang (or hide) one's head** repent, be sorry, grieve; see REGRET 1. —**head off** block off, interfere with, intervene; see STOP 1.

—**head over heels** entirely, precipitately, unreservedly; see COMPLETELY. —**keep one's head** remain calm, keep one's self-control, hold one's emotions in check; see RESTRAIN. —**lose one's head** become excited, become angry, rave; see RAGE 1. —**make head or tail of** comprehend, apprehend, see; see UNDERSTAND 1. —**one's head off** greatly, extremely, considerably; see MUCH. —**on (or upon) one's head** burdensome, taxing, strenuous; see DIFFICULT 1. —**out of (or off) one's head** crazy, delirious, raving; see INSANE. —**over one's head** incomprehensible, not understandable, hard; see DIFFICULT 2.

head *v.* direct, oversee, supervise; see COMMAND 2, MANAGE 1.

headache *n.* 1 [A pain in the head] migraine, sick headache, neuralgia; see PAIN 2. 2 [*A source of vexation and difficulty] problem, jumble, mess; see DIFFICULTY 1, 2, TROUBLE 1.

headed *a.* in transit, in motion, en route, going, directed, started, aimed, slated for, on the way to, pointed toward, consigned to, on the road to.

head′ing *n.* **1** something forming the head, top, or front **2** the title, topic, etc., as of a chapter **3** the direction in which a ship, plane, etc. is moving

head′land′ *n.* a point of land reaching out into the water; promontory

head′light′ *n.* a light with a reflector and lens, at the front of a vehicle

head′line′ *n.* printed lines at the top of a newspaper article, giving the topic — *vt.* **-lined′, -lin′ing** to give featured billing or publicity to

head′long (-lôn′) *adv., adj.* [ME *hedelinge(s)*] **1** with the head first **2** with uncontrolled speed or force **3** reckless(ly); rash(ly)

head′mas′ter *n.* the principal of a private school —**head′mis′tress** *n.fem.*

head′-on′ *adj., adv.* with the head or front foremost [a *head-on* collision]

head′phone′ *n.* [*often pl.*] a listening device for a radio, stereo, etc. worn over the head to position its tiny speakers over the ears

head′pin′ *n.* the pin at the front of a triangle of bowling pins

head′quarters (hed′kwôrt′ərz) *n.pl.* [*often with sing. v.*] **1** the main office, or center of operations, of one in command, as in an army **2** the main office in any organization

head′rest′ *n.* a support for the head

head′room′ *n.* space overhead, as in a doorway, tunnel, etc.

head start an early start or other competitive advantage

head′stone′ *n.* a stone marker placed at the head of a grave

head′strong′ *adj.* determined to do as one pleases

head′wa′ters *n.pl.* the small streams that are the sources of a river

head′way′ *n.* **1** forward motion **2** progress or success

heady (hed′ē) *adj.* **-i·er, -i·est** **1** impetuous; rash **2** intoxicating [*heady* wine] —**head′i·ness** *n.*

heal (hēl) *vt., vi.* [OE *hælan*] **1** to make or become well or healthy again **2** to cure (a disease) or mend, as a wound —**heal′er** *n.*

health (helth) *n.* [OE *hælth*] **1** physical and mental well-being; freedom from disease, etc. **2** condition of body or mind [poor *health*] **3** a wish for one's health and happiness, as in a toast **4** soundness, as of a society or culture

health food food thought to be very healthful, as food grown with natural fertilizers and free of additives

health′ful *adj.* helping to produce or maintain health; wholesome —**health′fully** *adv.* —**health′ful·ness** *n.*

healthy (hel′thē) *adj.* **-i·er, -i·est** **1** having good health **2** showing or resulting from good health [a *healthy* color] **3** HEALTHFUL —**health′i·ness** *n.*

heap (hēp) *n.* [< OE *heap,* a troop] **1** a pile or mass of jumbled things **2** [*often pl.*] [Colloq.] a large amount — *vt.* **1** to make a heap of **2** to give in large amounts **3** to fill (a plate, etc.) full or to overflowing — *vi.* to rise in a heap

hear (hir) *vt.* **heard** (hurd) **hear′ing** [OE *hieran*] **1** to be aware of (sounds) by the ear **2** to listen to **3** to conduct a hearing of (a law case, etc.) **4** to be informed of; learn — *vi.* **1** to be able to hear sounds **2** to be told (*of* or *about*) —**hear from** to get a letter, etc. from —**not hear of** to refuse to consider —**hear′er** *n.*

hear′ing *n.* **1** the act or process of perceiving sounds **2** the ability to hear **3** an opportunity to be heard **4** an appearance before a judge, investigative committee, etc. **5** the distance a sound will carry [within *hearing*]

hearken (härk′ən) *vi.* [OE *heorcnian*] to listen carefully; pay heed

hear′say′ (hir′sā′) *n.* rumor; gossip

hearse (hurs) *n.* [< L *hirpex,* a harrow] a vehicle used in a funeral for carrying the corpse

heart (härt) *n.* [OE *heorte*] **1** the hollow, muscular organ that circulates the blood by alternate dilation and contraction **2** the central, vital, or main part; core **3** the human

THESAURUS

heading *n.* headline, subtitle, address, caption, legend, head, banner head, subject, capital, superscription, ticket, headnote, display line, preface, prologue, streamer, preamble, topic, designation, specification.

headless *a.* **1** [Unthinking] witless, fatuous, brainless; see DULL 3, STUPID. **2** [Without a head] decapitated, lifeless, truncated; see DEAD 1.

headlight *n.* searchlight, beacon, spotlight; see LIGHT 3.

headline *n.* heading, caption, title; see HEADING.

headquarters *n.* main office, home office, chief office, central station, central place, distributing center, police station, meeting place, meeting house, manager's office, quarters, base, military station, military town, post, center of operations, base of operations, HQ.

headstone *n.* gravestone, marker, stone; see GRAVE.

headstrong *a.* determined, strong-minded, stubborn; see STUBBORN.

headway *n.* advance, increase, promotion; see PROGRESS 1.

heal *v.* restore, renew, treat, attend, make healthy, return to health, fix, repair, regenerate, bring around, remedy, purify, rejuvenate, medicate, make clean, dress a wound, rebuild, revive, rehabilitate, work a cure, cause to heal, resuscitate, salve, help to get well, ameliorate, doctor*, put one on his feet again, breathe new life into*.—*Ant.* EXPOSE, make ill, infect.

healing *a.* restorative, invigorating, medicinal; see HEALTHFUL.

health *n.* vigor, wholeness, good condition, healthfulness, good health, fitness, bloom, soundness of body, physical fitness, tone, hardiness, well-being, stamina, energy, full bloom, rosy cheeks*, good shape*, clean bill of health*; see also STRENGTH.

healthful *a.* nutritious, restorative, body-building, sanitary, hygienic, salutary, invigorating, tonic, stimulating, bracing, salubrious, wholesome, beneficial, health-giving, nutritive, nourishing, energy-giving, fresh, pure, clean, corrective, cathartic, sedative, regenerative, substantial, sustaining, benign, good for one, desirable, harmless, innocuous, healing, preventive, disease-free, unpolluted, unadulterated, favorable.—*Ant.* UNHEALTHY, sickly, unwholesome.

healthy *a.* sound, trim, all right, normal, robust, hale, vigorous, well, hearty, athletic, rosy-cheeked, hardy, able-bodied, virile, muscular, blooming, sturdy, safe and sound, in good condition, in full possession of one's faculties, in good health, full of pep*, never feeling better, fresh, whole, firm, lively, undecayed, flourishing, good, physically fit, clear-eyed, in fine fettle, youthful, free from disease, fine, fine and dandy*, hunky-dory*, in the pink of condition*, rugged, fit as a fiddle, feeling one's oats*; see also SANE 1, STRONG 1.—*Ant.* UNHEALTHY, ill, diseased.

heap *n.* pile, mass, stack; see QUANTITY.

heap *v.* pile, add, lump; see LOAD 1, PACK 2.

hear *v.* **1** [To perceive by ear] listen to, give attention, attend to, make out, become aware of, catch, apprehend, take in, eavesdrop, detect, perceive by the ear, overhear, take cognizance of, keep one's ears open, have the sense of hearing, read loud and clear, strain one's ears, listen in, get an earful*. **2** [To receive information aurally] overhear, eavesdrop, find out; see LISTEN. **3** [To hold a hearing] preside over, put on trial, summon to court; see JUDGE. —**hear from** get word from, be informed,

learn through; see RECEIVE 1. —**hear of** know about, be aware of, discover; see KNOW 1, 3. —**not hear of** not allow, refuse to consider, reject; see FORBID.

heard *a.* perceived, listened, witnessed, caught, made out, understood, heeded, noted, made clear.

hearer *n.* listener, witness, bystander; see LISTENER.

hearing *n.* **1** [An opportunity to be heard] audition, interview, test, fair hearing, tryout, attendance, conference, audit, notice, performance, presentation, audience, attention; see also TRIAL 2. **2** [The act of hearing] detecting, recording, distinguishing; see LISTENING. **3** [The faculty for hearing] ear, auditory faculty, perception, listening ear, sense of hearing, audition, act of perceiving sound, acoustic sensation. **4** [Range of hearing] earshot, hearing distance, reach, sound, carrying distance, range, auditory range; see also EXTENT.

hearsay *n.* noise, scandal, report; see GOSSIP 1, RUMOR.

heart *n.* **1** [The pump in the circulatory system] vital organ, vascular organ, blood pump, cardiac organ, ventricle, ticker*, clock*; see also ORGAN 2. **2** [Feeling] response, sympathy, sensitivity; see EMOTION, FEELING 4, PITY. **3** [The center] core, middle, pith; see CENTER 1. **4** [The most important portion] gist, essence, root; see SOUL 1. **5** [Courage] fortitude, gallantry, spirit; see COURAGE, MIND 1, SOUL 2. —**after one's own heart** suitable, pleasing, lovable; see PLEASANT 2. —**break one's heart** grieve, disappoint, pain; see HURT. —**by heart** from memory, memorized, learned; see REMEMBERED. —**change of heart** change of mind, reversal, alteration; see CHANGE 1. —**do one's heart**

heart considered as the center of emotions, personality attributes, etc.; specif., *a*) inmost thought and feeling *b*) love, sympathy, etc. *c*) spirit or courage **4** a conventionalized design of a heart (♥) **5** any of a suit of playing cards marked with such symbols in red —**after one's own heart** that pleases one perfectly —**at heart** in one's innermost nature —**by heart** by or from memorization —**set one's heart on** to have a fixed desire for —**take to heart 1** to consider seriously **2** to be troubled by

heart'ache' *n.* sorrow or grief

heart attack any sudden instance of heart failure; esp., a coronary

heart'beat' *n.* one full contraction and dilation of the heart

heart'break' *n.* overwhelming sorrow or grief —**heart'break'ing** *adj.* —**heart'bro'ken** *adj.*

heart'burn' *n.* a burning, acid sensation beneath the breastbone

-hearted (härt'id) [ME] *combining form* having a (specified kind of) heart *[stouthearted]*

heart'en (härt''n) *vt.* to encourage

heart failure the inability of the heart to pump enough blood to supply the body tissues adequately

heart'felt' *adj.* sincere; genuine

hearth (härth) *n.* [OE *heorth*] **1** the stone or brick floor of a fireplace **2** *a*) the fireside *b*) family life; home

heart'land' *n.* a geographically central area having crucial importance

heart'less *adj.* unkind; unfeeling —**heart'lessly** *adv.* —**heart'less·ness** *n.*

heart'-rend'ing *adj.* causing much grief or mental anguish

heart'sick' *adj.* sick at heart; extremely unhappy or despondent

heart'strings' *n.pl.* deepest feelings or affections

heart'-to-heart' *adj.* intimate and candid

heart'warm'ing *adj.* such as to cause genial feelings

heart'y *adj.* -**i·er**, -**i·est 1** warm and friendly; cordial **2** strongly felt; unrestrained *[hearty laughter]* **3** strong and healthy **4** nourishing and plentiful *[a hearty meal]* —*n.*, *pl.* **heart'ies** [Archaic] a fellow sailor —**heart'i·ly** *adv.* —**heart'i·ness** *n.*

heat (hēt) *n.* [OE *hætu*] **1** the quality of being hot; hotness, or the perception of this **2** much hotness **3** hot weather or climate **4** the warming of a house, etc. **5** *a*) strong feeling; ardor, anger, etc. *b*) the period of this **6** a

285   **heartache / heavenward**

single bout, round, or trial **7** the period of sexual excitement in animals, esp. females **8** [Slang] coercion —*vt.*, *vi.* **1** to make or become warm or hot **2** to make or become excited

heat'ed *adj.* **1** hot **2** vehement or angry —**heat'edly** *adv.*

heat'er *n.* an apparatus for giving heat; stove, furnace, radiator, etc.

heath (hēth) *n.* [OE *hæth*] **1** a tract of open wasteland, esp. in the British Isles **2** any of various shrubs that grow on heaths, as heather

hea·then (hē'thən) *n., pl.* -**thens** or -**then** [OE *hæthen*] **1** anyone not a Jew, Christian, or Muslim **2** a person regarded as irreligious, uncivilized, etc. —*adj.* **1** pagan **2** irreligious, uncivilized, etc. —**hea'then·ish** *adj.*

heather (heth'ər) *n.* [ME *haddyr*] a plant of the heath family, esp. common in the British Isles, with small, bell-shaped, purplish-pink flowers

heating pad a pad consisting of an electric heating element covered with fabric, for applying heat to the body

heat lightning lightning without thunder, seen on hot evenings

heat'stroke' *n.* a condition of high fever, collapse, etc. resulting from exposure to intense heat

heat wave 1 unusually hot weather **2** a period of such weather

heave (hēv) *vt.* **heaved** or (esp. *Naut.*) **hove, heav'ing** [OE *hebban*] **1** to lift, esp. with effort **2** to lift in this way and throw **3** to utter (a sigh, etc.) with effort **4** *Naut.* to raise, haul, etc. by pulling as with a rope —*vi.* **1** to swell up **2** to rise and fall rhythmically **3** *a*) to vomit *b*) to pant; gasp **4** *Naut.* to haul (on or at a rope, etc.) —*n.* the act or effort of heaving —**heave to** *Naut.* to stop —**heav'er** *n.*

heave'-ho' (-hō') *n.* [Colloq.] dismissal, as from a job: chiefly in **give** (or **get**) **the** (**old**) **heave-ho**

heaven (hev'ən) *n.* [OE *heofon*] **1** [*usually pl.*] the visible sky; firmament **2** [*often* H-] *Theol. a*) a state or place of complete happiness, etc. attained by the good after death *b*) the abode of God, his angels, and the blessed *c*) God **3** any place of great beauty or state of great happiness —**heav'enly** *adj.*

heav'en·ward (-wərd) *adv., adj.* toward heaven Also **heav'en·wards** *adv.*

═══ **THESAURUS** ═══

good please, make content, delight; see SATISFY 1. —**eat one's heart out** worry, regret, nurse one's troubles; see BROOD 2. —**from the bottom of one's heart** deeply, honestly, frankly; see SINCERELY. —**have a heart** be kind, empathize, take pity; see SYMPATHIZE. —**lose one's heart to** love, cherish, adore; see FALL IN LOVE (WITH). —**set one's heart at rest** calm, placate, soothe; see COMFORT 1. —**set one's heart on** long for, need, desire; see WANT 1. —**take to heart** think about, take into account, believe; see CONSIDER. —**wear one's heart on one's sleeve** disclose, divulge, confess; see REVEAL. —**with all one's heart** honestly, deeply, frankly; see SINCERELY.

heartache *n.* sorrow, despair, anguish; see GRIEF, REGRET.

heartbeat *n.* pulsation, throb of the heart, cardiovascular activity; see BEAT 1.

heartbreaking *a.* cheerless, deplorable, joyless; see PITIFUL, TRAGIC.

heartbroken *a.* melancholy, sorrowful, doleful; see SAD 1.

heartburn *n.* indigestion, nervous stomach, stomach upset; see ILLNESS 2.

hearth *n.* **1** [A fireplace] grate, fireside, hearthstone; see FIREPLACE. **2** [Home] dwelling, abode, residence; see HOME 1.

heartily *a.* enthusiastically, earnestly, cordially; see SERIOUSLY 2, SINCERELY.

heartless *a.* unkind, unthinking, insensitive; see CRUEL, RUTHLESS.

hearty *a.* warm, zealous, sincere, cheery, cheerful, jovial, wholehearted, neighborly, well-meant, animated, jolly, ardent, genial, glowing, enthusiastic, genuine, avid, deepest, passionate, deep, intense, exuberant, profuse, eager, devout, deep-felt, unfeigned, fervent, warm-hearted, authentic, impassioned, heartfelt, responsive; see also FRIENDLY.—*Ant.* FALSE, mock, sham.

heat *n.* **1** [Warmth] torridity, high temperature, hot wind, heat wave, fever, hot weather, temperature, hotness, warmness, sultriness, white heat, torridness, tropical heat, dog days; see also WARMTH.—*Ant.* COLD, frost, frigidity. **2** [Fervor] ardor, passion, excitement; see DESIRE 2. **3** [Sources of heat] flame, radiation, solar energy; see ENERGY 2, FIRE 1, 2.

heat *v.* **1** [To make hot] warm, fire, heat up, inflame, kindle, enkindle, subject to heat, put on the fire, make hot, make warm, scald, thaw, boil, char, roast, chafe, seethe, toast, oxidize, set fire to, melt, cauterize, reheat, steam, incinerate, sear, singe, scorch, fry, turn on the heat; see also BURN, COOK, IGNITE.—*Ant.* COOL, freeze. **2** [To become hot] glow, warm up, rise in temperature, grow hot, blaze, flame, seethe, burst into flame, kindle, ignite, thaw, swelter, perspire.

heated *a.* **1** [Warmed] cooked, fried, burnt; see BAKED, BURNED. **2** [Fervent] fiery, ardent, avid; see EXCITED, PASSIONATE 2.

heater *n.* radiator, car heater, electric heater; see FURNACE.

heathen *n.* infidel, non-Christian, atheist; see BARBARIAN.

heave *n.* throw, hurl, fling, cast, wing, toss; see also PITCH 2.

heave *v.* rock, bob, pitch, go up and down, lurch, roll, reel, sway, swell, dilate, expand, be raised, swirl, throb, waft, ebb and flow, wax and wane, puff, slosh, wash; see also WAVE 3.—*Ant.* REST, lie still, quiet.

heaven *n.* **1** [The sky; *often plural*] firmament, stratosphere, heights, atmosphere, azure, beyond, heavenly spheres, upstairs. **2** [The abode of the blessed] Paradise, Great Beyond, Abode of the Dead, Home of the Gods, Heavenly Home, God's Kingdom, Valhalla, Holy City, Nirvana, throne of God, the New Jerusalem, afterworld, heavenly city, the city of God, our eternal home, Kingdom of Heaven, next world, world to come, our Father's house, world beyond the grave, happy hunting grounds*, the eternal rest*, Kingdom Come, the hereafter.—*Ant.* HELL, underworld, inferno. **3** [A state of great comfort] bliss, felicity, harmony; see HAPPINESS.

heavenly *a.* **1** [Concerning heaven] divine, celestial, supernal; see ANGELIC, DIVINE, HOLY 1. **2** [*Much approved of or liked] blissful, sweet, enjoyable; see EXCELLENT, PLEASANT 1, 2.

heavily *a.* laboriously, tediously, weightily, massively, ponderously, gloomily, with difficulty, wearily, profoundly, densely; see also GRADUALLY.—*Ant.* LIGHTLY, gently, easily.

heavy (hev'ē) *adj.* **-i·er, -i·est** ⟦OE *hefig*⟧ **1** hard to lift because of great weight **2** of more than the usual, expected, or defined weight **3** larger, greater, or more intense than usual *[a heavy blow, a heavy vote, heavy applause]* **4** to an unusual extent *[a heavy drinker]* **5** hard to do *[heavy work]* **6** sorrowful *[a heavy heart]* **7** burdened with sleep *[heavy eyelids]* **8** hard to digest *[a heavy meal]* **9** clinging; penetrating *[a heavy odor]* **10** cloudy; gloomy *[a heavy sky]* **11** using massive machinery to produce basic materials, as steel — *adv.* in a heavy manner — *n., pl.* **-ies** *Theater* a villain —**heav'i·ly** *adv.* —**heav'i·ness** *n.*

heav'y-du'ty *adj.* made to withstand great strain, bad weather, etc.

heav'y-hand'ed *adj.* **1** clumsy or tactless **2** oppressive or tyrannical

heav'y-heart'ed *adj.* sad; depressed

heav'y·set' *adj.* having a stout or stocky build

heav'y·weight' *n.* **1** one weighing more than average; esp., a boxer in the heaviest weight class **2** [Colloq.] a very influential or important person

Heb. 1 Hebrew **2** *Bible* Hebrews

He·bra·ic (hē brā'ik, hi-) *adj.* of or characteristic of the Hebrews, their language, or culture; Hebrew

He·brew (hē'brōō') *n.* **1** *a*) a member of an ancient Semitic people; Israelite *b*) a Jew **2** *a*) the ancient Semitic language of the Israelites *b*) its modern form, the language of Israel — *adj.* **1** of Hebrew or the Hebrews **2** JEWISH

heck (hek) *interj., n.* [Colloq.] *a euphemism for* HELL

heckle (hek'əl) *vt.* **-led, -ling** ⟦ME *hechele*⟧ to harass (a speaker) with questions or taunts —**heck'ler** *n.*

hec·tare (hek'ter') *n.* ⟦Fr⟧ a metric unit of area, 10,000 square meters

hec·tic (hek'tik) *adj.* ⟦< Gr *hektikos*, habitual⟧ **1** feverish; flushed **2** confused, rushed, excited, etc. —**hec'ti·cally** *adv.*

Hec·tor (hek'tər) in Homer's *Iliad*, a Trojan hero, killed by Achilles — *vt.* [h-] to browbeat; bully

hedge (hej) *n.* ⟦OE *hecg*⟧ **1** a dense row of shrubs, etc. forming a boundary **2** any fence or barrier **3** a hedging — *vt.* **hedged, hedg'ing 1** to put a hedge around **2** to hinder or guard as with a barrier: often with *in* **3** to try to avoid loss in (a bet, etc.) by making counterbalancing bets, etc. — *vi.* to refuse to commit oneself or give a direct answer

hedge fund a partnership of investors who pool large sums for speculating in securities

hedge'hog' *n.* **1** a small, insect-eating mammal of the Old World, with sharp spines on the back **2** the American porcupine

hedge'hop' *vi.* **-hopped', -hop'ping** [Colloq.] to fly an airplane very close to the ground

he·don·ism (hē'dən iz'əm, hēd'n-) *n.* ⟦< Gr *hēdonē*, pleasure + -ISM⟧ the self-indulgent pursuit of pleasure as a way of life —**he'don·ist** *n.* —**he·do·nis·tic** (hē'də nis'tik, hēd''n is'-) *adj.*

-hedron (hē'drən) ⟦< Gr⟧ *combining form* a geometric figure or crystal having (a specified number of) surfaces

heed (hēd) *vt., vi.* ⟦OE *hēdan*⟧ to pay close attention (to)

— *n.* close attention —**heed'ful** *adj.* —**heed'less** *adj.* — **heed'less·ly** *adv.* —**heed'less·ness** *n.*

hee-haw (hē'hô') *n., vi.* ⟦echoic⟧ bray

heel[1] (hēl) *n.* ⟦OE *hela*⟧ **1** the back part of the foot, under the ankle **2** that part of a stocking, shoe, etc. at the heel **3** anything like a heel in location, shape, crushing power, etc. **4** [Colloq.] a despicable person — *vt.* **1** to furnish with a heel **2** to follow closely **3** [Colloq.] to provide with money, arms, etc. — *vi.* to follow along at the heels of someone —**down at (the) heel (or heels)** shabby; seedy —**kick up one's heels** have fun —**on** (or **upon**) **the heels of** close behind

heel[2] (hēl) *vi.* ⟦OE *hieldan*⟧ to lean to one side, as a ship — *vt.* to cause (a vessel) to heel

heft (heft) *n.* ⟦< base of HEAVE⟧ [Colloq.] **1** weight; heaviness **2** importance; influence — *vt.* [Colloq.] to try to judge the weight of by lifting

hefty (hef'tē) *adj.* **-i·er, -i·est** [Colloq.] **1** heavy **2** large and powerful **3** big —**heft'i·ness** *n.*

he·gem·o·ny (hi jem'ə nē) *n., pl.* **-nies** ⟦< Gr *hēgeisthai*, to lead⟧ leadership or dominance, esp. that of one state or nation over others

he·gi·ra (hi ji'rə) *n.* ⟦< Ar *hijrah*, flight⟧ **1** [*often* H-] Mohammed's flight from Mecca in 622 A.D. **2** a journey, esp. one made to escape

heifer (hef'ər) *n.* ⟦OE *heahfore*⟧ a young cow that has not borne a calf

height (hīt) *n.* ⟦< OE *heah*, high⟧ **1** the topmost point **2** the highest limit; extreme **3** the distance from the bottom to the top **4** elevation above a given level; altitude **5** a relatively great distance above a given level **6** [*often pl.*] an elevation; hill

height'en (-'n) *vt., vi.* **1** to bring or come to a higher position **2** to make or become larger, greater, etc.

Heim·lich maneuver (hīm'lik) [after H. J. *Heimlich*, 20th-c. U.S. surgeon] an emergency technique for dislodging an object stuck in the windpipe, using air forced out from the victim's lungs

hei·nous (hā'nəs) *adj.* ⟦< OFr *hair*, to hate⟧ outrageously evil —**hei'nous·ly** *adv.* —**hei'nous·ness** *n.*

heir (er) *n.* ⟦< L *heres*⟧ one who inherits or is entitled to inherit another's property, title, etc.

heir apparent *pl.* **heirs apparent** the heir whose right to inherit cannot be denied if he outlives the ancestor

heir'ess (-is) *n.* a female heir, esp. to great wealth

heir'loom' *n.* ⟦see HEIR & LOOM[1]⟧ any treasured possession handed down from generation to generation

heist (hīst) *n.* ⟦< HOIST⟧ [Slang] a robbery — *vt.* [Slang] to rob or steal

held (held) *vt., vi. pt. & pp. of* HOLD[1]

Helen of Troy *Gr. Legend* the beautiful wife of the king of Sparta: the Trojan War is started because of her abduction by Paris to Troy

hel·i·cal (hel'i kəl) *adj.* ⟦< Gr *helix*, spiral⟧ shaped like a helix; spiral

hel·i·cop·ter (hel'i käp'tər, hē'li-) *n.* ⟦< Gr *helix*, spiral + *pteron*, wing⟧ a vertical-lift aircraft, capable of hovering or moving in any direction, having a motor-driven, horizontal rotor — *vi., vt.* to travel or convey by helicopter

he·li·o·cen·tric (hē'lē ō sen'trik) *adj.* ⟦< Gr *hēlios*, the sun + *kentron*, a point⟧ having or regarding the sun as the center

he·li·o·trope (hē'lē ə trōp') *n.* ⟦< Gr *hēlios*, the sun + *trepein*, to turn⟧ **1** a plant with fragrant clusters of small,

---

THESAURUS

heaviness *n.* burden, denseness, ballast; see DENSITY, MASS 1, WEIGHT 1.

heavy *a.* **1** [Weighty] bulky, massive, unwieldy, ponderous, huge, overweight, top-heavy, of great weight, burdensome, weighty, stout, big, hard to carry, dense, fat, substantial, ample, hefty*, chunky*; see also LARGE 1.—*Ant.* LIGHT, buoyant, feather-light. **2** [Burdensome] troublesome, oppressive, vexatious; see DIFFICULT 1, DISTURBING. **3** [Dull] listless, slow, apathetic; see DULL 4, INDIFFERENT. **4** [Gloomy] dejected, cloudy, overcast; see DARK 1, DISMAL, SAD 1.

heavy-handed *a.* oppressive, harsh, coercive; see CRUEL, SEVERE 2.

heckle *v.* torment, disturb, pester; see BOTHER 2, RIDICULE.

hectic *a.* unsettled, boisterous, restless; see CONFUSED 2, DISORDERED.

hedge *n.* shrubbery, bushes, thicket;

see PLANT.

heel[1] *n.* **1** [Hind part of the foot] hock, hind toe, Achilles' tendon; see FOOT 2. **2** [The portion of the shoe under the heel] low, spring, wedge sole; see BOTTOM, FOUNDATION 2, SHOE. **3** [*A worthless individual]* scamp, skunk, trickster; see RASCAL. —**down at the heel(s)** shabby, seedy, rundown; see WORN 2. —**kick up one's heels** be lively, have fun, enjoy oneself; see PLAY 1, 2. —**on** (or **upon**) **the heels of** close behind, in back of, behind; see FOLLOWING. — **take to one's heels** run away, flee, take flight; see ESCAPE.

heel[1] *v.* follow, stay by one's heel, attend; see OBEY.

hefty* *a.* sturdy, husky, stout, beefy, strapping, substantial, massive; see also STRONG 1.

heifer *n.* yearling, baby cow, calf; see ANIMAL, COW.

height *n.* elevation, extent upward, prominence, loftiness, highness, perpendicular distance, upright distance, tallness, stature; see also EXPANSE, EXTENT, LENGTH 1.—*Ant.* DEPTH, breadth, width.

heighten *v.* **1** [Increase] sharpen, redouble, emphasize; see INCREASE, STRENGTHEN. **2** [Raise] uplift, elevate, lift; see RAISE 1.

heir *n.* future possessor, legal heir, heir apparent, successor, descendent, one who inherits, heiress, beneficiary, inheritor, crown prince.

heiress *n.* female inheritor, crown princess, inheritress; see HEIR.

heirloom *n.* inheritance, legacy, bequest; see GIFT 1.

held *a.* grasped, controlled, occupied, guarded, taken, gripped, clutched, defended, stuck, detained, sustained, believed.—*Ant.* LOST, released, freed.

white or reddish-purple flowers 2 reddish purple —*adj.* reddish-purple

heli·port (hel′i pôrt′) *n.* 〖HELI(COPTER) + (AIR)PORT〗 an airport for helicopters

he·lium (hē′lē əm) *n.* 〖< Gr *hēlios*, the sun〗 a chemical element, a colorless, odorless, very light inert gas having the lowest known boiling and melting points

he·lix (hē′liks′) *n., pl.* **-lixes′** (-iz′) or **heli·ces** (hel′i sēz′) 〖L & Gr〗 a spiral

hell (hel) *n.* 〖< OE *helan*, to hide〗 1 [*often* H-] *Theol.* the state or place of total and final separation from God and so of eternal misery and suffering, arrived at by those who die unrepentant in grave sin 2 any place or condition of evil, pain, etc. —**catch** (or **get**) **hell** [Slang] to receive a severe scolding, punishment, etc.

hell′bent′ *adj.* [Slang] 1 recklessly determined 2 moving fast

hell′cat′ *n.* an evil, spiteful woman

hel·le·bore (hel′ə bôr′) *n.* 〖< Gr *helleboros*〗 a plant of the buttercup family whose rhizomes were used in medicine

Hel·len·ic (hə len′ik, he-) *adj.* 1 Greek 2 of the history, language, or culture of the ancient Greeks —**Hel·len·ism** (hel′ən iz′əm) *n.* —**Hel′len·is′tic** *adj.*

hel·lion (hel′yən) *n.* 〖< Scot dial. *hallion*, a low fellow〗 [Colloq.] a person fond of deviltry; troublemaker

hell′ish *adj.* 1 devilish; fiendish 2 [Colloq.] very unpleasant —**hell′ishly** *adv.* —**hell′ish·ness** *n.*

hello (he lō′, hə lō′; hel′ō′) *interj.* an exclamation of greeting

helm (helm) *n.* 〖OE *helma*〗 1 the wheel or tiller by which a ship is steered 2 the control or leadership of an organization, government, etc.

hel·met (hel′mət) *n.* 〖< OFr *helme*〗 a protective, rigid head covering for use in combat, certain sports, etc.

helms·man (helmz′mən) *n., pl.* **-men** one who steers a ship

helot (hel′ət) *n.* 〖after *Helos*, ancient Greek town〗 a serf or slave

help (help) *vt.* 〖OE *helpan*〗 1 to make things easier or better for; aid; assist 2 to remedy /to *help* a cough/ 3 to keep from; avoid /can′t *help* crying/ 4 to serve or wait on (a customer, etc.) —*vi.* to give aid; be useful —*n.* 1 a helping; aid; assistance 2 a remedy 3 one that helps; esp., a hired person or persons; servant(s), farmhand(s), etc. —**help oneself to** to take without asking —**help out** to help in getting or doing something —**help′er** *n.*

help′ful (-fəl) *adj.* giving help; useful —**help′fully** *adv.* —**help′ful·ness** *n.*

help′ing (-iŋ) *n.* a portion of food served to one person

help′less (-lis) *adj.* 1 not able to help oneself; weak 2 lacking help or protection 3 incompetent —**help′lessly** *adv.* —**help′less·ness** *n.*

help′mate′ *n.* 〖< fol.〗 a helpful companion; specif., a wife or husband

help′meet′ *n.* 〖misreading of "an *help meet* for him" (Genesis 2:18)〗 HELPMATE

helter-skelter (hel′tər skel′tər) *adv.* in haste and confusion —*adj.* disorderly

helve (helv) *n.* 〖OE *helfe*〗 the handle of a tool, esp. of an ax

hem[1] (hem) *n.* 〖OE〗 the border on a garment, etc. made by folding the edge and sewing it down —*vt.* **hemmed**, **hem′ming** to fold back the edge of and sew down —**hem in** (or **around** or **about**) 1 to encircle 2 to confine

hem[2] (hem) *interj., n.* the sound made in clearing the throat —*vi.* **hemmed**, **hem′ming** 1 to make this sound, as in trying to get attention 2 to grope about in speech for the right words: usually used in the phrase **hem and haw**

he′-man′ *n.* [Colloq.] a strong, virile man

hema·tite (hem′ə tit′, hē′mə-) *n.* 〖< Gr *haimatitēs*, bloodlike〗 native ferric oxide, an important iron ore

hema·tol·ogy (hē′mə täl′ə jē) *n.* 〖< Gr *haima*, blood + -LOGY〗 the study of blood and blood diseases —**he′ma·tol′o·gist** *n.*

he′ma·to′ma (-tō′mə) *n., pl.* **-mas** or **-mata** (-mə tə) 〖< Gr *haima*, blood + -ōma, a mass〗 a tumorlike collection of blood outside a blood vessel

heme (hēm) *n.* 〖< Gr *haima*, blood〗 the iron-containing pigment in hemoglobin

hemi- 〖Gr *hēmi-*〗 *prefix* half [*hemisphere*]

hemi·sphere (hem′i sfir′) *n.* 〖< Gr *hēmisphairion*〗 1 half of a sphere, globe, celestial body, etc. 2 any of the halves (northern, southern, eastern, or western) of the earth —**hem′i·spher′i·cal** (-sfer′i kəl) or **hem′i·spher′ic** *adj.*

hem′line′ *n.* the bottom edge of a dress, skirt, coat, etc.

hem·lock (hem′läk′) *n.* 〖OE *hemlic*〗 1 *a*) a poisonous European plant related to parsley *b*) a poison made from this plant 2 *a*) an evergreen tree of the pine family *b*) the wood of this tree

hemo- 〖< Gr *haima*〗 *combining form* blood Also **hema-**

hemo·glo·bin (hē′mō glō′bin, -mə-) *n.* 〖< prec. + GLOB-ULE〗 the red coloring matter of the red blood corpuscles

hemo·philia (hē′mō fil′ē ə, -mə-) *n.* 〖< HEMO- + -PHILE〗

◼◼◼ THESAURUS ◼◼◼

hell *n.* 1 [Place of the dead, especially of the wicked dead; *often capitalized*] underworld, inferno, place of departed spirits, the lower world, the grave, infernal regions, abyss, Satan's Kingdom, purgatory, nether pit, perdition, place of the lost, place of torment, limbo, the hereafter.—*Ant.* HEAVEN, earth, paradise. 2 [A condition of torment] trial, agony, ordeal; see CRISIS, DIFFICULTY 1, 2, EMERGENCY. —**catch** (or **get**) **hell*** get into trouble, be scolded, receive punishment; see GET IT 2. —**for the hell of it*** for no reason, for the fun of it, playfully; see LIGHTLY. —**hell of a*** helluva*, extremely, very bad or good; see POOR 2, EXCELLENT. —**hell on*** hard on, prejudiced against, strict with; see CRUEL, HARMFUL.

hellish *a.* diabolical, fiendish, destructive; see BAD 1.

hello *interj.* how do you do, greetings, welcome, how are you, good morning, good day, hi*, hey*, howdy*, lo*, hyah*, how goes it.—*Ant.* GOODBYE, farewell, so long.

helmet *n.* football helmet, diver's helmet, hard hat; see HAT.

help *n.* 1 [Assistance] advice, comfort, aid, favor, support, gift, reward, charity, encouragement, advancement, advice, subsidy, service, relief, care, endowment, cooperation, guidance. 2 [Employees] aides, representatives, hired help; see ASSISTANT, FACULTY 2, STAFF 2. 3 [Physical relief] maintenance, sustenance,

nourishment; see RELIEF 4, REMEDY. —**cannot help but** be obliged to, cannot fail to, have to; see MUST. —**cannot help oneself** be compelled to, have a need to, be the victim of habit; see MUST. —**so help me (God)** as God is my witness, by God, I swear; see OATH 1.

help *v.* assist, uphold, advise, encourage, stand by, cooperate, intercede for, befriend, accommodate, work for, back up, maintain, sustain, benefit, bolster, lend a hand, do a service, see through, do one's part, give a hand, be of use, come to the aid of, be of some help, help along, do a favor, promote, back, advocate, abet, stimulate, uphold, further, work for, stick up for*, take under one's wing, go to bat for*, side with, give a lift, boost, pitch in*; see also SUPPORT 2.—*Ant.* OPPOSE, rival, combat. —**help oneself** aid oneself, promote oneself, further oneself, live by one's own efforts, get on, get along; see also HELP. —**help oneself to** take, grab, pick up; see SEIZE 1, 2, STEAL.

helped *a.* aided, maintained, supported, advised, befriended, relieved, sustained, nursed, encouraged, assisted, accompanied, taken care of, subsidized, upheld.—*Ant.* HURT, impeded, harmed.

helpful *a.* 1 [Useful] valuable, important, significant, crucial, essential, cooperative, symbiotic, serviceable, profitable, advantageous, favorable, convenient, suitable, practical, operative, usable, applicable,

conducive, improving, bettering, of service, all-purpose, desirable, instrumental, contributive, good for, to one's advantage, at one's command; see also CONVENIENT 1.—*Ant.* USELESS, ineffective, impractical. 2 [Curative] healthy, salutary, restorative; see HEALTHFUL. 3 [Obliging] accommodating, considerate, neighborly; see KIND.

helping *n.* serving, plateful, portion; see FOOD, MEAL 2, SHARE.

helping *a.* aiding, assisting, cooperating, collaborating, synergistic, working, cooperating, being assistant to, being consultant to, in cooperation with, in combination with, contributing to, accessory to, going along with, in cahoots with*, thick as thieves*, in the same boat with; see also HELPFUL 1.

helpless *a.* 1 [Dependent] feeble, unable, invalid; see DEPENDENT 2, DISABLED, WEAK 1, 5. 2 [Incompetent] incapable, unfit, inexpert; see INCOMPETENT.

helplessness *n.* 1 [Disability] poor health, disorder, convalescence; see ILLNESS 1, WEAKNESS 1. 2 [Incompetence] incapacity, weakness, failure; see WEAKNESS 1.

hem[1] *n.* border, skirting, edging; see EDGE 1, FRINGE, RIM.

hemisphere *n.* half of the globe, Western Hemisphere, Eastern Hemisphere, Northern Hemisphere, Southern Hemisphere, territory; see also EARTH 1.

a hereditary disorder in which the blood fails to clot normally, causing prolonged bleeding from even minor injuries —**he′mo·phil′i·ac′** (-ak′) *n.*

hem·or·rhage (hem′ər ij′, hem′rij′) *n.* ⟦< Gr *haima*, blood + *rhēgnynai*, to break⟧ the escape of large quantities of blood from a blood vessel; heavy bleeding — *vi.* **-rhaged′, -rhag′ing** (-ij iŋ′) to have a hemorrhage —**hem′or·rhag′ic** (-aj′ik) *adj.*

hem·or·rhoid (hem′ər oid′, hem′roid′) *n.* ⟦< Gr *haima*, blood + *rheein*, to flow⟧ a painful swelling of a vein in the region of the anus, often with bleeding: *usually used in pl.* —**hem′or·rhoi′dal** *adj.*

hemo·stat (hē′mō stat′) *n.* ⟦see HEMO- & STATIC⟧ anything used to stop bleeding, as a surgical clamp

hemp (hemp) *n.* ⟦OE *hænep*⟧ **1** a tall Asiatic plant having tough fiber **2** the fiber, used to make rope, sailcloth, etc. **3** a substance, as marijuana, made from its leaves and flowers

hempen (hemp′ən) *adj.* of or like hemp

hem′stitch′ *n.* an ornamental stitch, used esp. at a hem, made by pulling out several parallel threads and tying the cross threads into small bunches — *vt.* to put hemstitches on

hen (hen) *n.* ⟦OE *henn*⟧ **1** the female of the domesticated chicken **2** the female of various other birds

hence (hens) *adv.* ⟦< OE *heonan*, from here⟧ **1** from this place; away [go *hence*] **2** from this time [a year *hence*] **3** as a result; therefore **4** [Archaic] from this origin or source

hence·forth′ *adv.* from this time on Also **hence′for′ward**

hench·man (hench′mən) *n., pl.* **-men** ⟦< OE *hengest*, stallion + *-man*⟧ a trusted helper or follower

henna (hen′ə) *n.* ⟦Ar *ḥinnā′*⟧ **1** an Old World plant with minute flowers **2** a dye extracted from its leaves, used to tint the hair auburn **3** reddish brown — *adj.* reddish-brown — *vt.* **-naed, -na·ing** to tint with henna

hen·peck (hen′pek′) *vt.* to nag and domineer over (one's husband) —**hen′pecked′** *adj.*

hep (hep) *adj. early form of* HIP²

hepa·rin (hep′ə rin) *n.* ⟦Gr *hēpar*, liver + -IN⟧ a substance in body tissues, esp. in the liver, that slows the clotting of blood

he·patic (hi pat′ik) *adj.* ⟦< Gr *hēpar*, liver⟧ of or like the liver

hepa·ti·tis (hep′ə tīt′is) *n.* ⟦< Gr *hēpar*, liver + -ITIS⟧ inflammation of the liver

her (hur) *pron.* ⟦OE *hire*⟧ *objective case of* SHE — *poss. pronominal adj.* of, belonging to, or done by her

Hera (hir′ə) *Gr. Myth.* the wife of Zeus and queen of the gods

her·ald (her′əld) *n.* ⟦< OFr *heralt*⟧ **1** [Historical] an official who made proclamations, carried state messages, etc. **2** one who announces significant news, etc. **3** a forerunner; harbinger — *vt.* to announce, foretell, etc.

he·ral·dic (hə ral′dik) *adj.* of heraldry or heralds

her′aldry *n., pl.* **-ries 1** the art or science having to do with coats of arms, genealogies, etc. **2** ceremony or pomp

herb (urb, hurb) *n.* ⟦< L *herba*⟧ **1** any seed plant whose stem withers away annually **2** any plant used as a medi-

cine, seasoning, etc. —**her·ba·ceous** (hər bā′shəs, ər-) *adj.* —**herb′al** *adj.*

herb·age (ur′bij, hur′-) *n.* herbs collectively, esp. pasturage; grass

herb·al·ist (hur′bəl ist, ur′-) *n.* one who grows or deals in herbs

her·bi·cide (hur′bə sīd′, ur′-) *n.* any chemical substance used to destroy plants, esp. weeds —**her′bi·ci′dal** *adj.*

her·bi·vore′ (-vôr′) *n.* ⟦Fr⟧ a herbivorous animal

her·bivo·rous (hər biv′ər əs) *adj.* ⟦< L *herba*, herb + *vorare*, to devour⟧ feeding chiefly on grass or other plants

her·cu·lean (hər kyōō′lē ən, hur′kyoo lē′ən) *adj.* [*sometimes* H-] **1** having the great size or strength of Hercules **2** calling for great strength, size, or courage

Her·cu·les (hur′kyōō lēz′) *Gr. & Rom. Myth.* a hero famous for feats of strength — *n.* [h-] a very strong man

herd (hurd) *n.* ⟦OE *heord*⟧ **1** a number of cattle or other large animals feeding or living together **2** *a)* a crowd *b)* the common people; masses (a contemptuous term) — *vt., vi.* to gather or move as a herd

herds·man (hurdz′mən) *n., pl.* **-men** one who keeps or tends a herd

here (hir) *adv.* ⟦OE *her*⟧ **1** at or in this place: often used as an intensive [John *here* is an actor] **2** to or into this place [come *here*] **3** at this point; now **4** on earth — *n.* this place —**neither here nor there** irrelevant

here′about′ *adv.* in this general vicinity Also **here′abouts′**

here·af′ter *adv.* **1** from now on; in the future **2** following this — *n.* **1** the future **2** the state after death

here·by′ *adv.* by this means

he·redi·tary (hə red′i ter′ē) *adj.* **1** *a)* of, or passed down by, inheritance from an ancestor *b)* having title, etc. by inheritance **2** of, or passed down by, heredity

he·red·ity (hə red′i tē) *n., pl.* **-ties** ⟦< L *heres*, heir⟧ the transmission of characteristics from parent to offspring by means of genes

here·in′ (hir in′, hir′in′) *adv.* **1** in here **2** in this writing

here·of′ *adv.* of or concerning this

here′s (hirz) here is

her·esy (her′i sē) *n., pl.* **-sies** ⟦< Gr *hairesis*, selection, sect⟧ **1** a religious belief opposed to the orthodox doctrines of a church **2** any opinion opposed to official or established views

her′etic (-tik) *n.* one who professes a heresy; esp., a church member who holds beliefs opposed to church dogma —**he·reti·cal** (hə ret′i kal) *adj.*

here·to·fore′ *adv.* up until now

here·upon′ *adv.* **1** immediately following this; at once **2** concerning this subject, etc.

here·with′ *adv.* **1** along with this **2** by this method or means

her·it·able (her′it ə bəl) *adj.* that can be inherited

her·it·age (her′i tij) *n.* **1** property that is or can be inherited **2** tradition, etc. handed down from one's ancestors or the past

her·maph·ro·dite (hər maf′rō dit′, -rə-) *n.* ⟦after *Hermaphroditos*, son of Hermes and Aphrodite, united in a single body with a nymph⟧ a person, animal, or plant with the sexual organs of both the male and the female — **her·maph′ro·dit′ic** (-dit′ik) *adj.*

Her·mes (hur′mēz′) *Gr. Myth.* the god who was the messenger of the other gods

---

THESAURUS

hemorrhage *n.* discharge, bleeding, bloody flux; see ILLNESS 1, INJURY.

hen *n.* female chicken, pullet, egger*; see BIRD, FOWL.

hence *a.* **1** [Therefore] consequently, for that reason, on that account; see SO 2, THEREFORE. **2** [From now] henceforth, henceforward, from here; see HEREAFTER.

henpeck *v.* bully, suppress, intimidate; see BOTHER 2, THREATEN.

henpecked *a.* dominated by a wife, subjected to nagging, browbeaten, intimidated, passive, constrained, compliant, in bondage, yielding, without freedom or independence, acquiescent, in subjection, subject, obedient, resigned, submissive, docile, meek, cringing, unresisting, unassertive, led by the nose, under one's thumb, at one's beck and call, tied to one's apron strings, nagged, in harness; see also OBEDIENT 1.

herb *n.* seasoning, flavoring, spice,

medicine. *Herbs include the following:* ginger, peppermint, thyme, savory, mustard, chicory, chives, cardamom, coriander, sweet basil, parsley, anise, cumin, fennel, caraway, rosemary, tarragon, oregano, wintergreen; see also SPICE.

herd *n.* flock, drove, pack, brood, swarm, lot, bevy, covey, gaggle, nest, brood, flight, school, clan; see also GATHERING.

herdsman *n.* shepherd, herder, sheepherder; see COWBOY, RANCHER.

here *a.* in this place, hereabout, in this direction, on this spot, over here, up here, down here, right here, on hand, on board, on deck*, in the face of, within reach. —**here and there** often, patchily, sometimes; see EVERYWHERE, SCATTERED.

hereafter *a.* hence, henceforth, from now on, after this, in the future, hereupon, in the course of time.

hereafter *n.* underworld, abode of

the dead, the great beyond; see HEAVEN 2, HELL 1.

hereby *a.* at this moment, with these means, with this, thus, herewith.

hereditary *a.* inherited, genetic, paternal; see GENETIC.

heredity *n.* inheritance, ancestry, hereditary transmission, genetics, eugenics.

heresy *n.* nonconformity, dissidence, protestantism, dissent, heterodoxy, sectarianism, agnosticism, schism, unorthodoxy, secularism.

heretic *n.* schismatic, apostate, sectarian; see CYNIC.

heritage *n.* **1** [Inheritance] legacy, birthright, heirloom, ancestry, right, dowry; see also DIVISION 2, HEREDITY, SHARE. **2** [Tradition] convention, endowment, cultural inheritance; see CULTURE 1, CUSTOM, FASHION 2, METHOD, SYSTEM.

her·metic (hər met′ik) *adj.* ⟦after prec. (reputed founder of alchemy)⟧ airtight Also **her·met′i·cal** —**her·met′i·cally** *adv.*

her·mit (hur′mit) *n.* ⟦< Gr erēmos, desolate⟧ one who lives alone in a secluded spot; recluse

her′mit·age (-mi tij) *n.* a secluded retreat, as the place where a hermit lives

hermit crab a soft-bodied crab that lives in an empty mollusk shell

her·nia (hur′nē ə) *n., pl.* **-as** or **-ae′** (-ē′, -i′) ⟦L⟧ the protrusion of all or part of an organ through a tear in the wall of the surrounding structure; rupture —**her′nial** *adj.*

her′ni·ate′ (-āt′) *vi.* -at′ed, -at′ing to protrude so as to form a hernia —**her′nia′tion** *n.*

hero (hir′ō, hē′rō′) *n., pl.* **-roes** ⟦< Gr hērōs⟧ 1 any person, esp. a man, admired for courage, nobility, etc. 2 the central male character in a novel, play, etc.

he·roic (hi rō′ik) *adj.* 1 of or like a hero 2 of or about a hero and his deeds 3 daring and risky —*n.* [pl.] heroic behavior, talk, or deeds —**he·ro′i·cally** *adv.*

her·o·in (her′ō in) *n.* ⟦Ger, orig. a trademark⟧ a habit-forming narcotic derived from morphine

her·o·ine (her′ō in) *n.* a female hero in life or literature

her′o·ism′ (-iz′əm) *n.* the qualities and actions of a hero or heroine

her·on (her′ən) *n.* ⟦< OFr hairon⟧ a wading bird with a long neck, long legs, and a long, tapered bill

hero sandwich a large, sliced roll filled with meats, cheeses, etc.

her·pes (hur′pēz′) *n.* ⟦L < Gr herpein, to creep⟧ a viral disease causing small blisters on the skin and mucous membranes

herpes sim·plex (sim′pleks′) a recurrent, incurable form of herpes usually affecting the mouth, lips, face, or genitals

herpes zos·ter (zäs′tər) ⟦< HERPES + Gr zōstēr, a girdle⟧ a viral infection of certain sensory nerves, causing pain and an eruption of blisters; shingles

her·pe·tol·ogy (hur′pə täl′ə jē) *n.* ⟦< Gr herpeton, reptile⟧ the branch of zoology having to do with the study of reptiles and amphibians —**her′pe·tol′o·gist** *n.*

Herr (her) *n., pl.* **Her′ren** (-ən) ⟦Ger⟧ in Germany, a man; gentleman: title corresponding to *Mr.* or *Sir*

her·ring (her′iŋ) *n.* ⟦OE hæring⟧ a small food fish of the North Atlantic

her′ring·bone′ *n.* 1 the spine of a herring, having numerous sweptback, thin, parallel bony extensions on each side 2 such a pattern or anything having such a pattern

hers (hurz) *pron.* that or those belonging to her [hers are better]

her·self′ (hər-) *pron.* a form of the 3d pers. sing., fem. pronoun, used as an intensive [she went herself], as a reflexive [she hurt herself], or as a quasi-noun meaning "her true self" [she is not herself today]

hertz (herts, hurts) *n., pl.* **hertz** ⟦after H. R. Hertz, 19th-c. Ger physicist⟧ the international unit of frequency, equal to one cycle per second

Hertz·ian waves (hert′sē ən, hurt′-) ⟦see prec.⟧ [sometimes h- w-] radio waves or other electromagnetic radiation resulting from the oscillations of electricity in a conductor

he's (hēz) 1 he is 2 he has

hes·i·tant (hez′i tənt) *adj.* hesitating or undecided; doubtful —**hes′i·tancy** *n.* —**hes′i·tantly** *adv.*

hes′i·tate′ (-tāt′) *vi.* -tat′ed, -tat′ing ⟦< L haerere, to stick⟧ 1 to stop because of indecision 2 to pause 3 to be

reluctant [hesitating to ask] 4 to pause continually in speaking —**hes′i·tat′ingly** *adv.* —**hes′i·ta′tion** *n.*

hetero- ⟦Gr hetero-⟧ combining form other, another, different Also **heter-**

hetero·dox (het′ər ō däks′, -ər ə-) *adj.* ⟦< prec. + Gr doxa, opinion⟧ opposed to the usual beliefs, esp. in religion; unorthodox —**het′ero·dox′y**, *pl.* **-ies**, *n.*

hetero·geneous (het′ər ō′jē′nē əs, -ər ə-) *adj.* ⟦< HETERO- + Gr genos, a kind⟧ 1 differing in structure, quality, etc.; dissimilar 2 composed of unlike parts

het′ero·sex′ual (-sek′shōō əl) *adj.* 1 of or having sexual desire for those of the opposite sex 2 of different sexes —*n.* a heterosexual individual

heu·ris·tic (hyōō ris′tik) *adj.* ⟦< Gr heuriskein, to invent⟧ helping to learn, as by a method of education based on following rules to find answers

hew (hyōō) *vt.* **hewed**, **hewed** or **hewn**, **hew′ing** ⟦OE heawan⟧ 1 to chop or cut with an ax, knife, etc. 2 to make or shape in this way —*vi.* to conform (to a rule, principle, etc.)

hex (heks) *n.* ⟦< Ger hexe, witch⟧ a sign, spell, etc. supposed to bring bad luck —*vt.* [Dial.] to cause to have bad luck

hexa- ⟦< Gr hex, six⟧ combining form six Also **hex-**

hexa·gon (hek′sə gän′) *n.* ⟦< Gr hex, six + gōnia, an angle⟧ a plane figure with six angles and six sides —**hex·ag·o·nal** (heks ag′ə nəl) *adj.*

hex·am·eter (heks am′ə tər) *n.* ⟦see HEXA- & METER¹⟧ 1 a line of verse containing six metrical feet 2 verse consisting of hexameters

hey (hā) *interj.* an exclamation used to attract attention, etc.

hey·day (hā′dā′) *n.* the time of greatest health, vigor, etc.; prime

Hg ⟦L hydrargyrum⟧ Chem. symbol for mercury

HHS (Department of) Health and Human Services

hi (hī) *interj.* an informal exclamation of greeting

hi·a·tus (hī āt′əs) *n., pl.* **-tuses** or **-tus** ⟦L < hiare, to gape⟧ a gap or break, as where a part is missing

hi·ba·chi (hē bä′chē, hi-) *n., pl.* **-chis** ⟦Jpn < hi, fire + bachi, bowl⟧ a small, charcoal-burning grill

hi·ber·nate (hī′bər nāt′) *vi.* -nat′ed, -nat′ing ⟦< L hibernus, wintry⟧ to spend the winter in a dormant state —**hi′ber·na′tion** *n.*

hi·bis·cus (hī bis′kəs, hi-) *n.* ⟦< L⟧ a plant of the mallow family, with large, colorful flowers

hic·cup (hik′up′, -əp) *n.* ⟦echoic⟧ a sudden, involuntary contraction of the diaphragm as air enters the lungs, causing the glottis to close, producing an abrupt sound —*vi.* **-cuped′** or **-cupped′**, **-cup′ing** or **-cup′ping** to make a hiccup Also **hic·cough** (hi′kôf′; hik′up′, -əp)

hick (hik) *n.* ⟦< Richard⟧ an awkward, unsophisticated person regarded as typical of rural areas

hickey (hik′ē) *n., pl.* **-eys** or **-ies** [Colloq.] any device or gadget

hicko·ry (hik′ə rē, hik′rē) *n., pl.* **-ries** ⟦< AmInd pawcohiccora⟧ 1 a North American tree of the walnut family 2 its hard, tough wood 3 its smooth-shelled, edible nut: usually **hickory nut**

hid·den (hid′′n) *vt., vi.* ⟦OE gehydd⟧ alt. pp. of HIDE¹ —*adj.* concealed; secret

---

THESAURUS

hermit *n.* holy man, ascetic, anchorite, solitary, recluse, solitarian, anchoress, pillar saint.

hero *n.* 1 [One distinguished for action] brave man, model, conqueror, victorious general, god, martyr, champion, prize athlete, master, brave, warrior, saint, man of courage, star, popular figure, great man, knight-errant, a man among men, man of the hour; see also HEROINE 1. 2 [Principal male character in a literary composition] protagonist, male lead, leading man; see also ACTOR.

heroic *a.* valiant, valorous, fearless; see BRAVE, NOBLE 1, 5.

heroine *n.* 1 [A female hero] courageous woman, champion, goddess, ideal, intrepid woman, resourceful woman, supremely courageous woman, woman of heroic character,

woman of the hour; see also HERO 1. 2 [Leading female character in a literary composition] protagonist, leading lady, prima donna; see ACTOR.

heroism *n.* rare fortitude, valor, bravery; see COURAGE, STRENGTH.

hesitancy *n.* wavering, delaying, procrastination; see DELAY, PAUSE.

hesitant *a.* 1 [Doubtful] skeptical, unpredictable, irresolute; see DOUBTFUL, UNCERTAIN. 2 [Slow] delaying, wavering, dawdling; see LAZY 1, SLOW 2.

hesitantly *a.* dubiously, falteringly, shyly; see CAUTIOUSLY.

hesitate *v.* falter, fluctuate, vacillate, pause, stop, hold off, hold back, be dubious, be uncertain, flounder, alternate, ponder, think about, defer, delay, think it over, change one's

mind, recoil, not know what to do, pull back, catch one's breath, weigh, consider, hang back, swerve, debate, shift, wait, deliberate, linger, balance, think twice, drag one's feet, hem and haw, blow hot and cold, dillydally, straddle the fence, leave up in the air.—*Ant.* RESOLVE, decide, conclude.

hesitation *n.* 1 [Doubt] equivocation, skepticism, irresolution; see DOUBT, UNCERTAINTY 2. 2 [Delay] wavering, delaying, dawdling; see DELAY, PAUSE.

hey *interj.* you there, say, hey there; see HALT, HELLO.

heyday *n.* adolescence, bloom, prime of life; see YOUTH 1.

hibernate *v.* sleep through the winter, lie dormant, hole up*; see SLEEP.

hidden *a.* secluded, out of sight, pri-

hide[1] (hīd) *vt.* **hid** (hid), **hid′den** or **hid**, **hid′ing** ⟦ OE *hȳdan* ⟧ 1 to put or keep out of sight; conceal 2 to keep secret 3 to keep from sight by obscuring, etc. — *vi.* 1 to be concealed 2 to conceal oneself

hide[2] (hīd) *n.* ⟦ OE *hīd* ⟧ an animal skin or pelt, either raw or tanned

hide′away′ *n.* [Colloq.] a place where one can hide, be secluded, etc.

hide′bound′ *adj.* obstinately narrow-minded and conservative

hid·eous (hid′ē əs) *adj.* ⟦ < OFr *hide*, fright ⟧ horrible; very ugly —**hid′eous·ly** *adv.* —**hid′eous·ness** *n.*

hide′-out′ *n.* [Colloq.] a hiding place

hie (hī) *vi., vt.* **hied**, **hie′ing** or **hy′ing** ⟦ OE *higian* ⟧ to hasten

hi·er·ar·chy (hī′ər är′kē) *n., pl.* **-chies** ⟦ < Gr *hieros*, sacred + *archos*, ruler ⟧ 1 church government by clergy in graded ranks 2 the highest officials in such a system 3 a group of persons or things arranged in order of rank, grade, etc. —**hi′er·ar′chi·cal** (-ki kəl) *adj.*

hi·ero·glyphic (hī′ər ō′glif′ik, -ər ə-; hī′rō-, -rə-) *n.* ⟦ < Gr *hieros*, sacred + *glyphein*, to carve ⟧ 1 a picture or symbol representing a word, syllable, or sound, used by the ancient Egyptians and others 2 a symbol, etc. hard to understand — *adj.* of or like hieroglyphics

hi·ero·phant (hī′ər ō fant′) *n.* ⟦ < Gr *hieros*, sacred + *phainein*, to show ⟧ in ancient Greece, a priest of a mystery cult

hi-fi (hī′fī′) *n.* a radio, phonograph, etc. having high fidelity — *adj.* of or having high fidelity of sound reproduction

high (hī) *adj.* ⟦ OE *heah* ⟧ 1 lofty; tall 2 extending upward a (specified) distance 3 reaching to, situated at, or done from a height 4 above others in rank, position, etc.; superior 5 grave *[high* treason*]* 6 greater in size, amount, degree, etc. than usual *[high* prices*]* 7 luxurious *[high* living*]* 8 acute in pitch; shrill 9 slightly tainted, as meat 10 elated *[high* spirits*]* 11 [Slang] *a)* drunk *b)* under the influence of a drug — *adv.* in or to a high level, place, degree, etc. — *n.* 1 a high level, place, etc. 2 an area of high barometric pressure 3 that gear of a motor vehicle, etc. producing the greatest speed 4 [Slang] a condition of euphoria induced as by drugs —**high and low** everywhere —**high on** [Colloq.] enthusiastic about —**on high** in heaven

high′ball′ *n.* whiskey or brandy mixed with water, soda water, ginger ale, etc.

high′born′ *adj.* of noble birth

high′boy′ *n.* a high chest of drawers mounted on legs

high′brow′ *n.* [Colloq.] one having or affecting highly cultivated tastes; intellectual — *adj.* [Colloq.] of or for a highbrow

high′chair′ *n.* a baby's chair with long legs used esp. during meals

high′er-up′ *n.* [Colloq.] a person of higher rank or position

high′fa·lu′tin(g) (-fə lōōt′'n) *adj.* [Colloq.] pretentious or pompous

high fidelity in radio, sound recording, etc., nearly exact reproduction of sound

high′-flown′ *adj.* 1 extravagantly ambitious 2 bombastic

high frequency any radio frequency between 3 and 30 megahertz

High German the West Germanic dialects spoken in central and N Germany

high′-grade′ *adj.* of fine or superior quality

high′hand′ed *adj.* overbearing —**high′hand′ed·ly** *adv.* —**high′hand′ed·ness** *n.*

high′-hat′ *adj.* [Slang] snobbish — *vt.* **-hat′ted**, **-hat′ting** [Slang] to snub

high′land (-lənd) *n.* region with many hills or mountains —**High′lander** *n.*

high′-lev′el *adj.* 1 of or by persons of high office 2 in a high office

high′light′ *n.* 1 a part on which light is brightest: also **high light** 2 the most important or interesting part, scene, etc. — *vt.* 1 to give highlights to 2 to give prominence to; emphasize

high′ly *adv.* 1 very much 2 favorably 3 at a high level, wage, etc.

high′-mind′ed *adj.* having high ideals, principles, etc. —**high′-mind′edly** *adv.*

high′ness *n.* 1 height 2 [H-] a title used in speaking to or of royalty

high′-pres′sure *adj.* 1 having or withstanding high pressure 2 using forcefully persuasive or insistent methods — *vt.* **-sured**, **-suring** [Colloq.] to urge with such methods

high′-rise′ *adj.* designating or of a tall apartment house, office building, etc. — *n.* a high-rise building

high′road′ *n.* 1 [Chiefly Brit.] a highway 2 an easy or direct way

high school a secondary school that includes grades 10, 11, and 12, and sometimes grade 9

high seas open ocean waters outside the territorial limits of any nation

high sign a secret signal, as in a warning

■ THESAURUS ■

vate, covert, concealed, undercover, occult, in the dark, in a haze, in a fog, in darkness, masked, screened, veiled, cloaked, obscured, disguised, invisible, clouded, sealed, unobserved, blotted, impenetrable, unseen, eclipsed, camouflaged, shrouded, shadowy, unknown, buried, undetected, deep, unsuspected, inscrutable, illegible, puzzling, unobserved, out of view, dim, clandestine, subterranean, cloistered, suppressed, dark, inward, underground, unrevealed, withheld, surreptitious, underhand, kept in the dark, under wraps; see also PRIVATE.—*Ant.* OBVIOUS, open, apparent.

hide[1] *v.* 1 [To conceal] shroud, curtain, veil, camouflage, cover, mask, cloak, not give away, screen, blot out, bury, suppress, withhold, keep underground, stifle, keep secret, hush up, shield, eclipse, not tell, lock up, confuse, put out of sight, put out of the way, hold back, keep from, secrete, smuggle, shadow, conceal from sight, keep out of sight, stow away, protect, hoard, store, seclude, closet, conceal, hush, obscure, wrap, shelter, throw a veil over, keep in the dark, keep under one's hat*, seal one's lips*, put the lid on*, salt away*; see also DISGUISE.—*Ant.* EXPOSE, lay bare, uncover. 2 [To keep oneself concealed] disguise oneself, change one's identity, cover one's traces, keep out of sight, go

underground, lie in ambush, sneak, prowl, burrow, skulk, avoid notice, lie in wait, hibernate, lie concealed, lie low, conceal oneself, lurk, shut oneself up, seclude oneself, lie hidden, hide out, cover up, duck*, keep in the background; see also DECEIVE.

hide[2] *n.* pelt, rawhide, pigskin, chamois, bearskin, goatskin, jacket, sheepskin, sealskin, snakeskin, alligator skin, calfskin; see also FUR, LEATHER, SKIN. —**neither hide nor hair** nothing whatsoever, no indication, not at all; see NOTHING.

hideous *a.* ghastly, grisly, frightful; see UGLY 1.

hiding *a.* concealing, in concealment, out of sight; see HIDDEN.

hierarchy *n.* ministry, regime, theocracy; see GOVERNMENT 1, 2.

high *a.* 1 [Tall] towering, gigantic, big, colossal, tremendous, great, giant, huge, formidable, immense, long, sky-scraping, steep, sky-high; see also LARGE 1.—*Ant.* SHORT, diminutive, undersized. 2 [Elevated] lofty, uplifted, soaring, aerial, high-reaching, flying, hovering, overtopping, jutting; see also RAISED 1.—*Ant.* LOW, depressed, underground. 3 [Exalted] eminent, leading, powerful; see DISTINGUISHED 2, NOBLE 1, 2. 4 [Expensive] high-priced, costly, precious; see EXPENSIVE. 5 [To an unusual degree] great, extraordinary,

special; see UNUSUAL 1, 2. 6 [Shrill] piercing, sharp, penetrating; see LOUD 1, SHRILL. 7 [*Drunk] intoxicated, tipsy, inebriated; see DRUNK. 8 [*Under the influence of drugs] stoned*, freaked-out*, wasted*, turned-on*, on a trip*, tripping*, hyped-up*, spaced-out*, zonked out*. —**high and low** in every nook and corner, in all possible places, exhaustively; see COMPLETELY, EVERYWHERE.

higher *a.* taller, more advanced, superior to, over, larger than, ahead, surpassing, bigger, greater; see also ABOVE 1, BEYOND.—*Ant.* SHORTER, smaller, inferior.

highest *a.* topmost, superlative, supreme, maximal, most, top, maximum, head, preeminent, capital, chief, paramount, tiptop, crown.

highly *a.* extremely, profoundly, deeply; see VERY.

highness *n.* 1 [Quality of being high] length, tallness, loftiness; see HEIGHT. 2 [Term of respect, usually to royalty; *often capitalized*] majesty, lordship, ladyship; see ROYALTY.

high-pressure *a.* forceful, potent, compelling; see POWERFUL 1.

high school *n.* public school, secondary school, preparatory school, private academy, military school, upper grades, trade school, seminary, junior high school, vocational school; see also SCHOOL 1.

high'-spir'ited (-spir'i tid) *adj.* 1 courageous 2 lively; fiery
high'-strung' *adj.* highly sensitive or nervous and tense
high'-tech' (-tek') *adj.* 1 of specialized, complex technology: in full **high'-technol'ogy** 2 of furnishings, fashions, etc. industrial in design
high'-ten'sion *adj.* having or carrying a high voltage
high tide the highest level to which the tide rises
high time time beyond the proper time but before it is too late
high'way' *n.* 1 a public road 2 a main road; thoroughfare
high'way·man (-mən) *n., pl.* **-men** one who robs travelers on a highway
high wire a cable stretched high above the ground, on which aerialists perform
hi·jack (hī'jak') *vt.* [Colloq.] 1 to steal (goods in transit, etc.) by force 2 to seize control forcibly of (an aircraft, etc.), esp. to go to a nonscheduled destination —**hi'jack'er** *n.*
hike (hīk) *vi.* **hiked, hik'ing** [< dial. *heik*] to take a long walk — *vt.* [Colloq.] 1 to pull up; hoist 2 to raise (prices, etc.) — *n.* 1 a long walk 2 [Colloq.] a rise —**hik'er** *n.*
hi·lari·ous (hi ler'ē əs, hī-) *adj.* [< Gr *hilaros*, cheerful] noisily merry; very funny —**hi·lar'ity** (-i tē) *n.*
hill (hil) *n.* [OE *hyll*] 1 a natural raised part of the earth's surface, smaller than a mountain 2 a small pile, heap, or mound
hill'bil'ly *n., pl.* **-lies** [prec. + *Billy*] [Colloq.] one who lives in or comes from the mountains or backwoods, esp. of the South: now often offensive
hill'side' *n.* the side of a hill
hill'top' *n.* the top of a hill
hill'y *adj.* **-i·er, -i·est** 1 full of hills 2 like a hill; steep — **hill'i·ness** *n.*
hilt (hilt) *n.* [OE] the handle of a sword, tool, etc.
him (him) *pron.* [OE] *objective case of* HE
him·self' *pron.* a form of the 3d pers. sing., masc. pronoun, used as an intensive [he went *himself*], as a reflexive [he hurt *himself*], and as a quasi-noun meaning "his true self" [he is not *himself* today]
hind[1] (hīnd) *adj.* **hind'er, hind'most'** or **hind'er·most'** [prob. < HINDER[2]] back; rear; posterior
hind[2] (hīnd) *n.* [OE] the female of the red deer
hin·der[1] (hin'dər) *vt.* [OE *hindrian*] 1 to keep back; stop 2 to impede; thwart
hinder[2] (hīn'dər) *adj.* [OE] [Now Rare] rear
Hindi (hin'dē) *n.* the main (and official) language of India

hind'most' *adj.* farthest back; last
hind'quar'ter *n.* either of the two hind legs and the adjoining part of a carcass of veal, beef, etc.
hin·drance (hin'drəns) *n.* 1 the act of hindering 2 an obstacle
hind'sight' *n.* ability to see, after the event, what should have been done
Hindu (hin'dōō') *n.* 1 [Archaic] a native or inhabitant of India 2 a follower of Hinduism — *adj.* designating or of the Hindus or Hinduism
Hin'du·ism' *n.* the religion and social system of the Hindus
hinge (hinj) *n.* [< ME *hengen*, to hang] 1 a joint on which a door, lid, etc. swings 2 a natural joint, as of the shell of a clam — *vt.* **hinged, hing'ing** to attach by a hinge — *vi.* to hang as on a hinge; depend
hint (hint) *n.* [prob. < OE *hentan*, to grasp] a slight indication; indirect suggestion — *vt., vi.* to give a hint (of)
hinter·land (hin'tər land') *n.* [Ger] 1 the land behind that bordering a coast or river 2 a remote area
hip[1] (hip) *n.* [OE *hype*] the part of the body around the joint formed by each thighbone and the pelvis
hip[2] (hip) *adj.* **hip'per, hip'pest** [< ? HEP] [Slang] 1 sophisticated; aware; fashionable 2 of hippies —**get** (or **be**) **hip to** [Slang] to become (or be) informed about
hip'-hop' *n.* a style of music and dance, orig. among inner-city youths of the 1980's
hip'pie *n.* [Slang] a young person, esp. in the 1960's, who, in a state of alienation from conventional society, turned variously to mysticism, psychedelic drugs, communal living, etc. Also **hip'py,** *pl.* **-pies**
hippo (hip'ō') *n., pl.* **-pos** [Colloq.] HIPPOPOTAMUS
Hippo·cratic oath (hip'ə krat'ik) the oath, attributed to Hippocrates, ancient Greek physician, generally taken by medical graduates: it sets forth their ethical code
hippo·drome (hip'ə drōm') *n.* [< Gr *hippos*, horse + *dromos*, course] an arena for a circus, game, etc.
hippo·pota·mus (hip'ə pät'ə məs) *n., pl.* **-mus·es** or **-a·mi'** [< Gr *hippos*, a horse + *potamos*, river] a large, plant-eating mammal with a heavy, thick-skinned body and short legs: it lives chiefly in or near African rivers
hire (hīr) *n.* [< OE *hyr*, wages] 1 the amount paid in hiring 2 a hiring — *vt.* **hired, hir'ing** to pay for the services of (a person) or the use of (a thing) —**hire out** to work for pay

---

■■■■■■ THESAURUS ■■■■■■

high-spirited *a.* daring, dauntless, reckless; see BRAVE.
high-strung *a.* nervous, tense, impatient; see RESTLESS.
highway *n.* roadway, parkway, superhighway, freeway, turnpike, toll road, state highway, national highway; see also ROAD 1.
hijack* *v.* highjack, privateer, capture; see SEIZE 2.
hike *n.* trip, backpack, tour; see JOURNEY, WALK 3.
hike *v.* 1 [To tramp] take a hike, tour, explore; see TRAVEL, WALK 1. 2 [*To raise] lift, advance, pull up; see INCREASE.
hiking *a.* hitchhiking, backpacking, exploring; see WALKING.
hilarious *a.* amusing, lively, witty; see ENTERTAINING, FUNNY 1.
hill *n.* mound, knoll, butte, bluff, promontory, precipice, cliff, range, rising ground, headland, upland, downgrade, inclination, descent, slope, ascent, slant, grade, incline, height, highland, rise, foothill, dune, climb, elevation, ridge, heap, hillside, upgrade, hilltop, vantage point, gradient, summit; see also MOUNTAIN 1.
hillside *n.* grade, gradient, acclivity; see HILL.
hilltop *n.* peak, height, elevation; see HILL, TOP 1.
hilly *a.* steep, sloping, rugged; see MOUNTAINOUS, ROUGH 1, STEEP.— *Ant.* LEVEL, even, regular.
hinder[1] *v.* impede, obstruct, interfere with, check, retard, fetter, block, thwart, bar, clog, encumber, burden,

cripple, handicap, cramp, preclude, inhibit, shackle, interrupt, arrest, curb, resist, oppose, baffle, deter, hamper, frustrate, outwit, stop, counteract, offset, neutralize, tie up, hold up, embarrass, delay, postpone, keep back, set back, dam, close, box in, end, terminate, shut out, choke, intercept, bottleneck, defeat, trap, control, conflict with, deadlock, hold back, clash with, be an obstacle to, cross, exclude, limit, shorten, go against, prohibit, withhold, slow down, stall, bring to a standstill, smother, disappoint, spoil, gag, annul, silence, invalidate, detain, stalemate, taboo, suspend, set against, clip one's wings*, tie one's hands, get in the way of, hold up, throw a monkey wrench into the works*, knock the props from under*.—*Ant.* HELP, assist, aid.
hindrance *n.* obstacle, intervention, trammel; see BARRIER, INTERFERENCE 1.
hinge *n.* hook, pivot, juncture, articulation, link, elbow, ball-and-socket joint, knee, butt, strap, articulated joint, flap; see also JOINT 1.
hinge *v.* connect, add, couple; see JOIN 1.
hint *n.* allusion, inkling, insinuation, implication, reference, advice, observation, reminder, communication, notice, information, announcement, inside information, tip, clue, token, idea, omen, scent, cue, trace, notion, whisper, taste, suspicion, evidence, reminder, innuendo, symptom, sign,

bare suggestion, impression, supposition, inference, premonition, broad hint, gentle hint, word to the wise, indication, tip-off, pointer*; see also SUGGESTION 1.
hint *v.* touch on, allude to, intimate, inform, hint at, imply, acquaint, remind, impart, bring up, recall, cue, prompt, insinuate, indicate, wink, advise, cause to remember, make an allusion to, jog the memory, give a hint of, suggest, make mention of, remark in passing, drop a hint, whisper, give an inkling of, tip off*.—*Ant.* HIDE, conceal, cover. —**hinted at** signified, intimated, referred to; see IMPLIED, SUGGESTED.
hip[1] *n.* side, hipbone, pelvis; see BONE.
hip[2]* *a.* aware, informed, enlightened; see MODERN 1, OBSERVANT.
hippie *n.* dissenter, bohemian, nonconformist; see RADICAL.
hire *v.* engage, sign up, draft, obtain, secure, enlist, give a job to, take on, put to work, bring in, occupy, use, fill a position, appoint, delegate, authorize, retain, commission, empower, book, utilize, select, pick, contract, procure, fill an opening, find help, find a place for, exploit, make use of, use another's services, add to the payroll.—*Ant.* DISMISS, discharge, fire.
hired *a.* contracted, signed up, given work; see BUSY, EMPLOYED, ENGAGED 3.
hiring *n.* engaging, contracting, employing; see EMPLOYER.

hire'ling *n.* one who will follow anyone's orders for pay; mercenary

hir·sute (hʉr'sŏŏt', hər sŏŏt') *adj.* ⟦L *hirsutus*⟧ hairy

his (hiz) *pron.* ⟦OE⟧ that or those belonging to him [*his* are better] — *poss. pronominal adj.* of, belonging to, or done by him

His·panic (hi span'ik) *adj.* **1** Spanish or Spanish-and-Portuguese **2** of or relating to Hispanics — *n.* a Spanish-speaking person of Latin American origin who lives in the U.S.

hiss (his) *vi.* ⟦echoic⟧ **1** to make a sound like that of a prolonged *s* **2** to show disapproval by hissing — *vt.* to say or indicate by hissing — *n.* the act or sound of hissing

hist (st; hist) *interj.* be quiet!

his·ta·mine (his'tə mēn', -min') *n.* ⟦< Gr *histos*, web + AMMONIA⟧ an ammonia derivative in all organic matter: it is released in allergic reactions, lowers the blood pressure, etc.

his·tol·o·gy (his täl'ə jē) *n.* ⟦< Gr *histos*, web + -LOGY⟧ *Biol.* the microscopic study of tissue structure —**his·tol'o·gist** *n.*

his·to·rian (his tôr'ē ən) *n.* a writer of, or authority on, history

his·tor'ic (-ik) *adj.* historical; esp., famous in history

his·tor'i·cal (-i kəl) *adj.* **1** of or concerned with history **2** based on people or events of the past **3** established by history; factual —**his·tor'i·cally** *adv.*

historical present the present tense used for the narration of past events

his·to·ric·i·ty (his'tə ris'ə tē) *n.* historical authenticity

his·to·ri·og·ra·phy (his tôr'ē äg'rə fē) *n.* the study of the techniques of historical research

his·to·ry (his'tə rē, -trē) *n., pl.* **-ries** ⟦< Gr *histōr*, knowing⟧ **1** an account of what has happened, esp. in the life of a people, country, etc. **2** all recorded past events **3** the branch of knowledge that deals systematically with the past **4** a known or recorded past [the odd *history* of his coat]

his·tri·on·ic (his'trē än'ik) *adj.* ⟦< L *histrio*, actor⟧ **1** of acting or actors **2** overacted or overacting —**his'tri·on'i·cally** *adv.*

his'tri·on'ics *n.pl.* [*sometimes with sing. v.*] **1** dramatics **2** an artificial manner, display of emotion, etc.

hit (hit) *vt., vi.* **hit, hit'ting** ⟦< ON *hitta*, meet with⟧ **1** to come against (something) with force; knock **2** to give a blow (to); strike **3** to strike with a missile **4** to affect strongly [a town hard *hit* by floods] **5** to come (upon) by accident or after search **6** to arrive at [stocks *hit* a new high] **7** *Baseball* to get (a hit) — *n.* **1** a blow that strikes its mark **2** a collision **3** a successful and popular song, book, etc. **4** [Slang] a murder **5** [Slang] a dose of a drug, a drink of liquor, etc. **6** *Baseball* BASE HIT —**hit it off** to get along well together —**hit'ter** *n.*

hit-and-run (hit''n run') *adj.* hitting a person, car, etc. with a moving vehicle and fleeing the scene immediately Also **hit'-skip'**

hitch (hich) *vi.* ⟦ME *hicchen*⟧ **1** to move jerkily **2** to become fastened or caught — *vt.* **1** to move, pull, etc. with jerks **2** to fasten with a hook, knot, etc. **3** [Slang] to hitchhike — *n.* **1** a tug; jerk **2** a limp **3** a hindrance; obstacle **4** a fastening or catch **5** [Slang] a period of time served **6** a kind of knot

hitch'hike' *vi.* **-hiked', -hik'ing** to travel by asking for rides from passing drivers —**hitch'hik'er** *n.*

hither (hith'ər) *adv.* ⟦< OE *hider*⟧ to this place — *adj.* nearer

hith'er·to' *adv.* until this time

hit man [Colloq.] a hired murderer

hit'-or-miss' *adj.* haphazard; random

HIV *n.* a retrovirus that infects human T cells and causes AIDS

hive (hīv) *n.* ⟦< OE *hyfe*⟧ **1** a shelter for a colony of bees; beehive **2** a colony of bees; swarm **3** a crowd of busy people **4** a place of great activity — *vt.* **hived, hiv'ing** to gather (bees) into a hive — *vi.* to enter a hive

hives (hīvz) *n.pl.* ⟦orig. Scot dial.⟧ an allergic skin condition characterized by itching, burning, and the formation of smooth patches

HMO *n., pl.* **HMO's** ⟦*h(ealth) m(aintenance) o(rganization)*⟧ a health care system in which an organization hires medical professionals to provide services for its subscribers

HMS or **H.M.S. 1** Her (or His) Majesty's Service **2** Her (or His) Majesty's Ship

hoa·gie or **hoagy** (hō'gē) *n., pl.* **-gies** HERO SANDWICH

hoard (hôrd) *n.* ⟦OE *hord*⟧ a supply stored up and hidden — *vi., vt.* to accumulate and store away (money, goods, etc.) —**hoard'er** *n.* —**hoard'ing** *n.*

hoar·frost (hôr'frôst') *n.* FROST (sense 2)

hoarse (hôrs) *adj.* ⟦OE *has*⟧ **1** harsh and grating in sound **2** having a rough, husky voice —**hoarse'ness** *n.*

hoary (hôr'ē) *adj.* **-i·er, -i·est** ⟦< OE *har*⟧ **1** white or gray **2** having white or gray hair from old age **3** very old Also **hoar** —**hoar'i·ness** *n.*

hoax (hōks) *n.* ⟦< ? HOCUS-POCUS⟧ a trick or fraud; esp., a practical joke — *vt.* to deceive with a hoax

hob (häb) *n.* ⟦< *Robin* or *Robert*⟧ [Brit. Dial.] an elf or goblin —**play (or raise) hob with** to make trouble for

hob·ble (häb'əl) *vi.* **-bled, -bling** ⟦ME *hobelen*⟧ to go unsteadily; limp — *vt.* **1** to cause to limp **2** to hamper (a horse, etc.) by tying two feet together **3** to hinder — *n.* **1** a limp **2** a rope, etc. used to hobble a horse

hobby (häb'ē) *n., pl.* **-bies** ⟦ME *hobi*⟧ **1** HOBBYHORSE **2** something that one likes to do in one's spare time —**hob'by·ist** *n.*

hob'by·horse' *n.* **1** a child's toy consisting of a stick with a horse's head **2** ROCKING HORSE **3** an idea with which one is preoccupied

hob·gob·lin (häb'gäb'lin) *n.* ⟦HOB + GOBLIN⟧ **1** an elf **2** a bugbear

hob'nail' *n.* ⟦*hob*, a peg + NAIL⟧ a short nail with a broad head, put on the soles of heavy shoes to prevent wear or slipping — *vt.* to put hobnails on —**hob'nailed'** *adj.*

hob'nob' (-näb') *vi.* **-nobbed', -nob'bing** ⟦< ME *habben*, have + *nabben*, not to have⟧ to be on close terms

---

THESAURUS

hiss *n.* buzz, sibilance, escape of air; see NOISE 1.

hiss *v.* sibilate, fizz, seethe; see SOUND.

historical *a.* factual, traditional, chronicled; see OLD 3, PAST 1.

history *n.* annals, records, archives, recorded history, chronicle, historical knowledge, historical writings, historical evidence, historical development; see also RECORD 1, SOCIAL SCIENCE. —**make history** accomplish, do something important, achieve; see SUCCEED 1.

hit *a.* shot, struck, slugged, cuffed, slapped, smacked, clouted, punched, boxed, slammed, knocked, beaten, pounded, thrashed, spanked, banged, smashed, tapped, rapped, whacked, thwacked, thumped, kicked, swatted, mugged, pasted*, knocked out; see also HURT.—*Ant.* UNTOUCHED, unhurt, unscathed.

hit *n.* **1** [A blow] slap, rap, punch; see BLOW. **2** [A popular success] favorite, sellout*, smash; see SUCCESS 2. **3** [In baseball, a batted ball that cannot be fielded] base hit or single, two-base hit or double, three base-hit or triple, home run, Texas leaguer, two-bagger*, three-bagger*, homer*.

hit *v.* **1** [To strike] knock, beat, sock*, slap, jostle, butt, knock against, scrape, bump, run against, thump, collide with, bump into, punch, punish, hammer, strike down, bang, whack, thwack, jab, tap, smack, kick at, pelt, flail, thrash, cuff, kick, rap, clout*, club, bat around, lash out at, hit at, hit out at, let have it, crack, pop*, bash*; see also BEAT 1. **2** [To fire in time; *said of an internal combustion motor*] catch, go, run; see OPERATE 2. **3** [In baseball, to hit safely] make a hit, get on, get on base. —**hit it off** get along well, become friends, become friendly; see AGREE, LIKE 1, 2. —**hit upon** realize, come upon, stumble on; see DISCOVER, FIND, RECOGNIZE 1. —**hit or miss** at random, uncertainly, sometimes; see SCATTERED.

hit-and-run *a.* leaving without offering assistance, fugitive, illegally departed; see ILLEGAL.

hitch *n.* **1** [A knot] loop, noose, yoke; see KNOT 1, TIE 1. **2** [A difficulty] block, obstacle, tangle; see DIFFICULTY.

hitch *v.* tie up, strap, hook; see FASTEN, JOIN 1.

hitchhike *v.* take a lift, hitch a ride, thumb a ride; see RIDE 1, TRAVEL.

hive *n.* apiary, swarm, colony; see COLONY.

hoard *v.* store up, acquire, keep; see ACCUMULATE, SAVE 3.

hoarse *a.* grating, rough, uneven, harsh, raucous, discordant, gruff, husky, thick, growling, croaking, cracked, guttural, dry, piercing, scratching, indistinct, squawking, jarring, rasping.—*Ant.* PURE, sweet, mellifluous.

hoax *n.* falsification, fabrication, deceit; see DECEPTION, LIE.

hobby *n.* avocation, pastime, diversion, side interest, leisure-time activity, specialty, whim, fancy, whimsy, labor of love, play, craze, sport, amusement, craft, fun, art, game, sideline; see also ENTERTAINMENT.

hobo (hō′bō′) *n., pl.* **-bos′** or **-boes′** 1 a migratory worker 2 a tramp

hock¹ (häk) *n.* 〖< OE *hoh*, heel〗 the joint bending backward in the hind leg of a horse, ox, etc.

hock² (häk) *vt., n.* 〖< Du *hok*, prison〗 [Slang] PAWN¹

hockey (häk′ē) *n.* 〖prob. < OFr *hoquet*, bent stick〗 1 a team game played on ice skates, with curved sticks and a hard rubber disk (*puck*) 2 a similar game played on foot on a field, with a small ball

hock′shop′ *n.* [Slang] PAWNSHOP

hocus-pocus (hō′kəs pō′kəs) *n.* 〖imitation L〗 1 meaningless words used as a formula by conjurers 2 a magician's trick 3 trickery

hod (häd) *n.* 〖prob. < MDu *hodde*〗 1 a long-handled wooden trough used for carrying bricks, mortar, etc. on the shoulder 2 a coal scuttle

hodge·podge (häj′päj′) *n.* 〖< OFr *hochepot*, a stew〗 a jumbled mixture

Hodg·kin's disease (häj′kinz-) 〖after T. *Hodgkin* 19th-c. Eng physician〗 a chronic disease of unknown cause characterized by progressive enlargement of the lymph nodes

hoe (hō) *n.* 〖< OHG *houwan*, to cut〗 a tool with a thin blade set across the end of a long handle, for weeding, loosening soil, etc. — *vt., vi.* **hoed, hoe′ing** to cultivate with a hoe

hoe′cake′ *n.* a thin bread made of cornmeal

hoe′down′ *n.* 1 a lively, rollicking dance 2 a party with such dances

hog (hôg, häg) *n.* 〖OE *hogg*〗 1 any swine, esp. a domesticated adult ready for market 2 [Colloq.] a selfish, greedy, or filthy person — *vt.* **hogged, hog′ging** [Slang] to take all of or an unfair share of —**go (the) whole hog** [Slang] to go all the way —**high on** (or **off**) **the hog** [Colloq.] in a luxurious or costly way —**hog′gish** *adj.* —**hog′gishly** *adv.*

ho·gan (hō′gôn′, -gən) *n.* 〖< AmInd〗 a Navajo Indian dwelling, built of earth walls supported by timbers

hogs·head (hôgz′hed′) *n.* 1 a large barrel or cask holding from 63 to 140 gallons 2 a liquid measure, esp. one equal to 63 gallons

hog′tie′ *vt.* **-tied′, -ty′ing** or **-tie′ing** 1 to tie the four feet or the hands and feet of 2 [Colloq.] to make incapable of effective action

hog′wash′ *n.* 1 refuse fed to hogs; swill 2 insincere talk, writing, etc.

hoi pol·loi (hoi′pə loi′) 〖Gr, the many〗 the common people; the masses

hoist (hoist) *vt.* 〖< Du *hijschen*〗 to raise aloft; lift, esp. with a pulley, crane, etc. — *n.* 1 a hoisting 2 an apparatus for lifting; elevator; tackle

hoke (hōk) *vt.* **hoked, hok′ing** 〖< fol.〗 [Slang] to treat in a sentimental or crudely comic way: usually with *up* —**hok′ey** *adj.*

ho·kum (hō′kəm) *n.* 〖< HOCUS(-POCUS)〗 [Slang] 1 trite sentiment, crude humor, etc. 2 nonsense; humbug

hold¹ (hōld) *vt.* **held, hold′ing** 〖OE *haldan*〗 1 to keep in the hands, arms, etc.; grasp 2 to keep in a certain position or condition 3 to restrain or control; keep back 4 to possess; occupy /to hold an office/ 5 to guard; defend /hold the fort/ 6 to carry on (a meeting, etc.) 7 to contain /the jar holds a pint/ 8 to regard; consider /I hold the story to be true/ 9 *Law* to decide; decree — *vi.* 1 to go on being firm, loyal, etc. 2 to remain unbroken or unyielding /the rope held/ 3 to be true or valid /this rule holds for any case/ 4 to continue /the wind held steady/ — *n.* 1 a grasping or seizing; grip 2 a thing to hold on by 3 a thing for holding something else 4 a dominating force /she has a hold over him/ 5 a prison —**catch** (**get, lay,** or **take**) **hold of** to take, seize, acquire, etc. —**hold forth** 1 to preach; lecture 2 [Now Rare] to offer —**hold on** [Colloq.] stop! wait! —**hold out** 1 to last; endure 2 to stand firm 3 to offer 4 [Colloq.] to refuse to give (what is to be given) —**hold over** 1 to postpone 2 to stay for an additional period —**hold up** 1 to prop up 2 to show 3 to last; endure 4 to stop; delay 5 to stop forcibly and rob —**holder** *n.*

hold² (hōld) *n.* 〖< HOLE or < MDu *hol*〗 1 the interior of a ship below decks, where the cargo is carried 2 the compartment for cargo in an aircraft

hold′ing *n.* 1 land, esp. a farm, rented from another 2 [*usually pl.*] property owned, esp. stocks or bonds

hold′o′ver *n.* [Colloq.] one staying on from a previous period

hold′up′ *n.* 1 a delay 2 the act of stopping forcibly and robbing

hole (hōl) *n.* 〖OE *hol*〗 1 a hollow place; cavity 2 an animal's burrow; den 3 a small, dingy, squalid place 4 an opening in anything; break; gap; tear 5 *Golf a*) a small cup into which a ball is to be hit *b*) the tee, the fairway, etc. leading to this —**hole up** [Colloq.] to hibernate, as in a hole —**in the hole** [Colloq.] financially embarrassed or behind

-holic (häl′ik) *combining form* -AHOLIC

holi·day (häl′ə dā′) *n.* 1 a religious festival; holy day 2 a day of freedom from labor, often one set aside by law to

---

THESAURUS

hobo *n.* vagrant, vagabond, wanderer; see BEGGAR.

hock²* *v.* sell temporarily, pledge, deposit; see PAWN, SELL.

hockey *n.* ice hockey, field hockey, hockey game; see GAME 1, SPORT 3.

hodgepodge *n.* jumble, combination, mess; see MIXTURE 1.

hoe *n.* digger, scraper, garden hoe; see TOOL 1.

hog *n.* 1 [A pig] swine, sow, boar, shoat, razorback, wild boar, wart hog, peccary, porker, piggy, pork; see also ANIMAL. 2 [A person whose habits resemble a pig's] pig, glutton, filthy person; see SLOB. —**high on** (or **off**) **the hog*** luxuriously, extravagantly, richly; see EXPENSIVE.

hogtie *v.* fetter, shackle, tie up; see BIND.

hogwash *n.* foolishness, absurdity, ridiculousness; see NONSENSE 1.

hoist *n.* crane, lift, derrick; see ELEVATOR 1.

hold¹ *v.* 1 [To have in one's grasp] grasp, grip, clutch, carry, embrace, cling to, detain, enclose, restrain, confine, check, take hold of, contain, hold down, hold onto, not let go, hang on, squeeze, press, hug, handle, fondle, have in hand, keep in hand, get a grip on, retain, keep, clasp, hold fast, hold tight, keep a firm hold on, tie, take, catch; see also SEIZE 1.— *Ant.* DROP, let fall, release. 2 [To have in one's possession] keep, retain, possess; see HAVE 1. 3 [To

remain firm] resist, persevere, keep staunch; see CONTINUE 1, ENDURE 2. 4 [To adhere] attach, cling, take hold; see FASTEN, STICK 1. 5 [To be valid] exist, continue, operate; see BE 1.—*Ant.* STOP, expire, be out of date. 6 [To contain] have capacity for, carry, be equipped for; see INCLUDE 1. 7 [To support: *often used with "up"*] sustain, brace, buttress, prop, lock, stay, shoulder, uphold, bear up; see also SUPPORT 1. —**hold back** 1 [To restrain] inhibit, control, curb; see CHECK 1, PREVENT, RESTRAIN. 2 [To refrain] desist, hesitate, forbear; see ABSTAIN, AVOID. —**hold fast** clasp, lock, clamp; see FASTEN, STICK 1. —**hold off** be above, keep aloof, stave off; see AVOID, PREVENT. —**hold out** 1 [To offer] proffer, tempt with, grant; see GIVE 1, OFFER 1. 2 [To endure] suffer, hold on, withstand; see CONTINUE 1, ENDURE 2. —**hold out for** persist, go on supporting, stand firmly for; see CONTINUE 1. —**hold over** do again, show again, play over; see REPEAT 1. —**hold up** 1 [To show] exhibit, raise high, elevate; see DISPLAY. 2 [To delay] stop, pause, interfere with; see DELAY, HINDER, INTERRUPT. 3 [To rob at gunpoint] waylay, burglarize, steal from; see ROB. 4 [To support] brace, prop, shoulder; see HOLD 7, SUPPORT 1.

holder *n.* 1 [An instrument used in holding] sheath, container, holster,

bag, sack, fastener, clip, handle, rack, knob, stem; see also CONTAINER, FASTENER. 2 [An owner or occupant] leaseholder, renter, dweller; see OWNER, RESIDENT, TENANT.

holdings *n.* lands, possessions, security; see ESTATE, PROPERTY 1.

holdover *n.* remnant, relic, surplus; see REMAINDER.

holdup *n.* robbery, burglary, stickup*; see CRIME, THEFT.

hole *n.* 1 [A perforation or cavity] notch, puncture, slot, eyelet, keyhole, porthole, buttonhole, peephole, loophole, air hole, window, crack, rent, split, tear, rift, rupture, fracture, break, leak, aperture, space, chasm, breach, slit, nick, cut, chink, incision, orifice, eye, acupuncture, crater, mouth, gorge, throat, gullet, cranny, dent, opening, depression, indentation, impression, corner, pockmark, pocket, dimple, dip, drop, gulf, depth, pit, abyss, hollow, chasm, crevasse, mine, shaft, chamber, valley, ravine, burrow, rift, cell, niche. 2 [A cave] burrow, den, lair; see sense 1. 3 [*Serious difficulty] impasse, tangle, mess; see CRISIS, DIFFICULTY 1, EMERGENCY. —**in a hole*** in trouble, suffering, caught; see ABANDONED. —**in the hole*** broke, without money, in debt; see POOR 1.

holiday *n.* feast day, fiesta, legal holiday, holy day, festival, centennial, celebrate some event **3** [*often pl.*] [Chiefly Brit.] a vacation — *adj.* of or for a holiday; joyous; gay

holier-than-thou (hō′lē ər *th*ən thou′) *adj.* annoyingly self-righteous

ho·li·ness (hō′lē nis) *n.* **1** a being holy **2** [**H-**] a title of the pope

ho·lis·tic (hō lis′tik) *adj.* of or dealing with wholes or integrated systems rather than with their parts [*holistic* health care] — **ho·lis′ti·cal·ly** *adv.*

hol·lan·daise sauce (häl′ən dāz′) [Fr, of Holland] a creamy sauce made of butter, egg yolks, lemon juice, etc.

hol·ler (häl′ər) *vi., vt., n.* [Colloq.] shout or yell

hol·low (häl′ō) *adj.* [OE *holh*] **1** having a cavity inside; not solid **2** shaped like a bowl; concave **3** sunken [*hollow* cheeks] **4** empty or worthless [*hollow* praise] **5** hungry **6** deep-toned and muffled — *n.* **1** a hollow place; cavity **2** a valley — *vt., vi.* to make or become hollow — **hol′low·ness** *n.*

holly (häl′ē) *n., pl.* **-lies** [OE *holegn*] an evergreen shrub or tree with stiff, glossy, sharp-pointed leaves and bright-red berries

hol′ly·hock′ *n.* [< OE *halig*, holy + *hoc*, mallow] a tall plant of the mallow family, with large, showy flowers

holo·caust (häl′ə kôst′, hō′lə-) *n.* [< Gr *holos*, whole + *kaustos*, burnt] great destruction of life, esp. by fire — **the Holocaust** [*also* **the h-**] the killing of millions of European Jews by the Nazis

Holo·cene (häl′ō sēn′, hō′lə-) *adj.* [< Gr *holos*, whole + *kainos*, recent] designating the present epoch of geologic time

holo·graph (häl′ə graf′) *n.* [< Gr *holos*, whole + *graphein*, to write] a document, letter, etc. in the handwriting of the person under whose name it appears — **hol′o·graph′ic** *adj.*

ho·log·ra·phy (hō läg′rə fē) *n.* [< Gr *holos*, whole + -GRAPHY] a method of making three-dimensional photographs using a laser beam

Hol·stein (hōl′stēn′, -stin′) *n.* [after the region of Schleswig-*Holstein*, Germany] a breed of large, black-and-white dairy cattle

hol·ster (hōl′stər) *n.* [Du] a pistol case attached to a belt, saddle, etc.

holy (hō′lē) *adj.* **-li·er** or **-li·est** [OE *halig*] [*often* **H-**] **1** dedicated to religious use; sacred **2** spiritually pure; sinless **3** deserving deep respect, awe, etc.

Holy Communion a Christian rite in which bread and

wine are consecrated and received as the body and blood of Jesus or as symbols of them

Holy Spirit (or Ghost) the third person of the Trinity; spirit of God

hom·age (häm′ij, äm′-) *n.* [< L *homo*, man] anything given or done to show reverence, honor, etc.

hom·burg (häm′burg′) *n.* [after *Homburg*, Prussia] a man's felt hat with a crown dented front to back and a stiff, curved brim

home (hōm) *n.* [OE *hām*] **1** the place where one lives **2** the place where one was born or reared **3** a place thought of as home **4** a household and its affairs **5** an institution for orphans, the aged, etc. **6** the natural environment of an animal, plant, etc. **7** HOME PLATE — *adj.* **1** of one's home or country; domestic **2** central [*home* office] — *adv.* **1** at, to, or in the direction of home **2** to the point aimed at [to drive a nail *home*] — **at home 1** in one's home **2** at ease — **bring home to** impress upon — **home (in) on** to guide, or be guided as by radar, to (a target, etc.) — **home′less** *adj.* — **home′like** *adj.*

home′boy′ *n.* [Slang] **1** a boy or man from one's neighborhood, town, etc. **2** a close male friend — **home′girl′** *n.fem.*

home economics the science and art of homemaking, nutrition, etc.

home′land′ *n.* the country in which one was born or makes one's home

home′ly *adj.* **-li·er, -li·est 1** suitable for home life; everyday **2** crude **3** plain or unattractive — **home′li·ness** *n.*

home′made′ *adj.* made, or as if made, at home

home′mak′er *n.* one who manages a home — **home′mak′ing** *n.*

home plate *Baseball* the slab that the batter stands beside: it is the last base touched in scoring a run

home run *Baseball* a hit that allows the batter to touch all bases and score a run Also [Colloq.] **hom′er** *n.*

home′sick′ *adj.* longing for home — **home′sick′ness** *n.*

home′spun′ *n.* coarse, loosely woven cloth — *adj.* **1** made of homespun **2** plain; homely

home′stead′ (-sted′) *n.* **1** a place for a family's home, including the land and buildings **2** a tract of land granted by the U.S. government to a settler — **home′stead·er** *n.*

home′stretch′ *n.* **1** the part of a racetrack between the last turn and the finish line **2** the final part

home′town′ *n.* the town, city, etc. where one was born or grew up or where one presently lives

home′ward *adv., adj.* toward home Also **home′wards** *adv.*

THESAURUS

carnival, jubilee, red-letter day; see also ANNIVERSARY, CELEBRATION. *Common holidays include the following:* Sunday, Independence Day, Veterans Day, Memorial Day, Mardi Gras, New Year's Day, Saint Valentine's Day, Christmas, Easter Sunday, Lincoln's Birthday, Thanksgiving Day, Washington's Birthday, Presidents' Day, Columbus Day, Labor Day, Halloween, Election Day, Good Friday.

holiness *n.* devoutness, humility, saintliness; see DEVOTION, WORSHIP 1.

hollow *a.* **1** [Concave] curving inward, bell-shaped, curved, carved out, sunken, depressed, arched, vaulted, cup-shaped, excavated, hollowed-out, indented, cupped; see also BENT, ROUND 2.—*Ant.* RAISED, convex, elevated. **2** [Sounding as though from a cave] cavernous, echoing deep, resonant, booming, roaring, rumbling, reverberating, muffled, dull, resounding, sepulchral, vibrating, low, ringing, deep-toned, thunderous; see also LOUD 1.—*Ant.* DEAD, mute, silent.

hollow *n.* dale, bowl, basin; see VALLEY.

hollow (out) *v.* excavate, indent, remove earth; see DIG 1, SHOVEL.

holy *a.* **1** [Sinless] devout, pious, blessed, righteous, moral, just, good, angelic, godly, reverent, venerable, immaculate, pure, spotless, clean, humble, saintly, innocent, godlike, saintlike, perfect, faultless, undefiled, untainted, chaste, upright, virtuous,

revered, sainted, heavensent, pious, believing, profoundly good, sanctified, devotional, reverent, spiritual, unstained, pure in heart, dedicated, unspotted; see also FAITHFUL, RELIGIOUS 2.—*Ant.* BAD, wicked, sinful. **2** [Concerned with worship] devotional, religious, ceremonial; see DIVINE.

Holy Ghost *n.* Holy Spirit, the Dove, third person of the Holy Trinity; see GOD.

homage *n.* respect, adoration, deference; see DEVOTION, REVERENCE, WORSHIP 1.

home *a.* in one's home, at ease, at rest, homely, domestic, familiar, being oneself, homey, in the bosom of one's family, down home, in one's element; see also COMFORTABLE 1.

home *n.* **1** [A dwelling place] house, dwelling, residence, habitation, tenement, abode, lodging, quarters, homestead, domicile, dormitory, apartment house, flat, living quarters, chalet, shelter, asylum, hut, cabin, cottage, mansion, castle, summer home, rooming house, place, address, hovel, lodge, hotel, inn, farmhouse, tent, pad*, hang-out*, digs*, nest; see also APARTMENT. **2** [An asylum] orphanage, sanatorium, mental hospital; see HOSPITAL. —**at home** relaxed, at ease, familiar; see COMFORTABLE 1, HOME. —**bring home to** make clear to, convince, impress upon; see EMPHASIZE. —**come home** come back, return

home, regress; see RETURN 1. —**leave home** run off, play truant, depart; see LEAVE 1.

homeless *a.* desolate, outcast, destitute, vagrant, wandering, itinerant, friendless, banished, derelict, without a country, exiled, having no home, vagabond, forsaken, friendless, unsettled, unwelcome, dispossessed, disinherited, left to shift for oneself, without a roof over one's head; see also ABANDONED, POOR 1.—*Ant.* ESTABLISHED, at home, settled.

homely *a.* **1** [Unpretentious] snug, simple, cozy; see MODEST 2. **2** [Ill-favored] plain, unattractive, uncomely; see UGLY 1.

homemade *a.* homespun, domestic, do-it-yourself, self-made, made at home, home, not foreign.

home run *n.* inside-the-park home run, round-tripper*, homer*; see SCORE 1.

homesick *a.* nostalgic, pining, yearning for home, ill with longing, unhappy, alienated, rootless; see also LONELY.

homesickness *n.* nostalgia, isolation, unhappiness; see LONELINESS.

homespun *a.* handcrafted, domestic, handspun; see HOMEMADE.

homestead *n.* house, ranch, estate; see HOME 1, PROPERTY 2.

homeward *a.* toward home, back home, on the way home, homewards, home, homeward bound, to one's family, to one's native land.

home'work' *n.* **1** work, esp. piecework, done at home **2** lessons to be done outside the classroom **3** preparation for some project: usually in **do one's homework**

home'y (-ē) *adj.* **hom'i·er, hom'i·est** familiar, cozy, etc. —**home'y·ness** *n.*

homi·cide (häm'ə sīd', hō'mə-) *n.* ⟦< L *homo*, a man + *caedere*, to kill⟧ **1** the killing of one person by another **2** a person who kills another —**hom'i·ci'dal** *adj.*

homi·let·ics (häm'ə let'iks) *n.pl.* ⟦see fol.⟧ the art of preparing and delivering sermons

homi·ly (häm'ə lē) *n., pl.* **-lies** ⟦< Gr *homilos*, assembly⟧ **1** a sermon **2** a solemn, moralizing talk or writing

homing pigeon a pigeon trained to find its way home from distant places

homi·nid (häm'ə nid) *n.* ⟦< L *homo*, a man⟧ a human, extinct or living

homi·ny (häm'ə nē) *n.* ⟦< AmInd⟧ dry corn hulled and coarsely ground (**hominy grits**): it is boiled for food

homo- ⟦< Gr *homos*⟧ *combining form* same, equal, like

ho·mo·ge·neous (hō'mō jē'nē əs, -mə-; häm'ō-, -ə-) *adj.* ⟦see prec. & GENUS⟧ **1** the same in structure, quality, etc.; similar **2** composed of similar parts —**ho'mo·ge·ne'i·ty** (-jə nē'ə tē; -nā'-) *n.*

ho·mog·e·nize (hə mäj'ə nīz') *vt.* **-nized', -niz'ing** to make homogeneous, or more uniform throughout; specif., to process (milk) so that fat particles are so finely emulsified that the cream does not separate —**ho·mog'eni·za'tion** *n.*

homo·graph (häm'ə graf', hō'mə-) *n.* ⟦HOMO- + -GRAPH⟧ a word with the same spelling as another but with a different meaning and origin

ho·mol·o·gous (hō mäl'ə gəs) *adj.* ⟦Gr *homologos*, agreeing⟧ matching in structure, position, etc.

homo·nym (häm'ə nim') *n.* ⟦< Gr *homos*, same + *onyma*, name⟧ a word with the same pronunciation as another but with a different meaning, origin, and, usually, spelling

ho·mo·pho·bi·a (hō'mə fō'bē ə) *n.* ⟦HOMO(SEXUAL) + -PHOBIA⟧ hatred or fear of homosexuals or homosexuality —**ho'mo·pho'bic** (-fō'bik) *adj.*

Homo sa·pi·ens (hō'mō sā'pē enz') ⟦ModL *homo*, man + *sapiens*, prp. of *sapere*, to know⟧ human being

homo·sex·ual (hō'mō sek'shōō əl, -mə-) *adj.* of or having sexual desire for those of the same sex — *n.* a homosexual person —**ho'mo·sex'ual'i·ty** (-al'ə tē) *n.*

homy (hōm'ē) *adj.* **-i·er, -i·est** HOMEY —**hom'i·ness** *n.*

hone (hōn) *n.* ⟦OE *han*, a stone⟧ a hard stone used to sharpen cutting tools — *vt.* **honed, hon'ing** to sharpen, as with a hone

hon·est (än'ist) *adj.* ⟦< L *honor*, honor⟧ **1** truthful; trustworthy **2** *a*) sincere or fair *[honest effort]* *b*) gained by fair means *[an honest living]* **3** frank and open *[an honest face]* —**hon'estly** *adv.* —**hon'esty** *n.*

honey (hun'ē) *n., pl.* **-eys** ⟦OE *hunig*⟧ **1** a sweet, syrupy substance that bees make as food from the nectar of flowers **2** sweetness **3** darling

hon'ey·comb' *n.* **1** the structure of six-sided wax cells made by bees to hold their honey or eggs **2** anything like this — *vt.* to cause to have holes like a honeycomb — *adj.* of or like a honeycomb: also **hon'ey·combed'**

hon'ey·dew' melon a variety of melon with a smooth, whitish rind and sweet, greenish flesh

hon'ey·lo'cust *n.* a North American tree having featherlike foliage and large, twisted pods

hon'ey·moon' *n.* the vacation spent together by a newly married couple — *vi.* to have or spend a honeymoon

hon'ey·suck'le *n.* a plant with small, fragrant flowers of red, yellow, or white

honk (hôŋk, häŋk) *n.* ⟦echoic⟧ **1** the call of a wild goose **2** a similar sound, as of an automobile horn — *vi., vt.* to make or cause to make such a sound

honky-tonk (hôŋ'kē tôŋk') *n.* [Old Slang] a cheap, noisy nightclub — *adj.* designating music played on a piano with a tinkling sound

honor (än'ər) *n.* ⟦L⟧ **1** high regard or respect; esp., *a*) glory; fame *b*) good reputation **2** adherence to principles considered right; integrity **3** chastity **4** high rank; distinction **5** [H-] a title of certain officials, as judges **6** something done or given as a token of respect **7** a source of respect and fame — *vt.* **1** to respect greatly **2** to show high regard for **3** to do or give something in honor of **4** to accept and pay *[to honor a check]* Brit. sp. **hon'our** — **do the honors** to act as host

hon'or·able *adj.* **1** worthy of being honored **2** honest; upright **3** bringing honor —**hon'or·ably** *adv.*

hono·ra·rium (än'ə rer'ē əm) *n., pl.* **-ri·ums** or **-ria** (-ə) ⟦L⟧ a payment as to a professional person for services on which no fee is set

hon'or·ar'y (-ər er'ē) *adj.* **1** given as an honor **2** designating or in an office held as an honor, without service or pay —**hon'or·ar'i·ly** *adv.*

hon'or·if'ic (-ə rif'ik) *adj.* ⟦< L *honor* + *facere*, to make⟧ conferring honor *[an honorific title]*

hood (hood) *n.* ⟦OE *hod*⟧ **1** a covering for the head and neck, often part of a coat, etc. **2** anything resembling a hood, as the metal cover over an automobile engine — *vt.* to cover as with a hood —**hood'ed** *adj.*

-hood (hood) ⟦OE *had*⟧ *suffix* **1** state or quality *[childhood]* **2** the whole group of *[priesthood]*

hood·lum (hood'ləm, hood'-) *n.* ⟦prob. < Ger dial. *hudilump*, wretch⟧ a lawless person, as a member of a gang

hoo·doo (hoo'doo') *n., pl.* **-doos** ⟦var. of VOODOO⟧ **1** VOODOO **2** [Colloq.] bad luck or a person or thing that causes it

hood'wink' *vt.* ⟦HOOD + WINK⟧ to mislead by trickery; dupe

hooey (hoo'ē) *interj., n.* ⟦echoic⟧ [Slang] nonsense; bunk

THESAURUS

homework *n.* outside assignment, library assignment, preparation; see EDUCATION 1.

homey *a.* enjoyable, livable, familiar; see COMFORTABLE 2, PLEASANT 2.

homosexual *a.* monoclinius, gynandrous, hermaphroditic, lesbian, Sapphic, androgynous, homoerotic, epicene, gay.

homosexual *n.* lesbian, gay, gynandroid, androgyne, hermaphrodite, transvestite.

honest *a.* **1** [Truthful] true, trustworthy, correct, exact, verifiable, undisguised, candid, straightforward, aboveboard, just, frank, impartial, respectful, factual, sound, reasonable, unimpeachable, legitimate, unquestionable, realistic, true-to-life, naked, plain, square, honest as the day is long, on the level*, kosher*, fair and square*, straight.—*Ant.* deceptive, false, misleading. **2** [Frank] candid, straightforward, aboveboard; see sense 1 and FRANK. **3** [Fair] just, equitable, impartial; see FAIR 1.

honestly *a.* **1** [In an honest manner] uprightly, fairly, genuinely; see JUSTLY 1, SINCERELY. **2** [Really] indeed, truly, naturally; see REALLY 1.

honesty *n.* honor, fidelity, scrupulousness, trustworthiness, self-respect, straightforwardness, confidence, soundness, right, principle, truthfulness, candor, frankness, openness, morality, goodness, responsibility, loyalty, faithfulness, good faith, probity, courage, moral strength, virtue, reliability, character, conscience, worth, conscientiousness, trustiness, faith, justice, respectability.—*Ant.* DISHONESTY, deception, deceit.

honey *n.* comb honey, extracted honey, wild honey; see FOOD.

honk *n.* croak, quack, blare; see NOISE 1.

honk *v.* blare, trumpet, bellow; see SOUND.

honor *n.* **1** [Respect] reverence, esteem, worship, adoration, veneration, high regard, trust, faith, confidence, righteousness, recognition, praise, attention, deference, notice, consideration, renown, reputation, elevation, credit, tribute, popularity; see also ADMIRATION.—*Ant.* DISGRACE, opprobrium, disrepute. **2** [Integrity] courage, character, truthfulness; see HONESTY. —**do the honors** act as host or hostess, present, host; see SERVE. —**on** (or **upon**) **one's honor** by one's faith, on one's word, staking one's good name; see SINCERELY.

honor *v.* **1** [To treat with respect] worship, sanctify, venerate; see PRAISE 1. **2** [To recognize worth] esteem, value, look up to; see ADMIRE. **3** [To recognize as valid] clear, pass, accept; see ACKNOWLEDGE 2.

honorable *a.* proud, reputable, creditable; see DISTINGUISHED 2, FAMOUS, NOBLE 2, 3.

honorably *a.* nobly, fairly, virtuously; see JUSTLY 1.

honored *a.* respected, revered, decorated, privileged, celebrated, reputable, well-known, esteemed, eminent, distinguished, dignified, noble, recognized, highly regarded, venerated; see also FAMOUS.—*Ant.* CORRUPT, dishonored, shamed.

hood *n.* **1** [Covering worn over the head] cowl, shawl, bonnet, protector, veil, capuchin, kerchief, mantle; see also HAT. **2** [A covering for vehicles and the like] canopy, awning, auto top; see COVER 1. **3** [*A criminal] gangster, hoodlum, crook*; see CRIMINAL.

hoodlum *n.* outlaw, gangster, crook*; see CRIMINAL.

hoof (hoof, hŏŏf) *n., pl.* **hoofs** or **hooves** (hōōvz, hŏŏvz) ⟦OE *hof*⟧ the horny covering on the feet of cattle, horses, etc., or the entire foot — *vt., vi.* [Colloq.] to walk — **hoofed** *adj.*

hook (hŏŏk) *n.* ⟦OE *hoc*⟧ **1** a bent piece of metal, etc. used to catch, hold, or pull something **2** a fishhook **3** something shaped like a hook **4** something moving in a hook-like path, as a punch or pitch — *vt.* **1** to catch, fasten, throw, etc. with a hook **2** [Colloq.] to steal — *vi.* **1** to curve as a hook does **2** to be fastened or caught by a hook —**by hook or by crook** by any means, honest or dishonest —**hook up** to connect (a radio, etc.) —**off the hook** [Colloq.] out of trouble

hookah or **hooka** (hŏŏk'ə) *n.* ⟦Ar *ḥuqqa*⟧ a tobacco pipe of the Middle East, with a long tube for drawing the smoke through water to cool it

hooked (hŏŏkt) *adj.* **1** like a hook **2** made with a hook [*hooked* rug] **3** [Slang] *a)* obsessed with or addicted to (often with *on*) *b)* married

hook'er *n.* [Slang] a prostitute

hook'up' *n.* the arrangement and connection of parts, circuits, etc., as in a radio

hook'worm' *n.* a small, parasitic, intestinal roundworm with hooks around the mouth

hoo·li·gan (hŏŏ'li gən) *n.* ⟦< ? *Hooligan*, a family name⟧ [Slang] a hoodlum

hoop (hŏŏp) *n.* ⟦OE *hop*⟧ **1** a circular band for holding together the staves of a barrel, etc. **2** anything like this, as a metal basketball rim — *vt.* to bind or fasten as with a hoop

hoopla (hŏŏp'lä') *n.* ⟦< ?⟧ [Colloq.] **1** great excitement **2** showy publicity

hoop skirt a skirt worn over a framework of hoops

hoo·ray (hŏŏ rā', hə-; hŏŏ-) *interj., n., vi., vt.* HURRAH

hoose·gow (hŏŏs'gou') *n.* ⟦< Sp *juzgado*, court of justice⟧ [Slang] a jail

Hoo·sier (hŏŏ'zhər) *n.* [Colloq.] a native or inhabitant of Indiana

hoot (hŏŏt) *n.* ⟦echoic⟧ **1** the sound that an owl makes **2** any sound like this, as a shout of scorn — *vi.* to utter a hoot — *vt.* to express (scorn) of (someone) by hooting — **hoot'er** *n.*

hooten·anny (hŏŏt''n an'ē, hŏŏt''n an'ē) *n., pl.* **-nies** a meeting of folk singers, as for public entertainment

hop¹ (häp) *vi.* **hopped, hop'ping** ⟦OE *hoppian*⟧ **1** to make a short leap or leaps on one foot **2** to leap with both, or all, feet at once, as a frog **3** [Colloq.] to go briskly — *vt.* **1** to jump over **2** to get aboard — *n.* **1** a hopping **2** [Colloq.] *a)* a dance *b)* a short flight in an airplane

hop² (häp) *n.* ⟦< MDu *hoppe*⟧ **1** a twining vine with small, cone-shaped flowers **2** [*pl.*] the dried ripe cones, used for flavoring beer, ale, etc. —**hop up** **1** to stimulate, as by a drug **2** to supercharge (an automobile engine, etc.)

hope (hōp) *n.* ⟦OE *hopa*⟧ **1** a feeling that what is wanted will happen; desire accompanied by expectation **2** the object of this **3** a person or thing on which one may base some hope — *vt.* **hoped, hop'ing** to want and expect — *vi.* to have hope (*for*) —**hope'ful** *adj.* —**hope'fully** *adv.* —**hope'less** *adj.* —**hope'lessly** *adv.*

hop'head' *n.* [Slang] a drug addict

hop·per (häp'ər) *n.* **1** one that hops **2** any hopping insect **3** a container from which the contents can be emptied slowly and evenly

hop·sack·ing (häp'sak'iŋ) *n.* a sturdy fabric resembling coarse material used for bags, that is made into coats, suits, etc. Also **hop'sack'**

hop·scotch (häp'skäch') *n.* a children's game in which a player hops from section to section of a figure drawn on the ground

horde (hôrd) *n.* ⟦ult. < Tatar *urdu*, a camp⟧ a crowd or throng; swarm — *vi.* **hord'ed, hord'ing** to form or gather in a horde

hore·hound (hôr'hound') *n.* ⟦OE *harhune*⟧ **1** a bitter mint plant **2** medicine or candy made from its juice

ho·ri·zon (hə rī'zən) *n.* ⟦< Gr *horos*, boundary⟧ **1** the line where the sky seems to meet the earth **2** [*usually pl.*] the limit of one's experience, interest, etc.

hori·zon·tal (hôr'i zänt''l) *adj.* **1** parallel to the plane of the horizon; not vertical **2** flat and even; level —**hori'-zon'tally** *adv.*

hor·mone (hôr'mōn') *n.* ⟦< Gr *hormē*, impulse⟧ a substance formed in some organ of the body and carried to another part, where it takes effect —**hor·mo'nal** *adj.*

horn (hôrn) *n.* ⟦OE⟧ **1** a hard, bonelike projection growing on the head of a cow, goat, etc. **2** the substance horns are made of **3** anything like a horn in position, shape, etc. **4** any brass instrument; specif., FRENCH HORN **5** a device sounded to give a warning — *adj.* made of horn —**horn in (on)** to intrude or meddle (in) —**horned** *adj.* —**horn'less** *adj.* —**horn'like'** *adj.*

horn·blende (hôrn'blend') *n.* ⟦Ger⟧ a black, rock-forming mineral, common in some kinds of granite

---

THESAURUS

hoof *n.* ungula, animal foot, paw; see FOOT 2.

hook *n.* lock, catch, clasp; see FASTENER.

hook *v.* **1** [To curve in the shape of a hook] angle, crook, curve; see ARCH. **2** [To catch on a hook] pin, catch, secure; see FASTEN. —**hooked up** connected, linked together, attached; see JOINED. —**hook up** combine, connect, attach; see JOIN 1, UNITE.

hookup *n.* attachment, connection, consolidation; see LINK, UNION 1.

hoop *n.* wooden wheel, band, circlet; see CIRCLE 1.

hoot *n.* howl, whoo, boo; see CRY 2.

hop¹ *n.* spring, bounce, leap; see JUMP 1.

hop¹ *v.* leap, skip, jump on one leg; see BOUNCE, JUMP 1.

hope *n.* **1** [Reliance upon the future] faith, expectation, confidence; see ANTICIPATION, OPTIMISM 2. **2** [The object of hope] wish, goal, dream; see DESIRE 1, END 2, PURPOSE 1.

hope *v.* be hopeful, lean on, wish, desire, live in hope, rely, depend, count on, aspire to, doubt not, keep one's fingers crossed, hope for the best, be of good cheeer, pray, cherish the hope, look forward to, await, dream, presume, watch for, bank on, foresee, think to, promise oneself, suppose, deem likely, believe, suspect, surmise, hold, be assured, feel confident, anticipate, be prepared for, make plans for, have faith, rest assured, be sure of, be reassured, take heart, hope to hell*, knock on wood*;

see also EXPECT 1, TRUST 1.

hopeful *a.* **1** [Optimistic] expectant, assured, sanguine, buoyant, enthusiastic, trustful, reassured, emboldened, full of hope, cheerful, anticipating, trusting, expecting, in hopes of, forward-looking, light-hearted, serene, calm, poised, comfortable, eager, elated, looking through rose-colored glasses; see CONFIDENT, TRUSTING. **2** [Encouraging] promising, reassuring, favorable, bright, cheering, flattering, gracious, opportune, timely, fortunate, propitious, auspicious, well-timed, fit, suitable, convenient, beneficial, fair, uplifting, heartening, inspiring, exciting, pleasing, fine, lucky, stirring, making glad, helpful, rose-colored, rosy, animating, attractive, satisfactory, refreshing, probable, good, conducive, advantageous, pleasant, of promise, happy, cheerful.—*Ant.* UNFORTUNATE, discouraging, unfavorable.

hopefully *a.* **1** [Optimistically] confidently, expectantly, with confidence, with hope, trustingly, naively, with some reassurance, trustfully; see also BOLDLY 1, POSITIVELY 1, SURELY.—*Ant.* HOPELESSLY, doubtfully, gloomily. **2** [Probably] conceivably, expectedly, feasibly; see PROBABLY.

hopeless *a.* unfortunate, threatening, bad, sinister, unyielding, incurable, past hope, past cure, vain, irreversible, irreparable, without hope, with no hope, impracticable,

ill-fated, disastrous, menacing, foreboding, unfavorable, dying, worsening, past saving, tragic, fatal, desperate, helpless, lost, to no avail, gone, empty, idle, useless, pointless, worthless; see also ABANDONED, IMPOSSIBLE.—*Ant.* FAVORABLE, heartening, cheering.

hopelessly *a.* cynically, pessimistically, despondently, dejectedly, desperately, emptily, darkly, gloomily, dismally, desolately, down in the mouth*; see also SADLY.—*Ant.* HOPEFULLY, confidently, expectantly.

horde *n.* pack, throng, swarm; see CROWD, GATHERING.

horizon *n.* range, border, limit; see BOUNDARY, EXTENT.

horizontal *a.* **1** [Level] plane, aligned, parallel; see FLAT 1, LEVEL 3, STRAIGHT 1. **2** [Even] flush, uniform, regular; see FLAT 1, SMOOTH 1.

horn *n.* **1** [A hornlike sounding instrument] *Horns include the following:* bugle, trombone, saxophone, cornet, clarinet, bassoon, pipe, fife, flute, picolo, oboe, English horn, French horn, tuba; see also MUSICAL INSTRUMENT. **2** [Hard process protruding from the head of certain animals] tusk, antler, outgrowth, pronghorn, frontal bone, spine, spike, point; see also BONE, TOOTH. —**horn in (on)*** intrude, impose upon, get in on; see ENTER, MEDDLE 1. —**lock horns** disagree, conflict, defy; see OPPOSE 1.

horned toad a small, scaly, insect-eating lizard with horn-like spines

hor·net (hôr′nit) *n.* ⟦OE *hyrnet*⟧ a large, yellow and black wasp

horn of plenty CORNUCOPIA

horn′pipe′ *n.* ⟦ME⟧ a lively dance formerly popular with sailors

horny (hôrn′ē) *adj.* **-i·er, -i·est 1** made of horn **2** having horns **3** toughened and calloused [*horny* hands] **4** [Slang] sexually aroused

ho·rol·o·gy (hō räl′ə jē) *n.* ⟦< Gr *hōra*, hour + -LOGY⟧ the science of measuring time or making timepieces

horo·scope (hôr′ə skōp′) *n.* ⟦< Gr *hōra*, hour + *skopos*, watcher⟧ a chart of the zodiacal signs and positions of planets, etc., esp. at the time of a person's birth, used by an astrologer to make a forecast

hor·ren·dous (hô ren′dəs) *adj.* ⟦see HORRID⟧ horrible; frightful

hor·ri·ble (hôr′ə bəl) *adj.* ⟦see fol.⟧ **1** causing horror; terrible; dreadful **2** [Colloq.] very bad, ugly, unpleasant, etc. **—hor′ri·bly** *adv.*

hor·rid (hôr′id) *adj.* ⟦< L *horrere*, to bristle, shake, be afraid⟧ **1** causing horror; terrible **2** very bad, ugly, unpleasant, etc. **—hor′rid·ly** *adv.*

hor·rif·ic (hô rif′ik, hə-) *adj.* horrifying

hor·ri·fy (hôr′ə fī′) *vt.* **-fied′, -fy′ing 1** to cause to feel horror **2** [Colloq.] to shock or disgust

hor·ror (hôr′ər) *n.* ⟦see HORRID⟧ **1** the strong feeling caused by something frightful or shocking **2** strong dislike **3** something that causes horror, etc.

hors de com·bat (ôr də kōn bä′) ⟦Fr, out of combat⟧ disabled

hors d'oeu·vre (ôr′dʉrv′) *pl.* **hors d'oeu·vres** (ôr′dʉrvz′) ⟦Fr, lit., outside of work⟧ an appetizer, as olives, canapés, etc., served before a meal

horse (hôrs) *n.* ⟦OE *hors*⟧ **1** a large, four-legged, solid-hoofed animal with flowing mane and tail, domesticated for drawing loads, carrying riders, etc. **2** a frame with legs for supporting something **—** *vt.* **horsed, hors′ing** to supply with a horse or horses; put on horseback **—** *adj.* of or on horses **—hold one's horses** [Slang] to curb one's impatience **—horse around** [Slang] to engage in horseplay

horse′back′ *n.* the back of a horse **—** *adv.* on horseback

horse chestnut 1 a flowering tree with large leaves and glossy brown seeds **2** its seed

horse′feath′ers *n., interj.* [Slang] nonsense

horse′fly′ *n., pl.* **-flies′** a large fly that sucks the blood of horses, etc.

horse′hair′ *n.* **1** hair from the mane or tail of a horse **2** a stiff fabric made from this hair

horse′hide′ *n.* **1** the hide of a horse **2** leather made from this

horse′laugh′ *n.* a loud, derisive laugh; guffaw

horse′man (-mən) *n., pl.* **-men** a man skilled in the riding or care of horses **—horse′man·ship′** *n.* **—horse′wom′an,** *pl.* **-wom′en,** *n.fem.*

horse opera [Slang] WESTERN (*n.*)

horse′play′ *n.* rough, boisterous fun

horse′pow′er *n.* a unit for measuring the power of engines, etc., equal to 746 watts or 33,000 foot-pounds per minute

horse′rad·ish *n.* **1** a plant with a pungent, white, fleshy root **2** a relish made of the grated root

horse sense [Colloq.] common sense

horse′shoe′ *n.* **1** a flat, U-shaped metal plate nailed to a horse's hoof to protect the hoof **2** anything shaped like this **3** [*pl.*] a game in which players toss horseshoes at two stakes

horseshoe crab a sea arthropod shaped like the base of a horse's foot, with a long, spinelike tail

horse′tail′ *n.* a rushlike plant found in moist areas

horse′whip′ *n.* a whip for driving horses **—** *vt.* **-whipped′, -whip′ping** to lash with a horsewhip

horsy (hôrs′ē) *adj.* **-i·er, -i·est 1** of, like, or suggesting a horse **2** of or like people who are fond of horses, fox-hunting, horse racing, etc. Also **hors′ey**

hor·ta·tory (hôr′tə tôr′ē) *adj.* ⟦< L *hortari*, incite⟧ exhorting; advising

hor·ti·cul·ture (hôr′ti kul′chər) *n.* ⟦< L *hortus*, garden + *cultura*, cultivation⟧ the art or science of growing plants **—hor′ti·cul′tural** *adj.*

ho·san·na (hō zan′ə) *n., interj.* ⟦< Heb *hōshī'āh nnā*, lit., save, we pray⟧ an exclamation of praise to God

hose (hōz) *n., pl.* **hose** or, for 2, usually **hos′es** ⟦OE *hosa*⟧ **1** [*pl.*] *a*) stockings *b*) socks **2** a flexible tube used to convey fluids **—** *vt.* **hosed, hos′ing** to water with a hose

ho·siery (hō′zhər ē) *n.* stockings

hos·pice (häs′pis) *n.* ⟦< L *hospes*, host, guest⟧ **1** a shelter for travelers **2** a homelike facility for the care of terminally ill patients

hos·pi·ta·ble (häs′pit ə bəl, häs pit′-) *adj.* ⟦see prec.⟧ friendly and solicitous toward guests, new arrivals, etc. **—hos′pi·ta·bly** *adv.*

hos·pi·tal (häs′pit′l) *n.* ⟦< L *hospes*, host, guest⟧ an institution providing medical treatment for people who are ill, injured, pregnant, etc.

hos·pi·tal·i·ty (häs′pi tal′ə tē) *n., pl.* **-ties** the act, practice, or quality of being hospitable

hos·pi·tal·ize (häs′pit′l īz′) *vt.* **-ized′, -iz′ing** to put in, or admit to, a hospital **—hos′pi·tali·za′tion** *n.*

host¹ (hōst) *n.* ⟦< ML *hostia*⟧ a wafer of the bread used in the Eucharist

host² (hōst) *n.* ⟦< L *hospes*, host, guest⟧ **1** one who entertains guests, esp. at home **2** a person who keeps an inn or hotel **3** any organism on or in which a parasitic organism lives **—** *vi., vt.* to act as host (to)

host³ (hōst) *n.* ⟦< ML *hostis*, army⟧ **1** an army **2** a great number

hosta (häs′tə) *n.* a lily with broad, ribbed leaves and trumpet-shaped flowers

hos·tage (häs′tij) *n.* ⟦< OFr⟧ a person kept or given as a pledge until certain conditions are met

hos·tel (häs′təl) *n.* ⟦< L *hospes*, host, guest⟧ an inn Also **hos′telry** (-rē), *pl.* **-ries** **—hos′teler** *n.*

host·ess (hōs′tis) *n.* **1** a woman who entertains guests, esp. at home **2** a woman employed in a restaurant to supervise serving, seating, etc.

THESAURUS

horny *a.* **1** [Callous] hard, firm, bony; see TOUGH 2. **2** [*Sexually excited] sensual, aroused, lecherous; see EXCITED, LEWD 2.

horrendous *a.* horrible, frightful, terrible; see POOR 2, FAULTY.

horrible *a.* **1** [Offensive] repulsive, dreadful, disgusting; see OFFENSIVE 2. **2** [Frightful] shameful, shocking, awful; see FRIGHTFUL, TERRIBLE 1.

horrid *a.* hideous, disturbing, shameful; see OFFENSIVE 2, PITIFUL.

horror *n.* awe, terror, fright; see FEAR.

horse *n.* nag, draft animal, plow horse, racer, saddlehorse, steed, mount, charger, hunter, cutting horse, stallion, gelding, hack, mare, thoroughbred, pacer, trotter, courser; see also ANIMAL. **—from the horse's mouth*** originally, from an authority, according to the original source of the information; see OFFICIALLY 1. **—hold one's horses*** curb one's impatience, slow down,

relax; see RESTRAIN. **—horse around*** fool around, cavort, cause trouble; see MISBEHAVE, PLAY 2. **—on one's high horse*** arrogant, haughty, disdainful; see EGOTISTIC.

horseman *n.* equestrian, rider, jockey; see COWBOY, RIDER 1.

horseplay *n.* clowning, play, fooling around; see FUN, JOKE.

horsepower *n.* strength, pull, power; see ENERGY 2.

hose *n.* **1** [Stocking] men's or women's hose, tights, panty hose; see HOSIERY. **2** [A flexible conduit] garden hose, fire hose, line, tubing; see also PIPE 1, TUBE 1.

hosiery *n.* silk stockings, rayon stockings, nylon stockings, woolen stockings, seamless hose, full-fashioned hose, socks, anklets, tights, panty hose, leotards, knee socks, body stocking.

hospitable *a.* cordial, courteous, open; see FRIENDLY.

hospital *n.* clinic, infirmary, sanatorium, sanitarium, dispensary, mental hospital, army hospital, city hospital, public hospital, veteran's hospital, medical center, lying-in hospital, health service, outpatient ward, sick bay, rest home.

hospitality *n.* good cheer, companionship, good fellowship; see ENTERTAINMENT, WELCOME.

host² *v.* receive, treat, wine and dine; see ENTERTAIN 2.

host²,³ *n.* **1** [A person who entertains] man of the house, woman of the house, entertainer, toastmaster, master of ceremonies. **2** [A large group] throng, multitude, army; see CROWD, GATHERING. **3** [Organism on which a parasite subsists] host mother, host body, animal; see PARASITE 1.

hostage *n.* security, captive, victim of a kidnapping; see PRISONER.

hostess *n.* society lady, socialite, club-woman, social leader, social

hos·tile (häs′təl) *adj.* ⟦ < L *hostis*, enemy ⟧ **1** of or typical of an enemy **2** unfriendly —**hos′tilely** *adv.*

hos·til·i·ty (häs til′ə tē) *n., pl.* **-ties 1** a feeling of enmity, ill will, etc. **2** *a*) a hostile act *b*) [*pl.*] warfare

hos·tler (häs′lər, äs′-) *n.* ⟦contr. of HOSTELER⟧ one who takes care of horses at an inn, stable, etc.

hot (hät) *adj.* **hot′ter, hot′test** ⟦OE *hat*⟧ **1** *a*) having a temperature higher than that of the human body *b*) having a relatively high temperature **2** producing a burning sensation [*hot* pepper] **3** characterized by strong feeling or intense activity, etc., as *a*) impetuous [a *hot* temper] *b*) violent [a *hot* battle] *c*) lustful *d*) very controversial **4** following closely [in *hot* pursuit] **5** electrically charged [a *hot* wire] **6** [Colloq.] recent; fresh [*hot* news] **7** [Slang] *a*) recently stolen or smuggled *b*) excellent; good —**make it hot for** [Colloq.] to make things uncomfortable for — **hot′ly** *adv.* —**hot′ness** *n.*

hot air [Slang] empty talk

hot′bed′ *n.* **1** a bed of earth covered with glass and heated, as by manure, for forcing plants **2** any place that fosters rapid growth or extensive activity

hot′blood′ed *adj.* excitable; ardent, reckless, etc.

hot′box′ *n.* an overheated bearing on an axle or shaft

hot cake a pancake —**sell like hot cakes** [Colloq.] to be sold rapidly and in large quantities

hot dog [Colloq.] a wiener, esp. one served hot in a long, soft roll

ho·tel (hō tel′) *n.* ⟦ < OFr *hostel*, hostel ⟧ an establishment providing lodging and, usually, meals for travelers, etc.

ho·tel·ier (hōt′'l ir′, -yā′; hō′tel′-) *n.* ⟦Fr⟧ an owner or manager of a hotel

hot flash the sensation of a wave of heat passing over the body, often experienced by women during menopause

hot′head′ed *adj.* **1** quick-tempered **2** impetuous —**hot′head′** *n.*

hot′house′ *n.* GREENHOUSE

hot line a telephone line for immediate communication, as between heads of state in a crisis

hot plate a small, portable stove for cooking food

hot potato [Colloq.] a troubling problem that no one wants to handle

hot rod [Slang] an automobile, often an old one, whose engine has been supercharged —**hot rod·der**

hot seat [Slang] **1** ELECTRIC CHAIR **2** a difficult situation

hot′shot′ *n.* [Slang] one who is expert at something in an aggressive way

hot′-tem′pered *adj.* having a fiery temper

Hot·ten·tot (hät′'n tät′) *n.* **1** a member of a nomadic people of SW Africa **2** their language

hot tub a large wooden tub in which several people can soak in hot water

hound (hound) *n.* ⟦OE *hund*, dog⟧ **1** any of several breeds of hunting dog **2** any dog —*vt.* **1** to hunt or chase with or as with hounds **2** to urge on

hounds·tooth check (houndz′tooth′) a pattern of irregular broken checks, used in woven material

hour (our) *n.* ⟦ < Gr *hōra* ⟧ **1** one of the twenty-four parts of a day; sixty minutes **2** the time for a particular activity [lunch *hour*] **3** [*pl.*] a period fixed for work, etc. [office *hours*] **4** the time of day [the *hour* is 2:30] **5** *Educ.* a credit, equal to one hour spent in class per week —**after hours** after the regular hours for business, school, etc. —**hour after hour** every hour

hour′glass′ *n.* an instrument for measuring time by the trickling of sand, etc. from one part to another

hour hand the short hand of a clock or watch, which indicates the hours

hou·ri (hoo′rē, hou′-) *n., pl.* **-ris** ⟦ < Ar *hūrīyah*, black-eyed woman ⟧ a beautiful nymph of the Muslim Paradise

hour′ly *adj.* **1** happening every hour **2** done during an hour **3** frequent —*adv.* **1** once an hour **2** often

house (hous; *for v.* houz) *n., pl.* **houses** (hou′ziz) ⟦OE *hus*⟧ **1** a building to live in; specif., a building occupied by one family or person **2** the people who live in a house; household **3** [*often* H-] a family as including kin, ancestors, and descendants, etc. **4** a royal family **4** shelter, living or storage space, etc. **5** *a*) a theater *b*) the audience in a theater **6** a business firm **7** [*often* H-] a legislative assembly — *vt.* **housed, hous′ing 1** to provide a house or lodgings for **2** to cover, shelter, etc. —**keep house** to take care of a home —**on the house** at the expense of the establishment

house′boat′ *n.* a large, flat-bottomed boat used as a residence

house′break′ing *n.* the act of breaking into and entering another's house to commit theft or another felony

house′bro′ken *adj.* trained to live in a house (i.e., to urinate, etc. in a special place): said of a dog, cat, etc.

house′clean′ing *n.* a cleaning of the inside of a house — **house′clean′** *vi., vt.*

house′fly′ *n., pl.* **-flies′** a two-winged fly found in and around houses

house′hold′ *n.* **1** all those living in one house **2** the home and its affairs —**house′hold′er** *n.*

household word a common saying or thing, familiar to nearly everyone

house′hus′band *n.* a married man whose job is keeping house and taking care of domestic affairs

house′keep′er *n.* one who runs a home, esp. a person hired to do this

house′maid′ *n.* a maid for housework

house′moth′er *n.* a woman in charge of a sorority house, dormitory, etc., often as housekeeper

House of Commons the lower house of the legislature of Great Britain or Canada

House of Lords the upper house of the legislature of Great Britain

House of Representatives the lower house of the legislature of the U.S. and most of the States of the U.S.

house′plant′ *n.* an indoor plant used mainly for decoration

house′wares′ (-werz′) *n.pl.* articles for household use, esp. in the kitchen

house′warm′ing *n.* a party to celebrate moving into a new home

house′wife′ *n., pl.* **-wives′** a married woman whose job is keeping house and taking care of domestic affairs

---

◼ THESAURUS ◼

climber, entertainer, lady of the house, mistress of the household, toastmistress, mistress of ceremonies.

hostile *a.* antagonistic, hateful, opposed; see UNFRIENDLY.

hostility *n.* abhorrence, aversion, bitterness; see HATRED.

hot *a.* **1** [Having a high temperature] torrid, burning, fiery, flaming, blazing, very warm, baking, roasting, smoking, scorching, blistering, searing, sizzling, tropical, warm, broiling, red-hot, grilling, piping hot, white-hot, scalding, parching, sultry, on fire, at high temperature, incandescent, smoldering, thermal, toasting, simmering, blazing hot*, boiling hot*, like an oven*, hotter than blazes*; see also BOILING, COOKING, MOLTEN.—*Ant.* COLD, frigid, chilly. **2** [Aroused] furious, ill-tempered, indignant; see ANGRY. **3** [*Erotic] spicy, salacious, carnal; see SENSUAL 2. —**get hot*** become excited, become enthusiastic, burn with fervor, get angry, rave; see also RAGE 1.

—**hot under the collar*** furious, mad, resentful; see ANGRY. —**make it hot for*** create discomfort for, cause trouble for, vex; see DISTURB.

hotel *n.* stopping place, inn, lodging house, halfway house, boarding house, hostel, motel, motor hotel, resort, tavern, spa, rooming house, flop-house*.

hotheaded *a.* unmanageable, wild, reckless; see RASH, UNRULY.

hound *n.* greyhound, bloodhound, beagle; see ANIMAL, DOG.

hound *v.* badger, provoke, annoy; see BOTHER 2.

hour *n.* time unit, sixty minutes, man-hour, planetary hour, horse-power hour, class hour, supper hour, study hour, rush hour; see also TIME 1. —**hour after hour** continually, steadily, on and on; see REGULARLY.

hourly *a.* each hour, every hour, every sixty minutes; see FREQUENTLY, REGULARLY.

house *n.* **1** [A habitation] dwelling, apartment house, residence; see

APARTMENT, HOME **1**. **2** [A family] line, family tradition, ancestry; see FAMILY. **3** [A legislative body] congress, council, parliament; see LEGISLATURE. —**bring down the house*** receive applause, create enthusiasm, please; see EXCITE. —**clean house** arrange, put in order, tidy up; see CLEAN. —**keep house** manage a home, run a house, be a housekeeper; see MANAGE 1. —**like a house on fire** actively, vigorously, energetically; see QUICKLY. —**on the house*** without expense, gratis, complimentary; see FREE 4.

household *n.* family unit, house, domestic establishment; see FAMILY, HOME 1.

housekeeper *n.* wife and mother, caretaker, serving woman; see SERVANT.

housewife *n.* mistress, lady of the house, housekeeper, home economist, homemaker, family manager, wife and mother, stay-at-home*; see also WIFE.

house'work' *n.* the work involved in keeping house; cleaning, cooking, etc.

hous·ing (hou'ziŋ) *n.* **1** the providing of shelter or lodging **2** shelter or lodging **3** houses collectively **4** *Mech.* a frame, box, etc. for containing some part, mechanism, etc.

hove (hōv) *vt., vi. alt. pt. & pp. of* HEAVE

hovel (huv'əl, häv'-) *n.* ⟦ME⟧ any small, miserable dwelling; hut

hover (huv'ər, häv'-) *vi.* ⟦< ME *hoven*, to stay (suspended)⟧ **1** to flutter in the air near one place **2** to linger close by **3** to waver (*between*)

how (hou) *adv.* ⟦OE *hu*⟧ **1** in what manner or way **2** in what state or condition **3** for what reason **4** to what extent, degree, etc. *How* is also used as an intensive — **how about?** what is your thought concerning?

how·beit (hou bē'it) *adv.* [Archaic] however it may be; nevertheless

how·dah (hou'də) *n.* ⟦Hindi *hauda*⟧ a seat for riding on the back of an elephant or camel

how·ev·er (hou ev'ər) *adv.* **1** in whatever manner **2** to whatever degree **3** nevertheless Also [Old Poet.] **how·e·er'**

how·itzer (hou'it sər) *n.* ⟦< Czech *houfnice*, orig., a sling⟧ a short cannon, firing shells in a high trajectory

howl (houl) *vi.* ⟦ME *hulen*⟧ **1** to utter the long, wailing cry of wolves, dogs, etc. **2** to utter a similar cry of pain, anger, etc. **3** to shout or laugh in scorn, mirth, etc. — *vt.* **1** to utter with a howl **2** to drive by howling — *n.* **1** the wailing cry of a wolf, dog, etc. **2** any similar sound **3** [Colloq.] a joke

howl'er *n.* **1** one that howls **2** [Colloq.] a ludicrous blunder

howl'ing *adj.* **1** that howls **2** [Slang] great *[a howling success]*

how·so·ever (hou'sō ev'ər) *adv.* **1** to whatever degree or extent **2** by whatever means

hoy·den (hoi'dən) *n.* ⟦< ? Du⟧ a bold, boisterous girl; tomboy

Hoyle (hoil) *n.* a book of rules for card games, orig. compiled by E. Hoyle (1672-1769) —**according to Hoyle** according to the rules

HP or **hp** horsepower

HQ or **hq** headquarters

hr. hour

HR or **H.R.** House of Representatives

HRH or **H.R.H.** Her (or His) Royal Highness

HS or **H.S.** high school

ht. height

hua·ra·ches (wä rä'chēz', -chäz') *n.pl.* ⟦MexSp⟧ flat sandals with uppers made of straps or woven leather strips

hub (hub) *n.* ⟦< ?⟧ **1** the center part of a wheel **2** a center of activity

hub·bub (hub'bub') *n.* ⟦prob. < Gael exclamation⟧ an uproar; tumult

hub'cap' *n.* a tight cap over the hub of a wheel, esp. on an automobile

hu·bris (hyōō'bris) *n.* ⟦Gr *hybris*⟧ arrogance caused by excessive pride

huckle·berry (huk'əl ber'ē) *n., pl.* **-ries** ⟦prob. < ME *hurtilberye*⟧ **1** a shrub with blue berries **2** this berry

huck·ster (huk'stər) *n.* ⟦< MDu *hoeken*, peddle⟧ a peddler, esp. of fruits, vegetables, etc. — *vt.* to peddle

HUD (Department of) Housing and Urban Development

hud·dle (hud'l) *vi., vt.* **-dled, -dling** ⟦< ?⟧ **1** to crowd close together **2** to draw (oneself) up — *n.* **1** a confused crowd or heap **2** [Colloq.] a private conference **3** *Football* a grouping of a team to get signals before a play

hue¹ (hyōō) *n.* ⟦< OE *heow*⟧ **1** color **2** a particular shade or tint of a color

hue² (hyōō) *n.* ⟦< OFr *hu*, outcry⟧ a shouting: now only in **hue and cry**

huff (huf) *vi.* to blow; puff — *n.* a state of smoldering anger or resentment —**huff'y**, **-i·er**, **-i·est**, *adj.*

hug (hug) *vt.* **hugged, hug'ging** ⟦prob. < ON *hugga*, to comfort⟧ **1** to clasp closely and fondly in the arms; embrace **2** to cling to (a belief, etc.) **3** to keep close to — *vi.* to embrace each other — *n.* a close embrace

huge (hyōōj) *adj.* **hug'er, hug'est** ⟦< OFr *ahuge*⟧ very large; gigantic; immense —**huge'ly** *adv.* —**huge'ness** *n.*

Hu·gue·not (hyōō'gə nät') *n.* a 16th or 17th-c. French Protestant

huh (hu, hun) *interj.* an exclamation used to express contempt, surprise, etc., or to ask a question

hula (hōō'lə) *n.* ⟦Haw⟧ a native Hawaiian dance Also **hu'la-hu'la**

hulk (hulk) *n.* ⟦< Gr *holkas*, towed ship⟧ **1** the hull of an old, dismantled ship **2** a big, clumsy person or thing

hulk'ing *adj.* bulky and clumsy

hull (hul) *n.* ⟦OE *hulu*⟧ **1** the outer covering of a seed or fruit, as the husk of grain, shell of a nut, etc. **2** the frame or main body of a ship, airship, etc. **3** any outer covering — *vt.* to take the hulls off (nuts, etc.) —**hull'er** *n.*

hulla·ba·loo (hul'ə bə lōō') *n.* ⟦echoic⟧ clamor; hubbub

hum (hum) *vi.* **hummed, hum'ming** ⟦echoic⟧ **1** to make a low, continuous, murmuring sound **2** to sing with closed lips **3** [Colloq.] to be full of activity — *vt.* to sing (a tune) with closed lips — *n.* a continuous murmur

hu·man (hyōō'mən) *adj.* ⟦< L *humanus*⟧ of, characteristic of, or having the qualities typical of mankind — *n.* a person: also **human being** —**hu'man·ness** *n.*

hu·mane (hyōō mān') *adj.* ⟦var. of prec.⟧ **1** kind, tender, merciful, etc. **2** civilizing; refining —**hu·mane'ly** *adv.* — **hu·mane'ness** *n.*

hu·man·ism (hyōō'mə niz'əm) *n.* **1** any system of thought based on the interests and ideals of man **2** [H-] the intellectual movement that stemmed from the study of the Greek and Latin classics during the Middle Ages —**hu'man·ist** *n., adj.* —**hu'man·is'tic** *adj.* —**hu'man·is'ti·cally** *adv.*

housework *n.* house cleaning, spring cleaning, window-washing, sweeping, cooking, baking, dusting, mopping, washing, laundering, bed-making, sewing, ironing, mending; see also JOB 2.

housing *n.* habitation, home construction, housing development, low-cost housing, house-building program, sheltering, installation, abode, domicile, house, accommodations, quarters, roof, dwelling, lodging, pad*, residence, headquarters; see also HOME 1, SHELTER.

hover *v.* float, flutter, be in midair; see FLY 1, HANG 2.

how *a., conj.* in what way, to what degree, by what method, in what manner, according to what specifications, from what source, by whose help, whence, wherewith, by virtue of what, whereby, through what agency, by what means.

however *a., conj.* **1** [But] still, though, nevertheless; see BUT 1, YET 1. **2** [In spite of] despite, without regard to, nonetheless; see NOTWITH-STANDING.

howl *n.* wail, lament, shriek; see CRY 1, YELL.

howl *v.* bawl, wail, lament; see CRY 1,

YELL.

hub *n.* core, heart, middle; see CENTER 1.

hubbub *n.* turmoil, fuss, disorder; see CONFUSION, NOISE 2, UPROAR.

huddle *v.* crouch, press close, crowd, bunch, draw, together, mass, cluster, throng, nestle, cuddle, hug, curl up, snuggle.

hue¹ *n.* hue, shade, dye; see TINT.

huff *n.* annoyance, offense, perturbation; see ANGER, RAGE 1.

huffy *a.* offended, piqued, huffish; see ANGRY, INSULTED, IRRITABLE.

hug *n.* embrace, squeeze, tight grip, caress, clinch, bearhug; see also TOUCH 2.

hug *v.* embrace, squeeze, clasp, press, love, hold, be near to, cling, fold in the arms, clutch, seize, envelop, enfold, nestle, welcome, cuddle, lock, press to the bosom, snuggle.

huge *a.* tremendous, enormous, immense; see LARGE 1.

hulk *n.* bulk, hunk, lump; see MASS 1, PART 1.

hull *n.* **1** [The body of a vessel] framework, skeleton, main structure; see FRAME 1. **2** [A shell] peeling, husk, shuck; see SHELL 1.

hullabaloo *n.* tumult, chaos, clamor; see CONFUSION, NOISE 2, UPROAR.

hum *v.* buzz, drone, murmur, sing low, hum a tune, croon, whisper, moan, make a buzzing sound, whir, vibrate, purr.

human *a.* anthropoid, animal, biped, civilized, man-made, anthropomorphic, manlike, of man, belonging to man, humanistic, individual, man's, personal, humane; see also ANIMAL.— *Ant.* DIVINE, bestial, nonhuman.

human being *n.* being, mortal, individual; see MAN 1, PERSON 1, WOMAN 1.

humane *a.* benevolent, sympathetic, understanding, pitying, compassionate, kindhearted, human, tender-hearted, forgiving, gracious, charitable, gentle, tender, friendly, generous, lenient, tolerant, democratic, good-natured, liberal, open-minded, broad-minded, altruistic, philanthropic, helpful, magnanimous, amiable, genial, cordial, unselfish, warmhearted, bighearted, softhearted, good, soft, easy; see also KIND.—*Ant.* CRUEL, barbaric, inhuman.

hu·mani·tar·ian (hyōō man′ə ter′ē ən) *n.* a person devoted to promoting the welfare of humanity; philanthropist —*adj.* helping humanity —**hu·man′i·tar′i·an·ism′** *n.*

hu·man·ity (hyōō man′ə tē) *n.*, *pl.* **-ties** 1 the fact or quality of being human or humane 2 mankind; people — **the humanities** literature, philosophy, the fine arts, etc. as distinguished from the sciences

hu·man·ize (hyōō′mə niz′) *vt.* **-ized′, -iz′ing** to make or become human or humane —**hu′mani·za′tion** *n.* —**hu′man·iz′er** *n.*

hu′man·kind′ *n.* mankind; people

hu′manly *adv.* 1 in a human manner 2 by human means

hu′man·oid′ (-mə noid′) *adj.* nearly human —*n.* a nearly human creature

hum·ble (hum′b′l, um′-) *adj.* **-bler, -blest** 〚< L *humilis*, low〛 1 having or showing a consciousness of one's shortcomings; modest 2 lowly; unpretentious —*vt.* **-bled, -bling** 1 to lower in condition or rank 2 to lower in pride; make modest —**hum′ble·ness** *n.* —**hum′bly** *adv.*

hum·bug (hum′bug′) *n.* 〚< ?〛 1 fraud; sham; hoax 2 an impostor —*vt.* **-bugged′, -bug′ging** to dupe; deceive — *interj.* nonsense!

hum·dinger (hum′diŋ′ər) *n.* [Slang] a person or thing considered excellent

hum·drum (hum′drum′) *adj.* 〚echoic〛 dull; monotonous

hu·merus (hyōō′mər əs) *n.*, *pl.* **-meri** (-i′) 〚L〛 the bone of the upper arm or forelimb —**hu′meral** *adj.*

hu·mid (hyōō′mid) *adj.* 〚< L *umere*, be moist〛 damp; moist

hu·midi·fy (hyōō mid′ə fi′) *vt.* **-fied′, -fy′ing** to make humid; dampen —**hu·mid′i·fi′er** *n.*

hu·mid′ity *n.* 1 moistness; dampness 2 amount of moisture in the air

hu·mi·dor (hyōō′mə dôr′) *n.* a case or jar for keeping tobacco moist

hu·mili·ate (hyōō mil′ē āt′) *vt.* **-at′ed, -at′ing** 〚< L *humilis*, humble〛 to hurt the pride or dignity of; mortify —**hu·mil′ia′tion** *n.*

hu·mil′ity (-ə tē) *n.* the state or quality of being humble

humming·bird (hum′iŋ burd′) *n.* a very small, brightly colored bird with narrow wings that vibrate rapidly, often with a humming sound

hum·mock (hum′ək) *n.* 〚< ?〛 a low, rounded hill; knoll — **hum′mocky** *adj.*

hu·mon·gous (hyōō mäŋ′gəs, -muŋ′-) *adj.* 〚? a blend of *huge, monstrous*, etc.〛 [Slang] enormous

hu·mor (hyōō′mər, yōō′-) *n.* 〚< L *humor*, fluid: after former belief in four body fluids (humors) held responsible for one's disposition〛 1 mood; state of mind 2 whim; caprice 3 a comical quality 4 *a*) the ability to appreciate or express what is funny, amusing, etc. *b*) the expression of this —*vt.* to comply with the mood or whim of; indulge Brit. sp. **hu′mour** —**out of humor** not in a good mood; disagreeable —**hu′mor·ist** *n.* —**hu′mor·less** *adj.*

hu′mor·ous *adj.* funny; amusing; comical —**hu′mor·ously** *adv.*

hump (hump) *n.* 〚< ?〛 a rounded, protruding lump, as on a camel's back —*vt.* to hunch; arch —**over the hump** [Colloq.] past the most difficult part

hump′back′ *n.* 1 a humped, deformed back 2 a person having this 3 a large whale with long flippers and a raised, rounded back —**hump′backed′** *adj.*

hu·mus (hyōō′məs) *n.* 〚L, earth〛 the dark part of the soil, resulting from the partial decay of leaves, etc.

Hun (hun) *n.* a member of a warlike Asiatic people who invaded Europe in the 4th and 5th c. A.D.

hunch (hunch) *vt.* 〚< ?〛 to arch into a hump —*vi.* to move forward jerkily —*n.* 1 a hump 2 a feeling not based on known facts; premonition

hunch·back (hunch′bak′) *n.* HUMPBACK (senses 1 & 2) — **hunch′backed′** *adj.*

hun·dred (hun′drəd) *n.*, *adj.* 〚OE〛 ten times ten; 100; C —**hun′dredth** (-drədth) *adj.*, *n.*

hun′dred·fold′ *adj.*, *adv.* a hundred times as much or as many

hun′dred·weight′ *n.* a unit of weight equal to 100 pounds in the U.S. and 112 pounds in Great Britain

hung (hun) *vt.*, *vi. pt. & pp. of* HANG —**hung over** [Slang] having a hangover —**hung up (on)** [Slang] emotionally disturbed, frustrated, or obsessed (by)

Hung. 1 Hungarian 2 Hungary

Hun·gar·ian (huŋ ger′ē ən) *n.* 1 the language of Hungary 2 a native or inhabitant of Hungary —*adj.* of Hungary

THESAURUS

humanitarian *n.* altruist, philanthropist, benefactor; see PATRON.

humanity *n.* 1 [The human race] man, mankind, men; see MAN 1. 2 [An ideal of human behavior] tolerance, sympathy, understanding; see KINDNESS 1, VIRTUE 1, 2.

humble *a.* 1 [Meek] lowly, submissive, gentle, quiet, unassuming, diffident, simple, retiring, bashful, shy, timid, reserved, deferential, self-conscious, soft-spoken, sheepish, mild, withdrawn, unpretentious, hesitant, fearful, tentative, poor in spirit, sedate, unpresuming, manageable, ordinary, unambitious, commonplace, free from pride, without arrogance, peaceable, obedient, passive, tame, restrained, unostentatious, unimportant, gentle as a lamb, resigned, subdued, tolerant, content, eating humble pie; see also MODEST 2.—*Ant.* PROUD, haughty, conceited. 2 [Lowly] unpretentious, unassuming, modest, seemly, becoming, homespun, natural, low, proletarian, servile, undistinguished, pitiful, sordid, shabby, underprivileged, meager, beggarly, commonplace, unimportant, insignificant, small, poor, rough, hard, base, meek, little, of low birth, obscure, inferior, plain, common, homely, simple, uncouth, miserable, scrubby, ordinary, humdrum, trival, vulgar.—*Ant.* NOBLE, upperclass, privileged.

humble *v.* shame, mortify, chasten, demean, demote, lower, crush, bring low, put to shame, silence, reduce, humiliate, degrade, overcome, strike dumb, put down, pull down, bring down, snub, discredit, deflate, upset, make ashamed, take down a peg, pull rank on*, squelch*, squash*.—*Ant.* PRAISE, exalt, glorify.

humbly *a.* meekly, submissively, simply, obscurely, apologetically.

humbug *n.* lie, fraud, faker; see DECEPTION, NONSENSE 1.

humdrum *a.* monotonous, common, uninteresting; see DULL 4.

humid *a.* stuffy, sticky, muggy; see CLOSE 5, WET 1.

humidity *n.* moisture, wetness, dampness, mugginess, dankness, heaviness, sogginess, thickness, fogginess, wet, sultriness, steaminess, steam, evaporation, dewiness, stickiness, moistness; see also RAIN 1.

humiliate *v.* debase, chasten, mortify, make a fool of, put to shame, humble, degrade, crush, shame, confuse, snub, confound, lower, dishonor, depress, fill with shame, break, demean, bring low, conquer, make ashamed, vanquish, take down a peg; see also DISGRACE, EMBARRASS.

humiliation *n.* chagrin, mortification, degradation; see DISGRACE, EMBARRASSMENT, SHAME 2.

humility *n.* meekness, timidity, submissiveness, servility, reserve, subservience, subjection, humbleness, submission, obedience, passiveness, nonresistance, resignation, bashfulness, shyness, inferiority complex.— *Ant.* PRIDE, vainglory, conceit.

humor *n.* 1 [Comedy] amusement, jesting, raillery, joking, merriment, clowning, farce, facetiousness, whimsy, black humor; see also ENTERTAINMENT, FUN. 2 [An example of humor] witticism, pleasantry, banter; see JOKE. 3 [The ability to appreciate comedy] good humor, sense of humor, wittiness, high spirits, jolliness, gaiety, joyfulness, playfulness, happy frame of mind.

humor *v.* indulge, pamper, baby, play up to, gratify, please, pet, coddle, spoil, comply with, appease, placate, soften, be playful with; see also COMFORT 1.—*Ant.* ANGER, provoke, enrage.

humorous *a.* comical, comic, entertaining; see FUNNY 1.

humorously *a.* comically, ridiculously, playfully, absurdly, ludicrously, amusingly, jokingly, ironically, satirically, facetiously, merrily, genially, jovially, in a comical manner, in an amusing manner, just for fun.

hump *n.* protuberance, mound, bump, swelling, camel hump, humpback, hunchback, hummock, protrusion, knob, prominence, eminence, projection, swell, hunch, lump, dune.

hunch *n.* idea, notion, feeling, premonition, forecast, presentiment, instinct, expectation, anticipation, precognition, prescience, forewarning, clue, foreboding, hint, portent, apprehension, misgiving, qualm, suspicion, inkling, glimmer; see also THOUGHT 2.

hundred *n.* ten tens, five score, century; see NUMBER.

hung *a.* suspended, swaying, dangling; see HANGING. —**hung up*** 1 [Troubled] disturbed, psychotic, psychopathic; see TROUBLED. 2 [Intent] absorbed, engrossed, preoccupied; see THOUGHTFUL 1.

hun·ger (huŋ′gər) *n.* ⟦OE *hungor*⟧ **1** discomfort caused by a need for food **2** starvation **3** a desire for food **4** any strong desire — *vi.* **1** to be hungry **2** to desire —**hun′gry, -grier, -gri·est,** *adj.* —**hun′grily** *adv.*

hunger strike the refusal of a prisoner, demonstrator, etc. to eat until certain demands are met

hunk (huŋk) *n.* ⟦Fl *hunke*⟧ [Colloq.] a large piece, lump, etc.

hun·ker (huŋ′kər) *vi.* ⟦< dial.⟧ to squat —*n.* [*pl.*] haunches or buttocks

hunt (hunt) *vt., vi.* ⟦OE *huntian*⟧ **1** to kill or catch (game) for food or sport **2** to try to find; search **3** to chase —*n.* **1** a hunting **2** a group of people who hunt together **3** a search —**hunt′er** or **hunts′man** (-mən), *pl.* **-men,** *n.* —**hunt′ress** *n.fem.*

hur·dle (hurd′l) *n.* ⟦OE *hyrdel*⟧ **1** a framelike barrier which horses or runners must leap in a race **2** an obstacle —*vt.* **-dled, -dling 1** to jump over **2** to overcome (an obstacle) —**hur′dler** *n.*

hur·dy-gur·dy (hur′dē gur′dē) *n., pl.* **-dies** ⟦? echoic⟧ BARREL ORGAN

hurl (hurl) *vt.* ⟦prob. < ON⟧ **1** to throw with force or violence **2** to cast down **3** to utter vehemently — *vi.* [Colloq.] *Baseball* to pitch —**hurl′er** *n.*

hurly-burly (hurl′ē burl′ē) *n., pl.* **-burl′ies** a turmoil; uproar

hur·rah (hə rä′, -rô′) *interj., n.* ⟦echoic⟧ a shout of joy, approval, etc. — *vi., vt.* to shout "hurrah" (for); cheer Also **hur·ray′** (-rā′)

hur·ri·cane (hur′i kān′) *n.* ⟦< WInd *huracan*⟧ a violent tropical cyclone

hurricane lamp 1 an oil lamp or candlestick with a glass chimney to protect the flame **2** an electric lamp like this

hurry (hur′ē) *vt.* **-ried, -ry·ing** ⟦prob. akin to HURL⟧ **1** to move or send with haste **2** to cause to occur or be done more rapidly or too rapidly **3** to urge to act soon or too soon — *vi.* to move or act with haste —*n.* **1** rush; urgency **2** eagerness to do, go, etc. quickly —**hur′riedly** *adv.*

hurt (hurt) *vt.,* **hurt, hurt′ing** ⟦< OFr *hurter,* to hit⟧ **1** to cause pain or injury to **2** to harm **3** to offend — *vi.* **1** to cause injury, pain, etc. **2** to have pain; be sore —*n.* **1** a pain or injury **2** harm; damage —*adj.* injured; damaged

hurt′ful *adj.* causing hurt; harmful

hur·tle (hurt′l) *vi., vt.* **-tled, -tling** ⟦ME *hurtlen*⟧ to move or throw with great speed or much force

hus·band (huz′bənd) *n.* ⟦< ON *hūs,* house + *bondi,* freeholder⟧ a married man — *vt.* to manage economically; conserve

hus′band·man (-mən) *n., pl.* **-men** [Archaic] a farmer

hus′bandry *n.* **1** careful, thrifty management **2** farming

hush (hush) *vt.* ⟦< ME *huscht,* quiet (adj.)⟧ **1** to make quiet or silent **2** to soothe; lull — *vi.* to become quiet or silent —*n.* quiet; silence — *interj.* an exclamation calling for silence

hush′-hush′ *adj.* [Colloq.] very secret

Hush Puppies *trademark for* a kind of shoe with soft leather or suede uppers —[**h- p-**] such a pair of shoes

hush puppy a small ball of fried cornmeal dough

husk (husk) *n.* ⟦prob. < MDu *huus,* house⟧ **1** the dry outer covering of various fruits or seeds, as of an ear of corn **2** any dry, rough, or useless covering — *vt.* to remove the husk from

husky[1] (hus′kē) *n., pl.* **-kies** ⟦< a var. of ESKIMO⟧ [*also* H-] a dog of any of several breeds for pulling sleds in the Arctic

husky[2] (hus′kē) *adj.* **-i·er, -i·est 1** dry in the throat; hoarse **2** ⟦< toughness of a *husk*⟧ big and strong — **husk′i·ly** *adv.* —**husk′i·ness** *n.*

hus·sar (hoo zär′) *n.* ⟦< Serb *husar*⟧ a European lightarmed cavalryman, usually with a brilliant dress uniform

hussy (huz′ē, hus′-) *n., pl.* **-sies** ⟦< ME *huswif,* housewife⟧ **1** a woman of low morals **2** a bold, saucy girl

hus·tings (hus′tiŋz) *n.pl.* ⟦< ON *hūsthing,* house council⟧ [*usually with sing. v.*] the process of, or a place for, political campaigning

hus·tle (hus′əl) *vt.* **-tled, -tling** ⟦Du *husselen,* shake up⟧ **1** to push about; jostle **2** to force in a rough, hurried manner — *vi.* **1** to move hurriedly **2** [Colloq.] to work energetically **3** [Slang] to obtain money aggressively or

THESAURUS

hunger *n.* craving, longing, yearning, mania, lust, desire for food, famine, gluttony, hungriness, panting, drought, want, vacancy, void, greed, sweet tooth*.—*Ant.* SATISFACTION, satiety, glut.

hungry *a.* starved, famished, ravenous, desirous, hankering, unsatisfied, unfilled, starving, insatiate, voracious, half-starved, omnivorous, piggish, hoggish, on an empty stomach*, hungry as a wolf*, empty*.— *Ant.* FULL, satisfied, fed.

hunk *n.* lump, large piece, good-sized bit, portion, a fair quantity, a good bit, chunk, bunch, mass, clod, a pile, thick slice, morsel, a lot, slice, gob, loaf, wad; see also PIECE 1.

hunt *n.* chase, shooting, field sport; see HUNTING, SPORT 3.

hunt *v.* **1** [To pursue with intent to kill] follow, give chase, stalk, hound, trail, dog, seek, capture, kill, shoot, track, heel, shadow, chase, hunt out, snare, look for, fish, fish for, poach, gun for*, go gunning for*; see TRACK 1. **2** [To try to find] investigate, probe, look for; see SEEK.

hunted *a.* pursued, followed, tracked, sought, trailed, chased, stalked, hounded, tailed, wanted, driven out, searched for.

hunter *n.* huntsman, stalker, chaser, sportsman, pursuer, big-game hunter, gunner, poacher, horsewoman, huntress, horseman, archer, deerstalker, angler, fisherman, bowman, shooter.

hunting *n.* the chase, the hunt, sporting, shooting, stalking, preying, trapping, big-game hunting, deer hunting, fox hunting, pheasant shooting, angling, fishing, steeplechase, riding to hounds, gunning; see also SPORT 3.

hurdle *n.* barricade, obstacle, blockade; see BARRIER.

hurdle *v.* jump over, scale, leap over; see JUMP 1.

hurl *v.* cast, fling, heave; see THROW 1.

hurrah *interj.* three cheers, hurray, yippee; see CHEER 2, CRY 1, ENCOURAGEMENT, YELL 1.

hurricane *n.* typhoon, tempest, monsoon; see STORM.

hurry *interj.* run, hasten, move, hustle, gain time, get a move on*, on the double*.

hurry *n.* dispatch, haste, rush; see SPEED.

hurry *v.* **1** [To act hastily] hasten, be quick, make haste, scurry, scuttle, fly, tear, dash, sprint, be in a hurry, lose no time, move quickly, move rapidly, bolt, bustle, rush, make short work of, scoot*, work at high speed, dash on, hurry about, hurry off, hurry up, run off, waste no time, plunge, skip, gallop, zoom, dart, spring, make haste, make good time, whip, go by forced marches, speed, work under pressure, run like mad*, go at full tilt, make strides, act on a moment's notice, turn on the steam*, floor it*, get cracking*, step on it*, shake a leg*.—*Ant.* DELAY, lose time, procrastinate. **2** [To move rapidly] fly, bustle, dash off; see RACE 1, RUN 1. **3** [To urge others] push, spur, goad on; see DRIVE 1, URGE 2.

hurrying *a.* speeding, in a hurry, running; see FAST.

hurt *a.* injured, damaged, harmed, marred, wounded, in critical condition, impaired, shot, struck, bruised, stricken, battered, mauled, hit, stabbed, mutilated, disfigured, in pain, suffering, distressed, tortured, unhappy, grazed, scratched, nicked, winged*; see also WOUNDED.

hurt *n.* **1** [A wound] blow, gash, ache; see INJURY, PAIN 1. **2** [Damage] ill-treatment, harm, persecution; see DAMAGE 1, DISASTER, MISFORTUNE.

hurt *v.* **1** [To cause pain] cramp, squeeze, cut, bruise, tear, torment, afflict, kick, puncture, do violence to, slap, abuse, flog, whip, torture, gnaw, stab, pierce, maul, cut up, harm, injure, wound, lacerate, sting, bite, inflict pain, burn, crucify, tweak, thrash, punch, pinch, spank, punish, trounce, scourge, lash, cane, switch, work over*, wallop*, slug*.—*Ant.* EASE, comfort, soothe. **2** [To harm] maltreat, injure, spoil; see DAMAGE, DESTROY. **3** [To give a feeling of pain] ache, throb, sting; see sense 1.

hurtful *a.* aching, injurious, bad; see DANGEROUS, DEADLY, HARMFUL.

husband *n.* spouse, married man, mate, bedmate, helpmate, consort, bridegroom, breadwinner, provider, man, common-law husband, hubby*, lord and master*, the man of the house*, old man*; see also MAN 2.

hush *interj.* quiet, be quiet, pipe down*; see SHUT UP 1.

hush *n.* peace, stillness, quiet; see SILENCE 1.

hush *v.* silence, gag, stifle; see QUIET 2.

hush (up) *v.* cover, conceal, suppress; see HIDE 1.

husk *n.* shuck, covering, outside; see COVER 1, SHELL 1.

husky[2] *a.* **1** [Hoarse] throaty, growling, gruff; see HOARSE. **2** [Strong] muscular, sinewy, strapping; see STRONG 1.

hustle* *v.* act quickly, rush, push; see HURRY 1, RACE 1, RUN 1, SPEED.

immorally — *n.* **1** a hustling **2** [Colloq.] energetic action; drive —**hus′tler** *n.*

hut (hut) *n.* 〖< OHG *hutta*〗 a very plain or crude little house or cabin

hutch (huch) *n.* 〖< ML *hutica*, chest〗 **1** a chest or cupboard **2** a pen or coop for small animals **3** a hut

hutz·pah (hoots′pə) *n.* CHUTZPAH

huz·zah or **huzza** (hə zä′) *interj., n., vi., vt.* archaic var. of HURRAH

hwy. highway

hya·cinth (hī′ə sinth′) *n.* 〖< Gr *hyakinthos*〗 a plant of the lily family, with spikes of bell-shaped flowers

hy·brid (hī′brid) *n.* 〖L *hybrida*〗 **1** the offspring of two animals or plants of different varieties, species, etc. **2** anything of mixed origin — *adj.* of or like a hybrid —**hy′brid·ism′** *n.*

hy·brid·ize (hī′bri dīz′) *vt., vi.* **-ized′, -iz′ing** to produce or cause to produce hybrids; crossbreed

hy·dra (hī′drə) *n., pl.* **-dras** or **-drae′** (-drē′) 〖< Gr, water serpent〗 a small, freshwater polyp with a soft, tubelike body

hy·dran·gea (hī drān′jə, -dran′-; -jē ə) *n.* 〖< HYDR(O)- + Gr *angeion*, vessel〗 a shrub with large, showy clusters of white, blue, or pink flowers

hy·drant (hī′drənt) *n.* 〖< Gr *hydōr*, water〗 a large pipe with a valve for drawing water from a water main

hy·drate (hī′drāt′) *n.* 〖HYDR(O)- + -ATE¹〗 a chemical compound of water and some other substance

hy·drau·lic (hī drô′lik) *adj.* 〖ult. < Gr *hydōr*, water + *aulos*, tube〗 **1** of hydraulics **2** operated by the movement and force of liquid [hydraulic brakes] —**hy·drau′li·cally** *adv.*

hy·drau·lics *n.pl.* [with sing. v.] the science dealing with the mechanical properties of liquids, as water, and their application in engineering

hydro- 〖< Gr *hydōr*, WATER〗 *combining form* **1** water [hydrometer] **2** hydrogen

hydro·car·bon (hī′drō kär′bən) *n.* any compound containing only hydrogen and carbon

hydro·chlo·ric acid (hī′drō klôr′ik) a strong, highly corrosive acid that is a water solution of the gas hydrogen chloride

hy′dro·elec′tric (-ē lek′trik) *adj.* producing, or relating to the production of, electricity by water power —**hy′dro·e′lec′tric′i·ty** *n.*

hydro·foil (hī′drō foil′) *n.* 〖HYDRO- + (AIR)FOIL〗 **1** a winglike structure that lifts and carries a watercraft just above the water at high speed **2** such a watercraft

hydro·gen (hī′drə jən) *n.* 〖see HYDRO- & -GEN〗 a flammable, colorless, odorless, gaseous chemical element: the lightest known substance

hy·drog·enate (hī dräj′ə nāt′) *vt.* **-nat′ed, -nat′ing** to combine with or treat with hydrogen [oil is *hydrogenated* to make a solid fat]

hydrogen bomb an extremely destructive nuclear bomb in which an atomic bomb explosion starts a nuclear fusion explosion of heavy hydrogen atoms

hydrogen peroxide a colorless liquid used as a bleach or disinfectant

hy·drol·ogy (hī dräl′ə jē) *n.* 〖see HYDRO- & -LOGY〗 the study of the earth's waters, their distribution, and the cycle involving evaporation, precipitation, etc.

hy·drol′y·sis (-i sis) *n., pl.* **-ses′** (-sēz′) 〖HYDRO- + -LYSIS〗 a chemical reaction in which a substance reacts with water so as to be changed into one or more other substances

hy·drom·eter (hī dräm′ət ər) *n.* 〖HYDRO- + -METER〗 an instrument for measuring the specific gravity of liquids — **hy·drom′etry** *n.*

hydro·pho·bia (hī′drō fō′bē ə) *n.* 〖see HYDRO- & -PHOBIA〗 **1** abnormal fear of water **2** 〖from symptomatic inability to swallow liquids〗 RABIES

hy′dro·plane′ (-plān′) *n.* **1** a small, high-speed motorboat with hydrofoils or a flat bottom **2** SEAPLANE

hy′dro·pon′ics (-pän′iks) *n.pl.* 〖< HYDRO- & Gr *ponos*, labor〗 [with sing. v.] the science of growing plants in nutrient-rich solutions instead of soil

hy′dro·sphere′ (-sfir′) *n.* 〖HYDRO- + *-sphere*, a layer of the earth's atmosphere〗 all the water on the surface of the earth, as oceans, glaciers, etc.

hy′dro·ther′a·py *n.* the treatment of disease, etc. by the use of water

hy·drous (hī′drəs) *adj.* 〖HYDR(O)- + -OUS〗 containing water, esp. in chemical combination

hy·drox·ide (hī dräks′īd′) *n.* 〖HYDR(O)- + OXIDE〗 a compound consisting of an element or radical combined with the radical OH

hy·e·na (hī ē′nə) *n.* 〖< Gr *hyaina*〗 a wolflike, flesh-eating animal of Africa and Asia, with a shrill cry

hy·giene (hī′jēn′) *n.* 〖< Gr *hygiēs*, healthy〗 **1** a system of principles for preserving health **2** cleanliness

hy·gien·ic (hī′jē en′ik, hī jēn′ik, -jen′-) *adj.* **1** of hygiene or health **2** sanitary —**hy·gien′i·cally** *adv.*

hy·gien·ist (hī jēn′ist, hī′jēn′-, hī′jē en′-) *n.* **1** an expert in hygiene **2** an assistant to a dentist, trained to clean teeth, take x-rays, etc.

hy·grom·eter (hī gräm′ət ər) *n.* 〖< Gr *hygros*, wet + *metron*, a measure〗 an instrument for measuring humidity

hy·men (hī′mən) *n.* 〖Gr *hymēn*, membrane〗 the thin mucous membrane that closes part or sometimes all of the opening of the vagina

hy·meneal (hī′mə nē′əl) *adj.* 〖< Gr *Hymēn*, god of marriage〗 of a wedding or marriage

hymn (him) *n.* 〖< Gr *hymnos*〗 a song of praise, esp. in honor of God

hym·nal (him′nəl) *n.* a collection of hymns Also **hymn′book′**

hype¹ (hīp) *n.* [Slang] **1** short for HYPODERMIC **2** a drug addict — *vt.* **hyped, hyp′ing** [Slang] to stimulate, excite, etc. as by a drug injection: usually with *up*

hype² (hīp) *n.* 〖? < HYPERBOLE〗 [Slang] deception, esp. excessive promotion, as of a product — *vt.* **hyped, hyp′ing** [Slang] to promote in a sensational way

hyper (hī′pər) *adj.* [Slang] high-strung; keyed up

hyper- 〖< Gr *hyper*〗 *prefix* over, above, excessive

hy·per·bola (hī pur′bə lə) *n., pl.* **-las** or **-lae′** (-lē′) 〖< Gr *hyperbolē*, a throwing beyond, excess〗 *Geom.* a curve formed by the intersection of a cone with a plane more steeply inclined than its side

hy·per·bole (hī pur′bə lē) *n.* [see prec.] exaggeration for effect, not meant to be taken literally —**hy·per·bolic** (hī′pər bäl′ik) *adj.*

hyper·crit·i·cal (hī′pər krit′i kəl) *adj.* too critical

hy′per·gly·ce′mia (-glī sē′mē ə) *n.* 〖< HYPER- + Gr *glykys*, sweet + -EMIA〗 an abnormally high amount of sugar in the blood

hy′per·sen′si·tive (-sen′sə tiv) *adj.* excessively sensitive —**hy′per·sen·si·tiv′i·ty** *n.*

hy′per·ten′sion (-ten′shən) *n.* abnormally high blood pressure

hy′per·text (-tekst′) *n.* computer data organized so that related items can be easily accessed

hy′per·thy′roid·ism′ (-thī′roid iz′əm) *n.* excessive activity of the thyroid gland, causing nervousness, rapid pulse, etc. —**hy′per·thy′roid′** *adj., n.*

hyper·tro·phy (hī pur′trə fē) *n.* 〖< HYPER- + Gr *trophein*, nourish〗 an abnormal increase in the size of an organ or tissue — *vi., vt.* **-phied, -phy·ing** to undergo or cause to undergo hypertrophy

hyper·ven·ti·la·tion (hī′pər vent″l ā′shən) *n.* extremely rapid or deep breathing that may cause dizziness, fainting, etc. —**hy′per·ven′ti·late′** (-āt′), **-lat′ed, -lat′ing,** *vi., vt.*

hy·phen (hī′fən) *n.* 〖< Gr *hypo-*, under + *hen*, one〗 a mark (-) used between the parts of a compound word or

---

THESAURUS

hustler* *n.* **1** [A professional gambler] gamester, bookmaker, plunger*; see GAMBLER. **2** [A prostitute] whore, harlot, call girl; see PROSTITUTE. **3** [An energetic worker] dynamo, go-getter, workaholic; see EXECUTIVE, ZEALOT.

hut *n.* shanty, lean-to, shack, bungalow, bunkhouse, refuge, lodge, dugout, hovel, cottage, cabin, hogan, tepee, log cabin, wigwam, dump*; see also HOME 1, SHELTER.

hybrid *a.* crossed, alloyed, crossbred,

cross, half-blooded, half-breed*, half-caste*, heterogeneous, intermingled, half-and-half.

hybrid *n.* crossbreed, cross, mixture, composite, half-breed, half-blood, half-caste, combination, mestizo, mulatto, outcross; see also MIXTURE 1.

hydrant *n.* fire hydrant, fireplug, spigot; see FAUCET.

hydraulics *n.* science of liquids in motion, hydrodynamics, hydrology;

see SCIENCE 1.

hygiene *n.* cleanliness, hygienics, preventive medicine, public health, sanitary measures; see also HEALTH, CLEANLINESS.

hygienic *a.* healthful, sanitary, clean; see PURE 2, STERILE 3.

hymn *n.* chant, psalm, spiritual; see SONG.

hyperbole *n.* overstatement, metaphor, distortion; see EXAGGERATION.

the syllables of a divided word, as at the end of a line — **vt.**

hy·phen·ate (hī′fə nāt′) **vt.** **-at′ed, -at′ing** to connect or write with a hyphen —**hy′phen·a′tion** **n.**

hyp·no·sis (hip nō′sis) **n., pl.** **-ses′** (-sēz′) ⟦ < Gr *hypnos,* sleep + -OSIS ⟧ a trancelike condition usually induced by another person, in which the subject responds to the suggestions of the hypnotist

hyp·not′ic (-nät′ik) **adj.** **1** causing sleep; soporific **2** of, like, or inducing hypnosis — **n.** any agent causing sleep — **hyp·not′i·cally** **adv.**

hyp·no′tism′ (-nə tiz′əm) **n.** the act or practice of inducing hypnosis —**hyp′no·tist** **n.**

hyp′no·tize′ (-tīz′) **vt.** **-tized′, -tiz′ing** to induce hypnosis in

hypo (hī′pō) **n., pl.** **-pos** short for HYPODERMIC

hypo- ⟦Gr < *hypo,* less than⟧ **prefix** **1** under, beneath *[hypodermic]* **2** less than

hypo·chon·dria (hī′pō kän′drē ə, -pə-) **n.** ⟦LL., pl., abdomen (supposed seat of the condition)⟧ abnormal anxiety over one's health, often with imaginary illnesses —**hy′po·chon′driac′** (-ak′) **adj., n.**

hy·poc·ri·sy (hi päk′rə sē) **n., pl.** **-sies** ⟦ < Gr *hypokrisis,* acting a part ⟧ a pretending to be what one is not, or to feel what one does not feel; esp., a pretense of virtue, piety, etc.

hypo·crite (hip′ə krit′) **n.** ⟦see prec.⟧ one who pretends to be pious, virtuous, etc. without really being so —**hyp′o·crit′i·cal** **adj.** —**hyp′o·crit′i·cally** **adv.**

hypo·der·mic (hī′pō dur′mik, -pə-) **adj.** ⟦ < HYPO- + Gr *derma,* skin ⟧ injected under the skin — **n.** a hypodermic syringe or injection

hypodermic syringe a syringe attached to a hollow needle (**hypodermic needle**) and used for the injection of a medicine or drug under the skin

hypo·gly·cemia (hī′pō glī sē′mē ə) **n.** ⟦ < HYPO- + Gr

glykys, sweet + -EMIA ⟧ an abnormally low amount of sugar in the blood

hy·pot·enuse (hi pät′i nōōs′) **n.** ⟦ < Gr *hypo-,* under + *teinein,* to stretch ⟧ the side of a right-angled triangle located opposite the right angle

hypo·thal·a·mus (hī′pō thal′ə məs) **n., pl.** **-mi′** (-mī′) ⟦see HYPO- & THALAMUS⟧ a portion of the brain that regulates certain basic body functions, as temperature

hy′po·ther′mia (-thur′mē ə) **n.** ⟦ < HYPO- + Gr *thermē,* heat⟧ a subnormal body temperature

hy·poth·e·sis (hī päth′ə sis, hi-) **n., pl.** **-ses′** (-sēz′) ⟦ < Gr *hypo-,* under + *tithenai,* to place⟧ an unproved theory, etc. tentatively accepted to explain certain facts —**hy′poth′e·size′** (-sīz′), **-sized′, -siz′ing, vi., vt.**

hypo·thet·i·cal (hī′pō thet′i kəl) **adj.** based on a hypothesis; supposed —**hy′po·thet′i·cally** **adv.**

hypo·thy·roid·ism (hī′pō thī′roid iz′əm) **n.** deficient activity of the thyroid gland, causing sluggishness, puffiness, etc. —**hy′po·thy′roid′** **adj., n.**

hys·sop (his′əp) **n.** ⟦ < Heb *ēzōbh* ⟧ a fragrant, blue-flowered plant of the mint family

hys·ter·ec·tomy (his′tər ek′tə mē) **n., pl.** **-mies** ⟦ < Gr *hystera,* uterus + -ECTOMY⟧ surgical removal of all or part of the uterus

hys·teria (hi ster′ē ə, -stir′-) **n.** ⟦ < Gr *hystera,* uterus: orig. thought to occur more often in women than in men⟧ **1** a psychiatric condition characterized by excitability, anxiety, the simulation of organic disorders, etc. **2** any outbreak of wild, uncontrolled feeling: also **hys·ter′ics** — **hys·ter′i·cal** (-ster′-) or **hys·ter′ic** **adj.** —**hys·ter′i·cally** **adv.**

Hz or **hz** hertz

THESAURUS

hypnosis **n.** trance, anesthesia, lethargy; see SLEEP.

hypnotic **a.** sleep-inducing, opiate, narcotic, anesthetic, soporific, sleep-producing, soothing, calmative, trance-inducing.

hypnotism **n.** bewitchment, suggestion, hypnotherapy, deep sleep, self-hypnosis, autohypnosis, hypnotic, suggestion, charm, fascination.

hypnotize **v.** mesmerize, lull to sleep, dull the will, hold under a spell, bring under one's control, stupefy, drug, soothe, fascinate, anesthetize, subject to suggestion, make drowsy.

hypnotized **a.** entranced, mesmerized, enchanted; see CHARMED.

hypochondria **n.** depression, imagined ill-health, hypochondriasis; see PRETENSE 1.

hypochondriac **n.** malingerer, melancholic, self-tormentor; see FAKE.

hypocrisy **n.** affectation, deception, bad faith, hollowness, display, lip service, bigotry, sham, fraud, pretense of virtue, quackery, empty ceremony, sanctimony, cant; see also DISHONESTY, LIE.—*Ant.* VIRTUE, devotion, piety.

hypocrite **n.** pretender, fraud, faker, fake, deceiver, charlatan, bigot, quack, pharisee, sham, actor, cheat, informer, trickster, confidence man, malingerer, humbug, imposter, swindler, informer, rascal, traitor, wolf in sheep's clothing, masquerader, four-flusher*, two-timer*, two-face*; see also FAKE.

hypocritical **a.** deceptive, double-dealing, insincere; see DISHONEST.

hypothesis **n.** supposition, theory, assumption; see GUESS, OPINION 1.

hypothetical **a.** **1** [Supposed] imagined, uncertain, vague; see ASSUMED,

LIKELY **1.** **2** [Characterized by hypothesis] postulated, academic, philosophical; see LOGICAL.

hysteria **n.** delirium, agitation, feverishness; see CONFUSION, EXCITEMENT, NERVOUSNESS.

hysterical **a.** convulsed, uncontrolled, raving, delirious, unnerved, neurotic, emotional, rabid, emotionally disordered, distracted, fuming, distraught, unrestrained, possessed, fanatical, irrepressible, convulsive, carried away, seething, beside oneself, rampant, out of one's wits, mad, uncontrollable, agitated, raging, frenzied, spasmodic, confused, tempestuous, maddened, crazy, impetuous, crazed, furious, violent, impassioned, panic-stricken, nervous, vehement, overwrought, fiery, passionate, jittery*, wild-eyed, on a crying jag*; see also ANGRY, EXCITED, TROUBLED.

I

i or **I** (ī) *n.*, *pl.* **i's, I's** the ninth letter of the English alphabet

I¹ (ī) *n.* a Roman numeral for 1

I² (ī) *pron.* ⟦OE *ic*⟧ the person speaking or writing

I *Chem. symbol for* iodine

I, I., i, or **i. 1** island(s) **2** isle(s)

-ial (ē əl, yəl) ⟦L *-ialis*⟧ *suffix* -AL

iamb (ī'amb', -am') *n.* ⟦< Gr *iambos*⟧ a metrical foot of one unaccented syllable followed by one accented one

iam·bic (ī am'bik) *adj.* ⟦< Gr *iambikos*⟧ of or made up of iambs —*n.* an iamb

-iatrics (ē a'triks') ⟦< Gr *iatros*, physician⟧ *combining form* treatment of disease *[pediatrics]*

-iatry (ī'ə trē) ⟦< Gr *iatreia*, healing⟧ *combining form* medical treatment *[psychiatry]*

ibex (ī'beks') *n.*, *pl.* **i'bex'es** or **ibi·ces** (ī'bə sēz') ⟦L⟧ a wild goat of the Old World, with large, backward-curved horns

ibid. ⟦L *ibidem*⟧ in the same place, i.e., the book, page, etc. just cited

ibis (ī'bis) *n.* ⟦Egypt *hb*⟧ a large wading bird found chiefly in tropical regions

-ible (i bəl, ə bəl) ⟦L *-ibilis*⟧ *suffix* -ABLE

ibu·pro·fen (ī'byoo prō'fən) *n.* a white powder used for reducing fever and relieving pain, esp. for arthritis

-ic (ik) ⟦< Gr *-ikos*⟧ *suffix* **1** of, having to do with *[volcanic]* *b)* like *[angelic]* *c)* produced by *[anaerobic]* *d)* consisting of, containing *[dactylic]* *e)* having, showing *[lethargic]* **2** a person or thing: *a)* having *[paraplegic]* *b)* supporting *c)* producing *[hypnotic]* Also **-ical** (i kəl, ə kəl)

ICBM *n.* intercontinental ballistic missile

ICC Interstate Commerce Commission

ice (īs) *n.* ⟦OE *īs*⟧ **1** water frozen solid by cold **2** a frozen dessert of fruit juice, sugar, etc. **3** [Slang] diamonds —*vt.* **iced, ic'ing 1** to change into ice; freeze **2** to cool with ice **3** to cover with icing —*vi.* to freeze: often with *up* or *over* —**break the ice** to make a start, as in getting acquainted —**cut no ice** [Colloq.] to have no influence —**on thin ice** [Colloq.] in danger

Ice. 1 Iceland **2** Icelandic

ice'berg' (-burg') *n.* ⟦prob. < Du *ijsberg*, ice mountain⟧ a great mass of ice broken off from a glacier and floating in the sea

ice'bound' (-bound') *adj.* held fast or shut in by ice

ice'box' (-bäks') *n.* a refrigerator, esp. one in which ice is used

ice'break'er *n.* a sturdy boat for cutting channels through ice

ice'cap' *n.* a mass of glacial ice that spreads slowly from a center

ice cream ⟦orig., *iced cream*⟧ a sweet, frozen food made from flavored cream or milk —**ice'-cream'** *adj.*

ice floe a piece of floating sea ice

ice hockey *see* HOCKEY (sense 1)

Ice·lan·dic (īs lan'dik) *n.* the Germanic language of Iceland —*adj.* of Iceland

ice·man (īs'man', -mən) *n.*, *pl.* **-men'** one who sells or delivers ice

ice milk a frozen dessert like ice cream, but with less butterfat

ice skate *see* SKATE¹ (*n.* 1) —**ice'-skate', -skat'ed, -skat'ing,** *vi.*

ich·thy·ol·ogy (ik'thē äl'ə jē) *n.* ⟦< Gr *ichthys*, a fish + -LOGY⟧ the branch of zoology dealing with fishes —**ich'thy·ol'o·gist** *n.*

ici·cle (ī'sik'əl, -si kəl) *n.* ⟦< OE *is*, ice + *gicel*, piece of ice⟧ a hanging piece of ice, formed by the freezing of dripping water

ic·ing (īs'iŋ) *n.* a mixture variously of sugar, butter, flavoring, egg whites, etc. for covering a cake; frosting

icky (ik'ē) *adj.* **-i·er, -i·est** ⟦< STICKY⟧ [Slang] **1** unpleasantly sticky or sweet **2** very distasteful

icon (ī'kän') *n.* ⟦< Gr *eikōn*, image⟧ **1** an image; figure **2** *Eastern Orthodox Ch.* a sacred image or picture of Jesus, Mary, etc.

icono·clast (ī kän'ə klast') *n.* ⟦< c. 6th-c. Gr *eikōn*, image + *klaein*, to break⟧ one who attacks widely accepted ideas, beliefs, etc. —**icon'o·clas'tic** *adj.*

-ics (iks) ⟦-IC + -s (pl.)⟧ *suffix* [*usually with sing. v.*] art, science, study *[mathematics]*

icy (ī'sē) *adj.* **i'ci·er, i'ci·est 1** full of or covered with ice **2** of or like ice; specif., *a)* slippery *b)* very cold **3** cold in manner; unfriendly —**i'ci·ly** *adv.* —**i'ci·ness** *n.*

id (id) *n.* ⟦L, it⟧ *Psychoanalysis* that part of the psyche which is the source of psychic energy

ID identification

idea (ī dē'ə) *n.* ⟦L < Gr, appearance of a thing⟧ **1** a thought; mental conception or image **2** an opinion or belief **3** a plan; scheme **4** meaning or significance

ideal (ī dē'əl, -dēl') *adj.* ⟦see prec.⟧ **1** existing as an idea, model, etc. **2** thought of as perfect **3** existing only in the mind; imaginary —*n.* **1** a conception of something in its most excellent form **2** a perfect model **3** a goal or principle

ide·al·ism' *n.* **1** behavior or thought based on a conception of things as one thinks they should be **2** a striving to achieve one's ideals —**ide'al·ist** *n.* —**i'deal·is'tic** *adj.* —**i'deal·is'ti·cal·ly** *adv.*

ideal·ize (ī dē'əl īz') *vt.* **-ized', -iz'ing** to regard or show as perfect or more nearly perfect than is true —**ide'ali·za'tion** *n.* —**ide'al·iz'er** *n.*

ide·al·ly *adv.* **1** in an ideal manner; perfectly **2** in theory

iden·ti·cal (ī den'ti kəl) *adj.* ⟦< L *idem*, the same⟧ **1** the very same **2** exactly alike —**iden'ti·cal·ly** *adv.*

iden·ti·fi·ca·tion (ī den'tə fi kā'shən) *n.* **1** an identifying or being identified **2** anything by which one can be identified

iden·tify (ī den'tə fī') *vt.* **-fied', -fy'ing 1** to make identical; treat as the same **2** to fix the identity of *[to identify a biological specimen]* **3** to connect or associate closely —**iden'ti·fi'able** *adj.*

iden·tity (ī den'tə tē) *n.*, *pl.* **-ties 1** the state or fact of being the same **2** *a)* the state or fact of being a specific person or thing; individuality *b)* the state of being as described

identity crisis the state of being uncertain about oneself regarding character, goals, etc., esp. in adolescence

ideo·gram (id'ē ō gram', ī'dē-) *n.* ⟦see IDEA & -GRAM⟧ a

THESAURUS

I² *pron.* myself, ego (Latin), self; see CHARACTER 2.

ICBM *n.* Intercontinental Ballistic Missile, guided missile, strategic deterrent; see ROCKET, WEAPON.

ice *n.* crystal, hail, floe, glacier, icicle, ice cube, cube ice, dry ice, black ice, white ice, chunk ice, iceberg, permafrost; see also FROST. —**break the ice** make a start, initiate, commence; see BEGIN 1. —**on ice*** in reserve, held, in abeyance; see SAVED 2. —**on thin ice*** in a dangerous situation, imperiled, insecure; see ENDANGERED.

ice *v.* frost, coat, mist; see FREEZE 1.

iceberg *n.* ice field, berg, icecap; see ICE.

icebox *n.* cooler, freezer, fridge*; see REFRIGERATOR.

ice cream *n.* mousse, spumoni, *glacé* (French), sherbet, ice, ice milk, soft serve, frozen custard, parfait, frozen dessert; see also DESSERT.

icy *a.* frozen over, iced, freezing, glacial, frostbound, frosted, frosty, smooth as glass; see also SLIPPERY.

idea *n.* **1** [A concept] conception, plans, view, fancy, impression, image, understanding, conception, observation, belief, feeling, opinion, guess, inference, theory, hypothesis, supposition, assumption, intuition, conjecture, design, approach, mental impression, notion. **2** [Fancy] whimsy, whim, fantasy; see FANCY 1, IMAGINATION. **3** [Meaning] sense, import, purport; see MEANING.

ideal *a.* **1** [Typical] prototypical, model, archetypal; see TYPICAL. **2** [Perfect] supreme, fitting, exemplary; see EXCELLENT, PERFECT.

ideal *n.* paragon, goal, prototype; see MODEL 1.

idealism *n.* principle, conscience, philosophy; see ETHICS.

idealistic *a.* lofty, noble, exalted; see IMPRACTICAL, NOBLE 1.

idealize *v.* romanticize, glorify, build castles in the air; see DREAM 2, INVENT 1.

identical *a.* like, twin, indistinguishable; see ALIKE.

identification *n.* **1** [The act of identifying] classifying, naming, cataloging; see CLASSIFICATION, DESCRIPTION. **2** [Means of identifying] credentials, letter of introduction, testimony, letter of credit, badge, papers, ID; see also PASSPORT.

identify *v.* classify, catalog, analyze; see DESCRIBE, NAME 1, 2.

identity *n.* identification, character, individuality, uniqueness, antecedents, true circumstances, parentage, status, citizenship, nationality, connections; see also NAME 1.

symbol representing an object or idea without expressing the word for it Also **id′eo·graph′**

ideo·logue (id′ē ə lôg′, i′dē-) *n.* 〚see fol.〛 a zealous advocate of a specified ideology

ideol·ogy (i′dē äl′ə jē, id′ē-) *n.*, *pl.* **-gies** 〚see IDEA & -LOGY〛 the doctrines, opinions, etc. of an individual, class, etc. —**i′deo·log′i·cal** *adj.* —**i′deol′o·gist** *n.*

ides (īdz) *n.pl.* 〚< L *idus*〛 in the ancient Roman calendar, the 15th day of March, May, July, or October, or the 13th of the other months

idio·cy (id′ē ə sē) *n.* **1** great foolishness or stupidity **2** *pl.* **-cies** an idiotic act or remark

idi·om (id′ē əm) *n.* 〚< Gr *idios*, one's own〛 **1** the language or dialect of a people, region, class, etc. **2** the usual way that the words of a language are joined to express thought **3** a phrase or expression with an unusual syntactic pattern or with a meaning differing from the literal **4** a characteristic style, as in art or music —**id′io·mat′ic** (-ə mat′ik) *adj.* —**id′io·mat′i·cally** *adv.*

idio·pathic (id′ē ō′path′ik, -ē ə-) *adj.* 〚< Gr *idiopatheia*, feeling for oneself alone〛 of a disease whose cause is unknown

idio·syn·crasy (id′ē ō′ siŋ′krə sē) *n.*, *pl.* **-sies** 〚< Gr *idio-*, one's own + *synkrasis*, a mixing〛 any personal peculiarity, mannerism, etc. —**id′io·syn·crat′ic** (-sin krat′ik) *adj.*

idi·ot (id′ē ət) *n.* 〚< Gr *idiōtēs*, ignorant person〛 **1** [Obs.] a retarded person mentally equal or inferior to a child two years old **2** a very foolish or stupid person —**id′i·ot′ic** (-ät′ik) *adj.* —**id′i·ot′i·cally** *adv.*

idle (īd′'l) *adj.* **i′dler, i′dlest** 〚OE *idel*, empty〛 **1** useless; futile **2** unfounded 〚*idle* rumors〛 **3** *a)* unemployed; not busy *b)* inactive; not in use **4** lazy — *vi.* **i′dled, i′dling 1** to move slowly or aimlessly **2** to be unemployed or inactive **3** to operate without transmitting power 〚the motor *idled*〛 — *vt.* **1** to waste: usually with *away* **2** to cause (a motor, etc.) to idle —**i′dle·ness** *n.* —**i′dler** *n.* —**i′dly** *adv.*

idol (īd′'l) *n.* 〚< Gr *eidōlon*, image〛 **1** an image of a god, used as an object of worship **2** any object of ardent or excessive devotion

idola·try (ī däl′ə trē) *n.*, *pl.* **-tries 1** worship of idols **2** excessive devotion to or reverence for some person or thing —**idol·a·ter** *n.* —**idol′a·trous** *adj.*

idol·ize (īd′'l īz′) *vt.* **-ized′, -iz′ing 1** to make an idol of **2** to love or admire excessively —**i′doli·za′tion** *n.*

idyll or **idyl** (īd′'l) *n.* 〚< Gr *eidos*, a form〛 **1** a short poem or prose work describing a simple, peaceful scene of rural or pastoral life **2** a scene or incident suitable for such a work —**idyl′lic** (ī dil′ik) *adj.*

-ie (ē) 〚earlier form of -Y¹〛 *suffix* **1** small or little (one, as specified) 〚*lassie*〛 **2** *a)* one that is as specified 〚*softie*〛 *b)* one connected with 〚*groupie*〛

i.e. 〚L *id est*〛 that is (to say)

IE Indo-European

-ier (ē′ər, yər; ir, ər) 〚< L *-arius*〛 *suffix* a person concerned with (a specified action or thing) 〚*bombardier*〛

if (if) *conj.* 〚OE *gif*〛 **1** on condition that; in case that 〚*if* I were you, I would quit〛 **2** allowing that 〚*if* she was there, I didn't see her〛 **3** whether 〚ask him *if* he knows her〛

iffy (if′ē) *adj.* [Colloq.] not definite; containing doubtful elements

ig·loo (ig′lōō′) *n.*, *pl.* **-loos′** 〚Esk *igdlu*, snow house〛 an Eskimo hut, usually dome-shaped and built of blocks of packed snow

ig·ne·ous (ig′nē əs) *adj.* 〚< L *ignis*, a fire〛 **1** of fire **2** produced by volcanic action or intense heat 〚*igneous* rock〛

ig·nite (ig nīt′) *vt.* **-nit′ed, -nit′ing** 〚see prec.〛 to set fire to — *vi.* to catch on fire; start burning —**ig·nit′able** or **ig·nit′ible** *adj.*

ig·ni·tion (ig nish′ən) *n.* **1** an igniting or being ignited **2** the system for igniting the explosive mixture in the cylinder of an internal-combustion engine

ig·no·ble (ig nō′bəl) *adj.* 〚< L *in-*, not + *nobilis* (< earlier *gnobilis*, known)〛 not noble; base; mean —**ig·no′bly** *adv.*

ig·no·miny (ig′nə min′ē) *n.*, *pl.* **-ies** 〚< L *in-*, no, not + *nomen*, name〛 loss of reputation; shame; disgrace —**ig′no·min′i·ous** *adj.* —**ig′no·min′i·ously** *adv.*

ig·no·ra·mus (ig′nə rā′məs) *n.*, *pl.* **-muses** an ignorant person

ig·no·rant (ig′nə rənt) *adj.* 〚see fol.〛 **1** lacking knowledge or experience **2** caused by or showing lack of knowledge **3** unaware (*of*) —**ig′no·rance** *n.* —**ig′no·rantly** *adv.*

ig·nore (ig nôr′) *vt.* **-nored′, -nor′ing** 〚< L *in-*, not + *gnarus*, knowing〛 to disregard; pay no attention to

igua·na (i gwä′nə) *n.* 〚Sp < WInd〛 a large tropical American lizard

il- *prefix* **1** IN-¹ **2** IN-² Used before *l*

Ili·ad (il′ē əd) *n.* 〚< Gr *Ilios*, Troy〛 a Greek epic poem, ascribed to Homer, about the Trojan War

ilk (ilk) *n.* 〚< OE *ilca*, same〛 kind; sort; class: only in **of that** (or **his, her,** etc.) **ilk**

ill (il) *adj.* **worse, worst** 〚< ON *illr*〛 **1** bad 〚*ill* repute, *ill* will, *ill* omen〛 **2** not well; sick — *n.* an evil or a disease — *adv.* **worse, worst 1** badly **2** scarcely 〚I can *ill* afford it〛 —**ill at ease** uneasy; uncomfortable

ill-advised (il′əd vīzd′) *adj.* showing or resulting from poor advice; unwise

ill′-bred′ *adj.* rude; impolite

il·legal (il lē′gəl) *adj.* prohibited by law; against the law — **il·legal·ity** (il′lē gal′i tē), *pl.* **-ties,** *n.* —**il·le′gal·ly** *adv.*

═ THESAURUS ═

ideology *n.* beliefs, ideas, philosophy; see CULTURE 2, ETHICS.

idiot *n.* simpleton, nincompoop, booby; see FOOL.

idiotic *a.* thickwitted, dull, moronic; see STUPID.

idle *a.* unoccupied, fallow, vacant, deserted, not in use, barren, void, empty, abandoned, still, quiet, motionless, inert, dead, rusty, dusty, out of action, out of a job, out of work, resting; see also UNEM-PLOYED.—*Ant.* ACTIVE, busy, engaged.

idle *v.* slack, shirk, slow down; see LOAF.

idleness *n.* loitering, time-killing, dawdling, inertia, inactivity, indolence, sluggishness, unemployment, dormancy, lethargy, stupor, loafing.—*Ant.* ACTION, industry, occupation.

idol *n.* icon, graven image, god, Buddha, false god, figurine, fetish, totem, golden calf, pagan deity.

idolatry *n.* infatuation, fervor, transport; see ZEAL.

idolize *v.* glorify, adore, canonize; see WORSHIP.

if *conj.* provided that, with the condition that, supposing that, conceding that, on the assumption that, granted that, assuming that, whenever, wherever. —**as if** as though,

assuming that, in a way; see AS IF.

iffy *a.* unsettled, doubtful, uncertain; see UNCERTAIN.

ignite *v.* enkindle, light, strike a light, start up, burst into flames, touch off, touch a match to, set off; see also BURN.

ignition *n.* **1** [Igniting] combustion, bursting into flame, kindling; see FIRE 1. **2** [A system for igniting] distributor, firing system, wiring system; see ENGINE, MACHINE, MOTOR.

ignorance *n.* unconsciousness, incomprehension, bewilderment, incapacity, inexperience, disregard, illiteracy, denseness, stupidity, dumbness, empty-headedness, unintelligence, rawness, blindness, simplicity, insensitivity, shallowness, fog, vagueness, half-knowledge, lack of education, a little learning.—*Ant.* ABILITY, learning, erudition.

ignorant *a.* **1** [Unaware] unconscious of, uninformed about, unknowing, uninitiated, inexperienced, unwitting, unmindful, disregardful, misinformed, unsuspecting, unaware of, unmindful of, unconscious of, mindless, witless, not conversant with, unintelligent, obtuse, thick, dense, unscientific, birdbrained*, lowbrow*, sappy*, green; see also sense 2 and DULL 3, SHALLOW

2, STUPID.—*Ant.* INTELLIGENT, alert, aware. **2** [Untrained] illiterate, uneducated, unlettered, untaught, uninstructed, uncultivated, unenlightened, untutored, unschooled, unread, benighted, shallow, superficial, gross, coarse, vulgar, crude, green, knowing nothing, misinformed, misguided, just beginning, apprenticed, unbriefed; see also INEX-PERIENCED, NAIVE, UNAWARE.—*Ant.* LEARNED, cognizant, tutored.

ignore *v.* disregard, overlook, pass over; see DISCARD, NEGLECT 2.

ill *a.* **1** [Bad] harmful, evil, noxious; see BAD 1. **2** [Sick] unwell, unhealthy, ailing; see SICK. —**ill at ease** anxious, uneasy, uncomfortable; see DOUBTFUL, RESTLESS, SUSPI-CIOUS 1, 2.

ill *n.* depravity, misfortune, mischief; see EVIL 2, INSULT, WRONG.

illegal *a.* illicit, unlawful, contraband, unwarranted, banned, unconstitutional, outside the law, extralegal, outlawed, not legal, unauthorized, unlicensed, lawless, actionable, illegitimate, prohibited, forbidden, criminal, against the law, not approved, uncertified, unlicensed, smuggled, bootlegged, hot*.—*Ant.* LEGAL, lawful, authorized.

il·leg·ible (il lej′ə bəl) *adj.* hard or impossible to read because badly written or printed —il·leg·ibil′i·ty *n.* —il·leg′ibly *adv.*

il·legit·imate (il′lə jit′ə mət) *adj.* 1 born of parents not married to each other 2 contrary to law, rules, or logic — il′legit′i·macy (-mə sē), *pl.* -cies, *n.*

ill-fated (il′fāt′id) *adj.* 1 certain to have an evil fate or unlucky end 2 unlucky

ill′-fa′vored *adj.* ugly or unpleasant

ill′-got′ten *adj.* obtained by evil, unlawful, or dishonest means

il·lib·eral (il lib′ər əl) *adj.* 1 narrow-minded 2 not generous

il·licit (il lis′it) *adj.* ⟦< L *illicitus*, not allowed⟧ unlawful; improper —il·lic′itly *adv.* —il·lic′it·ness *n.*

il·lim·it·able (il lim′i tə bəl) *adj.* without limit; immeasurable

il·liquid (il lik′wid) *adj.* not readily convertible into cash

il·lit·er·ate (il lit′ər it) *adj.* uneducated; esp., not knowing how to read or write — *n.* an illiterate person —il·lit′era·cy (-ə sē) *n.*

ill-mannered (il′man′ərd) *adj.* having bad manners; rude; impolite

ill nature a disagreeable or mean disposition —ill-natured (il′nā′chərd) *adj.*

ill′ness *n.* the condition of being in poor health; sickness; disease

il·logi·cal (il läj′i kəl) *adj.* not logical or reasonable —il·log′i·cally *adv.*

ill-starred (il′stärd′) *adj.* unlucky

ill′-suit′ed *adj.* not suited or appropriate

ill′-tem′pered *adj.* sullen; irritable

ill′-timed′ *adj.* inopportune

ill′-treat′ *vt.* to treat unkindly, unfairly, etc. —ill′-treat′ment *n.*

il·lu·mi·nate (i loo′mə nāt′) *vt.* -nat′ed, -nat′ing ⟦< L *in-*, in + *luminare*, to light⟧ 1 to give light to; light up 2 *a*) to make clear; explain *b*) to inform 3 to decorate as with lights —il·lu′mi·nable *adj.*

il·lu·mi·na′tion *n.* 1 an illuminating 2 the intensity of light per unit of area

il·lu′mine (-mən) *vt.* -mined, -min·ing to light up

illus. 1 illustrated 2 illustration

ill-usage (il′yoo′sij) *n.* unkind or cruel treatment; abuse Also ill usage

ill′-use′ (-yooz′; *for n.*, -yoos′) *vt.* -used′, -us′ing to treat unkindly; abuse — *n.* ILL-USAGE

il·lu·sion (i loo′zhən) *n.* ⟦< L *illudere*, to mock⟧ 1 a false idea or conception 2 an unreal or misleading appearance or image —il·lu′sory (-sə rē) or il·lu′sive (-siv) *adj.*

il·lus·trate (il′əs trāt′) *vt.* -trat′ed, -trat′ing ⟦< L *in-*, + *lustrare*, illuminate⟧ 1 to explain; make clear, as by examples 2 to furnish (books, etc.) with explanatory or decorative pictures, etc. —il′lus·tra′tor *n.*

il′lus·tra′tion *n.* 1 an illustrating 2 an example, etc. used to help explain 3 a picture, diagram, etc. used to decorate or explain

il·lus·tra·tive (i lus′trə tiv) *adj.* serving as an illustration or example

il·lus·tri·ous (i lus′trē əs) *adj.* ⟦< L *illustris*, clear⟧ distinguished; famous; outstanding —il·lus′tri·ously *adv.* —il·lus′tri·ous·ness *n.*

ill will hostility; hate; dislike

I'm (im) I am

im- *prefix* 1 IN-¹ 2 IN-² Used before *b, m,* or *p*

im·age (im′ij) *n.* ⟦< L *imago*⟧ 1 a representation of a person or thing; esp., a statue 2 the visual impression of something in a mirror, through a lens, etc. 3 a copy 4 *a*) a mental picture; idea *b*) the concept of a person, product, etc. held by the general public 5 a metaphor or simile — *vt.* -aged, -ag·ing 1 to make a representation of 2 to reflect 3 to imagine

im·agery (im′ij rē) *n.* 1 mental images 2 figurative language

imagi·nable (i maj′i nə bəl) *adj.* that can be imagined — **imag′i·nably** *adv.*

imag′i·nar′y (-ner′ē) *adj.* existing only in the imagination; unreal

imag′i·na′tion (-nā′shən) *n.* 1 *a*) the act or power of forming mental images of what is not present *b*) the act or power of creating new ideas by combining previous experiences 2 the ability to understand the imaginative creations of others 3 resourcefulness

imag′i·na·tive (-nə tiv) *adj.* 1 having, using, or showing imagination 2 of or resulting from imagination —**imag′i·na·tively** *adv.*

imag·ine (i maj′in) *vt., vi.* -ined, -in·ing ⟦< L *imago, image*⟧ 1 to make a mental image (of); conceive in the mind 2 to suppose; think

---

THESAURUS

illegible *a.* faint, unintelligible, difficult to read; see CONFUSED 2, OBSCURE 1.

illegibly *a.* faintly, unintelligibly, indistinctly; see CONFUSED 2.

illegitimate *a.* 1 [Unlawful] contraband, wrong, illicit; see BAD 1, ILLEGAL. 2 [Misbegotten] born out of wedlock, unlawfully begotten, unfathered; see BASTARD.

illicit *a.* unlawful, prohibited, unauthorized; see BAD 1, ILLEGAL, WRONG 1.

illiteracy *n.* lack of education, stupidity, idiocy; see IGNORANCE.

illiterate *a.* uneducated, unenlightened, dumb*; see IGNORANT 2.

ill-mannered *a.* impolite, uncouth, rough; see RUDE 2.

illness *n.* 1 [Poor health] sickness, failing health, seizure, ailing, infirmity, disorder, relapse, attack, fit, convalescence, complaint, delicate health, collapse, breakdown, confinement, disturbance, ill health; see also WEAKNESS 1. 2 [A particular disease] sickness, ailment, malady, ache, infection, stroke, allergy; see also COLD 2, IMPEDIMENT 2, INSANITY, PAIN 2.

illogical *a.* irrational, unreasonable, absurd, fallacious, unsubstantial, incorrect, inconsistent, false, unscientific, contradictory, untenable, unsound, preposterous, invalid, self-contradictory, unproved, groundless, implausible, hollow, irrelevant, inconclusive, prejudiced, biased, unconnected, without foundation, not following, without rhyme or reason; see also WRONG 2.—*Ant.* LOGICAL, sound, reasonable.

ill-suited *a.* inappropriate, unsuitable, mismatched; see UNSUITABLE.

ill-tempered *a.* cross, touchy, querulous; see IRRITABLE, SULLEN.

illuminate *v.* 1 [To make light(er)] lighten, irradiate, illume; see BRIGHTEN 1, LIGHT 1. 2 [To explain] interpret, elucidate, clarify; see EXPLAIN.

illumination *n.* 1 [A light] gleam, flame, brilliance, lighting; see also FLASH, LIGHT 1, 3. 2 [Instruction] teaching, education, information; see KNOWLEDGE 1.

illusion *n.* fancy, hallucination, mirage, apparition, ghost, delusion, figment of the imagination, image, trick of vision, myth, make-believe; see also DREAM.

illustrate *v.* picture, represent, portray, depict, imitate; see also DRAW 2, PAINT 1.

illustrated *a.* engraved, decorated, portrayed; see DESCRIPTIVE.

illustration *n.* engraving, tailpiece, frontispiece, cartoon, vignette, etching, inset picture, newsphoto; see also PICTURE 3.

illustrative *a.* symbolic, representative, pictorial; see DESCRIPTIVE, EXPLANATORY, GRAPHIC 1, 2.

ill will *n.* malevolence, dislike, hostility; see BLAME, HATRED, OBJECTION.

image *n.* 1 [Mental impression] concept, conception, perception; see IDEA 1, THOUGHT 2. 2 [Representation] idol, carved figure, effigy, form, drawing, model, illustration, portrait, photograph, reproduction, copy, likeness, facsimile, counterpart, replica; see also PICTURE 2.

imagery *n.* illustration, metaphor, representation; see COMPARISON.

imaginable *a.* conceivable, comprehensible, credible, thinkable, sensible, possible, plausible, believable, reasonable; see also LIKELY 1.—*Ant.* UNBELIEVABLE, unimaginable, inconceivable.

imaginary *a.* fancied, illusory, visionary, shadowy, dreamy, dreamlike, hypothetical, theoretical, deceptive, imagined, hallucinatory, ideal, whimsical, fabulous, nonexistent, apocryphal, fantastic, mythological, legendary, fictitious, imaginative; see also UNREAL.—*Ant.* REAL, factual, existing.

imagination *n.* intelligence, thoughtfulness, inventiveness, conception, mental agility, wit, sensitivity, fancy, visualization, realization, cognition, awareness, dramatization, pictorialization, insight; see also MIND 1.

imaginative *a.* creative, inventive, originative; see ARTISTIC, ORIGINAL 2.

imagine *v.* conceive, picture, conjure up, envisage, envision, see in one's mind, invent, fabricate, formulate, devise, think of, make up, conceptualize, dream, dream up*, perceive, dramatize, create.

imagined *a.* not real, insubstantial, thought-up; see FALSE 1, 2, 3, IMAGINARY.

im·bal·ance (im bal′əns) *n.* lack of balance, as in proportion or force

im·be·cile (im′bə sil) *n.* ⟦< L *imbecilis,* feeble⟧ **1** [Obs.] a retarded person mentally equal to a child between three and eight years old **2** a foolish or stupid person — *adj.* foolish or stupid: also **im′becil′ic** (-sil′ik) —**im′becil′ity** *n.*

im·bed (im bed′) *vt.* EMBED

im·bibe (im bīb′) *vt.* **-bibed′, -bib′ing** ⟦< L *in-,* in + *bibere,* to drink⟧ **1** to drink (esp. alcoholic liquor) **2** to take into the mind and keep, as ideas — *vi.* to drink, esp. alcoholic liquor

im·bro·glio (im brōl′yō) *n., pl.* **-glios** ⟦It < *imbrogliare,* embroil⟧ **1** an involved and confusing situation **2** a confused misunderstanding

im·bue (im byōō′) *vt.* **-bued′, -bu′ing** ⟦< L *imbuere,* to wet⟧ **1** to dye **2** to permeate (*with* ideas, emotions, etc.)

imi·tate (im′i tāt′) *vt.* **-tat′ed, -tat′ing** ⟦< L *imitari*⟧ **1** to seek to follow the example of **2** to mimic **3** to reproduce in form, color, etc. **4** to resemble —**im′i·ta′tor** *n.*

im′i·ta′tion *n.* **1** an imitating **2** the result of imitating; copy — *adj.* not real; sham [*imitation* leather] —**im′i·ta′tive** *adj.*

im·macu·late (im mak′yoo lit, -yə-) *adj.* ⟦< L *in-,* not + *macula,* a spot⟧ **1** perfectly clean **2** without a flaw or error **3** pure; innocent; sinless —**im·mac′u·lately** *adv.* —**im·mac′u·late·ness** *n.*

im·ma·nent (im′ə nənt) *adj.* ⟦< L *in-,* in + *manere,* remain⟧ **1** operating within; inherent **2** present throughout the universe: said of God —**im′ma·nence** *n.* —**im′ma·nently** *adv.*

im·ma·teri·al (im′mə tir′ē əl) *adj.* **1** spiritual **2** unimportant

im·ma·ture (im′mə toor′, -tyoor′, -choor′) *adj.* **1** not mature; not completely developed **2** not finished or perfected —**im′ma·tu′rity** *n.*

im·meas·ur·able (im mezh′ər ə bəl) *adj.* that cannot be measured; boundless; vast —**im·meas′ur·ably** *adv.*

im·media·cy (i mē′dē ə sē) *n.* a being immediate; esp., direct relevance to the present time, purpose, etc.

im·medi·ate (i mē′dē it) *adj.* ⟦see IN-² & MEDIATE⟧ **1** not separated in space; closest **2** without delay; instant **3** next in order or relation **4** direct; firsthand —**im·me′di·ately** *adv.*

im·memo·rial (im′me môr′ē əl) *adj.* extending back beyond memory or record; ancient

im·mense (im mens′) *adj.* ⟦< L *in-,* not + *metiri,* to measure⟧ very large; vast; huge —**im·mense′ly** *adv.* —**im·men′sity** *n.*

im·merse (im murs′) *vt.* **-mersed′, -mers′ing** ⟦< L *immergere*⟧ **1** to plunge into or as if into a liquid **2** to baptize by submerging in water **3** to absorb deeply; engross [*immersed* in study] —**im·mer′sion** (-mur′shən, -mur′zhən) *n.*

immersion heater an electric coil or rod immersed in water to heat it

im·mi·grant (im′ə grənt) *n.* one who immigrates — *adj.* immigrating

im′mi·grate′ (-grāt′) *vi.* **-grat′ed, -grat′ing** ⟦see IN-¹ & MIGRATE⟧ to come into a new country, etc., esp. to settle there —**im′mi·gra′tion** *n.*

im·mi·nent (im′ə nənt) *adj.* ⟦< L *in-,* on + *minere,* to project⟧ likely to happen without delay; impending —**im′mi·nence** *n.*

im·mo·bile (im mō′bəl) *adj.* **1** firmly placed; stable **2** motionless —**im′mo·bil′ity** *n.* —**im·mo′bi·lize′** (-bə līz′), -**lized′, -liz′ing,** *vt.*

im·mod·er·ate (im mäd′ər it) *adj.* without restraint; excessive

im·mod·est (im mäd′ist) *adj.* **1** indecent **2** not shy; forward —**im·mod′estly** *adv.* —**im·mod′esty** *n.*

im·mo·late (im′ə lāt′) *vt.* **-lat′ed, -lat′ing** ⟦< L *immolare,* sprinkle with sacrificial meal⟧ to kill as a sacrifice —**im′mo·la′tion** *n.*

im·moral (im môr′əl) *adj.* **1** not moral **2** lewd —**im·mor′ally** *adv.*

im·mo·ral·ity (im′mō ral′i tē, im′ə-) *n.* **1** a being immoral **2** *pl.* **-ties** an immoral act or practice; vice

im·mor·tal (im môrt′'l) *adj.* **1** not mortal; living forever **2** enduring **3** having lasting fame — *n.* an immortal being — **im·mor·tal′ity** (im′môr tal′i tē) *n.*

im·mor·tal·ize (im môrt′'l īz′) *vt.* **-ized′, -iz′ing** to make immortal, as in fame

im·mov·able (im mōōv′ə bəl) *adj.* **1** firmly fixed **2** unyielding; steadfast

im·mune (im myōōn′, i myōōn′) *adj.* ⟦< L *in-,* without + *munia,* duties⟧ **1** exempt from or protected against something disagreeable or harmful **2** not susceptible to some specified disease

im·mu·nity (im myōōn′i tē) *n., pl.* **-ties 1** exemption from something burdensome, as a legal obligation **2** resistance to infection or a specified disease

im·mu·nize (im′myōō nīz′) *vt.* **-nized′, -niz′ing** to make immune, as by inoculation —**im′mu·ni·za′tion** *n.*

im·mu·nol·ogy (im′myōō näl′ə jē) *n.* the branch of science

THESAURUS

imbalance *n.* lack of balance, unevenness, inequality; see IRREGULARITY.

imbibe *v.* ingest, gorge, guzzle; see DRINK 1, SWALLOW.

imitate *v.* **1** [To mimic] impersonate, mirror, copy, mime, ape, simulate, duplicate, act, repeat, echo, parody, emulate, do like, reflect, pretend, play a part, take off*. **2** [To copy] duplicate, counterfeit, falsify; see COPY, REPRODUCE 2. **3** [To resemble] be like, simulate, parallel; see RESEMBLE.

imitated *a.* copied, duplicated, mimicked, mocked, aped, counterfeited, caricatured, parodied.

imitation *a.* copied, feigned, bogus; see FALSE 3.

imitation *n.* **1** [The act of imitating] simulation, counterfeiting, copying, duplication, patterning after, picturing, representing, mimicry, aping, impersonation, echoing, matching, mirroring, paralleling; see also COPY. **2** [An object made by imitating] counterfeit, mime, sham, fake, picture, replica, echo, reflection, match, parallel, resemblance, transcription, image, mockery, takeoff*, caricature, parody, satire, substitution, forgery; see also COPY.—*Ant.* ORIGINAL, novelty, pattern.

imitative *a.* forged, sham, deceptive; see FALSE 2, 3.

imitator *n.* follower, copier, impersonator, mime, mimic, pretender, counterfeiter, forger, copycat.

immaculate *a.* unsullied, spotless, stainless; see BRIGHT 1, CLEAN 1.

immature *a.* youthful, sophomoric, half-grown; see NAIVE.

immaturity *n.* imperfection, incompleteness, childlike behavior; see INSTABILITY.

immediate *a.* at once, instant, now, on the moment, at this moment, at the present time, next, prompt; see also FOLLOWING.—*Ant.* SOMEDAY, later, any time.

immediately *a.* at once, without delay, instantly, directly, right away, at the first opportunity, at short notice, now, this instant, speedily, quickly, promptly, on the spot, on the dot, rapidly, instantaneously, shortly, on the double*, in a jiffy*; see also URGENTLY.—*Ant.* LATER, in the future, in a while.

immense *a.* gigantic, tremendous, enormous; see LARGE 1.

immensity *n.* infinity, vastness, greatness; see EXTENT.

immerse *v.* submerge, dip, douse, plunge, duck, cover with water, drown, bathe, steep, soak, drench, dunk, souse; see also SOAK 1.

immersed *a.* drowned, plunged, bathed; see DIPPED, SOAKED, WET 1.

immigrant *n.* newcomer, naturalized citizen, adoptive citizen; see ALIEN, EMIGRANT.

immigrate *v.* migrate, colonize, seek political asylum; see ENTER.

immigration *n.* colonization, settlement, migration; see ENTRANCE 1.

imminent *a.* approaching, in store, about to happen; see COMING 1, DESTINED.

immodest *a.* brazen, shameless, bold; see EGOTISTIC, RUDE 2.

immoral *a.* sinful, corrupt, shameless; see BAD 1.

immorality *n.* vice, depravity, dissoluteness; see EVIL 1.

immorally *a.* sinfully, wickedly, unrighteously; see WRONGLY.

immortal *a.* **1** [Deathless] undying, permanent, imperishable, endless, timeless, everlasting, death-defying, unfading, never-ending, perennial, constant, ceaseless, indestructible, enduring; see also ETERNAL.—*Ant.* MORTAL, perishable, corrupt. **2** [Illustrious] celebrated, eminent, glorious; see FAMOUS.

immortality *n.* deathlessness, everlasting life, permanence, endlessness, timelessness, divinity, indestructibility, continuity, perpetuation, endless life, unlimited existence, perpetuity; see also ETERNITY.—*Ant.* DEATH, mortality, decease.

immovable *a.* solid, stable, fixed; see FIRM 1.

immune *a.* free, unaffected by, hardened to, unsusceptible, privileged, not liable, excused; see also SAFE 1.

immunity *n.* **1** [Exemption] favor, privilege, license; see FREEDOM 2. **2** [Freedom from disease] resistance, immunization, protection, active dealing with immunity, as to infection or a disease, and with the body mechanisms producing it —**im'munol'o·gist** *n.*

im·mure (im myoor') *vt.* **-mured', -mur'ing** 〚< L *in-*, in + *murus*, wall 〛 to shut up within walls; confine

im·mu·ta·ble (im myoōt'ə bəl) *adj.* unchangeable —**im·mu'ta·bly** *adv.*

imp (imp) *n.* 〚< Gr *em-*, in + *phyton*, growth 〛 1 a young demon 2 a mischievous child —**imp'ish** *adj.*

im·pact (im pakt'; *for n.* im'pakt') *vt.* 〚< L *impingere*, press firmly together 〛 1 to force tightly together 2 [Colloq.] to affect —*vi.* 1 to hit with force 2 [Colloq.] to have an effect (*on*) —*n.* 1 a violent contact 2 the power to move feelings, influence thinking, etc.

im·pact'ed (-pakt'id) *adj.* abnormally lodged in the jaw: said of a tooth

im·pair (im per') *vt.* 〚< L *in-*, intens. + *pejor*, worse 〛 to make worse, less, etc. —**im·pair'ment** *n.*

im·pa·la (im pä'lə) *n., pl.* **-la** or **-las** a reddish antelope of central and S Africa

im·pale (im pāl') *vt.* **-paled', -pal'ing** 〚< L *in-*, on + *palus*, a pole 〛 to pierce through with, or fix on, something pointed —**im·pale'ment** *n.*

im·pal·pa·ble (im pal'pə bəl) *adj.* 1 not perceptible to the touch 2 too subtle to be easily understood

im·pan·el (im pan'əl) *vt.* **-eled** or **-elled, -el·ing** or **-el·ling** to choose (a jury) in a law case —**im·pan'el·ment** *n.*

im·part (im pärt') *vt.* [see IN-¹ & PART] 1 to give a share of; give 2 to make known; reveal

im·par·tial (im pär'shəl) *adj.* without bias; fair —**im·par'ti·al'ity** (-shē al'i tē) *n.* —**im·par'tially** *adv.*

im·pass·able (im pas'ə bəl) *adj.* that cannot be passed or traveled over

im·passe (im'pas', im pas') *n.* 〚Fr〛 a situation offering no escape or resolution, as a deadlocked argument

im·pas·sioned (im pash'ənd) *adj.* passionate; fiery; ardent

im·pas·sive (im pas'iv) *adj.* not feeling or showing emotion; calm —**im·pas·siv'ity** (im'pa siv'i tē) *n.*

im·pas·to (im päs'tō) *n.* 〚It〛 1 painting in which the paint is laid thickly on the canvas 2 such paint

im·pa·tient (im pā'shənt) *adj.* lacking patience; specif., *a*) annoyed because of delay, opposition, etc. *b*) restlessly eager to do something, etc. —**im·pa'tience** *n.* —**im·pa'tiently** *adv.*

im·peach (im pēch') *vt.* 〚< L *in-*, in + *pedica*, a fetter 〛 1 to discredit (a person's honor, etc.) 2 to try (a public official) on charges of wrongdoing —**im·peach'ment** *n.*

im·pec·ca·ble (im pek'ə bəl) *adj.* 〚< L *in-*, not + *peccare*, to sin 〛 without defect or error; flawless —**im·pec·cabil'ity** *n.* —**im·pec'cably** *adv.*

im·pe·cu·ni·ous (im'pi kyoo'nē əs) *adj.* 〚< L *in-*, not + *pecunia*, money 〛 having no money; poor

im·ped·ance (im pēd'ns) *n.* 〚< fol. + -ANCE 〛 the resistance in an electric circuit to a flow of alternating current

im·pede (im pēd') *vt.* **-ped'ed, -ped'ing** 〚< L *in-*, in + *pes*, foot 〛 to hinder the progress of; obstruct

im·pedi·ment (im ped'ə mənt) *n.* anything that impedes; specif., a speech defect

im·ped'i·men'ta (-men'tə) *n.pl.* encumbrances, as baggage or supplies

im·pel (im pel') *vt.* **-pelled', -pel'ling** 〚< L *in-*, in + *pellere*, to drive 〛 1 to drive or move forward 2 to force, compel, or urge —**im·pel'ler** *n.*

im·pend (im pend') *vi.* 〚< L *in-*, in + *pendere*, hang 〛 to be about to happen; be imminent *[impending disaster]* —**im·pend'ing** *adj.*

im·pen·e·tra·ble (im pen'i trə bəl) *adj.* 1 that cannot be penetrated 2 that cannot be solved or understood —**im·pen'etrabil'ity** *n.* —**im·pen'etrably** *adv.*

im·peni·tent (im pen'ə tənt) *adj.* without regret, shame, or remorse

im·pera·tive (im per'ə tiv) *adj.* 〚< L *imperare*, to command 〛 1 indicating authority or command 2 necessary; urgent 3 designating or of the mood of a verb that expresses a command, etc. —*n.* a command

im·per·cep·ti·ble (im'pər sep'tə bəl) *adj.* not easily perceived by the senses or the mind; very slight, subtle, etc. —**im'per·cep'tibly** *adv.*

im'per·cep'tive (-tiv) *adj.* not perceiving —**im'per·cep'tive·ness** *n.*

im·per·fect (im pur'fikt) *adj.* 1 not complete 2 not perfect 3 designating a verb tense that indicates a past action or state as uncompleted or continuous —**im·per'fectly** *adv.*

im·per·fec·tion (im'pər fek'shən) *n.* 1 a being imperfect 2 a defect; fault

im·peri·al (im pir'ē əl) *adj.* 〚< L *imperium*, empire 〛 1 of an empire, emperor, or empress 2 having supreme authority 3 majestic; august 4 of great size or superior quality —*n.* a small, pointed chin beard

imperial gallon the standard British gallon, equal to 4.546 liters

im·pe'ri·al·ism' *n.* 1 imperial state or authority 2 the policy of forming and maintaining an empire, as by establishing colonies, etc. 3 the policy of seeking to dominate the affairs of weaker countries —**im·pe'ri·al·ist** *n., adj.* —**im·pe'ri·al·is'tic** *adj.*

im·peril (im per'əl) *vt.* **-iled** or **-illed, -il·ing** or **-il·ling** to put in peril; endanger

im·peri·ous (im pir'ē əs) *adj.* 〚< L *imperium*, empire 〛 1 overbearing, arrogant, etc. 2 urgent; imperative —**im·pe'ri·ously** *adv.*

im·per·ish·a·ble (im per'ish ə bəl) *adj.* not perishable; indestructible

im·per·ma·nent (im pur'mə nənt) *adj.* not permanent; temporary —**im·per'ma·nently** *adv.*

im·per·me·a·ble (im pur'mē ə bəl) *adj.* not permeable; not permitting passage, esp. of fluids —**im·per'meabil'ity** *n.*

im·per·sonal (im pur'sə nəl) *adj.* 1 without reference to any particular person 2 not existing as a person *[an impersonal force]* 3 designating or of a verb occurring only in the third person singular, usually with *it* as subject —**im·per'son·ally** *adv.*

im·per·son·ate (im pur'sə nāt') *vt.* **-at'ed, -at'ing** to assume the role of, for purposes of entertainment or fraud —**im·per'sona'tion** *n.* —**im·per'sona'tor** *n.*

im·per·ti·nent (im purt''n ənt) *adj.* 1 not pertinent 2 insolent; impudent —**im·per'ti·nence** *n.*

im·per·turb·a·ble (im'pər tur'bə bəl) *adj.* that cannot be disconcerted, disturbed, or excited; impassive

im·per·vi·ous (im pur'vē əs) *adj.* 1 incapable of being penetrated, as by moisture 2 not affected by: with *to*

im·peti·go (im'pə ti'gō) *n.* [see IMPETUS] a contagious skin disease with eruption of pustules

---

THESAURUS

immunity, passive immunity; see also SAFETY 1.

impact *n.* shock, impression, contact; see COLLISION.

impair *v.* spoil, injure, hurt; see BREAK 2, DAMAGE, DESTROY.

impart *v.* 1 [To give] bestow, grant, present; see ALLOW, GIVE 1. 2 [To inform] tell, announce, divulge; see ADMIT 2, REVEAL.

impartial *a.* unbiased, unprejudiced, disinterested; see EQUAL, FAIR 1.

impartiality *n.* objectivity, candor, justice; see EQUALITY, FAIRNESS.

impasse *n.* deadlock, standstill, cessation; see PAUSE.

impatience *n.* agitation, restlessness, anxiety; see EXCITEMENT, NERVOUSNESS.

impatient *a.* anxious, eager, feverish; see RESTLESS.

impeach *v.* criticize, charge, arraign, denounce, indict, discredit, reprimand, blame, incriminate, try, bring charges against, question; see also BLAME.—*Ant.* FREE, acquit, absolve.

impediment *n.* 1 [An obstruction] hindrance, obstacle, difficulty; see BARRIER. 2 [An obstruction in speech] speech impediment, speech difficulty, stutter, stammer, lisp, halting, harelip, cleft palate.

impending *a.* in the offing, threatening, menacing; see OMINOUS.

impenetrable *a.* 1 [Dense] impervious, hard, compact; see FIRM 2, THICK 3. 2 [Incomprehensible] unintelligible, inscrutable, unfathomable; see OBSCURE 1.

imperative *a.* 1 [Necessary] inescapable, immediate, crucial; see IMPORTANT 1, NECESSARY, URGENT 1. 2 [Authoritative] masterful, commanding, dominant; see AGGRESSIVE, POWERFUL 1.

imperfect *a.* flawed, incomplete, deficient; see FAULTY.

imperfection *n.* fault, flaw, stain; see BLEMISH.

imperialism *n.* empire, international domination, power politics; see POWER 2.

impersonal *a.* detached, disinterested, cold; see INDIFFERENT.

impersonate *v.* mimic, portray, act out, pose as, pass for, double for, put on an act, pretend to be, act the part of, take the part of, act a part, dress as, represent; see also IMITATE 1.

impersonation *n.* imitation, role, enactment; see PERFORMANCE.

impertinence *n.* impudence, insolence, disrespectfulness; see RUDENESS.

impertinent *a.* saucy, insolent, impudent; see RUDE 2.

impervious *a.* impenetrable, watertight, hermetic; see TIGHT 2.

im·petu·ous (im pech′ōō əs) *adj.* [see fol.] acting or done suddenly with little thought; rash —**im·pet′u·os′i·ty** (-äs′i tē) *n.* —**im·pet′u·ous·ly** *adv.*

im·petus (im′pə təs) *n.* [< L *in-*, in + *petere*, rush at] 1 the force with which a body moves against resistance 2 driving force or motive

im·pi·ety (im pī′ə tē) *n.* 1 lack of reverence for God 2 disrespect

im·pinge (im pinj′) *vi.* **-pinged′, -ping′ing** [< L *in-*, in + *pangere*, to strike] 1 to strike, hit, etc. (on or upon) 2 to encroach (on or upon) —**im·pinge′ment** *n.*

im·pi·ous (im′pē əs) *adj.* not pious; specif., lacking reverence for God

im·pla·ca·ble (im plā′kə bəl, -plak′ə-) *adj.* not to be placated or appeased; relentless —**im·pla·cabil′i·ty** *n.* —**im·pla′cably** *adv.*

im·plant (im plant′; *for n.* im′plant′) *vt.* 1 to plant firmly 2 to fix firmly in the mind 3 to insert surgically — *n.* an implanted organ, etc.

im·plau·sible (im plô′zə bəl) *adj.* not plausible —**im·plau′sibly** *adv.*

im·ple·ment (im′plə mənt; *for v.*, -ment′) *n.* [< L *in-*, in + *plere*, to fill] something used in a given activity; tool, instrument, etc. — *vt.* to carry into effect; accomplish —**im′ple·men·ta′tion** (-mən tā′shən) *n.*

im·pli·cate (im′pli kāt′) *vt.* **-cat′ed, -cat′ing** [see IMPLY] to show to be party to a crime, etc. —**im′pli·ca′tive** *adj.*

im′pli·ca′tion *n.* 1 an implicating or being implicated 2 an implying or being implied 3 something implied

im·plicit (im plis′it) *adj.* [see IMPLY] 1 suggested though not plainly expressed; implied 2 necessarily involved though not apparent; inherent 3 without reservation —**im·plic′itly** *adv.*

im·plode (im plōd′) *vt.*, *vi.* **-plod′ed, -plod′ing** [< IN-¹ + (EX)PLODE] to burst or cause to burst inward —**im·plo′sion** (-plō′zhən) *n.* —**im·plo′sive** (-plō′siv) *adj.*

im·plore (im plôr′) *vt.* **-plored′, -plor′ing** [< L *in-*, intens. + *plorare*, cry out] 1 to ask earnestly for 2 to beg (a person) to do something —**im·plor′ingly** *adv.*

im·ply (im plī′) *vt.* **-plied′, -ply′ing** [< L *in-*, in + *plicare*, to fold] 1 to have as a necessary part, condition, etc. 2 to indicate indirectly; hint; suggest

im·po·lite (im′pə līt′) *adj.* not polite; discourteous —**im′po·lite′ly** *adv.*

im·poli·tic (im päl′ə tik′) *adj.* not politic; unwise

im·pon·der·a·ble (im pän′dər ə bəl) *adj.* that cannot be weighed or measured — *n.* anything imponderable

im·port (im pôrt′, *also, and for n. always* im′pôrt′) *vt.* [< L *in-*, in + *portare*, carry] 1 to bring (goods) from another country, esp. for sale 2 to mean; signify — *vi.* to be of importance; matter — *n.* 1 something imported 2 meaning; signification 3 importance —**im·por·ta′tion** *n.* —**im·port′er** *n.*

im·por·tant (im pôrt′′nt) *adj.* [see IMPORT] 1 meaning a great deal; having much significance or value 2 having, or acting as if having, power, authority, etc. —**im·por′tance** *n.* —**im·por′tantly** *adv.*

im·por·tu·nate (im pôr′choo nit) *adj.* persistent in asking or demanding

im·por·tune (im′pôr tōōn′) *vt.*, *vi.* **-tuned′, -tun′ing** [< L *importunus*, troublesome] to urge or entreat persistently or repeatedly —**im′por·tu′ni·ty**, pl. **-ties**, *n.*

im·pose (im pōz′) *vt.* **-posed′, -pos′ing** [< L *in-*, on + *ponere*, to place] 1 to place (a burden, tax, etc. on or upon) 2 to force (oneself) on others —**impose on (or upon)** 1 to take advantage of 2 to cheat or defraud —**im′po·si′tion** (-pə zish′ən) *n.*

im·pos′ing *adj.* impressive because of great size, strength, dignity, etc. —**im·pos′ingly** *adv.*

im·pos·sible (im päs′ə bəl) *adj.* 1 not capable of being, being done, or happening 2 not capable of being endured, used, etc. because disagreeable or unsuitable —**im·pos′sibil′ity**, pl. **-ties**, *n.* —**im·pos′sibly** *adv.*

im·post (im′pōst′) *n.* [see IMPOSE] a tax; esp., a duty on imported goods

im·pos·tor or **im·post′er** (im päs′tər) *n.* [see IMPOSE] one who deceives or cheats others by pretending to be what he is not

im·pos′ture (-chər) *n.* the act or practice of an impostor; fraud

im·po·tent (im′pə tənt) *adj.* 1 lacking physical strength 2 ineffective; powerless 3 unable to engage in sexual intercourse: said of males —**im′po·tence** or **im′po·tency** *n.* —**im′po·tently** *adv.*

im·pound (im pound′) *vt.* 1 to shut up (an animal) in a pound 2 to take and hold in legal custody 3 to gather and enclose (water), as for irrigation

im·pov·er·ish (im päv′ər ish) *vt.* [< L *in-*, in + *pauper*, poor] 1 to make poor 2 to deprive of strength, resources, etc. —**im·pov′er·ish·ment** *n.*

═══════════ **THESAURUS** ═══════════

impetus *n.* force, cause, stimulus; see INCENTIVE, PURPOSE 1, REASON 3.

impious *a.* sinful, profane, blasphemous; see BAD 1.

implant *v.* stick in, insert, root; see PLANT.

implement *n.* utensil, device, instrument; see EQUIPMENT, MACHINE, TOOL 1.

implicate *v.* connect, cite, associate, tie up with, charge, link, catch up in, relate, compromise; see also BLAME.

implicated *a.* under suspicion, suspected, known to have been associated with; see GUILTY, INVOLVED, SUSPICIOUS 1, 2.

implication *n.* 1 [Assumption] reference, indication, inference; see ASSUMPTION 1, GUESS. 2 [A link] connection, involvement, entanglement; see JOINT 1, LINK, UNION 1.

implicit *a.* unquestioned, certain, absolute; see ACCURATE 2, DEFINITE 1, INEVITABLE.

implied *a.* implicit, indicated, foreshadowed, involved, tacit, signified, figured, intended, meant, alluded to, latent, hidden, insinuated, hinted at, understood, symbolized, indicative, potential, indirectly meant, inferred, inferential, undeclared; see also SUGGESTED.

imply *v.* 1 [To indicate] intimate, hint at, suggest; see HINT, MENTION, REFER 2. 2 [To mean] import, indicate, signify; see INTEND 2, MEAN 1.

impolite *a.* discourteous, moody, churlish; see IRRITABLE, RUDE 2, SULLEN.

import *v.* introduce, bring in, buy abroad; see CARRY 1, SEND 1.

importance *n.* import, force, sense, consequence, bearing, denotation, gist, effect, distinction, influence, usefulness, moment, weightiness, momentousness, emphasis, standing, stress, accent, weight, concern, attention, interest, seriousness, point, substance, relevance, sum and substance; see also MEANING.—*Ant.* INSIGNIFICANCE, triviality, emptiness.

important *a.* 1 [Weighty; *said usually of things*] significant, considerable, momentous, essential, great, decisive, critical, determining, chief, paramount, primary, foremost, principal, influential, marked, of great consequence, ponderous, of importance, never to be overlooked, of note, valuable, crucial, substantial, vital, serious, grave, relevant, pressing, far-reaching, extensive, conspicuous, heavy, big-league*, big*; see also NECESSARY.—*Ant.* TRIVIAL, inconsequential, unimportant. 2 [Eminent; *said usually of persons*] illustrious, well-known, influential; see FAMOUS. 3 [Relevant] material, influential, significant; see FIT 1, RELATED 2, RELEVANT.

imported *a.* shipped in, produced abroad, exotic, alien; see also FOREIGN.—*Ant.* NATIVE, domestic, made in America.

impose *v.* force upon, compel, fix; see FORCE. —**impose on (or upon)** intrude, interrupt, presume; see BOTHER 2, DISTURB.

imposing *a.* stirring, exciting, overwhelming; see IMPRESSIVE.

imposition *n.* demand, restraint, encumbrance; see COMMAND, PRESSURE 2.

impossibility *n.* hopelessness, impracticality, impractibility, difficulty, unworkability, unlikelihood, failure; see also FUTILITY.

impossible *a.* inconceivable, vain, unachievable, unattainable, out of the question, too much, insurmountable, useless, inaccessible, unworkable, preposterous, unimaginable, unobtainable, not to be thought of, hardly possible, like finding a needle in a haystack*, a hundred to one*, out of the question; see also FUTILE, HOPELESS.—*Ant.* REASONABLE, possible, likely.

impostor *n.* pretender, charlatan, quack; see CHEAT.

impotence *n.* 1 [Sterility] unproductiveness, frigidity, infecundity; see EMPTINESS. 2 [Weakness] inability, feebleness, infirmity; see WEAKNESS 1.

impotent *a.* 1 [Weak] powerless, inept, infirm; see UNABLE, WEAK 1. 2 [Sterile] barren, frigid, unproductive; see STERILE 1.

impound *v.* appropriate, take, usurp; see SEIZE 1.

impounded *a.* kept, seized, confiscated; see HELD, RETAINED 1.

impoverish *v.* make poor, bankrupt, exhaust; see DESTROY.

impoverished *a.* poverty-stricken, bankrupt, broke*; see POOR 1, RUINED 3.

im·prac·ti·ca·ble (im prak′ti kə bəl) *adj.* not capable of being carried out in practice

im·prac·ti·cal (im prak′ti kəl) *adj.* not practical —**im·prac′ti·cal′i·ty** *n.*

im·pre·cate (im′pri kāt′) *vt.* -cat′ed, -cat′ing 〚< L *in-*, on + *precari*, pray〛 to invoke (evil, a curse, etc.) —**im′pre·ca′tion** *n.*

im·pre·cise (im′pri sīs′) *adj.* not precise; vague —**im′pre·cise′ly** *adv.* —**im′pre·ci′sion** (-sizh′ən) *n.*

im·preg·na·ble (im preg′nə bəl) *adj.* 1 that cannot be captured or entered by force 2 unyielding —**im·preg′nabil′ity** *n.* —**im·preg′nably** *adv.*

im·preg·nate (im preg′nāt′) *vt.* -nat′ed, -nat′ing 1 to make pregnant; fertilize 2 to saturate 3 to imbue (*with* ideas, etc.) —**im′preg·na′tion** *n.*

im·pre·sa·rio (im′prə sä′rē ō′) *n.*, *pl.* -os 〚It〛 one who manages an opera, organizes concert series, etc.

im·press[1] (im pres′) *vt.* 〚< IN-[1] + PRESS[2]〛 1 to force into military service 2 to seize for public use

im·press[2] (im pres′; *for n.* im′pres′) *vt.* 〚see IMPRINT〛 1 to stamp; imprint 2 to affect strongly the mind or emotions of 3 to fix in the memory: with *on* or *upon* —*n.* 1 an impressing 2 an imprint

im·press′i·ble (-ə bəl) *adj.* that can be impressed —**im·press′ibil′ity** *n.*

im·pres·sion (im presh′ən) *n.* 1 an impressing 2 *a*) a mark, imprint, etc. *b*) an effect produced on the mind 3 a vague notion 4 an amusing impersonation; mimicking

im·pres′sion·a·ble *adj.* easily impressed or influenced; sensitive

im·pres′sion·ism′ *n.* a theory of art, music, etc. whose aim is to capture a brief, immediate impression —**im·pres′sion·ist** *n.* —**im·pres′sion·is′tic** *adj.*

im·pres·sive (im pres′iv) *adj.* tending to impress the mind or emotions; eliciting wonder or admiration —**im·pres′sively** *adv.*

im·pri·ma·tur (im′pri mät′ər) *n.* 〚ModL, lit., let it be printed〛 permission to publish a book, etc., as granted by a Catholic bishop

im·print (im print′; *for n.* im′print′) *vt.* 〚< L *in-*, on + *premere*, to press〛 to mark or fix as by pressing or stamping —*n.* 1 a mark made by imprinting 2 a lasting effect 3 a note in a book giving facts of its publication

im·prison (im priz′ən) *vt.* to put in or as in prison —**im·pris′on·ment** *n.*

im·prob·a·ble (im präb′ə bəl) *adj.* not probable; unlikely —**im′prob·abil′ity** *n.* —**im·prob′ably** *adv.*

im·promp·tu (im prämp′tōō′) *adj.*, *adv.* 〚< L *in promptu*, in readiness〛 without preparation; offhand

im·prop·er (im präp′ər) *adj.* 1 not suitable; unfit 2 incorrect 3 not in good taste —**im·prop′erly** *adv.*

im·pro·pri·e·ty (im′prō prī′ə tē) *n.*, *pl.* -ties 1 a being improper 2 an improper act, word usage, etc.

im·prove (im prōōv′) *vt.* -proved′, -prov′ing 〚< Anglo-Fr *en-*, in + *prou*, gain〛 1 to make better 2 to make (real estate) more valuable by cultivation, construction, etc. —*vi.* to become better —**improve on** (or **upon**) to do or make better than —**im·prov′able** *adj.*

im·prove′ment *n.* 1 an improving or being improved 2 an addition or change that improves something

im·prov·i·dent (im präv′ə dənt) *adj.* lacking foresight or thrift —**im·prov′i·dence** *n.* —**im·prov′i·dently** *adv.*

im·pro·vise (im′prə vīz′) *vt.*, *vi.* -vised′, -vis′ing 〚< L *in-*, not + *providere*, foresee〛 1 to compose and perform without preparation 2 to make or do with whatever is at hand —**im·prov′i·sa′tion** (-präv′i zā′shən) *n.* —**im·prov′i·sa′tional** *adj.*

im·pru·dent (im prōōd′nt) *adj.* not prudent; rash —**im·pru′dence** *n.*

im·pu·dent (im′pyōō dənt) *adj.* 〚< L *in-*, not + *pudere*, feel shame〛 shamelessly bold; insolent —**im′pu·dence** *n.* —**im′pu·dently** *adv.*

im·pugn (im pyōōn′) *vt.* 〚< L *in-*, against + *pugnare*, to fight〛 to oppose or challenge as false

im·pulse (im′puls′) *n.* 〚see IMPEL〛 1 *a*) a driving forward *b*) an impelling force; impetus *c*) the motion or effect

---

THESAURUS

impractical *a.* unreal, unrealistic, unworkable, improbable, illogical, unreasonable, absurd, wild, abstract, impossible, idealistic, unfeasible, out of the question.—*Ant.* PRACTICAL, logical, reasonable.

impregnate *v.* 1 [To permeate] fill up, pervade, overflow; see FILL 2, SOAK 1. 2 [To beget] procreate, conceive, reproduce; see FERTILIZE 2.

impregnated *a.* 1 [Full] saturated, shot through and through, full of; see FULL 1. 2 [Pregnant] bred, in a family way*, with child; see PREGNANT.

impress[2] *v.* 1 [To make an impression] indent, emboss, imprint; see DENT, MARK 1, PRINT 2. 2 [To attract attention] stand out, be conspicuous, cause a stir, create an impression, make an impression on, direct attention to, make an impact upon, engage the thoughts of, engage the attention of, be listened to, find favor with, make a hit*, make a dent in; see also FASCINATE.

impressed *a.* aroused, awakened, awed; see AFFECTED 1, EXCITED.

impression *n.* 1 [An imprint] print, footprint, fingerprint, dent, mold, indentation, depression, cast, form, track, pattern; see also MARK 1. 2 [An effect] response, consequence, reaction; see RESULT. 3 [A notion based on scanty evidence] theory, conjecture, supposition; see GUESS, OPINION 1.

impressionable *a.* perceptive, impressible, receptive; see AFFECTED 1.

impressive *a.* stirring, moving, inspiring, effective, affecting, eloquent, impassioned, thrilling, excited, intense, well-done, dramatic, absorbing, deep, profound, penetrating, remarkable, extraordinary, notable, important, momentous, vital; see also PROFOUND.—*Ant.* DULL,

uninteresting, common.

imprint *n.* 1 [A printed identification] firm name, banner, trademark, direction, heading; see also EMBLEM, SIGNATURE. 2 [An impression] dent, indentation, print; see MARK 1.

imprint *v.* print, stamp, designate; see MARK 1, 2.

imprison *v.* jail, lock up, confine, incarcerate, immure, impound, detain, keep in, hold, intern, shut in, lock in, box in, fence in, cage, send to prison, keep as captive, hold captive, hold as hostage, enclose, keep in custody, put behind bars, put away*, send up*.—*Ant.* FREE, liberate, release.

imprisoned *a.* arrested, jailed, incarcerated; see CONFINED 3.

imprisonment *n.* captivity, isolation, incarceration, duress, durance, bondage; see also CONFINEMENT.—*Ant.* FREEDOM, liberty, emancipation.

improbable *a.* not likely, doubtful, not to be expected; see UNLIKELY.

improper *a.* at odds, ill-advised, unsuited, incongruous, out of place, ludicrous, incorrect, preposterous, unwarranted, undue, imprudent, abnormal, irregular, inexpedient, unseasonable, inadvisable, untimely, inopportune, unfit, malapropos, unfitting, inappropriate, unbefitting, ill-timed, awkward, inharmonious, inapplicable, odd; see also UNSUITABLE.

improperly *a.* poorly, inappropriately, clumsily; see AWKWARDLY, BADLY 1, INADEQUATELY.

improve *v.* 1 [To make better] mend, update, refine; see CHANGE 1, REPAIR. 2 [To become better] regenerate, advance, progress, renew, enrich, enhance, augment, gain strength, develop, get better, grow better, grow, make progress, widen, increase, mellow, mature, come

along, get on, look up, shape up*, pick up, perk up, come around, make headway, snap out of*; see also CHANGE 2, RECOVER 3.—*Ant.* WEAKEN, worsen, grow worse. —**improve on** (or **upon**) make better, develop, refine; see CORRECT, REPAIR.

improved *a.* corrected, bettered, amended, mended, reformed, elaborated, refined, modernized, brought up-to-date, enhanced, repaired, bolstered up, rectified, remodeled, reorganized, made-over, better for, doctored up*, polished up*; see also CHANGED 2.

improvement *n.* 1 [The process of becoming better] amelioration, betterment, rectification, change, alteration, reformation, progression, advance, advancement, development, growth, rise, civilization, gain, cultivation, increase, enrichment, promotion, elevation, regeneration, recovery, renovation, reorganization, amendment, reform, revision, elaboration, refinement, modernization, enhancement, remodeling.—*Ant.* DECAY, deterioration, retrogression. 2 [That which has been improved] addition, supplement, repair, extra, attachment, correction, reform, remodeling, repairing, refinement, luxury, advance, latest thing, last word; see also CHANGE 1.

improving *a.* reconstructing, repairing, elaborating, bettering, correcting, developing, remodeling, fixing, on the mend.

impudence *n.* insolence, impertinence, effrontery; see RUDENESS.

impudent *a.* forward, insolent, shameless; see RUDE 2.

impugn *v.* question, attack, challenge, call into question, contradict, assail, knock*; see also DOUBT.

impulse *n.* 1 [A throb] surge, pulse, pulsation; see BEAT 1. 2 [A sudden caused by such a force **2** *a*) incitement to action by a stimulus *b*) a sudden inclination to act **3** a brief surge in an electric current

im·pul·sion (im pul′shən) *n.* **1** an impelling or being impelled **2** IMPULSE (sense 1*b*) **3** IMPULSE (sense 2)

im·pul·sive (im pul′siv) *adj.* **1** driving forward **2** likely to act on impulse —**im·pul′sive·ly** *adv.*

im·pu·ni·ty (im pyōo′ni tē) *n.* ⟦< L *in-*, without + *poena*, punishment⟧ freedom from punishment, harm, etc.

im·pure (im pyoor′) *adj.* **1** unclean; dirty **2** immoral; obscene; **3** mixed with foreign matter; adulterated —**im·pure′ly** *adv.* —**im·pure′ness** *n.*

im·pu·ri·ty (-ə tē) *n.* **1** a being impure **2** *pl.* -ties an impure thing or part

im·pute (im pyōot′) *vt.* -put′ed, -put′ing ⟦< L *in-*, in, to + *putare*, to think⟧ to attribute (esp. a fault or misconduct) to another —**im′pu·ta′tion** (-pyōo tā′shən) *n.*

in (in) *prep.* ⟦OE⟧ **1** contained by [*in* the room] **2** wearing [dressed *in* furs] **3** during [done *in* a day] **4** at the end of [due *in* an hour] **5** not beyond [*in* sight] **6** employed, enrolled, etc. at [*in* college] **7** out of a group of [one *in* ten] **8** amidst [*in* a storm] **9** affected by [*in* trouble] **10** with regard to [to vary *in* size] **11** using [speak *in* English] **12** because of; for [to cry *in* pain] **13** into [come *in* the house] — *adv.* **1** to the inside [he went *in*] **2** to or at a certain place **3** so as to be contained by a certain space, condition, etc. — *adj.* **1** that is in power [the *in* group] **2** inner; inside **3** gathered, counted, etc. **4** [Colloq.] currently smart, popular, etc. — *n.* **1** one that is in power: *usually used in pl.* **2** [Colloq.] special influence or favor —**have it in for** [Colloq.] to hold a grudge against —**ins and outs** all the details and intricacies —**in that** because; since —**in with** associated with

in-[1] ⟦< the prep. IN or L *in*, in⟧ *prefix* in, into, within, on, toward [*inbreed*]

in-[2] ⟦L⟧ *prefix* no, not, without, NON- The following list includes some common compounds formed with *in-*, with no special meanings; they will be understood if "not" or "lack of" is used with the meaning of the base word:

inability	inapt
inaccessible	inaudible
inaccuracy	inauspicious
inaccurate	incapable
inaction	incautious
inactive	incivility
inadequacy	incombustible
inadequate	incommensurate
inadequately	incommunicable
inadmissible	incomprehensible
inadvisable	inconceivable
inanimate	inconclusive
inapplicable	inconsistency
inappropriate	inconsistent

incorrect	inexact
incorrectly	inexcusable
incurable	inexpensive
indecorous	infertile
indefinable	inharmonious
indiscernible	inhospitable
indisputable	inhumane
indistinct	injudicious
indistinguishable	inopportune
indivisible	inseparable
inedible	insignificance
ineffective	insignificant
ineffectual	insolvable
inefficacy	insufficient
inelastic	insufficiently
ineligible	insurmountable
inequality	insusceptible
inequitable	invariable
inequity	invariably

-in (in) *combining form* a mass action or gathering of a (specified) type [pray-*in*, be-*in*]

in. inch(es)

in ab·sen·tia (in ab sen′shə, -shē ə) ⟦L⟧ although not present [to receive an award *in absentia*]

in·ac·ti·vate (in ak′tə vāt′) *vt.* -vat′ed, -vat′ing to make inactive —**in·ac′ti·va′tion** *n.*

in·ad·vert·ent (in′ad vurt′nt, -əd-) *adj.* **1** not attentive or observant **2** due to oversight —**in′ad·vert′ence** *n.* —**in′ad·vert′ently** *adv.*

in·alien·able (in āl′yən ə bəl) *adj.* ⟦see ALIEN⟧ that may not be taken away or transferred —**in·al′ien·ably** *adv.*

in·amo·rata (in am′ə rät′ə) *n.* ⟦It⟧ a sweetheart or lover: said of a woman

in·ane (in ān′) *adj.* ⟦L *inanis*⟧ **1** empty **2** lacking sense; silly —**in·an′ity** (-an′i tē) *n.*

in·ar·ticu·late (in′är tik′yōo lit, -yə-) *adj.* **1** without the articulation of normal speech [an *inarticulate* cry] **2** mute **3** unable to speak clearly or coherently **4** unexpressed or unexpressible

inasmuch as (in′əz much′ az′) **1** since; because **2** to the extent that

in·at·ten·tion (in′ə ten′shən) *n.* failure to pay attention; negligence —**in′at·ten′tive** *adj.*

in·au·gu·ral (in ô′gyoo rəl) *adj.* ⟦Fr⟧ **1** of an inauguration **2** first in a series — *n.* **1** a speech made at an inauguration **2** an inauguration

in·au′gu·rate′ (-rāt′) *vt.* -rat′ed, -rat′ing ⟦< L *inaugurare*, to practice augury⟧ **1** to induct into office with a formal ceremony **2** to make a formal beginning of **3** to dedicate formally —**in·au′gu·ra′tion** *n.*

in·au·then·tic (in′ô then′tik) *adj.* not authentic

in·board (in′bôrd′) *adv.*, *adj.* **1** inside the hull of a ship or

---

THESAURUS

urge] fancy, whim, caprice, motive, motivation, spontaneity, drive, appeal, notion, inclination, disposition, wish, whimsy, inspiration, hunch, flash, thought.

impulsive *a.* offhand, unpremeditated, extemporaneous; see AUTOMATIC, SPONTANEOUS.

impulsively *a.* imprudently, hastily, abruptly; see CARELESSLY, RASHLY.

impure *a.* **1** [Adulterated] not pure, loaded, weighted, salted, diluted, debased, contaminated, mixed, watered down, polluted, corrupted, raw, tainted, cut, adulterated, doctored*, tampered with; see also UNCLEAN. **2** [Not chaste] unclean, unchaste, corrupt; see BAD 1, LEWD 2.

impurity *n.* **1** [Lewdness] indecency, profligacy, pornography; see LEWDNESS. **2** [Filth] dirt, defilement, excrement; see FILTH, POLLUTION.

in *prep.* **1** [Within] surrounded by, in the midst of, within the boundaries of, in the area of, within the time of, concerning the subject of, as a part of, inside of, enclosed in, not out of; see also WITHIN. **2** [Into] to the center of, to the midst of, in the direction of, within the extent of, under, near, against; see also INTO, TOWARD. **3** [While engaged in] in the act of, during the process of, while occupied with; see DURING, MEANWHILE, WHILE 1. —**have it in for*** wish to harm, be out to destroy, detest; see HATE 1.

inability *n.* **1** [Lack of competence] incapacity, incompetence, shortcoming; see FAILURE 1, WEAKNESS 1. **2** [A temporary lack] disability, failure, frailty; see LACK 2, NECESSITY 2.

inaccessible *a.* unobtainable, unworkable, out of reach; see AWAY, BEYOND, DIFFICULT 2, DISTANT, RARE 2, REMOTE 1, SEPARATED.

inaccuracy *n.* exaggeration, mistake, deception; see ERROR.

inaccurate *a.* fallacious, in error, incorrect; see MISTAKEN 1, WRONG 2.

inactive *a.* dormant, stable, still; see IDLE, MOTIONLESS 1.

inadequacy *n.* **1** [Inferiority] ineptitude, incompetence, insufficiency; see WEAKNESS 1. **2** [A defect] flaw, drawback, shortcoming; see BLEMISH, DEFECT, LACK 2.

inadequate *a.* lacking, scanty, short, meager, failing, unequal, not enough, sparing, stinted, stunted, feeble, sparse, too little, small, thin, deficient, incomplete, inconsiderable, spare, bare, niggardly, miserly, scarce, barren, depleted, low, weak, impotent, unproductive, dry, sterile, imperfect, defective, lame, skimpy*; see also UNSATISFACTORY.—*Ant.* ENOUGH, adequate, sufficient.

inadequately *a.* insufficiently, not enough, partly, partially, incompletely, scantily, deficiently, perfunc-

torily, ineffectively, inefficiently, ineptly, not up to standards, not up to specifications, not up to requirements, meagerly, not in sufficient quantity, not in sufficient quality, to a limited degree, below par, not up to snuff*; see also BADLY 1.

inadvisable *a.* unsuitable, inappropriate, inconvenient; see IMPROPER, WRONG 2.

inane *a.* pointless, foolish, ridiculous; see ILLOGICAL, SILLY, STUPID.

inanimate *a.* dull, inert, inoperative; see IDLE, MOTIONLESS 1.

inappropriate *a.* improper, irrelevant, inapplicable; see UNSUITABLE.

inarticulate *a.* **1** [Mute] reticent, wordless, mute; see DUMB 1. **2** [Indistinct] unintelligible, inaudible, vague; see OBSCURE 1.

inasmuch as *conj.* in view of, making allowance for, while; see BECAUSE, SINCE 1.

inattentive *a.* indifferent, preoccupied, negligent; see CARELESS, DIVERTED.

inaudible *a.* low, indistinct, silent; see OBSCURE 1, VAGUE.

inaugurate *v.* introduce, initiate, originate; see BEGIN 1.

inauguration *n.* initiation, commencement, installment; see INSTALLATION 1.

boat **2** close to the fuselage of an aircraft — *n.* a boat with an inboard motor

in·born (in′bôrn′) *adj.* present in the organism at birth; innate

in·bound (in′bound′) *adj.* traveling or going inward — *vt., vi.* *Basketball* to put (the ball) in play from out of bounds

in·bred (in′bred′) *adj.* **1** innate; inborn **2** resulting from inbreeding

in·breed (in′brēd′) *vt.* **-bred′, -breed′ing** to breed by continual mating of individuals of the same or closely related stocks — *vi.* **1** to engage in such breeding **2** to become too refined, effete, etc.

inc. **1** incorporated: also **Inc.** **2** increase

Inca (iŋ′kə) *n.* a member of the highly civilized Indian people that dominated ancient Peru until the Spanish conquest

in·cal·cu·la·ble (in kal′kyo͞o lə bəl) *adj.* **1** that cannot be calculated; too great or too many to be counted **2** unpredictable —**in·cal′cu·la·bly** *adv.*

in·can·des·cent (in′kən des′ənt) *adj.* [< L *in-*, in + *candere*, to shine] **1** glowing with intense heat **2** very bright —**in′can·des′cence** *n.*

incandescent lamp a lamp with a filament in a vacuum heated to incandescence by an electric current

in·can·ta·tion (in′kan tā′shən) *n.* [< L *in-*, intens. + *cantare*, to sing] words chanted in magic spells or rites

in·ca·pac·i·tate (in′kə pas′ə tāt′) *vt.* **-tat′ed, -tat′ing 1** to make unable or unfit **2** *Law* to disqualify

in′ca·pac′i·ty *n.* **1** lack of capacity, power, or fitness **2** legal ineligibility

in·car·cer·ate (in kär′sər āt′) *vt.* **-at′ed, -at′ing** [< L *in-*, in + *carcer*, prison] to imprison —**in·car′cer·a′tion** *n.*

in·car·na·dine (in kär′nə din′) *vt.* **-dined′, -din′ing** to make red

in·car·nate (in kär′nit, -nāt′; *for v. always,* -nāt′) *adj.* [< L *in-*, in + *caro*, flesh] endowed with a human body; personified — *vt.* **-nat′ed, -nat′ing 1** to give bodily form to **2** to be the type or embodiment of —**in′car·na′tion** *n.*

in·cen·di·ary (in sen′dē er′ē) *adj.* [< L *incendium*, a fire] **1** having to do with the willful destruction of property by fire **2** designed to cause fires, as certain bombs **3** willfully stirring up strife, riot, etc. — *n., pl.* **-ar′ies** one who willfully stirs up strife, riot, etc.

in·cense¹ (in′sens) *n.* [< L *in-*, in + *candere*, to burn] **1** any substance burned to produce a pleasant odor **2** the odor from this **3** any pleasant odor

in·cense² (in sens′) *vt.* **-censed′, -cens′ing** [see prec.] to make very angry —**in·cense′ment** *n.*

in·cen·tive (in sent′iv) *n.* [< L *in-*, in, on + *canere*, sing] a stimulus; motive

in·cep·tion (in sep′shən) *n.* [see INCIPIENT] the beginning of something; start

in·cer·ti·tude (in sʉrt′ə to͞od′, -tyo͞od′) *n.* **1** doubt **2** insecurity

in·ces·sant (in ses′ənt) *adj.* [< L *in-*, not + *cessare*, cease] never ceasing; continuing without stopping; constant —**in·ces′sant·ly** *adv.*

in·cest (in′sest′) *n.* [< L *in-*, not + *castus*, chaste] sexual intercourse between persons too closely related to marry legally —**in·ces·tu·ous** (in ses′tyo͞o əs) *adj.* —**in·ces′tu·ously** *adv.* —**in·ces′tu·ous·ness** *n.*

inch (inch) *n.* [< L *uncia*, twelfth part] a measure of length equal to $\frac{1}{12}$ foot: symbol, ″ — *vt., vi.* to move very slowly, or by degrees —**every inch** in all respects —**inch by inch** gradually: also **by inches** —**within an inch of** very close to

in·cho·ate (in kō′it) *adj.* [< L *inchoare*, begin] **1** just begun; rudimentary **2** not yet clearly formed

in·ci·dence (in′sə dəns) *n.* the degree or range of occurrence or effect

in′ci·dent (-dənt) *adj.* [< L *in-*, on + *cadere*, to fall] **1** likely to happen as a result **2** falling upon or affecting [*incident* rays] — *n.* **1** something that happens; an event, esp. a minor one **2** a minor conflict

in′ci·den′tal (-dent″l) *adj.* **1** happening in connection with something more important; casual **2** secondary or minor — *n.* **1** something incidental **2** [*pl.*] miscellaneous items

in′ci·den′tally *adv.* **1** in an incidental manner **2** by the way

in·cin·er·ate (in sin′ər āt′) *vt., vi.* **-at′ed, -at′ing** [< L *in*, in + *cinis*, ashes] to burn to ashes; burn up —**in·cin·era′tion** *n.*

in·cin′era′tor *n.* a furnace for burning trash

in·cip·i·ent (in sip′ē ənt) *adj.* [< L *in-*, in + *capere*, to take] just beginning to exist or appear —**in·cip′i·ence** *n.*

in·cise (in sīz′) *vt.* **-cised′, -cis′ing** [< L *in-*, into + *caedere*, to cut] to cut into with a sharp tool; specif., to engrave or carve

in·ci·sion (in sizh′ən) *n.* **1** an incising **2** a cut; specif., one made surgically **3** incisive quality

in·ci·sive (in sī′siv) *adj.* **1** cutting into **2** sharp; penetrating —**in·ci′sively** *adv.* —**in·ci′sive·ness** *n.*

in·ci·sor (in sī′zər) *n.* any of the front cutting teeth between the canines

in·cite (in sīt′) *vt.* **-cit′ed, -cit′ing** [< L *in-*, on + *citare*, to urge] to urge to action; rouse —**in·cite′ment** *n.*

incl. **1** including **2** inclusive

in·clem·ent (in klem′ənt) *adj.* [< L *in-*, on + *clemens*, lenient] **1** rough; stormy **2** lacking mercy; harsh —**in·clem′ency,** *pl.* **-cies,** *n.*

in·cli·na·tion (in′klə nā′shən) *n.* **1** a bending, leaning, or sloping **2** an inclined surface; slope **3** *a*) a bias; tendency *b*) a preference

in·cline (in klīn′; *for n., usually* in′klīn′) *vi.* **-clined′, -clin′ing** [< L *in-*, on + *clinare*, to lean] **1** to lean; slope **2** to have a tendency **3** to have a preference or liking — *vt.* **1**

THESAURUS

inborn *a.* essential, intrinsic, inbred; see NATIVE 1.

inbred *a.* innate, inborn, ingrained; see NATIVE 1.

incalculable *a.* unpredictable, unforeseen, unfixed; see UNCERTAIN.

incandescent *a.* radiant, glowing, brilliant; see BRIGHT 1.

incapable *a.* unsuited, poor, inadequate; see INCOMPETENT, INEXPERIENCED, NAIVE.

incapacity *n.* inadequacy, insufficiency, uselessness; see WEAKNESS 1.

incense¹ *n.* scent, fragrance, essence; see PERFUME.

incentive *n.* spur, inducement, motive, stimulus, stimulation, impetus, provocation, enticement, temptation, bait, consideration, excuse, rationale, urge, influence, lure, persuasion, inspiration, encouragement, insistence, instigation, incitement, reason why; see also PURPOSE 1.

incessant *a.* ceaseless, continuous, monotonous; see CONSTANT.

incessantly *a.* steadily, monotonously, perpetually; see REGULARLY.

inch *n.* **1** [Twelfth of a foot] fingerbreadth, measurement, 1/36 yard; see MEASURE 1. **2** [Small degree] jot,

little bit, iota; see BIT 2. —**by inches** slowly, by degrees, step by step; see GRADUALLY. —**every inch** in all respects, thoroughly, entirely; see COMPLETELY.

inch *v.* creep, barely move, make some progress; see CRAWL.

inchoate *a.* incipient, rudimentary, preliminary, beginning; see also UNFINISHED 1.

incident *n.* episode, happening, occurrence; see EVENT.

incidental *a.* subsidiary, relative to, contributing to; see RELATED 2, SUBORDINATE.

incidentally *a.* subordinately, by chance, by the way, as a side effect, as a by-product, unexpectedly, not by design, remotely; see also ACCIDENTALLY.

incidentals *n.* minor needs, incidental expenses, per diem; see EXPENSES, NECESSITY 2.

incinerate *v.* cremate, parch, burn up; see BURN.

incise *v.* dissect, chop, split; see CUT 1, DIVIDE.

incision *n.* gash, slash, surgery; see CUT 1, HOLE 1.

incite *v.* arouse, rouse, impel, stimulate, instigate, provoke, excite, spur,

goad, persuade, influence, induce, taunt, activate, animate, inspirit, coax, stir up, motivate, prompt, urge on, inspire, force, work up*, talk into*, egg on, fan the flame*; see also URGE 2.—*Ant.* DISCOURAGE, dissuade, check.

incited *a.* driven, pushed, motivated; see URGED 2.

inclination *n.* **1** [A tendency] bias, bent, propensity, predilection, penchant, attachment, capability, capacity, aptness, leaning, fondness, disposition, liking, preference, movement, susceptibility, weakness, drift, trend, turn, slant, impulse, attraction, affection, desire, temperament, whim, idiosyncrasy, urge, persuasion. **2** [A slant] pitch, slope, incline, angle, ramp, bank, lean, list; see also GRADE 1.

incline *n.* slope, inclined plane, approach; see GRADE 1, INCLINATION 2.

incline *v.* **1** [To lean] bow, nod, cock; see LEAN 1. **2** [To tend toward] prefer, be disposed, be predisposed; see FAVOR.

inclined *a.* prone, slanted, willing; see LIKELY 4.

inclined plane a sloping plane surface, esp. one sloping slightly, as for raising heavy objects

in·close (in klōz′) *vt.* **-closed′, -clos′ing** ENCLOSE —**in·clo′sure** (-klō′zhər) *n.*

in·clude (in klōōd′) *vt.* **-clud′ed, -clud′ing** ⟦< L *in-*, in + *claudere*, to close⟧ **1** to enclose **2** to have as part of a whole; contain; comprise **3** to take into account —**in·clu′sion** (-klōō′zhən) *n.*

in·clu·sive (-klōō′siv) *adj.* **1** taking everything into account **2** including the terms or limits mentioned ⟦the third to the fifth *inclusive*⟧ —**inclusive of** including —**in·clu′sively** *adv.*

in·cog·ni·to (in käg′ni tō′, in′käg nē′-) *adv., adj.* ⟦It < L *in-*, not + *cognitus*, known⟧ with true identity unrevealed or disguised

in·co·her·ent (in′kō hir′ənt, -her′-) *adj.* **1** not logically connected; rambling **2** characterized by speech, etc. like this —**in′co·her′ence** *n.* —**in′co·her′ently** *adv.*

in·come (in′kum′, -kəm) *n.* money, etc. received in a given period, as wages, rent, interest, etc.

in′com′ing *adj.* coming in or about to come in

in·com·mode (in′kə mōd′) *vt.* **-mod′ed, -mod′ing** ⟦< Fr < L *in-*, not + *commodus*, convenient⟧ to inconvenience; bother

in·com·mu·ni·ca·do (in′kə myōō′ni kä′dō) *adj., adv.* ⟦Sp⟧ not allowed to communicate with others

in·com·pa·ra·ble (in käm′pə rə bəl) *adj.* **1** having no basis of comparison **2** beyond comparison; matchless

in·com·pat·i·ble (in′kəm pat′ə bəl) *adj.* not compatible; specif., unable to live together harmoniously —**in′com·pat′ibil′ity,** *pl.* **-ties,** *n.*

in·com·pe·tent (in käm′pə tənt) *adj.* without adequate ability, knowledge, fitness, etc. — *n.* an incompetent person —**in·com′pe·tence** *n.* —**in·com′pe·tently** *adv.*

in·com·plete (in′kəm plēt′) *adj.* **1** lacking a part or parts **2** unfinished **3** not perfect

in·con·gru·ous (in kän′grōō əs) *adj.* **1** lacking harmony or agreement of parts, etc. **2** unsuitable; inappropriate —**in′con·gru′ity** (-kän grōō′i tē) *n.*

in·con·se·quen·tial (in kän′si kwen′shəl) *adj.* of no consequence

in·con·sid·er·able (in′kən sid′ər ə bəl) *adj.* trivial; small

in′con·sid′er·ate (-it) *adj.* without thought or consideration for others; thoughtless —**in′con·sid′er·ately** *adv.* —**in′con·sid′er·ate·ness** or **in′con·sid′er·a′tion** (-ər ā′shən) *n.*

in·con·sol·able (in′kən sōl′ə bəl) *adj.* that cannot be consoled

in·con·spic·u·ous (in′kən spik′yōō əs) *adj.* attracting little attention —**in′con·spic′u·ously** *adv.*

in·con·stant (in kän′stənt) *adj.* not constant; changeable, fickle, irregular, etc. —**in·con′stancy** *n.*

in·con·test·able (in′kən tes′tə bəl) *adj.* unquestionable; indisputable —**in′con·test·abil′ity** *n.* —**in′con·test′ably** *adv.*

in·con·ti·nent (in kän′tə nənt) *adj.* **1** without self-restraint, esp. in sexual activity **2** unable to restrain a natural discharge, as of urine —**in·con′ti·nence** *n.*

in·con·ven·ience (in′kən vēn′yəns) *n.* **1** lack of comfort, ease, etc. **2** anything inconvenient — *vt.* **-ienced, -ienc·ing** to cause inconvenience to

in′con·ven′ient *adj.* not favorable to one's comfort; causing bother, etc.

in·cor·po·rate (in kôr′pə rāt′) *vt.* **-rat′ed, -rat′ing** ⟦see IN-[1] & CORPORATE⟧ **1** to combine; include; embody **2** to bring together into a single whole; merge **3** to form into a corporation — *vi.* **1** to combine into a single whole **2** to form a corporation —**in·cor′po·ra′tion** *n.*

in·cor·ri·gi·ble (in kôr′ə jə bəl) *adj.* ⟦< LL *incorrigibilis*⟧ that cannot be corrected or reformed, esp. because set in bad habits —**in·cor′ri·gibil′ity** *n.* —**in·cor′ri·gibly** *adv.*

in·cor·rupt·ible (in′kə rup′tə bəl) *adj.* that cannot be corrupted, esp. morally

in·crease (in krēs′, in′krēs′) *vi.* **-creased′, -creas′ing** ⟦< L *in-*, in + *crescere*, grow⟧ to become greater in size, amount, degree, etc. — *vt.* to make greater in size, etc. —

THESAURUS

include *v.* **1** [To contain] hold, admit, cover, embrace, involve, consist of, take in, entail, incorporate, constitute, accommodate, be comprised of, be composed of, embody, be made up of, number among, carry, bear; see also COMPOSE 1.—*Ant.* BAR, omit, stand outside of. **2** [To place into or among] enter, introduce, take in, incorporate, make room for, build, work in, inject, interject, add on, insert, combine, make a part of, make allowance for, give consideration to, count in.—*Ant.* DISCARD, exclude, reject.

included *a.* counted, numbered, admitted, covered, involved, constituted, embodied, inserted, entered, incorporated, combined, placed, fused, merged; see also WITHIN.—*Ant.* REFUSED, excluded, left out.

including *a.* together with, along with, as well as, in conjunction with, not to mention, to say nothing of, among other things, with the addition of, in addition to, counting, made up of; see also PLUS.—*Ant.* BESIDES, not counting, aside from.

incoherence *n.* disagreement, dissimilarity, incongruity; see INCONSISTENCY.

incoherent *a.* mumbling, stammering, confused, speechless, puzzling, indistinct, faltering, stuttering, unintelligible, muttered, mumbled, jumbled, gasping, breathless, tongue-tied, muffled, indistinguishable, incomprehensible, disconnected, muddled.—*Ant.* CLEAR, eloquent, distinct.

incoherently *a.* frantically, drunkenly, confusedly, spasmodically, chaotically, randomly, ineptly, unsystematically, aimlessly, casually, sloppily, ambiguously, equivocally, illegibly, incomprehensibly, unrecog-

nizably, uncertainly, inaudibly; see also WILDLY.

income *n.* earnings, salary, wages, returns, profit, dividends, assets, proceeds, benefits, receipts, gains, commission, drawings, rent, royalty, honorarium, net income, gross income, taxable income, cash, take; see also PAY 2.—*Ant.* EXPENSE, expenditures, outgo.

incomparable *a.* unequaled, exceptional, superior; see EXCELLENT, PERFECT.

incompatibility *n.* variance, conflict, animosity; see DISAGREEMENT 1.

incompatible *a.* inconsistent, contrary, clashing, inappropriate, contradictory, disagreeing, inconstant, unadapted, opposite, jarring, discordant, incoherent, inadmissible; see also OPPOSED, UNSUITABLE.

incompetence *n.* inadequacy, inexperience, worthlessness; see WEAKNESS 1.

incompetent *a.* incapable, inefficient, unskillful, not qualified, inadequate, unfit, unskilled, bungling, inexpert, ineffectual, unsuitable, untrained, clumsy, awkward, uninitiated, raw, inexperienced, unadapted, not equal to, amateurish; see also UNABLE.—*Ant.* ABLE, fit, qualified.

incomplete *a.* rough, half-done, under construction; see UNFINISHED 1.

inconceivable *a.* unimaginable, fantastic, incredible; see IMPOSSIBLE.

inconclusive *a.* indecisive, deficient, lacking; see FAULTY, INADEQUATE, UNSATISFACTORY.

incongruous *a.* uncoordinated, unconnected, contradictory; see ILLOGICAL, UNSUITABLE.

inconsequential *a.* unimportant, immaterial, insignificant; see IRREL-

EVANT, TRIVIAL, UNNECESSARY.

inconsiderate *a.* boorish, impolite, discourteous; see RUDE 2, THOUGHTLESS 2.

inconsistency *n.* discrepancy, disagreement, dissimilarity, disparity, variance, incongruity, inequality, divergence, deviation, disproportion, paradox; see also DIFFERENCE 1.—*Ant.* SIMILARITY, consistency, congruity.

inconsistent *a.* contradictory, illogical, incoherent; see ILLOGICAL.

inconspicuous *a.* concealed, indistinct, retiring; see HIDDEN, OBSCURE 1, 3, SECRETIVE.

inconspicuously *a.* slyly, surreptitiously, not openly; see SLYLY.

inconvenience *n.* bother, trouble, awkward detail; see DIFFICULTY 1.

inconvenient *a.* bothersome, awkward, badly arranged; see DISTURBING.

incorporate *v.* add to, combine, fuse; see INCLUDE 2, JOIN 1.

incorporated *a.* entered, placed, fused; see INCLUDED, JOINED.

incorporation *n.* embodiment, adding, fusion; see ADDITION 1.

incorrect *a.* inaccurate, not trustworthy, false; see MISTAKEN 1, UNRELIABLE, WRONG 2.

incorrectly *a.* mistakenly, inaccurately, clumsily; see BADLY 1, WRONGLY.

increase *n.* development, spread, enlargement, expansion, escalation, elaboration, swelling, addition, incorporation, merger, inflation, extension, heightening, dilation, multiplication, rise, broadening, advance, intensification, deepening, swell, amplification, progression, improvement, boost, hike*, jump,

n. 1 an increasing or becoming increased 2 the result or amount of an increasing —**on the increase** increasing

in·creas′ing·ly *adv.* more and more

in·cred·ible (in kred′ə bəl) *adj.* 1 not credible 2 seeming too unusual to be possible —**in·cred′ibil′i·ty** *n.* —**in·cred′ibly** *adv.*

in·cred·u·lous (in krej′oo ləs) *adj.* 1 unwilling to believe 2 showing doubt or disbelief —**in·cre·du·li·ty** (in′krə doo′lə tē) *n.*

in·cre·ment (in′krə mənt, iŋ′-) *n.* [< L *incrementum*] 1 an increase 2 amount of increase —**in′cre·men′tal** *adj.*

in·crim·i·nate (in krim′i nāt′) *vt.* -nat′ed, -nat′ing [< L *in-*, in + *crimen*, offense] 1 to accuse of a crime 2 to involve in, or make appear guilty of, a crime or fault —**in·crim′i·na′tion** *n.*

in·crust (in krust′) *vt.*, *vi.* ENCRUST —**in·crus·ta·tion** (in′krus tā′shən) *n.*

in·cu·bate (in′kyoo bāt′, iŋ′-) *vt.* -bat′ed, -bat′ing [< L *in-*, on + *cubare*, to lie] 1 to sit on and hatch (eggs) 2 to heat, etc. so as to hatch or grow, as in an incubator 3 to develop, as by planning — *vi.* to undergo incubation —**in′cu·ba′tion** *n.*

in′cu·ba′tor *n.* 1 a heated container for hatching eggs 2 any similar device, as for protecting premature babies, growing cell cultures, etc.

in·cu·bus (in′kyoo bəs) *n.* [LL] 1 a nightmare 2 an oppressive burden

in·cul·cate (in kul′kāt, in′kul-) *vt.* -cat′ed, -cat′ing [< L *in-*, in + *calcare*, trample underfoot] to impress upon the mind, as by persistent urging —**in′cul·ca′tion** *n.*

in·cul·pate (in kul′pāt, in′kul-) *vt.* -pat′ed, -pat′ing [< L *in*, on + *culpa*, blame] INCRIMINATE

in·cum·ben·cy (in kum′bən sē) *n.*, *pl.* -cies 1 a duty or obligation 2 tenure of office

in·cum′bent (-bənt) *adj.* [< L *in-*, on + *cubare*, lie down] currently in office — *n.* one currently in office —**incum·bent on** (or **upon**) resting upon as a duty or obligation

in·cum·ber (in kum′bər) *vt.* ENCUMBER —**in·cum′brance** *n.*

in·cu·nab·u·la (in′kyoo nab′yoo lə) *n.pl.*, *sing.* -**lum** (-ləm) [< L *in-*, in + *cunabula*, pl., a cradle] 1 infancy; beginnings 2 books printed before 1500

in·cur (in kur′) *vt.* -curred′, -cur′ring [< L *in-*, in + *currere*, to run] 1 to acquire (something undesirable) 2 to bring upon oneself

in·cu·ri·ous (in kyoor′ē əs) *adj.* not curious; uninterested

in·cur·sion (in kur′zhən) *n.* [see INCUR] an invasion or raid

ind. 1 independent 2 index

Ind. 1 India 2 Indian 3 Indiana

in·debted (in det′id) *adj.* 1 in debt 2 owing gratitude, as for a favor

in·debt′ed·ness *n.* 1 a being indebted 2 the amount owed

in·de·cent (in dē′sənt) *adj.* not decent; specif., *a)* improper *b)* morally offensive; obscene —**in·de′cen·cy** *n.* —**in·de′cent·ly** *adv.*

in·de·ci·pher·able (in′dē sī′fər ə bəl) *adj.* that cannot be deciphered

in·de·ci·sion (in′dē sizh′ən) *n.* inability to decide; vacillation

in′de·ci′sive (-sī′siv) *adj.* 1 not conclusive or final 2 showing indecision —**in′de·ci′sive·ly** *adv.* —**in′de·ci′sive·ness** *n.*

in·deed (in dēd′) *adv.* certainly; truly —*interj.* an exclamation of surprise, doubt, sarcasm, etc.

in·de·fat·i·ga·ble (in′di fat′i gə bəl) *adj.* [< L *in-*, not + *defatigare*, tire out] that cannot be tired out

in·de·fen·si·ble (in′dē fen′sə bəl) *adj.* 1 that cannot be defended 2 that cannot be justified

in·def·i·nite (in def′ə nit) *adj.* not definite; specif., *a)* having no exact limits *b)* not precise in meaning; vague *c)* uncertain *d) Gram.* not limiting or specifying ["a" and "an" are *indefinite* articles] —**in·def′i·nite·ly** *adv.*

in·del·i·ble (in del′ə bəl) *adj.* [< L *in-*, not + *delere*, destroy] 1 that cannot be erased, blotted out, etc. 2 leaving an indelible mark —**in·del′i·bly** *adv.*

in·del·i·cate (in del′i kit) *adj.* lacking propriety or modesty; coarse —**in·del′i·cacy**, *pl.* -**cies**, *n.*

in·dem·ni·fy (in dem′ni fī′) *vt.* -fied′, -fy′ing [< L *indemnis*, unhurt + -FY] 1 to insure against loss, damage, etc. 2 to repay for (loss or damage) —**in·dem′ni·fi·ca′tion** *n.*

in·dem′ni·ty *n.*, *pl.* -**ties** 1 insurance against loss, damage, etc. 2 repayment for loss, damage, etc.

in·dent[1] (in dent′) *vt.* [< L *in*, in + *dens*, tooth] 1 to notch 2 to space (a line, paragraph, etc.) in from the margin of a page — *vi.* 1 to form or be marked by notches or a jagged border 2 to space in from the margin

in·dent[2] (in dent′) *vt.* [IN-[1] + DENT] to make a dent in

in·den·ta·tion (in′den tā′shən) *n.* 1 a being indented 2 a notch, cut, inlet, etc. 3 a dent 4 a spacing in from a margin, or a blank space so made: usually **in·den′tion**

in·den·ture (in den′chər) *n.* 1 a written contract 2 [*often pl.*] a contract binding one to work for another 3 a document listing the terms of a bond issue — *vt.* -tured, -tur·ing to bind by indenture

in·de·pend·ence (in′dē pen′dəns) *n.* a being independent; freedom from the influence or control of others

Independence Day the anniversary of the adoption of the Declaration of Independence on July 4, 1776

in′de·pend′ent (-dənt) *adj.* 1 free from the influence or control of others; specif., *a)* self-governing *b)* self-reliant *c)* not adhering to any political party *d)* not connected with others [an *independent* grocer] 2 not depending on another for financial support — *n.* one who is independent in thinking, action, etc. —**in′de·pend′ent·ly** *adv.*

THESAURUS

boom; see also PROGRESS 1.—*Ant.* REDUCTION, decline, decrease. —**on the increase** growing, developing, spreading; see INCREASING.

increase *v.* extend, enlarge, expand, dilate, broaden, widen, thicken, deepen, heighten, build, lengthen, magnify, add on, augment, escalate, let out, branch out, further, mark up, sharpen, build up, raise, enhance, amplify, reinforce, supplement, annex, double, triple, stretch, multiply, intensify, exaggerate, prolong, redouble, boost, step up, rev up*.—*Ant.* DECREASE, reduce, abridge.

increased *a.* marked up, raised, heightened, elevated, added on, doubled.

increasing *a.* developing, maturing, multiplying, broadening, widening, intensifying, heightening, growing, dominant, advancing, growing louder, sharpening, accentuating, aggravating, emphasizing, accelerating, deepening, flourishing, rising, expanding, enlarging, accumulating, piling up, shooting up, getting big, swelling, on the rise, on the increase, booming; see also GROWING.

increasingly *a.* with continual acceleration, more and more, with steady increase; see MORE 1, 2.

incredible *a.* unbelievable, improbable, ridiculous; see IMPOSSIBLE.

incriminate *v.* implicate, blame, charge; see IMPLICATE.

incriminating *a.* damning, damaging, accusatory; see SUSPICIOUS 2.

inculcate *v.* instill, implant, impress; see INSTILL, TEACH.

incurable *a.* fatal, serious, hopeless; see DEADLY.

indebted *a.* obligated, grateful, appreciative; see RESPONSIBLE 1, THANKFUL.

indebtedness *n.* deficit, responsibility, obligation; see DEBT.

indecency *n.* impurity, immodesty, vulgarity, impropriety, obscenity, raciness, four-letter word, lewdness, foulness; see also EVIL 1.—*Ant.* CHASTITY, purity, delicacy.

indecent *a.* immoral, shocking, shameless; see BAD 1, LEWD 2, SHAMEFUL 1, 2.

indecision *n.* hesitation, question, irresolution; see DOUBT, UNCERTAINTY 2.

indecisive *a.* irresolute, unstable, wishy-washy*; see DOUBTFUL.

indeed *a.* 1 [Surely] naturally, of course, certainly; see REALLY 1,

SURELY. 2 [Really] For sure?, Honestly?, So?; see OH.

indefensible *a.* bad, unforgivable, unpardonable; see WRONG 1.

indefinite *a.* unsure, unsettled, loose; see UNCERTAIN, VAGUE 2.

indefinitely *a.* 1 [Vaguely] loosely, unclearly, ambiguously, indistinctly, incoherently, obscurely, indecisively, incompletely, lightly, briefly, momentarily, generally; see also VAGUELY.—*Ant.* POSITIVELY, clearly, exactly. 2 [Without stated limit] endlessly, continually, considerably; see FREQUENTLY, REGULARLY.

indelible *a.* ingrained, enduring, strong; see PERMANENT.

indent[1] *v.* make a margin, range, space inward; see ORDER 3.

indentation *n.* imprint, recession, depression; see DENT.

independence *n.* sovereignty, autonomy, license; see FREEDOM 1, 2.

independent *a.* self-ruling, autonomous, unregimented; see FREE 1.

independently *a.* alone, autonomously, unilaterally, without support, separately, exclusively, regardlessly, by oneself, on one's own*; see also FREELY 2.

independent clause a clause that can function as a complete sentence

in'-depth' *adj.* profound; thorough

in·de·scrib·able (in'di skrīb'ə bəl) *adj.* beyond the power of description —**in'de·scrib'ably** *adv.*

in·de·struct·ible (in'di struk'tə bəl) *adj.* that cannot be destroyed

in·de·ter·mi·nate (in'dē tur'mi nit, -di-) *adj.* 1 indefinite; vague 2 unsettled; inconclusive

in·dex (in'deks') *n., pl.* **-dex·es** or **-di·ces'** (-di sēz') [L, indicator] 1 forefinger: in full, **index finger** 2 a pointer or indicator 3 an indication [an *index* of ability] 4 an alphabetical list of names, subjects, etc. indicating pages where found, as in a book 5 a number used to measure change in prices, wages, etc. — *vt.* to make or be an index of or for

In·dia ink (in'dē ə) a black liquid ink

In·dian (in'dē ən, -dyən) *n.* 1 a native of India or the East Indies 2 a member of any of the aboriginal peoples of North America, South America, or the West Indies: also **American Indian** — *adj.* 1 of India or the East Indies, their people, etc. 2 of the American Indians, their culture, etc.

Indian corn CORN[1] (sense 2)

Indian file SINGLE FILE

Indian summer mild, warm weather following the first frosts of late autumn

India paper 1 a thin, absorbent paper for taking proofs from engraved plates 2 a thin, opaque printing paper, as for Bibles

in·di·cate (in'di kāt') *vt.* **-cat'ed, -cat'ing** [< L *in-,* in + *dicare,* declare] 1 to direct attention to; point out 2 to be a sign of; signify 3 to show the need for 4 to express briefly or generally —**in'di·ca'tion** *n.*

in·dic·a·tive (in dik'ə tiv) *adj.* 1 giving an indication 2 designating the mood of a verb used to express an act, state, etc. as actual, or to ask a question of fact — *n.* the indicative mood

in'di·ca'tor *n.* a person or thing that indicates; specif., a gauge, dial, etc. that measures something

in·dict (in dīt') *vt.* [ult. < L *in,* against + *dicere,* speak] to charge with a crime —**in·dict'ment** *n.*

in·dif·fer·ent (in dif'ər ənt, -dif'rənt) *adj.* 1 neutral 2 unconcerned; apathetic 3 of no importance 4 average — **in·dif'fer·ence** *n.* —**in·dif'fer·ently** *adv.*

in·dig·e·nous (in dij'ə nəs) *adj.* [< L *indigena,* a native] existing or growing naturally in a region or country; native

in·di·gent (in'di jənt) *adj.* [< L *indegere,* to be in need] poor; needy — *n.* an indigent person —**in'di·gence** *n.* — **in'di·gently** *adv.*

in·di·gest·ible (in'di jes'tə bəl) *adj.* not easily digested

in·di·ges·tion (-jes'chən) *n.* difficulty in digesting food

in·dig·nant (in dig'nənt) *adj.* [< L *in-,* not + *dignus,* worthy] feeling or expressing anger, esp. at unjust or mean action —**in·dig'nantly** *adv.*

in·dig·na·tion (in'dig nā'shən) *n.* righteous anger

in·dig·ni·ty (in dig'nə tē) *n., pl.* **-ties** an insult or affront to one's dignity or self-respect

in·di·go (in'di gō') *n., pl.* **-gos'** or **-goes'** [Sp < Gr *Indikos,* Indian] 1 a blue dye obtained from certain plants or made synthetically 2 a deep violet blue — *adj.* of this color

in·di·rect (in'də rekt', -di-) *adj.* 1 not straight 2 not straight to the point 3 dishonest [indirect dealing] 4 not immediate; secondary [an *indirect* result] —**in'di·rect'ly** *adv.* —**in'di·rect'ness** *n.*

in'di·rec'tion *n.* 1 roundabout act, procedure, or means 2 deceit; dishonesty

indirect object the word or words denoting the person or thing indirectly affected by the action of the verb (Ex.: *him* in "give *him* the ball")

in·dis·creet (in'di skrēt') *adj.* not prudent, as in speech or action; unwise

in'dis·cre'tion (-skresh'ən) *n.* 1 lack of discretion; imprudence 2 an indiscreet act or remark

in·dis·crim·i·nate (in'di skrim'i nit) *adj.* 1 mixed or random 2 making no distinctions —**in'dis·crim'i·nately** *adv.*

in·dis·pen·sa·ble (in'di spen'sə bəl) *adj.* absolutely necessary

in·dis·posed (in'di spōzd') *adj.* 1 slightly ill 2 unwilling; disinclined —**in·dis·po·si·tion** (in'dis pə zish'ən) *n.*

in·dis·sol·u·ble (in'di säl'yōō bəl) *adj.* that cannot be dissolved or destroyed; lasting

---

THESAURUS

indestructible *a.* unchangeable, durable, immortal; see PERMANENT.

index *n.* 1 [An indicator] formula, rule, average; see MODEL 2. 2 [An alphabetic arrangement] tabular matter, book index, guide to publications, bibliography, bibliographical work, card file, book list, appendix, end list, directory, dictionary; see also FILE 1, LIST, RECORD 1.

index *v.* alphabetize, arrange, tabulate; see FILE 1, LIST 1, RECORD 1.

Indian *a.* native-American, pre-Columbian, Amerindian; see INDIAN, *n.* 1.

Indian *n.* 1 [American native] American aborigine, American Indian, Amerindian, red man. *Terms for Indian groups having had historical or social importance include the following—United States and Canada: Arctic Indians:* Eskimo, Aleut; *eastern or Woods Indians;* Iroquois *or* Six Nations, Mohawk, Oneida, Seneca, Cayuga, Huron, Algonquin, Mohican, Delaware, Ojibway *or* Chippewa, Sauk, Fox, Pottawattamic, Seminole, Cherokee, Choctaw, Chicasaw, Creek, Natchez, Winnebago; *Plains Indians:* Sioux, Oglala, Mandan, Iowa, Omaha, Comanche, Dakota, Crow, Osage, Apache, Kiowa, Arapahoe, Cheyenne, Pawnee; *Great Basin Indians:* Blackfoot, Ute, Paiute, Shoshone, Bannock, Modoc, Digger, Pueblo, Hopi, Navajo, Zuni; *west coast Indians;* Athabascan, Costanoca, Chinook, Nez Perce, Tlingit, Flathead, Kwakiutl, Bella Coola, Klamath, Luiseno, Pomo; *Mexico and Central America:* Maya, Aztec, Toltec, Nahuatl, Zacateca, Quiche; *South America:* Inca,

Quechua, Carib, Tupi, Arawak. 2 [A native of India] Hindu, Muslim, Brahmin; see ORIENTAL.

indicate *v.* 1 [To signify] symbolize, betoken, intimate; see MEAN 1. 2 [To designate] show, point to, register; see NAME 2.

indication *n.* evidence, sign, implication; see HINT, SUGGESTION 1.

indicator *n.* notice, pointer, symbol; see SIGN 1.

indict *v.* charge, face with charges, arraign; see BLAME.

indictment *n.* detention, censure, incrimination; see BLAME.

indifference *n.* unconcern, nonchalance, aloofness, coldness, insensitivity, callousness, alienation, disregard, neutrality, isolationism, heedlessness, detachment, dullness, sluggishness, stupor, coldbloodedness, disdain, cool*.

indifferent *a.* listless, cold, cool, unemotional, unsympathetic, heartless, unresponsive, unfeeling, uncommunicative, nonchalant, impassive, detached, callous, uninterested, stony, reticent, remote, reserved, distant, unsocial, scornful, apathetic, heedless, unmoved, not inclined toward, neutral, uncaring, aloof, silent, disdainful, haughty, superior, condescending, snobbish, arrogant, not caring about; see also UNMOVED 2.—*Ant.* EXCITED, aroused, warm.

indifferently *a.* 1 [Rather badly] poorly, not very well done, in a mediocre manner; see BADLY 1, INADEQUATELY. 2 [In an indifferent manner] nonchalantly, coolly, detached; see CALMLY.

indigestible *a.* inedible, rough, hard, unripe, green, tasteless, unhealthy, undercooked, raw, poisonous, toxic, moldy, bad-smelling, rotten, uneatable, icky*.—*Ant.* DELICIOUS, appetizing, tasty.

indigestion *n.* heartburn, nausea, acid indigestion; see ILLNESS 1, PAIN 2.

indignant *a.* upset, displeased, piqued; see ANGRY.

indirect *a.* roundabout, out-of-the-way, tortuous, twisting, long, complicated, devious, erratic, sidelong, zigzag, crooked, backhanded, obscure, sinister, rambling, long-winded, secondary, implied, oblique.—*Ant.* DIRECT, straight, immediate.

indirectly *a.* by implication, by indirection, in a roundabout way, secondhand, from a secondary source, not immediately, discursively, obliquely.—*Ant.* IMMEDIATELY, directly, primarily.

indiscreet *a.* naive, inopportune, misguided; see RASH, TACTLESS.

indiscretion *n.* recklessness, tactlessness, rashness; see CARELESSNESS.

indiscriminate *a.* random, confused, chaotic; see AIMLESS.

indispensable *a.* required, needed, essential; see NECESSARY.

indisputable *a.* undoubted, undeniable, unquestionable; see CERTAIN 2.

indistinct *a.* vague, confused, indefinite; see OBSCURE 1.

indistinguishable *a.* 1 [Identical] like, same, equivalent; see ALIKE, EQUAL. 2 [Indistinct] vague, invisible, dull; see OBSCURE 1, UNCERTAIN.

in·dite (in dīt′) *vt.* **-dit′ed, -dit′ing** [see INDICT] to compose and write

in·di·vid·ual (in′də vij′o͞o əl) *adj.* [< L < *in-*, not + *dividere*, to divide] 1 existing as a separate thing or being; single 2 of, for, by, or relating to a single person or thing — *n.* 1 a single thing or being 2 a person

in′di·vid′u·al·ism′ *n.* 1 individuality 2 the doctrine that the state exists for the individual 3 the leading of one's life in one's own way —**in′di·vid′u·al·ist** *n., adj.* —**in′di·vid′u·al·is′tic** *adj.*

in′di·vid′u·al′i·ty (-al′ə tē) *n., pl.* **-ties** 1 the sum of the characteristics that set one person or thing apart 2 existence as an individual

in′di·vid′u·al·ize′ (-əl īz′) *vt.* **-ized′, -iz′ing** 1 to make individual 2 to treat as an individual —**in′di·vid′u·ali·za′tion** *n.*

in′di·vid′u·al·ly *adv.* 1 as individuals; separately 2 distinctively

in·doc·tri·nate (in däk′trə nāt′) *vt.* **-nat′ed, -nat′ing** to instruct in, or imbue with, doctrines, theories, etc. —**in·doc′tri·na′tion** *n.*

Indo-European (in′dō yo͝or′ə pē′ən) *adj.* designating a family of languages including most of those of Europe and many of those of Asia

in·do·lent (in′də lənt) *adj.* [< L *in-*, not + *dolere*, feel pain] idle; lazy —**in′do·lence** *n.* —**in′do·lently** *adv.*

in·dom·i·ta·ble (in däm′i tə bəl) *adj.* [< L *in-*, not + *domitare*, to tame] not easily discouraged or defeated

In·do·ne·sian (in′də nē′zhən) *n.* 1 a native or inhabitant of Indonesia 2 the official Malay language of Indonesia — *adj.* of Indonesia, its people, language, etc.

in′door′ *adj.* living, belonging, etc. in a building

in′doors′ *adv.* in or into a building

in·dorse (in dôrs′) *vt.* **-dorsed′, -dors′ing** ENDORSE

in·du·bi·ta·ble (in do͞o′bi tə bəl) *adj.* that cannot be doubted —**in·du′bi·tably** *adv.*

in·duce (in do͞os′) *vt.* **-duced′, -duc′ing** [< L *in-*, in + *ducere*, to lead] 1 to persuade 2 to bring on or about; cause 3 to draw (a conclusion) from particular facts 4 to bring about (an electric or magnetic effect) in a body by placing it within a field of force —**in·duc′er** *n.*

in·duce′ment *n.* 1 an inducing or being induced 2 a motive; incentive

in·duct (in dukt′) *vt.* [see INDUCE] 1 to place formally in an office, a society, etc. 2 to enroll (esp. a draftee) in the armed forces

in·duct′ance (-əns) *n.* the property of an electric circuit by which a varying current in it produces a magnetic field that induces voltages in the same or a nearby circuit

in·duct·ee (in′duk tē′) *n.* a person inducted, esp. into the armed forces

in·duc′tion (-shən) *n.* 1 an inducting or being inducted 2 reasoning from particular facts to a general conclusion 3 the inducing of an electric or magnetic effect by a field of force —**in·duc′tive** *adj.*

in·due (in do͞o′, -dyo͞o′) *vt.* **-dued′, -du′ing** ENDUE

in·dulge (in dulj′) *vt.* **-dulged′, -dulg′ing** [L *indulgere*, be kind to] 1 to satisfy (a desire) 2 to gratify the wishes of; humor — *vi.* to give way to one's own desires —**in·dulg′er** *n.*

in·dul·gence (in dul′jəns) *n.* 1 an indulging or being indulgent 2 a thing indulged in 3 a favor or privilege 4 *R.C.Ch.* remission of punishment still due for a sin committed but forgiven

in·dul′gent (-jənt) *adj.* indulging or inclined to indulge; kind or lenient, often to excess —**in·dul′gently** *adv.*

in·dus·trial (in dus′trē əl) *adj.* having to do with industry or its workers, products, etc. —**in·dus′tri·ally** *adv.*

industrial arts the mechanical and technical skills used in industry

in·dus·tri·al·ism′ *n.* social and economic structure characterized by large industries, machine production, etc.

in·dus′tri·al·ist *n.* one who owns or controls an industrial enterprise

in·dus′tri·al·ize′ (-īz′) *vt.* **-ized′, -iz′ing** 1 to establish or develop industrialism in 2 to organize as an industry —**in·dus′tri·ali·za′tion** *n.*

industrial park a planned area for industrial use, usually on the outskirts of a city

in·dus·tri·ous (in dus′trē əs) *adj.* hard-working; diligent —**in·dus′tri·ously** *adv.* —**in·dus′tri·ous·ness** *n.*

in·dus·try (in′dəs trē) *n., pl.* **-tries** [< L *industrius*, active] 1 earnest, steady effort 2 any particular branch of productive, esp. manufacturing, enterprise, or all of these collectively 3 any large-scale business activity 4 the owners and managers of industry

-ine[1] (*variously* in, īn, ēn, ən) [< L *-inus*] suffix of, having the nature of, like [*aquiline, crystalline*]

-ine[2] (in, ən) [< L *-ina*] suffix forming abstract nouns [*discipline, doctrine*]

-ine[3] (*variously* ēn, in, īn, ən) [< L *-inus*] suffix forming chemical names, as of *a*) halogens [*iodine*] *b*) alkaloids or nitrogenous bases [*morphine*] Often forming commercial names [*Vaseline*]

in·ebri·ate (in ē′brē āt′; *for n. also,* -it′) *vt.* **-at′ed, -at′ing** [< L *in-*, intens. + *ebrius*, drunk] to make drunk — *n.* a drunkard —**in·e′bria′tion** *n.*

in·edu·ca·ble (in ej′o͞o kə bəl) *adj.* thought to be incapable of being educated

in·ef·fa·ble (in ef′ə bəl) *adj.* [< L *in-*, not + *effabilis*, utterable] 1 inexpressible 2 too sacred to be spoken

---

THESAURUS

individual *a.* specific, personal, special, proper, own, particular, definite, lone, alone, solitary, secluded, original, distinct, distinctive, personalized, individualized, exclusive, select, single, only, reserved, separate, sole; see PRIVATE, SPECIAL.—*Ant.* PUBLIC, collective, social.

individual *n.* human being, self, somebody; see CHILD, MAN 2, PERSON 1, WOMAN 1.

individuality *n.* personality, distinctiveness, particularity, separateness, dissimilarity, singularity, idiosyncrasy, air, manner, habit, eccentricity, oddity, rarity, way of doing things; see also ORIGINALITY.

individually *a.* separately, severally, one by one, one at a time, personally, exclusively, singly, by oneself, alone, independently, without help, distinctively, apart; see also ONLY 1.—*Ant.* TOGETHER, collectively, cooperatively.

indoctrinate *v.* inculcate, imbue, implant; see CONVINCE, INFLUENCE, TEACH.

indoctrination *n.* propagandism, instruction, brainwashing; see EDUCATION 1, TRAINING.

indoors *a.* in the house, at home, under a roof; see INSIDE 2, WITHIN.

induce *v.* produce, effect, make; see

BEGIN 1.

induced *a.* 1 [Brought about] effected, achieved, caused; see FINISHED 1. 2 [Inferred] thought, concluded, reasoned; see ASSUMED, CONSIDERED, DETERMINED 1.

induct *v.* conscript, initiate, draft; see ENLIST 1, RECRUIT 1.

inducted *a.* conscripted, called up, drafted; see INITIATED 2.

induction *n.* 1 [Logical reasoning] inference, rationalization, generalization, conclusion, judgment, conjecture; see also REASON 2. 2 [The process of electrical attraction] electric induction, magnetic induction, electromagnetic action; see ELECTRICITY. 3 [The process of being initiated] initiation, introduction, ordination, consecration, entrance into service.

indulge *v.* 1 [To humor] tickle, nourish, coddle; see ENTERTAIN 1, HUMOR. 2 [To take part in] go in for, revel, give way to; see JOIN 2.

indulgence *n.* 1 [Humoring] coddling, pampering, petting, fondling, babying, spoiling, placating, pleasing, toadying, favoring, kowtowing, gratifying. 2 [Revelry] intemperance, overindulgence, self-indulgence; see GREED, WASTE 1.

indulgent *a.* fond, considerate, tolerant; see KIND.

industrial *a.* manufacturing, manufactured, mechanized, automated, industrialized, in industry, factory-made, machine-made, modern, streamlined, technical; see also MECHANICAL 1.—*Ant.* HOMEMADE, handmade, domestic.

industrious *a.* intent, involved, diligent; see ACTIVE, BUSY 1.

industriously *a.* diligently, energetically, busily; see CAREFULLY 1, VIGOROUSLY.

industry *n.* 1 [Attention to work] activity, persistence, application, patience, intentness, perseverance, enterprise, hard work, zeal, energy, dynamism, pains, inventiveness; see also ATTENTION.—*Ant.* LAZINESS, lethargy, idleness. 2 [Business as a division of society] big business, management, corporation officers, shareholders, high finance, entrepreneurs, capital, private enterprise, monied interests, stockholders.

inebriated *a.* intoxicated, tipsy, plastered*; see DRUNK.

ineffective *a.* not effective, worthless, neutralized; see INCOMPETENT, WEAK 1, 2.

inefficiency *n.* incompetence, incapability, incapacity; see FAILURE 1, WEAKNESS 1.

in·ef·fi·cient (in′e fish′ənt) *adj.* **1** not producing the desired effect with a minimum use of energy, time, etc. **2** incapable —**in′ef·fi′cien·cy** *n.* —**in′ef·fi′cient·ly** *adv.*

in·el·e·gant (in el′ə gənt) *adj.* not elegant; crude —**in·el′e·gant·ly** *adv.*

in·e·luc·ta·ble (in′ē′luk′tə bəl) *adj.* ⟦< L *in-*, not + *eluctari*, to struggle⟧ not to be avoided or escaped —**in′e·luc′ta·bly** *adv.*

in·ept (in ept′) *adj.* ⟦< L *in-*, not + *aptus*, apt⟧ **1** unsuitable; unfit **2** foolish **3** awkward; clumsy —**in·ep′ti·tude′** (-ep′tə tōōd′) *n.* —**in·ept′ness** *n.*

in·ert (in ʉrt′) *adj.* ⟦< L *in-*, not + *ars*, skill⟧ **1** without power to move or to resist **2** inactive; dull; slow **3** with few or no active properties

in·er·tia (in ʉr′shə) *n.* ⟦see prec.⟧ **1** *Physics* the tendency of matter to remain at rest or to continue in a fixed direction unless affected by some outside force **2** a disinclination to move or act —**in·er′tial** *adj.*

in·es·cap·able (in′e skāp′ə bəl) *adj.* that cannot be escaped or avoided

in·es·ti·ma·ble (in es′tə mə bəl) *adj.* too great to be properly measured

in·ev·i·ta·ble (in ev′i tə bəl) *adj.* ⟦< L *in-*, not + *evitabilis*, avoidable⟧ certain to happen; unavoidable —**in·ev′i·tabil′i·ty** *n.* —**in·ev′i·ta·bly** *adv.*

in·ex·haust·i·ble (in′eg zôs′tə bəl) *adj.* **1** that cannot be used up or emptied **2** tireless

in·ex·o·ra·ble (in eks′ə rə bəl) *adj.* ⟦< L *in-*, not + *exorare*, move by entreaty⟧ **1** that cannot be influenced by persuasion or entreaty; unrelenting **2** that cannot be altered, checked, etc. —**in·ex′o·ra·bly** *adv.*

in·ex·pe·ri·ence (in′ek spir′ē əns) *n.* lack of experience or of the knowledge or skill resulting from experience —**in′ex·pe′ri·enced** *adj.*

in·ex·pert (in ek′spərt; *also* in′ek spʉrt′) *adj.* not expert; unskillful

in·ex·pi·a·ble (in eks′pē ə bəl) *adj.* that cannot be expiated or atoned for

in·ex·pli·ca·ble (in eks′pli kə bəl) *adj.* that cannot be explained —**in·ex′pli·ca·bly** *adv.*

in·ex·press·i·ble (in′eks pres′ə bəl) *adj.* that cannot be expressed

in·ex·tin·guish·a·ble (in′ek stiŋ′gwish ə bəl) *adj.* that cannot be put out or stopped

in ex·tre·mis (in′ eks trē′mis) ⟦L, in extremity⟧ at the point of death

in·ex·tri·ca·ble (in eks′tri kə bəl) *adj.* **1** that one cannot extricate oneself from **2** that cannot be disentangled or untied **3** insolvable —**in·ex′tri·ca·bly** *adv.*

in·fal·li·ble (in fal′ə bəl) *adj.* ⟦see IN-² & FALLIBLE⟧ **1** incapable of error **2** dependable; reliable —**in·fal′libil′i·ty** *n.* —**in·fal′li·bly** *adv.*

in·fa·mous (in′fə məs) *adj.* **1** having a bad reputation; notorious **2** causing a bad reputation; scandalous

in·fa·my (-mē) *n., pl.* **-mies** **1** very bad reputation; disgrace **2** great wickedness **3** an infamous act

in·fan·cy (in′fən sē) *n., pl.* **-cies** **1** the state or period of being an infant **2** the earliest stage of anything

in·fant (in′fənt) *n.* ⟦< L *in-*, not + *fari*, speak⟧ a very young child; baby —*adj.* **1** of or for infants **2** in a very early stage

in·fan·ti·cide (in fan′tə sīd′) *n.* **1** the murder of a baby **2** a person guilty of this

in·fan·tile (in′fən tīl′) *adj.* **1** of infants **2** like an infant; babyish

infantile paralysis POLIOMYELITIS

in·fan·try (in′fən trē) *n., pl.* **-tries** ⟦< L *infans*, child⟧ that branch of an army consisting of soldiers trained to fight on foot —**in′fantry·man** (-mən) *pl.* **-men,** *n.*

in·farct (in färkt′) *n.* ⟦< L *in-*, in + *farcire*, to stuff⟧ an area of dying or dead tissue resulting from inadequate blood flow to that area Also **in·farc′tion** (-färk′shən)

in·fat·u·ate (in fach′ōō āt′) *vt.* **-at′ed, -at′ing** ⟦< L *in-*, intens. + *fatuus*, foolish⟧ to inspire with foolish love or affection —**in·fat′u·a′tion** *n.*

in·fect (in fekt′) *vt.* ⟦< L *inficere*, to stain⟧ **1** to contaminate or cause to become diseased by contact with disease-producing matter **2** to imbue with one's feelings, beliefs, etc. esp. so as to harm

in·fec·tion (in fek′shən) *n.* **1** an infecting or being infected **2** an infectious disease

in·fec·tious (-shəs) *adj.* **1** likely to cause infection **2** designating a disease caused by the presence in the body of certain bacteria, viruses, etc. **3** tending to affect others, as a laugh —**in·fec′tious·ly** *adv.* —**in·fec′tious·ness** *n.*

in·fe·lic·i·tous (in′fə lis′ə təs) *adj.* not felicitous; unsuitable; not apt —**in·fe·lic′i·ty,** *pl.* **-ties,** *n.*

in·fer (in fʉr′) *vt.* **-ferred′, -fer′ring** ⟦< L *in-*, in + *ferre*, to carry⟧ **1** to conclude by reasoning from something known or assumed **2** to imply: still sometimes regarded as a loose usage —**in·fer·ence** (in′fər əns) *n.*

in·fer·en·tial (in′fər en′shəl) *adj.* based on or having to do with inference

in·fe·ri·or (in fir′ē ər) *adj.* ⟦< L *inferus*, low⟧ **1** lower in space **2** lower in order, status, etc. **3** lower in quality than: with *to* **4** poor in quality — *n.* an inferior person or thing —**in·fe′ri·or′i·ty** (-ôr′ə tē) *n.*

in·fer·nal (in fʉr′nəl) *adj.* ⟦< L *inferus*, below⟧ **1** of hell or Hades **2** hellish; fiendish

in·fer·no (in fʉr′nō′) *n., pl.* **-nos′** ⟦see prec.⟧ HELL

in·fest (in fest′) *vt.* ⟦< L *infestus*, hostile⟧ **1** to overrun in large numbers, usually so as to be harmful **2** to be parasitic in or on —**in′fes·ta′tion** *n.* —**in·fest′er** *n.*

in·fi·del (in′fə del′) *n.* ⟦< L *in-*, not + *fidelis*, faithful⟧ **1**

═══ THESAURUS ═══

inefficient *a.* extravagant, prodigal, improvident; see WASTEFUL.

ineligible *a.* inappropriate, unavailable, unsuitable; see INCOMPETENT, UNFIT.

ineluctable *a.* certain, inevitable, unavoidable; see INEVITABLE.

inept *a.* clumsy, gauche, ungraceful; see AWKWARD.

inequality *n.* disparity, dissimilarity, irregularity; see CONTRAST, DIFFERENCE 1, VARIATION 2.

inert *a.* still, dormant, inactive; see IDLE.

inertia *n.* passivity, indolence, inactivity; see LAZINESS.

inevitable *a.* faded, sure, unavoidable, impending, inescapable, necessary, unpreventable, irresistible, destined, assured, unalterable, compulsory, obligatory, binding, irrevocable, inexorable, without fail, undeniable, fateful, doomed, determined, decreed, fixed, ordained, foreordained, decided, sure as shooting*, in the cards, come rain or shine*.—*Ant.* DOUBTFUL, contingent, indeterminate.

inevitably *a.* unavoidably, inescapably, surely; see NECESSARILY.

inexcusable *a.* unpardonable, reprehensible, indefensible; see WRONG 1.

inexpensive *a.* thrifty, low-priced,

modest; see CHEAP 1, ECONOMICAL 2.

inexperience *n.* naiveté, inability, incompetence; see IGNORANCE.

inexperienced *a.* unused, unaccustomed, unadapted, unskilled, common, ordinary, unlicensed, untried, youthful, undeveloped, naive, amateur, untrained, untutored, inefficient, fresh, ignorant, innocent, uninformed, unacquainted, undisciplined, new, immature, tender, not dry behind the ears, soft, raw, green.—*Ant.* EXPERIENCED, seasoned, hardened.

inexplicable *a.* unexplainable, incomprehensible, puzzling; see OBSCURE 1.

infallibility *n.* supremacy, impeccability, consummation; see PERFECTION.

infallible *a.* perfect, reliable, unquestionable; see ACCURATE 1, 2, CERTAIN 2.

infamous *a.* shocking, disgraceful, heinous; see OFFENSIVE 2, SHAMEFUL 2.

infancy *n.* cradle, babyhood, early childhood; see CHILDHOOD.

infant *n.* small child, tot, little one; see BABY, CHILD.

infantile *a.* babyish, childlike, juvenile; see CHILDISH, NAIVE.

infantry *n.* foot soldiers, infantry-

men, combat troops; see ARMY 1, 2.

infect *v.* defile, taint, spoil; see POISON.

infection *n.* **1** [The spread of disease] contagion, communicability, epidemic, taint, corruption; see also POLLUTION. **2** [Disease] virus, impurity, germs; see GERM.

infectious *a.* transferable, diseased, communicable; see CATCHING, CONTAGIOUS, DANGEROUS.

infer *v.* deduce, gather, reach the conclusion that; see ASSUME, UNDERSTAND 1.

inference *n.* deduction, conclusion, answer; see JUDGMENT 3, RESULT.

inferior *a.* mediocre, common, second-rate; see POOR 2.

inferiority *n.* deficiency, mediocrity, inadequacy; see FAILURE 1, WEAKNESS 1.

infest *v.* **1** [To contaminate] pollute, infect, defile; see CORRUPT, DIRTY. **2** [To swarm] overrun, swarm about, crowd, press, harass, jam, pack, teem, fill, flood, throng, flock, be thick as flies*; see also SWARM.

infested *a.* **1** [Overrun] swarming with, full of, overwhelmed; see FULL 1. **2** [Diseased] wormy, lousy, grubby; see SICK.

one who does not believe in a particular religion **2** one who has no religion

in·fi·del·i·ty (in'fə del'ə tē) *n.* unfaithfulness, esp. in marriage

in·field (in'fēld') *n.* **1** the area enclosed by the four base lines on a baseball field **2** the players (**infielders**) whose field positions are there

in·fight·ing (in'fīt'iŋ) *n.* **1** fighting, esp. boxing, at close range **2** personal conflict within a group —**in'fight'er** *n.*

in·fil·trate (in fil'trāt, in'fil trāt') *vi., vt.* **-trat'ed, -trat' ing 1** to filter or pass gradually through or into **2** to penetrate (enemy lines, a region, etc.) gradually or stealthily, so as to attack or to seize control from within — **in'fil·tra'tion.** *n.* —**in'fil·tra'tor** *n.*

in·fi·nite (in'fə nit) *adj.* ⟦see IN-² & FINITE⟧ **1** lacking limits or bounds; endless **2** very great; vast — *n.* something infinite —**in'fi·nitely** *adv.*

in·fin·i·tes·i·mal (in'fin i tes'i məl) *adj.* ⟦< L *infinitus*, infinite⟧ too small to be measured; infinitely small —**in' fini·tes'i·mally** *adv.*

in·fin·i·tive (in fin'i tiv) *n.* ⟦see INFINITE⟧ the form of a verb without reference to person, number, or tense Usually with *to* as in "I want *to go*" —**in·fin'i·ti'val** (-tī'vəl) *adj.*

in·fin'i·tude (-tōōd', -tyōōd') *n.* ⟦< L *infinitus*, INFINITE, prob. infl. by MAGNITUDE⟧ **1** a being infinite **2** an infinite quantity

in·fin'i·ty (-tē) *n., pl.* **-ties** ⟦< L *infinitas*⟧ **1** the quality of being infinite **2** unlimited space, time, etc. **3** an indefinitely large quantity

in·firm (in furm') *adj.* **1** weak; feeble **2** not firm; unstable; frail; shaky —**in·firm'ly** *adv.* —**in·firm'ness** *n.*

in·fir·ma·ry (in fur'mə rē) *n., pl.* **-ries** a place for the care of the sick, injured, or infirm; hospital

in·fir'mi·ty (-mə tē) *n., pl.* **-ties** physical weakness or defect

in·flame (in flame') *vt., vi.* **-flamed', -flam'ing** ⟦see IN-¹ & FLAME⟧ **1** to arouse, excite, etc. or become aroused, excited, etc. **2** to undergo or cause to undergo inflammation

in·flam·ma·ble (in flam'ə bəl) *adj.* **1** FLAMMABLE **2** easily excited —**in·flam'mabil'ity** *n.*

in·flam·ma·tion (in'flə mā'shən) *n.* **1** an inflaming or being inflamed **2** redness, pain, heat, and swelling in the body, due to injury or disease

in·flam·ma·tory (in flam'ə tôr'ē) *adj.* **1** rousing excitement, anger, etc. **2** of or caused by inflammation

in·flate (in flāt') *vt.* **-flat'ed, -flat'ing** ⟦< L *in-*, in + *flare*, to blow⟧ **1** to blow full as with air or gas **2** to puff up with pride **3** to increase beyond what is normal; specif., to cause inflation of (money, credit, etc.) — *vi.* to become inflated —**in·flat'able** *adj.*

in·fla'tion *n.* **1** an inflating or being inflated **2** *a*) an increase in the amount of money and credit in relation to the supply of goods and services *b*) an excessive or persistent increase in the general price level as a result of this, causing a decline in purchasing power —**in·fla'tion·ar'y** *adj.*

in·flect (in flekt') *vt.* ⟦< L *in-*, in + *flectere*, to bend⟧ **1** to vary the tone of (the voice) **2** *Gram.* to change the form of (a word) by inflection

in·flec·tion (in flek'shən) *n.* **1** a change in the tone of the voice **2** the change of form in a word to indicate number, case, tense, etc. Brit. sp. **in·flex'ion** —**in·flec'tional** *adj.*

in·flex·i·ble (in flek'sə bəl) *adj.* not flexible; stiff, rigid, fixed, unyielding, etc. —**in·flex'ibil'ity** *n.*

in·flict (in flikt') *vt.* ⟦< L *in-*, on + *fligere*, to strike⟧ **1** to cause (pain, wounds, etc.) as by striking **2** to impose (a punishment, etc. *on* or *upon*) —**in·flic'tion** *n.* —**in·flic' tive** *adj.*

in-flight (in'flīt') *adj.* done, shown, etc. while an aircraft is in flight

in·flo·res·cence (in'flō res'əns, -flō-) *n.* **1** the producing of blossoms **2** the arrangement of flowers on a stem **3** a flower cluster **4** flowers collectively

in·flu·ence (in'flōō əns) *n.* ⟦< L *in-*, in + *fluere*, to flow⟧ **1** power to affect others **2** power to produce effects because of wealth, position, ability, etc. **3** one that has influence — *vt.* **-enced, -encing** to have influence or effect on

in'flu·en'tial (-en'shəl) *adj.* exerting influence, esp. great influence

in·flu·en·za (in'flōō en'zə) *n.* ⟦It, an influence⟧ an acute, contagious viral disease, characterized by inflammation of the respiratory tract, fever, and muscular pain

in·flux (in'fluks') *n.* ⟦see INFLUENCE⟧ a flowing in or streaming in

info (in'fō) *n.* [Slang] *short for* INFORMATION (senses 1 & 2)

in·fold (in fōld') *vt. var. of* ENFOLD

in·form (in fôrm') *vt.* ⟦see IN-¹ & FORM⟧ to give knowledge of something to — *vi.* to give information, esp. in accusing another —**in·form'er** *n.*

in·for·mal (in fôr'məl) *adj.* not formal; specif., *a*) not according to fixed customs, rules, etc. *b*) casual, relaxed,

THESAURUS

infielder *n.* first baseman, second baseman, third baseman; see BASEBALL PLAYER.

infiltrate *v.* permeate, pervade, penetrate; see JOIN 2.

infinite *a.* unlimited, incalculable, unbounded, boundless, unconfined, countless, interminable, measureless, inexhaustible, bottomless, without end, limitless, tremendous, immense, having no limit, never-ending, immeasurable; see also ENDLESS, UNLIMITED.—*Ant.* RESTRICTED, limited, bounded.

infinite *n.* boundlessness, infinity, the unknown; see ETERNITY, SPACE 1.

infinitely *a.* extremely, very much, unbelievably; see VERY.

infinity *n.* boundlessness, endlessness, the beyond, limitlessness, expanse, extent, continuum, continuity, eternity, infinite space; see also SPACE 1.

infirmary *n.* clinic, sickroom, sick bay; see HOSPITAL.

infirmity *n.* frailty, deficiency, debility; see WEAKNESS 1.

inflame *v.* **1** [To arouse emotions] incense, aggravate, disturb; see EXCITE. **2** [To cause physical soreness] redden, break into a rash, swell; see HURT 1. **3** [To burn] kindle, set on fire, scorch; see BURN, IGNITE.

inflamed *a.* **1** [Stirred to anger] aroused, incited, angered; see ANGRY. **2** [Congested] raw, blistered, swollen; see HURT, PAINFUL 1, SORE 1.

inflammable *a.* combustible, burnable, liable to burn, risky, hazardous, dangerous, unsafe, flammable.—*Ant.* SAFE, fireproof, nonflammable.

inflammation *n.* congestion, soreness, infection; see PAIN 2, SORE.

inflate *v.* **1** [To fill with air or gas] pump up, expand, swell; see FILL 1. **2** [To swell] exaggerate, bloat, cram, expand, balloon, distend, swell up, widen, augment, spread out, enlarge, magnify, exalt, build up, raise, maximize, overestimate; see also STRETCH 1, SWELL.

inflated *a.* distended, swollen, extended, dilated, puffed, filled, grown, stretched, spread, enlarged, amplified, augmented, pumped up, exaggerated, bloated, crammed, magnified, overestimated, pompous, verbose.—*Ant.* REDUCED, deflated, minimized.

inflation *n.* **1** [Increase] expansion, extension, buildup; see INCREASE. **2** [General rise in price levels] financial crisis, boom, move toward higher price levels; see RISE 3.

inflection *n.* pronunciation, enunciation, intonation; see ACCENT, SOUND 2.

inflexibility *n.* stability, toughness, rigidity, stiffness, ossification, fossilization, solidity, crystallization; see also FIRMNESS.

inflexible *a.* rigid, hardened, taut; see FIRM 2, STIFF 1.

inflict *v.* deliver, strike, dispense; see CAUSE.

influence *n.* control, weight, authority, supremacy, command, domination, esteem, political influence, monopoly, rule, fame, prominence, prestige, character, reputation, force, importance, money, power behind the throne*, pull*, clout*; see also LEADERSHIP, POWER 2.

influence *v.* sway, affect, impress, carry weight, be influential, determine, make oneself felt, have influence over, lead to believe, bring pressure to bear, bribe, seduce, talk one into, alter, change, act upon, act on, lead, brainwash, direct, modify, regulate, rule, compel, urge, incite, bias, prejudice, train, channel, mold, form, shape, carry weight, exert influence, get at, be recognized, induce, convince, cajole, persuade, motivate, have an in*, pull strings, have a finger in the pie*, lead by the nose, fix*.

influenced *a.* changed, swayed, persuaded; see AFFECTED 1.

influential *a.* prominent, substantial, powerful; see FAMOUS.

influx *n.* introduction, penetration, coming in; see ENTRANCE 1.

inform *v.* instruct, relate, teach; see TELL 1.

informal *a.* intimate, relaxed, frank, open, straightforward, ordinary, everyday, inconspicuous, habitual, free, extemporaneous, spontaneous, congenial, easygoing, unrestrained, etc. *c)* not requiring formal dress *d)* COLLOQUIAL —**in′·for·mal′i·ty** (-mal′ə tē), *pl.* **-ties,** *n.* —**in·for′mal·ly** *adv.*

in·form·ant (in fôrm′ənt) *n.* a person who gives information

in·for·ma·tion (in′fər mā′shən) *n.* **1** an informing or being informed **2** something told or facts learned; news or knowledge **3** data stored in or retrieved from a computer

information science the science dealing with the collection, storage, and retrieval of information

in·form·a·tive (in fôrm′ə tiv) *adj.* giving information; instructive

infra- ⟦< L⟧ *prefix* below, beneath

in·frac·tion (in frak′shən) *n.* ⟦see INFRINGE⟧ a violation of a law, pact, etc.

in·fran·gi·ble (in fran′jə bəl) *adj.* ⟦see IN-² & FRANGIBLE⟧ unbreakable or inviolable —**in·fran′gi·bly** *adv.*

infra·red (in′frə red′) *adj.* designating or of those invisible rays just beyond the red of the visible spectrum: they have a penetrating heating effect

in′fra·son′ic (-sän′ik) *adj.* of a frequency of sound below the range audible to the human ear

in′fra·struc′ture (-struk′chər) *n.* basic installations and facilities, as roads, power plants, transportation and communication systems, etc.

in·fre·quent (in frē′kwənt) *adj.* not frequent; happening seldom; rare —**in·fre′quency** or **in·fre′quence** *n.* —**in·fre′quently** *adv.*

in·fringe (in frinj′) *vt.* **-fringed′, -fring′ing** ⟦< L *in*-, in + *frangere*, to break⟧ to break (a law or pact) —**infringe on** (or **upon**) to encroach on (the rights, etc. of others) —**in·fringe′ment** *n.*

in·fu·ri·ate (in fyoor′ē āt′) *vt.* **-at′ed, -at′ing** ⟦< L *in*-, in + *furia*, rage⟧ to make very angry; enrage

in·fuse (in fyōōz′) *vt.* **-fused′, -fus′ing** ⟦< L *in*-, in + *fundere*, pour⟧ **1** to instill or impart (qualities, etc.) **2** to fill; inspire **3** to steep (tea leaves, etc.) to extract the essence —**in·fus′er** *n.* —**in·fu′sion** *n.*

-ing ⟦< OE⟧ *suffix* used to form the present participle or verbal nouns *[talking, painting]*

in·gen·ious (in jēn′yəs) *adj.* ⟦< L *in*-, in + *gignere*, to produce⟧ **1** clever, resourceful, etc. **2** made or done in a clever or original way —**in·gen′iously** *adv.*

in·gé·nue (an′zhə nōō′, -jə-) *n.* ⟦Fr, ingenuous⟧ *Theater* the role of an inexperienced young woman, or an actress in this role

in·ge·nu·i·ty (in′jə nōō′ə tē, -nyōō′-) *n.* the quality of being ingenious; cleverness

in·gen·u·ous (in jen′yōō əs) *adj.* ⟦< L *in*-, in + *gignere*, to produce⟧ **1** frank; open **2** simple; naive —**in·gen′u·ously** *adv.* —**in·gen′u·ous·ness** *n.*

in·gest (in jest′) *vt.* ⟦< L *in*-, into + *gerere*, carry⟧ to take (food, etc.) into the body —**in·ges′tion** *n.*

in·glo·ri·ous (in glôr′ē əs) *adj.* shameful; disgraceful

in·got (iŋ′gət) *n.* ⟦prob. < OFr *lingo*, tongue⟧ a mass of metal cast into a bar or other convenient shape

in·grained (in′grānd′) *adj.* **1** firmly established, as habits **2** inveterate *[an ingrained liar]*

in·grate (in′grāt′) *n.* ⟦< L *in*-, not + *gratus*, grateful⟧ an ungrateful person

in·gra·ti·ate (in grā′shē āt′) *vt.* **-at′ed, -at′ing** ⟦< L *in*-, in + *gratia*, favor⟧ to bring (oneself) into another's favor —**in·gra′tia′tion** *n.*

in·grati·tude (in grat′i tōōd′, -tyōōd′) *n.* lack of gratitude; ungratefulness

in·gre·di·ent (in grē′dē ənt) *n.* ⟦see fol.⟧ any of the things that a mixture is made of; component

in·gress (in′gres′) *n.* ⟦< L *in*-, into + *gradi*, to go⟧ entrance

in·grown (in′grōn′) *adj.* grown inward, esp. into the flesh, as a toenail

in·gui·nal (iŋ′gwi nəl) *adj.* ⟦< L *inguen*, groin⟧ of or near the groin

in·habit (in hab′it) *vt.* ⟦< L *in*-, in + *habitare*, dwell⟧ to live in —**in·hab′it·able** *adj.*

in·hab·it·ant (-i tənt) *n.* a person or animal inhabiting a specified place

in·hal·ant (in hāl′ənt) *n.* a medicine, etc. to be inhaled

in·ha·la·tor (in′hə lāt′ər) *n.* **1** an apparatus used in inhaling medicinal vapors **2** RESPIRATOR (sense 2)

in·hale (in hāl′) *vt., vi.* **-haled′, -hal′ing** ⟦< L *in*-, in + *halare*, breathe⟧ to breathe in (air, vapor, etc.) —**in·ha·la′tion** (in′hə lā′shən) *n.*

in·haler (in hāl′ər) *n.* **1** one who inhales **2** RESPIRATOR (sense 1) **3** INHALATOR (sense 1)

in·here (in hir′) *vi.* **-hered′, -her′ing** ⟦< L *in*-, in + *haerere*, to stick⟧ to be inherent

in·her·ent (in hir′ənt, -her′-) *adj.* existing in someone or something as a natural and inseparable quality —**in·her′ently** *adv.*

in·herit (in her′it) *vt., vi.* ⟦< L *in*, in + *heres*, heir⟧ **1** to receive (property, etc.) as an heir **2** to have (certain characteristics) by heredity —**in·her′i·tor** *n.*

in·her·it·ance (in her′i təns) *n.* **1** the action of inheriting **2** something inherited

in·hibit (in hib′it) *vt.* ⟦< L *in*-, in, on + *habere*, to hold⟧ to check or repress

in·hi·bi·tion (in′hi bish′ən, in′i-) *n.* **1** an inhibiting or being inhibited **2** a mental process that restrains an action, emotion, or thought

in·hu·man (in hyōō′mən) *adj.* not having worthy human characteristics; heartless, cruel, brutal, etc. —**in′hu·man′i·ty** (-man′ə tē) *n.*

in·im·i·cal (i nim′i kəl) *adj.* ⟦< L *in*-, not + *amicus*, friend⟧ **1** hostile; unfriendly **2** in opposition; adverse

in·im·i·table (in im′i tə bəl) *adj.* that cannot be imitated; matchless

in·iq·ui·ty (i nik′wi tē) *n.* ⟦< L *in*-, not + *aequus*, equal⟧ **1** wickedness **2** *pl.* **-ties** a wicked or unjust act —**in·iq′ui·tous** *adj.*

ini·tial (i nish′əl) *adj.* ⟦< L *in*-, into, in + *ire*, go⟧ of or at the beginning; first — *n.* the first letter of a name — *vt.*

THESAURUS

unconventional; see also FRIENDLY.—*Ant.* RESTRAINED, ceremonial, ritualistic.

informality *n.* casualness, familiarity, ease; see COMFORT.

information *n.* **1** [Derived knowledge] acquired facts, evidence, knowledge, reports, details, results, notes, documents, testimony, facts, figures, statistics, measurements, conclusions, deductions, plans, field notes, lab notes, learning, erudition; see also KNOWLEDGE 1. **2** [News] report, notice, message; see NEWS 1, 2.

informative *a.* instructive, informing, accurate; see DETAILED.

infraction *n.* violation, infringement, breach; see VIOLATION.

infrastructure *n.* foundation, basic structure, base; see FOUNDATION 2.

infrequent *a.* sparse, occasional, scarce; see RARE 2.

infrequently *a.* occasionally, rarely, hardly ever; see SELDOM.

infringe *v.* transgress, violate, trespass; see MEDDLE 1.

infuriate *v.* aggravate, enrage, provoke; see ANGER.

infuriated *a.* furious, enraged,

incensed; see ANGRY.

ingenious *a.* original, skillful, gifted; see ABLE, INTELLIGENT.

ingenuity *n.* inventiveness, imagination, productiveness; see ORIGINALITY.

ingrained *a.* congenital, inborn, indelible; see NATIVE 1.

ingratitude *n.* thanklessness, disloyalty, ungratefulness, callousness, boorishness, lack of appreciation, inconsiderateness, thoughtlessness; see also RUDENESS.—*Ant.* GRATITUDE, appreciation, consideration.

ingredient *n.* constituent, component, element; see FUNDAMENTAL.

ingredients *n.* parts, elements, additives, constituents, pieces, components, makings, fixings*.

inhabit *v.* occupy, stay, live in; see DWELL.

inhabitant *n.* occupant, dweller, settler, denizen, lodger, permanent resident, roomer, boarder, occupier, householder, addressee, inmate, tenant, settler, colonist, squatter, native; see also CITIZEN, RESIDENT.—*Ant.* ALIEN, transient, nonresident.

inhabited *a.* settled, owned, lived in, dwelt in, sustaining human life, peo-

pled, occupied, colonized, developed, pioneered.

inhale *v.* gasp, smell, sniff; see BREATHE.

inherent *a.* innate, inborn, inbred; see NATURAL 1, NATIVE 1.—*Ant.* SUPERFICIAL, incidental, extrinsic.

inherently *a.* naturally, intrinsically, by birth; see ESSENTIALLY.

inherit *v.* succeed to, acquire, receive, obtain, get one's inheritance, fall heir to, come into, come in for*, take over, receive an endowment; see also GET 1.—*Ant.* LOSE, be disowned, miss.

inheritance *n.* bequest, legacy, heritage; see GIFT 1.

inhibit *v.* repress, frustrate, hold back; see HINDER, RESTRAIN.

inhibition *n.* prevention, restraint, hindrance; see BARRIER, INTERFERENCE 1.

inhuman *a.* mean, heartless, cold-blooded; see CRUEL, FIERCE, RUTHLESS.

inhumanity *n.* savagery, barbarity, brutality; see CRUELTY, EVIL 1, TYRANNY.

initial *a.* basic, primary, elementary;

-tialed or **-tialled**, **-tial·ing** or **-tial·ling** to mark with initials —**ini'tial·ly** *adv.*

ini·ti·ate (i nish'ē āt') *vt.* **-at'ed, -at'ing** ⟦see prec.⟧ **1** to bring into practice or use **2** to teach the fundamentals of a subject to **3** to admit as a member into a fraternity, club, etc., esp. with a special or secret ceremony —**ini'tia'tion** *n.* —**ini'tia·to'ry** (-ə tôr'ē) *adj.*

ini·tia·tive (i nish'ə tiv, -ē ə tiv) *n.* **1** the action of taking the first step or move **2** ability in originating new ideas or methods **3** the introduction of proposed legislation, as to popular vote, by voters' petitions

in·ject (in jekt') *vt.* ⟦< L *in-*, in + *jacere*, to throw⟧ **1** to force (a fluid) into a vein, tissue, etc. with a syringe or the like **2** to introduce (a remark, quality, etc.) —**in·jec'tion** *n.* —**in·jec'tor** *n.*

in·junc·tion (in juŋk'shən) *n.* ⟦< L *in-*, in + *jungere*, join⟧ **1** a command; order **2** a court order prohibiting or ordering a given action

in·jure (in'jər) *vt.* **-jured, -jur·ing** ⟦see INJURY⟧ **1** to do harm or damage to; hurt **2** to wrong or offend

in·ju·ri·ous (in joor'ē əs) *adj.* injuring or likely to injure; harmful

in·ju·ry (in'jə rē) *n., pl.* **-ries** ⟦< L *in-*, not + *jus*, right⟧ **1** harm or damage **2** an injurious act

in·jus·tice (in jus'tis) *n.* **1** a being unjust **2** an unjust act; wrong

ink (iŋk) *n.* ⟦< Gr *en-*, in + *kaiein*, to burn⟧ **1** a colored liquid used for writing, printing, etc. **2** a dark, liquid secretion ejected by cuttlefish, squid, etc. —*vt.* to cover, mark, or color with ink

ink'blot' *n.* any of the patterns made by blots of ink that are used in the RORSCHACH TEST

ink'ling (iŋk'liŋ) *n.* ⟦ME *ingkiling*⟧ **1** a hint **2** a vague notion

ink'well' *n.* a container for ink

ink'y *adj.* **-i·er, -i·est** **1** like ink in color; dark; black **2** covered with ink —**ink'i·ness** *n.*

in·laid (in'lād', in lād') *adj.* set into a surface or formed, decorated, etc. by inlaying

in·land (*for adj.* in'lənd; *for n. & adv.,* -land', -lənd) *adj.* of or in the interior of a country — *n.* inland region — *adv.* into or toward this region

in-law (in'lô') *n.* ⟦< *mother-* (or *father-*, etc.) *in-law*⟧ [Colloq.] a relative by marriage

in·lay (*for v.* in'lā', in lā'; *for n.* in'lā') *vt.* **-laid', -lay'ing 1** to set (pieces of wood, etc.) into a surface, specif. for decoration **2** to decorate thus — *n., pl.* **-lays'** **1** inlaid

decoration or material **2** a shaped filling, as of gold, cemented into the cavity of a tooth

in·let (in'let') *n.* a narrow strip of water extending into a body of land

in·mate (in'māt') *n.* a person confined with others in a prison or mental institution

in me·mo·ri·am (in mə môr'ē əm) ⟦L⟧ in memory (of)

in·most (in'mōst) *adj.* **1** farthest within **2** most secret

inn (in) *n.* ⟦OE⟧ **1** a small hotel **2** a restaurant or tavern: now usually only in the names of such places

in·nards (in'ərdz) *n.pl.* ⟦< INWARDS⟧ [Colloq. or Dial.] the inner organs or parts

in·nate (in'āt', i nāt') *adj.* ⟦< L *in-*, in + *nasci*, be born⟧ inborn; natural

in·ner (in'ər) *adj.* **1** farther within **2** more secret

inner circle the small, exclusive, most influential part of a group

inner city the crowded or blighted central sections of a large city

inner ear the part of the ear consisting of the semicircular canal, vestibule, and cochlea

in'ner·most' *adj.* INMOST

in'ner·sole' *n.* INSOLE

in'ner·spring' mat'tress a mattress with built-in coil springs

in·ner·vate (i nur'vāt', in'ər vāt') *vt.* **-vat'ed, -vat'ing** *Med.* **1** to supply (a part) with nerves **2** to stimulate (a muscle, etc.) —**in'ner·va'tion** *n.*

in·ning (in'iŋ) *n.* ⟦< OE *innung*, getting in⟧ [*pl. for Cricket*] *Baseball, Cricket* **1** a team's turn at bat **2** a numbered round of play in which both teams have a turn at bat

inn'keep'er *n.* the owner of an inn

in·no·cent (in'ə sənt) *adj.* ⟦< L *in-*, not + *nocere*, to harm⟧ **1** free from sin, evil, etc.; specif., not guilty of a specific crime **2** harmless **3** knowing no evil **4** without guile — *n.* an innocent person, as a child —**in'no·cence** *n.* —**in'no·cent·ly** *adv.*

in·noc·u·ous (in näk'yōō əs) *adj.* ⟦see prec.⟧ harmless —**in·noc'u·ous·ly** *adv.* —**in·noc'u·ous·ness** *n.*

in·no·va·tion (in'ə vā'shən) *n.* ⟦< L *in-*, in + *novus*, new⟧ **1** the process of making changes **2** a new method, custom, device, etc. —**in'no·vate', -vat'ed, -vat'ing**, *vi., vt.* —**in'no·va'tive** *adj.* —**in'no·va'tor** *n.*

in·nu·en·do (in'yōō en'dō') *n., pl.* **-does'** or **-dos'** ⟦< L *in-*, in + *-nuere*, to nod⟧ a hint or sly remark, usually derogatory; insinuation

in·nu·mer·a·ble (in nōō'mer ə bəl) *adj.* too numerous to be counted

in·ocu·late (i näk'yōō lāt') *vt.* **-lat'ed, -lat'ing** ⟦< L *in-*, in + *oculus*, eye⟧ to inject a serum, vaccine, etc. into, esp. in order to create immunity —**in·oc'u·la'tion** *n.*

■ THESAURUS ■

see FIRST, FUNDAMENTAL.

initially *a.* at first, in the beginning, originally; see FIRST.

initiate *v.* open, start, inaugurate; see BEGIN 1.

initiated *a.* **1** [Introduced into] proposed, sponsored, originated, entered, brought into, admitted, inserted, put into, instituted; see also PROPOSED. **2** [Having undergone initiation] installed, inducted, confirmed, instructed, grounded, passed, admitted, approved, made part of, made a member of, received, introduced, acknowledged, accepted, drafted, called up, levied.

initiation *n.* baptism, induction, indoctrination; see INTRODUCTION 3.

initiative *n.* action, enterprise, first step; see RESPONSIBILITY 1.

inject *v.* inoculate, shoot, mainline*; see VACCINATE.

injection *n.* dose, vaccination, inoculation; see TREATMENT 2.

injure *v.* harm, damage, wound; see HURT 1.

injured *a.* spoiled, damaged, harmed; see HURT, WOUNDED.

injurious *a.* detrimental, damaging, bad; see DANGEROUS, DEADLY, HARMFUL, POISONOUS.

injury *n.* harm, sprain, damage, mutilation, blemish, cut, gash, scratch, stab, impairment, bite, fracture, hemorrhage, sting, bruise, sore, cramp, trauma, abrasion, burn,

lesion, swelling, wound, scar, laceration, affliction, deformation; see also PAIN 1.

injustice *n.* wrongdoing, malpractice, offense, crime, villainy, injury, unfairness, miscarriage, infringement, violation, abuse, criminal negligence, transgression, grievance, breach, damage, infraction, a crying shame*; see also EVIL 1, WRONG.— *Ant.* RIGHT, just decision, honest verdict.

ink *n.* dye, paint, watercolor; see COLOR.

inkling *n.* indication, clue, suspicion; see HINT, SUGGESTION 1.

inland *a.* toward the interior, backcountry, backland, hinterland, interior, midland, provincial, domestic, inward; see also CENTRAL.— *Ant.* FOREIGN, international, outlying.

inmate *n.* patient, convict, captive; see PATIENT, PRISONER.

inn *n.* tavern, hostel, saloon; see BAR 2, HOTEL, MOTEL, RESORT 2.

inner *a.* innate, inherent, essential, inward, internal, interior, inside, nuclear, central, spiritual, private, subconscious, intrinsic, deep-seated, deep-rooted, intuitive.— *Ant.* OUTER, surface, external.

innocence *n.* **1** [Freedom from guilt] guiltlessness, blamelessness, integrity, clear conscience, faultlessness, clean hands; see also HONESTY.— *Ant.* GUILT, culpability,

dishonesty. **2** [Freedom from guile] frankness, candidness, sincerity, simple-mindedness, plainness, forthrightness, inoffensiveness; see also SIMPLICITY 1. **3** [Lack of experience] purity, virginity, naiveté; see CHASTITY, IGNORANCE, VIRTUE 1.

innocent *a.* **1** [Guiltless] not guilty, blameless, impeccable, faultless, safe, upright, free of, uninvolved, above suspicion, clean*; see also HONEST 1.— *Ant.* GUILTY, culpable, blameworthy. **2** [Without guile] open, fresh, guileless; see FRANK, CHILDISH, NAIVE, NATURAL 3, SIMPLE 1. **3** [Morally pure] sinless, unblemished, pure, unsullied, undefiled, spotless, wholesome, upright, unimpeachable, clean, virtuous, virginal, immaculate, impeccable, righteous, uncorrupted, irreproachable, unstained, stainless, moral, angelic.— *Ant.* DISHONEST, sinful, corrupt. **4** [Harmless] innocuous, powerless, inoffensive; see HARMLESS, SAFE 1.

innocently *a.* without guilt, with good intentions, ignorantly, with the best of intentions; see also NICELY 1, POLITELY.

innovation *n.* change, alteration, addition; see CHANGE 1.

innuendo *n.* aside, intimation, insinuation; see HINT, SUGGESTION 1.

inoculate *v.* immunize, inject, vaccinate; see TREAT 3.

inoculation *n.* vaccination, injec-

in·of·fen·sive (in′ə fen′siv) *adj.* causing no harm or annoyance; not objectionable —**in′of·fen′sive·ly** *adv.*

in·op·er·a·ble (in äp′ər ə bəl) *adj.* not operable; specif., *a)* not practical *b)* incapable of being treated by surgery

in·op·er·a·tive (in äp′ər ə tiv, -ər āt′iv) *adj.* not working or functioning

in·or·di·nate (in ôr′də nit, -ôrd′'n it) *adj.* ⟦< L *in-*, not + *ordino*, to order⟧ excessive; immoderate —**in·or′di·nately** *adv.*

in·or·gan·ic (in′ôr gan′ik) *adj.* not organic; specif., designating or of matter not animal or vegetable; not living

in·pa·tient (in′pā′shənt) *n.* a patient who stays in a hospital, etc. while receiving treatment

in·put (in′poot′) *n.* 1 what is put in; specif., *a)* power into a machine, etc. *b)* data or programs into a computer 2 opinion; advice —*vt.* -**put′**, -**put′ting** to feed (data) into a computer

in·quest (in′kwest′) *n.* ⟦see INQUIRE⟧ a judicial inquiry, esp. before a jury, as a coroner's inquiry of a death

in·qui·etude (in kwī′ə tood′, -tyōōd′) *n.* restlessness; uneasiness

in·quire (in kwīr′) *vi.* -**quired′**, -**quir′ing** ⟦< L *in-*, into + *quaerere*, seek⟧ 1 to ask a question or questions 2 to investigate: usually with *into* —*vt.* to seek information about —**in·quir′er** *n.*

in·quir·y (in′kwə rē, in kwīr′ē) *n., pl.* -**ies** 1 an inquiring; investigation 2 a question

in·qui·si·tion (in′kwə zish′ən) *n.* 1 an investigation or inquest 2 [I-] *R.C.Ch.* the tribunal established in the 13th c. for suppressing heresy and heretics 3 any relentless questioning or harsh suppression —**in′qui·si′tion·al** *adj.* —**in·quis′i·tor** *n.*

in·quis·i·tive (in kwiz′ə tiv) *adj.* 1 inclined to ask many questions 2 unnecessarily curious; prying —**in·quis′i·tive·ness** *n.*

in re (in rē′, -rā′) ⟦L⟧ in the matter (of)

-in-res·i·dence *combining form* appointed to work and usually residing at an institution, as a college, for a certain period

in·road (in′rōd′) *n.* 1 a raid 2 [*usually pl.*] any injurious encroachment

in·sane (in sān′) *adj.* 1 not sane; mentally ill or deranged 2 of or for insane people 3 very foolish —**in·sane′ly** *adv.* —**in·san′ity** (-san′ə tē) *n.*

in·sa·tia·ble (in sā′shə bəl, -shē ə-) *adj.* ⟦see IN-² & SATIATE⟧ that cannot be satisfied —**in·sa′tia·bly** *adv.*

in·scribe (in skrīb′) *vt.* -**scribed′**, -**scrib′ing** ⟦< L *in-*, in + *scribere*, write⟧ 1 to mark or engrave (words, etc.) on (a surface) 2 to add (a person's name) to a list 3 *a)* to dedicate (a book, etc.) to someone *b)* to autograph 4 to fix in the mind —**in·scrip′tion** (-skrip′shən) *n.*

in·scru·ta·ble (in skrōōt′ə bəl) *adj.* ⟦< L *in-*, not +

scrutari, examine⟧ not easily understood; enigmatic —**in·scru′ta·bly** *adv.*

in·seam (in′sēm′) *n.* an inner seam; specif., the seam from the crotch to the bottom of a trouser leg

in·sect (in′sekt′) *n.* ⟦< L *insectum*, lit., notched⟧ any of a large class of small, usually winged, invertebrates, as beetles, flies, wasps, etc., having three pairs of legs

in·sec·ti·cide (in sek′tə sīd′) *n.* any substance used to kill insects —**in·sec′ti·ci′dal** *adj.*

in·sec·ti·vore (in sek′tə vôr′) *n.* ⟦see fol.⟧ any of various small mammals that are active mainly at night and that feed principally on insects, as moles, shrews, etc.

in·sec·tiv·o·rous (in′sek tiv′ə rəs) *adj.* ⟦< INSECT + L *vorare*, devour⟧ feeding chiefly on insects

in·se·cure (in′si kyoor′) *adj.* 1 not safe from danger 2 feeling anxiety 3 not firm or dependable —**in′se·cure′ly** *adv.* —**in′se·cu′ri·ty**, *pl.* -**ties**, *n.*

in·sem·i·nate (in sem′ə nāt′) *vt.* -**nat′ed**, -**nat′ing** ⟦< L *in-*, in + *semen*, seed⟧ 1 to sow seeds in; esp., to impregnate 2 to imbue (with ideas, etc.) —**in·sem′i·na′tion** *n.*

in·sen·sate (in sen′sāt′, -sit) *adj.* 1 not feeling sensation 2 foolish; stupid 3 without regard or feeling; cold

in·sen·si·ble (in sen′sə bəl) *adj.* 1 unable to perceive with the senses 2 unconscious 3 unaware; indifferent 4 so small as to be virtually imperceptible —**in·sen′si·bil′i·ty** *n.*

in·sen·si·tive (-sə tiv) *adj.* not sensitive; not responsive —**in·sen′si·tive·ly** *adv.* —**in·sen′si·tiv′i·ty** *n.*

in·sen·tient (in sen′shənt, -shē ənt) *adj.* not sentient; without life or consciousness —**in·sen′tience** *n.*

in·sert (in surt′; *for n.* in′surt′) *vt.* ⟦< L *in-*, in + *serere*, join⟧ to put or fit (something) into something else —*n.* anything inserted or for insertion —**in·ser′tion** *n.*

in·set (in set′; *for n.* in′set′) *vt.* -**set′**, -**set′ting** to set in; insert —*n.* something inserted

in·shore (in′shôr′, in shôr′) *adv., adj.* in, near, or toward the shore

in·side (in′sīd′, in′sīd′, in sīd′) *n.* 1 the inner side, surface, or part 2 [*pl.*] [Colloq.] the viscera —*adj.* 1 internal 2 known only to insiders; secret —*adv.* 1 on or to the inside; within 2 indoors —*prep.* in or within —**inside of** within the space or time of —**inside out** 1 reversed 2 [Colloq.] thoroughly

in·sid′er *n.* 1 one inside a given place or group 2 one having secret or confidential information

in·sid·i·ous (in sid′ē əs) *adj.* ⟦< L *insidiae*, an ambush⟧ 1 characterized by treachery or slyness 2 more dangerous than seems evident

in·sight (in′sīt′) *n.* 1 the ability to see and understand clearly the inner nature of things, esp. by intuition 2 an instance of such understanding

---

THESAURUS

tion, shot; see TREATMENT 2.

inoffensive *a.* innocuous, pleasant, peaceable; see CALM 1, FRIENDLY.

input *n.* information, knowledge, facts; see DATA.

inquire *v.* make an inquiry, probe, interrogate; see ASK, QUESTION.

inquiry *n.* probe, analysis, hearing; see EXAMINATION.

inquisitive *a.* curious, inquiring, speculative, questioning, meddling, searching, intrusive, challenging, analytical, scrutinizing, prying, forward, presumptuous, impertinent, snoopy*, nosy*; see also INTERESTED 1.—*Ant.* INDIFFERENT, unconcerned, aloof.

insane *a.* 1 [Deranged] crazy, crazed, wild, raging, frenzied, lunatic, balmy, schizophrenic, psychotic, psychopathic, paranoid, maniacal, raving, demented, rabid, unhinged, mentally unsound, mentally ill, suffering from hallucinations, deluded, daft, possessed, stark mad, out of one's mind, obsessed, touched, cracked*, screwy*, nutty*, nuts*, schizo*, loco*, wacko*, wacky*, haywire*, batty*, unglued*, off one's rocker*, not all there*; see also SICK.—*Ant.* SANE, rational, sensible. 2 [Utterly foolish] madcap, daft, idiotic; see STUPID.

insanely *a.* furiously, psychopathi-

cally, fiercely; see CRAZILY, VIOLENTLY, WILDLY.

insanity *n.* mental derangement, delusions, hysteria, anxiety, obsession, compulsion, madness, dementia, lunacy, psychosis, alienation, neurosis, phobia, mania.—*Ant.* SANITY, reason, normality.

inscription *n.* engraving, saying, legend; see WRITING 2.

insect *n.* bug, beetle, mite, vermin, arthropod, cootie*; see also PEST 1. *Creatures commonly called insects include the following:* spider, ant, bee, flea, fly, mosquito, gnat, silverfish, hornet, leafhopper, squash bug, earwig, mayfly, walking stick, dragonfly, termite, cicada, aphid, aphis, mantis, beetle, butterfly, moth, wasp, locust, bedbug, caterpillar, grasshopper, cricket, bumblebee, honeybee, cockroach, potato bug, corn borer, boll weevil, stinkbug, firefly, Japanese beetle, yellow jacket; see also FLY 1, SPIDER.

insecticide *n.* DDT, insect poison, pesticide; see POISON.

insecure *a.* anxious, vague, uncertain; see TROUBLED.

insecurity *n.* 1 [Anxiety] vacillation, indecision, instability; see DOUBT, UNCERTAINTY 2. 2 [Danger] risk, hazard, vulnerability; see

CHANCE 1, DANGER.

inseparable *a.* indivisible, as one, tied up, intertwined, integrated, integral, interwoven, entwined, whole, connected, attached, conjoined, united; see also JOINED, UNIFIED.—*Ant.* DIVISIBLE, separable, apart.

insert *n.* inclusion, insertion, new material; see ADDITION 1.

insert *v.* enter, introduce, inject; see INCLUDE 2.

inserted *a.* introduced, added, stuck in; see INCLUDED.

insertion *n.* insert, injection, inclusion; see ADDITION 1.

inside *a.* 1 [Within] inner, in, within the boundaries of, bounded, surrounded by; see also INNER, UNDER.—*Ant.* BEYOND, after, outside. 2 [Within doors] indoors, under a roof, in a house, out of the open, behind closed doors, under a shelter, in the interior; see also WITHIN.—*Ant.* OUTSIDE, out-of-doors, in the open.

inside *n.* inner wall, sheathing, plaster, facing, wadding; see also LINING.

insides *n.* interior, inner portion, bowels, recesses, inland, middle, belly, womb, heart, soul, breast; see also CENTER 1, STOMACH.

insight *n.* intuition, acuteness, shrewdness; see JUDGMENT 1.

in·sig·nia (in sig'nē ə) *n.pl.*, *sing.* **in·sig'ne** (-nē) or **in·sig'nia** [ult. < L *in-*, in + *signum*, a mark] distinguishing marks, as emblems of rank, membership, etc.

in·sin·cere (in'sin sir') *adj.* not sincere; deceptive or hypocritical —**in'sin·cere'ly** *adv.* —**in'sin·cer'ity** (-ser'ə tē), *pl.* **-ties,** *n.*

in·sin·u·ate (in sin'yōō āt') *vt.* **-at'ed, -at'ing** [< L *in-*, in + *sinus*, a curve] 1 to introduce or work into gradually, indirectly, etc. 2 to hint or suggest indirectly; imply —**in·sin'u·a'tion** *n.* —**in·sin'u·a'tive** *adj.* —**in·sin'u·a'tor** *n.*

in·sip·id (in sip'id) *adj.* [< L *in-*, not + *sapidus*, savory] 1 without flavor; tasteless 2 not exciting; dull

in·sist (in sist') *vi.* [< L *in-*, in, on + *sistere*, to stand] to take and maintain a stand: often with *on* or *upon* —*vt.* 1 to demand strongly 2 to declare firmly —**in·sist'ingly** *adv.*

in·sist'ent *adj.* insisting or demanding —**in·sist'ence** *n.*

in situ (in sī'tōō') [L] in position; in its original place

in·so·far (in'sō fär') *adv.* to such a degree or extent: usually with *as*

in·sole (in'sōl') *n.* 1 the inside sole of a shoe 2 a removable inside sole put in for comfort

in·so·lent (in'sə lənt) *adj.* [< L *in-*, not + *solere*, be accustomed] boldly disrespectful; impudent —**in'so·lence** *n.*

in·sol·uble (in säl'yōō bəl) *adj.* 1 that cannot be solved 2 that cannot be dissolved —**in·sol'ubil'ity** *n.*

in·sol·vent (in säl'vənt) *adj.* not solvent; unable to pay debts; bankrupt —**in·sol'vency** *n.*

in·som·nia (in säm'nē ə) *n.* [< L *in-*, without + *somnus*, sleep] abnormal inability to sleep —**in·som'niac'** (-ak') *n., adj.*

in·so·much (in'sō much') *adv.* 1 to such a degree or extent; so: with *that* 2 inasmuch (as)

in·sou·ci·ant (in sōō'sē ənt) *adj.* [Fr < *in-*, not + *soucier*, to care] calm and untroubled; carefree —**in·sou'ci·ance** *n.*

in·spect (in spekt') *vt.* [< L *in-*, at + *specere*, look at] 1 to look at carefully 2 to examine or review officially —**in·spec'tion** *n.*

in·spec'tor *n.* 1 one who inspects 2 an officer on a police force, ranking next below a superintendent

in·spi·ra·tion (in'spə rā'shən) *n.* 1 an inhaling 2 an inspiring or being inspired mentally or emotionally 3 *a*) any stimulus to creative thought or action *b*) an inspired idea, action, etc. —**in'spi·ra'tional** *adj.*

in·spire (in spīr') *vt.* **-spired', -spir'ing** [< L *in-*, in, on + *spirare*, breathe] 1 to inhale 2 to stimulate or impel, as to some creative effort 3 to motivate as by divine influence 4 to arouse (a thought or feeling) in (someone) 5 to occasion or cause — *vi.* 1 to inhale 2 to give inspiration

in·spirit (in spir'it) *vt.* to put spirit into; cheer; hearten

Inst. 1 Institute 2 Institution

in·sta·bil·ity (in'stə bil'ə tē) *n.* lack of firmness, determination, etc.

in·stall or **in·stal** (in stôl') *vt.* **-stalled', -stall'ing** [< ML *in-*, in + *stallum*, a place] 1 to place in an office, rank, etc., with formality 2 to establish in a place 3 to fix in position for use [*to install* new fixtures] —**in·stal·la·tion** (in'stə lā'shən) *n.* —**in·stall'er** *n.*

in·stall'ment or **in·stal'ment** *n.* 1 an installing or being installed 2 any of the parts of a sum of money to be paid at regular specified times 3 any of several parts, as of a serial

installment plan a credit system by which debts, as for purchased articles, are paid in installments

in·stance (in'stəns) *n.* [see fol.] 1 an example; case 2 a step in proceeding; occasion [in the first *instance*] — *vt.* **-stanced, -stanc·ing** to give as an example; cite —**at the instance** of at the suggestion or instigation of

in·stant (in'stənt) *adj.* [< L *in-*, in, upon + *stare*, to stand] 1 urgent; pressing 2 imminent 3 immediate 4 concentrated or precooked for quick preparation, as a food or beverage 5 [Archaic] present; current — *n.* 1 a moment 2 a particular moment —**the instant** as soon as

in·stan·ta·neous (in'stən tā'nē əs) *adj.* done or happening in an instant —**in'stan·ta'neous·ly** *adv.*

in·stan·ter (in stan'tər) *adv.* [L] *Law* immediately

in·stan·ti·ate (in stan'shē āt') *vt.* **-at'ed, -at'ing** to represent by a concrete example; instance

in'stantly *adv.* immediately

in·state (in stāt') *vt.* **-stat'ed, -stat'ing** [IN-¹ + STATE] to put in a particular rank, etc.; install

in·stead (in sted') *adv.* [IN + STEAD] in place of the one mentioned —**instead of** in place of

in·step (in'step') *n.* the upper part of the arch of the foot, between the ankle and the toes

in·sti·gate (in'stə gāt') *vt.* **-gat'ed, -gat'ing** [< L *in-*, on + *-stigare*, to prick] 1 to urge on to some action 2 to foment (rebellion, etc.) —**in'sti·ga'tion** *n.* —**in'sti·ga'tor** *n.*

in·still or **in·stil** (in stil') *vt.* **-stilled', -still'ing** [< L *in-*, in + *stilla*, a drop] 1 to put in drop by drop 2 to put (an idea, etc.) *in* or *into* gradually

---

THESAURUS

insignia *n.* ensign, coat of arms, symbol; see EMBLEM.

insignificance *n.* unimportance, worthlessness, indifference, triviality, nothingness, smallness, pettiness, matter of no consequence, nothing to speak of, nothing particular, trifling matter, drop in the bucket*, molehill*.

insignificant *a.* irrelevant, petty, trifling; see TRIVIAL, UNIMPORTANT.

insincere *a.* deceitful, pretentious, shifty; see DISHONEST, FALSE 1, HYPOCRITICAL, SLY.

insincerity *n.* deceit, treachery, lies; see DECEPTION, DISHONESTY, HYPOCRISY.

insinuate *v.* imply, suggest, purport; see HINT, MENTION, PROPOSE 1, REFER 2.

insinuation *n.* implication, veiled remark, innuendo; see HINT, SUGGESTION 1.

insistence *n.* persistence, perseverance, obstinacy; see DETERMINATION.

insistent *a.* persistent, obstinate, continuous; see STUBBORN.

insist upon *v.* expect, request, order; see ASK.

insolvent *a.* bankrupt, failed, broke*; see RUINED 3.—*Ant.* RUNNING, solvent, in good condition.

inspect *v.* scrutinize, probe, investigate; see EXAMINE.

inspected *a.* tested, checked, authorized; see APPROVED, INVESTIGATED.

inspection *n.* inventory, investiga-tion, inquiry; see EXAMINATION 1.

inspector *n.* police inspector, chief detective, investigating officer, customs officer, immigration inspector, government inspector, checker, FBI agent, narc*, postal inspector; see also POLICEMAN.

inspiration *n.* 1 [An idea] notion, hunch, whim; see FANCY 1, IMPULSE 2, THOUGHT 2. 2 [A stimulant to creative activity] stimulus, motivation, influence; see INCENTIVE.

inspire *v.* fire, be the cause of, start off, urge, stimulate, cause, put one in the mood, give one the idea for, motivate, give an impetus.

inspired *a.* roused, animated, motivated, stimulated, energized, stirred, excited, exhilarated, influenced, set going, started, activated, moved; see also ENCOURAGED.

inspiring *a.* illuminating, encouraging, revealing; see EXCITING, STIMULATING.

instability *n.* inconstancy, changeability, immaturity, variability, inconsistency, irregularity, imbalance, unsteadiness, restlessness, anxiety, fluctuation, alternation, disquiet, fitfulness, impermanence, transience, vacillation, hesitation, oscillation, flightiness, capriciousness, wavering, fickleness; see also CHANGE 1, UNCERTAINTY 2.

install *v.* set up, establish, build in, put in, place, invest, introduce, inaugurate, furnish with, fix up.

installation *n.* 1 [The act of install-ing] placing, induction, ordination, inauguration, launching, coronation, establishment. 2 [That which has been installed] machinery, wiring, lighting, insulation, power, power plant, heating system, furnishings, foundation, base.

installed *a.* set up, started, put in; see ESTABLISHED 1, FINISHED 1.

installment *n.* partial payment, periodic payment, down payment; see PART 1, PAYMENT 1.

instance *n.* case, situation, occurrence; see EXAMPLE. —**for instance** as an example, by way of illustration, in this fashion; see FOR EXAMPLE.

instant *n.* short while, second, flash, split second, wink of the eye, jiffy*; see also MOMENT 1. —**on the instant** instantly, without delay, simultaneously; see IMMEDIATELY.

instantly *a.* directly, at once, without delay; see IMMEDIATELY.

instead *a.* in place of, as a substitute, alternative, on second thought, in lieu of, on behalf of, alternatively; see also RATHER 2. —**instead of** rather than, in place of, as a substitute for, in lieu of, as an alternative for.

instill *v.* inject, infiltrate, inoculate, impregnate, inseminate, implant, inspire, impress, brainwash, introduce, inculcate, indoctrinate, impart, insert, force in, imbue, put into someone's head*; see also TEACH.—*Ant.* REMOVE, draw out, extract.

in·stinct (in'stiŋkt') *n.* ‖ < L *instinguere*, to impel ‖ **1** (an) inborn tendency to behave in a way characteristic of a species **2** a natural or acquired tendency; knack —**in·stinc'tive** *adj.* —**in·stinc'tively** *adv.* —**in·stinc'tual** *adj.*

in·sti·tute (in'stə to͞ot', -tyo͞ot') *vt.* -**tut'ed**, -**tut'ing** ‖ < L *in-*, in, on + *statuere*, to cause to set up ‖ **1** to set up; establish **2** to start; initiate — *n.* something instituted; specif., *a*) an organization for the promotion of art, science, etc. *b*) a school or college specializing in some field —**in'sti·tut'er** or **in'sti·tu'tor** *n.*

in·sti·tu·tion (in'stə to͞o'shən, -tyo͞o'-) *n.* **1** an instituting or being instituted **2** an established law, custom, etc. **3** *a*) an organization having a social, educational, or religious purpose *b*) the building housing it **4** a person or thing long established in a place —**in'sti·tu'tional** *adj.*

in·sti·tu·tion·al·ize (-īz') *vt.* -**ized'**, -**iz'ing 1** to make into an institution **2** to place in an institution, as for treatment —**in'sti·tu'tion·al·i·za'tion** *n.*

in·struct (in strukt') *vt.* ‖ < L *in-*, in + *struere*, pile up ‖ **1** to teach; educate **2** to inform **3** to order or direct

in·struc·tion (-struk'shən) *n.* **1** an instructing; education **2** something taught **3** [*pl.*] orders or directions

in·struc·tive *adj.* giving knowledge

in·struc·tor *n.* **1** a teacher **2** a college teacher of the lowest rank

in·stru·ment (in'strə mənt) *n.* ‖ see INSTRUCT ‖ **1** a thing by means of which something is done **2** a tool or implement **3** any of various devices for indicating, measuring, controlling, etc. **4** any of various devices producing musical sound **5** *Law* a formal document

in·stru·men·tal (-mənt″l) *adj.* **1** serving as a means; helpful **2** of, performed on, or written for a musical instrument or instruments

in·stru·men·tal·ist *n.* a person who performs on a musical instrument

in·stru·men·tal·ity (-men'tal'ə tē) *n.*, *pl.* -**ties** a means; agency

in·stru·men·ta·tion (-tā'shən) *n.* **1** the writing or scoring of music for instruments **2** the use of or equipment with instruments

instrument flying the flying of an aircraft by instruments only

in·sub·or·di·nate (in'sə bôrd″n it) *adj.* not submitting to authority; disobedient —**in'sub·or'di·na'tion** *n.*

in·sub·stan·tial (in'səb stan'shəl) *adj.* not substantial; specif., *a*) not real; imaginary *b*) weak or flimsy

in·suf·fer·able (in suf'ər ə bəl) *adj.* not sufferable; intolerable; unbearable —**in·suf'fer·ably** *adv.*

in·su·lar (in'sə lər, -so͞o-, -syo͞o-) *adj.* ‖ < L *insula*, island ‖ **1** of or like an island or islanders **2** narrow-minded; illiberal

in·su·late (-lāt') *vt.* -**lat'ed**, -**lat'ing** ‖ < L *insula*, island ‖ **1** to set apart; isolate **2** to cover with a nonconducting material in order to prevent the escape of electricity, heat, sound, etc. —**in'su·la'tor** *n.*

in·su·la·tion *n.* **1** an insulating or being insulated **2** material for this

in·su·lin (in'sə lin; -soo-, -syoo-) *n.* ‖ < L *insula*, island ‖ **1** a hormone vital to carbohydrate metabolism, secreted by islets of tissue in the pancreas **2** an extract from the pancreas of sheep, oxen, etc., used in the treatment of diabetes

insulin shock the abnormal condition caused by an excess of insulin: it is characterized by tremors, cold sweat, convulsions, and coma

in·sult (in sult'; *for n.* in'sult') *vt.* ‖ < L *in-*, on + *salire*, to leap ‖ to subject to an act, remark, etc. meant to hurt the feelings or pride — *n.* an insulting act, remark, etc.

in·su·per·able (in so͞o'pər ə bəl) *adj.* ‖ < L *insuperabilis* ‖ that cannot be overcome

in·sup·port·able (in'sə pôrt'ə bəl) *adj.* not supportable; incapable of being borne, upheld, proved, etc.

in·sur·ance (in shoor'əns) *n.* **1** an insuring or being insured **2** a contract (**insurance policy**) purchased to guarantee compensation for a specified loss by fire, death, etc. **3** the amount for which something is insured **4** the business of insuring against loss

in·sure (in shoor') *vt.* -**sured'**, -**sur'ing** ‖ ME *ensuren*: see ENSURE ‖ **1** to take out or issue insurance on **2** ENSURE —**in·sur'able** *adj.*

in·sured' *n.* a person whose life, property, etc. is insured against loss

in·sur'er *n.* a person or company that insures others against loss

in·sur·gent (in sur'jənt) *adj.* ‖ < L *in-*, upon + *surgere*, rise ‖ rising up against established authority — *n.* an insurgent person —**in·sur'gence** *n.*

in·sur·rec·tion (in'sə rek'shən) *n.* ‖ see INSURGENT ‖ a rising up against established authority; rebellion —**in'sur·rec'tion·ist** *n.*

int. 1 interest **2** international

in·tact (in takt') *adj.* ‖ < L *in-*, not + *tactus*, touched ‖ unimpaired or uninjured; kept or left whole

in·ta·glio (in tal'yō') *n.*, *pl.* -**glios'** ‖ It < *in-*, in + *tagliare*, to cut ‖ a design carved or engraved below the surface

in·take (in'tāk') *n.* **1** a taking in **2** amount taken in **3** the place in a pipe, etc. where a fluid is taken in

in·tan·gi·ble (in tan'jə bəl) *adj.* **1** that cannot be touched; incorporeal **2** representing value, but either without intrinsic value or without material being [goodwill is an

---

THESAURUS

instinct *n.* drive, sense, intuition; see FEELING 4.
instinctive *a.* spontaneous, accustomed, normal; see NATURAL 2.
instinctively *a.* inherently, intuitively, by instinct; see NATURALLY 2.
institute *v.* found, organize, launch; see ESTABLISH 2.
institution *n.* system, company, association; see BUSINESS 4, OFFICE 3, UNIVERSITY.
institutionalize *v.* standardize, incorporate into a system, make official; see ORDER 3, REGULATE 2, SYSTEMATIZE.
instruct *v.* educate, give lessons, guide; see TEACH.
instructed *a.* told, advised, informed; see EDUCATED, LEARNED 1.
instruction *n.* guidance, preparation, direction; see EDUCATION 1.
instructions *n.* orders, plans, directive; see ADVICE, DIRECTIONS.
instructor *n.* professor, tutor, lecturer; see TEACHER.
instrument *n.* means, apparatus, implement; see DEVICE 1, MACHINE, TOOL 1.
instrumental *a.* partly responsible for, contributory, conducive; see EFFECTIVE, HELPFUL 1, NECESSARY.
insubordinate *a.* disobedient, dissident, defiant; see REBELLIOUS.
insubordination *n.* disobedience,

defiance, disregard; see DISOBEDIENCE.
insubstantial *a.* petty, slight, inadequate; see FLIMSY, POOR 2.
insufficient *a.* skimpy, meager, thin; see INADEQUATE, UNSATISFACTORY.
insufficiently *a.* barely, incompletely, partly; see BADLY 1, INADEQUATELY.
insulate *v.* protect, coat, treat, apply insulation, tape up, glass in, pad, caulk, weatherstrip, paint.
insulation *n.* nonconductor, protector, covering, packing, lining, resistant material, weatherstripping, padding, caulking.
insult *n.* indignity, offense, affront, abuse, outrage, impudence, insolence, blasphemy, mockery, derision, impertinence, discourtesy, invective, disrespect, slight, slander, libel, slap in the face, black eye*; see also RUDENESS.—*Ant.* PRAISE, tribute, homage.
insult *v.* revile, libel, offend, outrage, vilify, humiliate, mock, vex, tease, irritate, annoy, aggravate, provoke, taunt, ridicule, abuse, deride, jeer, step on one's toes; see also CURSE, SLANDER.
insulted *a.* slandered, libeled, reviled, disgraced, defamed, vilified, cursed, dishonored, mocked, ridiculed, jeered at, humiliated, mistreated, offended, hurt, outraged,

affronted, slighted, shamed; see also HURT.—*Ant.* PRAISED, admired, extolled.
insulting *a.* outrageous, offensive, degrading, humiliating, debasing, embarrassing, humbling, deriding, contemptuous.—*Ant.* RESPECTFUL, complimentary, honoring.
insurance *n.* indemnity, assurance, warrant, backing, allowance, safeguard, protection, coverage, support, something to fall back on*; see also SECURITY 2.
insure *v.* warrant, protect, cover; see GUARANTEE.
insured *a.* safeguarded, defended, warranteed; see GUARANTEED, PROTECTED.
insurmountable *a.* unconquerable, unbeatable, hopeless; see IMPOSSIBLE.
insurrection *n.* riot, revolt, rebellion; see DISORDER, REVOLUTION 2.
intact *a.* together, entire, uninjured; see WHOLE 2.
intake *n.* **1** [Contraction] alteration, shortening, constriction; see ABBREVIATION, REDUCTION 1. **2** [Profit] harvest, gain, accumulation; see PROFIT 2.
intangible *a.* indefinite, unsure, hypothetical; see UNCERTAIN, VAGUE 2.

intangible asset/ **3** that cannot be easily defined; vague — **n.** something intangible

in·te·ger (in'tə jər) **n.** ⟦ L, whole ⟧ a whole number (e.g., 5, -10) or zero

in·te·gral (in'tə grəl; *often* in teg'rəl) **adj.** ⟦see prec.⟧ **1** necessary for completeness; essential **2** whole or complete **3** made up of parts forming a whole

in·te·grate (-grāt') **vt., vi.** **-grat'ed, -grat'ing** ⟦ < L *integer*, whole ⟧ **1** to make or become whole or complete **2** to bring (parts) together into a whole **3** *a)* to remove barriers imposing segregation upon (racial groups) *b)* to abolish segregation in —**in'te·gra'tion n.** —**in'te·gra'tive adj.**

integrated circuit an electronic circuit with many interconnected circuit elements formed on a single body, or chip, of semiconductor material

in·teg·ri·ty (in teg'rə tē) **n.** ⟦see INTEGER⟧ **1** completeness; wholeness **2** unimpaired condition; soundness **3** honesty, sincerity, etc.

in·teg·u·ment (in teg'yōo mənt) **n.** ⟦ < L *in-*, upon + *tegere*, to cover ⟧ an outer covering; skin, shell, etc.

in·tel·lect (in'tə lekt', int''l ekt') **n.** ⟦ < L *inter-*, between + *legere*, choose ⟧ **1** the ability to reason or understand **2** high intelligence **3** a very intelligent person

in·tel·lec·tual (in'tə lek'chōo əl, int''l ek'-) **adj.** **1** of, involving, or appealing to the intellect **2** requiring intelligence **3** showing high intelligence — **n.** one with intellectual interests or tastes —**in'tel·lec'tu·al·ly adv.**

in·tel·lec·tu·al·ize (-īz') **vt.** **-ized', -iz'ing** to examine or interpret rationally, often without proper regard for emotional considerations

intellectual property something produced by the mind, the rights to which may be protected by a copyright, patent, etc.

in·tel·li·gence (in tel'ə jəns) **n.** ⟦see INTELLECT⟧ **1** *a)* the ability to learn or understand *b)* the ability to cope with a new situation **2** news or information **3** those engaged in gathering secret, esp. military, information

intelligence quotient a number intended to indicate a person's level of intelligence, based on a test

in·tel·li·gent (-jənt) **adj.** having or showing intelligence; clever, wise, etc. —**in·tel'li·gent·ly adv.**

in·tel·li·gent'si·a (-jənt'sē ə) **n.pl.** ⟦ < Russ ⟧ [*also with sing. v.*] intellectuals collectively

in·tel·li·gi·ble (in tel'i jə bəl) **adj.** that can be understood; clear —**in·tel'li·gi·bil'i·ty n.** —**in·tel'li·gi·bly adv.**

in·tem·per·ate (in tem'pər it) **adj.** **1** not temperate or moderate; excessive **2** drinking too much alcoholic liquor —**in·tem'per·ance n.**

in·tend (in tend') **vt.** ⟦ < L *in-*, at + *tendere*, to stretch ⟧ **1** to plan; purpose **2** to mean (something) to be or be used (*for*) **3** to mean; signify

in·tend'ed n. [Colloq.] one's future spouse; fiancé(e)

in·tense (in tens') **adj.** ⟦see INTEND⟧ **1** very strong /an *intense* light/ **2** strained to the utmost; strenuous /intense thought/ **3** characterized by much action, strong emotion, etc. —**in·tense'ly adv.**

in·ten·si·fy (in ten'sə fī') **vt., vi.** **-fied', -fy'ing** to make or become more intense —**in·ten'si·fi·ca'tion n.**

in·ten·si·ty n., pl. **-ties 1** a being intense **2** great energy or vehemence, as of emotion **3** the amount of force or energy of heat, light, sound, etc.

in·ten·sive adj. **1** of or characterized by intensity; thorough **2** designating very attentive care given to patients right after surgery, etc. **3** *Gram.* giving force or emphasis /"very" is an *intensive* adverb/ — **n.** *Gram.* an intensive word, prefix, etc. —**in·ten'sive·ly adv.** —**in·ten'sive·ness n.**

-intensive (in ten'siv) *combining form* intensively using or requiring large amounts of (a specified thing) /energy-*intensive*/

in·tent (in tent') **adj.** ⟦see INTEND⟧ **1** firmly directed; earnest **2** having one's attention or purpose firmly fixed /intent on going/ — **n.** **1** an intending **2** something intended; purpose or meaning —**to all intents and purposes** in almost every respect; practically; virtually —**in·tent'ly adv.** —**in·tent'ness n.**

in·ten·tion (in ten'shən) **n.** **1** a determination to act in a specified way **2** anything intended; purpose

in·ten'tion·al adj. done purposely —**in·ten'tion·al·ly adv.**

in·ter (in tur') **vt.** **-terred', -ter'ring** ⟦ < L *in*, in + *terra*, earth ⟧ to put (a dead body) into a grave or tomb

inter- ⟦ L ⟧ *prefix* **1** between or among: the second element of the compound is singular in form /interstate/ **2** with or on each other (or one another) /interact/

inter·act (in'tər akt') **vi.** to act on one another —**in'ter·ac'tion n.**

in'ter·ac'tive (-ak'tiv) **adj.** **1** acting on one another **2** designating or of programming or electronic equipment, as for TV, which allows viewers to participate, as by making a response **3** of or involving exchange of information between the computer and the user at a video screen

inter·breed (in'tər brēd', in'tər brēd') **vt., vi.** **-bred', -breed'ing** HYBRIDIZE

in'ter·cede' (-sēd') **vi.** **-ced'ed, -ced'ing** ⟦ < L *inter-*, between + *cedere*, go ⟧ **1** to plead in behalf of another **2** to mediate

in'ter·cept' (-sept') **vt.** ⟦ < L *inter-*, between + *capere*, take ⟧ **1** to seize or stop in its course /to *intercept* a mes-

THESAURUS

integrate *v.* unify, combine, desegregate; see MIX 1, UNITE.

integrated *a.* nonsegregated, not segregated, for both black and white, interracial, nonracial, for all races, nonsectarian, without restriction as to race, creed or color, combined; see also FREE 1, 2, OPEN 3.

integration *n.* unification, combination, cooperation; see ALLIANCE 1, MIXTURE 1, UNION 1.

integrity *n.* uprightness, honor, probity; see HONESTY.

intellect *n.* intelligence, brain, mentality; see MIND 1.

intellectual *a.* mental, inventive, creative; see INTELLIGENT, LEARNED 1.

intellectual *n.* genius, philosopher, academician, highbrow, member of the intelligentsia, egghead*, brain*, Einstein*; see also ARTIST, PHILOSOPHER, SCIENTIST, WRITER.

intelligence *n.* **1** [Understanding] perspicacity, discernment, comprehension; see JUDGMENT 1. **2** [Secret information] report, statistics, facts, inside information, account, info*, the dope*; see also KNOWLEDGE 1, NEWS 1, SECRET. **3** [The mind] intellect, brain, mentality; see MIND 1.

intelligent *a.* clever, bright, exceptional, astute, smart, brilliant, perceptive, well-informed, resourceful, profound, penetrating, original, keen, imaginative, inventive, reasonable, capable, able, ingenious, knowledge-able, creative, responsible, understanding, alert, quick-witted, clear-headed, quick, sharp, witty, ready, calculating, comprehending, discerning, discriminating, knowing, intellectual, studious, contemplative, having a head on one's shoulders, talented, apt, wise, shrewd, smart as a whip*, on the ball*, on the beam*, not born yesterday*.—*Ant.* DULL, slow-minded, shallow.

intelligently *a.* skillfully, admirably, reasonably, logically, judiciously, capably, diligently, sharply, astutely, discerningly, knowingly, knowledgeably, farsightedly, sensibly, prudently, alertly, keenly, resourcefully, aptly, discriminatingly; see also EFFECTIVELY.—*Ant.* BADLY, foolishly, stupidly.

intelligible *a.* plain, clear, obvious; see UNDERSTANDABLE.

intend *v.* **1** [To propose] plan, purpose, aim, expect, be resolved, be determined to, aspire to, have in mind, hope to, contemplate, think, aim at, take into one's head. **2** [To destine for] design, mean, devote to, reserve, appoint, set apart, aim at, aim for; see also ASSIGN, DEDICATE. **3** [To mean] indicate, signify, denote; see MEAN 1.

intended *a.* designed, advised, expected, predetermined, calculated, prearranged, predestined, meant; see also PLANNED, PROPOSED.

intense *a.* intensified, deep, profound, extraordinary, exceptional, heightened, marked, vivid, ardent, powerful, passionate, impassioned, diligent, hard, full, great, exaggerated, violent, excessive, acute, keen, piercing, cutting, bitter, severe, concentrated, intensive, forceful, sharp, biting, stinging, shrill, high-pitched, strenuous, fervent, earnest, zealous, vehement, harsh, strong, brilliant.

intensely *a.* deeply, profoundly, strongly; see VERY.

intensify *v.* heighten, sharpen, emphasize; see STRENGTHEN, INCREASE.

intensity *n.* strain, force, concentration, power, vehemence, passion, fervor, ardor, severity, acuteness, depth, deepness, forcefulness, high pitch, sharpness, emphasis, magnitude.

intensive *a.* accelerated, speeded up, hard; see FAST 1, SEVERE 1, 2.

intention *n.* aim, end, plan; see PURPOSE 1.

intentional *a.* intended, meditated, prearranged; see DELIBERATE.

intentionally *a.* specifically, with malice aforethought, in cold blood; see DELIBERATELY.

intently *a.* hard, with concentration, keenly; see CLOSELY.

intercept *v.* cut off, stop, ambush, block, catch, take away, appropriate, hijack*, head off; see also PREVENT.

sage*] 2 *Math.* to cut off or mark off between two points, lines, etc. —**in′ter·cep′tion** *n.* —**in′ter·cep′tor** *n.*

in′ter·ces′sion (-sesh′ən) *n.* mediation or prayer in behalf of another —**in′ter·ces′sor** (-ses′ər) *n.*

inter·change (in′tər chānj′; *for n.* in′tər chānj′) *vt.* **-changed′, -chang′ing 1** to give and take mutually; exchange **2** to put (each of two things) in the other's place **3** to alternate — *n.* **1** an interchanging **2** a junction which allows movement on traffic between highways on different levels, as a cloverleaf —**in′ter·change′able** *adj.*

in′ter·col·le′gi·ate *adj.* between or among colleges and universities

inter·com (in′tər käm′) *n.* a radio or telephone intercommunication system, as between rooms

in′ter·com·mu′ni·cate′ *vt., vi.* **-cat′ed, -cat′ing** to communicate with or to each other or one another —**in′ter·com·mu′ni·ca′tion** *n.*

in′ter·con·nect′ (′-kə nekt′) *vt., vi.* to connect or be connected with one another —**in′ter·con·nec′tion** *n.*

in′ter·con′ti·nen′tal *adj.* **1** between or among continents **2** able to travel from one continent to another, as a missile, etc.

inter·course (in′tər kôrs′) *n.* 〚see INTER- & COURSE〛 **1** communication or dealings between or among people, countries, etc. **2** SEXUAL INTERCOURSE

in′ter·denom′i·na′tional *adj.* between or among religious denominations

in′ter·depend′ence *n.* mutual dependence —**in′ter·depend′ent** *adj.*

in·ter·dict (in′tər dikt′; *for n.* in′tər dikt′) *vt.* 〚< L *inter*-, between + *dicere*, say〛 **1** to prohibit (an action) **2** to restrain from doing or using something — *n.* an official prohibition —**in′ter·dic′tion** *n.*

in′ter·dis′ci·pli·nar′y *adj.* involving two or more disciplines, or branches of learning

in·ter·est (in′trist, -trəst, -tər ist) *n.* 〚< L *inter*-, between + *esse*, be〛 **1** a right to, or a share in, something **2** anything in which one has a share **3** [*often pl.*] advantage; benefit **4** [*usually pl.*] those having a common concern or power in some industry, cause, etc. *[the steel interests]* **5** *a)* a feeling of concern, curiosity, etc. about something *b)* the power of causing this feeling *c)* something causing this feeling **6** *a)* money paid for the use of money *b)* the rate of such payment — *vt.* **1** to involve or excite the interest or attention of **2** to cause to have an interest, or share, in —**in the interest(s) of** for the sake of

in′ter·ested *adj.* **1** having an interest or share **2** influenced by personal interest; biased **3** feeling or showing interest

in′ter·est·ing *adj.* exciting curiosity or attention

inter·face (in′tər fās′) *n.* **1** a plane forming the common boundary between two parts of matter or space **2** a point or means of interaction between two systems, groups, etc. — *vt., vi.* **-faced′, -fac′ing** to interact with (another system, group, etc.)

in·ter·fere (in′tər fir′) *vt.* **-fered′, -fer′ing** 〚ult. < L *inter*-, between + *ferire*, to strike〛 **1** to clash; collide **2** *a)* to come between; intervene *b)* to meddle **3** *Sports* to hinder an opposing player in any of various illegal ways **4** *Radio, TV* to create static, unwanted signals, etc., resulting in distorted reception —**interfere with** to hinder -- —**in′ter·fer′ence** *n.*

in·ter·feron (in′tər fir′än′) *n.* 〚INTERFER(E) + *-on*, arbitrary suffix〛 a cellular protein produced in response to infection by a virus and acting to inhibit viral growth

inter·file (in′tər fīl′) *vt.* to place (papers, etc.) in order in a file, set, etc., esp., to combine such sets

in·terim (in′tər im) *n.* 〚< L *inter*, between〛 the period of time between; meantime — *adj.* temporary

in·teri·or (in tir′ē ər) *adj.* 〚< L *inter*, between〛 **1** situated within; inner **2** inland **3** private — *n.* **1** the interior part, as of a room, country, etc. **2** the internal, or domestic, affairs of a country

interior decoration the art or business of decorating and furnishing the interiors of houses, offices, etc. — **interior decorator**

in·te′ri·or·ize′ (-īz′) *vt.* **-ized′, -iz′ing** to make (a concept, value, etc.) part of one's inner nature

interj. interjection

in·ter·ject (in′tər jekt′) *vt.* 〚< L *inter*-, between + *jacere*, to throw〛 to throw in between; interrupt with

in′ter·jec′tion (-jek′shən) *n.* **1** an interjecting **2** something interjected **3** *Gram.* an exclamation

in′ter·lace′ *vt., vi.* **-laced′, -lac′ing** to lace or weave together

in′ter·lard′ (-lärd′) *vt.* 〚see INTER- & LARD〛 to intersperse; diversify *[to interlard a talk with quotations]*

inter·leu·kin (in′tər lōō′kin) *n.* any of several proteins derived from many cell types and having an effect on the activity of other cells, as stimulating the growth of T cells, etc.

in′ter·line′[1] *vt.* **-lined′, -lin′ing** to write (something) between the lines of (a text, etc.) —**in′ter·lin′ear** *adj.*

in′ter·line′[2] *vt.* **-lined′, -lin′ing** to put an inner lining under the ordinary lining of (a garment)

in′ter·lock′ *vt., vi.* to lock together; join with one another

inter·locu·tory (in′tər läk′yōō tôr′ē, -yə-) *adj. Law* not final, as a decree

inter·loper (in′tər lō′pər) *n.* 〚INTER- + *-loper* < Du *lopen*, to run〛 one who meddles

inter·lude (in′tər lōōd′) *n.* 〚< L *inter*, between + *ludus*, play〛 anything that fills time between two events, as music between acts of a play

in′ter·mar′ry *vi.* **-ried, -ry·ing 1** to become connected by marriage: said of different clans, races, etc. **2** to marry: said of closely related persons —**in′ter·mar′riage** *n.*

in′ter·me′di·ar′y (-mē′dē er′ē) *adj.* **1** acting as a go-between or mediator **2** intermediate — *n., pl.* **-ar′ies** a go-between; mediator

in′ter·me′di·ate (-mē′dē it) *adj.* 〚< L *inter*-, between + *medius*, middle〛 **1** in the middle; in between **2** of an automobile larger than a compact but smaller than the standard size — *n.* an intermediate automobile

in·ter·ment (in tur′mənt) *n.* the act of interring; burial

in·ter·mezzo (in′tər met′sō′) *n., pl.* **-zos′** or **-zi′** (-sē′) 〚It < L: see INTERMEDIATE〛 a short piece of music, as between parts of a composition

THESAURUS

interception *n.* blocking, interfering with, interposing; see INTERFERENCE 1.

interchange *n.* **1** [The act of giving and receiving reciprocally] barter, trade, reciprocation; see EXCHANGE 1. **2** [A highway intersection] cloverleaf, intersection, off-ramp; see HIGHWAY, ROAD 1.

intercourse *n.* **1** [Communication] association, dealings, interchange; see COMMUNICATION. **2** [Sex act] coitus, coition, sexual relations; see COPULATION, SEX 4.

interest *n.* **1** [Concern] attention, curiosity, excitement; see ATTENTION. **2** [Advantage] profit, benefit, gain; see ADVANTAGE. **3** [Premium] credit, gain, earnings; see ADDITION 1, PROFIT 2. —**in the interest(s) of** for the sake of, on behalf of, in order to promote; see FOR.

interest *v.* intrigue, amuse, please; see ENTERTAIN 1, FASCINATE.

interested *a.* **1** [Having one's interest aroused] stimulated, attentive, curious, drawn, touched, moved, affected, inspired, sympathetic to, responsive, struck, impressed, roused, awakened, stirred, open to suggestion, all for, all wrapped up in.—*Ant.* BORED, tired, annoyed. **2** [Concerned with or engaged in] occupied, engrossed, partial, prejudiced, biased, taken, obsessed with, absorbed in; see also INVOLVED.—*Ant.* INDIFFERENT, impartial, disinterested.

interesting *a.* pleasing, pleasurable, fine, satisfying, fascinating, arresting, engaging, readable, absorbing, stirring, affecting, exotic, unusual, lovely, gracious, impressive, attractive, captivating, enchanting, beautiful, inviting, winning, magnetic, delightful, amusing, genial, refreshing; see also EXCITING.—*Ant.* DULL, shallow, boring.

interfere *v.* intervene, interpose, interlope; see MEDDLE 1.

interference *n.* **1** [Taking forcible part in the affairs of others] meddling, interruption, prying, trespassing, tampering, barging in, back-seat driving; see also INTERRUPTION. **2** [That which obstructs] obstruction, check, obstacle; see BARRIER, RESTRAINT 2.

interior *a.* inner, internal, inward; see CENTRAL, INSIDE 2.

interior *n.* **1** [Inside] inner part, lining, heart; see CENTER 1, INSIDE. **2** [The inside of a building] rooms, halls, stairway, vestibule, lobby, chapel, choir, gallery, basement.

interjection *n.* **1** [Insertion] interpolation, insinuation, inclusion; see ADDITION 1. **2** [Exclamation] utterance, ejaculation, exclamation; see CRY 1.

intermediate *a.* mean, between, medium, half-way, compromising, intermediary, neutral, standard, median, moderate, average; see also CENTRAL, COMMON 1, MIDDLE.

in·ter·mi·na·ble (in tʉr′mi nə bəl) *adj.* lasting, or seeming to last, forever; endless —**in·ter′mi·na·bly** *adv.*

in·ter·min′gle *vt., vi.* **-gled, -gling** to mix together; mingle

in·ter·mis′sion (in′tər mish′ən) *n.* ⟦< L *inter-*, between + *mittere*, send⟧ an interval of time between periods of activity, as between acts of a play

in′ter·mit′tent (-mit′′nt) *adj.* ⟦see prec.⟧ stopping and starting again at intervals; periodic —**in′ter·mit′tently** *adv.*

in·tern (*for n. & vi.* in′tʉrn; *for vt.* in tʉrn′, in′tʉrn) *n.* ⟦< L *internus*, inward⟧ **1** a doctor serving as assistant resident in a hospital generally just after graduation from medical school **2** an apprentice teacher, journalist, etc. — *vi.* to serve as an intern — *vt.* to detain or confine (foreign persons, etc.), as during a war —**in·tern′ment** *n.* —**in′tern′ship** *n.*

in·ter′nal (in tʉr′nəl, -tʉrn′′l) *adj.* ⟦< L *internus*⟧ **1** of or on the inside; inner **2** to be taken inside the body [*internal* remedies] **3** intrinsic [*internal* evidence] **4** domestic [*internal* revenue] —**in·ter′nal·ly** *adv.*

inter·nal-combus′tion engine an engine, as in an automobile, powered by the explosion of a fuel-and-air mixture within the cylinders

in·ter′nal·ize′ (-īz′) *vt.* **-ized′, -iz′ing** to make (others′ ideas, etc.) a part of one′s own way of thinking

internal medicine the branch of medicine that deals with the diagnosis and nonsurgical treatment of diseases

internal revenue governmental income from taxes on income, profits, etc.

inter·na·tional (in′tər nash′ə nəl) *adj.* **1** between or among nations **2** concerned with the relations between nations **3** for the use of all nations **4** of or for people in various nations —**in′ter·na′tion·al·ize′, -ized′, -iz′ing,** *vt.* —**in′ter·na′tion·al·ly** *adv.*

International Phonetic Alphabet a set of phonetic symbols for international use: each symbol represents a single sound, whether the sound occurs in only one language or in more than one

inter·ne′cine (in′tər nē′sin) *adj.* ⟦< L *inter-*, between + *necare*, kill⟧ deadly or harmful to both sides

in·tern·ist (in′tʉrn·ist, in tʉrn′ist) *n.* a doctor who specializes in the nonsurgical treatment of diseases

inter·office (in′tər ôf′is) *adj.* between the offices of an organization

in′ter·per′sonal (-pʉr′sən əl) *adj.* between persons

in′ter·plan′etar′y *adj.* between planets

in′ter·play′ *n.* action, effect, or influence on each other

in·ter·po·late (in tʉr′pə lāt′) *vt.* **-lat′ed, -lat′ing** ⟦< L *inter-*, among + *polire*, to polish⟧ **1** to change (a text, etc.) by inserting new material **2** to insert between or among others —**in·ter·po·la′tion** *n.*

in·ter·pose (in′tər pōz′) *vt., vi.* **-posed′, -pos′ing** **1** to place or come between **2** to intervene (with) **3** to interrupt (with) —**in′ter·po·si′tion** (-pə zish′ən) *n.*

in·ter·pret (in tʉr′prət) *vt.* ⟦< L *interpres*, agent, broker⟧ **1** to explain or translate **2** to construe [to *interpret* a silence as contempt] **3** to give one′s own conception of, as a role in a play — *vi.* to explain or translate —**in·ter′pre·ta′tion** *n.* —**in·ter′preter** *n.*

in·ter′pre·tive (-prə tiv) *adj.* that interprets; explanatory Also **in·ter′pre·ta′tive** (-tāt′iv)

inter·ra·cial (in′tər rā′shəl) *adj.* between, among, or for members of different races Also **in′ter·race′**

inter·reg′num (in′tər reg′nəm) *n., pl.* **-nums** or **-na** (-nə) ⟦< L *inter-*, between + *regnum*, a reign⟧ **1** an interval between two successive reigns, when the country has no sovereign **2** any break in a series

in′ter·re·late′ (-ri lāt′) *vt., vi.* **-lat′ed, -lat′ing** to make or be mutually related —**in′ter·re·lat′ed** *adj.*

in·ter·ro·gate (in ter′ə gāt′) *vt., vi.* **-gat′ed, -gat′ing** ⟦< L *inter-*, between + *rogare*, ask⟧ to ask questions, esp. formally —**in·ter′ro·ga′tion** *n.* —**in·ter′ro·ga′tor** *n.*

in·ter·rog·a·tive (in′tə räg′ə tiv) *adj.* asking a question Also **in′ter·rog′a·to′ry** (-ə tôr′ē)

in·ter·rupt (in′tə rupt′, -tər rupt′) *vt.* ⟦< L *inter-*, between + *rumpere*, to break⟧ **1** to break into (a discussion, etc.) or to break in upon (a speaker, worker, etc.) **2** to make a break in the continuity of — *vi.* to interrupt an action, talk, etc. —**in′ter·rup′tion** *n.*

inter·scho·las·tic (in′tər skə las′tik) *adj.* between or among schools

inter·sect (in′tər sekt′) *vt.* ⟦< L *inter-*, between + *secare*, to cut⟧ to divide into two parts by passing through — *vi.* to cross each other

in′ter·sec′tion (-sek′shən) *n.* **1** an intersecting **2** the place where two lines, roads, etc. meet or cross

in′ter·serv′ice *adj.* between or among branches of the armed forces

in′ter·ses′sion *n.* a short session between regular college sessions, for concentration on specialized projects

in·ter·sperse (in′tər spʉrs′) *vt.* **-spersed′, -spers′ing** ⟦< L *inter-*, among + *spargere*, scatter⟧ **1** to put here and there; scatter **2** to vary with things scattered here and there

in′ter·state′ *adj.* between or among states, esp. of the U.S.

in′ter·stel′lar *adj.* between or among the stars

in·ter·stice (in tʉr′stis) *n., pl.* **-sti·ces** (-stə siz′, -sēz′) ⟦< L *inter-*, between + *sistere*, to set⟧ a crack; crevice

in′ter·twine′ *vt., vi.* **-twined′, -twin′ing** to twine together

in′ter·ur′ban (-ʉr′bən) *adj.* between cities or towns

in·ter·val (in′tər val) *n.* ⟦< L *inter-*, between + *vallum*, wall⟧ **1** a space between things; gap **2** the time between events **3** the difference in pitch between two tones —**at intervals 1** once in a while **2** here and there

in·ter·vene (in′tər vēn′) *vi.* **-vened′, -ven′ing** ⟦< L *inter-*, between + *venire*, come⟧ **1** to come or be between **2** to occur between two events, etc. **3** to come between to modify, settle, or hinder some action, etc.

in′ter·ven′tion (-ven′shən) *n.* **1** an intervening **2** interference, esp. of one state in the affairs of another

---

THESAURUS

intermission *n.* interim, wait, respite; see PAUSE, RECESS 1.

intermittent *a.* periodic, coming and going, recurrent; see CHANGING, IRREGULAR 1.

internal *a.* **1** [Within] inside, inward, interior, private, intrinsic, innate, inherent, under the surface, intimate, subjective, enclosed, circumscribed; see also INNER.—*Ant.* OUTER, external, outward. **2** [Within the body] intestinal, physiological, physical, neurological, abdominal, visceral.—*Ant.* FOREIGN, alien, external.

internally *a.* within the body, beneath the surface, inwardly, deep down, spiritually, mentally, invisibly, by injection, out of sight; see also INSIDE 1, WITHIN.

international *a.* world-wide, worldly, world, intercontinental, between nations, all over the world, universal, all-embracing, foreign, cosmopolitan; see also UNIVERSAL 3.—*Ant.* DOMESTIC, national, internal.

internationally *a.* interculturally, interracially, cooperatively, globally,

universally, concerning the intercourse of nations, not provincial; see also ABROAD, EVERYWHERE.

interpret *v.* give one′s impression of, render, play, perform, depict, delineate, enact, portray, make sense of, read into, improvise on, re-enact, mimic, gather from, view as, give one an idea about, make something of*; see also DEFINE, DESCRIBE.

interpretation *n.* account, rendition, exposition, statement, diagnosis, description, representation, definition, presentation, argument, answer, solution; see also EXPLANATION.

interpreter *n.* commentator, writer, artist, editor, reviewer, biographer, analyst, scholar, spokesman, delegate, speaker, exponent, demonstrator, philosopher, professor, translator, linguist, language expert.

interrogate *v.* cross-examine, ask, give the third degree; see EXAMINE, QUESTION.

interrogation *n.* inquiry, query, investigation; see EXAMINATION 1.

interrupt *v.* intrude, intervene, cut

in on, break into, interfere, infringe, cut off, break someone′s train of thought, come between, butt in*, burst in, crash*.

interrupted *a.* stopped, checked, held up, obstructed, delayed, interfered with, disordered, hindered, suspended, cut short.

interruption *n.* check, break, gap, hiatus, suspension, intrusion, obstruction; see also DELAY, INTERFERENCE 1.

intersect *v.* cut across, break in two, intercross; see DIVIDE.

interstate *a.* internal, interior, domestic; see LOCAL 1.

interval *n.* period, interlude, interim; see PAUSE.

intervene *v.* step in, intercede, mediate; see NEGOTIATE 1, RECONCILE 2.

intervention *n.* **1** [The act of intervening] intercession, interruption, breaking in; see INTERFERENCE 1, INTRUSION. **2** [Armed interference] invasion, military occupation, armed aggression; see ATTACK.

in'ter·view' (-vyōō') *n.* **1** a meeting of people face to face to confer **2** *a)* a meeting in which a person is asked about personal views, etc., as by a reporter *b)* a published, taped, or filmed account of this — *vt.* to have an interview with —**in'ter·viewee'** *n.* —**in'ter·view'er** *n.*
in'ter·weave' *vt., vi.* **-wove', -wo'ven, -weav'ing 1** to weave together **2** to connect closely
in·tes·tacy (in tes'tə sē) *n.* the fact or state of dying intestate
in·tes·tate (in tes'tāt', -tit) *adj.* [< L *in-*, not + *testari*, make a will] having made no will
in·tes·tine (in tes'tən) *n.* [< L *intus*, within] [*usually pl.*] the lower part of the alimentary canal, extending from the stomach to the anus and consisting of a long, winding upper part (*small intestine*) and a shorter, thicker lower part (*large intestine*); bowels —**in·tes'ti·nal** *adj.*
in·ti·mate (in'tə mət; *for v.*, -māt') *adj.* [< L *intus*, within] **1** most private or personal **2** very close or familiar **3** deep and thorough — *n.* an intimate friend — *vt.* **-mat'ed, -mat'ing** to hint or imply —**in'ti·macy** (-ma sē), *pl.* **-cies,** *n.* —**in'ti·mate·ly** *adv.* —**in'ti·ma'tion** *n.*
in·tim·i·date (in tim'ə dāt') *vt.* **-dat'ed, -dat'ing** [< L *in-*, in + *timidus*, afraid] to make afraid, as with threats —**in·tim'i·da'tion** *n.*
into (in'tōō, -too) *prep.* [OE] **1** toward and within [*into* a room] **2** continuing to the midst of [to talk *into* the night] **3** to the form, substance, or condition of [divided *into* parts] **4** so as to strike [to run *into* a wall] **5** [Colloq.] involved in [she's *into* jazz now]
in·tol·er·a·ble (in tãl'ər ə bəl) *adj.* unbearable; too severe, painful, etc. to be endured —**in·tol'er·a·bly** *adv.*
in·tol·er·ant (-ənt) *adj.* unwilling to tolerate others' beliefs, etc. —**intolerant of** not able or willing to tolerate —**in·tol'er·ance** *n.*
in·to·na·tion (in'tō nā'shən, -tə-) *n.* **1** an intoning **2** the manner of producing tones with regard to a given standard of pitch **3** variations in pitch within an utterance
in·tone (in tōn') *vt., vi.* **-toned', -ton'ing** to speak or recite in a singing tone; chant —**in·ton'er** *n.*
in toto (in tō'tō) [L] as a whole
in·tox·i·cate (in tãks'i kāt') *vt.* **-cat'ed, -cat'ing** [< L *in-*, in + *toxicum*, poison] **1** to make drunk **2** to excite greatly —**in·tox'i·cant** *n.* —**in·tox'i·ca'tion** *n.*
intra- [L, within] *prefix* within, inside
intra·city (in'trə sit'ē) *adj.* of or within a large municipality, often specif. the inner city
in·trac·ta·ble (in trak'tə bəl) *adj.* hard to manage; unruly or stubborn
intra·der·mal (in'trə dur'məl) *adj.* within the skin or between the layers of the skin

in'tra·mu'ral (-myoor'əl) *adj.* [INTRA- + MURAL] between or among members of the same school, college, etc. [*intramural* athletics]
in·tran·si·gent (in tran'sə jənt) *adj.* [< L *in-*, not + *transigere*, to settle] refusing to compromise —**in·tran'si·gence** *n.*
in·tran·si·tive (in tran'sə tiv) *adj.* not transitive; designating a verb that does not require a direct object —**in·tran'si·tive·ly** *adv.*
in·tra·uter·ine (contraceptive) device (in'trə yōōt'ər in) any of various devices, as a plastic loop, inserted in the uterus as a contraceptive
in'tra·ve'nous (-vē'nəs) *adj.* [INTRA- + VENOUS] directly into a vein —**in'tra·ve'nous·ly** *adv.*
in·trench (in trench') *vt., vi.* ENTRENCH
in·trep·id (in trep'id) *adj.* [< L *in-*, not + *trepidus*, alarmed] bold; fearless; brave —**in·tre·pid'i·ty** (-trə pid'ə tē) *n.* —**in·trep'id·ly** *adv.*
in·tri·cate (in'tri kit) *adj.* [< L *in-*, in + *tricae*, vexations] **1** hard to follow or understand because full of puzzling parts, details, etc. **2** full of elaborate detail —**in'tri·cacy** (-kə sē), *pl.* **-cies,** *n.* —**in'tri·cate·ly** *adv.*
in·trigue (in trēg'; *for n., also* in'trēg') *vi.* **-trigued', -trigu'ing** [see prec.] to plot secretly or underhandedly — *vt.* to excite the interest or curiosity of — *n.* **1** a secret or underhanded plotting **2** a secret or underhanded plot or scheme **3** a secret love affair —**in·trigu'er** *n.* —**in·trigu'ing·ly** *adv.*
in·trin·sic (in trin'sik) *adj.* [< L *intra-*, within + *secus*, following] belonging to the real nature of a thing; inherent —**in·trin'si·cal·ly** *adv.*
intro- [L] *prefix* into, within, inward
in·tro·duce (in'trə dōōs, -dyōōs') *vt.* **-duced', -duc'ing** [< L *intro-*, in + *ducere*, to lead] **1** to put in; insert **2** to bring in as a new feature **3** to bring into use or fashion **4** *a)* to make acquainted; present [*introduce* me to her] *b)* to give experience of [they *introduced* him to music] **5** to bring forward **6** to start; begin [to *introduce* a talk with a joke]
in'tro·duc'tion (-duk'shən) *n.* **1** an introducing or being introduced **2** the preliminary section of a book, speech, etc.; preface
in'tro·duc'tory (-duk'tə rē) *adj.* serving to introduce; preliminary
in·troit (in trō'it, in'troit') *n.* [< L *intro-*, in + *ire*, to go] **1** a psalm or hymn at the opening of a Christian worship service **2** [I-] *R.C.Ch.* the first variable part of the Mass
in·tro·spec·tion (in'trə spek'shən) *n.* [< L *intro-*, within

---

THESAURUS

interview *n.* meeting, audience, conference; see COMMUNICATION, CONVERSATION.
interview *v.* converse with, get someone's opinion, consult with, interrogate, hold an inquiry, give an oral examination to, get something for the record.
intestines *n.* entrails, bowels, viscera, vitals, digestive organs, guts*; see also INSIDES.
intimacy *n.* closeness, familiarity, confidence; see AFFECTION, FRIENDSHIP.
intimate *a.* close, near, trusted; see PRIVATE, SECRET 1, SPECIAL.
intimate *n.* associate, constant companion, close friend; see FRIEND, LOVER 1.
intimate *v.* suggest, imply, hint; see HINT.
intimately *a.* closely, personally, informally, familiarly, confidentially, without reserve, privately; see also LOVINGLY, SECRETLY.—*Ant.* OPENLY, reservedly, publicly.
into *prep.* inside, in the direction of, through, to, to the middle of; see also IN 1, 2, TOWARD, WITHIN.
intolerable *a.* insufferable, unendurable, unbearable; see IMPOSSIBLE, OFFENSIVE 2, PAINFUL 1, UNDESIRABLE.
intolerance *n.* racism, chauvinism, nationalism; see FANATICISM, PREJUDICE.
intolerant *a.* dogmatic, narrow, big-

oted; see PREJUDICED, STUPID.
intoxicant *n.* **1** [Alcohol] alcoholic drink, liquor, booze*; see DRINK 2. **2** [Drug] narcotic, hallucinogen, dope*; see DRUG.
intoxicate *v.* befuddle, inebriate, muddle; see CONFUSE.
intoxicated *a.* inebriated, high*, stoned*; see DIZZY, DRUNK.
intoxication *n.* infatuation, inebriation, intemperance; see DRUNKENNESS.
intricacy *n.* complication, elaborateness, complexity; see CONFUSION, DIFFICULTY 1, 2.
intricate *a.* involved, tricky, abstruse; see COMPLEX 2, DIFFICULT 1, 2, OBSCURE 1.
intrigue *n.* scheme, conspiracy, ruse; see TRICK 1.
intrigue *v.* delight, please, attract; see CHARM, ENTERTAIN 1, FASCINATE.
intrigued *a.* attracted, delighted, pleased; see CHARMED, ENTERTAINED, FASCINATED.
intriguing *a.* engaging, attractive, delightful; see BEAUTIFUL, CHARMING, HANDSOME, PLEASANT 1.
introduce *v.* **1** [To bring in] freight, carry in, transport; see CARRY, SEND 1. **2** [To present] set forth, submit, advance; see OFFER 1, PROPOSE 1. **3** [To make strangers acquainted] present, give an introduction, make known, put on speaking terms with,

do the honors, break the ice. **4** [To insert] put in, add, enter; see INCLUDE 2.
introduced *a.* **1** [Brought in] made known, put on the market, advanced, proposed, offered, imported, popularized; see also RECEIVED. **2** [Made acquainted] acquainted with, befriended, acknowledged, recognized, on speaking terms, not unknown to one another; see also FAMILIAR WITH.
introduction *n.* **1** [The act of bringing in] admittance, initiation, installation; see ENTRANCE 1. **2** [The act of making strangers acquainted] presentation, debut, meeting, formal acquaintance, preliminary encounter. **3** [Introductory knowledge] first acquaintance, elementary statement, first contact, start, awakening, first taste, baptism, preliminary training, basic principles; see also KNOWLEDGE 1. **4** [An introductory explanation] preface, preamble, foreword, prologue, prelude, overture; see also EXPLANATION. **5** [A work supplying introductory knowledge] primer, manual, handbook; see BOOK.
introductory *a.* initial, opening, early, prior, starting, beginning, preparatory, primary, original, provisional.—*Ant.* PRINCIPAL, substantial, secondary.

+ *specere*, to look] a looking into one's own mind, feelings, etc. —**in′tro·spec′tive** *adj.*

in·tro·vert (in′trō vʉrt′, -trə-) *n.* ⟦ < L *intro-*, within + *vertere*, to turn ⟧ one whose interest is more in oneself than in external objects or other people —**in′tro·ver′sion** (-vʉr′zhən) *n.* —**in′tro·vert′ed** *adj.*

in·trude (in trōōd′) *vt.* **-trud′ed, -trud′ing** ⟦ < L *in-*, in + *trudere*, to push ⟧ to force (oneself) upon others unasked —**in·trud′er** *n.*

in·tru·sion (in trōō′zhən) *n.* an intruding —**in·tru′sive** (-siv) *adj.* —**in·tru′sive·ly** *adv.* —**in·tru′sive·ness** *n.*

in·trust (in trust′) *vt.* ENTRUST

in·tu·bate (in′tōō bāt′) *vt.* **-bat′ed, -bat′ing** to insert a tube into (a hollow organ, etc.) to admit air, etc.

in·tu·i·tion (in′tōō ish′ən) *n.* ⟦ < L *in-*, in + *tueri*, look at ⟧ the immediate knowing of something without the conscious use of reasoning —**in·tu·i·tive** (in tōō′i tiv) *adj.*

In·u·it (in′ōō wit) *n.* ⟦Esk⟧ ESKIMO: now the preferred term, esp. in Canada

in·un·date (in′ən dāt′) *vt.* **-dat′ed, -dat′ing** ⟦ < L *in-*, in + *unda*, a wave ⟧ to cover with or as with a flood; deluge —**in′un·da′tion** *n.*

in·ure (in yoor′) *vt.* **-ured′, -ur′ing** ⟦ME *in ure*, in practice ⟧ to accustom to pain, trouble, etc.

in·vade (in vād′) *vt.* **-vad′ed, -vad′ing** ⟦ < L *in-*, in + *vadere*, to go ⟧ 1 to enter forcibly or hostilely 2 to intrude upon; violate —**in·vad′er** *n.*

in·va·lid[1] (in′və lid) *adj.* ⟦ < L *in-*, not + *validus*, strong ⟧ 1 weak and sickly 2 of or for invalids — *n.* one who is ill or disabled —**in′va·lid·ism′** *n.*

in·val·id[2] (in val′id) *adj.* not valid

in·val′i·date (-ə dāt′) *vt.* **-dat′ed, -dat′ing** to make invalid; deprive of legal force —**in·val′i·da′tion** *n.*

in·val·u·a·ble (in val′yōō ə bəl) *adj.* too valuable to be measured; priceless —**in·val′u·a·bly** *adv.*

in·va·sion (in vā′zhən) *n.* an invading or being invaded, as by an army

in·vec·tive (in vek′tiv) *n.* ⟦see fol.⟧ a violent verbal attack; vituperation

in·veigh (in vā′) *vi.* ⟦ < L *in-*, in + *vehere*, carry ⟧ to make a violent verbal attack; rail (*against*)

in·vei·gle (in vē′g'l, -vā′-) *vt.* **-gled, -gling** ⟦ < MFr *aveugler*, to blind ⟧ to entice or trick into doing or giving something —**in·vei′gler** *n.*

in·vent (in vent′) *vt.* ⟦ < L *in-*, in + *venire*, come ⟧ 1 to think up [to invent excuses] 2 to think out or produce (a new device, process, etc.); originate —**in·ven′tor** *n.*

in·ven′tion (-ven′shən) *n.* 1 an inventing 2 the power of inventing 3 something invented

in·ven′tive (-tiv) *adj.* 1 of invention 2 skilled in inventing —**in·ven′tive·ly** *adv.* —**in·ven′tive·ness** *n.*

in·ven·to·ry (in′vən tôr′ē) *n.*, *pl.* **-ries** ⟦see INVENT⟧ 1 an itemized list of goods, property, etc., as of a business 2 the store of goods, etc. for such listing; stock — *vt.* **-ried, -ry·ing** to make an inventory of

in·verse (in vʉrs′, in′vʉrs′) *adj.* inverted; directly opposite — *n.* any inverse thing —**in·verse′ly** *adv.*

in·ver·sion (in vʉr′zhən) *n.* 1 an inverting or being inverted 2 something inverted; reversal 3 *Meteorol.* a temperature reversal in which a layer of warm air traps cooler air near the surface of the earth

in·vert (in vʉrt′) *vt.* ⟦ < L *in-*, to + *vertere*, to turn ⟧ 1 to turn upside down 2 to reverse the order, position, direction, etc. of

in·ver·te·brate (in vʉr′tə brit, -brāt′) *adj.* not vertebrate; having no backbone — *n.* any invertebrate animal

in·vest (in vest′) *vt.* ⟦ < L *in-*, in + *vestis*, clothing ⟧ 1 to clothe 2 to install in office with ceremony 3 to furnish with power, authority, etc. 4 to put (money) into business, stocks, etc. in order to get a profit — *vi.* to invest money —**in·ves′tor** *n.*

in·ves·ti·gate (in ves′tə gāt′) *vt.*, *vi.* **-gat′ed, -gat′ing** ⟦ < L *in-*, in + *vestigare*, to track ⟧ to search (into); inquire —**in·ves′ti·ga′tive** *adj.* —**in·ves′ti·ga′tor** *n.*

in·ves′ti·ga′tion *n.* an investigating; careful search; systematic inquiry

in·ves′ti·ture (-chər) *n.* a formal investing, as with an office

in·vest·ment (in vest′mənt) *n.* 1 an investing or being invested 2 *a)* money invested *b)* anything in which money is or may be invested

in·vet·er·ate (in vet′ər it) *adj.* ⟦ < L *inveterare*, to age ⟧ firmly established; habitual —**in·vet′era·cy** *n.*

in·vid·i·ous (in vid′ē əs) *adj.* ⟦ < L *invidia*, envy ⟧ such as to excite ill will; giving offense, as by discriminating unfairly —**in·vid′i·ous·ly** *adv.* —**in·vid′i·ous·ness** *n.*

in·vig·or·ate (in vig′ər āt′) *vt.* **-at′ed, -at′ing** to give vigor to; fill with energy —**in·vig′ora′tion** *n.*

in·vin·ci·ble (in vin′sə bəl) *adj.* ⟦ < L *in-*, not + *vincere*, overcome ⟧ that cannot be overcome; unconquerable —**in·vin′cibil′i·ty** *n.*

in·vi·o·la·ble (in vī′ə lə bəl) *adj.* 1 not to be violated; not to be profaned or injured; sacred 2 indestructible —**in·vi′o·labil′i·ty** *n.*

in·vi′o·late (-lit) *adj.* not violated; kept sacred or unbroken

---

THESAURUS

intrude *v.* interfere, interrupt, interpose; see MEDDLE 1.

intruder *n.* prowler, thief, unwelcome guest, meddler, invader, snooper, unwanted person, interferer, interrupter, trespasser; see also ROBBER, TROUBLE 1.

intrusion *n.* interruption, forced entrance, trespass, intervention, meddling, encroachment, invasion, infraction, overstepping, transgression, nose-in*, horn-in*, muscle-in*; see also INTERFERENCE 1.

intuition *n.* presentiment, foreknowledge, inspiration; see FEELING 4.

intuitive *a.* instantaneously apprehended, emotional, instinctive; see AUTOMATIC, NATURAL 1, SPONTANEOUS.

invade *v.* 1 [To enter with armed force] force a landing, penetrate, fall on; see ATTACK. 2 [To encroach upon] infringe on, trespass, interfere with; see MEDDLE 1.

invader *n.* trespasser, alien, attacking force; see ATTACKER, ENEMY.

invalid[1] *n.* disabled person, incurable, paralytic, cripple, tubercular, leper, inmate; see also PATIENT.

invalid[2] *a.* irrational, unreasonable, fallacious; see ILLOGICAL, WRONG 2.

invalidate *v.* annul, refute, nullify; see CANCEL.

invaluable *a.* priceless, expensive, dear; see VALUABLE.

invariable *a.* unchanging, uniform, static; see CONSTANT, REGULAR 3.

invariably *a.* perpetually, constantly, habitually; see CUSTOMARILY, REGULARLY.

invasion *n.* forced entrance, intrusion, aggression; see ATTACK.

invent *v.* 1 [To create or discover] originate, devise, fashion, form, project, design, find, improvise, contrive, author, plan, think up, make up, bear, turn out, forge, make, hatch, dream up*, cook up*. 2 [To fabricate] misrepresent, fake, make believe; see LIE 1.

invention *n.* contrivance, contraption, design; see DISCOVERY.

inventive *a.* productive, imaginative, fertile; see ARTISTIC, ORIGINAL 2.

inventor *n.* author, originator, creator; see ARCHITECT, ARTIST.

inventory *n.* 1 [A list] stock book, itemization, register; see INDEX 2, LIST, RECORD 1. 2 [The act of taking stock] inspection, examination, investigation; see SUMMARY.

inventory *v.* take stock of, count, audit; see FILE 1, LIST 1, RECORD 1.

invert *v.* 1 [To upset] overturn, turn upside-down, tip; see UPSET 1. 2 [To reverse] change, rearrange, transpose; see EXCHANGE.

invest *v.* lay out, spend, put one's money into, advance, give money over, buy stocks, make an investment, loan, buy into, sink money in*, put up the dough*; see also BUY.

investigate *v.* look into, interrogate, review; see EXAMINE, STUDY.

investigated *a.* examined, tried, tested, inspected, searched, questioned, probed, considered, measured, checked, studied, researched, made the subject of an investigation, worked on, thought out, thought through, scrutinized, put to the test, gone over, gone into, cross-examined.

investigation *n.* inquiry, search, research; see EXAMINATION 1.

investigator *n.* reviewer, spy, auditor; see DETECTIVE, INSPECTOR.

investment *n.* grant, loan, expenditure, expense, backing, speculation, financing, finance, purchase, advance, bail, interest. *Types of investment include the following:* stocks, bonds, shares, securities, property, real estate, mortgage, capital, goods, property liens, debentures, futures, gold, grain.

invigorate *v.* stimulate, freshen, exhilarate; see ANIMATE, EXCITE.

invigorating *a.* refreshing, exhilarating, bracing; see STIMULATING.

invincible *a.* unconquerable, insuperable, impregnable; see POWERFUL 1, STRONG 1, 2.

invisibility *n.* obscurity, concealment, camouflage, indefiniteness, seclusion, cloudiness, haziness, fogginess, mistiness, duskiness, darkness, gloom, intangibility, disappearance, vagueness, indefiniteness.

in·vis·ible (in viz′ə bəl) *adj.* **1** not visible; that cannot be seen **2** out of sight **3** imperceptible —**in·vis′ibil′ity** *n.* —**in·vis′ibly** *adv.*

in·vi·ta·tion (in′və tā′shən) *n.* **1** an inviting **2** a message used in inviting

in′vi·ta′tional *adj.* only for those invited to take part, as an art show

in·vite (in vīt′; *for n.* in′vīt′) *vt.* **-vit′ed, -vit′ing** ⟦< L *invitare*⟧ **1** to ask to come somewhere or do something **2** to ask for **3** to give occasion for [action that *invites* scandal] **4** to tempt; entice — *n.* [Colloq.] an invitation —**in′vitee′** *n.*

in·vit′ing *adj.* tempting; enticing

in vi·tro (in vē′trō) ⟦L, in glass⟧ isolated from the living organism and artificially maintained, as in a test tube

in·vo·ca·tion (in′və kā′shən) *n.* an invoking of God, the Muses, etc.

in·voice (in′vois′) *n.* ⟦prob. < ME *envoie*, message⟧ a list of goods shipped or services rendered, stating prices, etc.; bill — *vt.* **-voiced′, -voic′ing** to present an invoice for or to

in·voke (in vōk′) *vt.* **-voked′, -vok′ing** ⟦< L *in-*, in, on + *vocare*, to call⟧ **1** to call on (God, the Muses, etc.) for blessing, help, etc. **2** to resort to (a law, ruling, etc.) as pertinent **3** to conjure **4** to beg for; implore

in·vol·un·tary (in väl′ən ter′ē) *adj.* **1** not done by choice **2** not consciously controlled —**in·vol′un·tar′i·ly** *adv.* —**in·vol′un·tar′i·ness** *n.*

in·vo·lu·tion (in′və lōō′shən) *n.* **1** an involving or being involved; entanglement **2** a complication; intricacy

in·volve (in välv′, -vôlv′) *vt.* **-volved′, -volv′ing** ⟦< L *in-*, in + *volvere*, to roll⟧ **1** to make intricate or complicated **2** to entangle in difficulty, danger, etc.; implicate **3** to affect or include [the riot *involved* thousands] **4** to require [saving *involves* thrift] **5** to make busy; occupy [*involved* the class in research] —**in·volved′** *adj.* —**in·volve′ment** *n.*

in·vul·ner·able (in vul′nər ə bəl) *adj.* **1** that cannot be wounded or injured **2** proof against attack

in·ward (in′wərd) *adj.* **1** situated within; internal **2** mental or spiritual **3** directed toward the inside **4** sensitive, subtle, reticent, etc. — *adv.* **1** toward the inside **2** into the mind or soul Also **in′wards** *adv.*

in′wardly *adv.* **1** in or on the inside **2** in the mind or spirit **3** toward the inside

I/O input/output

iodine (ī′ə dīn′, -din) *n.* ⟦< Gr *iōdēs*, violetlike⟧ **1** a nonmetallic chemical element, used in medicine, etc. **2** a tincture of iodine, used as an antiseptic

i′odize′ (-dīz′) *vt.* **-dized′, -diz′ing** to treat with iodine

ion (ī′ən, -än′) *n.* ⟦< Gr *ienai*, to go⟧ an electrically charged atom or group of atoms

-ion ⟦< L *-io*⟧ *suffix* **1** the act or condition of **2** the result of

Ion·ic (ī än′ik) *adj.* designating or of a Greek or Roman style of architecture, distinguished by ornamental scrolls on the capitals

ion·ize (ī′ən īz′) *vt., vi.* **-ized′, -iz′ing** to dissociate into ions, as a salt dissolved in water, or become electrically

charged, as a gas under radiation —**i′oni·za′tion** *n.* —**i′on·iz′er** *n.*

iono·sphere (ī än′ə sfir′) *n.* the outer layers of the earth's atmosphere, with some electron and ion content

iota (ī ōt′ə) *n.* **1** the ninth letter of the Greek alphabet (I, ι) **2** a very small quantity; jot

IOU (ī′ō′yōō′) *n., pl.* **IOU's** ⟦for *I owe you*⟧ a signed paper bearing the letters *IOU*, acknowledging a specified debt

-ious (ē əs, yəs, əs) ⟦see **-ous**⟧ *suffix* characterized by [furious]

ip·ecac (ip′i kak′) *n.* ⟦< AmInd (Brazil) name⟧ an emetic made as from the dried roots of a South American plant

ipso facto (ip′sō fak′tō) ⟦L⟧ by that very fact

IQ or **I.Q.** intelligence quotient

ir- *prefix* **1** IN-[1] **2** IN-[2] Used before *r*

Ir *Chem. symbol for* iridium

Ir. **1** Ireland: also **Ire.** **2** Irish

IRA (ī′är′ā′; ī′rə) *n., pl.* **IRA's** ⟦I(ndividual) R(etirement) A(ccount)⟧ a personal retirement plan with taxes on the earnings deferred until funds are withdrawn

Ira·nian (i rā′nē ən) *adj.* of Iran, its people, etc. — *n.* **1** a native of Iran; Persian **2** a group of languages, including Persian

Iraqi (i rä′kē, -rak′ē) *n., pl.* **-qis** a native or inhabitant of Iraq — *adj.* of Iraq, its people, etc.

iras·cible (i ras′ə bəl, ī-) *adj.* ⟦see fol.⟧ easily angered; hot-tempered

irate (ī rāt′, ī′rāt′) *adj.* ⟦< L *ira*, anger⟧ angry; wrathful; incensed —**irate′ly** *adv.* —**irate′ness** *n.*

ire (īr) *n.* ⟦< L *ira*⟧ anger; wrath

iren·ic (ī ren′ik) *adj.* ⟦< Gr *eirēnē*, peace⟧ promoting peace

iri·des·cent (ir′i des′ənt) *adj.* ⟦< Gr *iris*, rainbow⟧ having or showing an interplay of rainbowlike colors —**ir′i·des′cence** *n.*

irid·i·um (i rid′ē əm) *n.* ⟦see fol.⟧ a white, metallic chemical element

iris (ī′ris) *n., pl.* **i′ris·es** ⟦Gr, rainbow⟧ **1** the round, pigmented membrane surrounding the pupil of the eye **2** a plant with sword-shaped leaves and a showy flower

Irish (ī′rish) *adj.* of Ireland, its people, language, etc. — *n.* **1** the Celtic language of Ireland **2** the English dialect of Ireland —**the Irish** the people of Ireland —**I′rish·man**, *pl.* **-men**, *n.* —**I′rish·wom′an**, *pl.* **-wom′en**, *n.fem.*

Irish coffee brewed coffee with Irish whiskey, topped with whipped cream

irk (ʉrk) *vt.* ⟦ME *irken*, be weary of⟧ to annoy, irritate, tire out, etc.

irk′some (-səm) *adj.* that tends to irk; tiresome or annoying

iron (ī′ərn) *n.* ⟦OE *iren*⟧ **1** a metallic chemical element, the most common of all metals **2** any device of iron; esp., such a device with a flat undersurface, heated for pressing cloth **3** [*pl.*] iron shackles **4** firm strength; power **5** any of certain golf clubs with angled metal heads — *adj.* **1** of

---

▪ THESAURUS ▪

invisible *a.* intangible, out of sight, microscopic, beyond the visual range, unseen, undisclosed, vaporous, gaseous.—*Ant.* REAL, substantial, material.

invisibly *a.* imperceptibly, undetectibly, out of sight; see VAGUELY.

invitation *n.* note, card, message, encouragement, proposition, proposal, call, petition, overture, offer, temptation, attraction, lure, prompting, urge, pressure, reason, motive, ground.

invite *v.* bid, request, beg, suggest, encourage, entice, solicit, pray, petition, persuade, insist, press, ply, propose, appeal to, implore, call upon, ask, have over, have in, formally invite, send an invitation; see also ASK.

invited *a.* asked, requested, solicited, persuaded, bade, summoned; see also WELCOME.

inviting *a.* appealing, alluring, tempting, attractive, captivating, agreeable, open, encouraging, delightful, pleasing, persuasive, magnetic, fascinating, provocative, bewitching.—*Ant.* PAINFUL, unbearable, insufferable.

invoice *n.* bill of lading, receipt, bill of shipment; see STATEMENT 2.

involuntary *a.* unintentional, uncontrolled, instinctive; see AUTOMATIC, HABITUAL.

involve *v.* draw into, compromise, implicate, entangle, link, connect, incriminate, associate, relate, suggest, prove, comprise, point to, commit, bring up.

involved *a.* brought into difficulties, entangled in a crime, incriminated, embarrassed, embroiled, caught up in; see also INCLUDED.

involvement *n.* **1** [Difficulty] quandary, crisis, embarrassment; see DIFFICULTY 1, 2. **2** [Engrossment] intentness, study, preoccupation; see REFLECTION 1.

invulnerable *a.* strong, invincible, secure; see SAFE 1.

inward *a.* **1** [Moving into] penetrating, ingoing, through, incoming, entering, inbound, infiltrating, inflowing. **2** [Placed within] inside, internal, interior; see IN 1, WITHIN. **3**

[Private] spiritual, intellectual, intimate; see PRIVATE, RELIGIOUS 2.

inwardly *a.* from within, fundamentally, basically; see NATURALLY, WITHIN.

iota *n.* grain, particle, speck; see BIT 1.

irate *a.* enraged, furious, incensed; see ANGRY.

Irish *a.* Celtic, Gaelic, from the old sod*; see EUROPEAN.

irk *v.* annoy, harass, disturb; see BOTHER 1, 2.

iron *a.* ferrous, ironclad, hard, robust, strong, unyielding, dense, inflexible, heavy; see also FIRM 2, THICK 3.

iron *n.* **1** [A metallic element] pig iron, cast iron, wrought iron, sheet iron, coke; see also METAL. **2** [An appliance] pressing device, presser, steam iron; see APPLIANCE.

iron *v.* use as steam iron on, press, mangle, roll, finish, smooth out; see also SMOOTH. —**iron out** compromise, settle differences, reach an agreement about; see AGREE, NEGOTIATE 1.

iron 2 like iron; strong; firm — *vt.*, *vi.* to press with a hot iron —**iron out** to smooth out; eliminate

i'ron·clad' (-klad') *adj.* 1 covered or protected with iron 2 difficult to change or break *[an ironclad lease]*

iron curtain a barrier of secrecy and censorship, esp. around the U.S.S.R.

ironic (ī rän'ik) *adj.* 1 meaning the contrary of what is expressed 2 using irony 3 opposite to what might be expected Also **iron'i·cal** —**iron'i·cally** *adv.*

i'ron·stone' *n.* a hard, white ceramic ware

i'ron·ware' *n.* things made of iron

irony (ī'rə nē, ī'ər nē) *n., pl.* **-nies** ⟦< Gr *eirōn*, dissembler in speech⟧ 1 expression in which the intended meaning of the words is the direct opposite of their usual sense 2 an event or result that is the opposite of what is expected

Iro·quois (ir'ə kwoi') *n., pl.* **-quois** (-kwoi', -kwoiz') a member of a confederation of North American Indian peoples that lived in upstate New York — *adj.* of the Iroquois —**Ir'o·quoi'an** *n., adj.*

ir·ra·di·ate (ir rā'dē āt') *vt.* **-at'ed, -at'ing** 1 to shine upon; light up 2 to enlighten 3 to radiate 4 to expose to X-rays or other radiant energy — *vi.* to emit rays; shine — **ir·ra'di·a'tion** *n.*

ir·ra·tional (ir rash'ə nəl) *adj.* 1 lacking the power to reason 2 senseless; unreasonable; absurd —**ir·ra'tion·al'ity** (-ə nal'ə tē), *pl.* **-ties,** *n.* —**ir·ra'tion·ally** *adv.*

ir·re·claim·able (ir'ri klām'ə bəl) *adj.* that cannot be reclaimed

ir·rec·on·cil·able (ir rek'ən sīl'ə bəl) *adj.* that cannot be brought into agreement; incompatible

ir·re·cov·er·able (ir'ri kuv'ər ə bəl) *adj.* that cannot be recovered, rectified, or remedied

ir·re·deem·able (ir'ri dēm'ə bəl) *adj.* 1 that cannot be bought back 2 that cannot be converted into coin, as certain paper money 3 that cannot be changed or reformed

ir·ref·u·table (ir ref'yōō tə bəl, ir'ri fyōōt'ə-) *adj.* indisputable

ir·re·gard·less (ir'i gärd'lis) *adj., adv.* REGARDLESS: a nonstandard or humorous usage

ir·reg·u·lar (ir reg'yōō lər) *adj.* 1 not conforming to established rule, standard, etc. 2 not straight, even, or uniform 3 *Gram.* not inflected in the usual way —**ir·reg'u·lar'ity,** *pl.* **-ties,** *n.* —**ir·reg'u·larly** *adv.*

ir·rel·evant (ir rel'ə vənt) *adj.* not pertinent; not to the point —**ir·rel'evance** or **ir·rel'evancy** *n.* —**ir·rel'evantly** *adv.*

ir·re·li·gious (ir'ri lij'əs) *adj.* 1 not religious 2 indifferent or hostile to religion 3 profane; impious

ir·re·medi·able (ir'ri mē'dē ə bəl) *adj.* that cannot be remedied or corrected —**ir're·me'di·ably** *adv.*

ir·repa·rable (ir rep'ə rə bəl) *adj.* that cannot be repaired, mended, etc.

ir·re·place·able (ir'ri plās'ə bəl) *adj.* that cannot be replaced

ir're·press'ible (-pres'ə bəl) *adj.* that cannot be repressed

ir're·proach'able (-prō'chə bəl) *adj.* blameless; faultless

ir're·sist'ible (-zis'tə bəl) *adj.* that cannot be resisted; too strong, fascinating, etc. to be withstood —**ir're·sist'ibly** *adv.*

ir·reso·lute (ir rez'ə lōōt') *adj.* not resolute; wavering; indecisive —**ir·res'o·lu'tion** (-lōō'shən) *n.*

ir·re·spec·tive (ir'ri spek'tiv) *adj.* regardless (*of*)

ir're·spon'sible (-spän'sə bəl) *adj.* 1 not responsible for actions 2 lacking a sense of responsibility —**ir're·spon'sibil'ity** *n.*

ir're·triev'able (-trēv'ə bəl) *adj.* that cannot be retrieved

ir·rev·er·ence (ir rev'ər əns) *n.* lack of reverence; disrespect —**ir·rev'er·ent** *adj.*

ir·re·vers·ible (ir'ri vʉr'sə bəl) *adj.* that cannot be reversed; esp., that cannot be annulled or turned back

ir·revo·cable (ir rev'ə kə bəl) *adj.* that cannot be revoked or undone —**ir·rev'o·cably** *adv.*

ir·ri·gable (ir'i gə bəl) *adj.* that can be irrigated

ir·ri·gate (ir'ə gāt') *vt.* **-gat'ed, -gat'ing** ⟦< L *in-*, in + *rigare*, to water⟧ 1 to supply (land) with water, as by means of artificial ditches 2 *Med.* to wash out (a cavity, wound, etc.) —**ir'ri·ga'tion** *n.*

ir·ri·table (ir'i tə bəl) *adj.* 1 easily irritated or provoked 2 *Med.* excessively sensitive to a stimulus —**ir·ri·tabil'ity** *n.* —**ir'ri·tably** *adv.*

ir·ri·tant (-tənt) *adj.* causing irritation — *n.* a thing that irritates

ir·ri·tate' (-tāt') *vt.* **-tat'ed, -tat'ing** ⟦< L *irritare*, excite⟧ 1 to provoke to anger; annoy 2 to make inflamed or sore —**ir'ri·ta'tion** *n.*

ir·rupt (ir rupt') *vi.* ⟦< L *in-*, in + *rumpere*, to break⟧ to burst suddenly or violently (*into*) —**ir·rup'tion** *n.* —**ir·rup'tive** *adj.*

IRS Internal Revenue Service

is (iz) *vi.* ⟦OE⟧ 3d pers. sing., pres. indic., of BE

THESAURUS

ironical *a.* contradictory, twisted, ridiculous, mocking, satiric, paradoxical, critical, derisive, exaggerated, caustic, biting, incisive, scathing, satirical, bitter; see also SARCASTIC.

irony *n.* satire, wit, ridicule, mockery, quip, banter, derision, criticism, paradox, twist, humor, reproach, repartee, back-handed compliment; see also SARCASM.

irrational *a.* 1 [Illogical] unreasonable, specious, fallacious; see ILLOGICAL, WRONG 2. 2 [Stupid] senseless, silly, ridiculous; see STUPID.

irrationally *a.* illogically, unreasonably, stupidly; see FOOLISHLY.

irregular *a.* 1 [Not even] uneven, spasmodic, fitful, uncertain, random, unsettled, inconstant, unsteady, fragmentary, unsystematic, occasional, infrequent, fluctuating, wavering, intermittent, sporadic, changeable, capricious, variable, shifting, unmethodical, jerky, up and down.—*Ant.* REGULAR, even, punctual. 2 [Not customary] unique, extraordinary, abnormal; see UNUSUAL 2. 3 [Questionable] strange, overt, debatable; see QUESTIONABLE 2, SUSPICIOUS 2. 4 [Not regular in form or in outline] not uniform, unsymmetrical, uneven, asymmetrical, unequal, craggy, hilly, broken, jagged, notched, eccentric, bumpy, meandering, variable, wobbly, lumpy, off balance, off center, lopsided, pock-marked, scarred, bumpy, sprawling, out of proportion; see also BENT.

irregularity *n.* peculiarity, singularity, abnormality, strangeness, uniqueness, exception, excess, malformation, deviation, allowance, exemption, privilege, nonconformity, innovation, oddity, eccentricity, anomaly, rarity; see also CHARACTERISTIC.—*Ant.* CUSTOM, regularity, rule.

irregularly *a.* periodically, at irregular intervals, intermittently, fitfully, off and on; see also UNEXPECTEDLY.

irrelevant *a.* inapplicable, impertinent, off the topic, inappropriate, unrelated, extraneous, inapropos, unconnected, off the point, foreign, beside the question, out of order, out of place, pointless, beside the point, not pertaining to, without reference to, out of the way, remote, neither here nor there; see also TRIVIAL, UNNECESSARY.

irreparable *a.* incurable, hopeless, irreversible; see BROKEN 1, DESTROYED, RUINED 1.

irresistible *a.* compelling, overpowering, invincible; see OVERWHELMING, POWERFUL 1.

irresponsible *a.* untrustworthy, capricious, flighty, fickle, thoughtless, rash, undependable, unstable, loose, lax, immoral, shiftless, unpredictable, wild, devil-may-care; see also UNRELIABLE.—*Ant.* RESPONSIBLE, trustworthy, dependable.

irrevocable *a.* permanent, indelible, lost; see CERTAIN 2, INEVITABLE.

irrigate *v.* water, pass water through, inundate; see FLOOD.

irrigation *n.* watering, flooding,

inundation; see FLOOD.

irritability *n.* anger, peevishness, impatience; see ANGER, ANNOYANCE.

irritable *a.* sensitive, touchy, testy, peevish, ill-tempered, huffy, petulant, tense, resentful, fretting, carping, crabbed, hypercritical, quick-tempered, easily offended, glum, complaining, brooding, dissatisfied, snarling, grumbling, surly, gloomy, ill-natured, morose, moody, snappish, waspish, in bad humor, cantankerous, fretful, hypersensitive, annoyed, cross, churlish, grouchy, sulky, sullen, high-strung, thin-skinned, grumpy; see also ANGRY.—*Ant.* PLEASANT, agreeable, good-natured.

irritant *n.* bother, burden, nuisance; see ANNOYANCE.

irritate *v.* 1 [To bother] provoke, exasperate, pester; see BOTHER 1, CONFUSE, DISTURB. 2 [To inflame] redden, chafe, swell, erupt, pain, sting; see also BURN, HURT 1, ITCH.

irritated *a.* disturbed, upset, bothered; see TROUBLED.

irritating *a.* annoying, bothersome, trying; see DISTURBING.

irritation *n.* 1 [The result of irritating] soreness, tenderness, rawness; see FEELING 4. 2 [A disturbed mental state] excitement, upset, provocation; see ANGER, ANNOYANCE.

is *v.* lives, breathes, transpires, happens, amounts to, equals, comprises, signifies, means.

Isaac (ī′zək) *Bible* one of the patriarchs, son of Abraham, and father of Jacob and Esau

Isa·iah (ī zā′ə) *Bible* **1** a Hebrew prophet of the 8th c. B.C. **2** the book containing his teachings

-ise (īz) *suffix chiefly Brit. sp. of* -IZE

-ish (ish) 〖< OE *-isc*〗 *suffix* **1** of (a specified people) *[Irish]* **2** somewhat *[tallish]* **3** [Colloq.] approximately *[thirtyish]*

Ish·tar (ish′tär′) the Babylonian and Assyrian goddess of fertility

isin·glass (ī′zin glas′; *also,* -ziŋ-) *n.* 〖< MDu *huizen*, sturgeon + *blas*, bladder〗 mica, esp. in thin sheets

Isis (ī′sis) the Egyptian goddess of fertility

isl. **1** island **2** isle

Is·lam (is′läm′, iz′-; is läm′) *n.* 〖Ar *islām*, lit., submission (to God's will)〗 **1** the Muslim religion, a monotheistic religion founded by Mohammed **2** Muslims collectively or the lands in which they predominate —**Is·lam′ic** (-läm′ik, -lam′-) *adj.*

is·land (ī′lənd) *n.* 〖< OE *igland*, lit., island land: sp. after *isle*〗 **1** a land mass smaller than a continent and surrounded by water **2** anything like this in position or isolation

is′land·er *n.* a native or inhabitant of an island

isle (īl) *n.* 〖< L *insula*〗 an island, esp. a small island

is·let (ī′lit) *n.* a very small island

islets (or islands) of Lang·er·hans (läŋ′ər häns′) 〖after P. *Langerhans* (1847-88), Ger histologist〗 endocrine cells in the pancreas that produce the hormone insulin

ism (iz′əm) *n.* a doctrine, theory, system, etc. whose name ends in *-ism*

-ism (iz′əm) 〖< Gr *-ismos*〗 *suffix* **1** act or result of *[terrorism]* **2** condition, conduct, or qualities of *[patriotism]* **3** theory of *[socialism]* **4** devotion to *[nationalism]* **5** an instance of *[witticism]*

isn't (iz′ənt) is not

iso- 〖< Gr *isos*〗 *combining form* equal, similar, identical *[isomorph]*

iso·bar (ī′sō bär′) *n.* 〖< prec. + Gr *baros*, weight〗 a line on a map connecting points of equal barometric pressure

iso·late (ī′sə lāt′; *for n., usually,* -lit) *vt.* **-lat′ed, -lat′ing** 〖< It *isola* (< L *insula*), island〗 to set apart from others; place alone — *n.* a person or thing that is isolated —**i′so·la′tion** *n.* —**i′so·la′tor** *n.*

i′so·la′tion·ist *n.* one who opposes the involvement of a country in international alliances, etc. — *adj.* of isolationists —**i′so·la′tion·ism′** *n.*

iso·mer (ī′sō mər) *n.* 〖< Gr *isos*, equal + *meros*, a part〗 any of two or more chemical compounds whose molecules contain the same atoms but in different arrangements —**i′so·mer′ic** (-mer′ik) *adj.*

i′so·met′ric (-met′rik) *adj.* 〖< Gr *isos*, equal + *metron*, measure〗 **1** equal in measure **2** of isometrics — *n.* [*pl.*] exercise in which muscles are briefly tensed in opposition to other muscles or to an immovable object —**i′so·met′ri·cally** *adv.*

isos·celes (ī säs′ə lēz′) *adj.* 〖< Gr *isos*, equal + *skelos*, leg〗 designating a triangle with two equal sides

iso·tope (ī′sə tōp′) *n.* 〖< ISO- + Gr *topos*, place〗 any of two or more forms of an element having the same atomic number but different atomic weights

Is·raeli (iz rā′lē) *n.* a native or inhabitant of modern Israel — *adj.* of modern Israel or its people

Is·ra·el·ite (iz′rē ə līt′) *n.* any of the people of ancient Israel

is·su·ance (ish′ŏŏ əns) *n.* an issuing; issue

is·sue (ish′ŏŏ) *n.* 〖< L *ex-*, out + *ire*, go〗 **1** an outgoing; outflow **2** an exit; outlet **3** a result; consequence **4** offspring **5** a point under dispute **6** a sending or giving out **7** all that is put forth at one time *[an issue* of bonds, a periodical, etc.*]* — *vi.* **-sued, -su·ing** **1** to go or flow out; emerge **2** to result *(from)* or end *(in)* **3** to be published — *vt.* **1** to let out; discharge **2** to give or deal out *[to issue* supplies*]* **3** to publish —**at issue** in dispute —**take issue** to disagree

-ist (ist, əst) 〖< Gr *-istēs*〗 *suffix* **1** one who does, makes, or practices *[satirist]* **2** one skilled in or occupied with *[druggist, violinist]* **3** an adherent of *[anarchist]*

isth·mus (is′məs) *n., pl.* **-muses** or **-mi** (-mī′) 〖< Gr *isthmos*, a neck〗 a narrow strip of land having water at each side and connecting two larger bodies of land

it (it) *pron., pl. see* THEY 〖< OE *hit*〗 **1** the animal or thing previously mentioned **2** *It* is also used as: *a)* the subject of an impersonal verb *[it* is snowing*]* *b)* a subject or object of indefinite sense in various idiomatic constructions *[it's* all right, he lords *it* over us*]* — *n.* the player, as in tag, who must try to catch another —**with it** [Slang] alert, informed, or hip

It. or **Ital.** **1** Italian **2** Italy

Ital·ian (i tal′yən) *adj.* of Italy, its people, language, etc. — *n.* **1** a native or inhabitant of Italy **2** the Romance language of Italy

ital·ic (i tal′ik) *adj.* 〖< its early use in *Italy*〗 designating a type in which the characters slant upward to the right (Ex.: *this is italic type*) — *n.* [*usually pl., sometimes with sing. v.*] italic type or print: abbrev. **ital.**

ital·i·cize (i tal′ə sīz′, ī-) *vt.* **-cized′, -ciz′ing** to print in italics

itch (ich) *vi.* 〖OE *giccan*〗 **1** to feel a tingling of the skin, with the desire to scratch **2** to have a restless desire — *vt.* [Colloq.] SCRATCH — *n.* **1** an itching **2** a restless desire —**itch′y, -i·er, -i·est,** *adj.*

-ite (it) 〖< Gr *-itēs*〗 *suffix* **1** an inhabitant of *[Akronite]* **2** an adherent of *[laborite]* **3** a manufactured product *[dynamite]*

item (ī′təm) *n.* 〖< L *ita*, so, thus〗 **1** an article; unit; separate thing **2** a bit of news or information

i′tem·ize′ (-īz′) *vt.* **-ized′, -iz′ing** to specify the items of; set down by items —**i′tem·i·za′tion** *n.*

it·er·ate (it′ər āt′) *vt.* **-at′ed, -at′ing** 〖< L *iterum*, again〗 to utter or do again —**it′era′tion** *n.*

itin·er·ant (i tin′ər ənt) *adj.* 〖< L *iter*, a walk〗 traveling from place to place — *n.* a traveler

itin′er·ar′y (-er′ē) *n., pl.* **-ar′ies** **1** a route **2** a record of a journey **3** a detailed plan of a journey

-itis (īt′is) 〖< Gr *-itis*〗 *suffix* inflammation of (a specified part or organ) *[neuritis]*

its (its) *pron.* of, or those belonging to it — *poss. pronominal adj.* of, belonging to, or done by it

it's (its) **1** it is **2** it has

it·self (it self′) *pron.* a form of *it* used: *a)* as an intensive *[the work itself* is easy*]* *b)* as a reflexive *[the dog bit*

THESAURUS

island *n.* **1** [Land surrounded by water] isle, sandbar, archipelago; see LAND 1. **2** [An isolated spot] haven, retreat, sanctuary; see REFUGE 1, SHELTER.

isolate *v.* confine, detach, seclude; see DIVIDE.

isolated *a.* secluded, apart, backwoods, insular, segregated, confined, withdrawn, rustic, separate, lonely, forsaken, hidden, remote, out-of-the-way, lonesome, God-forsaken; see also ALONE, PRIVATE, SOLITARY.

isolation *n.* detachment, solitude, loneliness, seclusion, segregation, confinement, separation, self-sufficiency, obscurity, retreat, privacy; see also WITHDRAWAL.

issue *n.* **1** [Question] point, matter, problem, concern, point in question, argument; see also MATTER. **2** [Result] upshot, culmination, effect; see RESULT. **3** [Edition] number,

copy, impression; see COPY. —**at issue** in dispute, unsettled, controversial; see CONTROVERSIAL. —**take issue** differ, disagree, take a stand against; see OPPOSE 1.

issue *v.* **1** [To emerge] flow out, proceed, come forth; see APPEAR 1. **2** [To be a result of] rise from, spring, originate; see BEGIN 2, RESULT. **3** [To release] circulate, send out, announce; see ADVERTISE, DECLARE, PUBLISH 1.

issued *a.* circulated, broadcast, televised, made public, announced, published, sent out, spread; see also DISTRIBUTED.

it *pron.* such a thing, that which, that object, this thing, the subject; see also THAT, THIS. —**with it*** alert, aware, up-to-date; see READY 2.

Italian *a.* Latin, Etruscan, Roman, Florentine, Milanese, Venetian, Neapolitan, Sicilian.

italicize *v.* stress, underline, print in italic type, draw attention to; see also DISTINGUISH 1, EMPHASIZE.

itch *n.* tingling, prickling, crawling, creeping sensation, rawness, psoriasis, scabbiness.

itch *v.* creep, prickle, be irritated, crawl, tickle; see also TINGLE.

item *n.* piece, article, matter; see DETAIL, PART 1.

itemize *v.* inventory, enumerate, number; see DETAIL, LIST 1.

itemized *a.* counted, particularized, enumerated; see DETAILED.

itinerant *a.* roving, nomadic, peripatetic; see VAGRANT, WANDERING 1.

itinerant *n.* nomad, wanderer, vagrant; see TRAMP 1.

itinerary *n.* course, travel plans, route; see PATH, PLAN 2, PROGRAM 2, WAY 2.

itself] c) as a quasi-noun meaning "its real, true self" *[the bird is not* itself *today]*

itty-bitty (it′ē bit′ē) *adj.* ⟦baby talk < *little bit*⟧ [Colloq.] very small; tiny   Also **itsy-bitsy** (it′sē bit′sē)

-ity (ə tē, i-) ⟦< L *-itas*⟧ *suffix* state, quality, or instance *[chastity]*

IUD intrauterine (contraceptive) device

IV intravenous

-ive (iv) ⟦< L *-ivus*⟧ *suffix* **1** of or having the nature of *[sportive]* **2** tending to *[retrospective]*

ivied (ī′vēd) *adj.* covered or overgrown with ivy

ivo·ry (ī′və rē) *n., pl.* **-ries** ⟦ult. < Egypt 3*bw*⟧ **1** the hard, white substance forming the tusks of elephants, walruses, etc. **2** any substance like ivory **3** creamy white **4** [*pl.*] [Slang] *a)* piano keys *b)* dice — *adj.* **1** of or like ivory **2** creamy-white

ivory tower a retreat away from reality or action

ivy (ī′vē) *n., pl.* **i′vies** ⟦OE *ifig*⟧ **1** a climbing vine with a woody stem and evergreen leaves **2** any of various similar climbing plants

-ize (īz) ⟦< Gr *-izein*⟧ *suffix* **1** to cause to be *[sterilize]* **2** to become (like) *[crystallize]* **3** to combine with *[oxidize]* **4** to engage in *[soliloquize]*

j or **J** (jā) *n., pl.* **j's, J's** the tenth letter of the English alphabet

jab (jab) *vt., vi.* **jabbed, jab′bing** [< ME *jobben*, to peck] **1** to poke, as with a sharp instrument **2** to punch with short, straight blows — *n.* a quick thrust or blow

jab·ber (jab′ər) *vi., vt.* [prob. echoic] to speak or say quickly, incoherently, or foolishly; chatter — *n.* chatter — **jab′berer** *n.*

ja·bot (zha bō′) *n.* [Fr, bird's crop] a ruffle or frill down the front of a blouse, etc.

jack (jak) *n.* [< the name *Jack*] **1** [*often* J-] a man or boy **2** any of various machines used to lift something heavy a short distance [an automobile *jack*] **3** a playing card with a picture of a royal male servant or soldier **4** a small flag flown on a ship's bow to show nationality **5** any of the small 6-pronged metal pieces tossed and picked up in a game (**jacks**) **6** *Elec.* a plug-in receptacle used to make electrical contact — *vt.* to raise by means of a jack: usually with *up* —**jack up** [Colloq.] to raise (prices, wages, etc.)

jack- [see prec.] *combining form* **1** male [*jackass*] **2** large or strong [*jackknife*] **3** boy; fellow [*jack*-in-the-box]

jackal (jak′əl) *n.* [< Sans] a wild dog of Asia and N Africa

jack·ass (jak′as′) *n.* [JACK- + ASS] **1** a male donkey **2** a fool

jack′daw′ (-dô′) *n.* [JACK- + ME *dawe*, jackdaw] a small European crow

jacket (jak′it) *n.* [< Ar *shakk*] **1** a short coat **2** an outer covering, as the removable paper cover on a book, the cardboard holder of a phonograph record, the skin of a potato, etc.

Jack Frost frost or cold weather personified

jack′ham′mer *n.* a portable type of pneumatic hammer, used for breaking up concrete, rock, etc.

jack′-in-the-box′ *n., pl.* **-box′es** a toy consisting of a box from which a figure on a spring jumps up when the lid is lifted Also **jack′-in-a-box′**

jack′-in-the-pul′pit (-pool′pit) *n., pl.* **-pits** a plant with a flower spike partly arched over by a hoodlike covering

jack′knife′ *n., pl.* **-knives′ 1** a large pocketknife **2** a dive in which the diver keeps knees unbent, touches the feet, and then straightens out — *vi., vt.* **-knifed′, -knif′ing** to bend or fold at the middle or at a connection

jack′-of-all′-trades′ *n., pl.* **jacks′-** [*often* J-] one who can do many kinds of work acceptably

jack-o′-lantern (jak′ə lant′ərn) *n., pl.* **-terns** a hollow pumpkin cut to look like a face and used as a lantern

jack′pot′ *n.* [*jack*, playing card + *pot*] cumulative stakes, as in poker

jack rabbit a large hare of W North America, with strong hind legs

Ja·cob (jā′kəb) *Bible* a son of Isaac

Jac·quard (jə kärd′) *n.* [after J. M. *Jacquard* (1752-1834), Fr inventor] a fabric with a figured weave

Ja·cuzzi (jə kōō′zē) [< *Jacuzzi*, U.S. developers] *trademark for* a kind of whirlpool bath

jade¹ (jād) *n.* [< Sp (*piedra de*) *ijada*, (stone of) the side: supposed to cure pains in the side] **1** a hard, greenish, ornamental gemstone **2** a medium green color

jade² (jād) *n.* [< ON *jalda*, a mare] **1** a worn-out, worthless horse **2** a disreputable woman — *vt., vi.* **jad′ed, jad′ing 1** to tire **2** to satiate —**jad′edly** *adv.* —**jad′ed·ness** *n.*

jade·ite (jād′īt) *n.* a hard, translucent type of jade

jade plant a thick-leaved plant native to S Africa and Asia

jag¹ (jag) *n.* [ME *jagge*] a sharp, toothlike projection

jag² (jag) *n.* [< ?] a drunken spree

jag·ged (jag′id) *adj.* having sharp projecting points; notched or ragged —**jag′gedly** *adv.* —**jag′ged·ness** *n.*

jag·uar (jag′wär′) *n.* [Port < AmInd (Brazil)] a large, leopardlike cat found from SW U.S. to Argentina

jai alai (hī′lī′, hī′ə lī′) [< Basque *jai*, celebration + *alai*, merry] a game like handball, played with a basketlike racket

jail (jāl) *n.* [ult. < L *cavea*, cage] a prison, esp. for minor offenders or persons awaiting trial — *vt.* to put or keep in jail

jail′break′ *n.* a breaking out of jail

jail′er or **jail′or** *n.* a person in charge of a jail or of prisoners

ja·la·peño (häl′ə pān′yō) *n.* [Mex] a kind of hot pepper, orig. from Mexico

ja·lopy (jə läp′ē) *n., pl.* **-lop′ies** [< ?] [Slang] an old, ramshackle car

jal·ou·sie (jal′ə sē′) *n.* [Fr < It *gelosia*, jealousy] a window, shade, or door formed of adjustable horizontal slats of wood, metal, or glass

jam¹ (jam) *vt.* **jammed, jam′ming** [< ?] **1** to squeeze into a confined space **2** to crush **3** to crowd **4** to crowd into or block (a passageway, etc.) **5** to make stick so that it cannot move or work **6** to make (radio broadcasts, etc.) unintelligible, as by sending out other signals on the same wavelength — *vi.* **1** *a*) to become stuck fast *b*) to become unworkable because of jammed parts **2** to become squeezed into a confined space **3** [Slang] *Jazz* to improvise, as in a gathering of musicians (**jam session**) — *n.* **1** a jamming or being jammed [a traffic *jam*] **2** [Colloq.] a difficult situation

jam² (jam) *n.* [< ? prec.] fruit boiled with sugar to a thick mixture

jamb (jam) *n.* [< LL *gamba*, hoof] a side post of a doorway

jam·bo·ree (jam′bə rē′) *n.* [< ?] **1** [Colloq.] a noisy revel **2** a large assembly of Boy Scouts from many places

jam′packed′ (jam′pakt′) *adj.* [Colloq.] tightly packed

jan·gle (jaŋ′gəl) *vi.* **-gled, -gling** [< OFr *jangler*] to make a harsh, usually metallic sound — *vt.* **1** to cause to jangle **2** to irritate [*jangled* nerves] — *n.* a jangling —**jan′gler** *n.*

jani·tor (jan′i tər) *n.* [L, doorkeeper] one who takes care of a building, doing routine repairs, etc. —**jan′i·to′rial** (-i tôr′ē əl) *adj.*

Janu·ary (jan′yōō er′ē) *n., pl.* **-ar′ies** [< L < *Janus*, Roman god who was a patron of beginnings and endings] the first month of the year, having 31 days: abbrev. **Jan.**

ja·pan (jə pan′) *n.* [orig. made in Japan] a lacquer giving a hard, glossy finish

Japa·nese (jap′ə nēz′) *adj.* of Japan, its people, language, etc. — *n.* **1** *pl.* **-nese′** a native of Japan **2** the language of Japan

Japanese beetle a shiny, green-and-brown scarab beetle, orig. from Japan, damaging to crops

jape (jāp) *n.* [< OFr *japer*, to howl] **1** to joke **2** to play tricks — *n.* **1** a joke **2** a trick

jar¹ (jär) *vi.* **jarred, jar′ring** [ult. echoic] **1** to make a harsh sound; grate **2** to have an irritating effect (*on* one)

THESAURUS

jab *n.* poke, punch, hit; see BLOW.

jabber *v.* gibber, babble, mutter; see MURMUR 1, SOUND.

jack *n.* automobile jack, pneumatic jack, hydraulic jack; see DEVICE 1, TOOL 1. —**jack up** lift, add to, accelerate; see INCREASE, RAISE 1.

jacket *n.* tunic, jerkin, parka; see CAPE 2, CLOTHES, COAT 1.

jackknife *n.* clasp knife, case knife, Barlow knife; see KNIFE.

jack-of-all-trades *n.* handyman, factotum, versatile person; see LABORER, WORKMAN.

jackpot *n.* bonanza, find, winnings; see LUCK 1, PROFIT 2, SUCCESS 2.

jagged *a.* serrated, ragged, rugged; see IRREGULAR 4, ROUGH 1.

jail *n.* penitentiary, cage, cell, dungeon, bastille, pound, reformatory, stockade, detention camp, gaol, concentration camp, penal institution, house of detention, prison, lockup, death house, pen*, stir*, clink*, jug*, can*; see also PRISON.

jail *v.* confine, lock up, incarcerate, sentence, impound, detain, put behind bars, put in the clink*, throw away the keys*; see also IMPRISON.— *Ant.* FREE, liberate, discharge.

jailed *a.* arrested, incarcerated, in jail; see CONFINED 3, HELD, UNDER ARREST.

jam¹ *v.* **1** [To force one's way] jostle, squeeze, crowd, throng, press, thrust, pack; see also PUSH 1. **2** [To compress] bind, squeeze, push; see COMPRESS, PACK 2, PRESS 1.

jam¹·² *n.* **1** [Preserves] conserve, fruit butter, spread, marmalade, candied fruit; blackberry jam, plum jam, strawberry jam, etc.; see also JELLY. **2** [*A troublesome situation] trouble, dilemma, problem; see DIFFICULTY 1.

jammed *a.* **1** [Stuck fast] wedged, caught, frozen; see TIGHT 2. **2** [Thronged] crowded, busy, congested; see FULL 1.

janitor *n.* building custodian, watchman, doorman; see ATTENDANT, CUSTODIAN.

January *n.* New Year, the new year, first month of the year; see MONTH, WINTER.

Japanese *a.* Ainu, Nipponese, East Asiatic; see ORIENTAL.

jar¹ *v.* jolt, bounce, bump; see CRASH 4, HIT 1.

jar¹·² *n.* **1** [A glass or earthen con-

3 to vibrate from an impact **4** to clash; conflict — *vt.* to jolt — *n.* **1** a grating sound **2** a vibration due to impact **3** a jolt

jar[2] (jär) *n.* ⟦< Ar *jarrah*, earthen container⟧ **1** a container made of glass, earthenware, etc., with a large opening **2** as much as a jar will hold: also **jar′ful′**

jar·di·niere (jär′də nir′) *n.* ⟦< Fr < *jardin*, a garden⟧ an ornamental pot or stand for flowers or plants

jar·gon (jär′gən) *n.* ⟦< MFr, a chattering⟧ **1** unintelligible talk **2** the specialized vocabulary of those in the same work, way of life, etc.

jas·mine (jaz′min, jas′-) *n.* ⟦< Pers *yāsamin*⟧ any of certain plants of warm regions, with fragrant flowers of yellow, red, or white

Ja·son (jā′sən) *Gr. Myth.* the leader of the Argonauts: cf. ARGONAUT

jas·per (jas′pər) *n.* ⟦< Gr *iaspis*⟧ an opaque variety of colored quartz

jaun·dice (jôn′dis) *n.* ⟦< L *galbus*, yellow⟧ a diseased condition in which the eyeballs, skin, and urine become abnormally yellowish as a result of increased bile in the blood — *vt.* **-diced, -dic·ing 1** to cause to have jaundice **2** to make bitter through envy, etc.

jaunt (jônt) *vi.* ⟦< ?⟧ to take a short pleasure trip — *n.* such a trip

jaunty (jôn′tē) *adj.* **-ti·er, -ti·est** ⟦< Fr *gentil*, genteel⟧ showing an easy confidence; sprightly or perky —**jaun′ti·ly** *adv.* —**jaun′ti·ness** *n.*

Java (jä′və, jav′ə) *n.* ⟦after *Java*, island of Indonesia⟧ [*often* j-] [Slang] coffee

jav·elin (jav′lin, -ə lin) *n.* ⟦MFr *javeline*⟧ a light spear, esp. one thrown for distance in a contest

jaw (jô) *n.* ⟦< OFr *joue*, cheek⟧ **1** either of the two bony parts that hold the teeth and frame the mouth **2** either of two movable parts that grasp or crush something, as in a vise — *vi.* [Slang] to talk

jaw′bone′ *n.* a bone of a jaw, esp. of the lower jaw — *vt., vi.* **-boned′, -bon′ing** to try to persuade by using the influence of one's office

jaw′break′er (-brā′kər) *n.* **1** a hard, usually round candy **2** [Slang] a word hard to pronounce

jaw′less fish a jawless fish with an eel-like body and a circular sucking mouth, as the lamprey

jay (jā) *n.* ⟦< LL *gaius*, jay⟧ any of several birds, usually strikingly colored, as the blue jay

jay′walk′ *vi.* to walk across a street without obeying traffic rules and signals —**jay′walk′er** *n.*

jazz (jaz) *n.* ⟦< ?⟧ **1** a kind of syncopated, highly rhythmic music originated by Southern blacks in the late 19th c. **2** [Slang] talk, acts, etc. regarded disparagingly — *vt.* [Slang] to enliven or embellish: with *up*

jazz′y *adj.* **-i·er, -i·est 1** of or like jazz **2** [Slang] lively, flashy, etc.

jeal·ous (jel′əs) *adj.* ⟦see ZEAL⟧ **1** watchful in guarding [*jealous* of one's rights] **2** *a*) resentfully suspicious of rivalry [a *jealous* lover] *b*) resentfully envious *c*) resulting from such feelings [a *jealous* rage] —**jeal′ous·ly** *adv.*

jeal′ous·y *n.* **1** the quality or condition of being jealous **2** *pl.* **-ous·ies** a jealous feeling

jean (jēn) *n.* ⟦< L *Genua*, Genoa, city in Italy⟧ **1** a

durable, twilled cotton cloth **2** [*pl.*] trousers of this or of denim

jeep (jēp) *n.* ⟦< creature in comic strip by E. C. Segar (1894-1938)⟧ a small, rugged military vehicle of World War II —[J-] *trademark for* a similar vehicle for civilian use

jeer (jir) *vt., vi.* ⟦< ? CHEER⟧ to make fun of in a rude, sarcastic manner; scoff (at) — *n.* a jeering remark —**jeer′ingly** *adv.*

Je·ho·vah (ji hō′və) ⟦< Heb⟧ God

je·june (ji jōōn′) *adj.* ⟦L *jejunus*, empty⟧ **1** not interesting or satisfying **2** not mature; childish

je·ju·num (jē jōō′nəm) *n., pl.* **-na** (-nə) ⟦< L *jejunus*, empty⟧ the middle part of the small intestine

jell (jel) *vi., vt.* ⟦< fol.⟧ **1** to become, or make into, jelly **2** [Colloq.] to crystallize [plans haven't *jelled* yet]

jelly (jel′ē) *n., pl.* **-lies** ⟦< L *gelare*, freeze⟧ **1** a soft, gelatinous food made from cooked fruit syrup or meat juice **2** any substance like this — *vi., vt.* **-lied, -ly·ing** JELL (sense 1)

jelly bean a small, bean-shaped, gelatinous candy Also **jel′ly·bean′**

jel′ly·fish′ *n., pl.* **-fish′** or (for different species) **-fish′es 1** a sea animal with an umbrella-shaped, jellylike body and long tentacles **2** [Colloq.] a weak-willed person

jel′ly·roll′ *n.* a thin sheet of sponge cake spread with jelly and rolled up

jeop·ard·ize (jep′ər dīz′) *vt.* **-ized′, -iz′ing** to put in jeopardy

jeop′ardy (-dē) *n.* ⟦< OFr *jeu parti*, lit., a game with even chances⟧ great danger or risk

jer·emi·ad (jer′ə mī′ad′, -əd) *n.* a long lamentation or complaint: in allusion to the *Lamentations of Jeremiah*

Jer′emi·ah (-ə) *Bible* a Hebrew prophet of the 7th and 6th c. B.C.

jerk (jurk) *n.* ⟦< ?⟧ **1** a sharp, abrupt pull, twist, etc. **2** a sudden muscular contraction **3** [Slang] a person regarded as disagreeable, contemptible, etc. — *vi., vt.* **1** to move with a jerk; pull sharply **2** to twitch

jer·kin (jur′kin) *n.* ⟦< ?⟧ a short, closefitting jacket, often sleeveless

jerk′wa′ter *adj.* [Colloq.] small, unimportant, etc. [a *jerkwater* town]

jerky[1] (jur′kē) *adj.* **jerk′i·er, jerk′i·est 1** moving by jerks; spasmodic **2** [Slang] foolish, mean, etc. —**jerk′i·ly** *adv.*

jerky[2] (jur′kē) *n.* ⟦< Sp *charqui*⟧ meat preserved by being sliced into strips and dried in the sun

jerry-built (jer′ē bilt′) *adj.* built poorly, of cheap materials

jer·sey (jur′zē) *n., pl.* **-seys** ⟦after *Jersey*, one of the Channel Islands⟧ **1** [J-] any of a breed of reddish-brown dairy cattle, orig. from Jersey **2** a soft, knitted cloth **3** a closefitting, knitted upper garment

jest (jest) *n.* ⟦< L *gerere*, perform⟧ **1** a mocking remark; taunt **2** a joke **3** fun; joking **4** something to be laughed at — *vi.* **1** to jeer **2** to joke

jest′er *n.* one who jests; esp., a man kept by a medieval ruler to amuse him by joking and clowning

Jesu·it (jezh′ōō it, jez′-) *n.* a member of the Society of Jesus, a Roman Catholic religious order for men, founded in 1534

THESAURUS

tainer] crock, pot, fruit jar, can, vessel, basin, beaker, jug, cruet, vat, decanter, pitcher, bottle, flagon, flask, phial, vase, chalice, urn; see also CONTAINER. **2** [A jolt] jounce, thud, thump; see BUMP 1.

jargon *n.* **1** [Trite speech] banality, patter, hackneyed terms, overused words, commonplace phrases, shopworn language, trite vocabulary, hocus-pocus; see also LANGUAGE 1. **2** [Specialized vocabulary or pronunciation, etc.] argot, patois, lingo, broken English, idiom, pidgin English, vernacular, colloquialism, coined words, pig Latin, localism, rhyming slang, doubletalk, officialese, newspeak, journalese; see also DIALECT, SLANG.

jarring *a.* **1** [Discordant] unharmonious, grating, rasping; see HARSH, LOUD 1, 2, SHRILL. **2** [Jolting] bumpy, rough, uneven; see UNSTABLE 1.

jaunt *n.* excursion, trip, tour; see

JOURNEY, WALK 3.

jaw *n.* jawbone, muzzle, jowl, mandible, maxilla, chops; see also BONE.

jaywalk *v.* cross a street obliquely, walk in a forbidden traffic zone, cross against a light, cut across, cross illegally.

jazz *n.* Dixieland, ragtime, modern jazz, traditional jazz, improvisation, hot music, bop, hard bop, mainstream, fusion, free jazz, swing, boogie-woogie; see also MUSIC 1.

jealous *a.* possessive, demanding, monopolizing, envious, watchful, resentful, mistrustful, doubting, apprehensive; see also SUSPICIOUS 1.—*Ant.* TRUSTING, confiding, believing.

jealousy *n.* resentment, possessiveness, suspicion; see DOUBT, ENVY.

jeep *n.* four-wheel-drive vehicle, army car, general-purpose vehicle; see AUTOMOBILE, VEHICLE.

jell *v.* set, crystallize, condense; see

FREEZE 1, HARDEN, STIFFEN, THICKEN.

jelly *n.* jell, extract, preserve, gelatin; apple jelly, currant jelly, raspberry jelly, etc.; see also JAM 1.

jellyfish *n.* medusa, coelenterate, hydrozoan; see FISH.

jeopardize *v.* imperil, expose, venture; see ENDANGER, RISK.

jeopardy *n.* risk, peril, exposure; see CHANCE 1, DANGER.

jerk *n.* **1** [A twitch] tic, shrug, wiggle, shake, quiver, flick, jiggle; see also BUMP 1. **2** [*A contemptible person] scoundrel, rat*, twerp*; see FOOL, RASCAL.

jerk *v.* **1** [To undergo a spasm] have a convulsion, quiver, shiver; see SHAKE 1, TWITCH 2. **2** [To move an object with a quick tug] snatch, grab, flick; see SEIZE 1, 2.

jester *n.* comedian, buffoon, joker; see ACTOR, CLOWN, FOOL.

Je·sus (jē′zəz, -zəs) founder of the Christian religion: also **Jesus Christ**

jet[1] (jet) *vt., vi.* **jet′ted, jet′ting** [< L *jacere,* to throw] 1 to gush out in a stream 2 to travel or convey by jet airplane — *n.* 1 a stream of liquid or gas suddenly emitted 2 a spout or nozzle for emitting a jet 3 a jet-propelled airplane: in full, **jet (air)plane** — *adj.* driven by jet propulsion

jet[2] (jet) *n.* [after *Gagas,* town in Asia Minor] 1 a hard, black mineral like coal, polished and used in jewelry 2 a lustrous black — *adj.* black

jet lag a disruption of the daily body rhythms, associated with high-speed travel by jet airplane to distant time zones

jet′lin′er *n.* a commercial jet aircraft for carrying passengers

jet′port′ *n.* a large airport with long runways, for use by jetliners

jet propulsion propulsion of airplanes, boats, etc. by forcing compressed outside air and hot exhaust gases through a jet nozzle —**jet′-propelled′** (-prō peld′) *adj.*

jet·sam (jet′səm) *n.* [var. of JETTISON] cargo thrown overboard to lighten a ship in danger

jet set fashionable people who frequently travel, often by jet, as for pleasure —**jet′-set′ter** *n.*

jet stream high-velocity winds moving from west to east, high above the earth

jet·ti·son (jet′ə sən) *vt.* [< L *jactare,* to throw] 1 to throw (goods) overboard so as to lighten a ship in danger 2 to discard

jet·ty (jet′ē) *n., pl.* **-ties** [see JET[1]] 1 a wall built out into the water to restrain currents, protect a harbor, etc. 2 a landing pier

Jew (jōō) *n.* [< Heb *yehūdī,* citizen of Judah] 1 a person descended, or regarded as descended, from the ancient Hebrews 2 a person whose religion is Judaism

jewel (jōō′əl) *n.* [ult. < L *jocus,* a joke] 1 a valuable ring, necklace, etc., esp. one set with gems 2 a precious stone; gem 3 any person or thing very dear to one 4 a small gem used as a bearing in a watch — *vt.* **-eled** or **-elled, -el·ing** or **-el·ling** to decorate or set with jewels

jew′eler or **jew′el·ler** (-ər) *n.* [ME *jueler* < OFr *joieleor* < *joel:* see prec.] one who makes or deals in jewelry

jew′elry *n.* ornaments such as rings, bracelets, etc., collectively

Jew·ish (jōō′ish) *adj.* of or having to do with Jews or Judaism — *n.* loosely, Yiddish —**Jew′ish·ness** *n.*

Jewry (jōō′rē) *n.* the Jewish people

jew′s-harp (jōōz′härp′) *n.* [< Du *jeugdtromp,* child′s trumpet] a small, metal musical instrument held between the teeth and plucked to produce twanging tones

Jez·ebel (jez′ə bel′) *Bible* a wicked queen of Israel

jib (jib) *n.* [Dan *gib*] a triangular sail secured forward of the mast or foremast

jibe[1] (jib) *vi.* **jibed, jib′ing** [< Du *gijpen*] 1 to shift from one side of a ship to the other, as a fore-and-aft sail 2 to change the course of a ship so that the sails jibe 3 [Colloq.] to be in agreement or accord

jibe[2] (jib) *vi., vt., n.* GIBE

jiffy (jif′ē) *n., pl.* **-fies** [< ?] a very short time Also **jiff**

jig (jig) *n.* [prob. < MFr *giguer,* to dance] 1 a fast, springy dance in triple time, or music for this 2 a device used to guide a tool — *vi., vt.* **jigged, jig′ging** to dance (a jig) — **in jig time** [Colloq.] very quickly —**the jig is up** [Slang] no chance is left

jig·ger (jig′ər) *n.* 1 a small glass, usually of 1½ ounces, used to measure liquor 2 the contents of a jigger

jig·gle (jig′əl) *vt., vi.* **-gled, -gling** [< JIG] to move in quick, slight jerks — *n.* a jiggling

jig·saw (jig′sô′) *n.* a saw with a narrow blade set in a frame, for cutting curves, etc.

jigsaw puzzle a puzzle consisting of a picture cut up into irregularly shaped pieces, which must be put together again

jilt (jilt) *vt.* [< *Jill,* sweetheart] to reject or cast off (a previously accepted lover, etc.)

Jim Crow [name of an early black minstrel song] [*also* j-c-] [Colloq.] discrimination against or segregation of blacks —**Jim′-Crow′** *vt., adj.*

jimmy (jim′ē) *n., pl.* **-mies** [< *James*] a short crowbar, used as by burglars to pry open windows, etc. — *vt.* **-mied, -my·ing** to pry open with or as with a jimmy

jim·son weed (jim′sən) [< *Jamestown weed*] a poisonous weed with white or purplish, trumpet-shaped flowers

jin·gle (jiŋ′gəl) *vi.* **-gled, -gling** [echoic] to make light, ringing sounds, as small bells — *vt.* to cause to jingle — *n.* 1 a jingling sound 2 a catchy verse or song with easy rhythm, simple rhymes, etc.

jin·go·ism (jiŋ′gō iz′əm) *n.* [< phrase *by jingo* in patriotic Brit song] chauvinistic advocacy of an aggressive, warlike foreign policy —**jin′go·ist** *n.* —**jin′go·is′tic** *adj.*

jinni (ji nē′, jin′ē) *n., pl.* **jinn** [Ar] *Muslim Folklore* a supernatural being that can influence human affairs

jin·riki·sha (jin rik′shô′) *n.* [Jpn < *jin,* a man + *riki,* power + *sha,* carriage] a small, two-wheeled carriage, pulled by a man, esp. formerly in the Orient Also sp. **jin·rick′sha′** or **jin·rik′sha′**

jinx (jiŋks) *n.* [< Gr *iynx,* the wryneck (bird used in black magic)] [Colloq.] a person or thing supposed to bring bad luck — *vt.* [Colloq.] to be a jinx to

jit·ney (jit′nē) *n., pl.* **-neys** [< ? Fr *jeton,* a token] a small bus or a car carrying passengers for a low fare

jit·ter·bug (jit′ər bug′) *n.* a fast, acrobatic dance for couples, esp. in the 1940′s — *vi.* **-bugged′, -bug′ging** to do this dance

jit·ters (jit′ərz) *n.pl.* [Colloq.] an uneasy, nervous feeling; fidgets: with *the* —**jit′tery** *adj.*

jive (jiv) *n.* [< JIBE[2]] [Slang] foolish, exaggerated, or insincere talk — *adj.* [Slang] insincere, fraudulent, etc.

job (jäb) *n.* [< ?] 1 a piece of work done for pay 2 a task; duty 3 the thing or material being worked on 4 employment; work — *adj.* hired or done by the job — *vt., vi.* **jobbed, job′bing** 1 to deal in (goods) as a jobber 2 to sublet (work, etc.) —**job′hold′er** *n.* —**job′less** *adj.*

Job (jōb) *Bible* a man who suffered much but kept his faith in God

job action a refusal by a group of employees (esp. a group forbidden by law to strike) to perform their duties in an effort to win certain demands

job·ber (jäb′ər) *n.* 1 one who buys goods in quantity and sells them to dealers 2 one who does piecework

job lot an assortment of goods for sale as one quantity

jock (jäk) *n.* 1 *short for: a)* JOCKEY *b)* JOCKSTRAP 2 [Slang] a male athlete

jockey (jäk′ē) *n., pl.* **-eys** [< Scot dim. of JACK] one whose work is riding horses in races — *vt., vi.* **-eyed, -ey·ing** 1 to cheat; swindle 2 to maneuver for position or advantage

jock·strap (jäk′strap′) *n.* [*jock,* penis + STRAP] an elastic belt with a pouch for supporting the genitals, worn by male athletes

jo·cose (jō kōs′) *adj.* [< L *jocus,* a joke] joking or playful

---

THESAURUS

jet[1] *n.* 1 [A stream of liquid or gas] spray, stream, spurt; see FOUNTAIN 1. 2 [A jet-propelled airplane] jet plane, twin jet, supersonic transport; see PLANE 3.

jet[1] *v.* 1 [To gush out in a stream] spout, squirt, spurt; see FLOW. 2 [To travel by jet airplane] take a jet, go by jet, fly; see TRAVEL.

Jew *n.* Hebrew, Israelite, Semite.

jewel *n.* bauble, gem, trinket; see DIAMOND. *Jewels include the following:* emerald, amethyst, sapphire, opal, pearl, jade, aquamarine, moonstone, agate, ruby, turquoise, topaz, garnet, jasper, coral, peridot, lapis lazuli, bloodstone, onyx, zircon.

jeweler *n.* goldsmith, diamond setter, lapidary; see ARTIST, CRAFTSMAN,

SPECIALIST.

jewelry *n.* gems, jewels, baubles, trinkets, adornments, frippery, ornaments, costume jewelry, bangles; see also JEWEL.

Jewish *a.* Hebrew, Semitic, Yiddish.

jibe[1]* *v.* agree, match, correspond; see RESEMBLE, AGREE.

jiggle *v.* shake, twitch, wiggle; see JERK 2.

jingle *n.* tinkle, jangle, clank; see NOISE 1.

jingle *v.* tinkle, clink, rattle; see SOUND.

jinx *n.* evil eye, hex, spell; see CHANCE 1.

job *n.* 1 [Gainful employment] situation, place, position, appointment,

operation, task, line, calling, vocation, handicraft, career, craft, pursuit, office, function, means of livelihood; see also BUSINESS 1, PROFESSION 1, TRADE 2, WORK 2. 2 [Something to be done] task, business, action, act, mission, assignment, affair, concern, obligation, enterprise, undertaking, project, chore, errand, care, matter in hand, commission, function, responsibility, office, tour of duty, operation; see also DUTY 1. 3 [The amount of work done] assignment, day′s work, output; see DUTY 1. —**odd jobs** miscellaneous duties, chores, occasional labor; see WORK 2. —**on the job** busy, engaged, occupied; see BUSY 1.

—**jo·cose′ly** *adv.* —**jo·cos′i·ty** (-käs′ə tē), *pl.* **-ties,** or **jo·cose′ness** *n.*

jocu·lar (jäk′yōō lər) *adj.* ⟦ < L *jocus,* a joke ⟧ joking; full of fun —**joc′u·lar′i·ty** (-lar′ə tē), *pl.* **-ties,** *n.*

joc·und (jäk′ənd) *adj.* ⟦ < L *jucundus,* pleasant ⟧ cheerful; genial —**joc′und·ly** *adv.*

jodh·purs (jäd′pərz) *n.pl.* ⟦ after *Jodhpur,* former state in India ⟧ riding breeches made loose and full above the knees and closefitting below

jog¹ (jäg) *vt.* **jogged, jog′ging** ⟦ME *joggen,* to spur (a horse) ⟧ 1 to give a little shake to; nudge 2 to rouse (the memory) — *vi.* to move along at a slow, steady, jolting pace; specif., to engage in jogging — *n.* 1 a little shake or nudge 2 a slow, steady, jolting motion —**jog′ger** *n.*

jog² (jäg) *n.* ⟦var. of JAG¹⟧ 1 a projecting or notched part in a surface or line 2 a sharp change of direction

jog′ging *n.* trotting slowly and steadily as a form of exercise

jog·gle (jäg′əl) *vt., vi.* **-gled, -gling** ⟦ < JOG¹⟧ to shake or jolt slightly — *n.* a slight jolt

john (jän) *n.* [Slang] 1 a toilet 2 [*also* J-] a prostitute's customer

John (jän) *Bible* 1 a Christian apostle, the reputed author of the fourth Gospel 2 this book

John Bull *personification of* England or an Englishman

John Doe (dō) a fictitious name used in legal papers for an unknown person

John the Baptist *Bible* the forerunner and baptizer of Jesus

join (join) *vt., vi.* ⟦ < L *jungere* ⟧ 1 to bring or come together (with); connect; unite 2 to become a part or member of (a club, etc.) 3 to participate (*in* a conversation, etc.)

join′er *n.* 1 a carpenter who finishes interior woodwork 2 [Colloq.] one who joins many organizations

joint (joint) *n.* ⟦ < L *jungere* ⟧ 1 a place where, or way in which, two things are joined 2 any of the parts of a jointed whole 3 a large cut of meat with the bone still in it 4 [Slang] a cheap bar, restaurant, etc., or any house, building, etc. 5 [Slang] a marijuana cigarette — *adj.* 1 common to two or more *[joint* property*]* 2 sharing with another *[a joint* owner*]* — *vt.* 1 to connect by or provide with a joint or joints 2 to cut (meat) into joints —**out of joint** 1 dislocated 2 disordered

joint′ly *adv.* in common

joist (joist) *n.* ⟦ < OFr *giste,* a bed ⟧ any of the parallel beams that hold up the planks of a floor or the laths of a ceiling

joke (jōk) *n.* ⟦L *jocus* ⟧ 1 anything said or done to arouse laughter, as a funny anecdote 2 a thing done or said merely in fun 3 a person or thing to be laughed at — *vi.* **joked, jok′ing** to make jokes —**jok′ing·ly** *adv.*

jok′er *n.* 1 one who jokes: also **joke′ster** 2 a hidden provision put into a legal document, etc. to make it different from what it seems to be 3 an extra playing card

jok′ey *adj.* comical or lighthearted Also **jok′y**

jol·lity (jäl′ə tē) *n.* a being jolly

jolly (jäl′ē) *adj.* **-lier, -li·est** ⟦OFr *joli* ⟧ 1 full of high spirits and good humor; merry 2 [Colloq.] enjoyable — *vt., vi.* **-lied, -ly·ing** [Colloq.] 1 to try to make (a person) feel good, as by coaxing: often with *along* 2 to make fun of (someone) —**jol′lily** *adv.* —**jol′li·ness** *n.*

jolt (jōlt) *vt.* ⟦ < earlier *jot* ⟧ 1 to shake up, as with a bumpy ride 2 to shock or surprise — *vi.* to move along in a bumpy manner — *n.* 1 a sudden jerk, bump, etc. 2 a shock or surprise

Jo·nah (jō′nə) *Bible* a Hebrew prophet: cast overboard and swallowed by a big fish, he was later cast up unharmed — *n.* one who brings bad luck

jon·quil (jän′kwil, jän′-) *n.* ⟦ < L *juncus,* a rush ⟧ a species of narcissus with small, yellow flowers

Jo·seph (jō′zəf) *Bible* 1 one of Jacob's sons, who became a high official in Egypt 2 the husband of Mary, mother of Jesus

josh (jäsh) *vt., vi.* ⟦ < ? ⟧ [Colloq.] to tease; banter — **josh′er** *n.*

Joshua (jäsh′yōō ə) *Bible* Moses' successor, who led the Israelites into the Promised Land

jos·tle (jäs′əl) *vt., vi.* **-tled, -tling** ⟦see JOUST ⟧ to push, as in a crowd; shove roughly — *n.* a jostling

jot (jät) *n.* ⟦ < Gr *iōta,* the smallest letter ⟧ a very small amount — *vt.* **jot′ted, jot′ting** to make a brief note of: usually with *down* —**jot′ter** *n.*

joule (jōōl) *n.* ⟦after J. P. *Joule,* 19th-c. Eng physicist ⟧ the unit of work or energy in the metric system

jounce (jouns) *vt., vi.* **jounced, jounc′ing** ⟦ < ? ⟧ to jolt or bounce — *n.* a jolt —**jounc′y** *adj.*

jour·nal (jur′nəl) *n.* ⟦ < L *diurnalis,* daily ⟧ 1 a daily record of happenings, as a diary 2 a newspaper or periodical 3 *Bookkeeping* a book of original entry for recording transactions 4 ⟦orig. Scot ⟧ the part of an axle or shaft that turns in a bearing

jour·nal·ese (jur′nəl ēz′) *n.* a facile style of writing found in many newspapers, magazines, etc.

jour′nal·ism′ (-iz′əm) *n.* the work of gathering news for, or producing, a newspaper, etc. —**jour′nal·ist** *n.* —**jour′nal·is′tic** *adj.*

jour·ney (jur′nē) *n., pl.* **-neys** ⟦ < OFr *journee;* ult. < L *dies,* day ⟧ a traveling from one place to another; trip — *vi.* **-neyed, -ney·ing** to travel —**jour′ney·er** *n.*

jour′ney·man (-mən) *n., pl.* **-men** ⟦ME < *journee,* day's work + *man* ⟧ 1 a worker qualified to work at a specified

THESAURUS

jog¹ *n.* 1 [A slow run] trot, amble, pace; see RUN 1. 2 [A bump] nudge, poke, shake; see BLOW, BUMP 1.

jog¹ *v.* jog along, take one's exercise, trot; see RUN 1.

jog someone's memory *v.* bring up, recall, suggest; see REMIND.

John Doe *n.* the average citizen, John Q. Public, anyone; see MISTER.

join *v.* 1 [To unite] put together, blend, combine, bring in contact with, touch, connect, couple, mix, assemble, bind together, fasten, marry, wed, copulate, cement, weld, clasp, fuse, lock, grapple, clamp, entwine; see also UNITE.—*Ant.* SEPARATE, sunder, sever. 2 [To enter the company of] go to, seek, associate with, join forces, go to the aid of, place by the side of, follow, register, team up with, take up with, be in, sign on, sign up, go in with, fall in with, consort, enlist, fraternize, throw in with*, pair with, affiliate, side with, make one of, take part in, seek a place among, advance toward, seek reception, go to meet.—*Ant.* DESERT, leave, abandon. 3 [*To adjoin] lie next to, neighbor, border, fringe, verge upon, be adjacent to, open into, be close to, bound, lie beside, be at hand, touch, skirt, parallel, rim, hem.

joined *a.* linked, yoked, coupled, allied, akin, intertwined, blended, connected, united, federated, banded, wedded, married, mixed, tied together, combined, touching, cemented, welded, fused, locked, grappled, clipped together, accompanying, associated, confederated, mingled, spliced, affixed, attached, joint, incorporated, involved, inseparable, affiliated, related, pieced together, coupled with, bound up with; see also UNIFIED.—*Ant.* SEPARATED, disparate, apart.

joint *n.* 1 [A juncture] union, coupling, hinge, tie, swivel, link, connection, point of union, bond, splice, bend, hyphen, junction, bridge; see also BOND 1. 2 [A section] piece, unit, portion; see LINK, PART 3. 3 [*An establishment, particularly one providing entertainment] hangout*, dive*, hole in the wall*; see BAR 2, RESTAURANT. 4 [*A marijuana cigarette] roach*, doobie*, reefer*, stick*; see also DRUG. —**out of joint** dislocated, disjointed, wrong; see DISORDERED.

jointly *a.* conjointly, mutually, combined; see TOGETHER.

joke *n.* prank, put-on*, game, sport, frolic, practical joke, jest, pun, witticism, play on words, quip, pleasantry, banter, drollery, retort, repartee, crack*, wisecrack*, clowning, caper, mischief, escapade, tom-foolery, play, antic, spree, farce, monkeyshine*, shenanigan*, horseplay, stunt, gag*; see also TRICK 1.

joke *v.* jest, quip, banter, laugh, raise laughter, poke fun, play, frolic, play tricks, pun, twit, trick, fool, make merry, play the fool, wisecrack*, pull someone's leg*.

joking *a.* humorous, facetious, not serious; see FUNNY 1.

jokingly *a.* facetiously, amusingly, not seriously; see HUMOROUSLY.

jolly *a.* gay, merry, joyful; see HAPPY.

jolt *n.* 1 [A bump] jar, punch, bounce; see BLOW, BUMP 1. 2 [A surprise] jar, start, shock; see SURPRISE 2, WONDER 1.

jostle *v.* nudge, elbow, shoulder; see PRESS 1, PUSH 1.

jot *v.* scribble, indicate, list; see RECORD 1, WRITE 1.

journal *n.* 1 [A daily record] diary, almanac, chronicle; see RECORD 1. 2 [A periodical] publication, annual, daily; see MAGAZINE, NEWSPAPER.

journalism *n.* reportage, news coverage, the fourth estate; see WRITING 3.

journalist *n.* commentator, publicist, member of the fourth estate; see ANNOUNCER, REPORTER, WRITER.

journey *n.* trip, visit, run, passage, tour, excursion, jaunt, pilgrimage, voyage, crossing, expedition, patrol, trade **2** any sound, experienced, but not brilliant performer

joust (joust, just) *n.* ⟦ult. < L *juxta*, close to⟧ a combat with lances between two knights on horseback —*vi.* to engage in a joust

jo·vial (jō'vē əl) *adj.* ⟦< LL *Jovialis*, of Jupiter: from astrological notion of planet's influence⟧ full of playful good humor —**jo'vi·al'ity** (-al'ə tē) *n.* —**jo'vi·al·ly** *adv.*

jowl[1] (joul) *n.* ⟦OE *ceafl*, jaw⟧ **1** the lower jaw **2** the cheek, esp. of a hog

jowl[2] (joul) *n.* ⟦OE *ceole*, throat⟧ [*usually pl.*] the fleshy hanging part under the jaw —**jowl'y** *adj.*

joy (joi) *n.* ⟦ult. < L *gaudium*, joy⟧ **1** a very glad feeling; happiness; delight **2** anything causing this —**joy'less** *adj.*

joy'ful *adj.* feeling, expressing, or causing joy; glad —**joy'fully** *adv.*

joy'ous (-əs) *adj.* joyful; happy —**joy'ously** *adv.* —**joy'ous·ness** *n.*

joy ride [Colloq.] an automobile ride, often at a reckless speed, just for pleasure —**joy rider** —**joy riding**

joy'stick' *n.* **1** [Slang] the control stick of an airplane **2** a manual device with a control lever for positioning a lighted indicator, as on a video screen

JP or **J.P.** Justice of the Peace

Jpn. **1** Japan **2** Japanese

Jr. or **jr.** junior

ju·bi·lant (jōō'bə lənt) *adj.* ⟦< L *jubilum*, wild shout⟧ joyful and triumphant; elated; rejoicing

ju·bi·la·tion (jōō'bə lā'shən) *n.* **1** a rejoicing **2** a happy celebration

ju·bi·lee (jōō'bə lē') *n.* ⟦< Heb *yōbēl*, a ram's horn (trumpet)⟧ **1** a 50th or 25th anniversary **2** a time of rejoicing **3** jubilation

Ju·dah (jōō'də) *Bible* one of Jacob's sons

Ju·da·ism (jōō'də iz'əm, -dē-, -də-) *n.* the Jewish religion —**Ju·da'ic** (-dā'ik) *adj.*

Judas (jōō'dəs) *Bible* the disciple who betrayed Jesus for money: in full **Judas Is·car·iot** (is ker'ē ət) —*n.* a traitor or betrayer

Judeo- *combining form* Jewish

judge (juj) *n.* ⟦< L *jus*, law + *dicere*, say⟧ **1** a public official with authority to hear and decide cases in a court of law **2** a person designated to determine the winner, settle a controversy, etc. **3** a person qualified to decide on the relative worth of anything —*vt., vi.* **judged, judg'ing** **1** to hear and pass judgment on in a court of law **2** to determine the winner of (a contest) or settle (a controversy) **3** to form an opinion about **4** to criticize or censure **5** to think; suppose —**judge'ship'** *n.*

judg·ment (juj'mənt) *n.* **1** a judging; deciding **2** a legal decision; order given by a judge, etc. **3** an opinion **4** the ability to come to an opinion **5** [**J-**] *short for* LAST JUDGMENT Also **judge'ment**

judg·men'tal (-ment''l) *adj.* making judgments as to value, etc., often, specif., judgments considered to be lacking in tolerance, objectivity, etc.

Judgment Day *Theol.* the time of God's final judgment of all people

ju·di·ca·tory (jōō'di kə tôr'ē) *adj.* ⟦see JUDGE⟧ having to do with administering justice —*n., pl.* **-ries** a law court, or law courts collectively

ju·di·ca·ture (-chər) *n.* **1** the administering of justice **2** jurisdiction **3** judges or courts collectively

ju·di·cial (jōō dish'əl) *adj.* **1** of judges, courts, or their functions **2** allowed, enforced, etc. by a court **3** befitting a judge **4** fair; impartial —**ju·di'cially** *adv.*

ju·di·ci·ary (jōō dish'ē er'ē) *adj.* of judges or courts —*n., pl.* **-ar'ies** **1** the part of government that administers justice **2** judges collectively

ju·di·cious (-dish'əs) *adj.* having or showing sound judgment —**ju·di'ciously** *adv.*

judo (jōō'dō) *n.* ⟦Jpn < *jū*, soft + *dō*, way⟧ a form of jujitsu

jug (jug) *n.* ⟦a pet form of *Judith* or *Joan*⟧ **1** a container for liquids, with a small opening and a handle **2** [Slang] a jail

jug·ger·naut (jug'ər nôt') *n.* ⟦< Sans *Jagannātha*, lord of the world⟧ a terrible, irresistible force

jug·gle (jug'əl) *vt.* **-gled, -gling** ⟦< L *jocus*, a joke⟧ **1** to perform skillful tricks of sleight of hand with (balls, etc.) **2** to manipulate so as to deceive —*vi.* to toss up balls, etc. and keep them in the air —**jug'gler** (jug'lər) *n.* —**jug'glery** *n.*

jugu·lar (jug'yōo lər, jug'lər) *adj.* ⟦< L *jugum*, a yoke⟧ of the neck or throat —*n.* JUGULAR VEIN

jugular vein either of two large veins in the neck carrying blood from the head

juice (jōōs) *n.* ⟦< L *jus*, broth, juice⟧ **1** the liquid part of a plant, fruit, etc. **2** a liquid in or from animal tissue **3** [Colloq.] vitality **4** [Slang] *a*) electricity *b*) alcoholic liquor *c*) power or influence —*vt.* **juiced, juic'ing** to extract juice from —*vi.* [Slang] to drink alcoholic beverages to excess

juiced (jōōst) *adj.* drunk; intoxicated

juicer (jōō'sər) *n.* **1** a device for extracting juice from fruit **2** [Slang] one who drinks alcoholic beverages to excess

juicy (jōō'sē) *adj.* **-i·er, -i·est** **1** full of juice **2** [Colloq.] *a*) very interesting *b*) highly profitable —**juic'i·ness** *n.*

ju·jitsu (jōō jit'sōō') *n.* ⟦< Jpn *jū*, soft, pliant + *jutsu*, art⟧

THESAURUS

beat, venture, adventure, drive, flight, cruise, course, route, sojourn, traveling, travels, trek, migration, caravan, roaming, quest, safari, exploration, hike, airing, outing, march, picnic, survey, mission, ride.

journey *v.* tour, jaunt, take a trip; see TRAVEL.

jovial *a.* affable, amiable, merry; see HAPPY.

jowl[1] *n.* mandible, chin, cheek; see JAW.

joy *n.* mirth, cheerfulness, delight, pleasure, gratification, treat, diversion, sport, refreshment, revelry, frolic, playfulness, gaiety, geniality, good humor, merriment, merrymaking, levity, rejoicing, liveliness, high spirits, good spirits, jubilation, celebration; see also LAUGHTER.— *Ant.* COMPLAINING, weeping, wailing.

joyful *a.* joyous, cheery, glad; see HAPPY.

joyous *a.* blithe, glad, gay; see HAPPY.

joy ride* *n.* reckless trip, car theft, pleasure trip; see DRIVE 1, RACE 3.

Judaism *n.* Jewish religion, Hebraism, Zionism; see RELIGION 2.

Judas *n.* betrayer, fraud, informer; see HYPOCRITE, TRAITOR.

judge *n.* **1** [A legal official] justice, executive judge, magistrate, justice of the peace, chief justice, associate justice, judiciary, circuit judge, county judge, judge of the district court, appellate judge. **2** [A connoisseur]

expert, man of taste, professional; see CRITIC 2, SPECIALIST.

judge *v.* adjudge, adjudicate, rule on, pass on, sit in judgment, sentence, give a hearing to, hold the scales; see also CONDEMN, CONVICT.

judged *a.* found guilty or innocent, convicted, settled; see DETERMINED 1, GUILTY.

judgment *n.* **1** [Discernment] discrimination, taste, shrewdness, sapience, understanding, knowledge, wit, keenness, sharpness, critical faculty, rational faculty, reason, rationality, intuition, mentality, acuteness, intelligence, awareness, experience, profundity, depth, brilliance, mentality, sanity, intellectual power, capacity, comprehension, mother wit, quickness, readiness, grasp, apprehension, perspicacity, soundness, genius, good sense, common sense, astuteness, prudence, wisdom, gray matter*, brains, savvy*, horse sense*.—*Ant.* STUPIDITY, simplicity, naiveté. **2** [The act of judging] decision, consideration, appraisal, examination, weighing, sifting the evidence, determination, inspection, assessment, estimate, estimation, probing, appreciation, evaluation, review, contemplation, analysis, inquiry, inquisition, inquest, search, quest, pursuit, scrutiny, exploration, close study, observation, exhaustive inquiry; see also EXAMINATION 1. **3** [A pronounce-

ment] conclusion, appraisal, estimate, opinion, report, view, summary, belief, idea, conviction, inference, resolution, deduction, induction, determination, decree, opinion, supposition, commentary, finding, recommendation; see also VERDICT.

Judgment Day *n.* doomsday, Day of Judgment, retribution, visitation, chastisement, correction, castigation, mortification, end of the world, last day, particular judgment; see also JUDGMENT 1, 2.

judicial *a.* legalistic, authoritative, administrative; see LAWFUL.

judiciary *n.* justices, bench, bar; see COURT 2.

judicious *a.* well-advised, prudent, sensible; see DISCREET, RATIONAL 1.— *Ant.* RASH, ill-advised, hasty.

jug *n.* crock, flask, pitcher; see CONTAINER.

juggle *v.* **1** [To keep in the air by tossing] toss, keep in motion, perform sleight of hand; see BALANCE 2. **2** [To alter, usually so as to deceive] shuffle, trick, delude; see DECEIVE.

juice *n.* sap, extract, fluid; see LIQUID.

juicy *a.* **1** [Succulent] moist, wet, watery, humid, dewy, sappy, dank, dripping, sodden, soaked, liquid, oily, sirupy; see also WET.—*Ant.* DRY, dehydrated, bone-dry. **2** [*Full of interest] spicy, piquant, intriguing, a Japanese system of wrestling in which an opponent's strength and weight are used against him

ju·jube (jōō'jōō bē') *n.* ⟦< Gr⟧ a fruit-flavored, jellylike lozenge

ju·jutsu (jōō joot'sōō', -jut'-) *n.* JUJITSU

juke·box (jōōk'bäks') *n.* ⟦< Am black *juke*, wicked⟧ a coin-operated record player

ju·lep (jōō'ləp) *n.* ⟦< Pers *gul*, rose + *āb*, water⟧ MINT JULEP

ju·li·enne (jōō'lē en') *adj.* ⟦Fr⟧ cut into strips: said of vegetables, etc.

Ju·liet (jōō'lē et', jōō'lē et') the heroine of Shakespeare's tragedy *Romeo and Juliet*

July (jōō lī', jōō-) *n.* ⟦< L < *Julius* Caesar, Rom. dictator⟧ the seventh month of the year, having 31 days: abbrev. **Jul.**

jum·ble (jum'bəl) *vt., vi.* **-bled, -bling** ⟦? blend of JUMP + TUMBLE⟧ to mix or be mixed in a confused heap — *n.* a confused mixture or heap

jumbo (jum'bō) *n., pl.* **-bos** ⟦< Am black *jamba*, elephant⟧ a large person, animal, or thing — *adj.* very large

jump (jump) *vi.* ⟦< ?⟧ **1** to spring or leap from the ground, a height, etc. **2** to jerk; bob **3** to move or act eagerly: often with *at* **4** to pass suddenly, as to a new topic **5** to rise suddenly, as prices **6** [Slang] to be lively — *vt.* **1** *a)* to leap over *b)* to pass over **2** to cause to leap **3** to leap upon **4** to cause (prices, etc.) to rise **5** [Colloq.] *a)* to attack suddenly *b)* to react to prematurely **6** [Slang] to leave suddenly *[to jump town]* — *n.* **1** a jumping **2** a distance jumped **3** a sudden transition **4** a sudden rise, as in prices **5** a sudden, nervous start — **get (or have) the jump on** [Slang] to get (or have) an advantage over — **jump bail** to forfeit bail by running away

jumper[1] (jump'ər) *n.* **1** one that jumps **2** a short wire to make a temporary electrical connection

jumper[2] (jump'ər) *n.* ⟦< dial. *jump*, short coat⟧ **1** a loose jacket **2** a sleeveless dress for wearing over a blouse, etc. **3** [*pl.*] rompers: see ROMPER (sense 2)

jumper cables a pair of thick, insulated electrical wires with clamplike terminals, used to connect a live battery to a dead one

jump'-start' *vt.* to start (the engine of a motor vehicle) with jumper cables — *n.* a starting in such a way

jump·suit (jump'sōōt) *n.* **1** a coverall worn by paratroops, etc. **2** any one-piece garment like this

jumpy (jum'pē) *adj.* **-i·er, -i·est 1** moving in jumps, etc. **2** easily startled —**jump'i·ly** *adv.* —**jump'i·ness** *n.*

junco (jun'kō') *n., pl.* **-cos** ⟦< Sp⟧ a small bird with a gray or black head

junc·tion (junk'shən) *n.* ⟦< L *jungere*, join⟧ **1** a joining or being joined **2** a place of joining, as of roads —**junc'tion·al** *adj.*

junc·ture (junk'chər) *n.* **1** a junction **2** a point of time **3** a crisis

June (jōōn) *n.* ⟦< L < *Junius*, of *Juno*⟧ the sixth month of the year, having 30 days: abbrev. **Jun.**

jun·gle (jun'gəl) *n.* ⟦< Sans *jaṅgala*, wasteland⟧ **1** land densely covered with trees, vines, etc., as in the tropics **2**

[Slang] a situation in which people struggle fiercely for survival

jun·ior (jōōn'yər) *adj.* ⟦L < *juvenis*, young⟧ **1** the younger: written *Jr.* after a son's name if it is the same as his father's **2** of more recent position or lower status *[a junior partner]* **3** of juniors — *n.* **1** one who is younger, of lower rank, etc. **2** a student in the next-to-last year, as of college

junior college a school offering courses two years beyond high school

junior high school a school usually including grades 7, 8, and 9

ju·ni·per (jōō'ni pər) *n.* ⟦L *juniperus*⟧ a small evergreen shrub or tree with berrylike cones

junk[1] (junk) *n.* ⟦< ?⟧ **1** old metal, paper, rags, etc. **2** [Colloq.] trash **3** [Slang] heroin — *vt.* [Colloq.] to scrap —**junk'y, -i·er, -i·est,** *adj.*

junk[2] (junk) *n.* ⟦< Malay *adjong*⟧ a Chinese or Japanese flat-bottomed ship

junk bond [Colloq.] a speculative BOND (*n.* 6), often issued to finance the takeover of a corporation

junker (jun'kər) *n.* [Slang] an old, dilapidated car or truck

Jun·ker (yoon'kər) *n.* ⟦Ger⟧ [Historical] a Prussian of the militaristic landowning class

jun·ket (junk'it) *n.* ⟦ME *joncate*, cream cheese⟧ **1** milk sweetened, flavored, and thickened into curd **2** a picnic **3** an excursion, esp. one by an official at public expense — *vi.* to go on a junket —**jun'keteer'** (-i tir') or **jun'keter** *n.*

junk food snack food with chemical additives and little food value

junkie or **junky** (junk'ē) *n., pl.* **-ies** ⟦< JUNK[1], *n.* 3⟧ [Slang] **1** a narcotics addict **2** one who is addicted to a specified activity, food, etc. *[a TV junkie]*

Juno (jōō'nō) *Rom. Myth.* the wife of Jupiter and queen of the gods

junta (hoon'tä, jun'-) *n.* ⟦Sp < L *jungere*, join⟧ a group of political intriguers, esp. military men, in power after a coup d'état Also **junto** (jun'tō), *pl.* **-tos**

Ju·pi·ter (jōō'pit ər) **1** the chief Roman god **2** the largest planet of the solar system: see PLANET

Ju·ras·sic (jōō ras'ik) *adj.* ⟦< Fr, after *Jura* Mountains, between France and Switzerland⟧ of the geologic period characterized by the dominance of dinosaurs

ju·rid·i·cal (jōō rid'i kəl, joo-) *adj.* ⟦< L *jus*, law + *dicere*, declare⟧ of judicial proceedings or law —**ju·rid'i·cally** *adv.*

ju·ris·dic·tion (joor'is dik'shən) *n.* ⟦see prec.⟧ **1** the administering of justice **2** authority or its range —**ju'ris·dic'tional** *adj.*

juris·pru·dence (joor'is prōōd''ns) *n.* ⟦< L *jus*, law + *prudentia*, a foreseeing⟧ **1** the science or philosophy of law **2** a division of law

ju·rist (joor'ist) *n.* ⟦< L *jus*, law⟧ an expert in law or writer on law

ju·ror (joor'ər) *n.* a member of a jury

jury (joor'ē) *n., pl.* **-ries** ⟦L *jurare*, to swear⟧ **1** a group of people sworn to hear evidence in a law case and to give a decision **2** a committee that decides winners in a contest

just (just) *adj.* ⟦< L *jus*, law⟧ **1** right or fair *[a just decision]* **2** righteous *[a just man]* **3** deserved *[just praise]* **4** lawful **5** proper **6** correct or true **7** accurate; exact —

THESAURUS

---

racy, risqué, fascinating, colorful. **3** [*Profitable] lucrative, remunerative, fruitful; see PROFITABLE.

July *n.* summer month, midsummer, baseball season; see MONTH, SUMMER.

jumble *n.* clutter, mess, hodgepodge; see CONFUSION, MIXTURE 1.

jumbo *a.* immense, mammoth, gigantic; see LARGE 1.

jump *n.* **1** [A leap up or across] skip, hop, rise, pounce, lunge, jumping, broad jump, high jump, vault, bounce, hurdle, spring, bound, caper. **2** [A leap down] plunge, plummet, fall; see DIVE, DROP 2. **3** [Distance jumped] leap, stretch, vault; see HEIGHT, LENGTH 1. **4** [*An advantage] upper hand, handicap, head start; see ADVANTAGE. **5** [A sudden rise] ascent, spurt, inflation; see INCREASE, RISE 3.

jump *v.* **1** [To leap across or up] vault, leap over, spring, lurch, lunge, pop up, bound, hop, skip, high-jump, broad-jump, hurdle, top. **2** [To leap down] drop, plummet, plunge; see

DIVE, FALL 1. **3** [To pass over] cover, take, skip, traverse, remove, nullify; see also CANCEL, CROSS 1. **4** [To vibrate] jiggle, wobble, rattle; see BOUNCE. **5** [*To accost belligerently] attack suddenly, assault, mug*; see ATTACK.

jumping *a.* vaulting, hopping, skipping; see ACTIVE.

jumpy *a.* sensitive, restless, nervous; see EXCITED.

junction *n.* **1** [A meeting] joining, coupling, reunion; see JOINT 1, UNION 1. **2** [A place of meeting, especially of roads] crossroads, crossing, intersection; see ROAD 1.

June *n.* spring or summer month, month of brides, month of roses, beginning of summer; see also MONTH, SUMMER.

jungle *n.* wilderness, undergrowth, wood; see FOREST.

junior *a.* subordinate, lesser, lower; see SUBORDINATE.

junk[1] *n.* waste, garbage, filth; see

TRASH 1.

junk[1]* *v.* dump, scrap, wreck; see DISCARD.

junkie* *n.* dope addict, doper*, head*; see ADDICT.

jurisdiction *n.* authority, range, supervision, control, discretion, province, commission, inquisition, scope, arbitration, reign, domain, extent, empire, sovereignty.

jurist *n.* attorney, judge, legal advisor; see LAWYER.

jury *n.* tribunal, panel, board; see COURT 2.

just *a.* **1** [Precisely] exactly, correctly, perfectly; see ACCURATE. **2** [Hardly] barely, scarcely, by very little; see HARDLY. **3** [Only] merely, simply, no more than; see ONLY 2. **4** [Recently] just a while ago, lately, a moment ago; see RECENTLY. **5** [Fair] impartial, equal, righteous; see FAIR 1. —**just the same** nevertheless, however, in spite of that; see BUT 1.

adv. 1 exactly *[just* one o'clock*]* 2 nearly 3 only *[just* a taste*]* 4 barely *[just* missed him*]* 5 a very short time ago *[*she's *just* left*]* 6 immediately *[just* east of here*]* 7 [Colloq.] really *[just* beautiful*]* —**just the same** [Colloq.] nevertheless —**just'ly** *adv.* —**just'ness** *n.*

jus·tice (jus'tis) *n.* 1 a being righteous 2 fairness 3 rightfulness 4 reward or penalty as deserved 5 the use of authority to uphold what is just 6 the administration of law 7 *a)* JUDGE (*n.* 1) *b)* JUSTICE OF THE PEACE —**do justice to** to treat fairly

justice of the peace a local magistrate who decides minor cases, performs marriages, etc.

jus·tify (jus'tə fī') *vt.* -**fied'**, -**fy'ing** ⟦< L *justus*, just + *facere*, to do⟧ 1 to show to be just, right, etc. 2 *Theol.* to free from blame or guilt 3 to supply grounds for —**jus'ti·fi'able** *adj.* —**jus'ti·fi'ably** *adv.* —**jus'ti·fi·ca'tion** (-fi kā' shən) *n.*

jut (jut) *vi., vt.* **jut'ted, jut'ting** ⟦prob. var. of JET¹⟧ to stick out; project — *n.* a part that juts

jute (jo͞ot) *n.* ⟦< Sans *jūta*, matted hair⟧ 1 a strong fiber used for making burlap, rope, etc. 2 a S Asian plant yielding this fiber

ju·venile (jo͞o'və nil', -nəl) *adj.* ⟦< L *juvenis*, young⟧ 1 young; immature 2 of or for young persons — *n.* 1 a young person 2 an actor who plays youthful roles 3 a book for children

juvenile delinquency antisocial or illegal behavior by minors, usually 18 years of age or younger —**juvenile delinquent**

juxta·pose (juks'tə pōz', juks'tə pōz') *vt.* -**posed', -pos'ing** ⟦< Fr < L *juxta*, beside + POSE⟧ to put side by side —**jux'ta·po·si'tion** *n.*

JV junior varsity

THESAURUS

justice *n.* 1 [Fairness] right, truth, equity; see FAIRNESS. 2 [Lawfulness] legality, equity, prescriptive right, statutory right, established right, legitimacy, sanction, legalization, constitutionality, authority, code, charter, decree, rule, legal process, authorization; see also CUSTOM, LAW 1, POWER 2.—*Ant.* WRONG, illegality, illegitimacy. 3 [The administration of law] adjudication, settlement, arbitration, hearing, legal process, due process, judicial procedure, jury trial, trial by jury, regulation, decision, pronouncement, review, appeal, sentence, consideration, taking evidence, litigation, prosecution; see also JUDGMENT 2, LAW 1, TRIAL 2.—*Ant.* DISORDER, lawlessness, despotism. 4 [A judge] magistrate, umpire, chancellor; see JUDGE 1. —**do justice to** esteem, pay tribute, honor; see ADMIRE, CONSIDER, RESPECT 2. —**do oneself justice** be fair to oneself, give oneself credit, behave in a worthy way; see APPROVE.

justifiable *a.* proper, suitable, probable; see FIT 1, LOGICAL.

justification *n.* excuse, defense, reason; see APPEAL 1, EXPLANATION.

justify *v.* 1 [To vindicate] absolve, acquit, clear; see EXCUSE. 2 [To give reasons for] support, apologize for, excuse; see DEFEND, EXPLAIN.

justly *a.* 1 [Honorably] impartially, honestly, frankly, candidly, straightforwardly, reasonably, fairly, moderately, temperately, even-handedly, rightly, equitably, equably, tolerantly, charitably, respectably, lawfully, legally, legitimately, rightfully, properly, duly, in justice, as it ought to be. 2 [Exactly] properly, precisely, rationally; see ACCURATELY.

jut *v.* extend, bulge, stick out; see PROJECT 1.

juvenile *a.* youthful, adolescent, teenage; see YOUNG 1.

K

k or **K** (kā) *n., pl.* **k's, K's** the eleventh letter of the English alphabet

K *symbol for* **1** *Baseball* strikeout **2** 〚ModL *kalium*〛 *Chem.* potassium **3** *Electronics* the number 1,024, or 2^{10}

K *abbrev.* **1** karat (carat) **2** kilometer **3** kindergarten Also, for 1 & 2, **k**

kad·dish (käd′ish) *n.* 〚Aram *kadish*, lit., holy〛 *Judaism* a hymn in praise of God, recited at the daily service or as a mourner's prayer

kaffee·klatsch (kä′fä kläch′, kô′fē klach′) *n.* 〚Ger < *kaffee*, coffee + *klatsch*, gossip〛 [*also* **K-**] an informal gathering to drink coffee and chat

Kai·ser (kī′zər) *n.* 〚ME *caiser*, emperor < L *Caesar*〛 the title of the former rulers of Austria and Germany

kale (kāl) *n.* 〚var. of COLE〛 a hardy cabbage with spreading leaves

ka·lei·do·scope (kə lī′də skōp′) *n.* 〚< Gr *kalos*, beautiful + *eidos*, form + -SCOPE〛 **1** a small tube containing bits of colored glass reflected by mirrors to form symmetrical patterns as the tube is rotated **2** anything that constantly changes —**ka·lei·do·scop·ic** (-skäp′ik) *adj.*

ka·mi·kaze (kä′mə kä′zē) *adj.* 〚Jpn, divine wind〛 of a suicidal attack by a WWII Japanese airplane pilot

kan·ga·roo (kaŋ′gə rōō′) *n.* 〚< ?〛 a leaping marsupial of Australia and nearby islands, with short forelegs and strong, large hind legs

kangaroo court [Colloq.] a mock court illegally passing and executing judgment, as among frontiersmen

kao·lin (kā′ə lin) *n.* 〚Fr < Chin name of hill where found〛 a white clay used in porcelain, etc.

ka·pok (kā′päk′) *n.* 〚Malay〛 the silky fibers around the seeds of certain tropical trees, used for stuffing mattresses, etc.

kappa (kap′ə) *n.* the tenth letter of the Greek alphabet (K, κ)

ka·put (kə poot′, -pōōt′) *adj.* 〚Ger *kaputt*〛 [Slang] ruined, destroyed, etc.

kara·kul (kar′ə kul′, -kəl) *n.* 〚ult. < Turkic *qara köl*, dark lake〛 **1** a sheep native to central Asia **2** the curly black fur from the fleece of its lambs: usually sp. *caracul*

karat (kar′ət) *n.* 〚var. of CARAT〛 one 24th part (of pure gold)

ka·rate (kə rät′ē) *n.* 〚Jpn〛 a Japanese system of self-defense by sharp, quick blows with the hands and feet

karma (kär′mə) *n.* 〚Sans., act〛 **1** *Buddhism, Hinduism* the totality of one's acts in each state of one's existence **2** loosely, fate

kart (kärt) *n.* 〚< CART〛 a small, flat, motorized vehicle, used in racing

katy·did (kāt′ē did′) *n.* 〚echoic of its shrill sound〛 a large, green tree insect resembling the grasshopper

kayak (kī′ak′) *n.* 〚Esk〛 an Eskimo canoe made of skins completely covering a wooden frame except for a small opening for the paddler

kayo (kā′ō′) *vt.* **-oed′, -o′ing** 〚< KO〛 [Slang] *Boxing* to knock out —*n.* [Slang] *Boxing* a knockout

ka·zoo (kə zōō′) *n.* 〚echoic〛 a toy musical instrument consisting of a small tube with a paper-covered hole: it makes buzzing tones when hummed into

KB kilobyte(s)

kc kilocycle(s)

ke·bab or **ke·bob** (kə bäb′) *n.* 〚Ar *kabāb*〛 any of the small pieces of marinated meat used in making shish kebab

keel (kēl) *n.* 〚< ON *kjolr*〛 the chief timber or piece extending along the length of the bottom of a boat or ship —**keel over 1** to capsize **2** to fall over suddenly —**on an even keel** in an upright, level position

keen¹ (kēn) *adj.* 〚OE *cene*, wise〛 **1** having a sharp edge or point /a *keen* knife/ **2** cutting; piercing /a *keen* wind/ **3** very perceptive /*keen* eyes/ **4** shrewd **5** eager **6** strongly felt; intense —**keen′ly** *adv.* —**keen′ness** *n.*

keen² (kēn) *n.* 〚< Ir *caoinim*, I wail〛 [Irish] a wailing for the dead —*vt., vi.* [Irish] to lament or wail for (the dead)

keep (kēp) *vt.* **kept, keep′ing** 〚OE *cœpan*, behold〛 **1** to celebrate; observe /to *keep* the Sabbath/ **2** to fulfill (a promise, etc.) **3** to protect; guard; take care of; tend **4** to preserve **5** to provide for; support **6** to make regular entries in /to *keep* books/ **7** to maintain in a specified state, position, etc. /to *keep* prices down/ **8** to hold for the future; retain **9** to hold and not let go; detain, withhold, restrain, etc. **10** to stay in or on (a course, place, etc.) —*vi.* **1** to stay in a specified state, position, etc. **2** to continue; go on **3** to refrain /to *keep* from eating/ **4** to stay fresh; not spoil —*n.* **1** care or custody **2** food and shelter; support **3** the inner stronghold of a castle —**for keeps** [Colloq.] **1** with the winner keeping what he wins **2** permanently —**keep to oneself 1** to avoid others **2** to refrain from telling —**keep up 1** to maintain in good condition **2** to continue **3** to maintain the pace: also with *with* **4** to remain informed about: with *on* or *with*

keep′er *n.* one that keeps; specif., *a*) a guard *b*) a guardian *c*) a custodian

keep′ing *n.* **1** observance (of a rule, etc.) **2** care; charge —**in keeping with** in conformity or accord with

keep′sake′ *n.* something kept, or to be kept, in memory of the giver

keg (keg) *n.* 〚< ON *kaggi*, keg〛 **1** a small barrel **2** a unit of weight for nails, equal to 100 lb.

kelp (kelp) *n.* 〚ME *culp*〛 a large, coarse, brown seaweed, rich in iodine

Kelt (kelt) *n. var. of* CELT

Kel·vin (kel′vin) *adj.* 〚after 1st Baron *Kelvin*, 19th-c. Brit physicist〛 designating a scale of temperature measured from absolute zero (-273.15°C)

ken (ken) *vt.* kenned, ken′ning 〚OE *cennan*, cause to know〛 [Scot.] to know —*n.* range of knowledge

ken·nel (ken′əl) *n.* 〚< L *canis*, dog〛 **1** a doghouse **2** [*often pl.*] a place where dogs are bred or kept —*vt.* **-neled** or **-nelled, -nel·ing** or **-nel·ling** to keep in a kennel

kept (kept) *vt., vi. pt. & pp. of* KEEP —*adj.* maintained as a mistress /a *kept* woman/

◼◼◼◼ THESAURUS ◼◼◼◼

keen¹ *a.* **1** [Sharp] pointed, edged, acute; see SHARP 1. **2** [Astute] bright, clever, shrewd; see INTELLIGENT. **3** [Eager] ardent, interested, intent; see ZEALOUS.

keenly *a.* acutely, sharply, penetratingly; see CLEARLY 1, 2, VERY, VIGOROUSLY.

keep *v.* **1** [To hold] retain, grip, own, possess, have, take, seize, save, grasp; see also HOLD 1. **2** [To maintain] preserve, conserve, care for; see MAINTAIN 3. **3** [To continue] keep going, carry on, sustain; see CONTINUE 1, ENDURE 1. **4** [To operate] administer, run, direct; see MANAGE 1. **5** [To tend] care for, minister to, attend; see TEND 1. **6** [To remain] stay, continue, abide; see SETTLE 5, 6. **7** [To store] deposit, hoard, retain, store, preserve, reserve, put away, conserve, warehouse, stash away*, put away, cache; see also SAVE 3, STORE. **8** [To prevent] *used with* "*from*"] stop, block, avert; see HINDER, PREVENT. **9** [To retain] not

spoil, season, put up; see PRESERVE 3. —**for keeps*** permanently, changelessly, perpetually; see FOREVER. — **keep after 1** [To pursue] track, trail, follow; see PURSUE 1. **2** [To nag] push, remind, pester; see BOTHER 2, DISTURB. —**keep at** persist, persevere, endure; see CONTINUE 1. —**keep away 1** [To remain] stay away, hold back, not come; see WAIT 1. **2** [To restrain] keep off, hold back, defend oneself from; see HINDER, PREVENT, RESTRICT. —**keep back 1** [To delay] check, hold, postpone; see DELAY, HINDER, SUSPEND. **2** [To restrict] enclose, inhibit, oppose; see FORBID, RESTRICT. — **keep down** reduce, deaden, muffle; see DECREASE 2, SOFTEN. —**keep from 1** [To abstain] desist, refrain, avoid; see ABSTAIN. **2** [To prevent] prohibit, forestall, impede; see HINDER, PREVENT. —**keep on** finish, repeat, pursue; see CONTINUE 1, ENDURE 1. —**keep to oneself** be a recluse, be a hermit, cultivate soli-

tude, avoid human companionship, stay away, keep one's own counsel; see also HIDE. —**keep up** support, care for, safeguard; see SUSTAIN 2. — **keep up with** keep step with, keep pace with, run with; see COMPETE.

keeper *n.* guard, official, attendant; see WARDEN, WATCHMAN.

keeping *n.* care, custody, guard; see PROTECTION 2. —**in keeping with** similar to, much the same as, in conformity with; see ALIKE.

keepsake *n.* memento, token, remembrance; see REMINDER.

keg *n.* cask, drum, vat; see BARREL, CONTAINER.

kennel *n.* doghouse, den, pound; see ENCLOSURE 1, PEN 1.

kept *a.* **1** [Preserved] put up, pickled, stored; see PRESERVED 2. **2** [Retained] maintained, withheld, held, guarded, watched over, reserved, on file, at hand; see also SAVED 2. **3** [Observed] obeyed, honored, continued, discharged,

kera·tin (ker′ə tin) *n.* ⟦< Gr *keras*, horn⟧ a tough, fibrous protein, the basic substance of hair, nails, etc.

kerb (kʉrb) *n. Brit. sp. of* CURB (*n.* 3)

ker·chief (kʉr′chif) *n.* ⟦< OFr *couvrir*, to cover + *chef*, head⟧ 1 a piece of cloth worn over the head or around the neck 2 a handkerchief

ker·nel (kʉr′nəl) *n.* ⟦< OE *cyrnel*⟧ 1 a grain or seed, as of corn 2 the inner, softer part of a nut, etc. 3 the central, most important part; essence

kero·sene (ker′ə sēn′) *n.* ⟦Gr *kēros*, wax⟧ a thin oil distilled from petroleum, used as a fuel, solvent, etc. Also **kerosine**

kes·trel (kes′trəl) *n.* ⟦echoic of its cry⟧ a small European falcon

ketch (kech) *n.* ⟦ME *cache*⟧ a fore-and-aft rigged sailing vessel

ketch·up (kech′əp) *n.* ⟦? Malay *kēchap*, sauce⟧ a sauce for meat, fish, etc.; esp., a thick sauce (**tomato ketchup**) of tomatoes, onions, spices, etc.

ket·tle (ket′'l) *n.* ⟦< L *catinus*, container for food⟧ 1 a metal container for boiling or cooking things 2 a teakettle

ket′tle·drum′ *n.* a hemispheric percussion instrument of copper with a parchment top that can be tightened or loosened to change the pitch

Kev·lar (kev′lär′) *trademark for* a tough, light, synthetic fiber used in bulletproof vests, boat hulls, etc.

key[1] (kē) *n., pl.* **keys** ⟦OE *cæge*⟧ 1 a device for moving the bolt of a lock and thus locking or unlocking something 2 any somewhat similar device, as a lever pressed in operating a piano, typewriter, etc. 3 a thing that explains or solves something else, as a code, the legend of a map, etc. 4 a controlling person or thing 5 tone or style of expression 6 *Music* a system of related tones based on a keynote and forming a given scale — *adj.* controlling; important — *vt.* **keyed, key′ing** 1 to furnish with a key 2 to regulate the tone or pitch of 3 to bring into harmony —**key in** to input (data) by means of a keyboard —**key up** to make nervous

key[2] (kē) *n., pl.* **keys** ⟦Sp *cayo*⟧ a reef or low island

key·board (kē′bôrd′) *n.* 1 the row or rows of keys of a piano, typewriter, computer terminal, etc. 2 an instrument with a keyboard — *vt., vi.* to write (text) or input (data) by means of a keyboard —**key′board′er** *n.*

key′hole′ *n.* an opening (in a lock) into which a key is inserted

key′note′ *n.* 1 the lowest, basic note or tone of a musical scale 2 the basic idea or ruling principle — *vt.* **-not′ed, -not′ing** 1 to give the keynote of 2 to give the keynote speech at —**key′not′er** *n.*

keynote speech (or **address**) a speech, as at a convention, setting forth the main line of policy

key punch a machine with a keyboard for recording data by punching holes in cards for use in data processing

key′stone′ *n.* 1 the central, topmost stone of an arch 2 an essential part

key′stroke′ *n.* any of the strokes made in operating a keyboard

kg kilogram(s)

khaki (kak′ē, kä′kē) *adj.* ⟦< Pers *khāk*, dust⟧ 1 dull yellowish-brown 2 made of khaki (cloth) —*n., pl.* **-kis** 1 a dull yellowish brown 2 strong, twilled cloth of this color 3 [*often pl.*] a khaki uniform or pants

khan (kän, kan) *n.* ⟦< Mongolian *qan*, lord⟧ 1 a title of Tatar or Mongol rulers in the Middle Ages 2 a title of various dignitaries in Iran, Afghanistan, etc.

kHz or **khz** kilohertz

kib·butz (ki bōōts′, -boots′) *n., pl.* **kib·but·zim** (kē′bōō tsēm′) ⟦ModHeb⟧ an Israeli collective settlement, esp. a collective farm

kib·itzer (kib′its ər) *n.* ⟦Yidd < Ger *kiebitz*⟧ [Colloq.] 1 an onlooker at a card game, etc., esp. one who volunteers advice 2 a giver of unwanted advice or meddler in others' affairs —**kib′itz** *vi.*

ki·bosh (kī′bäsh′, ki bäsh′) *n.* ⟦< ?⟧ end: now usually in **put the kibosh on**, to check, squelch, etc.

kick (kik) *vi.* ⟦ME *kiken*⟧ 1 to strike out with the foot 2 to recoil, as a gun 3 [Colloq.] to complain 4 *Football* to kick the ball — *vt.* 1 to strike with the foot 2 to drive, force, etc., as by kicking 3 to score (a goal, etc.) by kicking 4 [Slang] to get rid of (a habit) — *n.* 1 an act or method of kicking 2 a sudden recoil 3 a complaint 4 [Colloq.] an intoxicating effect 5 [*often pl.*] [Colloq.] pleasure —**kick in** [Slang] to pay (one's share) —**kick over** to start up, as an automobile engine —**kick′er** *n.*

kick′back′ *n.* [Slang] 1 a giving back of part of money received as payment 2 the money so returned

kick′off′ *n.* 1 *Football* a kick that puts the ball into play 2 a beginning, as of a campaign

kick′stand′ *n.* a pivoted metal bar that can be kicked down to support a bicycle, etc. in an upright position

kicky (kik′ē) *adj.* **-i·er, -i·est** [Slang] 1 fashionable 2 exciting

kid (kid) *n.* ⟦ME *kide*⟧ 1 a young goat 2 leather from the skin of young goats: also **kid′skin′** 3 [Colloq.] a child — *vt., vi.* **kid′ded, kid′ding** [Colloq.] to tease or fool playfully —**kid′der** *n.*

kid′die or **kid′dy** (-ē) *n., pl.* **-dies** ⟦dim. of prec., *n.* 3⟧ [Colloq.] a child

kid·nap (kid′nap′) *vt.* **-napped′** or **-naped′, -nap′ping** or **-nap′ing** ⟦KID, *n.* 3 + dial. *nap*, to snatch⟧ to seize and hold (a person) by force or fraud, as for ransom —**kid′nap′per** or **kid′nap′er** *n.*

kid·ney (kid′nē) *n., pl.* **-neys** ⟦< ?⟧ 1 either of a pair of glandular organs that separate waste products from the blood and excrete them as urine 2 an animal's kidney, used as food 3 *a*) disposition *b*) class; kind

kidney bean the kidney-shaped seed of the common garden bean

kidney stone a hard mineral deposit sometimes formed in the kidney

kiel·basa (kēl bä′sə, kil-) *n., pl.* **-si** (-sē) or **-sas** ⟦Pol⟧ a Polish smoked sausage

kill (kil) *vt.* ⟦< ? OE *cwellan*⟧ 1 to cause the death of; slay 2 to destroy; put an end to 3 to defeat or veto (legislation) 4 to spend (time) on trivial matters 5 to turn off (an

---

◼ THESAURUS ◼

maintained, carried on; see also FUL-FILLED.—*Ant.* ABANDONED, dishonored, forgotten.

kernel *n.* nut, core, germ; see GRAIN 1, SEED.

ketchup *n.* tomato sauce, mushroom sauce, condiment; see RELISH.

kettle *n.* cauldron, saucepan, stewpot; see POT 1.

key[1] *n.* 1 [Instrument to open a lock] latchkey, opener, master key, passkey, skeleton key. 2 [A means of solution] clue, code, indicator; see ANSWER 2.

keyed up* *a.* stimulated, spurred on, nervous; see EXCITED.

keynote *a.* main, leading, official; see IMPORTANT 1, PRINCIPAL.

kick *n.* 1 [*A blow with the foot] boot, swift kick, jolt, jar, hit; see also BLOW. 2 [In sports, a kicked ball] punt, drop kick, place kick; see sense 1. 3 [*Pleasant reaction] joy, pleasant sensation, refreshment; see ENJOYMENT.

kick *v.* 1 [To give a blow with the foot] boot, jolt, punt, drop-kick, place-kick, kick off; see also BEAT 1,

HIT 1. 2 [*To object] make a complaint, criticize, carp; see COMPLAIN, OPPOSE 1. —**kick about** (or **around**) mistreat, treat badly, misuse; see ABUSE. —**kick off** start, open, get under way; see BEGIN 1. — **kick out*** reject, throw out, eject; see DISMISS, REMOVE 1.

kickoff *n.* opening, beginning, launching; see ORIGIN 2.

kid *n.* 1 [The young of certain animals] lamb, lambkin, fawn, calf, yearling; see also ANIMAL. 2 [*A child] son, daughter, tot; see BOY, CHILD, GIRL.

kid* *v.* tease, pretend, fool; see BOTHER 2, JOKE.

kidnap *v.* abduct, ravish, capture, steal, rape, carry away, hold for ransom, shanghai, carry off, make off with, make away with, grab, spirit away, pirate, snatch*, bundle off.— *Ant.* RESCUE, ransom, release.

kidnapped *a.* made off with, abducted, ravished, stolen, carried away, held for ransom, shanghaied, waylaid, manhandled, seized, held under illegal restraint; see also CAP-

TURED.—*Ant.* FREE, rescued, freed.

kidney *n.* excretory organ, urinary organ, abdominal gland; see ORGAN 2.

kill *v.* 1 [To deprive of life] slay, slaughter, murder, assassinate, massacre, butcher, hang, lynch, electrocute, dispatch, execute, knife, sacrifice, shoot, strangle, poison, choke, smother, suffocate, asphyxiate, drown, behead, guillotine, crucify, dismember, decapitate, disembowel, quarter, tear limb from limb, destroy, give the death blow, give the *coup de grâce*, put to death, deprive of life, put an end to, exterminate, stab, cut the throat, shoot down, mangle, cut down, bring down, mow down, machine-gun, pick off, liquidate, put someone out of his misery, starve, do away with, commit murder, bump off*, rub out*, wipe out*, do in*, knock off*, finish off*, blow someone's brains out*, put to sleep*, brain*, zap*.—*Ant.* RESCUE, resuscitate, animate. 2 [To cancel] annul, nullify, counteract; see CANCEL. 3 [To turn off] turn out, shut off, stop; see HALT, TURN OFF. 4 [To engine, etc.) **6** to stop publication of — *n.* **1** the act of killing **2** an animal or animals killed —**kill′er** *n.*

kill·deer (kil′dir′) *n.* ⟦echoic⟧ a medium-sized North American plover

killer whale a large dolphin that hunts in packs and preys on large fish, seals, etc.

kill′ing *adj.* **1** causing death; deadly **2** exhausting; fatiguing — *n.* **1** slaughter; murder **2** [Colloq.] a sudden great profit

kill′joy′ *n.* one who destroys or lessens other people's enjoyment Also **kill-joy**

kiln (kil, kiln) *n.* ⟦< L *culina*, cookstove⟧ a furnace or oven for drying, burning, or baking bricks, pottery, etc.

kilo (kē′lō, kil′ō) *n., pl.* **-los** ⟦Fr⟧ **1** KILOGRAM **2** KILOMETER

kilo- ⟦< Gr *chilioi*⟧ *combining form* one thousand

kilo·byte (kil′ō bit′, kil′ə-) *n.* 1,024 bytes, or, loosely, 1,000 bytes

kil′o·cy′cle (-sī′kəl) *n.* old term for KILOHERTZ

kil′o·gram′ (-gram′) *n.* a metric unit of weight equal to 1,000 grams

kil′o·hertz′ (-herts′, -hurts′) *n., pl.* **-hertz′** 1,000 hertz

kilo·meter (kil′ə mēt′ər, kə läm′ət ər) *n.* a metric unit of linear measure equal to 1,000 meters

kilo·ton (kil′ō tun′, kil′ə-) *n.* the explosive force of 1,000 tons of TNT

kil′o·watt′ (-wät′) *n.* a unit of electrical power, equal to 1,000 watts

kilt (kilt) *n.* ⟦prob. < ON⟧ a knee-length, pleated tartan skirt worn sometimes by men of the Scottish Highlands

kil·ter (kil′tər) *n.* ⟦< ?⟧ [Colloq.] good condition; proper order: now chiefly in **out of kilter**

ki·mono (kə mō′nə) *n., pl.* **-nos** ⟦Jpn⟧ **1** a robe with wide sleeves and a sash, part of the traditional Japanese costume **2** a woman's dressing gown

kin (kin) *n.* ⟦OE *cynn*⟧ relatives; family

-kin (kin) ⟦< MDu *-ken*⟧ *suffix* little *[lambkin]*

kind (kīnd) *n.* ⟦OE *cynd*⟧ **1** a natural group or division **2** essential character **3** sort; variety; class — *adj.* sympathetic, gentle, benevolent, etc. —**in kind** in the same way —**kind of** [Colloq.] somewhat; rather —**of a kind** alike

kinder·gar·ten (kin′dər gärt′'n) *n.* ⟦Ger < *kinder*, child + *garten*, garden⟧ a school or class for young children, usually four to six years old, that develops basic skills and social behavior by games, handicraft, etc. —**kin′der·gart′-ner** or **kin′der·gar′tener** (-gärt′nər) *n.*

kind′heart′ed *adj.* kind

kin·dle (kin′dəl) *vt.* **-dled, -dling** ⟦< ON *kynda*⟧ **1** to set on fire; ignite **2** to excite (interest, feelings, etc.) — *vi.* **1** to catch fire **2** to become aroused or excited

kindling (kind′liŋ) *n.* material, as bits of dry wood, for starting a fire

kindly (kīnd′lē) *adj.* **-lier, -li·est** **1** kind; gracious **2** agreeable; pleasant — *adv.* **1** in a kind, gracious manner **2** agreeably; favorably **3** please *[kindly* shut the door*]* —**kind′li·ness** *n.*

kind′ness *n.* **1** the state, quality, or habit of being kind **2** a kind act

kin·dred (kin′drid) *n.* ⟦< OE *cynn*, kin + *ræden*, condition⟧ relatives or family — *adj.* similar *[kindred* spirits*]*

kine (kīn) *n.pl.* ⟦< OE *cy*, cows⟧ [Archaic] cattle; cattle

ki·netic (ki net′ik) *adj.* ⟦< Gr *kinein*, to move⟧ of or resulting from motion

kin·folk (kin′fōk′) *n.pl.* family; relatives Also **kin′folks′**

king (kiŋ) *n.* ⟦< OE *cyning*⟧ **1** a male ruler of a state **2** a man who is supreme in some field **3** something supreme in its class **4** a playing card with a picture of a king on it **5** *Chess* the chief piece — *adj.* chief (in size, importance, etc.) —**king′ly** *adj.* —**king′ship′** *n.*

king′dom (-dəm) *n.* **1** a country headed by a king or queen; monarchy **2** a realm; domain *[the kingdom of poetry]* **3** any of three divisions into which all natural objects have been classified (the animal, vegetable, and mineral kingdoms)

king′fish′er *n.* a short-tailed diving bird that feeds chiefly on fish

King James Version AUTHORIZED VERSION

King Lear (lir) the title character of a tragedy by Shakespeare

king′pin′ *n.* **1** the pin at the front of a triangle of bowling pins **2** the essential person or thing

king′-size′ *adj.* larger than the regular kind Also **king′-sized′**

kink (kiŋk) *n.* ⟦< Scand⟧ **1** a short twist or curl in a rope, hair, etc. **2** a painful cramp in the neck, back, etc. **3** a mental twist; queer notion; whim — *vi., vt.* to form or cause to form a kink or kinks —**kink′y, -i·er, -i·est,** *adj.*

kin·ship (kin′ship′) *n.* **1** family relationship **2** close connection

kins·man (kinz′mən) *n., pl.* **-men** a relative; esp., a male relative —**kins′wom′an,** *pl.* **-wom′en,** *n.*

ki·osk (kē′äsk′, kē äsk′) *n.* ⟦< Pers *kūshk*, palace⟧ a small, open structure used as a newsstand, etc.

kip·per (kip′ər) *vt.* ⟦< ?⟧ to cure (herring, salmon, etc.) by salting and drying or smoking — *n.* a kippered herring, etc.

kirk (kurk, kirk) *n.* [Scot. or North Eng.] a church

kis·met (kiz′met) *n.* ⟦< Ar *qasama*, to divide⟧ fate; destiny

kiss (kis) *vt., vi.* ⟦OE *cyssan*⟧ **1** to touch or caress with the lips as an act of affection, greeting, etc. **2** to touch lightly or gently — *n.* **1** an act of kissing **2** a light, gentle touch **3** any of various candies —**kiss′able** *adj.*

■■■■ THESAURUS ■■■■

veto] cancel, prohibit, refuse; see FORBID.

killer *n.* murderer, manslayer, gunman, gangster, shooter, butcher, hangman, assassin, slayer, sniper, cutthroat, thug, Cain; see also CRIMINAL.

killing *a.* mortal, lethal, fatal; see DEADLY.

killing *n.* slaying, assassination, slaughter; see CRIME.

kin *n.* blood relation, member of the family, sibling; see FAMILY, RELATIVE.

kind *a.* tender, well-meaning, considerate, charitable, loving, pleasant, amiable, soft, softhearted, compassionate, sympathetic, understanding, solicitous, sweet, generous, helpful, obliging, neighborly, accommodating, indulgent, delicate, tactful, gentle, tenderhearted, kindhearted, good-natured, inoffensive, benevolent, altruistic, other-directed, lenient, easy-going, patient, tolerant, mellow, genial, sensitive, courteous, agreeable, thoughtful, well-disposed.— *Ant.* ROUGH, brutal, harsh.

kind *n.* **1** [Class] classification, species, genus; see CLASS 1. **2** [Type] sort, variety, description, stamp, character, tendency, gender, habit, breed, set, tribe, denomination, persuasion, manner, connection, designation. —**kind of*** somewhat,

having the nature of, sort of*; see MODERATELY.

kindergarten *n.* class for small children, pre-elementary grade, pre-school training; see SCHOOL 1.

kindhearted *a.* amiable, generous, good; see HUMANE, KIND.

kindle *v.* light, catch fire, set fire; see BURN, IGNITE.

kindling *n.* firewood, tinder, coals; see FUEL, WOOD 2.

kindly *a.* generous, helpful, good; see HUMANE, KIND.

kindness *n.* **1** [The quality of being kind] tenderness, good intention, consideration, sympathy, sweetness, helpfulness, tact, benignity, mildness, courtesy, thoughtfulness, humanity, courteousness, understanding, compassion, unselfishness, altruism, warmheartedness, softheartedness, politeness, kindliness, clemency, benevolence, goodness, philanthropy, charity, friendliness, affection, loving kindness, cordiality, mercy, amiability, forbearance, graciousness, kindheartedness, virtue.— *Ant.* CRUELTY, brutality, selfishness. **2** [A kindly act] good service, relief, charity, benevolence, philanthropy, favor, good deed, good turn, self-sacrifice, mercy, lift, boost; see also HELP 1.— *Ant.* INJURY, transgression, wrong.

kindred *n.* kin, relations, relatives; see FAMILY, RELATIVE.

king *n.* **1** [A male sovereign] monarch, tyrant, prince, autocrat, czar, caesar, lord, emperor, overlord, crowned head, imperator, majesty, regal personage, sultan, caliph, shah, rajah, maharajah; see also RULER 1.— *Ant.* SERVANT, slave, subordinate. **2** [A very superior being] lord, chief, head; see LEADER 2.

kingdom *n.* realm, domain, country, empire, lands, possessions, principality, state, dominions, sway, rule, crown, throne, subject territory.

kingship *n.* supremacy, divinity, majesty; see POWER 2, ROYALTY.

king-size *a.* big, large-size, giant; see BROAD 1, LARGE 1.

kink *n.* **1** [A twist] tangle, crimp, crinkle; see CURL, CURVE. **2** [A difficulty] hitch, defect, complication; see DIFFICULTY 1.

kinky *a.* **1** [Full of kinks] fuzzy, curled, crimped; see CURLY. **2** [*Bizarre] weird, odd, sick*; see UNUSUAL 2.

kinship *n.* affiliation, kindred, relationship, affinity, cohesion, unity, familiarity, intimacy, connection, alliance; see also FAMILY, RELATIONSHIP.

kiss *n.* embrace, endearment, touch

kiss′er *n.* **1** a person who kisses **2** [Slang] *a)* the mouth or lips *b)* the face

kit (kit) *n.* ⟦ME *kyt, tub*⟧ **1** *a)* personal equipment, esp. as packed for travel *b)* a set of tools *c)* equipment for some particular activity, etc. *d)* a set of parts to be assembled **2** a box, bag, etc. for carrying such parts, equipment, or tools —**the whole kit and caboodle** [Colloq.] the whole lot

kitchen (kich′ən) *n.* ⟦ult. < L *coquere,* to cook⟧ a room or place for the preparation and cooking of food

kitch′en·ette′ or **kitch′enet′** (-et′) *n.* a small, compact kitchen

kitch′en·ware′ (-wer′) *n.* kitchen utensils

kite (kit) *n.* ⟦< OE *cyta*⟧ **1** any of several long-winged birds of prey **2** a light, wooden frame covered with paper or cloth, to be flown in the wind at the end of a string

kith (kith) *n.* ⟦< OE *cyth*⟧ friends: now only in **kith and kin,** friends and relatives; also, relatives, or kin

kitsch (kich) *n.* ⟦Ger, gaudy trash⟧ pretentious but shallow art or writing —**kitsch′y** *adj.*

kit·ten (kit′'n) *n.* ⟦< OFr dim. of *chat,* cat⟧ a young cat —**kit′ten·ish** *adj.*

kitty[1] (kit′ē) *n., pl.* **-ties 1** a kitten **2** a pet name for a cat

kitty[2] (kit′ē) *n., pl.* **-ties** ⟦prob. < KIT⟧ **1** the stakes in a poker game **2** money pooled for some purpose

kitty-cornered (kit′ē kôr′nərd) *adj., adv.* CATER-COR-NERED Also **kit′ty-cor′ner**

kiwi (kē′wē) *n., pl.* **-wis** ⟦echoic of its cry⟧ a flightless bird of New Zealand

KKK Ku Klux Klan

Klee·nex (klē′neks′) *trademark for* soft tissue paper used as a handkerchief, etc. —*n.* [*occas.* **k-**] a piece of such paper

klepto·ma·nia (klep′tō mā′nē ə) *n.* ⟦< Gr *kleptēs,* thief + MANIA⟧ an abnormal, persistent impulse to steal —**klep′to·ma′niac′** *n., adj.*

klieg light (klēg) ⟦after A. & J. *Kliegl,* who developed it in 1911⟧ a very bright arc light used on motion picture sets

klutz (kluts) *n.* ⟦< Yidd *klots,* lit., wooden block⟧ [Slang] a clumsy or stupid person

km kilometer(s)

knack (nak) *n.* ⟦ME *knak,* sharp blow⟧ **1** a clever expedient **2** ability to do something easily

knack·wurst (näk′wurst′) *n.* ⟦Ger < *knacken,* to burst + *wurst,* sausage⟧ a thick, highly seasoned sausage

knap·sack (nap′sak′) *n.* ⟦< Du *knappen,* eat + *zak,* sack⟧ a leather or canvas bag for carrying equipment or supplies on the back

knave (nāv) *n.* ⟦< OE *cnafa,* boy⟧ **1** a dishonest, deceitful person; rogue **2** JACK (*n.* 3) —**knav′ish** *adj.*

knav·ery (nāv′ər ē) *n., pl.* **-ies** rascality; dishonesty

knead (nēd) *vt.* ⟦< OE *cnedan*⟧ **1** to work (dough, clay, etc.) into a pliable mass by pressing and squeezing **2** to massage —**knead′er** *n.*

knee (nē) *n.* ⟦< OE *cneow*⟧ **1** the joint between the thigh and the lower leg **2** anything shaped like a bent knee —*vt.* **kneed, knee′ing** to hit or touch with the knee

knee′cap′ *n.* a movable bone at the front of the human knee

knee′-deep′ *adj.* **1** up to the knees **2** very much involved

knee′-jerk′ *adj.* ⟦< the reflex when the knee is tapped⟧ [Colloq.] characterized by or reacting with an automatic, predictable response

kneel (nēl) *vi.* **knelt** or **kneeled, kneel′ing** ⟦< OE *cneow,* knee⟧ to bend or rest on one's knee or knees

knell (nel) *vi.* ⟦< OE *cnyllan*⟧ **1** to ring slowly; toll **2** to sound ominously —*vt.* to call or announce as by a knell —*n.* **1** the sound of a bell rung slowly, as at a funeral **2** an omen of death, failure, etc.

knelt (nelt) *vi. alt. pt. and pp. of* KNEEL

knew (nōō, nyōō) *vt., vi. pt. of* KNOW

knick·ers (nik′ərz) *n.* ⟦< D. *Knickerbocker,* fictitious Du author of W. Irving's *History of New York*⟧ loose breeches gathered just below the knees: also **knick′er·bock·ers** (-ər bäk′ərz)

knick·knack (nik′nak′) *n.* ⟦< KNACK⟧ a small ornamental article

knife (nif) *n., pl.* **knives** ⟦< OE *cnif*⟧ **1** a cutting instrument with a sharp-edged blade set in a handle **2** a cutting blade, as in a machine —*vt.* **knifed, knif′ing 1** to cut or stab with a knife **2** [Colloq.] to injure or defeat by treachery —**under the knife** [Colloq.] undergoing surgery

knight (nit) *n.* ⟦< OE *cniht,* boy⟧ **1** in medieval times, a man formally raised to special military rank and pledged to chivalrous conduct **2** in Great Britain, a man who for some achievement is given honorary rank entitling him to use *Sir* before his given name **3** a chessman shaped like a horse's head —*vt.* to make (a man) a knight

knight′-er′rant (-er′ənt) *n., pl.* **knights′-er′rant 1** a medieval knight wandering in search of adventure **2** a chivalrous or quixotic person —**knight′-er′rantry** (-rē) *n.*

knight′hood′ (-hood′) *n.* **1** the rank, status, or vocation of a knight **2** chivalry **3** knights collectively

knight′ly *adj.* of or like a knight; chivalrous, brave, etc.

knit (nit) *vt., vi.* **knit′ted** or **knit, knit′ting** ⟦< OE *cnotta,* a knot⟧ **1** to make (a fabric) by looping yarn or thread together with special needles **2** to join or grow together closely and firmly, as a broken bone **3** to draw or become drawn together in wrinkles, as the brows —**knit′ter** *n.*

knit′ting *n.* knitted work

knit′wear′ (-wer′) *n.* knitted clothing

knob (näb) *n.* ⟦ME *knobbe*⟧ **1** a rounded lump or protuberance **2** *a)* a handle, usually round, of a door, drawer, etc. *b)* a similar device used to control a radio, TV, etc.

knob′by *adj.* **-bier, -bi·est 1** covered with knobs **2** like a knob

knock (näk) *vi.* ⟦< OE *cnocian*⟧ **1** to strike a blow **2** to rap on a door **3** to bump; collide **4** to make a thumping noise: said of an engine, etc. —*vt.* **1** to hit; strike **2** to

---

THESAURUS

of the lips, butterfly kiss, caress, smack*, peck*; see also TOUCH 2.

kiss *v.* salute, osculate, make love, play post office*, smack*, smooch*, pet*, neck*, make out*, blow a kiss*; see also LOVE 2.

kit *n.* **1** [Equipment] material, tools, outfit; see EQUIPMENT. **2** [A pack] poke*, knapsack, satchel; see BAG, CONTAINER.

kitchen *n.* scullery, galley, canteen, cook's room, kitchenette, mess.

kite *n.* box kite, Chinese kite, tailless kite; see TOY 1.

kitten *n.* pussy, kitty, baby cat; see ANIMAL, CAT.

knack *n.* trick, skill, faculty; see ABILITY.

knapsack *n.* backpack, kit, rucksack; see BAG, CONTAINER.

knead *v.* work, shape, twist; see PRESS 1.

knee *n.* knee joint, crook, bend, hinge, kneecap, articulation of the femur and the tibia; see also BONE.

kneel *v.* bend the knee, rest on the knees, genuflect, bend, stoop, bow down, curtsey.

knickknack *n.* gadget, bric-a-brac, curio, ornament, trifle, bauble, trin-ket, toy, plaything, showpiece, gewgaw*; see also TOY 1.

knife *n.* blade, cutter, sword, bayonet, cutting edge, dagger, stiletto, lance, machete, poniard, scalpel, edge, dirk, sickle, scythe, sabre, scimitar, broadsword, point, pigsticker*, toad-stabber*, shiv*; see also RAZOR. *Knives include the following:* carving, chopping, table, dinner, breakfast, dessert, grapefruit, fish, pocket, hunting, Bowie, cane, butcher, skinning, surgical, paper, pruning, oyster, putty, palette, bread, cake, serving, Boy Scout, Swiss Army.

knife *v.* **1** [To stab] spit, lance, thrust through; see HURT 1, KILL 1, STAB. **2** [*To injure in an underhanded way*] trick, give a coward's blow, strike below the belt; see DECEIVE.

knight *n.* cavalier, champion, knight-errant; see ARISTOCRAT.

knit *v.* **1** [To form by knitting] spin, crochet, web, cable, net; see also SEW, WEAVE 1. **2** [To combine or join closely] intermingle, connect, affiliate; see JOIN 1.

knitted *a.* knit, crocheted, stitched; see WOVEN.

knob *n.* **1** [A projection] hump, bulge, knot, node, bend, bump, protuberance; see also BENT, CROOKED 1. **2** [A door handle] doorknob, latch, door latch; see HANDLE 1.

knobby *a.* knobbed, lumpy, bumpy; see BENT, CROOKED 1.

knock *n.* rap, thump, whack; see BEAT 1, BLOW, INJURY.

knock *v.* tap, rap, thump; see BEAT 2, HIT 1, HURT 1. —**knock down** thrash, drub, kayo*; see BEAT 1, HIT 1, KNOCK OUT 2. —**knock off*** **1** [To kill] murder, stab, shoot; see KILL 1. **2** [To accomplish] complete, finish, eliminate; see ACHIEVE, SUCCEED 1. **3** [To stop] quit, leave, halt; see STOP 2. —**knock oneself out*** slave, labor, do one's utmost; see WORK 1. —**knock out** **1** [To anesthetize] etherize, put to sleep, stupefy; see DEADEN. **2** [To strike down] strike senseless, render unconscious, knock a person out of his senses, knock cold*, kayo*, knock for a loop*, put out like a light*; see also HIT 1. —**knock up*** impregnate, make pregnant, inseminate; see FERTILIZE 2.

make by hitting *[to knock a hole in a wall]* **3** [Colloq.] to find fault with — *n.* **1** a knocking **2** a hit; rap **3** a thumping noise in an engine, etc., as because of faulty combustion **4** [Colloq.] an adverse criticism —**knock about (or around)** [Colloq.] to wander about —**knock down 1** to hit so as to cause to fall **2** to take apart **3** to indicate the sale of (an article) at an auction —**knock off 1** [Colloq.] to stop working **2** [Colloq.] to deduct **3** [Slang] to kill, overcome, etc. —**knock out** to make unconscious or exhausted —**knock together** to make or compose hastily

knock′er *n.* one that knocks; esp., a small ring, knob, etc. on a door for use in knocking

knock′-kneed′ (-nēd′) *adj.* having legs that bend inward at the knees

knock′out′ (-out′) *n.* **1** a knocking out or being knocked out **2** [Slang] a very attractive person or thing **3** *Boxing* a victory won when the opponent is unable to continue to fight, as by being knocked unconscious

knock·wurst (näk′wurst′) *n.* alt. sp. of KNACKWURST

knoll (nōl) *n.* [OE *cnoll*] a hillock; mound

knot (nät) *n.* [< OE *cnotta*] **1** a lump in a thread, etc., formed by a tightened loop or tangle **2** a fastening made by tying together pieces of string, rope, etc. **3** an ornamental bow of ribbon, etc. **4** a small group or cluster **5** something that ties closely; esp., the bond of marriage **6** a problem; difficulty **7** a hard lump on a tree where a branch grows out, or a cross section of such a lump in a board **8** *Naut.* a unit of speed of one nautical mile (6,076.12 feet) an hour — *vt., vi.* **knot′ted, knot′ting 1** to make or form a knot (in) **2** to entangle or become entangled —**tie the knot** [Colloq.] to get married

knot′hole′ *n.* a hole in a board, etc. where a knot has fallen out

knot′ty *adj.* **-tier, -ti·est** [ME] **1** full of knots *[knotty pine]* **2** hard to solve; puzzling *[a knotty problem]*

know (nō) *vt.* **knew, known, know′ing** [< OE *cnawan*] **1** to be well informed about **2** to be aware of *[to know that one is loved]* **3** to be acquainted with **4** to recognize or distinguish *[to know right from wrong]* — *vi.* **1** to have knowledge **2** to be sure or aware —**in the know** [Colloq.] having confidential information —**know′able** *adj.*

know′-how′ *n.* [Colloq.] technical skill

know′ing *adj.* **1** having knowledge **2** shrewd; clever **3** implying shrewd or secret understanding *[a knowing look]* —**know′ingly** *adv.*

know′-it-all′ *n.* [Colloq.] one who acts as if he knows much about nearly everything

knowl·edge (näl′ij) *n.* **1** the fact or state of knowing **2** range of information or understanding **3** what is known; learning **4** the body of facts, etc. accumulated by mankind —**to (the best of) one's knowledge** as far as one knows

knowl′edge·able (-ə bəl) *adj.* having knowledge or intelligence —**knowl′edge·ably** *adv.*

known (nōn) *vt., vi. pp. of* KNOW — *adj.* **1** familiar **2** recognized, proven, etc. *[a known expert]*

knuckle (nuk′əl) *n.* [< or akin to MDu & LowG *knokel*, dim. of *knoke*, bone] **1** a joint of the finger; esp., the joint connecting a finger to the rest of the hand **2** the knee or

hock joint of an animal, used as food —**knuckle down** to work hard —**knuckle under** to yield; give in

knuck′le·head′ (-hed′) *n.* [Colloq.] a stupid person

knurl (nurl) *n.* [prob. < ME *knur*, a knot + GNARL] **1** a knot, knob, etc. **2** any of a series of small beads or ridges, as along the edge of a coin — *vt.* to make knurls on

KO (kā′ō′) *vt.* **KO′d, KO′ing** [Slang] *Boxing* to knock out — *n., pl.* **KO′s** [Slang] *Boxing* a knockout Also **K.O.** or **k.o.**

koa·la (kō ä′lə) *n.* [< native name] a tree-dwelling Australian marsupial with thick, gray fur

kohl·ra·bi (kōl′rä′bē) *n., pl.* **-bies** [< It *cavolo rapa*] a vegetable related to the cabbage, with an edible, turniplike stem

kola (kō′lə) *n.* COLA

kook (ko̅o̅k) *n.* [prob. < CUCKOO] [Slang] a person regarded as silly, eccentric, etc. —**kook′y** or **kook′ie** *adj.*

kooka·burra (kook′ə bur′ə) *n.* [< native name] an Australian kingfisher with a harsh cry like loud laughter

ko·peck or **ko·pek** (kō′pek′) *n.* [Russ < *kopye*, a lance] a 100th part of a ruble

Ko·ran (kə ran′, kôr′an′) [< Ar *qur'ān*, book] the sacred book of Islam

Ko·rean (kə rē′ən, kô-) *adj.* of Korea, its people, their language, etc. — *n.* **1** a native or inhabitant of Korea **2** the language of the Koreans

ko·sher (kō′shər) *adj.* [< Heb *kāshēr*, proper] *Judaism* clean or fit to eat according to the dietary laws

kow·tow (kou′tou′) *vi.* [Chin *k'o-t'ou*, lit., bump head] to show great deference, respect, etc. *(to)*

KP kitchen police, a detail to assist the cooks in an army kitchen

kraal (kräl) *n.* [Afrik] **1** a village of South African natives **2** an enclosure for cattle or sheep in South Africa

Krem·lin (krem′lin) *n.* [< Russ *kryeml′*] **1** the citadel of Moscow, housing many Russian, or, formerly, Soviet government offices **2** the Russian, or formerly, Soviet, government

Krem·lin·ol·ogy (krem′lin äl′ə jē) *n.* the study of the policies, etc. of the Soviet Union —**Krem′lin·ol′o·gist** *n.*

Krishna (krish′nə) *n.* a Hindu god, an incarnation of Vishnu

krona (krō′nə) *n., pl.* **-nor** (-nôr′) [ult. < L *corona*, crown] the monetary unit of Sweden

króna (krō′nə) *n., pl.* **-nur** (-nər) [see prec.] the monetary unit of Iceland

krone (krō′nə) *n., pl.* **-ner** (-nər) [see KRONA] the monetary unit of *a)* Denmark *b)* Norway

Kru·ger·rand (kro̅o̅′gə rand′) *n.* a gold coin of South Africa

kryp·ton (krip′tän′) *n.* [< Gr *kryptein*, to hide] a rare, inert gaseous chemical element Symbol, **Kr**

ku·chen (ko̅o̅′kən) *n.* [Ger, cake] a kind of cake made of yeast dough, often with raisins, nuts, etc.

ku·dos (kyo̅o̅′däs′, ko̅o̅′-) *n.* [Gr *kydos*] credit for an achievement; glory; fame: often wrongly taken to be the plural *(pron.* -dōz) of an assumed word "kudo"

kudzu (kood′zo̅o̅′) *n.* [Jpn] a fast-growing, perennial vine with large, three-part leaves

Ku Klux Klan (ko̅o̅′ kluks′ klan′, kyo̅o̅′-) [< Gr *kyklos*,

THESAURUS

knockout *n.* **1** [A blow that knocks unconscious] knockout blow, final blow, kayo*; see BLOW. **2** [*A success] excellent thing, sensation, perfection; see SUCCESS 1.

knot *n.* **1** [An arrangement of strands] tie, clinch, hitch, splice, ligature, bond. **2** [A hard or twisted portion] snarl, gnarl, snag, bunch, coil, entanglement, tangle, twist, twirl, whirl.

knot *v.* bind, tie, cord; see FASTEN.

knotted *a.* tied, twisted, tangled, snarled, entangled, bunched, clustered, whirled, looped, hitched, spiced, fastened, bent, warped, clinched, banded, lassoed, braided, linked, involved.—*Ant.* FREE, loose, separate.

know *v.* **1** [To possess information] be cognizant, be acquainted, be informed, be in possession of the facts, have knowledge of, be schooled in, be versed in, be conversant with, recognize, know full well, have at one's fingertips, be master of, know

by heart, know inside and out, be instructed, awaken to, keep up on, have information about, know what's what*, know all the answers, have someone's number*, have the jump on*, have down cold*, know one's stuff*, know the score*, know the ropes*.—*Ant.* NEGLECT, be oblivious of, overlook. **2** [To understand] comprehend, apprehend, see into; see UNDERSTAND 1. **3** [To recognize] perceive, discern, be familiar with, have the friendship of, acknowledge, be accustomed to, associate with, get acquainted. —**know how** be able, have the necessary background, be trained for; see UNDERSTAND 1.

know-how* *n.* skill, background, wisdom; see ABILITY, EXPERIENCE, KNOWLEDGE 1.

knowing *a.* sharp, clever, acute; see INTELLIGENT, REASONABLE 1.

knowingly *a.* intentionally, purposely, consciously; see DELIBERATELY.

knowledge *n.* **1** [Information]

learning, lore, scholarship, facts, wisdom, instruction, book learning, enlightenment, expertise, intelligence, light, theory, science, principles, philosophy, awareness, insight, education, substance, store of learning, know-how*; see also INFORMATION 1.—*Ant.* IGNORANCE, emptiness, pretension. **2** [Culture] dexterity, cultivation, learning; see EXPERIENCE, REFINEMENT 2.

known *a.* **1** [Open] discovered, disclosed, revealed; see OBVIOUS 1, PUBLIC 1. **2** [Established] well-known, published, recognized, notorious, received, accepted, noted, proverbial, certified, down pat*; see also FAMILIAR.

knuckle under *v.* give in, give up, acquiesce; see YIELD 1.

kook* *n.* eccentric, crackpot*, loony*, cuckoo*, ding-a-ling*, nut*, screwball*, crazy*, weirdo*, wacko*, flake*, dingbat*.

kudos *n.* praise, credit, glory, fame, honor; see also PRAISE 2, HONOR 1.

circle] a U.S. secret society that is anti-black, anti-semitic, anti-Catholic, etc., and uses terrorist methods

küm·mel (kim′əl) *n.* ⟦Ger, caraway⟧ a liqueur flavored with caraway seeds, anise, etc.

kum·quat (kum′kwät′) *n.* ⟦< Mandarin *chin-chü*, lit., golden orange⟧ a small, orange-colored, oval fruit with a sour pulp and a sweet rind

kung fu (kooŋ′ foo′, gooŋ′-) ⟦< Chin⟧ a Chinese system of self-defense, like karate but with circular movements

kW or **kw** kilowatt(s)

L

l or **L** (el) *n., pl.* **l's, L's** the 12th letter of the English alphabet

L (el) *n., pl.* **L's** **1** an extension forming an L with the main structure **2** a Roman numeral for 50

l or **l.** **1** latitude **2** left **3** length **4** line **5** long

L or **L.** **1** Lake **2** large **3** Latin **4** left **5** length **6** longitude **7** 〖L *libra,* pl. *librae*〗 pound(s): now usually £

l liter(s)

la (lä) *n.* 〖< L〗 *Music* the sixth tone of the diatonic scale

lab (lab) *n.* [Colloq.] a laboratory

la·bel (lā′bəl) *n.* 〖OFr, a rag〗 **1** a card, paper, etc. marked and attached to an object to indicate its contents, owner, destination, etc. **2** a term of generalized classification — *vt.* **-beled** or **-belled, -bel·ing** or **-bel·ling** **1** to attach a label to **2** to classify as; call

la·bial (lā′bē əl) *adj.* 〖< L *labium,* lip〗 **1** of the lips **2** *Phonetics* articulated with one or both lips, as (f), (b), and (ü)

la′bium (-əm) *n., pl.* **-bia** (-ə) 〖L, lip〗 any one of two pairs of liplike folds of the vulva

la·bor (lā′bər) *n.* 〖< L〗 **1** physical or mental exertion; work **2** a specific task **3** all wage-earning workers **4** labor unions collectively **5** the process of childbirth — *vi.* **1** to work **2** to work hard **3** to move slowly and with difficulty **4** to suffer (*under* a false idea, etc.) **5** to be in childbirth — *vt.* to develop in too great detail *[to labor a point]*

labo·ra·tory (lab′ə rə tôr′ē, lab′rə-) *n., pl.* **-ries** [see prec.] a room, building, etc. for scientific work or research

Labor Day the first Monday in September, a legal holiday honoring labor

la·bored (lā′bərd) *adj.* made or done with great effort; strained

la′borer *n.* one who labors; esp., a wage-earning worker whose work is largely hard physical labor

la·bo·ri·ous (lə bôr′ē əs) *adj.* **1** involving much hard work; difficult **2** hard-working **3** LABORED **—la·bo′ri·ously** *adv.*

labor union an association of workers to promote and protect the welfare, rights, etc. of its members

la·bour (lā′bər) *n., vi., vt. Brit. sp. of* LABOR

la·bur·num (lə bʉr′nəm) *n.* 〖< L〗 a small tree or shrub of the pea family, with drooping yellow flowers

lab·y·rinth (lab′ə rinth′) *n.* 〖< Gr *labyrinthos*〗 a structure containing winding passages hard to follow without losing one's way; maze

lac (lak) *n.* 〖< Sans *lākṣā*〗 a resinous substance secreted on certain Asiatic trees by a certain kind of insect: source of shellac

lace (lās) *n.* 〖< L *laqueus,* noose〗 **1** a string, etc. used to draw together and fasten the parts of a shoe, corset, etc. **2** a fine netting of cotton, polyester, silk, etc., woven in ornamental designs — *vt.* **laced, lac′ing** **1** to fasten with a lace **2** to weave together; intertwine **3** to thrash; whip

lac·er·ate (las′ər āt′) *vt.* **-at′ed, -at′ing** 〖< L *lacer,* lacerated〗 to tear jaggedly; mangle **—lac′er·a′tion** *n.*

lace′work′ *n.* lace, or any openwork decoration like lace

lach·ry·mal (lak′ri məl) *adj.* 〖< L *lacrima,* TEAR²〗 **1** of or producing tears **2** LACRIMAL (sense 1)

lach′ry·mose′ (-mōs′) *adj.* [see prec.] shedding, or causing to shed, tears; tearful or sad

lack (lak) *n.* 〖< or akin to Medieval LowG *lak*〗 **1** the fact or state of not having enough or not having any **2** the thing that is needed — *vi., vt.* to be deficient in or entirely without

lacka·dai·si·cal (lak′ə dā′zi kəl) *adj.* 〖< archaic *lackaday,* an exclamation of regret, etc.〗 showing lack of interest or spirit; listless

lackey (lak′ē) *n., pl.* **-eys** 〖< Sp *lacayo*〗 **1** a male servant of low rank, usually in some sort of livery or uniform **2** a servile follower; toady

lack·lus·ter (lak′lus′tər) *adj.* lacking brightness; dull Also, chiefly Brit. sp., **lack′lus′tre**

la·conic (lə kän′ik) *adj.* 〖< Gr *Lakōn,* a Spartan〗 terse in expression; concise **—la·con′i·cally** *adv.*

lac·quer (lak′ər) *n.* 〖< Fr < Port *laca,* lac〗 **1** a coating substance made of shellac, gum resins, etc. dissolved in ethyl alcohol or other solvent that evaporates rapidly **2** a resinous varnish obtained from certain Oriental trees **3** a wooden article coated with this — *vt.* to coat with lacquer

lac·ri·mal (lak′ri məl) *adj.* **1** of or near the glands that secrete tears **2** LACHRYMAL (sense 1)

la·crosse (lə krôs′) *n.* 〖CdnFr < Fr *la,* the + *crosse,* crutch〗 a ballgame played by two teams using long-handled, pouched rackets

lac·ta·tion (lak tā′shən) *n.* 〖< L *lac,* milk〗 **1** the secretion of milk by a mammary gland **2** the period during which milk is secreted

lac·teal (lak′tē əl) *adj.* 〖< L *lac,* milk〗 of or like milk; milky

lac·tic (lak′tik) *adj.* 〖< L *lac,* milk〗 of or obtained from milk

lactic acid a clear, syrupy acid formed when milk sours

lac·tose (lak′tōs′) *n.* 〖< L *lac,* milk〗 a sugar found in milk: used in foods

la·cuna (lə kyōō′nə) *n., pl.* **-nas** or **-nae** (-nē) 〖L, a ditch〗 a blank space; esp., a missing portion in a text, etc.

lacy (lās′ē) *adj.* **-i·er, -i·est** of or like lace **—lac′i·ness** *n.*

lad (lad) *n.* 〖ME *ladde*〗 a boy; youth

lad·der (lad′ər) *n.* 〖OE *hlæder*〗 **1** a framework consisting of two sidepieces connected by a series of rungs, for use in climbing up or down **2** any means of climbing

lad·die (lad′ē) *n.* [Chiefly Scot.] a lad

lade (lād) *vt., vi.* **lad′ed, lad′ed** or **lad′en, lad′ing** 〖OE *hladan*〗 **1** to load **2** to bail; ladle

lad′en *adj.* **1** loaded **2** burdened; afflicted

la-di-da (lä′dē dä′) *adj.* 〖imitative〗 [Colloq.] affectedly refined

lad′ing *n.* a load; cargo; freight

la·dle (lād′'l) *n.* 〖OE *hlædel*〗 a long-handled, cuplike spoon — *vt.* **-dled, -dling** to dip out with a ladle

---

◼ THESAURUS ◼

label *n.* tag, marker, mark, stamp, hallmark, insignia, design, number, identification, description, classification; see also NAME 1.

label *v.* specify, mark, identify; see NAME 1, 2.

labeled *a.* identified, provided with identification, stamped; see MARKED 1, 2.

labor *n.* **1** [The act of doing work] activity, toil, operation; see WORK 2. **2** [Work to be done] task, employment, undertaking; see JOB 2. **3** [Exertion required in work] exertion, energy, industry, diligence, strain, stress, drudgery; see also EFFORT, EXERCISE 1. **4** [The body of workers] laborers, workers, workingmen, proletariat, work force, labor force, working people, employees.—*Ant.* EMPLOYER, capitalist, businessman. **5** [Childbirth] parturition, giving birth, labor pains; see BIRTH.

labor *v.* toil, strive, get cracking*; see WORK 1.

laboratory *n.* workroom, lab*, research room, testing room; see also

OFFICE 3.

laborer *n.* day laborer, unskilled worker, hand, manual laborer, ranch hand, farm hand, apprentice, hired man, transient worker, toiler, seasonal laborer, ditchdigger, pick and shovel man, roustabout, stevedore, miner, street cleaner, instrument, peon, flunky, lackey, hireling, hack, beast of burden*, doormat*.

labor union *n.* organized labor, American Federation of Labor and Congress of Industrial Organizations (AFL-CIO), independent union, local, labor party; see also ORGANIZATION 2.

lace *n.* **1** [Ornamental threadwork] border, tissue, net; see DECORATION 2. **2** [Material for binding through openings] thong, cord, band; see ROPE.

lace *v.* strap, bind, close; see FASTEN, TIE 2.

lacing *n.* bond, hitch, tie; see FASTENER, KNOT 1.

lack *n.* **1** [The state of being lacking]

destitution, absence, need, shortage, paucity, deprivation, deficiency, scarcity, insufficiency, inadequacy, privation, poverty, distress, scantiness.—*Ant.* PLENTY, sufficiency, abundance. **2** [That which is lacking] need, decrease, want, loss, depletion, shrinkage, shortage, defect, inferiority, paucity, stint, curtailment, reduction; see also NECESSITY 2.—*Ant.* WEALTH, overflow, satisfaction.

lack *v.* want, require, have need of; see NEED.

lacking *a.* needed, deprived of, missing; see WANTING.

lacy *a.* sheer, thin, gauzy; see TRANSPARENT 1.

lad *n.* fellow, youth, stripling; see BOY, CHILD.

ladder *n.* Ladders include the following: stepladder, rope ladder, ship's ladder, aerial ladder, extension ladder, step-stool, gangway, fire escape; see also STAIRS.

ladle *n.* skimmer, scoop, vessel; see SILVERWARE.

lady (lād′ē) *n., pl.* **-dies** ⟦< OE *hlaf*, loaf + *dæge*, kneader⟧ **1** *a)* a woman of high social position *b)* a woman who is polite, refined, etc. **2** any woman: used to address a group **3** [L-] a British title given to women of certain ranks — *adj.* [Colloq.] female
la′dy·bug′ *n.* a small, roundish beetle with a spotted back Also **la′dy·bird′**
la′dy·fin′ger *n.* a small spongecake shaped somewhat like a finger
la·dy-in-wait′ing *n., pl.* **la′dies-in-wait′ing** a woman waiting upon a queen or princess
la′dy·like′ *adj.* like or suitable for a lady; refined; well-bred
la′dy·love′ *n.* a female sweetheart
la′dy·ship′ *n.* **1** the rank or position of a lady **2** [*usually* L-] a title used in speaking to or of a titled Lady
la′dy-slip′per *n.* an orchid with flowers somewhat like slippers Also **la′dy's-slip′per**
la·etrile (lā′ə tril′) *n.* any of several compounds obtained from certain substances, as almond seeds, and claimed to be effective in treating cancer
lag (lag) *vi.* **lagged, lag′ging** ⟦< ?⟧ **1** to fall behind or move slowly; loiter **2** to become less intense — *n.* **1** a falling behind **2** the amount of this
la·ger (beer) (lä′gər) ⟦Ger *lagerbier*, storehouse beer⟧ a beer that has been aged for several months
lag·gard (lag′ərd) *n.* ⟦< LAG + -ARD⟧ a slow person, esp. one who falls behind — *adj.* slow; falling behind
lagniappe or **lagnappe** (lan yap′, lan′yap′) *n.* ⟦Creole < Fr & Sp⟧ **1** [*Chiefly South*] a small present given to a customer with a purchase **2** a gratuity
la·goon (lə gōōn′) *n.* ⟦< L *lacuna*, pool⟧ **1** a shallow lake or pond, esp. one connected with a larger body of water **2** the water enclosed by a circular coral reef **3** shallow water separated from the sea by sand dunes
laid (lād) *vt., vi. pt. & pp. of* LAY[1]
laid′-back′ (-bak′) *adj.* [Slang] relaxed, easygoing, etc.; not hurried
lain (lān) *vi. pp. of* LIE[1]
lair (ler) *n.* ⟦OE *leger*⟧ a resting place of a wild animal; den
laird (lerd) *n.* ⟦Scot form of LORD⟧ in Scotland, a land-owner, esp. a wealthy one
lais·sez faire (les′ā fer′) ⟦Fr, allow to do⟧ noninterference; specif., absence of government control over industry and business
la·ity (lā′i tē) *n., pl.* **-ties** ⟦< LAY[3]⟧ laymen collectively
lake (lāk) *n.* ⟦< L *lacus*⟧ **1** a large inland body of usually fresh water **2** a pool of oil or other liquid
lal·ly·gag (läl′ē gag′) *vi.* **-gagged′, -gag′ging** [Colloq.] LOLLYGAG
lam (lam) *n.* ⟦< ?⟧ [Slang] headlong flight — *vi.* **lammed, lam′ming** [Slang] to flee; escape —**on the lam** [Slang] in flight, as from the police
lama (lä′mə) *n.* ⟦Tibetan *blama*⟧ a priest or monk in Lamaism
La·ma·ism (lä′mə iz′əm) *n.* a form of Buddhism in Tibet and Mongolia
la·ma·sery (lä′mə ser′ē) *n., pl.* **-ies** a monastery of lamas
La·maze (lə mäz′) ⟦after F. *Lamaze*, 20th-c. Fr physician⟧ a training program in natural childbirth, involving the help of the father
lamb (lam) *n.* ⟦OE⟧ **1** a young sheep **2** its flesh, used as food **3** a gentle, innocent, or gullible person

lam·baste (lam bāst′, -bast′) *vt.* **-bast′ed, -bast′ing** ⟦< *lam*, to beat + *baste*, to flog⟧ [Colloq.] **1** to beat soundly **2** to scold severely
lambda (lam′də) *n.* the 11th letter of the Greek alphabet (Λ, λ)
lam·bent (lam′bənt) *adj.* ⟦< L *lambere*, to lick⟧ **1** playing lightly over a surface: said of a flame, etc. **2** giving off a soft glow **3** light and graceful [*lambent* wit] —**lam′bency** *n.*
lamb′kin *n.* a little lamb
lamb′skin′ *n.* the skin of a lamb, esp. with the fleece left on it
lame (lām) *adj.* ⟦OE *lama*⟧ **1** crippled; esp., having an injury that makes one limp **2** stiff and painful **3** poor; ineffectual [a *lame* excuse] — *vt.* **lamed, lam′ing** to make lame —**lame′ly** *adv.* —**lame′ness** *n.*
lamé (la mā′, lä-) *n.* ⟦< Fr *lame*, metal plate⟧ a cloth interwoven with metal threads, as of gold or silver
lame duck an elected official whose term ends after some-one else has been elected to the office
la·mella (lə mel′ə) *n., pl.* **-lae** (-ē) or **-las** ⟦L⟧ a thin plate, scale, or layer
la·ment (lə ment′) *vi., vt.* ⟦< L *lamentum*, a wailing⟧ to feel or express deep sorrow (for); mourn — *n.* **1** a lamenting **2** an elegy, dirge, etc. mourning some loss or death — **lam·en·table** (lam′ən tə bəl, lə men′-) *adj.* —**lam·en·ta·tion** (lam′ən tā′shən) *n.*
lami·na (lam′i nə) *n., pl.* **-nae** (-nē′) or **-nas** ⟦L⟧ a thin scale or layer, as of metal, tissue, etc.
lami·nate (lam′i nāt′; *for adj. usually*, -nit) *vt.* **-nat′ed, -nat′ing** [*see prec.*] **1** to cover with one or more thin layers **2** to make by building up in layers — *adj.* LAMI-NATED —**lam′i·na′tion** *n.*
lam′i·nat′ed (-nāt′id) *adj.* **1** built in thin sheets or layers **2** covered with a thin protective layer, as of clear plastic
lamp (lamp) *n.* ⟦< Gr *lampein*, to shine⟧ **1** a container with a wick for burning oil, etc. to produce light or heat **2** any device for producing light or heat, as an electric light bulb **3** a holder or base for such a device
lamp′black′ *n.* fine soot used as a black pigment
lam·poon (lam pōōn′) *n.* ⟦< Fr *lampons*, let us drink: used as a refrain⟧ a satirical writing attacking someone — *vt.* to attack in a lampoon
lamp′post′ (lamp′pōst′, lam′-) *n.* a post supporting a street lamp
lam·prey (lam′prē) *n., pl.* **-preys** ⟦< ML *lampreda*⟧ an eel-like fish with a jawless, sucking mouth
la·nai (lə nä′ē, -nī′) *n.* ⟦Haw⟧ a veranda or open-sided living room
lance (lans, läns) *n.* ⟦< L *lancea*⟧ **1** a long, wooden spear with a sharp metal head **2** *a)* LANCER *b)* LANCET **3** any instrument like a lance — *vt.* **lanced, lanc′ing** **1** to pierce with a lance **2** to cut open with a lancet
Lan·celot (län′sə lət, -lät′) the most celebrated of the Knights of the Round Table
lancer (lans′ər) *n.* a cavalry soldier armed with a lance
lan·cet (lan′sit) *n.* ⟦< OFr dim. of *lance*, lance⟧ a small, pointed surgical knife, usually two-edged
land (land) *n.* ⟦OE⟧ **1** the solid part of the earth's surface **2** a country or nation **3** ground or soil **4** real estate — *vt.* **1** to put on shore from a ship **2** to bring to a particular

---

THESAURUS

lady *n.* **1** [A woman] female, adult, matron; see WOMAN 1. **2** [A woman of gentle breeding] gentlewoman, well-bred woman, woman of quality, cultured woman, high-born lady, mistress of an estate, noblewoman, titled lady; see also WOMAN 1.
ladylike *a.* womanly, cultured, well-bred; see POLITE, REFINED 2.
lag *n.* slack, slowness, tardiness, falling behind, sluggishness, backward-ness.—*Ant.* PROGRESS, progression, advance.
lag *v.* dawdle, linger, fall back, loiter, tarry, straggle, get behind, slacken, slow up, fall behind, procrastinate, plod, trudge, lounge, shuffle, falter, stagger, limp, get no place fast*; see also DELAY.—*Ant.* HURRY, hasten, keep pace with.
lagoon *n.* inlet, sound, pool; see BAY, LAKE.
lair *n.* cave, home, den; see PEN 1.

lake *n.* pond, creek, loch, pool, inland sea; see also SEA. *Famous lakes include the following:* Yellowstone, Geneva, Lucerne, Arrowhead, Great Salt, Superior, Huron, Michigan, Erie, Ontario, Champlain, Tahoe, Tanganyika, Nyasa, Como, Loch Lomond.
lamb *n.* young sheep, young one, yeanling; see ANIMAL.
lame *a.* **1** [Forced to limp] crippled, unable to walk, halt, weak, paralyzed, impaired, handicapped, defective, limping; see also DEFORMED, DIS-ABLED. **2** [Weak; *usually used figuratively*] inefficient, ineffective, faltering; see UNSATISFACTORY, WANT-ING.
lamp *n.* light, light bulb, lighting device; see LIGHT 3. *Types and forms of lamps include the following:* wick, oil, gas, electric, sun, hanging, bracket, portable, table, standing,

floor, miner's, street, arc, incandescent, gasoline, night, chandelier, lantern, torch.
lampoon *n.* satire, pasquinade, travesty, parody, burlesque.
lance *n.* lancet, foil, point; see SPEAR, WEAPON.
land *n.* **1** [The solid surface of the earth] ground, soil, dirt, clay, loam, gravel, subsoil, clod, sand, rock, mineral, metal, pebble, stone, dry land, valley, desert, hill, bank, seaside, shore, beach, crag, cliff, boulder, ledge, peninsula, delta, promontory; see also EARTH 2, MOUNTAIN 1, PLAIN. **2** [The SEA, stream, ocean. **2** [Land as property] estate, tract, ranch, farm, home, lot, real estate; see also AREA, PROPERTY 2. **3** [A country] continent, province, region; see NATION 1.
land *v.* **1** [To come into port; *said of a ship*] dock, berth, make port, tie

place [it **landed** him in jail] **3** to set (an aircraft) down on land or water **4** to catch [to **land** a fish] **5** [Colloq.] to get or secure [to **land** a job] **6** [Colloq.] to deliver (a blow) — **vi. 1** to leave a ship and go on shore **2** to come to a port, etc.: said of a ship **3** to arrive at a specified place **4** to come to rest

land contract a contract in which the seller of real estate transfers his interest to the buyer only after the purchase price is fully paid in regular payments over a specified period

landed (lan'did) *adj.* owning land [*landed* gentry]

land′fall′ *n.* **1** a sighting of land from a ship at sea **2** the land sighted

land′fill′ *n.* disposal of garbage, rubbish, etc. by burying it in the ground

land grant a grant of land by the government for a railroad, college, etc.

land′hold′er *n.* an owner of land —**land′hold′ing** *adj., n.*

land·ing (lan'diŋ) *n.* **1** the act of coming to shore **2** a place where a ship or boat is loaded or unloaded **3** a platform at the end of a flight of stairs **4** the act of alighting

landing gear the system of parts on an aircraft or spacecraft used for support or mobility on land or water

land′locked′ *adj.* **1** surrounded by land, as a bay **2** cut off from the sea and confined to fresh water [*landlocked* salmon]

land′lord′ *n.* **1** a person who leases land, houses, etc. to others **2** a man who keeps a rooming house, inn, etc. —**land′la′dy,** *pl.* **-dies,** *n.fem.*

land′lub′ber (-lub'ər) *n.* one who has had little experience at sea

land′mark′ *n.* **1** an object that marks the boundary of a piece of land **2** any prominent feature of the landscape, distinguishing a locality **3** an important event or turning point

land′mass′ *n.* a very large area of land; esp., a continent

land office a government office that handles the sales of public lands

land′-of′fice business [Colloq.] a booming business

land′scape′ (-skāp') *n.* [< Du *land,* land + *-schap,* -ship] **1** a picture of natural, inland scenery **2** an expanse of natural scenery seen in one view — *vt.* **-scaped′, -scap′ing** to make (a plot of ground) more attractive, as by adding lawns, bushes, etc. —**land′scap′er** *n.*

land′slide′ *n.* **1** the sliding of a mass of earth or rocks down a slope **2** the mass sliding down **3** an overwhelming victory, esp. in an election

land′ward (-wərd) *adv., adj.* toward the land   Also **land′wards** *adv.*

lane (lān) *n.* [OE *lanu*] **1** a narrow way, path, road, etc. **2** a path or route designated, for reasons of safety, for ships, aircraft, automobiles, etc.

lan·guage (laŋ'gwij) *n.* [< L *lingua,* tongue] **1** human speech or the written symbols for speech **2** *a)* any means of communicating *b)* a special set of symbols used in a computer **3** the speech of a particular nation, etc. [the French *language*] **4** the particular style of verbal expression characteristic of a person, group, profession, etc.

lan·guid (laŋ'gwid) *adj.* [< L *languere,* be weary] **1** without vigor or vitality; weak **2** listless; indifferent **3** slow; dull —**lan′guidly** *adv.*

lan′guish (-gwish) *vi.* [see prec.] **1** to become weak; droop **2** to live under distressing conditions [to *languish* in poverty] **3** to long; pine **4** to put on a wistful air

lan·guor (laŋ'gər) *n.* [see LANGUID] lack of vigor or vitality; weakness; listlessness —**lan′guor·ous** *adj.*

lank (laŋk) *adj.* [OE *hlanc*] **1** long and slender; lean **2** straight and limp: said of hair —**lank′ness** *n.*

lanky (laŋk'ē) *adj.* **-i·er, -i·est** awkwardly tall and lean

lano·lin (lan'ə lin') *n.* [< L *lana,* wool + *oleum,* oil] a fatty substance obtained from wool and used in ointments, cosmetics, etc.

THESAURUS

up, come to land, drop anchor, put in; see also ARRIVE.—*Ant.* LEAVE, weigh anchor, cast off. **2** [To go ashore] disembark, come ashore, arrive, alight, leave the boat or ship, go down the gangplank, hit the beach*. **3** [To bring an airplane to earth] touch down, ground, take down, alight, come in, settle, level off, come down, descend upon, make a forced landing, crash-land, nose over, overshoot, splash down, check in, undershoot, pancake, settle her down hot*, fishtail down; see also ARRIVE.

landing *n.* **1** [The act of reaching shore] arriving, docking, making port, anchoring, dropping anchor; see also ARRIVAL 1. **2** [The place where landing on the shore is possible] marina, pier, wharf; see DOCK. **3** [The act of reaching the earth] setting down, grounding, getting in, arriving, deplaning, reaching an airport, splashing down, completing a mission, settling, splashdown.

landlady *n.* homeowner, apartment manager, innkeeper; see OWNER.

landlord *n.* homeowner, apartment manager, realtor, landowner, lessor, property owner, innkeeper; see also OWNER.

landmark *n.* **1** [A notable relic] remnant, vestige, souvenir; see MONUMENT 1, RELIC. **2** [A point from which a course may be taken] vantage point, mark, blaze, guide, marker, stone, tree, hill, mountain, bend, promontory, duck on a rock*.

landscape *n.* scene, scenery, panorama; see VIEW.

landscape *v.* do the landscaping, finish up, put in the lawn and shrubbery; see DECORATE.

landscaping *n.* lawn, shrubbery, garden; see DECORATION 2.

landslide *n.* slide, avalanche, rock slide; see DESCENT 2.

lane *n.* way, alley, passage; see PATH, ROAD 1.

language *n.* **1** [A means of communication] voice, utterance, expression, vocalization, sound, phonation, tongue, mother tongue, articulation, metalanguage, physical language; language of diplomacy, language of chemistry, language of flowers, etc.; accent, word, sign, signal, pantomime, gesture, vocabulary, diction, dialect, idiom, local speech, broken English, pidgin English, polyglot, patois, vernacular, lingua franca, gibberish, pig Latin, debased speech; see also DIALECT, JARGON 2, WRITING 1, 2. **2** [The study of language] morphology, phonology, phonemics, morphemics, phonics, phonetics, letters, linguistic studies, history of language, etymology, dialectology, linguistic geography; see also GRAMMAR, LINGUISTICS, LITERATURE 1. *Types of languages include the following:* synthetic, inflectional, analytic, distributive, incorporating, agglutinative, computer, artificial, polysynthetic. *Indo-European languages include the following—Germanic:* Gothic, Old Saxon, Old English or Anglo-Saxon, English, Frisian, Old High German, German, Yiddish, Dutch, Afrikaans, Flemish, Old Norse, Danish, Swedish, Norwegian, Icelandic; *Celtic:* Breton, Welsh or Cymric, Cornish, Irish or Erse, Scots Gaelic, Manx; *Italic:* Oscan, Umbrian, Venetic, Latin; *Romance:* Portuguese, Galician, Spanish, Catalan, Provençal, French, Haitian Creole, Walloon, Italian, Sardinian, Romanian, Rhaeto-Romantic or Romansh or Ladin; *Greek:* Attic, Ionic, Doric, Koine; *Slavic:* Old Church Slavonic, Russian, Byelorussian, Ukrainian, Polish, Czech, Slovak, Slovene, Serbo-Croatian, Bulgarian; *Baltic:* Old Prussian, Lithuanian, Latvian or Lettish; Albanian; Armenian; *Iranian:* Old Persian, Avestan, Pahlavi, Kurdish, Persian, Pushtu or Afghan;

Indic: Sanskrit, Pali, Prakrit, Hindi, Urdu; Tocharian; Hittite. *Other Eurasian languages include the following—Uralic:* Finnish, Estonian, Hungarian, Samoyed; *Altaic:* Turkish, Mongolian; Georgian; Abkhasian, Kabardian, Chechen; Basque; Etruscan. *North American languages include the following—Algonquian:* Massachusetts, Delaware, Mohegan, Pasamaquoddy, Fox-Sauk-Kickapoo, Cree, Penobscot, Menomini, Shawnee, Blackfoot, Arapaho, Cheyenne; Wiyot, Yorok; Kutenai; *Salishan:* Tillamook, Lillooet; *Wakashan:* Nootka, Kwakiutl; *Muskogean:* Creek, Choctaw-Chickasaw, Seminole; Natchez, Chitimacha; *Iroquoian:* Cherokee, Huron or Wayondot, Erie, Oneida, Mohawk, Seneca, Cayuga, Susquehanna or Conestoga; *Siouan:* Biloxi, Dakota, Mandan, Winnebago, Hidatsa, Crow; *Caddoan:* Caddo, Wichita, Pawnee; Yuchi; Aleut, Eskimo; *Penutian:* Tsimshian, Maidu, Miwok, Klamath-Modoc; Zuni; *Hokan:* Karok, Shasta, Washo, Pomo; *Mayan:* Kekchi, Quiche, Yucatec; Totonac; Mixe, Zoque, Vera Cruz; Huave; Zapotec, Chatino; Mixtec; Pueblo or Populoca; Otomi, Pame; Tarascan; *Uto-Aztecan:* Tubatulabal, Luiseño, Tepehuan, Pima-Papago, Hopi, Huichol, Nahuatl or Aztec, Northern Paiute or Paviotso, Southern Paiute-Ute, Mono, Shoshoni-Comanche, Chemehuevi; Kiowa-Tanoan; Keresan; *Na-Dene:* Haida, Tlingit, Athabaskan; Chippewayan, Apachean, Navajo, Hupa. **—speak the same language** understand one another, communicate, get along; see AGREE.

languor *n.* lethargy, listlessness, lassitude; see INDIFFERENCE, LAZINESS.

lanky *a.* lean, bony, rangy; see THIN 2.

lan·tern (lan'tərn) *n.* ⟦ult. < Gr *lampein*, to shine⟧ a transparent case for holding and shielding a light

lan'tern-jawed' *adj.* having long, thin jaws and sunken cheeks

lan·yard (lan'yərd) *n.* ⟦ < OFr *lasne*, noose⟧ a short rope used on board ship for holding or fastening something

lap[1] (lap) *n.* ⟦OE *læppa*⟧ 1 the front part from the waist to the knees of a sitting person 2 the part of the clothing covering this 3 that in which a person or thing is cared for 4 *a*) an overlapping *b*) a part that overlaps 5 one complete circuit of a racetrack — *vt.* **lapped, lap'ping** 1 to fold (*over* or *on*) 2 to wrap; enfold 3 to overlap 4 to get a lap ahead of (an opponent) in a race — *vi.* 1 to overlap 2 to extend beyond something in space or time: with *over*

lap[2] (lap) *vi., vt.* **lapped, lap'ping** ⟦OE *lapian*⟧ 1 to drink (a liquid) by dipping it up with the tongue as a dog does 2 to strike gently with a light splash: said of waves — *n.* 1 a lapping 2 the sound of lapping — **lap up** to accept eagerly

lap'board' *n.* a board placed on the lap for use as a table or desk

lap dog any pet dog small enough to be held in the lap

la·pel (lə pel') *n.* ⟦dim. of LAP[1]⟧ the front part of a coat folded back, forming an extension of the collar

lapi·dary (lap'ə der'ē) *n., pl.* **-dar·ies** ⟦ < L *lapis*, a stone⟧ one who cuts and polishes precious stones

lapin (lap'in) *n.* ⟦Fr, rabbit⟧ rabbit fur, often dyed to resemble other skins

lapis lazu·li (lap'is laz'yoo lī', -lazh'-; -lē') ⟦ < L *lapis*, a stone + ML *lazulus*, azure⟧ an azure, opaque, semi-precious stone

Lapp (lap) *n.* a member of a people living in Lapland, region in N Europe Also **Lap'land'er**

lap·pet (lap'it) *n.* ⟦dim. of LAP[1]⟧ a loose flap or fold of a garment or head covering

lap robe a heavy blanket, fur covering, etc. laid over the lap for warmth

lapse (laps) *n.* ⟦ < L *labi*, to slip⟧ 1 a small error 2 *a*) a moral slip *b*) a falling into a lower condition 3 a passing, as of time 4 the termination as of a privilege through failure to meet requirements — *vi.* **lapsed, laps'ing** 1 to fall into a specified state *[he lapsed* into silence*]* 2 to backslide 3 to elapse 4 to come to an end; stop 5 to become void because of failure to meet requirements

lap'top' *n.* a small, light, portable microcomputer having, in a single unit, a CPU, keyboard, screen, etc., and, usually, a rechargeable battery

lar'board (lär'bôrd') *n.* ⟦ < OE *hladan*, lade + *bord*, side⟧ port; left

lar·ceny (lär'sə nē) *n., pl.* **-nies** ⟦ult. < L *latro*, robber⟧ the unlawful taking of another's property; theft — **lar'cenist** *n.* — **lar'cenous** *adj.*

larch (lärch) *n.* ⟦ < L *larix*⟧ 1 a tree of the pine family that sheds its needles annually 2 its tough wood

lard (lärd) *n.* ⟦ < L *lardum*⟧ the fat of hogs, melted and clarified — *vt.* 1 to put strips of fat pork, bacon, etc. on (meat, etc.) before cooking 2 to embellish

lard'er *n.* 1 a place where food supplies are kept 2 food supplies

la·res and pe·na·tes (lā'rēz' ənd pē nā'tēz) the household gods of the ancient Romans

large (lärj) *adj.* **larg'er, larg'est** ⟦ < L *largus*⟧ 1 of great extent or amount; big, bulky, spacious, etc. 2 bigger than

others of its kind 3 operating on a big scale *[a large* producer*]* — *adv.* in a large way *[write large]* — **at large** 1 free; not confined 2 representing no particular district *[a* congressman *at large]* — **large'ness** *n.* — **larg'ish** *adj.*

large'heart'ed *adj.* generous; kindly

large intestine the relatively large section of the intestines of vertebrates, including the cecum, colon, and rectum

large'ly *adv.* 1 much; in great amounts 2 for the most part; mainly

large'-scale' *adj.* 1 drawn to a large scale 2 of wide scope; extensive

lar·gess or **lar·gesse** (lär jes', lär'jis) *n.* ⟦see LARGE⟧ 1 generous giving 2 a gift generously given

largo (lär'gō) *adj., adv.* ⟦It, slow⟧ *Musical Direction* slow and stately

lar·i·at (lar'ē ət) *n.* ⟦Sp *la reata*, the rope⟧ 1 a rope used for tethering grazing horses, etc. 2 LASSO

lark[1] (lärk) *n.* ⟦ < OE *læwerce*⟧ any of a large family of chiefly Old World birds, esp. the skylark

lark[2] (lärk) *vi.* ⟦? < ON *leika*⟧ to play or frolic — *n.* a frolic or spree

lark·spur (lärk'spur') *n.* DELPHINIUM

larva (lär'və) *n., pl.* **-vae** (-vē') or **-vas** ⟦L, ghost⟧ the early form of any animal that changes structurally when it becomes an adult *[the tadpole is the larva* of the frog*]* — **lar'val** *adj.*

laryn·gi·tis (lar'in jīt'is) *n.* an inflammation of the larynx, often with a temporary loss of voice

larynx (lar'inks) *n., pl.* **lar'ynx·es** (-iz') or **la·ryn·ges** (lə rin'jēz') ⟦ < Gr⟧ the structure at the upper end of the trachea, containing the vocal cords

la·sa·gna (lə zän'yə) *n.* ⟦It⟧ wide noodles baked in layers with tomato sauce, ground meat, and cheese

las·civ·i·ous (lə siv'ē əs) *adj.* ⟦ < L *lascivus*, wanton⟧ 1 characterized by or expressing lust 2 exciting lust

la·ser (lā'zər) *n.* ⟦*l(ight) a(mplification by) s(timulated) e(mission of) r(adiation)*⟧ a device that raises the energy state of a substance so that it emits light in an intense, narrow beam

laser disc (or **disk**) a videodisc for recording audio and video data to be read by a laser beam

lash[1] (lash) *n.* ⟦ < ?⟧ 1 the flexible striking part of a whip 2 a stroke as with a whip 3 an eyelash — *vt.* 1 to strike or drive as with a lash 2 to switch energetically *[the cat lashed* her tail*]* 3 to censure or rebuke — *vi.* to make strokes as with a whip — **lash out** 1 to strike out violently 2 to speak angrily

lash[2] (lash) *vt.* ⟦see LACE⟧ to fasten or tie with a rope, etc.

lass (las) *n.* ⟦prob. < ON *lǫskr*, weak⟧ a young woman

las·sie (las'ē) *n.* [Scot.] a young woman

las·si·tude (las'i tood') *n.* ⟦ < L *lassus*, faint⟧ weariness; languor

lasso (las'ō') *n., pl.* **-sos'** or **-soes'** ⟦ < Sp < L *laqueus*, noose⟧ a rope with a sliding noose used to catch cattle, etc. — *vt.* **-soed', -so'ing** to catch with a lasso

last[1] (last) *adj.* 1 *alt. superl. of* LATE 2 being or coming after all others in place or time; final 3 only remaining 4 most recent *[last* month*]* 5 least likely *[the last* person to

THESAURUS

lantern *n.* torch, lamp, lighting device; see LIGHT 3.

lap[1] *n.* 1 [That portion of the body that is formed when one sits down] knees, legs, thighs, front. 2 [The portion that overlaps] extension, projection, fold; see FLAP. 3 [Part of a race] circuit, round, course; see DISTANCE 3, RACE 3. —**drop into someone's lap** transfer responsibility, shift blame, pass the buck*; see GIVE 1. —**in the lap of luxury** surrounded by luxury, living elegantly, prospering; see RICH 1.

lapse *n.* slip, mistake, failure; see ERROR.

lapse *v.* slip, deteriorate, decline; see WEAKEN 1.

larceny *n.* burglary, thievery, robbery; see CRIME, THEFT.

large *a.* 1 [Of great size] huge, big, wide, grand, great, considerable, substantial, vast, massive, immense, spacious, bulky, colossal, gigantic, mountainous, immeasurable, exten-

sive, plentiful, copious, populous, ample, abundant, liberal, comprehensive, lavish, swollen, bloated, puffy, obese, monstrous, towering, mighty, magnificent, enormous, giant, tremendous, monumental, stupendous, voluminous, cumbersome, ponderous, gross, immoderate, extravagant, super*, booming, bumper, whopping*; see also BIG 1, BROAD 1, DEEP 2, EXTENSIVE, HIGH 1.—*Ant.* LITTLE, small, tiny. 2 [Involving great plans] extensive, extended, considerable; see GENERAL 1.

largely *a.* 1 [In large measure] mostly, mainly, chiefly; see PRINCIPALLY. 2 [In a large way] extensively, abundantly, comprehensively; see WIDELY.

largeness *n.* magnitude, proportion, breadth; see MEASURE 1, MEASUREMENT 2, QUANTITY, SIZE.

lariat *n.* lasso, tether, line; see ROPE.

lark[1] *n.* songbird, warbler, philomel; see BIRD.

larva *n.* maggot, grub, caterpillar; see WORM.

lash[1] *v.* cane, scourge, strap; see BEAT 1, HIT 1.

lass *n.* young woman, damsel, maiden; see GIRL, WOMAN.

lasso *n.* tether, lariat, noose; see ROPE.

last[1] *a.* 1 [Final] ultimate, utmost, lowest, meanest, least, end, extreme, remotest, furthest, outermost, farthest, uttermost, concluding, hindmost, far-off, ulterior, once and for all, definitive, after all others, ending, at the end, terminal, eventual, settling, resolving, decisive, crowning, climactic, closing, ending, finishing, irrefutable.—*Ant.* FIRST, foremost, beginning. 2 [Most recent] latest, newest, current, freshest, immediate, in the fashion, modish, the last word*, trendy*; see also FASHIONABLE, MODERN 1.—*Ant.* OLD, stale, outmoded.

suspect/ 6 conclusive [the *last* word/ — *adv.* 1 after all others 2 most recently 3 finally — *n.* the one coming last —**at (long) last** finally

last[2] (last) *vi.* 〖OE *læstan*〗 to remain in existence, use, etc.; endure — *vt.* 1 to continue during 2 to be enough for

last[3] (last) *n.* 〖< OE *last*, footstep〗 a form shaped like the foot, used in making or repairing shoes

last hurrah a final attempt or appearance, as in politics

last'ing *adj.* that lasts a long time —**last'ingly** *adv.*

Last Judgment *Theol.* the final judgment at the end of the world

last'ly *adv.* in conclusion; finally

last straw 〖< the straw that broke the camel's back〗 a final trouble that results in a defeat, loss of patience, etc.

lat. latitude

latch (lach) *n.* 〖< OE *læccan*〗 a fastening for a door, gate, or window; esp., a bar that fits into a notch — *vt., vi.* to fasten with a latch —**latch onto** [Colloq.] to get or obtain

late (lāt) *adj.* **lat'er** or **lat'ter, lat'est** or **last** 〖OE *læt*〗 1 happening, coming, etc. after the usual or expected time, or at a time far advanced in a period [*late* to class, *late* Victorian/ 2 recent 3 having recently died — *adv.* **lat'er, lat'est** or **last** 1 after the expected time 2 at or until an advanced time of the day, year, etc. 3 toward the end of a period 4 recently —**of late** recently —**late'ness** *n.*

lately (lāt'lē) *adv.* recently; not long ago

la·tent (lāt''nt) *adj.* 〖< L *latere*, lurk〗 lying hidden and undeveloped in a person or thing —**la'tency** *n.*

lat·eral (lat'ər əl) *adj.* 〖< L *latus*, a side〗 of, at, from, or toward the side; sideways —**lat'er·ally** *adv.*

la·tex (lā'teks') *n.* 〖L, a fluid〗 a milky liquid in certain plants and trees: used esp. as the basis of rubber

lath (lath) *n., pl.* **laths** (la*th*z, laths) 〖< ME〗 1 any of the thin, narrow strips of wood used as a foundation for plaster, etc. 2 any foundation for plaster

lathe (lā*th*) *n.* 〖prob. < MDu *lade*〗 a machine for shaping wood, metal, etc. by holding and turning it rapidly against a cutting tool — *vt.* **lathed, lath'ing** to shape on a lathe

lather (la*th*'ər) *n.* 〖OE *leathor*, soap〗 1 the foam formed by soap and water 2 foamy sweat 3 [Slang] an excited state — *vt., vi.* to cover with or form lather —**lath'ery** *adj.*

Latin (lat''n) *adj.* 〖< *Latium*, ancient country in central Italy〗 1 of ancient Rome, its people, their language, etc. 2 designating or of the languages derived from Latin, the peoples who speak them, their countries, etc. — *n.* 1 a native or inhabitant of ancient Rome 2 the language of ancient Rome 3 a person whose language is derived from Latin, as a Spaniard or Italian

lat·ish (lāt'ish) *adj., adv.* somewhat late

lati·tude (lat'ə tood') *n.* 〖< L *latus*, wide〗 1 freedom from narrow restrictions 2 *a)* distance, measured in degrees, north or south from the equator *b)* a region with reference to this distance

la·trine (lə trēn') *n.* 〖< L *lavare*, to wash〗 a toilet for the use of a large number of people, as in an army camp

lat·ter (lat'ər) *adj.* 〖orig. compar. of LATE〗 1 *alt. compar. of* LATE 2 *a)* later; more recent *b)* nearer the end or close 3 being the last mentioned of two

lat'terly *adv.* lately; recently

lat·tice (lat'is) *n.* 〖< OHG *latta*, lath〗 an openwork structure of crossed strips of wood, metal, etc. used as a screen, support, etc.

lat'tice·work' (-wurk') *n.* 1 a lattice 2 lattices collectively

laud (lôd) *vt.* 〖< L *laus*, glory〗 to praise; extol

laud'able *adj.* praiseworthy; commendable

lau·da·num (lôd''n əm) *n.* 〖< L *ladanum*, a dark resin〗 1 [Archaic] any of various opium preparations 2 a solution of opium in alcohol

lauda·tory (lôd'ə tôr'ē) *adj.* expressing praise; commendatory

laugh (laf) *vi.* 〖< OE *hleahhan*〗 to make the sounds and facial movements that express mirth, ridicule, etc. — *n.* 1 the act or sound of laughing 2 a cause of laughter —**laugh at** 1 to be amused by 2 to make fun of

laugh'able *adj.* amusing or ridiculous —**laugh'ably** *adv.*

laugh'er *n.* 1 one that laughs 2 [Colloq.] a contest won by a wide margin; easy victory

laughing gas nitrous oxide used as an anesthetic: inhaling it may cause a reaction of laughter

laugh'ing·stock' (-stäk') *n.* an object of ridicule

laugh'ter *n.* the action or sound of laughing

launch[1] (lônch) *vt.* 〖< L *lancea*, a lance〗 1 to hurl or send forth with some force [to *launch* a rocket/ 2 to slide (a new vessel) into the water 3 to set in operation or on some course; start [to *launch* an attack/ — *vi.* 1 to start something new: often with *out* or *forth* 2 to plunge (*into*) — *n.* a launching — *adj.* designating or of vehicles, sites, etc. used in launching spacecraft or missiles

launch[2] (lônch) *n.* 〖Sp or Port *lancha*〗 an open, or partly enclosed, motorboat

launch pad the platform from which a rocket, guided missile, etc. is launched Also **launching pad**

launch window a favorable time period for launching a spacecraft, etc.

laun·der (lôn'dər) *vt.* 〖< L *lavare*, to wash〗 1 to wash, or wash and iron (clothes, etc.) 2 to exchange or invest (illegally gotten money) so as to conceal its source —**laun'derer** *n.* —**laun'dress** (-dris) *n.fem.*

THESAURUS

last[1] *n.* tail end, last one, ending; see END 4. —**at (long) last** after a long time, in the end, ultimately; see FINALLY 2. —**see the last of** see for the last time, dispose of, get rid of; see END 1.

last[2] *v.* 1 [To endure] remain, carry on, survive, hold out, suffer, stay, overcome, persist, sustain, maintain, stick it out*, stick with it*, go on; see also CONTINUE 1, ENDURE 1, 2. 2 [To be sufficient] hold out, be adequate, be enough, serve, do, accomplish the purpose, answer; see also SATISFY 3.

lasting *a.* enduring, abiding, constant; see PERMANENT.

latch *n.* catch, hook, bar; see FASTENER, LOCK 1.

latch *v.* lock, cinch, close up; see CLOSE 4, FASTEN.

late *a.* 1 [Tardy] too late, held up, overdue, stayed, postponed, put off, not on time, belated, behind time, lagging, delayed, backward, not in time; see also SLOW 2, 3.—*Ant.* EARLY, punctual, on time. 2 [Recently dead] defunct, deceased, departed; see DEAD 1. 3 [Recent] new, just out, recently published; see FRESH 1. 4 [Far into the night] nocturnal, night-loving, advanced, tardy, toward morning, after midnight. —**of late** lately, in recent times, a short time ago; see RECENTLY.

lately *a.* a short time ago, in recent times, of late; see RECENTLY.

lateness *n.* belatedness, procrastination, hesitation, tardiness, retardation, protraction, prolongation, slowness, backwardness, advanced hour, late date.—*Ant.* ANTICIPATION, earliness, promptness.

latent *a.* underdeveloped, potential, dormant, inactive.

later *a.* succeeding, next, more recent; see FOLLOWING.

lateral *a.* oblique, sidelong, side by side; see SIDE.

latest *a.* most recent, immediately prior, just finished; see LAST 1, 2.

lather *n.* suds, foam, bubbles; see FROTH.

Latin *a.* 1 [Pertaining to ancient Rome or to its language] Roman, Romanic, Latinic. 2 [Pertaining to southwestern Europe] Roman, Mediterranean, Italian; see EUROPEAN.

Latin *n.* Romance language, Classical Latin, Late Latin; see LANGUAGE 2.

latitude *n.* meridional distance, degree, measure, degrees of latitude; see also MEASURE 1.

latter *a.* late, last, recent; see FOLLOWING, LAST 1.

laugh *n.* mirth, merriment, amusement, rejoicing, gesture, crow, shout, chuckle, chortle, cackle, peal of laughter, horselaugh, guffaw, titter,

snicker, giggle, roar, snort; see also LAUGHTER.—*Ant.* CRY, sob, whimper. —**have the last laugh** defeat finally, beat in the end, overcome all obstacles; see WIN 1.

laugh *v.* chuckle, chortle, guffaw, laugh off, snicker, titter, giggle, burst out laughing, shriek, roar, beam, grin, smile, smirk, shout, die laughing*, break up*, crack up*, howl, roll in the aisles*, be in stitches; see also SMILE.—*Ant.* CRY, sob, weep. —**laugh at** deride, taunt, make fun of; see RIDICULE.

laughable *a.* ludicrous, comic, comical; see FUNNY 1.

laughing *a.* chortling, giggling, chuckling; see HAPPY. —**no laughing matter** serious, grave, significant; see IMPORTANT 1.

laughter *n.* chortling, chuckling, guffawing, tittering, giggling, shouting, roaring, howling, snorting; see also LAUGH.—*Ant.* CRY, weeping, wailing.

launch[1] *v.* 1 [To initiate] originate, start, set going; see BEGIN 1. 2 [To send off] set in motion, propel, drive, thrust, fire off, send forth, eject; see also DRIVE 1, 2, PROPEL.

launched *a.* started, sent, set in motion; see BEGIN, DRIVEN, SENT.

launder *v.* cleanse, do the wash, wash and iron; see CLEAN, WASH 2.

Laun·dro·mat (lôn′drō mat′, -drə-) *service mark for* a self-service laundry — *n.* [l-] such a laundry
laun·dry (lôn′drē) *n., pl.* **-dries 1** a place for laundering **2** clothes, etc. laundered or to be laundered
laun′dry·man′ *n., pl.* **-men′** a man who works in or for a laundry, esp. one who collects and delivers laundry — **laun′dry·wom′an,** *pl.* **-wom′en,** *n.fem.*
lau·re·ate (lôr′ē it) *adj.* [< L *laurus*, laurel] honored, as with a crown of laurel — *n.* POET LAUREATE
lau·rel (lôr′əl) *n.* [< L *laurus*] **1** an evergreen tree or shrub of S Europe, with large, glossy leaves **2** its foliage, esp. as woven into crowns **3** [*pl.*] fame; honor **4** any of various trees and shrubs resembling the true laurel
lava (lä′və, lav′ə) *n.* [It < L *labi*, to slide] **1** melted rock issuing from a volcano **2** such rock when solidified by cooling
lava·liere or **lava·lier** (lav′ə lir′, lä′və-) *n.* [< Fr] an ornament on a chain, worn around the neck
lava·tory (lav′ə tôr′ē) *n., pl.* **-ries** [< L *lavare*, to wash] a room with a washbowl and a toilet
lave (lāv) *vt., vi.* **laved, lav′ing** [< L *lavare*] [Old Poet.] to wash or bathe
lav·en·der (lav′ən dər) *n.* [< ML *lavandria*] **1** a fragrant European mint, with spikes of pale-purplish flowers **2** its dried flowers and leaves, used to perfume clothes, etc. **3** a pale purple — *adj.* pale-purple
lav·ish (lav′ish) *adj.* [< OFr *lavasse*, downpour] **1** very generous; prodigal **2** very abundant — *vt.* to give or spend generously —**lav′ishly** *adv.*
law (lô) *n.* [OE *lagu*] **1** *a*) all the rules of conduct established by the authority or custom of a nation, etc. *b*) any one of such rules **2** obedience to such rules **3** the study of such rules; jurisprudence **4** the seeking of justice in courts under such rules **5** the profession of lawyers, judges, etc. **6** *a*) a sequence of natural events occurring with unvarying uniformity under the same conditions *b*) the stating of such a sequence **7** any rule expected to be observed [the *laws* of health] —**the Law 1** the Mosaic law, or the part of the Jewish Scriptures containing it **2** [the l-] [Colloq.] a policeman or the police
law′-abid′ing *adj.* obeying the law
law′break′er *n.* one who violates the law —**law′break′ing** *adj., n.*
law′ful *adj.* **1** in conformity with the law **2** recognized by law [*lawful* debts] —**law′fully** *adv.*

law′giv′er *n.* a lawmaker; legislator
law′less *adj.* **1** not regulated by the authority of law **2** not in conformity with law; illegal **3** not obeying the law; unruly —**law′less·ness** *n.*
law′mak′er *n.* one who makes or helps to make laws; esp., a legislator
lawn[1] (lôn) *n.* [< OFr *launde*, heath] land covered with grass kept closely mowed, esp. around a house
lawn[2] (lôn) *n.* [after *Laon*, city in France] a fine, sheer cloth of linen or cotton
law·ren·cium (lô ren′sē əm) *n.* [after E.O. *Lawrence* (1901-58), U.S. physicist] a radioactive chemical element produced by nuclear bombardment
law′suit′ *n.* a suit between private parties in a law court
law·yer (lô′yər) *n.* one whose profession is advising others in matters of law or representing them in lawsuits
lax (laks) *adj.* [< L *laxus*] **1** loose; slack; not tight **2** not strict or exact —**lax′ly** *adv.*
laxa·tive (laks′ə tiv) *adj.* [see prec.] making the bowels loose and relieving constipation — *n.* any laxative medicine
lax·ity (laks′i tē) *n.* lax quality or condition
lay[1] (lā) *vt.* **laid, lay′ing** [< OE *lecgan*] **1** to cause to fall with force; knock down **2** to place or put in a resting position: often with *on* or *in* **3** to put down (bricks, carpeting, etc.) in the correct position or way **4** to place; put; set [to *lay* emphasis on accuracy] **5** to produce (an egg) **6** to allay, suppress, etc. **7** to bet (a specified sum, etc.) **8** to devise [to *lay* plans] **9** to present or assert [to *lay* claim to property] — *n.* the way or position in which something is situated [the *lay* of the land] —**lay aside** to put away for future use; save: also **lay away** or **lay by** —**lay in** to get and store away —**lay off 1** to discharge (an employee), esp. temporarily **2** [Slang] to cease —**lay open 1** to cut open **2** to expose —**lay out 1** to spend **2** to arrange according to a plan **3** to spread out (clothes, etc.) ready for wear, etc. —**lay over** to stop a while in a place before going on —**lay up 1** to store for future use **2** to confine to a sickbed
lay[2] (lā) *vi. pt. of* LIE[1]
lay[3] (lā) *adj.* [< Gr *laos*, the people] **1** of a layman **2** not belonging to a given profession

THESAURUS

laundry *n.* ironing, washing, clothes; see WASH 1.
lavatory *n.* privy, bathroom, washroom; see BATH 2, TOILET.
lavender *a., n.* lilac, lilac-purple, bluish-red; see COLOR, PURPLE.
lavish *a.* generous, unstinted, unsparing; see PLENTIFUL 1, 2.
lavish *v.* scatter freely, give generously, squander; see SPEND, WASTE 2.
lavishly *a.* profusely, richly, expensively; see CARELESSLY, FOOLISHLY, WASTEFULLY.
law *n.* **1** [The judicial system] judicial procedure, legal process, the legal authorities, the police, due process, precept, summons, notice, warrant, search warrant, warrant of arrest, subpoena. **2** [Bodies of law] code, constitution, criminal law, statute law, civil law, martial law, military law, private law, public law, commercial law, probate law, statutory law, statutes, civil code, ordinances, equity, cases, common law, canon law, decisions, unwritten law, natural law. **3** [An enactment] statute, edict, decree, order, ordinance, judicial decision, ruling, injunction, summons, act, enactment, requirement, demand, canon, regulation, bylaw, instruction, legislation; see also COMMAND, ORDER 1. **4** [A principle] foundation, fundamental, origin, source, ultimate cause, truth, axiom, maxim, ground, base, reason, rule, theorem, guide, precept, usage, postulate, proposition, generalization, assumption, hard and fast rule; see also REASON 3. **5** [Officers appointed to enforce the law] sheriff, state police,

city police; see JUDGE 1, LAWYER, POLICE. —**lay down the law** establish rules, order, prohibit; see ORDER 1.
lawbreaker *n.* felon, offender, violator; see CRIMINAL.
lawful *a.* legalized, legitimate, statutory, passed, decreed, judged, judicial, juridical, commanded, ruled, ordered, constitutional, legislated, enacted, official, enforced, protected, vested, within the law, legitimatized, established; see also LEGAL, PERMITTED.—*Ant.* ILLEGAL, unlawful, illegitimate.
lawfully *a.* licitly, in accordance with the law, by law; see LEGALLY.
lawless *a.* **1** [Without law] wild, untamed, uncivilized, savage, native, uncultivated, barbarous, fierce, violent, barbarous, fierce, violent, tempestuous, disordered, agitated, disturbed, warlike; see also UNCONTROLLED.—*Ant.* CULTURED, cultivated, controlled. **2** [Not restrained by law] riotous, insubordinate, disobedient; see UNRULY.
lawlessness *n.* irresponsibility, terrorism, chaos; see DISORDER, DISTURBANCE 2.
lawmaker *n.* lawgiver, congressman, councilman; see GOVERNOR.
lawn[1] *n.* green, grassplot, grassland; see GRASS 2, YARD 1.
lawsuit *n.* action, prosecution, suit; see CLAIM, TRIAL 2.
lawyer *n.* professional man, legal adviser, jurist, defender, prosecuting attorney, prosecutor, attorney, solicitor, counsel, counselor, counselor-at-law, barrister, advocate, professor of

law, attorney at law, public attorney, private attorney, attorney general, district attorney, Philadelphia lawyer*, legal eagle*, shyster*, mouthpiece*.
lax *a.* slack, remiss, soft; see CARELESS, INDIFFERENT.
laxative *n.* physic, purgative, diuretic, cathartic, purge, remedy, cure, dose; see also MEDICINE 2. *Common laxatives include the following;* castor oil, mineral oil, agar-agar, cascara sagrada, flaxseed, milk of magnesia, croton oil, epsom salts, cascarin compound.
lay[1] *v.* **1** [To knock down] trounce, defeat, club; see BEAT 1, HIT 1. **2** [To place] put, locate, settle, deposit, plant, lodge, store, stow, situate, deposit, set; see also SET 1. **3** [To put in order] arrange, organize, systematize; see ORDER 3. —**lay aside 1** [To place] deposit, put, set; see SET 1. **2** [To save] lay away, collect, keep; see SAVE 3, STORE. —**lay away** lay aside, keep, collect; see STORE. —**lay down 1** [To declare] assert, state, affirm; see DECLARE, REPORT 1, SAY. **2** [To bet] game, put up, wager; see BET, GAMBLE. —**lay off 1** [To discharge employees, usually temporarily] fire, discharge, let go; see DISMISS, OUST. **2** [*To stop] cease, halt, desist; see END 1, STOP 2. —**lay out** lend, put out at interest, put up; see INVEST, SPEND. —**lay over** delay, stay over, break a journey; see STOP 1. —**lay up 1** [To save] conserve, preserve, hoard; see SAVE 3, STORE. **2** [To disable] injure, harm, beat up*; see HURT.

lay⁴ (lā) *n.* 〖ME & OFr *lai*〗 **1** a short poem, esp. a narrative poem, orig. for singing **2** [Obs.] a song

lay′a·way′ *n.* a method of buying by making a deposit on something which is delivered only after full payment

lay′er *n.* **1** a person or thing that lays **2** a single thickness, fold, etc.

lay·ette (lā et′) *n.* 〖< MDu *lade*, chest〗 a complete outfit of clothes, bedding, etc. for a newborn baby

lay·man (lā′mən) *n.*, *pl.* **-men** a person not a clergyman or one not belonging to a given profession

lay′off′ *n.* temporary unemployment, or the period of this

lay′out′ *n.* **1** the manner in which anything is laid out; specif., the makeup of a newspaper, advertisement, etc. **2** the thing laid out

lay′o′ver *n.* a stop during a journey

Laza·rus (laz′ə rəs) *Bible* a man raised from the dead by Jesus

laze (lāz) *vi.*, *vt.* **lazed, laz′ing** to idle or loaf

lazy (lā′zē) *adj.* **-zier, -zi·est** 〖prob. < Medieval LowG or MDu〗 **1** not eager or willing to work or exert oneself **2** sluggish — *vi.*, *vt.* **-zied, -zy·ing** LAZE —**la′zily** *adv.* —**la′zi·ness** *n.*

la′zy·bones′ *n.* [Colloq.] a lazy person

Lazy Su·san (sōō′zən) a rotating tray for food

lb. 〖L *libra*, pl. *librae*〗 pound; pounds

l.c. 〖L *loco citato*〗 in the place cited

LCD 〖*l(iquid-)c(rystal) d(isplay)*〗 a device for alphanumeric displays, as on digital watches, using a crystalline liquid

lea (lē) *n.* 〖OE *leah*〗 [Old Poet.] a meadow

leach (lēch) *vt.* 〖prob. < OE *leccan*, to water〗 **1** to wash (some material) with a filtering liquid **2** to extract (a soluble substance) from some material — *vi.* to dissolve and be washed away

lead¹ (lēd) *vt.* **led, lead′ing** 〖OE *lædan*〗 **1** to direct, as by going before or along with, by physical contact, pulling a rope, etc.; guide **2** to guide by influence **3** to be the head of (an expedition, orchestra, etc.) **4** to be at the head of [to lead one's class] **5** to be ahead of in a contest **6** to live; spend [to lead a hard life] — *vi.* **1** to show the way, as by going before **2** to tend in a certain direction: with *to, from*, etc. **3** to bring as a result: with *to* [hate led to war] **4** to be or go first — *n.* **1** the role or example of a leader **2** first or front place **3** the amount or distance ahead [to hold a safe

lead] **4** anything that leads, as a clue **5** the leading role in a play, etc. **6** the right of playing first in cards or the card played —**lead off** to begin —**lead on** to lure —**lead up to** to prepare the way for

lead² (led) *n.* 〖OE〗 **1** a heavy, soft, bluish-gray metallic chemical element **2** a weight for measuring depth at sea **3** bullets **4** a stick of graphite, used in pencils — *adj.* of or containing lead — *vt.* to cover, line, or weight with lead

lead·ed (led′əd) *adj.* containing a lead compound: said of gasoline

lead·en (led′'n) *adj.* **1** of lead **2** heavy **3** sluggish **4** gloomy **5** gray

lead·er (lēd′ər) *n.* one that leads; guiding head —**lead′er·ship′** *n.*

lead·ing (lēd′iŋ) *adj.* **1** that leads; guiding **2** principal; chief

leading question a question put in such a way as to suggest the answer sought

lead time (lēd) the period of time between the decision to make a product and the start of production

leaf (lēf) *n.*, *pl.* **leaves** 〖OE〗 **1** any of the flat, thin parts, usually green, growing from the stem of a plant **2** a sheet of paper **3** a very thin sheet of metal **4** a hinged or removable section of a table top — *vi.* **1** to bear leaves **2** to turn the pages of a book: with *through* —**leaf′less** *adj.*

leaf·let (-lit) *n.* **1** a small or young leaf **2** a separate sheet of printed matter, often folded

leaf′stalk′ (-stôk′) *n.* the part of a leaf that supports the blade and is attached to the stem

leaf′y *adj.* **-i·er, -i·est** having many or broad leaves [a leafy vegetable]

league¹ (lēg) *n.* 〖< L *ligare*, bind〗 **1** an association of nations, groups, etc. for promoting common interests **2** *Sports* a group of teams organized to play one another — *vt.*, *vi.* **leagued, leagu′ing** to form into a league

league² (lēg) *n.* 〖ult. < OE *leowe*, mile〗 a measure of distance, about three miles

leak (lēk) *vi.* 〖< ON *leka*, to drip〗 **1** to let a fluid out or in accidentally **2** to pass in or out of a container thus **3** to become known gradually, by accident, etc. — *vt.* to allow to leak — *n.* **1** an accidental crack, etc. that lets something out or in **2** any accidental means of escape **3** leakage —**leak′y, -i·er, -i·est,** *adj.*

leak′age (-ij) *n.* **1** a leaking **2** that which or the amount that leaks

lean¹ (lēn) *vi.* **leaned** or **leant** (lent), **lean′ing** 〖OE *hlinian*〗 **1** to bend or slant from an upright position **2** to

---

THESAURUS

layer *n.* thickness, fold, band, overlay, lap, overlap, seam, floor, story, tier, zone, stripe, coating, flap, panel.

layman *n.* nonprofessional, novice, dilettante; see AMATEUR, RECRUIT.

laymen *n.* laity, converts, congregation, neophytes, parish, parishioners, the faithful, communicants, members, believers; see also FOLLOWING.

layout *n.* arrangement, design, draft; see ORGANIZATION 2, PLAN 1, PURPOSE 1.

layover *n.* break, stop, rest; see DELAY, PAUSE.

lazily *a.* indolently, nonchalantly, slackly; see GRADUALLY, SLOWLY.

laziness *n.* indolence, sloth, lethargy, inactivity, slackness, sluggishness, dullness, heaviness, inertia, drowsiness, passivity, listlessness, laxness, negligence, sleepiness, dullness, stupidity, dreaminess, weariness, apathy, indifference, tardiness, shiftlessness, procrastination; see also IDLENESS.—*Ant.* ACTION, promptitude, agility.

lazy *a.* **1** [Indolent] indolent, idle, remiss, sluggish, lagging, apathetic, loafing, dallying, passive, asleep on the job, procrastinating, neglectful, indifferent, dilatory, tardy, slack, inattentive, careless, flagging, weary, tired.—*Ant.* ACTIVE, businesslike, indefatigable. **2** [Slow] slothful, inactive, lethargic; see SLOW 1, 2.

lead¹ *a.* leading, head, foremost; see BEST, FIRST, PRINCIPAL.

lead¹ *n.* **1** [The position at the front] head, advance, first place, point, edge, front rank, first line, scout, out-

post, scouting party, patrol, advance position, forerunner; see also FRONT.—*Ant.* END, rear, last place. **2** [Leadership] direction, guidance, headship; see LEADERSHIP. **3** [A clue] evidence, trace, hint; see PROOF 1, SIGN 1. **4** [A leading role] principal part, important role, chief character; see ROLE. —**in the lead** ahead, winning, leading; see TRIUMPHANT. — **take the lead** direct, guide, head; see LEAD 1.

lead¹ *v.* **1** [To conduct] guide, steer, pilot, show the way, point the way, show in, point out, escort, accompany, protect, guard, safeguard, watch over, drive, discover the way, find a way through, be responsible for.—*Ant.* FOLLOW, be conveyed, be piloted. **2** [To exercise leadership] direct, manage, supervise; see MANAGE 1. **3** [To extend] traverse, pass along, span; see REACH 1. —**lead on** lure, entice, intrigue; see DECEIVE. —**lead up to** prepare for, introduce, make preparations for; see BEGIN 2, PROPOSE 1.

lead² *n.* metallic lead, galena, blue lead; see ELEMENT 2, METAL.

leaden *a.* **1** [Made of lead] metal, pewter, galena; see METALLIC 1. **2** [Heavy] burdensome, oppressive, weighty; see HEAVY 1. **3** [Lead-colored] dull, pewter, blue-gray; see GRAY.

leader *n.* **1** [A guide] conductor, lead, pilot; see GUIDE. **2** [One who provides leadership] general, commander, director, manager, head, officer, captain, master, chieftain,

governor, ruler, executor, boss, brains*; see also EXECUTIVE.

leadership *n.* authority, control, administration, effectiveness, superiority, supremacy, skill, initiative, foresight, energy, capacity; see also INFLUENCE, POWER 2.

leading *a.* foremost, chief, dominating; see BEST, PRINCIPAL.

leaf *n.* leaflet, needle, blade, stalk, scale, floral leaf, seed leaf, sepal, petal. —**turn over a new leaf** make a new start, redo, begin again; see CHANGE 2.

leaflet *n.* handbill, circular, broadside; see PAMPHLET.

leafy *a.* leafed out, in leaf, shaded; see SHADY.

league¹ *n.* band, group, unit; see ORGANIZATION 2.

leak *n.* **1** [Loss through leakage] leakage, loss, flow, seepage, escape, falling off, expenditure, decrease; see also WASTE 1. **2** [An aperture through which a leak may take place] puncture, chink, crevice; see HOLE 1. **3** [Surreptitious news] news leak, exposé, slip; see NEWS 1, 2.

leak *v.* **1** [To escape by leaking] drip, ooze, drool; see FLOW. **2** [To permit leakage] be cracked, be split, have a fissure, be out of order, have a slow leak.

leaky *a.* punctured, cracked, split; see BROKEN 1, OPEN 4.

lean¹ *v.* **1** [To incline] slope, slant, sag, sink, decline, list, tip, bow, roll, veer, droop, drift, pitch, bend, be slanted, be off; see also BEND, TILT. **2**

bend the body and rest part of one's weight on something 3 to rely (*on* or *upon*) 4 to tend (*toward* or *to*) — *vt.* to cause to lean —**lean′er** *n.*

lean[2] (lēn) *adj.* ⟦OE *hlæne*⟧ 1 with little flesh or fat; thin; spare 2 meager —**lean′ness** *n.*

lean′ing *n.* a tendency; inclination

lean′-to′ *n., pl.* **-tos′** a structure whose sloping roof abuts a wall, etc.

leap (lēp) *vi.* **leapt** (lept, lēpt) or **lept** or **leaped, leap′ing** ⟦OE *hleapan*⟧ 1 to jump; spring; bound 2 to accept eagerly something offered: with *at* — *vt.* 1 to pass over by a jump 2 to cause to leap — *n.* 1 a jump; spring 2 the distance covered in a jump 3 a sudden transition — **leap′er** *n.*

leap′frog′ *n.* a game in which each player in turn leaps over the bent backs of the other players — *vt., vi.* **-frog′ged′, -frog′ging** to leap or jump in or as in this way; skip (*over*)

leap year every fourth year, containing an extra day in February

learn (lurn) *vt., vi.* **learned** (lurnd) or **learnt** (lurnt), **learn′ing** ⟦OE *leornian*⟧ 1 to get knowledge of or skill in (an art, trade, etc.) by study, experience, etc. 2 to come to know; hear (*of* or *about*) 3 to memorize —**learn′er** *n.*

learned (lurn′id; *for 2* lurnd) *adj.* 1 having or showing much learning 2 acquired by study, experience, etc.

learn′ing *n.* 1 the acquiring of knowledge or skill 2 acquired knowledge or skill

learning disability any of several conditions, believed to involve the nervous system, which limit the ability to read, write, etc.

lease (lēs) *n.* ⟦< L *laxus*, loose⟧ a contract by which a landlord rents lands, buildings, etc. to a tenant for a specified time — *vt.* **leased, leas′ing** to give or get by a lease — **leas′er** *n.*

lease′hold′ *n.* 1 the act of holding by lease 2 land, buildings, etc. held by lease —**lease′hold′er** *n.*

leash (lēsh) *n.* ⟦< L *laxus*, loose⟧ a cord, strap, etc. by which a dog or the like is held in check — *vt.* to check or control as by a leash

least (lēst) *adj.* ⟦OE *læst*⟧ 1 *alt. superl. of* LITTLE 2 smallest or slightest in size, degree, etc. — *adv.* in the smallest degree — *n.* the smallest in amount, importance, etc. —**at (the) least** 1 at the lowest 2 at any rate —**not in the least** not at all

least′wise′ *adv.* [Colloq.] at least; anyway Also **least′ ways′**

leather (leth′ər) *n.* ⟦< OE *lether-*⟧ animal skin prepared for use by removing the hair and tanning — *adj.* of leather

leath′er·neck′ *n.* ⟦< former leather-lined uniform collar⟧ [Slang] a U.S. Marine

leath′ery *adj.* like leather; tough and flexible —**leath′eri· ness** *n.*

leave[1] (lēv) *vt.* **left, leav′ing** ⟦OE *læfan*, let remain⟧ 1 to allow to remain or remain (*leave* it open) 2 to have remaining behind or after one 3 to bequeath 4 to go away from 5 to abandon 6 [Chiefly Dial.] to let (*leave* us go) — *vi.* to go away or set out —**leave off** to stop —**leave out** to omit —**leav′er** *n.*

leave[2] (lēv) *n.* ⟦OE *leaf*⟧ 1 permission 2 *a*) permission to be absent from duty *b*) the period for which this is granted —**take leave of** to say goodbye to —**take one's leave** to depart

leave[3] (lēv) *vi.* **leaved, leav′ing** to put forth, or bear, leaves; leaf

leaven (lev′ən) *n.* ⟦< L *levare*, raise⟧ 1 a substance, as fermenting dough from a previous baking, yeast, etc., used to make dough rise 2 a tempering or modifying quality or thing — *vt.* 1 to make (dough) rise 2 to spread through, causing gradual change

leav′en·ing (-iŋ) *n.* 1 LEAVEN 2 a causing to be leavened

leave of absence permission to be absent from work or duty, esp. for a long time; also, the period for which this is granted

leaves (lēvz) *n. pl. of* LEAF

leave′-tak′ing *n.* a parting; farewell

leav·ings (lēv′iŋz) *n.pl.* leftovers, remnants, refuse, etc.

lecher (lech′ər) *n.* ⟦OFr *lechier*, live debauchedly⟧ a lewd, grossly sensual man —**lech′er·ous** *adj.* —**lech′ery** *n.*

leci·thin (les′i thin) *n.* ⟦< Gr *lekithos*, egg yolk⟧ a nitrogenous, fatty compound found in animal and plant cells: used in medicine, foods, etc.

lec·tern (lek′tərn) *n.* ⟦< L *legere*, to read⟧ a reading stand

lec·ture (lek′chər) *n.* ⟦< L *legere*, read⟧ 1 an informative talk to a class, etc. 2 a lengthy scolding — *vt., vi.* **-tured, -tur·ing** 1 to give a lecture (to) 2 to scold —**lec′turer** *n.*

led (led) *vt., vi. pt. & pp. of* LEAD[1]

LED *n.* ⟦*l(ight-)e(mitting) d(iode)*⟧ a semiconductor diode that emits light when voltage is applied: used as in lamps and digital watches

ledge (lej) *n.* ⟦ME *legge*⟧ 1 a shelf 2 a projecting ridge of rocks

■ THESAURUS ■

[To tend] favor, be disposed, incline; see TEND 2. —**lean on** 1 [To be supported by] rest on, be upheld by, bear on, put one's weight on, hang on, fasten on; see also LEAN 1. 2 [To rely upon] believe in, count on, put faith in; see TRUST 1.

lean[2] *a.* 1 [Thin] lank, meager, slim; see THIN 2. 2 [Containing little fat] fibrous, muscular, sinewy, meaty, free from fat, all-meat, protein-rich.

leaning *a.* inclining, tilting, out of perpendicular; see OBLIQUE.

lean-to *n.* shelter, shanty, cabin; see HUT.

leap *v.* spring, vault, bound; see BOUNCE, JUMP 1.

learn *v.* acquire, receive, get, take in, drink in, pick up, read, master, ground oneself in, pore over, gain information, ascertain, determine, unearth, hear, find out, learn by heart, memorize, be taught a lesson, improve one's mind, build one's background, get up on*, get the signal*; see also STUDY.

learned *a.* 1 [Having great learning; *said of people*] scholarly, erudite, academic, accomplished, conversant with, lettered, instructed, collegiate, well-informed, bookish, pedantic, professorial; see also CULTURED, EDUCATED.—*Ant.* IGNORANT, incapable, illiterate. 2 [Showing evidence of learning; *said of productions*] deep, sound, solemn; see PROFOUND.

learned *a.* memorized, word for word, by heart; see KNOWN 2.

learning *n.* lore, scholarship, train-

ing; see EDUCATION 1, KNOWLEDGE 1.

lease *n.* document of use, permission to rent, charter; see CONTRACT, RECORD 1.

lease *v.* let, charter, rent out; see RENT 1.

leash *n.* cord, chain, strap; see ROPE.

least *a.* 1 [Smallest] tiniest, infinitesimal, microscopic; see MINUTE 1. 2 [Least important] slightest, piddling, next to nothing; see TRIVIAL, UNIMPORTANT. 3 [In the lowest degree] minimal, most inferior, bottom; see LOWEST, MINIMUM. —**at (the) least** in any event, with no less than, at any rate; see ANYHOW. —**not in the least** not at all, in no way, not in the slightest degree; see NEVER.

leather *n.* tanned hide, parchment, calfskin, horsehide, buckskin, deerskin, elk hide, goatskin, sheepskin, rawhide, cowhide, snakeskin, sharkskin, lizard, shoe leather, glove leather, chamois skin, alligator hide; see also HIDE, SKIN.

leave[1] *v.* 1 [To go away] go, depart, take leave, withdraw, move, set out, come away, go forth, take off, start, step down, quit a place, part company, defect, vanish, walk out, walk away, get out, get away, slip out, slip away, break away, break out, ride off, ride away, go off, go out, go away, move out, move away, vacate, abscond, flee, flit, migrate, fly, run along, embark, say goodbye, emigrate, clear out*, cut out, pull out, push off*, cast off*, scram*, split*, sign out, check out, beat it*, take a

powder*, pull up stakes*.—*Ant.* ARRIVE, get to, reach. 2 [To abandon] back out, forsake, desert; see ABANDON 2. 3 [To allow to remain] let stay, leave behind, let continue, let go, drop, lay down, omit, forget; see also NEGLECT 1, 2.—*Ant.* SEIZE, take away, keep. 4 [To allow to fall to another] bequeath, hand down, transmit; see GIVE 1. —**leave out** cast aside, reject, dispose of; see DISCARD, ELIMINATE. —**leave to** bequeath, hand down, pass on; see GIVE 1.

leave[2] *n.* 1 [Permission] consent, dispensation, allowance; see PERMISSION. 2 [Authorized absence] leave of absence, holiday, furlough; see VACATION. —**on leave** away, gone, on a vacation; see ABSENT. —**take one's leave** go away, depart, remove oneself; see LEAVE 1.

leavings *n.* remains, residue, garbage; see TRASH 1.

lecture *n.* 1 [A speech] discourse, instruction, lesson; see EDUCATION 1, SPEECH 3. 2 [A reprimand] rebuke, talking to, dressing down.

lecture *v.* 1 [To give a speech] talk, instruct, teach; see ADDRESS 2, TEACH. 2 [To rebuke] scold, reprimand, admonish, give a going-over*, give a piece of one's mind*; see also SCOLD.

led *a.* taken, escorted, guided; see ACCOMPANIED.

ledge *n.* shelf, mantle, strip, bar, step, ridge, reef, rim, bench, edge, path, route, way, walk, track, trail.

ledger (lej′ər) *n.* ⟦ME *legger*⟧ a book of final entry, in which a record of debits and credits is kept

lee (lē) *n.* ⟦OE *hleo*, shelter⟧ **1** shelter **2** *Naut.* the side or direction away from the wind —*adj.* of or on the lee

leech (lēch) *n.* ⟦OE *læce*⟧ **1** a bloodsucking worm living in water and used, esp. formerly, to bleed patients **2** one who clings to another for personal advantage —*vi.* to cling (*onto*) thus

leek (lēk) *n.* ⟦OE *leac*⟧ a vegetable that resembles a thick green onion

leer (lir) *n.* ⟦OE *hleor*⟧ a sly, sidelong look showing lust, malicious triumph, etc. —*vi.* to look with a leer —**leer′ingly** *adv.*

leery (lir′ē) *adj.* **-i·er, -i·est** wary; suspicious

lees (lēz) *n.pl.* ⟦< ML *lia*⟧ dregs or sediment, as of wine

lee·ward (lē′wərd; *naut.* lōō′ərd) *adj.* away from the wind —*n.* the side or direction away from the wind —*adv.* toward the lee

lee·way (lē′wā′) *n.* **1** the leeward drift of a ship or aircraft from its course **2** [Colloq.] *a*) margin of time, money, etc. *b*) room for freedom of action

left[1] (left) *adj.* ⟦< OE *lyft*, weak⟧ **1** of or on the side that is toward the west when one faces north **2** closer to the left side of one facing the thing mentioned —*n.* **1** the left side **2** [*often* L-] *Politics* a liberal or radical position, party, etc.: often with *the* —*adv.* on or toward the left hand or side

left[2] (left) *vt., vi. pt. & pp. of* LEAVE[1]

left′-hand′ *adj.* **1** on the left **2** of, for, or with the left hand

left′-hand′ed *adj.* **1** using the left hand more skillfully than the right **2** done with or made for use with the left hand **3** ambiguous or backhanded /a *left-handed* compliment/ —*adv.* with the left hand /to write *left-handed*/

left′ist *n., adj.* liberal or radical

left′o′ver *n.* something left over

left wing the more liberal or radical section of a political party, group, etc. —**left′-wing′** *adj.* —**left′-wing′er** *n.*

left′y *n., pl.* **-ies** [Slang] a left-handed person: often a nickname

leg (leg) *n.* ⟦ON *leggr*⟧ **1** one of the parts of the body by means of which humans and animals stand and walk **2** the part of a garment covering the leg **3** anything like a leg in shape or use **4** a stage, as of a trip —*vi.* **legged, leg′ging** [Colloq.] to walk or run: chiefly in the phrase **leg it**

lega·cy (leg′ə sē) *n., pl.* **-cies** ⟦ult. < L *lex*, law⟧ **1** money or property left to someone by a will **2** anything handed down as from an ancestor

le·gal (lē′gəl) *adj.* ⟦< L *lex*, law⟧ **1** of or based on law **2** permitted by law **3** of or for lawyers —**le′gally** *adv.*

le′gal·ese′ (-ēz′) *n.* the special language of legal forms, documents, etc.

legal holiday a holiday set by law

le′gal·ism′ *n.* strict or too strict adherence to the law —**le′gal·is′tic** *adj.*

le·gal·ity (li gal′i tē) *n., pl.* **-ties** quality, condition, or instance of being legal or lawful

le·gal·ize (lē′gəl īz′) *vt.* **-ized′, -iz′ing** to make legal or lawful

legal tender money acceptable by law in payment of an obligation

leg·ate (leg′it) *n.* ⟦< L *lex*, law⟧ an envoy or ambassador

lega·tee (leg′ə tē′) *n.* one to whom a legacy is bequeathed

le·ga·tion (li gā′shən) *n.* **1** a diplomatic minister and staff collectively **2** the headquarters of such a group

le·gato (li gät′ō) *adj., adv.* ⟦< L *ligare*, to tie⟧ *Music* in a smooth, even style, with no breaks between notes

leg·end (lej′ənd) *n.* ⟦< L *legere*, read⟧ **1** a story or body of stories handed down for generations and popularly believed to have a historical basis **2** a notable person or the stories told about his exploits **3** an inscription on a coin, etc. **4** a title, key, etc. accompanying an illustration or map

leg·end·ary (lej′ən der′ē) *adj.* of, based on, or presented in legends

leger·demain (lej′ər di mān′) *n.* ⟦< Fr *leger de main*, light of hand⟧ **1** sleight of hand **2** trickery

-leg·ged (leg′id, legd) *combining form* having (a specified number or kind of) legs /long-*legged*/

leg·ging (leg′iŋ, -in) *n.* a covering for the lower leg: *usually used in pl.*

leggy (leg′ē) *adj.* **-gier, -gi·est 1** having long legs **2** [Colloq.] having long, spindly stems

leg·horn (leg′hôrn′, -ərn) *n.* [after *Leghorn*, It seaport] [*often* L-] any of a breed of small chicken

leg·ible (lej′ə bəl) *adj.* ⟦< L *legere*, read⟧ that can be read, esp. easily —**leg·ibil′ity** *n.* —**leg′ibly** *adv.*

le·gion (lē′jən) *n.* ⟦< L *legere*, choose⟧ **1** a large group of soldiers; army **2** a large number; multitude —**le′gion·naire′** (-jə ner′) *n.*

leg·is·late (lej′is lāt′) *vi.* **-lat′ed, -lat′ing** ⟦see fol.⟧ to make or pass a law or laws —*vt.* to cause to be, go, etc. by making laws —**leg′is·la′tor** *n.*

leg·is·la·tion *n.* ⟦< L *lex*, law + *latio*, a bringing⟧ **1** the making of laws **2** the laws made

leg′is·la′tive *adj.* **1** of legislation or a legislature **2** having the power to make laws —**leg′is·la′tively** *adv.*

leg′is·la′ture (-lā′chər) *n.* a body of persons given the power to make laws

▬ THESAURUS ▬

leech *n.* **1** [A parasite] tapeworm, hookworm, bloodsucker; see PARASITE 1. **2** [Dependent] parasite, hanger-on, sponger*; see WEAKLING.

leeward *a.* protected, screened, safe; see CALM 2.

leeway *n.* space, margin, latitude; see EXTENT.

left[1] *n.* left hand, left side, left part, port, not the right, not the center; see also POSITION 1.

left[1,2] *a.* **1** [Opposite to right] leftward, left-hand, near, sinister, larboard, port, portside.—*Ant.* RIGHT, right-hand, starboard. **2** [Remaining] staying, continuing, over; see EXTRA. **3** [Radical] left-wing, liberal, progressive; see RADICAL 2, REVOLUTIONARY 1. **4** [Departed] gone out, absent, lacking; see GONE 1. —**left out** lost, neglected, removed; see LOST 1.

leftist *n.* socialist, anarchist, communist; see LIBERAL, RADICAL.

leftover *a.* remaining, unwanted, unused, residual, uneaten, unconsumed, untouched, perfectly good; see also EXTRA.

leftovers *n.* leavings, scraps, debris; see FOOD, TRASH 1.

left-wing *a.* leftist, not conservative, reform; see LIBERAL, RADICAL 2.

leg *n.* part, member, lower appendage, hind leg, foreleg, back leg, front leg, left leg, right leg, shank; see also LIMB

2. —not have a leg to stand on* be unreasonable, make rash statements, have no defense; see MISTAKE. —**on one's** (or **its**) **last legs*** decaying, not far from breakdown, old; see DYING 2, WORN 2. —**pull someone's leg*** make fun of, fool, play a trick on; see DECEIVE.

legal *a.* lawful, constitutional, permissible, allowable, allowed, proper, legalized, sanctioned, legitimate, right, just, justifiable, justified, fair, authorized, accustomed, due, rightful, warranted, admitted, sound, granted, acknowledged, equitable, within the law, protected, enforced, judged, decreed, statutory, contractual, customary, chartered, clean*, legit*, straight*, on the up and up*; see also LAWFUL, PERMITTED.—*Ant.* ILLEGAL, unlawful, prohibited.

legality *n.* legitimacy, lawfulness, authority; see LAW 1.

legalize *v.* authorize, formulate, sanction; see APPROVE.

legally *a.* lawfully, legitimately, permissibly, licitly, enforcibly, allowably, admittedly, juridically, constitutionally, with due process of law, by statute, by law, in the eyes of the law, in accordance with law, in accordance with the constitution; see also RIGHTFULLY.—*Ant.* illegally, unconstitutionally, illicitly.

legend *n.* folk tale, saga, fable; see MYTH, STORY.

legendary *a.* fabulous, mythical, mythological, fanciful, imaginative, created, invented, allegorical, apocryphal, improbable, imaginary, dubious, not historical, doubtful, romantic, storied, unverifiable; see also IMAGINARY.

legerdemain *n.* deceit, trickery, deception; see DECEPTION, TRICK 1.

legible *a.* distinct, plain, sharp; see CLEAR 2.

legion *n.* multitude, body, group; see CROWD, GATHERING.

legislate *v.* make laws, pass, constitute; see ENACT.

legislation *n.* bill, enactment, act; see LAW 3.

legislative *a.* lawmaking, enacting, decreeing, ordaining, lawgiving, congressional, parliamentary, parliamentarian, senatorial, by the legislature.

legislator *n.* lawmaker, lawgiver, assemblyman, representative, congressman, congresswoman, senator, member of parliament, floor leader, councilman, councilwoman, alderman; see also EXECUTIVE.

legislature *n.* lawmakers, congress, parliament, chamber, assembly, senate, house, congress, elected representatives, soviet, plenum, lawmaking body, voice of the people.

le·giti·mate (lə jit'ə mət; *for v.*, -māt') *adj.* [< L *lex*, law] 1 born of parents married to each other 2 lawful 3 *a*) reasonable *b*) justifiable 4 conforming to accepted rules, standards, etc. 5 of stage plays, as distinguished from films, vaudeville, etc. — *vt.* -**mat'ed, -mat'ing** LEGITIMIZE —**le·git'i·macy** (-mə sē) *n.* —**le·git'i·mately** *adv.*

le·git'i·ma·tize' (-mə tīz') *vt.* -**tized', -tiz'ing** LEGITIMIZE

le·git'i·mize' (-mīz') *vt.* -**mized', -miz'ing** to make or declare legitimate —**le·git'i·mi·za'tion** *n.*

leg·man (leg'man') *n., pl.* -**men'** 1 a news reporter who transmits information from the scene 2 an assistant who does routine tasks outside the office

leg'room' *n.* adequate space for the legs while seated, as in a car

leg·ume (leg'yōōm') *n.* [< L *legere*, gather] 1 any of an order of plants having seeds growing in pods, including peas, beans, etc. 2 the pod or seed of such a plant —**le·gu·mi·nous** (lə gyōō'mə nəs) *adj.*

leg'work' *n.* [Colloq.] necessary, routine work, typically involving walking, as part of a job

lei (lā, lā'ē) *n., pl.* **leis** [Haw] a garland of flowers

lei·sure (lē'zhər, lezh'ər) *n.* [< L *licere*, be permitted] free time during which one may indulge in rest, recreation, etc. — *adj.* free and unoccupied

lei'surely *adj.* without haste; slow — *adv.* in an unhurried manner

leit·mo·tif or **leit·mo·tiv** (līt'mō tēf') *n.* [Ger *leitmotiv* < *leiten*, to guide + *motiv*, motive] a dominant theme

lem·ming (lem'iŋ) *n.* [< ON *læmingi*] a small arctic rodent with a short tail

lemon (lem'ən) *n.* [< Pers *līmūn*] 1 a small, sour, pale-yellow citrus fruit 2 the spiny, semitropical tree that it grows on 3 [Slang] something that is defective — *adj.* pale-yellow

lem'on·ade' (-ād') *n.* a drink made from lemon juice, sugar, and water

le·mur (lē'mər) *n.* [< L *lemures*, ghosts] a small tree-dwelling primate with large eyes

lend (lend) *vt.* **lent, lend'ing** [< OE *læn*, a loan] 1 to let another use or have (a thing) temporarily 2 to let out (money) at interest 3 to give; impart — *vi.* to make loans —**lend itself** (or **oneself**) **to** to be useful for or open to — **lend'er** *n.*

length (leŋkth) *n.* [< OE *lang*, long] 1 the distance from end to end of a thing 2 extent in space or time 3 a long stretch or extent 4 a piece of a certain length —**at length** 1 finally 2 in full

length'en *vt., vi.* to make or become longer

length'wise' *adv., adj.* in the direction of the length Also **length'ways'**

length'y *adj.* -**i·er, -i·est** long; esp., too long —**length'i·ly** *adv.*

le·ni·ent (lēn'yənt, lē'nē ənt) *adj.* [< L *lenis*, soft] not harsh or severe; merciful —**le'ni·ency** *n.* —**le'ni·ently** *adv.*

leni·tive (len'ə tiv) *adj.* [< L *lenire*, to soften] lessening pain or distress

lens (lenz) *n.* [L, lentil: < its shape] 1 a curved piece of glass, plastic, etc. for bringing together or spreading rays of light passing through it: used in optical instruments to form an image 2 any device used to focus microwaves, sound waves, etc. 3 a similar transparent part of the eye: it focuses light rays upon the retina

lent (lent) *vt., vi. pt. & pp. of* LEND

Lent (lent) *n.* [OE *lengten*, the spring] *Christianity* the forty weekdays of fasting and penitence from Ash Wednesday to Easter —**Lent'en** or **lent'en** *adj.*

len·til (lent'l) *n.* [< L *lens*] 1 a kind of legume, with small, edible seeds 2 this seed

Leo (lē'ō) [L, lion] the fifth sign of the zodiac

leo·nine (lē'ə nīn') *adj.* [< L *leo*, lion] of or like a lion

leop·ard (lep'ərd) *n.* [< Gr *leōn*, lion + *pardos*, panther] any of various large, ferocious cats, including the jaguar; esp., one with a black-spotted, tawny coat, found in Africa and Asia

leo·tard (lē'ə tärd') *n.* [after J. *Léotard*, 19th-c. Fr aerial performer] a tightfitting garment for acrobats, dancers, etc.

leper (lep'ər) *n.* [< Gr *lepros*, scaly] a person having leprosy

lep·re·chaun (lep'rə kôn') *n.* [< Old Ir *lu*, little + *corp*, body] *Ir. Folklore* a fairy who can reveal hidden treasure

lep·rosy (lep'rə sē) *n.* [see LEPER] a progressive infectious disease of the skin, flesh, nerves, etc., characterized by ulcers, white scaly scabs, deformities, etc. —**lep'rous** *adj.*

lept (lept) *vi., vt. alt. pt. of* LEAP

lep·ton (lep'tän') *n.* [< Gr *leptos*, thin] any of certain light atomic particles

les·bian (lez'bē ən) *n.* [after *Lesbos*, Gr. island home of the poetess Sappho] a homosexual woman —**les'bi·an·ism'** *n.*

lèse-majesté (lez'ma'zhes tā', -maj'is tē) *n.* [Fr < L *laesa majestas*, injured majesty] 1 a crime against the sovereign 2 any lack of proper respect as toward one in authority

le·sion (lē'zhən) *n.* [< L *laedere*, to harm] an injury of an organ or tissue resulting in impairment of function

less (les) *adj.* [OE *læs(sa)*] 1 *alt. compar. of* LITTLE 2 not so much 3 fewer — *adv.* 1 *compar. of* LITTLE 2 to a smaller extent — *n.* a smaller amount — *prep.* minus — **less and less** decreasingly

-less (lis, ləs) [OE *leas*, free] *suffix* 1 without 2 not able to 3 not able to be _____ed

les·see (les ē') *n.* [see LEASE] one to whom a lease is given; tenant

lessen (les'ən) *vt., vi.* to make or become less; decrease

THESAURUS

legitimate *a.* 1 [In accordance with legal provisions] licit, statutory, authorized; see LAWFUL, LEGAL. 2 [Logical] reasonable, probable, consistent; see LOGICAL, UNDERSTANDABLE. 3 [Authentic] verifiable, valid, reliable; see GENUINE 1, 2.

leisure *n.* freedom, free time, spare time, spare moments, relaxation, recreation, ease, recess, holiday, leave of absence, convenience, idle hours, opportunity; see also REST 1, VACATION.—*Ant.* WORK, toil, travail. —**leisure** idle, resting, not busy; see RESTING 1. —**at one's leisure** when one has time, at one's convenience, at an early opportunity; see WHENEVER.

leisurely *a.* slowly, unhurriedly, lazily, deliberately, calmly, inactively, taking one's time, gradually, sluggishly, lethargically, indolently, listlessly.—*Ant.* QUICKLY, rapidly, hastily.

lemon *n.* citrus fruit, citron, food; see FRUIT.

lend *v.* advance, provide with, let out, furnish, permit to borrow, allow, trust with, lend on security, extend credit, entrust, accommodate.—*Ant.* BORROW, repay, pay back.

lender *n.* moneylender, bank, loan company; see BANKER, DONOR.

length *n.* 1 [Linear distance] space, measure, span, reach, range, longitude, remoteness, magnitude, compass, portion, dimension, unit, radius, diameter, longness, mileage, stretch, extensiveness, spaciousness, tallness, height, expansion; see also EXPANSE, EXTENT.—*Ant.* NEARNESS, shortness, closeness. 2 [Duration] period, interval, season, year, month, week, day, minute, limit; see also TIME 1. —**at length** 1 [Finally] after a while, at last, in the end; see FINALLY 2. 2 [Fully] in full, extensively, without omission; see COMPLETELY.

lengthen *v.* 1 [To make longer] extend, stretch, protract; see INCREASE. 2 [To grow longer] produce, increase, expand; see GROW 1.

lengthwise *a.* longitudinally, the long way, along, endlong, from end to end, from stem to stern, overall, from head to foot, from top to bottom; see also ALONGSIDE.

lengthy *a.* tedious, not brief, long; see DULL 4.

lenient *a.* soft, mild, tolerant; see KIND.

lens *n.* microscope, camera, spectacles; see GLASS.

leopard *n.* panther, hunting leopard, jaguar; see ANIMAL, CAT 2.

lesbian *n.* gay, Sapphist, homosexual; see HOMOSEXUAL.

less *a.* smaller, lower, not so much as, not as much, lesser, minor, fewer, reduced, declined, in decline, depressed, inferior, secondary, subordinate, beneath, minus, deficient, diminished, shortened, limited; see also SHORTER.—*Ant.* MORE, more than, longer.

lessen *v.* 1 [To grow less] diminish, dwindle, decline; see DECREASE 1. 2 [To make less] reduce, diminish, slack up; see DECREASE 2.

lessening *a.* decreasing, declining, waning, dropping, diminishing, abating, slowing down, dwindling, sinking, sagging, subsiding, moderating, slackening, ebbing, lowering, shrinking, drying up, shriveling up, softening, weakening, decaying, narrowing down, drooping, wasting, running low, running down, dying away, dying down, wearing off, wearing out, wearing away, wearing down, falling off, slacking off, growing less and less, losing momentum, slumping, plunging, plummeting, going down, in reverse, getting worse, getting slower.

lesser (les′ər) *adj.* **1** *alt. compar. of* LITTLE **2** smaller, less, or less important

les·son (les′ən) *n.* ⟦< L *legere*, to read⟧ **1** an exercise for a student to learn **2** something learned for one's safety, etc. **3** [*pl.*] course of instruction **4** a selection read from the Bible

les·sor (les′ôr) *n.* ⟦see LEASE⟧ one who gives a lease

lest (lest) *conj.* ⟦< OE *thy læs the*, lit., by the less that⟧ for fear that

let¹ (let) *vt.* **let, let′ting** ⟦OE *lætan*, leave behind⟧ **1** to leave: now only in **let alone, let be** (**2** *a*) to rent *b*) to assign (a contract) **3** to cause to escape [to *let* blood] **4** to allow; permit Also used as an auxiliary in commands or suggestions [*let* us go] — *vi.* to be rented —**let down 1** to lower **2** to slow up **3** to disappoint —**let off 1** to give forth **2** to deal leniently with —**let on** [Colloq.] **1** to indicate one's awareness **2** to pretend —**let out 1** to release **2** to rent out **3** to make a garment larger —**let up 1** to relax **2** to cease

let² (let) *n.* ⟦< OE *lettan*, make late⟧ an obstacle: in **without let or hindrance**

-let (lit, lət) ⟦Fr *-el* + *-et*, dim. suffixes⟧ *suffix* small [*piglet*]

let′down′ *n.* **1** a slowing up **2** a disappointment

le·thal (lē′thəl) *adj.* ⟦< L *letum*, death⟧ causing death; fatal

leth·ar·gy (leth′ər jē) *n.*, *pl.* **-gies** ⟦< Gr *lēthē*, oblivion + *argos*, idle⟧ **1** an abnormal drowsiness **2** sluggishness, apathy, etc. —**le·thar·gic** (li thär′jik) *adj.* —**le·thar′gi·cal·ly** *adv.*

let's (lets) let us

let·ter (let′ər) *n.* ⟦< L *littera*⟧ **1** any character in an alphabet **2** a written or printed message, usually sent by mail **3** [*pl.*] *a*) literature *b*) learning; knowledge **4** literal meaning — *vt.* to mark with letters —**let′ter·er** *n.*

letter carrier a postal employee who delivers mail

let′tered *adj.* **1** literate **2** highly educated **3** marked with letters

let′ter·head′ *n.* the name, address, etc. as a heading on stationery

let′ter·ing *n.* the act of making or inscribing letters, or such letters

let′ter-per′fect *adj.* entirely correct

let′ter-qual′ity *adj.* of or producing printed characters similar in quality to typewritten characters

letters patent a document granting a patent

let·tuce (let′əs) *n.* ⟦< L *lac*, milk⟧ **1** a plant with crisp, green leaves **2** the leaves, much used for salads

let·up (let′up′) *n.* [Colloq.] **1** a slackening **2** a stop or pause

leu·kemia (lōō kē′mē ə) *n.* ⟦see fol. & -EMIA⟧ a disease characterized by an abnormal increase in the number of leukocytes Also sp. **leu·kae′mia**

leuko·cyte (lōō′kō sīt′, -kə-) *n.* ⟦< Gr *leukos*, white + *kytos*, hollow⟧ a white corpuscle in the blood: it destroys disease-causing organisms

levee (lev′ē) *n.* ⟦ult. < L *levare*, to raise⟧ an embankment to prevent a river from flooding bordering land

level (lev′əl) *n.* ⟦< L *libra*, a balance⟧ **1** an instrument for determining the horizontal **2** a horizontal plane or line [sea *level*] **3** a horizontal area **4** normal position with reference to height [water seeks its *level*] **5** position in a scale of values [income *level*] — *adj.* **1** perfectly flat and even **2** not sloping **3** even in height (*with*) **4** equal in importance, advancement, quality, etc. **5** calm or steady — *vt.*, *vi.* **-eled** or **-elled**, **-el·ing** or **-el·ling 1** to make or become level **2** to demolish **3** to aim (a gun, etc.) —**level with** [Slang] to be honest with —**lev′el·er** or **lev′el·ler** *n.*

lev′el·head′ed *adj.* having an even temper and sound judgment —**lev′el·head′ed·ness** *n.*

lever (lev′ər, lē′vər) *n.* ⟦< L *levare*, to raise⟧ **1** a bar used as a pry **2** a means to an end **3** a device consisting of a bar turning about a fixed point, using force at a second point to lift a weight at a third

lev′er·age (-ij) *n.* the action or mechanical power of a lever

leveraged buyout the acquisition of a corporation using borrowed funds which are secured by the corporation's assets

le·via·than (lə vī′ə thən) *n.* ⟦< Heb *liwyāthān*⟧ **1** *Bible* a sea monster **2** anything huge

Levi's (lē′vīz′) ⟦after *Levi* Strauss, U.S. manufacturer⟧ *trademark for* closefitting trousers of heavy denim — *n.pl.* such trousers: usually written **Le′vis** or **le′vis**

levi·ta·tion (lev′ə tā′shən) *n.* ⟦< L *levis*, light⟧ the illusion of raising a body in the air with no support —**lev′i·tate′, -tat′ed, -tat′ing,** *vt.*, *vi.*

Le·viti·cus (lə vit′i kəs) the third book of the Pentateuch

lev·ity (lev′i tē) *n.*, *pl.* **-ties** ⟦< L *levis*, light⟧ frivolity; improper gaiety

levy (lev′ē) *n.*, *pl.* **lev′ies** ⟦< L *levare*, to raise⟧ **1** an imposing and collecting of a tax, fine, etc. **2** the amount collected **3** compulsory enlistment for military service **4** a group so enlisted — *vt.* **-ied, -y·ing 1** to impose (a tax, fine, etc.) **2** to enlist (troops) **3** to wage (war)

lewd (lōōd) *adj.* ⟦OE *læwede*, unlearned⟧ indecent; lustful; obscene —**lewd′ly** *adv.* —**lewd′ness** *n.*

lexi·cog·ra·phy (leks′i käg′rə fē) *n.* ⟦see fol. & -GRAPHY⟧

◼ THESAURUS ◼

lesser *a.* inferior, minor, secondary; see SUBORDINATE.

lesson *n.* drill, assignment, reading; see JOB 2.

let¹ *v.* **1** [To permit] suffer, give permission, allow, condone, approve, authorize, consent, permit, tolerate; see also ALLOW. **2** [To rent] lease, hire, sublet; see RENT 1. —**let down** disappoint, disillusion, not support; see ABANDON 2, FAIL 1. —**let in** admit, allow to enter, give admission to; see RECEIVE 4. —**let off** leave, excuse, let go, remove; see also ABANDON 1. —**let on*** imply, indicate, suggest; see HINT. —**let out** liberate, let go, eject; see FREE. —**let up** cease, release, slow down; see SLOW 1, STOP 2.

letdown *n.* frustration, setback, disillusionment; see DISAPPOINTMENT 1.

lethal *a.* fatal, mortal, malignant; see DEADLY, HARMFUL, POISONOUS.

letter *n.* **1** [A unit of the alphabet] capital, upper case, lower case, small letter, vowel, consonant, digraph, rune, stop, plosive, fricative, diphthong, nasal, dental, glottal, gutteral; see also CONSONANT, VOWEL. **2** [A written communication] note, epistle, missive, message, memorandum, report, line. *Types of letters include the following:* business, form, circular, drop, open, personal; billet-doux, postcard, postal, direct mail advertising, junk mail*. —**to the letter** just as directed, perfectly, precisely; see

PERFECTLY.

letup *n.* interval, recess, respite; see PAUSE.

level *a.* **1** [Smooth] polished, rolled, planed; see FLAT 1, SMOOTH 1. **2** [Of an even height] regular, equal, uniform, flush, of the same height, same, constant, straight, balanced, steady, stable, trim, precise, exact, matched, unbroken, on a line, lined up, aligned, uninterrupted, continuous; see also SMOOTH 1.—*Ant.* IRREGULAR, uneven, crooked. **3** [Horizontal] plane, leveled, lying prone, in the same plane, on one plane; see also FLAT 1. —**one's level best*** one's best, the best one can do, all one's effort; see BEST. —**on the level*** fair, sincere, truthful; see HONEST 1.

level *v.* **1** [To straighten] surface, bulldoze, equalize; see SMOOTH, STRAIGHTEN. **2** [To demolish] ruin, waste, wreck; see DESTROY. **3** [*To be honest with] be frank with, come to terms, be open and aboveboard; see DECLARE. —**level off** level out, find a level, reach an equilibrium; see DECREASE 1, STRAIGHTEN.

levelheaded *a.* wise, practical, prudent; see RATIONAL 1, REASONABLE 1.

lever *n.* lifter, pry, leverage, pry bar, pinch bar, crowbar, handspike, arm, advantage; see also TOOL 1.

leverage *n.* purchase, lift, hold; see SUPPORT 2.

levied *a.* exacted, taken, collected;

see TAXED 1.

levy *n.* toll, duty, custom; see TAX 1.

lewd *a.* **1** [Suggestive of lewdness] ribald, smutty, indecent; see sense 2 and SENSUAL 2. **2** [Inclined to lewdness] lustful, wanton, lascivious, libidinous, licentious, lecherous, profligate, dissolute, carnal, sensual, debauched, corrupt, unchaste, depraved, unbridled, ruttish, nymphomaniacal, prurient, concupiscent, incontinent, incestuous, goatish, horny*, in heat*; see also VULGAR.—*Ant.* PURE, chaste, modest.

lewdly *a.* wantonly, shockingly, indecently, lasciviously, lecherously, libidinously, unchastely, carnally, dissolutely, immodestly, voluptuously, sensually, incontinently, indelicately, in a lewd manner, with lewd gestures, in a suggestive manner.

lewdness *n.* indecency, unchastity, incontinence, vulgarity, lechery, wantonness, lasciviousness, sensuality, licentiousness, voluptuousness, lecherousness, profligacy, dissoluteness, obscenity, scurrility, coarseness, carnal passion, grossness, sensuous desire, salaciousness, pornography, lust, depravity, carnality, nymphomania, corruption, raunchiness*, dirtiness, incest, indelicacy, eroticism, erotism, smut, impurity, debauchery.—*Ant.* MODESTY, continency, decency.

lexi·con (leks′i kän′) *n.* ⟦< Gr *lexis*, word⟧ 1 a dictionary 2 a special vocabulary

Li *Chem. symbol for* lithium

liabil·ity (lī′ə bil′ə tē) *n., pl.* **-ties** 1 the state of being liable 2 anything for which a person is liable 3 [*pl.*] the debts of a person or business 4 something that works to one's disadvantage

liable (lī′ə bəl) *adj.* ⟦< L *ligare*, bind⟧ 1 legally bound or responsible 2 subject to [*liable* to heart attacks] 3 likely to [*liable* to get hurt]

li·ai·son (lē ā′zän′, -zən) *n.* ⟦< L *ligare*, bind⟧ 1 intercommunication as between units of a military force 2 an illicit love affair

liar (lī′ər) *n.* one who tells lies

lib (lib) *n. short for* LIBERATION

li·ba·tion (lī bā′shən) *n.* ⟦< L *libare*, pour out⟧ 1 the ritual of pouring out wine or oil in honor of a god 2 this liquid 3 an alcoholic drink

li·bel (lī′bəl) *n.* ⟦< L *liber*, book⟧ 1 any written or printed matter tending to injure a person's reputation unjustly 2 the act or crime of publishing such a thing — *vt.* **-beled** or **-belled, -bel·ing** or **-bel·ling** to make a libel against —**li′beler** or **li′bel·ler** *n.* —**li′bel·ous** or **li′bel·lous** *adj.*

lib·eral (lib′ər əl) *adj.* ⟦< L *liber*, free⟧ 1 generous 2 ample; abundant 3 not literal or strict 4 tolerant; broadminded 5 favoring reform or progress — *n.* one who favors reform or progress —**lib′er·al·ism′** *n.* —**lib′er·ally** *adv.* —**lib′er·al·ness** *n.*

liberal arts literature, languages, history, etc. as courses of study

lib′er·al′ity (-al′i tē) *n., pl.* **-ties** 1 generosity 2 broadmindedness

lib′er·al·ize′ (-əl īz′) *vt., vi.* **-ized′, -iz′ing** to make or become liberal —**lib′er·al·i·za′tion** *n.*

lib·er·ate (lib′ər āt′) *vt.* **-at′ed, -at′ing** ⟦< L *liber*, free⟧ 1 to release from slavery, enemy occupation, etc. 2 to secure equal rights for (women, etc.) —**lib′era′tion** *n.* —**lib′era′tor** *n.*

lib·er·tar·ian (lib′ər ter′ē ən) *n.* an advocate of full individual freedom of thought and action

lib·er·tine (lib′ər tēn′) *n.* ⟦< L *liber*, free⟧ a man who is sexually promiscuous — *adj.* licentious

lib·erty (lib′ər tē) *n., pl.* **-ties** ⟦< L *liber*, free⟧ 1 freedom from slavery, captivity, etc. 2 a particular right, freedom, etc. 3 an impertinent action or attitude 4 permission given to a sailor to go ashore See also CIVIL LIBERTIES — **at liberty** 1 not confined 2 permitted (to do or say something) 3 not busy or in use —**take liberties** 1 to be too familiar or impertinent 2 to deal inaccurately (*with* facts, data, etc.)

li·bidi·nous (li bid′'n əs) *adj.* ⟦see fol.⟧ lustful; lascivious

li·bido (li bē′dō, -bī′-) *n.* ⟦< L, pleasure⟧ 1 the sexual urge 2 *Psychoanalysis* psychic energy generally; specif., that comprising the positive, loving instincts

Li·bra (lī′brə, lē′-) ⟦L, a balance⟧ the seventh sign of the zodiac

li·brar·ian (lī brer′ē ən) *n.* one in charge of a library or trained in library management

li·brary (lī′brer′ē) *n., pl.* **-ies** 1 a collection of books, etc. 2 a room or building for, or an institution in charge of, such a collection

li·bretto (li bret′ō) *n., pl.* **-tos** or **-ti** (-ē) ⟦It < L *liber*, book⟧ the words, or text, of an opera, oratorio, etc. —**li·bret′tist** *n.*

lice (līs) *n. pl. of* LOUSE

li·cense (lī′səns) *n.* ⟦< L *licere*, be permitted⟧ 1 formal or legal permission to do something specified 2 a document indicating such permission 3 freedom to deviate from rule, practice, etc. [*poetic license*] 4 excessive freedom, constituting an abuse of liberty Brit. sp. **li′cence** — *vt.* **-censed, -cens·ing** to permit formally

li·cen·see (lī′səns ē′) *n.* a person to whom a license is granted

li·cen·tiate (lī sen′shē it, -āt′) *n.* a person having a professional license

li·cen·tious (lī sen′shəs) *adj.* ⟦see LICENSE⟧ sexually unrestrained; lascivious —**li·cen′tious·ness** *n.*

li·chen (lī′kən) *n.* ⟦< Gr *leichein*, to lick⟧ a mosslike plant growing in patches on rock, wood, soil, etc.

licit (lis′it) *adj.* ⟦< L *licitus*, permitted⟧ lawful —**lic′itly** *adv.*

lick (lik) *vt.* ⟦OE *liccian*⟧ 1 to pass the tongue over 2 to pass lightly over like a tongue 3 [Colloq.] *a*) a whip *b*) to vanquish — *vi.* to move lightly, as a flame — *n.* 1 a licking with the tongue 2 a small quantity 3 *short for* SALT LICK 4 [Colloq.] *a*) a sharp blow *b*) a short, rapid burst of activity (also **lick and a promise**) —**lick up** to consume as by licking

lico·rice (lik′ər ish, -ə ris) *n.* ⟦< Gr *glykys*, sweet + *rhiza*, root⟧ 1 a black flavoring extract made from the root of a European plant 2 candy flavored with this extract

lid (lid) *n.* ⟦OE *hlid*⟧ 1 a movable cover, as for a box, etc. 2 *short for* EYELID 3 [Colloq.] a restraint —**lid′ded** *adj.*

lie¹ (lī) *vi.* **lay, lain, ly′ing** ⟦OE *licgan*⟧ 1 to be or put oneself in a reclining or horizontal position 2 to rest on a support in a horizontal position 3 to be in a specified condition 4 to be situated [Canada *lies* to the north] 5 to exist [love *lies* in her eyes] — *n.* the way in which something is situated; lay

---

THESAURUS

liability *n.* obligation, indebtedness, answerability; see RESPONSIBILITY 2.

liable *a.* 1 [Responsible] answerable, subject, accountable; see RESPONSIBLE 1. 2 [Likely] tending, apt, inclined; see LIKELY 4.

liar *n.* prevaricator, false witness, deceiver, perjurer, trickster, cheat, misleader, falsifier, storyteller*, equivocator, fibber, fabricator; see also CHEAT.

libel *n.* calumny, slander, lying; see LIE.

liberal *a.* tolerant, receptive, nonconformist, progressive, advanced, left, radical, interested, wide-awake, broad-minded, understanding, permissive, indulgent, impartial, unprejudiced, reasonable, rational, unbiased, detached, dispassionate, unconventional, avant-garde, left-wing, objective, magnanimous; see also FAIR 1.—*Ant.* PREJUDICED, intolerant, biased.

liberal *n.* individualist, insurgent, rebel, revolutionary, nonconformist, nonpartisan, independent; believer in civil rights, welfare, reform, etc.; socialist, eccentric, freethinker, left-winger; see also RADICAL.

liberate *v.* set free, loose, release; see FREE.

liberation *n.* rescue, freedom, deliverance; see RESCUE 1.

liberty *n.* 1 [Freedom from bondage] deliverance, emancipation, enfranchisement; see RESCUE 1. 2 [Freedom from occupation] rest, leave, relaxation; see FREEDOM 2, LEISURE, RECREATION. 3 [Freedom to choose] permission, alternative, decision; see CHOICE, SELECTION 1. 4 [The rights supposedly natural to man] freedom, independence, power of choice; see DEMOCRACY. —**at liberty** unrestricted, unlimited, not confined; see FREE 1, 2. —**take liberties** be too impertinent, act too freely, use carelessly; see ABUSE.

librarian *n.* keeper, caretaker, curator; see EXECUTIVE.

library *n.* books, book collection, manuscripts, manuscript collection, institution, public library, private library, book room, lending library, reference collection, archives, museum, treasury, memorabilia, rare books, reading room.

license *n.* 1 [Unbridled use of freedom] looseness, excess, immoderation; see FREEDOM 2. 2 [A formal permission] permit, form, identification, tag, card, consent, grant; see also PERMISSION.

license *v.* permit, authorize, privilege; see ALLOW.

lick *v.* 1 [To pass the tongue over] stroke, rub, touch, pass over, pass across, caress, wash, graze, brush, glance, tongue, fondle, soothe, tranquilize, calm, quiet. 2 [To play over; *said of flames*] rise and fall, fluctuate, leap; see BURN, DART, WAVE 3. 3 [*To beat*] whip, trim*, thrash; see BEAT 1. 4 [*To defeat*] overcome, vanquish, frustrate; see DEFEAT 3.

lid *n.* cap, top, roof; see COVER 1, HOOD 1.

lie¹,² *v.* 1 [To utter an untruth] falsify, prevaricate, tell a lie, lie out of, deceive, mislead, misinform, exaggerate, distort, concoct, equivocate, be untruthful, be a liar, break one's word, bear false witness, go back on, say one thing and mean another, misrepresent, dissemble, perjure oneself, delude, invent.—*Ant.* DECLARE, tell the truth, be honest. 2 [To be situated] extend, be on, be beside, be located, be fixed, be established, be placed, be seated, be set, be level, be smooth, be even, exist in space, stretch along, reach along, spread along. 3 [To be prostrate] be flat, be prone, sprawl, loll, be stretched out; see also REST 1.—*Ant.* STAND, be upright, sit. 4 [To assume a prostrate position] lie down, recline, stretch out, go to bed, turn in, retire, take a nap, take a siesta, hit the sack*, hit the hay*; see also REST 1, SLEEP.—*Ant.* RISE, get up, arise. — **take lying down** submit, surrender, be passive; see YIELD 1.

lie[2] (lī) *vi.* **lied, ly'ing** 〚OE *leogan*〛 to make a statement that one knows is false — *vt.* to bring, put, accomplish, etc. by lying — *n.* a false statement made with intent to deceive

Lieb·frau·milch (lēb'frou milk') *n.* 〚Ger〛 a white wine

lie detector a polygraph used on persons suspected of lying

lief (lēf) *adv.* 〚< OE *leof*, dear〛 willingly; gladly: only in **would** (or **had**) **as lief**

liege (lēj) *adj.* 〚OFr〛 loyal; faithful — *n. Feudal Law* **1** a lord or sovereign **2** a subject or vassal

lien (lēn, lē'ən) *n.* 〚Fr < L *ligare*, to bind〛 a legal claim on another's property as security for the payment of a just debt

lieu (lōō) *n.* 〚< L *locus*〛 place: chiefly in **in lieu of**, instead of

lieu·ten·ant (lōō ten'ənt) *n.* 〚< Fr *lieu*, place + *tenant*, holding〛 **1** one who acts for a superior **2** *U.S. Mil.* an officer ranking below a captain: see FIRST LIEUTENANT, SECOND LIEUTENANT **3** *U.S. Navy* an officer ranking just above a lieutenant junior grade Abbrev. **Lieut.** —**lieu·ten'an·cy** *n.*

lieutenant colonel *U.S. Mil.* an officer ranking just above a major

lieutenant commander *U.S. Navy* an officer ranking just above a lieutenant

lieutenant general *U.S. Mil.* an officer ranking just above a major general

lieutenant governor an elected official of a State who ranks below and substitutes for the governor

lieutenant junior grade *U.S. Navy* an officer ranking just above an ensign

life (līf) *n., pl.* **lives** 〚OE *lif*〛 **1** that property of plants and animals (ending at death) which makes it possible for them to take in food, get energy from it, grow, etc. **2** the state of having this property **3** a human being *[100 lives were lost]* **4** living things collectively *[plant life]* **5** the time a person or thing is alive or exists **6** one's manner of living *[a life of ease]* **7** the people and activities of a given time, place, etc. *[military life]* **8** *a*) one's animate existence *b*) a biography **9** the source of liveliness *[the life of the party]* **10** vigor; liveliness

life belt a life preserver in belt form

life'blood' *n.* **1** the blood necessary to life **2** a vital element

life'boat' *n.* one of the small rescue boats carried by a ship

life buoy a life preserver in the shape of a ring

life'guard' *n.* a swimmer employed as at a beach to prevent drownings

life insurance insurance in which a stipulated sum is paid at the death of the insured

life jacket (or **vest**) a life preserver like a sleeveless jacket or vest

life'less *adj.* **1** without life; specif., *a*) inanimate *b*) dead **2** dull

life'like' *adj.* resembling real life or a real person or thing

life'line' *n.* **1** the rope for raising or lowering a diver **2** a very important commercial route

life'long' *adj.* lasting or not changing during one's whole life

life net a strong net used as by firefighters to catch people jumping from a burning building

life preserver a buoyant device for saving a person from drowning by keeping the body afloat

lif'er *n.* [Slang] a person sentenced to prison for life

life raft a small, inflatable raft for emergency use at sea

life'sav'er *n.* **1** a lifeguard **2** [Colloq.] a help in time of need

life'-size' *adj.* as big as the person or thing represented: said of a picture, sculpture, etc. Also **life'-sized'**

life'style' *n.* an individual's whole way of living

life'time' *n.* **1** the period of time that someone lives or that a thing lasts **2** a very long time

life'work' *n.* the work to which a person's life is devoted

lift (lift) *vt.* 〚< ON *lopt*, air〛 **1** to bring up to a higher position; raise **2** to raise in rank, condition, etc.; exalt **3** to pay off (a mortgage, debt, etc.) **4** to end (a blockade, etc.) **5** [Slang] to steal — *vi.* **1** to exert strength in raising something **2** to rise; go up — *n.* **1** a lifting or rising **2** the amount lifted **3** the distance something is lifted **4** lifting power or influence **5** elevation of mood **6** elevated position or carriage **7** a ride in the direction one is going **8** help of any kind **9** [Brit.] ELEVATOR

lift'off' *n.* **1** the initial vertical takeoff of a rocket, helicopter, etc. **2** the time this occurs

lig·a·ment (lig'ə mənt) *n.* 〚< L *ligare*, bind〛 a band of tissue connecting bones or holding organs in place

lig·a·ture (lig'ə chər) *n.* 〚< L *ligare*, bind〛 **1** a tying or binding together **2** a tie, bond, etc. **3** two or more letters united, as *æ*, *th* **4** *Surgery* a thread used to tie up an artery, etc.

light[1] (līt) *n.* 〚OE *leoht*〛 **1** *a*) the form of radiant energy acting on the retina of the eye to make sight possible *b*) ultraviolet or infrared radiation **2** brightness; illumination

---

◄══ THESAURUS ══►

lie[2] *n.* falsehood, untruth, fiction, inaccuracy, misstatement, myth, fable, deceptiveness, misrepresentation, lying, prevarication, falsification, falseness, defamation, tall story*, fabrication, deception, slander, aspersion, tale, perjury, libel, forgery, distortion, fib, white lie, fish story*, whopper*.—*Ant.* TRUTH, veracity, truthfulness.

life *n.* **1** [The fact or act of living] being, entity, growth, animation, endurance, survival, presence, living, consciousness, breath, continuance, flesh and blood, viability, metabolism, vitality, vital spark; see also EXPERIENCE.—*Ant.* DEATH, discontinuance, nonexistence. **2** [The sum of one's experiences] life experience, conduct, behavior, way of life, reaction, response, participation, enjoyment, joy, suffering, happiness, tide of events, circumstances, realization, knowledge, enlightenment, attainment, development, growth, personality. **3** [A biography] life story, memoir, memorial; see BIOGRAPHY, STORY. **4** [Duration] lifetime, one's natural life, period of existence, duration of life, endurance, continuance, span, history, career, course, era, epoch, century, decade, days, generation, time, period, life span, season, cycle, record; see also TIME 1. **5** [One who promotes gaiety] animator, entertainer, life of the party*; see HOST 1, HOSTESS. **6** [Vital spirit] vital force, vital principle, *élan vital* (French); see EXCITEMENT, ZEAL. —

as large (or **big**) **as life** actually, truly, in actual fact; see TRULY. — **for dear life** intensely, desperately, for all one is worth; see STRONGLY. —**for life** for the duration of one's life, for a long time, as long as one lives; see FOREVER. —**for the life of me*** by any means, as if one's life were at stake, whatever happens; see ANYHOW. —**life or death** decisive, necessary, critical; see IMPORTANT 1. —**matter of life and death** crisis, grave concern, something vitally important; see IMPORTANCE. —**not on your life*** by no means, certainly not, never; see NO. —**take one's own life** kill oneself, die by one's own hand, murder; see COMMIT SUICIDE. —**true to life** true to reality, realistic, representational; see GENUINE 1.

lifeless *a.* **1** [Without life] inert, inanimate, departed; see DEAD 1. **2** [Lacking spirit] lackluster, listless, heavy; see DULL 3, 4, SLOW 2.

lifelike *a.* simulated, exact, imitative; see GRAPHIC 1, 2.

lifetime *a.* lifelong, continuing, enduring; see PERMANENT.

lifetime *n.* existence, endurance, continuance; see LIFE 4, RECORD 2.

lift *n.* **1** [The work of lifting] pull, lifting, ascension, raising, weight, foot pounds, elevation, escalation, ascent, mounting. **2** [A ride] transportation, drive, passage; see JOURNEY. **3** [Aid] help, assistance, support; see HELP 1.

lift *v.* hoist, elevate, upheave; see RAISE 1.

light[1] *n.* **1** [The condition opposed to darkness] radiance, brilliance, splendor, glare, brightness, clearness, lightness, incandescence, shine, luster, sheen, sparkle, glitter, glimmer, flood of light, blare, radiation, gleam.—*Ant.* DARKNESS, blackness, blankness. **2** [Emanations from a source of light] radiation, stream, blaze; see FLASH, RAY. **3** [A source of light] match, wick, sun, planet, star, moon, lightning, torch, flashlight, chandelier, spotlight, halo, corona. **4** [Day] daylight, sun, sunrise; see DAY 1. **5** [Aspect] point of view, condition, standing; see CIRCUMSTANCES 2. —**in (the) light of** with knowledge of, because of, in view of; see CONSIDERING. —**see the light (of day)** **1** come into being, exist, begin; see BE. **2** comprehend, realize, be aware; see UNDERSTAND 1.

light[1,2] *a.* **1** [Having illumination] illuminated, radiant, luminous; see BRIGHT 1. **2** [Having color] vivid, rich, clear; see CLEAR 2. **3** [Having little content] superficial, slight, frivolous; see TRIVIAL, UNIMPORTANT. **4** [Having gaiety and spirit] lively, merry, animated; see ACTIVE. **5** [Having little weight] airy, fluffy, feathery, slender, downy, floating, lighter than air, light as air, floatable, light as a feather, frothy, buoyant, dainty, thin, sheer, insubstantial, ethereal, graceful, weightless, atmos-

3 a source of light, as the sun, a lamp, etc. 4 daylight 5 a thing used to ignite something 6 a window or windowpane 7 knowledge; enlightenment 8 public view /to bring new facts to *light/* 9 aspect /viewed in another *light/* 10 an outstanding person — *adj.* 1 having light; bright 2 pale in color; fair — *adv.* palely /a *light* blue color/ — *vt.* **light′ed** or **lit, light′ing** 1 to ignite /to *light* a bonfire/ 2 to cause to give off light 3 to furnish with light 4 to brighten; animate — *vi.* 1 to catch fire 2 to be lighted: usually with *up* —**in the light of** considering —**see the light (of day)** 1 to come into existence 2 to come to public view 3 to understand

light² (līt) *adj.* [OE *leoht*] 1 having little weight; not heavy, esp. for its size 2 less than usual in weight, amount, force, etc. /a *light* blow/ 3 of little importance 4 easy to bear /a *light* tax/ 5 easy to do /light *work/* 6 gay; happy 7 dizzy; giddy 8 not serious /light *reading/* 9 containing fewer calories 10 moderate /a *light* meal/ 11 moving with ease /light *on one's feet/* 12 producing small products /light *industry/* — *adv.* LIGHTLY — *vi.* **light′ed** or **lit, light′ing** 1 to come to rest after traveling through the air 2 to come or happen (*on* or *upon*) —**light into** [Colloq.] to attack —**light out** [Colloq.] to depart suddenly —**make light of** to treat as unimportant

light′en¹ *vt., vi.* 1 to make or become light or brighter 2 to shine; flash

light′en² *vt., vi.* 1 to make or become lighter in weight 2 to make or become more cheerful

light′er¹ *n.* a person or thing that starts something burning

light′er² *n.* [< MDu *licht*, LIGHT²] a large barge used to load or unload ships anchored in a harbor

light′face′ *n.* *Printing* type with thin, light lines

light′-fin′gered *adj.* 1 skillful at stealing 2 likely to steal

light′-foot′ed *adj.* stepping lightly and gracefully

light′head′ed *adj.* 1 giddy; dizzy 2 flighty; frivolous

light′heart′ed *adj.* gay; cheerful —**light′heart′ed·ly** *adv.* —**light′heart′ed·ness** *n.*

light heavyweight a boxer with a maximum weight of 175 lb.

light′house′ *n.* a tower with a very bright light to guide ships at night

light′ing *n.* the act or manner of giving light, or illuminating

---

light′ly *adv.* 1 with little weight or pressure; gently 2 to a small degree or amount 3 nimbly; deftly 4 cheerfully 5 with indifference

light meter an instrument to measure intensity of light, used in photography

light′-mind′ed *adj.* silly; frivolous

light′ness¹ (līt′nis) *n.* 1 the amount of light; brightness 2 paleness in color

light′ness² *n.* 1 a being light, not heavy 2 mildness, nimbleness, cheerfulness, etc.

light′ning (-niŋ) *n.* a flash of light in the sky caused by the discharge of atmospheric electricity

lightning bug FIREFLY

lightning rod a metal rod placed high on a building and grounded to divert lightning from the structure

light opera OPERETTA

light′weight′ *n.* a boxer with a maximum weight of 135 lb. — *adj.* light in weight

light′-year′ *n.* a unit of distance equal to the distance light travels in one year, *c.* 6 trillion miles

lig·nite (lig′nīt) *n.* [< L *lignum*, wood] a soft coal, brownish-black in color and retaining the texture of the original wood

lik·able (līk′ə bəl) *adj.* attractive, pleasant, genial, etc. Also **like′able** —**lik′able·ness** or **lik′abil′ity** *n.*

like¹ (līk) *adj.* [OE *gelic*] having the same characteristics; similar; equal — *adv.* [Colloq.] likely /like as not, he'll go/ — *prep.* 1 similar to 2 similarly to /to sing *like* a bird/ 3 characteristic of /not *like* her to cry/ 4 in the mood for /to feel *like* sleeping/ 5 indicative of /it looks *like* rain/ 6 as for example /fruit, *like* pears and plums/ — *conj.* [Colloq.] 1 as /it's just *like* he said/ 2 as if /it looks *like* he's late/ — *n.* an equal or counterpart /I've never met her *like/* —**and the like** and others of the same kind —**nothing like** not at all like —**something like** almost like —**the like** (or **likes**) **of** [Colloq.] any person or thing like

like² (līk) *vi.* **liked, lik′ing** [OE *lician*] to be inclined /do as you *like/* — *vt.* 1 to be pleased with; enjoy 2 to wish /I'd *like* to go/ — *n.* [*pl.*] preferences or tastes —**lik′er** *n.*

-like (līk) *suffix forming adjectives* like, characteristic of /homelike, bull-*like/*

like·li·hood (līk′lē hood′) *n.* a being likely to happen; probability

---

▬▬ THESAURUS ▬▬

pheric.—*Ant.* HEAVY, ponderous, weighty. 6 [Digestible] slight, edible, moderate; see EATABLE. 7 [Small in quantity or number] wee, small, tiny, minute, thin, inadequate, insufficient, hardly any, not much, hardly any, not many, slender, scanty, slight, sparse, fragmentary, fractional; see also FEW.—*Ant.* LARGE, great, immense.

light¹,² *v.* 1 [To provide light] illuminate, illumine, lighten, give light to, shine upon, furnish with light, light up, turn on the electricity, make a light, make visible, provide adequate illumination, switch on a light, floodlight, make bright, flood with light, fill with light; see also BRIGHTEN 1.— *Ant.* SHADE, put out, darken. 2 [To cause to ignite] inflame, spark, kindle; see BURN, IGNITE. 3 [To become ignited] take fire, become inflamed, flame; see BURN, IGNITE. 4 [To come to rest from flight or travel] rest, come down, stop; see ARRIVE. — **light into** rebuke, blame, assault; see SCOLD. —**make light of** make fun of, mock, belittle; see NEGLECT 1, RIDICULE.

lighted *a.* 1 [Illuminated] brilliant, alight, glowing; see BRIGHT 1. 2 [Burning] blazing, flaming, aflame; see BURNING.

lighten² *v.* unburden, make lighter, reduce the load of, lessen the weight of, uplift, buoy up, alleviate, take off a load, remove, take from, pour out, throw overboard, reduce, cut down, put off, make buoyant, take off weight, eradicate, shift, change; see also UNLOAD.—*Ant.* LOAD, burden,

overload.

lighter¹ *n.* cigarette lighter, igniter, flame; see LIGHT 3, MATCH 1.

lightheaded *a.* 1 [Giddy] inane, fickle, frivolous; see SILLY. 2 [Faint] tired, delirious, dizzy; see WEAK 1.

lighthearted *a.* gay, joyous, cheerful; see HAPPY.

lighting *n.* brilliance, flame, brightness; see FLASH, LIGHT 1, 3.

lightly *a.* delicately, airily, buoyantly, daintily, readily, gently, subtly, mildly, softly, tenderly, carefully, leniently, effortlessly, smoothly, blandly, sweetly, comfortably, restfully, peacefully, quietly; see also EASILY.—*Ant.* HEAVILY, ponderously, roughly.

lightness¹,² *n.* 1 [Illumination] sparkle, blaze, shine; see FLASH, LIGHT 1, 3. 2 [The state of being light] airiness, etherealness, downiness, thinness, sheerness, fluffiness. 3 [Agility] balance, deftness, nimbleness; see AGILITY, GRACE 1.

lightning *n.* electrical discharge, bolt, streak of lightning, thunderstroke, firebolt, fireball, thunderbolt; see also ELECTRICITY.

likable *a.* agreeable, amiable, attractive; see FRIENDLY.

like¹ *a.* similar, same, alike, near, resembling, close, not far from, according to, conforming with, matching, equaling, not unlike, akin, related, analogous, twin, corresponding, allied to, much the same, the same form, comparable, identical, in the manner of, parallel, homologous, to the effect that, consistent,

approximating.—*Ant.* UNLIKE, different, unrelated.

like¹ *prep.* similar to, same, near to; see ALIKE, LIKE.

like¹ *n.* counterpart, resemblance, parallelism; see SIMILARITY. —**and the like** and so forth, and so on, similar kinds; see OTHERS. —**more like it*** acceptable, good, improved; see BETTER 1. —**nothing like** dissimilar, contrasting, opposed; see UNLIKE. —**something like** similar, resembling, akin; see LIKE *a.*

like² *v.* 1 [To enjoy] take delight in, relish, derive pleasure from, be keen on, be pleased by, revel in, indulge in, rejoice in, find agreeable, find appealing, be gratified by, take satisfaction in, savor, fancy, dote on, take an interest in, develop interest for, delight in, regard with favor, have a liking for, love, have a taste for, care to, get a kick out of*, be tickled by, eat up*, go in for.—*Ant.* ENDURE, detest, dislike. 2 [To be fond of] have a fondness for, admire, take a fancy to, feel affectionately toward, prize, esteem, hold dear, care about, care for, approve, be pleased with, take to, have a soft spot in one's heart for, hanker for, dote on, have a yen for*, become attached to, be sweet on*, have eyes for*; see also LOVE 1.—*Ant.* HATE, disapprove, dislike. 3 [To be inclined] choose, feel disposed to, wish, desire, have a preference for, prefer, fancy, feel like, incline toward, want.

liked *a.* popular, loved, admired; see BELOVED, HONORED.

likely (līk′lē) *adj.* **-lier, -li·est** ⟦OE *geliclic*⟧ **1** credible *[a likely cause]* **2** reasonably to be expected *[likely* to rain*]* **3** suitable *[a likely* place to swim*]* — *adv.* probably *[she'll likely go]*

like′-mind′ed *adj.* having the same ideas, plans, tastes, etc. **—like′-mind′edness** *n.*

liken (līk′ən) *vt.* to compare

like′ness *n.* **1** a being like **2** (the same) form **3** a copy, portrait, etc.

like′wise′ *adv.* ⟦< *in like wise*⟧ **1** in the same manner **2** also; too

lik·ing (līk′iŋ) *n.* **1** fondness; affection **2** preference; taste; pleasure

li·lac (lī′lak′, -lək, -läk′) *n.* ⟦ult. < Pers *lilak*, bluish⟧ **1** a shrub with large clusters of tiny, fragrant flowers **2** pale purple — *adj.* pale-purple

Lil·li·pu·tian (lil′ə pyōō′shən) *adj.* ⟦after *Lilliput*, place in J. Swift's *Gulliver's Travels*⟧ **1** tiny **2** petty

lilt (lilt) *n.* ⟦ME *lilten*, to sound⟧ a light, swingy rhythm or tune **—lilt′ing** *adj.*

lily (lil′ē) *n., pl.* **lil′ies** ⟦< L *lilium*⟧ **1** a plant grown from a bulb and having typically trumpet-shaped flowers **2** its flower **3** any similar plant, as the waterlily — *adj.* like a lily, as in whiteness, purity, etc.

lil′y-liv′ered *adj.* cowardly; timid

lily of the valley *pl.* **lilies of the valley** a low plant with a spike of fragrant, white, bell-shaped flowers

lima bean (lī′mə) ⟦after *Lima*, Peru⟧ **1** a bean with broad pods **2** its broad, flat, edible seed

limb (lim) *n.* ⟦OE *lim*⟧ **1** an arm, leg, or wing **2** a large branch of a tree **—out on a limb** [Colloq.] in a precarious position **—limb′less** *adj.*

lim·ber (lim′bər) *adj.* ⟦< ? prec.⟧ **1** easily bent; flexible **2** able to bend the body easily; supple — *vt., vi.* to make or become limber

Limbo (lim′bō′) *n.* ⟦< L (*in*) *limbo*, (on) the border⟧ [*often* l-] in some Christian theologies, the abode after death of unbaptized children, etc. — *n., pl.* **-bos′** [l-] **1** a vague condition **2** a place of oblivion

Lim·burger (cheese) (lim′bʉrg′ər) ⟦after *Limburg*, Belgian province⟧ a semisoft cheese with a strong odor

lime¹ (līm) *n.* ⟦OE *lim*⟧ a white substance, calcium oxide, obtained from limestone, etc. and used in mortar and cement and to neutralize acid soil — *vt.* **limed, lim′ing** to treat with lime

lime² (līm) *n.* ⟦< Ar *limah*⟧ a small, lemon-shaped, greenish-yellow citrus fruit with a juicy, sour pulp

lime′ade′ (-ād′) *n.* a drink made of lime juice, sugar, and water

lime′light′ *n.* **1** a brilliant light created by the incandescence of lime, formerly used in theaters **2** a prominent position before the public

lim·er·ick (lim′ər ik) *n.* ⟦prob. after *Limerick*, Ir county⟧ a rhymed nonsense poem of five lines

lime′stone′ *n.* rock consisting mainly of calcium carbonate

limit (lim′it) *n.* ⟦< L *limes*⟧ **1** the point, line, etc. where something ends; boundary **2** [*pl.*] bounds **3** the greatest amount allowed — *vt.* to set a limit to; restrict **—lim′i·ta′tion** *n.* **—lim′iter** *n.* **—lim′it·less** *adj.*

lim′ited *adj.* **1** confined within bounds **2** making a restricted number of stops: said of a train, bus, etc.

limn (lim) *vt.* **limned, limn·ing** (lim′iŋ, -niŋ) ⟦< L *illuminare*, to illuminate⟧ **1** to paint or draw **2** to describe

lim·nol·ogy (lim näl′ə jē) *n.* ⟦< Gr *limnē*, marsh + -LOGY⟧ the science that deals with the physical, etc. properties and features of fresh waters, esp. lakes, etc.

limo (lim′ō) *n., pl.* **lim′os** [Colloq.] LIMOUSINE

limou·sine (lim′ə zēn′) *n.* ⟦Fr, lit., cloak⟧ a large, luxurious sedan, esp. one driven by a chauffeur

limp (limp) *vi.* ⟦< OE *limpan*⟧ to walk with or as with a lame leg — *n.* a halt or lameness in walking — *adj.* lacking firmness; wilted, flexible, etc. **—limp′ly** *adv.* **—limp′ness** *n.*

limpet (lim′pit) *n.* ⟦< ML *lempreda*⟧ a mollusk that clings to rocks, etc.

lim·pid (lim′pid) *adj.* ⟦< L *limpidus*⟧ perfectly clear; transparent **—lim·pid′ity** *n.* **—lim′pidly** *adv.*

limy (lī′mē) *adj.* **-i·er, -i·est** of, like, or containing lime

lin·age (līn′ij) *n.* the number of written or printed lines, as on a page

linch·pin (linch′pin′) *n.* ⟦OE *lynis*, linchpin⟧ a pin in an axle to keep the wheel from coming off

lin·den (lin′dən) *n.* ⟦OE⟧ a tree with dense, heart-shaped leaves

line¹ (līn) *n.* ⟦< L *linea*, lit., linen thread⟧ **1** a cord, rope, wire, etc. **2** any wire, pipe, etc., or system of these, conducting fluid, electricity, etc. **3** a thin, threadlike mark **4**

THESAURUS

likely *a.* **1** [Probable] apparent, probable, seeming, credible, possible, feasible, presumable, conceivable, reasonable, workable, attainable, achievable, believable, rational, thinkable, imaginable, ostensible, plausible, anticipated, expected, imminent.—*Ant.* IMPOSSIBLE, doubtful, questionable. **2** [Promising] suitable, apt, assuring; see FIT 1, HOPEFUL 2. **3** [Believable] plausible, true, acceptable; see CONVINCING. **4** [Apt] inclined, tending, disposed, predisposed, prone, liable, subject to, on the verge of, in the habit of, given to, in favor of, having a weakness for.

likeness *n.* **1** [Similarity] resemblance, correspondence, affinity; see SIMILARITY. **2** [A representation] image, effigy, portrait; see COPY, PICTURE 3.

likewise *a.* in like manner, furthermore, moreover; see BESIDES.

liking *n.* desire, fondness, devotion; see AFFECTION, LOVE 1.

limb *n.* **1** [A tree branch] arm, bough, offshoot; see BRANCH 2. **2** [A bodily appendage] arm, leg, part, wing, fin, flipper, member; see also ARM 1, LEG.

limber *a.* nimble, spry, deft; see AGILE, GRACEFUL 1.

limit *n.* **1** [The boundary] end, frontier, border; see BOUNDARY. **2** [The ultimate] utmost, farthest point, farthest reach, destination, goal, conclusion, extremity, eventuality, termination, absolute, the bitter end, deadline, cut-off point; see also END 4.—*Ant.* ORIGIN, start.

limit *v.* bound, confine, curb; see DEFINE 1, RESTRICT.

limitation *n.* **1** [The act of limiting] restriction, restraint, control; see ARREST, INTERFERENCE 1, INTERRUPTION, PREVENTION. **2** [That which limits] condition, definition, qualification, reservation, control, curb, check, injunction, bar, obstruction, stricture, taboo, inhibition, modification; see also ARREST, BARRIER, BOUNDARY, REFUSAL, RESTRAINT 2.—*Ant.* FREEDOM, latitude, liberty. **3** [A shortcoming] inadequacy, insufficiency, deficiency, shortcoming, weakness, want, blemish, defect, lack, imperfection, failing, fault, frailty, flaw; see also FAULT 1.—*Ant.* STRENGTH, perfection, ability.

limited *a.* **1** [Restricted] confined, checked, curbed; see BOUND 1, 2, RESTRICTED. **2** [Having only moderate capacity] cramped, insufficient, short; see FAULTY, INADEQUATE, POOR 2, UNSATISFACTORY.

limitless *a.* unending, boundless, immeasurable; see ENDLESS, INFINITE, UNLIMITED.

limp *a.* pliant, soft, flaccid, flabby, supple, pliable, limber, relaxed, flexible, droopy, unsubstantial, bending readily, plastic, yielding, lax, slack, loose, flimsy.—*Ant.* STIFF, rigid, wooden.

limp *v.* walk lamely, proceed slowly, shuffle, lag, stagger, totter, dodder, hobble, falter.

line¹ *n.* **1** [A row] array, list, rank, file, catalogue, order, group, arrangement, ridge, range, seam, series, sequence, succession, procession, chain, train, string, column, formation, division, queue, channel, furrow, scar, trench, groove, mark, thread, fissure, crack, straight line. **2** [A mark] outline, tracing, stroke; see MARK 1. **3** [A rope] string, cable, towline; see ROPE, WIRE 1. **4** [Lineal descent] ancestry, pedigree, lineage; see FAMILY, HEREDITY. **5** [A border line] border, mark, limit; see BOUNDARY, EDGE 1. **6** [Matter printed in a row of type] row, words, letters; see COPY. **7** [A military front] disposition, formation, position; see FRONT 2. **8** [A transportation system] trunk line, bus line, steamship line, railroad line, airline. **9** [Goods handled by a given company] wares, merchandise, produce; see MATERIAL 2. **10** [*Talk intended to influence another] sermon, rhetoric, lecture, propaganda, advertising; see also CONVERSATION, SPEECH 3. **—all along the line** at every turn, completely, constantly; see EVERYWHERE. **—bring** (or **come** or **get**) **into line** align, make uniform, regulate; see ORDER 3. **—draw the** (or **a**) **line** set a limit, prohibit, restrain; see RESTRICT. **—get a line on*** find out about, investigate, expose; see DISCOVER. **—in line** agreeing, conforming, uniform; see REGULAR 3. **—in line for** being considered for, ready, thought about; see CONSIDERED. **—in line with** similar to, in accord with, consonant; see HARMONIOUS 2, FIT 1. **—keep in line** [To behave] obey, be good, restrain oneself; see BEHAVE. **—lay** (or **put**) **it on the line** elucidate, define, clarify; see EXPLAIN. **—on a line** straight, even, level; see a border or boundary **5** a limit **6** outline; contour **7** a row of persons or things, as of printed letters across a page **8** a succession of persons or things **9** lineage **10** a transportation system of buses, ships, etc. **11** the course a moving thing takes **12** a course of conduct, action, explanation, etc. **13** a person's trade or occupation **14** a stock of goods **15** a piece of information **16** a short letter, note, etc. **17** [*pl.*] all the speeches of a character in a play **18** the forward combat position in warfare **19** *Football* the players in the forward row **20** *Math.* the path of a moving point — *vt.* **lined, lin′ing 1** to mark with lines **2** to form a line along —**bring (or come) into line** to bring (or come) into alignment or conformity —**draw (or the) line** to set a limit —**hold the line** to stand firm —**in line for** being considered for —**line up** to form, or bring into, a line

line² (līn) *vt.* **lined, lin′ing** [[< L *linum*, flax]] to put, or serve as, a lining in

lin·eage (lin′ē ij) *n.* [[see LINE¹]] **1** direct descent from an ancestor **2** ancestry; family

lin·eal (lin′ē əl) *adj.* **1** in the direct line of descent from an ancestor **2** hereditary **3** of lines; linear

linea·ment (lin′ē ə mənt) *n.* [[< L *linea*, line]] a distinctive feature, esp. of the face　*Usually used in pl.*

lin·ear (lin′ē ər) *adj.* **1** of, made, or using a line or lines **2** narrow and long **3** in relation to length only

line·backer (līn′bak′ər) *n. Football* a defensive player directly behind the line

line drive a baseball hit in a straight line parallel to the ground

line′man (-mən) *n., pl.* **-men 1** one who sets up and repairs telephone lines, electric power lines, etc. **2** *Football* a player in the line

linen (lin′ən) *n.* [[< OE *lin*, flax: see LINE²]] **1** thread or cloth made of flax **2** [*often pl.*] sheets, cloths, etc. of linen, or of cotton, etc.

liner (līn′ər) *n.* **1** a steamship, airplane, etc. in regular service for a specific line **2** a cosmetic applied in a fine line, as along the eyelid

lines·man (līnz′mən) *n., pl.* **-men 1** *Football* an official who marks the gains or losses in ground **2** *Tennis* an official who reports whether the ball is inside or outside the lines

line′up′ *n.* an arrangement of persons or things in or as in a line

-ling (liŋ) [[OE]] *suffix* **1** small [*duckling*] **2** unimportant or contemptible [*princeling*]

lin·ger (liŋ′gər) *vi.* [[OE *lengan*, to delay]] **1** to continue to stay, esp. through reluctance to leave **2** to loiter —**lin′gerer** *n.* —**lin′ger·ing** *adj.*

lin·ge·rie (lan′zhə rē′, -rā′; -jə-) *n.* [[Fr]] women's underwear

lingo (liŋ′gō) *n., pl.* **-goes′** [[< L *lingua*, tongue]] [Colloq.] a dialect, jargon, etc. that one is not familiar with

lin·gua franca (liŋ′gwə fraŋ′kə) a hybrid language used for communication by speakers of different languages

lin·gual (liŋ′gwəl) *adj.* [[see LANGUAGE]] of, or pronounced with, the tongue

lin·guine (liŋ gwē′nē) *n.* [[< It *lingua*, tongue]] pasta in thin, flat, narrow strips　Also sp. **lin·gui′ni** (-nē)

lin·guist (liŋ′gwist) *n.* [[< L *lingua*, tongue]] **1** a specialist in linguistics **2** loosely, POLYGLOT (*n.* 1)

lin·guis′tics (-gwis′tiks) *n.pl.* [*with sing. v.*] **1** the science of language **2** the study of a particular language —**lin·guis′tic** *adj.*

lini·ment (lin′ə mənt) *n.* [[< L *linere*, to smear]] a soothing medicated liquid to be rubbed on the skin

lin·ing (līn′iŋ) *n.* the material covering an inner surface

link (liŋk) *n.* [[< Scand]] **1** any of the loops making up a chain **2** *a*) a section of something like a chain [*a link* of sausage] *b*) an element in a series [*a weak link* in evidence] **3** anything that connects [*a link* with the past] — *vt., vi.* to join; connect

link·age (liŋk′ij) *n.* **1** a linking **2** a series or system of links

linking verb a verb that functions chiefly as a connection between a subject and a predicate (Ex.: *be, seem, become*)

links (liŋks) *n.pl.* [[OE *hlinc*, a slope]] GOLF COURSE

link′up′ *n.* a linking together

lin·net (lin′it) *n.* [[< L *linum*, flax: it feeds on flaxseed]] either of two small finches of the Old World or the New World

li·no·leum (li nō′lē əm) *n.* [[< L *linum*, flax + *oleum*, oil]] **1** a smooth, washable floor covering, formerly much used, esp. in kitchens **2** any floor covering like linoleum

lin·seed (lin′sēd′) *n.* [[OE *linsæd*]] the seed of flax; flaxseed

linseed oil a yellowish oil extracted from flaxseed, used in oil paints, etc.

lint (lint) *n.* [[< L *linum*, flax]] bits of thread, fluff, etc. from cloth or yarn —**lint′y, -i·er, -i·est,** *adj.*

lin·tel (lint′'l) *n.* [[ult. < L *limen*, threshold]] the horizontal crosspiece over a door, window, etc.

liny (līn′ē) *adj.* **-i·er, -i·est 1** like a line; thin **2** marked with lines

lion (lī′ən) *n.* [[< Gr *leōn*]] **1** a large, powerful cat, found in Africa and SW Asia **2** a person of great courage or strength **3** a celebrity —**li′on·ess** *n.fem.*

li′on·heart′ed *adj.* very brave

lion·ize (lī′ən īz′) *vt.* **-ized′, -iz′ing** to treat as a celebrity

lip (lip) *n.* [[OE *lippa*]] **1** either of the two fleshy folds forming the edges of the mouth **2** anything like a lip, as the rim of a pitcher **3** [Slang] insolent talk — *adj.* spoken, but insincere [*lip* service] —**keep a stiff upper lip** [Colloq.] to bear pain or distress bravely

lipid (lip′id) *n.* [[< Gr *lipos*, fat]] any of a group of organic compounds consisting of the fats and other similar substances　Also **lip·ide** (lip′id′, -id)

lip·o·suc·tion (lip′ō suk′shən) *n.* [[< LIPID + SUCTION]] surgical removal of fatty tissue under the skin by means of suction

lippy (lip′ē) *adj.* **-pier, -pi·est** [Slang] impudent; insolent —**lip′pi·ness** *n.*

lip reading the act or skill of recognizing a speaker's words by watching the lip movements: it is taught esp. to the deaf —**lip′-read′** *vt., vi.* —**lip reader**

■ THESAURUS ■

DIRECT 1, STRAIGHT 1. —out of line misdirected, not uniform, not even; see IRREGULAR 1, 4. —**read between the lines** read meaning into, discover a hidden meaning, expose; see UNDERSTAND 1.

line¹,² *v.* **1** [To provide a lining] interline, stuff, wad, panel, pad, quilt, fill. **2** [To provide lines] trace, delineate, outline; see DRAW 2, MARK 1. **3** [To be in a line] border, edge, outline, rim, bound, fall in, fall into line, fringe, follow. **4** [To arrange in a line] align, queue, marshal, arrange, range, array, group, set out, bring into a line with others, fix, place, draw up; see also LINE UP.—*Ant.* SCATTER, disarrange, disperse. —**line up** fall in, form in line, take one's proper place in line, queue up, form ranks, get in line, get set, get into formation.

linear *a.* long, elongated, successive; see DIRECT 1, STRAIGHT 1.

lined *a.* interlined, stuffed, coated; see FULL 1.

linen *n.* material, sheeting, linen cloth; see GOODS. *Articles called lin-*

ens include the following: handkerchiefs, towels, bedding, sheets, pillowcases, underwear, shirts, dishtowels, tablecloths, napkins, doilies.

lineup *n.* starters, entrants, first string; see LIST.

linger *v.* tarry, saunter, lag, hesitate, trail, vacillate, delay, plod, trudge, falter, dawdle, procrastinate, slouch, shuffle, crawl, loll, take one's time, wait, putter, be tardy, be long, sit around, hang around*; see also LOITER.—*Ant.* HURRY, hasten, speed.

lingerie *n.* women's underwear, undergarmets, unmentionables*; see CLOTHES, UNDERWEAR.

linguist *n.* student of language, language expert, philologist, lexicographer, polyglot, translator, grammarian, etymologist; see also SCIENTIST.

linguistics *n.* grammar, semantics, phonology, etymology, prosody, morphology, syntax, philology; see also GRAMMAR, LANGUAGE 2.

liniment *n.* ointment, cream, lotion;

see MEDICINE 2, SALVE.

lining *n.* interlining, inner coating, inner surface, filling, quilting, stuffing, wadding, padding, sheathing, covering, wall, reinforcement, partition, paneling.

link *n.* ring, loop, coupling, coupler, section, seam, weld, hitch, intersection, copula, connective, connection, fastening, splice, interconnection, junction, joining, ligature, articulation; see also JOINT 1.

link *v.* connect, associate, combine; see JOIN 1.

linked *a.* connected, combined, associated; see JOINED.

linking *a.* combining, joining, associating; see CONNECTING.

lint *n.* thread, fluff, fiber; see DUST.

lion *n.* king of beasts, king of the jungle, lioness; see ANIMAL, CAT 2.

lip *n.* edge of the mouth, liplike part, labium; see MOUTH 1. —**keep a stiff upper lip*** take heart, be encouraged, remain strong; see ENDURE 2.

lip'stick' *n.* a small stick of cosmetic paste for coloring the lips

lip'-sync' or **lip'-synch'** (-siŋk′) *vt., vi.* ⟦ < *lip sync(hronization)* ⟧ to move the lips silently so as to seem to be speaking or singing (something recorded)

lique·fy (lik′wi fī′) *vt., vi.* **-fied′, -fy′ing** ⟦ < L *liquere*, be liquid + *facere*, make ⟧ to change into a liquid —**liq′ue·fac′tion** (-fak′shən) *n.*

li·queur (lē kur′, li kur′) *n.* ⟦Fr⟧ a sweet, syrupy, flavored alcoholic liquor

liquid (lik′wid) *adj.* ⟦ < L *liquidus* ⟧ **1** readily flowing; fluid **2** clear; limpid **3** flowing smoothly and musically, as verse **4** readily convertible into cash — *n.* a substance that, unlike a solid, flows readily but, unlike a gas, does not expand indefinitely —**liquid′ity** *n.*

liqui·date (lik′wi dāt′) *vt.* **-dat′ed, -dat′ing** ⟦see prec.⟧ **1** to settle the accounts of (a business) by apportioning assets and debts **2** to pay (a debt) **3** to convert into cash **4** to get rid of, as by killing —**liq′ui·da′tion** *n.* —**liq′ui·da′tor** *n.*

liq′uid·ize′ (-wid īz′) *vt.* **-ized′, -iz′ing** to cause to become liquid

liquor (lik′ər) *n.* ⟦L⟧ **1** any liquid **2** an alcoholic drink, esp. a distilled drink, as whiskey or rum

lira (lir′ə) *n., pl.* **li′re** (-ā) or **li′ras** ⟦ < L *libra*, a pound ⟧ the monetary unit of Italy

lisle (līl) *n.* ⟦after *Lisle* (now *Lille*), city in France⟧ **1** a fine, hard, extra-strong cotton thread **2** a fabric, or stockings, gloves, etc., woven of lisle

lisp (lisp) *vi.* ⟦ < OE *wlisp*, a lisping⟧ **1** to substitute the sounds (th) and (*th*) for the sounds of *s* and *z*, respectively **2** to speak imperfectly — *vt.* to utter with a lisp — *n.* the act or sound of lisping

lis·some or **lis·som** (lis′əm) *adj.* ⟦ < *lithesome*⟧ lithe, supple, limber, agile, etc.

list¹ (list) *n.* ⟦ < OE *liste*, border⟧ a series of names, words, numbers, etc. set forth in order — *vt.* to set forth or enter in a list, directory, etc.

list² (list) *vt., vi.* ⟦prob. ult. < OE *lust*, desire⟧ to tilt to one side, as a ship — *n.* such a tilting

lis·ten (lis′ən) *vi.* ⟦ < OE *hlysnan*⟧ **1** to make a conscious effort to hear **2** to give heed; take advice —**lis′tener** *n.*

list·ing (lis′tiŋ) *n.* **1** the making of a list **2** an entry in a list

list·less (list′lis) *adj.* ⟦ < OE *lust*, desire + -LESS⟧ **1** indifferent because of illness, dejection, etc.; languid —**list′lessly** *adv.* —**list′less·ness** *n.*

list price retail price as given in a list or catalog

lists (lists) *n.pl.* ⟦ < ME *liste*, border⟧ a fenced area in which knights jousted

lit (lit) *vt., vi. alt. pt. & pp. of* LIGHT¹

lit. **1** literally **2** literature

lita·ny (lit′'n ē) *n., pl.* **-nies** ⟦ < Gr *litē*, a request⟧ a series of fixed invocations and responses, used as a prayer

li·tchi (lē′chē′) *n.* ⟦ < Chin⟧ the raisinlike fruit of a Chinese evergreen tree, enclosed in a papery shell

li·ter (lēt′ər) *n.* ⟦ < Gr *litra*, a pound⟧ the basic metric unit of capacity equal to 1 cubic decimeter or 61.025 cubic inches Brit. sp. **li′tre**

lit·er·a·cy (lit′ər ə sē) *n.* the ability to read and write

lit·eral (lit′ər əl) *adj.* ⟦ < L *littera*, a letter⟧ **1** following the exact words of the original /a *literal* translation/ **2** in a basic or strict sense /the *literal* meaning/ **3** prosaic; matter-of-fact /a *literal* mind/ **4** real /the *literal* truth/ —**lit′er·al·ly** *adv.*

lit·er·ary (lit′ər er′ē) *adj.* **1** of or dealing with literature **2** familiar with or versed in literature

lit·er·ate (lit′ər it) *adj.* ⟦ < L *littera*, a letter⟧ **1** able to read and write **2** well-educated — *n.* a literate person

lit·er·a·ti (lit′ə rä′tē, -rä′tē) *n.pl.* ⟦It < L *litterati*: see prec.⟧ scholarly people

lit·er·a·ture (lit′ər ə choor′) *n.* ⟦ < L *littera*, a letter⟧ **1** *a)* all writings in prose or verse of an imaginative character *b)* all such writings having permanent value, excellence of form, etc. *c)* all the writings of a particular time, country, etc. *d)* all the writings on a particular subject **2** [Colloq.] any printed matter

lithe (līth) *adj.* **lith′er, lith′est** ⟦OE *lithe*, soft⟧ flexible; supple: also **lithe′some** (-səm) —**lithe′ness** *n.*

lith·i·um (lith′ē əm) *n.* ⟦ < Gr *lithos*, stone⟧ a soft, silver-white, chemical element

lithium carbonate a white, powdery salt, used in making glass, dyes, etc. and in treating manic-depressive disorders

litho·graph (lith′ə graf′) *n.* a print made by lithography — *vi., vt.* to make (prints or copies) by this process —**li·thog·ra·pher** (li thäg′rə fər) *n.*

li·thog·ra·phy (li thäg′rə fē) *n.* ⟦ < Gr *lithos*, stone + -GRAPHY⟧ printing from a flat stone or metal plate, parts of which have been treated to repel ink —**litho·graphic** (lith′ə graf′ik) *adj.*

litho·sphere (lith′ō sfir′) *n.* ⟦ < Gr *lithos*, stone + *sphaira*, sphere⟧ the solid, rocky part of the earth; earth's crust

liti·gant (lit′i gənt) *n.* ⟦see fol.⟧ a party to a lawsuit

lit′i·gate′ (-gāt′) *vt., vi.* **-gat′ed, -gat′ing** ⟦ < L *lis*, dispute + *agere*, do⟧ to contest in a lawsuit —**lit′i·ga′tion** *n.* —**lit′i·ga′tor** *n.*

li·ti·gious (li tij′əs) *adj.* ⟦see prec.⟧ **1** *a)* given to carrying on lawsuits *b)* quarrelsome **2** of lawsuits —**li·ti′gious·ness** *n.*

lit·mus (lit′məs) *n.* ⟦ < ON *litr*, color + *mosi*, moss⟧ a purple coloring matter obtained from various lichens: paper treated with it (**litmus paper**) turns blue in bases and red in acids

LittD or **Litt.D.** Doctor of Letters

lit·ter (lit′ər) *n.* ⟦ < L *lectus*, a couch⟧ **1** a framework enclosing a couch on which a person can be carried **2** a stretcher for carrying the sick or wounded **3** straw, hay,

---

THESAURUS

liquid *a.* **1** [In a state neither solid nor gaseous] watery, molten, damp, moist, aqueous, liquefied, dissolved, melted, thawed; see also FLUID, WET 1. **2** [Having qualities suggestive of fluids] flowing, running, splashing, thin, moving, viscous, diluting; see also FLUID, JUICY.

liquid *n.* liquor, fluid, juice, sap, extract, secretion, flow; see also WATER 1.

liquidate *v.* **1** [To change into money] sell, convert, change; see EXCHANGE. **2** [To abolish] annul, cancel, destroy; see ABOLISH, ELIMINATE.

liquor *n.* whiskey, booze*, alcohol; see COCKTAIL, DRINK 2.

lisp *v.* mispronounce, sputter, stutter; see UTTER.

lissome *a.* lithe, supple, flexible; see AGILE, FLEXIBLE.

list¹ *n.* roll, record, schedule, agenda, arrangement, enrollment, slate, draft, panel, brief, invoice, register, memorandum, inventory, account, outline, tally, bulletin, directory, roster, subscribers, subscription list, muster, poll, ballot, table of contents, menu, dictionary, thesaurus, glossary, lexicon, vocabulary, docket.

list¹,² *v.* **1** [To enter in a list] set down, arrange, bill, catalogue, schedule, enter, note, add, place, file, record, insert, enroll, register, tally, inventory, index, draft, enumerate, tabulate, book, take a census, poll, slate, keep count of, run down, call the roll.—*Ant.* REMOVE, wipe out, obliterate. **2** [To lean] pitch, slant, incline; see LEAN 2.

listed *a.* filed, cataloged, indexed; see RECORDED.

listen *v.* attend, keep one's ears open, be attentive, listen in, pick up, overhear, monitor, tap, give attention to, give ear, listen to, pay attention, hear, tune in*, lend an ear*, strain one's ears*.—*Ant.* IGNORE, be deaf to, turn a deaf ear to.

listener *n.* spy, student, monitor, spectator, audience, eavesdropper, witness.

listening *a.* hearing, paying attention, interested, involved, attentive, heeding, overhearing, straining to hear, receiving, lending an ear*.—*Ant.* INDIFFERENT, giving no attention, inattentive.

listless *a.* passive, sluggish, lifeless; see INDIFFERENT, SLOW 2.

lit *a.* illuminated, lighted, resplendent; see BRIGHT 1, BURNING.

literacy *n.* scholarship, ability to read and write, verbal competence; see EDUCATION 1, KNOWLEDGE 1.

literal *a.* true, verbatim, methodical; see ACCURATE 2.

literally *a.* really, actually, precisely, exactly, completely, indisputably, correctly, completely, to the letter, faithfully, rigorously, straight, unmistakably, truly, not metaphorically, not figuratively, word for word, verbatim, letter by letter.—*Ant.* FREELY, figuratively, fancifully.

literary *a.* scholarly, bookish, literate; see LEARNED 1.

literate *a.* informed, scholarly, able to read and write; see EDUCATED, INTELLIGENT, LEARNED 1.

literature *n.* **1** [Artistic production in language] letters, lore, belles lettres, literary works, literary productions, the humanities, classics, books, writings. **2** [Written matter treating a given subject] discourse, composition, treatise, dissertation, thesis, paper, treatment, essay, discussion, research, observation, comment, critique, findings, abstract, report, summary.

litter *n.* **1** [Trash] rubbish, debris, waste; see TRASH 1. **2** [The young of certain animals] piglets, puppies, kittens; see OFFSPRING.

etc. used as bedding for animals **4** granular clay used in an indoor receptacle (**litter box**) to absorb cat waste **5** the young borne at one time by a dog, cat, etc. **6** things lying about in disorder, esp. bits of rubbish — *vt.* **1** to make untidy **2** to scatter about carelessly

lit′ter·bug′ (-bug′) *n.* one who litters public places with rubbish, etc.

lit·tle (lit′'l) *adj.* **lit′tler** or **less** or **less′er, lit′tlest** or **least** ⟦OE *lytel*⟧ **1** small in size, amount, degree, etc. **2** short in duration; brief **3** small in importance or power /the *little* man/ **4** narrow-minded /a *little* mind/ — *adv.* **less, least 1** slightly; not much **2** not in the least — *n.* a small amount, degree, etc. —**little by little** gradually —**make** (or **think**) **little of** to consider as not very important —**lit′tle·ness** *n.*

little slam *Bridge* the winning of all but one trick in a deal

lit·to·ral (lit′ə rəl) *adj.* ⟦< L *litus*, seashore⟧ of or along the shore

lit·ur·gy (lit′ər jē) *n., pl.* **-gies** ⟦ult. < Gr *leōs, laos*, people + *ergon*, work⟧ prescribed ritual for public worship —**li·tur·gi·cal** (lə tʉr′ji kəl) *adj.* —**lit′ur·gist** *n.*

liv·able (liv′ə bəl) *adj.* **1** fit or pleasant to live in /a *livable* house/ **2** endurable Also **live′able**

live[1] (liv) *vi.* **lived, liv′ing** ⟦OE *libban*⟧ **1** to have life **2** *a)* to remain alive *b)* to endure **3** to pass one's life in a specified manner **4** to enjoy a full life **5** to feed /to *live* on fruit/ **6** to reside /I *live* at 15 Elm Lane; she *lives* nearby/ — *vt.* **1** to carry out in one's life /to *live* one's faith/ **2** to spend; pass /to *live* a useful life/ —**live down** to live so as to wipe out the shame of (a misdeed, etc.) —**live up to** to live or act in accordance with (one's ideals, etc.)

live[2] (liv) *adj.* ⟦< ALIVE⟧ **1** having life **2** of the living state or living beings **3** of present interest /a *live* issue/ **4** still burning /a *live* spark/ **5** unexploded /a *live* shell/ **6** carrying electrical current /a *live* wire/ **7** *a)* in person *b)* broadcast, recorded, etc. during the actual performance **8** *Sports* in play /a *live* ball/

live·bear·er (liv′ber′ər) *n.* any of various small, tropical, American, freshwater aquarium fishes, as the guppy, swordtail, etc.

-lived (livd; *often* livd) *combining form* having (a specified kind of) life /long-*lived*/

live·li·hood (liv′lē hood′) *n.* ⟦< OE *lif*, life + *-lad*, course⟧ means of living or of supporting life

live·long (liv′lôŋ′, liv′-) *adj.* ⟦ME *lefe longe*, lit., lief long: *lief* is merely intens.⟧ long in passing; whole /the *livelong* day/

lively (liv′lē) *adj.* **-lier, -li·est** ⟦OE *liflic*⟧ **1** full of life; vigorous **2** full of spirit; exciting **3** animated, cheerful, vivacious, etc. **4** vivid; keen **5** bounding back with great resilience /a *lively* ball/ —**live′li·ness** *n.*

liven (liv′ən) *vt., vi.* to make or become lively; cheer Often with *up*

liver (liv′ər) *n.* ⟦OE *lifer*⟧ **1** the largest glandular organ in vertebrate animals: it secretes bile and is important in metabolism **2** this organ of an animal used as food

liver·wurst (liv′ər wʉrst′) *n.* ⟦< Ger *leber*, liver + *wurst*, sausage⟧ a sausage containing ground liver

liv·ery (liv′ər ē) *n., pl.* **-er·ies** ⟦ME, gift of clothes to a servant⟧ **1** an identifying uniform as of a servant **2** *a)* the care and feeding of horses for a fee *b)* the keeping of horses or vehicles for hire

lives (livz) *n. pl. of* LIFE

live·stock (liv′stäk′) *n.* domestic animals raised for use and sale

livid (liv′id) *adj.* ⟦< L *lividus*⟧ **1** discolored by a bruise; black-and-blue **2** grayish-blue or pale /*livid* with rage/

liv·ing (liv′iŋ) *adj.* **1** alive; having life **2** in active operation or use /a *living* institution/ **3** of persons alive /within *living* memory/ **4** true; lifelike **5** of life /*living* conditions/ — *n.* **1** a being alive **2** livelihood **3** manner of existence —**the living** those that are still alive

living room a room in a home, with sofas, chairs, etc., used for social activities, entertaining guests, etc.

living wage a wage sufficient to maintain a reasonable level of comfort

living will a document directing that the signer's life not be artificially supported during a terminal illness

liz·ard (liz′ərd) *n.* ⟦< L *lacerta*⟧ any of a group of slender, scaly reptiles with four legs and a tail

'll will or shall Used in contractions /she'll sing/

ll. lines

LL Late Latin

lla·ma (lä′mə) *n.* ⟦Sp < AmInd (Peru)⟧ a South American beast of burden related to the camel but smaller

lla·no (lä′nō) *n., pl.* **-nos** ⟦Sp < L *planus*, plain⟧ any of the level, grassy plains of Spanish America

LLB or **LL.B.** Bachelor of Laws

LLD or **LL.D.** Doctor of Laws

lo (lō) *interj.* ⟦OE *la*⟧ look! see!

load (lōd) *n.* ⟦< OE *lad*, a course⟧ **1** an amount carried at one time **2** something borne with difficulty; burden **3**

THESAURUS

litter *v.* scatter, discard, spread; see DIRTY.

litterbug *n.* slob*, pig, polluter; see SLOB.

little *a.* **1** [Small in size] diminutive, small, tiny, wee, undersized, stubby, truncated, stunted, limited, cramped, imperceptible, light, slight, microscopic, short, runty, shriveled, toy, miniature, puny, pygmy, dwarfed, bantam, half-pint*, pocket-sized*, pint-sized*.—*Ant.* LARGE, big, huge. **2** [Inadequate] a lack of, deficient, insufficient; see INADEQUATE. **3** [Few in number] scarce, not many, hardly any; see FEW. **4** [Brief] concise, succinct, abrupt; see SHORT 2. **5** [Small in importance] trifling, shallow, petty, superficial, frivolous, irrelevant, meaningless, slight, paltry, insignificant, inconsiderable; see also TRIVIAL, UNIMPORTANT. **6** [Small in character] base, weak, shallow, small-minded, prejudiced, bigoted, low, sneaky, mean, petty; see also VULGAR. **7** [Weak] stunted, runty, undersized; see WEAK 1. —**make little of** make fun of, mock, abuse; see RIDICULE.

little *n.* some, a few, trifle; see BIT 1.

livable *a.* habitable, endurable, inhabitable; see BEARABLE, COMFORTABLE 2.

live[1] *v.* **1** [To have life] exist, continue, subsist, prevail, survive, breathe, be alive; see also BE 1. **2** [To enjoy life] relish, savor, experience, love, delight in, make every moment count, experience life to the full, live

it up*, make the most of life, take pleasure in, get a great deal from life.—*Ant.* SUFFER, endure pain, be discouraged. **3** [To dwell] live in, inhabit, settle; see DWELL. **4** [To gain subsistence] earn a living, support oneself, earn money, get ahead, provide for one's needs, make ends meet, subsist, maintain oneself; see also SURVIVE 1. **5** [To persist in human memory] remain, be remembered, last; see ENDURE 1. —**live and let live** be tolerant, accept, ignore; see ALLOW. —**live at** inhabit, reside, occupy; see DWELL. —**live down** overcome, survive, outgrow; see ENDURE 2. —**live on** be supported, earn, subsist on; see LIVE 4. —**live up to** meet expectations, do well, give satisfaction; see SATISFY 3. —**where one lives*** personally, in a vulnerable area, at one's heart; see PERSONALLY 2.

live[2] *a.* **1** [Active] energetic, lively, dynamic; see ACTIVE. **2** [Not dead] aware, conscious, existing; see ALIVE. **3** [Not taped or filmed] broadcast direct, unrehearsed, on stage; see REAL 2.

livelihood *n.* career, occupation, job; see PROFESSION 1.

lively *a.* vigorous, brisk, industrious; see ACTIVE.

livestock *n.* cows, sheep, domestic animals; see CATTLE, HERD.

living *a.* **1** [Alive] existing, breathing, having being; see ALIVE. **2** [Vigorous] awake, brisk, alert; see ACTIVE.

living *n.* **1** [A means of survival] existence, sustenance, maintenance; see SUBSISTENCE 2. **2** [Those not dead; *usually used with "the"*] the world, everyone, people; see ANIMAL, PERSON, PLANT.

living room *n.* lounge, front room, den; see ROOM 2.

load *n.* **1** [A physical burden] weight, encumbrance, truckload, carload, wagonload, shipload, cargo, haul, charge, pack, mass, payload, shipment, contents, capacity, bundle.—*Ant.* LIGHTNESS, buoyancy, weightlessness. **2** [Responsibility] charge, obligation, trust; see DUTY 1. **3** [A charge; *said especially of firearms*] shot, clip, round; see AMMUNITION. **4** [A measure] quantity, portion, amount; see MEASUREMENT 2, QUANTITY.

load *v.* **1** [To place a load] arrange, stow away, store, burden, stuff, put goods in, put goods on, freight, weight, pile, heap, fill, cram, put aboard, stack, pour in, take on cargo; see also PACK 1.—*Ant.* UNLOAD, unpack, take off cargo. **2** [To overload] encumber, saddle, weigh down; see BURDEN. **3** [To charge; *said especially of firearms*] prime, ready, make ready to fire; see SHOOT 1.

loaded *a.* **1** [Supplied with a load] laden, burdened, weighted; see FULL 1. **2** [Ready to discharge; *said of firearms*] charged, primed, ready to shoot. **3** [*Intoxicated] inebriated, drunken, smashed*; see DRUNK.

[often pl.] [Colloq.] a great amount **4** *Finance* an amount added to the price of mutual fund shares to cover costs, etc. —*vt.* **1** to put (a load) into or upon (a carrier) **2** to burden; oppress **3** to supply in large quantities **4** to put a charge of ammunition into (a firearm) **5** *Comput.* to transfer (a program or data) into main memory from a disk, etc. —**load′er** *n.* —**load′ing** *n.*

load·star (lōd′stär′) *n.* LODESTAR

load·stone (lōd′stōn′) *n.* LODESTONE

loaf¹ (lōf) *n., pl.* **loaves** (lōvz) [OE *hlaf*] **1** a portion of bread baked in one piece **2** any food baked in this shape

loaf² (lōf) *vi.* [prob. < fol.] to spend time idly; idle, dawdle, etc.

loaf′er *n.* [prob. < Ger *landläufer*, a vagabond] one who loafs; idler

loam (lōm) *n.* [OE *lam*] a rich soil, esp. one composed of clay, sand, and some organic matter —**loam′y, -i·er, -i·est, adj.**

loan (lōn) *n.* [< ON *lān*] **1** the act of lending **2** something lent, esp. money at interest —*vt., vi.* to lend

loan′er (-ər) *n.* **1** one who loans something **2** an automobile, TV, etc. lent in place of one left for repair

loan shark [Colloq.] one who lends money at illegal rates of interest

loan′word′ (-wurd′) *n.* a word of one language taken into and used in another

loath (lōth) *adj.* [< OE *lath*, hostile] reluctant [to be *loath* to depart]

loathe (lōth) *vt.* **loathed, loath′ing** [< OE *lathian*, be hateful] to feel intense dislike or disgust for; abhor

loath′ing (-iŋ) *n.* intense dislike, disgust, or hatred; abhorrence

loath′some (-səm) *adj.* causing loathing; disgusting; abhorrent

loaves (lōvz) *n. pl. of* LOAF¹

lob (läb) *vt., vi.* **lobbed, lob′bing** [ME *lobbe*, heavy] to toss or hit (a ball) in a high curve —**lob′ber** *n.*

lobby (läb′ē) *n., pl.* **-bies** [LL *lobia*] **1** an entrance hall, as of a hotel, theater, etc. **2** a group of lobbyists representing the same interest —*vi.* **-bied, -by·ing** to act as a lobbyist

lob′by·ist (-ist) *n.* one who tries to get legislators to support certain measures

lobe (lōb) *n.* [< Gr *lobos*] a rounded projection, as the lower end of the ear or any of the divisions of the lung

lo·bot′o·mize′ (-mīz′) *vt.* **-mized′, -miz′ing** **1** to perform a lobotomy on **2** to cause to behave in a machinelike way, as without emotion or independent thought

lo·bot·o·my (lō bät′ə mē) *n., pl.* **-mies** [< LOBE + -TOMY] a surgical operation in which a lobe of the brain is cut into or across: now rarely used

lob·ster (läb′stər) *n.* [< OE *loppe*, spider + -*estre*, -ster] an edible sea crustacean with four pairs of legs and a pair of large pincers

lobster tail the edible tail of any of various crustaceans

lo·cal (lō′kəl) *adj.* [< L *locus*, a place] **1** of, characteristic of, or confined to a particular place **2** of or for a particular part of the body **3** making all stops along its run *[a local bus]* —*n.* **1** a local train, bus, etc. **2** a branch, as of a labor union —**lo′cally** *adv.*

lo·cale (lō kal′) *n.* [OFr *local*] a locality, esp. with reference to events, etc. associated with it

lo·cal·ity (lō kal′ə tē) *n., pl.* **-ties** **1** position with regard to surrounding objects, etc. **2** a place or district

lo·cal·ize (lō′kəl īz′) *vt.* **-ized′, -iz′ing** to limit, confine, or trace to a particular place —**lo′cal·i·za′tion** *n.*

lo·cate (lō′kāt′, lō kāt′) *vt.* **-cat·ed, -cat·ing** [< L *locus*, a place] **1** to establish in a certain place *[offices located downtown]* **2** to discover the position of **3** to show the position of *[to locate Guam on a map]* —*vi.* [Colloq.] to settle *[she located in Ohio]*

lo·ca′tion *n.* **1** a locating or being located **2** position; place —**on location** *Film* away from the studio

loc. cit. [L *loco citato*] in the place cited

loch (läk, läkh) *n.* [< Gael & OldIr] [Scot.] **1** a lake **2** an arm of the sea

lock¹ (läk) *n.* [< OE *loc*, a bolt] **1** a mechanical device for fastening a door, strongbox, etc. as with a key or combination **2** an enclosed part of a canal, etc. equipped with gates for raising or lowering the level of the water **3** the mechanism of a firearm that explodes the charge —*vt.* **1** to fasten with a lock **2** to shut (*up*, *in*, or *out*); confine **3** to fit; link *[to lock arms]* **4** to jam together so as to make immovable —*vi.* **1** to become locked **2** to interlock

lock² (läk) *n.* [OE *loc*] **1** a curl of hair **2** a tuft of wool, cotton, etc.

lock′box′ *n.* **1** a box with a lock for securing items of value **2** an electronic device which prevents unauthorized viewing of designated cable TV channels Also **lock box**

lock′er *n.* **1** a chest, closet, etc. which can be locked **2** a large compartment for freezing and storing foods

locker room a room, as at a gymnasium, equipped with lockers for storing a person's clothes and equipment

locket (läk′it) *n.* [< OFr *loc*, a lock] a small, hinged case of gold, etc. for holding a picture, lock of hair, etc.: usually worn on a necklace

lock′jaw′ *n.* a form of tetanus, in which the jaws become firmly closed

lock′out′ *n.* the shutdown of a plant to bring the workers to terms

lock′smith′ *n.* one whose work is making or repairing locks and keys

lock′up (läk′up′) *n.* a jail

loco (lō′kō) *adj.* [Sp, mad] [Slang] crazy; demented

loco disease (lō′kō) a nervous disease of horses and cattle caused by locoweed poison

lo·co·mo·tion (lō′kə mō′shən) *n.* [< L *locus*, a place + MOTION] motion, or the power of moving, from one place to another

lo′co·mo′tive (-mōt′iv) *adj.* of locomotion —*n.* an electric, steam, or diesel engine on wheels, designed to push or pull a railroad train

---

THESAURUS

loaf¹ *n.* roll, bun, pastry; see BREAD, CAKE 2.

loaf² *v.* idle, trifle, lounge, kill time, be inactive, be slothful, be lazy, take it easy, not lift a finger, putter, rest, dally, let down, slack off, vegetate, loll, malinger, drift, relax, slack, shirk, waste time, slow down, evade, dilly-dally, stand around, dream, goof off*, bum*, stall, piddle.

loafer *n.* idler, lounger, lazy person, ne'er-do-well, good-for-nothing, lazybones, malinger, waster, slacker, shirker, wanderer, bum*, goldbrick*.

loafing *a.* careless, apathetic, shirking; see LAZY 1.

loan *n.* lending, trust, advance, giving credit, mortgage, time payment, installment loan, student loan, car loan, home equity loan, personal loan.

loan *v.* provide with, share, furnish; see LEND.

loaned *a.* lent, advanced, invested, granted, furnished, put out at interest, let, risked, leased; see also GIVEN.—*Ant.* BORROWED, pledged, pawned.

lobby *n.* vestibule, entryway, foyer; see HALL 1, ROOM 2.

lobby *v.* induce, put pressure on, promote; see INFLUENCE.

local *a.* **1** [Associated with a locality] sectional, divisional, territorial, district, provincial, neighborhood, town, civic, small-town, grass-roots, parochial, geographical; see also REGIONAL. **2** [Restricted to a locality] limited, confined, bounded; see RESTRICTED.

locale *n.* vicinity, territory, district; see AREA, REGION 1.

locality *n.* **1** [Area] district, section, sector; see AREA, REGION 1. **2** [Position] spot, location, site; see POSITION 1. **3** [Neighborhood] block, vicinity, district; see NEIGHBORHOOD.

locally *a.* regionally, sectionally, provincially, in the neighborhood, in the town, close by, nearby.

locate *v.* **1** [To determine a location] discover, search out, find, come across, position, ferret out, stumble on, discover the location of, get at, hit upon, come upon, lay one's hands on, track down, unearth, establish, determine, station, place; see also FIND. **2** [To take up residence] settle down, establish oneself, inhabit; see DWELL, SETTLE 5.

located *a.* **1** [Discovered] traced, found, happened on; see DISCOVERED. **2** [Situated] positioned, seated, fixed; see PLACED.

location *n.* **1** [A position] place, spot, section; see POSITION 1. **2** [A site] situation, place, scene; see AREA, NEIGHBORHOOD.

lock¹ *v.* bolt, bar, turn the key; see FASTEN. —**lock up** confine, put behind bars, shut up; see IMPRISON.

lock¹,² *n.* **1** [A device for locking] hook, catch, latch, bolt, bar, hasp, bond, fastening, padlock, safety catch, clamp, clasp, tumblers, barrier, device, fixture, grip; see also FASTENER. **2** [A tuft of hair] tress, ringlet, curl; see HAIR 1. —**under lock and key** locked up, imprisoned, in jail; see CONFINED 3.

locked *a.* secured, padlocked, closed; see TIGHT 3.

locker *n.* cabinet, footlocker, cupboard; see CLOSET, FURNITURE.

locket *n.* memento case, pendant, keepsake; see JEWELRY, NECKLACE.

lockup *n.* prison, jail, penitentiary; see JAIL.

lo·co·weed (lō′kō wēd′) *n.* a plant of W North America that causes the loco disease of cattle, horses, etc.

lo·cus (lō′kəs) *n., pl.* **lo′ci** (-sī′) ⟦L⟧ **1** a place **2** *Math.* a line, plane, etc. every point of which satisfies a given condition

lo·cust (lō′kəst) *n.* ⟦< L *locusta*⟧ **1** a large grasshopper often traveling in swarms and destroying crops **2** SEVENTEEN-YEAR LOCUST **3** a tree of the E or Central U.S., with clusters of fragrant white flowers

lo·cu·tion (lō kyōō′shən) *n.* ⟦< L *loqui*, speak⟧ a word, phrase, etc.

lode (lōd) *n.* ⟦< OE *lad*, course⟧ a vein, stratum, etc. of metallic ore

lode′star′ *n.* a star by which one directs one's course; esp., the North Star

lode′stone′ *n.* a strongly magnetic variety of iron ore

lodge (läj) *n.* ⟦< OFr *loge*, arbor⟧ **1** *a)* a small house for some special use *[a hunting lodge] b)* a resort hotel or motel **2** the local chapter or hall of a fraternal society — *vt.* **lodged, lodg′ing 1** to house temporarily **2** to shoot, thrust, etc. firmly (*in*) **3** to bring (a complaint, etc.) before legal authorities **4** to confer (powers) upon: with *in* — *vi.* **1** to live in a place for a time **2** to live (*with* or *in*) as a paying guest **3** to come to rest and stick firmly (*in*)

lodg′er *n.* one who lives in a rented room in another's home

lodg′ing *n.* **1** a place to live in, esp. temporarily **2** [*pl.*] a room or rooms rented in a private home

loft (lôft, läft) *n.* ⟦< ON *lopt*, upper room, air⟧ **1** the space just below the roof of a house, barn, etc. **2** an upper story of a warehouse or factory; specif., a dwelling space, artist's studio, etc. in such an upper story **3** a gallery *[a choir loft]* **4** height given to a ball hit or thrown — *vt.* to send (a ball) into a high curve

loft bed a bed on a platform or balcony allowing the use of the floor area below as living room, etc.

loft′y *adj.* **-i·er, -i·est 1** very high **2** elevated; noble **3** haughty; arrogant —**loft′i·ness** *n.*

log[1] (lôg, läg) *n.* ⟦ME *logge*⟧ **1** a section of the trunk or of a large branch of a felled tree **2** a device for measuring the speed of a ship **3** a record of progress, speed, etc., specif. one kept on a ship's voyage or aircraft's flight — *vt.* **logged, log′ging 1** to saw (trees) into logs **2** to record in a log **3** to sail or fly (a specified distance) — *vi.* to cut down trees and remove the logs —**log on** (or **off**) to enter the necessary information to begin (or end) a session on a computer terminal —**log′ger** *n.*

log[2] (lôg, läg) *n. short for* LOGARITHM

-log (lôg, läg) *combining form* -LOGUE

lo·gan·ber·ry (lō′gən ber′ē) *n., pl.* **-ries** ⟦after J. H. *Logan*, who developed it (1881)⟧ **1** a hybrid developed from the blackberry and the red raspberry **2** its purplish-red fruit

log·a·rithm (lôg′ə rith əm, läg′-) *n.* ⟦< Gr *logos*, ratio + *arithmos*, number⟧ *Math.* the exponent expressing the power to which a fixed number must be raised to produce a given number —**log·a·rith′mic** *adj.*

loge (lōzh) *n.* ⟦OFr: see LODGE⟧ a theater box or mezzanine section

log·ger·head (lôg′ər hed′, läg′-) *n.* ⟦dial. *logger*, block of wood + HEAD⟧ a blockhead —**at loggerheads** in sharp disagreement

log′ging *n.* the work of felling trees, cutting them into logs, and transporting the logs to as sawmill

logic (läj′ik) *n.* ⟦ult. < Gr *logos*, word⟧ **1** correct reasoning, or the science of this **2** way of reasoning *[bad logic]* **3** what is expected by the working of cause and effect **4** *Comput.* the system of switching functions, circuits, or devices —**lo·gi·cian** (lō jish′ən) *n.*

log′i·cal (-i kəl) *adj.* ⟦ML *logicalis*⟧ **1** based on or using logic **2** expected because of what has gone before —**log′i·cally** *adv.*

lo·gis·tics (lō jis′tiks) *n.pl.* ⟦< Fr *loger*, to quarter⟧ [*with sing. v.*] the military science of procuring, maintaining, and transporting materiel and personnel —**lo·gis′tic** or **lo·gis′ti·cal** *adj.* —**lo·gis′ti·cally** *adv.*

log′jam′ *n.* **1** an obstacle of logs jamming together in a stream **2** piled-up work, etc. that obstructs progress **3** a deadlock

logo·type (lôg′ə tip′, läg′-) *n.* ⟦< Gr *logos*, a word + -TYPE⟧ a distinctive company signature, trademark, etc. Also **logo** (lō′gō′, lô′gō, läg′ō)

log′roll′ing *n.* **1** mutual exchange of favors, esp. among legislators **2** the sport of balancing oneself while revolving a floating log with one's feet

-logue (lôg, läg) ⟦see LOGIC⟧ *combining form* a (specified kind of) speaking or writing *[Decalogue]*

logy (lō′gē) *adj.* **-gier, -gi·est** ⟦< ? Du *log*, dull⟧ [Colloq.] dull or sluggish

-logy (lə jē) ⟦see LOGIC⟧ *combining form* **1** a (specified kind of) speaking *[eulogy]* **2** science, doctrine, or theory of *[biology]*

loin (loin) *n.* ⟦< L *lumbus*⟧ **1** [*usually pl.*] the lower part of the back between the hipbones and the ribs **2** the front part of the hindquarters of beef, lamb, etc. **3** [*pl.*] the hips and the lower abdomen regarded as the region of strength, etc.

loin′cloth′ *n.* a cloth worn about the loins, as by some peoples in the tropics

loi·ter (loit′ər) *vi.* ⟦< MDu *loteren*⟧ **1** to spend time idly; linger **2** to move slowly and idly —**loi′terer** *n.*

loll (läl) *vi.* ⟦< MDu *lollen*⟧ **1** to lean or lounge about lazily **2** to hang loosely; droop *[the camel's tongue lolled out]* — *vt.* to let hang loosely

lol·li·pop or **lol·ly·pop** (läl′ē päp′) *n.* ⟦prob. < dial. *lolly*, the tongue + *pop*⟧ a piece of candy on the end of a stick

lol·ly·gag (läl′ē gag′) *vi.* **-gagged′, -gag′ging** ⟦var. of *lallygag* < ?⟧ [Colloq.] to waste time in trifling or aimless activity

lone (lōn) *adj.* ⟦< *alone*⟧ **1** by oneself; solitary **2** isolated

lone′ly *adj.* **-lier, -li·est 1** solitary or isolated **2** unhappy at being alone —**lone′li·ness** *n.*

loner (lōn′ər) *n.* [Colloq.] one who prefers to be independent of others, as by living or working alone

lone′some *adj.* **1** having or causing a lonely feeling **2** unfrequented

long[1] (lôŋ) *adj.* ⟦< OE⟧ **1** measuring much in space or time **2** in length *[six feet long]* **3** of greater than usual length, quantity, etc. *[a long list]* **4** tedious; slow **5** far-reaching *[a long view of the matter]* **6** well-supplied *[long

---

THESAURUS

lodge *n.* inn, hostel, ski lodge; see HOTEL, MOTEL, RESORT 2.

lodge *v.* **1** [To become fixed] catch, stay, abide; see STICK 1. **2** [To take (temporary) residence] room, stay over, board; see DWELL.

lodger *n.* guest, roomer, resident; see TENANT.

lodging *n.* **1** [Place of protection] sanctuary, retreat, asylum; see REFUGE 1, SHELTER. **2** [A (temporary) living place; *usually plural*] room, apartment, suite; see HOTEL, MOTEL, RESORT 2.

lofty *a.* tall, elevated, towering; see HIGH 2, RAISED 1.

log[1] *n.* **1** [The main stem of a fallen or cut tree] timber, trunk, lumber; see WOOD 2. **2** [The record of a voyage] journal, account, diary; see RECORD 1.

logic *n.* reasoning, deduction, induction; see PHILOSOPHY 1, THOUGHT 1.

logical *a.* coherent, consistent, probable, sound, pertinent, germane, legitimate, cogent, relevant, congru-

ent with, as it ought to be; see also REASONABLE 1.

logically *a.* rationally, by reason, inevitably; see REASONABLY 1, 2.

logy* *a.* dull, sluggish, drowsy; see LAZY 1.

loiter *v.* saunter, stroll, dawdle, delay, lag, shuffle, waste time, procrastinate, tarry, fritter away time, loll, loaf, dabble, wait, pause, dillydally, hang back, trail, drag, ramble, idle; see also LINGER.—*Ant.* HURRY, hasten, stride along.

lone *a.* solitary, lonesome, deserted; see ALONE.

loneliness *n.* detachment, separation, solitude, desolation, isolation, aloneness, lonesomeness, forlornness.

lonely *a.* abandoned, homesick, forlorn, forsaken, friendless, deserted, desolate, homeless, left, lone, lonesome, solitary, empty, companionless, renounced, withdrawn, secluded, unattended, by oneself, apart, reclusive, single, rejected,

unaccompanied; see also ALONE.— *Ant.* ACCOMPANIED, joined, associated.

lonesome *a.* solitary, forlorn, alone; see HOMESICK, LONELY.

long[1] *a.* **1** [Extended in space] lengthy, extended, outstretched, elongated, interminable, boundless, endless, unending, limitless, stretching, great, high, deep, drawn out, enlarged, expanded, spread, tall, lofty, towering, lengthened, stringy, rangy, lanky, gangling, far-reaching, distant, running, faraway, far-off, remote; see also LARGE 1.—*Ant.* SHORT, small, stubby. **2** [Extended in time] protracted, prolonged, enduring, unending, meandering, long-winded, spun out, lengthy, for ages, without end, perpetual, forever and a day, lasting, continued, long-lived, sustained, lingering; day after day, hour after hour, etc.—*Ant.* SHORT, brief, uncontinued. **3** [Tedious] hard, boring, long-drawn; see DULL 4. **4** [Having (a certain commodity) in on excuses] —*adv.* 1 for a long time 2 from start to finish *[all day long]* 3 at a remote time *[long* ago] —**as** (or **so**) **long as** 1 during the time that 2 since 3 provided that —**before long** soon

long² (lôṇ) *vi.* ⟦ < OE *langian* ⟧ to feel a strong yearning; wish earnestly

long. longitude

long distance a telephone service for calls to and from distant places —**long′-dis′tance** *adj., adv.*

lon·gev′i·ty (län jev′ə tē, lôn-) *n.* ⟦ < L *longus*, long + *aevum*, age ⟧ long life

long′-faced′ *adj.* glum

long′hair′ *adj.* of intellectuals or intellectual tastes

long′hand′ *n.* ordinary handwriting, as distinguished from shorthand

long′horn′ *n.* any of a breed of long-horned cattle formerly raised in the Southwest

long′ing *n.* strong desire; yearning —*adj.* feeling or showing a yearning

lon·gi·tude′ (län′jə tōōd′) *n.* ⟦ < L *longus*, long ⟧ distance east or west of the prime meridian, expressed in degrees or time

lon·gi·tu′di·nal (-tōōd′′n əl) *adj.* 1 of or in length 2 running or placed lengthwise 3 of longitude

long jump *Sports* a jump for distance made either from a stationary position or with a running start

long′-lived′ (-līvd′, -livd′) *adj.* having or tending to have a long life span

long′-range′ *adj.* reaching over a long distance or period of time

long·shore·man (lôṇ′shôr′mən) *n., pl.* **-men** ⟦ < *alongshore* + MAN ⟧ a person who works on a waterfront loading and unloading ships; stevedore

long shot [Colloq.] in betting, a choice that is little favored and, hence, carries great odds

long′-stand′ing *adj.* having continued for a long time

long′-suf′fering *adj.* bearing trouble, etc. patiently for a long time

long′-term′ *adj.* for or extending over a long time

long ton TON (sense 2)

long′-wind′ed (-win′did) *adj.* 1 speaking or writing at great length 2 tiresomely long

look (look) *vi.* ⟦ < OE *locian* ⟧ 1 to direct one's eyes in order to see 2 to search 3 to appear; seem 4 to be facing in a specified direction — *vt.* 1 to direct one's eyes on 2 to have an appearance befitting *[to look* the part] — *n.* 1 a looking; glance 2 appearance; aspect 3 [Colloq.] *a)* [*usually pl.*] appearance *b)* [*pl.*] personal appearance — *interj.* 1 see! 2 pay attention! —**look after** to take care of — **look down on** (or **upon**) to regard with contempt —**look**

for to expect —**look forward to** to anticipate —**look in** (**on**) to pay a brief visit (to) —**look into** to investigate — **look out** to be careful —**look over** to examine —**look to** 1 to take care of 2 to rely on —**look up** 1 to search for as in a reference book 2 [Colloq.] to call on —**look up to** to admire —**look′er** *n.*

look′er-on′ *n., pl.* **look′ers-on′** an observer or spectator; onlooker

looking glass a (glass) mirror

look′out′ *n.* 1 a careful watching 2 a place for keeping watch 3 a person detailed to watch 4 [Colloq.] concern

look′-see′ *n.* [Colloq.] a quick look

loom¹ (lōōm) *n.* ⟦ < OE (*ge*)*loma*, tool ⟧ a machine for weaving thread or yarn into cloth — *vt.* to weave on a loom

loom² (lōōm) *vi.* ⟦ < ? ⟧ to come into sight indistinctly, esp. threateningly

loon¹ (lōōn) *n.* ⟦ < ON *lomr* ⟧ a fish-eating, diving bird, similar to a duck

loon² (lōōn) *n.* ⟦ < ? ⟧ 1 a clumsy, stupid person 2 a crazy person

loony (lōōn′ē) *adj.* **-i·er, -i·est** ⟦ < LUNATIC ⟧ [Slang] crazy; demented

loop (lōōp) *n.* ⟦ ME *loup* ⟧ 1 the figure made by a line, thread, etc. that curves back to cross itself 2 anything forming this figure 3 an intrauterine contraceptive device 4 a segment of movie film or magnetic tape — *vt.* 1 to make a loop of 2 to fasten with a loop — *vi.* to form a loop or loops

loop′hole′ *n.* ⟦ prob. < MDu *lupen*, to peer + HOLE ⟧ 1 a hole in a wall for looking or shooting through 2 a means of evading an obligation, etc.

loopy (lōō′pē) *adj.* **-i·er, -i·est** [Slang] 1 slightly crazy 2 confused

loose (lōōs) *adj.* **loos′er, loos′est** ⟦ < ON *lauss* ⟧ 1 not confined or restrained; free 2 not firmly fastened 3 not tight or compact 4 not precise; inexact 5 sexually immoral 6 [Colloq.] relaxed — *adv.* loosely — *vt.* **loosed, loos′ing** 1 to set free; unbind 2 to make less tight, compact, etc. 3 to relax 4 to release (an arrow, etc.) — *vi.* to become loose —**on the loose** not confined; free —**loose′ly** *adv.* —**loose′ness** *n.*

loose ends unsettled details —**at loose ends** unsettled, idle, etc.

loose′-leaf′ *adj.* having leaves, or sheets, that can easily be removed or replaced

loosen (lōōs′ən) *vt., vi.* to make or become loose or looser

loot (lōōt) *n.* ⟦ Hindi *lūt* ⟧ 1 goods stolen or taken by force; plunder 2 [Slang] money, presents, etc. — *vt., vi.* to plunder

lop¹ (läp) *vt.* **lopped, lop′ping** ⟦ < OE *loppian* ⟧ 1 to trim (a tree, etc.) by cutting off branches, etc. 2 to remove as by cutting off —**lop′per** *n.*

THESAURUS

excess] rich, profuse, abundant; see PLENTIFUL 1. —**as** (or **so**) **long as** seeing that, provided, since; see BECAUSE. —**before long** in the near future, immediately, shortly; see SOON. —**long and short of** gist, totality, outcome; see RESULT, WHOLE.

long² *v.* desire, yearn for, wish; see WANT 1.

longing *n.* yearning, pining, hunger; see DESIRE 1, WISH.

long-lived *a.* long-lasting, perpetual, enduring; see PERMANENT.

look *n.* 1 [Appearance] features, demeanor, shape; see EXPRESSION 4, LOOKS. 2 [An effort to see] gaze, stare, scrutiny, inspection, examination, contemplation, speculation, attending, noticing, regarding, marking, observation, reconnaissance, keeping watch, once-over*; see also ATTENTION. 3 [A quick use of the eyes] glance, survey, squint, glimpse, peek, peep, leer, flash.

look *v.* 1 [To appear] seem to be, look like, resemble; see SEEM. 2 [To endeavor to see] view, gaze, glance at, scan, stare, behold, contemplate, watch, survey, scrutinize, regard, inspect, discern, spy, observe, attend, examine, mark, gape, give attention, peer, ogle, have an eye on, study, peep, look at, take a gander at*, get a

load of*; see also SEE 1. —**it looks like** probably, it seems that there will be, it seems as if; see SEEM. — **look after** look out for, support, watch; see GUARD. —**look into** investigate, study, probe; see EXAMINE. —**look up** come upon, research, find; see DISCOVER, SEARCH, SEEK. — **look up to** respect, idolize, honor; see ADMIRE.

lookout *n.* 1 [A place of vantage] watchtower, observatory, patrol station, post, crow's nest, observation tower. 2 [One stationed at a lookout] observer, sentinel, scout; see WATCHMAN.

looks* *n.* appearance, countenance, aspect, manner, demeanor, face, expression, features, form, shape, posture, bearing, presence.

loom² *v.* 1 [To appear] come into view, come on the scene, rise; see APPEAR 1. 2 [To appear large or imposing] menace, overshadow, hulk, emerge, shadow, top, tower, impress, hang over, rise gradually, seem huge, be near, hover, approach, come forth; see also THREATEN.

loop *n.* ring, eye, circuit; see CIRCLE 1. —**knock** (or **throw**) **for a loop*** confuse, disturb, startle; see SHOCK 2.

loop *v.* curve, connect, tie together; see BEND.

loophole *n.* avoidance, means of escape, deception; see LIE, TRICK 1.

loose *a.* 1 [Unbound] unfastened, undone, untied, insecure, relaxed, unattached, unconnected, disconnected, untethered, unbuttoned, unclasped, unhooked, unsewed, unstuck, slack, loosened, baggy, unconfined, unlatched, unlocked, unbolted, unscrewed, unhinged, worked free; see also FREE 3.—*Ant.* TIGHT, confined, bound. 2 [Movable] unattached, free, wobbly; see MOVABLE. 3 [Vague] disconnected, random, detached; see OBSCURE 1, VAGUE 2. 4 [Wanton] dissolute, licentious, disreputable; see LEWD 2. —**on the loose*** unconfined, unrestrained, wild; see FREE. —**set** (or **turn**) **loose** set free, release, untie; see FREE.

loosen *v.* 1 [To make loose] extricate, untie, unbind, undo, disentangle, let go, unlock, release, unfix; see also FREE. 2 [To become loose] relax, slacken, work free, break up, let go, become unstuck.—*Ant.* TIGHTEN, tighten up, become rigid.

loot *n.* spoils, plunder, take*; see BOOTY.

loot *v.* plunder, thieve, rifle; see ROB, STEAL.

lop¹ *v.* trim, prune, chop; see CUT 1.

lop² (läp) *vi.* **lopped, lop′ping** [prob. akin to LOB] to hang down loosely

lope (lōp) *vi.* **loped, lop′ing** [< ON *hlaupa*, to leap] to move with a long, swinging stride —*n.* such a stride

lop·sided (läp′sīd′id) *adj.* noticeably heavier, bigger, or lower on one side

lo·qua·cious (lō kwā′shəs) *adj.* [< L *loqui*, speak] very talkative —**lo·quac′i·ty** (-kwas′ə tē) *n.*

lord (lôrd) *n.* [< OE *hlaf*, loaf + *weard*, keeper] **1** a ruler; master **2** the head of a feudal estate **3** [L-] in Great Britain, a titled nobleman —[L-] **1** God **2** Jesus Christ — **lord it (over)** to be overbearing toward

lord′ly (-lē) *adj.* **-lier, -li·est 1** noble; magnificent **2** haughty —*adv.* in the manner of a lord

Lord′s Sunday

lord′ship′ *n.* **1** the rank or authority of a lord **2** rule; dominion **3** the territory of a lord **4** [often L-] a title used in speaking to or of a lord

Lord's Prayer the prayer beginning *Our Father:* Matt. 6:9-13

lore (lôr) *n.* [< OE *lar*] knowledge; learning, esp. of a traditional nature

lor·gnette (lôrn yet′) *n.* [Fr < OFr *lorgne*, squinting] eyeglasses, or opera glasses, attached to a handle

lo·ris (lô′ris, lôr′is) *n.* [ult. < Du *loer*, a clown] a small, slow-moving, large-eyed Asiatic lemur that lives in trees and is active at night

lorn (lôrn) *adj.* [ME < *losen*, lose] [Old Poet.] forsaken, forlorn, etc.

lorry (lôr′ē) *n., pl.* **-ries** [prob. < dial. *lurry*, to pull] [Brit.] a motor truck

lose (lōōz) *vt.* **lost, los′ing** [OE *losian*] **1** to become unable to find [to *lose* one's keys] **2** to have taken from one by accident, death, removal, etc. **3** to fail to keep [to *lose* one's temper] **4** to fail to see, hear, or understand **5** to fail to have, get, etc. [to *lose* one's chance] **6** to fail to win **7** to cause the loss of **8** to wander from (one's way, etc.) **9** to squander —*vi.* to suffer (a) loss —**lose oneself** to become absorbed —**los′er** *n.*

loss (lôs, läs) *n.* [ME *los*] **1** a losing or being lost **2** the damage, trouble, etc. caused by losing **3** the person, thing, or amount lost —**at a loss to** uncertain how to

lost (lôst, läst) *vt., vi. pt. & pp. of* LOSE —*adj.* **1** ruined; destroyed **2** not to be found; missing **3** no longer held, seen, heard, etc. **4** not gained or won **5** having wandered astray **6** wasted

lot (lät) *n.* [< OE *hlot*] **1** the deciding of a matter by chance, as by drawing counters **2** the decision thus arrived at **3** one's share by lot **4** fortune [her unhappy *lot*] **5** a plot of ground **6** a group of persons or things **7** [often *pl.*] [Colloq.] a great amount **8** [Colloq.] sort [he's a bad *lot*] —*adv.* very much Also **lots** —**draw (or cast) lots** to decide by lot

Lo·thario (lō ther′ē ō′) *n., pl.* **-i·os′** [after the rake in the play *The Fair Penitent*] [often l-] a seducer of women; rake

lo·tion (lō′shən) *n.* [< L *lavare*, to wash] a liquid preparation used, as on the skin, for cleansing, healing, etc.

lot·tery (lät′ər ē) *n., pl.* **-ies** [< MDu *lot*, lot] **1** a game of chance in which people buy numbered tickets on prizes, winners being chosen by lot **2** a drawing, event, etc. based on chance

lotto (lät′ō) *n.* [It < MDu: see LOT] a game resembling bingo

lo·tus (lōt′əs) *n.* [< Gr *lōtos*] **1** *Gr. Legend* a plant whose fruit induced forgetfulness **2** any of several tropical water-lilies

lotus position an erect sitting position in yoga, with the legs crossed close to the body

loud (loud) *adj.* [< OE *hlud*] **1** strongly audible: said of sound **2** sounding with great intensity **3** noisy **4** emphatic [loud *denials*] **5** [Colloq.] *a)* flashy *b)* vulgar — *adv.* in a loud manner —**loud′ly** *adv.* —**loud′ness** *n.*

loud·hailer (loud′hāl′ər) *n.* BULLHORN

loud′mouthed′ (-mouthd′, -moutht′) *adj.* talking in a loud, irritating voice

loud′speak′er *n.* a device for converting electrical signals to sound waves which are radiated into the air

lounge (lounj) *vi.* **lounged, loung′ing** [Scot dial. < ? *lungis*, a laggard] **1** to move, sit, lie, etc. in a relaxed way **2** to spend time in idleness —*n.* **1** a room with comfortable furniture for lounging **2** a couch or sofa

---

THESAURUS

lopsided *a.* uneven, unbalanced, crooked; see IRREGULAR 4.

lord *n.* **1** [A master] ruler, governor, prince; see LEADER 2. **2** [A member of the nobility] nobleman, count, titled person; see ARISTOCRAT, ROYALTY.

Lord *n.* Divinity, the Supreme Being, Jehovah; see GOD 1.

lordly *a.* grand, dignified, honorable; see NOBLE 1, 2, 3.

lore *n.* enlightenment, wisdom, learning; see KNOWLEDGE 1.

lose *v.* **1** [To bring about a loss] mislay, misfile, disturb, disorder, confuse, mix, scatter, mess, muss, disorganize, forget, be careless with. **2** [To incur loss] suffer, miss, be deprived of, fail to keep, suffer loss, be impoverished from, become poorer by, let slip through the fingers*; see also WASTE 1.—*Ant.* PROFIT, gain, improve. **3** [To fail to win] be defeated, suffer defeat, go down in defeat, succumb, fall, be the loser, miss, have the worst of it, be humbled, take defeat at the hands of, go down for the count*, be sunk*; see also FAIL 1.—*Ant.* WIN, triumph, be victorious. **4** [To suffer financially] squander, expend, dissipate; see SPEND, WASTE 2.

loser *n.* sufferer, victim, prey, failure, defeated, forfeiter, dispossessed, underdog, disadvantaged, underprivileged, fallen.—*Ant.* WINNER, gainer, conqueror.

losing *a.* **1** [Said of one who loses] failing, having the worst of it, on the way out; see RUINED 1. **2** [Said of an activity in which one must lose] futile, desperate, lost; see HOPELESS.

loss *n.* **1** [The act or fact of losing] ruin, destruction, mishap, misfortune, giving up, ill fortune, accident,

calamity, trouble, disaster, sacrifice, catastrophe, trial, failure. **2** [Damage caused by losing something] hurt, injury, wound; see DAMAGE 1, 2. **3** [The result of unprofitable activity] privation, want, bereavement, deprivation, need, destitution, being without, lack, waste, deterioration, impairment, degeneration, decline, disadvantage, wreck, wreckage, undoing, annihilation, bane, end, undoing, disorganization, breaking up, suppression, relapse.—*Ant.* ADVANTAGE, advancement, supply. — **at a loss** confused, puzzled, unsure; see UNCERTAIN.

losses *n.* casualties, damage, deaths; see DESTRUCTION 2.

lost *a.* **1** [Not to be found] misplaced, mislaid, missing, hidden, obscured, gone astray, nowhere to be found, strayed, lacking, wandered off, absent, forfeited, vanished, wandering, without, gone out of one's possession.—*Ant.* FOUND, come back, returned. **2** [Ignorant of the way] perplexed, bewildered, ignorant; see DOUBTFUL 1. **3** [Destroyed] demolished, devastated, wasted; see DESTROYED, RUINED 1. **4** [No longer to be gained] gone, passed, costly; see UNPROFITABLE. **5** [Helpless] feeble, sickly, disabled; see WEAK 1, 3. —**get lost*** go away!, leave!, begone!.

lot *n.* **1** [A small parcel of land] parcel, part, division, patch, clearing, piece of ground, plat, plot, field, tract, block, portion, parking lot, piece, property, acreage. **2** [A number of individual items, usually alike] batch, consignment, requisition; see LOAD 1. **3** [Destiny] doom, portion, fate; see CHANCE 1. **4** [*A great quantity] large amount, abundance,

plenty, considerable amount, great numbers, bundle, bunch, cluster, group, pack, large numbers, very much, very many, quite a lot, quite a bit, a good deal, a whole bunch*, loads*, oodles*; see also PLENTY.

lotion *n.* liniment, hand lotion, cream, wash, unguent; see also COSMETIC, MEDICINE 2, SALVE.

loud *a.* **1** [Having volume of sound] deafening, ringing, ear-piercing, ear-splitting, booming, intense, resounding, piercing, blaring, sonorous, resonant, crashing, deep, full, powerful, emphatic, thundering, heavy, big, deep-toned, full-tongued, roaring, enough to wake the dead; see also SHRILL.—*Ant.* SOFT, faint, feeble. **2** [Producing loud sounds] clamorous, noisy, uproarious, blatant, vociferous, turbulent, tumultuous, blustering, lusty, loud-voiced, boisterous, cacophonous, raucous; see also HARSH.—*Ant.* QUIET, soft-voiced, calm. **3** [*Lacking manners and refinement] loud-mouthed, brash, offensive; see RUDE 2, VULGAR. **4** [*Lacking good taste, especially in colors] garish, flashy, tawdry; see ORNATE.

loudly *a.* audibly, fully, powerfully, crashingly, shrilly, deafeningly, piercingly, resonantly, emphatically, vehemently, thunderingly, in full cry, clamorously, noisily, uproariously, blatantly, at the top of one's lungs.

loudspeaker *n.* speaker, amplifier, public address system, PA, high-fidelity speaker, high-frequency speaker, low-frequency speaker, tweeter, woofer, bullhorn.

lounge *v.* idle, repose, kill time; see LOAF, REST 1.

louse (lous) *n., pl.* **lice** ⟦< OE *lus*⟧ **1** a small, wingless insect parasitic on man and other animals **2** any similar insect parasitic on plants **3** [Slang] a mean, contemptible person —**louse up** [Slang] to spoil; ruin

lousy (lou′zē) *adj.* **-i·er, -i·est 1** infested with lice **2** [Slang] *a)* disgusting *b)* poor; inferior **3** well supplied (*with*) —**lous′i·ness** *n.*

lout (lout) *n.* ⟦prob. < or akin to ME *lutien*, to lurk⟧ a clumsy, stupid fellow —**lout′ish** *adj.*

lou·ver (lōō′vər) *n.* ⟦< MDu *love*, gallery⟧ **1** an opening, window, etc. fitted with a series of sloping slats arranged so as to admit light and air but shed rain **2** any of these slats

love (luv) *n.* ⟦< OE *lufu*⟧ **1** strong affection or liking for someone or something **2** a passionate affection of one person for another **3** the object of such affection; a sweetheart or lover **4** *Tennis* a score of zero — *vt., vi.* to feel love (for) —**fall in love (with)** to begin to feel love (for) —**in love** feeling love **1** to woo, embrace, etc. **2** to have sexual intercourse —**lov′able** or **love′able** *adj.* —**love′less** *adj.*

love′bird′ (-burd′) *n.* any of various small, Old World parrots often kept as cage birds

love′lorn′ *adj.* pining from love

love′ly *adj.* **-lier, -li·est 1** beautiful **2** [Colloq.] highly enjoyable —**love′li·ness** *n.*

lover (luv′ər) *n.* one who loves; specif., *a)* a sweetheart *b)* a paramour *c)* [*pl.*] a couple in love with each other *d)* a devotee, as of music

love seat a small sofa for two people

lov′ing *adj.* feeling or expressing love —**lov′ing·ly** *adv.*

loving cup a large drinking cup with two handles, often given as a prize

low¹ (lō) *adj.* ⟦< ON *lagr*⟧ **1** not high or tall **2** below the normal level *[low ground]* **3** shallow **4** less in size, degree, etc. than usual *[low speed]* **5** deep in pitch **6** depressed in spirits **7** not of high rank; humble **8** vulgar; coarse **9** poor; inferior **10** not loud — *adv.* in or to a low level, degree, etc. — *n.* **1** a low level, degree, etc. **2** an arrangement of gears giving the lowest speed and greatest power **3** *Meteorol.* an area of low barometric pressure —**lay low** to overcome or kill —**lie low** to keep oneself hidden —**low′ness** *n.*

low² (lō) *vi., n.* ⟦< OE *hlowan*⟧ MOO

low′born′ *adj.* of humble birth

low′boy′ *n.* a chest of drawers mounted on short legs

low′brow′ *n.* [Colloq.] one considered to lack cultivated tastes

low·down (lō′doun′; *for adj.,* -doun′) *n.* [Slang] the true, pertinent facts: with *the* — *adj.* [Colloq.] mean; contemptible

lower¹ (lō′ər) *adj.* ⟦compar. of LOW¹⟧ **1** below in place, rank, etc. **2** less in amount, degree, etc. — *vt.* **1** to let or put down *[lower* the window*]* **2** to reduce in height, amount, etc. **3** to bring down in respect, etc. — *vi.* to become lower

lower² (lou′ər) *vi.* ⟦ME *louren*⟧ **1** to scowl or frown **2** to appear dark and threatening, as the sky —**low′er·ing** *adj.* —**low′er·ing·ly** *adv.*

lower case (lō′ər kās′) *n.* small-letter type used in printing, as distinguished from capital letters —*adj.* of or in lowercase

low′er·class′man (-klas′mən) *n., pl.* **-men** a student in the freshman or sophomore class of a high school or college

low frequency any radio frequency between 30 and 300 kilohertz

Low German 1 the vernacular dialects of N Germany **2** the branch of Germanic languages including English, Dutch, Flemish, etc.

low′-grade′ *adj.* of low quality, degree, etc.

low′-key′ *adj.* of low intensity, tone, etc.; subdued Also **low′-keyed′**

low′land′ *n.* land below the level of the surrounding land

low′ly *adj.* **-lier, -li·est 1** of low position or rank **2** humble; meek — *adv.* humbly —**low′li·ness** *n.*

low′-mind′ed *adj.* having or showing a coarse, vulgar mind

low profile a barely noticeable presence or concealed activity

low′-spir′ited *adj.* sad; depressed

low tide the lowest level reached by the ebbing tide

lox¹ (läks) *n.* ⟦< Yidd < Ger *lachs*, salmon⟧ a kind of smoked salmon

lox² (läks) *n.* ⟦*l(iquid) ox(ygen)*⟧ liquid oxygen, esp. when used in rockets Also **LOX**

■ THESAURUS ■

lousy *a.* **1** [Having lice] infested with lice, crawling with lice, pediculous, pedicular; see also CREEPING. **2** [*Bad] horrible, disliked, unwelcome; see OFFENSIVE 2.

lovable *a.* winning, winsome, lovely; see FRIENDLY.

love *n.* **1** [Passionate and tender devotion] attachment, devotedness, passion, infatuation, yearning, flame, rapture, enchantment, ardor, emotion, sentiment, fondness, tenderness, adoration, crush*; see also AFFECTION.—*Ant.* HATE, aversion, antipathy. **2** [Affection based on esteem] respect, regard, appreciation; see ADMIRATION. **3** [A lively and enduring interest] involvement, concern, enjoyment; see DEVOTION. **4** [A beloved] dear one, loved one, cherished one; see LOVER 1. —**fall in love (with)** become enamoured, lose one's heart, take a fancy to, have eyes for, take a liking to, become attached to, become fond of, fancy. —**for the love of** for the sake of, with fond concern for, because of; see FOR. —**in love** enamored, infatuated, charmed; see LOVING. —**make love** fondle, embrace, kiss; see COPULATE, LOVE 2. —**not for love or money** under no conditions, by no means, no; see NEVER.

love *v.* **1** [To be passionately devoted] adore, be in love with, care for, hold dear, choose, fancy, be enchanted by, be passionately attached to, have affection for, dote on, glorify, idolize, prize, be fascinated by, hold high, think the world of, treasure, prefer, yearn for, be fond

of, admire, long for, flip over*, fall for*, be nuts about*, be crazy about*, go for*.—*Ant.* HATE, detest, loathe. **2** [To express love by caresses] cherish, fondle, kiss, make love to, embrace, cling to, clasp, hug, take into one's arms, hold, pet, stroke, draw close, bring to one's side; see also KISS.—*Ant.* REFUSE, exclude, spurn. **3** [To possess a deep and abiding interest] enjoy, delight in, relish; see ADMIRE, LIKE 1.

loved *a.* desired, cherished, well beloved; see BELOVED.

loveliness *n.* appeal, charm, fairness; see BEAUTY 1.

lovely *a.* **1** [Beautiful] attractive, comely, fair; see sense 2 and BEAUTIFUL, HANDSOME. **2** [Charming] engaging, enchanting, captivating; see CHARMING. **3** [*Very pleasing] nice, splendid, delightful; see PLEASANT 1, 2.

lover *n.* **1** [A suitor] sweetheart, admirer, escort, paramour, fiancé, fiancée, gentleman friend, boyfriend*, girlfriend*, steady*. **2** [A willing student or practitioner] practitioner, fan, hobbyist; see ZEALOT. **3** [An epithet for a beloved] beloved, sweetheart, dear; see DARLING.

loving *a.* admiring, respecting, valuing, liking, fond, tender, kind, enamored, attached, devoted, appreciative, attentive, thoughtful, passionate, ardent, amiable, warm, amorous, affectionate, anxious, concerned, sentimental, earnest, benevolent, cordial, caring, considerate, loyal,

generous.

lovingly *a.* tenderly, devotedly, adoringly, warmly, ardently, fervently, zealously, earnestly, loyally, generously, kindly, thoughtfully, dotingly, fondly, affectionately, passionately, longingly, rapturously, admiringly, respectfully, reverently, with love, attentively.

low¹ *a.* **1** [Close to the earth] squat, flat, level, low-lying, prostrate, crouched, below, not far above the horizon, low-hanging, knee-high, beneath, under, depressed, sunken, nether, inferior, lying under.—*Ant.* HIGH, lofty, elevated. **2** [Far down on a scale] muffled, hushed, quiet; see FAINT 3. **3** [Low in spirits] dejected, moody, blue; see SAD 1. **4** [Vulgar] base, mean, coarse; see VULGAR. **5** [Faint] ill, dizzy, feeble; see SICK, WEAK 1. **6** [Simple] economical, moderate, inexpensive; see CHEAP 1. —**lay low** bring to ruin, overcome, kill; see DESTROY. —**lie low** wait, conceal oneself, take cover; see HIDE 2.

lower¹ *a.* beneath, inferior, under; see LOW 1.

lower¹ *v.* bring low, cast down, depress; see DECREASE 1, 2, DROP 2.

lowest *a.* shortest, littlest, smallest, slightest, least, rock-bottom, ground, base; see also MINIMUM.

low-key *a.* subdued, relaxed, laid-back*; see CALM.

lowly *a.* unpretentious, cast down, meek; see HUMBLE 2.

loyal (loi′əl) *adj.* ⟦see LEGAL⟧ 1 faithful to one's country, friends, ideals, etc. 2 showing such faithfulness —**loy′ally** *adv.* —**loy′alty,** *pl.* **-ties,** *n.*

loy′al·ist *n.* one who supports the government during a revolt —**loy′al·ism′** *n.*

loz·enge (läz′ənj) *n.* ⟦< OFr *losenge*⟧ a cough drop, candy, etc., orig. diamond-shaped

LP (el′pē′) *n.* ⟦*L(ong) P(laying)*⟧ a phonograph record having microgrooves, for playing at 33⅓ revolutions per minute

LPN. or **L.P.N.** Licensed Practical Nurse

Lr *Chem.* lawrencium

LSD ⟦*l(y)s(ergic acid) d(iethylamide)*⟧ a chemical compound used in the study of mental disorders and as a psychedelic drug

Lt. Lieutenant

Ltd. or **ltd.** limited

luau (lōō′ou′) *n.* a Hawaiian feast

lub·ber (lub′ər) *n.* ⟦< ME *lobbe*-, heavy⟧ 1 a big, slow, clumsy person 2 an inexperienced, clumsy sailor

lube (lōōb) *n.* 1 a lubricating oil for machinery: also **lube oil** 2 [Colloq.] a lubrication

lu·bri·cant (lōō′bri kənt) *adj.* reducing friction by providing a smooth film over parts coming into contact — *n.* a lubricant oil, etc.

lu′bri·cate′ (-kāt′) *vt.* **-cat′ed, -cat′ing** ⟦< L *lubricus,* smooth⟧ 1 to make slippery or smooth 2 to apply a lubricant to machinery, etc. — *vi.* to serve as a lubricant —**lu′bri·ca′tion** *n.* —**lu′bri·ca′tor** *n.*

lu·cid (lōō′sid) *adj.* ⟦< L *lucere,* to shine⟧ 1 [Old Poet.] shining 2 transparent 3 sane 4 clear; readily understood —**lu·cid′i·ty** *n.* —**lu′cid·ly** *adv.*

Lu·ci·fer (lōō′sə fər) *n.* Satan

luck (luk) *n.* ⟦prob. < MDu *gelucke*⟧ 1 the seemingly chance happening of events which affect one; fortune; lot 2 good fortune —**luck out** [Colloq.] to be lucky —**luck′less** *adj.*

luck′y *adj.* **-i·er, -i·est** 1 having good luck 2 resulting fortunately 3 believed to bring good luck —**luck′i·ly** *adv.* —**luck′i·ness** *n.*

lu·cra·tive (lōō′krə tiv) *adj.* ⟦< L *lucrum,* riches⟧ producing wealth or profit; profitable

lu·cre (lōō′kər) *n.* ⟦< L *lucrum,* riches⟧ riches; money: chiefly derogatory

lu·cu·brate (lōō′kə brāt′, -kyōō-) *vi.* **-brat′ed, -brat′ing** ⟦< L *lucubrare,* to work by candlelight⟧ to work, study, or write laboriously, esp. late at night —**lu′cu·bra′tion** *n.*

lu·dic (lōō′dik) *adj.* ⟦see fol.⟧ expressive of a playful but aimless outlook ⟦the *ludic* uses of rhyme⟧

lu·di·crous (lōō′di krəs) *adj.* ⟦< L *ludus,* a game⟧ causing laughter because absurd or ridiculous —**lu′di·crously** *adv.* —**lu′di·crous·ness** *n.*

luff (luf) *vi.* ⟦ME *lof*⟧ to turn the bow of a ship toward the wind

lug (lug) *vt.* **lugged, lug′ging** ⟦prob. < Scand⟧ to carry or drag with effort — *n.* 1 an earlike projection by which a thing is held or supported 2 a heavy nut for securing a wheel to an axle

lug·gage (lug′ij) *n.* ⟦< prec.⟧ suitcases, trunks, etc.; baggage

lu·gu·bri·ous (lə gōō′brē əs) *adj.* ⟦< L *lugere,* mourn⟧ very sad or mournful, esp. in an exaggerated way —**lu·gu′bri·ously** *adv.* —**lu·gu′bri·ous·ness** *n.*

Luke (lōōk) *Bible* 1 an early Christian, the reputed author of the third Gospel 2 this book

luke·warm (lōōk′wôrm′) *adj.* ⟦< ME *luke,* tepid + *warm,* warm⟧ 1 barely warm; tepid 2 lacking enthusiasm —**luke′warm′ly** *adv.* —**luke′warm′ness** *n.*

lull (lul) *vt.* ⟦ME *lullen*⟧ 1 to calm by gentle sound or motion 2 to bring into a specified condition by soothing and reassuring — *vi.* to become calm — *n.* a short period of calm

lull′a·by′ (-ə bī′) *n., pl.* **-bies′** a song for lulling a baby to sleep

lum·bago (lum bā′gō) *n.* ⟦L < *lumbus,* loin⟧ pain in the lower back

lum·bar (lum′bər, -bär′) *adj.* ⟦< L *lumbus,* loin⟧ of or near the loins

lum·ber¹ (lum′bər) *n.* ⟦< ? pawnbrokers of *Lombardy,* Italy; hence, stored articles⟧ 1 discarded household articles, furniture, etc. 2 timber sawed into boards, etc. — *vi.* to cut down timber and saw it into lumber —**lum′berer** *n.* —**lum′ber·ing** *n.*

lum·ber² (lum′bər) *vi.* ⟦< ? Scand⟧ to move heavily and noisily —**lum′ber·ing** *adj.*

lum′ber·jack′ (-jak′) *n.* one whose work is cutting down timber and preparing it for the sawmill

lum′ber·man (-mən) *n., pl.* **-men** one who deals in lumber

lu·mi·naria (lōō′mə ner′ē ə) *n.* a lighted candle held within an open paper bag, used as an outdoor Christmas ornament

lu·mi·nary (lōō′mə ner′ē) *n., pl.* **-nar′ies** ⟦< L *lumen,* light⟧ 1 a body that gives off light, such as the sun 2 a famous or notable person

lu·mi·nes·cence (lōō′mə nes′əns) *n.* ⟦< L *lumen,* LIGHT¹ + -ESCENCE⟧ the giving off of light without heat, as in fluorescence or phosphorescence —**lu′mi·nes′cent** *adj.*

lu·mi·nous (lōō′mə nəs) *adj.* ⟦< L *lumen,* light⟧ 1 giving off light; bright 2 clear; readily understood —**lu′mi·nos′ity** (-näs′ə tē) *n.*

lum·mox (lum′əks) *n.* ⟦< ?⟧ [Colloq.] a clumsy, stupid person

lump¹ (lump) *n.* ⟦ME *lompe*⟧ 1 an indefinitely shaped mass of something 2 a swelling 3 [*pl.*] [Colloq.] hard blows, criticism, etc. — *adj.* in a lump or lumps — *vt.* 1 to put together in a lump or lumps 2 to treat or deal with in a mass — *vi.* to become lumpy —**lump′i·ness** *n.* —**lump′y, -i·er, -i·est,** *adj.*

lump² (lump) *vt.* ⟦< ?⟧ [Colloq.] to have to put up with (something disagreeable)

lump sum a gross, or total, sum paid at one time

lu·nacy (lōō′nə sē) *n.* ⟦< LUNATIC⟧ 1 insanity 2 utter folly

lu·nar (lōō′nər) *adj.* ⟦< L *luna,* the moon⟧ of or like the moon

---

THESAURUS

loyal *a.* true, dependable, firm; see FAITHFUL.

loyally *a.* faithfully, conscientiously, truly, devotedly, constantly, sincerely, obediently, resolutely, earnestly, steadfastly, in good faith.

loyalty *n.* allegiance, faithfulness, fidelity, trustworthiness, constancy, integrity, attachment, sincerity, adherence, bond, tie, honor, reliability, good faith, conscientiousness, dependability, devotedness, support, zeal, ardor, earnestness, resolution, obedience, duty, honesty, truthfulness; see also DEVOTION.—*Ant.* DISHONESTY, disloyalty, faithlessness.

lubricant *n.* cream, ointment, oil; see GREASE.

lubricate *v.* oil, daub, put grease on or in; see GREASE.

luck *n.* 1 [Good fortune] good luck, prosperity, wealth, streak of luck, windfall, advantage, profit, triumph, victory, win, happiness, blessings, opportunity, lucky break, break*, the breaks*.—*Ant.* FAILURE, ill-fortune, bad luck. 2 [Chance] unforeseen occurrence, happenstance*, fate; see ACCIDENT, CHANCE 1. —**crowd (or push) one's luck*** gamble, take risks, chance; see RISK. —**good luck** prosperity, fortune, affluence; see SUCCESS 2. —**in luck** lucky, successful, prosperous; see FORTUNATE. —**out of luck** unlucky, in misfortune, in trouble; see UNFORTUNATE. —**try one's luck** attempt, risk, endeavor; see TRY 1.

luckily *a.* opportunely, happily, favorably; see FORTUNATELY.

lucky *a.* 1 [Enjoying good luck] blessed, wealthy, victorious, happy, favored, winning, in luck, successful, prosperous; see also FORTUNATE. 2 [Supposed to bring good luck] providential, propitious, auspicious; see MAGIC.

lucrative *a.* fruitful, productive, gainful; see PROFITABLE.

ludicrous *a.* comical, odd, farcical; see FUNNY 1.

lug *v.* carry, tug, lift; see DRAW 1.

luggage *n.* trunks, bags, valises; see BAGGAGE.

lukewarm *a.* cool, tepid, room-temperature; see WARM 1.

lull *n.* quiet, stillness, calm; see SILENCE 1, PAUSE.

lull *v.* calm, quiet down, bring repose; see QUIET 1, 2.

lullaby *n.* good-night song, bedtime song, cradlesong; see SONG.

lumber¹ *n.* cut timber, logs, sawed timber, forest products, boards, hardwood, softwood, lumbering products; see also WOOD 2.

luminescence *n.* fluorescence, incandescence, radiance; see LIGHT 1.

luminous *a.* lighted, glowing, radiant; see BRIGHT 1.

lump¹ *n.* handful, protuberance, bunch, bump, hump, block, bulk, chunk, piece, portion, section; see also HUNK.

lumpy *a.* knotty, clotty, uneven; see IRREGULAR 4, THICK 1, 3.

lunacy *n.* madness, dementia, mania; see INSANITY.

lu·na·tic (lōō′nə tik) *adj.* ⟦< L *luna*, the moon⟧ 1 insane or for the insane 2 utterly foolish — *n.* an insane person

lunch (lunch) *n.* ⟦< ? Sp *lonja*, slice of ham⟧ a light meal; esp., the midday meal between breakfast and dinner — *vi.* to eat lunch

lunch·eon (lunch′ən) *n.* a lunch; esp., a formal lunch

lunch·eon·ette (lun′chən et′) *n.* a place where light lunches are served

luncheon meat meat processed in loaves, sausages, etc. and ready to eat

lung (luŋ) *n.* ⟦OE *lungen*⟧ either of the two spongelike breathing organs in the thorax of vertebrates

lunge (lunj) *n.* ⟦< Fr *allonger*, lengthen⟧ 1 a sudden thrust as with a sword 2 a sudden plunge forward — *vi., vt.* **lunged, lung′ing** to move, or cause to move, with a lunge

lung·fish (luŋ′fish′) *n., pl.* **-fish′** or (for different species) **-fish′es** any of various fishes having lungs as well as gills

lunk·head (luŋk′hed′) *n.* ⟦prob. echoic alteration of LUMP[1] + HEAD⟧ [Colloq.] a stupid person Also **lunk**

lu·pine (lōō′pin′; *for n.,* -pin) *adj.* ⟦< L *lupus*, wolf⟧ of or like a wolf — *n.* a plant with long spikes of white, rose, or blue flowers

lu·pus (lōō′pəs) *n.* ⟦< L, a wolf⟧ any of various diseases with skin lesions

lurch[1] (lurch) *vi.* ⟦< ?⟧ 1 to pitch or sway suddenly to one side 2 to stagger — *n.* a lurching movement

lurch[2] (lurch) *n.* ⟦prob. < OFr *lourche*, duped⟧ a difficult situation Only in **leave in the lurch**

lure (loor) *n.* ⟦< OFr *loirre*⟧ 1 anything that tempts or entices 2 a bait used in fishing — *vt.* **lured, lur′ing** to attract; tempt; entice

lu·rid (loor′id) *adj.* ⟦L *luridus*, ghastly⟧ 1 glowing through a haze, as flames enveloped by smoke 2 shocking; sensational —**lu′rid·ness** *n.*

lurk (lurk) *vi.* ⟦ME *lurken*⟧ 1 to stay hidden, ready to attack, etc. 2 to move furtively

lus·cious (lush′əs) *adj.* ⟦ME *lucius*⟧ 1 highly gratifying to taste or smell; delicious 2 delighting any of the senses — **lus′cious·ness** *n.*

lush[1] (lush) *adj.* ⟦< ? OFr *lasche*, lax⟧ 1 of or showing luxuriant growth 2 rich, abundant, extravagant, etc. — **lush′ness** *n.*

lush[2] (lush) *n.* [Slang] an alcoholic

lust (lust) *n.* ⟦OE, pleasure⟧ 1 bodily appetite; esp., excessive sexual desire 2 overmastering desire *[a lust for power]* — *vi.* to feel an intense desire —**lust′ful** *adj.* —**lust′fully** *adv.*

lus·ter (lus′tər) *n.* ⟦< L *lustrare*, illumine⟧ 1 gloss; sheen 2 brightness; radiance 3 brilliant beauty or fame; glory Also, chiefly Brit., **lus′tre**

lus′trous *adj.* having luster; shining

lusty (lus′tē) *adj.* **-i·er, -i·est** full of vigor; robust —**lust′i·ly** *adv.* —**lust′i·ness** *n.*

lute (lōōt′) *n.* ⟦ult. < Ar *al′ūd*, the wood⟧ an old stringed instrument like the guitar, with a rounded body

lu·tenist (lōōt′'n ist) *n.* a lute player Also **lu′ta·nist**

Lu·theran (lōō′thər ən) *adj.* of the Protestant denomination founded by Martin Luther (1483-1546), leader of the German Reformation — *n.* a member of a Lutheran Church —**Lu′ther·an·ism′** *n.*

lut·ist (lōōt′ist) *n.* 1 LUTENIST 2 a maker of lutes

luxu·ri·ant (lug zhoor′ē ənt) *adj.* ⟦see LUXURY⟧ 1 growing with vigor and in abundance 2 having rich ornamentation, etc. —**luxu′ri·ance** *n.* —**luxu′ri·antly** *adv.*

luxu·ri·ate (-āt′) *vi.* **-at·ed, -at·ing** 1 to live in great luxury 2 to revel (*in*) —**luxu′ri·a′tion** *n.*

luxu·ri·ous (-əs) *adj.* 1 fond of or indulging in luxury 2 constituting luxury; rich, comfortable, etc. —**luxu′ri·ously** *adv.*

luxu·ry (luk′shə rē, lug′zhə rē) *n., pl.* **-ries** ⟦< L *luxus*⟧ 1 the enjoyment of the best and most costly things 2 anything contributing to such enjoyment, usually something not necessary

-ly[1] (lē) ⟦< OE *-lic*⟧ *suffix* 1 like or characteristic of *[manly]* 2 happening (once) every (specified period of time) *[monthly]*

-ly[2] (lē) ⟦< OE *-lic*⟧ *suffix* 1 in a (specified) manner or direction, to a (specified) extent, in or at a (specified) time or place *[harshly, inwardly, hourly]* 2 in the (specified) order *[thirdly]*

ly·ceum (lī sē′əm) *n.* ⟦< Gr *Lykeion*, grove at Athens where Aristotle taught⟧ 1 a lecture hall 2 an organization presenting lectures, etc.

lye (lī) *n.* ⟦OE *leag*⟧ any strongly alkaline substance, used in cleaning, making soap, etc.

ly·ing[1] (lī′iŋ) *vi. prp. of* LIE[1]

ly·ing[2] (lī′iŋ) *vt., vi. prp. of* LIE[2] — *adj.* false; not truthful — *n.* the telling of a lie or lies

ly′ing-in′ (-in′) *n.* confinement in childbirth — *adj.* of or for childbirth

lymph (limf) *n.* ⟦L *lympha*, spring water⟧ a clear, yellowish body fluid resembling blood plasma, found in intercellular spaces and in the lymphatic vessels

lym·phatic (lim fat′ik) *adj.* 1 of or containing lymph 2 sluggish

lymph node any of the small, compact structures lying in groups along the course of the lymphatic vessels

lymph·oid (limf′oid′) *adj.* of or like lymph or tissue of the lymph nodes

lym·phoma (lim fō′mə) *n.* any of a group of diseases resulting from the proliferation of malignant lymphoid cells

lynch (linch) *vt.* ⟦after W. *Lynch*, vigilante in Va. in 1780⟧ to murder (an accused person) by mob action and without lawful trial, as by hanging —**lynch′ing** *n.*

lynx (liŋks) *n.* ⟦< Gr *lynx*⟧ a wildcat found throughout the Northern Hemisphere, having a short tail and tufted ears

lynx′-eyed′ (-īd′) *adj.* keen-sighted

lyon·naise (lī′ə nāz′) *adj.* ⟦Fr⟧ prepared with sliced onions

lyre (lir) *n.* ⟦< Gr *lyra*⟧ a small stringed instrument of the harp family, used by the ancient Greeks

lyric (lir′ik) *adj.* ⟦< Gr *lyrikos*⟧ 1 suitable for singing; specif., designating or of poetry expressing the poet's personal emotion 2 of or having a high voice with a light, flexible quality *[a lyric tenor]* — *n.* 1 a lyric poem 2 *[usually pl.]* the words of a song

═══ THESAURUS ═══

lunatic *a.* 1 [Insane] demented, deranged, psychotic; see INSANE. 2 [Foolish] irrational, idiotic, daft; see STUPID.

lunatic *n.* crazy person, psychotic, insane person; see MADMAN.

lunch *n.* meal, luncheon, brunch, refreshment, sandwich, snack, high tea.

lunch *v.* dine, have lunch, take a lunch break; see EAT 1.

lunge *v.* surge, lurch, bound; see JUMP 1.

lurch[1] *v.* stagger, weave, lunge; see TOTTER.

lure *n.* bait, decoy, fake; see CAMOUFLAGE, TRICK 1.

lure *v.* enchant, bewitch, allure; see CHARM, FASCINATE.

lurid *a.* 1 [Shocking] startling, ghastly, sensational; see UNUSUAL, OFFENSIVE 2. 2 [Vivid] distinct, extreme, deep; see INTENSE.

lurk *v.* wait, crouch, conceal oneself; see HIDE 2.

lurking *a.* hiding out, sneaking, hidden; see HIDDEN.

luscious *a.* sweet, toothsome, palatable; see DELICIOUS.

lush[1] *a.* 1 [Green] verdant, dense, grassy; see GREEN 2. 2 [Delicious] rich, juicy, succulent; see DELICIOUS. 3 [Elaborate] extensive, luxurious, ornamental; see ELABORATE 1, ORNATE.

lust *n.* appetite, passion, sensuality; see DESIRE 2.

lust (after) *v.* long for, desire, hunger for; see WANT 1.

luster *n.* glow, brilliance, radiance; see LIGHT 1.

lustrous *a.* shiny, radiant, glowing; see BRIGHT 1.

lusty *a.* hearty, robust, vigorous; see HEALTHY.

luxuriant *a.* lush, dense, rank; see GREEN 2.

luxurious *a.* comfortable, easy, affluent; see EXPENSIVE, RICH 2.

luxury *n.* 1 [Indulgence of the senses, regardless of the cost] gratification, costliness, expensiveness, richness, idleness, leisure, high-living, lavishness; see also INDULGENCE 1.—*Ant.* POVERTY, poorness, lack. 2 [An indulgence beyond one's means] extravagance, exorbitance, wastefulness; see EXCESS 1, WASTE 1.

lying[1,2] *a.* 1 [In the act of lying] falsifying, prevaricating, swearing falsely, committing perjury, fibbing, misrepresenting, inventing.—*Ant.* FRANK, truthful, veracious. 2 [Given to lying] deceitful, unreliable, doubledealing; see DISHONEST. 3 [Not reliable] unsound, tricky, treacherous; see FALSE 2. 4 [Prostrate] supine, reclining, resting, horizontal, reposing, recumbent, flat, fallen, prone, powerless.

lynch *v.* hang, string up*, murder; see KILL 1.

lyric *n.* 1 [Verses set to music] the words, the lyrics, the verse; see POEM. 2 [A short, songlike poem] lyrical poem, ode, sonnet, hymn, roundel; see also POETRY, SONG, VERSE 1.

lyr′i·cal (-i kəl) *adj.* 1 LYRIC 2 expressing rapture or great enthusiasm

lyr′i·cism′ (-ə siz′əm) *n.* 1 lyric quality or style 2 emotional and poetic expression

lyr′i·cist (-ə sist) *n.* a writer of lyrics, esp. lyrics for popular songs

lyser·gic acid (li sur′jik) *see* LSD

-lysis (lə sis, li-) ⟦ < Gr *lysis*, a loosening⟧ *combining form* a loosening, dissolution, dissolving, destruction [*catalysis, electrolysis*]

-lyte (lit) ⟦ < Gr *lyein*, dissolve⟧ *combining form* a substance undergoing decomposition [*electrolyte*]

M

m or **M** (em) *n.*, *pl.* **m's, M's** the 13th letter of the English alphabet

M (em) *n.* a Roman numeral for 1,000

m meter(s)

m or **m.** 1 married 2 masculine 3 medium 4 mile(s) 5 minute(s)

M or **M.** 1 male 2 married 3 medium 4 Monday 5 Monsieur 6 month

ma (mä) *n.* [Colloq.] mother

MA [L *Magister Artium*] Master of Arts Also **M.A.**

ma'am (mam, mäm, məm) *n.* [Colloq.] madam: used in direct address

ma·ca·bre (mə käb′rə, mə käb′) *adj.* [< OFr (*danse*) *Macabré*, (dance) of death] grim and horrible; gruesome

mac·adam (mə kad′əm) *n.* [after J. L. *McAdam* (1756-1836), Scot engineer] small broken stones, or a road made by rolling successive layers of these, often with tar or asphalt

maca·roni (mak′ə rō′nē) *n.* [It *maccaroni*, ult. < Gr *makar*, blessed] pasta in the form of tubes, etc.

maca·roon (mak′ə rōōn′) *n.* [see prec.] a small, chewy cookie made with crushed almonds or coconut

ma·caw (mə kô′) *n.* [prob. < AmInd (Brazil)] a large, bright-colored parrot of Central and South America

Mac·beth (mək beth′) the title character of a tragedy by Shakespeare

Mac·ca·bees (mak′ə bēz′) a family of Jewish patriots who headed a successful revolt against the Syrians (175-164 B.C.)

mace[1] (mās) *n.* [OFr *masse*] 1 a heavy, spiked war club, used in the Middle Ages 2 a staff used as a symbol of authority by certain officials

mace[2] (mās) *n.* [< ML *macis*] a spice made from the husk of the nutmeg

Mace (mās) [< MACE[1]] *trademark for* a gas, sold in aerosol containers, that temporarily stuns its victims — *n.* [often **m-**] such a substance, or a container of it — *vt.* **Maced, Mac′ing** [often **m-**] to spray with Mace

mac·er·ate (mas′ər āt′) *vt.* **-at′ed, -at′ing** [< L *macerare*, soften] 1 to soften and separate into parts by soaking in liquid 2 to steep (fruit or vegetables), as in wine 3 loosely, to tear, chop, etc. into bits —**mac′era′tion** *n.*

ma·chete (mə shet′ē, -chet′ē) *n.* [Sp < L *marcus*, hammer] a large knife used for cutting sugar cane, underbrush, etc., esp. in Central and South America

Machia·vel·lian (mak′ē ə vel′ē ən) *adj.* [after N. *Machiavelli* (1469-1527), It statesman] crafty; deceitful

mach·i·na·tion (mak′ə nā′shən) *n.* [< L *machinari*, to plot] a plot or scheme, esp. one with evil intent

ma·chine (mə shēn′) *n.* [< Gr *mēchos*, contrivance] 1 [Old-fashioned] a vehicle, as an automobile 2 a structure consisting of a framework with various moving parts, for doing some kind of work 3 an organization functioning like a machine 4 the controlling group in a political party 5 *Mech.* a device, as the lever, that transmits, or changes the application of, energy — *adj.* 1 of machines 2 done by machinery — *vt.* **-chined′, -chin′ing** to shape, etc. by machinery

machine gun an automatic gun, firing a rapid stream of bullets

machine language a language entirely in binary digits, used directly by a computer

ma·chin·ery (mə shēn′ər ē, -shēn′rē) *n.*, *pl.* **-ies** 1 machines collectively 2 the working parts of a machine 3 the means for keeping something going

ma·chin·ist *n.* one who makes, repairs, or operates machinery

ma·chismo (mä chēz′mō) *n.* [Sp < *macho*, masculine + *-ismo*, -ISM] overly assertive or exaggerated masculinity

Mach number (mäk) [after E. *Mach* (1838-1916), Austrian physicist] [*also* **m- n-**] a number indicating the ratio of an object's speed to the speed of sound in the surrounding medium

ma·cho (mä′chō) *adj.* [Sp, masculine] exhibiting or characterized by machismo

mack·erel (mak′ər əl) *n.*, *pl.* **-el** or **-els** [< OFr *maquerel*] an edible fish of the North Atlantic

Macki·naw (coat) (mak′ə nô′) [after *Mackinac* Island in N Lake Huron] [*also* **m-**] a short, heavy, double-breasted woolen coat, usually plaid

mack·in·tosh (mak′in täsh′) *n.* [after C. *Macintosh*, 19th-c. Scot inventor] a raincoat of rubberized cloth

mac·ramé (mak′rə mā′) *n.* [Fr, ult. < Ar *miqramah*, a veil] coarse lace made as of cord knotted in designs

macro- [< Gr *makros*, long] *combining form* long, large, enlarged

macro·bi·ot·ics (mak′rō bī ät′iks) *n.pl.* [< prec. + Gr *bios*, life] [*with sing. v.*] the study of prolonging life, as by special diets —**mac′ro·bi·ot′ic** *adj.*

mac′ro·cosm′ (-käz′əm) *n.* [see MACRO- & COSMOS] 1 the universe 2 any large, complex entity —**mac′ro·cos′mic** *adj.*

ma·cron (mā′krən) *n.* [< Gr *makros*, long] a mark (-) placed over a vowel to indicate its pronunciation

mad (mad) *adj.* **mad′der, mad′dest** [< OE (*ge*)*mædan*, make mad] 1 mentally ill; insane 2 frantic [*mad* with fear] 3 foolish and rash 4 infatuated [he's *mad* about her] 5 wildly amusing 6 having rabies [a *mad* dog] 7 angry — *n.* an angry mood —**mad′ly** *adv.* —**mad′ness** *n.*

madam (mad′əm) *n.*, *pl.* **mes·dames** (mā däm′, -dam′); for 1, usually **mes·dames** (mā däm′, -dam′) [Fr *madame*, orig. *ma dame*, my lady] 1 a woman; lady: a polite term of address 2 a woman in charge of a brothel

ma·dame (mə dam′, -däm′; mad′əm; Fr mä däm′) *n.*, *pl.* **mes·dames** (mā′dam′, -däm′; Fr mā däm′) [Fr: see prec.] 1 a married woman: equivalent to *Mrs.* 2 a distinguished woman: a title of respect

mad·cap (mad′kap′) *n.* [MAD + CAP, figurative for head] a reckless, impulsive person — *adj.* reckless and impulsive

mad·den (mad′n) *vt., vi.* to make or become insane, angry, or wildly excited —**mad′den·ing** *adj.*

mad·der (mad′ər) *n.* [OE *mædere*] 1 any of various related plants, esp. a vine with yellow flowers and a red root 2 a red dye made from this root

made (mād) *vt., vi. pt. & pp.* of MAKE

ma·demoi·selle (mad′ə mə zel′; Fr mäd mwä zel′) *n.*, *pl.* **Fr. mes·demoi·selles** (mād mwä zel′) [Fr < *ma*, my + *demoiselle*, young lady] an unmarried woman or girl: equivalent to *Miss*

made′-to-or′der *adj.* made to conform to the customer's specifications

made′-up′ *adj.* 1 put together 2 invented; false [a *made-up* story] 3 with cosmetics applied

mad′house′ *n.* 1 an insane asylum 2 any place of turmoil, noise, etc.

mad′man′ *n.*, *pl.* **-men′** an insane person; lunatic —**mad′wom′an**, *pl.* **-wom′en**, *n.fem.*

Ma·donna (mə dän′ə) [It < *ma*, my + *donna*, lady] Mary, mother of Jesus — *n.* a picture or statue of Mary

ma·dras (ma′drəs; mə dras′, -dräs′) *n.* [after *Madras*, city in SE India] a fine, firm cotton cloth, usually striped or plaid

---

THESAURUS

ma* *n.* mama*, mommy*, mom*; see MOTHER 1.

machine *n.* instrument, appliance, vehicle, implement, gadget; see also DEVICE 1, ENGINE, MOTOR, TOOL 1.

machine gun *n.* automatic rifle, semiautomatic rifle, automatic arms, light ordnance, Tommy gun*, burp gun*, Gatling gun; see also GUN, WEAPON.

machinery *n.* appliances, implements, tools; see APPLIANCE, DEVICE 1, ENGINE, MACHINE, MOTOR.

mad *a.* 1 [Insane] demented, deranged, psychotic; see INSANE. 2 [Angry] provoked, enraged, exasper-ated; see ANGRY. 3 [Afflicted with rabies] frenzied, raging, foaming at the mouth; see SICK. —**get mad** lose one's temper, become angry, rant and rave; see GET ANGRY.

madden *v.* craze, infuriate, enrage; see ANGER.

maddening *a.* annoying, infuriating, offensive; see DISTURBING.

made *a.* fashioned, shaped, finished; see BUILT, FORMED, MANUFACTURED. —**have (or have got) it made*** succeed, be assured, be prosperous; see SUCCEED 1.

made-up *a.* 1 [False] invented, concocted, devised, fabricated, exagger-ated, prepared, fictitious; see also FALSE 2, 3, UNREAL. 2 [Marked by the use of make-up] rouged, powdered, painted, colored, freshened, reddened, cosmeticized.

madhouse *n.* mental hospital, asylum, bedlam; see HOSPITAL.

madly *a.* rashly, crazily, hastily; see VIOLENTLY, WILDLY.

madman *n.* lunatic, psychopath, maniac, raver, insane person, deranged person, psychiatric patient, nut*, screwball*, oddball*, psycho*, wacko*, schizo*, cuckoo*.

madness *n.* derangement, aberration, delusion; see INSANITY.

mad·ri·gal (ma′dri gəl) *n.* 〚< It〛 a part song, without accompaniment, popular in the 15th to 17th c.

mael·strom (māl′strəm) *n.* 〚< Du *malen*, to grind + *stroom*, a stream〛 **1** a large or violent whirlpool **2** an agitated state of mind, affairs, etc.

maes·tro (mis′trō, mä es′trō′) *n., pl.* **-tros** or **-tri** (-trē) 〚It < L *magister*, master〛 a master in any art; esp., a great composer or conductor of music

Ma·fia (mä′fē ə) *n.* 〚It *maffia*〛 a secret society engaged in illegal activities —**Ma·fio·so** (mä′fē ō′sō′), *pl.* **-si** (-sē), *n.*

maga·zine (mag′ə zēn′) *n.* 〚< Ar *makhzan*, storehouse〛 **1** a warehouse or military supply depot **2** a space in which explosives are stored, as in a fort **3** a supply chamber, as in a rifle, camera, etc. **4** a periodical publication containing stories, articles, etc.

ma·genta (mə jen′tə) *n.* 〚after *Magenta*, town in Italy〛 **1** a purplish-red dye **2** purplish red — *adj.* purplish-red

mag·got (mag′ət) *n.* 〚ME *magotte*〛 a wormlike insect larva, as of the housefly —**mag′goty** *adj.*

Magi (mā′jī′) *n.pl., sing.* **-gus** (-gəs) 〚< old Pers *magus*, magician〛 the wise men who came bearing gifts to the infant Jesus

magic (maj′ik) *n.* 〚< Gr *magikos*, of the Magi〛 **1** the use of charms, spells, etc. in seeking or pretending to control events **2** any mysterious power *[the magic of love]* **3** the art of producing illusions by sleight of hand, etc. — *adj.* **1** of, produced by, or using magic **2** producing extraordinary results, as if by magic —**mag′i·cal** *adj.* —**mag′i·cally** *adv.*

ma·gi·cian (mə jish′ən) *n.* 〚< OFr *magicien*〛 an expert in magic

mag·is·te·rial (maj′is tir′ē əl) *adj.* **1** of or suitable for a magistrate **2** authoritative —**mag′is·te′ri·ally** *adv.*

mag·is·trate (maj′is trāt′) *n.* 〚< L *magister*, master〛 **1** a civil officer empowered to administer the law **2** a minor official, as a justice of the peace

magma (mag′mə) *n.* 〚< Gr *massein*, knead〛 liquid or molten rock in the earth, which solidifies to produce igneous rock

Magna Carta or **Magna Charta** (mag′nə kär′tə) 〚ML, great charter〛 the charter, granted in 1215, that guarantees certain civil and political liberties to the English people

mag·nani·mous (mag nan′ə məs) *adj.* 〚< L *magnus*, great + *animus*, soul〛 generous in overlooking injury or insult; rising above pettiness; noble —**mag′na·nim′i·ty** (-nə nim′ə tē) *n.* —**mag·nan′i·mously** *adv.*

mag·nate (mag′nāt) *n.* 〚< L *magnus*, great〛 a very influential person, esp. in business

mag·ne·sia (mag nē′zhə, -shə) *n.* 〚ModL, ult. < Gr *Magnēsia*, ancient Gr city〛 magnesium oxide, a white powder, used as a mild laxative and antacid

mag·ne′sium (-zē əm, -zhē-) *n.* 〚ModL: see prec.〛 a light metallic chemical element

mag·net (mag′nit) *n.* 〚see MAGNESIA〛 **1** any piece of iron or certain other materials that has the property of attracting similar material **2** one that attracts

mag·netic (mag net′ik) *adj.* **1** having the properties of a magnet **2** of, producing, or caused by magnetism **3** of the earth's magnetism **4** that can be magnetized **5** powerfully attractive —**mag·net′i·cally** *adv.*

magnetic field a physical field arising from an electric

charge in motion, producing a force on a moving electric charge

magnetic tape a thin plastic ribbon with a magnetized coating for recording sounds, digital computer data, etc.

mag·net·ism (mag′nə tiz′əm) *n.* **1** the property, quality, or condition of being magnetic **2** the force to which this is due **3** personal charm

mag′net·ite′ (-tīt′) *n.* 〚< Ger〛 black iron oxide, an important iron ore

mag′net·ize′ (-tīz′) *vt.* **-ized′, -iz′ing 1** to give magnetic properties to (steel, iron, etc.) **2** to charm (a person) — **mag′neti·za′tion** *n.*

mag·neto (mag nēt′ō) *n., pl.* **-tos** a small generator in which one or more permanent magnets produce the magnetic field

mag·ne·tom·eter (mag′nə täm′ət ər) *n.* **1** an instrument for measuring magnetic forces **2** such an instrument used as to detect concealed metal weapons at airports, etc.

magnet school a public school offering new and special courses to attract students from a broad urban area so as to bring about desegregation

mag·nifi·cent (mag nif′ə sənt) *adj.* 〚< L *magnus*, great + *facere*, do〛 **1** splendid, stately, or sumptuous, as in form **2** exalted: said of ideas, etc. **3** [Colloq.] excellent —**mag·nif′i·cence** *n.* —**mag·nif′i·cently** *adv.*

mag·nify (mag′nə fī′) *vt.* **-fied′, -fy′ing** [see prec.] **1** to exaggerate **2** to increase the apparent size of, esp. with a lens **3** [Archaic] to praise — *vi.* to have the power of increasing the apparent size of an object —**mag′ni·fi·ca′tion** *n.* —**mag′ni·fi′er** *n.*

mag′ni·tude′ (-tōōd′, -tyōōd′) *n.* 〚< L *magnus*, great〛 **1** greatness of size, extent, etc. **2** *a*) size *b*) loudness (of sound) *c*) importance **3** the degree of brightness of a star, etc.

mag·no·lia (mag nō′lē ə, -nōl′yə) *n.* 〚after P. *Magnol* (1638-1715), Fr botanist〛 a tree with large, fragrant flowers of white, pink, or purple

mag·num (mag′nəm) *n.* 〚< L *magnus*, great〛 **1** a wine bottle holding 1.5 liters **2** [*usually* M-] a firearm, esp. a revolver, that fires magnum cartridges — *adj.* of or pertaining to a cartridge having great explosive force for its size

mag·num opus (mag′nəm ō′pəs) 〚L〛 a great work; masterpiece

mag·pie (mag′pī′) *n.* 〚< *Mag*, dim. of *Margaret* + *pie*, magpie〛 **1** a noisy, black-and-white bird related to the jay **2** a person who chatters

mag (wheel) a shiny, lightweight motor vehicle wheel with a pattern of holes or spokes around the hub

Mag·yar (mag′yär′) *n.* **1** the Hungarian language **2** a member of the main ethnic group in Hungary

maha·ra·jah or **maha·raja** (mä′hə rä′jə) *n.* 〚< Sans *mahā*, great + *rājā*, king〛 [Historical] in India, a prince, specif. the ruler of a native state —**ma′ha·ra′ni** or **ma′ha·ra′nee** (-nē) *n.fem.*

maha·ri·shi (mä′hä rish′ē) *n.* 〚Hindi < *mahā*, great + *ṛshi*, sage〛 a Hindu teacher of mysticism

ma·hatma (mə hat′mə, -hät′-) *n.* 〚< Sans *mahā*, great + *ātman*, soul〛 *Buddhism* any of a class of wise and holy persons held in special regard

---

THESAURUS

magazine *n.* publication, broadside, pamphlet, booklet, manual, circular, journal, periodical, weekly, monthly, quarterly, annual, bulletin, transactions, review, supplement, gazette, report, brochure, pulp, glossy*, slick*.

maggot *n.* grub, slug, larva; see PARASITE 1, WORM.

magic *a.* magical, mystic, diabolic, Satanic, necromantic, fiendish, demoniac, malevolent, shamanist, voodooistic, conjuring, spellbinding, enchanting, fascinating, cryptic, transcendental, supernatural, alchemistic, spooky, ghostly, haunted, weird, uncanny, eerie, disembodied, immaterial, astral, spiritualistic, psychic, supersensory, otherworldly, fairylike, mythical, mythic, charmed, enchanted, bewitched, entranced, spellbound, under a spell, cursed, prophetic, telepathic, clairvoyant, telekinetic, parapsychological; see also MYSTERIOUS 2.

magic *n.* **1** [The controlling of supernatural powers] occultism, legerdemain, necromancy, incantation, spell, wizardry, alchemy, superstition, enchantment, sorcery, prophecy, divination, astrology, taboo, witchcraft, black magic, voodooism, fire worship; see also WITCHCRAFT. **2** [An example of magic] incantation, prediction, soothsaying, fortunetelling, foreboding, exorcism, ghost dance.

magical *a.* occult, enchanting, mystic; see MAGIC, MYSTERIOUS 2.

magician *n.* enchanter, necromancer, conjurer, seer, soothsayer, diviner, sorcerer, wizard, warlock, medicine man, shaman, exorcist; see also PROPHET, WITCH.

magnet *n.* lodestone, magnetite, magnetic iron ore, natural magnet, artificial magnet, bar magnet, electromagnet, horseshoe magnet.

magnetic *a.* irresistible, captivating, fascinating; see CHARMING.

magnetism *n.* lure, influence, charm; see ATTRACTION.

magnificence *n.* grandeur, majesty, stateliness, nobleness, glory, radiance, grace, beauty, style, flourish, luxuriousness, glitter, nobility, greatness, lavishness, brilliance, splendor, richness, pomp, swank*; see also GRANDEUR.—*Ant.* DULLNESS, simplicity, unostentatiousness.

magnificent *a.* exalted, great, majestic; see GRAND.

magnify *v.* amplify, blow up, expand; see INCREASE.

magnitude *n.* **1** [Size] extent, breadth, dimension; see MEASURE 1, MEASUREMENT 2, QUANTITY, SIZE. **2** [Importance] greatness, consequence, significance; see DEGREE 2, IMPORTANCE.

mah-jongg or **mah·jong** (mä′jôŋ′) *n.* ⟦< Chin *ma-ch'iao*, sparrow, a figure on one of the tiles⟧ a game of Chinese origin played with small pieces called *tiles*

ma·hoga·ny (mə häg′ə nē, -hôg′-) *n., pl.* **-nies** ⟦< ?⟧ 1 *a)* a tropical American tree *b)* the reddish-brown wood of this tree 2 reddish brown

ma·hout (mə hout′) *n.* ⟦< Hindi⟧ in India, an elephant driver or keeper

maid (mād) *n.* 1 MAIDEN 2 a girl or woman servant

maid′en (-'n) *n.* ⟦OE *mægden*⟧ [Now Rare] a girl or young unmarried woman 3 untried 4 first *[a maiden voyage]* —**maid′en·hood′** *n.* —**maid′enly** *adj.*

maid′en·hair′ *n.* a delicate fern

maid′en·head′ (-hed′) *n.* the hymen

maiden name the surname that a married woman had when not yet married

maid of honor an unmarried woman acting as chief attendant to a bride

maid′ser′vant *n.* a female servant

mail¹ (māl) *n.* ⟦< OHG *malaha*, wallet⟧ 1 letters, packages, etc. transported and delivered by the post office 2 a postal system — *adj.* of mail — *vt.* to send by mail — **mail′er** *n.*

mail² (māl) *n.* ⟦< L *macula*, mesh of a net⟧ flexible body armor made of small metal rings, scales, etc. —**mailed** *adj.*

mail′box′ *n.* 1 a box into which mail is delivered 2 a box for depositing outgoing mail Also **mail box**

mail′man′ *n., pl.* **-men′** a man who carries and delivers mail

mail order an order for goods to be sent by mail —**mail′-or′der** *adj.*

maim (mām) *vt.* ⟦OFr *mahaigner*⟧ to cripple; mutilate

main (mān) *n.* ⟦OE *mægen*, strength⟧ 1 a principal pipe in a distributing system for water, gas, etc. 2 [Old Poet.] the ocean — *adj.* chief in size, importance, etc.; principal —**by main force** (or **strength**) by sheer force (or strength) —**in the main** mostly; chiefly —**with might and main** with all one's strength

main clause *Gram.* INDEPENDENT CLAUSE

main drag [Slang] the principal street of a city or town

main·frame (mān′frām′) *n.* 1 the central processing unit of a large computer 2 a very large computer, to which several terminals may be connected

main′land′ (-land′, -lənd) *n.* the principal land mass of a continent, as distinguished from nearby islands

main′line′ *n.* the principal road, course, etc. — *vt.* **-lined′, -lin′ing** [Slang] to inject (a narcotic drug) directly into a large vein

main′ly *adv.* chiefly; principally

main′mast′ (-mast′, -məst) *n.* the principal mast of a vessel

main′sail′ (-sāl′, -səl) *n.* the principal sail of a vessel, set from the mainmast

main′spring′ *n.* 1 the principal spring in a clock, watch, etc. 2 the chief motive or cause

main′stay (-stā′) *n.* 1 the supporting line extending forward from the mainmast 2 a chief support

main′stream′ (-strēm′) *n.* a major trend or line of thought, action, etc. — *vt.* to cause to undergo mainstreaming

main′stream′ing *n.* the placement of disabled people into regular school classes, work places, etc.

main·tain (mān tān′) *vt.* ⟦< L *manu tenere*, hold in the hand⟧ 1 to keep or keep up; carry on 2 to keep in continuance or in a certain state, as of repair 3 to defend 4 to affirm or assert 5 to support by providing what is needed —**main·tain′able** *adj.*

main·te·nance (mān′tə nəns) *n.* a maintaining or being maintained

mai tai (mī′ tī′) ⟦Tahitian, lit., good⟧ *[often* M- T-] a cocktail of rum, fruit juices, etc.

maî·tre d'hô·tel (me tr′ dô tel′) ⟦Fr, master of the house⟧ a supervisor of waiters and waitresses Also [Colloq.] **maî·tre d'** (māt′ər dē′)

maize (māz) *n.* ⟦< WInd *mahiz*⟧ 1 *chiefly Brit. name for* CORN¹ (*n.* 2) 2 yellow

Maj. Major

ma·jes·tic (mə jes′tik) *adj.* grand; stately —**ma·jes′ti·cally** *adv.*

maj·esty (maj′is tē) *n., pl.* **-ties** ⟦< L *magnus*, great⟧ 1 [M-] a title used in speaking to or of a sovereign 2 grandeur

ma·joli·ca (mə jäl′i kə) *n.* ⟦It⟧ Italian glazed pottery

ma·jor (mā′jər) *n.* ⟦L, compar. of *magnus*, great⟧ 1 greater in size, amount, importance, etc. 2 *Music* designating an interval greater than the corresponding minor by a half tone — *vi. Educ.* to specialize (*in* a field of study) —*n.* 1 *U.S. Mil.* an officer ranking just above a captain 2 *Educ.* a principal field of study

ma′jor-do′mo (-dō′mō) *n., pl.* **-mos** ⟦< L *major*, greater + *domus*, house⟧ a man in charge of a great household

major general *pl.* **major generals** *U.S. Mil.* an officer ranking just above a brigadier general

ma·jor·ity (mə jôr′ə tē) *n., pl.* **-ties** ⟦see MAJOR⟧ 1 the greater number; more than half of a total 2 the number by which the votes cast for the candidate who receives more than half the votes, exceed the sum of all the other votes cast 3 full legal age 4 the military rank of a major

major scale a musical scale with half steps between the third and fourth and the seventh and eighth tones, and whole steps in all other positions

make (māk) *vt.* **made, mak′ing** ⟦OE *macian*⟧ 1 to bring into being; build, create, produce, etc. 2 to cause to be or

---

■ THESAURUS ■

maid *n.* 1 [A female servant] maidservant, nursemaid, housemaid, chambermaid, barmaid; see also SERVANT. 2 [A girl] child, maiden, kid*; see GIRL, WOMAN 1.

maiden *a.* earliest, beginning, virgin; see FIRST.

maiden name *n.* family name, inherited name, surname; see NAME 1.

mail¹ *n.* letter, post, communication, correspondence, airmail letters, postal*, junk mail, postcard, printed matter; see also LETTER 2.

mail¹ *v.* post, send by mail, drop into a mailbox; see SEND 1.

mailed *a.* posted, sent by post, transmitted by post, in the mail, shipped, consigned, dispatched, sent by mail, dropped in a mailbox; see also SENT.

maim *v.* mutilate, disable, disfigure; see DAMAGE, HURT.

main *a.* 1 [Principal] chief, dominant, first, authoritative, significant, most important, superior, foremost, leading; see also MAJOR 1. 2 [Only] utter, pure, simple; see ABSOLUTE.

mainland *n.* shore, beach, dry land; see LAND 1, REGION 1.

mainly *a.* chiefly, largely, essentially; see PRINCIPALLY.

maintain *v.* 1 [To uphold] hold up, advance, keep; see SUPPORT 2, SUS-

TAIN 1. 2 [To assert] state, affirm, attest; see DECLARE, REPORT 1, SAY. 3 [To keep ready for use] preserve, keep, conserve, repair, withhold, renew, reserve, defer, hold back, have in store, care for, save, put away, set aside, store up, keep for, lay aside, lay away, set by, keep on hand, keep in reserve, set apart, keep up, keep aside, control, hold over, manage, direct, have, own, sustain, secure, stick to, stand by; see also KEEP 1.— *Ant.* WASTE, neglect, consume. 4 [To continue] carry on, persevere, keep on; see CONTINUE 1. 5 [To support] provide for, take care of, keep; see SUPPORT 3, SUSTAIN 3.

maintenance *n.* sustenance, livelihood, resources; see PAY 1, 2, SUBSISTENCE 2.

majestic *a.* dignified, sumptuous, exalted; see GRAND, NOBLE 1, 3.

majesty *n.* 1 [Grandeur] nobility, illustriousness, greatness; see GRANDEUR. 2 [A form of address; *usually capital*] Lord, King, Emperor, Prince, Royal Highness, Highness, Sire, Eminence, Queen.

major *a.* 1 [Greater] higher, larger, dominant, primary, upper, exceeding, extreme, ultra, over, above; see also SUPERIOR. 2 [Important] significant, main, influential; see IMPOR-

TANT 1, PRINCIPAL.

majority *n.* 1 [The larger part] more than half, preponderance, most, best, gross, lion's share*, greater number. 2 [Legal maturity] legal age, adulthood, voting age; see MANHOOD 1.

make *v.* 1 [To manufacture] construct, fabricate, assemble, fashion, compose, compile, create, effect, produce; see also BUILD, MANUFACTURE. 2 [To total] add up to, come to, equal; see AMOUNT TO. 3 [To create] originate, actualize, effect, generate, compose, plan, devise, construct, cause, conceive; see also COMPOSE 2, CREATE , INVENT 1, PRODUCE 2. 4 [To acquire] gain, get, secure; see GET 1. 5 [To force] constrain, compel, coerce; see FORCE. 6 [To cause] start, effect, initiate; see BEGIN 1, CAUSE. 7 [To wage] carry on, conduct, engage in; see ACT 2. 8 [To prepare] get ready, arrange, adjust; see COOK, PREPARE 1. —**make believe** feign, simulate, counterfeit; see DREAM 2, PRETEND 1, 2. —**make do** employ, suffice, accept; see ENDURE 2, SURVIVE 1, USE 1. —**make it*** achieve, triumph, accomplish; see SUCCEED 1. —**make off with** abduct, rob, kidnap; see STEAL. —**make out** 1 [To understand] perceive, recognize, see;

become [made king, made sad] **3** to prepare for use [make the beds] **4** to amount to [two pints make a quart] **5** to have the qualities of [to make a fine leader] **6** to acquire; earn **7** to cause the success of [that venture made her] **8** to understand [what do you make of that?] **9** to execute, do, etc. [to make a speech] **10** to cause or force: with an infinitive without to [make him go] **11** to arrive at; reach [the ship made port] **12** [Colloq.] to get on or in [to make the team] —**vi. 1** to start (to do something) **2** to behave as specified [make bold] **3** to cause something to be as specified [make ready] —**n. 1** the way in which something is made; style **2** type; brand —**make away with 1** to steal **2** to kill —**make believe** to pretend —**make one's day** [Slang] to give pleasure that will be the high point of one's day —**make do** to manage with what is available —**make for 1** to go toward **2** to help effect —**make it** [Colloq.] to achieve a certain thing —**make off with** to steal —**make out 1** to see with difficulty **2** to understand **3** to fill out (a blank form, etc.) **4** to (try to) show or prove to be **5** to succeed; get along **6** [Slang] *a*) to kiss and caress as lovers *b*) to have sexual intercourse —**make over 1** to change; renovate **2** to transfer the ownership of —**make up 1** to put together **2** to form; constitute **3** to invent **4** to complete by providing what is lacking **5** to compensate (*for*) **6** to become friendly again after a quarrel **7** to put on cosmetics, etc. **8** to decide (one's mind) —**make up to** to try to win over, as by flattering —**mak′er** *n.*

make′-believe′ *n.* pretense; feigning —*adj.* pretended; feigned

make′shift′ *n.* a temporary substitute or expedient —*adj.* that will do as a temporary substitute

make′up′ or **make′-up′** *n.* **1** the way something is put together; composition **2** nature; disposition **3** the cosmetics, etc. used by an actor **4** cosmetics generally

make′-work′ *adj.* that serves no other purpose than to give an idle or unemployed person something to do [a *make-work* project]

mak′ing *n.* the act of one that makes or the process of being made

mal- [< L *malus*, bad] *prefix* bad or badly, wrong, ill

mal·ad·just·ed (mal′ə jus′tid) *adj.* poorly adjusted; esp., unable to adapt oneself psychologically to one's environment or circumstances —**mal′ad·just′ment** *n.*

mal·adroit (mal′ə droit′) *adj.* [Fr: see MAL- & ADROIT] awkward; clumsy; bungling —**mal′adroit′ly** *adv.*

mala·dy (mal′ə dē) *n., pl.* **-dies** [< VL *male habitus*, badly kept] a disease; illness

ma·laise (ma lāz′) *n.* [Fr < *mal*, bad + *aise*, ease] a vague feeling of physical discomfort or of uneasiness

mala·mute (mal′ə myo͞ot′) *n.* [< *Malemute*, an Eskimo tribe] a strong dog developed as a sled dog by Eskimos

mala·prop·ism (mal′ə präp′iz′əm) *n.* [after Mrs. *Malaprop* in Sheridan's *The Rivals* (1775)] a ludicrous misuse of words that sound alike

ma·laria (mə ler′ē ə) *n.* [It < *mala aria*, bad air] an infectious disease transmitted by the anopheles mosquito, characterized by severe chills and fever —**ma·lar′ial** *adj.*

ma·lar·key or **ma·larky** (mə lär′kē) *n.* [< ?] [Slang] nonsensical talk

mala·thion (mal′ə thī′än′) *n.* [< chemical names] an organic insecticide

Ma·lay (mā′lā′, mə lā′) *n.* **1** the language of a large group of indigenous peoples of the Malay Peninsula and the

Malay Archipelago, now the official language of Malaysia and Indonesia **2** a member of any of these peoples —*adj.* of these peoples, their language, etc. Also **Ma′lay′an**

Mala·ya·lam (mal′ə yä′ləm) *n.* a language of the SW coast of India

mal·con·tent (mal′kən tent′) *adj.* [OFr: see MAL- & CONTENT¹] dissatisfied; rebellious —*n.* a malcontent person

male (māl) *adj.* [< L *mas*, a male] **1** designating or of the sex that fertilizes the ovum **2** of, like, or suitable for men or boys; masculine **3** having a part shaped to fit into a corresponding hollow part (called *female*): said of electric plugs, etc. —*n.* a male person, animal, or plant

mal·edic·tion (mal′ə dik′shən) *n.* [see MAL- & DICTION] a curse

mal′efac′tor (-fak′tər) *n.* [< L *male*, evil + *facere*, do] an evildoer or criminal —**mal′efac′tion** *n.*

ma·lefi·cent (mə lef′ə sənt) *adj.* [< L: see prec.] harmful; evil —**ma·lef′i·cence** *n.*

ma·levo·lent (mə lev′ə lənt) *adj.* [< L *male*, evil + *velle*, to wish] wishing evil or harm to others; malicious —**ma·lev′o·lence** *n.*

mal·fea·sance (mal fē′zəns) *n.* [< Fr *mal*, evil + *faire*, do] wrongdoing, esp. by a public official

mal·for·ma·tion (mal′fôr mā′shən) *n.* faulty or abnormal formation of a body or part —**mal·formed′** *adj.*

mal·func′tion *vi.* to fail to function as it should —*n.* an instance of malfunctioning

mal·ice (mal′is) *n.* [< L *malus*, bad] **1** active ill will; desire to harm another **2** *Law* evil intent

ma·li·cious (mə lish′əs) *adj.* having, showing, or caused by malice; spiteful —**ma·li′ciously** *adv.*

ma·lign (mə līn′) *vt.* [< L *male*, ill + *genus*, born] to speak evil of; slander —*adj.* **1** malicious **2** evil; baleful **3** very harmful

ma·lig·nant (mə lig′nənt) *adj.* [see prec.] **1** having an evil influence **2** wishing evil **3** very harmful **4** causing or likely to cause death [a *malignant* tumor] —**ma·lig′nancy,** *pl.* **-cies,** *n.* —**ma·lig′nity** (-nə tē), *pl.* **-ties,** *n.*

ma·lin·ger (mə lin′gər) *vi.* [< Fr *malingre*, sickly] to feign illness so as to escape duty —**ma·lin′gerer** *n.*

mall (môl) *n.* [< *maul*, mallet: from use in a game on outdoor lanes] **1** a shaded walk or public promenade **2** *a*) a shop-lined street for pedestrians only *b*) an enclosed shopping center

mal·lard (mal′ərd) *n.* [< OFr *malart*] the common wild duck

mal·le·able (mal′ē ə bəl) *adj.* [< L *malleus*, a hammer] **1** that can be hammered, pounded, or pressed into various shapes without breaking **2** adaptable —**mal′le·abil′ity** *n.*

mal·let (mal′ət) *n.* [< L *malleus*, a hammer] **1** a short-handled hammer with a wooden head, for driving a chisel, etc. **2** any similar long-handled hammer, as for use in croquet or polo **3** a small hammer for playing a xylophone, etc.

mal·low (mal′ō) *n.* [< L *malva*] any of a family of plants, including the hollyhock, cotton, and okra, with large, showy flowers

mal·nour·ished (mal nur′isht) *adj.* improperly nourished

mal′nu·tri′tion *n.* faulty or inadequate nutrition; poor nourishment

---

THESAURUS

see UNDERSTAND 1. **2** [To succeed] accomplish, achieve, prosper; see SUCCEED 1. **3** [To see] discern, perceive, detect; see DISCOVER, SEE 1. — **make over 1** [To improve] amend, correct, restore; see IMPROVE 1, REDECORATE, REMODEL. **2** [To rebuild] renovate, refashion, refurbish; see REPAIR, RESTORE 3. —**make up 1** [To compose] compound, combine, mingle; see JOIN 1, MIX 1. **2** [To constitute] comprise, belong to, go into the making of, be contained in, be an element of, be a portion of, include, consist of; see also COMPOSE 1. **3** [To invent] fabricate, devise, fashion; see COMPOSE 2, CREATE, INVENT 1. **4** [To reconcile] conciliate, pacify, accommodate; see RECONCILE 2. **5** [To apply cosmetics] powder; apply face powder, apply lipstick, apply eye shadow, etc.; beautify, do up*, put one's face on. —**make up**

one's mind choose, pick, elect; see DECIDE, RESOLVE.

make-believe *a.* pretended, fraudulent, acted; see FALSE 3, FANTASTIC, UNREAL.

make-believe *n.* sham, unreality, fairy tale; see FANTASY, PRETENSE 2.

makeshift *a.* substitute, alternative, stopgap; see TEMPORARY.

makeup *n.* **1** [Cosmetics] greasepaint, mascara, eyeliner, powder, foundation, eye shadow, lipstick, war paint*; see also COSMETIC. **2** [*Anything offered to make good a shortage] atonement, compensation, conciliation; see PAYMENT. **3** [Composition] scheme, structure, arrangement; see COMPOSITION, DESIGN, FORMATION.

making *n.* imagination, conception, formulation, devising, producing, constituting, causation, fashioning,

building, origination, shaping, forging, designing, planning, fabrication, composition; see also PRODUCTION 1.

male *a.* manlike, virile, powerful; see MASCULINE.

male *n.* male sex, man, he; see BOY, FATHER 1.

malformed *a.* distorted, grotesque, abnormal; see DEFORMED, TWISTED 1.

malfunction *n.* slip, bad performance, failure to function; see FAILURE 1.

malice *n.* spite, animosity, resentment; see EVIL 1, HATRED.

malicious *a.* ill-disposed, spiteful, hateful; see BAD 1.

malignant *a.* **1** [Diseased] cancerous, lethal, poisonous; see DEADLY. **2** [Harmful] deleterious, corrupt, sapping; see DANGEROUS, HARMFUL.

mal·oc·clu'sion (-ə klōō'zhən) *n.* improper meeting of the upper and lower teeth

mal·o'dor·ous (-ō'dər əs) *adj.* having a bad odor; stinking

mal·prac'tice *n.* professional misconduct or improper practice, esp. by a physician

malt (môlt) *n.* ⟦OE *mealt*⟧ 1 barley or other grain soaked until it sprouts and then dried in a kiln: used in brewing and distilling 2 beer, ale, etc. — *adj.* made with malt — **malt'y, -i·er, -i·est,** *adj.*

malted milk 1 powdered malt and dried milk, used in a drink with milk, ice cream, etc. 2 this drink: also **malt'ed** *n.*

Mal·tese (môl tēz') *n.* 1 the variety of Arabic spoken in Malta 2 *pl.* **Mal·tese'** a native or inhabitant of Malta — *adj.* of Malta, its inhabitants, etc.

malt liquor beer, ale, or the like made from malt by fermentation

mal·treat (mal trēt') *vt.* ⟦see MAL- & TREAT⟧ to treat roughly or unkindly; abuse —**mal·treat'ment** *n.*

mama or **mam'ma** (mä'mə; *also* mə mä') *n.* child's term for MOTHER

mam·mal (mam'əl) *n.* ⟦< L *mamma*, breast⟧ any of a large group of vertebrates the females of which have milk-secreting glands (**mam'mary glands**) for feeding their offspring —**mam·ma·lian** (mə mā'lē ən) *adj., n.*

mam·mo·gram (mam'ə gram') *n.* an X-ray obtained from mammography

mam·mog·ra·phy (mə mäg'rə fē) *n.* ⟦< L *mamma*, breast + -GRAPHY⟧ an X-ray technique for detecting breast tumors before they can be seen or felt

mam·mon (mam'ən) *n.* ⟦< Aram⟧ [*often* M-] riches regarded as an object of worship and greedy pursuit

mam·moth (mam'əth) *n.* ⟦< Russ *mamont*⟧ an extinct elephant with long tusks — *adj.* very big; huge

man (man) *n., pl.* **men** (men) ⟦OE *mann*⟧ 1 a human being; person 2 the human race; mankind 3 an adult male person 4 an adult male servant, employee, etc. 5 a husband 6 any of the pieces used in chess, checkers, etc. — *vt.* **manned, man'ning** 1 to furnish with a labor force for work, defense, etc. 2 to strengthen; brace ⟦*to man oneself for an ordeal*⟧ —**as a** (or **one**) **man** in unison; unanimously —**to a man** with no exception

-man (mən, man) *combining form* man or person of a (specified) kind, in a (specified) activity, etc. Now often replaced by -PERSON or -WOMAN

mana·cle (man'ə kəl) *n.* ⟦< L *manus*, hand⟧ a handcuff: usually used in pl. — *vt.* **-cled, -cling** 1 to put handcuffs on 2 to restrain

man·age (man'ij) *vt.* **-aged, -ag·ing** ⟦< L *manus*, hand⟧ 1 to control the movement or behavior of 2 to have charge of; direct ⟦*to manage a hotel*⟧ 3 to succeed in accomplishing — *vi.* 1 to carry on business 2 to contrive to get along —**man'age·able** *adj.*

man'age·ment *n.* 1 a managing or being managed 2 the persons managing a business, institution, etc.

man'ager *n.* one who manages; esp., one who manages a business, etc.

mana·gerial (man'ə jir'ē əl) *adj.* of a manager or management

man'ag·ing *n.* the activity of one who manages

ma·ñana (mä nyä'nä) *n., adv.* ⟦Sp⟧ tomorrow or an indefinite future time

mana·tee (man'ə tē') *n.* ⟦< WInd native name⟧ a large, plant-eating aquatic mammal of tropical waters

Man·chu (man chōō', man'chōō) *n.* 1 *pl.* **-chus'** or **-chu'** a member of a Mongolian people of Manchuria who ruled China from 1644 to 1912 2 their language — *adj.* of the Manchus, their language, etc.

man·da·rin (man'də rin) *n.* ⟦< Sans *mantrin*, counselor⟧ 1 a high official in the Chinese empire 2 [M-] the main dialect of Chinese

man·date (man'dāt) *n.* ⟦< L *mandare*, to command⟧ 1 an order or command 2 [Historical] *a*) a League of Nations commission to a country to administer some region *b*) this region 3 the will of constituents expressed to their representative, legislature, etc.

man·da·tory (man'də tôr'ē) *adj.* 1 of or containing a mandate 2 authoritatively commanded; obligatory

man·di·ble (man'də bəl) *n.* ⟦< L *mandere*, chew⟧ the jaw; specif., *a*) the lower jaw of a vertebrate *b*) either jaw of a beaked animal —**man·dib'u·lar** (-dib'yōō lər) *adj.*

man·do·lin (man'də lin') *n.* ⟦< Gr *pandoura*, kind of lute⟧ a musical instrument with four to six pairs of strings

man·drake (man'drāk') *n.* ⟦< Gr *mandragoras*⟧ a poisonous plant of the nightshade family, with a thick, forked root suggesting the human form

man·drill (man'dril) *n.* ⟦MAN + *drill*, kind of monkey⟧ a large, strong baboon of W Africa: the male has blue and scarlet patches on the face and rump

mane (mān) *n.* ⟦OE *manu*⟧ the long hair growing on the neck of the horse, lion, etc. —**maned** *adj.*

man'-eat'er *n.* an animal that eats human flesh —**man'-eat'ing** *adj.*

ma·nège or **ma·nege** (ma nezh') *n.* ⟦Fr < It *maneggiare*, manage⟧ the art of riding and training horses

ma·neu·ver (mə nōō'vər) *n.* ⟦< L *manu operare*, to work by hand⟧ 1 a planned and controlled movement of troops, warships, etc. 2 a skillful or shrewd move; stratagem —

◼ THESAURUS ◼

malpractice *n.* negligence, misbehavior, neglect; see CARELESSNESS, VIOLATION.

mama* *n.* female progenitor, mamma*, parent; see MOTHER 1.

mammal *n.* vertebrate, creature, beast; see ANIMAL.

man *n.* 1 [The human race] mankind, human beings, race, humanity, human species, human nature, persons, mortals, individuals, earthlings, civilized society, creatures, fellow creatures, people, folk, society, *Homo sapiens* (Latin). 2 [An adult male] he, gentleman, Sir, Mr., fellow, mister, master, chap*, guy*; see also BOY. 3 [Anyone] human being, an individual, fellow creature; see PERSON 1. 4 [An employee] hand, worker, representative; see EMPLOYEE. 5 [*Husband] married man, spouse, partner; see HUSBAND. —**as a man** in unison, united, all together; see UNANIMOUSLY. —**be one's own man** be independent, stand alone, be free; see ENDURE 1. —**to a man** all, everyone, with no exception; see EVERYBODY.

man *v.* garrison, protect, fortify; see DEFEND 1, GUARD.

manage *v.* 1 [To direct] lead, oversee, indicate, designate, instruct, mastermind, engineer, show, disburse, distribute, execute, handle, watch, guide, supervise, conduct, engage in, officiate, pilot, steer, run, minister, regulate, administer, manipulate, officiate, superintend, preside, suggest, advocate, counsel, request, call upon, maintain, care for, take over, take care of, carry on, watch over, look after, see to, run the show*, call the shots*, run a tight ship*.—*Ant.* OBEY, follow, take orders. 2 [To contrive] accomplish, bring about, effect; see ACHIEVE, SUCCEED 1. 3 [To get along] bear up, survive, get by; see ENDURE 2.

manageable *a.* controllable, docile, compliant, governable, teachable, tractable, willing, obedient, submissive, yielding, adaptable, flexible, dutiful, humble, meek, easy; see also GENTLE 3, OBEDIENT 1, WILLING.—*Ant.* REBELLIOUS, ungovernable, unruly.

managed *a.* 1 [Trained] handled, guided, persuaded, influenced, driven, counselled, urged, taught, instructed, coached, groomed, primed, given a workout; see also EDUCATED, TRAINED.—*Ant.* WILD, undisciplined, uneducated. 2 [Governed] ruled, controlled, dominated, commanded, directed, swayed, mastered, run, regulated, ordered, compelled, supervised, piloted, cared for, taken care of; see also GOVERNED.—*Ant.* FREE, ungoverned, unsupervised.

management *n.* 1 [Direction] supervision, superintendence, government, command, guidance, conduct, organization, handling, policy, order, power, control; see also COMMAND. 2 [Those who undertake management; *usually preceded by "the"*] directors, administrators, executives; see ADMINISTRATION 2.

manager *n.* director, handler, superintendent, supervisor; see also EXECUTIVE.

managing *n.* directing, supervising, superintending, advising, overseeing, controlling, taking charge of, caring for, administering, executing, organizing, regulating, leading, piloting, steering, handling, charging, manipulating; see also OPERATING.

mandate *n.* command, decree, order; see COMMAND.

mandatory *a.* compulsory, forced, obligatory; see NECESSARY.

man-eating *a.* cannibal, carnivorous, omnivorous; see DANGEROUS, DEADLY.

maneuver *n.* 1 [A movement, usually military] stratagem, movement, procedure; see PLAN 2, TACTICS. 2 [A trick] subterfuge, finesse, ruse; see TRICK 1. 3 [Extensive practice in arms; *plural*] imitation war, exercise, war games; see DRILL 3, EXERCISE 1, PARADE 1.

maneuver *v.* plot, scheme, move, manage, contrive, design, devise, trick, cheat, conspire, sham, angle for*; see also PLAN 1.

vi., *vt.* **1** to perform or cause to perform a maneuver or maneuvers **2** to manage or plan skillfully **3** to move, get, make, etc. by some scheme —**ma·neu′ver·a·ble** *adj.*

man·ful (man′fəl) *adj.* manly; brave, resolute, etc. —**man′ful·ly** *adv.*

man·ga·nese (maŋ′gə nēs′, -nēz′) *n.* [ult. < ML *magnesia*: see MAGNESIA] a grayish-white, metallic chemical element, used in alloys

mange (mānj) *n.* [< OFr *mangeue*, an itch] a skin disease of mammals, causing itching, hair loss, etc.

man·ger (mān′jər) *n.* [< L *mandere*, chew] a box or trough to hold fodder for horses or cattle to eat

man·gle[1] (maŋ′gəl) *vt.* **-gled, -gling** [prob. < OFr *mehaigner*, maim] **1** to mutilate by roughly cutting, tearing, crushing, etc. **2** to spoil; botch; mar

man·gle[2] (maŋ′gəl) *n.* [< Gr *manganon*, war machine] a machine for pressing and smoothing sheets, etc. between rollers

man·go (maŋ′gō) *n., pl.* **-goes** or **-gos** [< Tamil *mān-kāy*] **1** the yellow-red, somewhat acid fruit of a tropical tree **2** this tree

man·grove (maŋ′grōv) *n.* [< WInd name] a tropical tree with branches that spread and send down roots, forming additional trunks

mangy (mān′jē) *adj.* **-gier, -gi·est 1** having mange **2** filthy, low, etc. —**man′gi·ly** *adv.* —**man′gi·ness** *n.*

man′han·dle (man′-) *vt.* **-dled, -dling** to handle roughly

man′hole′ *n.* a hole through which one can enter a sewer, conduit, etc.

man′hood′ *n.* **1** the state or time of being a man **2** manly qualities; manliness **3** men collectively

man′-hour′ *n.* a time unit equal to one hour of work done by one person

man′hunt′ *n.* a hunt for a fugitive

ma·nia (mā′nē ə) *n.* [Gr, madness] **1** wild or violent mental disorder **2** an excessive enthusiasm; obsession; craze

-mania (mā′nē ə) [see prec.] *combining form* a (specified) type of mental disorder

ma·niac (mā′nē ak′) *adj.* wildly insane —*n.* a violently insane person —**ma·ni·a·cal** (mə nī′ə kəl) *adj.*

manic (man′ik) *adj.* having, characterized by, or like mania

man′ic-depres′sive (-dē pres′iv) *adj.* characterized by alternating periods of extreme excitability, excessive activity, etc., and severe mental depression

mani·cure (man′i kyoor′) *n.* [< L *manus*, a hand + *cura*, care] a trimming, polishing, etc. of the fingernails —*vt.* **-cured′, -cur′ing** to trim, polish, etc. (fingernails) —**man′i·cur′ist** *n.*

mani·fest (man′ə fest′) *adj.* [< L *manifestus*, lit., struck by the hand] apparent to the senses or the mind; obvious —*vt.* to show plainly; reveal —*n.* an itemized list of a craft's cargo or passengers —**man′i·fest′ly** *adv.*

man′i·fes·ta′tion (-fes tā′shən) *n.* **1** a manifesting or being manifested **2** something that manifests

man′i·fes′to (-fes′tō) *n., pl.* **-toes** or **-tos** [It < *manifestare*, to manifest] a public declaration of intention by an important person or group

mani·fold (man′ə fōld′) *adj.* [see MANY & -FOLD] **1** having many forms, parts, etc. **2** of many sorts **3** being such in many ways [a *manifold* villain] **4** operating several parts of one kind —*n.* a pipe with several outlets, as for conducting cylinder exhaust from an engine —*vt.* to make copies of, as with carbon paper

mani·kin or **man·ni·kin** (man′i kin) *n.* [Du *manneken* < *man*, man + *-ken*, -KIN] **1** a little man; dwarf **2** an anatomical model of the human body, used as in art classes **3** MANNEQUIN

Ma·nila hemp (mə nil′ə) [after *Manila*, capital of the Philippines] [*often* **m- h-**] a strong fiber from the leafstalks of a Philippine plant, used for making rope, paper, etc.

Manila paper [*often* **m- p-**] a strong, buff-colored paper, orig. made of Manila hemp

man in the street the average person

ma·nipu·late (mə nip′yōo lāt′, -yə-) *vt.* **-lat′ed, -lat′ing** [ult. < L *manus*, a hand + *plere*, to fill] **1** to work or handle skillfully **2** to manage artfully or shrewdly, often in an unfair way **3** to alter (figures, etc.) for one's own purposes —**ma·nip′u·la′tion** *n.* —**ma·nip′u·la′tor** *n.*

man·kind (man′kīnd′; *also, & for 2 always,* man′kīnd′) *n.* **1** the human race **2** all human males

manly (man′lē) *adj.* **-lier, -li·est** having the qualities regarded as suitable for a man; virile, brave, etc. —*adv.* in a manly way —**man′li·ness** *n.*

man′-made′ *adj.* artificial; synthetic

manna (man′ə) *n.* [< Heb *mān*] **1** *Bible* food miraculously provided for the Israelites in the wilderness **2** any help that comes unexpectedly

man·ne·quin (man′i kin) *n.* [see MANIKIN] **1** a model of the human body, used as by tailors **2** a woman who models clothes in stores, etc.

man·ner (man′ər) *n.* [< L *manus*, a hand] **1** a way of doing something; mode of procedure **2** a way, esp. a usual way, of acting; habit **3** [*pl.*] *a)* ways of social behavior [bad *manners*] *b)* polite ways of social behavior [to learn *manners*] **4** kind; sort

man′nered (-ərd) *adj.* **1** having manners of a specified sort [ill-*mannered*] **2** artificial, stylized, etc.

man′ner·ism′ *n.* **1** excessive use of some distinctive manner or style in art, literature, etc. **2** a peculiarity of manner in behavior, speech, etc.

man′nerly *adj.* polite

man·nish (man′ish) *adj.* like a man or man's: said of a woman having characteristics generally attributed to men

ma·noeu·vre (mə nōō′vər) *n., vi., vt.* **-vred, -vring** *chiefly Brit., etc. sp. of* MANEUVER

man of letters a writer, scholar, editor, etc., esp. in the field of literature

man′-of-war′ *n., pl.* **men′-of-war′** an armed naval vessel; warship

ma·nom·eter (mə näm′ət ər) *n.* [Fr < Gr *manos*, rare (as in "thin, sparse") + Fr *-mètre*, -METER] an instrument for measuring the pressure of gases or liquids

manor (man′ər) *n.* [< L *manere*, remain, dwell] **1** in England, a landed estate **2** the main house on an estate —**ma·no·rial** (mə nôr′ē əl) *adj.*

man′pow′er *n.* **1** power furnished by human strength **2** the collective strength or availability for work of the people in any given area, nation, etc.

man·qué (män kā′) *adj.* [Fr < *manquer*, be lacking] unfulfilled; would-be [a poet *manqué*]

man·sard (roof) (man′särd) [after F. *Mansard*, 17th-c. Fr architect] a roof with two slopes on each of four sides, the lower slope being steeper than the upper

manse (mans) *n.* [see MANOR] the residence of a minister; parsonage

man′ser′vant *n., pl.* **men′ser′vants** a male servant Also **man servant**

-manship (man ship) *combining form* talent or skill (esp. in gaining advantage) in [grantsmanship]

man·sion (man′shən) *n.* [< L *manere*, remain, dwell] a large, imposing house

---

THESAURUS

mangle[1] *v.* tear, lacerate, wound, injure, cripple, maim, rend, disfigure, cut, slit, butcher, slash, slice, carve, bruise, mutilate; see also HURT 1.

manhandle *v.* damage, maul, mistreat; see ABUSE, BEAT 1.

manhood *n.* **1** [Male maturity] legal age, post-pubescence, coming of age, prime of life, middle age, voting age, adulthood. **2** [Manly qualities] virility, resoluteness, honor, gallantry, nobility, forcefulness, daring, boldness, tenacity, self-reliance, potency.

mania *n.* craze, lunacy, madness; see DESIRE 1, INSANITY, OBSESSION.

maniac *n.* lunatic, insane person, crazy person; see MADMAN.

manipulate *v.* handle, shape, mold; see FORM 1, MANAGE 1, PLAN 1.

manipulation *n.* guidance, use, direction; see MANAGEMENT 1.

mankind *n.* humanity, human race, society; see MAN 1.

manly *a.* masculine, courageous, fearless, firm, noble, valiant, highspirited, intrepid, gallant, resolute, bold, confident, dauntless, self-reliant; see also MASCULINE.—*Ant.* COWARDLY, timid, effeminate.

man-made *a.* manufactured, artificial, synthetic, unnatural, counterfeit, not organic, ersatz, false, faux, not genuine.

manner *n.* **1** [Personal conduct] mien, deportment, demeanor; see BEHAVIOR. **2** [Customary action] use, way, practice; see CUSTOM, HABIT 1. **3** [Method] mode, fashion, style; see METHOD. —**in a manner of speaking** in a way, so to speak, so to say; see RATHER.

mannerism *n.* idiosyncrasy, pretension, peculiarity; see CHARACTERISTIC, QUIRK.

mannerly *a.* polished, considerate, charming; see POLITE.

manners *n.* **1** [Personal behavior] conduct, deportment, bearing; see BEHAVIOR. **2** [Culture] urbanity, taste, refinement; see COURTESY 1, CULTURE 2, ELEGANCE.

manpower *n.* youth, men of military age, males; see LABOR 4.

mansion *n.* villa, house, hall; see ESTATE, HOME 1.

man′-sized *adj.* [Colloq.] of a size fit for a man; big Also **man′-size′**

man′slaugh′ter (-slôt′ər) *n.* the killing of a human being by another, esp. when unlawful but without malice

manta (man′tə) *n.* [Sp < LL *mantum*, a cloak] a giant RAY², with winglike pectoral fins Also **manta ray**

man·tel (man′təl) *n.* [var. of MANTLE] 1 the facing of stone, etc. about a fireplace, including a projecting shelf 2 this shelf: also **man′tel·piece′**

man·tilla (man til′ə, -tē′ə) *n.* [Sp: see MANTA] a woman's scarf, as of lace, worn over the hair and shoulders

man·tis (man′tis) *n., pl.* **-tises** or **-tes′** (-tēz′) [< Gr, prophet] an insect with forelegs held up together as if praying

man·tissa (man tis′ə) *n.* [L, (useless) addition] the decimal part of a logarithm

man·tle (man′təl) *n.* [< L *mantellum*] 1 a loose, sleeveless cloak 2 anything that envelops or conceals 3 a small hood which when placed over a flame gives off a brilliant incandescent light — *vt.* **-tled, -tling** to cover as with a mantle — *vi.* 1 to be or become covered 2 to blush or flush

man·tra (man′trə, mun′-) *n.* [Sans] a chant of a Vedic hymn, text, etc.

manu·al (man′yōō əl) *adj.* [< L *manus*, a hand] 1 of the hands 2 made, done, or worked by hand 3 involving skill or hard work with the hands — *n.* 1 a handy book for use as a guide, reference, etc. 2 prescribed drill in the handling of a weapon — **man′u·ally** *adv.*

manual training training in practical arts and crafts, as metalworking, etc.

manu·fac·ture (man′yōō fak′chər, -yə-) *n.* [< L *manus*, a hand + *facere*, make] 1 the making of goods, esp. by machinery and on a large scale 2 the making of any product, esp. when regarded as merely mechanical — *vt.* **-tured, -tur·ing** 1 to make, esp. by machinery 2 to make up (excuses, etc.); invent — **man′u·fac′turer** *n.*

manu·mit (man′yōō mit′) *vt.* **-mit′ted, -mit′ting** [< L *manus*, a hand + *mittere*, send] to free from slavery — **man′u·mis′sion** *n.*

ma·nure (mə noor′, -nyoor′) *vt.* **-nured′, -nur′ing** [< OFr *manouvrer*, work with the hands] to put manure on or into — *n.* animal excrement, etc. used to fertilize soil

manu·script (man′yōō skript′, -yə-) *adj.* [< L *manus*, hand + *scriptus*, written] 1 written by hand or typewritten 2 designating writing that consists of unconnected letters like print — *n.* 1 a written or typewritten document, book, etc., as submitted to a publisher 2 writing as opposed to print

Manx (maŋks) *n.* the language spoken on the Isle of Man,

now nearly extinct — *adj.* of the Isle of Man, its people, etc.

many (men′ē) *adj.* **more, most** [OE *manig*] numerous — *n.* a large number (of persons or things) — *pron.* many persons or things

man′y-sid′ed *adj.* having many sides, qualities, etc.

Mao·ri (mä′ō rē, mou′rē) *n.* 1 *pl.* **-ris** or **-ri** a member of a Polynesian people native to New Zealand 2 their language — *adj.* of the Maoris, their language, etc.

map (map) *n.* [< L *mappa*, napkin, cloth] 1 a representation of all or part of the earth's surface, showing countries, bodies of water, etc. 2 a representation of the sky, showing the stars, etc. — *vt.* **mapped, map′ping** 1 to make a map of 2 to plan

ma·ple (mā′pəl) *n.* [OE *mapel*] 1 any of a large group of trees with two-winged fruits, grown for wood, sap, or shade 2 the hard, light-colored wood 3 the flavor of the syrup or sugar made from the sap

maple sugar sugar made by a further boiling down of maple syrup

maple syrup syrup made by boiling down the sap of any of various maples

mar (mär) *vt.* **marred, mar′ring** [OE *mierran*, hinder] to injure so as to make imperfect, etc.; spoil

mara·bou (mar′ə bōō) *n.* [Fr < Ar *murābit*, hermit] 1 a large-billed African stork 2 its plumes

ma·raca (mə rä′kə) *n.* [Port *maracá* < native name in Brazil] a percussion instrument that is a dried gourd or a gourd-shaped rattle with pebbles in it

mara·schino (mar′ə skē′nō, -shē′-) *n.* [It < *marasca*, kind of cherry] a liqueur made from a dark sour cherry

maraschino cherries cherries in a syrup flavored with maraschino or imitation maraschino

mara·thon (mar′ə thän′) *n.* [after *Marathon*, plain in ancient Greece] 1 a race on foot, 26 miles and 385 yards in length 2 any endurance contest

ma·raud (mə rôd′) *vi., vt.* [< Fr *maraud*, vagabond] to raid and plunder — **ma·raud′er** *n.*

mar·ble (mär′bəl) *n.* [< Gr *marmaros*, white stone] 1 a hard limestone, white or colored, which takes a high polish 2 a piece of this stone, used in sculpture, etc. 3 anything like marble in hardness, coldness, etc. 4 *a*) a little ball of stone, glass, etc. *b*) [*pl., sing. v.*] a children's game played with such balls 5 [*pl.*] [Slang] mental soundness; wits — *adj.* of or like marble — *vt.* **-bled, -bling** 1 to make (book edges) look mottled like marble 2 to cause (meat) to be streaked with fat

mar′ble·ize′ (-bəl īz′) *vt.* **-ized′, -iz′ing** to make look like marble

march¹ (märch) *vi.* [Fr *marcher*] 1 to walk with regular steps, as in military formation 2 to advance steadily — *vt.* to cause to march — *n.* 1 a marching 2 a steady advance;

THESAURUS

manslaughter *n.* killing, homicide, assassination; see CRIME, MURDER.

mantle *n.* fireplace, mantlepiece, chimney piece; see SHELF 2.

manual *a.* hand-operated, not automatic, standard; see OLD-FASHIONED.

manual *n.* guidebook, reference book, textbook; see BOOK.

manufacture *n.* fashioning, forming, assembling; see PRODUCTION 1.

manufacture *v.* make, construct, fabricate, produce, form, fashion, carve, mold, cast, frame, put together, turn out, stamp out, print out, cut out, have in production, have on the assembly line, print, shape, execute, accomplish, complete, tool, machine, mill, make up; see also BUILD.—*Ant.* DESTROY, demolish, tear down.

manufactured *a.* made, produced, constructed, fabricated, erected, fashioned, shaped, forged, turned out, tooled, executed, done, assembled, ready for the market, in shape, complete, completed; see also BUILT, FORMED.

manufacturer *n.* maker, producer, fabricator, constructor, builder, operator, craftsman, corporation, entrepreneur, company.

manufacturing *n.* fabrication, building, construction, assembling, preparing for market, putting in production, continuing production,

keeping in production, forging, formation, erection, composition, accomplishment, completion, finishing, doing, turning out; see also PRODUCTION 1.—*Ant.* DESTRUCTION, wreck, demolition.

manure *n.* guano, plant-food, compost; see DUNG, FERTILIZER.

manuscript *n.* composition, parchment, tablet, paper, document, original, copy, letterpress, autograph, translation, facsimile, book, script; see also WRITING 2.

many *a.* numerous, multiplied, manifold, multitudinous, multifarious, diverse, sundry, profuse, innumerable, not a few, numberless, a world of, countless, uncounted, alive with, teeming, in heaps, several, of every description, prevalent, no end of, no end to, everywhere, crowded, common, usual, plentiful, abundant, galore; see also VARIOUS.—*Ant.* FEW, meager, scanty.

many *n.* a great number, abundance, thousands*; see PLENTY. —**a good (or great) many** a great number, abundance, thousands*; see PLENTY. —**as many (as)** as much as, an equal number, a similar amount; see SAME.

many-sided *a.* 1 [Multilateral] polyhedral, geometric, bilateral, dihedral, trilateral, quadrilateral, tetrahedral; see also GEOMETRICAL. 2

[Gifted] endowed, talented, adaptable; see ABLE, VERSATILE.

map *n.* chart, graph, plat, sketch, delineation, drawing, picture, portrayal, draft, tracing, outline, ground plan. —**put on the map** make famous, bring fame to, glorify; see ESTABLISH 2. —**wipe off the map** eliminate, put out of existence, ruin; see DESTROY.

map *v.* outline, draft, chart; see PLAN 2.

mar *v.* 1 [To damage slightly] harm, bruise, scratch; see BREAK 2, DAMAGE. 2 [To impair] deform, deface, warp; see DESTROY.

marble *a.* petrified, granitelike, unyielding; see ROCK n. 1, STONE.

marble *n.* 1 [Metamorphic limestone] *Marbles include the following:* Parian, Pentelic, Carrian, Serpentine, Algerian, Tecali (onyx marbles), Tuscan, Gibraltar, Vermont, Georgia, fire, black, ophicalcite; see also STONE. 2 [A piece of carved marble] carving, figurine, figure; see ART, SCULPTURE, STATUE. 3 [A ball used in marbles] nib*, shooter*, aggie; see TOY 1.

march¹ *n.* 1 [The act of marching] progression, movement, advancing, advancement, countermarch, goose step, military parade; see also STEP 1, WALK 3. 2 [The distance or route progress **3** a regular, steady step **4** the distance covered in marching **5** a piece of music for marching —**on the march** marching —**steal a march on** to get an advantage over secretly —**march'er** *n.*

march² (märch) *n.* ⟦< OFr⟧ a boundary, border, or frontier

March (märch) *n.* ⟦< L *Mars*, the god Mars⟧ the third month of the year, having 31 days: abbrev. **Mar.**

March hare a hare in breeding time, proverbially an example of madness

marching orders 1 orders to march, go, or leave **2** notice of dismissal

mar·chion·ess (mär'shən is) *n.* **1** the wife or widow of a marquess **2** a lady of the rank of a marquess

Mardi Gras (mär'dē grä') ⟦Fr, fat Tuesday⟧ [*sometimes* **M- g-**] the last day before Lent: a day of carnival in New Orleans, etc.

mare¹ (mar, mer) *n.* ⟦< OE *mere*⟧ a mature female horse, mule, donkey, etc.

mare² (mä'rä', mar'ē) *n., pl.* **ma·ria** (mä'rē ə, mar'ē ə) ⟦L, sea⟧ a large, dark area on the moon

mare's-nest (marz'nest', merz'-) *n.* **1** a hoax **2** a jumble; mess

mar·ga·rine (mär'jə rin) *n.* ⟦Fr⟧ a spread or cooking fat of vegetable oils processed, often with milk or whey, to the consistency of butter

mar·gin (mär'jən) *n.* ⟦< L *margo*⟧ **1** a border; edge **2** the blank border of a printed or written page **3** an amount beyond what is needed **4** provision for increase, error, etc. **5** the difference between the cost and the selling price of goods **6** collateral deposited with a broker, either to meet legal requirements or to insure against loss on contracts as for buying stocks —**mar'gin·al** *adj.*

mar·gin·al·ia (mär'jə nā'lē ə) *n.pl.* marginal notes

mar'gin·al·ize' *vt.* to exclude or ignore

ma·ria·chi (mär'ē ä'chē) *n., pl.* **-chis** ⟦MexSp < Fr *mariage*, marriage: from playing at wedding celebrations⟧ **1** a member of a strolling band of musicians in Mexico **2** such a band **3** its music

Mar·ian (mer'ē ən, mar'-) *adj.* of the Virgin Mary

mari·gold (mar'i gōld') *n.* ⟦< *Marie* (prob. the Virgin Mary) + GOLD⟧ a plant of the composite family, with yellow or orange flowers

mari·juana *or* **mari·huana** (mar'i wä'nə) *n.* ⟦AmSp⟧ **1** HEMP (*n.* 1) **2** its dried leaves and flowers, smoked, esp. as cigarettes, for euphoric effects

ma·rimba (mə rim'bə) *n.* ⟦< native name in Africa⟧ a kind of xylophone with a resonant tube beneath each bar

ma·rina (mə rē'nə) *n.* ⟦< L *mare*, sea⟧ a small harbor with docks, services, etc. for pleasure craft

mari·nade (mar'ə nād') *n.* ⟦Fr < Sp *marinar*, to pickle⟧ **1** a spiced pickling solution for steeping meat, fish, etc., often before cooking **2** meat or fish thus steeped —*vt.* **-nad'ed, -nad'ing** MARINATE

mari·nate (mar'i nāt') *vt.* **-nat'ed, -nat'ing** ⟦< It

marinare, to pickle⟧ to steep (meat, fish, etc.) in a marinade

ma·rine (mə rēn') *adj.* ⟦< L *mare*, sea⟧ **1** of or found in the sea **2** *a*) maritime; nautical *b*) naval —*n.* **1** a member of a military force trained for service at sea **2** [*often* **M-**] a member of the MARINE CORPS **3** naval or merchant ships

Marine Corps a branch of the United States armed forces trained for land, sea, and aerial combat

mari·ner (mar'i nər) *n.* a sailor

mario·nette (mar'ē ə net', mer'-) *n.* ⟦Fr < *Marie*, Mary⟧ a jointed puppet moved by strings or wires

mari·tal (mar'i təl) *adj.* ⟦< L *maritus*, a husband⟧ of marriage; matrimonial —**mar'i·tally** *adv.*

mari·time (mar'i tim') *adj.* ⟦< L *mare*, sea⟧ **1** on, near, or living near the sea **2** of sea navigation, shipping, etc.

mar·jo·ram (mär'jə rəm) *n.* ⟦prob. ult. < Gr *amarakos*⟧ a fragrant plant of the mint family, used in cooking

mark¹ (märk) *n.* ⟦OE *mearc*, boundary⟧ **1** a line, dot, spot, scratch, etc. on a surface **2** a printed or written symbol [*punctuation marks*] **3** a brand or label on an article showing the maker, etc. **4** an indication of some quality **5** a grade [*a mark* of B in Latin] **6** a standard of quality **7** impression, influence, etc. **8** an object of known position, serving as a guide **9** a line, dot, etc. indicating position, as on a graduated scale **10** an object aimed at; target **11** an object desired or worked for; goal end; aim —*vt.* **1** to put or make a mark or marks on **2** to identify as by a mark **3** to indicate by a mark **4** to show plainly [*her smile marked* her joy] **5** to set off; characterize **6** to take notice of; heed [*mark* my words] **7** to grade; rate **8** to put a price on —**make one's mark** to achieve fame —**mark down** (or **up**) to mark for sale at a reduced (or an increased) price —**mark time 1** to keep time while at a halt by lifting the feet as if marching **2** to suspend progress for a time —**mark'er** *n.*

mark² (märk) *n.* ⟦< ON *mǫrk*⟧ DEUTSCHE MARK

Mark (märk) *Bible* **1** one of the four Evangelists, the reputed author of the second Gospel **2** this Gospel

mark'down' *n.* **1** a selling at a reduced price **2** the amount of reduction

marked (märkt) *adj.* **1** having a mark or marks **2** noticeable; obvious —**mark·edly** (märk'id lē) *adv.*

mar·ket (mär'kit) *n.* ⟦ult. < L *merx*, merchandise⟧ **1** a gathering of people for buying and selling things **2** an open space or a building where goods are shown for sale: also **mar'ket·place' 3** a shop for the sale of provisions [*a meat market*] **4** a region in which goods can be bought and sold [*the European market*] **5** trade; buying and selling **6** demand (for goods, etc.) [*a good market for tea*] —*vt.* **1** to offer for sale **2** to sell —*vi.* **1** to buy provisions —**mar'ket·able** *adj.* —**mar'ket·abil'ity** *n.* —**mar'ket·eer'** (-kə tir') *n.* —**mar'keter** *n.*

mar·ket·ing (-iŋ) *n.* **1** a buying or selling in a market **2**

THESAURUS

marched] walk, trek, hike; see JOURNEY. **3** [Music for marching] martial music, wedding march, processional; see MUSIC.

march¹ *v.* move, advance, step out, go on, proceed, step, tread, tramp, patrol, prowl, parade, goose step, file, range, strut, proceed, progress, go ahead, forge ahead.—*Ant.* PAUSE, halt, retreat. —**on the march** proceeding, advancing, tramping; see MOVING 1.

March *n.* spring month, beginning of spring, month that comes in like a lion and goes out like a lamb; see MONTH, SPRING 2.

mare¹ *n.* female horse, brood mare, breeding stock; see ANIMAL, HORSE.

margin *n.* border, lip, shore; see BOUNDARY, EDGE 1.

marginal *a.* rimming, edging, verging; see BORDERING.

marijuana *n.* *cannabis sativa*, grass*, pot*; see DRUG.

marine *a.* maritime, of the sea, oceanic; see MARITIME, NAUTICAL.

marital *a.* conjugal, connubial, nuptial; see MARRIED.

maritime *a.* naval, marine, oceanic, seagoing, hydrographic, seafaring, aquatic, natatorial, Neptunian; see

also NAUTICAL.

mark¹ *n.* **1** [The physical result of marking] brand, stamp, blaze, imprint, impression, line, trace, check, stroke, streak, dot, point, nick. **2** [A target] butt, prey, bull's-eye. **3** [Effect] manifestation, consequence, value; see RESULT. —**hit the mark** achieve, accomplish, do well; see SUCCEED 1. —**make one's mark** accomplish, prosper, become famous; see SUCCEED 1. —**miss the mark** be unsuccessful, err, mistake; see FAIL 1.

mark¹ *v.* **1** [To make a mark] brand, stamp, imprint, blaze, print, check, chalk, label, sign, identify, check off, trace, stroke, streak, dot, point, nick, x, underline. **2** [To designate] earmark, point out, stake out, indicate, check off, mark off, signify, denote; see also MEAN 1. **3** [To distinguish] characterize, signalize, qualify; see DISTINGUISH 1. **4** [To put prices upon] ticket, label, tag; see PRICE. —**mark down** reduce, put on sale, cut the price of; see PRICE. —**mark time** cool off, postpone, kill time; see DELAY, WAIT 1. —**mark up** raise the price, adjust, add to; see INCREASE.

marked *a.* **1** [Carrying a mark] branded, signed, sealed, stamped,

imprinted, inscribed, characterized by, distinguished by, recognized by, identified by. **2** [Priced] labeled, trade-marked, price-marked, marked down, marked up, ticketed, priced, tagged; see also COSTING.

marker *n.* ticket, price mark, trademark, seal, brand, stamp, boundary mark, inscription, pencil, pen; see also LABEL.

market *n.* **1** [A place devoted to sale] trading post, mart, shopping mall, shopper's square, emporium, exchange, city market, public market, supermarket, meat market, fish market, stock market, stock exchange, fair, dime store, drug store, discount store, department store, variety store, bazaar, warehouse, business, delicatessen; see also SHOP, STORE. **2** [The state of trade] supply and demand, sale, run; see BUSINESS 1, 4, DEMAND 2. —**be in the market (for)** want to buy, be willing to purchase, need; see WANT 1. —**on the market** salable, ready for purchase, available; see FOR (or ON or UP FOR) SALE.

market *v.* vend, exchange, barter; see SELL.

the total of activities involved in the moving of goods from the producer to the consumer, including selling, advertising, etc.

mark'ing *n.* 1 a mark or marks 2 the characteristic arrangement of marks, as of a plant or animal

marks·man (märks'mən) *n., pl.* **-men** one who shoots, esp. one who shoots well —**marks'man·ship** *n.*

mark'up' *n.* 1 a selling at an increased price 2 the amount of increase

mar·lin (mär'lin) *n., pl.* **-lin** or **-lins** 〚< fol.: from the shape〛 a large, slender, deep-sea fish

mar·line·spike (mär'lin spīk') *n.* 〚< Du *marlijn*, small cord + SPIKE¹〛 a pointed metal tool for splicing rope

mar·ma·lade (mär'mə lād') *n.* 〚ult. < Gr *meli*, honey + *mēlon*, apple〛 a jamlike preserve of oranges, etc.

mar·mo·set (mär'mə zet') *n.* 〚< OFr *marmouset*, grotesque figure〛 a small monkey of South and Central America

mar·mot (mär'mət) *n.* 〚prob. < L *mus montanus*, mountain mouse〛 any of a group of thick-bodied rodents, as the woodchuck

ma·roon¹ (mə rōōn') *n., adj.* 〚Fr *marron*, chestnut〛 dark brownish red

ma·roon² (mə rōōn') *vt.* 〚< AmSp *cimarrón*, wild〛 1 to put (a person) ashore in a lonely place and abandon that person 2 to leave helpless and alone

marque (märk) *n.* 〚Fr, a sign〛 a distinctive emblem on an automobile

mar·quee (mär kē') *n.* 〚< Fr *marquise*, awning〛 a rooflike projection over an entrance, as to a theater

mar·quess (mär'kwis) *n.* 〚var. of MARQUIS〛 1 a British nobleman ranking above an earl 2 MARQUIS

mar·que·try (mär'kə trē) *n.* 〚Fr, ult. < *marque*, a mark〛 decorative inlaid work, as in furniture

mar·quis (mär'kwis; *Fr* mär kē') *n.* 〚< ML *marchisus*, prefect〛 in some European countries, a nobleman ranking above an earl or count

mar·quise (mär kēz') *n.* 1 the wife or widow of a marquis 2 a lady of the rank of a marquis

mar·qui·sette (mär'ki zet', -kwi-) *n.* 〚see MARQUEE〛 a thin, meshlike fabric used for curtains, etc.

mar·riage (mar'ij) *n.* 1 the state of being married 2 a wedding 3 a close union —**mar'riage·able** *adj.*

mar·ried *adj.* 1 being husband and wife 2 having a husband or wife 3 of marriage — *n.* a married person

mar·row (mar'ō) *n.* 〚OE *mearg*〛 the soft, fatty tissue that fills the cavities of most bones

marry (mar'ē) *vt.* **-ried, -ry·ing** 〚< L *maritus*, husband〛 1 to join as husband and wife 2 to take as husband or wife 3 to unite — *vi.* to get married —**marry off** to give in marriage

Mars (märz) 1 the Roman god of war 2 a planet of the solar system: see PLANET

marsh (märsh) *n.* 〚OE *merisc*〛 a tract of low, wet, soft land; swamp —**marsh'y, -i·er, -i·est,** *adj.*

mar·shal (mär'shəl) *n.* 〚< OHG *marah*, horse + *scalh*, servant〛 1 in various foreign armies, a general officer of the highest rank 2 an official in charge of ceremonies, parades, etc. 3 in the U.S., a) a Federal officer appointed to a judicial district with duties like those of a sheriff b) the head of some police or fire departments — *vt.* **-shaled** or **-shalled, -shal·ing** or **-shal·ling** 1 to arrange (troops, ideas, etc.) in order 2 to guide

marsh·mal·low (märsh'mal'ō, -mel'ō) *n.* 〚orig. made of the root of a mallow found in marshes〛 a soft, spongy confection of sugar, gelatin, etc.

marsh marigold a marsh plant with bright-yellow flowers

mar·su·pial (mär sōō'pē əl) *adj.* 〚< Gr *marsypos*, pouch〛 of a group of mammals that carry their incompletely developed young in an external abdominal pouch on the mother — *n.* such an animal, as a kangaroo or opossum

mart (märt) *n.* 〚MDu *markt*〛 a market

mar·ten (mär't'n) *n.* 〚< OFr *martre*〛 1 a small mammal like a weasel, with soft, thick fur 2 the fur

mar·tial (mär'shəl) *adj.* 〚< L *martialis*, of Mars〛 1 of or suitable for war 2 warlike; bold 3 military —**mar'tially** *adv.*

martial arts systems of self-defense originating in the Orient, such as karate or kung fu

martial law rule by military authorities over civilians, as during a war

Mar·tian (mär'shən) *adj.* of Mars — *n.* an inhabitant of Mars, as in science fiction

mar·tin (märt'n) *n.* 〚Fr〛 any of several birds of the swallow family

mar·ti·net (märt'n et') *n.* 〚after *Martinet*, 17th-c. Fr general〛 a very strict disciplinarian

mar·ti·ni (mär tē'nē) *n., pl.* **-nis** 〚< ?〛 a cocktail made of gin (or vodka) and dry vermouth

mar·tyr (märt'ər) *n.* 〚< Gr *martyr*, a witness〛 1 one who chooses to suffer or die for one's faith or principles 2 one who suffers misery for a long time — *vt.* to kill or persecute for a belief —**mar'tyr·dom** *n.*

mar·vel (mär'vəl) *n.* 〚< L *mirari*, wonder at〛 a wonderful or astonishing thing — *vi.* **-veled** or **-velled, -vel·ing** or **-vel·ling** to be filled with wonder — *vt.* to wonder at or about: followed by a clause

mar'vel·ous (-və ləs) *adj.* 1 causing wonder; extraordinary, etc. 2 improbable; incredible 3 [Colloq.] fine; splendid Also [Chiefly Brit.] **mar'vel·lous** —**mar'vel·ously** *adv.*

Marx·ism (märks'iz'əm) *n.* the system of thought developed by Karl Marx (1818-83, the founder of modern socialism) and Friedrich Engels (1820-95, Ger. socialist leader & writer), serving as a basis for socialism and communism —**Marx'ist** or **Marx'ian** *adj., n.*

Mary (mer'ē) *Bible* mother of Jesus

Mary Mag·da·lene (mag'də lən) *Bible* a woman out of whom Jesus cast devils

mar·zi·pan (mär'zi pan') *n.* 〚Ger < It *marzapane*〛 a confection of ground almonds, sugar, and egg white

masc. or **mas.** masculine

mas·cara (mas kar'ə) *n.* 〚It *maschera*, mask〛 a cosmetic for coloring the eyelashes — *vt.* **-car'aed, -car'a·ing** to put mascara on

mas·cot (mas'kät') *n.* 〚< Prov *masco*, sorcerer〛 any person, animal, or thing supposed to bring good luck

mas·cu·line (mas'kyōō lin, -kyə-) *adj.* 〚< L *mas*, male〛 1 male; of men or boys 2 suitable to or having qualities regarded as characteristic of men; strong, vigorous, manly, etc. 3 mannish: said of women 4 *Gram.* designating or of the gender of words referring to males and many other words to which no sex is attributed —**mas'cu·lin'i·ty** *n.*

mash (mash) *n.* 〚< OE *mascwyrt*〛 1 crushed malt or meal soaked in hot water for making wort 2 a mixture of watered bran, meal, etc. for feeding horses, etc. 3 any soft mass — *vt.* 1 to change into a soft mass by beating, crushing, etc. 2 to crush and injure —**mash'er** *n.*

THESAURUS

markup *n.* raise, margin, gross profit; see INCREASE, PROFIT 2.

marriage *n.* wedding, espousal, spousal, nuptials, pledging, mating, matrimony, conjugality, union, match, wedlock, wedded state, wedded bliss, holy matrimony.

married *a.* wedded, mated, espoused, united, given in marriage, pledged in marriage, living in the married state, in the state of matrimony, hitched*.—*Ant.* SINGLE, unwedded, unmarried.

marry *v.* 1 [To take a spouse] wed, espouse, enter the matrimonial state, take wedding vows, pledge in marriage, mate, lead to the altar, tie the knot*, get hitched*, get hooked*.— *Ant.* DIVORCE, separate, reject. 2 [To join in wedlock] unite, give, join in

matrimony, pronounce man and wife; see also JOIN 1.—*Ant.* DIVORCE, annul, separate.

marsh *n.* morass, bog, quagmire; see SWAMP.

marshy *a.* swampy, wet, sloppy; see MUDDY 1, 2.

martial *a.* warlike, soldierly, combative; see AGGRESSIVE.

martyr *n.* sufferer, offering, scapegoat; see SAINT, VICTIM.

martyrdom *n.* agony, suffering, devotion; see TORTURE.

marvel *n.* miracle, phenomenon, curiosity; see WONDER 2.

marvel *v.* stare, stand in awe, stare with open mouth; see WONDER 1.

marvelous *a.* fabulous, astonishing, spectacular; see UNUSUAL 1.

masculine *a.* courageous, male, virile, potent, vigorous, forceful, aggressive, adult, honorable; see also MANLY.

masculinity *n.* virility, power, manliness; see MANHOOD 2, STRENGTH.

mash *n.* mix, pulp, paste; see FEED, MIXTURE 1.

mash *v.* crush, bruise, squash, chew, masticate, smash, pound, reduce, squeeze, brew, pulverize; see also GRIND, PRESS 1.

mashed *a.* crushed, pressed, mixed, pulpy, battered, pounded, smashed, squashed, softened, reduced, spongy, pasty, pulverized, masticated, chewed, bruised; made into a powder, made into a paste, etc.—*Ant.* WHOLE, hard, uncrushed.

mask (mask) *n.* ⟦< Fr < It *maschera*⟧ **1** a covering to conceal or protect the face **2** anything that conceals or disguises **3** a masquerade **4** *a*) a molded likeness of the face *b*) a grotesque representation of a face, worn to amuse or frighten — *vt.* to conceal or cover with or as with a mask —**masked** *adj.*

mask'er *n.* a participant in a masquerade

maso·chism (mas'ə kiz'əm) *n.* ⟦after L. von Sacher-*Masoch* (1835-95), Austrian writer⟧ the getting of pleasure, often sexual, from being hurt or humiliated — **mas'o·chist** *n.* —**mas'o·chis'tic** *adj.* —**mas'o·chis'ti· cally** *adv.*

ma·son (mā'sən) *n.* ⟦< ML *macio*⟧ **1** one whose work is building with stone, brick, etc. **2** [M-] FREEMASON

Ma·sonic (mə sän'ik) *adj.* [*also* m-] of Freemasons or Freemasonry

ma·sonry (mā'sən rē) *n.* **1** a mason's trade **2** *pl.* **-ries** something built, as by a mason, of stone, brick, etc. **3** [*usually* M-] FREEMASONRY

masque (mask) *n.* ⟦see MASK⟧ **1** MASQUERADE (*n.* 1) **2** a former kind of dramatic entertainment, with a mythical or allegorical theme —**masqu'er** *n.*

mas·quer·ade (mas'kər ād') *n.* ⟦see MASK⟧ **1** a ball or party at which masks and fancy costumes are worn **2** *a*) a disguise *b*) an acting under false pretenses — *vi.* **-ad'ed, -ad'ing 1** to take part in a masquerade **2** to act under false pretenses

mass (mas) *n.* ⟦< Gr *maza*, barley cake⟧ **1** a quantity of matter of indefinite shape and size; lump **2** a large quantity or number [*a* mass of bruises] **3** bulk; size **4** the main part **5** *Physics* the quantity of matter in a body as measured by its inertia — *adj.* of or for the masses or for a large number — *vt., vi.* to gather or form into a mass —**the masses** the common people; specif., the working people

Mass (mas) *n.* ⟦< L *missa* in the words said by the priest: *ite, missa est* (*contio*), go, (the meeting) is dismissed⟧ [*also* m-] *R.C.Ch.* the service that includes the Eucharist

mas·sa·cre (mas'ə kər) *n.* ⟦< OFr *maçacre*, shambles⟧ the indiscriminate, merciless killing of many people or animals — *vt.* **-cred, -cring** (-kər iŋ, -kriŋ) to kill in large numbers

mas·sage (mə säzh') *n.* ⟦Fr < Ar *massa*, to touch⟧ a rubbing, kneading, etc. of part of the body, as to stimulate circulation — *vt.* **-saged', -sag'ing** to give a massage to

mas·seur (ma sur', mə-) *n.* ⟦Fr⟧ a man whose work is giving massages —**mas·seuse** (ma suz', mə-) *n.fem.*

mas·sive (mas'iv) *adj.* **1** forming or consisting of a large mass; big and solid **2** large and imposing —**mas'sively** *adv.* —**mas'sive·ness** *n.*

mass media those means of communication that reach large numbers of people, as newspapers, radio, etc.

mass noun a noun denoting an abstraction or something that is uncountable (Ex.: *love, news*)

mass number the number of neutrons and protons in the nucleus of an atom

mass production quantity production of goods, esp. by machinery and division of labor

mast (mast) *n.* ⟦OE *mæst*⟧ **1** a tall vertical spar used to support the sails, yards, radar, etc. on a ship **2** a vertical pole

mas·tec·tomy (mas tek'tə mē) *n., pl.* **-mies** the surgical removal of a breast

mas·ter (mas'tər) *n.* ⟦< L *magister*⟧ **1** a man who rules others or has control over something; specif., *a*) one who is head of a household *b*) an employer *c*) one who owns a slave or an animal *d*) the captain of a merchant ship **2** *a*) a person very skilled and able in some work, profession, science, etc.; expert *b*) an artist regarded as great **3** [M-] a title applied to a boy too young to be addressed as *Mr.* — *adj.* **1** being a master **2** of a master **3** chief; main; controlling — *vt.* **1** to become master of **2** to become an expert in (an art, etc.)

mas'ter·ful *adj.* **1** acting the part of a master; domineering **2** expert; skillful —**mas'ter·fully** *adv.*

master key a key that will open every one of a set of locks

mas'terly *adj.* expert; skillful — *adv.* in a masterly manner

mas'ter·mind' *n.* a very clever person, esp. one who plans or runs a project — *vt.* to be the mastermind of

Master of Arts (or **Science**, etc.) a degree given by a college or university to one who has completed a prescribed course at the first level of graduate study Also **master's (degree)**

master of ceremonies one who supervises a ceremony, program, etc.

mas'ter·piece' *n.* **1** a thing made or done with masterly skill **2** the greatest work of a person or group

master sergeant *U.S. Mil.* a noncommissioned officer of high rank

mas'ter·stroke' *n.* a masterly action, move, or achievement

mas'ter·work' *n.* MASTERPIECE

mas'tery *n., pl.* **-ies 1** rule; control **2** ascendancy or victory **3** expert skill or knowledge

mast'head' *n.* **1** the top part of a ship's mast **2** a listing of the owner, editors, etc. of a newspaper or magazine

mas·ti·cate (mas'ti kāt') *vt.* **-cat'ed, -cat'ing** ⟦ult. < Gr *mastax*, mouth⟧ to chew up —**mas'ti·ca'tion** *n.*

mas·tiff (mas'tif) *n.* ⟦< L *mansuetus*, tame⟧ a large, powerful dog with a short, thick coat

mas·to·don (mas'tə dän') *n.* ⟦< Gr *mastos*, breast + *odous*, tooth: from the nipplelike processes on its molar⟧ a large, extinct mammal resembling the elephant but larger

mas·toid (mas'toid') *adj.* ⟦< Gr *mastos*, breast + *-eidēs*, -OID⟧ designating, of, or near a projection of the temporal bone behind the ear — *n.* the mastoid projection

mas·tur·bate (mas'tər bāt') *vi., vt.* **-bat'ed, -bat'ing** ⟦< L *masturbari*⟧ to manipulate the genitals for sexual gratification —**mas'tur·ba'tion** *n.*

mat[1] (mat) *n.* ⟦< LL *matta*⟧ **1** a flat piece of cloth, rubber, woven straw, etc. used for protection, as on a floor or under a vase **2** a thickly padded floor covering, esp. one used for wrestling, etc. **3** anything densely interwoven or

---

THESAURUS

mask *n.* **1** [A disguise] cover, false face, veil, hood, costume, theater device; see also CAMOUFLAGE, DISGUISE. **2** [A protection] gas mask, catcher's mask, fencing mask, fireman's mask, respirator; see also PROTECTION 2. **3** [A masquerade] revel, party, carnival; see PARTY 1.

mask *v.* cloak, conceal, veil; see DISGUISE, HIDE 1.

masquerade *n.* Mardi Gras, masked ball, pretense; see DANCE 1, ENTERTAINMENT, PARTY 1.

mass *n.* **1** [A body of matter] lump, bulk, piece, portion, section, batch, block, body, core, clot, coagulation, wad*, gob*; see also HUNK. **2** [A considerable quantity] heap, volume, crowd; see QUANTITY, SIZE 2. **3** [Size] magnitude, volume, span; see EXTENT, SIZE 2. —**the masses** the proletariat, the rank and file, the multitude; see PEOPLE 3.

Mass *n.* eucharistic rite, Catholic service, Eucharist, Lord's Supper, Holy Communion, ceremony, observance; see also CELEBRATION, WORSHIP 1. *Masses include the following:* High

Mass, Low Mass, Solemn High Mass, Requiem Mass, Votive Mass.

massacre *n.* butchering, killing, slaughter; see MURDER.

massacre *v.* exterminate, mass murder, annihilate; see KILL 1.

massage *v.* stimulate, caress, press; see RUB 1.

massive *a.* huge, heavy, cumbersome; see LARGE 1.

mass production *n.* automation, mass producing, assembly-line methods; see MANUFACTURING, PRODUCTION 1.

mast *n.* spar, pole, post, timber, trunk; see also POST.

master *a.* leading, supreme, main; see EXCELLENT, MAJOR 1, PRINCIPAL.

master *n.* **1** [One who directs others] chief, director, boss; see EXECUTIVE, LEADER 2. **2** [A teacher] instructor, preceptor, mentor; see TEACHER. **3** [One who possesses great skill] genius, maestro, sage, scientist, past master, champion, prima donna, connoisseur, fellow, doctor;

see also ARTIST.—*Ant.* DISCIPLE, beginner, undergraduate.

master *v.* **1** [To conquer] subdue, rule, humble; see SUCCEED 1. **2** [To become proficient in] gain mastery in, understand, comprehend; see LEARN, STUDY.

masterful *a.* commanding, expert, skillful; see EXCELLENT.

masterpiece *n.* perfection, model, standard, cream of the crop, masterwork, *magnum opus* (Latin).

mastery *n.* **1** [Control] dominance, sovereignty, government; see COMMAND, POWER 2. **2** [Ability to use to the full] skill, capacity, proficiency; see ABILITY, EDUCATION 1.

masturbation *n.* sexual self-gratification, onanism, self-love, self-abuse*.

mat[1] *n.* covering, floor covering, doormat, place mat, network, table mat, place setting, web, mesh, cloth, straw mat; see also COVER 1, RUG.

mat[1] *v.* braid, tangle, snarl; see TWIST, WEAVE 1.

growing in a thick tangle — *vt.*, *vi.* **mat′ted, mat′ting 1** to cover as with a mat **2** to interweave or tangle into a thick mass —**go to the mat** [Colloq.] to engage in a struggle or dispute

mat² (mat) *n.* ‖ < OFr ‖ **1** MATTE **2** a border, as of cardboard, put around a picture — *vt.* **mat′ted, mat′ting 1** to put a dull finish on **2** to frame with a mat

mat³ (mat) *n.* [Colloq.] *Printing* a matrix

mata·dor (mat′ə dôr′) *n.* ‖ < Sp *matar*, to kill ‖ a bullfighter whose specialty is killing the bull

match¹ (mach) *n.* ‖ < OFr *mesche* ‖ a slender piece of wood, cardboard, etc. tipped with a substance that catches fire by friction

match² (mach) *n.* [OE (*ge*)*mæcca*, mate] **1** any person or thing equal or similar to another **2** two persons or things that go well together **3** a contest or game **4** a marriage or mating — *vt.* **1** to join in marriage; mate **2** to put in opposition (*with* or *against*) **3** to be equal or similar to **4** to make or get a counterpart or equivalent to **5** to fit (one thing) to another — *vi.* to be equal, similar, suitable, etc.

match′book′ *n.* a folder of book matches

match′less *adj.* having no equal

match′mak′ing *n.* the arranging of marriages, boxing matches, etc. —**match′mak′er** *n.*

match′stick′ *n.* a thin piece of wood, cardboard, etc., as of a match

mate (māt) *n.* ‖ < MDu ‖ **1** a companion or fellow worker **2** one of a matched pair **3** *a*) a husband or wife *b*) the male or female of paired animals **4** an officer of a merchant ship, ranking below the captain — *vt.*, *vi.* **mat′ed, mat′ing 1** to join as a pair **2** to couple in marriage or sexual union

ma·teri·al (mə tir′ē əl) *adj.* ‖ < L *materia*, matter ‖ **1** of matter; physical [a *material* object] **2** of the body or bodily needs, comfort, etc.; not spiritual **3** important, essential, etc. — *n.* **1** what a thing is, or may be, made of; elements or parts **2** cloth; fabric **3** [*pl.*] tools, etc. needed to make or do something

ma·te′ri·al·ism′ (-iz′əm) *n.* **1** the doctrine that everything in the world, including thought, can be explained only in terms of matter **2** the tendency to be more concerned with material than with spiritual or intellectual values —**ma·te′ri·al·ist** *adj.*, *n.* —**ma·te′ri·al·is′tic** *adj.*

ma·te′ri·al·ize′ (-iz′) *vt.* **-ized′, -iz′ing** to give material form to — *vi.* **1** to become fact; be realized **2** to take on bodily form: said of spirits, etc. —**ma·te′ri·al·i·za′tion** *n.*

ma·te′ri·al·ly *adv.* **1** physically **2** to a great extent; substantially

ma·teri·el or **ma·té·riel** (mə tir′ē el′) *n.* ‖ Fr ‖ the neces-

sary materials and tools; specif., military weapons, equipment, etc.

ma·ter′nal (mə tur′nəl) *adj.* ‖ < L *mater*, mother ‖ **1** of, like, or from a mother **2** related through the mother's side of the family —**ma·ter′nally** *adv.*

ma·ter′nity (-nə tē) *n.* the state of being a mother; motherhood — *adj.* **1** for pregnant women **2** for the care of mothers and their newborn babies

math·emati·cal (math′ə mat′i kəl) *adj.* ‖ < Gr *manthanein*, learn ‖ **1** of, like, or concerned with mathematics **2** very precise, accurate, etc. Also **math′emat′ic** —**math′emat′i·cally** *adv.*

math·emat·ics (math′ə mat′iks) *n.pl.* ‖ see prec. & -ICS ‖ [*with sing. v.*] the science dealing with quantities, forms, etc. and their relationships, by the use of numbers and symbols Also **math** —**math′ema·ti′cian** (-mə tish′ən; math′mə-) *n.*

mati·nee or **mati·née** (mat′'n ā′) *n.* ‖ < Fr *matin*, morning ‖ an afternoon performance of a play, etc.

mat·ins (mat′'nz) *n.pl.* ‖ < L *matutinus*, of the morning ‖ [*often* M-] [*usually with sing. v.*] a church service of morning prayer

matri- ‖ < L *mater* ‖ *combining form* mother Also **matr-**

ma·tri·arch (mā′trē ärk′) *n.* ‖ prec. + -ARCH ‖ a woman who rules a family, tribe, etc. —**ma′tri·ar′chal** (-är′kəl) *adj.* —**ma′tri·arch′y** (-är′kē), *pl.* **-ies,** *n.*

ma·tricu·late (mə trik′yōō lāt′, -yə-) *vt.*, *vi.* **-lat′ed, -lat′ing** ‖ < LL: see MATRIX ‖ to enroll, esp. as a student in a college —**ma·tric′u·la′tion** *n.*

mat·ri·mony (ma′trə mō′nē) *n.*, *pl.* **-nies** ‖ < L *mater*, mother ‖ **1** the act or rite of marriage **2** married life —**mat′ri·mo′nial** *adj.*

ma·trix (mā′triks) *n.*, *pl.* **-tri·ces** (mā′trə sēz′, ma′trə-) or **-trix′es** ‖ < L *mater*, mother ‖ that within which something originates, takes form, etc., as a mold for a printing plate

ma·tron (mā′trən) *n.* ‖ < L *mater*, mother ‖ **1** a wife or widow, esp. one with a mature appearance and manner **2** a woman manager of the domestic arrangements of a hospital, prison, etc. —**ma′tronly** *adj.*

matron of honor a married woman acting as chief attendant to a bride

matte (mat) *n.* ‖ var. of MAT² ‖ a dull surface or finish — *adj.* not shiny Also **matt**

mat·ted (mat′id) *adj.* closely tangled in a dense mass

mat·ter (mat′ər) *n.* ‖ < L *materia* ‖ **1** what a thing is made of; material **2** whatever occupies space and is perceptible to the senses **3** any specified substance [*coloring matter*] **4** material of thought or expression **5** an amount or quantity **6** *a*) a thing or affair *b*) cause or occasion [no *laughing matter*] **7** importance; significance [it's of no *matter*]

---

match^1,2 *n.* **1** [An instrument to produce fire] safety match, sulphur match, matchstick, fuse; see also LIGHT 3. **2** [An article that is like another] peer, equivalent, mate, analogue, counterpart, approximation; see also EQUAL. **3** [A formal contest] race, event, rivalry; see COMPETITION, SPORT 3.

match² *v.* **1** [To find or make equals] equalize, liken, equate, make equal, pair, coordinate, level, even, match up, balance, mate, marry, unite; see also EQUAL. **2** [To be alike] harmonize, suit, be twins, be counterparts, be doubles, check with, go together, go with, rhyme with, take after; see also AGREE, RESEMBLE.—*Ant.* DIFFER, be unlike, bear no resemblance. **3** [To meet in contest] equal, meet, compete with; see COMPETE.

matched *a.* doubled, similar, equated, evened, coordinated, harmonized, paired, mated; see also ALIKE, BALANCED 1.—*Ant.* UNLIKE, unequal, different.

matching *a.* comparable, analogous, parallel; see EQUAL.

mate *n.* **1** [One of a pair] complement, analogue, counterpart; see MATCH 2. **2** [A companion] playmate, classmate, buddy; see FRIEND. **3** [A marriage partner] spouse, bride, groom, bedmate, the old man*, the old lady*; see also HUSBAND, WIFE.

material *a.* palpable, sensible, corpo-

real; see PHYSICAL 1, REAL 2, TANGIBLE.

material *n.* **1** [Matter] body, corporeality, substance; see ELEMENT 2, MATTER 1. **2** [Unfinished matter] *often plural*] raw material, stuff, stock, staple, ore, stockpile, crop, supply, accumulation; see also ALLOY, ELEMENT 2, GOODS, METAL, MINERAL, PLASTIC, ROCK 1, WOOL.

materialistic *a.* possessive, acquisitive, opportunistic; see GREEDY, WORLDLY.

materialize *v.* be realized, take on form, become real, actualize, become concrete, metamorphose, reintegrate; see also BECOME.—*Ant.* DISSOLVE, disintegrate, disperse.

maternal *a.* parental, sympathetic, protective; see MOTHERLY.

maternity *n.* parenthood, motherhood, motherliness; see PARENT.

mathematical *a.* arithmetical, numerical, computable; see NUMERICAL.

mathematics *n.* science of real numbers, science of numbers, language of numbers, computation, reckoning, calculation, new math, math. *Types of mathematics include the following:* arithmetic, algebra, plane geometry, spherical geometry, trigonometry, trig*, analytical geometry, differential calculus, integral

calculus, programming, applied mathematics, probability, statistics, topology, transforms, logarithms.

matriarch *n.* female ruler, dowager, matron; see QUEEN.

matrimony *n.* conjugality, wedlock, union; see MARRIAGE.

matron *n.* lady, wife, mother; see WOMAN 1.

matronly *a.* middle-aged, grave, sedate; see MATURE, MOTHERLY.

matted *a.* snarled, rumpled, disordered; see TANGLED, TWISTED 1.

matter *n.* **1** [Substance] body, material, substantiality, corporeality, constituents, stuff, object, thing, physical world; see also ELEMENT 2.— *Ant.* NOTHING, nothingness, immateriality. **2** [Subject] interest, focus, resolution; see SUBJECT, THEME 1. **3** [An affair] undertaking, circumstance, concern; see AFFAIR 1. —**as a matter of fact** in fact, in actuality, truly; see REALLY 1. —**for that matter** in regard to that, as far as that is concerned, concerning that; see AND. —**no matter** it doesn't matter, it is of no concern, regardless of; see REGARDLESS 2.

matter *v.* signify, be substantive, be important, have influence, imply, express, be of consequence, involve, be worthy of notice, cut ice*; see also MEAN 1.

8 trouble; difficulty: with *the* [what seems to be the *matter*] 9 mail — *vi.* to be of importance —**as a matter of fact** in fact; really —**no matter** 1 it is not important 2 regardless of

mat'ter-of-fact' *adj.* sticking to facts; literal, unimaginative, etc.

Mat·thew (math'yōō') *Bible* 1 a Christian apostle, reputed author of the first Gospel 2 this book: abbrev. **Matt.**

mat·ting (mat'iŋ) *n.* 1 a woven mat of fiber, as straw, for mats, etc. 2 mats collectively

mat·tock (mat'ək) *n.* [OE *mattuc*] a tool like a pickax, for loosening the soil, digging roots, etc.

mat·tress (ma'trəs) *n.* [< Ar *maṭraḥ*, cushion] a casing of strong cloth filled with cotton, foam rubber, coiled springs, etc., used on a bed

ma·ture (mə toor', -tyoor', -choor') *adj.* [< L *maturus*, ripe] 1 full-grown; ripe 2 fully developed, perfected, etc. 3 due: said of a note, bond, etc. — *vt., vi.* **-tured', -tur'ing** to make or become mature —**matu·ra·tion** (mach'ə rā'shən) *n.* —**ma·tu'ri·ty** *n.*

matzo (mät'sə, -sō) *n., pl.* **mat'zot, mat'zoth** (-sōt), or **mat'zos** [Heb *matstsāh*, unleavened] 1 flat, thin, unleavened bread eaten during the Passover 2 a piece of this

matzo ball a dumpling made of matzo meal, usually in chicken broth or soup

maud·lin (môd'lin) *adj.* [< ME *Maudeleyne*, (Mary) Magdalene (often represented as weeping)] foolishly, often tearfully, sentimental

maul (môl) *n.* [< L *malleus*, a hammer] a heavy hammer for driving stakes, etc. — *vt.* 1 to bruise or lacerate 2 to handle roughly; manhandle —**maul'er** *n.*

maun·der (môn'dər) *vi.* [< earlier *mander*, to grumble] to talk or move in a confused way

mau·so·leum (mô'sə lē'əm, -zə-) *n., pl.* **-le'ums** or **-le'a** (-ə) [after the tomb of King *Mausolus*, in ancient Asia Minor] a large, imposing tomb

mauve (mōv) *n.* [Fr, mallow] any of several shades of pale purple — *adj.* of such a color

mav·er·ick (mav'ər ik) *n.* [after S. *Maverick*, 19th-c. Texan whose cattle had no brand] 1 an unbranded animal, esp. a lost calf 2 [Colloq.] one who takes an independent stand, as in politics

maw (mô) *n.* [OE *maga*] 1 orig., the stomach 2 the throat, gullet, jaws, or oral cavity of a voracious animal

mawk·ish (môk'ish) *adj.* [< ON *mathkr*, maggot] sentimental in a weak, insipid way —**mawk'ishly adv.**

maxi- [< MAXI(MUM)] *combining form* maximum, very large, very long

max·illa (maks il'ə) *n., pl.* **-lae** (-ē) [L] the upper jawbone —**max'il·lar'y** (-i ler'ē) *adj.*

maxim (maks'im) *n.* [< LL *maxima* (*propositio*), the greatest (premise)] a concise rule of conduct

maxi·mize (maks'i miz') *vt.* **-mized', -miz'ing** to increase to the maximum

maxi·mum (maks'i məm) *n., pl.* **-mums** or **-ma** (-mə) [< L superl. of *magnus*, great] 1 the greatest quantity, number, etc. possible 2 the highest degree or point reached — *adj.* greatest possible, permissible, or reached —**max'i·mal** (-məl) *adj.*

may (mā) *v.aux. pt.* **might** [OE *mæg*] used to express: 1 possibility [it *may* rain] 2 permission [you *may* go]: see also CAN[1] 3 contingency [they died that we *may* be free] 4 a wish or hope [*may* he live!]

May (mā) *n.* [< L *Maius*] the fifth month of the year, having 31 days

Maya (mä'yə, mi'ə) *n., pl.* **Ma'yas** or **Ma'ya** [Sp < native name] 1 a member of a tribe of Indians of Central America that had a highly developed civilization 2 the language of the Mayas —**Ma'yan** *adj., n.*

maybe (mā'bē) *adv.* [ME (for *it may be*)] perhaps

May Day May 1: a traditional spring festival, now also a labor holiday in many countries

may'flow'er *n.* an early spring flower, as the trailing arbutus —[M-] the ship on which the Pilgrims came to America (1620)

may'fly' *n., pl.* **-flies'** [thought to be prevalent in May] a delicate, soft-bodied insect with gauzy wings

may·hem (mā'hem, -əm) *n.* [see MAIM] 1 *Law* the offense of maiming a person 2 any deliberate destruction

mayo (mā'ō) *n.* [Colloq.] short for MAYONNAISE

may·on·naise (mā'ə nāz') *n.* [after *Mahón*, port on a Sp island] a creamy sauce of egg yolks, oil, vinegar, etc. beaten together

mayor (mā'ər) *n.* [< L *major*, greater] the chief administrative official of a city, town, etc. —**may'or·al** (-ər əl, mā ôr'əl) *adj.*

may'or·alty (-əl tē) *n., pl.* **-ties** the office or term of office of a mayor

may·pole (mā'pōl) *n.* [often M-] a high pole with flowers, streamers, etc., for dancing around on May Day

maze (māz) *n.* [< OE *amasian*, amaze] 1 a confusing, intricate network of pathways 2 a confused state

mazel tov (mä'zəl tōv', -tôf') [Heb] good luck Also **maz'el·tov'**

ma·zurka or **ma·zourka** (mə zur'kə) *n.* [Pol] a lively Polish folk dance in 3/4 or 3/8 time

MBA or **M.B.A.** Master of Business Administration

MC or **M.C.** 1 Master of Ceremonies 2 Member of Congress

McCoy (mə koi') *n.* [< *Mackay*, Scot clan name] [Slang] the real person or thing, not a substitute: with *the* In full **the real McCoy**

MD [L *Medicinae Doctor*] Doctor of Medicine Also **M.D.**

me (mē) *pron.* [OE] objective case of I[2]

mead[1] (mēd) *n.* [OE *meodu*] an alcoholic liquor made of fermented honey and water

mead[2] (mēd) *n.* [Old Poet.] var. of MEADOW

meadow (med'ō) *n.* [< OE *mæd*] 1 a grassland where the grass is grown for hay 2 low, level grassland

mea·ger (mē'gər) *adj.* [< L *macer*, lean] 1 thin; lean 2 poor; not full or rich; inadequate Brit. sp. **mea'gre** —**mea'gerly adv.** —**mea'ger·ness n.**

meal[1] (mēl) *n.* [OE *mæl*] 1 any of the times for eating, as lunch or dinner 2 the food served at such a time

meal[2] (mēl) *n.* [OE *melu*] 1 any edible grain, coarsely

THESAURUS

matter-of-fact *a.* objective, prosaic, feasible; see PRACTICAL.

mattress *n.* innerspring, springs, box spring, bedding, cushion, crib mattress; see also BED.

mature *a.* full-grown, middle-aged, grown, grown-up, of age, in full bloom, womanly, manly, matronly, developed, prepared, settled, cultivated, cultured, sophisticated; see also EXPERIENCED.—*Ant.* YOUNG, adolescent, immature.

mature *v.* grow up, become a man, become a woman, come of age, become experienced, settle down, ripen, reach perfection, attain majority, culminate, become wise, become perfected, grow skilled, fill out; see also AGE, DEVELOP 1.

matured *a.* grown, full-grown, aged; see FINISHED.

maturity *n.* 1 [Mental competence] development, sophistication, cultivation, culture, civilization, advancement, mental power, capability. 2 [Physical development] prime of life, post-pubescence, adulthood; see

MAJORITY 2. 3 [Ripeness] readiness, mellowness, sweetness; see DEVELOPMENT.

maul *v.* pound, whip, trample; see BEAT 1, HIT 1.

maxim *n.* aphorism, adage, epithet; see PROVERB, SAYING.

maximum *a.* supreme, highest, greatest; see BEST.

maximum *n.* supremacy, height, pinnacle, pre-eminence, culmination, matchlessness, preponderance, apex, peak, greatest number, highest degree, summit; see also CLIMAX.—*Ant.* MINIMUM, foot, bottom.

may *v.* 1 [Grant permission] be permitted, be allowed, can, be privileged to, be authorized, be at liberty to. 2 [Concede possibility] will, shall, be going to, should, be conceivable, be practicable, be within reach, be obtainable; see also WILL 3.

May *n.* spring month, baseball season, fifth month; see MONTH, SPRING 2.

maybe *a.* perhaps, possibly, it might

be, it could be, maybe so, as it may be, conceivably, God willing.—*Ant.* HARDLY, scarcely, probably not.

mayor *n.* magistrate, Lord Mayor, burgomaster, president of a city council, civil administrator, civil judge, city father; see also EXECUTIVE.

maze *n.* tangle, entanglement, twist, winding, convolution, intricacy, confusion, meandering, puzzle.—*Ant.* ORDER, disentanglement, simplicity.

meadow *n.* grass, pasture, mountain meadow, upland pasture, meadow land, bottom land, bottoms, pasturage; hay meadow, clover meadow, bluegrass meadow, etc.; salt marsh, steppe, heath, pampa, savanna; see also FIELD 1.

meager *a.* lank, lanky, gaunt, starved, emaciated, lean, bony, slender, slim, spare, little, bare, scant, stinted, lacking, wanting, scrawny, withered, lithe, narrow, tenuous, slightly-made, skinny; see also THIN 2.—*Ant.* FAT, plump, stout.

meal[1,2] *n.* 1 [Ground feed] bran,

ground *[cornmeal]* **2** any substance similarly ground — **meal'y, -i·er, -i·est,** *adj.*

mealy-mouthed (mēl′ē mou*th*d′) *adj.* not outspoken or blunt; euphemistic

mean[1] (mēn) *vt.* **meant** (ment), **mean'ing** ‖ OE *mænan* ‖ **1** to have in mind; intend *[he means to go]* **2** to intend to express *[say what you mean]* **3** to signify; denote *["ja" means "yes"]* — *vi.* to have a (specified) degree of importance, effect, etc. *[honors mean little to him]* —**mean well** to have good intentions

mean[2] (mēn) *adj.* ‖ OE *(ge)mæne* ‖ **1** low in quality or value; paltry; inferior **2** poor in appearance; shabby **3** ignoble; petty **4** stingy **5** pettily bad-tempered, disagreeable, etc. **6** [Slang] *a)* hard to cope with *b)* skillful — **mean'ly** *adv.* —**mean'ness** *n.*

mean[3] (mēn) *adj.* ‖ < L *medius,* middle ‖ **1** halfway between extremes **2** average — *n.* **1** what is between extremes **2** *Math.* a number between the smallest and largest values of a set of quantities; esp., an average

me·an·der (mē an′dər) *vi.* ‖ < Gr *Maiandros,* a winding river in Asia Minor ‖ **1** to take a winding course: said of a stream **2** to wander idly

mean·ie or **mean·y** (mēn′ē) *n., pl.* **-ies** [Colloq.] one who is mean, selfish, etc.

mean'ing *n.* what is meant; what is intended to be signified or understood; sense *[the meaning of a word]* —**mean'ing·ful** *adj.* —**mean'ing·less** *adj.*

means (mēnz) *n.pl.* ‖ < MEAN[3], *n.* ‖ **1** *[with sing. or pl. v.]* that by which something is done or obtained; agency *[a means of travel]* **2** resources; wealth —**by all means 1** without fail **2** certainly —**by means of** by using —**by no means** not at all

meant (ment) *vt., vi. pt. & pp. of* MEAN[1]

mean'time' *adv.* **1** in or during the intervening time **2** at the same time — *n.* the intervening time Also **mean'while'**

mea·sles (mē′zəlz) *n.pl.* ‖ ME *maseles* ‖ *[with sing. v.]* **1** an acute, infectious, communicable viral disease, usually of children, characterized by small, red spots on the skin, high fever, etc. **2** a similar but milder disease; esp., rubella (*German measles*)

mea·sly (mēz′lē) *adj.* **-sli·er, -sli·est** [Colloq.] contemptibly slight or worthless

meas·ure (mezh′ər) *n.* ‖ < L *metiri,* to measure ‖ **1** the extent, dimensions, capacity, etc. of anything **2** a determining of this; measurement **3** *a)* a unit of measurement *b)* any standard of valuation **4** a system of measurement **5** an instrument for measuring **6** a definite quantity measured out **7** a course of action *[reform measures]* **8** a statute; law **9** a rhythmical pattern or unit; specif., the notes and rests between two bars on a musical staff — *vt.* **-ured, -ur·ing 1** to find out or estimate the extent, dimensions, etc. of, esp. by a standard **2** to mark off by measuring **3** to be a measure of — *vi.* **1** to take measurements **2** to be of a specified dimension, etc. —**beyond measure** exceedingly —**for good measure** as something extra —**in a measure** to some extent —**measure up to** prove to be competent —**meas'ur·able** *adj.* —**meas'ur·ably** *adv.* —**meas'ure·less** *adj.*

meas'ured *adj.* **1** determined or marked off by a standard **2** regular or steady *[measured steps]* **3** careful and guarded: said of speech, etc.

meas'ure·ment *n.* **1** a measuring or being measured **2** extent or quantity determined by measuring **3** a system of measuring or of measures

meat (mēt) *n.* ‖ OE *mete* ‖ **1** food: now archaic except in **meat and drink 2** the flesh of animals, esp. of mammals,

---

■ THESAURUS ■

farina, grits, fodder, provender, forage; see also FEED, FLOUR, GRAIN 1. *Types of meal include the following:* corn meal, corn grits, hominy, corn starch, barley meal, oatmeal, soybean meal, soybean flour. 2 [The quantity of food taken at one time] repast, feast, refreshment, mess, feed bag*, eats*, grub*, chow*, spread*, square meal*, snack. *Meals include the following:* breakfast, dinner, lunch, banquet, brunch, snack, tea, picnic, luncheon, dinner, midnight supper; see also BREAKFAST, DINNER, LUNCH.

mean[1] *v.* **1** [To have as meaning] indicate, spell, denote, signify, add up, determine, symbolize, imply, involve, speak of, touch on, stand for, drive at, point to, connote, suggest, express, designate, intimate, tell the meaning of, purport. 2 [To have in mind] anticipate, propose, expect; see INTEND 1. 3 [To design for] destine for, aim at, set apart; see INTEND 2.

mean[2] *a.* **1** [Small-minded] base, low, debased; see VULGAR. 2 [Of low estate] servile, pitiful, shabby; see HUMBLE 2. 3 [Vicious] shameless, dishonorable, degraded, contemptible, evil, infamous, treacherous, crooked, fraudulent, faithless, unfaithful, ill-tempered, dangerous, despicable, degenerate, knavish, unscrupulous, hard as nails.

mean[3] *n.* middle, median, midpoint; see AVERAGE, CENTER 1.

meander *v.* twist and turn, roam, flow; see RAMBLE 2, RUN 1, WALK 1.

meaning *n.* sense, import, purport, purpose, definition, object, implication, application, intent, suggestion, connotation, aim, drift, context, significance, essence, worth, intrinsic value, interest.—*Ant.* NONSENSE, aimlessness, absurdity.

meaningful *a.* significant, exact, essential; see IMPORTANT 1.

meaningless *a.* vague, absurd, insignificant; see TRIVIAL, UNIMPORTANT.

meanness *n.* **1** [The quality of being mean] small-mindedness, debase-

ment, degradation, degeneracy, unscrupulousness, stinginess, disrepute, malice, unworthiness, ill-temper, unkindness, covetousness, avarice, miserliness; see also GREED.—*Ant.* GENEROSITY, nobility, worthiness. 2 [A mean action] belittling, defaming, groveling, cheating, sneaking, quarreling, scolding, taking advantage of, deceiving, coveting, grudging, dishonoring, defrauding, shaming, degrading, stealing.

means *n.* **1** [An instrumentality or instrumentalities] machinery, mechanism, agency, organ, channel, medium, factor, agent, power, organization; see also METHOD, SYSTEM. 2 [Wealth] resources, substance, property; see WEALTH. —**by all means** of course, certainly, yes indeed; see SURELY, YES. —**by any means** in any way, at all, somehow; see ANYHOW. —**by means of** with the aid of, somehow, through; see BY 2. —**by no (manner of) means** in no way, not possible, definitely not; see NEVER, NO.

meanwhile *a.* meantime, during the interval, in the interim, ad interim, for the time being, until, till, up to, in the meantime, when; see also DURING.

measurable *a.* weighable, definite, limited, determinable, knowable, recognizable, detectable, calculable, real, present, fathomable, assessible.

measure *n.* **1** [A unit of measurement] dimension, capacity, weight, volume, distance, degree, quantity, area, mass, frequency, density, intensity, rapidity, speed, caliber, bulk, sum, duration, magnitude, amplitude, size, pitch, ratio, depth, scope, height, strength, breadth, amplification. *Common units of measure include the following:—linear:* inch, foot, yard, rod, mile, millimeter, centimeter, decimeter, meter, kilometer; *surface:* square inch, square foot, square yard, acre, square rod, square mile; *volume:* dram, pint, quart, gallon, centiliter, liter; *weight:* gram,

ounce, pound; milligram, gram, kilogram; *relationship:* revolutions per minute (r.p.m.), miles per hour (m.p.h.), feet per second (f.p.s.), per second per second, erg, foot-pound, kilowatt-hour, acre-foot, decibel, man-hour, ohm, watt, volt, octane number. 2 [Anything used as a standard] rule, test, trial, example, standard, yardstick, norm, pattern, type, model; see also CRITERION. 3 [A beat] rhythm, tempo, time, step, throb, stroke, accent, meter, cadence, tune, melody, stress, vibration, division; see also BEAT 2. —**for good measure** added, as a bonus, additionally; see EXTRA. —**in full measure** completely, sufficiently, amply; see ADEQUATELY. —**take measures** take action, do things to accomplish a purpose, employ; see ACT 1.

measure *v.* **1** [To apply a standard of measurement] rule, weigh, mark, lay out, grade, graduate, gauge, sound, pitch, beat, stroke, time, mark off, scale, rank, even, level, gradate, line, align, line out, regulate, portion, set a standard, average, equate, square, calibrate, block in, survey, map. 2 [To contain by measurement] hold, cover, contain; see INCLUDE 1.

measured *a.* **1** [Steady] orderly, systematic, deliberate; see REGULAR 3. 2 [Determined] checked, evaluated, calculated; see DETERMINED 1.

measurement *n.* **1** [The act of measuring] estimation, analysis, computation; see JUDGMENT 2. 2 [The result of measuring] distance, dimension, weight, degree, pitch, time, height, depth, density, volume, area, length, measure, thickness, quantity, magnitude, extent, range, scope, reach, amount, capacity, frequency, intensity, pressure, speed, caliber, grade, span, step, strength, mass. 3 [A set of measures] inch, foot, yard; see MEASURE 1.

meat *n.* veal, mutton, lamb, chicken, turkey, goose, duck, rabbit, venison, horsemeat; see also FOOD. *Cuts and* used as food **3** the edible, inner part *[the meat of a nut]* **4** the substance or essence —**meat'y, -i·er, -i·est,** *adj.*

meat'ball' *n.* a small ball of ground meat, seasoned and cooked

meat'pack'ing *n.* the process or industry of preparing the meat of animals for market

Mecca (mek'ə) *n.* ⟦after *Mecca*, Saudi Arabia: Muslim pilgrimage center⟧ *[often* **m-***]* **1** any place visited by many people **2** any place that one yearns to go to

me·chanic (mə kan'ik) *n.* ⟦< Gr *mēchanē*, machine⟧ a worker skilled in using tools, repairing machines, etc.

me·chan'i·cal *adj.* **1** having to do with machinery or tools **2** produced or operated by machinery or a mechanism **3** of the science of mechanics **4** machinelike; lacking warmth, etc. —**me·chan'i·cally** *adv.*

me·chan'ics *n.pl.* *[with sing. v.]* **1** the science of motion and of the action of forces on bodies **2** knowledge of machinery **3** the technical part *[the mechanics of writing]*

mecha·nism (mek'ə niz'əm) *n.* ⟦< Gr *mēchanē*, machine⟧ **1** the working parts of a machine **2** any system of interrelated parts **3** any physical or mental process by which a result is produced —**mech'a·nis'tic** *adj.*

mech'a·nize' (-nīz') *vt.* **-nized', -niz'ing 1** to make mechanical **2** to equip (an industry) with machinery or (an army, etc.) with motor vehicles, tanks, etc. —**mech'a·ni·za'tion** *n.*

medal (med'l) *n.* ⟦< LL *medialis*, medial⟧ **1** a small, flat piece of inscribed metal commemorating some event or awarded for some distinguished action, merit, etc. **2** a similar piece of metal with a religious figure

med'al·ist *n.* one awarded a medal

me·dal·lion (mə dal'yən) *n.* ⟦Fr *médaillon*⟧ **1** a large medal **2** a design, portrait, etc. resembling a medal

med·dle (med'l) *vi.* **-dled, -dling** ⟦< L *miscere*, to mix⟧ to interfere in another's affairs —**med'dler** *n.* —**med'dle·some** (-səm) *adj.*

me·dia (mē'dē ə) *n. alt. pl. of* MEDIUM: see MEDIUM (*n.* 3) — **the media** *[usually with sing. v.]* all the means of communication, as newspapers, radio, etc.

me·dial (mē'dē əl) *adj.* ⟦< L *medius*⟧ **1** middle **2** ordinary

me·dian (mē'dē ən) *adj.* **1** middle; intermediate **2** designating the middle number in a series —*n.* **1** a median

385

number, point, line, etc. **2** the strip of land separating the lanes of opposing traffic of a divided highway: in full **median strip**

me·di·ate (mē'dē āt') *vi.* **-at·ed, -at·ing** ⟦< L *medius*, middle⟧ **1** to be in an intermediate position **2** to be an intermediary — *vt.* to settle (differences) between persons, nations, etc. by intervention —**me'di·a'tion** *n.* —**me'di·a'tor** *n.*

medic (med'ik) *n.* [Colloq.] **1** a physician or surgeon **2** a medical officer who gives first aid in combat

Med'ic·aid' (-i kād') *n.* ⟦MEDIC(AL) + AID⟧ *[also* **m-***]* a State and Federal health program for paying certain medical expenses of persons of low income

med'i·cal (-i kəl) *adj.* of or connected with the practice or study of medicine —**med'i·cally** *adv.*

medical jurisprudence the application of medical knowledge to questions of law

Med'i·care' (-ker') *n.* ⟦MEDI(CAL) + CARE⟧ *[also* **m-***]* a Federal health program for paying certain medical expenses of the aged and the needy

med'i·cate' (-kāt') *vt.* **-cat·ed, -cat·ing** ⟦< L *medicari*, heal⟧ to treat with medicine —**med'i·ca'tion** *n.*

me·dici·nal (mə dis'ən əl) *adj.* of, or having the properties of, medicine

medi·cine (med'i sən) *n.* ⟦< L *medicus*, physician⟧ **1** the science and art of treating and preventing disease **2** any substance, as a drug, used in treating disease, relieving pain, etc.

medicine man among North American Indians, etc., a man supposed to have supernatural powers for healing the sick, etc.

me·di·eval (mē'dē ē'vəl) *adj.* ⟦< L *medius*, middle + *aevum*, age⟧ of or characteristic of the Middle Ages

me·dio·cre (mē'dē ō'kər) *adj.* ⟦< L *medius*, middle + *ocris*, peak⟧ **1** ordinary; average **2** inferior —**me'di·oc'rity** (-äk'rə tē) *n.*, pl. **-ties,** *n.*

medi·tate (med'ə tāt') *vt.* **-tat·ed, -tat·ing** ⟦< L *meditari*⟧ to plan or intend — *vi.* to think deeply —**med'i·ta'tion** *n.* —**med'i·ta'tive** *adj.*

me·dium (mē'dē əm) *n., pl.* **-di·ums** *or* **-dia** (-ə) ⟦L < *medius*, the middle⟧ **1** *a)* something intermediate *b)* a

---

THESAURUS

forms of meat include the following: roast, cutlet, steak, filet, leg, shoulder, loin, tenderloin, rib, round, rump, flank, chop, liver, brains, kidneys, heart, bacon, tripe, shank, sausage, frankfurter, ground meat, chipped meat, dried meat, salted meat, pickled meat.

mechanic *n.* machinist, repair man, skilled workman; see WORKMAN.

mechanical *a.* **1** [Concerning machinery] engineering, production, manufacturing, tooling, tuning, implementing, fabricating, forging, machining, building, construction, constructing. **2** [Like a machine] made to a pattern, machinelike, stereotyped, standardized, without variation, unchanging, monotonous.—*Ant.* ORIGINAL, varied, changing. **3** [Operated by the use of machinery] power-driven, involuntary, programmed; see AUTOMATED, AUTOMATIC.

mechanically *a.* automatically, unreasoningly, unchangeably; see REGULARLY.

mechanism *n.* working parts, mechanical action, system of parts; see DEVICE 1, TOOL 1.

mechanize *v.* equip, computerize, industrialize, motorize, automate, put on the assembly line, make mechanical, introduce machinery into.

medal *n.* reward, commemoration, badge; see DECORATION 3.

medallion *n.* ornament, emblem, necklace; see JEWELRY.

meddle *v.* **1** [To interfere in others' affairs] interfere, obtrude, interlope, intervene, pry, snoop, impose oneself, infringe, break in upon, make it one's business, abuse one's rights,

push in, chime in, force an entrance, encroach, intrude, be officious, obstruct, impede, hinder, encumber, busy oneself with, come uninvited, tamper with, inquire, be curious, stick one's nose in*, monkey with*, bust in*, muscle in*, barge in, have a finger on*, butt in*, horn in*; see also INTERRUPT.—*Ant.* NEGLECT, ignore, let alone. **2** [To handle others' things] tamper, molest, pry, fool with, trespass, snoop, nose, use improperly.

meddlesome *a.* obtrusive, interfering, officious, meddling, intrusive, impertinent, interposing, interrupting, obstructive, impeding, hindering, encumbering, curious, tampering, prying, snooping, troublesome, snoopy*, nosy*, kibitzing*, chiseling*.

meddling *n.* interfering, interrupting, snooping; see INTERFERENCE 1, RUDENESS.

media *n.* radio, television, newspaper, journalism, news, reporters, reportage, programming, audiovisual devices.

medic* *n.* physician, practitioner, surgeon; see DOCTOR.

medical *a.* healing, medicinal, curative, therapeutic, restorative, prophylactic, preventive, alleviating, medicating, pharmaceutical, sedative, narcotic, tonic, disinfectant, corrective, pathological, cathartic, health-bringing, demulcent, balsamic, emollient.—*Ant.* HARMFUL, destructive, disease-giving.

medication *n.* remedy, pill, vaccination; see MEDICINE 2.

medicinal *a.* curative, healing, therapeutic; see HEALTHFUL.

medicine *n.* **1** [The healing profes-

sion] medical men, healers, practitioners, doctors, physicians, surgeons, osteopaths, chiropractors. **2** [A medical preparation] drug, dose, potion, prescription, pills, tablet, capsule, draft, patent medicine, remedy, cure, antipoison, antibiotic, medication, vaccination, inoculation, injection, draught, herb, specific, nostrum, elixir, tonic, balm, salve, lotion, ointment, emetic, shot. **3** [The study and practice of medicine] medical science, physic, healing art, medical profession. *Branches of medicine include the following:* surgery, therapy, therapeutics, anesthesiology, internal medicine, general practice, psychiatry, psychotherapy, psychoanalysis, ophthalmology, obstetrics, gynecology, pediatrics, orthopedics, neurology, cardiology, dermatology, pathology, endocrinology, immunology, urology, hematology, inhalation therapy, diagnostics, radiotherapy, geriatrics, veterinary medicine.

medieval *a.* pertaining to the Middle Ages, feudal, antiquated; see OLD 3.

mediocre *a.* average, ordinary, standard; see COMMON 1, DULL 4.

mediocrity *n.* commonplaceness, commonness, normality; see REGULARITY.

meditate *v.* **1** [To muse] ponder, study, contemplate, muse over, revolve, say to oneself, reflect, view, brood over, dream; see also THINK 1. **2** [To think over] weigh, consider, speculate; see THINK 1.

meditation *n.* examination, contemplation, speculation; see REFLECTION 1, THOUGHT 1.

medium *a.* commonplace, mediocre, ordinary; see COMMON 1.

middle state or degree; mean **2** an intervening thing through which a force acts **3** any means, agency, etc.; specif., a means of communication that reaches the general public: a singular form **media** (*pl.* **medias**) is now sometimes used **4** any surrounding substance or environment **5** one through whom messages are supposedly sent from the dead — *adj.* intermediate in size, quality, etc.

med·ley (med′lē) *n., pl.* **-leys** [< L *miscere*, to mix] **1** a mixture of dissimilar things **2** a musical piece made up of various tunes or passages

me·dulla (mi dul′ə) *n., pl.* **-las** or **-lae** (-ē) [L, marrow] *Anat.* **1** a widening of the spinal cord forming the lowest part of the brain: in full **medulla ob·lon·gata** (äb′läŋ gät′ə) **2** the inner substance of an organ

meek (mēk) *adj.* [< ON *miukr*, gentle] **1** patient and mild **2** too submissive; spiritless —**meek′ly** *adv.* — **meek′ness** *n.*

meer·schaum (mir′shəm) *n.* [Ger, sea foam] **1** a white, claylike, heat-resistant mineral used for tobacco pipes, etc. **2** a pipe made of this

meet[1] (mēt) *vt.* **met**, **meet′ing** [OE *metan*] **1** to come upon; encounter **2** to be present at the arrival of [to meet a bus] **3** to come into contact with **4** to be introduced to **5** to contend with; deal with **6** to experience [to meet disaster] **7** to be perceived by (the eye, etc.) **8** *a)* to satisfy (a demand, etc.) *b)* to pay (a bill, etc.) — *vi.* **1** to come together **2** to come into contact, etc. **3** to be introduced **4** to assemble — *n.* a meeting [a track meet] — **meet with 1** to experience **2** to receive

meet[2] (mēt) *adj.* [OE (ge)*mæte*, fitting] [Now Rare] suitable; proper

meet′ing *n.* **1** a coming together **2** a gathering of people **3** a junction

mega- [Gr < *megas*, great] *combining form* **1** large, great, powerful **2** one million Also **meg-**

mega·byte (meg′ə bīt′) *n.* [prec. + BYTE] 2^{20} bytes, or, loosely, one million bytes

mega·dose *n.* an abnormally large dose, esp. of a vitamin

meg′a·hertz′ *n., pl.* **-hertz′** [MEGA- + HERTZ] one million hertz: formerly **meg′a·cy′cle**

megalo·ma·nia (meg′ə lō mā′nē ə) *n.* [< Gr *megas*, large + -MANIA] a mental disorder characterized by delusions of grandeur, power, etc.

mega·lopo·lis (meg′ə läp′ə lis) *n., pl.* **-lis·es** [Gr, great city] a vast, continuously urban area, including any number of cities

mega·phone (meg′ə fōn′) *n.* [MEGA- + -PHONE] a cone-shaped device for increasing the volume of the voice

meg′a·ton′ *n.* [MEGA- + TON] the explosive force of a million tons of TNT

mel·amine (mel′ə mēn′) *n.* [Ger *melamin*] a white, crystalline compound used in making synthetic resins

mel·an·cho·lia (mel′ən kō′lē ə) *n.* a mental disorder, often psychotic, characterized by extreme depression

mel·an·chol′y (-käl′ē) *n., pl.* **-ies** [< Gr *melas*, black + *cholē*, bile] sadness and depression of spirits — *adj.* **1** sad and depressed **2** causing sadness

Mela·nesian (mel′ə nē′zhən) *n.* a native or inhabitant of Melanesia — *adj.* of Melanesia

mé·lange (mā lônzh′, -lônj′) *n.* [Fr < *mêler*, to mix] a mixture; medley

mela·nin (mel′ə nin) *n.* [< Gr *melas*, black] a blackish pigment found in skin, hair, etc.

mel′a·no′ma (-nō′mə) *n., pl.* **-mas** or **-mata** (-mə tə) [< Gr *melas*, black + -*ōma*, mass] a skin tumor derived from cells capable of melanin formation

Melba toast (mel′bə) [after N. *Melba* (1861-1931), Australian soprano] [*also* **m- t-**] very crisp, thinly sliced toasted bread

meld (meld) *vt., vi.* [Ger *melden*, announce] *Card Games* to show (certain cards) for a score — *n.* the cards melded

me·lee or **mê·lée** (mā′lā′, mā lā′) *n.* [Fr] **1** a confused fight or hand-to-hand struggle **2** a confused conflict or mixture

melio·rate (mēl′yə rāt′) *vt., vi.* **-rat′ed**, **-rat′ing** [< L *melior*, better] to make or become better —**mel′io·ra′tion** *n.*

mel·lif·lu·ous (mə lif′lōō əs) *adj.* [< L *mel*, honey + *fluere*, to flow] sounding sweet and smooth Also **mel·lif′lu·ent** —**mel·lif′lu·ence** *n.*

mel·low (mel′ō) *adj.* [ME *melwe*, ripe] **1** soft, sweet, etc. because ripe: said of fruit **2** full-flavored: said of wine, etc. **3** full, rich, soft, etc.: said of sound, light, etc. **4** made gentle, understanding, etc. by age — *vt., vi.* to make or become mellow

me·lo·di·ous (mə lō′dē əs) *adj.* **1** producing melody **2** pleasing to hear; tuneful —**me·lo′di·ously** *adv.*

melo·drama (mel′ō drä′mə, -dram′ə; mel′ə-) *n.* [< Fr < Gr *melos*, song + LL *drama*, drama] a drama with exaggerated conflicts and emotions, stereotyped characters, etc. —**mel′o·dra·mat′ic** (-drə mat′ik) *adj.*

mel′o·dra·mat′ics (-drə mat′iks) *n.pl.* melodramatic behavior

melo·dy (mel′ə dē) *n., pl.* **-dies** [< Gr *melos*, song + *aeidein*, sing] **1** pleasing sounds in sequence **2** *Music a)* a tune, song, etc. *b)* the leading part in a harmonic composition —**me·lodic** (mə läd′ik) *adj.* —**me·lod′i·cally** *adv.*

melon (mel′ən) *n.* [< Gr *mēlon*, apple] the large, juicy, thick-skinned, many-seeded fruit of certain trailing plants, as the watermelon or cantaloupe

melt (melt) *vt., vi.* [OE *m(i)eltan*] **1** to change from a solid to a liquid state, generally by heat **2** to dissolve **3** to

---

THESAURUS

medium *n.* **1** [A means] mechanism, tool, factor; see MEANS 1, PART 3. **2** [A means of expression] symbol, sign, token, interpretation, manifestation, revelation, evidence, mark, statement; see also COMMUNICATION, SPEECH 2. **3** [A supposed channel of supernatural knowledge] oracle, seer, spiritualist; see PROPHET.

medley *n.* mingling, melee, conglomeration; see MIXTURE 1, VARIETY 1.

meek *a.* **1** [Humble] unassuming, plain, mild; see HUMBLE 1, MODEST 2. **2** [Long-suffering] passive, resigned, serene; see PATIENT 1. **3** [Lacking spirit] submissive, compliant, subdued; see DOCILE, RESIGNED.

meekness *n.* submission, mildness, timidity; see HUMILITY.

meet[1] *n.* match, athletic event, tournament; see COMPETITION, EVENT.

meet[1] *v.* **1** [To come together] converge, assemble, crowd, rally, convene, collect, associate, unite, swarm, get together, enter in; see also GATHER 1. **2** [To go to a place of meeting] resort, be present at, gather together, convene, congregate, muster, appear, go to the meeting; see also ASSEMBLE 1, ATTEND.—*Ant.* LEAVE, disperse, scatter. **3** [To touch] reach, coincide, adhere; see JOIN 1. **4** [To become acquainted] make the acquaintance of, be presented to, be introduced, present

oneself, make oneself known, get next to*, get to know; see also FAMILIARIZE (ONESELF WITH). **5** [To fulfill] answer, fit, suffice; see SATISFY 3. **6** [To encounter] fall in with, come upon, meet by accident, come across, meet face to face, face up to, bump into, touch shoulders with, meet at every turn, engage, join issue with, battle, match, push, brush against, shove; see also FACE 1, FIGHT.—*Ant.* ABANDON, turn one's back on, leave. —**meet with** observe, experience, suffer; see FIND.

meeting *n.* **1** [The act of coming together] encounter, juxtaposition, joining, juncture, unifying, unification, adherence, convergence, confrontation, contacting, connection, conflict, contention, accord, agreement, compromising.—*Ant.* SEPARATION, departure, dispersal. **2** [A gathering, usually of people] conference, assemblage, rally; see GATHERING.

melancholy *a.* depressed, unhappy, dispirited; see SAD 1.

melancholy *n.* wistfulness, despair, unhappiness; see DEPRESSION 2, GRIEF, SADNESS.

meld *v.* blend, merge, unite; see MIX 1, UNITE.

mellow *a.* **1** [Ripe] sweet, soft, perfected; see RIPE 1. **2** [Culturally mature] cultured, fully developed,

broad-minded; see MATURE.

mellowed *a.* mature, ripened, softened; see RIPE 1, SOFT 3.

melodious *a.* agreeable, pleasing, resonant; see HARMONIOUS 1, MUSICAL 1.

melodrama *n.* play, opera, theater; see DRAMA.

melodramatic *a.* artificial, spectacular, sensational; see EXAGGERATED.

melody *n.* **1** [The quality of being melodious] concord, unison, chime; see HARMONY 1. **2** [A melodious arrangement] air, lyric, strain; see SONG.

melon *n.* watermelon, cantaloupe, muskmelon; see FOOD, FRUIT.

melt *v.* **1** [To liquefy] thaw, fuse, blend, merge, soften, flow, run, disintegrate, waste away; see also DISSOLVE.—*Ant.* FREEZE, harden, coagulate. **2** [To relent] forgive, show mercy, become lenient; see YIELD 1. **3** [To decrease] vanish, pass away, go; see DECREASE 1.

melted *a.* softened, thawed, liquefied, dwindled, blended, merged, wasted away, disintegrated, vanished, decreased, diminished, tempered, relaxed.

melting *a.* softening, liquefying, reducing; see SOFT 2.

disappear or cause to disappear gradually **4** to soften; become gentle, tender, etc.

melt'down' *n.* a dangerous situation in which a nuclear reactor begins to melt its fuel rods

melting pot a country, etc. in which people of various nationalities and races are assimilated

mem·ber (mem'bər) *n.* 〖< L *membrum*〗 **1** a limb or other part of a person, animal, or plant **2** a distinct part of a whole **3** a person belonging to some group, society, etc.

mem'ber·ship' *n.* **1** the state of being a member **2** members collectively, as of a group **3** the number of members

mem·brane (mem'brān') *n.* 〖< L *membrum*, member〗 a thin, soft layer, esp. of animal or plant tissue, that covers or lines an organ, part, etc. —**mem'bra·nous** (-brə nəs) *adj.*

me·men·to (mə men'tō) *n., pl.* **-tos** or **-toes** 〖< L *meminisse*, remember〗 a reminder; esp., a souvenir

memo (mem'ō) *n., pl.* **-os** *short for* MEMORANDUM

mem·oirs (mem'wärz') *n.pl.* 〖< L *memoria*, memory〗 **1** an autobiography **2** a record of events based on the writer's personal observation or knowledge

memo·ra·bilia (mem'ə rə bil'ē ə, -bil'yə; -bēl'-) *n.pl.* 〖L〗 things worth remembering

memo·ra·ble (mem'ə rə bəl) *adj.* worth remembering; notable; remarkable —**memo·rably** *adv.*

memo·ran·dum (mem'ə ran'dəm) *n., pl.* **-dums** or **-da** (-də) 〖L〗 **1** a short note written to remind one of something **2** an informal written communication, as in an office **3** *Law* a short written statement of the terms of an agreement, contract, etc.

me·mo·rial (mə môr'ē əl) *adj.* 〖< L *memoria*, memory〗 serving to help people remember — *n.* anything meant to help people remember a person or event, as a monument or holiday —**me·mo'ri·al·ize'** (-īz'), **-ized'**, **-iz'ing**, *vt.*

Memorial Day a legal holiday in the U.S. (the last Monday in May in most States) in memory of members of the armed forces killed in war

memo·rize (mem'ə rīz') *vt.* **-rized'**, **-riz'ing** to commit to memory —**mem'o·ri·za'tion** *n.*

memo·ry (mem'ə rē, mem'rē) *n., pl.* **-ries** 〖< L *memor*, mindful〗 **1** the power or act of remembering **2** all that one remembers **3** something remembered **4** the period of remembering [within my *memory*] **5** commemoration **6** storage capacity, as of a computer

men (men) *n. pl. of* MAN

men·ace (men'əs) *n.* 〖< L *minari*, threaten〗 **1** a threat **2** [Colloq.] one who is a nuisance —*vt.*, *vi.* **-aced**, **-ac·ing** to threaten —**men'ac·ingly** *adv.*

mé·nage or **me·nage** (mā näzh', mə-) *n.* 〖Fr < L *mansio*, house〗 a household

me·nag·erie (mə naj'ər ē) *n.* 〖see prec.〗 a collection of wild animals kept in cages, etc. for exhibition

mend (mend) *vt.* 〖< ME *amenden*, amend〗 **1** to repair **2** to make better; reform — *vi.* **1** to improve, esp. in health **2** to heal, as a fracture — *n.* **1** a mending **2** a mended

place —**on the mend** improving, esp. in health —**mend'er** *n.*

men·da·cious (men dā'shəs) *adj.* 〖< L *mendax*〗 not truthful; lying —**men·dac'ity** (-das'ə tē), *pl.* **-ties**, *n.*

men·di·cant (men'di kənt) *adj.* 〖< L *mendicus*, needy〗 begging — *n.* **1** a beggar **2** a mendicant friar —**men'di·cancy** *n.*

men'folk' (-fōk') *n.pl.* [Colloq. or Dial.] men

men·ha·den (men hād'n) *n., pl.* **-den** or **-dens** 〖< AmInd〗 a common fish of the W Atlantic, used for bait or for making oil and fertilizer

me·nial (mē'nē əl) *adj.* 〖< L *mansio*, house〗 **1** of or fit for servants **2** servile; low — *n.* **1** a domestic servant **2** a servile, low person —**me'ni·ally** *adv.*

me·nin·ges (mə nin'jēz') *n.pl., sing.* **me·ninx** (mē'ninks') 〖< Gr *mēninx*, membrane〗 the three membranes that envelop the brain and the spinal cord —**me·nin'geal** (-jē əl) *adj.*

men·in·gi·tis (men'in jīt'is) *n.* 〖ModL: see prec. & -ITIS〗 inflammation of the meninges

me·nis·cus (mə nis'kəs) *n., pl.* **-nis'cuses** or **-nis'ci** (-nis'ī', -kī') 〖< Gr dim. of *mēnē*, the moon〗 **1** a crescent **2** the convex or concave upper surface of a column of liquid

Men·non·ite (men'ən it') *n.* 〖after *Menno* Simons, 16th-c. Du reformer〗 a member of an evangelical Christian sect that opposes military service, oaths, etc., and favors plain living and dress

meno·pause (men'ə pôz') *n.* 〖< Gr *mēn*, month + *pauein*, to end〗 the permanent cessation of menstruation

me·no·rah (mə nō'rə, -nôr'ə) *n.* 〖Heb *menora*, lamp stand〗 a candelabrum with seven (or nine) branches: a symbol of Judaism

men·ses (men'sēz') *n.pl.* 〖L, pl. of *mensis*, month〗 the periodic flow, usually monthly, of blood from the uterus

men·stru·ate (men'strāt', -strōō āt') *vi.* **-at'ed**, **-at'ing** 〖< L *mensis*, month〗 to have a discharge of the menses —**men'strual** *adj.* —**men'strua'tion** *n.*

men·su·ra·tion (men'shə rā'shən) *n.* 〖< L *mensura*, measure〗 a measuring —**men'sur·able** (-shər ə bəl) *adj.*

-ment (mənt, mint) 〖< L *-mentum*〗 *suffix* **1** a result **2** a means [*escapement*] **3** an act **4** a state [*enchantment*]

men·tal (ment'l) *adj.* 〖< L *mens*, the mind〗 **1** of, for, by, or in the mind **2** ill in mind [*mental* patients] **3** for the ill in mind —**men'tally** *adv.*

men'tal·ist *n.* MIND READER

men·tal·ity (men tal'ə tē) *n., pl.* **-ties** **1** mental capacity or power **2** mental attitude or outlook

mental reservation a qualification (of a statement) that one makes to oneself but does not express

mental retardation congenital disorder characterized by subnormal intelligence

men·ta·tion (men tā'shən) *n.* 〖< L *mens*, mind + -ATION〗 the act or process of using the mind

---

■ THESAURUS ■

member *n.* **1** [A person or group] constituent, charter member, active member, member in good standing, honorary member, affiliate, brother, sister, comrade, chapter, post, branch, lodge, district, county, town, township, state, country, countries, company, battalion, regiment, division. **2** [A part] portion, segment, fragment; see DIVISION 1, PART 1. **3** [A part of the body] organ, arm, leg; see LIMB 2.

membership *n.* club, society, association; see MEMBER 1.

memorable *a.* **1** [Historic] momentous, critical, unforgettable, crucial, famous, illustrious, distinguished, great, notable, significant, decisive, enduring, lasting, monumental, eventful, interesting; see also FAMOUS. **2** [Unusual] remarkable, exceptional, singular; see sense 1 and UNUSUAL 1.

memorandum *n.* notice, record, jotting; see NOTE 2, REMINDER.

memorial *a.* dedicatory, remembering, commemorating; see REMEMBERED.

memorial *n.* remembrance, testimonial, tablet, slab, pillar, tombstone, headstone, column, monolith, mau-

soleum, record, memento, inscription, statue; see also CELEBRATION, CEREMONY 2, MONUMENT.

memorize *v.* fix in the memory, make memorable, record, commemorate, memorialize, retain, commit to memory, imprint in one's mind, bear in mind, give word for word, get down pat*, have in one's head*, have at one's fingertips*, learn by heart; see also LEARN, REMEMBER 2.—*Ant.* NEGLECT, forget, fail to remember.

memory *n.* **1** [The power to call up the past] recollection, retrospection, reminiscence, thought, consciousness, subconsciousness, unconscious memory, retentive memory, photographic memory, visual memory, auditory memory; see also MIND 1. **2** [That which can be recalled] mental image, picture, vision; see THOUGHT 2. —**in memory** for, in honor of, in memoriam; see REMEMBERED.

menace *n.* **1** [A threat] caution, intimidation, foretelling; see WARNING. **2** [An imminent danger] hazard, peril, threat; see DANGER.

menace *v.* intimidate, portend, loom; see THREATEN.

menacing *a.* imminent, impending, threatening; see DANGEROUS, OMI-

NOUS, SINISTER.

mend *v.* **1** [To repair] heal, patch, fix; see REPAIR. **2** [To improve] aid, remedy, cure; see CORRECT.

mended *a.* restored, put in shape, patched up, renovated, refreshed, renewed, corrected, helped, bettered, lessened, remedied, cured, relieved, rectified, rejuvenated, remodeled, altered, changed, fixed, regulated, rebuilt, regenerated, reorganized, revived, touched up, doctored*; see also REPAIRED.

menial *a.* common, servile, abject; see HUMBLE 1, 2.

menstruation *n.* menses, lady's time, time of the month, monthlies*, the curse*; see also FLOW.

mental *a.* **1** [Concerning the mind] reasoning, cerebral, thinking; see RATIONAL 1, THOUGHTFUL 1. **2** [Existing only in the mind] subjective, subliminal, subconscious, telepathic, psychic, clairvoyant, imaginative; see also IMAGINARY.—*Ant.* OBJECTIVE, BODILY, SENSUAL.

mentality *n.* intellect, comprehension, reasoning; see MIND 1.

mentally *a.* rationally, psychically, intellectually; see REASONABLY 1.

men·thol (men'thôl', -thäl') *n.* 〖Ger < L *mentha*, MINT[2]〗 a white, crystalline alcohol obtained from oil of peppermint and used in medicine, cosmetics, etc. —**men'tho·lat'ed** (-thə lāt'id) *adj.*

men·tion (men'shən) *n.* 〖< L *mens*, the mind〗 1 a brief reference 2 a citing for honor — *vt.* to refer to briefly or incidentally —**make mention of** to mention —**not to mention** without even mentioning

men·tor (men'tər, -tôr') *n.* 〖after *Mentor*, friend and advisor of Odysseus〗 1 a wise advisor 2 a teacher or coach

menu (men'yōō) *n., pl.* **-us** 〖Fr, small, detailed〗 1 a detailed list of the foods served at a meal or those available at a restaurant 2 a list, as on a computer screen, of the various choices available to the user

meow or **meou** (mē ou') *n.* 〖echoic〗 the characteristic vocal sound made by a cat — *vi.* to make such a sound

mer·can·tile (mʉr'kən til', -til) *adj.* 〖Fr〗 of or characteristic of merchants or trade

mer·ce·nary (mʉr'sə ner'ē) *adj.* 〖< L *merces*, wages〗 working or done for payment only — *n., pl.* **-ies** a soldier hired to serve in a foreign army

mer·cer (mʉr'sər) *n.* 〖< L *merx*, wares〗 [Brit.] a dealer in textiles

mer'cer·ize *vt.* **-ized', -iz'ing** 〖after J. *Mercer* (1791-1866), Eng calico dealer〗 to treat (cotton thread or fabric) with an alkaline solution to strengthen it, give it a silky luster, etc.

mer·chan·dise (mʉr'chən dīz', -dīs') *n.* 〖see fol.〗 things bought and sold; wares — *vt., vi.* **-dised', -dis'ing** 1 to buy and sell 2 to promote the sale of (a product) Also, for v., **mer'chan·dize'** (-dīz') **-dized', -diz'ing** —**mer'chan·dis'er** or **mer'chan·diz'er** *n.*

mer·chant (mʉr'chənt) *n.* 〖ult. < L *merx*, wares〗 1 one whose business is buying and selling goods 2 a retail dealer; storekeeper — *adj.* mercantile

mer'chant·man (-mən) *n., pl.* **-men** a ship used in commerce

merchant marine 1 all of a nation's commercial ships 2 their personnel

merci (mer sē') *interj.* 〖Fr〗 thank you

mer·ci·ful (mʉr'sə fəl) *adj.* having or showing mercy —**mer'ci·ful·ly** *adv.*

mer'ci·less *adj.* without mercy; pitiless —**mer'ci·less·ly** *adv.*

mer·cu·rial (mər kyoor'ē əl) *adj.* 1 having qualities associated with Mercury; clever, shrewd, etc. 2 of or containing mercury 3 quick, changeable, fickle, etc.

Mer·cu·ry (mʉr'kyoo rē) 1 *Rom. Myth.* the messenger of the gods 2 a small planet in the solar system: see PLANET — *n.* [m-] a heavy, silver-white metallic chemical element, liquid at ordinary temperatures, used in thermometers, etc. —**mer·cu·ric** (mər kyoor'ik) *adj.* —**mer·cu'rous** *adj.*

mercy (mʉr'sē) *n., pl.* **-cies** 〖< L *merces*, payment〗 1 a refraining from harming offenders, enemies, etc. 2 imprisonment rather than death for a capital crime 3 a disposition to forgive or be kind 4 the power to forgive 5 a lucky thing; blessing —**at the mercy of** in the power of

mercy killing EUTHANASIA

mere (mir) *adj. superl.* **mer'est** 〖< L *merus*, pure〗 nothing more or other than 〖a *mere* boy〗

mere'ly *adv.* only; no more than

mer·e·tri·cious (mer'ə trish'əs) *adj.* 〖< L *meretrix*, a prostitute〗 1 attractive in a flashy way 2 specious

mer·gan·ser (mər gan'sər) *n.* 〖< L *mergus*, diver (bird) + *anser*, goose〗 a fish-eating, diving duck with a long bill

merge (mʉrj) *vi., vt.* **merged, merg'ing** 〖L *mergere*, to dip〗 1 to lose or cause to lose identity by being absorbed or combined 2 to unite

merg'er *n.* a merging; specif., a combining of two or more companies into one

me·rid·ian (mə rid'ē ən) *n.* 〖< L *meridies*, noon〗 1 the highest point of power, etc. 2 *a)* a circle on the earth's surface passing through the geographical poles and any given point *b)* any of the lines of longitude

me·ringue (mə raŋ') *n.* 〖Fr〗 egg whites beaten with sugar until stiff: used as a pie covering, etc.

me·ri·no (mə rē'nō) *n., pl.* **-nos** 〖Sp〗 1 any of a breed of hardy, white-faced sheep with long, fine wool 2 the wool 3 yarn or cloth made of it

merit (mer'it) *n.* 〖< L *merere*, deserve〗 1 worth; value; excellence 2 something deserving reward, praise, etc. 3 [*pl.*] intrinsic rightness or wrongness — *vt.* to deserve

mer·i·to·ri·ous (mer'i tôr'ē əs) *adj.* having merit; deserving reward, praise, etc. —**mer'i·to'ri·ous·ly** *adv.*

Mer·lin (mʉr'lin) *Arthurian Legend* a magician and seer, helper of King Arthur

mer·maid (mʉr'mād') *n.* 〖< OE *mere*, sea + MAID〗 an imaginary sea creature with the head and upper body of a woman and the tail of a fish —**mer'man'** (-man') *pl.* **-men'**, *n.masc.*

mer·ri·ment (mer'i mənt) *n.* a merrymaking; gaiety and fun; mirth

merry (mer'ē) *adj.* **-ri·er, -ri·est** 〖< OE *myrge*, pleasing〗 1 full of fun; lively 2 festive —**make merry** to be festive and have fun —**mer'ri·ly** *adv.* —**mer'ri·ness** *n.*

mer'ry-go-round' *n.* 1 a circular, revolving platform with forms of animals as seats on it, used at carnivals, etc. 2 a busy round, as of work

mer'ry·mak'ing *n.* a having fun; festivity —**mer'ry·mak'er** *n.*

mesa (mā'sə) *n.* 〖Sp < L *mensa*, a table〗 a small, high plateau with steep sides·

mes·cal (mes kal') *n.* 〖< Sp < AmInd(Mex)〗 a small cactus of N Mexico and the SW U.S.

mes·ca·line (mes'kə lēn', -lin) *n.* 〖< AmInd(Mex) *mexcalli*, a spineless cactus〗 a psychedelic drug obtained from the mescal

mes·dames (mā däm') *n. pl. of* MADAME, MADAM (sense 1), or MRS.

mes·demoi·selles (mād mwä zel') *n. pl. of* MADEMOISELLE

mesh (mesh) *n.* 〖prob. < MDu *mæsche*〗 1 any of the open spaces of a net, screen, etc. 2 a net or network 3 a netlike material, as for stockings 4 the engagement of the teeth of gears — *vt., vi.* 1 to entangle or become entangled 2 to engage or become engaged: said of gears 3 to interlock

mes·mer·ize (mez'mər iz', mes'-) *vt.* **-ized', -iz'ing** 〖after F. A. *Mesmer* (1734-1815), Ger physician〗 to hypnotize — **mes'mer·ism'** *n.* —**mes'mer·ist** *n.*

meson (mes'än', mez'-) *n.* 〖< Gr *mesos*, middle + (ELEC-

THESAURUS

mention *n.* notice, naming, specifying; see REMARK. —**not to mention** in addition, too, without even mentioning; see ALSO.

mention *v.* notice, specify, cite, introduce, state, declare, quote, refer to, discuss, touch on, instance, intimate, notify, communicate, suggest, make known, point out, speak of, throw out, toss off; see also TELL 1.— *Ant.* OVERLOOK, take no notice of, disregard.

mentioned *a.* noticed, cited, specified, named, quoted, introduced, referred to, discussed, declared, revealed, brought up, considered, communicated, made known, spoken of; see also TOLD.

menu *n.* bill of fare, cuisine, food; see LIST.

merchandise *n.* wares, commodities, stock; see COMMODITY.

merchandise *v.* market, distribute, promote; see SELL.

merchant *n.* trader, storekeeper, retailer, shopkeeper, wholesaler, exporter, shipper, dealer, jobber, tradesman; see also BUSINESSMAN.

merciful *a.* lenient, feeling, compassionate, softhearted, mild, tolerant, kindly, indulgent; see also KIND.— *Ant.* CRUEL, pitiless, unsparing.

merciless *a.* pitiless, unsparing, relentless; see CRUEL, FIERCE, RUTHLESS.

mercy *n.* leniency, lenience, softheartedness, mildness, clemency, tenderness, gentleness, compassion; see also GENEROSITY, TOLERANCE 1.— *Ant.* INDIFFERENCE, intolerance, selfishness. —**at the mercy of** in the power of, vulnerable to, controlled by; see SUBJECT.

mere *a.* small, minor, insignificant; see LITTLE 1, POOR 2.

merely *a.* slightly, solely, simply; see HARDLY, ONLY 3.

merge *v.* fuse, join, blend; see MIX 1, UNITE.

merger *n.* pool, consolidation, alliance; see ORGANIZATION 2.

merit *n.* 1 [Worth] credit, benefit, advantage; see QUALITY 3, VALUE 3. 2 [A creditable quality] worthiness, excellence, honor; see CHARACTER 2, VIRTUE 1.

merit *v.* be worth, warrant, justify; see DESERVE.

merited *a.* earned, proper, fitting; see DESERVED, FIT 1.

merrily *a.* joyfully, gleefully, genially; see CHEERFULLY, HAPPILY.

merriment *n.* joy, cheerfulness, gaiety; see HAPPINESS, HUMOR 3.

merry *a.* gay, joyous, mirthful; see HAPPY. —**make merry** frolic, revel, enjoy; see PLAY 1.

mesa *n.* plateau, table, tableland, butte, table mountain; see also HILL, MOUNTAIN 1.

mesh *v.* coincide, suit, be in gear; see AGREE, FIT 1.

TR)ON] an unstable boson with a mass between those of an electron and a proton

Meso·zo·ic (mes'ō zō'ik, mez'-) *adj.* ⟦< Gr *mesos*, middle + zo(o)- + -IC⟧ designating the geologic era (c. 225 to 65 million years ago) characterized by dinosaurs and by the appearance of flowering plants, grasses, birds, etc.

mes·quite or **mes·quit** (mes kēt') *n.* ⟦< AmInd(Mex) *mizquitl*⟧ a thorny tree or shrub of Mexico and the SW U.S.

mess (mes) *n.* ⟦< L *missus*, course (at a meal)⟧ 1 a portion of food for a meal 2 a group of people who regularly eat together, as in the army 3 the meal they eat 4 a jumble 5 a state of trouble, disorder, or confusion — *vt.* 1 to make dirty or untidy 2 to muddle; botch: often with *up* — *vi.* 1 to eat as one of a mess 2 to make a mess 3 to putter or meddle (*in* or *with*) —**mess'y, -i·er, -i·est,** *adj.* —**mess'i·ly** *adv.* —**mess'i·ness** *n.*

mes·sage (mes'ij) *n.* ⟦< L *mittere*, send⟧ 1 a communication sent by speech, in writing, etc. 2 the chief idea that an artist, writer, etc. seeks to communicate in a work — **get the message** [Colloq.] to understand a hint, etc.

mes·sen·ger (mes'ən jər) *n.* one who carries a message or goes on an errand

messenger RNA a form of RNA, derived from DNA, that carries the genetic code needed to form a protein

mess hall a room or building where soldiers, etc. regularly have meals

Mes·si·ah (mə sī'ə) ⟦< Heb *māshīaḥ*, anointed⟧ 1 *Judaism* the expected deliverer of the Jews 2 *Christianity* Jesus —**Mes·si·an·ic** (mes'ē an'ik) *adj.*

mes·sieurs (mes'ərz; Fr mā syö') *n. pl. of* MONSIEUR

Messrs. (mes'ərz) messieurs: now used chiefly as the pl. of Mr.

mes·ti·zo (mes tē'zō) *n., pl.* **-zos** or **-zoes** ⟦Sp < L *miscere*, to mix⟧ a person of mixed parentage, esp. Spanish and American Indian

met (met) *vt., vi. pt. & pp. of* MEET[1]

met. metropolitan

meta- ⟦< Gr *meta*, after⟧ *prefix* 1 changed [metathesis] 2 after, beyond, higher [metaphysics]

me·tab·o·lism (mə tab'ə liz'əm) *n.* ⟦< Gr *meta*, beyond + *ballein*, throw⟧ the chemical and physical processes continuously going on in living organisms and cells, including the changing of food into living tissue and the changing of living tissue into waste products and energy —**meta·bol·ic** (met'ə bäl'ik) *adj.* —**me·tab'o·lize'** (-līz'), **-lized', -liz'ing, vt., vi.**

meta·car·pus (met'ə kär'pəs) *n., pl.* **-pi** (-pī) ⟦< Gr *meta*, over + *karpos*, wrist⟧ the part of the hand between the wrist and the fingers —**met'a·car'pal** *adj., n.*

metal (met''l) *n.* ⟦< Gr *metallon*, a mine⟧ 1 *a*) any of a class of chemical elements, as iron or gold, that have luster, can conduct heat and electricity, etc. *b*) an alloy of such elements, as brass or bronze 2 anything consisting of metal —**me·tal·lic** (mə tal'ik) *adj.* —**me·tal'li·cally** *adv.*

met·al·lurgy (met'ə lur'jē, met''l ur'jē) *n.* ⟦< Gr *metallon*, metal + *ergon*, work⟧ the science of separating metals from their ores and preparing them for use, by smelting, refining, etc. —**met'al·lur'gi·cal** *adj.* —**met'al·lur'gist** *n.*

meta·mor·phose (met'ə môr'fōz', -fōs') *vt., vi.* **-phosed', -phos'ing** to change in form; transform

met'a·mor'pho·sis (-môr'fə sis, -môr fō'sis) *n., pl.* **-ses'** (-sēz') ⟦< Gr *meta*, over + *morphē*, form⟧ 1 a change of form, structure, substance, or function; specif., the physical change undergone by some animals, as of the tadpole

---

389

Mesozoic / methanol

to the frog 2 a marked change of character, appearance, condition, etc. —**met'a·mor'phic** *adj.*

meta·phor (met'ə fər, -fôr') *n.* ⟦< Gr *meta*, over + *pherein*, to bear⟧ a figure of speech in which one thing is spoken of as if it were another (Ex.: "all the world's a stage") —**met'a·phor'ic** or **met'a·phor'i·cal** *adj.* —**met'a·phor'i·cally** *adv.*

meta·physi·cal (met'ə fiz'i kəl) *adj.* 1 of, or having the nature of, metaphysics 2 very abstract or subtle 3 supernatural

met'a·phys'ics (-iks) *n.pl.* ⟦< Gr *meta* (ta) *physika*, after (the) *Physics* (of Aristotle)⟧ [with sing. v.] 1 the branch of philosophy that seeks to explain the nature of being and reality 2 speculative philosophy in general

me·tas·ta·sis (mə tas'tə sis) *n., pl.* **-ses'** (-sēz') ⟦< Gr *meta*, after + *histanai*, to place⟧ the spread of disease from one part of the body to another, esp. the spread of cancer cells by way of the bloodstream —**me·tas'ta·size'** (-sīz'), **-sized', -siz'ing,** *vi.*

meta·tar·sus (met'ə tär'səs) *n., pl.* **-si'** (-sī') ⟦< Gr *meta*, over + *tarsos*, flat of the foot⟧ the part of the human foot between the ankle and the toes —**met'a·tar'sal** *adj., n.*

me·tath·e·sis (mə tath'ə sis) *n., pl.* **-ses'** (-sēz') ⟦< Gr *meta*, over + *tithenai*, to place⟧ transposition, specif. of sounds in a word

mete (mēt) *vt.* **met'ed, met'ing** ⟦OE *metan*⟧ to allot; distribute: usually with *out*

metem·psy·cho·sis (mi tem'si kō'sis; met'əm si-) *n., pl.* **-ses'** (-sēz') ⟦< Gr *meta*, over + *en*, in + *psychē*, soul⟧ transmigration of souls

me·te·or (mēt'ē ər, -ē ôr') *n.* ⟦< Gr *meta*, beyond + *eōra*, a hovering⟧ 1 the streak of light, etc. observed when a meteoroid enters the earth's atmosphere 2 a meteoroid or meteorite

me'te·or'ic (-ôr'ik) *adj.* 1 of a meteor 2 like a meteor; momentarily brilliant, swift, etc.

me'te·or·ite' (-ər it') *n.* that part of a meteoroid that survives passage through the atmosphere

me'te·or·oid' (-ər oid') *n.* a small, solid body traveling through outer space, seen as a streak of light when in the earth's atmosphere

me'te·or·ol'o·gy (-ər äl'ə jē) *n.* ⟦see METEOR & -LOGY⟧ the science of the atmosphere and its phenomena; study of weather —**me'teoro·log'i·cal** (-ə läj'i kəl) *adj.* —**me'teor·ol'o·gist** *n.*

me·ter[1] (mēt'ər) *n.* ⟦< Gr *metron*, a measure⟧ 1 rhythm in verse; measured arrangement of syllables according to stress 2 the basic pattern of beats in music 3 ⟦Fr *mètre*⟧ the basic metric unit of length, equal to c. 39.37 inches

me·ter[2] (mēt'ər) *n.* ⟦< words ending in fol.⟧ 1 an apparatus for measuring and recording the quantity of gas, water, etc. passing through it 2 PARKING METER

-meter (mēt'ər, mi tər) ⟦< Gr *metron*, a measure⟧ *combining form* a device for measuring [barometer]

meter maid a woman employed by a police traffic department to issue tickets for illegal parking, jaywalking, etc.

metha·done (meth'ə dōn') *n.* ⟦< its chemical name⟧ a synthetic narcotic drug used in medicine to treat heroin and morphine addicts

meth·ane (meth'ān') *n.* ⟦< METHYL⟧ a colorless, odorless, flammable gas formed by the decomposition of vegetable matter, as in marshes

metha·nol (meth'ə nôl') *n.* ⟦< METHAN(E) + (ALCOH)OL⟧ a colorless, flammable, poisonous liquid used as a fuel, solvent, antifreeze, etc. Also **methyl alcohol**

═══ THESAURUS ═══

mess *n.* 1 [A mixture] combination, compound, blend; see MIXTURE 1. 2 [A confusion] jumble, muss, chaos, clutter, clog, congestion, snag, scramble, complexity, mayhem, hodgepodge; see also CONFUSION, DISORDER.

message *n.* tidings, information, intelligence; see ADVICE, BROADCAST, COMMUNICATION, DIRECTIONS. —**get the message** get the hint, comprehend, perceive; see UNDERSTAND 1.

messenger *n.* bearer, minister, herald, carrier, courier, runner, crier, errand boy, intermediary, envoy, emissary, angel, prophet, go-between; see also AGENT.

Messiah *n.* Saviour, Redeemer, Jesus Christ; see CHRIST, GOD 1.

mess up *v.* spoil, ruin, foul up*, damage; see also BOTCH, DESTROY.

messy *a.* rumpled, untidy, slovenly; see DIRTY, DISORDERED.

metal *n.* element, native rock, ore deposit, free metal, refined ore, smelted ore. *Types of metal include the following:* gold, silver, copper, iron, steel, aluminum, manganese, nickel, lead, cobalt, platinum, zinc, tin, barium, cadmium, chromium, tungsten, mercury, molybdenum, sodium, potassium, radium, magnesium, calcium, titanium, arsenic, uranium.

metallic *a.* 1 [Made of metal] hard, rocklike, iron, leaden, silvery, golden, metallurgic, mineral, geologic. 2 [Suggestive of metal; *said especially of sound*] ringing, resounding, resonant, bell-like, clanging.

metaphor *n.* trope, simile, implied comparison; see COMPARISON. —**mix metaphors** be inconsistent, garble, talk illogically; see CONFUSE.

metaphorical *a.* symbolical, allegorical, figurative; see DESCRIPTIVE, GRAPHIC 1, 2.

metaphysical *a.* mystical, abstract, spiritual; see DIFFICULT 2.

meteor *n.* falling star, shooting star, meteorite, fireball, meteoroid.

meteorology *n.* climate science, climatology, aerology; see SCIENCE 1, WEATHER.

meter[1] *n.* measure, rhythm, metrical feet, common meter, long meter, ballad meter, tetrameter, pentameter, sprung rhythm, dipodic rhythm.

me·thinks (mē thiŋks′) *v.impersonal pt.* **-thought′** ⟦OE *me,* to me + *thyncth,* it seems⟧ [Archaic] it seems to me
method (meth′əd) *n.* ⟦< Fr < Gr *meta,* after + *hodos,* a way⟧ **1** a way of doing anything; process **2** a system in doing things or handling ideas
me·thod·i·cal (mə thäd′i kəl) *adj.* characterized by method; orderly; systematic Also **me·thod′ic** —**me·thod′i·cal·ly** *adv.*
Meth·od·ist (meth′ə dist) *n.* a member of a Protestant Christian denomination that developed from the teachings of John Wesley —**Meth′od·ism′** *n.*
meth·od·ol·o·gy (-ə däl′ə jē) *n., pl.* **-gies** a system of methods, as in a science
Me·thu·se·lah (mə thōō′zə lə) *Bible* a patriarch who lived 969 years
meth·yl (meth′il) *n.* ⟦< Gr *methy,* wine + *hylē,* wood⟧ a hydrocarbon radical found in methanol
me·tic·u·lous (mə tik′yōō ləs, -yə-) *adj.* ⟦< L *metus,* fear⟧ extremely or excessively careful about details; scrupulous or finicky —**me·tic′u·lous·ly** *adv.*
mé·tier′ (mā tyā′) *n.* ⟦Fr, trade⟧ work that one is particularly suited for
me·tre (mē′tər) *n. Brit. sp. of* METER[1]
met·ric (me′trik) *adj.* **1** METRICAL **2** *a)* of the METER[1] (sense 3) *b)* of the metric system
met·ri·cal (me′tri kəl) *adj.* **1** of or composed in meter or verse **2** of or used in measurement —**met′ri·cal·ly** *adv.*
met·ri·cate (me′tri kāt′) *vt.* **-cat′ed, -cat′ing** to change over to the metric system —**met′ri·ca′tion** *n.*
metric system a decimal system of weights and measures in which the gram (.0022046 pound), the meter (39.37 inches), and the liter (61.025 cubic inches) are the basic units
metric ton a measure of weight equal to 1,000 kilograms or 2,204.62 pounds
metro (me′trō) *n., pl.* **-ros** ⟦ult. < *metro(politan)*⟧ [often M-] a subway
met·ro·nome (me′trə nōm′) *n.* ⟦< Gr *metron,* measure + *nomos,* law⟧ a device that beats time at a desired rate, as for piano practice
me·trop·o·lis (mə träp′əl is) *n., pl.* **-lises** ⟦< Gr *mētēr,* mother + *polis,* city⟧ **1** the main city, often the capital, of a country, state, etc. **2** any large or important city —**met·ro·pol·i·tan** (me′trō päl′i tən, -trə-) *adj.*
met·tle (met′'l) *n.* ⟦var. of METAL⟧ spirit; courage; ardor —**on one's mettle** prepared to do one's best
met′tle·some (-səm) *adj.* full of mettle; spirited; ardent, brave, etc.
mew[1] (myōō) *vt.* ⟦< L *mutare,* to change⟧ to confine
mew[2] *n.* ⟦echoic⟧ the characteristic vocal sound made by a cat — *vi.* to make this sound
mewl (myōōl) *vi.* ⟦< prec.⟧ to cry weakly, like a baby; whimper
mews (myōōz) *n.pl.* ⟦< MEW[1]⟧ [*usually with sing. v.*] [Chiefly Brit.] stables or carriage houses in a court or alley
Mex. **1** Mexican **2** Mexico
Mex·i·can (meks′i kən) *n.* a native or inhabitant of Mexico —*adj.* of Mexico
mez·za·nine (mez′ə nēn′, mez′ə nēn′) *n.* ⟦< It *mezzano,* middle⟧ **1** a low-ceilinged story between two main stories, as a balcony over the main floor **2** the first few rows of the balcony in some theaters
mezzo-soprano (met′sō sə pran′ō) *n., pl.* **-nos** or **-ni** (-ē) ⟦It < *mezzo,* medium + SOPRANO⟧ a voice or singer between soprano and contralto
mfg. manufacturing
mfr. manufacturer
Mg *Chem. symbol for* magnesium
mg milligram(s)
Mgr. manager

MHz or **Mhz** megahertz
mi (mē) *n.* ⟦ML⟧ *Music* the third tone of the diatonic scale
mi. **1** mile(s) **2** mill(s)
MI middle initial
mi·as·ma (mi az′mə, mē-) *n.* ⟦< Gr *miainein,* pollute⟧ **1** a vapor as from marshes, formerly supposed to poison the air **2** an unwholesome atmosphere or influence
mica (mi′kə) *n.* ⟦L, a crumb⟧ a mineral that crystallizes in thin, flexible layers, resistant to heat and electricity
mice (mis) *n. pl. of* MOUSE
micro- ⟦< Gr *mikros,* small⟧ *combining form* **1** little, small [*microcosm*] **2** enlarging [*microscope*] **3** microscopic [*microbiology*] **4** one millionth [*microsecond*] Also **micr-**
mi·crobe (mi′krōb′) *n.* ⟦< Gr *mikros,* small + *bios,* life⟧ a microorganism, esp. one causing disease
mi·cro·bi·ol·o·gy (mi′krō bi äl′ə jē) *n.* the branch of biology dealing with microorganisms —**mi′cro·bi·ol′o·gist** *n.*
mi′cro·chip′ *n.* INTEGRATED CIRCUIT
mi′cro·com·put′er *n.* a small, inexpensive computer having a microprocessor and used in the home, etc.
mi′cro·cosm′ (-käz′əm) *n.* ⟦see MICRO- & COSMOS⟧ something regarded as a world in miniature
mi′cro·ec′o·nom′ics *n.pl.* [*with sing. v.*] a branch of economics dealing with certain specific factors affecting an economy, as the behavior of individual consumers
mi′cro·fiche′ (-fēsh′) *n., pl.* **-fich′es** or **-fiche′** ⟦Fr < *micro-,* MICRO- + *fiche,* small card⟧ a small sheet of microfilm containing a group of microfilmed pages
mi′cro·film′ *n.* film on which documents, etc. are photographed in a reduced size for storage, etc. —*vt., vi.* to photograph on microfilm
mi′cro·groove′ *n.* the very narrow groove in an LP phonograph record
mi·crom·e·ter (mi kräm′ət ər) *n.* ⟦< Fr: see MICRO- & -METER⟧ an instrument for measuring very small distances, angles, etc.
mi·cron (mi′krän′) *n.* ⟦< Gr *mikros,* small⟧ one millionth of a meter
micro·organ·ism (mi′krō ôr′gən iz′əm) *n.* a microscopic organism, esp. a bacterium, protozoan, etc.
mi′cro·phone′ (mi′krə-) *n.* ⟦MICRO- + -PHONE⟧ an instrument for converting sound waves into an electric signal
mi′cro·proc′es′sor (mi′krō-) *n.* an integrated circuit that controls the operation of a microcomputer
mi′cro·scope′ (mi′krə-) *n.* ⟦see MICRO- & -SCOPE⟧ an instrument consisting of a combination of lenses, for making very small objects, as microorganisms, look larger
mi′cro·scop′ic (-skäp′ik) *adj.* **1** so small as to be invisible or obscure except through a microscope; minute **2** of, with, or like a microscope —**mi′cro·scop′i·cal·ly** *adv.*
mi′cro·sur′gery (mi′krō-) *n.* surgery performed using a microscope and minute instruments or laser beams
mi′cro·wave′ *adj.* **1** designating equipment, etc. using microwaves for radar, communications, etc. **2** designating an oven that cooks quickly using microwaves —*vt.* **-waved′, -wav′ing** to cook in a microwave oven —*n.* **1** an electromagnetic wave with a frequency of about 300,000 megahertz to 300 megahertz **2** a microwave oven
mid[1] (mid) *adj.* ⟦OE *midd-*⟧ middle
mid[2] (mid) *prep.* [Old Poet.] amid Also **'mid**
mid- *combining form* middle, middle part of [*mid-*May]
mid′air′ *n.* any point not in contact with the ground or any other surface
Mi·das (mi′dəs) *Gr. Myth.* a king granted the power of turning everything that he touched into gold
mid′day′ *n., adj.* ⟦OE *middæg*⟧ noon
mid·dle (mid′'l) *adj.* ⟦OE *middel*⟧ **1** halfway between two given points, times, etc. **2** intermediate **3** [M-] designating a stage in language development intermediate between *Old* and *Modern* [*Middle* English] —*n.* **1** a point or part

---

═══ THESAURUS ═══

method *n.* mode, style, standard procedure, fashion, way, means, process, proceeding, adjustment, disposition, practice, routine, technique, attack, mode of operation, manner of working, ways and means, habit, custom, manner, formula, process, course, rule; see also SYSTEM.
methodical *a.* well-regulated, systematic, exact; see ORDERLY 2, REGULAR 3.
métier *n.* trade, profession, occupation; see JOB 1, PROFESSION 1.
metropolis *n.* capital, megalopolis,

municipality; see CENTER 2, CITY.
metropolitan *a.* city, municipal, cosmopolitan; see MODERN 2, URBAN.
Mexican *a.* Latin American, south of the border, Hispanic; see AMERICAN 1.
microbe *n.* microorganism, bacterium, bacillus; see GERM.
microphone *n.* sound transmitter, receiver, pickup instrument, mike*, bug*, walkie-talkie.
microscope *n.* lens, magnifying glass, optical instrument, scope.

Microscopes include the following: high-powered, compound, photographic, electron, electronic.
microscopic *a.* diminutive, tiny, infinitesimal; see LITTLE 1, MINUTE 1.
middle *a.* mean, midway, medial, average, equidistant; see also CENTRAL, HALFWAY, INTERMEDIATE.
middle *n.* mean, focus, core, nucleus, heart, navel, midst, marrow, pivot, axis, medium, midpoint; see also CENTER 1.

halfway between extremes; middle point, time, etc. **2** something intermediate **3** the middle part of the body; waist

mid′dle age the time between youth and old age — **mid′dle-aged′** *adj.*

Middle Ages the period of European history between ancient and modern times, A.D. 476–c. 1450

Middle America the American middle class, seen as being conventional or conservative

mid′dle·brow′ (-brou′) *n.* [Colloq.] one regarded as having conventional, middle-class tastes or opinions

middle class the social class between the aristocracy or very wealthy and the lower working class —**mid′dle-class′** *adj.*

middle ear the part of the ear including the eardrum and the adjacent cavity containing three small bones

Middle English the English language between c. 1100 and c. 1500

mid′dle·man′ *n.*, *pl.* **-men′** **1** a trader who buys from a producer and sells at wholesale or retail **2** a go-between

mid′dle·most′ *adj.* MIDMOST

mid′dle-of-the-road′ *adj.* avoiding extremes, esp. political extremes

middle school a school with, usually, grades five through eight

mid′dle·weight′ *n.* a boxer with a maximum weight of 160 pounds

Middle West region of the north central U.S. —**Middle Western**

mid·dling (mid′liŋ) *adj.* of middle size, quality, etc.; medium — *adv.* [Colloq.] fairly; moderately

middy (mid′ē) *n.*, *pl.* **-dies** [< MIDSHIPMAN] a loose blouse with a sailor collar, worn by women and children

midge (mij) *n.* [OE *mycg*] a small, gnatlike insect

midget (mij′it) *n.* **1** a very small person **2** anything very small of its kind — *adj.* miniature

mid·land (mid′lənd) *n.* the middle region of a country; interior — *adj.* in or of the midland; inland

mid′most′ *adj.* exactly in the middle, or nearest the middle

mid′night′ (-nīt′) *n.* twelve o'clock at night — *adj.* **1** of or at midnight **2** like midnight; very dark

mid′point′ *n.* a point at or close to the middle or center

mid·riff (mid′rif) *n.* [< OE *midd-*, MID¹ + *hrif*, belly] **1** DIAPHRAGM (sense 1) **2** the middle part of the torso, between the abdomen and the chest

mid·ship·man (mid′ship′mən) *n.*, *pl.* **-men** a student in training to be a naval officer

mid-size or **mid·size** (mid′sīz′) *adj.* of a size intermediate between large and small [a *mid-size* car]

midst¹ (midst) *n.* the middle; central part —**in our** (or **your** or **their**) **midst** among us (or you or them) —**in the midst of 1** in the middle of **2** during

midst² (midst) *prep.* [Old Poet.] in the midst of; amidst Also **′midst**

mid·stream (mid′strēm′) *n.* the middle of a stream

mid′sum′mer *n.* **1** the middle of summer **2** the time of the summer solstice, about June 21

mid′term′ *adj.* in the middle of the term — *n.* [Colloq.] a midterm examination, as at a college

mid′way′ (-wā′) *n.* that part of a fair where sideshows, etc. are located — *adj.*, *adv.* in the middle of the way or distance; halfway

Mid·west (mid′west′) MIDDLE WEST —**Mid′west′ern** *adj.*

mid′wife′ (-wīf′) *n.*, *pl.* **-wives′** [< ME *mid*, with + *wif*, woman] a person who helps women in childbirth —**mid′wife′ry** (-wīf′rē) *n.*

mid′win′ter *n.* **1** the middle of winter **2** the time of the winter solstice, about Dec. 22

mid′year′ *adj.* in the middle of the year — *n.* [Colloq.] a midyear examination, as at a college

mien (mēn) *n.* [short for DEMEAN²] one's appearance, bearing, or manner

miff (mif) *vt.* [prob. orig. cry of disgust] [Colloq.] to offend

MIG (mig) [after Mikoyan & Gurevich, its Soviet designers] a high-speed, high-altitude jet fighter plane Also **MiG**

might¹ (mīt) *v.aux.* [OE *mihte*] **1** *pt.* of MAY **2** used as an auxiliary generally equivalent to MAY [it *might* rain]

might² (mīt) *n.* [OE *miht*] strength, power, or vigor

might′y (-ē) *adj.* **-i·er, -i·est 1** powerful; strong **2** remarkably large, etc.; great — *adv.* [Colloq.] very — **might′i·ly** *adv.* —**might′i·ness** *n.*

mi·gnon·ette (min′yə net′) *n.* [< Fr *mignon*, small] a plant with spikes of small, fragrant flowers

mi·graine (mī′grān′) *n.* [< Gr *hēmi-*, half + *kranion*, skull] an intense, periodic headache, usually limited to one side of the head

mi·grant (mī′grənt) *adj.* migrating — *n.* **1** one that migrates **2** a farm laborer who moves from place to place to harvest seasonal crops

mi·grate (mī′grāt′) *vi.* **-grat′ed, -grat′ing** [< L *migrare*] **1** to settle in another country or region **2** to move to another region with the change in seasons, as many birds —**mi·gra·tory** (mī′grə tôr′ē) *adj.*

mi·gra·tion (mī grā′shən) *n.* **1** a migrating **2** a group of people, birds, etc. migrating together

mi·ka·do (mi kä′dō) *n.*, *pl.* **-dos** [< Jpn *mi*, an honorific title + *kado*, gate] [often **M-**] the emperor of Japan: title no longer used

mike (mīk) *n.* [Colloq.] a microphone — *vt.* **miked, mik′ing** [Colloq.] to record, amplify, etc. with a microphone

mil (mil) *n.* [L *mille*, thousand] a unit of linear measure, equal to ¹⁄₁₀₀₀ inch

mi·lady or **mi·ladi** (mi lā′dē) *n.*, *pl.* **-dies** [Fr < Eng *my lady*] **1** a noblewoman **2** a woman of fashion: advertisers' term

milch (milch) *adj.* [ME *milche*] kept for milking [milch cows]

mild (mīld) *adj.* [OE *milde*] **1** gentle or kind; not severe **2** having a soft, pleasant flavor [a *mild* cheese] —**mild′ly** *adv.* —**mild′ness** *n.*

mil·dew (mil′dōō′) *n.* [OE *meledeaw*, honeydew] a fungus that attacks some plants or appears on damp cloth, etc. as a whitish coating — *vt.*, *vi.* to affect or be affected with mildew

mile (mīl) *n.* [< L *milia (passuum)*, thousand (paces)] a unit of linear measure equal to 5,280 feet

---

THESAURUS

middle age *n.* adulthood, prime, maturity; see MAJORITY 2.

middle-aged *a.* adult, in one's prime, matronly; see MATURE.

middle-class *a.* white-collar, bourgeois, substantial; see COMMON 1, POPULAR 3, 4.

midget *n.* pygmy, dwarf, manikin; see PERSON.

midnight *n.* dead of night, stroke of midnight, twelve midnight, noon of night, witching hour; see also NIGHT 1. —**burn the midnight oil** stay up late, work late, keep late hours; see STUDY, WORK 1.

midst¹ *n.* midpoint, nucleus, middle; see CENTER 1. —**in our** (or **your** or **their**) **midst** between us, with, accompanying; see AMONG. —**in the midst of** in the course of, engaged in, in the middle of; see CENTRAL.

midway *a.* in the thick of, between, in the middle of the way; see CENTRAL, HALFWAY, INTERMEDIATE, MIDDLE.

might² *n.* strength, force, sway; see STRENGTH.

mightily *a.* energetically, strongly, forcibly; see POWERFULLY, VIGOROUSLY.

mighty *a.* **1** [Strong] powerful, stalwart, muscular; see STRONG 1. **2** [Powerful through influence] great, all-powerful, omnipotent; see POWERFUL 1. **3** [Imposing] great, extensive, impressive, gigantic, magnificent, towering, dynamic, notable, extraordinary, grand, considerable, monumental, tremendous; see also LARGE 1.—*Ant.* PLAIN, unimpressive, ordinary. **4** [*To a high degree] exceedingly, greatly, extremely; see VERY.

migrate *v.* move, emigrate, immigrate; see LEAVE 1.

migration *n.* emigration, immigration, voyage; see DEPARTURE, JOURNEY, MOVEMENT 2.

migratory *a.* wandering, migrant, vagrant; see TEMPORARY.

mild *a.* **1** [Gentle; *said especially of* persons*] meek, easygoing, patient; see KIND. **2** [Temperate; *said especially of weather*] bland, untroubled, tropical, peaceful, summery, tepid, cool, balmy, breezy, gentle, soft, lukewarm, clear, moderate, mellow, fine, uncloudy, sunny, warm.—*Ant.* ROUGH, COLD, STORMY. **3** [Easy; *said especially of burdens or punishment*] soft, light, tempered; see MODERATE 4. **4** [Not irritating] bland, soothing, soft, smooth, gentle, moderate, easy, mellow, delicate, temperate.

mildly *a.* gently, meekly, calmly, genially, tranquilly, softly, lightly, moderately, tenderly, compassionately, tolerantly, patiently, temperately, indifferently, quietly.—*Ant.* VIOLENTLY, harshly, roughly.

mildness *n.* tolerance, tenderness, gentleness; see KINDNESS 1.

mile *n.* 5,280 feet, statute mile, geographical mile, nautical mile, Admiralty mile; see also DISTANCE 3, MEASURE 1.

mile′age (-ij) *n.* 1 an allowance per mile for traveling expenses 2 total miles traveled 3 the average number of miles that can be traveled, as per gallon of fuel

mile′post′ *n.* a signpost showing the distance in miles to or from a place

mil′er (-ər) *n.* one who competes in mile races

mile′stone′ *n.* 1 a stone set up to show the distance in miles to or from a place 2 a significant event

mi·lieu (mēl yʉ′, -yoo′, -yoo′; mil-) *n.* 〚Fr < L *medius*, middle + *locus*, a place〛 environment; esp., social setting

mili·tant (mil′i tənt) *adj.* 〚< L *miles*, soldier〛 1 fighting 2 ready to fight, esp. for some cause — *n.* a militant person —**mil′i·tancy** *n.* —**mil′i·tantly** *adv.*

mili·ta·rism (mil′ə tə riz′əm) *n.* 1 military spirit 2 a policy of aggressive military preparedness —**mil′i·ta·rist** *n.* —**mil′i·ta·ris′tic** *adj.*

mili·ta·rize (mil′i tə riz′) *vt.* -rized′, -riz′ing to equip and prepare for war

mili·tary (mil′ə ter′ē) *adj.* 〚< L *miles*, soldier〛 1 of, for, or done by soldiers 2 of, for, or fit for war 3 of the army —**the military** the armed forces

military police soldiers assigned to police duties in the army

mili·tate (mil′ə tāt′) *vi.* -tat′ed, -tat′ing 〚< L *militare*, be a soldier〛 to operate or work (*against*)

mi·li·tia (mə lish′ə) *n.* 〚< L *miles*, soldier〛 an army composed of citizens rather than professional soldiers, called up in time of emergency —**mi·li′tia·man** (-mən), *pl.* **-men**, *n.*

milk (milk) *n.* 〚OE *meolc*〛 1 a white fluid secreted by the mammary glands of female mammals for suckling their young 2 cow's milk, etc., drunk by humans as a food or used to make butter, cheese, etc. 3 any liquid like this, as coconut milk — *vt.* 1 to squeeze milk from (a cow, goat, etc.) 2 to extract money, ideas, etc. from as if by milking —**milk′er** *n.*

milk glass a nearly opaque whitish glass

milk′maid′ *n.* a girl or woman who milks cows or works in a dairy

milk′man′ *n.*, *pl.* **-men′** a man who sells or delivers milk for a dairy

milk of magnesia a milky-white suspension of magnesium hydroxide in water, used as a laxative and antacid

milk′shake′ *n.* a drink made of milk, flavoring, and ice cream, shaken until frothy

milk′sop′ (-säp′) *n.* one who is timid, ineffectual, effeminate, etc.

milk tooth any of the temporary, first teeth of a child or young animal

milk′weed′ *n.* any of a group of plants with a milky juice

milk′y (-ē) *adj.* -i·er, -i·est 1 like milk; esp., white as milk 2 of or containing milk —**milk′i·ness** *n.*

Milky Way a broad, faintly luminous band of very distant stars and interstellar gas, arching across the night sky

mill¹ (mil) *n.* 〚< L *mola*, millstone〛 1 a building with machinery for grinding grain into flour or meal 2 any of various machines for grinding, crushing, cutting, etc. 3 a factory 〔a textile *mill*〕 — *vt.* 1 to grind, form, etc. by or in a mill 2 to raise and ridge the edge of (a coin) — *vi.* to move (*around* or *about*) confusedly —**in the mill** in preparation —**through the mill** [Colloq.] through a hard, painful, instructive experience

mill² (mil) *n.* 〚< L *mille*, thousand〛 $\frac{1}{10}$ of a cent: unit used in calculating

mill·age (mil′ij) *n.* taxation in mills per dollar of valuation

mil·len·ni·um (mi len′ē əm) *n.*, *pl.* **-ni·ums** or **-ni·a** (-ə) 〚< L *mille*, thousand + *annus*, year〛 1 a thousand years 2 *Christian Theol.* the period of a thousand years during which Christ will reign on earth: with *the* 3 any period of great happiness, peace, etc. —**mil·len′ni·al** *adj.*

miller (mil′ər) *n.* one who owns or operates a mill, esp. a flour mill

mil·let (mil′it) *n.* 〚< L *milium*〛 1 a cereal grass whose grain is used for food in Europe and Asia 2 any of several similar grasses used for forage

milli- 〚< L *mille*, thousand〛 *combining form* one thousandth part of [*millimeter*]

milli·gram (mil′i gram′) *n.* one thousandth of a gram

mil′li·me′ter (-mēt′ər) *n.* one thousandth of a meter Brit. sp. **mil′li·me′tre**

mil·li·ner (mil′i nər) *n.* 〚< *Milaner*, vendor of dress wares from Milan, Italy〛 one who makes or sells women's hats

mil·li·nery (mil′i nerē) *n.* 1 women's hats, headdresses, etc. 2 the work or business of a milliner

mil·lion (mil′yən) *n.* 〚< L *mille*, thousand〛 a thousand thousands; 1,000,000 —**mil′lionth** *adj.*, *n.*

mil′lion·aire′ (-yə ner′) *n.* a person whose wealth comes to at least a million dollars, pounds, francs, etc.

milli·pede (mil′i pēd′) *n.* 〚< L *mille*, thousand + *pes*, foot〛 a many-legged arthropod with an elongated body

mill′race′ *n.* the channel in which water turning a wheel that drives the machinery in a mill runs

mill′stone′ *n.* 1 either of a pair of flat, round stones used for grinding grain, etc. 2 a heavy burden

mill′stream′ *n.* water flowing in a millrace

mill′wright′ (-rīt′) *n.* a worker who builds, installs, or repairs the machinery in a mill

milt (milt) *n.* 〚prob. < Scand〛 the sex glands or sperm of male fishes

mime (mīm) *n.* 〚< Gr *mimos*〛 1 the representation of an action, mood, etc. by gestures, not words 2 a mimic or pantomimist — *vt.* **mimed, mim′ing** to mimic or pantomime

mimeo·graph (mim′ē ə graf′) *n.* 〚< Gr *mimeomai*, I imitate〛 a machine for making copies of graphic matter by means of an inked stencil — *vt.* to make (such copies) of

mi·metic (mi met′ik, mī-) *adj.* 〚< Gr *mimeisthai*, to imitate〛 1 imitative 2 characterized by mimicry

mimic (mim′ik) *adj.* 〚< Gr *mimos*, actor〛 1 imitative 2 make-believe — *n.* an imitator; esp., an actor skilled in mimicry — *vt.* **-icked, -ick·ing** 1 to imitate, often so as to ridicule 2 to copy or resemble closely

mimic·ry (mim′ik rē) *n.*, *pl.* **-ries** the practice, art, or way of mimicking

mi·mosa (mi mō′sə) *n.* 〚see MIME〛 a tree, shrub, or herb growing in warm regions and usually having spikes of white or pink flowers

min. 1 minimum 2 minute(s)

mina·ret (min′ə ret′) *n.* 〚< Ar *manāra(t)*, lighthouse〛 a high, slender tower attached to a mosque

mina·tory (min′ə tôr′ē) *adj.* 〚< L *minari*, threaten〛 menacing

mince (mins) *vt.* **minced, minc′ing** 〚< L *minutus*, small〛 1 to cut up (meat, etc.) into small pieces 2 to express or do with affected daintiness 3 to lessen the force of 〔to *mince* no words〕 — *vi.* to speak or act with affected daintiness —**minc′ing** *adj.*

mince′meat′ *n.* a mixture of chopped apples, spices, raisins, etc., and sometimes meat, used as a pie filling

mind (mīnd) *n.* 〚< OE *(ge)mynd*〛 1 memory 〔to bring to *mind* a story〕 2 opinion 〔speak your *mind*〕 3 the seat of

---

THESAURUS

mileage *n.* rate, space, measure; see DISTANCE 3, LENGTH 1.

militant *a.* combative, belligerent, offensive; see AGGRESSIVE.

militant *n.* rioter, violent objector, demonstrator; see RADICAL.

military *a.* armed, militant, combative; see AGGRESSIVE.

militia *n.* military force, civilian army. National Guard; see ARMY 1.

milk *n.* fluid, juice, sap; see LIQUID. *Types of milk include the following:* whole, skim, raw, pasteurized, homogenized, certified; grade-A, grade-B, etc.; loose, condensed, dried, evaporated, powdered; two-percent, four-percent, etc.; goat's, mare's, mother's; cream, half-and-half, buttermilk, kefir. —**cry over spilt milk** mourn, lament, sulk; see

REGRET.

milky *a.* opaque, pearly, cloudy; see WHITE 1.

mill¹ *n.* 1 [A factory] manufactory, plant, millhouse; see FACTORY. 2 [A machine for grinding, crushing, pressing, etc.] *Types of mills include the following:* flour, coffee, cotton, weaving, spinning, powder, rolling, cider, cane, lapidary, sawmill, coin press.

millionaire *n.* man of means, capitalist, tycoon, rich man, plutocrat, Croesus, nabob, Midas, big-money man*, robber baron, fat cat*.—*Ant.* BEGGAR, poor man, pauper.

mimic *n.* mime, impersonator, comedian; see ACTOR, IMITATOR.

mimic *v.* 1 [To imitate] copy, simulate, impersonate; see IMITATE. 2 [To

mock] make fun of, burlesque, caricature; see RIDICULE.

mimicry *n.* mime, pretense, mockery; see IMITATION 2.

mind *n.* 1 [Intellectual potentiality] soul, spirit, intellect, brain, consciousness, thought, mentality, intuition, perception, conception, intelligence, intellectuality, capacity, judgment, understanding, wisdom, genius, talent, reasoning, instinct, wit, mental faculties, intellectual faculties, creativity, ingenuity, intellectual powers, gray matter*, brainpower. 2 [Purpose] intention, inclination, determination; see PURPOSE 1. —**bear** (or **keep**) **in mind** heed, recollect, recall; see REMEMBER 1. —**be in one's right mind** be mentally well, be rational, be sane;

consciousness, in which thinking, feeling, etc. takes place **4** intellect **5** PSYCHE (n. 2) **6** reason; sanity — *vt.* **1** to pay attention to; heed **2** to obey **3** to take care of /mind the baby/ **4** to be careful about /mind the stairs/ **5** to care about; object to /they don't mind the noise/ — *vi.* **1** to pay attention **2** to be obedient **3** to be careful **4** to care; object —**bear (or keep) in mind** to remember —**change one's mind** to change one's opinion, purpose, etc. —**have in mind** to intend —**make up one's mind** to reach a decision —**never mind** don't be concerned; it doesn't matter —**on one's mind 1** filling one's thoughts **2** worrying one —**out of one's mind** frantic

mind′ed *adj.* having a (specified kind of) mind: used in compounds /high-*minded*/

mind′ful (-fəl) *adj.* having in mind; aware or careful (*of*) —**mind′fully** *adv.* —**mind′ful·ness** *n.*

mind′less *adj.* **1** without intelligence **2** heedless (*of*) — **mind′lessly** *adv.*

mind reader one who professes ability to perceive another's thoughts

mind's eye the imagination

mine¹ (mīn) *pron.* ⟦OE min⟧ that or those belonging to me /this is *mine*/

mine² (mīn) *n.* ⟦< Fr⟧ **1** a large excavation made in the earth, from which to extract ores, coal, etc. **2** a deposit of ore, coal, etc. **3** any great source of supply **4** *Mil. a*) a tunnel dug under an enemy's fort, etc., in which an explosive is placed *b*) an explosive charge hidden underground or in the sea, for destroying enemy vehicles, ships, etc. — *vt., vi.* **mined, min′ing 1** to dig (ores, etc.) from (the earth) **2** to dig or lay military mines in or under **3** to undermine

min′er *n.* one whose work is digging coal, ore, etc. in a mine

min·er·al (min′ər əl) *n.* ⟦< ML minera, ore⟧ **1** an inorganic substance found naturally in the earth, as metallic ore **2** any substance that is neither vegetable nor animal — *adj.* of or containing a mineral

min·er·al·o·gy (min′ər al′ə jē) *n.* the scientific study of minerals —**min′er·al′o·gist** *n.*

mineral oil a colorless, tasteless oil from petroleum, used as a laxative

mineral water water impregnated with mineral salts or gases

Mi·nerva (mə nʉr′və) *Rom. Myth.* the goddess of wisdom

mi·nestro·ne (min′ə strō′nē) *n.* ⟦It.: ult. < L ministrare, serve⟧ a thick vegetable soup in a meat broth

min·gle (miŋ′gəl) *vt.* **-gled, -gling** ⟦< OE mengan, to mix⟧ to mix together; blend — *vi.* **1** to become mixed or blended **2** to join or unite with others

mini- ⟦< MINI(ATURE)⟧ *combining form* miniature, very small, very short /miniskirt/

min·ia·ture (min′ē ə chər, min′i chər) *n.* ⟦< L miniare, paint red⟧ **1** a small painting, esp. a portrait **2** a copy or model on a very small scale — *adj.* done on a very small scale

min·ia·tur·ize (-īz′) *vt.* **-ized′, -iz′ing** to make in a small and compact form —**min′ia·tur′i·za′tion** *n.*

mini·bike (min′ē bīk′) *n.* a compact motorcycle, usually used as an off-road vehicle

min′i·bus (-bus′) *n.* a very small bus

min′i·cam′ (-kam′) *n.* a portable TV camera for telecasting or videotaping news events, sports, etc.

min′i·com·put′er (-kəm pyōōt′ər) *n.* a computer intermediate in size, power, etc. between a mainframe and microcomputer

mini·mal (min′i məl) *adj.* **1** smallest or least possible **2** of minimalism —**min′i·mally** *adv.*

min′i·mal·ism′ (-iz′əm) *n.* a movement in art, music, etc. in which only the simplest design, forms, etc. are used, often repetitiously —**min′i·mal·ist** *adj., n.*

mini·mize (min′ə miz′) *vt.* **-mized′, -miz′ing** to reduce to or estimate at a minimum

min′i·mum (-məm) *n., pl.* **-mums** or **-ma** (-mə) ⟦L, least⟧ **1** the smallest quantity, number, etc. possible **2** the lowest degree or point reached — *adj.* smallest possible, permissible, or reached

min·ing (min′iŋ) *n.* the process or work of removing ores, coal, etc. from a mine

min·ion (min′yən) *n.* ⟦Fr mignon, darling⟧ **1** a favorite, esp. one who is a servile follower: term of contempt **2** a subordinate official

min·is·cule (min′i skyōōl′) *adj.* erroneous sp. of MINUSCULE

mini·series (min′ē sir′ēz) *n., pl.* **-ries** a TV drama broadcast serially in a limited number of episodes

mini·skirt (min′ē skʉrt′) *n.* a very short skirt ending well above the knee

min·is·ter (min′is tər) *n.* ⟦L, a servant⟧ **1** a person appointed to head a governmental department **2** a diplomat representing his or her government in a foreign nation **3** one authorized to conduct religious services in a

---

THESAURUS

see SANE. —**be of one mind** have the same opinion, concur, be in accord; see AGREE. —**call to mind** recall, recollect, bring to mind; see REMEMBER 1. —**change one's mind** alter one's opinion, change one's views, decide against, modify one's ideas. —**give someone a piece of one's mind** rebuke, confute, criticize; see SCOLD. —**have a good mind to** be inclined to, propose, tend to; see INTEND 1. —**have half a mind to** be inclined to, propose, tend to; see INTEND 1. —**have in mind 1** recall, recollect, think of; see REMEMBER 1. **2** purpose, propose, be inclined to; see INTEND 1. **3** expect, foresee, hope; see ANTICIPATE, THINK 1. —**know one's own mind** know oneself, be deliberate, have a plan; see KNOW 1. —**make up one's mind** form a definite opinion, choose, finalize; see DECIDE. —**meeting of the minds** concurrence, unity, harmony; see AGREEMENT 1. —**on one's mind** occupying one's thoughts, causing concern, worrying one; see IMPORTANT 1. —**out of one's mind** mentally ill, raving, mad; see INSANE. —**take one's mind off** turn one's attention from, divert, change; see DISTRACT.

mind *v.* **1** [To obey] be under the authority of, heed, do as told; see BEHAVE, OBEY. **2** [To give one's attention] heed, regard, be attentive to; see ATTEND. **3** [To be careful] tend, watch out for, take care, be wary, be concerned for, mind one's p's and q's*; see also CONSIDER.—

Ant. NEGLECT, ignore, be careless. **4** [*To remember] recollect, recall, bring to mind; see REMEMBER 1. **5** [To object to] complain, deplore, be opposed to; see DISLIKE. —**never mind** forget it, it doesn't matter, ignore it, don't bother, let it go, drop it*; see also STOP.

minded *a.* disposed, inclined, leaning toward; see WILLING.

mindful *a.* attentive, heedful, watchful; see CAREFUL.

mindless *a.* **1** [Careless] inattentive, oblivious, neglectful; see CARELESS, INDIFFERENT, RASH. **2** [Stupid] foolish, senseless, unintelligent; see STUPID.

mine¹ *a.* my own, belonging to me, possessed by me, mine by right, owned by me, left to me, from me, by me; see also OUR.

mine² *n.* **1** [A source of natural wealth] pit, well, shaft, diggings, excavation, workings, quarry, deposit, vein, lode, ore bed, placer, pay dirt, bonanza, strip mine, openpit mine, surface mine, hard-rock mine. **2** [An explosive charge] landmine, ambush, trap; see BOMB, EXPLOSIVE, WEAPON.

mine² *v.* **1** [To dig for minerals] excavate, work, quarry; see DIG 1. **2** [To lay mines] sow with mines, prepare mine fields, set booby traps; see DEFEND 1.

miner *n.* excavator, digger, driller, dredger, mine worker, prospector, mucker, driller, placer miner, hard-rock miner, mine superintendent,

mining engineer, desert rat*, sourdough*, forty-niner*; see also LABORER, WORKMAN.

mineral *a.* geologic, rock, metallurgic; see METALLIC 1.

mineral *n.* earth's crust, geologic formation, geologic rock, rock deposit, ore deposit, igneous rock, metamorphic rock, magma, petroleum, crystal; see also METAL.

mingle *v.* combine, blend, merge; see MIX 1.

miniature *a.* diminutive, small, tiny; see LITTLE 1.

minimize *v.* lessen, depreciate, reduce; see DECREASE 2.

minimum *a.* smallest, tiniest, merest, lowest.

minimum *n.* smallest, least, lowest, narrowest, atom, molecule, particle, dot, jot, iota, spark, shadow, gleam, grain, scruple.

mining *n.* excavating, hollowing, opening, digging, boring, drilling, delving, burrowing, tunneling, honeycombing, placer mining, hard-rock mining, prospecting.

minister *n.* **1** [One authorized to conduct Christian worship] pastor, parson, preacher, clergyman, rector, monk, abbot, prelate, canon, curate, vicar, deacon, chaplain, servant of God, shepherd, churchman, cleric, padre, ecclesiastic, bishop, archbishop, confessor, reverend, diocesan, divine, missionary; see also PRIEST.—*Ant.* LAYMAN, church member, parishioner. **2** [A high servant church **4** a pastor — *vi.* **1** to serve as a minister in a church **2** to give help (*to*) —**min′is·te′ri·al** (-tir′ē əl) *adj.* —**min′is·trant** (-trənt) *adj., n.*

min·is·tra′tion (-trā′shən) *n.* the act of giving help or care; service

min′is·try (-is trē) *n., pl.* **-tries 1** the act of ministering, or serving **2** *a*) the office or function of a minister of religion *b*) ministers of religion collectively; clergy **3** *a*) the department under a minister of government *b*) the minister's term of office *c*) the ministers of a particular government as a group

min·i·van (min′ē van′) *n.* a small van with windows all around and a back seat or back seats, used as a passenger vehicle: also **min′i-van**

mink (miŋk) *n.* 〚< Scand〛 **1** a slim, erminelike carnivore living in water part of the time **2** its valuable fur

min·now (min′ō) *n.* 〚< OE *myne*〛 any of various, usually small, freshwater fishes, often used as bait

Mi·noan (mi nō′ən) *adj.* 〚after *Minos*, mythical king of Crete〛 of an advanced prehistoric culture in Crete from *c.* 3000-*c.* 1100 B.C.

mi·nor (mi′nər) *adj.* 〚< L〛 **1** lesser in size, amount, importance, etc. **2** *Music* lower than the corresponding major by a half tone — *vi. Educ.* to have a secondary field of study (*in*) — *n.* **1** a person under full legal age **2** *Educ.* a secondary field of study

mi·nor·i·ty (mi nôr′ə tē, mi-) *n., pl.* **-ties 1** the lesser part or smaller number; less than half **2** a racial, religious, or political group that differs from the larger, controlling group **3** the state of being under full legal age

minor scale *Music* any of the twelve diatonic scales with a half step between the second and third tones

Mino·taur (min′ə tôr′) *Gr. Myth.* a monster with the body of a man and the head of a bull

min·strel (min′strəl) *n.* 〚see MINISTER〛 **1** a medieval traveling singer **2** a member of a comic variety show (**minstrel show**) in which the performers blacken their faces —**min′strelsy** (-sē), *pl.* **-sies,** *n.*

mint[1] (mint) *n.* 〚< L < Juno *Moneta*, whose temple was the mint〛 **1** a place where a government coins money **2** a large amount — *adj.* new, as if freshly minted — *vt.* to coin (money) —**mint′age** (-ij) *n.*

mint[2] (mint) *n.* 〚< Gr *mintha*〛 **1** an aromatic plant whose leaves are used for flavoring **2** a candy flavored with mint leaves

mint julep an iced drink of bourbon, sugar, and mint leaves

minu·end (min′yōō end′) *n.* 〚< L *minuere*, lessen〛 the number from which another is to be subtracted

minu·et (min′yōō et′) *n.* 〚< Fr < OFr *menu*, small〛 **1** a slow, stately dance **2** the music for this

mi·nus (mī′nəs) *prep.* 〚< L *minor*, less〛 **1** less 〔four *minus* two〕 **2** [Colloq.] without — *adj.* **1** involving subtraction 〔a *minus* sign〕 **2** negative **3** less than 〔a grade of A *minus*〕 — *n.* a sign (-), indicating subtraction or negative quantity: in full **minus sign**

mi·nus·cule (mi nus′kyōōl′; *commonly* min′i skyōōl′) *adj.* 〚L *minusculus*〛 very small; tiny

min·ute[1] (min′it) *n.* 〚see fol.〛 **1** the sixtieth part of an hour or of a degree of an arc **2** a moment **3** a specific point in time **4** [*pl.*] an official record of a meeting, etc. — **the minute (that)** just as soon as

mi·nute[2] (mī nōōt′) *adj.* 〚< L *minor*, less〛 **1** very small **2** of little importance **3** of or attentive to tiny details; precise —**mi·nute′ly** *adv.*

minute hand the longer hand of a clock, indicating the minutes

min′ute·man′ *n., pl.* **-men′** [*also* M-] a member of the American citizen army at the time of the American Revolution

min·ute steak (min′it) a small, thin steak that can be cooked quickly

mi·nu·tiae (mi nōō′shē ē′) *n.pl., sing.* **-tia** (-shē ə, -shə) 〚see MINUTE[2]〛 small or unimportant details

minx (miŋks) *n.* 〚< ?〛 a pert girl

mira·cle (mir′ə kəl) *n.* 〚< L *mirus*, wonderful〛 **1** an event or action that apparently contradicts known scientific laws **2** a remarkable thing

mi·racu·lous (mi rak′yōō ləs, -yə-) *adj.* **1** having the nature of, or like, a miracle **2** able to work miracles —**mi·rac′u·lously** *adv.*

mi·rage (mi räzh′) *n.* 〚< VL *mirare*, look at〛 an optical illusion, caused by the refraction of light, in which a distant object appears to be nearby

mire (mir) *n.* 〚< ON *myrr*〛 **1** an area of wet, soggy ground **2** deep mud; slush — *vt.* **mired, mir′ing 1** to cause to get stuck as in mire **2** to soil with mud, etc. — *vi.* to sink in mud —**mir′y, -i·er, -i·est,** *adj.*

mir·ror (mir′ər) *n.* 〚< L *mirare*, look at〛 **1** a smooth, reflecting surface; esp., a glass coated with silver **2** anything giving a true representation — *vt.* to reflect, as in a mirror

mirth (murth) *n.* 〚< OE *myrig*, pleasant〛 joyfulness or gaiety, esp. with laughter —**mirth′ful** *adj.* —**mirth′less** *adj.*

MIRV (murv) *n., pl.* **MIRV's** 〚m(ultiple) i(ndependently targeted) r(eentry) v(ehicle)〛 an intercontinental ballistic missile whose several warheads can be scattered

mis- 〚< OE *mis-* or OFr *mes-*〛 *prefix* **1** wrong(ly), bad(ly) **2** no, not

mis·ad·ven·ture (mis′əd ven′chər) *n.* a mishap; an instance of bad luck

mis·al·li′ance (-ə li′əns) *n.* an improper alliance; esp., an unsuitable marriage

mis·an·thrope (mis′ən thrōp′) *n.* 〚Gr *misein*, to hate + *anthrōpos*, man〛 a person who hates or distrusts all people Also **mis·an′thro·pist** (-an′thrə pist) —**mis′an·throp′ic** (-ən thräp′ik) *adj.* —**mis·an′thropy** *n.*

mis′ap·ply′ *vt.* **-plied′, -ply′ing** to apply badly or improperly

mis′ap·pre·hend′ (-ap rē hend′) *vt.* to misunderstand — **mis′ap·pre·hen′sion** *n.*

mis′ap·pro′pri·ate′ *vt.* **-at′ed, -at′ing** to appropriate to a wrong or dishonest use —**mis′ap·pro′pri·a′tion** *n.*

mis′be·got′ten *adj.* **1** wrongly or unlawfully begotten; illegitimate **2** wrongly or badly conceived

mis′be·have′ *vt., vi.* **-haved′, -hav′ing** to behave (oneself) wrongly —**mis′be·hav′ior** *n.*

THESAURUS

of the state] ambassador, consul, liaison officer; see DIPLOMAT, REPRESENTATIVE 2, STATESMAN.

minister *v.* administer to, tend, wait on; see HELP.

ministry *n.* **1** [The functions of the clergy] preaching, prayer, spiritual leadership; see RELIGION 2. **2** [The clergy] the cloth, clergymen, ecclesiastics, clerics, the clerical order, priesthood, clericals, prelacy, vicarage, clergy. **3** [A department of state] bureau, administrative agency, executive branch; see DEPARTMENT.

minor *a.* secondary, lesser, insignificant; see TRIVIAL, UNIMPORTANT.

minor *n.* person under eighteen or twenty-one, underage person, boy, girl, child, infant, little one, lad, schoolboy, schoolgirl; see also YOUTH 3.

minority *n.* **1** [An outnumbered group] opposition, less than half, the outvoted, the few, the outnumbered, the losing side, splinter group. **2** [The time before one is of legal age] childhood, immaturity, adolescence; see YOUTH 1.

mint[1] *v.* strike, coin, issue; see PRINT 2.

minus *a.* diminished, negative, deficient; see LESS.

minute[1] *n.* **1** [The sixtieth part of an hour] sixty seconds, unit of time, space of time; see TIME 1. **2** [A brief time] short time, second, flash, twinkling, breath, jiffy*, bat of an eye*.— *Ant.* FOREVER, eternity, long time. — **in a minute** before long, shortly, presently; see SOON. —**the minute that** as soon as, the second that, at the time that; see WHEN 2. —**up to the minute** modern, contemporary, in the latest style; see FASHIONABLE.

minute[2] *a.* **1** [Extremely small] microscopic, diminutive, wee, tiny, atomic, miniature, puny, microbic, molecular, exact, precise, fine, inconsiderable, teeny*, teeny*, teeny-weeny*, teensy*, itty-bitty*, invisible; see also LITTLE 1.—*Ant.* LARGE, huge, immense. **2** [Trivial] immaterial, nonessential, paltry; see TRIVIAL, UNIMPORTANT. **3** [Exact] particular,

circumstantial, specialized; see DETAILED, ELABORATE 2.

miracle *n.* marvel, revelation, supernatural occurrence; see WONDER 2.

miraculous *a.* **1** [Caused by divine intervention] supernatural, marvelous, superhuman, beyond understanding, phenomenal, awesome, unimaginable, stupendous, monstrous; see also MYSTERIOUS 2.—*Ant.* NATURAL, familiar, imaginable. **2** [So unusual as to suggest a miracle] extraordinary, freakish, wondrous; see UNUSUAL 1, 2.

mirage *n.* phantasm, delusion, hallucination; see FANTASY, ILLUSION.

mirror *n.* looking glass, speculum, reflector, polished metal, hand glass, pier glass, mirroring surface, camera finder, hand mirror, full-length mirror; see also GLASS.

mirth *n.* frolic, jollity, entertainment; see FUN.

misbehave *v.* do wrong, sin, fail, trip, blunder, offend, trespass, behave badly, misdo, err, lapse, be

misc. 1 miscellaneous 2 miscellany

mis·cal·cu·late′ *vt.*, *vi.* **-lat′ed, -lat′ing** to calculate incorrectly; misjudge **—mis′cal·cu·la′tion** *n.*

mis·call′ *vt.* to call by a wrong name

mis·car′ry (-kar′ē) *vi.* **-ried, -ry·ing** 1 to go wrong; fail: said of a plan, etc. 2 to fail to arrive: said of mail, etc. 3 to give birth to a fetus before it has developed enough to live **—mis·car′riage** (-ij) *n.*

mis·cast′ *vt.* **-cast′, -cast′ing** to cast (an actor or a play) unsuitably

mis·ce·gena·tion (mis′i jə nā′shən, mi sej′ə-) *n.* [< L *miscere*, to mix + *genus*, race] marriage or sexual relations between a man and woman of different races

mis·cel·la·ne·ous (mis′ə lā′nē əs) *adj.* [< L *miscere*, to mix] consisting of various kinds or qualities

mis·cel·lany (mis′ə lā′nē) *n.*, *pl.* **-nies** a miscellaneous collection, esp. of literary works

mis·chance′ *n.* bad luck

mis·chief (mis′chif) *n.* [< OFr *mes-*, MIS- + *chief*, end] 1 harm or damage 2 a cause of harm or annoyance 3 *a*) a prank *b*) playful teasing

mis·chie·vous (mis′chə vəs) *adj.* 1 causing mischief; specif., *a*) harmful *b*) prankish 2 inclined to annoy with playful tricks **—mis′chie·vously** *adv.*

mis·ci·ble (mis′ə bəl) *adj.* [< L *miscere*, to mix] that can be mixed **—mis′ci·bil′ity** *n.*

mis·con·ceive (mis′kən sēv′) *vt.*, *vi.* **-ceived′, -ceiv′ing** to misunderstand **—mis′con·cep′tion** (-sep′shən) *n.*

mis′con′duct′ *n.* 1 bad or dishonest management 2 improper behavior

mis·con·strue (mis′kən strōō′) *vt.* **-strued′, -stru′ing** to misinterpret **—mis′con·struc′tion** *n.*

mis′count′ *vt.*, *vi.* to count incorrectly **—** *n.* an incorrect count

mis·cre·ant (mis′krē ənt) *adj.* [< OFr *mes-*, MIS- + *croire*, believe] villainous; evil **—** *n.* a villain

mis′deal′ *vt.*, *vi.* **-dealt′, -deal′ing** to deal (playing cards) incorrectly **—** *n.* an incorrect deal

mis·deed′ (mis dēd′) *n.* a wrong or wicked act; crime, sin, etc.

mis·de·meanor (mis′di mēn′ər) *n. Law* any minor offense bringing a lesser punishment than a felony

mis′di·rect′ *vt.* to direct wrongly or badly **—mis′di·rec′tion** *n.*

mis′do′ *vt.* **-did′, -done′, -do′ing** to do wrongly

mis·do′ing *n.* wrongdoing

mi·ser (mī′zər) *n.* [< L, wretched] a greedy, stingy person who hoards money for its own sake **—mi′serly** *adv.* **—mi′ser·li·ness** *n.*

mis·er·able (miz′ər ə bəl) *adj.* 1 in misery 2 causing misery, discomfort, etc. 3 bad; inadequate 4 pitiable **—mis′er·ably** *adv.*

mis·ery (miz′ər ē) *n.*, *pl.* **-ies** [see MISER] 1 a condition of great suffering; distress 2 a cause of such suffering; pain, poverty, etc.

mis·fea·sance (mis fē′zəns) *n.* [< OFr *mes-*, mis- + *faire*, do] *Law* wrongdoing; specif., the doing of a lawful act in an unlawful manner

mis′file′ *vt.* **-filed′, -fil′ing** to file (papers, etc.) in the wrong place

mis′fire′ *vi.* **-fired′, -fir′ing** 1 to fail to go off or ignite properly 2 to fail to achieve a desired effect **—** *n.* a misfiring

mis·fit (mis′fit′; *for n.* mis′fit′) *vt.*, *vi.* **-fit′ted, -fit′ting** to fit badly **—** *n.* 1 an improper fit 2 a maladjusted person

mis′for′tune *n.* 1 ill fortune; trouble 2 a mishap, calamity, etc.

mis′giv′ing *n.* [*often pl.*] a disturbed feeling of fear, doubt, etc.

mis′gov′ern *vt.* to govern badly **—mis′gov′ern·ment** *n.*

mis′guide′ (-gīd′) *vt.* **-guid′ed, -guid′ing** to lead into error or misconduct; mislead **—mis′guid′ance** *n.*

mis′han′dle *vt.* **-dled, -dling** to handle badly or roughly; abuse

mis·hap (mis′hap′) *n.* an unlucky or unfortunate accident

mis′hear′ *vt.*, *vi.* **-heard′, -hear′ing** to hear wrongly

mish·mash (mish′mash′) *n.* a jumble

mis′in·form′ *vt.* to supply with false or misleading information **—mis′in·for·ma′tion** *n.*

mis′in·ter′pret *vt.* to interpret wrongly; understand or explain incorrectly **—mis′in·ter·pre·ta′tion** *n.*

mis′judge′ *vt.*, *vi.* **-judged′, -judg′ing** to judge wrongly or unfairly **—mis′judg′ment** *n.*

mis′la·bel *vt.* **-beled′** or **-belled′, -bel·ing** or **-bel·ling** to label incorrectly or improperly

mis′lay′ (-lā′) *vt.* **-laid′, -lay′ing** to put in a place afterward forgotten

mis′lead′ *vt.* **-led′, -lead′ing** 1 to lead in a wrong direction 2 to deceive or delude 3 to lead into wrongdoing

mis′man′age *vt.*, *vi.* **-aged, -ag·ing** to manage badly or dishonestly **—mis′man′age·ment** *n.*

mis·match (mis′mach′; *for n.* mis′mach′) *vt.* to match badly or unsuitably **—** *n.* a bad match

mis′mate′ *vt.*, *vi.* **-mat′ed, -mat′ing** to mate badly or unsuitably

---

◼ THESAURUS ◼

delinquent, be at fault, be culpable, be guilty, be bad, forget oneself, be dissolute, be indecorous, carry on*, be naughty, go astray, sow one's wild oats*, cut up*.—*Ant.* BEHAVE, be good, do well.

miscalculate *v.* blunder, miscount, err; see MISTAKE.

miscarriage *n.* 1 [Failure] malfunction, defeat, mistake; see FAILURE 1. 2 [A too premature delivery] unnatural birth, untimely delivery, birth interruption, premature delivery.

miscellaneous *a.* 1 [Lacking unity] diverse, disparate, unmatched; see UNLIKE. 2 [Lacking order] mixed, muddled, scattered; see CONFUSED 2, DISORDERED.

mischief *n.* troublesomeness, harmfulness, prankishness, playfulness, acting like a brat, impishness, misbehavior, misconduct, fault, transgression, wrongdoing, misdoing, naughtiness, mischiefmaking, friskiness.—*Ant.* DIGNITY, demureness, sedateness.

mischievous *a.* playful, roguish, prankish; see NAUGHTY, RUDE 2.

misconception *n.* delusion, blunder, fault; see ERROR, MISTAKE 2, MISUNDERSTANDING 1.

misconduct *n.* misbehavior, offense, wrongdoing; see EVIL 2, MISCHIEF.

misdemeanor *n.* misconduct, misbehavior, misdeed; see CRIME.

miser *n.* extortioner, usurer, misan-

thropist, stingy person, skinflint, Scrooge, money-grubber.—*Ant.* BEGGAR, spendthrift, waster.

miserable *a.* distressed, afflicted, sickly, ill, wretched, sick, ailing, unfortunate, uncomfortable, suffering, hurt, wounded, tormented, tortured, in pain, strained, injured, convulsed; see also TROUBLED.—*Ant.* HELPED, aided, comfortable.

miserably *a.* poorly, unsatisfactorily, imperfectly; see BADLY 1, INADEQUATELY.

miserly *a.* covetous, parsimonious, close-fisted; see STINGY.

misery *n.* 1 [Pain] distress, suffering, agony; see PAIN 2. 2 [Dejection] worry, despair, desolation; see DEPRESSION 2, GRIEF, SADNESS. 3 [Trouble] grief, anxiety, problem; see DIFFICULTY 2.

misfit *n.* paranoid, psychotic, maladjusted person; see PERVERT.

misfortune *n.* misadventure, ill luck, ill fortune, disadvantage, mischance, disappointment, adversity, discomfort, burden, annoyance, nuisance, unpleasantness, inconvenience, worry, anxiety; see also DIFFICULTY 1.—*Ant.* ADVANTAGE, good fortune, stroke of fortune.

misgiving *n.* distrust, mistrust, unbelief; see DOUBT, UNCERTAINTY 2.

misguided *a.* misled, deceived, confused; see MISTAKEN 1.

mishap *n.* accident, mischance, misadventure; see CATASTROPHE, DISAS-

TER, MISFORTUNE.

misinform *v.* mislead, report inaccurately, to misstate; see DECEIVE, LIE.

misinterpret *v.* falsify, distort, miscalculate; see MISTAKE, MISUNDERSTAND.

misinterpretation *n.* distortion, misreckoning, delusion; see MISTAKE 2, MISUNDERSTANDING 1.

misjudge *v.* 1 [To make a wrong judgment, usually of a person] be overcritical, be unfair, come to a hasty conclusion; see MISUNDERSTAND. 2 [To make an inaccurate estimate] miss, miscalculate, misconceive, misthink, misconstrue, overestimate, underestimate, bark up the wrong tree*; see also MISTAKE.—*Ant.* UNDERSTAND, estimate, calculate.

misjudgment *n.* distortion, misinterpretation, misconception; see MISTAKE 2.

mislead *v.* delude, cheat, defraud, bilk, take in, outwit, trick, entangle, advice badly, victimize, lure, beguile, hoax, dupe, bait, misrepresent, bluff, give a bum steer*, throw off the scent*, bamboozle, hoodwink, put on*; see also DECEIVE.

misled *a.* misguided, deluded, wronged; see DECEIVED, MISTAKEN 1.

mismanage *v.* bungle, blunder, mess up, foul up*; see also FAIL 1.

mismatched *a.* incompatible, discordant, inconsistent; see UNFIT.

mis·name' *vt.* **-named'**, **-nam'ing** to give an inappropriate name to

mis·no·mer (mis nō'mər) *n.* 〚< OFr < *mes-*, MIS- + *nomer*, to name〛 a wrong name

mi·sog·y·ny (mi säj'ə nē) *n.* 〚< Gr *misein*, to hate + *gynē*, woman〛 hatred of women —**mi·sog'y·nist** *n.* —**mi·sog'y·nous** *adj.*

mis·place (mis'plās') *vt.* **-placed'**, **-plac'ing** **1** to put in a wrong place **2** to bestow (one's trust, etc.) unwisely **3** MISLAY —**mis·place'ment** *n.*

mis·play (mis plā'; *for n.* mis'plā') *vt., vi.* to play wrongly or badly, as in games or sports — *n.* a wrong or bad play

mis·print (mis print'; *for n.* mis'print') *vt.* to print incorrectly — *n.* a printing error

mis·pri·sion (-prizh'ən) *n.* 〚< OFr *mesprendre*, take wrongly〛 misconduct or neglect of duty by a public official

mis·pro·nounce' *vt., vi.* **-nounced'**, **-nounc'ing** to pronounce differently from the accepted pronunciations —**mis'pro·nun·ci·a'tion** *n.*

mis·quote' *vt., vi.* **-quot'ed**, **-quot'ing** to quote incorrectly —**mis'quo·ta'tion** *n.*

mis·read' (-rēd') *vt., vi.* **-read'** (-red'), **-read'ing** (-rēd'iŋ) to read wrongly, esp. so as to misunderstand

mis'rep·re·sent' *vt.* to represent falsely; give an untrue idea of —**mis'rep·re·sen·ta'tion** *n.*

mis·rule (mis'rōōl'; *for n.* mis'rōōl') *vt.* **-ruled'**, **-rul'ing** to rule badly; misgovern — *n.* misgovernment

miss[1] (mis) *vt.* 〚OE *missan*〛 **1** to fail to hit, meet, do, attend, see, hear, etc. **2** to let (a chance, etc.) go by **3** to avoid 〔he *missed* being hit〕 **4** to notice or feel the absence or loss of **5** to lack 〔this book is *missing* a page〕 — *vi.* **1** to fail to hit **2** to fail to be successful **3** to misfire, as an engine — *n.* a failure to hit, obtain, etc.

miss[2] (mis) *n., pl.* **miss'es** 〚< MISTRESS〛 **1** [M-] a title used before the name of an unmarried woman or girl **2** a young unmarried woman or girl

mis·sal (mis'əl) *n.* 〚< LL *missa*, Mass〛 [*often* M-] a book of prayers, readings, etc. authorized by the Roman Catholic Church for the celebration of Mass

mis·shape' *vt.* **-shaped'**, **-shap'ing** to shape badly; deform —**mis·shap'en** *adj.*

mis·sile (mis'əl) *n.* 〚< L *mittere*, send〛 an object, as a spear, bullet, rocket, etc., designed to be thrown, fired, or launched toward a target

mis'sil·er·y or **mis'sil·ry** (-rē) *n.* **1** the science of building and launching guided missiles **2** such missiles

miss·ing (mis'iŋ) *adj.* absent; lost

mis·sion (mish'ən) *n.* 〚< L *mittere*, send〛 **1** a sending out or being sent out to perform a special service **2** *a*) a group of persons sent by a religious body to spread its religion, esp. in a foreign land *b*) its headquarters **3** a diplomatic delegation **4** a group of technicians, specialists, etc. sent to a foreign country **5** the special duty for which one is sent **6** a special task to which one devotes one's life; calling

mis'sion·ar'y (-er'ē) *adj.* of religious missions or missionaries — *n., pl.* **-ies** a person sent on a religious mission

mis·sive (mis'iv) *n.* 〚< L *mittere*, send〛 a letter or written message

mis·spell' *vt., vi.* **-spelled'** or **-spelt'**, **-spell'ing** to spell incorrectly

mis·spend' *vt.* **-spent'**, **-spend'ing** to spend improperly or wastefully

mis·state' *vt.* **-stat'ed**, **-stat'ing** to state incorrectly or falsely —**mis·state'ment** *n.*

mis·step' *n.* **1** a wrong or awkward step **2** a mistake in conduct

mist (mist) *n.* 〚OE〛 **1** a large mass of water vapor, less dense than a fog **2** anything that dims or obscures — *vt., vi.* to make or become misty

mis·take (mi stāk') *vt.* **-took'**, **-tak'en**, **-tak'ing** 〚< ON *mistaka*, take wrongly〛 to understand or perceive wrongly — *vi.* to make a mistake — *n.* an idea, answer, act, etc. that is wrong; error or blunder —**mis·tak'able** *adj.*

mis·tak'en *adj.* **1** wrong; having an incorrect understanding **2** incorrect: said of ideas, etc.

mis·ter (mis'tər) *n.* 〚< MASTER〛 **1** [M-] a title used before the name of a man or his office and usually written *Mr.* **2** [Colloq.] sir

mis·time (mis'tim', mis'-) *vt.* **-timed'**, **-tim'ing** to do or say at the wrong time

mis·tle·toe (mis'əl tō') *n.* 〚< OE *mistel*, mistletoe + *tan*, a twig〛 a parasitic evergreen plant with yellowish flowers and shiny, white, poisonous berries

mis·took (mis took') *vt., vi. pt. of* MISTAKE

mis·tral (mi sträl', mis'trəl) *n.* 〚Fr< Prov, master-wind〛 a cold, dry north wind that blows over the Mediterranean coast of France

mis·treat' *vt.* to treat wrongly or badly —**mis·treat'ment** *n.*

mis·tress (mis'tris) *n.* 〚< OFr, fem. of *maistre*, master〛 **1** a woman who is head of a household or institution **2** a woman, nation, etc. that has control, power, etc. **3** a woman with whom a man is having a prolonged affair **4** [Chiefly Brit.] a female schoolteacher **5** [M-] [Obs.] a title used before the name of a woman: now replaced by *Mrs.*, *Miss*, or *Ms.*

mis·tri·al *n.* *Law* a trial made void, as because of an error in the proceedings or the inability of the jury to reach a verdict

---

THESAURUS

misplace *v.* mislay, displace, shuffle, disarrange, remove, disturb, take out of its place, disorder, tumble, confuse, mix, scatter, unsettle, muss, disorganize; see also LOSE 2.—*Ant.* FIND, LOCATE, place.

misplaced *a.* displaced, mislaid, out of place; see LOST 1.

mispronounce *v.* falter, misspeak, mouth; see HESITATE, STAMMER.

misrepresent *v.* distort, falsify, understate; see DECEIVE, LIE 1, MISLEAD.

misrepresentation *n.* untruth, deceit, disguise; see DECEPTION, LIE.

miss[1] *v.* **1** [To feel a want] desire, crave, yearn; see NEED, WANT 1. **2** [To fail to catch] snatch at, drop, fumble, have butterfingers*, muff*, boot*.—*Ant.* CATCH, grab, hold. **3** [To fail to hit] miss one's aim, miss the mark, be wide of the mark, overshoot, undershoot, fan the air*.—*Ant.* HIT, shoot, get.

miss[1,2] *n.* **1** [A failure] slip, blunder, mishap; see MISTAKE 2. **2** [A young woman] lass, maid, female; see GIRL.

missed *a.* **1** [Not found or noticed] gone, misplaced, mislaid, forgotten, unrecalled, unnoticed, not in sight, put away, in hiding, strayed, moved, removed, unseen; see also LOST 1.—*Ant.* REMEMBERED, found, located. **2** [Longed for] needed, desired, wished for, pined for,

wanted, yearned for, clung to, craved for, hungered for.—*Ant.* HATED, disliked, unwanted.

missile *n.* cartridge, projectile, ammunition; see BULLET, SHOT 1, WEAPON. *Terms for types of missiles include the following:* Polaris, Poseidon, RPV or remotely piloted vehicle, Minuteman, guided missile, cruise missile, ICBM or intercontinental ballistic missile, ABM or antiballistic missile, ASW or antisubmarine warfare, MIRV or multiple independently targetable reentry vehicle.

missing *a.* disappeared, lacking, removed; see ABSENT, LOST 1.

mission *n.* charge, sortie, commission; see PURPOSE 1.

missionary *n.* apostle, evangelist, preacher; see MESSENGER, MINISTER 1.

misspent *a.* wasted, squandered, thrown away; see WASTED.

mist *n.* cloud, rain, haze; see FOG.

mistake *n.* **1** [A blunder] false step, blunder, slip, error, omission, failure, confusion, wrongdoing, sin, crime, goof*; see also ERROR. **2** [A misunderstanding] misapprehension, confusion, muddle, misconception, delusion, illusion, overestimation, underestimation, impression, confounding, misinterpretation, perversion, perplexity, bewilderment, misjudgment; see also EXAGGERATION,

MISUNDERSTANDING 1.—*Ant.* KNOWLEDGE, certainty, interpretation.

mistake *v.* err, blunder, slip, lapse, miss, overlook, omit, underestimate, overestimate, substitute, misjudge, misapprehend, misconceive, misunderstand, confound, misinterpret, confuse, botch, bungle, have the wrong impression, tangle, snarl, slip up, make a mess of*, miss the boat*, open one's mouth and put one's foot in it*.—*Ant.* SUCCEED, be accurate, explain.

mistaken *a.* **1** [In error] misinformed, deceived, confounded, confused, having the wrong impression, deluded, misinformed, misguided, at fault, off the track; see also WRONG 2. **2** [Ill-advised] unadvised, duped, fooled, misled, tricked, unwarranted; see also DECEIVED. **3** [Taken for another] wrongly identified, unrecognized, confused with, taken for, in a case of mistaken identity, misnamed, misconstrued.

mister *n.* Mr., man, sir, *monsieur* (French), *Herr* (German), *signor* (Italian), *señor* (Spanish).

mistreat *v.* harm, injure, wrong; see ABUSE.

mistress *n.* **1** [A woman in authority] housekeeper, chaperone, manager; see LADY 2. **2** [An illicit lover] courtesan, paramour, kept woman; see PROSTITUTE.

mis·trust' *n.* lack of trust or confidence — *vt.*, *vi.* to have no trust in; doubt —**mis·trust'ful** *adj.*

misty (mis'tē) *adj.* **-i·er**, **-i·est** 1 of, like, or covered with mist 2 blurred, as by mist; vague —**mist'i·ly** *adv.* —**mist'i·ness** *n.*

mis'un·der·stand' *vt.* **-stood'**, **-stand'ing** to fail to understand correctly; misinterpret

mis'un·der·stand'ing *n.* 1 a failure to understand; mistake of meaning, etc. 2 a quarrel or disagreement

mis·use (mis'yōōz'; *for n.*, -yōōs') *vt.* **-used'**, **-us'ing** 1 to use improperly 2 to treat badly or harshly — *n.* incorrect or improper use

mite (mīt) *n.* [OE] 1 a tiny arachnid, often parasitic upon animals or plants 2 a very small sum of money 3 a very small creature or object

mi·ter (mīt'ər) *n.* [< Gr *mitra*, headband] 1 a tall, ornamented cap worn by bishops and abbots 2 *Carpentry* a joint formed by fitting together two pieces beveled to form a corner: now usually **miter joint**

miti·gate (mit'ə gāt') *vt.*, *vi.* **-gat'ed**, **-gat'ing** [< L *mitis*, soft] 1 to make or become less severe, less painful, etc. 2 [< confusion with MILITATE] to operate or work (*against*): a loose usage —**mit'i·ga'tion** *n.*

mi·to·sis (mī tō'sis) *n.* [< Gr *mitos*, thread] the process by which a cell divides into two so that the nucleus of each new cell has the full number of chromosomes —**mi·tot'ic** (-tät'ik) *adj.*

mitt (mit) *n.* [< fol.] 1 a glove covering the hand and forearm, but only part of the fingers 2 [Slang] a hand 3 *a*) *Baseball* a padded glove, worn for protection *b*) a boxing glove

mit·ten (mit''n) *n.* [< OFr *mitaine*] a glove with a thumb but no separately divided fingers

mix (miks) *vt.* **mixed** or **mixt**, **mix'ing** [< L *miscere*] 1 to blend together in a single mass 2 to make by blending ingredients [to *mix* a cake] 3 to combine [to *mix* work and play] 4 to blend electronically (recorded sounds, etc.) on (a tape, etc.) — *vi.* 1 to be mixed or blended 2 to get along together — *n.* 1 a mixture 2 a beverage for mixing with alcoholic liquor 3 the blend of sounds in a recording, etc. —**mix up** 1 to mix thoroughly 2 to confuse 3 to involve or implicate (*in*): usually used in the passive —**mix'able** *adj.* —**mix'er** *n.*

mixed (mikst) *adj.* 1 blended 2 made up of different parts, classes, races, etc., or of both sexes 3 confused

mixed number a number consisting of a whole number and a fraction, as 3⅜

mix·ture (miks'chər) *n.* 1 a mixing or being mixed 2 something mixed

mix'-up' *n.* a confusion; tangle

miz·zen·mast (miz'ən mast'; *naut.*, -məst) *n.* [< L *medius*, middle] the mast third from the bow in a ship

ml milliliter(s)

Mlle Mademoiselle

mm millimeter(s)

MM Messieurs

Mme Madame

Mmes or **Mmes.** mesdames

Mn *Chem. symbol for* manganese

mne·monic (nē män'ik) *adj.* [< Gr *mnēmōn*, mindful] of or helping the memory

mo. month

Mo *Chem. symbol for* molybdenum

MO [L *modus operandi*] mode of operation Also **m.o.**

moan (mōn) *n.* [prob. < OE *mænan*, complain] a low, mournful sound, as of sorrow or pain — *vi.*, *vt.* 1 to utter or say with a moan 2 to complain (about)

moat (mōt) *n.* [< OFr *mote*, mound] a deep, broad ditch, often filled with water, around a fortress or castle

mob (mäb) *n.* [< L *mobile* (*vulgus*), movable (crowd)] 1 a disorderly, lawless crowd 2 any crowd 3 the masses: a contemptuous term 4 [Slang] a gang of criminals — *vt.* **mobbed**, **mob'bing** 1 to crowd around and attack, annoy, etc. 2 to throng

mo·bile (mō'bəl; *also*, -bil & *for n., usually*, -bēl' &, *chiefly Brit & Cdn*, -bīl') *adj.* [< L *movere*, to move] 1 moving or movable 2 movable by means of a motor vehicle [a *mobile* X-ray unit] 3 that can change rapidly or easily; adaptable 4 characterized by ease in change of social status — *n.* a piece of abstract sculpture which aims to depict movement, as by an arrangement of thin forms, rings, etc. suspended and set in motion by air currents —**mo·bil'ity** (-bil'ə tē) *n.*

-mobile (mō bēl') [< (AUTO)MOBILE] *combining form* motorized vehicle [bookmobile]

mobile home a movable dwelling set more or less permanently at a location: cf. MOTOR HOME

mo'bi·lize' (-bə līz') *vt.*, *vi.* **-lized'**, **-liz'ing** to make or become organized and ready, as for war —**mo'bi·li·za'tion** *n.*

Mö·bius strip (mā'bē əs, mō'-) [after A.F. *Möbius*, 19th-c. Ger mathematician] a one-edged geometric surface with only one continuous side, formed by giving a 180° twist to a narrow strip of paper and connecting the two ends

mob·ster (mäb'stər) *n.* [Slang] a gangster

moc·ca·sin (mäk'ə sən) *n.* [< AmInd] 1 a heelless slipper of soft, flexible leather 2 any similar heeled slipper

mo·cha (mō'kə) *n.* a choice grade of coffee grown orig. in Arabia — *adj.* flavored with coffee, and, often, chocolate

mock (mäk) *vt.* [< OFr *mocquer*] 1 to ridicule 2 to mimic, as in fun or derision 3 to defy and make futile — *vi.* to express scorn, ridicule, etc. — *adj.* sham; imitation — *adv.* falsely or insincerely [mock-sympathetic words]

THESAURUS

mistrust *v.* suspect, distrust, scruple; see DOUBT.

misty *a.* dim, foggy, hazy, murky, shrouded, obscure; see also DARK 1.

misunderstand *v.* err, misconceive, misinterpret, miscomprehend, misjudge, miscalculate, misconstrue, be perplexed, be bewildered, confuse, confound, have the wrong impression, fail to understand, misapprehend, overestimate, underestimate, be misled, be unfamiliar with, have the wrong slant on*, not register; see also MISTAKE.—*Ant.* UNDERSTAND, grasp, apprehend.

misunderstanding *n.* 1 [Misapprehension] delusion, miscalculation, confusion, misinterpretation, confounding; see also MISTAKE 2.—*Ant.* UNDERSTANDING, conception, apprehension. 2 [Mutual difficulty] debate, dissension, quarrel; see DISAGREEMENT 1, DISPUTE.

misunderstood *a.* misinterpreted, badly interpreted, misconceived; see MISTAKEN 1, WRONG 2.

mitt *n.* baseball glove, catcher's mitt, first baseman's mitt; see EQUIPMENT.

mitten *n.* mitt, gauntlet, glove; see CLOTHES.

mix *v.* 1 [To blend] fuse, merge, coalesce, brew, unite, combine, cross, interbreed, amalgamate, incorporate, alloy, mingle, compound, intermingle, weave, interweave, throw together, adulterate, infiltrate, twine, knead, stir, suffuse, instill, transfuse, synthesize, stir around, infuse, saturate, dye, season. 2 [To confuse] mix up, jumble, tangle; see CONFUSE. 3 [To associate] fraternize, get along, consort with; see JOIN 2.

mixed *a.* 1 [Commingled] blended, fused, mingled, compounded, combined, amalgamated, united, brewed, merged, transfused, crossed, assimilated, married, woven, kneaded, incorporated.—*Ant.* SEPARATED, severed, raveled. 2 [Various] miscellaneous, unselected, diverse; see VARIOUS. 3 [Confused] mixed up, jumbled, disordered; see CONFUSED 2.

mixer *n.* 1 [An instrument used to mix materials] blender, food processor, juicer, egg beater, cake mixer, food mixer, cocktail shaker, converter, carburetor, cement mixer, paint mixer; see also MACHINE. 2 [A substance used in a mixture] ingredient, component, combining element; see PART 1.

mixture *n.* 1 [A combination] blend, compound, composite, amalgam, miscellany, mishmash, mingling, medley, mix, potpourri, alloy, fusion, jumble, brew, merger, hybrid, crossing, infiltration, transfusion, infusion, mélange, saturation, assimilation, incorporation, hodgepodge. 2 [A mess] mix-up, muddle, disorder; see CONFUSION.

mix-up *n.* turmoil, chaos, commotion; see CONFUSION, DISORDER.

moan *n.* plaint, groan, wail; see CRY 1.

moan *v.* groan, wail, whine; see CRY 1.

mob *n.* 1 [A disorderly crowd of people] swarm, rabble, throng, press, multitude, populace, horde, riot, host, lawless element; see also CROWD, GATHERING. 2 [The lower classes] bourgeoisie, plebeians, proletariat; see PEOPLE 3.

mob *v.* hustle, crowd, swarm; see ATTACK, REBEL.

mobile *a.* unstationary, loose, free; see MOVABLE.

mobility *n.* changeability, versatility, flow; see MOVEMENT 2.

mobilize *v.* assemble, prepare, gather; see ENLIST 1.

moccasin *n.* heelless shoe, slipper, sandal; see SHOE.

mock *a.* counterfeit, sham, pretended; see FALSE 3, UNREAL.

mock *v.* 1 [To ridicule] deride, scorn, taunt; see RIDICULE. 2 [To mimic] mime, burlesque, caricature; see IMITATE.

mock′er·y *n., pl.* **-ies** 1 a mocking 2 one receiving or deserving ridicule 3 a false or derisive imitation

mock′ing·bird′ *n.* a bird of the U.S. that imitates the calls of other birds

mock′-up′ *n.* ⟦< Fr *maquette*⟧ a model built to scale, often full-sized, for teaching, testing, etc.

mod (mäd) *adj.* ⟦< MOD(ERN)⟧ up-to-date, fashionable, stylish, etc.

mode (mōd) *n.* ⟦< L *modus*⟧ 1 a manner or way of acting, doing, or being 2 customary usage or current fashion 3 *Gram.* MOOD²

model (mäd′'l) *n.* ⟦< L *modus*, a measure⟧ 1 a small representation of a planned or existing object 2 a hypothetical description, often based on an analogy, used in analyzing something 3 a person or thing regarded as a standard of excellence to be imitated 4 a style or design 5 *a*) one who poses for an artist or photographer *b*) one employed to display clothes by wearing them — *adj.* 1 serving as a model 2 representative of others of the same style, etc. [a *model* home] — *vt.* **-eled** or **-elled, -el·ing** or **-el·ling** 1 *a*) to make a model of *b*) to plan or form after a model 2 to display (clothes) by wearing — *vi.* to serve as a MODEL (*n.* 5)

mo·dem (mō′dem′; *also*, -dəm) *n.* ⟦MO(DULATOR) + DEM(ODULATION)⟧ a device that converts data for transmission, as by telephone, to data-processing equipment

mod·er·ate (mäd′ər it; *for v.*, -āt′) *adj.* ⟦< L *moderare*, restrain⟧ 1 within reasonable limits; avoiding extremes 2 mild; calm 3 of medium quality, amount, etc. — *n.* one holding moderate opinions — *vt., vi.* **-at′ed, -at′ing** 1 to make or become moderate 2 to preside over (a meeting, etc.) —**mod′er·ate·ly** *adv.*

mod′era′tion *n.* 1 a moderating 2 avoidance of extremes 3 calmness

mod′era′tor *n.* one who presides at an assembly, debate, etc.

mod·ern (mäd′ərn) *adj.* ⟦< L *modo*, just now⟧ 1 of the present or recent times; specif., up-to-date 2 [*often* **M-**] designating the most recent form of a language — *n.* a person living in modern times, with modern ideas, etc.

Modern English the English language since about the mid-15th c.

mod′ern·ism′ *n.* (a) modern usage, practice, thought, etc. —**mod′ern·ist** *n., adj.* —**mod′ern·is′tic** *adj.*

mo·der·ni·ty (mä dur′nə tē, mə-) *n.* a being modern

mod′ern·ize′ *vt., vi.* **-ized′, -iz′ing** to make or become modern —**mod′erni·za′tion** *n.*

mod·est (mäd′ist) *adj.* ⟦< L *modus*, a measure⟧ 1 not vain or boastful; unassuming 2 shy or reserved 3 decorous; decent 4 not extreme; unpretentious —**mod′estly** *adv.* —**mod′esty** *n.*

modi·cum (mäd′i kəm) *n.* ⟦< L, moderate⟧ a small amount; bit

modi·fy (mäd′ə fī′) *vt.* **-fied′, -fy′ing** ⟦< L *modificare*, to limit⟧ 1 to change partially in character, form, etc. 2 to limit slightly 3 *Gram.* to limit in meaning; qualify — **mod′i·fi·ca′tion** *n.* —**mod′i·fi′er** *n.*

mod·ish (mōd′ish) *adj.* fashionable; stylish —**mod′ish·ness** *n.*

modu·lar (mäj′ə lər) *adj.* of modules

mod′u·late′ (-lāt′) *vt.* **-lat′ed, -lat′ing** ⟦< L *modus*, a measure⟧ 1 to regulate or adjust 2 to vary the pitch, intensity, etc. of (the voice) 3 *Radio* to vary the frequency of (radio waves, etc.) —**mod′u·la′tion** *n.* —**mod′u·la′tor** *n.*

mod·ule (mäj′ōōl) *n.* ⟦Fr < L *modus*, a measure⟧ 1 a standard or unit of measurement, as of building materials 2 any of a set of units to be variously fitted together 3 a detachable unit with a specific function, as in a spacecraft

Moe·bius strip (mā′bē əs, mō′-) MÖBIUS STRIP Also **Moebius band**

mo·gul (mō′gul′) *n.* ⟦Pers *Mughul*, Mongol⟧ a powerful or important person

THESAURUS

mockery *n.* disparagement, imitation, sham; see RIDICULE.

model *n.* 1 [A person worthy of imitation] archetype, prototype, exemplar, paradigm, ideal, good man, good woman, good example, hero, demigod, saint. 2 [Anything that serves as a copy] original, text, guide, copy, tracing, facsimile, duplicate, pattern, design, gauge, ideal, shape, form, specimen, mold, principle, basis, standard, sketch, painting, precedent, archetype, prototype; see also CRITERION. 3 [A duplicate on a small scale] miniature, image, illustration, representation, reduction, statue, figure, figurine, effigy, mock-up, skeleton, portrait, photograph, relief, print, engraving; see also COPY, DUPLICATE. 4 [One who poses professionally] poser, sitter, mannequin; see NUDE.

model *v.* 1 [To form] shape, mold, fashion; see CREATE, FORM 1. 2 [To imitate a model] trace, duplicate, sketch, reduce, represent, print, counterfeit, caricature, parody; see also ILLUSTRATE, PAINT 1. 3 [To serve as a model] sit, act as model, set an example; see POSE 2. 4 [To demonstrate] show off, wear, parade in; see DISPLAY.

moderate *a.* 1 [Not expensive] inexpensive, low-priced, reasonable; see CHEAP 1, ECONOMICAL 2. 2 [Not violent] modest, cool, tranquil; see CALM 1, RESERVED 3. 3 [Not radical] tolerant, judicious, nonpartisan, liberal, middle-of-the-road, unopinionated, not given to extremes, measured, low-key, evenly balanced, neutral, impartial, straight, midway, in the mean, average, restrained, sound, cautious, considered, considerate, respectable, middle-class, compromising; see also CONSERVATIVE.—*Ant.* RADICAL, unbalanced, partial. 4 [Not intemperate] pleasant, gentle, soft, balmy, inexpensive, tepid, easy,

not rigorous, not severe, temperate, favorable, tolerable, bearable, tame, untroubled, unruffled, monotonous, even; see also FAIR 3, MILD 2.—*Ant.* SEVERE, rigorous, bitter. 5 [Not indulgent] sparing, frugal, regulated, self-denying, abstinent, non-indulgent, self-controlled, disciplined, careful, on the wagon*, sworn off*, teetotaling; see also SOBER.—*Ant.* WASTEFUL, excessive, self-indulgent.

moderate *v.* abate, modify, decline; see DECREASE 1.

moderately *a.* tolerantly, tolerably, temperately, somewhat, to a degree, enough, to some extent, to a certain extent, a little, to some degree, fairly, not exactly, in moderation, within reason, within bounds, within reasonable limits, as far as could be expected, within the bounds of reason, in reason; see also REASONABLY 2, SLIGHTLY.—*Ant.* MUCH, extremely, remarkably.

moderation *n.* 1 [Restraint] toleration, steadiness, sobriety, coolness, the golden mean, quiet, temperance, patience, fairness, justice, constraint, forbearance, poise, balance; see also RESTRAINT 1. 2 [The act of moderating] settlement, regulation, limitation; see RESTRAINT 2.

modern *a.* 1 [Up-to-date] stylish, modish, chic, smart, up-to-the-minute, late, current, recent, of the present, prevailing, prevalent, avant-garde, present-day, latest, most recent, advanced, streamlined, breaking with tradition, new, newest, untraditional, contemporary, in vogue, in use, common, newfangled, cool*, sharp*, smooth*, just out, mod*, jet-age; see also FASHIONABLE.—*Ant.* OLD-FASHIONED, out-of-date, out-of-style. 2 [Having the comforts of modern life] modernistic, modernized, renovated, functional, with modern conveniences, done over, having modern improvements;

see also CONVENIENT 1, IMPROVED. 3 [Concerning recent times] contemporary, contemporaneous, recent, concurrent, present-day, coincident, twentieth-century, latter-day, mechanical, of the Machine Age, automated, of modern times, modernist; see also NEW 1, 2, NOW 1.—*Ant.* OLD, medieval, primordial.

modest *a.* 1 [Humble] unassuming, meek, diffident; see HUMBLE 1, RESIGNED. 2 [Not showy] unpretentious, plain, unostentatious, unobtrusive, demure, quiet, seemly, proper, decorous, simple, natural, unassuming, humble, tasteful, unadorned, unaffected, homely. 3 [Moderate] reasonable, inexpensive, average; see CHEAP 1, ECONOMICAL 2. 4 [Proper] pure, chaste, seemly; see DECENT 2, HONEST 1. 5 [Lowly] plain, simple, unaffected; see HUMBLE 2.

modestly *a.* unobtrusively, retiringly, quietly, unpretentiously, diffidently, bashfully, unassumingly, chastely, virtuously, purely, shyly, demurely.—*Ant.* BOLDLY, boastfully, pretentiously.

modesty *n.* 1 [The attitude that leads one to make a modest self-estimate] humility, delicacy, reticence, constraint, unobtrusiveness, meekness; see also COURTESY 1, DIGNITY, RESTRAINT 1.—*Ant.* VANITY, conceit, egotism. 2 [Shyness] inhibition, timidity, diffidence; see SHYNESS. 3 [Chastity] decency, innocence, celibacy; see CHASTITY, VIRTUE 1.

modification *n.* qualification, alteration, correction; see ADJUSTMENT, CHANGE 2.

modified *a.* varied, mutated, adjusted; see CHANGED 2.

modify *v.* 1 [To change] alter, modify, vary; see BECOME, CHANGE 2. 2 [To moderate] mitigate, restrain, curb; see DECREASE 2, RESTRICT.

mo·hair (mō′her′) *n.* ⟦< Ar *mukhayyar*, fine cloth⟧ 1 the hair of the Angora goat 2 yarn or fabric made of this

Mo·ham·medan (mō ham′i dən) *adj.* of Mohammed or Islam — *n.* MUSLIM: term used mainly by non-Muslims — **Mo·ham′med·an·ism′** *n.*

moi·ety (moi′ə tē) *n., pl.* **-ties** ⟦< L *medius*, middle⟧ 1 a half 2 an indefinite part

moire (mwär, môr) *n.* ⟦Fr⟧ a fabric, esp. silk, etc., having a wavy pattern Also **moiré** (mwä rā′, mô-)

moist (moist) *adj.* ⟦< L *mucus*, mucus⟧ slightly wet; damp —**moist′ly** *adv.* —**moist′ness** *n.*

mois·ten (mois′ən) *vt., vi.* to make or become moist

mois′ture (-chər) *n.* water or other liquid causing a slight wetness

mois′tur·ize′ (-iz′) *vt., vi.* **-ized′, -iz′ing** to make (the skin, air, etc.) moist —**mois′tur·iz′er** *n.*

mojo (mō′jō) *n.* ⟦prob. of creole orig.⟧ 1 a charm or amulet thought to have magic powers 2 [Black Slang] magical power, luck, etc.

mo·lar (mō′lər) *adj.* ⟦< L *mola*, millstone⟧ designating a tooth or teeth adapted for grinding — *n.* a molar tooth

mo·las·ses (mə las′iz) *n.* ⟦< L *mel*, honey⟧ a thick, dark syrup produced during the refining of sugar

mold[1] (mōld) *n.* ⟦< L *modus*, a measure⟧ 1 a hollow form for giving a certain shape to something plastic or molten 2 a frame on which something is modeled 3 a pattern; model 4 something formed in or on a mold 5 distinctive character — *vt.* 1 to make in or on a mold 2 to form; shape

mold[2] (mōld) *n.* ⟦ME *moul*⟧ 1 a fungus producing a furry growth on the surface of organic matter 2 this growth — *vi.* to become moldy

mold[3] (mōld) *n.* ⟦OE *molde*⟧ loose, soft soil rich in decayed organic matter

mold·er (mōl′dər) *vi.* ⟦< OE *molde*, dust⟧ to crumble into dust

mold·ing (mōl′diŋ) *n.* 1 the act of one that molds 2 something molded 3 a shaped strip of wood, etc., as around the upper walls of a room

moldy (mōl′dē) *adj.* **-i·er, -i·est** 1 covered or overgrown with mold 2 musty or stale —**mold′i·ness** *n.*

mole[1] (mōl) *n.* ⟦OE *mal*⟧ a small, congenital spot on the human skin, usually dark-colored and raised

mole[2] (mōl) *n.* ⟦ME *molle*⟧ 1 a small, burrowing mammal with soft fur 2 *a*) a spy in an enemy intelligence agency, etc. who infiltrates long before engaging in spying *b*) DOUBLE AGENT

mole[3] (mōl) *n.* ⟦< L *moles*, dam⟧ a breakwater

mol·ecule (mäl′i kyōōl′) *n.* ⟦< L dim. of *moles*, a mass⟧ 1 the smallest particle of an element or compound that can exist in the free state and still retain the characteristics of the substance 2 a small particle —**mo·lecu·lar** (mō lek′yōō lər) *adj.*

mole′hill′ *n.* a small ridge of earth, formed by a burrowing mole

mole′skin′ *n.* 1 the fur of the mole 2 a napped cotton fabric

mo·lest (mə lest′) *vt.* ⟦< L *moles*, a burden⟧ 1 to annoy or to meddle with so as to trouble or harm 2 to make improper sexual advances to 3 to assault or attack (esp. a

child) sexually —**mo·les·ta·tion** (mō′les tā′shən) *n.* —**mo·lest′er** *n.*

mol·lify (mäl′ə fī′) *vt.* **-fied′, -fy′ing** ⟦< L *mollis*, soft + *facere*, make⟧ 1 to soothe; appease 2 to make less severe or violent

mol·lusk or **mol·lusc** (mäl′əsk) *n.* ⟦< L *mollis*, soft⟧ any of a group of invertebrates, as oysters, snails, squids, etc., characterized by a soft body often enclosed in a shell

molly (mäl′ē) *n., pl.* **-lies** ⟦after F. N. *Mollien* (1758-1850), Fr statesman⟧ any of various brightly colored fishes often kept in aquariums Also **mol′lie**

molly·cod·dle (mäl′ē käd′'l) *n.* ⟦< *Molly*, dim. of *Mary* + CODDLE⟧ a man or boy used to being coddled — *vt.* **-dled, -dling** to pamper; coddle

molt (mōlt) *vi.* ⟦< L *mutare*, to change⟧ to shed hair, skin, horns, etc. prior to replacement by a new growth, as reptiles, birds, etc.

mol·ten (mōl′tən) *vt., vi.* ⟦ME⟧ *archaic pp. of* MELT — *adj.* melted by heat

mo·lyb·de·num (mə lib′də nəm) *n.* ⟦< Gr *molybdos*, lead⟧ a silvery metallic chemical element, used in alloys

mom (mäm) *n.* [Colloq.] MOTHER

mo·ment (mō′mənt) *n.* ⟦< L *momentum*, movement⟧ 1 an indefinitely brief period of time; instant 2 a definite point in time 3 a brief time of importance 4 importance

mo·men·tari·ly (mō′mən ter′ə lē, mō′mən ter′-) *adv.* 1 for a short time 2 in an instant 3 at any moment

mo·men·tary (mō′mən ter′ē) *adj.* lasting for only a moment; passing

mo·men·tous (mō men′təs) *adj.* of great moment; very important

mo·men·tum (mō men′təm) *n., pl.* **-tums** or **-ta** (-tə) ⟦L: see MOMENT⟧ the impetus of a moving object, equal to the product of its mass and its velocity

mommy (mäm′ē) *n., pl.* **-mies** *child's term for* MOTHER

mon·arch (män′ərk) *n.* ⟦< Gr *monos*, alone + *archein*, to rule⟧ 1 a hereditary ruler; king, queen, etc. 2 a large butterfly of North America, having orange, black-edged wings —**mo·nar·chi·cal** (mō när′ki kəl) *adj.*

mon′ar·chist (-ər kist) *n.* one who favors monarchical government

mon′ar·chy (-kē) *n., pl.* **-chies** a government or state headed by a monarch

mon·as·tery (män′ə ster′ē) *n., pl.* **-ies** ⟦< Gr *monos*, alone⟧ the residence of a group of monks, etc. who have withdrawn from the world for religious reasons

mo·nas·tic (mō nas′tik) *adj.* of or like that of a monastery, monk, etc. Also **mo·nas′ti·cal** —**mo·nas′ti·cism′** (-tə siz′əm) *n.*

mon·au·ral (män ôr′əl) *adj.* of sound reproduction using a single channel to carry and reproduce sound

Mon·day (mun′dā, -dē) *n.* ⟦OE *monandæg*, moon's day⟧ the second day of the week: abbrev. **Mon.**

mon·etary (män′ə ter′ē, mun′-) *adj.* ⟦< L *moneta*, a MINT[1]⟧ 1 of the coinage or currency of a country 2 of money —**mon′etar′i·ly** *adv.*

money (mun′ē) *n., pl.* **-eys** or **-ies** ⟦< L *moneta*, a MINT[1]⟧ 1 stamped pieces of metal, or any paper notes, authorized

═══ **THESAURUS** ═══

moist *a.* humid, dank, moistened; see WET 1.

moisten *v.* sprinkle, dampen, saturate, drench, waterlog, steep, sog, sop, dip, rinse, wash over, wet down, water down, squirt, shower, rain on, splash, splatter, bathe, steam, spray, sponge.

moisture *n.* precipitation, mist, drizzle; see FOG, WATER 1.

mold[1,2] *n.* 1 [A form] matrix, womb, cavity, shape, frame, pattern, design, die, cast, cup, image, kind, molding, casting, reproduction, form, pottery, shell, core. 2 [A parasitic growth] rust, parasite, fungus, lichen; see also DECAY.

mold[1,2] *v.* 1 [To give physical shape to] make, round into, fashion; see FORM 1. 2 [To decay through the action of mold] rot, mildew, rust; see SPOIL.

moldy *a.* musty, mildewed, dank; see ROTTEN 1.

mole[1] *n.* flaw, birthmark, blotch; see BLEMISH.

molecular *a.* miniature, microscopic, atomic; see LITTLE 1, MINUTE 1.

molecule *n.* 1 [Unit] particle, fragment, unit; see BIT 1. 2 [Atom] electron, ion, particle; see ATOM.

molest *v.* 1 [To disturb objects] displace, meddle, disorganize; see DISTURB. 2 [To disturb people] bother, interrupt, break in upon, intrude, encroach upon, annoy, worry, irritate, plague, badger, bait, pester, hinder, tease, irk, vex, trouble, confuse, perturb, frighten, terrify, scare; see also BOTHER 2.

molten *a.* heated, melted, fused, liquefied, running, fluid, seething; see also HOT 1.—*Ant.* COLD, cool, solid.

moment *n.* 1 [A brief time] minute, instant, millisecond, trice, second, bit, while, flash, jiffy*; see also MINUTE 2. 2 [Importance] significance, note, consequence; see IMPORTANCE.

momentarily *a.* immediately, right now, instantly; see NOW 1.

momentary *a.* fleeting, quick, passing, flitting, flashing, transient, impermanent, shifting, ephemeral, vanishing, cursory, temporary, dreamlike, in the wink of an eye*.—*Ant.* ETERNAL, continual, ceaseless.

momentum *n.* impulse, force, drive; see ENERGY 2.

mommy* *n.* mom*, female parent, mama*; see MOTHER 1, PARENT.

monarch *n.* despot, sovereign, autocrat; see KING 1.

monarchy *n.* kingship, sovereignty, command; see POWER 2.

monastery *n.* abbey, priory, religious community; see CHURCH 1.

monetary *a.* pecuniary, financial, fiscal; see COMMERCIAL.

money *n.* 1 [A medium of exchange] gold, silver, cash, currency, check, bills, notes, specie, legal tender, Almighty Dollar*, gravy*, wampum*, shekels*, dough*, long green*, coins*, lucre, folding money*, wad*, bucks*, hard cash*, bread*. *Money includes by a government as a medium of exchange 2 property; wealth —**in the money** [Slang] 1 among the winners in a race, etc. 2 wealthy —**make money** to gain profits —**put money into** to invest money in

mon′ey·bag′ *n.* 1 a bag for money 2 [*pl., with sing. v.*] [Colloq.] a rich person

mon·eyed (mun′ēd) *adj.* rich; wealthy

mon′ey·mak′er *n.* 1 one good at acquiring money 2 something profitable —**mon′ey·mak′ing** *adj., n.*

money market the short-term system for lending and borrowing funds, especially by governments and large corporations

money order an order for payment of a specified sum of money, issued for a fee at one post office, bank, etc. and payable at another

mon·ger (muŋ′gər) *n.* [< OE *mangere*] [Chiefly Brit.] a dealer or trader

Mon·gol (mäŋ′gəl) *n., adj.* MONGOLIAN

Mon·go·lian (mäŋ gō′lē ən) *n.* 1 a native of Mongolia 2 a subfamily of languages spoken in Mongolia — *adj.* 1 of Mongolia, its peoples, or their cultures 2 [Obs.] affected with Down's syndrome

Mon·golic (mäŋ gäl′ik) *adj. var. of* MONGOLIAN — *n.* Mongolian, a language spoken in Mongolia

Mon·gol·oid (mäŋ′gəl oid′) *adj.* 1 *var. of* MONGOLIAN 2 designating or of one of the major geographical varieties of human beings, including most of the peoples of Asia 3 [*often* **m-**] [Obs.] affected with Down's syndrome — *n.* 1 a member of the Mongoloid population of human beings 2 [*often* **m-**] [Obs.] one affected with Down's syndrome

mon·goose (mäŋ′gōōs′) *n., pl.* **-goos′es** [< native name in India] a civetlike, Old World carnivore that kills snakes, rodents, etc.

mon·grel (muŋ′grəl, mäŋ′-) *n.* [< OE *gemong*, mixture] an animal or plant, esp. a dog, of mixed breed — *adj.* of mixed breed, origin, character, etc.

mon·ied (mun′ēd) *adj.* MONEYED

moni·ker or **mon·icker** (män′i kər) *n.* [< ?] [Slang] a person's name

mo·ni·tion (mō nish′ən) *n.* [< L *monere*, warn] admonition; warning

moni·tor (män′i tər) *n.* [< L *monere*, warn] 1 a student chosen to help the teacher 2 any device for regulating the performance of a machine, an aircraft, etc. 3 *Radio, TV* a receiver for checking the quality of transmission — *vt., vi.* to watch or check on (a person or thing)

monk (muŋk) *n.* [< Gr *monos*, alone] a man devoted to a religious life, usually in retirement from the general population

mon·key (muŋ′kē) *n., pl.* **-keys** [< ? Fr or Sp *mona*, ape + LowG *-ke*, -KIN] 1 a primate having a flat, hairless face and a long tail 2 a gibbon or chimpanzee — *vi.* [Colloq.] to play, trifle, or meddle

monkey business [Colloq.] foolishness, mischief, or deceit

mon′key·shines′ (-shīnz′) *n.pl.* [Colloq.] playful tricks or pranks

monkey wrench a wrench with an adjustable jaw — **throw a monkey wrench into** [Colloq.] to disrupt the orderly functioning of

monk's cloth a heavy cloth with a basket weave, used for drapes, etc.

monks·hood (muŋks′hood′) *n.* ACONITE

mono (män′ō) *adj. short for* MONOPHONIC — *n. short for* MONONUCLEOSIS

mono- [< Gr *monos*, single] *prefix* one, alone, single

mono·cle (män′ə kəl) *n.* [ult. < Gr *monos*, single + L *oculus*, eye] an eyeglass for one eye only

mon·o·clonal (män′ō klōn′əl) *adj.* of or cloned from one cell

mono·coty·ledon (män′ō kät′l ēd″n) *adj. Bot.* a plant having an embryo with only one seed leaf (cotyledon) — **mon′o·cot′y·le′don·ous** *adj.*

mo·noga·my (mō näg′ə mē) *n.* [ult. < Gr *monos*, single + *gamos*, marriage] the practice or state of being married to only one person at a time —**mo·nog′a·mous** *adj.*

mono·gram (män′ə gram′) *n.* [< Gr *monos*, single + *gramma*, letter] the initials of a name, combined in a single design — *vt.* **-grammed′, -gram′ming** to put a monogram on

mon′o·graph′ (-graf′) *n.* [MONO- + -GRAPH] a book or long article, esp. a scholarly one, on a single subject

mono·lin·gual (män′ō liŋ′gwəl) *adj.* using or knowing only one language

mono·lith (män′ə lith′) *n.* [< Gr *monos*, single + *lithos*, stone] 1 a single large block of stone, as one made into an obelisk, etc. 2 any massive, unyielding structure —**mon′o·lith′ic** *adj.*

mono·logue or **mono·log** (män′ə lôg′) *n.* [< Gr *monos*, single + *legein*, speak] 1 a long speech 2 a soliloquy 3 a skit, etc. for one actor only

mono·ma·nia (män′ō mā′nē ə) *n.* an excessive interest in or enthusiasm for some one thing; craze —**mon′o·ma′niac′** (-mā′nē ak′) *n.* —**mon′o·ma·ni′a·cal** (-mə nī′ə kəl) *adj.*

mono·nu·cleo·sis (män′ō nōō′klē ō′sis) *n.* [MONO- + NUCLE(US) + -OSIS] an acute disease, esp. of young people, with fever, swollen lymph nodes, etc.

mon′o·phon′ic (-fän′ik) *adj.* of sound reproduction using a single channel to carry and reproduce sounds

mo·nop·o·list (mə näp′ə list) *n.* one who has a monopoly or favors monopoly —**mo·nop′o·lis′tic** *adj.*

mo·nop′o·lize′ (-līz′) *vt.* **-lized′, -liz′ing** 1 to get, have, or exploit a monopoly of 2 to get full control of

mo·nop′o·ly (-lē) *n., pl.* **-lies** [< Gr *monos*, single + *pōlein*, sell] 1 exclusive control of a commodity or service in a given market 2 such control granted by a government 3 something held as a monopoly 4 a company that has a monopoly

mono·rail (män′ō rāl′) *n.* 1 a single rail that is a track for cars suspended from or balanced on it 2 a railway with such a track

mon′o·syl′la·ble (-sil′ə bəl) *n.* a word of one syllable — **mon′o·syl·lab′ic** (-si lab′ik) *adj.*

mon′o·theism′ (-thē iz′əm) *n.* [MONO- + THEISM] the belief that there is only one God —**mon′o·theist′** *n.* — **mon′o·theis′tic** *adj.*

mono·tone (män′ə tōn′) *n.* [see MONO- & TONE] 1 utterance of successive words without change of pitch or key 2 tiresome sameness of style, color, etc. 3 a single, unchanging tone

mo·noto·nous (mə nät′'n əs) *adj.* 1 going on in the same tone 2 having no variety 3 tiresome because unvarying —**mo·not′o·ny** *n.*

mon·ox·ide (mə näks′īd′) *n.* an oxide with one atom of oxygen in each molecule

mon·sieur (mə syʉr′; *Fr* mə syö′) *n., pl.* **mes·sieurs** (mes′ərz; *Fr* mā syö′) [Fr, lit., my lord] 1 a man; gentleman 2 [**M-**] French title, equivalent to *Mr.* or *Sir*

Mon·si·gnor (män sēn′yər) *n.* [It, lit., my lord] a title given to certain Roman Catholic prelates

mon·soon (män sōōn′) *n.* [< Ar *mausim*, a season]

■■■■■ THESAURUS ■■■■■

the following: cent, dollar, penny, pound, *centime, franc, centesimo, lira, centavo, peso, kopek, ruble, ore, krone, yuan, sen, yen, Pfennig, Mark.* 2 [Wealth] funds, capital, property; see WEALTH. 3 [Merged interest] financiers, corporate interests, capitalists; see BUSINESS 4. 4 [Pay] payment, salary, wages; see PAY 2. — **for one's money*** for one's choice, in one's opinion, to one's mind; see PERSONALLY 2. —**in the money*** wealthy, flush*, loaded*; see RICH 1. —**make money** gain profits, become wealthy, earn; see PROFIT 2. —**one's money's worth** full value, gain, benefit; see VALUE 1, 3. —**put money into** invest in, support, underwrite; see INVEST.

monk *n.* hermit, religious, ascetic,

solitary, recluse, abbot, prior; see also PRIEST.

monkey *n.* primate, lemur, anthropoid ape; see ANIMAL. *Monkeys include the following:* chimpanzee, orangutan, baboon, marmoset, gibbon, gorilla, mandrill; spider, squirrel, capuchin.

monkey* *v.* pry, fool around, tamper with; see MEDDLE 2.

monkey business* *n.* deceit, conniving, misconduct; see DECEPTION, LIE.

monologue *n.* talk, speech, discourse; see ADDRESS 1.

monopolize *v.* engross, acquire, exclude, own exclusively, absorb, consume, manage, have, hold, corner,

restrain, patent, copyright, corner the market*.—*Ant.* INCLUDE, give, invite.

monopoly *n.* trust, syndicate, cartel; see BUSINESS 1.

monotonous *a.* 1 [Tiresome] tedious, wearisome, wearying; see DULL 4. 2 [Having but one tone] monotonic, unvarying, lacking, variety, in one key, unchanged, reiterated, recurrent, single, uniform.—*Ant.* VARIOUS, varying, multiple.

monotony *n.* invariability, likeness, tediousness, similarity, continuity, continuance, oneness, evenness, levelness, flatness, the same old thing; see also BOREDOM.—*Ant.* VARIETY, difference, variability.

seasonal wind of the Indian Ocean and S Asia 2 the rainy season during which this wind blows from the southwest

mon·ster (män′stər) *n.* 〖< L *monere,* warn〗 1 any grotesque imaginary creature 2 a very wicked person 3 any huge animal or thing — *adj.* huge

mon·strance (män′strəns) *n.* 〖ult. < L *monstrare,* to show〗 R.C.Ch. a receptacle for displaying the consecrated Host

mon·strous (män′strəs) *adj.* 1 huge; enormous 2 greatly malformed 3 horrible; hideous; shocking 4 hideously evil —**mon·stros′i·ty** (-sträs′ə tē), *pl.* **-ties,** *n.*

mon·tage (mōn täzh′, män-) *n.* 〖Fr < *monter,* to mount〗 1 a composite picture 2 a rapid sequence of film scenes, often superimposed

Mon·tes·sori method (mänt′ə sôr′ē) 〖after M. *Montessori* (1870-1952), It educator〗 a method of teaching young children, emphasizing training of the senses

month (munth) *n.* 〖OE *monath*〗 1 any of the twelve divisions of the calendar year 2 a period of four weeks or 30 days 3 one twelfth of the solar year

month′ly *adj.* done, happening, payable, etc. every month — *n., pl.* **-lies** a periodical published once a month — *adv.* once a month; every month

monu·ment (män′yoo mənt) *n.* 〖< L *monere,* remind〗 1 something set up to keep alive the memory of a person or event, as a tablet, statue, etc. 2 a work of enduring significance

mon′u·men′tal (-ment′'l) *adj.* 1 of or serving as a monument 2 like a monument; massive, enduring, etc. 3 very great; colossal

moo (mōō) *n., pl.* **moos** 〖echoic〗 the vocal sound made by a cow — *vi.* **mooed, moo′ing** to make this sound

mooch (mōōch) *vi., vt.* 〖ult. < OFr *muchier,* to hide〗 [Slang] to get (food, money, etc.) by begging, imposition, etc. —**mooch′er** *n.*

mood[1] (mōōd) *n.* 〖< OE *mod,* mind〗 1 a particular state of mind or feeling 2 a predominant or pervading feeling or spirit

mood[2] (mōōd) *n.* 〖< MODE〗 a characteristic of verbs that indicates whether the action expressed is regarded as a fact, supposition, or command

mood′y *adj.* **-i·er, -i·est** characterized by gloomy or changing moods —**mood′i·ly** *adv.* —**mood′i·ness** *n.*

moon (mōōn) *n.* 〖OE *mona*〗 1 the celestial body that revolves around the earth once about every 29½ days 2 anything shaped like the moon (i.e., an orb or crescent) 3 any natural satellite of a planet — *vi.* to behave in an idle or abstracted way

moon′beam′ *n.* a ray of moonlight

moon′light′ *n.* the light of the moon

moon′light′ing *n.* the holding of a second job along with one's main job

moon′lit′ *adj.* lighted by the moon

moon′scape′ (-skāp′) *n.* 〖MOON + (LAND)SCAPE〗 the surface of the moon or a representation of it

moon′shine′ *n.* 1 MOONLIGHT 2 whiskey unlawfully distilled —**moon′shin′er** *n.*

moon′shot′ *n.* the launching of a spacecraft to the moon

moon′stone′ *n.* a feldspar with a pearly luster, used as a gem

moon′struck′ *adj.* 1 crazed; lunatic 2 romantically dreamy

moon′walk′ *n.* a walking about by an astronaut on the surface of the moon

moor[1] (moor) *n.* 〖OE *mor*〗 [Brit.] a tract of open wasteland, usually covered with heather and often marshy

moor[2] (moor) *vt.* 〖< ? MDu *maren,* to tie〗 1 to hold (a ship, etc.) in place by cables attached as to a pier, or by anchors 2 to secure — *vi.* to moor a ship, etc.

Moor (moor) *n.* any of a Muslim people of NW Africa — **Moor′ish** *adj.*

moor′ing *n.* 1 [*often pl.*] the cables, etc. by which a ship is moored 2 [*pl.*] a place where a ship is moored

moose (mōōs) *n., pl.* **moose** 〖< AmInd〗 a large deer of N regions, the male of which has broad, flat antlers

moot (mōōt) *adj.* 〖< OE *mot,* a meeting〗 1 debatable 2 resolved and thus not worthy of discussion

mop (mäp) *n.* 〖earlier *mappe*〗 1 a bundle of rags, or yarns, a sponge, etc. fastened to the end of a stick, as for washing floors 2 anything suggesting this, as a thick head of hair — *vt.* **mopped, mop′ping** to wash or wipe with a mop —**mop up** [Colloq.] 1 to finish 2 to clear of remnants of beaten enemy forces

mope (mōp) *vi.* **moped, mop′ing** 〖< ?〗 to be gloomy and apathetic —**mop′ey, mop′y,** or **mop′ish** *adj.*

mop·pet (mäp′it) *n.* 〖< ME *moppe,* rag doll〗 [Colloq.] a little child

mo·raine (mə rān′) *n.* 〖Fr〗 a mass of rocks, sand, etc. left by a glacier

moral (môr′əl, mär′-) *adj.* 〖< L *mos, pl. mores,* morals〗 1 dealing with, or capable of distinguishing between, right and wrong 2 of, teaching, or in accordance with the principles of right and wrong 3 good in conduct or character; specif., sexually virtuous 4 involving sympathy without action [*moral* support] 5 virtually such because of effects on thoughts or attitudes [a *moral* victory] 6 based on probability [a *moral* certainty] — *n.* 1 a moral lesson taught by a fable, event, etc. 2 [*pl.*] principles or standards with respect to right or wrong in conduct —**mor′ally** *adv.*

mo·rale (mə ral′, mô-) *n.* moral or mental condition with respect to courage, discipline, confidence, etc.

mor·al·ist (môr′əl ist) *n.* 1 a teacher of or writer on morals 2 one who seeks to impose personal morals on others —**mor·al·is′tic** *adj.*

■ THESAURUS ■

monster *n.* 1 [A great beast] beastlike creature, centaur, monstrosity, sphinx, chimera, unicorn, dragon, griffin, cyclops, phoenix, mermaid, sea serpent, rhinoceros, elephant, werewolf. 2 [An unnatural creation] abnormality, monstrosity, malformation; see FREAK. 3 [An inhuman person] brute, beast, cruel person; see CRIMINAL, RASCAL.

monstrous *a.* 1 [Huge] stupendous, prodigious, enormous; see LARGE 1. 2 [Unnatural] abnormal, preposterous, uncanny; see UNNATURAL 1, UNUSUAL 2.

month *n.* measure of time, thirty days, one-twelfth of a year, four weeks. *Months of the year are the following:* January, February, March, April, May, June, July, August, September, October, November, December.

monthly *a.* once a month, every month, menstrual, punctually, steadily, recurrent, cyclic, cyclical, repeated, rhythmic, methodically, periodically, from month to month; see also REGULARLY.

monument *n.* 1 [Anything erected to preserve a memory] tomb, shaft, column, pillar, headstone, tombstone, gravestone, mausoleum, obelisk, shrine, statue, building,

tower, monolith, tablet, slab, stone; see also MEMORIAL. 2 [A landmark in the history of creative work] work of art, magnum opus, permanent contribution; see ACHIEVEMENT, MASTERPIECE.

monumental *a.* lofty, impressive, majestic; see GRAND, GREAT 1.

mood[1,2] *n.* 1 [A state of mind] state, condition, frame of mind, temper, humor, disposition, inclination, caprice, whim, fancy, pleasure, freak, wish, desire. 2 [A quality of mind] bent, propensity, tendency; see ATTITUDE. 3 [Grammatical mode] aspect, inflection, mode. *Moods in English grammar include the following:* indicative, subjunctive, imperative, interrogative, conditional, potential.

moody *a.* pensive, unhappy, low-spirited; see SAD 1.

moon *n.* celestial body, heavenly body, planet, planetoid, crescent, new moon, half-moon, full moon, old moon, Luna, moon goddess, dry moon, wet moon.

moonlight *n.* effulgence, radiance, luminescence; see LIGHT 3.

moonshine *n.* 1 [Moonlight] effulgence, radiance, luminosity; see LIGHT 3. 2 [Whiskey distilled illic-

itly] mountain dew*, hooch*, white lightning*; see WHISKEY.

mop *n.* swab, duster, sweeper; see BROOM.

mop *v.* swab, wipe, rub, dab, pat, polish, wash, dust, wipe up; see also CLEAN. —**mop up** finish off, dispatch, clean up; see DEFEAT 2, ELIMINATE.

mope *v.* fret, pine away, grieve, sorrow, sink, lose heart, brood, pine, yearn, despair, grumble, chafe, lament, regret, look glum, sulk, pull a long face*.—*Ant.* CELEBRATE, revive, cheer up.

moral *a.* 1 [Characterized by conventional virtues] trustworthy, kindly, courteous, respectable, proper, scrupulous, conscientious, good, truthful, decent, just, honorable, honest, high-minded, saintly, pure, worthy, correct, seemly, aboveboard, dutiful, principled, conscientious, chaste, ethical; see also NOBLE 1, 2, RELIABLE.—*Ant.* LYING, DISHONEST, unscrupulous. 2 [Having to do with approved relationships between the sexes] virtuous, immaculate, decent; see CHASTE, INNOCENT 2.

morale *n.* assurance, resolve, spirit; see CONFIDENCE.

mo·ral·ity (mō ral′i tē, mə-) *n., pl.* **-ties** 1 rightness or wrongness, as of an action 2 right or moral conduct 3 moral principles

mor·al·ize (môr′əl īz′) *vi.* **-ized′, -iz′ing** to think, write, etc. about moral questions, often in a self-righteous or tedious way —**mor′al·iz′er** *n.*

mo·rass (mə ras′, mô-) *n.* [< OFr *maresc*] a bog; marsh; swamp

mora·to·rium (môr′ə tôr′ē əm) *n., pl.* **-ri·ums** or **-ria** (-ə) [< L *mora*, a delay] 1 a legal authorization to delay payment of money due 2 any authorized delay of a specified activity

mo·ray (eel) (môr′ā) [< Gr *myraina*] a voracious, brilliantly colored eel

mor·bid (môr′bid) *adj.* [< L *morbus*, disease] 1 of or caused by disease; diseased 2 resulting as from a diseased state of mind 3 gruesome [morbid details] —**mor·bid′ity** *n.* —**mor′bidly** *adv.*

mor·dant (môr′dənt) *adj.* [< L *mordere*, to bite] caustic; sarcastic —*n.* a substance that fixes colors in dyeing —**mor′dancy** *n.* —**mor′dantly** *adv.*

more (môr) *adj.* [OE *mara*] 1 greater in amount, degree, or number: comparative of MUCH or MANY 2 additional [take *more* tea] —*n.* 1 a greater amount or degree 2 [*with pl. v.*] a greater number (*of*) 3 something additional —*adv.* 1 in or to a greater degree or extent 2 in addition —**more or less** 1 somewhat 2 approximately

more·o′ver *adv.* in addition to what has been said; besides

mo·res (môr′ēz′, -āz′) *n.pl.* [L, customs] folkways so basic as to develop the force of law

morgue (môrg) *n.* [Fr] 1 a place where the bodies of unknown dead or those dead of unknown causes are temporarily kept 2 the file of back numbers, photographs, etc. kept as in a newspaper's office

mori·bund (môr′i bund′) *adj.* [< L *mori*, to die] dying

Mor·mon (môr′mən) *n.* a member of the Church of Jesus Christ of Latter-day Saints, founded (1830) in the U.S. — **Mor′mon·ism** *n.*

morn (môrn) *n.* [Old Poet.] morning

morn·ing (-iŋ) *n.* [OE *morgen*] the first or early part of the day, from midnight, or esp. dawn, to noon

morning glory a twining vine with trumpet-shaped flowers

morning sickness nausea, vomiting, etc. affecting many women early in pregnancy, occurring usually in the morning

mo·ron (môr′än′) *n.* [< Gr *mōros*, foolish] 1 an adult mentally equal to a child between eight and twelve years old: an obsolescent term 2 a very foolish or stupid person —**mo·ron′ic** *adj.*

mo·rose (mə rōs′) *adj.* [< L *mos*, manner] ill-tempered; gloomy, sullen, etc. —**mo·rose′ly** *adv.* —**mo·rose′ness** *n.*

mor·pheme (môr′fēm′) *n.* [< Gr *morphē*, form] the smallest meaningful language unit, as an affix or base

mor·phine (môr′fēn′) *n.* [after *Morpheus*, Gr god of dreams] an alkaloid derived from opium and used in medicine to relieve pain

mor·phol·ogy (môr fäl′ə jē) *n.* [Ger < Gr *morphē*, form + Ger -*logie*, -LOGY] the study of form and structure, as in biology or linguistics

mor·row (mär′ō, môr′-) *n.* [< OE *morgen*, morning] [Archaic] 1 morning 2 the next day

Morse (môrs) *adj.* [after S. *Morse*, 19th-c. U.S. inventor] [often **m-**] designating or of a code consisting of a system of dots and dashes, used in telegraphy

mor·sel (môr′səl) *n.* [< L *morsum*, a bite] 1 a small bite or portion of food 2 a small piece or amount

mor·tal (môr′təl) *adj.* [< L *mors*, death] 1 that must eventually die 2 of man as a being who must eventually die 3 of death 4 causing physical or spiritual death; deadly; fatal 5 very intense [mortal terror] —*n.* a human being —**mor′tally** *adv.*

mor·tal·ity (môr tal′ə tē) *n.* 1 the mortal nature of man 2 death on a large scale, as from war 3 the ratio of deaths to population; death rate

mor·tar (môrt′ər) *n.* [< L *mortarium*] 1 a bowl in which substances are pulverized with a pestle 2 a short-barreled cannon which hurls shells in a high trajectory 3 a mixture of cement or lime with sand and water, used to bind bricks or stones

mor′tar·board′ *n.* 1 a square board for holding mortar 2 an academic cap with a square, flat top

mort·gage (môr′gij) *n.* [< OFr *mort*, dead + *gage*, pledge] 1 the pledging of property to a creditor as security for the payment of a debt 2 the deed by which this is done — *vt.* **-gaged, -gag·ing** 1 to pledge (property) by a mortgage 2 to put an advance claim on [to *mortgage* one's future] — **mort′ga·gor** or **mort′gager** (-gi jər) *n.*

mort·ga·gee′ (-gə jē′) *n.* a person to whom property is mortgaged

mor·ti·cian (môr tish′ən) *n.* [< L *mors*, death] FUNERAL DIRECTOR

mor·ti·fy (môrt′ə fī′) *vt.* **-fied′, -fy′ing** [< L *mors*, death + *facere*, make] 1 to subdue (physical desires) by self-denial, fasting, etc. 2 to humiliate —**mor′ti·fi·ca′tion** *n.*

mor·tise (môrt′is) *n.* [< L *murtazza*, joined] a hole or recess cut in a piece of wood, to receive a projecting part (*tenon*) shaped to fit into it

mor·tu·ary (môr′chōō er′ē) *n., pl.* **-ies** a place where dead bodies are kept before burial or cremation

mo·sa·ic (mō zā′ik) *n.* [< L *musivus*, artistic] 1 the making of pictures or designs by inlaying small bits of colored stone, etc. in mortar 2 a picture or design so made

Mo·sa·ic (mō zā′ik) *adj.* of Moses or the laws, etc. attributed to him

Mo·ses (mō′zəz, -zəs) *Bible* the leader and lawgiver who brought the Israelites out of slavery in Egypt

mo·sey (mō′zē) *vi.* [prob. < VAMOOSE] [Slang] to amble along

Mos·lem (mäz′ləm) *n., adj.* MUSLIM

mosque (mäsk) *n.* [< Ar *masjid*, temple] a Muslim place of worship

mos·quito (mə skēt′ō) *n., pl.* **-toes** or **-tos** [Sp < L *musca*,

---

THESAURUS

morally *a.* 1 [In accordance with accepted standards of conduct] conscientiously, truthfully, honestly, honorably, appropriately, respectably, courteously, scrupulously, uprightly, righteously, trustworthily, decently, properly, in a manner approved by society; see also JUSTLY 1, SINCERELY.—*Ant.* WRONGLY, worthlessly, dishonorably. 2 [In a chaste manner] chastely, virtuously, purely; see MODESTLY.

morals *n.* ideals, customs, standards, mores, policies, beliefs, dogmas, social standards, principles; see also ETHICS.

morbid *a.* 1 [Diseased] sickly, unhealthy, ailing; see SICK. 2 [Pathological] gloomy, melancholic, depressed; see INSANE, SAD 1.

more *a.* 1 [Additional] also, likewise, and, over and above, more than that, in addition, further, besides, added; see also EXTRA.—*Ant.* LESS, less than, subtracted from. 2 [Greater in quantity, amount, degree, or quality] numerous, many, exceeding, extra, expanded, increased, major, aug-

mented, extended, enhanced, added to, larger, higher, wider, deeper, heavier, solider, stronger, above the mark.—*Ant.* weaker, lessened, decreased.

more or less *a.* about, somewhat, in general; see APPROXIMATE, APPROXIMATELY.

moreover *a.* further, by the same token, furthermore; see BESIDES.

morning *n.* 1 [Dawn] the East, morn, daybreak, break of day, first blush of morning, daylight, cockcrow, sun-up, the wee small hours*, crack of dawn*. 2 [The time before noon] forenoon, morningtide, after midnight, before noon, breakfast time, before lunch. —**good morning** good day, good morrow*, greetings; see HELLO.

mornings *a.* in the morning, every morning, before noon; see DAILY, REGULARLY.

moron *n.* feeble-minded person, imbecile, idiot, simpleton, goose, dullard, dunce, blockhead, cretin,

dunce, dunderhead*, numskull, loony*, dummy*; see also FOOL.—*Ant.* PHILOSOPHER, sage, scientist.

moronic *a.* foolish, mentally retarded, dumb*; see STUPID.

morsel *n.* bite, chunk, piece; see BIT 1, PART 1.

mortal *a.* 1 [Causing death] malignant, fatal, lethal; see DEADLY, POISONOUS. 2 [Subject to death] human, transient, temporal, passing, frail, impermanent, perishable, fading, passing away, momentary; see also TEMPORARY.—*Ant.* ETERNAL, perpetual, everlasting.

mortal *n.* creature, being, human; see ANIMAL, MAN 1.

mortality *n.* dying, extinction, fatality; see DEATH, DESTRUCTION 1.

mortgage *n.* lease, title, debt; see CONTRACT.

mortuary *n.* charnel house, funeral parlor, funeral home; see FUNERAL.

mosaic *a.* diapered, varied, inlaid; see ORNATE.

a fly] a two-winged insect, the female of which sucks blood from animals, including humans

moss (môs, mäs) *n.* ⟦OE *mos*, a swamp⟧ a very small, green plant that grows in velvety clusters on rocks, trees, etc. **—moss′y, -i·er, -i·est,** *adj.*

moss′back′ *n.* [Colloq.] an old-fashioned or very conservative person

most (mōst) *adj.* ⟦OE *mast*⟧ **1** greatest in amount, degree, or number: superlative of MUCH or MANY **2** in the greatest number of instances — *n.* **1** the greatest amount or degree **2** [*with pl. v.*] the greatest number (*of*) — *adv.* in or to the greatest degree or extent

most′ly *adv.* **1** for the most part **2** chiefly **3** usually

mot (mō) *n.* ⟦Fr, a word⟧ a witty remark

mote (mōt) *n.* ⟦OE *mot*⟧ a speck, as of dust

mo·tel (mō tel′) *n.* ⟦< MO(TOR) + (HO)TEL⟧ a hotel for motorists

moth (môth) *n., pl.* **moths** (môthz, môths) ⟦OE *moththe*⟧ a four-winged, chiefly night-flying insect, similar to the butterfly: the larvae of one kind feed on wool, etc.

moth′ball′ *n.* a small ball, as of naphthalene, the fumes of which repel moths from woolens, etc. **—in mothballs** put into storage or reserve

moth·er (mu*th*′ər) *n.* ⟦OE *modor*⟧ **1** a female parent **2** the origin or source of something **3** a woman who is the head (**mother superior**) of a religious establishment — *adj.* **1** of or like a mother **2** native [*mother* tongue] — *vt.* **1** to be the mother of **2** to be like a mother to **—moth′er·hood′** *n.* **—moth′er·less** *adj.*

Mother Goose the imaginary creator of a collection of nursery rhymes

moth′er-in-law′ *n., pl.* **moth′ers-in-law′** the mother of one's husband or wife

moth′er·land′ *n.* one's native land

moth′er·ly *adj.* of or like a mother; protective, nurturing, etc. **—moth′er·li·ness** *n.*

moth′er-of-pearl′ *n.* the hard internal layer of the shell of the pearl oyster, etc., used to make buttons, etc.

mother tongue one's native language

mo·tif (mō tēf′) *n.* ⟦Fr: see MOTIVE⟧ **1** *Art, Literature, Music* a main theme or subject for development **2** a repeated figure in a design

mo·tile (mōt′'l) *adj.* ⟦< L *movere*, to move⟧ *Biol.* capable of or exhibiting spontaneous motion **—mo·til′i·ty** *n.*

mo·tion (mō′shən) *n.* ⟦< L *movere*, to move⟧ **1** a moving from one place to another; movement **2** a moving of a part of the body; specif., a gesture **3** a proposal formally made in an assembly — *vi.* to make a meaningful movement of the hand, etc.; gesture — *vt.* to direct by a mean-

ingful gesture **—go through the motions** to do something as from habit, without enthusiasm, enjoyment, etc. **—in motion** moving **—mo′tion·less** *adj.*

motion picture FILM (*n.* 4)

motion sickness nausea, vomiting, etc. caused by the motion of a car, boat, etc.

mo·ti·vate (mōt′ə vāt′) *vt.* **-vat′ed, -vat′ing** to provide with, or affect as, a motive; incite **—mo′ti·va′tion** *n.*

mo·tive (mōt′iv) *n.* ⟦< L *movere*, to move⟧ **1** an inner drive, impulse, etc. that causes one to act; incentive **2** MOTIF (sense 1) — *adj.* of or causing motion

-motive (mōt′iv) *combining form* moving, of motion [*automotive*]

mot·ley (mät′lē) *adj.* ⟦< ?⟧ **1** of many colors **2** of many different or clashing elements [*a motley* group]

moto·cross (mō′tō krôs′) *n.* ⟦Fr⟧ a cross-country race for lightweight motorcycles

mo·tor (mōt′ər) *n.* ⟦L < *movere*, to move⟧ **1** anything that produces motion **2** an engine; esp., an internal-combustion engine **3** a machine for converting electric energy into mechanical energy — *adj.* **1** producing motion **2** of or powered by a motor **3** of, by, or for motor vehicles **4** of or involving muscular movements — *vi.* to travel by automobile

mo′tor·bike′ *n.* [Colloq.] **1** a motor-driven bicycle **2** a light motorcycle

mo′tor·boat′ *n.* a motor-driven boat, esp. a small one

mo′tor·cade′ (-kād′) *n.* ⟦MOTOR + -CADE⟧ an automobile procession

mo′tor·car′ *n.* an automobile

mo′tor·cy′cle (-sī′kəl) *n.* a two-wheeled vehicle propelled by an internal-combustion engine **—mo′tor·cy′clist** *n.*

motor home a motor vehicle with a truck chassis, outfitted as a traveling home

mo·tor·ist (mōt′ər ist) *n.* one who drives an automobile or travels by automobile

mo′tor·ize′ (-īz′) *vt.* **-ized′, -iz′ing** to equip with a motor or with motor-driven vehicles **—mo′tori·za′tion** *n.*

mo′tor·man (-mən) *n., pl.* **-men** one who drives an electric streetcar or electric locomotive

motor vehicle an automotive vehicle, esp. an automobile, truck, or bus

mot·tle (mät′'l) *vt.* **-tled, -tling** ⟦< MOTLEY⟧ to mark with blotches, etc. of different colors **—mot′tled** *adj.*

motto (mät′ō) *n., pl.* **-toes** or **-tos** ⟦It, a word⟧ a word or saying that expresses the goals, ideals, etc., as of a nation

---

THESAURUS

moss *n.* lichen, Iceland moss, peat moss; see PLANT.

mossy *a.* tufted, velvety, plushy, downy, smooth, fresh, damp, moist, resilient, soft, covered, overgrown.— *Ant.* DRY, bare, prickly.

most *a.* nearly all, all but, not quite all, close upon all, in the majority. — **at the most** in toto, not more than, at the outside; see MOST. —**make the most of** exploit, utilize, take advantage of; see USE 1.

mostly *a.* **1** [Frequently] often, many times, in many instances; see FREQUENTLY, REGULARLY. **2** [Largely] chiefly, essentially, for the most part; see PRINCIPALLY.

motel *n.* motor inn, inn, cabins, stopping place, road house, court, motor court; see also HOTEL, RESORT 2.

moth *n.* silkworm moth, gypsy moth, clothes moth; see INSECT.

mother *n.* **1** [A female parent] parent, matriarch, dam, mama, mammy*, mum*, ma*, mom*, mommy*, maw*, mater; see also PARENT, RELATIVE. **2** [The source] fountainhead, source, beginning; see ORIGIN 2.

mother-in-law *n.* husband's mother, wife's mother, mother by marriage; see RELATIVE.

motherly *a.* maternal, devoted, careful, watchful, kind, warm, gentle, tender, sympathetic, supporting, protective, nurturing, caretaking; see also LOVING.

motion *n.* **1** [A movement] change,

act, action; see MOVEMENT 2. **2** [The state of moving] passage, translating, changing; see MOVEMENT 1. **3** [An act formally proposed] suggestion, consideration, proposition; see PLAN 2. **—in motion** traveling, going, under way; see MOVING 1.

motionless *a.* **1** [Not moving] still, unmoving, dead, deathly still, inert, stock-still, stagnant, quiet.—*Ant.* MOVING, CHANGING, shifting. **2** [Firm] unmovable, fixed, stationary; see FIRM 1.

motion picture *n.* moving picture, cinema, the silver screen; see MOVIE.

motivate *v.* impel, inspire hope, stimulate, incite, propel, spur, goad, move, induce, prompt, arouse, whet, instigate, fire, provoke, cause, touch off*, egg on*, trigger*; see also DRIVE 1, EXCITE, URGE 2.

motive *n.* cause, purpose, idea; see REASON 3.

motor *n.* machine, device, instrument; see ENGINE. *Types of motors include the following:* internal combustion, diesel, spark diesel, compound, steam, external combustion, Wankel, piston, turbine, gas turbine, jet, rotary, radial, airplane, automobile, truck, AC electric, DC electric, high compression, low compression.

motorboat *n.* speedboat, putt-putt*, hop-up, skip-jack; see also BOAT. *Types of motorboats include the following:* open, outboard, electric-powered, gasoline-powered; cruiser, runabout.

motorcycle *n.* motorized two-wheeled vehicle, cycle, hog*, bike*, chopper*; see also VEHICLE.

motorist *n.* automobile operator, autoist*, gear grinder*; see DRIVER.

motorized *a.* motor-driven, motor-powered, electric-driven, gasoline-driven, oil-driven, motor-equipped, motor-operated.

motto *n.* maxim, adage, saw, epigram, aphorism, sentiment, slogan, catchword, axiom; see also PROVERB, SAYING. *Familiar mottoes include the following:* in God we trust, *e pluribus unum* (Latin), time flies, rest in peace, peace be with you, one for all and all for one, home sweet home, God bless our home, don't tread on me, give me liberty or give me death, all or nothing, you can't take it with you, all men are created free and equal; liberty, equality, fraternity; for God and country, what's worth doing is worth doing well, don't give up the ship, don't fire until you see the whites of their eyes; remember the Alamo, remember the Maine, remember Pearl Harbor, etc.; our Country, right or wrong; hew to the line and let the chips fall where they may, praise the Lord and pass the ammunition, put your trust in God and keep your powder dry; abandon hope, all ye who enter here; to err is human, to forgive, divine; make hay while the sun shines, Pike's Peak or bust*.

mould (mōld) *n., vt., vi. chiefly Brit., etc. sp. of* MOLD[1], MOLD[2], MOLD[3]
mould·ing *n. chiefly Brit., etc. sp. of* MOLDING
mouldy (mōl′dē) *adj. chiefly Brit., etc. sp. of* MOLDY
moult (mōlt) *vi. chiefly Brit. sp. of* MOLT
mound (mound) *n.* ⟦< ? MDu *mond*, protection⟧ a heap or bank of earth, sand, etc. — *vt.* to heap up
mount[1] (mount) *n.* ⟦< L *mons*⟧ a mountain
mount[2] (mount) *vi.* ⟦< L *mons*, mountain⟧ 1 to climb; ascend 2 to climb up on something, as a horse 3 to increase in amount — *vt.* 1 to go up; ascend *[to mount stairs]* 2 to get up on (a horse, platform, etc.) 3 to provide with horses *[mounted police]* 4 to place or fix (a jewel, picture, etc.) on or in the proper support, backing, etc. 5 to arrange (a dead animal, etc.) for exhibition 6 to place (a gun) into proper position for use 7 to prepare for and undertake (an expedition, etc.) — *n.* 1 a mounting 2 a horse, etc. for riding 3 the support, setting, etc. on or in which a thing is mounted
moun·tain (mount′'n) *n.* ⟦ult. < L *mons*⟧ 1 a natural raised part of the earth, larger than a hill 2 a large pile, amount, etc. — *adj.* of or in mountains
moun·tain·eer′ (-ir′) *n.* 1 one who lives in a mountainous region 2 a mountain climber
mountain goat a long-haired, goatlike antelope of the Rocky Mountains
mountain lion COUGAR
moun·tain·ous *adj.* 1 full of mountains 2 like a mountain; esp., huge
mountain sickness weakness, nausea, etc. caused by thin air at high altitudes
moun·te·bank (mount′ə baŋk′) *n.* ⟦< It *montambanco*, lit., mounted on a bench: orig. a person standing on a bench selling quack medicines⟧ a charlatan or quack
mount′ed *adj.* 1 on horseback 2 fixed firmly to a support or backing
mount′ing *n.* something serving as a backing, support, setting, etc.
mourn (môrn) *vi., vt.* ⟦OE *murnan*⟧ 1 to feel or express sorrow for (something regrettable) 2 to grieve for (someone who has died) — **mourn′er** *n.*
mourn′ful *adj.* 1 feeling or expressing grief or sorrow 2 causing sorrow

mourn′ing *n.* 1 the expression of grief, esp. at someone's death 2 black clothes, etc., worn as such an expression 3 the period during which one mourns
mouse (mous; *for v. also* mouz) *n., pl.* **mice** ⟦OE *mus*⟧ 1 any of many small rodents, esp. a species that commonly infests buildings 2 a timid person 3 [Slang] a black eye 4 a hand-held device for controlling the video display of a computer — *vi.* **moused, mous′ing** to hunt mice
mousse (mōōs) *n.* ⟦Fr, foam⟧ 1 a light, chilled dessert made with egg white, whipped cream, etc. 2 an aerosol foam used to keep hair in place, etc.
mous·tache (mus′tash′, məs tash′) *n. var. of* MUSTACHE
mousy (mous′ē, mouz′-) *adj.* **-i·er, -i·est** of or like a mouse; specif., quiet, timid, drab, etc. Also **mous′ey** — **mous′i·ness** *n.*
mouth (mouth; *for v.* mouth) *n., pl.* **mouths** (mouthz) ⟦OE *muth*⟧ 1 the opening in the head through which food is taken in and sounds are made 2 any opening regarded as like this *[the mouth of a jar, river, etc.]* — *vt.* 1 to say, esp. insincerely 2 to form (a word) with the mouth silently — **down in** (or **at**) **the mouth** [Colloq.] unhappy — **mouth off** [Slang] to talk loudly, impudently, etc.
mouth′ful′ *n., pl.* **-fuls′** 1 as much as the mouth can hold 2 as much as is usually taken into the mouth 3 a small amount 4 [Slang] a pertinent remark: chiefly in **say a mouthful**
mouth organ HARMONICA
mouth′piece′ *n.* 1 a part, as of a musical instrument, held in or to the mouth 2 a person, periodical, etc. which expresses the views as of a group
mouth′wash′ *n.* a flavored, often antiseptic liquid for rinsing the mouth
mouth′wa′ter·ing (-wôt′ər iŋ) *adj.* appetizing; tasty
mouth′y *adj.* **-i·er, -i·est** talkative, esp. in a bombastic or rude way — **mouth′i·ness** *n.*
mou·ton (mōō′tän′) *n.* ⟦Fr, sheep⟧ lambskin or sheepskin made to resemble beaver, seal, etc.
mov·able (mōōv′ə bəl) *adj.* that can be moved from one place to another — *n.* 1 something movable 2 *Law* personal property, esp. furniture: *usually used in pl.* Also **move′able**
move (mōōv) *vt.* **moved, mov′ing** ⟦< L *movere*⟧ 1 to change the place or position of 2 to set or keep in motion 3 to cause (*to do, say,* etc.) 4 to arouse the emotions, etc. of 5 to propose formally, as in a meeting — *vi.* 1 to

---

◼◼◼◼ THESAURUS ◼◼◼◼

mound *n.* pile, heap, knoll; see HILL.
mount[2] *v.* 1 [To rise] ascend, arise, uprise; see RISE 1. 2 [To climb] ascend, scale, clamber; see CLIMB.
mountain *n.* 1 [A lofty land mass] mount, elevation, peak, sierra, butte, hill, alp, range, ridge, pike, bluff, headland, volcano, crater, tableland, mesa, plateau, height, crag, precipice, cliff, earth mass.—*Ant.* VALLEY, ravine, flatland. *Famous chains of mountains include the following:* Alps, Himalayas, Caucasus, Urals, Pyrenees, Andes, Rockies, Canadian Rockies, Appalachians, Cascades, Adirondacks, White Mountains, Sierra Nevada, Sierra Madre, Cordillera, Apennine chain. *Famous peaks include the following:* Mont Blanc, Mt. Aetna, Vesuvius, the Matterhorn, Pike's Peak, Mt. Whitney, Mt. Shasta, Mt. Washington, the Jungfrau, the Grand Teton, Mt. McKinley, Krakatoa, Pelee, Popocatepetl, Mt. Cook, Mt. Everest, Annapurna, Mount of Olives, Mt. Sinai, Fujiyama, Mt. Kenya, Mt. Kilimanjaro. 2 [A pile] mass, mound, glob; see HEAP.
mountaineer *n.* mountain man, mountain dweller, hillman, highlander, uplander, native of mountains, mountain climber, rock climber, mountain guide, mountain scaler, hillbilly*.
mountainous *a.* mountainlike, with mountains, difficult, barbarous, wild, untamed, strange, remote, uncivilized, rude, unpopulated, solitary, unfamiliar, isolated, steep, lofty, hilly, alpine, upland, elevated, volcanic, towering, craggy, cliffy, rug-

ged.—*Ant.* LOW, small, flat.
mounted *a.* 1 [On horseback] seated, riding, in the saddle, cavalry, horsed*, up.—*Ant.* AFOOT, unhorsed, dismounted. 2 [Firmly fixed] supported, set, attached; see FIRM 1. 3 [Backed] based on, set off, strengthened; see REINFORCED.
mourn *v.* deplore, grieve, fret, sorrow, rue, regret, bemoan, sigh, long for, miss, droop, languish, yearn, pine, anguish, complain, agonize, weep, suffer, wring one's hands, be brokenhearted, be in distress, be sad.—*Ant.* CELEBRATE, rejoice, be happy.
mourner *n.* lamenter, griever, keener, weeper, wailer, sorrower, pallbearer, friend of the deceased, member of the family.
mournful *a.* sorrowful, mourning, unhappy; see SAD 1.
mourning *n.* 1 [The act of expressing grief] sorrowing, grieving, yearning, sorrow, lamentation, pining, sighing, regretting, deploring, weeping over, wailing, crying, moaning, murmuring, complaining, sobbing; see also DEPRESSION 2, GRIEF, SADNESS.—*Ant.* CELEBRATION, rejoicing, being glad. 2 [Symbols of mourning] black, mourning coach, arm band, mourning veil, widow's weeds, black suit, black tie.
mouse *n.* rodent, vermin, rat; see ANIMAL.
mouth *n.* 1 [The principal facial opening] *Parts of the mouth include the following:* lips, roof, floor, tongue, jaws, gums, teeth, soft palate, alveolar ridge, hard palate, uvula. 2 [Any

opening resembling a mouth] orifice, entrance, aperture; see ENTRANCE 2. 3 [The end of a river] estuary, firth, delta, portal, harbor, roads, sound, tidewater. —**down in** (or **at**) **the mouth*** depressed, discouraged, unhappy; see SAD 1. —**have a big mouth*** talk loudly, exaggerate, brag; see TALK 1.
mouthful *n.* portion, piece, morsel; see BITE 1.
movable *a.* not fastened, portable, adjustable, adaptable, not fixed, mobile, detachable, turnable, removable, separable, transferable, loose, unfastened, free, unattached, in parts, in sections, knocked down, on wheels.—*Ant.* FIXED, fastened, stationary.
move *n.* motility, transit, progress; see MOVEMENT 1, 2. —**get a move on*** go faster, start moving, get cracking*; see HURRY 1. —**on the move*** moving, busy, acting; see ACTIVE.
move *v.* 1 [To be in motion] go, walk, run, glide, travel, drift, budge, stir, shift, pass, cross, roll, flow, march, travel, progress, proceed, traverse, drive, ride, fly, hurry, head for, bustle, climb, crawl, leap, hop to it*, get a move on*, get going, get cracking*; see also ADVANCE 1.—*Ant.* STOP, remain stationary, stay quiet. 2 [To set in motion] impel, actuate, propel; see PUSH 2. 3 [To arouse the emotions of] influence, stir, instigate, stimulate, touch, play on, sway, induce, rouse, prevail upon, work upon, strike a sympathetic chord; see also DRIVE 1, ENCOURAGE, EXCITE.—

change place or position **2** to change one's residence **3** to be active **4** to make progress **5** to take action **6** to be, or be set, in motion **7** to make a formal application *(for)* **8** to evacuate: said of the bowels **9** to be sold: said of goods —*n.* **1** act of moving **2** an action toward some goal **3** a change of residence **4** *Chess, Checkers, etc.* the act of moving a piece, or one's turn to move —**move up** to promote or be promoted —**on the move** [Colloq.] moving about from place to place

move'ment *n.* **1** a moving or manner of moving **2** an evacuation (of the bowels) **3** a change in the location of troops, etc. **4** organized action by people working toward a goal **5** the moving parts of a mechanism, as of a clock **6** *Music* a) a principal division of a symphony, etc. b) rhythm

mov'er *n.* one that moves; specif., one whose work is moving furniture, etc. for those changing residence

movie (mōōv'ē) *n.* [< *moving picture*] FILM (*n.* 4) —**the movies 1** the film industry **2** a showing of a film

mov'ing *adj.* **1** in motion **2** changing place or position **3** stirring the emotions

mow[1] (mō) *vt., vi.* **mowed, mowed** or **mown** (mōn), **mow'ing** [OE *mawan*] to cut down (grass, etc.) from (a lawn, etc.) —**mow down 1** to cause to fall like cut grass **2** to overwhelm (an opponent) —**mow'er** *n.*

mow[2] (mou) *n.* [OE *muga*] **1** a heap of hay, etc., esp. in a barn **2** a haymow, or hayloft

MP 1 Member of Parliament: also **M.P. 2** Military Police

mpg miles per gallon

mph miles per hour

Mr. (mis'tər) mister: before a man's name or title: pl. *Messrs.*

Mrs. (mis'iz) mistress: before a married woman's name: pl. *Mmes.*

MS 1 manuscript: also **ms** or **ms. 2** Master of Science: also **M.S., MSc,** or **M.Sc. 3** multiple sclerosis

Ms. (miz) a title, free of reference to marital status, used in place of either *Miss* or *Mrs.*

Msgr. Monsignor

MST Mountain Standard Time

MSW or **M.S.W.** Master of Social Work

Mt. 1 Mount **2** Mountain

mu (mōō, myōō) *n.* the 12th letter of the Greek alphabet (M, μ)

much (much) *adj.* **more, most** [< OE *mycel*] great in quantity, degree, etc. —*adv.* **more, most 1** to a great degree or extent *[much* happier] **2** nearly *[much* the same] —*n.* **1** a great amount **2** something great or outstanding *[not much* to look at]

mu·ci·lage (myōō'si lij') *n.* [< L *mucere,* be moldy] **1** a thick, sticky substance in certain plants **2** any watery solution of gum, glue, etc. used as an adhesive —**mu'ci·lag'i·nous** (-laj'ə nəs) *adj.*

muck (muk) *n.* [ME *muk*] **1** moist manure **2** black earth with decaying matter, used as fertilizer **3** mud; dirt; filth —**muck'y, -i·er, -i·est,** *adj.*

muck'rake' *vi.* **-raked', -rak'ing** [see prec. & RAKE[1]] to search for and publicize real or alleged corruption in politics, etc. —**muck'rak'er** *n.*

mu·cous (myōō'kəs) *adj.* **1** of, containing, or secreting mucus **2** slimy

mucous membrane a mucus-secreting lining of certain body cavities

mu·cus (myōō'kəs) *n.* [L] the thick, slimy substance secreted by the mucous membranes for moistening and protection

mud (mud) *n.* [ME] **1** wet, soft, sticky earth **2** defamatory remarks

mud·dle (mud''l) *vt.* **-dled, -dling** [< prec.] **1** to mix up; bungle **2** to confuse mentally; befuddle —*vi.* to act or think confusedly —*n.* **1** a mess, jumble, etc. **2** mental confusion

mud'dle-head'ed *adj.* confused

mud'dy *adj.* **-dier, -di·est 1** full of or spattered with mud **2** not clear; cloudy *[muddy* coffee] **3** confused, obscure, etc. *[muddy* thinking] —*vt., vi.* **-died, -dy·ing** to make or become muddy —**mud'di·ness** *n.*

mud flat low, muddy land that floods at high tide

THESAURUS

Ant. QUIET, lull, pacify. **4** [To take up another residence] pack up, move out, move in; see LEAVE 1. **5** [To propose an action formally] suggest, introduce, submit; see PROPOSE 1. — **move up** go forward, do well, get ahead; see ADVANCE 1, RISE 1.

moved *a.* **1** [Transported] conveyed, carried, sent, taken, shifted, transferred, reassigned, changed, flown, driven, drawn, pushed, lifted, elevated, lowered, let down, displaced, withdrawn, replaced, sent abroad, trucked, hauled, dragged; see also SENT. **2** [Gone to a different residence] emigrated, migrated, vacated, removed, departed, gone away, changed residences, left, gone for good; see also GONE 1.—*Ant.* RESIDENT, remaining, still here. **3** [Proposed] recommended, submitted, introduced; see PROPOSED. **4** [Excited] disturbed, stimulated, upset; see EXCITED.

movement *n.* **1** [The act of moving] move, transit, passage, progress, journey, advance, mobility, change, shift, alteration, ascension, descension, propulsion, flow, flux, action, flight, wandering, journeying, voyaging, migration, emigration, transplanting, evolving, shifting, changing, locomotion, drive, evolution, undertaking, regression.—*Ant.* QUIET, rest, fixity. **2** [An example of movement] journey, trip, immigration, migration, march, crusade, patrol, sweep, emigration, evolution, unrest, transition, change, transfer, displacement, withdrawal, ascension, descension, progression, regression, transportation, removal, departure, shift, flight, slip, slide, step, foothold, stride, gesture, act, action, pilgrimage, expedition, locomotion. **3** [A trend] drift, tendency, bent; see INCLINATION 1.

movie *n.* moving picture, motion picture, photoplay, cinema, film, show, screenplay, cartoon, animated cartoon, serial, comedy, foreign film, travelogue, short, documentary, videotape, flick*; see also DRAMA.

movies *n.* **1** [A showing of a moving picture] motion picture, film, photoplay; see MOVIE. **2** [The motion picture industry] moving pictures, the cinematic industry, Hollywood, the screen world, the silver screen*, the industry*, pictures*, the flicks*, celluloids*.

moving *a.* **1** [In motion] going, changing, progressing, advancing, shifting, evolving, withdrawing, rising, going down, descending, ascending, getting up, traveling, journeying, on the march, moving up, starting, proceeding, flying, climbing, up-tempo, on the jump*, going great guns*. **2** [Going to another residence] migrating, emigrating, vacating, removing, departing, leaving, going away, changing residences. **3** [Exciting] affecting, emotional, touching; see EXCITING.

mow[1] *v.* scythe, reap, lay in swaths; see HARVEST.

much *a.* **1** [To a great degree or extent] important, weighty, notable, considerable, prominent, memorable, momentous, stirring, eventful, serious, urgent, pressing, critical, paramount, principal, leading, significant, telling, first-rate, in the front rank.— *Ant.* LITTLE, inconsiderable, trivial. **2** [In great quantity] full, many, very many, abundant, satisfying, enough, sufficient, adequate, considerable, substantial, ample, everywhere, copious, voluminous, plentiful, profuse, complete, lavish, generous, immeasurable, endless, countless, extravagant, hell of a lot*, all over the place*,

no end*.—*Ant.* INADEQUATE, insufficient, limited. **3** [Very] greatly, enormously, extremely; see VERY.

much *n.* a great quantity, abundance, quantities, a great deal, riches, wealth, volume, very much, breadth, plentifulness, fullness, completeness, lavishness, lot*, lots*, quite a bit*, gobs*, thousands*, tons*, oodles*; see also PLENTY.—*Ant.* LITTLE, penury, scarcity. —**as much as** practically, virtually, in effect; see ALMOST, EQUAL. —**make much of** treat with importance, expand, exaggerate; see OVERDO 1. —**not much of** a inferior, mediocre, unsatisfactory; see POOR 2. —**too much** excess, waste, extravagance, overabundance, superfluity, preposterousness, overcharge, ever so much, more than can be used, vastness, prodigiousness, immensity; see also EXCESS 1.—*Ant.* LACK, want, shortage.

muck *n.* refuse, dung, waste; see TRASH 1.

mud *n.* dirt, muck, clay, mire, slush, silt, muddiness, stickiness, ooze, bog, marsh, swamp.

muddle *n.* trouble, disarrangement, disarray; see CONFUSION, DISORDER.

muddle *v.* stir up, disarrange, entangle, foul, mix, jumble, derange, shake up, mess, botch, clutter, snarl, complicate, disorder; see also CONFUSE.

muddled *a.* uncertain, addled, stupid; see CONFUSED 2.

muddy *a.* **1** [Containing sediment] stirred, dull, dark, cloudy, murky, indistinct, roiled, roily, confused, obscure, opaque; see also DIRTY 1.— *Ant.* CLEAR, translucent, pellucid. **2** [Deep with mud] sloppy, swampy, soggy, sodden, slushy, watery, boggy, soaked.—*Ant.* DRY, barren, parched.

mud′room *n.* a room in a house for wet or muddy footwear and outerwear

mud′slide′ *n.* a massive flow of mud down a slope

mud′sling′ing *n.* the making of malicious verbal attacks, as against a political opponent —**mud′sling′er** *n.*

mu·ez·zin (myo͞o ez′in) *n.* ⟦< Ar *adhana*, proclaim⟧ a Muslim crier who calls the people to prayer

muff (muf) *n.* ⟦< Fr *moufle*, mitten⟧ **1** a cylindrical covering, as of fur, to warm the hands **2** any bungle — *vt.* to bungle; specif., to miss (a catch, etc.)

muf·fin (muf′ən) *n.* ⟦< ?⟧ a quick bread baked in a cup-shaped mold

muf·fle (muf′əl) *vt.* **-fled, -fling** ⟦prob. < OFr *moufle*, mitten⟧ **1** to wrap or cover so as to keep warm, deaden sound, etc. **2** to deaden (a sound)

muf′fler (-lər) *n.* **1** a warm scarf worn around the throat **2** a device for deadening sound, etc. of a car

mufti (muf′tē) *n., pl.* **-tis** ⟦< Ar⟧ ordinary clothes, esp. when worn by one usually wearing a uniform

mug (mug) *n.* ⟦prob. < Scand⟧ **1** a cup made of earthenware or metal, with a handle **2** as much as a mug will hold **3** [Slang] the face **4** a police photograph of a criminal suspect: in full **mug shot** — *vt.* **mugged, mug′ging** to assault, usually with intent to rob — *vi.* [Slang] to grimace, esp. in overacting —**mug′ger** *n.*

muggy (mug′ē) *adj.* **-gier, -gi·est** ⟦< dial. *mug*, mist⟧ hot, damp, and close —**mug′gi·ness** *n.*

mug·wump (mug′wump′) *n.* ⟦Algonquian *mugquomp*, chief⟧ an independent, esp. in politics

muk·luk (muk′luk′) *n.* ⟦Esk *muklok*, a seal⟧ an Eskimo boot of sealskin or reindeer skin

mu·lat·to (mə lät′ō, -lat′ō) *n., pl.* **-toes** or **-tos** ⟦Sp & Port *mulato*⟧ a person who has one black parent and one white parent

mul·berry (mul′ber′ē, -bər ē) *n., pl.* **-ries** ⟦< OE *morberie*⟧ **1** a tree with purplish-red, edible, berrylike fruit **2** the fruit **3** purplish red

mulch (mulch) *n.* ⟦ME *molsh*, soft⟧ leaves, straw, etc., spread around plants to prevent freezing of roots, etc. — *vt.* to apply mulch to

mulct (mulkt) *vt.* ⟦< L *mul(c)ta*, a fine⟧ **1** to fine **2** to take (money, etc.) from by fraud — *n.* a fine

mule[1] (myo͞ol) *n.* ⟦< L *mulus*⟧ **1** the (usually sterile) offspring of a jackass and a female horse **2** [Colloq.] a stubborn person

mule[2] (myo͞ol) *n.* ⟦< L *mulleus*, red shoe⟧ a lounging slipper that does not cover the heel

mu·leteer′ (-ə tir′) *n.* ⟦OFr *muletier*⟧ a driver of mules Also [Colloq.] **mule skin·ner** (skin′ər)

mul′ish *adj.* like a mule; stubborn, obstinate, etc.

mull[1] (mul) *vt., vi.* ⟦ME *mullen*, to grind⟧ to ponder (*over*)

mull[2] (mul) *vt.* ⟦< ?⟧ to heat, sweeten, and spice (wine, cider, etc.)

mul·lein (mul′in) *n.* ⟦< L *mollis*, soft⟧ a tall plant with spikes of variously colored flowers

mul·let (mul′it) *n.* ⟦< L *mullus*⟧ an edible, spiny-finned fish of fresh and salt waters

mul·li·gan stew (mul′i gən) a stew made of bits of meat and vegetables, esp. as by hobos

mul·li·ga·tawny (mul′i gə tô′nē) *n.* ⟦Tamil *miḷagutaṇṇir*, lit., pepper water⟧ an East Indian soup of meat, etc., flavored with curry

mul·lion (mul′yən) *n.* ⟦prob. < OFr *moien*, median⟧ a vertical dividing bar, as between windowpanes

multi- ⟦L < *multus*, many⟧ *combining form* **1** having **2** more than two **3** many times more than

mul·ti·cul·tur·al·ism (mul′tē kul′chər əl iz′əm) *n.* the practice of giving equal emphasis to the needs and contributions of all cultural groups, esp. traditionally underrepresented minority groups, in a society

multi·far·i·ous (mul′tə far′ē əs) *adj.* ⟦< L⟧ having many kinds of parts or elements; diverse

mul·ti·lin·gual (mul′ti liŋ′gwəl) *adj.* of, in, or capable of using several languages

mul′ti·mil′lion·aire′ *n.* one whose wealth amounts to many millions of dollars, pounds, etc.

mul·ti·na′tional *adj.* **1** of many nations **2** designating a corporation with branches in many nations — *n.* a multinational corporation

multi·ple (mul′tə pəl) *adj.* ⟦< L *multiplex*⟧ **1** having many parts, elements, etc. **2** shared by or involving many — *n.* a number which is a product of some specified number and another number

mul′tiple-choice′ *adj.* listing several answers from which the correct one is to be chosen

multiple sclerosis a disease of the central nervous system, with loss of muscular coordination, etc.

multi·plex (mul′tə pleks′) *adj.* ⟦L, multiple⟧ designating a system for sending two or more signals simultaneously over a common circuit, etc. —**mul′ti·plex′er** or **mul′ti·plex′or** *n.*

mul′ti·pli·cand′ (-pli kand′) *n.* a number to be multiplied by another

mul′ti·pli·ca′tion (-pli kā′shən) *n.* a multiplying or being multiplied; specif., the process of finding the quantity obtained by repeating a specified quantity a specified number of times

mul′ti·plic′i·ty (-plis′ə tē) *n.* a great number or variety (*of*)

mul′ti·pli′er (-plī′ər) *n.* one that multiplies; specif., the number by which another is to be multiplied

mul′ti·ply′ (-plī′) *vt., vi.* **-plied′, -ply′ing** ⟦see MULTIPLE⟧ **1** to increase in number, degree, etc. **2** to find the product (of) by multiplication

multi·proc·essor (mul′ti prä′ses′ər) *n.* a computer system capable of processing many programs at once

mul·ti·pur·pose (mul′ti pur′pəs) *adj.* having more than one purpose or use; esp., designating a room used for several activities

mul′ti·stage′ *adj.* having more than one stage, as a missile, process, etc.

multi·tude (mul′tə to͞od′) *n.* ⟦< L *multus*, many⟧ a large number; host

mul′ti·tu′di·nous (-to͞od′'n əs) *adj.* very numerous; many

mum[1] (mum) *n.* [Colloq.] a chrysanthemum

mum[2] (mum) *adj.* ⟦ME *momme*⟧ silent; not speaking

mum·ble (mum′bəl) *vt., vi.* **-bled, -bling** ⟦ME *momelen*⟧ to speak or say indistinctly; mutter — *n.* a mumbled utterance —**mum′bler** *n.*

mumbo jumbo (mum′bō jum′bō) ⟦of Afr orig.⟧ **1** an idol or fetish **2** meaningless ritual, talk, etc.

mum·mer (mum′ər) *n.* ⟦< OFr *momo*, grimace⟧ one who wears a mask or costume, esp. in a pantomime

mum′mery *n., pl.* **-ies 1** performance by mummers **2** any hypocritical display or ceremony

mum·mify (mum′ə fī′) *vt., vi.* **-fied′, -fy′ing** to make into or become (like) a mummy

mummy (mum′ē) *n., pl.* **-mies** ⟦ult. < Pers *mum*, wax⟧ a dead body preserved by embalming, as by the ancient Egyptians

mumps (mumps) *n.pl.* ⟦< obs. *mump*, a grimace⟧ [with

THESAURUS

muffle *v.* deaden, mute, stifle; see DECREASE 2, SOFTEN.

muffled *a.* suppressed, stifled, indistinct; see OBSCURE 1.

muffler *n.* chest protector, scarf, neckpiece, babushka, neckerchief, kerchief, neckband, neck cloth, Ascot, choker, mantle, stole; see also CLOTHES.

mug *n.* vessel, stein, flagon; see CUP.

muggy *a.* damp, humid, moist; see WET 1.

mule[1] *n.* hinney, army mule, Missouri mule; see ANIMAL.

mull[1] *v.* reflect, meditate, ponder; see THINK 1.

multiple *a.* **1** [Various] complicated, more than one, many, manifold, compound, having many uses, multi-fold, multitudinous, aggregated, many-sided, versatile, increased, varied, compound, added; see also VARIOUS.—*Ant.* SIMPLE, UNITED, centralized. **2** [Repeated] reoccurring, repetitious, duplicated; see MULTIPLIED.

multiplication *n.* duplication, reproduction, addition, increase, repetition, compounding, recurrence, amplification, making more, reproducing, repeating, augmenting; see also MATHEMATICS.—*Ant.* REDUCTION, subtraction, decrease.

multiplied *a.* compounded, added, reproduced, amplified, repeated, augmented, duplicated, reduplicated, made many.—*Ant.* REDUCED, divided, decreased.

multiply *v.* **1** [To increase] add, augment, double; see INCREASE. **2** [To bring forth young] generate, produce, populate; see REPRODUCE 3. **3** [To employ multiplication as an arithmetical process] square, cube, raise to a higher power; see INCREASE.

multitude *n.* throng, drove, mob; see CROWD, GATHERING, PEOPLE 3.

mumble *v.* mutter, utter, whine, whimper, grumble, murmur, maunder, ramble on, whisper, speak indistinctly, say to oneself; see also HESITATE, STAMMER.—*Ant.* SAY, articulate, enunciate.

mumbo jumbo *n.* gibberish, double talk, drivel; see NONSENSE 1.

sing. v.] an acute communicable disease characterized by swelling of the salivary glands

mun. municipal

munch (munch) *vt., vi.* ⟦ME *monchen*⟧ to chew steadily, often with a crunching sound

mun·dane (mun'dān', mun dān') *adj.* ⟦< L *mundus*, world⟧ 1 of the world; worldly 2 commonplace, ordinary, etc. —**mun'dane'ly** *adv.*

mu·nic·i·pal (myōō nis'ə pəl) *adj.* ⟦< L *municeps*, inhabitant of a free town⟧ of or having to do with a city, town, etc. or its local government

mu·nic'i·pal'i·ty (-pal'ə tē) *n., pl.* **-ties** a city, town, etc. having its own incorporated government

mu·nif·i·cent (myōō nif'ə sənt) *adj.* ⟦< L *munus*, a gift + *facere*, make⟧ very generous in giving; lavish —**mu·nif'i·cence** *n.*

mu·ni·tions (myōō nish'ənz) *n.pl.* ⟦< L *munire*, fortify⟧ war supplies; esp., weapons and ammunition

mu·ral (myoor'əl) *adj.* ⟦< L *murus*, wall⟧ of, on, or for a wall — *n.* a picture, esp. a large one, painted directly on a wall —**mu'ral·ist** *n.*

mur·der (mʉr'dər) *n.* ⟦OE *morthor*⟧ 1 the unlawful and malicious or premeditated killing of a person 2 [Colloq.] something very hard, unsafe, etc. to do or deal with — *vt.* 1 to kill (a person) unlawfully and with malice 2 to spoil, as in performance *[to murder a song]* —**mur'der·er** *n.* —**mur'der·ess** *n.fem.*

mur'der·ous *adj.* 1 of or characteristic of murder; brutal 2 capable or guilty of, or intending, murder —**mur'der·ously** *adv.*

murk (mʉrk) *n.* ⟦< ON *myrkr*, dark⟧ darkness; gloom

murk'y *adj.* **-i·er, -i·est** dark or gloomy —**murk'i·ness** *n.*

mur·mur (mʉr'mər) *n.* ⟦< L⟧ 1 a low, indistinct, continuous sound 2 a mumbled complaint 3 *Med.* an abnormal sound in the body, esp. in the heart — *vi.* to make a murmur — *vt.* to say in a murmur

mur·rain (mʉr'in) *n.* ⟦< L *mori*, to die⟧ 1 an infectious disease of cattle 2 [Archaic] a plague

mus·cat (mus'kət) *n.* ⟦< LL *muscus*, musk⟧ a sweet European grape

mus'ca·tel' (-kə tel') *n.* a sweet wine made from the muscat

mus·cle (mus'əl) *n.* ⟦< L *musculus*, lit., little mouse⟧ 1 any body organ consisting of fibrous tissue that can be contracted and expanded to produce bodily movements 2 this tissue 3 muscular strength — *vi.* **-cled, -cling** [Colloq.] to force one's way (*in*)

mus'cle-bound' *adj.* having some of the muscles enlarged and less elastic, as from too much exercise

mus·cu·lar (mus'kyōō lər, -kyə-) *adj.* 1 of or done by muscles 2 having well-developed muscles; strong —**mus'cu·lar'i·ty** (-lar'ə tē) *n.*

muscular dys·tro·phy (dis'trə fē) a chronic disease characterized by a progressive wasting of the muscles

mus·cu·la·ture (mus'kyōō lə chər, -kyə-) *n.* ⟦Fr⟧ the arrangement of the muscles of a body, limb, etc.; muscular system

muse (myōōz) *vi.* **mused, mus'ing** ⟦< OFr *muser*, ponder⟧ to meditate — *vt.* to think or say meditatively

Muse (myōōz) *n.* ⟦< Gr *mousa*⟧ 1 *Gr. Myth.* any of the nine goddesses of literature and of the arts and sciences 2 [m-] the spirit thought to inspire a poet, etc.

mu·sette (bag) (myōō zet') ⟦< OFr, bagpipe⟧ a bag with a shoulder strap, worn as by soldiers to carry supplies

mu·se·um (myōō zē'əm) *n.* ⟦< Gr *mousa*, Muse⟧ an institution, building, etc. for preserving and exhibiting artistic or historical objects

mush¹ (mush) *n.* ⟦prob. var. of MASH⟧ 1 a thick porridge of boiled meal 2 any thick, soft mass 3 [Colloq.] maudlin sentimentality —**mush'y, -i·er, -i·est,** *adj.*

mush² (mush) *interj.* ⟦prob. < Fr *marchons*, let's go⟧ a shout to urge on sled dogs — *vi.* to travel on foot over snow with a dog sled

mush'room' *n.* ⟦< LL *mussirio*⟧ any of various fleshy fungi, typically with a stalk capped by an umbrellalike top; esp., any edible variety — *adj.* of or like a mushroom — *vi.* to grow or spread rapidly

mu·sic (myōō'zik) *n.* ⟦< Gr *mousikē* (*technē*), art of the Muses⟧ 1 the art of combining tones to form expressive compositions 2 such compositions 3 any rhythmic sequence of pleasing sounds —**face the music** [Colloq.] to accept the consequences

mu'si·cal (-zi kəl) *adj.* 1 of or for music 2 melodious or harmonious 3 fond of or skilled in music 4 set to music — *n.* a play or film with a musical score featuring songs and dances —**mu'si·cally** *adv.*

◼ THESAURUS ◼

munch *v.* crunch, bite, crush; see CHEW, EAT.

mundane *a.* normal, ordinary, everyday; see WORLDLY.

municipal *a.* self-governing, metropolitan, city, town, community, local, civil, incorporated, corporate; see also PUBLIC.—*Ant.* PRIVATE, national, state.

municipality *n.* district, village, borough; see CITY, TOWN 1.

munitions *n.* materiel, weapons, ordnance; see AMMUNITION, BOMB, BULLET, CANNON, EXPLOSIVE, GUN, MACHINE GUN, ROCKET, SHOT 1.

murder *n.* killing, homicide, death, destruction, annihilation, carnage, putting an end to, slaying, shooting, knifing, assassination, lynching, crime, felony, killing with malice aforethought, murder in the first degree, first-degree murder, contract killing, murder in the second degree, murder in the third degree, massacre, genocide, butchery, patricide, matricide, infanticide, fratricide, genocide, suicide, foul play. —**get away with murder*** escape punishment, take flight, avoid punishment; see EVADE.

murder *v.* 1 [To kill unlawfully] slay, assassinate, butcher; see KILL 1. 2 [*To ruin, especially by incompetence] spoil, mar, misuse; see BOTCH, DESTROY, FAIL 1.

murdered *a.* killed, assassinated, massacred; see DEAD 1.

murderer *n.* slayer, assassin, butcher; see CRIMINAL, KILLER.

murderous *a.* killing, cruel, criminal; see DEADLY.

murky *a.* dim, dusky, dingy; see DARK 1, DIRTY 1.

murmur *v.* 1 [To make a low, continuous sound] ripple, moan, trickle, burble, babble, tinkle, gurgle, meander, flow gently; see also HUM, WHISPER.—*Ant.* SOUND, peal, clang. 2 [To mutter] mumble, rumble, growl; see MUTTER 2.

muscle *n.* fiber, flesh, protoplasm, brawn, beef*.

muscular *a.* brawny, powerful, husky; see STRONG 1.

museum *n.* institution, building, hall, place of exhibition, foundation, art gallery, library, picture gallery, archives, treasury, storehouse, depository, vault, aquarium, menagerie, zoological garden, zoo, botanical garden, herbarium, arboretum.

mush¹ *n.* 1 [Boiled meal] Indian meal, hasty pudding, hominy, cereal, grain; see also FOOD. 2 [*Sentimentality] sentimentalism, excessive sentiment, mawkishness, affectation, superficiality, romanticism, puppy love, heart and flowers*, sob story*.

mushroom *n.* toadstool, fungus, champignon (French); see FOOD, PLANT.

mushroom *v.* augment, spread, sprout; see GROW 1, INCREASE.

mushy *a.* 1 [Soft] pulpy, mashy, muddy; see SOFT 2. 2 [*Sentimental] romantic, maudlin, effusive; see EMOTIONAL, SENTIMENTAL.

music *n.* 1 [A combination of tone and rhythm] harmony, melody, tune, air, strain, harmonics, song, measure, refrain, phrasing; see also BEAT 2, HARMONY 1. *Terms used in music include the following:* scale, clef, note, tone, pitch, sharp, flat, major, minor, key, mode, bridge, theme, movement, orchestration, instrumentation, variation, improvisation,

rhythm, accent, beat, down-beat, up-beat, off-beat, chord, counterpoint, timbre, volume, resonance; see also SONG. *Musical forms for instruments include the following:* symphony (the conventional four movements of a symphony are sonata, andante, scherzo, finale), concerto, suite; trio, quartet, quintet, etc.; overture, prelude, sonata, mass, scherzo, nocturne, fugue, étude, tone poem, variations, rhapsody, serenade, ballade, march, rhythm and blues, dance; see also OVERTURE 2. *Musical dance forms include the following:* waltz, tango, foxtrot, rhumba, polka; see also DANCE 1. *General styles of music include the following:* classical, longhair*, serious, medieval, modern, folk, primitive, popular, national, sacred, baroque, modernistic, formal, romantic, jazz, blues, rhythm-and-blues, boogie-woogie, folk-rock, heavy metal, acid rock, rock-and-roll, pop, bebop, bop, soul, ragtime, swing; see also JAZZ. 2 [Responsiveness to music] musical appreciation, sensitivity, aesthetic sense; see APPRECIATION 2, FEELING 4. —**face the music*** accept the consequences of one's actions, suffer, undergo; see ENDURE 2.

musical *a.* 1 [Having the qualities of music] tuneful, sweet, pleasing, agreeable, symphonic, lyric, mellow, vocal, choral, consonant, rhythmical; see also HARMONIOUS 1.—*Ant.* HARSH, tuneless, discordant. 2 [Having aptitude for music] gifted, talented, musically inclined; see ARTISTIC.

musical *n.* musicale, musical comedy, burlesque; see PERFORMANCE, SHOW 1.

mu·si·cale (myōō'zi kal') *n.* [Fr] a social affair featuring a musical program

mu·si·cian (myōō zish'ən) *n.* one skilled in music; esp., a performer

mu'si·col'o·gy (-zi käl'ə jē) *n.* the study of the history, forms, etc. of music —**mu'si·col'o·gist** *n.*

musk (musk) *n.* [< Sans *muṣka,* testicle] a strong-smelling animal secretion, esp. from a type of male deer, used in perfume —**musk'y, -i·er, -i·est,** *adj.* —**musk'i·ness** *n.*

mus·kel·lunge (mus'kə lunj') *n.* [< AmInd] a very large, edible pike of North America Also **mus'kie** (-kē)

mus·ket (mus'kət) *n.* [< L *musca,* a fly] a former kind of firearm with a long barrel and smooth bore

mus·ket·eer (mus'kə tir') *n.* a soldier armed with a musket

musk'mel'on *n.* any of various sweet, juicy melons, as the cantaloupe

musk ox a hardy ox of arctic North America with a long, coarse coat and a musklike odor

musk·rat (musk'rat') *n.* 1 an American water rodent with webbed hind feet and a musklike odor 2 its fur

Mus·lim (muz'ləm, mooz'-, moos'-) *n.* [Ar, true believer < *aslama,* to resign oneself (to God)] an adherent of Islam — *adj.* of Islam or the Muslims

mus·lin (muz'lin) *n.* [after *Mosul,* city in Iraq] a strong cotton cloth; esp., a kind used for sheets, etc.

muss (mus) *n.* [prob. var. of MESS] [Colloq.] a mess; disorder — *vt.* to make messy or disordered: often with *up* — **muss'y, -i·er, -i·est,** *adj.*

mus·sel (mus'əl) *n.* [< OE *muscle*] any of various bivalve mollusks of fresh or salt waters; specif., an edible variety

must (must) *v.aux. pt.* **must** [< OE *moste*] used to express: 1 necessity [I *must* go] 2 probability [it *must* be Joe] 3 certainty [all men *must* die] — *n.* [Colloq.] something that must be done, had, etc.

mus·tache (mus'tash', məs tash') *n.* [ult. < Gr *mystax*] hair growing on the upper lip; esp., the hair that a man has let grow

mus·tang (mus'taŋ') *n.* [< L *mixtus,* a mingling] a small wild horse of the SW plains

mus·tard (mus'tərd) *n.* [< OFr] 1 an herb with yellow flowers and round seeds in slender pods 2 a pungent seasoning made from the ground seeds

mustard gas [< its mustardlike odor] an oily liquid used in warfare for its blistering and disabling effects

mus·ter (mus'tər) *vt.* [< L *monstrare,* to show] 1 to assemble (troops, etc.) 2 to collect; summon: often with *up* — *vi.* to assemble, as troops — *n.* 1 a gathering or assembling, as of troops for inspection 2 the persons or things assembled —**muster in** (or **out**) to enlist in (or discharge from) military service —**pass muster** to meet the required standards

musty (mus'tē) *adj.* **-tier, -ti·est** [< ? MOIST] 1 having a stale, moldy smell or taste 2 stale or trite; antiquated — **mus'ti·ly** *adv.* —**mus'ti·ness** *n.*

mu·ta·ble (myōōt'ə bəl) *adj.* [< L *mutare,* to change] 1 that can be changed 2 inconstant; fickle —**mu'ta·bil'i·ty** *n.* —**mu'ta·bly** *adv.*

mu·tant (myōōt'ənt) *adj.* of mutation — *n.* an animal or plant with inheritable characteristics that differ from those of the parents; sport

mu·ta·tion (myōō tā'shən) *n.* 1 a change, as in form, nature, etc. 2 a sudden variation in some inheritable characteristic of an animal or plant —**mu'tate', -tat'ed, -tat' ing,** *vi., vt.*

mute (myōōt) *adj.* [< L *mutus*] 1 not speaking; silent 2 unable to speak — *n.* 1 a deaf-mute 2 a device that softens the sound of a musical instrument — *vt.* **mut'ed, mut' ing** to soften the sound of (an instrument) —**mute'ly** *adv.* —**mute'ness** *n.*

mu·ti·late (myōōt''l āt') *vt.* **-lat'ed, -lat'ing** [< L *mutilus,* maimed] to cut off, damage, or spoil an important part of —**mu'ti·la'tion** *n.* —**mu'ti·la'tor** *n.*

mu·ti·ny (myōōt''n ē) *n., pl.* **-nies** [< L *movere,* to move] revolt against constituted authority; esp., rebellion of soldiers or sailors against their officers — *vi.* **-nied, -ny ing** to revolt in this way —**mu'ti·neer'** *n.* —**mu'ti·nous** *adj.*

mutt (mut) *n.* [Slang] a mongrel dog

mut·ter (mut'ər) *vi., vt.* [ME *moteren*] 1 to speak or say in low, indistinct tones 2 to grumble — *n.* 1 a muttering 2 something muttered

mut·ton (mut''n) *n.* [< OFr, a ram] the flesh of a sheep, esp. a grown sheep, used as food

mu·tual (myōō'chōō əl) *adj.* [< L *mutare,* to exchange] 1 *a)* done, felt, etc. by each of two or more for or toward the other or others *b)* of each other 2 shared in common [our *mutual* friend] —**mu'tu·ally** *adv.*

mutual fund a corporation which manages a diversified portfolio of investments for its shareholders

muu·muu (mōō'mōō') *n.* [< Haw] a long, loose dress of Hawaiian style

Mu·zak (myōō'zak') *trademark for* a system of transmitting recorded background music to stores, etc. — *n.* this music, variously regarded as unobtrusive, bland, etc.

muz·zle (muz'əl) *n.* [< ML *musum*] 1 the mouth, nose, and jaws of a dog, horse, etc. 2 a device put over the mouth of an animal to prevent its biting or eating 3 the front end of the barrel of a firearm — *vt.* **-zled, -zling** 1 to put a muzzle on (an animal) 2 to prevent from talking

MX missile [< *m*(*issile*), (*e*)*x*(*perimental*)] a U.S. ICBM armed with several nuclear warheads and capable of being concealed underground

my (mi) *poss. pronominal adj.* [< OE *min*] of, belonging to, or done by me

my·eli·tis (mi'ə lit'is) *n.* [< Gr *myelos,* marrow + -ITIS] inflammation of the spinal cord or the bone marrow

My·lar (mi'lär') *trademark for* a strong, thin polyester used for recording tapes, fabrics, etc. — *n.* [m-] this substance

my·na or **my·nah** (mi'nə) *n.* [Hindi *mainā*] any of vari-

---

THESAURUS

musical instrument *n. Types of musical instruments include the following:* recorder, grand piano, concert piano, lyre, bell, flute, piccolo, violin, fiddle*, oboe, clarinet, bassoon, fife, bagpipe, trombone, French horn, tuba, cornet, trumpet, saxophone, dulcimer, harpsichord, harmonica, organ, harp, tambourine, ukelele, guitar, electric guitar, banjo, mandolin, lute, viola, cello, double bass, xylophone, marimba, cymbal, drum, accordion, concertina, tom-tom, sitar, calliope.

musician *n.* player, performer, composer; see ARTIST. *Musicians include the following:* singer, instrumentalist, soloist, soprano, alto, contralto, tenor, baritone, bass, conductor, director, leader, basso profundo, folk singer, drummer, pianist, violinist, cellist; performer on a woodwind instrument, performer on a brass instrument, percussion performer, etc.; jazzman.

muss* *n.* chaos, disarrangement, turmoil; see CONFUSION, DISORDER.

muss *v.* rumble, tousle, dishevel, ruffle, crumple, jumble, disarrange, disturb, mess up; see also TANGLE.

mussy* *a.* messy, chaotic, rumpled; see TANGLED.

must* *n.* requirement, need, obligation; see NECESSITY 2.

must *v.* ought, should, have to, have got to, be compelled, be obliged, be required, be doomed, be destined, be ordered, be made, have no choice, be one's fate; see also NEED.

mustache *n.* moustachio, handlebar*, soup-strainer*; see BEARD, WHISKERS.

musty *a.* moldy, fusty, rank; see ROTTEN 1.

mutation *n.* modification, deviation, variation; see CHANGE 1, VARIETY 1, 2.

mute *a.* 1 [Without power of speech] tongueless, deaf-mute, deaf-and-dumb*, inarticulate, voiceless, tongue-tied; see also DUMB 1, QUIET.—*Ant.* VOCAL, noisy, unimpaired. 2 [Suddenly deprived of speech] speechless, wordless, silent; see BEWILDERED, SURPRISED.

mutilate *v.* 1 [To maim] cut, batter, scratch; see WEAKEN 2. 2 [To damage] injure, deface, ravage; see DAMAGE, HURT 1.

mutilated *a.* disfigured, distorted, maimed; see DEFORMED.

mutiny *n.* insurrection, revolt, resistance; see REVOLUTION 2.

mutter *v.* 1 [To make a low, mumbling sound] rumble, growl, snarl; see SOUND. 2 [To speak as if to oneself] murmur, grunt, grumble, sputter, whisper, speak inarticulately, speak indistinctly, speak in an undertone, swallow one's words*; see also MUMBLE, MURMUR, MURMUR 1. 3 [To complain] grumble, moan, groan; see COMPLAIN.

mutual *a.* 1 [Reciprocal] interchangeable, two-sided, given and taken; see COMPLEMENTARY. 2 [Common] joint, shared, belonging equally to each; see COMMON 5.

mutually *a.* commonly, cooperatively, jointly, reciprocally, in combination, by common consent, in conjunction; see also TOGETHER 2.

muzzle *v.* 1 [To fasten a muzzle upon] wrap, muffle, deaden; see BIND 1, GAG 1. 2 [To silence] gag, restrain, restrict, repress, suppress, check, stop, stop someone's mouth, hush, still, shush*; see also QUIET 2.

ous tropical birds of Southeast Asia: some can mimic speech

my·opia (mī ō′pē ə) *n.* ⟦< Gr *myein*, to close + *ōps*, eye⟧ nearsightedness —**my·op′ic** (-äp′ik) *adj.*

myri·ad (mir′ē əd) *n.* ⟦< Gr *myrios*, countless⟧ a great number of persons or things — *adj.* very many

myr·mi·don (mur′mə dän′, -dən) *n.* ⟦after name of a Gr tribe led by Achilles⟧ an unquestioning follower

myrrh (mur) *n.* ⟦< Ar *murr*⟧ a fragrant gum resin of Arabia and E Africa, used in incense, perfume, etc.

myr·tle (murt′'l) *n.* ⟦< Gr *myrtos*⟧ **1** an evergreen shrub with white or pink flowers and dark berries **2** any of various other plants, as the periwinkle

my·self (mī self′) *pron.* a form of the 1st pers. sing. pronoun, used as an intensive /I went *myself*/, as a reflexive /I hurt *myself*/, or as a quasi-noun meaning "my real, true, or actual self" /I am not *myself* today/

mys·teri·ous (mis tir′ē əs) *adj.* of, containing, implying, or characterized by mystery —**mys·te′ri·ously** *adv.* —**mys·te′ri·ous·ness** *n.*

mys·tery (mis′tə rē) *n., pl.* **-ies** ⟦< Gr *mystērion*, secret rite⟧ **1** something unexplained or secret **2** a story involving unknown persons, facts, etc. /a murder *mystery*/ **3** secrecy

mys·tic (mis′tik) *adj.* **1** of esoteric rites or doctrines **2** MYSTICAL **3** mysterious — *n.* one who professes to undergo profound spiritual experiences

mys′ti·cal *adj.* **1** spiritually significant or symbolic **2** of mystics or mysticism **3** occult —**mys′ti·cally** *adv.*

mys·ti·cism (mis′tə siz′əm) *n.* **1** belief in the possibility of attaining direct communion with God or knowledge of spiritual truths, as by meditation **2** obscure thinking or belief

mys′tify′ (-fī′) *vt.* **-fied′, -fy′ing 1** to puzzle or perplex **2** to involve in mystery —**mys′ti·fi·ca′tion** *n.*

mys·tique (mis tēk′) *n.* ⟦Fr, mystic⟧ a complex of quasi-mystical attitudes and feelings surrounding some person, etc.

myth (mith) *n.* ⟦< Gr *mythos*⟧ **1** a traditional story serving to explain some phenomenon, custom, etc. **2** mythology **3** any fictitious story, person, or thing —**myth′i·cal** *adj.*

my·thol·ogy (mi thäl′ə jē) *n., pl.* **-gies 1** the study of myths **2** myths collectively, as of a specific people —**mytho·logi·cal** (mith′ə läj′i kəl) *adj.* —**my·thol′o·gist** *n.*

myriad *a.* variable, infinite, innumerable; see ENDLESS, MULTIPLE 1.

myself *pron.* me, me personally; the speaker, the writer, etc.; on my own authority, on my own responsibility, yours truly*, your humble servant, me myself.

mysterious *a.* **1** [Puzzling] enigmatic, uncanny, strange; see DIFFICULT 2, OBSCURE 1, UNNATURAL 1. **2** [Concerning powers beyond those supposedly natural] mystic, occult, dark, mystifying, transcendental, spiritual, symbolic, subjective, mystical, magical, dark, veiled, strange, astrological, unknowable, unfathomable, esoteric, cryptic, oracular, unre-

vealed, incredible; see also MAGIC. **3** [Not generally known] obscure, hidden, ambiguous; see SECRET 1.

mystery *n.* **1** [The quality of being mysterious] inscrutability, occultism, cabalism; see MAGIC 1, 2, STRANGENESS. **2** [Something difficult to know] riddle, conundrum, enigma; see DIFFICULTY 2, PUZZLE 2. **3** [A trick] sleight-of-hand, trick of magic, juggle; see TRICK 1. **4** [A mystery story] detective story, mystery play, mystery movie; see STORY.

mystic *a.* occult, transcendental, spiritual; see MYSTERIOUS 2, SECRET 1.

mysticism *n.* occultism, cabala, qui-

etism, orphism.

mystify *v.* perplex, trick, hoodwink; see DECEIVE, LIE 1.

mystique *n.* attitude, complex, nature; see CHARACTER 1, TEMPERAMENT.

myth *n.* fable, folk tale, legend, lore, saga, folk ballad, allegory, parable, tale; see also STORY.

mythical *a.* mythological, fabricated, fictitious; see FALSE 3, UNREAL.

mythological *a.* whimsical, fictitious, chimerical; see FANTASTIC, IMAGINARY.

mythology *n.* belief, conviction, mythicism; see FAITH 2, RELIGION 1.

N

n or **N** (en) *n., pl.* **n's, N's** the 14th letter of the English alphabet

N *Chem. symbol for* nitrogen

n or **n.** 1 name 2 neuter 3 new 4 nominative 5 noun 6 number

N or **N.** 1 Navy 2 north 3 northerly 4 northern 5 November

Na [L *natrium*] *Chem. symbol for* sodium

N.A. North America

NAACP National Association for the Advancement of Colored People

nab (nab) *vt.* **nabbed, nab'bing** [prob. < dial. *nap*, to snatch] [Colloq.] 1 to snatch or seize 2 to arrest or catch (a felon or wrongdoer)

na·bob (nā'bäb') *n.* [< Ar *nā'ib*, deputy] a very rich or important man

na·cre (nā'kər) *n.* [Fr < Ar *naqqārah*, small kettledrum] MOTHER-OF-PEARL —**na'cre·ous** (-krē əs) *adj.*

na·dir (nā'dər, -dir') *n.* [< Ar *naẓīr*, opposite] 1 the point opposite the zenith and directly below the observer 2 the lowest point

nae (nā) [Scot.] *adv.* no; not —*adj.* no

nag[1] (nag) *vt., vi.* **nagged, nag'ging** [< ON *gnaga*] 1 to annoy (someone) by continual scolding, faultfinding, etc. 2 to keep troubling [nagged by doubts] —*n.* one who nags Also **nag'ger**

nag[2] (nag) *n.* [ME *nagge*] an old or inferior horse

naiad (nā'ad', nī'-) *n.* [< Gr *naein*, to flow] [also N-] *Gr. & Rom. Myth.* a nymph living in a spring, river, etc.

nail (nāl) *n.* [< OE *nægl*] 1 the thin, horny growth at the ends of fingers and toes 2 a tapered, pointed piece of metal driven with a hammer, as to join pieces of wood —*vt.* 1 to fasten, secure, etc. with or as with nails 2 [Colloq.] to catch or hit

na·ive or **na·ïve** (nä ēv') *adj.* [Fr < L *nativus*, natural] unaffectedly simple; artless —**na·ive'ly** or **na·ïve'ly** *adv.* —**na·iveté'** or **na·ïveté'** (-tā') *n.*

na·ked (nā'kid) *adj.* [OE *nacod*] 1 completely unclothed; nude 2 without covering [a naked sword] 3 without additions, disguises, etc.; plain [the naked truth] —**na'kedly** *adv.* —**na'ked·ness** *n.*

namby-pamby (nam'bē pam'bē) *adj.* [18th-c. play on name *Ambrose*] weak, insipid, indecisive, etc. —*n., pl.* **-bies** a namby-pamby person

name (nām) *n.* [OE *nama*] 1 a word or phrase by which a person, thing, or class is known; title 2 a word or words considered descriptive; epithet, often an abusive one 3 fame or reputation 4 appearance only, not reality [chief in *name* only] —*adj.* well-known —*vt.* **named, nam'ing** 1 to give a name to 2 to mention by name 3 to identify by the right name [name the oceans] 4 to appoint to an office, etc. 5 to specify (a date, price, etc.) —**in the name of** 1 in appeal to 2 by the authority of

name'less *adj.* 1 not having a name 2 left unnamed 3 indescribable

name'ly *adv.* that is to say; to wit

name'sake' *n.* a person with the same name as another, esp. if named after the other

nanny goat (nan'ē) [< fem. name *Nan*] a female goat

nap[1] (nap) *vi.* **napped, nap'ping** [OE *hnappian*] to sleep lightly for a short time —*n.* a brief, light sleep

nap[2] (nap) *n.* [ME *noppe*] the downy or hairy surface of cloth or suede formed by short hairs or fibers —**nap'less** *adj.* —**napped** *adj.*

na·palm (nā'päm') *n.* [*na*(phthene) + *palm*(itate)] a jelly-like substance used in flame throwers and fire bombs —*vt.* to attack or burn with napalm

nape (nāp) *n.* [ME] the back of the neck

naph·tha (naf'thə, nap'-) *n.* [< Pers *neft*, pitch] a flammable liquid distilled from petroleum, used as a fuel, solvent, etc.

naph'tha·lene' (-lēn') *n.* [< prec.] a white, crystalline hydrocarbon distilled from coal tar, used in moth repellents, dyes, etc.

nap·kin (nap'kin) *n.* [< L *mappa*] 1 a small piece of cloth or paper used while eating to protect the clothes and wipe the lips 2 any small cloth, towel, etc.

narc (närk) *n.* [< NARC(OTIC)] [Slang] a police agent who enforces laws dealing with narcotics Also **nark**

nar·cis·sism (när'sə siz'əm) *n.* [< fol.] self-love; specif., excessive interest in one's own appearance, etc. —**nar'cis·sist** *n., adj.* —**nar'cis·sis'tic** *adj.*

Nar·cis·sus (när sis'əs) *Gr. Myth.* a youth who falls in love with his reflection in a pool and changes into the narcissus

---

■ THESAURUS ■

nab *v.* grab, take, snatch; see SEIZE 2.

nag[1] *v.* vex, annoy, pester; see BOTHER 2.

nail *n.* brad, pin, peg, stud, spike; see also TACK 1.

nail *v.* 1 [To hammer] drive, pound, spike; see HIT 1. 2 [To fasten with nails] secure, hold, bind; see FASTEN. 3 [*To arrest] capture, detain, apprehend; see ARREST, SEIZE 2. —**hard as nails** callous, unfeeling, remorseless; see CRUEL. —**hit the nail on the head*** do what is exactly right, be accurate, come to the point; see DEFINE 2.

naive *a.* unaffected, childish, plain, artless, innocent, untrained, countrified, callow, natural, unschooled, ignorant, untaught, provincial, unsophisticated, unworldly, guileless, spontaneous, instinctive, impulsive, simple-minded, innocuous, unsuspecting, unsuspicious, harmless, gullible, credulous, trusting, original, fresh, unpolished, rude, primitive, ingenuous, sincere, open, candid, forthright, aboveboard, romantic, fanciful, unpretentious, transparent, straightforward, uncomplicated, easily imposed upon; see also INEXPERIENCED.—*Ant.* EXPERIENCED, sophisticated, complicated.

naively *a.* childishly, innocently, stupidly; see FOOLISHLY, OPENLY 1.

naiveté *n.* simplicity, childishness, inexperience; see INNOCENCE 2.

naked *a.* 1 [Nude] unclothed, undressed, stripped, unclad, unrobed, disrobed, leafless, hairless, bare, undraped, exposed, having nothing on, unappareled, denuded, unveiled, uncovered, uncloaked, stark naked, topless, bald, in one's birthday suit*, in the buff, peeled*, without a stitch, in the raw. 2 [Unadorned] plain, simple, artless; see MODEST 2, NATURAL 3.

nakedness *n.* nudity, bareness, undress, exposure, the raw, nudism.

name *n.* 1 [A title] proper name, Christian name, given name, cognomen, appellation, designation, first name, family name, title, denomination, surname, sign, handle*. 2 [Reputation] renown, honor, repute; see FAME. 3 [An epithet] nickname, pen name, pseudonym, sobriquet, stage name, *nom de plume* (French), *nom de guerre* (French), pet name, fictitious name, alias. *Insulting names include the following:* devil, imbecile, idiot, rat*, skunk*, dog*, pig*, fool, moron, brute, bum, boob*, oaf, goon, sourpuss*, dummy*, jerk*, swine, bigmouth*, schmuck*, weasel, beanpole*, bitch*, bastard*, four-eyes*, skinny, fatty*, windbag*. 4 [A famous person] star, hero, a person of renown; see CELEBRITY. —**call names** swear at, insult, slander; see SCOLD. —**in the name of** by authority of, in reference to, as representative of; see FOR. —**know only by name** be familiar with, not know personally, have heard of; see KNOW 3. —**to one's name** belonging to one, in one's possession, possessed by; see OWNED.

name *v.* 1 [To give a name] call, christen, baptize, style, term, label, identify, designate, classify, denominate, title, entitle, nickname, characterize, label, ticket, dub*; see also DESCRIBE, DEFINE. 2 [To indicate by name] refer to, specify, signify, denote, single out, mark, suggest, connote, point to, note, remark, index, list, cite; see also MENTION. 3 [To appoint] elect, nominate, select; see DELEGATE 1.

named *a.* 1 [Having as a name] called, designated, entitled, titled, termed, specified, styled, denominated, christened, baptized, nicknamed, labeled, tagged*, dubbed*. 2 [Chosen] appointed, commissioned, delegated, authorized, nominated, elected, invested, vested, assigned, ordained, entrusted, picked, selected, decided upon, settled on, picked out, preferred, favored, supported, approved, certified, called, anointed, consecrated, sanctioned, drafted, opted, declared, announced, singled out.

nameless *a.* inconspicuous, undistinguished, obscure; see UNKNOWN 2.

namely *a.* specifically, to wit, that is to say, particularly, by way of explanation, strictly speaking, in other words, in plain English.

nap[1,2] *n.* 1 [A short sleep] siesta, cat nap, doze; see SLEEP. 2 [The finish of certain goods, especially fabric] pile, shag, surface; see GRAIN 2, OUTSIDE 1, TEXTURE 1.

napkin *n.* paper napkin, paper towel, table linen; see TOWEL.

— *n., pl.* **-cis′sus, -cis′suses,** or **-cis′si** (-ī) [n-] any of various bulb plants whose flowers have tubelike projections

nar·co·sis (när kō′sis) *n., pl.* **-ses′** (-sēz′) unconsciousness caused by a narcotic

nar·cot·ic (när kät′ik) *n.* ⟦ < Gr *narkē*, numbness ⟧ a drug, as morphine, used to relieve pain and induce sleep: narcotics are often addictive — *adj.* of or having to do with narcotics

nar·co·tize (när′kə tīz′) *vt.* **-tized′, -tiz′ing** to subject to a narcotic — **nar′co·ti·za′tion** *n.*

nar·rate (nar′āt′, na rāt′) *vt., vi.* **-rat′ed, -rat′ing** ⟦ < L *narrare*, tell ⟧ to tell (a story), relate (events), etc. — **nar′ra′tor** *n.*

nar·ra·tion (na rā′shən) *n.* **1** a narrating **2** a narrative

nar·ra·tive (nar′ə tiv) *adj.* in story form — *n.* **1** a story; account **2** the art or practice of narrating

nar·row (nar′ō) *adj.* ⟦ OE *nearu* ⟧ **1** small in width; not wide **2** limited in meaning, size, amount, etc. [*a narrow majority*] **3** limited in outlook; not liberal **4** with limited margin [*a narrow escape*] — *vi., vt.* to decrease or limit in width, extent, etc. — *n.* [*usually pl.*] a narrow passage; strait — **nar′rowly** *adv.* — **nar′row·ness** *n.*

nar′row-mind′ed *adj.* limited in outlook; bigoted; prejudiced — **nar′row-mind′edness** *n.*

nar·whal (när′wəl) *n.* ⟦ < ON *nahvalr*, lit., corpse whale ⟧ a small arctic whale: the male has a long, spiral tusk

nary (ner′ē) *adj.* ⟦ < *ne′er a*, never a ⟧ [Dial.] not any; no: with *a* or *an*

NASA (nas′ə) National Aeronautics and Space Administration

na·sal (nā′zəl) *adj.* ⟦ < L *nasus*, nose ⟧ **1** of the nose **2** uttered so that the breath passes through the nose — **na′sally** *adv.*

na·sal·ize (nā′zəl īz′) *vt., vi.* **-ized′, -iz′ing** to pronounce or speak with a nasal sound — **na′sali·za′tion** *n.*

nas·cent (nas′ənt, nā′sənt) *adj.* ⟦ < L *nasci*, be born ⟧ **1** coming into being **2** beginning to form or develop: said of ideas, etc. — **nas′cence** *n.*

nas·tur·tium (nə stur′shəm, na-) *n.* ⟦ < L *nasus*, nose + *torquere*, to twist ⟧ **1** a plant with red, yellow, or orange trumpet-shaped flowers **2** its flower

nasty (nas′tē) *adj.* **-tier, -ti·est** ⟦ < ? ⟧ **1** filthy **2** morally offensive; indecent **3** very unpleasant [*nasty weather*] **4** mean; malicious — **nas′tily** *adv.* — **nas′ti·ness** *n.*

na·tal (nāt′′l) *adj.* ⟦ < L *nasci*, be born ⟧ of or relating to one's birth

na·tes (nā′tēz′) *n.pl.* ⟦ L ⟧ the buttocks

na·tion (nā′shən) *n.* ⟦ < L *natus*, born ⟧ **1** a stable community of people with a territory, history, culture, and language in common **2** people united under a single government; country

na·tional (nash′ə nəl) *adj.* of or affecting a nation as a whole — *n.* a citizen or subject — **na′tion·ally** *adv.*

National Guard the organized militia of each U.S. State: it is part of the U.S. Army

na′tion·al·ism′ *n.* **1** devotion to one's nation; patriotism **2** the advocacy of national independence — **na′tion·al·ist** *n., adj.* — **na′tion·al·is′tic** *adj.*

na·tion·al·ity (-nal′ə tē) *n., pl.* **-ties 1** the status of belonging to a nation by birth or naturalization **2** a national group, esp. of immigrants

na·tion·al·ize (-nə liz′) *vt.* **-ized′, -iz′ing 1** to make national **2** to transfer ownership or control of (land, industries, etc.) to the government — **na′tion·ali·za′tion** *n.*

na′tion·wide′ *adj.* by or throughout the whole nation; national

na·tive (nāt′iv) *adj.* ⟦ < L *natus*, born ⟧ **1** inborn **2** belonging to a locality or country by birth, production, growth **3** being, or connected with, the place of one's birth [*one's native land or language*] **4** as found in nature; natural **5** of or characteristic of the original inhabitants of a place — *n.* **1** a person born in the place indicated **2** an original inhabitant **3** an indigenous plant or animal

Native American AMERICAN INDIAN: now often the preferred term

na′tive-born′ *adj.* of a specified place by birth

na·tiv·ity (nə tiv′ə tē) *n., pl.* **-ties** ⟦ see NATIVE ⟧ birth — **the Nativity** the birth of Jesus

natl. national

NATO (nā′tō) *n.* North Atlantic Treaty Organization

natty (nat′ē) *adj.* **-tier, -ti·est** ⟦ < ? NEAT ⟧ trim and stylish — **nat′tily** *adv.*

natu·ral (nach′ər əl) *adj.* ⟦ < L *naturalis*, by birth ⟧ **1** of or dealing with nature **2** produced or existing in nature; not artificial **3** innate; not acquired **4** true to nature; lifelike **5** normal [*a natural result*] **6** free from affectation; at ease **7** *Music* neither sharped nor flatted — *n.* a person or thing sure to be successful — **nat′u·ral·ness** *n.*

natural childbirth childbirth without anesthesia through prior training

natural gas a mixture of gaseous hydrocarbons, chiefly methane, occurring naturally in the earth and used as fuel

---

THESAURUS

narcotic *n.* depressant, sedative, opiate; see DRUG.

narrate *v.* detail, describe, depict; see REPORT 1, TELL 1.

narrative *a.* storylike, historical, sequential; see CHRONOLOGICAL.

narrow *a.* **1** [Lacking breadth] close, cramped, tight, confined, shrunken, compressed, slender, thin, fine, linear, threadlike, tapering, tapered, slim, scant, scanty, lanky, small, meager; see also THIN 1.—*Ant.* BROAD, wide, extensive. **2** [Lacking tolerance] dogmatic, narrow-minded, parochial; see CONSERVATIVE, CONVENTIONAL 3, PREJUDICED. **3** [Lacking a comfortable margin] close, near, precarious; see DANGEROUS, ENDANGERED, UNSAFE.

narrowly *a.* nearly, closely, by a narrow margin; see ALMOST.

narrow-minded *a.* bigoted, biased, provincial; see CONSERVATIVE, CONVENTIONAL 3, PREJUDICED.

narrowness *n.* **1** [A physical restriction] confinement, slimness, restriction; see BARRIER, INTERFERENCE 1. **2** [A mental restriction] intolerance, bigotry, bias; see PREJUDICE, STUBBORNNESS.

nasty *a.* **1** [Offensive to the senses] foul, gross, revolting; see OFFENSIVE 2, VULGAR. **2** [Indecent] immoral, immodest, smutty; see LEWD 1, SHAMEFUL 3. **3** [Unkind] sarcastic, critical, mean; see CRUEL, FIERCE, RUTHLESS.

nation *n.* **1** [An organized state]

realm, country, commonwealth, republic, democracy, state, monarchy, dominion, body politic, land, domain, empire, kingdom, principality, sovereignty, colony; see also GOVERNMENT 1. **2** [A people having some unity] populace, community, public; see POPULATION, RACE 2, SOCIETY 2.

national *a.* **1** [Concerning a nation] racial, ethnic, political, sovereign, state, social, civic, societal, communal, royal, imperial, federal; see also GOVERNMENTAL, PUBLIC 2. **2** [Operative throughout a nation] nationwide, country-wide, interstate, internal, social, widespread, sweeping; see also GENERAL 1.

nationalism *n.* provincialism, chauvinism, allegiance; see LOYALTY, PATRIOTISM.

nationality *n.* native land, country, citizenship; see ORIGIN 2.

nationally *a.* politically, governmentally, as a state, as a country, publicly, of the people, throughout the country, transcending state boundaries, for the general welfare.

native *a.* **1** [Natural] innate, inherent, inborn, implanted, inbred, ingrained, congenital, fundamental, hereditary, inherited, essential, constitutional; see also NATURAL 1.—*Ant.* UNNATURAL, foreign, alien. **2** [Characteristic of a region] aboriginal, indigenous, original, primitive, primary, primeval, vernacular, domestic, local, found locally; see also REGIONAL.—*Ant.* IMPORTED, brought

in, transplanted.

native *n.* **1** [Aborigine] primitive, tribesman, hunter-gatherer; see MAN 1. **2** [Citizen] national, inhabitant, occupant; see CITIZEN, RESIDENT.

natural *a.* **1** [Rooted in nature] intrinsic, original, essential, true, fundamental, inborn, ingrained, inherent, instinctive, implanted, innate, inbred, incarnate, subjective, inherited, congenital, genetic; see also NATIVE 1.—*Ant.* FOREIGN, alien, acquired. **2** [To be expected] normal, typical, characteristic, usual, customary, habitual, accustomed, involuntary, spontaneous, uncontrolled, uncontrollable, familiar, common, universal, prevailing, prevalent, general, probable, uniform, constant, consistent, ordinary, logical, reasonable, anticipated, looked for, hoped for, counted on, relied on; see also REGULAR 3.—*Ant.* UNKNOWN, unexpected, unheard of. **3** [Not affected] ingenuous, simple, artless, innocent, unstudied, spontaneous, impulsive, childlike, unfeigned, open, frank, candid, unsophisticated, unpolished, homey, unpretentious, forthright, sincere, straightforward, being oneself, unsuspecting, credulous, trusting, plain, direct, rustic; see also NAIVE.—*Ant.* ORNATE, pretentious, sophisticated. **4** [Concerning the physical universe] actual, tangible, according to nature; see PHYSICAL 1, REAL.

natural history the study of the animal, vegetable, and mineral world

nat′u·ral·ism′ *n.* 1 action or thought based on natural desires 2 *Literature, Art, etc.* the portrayal of persons or things as they really are

nat′u·ral·ist *n.* 1 one who studies animals and plants 2 a proponent of naturalism —**nat′u·ral·is′tic** *adj.*

nat′u·ral·ize′ (-īz′) *vt.* -ized′, -iz′ing to confer citizenship upon (an alien) —**nat′u·rali·za′tion** *n.*

nat′u·rally *adv.* 1 in a natural manner 2 by nature 3 of course

natural number any positive integer, as 1, 2, 3, etc.

natural resources those forms of wealth supplied by nature, as land, minerals, water power, etc.

natural science the systematized knowledge of nature, including biology, chemistry, physics, etc.

natural selection the evolutionary process by which the most adaptable species survive

na·ture (nā′chər) *n.* 〖< L *natus*, born〗 1 the essential quality of a thing; essence 2 inherent tendencies of a person 3 kind; type 4 *a*) the physical universe *b*) [*sometimes* N-] the power, force etc. that seems to regulate this 5 the primitive state of humans 6 natural scenery —**by nature** naturally; inherently

Nauga·hyde (nôg′ə hīd′) 〖arbitrary coinage〗 *trademark for* an imitation leather, used for upholstery, luggage, etc. — *n.* [n-] this material

naught (nôt) *n.* 〖OE *nawiht*〗 1 nothing 2 *alt. sp. of* NOUGHT

naughty (nôt′ē) *adj.* -tier, -ti·est 〖ME *naugti*〗 1 mischievous or disobedient 2 indelicate; improper —**naugh′tily** *adv.* —**naugh′ti·ness** *n.*

nau·sea (nô′shə, -zhə; -sē ə, -zē ə) *n.* 〖< Gr *nausia*, seasickness〗 1 a sick feeling in the stomach, with an impulse to vomit 2 disgust; loathing

nau′seate′ (-shē āt′, -zhē-; -sē-, -zē-) *vt.* -at′ed, -at′ing to cause to feel nausea

nau·seous (nô′shəs, -zē əs, -sē-) *adj.* 1 causing nausea 2 [Colloq.] feeling nausea

nau·ti·cal (nôt′i kəl) *adj.* 〖< Gr *naus*, ship〗 of sailors, ships, or navigation —**nau′ti·cally** *adv.*

nautical mile a unit of linear measure used in navigation, equal to 1,852 m

nau·ti·lus (nôt′′l əs) *n., pl.* -luses or -li′ (-ī′) 〖< Gr *naus*, ship〗 a tropical mollusk with a spiral shell divided into many chambers —[N-] *trademark for* a type of mechanical weight-lifting equipment

Nava·jo (nav′ə hō′) *n. pl.* -jos′, -jo′, or -joes′ a member of an American Indian people of the SW U.S. Also sp. **Navaho**

na·val (nā′vəl) *adj.* 〖< L *navis*, a ship〗 of, having, characteristic of, or for a navy, its ships, etc.

nave (nāv) *n.* 〖< L *navis*, a ship〗 the main part of a church, from the chancel to the principal entrance

na·vel (nā′vəl) *n.* 〖OE *nafela*〗 the small scar in the abdomen, marking the place where the umbilical cord was attached to the fetus

navel orange a seedless orange with a navel-like hollow at its apex

navi·gable (nav′i gə bəl) *adj.* 1 wide or deep enough for the passage of ships 2 that can be steered —**navi·ga·bil′ity** *n.*

navi·gate (nav′ə gāt′) *vt., vi.* -gat′ed, -gat′ing 〖< L *navis*, a ship + *agere*, to lead〗 1 to steer or direct (a ship or aircraft) 2 to travel through or over (water, air, etc.) in a ship or aircraft 3 [Colloq.] to walk

nav′i·ga′tion (-gā′shən) *n.* the science of locating the position and plotting the course of ships and aircraft

nav′i·ga′tor *n.* one skilled in the navigation of a ship or aircraft

navy (nā′vē) *n., pl.* -vies 〖< L *navis*, a ship〗 1 all the warships of a nation 2 [*often* N-] a nation's entire sea force, including ships, men, stores, etc. 3 NAVY BLUE

navy bean 〖from use in U.S. *Navy*〗 a small, white variety of kidney bean

navy blue very dark, purplish blue

nay (nā) *adv.* 〖< ON *ne*, not + *ei*, ever〗 not that only, but also 〖I permit, nay encourage it〗 — *n.* 1 a denial 2 a negative vote or voter

Nazi (nät′sē) *adj.* 〖Ger contr. of the party name〗 designating or of the German fascist political party which ruled Germany under Hitler (1933-45) — *n.* a member of this party

n.b. or **N.B.** 〖L *nota bene*〗 note well

NCO noncommissioned officer

NC-17 *trademark for* a film rating indicating no one under 17 may be admitted

Ne *Chem. symbol for* neon

NE 1 northeast 2 northeasterly 3 northeastern Also **N.E.**

Ne·an·der·thal (nē an′dər thôl′) *adj.* 〖after a Ger Valley〗 1 designating or of a widespread form of early human of the Pleistocene Epoch 2 primitive or regressive — *n.* 1 a Neanderthal human 2 one who is crude, primitive, etc.

neap (nēp) *adj.* 〖OE *nep-* in *nepflod*, neap tide〗 designating either of the two lowest high tides in the month — *n.* neap tide

Nea·poli·tan (nē′ə päl′ət 'n) *adj.* of Naples — *n.* a native or inhabitant of Naples

Neapolitan ice cream brick ice cream in layers of different flavors

near (nir) *adv.* 〖OE compar. of *neah*, nigh〗 1 at a short distance in space or time 2 almost [*near* right] 3 closely;

naturalist *n.* botanist, zoologist, biologist; see SCIENTIST.

naturally *interj.* certainly, absolutely, of course; see SURELY, YES.

naturally *a.* 1 [In an unaffected manner] artlessly, spontaneously, innocently, candidly, openly, impulsively, freely, readily, easily, without restraint, directly; see also SIMPLY, SINCERELY.—*Ant.* AWKWARDLY, restrainedly, clumsily. 2 [As a matter of course] casually, according to expectation, as anticipated, characteristically, typically, normally, commonly, usually, ordinarily, habitually, by nature, instinctively, intuitively, by birth, uniformly, generally, consistently; see also REGULARLY.—*Ant.* STRANGELY, astonishingly, amazingly.

nature *n.* 1 [The external universe] cosmos, creation, macrocosm; see UNIVERSE. 2 [The complex of essential qualities] characteristics, quality, constitution; see CHARACTER 1, ESSENCE 1. 3 [Natural surroundings] outside, out-of-doors, scenery, natural setting, view, seascape, landscape, the outdoors, natural scenery, recreational facilities, the great outdoors; see also ENVIRONMENT, REALITY. 4 [Natural forces] natural law, natural order, underlying cause, cosmic process, physical energy, kinetic energy, potential energy, water power, fission, fusion, atomic power, the sun, radiation, rays; see also ENERGY 2. 5 [Vital forces in an organism] creation, generation, regeneration; see LIFE 1, 2, STRENGTH. 6 [Kind] species, sort, type; see KIND 2, VARIETY 1, 2. —**by nature** inherently, by birth, as a matter of course; see NATURALLY 2. —**of** (or **in**) **the nature of** similar to, having the essential character of, as compared to; see LIKE.

naughty *a.* wayward, disobedient, mischievous, impish, fiendish, badly behaved, roguish, bad, unmanageable, ungovernable, insubordinate, wanton, recalcitrant; see also RUDE 2, UNRULY.

nausea *n.* motion sickness, queasiness, vomiting; see ILLNESS 2.

nauseate *v.* sicken, offend, repulse; see BOTHER 2, DISGUST, DISTURB.

nauseous *a.* queasy, ill, squeamish; see SICK.

nautical *a.* ocean-going, marine, naval, oceanic, deep-sea, aquatic, sailing, seafaring, seaworthy, seagoing, boating, yachting, cruising, whaling, oceanographic, rowing, navigating; see also MARITIME.

naval *a.* seagoing, marine, aquatic; see MARITIME, NAUTICAL.

navel *n.* abdomen, depression, umbilicus; see CENTER 1.

navigable *a.* passable, deep enough, open; see SAFE 1.

navigate *v.* pilot, steer, lie to, head out for, ride out, lay a course, operate; see also DRIVE 2.

navigation *n.* navigating, seamanship, yachting, piloting, aeronautics, flying, sailing, seafaring, ocean travel, exploration, voyaging, shipping, cruising, plotting a course, boating, pilotage, dead reckoning.

navigator *n.* seaman, explorer, mariner; see PILOT 1, SAILOR.

navy *n.* fleet, carrier group, squadron, flotilla, armada, task force, submarine force, ships, amphibious force, coast guard.

near *a.* 1 [Not distant in space] proximate, adjacent, adjoining, neighboring, not remote, close at hand, contiguous, handy, near by, next door to, at close quarters, beside, side by side, in close proximity; see also BORDERING.—*Ant.* DISTANT, removed, far off. 2 [Not distant in relationship] touching, close, akin; see FRIENDLY, RELATED 3. 3 [Not distant in time] at hand, approaching, next; see COMING 1, EXPECTED.

intimately —**adj.** 1 close in distance or time 2 close in relationship; akin 3 close in friendship; intimate 4 close in degree *[a near escape]* 5 short or direct *[the near way]* —**prep.** close to —**vt., vi.** to draw near (to); approach —**near′ness** *n.*

near′by′ *adj., adv.* near; close at hand

near′ly *adv.* almost; not quite

near miss 1 a result that is nearly but not quite successful 2 a near escape

near′sight′ed *adj.* having better vision for near objects than for distant ones; myopic —**near′sight′ed·ness** *n.*

neat (nēt) *adj.* ⟦ < L *nitere*, to shine⟧ 1 unmixed; undiluted 2 trim; tidy 3 skillful and precise 4 shapely 5 cleverly said or done 6 [Slang] nice, pleasing, etc. —**neat′ly** *adv.* —**neat′ness** *n.*

'neath or **neath** (nēth) *prep. old poet. var. of* BENEATH

neb·u·la (neb′yə lə) *n., pl.* **-lae** (-lē′) or **-las** ⟦L, mist⟧ a cloud of interstellar gas or dust, or, formerly, any hazy, distant celestial object, as a star cluster —**neb′u·lar** *adj.*

neb′u·lous (-ləs) *adj.* unclear; vague

nec·es·sar·i·ly (nes′ə ser′ə lē) *adv.* 1 because of necessity 2 as a necessary result

nec′es·sar′y (-ser′ē) *adj.* ⟦ < L *ne-*, not + *cedere*, give way⟧ 1 essential; indispensable 2 inevitable 3 required —*n., pl.* **-sar′ies** something necessary

ne·ces·si·tate (nə ses′ə tāt′) *vt.* **-tat′ed, -tat′ing** to make necessary or unavoidable

ne·ces′si·ty (-tē) *n., pl.* **-ties** ⟦see NECESSARY⟧ 1 natural causation; fate 2 great need 3 something that cannot be done without 4 want; poverty —**of necessity** necessarily; inevitably

neck (nek) *n.* ⟦OE *hnecca*⟧ 1 that part of a human or animal joining the head to the body 2 that part of a garment near the neck 3 a necklike part; specif., *a*) a narrow strip of land *b*) the narrowest part of a bottle, etc. *c*) a strait —*vt., vi.* [Slang] to hug, kiss, and caress passionately —**neck and neck** very close, as in a race

neck·er·chief (nek′ər chif, -chēf′) *n.* ⟦see prec. & KERCHIEF⟧ a handkerchief or scarf worn around the neck

neck′lace (-lis) *n.* ⟦NECK + LACE⟧ an ornamental string of beads, chain of gold, etc., worn around the neck

neck′tie′ *n.* a band worn around the neck under a collar and tied in front

neck′wear′ *n.* articles worn about the neck, as neckties, scarves, etc.

necro- ⟦ < Gr *nekros*, dead body⟧ *combining form* death, corpse

ne·crol·o·gy (ne kräl′ə jē) *n., pl.* **-gies** ⟦ult. < Gr *nekros*, corpse + -LOGY⟧ a list of people who have died

necro·man·cy (nek′rə man′sē) *n.* ⟦ < Gr *nekros*, corpse + *manteia*, divination⟧ 1 divination by alleged communication with the dead 2 black magic; sorcery —**nec′ro·man′cer** *n.*

ne·cro·sis (ne krō′sis) *n., pl.* **-ses′** (-sēz′) ⟦ < Gr *nekros*, corpse⟧ the death or decay of tissue in a part of the body

nec·tar (nek′tər) *n.* ⟦ < Gr *nektar*⟧ 1 Gr. & Rom. Myth. the drink of the gods 2 any very delicious beverage 3 the sweetish liquid in many flowers, used by bees to make honey

nec·tar·ine (nek′tə rēn′, nek′tə rēn′) *n.* ⟦ < prec.⟧ a kind of smooth-skinned peach

nee or **née** (nā; *now often* nē) *adj.* ⟦Fr⟧ born *[Mrs. Helen Jones, nee Smith]*

need (nēd) *n.* ⟦OE *nied*⟧ 1 necessity 2 a lack of something required or desired *[the need of a rest]* 3 something required or desired that is lacking *[your daily needs]* 4 *a*) a condition in which help is required *[a friend in need]* *b*) poverty —*vt.* 1 to have need of; require 2 to be obliged; must *[I need to be careful]* —*vi.* to be in need —**have need to** to be required to —**if need be** if it is required

need′ful *adj.* necessary; required

nee·dle (nēd′'l) *n.* ⟦OE *nædl*⟧ 1 a small, slender, pointed piece of steel with a hole for thread, used for sewing 2 a slender rod of steel, bone, etc. used for crocheting or knitting 3 STYLUS (sense 2*b*) 4 the pointer of a compass, gauge, etc. 5 the thin, short, pointed leaf of the pine, spruce, etc. 6 the sharp, slender metal tube at the end of a hypodermic syringe —*vt.* **-dled, -dling** [Colloq.] 1 to goad; prod 2 to tease —**nee′dler** *n.*

nee′dle·point′ *n.* 1 embroidery of woolen threads upon canvas 2 lace made on a paper pattern, with a needle: in full **needlepoint lace**

need′less *adj.* not needed; unnecessary —**need′lessly** *adv.*

═══ THESAURUS ═══

nearly *a.* within a little, all but, approximately; see ALMOST.

nearness *n.* 1 [Nearness in time or space] closeness, proximity, vicinity, approximation, approach, intimacy, close quarters, resemblance, likeness, handiness, imminence, immediacy, loom, threat, menace.—*Ant.* DISTANCE, remoteness, difference. 2 [Nearness in feeling] familiarity, affection, intimacy; see ADMIRATION, FRIENDSHIP.

neat *a.* 1 [Clean and orderly] tidy, trim, prim, spruce, dapper, smart, correct, shipshape, methodical, regular, orderly, systematic, spotless, nice, meticulous, elegant, spick-and-span, immaculate, chic, well-groomed, exact, precise, proper, neat as a pin, in good order, spruced up; see also CLEAN 1.—*Ant.* DISORDERED, messy, slovenly. 2 [Clever; *said of something done*] dexterous, deft, skillful, expert, proficient, handy, apt, ready, artful, nimble, quick, agile, adept, speedy, finished, practiced, easy, effortless; see also ABLE.—*Ant.* AWKWARD, clumsy, fumbling.

neatly *a.* 1 [Arranged so as to present a neat appearance] tidily, orderly, systematically, methodically, correctly, exactly, uniformly, levelly, flatly, smoothly, regularly, precisely, immaculately; see also EVENLY 1, ORGANIZED. 2 [In an adroit manner] skillfully, deftly, agilely; see CLEVERLY, EASILY.

neatness *n.* cleanness, tidiness, orderliness; see CLEANLINESS.

necessarily *a.* vitally, fundamentally, importantly, indispensably, unavoidably, undeniably, certainly, as a matter of course, inescapably, irresistibly, inevitably, assuredly, significantly, undoubtedly, indubitably, positively, unquestionably, no doubt, without fail, of necessity, of course, by force, come what may, without recourse, beyond one's control, by its own nature, from within, by definition; see also SURELY.

necessary *a.* important, needed, requisite, expedient, needful, indispensable, required, urgent, wanted, imperative, prerequisite, pressing, vital, fundamental, quintessential, cardinal, significant, momentous, compulsory, mandatory, basic, paramount, obligatory, essential, compelling, incumbent upon, all-important, binding, specified, unavoidable, decisive, crucial, elementary, chief, principal, prime, intrinsic, fixed, constant, permanent, inherent, ingrained, innate, without choice.

necessitate *v.* compel, constrain, oblige; see FORCE.

necessity *n.* 1 [The state of being required] need, essentiality, indispensability; see REQUIREMENT 2. 2 [That which is needed] need, want, requisite, vital part, essential, demand, imperative, fundamental, claim; see also LACK 2. 3 [The state of being forced by circumstances] exigency, pinch, stress, urgency, destitution, extremity, privation, obligation, case of life or death; see also EMERGENCY, POVERTY 1. —**of necessity** inevitably, importantly, surely; see NECESSARILY.

neck *n.* 1 [The juncture of the head and the trunk] cervical vertebrae, nape, scruff; see THROAT. 2 [The part of a dress at the neck] neckband, neckline, collar line; see DRESS 1, 2. —**risk one's neck** endanger one-self, gamble, take a chance; see RISK. —**stick one's neck out** endanger oneself, take a chance, gamble; see RISK.

necklace *n.* ornament, accessory, string of beads, jewels, chain, neckband, pearls, diamonds, choker; see also JEWELRY.

necktie *n.* neckwear, knot, ascot; see TIE 2.

need *n.* 1 [Poverty] want, destitution, pennilessness; see POVERTY 1. 2 [Lack] insufficiency, shortage, inadequacy; see LACK 1, 2. 3 [A requirement] obligation, necessity, urgency; see REQUIREMENT 2. —**if need be** if it is required, if the occasion demands, if necessary; see IF.

need *v.* lack, require, feel the necessity for, be in need of, suffer privation, be in want, be destitute, be short, be inadequate, have occasion for, have use for, miss, be without, do without, be needy, be poor, be deficient, go hungry, live from hand to mouth, feel the pinch*, be down and out*, be hard up*, be up against it*; see also WANT 2.—*Ant.* OWN, have, hold. —**have need to** have to, be obligated to, have reason to; see MUST.

needed *a.* wanted, required, desired; see NECESSARY.

needle *n.* awl, spike, hypodermic needle, syringe, phonograph needle, stylus, electric needle, probe, skewer, pin, darning needle, sewing needle, knitting needle.

needle* *v.* provoke, goad, tease; see BOTHER 2, EXAMINE.

needless *a.* unwanted, excessive, groundless; see UNNECESSARY, USELESS 1.

nee'dle·work' *n.* work done with a needle; embroidery, needlepoint, etc.

needn't (nēd′′nt) need not

needs (nēdz) *adv.* [OE *nedes*] of necessity [he must *needs* obey]

need'y *adj.* **-i·er, -i·est** in need; very poor —**need'i·ness** *n.*

ne'er (ner) *adv.* [Old Poet.] never

ne'er'-do-well' *n.* a shiftless, irresponsible person

ne·fari·ous (nə fer′ē əs) *adj.* [< L *ne-*, not + *fas*, lawful] very wicked; villainous —**ne·far'i·ous·ly** *adv.* —**ne·far'i·ous·ness** *n.*

ne·gate (ni gāt′) *vt.* **-gat·ed, -gat·ing** [< L *negare*, deny] 1 to deny 2 to make ineffective

ne·ga'tion (ni gā′shən) *n.* 1 the act or an instance of denying 2 the lack or opposite of something positive

nega·tive (neg′ə tiv) *adj.* 1 expressing denial or refusal; saying "no" 2 opposite to or lacking in that which is positive [a *negative* force] 3 *Math.* designating a quantity less than zero, or one to be subtracted 4 *Med.* not proving the presence of bacteria, a fracture, etc. 5 *Photog.* reversing the relation of light and shade of the subject 6 *Elec. a)* of, generating, or charged with negative electricity *b)* having an excess of electrons — *n.* 1 a negative word, reply, etc. 2 the point of view that opposes the positive 3 the plate in a voltaic battery where the lower potential is 4 an exposed and developed photographic plate or film on which light and shadow are reversed — *vt.* **-tived, -tiv·ing** to reject or deny —**in the negative** in refusal or denial of a plan, etc. —**neg'a·tively** *adv.*

ne·glect (ni glekt′) *vt.* [< L *neg-*, not + *legere*, to gather] 1 to ignore or disregard 2 to fail to attend to properly 3 to leave undone — *n.* 1 a neglecting 2 lack of proper care 3 a being neglected —**ne·glect'ful** *adj.*

neg·li·gee (neg′lə zhā′, neg′lə zhā′) *n.* [< Fr *négliger*, to neglect] a woman's loosely fitting dressing gown

neg·li·gent (neg′lə jənt) *adj.* 1 habitually failing to do the required thing; neglectful 2 careless, inattentive, etc. — **neg'li·gence** *n.*

neg'li·gible (-jə bəl) *adj.* that can be neglected or disregarded; trifling

ne·go·tiate (ni gō′shē āt′) *vi.* **-at·ed, -at·ing** [< L *negotium*, business] to discuss with a view to reaching agreement — *vt.* 1 to settle (a business transaction, treaty, etc.) 2 to transfer or sell (bonds, stocks, etc.) 3 to succeed in crossing, passing, etc. —**ne·go'tiable** (-shē ə bəl, -shə bəl) *adj.* —**ne·go'tia'tion** *n.* —**ne·go'tia'tor** *n.*

neg·ri·tude (neg′rə tōōd′, nē′grə-) *n.* [Fr *négritude*] [*also* N-] an awareness and affirmation by blacks of their distinctive cultural heritage

Ne·gro (nē′grō) *n., pl.* **-groes** [Sp & Port *negro*, black] a member of any of the indigenous, dark-skinned peoples of Africa, or a person having some African ancestors; a black — *adj.* of or for Negroes

Ne'groid' (-grɔid′) *adj.* designating or of one of the major groups of human beings, including most of the peoples of Africa

neigh (nā) *vi.* [OE *hnægan*] to utter the characteristic cry of a horse — *n.* this cry; a whinny

neigh'bor (nā′bər) *n.* [OE *neah*, nigh + *gebur*, freeholder] 1 one who lives or is situated near another 2 a fellow man — *adj.* nearby — *vt., vi.* to live or be situated nearby Brit. sp. **neighbour** —**neigh'bor·ing** *adj.*

neigh'bor·hood' *n.* 1 a particular community, district, or area 2 the people living near one another —**in the neighborhood of** [Colloq.] 1 near 2 about; approximately

neigh'borly *adj.* like or appropriate to neighbors; friendly, helpful, etc. —**neigh'bor·li·ness** *n.*

nei·ther (nē′thər, nī′-) *adj., pron.* [OE *na-hwæther*, lit., not whether] not one or the other (of two); not either [*neither* boy went, *neither* of them was invited] — *conj.* not either [I could *neither* laugh nor cry]

nema·tode (nem′ə tōd′) *n.* [ult. < Gr *nēma*, thread] a long, cylindrical, unsegmented worm; roundworm

nem·esis (nem′ə sis) *n., pl.* **-ses'** (-sēz′) [< Gr *nemein*, deal out] 1 *a)* just punishment *b)* one who imposes it 2 anyone or anything that seems inevitably to defeat or frustrate one

neo- [< Gr *neos*] [*often* N-] combining form 1 new, recent 2 in a new or different way

neo·clas·sic (nē′ō klas′ik) *adj.* designating or of a revival of classic style and form in art, literature, etc. Also **ne'o·clas'si·cal** —**ne'o·clas'si·cism'** *n.*

ne'o·co·lo'ni·al·ism' *n.* exploitation by a foreign power of a region that has ostensibly achieved independence

ne·olo·gism (nē äl′ə jiz′əm) *n.* [see NEO-, -LOGY, & -ISM] a new word or a new meaning for an established word

neon (nē′än′) *n.* [< Gr *neos*, new] a rare, inert gaseous chemical element found in the earth's atmosphere

neo·nate (nē′ō nāt′, nē′ə-) *n.* [ModL < *neo-*, NEO- + L *natus*, born] a newborn infant —**ne'o·na'tal** *adj.*

neon lamp a tube containing neon, which glows red when an electric current is sent through it

■■■ THESAURUS ■■■

needy *a.* destitute, indigent, penniless; see POOR 1.

negate *v.* repeal, retract, nullify; see CANCEL.

negation *n.* opposition, contradiction, repudiation; see DENIAL, REFUSAL.

negative *a.* 1 [Involving a refusal] denying, contradictory, contrary, disavowing, repugnant, contravening, rejecting, disallowing.—*Ant.* FAVORABLE, encouraging, accepting. 2 [Lacking positive qualities] absent, removed, neutralizing, counteractive, annulling, invalidating.—*Ant.* EMPHATIC, validating, affirmative.

negative *n.* 1 [A refusal] contradiction, disavowal, refutation; see DENIAL, REFUSAL. 2 [A negative image] film, plate, developed film; see IMAGE 2, PICTURE 2.

neglect *n.* 1 [The act of showing indifference to a person] slight, disregard, thoughtlessness, disrespect, carelessness, scorn, oversight, heedlessness, inattention, unconcern, inconsideration, disdain, coolness; see also INDIFFERENCE. 2 [The act of neglecting duties or charges] negligence, slovenliness, neglectfulness; see CARELESSNESS.

neglect *v.* 1 [To treat with indifference] slight, scorn, overlook, disregard, disdain, detest, rebuff, affront, despise, ignore, depreciate, spurn, underestimate, undervalue, shake off, make light of, laugh off, keep one's distance, pass over, pass up, have nothing to do with, let alone, let go, not care for, pay no attention to, pay no heed, leave alone, not give a darn*, let the grass grow under one's feet, leave well enough alone, let it ride, play possum*, keep at arm's length.—*Ant.* CONSIDER, appreciate, value. 2 [To fail to attend to responsibilities] pass over, defer, procrastinate, suspend, dismiss, discard, let slip, miss, skip, omit, skimp, gloss over, be remiss, be derelict, let go, ignore, trifle, postpone, lose sight of, look the other way, let it go, not trouble oneself with, evade, be careless, be irresponsible.—*Ant.* WATCH, care for, attend.

neglected *a.* slighted, disregarded, scorned, disdained, despised, affronted, overlooked, ignored, spurned, omitted, undervalued, deferred, dismissed, passed over, postponed, evaded, deteriorated, underestimated, declined, lapsed, uncared for, unwatched, unheeded, depreciated, unconsidered, shaken off, unused, unwanted, tossed aside, abandoned, forgotten, out in the cold, dropped, put on the shelf.—*Ant.* CONSIDERED, cared for, heeded.

negligence *n.* disregard, inconsideration, disrespect; see CARELESSNESS, INDIFFERENCE NEGLECT 1.

negligent *a.* indifferent, inattentive, neglectful; see CARELESS.

negotiate *v.* 1 [To make arrangements for] arrange, bargain, confer, consult, parley, transact, mediate, make peace, contract, settle, adjust, conciliate, accomodate, arbitrate, referee, umpire, compromise, bring to terms, make terms, make the best of, treat with, moderate, work out, dicker*, haggle, bury the hatchet. 2 [To transfer] barter, allocate, transmit; see ASSIGN, SELL.

negotiation *n.* compromise, intervention, mediation; see AGREEMENT.

negro *a.* black, negroid, African, black-skinned, dark-skinned, Afro-American, Afro-Asian, Ethiopian, brown; see also BLACK 2.

Negro *n.* black, Ethiopian, African, African-American, Afro-American, Afro-Asian, colored person, Negroid person, black person, person of color.

neighbor *n.* acquaintance, companion, associate, next-door-neighbor, nearby resident; see also FRIEND.

neighborhood *n.* environs, block, vicinity, locality, proximity, district, area, parish, ward, precinct, community, region, zone, section, suburb, tract. —**in the neighborhood of** about, approximately, close to; see NEAR 1.

neighboring *a.* adjacent, adjoining, contiguous; see BORDERING, NEAR 1.

neighborly *a.* sociable, hospitable, helpful; see FRIENDLY.

neither *a., conj.* nor yet, also not, not either, not, not at all.

neither *pron.* no one, nobody, neither one, not this one, nor this nor that, no one of two, not the one, not any one; see also NONE 1, NOTHING.

ne·o·phyte (nē′ō fīt′, nē′ə-) *n.* [< Gr *neos*, new + *phyein*, to produce] 1 a new convert 2 a beginner; novice

ne·o·plasm (nē′ō plaz′əm) *n.* [< NEO- + Gr *plassein*, to form] an abnormal growth of tissue, as a tumor

ne′o·prene′ (-prēn′) *n.* a synthetic rubber resistant to oil, heat, etc.

ne·pen·the (nē pen′thē, ni-) *n.* [< Gr *ne-*, not + *penthos*, sorrow] anything that causes forgetfulness of sorrow

nephew (nef′yōō) *n.* [< L *nepos*] the son of one's brother or sister, or of one's brother-in-law or sister-in-law

neph·rite (nef′rīt′) *n.* [< Gr *nephros*, kidney] a hard, usually greenish type of jade

ne·phri·tis (nē frīt′əs, ni-) *n.* [< Gr *nephros*, kidney + -ITIS] a disease of the kidneys, characterized by inflammation

ne·phro·sis (nē frō′sis, ni-) *n.* [< Gr *nephros*, kidney + -OSIS] a degenerative disease of the kidneys, characterized by edema

ne plus ul·tra (nā plus ul′trə) [L, no more beyond] the ultimate

nepo·tism (nep′ə tiz′əm) *n.* [< L *nepos*, nephew] favoritism shown to relatives, esp. in securing jobs

Nep·tune (nep′tōōn′) 1 the Roman god of the sea 2 the planet eighth in distance from the sun: see PLANET

nep·tu·nium (nep tōō′nē əm) *n.* [after prec.] a radioactive chemical element produced by irradiating uranium atoms

nerd (nurd) *n.* [Slang] a person regarded as dull, ineffective, etc.

nerve (nurv) *n.* [< L *nervus*] 1 any of the cordlike fibers carrying impulses between body organs and the central nervous system 2 coolness in danger; courage 3 [*pl.*] nervousness 4 [Colloq.] impudent boldness — *vt.* **nerved, nerv′ing** to give strength or courage to —**get on someone's nerves** [Colloq.] to make someone irritable or exasperated —**nerve oneself** to collect one's energies or courage for an effort

nerve center a control center; headquarters

nerve gas a poisonous gas causing paralysis of the respiratory and nervous systems

nerve′less *adj.* 1 without strength, vigor, etc.; weak 2 not nervous; cool; controlled —**nerve′less·ly** *adv.*

nerve′-rack·ing or **nerve′-wrack·ing** (-rak′iŋ) *adj.* very trying to one's patience or equanimity

nerv·ous (nur′vəs) *adj.* 1 animated 2 of or made up of nerves 3 emotionally tense, restless, etc. 4 fearful — **nerv′ous·ly** *adv.* —**nerv′ous·ness** *n.*

nervous system all the nerve cells and nervous tissues in an organism, including, in the vertebrates, the brain, spinal cord, nerves, etc.

nerv′y *adj.* **-i·er, -i·est** 1 bold 2 [Colloq.] brazen; impudent

-ness (nis, nəs) [OE *-nes(s)*] *suffix* state, quality, or instance of being [*togetherness, sadness*]

nest (nest) *n.* [OE] 1 the structure or place where a bird lays its eggs and shelters its young 2 the place used by insects, fish, etc. for spawning or breeding 3 a cozy place; retreat 4 *a*) a resort, haunt, etc. *b*) the people who frequent such a place [a *nest* of criminals] 5 a set of things, each fitting within the one next larger — *vi., vt.* 1 to build or settle in (a nest) 2 to fit (an object) closely within another

nest egg money, etc. put aside as a reserve or to establish a fund

nes·tle (nes′əl) *vi.* **-tled, -tling** [OE *nestlian*] 1 to settle down comfortably 2 to press close for comfort or in affection 3 to lie sheltered, as a house among trees — *vt.* to rest snugly

nest·ling (nest′liŋ) *n.* a young bird not yet ready to leave the nest

net¹ (net) *n.* [OE *nett*] 1 an openwork fabric, as of string, used to snare birds, fish, etc. 2 a trap; snare 3 a meshed fabric, esp. one used to hold, protect, etc. [a *hairnet*] — *vt.* **net′ted, net′ting** to snare or enclose, as with a net

net² (net) *adj.* [Fr., clear] remaining after deductions or allowances have been made — *n.* a net amount, profit, weight, price, etc. — *vt.* **net′ted, net′ting** to clear as profit, etc.

nether (neth′ər) *adj.* [OE *neothera*] lower or under [the *nether* world]

neth′er·most′ *adj.* lowest

net′ting *n.* netted material

net·tle (net′'l) *n.* [OE *netele*] a weed with stinging hairs — *vt.* **-tled, -tling** to irritate; annoy; vex

net′tle·some *adj.* that nettles or irritates

net′work′ *n.* 1 an arrangement of parallel wires, etc. crossed at intervals by others so as to leave open spaces 2 anything like this, as a system of interconnected roads, individuals, computer terminals, etc. 3 *Radio, TV* a chain of transmitting stations — *adj.* broadcast over the stations of a network

net′work·ing *n.* 1 the developing of contacts or exchanging of information, as to further a career 2 the interconnection of computer systems

neu·ral (nōō′rəl) *adj.* [NEUR(O)- + -AL] of a nerve or the nervous system

neural·gia (nōō ral′jə) *n.* [see NEURO- & -ALGIA] severe pain along a nerve —**neu·ral′gic** (-jik) *adj.*

neuras·thenia (nōō′ras thē′nē ə) *n.* [< NEURO- + Gr *asthenia*, weakness] a former category of mental disorder, characterized by fatigue, anxiety, etc. —**neu·ras·then′ic** (-then′ik) *adj., n.*

neu·ri·tis (nōō rīt′əs) *n.* [fol. + -ITIS] inflammation of a nerve or nerves —**neu·rit′ic** (-rit′ik) *adj.*

neuro- [< Gr *neuron*, nerve] *combining form* of a nerve or the nervous system Also **neur-**

neurol·ogy (nōō räl′ə jē) *n.* [prec. + -LOGY] the branch of medicine dealing with the nervous system and its diseases —**neu·ro·logi·cal** (nōō′rō läj′i kəl) *adj.* —**neurol′o·gist** *n.*

neuro·mus·cu·lar (nōō′rō mus′kyōō lər) *adj.* of or involving both nerves and muscles

neu·ron (nōō′rän′) *n.* the nerve cell body and all its processes

neu·ro·sis (nōō rō′sis) *n., pl.* **-ses′** (-sēz′) [NEURO- + -OSIS] any of various mental disorders characterized by anxiety, compulsions, phobias, etc.

neuro·sur·gery (nōō′rō sur′jər ē) *n.* the branch of surgery involving the brain or spinal cord —**neu′ro·sur′geon** *n.*

neu·rotic (nōō rät′ik) *adj.* of, characteristic of, or having a neurosis — *n.* a neurotic person —**neu·rot′i·cally** *adv.*

THESAURUS

nephew *n.* brother's son, sister's son, grandnephew, son of a brother-in-law, son of a sister-in law, nephew by marriage; see also NIECE, RELATIVE.

nerve *n.* 1 [The structure that carries nervous impulses] nerve fiber, nerve tissue, nerve filament, nerve cord, nerve ending. *Types of nerves include the following:* motor, sensory, efferent, afferent, effector, receptors. 2 [Courage] resolution, spirit, mettle; see COURAGE. 3 [Impudence] temerity, audacity, effrontery; see RUDENESS.

nerve-racking *a.* exhausting, horrible, wearisome; see DIFFICULT 1, PAINFUL 1.

nerves *n.* strain, tension, hysteria, emotional stress, sleeplessness; see also NERVOUSNESS. **—get on one's nerves** exasperate, irritate, annoy; see BOTHER 2.

nervous *a.* 1 [Excitable] sensitive, irritable, impatient, moody, peevish, restless, uneasy, impulsive, rash, hasty, reckless, touchy, readily upset, high-strung, neurotic; see also UNSTABLE 2. 2 [Excited] agitated, bothered, annoyed; see EXCITED.

nervousness *n.* stimulation, agitation, animation, intoxication, sensitivity, delirium, excitability, irascibility, impulsiveness, impetuosity, moodiness, anger, elation, discomfiture, hastiness, vehemence, impatience, feverishness, stage fright, butterflies in the stomach*, the jitters*, the shakes; see also EMBARRASSMENT, EXCITEMENT.—*Ant.* REST, calm, relaxation.

nest *n.* den, cradle, incubator; see RETREAT 2.

nest egg* *n.* personal savings, personal property, real property, something for a rainy day*; see also MONEY 1, SAVINGS.

nestle *v.* cuddle, snuggle, settle down, take shelter, lie close, make oneself snug, huddle, move close to, lie against, curl up to.

net¹ *n.* screen, mesh, fabric; see WEB. *Varieties of nets include the following:* hair, mosquito, tennis, ping-pong, volleyball, goal, casting, bird, butterfly, fish, draw, drag, drop, hand, scoop.

net² *a.* clear, pure, remaining, excluding, exclusive, irreducible, undeductible.

net² *v.* make, clear, gain above expenses; see PROFIT 2.

network *n.* 1 [System of channels] tracks, circuitry, channels, system, labyrinth, artery, arrangement; see also CHAIN, WIRING. 2 [Netting] fiber, weave, mesh; see GOODS, WEB.

neurosis *n.* compulsion, instability, mental disorder; see INSANITY, NERVOUSNESS, OBSESSION.

neurotic *a.* disturbed, unstable, sick; see INSANE, TROUBLED.

neurotic *n.* paranoid, sick person, psychotic; see MADMAN.

neu·ro·trans·mit'ter *n.* a biochemical substance that transmits, or inhibits, nerve impulses at a synapse

neu·ter (nōōt'ər) *adj.* 〚< L *ne-*, not + *uter*, either〛 **1** *Biol.* *a)* having no sexual organ *b)* having undeveloped sexual organs in the adult **2** *Gram.* designating or of the gender of words neither masculine nor feminine — *vt.* to castrate or spay (an animal)

neu·tral (nōō'trəl) *adj.* 〚see prec.〛 **1** supporting neither side in a quarrel or war **2** of neither extreme in type, kind, etc.; indifferent **3** having little or no decided color — *n.* **1** a neutral person or nation **2** a neutral color **3** *Mech.* a disengaged position of gears —**neu'trally** *adv.*

neu·tral·ism' (-iz'əm) *n.* a policy of remaining neutral, esp. in international conflicts —**neu'tral·ist** *adj., n.*

neu·tral·i·ty (-tral'ə tē) *n.* **1** a being neutral **2** the status or policy of a neutral nation

neu·tral·ize (nōō'trə līz') *vt.* **-ized', -iz'ing** **1** to declare (a nation, etc.) neutral in war **2** to destroy or counteract the effectiveness, force, etc. of —**neu'tral·i·za'tion** *n.* —**neu'tral·iz'er** *n.*

neutral spirits ethyl alcohol of 190 proof or over, used in blended whiskeys, liqueurs, etc.

neu·tri·no (nōō trē'nō) *n., pl.* **-nos** 〚It, little neutron〛 either of two leptons having almost no mass

neu·tron (nōō'trän') *n.* 〚< NEUTRAL〛 one of the elementary, uncharged particles of an atom

neutron bomb a small thermonuclear bomb, that would release large numbers of neutrons that kill people without destroying buildings, etc.

neutron star a collapsed star of extremely high density composed almost entirely of neutrons

never (nev'ər) *adv.* 〚< OE *ne*, not + *æfre*, ever〛 **1** not ever; at no time **2** not at all; in no case

nev'er·more' *adv.* never again

nev·er-nev'er land an unreal or unrealistic place or situation

nev'er·the·less' (-thə les') *adv.* in spite of that; however

ne·vus (nē'vəs) *n., pl.* **ne'vi** (-vī') 〚< L *naevus*〛 a birthmark or mole

new (nōō) *adj.* 〚OE *niwe*〛 **1** appearing, thought of, developed, made, etc. for the first time **2** different from (the) one in the past 〚a *new* hairdo〛 **3** strange; unfamiliar **4** *a)* recently grown; fresh *b)* harvested early 〚*new* potatoes〛 **5** unused **6** modern; recent **7** more; additional **8** starting as a repetition of a cycle, series, etc. 〚the *new* moon〛 **9** having just reached a position, rank, etc. 〚a *new* arrival〛 — *adv.* **1** again **2** newly; recently —**new'ness** *n.*

New Age [*often* **n- a-**] **1** of or pertaining to a cultural movement variously combining belief in reincarnation, astrology, meditation, etc. **2** designating or of a style of popular instrumental music intended to effect a serene mood

new blood new people as a potential source of new ideas, vigor, etc.

new'born' *adj.* **1** recently born **2** reborn

new'com'er *n.* a recent arrival

New Deal the principles and policies adopted by President F. D. Roosevelt in the 1930's to advance economic recovery and social welfare

newel (nōō'əl) *n.* 〚ult. < L *nux*, nut〛 **1** the pillar around which the steps of a winding staircase turn **2** the post that supports the handrail of a flight of stairs: also **newel post**

new'fan'gled (-fan'gəld) *adj.* 〚ME *newe*, new + *-fangel* < OE *fon*, to take〛 new; novel: a humorously derogatory term

new'-fash'ioned *adj.* **1** recently come into fashion **2** new in form

new'ly *adv.* recently; lately

new'ly·wed' *n.* a recently married person

new moon the moon when it is between the earth and the sun, with its dark side toward the earth: it is followed by a thin crescent phase

news (nōōz) *n.pl.* [*with sing. v.*] **1** new information; information previously unknown **2** *a)* recent happenings *b)* reports of these **3** a newscast —**make news** to do something apt to be reported as news

news'boy' *n.* a boy who sells or delivers newspapers

news'cast' *n.* a radio or television news broadcast —**news'cast'er** *n.*

news'deal'er *n.* a retailer of newspapers, magazines, etc.

news'let'ter *n.* a bulletin issued regularly to subscribers, employees, or members of a group, containing news of upcoming events, etc.

news'man' (-man', -mən) *n., pl.* **-men'** (-men', -mən) a newscaster or reporter, esp. a male

news'pa'per *n.* a regular publication, usually daily or weekly, containing news, opinions, advertising, etc.

news'pa'per·man' *n., pl.* **-men'** **1** a person, esp. a man, who works for a newspaper, esp. as a reporter, editor, etc. **2** a newspaper owner or publisher —**news'pa'per·wom'an,** *pl.* **-wom'en,** *n.fem.*

news'print' *n.* a cheap paper used chiefly for newspapers

news'stand' *n.* a stand at which newspapers, magazines, etc. are sold

news'wor'thy (-wur'thē) *adj.* timely and important or interesting

news'y *adj.* **-i·er, -i·est** [Colloq.] containing much news

newt (nōōt, nyōōt) *n.* 〚by merging of ME (*a*)*n eute*, a newt〛 any of various small amphibious salamanders

New Testament the part of the Bible that contains the life and teachings of Jesus and his followers

new·ton (nōō'tən) *n.* 〚after Sir Isaac *Newton* (1642-1727), Eng mathematician〛 a unit of force

New World North and South America

New Year's (Day) Jan. 1

New Year's Eve the evening before New Year's Day

next (nekst) *adj.* 〚OE *neahst*, superl. of *neah*, nigh〛 nearest; immediately preceding or following — *adv.* **1** in the nearest time, place, rank, etc. **2** on the first subsequent occasion

---

■ THESAURUS ■

neutral *a.* **1** [Not fighting] noncombatant, nonpartisan, on the side lines, nonparticipating, inactive, disengaged, uninvolved, bystanding, standing by, inert, on the fence.— *Ant.* ENGAGED, involved, active. **2** [Without opinion] nonchalant, disinterested, impartial; see INDIFFERENT. **3** [Without distinctive color] drab, indeterminate, vague; see DULL 2.

never *a.* not ever, at no time, not at any time, not in the least, not in any way, in no way, not at all, not under any condition, nevermore, never again, no ways.

nevertheless *a.* not the less, nonetheless, notwithstanding; see ALTHOUGH, BUT 1.

new *a.* **1** [Recent] current, brand-new, newborn, young, new-fangled, latest, just out; see also FRESH 1. **2** [Modern] modish, popular, faddish, up to the minute, contemporary, latest; see also FASHIONABLE, MODERN 1. **3** [Novel] unique, original, bizarre; see UNUSUAL 1, 2. **4** [Different] unlike, dissimilar, distinct; see UNLIKE. **5** [Additional] further, increased, supplementary; see EXTRA. **6** [Inexperienced] unseasoned, unskilled, untrained; see INCOMPE-TENT, INEXPERIENCED. **7** [Recently] newly, freshly, lately; see RECENTLY.

newcomer *n.* immigrant, outsider, foreigner, tenderfoot, maverick*, Johnny-come-lately*; see also ALIEN, STRANGER.

newfangled *a.* novel, unique, new; see FASHIONABLE, MODERN 1.

newly *a.* lately, anew, afresh; see RECENTLY.

newlywed *n.* bride, bridegroom, honeymooner; see HUSBAND, WIFE.

newness *n.* uniqueness, modernity, recentness; see ORIGINALITY.

news *n.* **1** [Information] intelligence, tidings, advice, discovery, recognition, the scoop*, the goods*, headlines, front-page news; see also DATA, KNOWLEDGE 1. **2** [A specific report] telling, narration, recital, account, description, message, copy, communication, release, communiqué, telegram, cable, radiogram, broadcast, telecast, bulletin, dispatch, news story, scoop*, big news, eye opener*; see also ANNOUNCEMENT. —**make news** become famous, accomplish, create events; see EXPOSE, REVEAL.

newscast *n.* news broadcasting, telecast, newscasting; see ANNOUNCE-MENT, NEWS 2.

newscaster *n.* news analyst, commentator, broadcaster; see REPORTER, WRITER.

newspaper *n.* publication, daily paper, journal, press, fourth estate, public press, sheet, tabloid, gazette; see also RECORD 1. *Varieties of newspapers include the following:* daily, weekly, biweekly, metropolitan, rural, county, country, trade, provincial, community. *Parts of newspapers include the following:* front page section, news section, foreign news section, editorial page, state news section, city news section, local news section, domestic news section, magazine, business section, society section, family section, living section, women's section, sports section, entertainment section, amusement section, comics page, advertising section, syndicated section, boiler plate*.

newspaperman *n.* newsperson, journalist, member of the editorial department; see AUTHOR, EDITOR, REPORTER, WRITER.

next *a.* **1** [Following in order] succeeding, later, afterwards, presently,

next'-door' *adj.* in or at the next house, building, etc.

nexus (neks'əs) *n., pl.* **nex'uses** or **nex'us** ⟦L⟧ a connection, tie, or link

Ni *Chem. symbol for* nickel

nia·cin (nī'ə sin) *n.* ⟦NI(COTINIC) AC(ID) + -*in*⟧ NICOTINIC ACID

nib (nib) *n.* ⟦< ME *nebb*, a bird's beak⟧ a point, esp. a pen point

nib·ble (nib'əl) *vt., vi.* **-bled, -bling** ⟦ME *nebyllen*⟧ 1 to eat (food) with quick, small bites 2 to bite (*at*) lightly and intermittently — *n.* a small bite —**nib'bler** *n.*

nibs (nibz) *n.* ⟦< ?⟧ [Colloq.] a self-important person: preceded by *his* or *her*

nice (nīs) *adj.* **nic'er, nic'est** ⟦< L *nescius*, ignorant⟧ 1 fastidious; refined 2 delicate; precise; subtle ⟦*a nice* distinction⟧ 3 calling for care, tact, etc. 4 finely discriminating or minutely accurate 5 pleasant, attractive, kind, good, etc.: a generalized term of approval —**nice'ly** *adv.* —**nice'ness** *n.*

ni·cety (nī'sə tē) *n., pl.* **-ties** 1 precision; accuracy 2 fastidiousness; refinement 3 a subtle or minute detail, distinction, etc. 4 something choice or dainty

niche (nich) *n.* ⟦Fr < L *nidus*, a nest⟧ 1 a recess in a wall, for a statue, vase, etc. 2 an especially suitable place or position

nicht wahr? (nikht vär') ⟦Ger, not true?⟧ isn't that so?

nick (nik) *n.* ⟦ME *nyke*⟧ a small cut, chip, etc. made on a surface — *vt.* 1 to make a nick or nicks in 2 to wound superficially —**in the nick of time** exactly when needed

nickel (nik'əl) *n.* ⟦< Ger *kupfernickel*, copper devil: the copperlike ore contains no copper⟧ 1 a hard, silver-white, metallic chemical element, much used in alloys 2 a U.S. or Canadian coin of nickel and copper, equal to five cents

nickel·odeon (nik'əl ō'dē ən) *n.* ⟦prec. + (*mel*)*odeon*, a small keyboard organ⟧ a coin-operated player piano or early type of jukebox

nicker (nik'ər) *vi., n.* NEIGH

nick·name (nik'nām') *n.* ⟦by merging of ME (*a*)*n ekename*, a surname⟧ 1 a substitute, often descriptive, name given in fun, etc., as "Shorty" 2 a familiar form of a proper name, as "Dick" for "Richard" — *vt.* **-named'**, **-nam'ing** to give a nickname to

nico·tine (nik'ə tēn') *n.* ⟦Fr, after J. *Nicot*, 16th-c. Fr diplomat who introduced tobacco into France⟧ a poisonous alkaloid found in tobacco leaves

nic'o·tin'ic acid (-tin'ik) a member of the vitamin B complex

niece (nēs) *n.* ⟦< L *neptis*⟧ the daughter of one's brother or sister or of one's brother-in-law or sister-in-law

nifty (nif'tē) *adj.* **-tier, -ti·est** ⟦prob. < *magnificent*⟧ [Slang] attractive, smart, stylish, etc.

nig·gard (nig'ərd) *n.* ⟦prob. < Scand⟧ a stingy person; miser — *adj.* stingy; miserly —**nig'gardly** *adj., adv.* — **nig'gard·li·ness** *n.*

nig·gle (nig'əl) *vi.* **-gled, -gling** ⟦prob. akin to Norw *nigla*⟧ to work fussily; be finicky —**nig'gler** *n.* —**nig'gling** *adj., n.*

nigh (nī) *adv., adj., prep.* ⟦OE *neah*⟧ [Now Chiefly Dial.] NEAR

night (nīt) *n.* ⟦OE *niht*⟧ 1 the period of darkness from sunset to sunrise 2 any period or condition of darkness or gloom

night blindness imperfect vision in the dark or in dim light

night'cap' *n.* 1 a cap worn to bed 2 [Colloq.] an alcoholic drink taken just before going to bed

night'clothes' (-klōthz', -klōz') *n.* clothes to be worn in bed, as pajamas

night'club' *n.* a place of entertainment for drinking, dancing, etc. at night

night crawl'er a large earthworm that comes to the surface at night

night'dress' *n.* NIGHTGOWN

night'fall' *n.* the time in the evening when daylight is last visible; dusk

night'gown' *n.* a loose gown worn in bed by women or girls

night'hawk' *n.* 1 any of various nocturnal birds related to the whippoorwill 2 NIGHT OWL

night'ie (-ē) *n.* [Colloq.] a nightgown

night·in·gale (nīt'ʼn gāl') *n.* ⟦< OE *niht*, night + *galan*, sing⟧ a small European thrush: the male sings melodiously, esp. at night

night life pleasure-seeking activity at night, as in nightclubs

night'ly *adj.* done or occurring every night — *adv.* night after night; every night

night'mare' (-mer') *n.* ⟦ME < *niht*, night + *mare*, demon⟧ 1 a frightening dream 2 any frightening experience —**night'mar'ish** *adj.*

night owl a person who works at night or otherwise stays up late

night'shade' (-shād') *n.* 1 a chiefly tropical plant with five-lobed leaves and flowers of various colors 2 BELLADONNA

night'shirt' *n.* a kind of nightgown worn esp. by men or boys

night'spot' *n. colloq. var. of* NIGHTCLUB

night stand a small bedside table

night'stick' *n.* a policeman's club; billy

night'time' *n.* the time between dusk and dawn

night'wear' *n.* NIGHTCLOTHES

NIH National Institutes of Health

ni·hil·ism (nī'hi liz'əm, nī'ə-) *n.* ⟦< L *nihil*, nothing⟧ the general rejection of customary beliefs in morality, religion, etc. —**ni'hil·ist** *n.* —**ni'hil·is'tic** *adj.*

nil (nil) *n.* ⟦L, contr. of *nihil*⟧ nothing

nim·ble (nim'bəl) *adj.* **-bler, -blest** ⟦< OE *niman*, to take⟧ 1 quick-witted; alert 2 moving or acting quickly and lightly —**nim'bly** *adv.*

nim·bus (nim'bəs) *n., pl.* **-bi'** (-bī') or **-buses** ⟦L⟧ 1 orig., any rain-producing cloud 2 a halo around the head of a saint, etc., as on a picture

Nim·rod (nim'räd') *Bible* a mighty hunter

THESAURUS

resulting, subsequent, ensuing; see also FOLLOWING. 2 [Adjacent] beside, close, alongside, on one side, on the side, adjoining, neighboring, meeting, touching, bordering on, cheek by jowl, side by side, attached, abutting, back to back, to the left, to the right; see also NEAR 1.

nibble *n.* morsel, peck, cautious bite; see BIT 1, BITE 1.

nibble *v.* nip, gnaw, snack; see BITE 1, EAT 1.

nice *a.* 1 [Approved] likable, superior, admirable; see EXCELLENT. 2 [Behaving in a becoming manner] pleasing, agreeable, winning, refined, cultured, amiable, delightful, charming, inviting, pleasant, cordial, courteous, considerate, kind, kindly, helpful, gracious, obliging, genial, gentle, becoming, unassuming, modest, demure; see also FRIENDLY.— *Ant.* RUDE, indecorous, crude.

nicely *a.* 1 [In a welcome manner] pleasantly, perfectly, pleasingly, amiably, winningly, creditably, acceptably, excellently, distinctively, happily, admirably, desirably, pleas-

urably, attractively, likably, enjoyably, beautifully, graciously, finely; see also AGREEABLY.— *Ant.* BADLY, unfortunately, unsuccessfully. 2 [In a becoming manner] charmingly, winsomely, invitingly; see MODESTLY, POLITELY.

niceness *n.* discernment, taste, refinement; see CARE 1, DISCRETION, KINDNESS 1.

niche *n.* cranny, corner, cubbyhole; see HOLE 1.

nick *n.* indentation, notch, slit; see CUT 1, DENT.

nick *v.* indent, notch, slit; see CUT 1, DENT.

nickel *n.* 1 *Ni*, chemical element, plating material; see ELEMENT 2, METAL, MINERAL. 2 [A coin made of nickel] five-cent piece, coin, five cents; see MONEY 1.

niece *n.* sister's daughter, brother's daughter, niece by marriage, grandniece, daughter of a brother-in-law, daughter of a sister-in law; see also NEPHEW, RELATIVE.

niggling *a.* trifling, petty, piddling;

see TRIVIAL, UNIMPORTANT.

night *n.* 1 [The diurnal dark period] after dark, evening, from dusk to dawn, nightfall, after nightfall, twilight, nighttime, bedtime, midnight, before dawn, the dark hours, dead of night. 2 [The dark] blackness, duskiness, gloom; see DARKNESS 1. — **good night** sleep well, have a good evening, night-night; see GOODBYE.

nightclub *n.* casino, discotheque, cabaret; see BAR 2, RESTAURANT.

nightly *a.* nocturnal, in the hours of night, every twenty-four hours, during the hours of darkness, at night, each night, every night, by night; see also REGULARLY.—*Ant.* DAILY, by day, diurnal.

nightmare *n.* bad dream, horror, incubus; see DREAM.

nighttime *n.* darkness, bedtime, dark of night; see NIGHT 1.

nimble *a.* 1 [Agile] quick, spry, active; see AGILE, GRACEFUL 1. 2 [Alert] quick-witted, bright, clever; see INTELLIGENT.

nin·com·poop (nin′kəm po͞op′) *n.* 〖< ?〗 a stupid, silly person; fool

nine (nīn) *adj., n.* 〖OE *nigon* 〗 one more than eight; 9; IX —**ninth** (nīnth) *adj., n.*

nine′pins′ *n.pl.* [*with sing. v.*] a British version of the game of tenpins, played with nine wooden pins

nine′teen′ *adj., n.* nine more than ten; 19; XIX —**nine′ teenth′** (-tēnth′) *adj., n.*

ninety (nīnt′ē) *adj., n., pl.* **-ties** nine times ten; 90; XC (or LXXXX) —**the nineties** the numbers or years, as of a century, from 90 through 99 —**nine′ti·eth** (-ith) *adj., n.*

ninny (nin′ē) *n., pl.* **-nies** 〖< (a)n inn(ocent)〗 a fool; dolt

nip[1] (nip) *vt.* **nipped, nip′ping** 〖prob. < earlier LowG *nippen* 〗 1 to pinch or bite 2 to sever (shoots, etc.) by clipping 3 to check the growth of 4 to have a painful or injurious effect on because of cold — *n.* 1 a nipping; pinch; bite 2 a stinging, as in cold air 3 stinging cold; frost —**nip and tuck** so close as to leave the outcome in doubt

nip[2] (nip) *n.* 〖prob. < Du *nippen*, to sip 〗 a small drink of liquor — *vt., vi.* **nipped, nip′ping** to drink in nips

nip·per (nip′ər) *n.* 1 anything that nips 2 [*pl.*] pliers, pincers, etc. 3 the claw of a crab or lobster

nip·ple (nip′əl) *n.* 〖prob. < earlier *neb*, a beak 〗 1 the small protuberance on a breast or udder through which, in the female, the milk passes; teat 2 the teatlike part in the cap of a baby's bottle

Nip·pon·ese (nip′ə nēz′, -nēs′) *adj., n., pl.* **-ese′** 〖< Jpn *Nippon*, Japan 〗 Japanese

nippy (nip′ē) *adj.* **-pier, -pi·est** 1 sharp; biting 2 cold in a stinging way

nir·vana (nir vä′nə, nər-; -vän′ə) *n.* 〖< Sans 〗 [*also* N-] 1 *Buddhism* the state of perfect blessedness achieved by the absorption of the soul into the supreme spirit 2 great bliss

nit (nit) *n.* 〖OE *hnitu*〗 1 the egg of a louse or similar insect 2 a young louse, etc.

ni·ter (nīt′ər) *n.* 〖< Gr *nitron* 〗 potassium nitrate or sodium nitrate, used in making explosives, fertilizers, etc.; saltpeter Also [Chiefly Brit.] **ni′tre**

nit-picking (nit′pik′iŋ) *adj., n.* paying too much attention to petty details; niggling —**nit′-pick′er** *n.*

ni·trate (nī′trāt′) *n.* a salt of nitric acid, as sodium nitrate — *vt.* **-trat·ed, -trat·ing** to combine with nitric acid or, esp., to make into a nitrate

ni·tric acid (nī′trik) a colorless, corrosive acid containing nitrogen

nitro·cel·lu·lose (nī′trō sel′yo͞o lōs′) *n.* a substance obtained by treating cellulose with nitric acid, used in making explosives, lacquers, etc.

ni·tro·gen (nī′trə jən) *n.* 〖< Fr: see NITER & -GEN 〗 a colorless, odorless gaseous chemical element forming nearly four fifths of the atmosphere —**ni·trog′enous** (-träj′ə nəs) *adj.*

nitro·glyc·er·in or **nitro·glyc·er·ine** (nī′trō glis′ər in, -trə-) *n.* a thick, explosive oil, prepared by treating glycerin with nitric and sulfuric acids: used in making dynamite

ni·trous oxide (nī′trəs) a colorless gas containing nitrogen, used as an anesthetic and in aerosols

nitty-gritty (nit′ē grit′ē) *n.* [Slang] the actual, basic facts, issues, etc.

nit′wit′ *n.* 〖? NIT + WIT[1] 〗 a stupid or silly person

nix (niks) *adv.* 〖Ger *nichts* 〗 [Slang] 1 no 2 not at all — *interj.* [Slang] 1 stop! 2 I forbid, disagree, etc. — *vt.* [Slang] to disapprove of or put a stop to

no (nō) *adv.* 〖< OE *ne a*, not ever 〗 1 not at all [*no worse*] 2 nay; not so: used to deny, refuse, or disagree — *adj.* not any; not one [*no errors*] — *n., pl.* **noes** or **nos** 1 a refusal or denial 2 a negative vote or voter

no. 〖L *numero*〗 number

Noah (nō′ə) *Bible* the patriarch commanded by God to build the ARK (sense 3)

No·bel·ist (nō bel′ist) *n.* one who has won a Nobel prize

No·bel prizes (nō bel′) 〖after A. B. *Nobel*, 19th-c. Swed inventor who established them 〗 annual international prizes given for distinction in physics, chemistry, economics, medicine, and literature, and for promoting peace

no·bil·ity (nō bil′ə tē) *n., pl.* **-ties** 1 a being noble 2 high rank in society 3 the class of people of noble rank

no·ble (nō′bəl) *adj.* **-bler, -blest** 〖< L *nobilis*, well-known 〗 1 famous or renowned 2 having high moral qualities 3 excellent 4 grand; stately 5 of high hereditary rank — *n.* one having hereditary rank or title —**no′ble· ness** *n.* —**no′bly** (nō′blē) *adv.*

no′ble·man (-mən) *n., pl.* **-men** a member of the nobility; peer —**no′ble·wom′an**, *pl.* **-wom′en**, *n.fem.*

no·blesse oblige (nō bles′ ō blēzh′) 〖Fr, nobility obliges 〗 the inferred obligation of people of high rank to behave nobly toward others

no·body (nō′bäd′ē, -bud′ē, -bəd ē) *pron.* not anybody; no one — *n., pl.* **-ies** a person of no importance

noc·tur·nal (näk tur′nəl) *adj.* 〖< L *nox*, night 〗 1 of the night 2 functioning, done, or active during the night — **noc·tur′nally** *adv.*

noc·turne (näk′turn′) *n.* 〖Fr 〗 a romantic or dreamy musical composition thought appropriate to night

nod (näd) *vi.* **nod′ded, nod′ding** 〖ME *nodden* 〗 1 to bend the head forward quickly, as in agreement, greeting, etc. 2 to let the head fall forward because of drowsiness — *vt.* 1 to bend (the head) forward quickly 2 to signify (assent, etc.) by doing this — *n.* a nodding

node (nōd) *n.* 〖L *nodus* 〗 1 a knot; knob; swelling 2 that part of a stem from which a leaf starts to grow —**nodal** (nōd′l) *adj.*

nod·ule (näj′o͞ol′) *n.* 〖L *nodulus* 〗 a small knot or rounded lump

Noel or **Noël** (nō el′) *n.* 〖Fr < L *natalis*, natal 〗 CHRIST-MAS

no′-fault′ *adj.* 1 designating a form of automobile insurance in which those injured collect damages without blame being fixed 2 designating a form of divorce granted without blame being charged

nog·gin (näg′in) *n.* 〖prob. < Brit dial. *nog*, strong ale 〗 1 a small cup or mug 2 [Colloq.] the head

no′-good′ *adj.* [Slang] contemptible

noise (noiz) *n.* 〖< OFr 〗 1 clamor; din 2 sound; esp., any loud, disagreeable sound — *vt.* **noised, nois′ing** to spread (a report, rumor, etc.)

■ THESAURUS ■

nip[1] *v.* nibble, snap, munch; see BITE 1, PINCH.

nipple *n.* mamilla, mammary gland, teat; see BREAST 2.

nitwit *n.* blockhead, dummy*, dimwit*; see FOOL.

no *a., interj.* absolutely not, not at all, by no means, the answer is in the negative, not by any means, none, *nyet* (Russian), nix*; see also NEGATIVE 2, NEITHER, NEVER.

nobility *n.* [*Usually used with "the"*] ruling class, gentry, peerage; see ARISTOCRACY, ROYALTY.

noble *a.* 1 [Possessing an exalted mind and character] generous, princely, magnanimous, magnificent, courtly, lofty, elevated, splendid, excellent, supreme, eminent, lordly, dignified, great, good, superior, great-hearted, high-minded, honorable, distinguished, liberal, tolerant, gracious, humane, benevolent, charitable, sympathetic, bounteous, brilliant, extraordinary, remarkable, devoted, heroic, resolute, valorous;

see also WORTHY.—*Ant.* CORRUPT, low, ignoble. 2 [Possessing excellent qualities or properties] meritorious, virtuous, worthy, valuable, useful, first-rate, refined, cultivated, chivalrous, trustworthy, candid, liberal, gracious, princely, magnanimous, generous, sincere, truthful, constant, faithful, upright, honest, warm-hearted, true, incorruptible, distinctive, reputable, respectable, admirable, good, aboveboard, fair, just, estimable; see also EXCELLENT, PERFECT 2.—*Ant.* POOR, inferior, second-rate. 3 [Belonging to the nobility] titled, aristocratic, patrician, highborn, wellborn, blue-blooded, of gentle birth, imperial, lordly, high-bred, princely, of good breed, kingly; see also ROYAL.—*Ant.* COMMON, plebeian, lowborn. 4 [Grand] stately, impressive, imposing; see GRAND.

nobly *a.* 1 [Majestically] aristocratically, illustriously, royally; see GENEROUSLY 2, POLITELY. 2 [Honorably] fairly, respectably, honestly; see

JUSTLY 1.

nobody *n.* 1 [No one at all] no person, no one, not anybody; see NONE 1. 2 [A person of little importance] upstart, cipher, nonentity, whippersnapper, no great shakes*, nix*, zero.

nocturnal *a.* at night, night-loving, nighttime; see LATE 4, NIGHTLY.

nod *n.* dip, inclination, greeting; see GREETING.

nod *v.* 1 [To make a nodding movement] assent, sign, signal, greet, bend, curtsy, incline the head, bow, nod yes, acquiesce, consent, respond, fall in with, concur, acknowledge, recognize; see also AGREE, APPROVE.— *Ant.* DENY, dissent, disagree. 2 [To become sleepy or inattentive] drowse, nap, drift off; see SLEEP.

noise *n.* 1 [A sound] sound, something heard, impact of sound waves. *Kinds of noises include the following:—brief, loud noises:* bang, boom, crash, thud, blast, blast off, roar, bellow, blat, shout, peal, cry,

noise'less *adj.* with little or no noise; very quiet —**noise'lessly** *adv.*

noi·some (noi'səm) *adj.* ⟦see ANNOY & -SOME¹⟧ **1** injurious to health; harmful **2** foul-smelling

noisy (noiz'ē) *adj.* **-i·er, -i·est 1** making noise **2** full of noise —**nois'i·ly** *adv.* —**nois'i·ness** *n.*

no-load (nō'lōd') *adj.* designating mutual funds charging no commissions on sales

no·mad (nō'mad') *n.* ⟦< Gr *nemein*, to pasture⟧ **1** any of a people having no permanent home, but moving about constantly, as in search of pasture **2** a wanderer —**no·mad'ic** *adj.*

no man's land the unoccupied region separating opposing armies

nom de plume (näm' də plōōm') ⟦Fr⟧ a pen name

nomen·cla·ture (nō'mən klā'chər) *n.* ⟦< L *nomen*, a name + *calare*, to call⟧ the system of names used in a science, etc. or for the parts of a device

-nom·ics (näm'iks) *combining form* economics Also **-omics**

nomi·nal (näm'ə nəl) *adj.* ⟦< L *nomen*, a name⟧ **1** of or like a name **2** in name only, not in fact *[a nominal leader]* **3** relatively very small *[a nominal fee]* —**nom'i·nally** *adv.*

nom'i·nate (-nāt') *vt.* **-nat·ed, -nat·ing** ⟦< L *nomen*, a name⟧ **1** to appoint to an office or position **2** to name as a candidate for election —**nom'i·na'tion** *n.*

nom'i·na·tive (-nə tiv) *n. Gram.* the case of the subject of a verb

nom'i·nee' (-ə nē') *n.* a person who is nominated

non- ⟦< L *non*, not⟧ *prefix* not: less emphatic than IN-² and UN-, which often give a word a strong opposite or reverse meaning The terms in the following list will be understood if "not" is used before the meaning of the base word:

nonabrasive	noncontroversial
nonabsorbent	nonconvertible
nonactive	noncorroding
nonaddictive	noncorrosive
nonadministrative	noncriminal
nonaggression	noncritical
nonaggressive	noncrystalline
nonalcoholic	noncumulative
nonallergenic	nondeductible
nonallergic	nondelivery
nonassignable	nondepartmental
nonathletic	nondepreciating
nonattendance	nondestructive
nonautomotive	nondetachable
nonavailability	nondisciplinary
nonbasic	nondiscrimination
nonbeliever	nondramatic
nonbelligerent	nondrinker
nonbreakable	nondrying
non-Catholic	noneducational
nonchargeable	noneffective
nonclerical	nonenforceable
nonclinical	non-English
noncollectable	nonessential
noncombustible	nonexchangeable
noncommercial	nonexclusive
noncommunicable	nonexempt
non-Communist	nonexistence
noncompeting	nonexistent
noncompetitive	nonexplosive
noncompliance	nonfactual
noncomplying	nonfading
nonconducting	nonfat
nonconforming	nonfatal
nonconsecutive	nonfiction
nonconstructive	nonfictional
noncontagious	nonflammable
noncontributory	nonflowering
	nonfluctuating

nonflying	nonreciprocal
nonfreezing	nonreciprocating
nonfunctional	nonrecoverable
nongovernmental	nonrecurring
nongranular	nonredeemable
nonhazardous	nonrefillable
nonhereditary	nonreligious
nonhuman	nonrenewable
nonidentical	nonrepresentational
noninclusive	nonresidential
nonindependent	nonresidual
nonindustrial	nonresistant
noninfected	nonreturnable
noninflammatory	nonrhythmic
noninflationary	nonrigid
nonintellectual	nonsalaried
noninterchangeable	nonscientific
noninterference	nonscoring
nonintoxicating	nonseasonal
nonirritating	nonsecular
nonjudicial	nonsensitive
nonlegal	nonsmoker
nonliterary	nonsocial
nonmagnetic	nonspeaking
nonmalignant	nonspecializing
nonmember	nonspiritual
nonmigratory	nonstaining
nonmilitant	nonstandard
nonmilitary	nonsticking
nonnarcotic	nonstrategic
nonnegotiable	nonstriking
nonnumerical	nonstructural
nonobjective	nonsuccessive
nonobligatory	nonsupporting
nonobservance	nonsustaining
nonobservant	nonsympathizer
nonoccupational	nontaxable
nonoccurrence	nontechnical
nonofficial	nontheatrical
nonoperational	nonthinking
nonoperative	nontoxic
nonpaying	nontransferable
nonpayment	nontransparent
nonperishable	nontropical
nonphysical	nonuniform
nonpoisonous	nonuser
nonpolitical	nonvenomous
nonporous	nonverbal
nonprejudicial	nonvirulent
nonproductive	nonvocal
nonprofessional	nonvocational
nonprofitable	nonvoter
nonpunishable	nonvoting
nonracial	nonwhite
nonreactive	nonyielding

nona- *combining form* nine

non·age (nän'ij, nōn'ij) *n.* ⟦see NON- & AGE⟧ the state of being under full legal age

nona·genar·ian (nän'ə jə ner'ē ən) *n.* ⟦< L *nonaginta*, ninety⟧ a person between the ages of 90 and 100

non'aligned' *adj.* not aligned with either side in a conflict of power, especially power politics —**non'align'ment** *n.*

nonce (näns) *n.* ⟦by merging of ME (*for then*) *ones*, lit., (for the) once⟧ the present use, occasion, or time: chiefly in **for the nonce**

nonce word a word coined and used for a single occasion

non·cha·lant (nän'shə länt') *adj.* ⟦Fr, ult. < L *non*, not + *calere*, be warm⟧ **1** without warmth or enthusiasm **2** casually indifferent —**non'cha·lance'** *n.* —**non'cha·lant'ly** *adv.*

non·com (nän'käm') *n.* [Colloq.] short for NONCOMMISSIONED OFFICER

non·com·bat·ant (nän'käm'bə tənt) *n.* **1** a member of

THESAURUS

yelp, squawk, blare, clang; ring, shot, sonic boom, jangle, eruption, explosion, detonation; *brief, faint noises:* peep, squeak, squawk, cackle, cluck, tweet, clink, tinkle, pop, whisper, stage whisper, sigh, splash, swish, sob, whine, whimper, plunk, plop, pat, ping, rustle, murmur, beat, stir, purr, still small voice; *continuing noises:* reverberation, ringing, tone, tune, clanging, tinkling, resonance, cacophony, rattle, whir, whistle, dissonance, discord, shouting, roaring, bellowing, rumble, rumbling, grunting, murmuring, drone, droning, thundering, whine, screeching, screaming, banging, clanging, hum, humming, laughing, chuckle, swishing, rustling, ripple, strumming, beating, pattering, clattering, trilling,

whinneying, neighing, cawing, cackling. **2** [Clamor] racket, fracas, din; see UPROAR.

noiseless *a.* **1** [Containing no noise] silent, still, soundless; see QUIET. **2** [Making no noise] voiceless, speechless, wordless; see DUMB 1, MUTE 1.

noiselessly *a.* inaudibly, quietly, without a sound; see SILENTLY.

noisy *a.* clamorous, vociferous, boisterous; see LOUD 1, 2.

nomad *n.* wanderer, migrant, vagabond; see TRAVELER.

nominal *a.* professed, pretended, in effect only; see GIVEN, NAMED 1.

nominate *v.* propose as a candidate, designate for election, put up; see CHOOSE, DECIDE.

nominated *a.* designated, called,

suggested; see APPROVED, NAMED 2.

nomination *n.* naming, designation, proposal; see APPOINTMENT 1.

nonchalance *n.* apathy, disregard, insouciance; see INDIFFERENCE.

nonchalant *a.* **1** [Cool and casual] uncaring, unconcerned, untroubled, apathetic, cold, frigid, unfeeling, impassive, imperturbable, easygoing, listless, lackadaisical, unruffled, lukewarm, composed, collected, aloof, detached, calm, serene, placid, disinterested, easy, effortless, light, smooth, neutral; see also DIFFERENT.—*Ant.* WARM, ardent, enthusiastic. **2** [Careless] neglectful, negligent, trifling; see CARELESS.

nonchalantly *a.* coolly, indifferently, casually; see CALMLY.

the armed forces not engaged in actual combat **2** any civilian in wartime

non'com·mis'sioned officer an enlisted person of any of various grades in the armed forces: in the U.S. Army, from corporal to sergeant major inclusive

non'com·mit'tal (-kə mit'l) *adj.* not committing one to a definite point of view or course of action

non com·pos men·tis (nän' käm pōs men'tis) 〖L〗 *Law* not of sound mind

non'con·duc'tor *n.* a substance that does not readily transmit sound, heat, or, esp., electricity

non'con·form'ist *n.* **1** one who does not conform to prevailing attitudes, behavior, etc. **2** [N-] a British Protestant who is not Anglican —**non'con·form'i·ty** *n.*

non·dairy (nän'der'ē) *adj.* containing no milk or milk products

non·de·script (nän'di skript', nän'di skript') *adj.* 〖< *non*, not + *describere*, describe〗 belonging to no definite class or type; hard to classify or describe

none (nun) *pron.* 〖< OE *ne*, not + *an*, one〗 **1** no one; not anyone **2** [*with pl. v.*] not any [there are *none* on the table] —*n.* not any (of); no part [I want *none* of it] —*adv.* not at all [*none* the worse for wear]

non·en·ti·ty (nän'en'tə tē) *n., pl.* **-ties** a person or thing of little or no importance

none·such (nun'such') *n.* a person or thing unrivaled or unequaled

none·the·less (nun'thə les') *adv.* nevertheless Also **none the less**

non·event (nän'ē vent') *n.* [Colloq.] an event that is boring or deliberately staged, as for publicity

non'fer'rous (-fer'əs) *adj.* **1** not containing iron **2** designating or of metals other than iron

non'inter·ven'tion (-in'tər ven'shən) *n.* refusal to interfere; esp., a refusal by one nation to interfere in another's affairs

non'judg·men'tal *adj.* without bias; objective

non'met'al *n.* a chemical element, as oxygen, carbon, nitrogen, fluorine, etc., lacking the characteristics of a metal —**non'me·tal'lic** *adj.*

no'-non'sense *adj.* not indulging in or tolerating nonsense, impracticality, etc.

non·pa·reil (nän'pə rel') *adj.* 〖Fr < *non*, not + *pareil*, equal〗 unequaled; unrivaled; peerless

non'par'ti·san *adj.* not partisan; esp., not connected with any single political party

non·plus (nän'plüs', nän'plus') *vt.* **-plused'** or **-plussed'**, **-plus'ing** or **-plus'sing** 〖L *non*, not + *plus*, more〗 to greatly perplex or bewilder

non'prof'it *adj.* not intending or intended to earn a profit

non'res'i·dent *adj.* not residing in the locality where one works, attends school, etc. —*n.* a nonresident person

non're·stric'tive (-ri strik'tiv) *adj.* *Gram.* designating a clause, phrase, or word felt as not essential to the sense, usually set off by commas (Ex.: John, *who is tall*, is Bill's brother)

non'sched'uled *adj.* licensed for commercial air flights as demand warrants rather than on a schedule

non'sec·tar'ian (-sek ter'ē ən) *adj.* not confined to any specific religion

non·sense (nän'sens', -səns) *n.* words, actions, etc. that are absurd or meaningless —*interj.* how absurd!: an exclamation —**non·sen'si·cal** *adj.*

non se·qui·tur (nän' sek'wi tər) 〖L, it does not follow〗 **1** *Logic* a conclusion which does not follow from the premises **2** a remark having no bearing on what has just been said

non'skid' *adj.* having a surface so constructed as to reduce slipping or skidding: said of a tire, flooring, etc.

non'-start'er *n.* [Slang] **1** an expected occurrence, etc. that fails to materialize **2** a worthless idea

non'stop' *adj., adv.* without a stop

non'sup·port' *n.* failure to provide for a legal dependent

non'un'ion *adj.* **1** not belonging to a labor union **2** not made or serviced under labor-union conditions **3** refusing to recognize a labor union

non'vi·o·lence *n.* an abstaining from violence, as in efforts to obtain civil rights —**non'vi·o·lent** *adj.*

noo·dle[1] (nōod''l) *n.* 〖< ?〗 [Slang] the head

noo·dle[2] (nōod''l) *n.* 〖Ger *nudel*〗 a flat, narrow strip of dry dough, usually made with egg and served in soup, etc.

nook (nook) *n.* 〖ME *nok*〗 **1** a corner, esp. of a room **2** a small, secluded spot

noon (nōon) *n.* 〖< L *nona* (*hora*), ninth (hour)〗 twelve o'clock in the daytime; midday —*adj.* of or at noon Also **noon'time'** or **noon'day'**

no one not anybody; nobody

noose (nōos) *n.* 〖< L *nodus*, knot〗 a loop formed in a rope, etc., by means of a slipknot so that the loop tightens as the rope is pulled

nor (nôr) *conj.* 〖ME < *ne-*, not, + *or*, other〗 and not; and not either [I can neither go *nor* stay]

Nor·dic (nôr'dik) *adj.* 〖OE *north*, north〗 of a Caucasoid physical type exemplified by the tall, blond Scandinavians

norm (nôrm) *n.* 〖L *norma*, rule〗 a standard or model; esp., the standard of achievement of a large group

nor·mal (nôr'məl) *adj.* **1** conforming with an accepted standard or norm; natural; usual **2** average in intelligence, etc. —*n.* **1** anything normal **2** the usual state, amount, etc. —**nor'malcy** (-sē) or **nor·mal'ity** (-mal'ə tē) *n.* —**nor'mal·ize', -ized', -iz'ing,** *vt., vi.* —**nor'mali·za'tion** *n.*

nor'mally *adv.* **1** in a normal manner **2** under normal circumstances

Nor·man (nôr'mən) *n.* 〖< OFr〗 **1** any of the people of Normandy who conquered England in 1066 **2** a native of Normandy, France —*adj.* of Normandy, the Normans, their language, etc.

norma·tive (nôr'mə tiv) *adj.* of or establishing a norm

Norse (nôrs) *adj., n.* 〖prob. < Du *noord*, north〗 **1** SCANDINAVIAN **2** (of) the Scandinavian group of languages —**the Norse** the Scandinavians

Norse'man (-mən) *n., pl.* **-men** any of the ancient Scandinavian peoples

north (nôrth) *n.* 〖OE〗 **1** the direction to the right of one facing the sunset (0° or 360° on the compass) **2** a region

---

◼ THESAURUS ◼

nonconformist *n.* rebel, eccentric, maverick, malcontent, dissenter, demonstrator, hippie, protester, dissident, a different breed of cat; see also RADICAL.

nonconformity *n.* dissent, opposition, difference; see INDIVIDUALITY.

none *pron.* **1** [No person] no one, not one, not anyone, no one at all, not a person, not a soul, neither one nor the other; see also NEITHER.— *Ant.* MANY, some, a few. **2** [No thing] not a thing, not anything, not any; see NOTHING.

nonetheless *a.* nevertheless, in spite of that, anyway; see ALTHOUGH, BUT 1.

nonexistent *a.* missing, unsubstantial, fictitious; see IMAGINARY, UNREAL.

no-nonsense *a.* matter-of-fact, serious, purposeful, dedicated, resolute; see also PRACTICAL.

nonpartisan *a.* unprejudiced, unbiased, independent; see NEUTRAL 1.

nonpayment *n.* failure, delinquency, bankruptcy; see DEFAULT.

nonproductive *a.* unproductive, waste, not producing; see IDLE, USELESS 1.

nonprofit *a.* charitable, altruistic, humane; see GENEROUS.

nonresident *a.* absentee, out-of-state, living abroad; see FOREIGN.

nonsense *n.* **1** [Matter that has no meaning] balderdash, rubbish, trash, scrawl, inanity, senselessness, buncombe, idle chatter, prattle, rant, bombast, claptrap, bull*, baloney*, hooey*, bunk*, poppycock*, guff*, hot air*. **2** [Frivolous behavior] unsteadiness, flightiness, stupidity, thoughtlessness, fickleness, foolishness, giddiness, rashness, infatuation, extravagance, imprudence, madness, irrationality, senselessness, inconsistency, shallowness.—*Ant.* CONSIDERATION, steadiness, thoughtfulness. **3** [Pure fun] absurdity, jest, joke; see FUN.

nonstop *a.* uninterrupted, unbroken, continuous; see CONSTANT.

nonviolent *a.* passive, resistant, without violence; see CALM 1, QUIET.

nook *n.* niche, cubbyhole, cranny; see HOLE 1.

noon *n.* noontime, noontide, noonday, midday, twelve noon, meridian, noon hour; see also TIME 1, 2.

no one *pron.* no man, not one, nobody; see NEITHER, NONE 1.

noose *n.* hitch, running knot, lasso; see KNOT 1, ROPE.

nor *conj.* and not, not any, not either, not one, nor yet; see also NEITHER.

normal *a.* **1** [Usual] ordinary, run-of-the-mill, typical; see COMMON 1, CONVENTIONAL 1, 3. **2** [Regular] routine, orderly, methodical; see REGULAR 3. **3** [Sane] lucid, wholesome, right-minded; see RATIONAL, REASONABLE, SANE 1. **4** [Showing no abnormal bodily condition] in good health, whole, sound; see HEALTHY.

normally *a.* usually, commonly, in accordance with the norm; see FREQUENTLY, REGULARLY.

north *a.* **1** [Situated to the north] northward, northern, in the north, on the north side of, northerly, in or toward this direction — *adj.* **1** in, of, toward, or facing the north **2** from the north *[a north wind]* — *adv.* in or toward the north

north·east' *n.* **1** the direction halfway between north and east **2** a region in or toward this direction — *adj.* **1** in, of, or toward the northeast **2** from the northeast — *adv.* in, toward, or from the northeast —**north'east'erly** *adj., adv.* —**north'east'ern** *adj.* —**north'east'ward** *adj., adv.* —**north'east'wards** *adv.*

north'erly (-lē) *adj., adv.* **1** toward the north **2** from the north

north·ern (nôr'thərn) *adj.* **1** in, of, or toward the north **2** from the north

north'erner *n.* a native or inhabitant of the north

northern lights [*also* N- L-] the aurora borealis

North Pole the northern end of the earth's axis

North Star POLARIS

north'ward (-wərd) *adv., adj.* toward the north Also **north'wards** *adv.*

north'west' *n.* **1** the direction halfway between north and west **2** a region in or toward this direction — *adj.* **1** in, of, or toward the northwest **2** from the northwest — *adv.* in, toward, or from the northwest —**north'west'ern** *adj., adv.* —**north'west'ward** *adj., adv.* —**north'west'wards** *adv.*

Norw. **1** Norway **2** Norwegian

Nor·we·gian (nôr wē'jən) *n.* **1** the language of Norway **2** a native or inhabitant of Norway — *adj.* of Norway, its people, language, etc.

nose (nōz) *n.* [[OE *nosu*]] **1** the part of the face above the mouth, having two openings for breathing and smelling; in animals, the snout, muzzle, etc. **2** the sense of smell **3** anything like a nose in shape or position — *vt.* **nosed, nos'ing 1** to discover as by smell **2** to nuzzle **3** to push (a way, etc.) with the front forward — *vi.* **1** to pry inquisitively **2** to move forward —**look down one's nose at** [Colloq.] to be disdainful of —**nose out 1** to defeat by a very small margin **2** to discover, as by smelling —**on the nose** [Slang] precisely; exactly —**turn up one's nose at** to sneer at; scorn

nose'bleed' *n.* a bleeding from the nose

nose cone the cone-shaped foremost part of a rocket or missile

nose dive 1 a swift, steep downward plunge of an airplane, nose first **2** any sudden, sharp drop, as in profits — **nose'-dive', -dived', -div'ing,** *vi.*

nose drops medication administered through the nose with a dropper

nose·gay (nōz'gā') *n.* [[NOSE + GAY (obs. sense "bright object")]] a small bouquet

nos·tal·gia (näs tal'jə) *n.* [[< Gr *nostos*, a return + -ALGIA]] a longing for something far away or long ago —**nos·tal'gic** (-jik) *adj.*

nos·tril (näs'trəl) *n.* [[< OE *nosu*, the nose + *thyrel*, a hole]] either of the external openings of the nose

nos·trum (näs'trəm) *n.* [[L, ours]] **1** a quack medicine **2** a panacea

nosy or **nosey** (nō'zē) *adj.* **-i·er, -i·est** [Colloq.] prying; inquisitive

not (nät) *adv.* [[< ME *nought*]] in no manner, degree, etc.: a word expressing negation or the idea of *no*

no·table (nōt'ə bəl) *adj.* [[< L *notare*, to note]] worthy of notice; remarkable; outstanding — *n.* a person of distinction —**no'tably** *adv.*

no·ta·rize (nōt'ə rīz') *vt.* **-rized', -riz'ing** to certify or attest (a document) as a notary public

no'tary (-rē) *n., pl.* **-ries** [[< L *notare*, to note]] an official authorized to certify or attest documents, take affidavits, etc. In full **notary public**

no·ta·tion (nō tā'shən) *n.* **1** the use of signs or symbols to represent words, quantities, etc. **2** any such system of signs or symbols, as in mathematics, music, etc. **3** a brief note or noting

notch (näch) *n.* [prob. < ME *(a)n oche*, a notch] **1** a V-shaped cut in an edge or surface **2** a narrow pass with steep sides **3** [Colloq.] a step; degree — *vt.* to cut a notch or notches in

note (nōt) *n.* [[< L *nota*, a mark]] **1** a distinguishing feature *[a note of sadness]* **2** importance, distinction, etc. *[a person of note]* **3** a brief writing to aid the memory; memorandum **4** a comment or explanation; annotation **5** notice; heed *[worthy of note]* **6** a short, informal letter **7** a written acknowledgment of a debt **8** a cry or call, as of a bird **9** *Music a)* a tone of definite pitch *b)* a symbol for a tone, indicating its duration and pitch — *vt.* **not'ed, not'ing 1** to heed; observe **2** to set down in writing **3** to mention particularly —**compare notes** to exchange views; discuss

note'book' *n.* a book in which notes, or memorandums, are kept

noted (nōt'id) *adj.* distinguished; renowned; eminent

note'wor'thy *adj.* worthy of note; outstanding; remarkable —**note'wor'thi·ness** *n.*

noth·ing (nuth'iŋ) *n.* [[OE *na thing*]] **1** no thing; not anything **2** nothingness **3** a thing that does not exist **4** a person or thing considered of little or no importance **5** a zero; cipher — *adv.* not at all; in no way —**for nothing 1** free **2** in vain **3** without reason

---

THESAURUS

northmost, northernmost, toward the North Pole. **2** [Moving toward the north] northerly, northbound, northward, to the north, headed north, in a northerly direction; see also SOUTH 2. **3** [Coming from the north] northerly, southbound, headed south, out of the north, moving toward the equator, moving toward the South Pole; see also SOUTH 3. **4** [Associated with the north] polar, frozen, boreal; see COLD 1.

north *n.* the Barrens, tundra, northern section, northland, Northern Hemisphere, the north country, the north woods, Arctic regions, polar regions, the frozen north, land of ice and snow; see also DIRECTION 1.

northeast *a.* NE, northeastern, northeasterly, northeastward, northnortheast, northeast by east, northeast by north; see also DIRECTION 1.

northerly *a.* boreal, northern, polar; see NORTH 2.

northern *a.* northerly, arctic, polar; see NORTH 1.

northwest *a.* NW, nor'west, northwestern, northwesterly, northwestward, northwest by west, northnorth-west, northwest by north; see also DIRECTION 1.

nose *n.* **1** [The organ of smell] nasal organ, nasal cavity, nares, nasal passages, nostrils, olfactory nerves, snoot*, beak, bill; see also ORGAN 2. **2** [A projection] snout, nozzle, muzzle;

see BEAK. —**by a nose** by a very small margin, too close for comfort, barely; see ALMOST. —**look down one's nose at*** disdain, snub, be disgusted by; see ABUSE. —**on the nose*** precisely, to the point, correctly; see ACCURATE. —**turn up one's nose at** sneer at, refuse, scorn; see ABUSE. —**under one's very nose** in plain sight, visible, at one's fingertips; see OBVIOUS 1.

nostalgia *n.* remorse, wistfulness, sentimentality; see LONELINESS.

nostalgic *a.* lonesome, regretful, sentimental; see HOMESICK, LONELY.

nosy *a.* snoopy*, snooping*, unduly curious; see INQUISITIVE, INTERESTED 2.

not *a.* no, non-, un-, in-; see also NEGATIVE 2.

notable *a.* distinguished, important, striking; see FAMOUS, UNUSUAL 1.

notch *n.* nock, nick, indent; see CUT 1, DENT, GROOVE.

notch *v.* indent, nick, chisel; see CUT 1, DENT.

notched *a.* nicked, jagged, sawtoothed; see IRREGULAR 4, ROUGH 1.

note *n.* **1** [A representation] sign, figure, mark; see REPRESENTATION. **2** [A brief record] notation, jotting, scribble, reminder, scrawl, annotation, agenda, entry, memorandum, journal, inscription, calendar, diary; see also NOTES, SUMMARY. **3** [A brief communication] dispatch, epistle,

announcement; see LETTER 2. **4** [A musical tone, or its symbol] tone, key, scale, shape note, interval, degree, step, sharp, flat, natural; see also MUSIC 1.

note *v.* **1** [To notice] remark, heed, perceive; see REGARD 1, SEE 1. **2** [To record] write down, enter, transcribe; see RECORD 1, WRITE.

notebook *n.* memorandum book, record book, diary; see JOURNAL 1, RECORD 1.

noted *a.* well-known, celebrated, notorious; see FAMOUS.

notes *n.* commentary, interpretation, explanation, findings, recordings, field notes, observations; see also DATA, RECORDS. —**compare notes** exchange views, confer, go over; see DISCUSS.

nothing *n.* not anything, no thing, trifle, blank, emptiness, nothingness, nonexistence, inexistence, nonbeing, nullity, zero, extinction, oblivion, obliteration, annihilation, nonentity; neither hide nor hair. —**for nothing 1** gratis, without cost, unencumbered; see FREE 4. **2** in vain, for naught, emptily; see UNNECESSARY. —**have nothing on** have no evidence, be without proof, be only guessing; see GUESS. —**in nothing flat** in almost no time at all, speedily, rapidly; see QUICKLY. —**think nothing of** minimize, underplay, disregard; see NEGLECT 1.

noth'ing·ness *n.* 1 nonexistence 2 insignificance 3 unconsciousness or death

no·tice (nōt'is) *n.* ⟦see NOTE⟧ 1 announcement or warning 2 a brief article about a book, play, etc. 3 a sign giving some public information, warning, etc. 4 attention; heed 5 a formal warning of intention to end an agreement or contract at a certain time — *vt.* **-ticed, -tic·ing** 1 to mention; refer to 2 to observe; pay attention to —**take notice** to become aware; observe

no'tice·able *adj.* readily noticed; conspicuous —**no'tice·ably** *adv.*

no·ti·fy (nōt'ə fī') *vt.* **-fied', -fy'ing** ⟦< L *notus*, known + *facere*, make⟧ to give notice to; inform —**no'ti·fi·ca'tion** (-fi kā'shən) *n.*

no·tion (nō'shən) *n.* ⟦see NOTE⟧ 1 a general idea 2 a belief; opinion 3 an inclination; whim 4 [*pl.*] small, useful articles, as needles, thread, etc., sold in a store —**no'tional** *adj.*

no·to·ri·ety (nōt'ə rī'ə tē) *n.* a being notorious

no·to·ri·ous (nō tôr'ē əs) *adj.* ⟦see NOTE⟧ widely known, esp. unfavorably —**no·to'ri·ous·ly** *adv.*

no'-trump' *n. Bridge* a bid to play with no suit being trumps

not·with·stand·ing (nät'with stan'diŋ) *prep.* in spite of — *adv.* nevertheless — *conj.* although

nou·gat (nō'gət) *n.* ⟦< Prov *noga*, nut⟧ a confection of sugar paste with nuts

nought (nôt) *n.* ⟦< OE *ne*, not + *awiht*, aught⟧ *Arith.* the figure zero (0)

noun (noun) *n.* ⟦< L *nomen*, a name⟧ *Gram.* a word that names or denotes a person, thing, action, etc.

nour·ish (nur'ish) *vt.* ⟦< L *nutrire*⟧ 1 to provide with substances necessary to life and growth 2 to foster; promote —**nour'ish·ing** *adj.*

nour'ish·ment (-mənt) *n.* 1 a nourishing or being nourished 2 food

nou·veau riche (nō͞o'vō rēsh') *pl.* **nou·veaux riches** (nō͞o'vō rēsh') ⟦Fr⟧ a newly rich person, esp. one lacking cultural taste, or social grace

nou·velle cuisine (nō͞o vel') ⟦Fr⟧ a style of French cooking using a minimum of fat and starch, and very fresh ingredients, often in unusual combinations

nova (nō'və) *n., pl.* **-vae** (-vē) or **-vas** ⟦< L, new⟧ a star that brightens intensely and then gradually dims

novel (näv'əl) *adj.* ⟦< L *dim.* of *novus*, new⟧ new and unusual — *n.* a relatively long fictional prose narrative

nov'el·ette' (-əl et') *n.* a short novel

nov'el·ist *n.* one who writes novels

nov'el·ize' (-īz') *vt.* **-ized', -iz'ing** to make into or like a novel; specif., to use (a film script) as the basis of a novel

nov'elty (-tē) *n., pl.* **-ties** 1 the quality of being novel; newness 2 something new, fresh, or unusual 3 a small, often cheap, cleverly made article: *usually used in pl.*

No·vem·ber (nō vem'bər) *n.* ⟦< L *novem*, nine: ninth month in Roman year⟧ the 11th month of the year, having 30 days: abbrev. **Nov.**

no·vena (nō vē'nə) *n.* ⟦< L *novem*, nine⟧ *R.C.Ch.* special prayers and devotions for nine days

nov·ice (näv'is) *n.* ⟦< L *novus*, new⟧ 1 a person on probation in a religious order before taking final vows 2 a person new to something; beginner

no·vi·ti·ate (nō vish'ē it) *n.* the period or state of being a novice

No·vo·cain (nō'və kān') ⟦L *nov*(*us*), new + (C)OCAIN(E)⟧ *trademark for* PROCAINE   Also sp. **Novocaine**

now (nou) *adv.* 1 a) at the present time b) at once 2 at that time; then 3 with things as they are *[now we'll never know]* — *conj.* since; seeing that — *n.* the present time *[that's all for now]* — *adj.* of the present time — **just now** recently —**now and then** (or **again**) occasionally

now'a·days' (-ə dāz') *adv.* in these days; at the present time

no·way (nō'wā') *adv.* by no means; not at all: now often **no way**, used with the force of an interjection

no·where (nō'hwer', -wer') *adv.* not in, at, or to any place —**nowhere near** not by a wide margin

no-win (nō'win') *adj.* designating or of a situation, policy, etc. that cannot lead to success no matter what measures are taken

no'wise' (-wīz') *adv.* in no manner; noway

nox·ious (näk'shəs) *adj.* ⟦< L *nocere*, to hurt⟧ harmful to health or morals; injurious or unwholesome

noz·zle (näz'əl) *n.* ⟦dim. of *nose*⟧ the spout at the end of a hose, pipe, etc.

Np *Chem. symbol for* neptunium

-n't not   Used in combination with certain verbs *[aren't]*

NT or **N.T.** New Testament

nth (enth) *adj.* of the indefinitely large or small quantity represented by *n* —**to the nth degree** to an extreme

nt. wt. net weight

nu (nō͞o, nyō͞o) *n.* the 13th letter of the Greek alphabet (N, ν)

nu·ance (nō͞o'äns') *n.* ⟦Fr < *nuer*, to shade⟧ a slight variation in tone, color, meaning, etc. —**nu'anced** *adj.*

nub (nub) *n.* ⟦var. of *knub*, knob⟧ 1 a lump or small piece 2 [Colloq.] the main point; gist

nub·bin (nub'in) *n.* ⟦dim. of prec.⟧ 1 a small ear of corn 2 a small piece

nubby (nub'ē) *adj.* **-bier, -bi·est** having a rough, knotted surface *[a nubby fabric]*

nu·bile (nō͞o'bil, -bīl') *adj.* ⟦< L *nubere*, marry⟧ 1 marriageable 2 sexually attractive   Said of a young woman

nu·clear (nō͞o'klē ər) *adj.* 1 of, like, or forming a nucleus 2 of or relating to atomic nuclei *[nuclear energy]* 3 of or

---

THESAURUS

nothingness *n.* 1 [Void] vacuum, blank, hollowness; see EMPTINESS, NOTHING. 2 [Worthlessness] pettiness, unimportance, smallness; see INSIGNIFICANCE.

notice *n.* 1 [A warning] note, notification, intimation; see SIGN 1, WARNING. 2 [An announcement] remark, comments, enlightenment; see ANNOUNCEMENT, DECLARATION, REPORT 1. —**serve notice** give warning, notify, announce; see DECLARE. —**take notice** become aware, pay attention, observe; see SEE 1.

notice *v.* mark, remark, look at; see SEE 1.

noticeable *a.* observable, appreciable, conspicuous; see OBVIOUS 1.

noticed *a.* seen, remarked, observed; see RECORDED.

notify *v.* declare, announce, inform; see ADVERTISE, COMMUNICATE, TELL 1.

notion *n.* 1 [Opinion] idea, assumption, sentiment; see OPINION 1, THOUGHT 2. 2 [Conception] whim, fancy, imagination; see AWARENESS, KNOWLEDGE 1.

notoriety *n.* repute, renown, name; see FAME.

notorious *a.* ill-famed, infamous, disreputable; see BAD 1.

notwithstanding *a., prep.* despite, in spite of, in any case; see ALTHOUGH, BUT 1.

noun *n.* substantive, common noun, proper noun; see LABEL, NAME 1.

nourish *v.* feed, supply, sustain; see PROVIDE 1, SUPPORT 3.

nourishing *a.* healthy, nutritious, full of vitamins; see HEALTHFUL.

nourishment *n.* nurture, nutriment, provender; see FOOD.

novel *a.* new, odd, strange; see UNIQUE, UNUSUAL 1, 2.

novel *n.* paperback, best-seller, fiction; see BOOK, STORY. *Types of novels include the following:* romance, detective story, love story, novella, adventure story, ghost story, mystery, western, science fiction, fantasy; historical, regional, naturalistic, Gothic, biographical, psychological, pornographic, satirical, adventure, etc., novel; thriller, porn*.

novelist *n.* fiction writer, fictionist, story-teller, narrative writer, writer of novels, writer of prose fiction, hack; see also AUTHOR, WRITER.

novelty *n.* 1 [The quality of being novel] recentness, modernity, freshness; see ORIGINALITY. 2 [Something popular because it is new] innovation, origination, creation; see FAD.

November *n.* autumn month, Thanksgiving season, hunting season; see MONTH.

novice *n.* beginner, learner, neophyte; see AMATEUR.

now *a.* 1 [At the present] at this time, right now, at the moment, just now, momentarily, this day, these days, here and now. 2 [In the immediate future] promptly, in a moment, in a minute; see SOON. 3 [Immediately] at once, forthwith, instantly; see IMMEDIATELY. —**now and then** (or **again**) sometimes, infrequently, occasionally; see SELDOM.

nowadays *a.* in these days, in this age, in the present age; see NOW 1.

noway *a.* not at all, on no account, by no means, not a bit of it, nowhere near, in no respect.

nowhere *a.* not anywhere, not in any place, not at any place, nowhere at all, in no place, to no place.

nozzle *n.* spout, outlet, vent; see END 4.

nuance *n.* subtlety, refinement, distinction; see DIFFERENCE 1.

nub* *n.* essence, crux, core, nitty-gritty*; see also ESSENCE 1.

nuclear bomb *n.* nuclear warhead,

operated by the use of atomic energy [*nuclear* weapons] **4** of or involving nuclear weapons [*nuclear* warfare]

nuclear energy the energy released from an atom in nuclear reactions, esp. in nuclear fission or nuclear fusion

nuclear family a basic social unit consisting of parents and their children living in one household

nuclear fission the splitting of the nuclei of atoms, accompanied by conversion of part of the mass into energy: the principle of the atomic bomb

nuclear fusion the fusion of lightweight atomic nuclei into a nucleus of heavier mass with a resultant loss in the combined mass converted into energy: the principle of the hydrogen bomb

nuclear physics the branch of physics dealing with the structure of atomic nuclei, nuclear forces, etc.

nuclear reactor a device for creating a controlled nuclear chain reaction using atomic fuel, as for the production of energy

nuclear winter a hypothetical scenario following a major nuclear war in which the atmosphere will be clouded with radioactive smoke, dust, etc. for a long time causing loss of sunlight, frigid temperatures, destruction of life forms, etc.

nu·cle·ate (nōō′klē it; *for v.,* -āt′) *adj.* having a nucleus — *vt., vi.* **-at′ed, -at′ing** to form into a nucleus —**nu′clea′tion** *n.*

nu·cle·ic acid (nōō klē′ik) any of a group of essential complex organic acids found in all living cells: the two major types are DNA and RNA

nucleo- *combining form* **1** nucleus **2** nuclear **3** nucleic acid Also **nucle-**

nu·cle·o·lus (nōō klē′ə ləs) *n., pl.* **-li′** (-lī′) ⟦< LL, dim. of L *nucleus*⟧ a conspicuous, usually spherical, dense body in the nucleus of most cells, consisting of protein and RNA

nu·cle·us (nōō′klē əs) *n., pl.* **-clei′** (-ī′) or **-cleus·es** ⟦< L, kernel⟧ **1** a central thing or part around which others are grouped; core **2** any center of growth or development **3** the central part of an atom **4** the central mass of protoplasm in a cell

nude (nōōd) *adj.* ⟦L *nudus*⟧ naked; bare — *n.* **1** a nude human figure, esp. in a work of art **2** the state of being nude [*in the nude*] —**nu′di·ty** *n.*

nudge (nuj) *vt.* **nudged, nudg′ing** ⟦< ?⟧ to push gently, esp. with the elbow, in order to get the attention of, hint slyly, etc. — *n.* a gentle push

nud·ism′ *n.* the practice or cult of going nude —**nud′ist** *n., adj.*

nu·ga·tory (nōō′gə tôr′ē) *adj.* ⟦< L *nugari*, to trifle⟧ **1** trifling; worthless **2** not operative; invalid

nug·get (nug′ət) *n.* ⟦prob. < dial. *nug*, a lump⟧ a lump; esp. of native gold

nui·sance (nōō′səns, nyōō′-) *n.* ⟦< L *nocere*, annoy⟧ an act, thing, or person causing trouble, annoyance, etc.

null (nul) *adj.* ⟦< L *nullus*, none⟧ **1** without legal force; invalid: usually in the phrase **null and void 2** amounting to naught **3** of no value, effect, etc.

nul·li·fy (nul′ə fī′) *vt.* **-fied′, -fy′ing** ⟦< L *nullus*, none +

facere, to make⟧ **1** to make legally null or valueless **2** to cancel out —**nul′li·fi·ca′tion** *n.*

numb (num) *adj.* ⟦< ME *nimen*, to take⟧ deadened; insensible — *vt.* to make numb —**numb′ly** *adv.* —**numb′ness** *n.*

num·ber (num′bər) *n.* ⟦< L *numerus*⟧ **1** a symbol or word showing how many or which one in a series (Ex.: 2, 35, four, ninth) **2** [*pl.*] ARITHMETIC **3** the sum of persons or things; total **4** *a)* [*often pl.*] many *b)* [*pl.*] numerical superiority **5** quantity **6** *a)* a single issue of a periodical *b)* a single song, dance, etc. in a program of entertainment **7** [Colloq.] a person or thing singled out [*a smart number*] **8** *Gram.* the form of a word as indicating either singular or plural — *vt.* **1** to count; enumerate **2** to give a number to **3** to include as one of a group **4** to limit the number of **5** to have or comprise; total — *vi.* to be included —**a number of** several or many; some —**beyond** (or **without**) **number** too numerous to be counted —**the numbers** an illegal lottery based on certain numbers published in newspapers: also **numbers game** (or **racket**)

num′ber·less *adj.* countless

Num·bers (num′bərz) the fourth book of the Pentateuch in the Bible: abbrev. **Num.**

numb′skull′ *n.* NUMSKULL

nu·mer·al (nōō′mər əl) *adj.* ⟦< L *numerus*, number⟧ of or denoting a number or numbers — *n.* a figure, letter, or word expressing a number

nu′mer·ate′ (-mər āt′) *vt.* **-at′ed, -at′ing** to count one by one; enumerate

nu′mera′tor (-mər āt′ər) *n.* the part of a fraction above the line

nu·mer·i·cal (nōō mer′i kəl) *adj.* **1** of, or having the nature of, number **2** in or by numbers **3** expressed by numbers —**nu·mer′i·cally** *adv.*

nu·mer·ol·ogy (nōō′mər äl′ə jē) *n.* the attributing of occult meaning to numbers, as in birth dates

nu·mer·ous (nōō′mər əs) *adj.* **1** consisting of many persons or things **2** very many

nu·mis·mat·ics (nōō′miz mat′iks, -mis-) *n.pl.* ⟦< L *numisma*, a coin⟧ [*with sing. v.*] the study or collection of coins, medals, paper money, etc. —**nu·mis′ma·tist** (-mə tist) *n.*

num·skull (num′skul′) *n.* ⟦NUM(B) + SKULL⟧ a dunce

nun (nun) *n.* ⟦< L *nonna*⟧ a woman devoted to a religious life, esp. one living in a convent under vows

nun·cio (nun′shō′, -sē ō′) *n., pl.* **-cios′** ⟦< It < L *nuntius*, messenger⟧ a papal ambassador to a foreign state

nun·nery (nun′ər ē) *n., pl.* **-ies** *old term for* CONVENT

nup·tial (nup′shəl, -chəl) *adj.* ⟦< L *nubere*, marry⟧ of marriage or a wedding — *n.* [*pl.*] a wedding

nurse (nʉrs) *n.* ⟦< L *nutrire*, nourish⟧ **1** a woman hired to care for another's children **2** a person trained to care for the sick, assist surgeons, etc. — *vt.* **nursed, nurs′ing 1** to suckle (an infant) **2** to take care of (a child, invalid,

---

THESAURUS

hydrogen bomb, H-bomb, atomic bomb, A-bomb, cobalt bomb, atomic weapon, nuclear weapon; see also ARMS.

nucleus *n.* **1** [Essence] core, gist, kernel; see ESSENCE 1, MATTER 1. **2** [Center] hub, focus, pivot; see CENTER 1.

nude *a.* stripped, unclothed, bare; see NAKED 1.

nude *n.* naked body, naked man, naked woman, nudist, pinup, model, stripper*, peeler*.

nudge *n.* tap, poke, shove; see BUMP 1, PUSH, TOUCH 2.

nudge *v.* poke, bump, tap; see PUSH 1, TOUCH 1.

nudity *n.* bareness, nudeness, undress; see NAKEDNESS.

nugget *n.* ingot, bullion, chunk; see GOLD, ROCK 1.

nuisance *n.* **1** [A bother] annoyance, vexation, bore; see TROUBLE 2. **2** [An offense against the public] breach, infraction, affront; see CRIME. **3** [An unpleasant or unwelcome person] problem child, frump, bother, holy terror*, bad egg*, insect*, louse*, pain in the neck*, poor excuse*, bum*; see also TROUBLE 1.

null *a.* invalid, vain, unsanctioned; see VOID.

numb *a.* **1** [Insensible] deadened, dead, unfeeling, numbed, asleep, senseless, anesthetized, comatose; see also PARALYZED. **2** [Insensitive] apathetic, lethargic, phlegmatic; see INDIFFERENT.

numb *v.* paralyze, stun, dull; see DEADEN.

number *n.* amount, sum total, totality, aggregate, whole, whole number, product, measurable quantity, estimate, the lot, plenty, abundance; see also QUANTITY. —**get** (or **have**) **someone's number*** discover someone's true character, find out about, know; see UNDERSTAND 1. —**someone's number is up*** someone's time to die has arrived, someone's time has come, someone's destiny is fulfilled; see DOOMED. —**without number** too numerous to be counted, innumerable, countless; see MANY.

number *v.* count, calculate, enumerate; see ADD 1, TOTAL.

numbered *a.* designated, told, enumerated, checked, specified, indicated; see also MARKED 1.

numbness *n.* deadness, anesthesia, dullness, insensitivity, insensibility, paralysis, loss of sensation.

numeral *n.* character, cipher, digit; see NUMBER.

numerical *a.* arithmetical, statistical, fractional, exponential, logarithmic, differential, integral, digital, mathematical, binary.

numerous *a.* copious, various, diverse; see INFINITE, MANY.

nun *n.* sister, religious woman, one who has taken vows, anchorite, prioress, mother superior, ecclesiastic; see also MINISTRY.

nuptials *n.* wedding, matrimony, marriage ceremony; see MARRIAGE.

nurse *n.* **1** [One who cares for the sick] attendant, male nurse, practical nurse, private nurse, registered nurse, RN, floor nurse, night nurse, day nurse, doctor's assistant, student nurse, nurse's aide, therapist, Red Cross nurse, Florence Nightingale*. **2** [One who cares for the young] nursemaid, babysitter, tutor; see ATTENDANT.

nurse *v.* attend to, aid, medicate; see HEAL, SUSTAIN 2, TEND 1, TREAT 2.

etc.) **3** to nourish, foster, etc. **4** to try to cure *[to nurse a cold]* **5** to use or handle so as to protect or conserve — *vi.* **1** to feed at the breast; suckle **2** to serve as a nurse

nurse′maid′ *n.* a woman hired to care for a child or children

nurs·ery (nʉrs′ər ē) *n., pl.* **-ies 1** a room set aside for children **2** a place where parents may temporarily leave children to be cared for **3** a place where young trees or other plants are raised for transplanting, etc.

nurs′ery·man (-mən) *n., pl.* **-men** one who owns or works in a tree nursery

nursery rhyme a poem for children

nursery school a school for children, usually three to five years of age

nursing home a residence providing care for the infirm, chronically ill, disabled, etc.

nur·ture (nʉr′chər) *n.* ⟦ < L *nutrire*, nourish ⟧ **1** food **2** training; rearing — *vt.* **-tured, -tur·ing 1** to feed or nourish **2** to train, educate, rear, etc. —**nur′turer** *n.*

nut (nut) *n.* ⟦OE *hnutu*⟧ **1** a dry, one-seeded fruit, consisting of a kernel, often edible, in a woody shell, as the walnut **2** the kernel itself **3** any hard-shell, relatively nonperishable fruit, as the peanut **4** a small metal block with a threaded hole for screwing onto a bolt, etc. **5** [Slang] *a)* a crazy or eccentric person *b)* a devotee; fan

nut′crack′er *n.* **1** an instrument for cracking nutshells **2** a crowlike bird that feeds on nuts

nut′hatch′ *n.* a small nut-eating bird with a sharp beak

nut′meat′ *n.* the kernel of a nut

nut′meg′ (-meg′) *n.* ⟦ < L *nux*, nut + LL *muscus*, musk ⟧ the aromatic seed of an East Indian tree, grated and used as a spice

nut′pick′ *n.* a small, sharp instrument for digging out the kernels of cracked nuts

nu·tria (nōō′trē ə, nyōō′-) *n.* ⟦Sp < L *lutra*, otter⟧ the soft, brown fur of a South American rodent

nu·tri·ent (nōō′trē ənt) *adj.* ⟦ < L *nutrire*, nourish ⟧ nourishing — *n.* anything nutritious

nu′tri·ment (-trə mənt) *n.* anything that nourishes; food

nu·tri·tion (nōō trish′ən) *n.* ⟦see NUTRIENT⟧ **1** the process by which an organism takes in and assimilates food **2** anything that nourishes; food **3** the study of diet and health —**nu·tri′tional** *adj.* —**nu·tri′tion·ally** *adv.* —**nu′tri·tive** (-trə tiv) *adj.*

nu·tri′tious (-trish′əs) *adj.* nourishing

nuts (nuts) *adj.* [Slang] crazy; foolish — *interj.* [Slang] an exclamation of disgust, scorn, etc.: often in the phrase **nuts to someone** (or **something**) —**be nuts about** [Slang] **1** to be greatly in love with **2** to be very enthusiastic about

nut′shell′ *n.* the shell enclosing the kernel of a nut —**in a nutshell** in concise form; in a few words

nut′ty *adj.* **-tier, -ti·est 1** containing or producing nuts **2** having a nutlike flavor **3** [Slang] *a)* very enthusiastic *b)* foolish, crazy, etc. —**nut′ti·ness** *n.*

nuz·zle (nuz′əl) *vt., vi.* **-zled, -zling** ⟦ < NOSE ⟧ **1** to push (against) or rub with the nose, snout, etc. **2** to nestle; snuggle —**nuz′zler** *n.*

NW or **N.W. 1** northwest **2** northwesterly **3** northwestern

NWT Northwest Territories

ny·lon (nī′län′) *n.* ⟦arbitrary coinage⟧ **1** an elastic, very strong, synthetic material made into fiber, yarn, bristles, etc. **2** [*pl.*] stockings made of this

nymph (nimf) *n.* ⟦ < Gr *nymphē*⟧ **1** *Gr. & Rom. Myth.* any of a group of minor nature goddesses, living in rivers, trees, etc. **2** a lovely young woman **3** the young of an insect with incomplete metamorphosis

nympho·ma·nia (nim′fō mā′nē ə, -fə-) *n.* uncontrollable desire by a woman for sexual intercourse —**nym′pho·ma′niac′** (-ak′) *adj., n.*

THESAURUS

nursery *n.* **1** [A place for children] child's room, playroom, nursery school; see SCHOOL 1. **2** [A place for plants] hothouse, hotbed, greenhouse; see BUILDING.

nurture *v.* nourish, care for, provide for; see FEED, SUSTAIN 2.

nut *n.* **1** [The dry fruit] seed, kernel, stone; see FRUIT. *Common nuts include the following:* acorn, beechnut, peanut, hazelnut, black walnut, English walnut, almond, nutmeg, pecan, filbert, coconut, pistachio, cashew, pignut, chestnut, butternut, hickory, kola nut, Brazil nut, betel nut. **2** [A threaded metal block] bur, lock nut, cap, ratchet nut; see also BOLT. **3** [*An eccentric or insane person] eccentric, fanatic, maniac; see ZEALOT.

nutriment *n.* nourishment, provisions, sustenance; see FOOD.

nutrition *n.* diet, nourishment, victuals; see FOOD, SUBSISTENCE 1.

nutritive *a.* edible, wholesome, nutritious; see HEALTHFUL.

nuts * *a.* crazy, deranged, ridiculous; see INSANE, UNUSUAL 2.

nuzzle *v.* caress, cuddle, snuggle; see NESTLE.

nylon *n.* synthetic, polyamide product; synthetic fiber; see PLASTIC.

nymph *n.* nature goddess, sprite, mermaid; see FAIRY.

o or **O** (ō) *n.*, *pl.* **o's, O's** the 15th letter of the English alphabet

O¹ (ō) *n.*, *pl.* **O's** 1 the numeral zero 2 a blood type

O² (ō) *interj.* 1 an exclamation in direct address *[O Lord!]* 2 oh

O *symbol for* 1 *Physics* ohm 2 *Chem.* oxygen

-o (ō) *suffix* 1 forming slangy words *[cheapo, freako]* 2 forming slang nouns from adjectives *[weirdo, sicko]*

O or **O.** 1 Ocean 2 Ohio 3 Old

oaf (ōf) *n.* ⟦< ON *alfr*, elf⟧ a stupid, clumsy fellow; lout — **oaf'ish** *adj.*

oak (ōk) *n.* ⟦OE *ac*⟧ 1 a large hardwood tree with nuts called *acorns* 2 its wood — *adj.* of oak —**oak'en** *adj.*

oakum (ō'kəm) *n.* ⟦< OE *a-*, out + *camb*, a comb⟧ stringy hemp fiber gotten by taking apart old ropes, used as a caulking material

oar (ôr) *n.* ⟦OE *ar*⟧ a long pole with a broad blade at one end, used in rowing —**rest on one's oars** to stop to rest —**oars'man** (ôrz'mən), *pl.* **-men, n.**

oar'lock' *n.* a device, often U-shaped, for holding an oar in place in rowing

OAS Organization of American States

oasis (ō ā'sis) *n.*, *pl.* **-ses'** (-sēz') ⟦< Gr *ōasis*⟧ a fertile place in a desert, due to the presence of water

oat (ōt) *n.* ⟦OE *ate*⟧ *[usually pl.]* 1 a hardy cereal grass 2 its edible grain —**oat'en** *adj.*

oat'cake' *n.* a thin, flat cake made of oatmeal

oath (ōth) *n.*, *pl.* **oaths** (ōthz, ōths) ⟦OE *ath*⟧ 1 a declaration based on an appeal to God that one will speak the truth, keep a promise, etc. 2 the profane use of God's name, as in anger 3 a swearword; curse

oat'meal' *n.* 1 oats crushed into meal or flakes 2 a porridge of this

ob- ⟦< L *ob*⟧ *prefix* 1 to, toward, before *[obtrude]* 2 against *[obstinate]* 3 upon, over *[obscure]* 4 completely *[obdurate]*

ob. ⟦L *obiit*⟧ he (or she) died

OB or **O.B.** 1 obstetrician 2 obstetrics

ob·bli·gato (äb'li gät'ō) *n.*, *pl.* **-tos** or **-ti** (-ē) ⟦see OBLIGE⟧ an elaborate musical accompaniment, orig. thought necessary to the performance of a piece

ob·du·rate (äb'door it) *adj.* ⟦< L *obduratus* < *ob-*, intens. + *durus*, hard⟧ 1 hardhearted 2 stubborn; obstinate — **ob'du·racy** (-ə sē) *n.* —**ob'du·rately** *adv.*

obedi·ent (ō bē'dē ənt) *adj.* obeying or willing to obey — **obe'di·ence** *n.* —**obe'di·ently** *adv.*

obei·sance (ō bā'səns, -bē'-) *n.* ⟦< OFr *obeir*, obey⟧ 1 a gesture of respect, as a bow 2 homage; deference —**obei'sant** *adj.*

ob·elisk (äb'ə lisk, ō'bə-) *n.* ⟦< Gr *obelos*, needle⟧ a tall, four-sided stone pillar tapering to its pyramidal top

O

obese (ō bēs') *adj.* ⟦< L *obesus* < *ob-* (see OB-) + *edere*, to eat⟧ very fat; stout —**obe'si·ty** (-ə tē) *n.*

obey (ō bā', ə-) *vt.* ⟦< L *obedire* < *ob-* (see OB-) + *audire*, hear⟧ 1 to carry out the orders of 2 to carry out (an order, etc.) 3 to be guided by *[to obey one's conscience]* — *vi.* to be obedient

ob·fus·cate (äb fus'kāt', äb'fəs kāt') *vt.* **-cat'ed, -cat'ing** ⟦< L *obfuscatus* < *ob-* (see OB-) + *fuscus*, dark⟧ to obscure; confuse; bewilder —**ob·fus·ca'tion** *n.*

obitu·ary (ō bich'ōō er'ē) *n.*, *pl.* **-ar'ies** ⟦< L *obire*, die⟧ a notice of someone's death, usually with a brief biography Also **obit** (ō'bit)

obj. 1 object 2 objective

ob·ject (äb'jikt; *for v.* əb jekt', äb-) *n.* ⟦< ML *objectum*, thing thrown in the way < L *objectus* < *ob-* (see OB-) + *jacere*, to throw⟧ 1 a thing that can be seen or touched 2 a person or thing to which action, feeling, etc. is directed 3 purpose; goal 4 *Gram.* a noun or substantive that receives the action of a verb or is governed by a preposition — *vt.* to state by way of objection — *vi.* to feel or express disapproval or opposition —**ob·jec'tor** *n.*

ob·jec'tion (əb jek'shən) *n.* 1 a feeling or expression of opposition or disapproval 2 a reason for objecting

ob·jec'tion·able *adj.* 1 open to objection 2 disagreeable; offensive

ob·jec'tive *adj.* 1 existing as an object or fact, independent of the mind; real 2 concerned with the realities of the thing dealt with rather than the thoughts of the artist, writer, etc. 3 without bias or prejudice 4 *Gram.* designating or of the case of an object of a preposition or verb — *n.* something aimed at —**ob·jec'tively** *adv.* —**ob·jec·tiv·ity** (äb'jek tiv'ə tē) or **ob·jec'tive·ness** *n.*

object lesson an actual or practical demonstration or exemplification of some principle

ob·jet d'art (ôb'zhä där', äb'-) *pl.* **ob'jets d'art'** (-zhä) ⟦Fr⟧ a small object of artistic value, as a vase, etc.

ob·jur·gate (äb'jər gāt') *vt.* **-gat'ed, -gat'ing** ⟦< L *objurgatus* < *ob-* (see OB-) + *jurgare*, chide⟧ to upbraid sharply; rebuke —**ob'jur·ga'tion** *n.*

ob·late (äb'lāt') *adj.* ⟦ModL *oblatus*, thrust forward⟧ *Geom.* flattened at the poles *[an oblate spheroid]*

ob·la·tion (ə blā'shən) *n.* ⟦< L *oblatus*, offered⟧ an offering or sacrifice to God or a god

---

THESAURUS

oak *n.* 1 [An oak tree] willow, laurel, casuarina; see TREE. 2 [Oak woods] hardwood, oaken wood, oak paneling; see WOOD 2.

oar *n.* pole, sweep, scull; see TOOL 1.

oasis *n.* green area, fertile area, irrigated land, watered tract, garden spot, desert garden, water hole, watering place, desert resting place; see also REFUGE 1, RETREAT 1.

oath *n.* 1 [An attestation of the truth] affirmation, declaration, affidavit, vow, sworn statement, testimony, word, contract, pledge; see also PROMISE 1.—*Ant.* DENIAL, disavowal, lie. 2 [The name of the Lord taken in vain] malediction, swearword, blasphemy; see CURSE 1.

obedience *n.* docility, submission, compliance; see WILLINGNESS.

obedient *a.* 1 [Dutiful] loyal, lawabiding, governable, resigned, devoted, respectful, controllable, attentive, obliging, willing, tractable, deferential, under the control of, at one's command, at one's beck and call, on a string*, wrapped around one's little finger*; see also FAITHFUL.—*Ant.* UNRULY, disobedient, undutiful. 2 [Docile] pliant, acquiescent, compliant; see DOCILE.

obediently *a.* dutifully, submissively, loyally; see WILLINGLY.

obese *a.* corpulent, plump, stout; see FAT.

obey *v.* submit, answer to, respond, act upon, act on, bow to, surrender, yield, perform, do, carry out, attend to orders, do what one is told, accept, consent, do what is expected of one, do one's duty, do as one says, serve, concur, assent, conform, acquiesce, mind, take orders, do one's bidding, comply, fulfill; see also AGREE.—*Ant.* REBEL, disobey, mutiny.

obfuscate *v.* obscure, muddle, confuse; see MUDDLE, CONFUSE.

object *n.* 1 [A corporeal body] article, something, gadget; see THING 1. 2 [A purpose] objective, aim, wish; see PURPOSE 1. 3 [One who receives] recipient, target, victim; see RECEIVER.

object *v.* protest, take exception to, dispute; see COMPLAIN.

objection *n.* disapproval, scruple, hesitation, question, criticism, complaint, charge, accusation, reprimand, exception, admonition, reproach, dispute, opposition, adverse comment, rejection, ban, countercharge, grievance, contradiction, censure, abuse, scolding, denunciation, lecture, disagreement, difference, disdain, insistence, condemnation, grumbling, faultfinding, reproof, dissent, insinuation, complaining, frown, blame, sarcasm, wail, groan, murmur, lament, regret, aspersion, beef*, gripe*, demurring,

reluctance, unwillingness, rejection, dislike, dissatisfaction, discontent, displeasure, low opinion, abhorrence, dubiousness; see also DOUBT.—*Ant.* PERMISSION, acceptance, desire.

objectionable *a.* 1 [Revolting] gross, repugnant, abhorrent; see OFFENSIVE 2. 2 [Undesirable] unacceptable, unsatisfactory, inexpedient; see UNDESIRABLE.

objective *a.* 1 [Existing independently of the mind] actual, external, material, scientific, sure, extrinsic, measurable, extraneous, reified, tactile, corporeal, bodily, palpable, physical, sensible, outward, outside, determinable, unchangeable, invariable; see also REAL 2.—*Ant.* MENTAL, subjective, introspective. 2 [Free from personal bias] detached, impersonal, unbiased; see ACCURATE 2, FAIR 1.

objective *n.* goal, aim, aspiration; see PURPOSE 1.

objectively *a.* impartially, indifferently, neutrally, open-mindedly, dispassionately, justly, equitably, detachedly, soberly, accurately, candidly, considerately, not subjectively, with objectivity, with impartiality, with consideration, with good judgment, without prejudice, without bias, without partiality, without passion.

ob·li·gate (äb′lə gāt′) *vt.* **-gat′ed, -gat′ing** [see OBLIGE] to bind by a contract, promise, sense of duty, etc.

ob′li·ga′tion *n.* 1 an obligating or being obligated 2 a binding contract, promise, responsibility, etc. 3 the binding power of a contract, etc. 4 a being indebted for a favor, etc.

ob·lig·a·to·ry (əb lig′ə tôr′ē, äb′lə gə-) *adj.* legally or morally binding

oblige (ə blīj′, ō-) *vt.* **obliged′, oblig′ing** [< L *obligare* < *ob-* (see OB-) + *ligare*, to bind] 1 to compel by moral, legal, or physical force 2 to make indebted for a favor; do a favor for

oblig′ing *adj.* ready to do favors; helpful —**oblig′ingly** *adv.*

ob·lique (ə blēk′, ō-) *adj.* [< L *obliquus* < *ob-* (see OB-) + *liquis*, awry] 1 slanting 2 indirect or evasive —**ob·lique′ly** *adv.* —**ob·liqui·ty** (ə blik′wə tē) or **ob·lique′ness** *n.*

ob·lit·er·ate (ə blit′ər āt′) *vt.* **-at′ed, -at′ing** [< L *obliteratus* < *ob-* (see OB-) + *littera*, a letter] 1 to blot out; efface 2 to destroy —**ob·lit′era′tion** *n.*

ob·liv·i·on (ə bliv′ē ən) *n.* [< L *oblivisci*, to forget] 1 forgetfulness 2 the condition of being forgotten

ob·liv′i·ous *adj.* forgetful or unmindful: usually with *of* or *to*

ob·long (äb′lôŋ′) *adj.* [< L *oblongus*, rather long < *ob-* (see OB-) + *longus*, long] longer than broad; specif., rectangular and longer in one direction —*n.* an oblong figure

ob·lo·quy (äb′lə kwē) *n., pl.* **-quies** [< L *obloqui* < *ob-* (see OB-) + *loqui*, speak] 1 widespread censure or abuse 2 disgrace or infamy resulting from this

ob·nox·ious (əb näk′shəs, äb-) *adj.* [< L *obnoxiosus* < *ob-* (see OB-) + *noxa*, harm] very unpleasant; offensive —**ob·nox′iously** *adv.* —**ob·nox′ious·ness** *n.*

oboe (ō′bō) *n.* [< Fr *haut*, high (pitch) + *bois*, wood] a double-reed woodwind instrument having a high, penetrating tone —**o′bo·ist** *n.*

obs. obsolete

ob·scene (äb sēn′) *adj.* [< L *obscenus*, filthy] 1 offensive to modesty or decency; lewd 2 repulsive —**ob·scene′ly** *adv.* —**ob·scen′ity** (-sen′ə tē), *pl.* **-ties,** *n.*

ob·scure (əb skyoor′) *adj.* [< L *obscurus*, covered over] 1 dim; dark 2 not easily seen; faint 3 vague; ambiguous [an *obscure* answer] 4 inconspicuous; hidden 5 not well-known [an *obscure* actor] — *vt.* **-scured′, -scur′ing** to make obscure —**ob·scure′ly** *adv.* —**ob·scu′rity** *n.*

ob·se·quies (äb′si kwēz′) *n.pl.* [< L *obsequium*, compliance, substituted for L *exsequiae*, funeral] funeral rites

ob·se·qui·ous (əb sē′kwē əs) *adj.* [< L *obsequi*, to comply with] much too willing to serve or obey; fawning

ob·serv·ance (əb zurv′əns) *n.* 1 the observing of a law, duty, custom, etc. 2 a customary act, rite, etc.

ob·serv′ant *adj.* 1 strict in observing a law, custom, etc. 2 paying careful attention 3 perceptive or alert

ob·ser·va·tion (äb′zər vā′shən) *n.* 1 *a)* the act or power of noticing *b)* something noticed 2 a being seen 3 a noting and recording of facts, as for research 4 a comment or remark

ob·serva·tory (əb zurv′ə tôr′ē) *n., pl.* **-ries** a building equipped for astronomical research, esp. one with a large telescope

ob·serve (əb zurv′) *vt.* **-served′, -serv′ing** [< L *observare* < *ob-* (see OB-) + *servare*, to keep] 1 to adhere to (a law, custom, etc.) 2 to celebrate (a holiday, etc.) 3 *a)* to notice (something) *b)* to pay special attention to 4 to arrive at as a conclusion 5 to say casually; remark 6 to examine scientifically —**ob·serv′able** *adj.* —**ob·serv′er** *n.*

ob·sess (əb ses′) *vt.* [< L *obsessus* < *ob-* (see OB-) + *sedere*, sit] to haunt or trouble in mind; preoccupy —**ob·ses′sive** *adj.* —**ob·ses′sively** *adv.*

ob·ses′sion *n.* 1 a being obsessed 2 an idea, desire, etc. that obsesses one

ob·sid·i·an (əb sid′ē ən) *n.* [after one *Obsidius*, its alleged discoverer] a hard, dark, volcanic glass

ob·so·lesce (äb′sə les′) *vi.* **-lesced′, -lesc′ing** to be obsolescent

ob·so·les·cent (äb′sə les′ənt) *adj.* becoming obsolete —**ob′so·les′cence** *n.*

ob·so·lete (äb′sə lēt′, äb′sə lēt′) *adj.* [< L *obsoletus* < *ob-* (see OB-) + *exolescere*, to grow out of use] 1 no longer in use 2 out-of-date

THESAURUS

obligate *v.* bind, restrict, constrain; see FORCE.

obligation *n.* responsibility, burden, debt; see DUTY 1.

obligatory *a.* required, essential, binding; see NECESSARY.

oblige *v.* 1 [To accommodate] assist, aid, contribute; see ACCOMMODATE 1, HELP. 2 [To require] compel, coerce, bind; see FORCE, REQUIRE 2.

obliged *a.* compelled, obligated, required; see BOUND 2.

obliging *a.* amiable, accommodating, helpful; see KIND.

obligingly *a.* helpfully, thoughtfully, graciously; see AGREEABLY.

oblique *a.* inclined, inclining, diverging, leaning, sloping, angled, askew, asymmetrical, turned, twisted, awry, strained, askance, distorted, off level, sideways, slanted, tipping, tipped, at an angle, on the bias; see also BENT, CROOKED 1.—*Ant.* STRAIGHT, vertical, perpendicular.

oblivion *n.* nonexistence, obscurity, void; see EMPTINESS, NOTHING.

oblivious *a.* abstracted, preoccupied, absorbed; see ABSENT-MINDED, DREAMY.

oblong *a.* elongated, rectangular, oval, elliptical, egg-shaped.—*Ant.* SQUARE, circle, circular.

obnoxious *a.* annoying, disagreeable, displeasing; see OFFENSIVE 2.

obscene *a.* wanton, lustful, lascivious; see LEWD 2.

obscenity *n.* vulgarity, impropriety, smut; see INDECENCY, LEWDNESS.

obscure *a.* 1 [Vague] indistinct, ambiguous, indefinite, indecisive, unintelligible, impenetrable, inscrutable, unfathomable, unclear, vague, involved, intricate, illeg-

ible, incomprehensible, hazy, dark, dim, inexplicable, inconceivable, unbelievable, incredible, complicated, illogical, unreasoned, mixed up, doubtful, questionable, dubious, inexact, unreasoned, loose, ill-defined, unidentified, invisible, undisclosed, perplexing, cryptic, escaping notice, mystical, secret, enigmatic, concealed, mysterious, esoteric, puzzling, lacking clarity, unreadable, contradictory, out of focus, unrelated, clear as mud*, over one's head, deep, far out*; see also COMPLEX 2, CONFUSED 2, CONFUSING, DIFFICULT 2.—*Ant.* CLEAR, definite, distinct. 2 [Dark] cloudy, dense, hazy; see DARK 1. 3 [Little known] unknown, rare, hidden, covered, remote, reticent, secretive, seldom seen, unseen, inconspicuous, humble, invisible, mysterious, deep, cryptic, enigmatic, esoteric, arcane, undisclosed, dark; see also DISTANT, IRRELEVANT, PROFOUND.

obscure *v.* 1 [To dim] shadow, cloud, screen; see SHADE 2. 2 [To conceal] cover, veil, wrap up; see DISGUISE, HIDE 1.

obscurely *a.* dimly, darkly, thickly; see VAGUELY.

obscurity *n.* vagueness, dimness, fuzziness; see UNCERTAINTY 1, 2.

observable *a.* perceptible, noticeable, discernible; see OBVIOUS 1.

observance *n.* 1 [A custom] ritual, practice, rite; see CUSTOM. 2 [Attention] awareness, observation, notice; see ATTENTION.

observant *a.* keen, alert, penetrating, wide-awake, discerning, perceptive, sharp, eager, interested, discovering, detecting, discriminat-

ing, judicious, searching, understanding, questioning, deducing, sensitive, surveying, considering, clear-sighted, comprehending, bright, intelligent, on the ball*, on one's toes*; see also INTELLIGENT.—*Ant.* THOUGHTLESS, unobservant, insensitive.

observation *n.* 1 [The power of observing] seeing, recognizing, perception; see SIGHT 1. 2 [A remark] comment, note, commentary; see REMARK, SPEECH 3.

observe *v.* 1 [To watch] scrutinize, inspect, examine; see SEE, WATCH. 2 [To comment] note, remark, mention; see COMMENT. 3 [To commemorate] dedicate, solemnize, keep; see CELEBRATE 1. 4 [To abide by] conform to, comply, adopt; see FOLLOW 2, OBEY.

observed *a.* 1 [Noticed] seen, noted, marked; see RECOGNIZED. 2 [Commemorated] kept, celebrated, recalled; see REMEMBERED.

observer *n.* watcher, watchman, sentinel, lookout, sentry, guard, detective, policeman, spy, spectator, eyewitness, beholder, onlooker, bystander, passerby, meddler, peeper, voyeur, prying person, peeping Tom*; see also WITNESS.

obsess *v.* dominate, possess, hound; see HAUNT 2.

obsessed *a.* haunted, beset, controlled; see TROUBLED.

obsession *n.* fixation, fascination, passion, fancy, phantom, craze, delusion, mania, infatuation, fixed idea, compulsion, bee in one's bonnet*, hang-up*; see also FANTASY.

obsolete *a.* antiquated, archaic, out-of-date; see OLD 1, 2, OLD-FASHIONED.

ob·sta·cle (äb′stə kəl) *n.* [< L *obstaculum* < *ob-* (see OB-) + *stare*, to stand] anything that stands in the way; obstruction

ob·stet·rics (əb stet′riks) *n.pl.* [< L *obstetrix*, midwife] [*with sing. v.*] the branch of medicine concerned with the care and treatment of women during pregnancy and childbirth —**ob·stet′ric** or **ob·stet′ri·cal** *adj.* —**ob·ste·tri·cian** (äb′stə trish′ən) *n.*

ob·sti·nate (äb′stə nət) *adj.* [< L *obstinare*, to resolve on] **1** determined to have one's own way; stubborn **2** resisting treatment [an *obstinate* fever] —**ob′sti·nacy** (-nə sē) *n.* —**ob′sti·nately** *adv.*

ob·strep·er·ous (əb strep′ər əs, äb-) *adj.* [< L *obstreperus* < *ob-* (see OB-) + *strepere*, to roar] noisy or unruly, esp. in resisting —**ob·strep′er·ously** *adv.* —**ob·strep′er·ous·ness** *n.*

ob·struct (əb strukt′) *vt.* [< L *obstructus* < *ob-* (see OB-) + *struere*, to pile up] **1** to block or stop up (a passage) **2** to hinder (progress, etc.) **3** to cut off from view —**ob·struc′tive** *adj.* —**ob·struc′tively** *adv.* —**ob·struc′tive·ness** *n.*

ob·struc′tion *n.* **1** an obstructing **2** anything that obstructs; hindrance

ob·struc′tion·ist *n.* one who obstructs progress —*adj.* that obstructs

ob·tain (əb tān′) *vt.* [< L *obtinere* < *ob-* (see OB-) + *tenere*, to hold] to get possession of by trying; procure —*vi.* to prevail [peace will *obtain*] —**ob·tain′able** *adj.* —**ob·tain′ment** *n.*

ob·trude (əb trōōd′, äb-) *vt.* **-trud′ed, -trud′ing** [< L *obtrudere* < *ob-* (see OB-) + *trudere*, to thrust] **1** to push out; eject **2** to force (oneself, etc.) upon others unasked or unwanted —*vi.* to obtrude oneself —**ob·tru′sion** *n.* —**ob·tru′sive** *adj.* —**ob·tru′sively** *adv.* —**ob·tru′sive·ness** *n.*

ob·tuse (äb tōōs′, əb-) *adj.* [< L *obtundere*, to strike upon, blunt] **1** not sharp; blunt **2** greater than 90° and less than 180° [an *obtuse* angle] **3** slow to understand or perceive —**ob·tuse′ly** *adv.* —**ob·tuse′ness** *n.*

ob·verse (äb vurs′; *for n.* äb′vurs′) *adj.* [< L *obversus* < *ob-* (see OB-) + *vertere*, to turn] **1** turned toward the observer **2** forming a counterpart —*n.* **1** the side, as of a coin or medal, bearing the main design **2** a counterpart

ob·vi·ate (äb′vē āt′) *vt.* **-at′ed, -at′ing** [see fol.] to do away with or prevent by effective measures; make unnecessary —**ob′via′tion** *n.*

ob·vi·ous (äb′vē əs) *adj.* [L *obvius*, in the way] easy to see or understand; evident —**ob′vi·ously** *adv.* —**ob′vi·ous·ness** *n.*

oc- *prefix* OB-: used before *c* [*occur*]

oca·ri·na (äk′ə rē′nə) *n.* [It < LL *auca*, goose: from its shape] a small wind instrument with finger holes and a mouthpiece

occas. occasional(ly)

oc·ca·sion (ə kā′zhən) *n.* [< L *occasio* < *ob-* (see OB-) + *cadere*, to fall] **1** a favorable time; opportunity **2** an event, etc. that makes something else possible **3** *a*) a happening *b*) a particular time **4** a special time or event **5** need arising from circumstances —*vt.* to cause —**on occasion** sometimes

oc·ca′sional *adj.* **1** of or for special occasions **2** happening now and then; infrequent —**oc·ca′sion·ally** *adv.*

oc·ci·dent (äk′sə dənt, -dent′) *n.* [< L *occidere*, to fall: with reference to the setting sun] [Old Poet.] the west —[O-] Europe and the Americas —**oc′ci·den′tal** or **Oc′ci·den′tal** *adj., n.*

Oc′ci·den′tal·ize′ (-den′t'l īz′) *vt., vi.* **-ized′, -iz′ing** to turn to the ways of the Occident

oc·clude (ə klōōd′) *vt.* **-clud′ed, -clud′ing** [< L *occludere* < *ob-* (see OB-) + *claudere*, to shut] **1** to close or block (a passage) **2** to shut in or out —*vi.* Dentistry to meet with the cusps fitting closely —**oc·clu′sion** (-klōō′zhən) *n.* —**oc·clu′sive** *adj.*

oc·cult (ə kult′, ä′kult′) *adj.* [< L *occulere*, to conceal] **1** hidden **2** secret **3** mysterious **4** of mystic arts, such as magic, astrology, etc. —**the occult** the occult arts —**oc′cult′ism′** *n.*

oc·cu·pancy (äk′yōō pən sē) *n., pl.* **-cies** an occupying; a taking or keeping in possession

oc′cu·pant *n.* one who occupies

oc·cu·pa·tion (äk′yōō pā′shən) *n.* **1** an occupying or being occupied **2** that which occupies one's time; work; profession —**oc′cu·pa′tional** *adj.*

oc·cupy (äk′yōō pī′) *vt.* **-pied′, -py′ing** [< L *occupare* < *ob-* (see OB-) + *capere*, seize] **1** to take possession of by settlement or seizure **2** to hold possession of; specif., *a*) to dwell in *b*) to hold (a position or office) **3** to take up (space, time, etc.) **4** to employ (oneself, one's mind, etc.) —**oc′cu·pi′er** *n.*

oc·cur (ə kur′) *vi.* **-curred′, -cur′ring** [< L *occurrere* < *ob-* (see OB-) + *currere*, to run] **1** to be found; exist **2** to

---

THESAURUS

obstacle *n.* restriction, obstruction, hindrance; see BARRIER.
obstinate *a.* firm, headstrong, opinionated; see STUBBORN.
obstinately *a.* doggedly, bullheadedly, persistently; see STUBBORNLY.
obstruct *v.* stop, interfere, bar; see HINDER, PREVENT.
obstruction *n.* difficulty, trouble, roadblock; see BARRIER, IMPEDIMENT 1.
obtain *v.* **1** [To gain possession] take, acquire, seize; see GET 1. **2** [Pertain] be pertinent to, appertain to, bear upon; see CONCERN 1.
obtainable *a.* ready, attainable, achievable; see AVAILABLE.
obvious *a.* **1** [Clearly apparent to the eye] clear, visible, apparent, public, transparent, observable, perceptible, exposed, noticeable, plain, conspicuous, overt, glaring, prominent, standing out, light, bright, open, unmistakable, evident, recognizable, discernible, in evidence, in view, in sight, perceivable, discoverable, distinguishable, palpable, distinct, clear as a bell*, clear as day*, hitting one in the face*; see also DEFINITE 2.—*Ant.* OBSCURE, hidden, indistinct. **2** [Clearly apparent to the mind] lucid, apparent, conclusive, explicit, understood, intelligible, comprehensible, self-evident, indisputable, unquestionable, undeniable, proverbial, aphoristic, reasonable, broad, unambiguous, on the surface, as plain as the nose on one's face*, going without saying*, staring one in the face*, open-and-shut*; see also

UNDERSTANDABLE.—*Ant.* PROFOUND, ambiguous, equivocal.
obviously *interj.* of course, yes, evidently; see SURELY.
obviously *a.* without doubt, unmistakably, certainly; see CLEARLY 1, 2.
occasion *n.* **1** [An event] occurrence, incident, happening; see EVENT. **2** [An opportunity] chance, excuse, opening; see OPPORTUNITY 1, POSSIBILITY 2. —**on occasion** once in a while, sometimes, occasionally; see HARDLY, SELDOM.
occasional *a.* **1** [Occurring at odd times] sporadic, random, infrequent; see IRREGULAR 1. **2** [Intended for special use] especial, particular, specific; see EXCLUSIVE, SPECIAL.
occasionally *a.* infrequently, at random, irregularly; see HARDLY, SELDOM.
occult *a.* secret, magical, supernatural; see MYSTERIOUS 2.
occupancy *n.* possession, occupation, inhabitance; see DEED 2, OWNERSHIP.
occupant *n.* lessee, inhabitant, renter; see RESIDENT, TENANT.
occupation *n.* **1** [The act of occupying] seizure, entering, invasion; see ATTACK, CAPTURE. **2** [A vocation] calling, affair, chosen work; see JOB 1, PROFESSION 1, TRADE 2.
occupational *a.* professional, career, vocational, technical, workaday, official, industrial.
occupied *a.* **1** [Busy] engaged, working, engrossed; see BUSY 1. **2** [Full] in

use, leased, taken; see RENTED.
occupy *v.* **1** [To take possession] conquer, take over, invade; see GET 1, SEIZE 2. **2** [To fill space] remain, tenant, reside, live in, hold, take up, pervade, keep, own, command, be in command, extend, control, maintain, involve, permeate; see also FILL 2.—*Ant.* EMPTY, remove, move. **3** [To absorb attention] engage, engross, attend, monopolize, interest, immerse, arrest, absorb, take up, utilize, involve, keep busy, busy, be active with, be concerned with; see also FASCINATE.
occupying *a.* **1** [Filling a place] holding, remaining, situated, posted, assigned to, tenanting, residing, living in, taking up, possessing, pervading, covering, settled on, controlling, maintaining, commanding, sitting, staying, established in, established at, owning, set up*, running*; see also PLACED.—*Ant.* GONE, leaving, removing. **2** [Engaging attention] absorbing, engrossing, concerned with, monopolizing, engaging, arresting, working at, attracting, focusing, drawing, exacting, requiring; see also EXCITING, INTERESTING.
occur *v.* take place, transpire, befall; see HAPPEN 1, 2. —**occur to** come to mind, present itself, offer itself, suggest itself, spring, issue, rise, appear, catch one's attention, strike one, pass through one's mind, impress one, enter one's mind, cross one's mind, crop up.

come to mind *[an idea occurred to me]* **3** to take place; happen

oc·cur′rence *n.* **1** the act or fact of occurring **2** event; incident

ocean (ō′shən) *n.* ⟦< Gr *Ōkeanos*⟧ **1** the body of salt water that covers about 71% of the earth's surface **2** any of its four principal divisions: the Atlantic, Pacific, Indian, or Arctic Ocean **3** a great quantity —**ocean·ic** (ō′shē an′ ik) *adj.*

ocean·going (ō′shən gō′iŋ) *adj.* of, or made for, travel on the ocean

ocean·og·ra·phy (ō′shə näg′rə fē) *n.* the study of the environment in the ocean, its plants and animals, etc. — **o′ceano·graph′ic** (-nō′graf′ik) *adj.*

ocean·ol·ogy (-näl′ə jē) *n.* the study of the sea in all its aspects, including oceanography, undersea exploration, etc.

ocelot (äs′ə lət, -lät′) *n.* ⟦Fr < AmInd⟧ a spotted wildcat of North and South America

ocher or **ochre** (ō′kər) *n.* ⟦< Gr *ōchros*, pale-yellow⟧ **1** a yellow or reddish-brown clay containing iron, used as a pigment **2** its color

o′clock (ə kläk′, ō-) *adv.* of or according to the clock *[nine o'clock at night]*

octa- ⟦< Gr *oktō*, eight⟧ *combining form* eight *[octagon]*

oc·ta·gon (äk′tə gän′) *n.* ⟦< Gr: see prec. & -GON⟧ a plane figure with eight angles and eight sides —**oc·tag′o·nal** (-tag′ə nəl) *adj.*

octane number (or **rating**) (äk′tān) a number representing the antiknock properties of a gasoline, etc.

oc·tave (äk′tiv, -tāv′) *n.* ⟦< L *octavus*, eighth⟧ **1** any group of eight **2** *Music a)* the eighth tone of a diatonic scale, or a tone seven degrees above or below a given tone *b)* the interval of seven degrees between a tone and either of its octaves *c)* the series of tones within this interval, or the keys of an instrument producing such a series

oc·ta·vo (äk tā′vō, -tä′-) *n., pl.* **-vos** ⟦< L (*in*) *octavo*, (in) eight⟧ **1** the page size (about 6 by 9 in.) of a book made up of printer's sheets folded into eight leaves **2** a book of such pages

oc·tet or **oc·tette** (äk tet′) *n.* ⟦OCT(A)- + (DU)ET⟧ **1** a composition for eight voices or instruments **2** the eight performers of this

Oc·to·ber (äk tō′bər) *n.* ⟦< L *octo*, eight: eighth month in Rom. calendar⟧ the 10th month of the year, having 31 days: abbrev. **Oct.**

oc·to·ge·nar·ian (äk′tō ji ner′ē ən, -tə-) *adj.* ⟦< L *octoginta*, eighty⟧ between the ages of 80 and 90 — *n.* a person of this age

oc·to·pus (äk′tə pəs) *n., pl.* **-puses** or **-pi′** (-pī′) ⟦< Gr *oktō*, eight + *pous*, foot⟧ a mollusk with a soft body and eight arms covered with suckers

ocu·lar (äk′yōō lər) *adj.* ⟦< L *oculus*, eye⟧ **1** of, for, or like the eye **2** by eyesight

oc′u·list (-list) *n.* old term for OPHTHALMOLOGIST

OD (ō′dē′) *n., pl.* **ODs** or **OD's** [Slang] an overdose, esp. of a narcotic — *vi.* **OD'd** or **ODed, OD'ing** or **ODing** [Slang] to take an overdose, esp. a fatal overdose of a narcotic

OD or **O.D.** ⟦L⟧ Doctor of Optometry

oda·lisque or **oda·lisk** (ō′də lisk′, ōd′'l isk′) *n.* ⟦Fr <

Turk *ōdalik*, chambermaid⟧ a female slave or concubine in an Oriental harem

odd (äd) *adj.* ⟦< ON *oddi*⟧ **1** with the other of the pair missing *[an odd glove]* **2** having a remainder of one when divided by two **3** left over after taking a round number **4** with a few more: usually in hyphenated compounds *[sixty-odd years ago]* **5** occasional *[odd jobs]* **6** *a)* peculiar *b)* queer; eccentric —**odd′ly** *adv.* —**odd′ness** *n.*

odd′ball′ *adj.* [Slang] strange or eccentric — *n.* [Slang] one who is oddball

odd′ity (-ə tē) *n.* **1** strangeness **2** *pl.* **-ties** an odd person or thing

odds (ädz) *n.pl.* **1** difference in favor of one side over the other; advantage **2** an equalized advantage in betting, based on a bettor's assumed chance of winning and expressed as a ratio *[odds* of 3 to 1*]* —**at odds** quarreling —**by** (**all**) **odds** by far

odds and ends scraps; remnants

odds′-on′ *adj.* having a very good chance of winning *[an odds-on* favorite*]*

ode (ōd) *n.* ⟦< Gr *ōidē*, song⟧ a lyric poem characterized by lofty feeling, elaborate form, and dignified style

-ode (ōd) ⟦< Gr *hodos*⟧ *suffix* way, path *[electrode]*

Odin (ō′din) *Norse Myth.* the chief deity, god of art, war, and the dead

odi·ous (ō′dē əs) *adj.* ⟦< L *odium*, hatred⟧ disgusting; offensive —**o′di·ously** *adv.* —**o′di·ous·ness** *n.*

odi·um (ō′dē əm) *n.* ⟦< L *odi*, I hate⟧ **1** hatred **2** the disgrace brought on by hateful action

odom·eter (ō däm′ət ər) *n.* ⟦< Gr *hodometros* < *hodos*, way + *metron*, a measure⟧ an instrument for measuring the distance traveled by a vehicle

odor (ō′dər) *n.* ⟦L⟧ a smell; scent; aroma Brit. sp. **odour** —**be in bad** (or **ill**) **odor** to be in bad repute —**o′dor·less** *adj.* —**o′dor·ous** *adj.*

odor·if·er·ous (ō′dər if′ər əs) *adj.* ⟦< L *odor*, odor + *ferre*, to bear⟧ giving off an odor, now often, specif., a strong or offensive one

Odys·seus (ō dis′ē əs, ō dis′yōōs′) ⟦Gr⟧ the hero of the *Odyssey*, one of the Greek leaders in the Trojan War

Odys·sey (ō dis′ē sē) an ancient Greek epic poem, ascribed to Homer, about the wanderings of Odysseus after the fall of Troy — *n., pl.* **-seys** *[sometimes* o-*]* any extended journey

OE Old English

Oedi·pus (ed′i pəs, ē′di-) *Gr. Myth.* a king who unwittingly kills his father and marries his mother

oenol·ogy (ē näl′ə jē) *n.* ⟦< Gr *oinos*, wine + -LOGY⟧ the science or study of wines and winemaking —**oenol′o·gist** *n.*

oeno·phile (ē′nə fīl′) *n.* a connoisseur of wine

o′er (ō′ər, ôr) *prep., adv. chiefly old poet. contr. of* OVER

of (uv, äv, əv) *prep.* ⟦OE⟧ **1** from; specif., *a)* coming from *[men of Ohio]* *b)* resulting from *[to die of fever]* *c)* at a distance from *[east of the city]* *d)* by *[the poems of Poe]* *e)* separated from *[robbed of his money]* *f)* from the whole constituting *[one of her hats]* *g)* made from *[a sheet of paper]* **2** belonging to **3** *a)* possessing *[a man of wealth]* *b)* containing *[a bag of nuts]* **4** specified as *[a height of six feet]* **5** characterized by *[a man of honor]* **6** concerning; about **7** during *[of recent years]*

of- *prefix* OB-: used before *f [offer]*

off (ôf) *adv.* ⟦ME var. of *of*⟧ **1** so as to be away, at a distance, etc. **2** so as to be no longer on, attached, etc. *[take off* your hat*]* **3** (a specified distance) away in space

---

THESAURUS

occurrence *n.* happening, incident, episode; see EVENT.

ocean *n.* great sea, high seas, salt water, seashore, seaside, shores, the mighty deep, the main, the great waters, the Seven Seas; see also SEA.—*Ant.* EARTH, lake, river. *Oceans include the following:* Atlantic, Pacific, Arctic, Antarctic, Indian, North Atlantic, South Atlantic, North Pacific, South Pacific.

oceanic *a.* marine, aquatic, pelagic; see MARITIME, NAUTICAL.

October *n.* fall month, autumn month, harvest month, Indian summer, hunting season; see also AUTUMN, MONTH.

odd *a.* **1** [Unusual] queer, unique, strange; see UNUSUAL 2. **2** [Miscellaneous] fragmentary, odd-lot, varied; see VARIOUS. **3** [Single] unpaired, sole, unmatched; see ALONE. **4** [Not even] remaining, over and above,

leftover; see IRREGULAR 1, 4.

oddly *a.* curiously, ridiculously, inexplicably; see FOOLISHLY, STRANGELY.

odds *n.* **1** [An advantage] allowance, edge, benefit, difference, superiority, place money*, show money*; see also ADVANTAGE. **2** [A probability] favor, superiority, chances; see CHANCE 1. —**at odds** disagreeing, at variance, discordant; see QUARRELSOME.

odds and ends *n.* miscellany, scraps, particles; see REMNANTS.

odor *n.* perfume, fragrance, bouquet; see SMELL 1, 2.

odorless *a.* flat, scentless, unaromatic, unperfumed, unsmelling, unscented, without odor, odor-free, unfragrant, lacking fragrance.

odorous *a.* **1** [Having an offensive odor] smelly, stinking, putrid; see OFFENSIVE 2, ROTTEN 1. **2** [Having a pleasant odor] spicy, sweet-smelling,

fragrant; see SWEET 3.

of *prep.* from, out of, out from, away from, proceeding from, coming from, going from, about, concerning, as concerns, appropriate to, pertaining to, peculiar to, attributed to, characterized by, regarding, as regards, in regard to, referring to, in reference to, like, belonging to, related to, having relation to, native to, consequent to, based on, akin to, connected with; see also ABOUT 2.

off *a., prep.* **1** [Situated at a distance] ahead, behind, up front, to one side, divergent, beside, aside, below, beneath, above, far, absent, not here, removed, apart, in the distance, at a distance, gone, away; see also DISTANT.—*Ant.* HERE, at hand, present. **2** [Moving away] into the distance, away from, farther away, disappearing, vanishing, removing, or time *[20 yards off]* **4** so as to be no longer in operation, etc. *[turn the motor off]* **5** so as to be less, etc. *[5% off for cash]* **6** away from one's work — **prep. 1** (so as to be) no longer (or not) on, attached, etc. *[off the road]* **2** from the substance of *[live off the land]* **3** away from *[a mile off shore]* **4** branching out from *[an alley off Main Street]* **5** relieved from *[off duty]* **6** not up to the usual standard, etc. of *[off one's game]* — **adj. 1** not on or attached **2** not in operation **3** on the way *[off to bed]* **4** away from work *[we are off today]* **5** not up to the usual standard, etc. **6** more remote *[on the off chance]* **7** in (specified) circumstances *[to be well off]* **8** wrong *[his figures are off]* — **vt.** [Slang] to kill; murder — **interj.** go away! —**off and on** now and then

-off (ôf; *also* äf) *combining form* a contest of skill in a (specified) activity or field *[a chili cook-off]*

of·fal (ôf'əl) *n.* [ME *ofall,* lit., off-fall] **1** *[with sing. or pl. v.]* the entrails, etc. of a butchered animal **2** refuse; garbage

off·beat' *n. Music* a beat having a weak accent — *adj.* [Colloq.] unconventional, unusual, strange, etc.

off-color (ôf'kul'ər) *adj.* **1** varying from the standard color **2** improper; risqué

of·fend (ə fend') *vi.* [< L *offendere,* to strike against < *ob-* (see OB-) + *fendere,* to hit] **1** to commit a sin or crime **2** to create resentment, anger, etc. — *vt.* **1** to hurt the feelings of; insult **2** to be displeasing to (the taste, sense, etc.) —**of·fend'er** *n.*

of·fense (ə fens', ô'fens') *n.* **1** a sin or crime **2** a creating of resentment, displeasure, etc. **3** a feeling hurt, angry, etc. **4** something that causes anger, etc. **5** the act of attacking **6** the side that is attacking or seeking to score in any contest Brit. sp. **offence** —**take offense** to become offended

of·fen·sive *adj.* **1** attacking or for attack **2** unpleasant; disgusting **3** insulting **4** of the side that is seeking to

score in any contest — *n.* attitude or position of attack: often with *the* —**of·fen'sive·ly** *adv.* —**of·fen'sive·ness** *n.*

of·fer (ôf'ər, äf'-) *vt.* [< L *offerre* < *ob-* (see OB-) + *ferre,* to bear] **1** to present in worship *[to offer prayers]* **2** to present for acceptance *[to offer help]* **3** to suggest; propose **4** to show or give signs of *[to offer resistance]* **5** to bid (a price, etc.) — *vi.* to present itself — *n.* the act of offering or thing offered

of·fer·ing *n.* **1** the act of making an offer **2** something offered; specif., *a)* a gift *b)* presentation in worship

of·fer·to·ry (-tôr'ē) *n., pl.* **-ries** *[often* **O-**] **1** *a)* the part of a Eucharistic service in which the bread and wine are offered to God *b)* the prayers said, or music used, then **2** *a)* the part of a church service during which money offerings are collected *b)* the collection itself

off·hand' *adv.* without preparation — *adj.* **1** said or done offhand (this sense) Also **off'hand'ed**

of·fice (ôf'is, äf'-) *n.* [< L *officium*] **1** a service done for another **2** a duty, esp. as a part of one's work **3** a position of authority or trust, as in government **4** *a)* the place where the affairs of a business, etc. are carried on *b)* the people working there **5** a religious ceremony or rite

of'fice·hold'er *n.* a government official

of·fi·cer (ôf'i sər, äf'-) *n.* **1** anyone holding an office, or position of authority, in a government, business, club, etc. **2** a policeman **3** one holding a position of authority, esp. by commission, in the armed forces

officer of the day the military officer in charge of the security and guard at a military post for the day

of·fi·cial (ə fish'əl) *adj.* **1** of or holding an office, or position of authority **2** authorized or authoritative **3** formal — *n.* a person holding office —**of·fi'cial·dom** (-dəm) or **of·fi'cial·ism'** *n.* —**of·fi'cial·ly** *adv.*

═══ **THESAURUS** ═══

turning aside; see also AWAY.—*Ant.* APPROACHING, returning, coming. **3** [Started] initiated, commenced, originated; see BEGUN. **4** [Mistaken] erring, in error, confused; see MISTAKEN 1, WRONG 2. **5** [*Crazy] odd, peculiar, queer; see INSANE. **6** [*Not employed] not on duty, on vacation, gone; see UNEMPLOYED.

off and on *a.* now and then, sometimes, occasionally; see SELDOM.

off-color *a.* racy, spicy, indelicate; see RISQUÉ.

offend *v.* annoy, affront, outrage; see BOTHER 2.

offended *a.* vexed, provoked, exasperated; see ANGRY, INSULTED.

offense *n.* **1** [A misdeed] misdemeanor, malfeasance, transgression; see CRIME, SIN. **2** [An attack] assault, aggression, battery; see ATTACK. *Styles of offense in football include the following:* running attack, ground attack, passing attack, aerial attack, shotgun offense, T-formation, wishbone, power plays, flying wedge, razzle-dazzle. **3** [Resentment] umbrage, pique, indignation; see ANGER.

offensive *a.* **1** [Concerned with an attack] assaulting, attacking, invading; see AGGRESSIVE. **2** [Revolting] disgusting, horrid, repulsive, shocking, gross, dreadful, detestable, repugnant, obnoxious, hideous, horrible, displeasing, disagreeable, repellent, nauseating, invidious, nauseous, revolting, distasteful, unspeakable, accursed, unutterable, terrible, grisly, ghastly, bloody, gory, hateful, low, foul, corrupt, bad, indecent, nasty, dirty, unclean, filthy, sickening, malignant, rancid, putrid, vile, impure, beastly, monstrous, coarse, loathsome, obscene, smutty, damnable, reeking, abominable, stinking, distressing, irritating, unpleasant, contaminated, frightful, unattractive, forbidding, repelling, incompatible, unsavory, intolerable, unpalatable, disatisfactory, unpleasing, unsuited, objectionable, to one's disgust,

beneath contempt, icky*, lousy*; see also REVOLTING.—*Ant.* PLEASANT, agreeable, likable. **3** [Insolent] impertinent, impudent, insulting; see RUDE 2.

offensive *n.* position of attack, invasion, assault; see ATTACK.

offer *n.* proposal, presentation, proposition; see SUGGESTION 1.

offer *v.* **1** [To present] proffer, tender, administer, donate, put forth, advance, extend, submit, hold out, grant, allow, award, volunteer, accord, place at one's disposal, lay at one's feet, put up; see also CONTRIBUTE, GIVE 1.—*Ant.* REFUSE, withhold, keep. **2** [To propose] suggest, submit, advise; see PROPOSE 1.

offering *n.* contribution, donation, present; see GIFT 1.

offhand *a.* at the moment, unprepared, impromptu, improvised, by ear, informal, extemporaneous, extemporary, spontaneous, unpremeditated, unstudied, unrehearsed.

office *n.* **1** [A position involving responsibility] employment, occupation, business; see JOB 1, PROFESSION 1, TRADE 2. **2** [A function] performance, province, service; see DUTY 1. **3** [A place in which office work is done] room, office building, factory, bureau, agency, warehouse, facility, school building; see also BUILDING, DEPARTMENT. *Types of offices include the following:* governmental, school principal's, counseling, secretarial, insurance, data processing, real estate, brokerage, law, bank, foreign, consular, doctor's, dentist's, advertising agency, booking office, box office. —**hold office** be in office, direct, rule; see GOVERN, MANAGE 1.

officer *n.* **1** [An executive] manager, director, president; see EXECUTIVE, LEADER 2. **2** [One who enforces civil law] magistrate, military police, deputy; see POLICEMAN. **3** [One holding a responsible post in the armed

forces] *American officers include the following — Army commissioned and special officers:* Commander in Chief, Five-star General, Four-star General, Three-star General, Two-star General, General of the Army, Lieutenant General, Major General, Brigadier General, Colonel, Lieutenant Colonel, Major, Captain, First Lieutenant, Second Lieutenant, Chief of Staff; *Navy commissioned officers:* Admiral of the Fleet, Fleet Admiral, Admiral, Rear Admiral, Vice Admiral, Captain, Commander, Lieutenant Commander, Lieutenant; Lieutenant, junior grade; Ensign; *Army noncommissioned officers:* Chief Warrant Officer, Warrant Officer, junior grade; Master Sergeant, First Sergeant, Technical Sergeant, Staff Sergeant, Sergeant, Corporal.

official *a.* **1** [Having to do with one's office] formal, fitting, suitable, precise, established, according to precedent, according to protocol, proper, correct, accepted, recognized, customary; see also CONVENTIONAL 1, 3, FIT 1.—*Ant.* INFORMAL, ill-fitting, unceremonious. **2** [Authorized] ordered, endorsed, sanctioned; see APPROVED. **3** [Reliable] authoritative, authentic, trustworthy; see CERTAIN 3, GENUINE 1, RELIABLE.

official *n.* **1** [Administrator] comptroller, director, executive; see EXECUTIVE, LEADER 2. **2** [A sports official] referee, umpire, linesman; see UMPIRE.

officially *a.* **1** [In an official manner] regularly, formally, orderly, suitably, according to form, ceremoniously, in set form, precisely, according to precedent, conventionally, in an established manner, as prescribed, according to protocol, all in order, correctly, properly, customarily. **2** [With official approval] authoritatively, authorized, sanctioned; see APPROVED.

of·fi·ci·ant (ə fish′ənt, -ē ənt) *n.* an officiating priest, minister, etc.

of·fi·ci·ate (ə fish′ē āt′) *vi.* -at′ed, -at′ing **1** to perform the duties of an office **2** to perform the functions of a priest, minister, rabbi, etc.

of·fi·cious (ə fish′əs) *adj.* ⟦see OFFICE⟧ offering unwanted advice or services; meddlesome, esp. highhandedly so — **of·fi′ciously** *adv.* —**of·fi′cious·ness** *n.*

off·ing (ôf′iŋ) *n.* ⟦< OFF⟧ the distant part of the sea visible from the shore —**in the offing** **1** at a distance but in sight **2** at some vague future time

off′-key′ *adj.* **1** *Music* flat or sharp **2** not harmonious

off′-lim′its (-lim′its) *adj.* ruled to be a place that cannot be entered, etc. by a specified group

off′-line′ *adj.* designating or of equipment not directly connected to and controlled by the central processing unit of a computer

off′-put′ting *adj.* [Chiefly Brit.] distracting, annoying, etc.

off′-road′ *adj.* designating or of a vehicle, as a dune buggy, for use off regular highways, streets, etc.

off′-sea′son (-sē′zən) *n.* a time of the year when the usual activity is reduced or not carried on

off′set (ôf set′; *for n.* ôf′set′) *vt.* -set′, -set′ting to balance, compensate for, etc. — *n.* **1** a thing that offsets another **2** OFFSET PRINTING

offset printing a printing process in which the inked impression is first made on a rubber-covered roller, then transferred to paper

off′shoot′ *n.* anything that derives from a main source; specif., a shoot growing from the main stem of a plant

off′shore′ *adj.* **1** moving away from the shore **2** at some distance from the shore **3** engaged in outside the U.S. as by U.S. banks or manufacturers *[offshore* investments*]* — *adv.* **1** away from the shore **2** outside the U.S. *[*to borrow *offshore]*

off′side′ *adj.* *Sports* not in the proper position for play

off′spring′ *n., pl.* -spring′ or -springs′ a child or children; progeny; young

off′stage′ *n.* the part of the stage not seen by the audience — *adj.* in or from this — *adv.* to the offstage

off′-track′ *adj.* designating or of legalized betting on horse races, carried on away from the racetrack

off′-white′ *adj.* grayish-white or yellowish-white

off year **1** a year in which a major election does not take place **2** a year of little production

oft (ôft) *adv.* ⟦OE⟧ *chiefly poet. var. of* OFTEN

often (ôf′ən; *also,* -tən) *adv.* ⟦ME var. of prec.⟧ many times; frequently   Also **of′ten·times′**

ogle (ō′gəl) *vi., vt.* o′gled, o′gling ⟦prob. < LowG *oog,* an eye⟧ to keep looking (at) flirtatiously — *n.* an ogling look —**o′gler** *n.*

ogre (ō′gər) *n.* ⟦Fr⟧ **1** in fairy tales and folklore, a maneating giant **2** a hideous, cruel man —**o′gre·ish** or **o′grish** *adj.*

oh (ō) *interj., n., pl.* **oh's** or **ohs** an exclamation of surprise, fear, pain, etc.

ohm (ōm) *n.* ⟦after G. S. *Ohm* (1789-1854), Ger physicist⟧ unit of electrical resistance

oho (ō hō′) *interj.* an exclamation of surprise, taunting, triumph, etc.

-oholic (ə häl′ik) *combining form* -AHOLIC *[beeroholic]*

-oid (oid) ⟦< Gr *eidos,* a form⟧ *suffix* like or resembling *[crystalloid]*

oil (oil) *n.* ⟦< L *oleum*⟧ **1** any of various greasy, combustible, liquid substances obtained from animal, vegetable, and mineral matter **2** PETROLEUM **3** *a*) OIL COLOR *b*) OIL PAINTING — *vt.* to lubricate or supply with oil — *adj.* of, from, or like oil

oil′cloth′ *n.* cloth made waterproof by being treated with oil or paint

oil color paint made by grinding a pigment in oil   Also **oil paint**

oil painting **1** a picture painted in oil colors **2** painting in oil colors

oil shale shale from which oil can be extracted by distillation

oil′skin′ *n.* **1** cloth made waterproof by treatment with oil **2** *[often pl.]* a garment or outfit made of this

oil well a well bored through layers of rock, etc. to a supply of petroleum

oily (oil′ē) *adj.* -i·er, -i·est **1** of, like, or containing oil **2** greasy **3** too suave or smooth; unctuous —**oil′i·ness** *n.*

oink (oiŋk) *n.* ⟦echoic⟧ the grunt of a pig — *vi.* to make this sound

oint·ment (oint′mənt) *n.* ⟦< L *unguentum,* a salve⟧ a fatty substance used on the skin for healing or cosmetic purposes; salve

OK or **O.K.** (ō kā′; ō′kā′, ō′kā′) *adj., adv., interj.* ⟦< "oll korrect," facetious misspelling of *all correct*⟧ all right; correct — *n., pl.* **OK's** or **O.K.'s** approval — *vt.* **OK'd** or **O.K.'d, OK'ing** or **O.K.'ing** to put an OK on; approve   Also [Colloq.] **o′kay′**

okey-doke (ō′kē dōk′) *adj., interj. slang var. of* OK   Also **o′key-do′key** (-dō′kē)

okra (ō′krə) *n.* ⟦< WAfr name⟧ **1** a plant with sticky green pods **2** the pods, used in soups, stews, etc.

old (ōld) *adj.* **old′er** or **eld′er, old′est** or **eld′est** ⟦OE *ald*⟧ **1** having lived or existed for a long time **2** of aged people **3** of a certain age *[two years old]* **4** not new **5** worn out by age or use **6** former **7** experienced *[an old hand]* **8** ancient **9** *[often* O-*]* designating the earliest form of a language *[Old* English*]* **10** designating the earlier or earliest of two or more *[the Old* World*]* — *n.* **1** time long past *[days of old]* **2** something old: with *the* —**old′ness** *n.*

Old Church Slavonic (slə vän′ik) the South Slavic language now used only as a liturgical language by Orthodox Slavs: also called **Old Church Slavic** or **Old Bulgarian**

THESAURUS

offset *v.* counterbalance, compensate, allow for; see BALANCE 2.

offspring *n.* progeny, issue, descendants, children, kids, siblings, lineage, generation, brood, seed, family, heirs, offshoots, heredity, succession, successors, next generation; see also BABY, CHILD.

often *a.* usually, many times, oftentimes; see FREQUENTLY.

oh *interj.* indeed!, oh-oh!, oh, no!, oh, yes!, oops; see also NO, YES.

oil *n.* **1** [Liquid, greasy substance] melted fat, unction, lubricant; see GREASE. *Common oils include the following:* vegetable, animal, mineral, saturated, polyunsaturated, fatty, volatile, essential, machine, crude, lubricating, cottonseed, olive, castor, palm, corn, safflower, coconut, whale, cocoa, linseed, drying, nondrying, soybean, sesame, cod-liver, fish; lard, tallow, oleo, Vaseline (trademark), turpentine. **2** [Liquid substance used for power or illumination] petroleum, kerosene, coal oil, crude oil, liquid coal, fossil oil; see also FUEL.

oil *v.* lubricate, smear, coat with oil; see GREASE.

oily *a.* **1** [Rich with oil] fatty, greasy, buttery, oil-soaked, rich, lardy, bland, oleaginous, soapy, soothing, creamy, oil-bearing.—*Ant.* DRY, dried, gritty. **2** [Having a surface suggestive of oil] oiled, waxy, sleek, slippery, smooth, polished, lustrous, bright, brilliant, gleaming, glistening, shining; see also SMOOTH 1, 2.—*Ant.* ROUGH, dull, unpolished. **3** [Unctuous] fulsome, suave, flattering; see AFFECTED 2, TREACHEROUS.

ointment *n.* unguent, lotion, cream; see MEDICINE 2.

OK *interj.* all right, correct, surely; see YES.

OK *n.* approval, endorsement, affirmation; see PERMISSION.

OK *v.* confirm, condone, notarize; see APPROVE, ENDORSE 2.

old *a.* **1** [No longer vigorous] aged, elderly, patriarchal, gray, venerable, not young, of long life, past one's prime, far advanced in years, matured, having lived long, full of years, seasoned, infirm, inactive, enfeebled, decrepit, superannuated, exhausted, tired, impaired, broken down, wasted, doddering, senile, ancient, having one foot in the grave, gone to seed.—*Ant.* YOUNG, fresh, youthful. **2** [Worn] time-worn, worn-out, thin, patched, ragged, faded, used, in holes, rubbed off, mended, broken-down, fallen to pieces, fallen in, given way, out of use, rusted, crumbled, dilapidated, battered, shattered, shabby, castoff, decayed, decaying, stale, useless, tattered, in rags, torn, moth-eaten.—*Ant.* FRESH, new, unused. **3** [Ancient] archaic, time-honored, prehistoric, bygone, early, antique, forgotten, immemorial, antediluvian, olden, remote, past, distant, former, of old, gone by, classic, medieval, in the Middle Ages, out of the dim past, primordial, primeval, before history, dateless, unrecorded, handed down, of earliest time, of the old order, ancestral, traditional, time out of mind, in the dawn of history, old as the hills; see also senses 1, 2.—*Ant.* MODERN, recent, late.

older *a.* elder, senior, sooner, former, preceding, prior, more aged, less young, not so new, earlier, first, firstborn, having come before, more ancient, lower, of an earlier time, of an earlier vintage, of a former period; see also OLD 3.—*Ant.* YOUNG, newer, of a later vintage.

oldest *a.* most aged, initial, primeval; see FIRST, ORIGINAL 1.

old country the country, esp. in Europe, from which an immigrant came

olden (ōl′dən, old″n) *adj.* [Old Poet.] (of) old

Old English the Germanic language of the Anglo-Saxons, spoken in England from *c.* 400 to *c.* 1100 A.D.

old′-fash′ioned *adj.* suited to or favoring the styles, ideas, etc. of past times — *n.* [*also* O- F-] a cocktail made with whiskey, bitters, and bits of fruit

old fogy or **old fogey** *see* FOGY

Old French the French language from *c.* 800 to *c.* 1550 A.D.

Old Glory *name for* the flag of the United States

Old Guard [transl. < Fr] the conservative element of a group, party, etc.

old hat [Slang] old-fashioned or stale

Old High German the High German language before the 12th c.

oldie or **oldy** (ōl′dē) *n., pl.* **-ies** [Colloq.] an old joke, saying, song, movie, etc.

old lady [Slang] 1 one's mother 2 one's wife

old′-line′ *adj.* long-established, traditional, conservative, etc.

Old Low German the Low German language before the 12th c.

old maid 1 a woman, esp. an older woman, who has never married 2 a prim, prudish, fussy person

old man [Slang] 1 one's father 2 one's husband 3 [*usually* O- M-] any man in authority: with *the*

old master 1 any of the great European painters before the 18th c. 2 a painting by any of these

Old Norse the Germanic language of the Scandinavians before the 14th c.

Old Saxon the Low German dialect of the Saxons before the 10th c.

old school a group of people who cling to traditional or conservative ideas, customs

old′ster (-stər) *n.* [Colloq.] an old or elderly person

Old Testament *Christian designation for* the Holy Scriptures of Judaism, the first of the two general divisions of the Christian Bible

old′-time′ *adj.* 1 of past times 2 of long standing

old′-tim′er *n.* [Colloq.] a long-time resident, employee, member, etc.

Old World Europe, Asia, and Africa

olé (ō lā′) *interj., n.* [Sp] a shout of approval, triumph, joy, etc.

oleagi·nous (ō′lē aj′i nəs) *adj.* [< L *olea*, olive tree] oily; unctuous

olean·der (ō′lē an′dər) *n.* [ML] a poisonous evergreen shrub with fragrant white, pink, or red flowers and narrow, leathery leaves

oleo·mar·ga·rine or **oleo·mar·ga·rin** (ō′lē ō mär′jə rin) *n.* [< L *oleum*, oil + MARGARINE] *old term for* MARGARINE Also **o′leo′**

ol·fac·tory (äl fak′tə rē, ōl-) *adj.* [< L *olere*, have a smell + *facere*, make] of the sense of smell

oli·gar·chy (äl′i gär′kē) *n., pl.* **-chies** [< Gr *oligos*, few + -ARCHY] 1 a) government in which power belongs to a few persons b) a state so governed 2 the ruling persons — **ol′i·gar′chic** *adj.*

ol·ive (äl′iv) *n.* [< L *oliva*] 1 a) an evergreen tree of S Europe and the Near East b) its small, oval fruit, eaten as

a relish or pressed, when ripe, to extract its light-yellow oil (**olive oil**) 2 the yellowish-green color of the unripe fruit

olive branch the branch of the olive tree, a symbol of peace

Olym·pic games (ō lim′pik) [< *Olympia*, plain in Greece, site of ancient games] an international athletic competition now held every two years, alternating between summer and winter games Also **Olym′pics**

Olym·pus (ō lim′pəs), **Mount** mountain in N Greece: in Greek mythology, the home of the gods —**Olym′pian** (-pē ən) *n., adj.*

om (ōm) *n.* [Sans] *Hinduism* a word intoned as during meditation

om·buds·man (äm′bədz mən) *n., pl.* **-men** [Swed < *ombud*, a deputy] a public official appointed to investigate citizens' complaints

omega (ō mē′gə, -mä′-) *n.* name of the 24th & final letter of the Greek alphabet (Ω, ω)

om·elet or **om·elette** (äm′ə lət, -lit) *n.* [< L *lamella*, small plate] eggs beaten and cooked flat in a pan

omen (ō′mən) *n.* [L] a thing or happening supposed to foretell a future event, either good or evil

omi·cron or **omi·kron** (äm′i krän′, ō′mi-) *n.* name of the 15th letter of the Greek alphabet (O, o)

omi·nous (äm′ə nəs) *adj.* of or serving as an evil omen; threatening —**om′i·nously** *adv.*

omis·sion (ō mish′ən) *n.* 1 an omitting 2 something omitted

omit (ō mit′) *vt.* **omit′ted, omit′ting** [< L *omittere* < *ob-* (see OB-) + *mittere*, send] 1 to fail to include; leave out 2 to fail to do; neglect

omni- [L < *omnis*, all] *combining form* all, everywhere

om·ni·bus (äm′ni bəs) *n., pl.* **-bus·es** [< L, for all] BUS — *adj.* dealing with many things at once

om·nipo·tent (äm nip′ə tənt) *adj.* [< L *omnis*, all + *potens*, able] having unlimited power or authority; all-powerful —**om·nip′o·tence** *n.*

omni·pres·ent (äm′ni prez′ənt) *adj.* present in all places at the same time —**om′ni·pres′ence** *n.*

om·nis·cient (äm nish′ənt) *adj.* [< L *omnis*, all + *sciens*, knowing] knowing all things —**the Omniscient** God — **om·nis′cience** *n.*

om·nivo·rous (äm niv′ə rəs) *adj.* [< L *omnis*, all + *vorare*, devour] 1 eating any sort of food, esp. both animal and vegetable food 2 taking in everything indiscriminately [an *omnivorous* reader] —**om·niv′o·rously** *adv.* — **om·niv′o·rous·ness** *n.*

on (än, ôn) *prep.* [OE] 1 in contact with, supported by, or covering 2 in the surface of [scars *on* it] 3 *a*) near to [*on* my left] *b*) having as its location [a house *on* Main Street] 4 at the time of [*on* Monday] 5 connected with [*on* the team] 6 engaged in [*on* a trip] 7 in a state of [*on* parole] 8 as a result of [a profit *on* the sale] 9 in the direction of [light shone *on* us] 10 through the use of [live *on* bread] 11 concerning [an essay *on* war] 12 [Colloq.] at the expense of [a drink *on* the house] 13 [Slang] using; addicted to [*on* drugs] — *adv.* 1 in a situation of contacting, being supported by, or covering 2 in a direction toward [he looked *on*] 3 forward [move *on*] 4 without stopping [she sang *on*] 5 into action or operation [turn on the light] — *adj.* in action or operation [the TV is *on*] —

<hr>

THESAURUS

old-fashioned *a.* antiquated, out-of-date, obsolete, obsolescent, outmoded, *démodé* (French), unfashionable, traditional, unstylish, passé, before the War, Victorian, not modern, old-time, time-honored, not current, antique, ancient, no longer prevailing, bygone, archaic, grown old, primitive, quaint, amusing, odd, neglected, outworn, of long standing, unused, past, behind the times, gone by, of the old school, extinct, out, gone out, out of it*; see also OLD 3.— *Ant.* MODERN, fashionable, stylish.

old lady* *n.* female spouse, woman, female member of the family; see MOTHER 1, PARENT, WIFE.

old man* *n.* head of the house, male spouse, man; see FATHER 1, HUSBAND, PARENT.

Old Testament *n.* the Covenant, Hebrew Scripture, Jewish Law; see BIBLE.

old-time *a.* outmoded, ancient, obso-

lete; see OLD-FASHIONED.

Old World *n.* Europe, Asia, mother country; see EAST 2.

Olympics *n.* Olympic Games, world championships, international amateur athletic competion; see COMPETITION, SPORT 3.

omen *n.* portent, augury, indication; see SIGN 1.

ominous *a.* threatening, forbidding, foreboding, menacing, dark, suggestive, fateful, premonitory, dire, grim, gloomy, haunting, perilous, ill-starred, ill-fated, impending, fearful, prophetic; see also DANGEROUS, DISMAL, DOOMED.—*Ant.* FAVORABLE, encouraging, auspicious.

omission *n.* 1 [The act of omitting] overlooking, missing, leaving out; see CARELESSNESS, EXCLUSION, NEGLECT 1.—*Ant.* ADDITION, mention, insertion. 2 [Something omitted] need, want, imperfection; see LACK 2.

omit *v.* 1 [To fail to include] leave out, reject, exclude; see BAR 2, DISMISS, ELIMINATE. 2 [To neglect] ignore, slight, overlook; see DISREGARD, NEGLECT 2.

omitted *a.* unmentioned, left out, overlooked; see MISSED 1, NEGLECTED.

on *a., prep.* 1 [Upon] above, in contact with, touching, supported by, situated upon, resting upon, on top of, about, held by, moving across, moving over, covering; see also UPON 1.—*Ant.* UNDER, underneath, below. 2 [Against] in contact with, close to, leaning on; see NEXT 2. 3 [Toward] proceeding, at, moving; see APPROACHING, TOWARD. 4 [Forward] onward, ahead, advancing; see FORWARD 1. 5 [Near] beside, close to, adjacent to; see BORDERING, NEAR 1. **—and so on** and so forth, also, in addition; see AND.

and so on and more like the preceding —**on and off** intermittently —**on and on** for a long time; continuously —**on to** [Slang] aware of the real nature or meaning of
ON Old Norse
once (wuns) *adv.* ⟦ME *ones*⟧ **1** one time only **2** at any time; ever **3** formerly *[a once famous woman]* **4** by one degree *[a cousin once removed]* —*conj.* as soon as *[once he is tired, he will quit]* —*n.* one time *[go this once]* —**at once 1** immediately **2** at the same time —**once (and) for all** conclusively —**once in a while** now and then
once'-o'ver *n.* [Colloq.] a quick look
on·co·gene (äŋ'kə jēn') *n.* ⟦< Gr *onkos*, a mass + GENE⟧ a gene that, when activated as by a virus, may cause a normal cell to become cancerous
on·col·o·gy (än käl'ə jē, äŋ-) *n.* ⟦< Gr *onkos*, a mass + -LOGY⟧ the branch of medicine dealing with tumors
on·com·ing (än'kum'iŋ) *adj.* coming nearer in position or time
one (wun) *adj.* ⟦OE *an*⟧ **1** being a single thing or unit **2** united *[with one accord]* **3** a certain but unnamed *[take one path or the other, one day last week]* **4** the same **5** unique; only *[the one solution]* —*n.* **1** the first and lowest cardinal number; 1; I **2** a single person or thing —*pron.* **1** a certain person or thing **2** any person or thing —**at one** in accord —**one by one** individually in succession
one'ness (-nis) *n.* **1** singleness; unity **2** unity of mind, feeling, etc.
on·er·ous (än'ər əs) *adj.* ⟦< L *onus*, a load⟧ burdensome; oppressive
one·self' (wun'self') *pron.* a person's own self Also **one's self** —**be oneself 1** to function normally **2** to be natural —**by oneself** alone
one'-sid'ed *adj.* **1** on, having, or involving only one side **2** unfair **3** unequal *[a one-sided race]*
one'time' (-tim') *adj.* former
one'-track' *adj.* [Colloq.] limited in scope *[a one-track mind]*
one'-up' *adj.* [Colloq.] having an advantage (over another)
one-up'man·ship' *n.* skill in seizing an advantage over others
one'-way' *adj.* moving, or allowing movement, in one direction only
on'go'ing *adj.* going on; progressing
on·ion (un'yən) *n.* ⟦< L *unus*, one⟧ **1** a plant of the lily family with an edible bulb **2** this bulb, having a strong, sharp smell and taste
on'ion·skin' *n.* a tough, thin, translucent, glossy paper
on-line (än'lin') *adj.* designating or of equipment directly connected to and controlled by the central processing unit of a computer
on'look'er *n.* a spectator
only (ōn'lē) *adj.* ⟦< OE *an*, one + *-lic*, -ly⟧ **1** alone of its or their kind; sole **2** alone in superiority; best —*adv.* **1** and no other; and no more; solely **2** (but) in the end *[to meet one crisis, only to face another]* **3** as recently as —*conj.* [Colloq.] except that; but —**if only** I wish that —**only too** very; exceedingly
ono·mato·poeia (än'ō mat'ō pē'ə, -mät'-) *n.* ⟦< Gr *onoma*, a name + *poiein*, make⟧ the formation of words by imitating sounds (Ex.: *buzz*) —**on'o·mat'o·poe'ic** *adj.*
on'rush' *n.* a headlong dash forward
on'set' *n.* **1** an attack **2** a start
on·slaught (än'slôt') *n.* ⟦< Du *slagen*, to strike⟧ a violent attack
onto (än'tōo) *prep.* **1** to and upon; to a position on **2** [Slang] aware of Also **on to**
on·tog·eny (än täj'ə nē) *n.* ⟦ult. < Gr *einai*, to be + *-genēs*, born⟧ the life cycle of a single organism
onus (ō'nəs) *n.* ⟦L⟧ **1** a burden, unpleasant duty, etc. **2** blame
on·ward (än'wərd) *adv.* toward or at a position ahead; forward Also **on'wards** —*adj.* advancing
onyx (än'iks) *n.* ⟦< Gr, fingernail⟧ a type of agate with alternate colored layers
oo·dles (ōod'lz) *n.pl.* ⟦< ?⟧ [Colloq.] a great amount; very many
ooze¹ (ōoz) *n.* ⟦OE *wos*, sap⟧ something that oozes —*vi.* **oozed, ooz'ing** to flow or leak out slowly —*vt.* to exude
ooze² (ōoz) *n.* ⟦OE *wase*⟧ soft mud or slime, as at the bottom of a lake
op- *prefix* OB-: used before *p [oppress]*
opal (ō'pəl) *n.* ⟦< Sans *úpalaḥ*, (precious) stone⟧ an iridescent silica of various colors: some varieties are semiprecious —**opal·es·cent** (ō'pəl es'ənt) *adj.*
opaque (ō pāk') *adj.* ⟦< L *opacus*, shady⟧ **1** not transparent **2** not reflecting light; dull **3** hard to understand —**opac·ity** (ō pas'ə tē) or **opaque'ness** *n.* —**opaque'ly** *adv.*
op (art) (äp) a style of abstract painting creating optical illusions
op. cit. ⟦L *opere citato*⟧ in the work cited
OPEC (ō'pek') *n.* Organization of Petroleum Exporting Countries
Op-Ed (äp'ed') *adj.* ⟦*Op(posite) Ed(itorial page)*⟧ designating or on a page in a newspaper featuring a wide variety of columns, articles, letters, etc.
open (ō'pən) *adj.* ⟦OE⟧ **1** not closed, covered, clogged, or shut **2** not enclosed *[open fields]* **3** spread out; unfolded *[an open book]* **4** having gaps, holes, etc. **5** free to be

---

■ THESAURUS ■

on and off *a.* now and then, sometimes, infrequently; see SELDOM.
once *a.* **1** [One time] this time, but once, once only, before, one time before, already, one, just this once, not more than once, never again, a single time, one time previously, on one occasion, only one time.—*Ant.* FREQUENTLY, twice, many times. **2** [Formerly] long ago, previously, earlier; see FORMERLY. —**all at once** simultaneously, all at the same time, unanimously; see TOGETHER 2. —**at once** now, quickly, this moment; see IMMEDIATELY. —**for once** for at least one time, once only, uniquely; see ONCE 1. —**once and for all** with finality, permanently, unalterably; see FINALLY 1. —**once in a while** sometimes, occasionally, on occasion; see SELDOM.
once-over* *n.* look, inspection, checkup; see EXAMINATION 1.
oncoming *a.* impending, expected, imminent; see APPROACHING.
one *a.* individual, peculiar, special, specific, separate, single, singular, odd, one and only, precise, definite, sole, uncommon; see also SPECIAL, UNIQUE, UNUSUAL 2.—*Ant.* COMMON, several, imprecise.
one *n.* unit, whole, person, thing, identity, ace, integer, item, example, digit, singleness, individual, individuality, individuation.—*Ant.* MANY, plural, several. —**all one** making no

difference, insignificant, of no importance; see UNIMPORTANT. —**at one in** accord, agreeing, of the same opinion; see UNITED. —**tie one on*** go on a drinking spree, get drunk, imbibe; see DRINK 2.
oneness *n.* integrity, harmony, indivisibility; see UNITY 1.
one-sided *a.* **1** [Unilateral] single, uneven, partial; see IRREGULAR 4. **2** [Prejudiced] biased, partial, narrow-minded; see PREJUDICED, UNFAIR.
one-way *a.* directional, with no return, restricted; see NARROW 1.
ongoing *a.* open-ended, continuous, in process; see REGULAR 3.
only *a.* **1** [Solely] exclusively, uniquely, wholly, entirely, particularly, and no other, and no more, and nothing else, nothing but, totally, utterly, first and last, one and only; see also SINGLY 1. **2** [Merely] just, simply, plainly, barely, solely; see also HARDLY 3. **3** [Sole] single, companionless, without another, by oneself, isolated, apart, unaccompanied, exclusive, unique; see also ALONE.
onset *n.* incipience, opening, start; see ORIGIN 2.
onto *a., prep.* **1** [To] toward, in contact with, adjacent; see AGAINST 1. **2** [Upon] over, out upon, above; see UPON 1.
onward *a.* on ahead, beyond, in front of; see FORWARD 1, MOVING 1.

ooze¹ *v.* seep, exude, leak; see FLOW.
ooze² *n.* slime, fluid, mire; see MUD.
opaque *a.* not transparent, dim, dusky, darkened, murky, gloomy, smoky, thick, misty, cloudy, clouded, shady, muddy, dull, blurred, frosty, filmy, foggy, sooty, dirty, dusty, coated over, covered.—*Ant.* CLEAR, transparent, translucent.
open *a.* **1** [Not closed] unclosed, accessible, clear, open to view, uncovered, disclosed, divulged, introduced, initiated, begun, full-blown, unfurled, susceptible, ajar, gaping, wide, rent, torn, spacious, unshut, expansive, extensive, spread out, revealed; see also senses 2, 4.—*Ant.* CLOSED, tight, shut. **2** [Not obstructed] unlocked, unbarred, unbolted, unblocked, unfastened, cleared away, removed, made passable, unsealed, unobstructed, unoccupied, vacated, unburdened, emptied; see also sense 1.—*Ant.* TAKEN, barred, blocked. **3** [Not forbidden] free of entrance, unrestricted, permitted, allowable, free of access, public, welcoming, not posted; see also PERMITTED.—*Ant.* REFUSED, forbidden, restricted. **4** [Not protected] unguarded, unsecluded, liable, exposed, uncovered, apart, unshut, unroofed, insecure, unsafe, conspicuous, unhidden, unconcealed, subject, sensitive; see also sense 1 and

entered, used, etc. *[an open meeting]* **6** not decided *[an open question]* **7** not closed to new ideas, etc. *[an open mind]* **8** generous **9** free from legal or discriminatory restrictions *[open season, open housing]* **10** not conventional *[open marriage]* **11** not already taken *[the job is open]* **12** not secret; public **13** frank; candid *[an open manner]* —*vt.*, *vi.* **1** to cause to be, or to become, open **2** to spread out; expand; unfold **3** to make or become available for use, etc. without restriction **4** to begin; start **5** to start operating —**open to 1** willing to receive, discuss, etc. **2** available to —**the open 1** the outdoors **2** public knowledge —**o'pen·er** *n.* —**o'pen·ly** *adv.* —**o'pen·ness** *n.*

open air the outdoors —**o'pen-air'** *adj.*
o'pen-and-shut' *adj.* easily decided
o'pen-end'ed (-en'did) *adj.* broad, unlimited, or unrestricted
o'pen-eyed' *adj.* with the eyes wide open, as in surprise or watchfulness
o'pen-faced' *adj.* **1** having a frank, honest face **2** designating a sandwich without a top slice of bread: also **o'pen-face'**
o'pen·hand'ed *adj.* generous
o'pen-heart'ed *adj.* **1** not reserved; frank **2** kindly; generous
o'pen-hearth' *adj.* designating or using a furnace with a wide hearth and low roof, for making steel
o'pen-heart' surgery surgery on the heart during which the blood is diverted and circulated by mechanical means
open house 1 an informal reception at one's home **2** a time when an institution is open to visitors
o'pen·ing *n.* **1** an open place; hole; gap **2** a clearing **3** a beginning **4** start of operations **5** a favorable chance **6** an unfilled job
o'pen-mind'ed *adj.* having a mind open to new ideas; unprejudiced —**o'pen-mind'ed·ly** *adv.* —**o'pen-mind'ed·ness** *n.*

o'pen·work' *n.* ornamental work, as in cloth, with openings in it
op·er·a¹ (äp'ər ə) *n.* ⟦< L, a work⟧ a play having its text set to music and sung to orchestral accompaniment —**op'er·at'ic** (-ə rat'ik) *adj.*
ope·ra² (ō'pə rə, äp'ə rə) *n. pl. of* OPUS
op·er·a·ble (äp'ər ə bəl) *adj.* ⟦see OPERATE & -ABLE⟧ **1** feasible **2** that can be treated by a surgical operation
opera glasses a small binocular telescope used in theaters, etc.
op·er·ate (äp'ər āt') *vi.* **-at'ed, -at'ing** ⟦< L operari, to work⟧ **1** to be in action; act; work **2** to bring about a certain effect **3** to perform a surgical operation — *vt.* **1** to put or keep in action **2** to direct; manage
op'er·a'tion *n.* ⟦< L operatio⟧ **1** the act or method of operating **2** a being in action or at work **3** a process or action that is part of a series in some work **4** any surgical procedure to remedy a physical ailment
op'er·a'tion·al *adj.* **1** of or having to do with the operation of a device, system, process, etc. **2** *a)* that can be used or operated *b)* in use; operating
op'er·a·tive (-ə tiv') *adj.* **1** in operation **2** effective **3** connected with physical work or mechanical action
op'er·a·tor (-āt'ər) *n.* **1** one who operates a machine *[a telephone operator]* **2** one engaged in commercial or industrial operations
op·er·et·ta (äp'ər et'ə) *n.* ⟦It, dim. of opera, OPERA¹⟧ an amusing opera with spoken dialogue
oph·thal·mic (äf thal'mik) *adj.* ⟦< Gr ophthalmos, the eye⟧ of or connected with the eyes
oph·thal·mol·o·gy (äf'thal mäl'ə jē, -thəl-; äp'-) *n.* ⟦< Gr ophthalmos, the eye + -LOGY⟧ the branch of medicine dealing with the eye and its diseases —**oph'thal·mol'o·gist** *n.*
opi·ate (ō'pē it) *n.* ⟦ML opiatum⟧ **1** a drug containing, or

---

THESAURUS

UNSAFE.—*Ant.* SAFE, secluded, secure.
5 [Not decided] in question, up for discussion, debatable; see QUESTION-ABLE 1, UNCERTAIN. **6** [Frank] plain, candid, straightforward; see FRANK.
open *v.* **1** [To begin] start, inaugurate, initiate; see BEGIN 1, 2. **2** [To move aside a prepared obstruction] unbar, unlock, unclose, clear, admit, reopen, open the lock, lift the latch, free, loosen, disengage, unfasten, undo, unbolt, turn the key, turn the knob.—*Ant.* CLOSE, shut, lock. **3** [To make an opening] force an entrance, breach, cut in, tear down, push in, shatter, destroy, burst in, break open, cave in, burst out from, penetrate, pierce, force one's way into, smash, punch a hole into, slit, puncture, crack, muscle in*, jimmy*; see also FORCE, REMOVE 1.—*Ant.* REPAIR, seal, mend. **4** [To make available] make accessible, put on sale, put on view, open to the public, make public, put forward, free, make usable, prepare, present, make ready.—*Ant.* REMOVE, put away, lock up. **5** [To expose to fuller view] unroll, unfold, uncover; see EXPOSE 1, REVEAL.
opened *a.* unlocked, made open, not closed; see FREE 3, OPEN 2.
open-ended *a.* going on, without specified limits, optional; see CONSTANT, UNCERTAIN.
opening *a.* initial, beginning, primary; see FIRST.
opening *n.* **1** [A hole] break, crack, tear; see HOLE 1. **2** [An opportunity] chance, availability, occasion; see OPPORTUNITY 1, POSSIBILITY 2.
openly *a.* **1** [Frankly] naturally, simply, artlessly, naively, unsophisticatedly, out in the open, candidly, aboveboard, straightforwardly, honestly, unreservedly, fully, readily, willingly, without restraint, plainly, without reserve, to one's face, in public, face to face; see also SINCERELY.—*Ant.* SECRETLY, furtively, surrepti-

tiously. **2** [Shamelessly] immodestly, brazenly, not caring, regardlessly, insensibly, unconcernedly, crassly, insolently, flagrantly, wantonly, unblushingly, notoriously, without pretense, in defiance of the law; see also CARELESSLY, LEWDLY.—*Ant.* CAREFULLY, prudently, discreetly.
open-minded *a.* tolerant, fairminded, just; see FAIR 1, LIBERAL.
opera¹ *n.* musical drama, libretto, score, operetta, grand opera, light opera, comic opera, rock opera, opera performance; see also PERFORMANCE.
operate *v.* **1** [To keep in operation] manipulate, conduct, administer; see MANAGE 1. **2** [To be in operation] function, work, serve, carry on, run, revolve, act, behave, fulfill, turn, roll, spin, pump, lift, spark, burn, move, progress, advance, proceed, go, contact, hit, engage, transport, convey, contain, click*, tick*.—*Ant.* STOP, stall, break down. **3** [To produce an effect] react, act on, influence, bring about, determine, turn, bend, contrive, work, accomplish, fulfill, finish, complete, benefit, compel, promote, concern, enforce, take effect, have effect, work on, succeed, get results, get across; see also ACHIEVE, PRODUCE 1. **4** [To perform a surgical operation] remove diseased tissue, amputate, transplant; see TREAT 2.
operated *a.* conducted, handled, run, carried on, regulated, ordered, maintained, supervised, superintended, governed, administered, transacted, performed, conveyed, transported, moved, determined, achieved, contrived, accomplished, fulfilled, promoted, enforced, worked, served, guided, executed, sustained, used, practiced, put into effect, finished, driven, brought about, bent, manipulated, negotiated; see also DIRECTED, MANAGED 2.
operating *a.* managing, conducting, directing, executing, manipulating,

administering, ordering, regulating, supervising, running, wielding, transacting, guiding, putting into effect, sustaining, maintaining, performing, practicing, revolving, promoting, determining, moving, turning, spinning, driving, contriving, fulfilling, accomplishing, finishing, effecting, bringing about, serving, enforcing, in operation, at work; see also USING.
operation *n.* **1** [The act of causing to function] execution, guidance, superintendence, carrying out, ordering, order, maintenance, handling, manipulating, manipulation, supervision, control, conduct, agency, enforcement, advancement, regulating, running, supervising, directing, transacting, conducting; see also MANAGEMENT 1, REGULATION 1. **2** [An action] performance, act, employment, labor, service, carrying on, transaction, deed, doing, proceeding, handiwork, workmanship, enterprise, movement, progress, development, engagement, undertaking; see also ACTION 1, WORK 2. **3** [A method] process, formula, procedure; see METHOD, PLAN 2. **4** [Surgical treatment] surgery, transplant, amputation, dismemberment, vivisection, dissection, biopsy, emergency operation, acupuncture, exploratory operation, section, excision, removal, tonsillectomy, appendectomy, open-heart surgery, abortion, autopsy, the knife*; see also MEDICINE 3.
operator *n.* **1** [One who operates a machine] engineer, operative, skilled employee; see LABORER, WORKMAN. *Kinds of operators include the following:* telephone, computer, switchboard, PBX, information, long-distance, emergency. **2** [One who operates workable property] executive, supervisor, director; see EXECUTIVE. **3** [*Manipulator] speculator, scoundrel, fraud; see RASCAL.

derived from, opium **2** anything that quiets, soothes, or deadens

opine (ō pīn′) *vt., vi.* **opined′, opin′ing** ⟦ < L *opinari*, think ⟧ to hold (an opinion): usually humorous

opin·ion (ə pin′yən, ō-) *n.* ⟦ < L *opinari*, think ⟧ **1** a belief not based on certainty but on what seems true or probable **2** an evaluation, estimation, etc. **3** formal expert judgment

opin′ion·at′ed (-āt′id) *adj.* holding obstinately to one's opinions

opium (ō′pē əm) *n.* ⟦ < Gr *opos*, vegetable juice ⟧ a narcotic drug prepared from the seed of a certain poppy

opos′sum (ə päs′əm) *n.* ⟦ < AmInd, white beast ⟧ a small, nocturnal, tree-dwelling American marsupial

op·po·nent (ə pō′nənt) *n.* ⟦ < L *ob-* (see OB-) + *ponere*, to place ⟧ one who opposes, as in a game; adversary

op·por·tune (äp′ər tōōn′) *adj.* ⟦ < L *ob-* (see OB-) + *portus*, PORT[1] ⟧ **1** suitable: said of time **2** well-timed

op′por·tun′ism′ *n.* the adapting of one's actions, thoughts, etc. to circumstances, as in politics, without regard for principles —**op′por·tun′ist** *n., adj.* —**op′por· tun·is′tic** *adj.*

op·por·tu·ni·ty (äp′ər tōō′nə tē) *n., pl.* **-ties 1** a combination of circumstances favorable for the purpose **2** a good chance

op·pose (ə pōz′) *vt.* **-posed′, -pos′ing** ⟦ < L *ob-* (see OB-) + *ponere*, to place ⟧ **1** to place opposite **2** to contend with; resist

op·po·site (äp′ə zit) *adj.* ⟦ < L *ob-* (see OB-) + *ponere*, to place ⟧ **1** set against; in a contrary direction: often with *to* **2** entirely different; exactly contrary — *n.* anything opposed — *prep.* across from —**op′po·sitely** *adv.*

opposite number one whose position, rank, etc. parallels another's in a different place or organization

op′po·si′tion (-zish′ən) *n.* **1** an opposing **2** resistance, contrast, hostility, etc. **3** *a)* one that opposes *b)* [*often* O-] a political party opposing the party in power

op·press (ə pres′) *vt.* ⟦ < L *ob-* (see OB-) + *premere*, to press ⟧ **1** to weigh heavily on the mind of; worry **2** to keep down by the cruel or unjust use of authority —**op·pres′ sor** *n.*

op·pres·sion (ə presh′ən) *n.* **1** an oppressing or being oppressed **2** a thing that oppresses **3** physical or mental distress

op·pres·sive (ə pres′iv) *adj.* **1** causing discomfort **2** tyrannical **3** distressing —**op·pres′sively** *adv.*

op·pro·bri·ous (ə prō′brē əs) *adj.* expressing opprobrium; abusive

op·pro′bri·um (-əm) *n.* ⟦ < L *ob-* (see OB-) + *probrum*, a disgrace ⟧ **1** the disgrace attached to shameful conduct **2** anything bringing shame

opt (äpt) *vi.* ⟦ < L *optare*, to wish ⟧ to make a choice: often with *for* —**opt out (of)** to choose not to be or continue in (some activity, organization, etc.)

op·tic (äp′tik) *adj.* ⟦ < Gr *ōps*, an eye ⟧ of the eye or sense of sight

op·ti·cal (äp′ti kəl) *adj.* **1** of the sense of sight; visual **2** of optics **3** for aiding vision —**op′ti·cally** *adv.*

op·ti·cian (äp tish′ən) *n.* one who makes or sells eyeglasses, etc.

op·tics (äp′tiks) *n.pl.* [*with sing. v.*] the branch of physics dealing with light and vision

op·ti·mism (äp′tə miz′əm) *n.* ⟦ < L *optimus*, best ⟧ **1** the belief that good ultimately prevails over evil **2** the tendency to take the most hopeful view of matters —**op′ti· mist** (-mist) *n.* —**op′ti·mis′tic** (-mis′tik) *adj.* —**op′ti· mis′ti·cally** *adv.*

▬▬▬▬▬ THESAURUS ▬▬▬▬▬

opinion *n.* **1** [A belief] notion, view, point of view, sentiment, conception, idea, surmise, impression, inference, conjecture, inclination, fancy, imagining, supposition, suspicion, notion, assumption, guess, theory, thesis, theorem, postulate, hypothesis, persuasion, presumption, presupposition, mind; see also BELIEF. **2** [A considered judgment] estimation, estimate, view, summary, belief, idea, resolution, determination, recommendation, finding, conviction, conclusion; see also JUDGMENT 3, VERDICT.

opinionated *a.* bigoted, stubborn, unyielding; see OBSTINATE, PREJUDICED.

opium *n.* opiate, soporific, dope*; see DRUG.

opponent *n.* **1** [A rival] competitor, contender, challenger, candidate, equal, entrant, the opposition, aspirant, bidder.—*Ant.* SUPPORTER, defender, abettor. **2** [An opposing contestant] antagonist, contestant, litigant; see PLAYER 1. **3** [An enemy] foe, adversary, assailant; see ENEMY.

opportunity *n.* **1** [Favorable circumstances] chance, occasion, happening, event, excuse, suitable circumstance, probability, good fortune, luck, break; see also POSSIBILITY 2. **2** [A suitable time] occasion, moment, time and tide; see TIME 2.

oppose *v.* **1** [To hold a contrary opinion] object, disapprove, debate, dispute, disagree, contradict, argue, deny, run counter to, protest, defy, cross, speak against, confront, thwart, neutralize, reverse, turn the tables, be opposed to, oppose change, not have any part of, face down, interfere with, disapprove of, cry out against, disagree with, not conform, run against, run counter to, come in conflict with, go contrary to, frown at, not be good for, not accept, call into question, conflict with, grapple with, doubt, be against, be unwilling, reject, dislike, take exception, repudiate, question, probe, resist, con-

found, confute, refute, buck*, turn thumbs down*; see also sense 2 and DARE 2, FACE 1.—*Ant.* AGREE, approve, accept. **2** [To fight] resist, battle, encounter, assault, attack, assail, storm, protest, clash, meet, skirmish, engage, contest, face, restrain, go against, turn against, uphold, defend, rebel, revolt, mutiny, strike back, combat, run counter to, defy, snub, grapple with, fight off, withstand, repel, guard, counterattack, struggle, outflank, antagonize, retaliate, impede, overpower, take on all comers*, lock horns with; see also FIGHT.

opposed *a.* antagonistic to, averse, adverse, opposite, contrary, hostile to, at odds, disputed, counter to, at cross purposes, up against, against the grain; see also OPPOSITE 2.

opposing *a.* **1** [In the act of opposition] conflicting, unfriendly, clashing; see OPPOSED. **2** [Situated opposite] contrary, facing, fronting; see OPPOSITE 3.

opposite *a.* **1** [Contrary] antithetical, diametric, reversed; see UNLIKE. **2** [In conflict] adverse, inimical, antagonistic, rival, unfavorable, averse, argumentative, contradictory, hostile; see also AGAINST 1. **3** [So situated as to seem to oppose] facing, fronting, in front of, on different sides of, on opposite sides, in opposition to, contrasting, on the other side of, contrary, over against, front to front, back to back, nose to nose, on the farther side, opposing, diametrical, eyeball to eyeball*.—*Ant.* MATCHED, on the same side, side by side.

opposite *n.* contradiction, contrary, converse, direct opposite, opposition, vice versa, antithesis, antonym, counter term, counterpart, inverse, reverse, adverse, the opposite pole, the other extreme, the other side, the opposite idea.—*Ant.* EQUAL, like, similar thing.

opposition *n.* **1** [The act of oppos-

ing] hostilities, conflict, combat; see BATTLE, FIGHT 1. **2** [The attitude suggestive of opposition] dislike, disagreement, hostility, antagonism, defiance, antipathy, abhorrence, aversion, constraint, restriction, restraint, hindrance, discord, distaste, disfavor, dissatisfaction, discontent, displeasure, irritation, offense, chagrin, humiliation, anger, loathing, disapproval, complaint, repugnance; see also HATRED, RESENTMENT.—*Ant.* SUPPORT, enthusiasm, accord. **3** [The individual or group that opposes] antagonist, disputant, adversary; see ENEMY, OPPONENT 1.

oppress *v.* suppress, harass, maltreat; see ABUSE, BOTHER 2.

oppressed *a.* misused, downtrodden, enslaved; see HURT.

oppression *n.* tyranny, hardness, domination, coercion, dictatorship, fascism, persecution, severity, harshness, abuse, conquering, overthrowing, compulsion, force, torment, martial law; see also CRUELTY.—*Ant.* FREEDOM, liberalism, voluntary control.

opt (for) *v.* choose, decide, pick; see CHOOSE, DECIDE.

optical *a.* ocular, seeing, visible; see VISUAL.

optimism *n.* **1** [Belief in the essential goodness of the universe] mysticism, philosophy of goodness, belief in progress; see FAITH 1. **2** [An inclination to expect or to hope for the best] cheerfulness, hopefulness, confidence, assurance, encouragement, happiness, brightness, enthusiasm, good cheer, trust, calmness, elation, expectancy, expectation, anticipation, certainty.—*Ant.* GLOOM, despair, melancholy.

optimist *n.* Pollyanna, dreamer, positivist.

optimistic *a.* cheerful, sanguine, assured; see CONFIDENT, HOPEFUL 1, TRUSTING.

op·ti·mum (-məm) *n., pl.* **-mums** or **-ma** (-mə) ⟦see prec.⟧ the best or most favorable degree, condition, etc. — *adj.* most favorable; best: also **op'ti·mal** (-məl)

op·tion (äp'shən) *n.* ⟦< L *optare*, to wish⟧ 1 a choosing; choice 2 the right of choosing 3 something that is or can be chosen 4 the right to buy, sell, or lease at a fixed price within a specified time —**op'tional** *adj.*

op·tom·e·try (äp täm'ə trē) *n.* ⟦< Gr *optikos*, optic + *metron*, a measure⟧ the profession of testing and examining the eyes and prescribing glasses to correct vision problems —**op·tom'e·trist'** *n.*

opu·lent (äp'yōō lənt, -yə-) *adj.* ⟦< L *ops*, riches⟧ 1 very wealthy 2 abundant —**op'u·lence** *n.*

opus (ō'pəs) *n., pl.* **opera** (ō'pə rə, äp'ə rə) or **o'pus·es** ⟦L, a work⟧ a work; composition; esp., any of the numbered musical works of a composer

or (ôr) *conj.* ⟦OE *oththe*⟧ a coordinating conjunction introducing: *a)* an alternative [red *or* blue] or the last in a series of choices b) a synonymous word or phrase [oral, *or* spoken]

-or (ər, ôr) *suffix* 1 a person or thing that (does a specified thing) [*inventor*] 2 quality or condition [*favor*]

ora·cle (ôr'ə kəl, är'-) *n.* ⟦< L *orare*, pray⟧ 1 among the ancient Greeks and Romans, *a)* the place where, or medium by which, deities were consulted b) the revelation of a medium or priest 2 *a)* a person of great knowledge b) statements of such a person —**oracu·lar** (ō rak' yōō lər) *adj.*

oral (ôr'əl, ōr'-) *adj.* ⟦< L *os*, the mouth⟧ 1 uttered; spoken 2 of or near the mouth —**o'ral·ly** *adv.*

-orama (ə ram'ə, -räm'ə) *combining form* a greater-than-usual number, volume, etc. of a specified thing [*panorama*]

orange (ôr'inj, är'-) *n.* ⟦< Sans *naranga*⟧ 1 a round, edible, reddish-yellow citrus fruit, with a sweet, juicy pulp 2 the evergreen tree it grows on 3 reddish yellow

orange·ade (ôr'inj ād', ôrnj'äd') *n.* a drink made of orange juice, water, and sugar

orangu·tan (ō raŋ'ōō tan'; also raŋ'-, ə-) *n.* ⟦< Malay *oraṅ*, man + *utan*, forest⟧ an ape of Borneo and Sumatra with shaggy, reddish-brown hair and very long arms

orate (ō rāt', ô-) *vi.* **-rat'ed, -rat'ing** to make an oration; speak in a pompous or bombastic way

ora·tion (ō rā'shən, ô-) *n.* ⟦< L *orare*, speak⟧ a formal speech, esp. one given at a ceremony

ora·tor (ôr'ət ər, är'-) *n.* an eloquent public speaker

ora·to·rio (ôr'ə tôr'ē ō') *n., pl.* **-os'** ⟦It, small chapel⟧ a long, dramatic musical work, usually on a religious theme, but not acted out

ora·tory (ôr'ə tôr'ē, är'-) *n., pl.* **-ries** ⟦< L *oratoria*⟧ skill in public speaking —**or'a·tor'i·cal** *adj.*

orb (ôrb) *n.* ⟦L *orbis*, a circle⟧ a sphere, or globe

or·bit (ôr'bit) *n.* ⟦< L *orbis*, a circle⟧ 1 the path of a celestial body during its revolution around another 2 the path of an artificial satellite or spacecraft around a celestial body — *vi., vt.* to move in, or put into, an orbit —**or'bital** *adj.*

or·chard (ôr'chərd) *n.* ⟦OE *ortgeard*⟧ 1 land for growing fruit trees 2 the trees

or·ches·tra (ôr'kis trə, -kes'-) *n.* ⟦< Gr *orcheisthai*, to dance⟧ 1 the space in front of a theater stage, where the musicians sit: in full **orchestra pit** 2 the seats on the main floor of a theater 3 *a)* a group of musicians playing together b) their instruments —**or·ches'tral** (-kes'trəl) *adj.*

or'ches·trate' (-trāt') *vt., vi.* **-trat'ed, -trat'ing** to arrange (music) for an orchestra —**or'ches·tra'tion** *n.*

or·chid (ôr'kid) *n.* ⟦< Gr *orchis*, testicle: from the shape of the roots⟧ 1 a perennial plant having flowers with three petals, one of which is lip-shaped 2 this flower 3 pale purple

or·dain (ôr dān') *vt.* ⟦< L *ordo*, an order⟧ 1 to decree; establish; enact 2 to invest with the office of minister, priest, or rabbi — *vi.* to command —**or·dain'ment** *n.*

or·deal (ôr dēl', ôr'dēl') *n.* ⟦OE *ordal*⟧ any difficult or painful experience

or·der (ôr'dər) *n.* ⟦< L *ordo*, straight row⟧ 1 social position 2 a state of peace; orderly conduct 3 arrangement of things or events; series 4 a definite plan; system 5 a military, monastic, or social brotherhood 6 a condition in

---

THESAURUS

option *n.* 1 [A choice] selection, alternative, dilemma; see CHOICE. 2 [A privilege to purchase] right, prerogative, grant, claim, license, lease, franchise, advantage, security, immunity, benefit, title, prior claim, dibs*.

optional *a.* discretionary, elective, noncompulsory, free, unrestricted, arbitrary, not required, with no strings attached*, take it or leave it*; see also VOLUNTARY.—*Ant.* NECESSARY, compulsory, enforced.

or *conj.* 1 [A suggestion of choice] or only, or but, as an alternative, on the other hand, in turn, conversely, in other words, or else, in preference to; see also EITHER.—*Ant.* NOR, neither, without choice. 2 [A suggestion of correction] or not, or not exactly, in reverse, reversing it, on the contrary, contrary to, oppositely, or rather, instead of, correctly speaking; see also INSTEAD. 3 [A suggestion of approximation] roughly, about, practically; see APPROXIMATELY.

oral *a.* vocal, verbal, uttered, voiced, unwritten, phonetic, sounded, not written, by word of mouth; see also SPOKEN.—*Ant.* WRITTEN, PRINTED, unspoken.

orange *a.* reddish, ocherous, glowing; see ORANGE, *n.* 2.

orange *n.* 1 [Color] red-yellow, apricot, tangerine, burnt orange, peach, coral, salmon; see also COLOR. 2 [Fruit] citrus fruit, tropical fruit, sour orange; see FOOD, FRUIT.

orbit *n.* 1 [Path described by one body revolving around another] ellipse, circle, ring, circuit, apogee, course, perigee, lap, round, cycle, curve, flight path; see also REVOLUTION 1. 2 [Range of activity or influence] range, field, boundary; see AREA.

orbit *v.* 1 [To revolve around another body] encircle, encompass, ring, move in a circuit, go around, revolve; see also CIRCLE. 2 [To put into orbit] fire, lift off, project; see LAUNCH 2.

orbited *a.* sent into orbit, put up, rocketed; see DRIVEN, SENT.

orchard *n.* fruit trees, fruit farm, apple orchard; see FARM.

orchestra *n.* musical ensemble, symphony, trio, quartet, quintet; see also BAND.

ordain *v.* 1 [To establish] install, institute, appoint; see ENACT. 2 [To destine] determine, foreordain, intend; see INTEND 2. 3 [To invest with priestly functions] install, confer holy orders upon, consecrate, frock, delegate, invest; see also BLESS.

ordained *a.* 1 [Ordered] commanded, determined, established by law; see ESTABLISHED 2, ORDERED 2. 2 [Invested into the ministry] consecrated, anointed, received into the ministry; see NAMED 2.

ordeal *n.* tribulation, distress, calamity; see DIFFICULTY 1, 2.

order *n.* 1 [A command] direction, demand, decree, rule, edict, charge, requirement, ordinance, act, warrant, mandate, injunction; see also COMMAND, LAW 3. 2 [Sequence] progression, succession, procession; see LINE 1, SEQUENCE 1, SERIES. 3 [Orderly arrangement] regulation, plan, disposition, management, establishment, method, distribution, placement, scale, rule, computation, adjustment, adaptation, ordering, ranging, standardizing, lining up, trimming, grouping, composition, cast, assortment, disposal, scheme, form, routine, array, procedure, method, index, regularity, uniformity, symmetry,

harmony, placement, layout, lineup, setup; see also CLASSIFICATION, SYSTEM.—*Ant.* CONFUSION, disarray, displacement. 4 [Organization] society, sect, company; see ORGANIZATION 2. 5 [A formal agreement to purchase] engagement, reserve, application, requisition, request, stipulation, booking, layaway, arrangement; see also BUYING, RESERVATION 1. 6 [Kind] rank, hierarchy, degree; see CLASS 1, CLASSIFICATION. 7 [Customary method] ritual, rite, plan; see CUSTOM. —**in order** working, efficient, operative; see EFFECTIVE. —**in order to** for the purpose of, as a means to, so that; see FOR. —**in short order** rapidly, without delay, soon; see QUICKLY. —**on order** requested, on the way, sent for; see ORDERED 1. —**out of order** broken down, defective, faulty; see BROKEN 2.

order *v.* 1 [To give a command] direct, command, instruct, bid, tell, demand, impose, give directions, dictate, decree; see also REQUIRE 2. 2 [To authorize a purchase] secure, reserve, request; see BUY, OBTAIN 1. 3 [To put in order] arrange, plan, furnish, regulate, establish, manage, systematize, space, file, put away, classify, distribute, alphabetize, regularize, pattern, formalize, settle, fix, locate, dress up, sort out, index, put to rights, set guidelines for, adjust, adapt, set in order, assign, place, align, standardize, plan, group; see also ORGANIZE 1.—*Ant.* CONFUSE, disarrange, disarray.

ordered *a.* 1 [On order] requested, requisitioned, sent for, spoken for, engaged, booked, arranged for, retained, written for, telephoned for; see also RESERVED 1. 2 [Commanded] directed, ordained, comwhich everything is in its place and working properly 7 condition in general *[in good order]* 8 an authoritative command, instruction, etc. 9 a class; kind 10 an established method, as of conduct in meetings, etc. 11 *a)* a request to supply something *[an order for books]* *b)* the goods supplied 12 *[usually pl.]* the position of ordained minister, priest, etc. *[to take holy orders]* — *vt., vi.* 1 to put or keep (things) in order; arrange 2 to command 3 to request (something to be supplied) — **in** (or **out of**) **order** 1 in (or not in) proper position 2 in (or not in) good condition 3 in (or not in) accordance with the rules — **in order that** so that — **in order to** for the purpose of — **in short order** quickly — **on the order of** similar to — **to order** in accordance with the buyer's specifications

or·der·ly (ôr′dər lē) *adj.* 1 neat or tidy 2 well-behaved; law-abiding — *adv.* methodically — *n., pl.* **-lies** 1 an enlisted person assigned to perform personal services for an officer 2 a male hospital attendant — **or′der·li·ness** *n.*

or·di·nal (ôrd′'n əl) *adj.* *[< L ordo, order]* expressing order in a series — *n.* any number showing order in a series (e.g., first, tenth): in full **ordinal number**

or·di·nance (ôrd′'n əns) *n.* *[< L ordo, an order]* a statute or regulation, esp. a municipal one

or·di·nar·i·ly (ôrd′'n er′ə lē) *adv.* usually; as a rule

or·di·nary (ôrd′'n er′ē) *adj.* *[< L ordo, an order]* 1 customary; usual 2 familiar; unexceptional; common — **out of the ordinary** unusual

or·di·nate (ôrd′'n it, -āt′) *n.* *[< L (linea) ordinate (applicata), line applied in ordered manner] Math.* the vertical distance of a point from a horizontal axis

or·di·na·tion (ôrd′'n ā′shən) *n.* an ordaining or being ordained to the clergy

ord·nance (ôrd′nəns) *n.* *[< ORDINANCE]* 1 artillery 2 all military weapons, ammunition, vehicles, etc.

ordo (ôr′dō) *n., pl.* **-dos** or **-di·nes′** (-də nēz′) *[L, order] R.C.Ch.* an annual calendar giving directions for each day's Mass and Office

or·dure (ôr′jər) *n.* *[< L horridus, horrid]* dung; filth

ore (ôr) *n.* *[OE ar, brass]* a natural combination of minerals, esp. one from which a metal or metals can be profitably extracted

ore·ga·no (ô reg′ə nō, ə-) *n.* *[< Sp < Gr origanon]* a plant related to the mint, with fragrant leaves used for seasoning

or·gan (ôr′gən) *n.* *[< Gr organon, an implement]* 1 a keyboard musical instrument with sets of graduated pipes through which compressed air is passed, causing sound by vibration 2 in animals and plants, a part adapted to perform a specific function 3 a means for performing some action 4 a means of communicating ideas or opinions, as a periodical

or·gan·dy or **or·gan·die** (ôr′gən dē) *n., pl.* **-dies** *[Fr organdi]* a very sheer, crisp cotton fabric

or·gan·elle (ôr′gə nel′) *n.* *[< L organum, tool + dim. of -ellus]* a discrete structure within a cell, as a chloroplast, having specialized functions, a distinctive chemical composition, etc.

or·gan·ic (ôr gan′ik) *adj.* 1 of or having to do with a bodily organ 2 inherent; inborn 3 systematically arranged 4 designating or of any chemical compound containing carbon 5 of, like, or derived from living organisms — **or·gan′i·cal·ly** *adv.*

or·gan·ism (ôr′gə niz′əm) *n.* any living thing — **or′gan·is′mic** *adj.*

or′gan·ist *n.* an organ player

or·gan·i·za·tion (ôr′gə ni zā′shən) *n.* 1 an organizing or being organized 2 any organized group, as a club — **or′gan·i·za′tion·al** *adj.*

or·gan·ize (ôr′gə nīz′) *vt.* **-ized′, -iz′ing** 1 to provide with an organic structure 2 to arrange for 3 to institute; establish 4 to persuade to join a cause, group, etc. — *vi.* to become organized — **or′gan·iz′er** *n.*

or·ganza (ôr gan′zə) *n.* a thin, stiff fabric of rayon, silk, etc.

or·gasm (ôr′gaz′əm) *n.* *[< Gr organ, to swell]* the climax of a sexual act

orgy (ôr′jē) *n., pl.* **-gies** *[< Gr orgia, secret rites]* 1 a wild party, esp. with sexual activity 2 unrestrained indulgence in any activity — **or′gi·as′tic** (-jē as′tik) *adj.*

ori·el (ôr′ē əl, ôr′-) *n.* *[< ML oriolum, porch]* a bay window resting on a bracket or a corbel

ori·ent (ôr′ē ənt; *also, esp. for v.,* -ent′) *n.* *[< L oriri, arise: used of the rising sun]* *[Old Poet.]* the east — *vt.* to adjust

---

THESAURUS

manded, charged, dictated, regulated, decreed, ruled, enjoined, stipulated, bidden, imposed, authorized, exacted, forbidden, required, announced, by order, as ordered, under one's jurisdiction; see also APPROVED, REQUESTED.—*Ant.* NEGLECTED, omitted, revoked. 3 [Put in order] arranged, regulated, placed; see CLASSIFIED, ORGANIZED.

orderly *a.* 1 [Ordered; *said of objects and places]* neat, tidy, arranged; see CLEAN 1, NEAT 1. 2 [Methodical; *said of persons]* systematic, correct, formal, businesslike, systematical, exact, tidy, neat, thorough, precise; see also CAREFUL.—*Ant.* IRREGULAR, inaccurate, unmethodical.

ordinance *n.* direction, mandate, authorization; see LAW 3.

ordinarily *a.* usually, generally, habitually; see FREQUENTLY, REGULARLY.

ordinary *a.* 1 [In accordance with a regular order or sequence] customary, normal, regular, constant, usual, habitual, routine, mundane, everyday; see also COMMON 1, POPULAR 1, 3, TRADITIONAL. 2 [Lacking distinction] average, mediocre, familiar, natural, everyday, accepted, typical, commonplace, characteristic, prosaic, simple, banal, bland, trite, monotonous, stale, tedious, plain, normal; see also COMMON 1, CONVENTIONAL 3, DULL 4. — **out of the ordinary** extraordinary, uncommon, special; see UNUSUAL 2.

ore *n.* unrefined, rock, ore bed, native mineral; see also MINERAL.

organ *n.* 1 [An instrument] medium, means, way; see TOOL 1. 2 [A part of an organism having a specialized use] vital part, functional division,

process; see GLAND. *Human organs include the following:* brain, heart, eye, ear, nose, tongue, lung, kidney, stomach, intestine, pancreas, gall bladder, liver, penis, womb. 3 [A musical instrument] wind instrument, keyboard instrument, calliope, hurdy-gurdy, accordion; see also MUSICAL INSTRUMENT. *Types of organs include the following:* choir, orchestral, solo, pipe, echo, pedal, reed, electric, hand.

organic *a.* basic, vital, essential; see FUNDAMENTAL, NATURAL 1.

organically *a.* by nature, inevitably, wholly; see ESSENTIALLY, NATURALLY 2.

organism *n.* person, organic structure, physiological individual; see ANIMAL, BODY 1, PLANT.

organization *n.* 1 [The process or manner of organizing] establishment, plan, planning, ordering, creation, grouping, design, provision, working out, assembling, construction, regulation, systematization, system, method, coordination, adjustment, harmony, unity, correlation, standard, standardization, settlement, arrangement, disposition, classification, alignment, institution, foundation, preparation, rehearsal, direction, structure, situation, formation, association, uniformity; see also CLASSIFICATION, ORDER 3.—*Ant.* CONFUSION, bedlam, chance. 2 [An organized body] aggregation, association, federation, combine, corporation, union, institute, trust, cartel, confederation, monopoly, combination, machine, business, industry, company, society, league, club, fraternity, house, order, alliance, party,

cooperative, guild, profession, trade, coalition, syndicate, fellowship, lodge, brotherhood, confederacy, affiliation, body, band, team, squad, crew, clique, circle, set, troupe, group; see also SYSTEM.

organize *v.* 1 [To put in order] arrange, fix, straighten, standardize, compose, combine, systematize, methodize, coordinate, adjust, put in order, line up, regulate; see also CLASSIFY, ORDER 3. 2 [To form an organization] establish, build, found; see PLAN 2.

organized *a.* established, methodized, coordinated, systematized, systematic, constituted, directed, adjusted, assigned, distributed, grouped, fixed up, standardized, in order, in succession, in good form, placed, put away, orderly, in sequence, arranged, prepared, made ready, constructed, settled, composed, framed, planned, ranked, put in order, ordered, regulated, ranged, disposed, formulated, formed, fashioned, shaped, made, projected, designed, harmonized, related, correlated, founded, associated; see also CLASSIFIED.

Orient *n.* 1 [Eastern Asia] Far East, Asia, China, India, Japan, Vietnam, Thailand, Laos, Indo-China, Cambodia, Korea, Myanmar, the mysterious East, land of the rising sun.— *Ant.* Occident, Western World. 2 [Southwestern Asia] Near East, Middle East, Levant, Egypt, Mohammedan world, Turkey, Syria, Lebanon, Israel, Jordan, Iraq, Iran, Persia, Muslim world, Arabia, the Golden Crescent, the cradle of mankind; see also EAST 2.

(oneself) to a particular situation —[O-] the East, or Asia; esp., the Far East —**o′ri·en·ta′tion** *n.*

O′ri·en′tal (-ent′'l) *adj.* of the Orient, its people, etc. —*n.* a member of a people native to the Orient

ori·fice (ôr′ə fis, är′-) *n.* [< L *os*, a mouth + *facere*, make] a mouth of a tube, cavity, etc.; opening

orig. 1 origin 2 original 3 originally

ori·gami (ôr′ə gä′mē) *n.* [Jpn] the Japanese art of folding paper to form flowers, animal figures, etc.

ori·gin (ôr′ə jin, är′-) *n.* [< L *oriri*, to rise] 1 a coming into existence or use; beginning 2 parentage; birth 3 source; root; cause

origi·nal (ə rij′i nəl) *adj.* 1 first; earliest 2 never having been before; new; novel 3 capable of creating something new 4 being that from which copies are made —*n.* 1 a primary type that has given rise to varieties 2 an original work, as of art or literature —**orig′i·nal′i·ty** (-nal′ə tē) *n.* —**orig′i·nal·ly** *adv.*

orig′i·nate′ (-nāt′) *vt.* -nat′ed, -nat′ing to bring into being; esp., to invent — *vi.* to begin; start —**orig′i·na′tion** *n.* —**orig′i·na′tor** *n.*

ori·ole (ôr′ē ōl′) *n.* [< L *aurum*, gold] a bright-orange and black American bird that builds a hanging nest

Ori·on (ō rī′ən, ə-) a very bright equatorial constellation

Or·lon (ôr′län′) *trademark for* a synthetic acrylic fiber similar to nylon

or·molu (ôr′mə lōō′) *n.* [Fr < *moulu*, ground gold] an imitation gold made of a copper and tin alloy, used in ornaments, moldings, etc.

or·na·ment (ôr′nə mənt; *for v.*, -ment′) *n.* [< L *ornare*, adorn] 1 anything that adorns; decoration 2 one whose character or talent adds luster to the surroundings, etc. — *vt.* to decorate —**or′na·men′tal** *adj.* —**or′na·men·ta′tion** *n.*

or·nate (ôr nāt′) *adj.* [< L *ornare*, adorn] heavily ornamented; showy —**or·nate′ly** *adv.* —**or·nate′ness** *n.*

or·nery (ôr′nər ē) *adj.* [< ORDINARY] [Chiefly Dial.] 1 mean; nasty 2 obstinate —**or′neri·ness** *n.*

or·ni·thol·o·gy (ôr′nə thäl′ə jē) *n.* [< Gr *ornis*, bird + -LOGY] the branch of zoology dealing with birds —**or′ni·thol′o·gist** *n.*

oro·tund (ō′rō tund′, ôr′ə-) *adj.* [< L *os*, mouth + *rotundas*, round] 1 resonant: said of the voice 2 bombastic

or·phan (ôr′fən) *n.* [< Gr *orphanos*] a child whose parents are dead —*adj.* 1 being an orphan 2 of or for orphans — *vt.* to cause to become an orphan

or′phan·age (-ij) *n.* an institution that is a home for orphans

Or·pheus (ôr′fē əs) *Gr. Myth.* a poet-musician with magic musical powers

or·ris (ôr′is, är′-) *n.* [< Gr *iris*, iris] a European iris, esp. one with a root (**or′ris·root′**) pulverized for perfumery, etc.

ortho- [< Gr *orthos*, straight] *combining form* 1 straight

[*orthodontics*] 2 proper; correct [*orthography*] Also **orth-**

or·tho·don·tics (ôr′thō dän′tiks, -thə-) *n.pl.* [< ORTH(O)- + Gr *odōn*, tooth + -ICS] [*with sing. v.*] the branch of dentistry concerned with correcting tooth irregularities Also **or′tho·don′tia** (-dän′shə, -shē ə) —**or′tho·don′tist** *n.*

or·tho·dox (ôr′thə däks′) *adj.* [< Gr *orthos*, straight + *doxa*, opinion] conforming to the usual beliefs or established doctrines, as in religion; conventional —**or′tho·dox′y,** *pl.* **-ies,** *n.*

Orthodox (Eastern) Church the Christian church dominant in E Europe, W Asia, and N Africa

or·thog·ra·phy (ôr thäg′rə fē) *n.*, *pl.* **-phies** [< Gr: see ORTHO- & -GRAPHY] 1 correct spelling 2 spelling as a subject for study —**or′tho·graph′ic** (ôr′thō graf′ik, -thə-) *adj.*

ortho·pedics or **ortho·pae·dics** (ôr′thō pē′diks) *n.pl.* [< Gr *orthos*, straight + *pais*, child] [*with sing. v.*] the branch of surgery dealing with deformities, diseases, and injuries of the bones, joints, muscles, etc. —**or′tho·pe′dic** or **or′tho·pae′dic** *adj.* —**or′tho·pe′dist** or **or′tho·pae′dist** *n.*

-ory (ôr′ē, ər ē) [< L *-orius*] *suffix* 1 of, having the nature of [*sensory*] 2 a place or thing for [*crematory*]

OS Old Saxon

os·cil·late (äs′ə lāt′) *vi.* -lat′ed, -lat′ing [< L *oscillum*, a swing] 1 to swing to and fro 2 to vacillate 3 *Physics* to vary regularly between high and low values, as an electric current —**os′cil·la′tion** *n.* —**os′cil·la′tor** *n.*

os·cillo·scope (ə sil′ə skōp′) *n.* [< L *oscillare*, to swing + -SCOPE] an instrument that visually displays an electrical wave on a fluorescent screen

os·cu·late (äs′kyōō lāt′, -kyə-) *vt.*, *vi.* -lat′ed, -lat′ing [< L *osculum*, little mouth] to kiss —**os′cu·la′tion** *n.*

-ose¹ (ōs) [Fr < (*gluc*)*ose*] *suffix* 1 a carbohydrate [*sucrose*] 2 the product of a protein hydrolysis

-ose² (ōs) [L *-osus*] *suffix* full of, like

osier (ō′zhər) *n.* [< ML *auseria*, willow] a willow with lithe branches used for baskets and furniture

-osis (ō′sis) [< Gr] *suffix* 1 condition, action [*hypnosis*] 2 an abnormal or diseased condition [*psychosis*]

os·mo·sis (äs mō′sis, äz-) *n.* [< Gr *ōsmos*, impulse] 1 the tendency of fluids to pass through a membrane so as to equalize concentrations on both sides 2 an apparently effortless absorption of ideas, feelings, etc. —**os·mot′ic** (-mät′ik) *adj.*

os·prey (äs′prē, -prā) *n.*, *pl.* **-preys** [< L *os*, a bone + *frangere*, to break] a large, diving, hawklike bird that feeds mainly on fish

os·sify (äs′ə fī′) *vt.*, *vi.* **-fied′, -fy′ing** [< L *os*, a bone + -FY] 1 to change into bone 2 to fix rigidly in a custom, etc. —**os′si·fi·ca′tion** *n.*

▬▬ THESAURUS ▬▬

Oriental *a.* Far Eastern, Near Eastern, Asian, Chinese, Indian, Japanese, Vietnamese, Cambodian, Laotian, Thai, Korean, Siberian, Arabic, Jewish, Iraqi, Iranian, Malaysian, Hindustani, Ceylonese.

orientation *n.* familiarization, bearings, introduction; see ADJUSTMENT, INTRODUCTION 3, 4.

origin *n.* 1 [The act of beginning] rise, start, foundation; see BIRTH. 2 [The place or time of beginning] source, spring, issue, fountain, inlet, derivation, root, stem, shoot, twig, sapling, portal, door, gate, gateway, fountainhead, wellspring, font, fount, birthplace, cradle, nest, womb, reservoir, infancy, babyhood, childhood, youth.—*Ant.* RESULT, outcome, issue. 3 [Cause] seed, germ, stock, parentage, ancestry, parent, ancestor, egg, sperm, embryo, principle, element, nucleus, first cause, author, creator, prime mover, producer, causation, source, influence, generator, occasion, root, spring, antecedent, motive, inspiration; see also CAUSE.—*Ant.* RESULT, consequence, conclusion.

original *a.* 1 [Pertaining to the source] primary, primeval, primordial, rudimentary, elementary, incep-

tive, in embryo, fundamental, primitive, initial, beginning, commencing, starting, opening, dawning, incipient; see also FIRST.—*Ant.* LATE, recent, developed. 2 [Creative] originative, productive, causal, causative, generative, imaginative, inventive, formative, resourceful, ready, quick, seminal, envisioning, sensitive, archetypal, inspiring, devising, conceiving, fertile, fashioning, molding.—*Ant.* STUPID, imitative, unproductive. 3 [Not copied] primary, principal, first, genuine, new, firsthand, uncopied, fresh, novel, independent, one, sole, lone, single, solitary, authentic, unique, pure, rare, unusual, not translated, not copied, not imitated, real, absolute, sheer.—*Ant.* IMITATED, copied, repeated.

originality *n.* creativeness, inventiveness, invention, ingenuity, conception, authenticity, novelty, freshness, newness, individuality, brilliance; see also IMAGINATION.

originally *a.* 1 [In an original manner] imaginatively, creatively, ingeniously, inventively, startlingly, freshly, in a new fashion, independently, artistically. 2 [In the beginning] first, incipiently, basically; see

FORMERLY.

originate *v.* start, introduce, found; see BEGIN 1.

originated *a.* introduced, started, commenced; see BEGUN.

ornament *n.* embellishment, adornment, beautification; see DECORATION 2.

ornamental *a.* 1 [Intended for ornament] fancy, luxurious, showy; see ELABORATE 1, ORNATE. 2 [Beautiful] delicate, exquisite, spiritual; see BEAUTIFUL.

ornate *a.* showy, gaudy, sumptuous, lavish, bright, colored, tinseled, jeweled, embroidered, glossy, burnished, polished, gorgeous, pompous, stylish, magnificent, adorned, trimmed, gilded, embellished, inlaid, garnished, flowered, glowing, vivid, radiant, fine, alluring, dazzling, sparkling, shining, flashing, glistening, glamorous, artificial, pretentious, baroque, rococo, tawdry, flashy; see also ELABORATE 1.

orphan *n.* foundling, ragamuffin, parentless child, orphaned child, waif, stray; see also CHILD.

orphanage *n.* orphans' home, institution, foundling home; see SCHOOL 1.

os·ten·si·ble (ä sten′sə bəl) *adj.* 〚< L *ostendere,* to show〛 apparent; seeming —**os·ten′si·bly** *adv.*

os·ten·ta·tion (äs′tən tā′shən) *n.* 〚< L *ostendere,* to show〛 showy display; pretentiousness —**os′ten·ta′tious** *adj.*

osteo- 〚< Gr *osteon,* a bone〛 *combining form* bone or bones

oste·ar·thri·tis (äs′tē ō′är thrit′is) *n.* 〚prec. + ARTHRITIS〛 a common form of arthritis marked by degeneration of cartilage of the joints

oste·opa·thy (äs′tē äp′ə thē) *n.* 〚ModL: see OSTEO- & -PATHY〛 a school of medicine and surgery that emphasizes the interrelationship of muscles and bones —**osteo·path** (äs′tē ō path′, -tē ə-) *n.*

osteo·po·ro·sis (äs′tē ō′pə rō′sis) *n.* 〚< Gr *osteon,* a bone + L *porus,* a pore + -OSIS〛 a bone disorder characterized by porous, brittle bones

os·tomy (äs′tə mē) *n., pl.* **-mies** any surgery connecting a hollow organ to the outside of the body or to another hollow organ

os·tra·cize (äs′trə sīz′) *vt.* **-cized′, -ciz′ing** 〚< Gr *ostrakon,* a shell (cast as a ballot)〛 to banish from a group, society, etc. —**os′tra·cism′** *n.*

os·trich (äs′trich, ôs′-) *n.* 〚< L *avis,* bird + *struthio,* ostrich〛 a large, swift-running bird of Africa and SW Asia

OT or **O.T.** 1 Old Testament 2 overtime

Othel·lo (ō thel′ō) a tragedy by Shakespeare in which the title character, madly jealous, kills his wife

other (uth′ər) *adj.* 〚OE〛 1 being the remaining one or ones /Bill and the *other* boys/ 2 different or distinct from that or those implied /use your *other* foot/ 3 additional /he has no *other* coat/ —*pron.* 1 the other one 2 some other one /to do as *others* do/ —*adv.* otherwise /he can't do *other* than go/ —**the other day** (or **night,** etc.) not long ago; recently

oth·er·wise′ *adv.* 1 in another manner; differently /I believe *otherwise*/ 2 in all other respects /he is *otherwise* intelligent/ 3 in other circumstances —*adj.* different

oth′er·world′ly *adj.* being apart from earthly interests

oti·ose (ō′shē ōs′) *adj.* 〚< L *otium,* leisure〛 1 [Rare] idle 2 futile 3 useless

ot·ter (ät′ər) *n.* 〚OE *oter*〛 1 a furry, swimming, carnivorous mammal with webbed feet 2 its fur

otto·man (ät′ə mən) *n.* 〚Fr *ottomane*〛 a low, cushioned seat or footstool

ouch (ouch) *interj.* an exclamation of sudden pain

ought (ôt) *v.aux.* used with infinitives and meaning: 1 obligation, duty, or desirability /you *ought* to eat more/ 2 to be expected /it *ought* to be over·soon/

oui (wē) *adv.* 〚Fr〛 yes

Ouija (wē′jə, -jē) 〚< prec. + Ger *ja,* yes〛 *trademark for* a

supposedly spiritualistic device consisting of a board with the alphabet, and a sliding, three-legged pointer

ounce (ouns) *n.* 〚< L *uncia,* a twelfth〛 1 a unit of weight, $\frac{1}{16}$ pound avoirdupois or $\frac{1}{12}$ pound troy 2 fluid ounce, $\frac{1}{16}$ pint

our (our; är) *poss. pronominal adj.* 〚OE *ure*〛 of, belonging to, or done by us

ours (ourz, ärz) *pron.* that or those belonging to us /a friend of *ours*/

our·selves (our selvz′) *pron.* 1 *the intensive form of* WE /we went *ourselves*/ 2 *the reflexive form of* WE /we hurt *ourselves*/ 3 our true selves /we are not *ourselves* when sick/

-ous (əs) 〚< L *-osus*〛 *suffix* having, full of, characterized by /beauteous/

oust (oust) *vt.* 〚< L *ostare,* obstruct〛 to force out; expel; dispossess

oust′er *n.* an ousting or being ousted

out (out) *adv.* 〚OE *ut*〛 1 away or removed from a place, position, etc. 2 into the open air 3 into existence or activity /disease broke *out*/ 4 *a)* to a conclusion /argue it *out*/ *b)* completely /tired *out*/ 5 into sight or notice /the moon came *out*/ 6 from existence or activity /fade *out*/ 7 aloud /sing *out*/ 8 beyond a regular surface, condition, etc. /stand *out*/ 9 into disuse /long skirts went *out*/ 10 from a group or stock /pick *out*/ 11 [Slang] into unconsciousness 12 *Baseball* in a manner that results in an out /to fly *out*/ —*adj.* 1 external: usually in combination /outpost/ 2 beyond regular limits 3 away from work, etc. 4 in error /out in one's estimates/ 5 not in use, operation, etc. 6 [Colloq.] having suffered a financial loss /out one dollar/ 7 [Colloq.] outmoded 8 *Baseball* having failed to get on base —*prep.* 1 out of 2 along the way of —*n.* 1 something that is out 2 [Slang] a way out; excuse 3 *Baseball* the failure of a player to reach base safely —*vi.* to become known /the truth will *out*/ —**on the outs** [Colloq.] on unfriendly terms —**out for** making a determined effort to get or do —**out of** 1 from inside of 2 beyond 3 from (material, etc.) /made *out* of stone/ 4 because of /out of spite/ 5 having no /out of gas/ 6 so as to deprive —**out to** trying to

out- *combining form* 1 at or from a point away; outside /outpatient/ 2 going away or forth; outward /outbound/ 3 better or more than /outdo, outsmart/

out·age (out′ij) *n.* an interruption of operation, as of electric power

out′-and-out′ *adj.* thorough

out′back′ *n.* any remote, sparsely settled region viewed as uncivilized

out′bal′ance *vt.* **-anced, -anc·ing** to be greater than in weight, value, etc.

out′bid′ *vt.* **-bid′, -bid′ding** to bid or offer more than (someone else)

THESAURUS

other *a.* one of two, the remaining one, another, one beside, some beside, additional, different, separate, distinct, opposite, across from, lately, recently, not long ago, other than; see also EXTRA.

other *pron.* the one remaining, the part remaining, the alternate, the alternative; see also ANOTHER.—*Ant.* THIS, that, the first choice.

others *n.* unnamed persons, the remainder, some, a few, any others, a number, a handful, a small number, not many, hardly any, two or three, more than one, many, a great number, a great many, they, folks, the rest; see also EVERYBODY.—*Ant.* NONE, no one, not any.

otherwise *a.* 1 [In another way] in a different way, contrarily, in an opposed way, under other conditions, in different circumstances, on the other hand, in other respects, in other ways.—*Ant.* LIKE, so, in like manner. 2 [Introducing an alternative threat] unless you do, with this exception, except on these conditions, barring this, in any other circumstances, except that, without this, unless...then, other than; see also UNLESS.—*Ant.* THEREFORE, hence, as a result.

ought (to) *v.* should, have to, is nec-

essary, is fitting, is becoming, is expedient, behooves, is reasonable, is logical, is natural, requires, is in need of, is responsible for; see also MUST.

ounce *n.* measure, troy ounce, avoirdupois ounce, fluid ounce, one sixteenth of a pound (avoirdupois), one sixteenth of a pint, one twelfth of a pound (troy); see also MEASURE 1.

our *poss. pronominal adj.* ours, our own, belonging to us, owned by us, used by us, due to us, a part of us, of interest to us, done by us, accomplished by us, in our employ, with us, near us, of us.

ourselves *pron.* us, the speakers, individually, personally, privately, without help, our own selves*; see also WE.

oust *v.* eject, discharge, dispossess, evict, dislodge, remove, deprive, expel, drive out, force out, show the door, chase out, cast out, depose, dethrone, disinherit, banish, boot out*, bundle off*, send packing*, give the gate*, pack off*.

out *a., prep.* 1 [In motion from within] out of, away from, from, from within, out from, out toward, outward, on the way.—*Ant.* IN, in from, into. 2 [Not situated within] on the outer side, on the surface, external, extrinsic, outer, outdoors,

out-of-doors, unconcealed, open, exposed, in the open; see also OUTSIDE, WITHOUT.—*Ant.* WITHIN, inside, on the inner side. 3 [Beyond] distant, removed, removed from; see AWAY, BEYOND. 4 [Continued to the limit or near it] ended, accomplished, fulfilled; see DONE 1, FINISHED 1. 5 [Not at home or at one's office] not in, away, busy, on vacation, at lunch, gone, left; see also ABSENT.—*Ant.* IN, receiving, not busy. 6 [*Unconscious] insensible, out cold, blotto*; see UNCONSCIOUS. 7 [Wanting] lacking, missing, without; see WANTING 1. —**all out*** wholeheartedly, with great effort, entirely; see COMPLETELY. —**out of** 1 [Having none in stock] all out of stock, not in stock, gone; see SOLD OUT. 2 [From] out from, away from, from within; see FROM. 3 [Beyond] outside of, on the border of, in the outskirts; see BEYOND.

out* *n.* means of escape, way out, excuse; see ESCAPE, EXPLANATION.

outage *n.* interruption of service, blackout, dimout, brownout, failure of electrical service; see also INTERRUPTION.

out-and-out *a.* complete, entire, total; see COMPLETELY.

outbid *v.* offer higher than, raise the

out'board' *adj.* outside the hull of a ship or boat *[an outboard motor]*
out'bound' *adj.* outward bound
out'break' *n.* a breaking out; sudden occurrence, as of disease, rioting, etc.
out'build'ing *n.* a structure, as a barn, separate from the main building
out'burst' *n.* a sudden release, as of feeling, energy, etc.
out'cast' *adj.* driven out; rejected — *n.* a person rejected, as by society
out'class' *vt.* to surpass
out'come' *n.* result; consequence
out'crop' *n.* 1 the emergence of a mineral at the earth's surface 2 the mineral that so emerges
out'cry' *n., pl.* **-cries'** 1 a crying out 2 a strong protest
out'dat'ed *adj.* no longer current
out'dis'tance *vt.* **-tanced, -tanc·ing** to get ahead of, as in a race
out'do' *vt.* **-did', -done', -do'ing** to exceed or surpass — **outdo oneself** to do better than one expected to do
out'door' *adj.* 1 being or taking place outdoors 2 of or fond of the outdoors
out'doors' *adv.* in or into the open; outside — *n.* any area outside a building
out'er *adj.* farther out or away
out'er·most' *adj.* farthest out
outer space space beyond the earth's atmosphere or beyond the solar system
out'er·wear' *n.* garments, as overcoats, worn over the usual clothing
out'field' *n. Baseball* 1 the playing area beyond the infield 2 the players (**outfielders**) positioned there
out'fit' *n.* 1 the equipment used in an activity 2 clothing worn together; ensemble 3 a group of people associated in an activity — *vt.* **-fit'ted, -fit'ting** to furnish with an outfit —**out'fit'ter** *n.*
out'flank' *vt.* to go around and beyond the flank of (enemy troops)
out'fox' *vt.* to outsmart
out'go' *n., pl.* **-goes'** that which is paid out; expenditure
out'go'ing *adj.* 1 *a)* leaving *b)* retiring from office 2 sociable

out'grow' *vt.* **-grew', -grown', -grow'ing** 1 to grow faster or larger than 2 to lose in becoming mature *[to outgrow one's fear]* 3 to grow too large for
out'growth' *n.* 1 a growing out or that which grows out 2 a result, consequence, or development
out'guess' *vt.* to outwit
out'house' *n.* a small outdoor structure used as a toilet, having a seat with a hole over a deep pit
out'ing *n.* 1 a pleasure trip 2 an outdoor walk, ride, picnic, etc.
out'land'ish (-lan'dish) *adj.* very odd or strange; fantastic; bizarre
out'last' *vt.* to endure longer than
out'law' *n.* 1 orig., a person deprived by a court of law of legal rights and protection 2 a habitual or notorious criminal — *vt.* 1 orig., to declare to be an outlaw 2 to declare illegal
out'lay' *n.* 1 a spending (*of* money, etc.) 2 money, etc. spent
out'let' *n.* 1 a passage for letting something out 2 a means of expression *[an outlet for anger]* 3 a retail store selling defective or surplus goods at a discount: in full **outlet store** 4 a point in a wiring system at which current may be taken
out'line' *n.* 1 a line bounding the limits of an object 2 a sketch showing only contours 3 *[also pl.]* a general plan 4 a systematic summary — *vt.* **-lined', -lin'ing** 1 to draw in outline 2 to make an outline of
out'live' *vt.* **-lived', -liv'ing** to live or endure longer than; outlast
out'look' *n.* 1 the view from a place 2 viewpoint 3 expectation or prospect
out'ly'ing *adj.* relatively far out from a certain point; remote
out'ma·neu'ver or **out'ma·noeu'vre** *vt.* **-vered** or **-vred, -ver·ing** or **-vring** to outwit by maneuvering
out'match' (-mach') *vt.* to be superior to; outdo
out'mod'ed *adj.* no longer in fashion or accepted; obsolete
out'num'ber *vt.* to exceed in number
out'-of-date' *adj.* no longer in style or use; old-fashioned

---

THESAURUS

price, bid something up; see PAY 1.
outbreak *n.* 1 [A sudden violent appearance] eruption, explosion, outburst, disruption, burst, bursting forth, detonation, thunder, commotion, rending, break, breaking out, breaking forth, gush, gushing forth, outpouring, pouring forth, tumult, discharge, blast, blowup, crash, roar, earthquake, squall, paroxysm, spasm, convulsion, fit, effervescence, boiling, flash, flare, crack.—*Ant.* PEACE, tranquillity, quiet. 2 [Sudden violence] fury, mutiny, brawl; see DISORDER, REVOLUTION 2.
outburst *n.* discharge, upheaval, eruption; see DISTURBANCE 2, OUTBREAK 1.
outcast *a.* vagabond, driven out, hounded, untouchable, rejected, thrown aside, pushed out, disgraced, hunted, not accepted by society, cast out, degraded, expelled, outlawed, cast away, exiled, expatriated, serving a life sentence, having a price on one's head.
outcast *n.* fugitive, pariah, untouchable; see REFUGEE.
outcome *n.* issue, upshot, consequence; see END 2, RESULT.
outcrop *n.* bared soil, exposed surface, projecting land mass; see EARTH 2, LAND 1.
outcry *n.* complaint, clamor, scream; see OBJECTION.
outdated *a.* outmoded, out of fashion, antiquated; see OLD 3.
outdo *v.* surpass, best, beat; see EXCEED.
outdone *a.* defeated, bettered, improved upon; see BEATEN 1.
outdoor *a.* outside, airy, out-of-doors, open-air, out of the house, out in the open, free, unrestricted, rustic,

free and easy, healthful; see also OUT-DOORS.—*Ant.* interior, indoor, in the house.
outdoors *a.* out-of-doors, outdoor, without, out of the house, outside, on the outside, in the yard, in the open, in the garden, into the street.
outdoors *n.* the out-of-doors, natural scenery, fresh air, garden, patio, woods, hills, mountains, stream, Mother Nature, the great outdoors, countryside, the country.—*Ant.* INSIDE, domestic matters, household concerns.
outer *a.* outward, without, external, exterior, foreign, alien to, beyond, exposed; see also OUTSIDE.—*Ant.* INNER, inward, inside.
outer space *n.* infinity, the heavens, the universe; see SPACE 1.
outfield *n.* left field, deep left, center field, deep center, right field, deep right; see also BASEBALL, FIELD 2.
outfielder *n.* right fielder, center fielder, left fielder; see BASEBALL PLAYER.
outfit *n.* trappings, outlay, gear; see EQUIPMENT.
outfit *v.* equip, fit out, supply; see PROVIDE 1.
outflank *v.* bypass, surround, outmaneuver; see DEFEAT 2, PASS 1.
outgo *n.* costs, losses, outflow; see EXPENSES.
outgoing *a.* sociable, civil, kind; see FRIENDLY.
outgrowth *n.* end result, outcome, effect; see END 2, RESULT.
outing *n.* excursion, airing, drive; see VACATION.
outlast *v.* outlive, outwear, remain; see ENDURE 1, SURVIVE 1.
outlaw *n.* fugitive, bandit, badman;

see CRIMINAL.
outlaw *v.* make illegal, stop, ban; see BANISH, CONDEMN.
outlawed *a.* stopped, banned, made illegal; see ILLEGAL.
outlet *n.* 1 [An opening] break, crack, tear; see HOLE 1. 2 [An electric terminal] plug-in, socket, double socket, triple socket, wall plug, floor plug, electric service connection.
outline *n.* 1 [A skeletonized plan] frame, skeleton, framework; see PLAN 1. 2 [The line surrounding an object; *often plural*] contour, side, boundary; see EDGE 1, FRAME 2. 3 [A shape seen in outline] silhouette, profile, configuration, shape, figure, formation, aspect, appearance; see also FORM 1.
outline *v.* 1 [To draw] sketch, paint, describe; see DRAW 2. 2 [To plan] block out, draft, sketch; see PLAN 2.
outlined *a.* 1 [Marked in outline] bounded, edged, bordered, circumscribed, marked, zoned, girdled, banded, configurated. 2 [Given in summary] charted, summarized, surveyed; see PLANNED.
outlive *v.* live longer than, outlast, last; see ENDURE 1.
outlook *n.* 1 [Point of view] scope, vision, standpoint; see VIEWPOINT. 2 [Apparent future] probability, prospects, likelihood, possibility, chances, opportunity, appearances, probable future, openings, normal course of events, probabilities, risk, law of averages.
outlying *a.* afar, far-off, external; see DISTANT.
outnumbered *a.* exceeded, bested, overcome; see BEATEN 1.
out-of-date *a.* obsolete, passé, antiquated; see OLD-FASHIONED.

out'-of-door' *adj.* OUTDOOR

out'-of-doors' *adv., n.* OUTDOORS

out'-of-the-way' *adj.* 1 secluded 2 not common; unusual

out'-of-town'er *n.* a visitor from another town or city

out'pa'tient *n.* a patient treated at a hospital, etc. without becoming an inpatient

out'play' *vt.* to play better than

out'post' *n.* 1 *Mil. a)* a small group stationed at a distance from the main force *b)* the station so occupied *c)* a foreign base 2 a frontier settlement

out'put' *n.* 1 the work done or amount produced, esp. over a given period 2 information delivered by a computer 3 *Elec.* the useful voltage, current, or power delivered

out'rage' *n.* ⟦ult. < L *ultra*, beyond⟧ 1 an extremely vicious or violent act 2 a deep insult or offense 3 great anger, etc. aroused by this — *vt.* **-raged', -rag'ing** 1 to commit an outrage upon or against 2 to cause outrage in

out·ra'geous (-rā'jəs) *adj.* 1 involving or doing great injury or wrong 2 very offensive or shocking —**out·ra'geously** *adv.*

out'rank' *vt.* to exceed in rank

ou·tré (o͞o trā') *adj.* ⟦Fr⟧ 1 exaggerated 2 eccentric; bizarre

out·reach (*for v.* out'rēch'; *for n. & adj.* out'rēch') *vt., vi.* 1 to exceed; surpass 2 to reach out; extend — *n.* a reaching out — *adj.* designating of or a program extending services to those not usually accommodated

out'rid'er *n.* 1 a rider on horseback who accompanies a stagecoach, etc. 2 a cowboy riding a range, as to keep cattle from straying 3 a forerunner

out'rig'ger (-rig'ər) *n.* 1 a timber rigged out from the side of certain canoes to prevent tipping 2 a canoe of this type

out'right' *adj.* 1 without reservation 2 complete — *adv.* 1 entirely 2 openly 3 at once

out'run' *vt.* **-ran', -run', -run'ning** 1 to run faster than 2 to exceed

out'sell' *vt.* **-sold', -sell'ing** to sell in greater amounts than

out'set' *n.* a setting out; beginning

out'shine' *vt.* **-shone'** or **-shined', -shin'ing** 1 to shine brighter or longer than 2 to surpass; excel

out'side' *n.* 1 the outer side or part; exterior 2 outward appearance 3 any area not inside — *adj.* 1 of or on the outside; outer 2 extreme [an *outside* estimate] 3 slight [an *outside* chance] — *adv.* 1 on or to the outside 2 outdoors — *prep.* 1 on or to the outer side of 2 beyond the limits of —**outside of** 1 outside 2 [Colloq.] other than

out'sid'er *n.* one who is not included in a given group

out'size' *n.* an odd size, esp. an unusually large one

out'skirt' *n.* a part remote from the center, as of a city: usually used in *pl.*

out'smart' *vt.* to overcome by cunning or cleverness; outwit —**outsmart oneself** to have one's efforts at cunning or cleverness result in one's own disadvantage

out'sourc·ing (-sôr siŋ) *n.* the practice of purchasing parts, etc. from domestic nonunion shops or from foreign companies

out'spo'ken *adj.* 1 unrestrained in speech 2 spoken boldly or candidly

out'spread' *adj.* spread out; extended

out'stand'ing *adj.* 1 projecting 2 prominent; distinguished 3 unpaid; uncollected 4 issued and sold: said of stocks and bonds

out'sta'tion *n.* a post or station in a remote or unsettled area

out'stretch' *vt.* 1 to stretch out; extend 2 to stretch beyond

out'strip' *vt.* **-stripped', -strip'ping** 1 to go at a faster pace than 2 to excel; surpass

out'vote' *vt.* **-vot'ed, -vot'ing** to defeat in voting

out'ward (-wərd) *adj.* 1 having to do with the outside; outer 2 clearly apparent 3 away from the interior — *adv.* toward the outside: also **out'wards** —**out'wardly** *adv.*

out'wear' *vt.* **-wore', -worn', -wear'ing** 1 to wear out 2 to outlast

out'weigh' *vt.* 1 to weigh more than 2 to be more important than

out'wit' *vt.* **-wit'ted, -wit'ting** to get the better of by cleverness

ova (ō'və) *n. pl. of* OVUM

oval (ō'vəl) *adj.* ⟦< L *ovum*, egg⟧ egg-shaped; elliptical — *n.* anything oval

ova·ry (ō'və rē) *n., pl.* **-ries** ⟦< L *ovum*, egg⟧ 1 a female reproductive gland producing eggs 2 *Bot.* the enlarged, hollow part of the pistil, containing ovules —**ovar·ian** (ō ver'ē ən) *adj.*

ovate (ō'vāt') *adj.* egg-shaped; oval

ova·tion (ō vā'shən) *n.* ⟦< L *ovare*, celebrate a triumph⟧ enthusiastic applause or public welcome

oven (uv'ən) *n.* ⟦OE *ofen*⟧ a compartment or receptacle for baking, roasting, heating, etc.

over (ō'vər) *prep.* ⟦OE *ofer*⟧ 1 *a)* in, at, or to a position above *b)* across and down from [to fall *over* a cliff] 2 so as to cover [shutters *over* the windows] 3 upon, as an effect [to cast a spell *over* someone] 4 above in authority, power, etc. 5 on or to the other side of [fly *over* the lake] 6 throughout [*over* the whole city] 7 during [*over* the years] 8 more than [*over* ten cents] 9 in preference to 10 concerning — *adv.* 1 *a)* above or across *b)* across the brim or edge 2 more [three hours or *over*] 3 from start to finish [go *over* it] 4 *a)* from an upright position [to fall *over*] *b)* upside down [turn the cup *over*] 5 again [do it *over*] 6 at, on, to, or in a specified place [*over* in Spain] 7

■ THESAURUS ■

out-of-the-way *a.* far-off, secluded, isolated; see DISTANT.

outplay *v.* overcome, surpass, beat; see DEFEAT 3.

outpost *n.* forward position, listening post, point of attack; see BOUNDARY, POSITION 1.

output *n.* yield, amount, crop; see PRODUCE.

outrage *n.* indignity, abuse, affront; see INSULT.

outrage *v.* offend, wrong, affront; see ABUSE, INSULT.

outrageous *a.* wanton, notorious, shameless, disgraceful, brazen, barefaced, gross, scandalous, disorderly, insulting, affronting, abusive, oppressive, dishonorable, injurious, glaring, immoderate, extreme, flagrant, contemptible, ignoble, malevolent, odious, monstrous, atrocious, nefarious, vicious, iniquitous, wicked, shocking, violent, unbearable, villainous, infamous, corrupt, degenerate, criminal, sinful, abandoned, vile, abominable.—*Ant.* EXCELLENT, laudable, honorable.

outright *a.* out-and-out, unmitigated, unconditional; see COMPLETELY, OBVIOUS 1.

outset *n.* start, beginning, source; see ORIGIN 2.

outside *a.* extreme, outermost, farthest, apart from, external, away from, farther; see also OUTER.—*Ant.* INNER, inside, interior.

outside *n.* 1 [An outer surface] exterior, outer side, surface, skin, cover, covering, topside, upper side, front side, face, appearance, outer aspect, seeming.—*Ant.* INSIDE, interior, inner side. 2 [The limit] outline, border, bounds; see BOUNDARY, EDGE 1, END 4. —**at the outside** at the most, at the absolute limit, not more than; see MOST.

outsider *n.* foreigner, stranger, refugee; see ALIEN.

outskirts *n.* border, suburbs, limits; see BOUNDARY, EDGE 1.

outspoken *a.* blunt, candid, artless; see FRANK.

outspread *a.* spread out, expanded, extended; see WIDESPREAD.

outstanding *a.* conspicuous, leading, notable; see DISTINGUISHED 2.

outward *a.* 1 [In an outward direction] out, toward the edge, from within; see OUTER, OUTSIDE. 2 [To outward appearance] on the surface, visible, to the eye; see OBVIOUS 1, OPEN 1.

outwear *v.* sustain, last longer than, outlast; see CONTINUE 1, ENDURE 1, SURVIVE 1.

outweigh *v.* 1 [To exceed in weight] overbalance, overweigh, weigh more than, go beyond; see also BURDEN. 2 [To exceed in importance] excel, surpass, outrun; see EXCEED.

outwit *v.* baffle, trick, bewilder; see CONFUSE, DECEIVE.

outwitted *a.* tricked, outsmarted, taken*; see DECEIVED.

oval *a.* egg-shaped, elliptical, ellipsoid; see OBLONG.

oven *n.* hot-air chamber, oil burner, broiler; see FURNACE, STOVE.

over *a., prep.* 1 [Situated above] aloft, overhead, up beyond, covering, roofing, protecting, upper, higher than, farther up, upstairs, in the sky, straight up, high up, up there, in the clouds, among the stars, in heaven, just over, up from, outer, on top of; see also ABOVE.—*Ant.* under, below, beneath. 2 [Passing above] overhead, aloft, up high; see ACROSS. 3 [Again] once more, afresh, another time; see AGAIN. 4 [Beyond] past, farther on, out of sight; see BEYOND. 5 [Done] accomplished, ended, completed; see DONE 1, FINISHED 1. 6 [*In addition] over and above, extra, additionally; see BESIDES. 7 [Having authority] superior to, in authority, above; see HIGHER, SUPERIOR.

from one belief, etc. to another [win him *over*] — *adj.* 1 upper, outer, superior, excessive, or extra 2 finished; past 3 having reached the other side 4 [Colloq.] as a surplus

over- *combining form* 1 above in position, rank, etc. [*overlord*] 2 passing across or beyond [*overrun*] 3 excessively [*oversell*] The list below includes some common compounds formed with *over-* that can be understood if "too much" or "excessively" is added to the meaning of the base word:

overabundance	overgenerous
overactive	overheat
overambitious	overindulge
overanxious	overindulgence
overbid	overload
overburden	overpay
overcautious	overpopulate
overconfident	overproduce
overcook	overproduction
overcritical	overrefined
overcrowd	overripe
overdevelop	oversell
overeager	oversensitive
overeat	overspecialize
overemphasize	overspend
overenthusiastic	overstimulate
overexercise	overstock
overexert	overstrict
overexpose	oversupply
overextend	overtire

o'ver·act' *vt., vi.* to act with exaggeration

over·age¹ (ō'vər āj') *adj.* over the age fixed as a standard

over·age² (ō'vər ij) *n.* ⟦OVER + -AGE⟧ a surplus or excess

over·all (*for adj.* ō'vər ôl'; *for adv.* ō'vər ôl') *adj.* 1 from end to end 2 including everything; total — *adv.* 1 from end to end 2 in general

o'ver·alls' (-ôlz') *n.pl.* loose trousers extending up over the chest, worn over other clothing to protect against dirt

o'ver·awe' *vt.* **-awed', -aw'ing** to overcome or subdue by inspiring awe

o'ver·bal'ance *vt.* **-anced, -anc·ing** 1 OUTWEIGH 2 to throw off balance

o'ver·bear'ing *adj.* arrogant; domineering

o'ver·blown' (-blōn') *adj.* 1 overdone; excessive 2 pompous or bombastic

o'ver·board' *adv.* from a ship into the water — **go overboard** [Colloq.] to go to extremes

o'ver·book' *vt., vi.* to issue more reservations than there are seats for

o'ver·cast' *adj.* cloudy; dark: said of the sky

over·charge (ō'vər chärj'; *also & for n.* ō'vər chärj') *vt., vi.* **-charged', -charg'ing** 1 to charge too much 2 to overload — *n.* 1 an excessive charge 2 too full a load

o'ver·clothes' *n.pl.* OUTERWEAR

o'ver·cloud' *vt., vi.* to make or become cloudy, gloomy, etc.

o'ver·coat' *n.* a heavy coat worn over the usual clothing for warmth

o'ver·come' *vt.* **-came', -come', -com'ing** 1 to get the better of in competition, etc. 2 to master, prevail over, or surmount — *vi.* to win

o'ver·de·ter'mine *vt.* to bring about through many causes or factors

o'ver·do' *vt.* **-did', -done', -do'ing** 1 to do too much 2 to exaggerate 3 to overcook — *vi.* to exhaust oneself by doing too much

o'ver·dose' *n.* too large a dose

o'ver·draw' *vt.* **-drew', -drawn', -draw'ing** to draw on in excess of the amount credited to the drawer — **o'ver·draft'** *n.*

o'ver·dress' *vt., vi.* to dress too warmly, too showily, or too formally

o'ver·dub' *n.* a recording of sounds, music, etc. superimposed on another recording — *vt., vi.* **-dubbed', -dub'bing** to add (sounds, music, etc.) to (a recording)

o'ver·due' *adj.* past the time for payment, arrival, etc.

o'ver·es'ti·mate' *vt.* **-mat'ed, -mat'ing** to set too high an estimate on or for — **o'ver·es'ti·ma'tion** *n.*

o'ver·flight' *n.* the flight of an aircraft over a foreign territory, as in reconnaissance

over·flow (ō'vər flō'; *also & for n.* ō'vər flō') *vt.* 1 to flow across; flood 2 to flow over the brim of — *vi.* 1 to run over 2 to be superabundant — *n.* 1 an overflowing 2 the amount that overflows 3 an outlet for overflowing liquids

o'ver·grow' *vt.* **-grew', -grown', -grow'ing** to overspread with foliage so as to cover — *vi.* to grow too fast or beyond normal — **o'ver·grown'** *adj.* — **o'ver·growth'** *n.*

o'ver·hand' *adj., adv.* with the hand raised above the elbow or the arm above the shoulder

over·hang (ō'vər haŋ'; *also & for n.* ō'vər haŋ') *vt., vi.* **-hung', -hang'ing** to hang over or project beyond (something) — *n.* the projection of one thing over another

over·haul (ō'vər hôl'; *also & for n.* ō'vər hôl') *vt.* 1 *a)* to check thoroughly, as for needed repairs *b)* to restore (a motor, etc.) to good working order 2 to catch up with — *n.* an overhauling

over·head (*for adj. & adv.* ō'vər hed', ō'vər hed'; *for n.* ō'vər hed') *adj.* 1 above the head 2 in the sky 3 on a higher level, with reference to related objects — *n.* the general, continuing costs of a business, as of rent, taxes, etc. — *adv.* above the head; aloft

o'ver·hear' *vt.* **-heard', -hear'ing** to hear (something spoken or a speaker) without the speaker's knowledge

o'ver·joy' *vt.* to give great joy to; delight

o'ver·kill' *n.* much more of something than is necessary, appropriate, etc.

o'ver·land' *adv., adj.* by, on, or across land

o'ver·lap' *vt., vi.* **-lapped', -lap'ping** to extend over a part of (something) so as to coincide with this part — *n.* an overlapping part or amount

---

THESAURUS

overall *a.* complete, thorough, comprehensive; see GENERAL 1.

overalls *n.* an overall garment, jump suit, coveralls; see CLOTHES, PANTS 1.

overbearing *a.* despotic, tyrannical, dictatorial; see ABSOLUTE 3.

overboard *a.* over the side, out of the boat, into the water; see WET 1.

overcast *a.* cloudy, gloomy, not clear or fair; see DARK 1.

overcoat *n.* greatcoat, topcoat, raincoat; see CLOTHES, COAT 1.

overcome *a.* conquered, overwhelmed, overthrown; see BEATEN 1.

overcome *v.* overwhelm, best, vanquish, conquer, outdo, surpass, overpower, overwhelm, beat, trounce, subdue, master; see also DEFEAT 2, 3, WIN 1.

overconfident *a.* reckless, imprudent, heedless; see CARELESS, RASH.

overcritical *a.* domineering, harsh, hypercritical; see SEVERE 1, 2.

overcrowd *v.* crowd, stuff, fill; see PACK 2, PRESS 1.

overcrowded *a.* congested, overbuilt, crowded; see FULL 1.

overdo *v.* 1 [To do too much] magnify, amplify, overestimate, overreach, stretch, go too far, overrate, exaggerate, go to extremes, overstate, enlarge, enhance, exalt, bite off more

than one can chew*, run into the ground*, do to death, go overboard*, burn the candle at both ends, lay it on*, have too many irons in the fire, have one's cake and eat it too*; see also EXCEED.—*Ant.* NEGLECT, underdo, slack. 2 [To overtax oneself physically] tire, fatigue, exhaust; see WEARY 2.

overdone *a.* excessive, too much, pushed too far; see EXAGGERATED.

overdose *n.* excessive dose, too much, overtreatment; see EXCESS 1.

overdrawn *a.* exhausted, depleted, all paid out; see GONE 2.

overdue *a.* delayed, belated, tardy; see LATE 1.

overeat *v.* overindulge, stuff, gorge; see EAT 1.

overemphasize *v.* stress, make a big thing of*, make something out of*; see EMPHASIZE, EXCEED.

overestimate *v.* overvalue, overprice, overrate; see EXAGGERATE, EXCEED.

overflow *n.* 1 [The act of overflowing] redundancy, inundation, overproduction; see FLOOD. 2 [That which overflows] superfluity, surplus, surplusage; see EXCESS 1.

overflow *v.* 1 [To flow over the top, or out at a vent] spill over, run over,

pour out, waste, shed, cascade, spout forth, jet, spurt, drain, leak, squirt, spray, shower, gush, shoot, issue, rush, wave, surge, overtop, brim over, bubble over; see also LEAK 1. 2 [To flow out upon] inundate, water, wet; see FLOOD.

overflowing *a.* abundant, in plenty, bountiful; see PLENTIFUL 2.

overgrown *a.* disproportionate, excessive, huge; see LARGE 1.

overgrowth *n.* growth, abundance, luxuriance; see EXCESS 1.

overhang *v.* jut, be suspended, dangle over; see PROJECT 1.

overhaul *v.* modernize, fix, renew; see REPAIR.

overhead *a.* above, aloft, hanging; see OVER 1.

overhear *v.* hear intentionally, listen in on, catch; see EAVESDROP, HEAR 1.

overheard *a.* listened to, recorded, bugged*; see HEARD.

overheat *v.* heat too much, bake, blister; see HEAT 2.

overindulgence *n.* overeating, overdrinking, eating or drinking too much; see DRUNKENNESS, EATING, GREED.

overlap *n.* extension, overlay, addition; see FLAP.

o'ver·lay' *vt.* **-laid', -lay'ing** 1 to lay or spread over 2 to cover, as with a decorative layer

o'ver·lie' *vt.* **-lay', -lain', -ly'ing** to lie on or over

o'ver·look' *vt.* 1 to look at from above 2 to give a view of from above 3 *a)* to fail to notice *b)* to ignore; neglect 4 to excuse 5 to supervise

o'ver·lord' *n.* a lord ranking above other lords

o'ver·ly *adv.* too or too much

o'ver·mas'ter *vt.* to overcome

o'ver·much' *adj., adv., n.* too much

over·night (ō'vər nit', ō'-; ō'vər nit') *adv.* 1 during the night 2 suddenly — *adj.* 1 done or going on during the night 2 for one night *[an overnight guest]* 3 of or for a brief trip *[an overnight bag]*

o'ver·pass' *n.* a bridge, etc. over a road, railway, etc.

o'ver·play' *vt.* 1 to overact, overdo, or overemphasize 2 to overestimate the strength of (one's hand in cards)

o'ver·pow'er *vt.* to get the better of; subdue or overwhelm

o'ver·price' *vt.* **-priced', -pric'ing** to offer for sale at too high a price

o'ver·qual'i·fied *adj.* having more knowledge, education, etc. than needed to qualify

o'ver·rate' *vt.* **-rat'ed, -rat'ing** to rate or estimate too highly

o'ver·reach' *vt.* to reach beyond or above — **overreach oneself** to fail because of trying to do too much

o'ver·react' *vi.* to react in a highly emotional way

o'ver·ride' *vt.* **-rode', -rid'den, -rid'ing** 1 to ride over 2 to prevail over 3 to disregard or nullify

o'ver·rule' *vt.* **-ruled', -rul'ing** 1 to set aside or decide against by virtue of higher authority 2 to prevail over

o'ver·run' *vt.* **-ran', -run', -run'ning** 1 to spread out over so as to cover 2 to swarm over, as vermin 3 to extend beyond (certain limits)

o'ver·seas' *adv.* over or beyond the sea — *adj.* 1 foreign 2 over or across the sea Also [Chiefly Brit.] **o'ver·sea'**

o'ver·see' *vt.* **-saw', -seen', -see'ing** to supervise; superintend — **o'ver·se'er** (-sir', -sē'ər) *n.*

o'ver·sexed' *adj.* having exceptional sexual drive or interest

o'ver·shad'ow *vt.* 1 *a)* to cast a shadow over *b)* to darken 2 to be more important than by comparison

o'ver·shoe' *n.* a boot of rubber, etc. worn over the regular shoe to protect against cold or dampness

o'ver·shoot' *vt.* **-shot', -shoot'ing** 1 to shoot or pass over or beyond (a target, mark, etc.) 2 to exceed

o'ver·sight' *n.* a careless mistake or omission

o'ver·sim'plify' *vt., vi.* **-fied', -fy'ing** to simplify to the point of distortion — **o'ver·sim'pli·fi·ca'tion** *n.*

o'ver·size' *adj.* 1 too large 2 larger than the usual Also **o'ver·sized'**

o'ver·sleep' *vi.* **-slept', -sleep'ing** to sleep longer than intended

o'ver·spread' *vt.* **-spread', -spread'ing** to spread or cover over

o'ver·state' *vt.* **-stat'ed, -stat'ing** to exaggerate — **o'ver·state'ment** *n.*

o'ver·stay' *vt.* to stay beyond the time or limit of

o'ver·step' *vt.* **-stepped', -step'ping** to go beyond the limits of

o'ver·strung' *adj.* too highly strung; tense

o'ver·stuff' *vt.* 1 to stuff with too much of something 2 to upholster (furniture) with deep stuffing

overt (ō vurt', ō'vurt') *adj.* [< L *aperire*, to open] not hidden; apparent — **overt'ly** *adv.*

o'ver·take' *vt.* **-took', -tak'en, -tak'ing** 1 to catch up with 2 to come upon suddenly

o'ver·tax' *vt.* 1 to tax too heavily 2 to make excessive demands on

o'ver-the-count'er *adj.* 1 designating or of securities sold directly to buyers 2 sold legally without prescription, as some drugs

over·throw (ō'vər thrō'; *also & for n.* ō'vər thrō') *vt.* **-threw', -thrown', -throw'ing** 1 to throw or turn over 2 to conquer 3 to throw beyond — *n.* 1 an overthrowing or being overthrown 2 destruction; end

o'ver·time' *n.* 1 time beyond the established limit, as of working hours 2 pay for work done in such a time — *adj., adv.* of, for, or during overtime

o'ver·tone' *n.* 1 a faint, higher tone accompanying a fundamental tone produced by a musical instrument 2 an implication; nuance: *usually in pl.*

over·ture (ō'vər chər) *n.* [< L *apertura*, aperture] 1 an introductory proposal or offer 2 a musical introduction to an opera, etc.

o'ver·turn' *vt.* 1 to turn over 2 to conquer — *vi.* to tip over; capsize

o'ver·ween'ing (-wē'niŋ) *adj.* [< OE *ofer*, over + *wenan*, to think] 1 arrogant 2 excessive

o'ver·weight' *adj.* above the normal or allowed weight

o'ver·whelm' *vt.* 1 to pour down upon and bury beneath 2 to crush; overpower — **o'ver·whelm'ing** *adj.*

o'ver·work' *vt.* to work or use to excess — *vi.* to work too hard or too long — *n.* severe or burdensome work

---

■■■■ THESAURUS ■■■■

overlap *v.* overlie, overhang, lap over, fold over, extend alongside, flap, project upon, overlay; see also PROJECT 1.

overload *v.* oppress, weigh down, encumber; see BURDEN, LOAD 1.

overlook *v.* 1 [To occupy a commanding height] look over, top, survey, inspect, watch over, look out, view, give upon, give on, front on, have a prospect of. 2 [To ignore deliberately] slight, make light of, disdain; see NEGLECT 1. 3 [To fail to see] miss, leave out, neglect; see NEGLECT 2.

overlooked *a.* missed, left out, forgotten; see NEGLECTED.

overlooking *a.* 1 [Providing a view] looking over, looking out on, commanding; see SEEING. 2 [Disregarding] missing, neglecting, forgetting.

overnight *a.* one night, lasting one night, during the night; see LATE 4.

overpass *n.* span, footbridge, walkway; see BRIDGE 1.

overpower *v.* overwhelm, master, subjugate; see DEFEAT 2, 3.

overpowering *a.* irresistible, uncontrollable, overwhelming; see INTENSE.

overproduction *n.* excess, excessive production, overstock; see PRODUCTION 1.

overrate *v.* build up, magnify, overestimate; see EXAGGERATE, EXCEED.

overrated *a.* not very good, overblown, not satisfactory; see POOR 2, UNSATISFACTORY.

override *v.* 1 [To dismiss] pass over, not heed, take no account of; see DISREGARD, NEGLECT 1. 2 [To thwart] make void, reverse, annul; see CANCEL, REVOKE.

overrule *v.* 1 [To nullify] invalidate, rule against, override; see CANCEL, REVOKE. 2 [To rule] direct, control, manage; see GOVERN.

overrun *v.* 1 [To defeat] overwhelm, invade, occupy; see DEFEAT 2. 2 [To infest] ravage, invade, overwhelm; see INFEST 2.

overseas *a.* away, across, in foreign countries; see ABROAD.

oversee *v.* superintend, supervise, look after; see MANAGE 1.

overseer *n.* supervisor, manager, superintendent; see FOREMAN.

overshoes *n.* rubber shoes, galoshes, rubbers; see SHOE.

overshoot *v.* overreach, overdo, overact; see EXCEED.

oversight *n.* failure, overlooking, mistake; see ERROR.

oversleep *v.* sleep late, miss the alarm, stay in bed; see SLEEP.

overspecialize *v.* limit oneself, specialize too much, be a specialist; see RESTRAIN, RESTRICT.

overstay *v.* stay too long, stop, outstay one's welcome; see REMAIN 1.

overstep *v.* violate, encroach, trespass; see EXCEED, MEDDLE 1.

overtake *v.* overhaul, catch up with, get to; see REACH 1.

overtaken *a.* caught up with,

reached, apprehended; see BEATEN 1, CAPTURED.

overthrow *v.* overcome, overrun, overpower; see DEFEAT 2.

overthrown *a.* overcome, overwhelmed, vanquished; see BEATEN 1.

overtime *n.* extra pay, additional wages, late hours; see PAY 2.

overtone *n.* tone, implication, hint; see MEANING, SUGGESTION 1.

overture *n.* 1 [Preliminary negotiations; *sometimes plural*] approach, advance, tender; see SUGGESTION 1. 2 [A musical introduction] prelude, prologue, *Vorspiel* (German), voluntary, proem, preface; see also INTRODUCTION 3.

overturn *v.* reverse, upturn, overthrow; see UPSET 1.

overwhelm *v.* 1 [To defeat] overcome, overthrow, conquer; see DEFEAT 2, 3, WIN 1. 2 [To astonish] puzzle, bewilder, confound; see CONFUSE, SURPRISE.

overwhelmed *a.* beaten, worsted, submerged; see BEATEN 2.

overwhelming *a.* overpowering, ruinous, overthrowing, crushing, smashing, extinguishing, invading, ravaging, overriding, upsetting, inundating, drowning, deluging, surging, obliterating, dissolving, blotting out, wrecking, erasing, effacing, expunging, burying, immersing, engulfing, engrossing, covering; see also HARMFUL, TRIUMPHANT.

overwork *n.* extra work, overtime,

over·wrought (ō'vər rôt', ō'-) *adj.* **1** very nervous or excited **2** too elaborate

ovi·duct (ō'vi dukt') *n.* ⟦< L *ovum*, egg + DUCT⟧ a tube through which the ova pass from an ovary to the uterus

ovipa·rous (ō vip'ə rəs) *adj.* ⟦< L *ovum*, egg + *parere*, to bear⟧ producing eggs which hatch after leaving the body

ovoid (ō'void') *adj.* ⟦< L *ovum*, egg + -OID⟧ egg-shaped — *n.* anything ovoid

ovu·late (äv'yōō lāt', -yə-; ō'vyōō-, -vyə-) *vi.* **-lat'ed, -lat'ing** ⟦< L *ovum*, egg⟧ to produce and discharge ova from the ovary —**ov'u·la'tion** *n.*

ovule (äv'yōōl, ō'vyōōl') *n.* ⟦< L *ovum*, egg⟧ a small egg or seed, esp. one in an early stage of development —**ov'u·lar** *adj.*

ovum (ō'vəm) *n., pl.* **ova** (ō'və) ⟦L, egg⟧ a mature female germ cell

ow (ou) *interj.* a cry of pain

owe (ō) *vt.* **owed, ow'ing** ⟦OE *agan*, to own⟧ **1** to be indebted to the amount of **2** to have the need to do, give, etc., as because of gratitude **3** to be indebted *to* someone for —**owing to** because of

ow·ing (ō'iŋ) *adj.* ⟦ME *owynge*⟧ **1** that owes **2** due; unpaid —**owing to** because of

owl (oul) *n.* ⟦OE *ule*⟧ **1** a predatory night bird having a large, flat face, large eyes, and a short, hooked beak **2** a person of nocturnal habits, solemn appearance, etc. — **owl'ish** *adj.*

owl'et (-it) *n.* a young or small owl

own (ōn) *adj.* ⟦OE *agan*, possess⟧ belonging or relating to oneself or itself /his *own* book/ — *n.* that which belongs to oneself /that is her *own*/ — *vt.* **1** to possess; have **2** to admit; acknowledge — *vi.* to confess (*to*) —**on one's own** [Colloq.] by one's own efforts —**own'er** *n.* —**own'er·ship'** *n.*

ox (äks) *n., pl.* **ox'en** ⟦OE *oxa*⟧ any of certain cud-chewing, cattlelike mammals, esp. a castrated, domesticated bull used as a draft animal

ox'blood' *n.* a deep-red color

ox'bow' (-bō') *n.* the U-shaped part of an ox yoke which passes under and around the animal's neck

ox·ford (äks'fərd) *n.* ⟦after Oxford, England⟧ [*sometimes* O-] **1** a low shoe laced over the instep: also **oxford shoe 2** a cotton or rayon fabric with a basketlike weave: also **oxford cloth**

oxi·dant (äks'i dənt) *n.* an oxidizing agent

oxi·da·tion (äks'i dā'shən) *n.* an oxidizing or being oxidized

ox·ide (äks'id') *n.* ⟦Fr⟧ a compound of oxygen with another element or a radical

oxi·dize (äks'i dīz') *vt.* **-dized', -diz'ing** to unite with oxygen, as in burning or rusting — *vi.* to become oxidized — **ox'i·diz'er** *n.*

oxy·acety·lene (äks'ē ə set''l ēn') *adj.* of or using a mixture of oxygen and acetylene, as for producing a hot flame used in welding

oxy·gen (äks'i jən) *n.* ⟦Fr *oxygène*⟧ a colorless, odorless, gaseous chemical element: it is essential to life processes and to combustion

ox'y·gen·ate' (-jə nāt') *vt.* **-at'ed, -at'ing** to treat or combine with oxygen —**ox'y·gena'tion** *n.*

oxygen tent a transparent enclosure filled with oxygen, fitted around a bed patient to aid breathing

oys·ter (ois'tər) *n.* ⟦< Gr *ostreon*⟧ an edible bivalve mollusk with an irregular shell

oz. ounce(s)

ozone (ō'zōn') *n.* ⟦Fr < Gr *ozein*, to smell⟧ **1** an unstable, pale-blue form of oxygen with a strong odor, formed by an electrical discharge in air and used as a bleaching agent, water purifier, etc. **2** [Slang] pure, fresh air

ozone layer the layer of ozone in the stratosphere that absorbs much ultraviolet radiation

---

THESAURUS

exhaustion; see ABUSE.

overwork *v.* overdo, exhaust, wear out; see BURDEN, WEARY 1.

overworked *a.* overburdened, too busy, worked too hard; see TIRED.

owe *v.* be under obligation, be indebted to, be obligated to, have an obligation, ought to, be bound, get on credit, feel bound, be bound to pay, be contracted to, be in debt for, have signed a note for, have borrowed, have lost.

owed *a.* owing, becoming due, indebted; see DUE, UNPAID 1.

owl *n.* bird of prey, night bird, nocturnal bird; see BIRD.

own *a.* personal, individual, owned,

very own*; see also PRIVATE.

own *v.* **1** [To possess] hold, have, enjoy, fall heir to, have title to, have rights to, be master of, occupy, control, dominate, have claim upon, reserve, retain, keep, have in hand, have a deed for.—*Ant.* LACK, want, need. **2** [To acknowledge] assent to, grant, recognize; see ADMIT 2, DECLARE. —**come into one's own** receive what one deserves, gain proper recognition, thrive; see PROFIT 2. —**of one's own** personal, private, belonging to one; see OWNED. —**on one's own** by oneself, acting independently, singly; see INDEPENDENTLY.

owned *a.* possessed, had, bought, purchased, kept, inherited, enjoyed, in hand, bought over, in the possession of, among the possessions of.

owner *n.* one who has, keeper, buyer, purchaser, heir, heiress, proprietor, landlord, landlady, sharer, partner, title holder, master, heir-apparent.

ownership *n.* possession, having, holding, claim, deed, title, control, buying, purchasing, heirship, proprietorship, occupancy, use, residence, tenancy, dominion.

oyster *n.* bivalve, mollusk, seafood; see FISH, SHELLFISH.

P

p or **P** (pē) *n., pl.* **p's, P's** the 16th letter of the English alphabet

P *Chem. symbol for* phosphorus

p or **p.** 1 page 2 participle 3 past 4 per 5 pint

P or **P.** petite

pa (pä) *n.* [Colloq.] FATHER

PA public address (system) Also **P.A.**

PAC political action committee

pace (pās) *n.* [< L *passus*, a step] 1 a step in walking, etc. 2 the length of a step or stride 3 the rate of speed in walking, etc. 4 rate of progress, etc. 5 a gait 6 the gait of a horse in which both legs on the same side are raised together — *vt.* **paced, pac'ing** 1 to walk back and forth across 2 to measure by paces 3 to set the pace for (a runner, etc.) — *vi.* 1 to walk with regular steps 2 to move at a pace: said of a horse —**put through one's paces** to test one's ability, skills, etc. —**pac'er** *n.*

pace'mak·er *n.* 1 one that leads the way: also **pace'set'ter** 2 an electronic device placed in the body to regulate the heartbeat

pachy·derm (pak'ə durm') *n.* [< Gr *pachys*, thick + *derma*, skin] a large, thick-skinned, hoofed animal, as the elephant or rhinoceros

pachy·san·dra (pak'ə san'drə) *n.* [< ModL name of genus] a low, hardy evergreen plant often used for a ground cover in the shade

pa·cific (pə sif'ik) *adj.* [see PACIFY] 1 making peace 2 of a peaceful nature; tranquil; calm —**pa·cif'i·cally** *adv.*

paci·fier (pas'ə fi'ər) *n.* 1 one that pacifies 2 a nipple or teething ring for babies

pac'i·fism' (-fiz'əm) *n.* opposition to the use of force under any circumstances; specif., refusal to participate in war — **pac'i·fist** *n., adj.*

paci·fy (pas'ə fi') *vt.* **-fied', -fy'ing** [< L *pax*, peace + *facere*, make] to make peaceful, calm, nonhostile, etc. — **pac'i·fi·ca'tion** *n.*

pack[1] (pak) *n.* [< MDu *pak*] 1 a bundle of things tied up for carrying 2 a number of similar persons or things; specif., *a)* a group [a *pack* of lies] *b)* a package of a standard number [a *pack* of cigarettes] *c)* a number of wild animals living together — *vt.* 1 to make a pack of 2 *a)* to put together in a box, trunk, etc. *b)* to fill (a box, etc.) 3 to crowd; cram [the hall was *packed*] 4 to fill in tightly, as for prevention of leaks 5 to carry in a pack 6 to send (*off*) [to send him off to school] 7 [Slang] to carry (a gun, etc.) 8 [Slang] to deliver (a punch, etc.) with force — *vi.* 1 to make up packs 2 to put one's clothes, etc. into luggage for a trip 3 to crowd together 4 to settle into a compact mass — *adj.* used for carrying packs, loads, etc. [a *pack* animal] —**send packing** to dismiss abruptly

pack[2] (pak) *vt.* to choose (a jury, etc.) so as to get desired results

pack·age (pak'ij) *n.* 1 a wrapped or boxed thing or group of things; parcel 2 a number of items, plans, etc. offered as a unit — *vt.* **-aged, -ag·ing** to make a package of — **pack'ager** *n.*

package store a store where alcoholic beverages are sold by the bottle

pack'er *n.* one that packs; specif., one who operates a packing house

pack'et (-it) *n.* 1 a small package 2 a boat that travels a regular route carrying passengers, freight, and mail: in full **packet boat**

pack'ing *n.* 1 the act or process of a person or thing that packs 2 any material used to pack

pack'ing·house' *n.* a plant where meats, etc. are processed and packed for sale

pack rat a North American rat that often hides small articles in its nest

pack'sad'dle *n.* a saddle with fastenings to secure and balance the load carried by a pack animal

pact (pakt) *n.* [< L *pax*, peace] an agreement; compact

pad[1] (pad) *n.* [echoic] the dull sound of a footstep — *vi.* **pad'ded, pad'ding** to walk, esp. with a soft step

pad[2] (pad) *n.* [? var. of POD] 1 anything soft to protect against friction, pressure, etc.; cushion 2 the cushionlike sole of an animal's paw 3 the floating leaf of a water plant, as the waterlily 4 a number of sheets of paper glued along one edge; tablet 5 [Slang] the place where one lives — *vt.* **pad'ded, pad'ding** 1 to stuff or cover with soft material 2 to lengthen (a speech, etc.) with unnecessary material 3 to fill (an expense account, etc.) with invented or inflated entries

pad'ding *n.* anything used to pad

pad·dle[1] (pad''l) *n.* [ME *padell*, small spade] 1 a short pole with a wide blade at one or both ends, used in a canoe, kayak, etc. 2 an implement shaped like this, used to hit a ball, beat something, etc. — *vt., vi.* **-dled, -dling** 1 to propel (a canoe, etc.) by a paddle 2 to beat as with a paddle; spank

pad·dle[2] (pad''l) *vi.* **-dled, -dling** [prob. < PAD[1]] to move the hands or feet about in the water, as in playing

paddle wheel a wheel with paddles around it for propelling a steamboat

pad·dock (pad'ək) *n.* [OE *pearruc*, enclosure] 1 a small enclosure near a stable, in which horses are exercised 2 an enclosure at a racetrack, where horses are saddled

paddy (pad'ē) *n., pl.* **-dies** [Malay *padi*, rice in the husk] a rice field Often **rice paddy**

pad·lock (pad'läk') *n.* a removable lock with a hinged link to be passed through a staple, chain, or eye — *vt.* to fasten or close up as with a padlock

pa·dre (pä'drā') *n.* [< L *pater*] 1 father: the title of a priest in Italy, Spain, etc. 2 [Colloq.] a priest or chaplain

paean (pē'ən) *n.* [< Gr *paian*, hymn] a song of joy, triumph, etc.

THESAURUS

pa* *n.* sire, paterfamilias, dad*; see FATHER 1, PARENT.

pace *n.* step, velocity, movement; see SPEED. —**change of pace** variation, alteration, diversity; see CHANGE 1. —**keep pace (with)** go at the same speed, maintain the same rate of progress, keep up with; see EQUAL. —**set the pace** begin, initiate, establish criteria; see LEAD 1.

pace *v.* determine, pace off, step off; see MEASURE 1.

pacifist *n.* man of peace, peace-lover, conscientious objector; see RADICAL, RESISTER.

pacify *v.* conciliate, appease, placate; see QUIET 1.

pack[1] *n.* 1 [A package] bundle, parcel, load; see PACKAGE. 2 [Kit] outfit, baggage, luggage; see EQUIPMENT. 3 [A group] number, gang, mob; see CROWD. 4 [A medical dressing] application, hot pack, ice pack; see DRESSING 3. 5 [A set of cards] bridge deck, pinochle deck, set; see DECK 2.

pack[1] *v.* 1 [To prepare for transportation] prepare, gather, collect, ready, get ready, put in order, stow away, dispose, tie, bind, brace, fasten.—*Ant.* UNDO, untie, take out. 2 [To stow compactly] stuff, squeeze, bind, compress, condense, arrange, ram, cram, jam, insert, press, contract, put away.—*Ant.* SCATTER, loosen, fluff up.

package *n.* parcel, packet, burden, load, kit, bunch, sheaf, pack, batch, baggage, luggage, grip, suitcase, bag, handbag, valise, trunk, box, carton, crate, bundle, bale, can, tin, sack, bottle; see also CONTAINER.

packed *a.* 1 [Ready for storage or shipment] prepared, bundled, wrapped; see READY 2. 2 [Pressed together] compact, compressed, pressed down; see FULL 1.

packet *n.* pack, receptacle, parcel; see CONTAINER, PACKAGE.

packing *n.* preparation, arrangement, compression, consignment, disposal, disposition, sorting, grading, laying away.

pact *n.* settlement, compact, bargain; see TREATY.

pad[2] *n.* 1 [Material for writing] note pad, stationery, notebook, parchment; see also PAPER 4, TABLET 2. 2 [An article that cushions] mat, cushion, support; see PILLOW, MAT. 3 [*A residence] room, apartment, living quarters; see HOME.

pad[2] *v.* 1 [To stuff] pack, fill out, pad out; see FILL 1. 2 [To increase] inflate, build up, falsify; see DECEIVE, INCREASE.

padded *a.* stuffed, filled, quilted; see FULL 1.

padding *n.* stuffing, wadding, waste; see FILLING.

paddle[1] *n.* oar, pole, paddle wheel; see TOOL 1.

paddle[1] *v.* 1 [To propel by paddling] scull, boat, cruise, drift, navigate, cut water, shoot rapids, run rapids; see also DRIVE 2. 2 [To beat, usually rather lightly] spank, thrash, rap; see BEAT 1, PUNISH.

padlock *n.* latch, fastener, catch; see LOCK 1.

pa·gan (pā′gən) *n.* 〚< L *paganus,* peasant〛 1 a heathen 2 one who has no religion — *adj.* of pagans —**pa′gan·ism′** *n.*

page[1] (pāj) *n.* 〚< L *pangere,* fasten〛 1 *a)* one side of a leaf of a book, etc. *b)* an entire leaf in a book, etc. 2 [*often pl.*] a record of events — *vt.* **paged, pag′ing** to number the pages of

page[2] (pāj) *n.* 〚OFr〛 a boy attendant, esp. one who runs errands, etc., as in a hotel — *vt.* **paged, pag′ing** to try to find (a person) by calling his name, as a hotel page does

pag·eant (paj′ənt) *n.* 〚ME *pagent,* stage scene〛 1 a spectacular exhibition, parade, etc. 2 an elaborate outdoor drama celebrating a historical event

pag′eantry (-ən trē) *n., pl.* **-ries** 1 grand spectacle; gorgeous display 2 empty show or display

pager (pāj′ər) *n.* BEEPER

pagi·na·tion (paj′ə nā′shən) *n.* 1 the numbering of pages 2 the arrangement and number of pages

pa·go·da (pə gō′də) *n.* 〚prob. < Pers *but,* idol + *kadah,* house〛 in India and the Far East, a temple in the form of a pyramidal tower of several stories

paid (pād) *vt., vi. pt. & pp. of* PAY

pail (pāl) *n.* 〚< OE *pægel,* wine vessel〛 1 a container, usually with a handle, for holding liquids, etc.; bucket 2 the amount held by a pail: also **pail′ful′,** *pl.* **-fuls′**

pain (pān) *n.* 〚< Gr *poinē,* penalty〛 1 physical or mental suffering caused by injury, disease, grief, anxiety, etc. 2 [*pl.*] great care 〔take *pains* with one's work〕 — *vt.* to cause pain to; hurt —**on** (or **under**) **pain of** at the risk of a penalty —**pain′ful** *adj.* —**pain′fully** *adv.* —**pain′less** *adj.*

pain′kill′er *n.* [Colloq.] a medicine that relieves pain

pains·taking (pānz′tā′kiŋ) *adj.* requiring or showing great care; very careful —**pains′tak′ing·ly** *adv.*

paint (pānt) *vt.* 〚< L *pingere*〛 1 *a)* to make (a picture, etc.) in colors applied to a surface *b)* to depict with paints 2 to describe vividly 3 to cover or decorate with paint — *vi.* to paint pictures — *n.* 1 a mixture of a pigment with oil, water, etc., used as a covering or coloring 2 a dried coat of paint

paint′er *n.* 1 an artist who paints pictures 2 one whose work is covering surfaces, as walls, with paint

paint′ing *n.* a painted picture

pair (per) *n., pl.* **pairs** or **pair** 〚< L *par,* equal〛 1 two corresponding things associated or used together 〔a *pair* of shoes〕 2 a single unit of two corresponding parts 〔a *pair* of pants〕 3 any two persons or animals regarded as a unit — *vi., vt.* 1 to form a pair (of) 2 to mate

pais·ley (pāz′lē) *adj.* 〚after *Paisley,* Scotland〛 [*also* P-] having an intricate, multicolored pattern of swirls, etc.

pa·ja·mas (pə jä′məz, -jam′əz) *n.pl.* 〚< Pers *pāi,* a leg + *jāma,* garment〛 a loosely fitting sleeping or lounging suit consisting of jacket (or blouse) and trousers

Paki·stani (pak′i stan′ē, pä′ki stä′nē) *adj.* of Pakistan or its people — *n.* a native or inhabitant of Pakistan

pal (pal) *n.* 〚Romany, brother, ult. < Sans〛 [Colloq.] a close friend

pal·ace (pal′əs) *n.* 〚< L *Palatium,* one of the Seven Hills of Rome〛 1 the official residence of a king, etc. 2 any large, magnificent building

pal·at·able (pal′ə tə bəl) *adj.* pleasant or acceptable to the taste or mind

pal·ate (pal′ət) *n.* 〚< L *palatum*〛 1 the roof of the mouth 2 sense of taste —**pal′a·tal** (-ə təl) *adj.*

pa·la·tial (pə lā′shəl) *adj.* 〚see PALACE〛 1 of, suitable for, or like a palace 2 magnificent; stately

pala·tine (pal′ə tin′, -tin) *adj.* 〚see PALACE〛 designating or of a count or earl who ruled in his own territory

pa·laver (pə lav′ər) *n.* 〚Port *palavra,* a word〛 talk, esp. profuse or idle talk — *vi.* to talk idly or profusely

pale[1] (pāl) *adj.* **pal′er, pal′est** 〚< L *pallidus*〛 1 of a whitish or colorless complexion 2 lacking intensity, as color, light, etc.; dim — *vi., vt.* **paled, pal′ing** to become or make pale —**pale′ly** *adv.* —**pale′ness** *n.*

THESAURUS

pagan *a.* unchristian, idolatrous, heathenish.

pagan *n.* pantheist, heathen, doubter, scoffer, unbeliever, atheist, infidel.

paganism *n.* heathenism, agnosticism, idolatry; see ATHEISM.

page[1] *n.* leaf, sheet, folio, side, surface, recto, verso.

page[1,2] *v.* 1 [To call] hunt for, seek for, call the name of; see SUMMON. 2 [To mark the pages] number, check, paginate; see CHECK 2.

pageant *n.* exhibition, celebration, pomp; see PARADE 1.

paid *a.* rewarded, paid off, reimbursed, indemnified, remunerated, solvent, unindebted, unowed, recompensed, salaried, hired, out of debt, refunded; see also REPAID.

pail *n.* pot, receptacle, jug; see CONTAINER.

pain *n.* 1 [Suffering, physical or mental] hurt, anguish, distress, discomfort, disorder, agony, misery, martyrdom, wretchedness, shock, torture, torment, passion; see also INJURY.—*Ant.* HEALTH, well-being, ease. 2 [Suffering, usually physical] ache, twinge, catch, throe, spasm, cramp, torture, malady, sickness, laceration, soreness, fever, burning, torment, distress, agony, affliction, discomfort, hurt, wound, strain, sting, burn, crick; see also ILLNESS 1, INJURY. 3 [Suffering, usually mental] despondency, worry, anxiety; see DEPRESSION 2, GRIEF, SADNESS. — **feeling no pain*** intoxicated, inebriated, stoned*; see DRUNK. — **take pains** make an effort, care, endeavor; see TRY 1.

pain *v.* distress, grieve, trouble; see HURT 1.

painful *a.* 1 [Referring to physical anguish] raw, aching, throbbing, burning, torturing, hurtful, biting, piercing, sharp, severe, caustic, tormenting, smarting, extreme, grievous, stinging, bruised, sensitive, tender, irritated, distressing, inflamed, burned, unpleasant, ulcerated, abcessed, uncomfortable; see also SORE 1.—*Ant.* HEALTHY, comfortable, well. 2 [Referring to mental anguish] worrying, depressing, saddening; see DISTURBING.

paint *n.* 1 [Pigment] coloring material, chroma, chlorophyll; see COLOR. *Paints and colorings include the following—artist's materials:* oil, acrylic, pastel, crayon, charcoal, watercolor, tempera; *architectural finishes:* house paint, enamel, varnish, redwood stain, oil, wax, whitewash, tempera, fresco, luminous paint, plastic paint, cold-water paint, flat paint, high-gloss paint, metallic paint, barn paint, inside paint, outside paint, white lead. 2 [Covering] overlay, varnish, veneer; see FINISH 2.

paint *v.* 1 [To represent by painting] portray, paint in oils, sketch, outline, picture, depict, catch a likeness, design, shade, tint, fresco, wash; see also DRAW 2. 2 [To protect or decorate by painting] coat, decorate, apply, brush, tint, touch up, ornament, gloss over, swab, daub, slap on; see also COVER 1, SPREAD 3.

painted *a.* 1 [Portrayed] outlined, pictured, drawn, sketched, designed, depicted, washed on; see also COLORED 1. 2 [Finished] coated, covered, enameled, decorated, ornamented, brushed over, tinted, washed, daubed, touched up, smeared; see also FINISHED 1.

painter *n.* 1 [House painter] interior decorator, dauber, paintslinger*; see WORKMAN. 2 [An artist] craftsman, artisan, illustrator, draftsman, etcher, sketcher, cartoonist, animator; see also ARTIST. *Major painters include the following:* Giotto, Sandro Botticelli, Jan van Eyck, Albrecht Dürer, Hieronymus Bosch, Pieter Brueghel (the elder), Leonardo da Vinci, Raphael, Michelangelo, Titian, Tintoretto, El Greco, Peter Paul Rubens, Anthony Van Dyck, Rembrandt van Rijn, Jan Vermeer, Sir Joshua Reynolds, Thomas Gainsborough, Diego Velázquez, Francisco Goya, Eugène Delacroix, Auguste Renoir, Edgar Degas, James Whistler, Winslow Homer, Edouard Manet, Claude Monet, Paul Cézanne, Vincent van Gogh, Paul Gauguin, Henri de Toulouse-Lautrec, Pablo Picasso, Henri Matisse, Paul Klee, Salvador Dali, Jackson Pollock.

painting *n.* 1 [A work of art] oil painting, watercolor, abstract design, landscape, sketch, picture, likeness, artwork, canvas, mural, fresco, depiction, delineation; see also ART. 2 [The act of applying paint] enameling, covering, coating; see ART.

pair *n.* couple, mates, two, two of a kind, twosome, twins, fellows, duality, brace.

pair *v.* combine, match, balance; see JOIN 1, 2.

pajamas *n.* nightwear, lounging pajamas, lounging robe, PJ's*, jamas*, nightie*; see also CLOTHES.

pal* *n.* companion, bosom friend, buddy*; see FRIEND.

palace *n.* royal residence, manor, mansion; see CASTLE.

pale[1] *a.* 1 [Wan] pallid, sickly, anemic, bloodless, ghastly, cadaverous, haggard, deathlike, ghostly; see also DULL 2. 2 [Lacking color] white, colorless, bleached; see DULL 2.

pale[1] *v.* grow pale, lose color, blanch; see WHITEN 1.

paleness *n.* whiteness, anemia, colorlessness; see ILLNESS 1.

pale[2] (pāl) *n.* ⟦< L *palus*, a stake⟧ **1** a pointed stake used in fences **2** a boundary; restriction: now chiefly figurative

pale′face′ *n.* a white person: a term allegedly first used by North American Indians

paleon·tol·ogy (pā′lē ən täl′ə jē, -lē än-) *n.* ⟦< Fr⟧ the branch of geology studying prehistoric life by means of fossils —**pa′leon·tol′o·gist** *n.*

Pa′leo·zo′ic (-ō′zō′ik) *adj.* ⟦< Gr *palaios*, ancient + zo(o)- + -ic⟧ designating the geologic era (*c.* 570-225 million years ago) characterized by the first fishes, reptiles, and land plants

pal·ette (pal′it) *n.* ⟦Fr < L *pala*, a shovel⟧ a thin board on which an artist arranges and mixes paints

pal·frey (pôl′frē) *n., pl.* **-freys** ⟦ult. < Gr *para*, beside + L *veredus*, post horse⟧ [Archaic] a saddle horse, esp. a gentle one for a woman

pali·mony (pal′ə mō′nē) *n.* ⟦PAL + (AL)IMONY⟧ an allowance or a property settlement claimed by or granted to one member of an unmarried couple who separate after having lived together

pal·imp·sest (pal′imp sest′) *n.* ⟦< Gr *palimpsēstos*, lit., rubbed again⟧ a parchment previously written upon that bears traces of the erased texts

pal·in·drome (pal′in drōm′) *n.* ⟦< Gr *palindromos*, running back⟧ a word, phrase, or sentence that reads the same backward or forward (Ex.: madam)

pal·ing (pāl′iŋ) *n.* a fence made of pales

pali·sade (pal′ə sād′) *n.* ⟦< Fr < L *palus*, a stake⟧ **1** any of a row of large pointed stakes forming a fence as for fortification **2** such a fence **3** [*pl.*] a line of steep cliffs

pall[1] (pôl) *vi.* **palled, pall′ing** ⟦ME *pallen*, appall⟧ **1** to become cloying, insipid, boring, etc. **2** to become satiated

pall[2] (pôl) *n.* ⟦< L *pallium*, a cover⟧ **1** a cloth covering for a coffin **2** a dark or gloomy covering

pall·bearer (pôl′ber′ər) *n.* ⟦prec. + BEARER⟧ one of the persons who attend or carry the coffin at a funeral

pal·let[1] (pal′it) *n.* ⟦see PALETTE⟧ a low, portable platform used for stacking materials, as in a warehouse

pal·let[2] (pal′it) *n.* ⟦< L *palea*, chaff⟧ a small bed or a pad filled as with straw and used on the floor

pal·li·ate (pal′ē āt′) *vt.* **-at′ed, -at′ing** ⟦< L *pallium*, a cloak⟧ **1** to lessen the severity of without curing; alleviate **2** to make (an offense) appear less serious; excuse —**pal′·lia′tion** *n.* —**pal′lia′tive** *adj., n.*

pal·lid (pal′id) *adj.* ⟦L *pallidus*, pale⟧ faint in color; pale —**pal′lidly** *adv.*

pal·lor (pal′ər) *n.* ⟦< L *pallere*, be pale⟧ unnatural paleness

palm[1] (päm) *n.* ⟦< L *palma*: from its handlike leaf⟧ **1** any of a large group of tropical or subtropical trees or shrubs with a branchless trunk and a bunch of large leaves at the top **2** a leaf of such a tree carried as a symbol of victory, etc.

palm[2] (päm) *n.* ⟦< L *palma*⟧ the inner surface of the hand between the fingers and wrist — *vt.* to hide (something) in the palm, as in a sleight-of-hand trick —**palm off** [Colloq.] to pass off by fraud

pal·metto (pal met′ō) *n., pl.* **-tos** or **-toes** any of certain palms with fan-shaped leaves

palm·is·try (päm′is trē) *n.* ⟦prob. < ME *paume*, PALM[2] + *maistrie*, mastery⟧ fortunetelling by means of the lines, etc. on the palm of a person's hand —**palm′ist** *n.*

Palm Sunday common name for the Sunday before Easter, commemorating Jesus' entry into Jerusalem, when palm branches were strewn before him

palmy (päm′ē) *adj.* **-i·er, -i·est 1** of, like, or full of palm trees **2** prosperous

palo·mino (pal′ə mē′nō) *n., pl.* **-nos** ⟦AmSp < Sp, dove-colored⟧ a golden or cream-colored horse with a white tail

pal·pable (pal′pə bəl) *adj.* ⟦< L *palpare*, to touch⟧ **1** that can be touched, felt, etc. **2** easily perceived by the senses; perceptible **3** obvious; plain —**pal′pably** *adv.*

pal·pi·tate (pal′pə tāt′) *vi.* **-tat′ed, -tat′ing** ⟦< L *palpare*,

to feel⟧ **1** to beat rapidly, as the heart **2** to throb —**pal′pi·ta′tion** *n.*

palsy (pôl′zē) *n., pl.* **-sies** ⟦ult. < L *paralysis*, paralysis⟧ paralysis of any muscle, sometimes with involuntary tremors — *vt.* **-sied, -sy·ing** to paralyze

pal·try (pôl′trē) *adj.* **-tri·er, -tri·est** ⟦prob. < LowG *palte*, rag⟧ almost worthless; trifling —**pal′tri·ness** *n.*

pam·pas (päm′pəz, -pəs) *n.pl.* ⟦AmSp < AmInd *pámpa*, plain, field⟧ the extensive, treeless plains of Argentina

pam·per (pam′pər) *vt.* ⟦ME *pampren*, to feed too much < LowG⟧ to be overindulgent with; coddle; humor

pam·phlet (pam′flit) *n.* ⟦< OFr *Pamphilet*, shortened name of a ML poem⟧ a thin, unbound booklet, often on a topic of current interest —**pam′phlet·eer′** (-fli tir′) *n.*

pan[1] (pan) *n.* ⟦OE *panne*⟧ **1** any broad, shallow container used in cooking, etc. **2** a pan-shaped part or object — *vt.* **panned, pan′ning 1** [Colloq.] to criticize unfavorably **2** *Mining* to wash (gravel) in a pan, as to separate (gold) — *vi. Mining* to wash gravel in a pan, searching for gold —**pan out** [Colloq.] to turn out; esp., to turn out well; succeed

pan[2] (pan) *Film, TV, etc. vt., vi.* **panned, pan′ning** ⟦< PAN(ORAMA)⟧ to move (a camera) so as to get a panoramic effect — *n.* the act of panning

Pan (pan) *Gr. Myth.* a god of fields, forests, flocks, and shepherds, represented as having the legs of a goat

pan- ⟦< Gr *pan*, all, every⟧ *combining form* **1** all [*pantheism*] **2** [P-] of, comprising, or uniting every [*Pan-American*]

pana·cea (pan′ə sē′ə) *n.* ⟦< Gr *pan*, all + *akos*, healing, medicine⟧ a supposed remedy for all ills

pa·nache (pə nash′, -näsh′) *n.* ⟦Fr, ult. < L *pinna*, feather⟧ **1** a plume, esp. on a helmet **2** dashing elegance of manner or style

Panama hat [*also* p-] a hand-woven hat made with strawlike strips of the leaves of a tropical plant

Pan-American (pan′ə mer′i kən) *adj.* of North, South, and Central America, collectively

pan·cake (pan′kāk′) *n.* a flat cake of batter fried on a griddle or in a pan

pan·chro·matic (pan′krō mat′ik) *adj.* sensitive to light of all colors [*panchromatic* film]

pan·creas (pan′krē əs, paŋ′-) *n.* ⟦< Gr *pan*, all + *kreas*, flesh⟧ a large gland that secretes a digestive juice into the small intestine and produces insulin —**pan′creat′ic** (-at′ik) *adj.*

panda (pan′də) *n.* ⟦< native name in Nepal⟧ **1** a black-and-white, bearlike mammal of China: in full **giant panda 2** a reddish, raccoonlike mammal of the Himalayas: in full **lesser panda**

pan·demic (pan dem′ik) *adj.* ⟦< Gr *pan*, all + *dēmos*, people⟧ epidemic over a large region

pan·de·mo·nium (pan′də mō′nē əm) *n.* ⟦< name of demons' abode in Milton's *Paradise Lost* < Gr *pan*, all + *daimōn*, evil spirit⟧ wild disorder or noise

pan·der (pan′dər) *n.* ⟦< L *Pandarus*, lovers' go-between in Chaucer, etc.⟧ **1** a procurer; pimp **2** one who helps others to satisfy their vices, etc. Also **pan′derer** — *vi.* to act as a pander (*to*)

Pan·dora (pan dôr′ə) *n.* ⟦< Gr *pan*, all + *dōron*, gift⟧ *Gr. Myth.* the first mortal woman: she opens a box, letting all human ills into the world

pane (pān) *n.* ⟦< L *pannus*, piece of cloth⟧ a sheet of glass in a frame of a window, etc.

pan·egyr·ic (pan′ə jir′ik) *n.* ⟦< Gr *panēgyris*, public meeting⟧ **1** a formal speech or piece of writing praising a person or event **2** high praise

panel (pan′əl) *n.* ⟦see PANE⟧ **1** *a*) a section or division, usually rectangular, forming a part of a wall, door, etc. *b*) a board for instruments or controls **2** a lengthwise strip in a skirt, etc. **3** a list of persons summoned for jury duty **4** a group of persons selected for judging, discussing, etc. — *vt.* **-eled** or **-elled, -el·ing** or **-el·ling** to provide with panels

pan·el·ing or **pan·el·ling** *n.* **1** panels collectively **2** sheets of plastic, wood, etc. used for panels

---

▬▬ THESAURUS ▬▬

paltry *a.* small, insignificant, trifling; see UNIMPORTANT.

pamper *v.* spoil, indulge, pet, cater to, humor, gratify, yield to, coddle, overindulge, please, spare the rod and spoil the child*.

pamphlet *n.* booklet, brochure, pocketbook, chapbook, leaflet, bulletin, circular, broadside, handbill; see also ANNOUNCEMENT.

pan[1] *n.* vessel, kettle, container, pail,

bucket, baking pan, gold pan; see also CONTAINER. *Kitchen pans include the following:* kettle, stew pan, saucepan, double boiler, roaster, casserole, cake pan, bread pan, pie pan, cookie sheet, frying pan or skillet, dishpan.

pan[1]* *v.* criticize, review unfavorably, jeer at; see BLAME. —**pan out** turn out, work, be a success; see SUCCEED 1.

panacea *n.* relief, cure, elixir; see

REMEDY 2.

pancake *n.* flapjack, hot cake, griddlecake; see FOOD.

pandemonium *n.* uproar, anarchy, riot; see CONFUSION.

pane *n.* window glass, stained glass, mirror; see GLASS.

panel *n.* ornament, tablet, inset; see DECORATION 2.

pan·el·ist *n.* a member of a PANEL (*n.* 4)

panel truck an enclosed pickup truck

pang (paŋ) *n.* ⟦< ?⟧ a sudden, sharp pain, physical or emotional

pan·han·dle[1] (pan'han'dəl) *n.* [*often* P-] a strip of land projecting like the handle of a pan

pan·han·dle[2] (pan'han'dəl) *vt., vi.* **-dled, -dling** [Colloq.] to beg (from), esp. on the streets —**pan'han'dler** *n.*

panic (pan'ik) *n.* ⟦< Gr *panikos*, of Pan, as inspirer of sudden fear⟧ a sudden, unreasoning fear, often spreading quickly — *vt.* **-icked, -ick·ing** 1 to affect with panic 2 [Slang] to convulse (an audience, etc.) with laughter, etc. — *vi.* to show panic —**pan'icky** *adj.*

pan'ic-strick'en *adj.* badly frightened Also **pan'ic-struck'**

pan·nier or **pan·ier** (pan'yər, -ē ər) *n.* ⟦< L *panis*, bread⟧ a large basket for carrying loads on the back

pa·no·cha (pə nō'chə) *n.* ⟦AmSp, ult. < L *panis*, bread⟧ 1 a coarse Mexican sugar 2 *var. of* PENUCHE

pan·o·ply (pan'ə plē) *n., pl.* **-plies** ⟦< Gr *pan*, all + *hopla*, arms⟧ 1 a complete suit of armor 2 any magnificent covering or array

pan·o·rama (pan'ə ram'ə) *n.* ⟦< PAN- + Gr *horama*, a view⟧ 1 a wide view in all directions 2 a constantly changing scene —**pan'o·ram'ic** *adj.*

pansy (pan'zē) *n., pl.* **-sies** ⟦< Fr *penser*, think⟧ a small plant of the violet family, with velvety petals

pant (pant) *vi.* ⟦ult. < L *phantasia*, nightmare⟧ 1 to breathe rapidly and heavily, as from running fast 2 to yearn eagerly: with *for* or *after* — *vt.* to gasp out — *n.* any of a series of rapid, heavy breaths; gasp

pan·ta·loons (pan'tə lōōnz') *n.pl.* ⟦< It: ult. after St. *Pantalone*⟧ 1 orig., a kind of tight trousers 2 later, any trousers

pan·the·ism (pan'thē iz'əm) *n.* ⟦< Gr *pan*, all + *theos*, a god + -ISM⟧ 1 the doctrine that all forces, manifestations, etc. of the universe are God 2 the worship of all gods —**pan'theist** *n.* —**pan'theis'tic** *adj.*

pan·the·on (pan'thē än') *n.* ⟦< Gr *pan*, all + *theos*, a god⟧ 1 a temple for all the gods 2 [*often* P-] a building in which famous dead persons of a nation are entombed or commemorated

pan·ther (pan'thər) *n.* ⟦< Gr *panthēr*⟧ 1 a leopard, specif. one that is black 2 a cougar or a jaguar

pant·ies (pant'ēz) *n.pl.* women's or children's short underpants Also **pantie** (pant'ē) or **pant'y** *n.*

pan·to·mime (pan'tə mīm') *n.* ⟦ult. < Gr *pan*, all + *mimos*, a mimic⟧ 1 a drama played without words, using only action and gestures 2 action or gestures without words — *vt., vi.* **-mimed', -mim'ing** to express or act in pantomime —**pan'to·mim'ic** (-mim'ik) *adj.* —**pan'to·mim'ist** (-mīm'ist) *n.*

pan·to·then·ic acid (pan'tō then'ik) ⟦< Gr *pantothen*, from every side⟧ a viscous oil, part of the vitamin B complex, occurring widely in animal and plant tissues and thought essential for cell growth

pan·try (pan'trē) *n., pl.* **-tries** ⟦< L *panis*, bread⟧ a small room off the kitchen, where cooking ingredients and utensils, china, etc. are kept

pants (pants) *n.pl.* ⟦< PANTALOONS⟧ 1 trousers 2 drawers or panties

pant'suit' *n.* matched pants and jacket for women Also **pants suit**

panty·hose (pan'tē hōz') *n.* women's hose that extend to the waist, forming a one-piece garment

pant'y·waist' (-wāst') *n.* [Slang] a sissy

pap (pap) *n.* ⟦ME⟧ 1 any soft food for babies or invalids 2 any oversimplified or tasteless writing, ideas, etc.

papa (pä'pə) *n.* ⟦< baby talk⟧ *child's term for* FATHER

pa·pacy (pā'pə sē) *n., pl.* **-cies** ⟦LL *papa*, pope⟧ 1 the rank of pope 2 the term of office of a pope 3 the governing of the Roman Catholic Church by the pope, its head

pa·pal (pā'pəl) *adj.* of or relating to a pope or the papacy

pa·paw (pə pô', pô'pô') *n.* ⟦< fol.⟧ 1 PAPAYA 2 *a*) a tree of central and S U.S. with an oblong, yellowish, edible fruit *b*) its fruit

pa·pa·ya (pə pī'ə) *n.* ⟦Sp < WInd name⟧ 1 a tropical American tree with a large, yellowish-orange fruit 2 its fruit

pa·per (pā'pər) *n.* ⟦ult. < Gr *papyros*, papyrus⟧ 1 a thin, flexible material in sheets, made from rags, wood, etc. and used for writing or printing on, for packaging, etc. 2 a single sheet of this 3 an official document 4 an essay, dissertation, etc. 5 a newspaper 6 wallpaper 7 [*pl.*] credentials — *adj.* 1 of, or made of, paper 2 like paper; thin — *vt.* to cover with wallpaper —**pa'pery** *adj.*

pa'per·back' *n.* a book bound in paper covers

pa'per·boy' *n.* a boy who sells or delivers newspapers —**pa'per·girl'** *n.fem.*

paper clip a flexible clasp for holding loose sheets of paper together

pa'per·hang'er *n.* a person whose work is covering walls with wallpaper

paper tiger a person, nation, etc. that seems to pose a threat but is really powerless

pa'per·weight' *n.* any small, heavy object set on papers to keep them from being scattered

pa'per·work' *n.* the keeping of records, etc. incidental to some task

papier-mâché (pā'pər mə shā') *n.* ⟦Fr < *papier*, paper + *mâcher*, to chew⟧ a material made of paper pulp mixed with size, glue, etc., and molded into various objects when moist

pa·pil·la (pə pil'ə) *n., pl.* **-lae** (-ē) ⟦L < *papula*, pimple⟧ any small nipplelike projection of tissue, as on the tongue —**pap·il·lary** (pap'ə ler'ē) *adj.*

pa·poose (pa pōōs', pa-) *n.* ⟦< AmInd⟧ a North American Indian baby

pa·pri·ka (pa prē'kə) *n.* ⟦Hung, ult. < Gr *peperi*, pepper⟧ a mild or hot, red, powdered condiment ground from the fruit of certain pepper plants

Pap test (pap) ⟦after G. *Papanicolaou*, 20th-c. U.S. anatomist⟧ a test for uterine cancer

pa·py·rus (pə pī'rəs) *n., pl.* **-ri** (-rī') or **-ruses** ⟦< Gr

---

THESAURUS

pang *n.* throb, sting, bite; see PAIN 2.

panhandle[2]* *v.* solicit, ask alms, bum*; see BEG.

panhandler* *n.* vagrant, bum*, mendicant; see BEGGAR.

panic *n.* dread, alarm, fright; see FEAR.

panic-stricken *a.* terrified, hysterical, fearful; see AFRAID.

panorama *n.* spectacle, scenery, prospect; see VIEW.

pant *v.* wheeze, throb, palpitate; see BREATHE, GASP.

panties *n.* pants, underpants, briefs; see UNDERWEAR.

pantomime *n.* sign, sign language, dumb show, mimicry, play without words, acting without speech, charade, mime.

pantry *n.* storeroom, larder, cupboard; see CLOSET, ROOM 2.

pants *n.* 1 [Trousers] breeches, slacks, jeans, overalls, cords, shorts, corduroys, pantaloons, bell bottoms, riding breeches, chaps, short pants, knee pants, knickers, bloomers, rompers, sun suit; see also CLOTHES. 2 [Underclothing] shorts, briefs,

panties; see CLOTHES, UNDERWEAR.

papa* *n.* dad*, daddy*, male parent; see FATHER 1, PARENT.

paper *n.* 1 [A piece of legal or official writing] document, official document, legal paper; see RECORD 1. *Papers include the following:* abstract, affidavit, bill, certificate, citation, contract, credentials, data, deed, diploma, indictment, grant, orders, passport, visa, plea, records, safe-conduct, subpoena, summons, testimony, voucher, warrant, will. 2 [A newspaper] journal, daily, daily journal; see NEWSPAPER. 3 [A piece of writing] essay, article, theme; see WRITING 2. 4 [A manufactured product] *Paper products include the following—writing material:* typing paper, typewriter paper, stationery, bond paper, letterhead, personal stationery, ruled paper, second sheet, onion skin, carbon paper, note pad, note card, filing card; *printing paper:* coated stock, poster, linen finish, vellum, parchment, India; 50-pound, 60-pound, etc.; newsprint; *miscellaneous:* art, rice, Chinese or Japanese

rice, crêpe, butcher's, wrapping, tissue, brown, tar, roofing, tracing, graph, filter, toilet, wax, photographic; wallpaper, cellophane, paper towel, cleansing tissue. —**on paper** 1 recorded, signed, official; see WRITTEN 2. 2 in theory, assumed to be feasible, not yet in practice; see THEORETICAL.

paper *v.* hang, paste up, plaster; see COVER 1.

paperback *n.* softcover, pocket book, reprint; see BOOK.

papers *n.* 1 [Evidence of identity or authorization] naturalization papers, identification card, ID; see IDENTIFICATION 2, PASSPORT. 2 [Documentary materials] writings, documents, effects; see RECORD 1.

paperwork *n.* office work, desk work, keeping one's desk clear, keeping records, filing, preparing reports, taking dictation, typing, keeping books.

papery *a.* flimsy, insubstantial, slight; see POOR 2.

papyros] 1 a tall water plant of Egypt 2 a writing material made from the pith of this plant by the ancients

par (pär) *n.* [L, an equal] 1 the established value of a currency in terms of the money of another country 2 an equal status, level, etc.: usually in **on a par (with)** 3 the average state, condition, etc. [work that is above *par*] 4 the face value of stocks, etc. 5 *Golf* the number of strokes established as a skillful score for a hole or course — *adj.* 1 of or at par 2 average

par. 1 paragraph 2 parish

para- *prefix* 1 beside, beyond [*parapsychology*] 2 helping in a secondary way, accessory [*paramedical*]

para·ble (par'ə b'l) *n.* [< Gr *parabolē*, analogy < *para-*, beside + *ballein*, to throw] a short, simple story teaching a moral lesson

pa·rab·o·la (pə rab'ə lə) *n.* [see prec.] *Geom.* a curve formed by the intersection of a cone with a plane parallel to its side —**par·a·bolic** (par'ə bäl'ik) *adj.*

para·chute (par'ə shoot') *n.* [Fr < *para-*, protecting + *chute*, a fall] a cloth contrivance usually shaped like an umbrella when expanded, and used to retard the speed of one dropping from an airplane, etc. — *vt., vi.* **-chut'ed, -chut'ing** to drop by parachute —**par'a·chut'ist** *n.*

pa·rade (pə rād') *n.* [< L *parare*, prepare] 1 ostentatious display 2 a review of troops 3 any organized procession or march, as for display — *vt.* **-rad'ed, -rad'ing** 1 to march or walk through, as for display 2 to show off [to *parade* one's knowledge] — *vi.* 1 to march in a parade 2 to walk about ostentatiously

para·digm (par'ə dim', -dim') *n.* [< Gr *para-*, beside + *deigma*, example] 1 an example or model 2 *Gram.* an example of a declension or conjugation, giving all the inflections of a word

para·dise (par'ə dis') *n.* [< Gr *paradeisos*, garden] 1 [P-] the garden of Eden 2 heaven 3 any place or state of great happiness

para·dox (par'ə däks') *n.* [< Gr *para-*, beyond + *doxa*, opinion] 1 a statement that seems contradictory, etc. but may be true in fact 2 a statement that is self-contradictory and, hence, false —**par'a·dox'i·cal** *adj.* —**par'a·dox'i·cally** *adv.*

par·af·fin (par'ə fin) *n.* [Ger < L *parum*, too little + *affinis*, akin: from its inertness] a white, waxy substance used for making candles, sealing jars, etc. Also **par'af·fine** (-fin, -fēn')

para·gon (par'ə gän', -gən) *n.* [< It *paragone*, touchstone] a model of perfection or excellence

para·graph (par'ə graf') *n.* [< Gr *para-*, beside + *graphein*, write] 1 a distinct section of a writing, begun on a new line and often indented 2 a brief item in a newspaper, etc. — *vt.* to arrange in paragraphs

para·keet (par'ə kēt') *n.* [prob. < MFr *perrot*, parrot] a small, slender parrot with a long, tapering tail

para·legal (par'ə lē'gəl) *adj.* designating or of persons trained to aid lawyers but not licensed to practice law — *n.* such a person

par·al·lax (par'ə laks') *n.* [< Gr *para-*, beyond + *allassein*, to change] the apparent change in the position of an object resulting from a change in the viewer's position

par·al·lel (par'ə lel') *adj.* [< Gr *para-*, side by side + *allēlos*, one another] 1 extending in the same direction and at a constant distance apart, so as never to meet 2 similar or corresponding — *n.* 1 a parallel line, surface,

etc. 2 any person or thing similar to another; counterpart 3 any comparison showing likeness 4 any of the imaginary lines parallel to the equator and representing degrees of latitude: in full **parallel of latitude** — *vt.* **-leled'** or **-lelled', -lel'ing** or **-lel'ling** 1 to be parallel with [the road *parallels* the river] 2 to compare 3 to match; equal —**par'al·lel·ism'** (-iz'əm) *n.*

par·al·lel·o·gram' (-ə gram') *n.* a four-sided plane figure having the opposite sides parallel and equal

pa·ral·y·sis (pə ral'ə sis) *n., pl.* **-ses'** (-sēz') [< Gr *paralyein*, to loosen or weaken at the side] 1 partial or complete loss of voluntary motion or of sensation in part or all of the body 2 any condition of helpless inactivity —**par·a·lytic** (par'ə lit'ik) *adj., n.*

para·lyze (par'ə liz') *vt.* **-lyzed', -lyz'ing** 1 to cause paralysis in 2 to make ineffective or powerless

para·me·ci·um (par'ə mē'sē əm, -shē əm) *n., pl.* **-cia** (-ə) [< Gr *paramēkēs*, oval] an elongated protozoan that moves by means of cilia

para·medic (par'ə med'ik) *n.* a person in paramedical work

par'a·med'i·cal (-med'i kəl) *adj.* [PARA- + MEDICAL] of auxiliary medical personnel, as midwives, medics, nurses' aides, etc.

pa·ram·e·ter (pə ram'ət ər) *n.* [< Gr *para-*, beside + *metron*, a measure] 1 any of a set of interdependent variables 2 *a)* a boundary or limit *b)* a characteristic (*usually in pl.*)

para·mili·tary (par'ə mil'ə ter'ē) *adj.* [PARA- + MILITARY] of forces working along with, or in place of, a regular military organization

para·mount (par'ə mount') *adj.* [< OFr *par*, by + *amont*, uphill] ranking higher than any other; chief

par·amour (par'ə moor') *n.* [< OFr *par amour*, with love] a lover or mistress, esp. in an illicit relation

para·noia (par'ə noi'ə) *n.* [< Gr *para-*, beside + *nous*, the mind] a mental disorder characterized by delusions, as of grandeur or, esp., persecution —**par'a·noid'** *adj., n.*

para·pet (par'ə pet', -pət) *n.* [< It *parare*, to guard + *petto*, breast] 1 a wall or bank for screening troops from enemy fire 2 a low wall or railing

para·pher·na·lia (par'ə fər nāl'yə, -nā'lē ə) *n.pl.* [< Gr *para-*, beyond + *phernē*, dowry] 1 personal belongings 2 equipment

para·phrase (par'ə frāz') *n.* [< Gr *para-*, beside + *phrazein*, say] a rewording of the meaning of something spoken or written — *vt., vi.* **-phrased', -phras'ing** to express (something) in a paraphrase

para·plegia (par'ə plē'jē ə, -jə) *n.* [< Gr *para-*, beside + *plēgē*, a stroke] paralysis of the lower half of the body —**par·a·ple·gic** (-plē'jik) *adj., n.*

par·a·pro·fes'sional *n.* [see PARA-] a trained assistant to licensed professionals, as in medicine or education

par·a·psy·chol'ogy *n.* [see PARA-] psychology dealing with psychic phenomena, as telepathy

para·site (par'ə sit') *n.* [< Gr *para-*, beside + *sitos*, food] 1 one who lives at others' expense without making any useful return 2 a plant or animal that lives on or in another organism —**par·a·sit·ic** (-sit'ik) *adj.*

para·sol (par'ə sôl') *n.* [< It *parare*, ward off + *sole*, sun] a lightweight umbrella used as a sunshade

para·sym·pa·thetic (par'ə sim'pə thet'ik) *adj.* [PARA- + SYMPATHETIC] *Physiology* designating the part of the autonomic nervous system whose functions include constrict-

---

THESAURUS

par *n.* standard, level, norm; see MODEL 2.

parable *n.* fable, moral story, tale; see STORY.

parachute *n.* chute, seat pack parachute, lap pack parachute, harness and pack, umbrella*, bailer*, silk*.

parachute *v.* fall, bail out, hit the silk*; see DIVE.

parade *n.* 1 [A procession] spectacle, ceremony, demonstration, review, line of floats, line of march, pageant, ritual. 2 [An ostentatious show] show, ostentation, ceremony; see DISPLAY.

parade *v.* demonstrate, display, exhibit; see MARCH.

paradise *n.* 1 [Heaven] Kingdom Come, Celestial Home, the other world; see HEAVEN. 2 [The home of Adam and Eve] Garden of Eden, Eden, the Garden.

paradox *n.* mystery, enigma, ambiguity; see PUZZLE 2.

paragon *n.* ideal, perfection, best; see MODEL 1.

paragraph *n.* passage, section, division of thought, topic, statement, verse, article, item, notice.

parallel *a.* 1 [Equidistant at all points] side by side, never meeting, running parallel, coordinate, coextending, lateral, laterally, in the same direction, extending equally. 2 [Similar in kind, position, or the like] identical, equal, conforming; see ALIKE.

parallel *n.* resemblance, likeness, correspondence; see SIMILARITY.

parallel *v.* match, correspond, correlate; see EQUAL.

paralysis *n.* insensibility, loss of motion, loss of sensation; see ILLNESS 2.

paralytic *a.* inactive, paralyzed, crippled; see DISABLED, SICK.

paralytic *n.* paralysis victim, cripple, paralyzed person; see PATIENT.

paralyze *v.* strike with paralysis, make inert, render nerveless; see DEADEN.

paralyzed *a.* insensible, nerveless, benumbed, stupefied, inert, inactive, unmoving, helpless, torpid; see also DISABLED.

paranoid *a.* affected by paranoia, unreasonably distrustful, overly suspicious, having a persecution complex.

paraphernalia *n.* gear, material, apparatus; see EQUIPMENT.

parasite *n.* 1 [A plant or animal living on another] bacteria, parasitoid, saprophyte, epiphyte. 2 [A hanger-on] dependent, slave, sponger*; see SLAVE.

ing the pupils of the eyes, slowing the heartbeat, and stimulating some digestive glands

para·thion (par′ə thī′än′) *n.* ⟦PARA- + Gr *theion*, sulfur⟧ a highly poisonous insecticide

par·a·thy′roid′ (-thī′roid′) *adj.* ⟦PARA- + THYROID⟧ designating or of the small glands near the thyroid that regulate calcium and phosphorus metabolism

para·troops (par′ə trōōps′) *n.pl.* ⟦< PARA(CHUTE) + TROOP⟧ troops trained and equipped to parachute into a combat area —**par′a·troop′er** *n.*

par·boil (pär′boil′) *vt.* ⟦< L *per*, through + *bullire*, to boil: infl. by *part*⟧ to boil until partly cooked

par·cel (pär′səl) *n.* ⟦ult. < L *pars*, part⟧ 1 a small, wrapped bundle; package 2 a piece (of land) — *vt.* **-celed** or **-celled, -cel·ing** or **-cel·ling** to separate into parts and distribute: with *out*

parcel post a mail service for parcels of a specified total weight and size

parch (pärch) *vt.* ⟦< ?⟧ 1 to expose to great heat so as to dry or roast 2 to make very thirsty — *vi.* to become very dry, hot, thirsty, etc.

parch·ment (pärch′mənt) *n.* ⟦< L (*charta*) *Pergamena*, (paper) of Pergamum, city in Asia Minor⟧ 1 the skin of a sheep, goat, etc. prepared as a surface for writing 2 paper like parchment 3 a manuscript on parchment

par·don (pärd′n) *vt.* ⟦< L *per-*, through + *donare*, give⟧ 1 to release from further punishment 2 to forgive (an offense) 3 to excuse (a person) for a fault, etc. — *n.* 1 forgiveness 2 an official document granting a pardon — **par′don·able** *adj.* —**par′doner** *n.*

pare (per) *vt.* pared, par′ing ⟦< L *parare*, prepare⟧ 1 to cut or trim away (the rind, skin, etc.) of; peel 2 to reduce gradually: often with *down*

par·egor·ic (par′ə gôr′ik) *n.* ⟦< Gr *parēgoros*, soothing⟧ a tincture of opium, used to relieve diarrhea

par·ent (per′ənt) *n.* ⟦< L *parere*, beget⟧ 1 a person in relation to his or her offspring; a mother or father 2 any organism in relation to its offspring 3 a source; origin — *adj.* of a corporation in relation to a subsidiary that it owns —**pa·ren·tal** (pə rent′'l) *adj.* —**par′ent·hood′** *n.*

par′ent·age (-ij) *n.* descent from parents or ancestors; lineage

pa·ren·the·sis (pə ren′thə sis) *n., pl.* **-ses′** (-sēz′) ⟦< Gr *para-*, beside + *entithenai*, insert⟧ 1 a word, clause, etc. added as an explanation or comment within a sentence 2 either or both of the curved lines, ( ), used to set this off — **par·en·thet·i·cal** (par′ən thet′i kəl) or **par·en·thet′ic** *adj.*

par·ent·ing (per′ənt in) *n.* the work or skill of a parent in raising a child or children

pa·re·sis (pə rē′sis) *n., pl.* **-ses′** (-sēz′) ⟦Gr < *parienai*, relax⟧ 1 partial paralysis 2 a brain disease caused by syphilis of the central nervous system

par·fait (pär fā′) *n.* ⟦Fr, perfect⟧ a frozen dessert of cream, eggs, etc., or of ice cream with syrup, fruit, etc.

pa·riah (pə rī′ə) *n.* ⟦< Tamil *paṛaiyan*, drummer⟧ 1 a member of one of the lowest social castes in India 2 any outcast

pari·mu·tuel (par′ə myōō′chōō əl) *n.* ⟦Fr, lit., a mutual bet⟧ a system of betting on races in which the winning

bettors share the net of each pool in proportion to their wagers

par·ing (per′in) *n.* a piece pared off

Paris (par′is) *Gr. Legend* a prince of Troy: see HELEN OF TROY

par·ish (par′ish) *n.* ⟦< Gr *paroikia*, diocese⟧ 1 a part of a diocese, under the charge of a priest or minister 2 the congregation of a church 3 a civil division in Louisiana, like a county

pa·rish·ion·er (pə rish′ə nər) *n.* a member of a parish

par·ity (par′ə tē) *n.* ⟦< L *par*, equal⟧ 1 equality in power, value, etc. 2 equality of value at a given ratio between different kinds of money, etc.

park (pärk) *n.* ⟦< ML *parricus*⟧ 1 wooded land held as part of an estate or preserve 2 an area of public land, with walks, playgrounds, etc., for recreation 3 the system in an automatic transmission that locks the drive wheels of a motor vehicle — *vt., vi.* 1 to leave (a vehicle) in a place temporarily 2 to maneuver (a vehicle) into a parking space

parka (pär′kə) *n.* ⟦< Russ, fur coat⟧ a heavy, hooded jacket

parking meter a coin-operated device for indicating the length of time a parking space may be occupied

Par·kin·son's disease (pär′kin sənz) ⟦after J. *Parkinson* (1755-1824), Eng physician⟧ a degenerative disease of later life, causing rhythmic tremor and muscular rigidity

park′way′ *n.* a broad roadway landscaped with trees, bushes, etc.

par·lance (pär′ləns) *n.* ⟦< OFr *parler*, speak⟧ language or idiom

par·lay (pär′lā, -lē; *for v., also* pär lā′) *vt., vi.* ⟦< It *paro*, a pair⟧ to bet (an original wager plus its winnings) on another race, etc. — *n.* a parlayed bet

par·ley (pär′lē) *vi.* ⟦< Fr *parler*, speak⟧ to confer, esp. with an enemy — *n., pl.* **-leys** a conference, as to settle a dispute or discuss terms

par·lia·ment (pär′lə mənt) *n.* ⟦< OFr *parler*, speak⟧ 1 an official government council 2 [P-] the national legislative body of certain countries, esp. Great Britain

par·lia·men·tar·ian (-men ter′ē ən) *n.* one skilled in parliamentary rules

par·lia·men′tary (-men′tər ē) *adj.* 1 of or by a parliament 2 conforming to the rules of a parliament

par·lor (pär′lər) *n.* ⟦< OFr *parler*, speak⟧ 1 [Old-fashioned] any living room 2 any of certain establishments *[a beauty parlor]* Brit., etc. sp. **par′lour**

Par·me·san (cheese) (pär′mə zän′) ⟦after *Parma*, It city⟧ a very hard, dry cheese orig. of Italy

pa·ro·chial (pə rō′kē əl) *adj.* ⟦see PARISH⟧ 1 of or in a parish or parishes 2 narrow in scope; provincial —**pa·ro′chi·al·ism′** *n.*

parochial school a school supported and controlled by a church

par·o·dy (par′ə dē) *n., pl.* **-dies** ⟦< Gr *para-*, beside + *ōidē*, song⟧ a farcical imitation of a literary or musical work or

---

■■■ THESAURUS ■■■

parcel *n.* bundle, packet, carton; see PACKAGE.

parch *v.* dessicate, dehydrate, brown; see DRY 1.

parched *a.* burned, withered, dried; see DRY 1.

parchment *n.* vellum, goatskin, sheepskin; see PAPER 4.

pardon *n.* 1 [The reduction or removal of punishment] absolution, grace, remission, amnesty, exoneration, discharge; see also MERCY.— *Ant.* PUNISHMENT, condemnation, conviction. 2 [Forgiveness] excuse, forbearance, conciliation; see also FORGIVENESS, KINDNESS 1.

pardon *v.* 1 [To reduce punishment] exonerate, clear, absolve, reprieve, acquit, set free, liberate, discharge, rescue, justify, suspend charges, put on probation, grant amnesty to; see also FREE, RELEASE.—*Ant.* PUNISH, chastise, sentence. 2 [To forgive] condone, overlook, exculpate; see EXCUSE, FORGIVE.

pardoned *a.* forgiven, freed, excused, released, granted amnesty, given a

pardon, reprieved, granted a reprieve, acquitted, let off, sprung*, back in circulation; see also DISCHARGED, FREE 1.—*Ant.* ACCUSED, convicted, condemned.

pare *v.* scalp, strip, flay; see CUT 1, SHAVE, SKIN.

parent *n.* immediate forebear, procreator, progenitor, sire; see also FATHER 1, MOTHER 1.

parental *a.* paternal, maternal, familial; see GENETIC.

parentheses *n.* brackets, enclosure, punctuation marks; see PUNCTUATION.

parish *n.* archdiocese, congregation, diocese; see AREA, CHURCH 3.

park *n.* 1 [A place designated for outdoor recreation] square, plaza, lawn, green, village green, promenade, boulevard, tract, recreational area, pleasure ground, national park, national monument, enclosure, woodland, meadow. 2 [A place designed for outdoor storage] parking lot, parking space, lot; see GARAGE, PARKING LOT.

park *v.* mass, collect, order, place in order, station, place in rows, leave, store, impound, deposit; see also LINE UP.

parked *a.* stationed, standing, left, put, lined up, in rows, by the curb, in the parking lot, stored, halted, unmoving.

parking lot *n.* lot, parking, space, parking space, parking garage, parking area, parking facility, parking slot, off-street parking.

Parliament *n.* national legislative body of Great Britain, House of Commons, House of Lords; see GOVERNMENT 1, LEGISLATURE.

parliamentary *a.* congressional, administrative, lawmaking; see GOVERNMENTAL, LEGISLATIVE.

parochial *a.* provincial, insular, sectional; see LOCAL 1, REGIONAL.

parody *n.* travesty, burlesque, mimicry; see JOKE.

parody *v.* mimic, copy, caricature; see IMITATE 1, JOKE.

style — *vt.* **-died, -dy·ing** to make a parody of —**par'o·dist** *n.*

pa·role (pə rōl′) *n.* 〖< LL *parabola*, a speech〗 the release of a prisoner whose sentence has not expired, on condition of future good behavior — *vt.* **-roled′, -rol′ing** to release on parole —**on parole** at liberty under conditions of parole

par·ox·ysm (par′əks iz′əm) *n.* 〖< Gr *para-*, beyond + *oxynein*, sharpen〗 **1** a sudden attack of a disease **2** a sudden outburst as of laughter

par·quet (pär kā′) *n.* 〖Fr, < MFr *parchet*, dim. of *parc*, park〗 **1** the main floor of a theater: usually called *orchestra* **2** a flooring of parquetry — *vt.* **-queted′** (-kād′), **-quet′ing** (-kā′iŋ) to make of parquetry

parquet circle the part of a theater beneath the balcony and behind the parquet on the main floor

par·quetry (pär′kə trē) *n.* inlaid flooring in geometric forms

par·ri·cide (par′ə sīd′) *n.* 〖< L *paricida*: see -CIDE〗 **1** the act of murdering one's parent, close relative, etc. **2** one who does this

par·rot (par′ət) *n.* 〖Fr dial. *perrot*〗 **1** a bird with a hooked bill and brightly colored feathers: some parrots can learn to imitate human speech **2** one who parrots what others say — *vt.* to repeat without understanding

par·ry (par′ē) *vt.* **-ried, -ry·ing** 〖prob. ult. < L *parare*, prepare〗 **1** to ward off (a blow, etc.) **2** to evade (a question, etc.) — *n., pl.* **-ries** a parrying

parse (pärs) *vt., vi.* **parsed, pars′ing** 〖< L *pars* (*orationis*), part (of speech)〗 to break (a sentence) down, giving the form and function of each part

par·si·mony (pär′sə mō′nē) *n.* 〖< L *parcere*, to spare〗 stinginess; extreme frugality —**par'si·mo′ni·ous** *adj.*

pars·ley (pärs′lē) *n.* 〖< Gr *petros*, stone + *selinon*, celery〗 a plant with aromatic, often curled leaves used to flavor or garnish some foods

pars·nip (pärs′nip′) *n.* 〖< L *pastinare*, dig up〗 **1** a plant with a long, white root used as a vegetable **2** its root

par·son (pär′sən) *n.* 〖see PERSON〗 a minister, esp. one having a parish

par′son·age (-ij) *n.* the dwelling provided by a church for its minister

part (pärt) *n.* 〖< L *pars*〗 **1** a portion, segment, etc. of a whole 〖*a part* of a book〗 **2** an essential, separable element 〖automobile *parts*〗 **3** a portion or share; specif., *a*) duty 〖to do one's *part*〗 *b*) 〖*usually pl.*〗 talent; ability 〖a man of *parts*〗 *c*) a role in a play *d*) any of the voices or instruments in a musical ensemble, or the score for this **4** *a*) a region *b*) 〖*usually pl.*〗 a district **5** one of the sides in a conflict, etc. **6** a dividing line formed in combing the hair — *vt.* **1** to break or divide into parts **2** to comb (the hair) so as to leave a part **3** to break or hold apart — *vi.* **1** to

break or divide into parts **2** to separate and go different ways **3** to cease associating **4** to go away; leave: with *from* — *adj.* partial —**for one's part** as far as one is concerned —**for the most part** mostly —**in part** partly —**part with** relinquish —**take part** to participate

par·take (pär tāk′) *vi.* **-took′, -tak′en, -tak′ing** 〖< *part taker*〗 **1** to participate (*in* an activity) **2** to eat or drink something, esp. with others: usually with *of* —**par·tak′er** *n.*

parted (pärt′id) *adj.* separated

par·terre (pär ter′) *n.* 〖Fr < *par*, on + *terre*, earth〗 **1** a garden with flower beds and path in a pattern **2** PARQUET CIRCLE

par·theno·gen·esis (pär′thə nō′jen′ə sis) *n.* 〖see fol. & GENESIS〗 reproduction from an unfertilized ovum, seed, or spore

Par′thenon′ (-nän′) 〖< Gr *parthenos*, a virgin (i.e., Athena)〗 the Doric temple of Athena on the Acropolis

par·tial (pär′shəl) *adj.* 〖< L *pars*, a part〗 **1** favoring one person, faction, etc. more than another; biased **2** not complete —**partial to** fond of —**par'tial′i·ty** (-shē al′ə tē) *n.* —**par′tially** *adv.*

par·tic·i·pate (pär tis′ə pāt′, pər-) *vi.* **-pat′ed, -pat′ing** 〖< L *pars*, a part + *capere*, to take〗 to have or take a share with others (*in* some activity) —**par·tic′i·pant** *adj., n.* —**par·tic′i·pa′tion** *n.* —**par·tic′i·pa′tor** *n.* —**par·tic′i·pa·to′ry** (-pə tôr′ē) *adj.*

par·ti·ci·ple (pärt′i sip′əl) *n.* 〖see prec.〗 a verbal form having characteristics of both verb and adjective —**par'ti·cip′i·al** (-sip′ē əl) *adj.*

par·ti·cle (pärt′i kəl) *n.* 〖< L *pars*, a part〗 **1** a tiny fragment or trace **2** a short, usually invariable part of speech, as an article, preposition, etc. **3** *Physics* a piece of matter of negligible size though with other attributes, as mass

parti-colored (pär′ti kul′ərd) *adj.* 〖< Fr *parti*, divided + COLORED〗 having different colors in different parts

par·ticu·lar (pər tik′yə lər) *adj.* 〖< L *particula*, particle〗 **1** of or belonging to a single person, group, or thing **2** regarded separately; specific **3** unusual **4** exacting; fastidious — *n.* a distinct fact, item, detail, etc. —**in particular** especially —**par·tic'u·lar′ity** (-lar′ə tē) *n., pl.* **-ties,** *n.*

par·tic'u·lar·ize′ (-lər iz′) *vt., vi.* **-ized′, -iz′ing** to give particulars or details (of) —**par·tic′u·lari·za′tion** *n.*

par·tic'u·lar·ly *adv.* **1** in detail **3** specifically

par·tic'u·late (-yōō lit, -yōō lāt′) *adj.* of or formed of tiny, separate particles

part′ing *adj.* **1** dividing; separating **2** departing **3** given, spoken, etc. at parting — *n.* **1** a breaking or separating **2** a departure

par·ti·san (pärt′i zən) *n.* 〖< L *pars*, a part〗 **1** a strong supporter of a faction, party, etc. **2** a guerrilla fighter — *adj.* of or like a partisan Also **par′ti·zan** —**par'ti·san·ship′** *n.*

THESAURUS

parole *v.* discharge, pardon, liberate; see FREE, RELEASE.

parrot *n.* **1** [A bird] parakeet, lovebird, cockatoo; see BIRD. **2** [One who copies others] plagiarist, mimic, mimicker, ape, impersonator, imposter, mocker, copycat*; see also IMITATOR.

parson* *n.* clergyman, cleric, preacher; see MINISTER 1.

part *n.* **1** [A portion] piece, fragment, fraction, section, sector, member, segment, division, allotment, apportionment, ingredient, element, slab, subdivision, partition, particle, installment, component, constituent, bit, slice, scrap, chip, chunk, lump, sliver, splinter, shaving, molecule, atom, electron, proton, neutron; see also SHARE.—*Ant.* WHOLE, total, aggregate. **2** [A part of speech] modifier, preposition, conjunction; see NOUN, VERB. **3** [A machine part] molding, casting, fitting, lever, shaft, cam, spring, band, belt, chain, pulley, clutch, spare part, replacement; see also BOLT, GEAR, MACHINE, WHEEL 1. **4** [A character in a drama] hero, heroine, character; see ROLE. —**for the most part** mainly, mostly, to the greatest extent; see MOST. —**in part** partially, somewhat, to some extent;

see PARTLY, UNFINISHED 1. —**on one's part** privately, as far as one is concerned, coming from one; see PERSONALLY 2. —**play a part** share, join, take part; see PARTICIPATE 1. —**take part** associate, cooperate, follow; see JOIN 2, PARTICIPATE 1, SHARE 2.

part *v.* **1** [To put apart] separate, break, sever; see DIVIDE. **2** [To depart] withdraw, take leave, part company; see LEAVE 1. —**part from** separate, part, break up with; see LEAVE 1. —**part with** let go of, suffer loss, give up; see LOSE 2.

partake *v.* participate, divide, take; see SHARE 2.

parted *a.* divided, severed, sundered; see SEPARATED.

partial *a.* **1** [Not complete] unperformed, incomplete, half done; see UNFINISHED 1. **2** [Showing favoritism] unfair, influenced, biased; see PREJUDICED.

partiality *n.* fondness, inclination, preference; see AFFECTION.

partially *a.* partly, somewhat, in part; see PARTLY.

participant *n.* cooperator, partner, sharer; see ASSOCIATE.

participate *v.* **1** [To take part in]

share, partake, aid, cooperate, join in, come in, associate with, be a party to, have a hand in, concur, take an interest in, take part in, enter into, have to do with, get into the act*, go into, chip in*; see also JOIN 2.—*Ant.* RETIRE, withdraw, refuse. **2** [To engage in a contest] play, strive, engage; see COMPETE.

participation *n.* partnership, joining in, sharing, support, aid, assistance, encouragement, seconding, help, standing by, taking part; see also PARTNERSHIP.

particle *n.* jot, scrap, atom, molecule, fragment, piece, shred; see also BIT 1.

particular *a.* **1** [Specific] distinct, singular, appropriate; see SPECIAL. **2** [Accurate] precise, minute, exact; see ACCURATE 2. —**in particular** expressly, particularly, individually; see ESPECIALLY 1.

particular *n.* fact, specification, item; see DETAIL.

particularly *a.* unusually, expressly, individually; see ESPECIALLY 1.

parting *n.* leavetaking, goodbye, farewell; see DEPARTURE.

partisan *n.* adherent, supporter, disciple; see FOLLOWER.

par·ti·tion (pär tish'ən) *n.* ⟦< L *partitio*⟧ **1** division into parts **2** something that divides, as a wall separating rooms — *vt.* **1** to divide into parts; apportion **2** to divide by a partition —**par·ti'tioned** *adj.*

part'ly *adv.* not fully or completely

part·ner (pärt'nər) *n.* ⟦< ME⟧ **1** one who joins in an activity with another or others; specif., one of two or more persons jointly owning a business **2** a spouse **3** either of two persons dancing together **4** a player on the same team —**part'ner·ship'** *n.*

part of speech any of the classes to which a word can be assigned as by form, function, or meaning, as noun, verb, etc.

par·took (pär took') *vi. pt.* OF PARTAKE

par·tridge (pär'trij) *n.* ⟦< Gr *perdix*⟧ **1** any of several short-tailed game birds, esp. one with an orange-brown head and grayish neck **2** any of various birds resembling this

part song a song for several voices, usually without accompaniment

part'-time' *adj.* designating, of, or engaged in work, study, etc. for less than the usual time

par·tu·ri·tion (pär'too rish'ən) *n.* ⟦< L *parere*, bring forth⟧ childbirth

part'way' *adv.* to a degree, but not fully

party (pär'tē) *n., pl.* **-ties** ⟦< L *pars*, a part⟧ **1** a group of people working to promote a political platform or slate, a cause, etc. **2** a group acting together to accomplish a task **3** a gathering for social entertainment **4** one concerned in an action, plan, lawsuit, etc. ⟦a *party* to the action⟧ **5** [Colloq.] a person — *vi.* **-tied, -ty·ing** to attend or hold social parties

party line 1 a single circuit connecting two or more telephone users with the exchange **2** the policies of a political party

par·venu (pär'və noo') *n.* ⟦< L *pervenire*, arrive⟧ a newly rich person who is considered an upstart

Pas·cal (pas kal') ⟦after B. *Pascal* (1623-62), Fr mathematician & philosopher⟧ a computer language written in structured modules Also **PASCAL**

pas·chal (pas'kəl) *adj.* ⟦< LL < Gr < Heb *pesach*, Passover⟧ **1** of Passover **2** of Easter

pa·sha (pə shä', pä'shə) *n.* ⟦Turk⟧ [Historical] in Turkey, a title of rank or honor placed after the name

pass (pas) *vi.* ⟦< L *passus*, a step⟧ **1** to go or move forward, through, etc. **2** to go or be conveyed from one place,

form, condition, etc. to another **3** *a)* to cease *b)* to depart **4** to die: often with *away* or *on* **5** to go by **6** to elapse ⟦an hour *passed*⟧ **7** to make a way: with *through* or *by* **8** to be accepted without question **9** to be approved, as by a legislature **10** to go through a test, course, etc. successfully **11** to give a judgment, sentence, etc. **12** *Card Games* to decline a chance to bid — *vt.* **1** to go by, beyond, over, or through; specif., *a)* to leave behind *b)* to go through (a test, course, etc.) successfully **2** to cause or allow to go, move, or proceed; specif., *a)* to ratify; enact *b)* to spend (time) *c)* to excrete **3** to cause to move from place to place; circulate **4** to give (an opinion or judgment) — *n.* **1** an act of passing; passage **2** a state; situation ⟦a strange *pass*⟧ **3** *a)* a ticket, etc. giving permission to come or go freely or without charge *b)* *Mil.* a brief leave of absence **4** a motion of the hands **5** a tentative attempt **6** a narrow passage, etc., esp. between mountains **7** [Colloq.] an overly familiar attempt to embrace or kiss **8** *Sports* a transfer of a ball, etc. to another player during play — **come (or bring) to pass** to (cause to) happen —**pass for** to be accepted as —**pass off** to cause to be accepted through deceit —**pass out 1** to distribute **2** to faint — **pass over** to disregard; ignore —**pass up** [Colloq.] to refuse or let go by —**pass'er** *n.*

pass'able *adj.* **1** that can be passed, traveled over, etc. **2** barely adequate; fair —**pass'ably** *adv.*

pas·sage (pas'ij) *n.* **1** a passing; specif., *a)* migration *b)* transition *c)* the enactment of a law **2** permission or right to pass **3** a voyage **4** a means of passing; road, passageway, etc. **5** an exchange, as of blows **6** a portion of a book, musical composition, etc.

pass'age·way' *n.* a narrow way for passage, as a hall, alley, etc.

pass'book' *n.* BANKBOOK

passé (pä sā', pa-) *adj.* ⟦Fr, past⟧ **1** out-of-date; old-fashioned **2** rather old

pas·sel (pas'əl) *n.* ⟦< PARCEL⟧ [Colloq. or Dial.] a group, esp. a fairly large one

pas·sen·ger (pas'ən jər) *n.* ⟦< OFr *passage*, passage⟧ a person traveling in a train, boat, car, etc.

THESAURUS

partition *n.* **1** [Division] apportionment, separation, severance; see DISTRIBUTION. **2** [That which divides or separates] bar, obstruction, hindrance; see BARRIER, WALL 1.

partly *a.* in part, partially, to a degree, measurably, somewhat, noticeably, notably, in some part, incompletely, insufficiently, inadequately, up to a certain point, so far as possible, not entirely, as much as could be expected, to some extent, within limits, slightly, to a slight degree, in some ways, in certain particulars, only in details, in a general way, not strictly speaking, in bits and pieces, by fits and starts, carelessly, short of the end, at best, at worst, at most, at least, at the outside.—*Ant.* COMPLETELY, wholly, entirely.

partner *n.* co-worker, ally, comrade; see ASSOCIATE.

partnership *n.* alliance, union, cooperation, company, combination, corporation, connection, brotherhood, society, lodge, club, fellowship, fraternity, confederation, band, body, crew, clique, gang, ring, faction, party, community, conjunction, joining, companionship, friendship, help; see also ALLIANCE 1, UNION 1.

part of speech *n.* grammatical construction, word, lexeme; see ADJECTIVE, GRAMMAR, PRONOUN, VERB, WORD 1.

partway *a.* started, toward the middle, somewhat; see BEGUN, SOME.

party *n.* **1** [A social affair] at-home, tea, luncheon, dinner party, dinner, cocktail hour, surprise party, house party, social, reception, banquet,

feast, affair, gathering, function, fete, ball, recreation, amusement, entertainment, festive occasion, carouse, diversion, performance, high tea, binge*, spree*, blowout*, bash*. **2** [A group of people] multitude, mob, company; see CROWD, GATHERING. **3** [A political organization] organized group, body, electorate, combine, combination, bloc, ring, junta, partisans, cabal; see also FACTION. **4** [A specified but unnamed individual] party of the first part, someone, individual; see PERSON 1, SOMEBODY.

pass *n.* **1** [An opening through mountains] gorge, ravine, crossing, track, way, path, passageway; see also GAP 3. **2** [A document assuring permission to pass] ticket, permit, passport, visa, order, admission, furlough, permission, right, license. **3** [In sports, the passing of the ball from one player to another] toss, throw, fling; see PITCH 2. **4** [*An advance] approach, sexual overture, proposition; see SUGGESTION 1.

pass *v.* **1** [To move past] go by, run by, run past, flit by, come by, shoot ahead of, catch, come to the front, go beyond, roll on, fly past, reach, roll by, cross, flow past, glide by, go in opposite directions; see also MOVE 1. **2** [To elapse] transpire, slip away, slip by, pass away, pass by, fly, fly by, linger, glide by, run out, drag, crawl. **3** [To complete a course successfully] satisfy the requirements, be graduated, pass with honors; see SUCCEED 1. **4** [To hand to others] transfer, relinquish, hand over; see GIVE 1. **5** [To enact] legislate, establish, vote

in; see ENACT. **6** [To become enacted] carry, become law, become valid, be ratified, be established, be ordained, be sanctioned. **7** [To exceed] excel, transcend, go beyond; see EXCEED. **8** [To spend time] fill, occupy oneself, while away; see SPEND. **9** [To proceed] progress, get ahead, move on, go on; see also ADVANCE 1. **10** [To emit] give off, send forth, exude; see EMIT. —**bring to pass** bring about, initiate, start; see CAUSE. —**come to pass** occur, develop, come about; see HAPPEN 2. —**pass away** depart, expire, pass on; see DIE. —**pass by** travel, move past, depart from; see LEAVE 1, PASS 1. —**pass off** pass for, make a pretense of, palm off*; see PRETEND 1. —**pass on** expire, depart, succumb; see DIE. —**pass out 1** [To faint] swoon, lose consciousness, black out*; see FAINT. **2** [To distribute] hand out, circulate, deal out; see DISTRIBUTE, GIVE 1. —**pass over** dismiss, overlook, neglect; see DISREGARD. —**pass up** dismiss, send away, reject; see DENY, REFUSE.

passable *a.* open, fair, penetrable, navigable, accessible, traveled, easy, broad, graded; see also AVAILABLE.

passage *n.* **1** [A journey] voyage, crossing, trek; see JOURNEY. **2** [A passageway] way, exit, entrance; see ENTRANCE 2. **3** [A reading] section, portion, paragraph; see QUOTATION 1.

passé *a.* old-fashioned, out-of-date, outmoded; see OLD-FASHIONED.

passenger *n.* commuter, tourist, wanderer; see RIDER 1.

pass'er·by' *n.*, *pl.* **pass'ers·by'** one who passes by Also **pass'er-by'**, *pl.* **pass'ers·by'**

pass'-fail' *adj. Educ.* designating a grading system recording "pass" or "fail" instead of a letter or number grade

pass'ing *adj.* 1 going by, beyond, etc. 2 fleeting 3 casual *[a passing remark]* 4 satisfying given requirements *[a passing grade]* 5 current — *n.* the act of one that passes; specif., death —**in passing** incidentally

pas·sion (pash'ən) *n.* [< L *pati*, endure] 1 any emotion, as hate, love, fear, etc. 2 intense emotional excitement, as rage, enthusiasm, lust, etc. 3 the object of any strong desire —**[P-]** the sufferings of Jesus, from after the Last Supper through his death on the Cross

pas'sion·ate (-ə nit) *adj.* 1 having or showing strong feelings 2 hot-tempered 3 ardent; intense 4 sensual —**pas'sion·ately** *adv.*

pas·sive (pas'iv) *adj.* [see PASSION] 1 inactive, but acted upon 2 offering no resistance; submissive 3 *Gram.* denoting the voice of a verb whose subject is the recipient (object) of the action —**pas'sively** *adv.* —**pas·siv'i·ty** *n.*

passive resistance opposition to a government, etc. by refusal to comply or by nonviolent acts, as fasting

pass'key' *n.* 1 *a*) MASTER KEY *b*) SKELETON KEY 2 one's own key to something

Pass·over (pas'ō'vər) *n.* a Jewish holiday commemorating deliverance of the ancient Hebrews from slavery in Egypt

pass'port' *n.* a government document carried by a citizen traveling abroad, certifying identity and citizenship

pass'word' *n.* 1 a secret term used for identification, as in passing a guard 2 any means of admission

past (past) *vi.*, *vt. rare pp.* of PASS — *adj.* 1 gone by; ended 2 of a former time 3 immediately preceding 4 *Gram.* indicating an action completed, or a condition in existence, at a former time *[the past tense]* — *n.* 1 time gone by 2 the history of a person, group, etc. 3 a personal background that is hidden or questionable — *prep.* beyond in time, space, amount, etc. — *adv.* to and beyond

pas·ta (päs'tə) *n.* [It] 1 a flour paste or dough of which spaghetti, etc. is made 2 any food made of this

paste (pāst) *n.* [< Gr *pastē*, porridge] 1 dough for making pastry, etc. 2 any soft, moist, smooth preparation *[toothpaste]* 3 a mixture of flour, water, etc. used as an adhesive 4 the hard, brilliant glass of artificial gems — *vt.* **past'ed, past'ing** 1 to make adhere, as with paste 2 [Slang] to hit

paste'board' *n.* a stiff material made as of layers of paper pasted together — *adj.*

pas·tel (pas tel') *n.* [< LL *pasta*, paste] 1 a crayon of ground coloring matter 2 a picture drawn with such crayons 3 a soft, pale shade of color — *adj.* soft and pale: said of colors

pas·tern (pas'tərn) *n.* [< L *pastor*, shepherd] the part of the foot of a horse, dog, etc. just above the hoof or toes

pas·teur·ize (pas'tər iz', -chər-) *vt.* **-ized', -iz'ing** [after L. *Pasteur*, 19th-c. Fr bacteriologist] to destroy bacteria in (milk, etc.) by heating to a prescribed temperature for a specified time —**pas'teur·i·za'tion** *n.*

pas·tiche (pas tēsh') *n.* [Fr] 1 an artistic composition made up of bits from various sources 2 a hodgepodge

pas·time (pas'tim') *n.* a way of spending spare time; diversion

past master [for *passed master*] a person of long experience in an occupation, art, etc.; expert

pas·tor (pas'tər) *n.* [L, a shepherd] a priest or minister in charge of a congregation —**pas'tor·ate** (-it) *n.*

pas'to·ral *adj.* 1 of or relating to a pastor 2 of shepherds 3 of rustic life 4 peaceful; simple

past participle *Gram.* a participle used *a*) to express completed action (Ex.: *gone* in "he has gone") *b*) to form the passive voice (Ex.: *done* in "the deed was done") *c*) as an adjective (Ex.: *fried* in "fried fish")

pas·tra·mi (pə strä'mē) *n.* [E Yidd, ult. < Turk *basdyrma*, dried meat] highly spiced smoked beef

pas·try (pās'trē) *n.*, *pl.* **-tries** [see PASTE & -ERY] 1 pies, tarts, etc. with crusts baked from flour dough made with shortening 2 broadly, all fancy baked goods

pas·tur·age (pas'chər ij) *n.* PASTURE

pas·ture *n.* [< L *pascere*, to feed] 1 grass, etc. used as food by grazing animals 2 ground suitable for grazing — *vt.* **-tured, -tur·ing** to put (cattle, etc.) out to graze in a pasture

pas·ty (pās'tē) *adj.* **-i·er, -i·est** of or like paste in color or texture

pat (pat) *n.* [prob. echoic] 1 a gentle tap or stroke with a flat object 2 the sound made by this 3 a small lump, as of butter — *vt.* **pat'ted, pat'ting** 1 to tap or stroke gently, esp. with the hand 2 to shape or apply by patting — *adj.* 1 exactly suitable 2 so glibly plausible as to seem contrived —**have (down) pat** to know thoroughly —**pat on the back** 1 a compliment 2 to praise —**stand pat** to refuse to change an opinion, etc.

pat. 1 patent 2 patented

patch (pach) *n.* [ME *pacche*] 1 a piece of material applied to mend a hole or strengthen a weak spot 2 a bandage 3 an area or spot *[patches of blue sky]* 4 a small plot of land 5 a scrap; bit — *vt.* 1 to put a patch on 2 to produce crudely or hurriedly —**patch up** to settle (differences, a quarrel, etc.)

patch test *Med.* a test for allergy, made by attaching a sample of a substance to the skin and observing the reaction

patch'work' *n.* needlework, as a quilt, made of odd patches of cloth

patch'y *adj.* **-i·er, -i·est** 1 made up of patches 2 not consistent or uniform; irregular —**patch'i·ness** *n.*

pate (pāt) *n.* [< ?] the head, esp. the top of the head: a humorous term

pâ·té (pä tā') *n.* [Fr] a meat paste or pie

pa·tel·la (pə tel'ə) *n.*, *pl.* **-las** or **-lae** (-ē) [< L *patina*, a pan] KNEECAP

pat·ent (pat''nt; *also for adj.* 1 & 2, pāt'-) *adj.* [< L *patere*, be open] 1 open to all 2 obvious; plain 3 protected by a

THESAURUS

passerby *n.* witness, traveler, bystander; see OBSERVER.

passing *a.* 1 [In the act of going past] departing, crossing, going by, gliding by, flashing by, speeding by, going in opposite directions, passing in the night; see also MOVING 1. 2 [Of brief duration] fleeting, transitory, transient; see TEMPORARY.

passion *n.* lust, craving, sexual excitement; see DESIRE 2, EMOTION.

passionate *a.* 1 [Excitable] vehement, hotheaded, tempestuous; see sense 2. 2 [Ardent] intense, impassioned, loving, fervent, moving, inspiring, dramatic, melodramatic, romantic, poignant, swelling, enthusiastic, tragic, stimulating, wistful, stirring, thrilling, warm, burning, glowing, vehement, deep, affecting, eloquent, spirited, fiery, expressive, forceful, heated, hot. 3 [Intense] strong, vehement, violent; see INTENSE.

passive *a.* 1 [Being acted upon] receptive, stirred, influenced; see AFFECTED 1. 2 [Not active] inactive, inert, lifeless; see IDLE.

passport *n.* pass, license, permit, safeconduct, visa, travel permit, authorization, warrant, credentials; see also IDENTIFICATION 2.

password *n.* countersign, signal, phrase, secret word, watchword, identification, open sesame.

past *a.* 1 [Having occurred previously] former, preceding, gone by, foregoing, elapsed, anterior, antecedent, prior. 2 [No longer serving] ex-, retired, earlier; see PRECEDING.

past *n.* 1 [Past time] antiquity, long ago, the past, past times, old times, years ago, good old days, ancient times, former times, days gone by, auld lang-syne, days of old, yesterday.—*Ant.* FUTURE, the present, tomorrow. 2 [Past events] knowledge, happenings, events; see HISTORY.

past *prep.* through, farther than, behind; see BEYOND.

paste *n.* cement, glue, mucilage; see CEMENT.

paste *v.* glue, fix, affix, repair, patch; see also STICK 1.

pastime *n.* recreation, amusement, sport; see ENTERTAINMENT, HOBBY.

pastor *n.* priest, rector, clergyman; see MINISTER 1.

pastry *n.* baked goods, dainty, delicacy, bread, goodies*, fixings*, trimmings*; see also BREAD. *Pastries include the following:* French, Danish; tart, pie, turnover, oatcake, shortbread, pudding, eclair, cake, sweet roll.

pasture *n.* grazing land, pasturage, hayfield; see FIELD 1, MEADOW.

pasty *a.* wan, pallid, sickly, ashen, anemic; see also PALE 1, DULL 2.

pat *v.* 1 [To strike lightly] tap, beat, punch; see HIT 1. 2 [To strike lightly and affectionately] stroke, pet, rub; see TOUCH 2.

patch *n.* piece, mend, bit, scrap, spot, application.

patch *v.* darn, mend, cover; see REPAIR. —**patch up** appease, adjust, compensate; see SETTLE 7.

patchwork *n.* jumble, hodgepodge, muddle; see CONFUSION, DISORDER.

patent *n.* patent right, protection, concession, control, limitation, license, copyright, privilege; see also RIGHT 1.

patent *v.* license, secure, control, limit, monopolize, safeguard,

patent — *n.* **1** a document granting the exclusive right to produce or sell an invention, etc. for a specified time **2** *a)* the right so granted *b)* the thing protected by such a right — *vt.* to secure a patent for

patent leather (pat′′nt) leather with a hard, glossy finish: formerly leather

patent medicine (pat′′nt) a trademarked medical preparation

pa·ter·nal (pə tur′nəl) *adj.* ⟦< L *pater*, father⟧ **1** fatherly **2** inherited from a father **3** on the father's side

pa·ter′nal·ism *n.* the governing of a country, employees, etc. in a manner suggesting a father's relationship with his children — **pa·ter′nal·is′tic** *adj.*

pa·ter′ni·ty (-nə tē) *n.* **1** the state of being a father **2** male parentage

pater·nos·ter (pät′ər nôs′tər) *n.* ⟦L, our father⟧ the Lord's Prayer, esp. in Latin Often **Pater Noster**

path (path) *n.* ⟦OE *pæth*⟧ **1** a way worn by footsteps **2** a walk for the use of people on foot **3** a line of movement **4** a course of conduct, thought, etc. —**path′less** *adj.*

pa·thet·ic (pə thet′ik) *adj.* ⟦see PATHOS⟧ **1** arousing pity, sorrow, etc.; pitiful **2** pitifully unsuccessful, etc. —**pa·thet′i·cally** *adv.*

patho- ⟦< Gr: see PATHOS⟧ *combining form* suffering, disease, feeling Also **path-**

patho·gen (path′ə jən) *n.* ⟦prec. + -GEN⟧ a microorganism, etc. capable of causing disease —**path′o·gen′ic** (-jen′ik) *adj.*

pa·thol·ogy (pə thäl′ə jē) *n., pl.* **-gies** ⟦< Gr *pathologia:* see fol. & -LOGY⟧ **1** the branch of medicine that deals with the nature of disease, esp. with structural and functional effects **2** any abnormal variation from a sound condition —**patho·log·i·cal** (path′ə läj′i kəl) *adj.* —**pa·thol′o·gist** *n.*

pa·thos (pā′thäs′) *n.* ⟦Gr, suffering, disease, feeling⟧ the quality in something which arouses pity, sorrow, sympathy, etc.

path′way′ *n.* PATH

-pathy (pə thē) ⟦< Gr: see PATHOS⟧ *combining form* **1** feeling *[telepathy]* **2** (treatment of) disease *[osteopathy]*

pa·tience (pā′shəns) *n.* a being patient; calm endurance

pa′tient (-shənt) *adj.* ⟦< L *pati*, endure⟧ **1** enduring pain, trouble, etc. without complaining **2** calmly tolerating delay, confusion, etc. **3** diligent; persevering — *n.* one receiving medical care —**pa′tiently** *adv.*

pati·na (pat′′n ə, pə tē′nə) *n.* ⟦Fr < It⟧ a fine greenish crust on bronze or copper, formed by oxidation

pa·tio (pat′ē ō′, pät′-) *n., pl.* **-os′** ⟦Sp⟧ **1** a courtyard open to the sky **2** a paved area adjoining a house, for outdoor lounging, dining, etc.

pa·tois (pa′twä′) *n., pl.* **-tois′** (-twäz′) ⟦Fr⟧ a provincial or local dialect

pat. pend. patent pending

patri- ⟦< L *patēr*⟧ *combining form* father Also **patr-**

pa·tri·arch (pā′trē ärk′) *n.* ⟦< Gr *patēr*, father + *archein*, to rule⟧ **1** the father and head of a family or tribe, as Abraham, Isaac, or Jacob in the Bible **2** a man of great age and dignity **3** *[often* P-] a high-ranking bishop, as in the Eastern Orthodox Church —**pa′tri·ar′chal** *adj.*

pa′tri·arch′ate (-är′kit, -kāt′) *n.* the rank, jurisdiction, etc. of a patriarch

pa′tri·arch′y (-är′kē) *n., pl.* **-ies 1** a form of social organization in which the father is head of the family, descent being traced through the male line **2** rule or domination by men

pa·tri·cian (pə trish′ən) *n.* ⟦< L *pater*, father⟧ an aristocrat

pat′ri·mo′ny (-mō′nē) *n., pl.* **-nies** ⟦< L *pater*, father⟧ property inherited from one's father or ancestors —**pat′ri·mo′nial** *adj.*

pa·triot (pā′trē ət) *n.* ⟦< Gr *patris*, fatherland⟧ one who loves and zealously supports one's own country —**pa′tri·ot′ic** (-ät′ik) *adj.* —**pa′tri·ot′i·cally** *adv.* —**pa′tri·ot·ism′** *n.*

pa·trol (pə trōl′) *vt., vi.* **-trolled′, -trol′ling** ⟦Fr *patrouiller*⟧ to make a regular, repeated circuit (of) in guarding — *n.* **1** a patrolling **2** a person or group patrolling

patrol car a police car used to patrol an area, in radio contact with headquarters

patrol′man (-mən) *n., pl.* **-men** a police officer who patrols a certain area

patrol wagon an enclosed truck used by police to carry prisoners

pa·tron (pā′trən) *n.* ⟦< L *pater*, father⟧ **1** a protector; benefactor **2** one who sponsors and supports some person, activity, etc. **3** a regular customer —**pa′tron·ess** *n.fem.*

pa·tron·age (pā′trən ij, pa′-) *n.* **1** support, encouragement, etc. given by a patron **2** *a)* clientele *b)* business; trade **3** *a)* the power to grant political favors *b)* such favors

pa·tron·ize (pā′trən īz′, pa′-) *vt.* **-ized′, -iz′ing 1** to sponsor; support **2** to be kind or helpful to, but in a haughty or snobbish way **3** to be a regular customer of

patron saint a saint looked upon as a special guardian

pat·ro·nymic (pa′trō nim′ik, -trə-) *n.* ⟦< Gr *patēr*, father + *onyma*, name⟧ a name showing descent from a given person (Ex.: *Johnson*, son of John)

patsy (pat′sē) *n., pl.* **-sies** [Slang] a person easily imposed upon

pat·ter[1] (pat′ər) *vi.* ⟦< PAT⟧ to make, or move so as to make, a patter — *n.* a series of quick, light taps

pat·ter[2] (pat′ər) *vt., vi.* ⟦< PATERNOSTER⟧ to speak rapidly or glibly — *n.* glib, rapid speech, as of salespeople

pat·tern (pat′ərn) *n.* ⟦< OFr *patrun*, patron⟧ **1** a person or thing worthy of imitation **2** a model or plan used in making things **3** a design **4** a regular way of acting or doing **5** a predictable route, movement, etc. — *vt.* to make or do in imitation of a pattern

---

THESAURUS

exclude, copyright.

patented *a.* copyrighted, patent applied for, trademarked, under patent, under copyright, patent pending; see also RESTRICTED.

paternal *a.* patrimonial, fatherly, protective, benevolent.

paternity *n.* progenitorship, paternal parentage, fathership; see FATHER 1.

path *n.* trail, way, track, shortcut, footpath, crosscut, footway, roadway, cinder track, byway, path; see also ROUTE 1.

pathetic *a.* touching, affecting, moving; see PITIFUL.

patience *n.* **1** [Willingness to endure] forbearance, fortitude, composure, submission, endurance, nonresistance, self-control, passiveness, bearing, serenity, humility, yielding, poise, sufferance, long-suffering, moderation, leniency; see also RESIGNATION 1.—*Ant.* NERVOUSNESS, fretfulness, restlessness. **2** [Ability to continue] submission, perseverance, persistence; see ENDURANCE.

patient *a.* **1** [Enduring without complaint] submissive, meek, forbearing, mild-tempered, composed, tranquil, serene, long-suffering, unruffled, imperturbable, passive, coldblooded,

easy-going, tolerant, gentle, unresentful; see also RESIGNED.—*Ant.* IRRITABLE, violent, resentful. **2** [Quietly persistent in an activity] steady, dependable, calm, reliable, stable, composed, unwavering, quiet, serene, unimpassioned, enduring; see also RELIABLE.—*Ant.* RESTLESS, irrepressible, feverish.

patient *n.* case, inmate, victim, sufferer, sick individual, medical case, surgical case, patient, outpatient, bed patient, emergency ward patient, convalescent, hospital case, hospitalized person, subject.

patiently *a.* **1** [Suffering without complaint] enduringly, bravely, impassively, resignedly, numbly, forbearingly, tolerantly, submissively, meekly; see also CALMLY. **2** [Continuing without impatience] steadily, firmly, unabatingly; see REGULARLY.

patio *n.* porch, courtyard, square; see YARD 1.

patriarch *n.* master, head of family, ancestor; see CHIEF.

patriot *n.* lover of his country, good citizen, statesman, nationalist, volunteer, loyalist, jingoist, chauvinist.

patriotic *a.* devoted, zealous, publicspirited, consecrated, dedicated, jingoish, chauvinistic.

patriotism *n.* love of country, public spirit, good citizenship, nationality, nationalism; see also LOYALTY.

patrol *n.* guard, watch, protection; see ARMY 2.

patrol *v.* watch, walk, inspect; see GUARD.

patrolman *n.* police, police officer, constable; see POLICEMAN.

patron *n.* philanthropist, benefactor, helper, protector, encourager, champion, backer, advocate, defender, guide, leader, friend, ally, sympathizer, well-wisher, partisan, buyer, angel*, sugar daddy*, booster.—*Ant.* ENEMY, obstructionist, adversary.

patronage *n.* **1** [Trade] commerce, trading, shopping; see BUSINESS 1. **2** [Condescension] patronization, deference, toleration; see PRIDE 2.

patronize *v.* **1** [To trade with] frequent, buy from, shop with; see BUY, SELL. **2** [To assume a condescending attitude] talk down to, be overbearing, stoop, be gracious to, favor, pat on the back, play the snob, snub, lord it over; see also CONDESCEND.

patronizing *a.* condescending, gracious, stooping; see EGOTISTIC, POLITE.

pattern *n.* original, guide, copy; see

patty (pat′ē) *n.*, *pl.* **-ties** ⟦Fr *pâté*, pie⟧ **1** a small pie **2** a small, flat cake of ground meat, fish, etc., usually fried

patty shell a small pastry case for a single portion of creamed food, etc.

pau·city (pô′sə tē) *n.* ⟦< L *paucus*, few⟧ **1** fewness **2** scarcity

Paul (pôl) *Bible* the Apostle of Christianity to the Gentiles, author of many Epistles

Paul Bun·yan (bun′yən) *American Folklore* a giant lumberjack who performs superhuman feats

paunch (pônch) *n.* ⟦< L *pantex*, belly⟧ the abdomen, or belly; esp., a potbelly —**paunch′y** *adj.*

pau·per (pô′pər) *n.* ⟦L⟧ an extremely poor person, esp. one who lives on charity —**pau′per·ism′** *n.* —**pau′per·ize′, -ized′, -iz′ing,** *vt.*

pause (pôz) *n.* ⟦< Gr *pauein*, to bring to an end⟧ a temporary stop or rest — *vi.* **paused, paus′ing** to make a pause; stop

pave (pāv) *vt.* **paved, pav′ing** ⟦< L *pavire*, to beat⟧ to cover the surface of (a road, etc.), as with concrete —**pave the way (for)** to prepare the way (for)

pave′ment *n.* a paved surface, as of concrete; specif., a paved road, etc.

pa·vil·ion (pə vil′yən) *n.* ⟦< L *papilio*, tent⟧ **1** a large tent **2** a building, often partly open, for exhibits, etc., as at a fair or park **3** any of a group of related buildings

pav·ing (pāv′iŋ) *n.* a pavement

paw (pô) *n.* ⟦< OFr *poue*⟧ **1** the foot of a four-footed animal having claws **2** [Colloq.] a hand — *vt., vi.* **1** to touch, dig, hit, etc. with paws or feet **2** to handle clumsily or roughly

pawl (pôl) *n.* ⟦< ?⟧ a device, as a hinged tongue which engages cogs in a wheel, allowing rotation in only one direction

pawn[1] (pôn) *n.* ⟦< L *pannus*, cloth⟧ **1** anything given as security, as for a debt **2** the state of being pledged — *vt.* **1** to give as security **2** to wager or risk

pawn[2] (pôn) *n.* ⟦< ML *pedo*, foot soldier⟧ **1** a chess piece of the lowest value **2** a person used to advance another's purposes

pawn′bro′ker *n.* a person licensed to lend money at interest on personal property left as security —**pawn′bro′king** *n.*

pawn′shop′ *n.* a pawnbroker's shop

paw·paw (pô′pô′) *n. var. of* PAPAW

pay (pā) *vt.* **paid** or obs. (except in PAY OUT) **payed, pay′ing** ⟦< L *pacare*, pacify⟧ **1** to give to (a person) what is due, as for goods or services **2** to give (what is due) in return, as for goods or services **3** to settle (a debt, etc.) **4** *a)* to give (a compliment, etc.) *b)* to make (a visit, etc.) **5** to be profitable to — *vi.* **1** to give due compensation **2** to be profitable — *n.* money paid; esp., wages or salary — *adj.* **1** operated by the insertion of coins *[a pay phone]* **2** designating a service, etc. paid for by fees *[pay TV]* —**in the pay of** employed and paid by —**pay back 1** to repay **2** to retaliate upon —**pay down** to pay (part of the price) at purchase as an installment —**pay for** to suffer or atone for (a wrong) —**pay off 1** to pay all that is owed **2** to yield full recompense **3** [Colloq.] to succeed —**pay out** to let out (a rope, cable, etc.) —**pay up** to pay in full or on time —**pay′er** *n.*

pay′able *adj.* **1** that can be paid **2** due to be paid (*on a* specified date)

pay′check′ *n.* a check in payment of wages or salary

pay·day (pā′dā′) *n.* the day on which salary or wages are paid

payee (pā ē′) *n.* one to whom a payment is made or owed

pay′load′ *n.* **1** a cargo **2** a load, as a warhead, satellite, passengers, etc., carried by an aircraft, rocket, etc. but not essential to its flight operations

pay′mas′ter *n.* the official in charge of paying employees —**pay′mis′tress** *n.fem.*

pay′ment *n.* **1** a paying or being paid **2** something that is paid

pay′off′ *n.* **1** a settlement, reckoning, or payment **2** [Colloq.] a bribe **3** [Colloq.] an unexpected climax

payo·la (pā ō′lə) *n.* [Slang] a bribe, as to a disc jockey for promoting a song unfairly

pay′out′ *n.* **1** a paying out; disbursement **2** an amount paid out; dividend

pay phone (or station) a public telephone, usually coin-operated

pay′roll′ *n.* **1** a list of employees to be paid, with the amount due to each **2** the total amount needed for this

Pb ⟦L *plumbum*⟧ *Chem. symbol for* lead

PBX (pē′bē′eks′) *n.* ⟦ *p(rivate)* *b(ranch)* *ex(change)*⟧ a telephone system within an organization, having outside lines

PC (pē′sē′) *n.* PERSONAL COMPUTER

PC *abbrev.* politically correct or political correctness

pct. percent

PCV valve ⟦*p(ositive)* *c(rankcase)* *v(entilation)*⟧ a valve regulating the pollution control system of a motor vehicle

Pd *Chem. symbol for* palladium

pd. paid

pea (pē) *n.*, *pl.* **peas** ⟦< ME *pese*, a pea, taken as pl.; ult. < Gr *pison*⟧ **1** a climbing plant with green pods **2** its small, round seed, used as a vegetable

peace (pēs) *n.* ⟦< L *pax*⟧ **1** freedom from war **2** an agreement to end war **3** law and order **4** harmony; concord **5**

THESAURUS

MODEL 2.

pauper *n.* dependent, indigent, destitute person; see BEGGAR.

pause *v.* delay, halt, rest, catch one's breath, cease, hold back, reflect, deliberate, suspend, think twice, discontinue, interrupt; see also HESITATE.

pause *n.* lull, rest, stop, halt, truce, stay, respite, standstill, stand, deadlock, stillness, intermission, suspension, discontinuance, breathing space, hitch, hesitancy, interlude, hiatus, interim, lapse, cessation, stopover, interval, rest period, gap, stoppage.

pave *v.* lay concrete, asphalt, gravel; see COVER 1.

paved *a.* hard-surfaced, flagged, cobblestone, asphalt, concrete, brick, bricked, surfaced with wood blocks; see also COVERED 1.

pavement *n.* hard surface, paving, paving stone, paving tile, flagging, pave. *Road surfaces include the following:* concrete, asphalt, blacktop, stone, brick, tile, macadam, gravel, cobblestone, wood blocks, flagstone.

paving *n.* hard surface, concrete, paved highway; see PAVEMENT.

paw *n.* forefoot, talon, hand; see CLAW.

paw *v.* **1** [To strike wildly] clutch, grasp, smite; see HIT 1. **2** [To scrape with the front foot] scratch, rake,

claw; see DIG 1.

pawn[1] *v.* deposit, pledge, hock; see SELL.

pawned *a.* deposited, pledged, hocked; see SOLD OUT.

pay *n.* **1** [Monetary return] profit, proceeds, interest, return, recompense, indemnity, reparation, rake-off*, reward, consideration, defrayment.—*Ant.* EXPENSE, disbursement, outlay. **2** [Wages] compensation, salary, payment, hire, remuneration, commission, redress, fee, stipend, earnings, settlement, consideration, reimbursement, satisfaction, reward, time, time and a half, double time, overtime.

pay *v.* **1** [To give payment] pay up, compensate, recompense, make payment, reward, remunerate, charge, discharge, pay a bill, foot the bill*, refund, settle, get even with, reckon with, put down, make restitution, make reparation, hand over, repay, liquidate, handle, take care of, give, confer, bequeath, defray, meet, disburse, clear, adjust, satisfy, reimburse, kick in*, plunk down*, put up*, pay as you go, fork out*, fork over*, ante up, even the score*, chip in*.—*Ant.* DECEIVE, swindle, victimize. **2** [To produce a profit] return, pay off, pay out, show profit, yield profit, yield excess, show gain, pay dividends.—*Ant.* FAIL, lose, become

bankrupt. **3** [To retaliate] repay, punish, requite; see REVENGE. —**pay for** atone for, make amends for, do penance for, compensate for, make up for, make satisfaction for, expiate, make reparation for, give satisfaction for, pay the penalty for, make compensation for.

payment *n.* **1** [The act of paying] recompense, reimbursement, restitution, subsidy, return, redress, refund, remittance, reparation, disbursement, money down, amends, cash, salary, wage, sum, payoff, repayment, defrayment, retaliation; see also PAY 1. **2** [An installment] portion, part, amount; see DEBT.

payoff *n.* settlement, conclusion, reward; see PAY 1, PAYMENT 1.

payroll *n.* employees, workers, pay list; see FACULTY 2, STAFF 2.

peace *n.* **1** [The state of being without war] armistice, pacification, conciliation, order, concord, amity, union, unity, reconciliation, brotherhood, love, unanimity; see also AGREEMENT 1, FRIENDSHIP.—*Ant.* WAR, warfare, battle. **2** [State of being without disturbance] calm, repose, quiet, tranquillity, harmony, lull, hush, congeniality, equanimity, silence, stillness; see also REST 1.—*Ant.* FIGHT, noisiness, quarrel. **3** [Mental or emotional calm] calmness, repose, harmony, concord, conserenity, calm, or quiet —**hold** (or **keep**) **one's peace** to be silent —**peace′able** *adj.*

peace′ful *adj.* 1 not quarrelsome 2 free from disturbance; calm 3 of or in a time of peace —**peace′fully** *adv.*

peace′mak′er *n.* a person who makes peace, as by settling disagreements —**peace′mak′ing** *n.*, *adj.*

peace officer an officer entrusted with maintaining law and order, as like a sheriff

peace pipe CALUMET

peace′time′ *n.* a time of freedom from war — *adj.* of such a time

peach (pēch) *n.* ⟦< L *Persicum* (*malum*), Persian (apple)⟧ 1 a tree with round, juicy, orange-yellow fruit having a fuzzy skin and a rough pit 2 its fruit 3 [Slang] a well-liked person or thing

pea·cock (pē′käk′) *n.* ⟦< L *pavo*, peacock⟧ the male of a pheasantlike bird (**pea′fowl′**), with a long, showy tail that can be spread out like a fan —**pea′hen′** *n.fem.*

pea jacket (pē′) ⟦< Du *pijjekker*⟧ a hip-length, double-breasted coat of heavy woolen cloth, worn orig. by seamen

peak (pēk) *n.* ⟦var. of Brit dial. *pike*, prob. < ON *pic*⟧ 1 a pointed end or top, as of a cap, roof, etc. 2 *a*) the summit of a hill or mountain ending in a point *b*) a mountain with such a summit 3 the highest or utmost point of anything — *adj.* maximum — *vi., vt.* to come or bring to a peak

peaked (pēk′id) *adj.* ⟦< ?⟧ thin and drawn, as from illness

peal (pēl) *n.* ⟦ME *apele*, appeal⟧ 1 the loud ringing of a bell or bells 2 a set of tuned bells 3 a loud, prolonged sound, as of thunder, laughter, etc. — *vi., vt.* to sound in a peal; ring

pea′nut′ *n.* 1 a vine related to the pea, with underground pods containing edible seeds 2 the pod or any of its seeds 3 [*pl.*] [Slang] a trifling sum

peanut butter a food paste or spread made by grinding roasted peanuts

pear (per) *n.* ⟦< L *pirum*⟧ 1 a tree with greenish-yellow, brownish, or reddish fruit 2 the juicy fruit, round at the base and narrowing toward the stem

pearl (purl) *n.* ⟦< L *perna*, sea mussel⟧ 1 a smooth, hard, usually white or bluish-gray, roundish growth, formed within the shell of some oysters and other mollusks: used as a gem 2 MOTHER-OF-PEARL 3 anything like a pearl in shape, beauty, value, etc. 4 a bluish-gray —**pearl′y** *adj.*

peas·ant (pez′ənt) *n.* ⟦< LL *pagus*, district⟧ 1 a small farmer or farm laborer, as in Europe or Asia 2 a person regarded as boorish, ignorant, etc. —**peas′antry** *n.*

peat (pēt) *n.* ⟦< ML *peta*, piece of turf⟧ partly decayed plant matter from ancient swamps, used for fuel

peat moss peat composed of residues of mosses, used as mulch

peb·ble (peb′əl) *n.* ⟦< OE *papol-(stan)*, pebble (stone), prob. echoic⟧ a small stone worn smooth and round, as by running water —**peb′bly**, **-blier**, **-bliest**, *adj.*

pe·can (pē kän′, -kan′; pē-; pē′kän′, -kan′) *n.* ⟦< AmInd⟧ an edible nut with a thin, smooth shell 2 the tree it grows on

pec·ca·dillo (pek′ə dil′ō) *n., pl.* **-loes** or **-los** ⟦< Sp < L *peccare*, to sin⟧ a small fault or offense

pec·cary (pek′ə rē) *n., pl.* **-ries** ⟦< native name⟧ a piglike animal of North and South America, with sharp tusks

peck¹ (pek) *vt.* ⟦ME *picken*, to pick⟧ 1 to strike, as with a beak 2 to make by doing this ⟦*to peck a hole*⟧ 3 to pick up with the beak — *vi.* to make strokes as with a pointed object — *n.* 1 a stroke so made 2 [Colloq.] a quick, casual kiss —**peck at** [Colloq.] 1 to eat very little of 2 to criticize constantly

peck² (pek) *n.* ⟦< OFr *pek*⟧ a unit of dry measure, ¼ bushel, or eight quarts

pec·tin (pek′tin) *n.* ⟦< Gr *pēktos*, congealed⟧ a carbohydrate, obtained from certain fruits, which yields a gel that is the basis of jellies

pec·to·ral (pek′tə rəl) *adj.* ⟦< L *pectus*, breast⟧ of or located in or on the chest or breast

pecu·late (pek′yoo lāt′, -yə-) *vt., vi.* **-lat′ed**, **-lat′ing** ⟦< L *peculari*⟧ to embezzle —**pec′u·la′tion** *n.*

pe·cu·liar (pē kyool′yər, pi-) *adj.* ⟦< L *peculium*, private property⟧ 1 of only one person, thing, etc.; exclusive 2 particular; special 3 odd; strange —**pe·cu′liarly** *adv.*

pe·cu·li·ar·ity (pē kyōō′lē er′ə tē, pi-) *n.* 1 a being peculiar 2 *pl.* **-ties** something that is peculiar, as a trait

pe·cu·ni·ary (pi kyōō′nē er′ē, pē-) *adj.* ⟦< L *pecunia*, money⟧ of or involving money

peda·gogue or **peda·gog** (ped′ə gäg′) *n.* ⟦< Gr *pais*, child + *agein*, to lead⟧ a teacher, esp. a pedantic one

ped′a·gog′y (-gäj′ē, -gō′jē) *n.* the art or science of teaching —**ped′a·gog′ic** or **ped′a·gog′i·cal** *adj.*

pedal (ped′l) *adj.* ⟦< L *pes*, FOOT⟧ of the foot or feet — *n.* a lever operated by the foot, as on a bicycle, organ, etc. — *vt., vi.* **-aled** or **-alled**, **-al·ing** or **-al·ling** to operate by pedals

ped·ant (ped′nt) *n.* ⟦ult. < Gr *paidagōgos*, teacher⟧ 1 one who emphasizes trivial points of learning 2 a narrow-minded teacher who insists on exact adherence to rules — **pe·dan′tic** *adj.* —**pe·dan′ti·cally** *adv.* —**ped′antry** *n.*

ped·dle (ped′l) *vt., vi.* **-dled**, **-dling** ⟦< ? ME *ped*, basket⟧ to go from place to place selling (small articles) — **ped′dler** *n.*

-pede (pēd) ⟦< L *pes*⟧ *combining form* foot or feet [*centipede*]

ped·er·asty (ped′ər as′tē) *n.* ⟦< Gr *paiderastēs*, lover of boys⟧ sodomy between males, esp. between a man and a boy —**ped′er·ast′** *n.*

ped·estal (ped′əs təl) *n.* ⟦< It *piè*, foot + *di*, of + *stal*, a rest⟧ a bottom support of a pillar, statue, etc.

pe·destri·an (pi des′trē ən) *adj.* ⟦< L *pes*, foot⟧ 1 going or done on foot 2 of or for pedestrians 3 ordinary and dull; prosaic — *n.* a walker

pe·di·at·rics (pē′dē a′triks) *n.pl.* ⟦< Gr *pais*, child + *iatros*, physician⟧ [*with sing. v.*] the branch of medicine dealing with the care and treatment of infants and children —**pe′di·at′ric** *adj.* —**pe′dia·tri′cian** (-ə trish′ən) *n.*

pedi·cab (ped′i kab′) *n.* ⟦< L *pes*, foot + CAB⟧ a three-wheeled carriage, esp. formerly in SE Asia, pedaled by the driver

pedi·cure (ped′i kyoor′) *n.* ⟦< L *pes*, FOOT + *cura*, care⟧ a trimming, polishing, etc. of the toenails

pedi·gree (ped′i grē′) *n.* ⟦< MFr *pié de grue*, lit., crane's foot: from lines in genealogical tree⟧ 1 a list of ancestors 2 descent; lineage 3 a known line of descent, esp. of a purebred animal —**ped′i·greed′** *adj.*

pedi·ment (ped′i mənt) *n.* ⟦< earlier *periment*, prob. < PYRAMID⟧ an ornamental gable or triangular piece on the front of a building, over a doorway, etc.

pe·dom·eter (pi däm′ət ər, pi-) *n.* ⟦< L *pes*, foot + Gr *metron*, a measure⟧ an instrument carried to measure the distance walked

---

THESAURUS

tentment, sympathy; see also COMPOSURE, RESERVE 2, TRANQUILLITY.—*Ant.* DISTRESS, disturbance, agitation. —**at peace** peaceful, quiet, tranquil; see CALM 1, 2. —**hold** (or **keep**) **one's peace** be silent, keep quiet, not speak; see SHUT UP 1. —**make peace** end hostilities, settle, reconcile; see QUIET 1.

peaceable *a.* conciliatory, pacific, peaceful; see FRIENDLY.

peaceful *a.* 1 [At peace] quiet, tranquil, serene; see CALM 1, 2. 2 [Inclined to peace] well-disposed, sociable, amiable; see FRIENDLY.

peacefully *a.* 1 [Calmly] tranquilly, quietly, composedly; see CALMLY. 2 [Without making trouble] harmoniously, placatingly, inoffensively, temperately, civilly; see also MODESTLY.

peak *n.* 1 [A mountain] summit, top, crown; see MOUNTAIN 1. 2 [The maximum] zenith, highest point, greatest quantity; see HEIGHT, TIP 1, TOP 1.

peaked *a.* pointed, topped, triangle-topped; see SHARP 1.

pearl *n.* nacre, margarite, cultured pearl; see JEWEL.

peasant *n.* small farmer, farm laborer, farm worker; see FARMER, LABORER, WORKMAN.

pebble *n.* pebblestone, gravel, cobblestone; see ROCK 1, STONE.

peck¹ *v.* nip, pick, tap; see BITE 1, PINCH.

peck¹,² *n.* 1 [A slight, sharp blow] pinch, tap, rap; see BLOW. 2 [One fourth of a bushel] eight quarts, quarter-bushel, large amount; see MEASURE 1, QUANTITY.

peculiar *a.* 1 [Unusual] wonderful, singular, outlandish; see STRANGE, UNUSUAL 2. 2 [Characteristic of only one] strange, uncommon, eccentric; see CHARACTERISTIC, UNIQUE.

peculiarity *n.* distinctiveness, unusualness, singularity; see CHARACTERISTIC.

pedal *n.* treadle, foot lever, accelerator; see LEVER.

pedal *v.* treadle, operate, work; see DRIVE 2.

peddle *v.* hawk, vend, trade; see SELL.

peddler *n.* hawker, vender, seller; see BUSINESSMAN.

pedestal *n.* stand, foundation, footstall, plinth; see also COLUMN 1, SUPPORT 2.

pedestrian *n.* foot-traveler, walker, hiker; see WALKING *a.*

pe·duncle (pē duŋ′kəl, pē′duŋ′-) *n.* 〚< L *pes*, foot〛 a stalklike organ or part in some plants, animals, etc.

peek (pēk) *vi.* 〚ME *piken*〛 to look quickly and furtively — *n.* such a look

peel (pēl) *vt.* 〚< L *pilare*, make bald〛 to cut away (the rind, skin, etc.) of — *vi.* 1 to shed skin, etc. 2 to come off in layers or flakes — *n.* the rind or skin of fruit —**peel off** *Aeron.* to veer away from a flight formation abruptly

peel′ing *n.* a peeled-off strip

peen (pēn) *n.* 〚prob. < Scand〛 the end of a hammerhead opposite the flat striking surface, usually ball-shaped (**ball peen**) or wedge-shaped

peep[1] (pēp) *vi.* 〚echoic〛 to make the short, high-pitched cry of a young bird — *n.* a peeping sound

peep[2] (pēp) *vi.* 〚ME *pepen*〛 1 to look through a small opening or from a place of hiding 2 to show gradually or partially — *n.* a brief look; furtive glimpse —**peep′er** *n.*

peep′hole′ *n.* a hole to peep through

peeping Tom 〚after legendary peeper at Lady Godiva〛 one who gets sexual pleasure from furtively watching others

peer[1] (pir) *n.* 〚< L *par*, an equal〛 1 a person or thing of the same rank, ability, etc.; an equal 2 a British noble — **peer′age** (-ij) *n.* —**peer′ess** *n.fem.*

peer[2] (pir) *vi.* 〚< ? APPEAR〛 1 to look closely, as in trying to see more clearly 2 to show slightly

peer′less *adj.* without equal

peeve (pēv) *vt.* peeved, peev′ing [Colloq.] to make peevish — *n.* [Colloq.] an annoyance

pee·vish (pēv′ish) *adj.* 〚ME *pevische*〛 irritable; fretful; cross —**pee′vishly** *adv.* —**pee′vish·ness** *n.*

pee·wee (pē′wē′) *n.* 〚< ?〛 [Colloq.] an unusually small person or thing

peg (peg) *n.* 〚ME *pegge*〛 1 a short pin or bolt used to hold parts together, hang things on, etc. 2 a step or degree 3 [Colloq.] a throw — *vt.* **pegged, peg′ging** 1 to fasten, fix, secure, mark, etc., as with pegs 2 [Colloq.] to throw —**peg away (at)** to work steadily (at)

Peg·a·sus (peg′ə səs) *Gr. Myth.* a winged horse

peign·oir (pān wär′, pen-) *n.* 〚Fr〛 a woman's loose, full dressing gown

pein (pēn) *n. alt. sp. of* PEEN

pejo·ra·tion (pej′ə rā′shən, pē′jə-) *n.* 〚< L *pejor*, worse〛 a worsening —**pe·jo·ra·tive** (pi jôr′ə tiv) *adj.*

Pe·king·ese (pē′kə nēz′) *n., pl.* **-ese′** a small dog with a long, straight coat, short legs, and a short, wrinkled muzzle Also **Pe′kin·ese′** (-kə nēz′)

pe·koe (pē′kō) *n.* 〚< Chin *pek-ho*, white down (on the leaves used)〛 a black tea of Sri Lanka and India

pe·lagic (pi laj′ik) *adj.* 〚< Gr *pelagos*, sea〛 of the open sea or ocean

pelf (pelf) *n.* 〚< ? MFr *pelfre*, booty〛 money or wealth regarded with contempt

peli·can (pel′i kən) *n.* 〚< Gr *pelekan*〛 a large, web-footed water bird with an expandable pouch in the lower bill for scooping up fish

pel·la·gra (pə lā′grə, -lag′rə) *n.* 〚It ult. < L *pellis*, skin + Gr *agra*, seizure〛 a chronic disease caused by a lack of nicotinic acid in the diet, characterized by skin eruptions and mental disorders

pel·let (pel′it) *n.* 〚< L *pila*, a ball〛 1 a little ball, as of clay or medicine 2 a bullet, small lead shot, etc.

pell-mell (pel′mel′) *adv., adj.* 〚< OFr *mesler*, to mix〛 1 in a jumble 2 in wild, disorderly haste; headlong

pel·lu·cid (pə lōō′sid) *adj.* 〚< L *per*, through + *lucere*, to shine〛 1 transparent; clear 2 easy to understand

pelt[1] (pelt) *vt.* 〚ME *pelten*〛 1 to throw things at 2 to beat repeatedly — *vi.* to strike heavily or steadily, as hard rain

pelt[2] (pelt) *n.* 〚prob. < OFr *pel*, a skin〛 the skin of a fur-bearing animal, esp. when stripped from the carcass

pel·vis (pel′vis) *n., pl.* **-vises** or **-ves′** (-vēz′) 〚L, basin〛 1 the basinlike cavity in the posterior part of the trunk in humans and many other vertebrates 2 the bones forming this cavity —**pel′vic** *adj.*

pem·mi·can (pem′i kən) *n.* 〚< AmInd〛 a concentrated food of dried beef, suet, dried fruit, etc.

pen[1] (pen) *n.* 〚OE *penn*〛 1 a small enclosure for domestic animals 2 any small enclosure — *vt.* **penned** or **pent, pen′ning** to enclose as in a pen

pen[2] (pen) *n.* 〚< L *penna*, a feather〛 a device used in writing, etc. with ink; specif., *a*) a device with a metal point split into two nibs *b*) BALLPOINT (PEN) *c*) FOUNTAIN PEN — *vt.* **penned, pen′ning** to write with a pen

pen[3] (pen) *n.* [Slang] a penitentiary

Pen. or **pen.** peninsula

pe·nal (pēn′əl) *adj.* 〚< Gr *poinē*, penalty〛 of, for, constituting, or deserving punishment

pe·nal·ize (pē′nəl iz′, pen′əl-) *vt.* **-ized′, -iz′ing** to impose a penalty on; punish —**pe′nali·za′tion** *n.*

pen·alty (pen′əl tē) *n., pl.* **-ties** 1 a punishment 2 the handicap, etc. imposed on an offender, as a fine

pen·ance (pen′əns) *n.* 〚see PENITENT〛 voluntary self-punishment to show repentance for wrongdoing, sins, etc.

pena′tes *see* LARES AND PENATES

pence (pens) *n.* [Brit.] *pl. of* PENNY

pen·chant (pen′chənt) *n.* 〚Fr < L *pendere*, hang〛 a strong liking

pen·cil (pen′səl) *n.* 〚< L *penis*, a tail〛 a rod-shaped instrument with a core of graphite, crayon, etc. that is sharpened to a point for writing, etc. — *vt.* **-ciled** or **-cilled, -cil·ing** or **-cil·ling** to write, etc. with a pencil

pend (pend) *vi.* 〚< L *pendere*, hang〛 to await judgment or decision

pend·ant (pen′dənt) *n.* 〚see prec.〛 a hanging ornamental object, as a locket or earring

pend·ent (pen′dənt) *adj.* 〚see PEND〛 1 suspended 2 overhanging 3 undecided; pending

pend′ing *adj.* 〚prp. of PEND, infl. by Fr *pendant*, L *pendens*〛 1 not decided 2 impending — *prep.* 1 during 2 until

pen·du·lous (pen′dyōō ləs, -jōō-) *adj.* 〚see PEND〛 hanging freely; drooping

pen·du·lum (pen′dyōō ləm, -jōō-) *n.* 〚see PEND〛 a body hung so as to swing freely to and fro: used to regulate clock movements

pen·etrate (pen′i trāt′) *vt., vi.* **-trat′ed, -trat′ing** 〚< L *penitus*, inward〛 1 to enter by piercing 2 to have an

---

THESAURUS

peek *n.* sight, glimpse, glance; see LOOK 3.

peek *v.* glance, peep, glimpse; see SEE 1.

peel *n.* husk, bark, shell; see SKIN.

peel *v.* pare, strip, tear off, pull off, flay, uncover; see also SKIN.

peeling *n.* paring, strip, sliver; see SKIN.

peep[1,2] *n.* 1 [A peek] glimpse, glance, sight; see LOOK 3. 2 [A peeping sound] cheep, chirp, hoot; see CRY 2.

peep[1,2] *v.* 1 [To look cautiously] peek, glimpse, glance; see SEE 1. 2 [To make a peeping sound] cheep, chirp, squeak; see CRY 2.

peer[1] *n.* match, rival, companion; see EQUAL.

peer[2] *v.* gaze, inspect, scrutinize; see SEE 1.

peer group *n.* equals, social group, one's peers; see ASSOCIATE, EQUAL.

peeve* *v.* irritate, annoy, anger; see BOTHER 2.

peeved *a.* sullen, irritated, upset; see ANGRY.

peevish *a.* cross, fretful, fretting; see ANGRY.

peg *n.* pin, tack, fastener; see NAIL. — **take down a peg** humiliate, criticize, diminish; see HUMBLE.

pellet *n.* pill, bead, grain; see STONE.

pell-mell *a.* impetuously, hurriedly, indiscreetly; see FOOLISHLY.

pelt[2] *n.* fell, hair, wool; see HIDE.

pen[1,2] *v.* 1 [To enclose] close in, confine, coop up*; see ENCLOSE. 2 [To write] compose, indite, commit to writing; see WRITE 1, 2.

pen[1,2,3] *n.* 1 [An enclosed place] coop, cage, corral, sty, close, concentration camp, prison, penitentiary; see also ENCLOSURE 1. 2 [A writing instrument] Pens include the following: fountain, desk, drawing, ruling, artist's, reed, quill, steel, ballpoint, felt-tip.

penalize *v.* scold, chasten, castigate; see PUNISH.

penalty *n.* fine, mortification, discipline; see PUNISHMENT.

penance *n.* mortification, purgation, repentance, retribution, compensation, self-imposed atonement, fasting, suffering, sackcloth and ashes, hair shirt, reparation; see also PUNISHMENT.

pencil *n. Types of pencils include the following:* lead, mechanical, colored, drawing, indelible, charcoal, grease, eyebrow, cosmetic, drafting, chalk, crayon, stylus.

pendant *n.* earring, locket, lavaliere; see DECORATION 2, JEWELRY.

pending *a.* continuing, indeterminate, awaiting; see OMINOUS.

pendulum *n.* swing, pendant, suspended body; see DEVICE, MACHINE.

penetrable *a.* permeable, receptive, open, passable, accessible; see also POROUS.

penetrate *v.* bore, perforate, enter, insert, go through, make an entrance, stick into, jab, thrust, stab, force, make a hole, run into, run through, punch, puncture, drive into, stick, drill, eat through, spear, impale, wound, gore, sting, sink into, knife, effect throughout **3** to affect deeply **4** to understand — **pen′e·tra·ble** (-trə bəl) *adj.* —**pen′e·tra′tion** *n.*

pen·e·trat·ing (pen′i trāt′iŋ) *adj.* **1** that penetrates **2** sharp; piercing **3** acute; discerning Also **pen′e·tra′tive** (-trāt′iv)

pen·guin (peŋ′gwin, pen′-) *n.* [prob. < Welsh] a flightless bird of the Southern Hemisphere with webbed feet and flippers for swimming

pen·i·cil·lin (pen′i sil′in) *n.* [< L *penicillus*, brush] an antibiotic obtained from certain molds or produced synthetically

pen·in·su·la (pə nin′sə lə) *n.* [< L *paene*, almost + *insula*, isle] a land area almost surrounded by water —**penin′su·lar** *adj.*

pe·nis (pē′nis) *n., pl.* **-nises** or **-nes** (-nēz) [L] the male organ of sexual intercourse —**pe′nile** (-nil′) *adj.*

pen·i·tent (pen′i tənt) *adj.* [< L *paenitere*, repent] sorry for having done wrong and willing to atone — *n.* a penitent person —**pen′i·tence** *n.* —**pen′i·ten′tial** (-ten′shəl) *adj.* —**pen′i·tently** *adv.*

pen·i·ten·tia·ry (pen′i ten′shə rē) *adj.* making one liable to imprisonment in a penitentiary — *n., pl.* **-ries** a State or Federal prison for persons convicted of serious crimes

pen′knife′ *n., pl.* **-knives** (-nivz′) a small pocketknife

pen′light′ or **pen′lite′** *n.* a flashlight about the size of a fountain pen

pen′man (-mən) *n., pl.* **-men** one skilled in penmanship

pen′man·ship′ (-ship′) *n.* handwriting as an art or skill

pen name a pseudonym

pen·nant (pen′ənt) *n.* [< PENNON] **1** any long, narrow flag **2** such a flag symbolizing a championship

pen·ni·less (pen′ē lis, pen′i-) *adj.* without even a penny; extremely poor

pen·non (pen′ən) *n.* [< L *penna*, a feather] a flag or pennant

pen·ny (pen′ē) *n., pl.* **-nies** or **pence** (pens) [< OE *penig*] **1** in the United Kingdom, *a*) one 100th of a pound *b*) before 1971, 1/12 of a shilling **2** a U.S. or Canadian cent

penny arcade a public amusement hall with coin-operated games, etc.

penny pincher a miserly person —**pen′ny-pinch′ing** *n., adj.*

pen′ny·weight′ *n.* a unit of weight, equal to 1/20 ounce troy weight

pen′ny-wise′ *adj.* thrifty in small matters —**penny-wise and pound-foolish** thrifty in small matters but wasteful in major ones

pe·nol·o·gy (pē näl′ə jē) *n.* [< Gr *poinē*, punishment + -LOGY] the study of prison management and prison reform —**pe·nol′o·gist** *n.*

pen pal a person, esp. one abroad, with whom one exchanges letters

pen·sion (pen′shən) *n.* [< L *pensio*, a paying] a regular payment, not wages, as to one who is retired or disabled — *vt.* to grant a pension to —**pen′sioner** *n.*

pen·sive (pen′siv) *adj.* [< L *pensare*, consider] thoughtful or reflective, often in a melancholy way —**pen′sively** *adv.* —**pen′sive·ness** *n.*

pent (pent) *vt. alt. pt. & pp. of* PEN¹ — *adj.* held or kept in; penned Often with *up*

penta- [< Gr *pente*, FIVE] *combining form* five

pen·ta·cle (pen′tə kəl) *n.* [see prec.] a symbol, usually a five-pointed star, formerly used in magic

pen·ta·gon (pen′tə gän′) *n.* [< Gr *penta-*, five + *gōnia*, an angle] **1** a plane figure with five angles and five sides **2** [P-] the pentagonal office building of the Defense Department, near Washington, D.C. —**pen·tag′o·nal** (-tag′ə nəl) *adj.*

pen·tam·e·ter (pen tam′ət ər) *n.* [see PENTA- & METER¹] a line of verse containing five metrical feet; esp., English

iambic pentameter (Ex.: "Hĕ jĕst́s| ăt scaŕs| whŏ nĕv́| ĕr fĕlt́| ă wouńd")

Pen·ta·teuch (pen′tə tōōk′) *n.* [< Gr *penta-*, five + *teuchos*, book] the first five books of the Bible

pen·tath·lon (pen tath′län′) *n.* [PENTA- + Gr *athlon*, a contest] a contest in which each contestant takes part in five different events —**pen·tath′lete′** (-lēt′) *n.*

Pen·te·cost (pen′ti kôst′) *n.* [< Gr *pentēkostē* (*hēmera*), the fiftieth (day)] a Christian festival on the seventh Sunday after Easter

Pen·te·cos·tal (pen′tə kôs′təl) *adj.* **1** of Pentecost **2** designating or of any of various Protestant fundamentalist sects often stressing direct inspiration by the Holy Spirit —**Pen′tecos′tal·ism′** *n.*

pent·house (pent′hous′) *n.* [ult. < L *appendere*, append] an apartment on the roof of a building

pent-up (pent′up′) *adj.* held in check; curbed [pent-up emotion]

pe·nu·che or **pe·nu′chi** (pə nōō′chē) *n.* [var. of PANOCHA] a fudgelike candy

pen·ul·ti·mate (pē nul′tə mət) *adj.* [< L *paene*, almost + ULTIMATE] next to the last — *n.* the penultimate one

pe·nu·ri·ous (pe nyoor′ē əs, -noor′-) *adj.* [see fol.] miserly; stingy —**pe·nu′ri·ously** *adv.* —**pe·nu′ri·ous·ness** *n.*

pen·u·ry (pen′yoō rē, -yə-) *n.* [< L *penuria*, want] extreme poverty

pe·on (pē′ən, -än′) *n.* [< ML *pedo*, foot soldier] **1** in Spanish America, a member of the laboring class **2** in the SW U.S., a person forced into servitude to work off a debt — **pe′on·age** *n.*

pe·o·ny (pē′ə nē) *n., pl.* **-nies** [< Gr *Paiōn*, Apollo as god of medicine: from its former medicinal use] **1** a plant with large pink, white, red, or yellow, showy flowers **2** the flower

peo·ple (pē′pəl) *n., pl.* **-ples** [< L *populus*, nation, crowd] all the persons of a racial or ethnic group; nation, race, etc. — *n.pl.* **1** the persons of a certain place, group, or class **2** one's family; relatives **3** the populace **4** persons considered indefinitely [what will *people* say?] **5** human beings — *vt.* **-pled, -pling** to populate

pep (pep) *n.* [< fol.] [Colloq.] energy; vigor — *vt.* **pepped, pep′ping** [Colloq.] to fill with pep; invigorate: with *up* — **pep′py, -pier, -pi·est,** *adj.* —**pep′pi·ness** *n.*

pep·per (pep′ər) *n.* [< Gr *peperi*] **1** *a*) a pungent condiment ground from the dried fruits of an East Indian vine *b*) this vine **2** the fruit of the red pepper plant, red, yellow, or green, sweet or hot — *vt.* **1** to season with ground pepper **2** to pelt with small objects

pep′per·corn′ *n.* the dried berry of the pepper

pepper mill a hand mill used to grind peppercorns

pep′per·mint′ *n.* **1** a plant of the mint family that yields a pungent oil used for flavoring **2** the oil **3** a candy flavored with this oil

pep·per·o·ni (pep′ər ō′nē) *n., pl.* **-nis** or **-ni** [< It *peperoni*] a hard, highly spiced Italian sausage

pepper shaker a container for ground pepper, with a perforated top

pep′per·y *adj.* **1** of, like, or highly seasoned with pepper **2** sharp or fiery, as words **3** hot-tempered

pep·sin (pep′sin) *n.* [< L *peptein*, to digest] a stomach enzyme, aiding in the digestion of proteins

pep talk a talk, as to an athletic team by its coach, to instill enthusiasm, determination, etc.

pep·tic (pep′tik) *adj.* [see PEPSIN] **1** of or aiding digestion **2** caused by digestive secretions [a *peptic* ulcer]

per (pur, pər) *prep.* [L] **1** through; by; by means of **2** for each [fifty cents *per* yard] **3** [Colloq.] according to

---

THESAURUS

go through, pass through.—*Ant.* LEAVE, withdraw, turn aside.

penetrating *a.* **1** [Entering] piercing, going through, puncturing; see SHARP 1. **2** [Mentally keen] astute, shrewd, sharp; see INTELLIGENT.

penetration *n.* **1** [Act of entering] insertion, invasion, perforation; see ENTRANCE 1. **2** [Mental acuteness] discernment, perception, keen-sightedness; see INTELLIGENCE 1.

peninsula *n.* point, promontory, cape; see LAND 1.

penitentiary *n.* reformatory, penal institution, pen*; see JAIL, PRISON.

penniless *a.* poverty-stricken, lack-

ing means, indigent; see POOR 1.

penny *n.* cent, copper, red cent*; see MONEY 1.

pension *n.* annuity, premium, payment, grant, social security, gift, reward; see also ALLOWANCE.

pent-up *a.* held in check, repressed, restrained; see RESTRAINED, RESTRICTED.

people *n.* **1** [Humankind] humanity, mankind, the human race; see MAN 1. **2** [A body of persons having racial or social ties] nationality, tribe, community; see RACE 2. **3** [The middle and lower classes of society] mass, folk, proletariat, rabble, masses, the

multitude, the majority, democracy, crowd, common people, common herd, rank and file, the underprivileged, the public, the man in the street, bourgeoisie, riffraff, the herd*, the horde, the many, the great unwashed*, hoi polloi, John Q. Public, Jane Q. Public. **4** [Family] close relatives, kin, siblings; see FAMILY. **5** [Society in general] they, anybody, the public; see EVERYBODY.

peopled *a.* lived in, dwelt in, sustaining human life; see INHABITED.

pep* *n.* energy, vigor, liveliness; see ACTION 1.

per *prep.* to each, for each, contained

per- ⟦< prec.⟧ *prefix* **1** through, throughout **2** thoroughly

per·ad·ven·ture (pur′əd ven′chər) *adv.* ⟦< OFr *par*, by + *aventure*, chance⟧ [Archaic] possibly

per·am·bu·late (pər am′byōo lāt′) *vt., vi.* **-lat′ed, -lat′ing** ⟦< L *per*, through + *ambulare*, to walk⟧ to walk (through, over, etc.)

per·am′bu·la′tor (-lāt′ər) *n.* [Chiefly Brit., etc.] a baby carriage

per an·num (pər an′əm) ⟦L⟧ yearly

per·cale (pər kāl′) *n.* ⟦Fr < Pers *pargāla*, scrap⟧ fine, closely woven cotton cloth, used for sheets, etc.

per cap·i·ta (pər kap′i tə) ⟦ML, lit., by heads⟧ for each person

per·ceive (pər sēv′) *vt., vi.* **-ceived′, -ceiv′ing** ⟦< L *per*, through + *capere*, take⟧ **1** to understand **2** to become aware (of) through the senses —**per·ceiv′able** *adj.*

per·cent (pər sent′) *adv., adj.* ⟦< L *per centum*⟧ in, to, or for every hundred: symbol, % Also **per cent** — *n.* [Colloq.] percentage

per·cent′age (-ij) *n.* **1** a given part in every hundred **2** part; portion **3** advantage; profit

per·cen·tile (pər sen′tīl′, -sent″l) *n. Statistics* any of 100 divisions of a series, each of equal frequency

per·cep·ti·ble (pər sep′tə bəl) *adj.* that can be perceived — **per·cep′ti·bly** *adv.*

per·cep′tion (-shən) *n.* ⟦< L *percipere*, perceive⟧ **1** the mental grasp of objects, etc. through the senses **2** insight or intuition **3** the knowledge, etc. gotten by perceiving — **per·cep′tion·al** *adj.*

per·cep′tive *adj.* **1** of perception **2** able to perceive quickly —**per·cep′tive·ly** *adv.* —**per·cep′tive·ness** *n.*

per·cep′tu·al (-chōo əl) *adj.* of or involving perception

perch[1] (purch) *n., pl.* **-es** ⟦< Gr *perkē*⟧ **1** a small, spiny-finned, freshwater food fish **2** any of various other spiny-finned fishes

perch[2] (purch) *n.* ⟦< L *pertica*, pole⟧ **1** a horizontal pole, etc. serving as a roost for birds **2** any high resting place **3** a measure of length equal to 5½ yards — *vi., vt.* to rest or place on or as on a perch

per·chance (pər chans′) *adv.* ⟦< OFr *par*, by + *chance*, chance⟧ [Archaic] **1** by chance **2** perhaps

per·co·late (pur′kə lāt′) *vt.* **-lat′ed, -lat′ing** ⟦< L *per*, through + *colare*, to strain⟧ to pass (a liquid) through a porous substance; filter — *vi.* to ooze through a porous substance —**per′co·la′tion** *n.*

per′co·la′tor *n.* a coffeepot in which the boiling water bubbles up through a tube and filters back down through the ground coffee

per·cus·sion (pər kush′ən) *n.* ⟦< L *per-*, thoroughly + *quatere*, shake⟧ the hitting of one body against another, as the hammer of a firearm against a powder cap (**percussion cap**) — *adj.* designating, of, or for a musical instrument that produces a tone when struck, as a drum, cymbal, etc.

per·cus′sion·ist *n.* a musician who plays percussion instruments

per diem (pər dē′əm, dī′-) ⟦L⟧ daily

per·di·tion (pər dish′ən) *n.* ⟦< L *perdere*, to lose⟧ **1** *Theol.* the loss of the soul **2** HELL

per·dure (pər door′) *vi.* **-dured′, -dur′ing** ⟦< L *perdurare*, to endure⟧ to remain in existence; last

per·e·gri·nate (per′ə gri nāt′) *vt., vi.* **-nat′ed, -nat′ing** ⟦see PILGRIM⟧ to travel (along, over, or through) —**per′egri·na′tion** *n.*

per·e·grine (falcon) (per′ə grin) a swift falcon of nearly worldwide distribution, much used in falconry

per·emp·to·ry (pər emp′tə rē) *adj.* ⟦< L *perimere*, destroy⟧ **1** *Law* barring further action; final **2** that cannot be denied, delayed, etc., as a command **3** dogmatic; imperious

per·en·ni·al (pər en′ē əl) *adj.* ⟦< L *per-*, through + *annus*, year⟧ **1** lasting throughout the whole year **2** continuing for a long time **3** living more than two years: said of plants — *n.* a perennial plant —**per·en′ni·al·ly** *adv.*

per·es·troi·ka (per′ə stroi′kə) *n.* ⟦Russ, lit., a making over, rebuilding⟧ the Soviet official policy of economic and political reconstruction

per·fect (pur′fikt; *for v. usually* pər fekt′) *adj.* ⟦< L *per-*, through + *facere*, do⟧ **1** complete in all respects; flawless **2** excellent, as in skill or quality **3** completely accurate **4** utter; sheer; absolute *[a perfect fool]* **5** *Gram.* expressing a state or action completed at the time of speaking — *vt.* **1** to complete **2** to make perfect or nearly perfect — *n.* **1** the perfect tense **2** a verb form in this tense —**per′fectly** *adv.* —**per′fect·ness** *n.*

per·fec·ta (pər fek′tə) *n.* ⟦Sp, perfect⟧ a bet in which one wins if one correctly picks the first and second place finishers in a race

per·fect·i·ble (pər fek′tə bəl) *adj.* that can become, or be made, perfect

per·fec·tion (pər fek′shən) *n.* **1** the act of perfecting **2** a being perfect **3** a person or thing that is the perfect embodiment of some quality —**to perfection** perfectly

per·fec′tion·ism′ *n.* obsessive striving for perfection — **per·fec′tion·ist** *n., adj.*

per·fidy (pur′fə dē) *n., pl.* **-dies** ⟦< L *per*, through + *fides*, faith⟧ betrayal of trust; treachery —**per·fidi·ous** (pər fid′ē əs) *adj.*

per·fo·rate (pur′fə rāt′) *vt., vi.* **-rat′ed, -rat′ing** ⟦< L *per*, through + *forare*, to bore⟧ **1** to make a hole or holes through, as by boring **2** to pierce with holes in a row, as a pattern, etc. —**per′fo·ra′tion** *n.*

per·force (pər fôrs′) *adv.* ⟦< OFr: see PER & FORCE⟧ necessarily

per·form (pər fôrm′) *vt.* ⟦< OFr *parfournir*⟧ **1** to do (a task, etc.) **2** to fulfill (a promise, etc.) **3** to render or enact (a piece of music, dramatic role, etc.) — *vi.* to execute an action or process, esp. in a PERFORMANCE (sense 4) —**per·form′er** *n.*

═══════════════════ **THESAURUS** ═══════════════════

in each, according to, through, by, by means of.

perceive *v.* **1** [See] observe, note, notice; see LOOK 2, SEE 1. **2** [Understand] comprehend, sense, grasp; see UNDERSTAND 1.

perceived *a.* seen, felt, touched; see UNDERSTOOD 1.

percent *a.* by the hundred, reckoned on the basis of a hundred, in a hundred, percentaged, percentile.

percentage *n.* percent, rate, rate per cent, portion, section, allotment, duty, discount, commission, winnings, cut*, rake-off*, payoff, slice*; see also DIVISION 2.

perceptible *a.* perceivable, discernible, cognizable; see OBVIOUS 1.

perception *n.* **1** [The act of perceiving] realizing, understanding, apprehending; see ATTENTION, JUDGMENT 2. **2** [The result of perceiving] insight, knowledge, observation; see ATTITUDE, OPINION 1, VIEWPOINT.

perceptive *a.* alert, incisive, keen; see CONSCIOUS, OBSERVANT.

perch[2] *n.* seat, pole, landing place, resting place.

perch[2] *v.* roost, settle down, land; see REST 1, SIT.

perfect *a.* **1** [Having all necessary qualities] complete, sound, entire; see ABSOLUTE 1, WHOLE 1, 2. **2** [Without defect] excelling, faultless, flawless, impeccable, immaculate, unblemished, foolproof, untainted, unspotted, absolute, classical, stainless, spotless, crowning, culminating, supreme, ideal, sublime, beyond all praise, beyond compare; see also EXCELLENT, PURE 2, WHOLE 2.—*Ant.* RUINED, damaged, faulty. **3** [Exact] precise, sharp, distinct; see ACCURATE 2.

perfect *v.* fulfill, realize, develop; see ACHIEVE, COMPLETE.

perfected *a.* completed, developed, mature, conclusive, full, elaborate, thorough; see also FINISHED 1, FULFILLED.

perfection *n.* completion, fulfillment, finishing, consummation, supremacy, ideal, ending, realization; see also ACHIEVEMENT.—*Ant.* RUIN, destruction, neglect.

perfectly *a.* excellently, fitly, correctly, flawlessly, faultlessly, supremely, ideally.—*Ant.* BADLY, poorly, incorrectly.

perforate *v.* drill, slit, stab; see PEN-ETRATE.

perforation *n.* break, aperture, slit; see HOLE 1.

perform *v.* **1** [To accomplish an action] do, make, achieve, rehearse, accomplish, fulfill, execute, transact, carry out, carry through, discharge, effect, enforce, administer, complete, consummate, operate, finish, realize, go about, go through with, put through, work out, devote oneself to, come through, be engrossed in, be engaged in, saw it to, bring about, engage in, concern oneself with, have effect, fall to, do justice to, do one's part, make a move, follow through, apply oneself to, deal with, do something, look to, take measures, act on, lose oneself in, make it one's business, dispose of, bring to pass, do what is expected of one, put into effect, occupy oneself with, take action, address oneself to, put in action, lift a finger*, keep one's hand in*, pull off*. **2** [To present a performance] give, present, enact, play, offer, impersonate, show, exhibit, display, act out, dramatize, execute, put on the stage, produce, act the part of, put on an act, act one's part.

per·form·ance *n.* **1** the act of performing **2** functional effectiveness **3** deed or feat **4** *a*) a formal exhibition or presentation, as a play *b*) one's part in this

performance art an art form combining elements of several art forms, as dance, film, etc., in a presentation of juxtaposed images on various themes

performing arts arts, such as drama, for performance before an audience

per·fume (pər fyōōm'; *for n. usually* pur'fyōōm') *vt.* **-fumed'**, **-fum'ing** 〖< L *per-*, intens. + *fumare*, to smoke〗 **1** to scent **2** to put perfume on — *n.* a pleasing odor, or a substance producing this, as a volatile oil extracted from flowers

per·fum'er·y (-ər ē) *n.*, *pl.* **-ies** perfumes collectively

per·func·to·ry (pər funk'tə rē) *adj.* 〖< L *per-*, intens. + *fungi*, perform〗 **1** done merely as a routine; superficial **2** without concern; indifferent —**per·func'to·ri·ly** *adv.*

per·go·la (pur'gə lə) *n.* 〖< L *pergula*〗 an arbor with a latticework roof

per·haps (pər haps') *adv.* 〖PER + pl. of *hap*, chance〗 possibly; maybe

peri- 〖Gr〗 *prefix* **1** around; about **2** near

peri·car·dium (per'i kär'dē əm) *n.*, *pl.* **-dia** (-ə) 〖< Gr *peri-*, around + *kardia*, heart〗 in vertebrates, the thin, closed sac surrounding the heart and containing a serous liquid —**per'i·car'di·al** *adj.*

peri·gee (per'i jē') *n.* 〖< Gr *peri-*, near + *gē*, earth〗 the point nearest to the earth in the orbit of the moon or of a man-made satellite

peri·he·lion (per'i hē'lē ən) *n.*, *pl.* **-li·ons** or **-lia** (-ə) 〖< Gr *peri-*, around + *hēlios*, sun〗 the point nearest the sun in the orbit of a planet, comet, or man-made satellite

peril (per'əl) *n.* 〖< L *periculum*, danger〗 **1** exposure to harm or injury **2** something that may cause harm — *vt.* **-iled** or **-illed**, **-il·ing** or **-il·ling** to imperil

per'il·ous *adj.* involving peril or risk; dangerous —**per'il·ously** *adv.*

pe·rim·eter (pə rim'ə tər) *n.* 〖< Gr *peri-*, around + *metron*, measure〗 **1** the outer boundary of a figure or area **2** the total length of this

peri·neum (per'i nē'əm) *n.*, *pl.* **-ne'a** (-ə) 〖< Gr *perineon*〗 the small area between the anus and the genitals

pe·riod (pir'ē əd) *n.* 〖< Gr *periodos*, a cycle〗 **1** the interval between successive occurrences of an event **2** a portion of time characterized by certain processes, etc. *[a period of change]* **3** any of the portions of time into which a game, school day, etc. is divided **4** the menses **5** an end, conclusion **6** *a*) the pause in speaking or a mark of punctuation (.) used at the end of a sentence *b*) the dot (.) following many abbreviations — *interj.* an exclamation used for emphasis

pe·ri·od·ic (pir'ē äd'ik) *adj.* **1** appearing or recurring at regular intervals **2** intermittent

pe'ri·od'i·cal *adj.* **1** PERIODIC **2** published at regular intervals, as weekly, etc. **3** of a periodical — *n.* a periodical publication —**pe'ri·od'i·cally** *adv.*

periodic table an arrangement of the chemical elements according to their atomic numbers

pe·ri·odi·za·tion (pir'ē əd i zā'shən) *n.* the dividing, as of history, into chronological periods

perio·don·tal (per'ē ō dänt''l, -ē ə-) *adj.* 〖< PERI- + Gr *odōn*, tooth〗 occurring around a tooth or affecting the gums

peri·pa·tetic (per'i pə tet'ik) *adj.* 〖< Gr *peri-*, around + *patein*, walk〗 walking or moving about; itinerant

pe·riph·eral (pə rif'ər əl) *adj.* **1** of or forming a periphery **2** outer; external — *n.* a piece of equipment used with a computer to increase its range or efficiency, as a disk, etc.

pe·riph·ery (pə rif'ər ē) *n.*, *pl.* **-ies** 〖< Gr *peri-*, around + *pherein*, to bear〗 **1** an outer boundary, esp. of a rounded object **2** surrounding space or area

pe·riph·ra·sis (pə rif'rə sis) *n.*, *pl.* **-ses'** (-sēz') 〖< Gr *peri-*, around + *phrazein*, to speak〗 the use of many words where a few would do

peri·scope (per'i skōp') *n.* 〖PERI- + -SCOPE〗 an optical instrument which allows one to see around or over an obstacle: used on submarines, etc.

per·ish (per'ish) *vi.* 〖< L *per-*, through + *ire*, go〗 **1** to be destroyed or ruined **2** to die, esp. violently

per·ish·able (per'ish ə bəl) *adj.* that may perish; esp., liable to spoil, as some foods — *n.* something perishable, esp. food

peri·stal·sis (per'ə stal'sis, -stôl'-) *n.*, *pl.* **-ses'** (-sēz') 〖< Gr *peri-*, around + *stellein*, to place〗 the contractions and dilations of the alimentary canal, moving the contents onward —**peri·stal'tic** *adj.*

peri·to·neum (per'i tō nē'əm) *n.*, *pl.* **-ne'a** (-ə) or **-ne'ums** 〖< Gr *peri-*, around + *teinein*, to stretch〗 the serous membrane lining the abdominal cavity

per'i·to·ni'tis *n.* inflammation of the peritoneum

peri·wig (per'i wig') *n.* 〖altered < Fr *perruque*〗 a wig

peri·win·kle (per'i win'kəl) *n.* 〖< L *pervincire*, entwine〗 a creeping plant with blue, white, or pink flowers

peri·win·kle (per'i win'kəl) *n.* 〖OE *pinewincle*〗 a small saltwater snail with a thick, globular shell

per·jure (pur'jər) *vt.* **-jured**, **-jur·ing** 〖< L *per*, through + *jurare*, swear〗 to make (oneself) guilty of perjury —**per'jurer** *n.*

per·jury (pur'jə rē) *n.*, *pl.* **-ries** 〖< L *perjurus*, false〗 the willful telling of a lie while under oath

perk[1] (purk) *vt.* 〖ME *perken*〗 **1** to raise (the head, etc.) briskly **2** to give a smart, fresh, or vivacious look to: often with *up* — *vi.* to become lively: with *up* —**perk'y**, **-i·er**, **-i·est**, *adj.* —**perk'i·ness** *n.*

perk[2] (purk) *vt.*, *vi.* [Colloq.] *short for* PERCOLATE

perk[3] (purk) *n.* [Colloq.] *short for* PERQUISITE

perm (purm) *n.* [Colloq.] short for PERMANENT — *vt.* to give a permanent to

perma·frost (pur'mə frôst') *n.* permanently frozen subsoil

per·ma·nent (pur'mə nənt) *adj.* 〖< L *per*, through + *manere*, remain〗 lasting or intended to last indefinitely or for a long time — *n.* a long-lasting hair wave produced by use of chemicals or heat —**per'ma·nence** *n.* —**per'ma·nently** *adv.*

permanent wave PERMANENT (*n.*)

per·me·able (pur'mē ə bəl) *adj.* that can be permeated, as by fluids —**per'meabil'ity** *n.*

per·me·ate (pur'mē āt') *vt.*, *vi.* **-at'ed**, **-at'ing** 〖< L *per*, through + *meare*, to glide〗 to spread or diffuse; penetrate (*through* or *among*)

per·mis·si·ble (pər mis'ə bəl) *adj.* that can be permitted; allowable —**per·mis'si·bly** *adv.*

THESAURUS

performance *n.* appearance, rehearsal, exhibition, offering, representation, spectacle, review, revue, opera, play, concert, exhibit, display, show; see also DRAMA.

perfume *n.* scent, fragrance, aroma, odor, sweetness, bouquet, incense; see also SMELL 1. *Perfumes include the following:* attar of roses, sandalwood, bay, rosemary, frankincense, myrrh, eau de Cologne, musk, spice, sachet, lavender, rose geranium.

perhaps *a.* conceivably, possibly, reasonably; see MAYBE.

perilous *a.* precarious, unsafe, uncertain; see DANGEROUS.

perimeter *n.* margin, outline, border; see BOUNDARY, EDGE 1.

period *n.* **1** [A measure of time] epoch, time, era; see AGE 3. **2** [An end] limit, conclusion, close; see END 2. **3** [A mark of punctuation] point,

full stop, full pause, dot, ending-pitch; see also PUNCTUATION.

periodic *a.* rhythmic, regular, recurrent; see REGULAR 3.

periodical *n.* review, number, publication; see MAGAZINE, NEWSPAPER.

periodically *a.* rhythmically, systematically, annually; see REGULARLY.

peripheral *a.* external, outer, surface; see OUTSIDE.

periphery *n.* covering, perimeter, border; see OUTSIDE 1.

perish *v.* pass away, be lost, depart; see DIE.

perjure *v.* prevaricate, swear falsely, lie on the stand; see LIE 1.

perjury *n.* false statement, violation of an oath, willful falsehood; see LIE.

perk up *v.* **1** [Be refreshed] revive, recuperate, liven up; see RECOVER 3. **2** [Cheer or refresh] invigorate,

shake, enliven; see RENEW 1, REVIVE 1.

permanence *n.* continuity, dependability, durability; see STABILITY 1.

permanent *a.* durable, enduring, abiding, uninterrupted, stable, continuing, lasting, firm, hard, tough, strong, hardy, robust, sound, sturdy, steadfast, imperishble, surviving, living, long-lived, long-standing, invariable, persevering, unyielding, persisting, resistant, impenetrable, recurring, wearing, constant, changeless, persistent, perennial.

permanently *a.* for all time, enduringly, lastingly; see FOREVER.

permeate *v.* pervade, saturate, fill; see FILTER 1.

permissible *a.* allowable, sanctioned, to be permitted; see PERMITTED.

per·mis·sion (pər mish'ən) *n.* the act of permitting; esp., formal consent

per·mis·sive (-mis'iv) *adj.* 1 that permits 2 allowing freedom; lenient —**per·mis'sively** *adv.* —**per·mis'sive·ness** *n.*

per·mit (pər mit'; *for n. usually* pur'mit') *vt.* **-mit'ted, -mit'ting** ⟦< L *per*, through + *mittere*, send⟧ 1 to allow; consent to 2 to authorize — *vi.* to give opportunity ⟦if time *permits*⟧ — *n.* a license

per·mu·ta·tion (pur'myōō tā'shən) *n.* ⟦< L *per-*, intens. + *mutare*, change⟧ 1 any radical alteration 2 any of the total number of groupings possible within a group

per·ni·cious (pər nish'əs) *adj.* ⟦< L < *per*, thoroughly + *necare*, kill⟧ causing great injury, destruction, etc.; fatal — **per·ni'ciously** *adv.*

per·o·ra·tion (per'ə rā'shən) *n.* ⟦< L *per*, through + *orare*, speak⟧ the concluding part of a speech

per·ox·ide (pər äks'īd', pə räk'sīd') *n.* ⟦< L *per*, through + OXIDE⟧ any oxide containing the oxygen group linked by a single bond; specif., hydrogen peroxide — *vt.* **-id'ed, -id'ing** to bleach with hydrogen peroxide

per·pen·dic·u·lar (pur'pən dik'yōō lər, -yə-) *adj.* ⟦< L *perpendiculum*, plumb line⟧ 1 at right angles to a given plane or line 2 exactly upright; vertical — *n.* a line or plane at right angles to another line or plane

per·pe·trate (pur'pə trāt') *vt.* **-trat'ed, -trat'ing** ⟦< L *per*, thoroughly + *patrare*, to effect⟧ 1 to do (something evil, criminal, etc.) 2 to commit (a blunder, etc.) —**per'pe·tra'tion** *n.* —**per'pe·tra'tor** *n.*

per·pet·u·al (pər pech'ōō əl) *adj.* ⟦< L *perpetuus*, constant⟧ 1 lasting forever or for a long time 2 continuing without interruption; constant —**per·pet'ual·ly** *adv.*

per·pet'u·ate' (-āt') *vt.* **-at'ed, -at'ing** to make perpetual; cause to continue or be remembered —**per·pet'ua'tion** *n.*

per·pe·tu·ity (pur'pə tōō'ə tē) *n., pl.* **-ties** unlimited time; eternity —**in perpetuity** forever

per·plex (pər pleks') *vt.* ⟦< L *per*, through + *plectere*, twist⟧ to make (a person) uncertain, doubtful, etc.; confuse —**per·plex'ing** *adj.* —**per·plex'ity,** *pl.* **-ties,** *n.*

per·qui·site (pur'kwi zit) *n.* ⟦< L *per-*, intens. + *quaerere*, seek⟧ something in addition to regular pay for one's work, as a tip

per se (pur' sā', -sē') ⟦L⟧ by (or in) itself; intrinsically

per·se·cute (pur'si kyōōt') *vt.* **-cut'ed, -cut'ing** ⟦< L *per*, through + *sequi*, follow⟧ to afflict constantly so as to injure or distress, as for reasons of religion, race, etc. — **per'se·cu'tion** *n.* —**per'se·cu'tor** *n.*

per·se·vere (pur'sə vir') *vi.* **-vered', -ver'ing** ⟦< L *per-*, intens. + *severus*, severe⟧ to continue a course of action, etc. in spite of difficulty, opposition, etc. —**per'sev·er'ance** *n.*

Per·sian (pur'zhən, -shən) *adj.* of Persia, its people, language, etc.; Iranian — *n.* 1 a native or inhabitant of Persia 2 the Iranian language of Iran 3 a variety of domestic cat with a long, thick, glossy coat

Persian lamb the pelt of karakul lambs

per·si·flage (pur'si fläzh') *n.* ⟦Fr < L *per*, through + *sifilare*, to hiss⟧ frivolous talk or writing

per·sim·mon (pər sim'ən) *n.* ⟦< AmInd⟧ 1 a hardwood tree with plumlike fruit 2 the fruit

per·sist (pər sist', -zist') *vi.* ⟦< L *per*, through + *sistere*, cause to stand⟧ 1 to refuse to give up, esp. when faced with opposition 2 to continue insistently 3 to endure; remain

per·sist'ent *adj.* 1 continuing, esp. in the face of opposition, etc. 2 continuing to exist or endure 3 constantly repeated —**per·sist'ence** *n.*

per·snick·et·y (pər snik'ə tē) *adj.* ⟦< Scot dial.⟧ [Colloq.] 1 too particular; fussy 2 showing or requiring careful treatment

per·son (pur'sən) *n.* ⟦< L *persona*⟧ 1 a human being 2 the human body 3 personality; self 4 *Gram.* division into three sets of pronouns and corresponding verb forms: see FIRST PERSON, SECOND PERSON, THIRD PERSON 5 *Law* any individual or incorporated group having certain legal rights and responsibilities —**in person** actually present

-person (pur'sən) *combining form* person in a (specified) activity Used to avoid the masculine implication of *-man* [*chairperson*]

per·son·able (-ə bəl) *adj.* ⟦ME *personabilis*⟧ having a pleasing appearance and personality

per·son·age' (-ij') *n.* a person; esp., an important person; notable

per·sonal (-nəl) *adj.* 1 private; individual 2 done in person 3 involving human beings [*personal relationships*] 4 of the body or physical appearance 5 *a*) having to do with the character, conduct, etc. of a person [a *personal remark*] *b*) tending to make personal, esp. derogatory, remarks 6 *Gram.* indicating PERSON (sense 4) 7 *Law* of property (**personal property**) that is movable

personal computer MICROCOMPUTER

personal effects personal belongings, esp. those worn or carried

per·son·al·ity (pur'sə nal'ə tē) *n., pl.* **-ties** 1 the quality or fact of being a person or a particular person 2 distinctive individual qualities of a person, considered collectively 3 a notable person 4 [*pl.*] offensive remarks aimed at a person

per·son·al·ize (pur'sə nəl īz') *vt.* **-ized', -iz'ing** 1 to apply to a particular person, esp. to oneself 2 to have marked with one's name, etc.

per·son·al·ly *adv.* 1 in person 2 as a person [I dislike him *personally*] 3 in one's own opinion 4 as though directed at oneself

---

THESAURUS

permission *n.* leave, liberty, consent, assent, acceptance, letting, approbation, agreement, license, permit, allowance, authority, tolerance, toleration, authorization, approval, acknowledgment, recognition, concurrence, promise, avowal, support, corroboration, guarantee, guaranty, visa, encouragement, ratification, grace, authority, sanction, confirmation, endorsement, affirmation, assurance, empowering, legalization, grant, indulgence, trust, concession, adjustment, settlement, accord, nod*, OK, rubber stamp*, the go-ahead*, high sign, green light*.—*Ant.* DENIAL, injunction, interdiction.

permissive *a.* authorizing, allowing, agreeable; see PERMITTED.

permit *n.* license, grant, consent; see PERMISSION.

permit *v.* sanction, tolerate, let; see ALLOW.

permitted *a.* granted, allowed, licensed, authorized, legalized, tolerated, empowered, sanctioned, conceded, consented, favored, suffered, chartered, accorded, let, indulged, privileged; see also APPROVED.—*Ant.* REFUSED, denied, prohibited.

perpendicular *a.* vertical, plumb, straight; see STRAIGHT 1.

perpetrate *v.* commit, act, do; see

PERFORM 1.

perpetual *a.* 1 [Never stopping] continual, unceasing, constant; see ENDLESS. 2 [Continually repeating] repetitious, repeating, recurrent; see CONSTANT.

perpetually *a.* enduringly, permanently, unceasingly; see FOREVER.

perplex *v.* puzzle, confound, bewilder; see CONFUSE.

perplexed *a.* troubled, uncertain, bewildered; see DOUBTFUL.

perplexing *a.* bewildering, confusing, mystifying; see DIFFICULT 2.

per se *a.* as such, intrinsically, alone, singularly, fundamentally, in essence, in itself, by itself, virtually; see also ESSENTIALLY.

persecute *v.* afflict, harass, victimize; see ABUSE.

persecution *n.* torture, torment, teasing, provoking; see also ABUSE.

perseverance *n.* grit, resolution, pluck; see DETERMINATION.

persevere *v.* persist, remain, pursue; see ENDURE 1.

persist *v.* persevere, pursue, strive; see CONTINUE 1, ENDURE 1.

persistence *n.* constancy, resolution, stamina; see ENDURANCE.

persistent *a.* tenacious, steadfast, determined; see RESOLUTE.

person *n.* 1 [An individual] human

being, child, somebody, self, oneself, I, me, soul, spirit, character, individuality, personage, personality, identity; see also MAN 2, WOMAN 1. 2 [An individual enjoying distinction] distinguished person, personality, success; see CHARACTER 4. 3 [Bodily form] physique, frame, form; see BODY 1. —**in person** personally, in the flesh, present; see NEAR 1.

personable *a.* agreeable, pleasant, attractive; see CHARMING.

personage *n.* human being, someone, individual; see MAN 2, PERSON 1.

personal *a.* 1 [Private] secluded, secret, retired; see PRIVATE. 2 [Individual] claimed, peculiar, particular; see INDIVIDUAL, SPECIAL. 3 [Pertaining to one's person] fleshly, corporeal, corporal; see BODILY.

personality *n.* 1 [The total of one's nature] self, oneself, being; see CHARACTER 2. 2 [Individual characteristics] disposition, nature, temper; see CHARACTER 1. 3 [A notable person] celebrity, star, cynosure; see CHARACTER 4.

personally *a.* 1 [Viewed in a personal manner] narrowly, selfishly, with concern for self; see SELFISHLY. 2 [From the point of view of the speaker] for me, myself, for myself, for my part, as I see it, according to

per·sona non grata (pər sō′nə nän grät′ə) [L] an unwelcome person

per·soni·fy (pər sän′i fī′) vt. **-fied′, -fy′ing** 1 to think of or represent (a thing) as a person 2 to typify; embody — **per·son′i·fi·ca′tion** n.

per·son·nel (pur′sə nel′) n. [Fr] 1 persons employed in any work, enterprise, service, etc. 2 a personnel department or office — adj. of or relating to the division within a business, etc. responsible for hiring and training employees, etc.

per·spec·tive (pər spek′tiv) n. [< L per, through + specere, look] 1 the art of picturing objects so as to show relative distance or depth 2 the appearance of objects as determined by their relative distance and positions 3 sense of proportion 4 a) a specific point of view in understanding things or events b) the ability to see things in a true relationship

per·spi·ca·cious (pur′spi kā′shəs) adj. [see prec.] having keen judgment; discerning —**per′spi·ca′ciously** adv. — **per′spi·cac′ity** (-kas′ə tē) n.

per·spic·u·ous (pər spik′yōō əs) adj. [see PERSPECTIVE] easily understood; lucid —**per·spi·cu·ity** (pur′spi kyōō′ə tē) n.

per·spi·ra·tion (pur′spə rā′shən) n. 1 the act of perspiring 2 sweat

per·spire (pər spīr′) vt., vi. **-spired′, -spir′ing** [< L per-, through + spirare, breathe] to sweat

per·suade (pər swād′) vt. **-suad′ed, -suad′ing** [< L per-, intens. + suadere, to urge] to cause to do something, esp. by reasoning, urging, etc.; convince —**per·suad′able** adj. —**per·suad′er** n.

per·sua·sion (pər swā′zhən) n. 1 a persuading or being persuaded 2 power of persuading 3 a strong belief 4 a particular religious belief

per·sua·sive adj. having the power, or tending, to persuade —**per·sua′sively** adv.

pert (purt) adj. [< L apertus, open] bold; impudent; saucy —**pert′ly** adv.

per·tain (pər tān′) vi. [< L per-, intens. + tenere, hold] 1 to belong; be connected or associated 2 to be appropriate 3 to have reference

per·ti·na·cious (pur′tə nā′shəs) adj. [< L per-, intens. + tenax, holding fast] 1 holding firmly to some purpose, belief, etc. 2 hard to get rid of —**per′ti·nac′ity** (-nas′ə tē) n.

per·ti·nent (pur′tə nənt, purt′'n ənt) adj. [see PERTAIN] having some connection with the matter at hand —**per′ti·nence** n.

per·turb (pər turb′) vt. [< L per-, intens. + turbare, disturb] to cause to be alarmed, agitated, or upset —**per·tur·ba·tion** (pur′tər bā′shən) n.

pe·ruke (pə rook′) n. [Fr perruque] a wig

pe·ruse (pə rooz′) vt. **-rused′, -rus′ing** [prob. < L per-, intens. + ME usen, to use] 1 to read carefully; study 2 to read in a leisurely way —**pe·rus′al** n.

per·vade (pər vād′) vt. **-vad′ed, -vad′ing** [< L per, through + vadere, go] to spread or be prevalent throughout —**per·va′sive** adj.

per·verse (pər vurs′) adj. [see PERVERT] 1 deviating from what is considered right or good 2 stubbornly contrary 3 obstinately disobedient —**per·verse′ly** adv. — **per·verse′ness** or **per·ver′sity** n.

per·ver·sion (pər vur′zhən) n. 1 a perverting or being perverted 2 something perverted 3 any sexual act or practice considered abnormal

per·vert (pər vurt′; for n. pur′vurt′) vt. [< L per-, intens. + vertere, turn] 1 to lead astray; corrupt 2 to misuse 3 to distort 4 to debase — n. one practicing sexual perversion

pe·seta (pə sāt′ə) n. [Sp, dim. of peso, peso] the monetary unit of Spain

pesky (pes′kē) adj. **-kier, -ki·est** [prob. var. of pesty] [Colloq.] annoying; troublesome —**pes′ki·ness** n.

peso (pā′sō) n., pl. **-sos′** [Sp < L pensum, something weighed] the monetary unit of: a) Chile b) Colombia c) Cuba d) Mexico, etc.

pes·si·mism (pes′ə miz′əm) n. [< L pejor, worse] 1 the belief that the evil in life outweighs the good 2 the tendency to always expect the worst —**pes′si·mist** n. —**pes′si·mis′tic** adj. —**pes′si·mis′ti·cally** adv.

pest (pest) n. [< L pestis, plague] a person or thing that is troublesome, destructive, etc.; specif., a rat, fly, weed, etc.

pes·ter (pes′tər) vt. [< OFr empestrer, entangle] to annoy; vex

pest′hole′ n. a place infested with an epidemic disease

pes·ti·cide (pes′tə sīd′) n. any chemical for killing insects, weeds, etc.

pes·tif·er·ous (pes tif′ər əs) adj. [< L pestis, plague + ferre, to bear] 1 orig., infectious or diseased 2 noxious 3 [Colloq.] annoying

pes·ti·lence (pes′tə ləns) n. 1 a deadly epidemic disease; plague 2 anything regarded as harmful

pes·ti·lent (pes′tə lənt) adj. [< L pestis, plague] 1 likely to cause death 2 dangerous to society; pernicious [the pestilent threat of war] 3 annoying

pes·tle (pes′əl) n. [< L pinsere, to pound] a tool used to pound or grind substances, esp. in a mortar

pet[1] (pet) n. [orig. Scot dial.] 1 an animal that is domesticated and kept as a companion 2 a person treated with

---

THESAURUS

my opinion; see also INDIVIDUALLY.— Ant. CERTAINLY, objectively, scientifically.

personify v. 1 [To impersonate] represent, live as, act out; see IMPERSONATE. 2 [To represent] copy, symbolize, exemplify; see REPRESENT 3.

personnel n. workers, employees, group; see STAFF 2.

perspective n. aspect, attitude, outlook; see VIEWPOINT.

perspiration n. water, exudation, beads of moisture; see SWEAT.

perspire v. secrete, exude, lather; see SWEAT.

persuade v. convince, move, induce, assure, cajole, incline, talk someone into something, win over, bring around, lead to believe, lead to do something, gain the confidence of, prevail upon, overcome another's resistance, wear down, bring a person to his senses, win an argument, make one's point, gain the confidence of, make someone see the light; see also INFLUENCE.—Ant. NEGLECT, dissuade, dampen.

persuaded a. convinced, won over, moved to, led, influenced, motivated, lured, impelled, wheedled, having succumbed to pressure, brought to see the light.

persuasion n. 1 [The act of persuading] inducing, influencing, enticing; see INFLUENCE. 2 [A belief] creed, tenet, religion; see FAITH.

persuasive a. convincing, alluring, luring, seductive, influential, winning, enticing, impelling, moving, actuating, efficient, effective, effectual, compelling, touching, forceful, potent, powerful, swaying, pointed, strong, energetic, forcible, plausible, inveigling; see also CONVINCING.

pertain v. relate to, belong to, refer to; see CONCERN 1.

pertaining to a. belonging to, appropriate to, connected with, having to do with.

pertinence n. consistency, congruity, relevance; see IMPORTANCE.

pertinent a. appropriate, suitable, related; see RELEVANT.

perturb v. pester, worry, irritate; see BOTHER 2.

perturbed a. uneasy, anxious, restless; see TROUBLED.

pervade v. suffuse, permeate, spread through; see PENETRATE.

perverse a. wayward, delinquent, capricious; see BAD 1.

perversion n. 1 [A distortion] involution, regression, abuse; see CONTORTION. 2 [Sexual deviation] corruption, debasement, depravity, wickedness, depredation, degeneration, degradation, impairment, bestiality, self-defilement, vice; see also LEWDNESS.

pervert v. ruin, vitiate, divert; see CORRUPT.

pervert n. sex maniac, sex criminal, transvestite, rapist, autoeroticist, lecher, nymphomaniac, satyr.

perverted a. distorted, deviating, corrupt; see BAD 1.

pessimism n. unhappiness, gloom, low spirits; see DEPRESSION 2, GRIEF, SADNESS.

pessimistic a. 1 [Discouraging] worrisome, troublesome, troubling; see DISMAL. 2 [Inclined to a discouraging view] hopeless, gloomy, cynical; see SAD 1.

pest n. 1 [Anything destructive] virus, germ, insect pest, bug, harmful bird, bird of prey, destructive animal. Common pests include the following: house fly, mosquito, flea, louse, mite, gnat, bedbug, tick, aphid, Japanese beetle, corn borer, boll weevil, squash bug, peach moth, gypsy moth, cutworm, pear slug, mouse, rat, gopher, prairie dog, woodchuck, groundhog, rabbit, mole, weasel, coyote, hawk. 2 [A nuisance] bore, tease, annoyance; see TROUBLE 1.

pester v. annoy, harass, provoke; see BOTHER 2.

pestilence n. epidemic, endemic, sickness; see ILLNESS 1.

pet[1] n. 1 [A term of endearment] lover, dear, love; see DARLING. 2 [Favorite] darling, idol, adored one; see FAVORITE. 3 [A creature kept as an object of affection] Common pets particular indulgence — *adj.* 1 kept or treated as a pet 2 especially liked 3 particular *[a pet peeve]* 4 showing fondness *[a pet name]* — *vt.* **pet′ted, pet′ting** to stroke or pat gently; caress — *vi.* [Colloq.] to kiss, embrace, etc., passionately in making love

pet[2] (pet) *n.* ⟦ < ? ⟧ a sulky mood

petal (pet′'l) *n.* ⟦ < Gr *petalos*, outspread ⟧ any of the leaf-like parts of a blossom

pe·tard (pi tärd′) *n.* ⟦ < Fr ⟧ an explosive device formerly used to break down doors, walls, etc. —**hoist with (or by) one's own petard** destroyed by the very thing with which one meant to destroy others

pet·cock (pet′käk′) *n.* ⟦ < L *pedere*, break wind + *cock*, valve ⟧ a small valve for draining pipes, radiators, etc.

pe·ter (pēt′ər) *vi.* ⟦ < ? ⟧ [Colloq.] to become gradually smaller, weaker, etc. and then disappear With *out*

Peter (pēt′ər) *Bible* 1 one of the twelve Apostles; reputed author of two Epistles 2 either of these Epistles

pet·i·ole (pet′ē ōl′) *n.* ⟦ < L *pes*, FOOT ⟧ the part of a leaf supporting the blade and attached to the stem

pe·tite (pə tēt′) *adj.* ⟦Fr⟧ small and trim in figure: said of a woman

pe·tit four (pet′ē fôr′) *pl.* **pe′tits fours′** or **pe·tit fours** (pet′ē fôrz′) ⟦Fr, lit., small oven⟧ a tiny, frosted cake

pe·ti·tion (pə tish′ən) *n.* ⟦ < L *petere*, seek ⟧ 1 a solemn, earnest request; entreaty 2 a formal document embodying such a request, often signed by many people 3 *Law* a written formal request asking for a specific court action — *vt.* 1 to address a petition to 2 to ask for — *vi.* to make a petition —**pe·ti′tion·er** *n.*

petit jury a group of citizens picked to decide the issues of a trial in court

pet·rel (pe′trəl) *n.* ⟦ < ? ⟧ a small sea bird with long wings

pet·ri·fy (pe′tri fī′) *vt.* **-fied′, -fy′ing** ⟦ < L *petra*, rock + *facere*, make ⟧ 1 to turn into stone 2 to harden or deaden 3 to paralyze, as with fear —**pet′ri·fac′tion** *n.*

petro- ⟦ < Gr *petra*, rock ⟧ *combining form* 1 rock or stone 2 petroleum 3 of or relating to the petroleum business

petro·chemi·cal (pe′trō kem′i kəl) *n.* a chemical with a petroleum base

pet′ro·dol′lars *n.pl.* revenue from the sale of petroleum

pet·rol (pe′trəl) *n.* ⟦ see PETROLEUM ⟧ *Brit., etc.* (exc. Cdn.) term for GASOLINE

pet·ro·la·tum (pe′trə lāt′əm) *n.* ⟦ < fol. ⟧ a greasy, jellylike substance derived from petroleum and used in ointments, etc. Also **petroleum jelly**

pe·tro·leum (pə trō′lē əm) *n.* ⟦ < L *petra*, rock + *oleum*, oil ⟧ an oily, liquid solution of hydrocarbons, occurring naturally in certain rock strata: it yields kerosene, gasoline, etc.

PET scan (pet) ⟦*p*(*ositron*) *e*(*mission*) *t*(*omography*), an X-ray technique ⟧ a diagnostic X-raying of the metabolism of the body, esp. the brain, using many single-plane X-rays (*tomograms*) and radioactive tracers

petti·coat (pet′ē kōt′, pet′i-) *n.* ⟦ < PETTY + COAT ⟧ a woman's underskirt

petti·fog·ger (pet′i fäg′ər, -fôg′-; pet′ē-) *n.* ⟦ < PETTY + *fogger* < ? ⟧ a lawyer who handles petty cases, esp. unethically —**pet′ti·fog′, -fogged′, -fog′ging,** *vi.*

pet·tish (pet′ish) *adj.* ⟦ < PET[2] ⟧ peevish; petulant —**pet′-tishly** *adv.*

petty (pet′ē) *adj.* **-tier, -ti·est** ⟦ < OFr *petit* ⟧ 1 relatively unimportant 2 small-minded; mean 3 relatively low in rank —**pet′ti·ness** *n.*

petty cash a cash fund for incidentals

petty officer *U.S. Navy* a naval enlisted person who is a noncommissioned officer

petu·lant (pech′ə lənt) *adj.* ⟦ < L *petere*, to rush at ⟧ impatient or irritable, esp. over a petty annoyance —**pet′u·lance** *n.* —**pet′u·lantly** *adv.*

pe·tu·nia (pə tōōn′yə, -ē ə) *n.* ⟦ult. < AmInd (Brazil)⟧ a plant with showy, funnel-shaped flowers

pew (pyōō) *n.* ⟦ult. < Gr *pous*, foot ⟧ any of the benches with a back that are fixed in rows in a church

pew·ter (pyōōt′ər) *n.* ⟦OFr *peautre*⟧ 1 a dull, silvery-gray alloy of tin with copper, lead, etc. 2 articles made of this

pe·yote (pā ōt′ē) *n.* ⟦AmSp < AmInd (Mexico) *peyotl*, caterpillar⟧ the cactus plant mescal See MESCALINE

PFC or **Pfc.** Private First Class

pg. page

PG *trademark for* a film rating indicating parents may find some content unsuitable for children under 17

PG-13 *trademark for* a film rating indicating parents may find some content especially unsuitable for children under 13

pH (pē′āch′) ⟦ < Fr *p*(*ouvoir*) *h*(*ydrogène*), lit., hydrogen power ⟧ a symbol for the degree of acidity or alkalinity of a solution

pha·eton or **pha·ëton** (fā′ə tən) *n.* ⟦after *Phaetōn*, son of Helios, Gr sun god⟧ 1 a light, four-wheeled carriage 2 an early type of open automobile

phago·cyte (fag′ō sit′) *n.* ⟦ < Gr *phagein*, to eat + *kytos*, hollow⟧ any cell, esp. a leukocyte, that destroys foreign matter in the blood and tissues

pha·lan·ger (fā lan′jər, fə-) *n.* ⟦ < Gr *phalanx*, bone between fingers or toes⟧ any of various small, tree-dwelling Australian marsupials, often with bushy, prehensile tails

pha·lanx (fā′laŋks′) *n., pl.* **-lanx′es** or **pha·lan·ges** (fə lan′jēz′) ⟦Gr, line of battle⟧ 1 an ancient close-ranked infantry formation 2 any massed group 3 *pl.* **-lan′ges′** any of the bones forming the fingers or toes

phal·lus (fal′əs) *n., pl.* **-li** (-lī′) or **-luses** ⟦Gr *phallos*⟧ an image of the penis —**phal′lic** *adj.*

phan·tasm (fan′taz′əm) *n.* ⟦ < Gr *phantazein*, to show⟧ 1 a figment of the mind 2 a deceptive likeness

phan·tas·ma·go·ria (fan taz′mə gôr′ē ə) *n.* ⟦ < Gr *phantasma*, phantasm + *ageirein*, assemble⟧ a rapid sequence of images, as in a dream

phan·tasy (fan′tə sē) *n., pl.* **-sies** *alt. sp. of* FANTASY

phan·tom (fan′təm) *n.* ⟦see PHANTASM⟧ 1 an apparition; specter 2 an illusion — *adj.* of or like a phantom; illusory

Phar·aoh (far′ō, fer′ō) *n.* the title of the kings of ancient Egypt

Phari·see (far′i sē′) *n.* 1 a member of an ancient Jewish group that observed both the written and oral law 2 ⟦ < characterization in NT⟧ [**p-**] a self-righteous, hypocritical person —**Phar′i·sa′ic** (-sā′ik) *adj.*

phar·ma·ceu·ti·cal (fär′mə sōōt′i kəl) *adj.* ⟦ < Gr *pharmakon*, a drug⟧ of pharmacy or drugs Also **phar′ma·ceu′tic** — *n.* a drug or medicine

phar′ma·ceu′tics (-iks) *n.pl.* [*with sing. v.*] PHARMACY (sense 1)

phar·ma·cist (fär′mə sist) *n.* one licensed to practice pharmacy

phar·ma·col·ogy (-käl′ə jē) *n.* ⟦ < Gr *pharmakon*, a drug⟧ the science dealing with the effect of drugs on living organisms —**phar′ma·col′o·gist** *n.*

phar·ma·co·pe·ia or **phar·ma·co·poe·ia** (-kō pē′ə) *n.* ⟦ < Gr *pharmakon*, a drug + *poiein*, to make⟧ an official book of drugs and medicines

phar·macy (fär′mə sē) *n., pl.* **-cies** ⟦ < Gr *pharmakon*, a drug⟧ 1 the art or profession of preparing drugs and medicines 2 a drugstore

pharyn·gi·tis (far′in jīt′is) *n.* inflammation of the pharynx

phar·ynx (far′iŋks) *n., pl.* **phar′ynxes** or **pha·ryn·ges** (fə rin′jēz′) ⟦Gr *pharynx*⟧ the cavity leading from the mouth and nasal passages to the larynx and esophagus — **pha·ryn·geal** (fə rin′jē əl) *adj.*

phase (fāz) *n.* ⟦ < Gr *phainesthai*, to appear⟧ 1 any stage in a series or cycle of changes, as of the moon's illumination 2 an aspect or side, as of a problem — *vt.* **phased, phas′ing** to introduce or carry out in stages: often with *in* or *into* —**in (or out of) phase** in (or not in) a synchronized state —**phase out** to terminate (an activity) by stages

phase′out′ *n.* a phasing out; gradual termination or withdrawal

PhD or **Ph.D.** ⟦L *Philosophiae Doctor*⟧ Doctor of Philosophy

---

THESAURUS

include the following: pony, dog, cat, horse, goldfish, rabbit, hamster, guinea pig, mouse, canary, parrot.

pet[1] *v.* 1 [To caress] fondle, cuddle, kiss; see TOUCH 1. 2 [*To make love] embrace, hug, neck*; see CARESS, KISS, LOVE 2.

petal *n.* floral leaf, flower part, leaf; see FLOWER.

petition *n.* prayer, request, supplica-tion; see APPEAL 1.

petrified *a.* stone, hardened, miner-alized; see FIRM 2.

petrify *v.* mineralize, clarify, solidify; see HARDEN.

petroleum *n.* crude oil, fuel, coal oil; see OIL.

petty *a.* small, insignificant, frivo-lous; see TRIVIAL, UNIMPORTANT.

phantom *n.* apparition, specter, shade; see GHOST.

phase *n.* condition, stage, appearance, point, aspect; see also STATE 2.

phase out *v.* slowly get rid of, gradually dispose of, weed out*; see ELIMI-NATE.

pheas·ant (fez′ənt) *n.* 〚< Gr *phasianos*, (bird) of *Phasis*, river in Asia 〛 a large game bird with a long, sweeping tail and brilliant feathers

phenac·etin (fə nas′ə tin′, -tən; fi-) *n.* a white, crystalline powder used to reduce fever, relieve headaches, etc.

pheno·bar·bi·tal (fē′nō bär′bi tôl′) *n.* an odorless, white, crystalline powder, used as a sedative

phe·nol (fē′nōl′, -nôl′, -näl′) *n.* a white crystalline compound, corrosive and poisonous, used to make synthetic resins, etc. and, in dilute solution (*carbolic acid*) as an antiseptic

phenol·phthal·ein (fē′nōl thal′ēn′, -ē in) *n.* a white to pale-yellow, crystalline powder, used as a laxative, as an acid-base indicator in chemical analysis, etc.

phe·nom (fē′näm′) *n.* [Slang] one who is very talented or skilled, esp. a star in sports or popular music

phe·nom·enon (fə näm′ə nən′, -nän) *n., pl.* **-na** (-nə); also, esp. for 2 and usually for 3, **-nons** 〚< Gr *phainesthai*, appear 〛 1 any observable fact or event that can be scientifically described 2 anything very unusual 3 [Colloq.] an extraordinary person; prodigy —**phe·nom′enal** *adj.*

phero·mone (fer′ə mōn′) *n.* 〚< Gr *pherein*, to bear + (HOR)MONE 〛 a chemical substance secreted by certain animals, as ants, which conveys information to others of the same species

phi (fi, fē) *n.* the 21st letter of the Greek alphabet (Φ, φ)

phial (fī′əl) *n.* 〚< Gr *phialē*, shallow bowl 〛 a small glass bottle; vial

Phila·del·phia lawyer (fil′ə del′fē ə, -fyə) [Colloq.] a shrewd or tricky lawyer

phi·lan·der (fi lan′dər, fə-) *vi.* 〚< Gr *philos*, loving + *anēr*, man 〛 to engage lightly in love affairs: said of a man —**phi·lan′derer** *n.*

phi·lan·thropy (fə lan′thrə pē, fi-; -thrō-) *n.* 〚< Gr *philein*, to love + *anthrōpos*, man 〛 1 a desire to help mankind, esp. as shown by endowments to institutions, etc. 2 *pl.* **-pies** a philanthropic gift, institution, etc. —**phil·an·thropic** (fil′ən thräp′ik) *adj.* —**phi·lan′thro·pist** *n.*

phi·lat·ely (fə lat′′l ē, fi-) *n.* 〚< Fr < Gr *philos*, loving + *ateleia*, exemption from (further) tax (meaning "postage prepaid") 〛 the collection and study of postage stamps, postmarks, etc. —**phi·lat′elist** *n.*

-phile (fīl, fil) 〚< Gr *philos*, loving 〛 *combining form* one that loves, likes, etc. *[bibliophile]*

phil·har·monic (fil′här män′ik) *adj.* 〚< Gr *philos*, loving + *harmonia*, harmony 〛 devoted to music — *n.* 1 a society sponsoring a symphony orchestra 2 [Colloq.] such an orchestra

phi·lip·pic (fi lip′ik) *n.* 〚< Gr *Philippos*, Philip, Macedonian king denounced by Demosthenes 〛 a bitter verbal attack

Phil·ip·pine (fil′ə pēn′) *adj.* of the Philippine Islands or their people

Phil·is·tine (fi lis′tin, -tēn′; fə-; fil′is-; *also*, -tīn′) *n.* 1 any of a non-Semitic people of SW Palestine in Biblical times 2 [*often* p-] a person smugly conventional, narrow, lacking culture, etc.

Phil·lips (fil′ips) [after H. F. Phillips (?-1958), its U.S. developer 〛 *trademark* for a screwdriver (**Phillips screwdriver**) with a cross-shaped, pointed tip

philo- 〚< Gr *philos*, loving 〛 *combining form* loving, liking

philo·den·dron (fil′ō den′drən, fil′ə-) *n.* 〚< Gr *philos*, loving + *dendron*, tree 〛 a tropical American vine

phi·lol·ogy (fi läl′ə jē) *n.* 〚< Gr *philein*, to love + *logos*, word 〛 *old term for* LINGUISTICS —**philo·logi·cal** (fil′ō läj′i kəl, fil′ə-) *adj.* —**phi·lol′o·gist** *n.*

phi·loso·pher (fi läs′ə fər) *n.* 〚< Gr *philos*, loving + *sophos*, wise 〛 1 one who is learned in philosophy 2 one who lives by or expounds a system of philosophy 3 one who meets difficulties with calm composure

philo·sophic (fil′ō säf′ik, fil′ə-) *adj.* 1 of philosophy or philosophers 2 sensibly composed or calm Also **phil′o·soph′i·cal**

phi·loso·phize (fə läs′ə fīz′) *vi.* **-phized′, -phiz′ing** 1 to think or reason like a philosopher 2 to moralize, express truisms, etc.

phi·loso·phy (fə läs′ə fē) *n., pl.* **-phies** 〚see PHILOSOPHER 〛 1 the study of the principles underlying conduct, thought, and the nature of the universe 2 the general principles or laws of a field of knowledge 3 a particular system of ethics 4 composure; calmness

phil·ter (fil′tər) *n.* 〚< Gr *philein*, to love 〛 a magic potion, esp. one to arouse sexual love Also [Chiefly Brit.] **phil′tre** (-tər)

phle·bi·tis (flē bīt′is, fli-) *n.* 〚< Gr *phleps*, vein + -ITIS 〛 inflammation of a vein

phlegm (flem) *n.* 〚< Gr *phlegma*, inflammation 〛 1 thick mucus discharged from the throat, as during a cold 2 sluggishness or apathy

phleg·matic (fleg mat′ik) *adj.* 〚see prec. 〛 sluggish or unexcited —**phleg·mat′i·cally** *adv.*

phloem (flō′em′) *n.* 〚< Gr *phloos*, bark 〛 the vascular tissue through which food is distributed in a plant

phlox (fläks) *n.* 〚Gr, lit., a flame 〛 a North American plant with clusters of white, pink, or bluish flowers

-phobe (fōb) 〚< Gr *phobos*, fear 〛 *combining form* one who fears or hates

pho·bia (fō′bē ə) *n.* 〚see prec. 〛 an irrational, excessive, and persistent fear of some thing or situation

-phobia (fō′bē ə, fō′byə) 〚Gr *-phobia* < *phobos*, fear 〛 *combining form* fear, dread, hatred *[claustrophobia]*

phoebe (fē′bē) *n.* 〚echoic, with sp. after *Phoebe*, Gr goddess of the moon 〛 an American bird with a grayish or brown back that catches insects in flight

phoe·nix (fē′niks) 〚< Gr *phoinix*〛 *Egypt. Myth.* a bird which lives for 500 years and then sets itself on fire, rising renewed from the ashes

phone (fōn) *n., vt., vi.* **phoned, phon′ing** [Colloq] *short for* TELEPHONE

-phone (fōn) 〚< Gr *phōnē*, a sound 〛 *combining form* 1 a device producing or transmitting sound 2 telephone

pho·neme (fō′nēm′) *n.* 〚< Fr < Gr *phōnē*, voice 〛 *Linguistics* a set of language sounds with slight variations but heard as the same sound by native speakers —**pho·nemic** (fō nē′mik, fə-) *adj.*

pho·net·ics (fō net′iks, fə-) *n.pl.* 〚< Gr *phōnē*, a sound 〛 [*with sing. v.*] the study of the production and written representation of speech sounds —**pho·net′ic** *adj.* —**pho·neti·cian** (fō′nə tish′ən) *n.*

phon·ics (fän′iks) *n.pl.* 〚< Gr *phōnē*, sound 〛 [*with sing. v.*] a phonetic method of teaching reading —**phon′ic** *adj.* —**phon′i·cally** *adv.*

phono- 〚< Gr *phōnē*, a sound 〛 *combining form* sound, tone, speech *[phonology]*

pho·no·graph (fō′nə graf′) *n.* 〚prec. + -GRAPH 〛 a device for reproducing sound recorded in a spiral groove on a revolving disk —**pho′no·graph′ic** *adj.*

pho·nol·ogy (fō näl′ə jē, fə-) *n.* [PHONO- + -LOGY 〛 1 the

THESAURUS

phenomenal *a.* extraordinary, unique, remarkable; see UNUSUAL 1.

phenomenon *n.* aspect, appearance, happening; see EVENT.

philanthropic *a.* kindhearted, benevolent, humanitarian; see HUMANE, KIND.

philosopher *n.* logician, wise man, sage, savant, Sophist, Solon. *Major philosophers include the following:* Epicurus, Plato, Aristotle, Marcus Aurelius, St. Augustine, St. Thomas Aquinas, Thomas Hobbes, John Locke, Immanuel Kant, John Stuart Mill, Friedrich Schiller, Jean Jacques Rousseau, Arthur Schopenhauer, G.W.F. Hegel, Soren Kierkegaard, Friedrich Nietzsche, William James, Karl Marx, Ernst Cassirer, Jean-Paul Sartre.

philosophical *a.* 1 [Given to thought] reflective, cogitative, rational; see THOUGHTFUL 1. 2 [Embodying deep thought] erudite, thoughtful, deep; see LEARNED 1, PROFOUND.

philosophize *v.* ponder, weigh, deliberate; see THINK 1.

philosophy *n.* 1 [The study of knowledge] theory, reasoned doctrine, explanation of phenomena, logical concept, systematic view, theory of knowledge, early science, natural philosophy; see also KNOWLEDGE 1. *Fields of philosophy include the following:* aesthetics, logic, ethics, metaphysics, epistemology, psychology, axiology, ontology, teleology. *Philosophic attitudes include the following:* idealism, realism, existential-ism, nihilism, transcendentalism, mechanism, naturalism, determinism, natural realism, intuitionism, utilitarianism, nominalism, conceptualism, pragmatism, Kantianism, Hegelianism, absolutism, logical positivism. 2 [A fundamental principle] truth, axiom, conception; see BASIS, LAW 4, THEORY 1. 3 [A personal attitude or belief] outlook, view, position; see BELIEF, OPINION 1, VIEWPOINT.

phlegm *n.* spittle, discharge, spit; see SALIVA.

phobia *n.* fear, neurosis, aversion; see HATRED, RESENTMENT.

phone *n.* pay phone, home phone, wall phone, desk phone, car phone, cellular phone, fax; see also TELEPHONE.

study of speech sounds **2** a description of the sounds of a given language —**pho·no·log·i·cal** (-nō läj'i kəl, -nə-) *adj.* —**pho·nol'o·gist** *n.*

phony (fō'nē) *adj.* **-nier, -ni·est** ⟦< Brit thieves' argot *fawney,* gilt ring⟧ [Colloq.] not genuine; false — *n., pl.* **-nies** [Colloq.] something or someone not genuine; fraud; fake Also sp. **phoney** —**pho'ni·ness** *n.*

phooey (fōō'ē) *interj.* ⟦echoic⟧ an exclamation of scorn, disgust, etc.

phos·phate (fäs'fāt) *n.* ⟦Fr⟧ **1** a salt or ester of phosphoric acid **2** a fertilizer containing phosphates **3** a flavored carbonated beverage

phos·phor (fäs'fər, -fôr') *n.* ⟦see PHOSPHORUS⟧ a phosphorescent or fluorescent substance

phos·pho·res·cence (fäs'fə res'əns) *n.* **1** the property of giving off a lingering emission of light after exposure to radiant energy, as light **2** a continuing luminescence without noticeable heat, as from oxidizing phosphorus —**phos'pho·res'cent** *adj.*

phosphoric acid any of three colorless, crystalline acids with a phosphorus and oxygen radical

phos·pho·rus (fäs'fə rəs) *n.* ⟦< Gr *phōs,* a light + *pherein,* to bear⟧ a nonmetallic chemical element: a waxy solid that ignites spontaneously at room temperature

photo (fōt'ō) *n., pl.* **-tos** *short for* PHOTOGRAPH

photo- *combining form* **1** ⟦< Gr *phōs,* a light⟧ of or produced by light **2** ⟦< PHOTOGRAPH⟧ of photography

photo·copy (fōt'ō käp'ē) *n., pl.* **-ies** a photographic reproduction, as of a book page, made by a special device (**pho'to·cop'i·er**)

photo·elec·tric cell (fōt'ō ē lek'trik) any device in which light controls an electric circuit which operates a mechanical device, as for opening doors

pho'to·en·grav'ing *n.* **1** a process by which photographs are reproduced on relief printing plates **2** such a plate, or a print made from it —**pho'to·en·grave', -graved', -grav'ing,** *vt.* —**pho'to·en·grav'er** *n.*

photo finish a race finish so close that the winner can be determined only from a photograph of the finish

photo·fin·ish·ing (fōt'ō fin'ish iŋ) *n.* the process of developing photographic film, making prints, etc.

photo·flash (fōt'ō flash', fōt'ə-) *adj.* designating a flashbulb, etc. electrically synchronized with the camera shutter

photo·genic (fōt'ō jen'ik, fōt'ə-) *adj.* ⟦PHOTO- + *-genic,* suitable for⟧ likely to look attractive in photographs

photo·graph (fōt'ə graf') *n.* a picture made by photography — *vt.* to take a photograph of — *vi.* ₃o appear (as specified) in photographs —**pho·tog·ra·pher** (fə täg'rə fər) *n.*

pho·tog·ra·phy (fə täg'rə fē) *n.* ⟦PHOTO- + -GRAPHY⟧ the art or process of producing pictorial images on a surface sensitive to light or other radiant energy, as on film in a camera —**photo·graphic** (fōt'ə graf'ik) *adj.* —**pho'to·graph'i·cal·ly** *adv.*

pho·ton (fō'tän') *n.* ⟦PHOT(O)- + (ELECTR)ON⟧ a quantum of electromagnetic energy

photo-offset (fōt'ō ôf'set') *n.* offset printing in which the text or pictures are photographically transferred to a

metal plate from which inked impressions are made on the roller

Photo·stat (fōt'ō stat', fōt'ə-) *trademark for* a device for making photocopies on special paper — *n.* [p-] a copy so made — *vt.* **-stat'ed** or **-stat'ted, -stat'ing** or **-stat'ting** [p-] to make a photostat of —**pho'to·stat'ic** *adj.*

photo·syn·thesis (fōt'ō sin'thə sis, fōt'ə-) *n.* production of organic substances, esp. sugars, from carbon dioxide and water by the action of light on the chlorophyll in green plant cells

pho'to·syn'thesize' (-sīz') *vi., vt.* **-sized', -siz'ing** to carry on, or produce by, photosynthesis

phrase (frāz) *n.* ⟦< Gr *phrazein,* speak⟧ **1** a short, colorful expression **2** a group of words, not a full sentence or clause, conveying a single thought **3** a short, distinct musical passage — *vt., vi.* **phrased, phras'ing** to express in words or in a phrase —**phrasal** (frā'zəl) *adj.*

phra·seol·ogy (frā'zē äl'ə jē) *n., pl.* **-gies** choice and pattern of words

phre·net·ic (fri net'ik) *adj.* ⟦< Gr *phrenētikos,* mad⟧ *archaic sp. of* FRENETIC

phre·nol·ogy (fri näl'ə jē, frə-) *n.* ⟦< Gr *phrēn,* mind + -LOGY⟧ a system, now rejected, analyzing character from the shape of the skull

phy·lac·tery (fi lak'tər ē) *n., pl.* **-ies** ⟦< Gr *phylaktērion,* safeguard⟧ either of two small, leather cases holding Scripture texts, worn in prayer on the forehead and arm by orthodox Jewish men

phyllo (fē'lō, fī'-) *n.* ⟦< Gr *phyllon,* leaf⟧ dough in very thin sheets, becoming very flaky when baked

phy·log·eny (fi läj'ə nē) *n., pl.* **-nies** ⟦< Gr *phylon,* tribe + *-geneia,* origin⟧ the origin and evolution of a group or race of animals or plants

phy·lum (fī'ləm) *n., pl.* **-la** (-lə) ⟦< Gr *phylon,* tribe⟧ a main division of the animal kingdom or, loosely, of a plant division

physic (fiz'ik) *n.* ⟦< Gr *physis,* nature⟧ a medicine, esp. a cathartic — *vt.* **-icked, -ick·ing** to dose with this

physi·cal (fiz'i kəl) *adj.* **1** of nature and all matter; material **2** of or according to the laws of nature **3** of, or produced by the forces of, physics **4** of the body — *n.* a general medical examination —**phys'i·cally** *adv.*

physical anthropology a major division of anthropology that deals with the physical characteristics and evolution of humans

physical education instruction in the exercise and care of the body, including sports, calisthenics, and hygiene

physical science any science dealing with nonliving matter or energy, as physics, chemistry, or astronomy

physical therapy the treatment of disease, injury, etc. by physical means, as by exercise, massage, etc.

phy·si·cian (fi zish'ən) *n.* ⟦see PHYSIC⟧ a doctor of medicine

phys·ics (fiz'iks) *n.pl.* ⟦see PHYSIC⟧ [*with sing. v.*] the science dealing with the properties, changes, interactions, etc. of matter and energy —**phys'i·cist** (-ə sist) *n.*

physi·og·nomy (fiz'ē äg'nə mē) *n.* ⟦< Gr *physis,* nature + *gnōmōn,* judge⟧ facial features and expression

phys'i·og'ra·phy (-äg'rə fē) *n.* ⟦see prec. & -GRAPHY⟧ the study of the earth's surface and oceans, atmosphere, etc.

phys'i·ol'ogy (-äl'ə jē) *n.* ⟦< Gr *physis,* nature + -LOGY⟧ the science dealing with the functions and vital processes

---

THESAURUS

phony * *a.* counterfeit, imitation, artificial; see FALSE 3.

photograph *n.* photo, print, portrait, image, likeness, snapshot, microcopy, microfilm, radiograph, X-ray, photomontage, photomural, shot, pic*, close-up, candid; see also PICTURE 2, 3.

photograph *v.* take a picture, get a likeness, film, snapshot, copy, reproduce, illustrate, make an exposure, make a picture, catch a likeness, get a film, record, make a moving picture of, microfilm, snap, shoot, get a close-up.

photographer *n.* picture-taker, cameraman, cinematographer; see ARTIST.

photographic *a.* **1** [Of photography] camera, video, film, cinematographic. **2** [Precise] accurate, detailed, exact; see GRAPHIC 1.

photography *n.* picture-taking, portrait photography, view photogra-

phy, aerial photography, tactical photography, candid camera photography, microphotography, photomicrography, videotaping.

phrase *n.* group of words, expression, slogan, catchword, maxim, word group. *Grammatical phrases include the following:* prepositional, gerund, gerundive, participial, infinitive, noun, adjective, adjectival, adverbial, conjunctive, absolute, attributive.

phraseology *n.* style, manner, idiom; see DICTION.

physical *a.* **1** [Concerning matter] material, corporeal, visible, tangible, environmental, palpable, substantial, natural, sensible, concrete, materialistic; see also REAL 2. **2** [Concerning the body] corporal, corporeal, fleshly; see BODILY. **3** [Concerning physics] mechanical, motive, electrical, sonic, vibratory, vibrational, thermal, radioactive, atomic, relating to mat-

ter, dynamic.

physical *n.* medical checkup, health examination, exam, checkup.

physically *a.* corporally, really, actually; see BODILY.

physician *n.* practitioner, doctor of medicine, surgeon; see DOCTOR.

physicist *n.* biophysicist, geophysicist, nuclear physicist; see SCIENTIST.

physics *n.* natural philosophy, science of the material world, science of matter and motion; see SCIENCE 1. *Divisions of physics include the following:* heat, light, electricity, electronics, sound, mechanics, dynamics, kinetics, atomic structure, radiant energy, spectroscopy, supersonics, hydraulics, pneumatics, aerodynamics, engineering.

physiology *n.* anatomy, study of organic functions, biology; see SCIENCE 1.

of living organisms —**phys'io·log'i·cal** (-ō läj'i kəl) *adj.* —**phys'i·ol'o·gist** *n.*

physio·thera·py (fiz'ē ō'ther'ə pē) *n.* PHYSICAL THERAPY —**phys'io·ther'a·pist** *n.*

phy·sique (fi zēk') *n.* ⟦Fr⟧ the structure or form of the body; build

pi¹ (pī) *n., pl.* **pies** ⟦see PIE⟧ 1 jumbled printing type 2 any jumble — *vt.* **pied, pie'ing** or **pi'ing** to jumble

pi² (pī) *n.* 1 the 16th letter of the Greek alphabet (Π, π) 2 the symbol (π) designating the ratio of the circumference of a circle to its diameter, about 3.1416

pia·nis·simo (pē'ə nis'i mō') *adj., adv.* ⟦It⟧ *Musical Direction* very soft

pi·an·ist (pē'ə nist, pē an'ist, pyan'ist) *n.* one who plays the piano

pi·ano¹ (pē an'ō, pyan'ō) *adj., adv.* ⟦It⟧ *Musical Direction* soft

pia·no² (pē ä'nō, pyä'-) *n., pl.* **-nos** ⟦< fol.⟧ a large, stringed keyboard instrument: each key operates a felt-covered hammer that strikes a corresponding steel wire or wires

pi·ano·forte (pē an'ō fôrt', -an'ō fôrt'ē) *n.* ⟦It < *piano*, soft + *forte*, loud⟧ PIANO²

pi·as·ter (pē as'tər) *n.* ⟦ult. < L *emplastrum*, plaster⟧ one 100th of a pound in Egypt, Lebanon, Syria, and Sudan Brit., etc. sp. **pi·as'tre**

pi·azza (pē ät'sə, -sä'; *for 2* pē az'ə) *n., pl.* **-zas** or It. **-ze** (-tse) 1 in Italy, a public square 2 a large, covered porch

pi·broch (pē'bräk') *n.* ⟦< Gael *piob*, bagpipe⟧ music for the bagpipe, usually of a martial kind

pica (pī'kə) *n.* ⟦< ? ML, a directory⟧ a size of printing type, 12 point

pica·resque (pik'ə resk') *adj.* ⟦< Sp *pícaro*, rascal⟧ dealing with sharp-witted vagabonds or rogues and their adventures *[a picaresque novel]*

pica·yune (pik'ə yōōn', pik'ə yōōn') *adj.* ⟦< Fr *picaillon*, small coin⟧ trivial or petty

pic·ca·lilli (pik'ə lil'ē) *n.* ⟦prob. < PICKLE⟧ a relish, of chopped vegetables, mustard, and hot spices

pic·colo (pik'ə lō') *n., pl.* **-los** ⟦It, small⟧ a small flute, pitched an octave above the ordinary flute

pick¹ (pik) *n.* ⟦OE *pic*, PIKE²⟧ 1 any of several pointed tools or instruments used for picking, esp. a heavy one used in breaking up soil, rock, etc. 2 PLECTRUM

pick² (pik) *vt.* ⟦ME *picken*⟧ 1 to pierce, dig up, etc. with something pointed 2 to probe, scratch at, etc. so as to remove or clear something from 3 to gather (flowers, berries, etc.) 4 to prepare (a fowl) by removing the feathers 5 to pull (fibers, rags, etc.) apart 6 to choose; select 7 to provoke (a quarrel or fight) 8 to pluck (the strings) of (a guitar, etc.) 9 to open (a lock) with a wire, etc. instead of a key 10 to steal from (another's pocket, etc.) — *vi.* 1 to use a pick 2 to select, esp. in a fussy way — *n.* 1 the act of choosing or the choice made 2 the best —**pick at** to eat sparingly of —**pick off** 1 to remove by picking 2 to hit

with a carefully aimed shot —**pick on** [Colloq.] to single out for criticism or abuse; annoy; tease —**pick out** to choose —**pick up** 1 to grasp and lift 2 to get, find, or learn, esp. by chance 3 to stop for and take along 4 to gain (speed) 5 to improve 6 [Colloq.] to become acquainted with casually, esp. for lovemaking —**pick'er** *n.*

picka·back (pik'ə bak') *adv., adj., vt.* PIGGYBACK

pick·ax or **pick·axe** (pik'aks') *n.* ⟦< OFr *picquois*⟧ a pick with a point at one end of the head and a chisel-like edge at the other

pick·erel (pik'ər əl) *n., pl.* **-el** or **-els** ⟦< PIKE³⟧ any of various small, North American freshwater fishes

picket (pik'it) *n.* ⟦< Fr *pic*, PIKE²⟧ 1 a pointed stake used in a fence, as a hitching post, etc. 2 a soldier or soldiers stationed to guard against surprise attack 3 a person, as a member of a striking labor union, stationed outside a factory, etc. to demonstrate, keep workers out, etc. — *vt.* 1 to enclose with a picket fence 2 to hitch (an animal) to a picket 3 to post as a military picket 4 to place pickets, or serve as a picket, at (a factory, etc.)

picket line a line or cordon of people serving as pickets

pick'ings *n.pl.* something picked; specif., *a)* scraps; remains *b)* something got by effort, often dishonestly

pickle (pik'əl) *n.* ⟦< MDu *pekel*⟧ 1 any brine, vinegar, etc. used to preserve or marinate food 2 a vegetable, specif. a cucumber, preserved in this 3 [Colloq.] an awkward situation — *vt.* **-led, -ling** to put in or preserve in a pickle solution

pick'pock'et *n.* a thief who steals from pockets, as in a crowd

pick'up' *n.* 1 a picking up 2 the process or power of increasing in speed 3 a small, open delivery truck 4 [Colloq.] a casual acquaintance 5 [Colloq.] improvement 6 *a)* a device for producing electric currents from the vibrations of a phonograph needle *b)* the pivoted arm holding this device

picky (pik'ē) *adj.* **-i·er, -i·est** [Colloq.] overly fastidious; fussy

pic·nic (pik'nik) *n.* ⟦< Fr⟧ a pleasure outing at which a meal is eaten outdoors — *vi.* **-nicked, -nick·ing** to have a picnic —**pic'nick·er** *n.*

pi·cot (pē'kō) *n., pl.* **-cots** ⟦< Fr *pic*, a point⟧ any of the small loops forming a fancy edge as on lace

pic·to·graph (pik'tō graf', -tə-) *n.* 1 a picture or picture-like symbol used in a system of writing 2 a graph using pictures to give data

pic·to·rial (pik tôr'ē əl) *adj.* 1 of, containing, or expressed in pictures 2 suggesting a mental image; vivid —**pic·to'ri·ally** *adv.*

pic·ture (pik'chər) *n.* ⟦< L *pingere*, to paint⟧ 1 a likeness of a person, scene, etc. produced by drawing, painting, photography, etc. 2 a perfect likeness or image *[the pic-*

═══ **THESAURUS** ═══

physique *n.* build, structure, frame; see BODY 1.

pianist *n.* performer, piano player, virtuoso; see MUSICIAN.

piano² *n.* grand, baby grand, upright, cabinet, pianoforte, concert grand, spinet, clavichord, harpsichord, keyboard, electric piano, player piano; see also MUSICAL INSTRUMENT.

picayune *a.* trivial, petty, small; see TRIVIAL, UNIMPORTANT.

pick¹,² *n.* 1 [An implement for picking] pickax, mattock, ice pick; see TOOL 1. 2 [A blow with a pointed instrument] peck, nip, dent; see BLOW. 3 [A selection] choice, election, preference; see CHOICE.

pick¹,² *v.* 1 [To choose] select, pick out, separate; see CHOOSE. 2 [To gather] pluck, pull, choose; see ACCUMULATE. 3 [To use a pointed instrument] dent, indent, strike; see HIT 1. —**pick a fight** provoke, start, foment; see FIGHT. —**pick off** snipe, get, shoot; see KILL 1. —**pick out** select, make a choice of, notice; see CHOOSE. —**pick up** 1 [To acquire incidentally] happen upon, find, secure; see GET 1. 2 [To take up in the hand or arms] lift, elevate, hold up; see RAISE 1. 3 [To receive] get, take, acquire; see RECEIVE 1. 4 [To

increase] improve, do better, grow; see INCREASE. 5 [To improve physically] get better, get well, recover health; see RECOVER 3. 6 [*To call for] stop for, bring along, go to get, accompany, get, invite; see also INVITE.

picked *a.* elite, special, exclusive; see EXCELLENT.

picket *n.* 1 [A stake] stake, pole, pillar; see POST. 2 [A watchman] patrolman, guard, security person, scout, lookout, sentry.

picket *v.* 1 [To strike] walk out, blockade, boycott; see STRIKE 2. 2 [To enclose] imprison, fence, corral; see ENCLOSE.

pickings *n.* profits, earnings, proceeds; see BOOTY.

pickle *n.* 1 [A relish] *Varieties of pickles include the following:* cucumber, beet, green tomato, dill, bread-and-butter, sweet, gherkin, kosher, mustard, garlic, sour, pickled peppers, pickled beans, pickled apricots, pickled cherries, pickled peaches, pickled pears, piccalilli, chutney, spiced currants, spiced gooseberries, beet relish, chili sauce, catsup. 2 [*A troublesome situation] disorder, dilemma, evil plight; see DIFFICULTY 2.

pickpocket *n.* petty criminal, thief, purse snatcher; see CRIMINAL, ROBBER.

picnic *n.* barbecue, cookout, fish fry; see MEAL 2.

pictorial *a.* 1 [Having the quality of a picture] graphic, scenic, striking; see GRAPHIC 1. 2 [Making use of pictures] decorated, embellished, illustrated.

picture *n.* 1 [A scene before the eye or the imagination] spectacle, panorama, pageant; see VIEW. 2 [A human likeness] portrait, representation, photo, photograph, snapshot, cartoon, image, effigy, statue, statuette, figure, icon, figurine, close-up. 3 [A pictorial representation] illustration, engraving, etching, woodcut, cut, outline, cartoon, draft, hologram, fax, graph, halftone, still, ad*, crayon sketch, pastel, watercolor, poster, oil, chart, map, plot, mosaic, blueprint, advertisement, facsimile, animation, tracing, photograph, lithograph, print; see also DESIGN, DRAWING, PAINTING 1. *Types of pictures, as works of art, include the following:* landscape, seascape, genre painting, cityscape, historical work, religious work, battle scene, triumphal entry, detail, icon, illumination,

465   **physiotherapy / picture**

ture of health/ **3** anything suggestive of a beautiful painting, drawing, etc. **4** a vivid description **5** FILM (*n.* 4) **6** the image on a TV screen — *vt.* **-tured, -tur·ing 1** to make a picture of **2** to show visibly **3** to describe **4** to imagine — **in** (or **out of**) **the picture** considered (or not considered) as involved in a situation

pic′tur·esque′ (-chər esk′) *adj.* like or suggesting a picture; beautiful, vivid, quaint, etc.

picture tube a cathode-ray tube in a TV receiver, monitor, etc., that produces visual images on its screen

picture window a large window that seems to frame the outside view

pid·dle (pid′'l) *vi., vt.* **-dled, -dling** ⟦< ?⟧ to dawdle; trifle

pid·dling (pid′liŋ) *adj.* insignificant; trifling

pid·dly (pid′lē, pid′'lē) *adj.* PIDDLING

pidg·in (pij′in) *n.* ⟦supposed Chin pronunciation of **business**⟧ a jargon for trade purposes, using words and grammar from different languages: **pidgin English** uses English words and Chinese or Melanesian syntax

pie (pī) *n.* ⟦ME⟧ a baked dish of fruit, meat, etc. with an under crust or upper crust, or both — **(as) easy as pie** [Colloq.] extremely easy

pie·bald (pī′bôld′) *adj.* ⟦< *pie*, magpie + BALD⟧ covered with patches of two colors — *n.* a piebald horse, etc.

piece (pēs) *n.* ⟦OFr *pece*⟧ **1** a part broken or separated from the whole **2** a section of a whole regarded as complete in itself **3** any single thing, specimen, example, etc. [a *piece* of music] **4** a quantity, as of cloth, manufactured as a unit — *vt.* **pieced, piec′ing 1** to add pieces to, as in repairing **2** to join (*together*) the pieces of — **go to pieces 1** to fall apart **2** to lose self-control

pièce de ré·sis·tance (pyes də rā zēs täns′) ⟦Fr, piece of resistance⟧ **1** the principal dish of a meal **2** the main item in a series

piece goods YARD GOODS

piece′meal′ (-mēl′) *adv.* ⟦< ME *pece*, a piece + *-mele*, part⟧ piece by piece — *adj.* made or done piecemeal

piece′work′ *n.* work paid for at a fixed rate (**piece rate**) per piece of work done

pie chart a graph in the form of a circle divided into sectors in which relative quantities are indicated by the sizes of the sectors

pied (pīd) *adj.* ⟦< *pie*, magpie⟧ spotted with various colors

pie′-eyed′ *adj.* [Slang] intoxicated

pier (pir) *n.* ⟦< ML *pera*⟧ **1** a structure supporting the spans of a bridge **2** a structure built out over the water and supported by pillars: used as a landing place, pavilion, etc. **3** *Archit.* a heavy column used to support weight

pierce (pirs) *vt.* **pierced, pierc′ing** ⟦< OFr *percer*⟧ **1** to pass into or through as a pointed instrument does; stab **2** to make a hole in **3** to force a way into; break through **4** to sound sharply through **5** to penetrate with the sight or mind — *vi.* to penetrate

pi·ety (pī′ə tē) *n., pl.* **-ties** ⟦< L *pius*, pious⟧ **1** devotion to religious duties, etc. **2** devotion to parents, family, etc. **3** a pious act

pif·fle (pif′əl) *n.* [Colloq.] anything regarded as insignificant or nonsensical — **pif·fling** (pif′liŋ) *adj.*

pig (pig) *n.* ⟦ME *pigge*⟧ **1** any swine, esp. the unweaned young of the thick-bodied domesticated species; hog **2** a greedy or filthy person

pi·geon (pij′ən) *n.* ⟦< L *pipire*, to chirp⟧ any of various related birds with a small head, plump body, and short legs

pi′geon·hole′ *n.* a small open compartment, as in a desk, for filing papers — *vt.* **-holed′, -hol′ing 1** to put in the pigeonhole of a desk, etc. **2** to put aside indefinitely **3** to classify

pi′geon-toed′ (-tōd′) *adj.* having the toes or feet turned in

pig·gish (pig′ish) *adj.* like a pig; gluttonous or filthy — **pig′gish·ness** *n.*

pig·gy (pig′ē) *n., pl.* **-gies** a little pig — *adj.* **-gier, -gi·est** PIGGISH

pig′gy·back′ *adv., adj.* **1** on the shoulders or back **2** of or by a transportation system in which truck trailers are carried on flatcars

pig′head′ed *adj.* stubborn

pig iron crude iron, as it comes from the blast furnace

pig·ment (pig′mənt) *n.* ⟦< L *pingere*, to paint⟧ **1** coloring matter used to make paints **2** any coloring matter in the tissues of plants or animals

pig·men·ta·tion (pig′mən tā′shən) *n.* coloration in plants or animals due to pigment in the tissue

Pigmy (pig′mē) *adj., n., pl.* **-mies** PYGMY

pig′pen′ *n.* a pen where pigs are kept Also **pig′sty′** (-stī′), *pl.* **-sties′**

pig′skin′ *n.* **1** leather made from the skin of a pig **2** [Colloq.] a football

pig′tail′ (-tāl′) *n.* a long braid of hair hanging at the back of the head

pike¹ (pīk) *n.* [Colloq.] a highway: now chiefly in **come down the pike**, to happen or appear

pike² (pīk) *n.* ⟦Fr *pique*⟧ a former weapon consisting of a metal spearhead on a long wooden shaft (**pikestaff**)

pike³ (pīk) *n.* ⟦ME *pik*⟧ a slender, freshwater fish with a pointed head

pik·er (pīk′ər) *n.* ⟦< ? *Pike* County, Missouri⟧ [Slang] a person who does things in a petty or niggardly way

pi·laf or **pi·laff** (pi läf′, pē′läf′) *n.* ⟦Pers *pilāv*⟧ rice boiled in a seasoned liquid, and usually containing meat or fish Also **pi·lau′** (-lô′)

pi·las·ter (pi las′tər) *n.* ⟦< L *pila*, a pile⟧ a supporting column projecting partially from a wall

pil·chard (pil′chərd) *n.* ⟦< ?⟧ **1** a small, oily, marine fish, the commercial sardine of W Europe **2** any of several related fishes; esp., the **Pacific sardine** found off the W coast of the U.S.

pile¹ (pīl) *n.* ⟦< L *pila*, pillar⟧ **1** a mass of things heaped together **2** a heap of wood, etc. on which a corpse or sacrifice is burned **3** a large building **4** [Colloq.] a large

---

THESAURUS

miniature, portrait, illustration, self-portrait, nude, fresco, mural, collage, pin-up, figure, still life, center spread, animal picture, hunting print, fashion plate, photomural, poster, photomontage. **4** [A motion picture] cinema, film, show; see MOVIE. **5** [A description] depiction, delineation, portrayal; see DESCRIPTION. **6** [Adequate comprehension; *usually with "the"*] the idea, understanding, survey; see KNOWLEDGE 1.

picture *v.* **1** [To depict] sketch, delineate, portray; see DRAW 2. **2** [To imagine] envision, think of, conceive; see IMAGINE.

picturesque *a.* pictorial, scenic, graphic, striking, arresting.

pie *n.* *Varieties of pies include the following—meat pies:* fish, chicken, chicken pot, lamb, pork, beef, steak-and-kidney, cottage; *dessert pies:* apple, banana, banana cream, chiffon, apricot, peach, pear, raisin, custard, coconut cream, rice custard, pecan, rhubarb, caramel, caramel nut, chocolate, lemon, cranberry and raisin, orange, mince, prune, cherry, gooseberry, huckleberry, blueberry, strawberry, strawberry cream; see

also DESSERT. —**as easy as pie*** not difficult, simple, uncomplicated; see EASY 2.

piece *n.* **1** [Part] portion, share, section; see PART 1. **2** [Work of art] study, composition, creation; see ART. **3** [Musical, literary, or theatrical composition] suite, orchestration, production, opus, aria, song, study, arrangement, treatise, exposition, sketch, play, novel, thesis, dissertation, discourse, discussion, treatment, essay, article, paper, memoir, homily, poem, theme, monograph, commentary, review, paragraph, criticism, play, drama, melodrama, pageant, monologue, opera, overture, prelude, étude, ballet. —**go to pieces 1** come apart, break up, fail; see BREAK DOWN 2. **2** quit, collapse, lose control; see CRY 1, WORRY 2. — **in pieces** shattered, damaged, busted*; see BROKEN 1, DESTROYED, RUINED 1, 2. —**piece together** combine, make, create; see ASSEMBLE 2. —**speak one's piece** air one's opinions, talk, reveal; see TELL 1.

pier *n.* wharf, landing, quay; see DOCK.

pierce *v.* break into, stab, intrude; see PENETRATE.

piercing *a.* **1** [Shrill] deafening, ear-splitting, sharp; see LOUD 1, SHRILL. **2** [Penetrating] entering, boring, puncturing; see SHARP 1.

piety *n.* reverence, duty, zeal; see DEVOTION.

pig *n.* piglet, swine, shoat; see ANIMAL, HOG 1.

pigeon *n.* dove, homing pigeon, turtledove; see BIRD.

piggish *a.* selfish, dirty, ravenous; see GREEDY.

pigheaded *a.* recalcitrant, insistent, stubborn; see STUBBORN.

pigment *n.* paint, oil paint, dye; see COLOR.

pigskin* *n.* football, the ball, the sphere; see FOOTBALL 2.

pigtail *n.* plait, hairdo, braid; see HAIR 1.

piker* *n.* tightwad*, skinflint, cheapskate*; see MISER.

pile¹ *n.* collection, mass, quantity; see COLLECTION.

pile¹ *v.* heap, stack, gather; see ACCUMULATE, STORE.

amount — *vt.* **piled, pil′ing 1** to heap up **2** to load **3** to accumulate Often with *up* — *vi.* **1** to form a pile **2** to move confusedly in a mass: with *in, out, on, off,* etc.

pile² (pīl) *n.* ⟦< L *pilus,* hair⟧ a soft, velvety, raised surface of yarn loops, often sheared, as on a rug

pile³ (pīl) *n.* ⟦OE *pil*⟧ a long, heavy beam driven into the ground to support a bridge, dock, etc.

pile driver (or **engine**) a machine for driving piles by raising them and dropping a heavy weight on them

piles (pīlz) *n.pl.* ⟦< L *pila,* a ball⟧ hemorrhoids

pile′up′ *n.* **1** an accumulation of tasks, etc. **2** [Colloq.] a collision involving several vehicles

pil·fer (pil′fər) *vt., vi.* ⟦< MFr *pelfre,* booty⟧ to steal (esp. small sums, etc.) —**pil′fer·age** (-ij) *n.* —**pil′fer·er** *n.*

pil·grim (pil′grəm, -grim) *n.* ⟦< L *peregrinus,* foreigner⟧ **1** a wanderer **2** one who travels to a shrine or holy place as a religious act **3** [P-] any of the band of English Puritans who founded Plymouth Colony in 1620

pil′grim·age (-ij) *n.* **1** a journey made by a pilgrim, esp. to a shrine or holy place **2** any long journey

pill (pil) *n.* ⟦< L *pila,* a ball⟧ a small ball, tablet, etc. of medicine to be swallowed whole —**the pill** (or **Pill**) [Colloq.] any contraceptive drug for women, in the form of a pill

pil·lage (pil′ij) *n.* ⟦< MFr *piller,* to rob⟧ **1** a plundering **2** loot — *vt., vi.* **-laged, -lag·ing** to plunder

pil·lar (pil′ər) *n.* ⟦< L *pila,* column⟧ **1** a slender, vertical structure used as a support or monument; column **2** a main support of something

pill′box′ *n.* **1** a small box for holding pills **2** an enclosed gun emplacement of concrete and steel

pil·lion (pil′yən) *n.* ⟦< L *pellis,* a skin⟧ an extra seat behind the saddle on a horse or motorcycle

pil·lory (pil′ə rē) *n., pl.* **-ries** ⟦< OFr *pilori*⟧ a device with holes for the head and hands, in which petty offenders were formerly locked and exposed to public scorn — *vt.* **-ried, -ry·ing 1** to punish by placing in a pillory **2** to lay open to public scorn

pil·low (pil′ō) *n.* ⟦OE *pyle*⟧ a cloth case filled with feathers, down, etc., used as a support, as for the head in sleeping — *vt.* to rest as on a pillow

pil′low·case′ *n.* a removable covering for a pillow Also **pil′low·slip′**

pi·lot (pī′lət) *n.* ⟦< Gr *pēdon,* oar⟧ **1** *a)* orig., HELMSMAN *b)* a person licensed to direct ships into or out of a harbor or through difficult waters **2** a qualified operator of aircraft **3** a guide; leader — *vt.* **1** to act as a pilot of, on, etc. **2** to guide — *adj.* serving as a trial unit in testing

pilot film (or **tape**) a film (or videotape) of a single segment of a projected television series

pi′lot·house′ *n.* an enclosure for the helmsman on the upper deck of a ship

pilot light a small gas burner which is kept burning for use in lighting a main burner when needed

pi·men·to (pə men′tō) *n., pl.* **-tos** ⟦< Sp < L *pigmentum,* pigment⟧ a variety of sweet red pepper Also **pi·mien′to** (-myen′-, -men′-)

pimp (pimp) *n.* ⟦< ?⟧ a prostitute's agent — *vi.* to act as a pimp

pim·ple (pim′pəl) *n.* ⟦< OE *piplian,* to break out in pimples⟧ a small, often inflamed swelling of the skin —**pim′ply, -plier, -pli·est,** *adj.*

pin (pin) *n.* ⟦OE *pinn*⟧ **1** a peg, as of wood, or a pointed piece of stiff wire, for fastening things together, etc. **2**

anything like a pin **3** an ornament or badge with a pin or clasp for fastening to clothing **4** *Bowling* one of the clubs at which the ball is rolled — *vt.* **pinned, pin′ning 1** to fasten as with a pin **2** to hold firmly in one position —**pin down 1** to get (someone) to commit himself as to his plans, etc. **2** to establish (a fact, etc.) —**pin (something) on someone** [Colloq.] to lay the blame for (something) on someone

pin·a·fore (pin′ə fôr′) *n.* ⟦prec. + archaic *afore,* before⟧ a sleeveless garment worn over a dress

pin′ball′ machine a game machine with an inclined board having pins, holes, etc. for scoring automatically the contacts of a spring-driven ball

pince-nez (pans′nā′; pins′nā′) *n.* ⟦Fr, nose-pincher⟧ *pl.* **pince′-nez′** (-nāz′; -nā′) eyeglasses kept in place by a spring gripping the bridge of the nose

pin·cers (pin′sərz) *n.pl.* ⟦< OFr *pincier,* to pinch⟧ **1** a tool formed of two pivoted parts, used in gripping things **2** a grasping claw, as of a crab

pinch (pinch) *vt.* ⟦ME *pinchen*⟧ **1** to squeeze between two fingers, edges, etc. **2** to press painfully upon (a toe, etc.) **3** to make thin, cramped, etc., as by hunger **4** [Slang] *a)* to steal *b)* to arrest — *vi.* **1** to squeeze painfully **2** to be stingy or frugal — *n.* **1** a squeeze or nip **2** an amount grasped between finger and thumb **3** distress or difficulty **4** an emergency

pinch′-hit′ *vi.* **-hit′, -hit′ting 1** *Baseball* to bat in place of the batter whose turn it is **2** to substitute in an emergency (*for*) —**pinch hitter**

pin curl a strand of hair kept curled with a bobby pin while it sets

pin′cush′ion *n.* a small cushion to stick pins in to keep them handy

pine¹ (pīn) *n.* ⟦< L *pinus*⟧ **1** an evergreen tree with cones and needle-shaped leaves **2** its wood

pine² (pīn) *vi.* **pined, pin′ing** ⟦< L *poena,* a pain⟧ **1** to waste (*away*) through grief, etc. **2** to yearn

pin·e·al body (pin′ē əl) ⟦< L *pinea,* pine cone⟧ a small, cone-shaped body in the brain that produces a hormone

pine·ap·ple (pīn′ap′əl) *n.* ⟦ME *pinappel,* pine cone⟧ **1** a juicy, edible tropical fruit somewhat resembling a pine cone **2** the plant it grows on

pine tar a thick, dark liquid obtained from pine wood, used in disinfectants, paints, etc.

pin′feath′er *n.* an undeveloped, emerging feather

ping (piŋ) *n.* ⟦echoic⟧ the sound made as of a bullet striking something sharply — *vi., vt.* to strike with a ping

Ping-Pong (piŋ′pôŋ′) ⟦echoic⟧ *trademark for* table tennis equipment — *n.* [p- p-] TABLE TENNIS

pin′head′ *n.* **1** the head of a pin **2** a stupid or silly person

pin′hole′ *n.* **1** a tiny hole as from a pin **2** a hole to stick a pin into

pin·ion (pin′yən) *n.* ⟦< L *pinna,* feather⟧ **1** a small cogwheel which meshes with a larger one **2** the wing of a bird — *vt.* **1** to bind the wings or arms of **2** to shackle

pink¹ (piŋk) *n.* ⟦< ?⟧ **1** any of certain plants with white, pink, or red flowers, often clove-scented **2** the flower **3** pale red **4** the highest degree, finest example, etc. — *adj.* **1** pale-red **2** [Colloq.] somewhat leftist: a derogatory term —**in the pink** [Colloq.] healthy; fit

---

THESAURUS

pilgrim *n.* wayfarer, wanderer, sojourner; see TRAVELER.

pilgrimage *n.* travel, wayfaring, trip; see JOURNEY.

pill *n.* **1** [A tablet] capsule, gelcap, caplet; see MEDICINE 2. **2** [*A contraceptive tablet; usually with "the"*] birth control pill, oral contraceptive, prophylactic; see DRUG.

pillage *v.* plunder, loot, rob; see DESTROY, STEAL.

pillar *n.* **1** [A column] pedestal, mast, shaft; see COLUMN 1, POST. **2** [A support] mainstay, reinforcement, buttress; see SUPPORT 2.

pillow *n.* feather pillow, down pillow, foam rubber cushion, pad, padding, rest, cushion, support, headrest.

pillowcase *n.* pillow slip, pillow casing, pillow cover; see COVER 1.

pilot *n.* **1** [Flier] airman, fighter pilot, commercial pilot, bomber pilot, automatic pilot, mechanical pilot,

aeronaut, aerial navigator, navigator, aerialist. **2** [Guide] scout, leader, director; see GUIDE.

pilot *v.* guide, conduct, manage; see LEAD 1.

pimp *n.* procurer, whoremonger, pander; see CRIMINAL.

pimple *n.* pustule, swelling, acne, whitehead, blackhead, inflammation, bump, lump, boil, carbuncle, blister, zit*; see also BLEMISH.

pin *n.* **1** [A device to fasten goods by piercing or clasping] clip, catch, needle, bodkin, quill, clasp, nail; see also FASTENER. *Pins include the following:* common, safety, straight, hat, knitting, hair, clothes, bobby, cotter, push. **2** [A piece of jewelry] tiepin, stickpin, brooch, badge, stud, sorority pin, fraternity pin, school pin; see also JEWELRY.

pin *v.* close, clasp, bind; see FASTEN.

pinch *n.* squeeze, compression, nip,

nipping, grasp, grasping, pressure, cramp, contraction, confinement, limitation, hurt, torment. —**in a pinch** if necessary, in an emergency, under stress; see UNFORTUNATELY.

pinch *v.* **1** [To squeeze] nip, grasp, compress, press, cramp, grab, contract, confine, limit, torment; see also HURT 1. **2** [*To steal*] take, rob, pilfer; see STEAL. **3** [*To arrest*] apprehend, detain, hold; see ARREST.

pinch-hit *v.* replace, act for, succeed; see SUBSTITUTE.

pine¹ *n.* *Pines include the following:* white, jack, bristlecone, nut, loblolly, piñon. sugar, longleaf, lodgepole, Scotch; see also TREE, WOOD 2.

pink¹ *a.* rosy, reddish, pinkish, flushed, ruddy.

pink¹ *n.* rose, red, roseate, blush-rose, salmon, shocking pink, blushing pink; see also COLOR.

pink[2] (piŋk) *vt.* ⟦ME *pynken*⟧ **1** to cut a saw-toothed edge on (cloth, etc.) **2** to prick or stab

pink′eye′ *n.* a contagious eye infection in which the eyeball and the lining of the eyelid are red and inflamed

pinkie or **pinky** (piŋk′ē) *n.*, *pl.* **-ies** the smallest finger

pink′ing shears (piŋk′iŋ) shears with notched blades, for pinking edges of cloth

pin money a small sum of money, as for incidental minor expenses

pin·na·cle (pin′ə kəl) *n.* ⟦ < L *pinna*, feather⟧ **1** a small turret or spire **2** a slender, pointed formation, as a mountain peak **3** the highest point

pin·nate (pin′āt′, -it) *adj.* ⟦ < L *pinna*, feather⟧ *Bot.* with leaflets on each side of a common stem

pi·nochle or **pi·nocle** (pē′nuk′əl) *n.* ⟦ < Fr *binocle*, pincenez⟧ a card game played with a 48-card deck (two of every card above the eight)

pi·not noir (pē nō′ nwär) [*also* P- N-] **1** the main red-wine grape of the Burgundy region **2** a dry red wine made from this grape

pin′point′ *vt.* to locate precisely

pin′prick′ *n.* **1** a tiny puncture as by a pin **2** a minor annoyance

pins and needles a tingling feeling as in a numb limb — **on pins and needles** in anxious suspense

pin′set′ter *n.* a person or automatic device that sets up bowling pins on the alley Also **pin′spot′ter**

pin stripe a pattern of very narrow stripes in suit fabrics, etc.

pint (pīnt) *n.* ⟦ < ML⟧ a measure of capacity equal to ½ quart

pinto (pin′tō) *adj.* ⟦ < obs. Sp, spotted⟧ having patches of white and some other color — *n.*, *pl.* **-tos** a pinto horse

pinto bean a kind of mottled kidney bean grown in the SW U.S.

pin′up′ *adj.* **1** that is or can be fastened to a wall **2** [Colloq.] designating an attractive person whose picture is often pinned up on walls

pin′wheel′ *n.* **1** a small wheel with vanes of paper, etc., pinned to a stick so as to revolve in the wind **2** a revolving firework

Pin·yin (pin yin′) *n.* ⟦Chin *pinyin*, lit., phonetic sound⟧ [*also* p-] system for transliterating Chinese ideograms into the Latin alphabet

pio·neer (pī′ə nir′) *n.* ⟦ < OFr *peonier*, foot soldier⟧ one who goes before, preparing the way for others, as an early settler — *vi.* to be a pioneer — *vt.* to be a pioneer in or of

pi·os·ity (pī äs′ə tē) *n.* the quality of being excessively or insincerely pious

pi·ous (pī′əs) *adj.* ⟦ < L *pius*⟧ **1** having or showing religious devotion **2** seemingly virtuous **3** sacred —**pi′ously** *adv.*

pip[1] (pip) *n.* ⟦ < PIPPIN⟧ a small seed, as of an apple

pip[2] (pip) *n.* ⟦ < ?⟧ any of the figures or spots on playing cards, dice, etc.

pip[3] (pip) *n.* ⟦ < L *pituita*, phlegm⟧ a contagious disease of fowl

pipe (pīp) *n.* ⟦ < L *pipare*, chirp⟧ **1** a tube of wood, metal, etc. for making musical sounds **2** [*pl.*] the bagpipe **3** a long tube for conveying water, gas, etc. **4** a tube with a small bowl at one end in which tobacco is smoked **5** any tubular part, organ, etc. — *vi.* **piped, pip′ing 1** to play on a pipe **2** to utter shrill sounds — *vt.* **1** to play (a tune) on a pipe **2** to utter in a shrill voice **3** to bring, call, etc. by piping **4** to convey (water, gas, etc.) by pipes —**pipe down** [Slang] to shout or talk less —**pip′er** *n.*

pipe dream [Colloq.] a fantastic idea, vain hope or plan, etc.

pipe fitter a mechanic who installs and maintains plumbing pipes, etc.

pipe′line′ *n.* **1** a line of pipes for conveying water, gas, etc. **2** any means whereby something is passed on

pipe organ ORGAN (sense 1)

pip·ing (pīp′iŋ) *n.* **1** music made by pipes **2** a shrill sound **3** a pipelike fold of material for trimming seams, etc. — **piping hot** so hot as to sizzle

pipit (pip′it) *n.* ⟦echoic⟧ a small bird with a slender bill, streaked breast, and the habit of walking rather than hopping

pip·pin (pip′in) *n.* ⟦ < OFr *pepin*, seed⟧ any of several varieties of apple

pip·squeak (pip′skwēk′) *n.* [Colloq.] anyone or anything regarded as small or insignificant

pi·quant (pē′kənt) *adj.* ⟦Fr < *piquer*, to prick⟧ **1** agreeably pungent to the taste **2** exciting interest; stimulating —**pi′quancy** (-kən sē) *n.*

pique (pēk) *n.* ⟦see prec.⟧ resentment at being slighted — *vt.* **piqued, piqu′ing 1** to arouse such resentment in **2** to arouse; provoke

pi·qué or **pi·que** (pē kā′) *n.* ⟦see PIQUANT⟧ a cotton fabric with ribbed or corded wales

pi·racy (pī′rə sē) *n.*, *pl.* **-cies 1** robbery of ships on the high seas **2** the unauthorized use of copyrighted or patented work

pi·ra·nha (pə rän′yə, pi-; -rän′ə, -ran′ə) *n.* ⟦ < Brazilian Port < AmInd (Brazil) *pirá*, fish + *sainha*, tooth⟧ any of various small, voracious, freshwater South American fishes: they hunt in schools, attacking any animals

pi·rate (pī′rət) *n.* ⟦ < Gr *peirān*, to attack⟧ one who practices piracy — *vt.*, *vi.* **-rated, -rat′ing 1** to take (something) by piracy **2** to publish, reproduce, etc. (a book, recording, etc.) in violation of a copyright —**pi·rat′i·cal** (-rat′ i kəl) *adj.*

pi·rogi (pi rō′gē) *n.pl.* ⟦Russ⟧ small pastry turnovers filled with meat, cheese, etc. Also **pi·rosh′ki** (-räsh′kē)

pir·ou·ette (pir′ōō et′) *n.* ⟦Fr, spinning top⟧ a whirling on one foot or the point of the toe — *vi.* **-et′ted, -et′ting** to do a pirouette

pis·ca·to·rial (pis′kə tôr′ē əl) *adj.* ⟦ < L *piscator*, fisherman⟧ of fishes, fishermen, or fishing

Pis·ces (pī′sēz′; *also* pis′ēz′) ⟦ME < L, pl. of *piscis*, FISH⟧ the 12th sign of the zodiac

pis·mire (pis′mīr′, piz′-) *n.* ⟦ < ME *pisse*, urine + *mire*, ant⟧ [Archaic] an ant

pis·tachio (pis tash′ō′, -ē ō′; -täsh′ō, -ē ō′) *n.*, *pl.* **-os′** ⟦ < OPers *pistah*⟧ **1** a small tree of the cashew family **2** its edible, greenish seed (**pistachio nut**)

pis·til (pis′til, -təl) *n.* ⟦ < L *pistillum*, pestle⟧ the seed-bearing organ of a flower —**pis′til·late′** *adj.*

pis·tol (pis′təl) *n.* ⟦ < Czech *pišt'al*⟧ a small firearm operated with one hand

pis′tol-whip′ *vt.* **-whipped′, -whip′ping** to beat with a pistol, esp. about the head

pis·ton (pis′tən) *n.* ⟦ult. < L *pinsere*, to pound⟧ the snug-fitting engine part that is forced back and forth within a cylinder by the pressure of combustion, steam, etc. and a reciprocating connecting rod (**piston rod**)

piston ring a split ring fitted into a groove around a piston to seal the cylinder, transfer heat, etc.

pit[1] (pit) *n.* ⟦ < MDu *pitte*⟧ the hard stone, as of the plum, peach, etc. containing the seed — *vt.* **pit′ted, pit′ting** to remove the pit from

pit[2] (pit) *n.* ⟦ < L *puteus*, a well⟧ **1** a hole in the ground **2** an abyss **3** hell: used with *the* **4** a pitfall **5** any concealed danger **6** an enclosed area in which animals are kept or made to fight **7** a small hollow in a surface, as a scar left by smallpox **8** the section for the orchestra in front of the stage — *vt.* **pit′ted, pit′ting 1** to make pits or scars in **2** to set in competition (*against*) — *vi.* to become marked

---

THESAURUS

pinnacle *n.* zenith, crest, summit; see CLIMAX.

pioneer *a.* pioneering, initial, untried; see BRAVE, EARLY 1, EXPERIMENTAL.

pioneer *n.* **1** [One who prepares the way] pathfinder, scout, explorer; see GUIDE. **2** [One in the vanguard of civilization] early settler, colonist, pilgrim, immigrant, colonizer, homesteader, squatter.

pioneer *v.* discover, explore, found; see COLONIZE, ESTABLISH 2, SETTLE 1.

pious *a.* divine, holy, devout; see RELIGIOUS 2.

pipe *n.* **1** [A tube] pipeline, drain pipe, sewer, conduit, culvert, waterpipe, aqueduct, trough, passage, duct, canal, vessel. **2** [A device for smoking] *Varieties of smoking pipes include the following:* meerschaum, corncob, Missouri meerschaum, bulldog pipe, briar pipe, clay pipe, hookah, opium pipe, water pipe, churchwarden, calabash, calumet, hash pipe*. **3** [A musical instrument] wind instrument, flute, piccolo; see MUSICAL INSTRUMENT.

pipe down* *v.* become quiet, hush, speak lower; see STOP 2.

piracy *n.* pillage, holdup, robbery; see CRIME, THEFT.

pirate *n.* thief, freebooter, plunderer, pillager, marauder, privateer, soldier of fortune, buccaneer, sea rover; see also CRIMINAL, ROBBER.

pistol *n.* revolver, automatic, six-shooter, rod*, cannon*, six-gun*, Saturday night special*, iron*, forty-five*, thirty-eight*; see also GUN, WEAPON.

pit[2] *n.* abyss, cavity, depression; see HOLE 1.

with pits —**the pits** [Slang] the worst possible thing, place, etc.

469

pita / place

pi·ta (pē′tə, -tä) *n.* ⟦< Heb < Modern Greek⟧ a round, flat bread of the Middle East Also **pita bread**

pit·a·pat (pit′ə pat′) *adv.* with rapid beating —*n.* a rapid series of beats

pitch[1] (pich) *n.* ⟦< L *pix*⟧ a black, sticky substance formed from coal tar, etc. and used for roofing, etc.

pitch[2] (pich) *vt.* ⟦ME *picchen*⟧ 1 to set up [*pitch* a tent] 2 to throw or toss 3 to fix at a certain point, degree, key, etc. 4 *Baseball a)* to throw (the ball) to the batter *b)* to assign (a pitcher) *c)* to act as pitcher for (a game) —*vi.* 1 to pitch a ball, etc. 2 to plunge forward or dip downward 3 to rise and fall, as a ship in rough water —*n.* 1 act or manner of pitching 2 a throw or toss 3 anything pitched 4 a point or degree 5 the degree of slope 6 [Slang] a line of talk for persuading 7 *Music, etc.* the highness or lowness of a sound due to vibrations of sound waves —**pitch in** [Colloq.] 1 to begin working hard 2 to make a contribution —**pitch into** [Colloq.] to attack

pitch′-black′ *adj.* very black

pitch′blende′ (-blend′) *n.* ⟦< Ger *pech*, PITCH[1] + *blenden*, to blind⟧ a dark mineral, a major source of uranium

pitch′-dark′ *adj.* very dark

pitched battle (picht) 1 a battle in which troop placement is relatively fixed beforehand 2 a hard-fought battle

pitcher[1] (pich′ər) *n.* ⟦< OFr *pichier*⟧ a container, usually with a handle and lip, for holding and pouring liquids — **pitch′er·ful** *n.*

pitcher[2] (pich′ər) *n.* ⟦PITCH[2] + -ER⟧ one who pitches; specif., the baseball player who pitches the ball to the batters

pitcher plant a plant with pitcherlike leaves that trap and digest insects

pitch′fork′ *n.* a large, long-handled fork for lifting and tossing hay, etc.

pitch′man (-mən) *n., pl.* **-men** 1 a hawker of novelties, as at a carnival 2 [Colloq.] any high-pressure salesman

pitch pipe a small pipe which produces a fixed tone used as a standard in tuning instruments, etc.

pit·e·ous (pit′ē əs) *adj.* arousing or deserving pity —**pit′eous·ly** *adv.*

pit′fall′ (-fôl′) *n.* ⟦< PIT[2] + OE *fealle*, a trap⟧ 1 a lightly covered pit for trapping animals 2 an unsuspected danger, etc.

pith (pith) *n.* ⟦OE *pitha*⟧ 1 the soft, spongy tissue in the center of certain plant stems 2 the essential part; gist

pith′y (-ē) *adj.* **-i·er, -i·est** 1 of, like, or full of pith 2 terse and full of meaning —**pith′i·ly** *adv.*

piti·ful (pit′i fəl) *adj.* 1 arousing or deserving pity 2 contemptible Also **pit′i·able** (-ē ə bəl) —**pit′i·fully** *adv.*

pit′i·less (-lis) *adj.* without pity

pi·ton (pē′tän) *n.* ⟦Fr < MFr, a spike⟧ a metal spike with an eye for a rope, driven into rock or ice for support in mountain climbing

pit·tance (pit′ns) *n.* ⟦< OFr *pitance*, food allowed a monk⟧ 1 a meager allowance of money 2 any small amount or share

pitter-patter (pit′ər pat′ər) *n.* ⟦echoic⟧ a rapid succession of light tapping sounds

pi·tui·tary (pi tōō′ə ter′ē) *adj.* ⟦< L *pituita*, phlegm⟧ of a small, oval endocrine gland (**pituitary gland**) attached to the brain: it secretes hormones affecting growth, etc.

pit viper any of several poisonous vipers with a heat-sensitive pit on each side of the head, as the rattlesnake

pity (pit′ē) *n., pl.* **-ies** ⟦< L *pietas*, piety⟧ 1 sorrow for another's suffering or misfortune 2 a cause for sorrow —*vt., vi.* **-ied, -y·ing** to feel pity (for)

pivot (piv′ət) *n.* ⟦Fr⟧ 1 a point, shaft, etc. on which something turns 2 a person or thing on which something depends, etc. 3 a pivoting movement —*vt.* to provide with a pivot —*vi.* to turn as on a pivot —**piv′otal** *adj.*

pixel (piks′əl, -el′) *n.* ⟦< *pic(ture)s + el(ement)*⟧ any of the dots that make up an image, as on a TV screen

pixie or **pixy** (piks′ē) *n., pl.* **-ies** ⟦< Brit dial.⟧ a fairy, elf, or sprite

pi·zazz or **piz·zazz** (pi zaz′) *n.* [Colloq.] 1 vigor 2 style, flair, etc.

pizza (pēt′sə) *n.* ⟦It⟧ an Italian dish made by baking thin dough covered with tomatoes, cheese, etc.

piz·ze·ria (pēt′sə rē′ə) *n.* ⟦It⟧ a place where pizzas are made and sold

piz·zi·cato (pit′si kät′ō) *adj.* ⟦It⟧ *Musical Direction* plucked: a note to pluck the strings with the finger instead of bowing

pj's (pē′jāz′) *n.pl. colloq. var. of* PAJAMAS

pk. 1 park 2 peck

pkg. package(s)

Pkwy. or **Pky.** Parkway

pl. 1 place: also **Pl.** 2 plural

plac·ard (plak′ärd; *-ard; for v., also* plə kärd′, pla-) *n.* ⟦< MDu *placke*, a piece⟧ a notice for display in a public place —*vt.* to place placards on or in

pla·cate (plā′kāt′, plak′āt′) *vt.* **-cat·ed, -cat′ing** ⟦< L *placare*⟧ to appease; pacify —**pla·ca′tion** *n.*

place (plās) *n.* ⟦< Gr *plateia*, a street⟧ 1 a court or short street in a city 2 space; room 3 a region 4 *a)* the part of space occupied by a person or thing *b)* situation 5 a city, town, etc. 6 a residence 7 a building or space devoted to a special purpose [a *place* of amusement] 8 a particular point, part, position, etc. [a sore *place* on the leg, a *place* in history] 9 a step or point in a sequence 10 the customary or proper position, time, etc. 11 a space, seat, etc. reserved or occupied by a person 12 an office; employ-

---

THESAURUS

pitch[1,2] *n.* 1 [Slope] slant, incline, angle; see GRADE 1, INCLINATION 2. 2 [A throw] toss, fling, hurl, heave, cast, pitched ball, ball, strike, delivery, offering. 3 [Musical frequency] frequency of vibration, state of vibration, tone; see SOUND 2. 4 [A viscous liquid] resin, gum resin, rosin; see GUM, TAR.

pitch[2] *v.* 1 [To throw] hurl, fling, toss; see THROW 1. 2 [To fall forward] plunge, flop, vault; see DIVE, FALL 1. 3 [To slope abruptly] rise, fall, tilt; see BEND, LEAN 1. —**pitch in** volunteer, work, aid; see HELP. — **pitch into*** assault, blame, scold; see ATTACK, FIGHT.

pitcher[1,2] *n.* 1 [A utensil for pouring liquid] cream pitcher, milk pitcher, water pitcher, jug, vessel, amphora; see also CONTAINER. 2 [In baseball, one who pitches to the batter] right-hand pitcher, right-hander, left-hand pitcher, left-hander, southpaw*, lefty*, righty*, reliever*, fireballer*, hurler*, ace*.

pitchfork *n.* fork, hayfork, three-tined fork; see TOOL 1.

pitfall *n.* snare, pit, blind; see TRAP 1.

pitiful *a.* miserable, mournful, sorrowful, woeful, distressed, distressing, deplorable, cheerless, joyless, comfortless, dismal, touching, pathetic, affecting, stirring, arousing, lamentable, poignant, heart-breaking, human, dramatic, impressive, tearful, gratifying, heart-rending, depressing, afflicted, suffering, moving, vile; see also SAD 1.—*Ant.* HAPPY, cheerful, joyful.

pitiless *a.* unfeeling, heartless, cold; see INDIFFERENT.

pitter-patter *n.* thump, patter, tap; see NOISE 1.

pity *n.* sympathy, compassion, charity, softheartedness, tenderness, goodness, understanding, forbearance, mercy, kindness, warmheartedness, unselfishness, benevolence, favor, condolence, commiseration, clemency, humanity.—*Ant.* HATRED, severity, ferocity. —**have (or take) pity on** show pity to, spare, pardon; see FORGIVE, PITY 2.

pity *v.* 1 [To feel pity] feel for, sympathize with, commiserate, be sorry for, bleed for, be sympathetic to, show sympathy, express sympathy for, grieve with, weep for; see also COMFORT, SYMPATHIZE. 2 [To be merciful to] spare, take pity on, show pity to, show forgiveness to, be merciful to, give quarter, put out of one's misery, pardon, reprieve, grant amnesty to; see also FORGIVE.—*Ant.*

DESTROY, condemn, accuse.

pivot *v.* whirl, swivel, rotate; see TURN 1.

place *n.* 1 [Position] station, point, spot; see POSITION 1. 2 [Space] room, compass, stead, void, distance, area, seat, volume, berth, reservation, accommodation; see also EXTENT. 3 [Locality] spot, locus, site, community, district, suburb, country, section, habitat, home, residence, abode, house, quarters; see also AREA, NEIGHBORHOOD, REGION 1. 4 [Rank] status, position, station; see RANK 3. —**go places*** attain success, achieve, advance; see SUCCEED 1. —**in place** fitting, timely, appropriate; see FIT 1. —**in place of** as a substitute for, instead of, taking the place of, see INSTEAD. —**out of place** inappropriate, unsuitable, not fitting; see IMPROPER. —**put someone in his place** humiliate, reprimand, shame; see HUMBLE. —**take place** occur, come into being, be; see HAPPEN 2. — **take the place of** replace, act in one's stead, serve as proxy for; see SUBSTITUTE.

place *v.* 1 [To put in a place] locate, assign, deposit; see PUT 1. 2 [To put in order] fix, arrange, group; see ORDER 3.

ment **13** the duties of any position **14** the second position at the finish of a race — *vt.* **placed, plac′ing 1** a) to put in a particular place, condition, or relation b) to recognize or identify **2** to find employment for **3** to repose (trust) *in* a person or thing **4** to finish in (a specified position) in a race — *vi.* to finish second or among the first three in a race —**take place** to occur

pla·ce·bo (plə sē′bō) *n., pl.* **-bos** or **-boes** ⟦< L, I shall please⟧ a harmless, unmedicated preparation given as a medicine, as to humor a patient

place mat a small mat serving as an individual table cover for a person at a meal

place′ment *n.* **1** a placing or being placed **2** location or arrangement

pla·cen·ta (plə sen′tə) *n., pl.* **-tas** or **-tae** (-tē) ⟦ult. < Gr *plax*, a flat object⟧ the structure in the uterus through which the fetus is nourished: cf. AFTERBIRTH —**pla·cen′tal** *adj.*

placer (plas′ər) *n.* ⟦< Sp *placel*⟧ a deposit of gravel or sand containing particles of gold, platinum, etc., that can be washed out

placid (plas′id) *adj.* ⟦L *placidus*⟧ calm; quiet —**pla·cid·ity** (plə sid′ə tē) *n.* —**plac′idly** *adv.*

placket (plak′it) *n.* ⟦< ?⟧ a slit at the waist of a skirt or collar of a shirt, to make it easy to put on and take off

pla·gia·rize (plā′jə rīz′) *vt., vi.* **-rized′, -riz′ing** ⟦< L *plagiarius*, kidnapper⟧ to take (ideas, writings, etc.) from (another) and pass them off as one's own —**pla′gia·rism** (-riz′əm) *n.* —**pla′gia·ry** (-rē) *n.* —**pla′gia·rist** *n.*

plague (plāg) *n.* ⟦< Gr *plēgē*, a misfortune⟧ **1** any affliction or calamity **2** any deadly epidemic disease — *vt.* **plagued, plagu′ing 1** to afflict with a plague **2** to vex; torment

plaid (plad) *n.* ⟦Gael *plaide*, a blanket⟧ **1** cloth with a crossbarred pattern **2** any pattern of this kind

plain (plān) *adj.* ⟦< L *planus*, flat⟧ **1** open; clear ⟦in plain view⟧ **2** clearly understood; obvious **3** outspoken; straightforward **4** not luxurious or ornate **5** not complicated; simple **6** homely **7** pure; unmixed **8** common; ordinary ⟦a plain man⟧ — *n.* an extent of level country — *adv.* clearly —**plain′ly** *adv.* —**plain′ness** *n.*

plain′clothes′ man a detective or police officer who wears civilian clothes while on duty Also **plain′clothes′ man,** *pl.* **-men**

plains·man (plānz′mən) *n., pl.* **-men** an American frontiersman on the western Plains

plain′song′ *n.* a very old, plain kind of church music chanted in unison

plaint (plānt) *n.* ⟦< L *plangere*, to lament⟧ a complaint or lament

plain·tiff (plān′tif) *n.* ⟦see prec.⟧ one who brings a suit into a court of law

plain′tive (-tiv) *adj.* ⟦see PLAINT⟧ expressing sorrow or melancholy; mournful; sad —**plain′tively** *adv.*

plait (plāt) *n.* ⟦< L *plicare*, to fold⟧ **1** PLEAT **2** a braid of hair, etc. — *vt.* **1** PLEAT **2** to braid

plan (plan) *n.* ⟦Fr, plan, foundation⟧ **1** a diagram showing the arrangement of a structure, piece of ground, etc. **2** a scheme for making, doing, or arranging something **3** any outline or sketch — *vt.* **planned, plan′ning 1** to make a plan of (a structure, etc.) **2** to devise a scheme for doing, etc. **3** to have in mind as a project or purpose — *vi.* to make plans —**plan′ner** *n.*

plane[1] (plān) *adj.* ⟦L *planus*⟧ **1** flat; level **2** of or having to do with flat surfaces or points, lines, etc. on them ⟦plane geometry⟧ — *n.* **1** a flat, level surface **2** a level of achievement, etc. **3** *short for* AIRPLANE **4** a wing of an airplane

plane[2] (plān) *n.* ⟦< L *planus*, level⟧ a carpenter's tool for leveling or smoothing wood — *vt.* **planed, plan′ing** to smooth or level with a plane

planet (plan′it) *n.* ⟦< Gr *planan*, wander⟧ any celestial body that revolves about a star; esp., one of the sun's nine major planets: Mercury, Venus, Earth, Mars, Jupiter, Saturn, Uranus, Neptune, and Pluto —**plan′etar′y** (-i ter′ē) *adj.*

plan·e·tar·ium (plan′i ter′ē əm) *n., pl.* **-iums** or **-ia** (-ə) **1** the revolving projector used to simulate the past, present, or future motions or positions of the sun, planets, etc. on the inside of a large dome **2** the room in which this is contained

plane tree any of various trees with ball-shaped fruits and bark that sheds in large patches, as the sycamore

plank (plaŋk) *n.* ⟦< LL *planca*⟧ **1** a long, broad, thick board **2** an item in the platform of a political party — *vt.* **1** to cover with planks **2** to broil and serve (steak, fish, etc.) on a board **3** [Colloq.] to set (*down*) with force

plank′ing *n.* **1** planks in quantity **2** the planks of a structure

plank·ton (plaŋk′tən) *n.* ⟦< Gr *plazesthai*, wander⟧ the microscopic animal and plant life found floating in bodies of water

plant (plant, plänt) *n.* ⟦< L *planta*, a sprout⟧ **1** a living thing that cannot move voluntarily, has no sense organs,

THESAURUS

placed *a.* established, settled, fixed, located, rated, deposited, lodged, quartered, planted, set, arranged, stowed, stored, installed, situated, implanted, set up, ordered.

placement *n.* situation, position, arrangement; see ORGANIZATION 1.

plagiarism *n.* literary theft, forgery, fraud; see THEFT.

plague *n.* epidemic, pestilence, disease; see ILLNESS 2.

plague *v.* disturb, trouble, irk; see BOTHER 2.

plain *a.* **1** [Obvious] open, manifest, clear; see OBVIOUS 1, 2, UNDERSTANDABLE. **2** [Simple] unadorned, unostentatious, unpretentious; see MODEST 2. **3** [Ordinary] everyday, average, commonplace; see COMMON 1. **4** [Homely] plain-featured, coarse-featured, unattractive; see UGLY 1. **5** [In blunt language] outspoken, candid, impolite; see RUDE 2.

plain *n.* prairie, steppe, pampas, expanse, open country, lowland, flat, level land, mesa, savanna, moorland, moor, heath, tundra, veldt, downs, the High Plains; see also FIELD 1, MEADOW.

plainly *a.* evidently, visibly; see CLEARLY 1, 2.

plan *n.* **1** [A preliminary sketch] draft, diagram, map, chart, time line, design, outline, representation, form, drawing, view, projection, rough, rough draft, road map. **2** [A proposed sequence of action] plans, scheme, project, flow chart, scope, outline, idea, handling, manipulating,

projection, undertaking, method, design, tactics, procedure, treatment, intention, policy, course of action, plot, conspiracy, expedient, strategy, stratagem, arrangement, way of doing things, angle*, the picture; see also PROGRAM 2, PURPOSE 1. **3** [Arrangement] layout, method, disposition; see ORDER 3. —**lay plans (for)** draft, design, think out; see FORM 1, INTEND 1, PLAN 2.

plan *v.* **1** [To plot an action in advance] prepare, scheme, devise, invent, outline, project, contrive, shape, design, map, plot a course, form a plan, think out, concoct, engineer, figure on, intrigue, conspire, frame, steer one's course, establish guidelines, set parameters, work up, work out, line up, plan an attack, come through, calculate on, make arrangements, take measures, bargain for, cook up*, put on ice*. **2** [To arrange in a preliminary way] outline, draft, sketch, lay out, map out, preprint, organize, prepare a sketch, chart, map, draw, trace, design, illustrate, depict, delineate, represent, shape, chalk out, rough in, block out, block in. **3** [To have in mind] propose, think, contemplate; see INTEND 1.

plane[1,2] *n.* **1** [A plane surface] level, extension, horizontal, flat, sphere, face, stratum. **2** [A tool for smoothing wood] electric planer, jointer, foreplane; see TOOL 1. *Types include the following:* jack, smoothing, jointing, block, circular, rabbet, grooving,

routing, scraper, dado, trying, bullnose, toothing, chamfer. **3** [An airplane] aircraft, airliner, aeroplane, airship, heavier-than-air craft, shuttle, jet, jet plane. *Kinds of planes include the following:* propeller, jet, rocket, scout, observation, reconnaissance, transport, pursuit, commercial, passenger; biplane, triplane, monoplane, racer, glider, bomber, seaplane, hydroplane, fighter, fighter-bomber, dive bomber, interceptor, turbojet, stratojet, helicopter, gunship, gyroplane, amphibian, sailplane.

plane[2] *v.* finish, smooth, level; see FLATTEN.

planet *n.* celestial body, heavenly body, luminous body, wandering star, planetoid, asteroid, star. *The known planets are as follows:* Mercury, Venus, Earth, Mars, Jupiter, Saturn, Uranus, Neptune, Pluto, the asteroids.

plank *n.* board, planking, sheet; see LUMBER.

planned *a.* projected, budgeted, in the budget, provided for, on the drawing board, programmed, in the making, under consideration, on the docket, prospective, cut out, cut and dried, under advisement, prepared.

plant *n.* shrub, weed, bush, slip, shoot, cutting, sprout, seedling, plantlet, bulb, flower.

plant *v.* put in the ground, sow, farm, set out, pot, start, transplant, seed, stock, colonize, settle, establish, and synthesizes food from carbon dioxide 2 an herb, as distinguished from a tree or shrub 3 the machinery, buildings, etc. of a factory, etc. — *vt.* 1 to put into the ground to grow 2 to set firmly in position 3 to settle; establish 4 [Slang] to place (a person or thing) in such a way as to trick, trap, etc.

plan·tain¹ (plan′tin) *n.* [< L *plantago*] a plant with basal leaves and spikes of tiny, greenish flowers

plan·tain² (plan′tin) *n.* [< Sp *plátano*, banana tree] a tropical banana plant yielding a coarse fruit

plan·tar (plan′tər) *adj.* [< L *planta*, sole] of or on the sole of the foot

plan·ta·tion (plan tā′shən) *n.* [< L *plantare*, to plant] 1 an estate, as in a warm climate, cultivated by workers living on it 2 a large, cultivated planting of trees

planter (plant′ər) *n.* 1 the owner of a plantation 2 a machine that plants 3 a decorative container for plants

plant louse APHID

plaque (plak) *n.* [Fr < MDu *placke*, disk] 1 a thin, flat piece of metal, wood, etc. with decoration or lettering on it, hung on a wall, etc. 2 a thin film of matter on uncleaned teeth

plash (plash) *vt., vi., n.* [echoic] SPLASH

plasma (plaz′mə) *n.* [Ger < Gr, something molded] 1 the fluid part of blood, lymph, or milk 2 a high-temperature, ionized gas that is electrically neutral

plasma membrane a very thin living membrane surrounding a plant or animal cell

plas·ter (plas′tər, pläs′-) *n.* [< Gr *emplassein*, to daub over] 1 a pasty mixture, as of lime, sand, and water, hard when dry, for coating walls, etc. 2 PLASTER OF PARIS 3 a pasty preparation spread on cloth and applied to the body, as a medicine — *vt.* 1 to cover as with plaster 2 to apply like a plaster [to *plaster* posters on walls] 3 to make lie smooth and flat —**plas′terer** *n.*

plas′ter·board′ *n.* thin board formed of layers of plaster and paper, used in wide sheets for walls, etc.

plaster of Paris [from use of gypsum from *Paris*, France] a thick paste of gypsum and water that sets quickly: used for casts, statuary, etc.

plas·tic (plas′tik) *adj.* [< Gr *plassein*, to form] 1 molding or shaping matter; formative 2 that can be molded or shaped 3 made of plastic — *n.* 1 any of various nonmetallic compounds, synthetically produced, which can be molded and hardened for commercial use 2 [Colloq.] a credit card or credit cards, or credit based on their use —**plas·tic′i·ty** (-tis′ə tē) *n.*

plas′ti·cize′ (-ti siz′) *vt., vi.* -cized′, -ciz′ing to make or become plastic

plastic surgery surgery dealing with the repair of deformed or destroyed parts of the body, as by transferring skin, bone, etc. from other parts

plat (plat) *n.* [var. of PLOT] 1 a small piece of ground 2 a map or plan, as of a subdivision — *vt.* **plat′ted, plat′ting** to make a map or plan of

plate (plāt) *n.* [< Gr *platys*, broad] 1 a smooth, flat, thin piece of metal, etc., specif. one on which an engraving is cut 2 an impression taken from an engraved surface 3 dishes, utensils, etc. of, or plated with, silver or gold 4 a shallow dish 5 the food in a dish; a course 6 a denture, specif. that part of it which fits to the mouth 7 *Baseball*

short for HOME PLATE 8 *Photog.* a sheet of glass, metal, etc. coated with a film sensitive to light 9 *Printing* a cast made from a mold of set type — *vt.* **plat′ed, plat′ing** 1 to coat with gold, silver, etc. 2 to cover with metal plates

pla·teau (pla tō′) *n.* [Fr: see prec.] 1 an elevated tract of level land 2 a temporary halt in progress

plate glass polished, clear glass in thick sheets, for windows, mirrors, etc.

platen (plat′'n) *n.* [< OFr *plat*, flat] 1 in a printing press, a flat metal plate which presses the paper against the type 2 in a typewriter, the roller against which the keys strike

plate tec·ton·ics (tek tän′iks) *Geol.* the theory that the earth's surface consists of plates whose constant motion explains continental drift, etc.

plat·form (plat′fôrm′) *n.* [Fr *plate-forme*, lit., flat form] 1 a raised horizontal surface, as a stage for speakers, etc. 2 a statement of policy, esp. of a political party

plati·num (plat′'n əm) *n.* [< Sp *plata*, silver] a silvery, metallic chemical element, resistant to corrosion: used for jewelry, etc.

plati·tude (plat′ə tōōd′) *n.* [Fr < *plat*, flat, after *latitude*, etc.] a commonplace or trite remark

Pla·tonic (plə tän′ik) *adj.* 1 of Plato, an ancient Gr. philosopher, or his philosophy 2 [*usually* **p-**] not sexual but purely spiritual or intellectual [*platonic* love]

pla·toon (plə tōōn′) *n.* [Fr *peloton*, a group] 1 a military unit composed of two or more squads 2 *Sports* any of the specialized squads making up a team — *vt. Sports* to alternate (players) at a position

plat·ter (plat′ər) *n.* [< OFr *plat*, flat] a large, shallow dish, usually oval, for serving food

platy (plat′ē) *n., pl.* **plat′ies** [clipped < ModL *Platypoecilus*, a genus of fishes] a brightly colored, freshwater fish of Central America: used in aquariums

platy·pus (plat′i pəs) *n., pl.* **-puses** or **-pi′** (-pī′) [< Gr *platys*, flat + *pous*, foot] a small, egg-laying water mammal of Australia, with webbed feet and a ducklike bill; duckbill

plau·dit (plô′dit) *n.* [< L *plaudere*, applaud] [*usually pl.*] applause

plau·sible (plô′zə bəl) *adj.* [< L *plaudere*, applaud] seemingly true, trustworthy, honest, etc. —**plau·sibil′ity** *n.* — **plau′sibly** *adv.*

play (plā) *vi.* [OE *plegan*] 1 to move lightly, rapidly, etc. [sunlight *plays* on the water] 2 to engage in recreation 3 to take part in a game or sport 4 to trifle (*with* a thing or person) 5 to perform on a musical instrument 6 to give out sounds 7 to act in a specified way [to *play* dumb] 8 to act in a drama 9 to impose unscrupulously (*on* another's feelings) — *vt.* 1 to take part in (a game or sport) 2 to oppose (a person, etc.) in a game 3 to do, as in fun [to *play* tricks] 4 to bet on 5 to cause to move, etc.; wield 6 to cause [to *play* havoc] 7 to perform (music, a drama, etc.) 8 to perform on (an instrument) 9 to act the part of [to *play* Hamlet] — *n.* 1 motion or activity, esp. when free or rapid 2 freedom for motion or action 3 recreation; sport 4 fun; joking 5 the playing of a game 6 a move or act in a game 7 a dramatic composition or performance; drama —**play down** to attach little importance to —

THESAURUS

locate.

plantation *n.* acreage, estate, ranch; see FARM.

planted *a.* cultivated, sown, seeded, stocked, implanted, strewn, drilled.

plaster *n.* mortar, binding, plaster of Paris; see CEMENT.

plaster *v.* coat, bind, cement; see COVER 1.

plastic *a.* substitute, synthetic, cellulose; see SYNTHETIC.

plastic *n.* synthetic, artificial product, substitute, plastic material, processed material, polymerized substance, thermoplastic, cellophane, melamine, vinyl, nylon, PVC.

plate *n.* 1 [A flat surface] lamina, slice, stratum; see PLANE 1. 2 [A full-page illustration] photography, lithograph, etching; see ILLUSTRATION, PICTURE 3. 3 [A flattish dish] dinner plate, soup plate, salad plate, casserole, dessert plate, platter, trencher, 'china, serving dish; see also DISH 1. 4 [Food served on a plate] helping, serving, course; see MEAL 2. 5 [In

baseball, the base immediately before the catcher] home base, home plate, home; see BASE 4.

plate *v.* laminate, stratify, layer, scale, flake, overlay, gild, nickel, bronze, chrome, silver, enamel, encrust, cover.

plateau *n.* tableland, mesa, elevation; see HILL, PLAIN.

platform *n.* 1 [A stage] dais, pulpit, speaker's platform, rostrum, stand, floor, staging, terrace. 2 [A program] principles, policies, the party planks*; see PROGRAM 2.

platoon *n.* detachment, military unit, company; see ARMY 2.

platter *n.* tray, serving platter, meat platter; see DISH 1, PLATE 3.

plausible *a.* probable, credible, supposable; see LIKELY 1.

play *n.* 1 [Amusement] enjoyment, diversion, pleasure; see ENTERTAINMENT. 2 [Recreation] relaxation, game, sport; see ENTERTAINMENT. 3 [Fun] frolic, happiness, sportiveness; see FUN. 4 [A drama] performance,

musical, show; see DRAMA. 5 [Sport] exhibition, match, competition; see SPORT 1, 3. 6 [Action] activity, movement, working; see ACTION 1. — **make a play for*** make advances to, court, woo; see TRY 1.

play *v.* 1 [To amuse oneself] entertain oneself, revel, make merry, carouse, play games, rejoice, have a good time, idle away, horse around*.—*Ant.* MOURN, grieve, sulk. 2 [To frolic] frisk, sport, cavort, joke, dance, play games, make jokes, be a practical joker, show off, jump about, skip, gambol, caper.—*Ant.* DRAG, mope, droop. 3 [To produce music] perform, execute, work, cause to sound, finger, pedal, bow, plunk, tinkle, pipe, toot, mouth, pump, fiddle, sound, strike, saw, scrape, twang, pound, thump, tickle. 4 [To engage in sport] participate, engage, practice; see COMPETE. 5 [To pretend] imagine, suppose, think; see PRETEND 1. —**play down** belittle, hold back, minimize; see RESTRAIN.

played out exhausted —**play up** to give prominence to —**play up to** [Colloq.] to try to please by flattery

play'act' *vi.* 1 to pretend: make believe 2 to behave in an affected or dramatic manner —**play'act'ing** *n.*

play'back' *n.* 1 reproduction of sounds, images, etc. from a recorded disc, tape, etc. 2 the control or device for such reproduction on a player, recorder, etc.

play'bill' *n.* a program of a play

play'boy' *n.* a man of means who is given to pleasure-seeking

player (plā'ər) *n.* 1 one who plays a specified game, instrument, etc. 2 an actor

play'ful *adj.* 1 fond of play or fun 2 jocular —**play'fully** *adv.* —**play'ful·ness** *n.*

play'go'er *n.* one who goes to the theater frequently or regularly

play'ground' *n.* a place, often near a school, for outdoor recreation

play'house' *n.* 1 a theater for live dramatic productions 2 a small house for children to play in

playing cards cards used in playing various games, arranged in four suits

play'mate' *n.* a companion in games and recreation

play'off' (plā'ôf') *n.* a contest to break a tie or to decide a championship

play on words a pun or punning

play'pen' *n.* a portable enclosure for an infant to play or crawl in safely

play'thing' *n.* toy

play'wright' (-rīt') *n.* one who writes plays; dramatist

plaza (plä'zə, plaz'ə) *n.* [Sp < L *platea*, street] 1 a public square in a city or town 2 a shopping center 3 a service area along a superhighway

plea (plē) *n.* [< L *placere*, to please] 1 a statement in defense; excuse 2 a request; appeal 3 *Law* the response of a defendant to criminal charges

plea'-bar'gain *vi.* to engage in plea bargaining

plea bargaining pretrial negotiations in which the defendant agrees to plead guilty to a lesser charge if more serious charges are dropped

plead (plēd) *vi.* **plead'ed** or [Colloq.] **pled** or **plead** (pled), **plead'ing** [see PLEA] 1 to present a plea in a law court 2 to make an appeal; beg —*vt.* 1 to argue (a law case) 2 to answer (guilty or not guilty) to a charge 3 to offer as an excuse —**plead'er** *n.*

pleas·ant (plez'ənt) *adj.* [< Fr *plaisir*, to please] 1 agreeable to the mind or senses; pleasing 2 having an agreeable manner, look, etc. —**pleas'antly** *adv.* —**pleas'ant·ness** *n.*

pleas'ant·ry (-ən trē) *n., pl.* **-ries** 1 a humorous remark 2 a polite social remark [to exchange *pleasantries*]

please (plēz) *vt.* **pleased, pleas'ing** [< L *placere*] 1 to be agreeable to; satisfy 2 to be the wish of [it *pleased* him to go] —*vi.* 1 to be agreeable; satisfy 2 to have the wish; like [to do as one *pleases*] *Please* is also used in polite requests [*please* sit down]

pleas'ing *adj.* giving pleasure; agreeable —**pleas'ingly** *adv.*

pleas·ur·able (plezh'ər ə bəl) *adj.* pleasant; enjoyable —**pleas'ur·ably** *adv.*

pleas·ure (plezh'ər) *n.* 1 a pleased feeling; delight 2 one's wish, will, or choice 3 a thing that gives delight or satisfaction —**pleas'ure·ful** *adj.*

pleat (plēt) *n.* [ME *pleten*] a flat double fold in cloth, etc. pressed or stitched in place —*vt.* to lay and press (cloth) in a pleat or pleats

ple·beian (plē bē'ən, pli-) *n.* [< L *plebs*, common people] 1 one of the common people 2 a vulgar, coarse person —*adj.* vulgar or common

plebi·scite (pleb'ə sīt') *n.* [< L *plebs*, common people + *scitum*, decree] a direct vote of the people on a political issue, such as independent nationhood, annexation, etc.

plec·trum (plek'trəm) *n., pl.* **-trums** or **-tra** (-trə) [L < Gr *plēssein*, to strike] a thin piece of metal, etc., for plucking the strings of a guitar, etc.

pled (pled) *vi., vt.* [Colloq.] *pt. & pp. of* PLEAD

pledge (plej) *n.* [prob < OS *plegan*, to warrant] 1 the condition of being given or held as security for a contract, payment, etc. 2 a person or thing given or held as such security 3 a promise or agreement 4 something promised —*vt.* **pledged, pledg'ing** 1 to give as security 2 to bind by a promise 3 to promise to give

Pleis·to·cene (plīs'tō sēn', -tə-) *adj.* [< Gr *pleistos*, most + *kainos*, recent] designating an epoch in the Cenozoic Era, characterized by the appearance of modern humans

ple·nary (plē'nə rē, plen'ə-) *adj.* [< L *plenus*, full] 1 full; complete 2 for attendance by all members [a *plenary* session]

pleni·po·ten·ti·ary (plen'i pō ten'shē er'ē, -shə rē; -pə-) *adj.* [< L *plenus*, full + *potens*, powerful] having or conferring full authority —*n., pl.* **-ar'ies** a diplomat given full authority

pleni·tude (plen'i tōōd') *n.* [< L *plenus*, full] 1 fullness; completeness 2 abundance; plenty

plen·teous (plen'tē əs) *adj.* plentiful

plen·ti·ful (plen'ti fəl) *adj.* 1 having or yielding plenty 2 abundant —**plen'ti·fully** *adv.*

plenty (plen'tē) *n., pl.* **-ties** [< L *plenus*, full] 1 prosperity; opulence 2 a sufficient supply 3 a large number —*adv.* [Colloq.] very; quite

THESAURUS

player *n.* 1 [One who takes part in a game] member, athlete, sportsman, sportswoman, amateur, professional, gymnast, acrobat, swimmer, diver, trackman, champ*, pro*, semipro*, jock*; see also CONTESTANT. 2 [An actor] performer, entertainer, thespian; see ACTOR, ACTRESS.

playful *a.* joking, whimsical, comical; see FUNNY 1.

playground *n.* playing field, park, school ground, municipal playground, yard, school yard, diamond, gridiron.

playmate *n.* comrade, neighbor, companion; see FRIEND.

plaything *n.* gadget, amusement, trinket; see DOLL, GAME 1, TOY 1.

playwright *n.* scripter, scenarist, tragedian; see AUTHOR, WRITER.

plea *n.* 1 [An appeal] overture, request, supplication; see APPEAL 1. 2 [A form of legal defense] pleading, argument, case; see DEFENSE 2.

plead *v.* 1 [To beg] implore, beseech, solicit; see ASK, BEG. 2 [To enter a plea] present, allege, cite; see DECLARE. —**plead guilty** confess, repent, concede; see ADMIT 2.

pleading *a.* imploring, supplicating, desirous.

pleasant *a.* 1 [Affable] agreeable, attractive, obliging, charming, mild, amusing, kindly, mild-mannered, gracious, genial, amiable, polite,

urbane, cheerful, sympathetic, civil, cordial, engaging, social, bland, diplomatic, civilized, good-humored, good-natured, soft, fun, delightful, jovial, jolly.—*Ant.* SULLEN, unsympathetic, unkind. 2 [Giving pleasure; *said of occasions, experiences, and the like*] gratifying, pleasurable, agreeable, cheering, amusing, welcome, refreshing, satisfying, all right, satisfactory, adequate, acceptable, comfortable, diverting, fascinating, adorable, enjoyable, delightful, sociable, lively, exciting, glad, festive, cheerful, entertaining, relaxing, joyous, joyful, merry, happy, pleasing, favorable, bright, sunny, brisk, catchy, sparkling, enlivening, colorful, light, humorous, laughable, comforting.—*Ant.* SAD, disagreeable, unhappy.

pleasantly *a.* pleasingly, charmingly, welcomely; see AGREEABLY.

please *interj.* if you please, if it please you, may it please you, by your leave.

please *v.* 1 [To give pleasure] gratify, satisfy, make up to; see ENTERTAIN. 2 [To desire] wish, demand, command; see WANT 1. —**if you please** if you will, if I may, by your leave; see PLEASE.

pleased *a.* gratified, satisfied, charmed; see HAPPY.

pleasing *a.* charming, agreeable, delightful; see PLEASANT 1.

pleasure *n.* 1 [Enjoyment] bliss, delight, ease; see HAPPINESS. 2 [Will] want, preference, wish; see DESIRE 1.

pleat *n.* pleating, tuck, crease; see FOLD.

pleat *v.* ruffle, crease, gather; see FOLD.

pledge *n.* guarantee, token, agreement; see PROMISE 1.

pledge *v.* swear, vow, vouch; see PROMISE 1.

plentiful *a.* 1 [Bountiful] prolific, fruitful, profuse, lavish, liberal, unsparing, inexhaustible, replete, generous, abundant, extravagant, improvident, excessive, copious, superabundant, over-liberal, superfluous, overflowing, flowing.—*Ant.* STINGY, niggardly, skimpy. 2 [Existing in plenty] sufficient, abundant, copious, ample, overflowing, large, chock-full, teeming, unlimited, well-provided, flowing, full, flush, lush with, pouring, fruitful, swarming, swimming, abounding.—*Ant.* POOR, scant, scanty.

plenty *n.* abundance, fruitfulness, fullness, lavishness, deluge, torrent, sufficient, bounty, profusion, adequacy, flood, avalanche, good store, limit, capacity, adequate stock, enough and to spare, everything, all kinds of, all one wants, all one can eat and drink, more than one knows

pletho·ra (pleth'ə rə) *n.* ⟦< Gr *plēthein*, to be full⟧ an overabundance

pleura (ploor'ə) *n., pl.* **-rae** (-ē) ⟦< Gr, rib, side⟧ the thin membrane that covers a lung and lines the chest cavity in mammals

pleu·risy (ploor'ə sē) *n.* ⟦< Gr *pleura*, rib, side⟧ inflammation of the pleura, characterized by painful breathing

Plexi·glas (pleks'i glas') *trademark for* a lightweight, transparent, thermoplastic substance — *n.* this material: also **plex'i·glass'**

plexus (pleks'əs) *n., pl.* **-uses** or **-us** ⟦< L *plectere*, to twine⟧ a network, as of blood vessels, nerves, etc.

pli·able (plī'ə bəl) *adj.* ⟦< L *plicare*, to fold⟧ 1 easily bent; flexible 2 easily influenced or persuaded 3 adaptable — **pli·abil'i·ty** *n.*

pli·ant (plī'ənt) *adj.* 1 easily bent; pliable 2 compliant — **pli'an·cy** *n.*

pli·ers (plī'ərz) *n.pl.* ⟦< PLY[1]⟧ small pincers for gripping small objects, bending wire, etc. Often **pair of pliers**

plight[1] (plīt) *n.* ⟦< OFr *pleit*, a fold⟧ a distressing situation

plight[2] (plīt) *vt.* ⟦< OE *pliht*, danger⟧ to pledge, or bind by a pledge

plinth (plinth) *n.* ⟦< Gr *plinthos*, a brick⟧ the square block at the base of a column, pedestal, etc.

PLO Palestine Liberation Organization

plod (pläd) *vi.* **plod'ded, plod'ding** ⟦of echoic orig.⟧ 1 to move heavily and laboriously; trudge 2 to work steadily; drudge —**plod'der** *n.*

plop (pläp) *vt., vi.* **plopped, plop'ping** ⟦echoic⟧ to drop with a sound like that of something flat falling into water — *n.* such a sound

plot (plät) *n.* ⟦OE⟧ 1 a small area of ground 2 a secret, usually evil, scheme 3 the plan of action of a play, novel, etc. — *vt.* **plot'ted, plot'ting** 1 to mark or trace on a chart or map 2 to make secret plans for — *vi.* to scheme —**plot'ter** *n.*

plover (pluv'ər, plō'vər) *n.* ⟦< L *pluvia*, rain⟧ a shore bird with a short tail and long, pointed wings

plow (plou) *n.* ⟦OE *ploh*⟧ 1 a farm implement used to cut and turn up the soil 2 any implement like this, as a snow-plow — *vt.* 1 to cut and turn up (soil) with a plow 2 to make (one's way) through as if by plowing — *vi.* 1 to use a plow 2 to move (through, into, etc.) with force 3 to plod 4 to begin work vigorously: with *into* Also, chiefly Brit., **plough** —**plow'man** (-mən), *pl.* **-men,** *n.*

plow'share' (-sher') *n.* the cutting blade of a plow

ploy (ploi) *n.* ⟦? < (EM)PLOY⟧ an action intended to outwit someone

pluck (pluk) *vt.* ⟦OE *pluccian*⟧ 1 to pull off or out; pick 2 to snatch 3 to pull feathers or hair from 4 to pull at (a taut string, etc.) and release quickly — *vi.* to pull: often with *at* — *n.* 1 a pulling 2 courage

pluck'y *adj.* **-i·er, -i·est** brave; spirited —**pluck'i·ness** *n.*

plug (plug) *n.* ⟦MDu *plugge*⟧ 1 an object used to stop up a hole, etc. 2 a cake of tobacco 3 an electrical device, as with prongs, for making contact or closing a circuit 4 a kind of fishing lure 5 [Colloq.] a free boost, advertisement, etc. 6 [Slang] an old, worn-out horse — *vt.* **plugged, plug'ging** 1 to fill (a hole, etc.) with a plug 2 to insert a plug of 3 [Colloq.] to advertise with a plug 4

[Slang] to shoot a bullet into — *vi.* [Colloq.] to work doggedly

plug·o'la (-ō'lə) *n.* ⟦< PLUG, *n.* 5⟧ [Slang] a bribe for underhanded promotion on radio or TV

plum (plum) *n.* ⟦OE *plume*⟧ 1 *a*) a tree bearing a smooth-skinned fruit with a flattened stone *b*) the fruit 2 a raisin 3 the bluish-red color of some plums 4 something desirable

plum·age (ploo'mij) *n.* ⟦Fr < *plume*, a feather⟧ a bird's feathers

plumb (plum) *n.* ⟦< L *plumbum*, LEAD[2]⟧ a lead weight **(plumb bob)** hung at the end of a line **(plumb line)**, used to determine how deep water is or whether a wall, etc. is vertical — *adj.* perfectly vertical — *adv.* 1 straight down 2 [Colloq.] entirely — *vt.* 1 to test or sound with a plumb 2 to probe or fathom —**out of** (or **off**) **plumb** not vertical

plumber (plum'ər) *n.* ⟦see prec.⟧ a skilled worker who installs and repairs pipes, fixtures, etc., as of water systems

plumber's helper [Colloq.] PLUNGER (sense 2) Also **plumber's friend**

plumb·ing (plum'iŋ) *n.* 1 the work of a plumber 2 the pipes and fixtures with which a plumber works

plume (ploom) *n.* ⟦< L *pluma*⟧ 1 a feather, esp. a large, showy one 2 a group of these — *vt.* **plumed, plum'ing** 1 to adorn with plumes 2 to preen —**plum'y, -i·er, -i·est,** *adj.*

plum·met (plum'it) *n.* ⟦see PLUMB⟧ 1 a plumb 2 a thing that weighs heavily — *vi.* to fall straight downward

plump[1] (plump) *adj.* ⟦< MDu *plomp*, bulky⟧ full and rounded in form; chubby —**plump'ness** *n.*

plump[2] (plump) *vi., vt.* ⟦echoic⟧ to drop or bump suddenly or heavily — *n.* 1 a falling, bumping, etc. 2 the sound of this — *adv.* 1 suddenly; heavily 2 straight down

plun·der (plun'dər) *vt., vi.* ⟦< Ger *plunder*, baggage⟧ 1 to rob or pillage 2 to take (property) by force or fraud — *n.* 1 a plundering 2 things taken by force or fraud

plunge (plunj) *vt.* **plunged, plung'ing** ⟦see PLUMB⟧ to thrust or throw suddenly (*into* a liquid, condition, etc.) — *vi.* 1 to dive or rush 2 to move violently and rapidly downward or forward 3 [Colloq.] to gamble heavily — *n.* 1 a dive or fall 2 [Colloq.] a gamble

plung·er *n.* 1 one who plunges 2 a large, rubber suction cup used to free clogged drains 3 any cylindrical device that operates with a plunging motion, as a piston

plunk (pluŋk) *vt.* ⟦echoic⟧ 1 to strum (a banjo, etc.) 2 to throw or put down heavily — *vi.* 1 to give out a twanging sound 2 to fall heavily — *n.* the sound made by plunking —**plunk down** [Colloq.] to give in payment

plu·ral (ploor'əl) *adj.* ⟦< L *plus*, more⟧ more than one — *n. Gram.* the form of a word designating more than one (e.g., *hands, men*)

plu·ral·i·ty (ploo ral'ə tē) *n., pl.* **-ties** 1 a being plural or numerous 2 *a*) the excess of votes in an election that the leading candidate has over his nearest rival *b*) a majority

plural·ize (ploor'əl īz') *vt., vi.* **-ized', -iz'ing** to make plural

---

THESAURUS

what to do with, too much of a good thing, a good bit, all one needs, all one can use, a great deal, a lot*, lots*, oodles*.

pliable *a.* limber, supple, plastic; see FLEXIBLE.

pliant *a.* limber, supple, plastic; see FLEXIBLE.

pliers *n.* pinchers, wrench, pincers, tongs, forceps, tweezers.

plod *v.* trudge, hike, plug; see WALK 1.

plop *v.* thump, thud, bump; see SOUND.

plot *n.* 1 [An intrigue] conspiracy, scheme, artifice; see TRICK 1. 2 [The action of a story] plan, scheme, outline, design, development, progress, unfolding, movement, climax, events, incidents, enactment, suspense, structure, build-up, scenario. 3 [A piece of ground] parcel, land, division; see AREA, LOT 1.

plot *v.* 1 [To devise an intrigue] frame, contrive, scheme; see PLAN 1. 2 [To plan] sketch, outline, draft; see PLAN 2.

plow *n.* Plows include the following: moldboard, gang, steam, tractor, double, straddle, sulky, wheel, shovel, hand; lister, hoe plow or horse-hoe, garden plow or wheel hoe, (corn) cultivator; see also TOOL 1.

plow *v.* 1 [To use a plow] break, furrow, cultivate, turn, plow up, turn over, till, list, ridge, break ground, do the plowing; see also FARM. 2 [To act like a plow] smash into, rush through, shove apart; see DIG 1, PUSH 1.

plug *n.* 1 [An implement to stop an opening] cork, stopper, stopple, filling, stoppage, spigot, wedge. 2 [An electrical fitting] attachment plug, fitting, connection, wall plug, floor plug, plug fuse. 3 [A large pipe with a discharge valve] water plug, fire hydrant, fire plug; see PIPE 1.

plug *v.* stop, fill, obstruct, secure, ram, make tight, drive in; see also STOP 2.

plum *n.* Plums and plumlike fruits include the following: freestone, Damson, Satsuma, Green Gage, Reine Claude, Sugar plum, French prune, Stanley prune; see also FRUIT.

plumber *n.* tradesman, metal worker, handy man; see WORKMAN.

plumbing *n.* pipes, water pipes, sewage pipes, heating pipes, bathroom fixtures, sanitary provisions; see also PIPE 1.

plummet *v.* plunge, fall, nosedive; see DIVE, FALL 1.

plump[1] *a.* obese, stout, fleshy; see FAT.

plunder *v.* burn, steal, lay waste; see RAID, RAVAGE.

plunge *v.* fall, throw oneself, rush; see DIVE, JUMP 1.

plural *a.* few, a number of, abundant; see MANY h.

plurality *n.* majority, advantage in votes cast, favorable returns; see LEAD 1, MAJORITY 1.

plus (plus) *prep.* [L, more] **1** added to *[2 plus 2]* **2** in addition to — *adj.* **1** indicating addition **2** positive *[a plus quantity]* **3** somewhat higher than *[a grade of B plus]* **4** involving extra gain *[a plus factor]* **5** [Colloq.] and more *[personality plus]* — *n., pl.* **plus'es** or **plus'ses 1** a sign (**plus sign,** +) indicating addition or positive quantity **2** something added **3** an advantage; benefit

plush (plush) *n.* [< L *pilus,* hair] a fabric with a soft, thick pile — *adj.* [Colloq.] luxurious: also **plush'y**

Pluto (plōōt'ō) **1** *Gr. & Rom. Myth.* the god of the lower world **2** the outermost planet: see PLANET

plu·toc·ra·cy (plōō täk'rə sē) *n., pl.* **-cies** [< Gr *ploutos,* wealth + *kratein,* to rule] **1** government by the wealthy **2** a group of wealthy people who control a government

plu·to·crat (plōōt'ō krat', plōōt'ə-) *n.* **1** a member of a plutocracy **2** one whose wealth is the source of control or influence — **plu·to·crat'ic** *adj.*

plu·to·ni·um (plōō tō'nē əm) *n.* [after PLUTO (planet)] a radioactive, metallic chemical element

plu·vial (plōō'vē əl) *adj.* [< L *pluvia,* rain] of, or having much, rain

ply[1] (plī) *vt.* **plied, ply'ing** [< L *plicare,* to fold] [Now Rare] to twist, fold, etc. — *n., pl.* **plies 1** a thickness or layer, as of cloth, plywood, etc. **2** any of the twisted strands in rope, yarn, etc.

ply[2] (plī) *vt.* **plied, ply'ing** [contr. < APPLY] **1** to use (a tool, faculty, etc.), esp. with energy **2** to work at (a trade) **3** to keep supplying, assailing, etc. (*with*) **4** to sail back and forth across — *vi.* **1** to keep busy **2** to travel regularly (*between* places)

ply'wood' *n.* [PLY[1] + WOOD] a construction material made of thin layers of wood glued together

PM, P.M., p.m., or **pm** *abbrev.* [L *post meridiem*] after noon: used to designate the time from noon to midnight

PMS [*p(re)m(enstrual) s(yndrome)*] the physical and emotional disorders that may precede menstruation

pneu·matic (nōō mat'ik) *adj.* [< Gr *pneuma,* breath] **1** of or containing wind, air, or gases **2** filled with or worked by compressed air — **pneu·mat'i·cally** *adv.*

pneu·mo·nia (nōō mōn'yə) *n.* [< Gr *pneumōn,* lung < *pnem,* breathe] inflammation of the lungs caused as by bacteria or viruses

PO or **P.O. 1** Post Office **2** post office box

poach[1] (pōch) *vt.* [< MFr *poche,* pocket: the yolk is "pocketed" in the white] to cook (fish, an egg without its shell, etc.) in or over boiling water

poach[2] (pōch) *vt., vi.* [< MHG *puchen,* to plunder] **1** to trespass on (private property), esp. for hunting or fishing **2** to hunt or catch (game or fish) illegally **3** to steal (anything) — **poach'er** *n.*

pock (päk) *n.* [OE *pocc*] **1** a pustule caused by smallpox, etc. **2** POCKMARK — **pocked** *adj.*

pocket (päk'it) *n.* [< Fr *poque,* a pouch] **1** a little bag or pouch, esp. one sewn into clothing, for carrying small articles **2** a pouchlike cavity or hollow **3** a small area or group *[a pocket of poverty]* — *adj.* **1** that can be carried in a pocket **2** small — *vt.* **1** to put into a pocket **2** to envelop; enclose **3** to take (money, etc.) dishonestly **4** to suppress *[pocket one's pride]* — **pock'et·ful',** *pl.* **-fuls',** *n.*

pock'et·book' *n.* **1** a woman's purse or handbag **2** monetary resources

pock'et·knife' *n., pl.* **-knives'** a knife with a blade or blades that fold into the handle

pock'mark' *n.* a scar left by a pustule, as of smallpox

pod (päd) *n.* [< ?] a dry fruit or seed vessel, as of peas, beans, etc.

-pod (päd) [< Gr *pous,* foot] *combining form* **1** foot **2** (one) having (a specified number or kind of) feet Also **-pode** (pōd)

po·di·a·try (pō dī'ə trē) *n.* [< Gr *pous,* foot + -IATRY] the profession dealing with the care and treatment of the feet — **po·di'a·trist** *n.*

po·di·um (pō'dē əm) *n., pl.* **-dia** (-ə) [L < Gr *pous,* foot] **1** a small platform, as for an orchestra conductor **2** LECTERN

poem (pō'əm) *n.* [< Gr *poiein,* to make] an arrangement of words, esp. a rhythmical composition, sometimes rhymed, in a style more imaginative than ordinary speech

po·esy (pō'ə sē') *n.* old-fashioned var. of POETRY

poet (pō'ət) *n.* **1** one who writes poems or verses: often (see -ESS) **po'et·ess** *n.fem.* **2** one who displays beauty of thought, language, etc. in expression

poet·as·ter (pō'ət as'tər) *n.* [< prec. + Gr -*aster,* dim. suffix] a writer of mediocre verse

po·etic (pō et'ik) *adj.* **1** of or for poets or poetry **2** displaying the beauty, imaginative qualities, etc. found in poetry Also **po·et'i·cal** *adj.* — **po·et'i·cally** *adv.*

poetic license deviation from strict fact or rules, for artistic effect

poet laureate the official poet of a nation, appointed to write poems celebrating national events, etc.

po·etry (pō'ə trē) *n.* **1** the writing of poems **2** poems **3** poetic qualities

po·grom (pō gräm', pō'grəm) *n.* [< Russ., earlier, riot, storm] an organized massacre, as of Jews in czarist Russia

poi (poi) *n.* [Haw] a pastelike Hawaiian food made of taro root

poign·ant (poin'yənt) *adj.* [< L *pungere,* to prick] **1** pungent **2** *a)* sharply painful to the feelings *b)* emotion-

---

THESAURUS

plus *a., prep.* added to, additional, additionally, increased by, with the addition of, surplus, positive; see also EXTRA. —*Ant.* LESS, minus, subtracted from.

plush* *a.* elegant, luxurious, sumptuous; see RICH 2.

PM or **P.M.** *abbrev.* after noon, afternoon, evening, before midnight, shank of the evening, sunset.

pneumonia *n.* pneumonitis, lobar pneumonia, croupous pneumonia; see ILLNESS 2.

poach[2] *v.* filch, pilfer, smuggle; see STEAL.

pock *n.* flaw, hole, mark; see BLEMISH, SCAR.

pocket *a.* small, tiny, miniature; see LITTLE 1, MINUTE 1.

pocket *n.* **1** [A cavity] hollow, opening, air pocket; see HOLE 1. **2** [A pouch sewed into a garment] pouch, poke, sac, pod. *Kinds of pockets include the following:* patch, slash, inset, watch, coin, invisible, pants, jacket, coat, vest, inner, outer, inside. **3** [Small area] isolated group, enclave, survival; see AREA. —**in someone's pocket*** controlled, under control, regulated; see MANAGED.

pocket *v.* conceal, hide, enclose; see STEAL.

pocketbook *n.* wallet, pouch, coin purse; see BAG, PURSE.

pod *n.* seed vessel, bean pod, pea pod; see SEED.

poem *n.* poetry, lyric, sonnet, ballad, quatrain, blank verse, free verse, song, composition, creation; see also WRITING 2.

poet *n.* writer, poemwriter, bard, versifier, minstrel, troubadour, verse maker, maker of verses, lyrist, author of the lyric, dramatic poet, dramatist, lyric poet, writer of lyrics, lyricist, poetaster; see also ARTIST, WRITER. *Major poets include the following—British:* Geoffrey Chaucer, Edmund Spenser, William Shakespeare, John Donne, John Milton, John Dryden, Alexander Pope, Samuel Johnson, Robert Burns, William Blake, William Wordsworth, Samuel Taylor Coleridge, Lord Byron, John Keats, Percy Bysshe Shelley, Alfred, Lord Tennyson, Robert Browning, Gerard Manley Hopkins, William Butler Yeats, T.S. Eliot, Dylan Thomas, Philip Larkin; *American:* Edgar Allan Poe, Walt Whitman, Emily Dickinson, Edwin Arlington Robinson, Robert Frost, Carl Sandburg, Ezra Pound, Wallace Stevens, E.E. Cummings, Robert Lowell, Marianne Moore; *Classical Greek:* Homer, Pindar, Aeschylus, Sophocles, Euripides; *Latin:* Virgil, Lucretius, Ovid, Horace, Catullus, Juvenal; *European:* Dante Alighieri, Petrarch, Ludovico Ariosto, François Villon, Jean de La Fontaine, Charles Baudelaire, Stéphane Mallarmé, Paul Verlaine, Arthur Rimbaud, Victor Hugo, Pedro Calderón, Federico Garcia Lorca, Pablo Neruda, Luis Vaz de Camões, Wolfgang von Goethe, Friedrich Schiller, Heinrich Heine, Rainer Maria Rilke, Bertolt Brecht, Alexander Pushkin, Boris Pasternak, Vladimir Mayakovski.

poetic *a.* poetical, lyric, lyrical, metrical, tuneful, elegiac, romantic, dramatic, iambic, dactylic, spondaic, trochaic, anapestic, imaginative.

poetry *n.* poem, song, versification, metrical composition, rime, rhyme, poesy, stanza, rhythmical composition, poetical writings. *Forms of verse include the following:* sonnet, Shakespearean sonnet, Italian sonnet, Miltonic sonnet, Wordsworthian sonnet, Chaucerian stanza, Spenserian stanza, heroic couplet, Alexandrine, iambic pentameter, rhyme royal, ottava rima, couplet, distich, ode, epode, triolet, rondeau, rondel, rondelet, tanka, haiku, ballade, sestine, villanelle, limerick, blank verse, free verse, stop-short, strophic verse, stanzaic verse, assonance, accentual verse, alliterative verse.

pogrom *n.* slaughter, mass murder, massacre, genocide; see also MURDER.

poin·ci·ana (poin′sē an′ə) *n.* ⟦after M. de *Poinci*, governor of the Fr West Indies⟧ a small, tropical tree or shrub with showy red or yellow flowers

poin·set·tia (poin set′ē ə; *widely*, -set′ə) *n.* ⟦after J. R. *Poinsett*, 19th-c. U.S. ambassador to Mexico⟧ a tropical shrub with yellow flowers and petal-like, red leaves

point (point) *n.* ⟦ < L *pungere*, to prick⟧ **1** a dot in writing, etc. ⟦a decimal *point*⟧ **2** a position or location **3** the exact moment **4** a condition reached ⟦boiling *point*⟧ **5** a detail; item ⟦*point* by *point*⟧ **6** a distinguishing feature **7** a unit, as of value, game scores, etc. **8** a sharp end **9** a projecting piece of land; cape **10** the essential fact or idea ⟦the *point* of a joke⟧ **11** a purpose; object **12** a convincing idea or fact **13** a helpful hint **14** a mark showing direction on a compass **15** *Finance a)* a $1 change in the price of a stock *b)* a unit or amount equal to one percent **16** *Printing* a measuring unit for type, about $\frac{1}{72}$ of an inch — *vt.* **1** to sharpen to a point **2** to give (a story, etc.) emphasis: usually with *up* **3** to show: usually with *out* ⟦point out the way⟧ **4** to aim — *vi.* **1** to direct one's finger (*at* or *to*) **2** to call attention (*to*) **3** to be directed (*to* or *toward*) —**at the point of** very close to —**beside the point** irrelevant —**to the point** pertinent; apt: also **in point**

point′-blank′ *adj., adv.* ⟦prec. + *blank* (white center of a target)⟧ **1** (aimed) straight at a mark **2** direct(ly); blunt(ly)

point′ed *adj.* **1** having a sharp end **2** sharp; incisive **3** aimed at someone, as a remark **4** very evident —**point′edly** *adv.*

poin·telle (poin tel′) *n.* a lacy, openwork fabric, often of acrylic, used for blouses, sweaters, etc.

point′er *n.* **1** a long, tapered rod for pointing to things **2** an indicator on a meter, etc. **3** a large, muscular hunting dog with a smooth coat **4** [Colloq.] a helpful hint or suggestion

poin·til·lism (pwan′tə liz′əm) *n.* ⟦Fr⟧ a style of painting using dots of color that blend together when seen from a distance —**poin′til·list** *n., adj.*

point′less *adj.* **1** without a point **2** without meaning or force; senseless

point man 1 the soldier in the front position in a patrol **2** anyone in the forefront of attacking or supporting a political program, etc.

point of view 1 the way in which something is viewed **2** a mental attitude or opinion

point′y *adj.* **-i·er**, **-i·est 1** coming to a sharp point **2** many-pointed

poise (poiz) *n.* ⟦ < L *pendere*, weigh⟧ **1** balance; stability **2** ease and dignity of manner **3** carriage, as of the body — *vt., vi.* **poised, pois′ing** to balance or be balanced

poi·son (poi′zən) *n.* ⟦ < L *potio*, potion⟧ a substance which in small quantities can cause illness or death — *vt.* **1** to harm or kill with poison **2** to put poison into **3** to influence wrongfully — *adj.* poisonous

poison ivy a plant having leaves of three leaflets and ivory-colored berries: it can cause a severe rash

poi′son·ous *adj.* that can injure or kill by or as by poison —**poi′son·ously** *adv.*

poison pill any defensive measure which makes the takeover of a corporation prohibitively expensive

poke[1] (pōk) *vt.* **poked, pok′ing** ⟦ < MDu *poken*⟧ **1** *a)* to prod, as with a stick *b)* [Slang] to hit **2** to make (a hole, etc.) by poking — *vi.* **1** to jab (*at*) **2** to pry or search (*about* or *around*) **3** to move slowly (*along*) — *n.* **1** a jab; thrust **2** [Slang] a blow with the fist —**poke fun (at)** to ridicule

poke[2] (pōk) *n.* ⟦OFr⟧ [Dial.] a sack

poker[1] (pōk′ər) *n.* ⟦ < ? Ger *pochspiel*, lit., game of defiance⟧ a card game in which the players bet on the value of their hands

poker[2] (pōk′ər) *n.* a bar, usually of iron, for stirring a fire

poker face an expressionless face, as of a poker player trying to conceal the nature of his or her hand

poky (pōk′ē) *adj.* **-i·er**, **-i·est** ⟦POKE[1] + -y[2]⟧ **1** slow, dull, etc. **2** small and uncomfortable, as a room Also **pok′ey**

pol (päl) *n.* [Slang] a politician

Pol. 1 Poland **2** Polish

po·lar (pō′lər) *adj.* **1** of or near the North or South pole **2** of a pole

polar bear a large, white bear of coastal arctic regions

Po·la·ris (pō lar′is) *n.* the bright star almost directly above the North Pole

po·lar·ity (pō lar′ə tē) *n., pl.* **-ties 1** the tendency of having opposite magnetic poles **2** the tendency to turn, grow, think, etc. in contrary directions, as if because of magnetic repulsion

po·lar·i·za·tion (pō′lər i zā′shən) *n.* **1** a polarizing or being polarized **2** *Optics* a condition, or the production of a condition, of electromagnetic waves in which the motion of the wave is confined to one plane or one direction

po·lar·ize (pō′lər īz′) *vt.* **-ized′, -iz′ing** to give polarity to — *vi.* to acquire polarity; specif., to separate into opposed or antagonistic groups, viewpoints, etc.

Po·lar·oid (pō′lər oid′) *trademark for:* **1** a transparent material capable of polarizing light **2** a camera that produces a print within seconds: in full **Polaroid (Land) camera**

pole[1] (pōl) *n.* ⟦ < L *palus*, a stake⟧ a long, slender piece of wood, metal, etc. — *vt., vi.* **poled, pol′ing** to push along (a boat or raft) with a pole —**pol′er** *n.*

pole[2] (pōl) *n.* ⟦ < Gr *polos*⟧ **1** either end of any axis, as of the earth **2** either of two opposed forces, parts, etc., as the ends of a magnet, the terminals of a battery, etc.

Pole (pōl) *n.* a native or inhabitant of Poland

pole·cat (pōl′kat′) *n.* ⟦prob. < OFr *poule*, hen + CAT⟧ **1** a small, weasel-like Old World carnivore **2** SKUNK

THESAURUS

point *n.* **1** [A position having no extent] location, spot, locality; see POSITION 1. **2** [A sharp, tapered end] end, pointed end, needle point, pin point, barb, prick, spur, spike, snag, spine, claw, tooth, calk, sticker; see also TIP 1. **3** [Anything having a point] sword, dagger, stiletto; see KNIFE, NEEDLE. **4** [Purpose] aim, object, intent; see PURPOSE 1. **5** [Meaning] force, drift, import; see MEANING. **6** [A detail] case, feature, point at issue; see CIRCUMSTANCE 1, DETAIL. —**at (or on) the point of** on the verge of, close to, almost; see NEAR 1. —**beside the point** immaterial, not pertinent, not germane; see IRRELEVANT. —**make a point of** stress, emphasize, make an issue of; see DECLARE. —**to the point** pertinent, apt, exact; see RELEVANT.

point *v.* **1** [To indicate] show, name, denote; see NAME 2. **2** [To direct] guide, steer, influence; see LEAD 1. —**point out** indicate, show, denote; see NAME 1.

pointed *a.* **1** [Sharp] fine, keen, spiked; see SHARP 1. **2** [Biting or insinuating] caustic, tart, trenchant; see SARCASTIC.

pointer *n.* **1** [A pointing instrument] hand, rod, indicator, dial, gauge, director, index, mark, signal-needle, register. **2** [A variety of dog] hunting dog, gun dog, game dog; see DOG. **3** [*A hint] clue, tip, warning; see HINT.

pointless *a.* **1** [Dull] uninteresting, prosaic, not pertinent; see IRRELEVANT, TRIVIAL, UNNECESSARY. **2** [Blunt] worn, obtuse, rounded; see DULL 1. **3** [Ineffective] useless, powerless, impotent; see INCOMPETENT, WEAK 1, 2.

point of view *n.* outlook, position, approach; see ATTITUDE.

poise *n.* balance, gravity, equilibrium; see COMPOSURE, DIGNITY.

poison *n.* virus, bane, toxin, infection, germ, bacteria, oil, vapor, gas. *Poisons include the following:* rattlesnake, copperhead, black-widow-spider, tarantula venom; smallpox, yellow-fever, common-cold, flu virus; poison oak, poison ivy, carbon monoxide gas, cooking gas, arsenic, lead, strychnine, oxalic, sulfuric, hydrochloric, nitric, carbolic, prussic, hydrocyanic acid; cantharides, caustic soda, lye, belladonna, aconite, lead arsenate, blue vitriol or copper sulfate, nicotine.

poison *v.* infect, injure, kill, murder, destroy, corrupt, pervert, undermine, defile, harm, taint, make ill, cause violent illness.—*Ant.* HELP, benefit, purify.

poisoned *a.* **1** [Suffering from poisoning] infected, indisposed, diseased; see SICK. **2** [Dying of poison] fatally poisoned, beyond recovery, succumbing; see DYING 1. **3** [Polluted with poison] contaminated, tainted, defiled, corrupted, venomous, virulent, impure, malignant, noxious, deadly, toxic; see also POISONOUS.—*Ant.* PURE, fresh, untainted.

poisonous *a.* bad, noxious, hurtful, dangerous, malignant, infective, venomous, virulent, vicious, corrupt, morbid, fatal, pestilential, toxic, deadly, destructive; see also HARMFUL.—*Ant.* HEALTHY, wholesome, nourishing.

poke[1] *n.* jab, thrust, punch; see BLOW.

poke[2] *v.* jab, punch, crowd; see PUSH 1.

polar *a.* glacial, frozen, frigid; see COLD 1.

pole[1] *n.* shaft, flagpole, flagstaff; see POST.

po·lemic (pō lem′ik) *adj.* [< Gr *polemos*, war] of or involving dispute Also **po·lem′i·cal** — *n.* (a) controversy

po·lem′ics *n.pl.* [*with sing. v.*] the art or practice of disputation —**po·lem′i·cist** (-i sist) *n.*

pole′star′ Polaris, the North Star: also **Pole Star** — *n.* a guiding principle

pole vault a leap for height by vaulting over a bar with the aid of a long pole —**pole′-vault′** *vi.* —**pole′-vault′er** *n.*

po·lice (pə lēs′) *n.* [Fr: ult. < Gr *polis*, city] 1 the governmental department (of a city, state, etc.) for keeping order, detecting crime, etc. 2 [*with pl. v.*] the members of such a department — *vt.* **-liced′, -lic′ing** 1 to control, protect, etc. with police or a similar force 2 to keep (a military camp, etc.) clean and orderly

police′man (-mən) *n., pl.* **-men** a member of a police force —**police′wom′an**, *pl.* **-wom′en**, *n.fem.*

police officer a member of a police force

police state a government that seeks to suppress political opposition by means of police

poli·cy[1] (päl′ə sē) *n., pl.* **-cies** [see POLICE] 1 wise management 2 a principle, plan, etc., as of a government

poli·cy[2] (päl′ə sē) *n., pl.* **-cies** [< Gr *apodeixis*, proof] a written insurance contract In full **insurance policy**

pol′icy·hold′er *n.* a person to whom an insurance policy is issued

po·lio·my·eli·tis (pō′lē ō′mī′ə līt′is) *n.* [< Gr *polios*, gray + MYELITIS] an acute infectious disease caused by a virus inflammation of the gray matter of the spinal cord, often resulting in muscular paralysis Also **po′lio′**

pol·ish (päl′ish) *vt.* [< L *polire*] 1 to smooth and brighten, as by rubbing 2 to refine (manners, style, etc.) — *vi.* to take a polish — *n.* 1 surface gloss 2 elegance, refinement, etc. 3 a substance used to polish —**polish off** [Colloq.] to finish (a meal, job, etc.) completely — *n.* the Slavic language of the Poles

Pol·ish (pōl′ish) *adj.* of Poland, its people, language, etc.

po·lite (pə līt′) *adj.* [< L *polire*, to polish] 1 cultured; refined 2 having good manners; courteous —**po·lite′ly** *adv.* —**po·lite′ness** *n.*

poli·tesse (päl′i tes′) *n.* [Fr] politeness

poli·tic (päl′i tik′) *adj.* [see POLICE] 1 having practical wisdom; prudent 2 expedient, as a plan — *vi.* **-ticked′, -tick′ing** to campaign in politics

po·liti·cal (pə lit′i kəl) *adj.* 1 of, concerned with, or engaged in government, politics, etc. 2 of or characteristic of political parties or politicians —**po·lit′i·cally** *adv.*

politically correct holding orthodox liberal political views: usually used to connote dogmatism, excessive sensitivity to minority causes, etc. —**political correctness**

political science the science of the principles, organization, and methods of government —**political scientist**

poli·ti·cian (päl′i tish′ən) *n.* one actively engaged in politics: often used with implications of seeking personal or partisan gain, scheming, etc.

po·liti·cize (pə lit′ə sīz′) *vt.* **-cized′, -ciz′ing** to make political

po·liti·co (pə lit′i kō′) *n., pl.* **-cos′** [< Sp or It] POLITICIAN

poli·tics (päl′i tiks) *n.pl.* [*with sing. or pl. v.*] 1 the science of government 2 political affairs 3 political methods, tactics, etc. 4 political opinions, etc. 5 factional scheming for power

pol·ity (-ə tē) *n., pl.* **-ties** [see POLICE] 1 governmental organization 2 a society with a government; state

polka (pōl′kə) *n.* [Czech, Polish dance] 1 a fast dance for couples 2 music for this dance

polka dot (pō′kə; *also* pōl′-) any of a pattern of small, round dots on cloth

poll (pōl) *n.* [ME *pol*] 1 the head 2 a counting, listing, etc. of persons, esp. of voters 3 the number of votes recorded 4 [*pl.*] a place where votes are cast 5 a canvassing of people's opinions on some question — *vt.* 1 to cut off or cut short the wool, hair, horns, etc. of 2 to register the votes of 3 to require each member of (a jury, etc.) to declare individual votes 4 to receive (a specified number of votes) 5 to cast (a vote) 6 to canvass in a POLL (sense 5)

pol·len (päl′ən) *n.* [L, dust] the fine, dustlike mass of grains in the anthers of seed plants

pollen count the number of grains of pollen, esp. of ragweed, in a given volume of air at a specified time and place

pol·li·nate (päl′ə nāt′) *vt.* **-nat′ed, -nat′ing** to transfer pollen to the pistil of (a flower) —**pol′li·na′tion** *n.*

pol·li·wog (päl′ē wäg′, -wôg′) *n.* [< ME: see POLL + WIGGLE] TADPOLE Also **pol′ly·wog′**

poll·ster (pōl′stər) *n.* one whose work is taking public-opinion polls

pol·lute (pə lōōt′) *vt.* **-lut′ed, -lut′ing** [< L *polluere*] to make unclean or impure —**pol·lu′tant** *n.* —**pol·lut′er** *n.* —**pol·lu′tion** *n.*

polo (pō′lō) *n.* [ult. < Tibetan *pulu*, ball] a game played on horseback by two teams, using a wooden ball and long-handled mallets

polo·naise (päl′ə nāz′) *n.* [Fr (fem.), Polish] a stately Polish dance

pol·ter·geist (pōl′tər gīst′) *n.* [Ger < *poltern*, to rumble + *geist*, ghost] a ghost supposed to be responsible for mysterious noisy disturbances

pol·troon (päl trōōn′) *n.* [< It *poltrone*] a thorough coward

poly- [< Gr] *combining form* much, many

◼ THESAURUS ◼

police *n.* arm of the law, law enforcement body, FBI, police officers, policemen, police force, detective force, military police, Royal Canadian Mounted Police, New York's Finest*.

police *v.* watch, control, patrol; see GUARD.

policeman *n.* patrolman, officer, magistrate, process server, constable, cop*, copper*, flatfoot*, fuzz*, the Man*, speed cop*, bobby*, pig*. *Police officers include the following:* beat patrolman, mounted police, motorcycle police, traffic police, squad-car police, municipal police, state police, highway patrol, detective, federal agent, federal investigator, fed*, narc*, FBI agent, prefect, inspector, member of the homicide squad, member of the vice squad.

police state *n.* dictatorship, autocracy, authoritarian government; see TYRANNY.

policy[1] *n.* course, procedure, method, system, strategy, tactics, administration, management, theory, doctrine, behavior, scheme, design, arrangement, organization, plan, order.

polish *n.* shine, burnish, glaze; see FINISH 2.

polish *v.* burnish, furbish, finish; see SHINE 3.

polished *a.* 1 [Bright] glossy, shining, gleaming; see BRIGHT 1. 2

[Refined] polite, well-bred, cultured; see REFINED 2.

polite *a.* obliging, thoughtful, mannerly, attentive, pleasant, gentle, mild, nice, concerned, considerate, solicitous, bland, condescending, honey-tongued, amiable, gracious, cordial, considerate, good-natured, sympathetic, interested, smooth, diplomatic, kindly, kind, kindly disposed, affable, agreeable, civil, complacent, respectful, amenable, gallant, genteel, gentlemanly, mannered, sociable, ingratiating, neighborly, friendly, respectful.—*Ant.* EGOTISTIC, insolent, pompous.

politely *a.* thoughtfully, considerately, attentively, solicitously, cordially, graciously, kindheartedly, amiably, compassionately, gently, urbanely, affably, agreeably, civilly, gallantly, complacently, sociably, elegantly, gracefully, charmingly, ingratiatingly, winningly, tactfully, in good humor, with good grace; see also RESPECTFULLY.

politeness *n.* refinement, culture, civility; see COURTESY 1.

political *a.* legislative, executive, administrative; see GOVERNMENTAL.

politician *n.* officeholder, office seeker, party man, partisan, legislator, congressman, member of parliament, politico.

politics *n.* practical government, functional government, systematic government, domestic affairs, internal affairs, foreign affairs, matters of state, campaigning, getting votes, seeking nomination, electioneering, being up for election, running for office.

poll *n.* 1 [A census] vote, consensus, ballot; see CENSUS. 2 [A voting place; *usually plural*] ballot box, voting machines, polling place, polling area.

poll *v.* question, register, enroll; see EXAMINE, LIST 1.

pollute *v.* deprave, soil, stain; see DIRTY, POISON.

polluted *a.* corrupted, defiled, poisoned; see DIRTY 1.

pollution *n.* corruption, defilement, adulteration, blight, soiling, fouling, foulness, taint, tainting, polluting, decomposition, desecration, profanation, abuse, deterioration, rottenness, impairment, misuse, infection, besmearing, besmirching, smirching. *Some common pollutants of the air and water include the following:* sewage, soapsuds, garbage, factory waste, detergent, carbon monoxide, automobile or bus or truck exhaust, pesticides, factory smoke.

poltergeist *n.* spirit, spook, supernatural visitant; see GHOST.

poly·clin·ic (päl'i klin'ik) *n.* 〖POLY- + CLINIC〗 a clinic or hospital for treating various kinds of diseases

poly·es·ter (päl'ē es'tər) *n.* 〖POLY(MER) + ESTER〗 a polymeric resin used in making plastics, fibers, etc.

poly·eth·yl·ene (päl'ē eth'ə lēn') *n.* 〖POLY(MER) + ETHYL-ENE〗 a thermoplastic resin used in making plastics, films, etc.

po·lyg·a·my (pə lig'ə mē) *n.* 〖< Gr *poly-*, many + *gamos*, marriage〗 the practice of having two or more spouses at the same time —**po·lyg'a·mist** *n.* —**po·lyg'a·mous** *adj.*

poly·glot (päl'i glät') *adj.* 〖< Gr *poly-*, many + *glōtta*, tongue〗 1 speaking or writing several languages 2 written in several languages —*n.* 1 a polyglot person 2 a polyglot book

pol'y·gon' (-gän') *n.* 〖< Gr: see POLY- & -GON〗 a plane figure, esp. one with more than four sides and angles —**po·lyg·o·nal** (pə lig'ə nəl) *adj.*

pol'y·graph' (-graf') *n.* 〖see POLY- & -GRAPH〗 a device measuring changes in respiration, pulse rate, etc., used on persons suspected of lying

pol'y·math' (-ə math') *n.* 〖< Gr *poly-*, much + *manthanein*, learn〗 a person of great and varied learning

pol'y·mer (-mər) *n.* 〖Ger < Gr *poly-*, many + *meros*, part〗 a substance consisting of giant molecules formed from polymerization —**pol'y·mer'ic** (-mer'ik) *adj.*

po·lym·er·i·za·tion (pə lim'ər ə zā'shən) *n.* a chaining together of many simple molecules to form a more complex molecule with different properties —**po·lym'er·ize'** (-īz'), **-ized', -iz'ing,** *vt., vi.*

Poly·ne·sian (päl'i nē'zhən) *n.* 1 a member of any of the indigenous peoples of Polynesia 2 the languages of Polynesia —*adj.* of the Polynesians, their languages, etc.

poly·no·mial (päl'i nō'mē əl) *n.* 〖POLY- + (BI)NOMIAL〗 a mathematical expression containing three or more terms (Ex: $x^3 + 3x + 2$ or $x^2 - 2xy + y^2$)

polyp (päl'ip) *n.* 〖< Gr *poly-*, many + *pous*, foot〗 1 a cnidarian with many small tentacles at the top of a tube-like body 2 a growth of mucous membrane in the bladder, rectum, etc.

po·lyph·o·ny (pə lif'ə nē) *n.* 〖< Gr *poly-*, many + *phōnē*, a sound〗 *Music* a combining of independent, harmonizing tones, as in a fugue; counterpoint —**poly·phonic** (päl'i fän'ik) *adj.*

poly·syl·lab·ic (päl'i si lab'ik) *adj.* 1 having four or more syllables 2 characterized by polysyllabic words —**pol'y·syl'la·ble** (-sil'ə bəl) *n.*

pol'y·tech'nic (-tek'nik) *adj.* 〖< Gr *poly-*, many + *technē*, art〗 of or providing instruction in many scientific and technical subjects

pol'y·the·ism (-thē iz'əm) *n.* 〖< Gr *poly*, many + *theos*, god〗 belief in more than one god —**pol'y·theist** *adj., n.* —**pol'y·theis'tic** *adj.*

poly·un·satu·rated (päl'ē un sach'ə rāt'id) *adj.* designating any of certain plant and animal fats and oils with a low cholesterol content

poly·vi·nyl (päl'i vī'nəl) *adj.* designating or of any of a group of polymerized vinyl compounds: see VINYL

po·made (päm äd', *also* pō mäd'; *chiefly Brit* pō mäd') *n.* 〖< It *pomo*, apple (orig. an ingredient)〗 a perfumed ointment, as for the hair

pome·gran·ate (päm'gran'it, päm'ə-; *also* pum-) *n.* 〖ult. < L *pomum*, fruit + *granum*, seed〗 1 a round, red fruit with a hard rind and many seeds 2 the bush or tree it grows on

pom·mel (pum'əl; *also* päm'-) *n.* 〖< L *pomum*, fruit〗 1 the knob on the end of the hilt of some swords and daggers 2 the rounded, upward-projecting front part of a saddle —*vt.* **-meled** *or* **-melled, -mel·ing** *or* **-mel·ling** PUMMEL

pomp (pämp) *n.* 〖< Gr *pompē*, solemn procession〗 1 stately display 2 ostentatious show or display

pom·pa·dour (päm'pə dôr') *n.* 〖after Mme. *Pompadour*, mistress of Louis XV, 18th-c. king of France〗 a hairdo in which the hair is brushed up high from the forehead

pom·pano (päm'pə nō') *n.* 〖< Sp〗 a spiny-finned food fish of North America and the West Indies

pom·pom (päm'päm') *n.* 〖see POMP〗 an ornamental tuft of silk, etc., as on clothing: also **pom'pon'** (-pän')

pom·pous (päm'pəs) *adj.* 1 full of pomp 2 pretentious; self-important —**pom·pos'i·ty** (-päs'ə tē) *n.*

pon·cho (pän'chō) *n., pl.* **-chos** 〖AmSp < AmInd, woolen cloth〗 a cloak like a blanket with a hole in the middle for the head, esp. a waterproof one worn as a raincoat

pond (pänd) *n.* 〖< ME *pounde*, enclosure〗 a body of water smaller than a lake

pon·der (pän'dər) *vt., vi.* 〖< L *ponderare*, weigh〗 to think deeply (about); consider carefully

pon·dero·sa (pine) (pän'dər ō'sə) 〖< L *ponderosus*, very heavy〗 a yellow pine of W North America

pon'der·ous *adj.* 1 very heavy 2 unwieldy 3 labored and dull

pone (pōn) *n.* 〖< AmInd〗 〖Chiefly South〗 corn bread in the form of small ovals

pon·gee (pän jē', pun-) *n.* 〖< Mandarin Chin dial. *pen-chi*, one's own loom〗 a soft, thin silk cloth, usually in its natural tan

pon·iard (pän'yərd) *n.* 〖ult. < L *pugnus*, fist〗 a dagger

pon·tiff (pän'tif) *n.* 〖< L *pontifex*, high priest〗 1 a bishop 2 [P-] the pope —**pon·tif'i·cal** *adj.*

pon·tif'i·cate (-i kit; *for v.*, -kāt') *n.* the office or term of a pontiff —*vi.* **-cat'ed, -cat'ing** 1 to officiate as a pontiff 2 to be pompous or dogmatic

pon·toon (pän tōōn') *n.* 〖< L *pons*, a bridge〗 1 a flat-bottomed boat 2 any of a row of boats or floating objects used to support a temporary bridge 3 a boatlike float on an aircraft's landing gear

pony (pō'nē) *n., pl.* **-nies** 〖prob. < L *pullus*, foal〗 1 a horse of any small breed 2 a small liqueur glass 3 [Colloq.] a literal translation of a foreign work, used in doing schoolwork

po'ny·tail' *n.* a hair style in which the hair is tied tightly at the back and hangs down like a pony's tail

pooch (pōōch) *n.* 〖< ?〗 [Slang] a dog

poo·dle (pōōd'l) *n.* 〖Ger *pudel*〗 a dog with a thick, wiry coat of tight curls in a solid color

pooh (pōō) *interj.* an exclamation of disdain, disbelief, or impatience

pooh-pooh (pōō'pōō') *vt.* to treat disdainfully; make light of

pool[1] (pōōl) *n.* 〖OE *pol*〗 1 a small pond 2 a small collection of liquid, as a puddle 3 a tank for swimming

pool[2] (pōōl) *n.* 〖< LL *pulla*, hen〗 1 a game of billiards played on a table with six pockets 2 a combination of resources, funds, supplies, etc. for some common purpose 3 the parties forming such a combination —*vt., vi.* to contribute to a common fund

poop[1] (pōōp) *n.* 〖< L *puppis*, stern of a ship〗 a raised deck at the stern of a ship Also **poop deck**

poop[2] (pōōp) *vt.* [Slang] to tire

poop[3] (pōōp) *n.* [Slang] current inside information

poor (poor) *adj.* 〖< L *pauper*, poor〗 1 having little or no means of support; needy 2 lacking in some quality; specif., *a*) inadequate *b*) inferior or worthless *c*) con-

---

◼ THESAURUS ◼

polygamy *n.* polyandry, plural marriage, bigamy; see MARRIAGE.

pomp *n.* magnificence, affectation, splendor; see MAGNIFICENCE.

pompous *a.* arrogant, haughty, proud; see EGOTISTIC.

pond *n.* fishpond, millpond, lily pond; see LAKE, POOL 1.

ponder *v.* meditate, deliberate, consider; see THINK 1.

ponderous *a.* dull, weighty, lifeless; see HEAVY.

pony *n.* Shetland pony, bronco, mustang; see HORSE.

poodle *n.* French poodle, French barbet, fancy dog; see DOG.

pool[1,2] *n.* 1 [Small body of liquid, usually water] puddle, mud puddle, pond, fishpond, millpond; see also LAKE. 2 [Supply] funds, provisions,

amount available; see EQUIPMENT. 3 [Game] snooker, 8-ball, billiards; see GAME 1.

pool[2] *v.* combine, merge, blend; see JOIN 1.

poor *a.* 1 [Lacking worldly goods] indigent, penniless, moneyless, impecunious, destitute, needy, poverty-stricken, underprivileged, fortuneless, starved, pinched, reduced, beggared, emptyhanded, meager, scanty, insolvent, ill-provided, ill-furnished, in want, suffering privation, in need, poor as a church mouse, broke, hard up, down and out.—*Ant.* WEALTHY, well-to-do, affluent. 2 [Lacking excellence] pitiful, paltry, contemptible, miserable, pitiable, dwarfed, insignificant, diminutive, ordinary, common, mediocre, trashy,

shoddy, worthless, sorry, base, mean, coarse, vulgar, inferior, imperfect, smaller, lesser, below par, subnormal, under average; second-rate, third-rate, fourth-rate, etc.; reduced, defective, deficient, lower, subordinate, minor, secondary, humble, second-hand, pedestrian, beggarly, tawdry, petty, unimportant, bad, cheap, flimsy, threadbare, badly made, less than good, unwholesome, lacking in quality, dowdy, second-class, shabby, gaudy, mass-produced, squalid, trivial, sleazy, trifling, unsuccessful, second-best, tasteless, insipid, rustic, crude, odd, rock-bottom, garish, flashy, showy, loud, unsightly, affected, ramshackle, tumble-down, glaring, artificial, newfangled, out-of-date, crummy*, junky*, two-bit*, temptible **3** worthy of pity; unfortunate —**the poor** poor, or needy, people —**poor′ly** *adv.*

poor′house′ *n.* [Historical] a publicly supported institution for paupers

poor′-mouth′ *vi.* [Colloq.] to complain about one's lack of money

pop¹ (päp) *n.* [echoic] **1** a sudden, light, explosive sound **2** any carbonated, nonalcoholic beverage — *vi.* **popped, pop′ping 1** to make, or burst with, a pop **2** to move, go, etc. suddenly **3** to bulge: said of the eyes **4** *Baseball* to hit the ball high into the infield — *vt.* **1** to cause to pop, as corn by roasting **2** to put suddenly /*to pop* one's head in/

pop² (päp) *n.* [< PAPA] [Colloq.] FATHER

pop³ (päp) *adj.* **1** of music popular with the general public **2** intended for the popular taste, esp. as exploited commercially /*pop* culture/ **3** of a realistic art style using techniques and subjects adapted from commercial art, comic strips, posters, etc. — *n.* pop music

pop. 1 popular **2** popularly **3** population

pop′corn′ *n.* **1** a variety of corn with hard grains which pop open into a white, puffy mass when heated **2** the popped grains

pope (pōp) *n.* [< Gr *pappas*, father] [*usually* P-] *R.C.Ch.* the bishop of Rome and head of the Church

pop′gun′ *n.* a toy gun that shoots pellets by air compression, with a pop

pop·in·jay (päp′in jā′) *n.* [< Ar *babghō?*, a parrot] a conceited person

pop′lar (päp′lər) *n.* [< L *populus*] **1** a tall tree of the willow family having soft, fibrous wood **2** its wood

pop′lin (päp′lin) *n.* [prob. after *Poperinge*, city in Flanders] a sturdy ribbed fabric of cotton, silk, etc.

pop′o′ver *n.* a very light, puffy, hollow muffin

pop′per *n.* a person or thing that pops; specif., a covered pan, etc. for popping corn

poppy (päp′ē) *n., pl.* **-pies** [< L *papaver*] a plant with a milky juice and variously colored flowers

pop′py·cock′ (-käk′) *n.* [Colloq.] foolish talk; nonsense

poppy seed the small, dark seed of the poppy, used in baking, etc.

pops (päps) *adj.* of a symphony orchestra that plays light classical music or arrangements of popular music — *n.* a pops orchestra, concert, etc.

pop-top (päp′täp′) *n.* a container with a tab or ring pulled or pushed to make an opening in the top

popu·lace (päp′yōō lis) *n.* [< L *populus*] **1** the common people; the masses **2** POPULATION (sense 1*a*)

popu·lar (päp′yōō lər) *adj.* [< L *populus*, the people] **1** of, carried on by, or intended for people generally **2** not expensive /*popular* prices/ **3** commonly accepted; prevalent **4** liked by many people —**pop′u·lar′i·ty** (-lar′ə tē) *n.* —**pop′u·larly** *adv.*

popu·lar·ize (päp′yōō lə riz′) *vt.* **-ized′, -iz′ing** to make popular —**pop′u·lari·za′tion** *n.*

popu·late (päp′yōō lāt′) *vt.* **-lat′ed, -lat′ing** [< L *populus*, the people] **1** to inhabit **2** to supply with inhabitants

pop·u·la′tion *n.* **1** *a*) all the people in a country, region, etc. *b*) the number of these **2** a populating or being populated

population explosion the great and rapid increase in human population in modern times

popu·list (päp′yōō list) *n.* a politician, etc. who claims to represent the common people: often applied to someone demagogic — *adj.* of a populist —**pop′u·lism′** *n.*

popu·lous (päp′yōō ləs) *adj.* full of people; thickly populated

por·celain (pôr′sə lin) *n.* [< It *porcellana*] a hard, white, translucent variety of ceramic ware

porch (pôrch) *n.* [< L *porta*, gate] **1** a covered entrance to a building **2** an open or enclosed gallery or room on the outside of a building

por·cine (pôr′sin′, -sin) *adj.* [< L *porcus*, hog] of or like pigs or hogs

por·cu·pine (pôr′kyōō pīn′) *n.* [< L *porcus*, pig + *spina*, spine] a rodent having coarse hair mixed with long, stiff, sharp spines

pore¹ (pôr, pōr) *vi.* **pored, por′ing** [ME *poren*] **1** to study carefully: with *over* **2** to ponder: with *over*

pore² (pôr, pōr) *n.* [< Gr *poros*, passage] a tiny opening, as in plant leaves or skin, for absorbing or discharging fluids

pork (pôrk) *n.* [< L *porcus*, pig] the flesh of a pig, used as food

pork barrel [Colloq.] government appropriations for political patronage

pork′y *adj.* **-i·er, -iest 1** of or like pork **2** [Slang] saucy, cocky, etc.

porno (pôr′nō) *n., adj.* [Slang] *short for* PORNOGRAPHY, PORNOGRAPHIC Also **porn** (pôrn)

por·nog·ra·phy (pôr näg′rə fē) *n.* [< Gr *pornē*, a prostitute + *graphein*, write] writings, pictures, etc. intended primarily to arouse sexual desire —**por′no·graph′ic** (-nə graf′ik) *adj.*

po·rous (pôr′əs) *adj.* full of pores, through which fluids, air, or light may pass —**po·ros·ity** (pō räs′ə tē) *n.*

por·phy·ry (pôr′fər ē) *n., pl.* **-ries** [< Gr *porphyros*, purple] any igneous rock with large, distinct crystals

por·poise (pôr′pəs) *n.* [< L *porcus*, pig + *piscis*, a fish] **1** a small whale with a blunt snout **2** a dolphin

por·ridge (pôr′ij) *n.* [< POTTAGE by confusion with VL *porrata*, leek broth] [Chiefly Brit., etc.] a soft food of cereal or meal boiled in water or milk

por·rin·ger (-in jər) *n.* [< Fr *potager*, soup dish: infl. by prec.] a bowl for porridge, cereal, etc.

port¹ (pôrt) *n.* [< L *portus*, haven] **1** a harbor **2** a city with a harbor where ships load and unload cargo

port² (pôrt) *n.* [after *Oporto*, city in Portugal] a sweet, dark-red wine

port³ (pôrt) *vt.* [< L *portare*, carry] to hold (a rifle, etc.) diagonally in front of one, as for inspection

port⁴ (pôrt) *n.* [< PORT¹] the left side of a ship, etc. as one faces forward — *adj.* of or on this side — *vt., vi.* to turn (the helm) to the port side

port⁵ (pôrt) *n.* [< L *porta*, door] **1** PORTHOLE **2** an opening, as in a valve face, for the passage of steam, etc. **3** *Comput.* the circuit, outlet, etc. which connects a computer and its peripheral

---

THESAURUS

raunchy*, corny*, cheesy*; see also INADEQUATE, UNSATISFACTORY. **3** [Lacking strength] puny, feeble, infirm; see WEAK 1. **4** [Lacking vigor or health] indisposed, impaired, imperfect; see SICK. **5** [Lacking fertility] infertile, unproductive, barren; see STERILE 1, 2, WORTHLESS.

poor *n.* needy, forgotten man, the unemployed, underdogs, the underprivileged, beggars, the impoverished masses, second-class citizen, have-nots; see also PEOPLE 3.

poorly *a.* defectively, crudely, unsuccessfully; see BADLY 1, INADEQUATELY.

pop¹ *n.* [A slight explosive sound] report, burst, shot; see NOISE 1. **2** [A carbonated drink] soda pop, ginger pop, soda water, beverage, soft drink; see also DRINK 2.

pop¹ *v.* dart, leap, protrude; see JUMP 1.

Pope *n.* head of the Roman Catholic Church, bishop of Rome, the Holy Father; see PRIEST.

poppy *n.* bloom, blossom, herb; see DRUG, FLOWER.

populace *n.* masses, commonality, multitude; see MAN 1, PEOPLE 3.

popular *a.* **1** [Generally liked] favorite, well-liked, approved, pleasing, suitable, well-received, sought, fashionable, stylish, beloved, likable, lovable, attractive, praised, promoted, recommended, in the public eye, celebrated, noted, admired, famous, run after*.—*Ant.* UNKNOWN, in disrepute, out of favor. **2** [Cheap] low-priced, popular-priced, marked down; see CHEAP 1, ECONOMICAL 2. **3** [Commonly accepted] general, familiar, demanded, in demand, prevalent, prevailing, current, in use, widespread, ordinary, adopted, embraced, having caught on, in the majority; see also FASHIONABLE, MODERN 1. **4** [Pertaining to the common people] proletarian, accessible, neighborly; see DEMOCRATIC, REPUBLICAN.

popularity *n.* approval, general esteem, widespread acceptance, following, prevalence, universality, demand, fashionableness, the rage*.

popularly *a.* commonly, usually, ordinarily; see REGULARLY.

populated *a.* crowded, teeming, populous, peopled, urban, inhabited; see also INHABITED.

population *n.* inhabitants, dwellers, citizenry, natives, group, residents, culture, community, state, populace; see also SOCIETY 2.

porch *n.* entrance, doorstep, stoop; see ENTRANCE 2.

pore² *n.* opening, foramen, orifice, vesicle; see also HOLE 1.

pork *n.* ham, bacon, chops; see MEAT.

pornographic *a.* immoral, dirty, obscene; see LEWD 2.

pornography *n.* vulgarity, obscenity, smut; see LEWDNESS.

porous *a.* pervious, permeable, acceptable; see OPEN 1.

port¹ *n.* haven, anchorage, gate; see DOCK.

port·a·ble (pôr′ə bəl) *adj.* ⟦< L *portare*, carry⟧ 1 that can be carried 2 easily carried — *n.* something portable — **port′abil′ity** *n.*

por·tage (pôr′tij, pôr täzh′) *n.* ⟦< L *portare*, carry⟧ 1 a carrying of boats and supplies overland between navigable lakes, rivers, etc. 2 any route over which this is done — *vt., vi.* **-taged, -tag·ing** to carry (boats, etc.) over a portage

por·tal (pôrt′l) *n.* ⟦< L *porta*, door⟧ a doorway, gate, or entrance

port·cul·lis (pôrt kul′is) *n.* ⟦< MFr *porte*, gate + *coleïce*, sliding⟧ a heavy iron grating lowered to bar the gateway of a castle or fortified town

por·tend (pôr tend′) *vt.* ⟦< L *por-*, forth + *tendere*, to stretch⟧ 1 to be an omen of; presage 2 to signify

por·tent (pôr′tent′) *n.* 1 something that portends an event 2 significance

por·ten·tous (pôr ten′təs) *adj.* 1 portending evil; ominous 2 amazing 3 pompous; self-important —**por·ten′tously** *adv.*

por·ter[1] (pôr′tər) *n.* ⟦< L *porta*, gate⟧ a doorman or gatekeeper

por·ter[2] (pôr′tər) *n.* ⟦< L *portare*, carry⟧ 1 one who carries luggage, etc. for hire 2 an employee who sweeps, cleans, etc. in a bank, store, etc. 3 a railroad attendant for passengers as on a sleeper 4 a dark-brown beer

por′ter·house′ (-hous′) *n.* ⟦orig. a tavern: see PORTER[2], sense 4⟧ a choice cut of beef between the tenderloin and the sirloin 1 full **porterhouse steak**

port·fo·lio (pôrt fō′lē ō′) *n., pl.* **-lios′** ⟦< L *portare*, carry + *folium*, leaf⟧ 1 a flat, portable case, for loose papers; briefcase 2 the office of a minister of state 3 a list of an investor's securities

port·hole (pôrt′hōl′) *n.* an opening in a ship's side to admit light and air

por·ti·co (pôr′ti kō′) *n., pl.* **-coes′** or **-cos′** ⟦< L *porticus*, porch⟧ a porch or covered walk, consisting of a roof supported by columns

por·tiere or **por·tière** (pôr tyer′) *n.* ⟦Fr < *porte*, door⟧ a curtain hung in a doorway

por·tion (pôr′shən) *n.* ⟦< L *portio*⟧ 1 a part, esp. that allotted to a person; share 2 a dowry 3 one's lot; destiny — *vt.* 1 to divide into portions 2 to give as a portion to

portly (pôrt′lē) *adj.* **-lier, -li·est** 1 large and stately 2 stout; corpulent —**port′li·ness** *n.*

port·man·teau (pôrt man′tō′) *n., pl.* **-teaus′** or **-teaux′** (-tōz′) ⟦< Fr *porter*, carry + *manteau*, cloak⟧ a stiff suitcase that opens into two compartments

portmanteau word a word that is a combination of two other words (Ex.: *smog*, from *smoke* and *fog*)

port of entry a place where customs officials check people and goods entering a country

por·trait (pôr′trit, -trāt′) *n.* ⟦see PORTRAY⟧ 1 a painting, photograph, etc. of a person, esp. of the face 2 a description, portrayal, etc.

por′traiture (-tri chər) *n.* the practice or art of portraying

por·tray (pôr trā′) *vt.* ⟦< L *pro-*, forth + *trahere*, draw⟧ 1 to make a portrait of 2 to describe graphically 3 to play the part of as in a play or movie —**por·tray′al** *n.*

Por·tu·guese (pôr′chə gēz′, -gēs′) *adj.* of Portugal, its people, language, etc. — *n.* 1 *pl.* **-guese′** a native or inhabitant of Portugal 2 a Romance language of Portugal and Brazil

por·tu·laca (pôr′chə lak′ə) *n.* ⟦< L *portula*, small door: from the opening in its seed capsule⟧ a fleshy plant with yellow, pink, or purple flowers

pose (pōz) *vt.* **posed, pos′ing** ⟦< L *pausare*, to stop⟧ 1 to propose (a question, etc.) 2 to put (a model, etc.) in a certain attitude — *vi.* 1 to assume a certain attitude, as in modeling for an artist 2 to strike attitudes for effect 3 set oneself up (*as*) [*to pose* as an officer] — *n.* 1 a bodily attitude, esp. one held for an artist, etc. 2 behavior assumed for effect

Po·sei·don (pō sī′dən) the Greek god of the sea

poser (pōz′ər) *n.* 1 one who poses; esp., an affected person: also **po·seur** (pō zur′) 2 a baffling question

posh (päsh) *adj.* ⟦< ?⟧ [Colloq.] luxurious and fashionable

posit (päz′it) *vt.* ⟦see fol.⟧ to suppose to be a fact; postulate

po·si·tion (pə zish′ən) *n.* ⟦< L *ponere*, to place⟧ 1 the way in which a person or thing is placed or arranged 2 one's attitude or opinion 3 the place where one is; location 4 the usual or proper place 5 rank, esp. high rank 6 a post of employment; job — *vt.* to put in a certain position

pos·i·tive (päz′ə tiv) *adj.* ⟦see prec.⟧ 1 definitely set; explicit [*positive* instructions] 2 *a*) having the mind set; confident *b*) overconfident or dogmatic 3 showing agreement; affirmative 4 constructive [*positive* criticism] ·5 regarded as having real existence [a *positive* good] 6 based on facts [*positive* proof] 7 *Elec. a*) of electricity predominating in a glass body after it has been rubbed with silk *b*) charged with positive electricity *c*) having a deficiency of electrons 8 *Gram.* of an adjective or adverb in its uncompared degree 9 *Math.* greater than zero 10 *Med.* proving the presence of a condition, bacteria, etc. 11 *Photog.* with the light and shade corresponding to those of the subject — *n.* something positive, as a degree, quality, quantity, photographic print, etc. —**pos′i·tively** *adv.*

pos·i·tron (päz′i trän′) *n.* ⟦POSI(TIVE) + (ELEC)TRON⟧ the positive antiparticle of an electron, having the same mass and magnitude of charge

poss. 1 possessive 2 possibly

posse (päs′ē) *n.* ⟦< L, be able⟧ the body of men summoned to assist the sheriff in keeping the peace, etc.

pos·sess (pə zes′) *vt.* ⟦< L *possidere*⟧ 1 to have as belonging to one; own 2 to have as an attribute, quality, etc. 3 to gain control over [*possessed* by an idea] —**pos·ses′sor** *n.*

pos·sessed′ *adj.* 1 owned 2 controlled, as if by a demon; crazed

pos·ses′sion (-zesh′ən) *n.* 1 a possessing or being possessed 2 anything possessed 3 [*pl.*] wealth 4 territory ruled by an outside country

pos·ses′sive (-zes′iv) *adj.* 1 of possession 2 showing or desiring possession, domination, control, influence, etc. 3 *Gram.* designating or of a case, form, or construction expressing possession (Ex.: *my, Bill's*) — *n. Gram.* 1 the

---

THESAURUS

portable *a.* transportable, transferable, manageable; see MOVABLE.

portal *n.* gateway, opening, ingress; see DOOR, ENTRANCE 2, GATE.

portfolio *n.* 1 [A flat container] briefcase, attaché case, folder; see BAG, CONTAINER. 2 [Assets, especially stocks and bonds] holdings, selection, documents; see WEALTH.

portion *n.* section, piece, part; see DIVISION 2, SHARE.

portrait *n.* likeness, portraiture, representation; see PAINTING 1, PICTURE 4.

portray *v.* depict, characterize, reproduce; see DESCRIBE, REPRESENT 2.

portrayal *n.* depiction, replica, likeness; see DESCRIPTION, IMITATION 2.

pose *n.* artificial position, affectation, attitudinizing; see FAKE, PRETENSE 1.

pose *v.* 1 [To pretend] profess, feign, make believe; see ACT 1, PRETEND 1. 2 [To assume a pose for a picture] model, adopt a position, adopt a

stance; see SIT.

posh* *a.* elegant, stylish, opulent; see RICH 2, FASHIONABLE.

position *n.* 1 [A physical position] location, locality, spot, seat, ground, environment, post, whereabouts, bearings, station, point, place, stand, space, surroundings, situation, site, geography, region, tract, district, scene, setting; see also AREA, PLACE 3. 2 [An intellectual position] view, belief, attitude; see JUDGMENT 3, OPINION 1. 3 [An occupational position] office, employment, occupation; see JOB 1, PROFESSION 1. 4 [A social position] station, state, status; see RANK 3. 5 [Posture] pose, carriage, bearing; see POSTURE 1.

positive *a.* 1 [Definite] decisive, actual, concrete; see DEFINITE 1, REAL 2. 2 [Emphatic] peremptory, assertive, obstinate; see EMPHATIC, RESOLUTE. 3 [Certain] sure, convinced, confident; see CERTAIN 1.

positively *a.* 1 [In a positive man-

ner] assertively, uncompromisingly, dogmatically, arbitrarily, stubbornly, obstinately, emphatically, dictatorially, imperatively, decidedly, absolutely, insistently, authoritatively, assuredly, confidently, unhesitatingly, with conviction. 2 [Without doubt] undoubtedly, unmistakably, undeniably; see SURELY.

posse *n.* lynch mob, armed band, police force; see POLICE.

possess *v.* hold, occupy, control; see MAINTAIN 3, OWN 1.

possessed *a.* 1 [Insane] mad, crazed, violent; see INSANE. 2 [Owned] kept, enjoyed, in one's possession; see HELD, OWNED.

possession *n.* 1 [Ownership] proprietary rights, hold, mastery; see OWNERSHIP. 2 [Property] personal property, real estate, something possessed; see PROPERTY 1, 2.

possessions *n.* belongings, goods, effects; see ESTATE, PROPERTY 1.

possessive case 2 a word or phrase in this case —**pos·ses′sive·ly** *adv.* —**pos·ses′sive·ness** *n.*

pos·si·ble (päs′ə bəl) *adj.* 〖< L *posse*, be able〗 **1** that can be or exist **2** that may or may not happen **3** that can be done, selected, etc. **4** permissible —**pos·si·bil′i·ty** (-bil′ə tē), *pl.* **-ties**, *n.*

pos·si·bly (-blē) *adv.* **1** by any possible means **2** perhaps; maybe

pos·sum (päs′əm) *n.* [Colloq.] OPOSSUM —**play possum** to pretend to be asleep, dead, ill, etc.

post¹ (pōst) *n.* 〖< L *postis*〗 **1** a piece of wood, metal, etc. set upright to support a building, sign, etc. **2** the starting point of a horse race —*vt.* **1** to put up (a poster, etc.) on (a wall, etc.) **2** to announce by posting notices **3** to warn against trespassing on by posted notices **4** to put (a name) on a posted or published list

post² (pōst) *n.* 〖< Fr < It *posto*〗 **1** the place where a soldier, guard, etc. is stationed **2** *a*) a place where troops are garrisoned *b*) the troops at such a place **3** the place assigned to one **4** a job or duty —*vt.* **1** to assign to a post **2** to put up (a bond, etc.)

post³ (pōst) *n.* 〖< Fr < It *posta*〗 [Chiefly Brit.] (the) mail —*vi.* to travel fast; hasten —*vt.* **1** [Chiefly Brit.] to mail **2** to inform /keep me *posted*/

post- 〖L < *post*, after〗 *prefix* **1** after in time, later (than) /*postnatal*/ **2** after in space, behind

post·age (pōst′ij) *n.* the amount charged for mailing a letter, etc., esp. as represented by stamps

post·al (pōs′təl) *adj.* 〖Fr〗 of mail or post offices

post′card′ (-kärd′) *n.* **1** a card with a postage stamp printed on it, for sending short messages by mail: also **postal card 2** a similar card, usually with a picture on one side, to which a stamp is affixed

post′date′ *vt.* **-dat′ed, -dat′ing 1** to assign a later date to than the actual date **2** to be subsequent to

post·er (pōs′tər) *n.* a large advertisement or notice posted publicly

pos·te·ri·or (päs tir′ē ər) *adj.* 〖L < *post*, after〗 **1** later; following **2** at the rear; behind —*n.* the buttocks

pos·ter·i·ty (päs ter′ə tē) *n.* 〖see prec.〗 **1** all of a person's descendants **2** all succeeding generations

Post Exchange *trademark for* a nonprofit general store at an army post or camp

post′grad′u·ate *adj.* of or taking a course of study after graduation, esp. after receipt of the bachelor's degree

post′haste′ *adv.* with great haste

post·hu·mous (päs′tyōō məs, -choo-) *adj.* 〖< L *postumus*, last〗 **1** born after the father's death **2** published after the author's death **3** arising or continuing after one's death —**post′hu·mous·ly** *adv.*

post′hyp·not′ic (pōst′hip nät′ik) *adj.* in the time after a hypnotic trance /*posthypnotic* suggestion/

pos·til·ion or **pos·til·lion** (pōs til′yən, päs-) *n.* 〖Fr < It *posta*, a post〗 one who rides the leading left-hand horse of a team drawing a carriage

post′in·dus′tri·al *adj.* of a society in which the economy shifted from heavy industry to service industries, technology, etc.

post·lude (pōst′lōōd′) *n.* 〖POST- + (PRE)LUDE〗 a concluding musical piece

post′man (-mən) *n. pl.* **-men** MAILMAN

post′mark′ *n.* a post-office mark stamped on mail, canceling the postage stamp and recording the date and place —*vt.* to stamp with a postmark

post′mas·ter *n.* a manager of a post office —**post′mis′tress** *n.fem.*

postmaster general *pl.* **postmasters general** the head of a government's postal system

post me·ri′di·em (-mə rid′ē əm) 〖L〗 after noon Abbrev. *P.M., p.m., PM,* or *pm*

post′mod′ern *adj.* coming after, usually reacting to, 20th-c. modernism

post-mortem (pōst′môr′təm) *adj.* 〖L〗 **1** after death **2** of a post-mortem —*n.* **1** AUTOPSY **2** an evaluation of some event just ended

post′na·sal drip (pōst′nā′zəl) a discharge of mucus from behind the nose onto the pharynx, due to a cold, allergy, etc.

post′na·tal (-nāt′l) *adj.* after birth

post office 1 the governmental department in charge of the mails **2** a place where mail is sorted, postage stamps are sold, etc.

post′op′er·a·tive (-äp′ər ə tiv) *adj.* occurring after a surgical operation

post′paid′ *adj.* with postage prepaid

post′par·tum (-pär′təm) *adj.* 〖L < *post*-, after + *parere*, to bear〗 of the time after childbirth

post·pone (pōst pōn′) *vt.* **-poned′, -pon′ing** 〖< L *post*-, after + *ponere*, put〗 to put off until later; delay —**post·pone′ment** *n.*

post′script′ *n.* 〖< L *post*-, after + *scribere*, write〗 a note added below the signature in a letter

post time the scheduled starting time of a horse race

pos·tu·late (päs′tyōō lāt′, -chə-; *for n.*, -lit) *vt.* **-lat′ed, -lat′ing** 〖< L *postulare*, to demand〗 **1** to assume to be true, real, etc., esp. as a basis for argument **2** to take for granted —*n.* **1** something postulated **2** a prerequisite

pos·ture (päs′chər) *n.* 〖MFr < L *ponere*, to place〗 **1** the position or carriage of the body **2** a position assumed as in posing **3** an official stand or position /our national *posture*/ —*vi.* to pose or assume an attitude

post′war′ *adj.* after the (or a) war

po·sy (pō′zē) *n., pl.* **-sies** 〖< POESY〗 a flower or bouquet: old-fashioned term

pot¹ (pät) *n.* 〖OE *pott*〗 **1** a round vessel for holding liquids, cooking, etc. **2** a pot with its contents **3** [Colloq.] all the money bet at a single time —*vt.* **pot′ted, pot′ting 1** to put into a pot **2** to cook or preserve in a pot —**go to pot** to go to ruin —**pot′ful**, *pl.* **-fuls′**, *n.*

pot² (pät) *n.* 〖< AmSp *potiguaya*〗 [Slang] MARIJUANA

po·ta·ble (pōt′ə bəl) *adj.* 〖< L *potare*, to drink〗 drinkable —*n.* something drinkable —**po′ta·bil′i·ty** *n.*

pot′ash′ *n.* 〖< Du *pot*, POT¹ + *asch*, ASH¹〗 a potassium compound obtained from wood ashes, etc. and used in fertilizers, soaps, etc.

po·tas·si·um (pō tas′ē əm, pə-) *n.* 〖see prec.〗 a soft, silver-white, metallic chemical element

po·ta·to (pə tāt′ō) *n., pl.* **-toes** 〖< WInd〗 **1** the starchy tuber of a widely cultivated plant, eaten as a cooked vegetable **2** this plant

potato chip a very thin slice of potato fried crisp and then salted

pot′bel·ly *n., pl.* **-lies** a protruding belly —**pot′bel′lied** *adj.*

THESAURUS

possessor *n.* holder, proprietor, occupant; see OWNER.

possibility *n.* **1** [The condition of being possible] plausibility, feasibility, workableness; see CHANCE 2. **2** [A possible happening] hazard, chance, occasion, circumstance, hope, occurrence, hap, happening, outside chance, incident, instance; see also EVENT, OPPORTUNITY 1.

possible *a.* **1** [Within the realm of possibility] conceivable, imaginable, thinkable; see LIKELY 1. **2** [Acceptable] expedient, desirable, welcome; see PLEASANT 2. **3** [Contingent upon the future] indeterminate, fortuitous, adventitious; see LIKELY 1, UNCERTAIN.

possibly *a.* perhaps, by chance, potentially; see LIKELY 1, MAYBE, PROBABLY.

post¹ *n.* prop, support, pillar, pedestal, stake, stud, upright, doorpost; see also COLUMN 1, MAST.

postcard *n.* postal card, note, letter card; see LETTER 2.

poster *n.* placard, bill, sign, banner, sheet, billboard, handbill, broadside; see also ADVERTISEMENT.

posterior *a.* **1** [Subsequent] coming after, succeeding, next; see FOLLOWING. **2** [Behind] in back of, last, after; see BACK.

posterity *n.* descendants, breed, children; see FAMILY, OFFSPRING.

postman *n.* mailman, letter carrier, postal employee; see WORKMAN.

post office *n.* mail office, postal service, PO; see MAIL.

postpone *v.* defer, put off, hold over; see DELAY, SUSPEND 2.

postponed *a.* deferred, delayed, put off, set for a later time, to be done later, withheld, shelved, tabled, adjourned, suspended; see also LATE 1.

postponement *n.* respite, suspension, adjournment; see DELAY, PAUSE.

posture *n.* **1** [Stance] pose, carriage, demeanor, aspect, presence, condition. **2** [Attitude] way of thinking, feeling, sentiment; see ATTITUDE.

postwar *a.* peacetime, post-bellum, after the war, peaceful.

pot¹,² *n.* **1** [Container] vessel, kettle, pan, jug, jar, mug, tankard, cup, can, crock, canister, receptacle, bucket, urn, pitcher, bowl, cauldron, melting pot; see also CONTAINER. **2** [*Marijuana*] *cannabis sativa* (Latin), grass*, weed*; see DRUG. —**go to pot** deteriorate, go to ruin, fall apart; see SPOIL.

potato *n.* tuber, white potato, sweet potato, yam, spud*, tater*.

pot'boil'er *n.* a piece of writing, etc., done quickly and for money only

po·tent (pōt''nt) *adj.* ⟦< L *posse*, be able⟧ 1 having authority or power 2 convincing; cogent 3 effective, as a drug 4 able to have sexual intercourse: said of a male — **po'tency** *n.*

po·ten·tate (pōt''n tāt') *n.* a person having great power; ruler; monarch

po·ten·tial (pō ten'shəl) *adj.* ⟦see POTENT⟧ that can come into being; possible; latent — *n.* 1 something potential 2 the relative voltage at a point in an electric circuit with respect to some reference point in the same circuit —**po·ten'ti·al'ity** (-shē al'ə tē), *pl.* **-ties,** *n.* —**po·ten'tially** *adv.*

pother (päth'ər) *n.* ⟦< ?⟧ a fuss; commotion — *vt.,* *vi.* to fuss or bother

pot'herb' *n.* any herb whose leaves and stems are boiled and eaten or used as a flavoring

pot'hold'er *n.* a small pad, or piece of thick cloth, for handling hot pots, etc.

pot'hole' *n.* 1 a deep hole or pit 2 CHUCKHOLE

pot'hook' *n.* 1 an S-shaped hook for hanging a pot over a fire 2 a curved or S-shaped mark in writing

po·tion (pō'shən) *n.* ⟦< L *potare*, to drink⟧ a drink as of medicine, poison, or a supposedly magic substance

pot'luck' *n.* 1 whatever the family meal happens to be /to take *potluck*/ 2 a dinner to which everyone brings a dish to share: in full, **potluck dinner**

pot'pie' *n.* 1 a meat pie made in a deep dish 2 a stew with dumplings

pot·pourri (pō'pōō rē', pät'poor'ē) *n.* ⟦Fr < *pot*, a pot + *pourrir*, to rot⟧ a medley or miscellany; mixture

pot roast a large cut of beef cooked in one piece by braising

pot·sherd (pät'shurd') *n.* ⟦see POT¹ & SHARD⟧ a piece of broken pottery

pot'shot' (-shät') *n.* 1 an easy or random shot 2 a haphazard try 3 a random attack

pot·tage (pät'ij) *n.* ⟦< MFr *pot*, a pot⟧ a kind of thick soup or stew

pot'ter *n.* one who makes earthenware pots, dishes, etc.

potter's field (pät'ərz) a burial ground for paupers or unknown persons

potter's wheel a rotating disk, upon which clay is molded into bowls, etc.

pot'tery *n.,* *pl.* **-ies** 1 a potter's workshop 2 the art of a potter; ceramics 3 pots, dishes, etc. made of clay hardened by heat

pouch (pouch) *n.* ⟦< MFr *poche*⟧ 1 a small bag or sack /a tobacco *pouch*/ 2 a mailbag 3 a saclike structure, as that on the abdomen of the kangaroo, etc. for carrying young — *vt.,* *vi.* to form (into) a pouch

poul·tice (pōl'tis) *n.* ⟦< ML *pultes*, pap⟧ a hot, soft, moist

mass applied to a sore part of the body — *vt.* **-ticed, -tic·ing** to apply a poultice to

poul·try (pōl'trē) *n.* ⟦< L *pullus*, chicken⟧ domestic fowls; chickens, ducks, etc.

pounce (pouns) *n.* ⟦ME *pownce*, talon⟧ a pouncing — *vi.* **pounced, pounc'ing** to swoop down or leap (*on, upon,* or *at*) as if to seize

pound¹ (pound) *n., pl.* **pounds;** sometimes, after a number, **pound** ⟦< L *pondus*, weight⟧ 1 a unit of weight equal to 16 oz. avoirdupois or 12 oz. troy: abbrev. *lb.* 2 the monetary unit of the United Kingdom: symbol, £ 3 the monetary unit of various other countries, as Egypt, Syria, etc.

pound² (pound) *vt.* ⟦OE *punian*⟧ 1 to beat to a pulp, powder, etc. 2 to hit hard — *vi.* 1 to deliver repeated, heavy blows (*at* or *on*) 2 to move with heavy steps 3 to throb

pound³ (pound) *n.* ⟦< OE *pund-*⟧ a municipal enclosure for stray animals

pound'cake' *n.* a rich cake made (orig. with a pound each) of flour, butter, sugar, etc.

pour (pôr) *vt.* ⟦ME *pouren*⟧ 1 to cause to flow in a continuous stream 2 to emit, utter, etc. profusely or steadily — *vi.* 1 to flow freely, continuously, etc. 2 to rain heavily

pout (pout) *vi.* ⟦ME *pouten*⟧ 1 to thrust out the lips, as in sullenness 2 to sulk — *n.* a pouting —**pout'er** *n.*

pov·erty (päv'ər tē) *n.* ⟦< L *pauper*, poor⟧ 1 the condition or quality of being poor; need 2 deficiency; inadequacy 3 scarcity

pov'erty-strick'en *adj.* very poor

POW prisoner of war

pow·der (pou'dər) *n.* ⟦< L *pulvis*⟧ 1 any dry substance in the form of fine, dustlike particles, produced by crushing, grinding, etc. 2 a specific kind of powder /bath *powder*/ — *vt.* 1 to sprinkle, etc. with powder 2 to make into a powder —**pow'dery** *adj.*

powder keg 1 a keg for gunpowder 2 an explosive situation

powder room a lavatory for women

power (pou'ər) *n.* ⟦ult. < L *posse*, be able⟧ 1 ability to do or act 2 vigor; force; strength 3 *a*) authority; influence *b*) legal authority 4 physical force or energy /electric *power*/ 5 a person or thing having great influence, force, or authority 6 a nation with influence over other nations 7 the product of the multiplication of a quantity by itself 8 the degree of magnification of a lens — *vt.* to supply with a source of power — *adj.* 1 operated by electricity, a fuel engine, etc. /power tools/ 2 served by an auxiliary system that reduces effort /power steering/ 3 carrying electricity

---

▬ THESAURUS ▬

potency *n.* 1 [Strength] power, energy, vigor; see MANHOOD 2, STRENGTH. 2 [Authority] influence, control, dominion; see COMMAND, POWER 2.

potent *a.* 1 [Strong] vigorous, robust, sturdy; see STRONG 1, 2. 2 [Powerful] mighty, great, influential; see POWERFUL 1.

potential *a.* implied, inherent, dormant; see LIKELY 1.

potentially *a.* conceivably, imaginably, possibly; see LIKELY 1, MAYBE, PROBABLY.

potion *n.* dose, draft, liquor; see DRINK 1, LIQUID, MEDICINE 2.

pottery *n.* ceramics, porcelain, crockery, earthenware, clay ware; see also UTENSILS.

pouch *n.* sack, receptacle, poke; see BAG, CONTAINER.

poultry *n.* domesticated birds, pullets, barnyard fowls; see FOWL.

pounce *v.* bound, surge, dart; see DIVE, JUMP 1.

pound¹,³ *n.* 1 [Measure of weight] sixteen ounces, Troy pound, avoirdupois pound, commercial pound, pint; see also MEASURE 1, WEIGHT 1. 2 [Kennel] coop, doghouse, cage; see PEN 1.

pound² *v.* strike, crush, pulverize; see BEAT 1, HIT 1.

pour *v.* 1 [To flow] discharge, emit, issue; see DRAIN 3, FLOW. 2 [To allow to flow] replenish with, spill, splash; see EMPTY 2. 3 [To rain heavily] stream, flood, drench; see RAIN.

pouring *a.* streaming, gushing, spouting, rushing, raining, flooding, showering, discharging, emitting, issuing, escaping, emanating, welling out, spurting, spilling, shedding, draining, running down, running out; see also FLOWING.

pout *v.* make a long face, protrude the lips, sulk; see FROWN.

poverty *n.* 1 [Want of earthly goods] destitution, pennilessness, indigence, pauperism, want, need, insufficiency, starvation, famine, privation, insolvency, broken fortune, straits, scantiness, deficiency, meagerness, aridity, sparingness, stint, depletion, reduction, emptiness, vacancy, deficit, debt, wolf at the door*, pinch*, bite*, tough going*; see also LACK 1.—*Ant.* WEALTH, prosperity, comfort. 2 [Want of any desirable thing] shortage, inadequacy, scarcity; see LACK 1.

poverty-stricken *a.* penniless,

broke, bankrupt; see POOR 1, WANTING 1.

powder *n.* particles, film, powderiness, explosive powder, medicinal powder, cosmetic powder; see also COSMETIC, EXPLOSIVE, MEDICINE 2.

powdery *a.* sandy, gravelly, dusty; see GRITTY.

power *n.* 1 [Strength] vigor, energy, stamina; see STRENGTH. 2 [Controlling sway] authority, command, jurisdiction, dominion, ascendency, superiority, domination, dominance, mastery, control, sway, sovereignty, prerogative, prestige, omnipotence, supreme authority, the last word, rule, law, first-strike capability, warrant, supremacy, legal sanction, government, say-so*; see also INFLUENCE, LEADERSHIP. 3 [Ability] skill, endowment, capability; see ABILITY. 4 [Force] compulsion, coercion, duress; see PRESSURE 2, RESTRAINT 2. 5 [Energy] horsepower, potential, dynamism; see ENERGY 2. —**in power** ruling, authoritative, commanding; see POWERFUL 1. — **(the) powers that be** management, higher authorities, higher-ups*; see ADMINISTRATION 2.

pow′er·ful *adj.* strong, mighty, influential, etc. —**pow′er·fully** *adv.*

pow′er·house′ *n.* **1** a building where electric power is generated **2** [Colloq.] a powerful person, team, etc.

pow·er·less (pou′ər lis) *adj.* without power; weak, unable, etc. —**pow′er·lessly** *adv.*

power of attorney written legal authority to act for another person

pow′er·train′ *n.* DRIVETRAIN

pow·wow (pou′wou′) *n.* [< AmInd] **1** a conference of or with North American Indians **2** [Colloq.] any conference

pox (päks) *n.* [for *pocks*: see POCK] **1** a disease characterized by skin eruptions, as smallpox **2** syphilis

pp. 1 pages **2** past participle **3** postpaid **4** prepaid Also, for 3 & 4, **ppd.**

PP or **P.P.** parcel post

p.pr. or **ppr.** present participle

P.P.S., p.p.s., PPS, or **pps** [L *post postscriptum*] an additional postscript

pr. pair(s)

PR or **P.R. 1** public relations **2** Puerto Rico

Pr. Provençal

prac·ti·ca·ble (prak′ti kə bəl) *adj.* **1** that can be put into practice; feasible **2** that can be used; usable; useful —**prac′ti·ca·bil′i·ty** *n.* —**prac′ti·ca·bly** *adv.*

prac·ti·cal (prak′ti kəl) *adj.* **1** of or obtained through practice or action **2** useful **3** concerned with the application of knowledge to useful ends [*practical science*] **4** given to actual practice [a *practical* farmer] **5** that is so in practice, if not in theory, law, etc. **6** matter-of-fact —**prac′ti·cal′i·ty** (-kal′ə tē), *pl.* -**ties**, *n.*

practical joke a trick played on someone in fun —**practical joker**

prac′ti·cally *adv.* **1** in a practical manner **2** from a practical viewpoint **3** in effect; virtually

practical nurse a nurse with less training than a registered nurse, often one licensed by the State (**licensed practical nurse**) for specified duties

prac·tice (prak′tis) *vt.* **-ticed, -tic·ing** [< Gr *prassein*, do] **1** to do or engage in frequently; make a habit of **2** to do repeatedly so as to become proficient **3** to work at, esp. as a profession — *vi.* to do something repeatedly so as to become proficient; drill Chiefly Brit., etc. sp. **prac′tise** — *n.* **1** a practicing; habit, custom, etc. **2** *a*) repeated action to acquire proficiency *b*) proficiency so acquired **3**

the actual doing of something **4** *a*) the exercise of a profession *b*) a business based on this

prac′ticed *adj.* skilled

prac·ti·tioner (prak tish′ə nər) *n.* one who practices a profession

Prae·to·rian (prē tôr′ē ən) *adj.* [< L *praetor*, magistrate] of or belonging to the bodyguard (**Praetorian Guard**) of a Roman emperor — *n.* a member of the Praetorian Guard

prag·matic (prag mat′ik) *adj.* [< Gr *pragma*, thing done] **1** practical **2** testing the validity of all concepts by their practical results —**prag·mat′i·cally** *adv.* —**prag′ma·tism** (-mə tiz′əm) *n.* —**prag′ma·tist** *n.*

prai·rie (prer′ē) *n.* [Fr < L *pratum*, meadow] a large area of level or rolling grassy land

prairie dog a small, burrowing rodent of North America

prairie schooner a box-shaped covered wagon

praise (prāz) *vt.* **praised, prais′ing** [< L *pretium*, worth] **1** to commend the worth of **2** to glorify (God, a god, etc.), as in song — *n.* a praising or being praised; commendation

praise′wor·thy *adj.* worthy of praise —**praise′wor′thi·ly** *adv.* —**praise′wor′thi·ness** *n.*

pra·line (prā′lēn′, prä′-) *n.* [Fr] any of various soft or crisp candies made of nuts, sugar, etc.

prance (prans) *vi.* **pranced, pranc′ing** [< ?] **1** to rise up, or move along, on the hind legs, as a horse **2** to caper or strut — *n.* a prancing —**pranc′er** *n.* —**pranc′ingly** *adv.*

prank (praŋk) *n.* [< ?] a mischievous trick —**prank′ster** *n.*

prate (prāt) *vi., vt.* **prat′ed, prat′ing** [< MDu *praten*] to talk much and foolishly; chatter

prat·tle (prat′'l) *vi., vt.* **-tled, -tling** [LowG *pratelen*] to prate or babble — *n.* chatter or babble

prawn (prôn) *n.* [< ?] a large shrimp or other similar crustacean

pray (prā) *vt.* [< L *prex*, prayer] **1** to implore [(I) *pray* (you) tell me] **2** to ask for by prayer — *vi.* to say prayers, as to God

prayer[1] (prer) *n.* **1** the act of praying **2** an entreaty; supplication **3** *a*) a humble request, as to God *b*) any set formula for this **4** [*often pl.*] a devotional service chiefly of prayers **5** something prayed for —**prayer′ful** *adj.* —**prayer′fully** *adv.*

prayer[2] (prā′ər) *n.* one who prays

praying mantis MANTIS

■ THESAURUS ■

powerful *a.* **1** [Wielding power] mighty, all-powerful, almighty, superhuman, omnipotent, overpowering, great, invincible, dominant, influential, authoritative, overruling, potent, forceful, forcible, compelling, ruling, prevailing, preeminent, commanding, supreme, highest, important, authoritarian, ruthless, having the upper hand, in control.—*Ant.* WEAK, incompetent, impotent. **2** [Strong] robust, stalwart, sturdy; see STRONG 1, 2. **3** [Effective] efficacious, effectual, convincing; see PERSUASIVE.

powerfully *a.* forcibly, forcefully, effectively, severely, intensely, with authority; see also VIGOROUSLY.

powerless *a.* impotent, feeble, infirm; see WEAK 1, 2.

practical *a.* matter-of-fact, pragmatical, unimaginative, practicable, feasible, workable, functional, useful, sound, unromantic, sound-thinking, down-to-earth, realistic, sensible, sane, reasonable, rational, to one's advantage, operative, utilitarian, possible, usable, serviceable, efficient, effective, working, in action, in operation, with both feet on the ground.—*Ant.* UNREAL, imaginative, unserviceable.

practically *a.* **1** [In a practical manner] unimaginatively, pragmatically, efficiently, functionally, sensibly, rationally, reasonably, realistically, with regard to use, from a workable standpoint; see also EFFECTIVELY. **2** [Virtually] for ordinary purposes, nearly, just about; see

ALMOST.

practice *n.* **1** [A customary action] usage, use, wont; see CUSTOM. **2** [A method] mode, manner, fashion; see METHOD, SYSTEM. **3** [Educational repetition] exercise, drill, repetition, iteration, rehearsal, recitation, recounting, relating, tuneup*, prepping*. **4** [A practitioner's custom] work, patients, clients; see BUSINESS 4.

practice *v.* **1** [To seek improvement through repetition] drill, train, exercise, study, rehearse, repeat, recite, iterate, put in practice, make it one's business, work at, accustom oneself, act up to, polish up*, sharpen up*, build up. **2** [To employ one's professional skill] function, work at, employ oneself in; see WORK 2.

practiced *a.* trained, expert, exercised; see ABLE.

pragmatic *a.* realistic, utilitarian, logical; see PRACTICAL.

prairie *n.* steppe, savanna, grassland; see FIELD 1, MEADOW, PLAIN.

praise *n.* **1** [The act of praising] applause, approval, appreciation; see ADMIRATION. **2** [An expression of praise] laudation, eulogy, regard, applause, recommendation, handclapping, hurrahs, bravos, ovation, cheers, cries, whistling, tribute, compliment, acclaim, flattery, blessing, benediction, boost, rave.—*Ant.* BLAME, censure, condemnation.

praise *v.* **1** [To commend] recommend, applaud, cheer, acclaim,

endorse, sanction, admire, eulogize, adulate, elevate, smile on, cajole, give an ovation to, clap, pay tribute to, do credit to, have a good word for, make much of, extend credit, advocate, compliment, appreciate, admire, celebrate, honor, congratulate, flatter, rave over, boost, give a big hand, raise the roof*; see also APPROVE. **2** [To speak or sing in worship] glorify, adore, reverence; see WORSHIP.

praised *a.* admired, aided, helped, flattered, worshiped, glorified, exalted, blessed, celebrated, paid tribute to, magnified.

prance *v.* cavort, frisk, gambol; see DANCE.

prank *n.* game, escapade, caper; see JOKE.

pray *v.* **1** [To ask or beg] importune, petition, plead; see ASK, BEG. **2** [To call upon God] hold communion with God, supplicate, implore, petition, entreat, commend someone to God.

prayer[1] *n.* **1** [An earnest request] entreaty, request, petition; see APPEAL 1. **2** [An address to the deity] invocation, act of devotion, supplication, devotions, benediction, litany. *Prayers include the following:* Lord's Prayer, Pater Noster, Ave Maria, grace, kaddish, matins, vespers, Angelus, general confession, Miserere, collects, hours, stations of the cross, evensong.

prayer book *n.* liturgy, mass book, missal, missalette, hymnal, holy text, guide; see also BIBLE.

pre- ⟦< L *prae*, before⟧ *prefix* before in time, place, rank, etc.

preach (prēch) *vi.* ⟦< L *prae-*, before + *dicare*, proclaim⟧ 1 to give a religious sermon 2 to give moral advice, esp. in a tiresome manner — *vt.* 1 to urge as by preaching 2 to deliver (a sermon) —**preach′ment** *n.*

preach′er *n.* one who preaches: esp., a member of the clergy

preach′y *adj.* -i·er, -i·est [Colloq.] given to or marked by preaching

pre·am·ble (prē′am′bəl) *n.* ⟦< L *prae-*, before + *ambulare*, go⟧ an introduction, esp. one to a constitution, statute, etc., stating its purpose

pre·ar·range′ (-ə ränj′) *vt.* -ranged′, -rang′ing to arrange beforehand

pre·can·cer·ous (prē′kan′sər əs) *adj.* likely to become cancerous

pre·car·i·ous (prē ker′ē əs) *adj.* ⟦see PRAY⟧ dependent upon circumstances or chance; uncertain; risky —**pre·car′i·ous·ly** *adv.*

pre·cau·tion (prē kô′shən) *n.* ⟦< L *prae-*, before + *cavere*, take care⟧ care taken beforehand, as against danger, failure, etc. —**pre·cau′tion·ar·y** *adj.*

pre·cede (prē sēd′) *vt., vi.* -ced′ed, -ced′ing ⟦< L *prae-*, before + *cedere*, to move⟧ to be, come, or go before in time, place, rank, etc.

prec·e·dence (pres′ə dəns; prē sēd′′ns) *n.* the act, right, or fact of preceding in time, order, rank, etc.

pre·ced·ent (prē sēd′′nt; *for n.* pres′ə dənt) *adj.* preceding — *n.* **prec′e·dent** an act, statement, etc. that may serve as an example or justification for a later one

pre·ced′ing *adj.* that precedes

pre·cept (prē′sept′) *n.* ⟦< L *prae-*, before + *capere*, take⟧ a rule of moral conduct; maxim

pre·cep·tor (prē sep′tər) *n.* a teacher

pre·cinct (prē′siŋkt′) *n.* ⟦< L *prae-*, before + *cingere*, surround⟧ 1 [*usually pl.*] an enclosure between buildings, walls, etc. 2 [*pl.*] environs 3 *a*) police district *b*) a subdivision of a voting ward 4 limited area

pre·ci·os·i·ty (presh′ē äs′ə tē, pres′-) *n., pl.* -ties ⟦see fol.⟧ affectation, esp. in language

pre·cious (presh′əs) *adj.* ⟦< L *pretium*, a price⟧ 1 of great price or value; costly 2 beloved; dear 3 very fastidious, affected, etc. —**pre′cious·ly** *adv.* —**pre′cious·ness** *n.*

precious stone a rare and costly gem: applied to the diamond, emerald, ruby, and sapphire

prec·i·pice (pres′ə pis) *n.* ⟦< L *prae-*, before + *caput*, a head⟧ a vertical or overhanging rock face

pre·cip·i·tant (prē sip′ə tənt) *adj.* [see prec.] PRECIPITATE

pre·cip·i·tate (prē sip′ə tāt′; *for adj. & n.,* -tit, *also,* -tāt′) *vt.* -tat′ed, -tat′ing [see PRECIPICE] 1 to hurl downward 2 to cause to happen before expected, needed, etc. 3 *Chem.* to separate (a soluble substance) out of a solution — *vi.* 1 *Chem.* to be precipitated 2 *Meteorol.* to condense and fall as rain, snow, etc. — *adj.* 1 acting or done hastily or rashly 2 very sudden or abrupt — *n.* a substance precipitated out from a solution —**pre·cip′i·tate·ly** *adv.*

pre·cip·i·ta·tion *n.* 1 a headlong fall or rush 2 rash haste; impetuosity 3 a bringing on suddenly 4 *Chem.* a precipitating or being precipitated from a solution 5 *Meteorol. a*) rain, snow, etc. *b*) the amount of this

pre·cip·i·tous (-ə təs) *adj.* 1 steep like a precipice 2 rash; impetuous

pré·cis (prā sē′, prā′sē′) *n., pl.* -cis′ (-sēz′, -sēz′) ⟦Fr: see fol.⟧ a concise abridgment; summary

pre·cise (prē sis′, pri-) *adj.* ⟦< L *prae-*, before + *caedere*, to cut⟧ 1 accurately stated; definite 2 minutely exact 3 strict; scrupulous; fastidious —**pre·cise′ly** *adv.* —**pre·cise′ness** *n.*

pre·ci·sion (prē sizh′ən) *n.* the quality of being precise; exactness —*adj.* requiring exactness [*precision work*]

pre·clude (prē klōōd′) *vt.* -clud′ed, -clud′ing ⟦< L *prae-*, before + *claudere*, to close⟧ to make impossible, esp. in advance; prevent —**pre·clu′sion** (-klōō′zhən) *n.*

pre·co·cious (prē kō′shəs) *adj.* ⟦< L *prae-*, before + *coquere*, to cook⟧ matured earlier than usual [*a precocious child*] —**pre·coc′i·ty** (-käs′ə tē) *n.*

pre·cog·ni·tion (prē′käg nish′ən) *n.* ⟦see PRE- & COGNITION⟧ the supposed extrasensory perception of a future event —**pre·cog′ni·tive** (-nə tiv) *adj.*

pre-Columbian (prē′kə lum′bē ən) *adj.* of any period in the Americas before Columbus's voyages

pre·con·ceive (prē′kən sēv′) *vt.* -ceived′, -ceiv′ing to form (an opinion) in advance —**pre′con·cep′tion** *n.*

pre·con·di·tion (-dish′ən) *vt.* to prepare to behave, react, etc. in a certain way under certain conditions — *n.* a condition required beforehand

pre·cur·sor (prē kur′sər, prē′kur′-) *n.* ⟦< L *praecurrere,* run ahead⟧ 1 a forerunner 2 a predecessor —**pre·cur′sory** *adj.*

pred·a·to·ry (pred′ə tôr′ē) *adj.* ⟦< L *praeda*, a prey⟧ 1 of or living by plundering or robbing 2 preying on other animals —**pred′a·tor** (-tər) *n.*

pre·de·cease (prē′dē sēs′) *vt.* -ceased′, -ceas′ing to die before (someone else)

pred·e·ces·sor (pred′ə ses′ər) *n.* ⟦< L *prae-*, before + *decedere*, go away⟧ a person preceding another, as in office

pre·des·ti·na·tion (prē des′tə nā′shən) *n.* 1 *Theol.* the doctrine that *a*) God foreordained everything that would happen *b*) God predestines souls to salvation or to damnation 2 destiny

pre·des·tine (-tin) *vt.* -tined, -tin·ing to destine beforehand; foreordain

pre·de·ter′mine *vt.* -mined, -min·ing to determine beforehand

pre·dic·a·ment (prē dik′ə mənt) *n.* ⟦see PREACH⟧ an unpleasant or embarrassing situation

pred·i·cate (pred′i kāt′; *for n. & adj.,* -kit) *vt.* -cat′ed, -cat′ing ⟦see PREACH⟧ 1 to affirm as a quality or attribute 2 to base (something) *on* or *upon* facts, conditions, etc. — *n.* *Gram.* the word or words that make a statement about the subject — *adj.* *Gram.* of a predicate —**pred′i·ca′tion** *n.*

THESAURUS

preach *v.* exhort, discourse, moralize, teach, lecture, talk, harangue, inform, address.

preacher *n.* missionary, parson, evangelist; see MINISTER 1.

preamble *n.* prelude, preface, introductory part; see INTRODUCTION 4.

precarious *a.* doubtful, uncertain, dubious; see DANGEROUS.

precaution *n.* anticipation, forethought, regard; see CARE 1. —**take precautions** foresee, mind, adjust; see PREPARE 1, WATCH OUT.

precede *v.* go before, come first, be ahead of, move ahead of, take precedence over, preface, introduce, usher in, ring in, herald, forerun, head, lead, go ahead, scout, light the way, go in advance, come before, come to the front, forge ahead, head up.—*Ant.* SUCCEED, come after, come last.

precedence *n.* preference, precession, the lead; see ADVANTAGE.

precedent *n.* authoritative example, exemplar, pattern; see EXAMPLE 1, MODEL 1.

preceding *a.* antecedent, precedent,

previous, other, prior, aforesaid, ahead of, earlier, former, forerunning, past, foregoing, above-mentioned, above-named, above-cited, aforementioned, before-mentioned, above, before, prefatory, front, forward, anterior, preliminary, preparatory, introductory, aforeknown, already indicated, previously mentioned.

precious *a.* 1 [Valuable] high-priced, costly, dear; see EXPENSIVE, VALUABLE. 2 [Beloved] cherished, inestimable, prized; see BELOVED, FAVORITE. 3 [Refined and delicate] overrefined, overnice, fragile; see DAINTY.

precipice *n.* crag, cliff, bluff; see HILL, MOUNTAIN.

precipitate *v.* accelerate, press, hurry; see HASTEN 1, SPEED.

precipitation *n.* 1 [Carelessness] rashness, presumption, impetuosity; see CARELESSNESS, RUDENESS. 2 [Condensation] hail, rain, snow; see STORM.

precise *a.* 1 [Exact] decisive, well-

defined, strict; see ACCURATE 2, DEFINITE 1, 2. 2 [Fussily or prudishly careful] rigid, inflexible, uncompromising; see CAREFUL, SEVERE 1.

precisely *a.* correctly, exactly, definitely; see ACCURATE 2.

precision *n.* exactness, correctness, sureness; see ACCURACY.

preconception *n.* prejudice, bias, assumption; see INCLINATION 1.

predatory *a.* voracious, carnivorous, bloodthirsty; see GREEDY, HUNGRY.

predecessor *n.* antecedent, forerunner, ancestor; see PARENT.

predicament *n.* strait, quandary, plight, puzzle, perplexity, dilemma, scrape, corner, hole, impasse, tight situation, state, condition, position, lot, circumstance, mess, muddle, deadlock, pinch, crisis, bind*, fix*, pickle*, hot water*, jam*; see also DIFFICULTY 1, 2.

predicate *n.* verbal phrase, part of speech, word; see VERB.

predicate *v.* assert, declare, state; see MEAN 1.

pre·dict (prē dikt′) *vt., vi.* ⟦< L *prae-*, before + *dicere*, tell⟧ to say in advance (what one believes will happen); foretell —**pre·dict′a·ble** *adj.* —**pre·dic′tion** *n.* —**pre·dic′tor** *n.*

pre·di·gest (prē′di jest′, -dī-) *vt.* to treat (food) as with enzymes for easier digestion when eaten

predi·lec·tion (pred′'l ek′shən, prēd′-) *n.* ⟦< L *prae-*, before + *diligere*, prefer⟧ a partiality or preference

pre·dis·pose (prē′dis pōz′) *vt.* -**posed′**, -**pos′ing** to make susceptible (*to*); incline —**pre′dis·po·si′tion** *n.*

pre·dom·i·nant (prē däm′ə nənt) *adj.* 1 having authority or influence over others; superior 2 most frequent; prevailing —**pre·dom′i·nance** *n.* —**pre·dom′i·nantly** *adv.*

pre·dom·i·nate (prē däm′ə nāt′) *vi.* -**nat′ed**, -**nat′ing** 1 to have authority or influence (*over* others) 2 to be dominant in amount, number, etc.; prevail

pre·em·i·nent (prē em′ə nənt) *adj.* eminent above others; surpassing —**pre·em′i·nence** *n.* —**pre·em′i·nently** *adv.*

pre·empt or **pre·empt′** (prē empt′) *vt.* ⟦< L *prae-*, before + *emere*, buy⟧ 1 to gain the right to buy (public land) by settling on it 2 to seize before anyone else can 3 *Radio, TV* to replace (a scheduled program)

pre·emp′tion *n.* 1 a preempting 2 action taken to check other action beforehand —**pre·emp′tive** *adj.*

preen (prēn) *vt.* ⟦< ME *proinen*, to dress up⟧ 1 to clean and trim (the feathers) with a beak 2 to dress up or adorn (oneself) 3 to pride (oneself)

pre·exist (prē′eg zist′) *vt., vi.* to exist previously or before (another person or thing) —**pre′exist′ence** *n.*

pref. 1 preface 2 preferred

pre·fab (prē′fab′) *n.* [Colloq.] a prefabricated building

pre·fab·ri·cate (prē fab′ri kāt′) *vt.* -**cat′ed**, -**cat′ing** to build (a house, etc.) in standardized sections for shipment and quick assembly —**pre′fab·ri·ca′tion** *n.*

pref·ace (pref′is) *n.* ⟦< L *prae-*, before + *fari*, speak⟧ an introduction to a book, speech, etc. — *vt.* -**aced**, -**ac·ing** 1 to furnish with a preface 2 to introduce —**pref′a·to′ry** (-ə tôr′ē) *adj.*

pre·fect (prē′fekt′) *n.* ⟦< L *praeficere*, to set over⟧ any of various administrators —**pre′fec′ture** (-fek′chər) *n.*

pre·fer (prē fur′, pri-) *vt.* -**ferred′**, -**fer′ring** ⟦< L *prae-*, before + *ferre*, to bear⟧ 1 to promote; advance 2 to put before a court, etc. for consideration 3 to like better

pref·er·a·ble (pref′ər ə bəl) *adj.* more desirable —**pref′er·a·bly** *adv.*

pref′er·ence (-əns) *n.* 1 a preferring or being preferred 2 something preferred 3 advantage given to one person, country, etc. over others —**pref′er·en′tial** (-ər en′shəl) *adj.*

pre·fer·ment (prē fur′mənt) *n.* an advancement in rank, etc.; promotion

pre·fig·ure (prē fig′yər, -yoor) *vt.* -**ured**, -**ur·ing** to foreshadow

pre·fix (prē′fiks′; *also for v.* prē fiks′) *vt.* ⟦< L *prae-*, before + *figere*, fix⟧ to fix to the beginning; esp., to add as a prefix — *n.* a syllable, group of syllables, or word joined to the beginning of another word to alter its meaning

preg·nant (preg′nənt) *adj.* ⟦< L *pregnans*⟧ 1 having (an) offspring developing in the uterus; with child 2 mentally fertile; inventive 3 full of meaning, etc. [*a pregnant silence*] 4 filled (*with*); abounding —**preg′nancy**, *pl.* -**cies**, *n.* —**preg′nantly** *adv.*

pre·hen·sile (prē hen′sil, -səl) *adj.* ⟦< L *prehendere*, take⟧ adapted for seizing or grasping, esp. by wrapping around something, as a monkey's tail

pre·his·toric (prē′his tôr′ik) *adj.* of the period before recorded history

pre·igni·tion (prē′ig nish′ən) *n.* in an internal-combustion engine, ignition occurring before the intake valve is closed or before the spark plug fires

pre·judge′ *vt.* -**judged′**, -**judg′ing** to judge beforehand or without all the evidence —**pre′judg′ment** *n.*

preju·dice (prej′ə dis) *n.* ⟦< L *prae-*, before + *judicium*, judgment⟧ 1 a preconceived, usually unfavorable idea 2 an opinion held in disregard of facts that contradict it; bias 3 intolerance or hatred of other races, etc. 4 injury or harm — *vt.* -**diced**, -**dic·ing** 1 to injure or harm 2 to cause to have prejudice; bias —**prej′u·di′cial** (-dish′əl) *adj.*

prel·ate (prel′it) *n.* ⟦< L *praelatus*, placed before⟧ a high-ranking ecclesiastic, as a bishop —**prel′a·cy**, *pl.* -**cies**, *n.*

pre·limi·nary (prē lim′ə ner′ē, pri-) *adj.* ⟦< L *prae-*, before + *limen*, threshold⟧ leading up to the main action, etc.; introductory — *n.*, *pl.* -**ies** [*often pl.*] a preliminary step, procedure, etc.

pre·lit·er·ate (prē′lit′ər it) *adj.* of a society not having a written language

prel·ude (prel′yōōd′, prā′lōōd′) *n.* ⟦< L *prae-*, before + *ludere*, to play⟧ 1 a preliminary part 2 *Music a*) an introductory instrumental composition, as the overture to an opera *b*) a short, romantic composition

pre·mari·tal (prē mar′i təl, -it′l) *adj.* occurring before marriage

pre·ma·ture (prē′mə toor′, -tyoor′) *adj.* ⟦< L *prae-*, before + *maturus*, ripe⟧ happening, done, arriving, etc. before the proper or usual time; too early —**pre′ma·ture′ly** *adv.*

pre·med′i·tate′ (-med′i tāt′) *vt., vi.* -**tat′ed**, -**tat′ing** to think out or plan beforehand —**pre·med′i·ta′tion** *n.*

pre·men·strual (prē men′strəl) *adj.* occurring before a menstrual period

pre·mier (pri mir′, -myir′) *adj.* ⟦< L *primus*, first⟧ first in importance; foremost — *n.* a chief official; specif., a prime minister —**pre·mier′ship** *n.*

━━━━━━━ **THESAURUS** ━━━━━━━

predict *v.* prophesy, prognosticate, divine; see FORETELL.

predictable *a.* anticipated, foreseen, prepared for; see EXPECTED, LIKELY 1.

prediction *n.* prophecy, foresight, prognostication; see GUESS.

predominance *n.* reign, supremacy, control; see COMMAND, POWER 2.

predominant *a.* 1 [Supreme in power] mighty, almighty, supreme; see POWERFUL 1. 2 [Of first importance] transcendent, surpassing, superlative; see PRINCIPAL.

predominate *v.* dominate, prevail, rule; see GOVERN, MANAGE 1.

prefab* *n.* prefabricated building, temporary structure, standardized housing; see BUILDING.

prefabricate *v.* fabricate, preform, set up, coordinate, pre-assemble; see also ASSEMBLE 2.

preface *n.* prelude, prolegomenon, preliminary; see EXPLANATION, INTRODUCTION 4.

preface *v.* introduce, commence, precede; see BEGIN 1.

prefer *v.* single out, fix upon, fancy; see FAVOR.

preferable *a.* more eligible, more desirable, good; see EXCELLENT.

preferably *a.* by preference, by choice, by selection, in preference, first, sooner, before, optionally, at pleasure, willingly, at will; see also RATHER 2.

preference *n.* favorite, election, option, decision, selection, pick; see also CHOICE.

preferred *a.* chosen, selected, fancied, adopted, picked out, taken, elected, liked, favored, set apart, handpicked, singled out, endorsed, settled upon, sanctioned, decided upon.—*Ant.* NEGLECTED, unpreferred, overlooked.

prefix *n.* 1 [An addition] affix, adjunct, introductory word part, prefixion. 2 [A designation] title, cognomen, designation; see NAME 1.

pregnancy *n.* reproduction, fertilization, gestation; see BIRTH.

pregnant *a.* gestating, gravid, fruitful, with child, big with child, hopeful, anticipating, in a family way*, expecting*.

prehistoric *a.* preceding history, very early, unknown; see OLD 3.

prejudge *v.* presuppose, forejudge, presume; see DECIDE.

prejudice *n.* partiality, unfairness, spleen, bias, detriment, enmity, prejudgment, dislike, disgust, aversion, antipathy, race prejudice, apartheid, misjudgment, pique, coolness, animosity, contemptuousness, bad opinion, displeasure, repugnance, revulsion, preconception, foregone conclusion, quirk, warp, twist.—*Ant.* ADMIRATION, appreciation, good opinion.

prejudiced *a.* preconceived, prepossessed, biased, directed against, influenced, inclined, leaning, conditioned, presupposing, predisposed, dogmatic, opinionated, partisan, extreme, hidebound, narrow, intolerant, canting, racist, sexist, chauvinistic, blind, partial, narrow-minded, parochial, provincial, one-sided, not seeing an inch beyond one's nose, squint-eyed, intolerant of, disliking, having a predilection, closed against, judging on slight knowledge, smug.—*Ant.* GENEROUS, open-minded, receptive.

preliminary *a.* preparatory, preceding, prefatory; see INTRODUCTORY.

prelude *n.* preface, preliminary preparation, prelusion; see INTRODUCTION 3.

premarital *a.* before the vows, before marriage, during courtship; see BEFORE.

premature *a.* unanticipated, precipitate, rash; see EARLY 2, UNTIMELY.

prematurely *a.* too early, rash, precipitately; see EARLY 2, UNTIMELY.

pre·mière or **pre·miere** (pri mir′, -myer′) *n.* 〖Fr: see prec.〗 a first performance of a play, movie, etc.

prem·ise (prem′is) *n.* 〖< L *prae-*, before + *mittere*, send〗 1 a previous statement serving as a basis for an argument 2 [*pl.*] a piece of real estate — *vt.* **-ised, -is·ing** to state as a premise; postulate

pre·mium (prē′mē əm) *n., pl.* **-ums** 〖< L *prae-*, before + *emere*, take〗 1 a reward or prize, esp. as an inducement to buy 2 an additional amount paid or charged 3 a payment, as for an insurance policy 4 very high value 〖to put a *premium* on wit〗 —**at a premium** very valuable because of scarcity

pre·mo·ni·tion (prēm′ə nish′ən, prē′-) *n.* 〖< L *prae-*, before + *monere*, warn〗 1 a forewarning 2 a foreboding —**pre·mon·i·to·ry** (prē män′ə tôr′ē) *adj.*

pre·na·tal (prē nāt′′l) *adj.* 〖PRE- + NATAL〗 before birth

pre·oc·cu·py (prē äk′yoo pī′) *vt.* **-pied, -py′ing** 〖< L *prae-*, before + *occupare*, seize〗 1 to wholly occupy the thoughts of; engross 2 to take possession of before someone else or beforehand —**pre·oc·cu·pa′tion** (-pā′shən) *n.* —**pre·oc′cu·pied′** *adj.*

pre·or·dain (prē′ôr dān′) *vt.* to ordain or decree beforehand

prep (prep) *adj. short for* PREPARATORY 〖a *prep* school〗 — *vt.* **prepped, prep′ping** to prepare (a patient) for surgery, etc.

prep. 1 preparatory 2 preposition

pre·pack·age (prē′pak′ij) *vt.* **-aged, -ag·ing** to package (foods, etc.) in standard units before selling

pre·paid (prē′pād′) *vt. pt. & pp. of* PREPAY

prepa·ra·tion (prep′ə rā′shən) *n.* 1 a preparing or being prepared 2 a preparatory measure 3 something prepared, as a medicine, cosmetic, etc.

pre·para·to·ry (prē par′ə tôr′ē, pri-) *adj.* serving to prepare; introductory

preparatory school a private secondary school that prepares students for college

pre·pare (prē par′, pri-) *vt.* **-pared′, -par′ing** 〖< L *prae-*, before + *parare*, get ready〗 1 to make ready 2 to equip or furnish 3 to put together 〖to *prepare* dinner〗 — *vi.* 1 to make things ready 2 to make oneself ready

pre·par′ed·ness *n.* the state of being prepared, esp. for waging war

pre·pay′ *vt.* **-paid′, -pay′ing** to pay or pay for in advance —**pre′pay′ment** *n.*

pre·pon·der·ate (prē pän′dər āt′, pri-) *vi.* **-at′ed, -at′ing** 〖< L *prae-*, before + *ponderare*, weigh〗 to be superior in amount, power, etc. —**pre·pon′der·ance** *n.* —**pre·pon′der·ant** *adj.*

prepo·si·tion (prep′ə zish′ən) *n.* 〖< L *prae-*, before + *ponere*, to place〗 a word, as *in, by, to*, etc. that connects a noun or pronoun to another word —**prep′o·si′tional** *adj.*

pre·pos·sess (prē′pə zes′) *vt.* 1 to bias, esp. favorably 2 to impress favorably

pre′pos·sess′ing (-iŋ) *adj.* that impresses favorably

pre·pos·ter·ous (prē päs′tər əs, pri-) *adj.* 〖< L *prae-*, before + *posterus*, following〗 absurd; ridiculous; laughable

preppy or **preppie** (prep′ē) *n., pl.* **-pies** a (former) student at a preparatory school — *adj.* **-pier, -pi·est** of or like the clothes worn by such students

pre·puce (prē′pyoos′) *n.* 〖< L *praeputium*〗 FORESKIN

pre·record (prē′ri kôrd′) *vt. Radio, TV* to record (music, a program, etc.) for later use, as for a broadcast

pre·re·corded (prē′ri kôr′did) *adj.* designating or of a magnetic tape, as in a cassette, on which sound, etc. has been recorded before its sale

pre·requi·site (pri rek′wə zit) *adj.* required beforehand as a necessary condition — *n.* something prerequisite

pre·roga·tive (prē räg′ə tiv, pri-) *n.* 〖< L *prae-*, before + *rogare*, ask〗 an exclusive right or privilege

pres. present

Pres. President

pres·age (pres′ij; *for v., usually* prē sāj′, pri-) *n.* 〖< L *prae-*, before + *sagire*, perceive〗 1 an omen; portent 2 a foreboding — *vt.* **-aged′, -ag′ing** to give warning of

pres·by·ter (prez′bi tər) *n.* 〖see PRIEST〗 1 in the Presbyterian Church, an elder 2 in the Episcopal Church, a priest

Pres·by·te·ri·an (-ē ən) *adj.* designating or of a church of a traditionally Calvinistic denomination governed by presbyters — *n.* a member of a Presbyterian church

pre·school′ *adj.* of or for a child between infancy and school age — *n.* NURSERY SCHOOL —**pre′school′er** *n.*

pre·science (prē′shəns, -shē əns) *n.* 〖< L *prae-*, before + *scire*, know〗 foreknowledge; foresight —**pres′cient** *adj.*

pre·scribe (prē skrīb′, pri-) *vt.* **-scribed′, -scrib′ing** 〖< L *prae-*, before + *scribere*, write〗 1 to order; direct 2 to order or advise as a medicine or treatment: said of physicians, etc.

pre·script (prē′skript′) *n.* a prescribed rule —**pre·scrip′tive** *adj.*

pre·scrip·tion (prē skrip′shən, pri-) *n.* 1 something prescribed 2 *a)* a written direction for the preparation and use of medicine *b)* such a medicine

pres·ence (prez′əns) *n.* 1 the fact or state of being present 2 immediate surroundings 〖in his *presence*〗 3 *a)* a person's bearing or appearance *b)* impressive bearing, personality, etc.

presence of mind ability to think and act quickly in an emergency

pres·ent (prez′ənt; *for v.* prē zent′, pri-) *adj.* 〖< L *prae-*, before + *esse*, be〗 1 being at the specified place 2

THESAURUS

premiere *n.* first night, beginning, opening; see PERFORMANCE.

premise *n.* proposition, evidence, assumption; see BASIS, PROOF 1.

premises *n.* bounds, limits, land; see PROPERTY 2.

premium *a.* prime, superior, select; see EXCELLENT.

premium *n.* remuneration, bonus, installment; see PRIZE.

premonition *n.* omen, portent, forewarning; see SIGN 1, WARNING.

preoccupation *n.* absorption, daydreaming, amusement; see FANTASY, THOUGHT 1.

preoccupied *a.* removed, absorbed, distracted; see RAPT.

preparation *n.* 1 [The act of preparing] preparing, fitting, making ready, manufacture, readying, putting in order, establishment, compounding, adapting, rehearsal, incubation, gestation, building, construction, formation, maturing, anticipation, development, evolution, furnishing, buildup*. 2 [The state of being prepared] preparedness, readiness, fitness, adaptation, suitability, capacity, qualification, background, ripeness, mellowness, maturity, training, education, equipment. 3 [Something that is prepared] arrangement, product, compound; see MIXTURE 1.

prepare *v.* 1 [To make oneself ready] get ready, foresee, arrange, make preparations, make arrangements, fit, adapt, qualify, put in order, adjust, set one's house in order, prime, fix, settle, fabricate, appoint, furnish, elaborate, perfect, develop, prepare the ground, lay the foundations, block out, smooth the way, man, arm, cut out, warm up, lay the groundwork, contrive, devise, make provision, put in readiness, build up, provide for, provide against, make snug, be prepared, be ready; see also ANTICIPATE, PLAN 1. 2 [To make other persons or things ready] outfit, equip, fit out; see PROVIDE 1. 3 [To cook and serve] concoct, dress, brew; see COOK, SERVE.

prepared *a.* 1 [Fitted] adapted, qualified, adjusted; see ABLE, FIT 1. 2 [Subjected to a special process or treatment] frozen, precooked, processed; see PRESERVED 2. 3 [Ready] available, on hand, in order; see READY 2.

preposition *n.* part of speech, function word, form word; see GRAMMAR, WORD 1.

prepossessing *a.* handsome, captivating, attractive; see CHARMING, PLEASANT 1.

prerequisite *n.* essential, necessity, need; see REQUIREMENT 2.

prerogative *n.* privilege, advantage, exemption; see RIGHT 1.

prescribe *v.* guide, order, give directions; see ORDER 1.

prescription *n.* direction, medical recipe, formula; see MEDICINE 2.

presence *n.* 1 [The fact of being present] occupancy, occupation, residence, inhabitance, habitancy; see also ATTENDANCE 1. 2 [The vicinity of a person] propinquity, nearness, closeness; see NEIGHBORHOOD. 3 [One's appearance and behavior] carriage, port, demeanor; see APPEARANCE 1, BEHAVIOR.

presence of mind *n.* sensibility, alertness, acumen; see ATTENTION.

present *a.* 1 [Near in time] existing, being, in process, in duration, begun, started, commenced, going on, under consideration, at this time, contemporary, immediate, instant, prompt, at this moment, at present, today, nowadays, these days, already, even now, but now, just now, for the time being, for the occasion; see also NOW 1.—*Ant.* PAST, over, completed. 2 [Near in space] in view, at hand, within reach; see NEAR 1.

present *n.* 1 [The present time] instant, this time, present moment; see TODAY. 2 [A gift] grant, donation, offering; see GIFT 1.

existing or happening now **3** *Gram.* indicating action or state now or action that is always true *[present tense]* — *n.* **1** the present time or occasion **2** the present tense **3** a gift — *vt.* **1** to introduce (a person) **2** to exhibit; show **3** to offer for consideration **4** to give (a gift, etc.) to (a person, etc.) —**present arms** to hold a rifle vertically in front of the body

pre·sent·a·ble (prē zent′ə bəl, pri-) *adj.* **1** suitable for presentation **2** suitably groomed for meeting people

pres·en·ta·tion (prez′ən tā′shən, prē′zen-) *n.* **1** a presenting or being presented **2** something presented

pres′ent-day′ *adj.* of the present time

pre·sen·ti·ment (prē zent′ə mənt, pri-) *n.* ⟦see PRE- & SENTIMENT⟧ a feeling that something, esp. of an unfortunate nature, is about to take place

pres′ent·ly *adv.* **1** soon; shortly **2** at present; now

pre·sent·ment (prē zent′mənt, pri-) *n.* presentation

present participle a participle used to express present or continuing action or existence, as in "he is *growing*"

pre·ser·va·tive (prē zurv′ə tiv, pri-) *adj.* preserving — *n.* anything that preserves *[a preservative added to foods]*

pre·serve (prē zurv′, pri-) *vt.* **-served′, -serv′ing** ⟦< L *prae-*, before + *servare*, keep⟧ **1** to protect from harm, damage, etc. **2** to keep from spoiling **3** to prepare (food), as by canning, for future use **4** to carry on; maintain — *n.* **1** *[usually pl.]* fruit preserved by cooking with sugar **2** a place where game, fish, etc. are maintained —**pres·er·va·tion** (prez′ər vā′shən) *n.* —**pre·serv′er** *n.*

pre·set (prē′set′) *vt.* **-set′, -set′ting** to set (automatic controls) beforehand

pre·shrink (prē′shriŋk′) *vt.* **-shrank′ or -shrunk′, -shrunk′ or -shrunk′en, -shrink′ing** to shrink by a special process in manufacture, to minimize further shrinkage in laundering —**pre′shrunk′** *adj.*

pre·side (prē zīd′, pri-) *vi.* **-sid′ed, -sid′ing** ⟦< L *prae-*, before + *sedere*, sit⟧ **1** to serve as chairman **2** to have control or authority (*over*)

presi·dent (prez′ə dənt, -dent′) *n.* ⟦see PRESIDE⟧ **1** the highest executive officer of a company, club, etc. **2** *[often* P-] the chief executive (as in the U.S.), or the nominal head (as in Italy), of a republic —**pres′i·dency,** *pl.* **-cies,** *n.* —**pres′i·den′tial** (-den′shəl) *adj.*

press¹ (pres) *vt.* ⟦< L *premere*⟧ **1** to act on with steady force or weight; push against, squeeze, compress, etc. **2** to squeeze (juice, etc.) from **3** to iron (clothes, etc.) **4** to embrace closely **5** to force; compel **6** to urge persistently; entreat **7** to try to force **8** to emphasize **9** to distress or trouble *[pressed* for time*]* **10** to urge on — *vi.* **1** to weigh

down **2** to go forward with determination **3** to crowd — *n.* **1** pressure, urgency, etc. **2** a crowd **3** a machine for crushing, stamping, etc. **4** smoothness, etc. of clothes after pressing **5** *a) short for* PRINTING PRESS *b)* a printing establishment *c)* newspapers, magazines, etc., or the persons who write for them *d)* publicity, etc. in newspapers, etc. **6** an upright closet for storing clothes, etc. — **press′er** *n.*

press² (pres) *vt.* ⟦< L *praes*, surety + *stare*, to stand⟧ to force into service, esp. military or naval service

press agent one whose work is to get publicity for a client

press box a place for reporters at sports events, etc.

press conference a group interview granted to media personnel as by a celebrity

press′ing *adj.* calling for immediate attention; urgent

press′man (-mən) *n., pl.* **-men** an operator of a printing press

pres·sure (presh′ər) *n.* **1** a pressing or being pressed **2** a state of distress **3** a compelling influence *[social pressure]* **4** urgent demands; urgency **5** *Physics* force per unit of area exerted upon a surface, etc. — *vt.* **-sured, -sur·ing** to exert pressure on

pressure cooker a container for quick cooking by steam under pressure

pres′sur·ize′ (-īz′) *vt.* **-ized′, -iz′ing** to keep nearly normal atmosphere pressure inside (an airplane, etc.), as at high altitudes —**pres′suri·za′tion** *n.* —**pres′sur·iz′er** *n.*

pres·ti·dig·i·ta·tion (pres′tə dij′i tā′shən) *n.* ⟦Fr < *preste*, quick + L *digitus*, finger⟧ sleight of hand

pres·tige (pres tēzh′, -tēj′) *n.* ⟦< L *praestrigiae*, deceptions⟧ **1** the power to impress or influence **2** reputation based on high achievement, character, etc. —**pres·tige′ful** *adj.*

pres·ti′gious (-tij′əs, -tē′jəs) *adj.* having or imparting prestige or distinction

pres·to (pres′tō) *adv., adj.* ⟦It, quick⟧ **1** fast or at once **2** *Musical Direction* in fast tempo

pre′stressed′ concrete concrete containing tensed steel cables for strength

pre·sume (prē zoom′, pri-) *v.* **-sumed′, -sum′ing** ⟦< L *prae-*, before + *sumere*, take⟧ **1** to dare (to say or do something); venture **2** to take for granted; suppose — *vi.* to act presumptuously; take liberties —**pre·sum′able** *adj.* —**pre·sum′ably** *adv.*

pre·sump·tion (prē zump′shən, pri-) *n.* **1** a presuming; specif., *a)* an overstepping of proper bounds *b)* a taking of something for granted **2** the thing presumed **3** a reason for presuming —**pre·sump′tive** *adj.*

pre·sump′tu·ous (-choo əs, -chə wəs) *adj.* too bold or forward

---

THESAURUS

present *v.* **1** [To introduce] make known, acquaint with, give an introduction; see INTRODUCE 3. **2** [To submit] donate, proffer, put forth; see OFFER 1. **3** [To give] grant, bestow, confer; see GIVE 1. **4** [To give a play, etc.] put on, do, offer; see ACT 3, PERFORM 2.

presentable *a.* attractive, prepared, satisfactory; see FIT 1.

presentation *n.* **1** [The act of presenting] bestowal, donation, delivering; see GIVING. **2** [Something presented] present, offering, remembrance; see GIFT 1.

presented *a.* bestowed, granted, conferred; see GIVEN.

presently *a.* directly, without delay, shortly; see IMMEDIATELY, SOON.

preservation *n.* security, safety, protection, conservation, maintenance, saving, keeping, storage, curing, tanning, freezing, sugaring, pickling, evaporation, canning, refrigeration.

preserve *v.* **1** [To guard] protect, shield, save; see DEFEND 2. **2** [To maintain] keep up, care for, conserve; see MAINTAIN 3. **3** [To keep] can, conserve, process, save, put up, put down, store, cure, bottle, do up, season, salt, pickle, put in brine, put in vinegar, pot, tin, dry, smoke, corn, dry-cure, smoke-cure, freeze, quick freeze, keep up, cold-pack, refrigerate, dehydrate, seal up, kipper, marinate, evaporate, embalm, mummify,

mothball, fill.—*Ant.* WASTE, allow to spoil, let spoil.

preserved *a.* **1** [Saved] rescued, guarded, secured; see SAVED 1. **2** [Prepared for preservation] canned, corned, dried, freeze-dried, dehydrated, evaporated, smoked, seasoned, pickled, salted, brined, put up, conserved, cured, marinated, tinned, potted, bottled, embalmed, mummified.

preserves *n.* spread, sweet, jell*; see JAM 1, JELLY.

preside *v.* direct, lead, control; see ADVISE, MANAGE 1.

presidency *n.* office of the president, chairmanship, position; see ADMINISTRATION 2.

president *n.* presiding officer, chief director, prez*; see EXECUTIVE.

presidential *a.* official, regulatory, of the chief executive; see MANAGING.

press¹ *n.* **1** [The pressure of circumstances] rush, confusion, strain; see HASTE. **2** [Publishing as a social institution] the Fourth Estate, publishers, publicists, newsmen, newspapermen, journalists, journalistic writers, editors, correspondents, political writers, columnists, periodicals, papers, newspapers.

press¹ *v.* **1** [To subject to pressure] thrust, crowd, bear upon, bear down on, squeeze, hold down, pin down, force down, crush, drive, weight, urge; see also PUSH 1.—*Ant.* RAISE,

release, relieve. **2** [To smooth, usually by heat and pressure] finish, mangle, roll; see IRON, SMOOTH.

press conference *n.* interview, public report, briefing; see ANNOUNCEMENT, HEARING 1.

pressing *a.* importunate, constraining, distressing; see IMPORTANT 1, URGENT 1.

pressure *n.* **1** [Physical pressure] force, burden, mass, load, encumbrance, stress, thrust, tension, squeeze; see also WEIGHT 1.—*Ant.* RELEASE, relief, deliverance. **2** [Some form of social pressure] compulsion, constraint, urgency, persuasion, stress, affliction, coercion, trouble, hardship, humiliation, misfortune, necessity, repression, confinement, unnaturalness, obligation, discipline.—*Ant.* AID, assistance, encouragement.

pressure *v.* press, compel, constrain; see URGE 2, 3.

prestige *n.* renown, effect, influence; see FAME.

presumably *a.* in all probability, credibly, likely; see PROBABLY.

presume *v.* consider, suppose, take for granted; see ASSUME.

presumption *n.* **1** [An assumption] conjecture, guess, hypothesis; see ASSUMPTION 1. **2** [Impudence] arrogance, audacity, effrontery; see RUDENESS.

pre·sup·pose (prē′sə pōz′) *vt.* **-posed′, -pos′ing** 1 to suppose or assume beforehand 2 to require or imply as a preceding condition —**pre′sup·po·si′tion** (-sup ə zish′ən) *n.*

pre·teen (prē′tēn′) *n.* a child nearly a teenager

pre·tend (prē tend′, pri-) *vt.* ⟦< L *prae-*, before + *tendere*, to stretch⟧ 1 to profess [to *pretend* ignorance] 2 to feign; simulate [to *pretend* anger] 3 to make believe [to *pretend* to be astronauts] — *vi.* to lay claim (to) —**pre·tend′er** *n.*

pre·tense (prē tens′, pri-; prē′tens′) *n.* 1 a claim; pretension 2 a false claim 3 a false show of something 4 a pretending, as at play Also [Brit., etc.] **pre·tence′**

pre·ten·sion (prē ten′shən, pri-) *n.* 1 a pretext 2 a claim 3 assertion of a claim 4 pretentiousness

pre·ten′tious (-shəs) *adj.* 1 making claims to some distinction, importance, etc. 2 affectedly grand; ostentatious —**pre·ten′tiously** *adv.* —**pre·ten′tious·ness** *n.*

pret·er·it or **pret·er·ite** (pret′ər it) *adj.* ⟦< L *praeter-*, beyond + *ire*, go⟧ *Gram.* expressing past action or state — *n.* the past tense

preter·nat·u·ral (prēt′ər nach′ər əl) *adj.* ⟦ML *praeternaturalis*⟧ 1 differing from or beyond what is natural; abnormal 2 SUPERNATURAL

pre·test (prē′test′) *n., vi.* to test in advance

pre·text (prē′tekst′) *n.* ⟦< L *prae-*, before + *texere*, weave⟧ a false reason put forth to hide the real one

pret·ti·fy (prit′i fī′) *vt.* **-fied′, -fy′ing** to make pretty

pret·ty (prit′ē) *adj.* **-ti·er, -ti·est** ⟦OE *prættig*, crafty⟧ attractive in a dainty, graceful way — *adv.* fairly; somewhat — *vt.* **-tied, -ty·ing** to make pretty: usually with *up* —**pret′ti·ly** *adv.* —**pret′ti·ness** *n.*

pret·zel (pret′səl) *n.* ⟦< L *brachium*, an arm⟧ a hard, brittle, salted biscuit, often formed in a loose knot

pre·vail (prē vāl′, pri-) *vi.* ⟦< L *prae-*, before + *valere*, strong⟧ 1 to be victorious; triumph: often with *over* or *against* 2 to succeed 3 to be or become more widespread 4 to be prevalent —**prevail on** (or **upon** or **with**) to persuade

pre·vail′ing *adj.* 1 superior in strength or influence 2 prevalent

preva·lent (prev′ə lənt) *adj.* ⟦see PREVAIL⟧ widely existing; generally accepted, used, etc. —**prev′a·lence** *n.*

pre·vari·cate (pri var′i kāt′) *vi.* **-cat′ed, -cat′ing** ⟦< L

prae-, before + *varicare*, straddle⟧ 1 to evade the truth 2 to lie —**pre·var′i·ca′tion** *n.* —**pre·var′i·ca′tor** *n.*

pre·vent (prē vent′, pri-) *vt.* ⟦< L *prae-*, before + *venire*, come⟧ to stop or keep from doing or happening; hinder —**pre·vent′a·ble** or **pre·vent′i·ble** *adj.* —**pre·ven′tion** *n.*

pre·ven′tive (-vent′iv) *adj.* preventing or serving to prevent — *n.* anything that prevents Also **pre·vent′a·tive**

pre·view (prē′vyoo′) *n.* 1 an advance, restricted showing, as of a movie 2 a showing of scenes from a movie, etc. to advertise it Also **pre′vue** (-vyoo′)

pre·vi·ous (prē′vē əs) *adj.* ⟦< L *prae-*, before + *via*, a way⟧ occurring before; prior —**previous to** before —**pre′vi·ously** *adv.*

pre·war (prē′wôr′) *adj.* before a (or the) war

prexy (preks′ē) *n., pl.* **-ies** [Slang] the president, esp. of a college, etc.

prey (prā) *n.* ⟦< L *prehendere*, seize⟧ 1 an animal hunted for food by another animal 2 a victim 3 the mode of living by preying on other animals [a bird of *prey*] — *vi.* 1 to plunder 2 to hunt other animals for food 3 to weigh as an obsessor Generally used with *on* or *upon*

pri·apic (prī ap′ik) *adj.* ⟦after *Priapos*, Gr god of procreation⟧ of or relating to the phallus; phallic

price (prīs) *n.* ⟦< L *pretium*⟧ 1 the amount of money, etc. asked or paid for something; cost 2 value or worth 3 the cost, as in life, labor, etc., of obtaining some benefit — *vt.* **priced, pric′ing** 1 to fix the price of 2 [Colloq.] to find out the price of

price′less *adj.* of inestimable value; invaluable

prick (prik) *n.* ⟦OE *prica*, a point⟧ 1 a tiny puncture made by a sharp point 2 a sharp pain caused as by being pricked — *vt.* 1 to make (a hole) in (something) with a sharp point 2 to pain sharply —**prick up one's ears** 1 to raise the ears erect 2 to listen closely

prickle (prik′əl) *n.* ⟦OE *prica*, a point⟧ 1 a small, sharply pointed growth, as a thorn: also **prick′er** 2 a tingling sensation — *vt., vi.* **-led, -ling** to tingle —**prick′ly, -lier, -li·est,** *adj.*

prickly heat a skin eruption caused by inflammation of the sweat glands

pride (prīd) *n.* ⟦< OE *prut*, proud⟧ 1 *a)* an unduly high opinion of oneself *b)* haughtiness; arrogance 2 dignity

---

THESAURUS

pretend *v.* 1 [To feign] affect, simulate, claim falsely, imitate, counterfeit, sham, make as if, make as though, mislead, beguile, delude, pass off for, cheat, dupe, hoodwink, be deceitful, bluff, falsify, be hypocritical, fake, put on*, let on*, go through the motions, keep up appearances; see also DECEIVE. 2 [To make believe] mimic, fill a role, take a part, represent, portray, put on a front, play, make believe, act the part of, put on an act*, act a part, put on airs*, playact.

pretended *a.* feigned, counterfeit, assumed, affected, shammed, bluffing, simulated, lying, falsified, put on, concealed, covered, masked, cheating; see also FALSE 3.

pretense *n.* 1 [The act of pretending] affectation, misrepresentation, falsification, act, deceit, fabrication, trickery, double-dealing, misstatement, falsifying, simulation, excuse, insincerity, profession, ostentation, assumption, dissimulation, evasion, equivocation, prevarication, egotism, brazenness, arrogance, dandyism, foppery, servility, complacency, smugness, prudishness, coyness, formality, stiffness, blind, smoke screen; see also DISHONESTY, IMITATION.— *Ant.* HONESTY, candor, sincerity. 2 [Something pretended] falsehood, lie, falseness, affectation, mask, cloak, show, excuse, subterfuge, pretext, fraud, appearance, seeming, semblance, wile, ruse, sham, airs, claim, mannerism; see also DECEPTION, IMITATION 2.

prettily *a.* pleasingly, gently, quietly; see POLITELY.

pretty *a.* 1 [Attractive] comely,

lovely, good-looking; see BEAUTIFUL. 2 [Pleasant] delightful, cheerful, pleasing; see PLEASANT 2. 3 [*Considerable] ample, sizable, notable; see LARGE 1, MUCH 1, 2. 4 [Somewhat] rather, tolerably, a little; see MODERATELY.

prevalence *n.* dissemination, occurrence, currency; see REGULARITY.

prevalent *a.* widespread, accepted, frequently met; see COMMON 1.

prevent *v.* preclude, obviate, forestall, anticipate, block, arrest, stop, thwart, repress, interrupt, halt, impede, check, avert, frustrate, balk, foil, retard, obstruct, counter, countercheck, counteract, inhibit, restrict, block off, limit, hold back, hold off, stop from, deter, intercept, override, circumvent, bar, ward off, keep from happening, nip in the bud, put a stop to, stave off, keep off, turn aside; see also HINDER, RESTRAIN.— *Ant.* HELP, aid, encourage.

prevented *a.* obviated, stopped, interfered with; see INTERRUPTED.

prevention *n.* anticipation, forestalling, arresting, obviating, bar, debarring, halt, impeding, retardation, repression, restraint, restriction, inhibition, interception, overriding, circumvention, hindering, counteraction, obstruction, opposition, warding off, staving off, keeping off, stopping, thwarting, blocking; see also REFUSAL.— *Ant.* AID, encouragement, help.

preventive *a.* deterrent, precautionary, tending to prevent, averting, defensive.

previous *a.* antecedent, prior, former; see PRECEDING.

previously *a.* long ago, earlier, beforehand; see BEFORE.

prey *n.* spoil, pillage, loot; see VICTIM.

prey on *v.* 1 [To destroy] seize, raid, pillage; see DESTROY. 2 [To eat] feed on, devour, consume; see EAT 1.

price *n.* expenditure, outlay, expense, cost, value, worth, figure, dues, tariff, valuation, quotation, fare, hire, wages, return, disbursement, rate, appraisal, reckoning, equivalent, payment, demand, barter, consideration, amount, marked price, asking price, estimate, output, ransom, reward, pay, prize, return, par value, money's worth, price ceiling, ceiling; see also VALUE 1. —**at any price** whatever the cost, expense no object, anyhow; see REGARDLESS 2.

price *v.* fix the price of, appraise, assess; see RATE, VALUE 2.

priced *a.* valued, estimated, worth; see COSTING.

priceless *a.* invaluable, inestimable, without price; see VALUABLE.

prick *n.* tap, stab, stick; see CUT.

prick *v.* pierce, puncture, stick; see CUT, HURT 1.

prickly *a.* thorny, pointed, spiny; see SHARP 1.

pride *n.* 1 [The quality of being vain] conceit, vainglory, egoism, egotism, self-esteem, self-love, self-exaltation, self-glorification, self-admiration, pretension.— *Ant.* HUMILITY, self-effacement, unpretentiousness. 2 [Conduct growing from pride or conceit] haughtiness, vanity, disdain, condescension, patronizing, patronage, superiority; see also sense 1. 3 [Sense of personal satisfaction] and self-respect **3** satisfaction in something done, owned, etc. **4** a person or thing in which pride is taken —**pride′** **oneself on** to be proud of —**pride′ful** *adj.* —**pride′fully** *adv.*

prier (prī′ər) *n.* one who pries

priest (prēst) *n.* [< Gr *presbys*, old] **1** a person of special rank who performs religious rites in a temple of God or a god **2** *R.C.Ch.* a clergyman ranking next below a bishop —**priest′ess** *n.fem.* —**priest′hood′** *n.* —**priest′ly**, **-li·er**, **-li·est**, *adj.*

prig (prig) *n.* [< 16th-c. cant] one who smugly affects great propriety or morality —**prig′gish** *adj.*

prim (prim) *adj.* **prim′mer**, **prim′mest** [< ?] stiffly formal, precise, or moral —**prim′ly** *adv.* —**prim′ness** *n.*

pri·ma·cy (prī′mə sē) *n.*, *pl.* **-cies** [< L *primus*, first] **1** a being first in time, rank, etc.; supremacy **2** the rank or office of a primate

prima donna (prē′mə dän′ə, prim′ə) *pl.* **pri′ma don′nas** [It, lit., first lady] the principal woman singer in an opera

prima facie (prī′mə fā′shē ē′, -shi ē′) [L, lit., at first sight] adequate to establish a fact unless refuted Said of evidence

pri·mal (prī′məl) *adj.* [< L *primus*, first] **1** first in time; original **2** first in importance; chief

pri·mari·ly (prī mer′ə lē, prī′mer′-) *adv.* **1** at first; originally **2** mainly; principally

pri·mary (prī′mer′ē, -mə rē) *adj.* [< L *primus*, first] **1** first in time or order; original **2** from which others are derived; fundamental *[primary colors]* **3** first in importance; chief —*n.*, *pl.* **-ries 1** something first in order, importance, etc. **2** a preliminary election at which candidates are chosen for the final election

primary school 1 ELEMENTARY SCHOOL **2** a school including the first three elementary grades and, sometimes, kindergarten

primary stress (or **accent**) the heaviest stress (ʹ) in pronouncing a word

pri·mate (prī′māt′; *for 1*, -mit) *n.* [< L *primus*, first] **1** an archbishop, or the highest-ranking bishop in a province, etc. **2** any of the most highly developed order of animals, including man, the apes, etc.

prime (prīm) *adj.* [< L *primus*, first] **1** first in time; original **2** first in rank or importance; chief; principal **3** first in quality **4** fundamental **5** *Math.* that can be evenly divided by no other whole number than itself and 1 —*n.* **1** the first or earliest part **2** the most vigorous period **3** the best part —*vt.* **primed**, **prim′ing 1** to make ready; prepare **2** to get (a pump) into operation by pouring water into it **3** to undercoat, size, etc. before painting **4** to provide with facts, answers, etc. beforehand

prime meridian the meridian at Greenwich, England, from which longitude is measured east and west

prime minister in some countries, the chief executive of the government

prim·er[1] (prim′ər) *n.* [< L *primus*, first] **1** a simple book for teaching reading **2** any elementary textbook

prim·er[2] (prim′ər) *n.* a thing that primes; specif., *a*) an explosive cap, etc. used to set off a main charge *b*) a preliminary coat of paint, etc.

prime rate *Finance* the most favorable interest rate charged on bank loans to large corporations Also **prime interest rate** or **prime lending rate**

prime time *Radio, TV* the hours when the largest audience is available

pri·meval (prī mē′vəl) *adj.* [< L *primus*, first + *aevum*, an age] of the earliest times or ages; primordial

primi·tive (prim′i tiv) *adj.* [< L *primus*, first] **1** of the earliest times; original **2** crude; simple **3** primary; basic —*n.* a primitive person or thing

primo·geni·ture (prī′mō jen′i chər, -mə-) *n.* [< L *primus*, first + *genitura*, a begetting] **1** the condition of being the firstborn of the same parents **2** the right of inheritance of the eldest son

pri·mor·dial (prī môr′dē əl) *adj.* [< L *primus*, first + *ordiri*, begin] primitive; fundamental; original

primp (primp) *vt.*, *vi.* [prob. < PRIM] to groom or dress up in a fussy way

prim·rose (prim′rōz′) *n.* [altered (after *rose*) < ML *primula*] a plant with tubelike, often yellow flowers

primrose path 1 the path of pleasure, self-indulgence, etc. **2** a course of action that seems easy but that can lead to disaster

prince (prins) *n.* [< L *princeps*, chief] **1** a ruler ranking below a king; head of a principality **2** a son of a sovereign **3** any preeminent person

prince consort the husband of a reigning queen

prince′ly *adj.* **-lier**, **-li·est 1** of a prince **2** magnificent; generous —**prince′li·ness** *n.*

prin·cess (prin′sis, -ses′) *n.* **1** a daughter of a sovereign **2** the wife of a prince

prin·ci·pal (prin′sə pəl) *adj.* [see PRINCE] first in rank, importance, etc. —*n.* **1** a principal person or thing **2** the head of a school **3** the amount of a debt, etc. minus the interest —**prin′ci·pally** *adv.*

prin·ci·pal·ity (-pal′ə tē) *n.*, *pl.* **-ties** the territory ruled by a prince

principal parts the principal inflected forms of a verb: in English, the infinitive, past tense, and past participle (Ex: *drink, drank, drunk*)

prin·ci·ple (prin′sə pəl) *n.* [see PRINCE] **1** a fundamental truth, law, etc. upon which others are based **2** *a*) a rule of conduct *b*) adherence to such rules; integrity **3** a basic part **4** *a*) the scientific law explaining a natural action *b*) the method of a thing's operation —**prin′ci·pled** *adj.*

print (print) *n.* [< L *premere*, to press] **1** a mark made on a surface by pressing or stamping **2** cloth printed with

---

THESAURUS

self-respect, self-satisfaction, self-sufficiency; see HAPPINESS. **4** [A source of satisfaction] enjoyment, repletion, sufficiency; see SATISFACTION 2.

pride oneself on *v.* take pride in, flatter oneself that, be proud of; see BOAST.

priest *n.* *Names for priests in various sects include the following:* father confessor, spiritual father, priestvicar, high priest, minor canon, pontiff, vicar, care of souls, clergyman, rector, preacher, presbyter, elder, rabbi, lama, monk, friar; see also MINISTER 1.

priesthood *n.* clergy, Holy Orders, monasticism; see MINISTRY 2.

priestly *a.* ecclesiastic, episcopal, ministerial; see CLERICAL 2.

prim *a.* stiff, formal, precise, demure, decorous, nice, orderly, tidy, cleanly, trim, spruce, pat; see also POLITE.

primarily *a.* mainly, fundamentally, in the first place; see PRINCIPALLY.

primary *a.* **1** [Earliest] primitive, initial, first; see ORIGINAL 1. **2** [Fundamental] elemental, basic, central; see FUNDAMENTAL. **3** [Principal] chief, prime, main; see PRINCIPAL.

primate *n.* gorilla, chimpanzee, orangutan, gibbon, great ape; see also MAN 1, MONKEY.

prime *a.* **1** [Principal] main, first, chief; see PRINCIPAL. **2** [Excellent] top, choice, superior; see EXCELLENT.

primitive *a.* **1** [Simple] rudimentary, elementary, first; see FUNDAMENTAL. **2** [Ancient] primeval, archaic, primordial; see OLD 3. **3** [Uncivilized] crude, rough, simple, rude, atavistic, uncultured, savage, uncultured, natural, barbaric, barbarous, barbarian, fierce, untamed, uncouth, ignorant, undomesticated, wild, animal, brutish, raw, untaught, green, unlearned, untutored, underdeveloped.

primp* *v.* make one's toilet, paint and powder, get dressed up; see DRESS, PREPARE 1.

prince *n.* sovereign, ruler, monarch, potentate; see also ROYALTY.

princely *a.* **1** [Royal] sovereign, regal, august; see ROYAL. **2** [Suited to a prince] lavish, sumptuous, luxurious; see EXPENSIVE, HANDSOME, RICH 1, 2.

princess *n.* sovereign, monarch, infanta; see ROYALTY.

principal *a.* leading, chief, first, head, prime, main, foremost, cardinal, essential, capital, important, preeminent, highest, supreme, prominent, dominant, predominant, controlling, superior, prevailing,

paramount, greatest, incomparable, unapproachable, peerless, matchless, unequaled, unrivaled, maximum, crowning, unparalleled, sovereign, second to none.—*Ant.* UNIMPORTANT, secondary, accessory.

principal *n.* chief, head, governing officer, master; see also EXECUTIVE.

principally *a.* chiefly, mainly, essentially, substantially, materially, eminently, preeminently, superlatively, supremely, vitally, especially, particularly, peculiarly, notably, importantly, fundamentally, dominantly, predominantly, basically, largely, first and foremost, in large measure, first of all, to a great degree, prevalently, generally, universally, mostly, above all, in the first place, for the most part, for the greatest part, before anything else, in the main.—*Ant.* SLIGHTLY, somewhat, tolerably.

principle *n.* **1** [A fundamental law] underlying truth, basic doctrine, postulate; see LAW 4. **2** [A belief or set of beliefs; *often plural*] system, opinion, teaching; see BELIEF, FAITH 2, POLICY.

print *n.* **1** [Printed matter] impression, reprint, issue; see COPY. **2** [A printed picture] engraving, lithograph, photograph; see PICTURE 3, SKETCH. —**in print** printed, availa design 3 the impression of letters, designs, etc. made by inked type or from a plate, block, etc. 4 a photograph, esp. one made from a negative — *vt., vi.* 1 to stamp (a mark, letter, etc.) on a surface 2 to produce on (paper, etc.) the impression of inked type, etc. 3 to produce (a book, etc.) 4 to write in letters resembling printed ones 5 to make (a photographic print) —**in** (or **out of**) **print** still (or no longer) being sold by the publisher: said of books, etc. — **print'er** *n.*

printed circuit an electrical circuit of conductive material, as in fine lines, applied to an insulating sheet

print'ing *n.* 1 the act of one that prints 2 something printed 3 all the copies printed at one time

printing press a machine for printing from inked type, plates, or rolls

print·out (print'out') *n.* the printed or typewritten output of a computer

prior (prī'ər) *adj.* [L] 1 earlier; previous 2 preceding in order or importance — *n.* the head of a priory —**prior to** before in time

pri'or·ess (-is) *n.* the woman head of a priory of nuns, etc.

pri·or·i·tize (prī ôr'ə tīz') *vt.* -tized', -tiz'ing to arrange (items) in order of importance

pri·or·i·ty (prī ôr'ə tē) *n., pl.* -ties 1 a being prior; precedence 2 a prior right to get, buy, or do something 3 something to be given prior attention

pri'o·ry *n., pl.* -ries a monastery governed by a prior, or a convent governed by a prioress

prism (priz'əm) *n.* [< Gr *prizein*, to saw] 1 *Geom.* a solid figure whose ends are parallel, polygonal, and equal in size and shape, and whose sides are parallelograms 2 a transparent prism whose ends are triangles: used to disperse light into the spectrum —**pris·matic** (priz mat'ik) *adj.* — **pris·mat'i·cal·ly** *adv.*

prison (priz'ən) *n.* [< L *prehendere*, take] a place of confinement for those convicted or awaiting trial

prison camp 1 a camp with minimum security for holding reliable prisoners 2 a camp for confining prisoners of war

pris'on·er *n.* one held captive or confined, esp. in prison

prissy (pris'ē) *adj.* -sier, -si·est [prob. PR(IM) + (S)ISSY] [Colloq.] very prim or prudish —**pris'si·ness** *n.*

pris·tine (pris'tēn, pris tēn') *adj.* [L *pristinus*, former] 1 characteristic of the earliest period 2 unspoiled

prithee (prith'ē) *interj.* [< *pray thee*] [Archaic] I pray thee; please

pri·va·cy (prī'və sē) *n., pl.* -cies 1 a being private; seclusion 2 secrecy 3 one's private life

pri·vate (prī'vət) *adj.* [< L *privus*, separate] 1 of or concerning a particular person or group 2 not open to or controlled by the public [a *private* school] 3 for an individual person [a *private* room] 4 not holding public office [a *private* citizen] 5 secret [a *private* matter] — *n.* 1 [pl.] the genitals: also **private parts** 2 an enlisted man of either of the lowest ranks in the U.S. Army or of the

lowest rank in the U.S. Marine Corps —**go private** to restore private corporate ownership by buying back publicly held stock —**in private** not publicly —**pri'vately** *adv.*

pri·va·teer (prī'və tir') *n.* 1 a privately owned ship commissioned in war to capture enemy ships 2 a commander or crew member of a privateer

private eye [Slang] a private detective

pri·va·tion (prī vā'shən) *n.* the lack of ordinary necessities or comforts

privet (priv'it) *n.* [< ?] an evergreen shrub used for hedges

priv·i·lege (priv'ə lij, priv'lij) *n.* [< L *privus*, separate + *lex*, law] a special right, favor, etc. granted to some person or group — *vt.* -leged, -leg·ing to grant a privilege to

privy (priv'ē) *adj.* private: now only in such phrases as **privy council**, a body of confidential advisers named by a ruler — *n., pl.* **priv'ies** an outhouse —**privy to** privately informed about

prize[1] (prīz) *vt.* **prized, priz'ing** [see PRICE] to value highly; esteem — *n.* 1 something given to the winner of a contest, etc. 2 anything worth striving for — *adj.* 1 that has won or is worthy of a prize 2 given as a prize

prize[2] (prīz) *n.* [< L *prehendere*, to take] something taken by force, as in war — *vt.* **prized, priz'ing** to pry, as with a lever

prize'fight' *n.* a professional boxing match —**prize'fight'er** *n.*

pro[1] (prō) *adv.* [L, for] favorably — *adj.* favorable — *n., pl.* **pros** 1 a person or vote on the affirmative side 2 an argument in favor of something

pro[2] (prō) *adj., n., pl.* **pros** short for PROFESSIONAL

pro-[1] [Gr < *pro*, before] *prefix* before in place or time

pro-[2] [L < *pro*, forward] *prefix* 1 moving forward or ahead of [*proclivity*] 2 forth [*produce*] 3 substituting for [*pronoun*] 4 supporting [*prolabor*]

pro-am (prō'am') *n.* a sports competition for both amateurs and professionals

prob. 1 probably 2 problem

prob·a·bil·i·ty (präb'ə bil'ə tē) *n., pl.* -ties 1 a being probable; likelihood 2 something probable

prob·a·ble (präb'ə bəl) *adj.* [< L *probare*, prove] 1 likely to occur or be 2 reasonably so, but not proved —**prob'ably** *adv.*

pro·bate (prō'bāt) *n.* [see PROBE] the act or process of probating — *adj.* having to do with probating [*probate court*] — *vt.* -bat'ed, -bat'ing to establish officially that (a document, esp. a will) is genuine

pro·ba·tion (prō bā'shən) *n.* [see PROBE] 1 a testing, as of one's character, ability, etc. 2 the conditional suspension of a convicted person's sentence —**pro·ba'tion·ar'y** or **pro·ba'tion·al** *adj.*

THESAURUS

able, obtainable; see PUBLISHED. — **out of print** O.P., unavailable, remaindered; see SOLD OUT.

print *v.* 1 [To make an impression] impress, imprint, indent; see MARK 1. 2 [To reproduce by printing] run off, print up, issue, reissue, reprint, bring out, go to press, set type, compose, start the presses; see also PUBLISH 1.—*Ant.* TALK, write, inscribe. 3 [To simulate printing] letter, do lettering, hand-letter; see WRITE 2.

printed *a.* impressed, imprinted, engraved, stamped, lithographed, multiditioned, xeroxed, printed by photo-offset, silkscreened; see also REPRODUCED.

printer *n.* typesetter, compositor, linotype operator; see WORKMAN.

printing *n.* 1 [A process of reproduction] typography, composition, typesetting, presswork. 2 [Printed matter] line, page, sheet; see PAGE. 3 [Publication] issuing, issuance, distribution; see PUBLICATION 1.

prior *a.* antecedent, above-mentioned, foregoing; see PRECEDING.

priority *n.* superiority, preference, precedence; see ADVANTAGE.

prison *n.* penitentiary, reformatory, prison house, guardhouse, stockade; see also JAIL.

prisoner *n.* captive, convict, culprit, jailbird, detainee, escapee, hostage, con*; see also DEFENDANT.

prisoner of war *n.* captive person, captured person, interned person, person in captivity, POW; see also PRISONER.

privacy *n.* seclusion, solitude, retreat, isolation, separateness, aloofness, separation, concealment; see also SECRECY.

private *a.* special, separate, retired, secluded, withdrawn, removed, not open, behind the scenes, off the record, privy, clandestine, single; see also INDIVIDUAL, OWN.—*Ant.* PUBLIC, open, exposed. —**in private** privately, personally, not publicly; see SECRETLY.

private *n.* enlisted man, infantryman; private first class, second class, etc.; see also SAILOR, SOLDIER.

privately *a.* confidentially, clandestinely, alone; see PERSONALLY 1, SECRETLY.

private parts *n.* genital organs, organs of reproduction, privates; see GENITALS.

privilege *n.* 1 [A customary concession] due, perquisite, prerogative; see RIGHT 1. 2 [An opportunity] chance,

fortunate happening, event; see OPPORTUNITY 1.

privileged *a.* free, vested, furnished; see EXEMPT.

prize[1] *n.* reward, advantage, privilege, possession, honor, inducement, premium, bounty, bonus, spoil, booty, plunder, pillage, loot, award, accolade, recompense, requital, acquisitions, laurel, decoration, medal, trophy, palm, crown, citation, scholarship, fellowship, feather in one's cap, title, championship, first place, pay-off*, cake*, plum.

prize[1] *v.* regard highly, value, esteem; see VALUE 2.

probability *n.* likelihood, possibility, chance; see CHANCE, POSSIBILITY 2.

probable *a.* seeming, presumable, feasible; see LIKELY 1.

probably *a.* presumably, seemingly, apparently, believably, reasonably, imaginably, feasibly, practicably, expediently, plausibly, most likely, everything being equal, as like as not, as the case may be, one can assume, like enough, no doubt, to all appearance, in all probability.—*Ant.* UNLIKELY, doubtfully, questionably.

pro·ba'tion·er (-ər) *n.* a person on probation

probation officer an officer who watches over persons on probation

probe (prōb) *n.* ⟦< L *probare*, to test⟧ 1 a surgical instrument for exploring a wound, etc. 2 a searching examination 3 a device, as a spacecraft with instruments, used to get information about an environment — *vt.* **probed, prob'ing** 1 to explore (a wound, etc.) with a probe 2 to investigate thoroughly — *vi.* to search

pro·bity (prō'bə tē, präb'ə-) *n.* ⟦< L *probus*, good⟧ honesty; integrity

prob·lem (präb'ləm) *n.* ⟦< Gr *problēma*⟧ 1 a question proposed for solution 2 a perplexing or difficult matter, person, etc.

prob·lem·at·ic (präb'lə mat'ik) *adj.* 1 of the nature of a problem 2 uncertain Also **prob'lem·at'i·cal** —**prob'lem·at'i·cal·ly** *adv.*

pro·bos·cis (prō bäs'is) *n., pl.* **-cises** ⟦< Gr *pro-*, before + *boskein*, to feed⟧ an elephant's trunk, or any similar long, flexible snout

pro·caine (prō'kān') *n.* ⟦PRO-² + (CO)CAINE⟧ a synthetic compound used as a local anesthetic

pro·ce·dure (prō sē'jər, prə-) *n.* the act or method of proceeding in an action —**pro·ce'dur·al** *adj.*

pro·ceed (prō sēd', prə-) *vi.* ⟦< L *pro-*, forward + *cedere*, go⟧ 1 to go on, esp. after stopping 2 to carry on some action 3 to take legal action (*against*) 4 to come forth or issue (*from*)

pro·ceed'ing *n.* 1 a going on with what one has been doing 2 a course of action 3 [*pl.*] a record of the business carried on, as by a learned society 4 [*pl.*] legal action

pro·ceeds (prō'sēdz') *n.pl.* the sum derived from a sale, business venture, etc.

proc·ess (prä'ses') *n.* ⟦see PROCEED⟧ 1 the course of being done: chiefly in **in process** 2 course (*of* time, etc.) 3 a continuing development involving many changes [*the process* of digestion*]* 4 a method of doing something, with all the steps involved 5 *Biol.* a projecting part 6 *Law* a court summons — *vt.* to prepare by or subject to a special process —**pro'ces·sor** *n.*

pro·ces·sion (prō sesh'ən, prə-) *n.* ⟦see PROCEED⟧ a number of persons or things moving forward, as in a parade

pro·ces'sion·al *n.* a hymn sung at the beginning of a church service during the entrance of the clergy

pro'-choice' *adj.* advocating the right to legal abortion —**pro'-choic'er** *n.*

pro·claim (prō klām') *vt.* ⟦< L *pro-*, before + *clamare*, cry out⟧ to announce officially; announce to be

proc·la·ma·tion (präk'lə mā'shən) *n.* 1 a proclaiming 2 something that is proclaimed

pro·cliv·ity (prō kliv'ə tē) *n., pl.* **-ties** ⟦< L *pro-*, before + *clivus*, a slope⟧ a tendency or inclination

pro·cras·ti·nate (prō kras'tə nāt', prə-) *vi., vt.* **-nat'ed, -nat'ing** ⟦< L *pro-*, forward + *cras*, tomorrow⟧ to put off doing (something) until later; delay —**pro·cras'ti·na'tion** *n.* —**pro·cras'ti·na'tor** *n.*

pro·create (prō'krē āt') *vt., vi.* **-at'ed, -at'ing** ⟦< L *pro-*, before + *creare*, create⟧ to produce (young); beget (offspring) —**pro'crea'tion** *n.* —**pro'crea'tive** *adj.*

proc·tor (präk'tər) *n.* ⟦see PROCURE⟧ one who supervises or monitors students, as at an examination — *vt.* to supervise (an academic examination)

pro·cu·ra·tor (präk'yoō rāt'ər, -yə-) *n.* ⟦see fol.⟧ in the Roman Empire, the governor of a lesser province

pro·cure (prō kyoor') *vt.* **-cured', -cur'ing** ⟦< L *pro-*, before + *curare*, attend to⟧ to obtain; get —**pro·cur'able** *adj.* —**pro·cure'ment** *n.*

pro·cur'er *n.* a pimp

prod (präd) *vt.* **prod'ded, prod'ding** ⟦< ?⟧ 1 to jab as with a pointed stick 2 to goad into action — *n.* 1 a jab or thrust 2 something that prods

prod·i·gal (präd'i gəl) *adj.* ⟦< L *pro-*, forth + *agere*, to drive⟧ 1 exceedingly or recklessly wasteful 2 extremely abundant — *n.* a spendthrift —**prod'i·gal'ity** (-gal'ə tē), *pl.* **-ties,** *n.*

pro·di·gious (prō dij'əs, prə-) *adj.* ⟦see fol.⟧ 1 wonderful; amazing 2 enormous —**pro·di'gious·ly** *adv.*

prod·i·gy (präd'ə jē) *n., pl.* **-gies** ⟦< L *prodigium*, omen⟧ an extraordinary person, thing, or act; specif., a child of genius

pro·duce (prō doōs'; *for n.* prä'doōs, prō'-) *vt.* **-duced', -duc'ing** ⟦< L *pro-*, forward + *ducere*, to lead⟧ 1 to bring to view; show [*to produce* identification*]* 2 to bring forth; bear 3 to make or manufacture 4 to cause 5 to get (a play, etc.) ready for presentation — *vi.* to yield something — *n.* something produced; esp., fruit and vegetables — **pro·duc'er** *n.*

prod·uct (präd'ukt', -əkt) *n.* 1 something produced by nature, industry, or art 2 result; outgrowth 3 *Math.* the quantity obtained by multiplying two or more quantities together

pro·duc·tion (prō duk'shən, prə-) *n.* a producing or something produced

pro·duc'tive *adj.* 1 fertile 2 marked by abundant production 3 bringing as a result (with *of*) [*war is productive* of misery*]* —**pro·duc'tively** *adv.* —**pro·duc·tiv·ity** (prō'dək tiv'ə tē) or **pro·duc'tive·ness** *n.*

prof (präf) *n.* [Colloq.] *short for* PROFESSOR

Prof. Professor

pro·fane (prō fān', prə-) *adj.* ⟦< L *pro-*, before + *fanum*, temple⟧ 1 not connected with religion; secular 2 showing disrespect or contempt for sacred things — *vt.* **-faned', -fan'ing** 1 to treat (sacred things) with irreverence or contempt 2 to debase; defile —**prof·a·na·tion** (präf'ə nā'shən) *n.* —**pro·fane'ly** *adv.* —**pro·fane'ness** *n.*

pro·fan·ity (-fan'ə tē) *n.* 1 a being profane 2 *pl.* **-ties** profane language; swearing

pro·fess (prō fes', prə-) *vt.* ⟦< L *pro-*, before + *fateri*, avow⟧ 1 to declare openly; affirm 2 to claim to have

---

THESAURUS

problem *n.* 1 [A difficulty] dilemma, quandary, obstacle; see DIFFICULTY 1, 2. 2 [A question to be solved] query, intricacy, enigma; see PUZZLE 2.

procedure *n.* fashion, style, mode; see METHOD, SYSTEM.

proceed *v.* move, progress, continue; see ADVANCE 1.

proceeding *n.* [*Often plural*] process, transaction, deed, experiment, performance, measure, step, course, undertaking, venture, adventure, occurrence, incident, circumstance, happening, movement, operation, procedure, exercise, maneuver; see also ACTION 1.

proceeds *n.* gain, profit, yield; see RETURN 3.

process *n.* means, rule, manner; see METHOD. —**in (the) process of** while, when, in the course of; see DURING.

process *v.* treat, make ready, concoct; see PREPARE 1.

processed *a.* treated, handled, fixed; see PRESERVED 2.

prod *v.* provoke, crowd, shove; see PUSH 1.

prodigy *n.* marvel, portent, miracle, monster, enormity, spectacle, freak, curiosity; see also WONDER 2. —

(child) **prodigy** genius, gifted child, boy or girl wonder; see ARTIST, MUSICIAN, SCIENTIST, WRITER.

produce *n.* product, harvest, result, crop, return, effect, consequence, amount, profit, outcome, outgrowth, aftermath, gain, realization; see also BUTTER, CHEESE, CREAM 1, FOOD, FRUIT, GRAIN 1, MILK, VEGETABLE.

produce *v.* 1 [To bear] yield, bring forth, give birth to, propagate, bring out, come through, blossom, flower, deliver, generate, engender, breed, contribute, give, afford, furnish, return, render, show fruit, fetch, bring in, present, offer, provide, contribute, sell for, bear fruit, accrue, allow, admit, proliferate, be delivered of, bring to birth, reproduce, foal, lamb, drop, calve, fawn, whelp, kitten, litter, hatch, usher into the world, spawn. 2 [To create by mental effort] originate, author, procreate, bring forth, conceive, engender, write, design, fabricate, imagine, turn out, churn out, devise; see also COMPOSE 2, CREATE, INVENT 1. 3 [To cause] effect, occasion, bring about; see BEGIN 1. 4 [To show] exhibit, present, unfold; see DISPLAY. 5 [To make] assemble,

build, construct; see MANUFACTURE. 6 [To present a performance] present, play, prepare for public presentation; see ACT 3, PERFORM 2.

produced *a.* 1 [Created] originated, composed, made; see FORMED. 2 [Presented] performed, acted, put on; see SHOWN 1. 3 [Caused] occasioned, propagated, begot, bred, engendered, generated, hatched, induced.

product *n.* 1 [A result] output, outcome, outgrowth; see RESULT. 2 [Goods produced; *often plural*] stock, goods, merchandise; see GOODS 1.

production *n.* 1 [The act of producing] origination, creation, authoring, reproduction, yielding, giving, bearing, rendering, giving forth, increasing, return, procreation, generation, engendering, blooming, blossoming; see also MAKING. 2 [The amount produced] crop, result, stock; see QUANTITY.

productive *a.* rich, fruitful, prolific; see FERTILE.

productivity *n.* richness, potency, fecundity; see FERTILITY.

profanity *n.* abuse, cursing, swearing; see CURSE 1.

(some feeling, etc.): often insincerely **3** to declare one's belief in —**pro·fessed′** *adj.*

pro·fes·sion (prō fesh′ən, prə-) *n.* **1** a professing, or declaring; avowal **2** an occupation requiring advanced academic training, as medicine, law, etc. **3** all the persons in such an occupation

pro·fes′sion·al *adj.* **1** of or engaged in a profession **2** engaged in some sport or in a specified occupation for pay —*n.* a person who is professional (esp. in sense 2) —**pro· fes′sion·al·ly** *adv.*

pro·fes·sor (prō fes′ər, prə-) *n.* **1** a college or university teacher of the highest rank **2** loosely, a teacher —**pro·fes· so′ri·al** (prō′fə sôr′ē əl) *adj.* —**pro·fes′sor·ship′** *n.*

prof·fer (präf′ər) *vt.* ⟦< OFr: see PRO-² & OFFER⟧ to offer (usually something intangible) *[to proffer friendship]* —*n.* an offer

pro·fi·cient (prō fish′ənt, prə-) *adj.* ⟦< L *pro-*, forward + *facere*, make⟧ highly competent; skilled —**pro·fi′ciency** *n.* —**pro·fi′cient·ly** *adv.*

pro·file (prō′fīl′) *n.* ⟦< It *profilare*, to outline⟧ **1** a side view of the face **2** a drawing of this **3** an outline **4** a short, vivid biography

profit (präf′it) *n.* ⟦see PROFICIENT⟧ **1** advantage; gain **2** *[often pl.]* financial gain; esp. the sum remaining after deducting costs —*vt., vi.* **1** to be of advantage (to) **2** to benefit —**prof′it·a·ble** *adj.* —**prof′it·a·bly** *adv.* —**prof′it· less** *adj.*

prof·it·eer (präf′i tir′) *n.* one who makes excessive profits by charging exorbitant prices —*vi.* to be a profiteer

pro·fi·te·role (prə fit′ə rōl′) *n.* a small cream puff, variously filled

prof·li·gate (präf′li git) *adj.* ⟦< L *pro-*, forward + *fligere*, to drive⟧ **1** dissolute **2** recklessly wasteful —**prof′li·gacy** (-gə sē) *n.*

pro forma (prō fôr′mə) ⟦L⟧ for (the sake of) form; as a matter of form

pro·found (prō found′, prə-) *adj.* ⟦< L *pro-*, forward + *fundus*, bottom⟧ **1** very deep *[a profound sigh, sleep, etc.]* **2** marked by intellectual depth **3** deeply felt *[profound grief]* **4** thoroughgoing *[profound changes]* —**pro· found′ly** *adv.* —**pro·fun′dity** (-fun′də tē), *pl.* -**ties**, *n.*

pro·fuse (prō fyōōs′, prə-) *adj.* ⟦< L *pro-*, forth + *fundere*, pour⟧ giving or given freely and abundantly —**pro·fuse′ly** *adv.* —**pro·fu′sion** (-fyōō′zhən) *n.*

pro·gen·i·tor (prō jen′ə tər) *n.* ⟦< L *pro-*, forth + *gignere*, beget⟧ **1** an ancestor in direct line **2** a precursor

prog·e·ny (präj′ə nē) *n., pl.* -**nies** ⟦see prec.⟧ children; offspring

pro·ges·ter·one (prō jes′tər ōn′) *n.* a female hormone secreted by the ovary or prepared synthetically

prog·na·thous (präg′nə thəs) *adj.* ⟦PRO-¹ + Gr *gnathos*, jaw⟧ having the jaws projecting beyond the upper face

prog·no·sis (präg nō′sis) *n., pl.* -**no′ses′** (-sēz′) ⟦< Gr *pro-*, before + *gignōskein*, know⟧ a prediction, esp. of the course of a disease

prog·nos·tic (-näs′tik) *n.* ⟦see prec.⟧ **1** an omen **2** a prediction —*adj.* predictive

prog·nos′ti·cate′ (-näs′ti kāt′) *vt.* -**cat′ed**, -**cat′ing** ⟦see PROGNOSIS⟧ to foretell —**prog·nos′ti·ca′tion** *n.* —**prog· nos′ti·ca′tor** *n.*

pro·gram (prō′gram′, -grəm) *n.* ⟦< Gr *pro-*, before + *graphein*, write⟧ **1** a list of the acts, speeches, musical pieces, etc. as of an entertainment **2** a plan or procedure **3** a scheduled radio or TV broadcast **4** a logical sequence of coded instructions specifying the operations to be performed by a computer **5** a series of operations used to control an electronic device —*vt.* -**grammed′** or -**gramed′**, -**gram′ming** or -**gram′ing** **1** to schedule in a program **2** to prepare (a textbook, etc.) for use in program grammed instruction **3** to plan a computer program for **4** to furnish (a computer) with a program ☆ Chiefly Brit., etc. sp. **pro′gramme** —**pro·gram·ma·ble** (prō′gram′ə bəl, prō gram′-) *adj., n.* —**pro′gram·mer** or **pro′gramer** *n.*

programmed instruction instruction in which individual students answer questions about a unit of study at their own rate, checking their own answers and advancing only after answering correctly Also **programmed learning**

prog·ress (präg′res; *for v.* prō gres′, prə-) *n.* ⟦< L *pro-*, before + *gradi*, to step⟧ **1** a moving forward **2** development **3** improvement —*vi.* **1** to move forward **2** to move forward toward completion **3** to improve

pro·gres·sion (prō gresh′ən, prə-) *n.* **1** a moving forward **2** a succession, as of events **3** *Math.* a series of numbers increasing or decreasing by a constant difference between terms

---

◼ THESAURUS ◼

profession *n.* **1** [A skilled or learned occupation] calling, business, avocation, vocation, employment, occupation, engagement, office, situation, position, lifework, chosen work, role, service, pursuit, undertaking, concern, post, berth, craft, sphere, field, walk of life; see also CHURCH 3, EDUCATION 3, JUDICIARY, MEDICINE 3, TRADE 2, WRITING 3. **2** [A declaration] pretense, avowal, vow; see DECLARATION, OATH 1.

professional *a.* **1** [Skillful] expert, learned, adept; see ABLE. **2** [Well-qualified] acknowledged, known, licensed; see ABLE.

professional *n.* expert, trained personnel, specially trained person; see SPECIALIST.

professor *n.* educator, faculty member, sage; see TEACHER. *Teachers popularly called professors include the following:* full professor, associate professor, assistant professor, instructor, lecturer, graduate assistant, teaching assistant, tutor, school principal, fellow, teaching fellow, master docent.

proficiency *n.* learning, skill, knowledge; see ABILITY.

proficient *a.* skilled, expert, skillful; see ABLE.

profile *n.* silhouette, shape, figure; see FORM 1, OUTLINE 3.

profit *n.* **1** [Advantage] avail, good, value; see ADVANTAGE. **2** [Excess of receipts over expenditures] gain, returns, proceeds, receipts, take*, gate, acquisition, rake-off*, accumulation, saving, interest, remuneration, earnings.—*Ant.* LOSS, debits, costs.

profit *v.* **1** [To be of benefit] benefit, assist, avail; see HELP. **2** [To derive gain] benefit, capitalize on, cash in on, realize, clear, gain, reap profits, make a profit, recover, thrive, prosper, harvest, make money.—*Ant.* LOSE, lose out on, miss out on.

profitable *a.* lucrative, useful, sustaining, aiding, remunerative, beneficial, gainful, advantageous, paying, successful, favorable, assisting, productive, serviceable, valuable, instrumental, practical, pragmatic, effective, to advantage, effectual, sufficient, paying its way, bringing in returns, making money, paying well, paying out, in the black; see also HELPFUL 1.—*Ant.* UNPROFITABLE, UNSUCCESSFUL, unproductive.

profitably *a.* lucratively, remuneratively, gainfully, usefully, advantageously, successfully, favorably, for money, productively, practically, effectively, effectually, sufficiently, sustainingly.

profiteer *n.* exploiter, chiseler, cheater; see CHEAT.

profound *a.* **1** [Physically deep] fathomless, bottomless, subterranean; see DEEP 1. **2** [Intellectually deep] heavy, erudite, scholarly, mysterious, sage, serious, sagacious, penetrating, discerning, knowing, wise, knowledgeable, intellectual, enlightened, thorough, informed; see also LEARNED 1, SOLEMN.—*Ant.* SUPERFICIAL, shallow, flighty. **3** [Emotionally deep] heartfelt, deep-felt, great; see INTENSE.

profoundly *a.* deeply, extremely, thoroughly; see VERY.

program *n.* **1** [A list of subjects] schedule, memoranda, printed program; see LIST. **2** [A sequence of events] happenings, schedule, agenda, order of business, calendar, plans, business, affairs, details, arrangements, catalogue, curriculum, order of the day, series of events, appointments, things to do, chores, preparations, meetings, getting and spending, all the thousand and one things; see also PLAN 2. **3** [An entertainment] performance, show, presentation; see PERFORMANCE.

program *v.* **1** [To schedule] slate, book, bill; see sense 2. **2** [To work out a sequence to be performed] feed in, activate a computer, compute, reckon, figure, calculate, estimate, enter, compile, feed, edit, process, extend, delete, add.

programmed *a.* scheduled, slated, lined up; see PLANNED.

progress *n.* **1** [Movement forward] progression, advance, headway, impetus, forward course, development, velocity, pace, momentum, motion, rate, step, stride, current, flow, tour, circuit, transit, journey, voyage, march, expedition, locomotion, passage, course, procession, process, march of events, course of life, movement of the stars, motion through space.—*Ant.* STOP, stay, stand. **2** [Improvement] advancement, development, growth; see IMPROVEMENT 1. —**in progress** advancing, going on, continuing; see MOVING 1.

progress *v.* proceed, move onward, move on; see ADVANCE 1.

pro·gres'sive (-gres'iv, prə-) *adj.* 1 moving forward 2 continuing by successive steps 3 of or favoring progress, reform, etc. 4 *Gram.* indicating continuing action or state, as certain verb forms — *n.* one who is progressive —**pro·gres'sively** *adv.*

pro·hibit (prō hib'it, prə-) *vt.* ⟦< L *pro-*, before + *habere*, have⟧ 1 to forbid by law or an order 2 to prevent; hinder —**pro·hib'i·tive** or **pro·hib'i·to'ry** *adj.*

pro·hi·bi·tion (prō'i bish'ən) *n.* 1 a prohibiting 2 the forbidding by law of the manufacture or sale of alcoholic beverages —**pro'hi·bi'tion·ist** *n.*

proj·ect (prä'jekt'; *for v.* prō jekt', prə-) *n.* ⟦< L *pro-*, before + *jacere*, to throw⟧ 1 a proposal; scheme 2 an organized undertaking — *vt.* **pro·ject'** 1 to propose (a plan) 2 to throw forward 3 to cause to jut out 4 to cause (a shadow, image, etc.) to fall upon a surface — *vi.* to jut out —**pro·jec'tion** *n.*

pro·jec·tile (prō jek'təl, prə-) *n.* 1 an object designed to be shot forward, as a bullet 2 anything thrown or hurled forward

projection booth a small chamber, as in a theater, from which images on film, slides, etc. are projected

pro·jec'tion·ist *n.* the operator of a film or slide projector

pro·jec'tor *n.* a machine for projecting images on a screen

pro·le·tar·i·at (prō'lə ter'ē ət) *n.* ⟦< L *proletarius*, a citizen of the lowest class⟧ the working class; esp., the industrial working class —**pro'letar'ian** *adj., n.*

pro'-life' *adj.* opposing the right to legal abortion —**pro'-lif'er** *n.*

pro·lif·er·ate (prō lif'ər āt', prə-) *vi.* **-at'ed, -at'ing** ⟦< L *proles*, offspring + *ferre*, to bear⟧ to increase rapidly —**pro·lif'era'tion** *n.*

pro·lific (prō lif'ik, prə-) *adj.* ⟦< L *proles*, offspring + *facere*, make⟧ 1 producing many young or much fruit 2 turning out many products of the mind —**pro·lif'i·cally** *adv.*

pro·lix (prō liks') *adj.* ⟦< L *prolixus*, extended⟧ wordy or long-winded —**pro·lix'i·ty** *n.* —**pro·lix'ly** *adv.*

pro·logue (prō'lôg') *n.* ⟦< Gr *pro-*, before + *logos*, discourse⟧ 1 an introduction to a poem, play, etc. 2 any preliminary act, event, etc.

pro·long (prō lôŋ', prə-) *vt.* ⟦< L *pro-*, forth + *longus*, long⟧ to lengthen in time or space Also **pro·lon'gate'** (-gāt'), **-gat'ed, -gat'ing** —**pro·lon·ga·tion** (prō'lôŋ gā'shən) *n.*

prom (präm) *n.* ⟦< fol.⟧ a dance, as of a particular school class

prom·enade (präm'ə nād', -näd') *n.* ⟦Fr < L *pro-*, forth + *minare*, to herd⟧ 1 a leisurely walk taken for pleasure, display, etc. 2 a public place for walking 3 a ball or dance — *vi., vt.* **-nad'ed, -nad'ing** to take a promenade along or through

Pro·me·theus (prō mē'thē əs) *Gr. Myth.* a Titan who steals fire from heaven for the benefit of mankind

prom·i·nent (präm'ə nənt) *adj.* ⟦< L *prominere*, to project⟧ 1 sticking out; projecting 2 noticeable; conspicuous 3 widely and favorably known —**prom'i·nence** *n.* —**prom'i·nently** *adv.*

pro·mis·cu·ous (prō mis'kyōō əs, prə-) *adj.* ⟦< L *pro-*, forth + *miscere*, to mix⟧ 1 consisting of different elements indiscriminately mingled 2 characterized by a lack of discrimination, esp. in sexual liaisons —**prom·is·cu·i·ty** (präm'is kyōō'ə tē), *pl.* **-ties,** *n.* —**pro·mis'cu·ously** *adv.*

prom·ise (präm'is) *n.* ⟦< L *pro-*, forth + *mittere*, send⟧ 1 an agreement to do or not to do something 2 indication, as of a successful future 3 something promised — *vi., vt.* **-ised, -is·ing** 1 to make a promise of (something) 2 to give a basis for expecting

Promised Land *Bible* Canaan, promised by God to Abraham and his descendants: Genesis 17:8

prom·is·sory (präm'i sôr'ē) *adj.* containing a promise

pro·mo (prō'mō) *adj.* [Colloq.] of or engaged in the promotion or advertisement of a product, etc. — *n., pl.* **-mos** [Colloq.] a recorded announcement, radio or TV commercial, etc. used in advertising, etc.

prom·on·tory (präm'ən tôr'ē) *n., pl.* **-ries** ⟦prob. < L *prominere*, to project⟧ a peak of high land that juts out into a body of water; headland

pro·mote (prō mōt', prə-) *vt.* **-mot'ed, -mot'ing** ⟦< L *pro-*, forward + *movere*, to move⟧ 1 to raise to a higher position or rank 2 to further the growth, establishment, sales, etc. of —**pro·mo'tion** *n.* —**pro·mo'tional** *adj.*

pro·mot'er *n.* one who begins, organizes, and furthers an undertaking

prompt (prämpt) *adj.* ⟦< L *pro-*, forth + *emere*, take⟧ 1 ready, punctual, etc. 2 done, spoken, etc. without delay — *vt.* 1 to urge into action 2 to remind (a person) of something he or she has forgotten; specif., to help (an actor, etc.) with a cue 3 to inspire —**prompt'er** *n.* —**prompt'ly** *adv.* —**prompt'ness** or **promp'ti·tude'** *n.*

prom·ul·gate (präm'əl gāt', prō mul'gāt') *vt.* **-gat'ed, -gat'ing** ⟦< L *promulgare*, publish⟧ 1 to make known officially 2 to make widespread —**prom'ul·ga'tion** *n.*

THESAURUS

progressive *a.* 1 [In mounting sequence] advancing, mounting, rising; see MOVING 1. 2 [Receptive to new ideas] tolerant, lenient, open-minded; see LIBERAL.

prohibit *v.* interdict, put under the ban, obstruct; see FORBID, PREVENT.

prohibited *a.* forbidden, restricted, not approved; see ILLEGAL, REFUSED.

project *n.* outline, design, scheme; see PLAN 2.

project *v.* 1 [To thrust out] protrude, hang over, extend, jut, bulge, stick out, hang out, jut out, be prominent, be conspicuous.—*Ant.* WITHDRAW, regress, revert. 2 [To throw] pitch, heave, propel; see THROW 1.

projection *n.* 1 [Bulge] prominence, jut, protuberance, step, ridge, rim; see also BULGE. 2 [Forecast] prognostication, prediction, guess; see GUESS.

prolong *v.* continue, hold, draw out; see INCREASE.

prolonged *a.* extended, lengthened, continued; see DULL 4.

prominence *n.* 1 [A projection] jut, protrusion, bump; see BULGE, PROJECTION 1. 2 [Notability] renown, influence, distinction; see FAME.

prominent *a.* 1 [Physically prominent] protuberant, extended, jutting, conspicuous, protruding, projecting, noticeable, rugged, rough, obtrusive, standing out, sticking out, hilly, raised, relieved, rounded.—*Ant.* HOLLOW, depressed, sunken. 2 [Socially prominent] notable, preeminent, leading; see FAMOUS. 3 [Conspicu-

ous] remarkable, striking, noticeable; see CONSPICUOUS.

promiscuity *n.* lechery, looseness, sexual immorality; see LEWDNESS.

promiscuous *a.* indiscriminate, sexually immoral, loose; see LEWD 2.

promise *n.* 1 [A pledge] assurance, agreement, pact, oath, engagement, covenant, consent, warrant, affirmation, swearing, plight, word, troth, vow, profession, guarantee, insurance, obligation, commitment, betrothal, espousal, plighted faith, marriage contract, giving one's word, gentleman's agreement, word of honor. 2 [Hope] outlook, good omen, good appearance; see ENCOURAGEMENT.

promise *v.* 1 [To give one's word] engage, declare, agree, vow, swear, consent, affirm, profess, undertake, pledge, covenant, contract, bargain, espouse, betroth, assure, guarantee, warrant, give assurance, give warranty, insure, cross one's heart, plight one's troth, bind oneself, commit oneself, obligate oneself, make oneself answerable, give security, underwrite, subscribe, lead someone to expect, answer for, pledge one's honor.—*Ant.* DECEIVE, deny, break faith. 2 [To appear promising] ensure, insure, assure; see ENCOURAGE.

promised *a.* pledged, sworn, vowed, agreed, covenanted, as agreed upon, undertaken, professed, consented, affirmed, insured, warranted,

vouched for, underwritten, subscribed, stipulated, assured, ensured; see also GUARANTEED.

promising *a.* likely, assuring, encouraging; see HOPEFUL 2.

promote *v.* 1 [To further] forward, urge, encourage, profit, patronize, help, aid, assist, develop, support, boom, back, uphold, champion, advertise, advocate, cultivate, improve, push, bolster, develop, speed, foster, nourish, nurture, subsidize, befriend, benefit, subscribe to, favor, expand, improve, better, cooperate, get behind, boost.—*Ant.* DISCOURAGE, weaken, enfeeble. 2 [To advance in rank] raise, advance, elevate, graduate, move up, exalt, aggrandize, magnify, prefer, favor, increase, better, dignify.—*Ant.* HUMBLE, demote, reduce.

promotion *n.* 1 [Advancement in rank] preferment, elevation, raise, improvement, advance, lift, betterment, ennobling, favoring.—*Ant.* REMOVAL, demotion, lowering. 2 [Improvement] advancement, progression, development; see IMPROVEMENT 1, INCREASE.

prompt *a.* early, timely, precise; see PUNCTUAL.

prompt *v.* 1 [To instigate] arouse, provoke, inspire; see INCITE, URGE 2. 2 [To suggest] bring up, indicate, imply; see PROPOSE 1.

promptly *a.* on time, punctually, hastily; see IMMEDIATELY, QUICKLY.

pron. 1 pronoun 2 pronunciation

prone (prōn) *adj.* ⟦< L *pronus*⟧ 1 lying face downward or prostrate 2 disposed or inclined (*to*) [*prone to error*]

prong (prôŋ) *n.* ⟦ME *pronge*⟧ 1 any of the pointed ends of a fork; tine 2 any projecting part —**pronged** *adj.*

prong′horn′ *n.* a deerlike animal of the W U.S., having curved horns: it also resembles the antelope

pro·noun (prō′noun′) *n.* ⟦< L *pro*, for + *nomen*, noun⟧ *Gram.* a word used in place of a noun (Ex.: *I, he, it,* etc.) — **pro·nom′i·nal** (-näm′i nəl) *adj.*

pro·nounce (prō nouns′, prə-) *vt.* **-nounced′, -nounc′ing** ⟦< L *pro*-, before + *nuntiare*, announce⟧ 1 to declare officially, solemnly, etc. [*to pronounce* a couple man and wife] 2 utter or articulate (a sound or word) —**pro·nounce′a·ble** *adj.*

pro·nounced′ *adj.* clearly marked; decided [*a pronounced change*]

pro·nounce′ment *n.* a formal statement, as of an opinion

pronto (prän′tō) *adv.* ⟦Sp: see PROMPT⟧ [Slang] at once; quickly

pro·nun·ci·a·tion (prō nun′sē ā′shən, prə-) *n.* 1 the act or manner of pronouncing words 2 the way a word is usually pronounced, esp. in phonetic symbols

proof (prōōf) *n.* ⟦see PROBE⟧ 1 a proving or testing of something 2 evidence that establishes the truth of something 3 the relative strength of an alcoholic liquor 4 *Photog.* a trial print of a negative 5 a sheet printed from set type, for checking errors, etc. — *adj.* of tested strength in resisting: with *against*

-proof (prōōf) ⟦< prec.⟧ *combining form* 1 impervious to [*waterproof*] 2 protected from [*rustproof*] 3 resistant to [*fireproof*]

proof′read′ *vt., vi.* to read and mark corrections on (printers' proofs, etc.) —**proof′read′er** *n.*

prop[1] (präp) *n.* ⟦< MDu *proppe*⟧ a support, as a pole, placed under or against something: often used figuratively — *vt.* **propped, prop′ping** 1 to support, as with a prop: often with *up* 2 to lean (something) *against* a support

prop[2] (präp) *n.* PROPERTY (sense 4)

prop[3] (präp) *n. short for* PROPELLER

prop. 1 proper(ly) 2 property 3 proposition 4 proprietor

propa·ganda (präp′ə gan′də) *n.* ⟦ModL: see fol.⟧ 1 any widespread promotion of particular ideas, doctrines, etc. 2 ideas, etc. so spread —**prop′a·gan′dist** *n., adj.* — **prop′a·gan′dize** (-dīz′) *vt., vi.*

propa·gate (präp′ə gāt′) *vt.* **-gat′ed, -gat′ing** ⟦< L *propago*, slip (of a plant)⟧ 1 to cause (a plant or animal) to reproduce itself 2 to reproduce (itself): said of a plant or animal 3 to spread (ideas, customs, etc.) — *vi.* to reproduce, as plants or animals —**prop′a·ga′tion** *n.*

pro·pane (prō′pān′) *n.* a gaseous hydrocarbon from petroleum, used as a fuel

pro·pel (prō pel′, prə-) *vt.* **-pelled′, -pel′ling** ⟦< L *pro*-, forward + *pellere*, drive⟧ to drive onward or forward

pro·pel′lant or **pro·pel′lent** *n.* one that propels; specif., the fuel for a rocket

pro·pel′ler *n.* a device having two or more blades in a revolving hub, for propelling a ship or aircraft

pro·pen·sity (prə pen′sə tē) *n., pl.* **-ties** ⟦< L *propendere*, hang forward⟧ a natural inclination or tendency

proper (präp′ər) *adj.* ⟦< L *proprius*, one's own⟧ 1 specially suitable; appropriate; fitting 2 naturally belonging (*to*) 3 conforming to a standard; correct 4 decent; decorous 5 in the most restricted sense [*Chicago proper* (i.e., apart from its suburbs)] 6 designating a noun that names a specific individual, place, etc. (Ex.: *Bill, Paris*) —**prop′erly** *adv.*

prop·erty (präp′ər tē) *n., pl.* **-ties** ⟦see prec.⟧ 1 ownership 2 something owned, esp. real estate 3 a characteristic or attribute 4 any of the movable articles used in a stage setting —**prop′er·tied** (-tēd) *adj.*

proph·ecy (präf′ə sē) *n., pl.* **-cies** ⟦see PROPHET⟧ 1 prediction of the future 2 something predicted

proph′esy′ (-sī′) *vt., vi.* **-sied′, -sy′ing** 1 to predict as by divine guidance 2 to predict in any way —**proph′esi′er** *n.*

prophet (präf′ət, -it) *n.* ⟦< Gr *pro*-, before + *phanai*, speak⟧ 1 a religious leader regarded as, or claiming to be, divinely inspired 2 one who predicts the future —**proph′et·ess** *n.fem.*

pro·phetic (prō fet′ik, prə-) *adj.* 1 of or like a prophet 2 like or containing a prophecy —**pro·phet′i·cally** *adv.*

pro·phy·lac·tic (prō′fə lak′tik) *adj.* ⟦< Gr *pro*-, before + *phylassein*, to guard⟧ preventive or protective; esp., preventing disease — *n.* a prophylactic medicine, device, etc.

pro·phy·lax·is (-laks′is) *n., pl.* **-lax·es′** (-ēz′) prophylactic treatment; specif., in dentistry, a cleaning of the teeth to remove plaque and tartar

pro·pin·quity (prō piŋ′kwə tē) *n.* ⟦< L *propinquus*, near⟧ nearness

pro·pi·ti·ate (prō pish′ē āt′, prə-) *vt.* **-at′ed, -at′ing** ⟦see fol.⟧ to win the good will of; appease —**pro·pi′tia′tion** *n.* —**pro·pi′tia·to′ry** (-ə tôr′ē) *adj.*

pro·pi·tious (prō pish′əs, prə-) *adj.* ⟦< L *pro*-, before + *petere*, seek⟧ 1 favorably inclined 2 favorable; auspicious

pro·po·nent (prō pō′nənt, prə-) *n.* ⟦see PROPOSE⟧ one who espouses or supports a cause, etc.

pro·por·tion (prō pôr′shən, prə-) *n.* ⟦< L *pro*, for + *portio*, a part⟧ 1 the comparative relation in size, amount, etc. between things; ratio 2 a part, share, etc. in its relation to the whole 3 balance or symmetry 4 [*pl.*] dimensions — *vt.* 1 to put in proper relation with something else 2 to arrange the parts of (a whole) so as to be harmonious —**pro·por′tional** or **pro·por′tion·ate** (-shə nit) *adj.*

pro·posal (prō pōz′əl, prə-) *n.* 1 a proposing 2 a proposed plan, etc. 3 an offer of marriage

---

◼ THESAURUS ◼

prone *a.* inclined, predisposed, disposed; see LIKELY 4.

prong *n.* spine, spur, spike; see FASTENER.

pronoun *n. Pronouns include the following:* personal, possessive, demonstrative, relative, definite, indefinite, interrogative, intensive, reflexive, reciprocal.

pronounce *v.* 1 [To speak formally] proclaim, say, assert; see DECLARE. 2 [To articulate] enunciate, phonate, vocalize; see UTTER.

pronounced *a.* notable, noticeable, clear; see DEFINITE 2, OBVIOUS 1, 2, UNUSUAL 1.

pronouncement *n.* report, declaration, statement; see ANNOUNCEMENT.

pronunciation *n.* articulation, utterance, voicing; see DICTION.

proof *n.* 1 [Evidence] demonstration, verification, case, reasons, exhibits, credentials, data, warrant, confirmation, substantiation, attestation, corroboration, affidavit, facts, witness, testimony, deposition, trace, record, criterion. 2 [Process of proving] test, attempt, assay; see TRIAL 2.

prop[1] *n.* aid, assistance, strengthener; see POST.

propaganda *n.* promotion, public-ity, advertisement, plug*, evangelism, proselytism, ballyhoo, handout.

propel *v.* impel forward, move, press onward; see DRIVE 2.

propellant *n.* charge, gunpowder, combustible; see EXPLOSIVE, FUEL.

propeller *n. Propellers include the following:* screw, Archimedean, fishtail, variable-pitch, feathering, marine, airplane, two-bladed, three-bladed, four-bladed, weedless, pusher, pulling.

propensity *n.* talent, capacity, competence; see ABILITY.

proper *a.* 1 [Suitable] just, decent, fitting; see FIT 1. 2 [Conventional] customary, usual, decorous; see CONVENTIONAL 1, 3. 3 [Prudish] prim, precise, strait-laced; see PRUDISH.

properly *a.* correctly, fitly, suitably; see WELL 3.

property *n.* 1 [Possessions] belongings, lands, assets, holdings, inheritance, capital, equity, investments, goods and chattels, earthly possessions, real property, personal property, taxable property, resources, private property, public property, wealth; see also BUSINESS 4, ESTATE, FARM, HOME 1. 2 [A piece of land] section, quarter section, estate, tract, part, farm, park, ranch, homestead, yard, grounds, frontage, acres, acreage, premises, campus, grant, landed property, field, claim, holding, plot; see also LOT 1.

prophecy *n.* prediction, prognostication, augury; see IDEA 1.

prophesy *v.* predict, prognosticate, divine; see FORETELL.

prophet *n.* seer, oracle, soothsayer, prophetess, seeress, clairvoyant, wizard, augur, sibyl, sorcerer, predictor, forecaster, prognosticator, diviner, medium, witch, palmist, fortuneteller, weather forecaster, meteorologist, magus, astrologer, horoscopist.

prophetic *a.* predictive, occult, clairvoyant, oracular, sibylline.

propitious *a.* 1 [Favorable] auspicious, encouraging, promising; see HOPEFUL 2. 2 [Kindly] benignant, helpful, generous; see KIND.

proponent *n.* defender, advocate, champion; see PROTECTOR.

proportion *n.* relationship, dimension, share; see BALANCE 2, PART 1.

proportional *a.* proportionate, equivalent, comparable; see EQUAL.

proposal *n.* 1 [Offer] overture, rec-

pro·pose (prō pōz′, prə-) *vt.* **-posed′, -pos′ing** ⟦< L *pro-*, forth + *ponere*, to place⟧ 1 to put forth for consideration, approval, etc. 2 to plan or intend 3 to present as a toast in drinking — *vi.* to offer marriage

propo·si·tion (präp′ə zish′ən) *n.* 1 something proposed; plan 2 [Colloq.] a proposed deal, as in business 3 [Colloq.] an undertaking, etc. to be dealt with 4 a subject to be discussed 5 *Math.* a problem to be solved

pro·pound (prō pound′, prə-) *vt.* ⟦see PROPOSE⟧ to put forward for consideration

pro·pri·etary (prō prī′ə tər ē, prə-) *adj.* ⟦see PROPERTY⟧ belonging to a proprietor, as under a patent or copyright

pro·pri′etor *n.* an owner —**pro·pri′etor·ship′** *n.* —**pro·pri′etress** (-tris) *n.fem.*

pro·pri′ety (-ə tē) *n., pl.* **-ties** ⟦see PROPER⟧ 1 the quality of being proper, fitting, etc. 2 conformity with accepted standards of behavior

pro·pul·sion (prō pul′shən, prə-) *n.* ⟦see PROPEL⟧ 1 a propelling or being propelled 2 something that propels — **pro·pul′sive** *adj.*

pro·rate (prō rāt′, prō′rāt′) *vt., vi.* **-rat′ed, -rat′ing** ⟦< L *pro rata*, in proportion⟧ to divide or assess proportionally

pro·saic (prō zā′ik) *adj.* ⟦< L *prosa*, prose⟧ commonplace; dull

pro·sceni·um (prō sē′nē əm) *n., pl.* **-ni·ums** or **-nia** (-ə) ⟦< Gr *pro-*, before + *skēnē*, tent⟧ the plane separating the stage proper from the audience and including the arch (**proscenium arch**) or the curtain within it

pro·scribe (prō skrīb′) *vt.* **-scribed′, -scrib′ing** ⟦< L < *pro-*, before + *scribere*, write⟧ 1 to outlaw 2 to banish; exile 3 to denounce or forbid the use, etc. of —**pro·scrip′tion** (-skrip′shən) *n.*

prose (prōz) *n.* ⟦< L *prorsus*, straight on⟧ ordinary language; not poetry

pros·ecute (präs′i kyōōt′) *vt.* **-cut′ed, -cut′ing** ⟦< L *pro-*, before + *sequi*, follow⟧ 1 to carry on 2 to conduct legal action against —**pros′ecu′tion** *n.* —**pros′ecu′tor** *n.*

pros·elyte (präs′ə lit′) *n.* ⟦< Gr *prosēlytos*, a stranger⟧ one who has been converted from one religion, sect, etc. to another — *vt., vi.* **-lyt′ed, -lyt′ing** to try to make a convert (of)

pros·elyt·ize (präs′ə li tiz′) *vi., vt.* **-ized′, -iz′ing** PROS·ELYTE —**pros′elyt·ism′** (-li tiz′əm) *n.* —**pros′elyt·iz′er** *n.*

pro·sim·ian (prō sim′ē ən) *n.* any of various small, arboreal primates

proso·dy (präs′ə dē) *n., pl.* **-dies** ⟦< Gr *prosōidia*, accent⟧ versification; study of meter, rhyme, etc.

pros·pect (prä′spekt′) *n.* ⟦< L *pro-*, forward + *specere*, look⟧ 1 a broad view; scene 2 viewpoint; outlook 3 anticipation 4 *a*) something expected *b*) [*usually pl.*] apparent chance for success 5 a likely customer, candidate, etc. — *vt., vi.* to explore or search (*for* gold, etc.) — **pros′pec′tor** *n.*

pro·spec·tive (prō spek′tiv, prə-) *adj.* expected; likely

pro·spec·tus (prō spek′təs, prə-) *n.* ⟦L: see PROSPECT⟧ a statement of the features of a new work, enterprise, etc.

pros·per (präs′pər) *vi.* ⟦< L *prospere*, fortunately⟧ to succeed; thrive

pros·per·ity (prä sper′ə tē) *n., pl.* **-ties** prosperous condition; wealth

pros·per·ous (präs′pər əs) *adj.* 1 prospering; successful 2 wealthy 3 favorable —**pros′per·ously** *adv.*

pros·tate (präs′tāt′) *adj.* ⟦< Gr *prostatēs*, one standing before⟧ of or designating a gland surrounding the male urethra at the base of the bladder

pros·thesis (präs′thə sis, präs thē′-) *n., pl.* **-ses′** (-sēz′) *Med.* 1 the replacement of a missing part of the body, as a limb, by an artificial substitute 2 such a substitute — **pros·thet′ic** (-thet′ik) *adj.*

pros·ti·tute (präs′tə tōōt′) *n.* ⟦< L *pro-*, before + *statuere*, cause to stand⟧ one who engages in promiscuous sexual activity for pay — *vt.* **-tut′ed, -tut′ing** 1 to offer (oneself) as a prostitute 2 to sell (oneself, one's talents, etc.) for base purposes —**pros′ti·tu′tion** *n.*

pros·trate (präs′trāt′) *adj.* ⟦< L *pro-*, before + *sternere*, stretch out⟧ 1 lying face downward 2 lying prone or supine 3 laid low; overcome — *vt.* **-trat′ed, -trat′ing** 1 to lay flat on the ground 2 to lay low; subjugate —**pros·tra′tion** *n.*

prosy (prō′zē) *adj.* **-i·er, -i·est** prosaic; commonplace, dull, etc.

pro·tago·nist (prō tag′ə nist) *n.* ⟦< Gr *prōtos*, first + *agōnistēs*, actor⟧ the main character in a drama, novel, etc.

pro·tean (prōt′ē ən; *also* prō tē′ən) *adj.* ⟦after *Proteus*, Gr god who changes his form at will⟧ readily taking on many forms

pro·tect (prō tekt′, prə-) *vt.* ⟦< L *pro-*, before + *tegere*, to cover⟧ to shield from injury, danger, etc.; defend —**pro·tec′tor** *n.*

pro·tec′tion *n.* 1 a protecting or being protected 2 a person or thing that protects

pro·tec′tive *adj.* 1 protecting 2 *Economics* intended to protect domestic industry from foreign competition [a *protective* tariff] —**pro·tec′tively** *adv.* —**pro·tec′tive·ness** *n.*

THESAURUS

ommendation, proposition; see SUG·GESTION 1. 2 [Plan] scheme, program, prospectus; see PLAN 2.

propose *v.* 1 [To make a suggestion] suggest, offer, put forward, move, set forth, come up with, state, proffer, advance, propound, introduce, put to, contend, assert, tender, recommend, advise, counsel, lay before, submit, affirm, volunteer, press, urge upon, hold out, make a motion, lay on the line.—*Ant.* OPPOSE, dissent, protest. 2 [To mean] purpose, intend, aim; see MEAN 1. 3 [To propose marriage] offer marriage, ask in marriage, make a proposal, ask for the hand of, pop the question*.

proposed *a.* projected, prospective, advised, scheduled, expected, arranged, advanced, suggested, moved, put forward, submitted, recommended, urged, volunteered, pressed, intended, determined, anticipated, designed, schemed, purposed, considered, referred to, contingent; see also PLANNED.

proposition *n.* proposal, scheme, project; see PLAN 1.

proprietor *n.* heritor, master, proprietary; see OWNER, POSSESSOR.

propriety *n.* aptness, suitability, advisability, accordance, agreeableness, compatibility, correspondence, consonance, appropriateness, congruity, modesty, seemliness, good breeding, dignity, concord, harmony, expedience, pleasantness, welcome-ness; see also FITNESS.—*Ant.* INCONSISTENCY, inappropriateness, incongruity.

prose *n.* fiction, nonfiction, composition; see LITERATURE 1, 2, STORY, WRITING 2.

prosecute *v.* contest, indict, involve in litigation; see SUE.

prosecution *n.* state, government, prosecuting attorney, state's attorney; see also LAWYER.

prospect *n.* 1 [A view] sight, landscape, vista; see VIEW. 2 [A probable future] expectancy, promise, hope; see OUTLOOK 2. 3 [A possible candidate] possibility, likely person, interested party; see CANDIDATE.

prospective *a.* considered, hoped for, promised; see PLANNED, PROPOSED.

prosper *v.* become rich, become wealthy, be enriched, thrive, turn out well, fare well, do well, be fortunate, have good fortune, flourish, get on, rise in the world, fatten, increase, bear fruit, bloom, blossom, flower, make money, make a fortune, benefit, advance, gain, make good*, do well by oneself*, make one's mark, roll in the lap of luxury*, come along*, do wonders*; see also SUCCEED 1.

prosperity *n.* accomplishment, victory, successfulness; see SUCCESS 2.

prosperous *a.* flourishing, well-off, well-to-do; see RICH 1.

prostitute *n.* harlot, strumpet, lewd woman, whore, bawd, streetwalker, loose woman, fallen woman, courtesan, abandoned woman, concubine, vice girl, hustler, call girl, tramp, slut, tart*, hooker*; see also CRIMINAL.

prostitution *n.* hustling, harlotry, hooking*; see LEWDNESS.

protagonist *n.* leading character, lead, combatant; see HERO 1, IDOL.

protect *v.* shield, guard, preserve; see DEFEND 1, 2.

protected *a.* shielded, safeguarded, cared for, watched over, preserved, defended, guarded, secured, kept safe, sheltered, harbored, screened, fostered, cherished, curtained, shaded, disguised, camouflaged; see also COVERED 1, SAFE 1.—*Ant.* WEAK, insecure, unsheltered.

protection *n.* 1 [A covering] shield, screen, camouflage; see SHELTER. 2 [A surety] certainty, safeguard, safekeeping, assurance, invulnerability, reassurance, security, stability, strength; see also GUARANTY.—*Ant.* WEAKNESS, insecurity, frailty.

protector *n.* champion, defender, patron, sponsor, safeguard, benefactor, supporter, advocate, guardian angel, guard, shield, savior, standby, promoter, mediator, counsel, second, backer, upholder, sympathizer, big brother*, big sister*, angel*, cover*, front*; see also GUARDIAN.

pro·tec′tor·ate (-tek′tər it) *n.* a weak state under the protection and control of a strong state

pro·té·gé (prōt′ə zhā′) *n.* [Fr: see PROTECT] a person guided and helped in his career by another person

pro·tein (prō′tēn′, prō′tē in) *n.* [< Gr *prōtos*, first] any of numerous nitrogenous substances occurring in all living matter and essential to diet

pro tem·pore (prō tem′pə rē′) [L] for the time (being); temporarily Shortened to **pro tem**

pro·test (prō test′, prə-; *for n.,* prō′test′) *vt.* [< L *pro-*, forth + *testari*, affirm] 1 to state positively 2 to speak strongly against — *vi.* to express disapproval; object — *n.* 1 an objection 2 a formal statement of objection —**prot·esta·tion** (prät′es tā′shən) *n.* —**pro·test′er** *n.*

Prot·estant (prät′əs tənt) *n.* [see prec.] any Christian not belonging to the Roman Catholic or Eastern Orthodox Church —**Prot′estant·ism′** *n.*

proto- [< Gr *prōtos*, first] *combining form* 1 first in time, original 2 first in importance, chief

pro·to·col (prōt′ə kôl′, prōt′ə-) *n.* [< Gr *prōtokollon*, contents page] 1 an original draft of a document, etc. 2 the ceremonial forms accepted as correct in official dealings, as between heads of states or diplomatic officials

pro·ton (prō′tän) *n.* [< Gr *prōtos*, first] an elementary particle in the nucleus of all atoms, carrying a unit positive charge of electricity

proto·plasm (prōt′ō plaz′əm, prōt′ə-) *n.* [see PROTO- & PLASMA] a semifluid viscous colloid, the essential living matter of all animal and plant cells —**pro′to·plas′mic** (-plaz′mik) *adj.*

proto·type (prōt′ō tīp′, prōt′ə-) *n.* the first thing or being of its kind; model

proto·zoan (prōt′ō zō′ən, prōt′ə-) *n.* [< Gr *protos*, first + *zōion*, an animal] *pl.* **-zo′a** (-ə) any of various, mostly microscopic, single-celled animals Also **pro′to·zo′on′** (-än′), *pl.* **-zo′a** (-ə)

pro·tract (prō trakt′, prə-) *vt.* [< L *pro-*, forward + *trahere*, draw] to draw out; prolong —**pro·trac′tion** *n.*

pro·trac′tor *n.* a graduated semicircular instrument for plotting and measuring angles

pro·trude (prō trōōd′, prə-) *vt., vi.* **-trud′ed, -trud′ing** [< L *pro-*, forth + *trudere*, to thrust] to jut out; project —**pro·tru′sion** (-trōō′zhən) *n.*

pro·tru′sile (-trōō′səl) *adj.* that can be protruded, or thrust out Also **pro·trac′tile** (-trak′təl)

pro·tu·ber·ance (prō tōō′bər əns, prə-) *n.* a part or thing that protrudes; bulge —**pro·tu′ber·ant** *adj.*

proud (proud) *adj.* [< LL *prode*, beneficial] 1 having a proper pride in oneself 2 arrogant; haughty 3 feeling great pride or joy 4 that is a cause of pride 5 caused by pride 6 stately; splendid [a proud fleet] —**proud of** highly pleased with —**proud′ly** *adv.*

proud flesh [from the notion of swelling up] an abnormal growth of flesh around a healing wound

prove (prōōv) *vt.* **proved, proved** or **prov′en, prov′ing** [< L *probare*, to test] 1 to test by experiment, a standard, etc. 2 to establish as true — *vi.* to be found by experience or trial —**prov′abil′ity** *n.* —**prov′able** *adj.*

prov·enance (präv′ə nəns) *n.* [< L *provenire*, come forth] origin; source Also **pro·veni·ence** (prō vē′nē əns)

Pro·ven·çal (prō′vän säl′, -vən-; präv′ən-) *n.* the vernacular of S France, a Romance language of literary importance in the Middle Ages

prov·ender (präv′ən dər) *n.* [< L *praebere*, give] 1 dry food for livestock 2 [Colloq.] food

prov·erb (präv′ʉrb′) *n.* [< L *pro-*, PRO-² + *verbum*, word] a short, popular saying expressing an obvious truth —**pro·ver′bial** (prō vʉr′bē əl) *adj.* —**pro·ver′bi·ally** *adv.*

Prov′erbs′ a book of the Bible containing maxims

pro·vide (prō vīd′) *vt.* **-vid′ed, -vid′ing** [< L *pro-*, PRO-² + *videre*, see] 1 to make available; supply 2 to furnish with 3 to stipulate — *vi.* 1 to prepare (*for* or *against* a possible situation, etc.) 2 to furnish support (*for*) —**pro·vid′er** *n.*

pro·vid′ed or **pro·vid′ing** *conj.* on the condition or understanding (*that*)

provi·dence (präv′ə dəns) *n.* 1 provident management 2 the benevolent guidance of God or nature —**[P-]** God

prov′i·dent *adj.* [see PROVIDE] 1 providing for the future 2 prudent or economical —**prov′i·dently** *adv.*

prov·i·den′tial (-den′shəl) *adj.* of, by, or as if decreed by divine providence —**prov′i·den′tially** *adv.*

prov·ince (präv′ins) *n.* [< L *provincia*] 1 an administrative division of a country; specif., of Canada 2 *a*) a district; territory *b*) [*pl.*] the parts of a country removed from the major cities 3 range of duties or work; sphere

pro·vin·cial (prō vin′shəl) *adj.* 1 of the provinces 2 having the ways, speech, etc. of a certain province 3 countrylike; rustic 4 narrow; limited —**pro·vin′cial·ism′** *n.*

proving ground a place for testing new equipment, new theories, etc.

pro·vi·sion (prō vizh′ən) *n.* 1 a providing or preparing 2 something provided for the future 3 [*pl.*] a stock of food 4 a stipulation; proviso — *vt.* to supply with provisions

pro·vi′sional *adj.* temporary —**pro·vi′sion·ally** *adv.*

pro·vi·so (prō vī′zō′) *n., pl.* **-sos′** or **-soes′** [see PROVIDE] a condition or stipulation, or a clause making one

provo·ca·tion (präv′ə kā′shən) *n.* 1 a provoking 2 something that provokes; incitement

THESAURUS

protest *n.* mass meeting, rally, demonstration, peace demonstration, draft demonstration, peace rally, race riot, clamor, tumult, turmoil, campus revolt, moratorium, sit-in, love-in*.

protest *v.* demur, disagree, object; see OPPOSE 1.

Protestant *n. Protestant sects include the following:* Evangelist, Adventist, Baptist, Congregational, Episcopal, Lutheran, Methodist, Presbyterian.

protester *n.* demonstrator, dissident, rebel; see RADICAL.

protrude *v.* come through, stick out, jut out; see PROJECT 1.

proud *a.* 1 [Having a creditable self-respect] self-respecting, self-sufficient, self-satisfied, ambitious, spirited, vigorous, high-spirited, greathearted, fiery, dignified, honorable, stately, lordly, lofty-minded, high-minded, impressive, imposing, fine, splendid, looking one in the eye, on one's high horse, high and mighty, holding up one's head.—*Ant.* HUMBLE, unpretentious, unassuming. 2 [Egotistic] egotistical, vain, vainglorious; see EGOTISTIC. —**do oneself proud*** achieve, prosper, advance; see SUCCEED 1.

proudly *a.* boastfully, haughtily, insolently; see ARROGANTLY.

prove *v.* justify, substantiate, authenticate, corroborate, testify, explain, attest, show, warrant, uphold, determine, settle, fix, certify, back, sustain, validate, bear out, affirm, confirm, make evident, convince, evidence, be evidence of, witness, declare, testify, have a case, manifest, demonstrate, document, establish, settle once and for all.

proved *a.* confirmed, established, demonstrated; see ESTABLISH 3.

proverb *n.* maxim, adage, aphorism, precept, saw, saying, motto, dictum, text, witticism, repartee, axiom, truism, byword, epigram, moral, folk wisdom, platitude.

proverbial *a.* current, general, unquestioned; see COMMON 1, DULL 4.

provide *v.* 1 [To supply] furnish, equip, grant, replenish, provide with, accommodate, care for, indulge with, favor with, contribute, give, outfit, stock, store, minister, administer, render, procure, afford, present, bestow, cater, rig up, fit out, fit up, provision, ration, implement.—*Ant.* REFUSE, take away, deny. 2 [To yield] render, afford, give; see PRODUCE 1. —**provide for (or against)** prepare for, arrange, plan ahead; see PREPARE 1.

provided *conj.* on the assumption that, in the event, in the case that; see IF, SUPPOSING. —**provided that** on condition, in the event, with that understood; see IF, SUPPOSING.

providence *n.* divine government, divine superintendence, Deity; see GOD.

providing *conj.* provided, in the event that, on the assumption that; see IF, SUPPOSING.

providing *n.* provision, supplying, furnishing, equipping, replenishing, replenishment, contributing, outfitting, stocking, filling, procurement, affording, presenting, preparing, preparation, arrangement, planning, putting by, laying in, putting in readiness, granting, bestowing, giving, offering, tendering, accumulating, storing, saving.

province *n.* area, region, dependency; see TERRITORY 2.

provincial *a.* rude, unpolished, countrified; see RURAL.

provision *n.* 1 [Arrangement] preparation, outline, procurement; see PLAN 2. 2 [Supplies; *usually plural*] stock, store, emergency; see EQUIPMENT. 3 [A proviso] stipulation, prerequisite, terms; see REQUIREMENT 1.

provisional *a.* transient, passing, ephemeral; see TEMPORARY.

provisionally *a.* conditionally, for certain conditions, for the time being; see TEMPORARILY.

provocation *n.* incitement, stimulus, inducement; see INCENTIVE.

pro·voca·tive (prō văk′ə tiv) *adj.* provoking or tending to provoke, as to action, thought, feeling, etc. —**pro·voc′a·tively** *adv.*

pro·voke (prō vōk′) *vt.* -voked′, -vok′ing 〚< L *pro-*, forth + *vocare*, to call〛 1 to excite to some action or feeling 2 to anger or irritate 3 to stir up (action or feeling) 4 to evoke —**pro·vok′er** *n.* —**pro·vok′ing** *adj.*

pro·vost (prō′vōst′) *n.* 〚< L *praepositus*, chief〛 a high executive official, as in some churches or colleges

pro′vost guard (prō′vō-) a detail of military police under the command of an officer (**provost marshal**)

prow (prou) *n.* 〚< Gr *prōira*〛 the forward part of a ship, etc.

prow·ess (prou′is) *n.* 〚< OFr *prouesse*〛 1 bravery; valor 2 superior ability, skill, etc.

prowl (proul) *vi.*, *vt.* 〚< ?〛 to roam about furtively, as in search of prey or loot — *n.* a prowling —**prowl′er** *n.*

prowl car PATROL CAR

prox·im·ity (präks im′ə tē) *n.* 〚< L *prope*, near〛 nearness

proxy (präks′ē) *n.*, *pl.* -ies 〚< ME *procuracie*, function of a procurator〛 1 the authority to act for another, as in voting 2 one so authorized

prude (prōōd) *n.* 〚Fr < *prudefemme*, excellent woman〛 one who is overly modest or proper in behavior, dress, etc. —**prud′ery** *n.* —**prud′ish** *adj.*

pru·dent (prōōd′′nt) *adj.* 〚< L *providens*, provident〛 1 exercising sound judgment in practical matters 2 cautious in conduct; not rash 3 managing carefully —**pru′dence** *n.* —**pru·den′tial** (prōō den′shəl) *adj.* —**pru′dently** *adv.*

prune[1] (prōōn) *n.* 〚< Gr *proumnon*, plum〛 a dried plum

prune[2] (prōōn) *vt.* pruned, prun′ing 〚< OFr *prooignier*〛 1 to trim dead or living parts from (a plant) 2 to cut out (unnecessary parts, etc.) —**prun′er** *n.*

pru·ri·ent (proor′ē ənt) *adj.* 〚< L *prurire*, to itch〛 tending to excite lust; lewd —**pru′ri·ence** *n.*

pry[1] (prī) *n.*, *pl.* **pries** 〚< PRIZE[2]〛 a lever or crowbar — *vt.* pried, pry′ing 1 to raise or move with a pry 2 to obtain with difficulty

pry[2] (prī) *vi.* pried, pry′ing 〚< ?〛 to look closely and inquisitively; snoop

pry′er *n.* PRIER

PS or **P.S.** 1 postscript: also **p.s.** or **ps** 2 Public School

psalm (säm) *n.* 〚< Gr *psallein*, to pluck (a harp)〛 1 a sacred song or poem 2 [*usually* P-] any of the songs in praise of God constituting the Book of Psalms —**psalm′ist** *n.*

Psalms (sämz) a book of the Bible consisting of 150 psalms

Psal·ter (sôl′tər) 〚< Gr *psaltērion*, a harp〛 Psalms — *n.* [*also* p-] a version of the Book of Psalms for use in religious services

pseudo (sōō′dō) *adj.* 〚ME: see fol.〛 sham; false; spurious

pseudo- 〚< Gr *pseudein*, deceive〛 *combining form* sham, counterfeit

pseudo·nym (sōō′də nim′) *n.* 〚< Gr *pseudēs*, false + *onyma*, a name〛 a fictitious name, esp. one assumed by an author; pen name

pshaw (shô) *interj.*, *n.* an exclamation of impatience, disgust, etc.

psi (psē, sī) *n.* the 23d letter of the Greek alphabet (Ψ, ψ)

psit·ta·co·sis (sit′ə kō′sis) *n.* 〚< Gr *psittakos*, parrot + -OSIS〛 a disease of birds, esp. parrots, often transmitted to humans

pso·ria·sis (sō rī′ə sis, sə-) *n.* 〚ult. < Gr *psōra*, an itch〛 a chronic skin disease characterized by scaly, reddish patches

psst (pst) *interj.* sound made to get another's attention quietly

PST Pacific Standard Time

psych (sīk) *vt.* psyched, psych′ing 〚< PSYCHOANALYZE〛 [Slang] 1 to outwit, overcome, etc. by psychological means: often with *out* 2 to prepare (oneself) mentally: usually with *up*

psych. psychology

psy·che (sī′kē) *n.* 〚Gr *psychē*〛 1 the soul 2 the mind regarded as an entity based ultimately upon physical processes but with its own complex processes —[P-] *Rom. Folklore* the wife of Cupid

psyche·delic (sī′kə del′ik) *adj.* 〚< prec. + Gr *dēloun*, make manifest〛 1 of or causing extreme changes in the conscious mind, as hallucinations 2 of or associated with psychedelic drugs

psy·chia·try (sī kī′ə trē) *n.* 〚see PSYCHO- & -IATRY〛 the branch of medicine dealing with disorders of the mind, including psychoses and neuroses —**psy·chi·at·ric** (sī′kē a′trik) *adj.* —**psy·chi′a·trist** *n.*

psy·chic (sī′kik) *adj.* 〚see PSYCHE〛 1 of the psyche, or mind 2 beyond known physical processes 3 apparently sensitive to forces beyond the physical world Also **psy′chi·cal** —**psy′chi·cally** *adv.*

psycho (sī′kō) *adj.*, *n.* [Colloq.] *short for* PSYCHOTIC, PSYCHOPATHIC, and PSYCHOPATH

psycho- 〚see PSYCHE〛 *combining form* the mind or mental processes Also **psych-**

psycho·analy·sis (sī′kō ə nal′ə sis) *n.* a method of treating some mental disorders by discovering and analyzing repressed feelings, emotional conflicts, etc. through the use of free association, dream analysis, etc. —**psy′cho·an′a·lyst** (-an′ə list) *n.* —**psy′cho·an′a·lyze** (-līz′), -lyzed′, -lyz′ing, *vt.*

psy′cho·bab′ble (-bab′əl) *n.* [Colloq.] talk or writing that uses psychological terms and concepts in a trite or superficial way

psy′cho·gen′ic (-jen′ik) *adj.* 〚see PSYCHO- & GENESIS〛 originating in the mind or caused by mental conflicts

psy·chol·ogy (sī käl′ə jē) *n.*, *pl.* -gies 〚see PSYCHO- & -LOGY〛 1 the science dealing with the mind and with mental and emotional processes 2 the science of human and animal behavior —**psy′cho·log′i·cal** (-kə läj′i kəl) *adj.* —**psy·chol′o·gist** *n.*

━━━━━━ **THESAURUS** ━━━━━━

provocative *a.* alluring, arousing, intriguing; see INTERESTING.

provoke *v.* 1 [To vex] irritate, put out, aggravate; see BOTHER 2. 2 [To incite] stir, rouse, arouse; see INCITE. 3 [To cause] make, produce, bring about; see BEGIN 1.

provoked *a.* exasperated, incensed, enraged; see ANGRY.

prowl *v.* slink, lurk, rove; see SNEAK.

proxy *n.* substitute, broker, representative; see AGENT, DELEGATE.

prude *n.* prig, puritan, old maid, prudish person, priss*, sourpuss*, stick-in-the-mud*, spoilsport, wet blanket*, goody-goody*.

prudence *n.* caution, circumspection, judgment, providence, considerateness, judiciousness, deliberation, wisdom, foresight, forethought, care, carefulness, frugality, watchfulness, precaution, heedfulness, heed, economy, husbandry, concern, conservatism, conservation, discrimination, cunning, vigilance, coolness, calculation, presence of mind.—*Ant.* CARELESSNESS, imprudence, rashness.

prudent *a.* 1 [Cautious and careful] cautious, circumspect, wary; see CAREFUL, DISCREET. 2 [Sensible and wise] discerning, sound, reasonable; see CAREFUL.

prudish *a.* narrow-minded, illiberal, bigoted, prissy, priggish, over-refined, fastidious, stiff, smug, stuffy, conventional, offish, straitlaced, demure, narrow, puritanical, affected, artificial, scrupulous, over-exact, pedantic, pretentious, strict, rigid, rigorous, simpering, finical, finicking, finicky, squeamish, like a maiden aunt, like an old maid; see also PRIM.—*Ant.* SOCIABLE, broad-minded, genial.

pry[1,2] *v.* 1 [To move, with a lever] push, lift, raise, pull, move, tilt, hoist, heave, uplift, upraise, elevate, turn out, jimmy*; see also FORCE, OPEN 2. 2 [To endeavor to discover; *often used with "into"*] search, ferret out, seek, ransack, reconnoiter, peep, peer, peek, snoop, gaze, look closely, spy, stare, gape, nose, be curious, inquire; see also MEDDLE 1.

pseudo *a.* imitation, quasi, sham; see FALSE 3.

psyche *n.* subconscious, mind, ego; see CHARACTER 2.

psychiatrist *n.* analyst, therapist,

shrink; see DOCTOR.

psychiatry *n.* psychopathology, psychotherapy, psychoanalysis; see MEDICINE 1, SCIENCE 1.

psychic *a.* 1 [Mental] analytic, intellectual, psychological; see MENTAL 2. 2 [Spiritual] telepathic, mystic, immaterial; see SUPERNATURAL.

psycho *a.* mad, crazy, psychopathic; see INSANE.

psychological *a.* directly experimental, subjective, experimental; see MENTAL 2.

psychologist *n.* psychiatrist, analyst, clinician; see DOCTOR, SCIENTIST.

psychology *n.* science of mind, study of personality, medicine, therapy; see also SCIENCE 1, SOCIAL SCIENCE. *Divisions and varieties of psychology include the following:* rational, existential, functional, structural, self, dynamic, motor, physiological, abnormal, differential, Gestalt, Freudian, Adlerian, Jungian, genetic, applied, popular, analytical, comparative, child, animal, mass, individual, social, behaviorism, parapsychology.

psy·cho·neu·ro·sis (sī′kō nŏŏ rō′sis) *n., pl.* **-ro′ses′** (-sēz′) NEUROSIS

psy′cho·path′ (-path′) *n.* [see PSYCHO- & -PATHY] one who has a severe mental disorder with antisocial behavior —**psy′cho·path′ic** *adj.*

psy·cho·sis (sī kō′sis) *n., pl.* **-ses** (-sēz′) [see PSYCHO- & -OSIS] a mental disorder in which the personality is seriously disorganized and contact with reality is usually impaired —**psy·chot′ic** (-kät′ik) *adj.*

psy·cho·so·mat′ic (-sō mat′ik) *adj.* [PSYCHO- + SOMATIC] designating or of a physical disorder brought on, or made worse, by one's emotional state

psy′cho·ther′a·py (-ther′ə pē) *n.* [PSYCHO- + THERAPY] treatment of mental disorder by counseling, psychoanalysis, etc. —**psy′cho·ther′a·pist** *n.*

pt. 1 part 2 pint(s) 3 point

Pt *Chem. symbol for* platinum

Pt. 1 Point 2 Port

PTA Parent-Teacher Association

ptar·mi·gan (tär′mi gən) *n.* [< Scot *tarmachan*] a grouse of northern regions

ptero- [< Gr *pteron*, wing] *combining form* feather, wing

ptero·dac·tyl (ter′ō dak′təl) *n.* [see prec. & DACTYL] an extinct flying reptile with wings of skin stretched from the hind limbs to the long digits of each forelimb

pto·maine (tō′mān′) *n.* [< Gr *ptōma*, corpse] an alkaloid substance, often poisonous, formed in decaying matter

Pu *Chem. symbol for* plutonium

pub (pub) *n.* [< *pub*(*lic house*)] [Colloq., Chiefly Brit., etc.] a bar or tavern

pu·ber·ty (pyōō′bər tē) *n.* [< L *puber*, adult] the stage of physical development when sexual reproduction first becomes possible —**pu′ber·tal** *adj.*

pu·bes′cent (-bes′ənt) *adj.* [see prec.] reaching or having reached puberty —**pu·bes′cence** *n.*

pu′bic (-bik) *adj.* of or in the region of the genitals

pub·lic (pub′lik) *adj.* [ult. < L *populus*, the people] 1 of people as a whole 2 for the use or benefit of all [a *public* park] 3 acting officially for the people [a *public* prosecutor] 4 known by, open to, or available to most or all people [to make *public*, a *public* company] —*n.* 1 the people as a whole 2 a specific part of the people [the reading *public*] —**in public** openly —**pub′lic·ly** *adv.*

pub·li·can (pub′li kən) *n.* 1 in ancient Rome, a tax collector 2 [Brit., etc. (exc. Cdn.)] a saloonkeeper; innkeeper

pub·li·ca·tion (pub′li kā′shən) *n.* [see PUBLISH] 1 public notification 2 the printing and distribution of books, magazines, etc. 3 something published, as a periodical or book

public domain the condition of being free from copyright or patent

pub·li·cist (pub′lə sist) *n.* a person whose business is publicity

pub·lic·i·ty (pub lis′ə tē) *n.* 1 *a*) any information or action that brings a person, cause, etc. to public notice *b*) work

concerned with such promotional matters 2 notice by the public

pub·li·cize (pub′lə sīz′) *vt.* **-cized′**, **-ciz′ing** to give publicity to

public relations relations of an organization, etc. with the general public as through publicity

public school 1 in the U.S., an elementary or secondary school maintained by public taxes and supervised by local authorities 2 in England, a private boarding school

public servant a government official or a civil-service employee

pub′lic-spir′ited *adj.* having or showing zeal for the public welfare

public utility an organization supplying water, electricity, transportation, etc. to the public

pub·lish (pub′lish) *vt.* [< L *publicare*] 1 to make publicly known; announce 2 to issue (a printed work) for sale — *vi.* 1 to issue books, newspapers, printed music, etc. to the public 2 to write books, etc. that are published —**pub′lisher** *n.*

puck (puk) *n.* [< dial. *puck*, to strike] the hard rubber disk used in ice hockey

pucker (puk′ər) *vt., vi.* [< POKE²] to gather into wrinkles — *n.* a wrinkle or small fold made by puckering

puck·ish (puk′ish) *adj.* [after elf in a Shakespeare play] mischievous

pud·ding (pood′iŋ) *n.* [ME *puddyng*] a soft, sweet food variously made with flour, eggs, milk, fruit, etc.

pud·dle (pud′′l) *n.* [dim. < OE *pudd*, a ditch] a small pool of water, esp. stagnant, spilled, or muddy water

pud′dling (-liŋ) *n.* the making of wrought iron from pig iron melted and stirred in an oxidizing atmosphere

pudgy (puj′ē) *adj.* **-i·er**, **-i·est** [< Scot *pud*, belly] short and fat —**pudg′i·ness** *n.*

pueblo (pweb′lō) *n., pl.* **-los** (-lōz′) or **-lo** [Sp < L *populus*, people] an Amerindian communal village, as in SW U.S., of terraced adobe dwellings

pu·er·ile (pyōō′ər il) *adj.* [< L *puer*, boy] childish; silly — **pu′er·il′i·ty** *n.*

puff (puf) *n.* [OE *pyff*] 1 a short, sudden gust or expulsion of air, breath, smoke, etc. 2 a draw at a cigarette, etc. 3 a light pastry filled with whipped cream, etc. 4 a soft pad [a powder *puff*] 5 a book review, etc. giving undue praise — *vi.* 1 to blow in puffs 2 to breathe rapidly 3 to fill or swell (*out* or *up*) 4 to take puffs at a cigarette, etc. — *vt.* 1 to blow, smoke, etc. in or with puffs 2 to swell; inflate 3 to praise unduly —**puff′y**, **-i·er**, **-i·est**, *adj.* —**puff′i·ness** *n.*

puff′ball′ *n.* a fungus that bursts at the touch and discharges a brown powder

puff′er *n.* a small saltwater fish that can expand its body by swallowing water or air

puf·fin (puf′in) *n.* [ME *poffin*] a northern sea bird with a brightly colored, triangular beak

---

■ THESAURUS ■

psychopath *n.* lunatic, antisocial personality, sociopath; see MADMAN.

psychotic *a.* insane, mad, psychopathic; see INSANE 1.

puberty *n.* boyhood, pubescence, adolescence; see YOUTH 1.

public *a.* 1 [Available to the public] free to all, without charge, open, unrestricted, not private, known; see also FREE 4. 2 [Owned by the public] governmental, government, civil, civic, common, communal, publicly owned, municipal, metropolitan, state, federal, county, city, township.—*Ant.* PRIVATE, personal, restricted.

public *n.* men, society, the community; see PEOPLE 3. —**in public** candidly, plainly, aboveboard; see OPENLY 1.

publication *n.* 1 [The act of making public] writing, printing, broadcasting, announcement, notification, promulgation, issuing, statement, acquaintance, advisement, advertisement, communication, revelation, disclosure, discovery, making current, making available. 2 [Something published] news, tidings, information; see BOOK, MAGAZINE, NEWSPAPER.

publicity *n.* 1 [Public distribution] notoriety, currency, publicness; see DISTRIBUTION. 2 [Free advertising] public relations copy, press release, report; see PROPAGANDA. 3 [Activity intended to advertise] promotion, publicizing, advertising; see ADVERTISEMENT.

publicize *v.* announce, broadcast, promulgate; see ADVERTISE.

publicly *a.* candidly, plainly, aboveboard; see OPENLY 1.

public relations *n.* promotion, public image, favorable climate of opinion; see ADVERTISEMENT, PROPAGANDA.

public-spirited *a.* altruistic, humanitarian, openhanded; see GENEROUS 1.

public utility *n.* public services, natural monopoly, light and power; see UTILITIES.

publish *v.* 1 [To print and distribute] reprint, issue, reissue, distribute, bring out, write, do publishing, become a publisher, get out, put to press, put forth, be in the newspaper business, be in the book business, own a publishing house, send forth, give out; see also PRINT 2. 2 [To

make known] announce, promulgate, proclaim; see ADVERTISE.

published *a.* written, printed, made public, circulated, proclaimed, promulgated, propagated, pronounced, ventilated, divulged, made current, made known, broadcast, circulated, spread abroad, disseminated, got out, appeared, released, coming forth, seeing the light, presented, offered, voiced, noised abroad, given publicity, brought before the public; see also ADVERTISED, ISSUED.—*Ant.* UNKNOWN, unpublished, unwritten.

publisher *n.* publicist, businessman, administrator; see EDITOR.

pudding *n.* mousse, custard, tapioca; see DESSERT.

puddle *n.* plash, mud puddle, rut; see POOL 1.

pudgy *a.* chubby, chunky, stout; see FAT.

puff *n.* whiff, sudden gust, quick blast; see WIND.

puff *v.* distend, enlarge, swell; see FILL 1, 2.

puffy *a.* 1 [Windy] airy, gusty, breezy; see WINDY. 2 [Swollen] distended, expanded, blown; see FULL 1.

puff pastry rich, flaky pastry made of many thin layers of dough

pug (pug) *n.* 〖< ? *Puck*, an elf〗 any of a breed of small, short-haired, snub-nosed dog

pu·gil·ism (pyōō′jil iz′əm) *n.* 〖L *pugil*, boxer〗 the sport of boxing —**pu′gil·ist** *n.* —**pu′gil·is′tic** *adj.*

pug·na·cious (pug nā′shəs) *adj.* 〖< L *pugnare*, to fight〗 eager and ready to fight; quarrelsome —**pug·na′ciously** *adv.* —**pug·nac′i·ty** (-nas′ə tē) *n.*

pug nose a short, thick, turned-up nose —**pug′-nosed′** *adj.*

puke (pyōōk) *n., vi., vt.* puked, puk′ing 〖< ?〗 [Colloq.] VOMIT

pukka (puk′ə) *adj.* 〖Hindi *pakka*, ripe〗 1 first-rate 2 genuine; real

pul·chri·tude (pul′krə tōōd′) *n.* 〖< L *pulcher*, beautiful〗 beauty

pule (pyōōl) *vi.* puled, pul′ing 〖echoic〗 to whimper or whine, as a sick or fretful child does

pull (pool) *vt.* 〖< OE *pullian*, to pluck〗 1 to exert force on so as to move toward the source of the force 2 to pluck out 〖to *pull* a tooth〗 3 to rip; tear 4 to strain (a muscle) 5 [Colloq.] to carry out; perform 〖to *pull* a raid〗 6 [Colloq.] to restrain 〖to *pull* a punch〗 7 to draw out (a gun, etc.) — *vi.* 1 to exert force in dragging, tugging, or attracting 2 to be capable of being pulled 3 to move (*away, ahead*, etc.) — *n.* 1 the act or force, of pulling; a tugging, attracting, etc. 2 a difficult, continuous effort 3 something to be pulled, as a handle 4 [Colloq.] *a)* influence *b)* drawing power —**pull for** to cheer on —**pull off** [Colloq.] to accomplish —**pull oneself together** to regain one's poise, etc. —**pull out** to depart or withdraw —**pull through** [Colloq.] to get over (an illness, difficulty, etc.) —**pull up** 1 to bring or come to a stop 2 to move ahead —**pull′er** *n.*

pull′back′ *n.* a pulling back; esp., a planned military withdrawal

pul·let (pool′it) *n.* 〖< L *pullus*, chicken〗 a young hen

pul·ley (pool′ē) *n., pl.* -leys 〖< Medieval Gr *polos*, pivot〗 a small wheel with a grooved rim in which a rope, belt, etc. runs, as to raise weights or transmit power

Pull·man (pool′mən) *n.* 〖after G. M. *Pullman* (1831-97), U.S. inventor〗 a railroad car with convertible berths for sleeping Also **Pullman car**

pull′out′ *n.* 1 a pulling out; esp. a removal, withdrawal, etc. 2 something to be pulled out, as a magazine insert

pull′o′ver *adj.* that is put on by being pulled over the head — *n.* a pullover sweater, shirt, etc.

pull′-up′ or **pull′up′** *n.* the act of chinning oneself

pul·mo·nary (pool′mə ner′ē) *adj.* 〖< L *pulmo*, lung〗 of the lungs

pul·mo·tor (pool′mō′tər) *n.* 〖< L *pulmo*, lung + MOTOR〗 an apparatus for applying artificial respiration

pulp (pulp) *n.* 〖< L *pulpa*, flesh〗 1 a soft, moist, sticky mass 2 the soft, juicy part of a fruit or the pith inside a plant stem 3 the soft, sensitive tissue in the center of a tooth 4 ground-up, moistened fibers of wood, rags, etc., used to make paper —**pulp′y** *adj.* —**pulp′i·ness** *n.*

pul·pit (pool′pit) *n.* 〖< L *pulpitum*, a stage〗 1 a raised platform from which a clergyman preaches in a church 2 preachers collectively

pul·sar (pul′sär′) *n.* 〖< PULSE〗 any of several celestial objects that emit radio waves at short, regular intervals

pul·sate (pul′sāt) *vi.* -sat′ed, -sat′ing 〖< L *pulsare*, to beat〗 1 to beat or throb rhythmically 2 to vibrate; quiver —**pul·sa′tion** *n.*

pulse (puls) *n.* 〖< L *pulsus*, a beating〗 1 the regular beating in the arteries, caused by the contractions of the heart 2 any regular beat 3 a brief, abnormal burst or surge, as of electric current — *vi.* **pulsed, puls′ing** to pulsate; throb

pul·ver·ize (pul′vər iz′) *vt., vi.* -ized′, -iz′ing 〖< L *pulvis*, powder〗 to grind or be ground into powder —**pul′ver·i·za′tion** *n.*

puma (pyōō′mə) *n.* 〖AmSp〗 COUGAR

pum·ice (pum′is) *n.* 〖< L *pumex*〗 a light, porous volcanic rock used for scouring, polishing, etc.

pum·mel (pum′əl) *vt.* -meled or -melled, -mel·ing or -mel·ling 〖< POMMEL〗 to hit with repeated blows

pump[1] (pump) *n.* 〖< Sp *bomba*〗 a machine that forces a liquid or gas into, or draws it out of, something — *vt.* 1 to move (fluids) with a pump 2 to remove water, etc. from 3 to drive air into with a pump 4 to draw out, move up and down, pour forth, etc. as a pump does 5 [Colloq.] to question persistently, or to elicit by this —**pump′er** *n.*

pump[2] (pump) *n.* 〖prob. < Fr *pompe*, boot〗 a low-cut shoe without straps or ties

pum·per·nickel (pum′pər nik′əl) *n.* 〖Ger〗 a coarse, dark, rye bread

pump·kin (pump′kin; *often* pun′-) *n.* 〖< Gr *pepōn*, ripe〗 a large, round, orange-yellow, edible gourdlike fruit that grows on a vine

pun (pun) *n.* 〖< ? It *puntiglio*, fine point〗 the humorous use of a word, or of different words sounded alike, so as to play on the various meanings — *vi.* **punned, pun′ning** to make puns

punch[1] (punch) *n.* 〖< ME *punchoun*, ult. < L *pungere*, to prick〗 a tool driven against a surface that is to be stamped, pierced, etc. — *vt.* 1 to pierce, stamp, etc. with a punch 2 to make (a hole) as with a punch

punch[2] (punch) *vt.* 〖ME *punchen*〗 1 to prod with a stick 2 to herd (cattle) as by prodding 3 to strike with the fist — *n.* 1 a thrusting blow with the fist 2 [Colloq.] effective force —**punch in** (or **out**) to record with a time clock one's arrival (or departure)

punch[3] (punch) *n.* 〖Hindi *pañca*, five〗 a sweet drink made with fruit juices, sherbet, etc., often mixed with wine or liquor

punch′-drunk′ *adj.* confused, unsteady, etc., as from many blows to the head in boxing

pun·cheon (pun′chən) *n.* 〖OFr *poinçon*〗 a large cask for beer, wine, etc.

punch line the surprise line carrying the point of a joke

punch′y *adj.* -i·er, -i·est 〖< PUNCH〗 1 forceful; vigorous 2 PUNCH-DRUNK

punc·til·i·ous (puŋk til′ē əs) *adj.* 〖see fol.〗 1 very careful about nice points of behavior 2 very exact; scrupulous

punc·tual (puŋk′chōō əl) *adj.* 〖< L *punctus*, a point〗 on time; prompt —**punc′tu·al′i·ty** (-al′ə tē) *n.* —**punc′tu·ally** *adv.*

punc·tu·ate (-chōō āt′) *vt.* -at′ed, -at′ing 〖see prec.〗 1 to use standardized marks (**punctuation marks**), as the period and comma, in (written matter) to clarify meaning

---

THESAURUS

puke* *v.* throw up, retch, upchuck*; see VOMIT.

pull *n.* 1 [The act of pulling] tow, drag, haul, jerk, twitch, wrench, extraction, drawing, rending, tearing, uprooting, weeding, row, paddle. 2 [Exerted force] work, strain, tug; see STRENGTH. 3 [*Influence] inclination, inducement, weight; see INFLUENCE.

pull *v.* 1 [To exert force] tug, pull at, draw in; see WORK 1. 2 [To move by pulling] draw, ease, drag, lift, stretch, move, jerk, haul, tear, rend, gather; see also DRAW 1. 3 [To incline] slope, tend, move toward; see LEAN 1. — **pull away** depart, pull off, go; see LEAVE 1. —**pull off** 1 [To remove] detach, separate, yank off; see REMOVE 1. 2 [*To achieve] accomplish, manage, succeed; see ACHIEVE. —**pull oneself together** recover, revive, get on one's feet; see IMPROVE 2. —**pull out** go, depart, stop par-

ticipating; see LEAVE 1, STOP 2. — **pull through*** get better, get over something, triumph; see SURVIVE 1. —**pull up** 1 [To remove] dislodge, elevate, dig out; see REMOVE 1. 2 [To stop] arrive, come to a stop, get there; see STOP 1.

pulley *n.* sheave, block, lift, lifter, crowbar, crow, pry; see also TOOL 1.

Pullman *n.* railroad sleeping car, chair car, sleeper, first-class accommodation, wagon-lit.

pulp *n.* pap, mash, sponge, paste, dough, batter, curd, jam, poultice.

pulpit *n.* 1 [The ministry] priesthood, clergy, ecclesiastics; see MINISTRY 2. 2 [A platform in a church] desk, rostrum, stage; see PLATFORM 1.

pulpy *a.* smooth, thick, fleshy; see SOFT 1.

pulse *n.* pulsation, vibration, throb; see BEAT 1.

pump[1] *n.* air pump, vacuum pump,

jet pump; see MACHINE, TOOL 1.

pump[1] *v.* elevate, draw out, tap; see DRAW 1.

pun *n.* witticism, quip, play on words; see JOKE.

punch[1,2] *v.* 1 [To hit] strike, knock, thrust against; see HIT. 2 [To perforate] pierce, puncture, bore; see PENETRATE.

punch[2] *n.* thrust, knock, stroke; see BLOW.

punched *a.* perforated, dented, pierced, punctured, needled, stamped, imprinted, bored, wounded, bitten, tapped, impaled, spiked, gored, speared, stabbed, stuck.

punctual *a.* prompt, precise, particular, on time, on schedule, exact, timely, seasonable, regular, cyclic, dependable, recurrent, constant, steady, scrupulous, punctilious, meticulous, on the nose.—*Ant.* CARELESS, unreliable, desultory.

punc·ture (puŋk′chər) *n.* 〖< L *pungere*, pierce〗 1 a piercing 2 a hole made by a sharp point — *vt., vi.* **-tured, -tur·ing** to pierce or be pierced as with a sharp point

pun·dit (pun′dit) *n.* 〖< Sans *paṇḍita*〗 a person of great learning

pun·gent (pun′jənt) *adj.* 〖< L *pungere*, pierce〗 1 producing a sharp sensation of taste and smell 2 sharp, biting, or stimulating *[pungent wit]* —**pun′gency** *n.* —**pun′gently** *adv.*

pun·ish (pun′ish) *vt.* 〖< L *punire*〗 1 to cause to undergo pain, loss, etc., as for a crime 2 to impose a penalty for (an offense) —**pun′ish·able** *adj.*

pun′ish·ment *n.* 1 a punishing or being punished 2 the penalty imposed 3 harsh treatment

pu·ni·tive (pyōō′ni tiv) *adj.* inflicting, or concerned with, punishment

punk[1] (puŋk) *n.* 〖prob. < SPUNK〗 1 decayed wood used as tinder 2 a fungous substance that smolders when ignited, used to light fireworks, etc.

punk[2] (puŋk) *n.* 〖< ?〗 1 [Slang] *a)* a young hoodlum *b)* a young person regarded as inexperienced, insignificant, etc. 2 PUNK ROCK — *adj.* 1 [Slang] poor; inferior 2 of punk rock

punk rock a loud, fast, and deliberately offensive style of rock music

pun·ster (pun′stər) *n.* one who is fond of making puns

punt[1] (punt) *n.* 〖< ? dial. *bunt*, to kick〗 *Football* a kick in which the ball is dropped and kicked before it hits the ground — *vt., vi.* to kick (a football) in this way

punt[2] (punt) *n.* 〖< L *pons*, a bridge〗 a flat-bottomed boat with square ends — *vt., vi.* to propel (a punt) with a long pole

puny (pyōō′nē) *adj.* **-nier, -ni·est** 〖< OFr *puis*, after + *né*, born〗 of inferior size, strength, or importance —**pu′ni·ness** *n.*

pup (pup) *n.* 1 a young dog; puppy 2 a young fox, seal, etc.

pupa (pyōō′pə) *n., pl.* **-pae** (-pē) or **-pas** 〖< L, a doll〗 an insect in the stage between the last larval and adult forms —**pu′pal** *adj.*

pu·pil[1] (pyōō′pəl) *n.* 〖< L *pupillus*, a ward〗 a person taught under the supervision of a teacher or tutor

pu·pil[2] (pyōō′pəl) *n.* 〖< L *pupilla*, figure reflected in the eye〗 the contractile circular opening, apparently black, in the center of the iris of the eye

pup·pet (pup′ət) *n.* 〖< L *pupa*, a doll〗 1 a small figure, as of a person, moved by strings or the hands, as in a performance (**puppet show**) 2 one whose actions, ideas, etc. are controlled by another —**pup′petry** *n.*

pup′pet·eer′ (-ə tir′) *n.* one who operates, designs, etc. puppets

puppy (pup′ē) *n., pl.* **-pies** 〖< MedievalFr *popee*, a doll〗 PUP

pup tent a small, portable tent

pur·blind (pur′blind′) *adj.* [ME *pur blind*, quite blind〗 1 partly blind 2 slow in understanding

pur·chase (pur′chəs) *vt.* **-chased, -chas·ing** 〖< OFr *pour*, for + *chacier*, to chase〗 to buy — *n.* 1 anything bought 2 the act of buying 3 a firm hold applied to move something heavy or to keep from slipping —**pur′chas·able** *adj.* —**pur′chaser** *n.*

pure (pyoor) *adj.* 〖< L *purus*〗 1 free from anything that adulterates, taints, etc.; unmixed 2 simple; mere 3 utter; absolute 4 faultless 5 blameless 6 virgin or chaste 7 abstract or theoretical *[pure physics]* —**pure′ly** *adv.* —**pure′ness** *n.*

pu·rée or **pu·ree** (pyōō rā′) *n.* 〖Fr: see prec.〗 1 cooked food pressed through a sieve or whipped in a blender to a soft, smooth consistency 2 a thick soup made of this — *vt.* **pu·réed′** or **-reed′, -rée′ing** or **-ree′ing** to make a purée of

pur·ga·tive (pur′gə tiv) *adj.* purging — *n.* a purging substance; cathartic

pur·ga·tory (pur′gə tôr′ē) *n., pl.* **-ries** 〖see fol.〗 *[often* P-] *Christian Theol.* a state or place after death for expiating sins by suffering —**pur′ga·to′rial** *adj.*

purge (purj) *vt.* **purged, purg′ing** 〖< L *purus*, clean + *agere*, do〗 1 to cleanse of impurities, etc. 2 to cleanse of sin 3 to rid (a nation, party, etc.) of (individuals held to be disloyal) 4 to empty (the bowels) — *n.* 1 a purging 2 that which purges; esp., a cathartic —**purg′er** *n.*

pu·ri·fy (pyoor′ə fī′) *vt.* **-fied′, -fy′ing** 〖see PURE & -FY〗 1 to rid of impurities, etc. 2 to free from guilt, sin, etc. — *vi.* to become purified —**pu′ri·fi·ca′tion** *n.*

Pu·rim (poor′im) *n.* 〖Heb〗 a Jewish holiday commemorating the deliverance of the Jews by Esther from a massacre

pu·rine (pyoor′ēn, -in) *n.* 〖Ger *purin*〗 1 a colorless, crystalline organic compound, from which is derived a group of compounds including uric acid and caffeine 2 any of several purine derivatives, as adenine

pur·ism (pyoor′iz′əm) *n.* strict or excessive observance of precise usage in language, style, etc. —**pur′ist** *n.*

Pu·ri·tan (pyoor′i tən) *n.* 〖see fol.〗 1 a member of a group in 16th-17th-c. England which wanted to purify the Church of England from elaborate forms 2 [p-] a person regarded as excessively strict in morals and religion —**pu′ri·tan′i·cal** (-tan′i kəl) *adj.* —**Pu′ri·tan·ism′** or **pu′ri·tan·ism′** *n.*

pu′ri·ty (-tē) *n.* 〖< LL *puritas*〗 a being pure; specif., *a)* freedom from adulterating matter *b)* cleanness *c)* freedom from sin; chastity

---

THESAURUS

punctuation *n.* Marks of punctuation include the following: period, colon, semicolon, comma, interrogation, exclamation, parentheses, dash, brackets, apostrophe, hyphen, quotation marks, brace, ellipsis.

puncture *n.* punctured tire, flat tire, flat; see HOLE, TROUBLE 1.

puncture *v.* prick, perforate, pierce; see PENETRATE.

punish *v.* correct, discipline, chasten, chastise, sentence, train, reprove, lecture, penalize, fine, incarcerate, expel, execute, exile, behead, hang, electrocute, dismiss, debar, whip, spank, paddle, trounce, switch, cuff, inflict penalty, come down on*, attend to, crack down on*, make it hot for*, pitch into*, give a dressing-down*, lower the boom on*, ground*, throw the book at*, blacklist*, blackball*; see also BEAT 1, IMPRISON, KILL 1, SCOLD.

punished *a.* corrected, disciplined, chastened, penalized, sentenced, trained, reproved, chastised, castigated, lectured, scolded, imprisoned, incarcerated, expelled, exiled, dismissed, disbarred, defrocked, whipped, switched, cuffed, cracked down on, pitched into, grounded, given one's just deserts; see also BEATEN 1, CONFINED 3, EXECUTED 2.— *Ant.* RELEASED, cleared, exonerated.

punishment *n.* correction, discipline, reproof, penalty, infliction, suffering, deprivation, unhappiness, trial, penance, retribution, mortification, disciplinary action, fine, reparation, forfeiture, forfeit, confiscation, rap on the knuckles*.—*Ant.* FREEDOM, exoneration, release.

puny *a.* feeble, inferior, diminutive; see WEAK 1.

pup *n.* puppy, whelp, young dog; see ANIMAL, DOG.

pupil[1] *n.* schoolboy, schoolgirl, learner; see STUDENT.

puppet *n.* manikin, figurine, moppet; see DOLL.

puppy *n.* pup, whelp, young dog; see ANIMAL, DOG.

purchase *n.* 1 [The act of buying] procurement, getting, obtaining, shopping, installment buying, bargaining, marketing, investing; see also BUYING. 2 [Something bought] buy, order, goods, shipment, acquisition, invoice, packages, delivery, articles, property, possession, gain, booty, acquirement, investment; see also BARGAIN, GOODS.

purchase *v.* obtain, acquire, buy up; see BUY.

purchaser *n.* shopper, obtainer, procurer; see BUYER.

pure *a.* 1 [Not mixed] unmixed, unadulterated, unalloyed, unmingled, simple, clear, genuine, undiluted, classic, real, true, fair, bright, unclouded, transparent, lucid, straight, neat; see also CLEAR 2, GENUINE 1, SIMPLE 1.—*Ant.* MIXED, mingled, blended. 2 [Clean] immaculate, spotless, stainless, unspotted, germ-free, unstained, unadulterated, unblemished, untarnished, unsoiled, disinfected, sterilized, uncontaminated, sanitary, unpolluted, purified, refined.—*Ant.* DIRTY, sullied, contaminated. 3 [Chaste] virgin, continent, celibate; see CHASTE. 4 [Absolute] sheer, utter, complete; see ABSOLUTE 1.

purely *a.* entirely, totally, essentially; see COMPLETELY.

purification *n.* purifying, cleansing, purgation; see CLEANING.—*Ant.* POLLUTION, defilement, contamination.

purify *v.* cleanse, clear, refine, wash, disinfect, fumigate, deodorize, clarify, sublimate, purge, filter; see also CLEAN.

purity *n.* 1 [The state of being pure] pureness, cleanness, cleanliness, immaculateness, stainlessness, whiteness, clearness. 2 [Innocence] artlessness, guilelessness, blamelessness; see INNOCENCE 2. 3 [Chastity] abstemiousness, continence, self-

purl[1] (purl) *vi.* [< ? Scand] to move in ripples or with a murmuring sound —*n.* the sound of purling water

purl[2] (purl) *vt., vi.* [earlier *pirl*, prob. ult. < It] to invert (stitches) in knitting so as to form ribbing

pur·lieu (purl′yōō′) *n.* [< OFr *pur-*, through + *aler*, go] 1 [*pl.*] environs 2 an outlying part, as of a city

pur·loin (pər loin′) *vt., vi.* [< OFr *pur-*, for + *loin*, far] to steal

pur·ple (pur′pəl) *n.* [< Gr *porphyra*, shellfish yielding a dye] 1 a dark bluish red 2 crimson cloth or clothing, esp. as a former emblem of royalty —*adj.* 1 bluish-red 2 imperial 3 ornate [*purple* prose] 4 profane or obscene [*purple* language] —**pur′plish** *adj.*

pur·port (pur pôrt′; *for n.* pur′pôrt′) *vt.* [< OFr *por-*, forth + *porter*, to bear] 1 to profess or claim as its meaning 2 to give the appearance, often falsely, of being, intending, etc. —*n.* 1 meaning; sense 2 intention —**pur′port′ed** *adj.* —**pur′port′edly** *adv.*

pur·pose (pur′pəs) *vt., vi.* **-posed, -pos·ing** [see PROPOSE] to intend or plan —*n.* 1 something one intends to get or do; aim 2 determination 3 the object for which something exists or is done —**on purpose** intentionally —**pur′pose·ful** *adj.* —**pur′pose·less** *adj.*

pur′pose·ly *adv.* with a definite purpose; intentionally; deliberately

purr (pur) *n.* [echoic] a low, vibratory sound made by a cat at ease —*vi., vt.* to make, or express by, such a sound

purse (purs) *n.* [< Gr *byrsa*, a hide] 1 a small bag for carrying money 2 finances; money 3 a sum of money for a present or prize 4 a woman's handbag —*vt.* **pursed, purs′ing** to pucker

purser (pur′sər) *n.* [ME, purse-bearer] a ship's officer in charge of accounts, tickets, etc.

pur·su·ance (pər sōō′əns) *n.* a pursuing of a project, plan, etc.

pur·su′ant *adj.* [Now Rare] pursuing —**pursuant to** in accordance with

pur·sue (pər sōō′, -syōō′) *vt.* **-sued′, -su′ing** [< L *pro-*, forth + *sequi*, follow] 1 to follow in order to overtake or capture; chase 2 to follow (a specified course, action, etc.) 3 to strive for 4 to continue to annoy —**pur·su′er** *n.*

pur·suit′ (-sōōt′) *n.* 1 a pursuing 2 an occupation; interest

pu·ru·lent (pyōō′rōō lənt, pyōōr′yōō-) *adj.* [< L *pus*, pus] of, like, or discharging pus —**pu′ru·lence** *n.*

pur·vey (pər vā′) *vt.* [see PROVIDE] to supply (esp. food) —**pur·vey′or** *n.*

pur·view (pur′vyōō′) *n.* [< OFr *pourveü*, provided] scope or extent, as of control, activity, etc.

pus (pus) *n.* [L] the yellowish-white matter produced by an infection

push (poosh) *vt.* [< L *pulsare*, to beat] 1 to press against so as to move 2 to press or urge on 3 to urge the use, sale, etc. of —*n.* 1 a pushing 2 a vigorous effort 3 an advance against opposition 4 [Colloq.] aggressiveness; drive —**push′er** *n.*

push button a small knob pushed to operate something electrically

push′o′ver *n.* [Slang] 1 anything very easy to do 2 a person, group, etc. easily persuaded, defeated, etc.

push′-up′ or **push′up′** *n.* an exercise in which a prone person, with the hands under the shoulders, raises the body by pushing down with the palms

push′y *adj.* **-i·er, -i·est** [Colloq.] annoyingly aggressive and persistent —**push′i·ness** *n.*

pu·sil·lani·mous (pyōō′si lan′ə məs) *adj.* [< L *pusillus*, tiny + *animus*, the mind] timid; cowardly —**pu·sil·la·nim′i·ty** (-si lə nim′ə tē) *n.*

puss (poos) *n.* [< ?] a cat Also **puss′y·cat′** or **puss′y**, *pl.* **-ies**

puss′y·foot′ *vi.* [Colloq.] 1 to move with stealth or caution, like a cat 2 to avoid committing oneself

pussy willow a willow bearing velvetlike, silvery catkins

pus·tule (pus′tyōōl′) *n.* [L *pustula*] a pus-filled blister or pimple —**pus′tu·lar** *adj.*

put (poot) *vt.* **put, put′ting** [< or akin to OE *potian*, to push] 1 *a*) to thrust; drive *b*) to propel with an overhand thrust [to *put* the shot] 2 to cause to be in a certain place, condition, relation, etc.; place; set 3 to impose (a tax, etc.) 4 to attribute; ascribe 5 to express [*put* it plainly] 6 to present for decision [*put* the question] 7 to bet (money) *on* —*n.* Finance an option to sell a stock, etc. —*adj.* [Colloq.] fixed [stay *put*] —**put across** [Colloq.] to cause to be understood or accepted —**put aside** (or **by**) to reserve for later use —**put down** 1 to crush; repress 2 to write down 3 [Slang] to belittle or humiliate —**put in for** to apply for —**put it** (or **something**) **over on** [Colloq.] to deceive; trick —**put off** 1 to postpone; delay 2 to evade; divert —**put on** 1 to clothe oneself with 2 to pretend 3 to stage (a play) 4 [Slang] to hoax —**put out** 1 to expel; dismiss 2 to extinguish (a fire or light) 3 to inconvenience 4 *Baseball* to retire (a batter or runner) —**put through** 1 to carry out 2 to cause to do or undergo —**put up** 1 to offer 2 to preserve fruits, etc. 3 to build 4 to provide lodgings for 5 to provide (money) 6 to arrange (the hair) with curlers, etc. 7 [Colloq.] to incite *to* some action —**put up with** to tolerate

pu·ta·tive (pyōōt′ə tiv) *adj.* [< L *putare*, suppose] generally considered or deemed such; reputed

put′-down′ *n.* [Slang] a belittling remark or crushing retort

put′-on′ *n.* [Slang] a hoax

pu·trefy (pyōō′trə fī′) *vt., vi.* **-fied′, -fy′ing** [see PUTRID & -FY] to make or become putrid; rot —**pu′tre·fac′tion** (-fak′shən) *n.*

═══════ THESAURUS ═══════

command; see CHASTITY, VIRTUE 1.
purple *a.* purpled, reddish blue, bluish red; see COLOR. *Tints and shades of purple include the following:* lilac, violet, mauve, heliotrope, magenta, plum, lavender, pomegranate, royal purple, wine.
purpose *n.* 1 [Aim] intention, end, goal, mission, objective, object, idea, design, hope, resolve, meaning, view, scope, desire, dream, expectation, ambition, intent, destination, direction, scheme, prospective, proposal, target, aspiration; see also PLAN 2. 2 [Resolution] tenacity, constancy, persistence; see CONFIDENCE, DETERMINATION, FAITH 1. —**on purpose** purposefully, intentionally, designedly; see DELIBERATELY. —**to the purpose** to the point, pertinent, apt; see RELEVANT.
purpose *v.* aim, plan, propose; see INTEND 1.
purposeful *a.* obstinate, stubborn, persistent; see RESOLUTE.
purr *v.* hum, drone, sigh; see SOUND.
purse *n.* pouch, pocketbook, receptacle, moneybag, wallet, pocket, coin purse, billfold, money belt, sack, vanity case.
pursue *v.* 1 [To chase] seek, hound, track down, dog, shadow, search for, search out, stalk, run after, go after,

hunt down, trail, tag with, follow close upon, move behind, scout out, nose around, poke around, keep on foot, follow up. 2 [To seek] strive for, aspire to, attempt; see TRY 1. 3 [To continue] persevere, proceed, carry on; see CONTINUE 1.
pursuit *n.* chase, race, pursuance; see HUNT.
pus *n.* infection, discharge, mucus; see MATTER 1.
push *n.* shove, force, bearing, propulsion, drive, exertion, weight, straining, shoving, thrusting, forcing, driving, inducement, mass, potential, reserve, impact, blow; see also PRESSURE.
push *v.* 1 [To press against] thrust, shove, butt, crowd, gore, ram, crush against, jostle, push out of one's way, lie on, shoulder, elbow, struggle, strain, exert, set one's shoulder to, rest one's weight on, put forth one's strength; see also FORCE. 2 [To move by pushing] impel, accelerate, drive onward, launch, start, set in motion, push forward, shift, start rolling, budge, stir, shove along; see also DRIVE 2. 3 [To promote] advance, expedite, urge; see PROMOTE 1. 4 [*To sell illegally] sell under the counter, bootleg, black-market,

moonshine; see also SELL.
pushover *n.* sucker, easy pickings, fool; see VICTIM.
pussyfoot* *v.* evade, avoid, dodge, sidestep, hedge; see also AVOID, EVADE.
put *v.* 1 [To place] set, locate, deposit, plant, lodge, store, situate, fix, put in a place, lay, pin down, seat, settle. 2 [To establish] install, quarter, fix; see ESTABLISH 2. 3 [To deposit] invest in, insert, embed; see PLANT. —**put aside** deposit, save, put out of the way; see STORE. —**put down** silence, repress, crush; see DEFEAT 2, 3. —**put off** postpone, defer, retard; see DELAY. —**put on** 1 [To pretend] feign, sham, make believe; see PRETEND 1. 2 [*To deceive] trick, confuse, confound; see DECEIVE. —**put through** do, manage, finish; see ACHIEVE. —**put up** 1 [To preserve] can, smoke, pickle; see PRESERVE 2. 2 [To build] erect, fabricate, construct; see BUILD. —**put up with** undergo, tolerate, stand; see ENDURE 2.
put-down* *n.* suppression, indignity, cut*; see INSULT.
put-on* *n.* deception, device, job*; see TRICK 1.

pu·tres·cent (pyōō tres′ənt) *adj.* putrefying; rotting —**pu·tres′cence** *n.*
pu·trid (pyōō′trid) *adj.* ⟦< L *putrere*, to rot⟧ rotten and foul-smelling
putt (put) *n.* ⟦< PUT, *v.*⟧ *Golf* a shot which attempts to roll the ball into the hole — *vt., vi.* to hit (the ball) with a putt
putter[1] (put′ər) *n. Golf* a short, straight-faced club used in putting
put·ter[2] (put′ər) *vi.* ⟦< OE *potian*, to push⟧ to busy oneself in an ineffective or aimless way (with *along, around,* etc.) — *vt.* to fritter (*away*)
putty (put′ē) *n.* ⟦Fr *potée*, lit., potful⟧ a soft, plastic mixture of powdered chalk and linseed oil, used to fill small cracks, etc. — *vt.* **-tied, -ty·ing** to cement or fill with putty
puz·zle (puz′əl) *vt.* **-zled, -zling** ⟦< ?⟧ to perplex; bewilder — *vi.* 1 to be perplexed 2 to exercise one's mind, as over a problem — *n.* 1 something that puzzles 2 a toy or problem for testing skill or ingenuity —**puzzle out** to solve by deep study —**puz′zle·ment** *n.* —**puz′zler** *n.*
PVC (pē′vē′sē′) *n.* ⟦*p(oly)v(inyl) c(hloride)*⟧ a type of polymer used in packaging materials, plumbing, etc.
Pvt. *Mil.* Private
PX Post Exchange
Pygmy[2] (pig′mē) *n., pl.* **-mies** ⟦< Gr *pygmaios*, of a forearm's length⟧ 1 a member of any of several races of small African or Asian peoples 2 [p-] a dwarf — *adj.* 1 of the Pygmies 2 [p-] very small
py·ja·mas (pə jä′məz, -jam′əz) *n.pl. Brit., etc. sp.* of PAJAMAS
py·lon (pī′län′) *n.* ⟦Gr *pylōn*, gateway⟧ 1 a gateway, as of an Egyptian temple 2 a towerlike structure supporting electric lines, marking a flight course, etc.
py·lo·rus (pī lō′rəs) *n., pl.* **-ri** (-rī) ⟦< Gr *pylōros*, gatekeeper⟧ the opening from the stomach into the duodenum —**py·lor′ic** *adj.*
py·or·rhea (pī′ə rē′ə) *n.* ⟦< Gr *pyon*, pus + *rheein*, to flow⟧ a periodontal infection with formation of pus and loosening of teeth —**py′or·rhe′al** *adj.*
pyra·mid (pir′ə mid) *n.* ⟦< Gr *pyramis*⟧ 1 a huge structure with a square base and four triangular sides meeting at the top, as a royal tomb of ancient Egypt 2 *Geom.* a solid figure with a polygonal base, the sides of which form the bases of triangular surfaces meeting at a common vertex —**py·rami·dal** (pi ram′i dəl) *adj.*
pyre (pīr) *n.* ⟦< Gr *pyr*, fire⟧ a pile of wood for burning a dead body
py·ret·ic (pī ret′ik) *adj.* ⟦< Gr *pyretos*, fever⟧ of, causing, or characterized by fever
Py·rex (pī′reks′) ⟦arbitrary coinage < *pie*⟧ *trademark for* a heat-resistant glassware used for cooking, lab work, etc.
py·rite (pī′rīt′) *n., pl.* **py·ri·tes** (pi rīt′ēz′, pī′rīts′) ⟦< Gr *pyritēs*, flint⟧ iron sulfide, a lustrous, yellow mineral used as a source of sulfur
pyro- ⟦< Gr *pyr*, fire⟧ *combining form* fire, heat
pyro·ma·nia (pī′rō mā′nē ə) *n.* ⟦ModL: see prec. & -MANIA⟧ a compulsion to start destructive fires —**py′ro·ma′niac′** *n., adj.*
pyro·tech·nics (pī′rō tek′niks) *n.pl.* ⟦< Gr *pyr*, fire + *technē*, art⟧ 1 a display of fireworks 2 a dazzling display, as of wit —**py′ro·tech′nic** *adj.*
Pyr·rhic victory (pir′ik) ⟦after *Pyrrhus*, Gr king who won such a victory over Romans, 279 B.C.⟧ a too costly victory
py·thon (pī′thän′, -thən) *n.* ⟦< Gr *Pythōn*, a serpent slain by Apollo⟧ a large, nonpoisonous snake of Asia, Africa, and Australia, that crushes its prey to death
pyx (piks) *n.* ⟦< Gr *pyxis*, a box⟧ a container for Eucharistic wafers

---

THESAURUS

putrid *a.* corrupt, putrified, decayed; see ROTTEN 1.
putter[2] *v.* dawdle, fritter, poke; see LOITER.
puzzle *n.* 1 [The state of being puzzled] uncertainty, hardship, vexation; see CONFUSION. 2 [A problem] tangle, bafflement, question, frustration, intricacy, maze, issue, enigma, proposition, mystification, bewilderment, query, mystery, dilemma, muddle, secret, riddle,
ambiguity, difficulty, perplexity, confusion, entanglement, stickler, paradox.—*Ant.* ANSWER, solution, development. 3 [A problem to be worked for amusement] *Varieties include the following:* riddle, cryptogram, logogram, crossword puzzle, jigsaw puzzle, anagram, acrostic, rebus, Chinese puzzle, puzzle-ring.
puzzle *v.* 1 [To perplex] obscure, bewilder, complicate; see CONFUSE. 2 [To wonder] marvel, be surprised, be
astonished; see WONDER 1. —**puzzle out** figure out, work out, decipher; see SOLVE.
puzzled *a.* perplexed, bewildered, mystified; see DOUBTFUL.
puzzling *a.* 1 [Obscure] uncertain, ambiguous, mystifying; see OBSCURE 1. 2 [Difficult] perplexing, abstruse, hard; see DIFFICULT 2.
pyramid *n.* tomb, shrine, remains; see MONUMENT 1.

Q

q or **Q** (kyōō) *n., pl.* **q's, Q's** the 17th letter of the English alphabet

q. 1 quart 2 question

Q.E.D. or **q.e.d.** ⟦L *quod erat demonstrandum*⟧ which was to be demonstrated or proved

qt. quart(s)

Q.T. or **q.t.** [Slang] quiet: usually in **on the Q.T.** (or **q.t.**), in secret

quack[1] (kwak) *vi.* ⟦echoic⟧ to utter the sound or cry of a duck —*n.* this sound

quack[2] (kwak) *n.* ⟦ult. < MDu *quacken*, to brag⟧ 1 an untrained person who practices medicine fraudulently 2 one who pretends to have knowledge or skill that he does not have —*adj.* fraudulent —**quack′ery** *n.*

quad (kwäd) *n. short for:* 1 QUADRANGLE 2 QUADRUPLET

quad *abbrev.* 1 quadrangle 2 quadrant 3 quadruplicate

quadran·gle (kwä′draŋ′gəl) *n.* ⟦see QUADRI- & ANGLE[1]⟧ 1 *Geom.* a plane figure with four angles and four sides 2 an area surrounded on its four sides by buildings —**quadran′gu·lar** *adj.*

quadrant (kwä′drənt) *n.* ⟦< L *quadrans*, fourth part⟧ 1 an arc of 90° 2 a quarter section of a circle 3 an instrument formerly used in measuring angular elevation and altitude in navigation, etc.

quadra·phonic (kwä′drə fän′ik) *adj.* ⟦< QUADRI- + Gr *phōnē*, a sound⟧ using four channels to record and reproduce sound

quadratic (kwä drat′ik) *adj. Algebra* involving a quantity or quantities that are squared but none that are raised to a higher power

quadren·nial (kwä dren′ē əl) *adj.* ⟦< L *quadri-* (see fol.) + *annus*, a year⟧ 1 happening every four years 2 lasting four years

quadri- ⟦L < *quattuor*, four⟧ *combining form* four, four times

quadri·ceps (kwä′dri seps′) *n.* ⟦< prec. + L *caput*, the head⟧ a muscle with four points of origin; esp., the large muscle at the front of the thigh

quadri·lat·eral (kwä′dri lat′ər əl) *adj.* ⟦see QUADRI- & LATERAL⟧ four-sided —*n. Geom.* a plane figure having four sides and four angles

qua·drille (kwə dril′, kwä-) *n.* ⟦Fr: ult. < L *quadra*, a square⟧ a square dance performed by four couples

quadri·plegia (kwä′dri plē′jē ə, -jə) *n.* ⟦ModL < QUADRI- + Gr *plēgē*, a stroke⟧ total paralysis of the body from the neck down —**quad′ri·ple′gic** (-plē′jik) *adj., n.*

quadru·ped (kwä′droo ped′) *n.* ⟦< L *quadru-*, four + *pes, foot*⟧ an animal, esp. a mammal, with four feet

quadru·ple (kwä′droo pəl, kwä drōō′-) *adj.* ⟦< L *quadru-*, four + -*plus*, -fold⟧ 1 consisting of four 2 four times as much or as many —*n.* an amount four times as much or as many —*vt., vi.* **-pled, -pling** to make or become four times as much or as many

quadru·plet (kwä drōō′plit, -drup′lit) *n.* 1 any of four

offspring born at a single birth 2 a collection or group of four, usually of one kind

quadru·pli·cate (kwä drōō′pli kāt′; *for adj. & n.,* -kit, -kāt′) *vt.* **-cat′ed, -cat′ing** to make four identical copies of —*adj.* 1 fourfold 2 being the last of four identical copies —*n.* any one of such copies —**in quadruplicate** in four such copies —**quadru′pli·ca′tion** *n.*

quaff (kwäf; *also* kwaf) *vt., vi.* ⟦prob. < LowG *quassen*, overindulge⟧ to drink deeply and heartily —*n.* a quaffing

quag·mire (kwag′mīr′) *n.* ⟦*quag*, a bog + MIRE⟧ wet, boggy ground

qua·hog or **qua·haug** (kwô′hôg′; *also* kō′-) *n.* [AmInd] an edible clam of the E coast

quail[1] (kwāl) *vi.* ⟦prob. < L *coagulare*, coagulate⟧ to recoil in fear

quail[2] (kwāl) *n.* ⟦< OFr *quaille*⟧ a small, short-tailed bird resembling a partridge

quaint (kwānt) *adj.* ⟦< OFr *cointe* < L *cognitus*, known⟧ 1 pleasingly odd or old-fashioned 2 unusual; curious 3 fanciful; whimsical —**quaint′ly** *adv.* —**quaint′ness** *n.*

quake (kwāk) *vi.* **quaked, quak′ing** ⟦< OE *cwacian*⟧ 1 to tremble or shake 2 to shiver, as from fear or cold —*n.* 1 a shaking or tremor 2 an earthquake —**quak′y, -i·er, -i·est,** *adj.*

Quaker (kwāk′ər) *n.* ⟦< founder's admonition to "quake" at the word of the Lord⟧ *name for* a member of the SOCIETY OF FRIENDS

quali·fi·ca·tion (kwôl′i fi kā′shən) *n.* 1 a qualifying or being qualified 2 a restriction; limiting condition 3 any skill, etc. that fits one for a job, office, etc.

quali·fied (kwôl′i fīd′) *adj.* 1 fit; competent 2 limited; modified

qual′i·fi′er (-fī′ər) *n.* 1 one that qualifies 2 an adjective or adverb

qual′i·fy′ (-fī′) *vt.* **-fied′, -fy′ing** ⟦< L *qualis*, of what kind + *facere*, make⟧ 1 to make fit for a job, etc. 2 to make legally capable 3 to modify; restrict 4 to moderate; soften —*vi.* to be or become qualified

qual′i·ta·tive (-tāt′iv) *adj.* having to do with quality or qualities —**qual′i·ta′tively** *adv.*

qual′ity (-tē) *n., pl.* **-ties** ⟦< L *qualis*, of what kind⟧ 1 that which makes something what it is; characteristic element 2 basic nature; kind 3 the degree of excellence of a thing 4 excellence —*adj.* of high quality

quality circle a small group of workers that meet regularly to discuss ways to improve production

qualm (kwäm) *n.* ⟦OE *cwealm*, disaster⟧ 1 a sudden, brief feeling of sickness, faintness, etc. 2 a doubt; misgiving 3 a twinge of conscience —**qualm′ish** *adj.*

quan·dary (kwän′də rē, -drē) *n., pl.* **-ries** ⟦prob. < L⟧ a state of uncertainty; dilemma

quan·tify (kwänt′ə fī′) *vt.* **-fied′, -fy′ing** ⟦< L *quantus*, how much + *facere*, make⟧ 1 to determine or express the quantity of 2 to express as a quantity or number

quan′ti·ta·tive (-tāt′iv) *adj.* having to do with quantity

quan′tity (-tē) *n., pl.* **-ties** ⟦< L *quantus*, how great⟧ 1 an amount; portion 2 any indeterminate bulk or number 3 [*also pl.*] a great amount 4 that property by which a thing can be measured 5 a number or symbol expressing this property

quan·tum (kwänt′əm) *n., pl.* **-ta** (-ə) ⟦L, how much⟧ a fixed, elemental unit of energy: the **quantum theory** states that energy is radiated discontinuously in quanta

quar·an·tine (kwôr′ən tēn) *n.* ⟦< L *quadraginta*, forty⟧

THESAURUS

quack[2] *a.* unprincipled, pretentious, dissembling; see DISHONEST.

quack[2] *n.* rogue, charlatan, humbug; see CHEAT, IMPOSTOR.

quadrangle *n.* geometrical four-sided figure, parallelogram, rhombus; see RECTANGLE.

quadrangular *a.* quadrilateral, plane, rectangular; see ANGULAR, SQUARE.

quadruped *n.* four-legged animal, domestic beast, mammal; see ANIMAL.

quadruple *a.* fourfold, four-way, four times as great, consisting of four parts, quadruplex, four-cycle, quadruplicate.

quaff *v.* gulp, swallow, guzzle; see DRINK 1, SWALLOW.

quaint *a.* fanciful, cute, pleasing, captivating, curious, ancient, antique, whimsical, affected, enchanting, baroque, Victorian, French Provincial, Early American,

Colonial; see also CHARMING.—*Ant.* MODERN, up-to-date, fashionable.

quake *n.* temblor, tremor, shock; see EARTHQUAKE.

quake *v.* tremble, shrink, cower; see SHAKE 1.

qualification *n.* need, requisite, essential; see REQUIREMENT 1.

qualifications *n.* endowments, acquirements, attainments; see EXPERIENCE.

qualified *a.* 1 [Limited] conditional, modified, confined; see RESTRICTED. 2 [Competent] adequate, equipped, fitted; see ABLE.

qualify *v.* 1 [To limit] reduce, restrain, temper; see ALTER 1. 2 [To fulfill requirements] fit, suit, pass, be capacitated for, have the requisites, meet the demands, be endowed by nature for, measure up, meet the specifications.—*Ant.* FAIL, become

unfit, be unsuited.

quality *n.* 1 [A characteristic] attribute, trait, endowment; see CHARACTERISTIC. 2 [Essential character] nature, essence, genius; see CHARACTER 2. 3 [Grade] class, kind, state, condition, merit, worth, excellence, stage, step, variety, standing, rank, group, place, position, repute.

qualm *n.* indecision, scruple, suspicion; see DOUBT, UNCERTAINTY 2.

quantity *n.* amount, number, bulk, mass, measure, extent, abundance, volume, capacity, lot, deal, pile, multitude, portion, carload, sum, profusion, mountain, load, barrel, shipment, consignment, bushel, supply, ton, ocean, flood, sea, flock, the amount of, score, swarm, quite a few, army, host, pack, crowd, bunch*, heap*, mess*, gob*, batch, all kinds of*, all sorts of*; see also SIZE 2.

1 the period, orig. 40 days, during which a vessel suspected of carrying contagious disease is detained in port 2 any isolation imposed to keep contagious diseases, etc. from spreading 3 a place for such isolation — *vt.* -tined', -tin' ing to place under quarantine

quark (kwôrk) *n.* ⟦arbitrary coinage⟧ any of six types of hypothetical particles assumed to be basic units of matter

quar·rel (kwôr'əl, kwär'-) *n.* ⟦< L *queri*, complain⟧ 1 a cause for dispute 2 a dispute, esp. an angry one — *vi.* -reled or -relled, -rel·ing or -rel·ling 1 to find fault 2 to dispute heatedly 3 to have a breach in friendship — quar'reler or quar'rel·ler *n.* —quar'rel·some *adj.*

quarry[1] (kwôr'ē) *n., pl.* -ries ⟦< OFr *cuiree*, parts of prey fed to dogs⟧ an animal, etc. being hunted down

quarry[2] (kwôr'ē) *n., pl.* -ries ⟦< L *quadrare*, to square⟧ a place where stone, slate, etc. is excavated — *vt.* -ried, -ry·ing to excavate from a quarry

quart (kwôrt) *n.* ⟦< L *quartus*, fourth⟧ 1 one fourth of a gallon in liquid measure 2 one eighth of a peck in dry measure

quar'ter (-ər) *n.* ⟦< L *quartus*, fourth⟧ 1 a fourth of something 2 one fourth of a year 3 any of the three terms of about eleven weeks each in an academic year 4 one fourth of a dollar; 25 cents, or a coin of this value 5 any leg of a four-legged animal, with the adjoining parts 6 a particular district or section 7 [*pl.*] lodgings 8 mercy 9 a particular source [news from high *quarters*] — *vt.* 1 to divide into four equal parts 2 to provide lodgings for — *adj.* constituting a quarter —at close quarters at close range

quar'ter·back' *n.* *Football* the back who calls the signals

quar'ter·deck' *n.* the after part of the upper deck of a ship, usually for officers

quar'ter·fi'nal *adj.* *Sports* coming just before the semifinals in a tournament — *n.* a quarterfinal match

quarter horse ⟦< its speed in a *quarter*-mile sprint⟧ any of a breed of muscular, solid-colored horse

quar'terly *adj.* occurring regularly four times a year — *adv.* once every quarter of the year — *n., pl.* -lies a publication issued every three months

quar'ter·mas'ter *n.* 1 *Mil.* an officer who provides troops with quarters, clothing, equipment, etc. 2 *Naut.* a petty officer or mate involved in steering and navigating a ship

quarter note *Music* a note having one fourth the duration of a whole note

quar·tet or **quar·tette** (kwôr tet') *n.* ⟦ult. < L *quartus*, fourth⟧ 1 a group of four 2 *Music* a) a composition for four voices or instruments b) the four performers of this

quarto (kwôrt'ō) *n., pl.* -tos ⟦< L (*in*) *quarto*, (in) a- fourth⟧ 1 the page size (about 9 by 12 in.) of a book made

up of sheets each of which is folded twice to form four leaves, or eight pages 2 a book with pages of this size

quartz (kwôrts) *n.* ⟦Ger *quarz*⟧ a crystalline mineral, a form of silica, usually colorless and transparent

qua·sar (kwā'zär') *n.* ⟦< *quas(i-stell)ar* (*radio source*)⟧ a distant, starlike, celestial object that emits immense quantities of light and radio waves

quash[1] (kwäsh) *vt.* ⟦< L *cassus*, empty⟧ *Law* to set aside (an indictment)

quash[2] (kwäsh) *vt.* ⟦< L *quatere*, to break⟧ to quell (an uprising)

quasi (kwā'sī', -zī'; kwä'sē, -zē) *adv.* ⟦L⟧ as if; seemingly — *adj.* seeming Often hyphenated as a prefix [*quasi*-le- gal]

quatrain (kwä'trān') *n.* ⟦< L *quattuor*, four⟧ a stanza of four lines

qua·ver (kwā'vər) *vi.* ⟦ME *cwafien*⟧ 1 to shake or trem- ble 2 to be tremulous: said of the voice — *n.* a tremulous quality in a voice or tone

quay (kē) *n.* ⟦ult. < Celt⟧ a wharf, usually of concrete or stone

queasy (kwē'zē) *adj.* -sier, -si·est ⟦ME *qwesye* < Gmc⟧ 1 affected with nausea 2 squeamish; easily nauseated — **quea'sily** *adv.* —**quea'si·ness** *n.*

queen (kwēn) *n.* ⟦< OE *cwen*⟧ 1 the wife of a king 2 a female monarch in her own right 3 a woman noted for her beauty or accomplishments 4 the fully developed, repro- ductive female in a colony of bees, ants, etc. 5 a playing card with a picture of a queen on it 6 *Chess* the most powerful piece —**queen'ly, -lier, -li·est,** *adj.*

queer (kwir) *adj.* ⟦< ? Ger *quer*, crosswise⟧ 1 different from the usual; strange 2 [Colloq.] eccentric — *vt.* [Slang] to spoil the success of — *n.* [Slang] a strange person

quell (kwel) *vt.* ⟦OE *cwellan*, kill⟧ 1 to subdue 2 to quiet; allay

quench (kwench) *vt.* ⟦OE *cwencan*⟧ 1 to extinguish [to *quench* fire with water] 2 to satisfy [to *quench* one's thirst] 3 to cool (hot steel, etc.) suddenly by plunging into water, etc. —**quench'less** *adj.*

queru·lous (kwer'yōō ləs, -ə-) *adj.* ⟦< L *queri*, complain⟧ 1 inclined to find fault 2 full of complaint; peevish — **quer'u·lously** *adv.*

query (kwir'ē) *n., pl.* -ries ⟦< L *quaerere*, ask⟧ 1 a ques- tion; inquiry 2 a question mark — *vt., vi.* -ried, -ry·ing to question

quest (kwest) *n.* ⟦see prec.⟧ 1 a seeking 2 a journey for adventure

ques·tion (kwes'chən) *n.* ⟦see QUERY⟧ 1 an asking; inquiry 2 something asked 3 doubt; uncertainty 4 mat-

---

◼ THESAURUS ◼

quarantined *a.* shut up, under quarantine, hospitalized, restrained, separated; see also ISOLATED.

quarrel *n.* 1 [An angry dispute] wrangle, squabble, dissension; see DISAGREEMENT 1, DISPUTE. 2 [Objec- tion] complaint, disapproval, dis- agreement; see OBJECTION.

quarrel *v.* wrangle, dispute, contend, fight, squabble, row, clash, altercate, dissent, bicker, struggle, strive, con- test, object, complain, disagree, argue, charge, allegate, feud, strike, engage in blows, mix it up with*, step on one's toes, get tough with*, lock horns, have words with, have a brush with*, have it out*, fall out with*, break with*; see also OPPOSE 1.—*Ant.* AGREE, accord, harmonize.

quarrelsome *a.* factious, irritable, combative, pugnacious, turbulent, unruly, passionate, violent, conten- tious, disputatious, fiery, cross, iras- cible, snappish, waspish, peevish, petulant, churlish, cantankerous, thin-skinned, touchy, huffy, pettish, peppery, impassioned, hotheaded, excitable, hasty, tempestuous, with a chip on one's shoulder*.—*Ant.* AGREEABLE, CALM, peaceful.

quart *n.* two pints, thirty-two ounces, one-fourth gallon; see MEASURE 1.

quarter *n.* 1 [One of four equal parts] fourth, one-fourth part, por- tion, farthing, division, three months, semester, school term, quar-

ter of an hour, quarter section; see also PART 1. 2 [One quarter of a dol- lar; *United States*] twenty-five cents, one-fourth of a dollar, coin, two bits*; see also MONEY 1. 3 [A section of a community] neighborhood, dis- trict, section; see AREA. —at close quarters at close range, cramped, restricted; see NEAR 1.

quarter *v.* 1 [To divide into quarters] cleave, dismember, cut up; see CUT 1, DIVIDE. 2 [To provide liv- ing quarters] lodge, shelter, house; see SHELTER.

quarterly *a.* by quarters, once every three months, periodically; see REGU- LARLY.

quarters *n.* house, apartment, room, barracks, tent, lodge, cabins, cottage, car trailer.

quartet *n.* four persons, four voices, four musicians, string quartet, prin- cipals, four-voice parts.

quartz *n.* *Types of quartz include the following:* amethyst, chalcedony, rock crystal, rose quartz, smoky quartz, bloodstone, agate, onyx, sardonyx, carnelian, chrysoprase, prase, flint, jasper; see also ROCK 1.

quasi *a.* supposedly, to a certain extent, apparently; see ALMOST.

queasy *a.* squeamish, sick, uneasy; see UNCOMFORTABLE 1.

queen *n.* ruler, female ruler, female sovereign, woman monarch, queen

mother, regent, wife of a king, con- sort, queen consort, queen dowager, queen regent, fairy queen, May Queen, matriarch.

queer *a.* 1 [Odd] odd, peculiar, uncommon; see UNUSUAL 2. 2 [*Sus- picious] strange, questionable, curi- ous; see SUSPICIOUS 2.

quench *v.* 1 [To satisfy] slake, glut, gorge; see DRINK 1. 2 [To smother] stifle, dampen, douse; see MOISTEN.

quest *n.* journey, search, crusade; see EXAMINATION 1.

question *n.* 1 [A query] inquiry, interrogatory, interrogation, inquisi- tion, feeler, catechism, inquest, rhe- torical question, burning question, crucial question, leading question, academic question.—*Ant.* ANSWER, solution, reply. 2 [A puzzle] enigma, mystery, problem; see PUZZLE 2. 3 [A subject] proposal, topic, discussion; see SUBJECT. —**beside the question** not germane, beside the point, unnecessary; see IRRELEVANT. — **beyond question** beyond dispute, without any doubt, sure; see CERTAIN 2. —**in question** open for discus- sion, in debate, at issue; see CONTRO- VERSIAL, QUESTIONABLE 1, UNCERTAIN. —**out of the question** not to be considered, by no means, no; see IMPOSSIBLE.

question *v.* 1 [To ask] inquire, interrogate, query, quest, seek, ter open to discussion **5** a difficult matter [not a *question* of money] **6** a point being debated before an assembly — **vt. 1** to ask questions of **2** to express doubt about **3** to dispute; challenge — **vi.** to ask questions —**out of the question** impossible

ques'tion·able *adj.* **1** that can be questioned **2** suspected of being immoral, dishonest, etc. **3** uncertain — **ques'tion·ably** *adv.*

question mark a mark of punctuation (?) put after a sentence, word, etc. to indicate a direct question or to express doubt, uncertainty, etc.

ques'tion·naire' (-chǝn ner') *n.* a written or printed set of questions used in gathering information from people

queue (kyōō) *n.* [< L *cauda*, tail] **1** a pigtail **2** [Chiefly Brit., etc.] a line, as of persons waiting to be served **3** stored computer data or programs waiting to be processed — **vi. queued, queu'ing** [Chiefly Brit., etc.] to line up in a queue: often with *up*

quib·ble (kwib'əl) *n.* [< L *qui*, who] a petty evasion; cavil — **vi. -bled, -bling** to evade the truth of a point under discussion by caviling —**quib'bler** *n.*

quiche (kēsh) *n.* a custard baked in a pastry shell with various ingredients, as bacon, cheese, or spinach

quick (kwik) *adj.* [< OE *cwicu*, living] **1** *a)* rapid; swift [a *quick* walk] *b)* prompt [a *quick* reply] **2** prompt to understand or learn [a *quick* mind] **3** easily stirred [a *quick* temper] — *adv.* quickly; rapidly — *n.* **1** the living, esp. in **the quick and the dead 2** the sensitive flesh under the nails **3** the deepest feelings [hurt to the *quick*] —**quick'ly** *adv.* —**quick'ness** *n.*

quick bread any bread leavened with baking powder, soda, etc. and baked as soon as the batter is mixed

quick'en *vt.* **1** to animate; enliven; revive **2** to cause to move more rapidly — *vi.* **1** to become enlivened; revive **2** to show signs of life, as a fetus **3** to become more rapid

quick'-freeze' *vt.* **-froze', -fro'zen, -freez'ing** to subject (food) to sudden freezing for long storage at low temperatures

quick'ie *n.* [Colloq.] anything done or made quickly and, often, cheaply

quick'lime' *n.* unslaked lime

quick'sand' *n.* [< ME: see QUICK & SAND] a loose, wet, deep, sand deposit, engulfing heavy objects easily

quick'sil'ver *n.* mercury

quick'-tem'pered *adj.* easily angered

quick'-wit'ted *adj.* nimble of mind

quid (kwid) *n.* [var. of *cud*] a piece, as of tobacco, to be chewed

quid pro quo (kwid' prō kwō') [L] one thing in return for another

qui·es·cent (kwi es'ənt) *adj.* [< L *quiescere*, become quiet] quiet; still; inactive —**qui·es'cence** *n.*

quiet (kwī'ət) *adj.* [< L *quies*, rest] **1** still; motionless **2** *a)* not noisy; hushed *b)* not speaking; silent **3** not easily excited **4** not showy [quiet clothes] **5** not forward; unobtrusive **6** peaceful and relaxing — *n.* **1** calmness, stillness, etc. **2** a quiet or peaceful quality — *vt.* to make quiet — *vi.* to become quiet: usually with *down* —**qui'etly** *adv.*

qui·etude (kwī'ǝ tōōd') *n.* a state of being quiet; calmness

qui·etus (kwi ēt'əs) *n.* [< ML *quietus (est)*, (he is) quit] **1** discharge from debt, etc. **2** death

quill (kwil) *n.* [prob. < LowG or MDu] **1** a large, stiff feather **2** *a)* the hollow stem of a feather *b)* anything made from this, as a pen **3** a spine of a porcupine or hedgehog

quilt (kwilt) *n.* [< L *culcita*, bed] a bedcover filled with down, cotton, etc. and stitched together in lines or patterns — *vt.* to stitch like a quilt — *vi.* to make a quilt — **quilt'er** *n.*

quince (kwins) *n.* [< Gr *kydōnion*] **1** a yellowish, apple-shaped fruit, used in preserves **2** the tree it grows on

qui·nine (kwī'nīn') *n.* [< *quina*, cinchona bark] a bitter, crystalline alkaloid extracted from cinchona bark, used esp. for treating malaria

quinsy (kwin'zē) *n.* [< Gr *kyōn*, dog + *anchein*, choke] *early term for* TONSILLITIS

quintes·sence (kwin tes'əns) *n.* [< ML *quinta essentia*] the pure essence or perfect type —**quin'tes·sen'tial** (-te sen'shəl) *adj.*

quin·tet or **quin·tette** (kwin tet') *n.* [ult. < L *quintus*, a fifth] **1** a group of five **2** *Music a)* a composition for five voices or instruments *b)* the five performers of this

quin·tu·ple (kwin'tǝ pǝl, kwin tōō'-) *adj.* [< L *quintus*, a fifth + *-plex*, -FOLD] consisting of five **2** five times as much or as many — *vt., vi.* **-pled, -pling** to make or become five times as much or as many

quin·tu·plet (kwin tup'lit, -tōō'plit) *n.* **1** any of five offspring born at a single birth **2** a group of five, usually of one kind

quip (kwip) *n.* [< L *quippe*, indeed] a witty or sarcastic remark; jest — *vi.* **quipped, quip'ping** to utter quips — **quip'ster** *n.*

quire (kwīr) *n.* [< L *quaterni*, four each] a set of 24 or 25 sheets of paper of the same size and stock

---

◼ THESAURUS ◼

search, sound out, petition, solicit, ask about, catechize, show curiosity, pry into, ask a leading question, challenge, raise a question, make inquiry, quiz, cross-examine, probe, investigate, put to the question, bring into question; see also ASK. **2** [To doubt] distrust, suspect, dispute; see DOUBT.

questionable *a.* **1** [Justifying doubt] doubtful, undefined, equivocal, disputable, obscure, occult, indecisive, controversial, vague, unsettled, open to doubt, indeterminate, debatable, unconfirmed, problematical, cryptic, apocryphal, hypothetical, mysterious, enigmatic, ambiguous, indefinite, contingent, provisional, paradoxical, under advisement, under examination, open to question, up for discussion, in question, to be voted on, to be decided, hard to believe, incredible; see also UNCERTAIN. —*Ant.* DEFINITE, undoubted, credible. **2** [Having a poor appearance or reputation] dubious, disreputable, notorious, opprobrious, obnoxious, of ill repute, unsatisfactory, of little account, thought ill of, under a cloud, illfavored, unpopular, unpleasing, ugly, unattractive, offensive, disagreeable, evil-looking, illegitimate, discreditable, unhonored, unliked, unloved; see also SUSPICIOUS 2.—*Ant.* HONORED, esteemed, liked.

questionnaire *n.* set of questions, inquiry, survey; see CENSUS.

quick *a.* **1** [Rapid] swift, expeditious, fleet; see FAST 1. **2** [Almost

immediate] posthaste, prompt, instantaneous; see IMMEDIATE. **3** [Hasty] impetuous, mercurial, quick-tempered; see RASH. **4** [Alert] ready, sharp, vigorous; see ACTIVE.

quicken *v.* **1** [To hasten] speed, hurry, make haste; see HASTEN 2. **2** [To cause to hasten] expedite, urge, promote; see HASTEN 2.

quickly *a.* speedily, swiftly, fleetly, flying, wingedly, with dispatch, scurrying, hurrying, rushing, shooting, bolting, darting, flashing, dashing, suddenly, in haste, in a hurry, just now, this minute, in a moment, in an instant, right away, at a greater rate, without delay, against the clock, racing, galloping, loping, sweeping, light-footedly, briskly, at once, like a bat out of hell*, on the double*, in a flash*, in a jiffy*, to beat the band*, at full blast*, hellbent for leather*, hand over fist*, like mad*, by leaps and bounds, like a house afire*.— *Ant.* SLOWLY, sluggishly, creepingly.

quick-tempered *a.* temperamental, quarrelsome, sensitive; see IRRITABLE.

quiet *a.* calm, peaceful, hushed, muffled, noiseless, still, stilled, mute, muted, soundless, dumb, quieted, speechless, unspeaking, quiescent, taciturn, reserved, reticent, not excited, not anxious, not disturbed, silent, unexpressed, closemouthed, close, tight-lipped, uncommunicative, secretive.

quiet *n.* **1** [Rest] calm, tranquillity,

relaxation; see PEACE 2. **2** [Silence] hush, stillness, speechlessness; see SILENCE 1.

quiet *v.* **1** [To make calm] calm, cool, relax, compose, tranquilize, satisfy, please, pacify, mollify, console, subdue, reconcile, gratify, calm down, soften, moderate, smooth, ameliorate, lull, appease, restrain, sober, slacken, soothe.—*Ant.* EXCITE, increase, agitate. **2** [To make silent] still, deaden, silence, lower the sound level, muffle, mute, stop, check, restrain, suppress, break in, confute, eliminate, repress, refute, confound, answer, quell, to stop the mouth*, put the lid on*, button up*, choke off*, put the stopper on*.—*Ant.* SOUND, ring, cause to sound. —**quiet down** grow silent, be hushed, hush, be subdued, be suppressed, become speechless, fall quiet, break off, be answered.

quietly *a.* **1** [Calmly] peacefully, unconcernedly, confidently; see CALMLY. **2** [Almost silently] noiselessly, speechlessly, as quietly as possible; see SILENTLY. **3** [Without attracting attention] humbly, unostentatiously, simply; see MODESTLY.

quilt *n.* bed covering, coverlet, comforter, feather bed, puff, down puff, batt, bed quilt, patchwork quilt, pieced quilt, bedspread, pad; see also COVER 1.

quip *n.* jest, repartee, banter; see LANGUAGE 1.

quirk (kwʉrk) *n.* 〖< ? 〗 **1** a sudden twist or turn **2** a peculiarity —**quirk′i·ness** *n.* —**quirk′y, -i·er, -i·est,** *adj.*

quirt (kwʉrt) *n.* 〖AmSp *cuarta*〗 a riding whip with a braided leather lash and a short handle

quis·ling (kwiz′liŋ) *n.* 〖after V. *Quisling*, Norw collaborator with the Nazis〗 a traitor

quit (kwit) *vt.* **quit, quit′ting** 〖< ML *quittus*, free〗 **1** to free (oneself) *of* **2** to give up **3** to leave; depart from **4** to stop or resign from — *vi.* **1** to stop doing something **2** to give up one's job

quit′claim′ *n.* a deed relinquishing a claim, as to property

quite (kwit) *adv.* 〖see QUIT〗 **1** completely **2** really; positively **3** very or fairly 〖*quite* warm〗 —**quite a few** (or **bit,** etc.) [Colloq.] more than a few (or bit, etc.)

quits (kwits) *adj.* 〖< ML *quittus*, free〗 on even terms, as by discharge of a debt, retaliation, etc. —**call it quits** [Colloq.] **1** to stop working, etc. **2** to stop being friendly

quit·tance (kwit′ns) *n.* 〖see QUIT〗 **1** discharge from a debt **2** recompense

quit′ter *n.* [Colloq.] one who quits or gives up easily, without trying hard

quiver[1] (kwiv′ər) *vi.* 〖< OE *cwifer-*, eager〗 to shake tremulously; tremble — *n.* a quivering; tremor

quiver[2] (kwiv′ər) *n.* 〖< OFr *coivre*〗 a case for holding arrows

quix·otic (kwiks ät′ik) *adj.* 〖after DON QUIXOTE〗 extravagantly chivalrous or foolishly idealistic

quiz (kwiz) *n.,* *pl.* **quiz′zes** 〖prob. < L *quis*, what〗 a questioning; esp., a short examination to test knowledge — *vt.* **quizzed, quiz′zing** to ask questions, or test the knowledge, of —**quiz′zer** *n.*

quiz′zi·cal (-i kəl) *adj.* **1** odd; comical **2** perplexed —**quiz′zi·cally** *adv.*

---

quoin (koin, kwoin) *n.* 〖var. of COIN〗 **1** the external corner of a building; esp., any of the large stones at such a corner **2** a wedge-shaped block

quoit (kwoit) *n.* 〖prob. < OFr *coite*, a cushion〗 **1** a ring thrown in quoits **2** [*pl., with sing. v.*] a game somewhat like horseshoes, in which rings are thrown at a peg

quon·dam (kwän′dəm) *adj.* 〖L〗 former 〖a *quondam* companion〗

Quon·set hut (kwän′sit) 〖< *Quonset*, a trademark〗 a prefabricated, metal shelter like a half cylinder on its flat side

quo·rum (kwôr′əm) *n.* 〖< L *qui*, who〗 the minimum number of members required to be present before an assembly can transact business

quot. quotation

quota (kwōt′ə) *n.* 〖< L *quota pars*, how large a part〗 a share or proportion assigned to each of a number

quotation mark either of a pair of punctuation marks (" ...") used to enclose a direct quotation

quote (kwōt) *vt.* **quot′ed, quot′ing** 〖< L *quotus*, of what number〗 **1** to repeat a passage from or statement of **2** to repeat (a passage, statement, etc.) **3** to state the price of (something) — *n.* [Colloq.] **1** something quoted **2** QUOTATION MARK —**quot′able** *adj.* —**quo·ta·tion** (kwō tā′shən) *n.*

quoth (kwōth) *vt.* 〖< OE *cwethan*, speak〗 [Archaic] said

quo·tid·i·an (kwō tid′ē ən) *adj.* 〖< L *quotidie*〗 **1** daily **2** ordinary

quo·tient (kwō′shənt) *n.* 〖< L *quot*, how many〗 *Math.* the result obtained when one number is divided by another

q.v. 〖L *quod vide*〗 which see

THESAURUS

quirk *n.* vagary, whim, caprice, fancy, whimsy, conceit, humor, turn, twist, knack, peculiarity, idiosyncrasy, foible, quibble, equivocation, subterfuge, bee in one's bonnet*; see also CHARACTERISTIC, IRREGULARITY.

quit *v.* **1** [Abandon] surrender, renounce, relinquish; see ABANDON 1. **2** [To cease] discontinue, cease, halt, pause, stop, end, desist; see also STOP 2. **3** [To leave] go away from, depart, vacate; see LEAVE 1. **4** [To resign] leave, resign, stop work, walk out, quit, change jobs, cease work, give notice; see also RESIGN 2.

quite *a.* **1** [Completely] entirely, wholly, totally; see COMPLETELY. **2** [Really] truly, positively, actually; see REALLY 1. **3** [To a considerable degree] pretty, more or less, considerably; see VERY.

quitter *n.* shirker, dropout, deserter, goldbrick*, piker*, slacker*.

quiver[1] *n.* shudder, shiver, tremble; see VIBRATION.

quiver[1] *v.* vibrate, shudder, shiver; see WAVE 3.

quiz *n.* test, questioning, query; see EXAMINATION 2.

quiz *v.* question, test, cross-examine; see EXAMINE.

quorum *n.* enough to transact business, majority of the membership, legal minimum; see MEMBER.

quota *n.* portion, part, division; see SHARE.

quotation *n.* **1** [Quoted matter] excerpt, passage, citation, cite*, citing, extract, recitation, repetition, sentence, quote, plagiarism. **2** [A quoted price] market price, current price, published price; see PRICE.

quote *v.* **1** [To repeat verbatim] recite, excerpt, extract; see SAY. **2** [To state a price] name a price, request, demand; see PRICE, VALUE 2.

quoted *a.* **1** [Repeated from someone else] recited, excerpted, extracted, cited, instanced, copied. **2** [Offered or mentioned at a stated price] asked, stated, announced, published, named, marked, given, priced, ticketed, tagged.

R

r or **R** (är) *n.*, *pl.* **r's, R's** the 18th letter of the English alphabet

r *Math. symbol for* radius

R (är) *trademark for* a film rating indicating that no one under 17 may be admitted unless accompanied by a parent or guardian

R or **R.** 1 [L *Rex*] king 2 [L *Regina*] queen 3 Republican 4 right 5 River 6 Road 7 route 8 *Baseball* run(s)

Ra *Chem. symbol for* radium

rab·bet (rab'it) *n.* [< OFr *rabattre*, beat down] a cut made in a board so that another may be fitted into it — *vt., vi.* to cut, or be joined by, a rabbet

rab·bi (rab'ī) *n.*, *pl.* **-bis** [< Heb *rabi*, my master] an ordained teacher of the Jewish law —**rab'bin·ate** (-i nit) *n.* —**rab·bin·i·cal** (rə bin'i kəl) *adj.*

rab·bit (rab'it) *n.* [ME *rabette*] a swift, burrowing mammal with soft fur, long ears, and a stubby tail

rabbit punch *Boxing* a short, sharp blow to the back of the neck

rab·ble (rab'əl) *n.* [< ?] a mob

rab'ble-rous'er *n.* one who tries to arouse people to violent action by appeals to emotions, prejudices, etc.

rab·id (rab'id) *adj.* [< L *rabere*, to rage] 1 violent; raging 2 fanatic 3 of or having rabies

ra·bies (rā'bēz) *n.* [L, madness] an infectious disease characterized by convulsions, etc., transmitted to people by the bite of an infected animal

rac·coon (ra kōōn') *n.* [< AmInd *aroughcun*] 1 a small, tree-climbing mammal of North America, with yellowish-gray fur and a black-ringed tail 2 its fur

race¹ (rās) *n.* [< ON *rās*, a running] 1 a competition of speed in running, etc. 2 any similar contest [the *race* for mayor] 3 a swift current of water, or its channel — *vi.* **raced, rac'ing** 1 to take part in a race 2 to go or move swiftly — *vt.* 1 to compete with in a race 2 to enter (a horse, etc.) in a race 3 to cause to go swiftly —**rac'er** *n.*

race² (rās) *n.* [Fr < It *razza*] 1 any of the different varieties of human beings distinguished by physical traits, blood types, etc. 2 any geographical population sharing the same habits, ideas, etc. 3 any distinct group of people

race'horse' *n.* a horse bred and trained for racing

ra·ceme (rā sēm', rə-) *n.* [L *racemus*, cluster of grapes] a flower cluster having a central stem along which individual flowers grow on small stalks

race'track' *n.* a course prepared for racing, esp. an oval track for horse races

race'way' *n.* 1 a narrow channel for water 2 a racetrack for harness racing, drag racing, etc.

ra·cial (rā'shəl) *adj.* of or characteristic of a race —**ra'cially** *adv.*

raci·ness (rā'sē nis) *n.* racy quality

rac·ism (rā'siz'əm) *n.* the practice of racial discrimination, segregation, etc. —**rac'ist** *n., adj.*

rack¹ (rak) *n.* [< LowG *rack*] 1 a framework, etc. for holding or displaying various things [pipe *rack*] 2 a toothed bar into which a pinion, etc. meshes 3 an instrument of torture which stretches the victim's limbs 4 any great torment — *vt.* 1 to arrange in or on a rack 2 to torture on a rack 3 to torment —**on the rack** in a difficult situation —**rack one's brains** to try hard to think of something —**rack up** [Slang] to score or achieve

rack² (rak) *n.* [var. of WRACK] destruction: now only in **go to rack and ruin**, to become ruined

racket¹ (rak'it) *n.* [prob. echoic] 1 a noisy confusion 2 *a)* an obtaining of money illegally *b)* [Colloq.] any dishonest practice

racket² (rak'it) *n.* [< Ar *rāha(t)*, palm of the hand] a light bat for tennis, etc., with a network, as of catgut, in a round frame attached to a handle Also **rac'quet**

racket·eer (rak'ə tir') *n.* one who obtains money illegally, as by fraud, extortion, etc. —**rack'et·eer'ing** *n.*

rac·on·teur (rak'än tur') *n.* [Fr < *raconter*, to recount] one skilled in telling stories or anecdotes

rac'quet·ball' *n.* a game played like handball, but with a racket

racy (rā'sē) *adj.* **-i·er, -i·est** [RACE² + -Y²] 1 having the taste or quality of the genuine type [racy *fruit*] 2 lively; spirited 3 pungent 4 risqué

rad (rad) *n.* [< RAD(IATION)] a dosage of absorbed ionizing radiation

ra·dar (rā'där) *n.* [*ra(dio) d(etecting) a(nd) r(anging)*] a system or device that transmits radio waves to a reflecting object, as an aircraft, to determine its location, speed, etc. by the reflected waves

ra'dar·scope' *n.* an oscilloscope that picks up radar waves

ra·dial (rā'dē əl) *adj.* [< L *radius*, ray] 1 of or like a ray or rays; branching out from a center 2 of a radius

radial (ply) tire an automobile tire with plies of rubberized cords at right angles to the center line of the tread

ra·di·ant (rā'dē ənt) *adj.* [< L *radius*, ray] 1 shining brightly 2 showing pleasure, etc.; beaming 3 issuing (from a source) in or as in rays —**ra'di·ance** *n.* —**ra'di·antly** *adv.*

▬ THESAURUS ▬

rabbi *n.* Jewish teacher, teacher, Hebrew theologian; see PRIEST.

rabbit *n.* hare, pika, bunny, Easter bunny; see also ANIMAL, RODENT. *Kinds of rabbits include the following:* jack rabbit, cottontail, snowshoe rabbit, Chinchilla hare, tapeti.

rabble *n.* mob, masses, riffraff; see CROWD, PEOPLE 3.

rabid *a.* 1 [Fanatical] obsessed, zealous, keen; see RADICAL 2. 2 [Insane] mad, raging, deranged; see INSANE. 3 [Affected with rabies] attacked by a mad dog, hydrophobic, foaming at the mouth; see SICK.

rabies *n.* canine madness, hydrophobia, lyssa; see ILLNESS 2.

race¹ *v.* 1 [To move at great speed] speed, hurry, run, pursue, chase, tear, bustle, spurt, post, press on, run swiftly, hasten, trip, fly, hustle, dash, rush, sprint, swoop, scuttle, dart, scamper, haste, plunge ahead, whiz, bolt, scramble, whisk, shoot, run like mad, burn up the road*, gun the motor*, skedaddle*. 2 [To compete] run a race, compete in a race, contend in running, follow a course, engage in a contest of speed, try to beat in a contest of speed, contend, enter a competition.

race¹,² *n.* 1 [A major division of mankind] species, culture, variety, type, kind, strain, breed, family, cultural group, color; see also MAN 1. 2 [Roughly, people united by blood or custom] nationality, caste, variety, type, the people, mankind, tribe, group, ethnic stock, human race, class, kind, nation, folk, gene pool, pedigree, lineage, community, inhabitants, population, populace, public, clan, breeding population; see also HEREDITY, SOCIETY 2. 3 [A contest, usually in speed] competition, run, sprint, clash, meet, event, engagement, competitive trail of speed, competitive action, pursuit, rush, steeplechase, handicap, chase, match, derby, regatta, sweepstakes, marathon, heat, time trial; see also SPORT 3.

racial *a.* lineal, hereditary, ancestral, genetic, ethnic, genealogical, ethnological, patriarchal, paternal, parental.

racism *n.* racial prejudice, racial bias, bigotry, racial discrimination, apartheid, segregation; see also PREJUDICE.

racist *a.* supremacist, favoring racism, bigoted; see CONSERVATIVE, PREJUDICED.

racist *n.* supremacist, believer in racism, supporter of the color line; see BIGOT, CONSERVATIVE.

rack¹ *n.* holder, receptacle, framework, stand, shelf, ledge, perch, frame, bracket, whatnot, arbor, box, counter, trestle, hat rack, clothes rack, bottle rack, gun rack, feed rack; see also FRAME 1.

racket¹ *n.* 1 [Disturbing noise] uproar, clatter, din; see DISTURBANCE 2, NOISE 2. 2 [Confusion accompanied by noise] squabble, scuffle, fracas, clash, row, wrangle, agitation, babel, pandemonium, turbulence, clamor, outcry, hullabaloo, tumult, hubbub, commotion, blare, turmoil, stir, noisy fuss, uproar, clatter, charivari, babble, roar, shouting, rumpus, riot, squall, brawl, fight, pitched battle, free-for-all, to-do*, fuss*. 3 [A means of extortion] illegitimate business, confidence game, con game*; see CORRUPTION 2, CRIME, THEFT.

racketeer *n.* gang leader, trickster, dealer in illicit goods; see CRIMINAL.

racy *a.* 1 [Full of zest] spicy, sharp, spirited; see EXCITING. 2 [Not quite respectable] indecent, erotic, indelicate; see LEWD 2, SENSUAL 2.

radar *n.* radio detecting and ranging, radar principle, Missile Site Radar; see ELECTRONICS.

radial *a.* branched, outspread, radiated; see SPIRAL, SPREADING.

radiance *n.* brightness, brilliance, effulgence; see LIGHT 1.

radiant *a.* shining, luminous, radiating; see BRIGHT 1.

ra·di·ate (rā′dē āt′) *vi.* **-at′ed, -at′ing** 〚< L *radius*, ray〛 **1** to send out rays of heat, light, etc. **2** to branch out in lines from a center — *vt.* **1** to send out (heat, light, etc.) in rays **2** to spread (happiness, love, etc.)

ra′di·a′tion *n.* **1** a radiating **2** the rays sent out **3** nuclear particles

radiation sickness sickness produced by overexposure to X-rays, radioactive matter, etc.

ra′di·a′tor *n.* an apparatus for radiating heat, as into a room or from an automobile engine

rad·i·cal (rad′i kal) *adj.* 〚< L *radix*, root〛 **1** of or from the root; fundamental **2** favoring basic change, as in the social or economic structure — *n.* **1** a person holding radical views **2** *Chem.* a group of two or more atoms acting as a single atom **3** *Math.* the sign (√) used with a quantity to show that its root is to be extracted —**rad′i·cal·ism′** *n.* —**rad′i·cally** *adv.*

ra·dii (rā′dē ī′) *n. alt. pl. of* RADIUS

ra·dio (rā′dē ō′) *n.* 〚< *radio(telegraphy)*〛 **1** the transmission of sounds or signals by electromagnetic waves directly through space to a receiving set **2** *pl.* **-os′** such a set **3** broadcasting by radio as an industry, entertainment, etc. — *adj.* of, using, used in, or sent by radio — *vt., vi.* **-oed′, -o′ing** to transmit, or communicate with, by radio

radio- 〚< L *radius*, ray〛 *combining form* **1** ray, raylike **2** by radio **3** using radiant energy **4** radioactive *[radiotherapy]*

ra′di·o·ac′tive *adj.* giving off radiant energy in the form of particles or rays by the disintegration of atomic nuclei — **ra′di·o·ac′tively** *adv.* —**ra′di·o·ac·tiv′i·ty** *n.*

radio astronomy astronomy dealing with radio waves in space in order to obtain information about the universe

ra′di·o·gram′ *n.* a message sent by radio

ra′di·o·i′so·tope′ *n.* a radioactive isotope of a chemical element

ra′di·ol′o·gy (-äl′ə jē) *n.* the use of radiant energy, as X-rays, in medical diagnosis and therapy —**ra′di·ol′o·gist** *n.*

ra′di·o·paque′ (-ō pāk′) *adj.* 〚RADIO- + (O)PAQUE〛 not allowing the passage of X-rays, etc.

radio telescope a radio antenna for receiving and measuring radio waves from stars, spacecraft, etc.

ra′di·o·ther′a·py *n.* the treatment of disease by the use of X-rays or rays from a radioactive substance

rad·ish (rad′ish) *n.* 〚< L *radix*, root〛 **1** an annual plant with an edible root **2** the pungent root, eaten raw

ra·dium (rā′dē əm) *n.* 〚< L *radius*, ray〛 a radioactive metallic chemical element, found in some uranium, which undergoes spontaneous atomic disintegration

ra·di·us (rā′dē əs) *n., pl.* **-di·i** (-ī′) or **-uses** 〚L, ray〛 **1** any straight line from the center to the periphery of a circle or sphere **2** the circular area limited by the sweep of such a line *[within a radius of two miles]*

ra·don (rā′dän) *n.* 〚< RADIUM〛 a radioactive, gaseous chemical element formed in the atomic disintegration of radium

RAF Royal Air Force

raf·fi·a (raf′ē ə) *n.* 〚< native name〛 **1** a palm tree of Madagascar with large leaves **2** fiber from its leaves, used as string or for weaving

raff·ish (raf′ish) *adj.* 〚(RIFF)RAFF + -ISH〛 **1** rakish **2** vulgar; low

raf·fle (raf′ʼl) *n.* 〚ME *rafle*〛 a lottery in which each participant buys a chance to win a prize — *vt.* **-fled, -fling** to offer as a prize in a raffle: often with *off*

raft¹ (raft) *n.* 〚< ON *raptr*, a log〛 **1** a flat, buoyant structure of logs, etc. fastened together **2** a flat-bottomed, inflatable boat

raft² (raft) *n.* 〚< Brit dial. *raff*, rubbish〛 [Colloq.] a large quantity

raf·ter (raf′tər) *n.* 〚OE *ræfter*〛 any of the beams that slope from the ridge of a roof to the eaves

rag¹ (rag) *n.* 〚< ON *rögg*, tuft of hair〛 **1** a waste piece of cloth, esp. one old or torn **2** a small piece of cloth for dusting, etc. **3** *[pl.]* old, worn clothes

rag² (rag) *vt.* **ragged, rag′ging** 〚< ?〛 [Slang] to tease or scold

rag³ (rag) *n.* a tune in ragtime

raga (rä′gə) *n.* 〚Sans *rāga*, color〛 any of various melody patterns improvised on by Hindu musicians

raga·muf·fin (rag′ə muf′in) *n.* 〚ME *Ragamoffyn*, name of a demon〛 a dirty, ragged person, esp. a poor child

rag′bag′ *n.* **1** a bag for rags **2** a collection of odds and ends

rage (rāj) *n.* 〚< LL *rabia*, madness〛 **1** a furious, uncontrolled anger **2** a great force, violence, etc. — *vi.* **raged, rag′ing 1** to show violent anger in action or speech **2** to be forceful, violent, etc. **3** to spread unchecked, as a disease —**(all) the rage** a fad

rag·ged (rag′id) *adj.* **1** shabby or torn from wear **2** wearing shabby or torn clothes **3** uneven; imperfect **4** shaggy

THESAURUS

radiate *v.* **1** [To send forth from a center] shed, diffuse, spread, disperse, shoot in all directions, irradiate, emit in straight lines, transmit, disseminate, broadcast, dispel, strew, sprinkle, circulate, send out in rays from a point, throw out. **2** [To shed light or heat] beam, light up, illumine, heat, warm, circulate, expand, widen, brighten, illuminate, irradiate, glitter, glisten, glow, glare, gleam, glimmer, flare, blaze, flicker, sparkle, flash, shimmer, reflect.

radiation *n.* **1** [Dissemination] propagation, dissipation, polarization, scattering, spread, diffraction, transmission, broadcast, emission, diffusion, dispersion, circulation, divergence, dispersal; see also DISTRIBUTION, EXTENT. **2** [Fallout] nuclear particles, radioactivity, radiant energy; see ENERGY 2.

radical *a.* **1** [Fundamental] original, primitive, native; see FUNDAMENTAL, ORGANIC. **2** [Advocating violent change] extreme, thorough, complete, insurgent, revolutionary, iconoclastic, advanced, forward, progressive, abolitionist, militant, extremist, recalcitrant, mutinous, seditious, riotous, lawless, racist, insubordinate, anarchistic, unruly, nihilistic, communistic, liberal, leftist, immoderate, freethinking, ultra*, red*; see also REBELLIOUS.—*Ant.* CONSERVATIVE, reformist, gradualist. **3** [Believing in violent political and social change] leftist, communistic, heretical; see REVOLUTIONARY 1.

radical *n.* insurgent, objector, revolutionist, revolutionary, insurrectionist, leftist, Bolshevik, anarchist, socialist, communist, pacifist, nihilist, traitor, mutineer, firebrand, renegade, extremeist, crusader, individualist, fascist, Nazi, misfit, iconoclast, eccentric, freethinker, rightist, hippie, fanatic, demonstrator, peace marcher, rioter, fifth columnist, nonconformist, left-winger, right-winger, pinko*, red*.

radically *a.* **1** [Completely] wholly, thoroughly, entirely; see COMPLETELY. **2** [Originally] basically, primitively, firstly; see ESSENTIALLY, FORMERLY.

radio *n.* **1** [The study and practice of wireless communication] radio transmission, radio reception, signaling; see BROADCASTING, COMMUNICATION. **2** [A receiving device] wireless, ship's radio, radio set, home radio, transistor radio, transistor, portable radio, pocket radio, auto radio, walkie-talkie, squawk box*; see also ELECTRONICS.

radioactive *a.* active, energetic, dangerous, hot*; see also POISONOUS.

radioactivity *n.* radiant energy, radioactive particles, Roentgen rays; see ENERGY 2.

radius *n.* space, sweep, range; see BOUNDARY, EXPANSE.

raffle *n.* sweepstakes, pool, lottery; see GAMBLING.

raft¹ *n.* flatboat, barge, float, catamaran, life raft, swimming raft, rubber raft; see also BOAT.

rag¹ *n.* remnant, wiper, dishrag, discarded material, hand rag, tatter, shred; see also GOODS 1. —**chew the rag*** chat, converse, have a talk; see TALK 1.

rage *n.* **1** [A fit of anger] frenzy, tantrum, uproar, hysterics, explosion, storm, outburst, spasm, convulsion, eruption, furor, excitement, extreme agitation, madness, vehemence, fury, rampage, huff, wrath, raving, violent anger, ire, resentment, bitterness, gall, irritation, animosity, exasperation, passion, indignation, apoplexy, heat, temper, blowup*, fireworks*, hemorrhage*. **2** [The object of enthusiasm and imitation] style, mode, fashion, vogue, craze, mania, the last word, the latest; see also FAD.

rage *v.* **1** [To give vent to anger] rant, fume, rave, foam, splutter, yell, scream, roar, rail at, boil over, shake, quiver, seethe, shout, scold, go into a tantrum, have a fit, run amok, run riot, fly apart, flare up, carry on, show violent anger, bluster, storm, be furious, fret, lose one's temper, work oneself into a sweat*, go berserk, go into a tailspin, go up in the air*, blow one's top*, gnash one's teeth, raise Cain*, raise the devil, take on*, throw a fit*, fly off the handle*, explode, vent one's spleen, snap at, blow up*, blow a fuse*, go off at a tangent, cut loose*, have a hemorrhage*, make a fuss over*, kick up a row*, have a nervous breakdown, let off steam*, get oneself into a lather*, lose one's head*.—*Ant.* CRY, be calm, pout. **2** [To be out of control] explode, flare, roar; see BURN, RUN 1.

ragged *a.* tattered, in shreds, patched, badly worn, rough, worn *[ragged* hair] —**run ragged** to tire out; exhaust —**rag′ged·ness** *n.*

rag′ged·y (-i dē) *adj.* tattered

rag·lan (rag′lən) *n.* [after Lord *Raglan*, 19th-c. Brit general] a loose coat with sleeves that continue in one piece to the collar —*adj.* designating such a sleeve

ra·gout (ra gōō′) *n.* [< Fr *ragoûter*, revive the appetite of] a highly seasoned stew of meat and vegetables

rag′time′ *n.* [prob. < *ragged time*] 1 a type of American music (*c.* 1890-1920), with strong syncopation in even time 2 its rhythm

rag′weed′ *n.* [< its ragged-looking leaves] a weed whose pollen is a common cause of hay fever

rah (rä) *interj.* hurrah

raid (rād) *n.* [dial. var. of ROAD] 1 a sudden, hostile attack, esp. by troops or bandits 2 a sudden invasion of a place by police, for discovering violations of the law — *vt., vi.* to make a raid (on) —**raid′er** *n.*

rail[1] (rāl) *n.* [< L *regula*, a rule] 1 a bar of wood, metal, etc. placed between posts as a barrier or support 2 any of the parallel metal bars forming a track for a railroad, etc. 3 a railroad — *vt.* to supply with rails

rail[2] (rāl) *vi.* [< LL *ragere*, to bellow] to speak bitterly; complain violently

rail[3] (rāl) *n.* [< Fr *raaler*, to screech] a marsh bird with a harsh cry

rail′ing *n.* 1 materials for rails 2 a fence, etc. made of rails and posts

rail·ler·y (rāl′ər ē) *n., pl.* **-ies** [see RAIL[2]] light, good-natured ridicule

rail′road′ *n.* 1 a track of parallel steel rails for a train 2 a complete system of such tracks, trains, etc. — *vt.* 1 to transport by railroad 2 [Colloq.] to rush through quickly, so as to prevent careful consideration — *vi.* to work on a railroad —**rail′road′er** *n.* —**rail′road′ing** *n.*

rail′way′ *n.* 1 any track with rails for guiding wheels 2 RAILROAD

rai·ment (rā′mənt) *n.* [see ARRAY & -MENT] [Archaic] clothing; attire

rain (rān) *n.* [OE *regn*] 1 water falling in drops condensed from the atmosphere 2 the falling of such drops 3 a rapid falling of many small objects — *vi.* 1 to fall: said of rain 2 to fall like rain — *vt.* 1 to pour down (rain, etc.) 2 to give in large quantities —**rain out** to cause (an event) to be postponed because of rain —**rain′y, -i·er, -i·est,** *adj.*

rain′bow′ (-bō′) *n.* [OE *regnboga*] an arc containing the colors of the spectrum formed in the sky by the refraction, reflection, and dispersion of light in rain or fog

rain check the stub of a ticket to a ballgame, etc. allowing future admission if the event is rained out

rain′coat′ *n.* a water-repellent coat

rain′drop′ *n.* a single drop of rain

rain′fall′ *n.* 1 a falling of rain 2 the amount of water falling over a given area during a given time

rain forest a dense, evergreen forest in a rainy tropical region

rain′storm′ *n.* a storm with a heavy rain

rain′wa′ter *n.* water that is falling or has fallen as rain

raise (rāz) *vt.* **raised, rais′ing** [< ON *reisa*] 1 to cause to rise; lift 2 to construct; build 3 to increase in size, intensity, amount, degree, etc. *[raise* prices, *raise* one's voice]* 4 to provoke; inspire 5 to present for consideration *[raise* a question] 6 to collect (an army, money, etc.) 7 to end *[raise* a siege] 8 *a)* to cause to grow *b)* to rear (children) — *n.* 1 a raising 2 an increase in salary or in a bet —**raise Cain** (or **hell,** etc.) [Slang] to create a disturbance

rai·sin (rā′zən) *n.* [< L *racemus*, cluster of grapes] a dried sweet grape

rai·son d′être (rā′zōn det′, det′rə) [Fr] reason for being

ra·jah or **raja** (rä′jə) *n.* [< Sans *rāj*, to rule] a prince in India

rake[1] (rāk) *n.* [OE *raca*] a long-handled tool with teeth at one end, for gathering loose hay, leaves, etc. — *vt.* **raked, rak′ing** 1 to gather or smooth with a rake 2 to search through minutely 3 to direct gunfire along (a line of troops, etc.) —**rake in** to gather a great amount of rapidly —**rake up** to uncover facts or gossip about (the past, a scandal, etc.)

rake[2] (rāk) *n.* [contr. of *rakehell*] a dissolute, debauched man

rake[3] (rāk) *vi., vt.* **raked, rak′ing** [< ?] to slant — *n.* a slanting

rake′-off′ *n.* [Slang] a commission or rebate, esp. when illegitimate

rak·ish (rāk′ish) *adj.* [< RAKE[3] + -ISH] 1 having a trim appearance suggesting speed: said of a ship 2 dashing; jaunty —**rak′ishly** *adv.* —**rak′ish·ness** *n.*

rally[1] (ral′ē) *vt., vi.* **-lied, -ly·ing** [< OFr *re-,* again + *alier,* join] 1 to bring back together in, or come back to, a state of order, as troops 2 to bring or come together for a common purpose 3 to recover; revive — *n., pl.* **-lies** 1 a rallying or being rallied; esp., a gathering of people for some purpose 2 an organized automobile run designed to test driving skills

rally[2] (ral′ē) *vt., vi.* **-lied, -ly·ing** [see RAIL[2]] to tease or ridicule

ram (ram) *n.* [OE *ramm*] 1 a male sheep 2 BATTERING RAM — *vt.* **rammed, ram′ming** 1 to strike against with great force 2 to force into place; press down

---

THESAURUS

out, broken, worn to rags, frayed, frazzled, threadbare, shoddy, out at the seams, shredded, battered, the worse for wear, worn to a thread, down at the heel, moth-eaten, full of holes, torn, badly dressed; see also SHABBY, WORN 2.—*Ant.* WHOLE, new, unworn.

raging *a.* furious, irate, enraged; see ANGRY.

raid *n.* 1 [A predatory attack] invasion, assault, forced entrance; see ATTACK. 2 [An armed investigation] seizure, surprise entrance, police raid, roundup, bust*; see also ARREST, CAPTURE.

raid *v.* assail, storm, plunder; see ATTACK.

raider *n.* bandit, thief, plunderer; see CRIMINAL, PIRATE, ROBBER.

rail[1] *n.* 1 [A polelike structure] post, railing, barrier, picket, rail fence, siding, banister, paling, rest, hand rail, guard rail, brass rail; see also BAR 1, FENCE. 2 [A track: *often plural*] railway, monorail, railroad track; see RAILROAD.

railroad *n.* track, line, railway, trains, rails, elevated, underground, subway, commuter line, sidetrack, siding, passing track, loading track, feeder line, main line, double track, single track, trunk line, transcontinental railroad; see also TRAIN.

railway *n.* track, line, route; see RAILROAD.

rain *n.* 1 [Water falling in drops] drizzle, mist, sprinkle, sprinkling, damp day, spring rain, rainfall, shower, precipitation, wet weather. 2 [A rainstorm] thunderstorm, tempest, cloudburst; see STORM.

rain *v.* pour, drizzle, drop, fall, shower, sprinkle, mist, mizzle, spit, lay the dust, patter, rain cats and dogs*, come down in bucketfuls; see also STORM.

raincoat *n.* oilskin, canvas coat, mackintosh; see COAT 1, CLOTHES.

rainy *a.* moist, coastal, drizzly; see STORMY, WET 2.

raise *n.* raising, salary increment, advance; see PROMOTION 1.

raise *v.* 1 [To lift] uplift, upraise, upheave, pull up, lift up, hold up, stand up, heave, set upright, put on its end, shove, boost, rear, mount, pry.—*Ant.* LOWER, bring down, take down. 2 [To nurture] bring up, rear, nurse, suckle, nourish, wean, breed, cultivate, train, foster; see also PROVIDE 1, SUPPORT 3. 3 [To collect or make available] gather, borrow, have ready; see ACCUMULATE, APPROPRIATE 2. 4 [To erect] construct, establish, put up; see BUILD. 5 [To ask] bring up, suggest, put; see ASK, PROPOSE 1. 6 [To advance in rank] exalt, dignify, honor; see PROMOTE 2. —**raise hell*** carry on*, celebrate, carouse; see

DRINK 2.

raised *a.* 1 [Elevated] lifted, hoisted, built high, heightened, set high, in relief, erected, constructed, set up; see also BUILT.—*Ant.* REDUCED, lowered, taken down. 2 [Nurtured] reared, brought up, trained, prepared, educated, fostered, bred, nourished, nursed. 3 [Produced] harvested, cultivated, massproduced; see MADE.

rake[1] *v.* 1 [To use a rake] clear up, collect, scratch, gather, scrape, clean up, weed, clear, grade, level. 2 [To sweep with gunfire] strafe, machine-gun, blister; see SHOOT 1.

rake[1,2] *n.* 1 [A debauched person] lecher, libertine, profligate; see DRUNKARD, RASCAL. 2 [A pronged implement] *Rakes include the following:* clam, lawn, garden, moss, hay, stubble, weeding, oyster, horse, revolving; leaf sweeper; see also TOOL 1.

rally[1] *n.* celebration, mass meeting, session; see GATHERING.

rally[1] *v.* unite against, renew, redouble; see RETURN 1, REVENGE.

ram *n.* 1 [An object used to deliver a thrust] plunger, pump, beam, prow, hammerhead, weight, pole, shaft, lever, spike, battering-ram, pile driver, tamping iron, punch, sledge hammer, rammer, tamper, monkey, bat, maul, hydraulic ram, spar, pis-

RAM (ram) *n.* a computer memory that allows data to be directly accessible Also **random-access memory**

-rama (ram′ə) *combining form* -ORAMA [*autorama*]

ram·ble (ram′bəl) *vi.* **-bled, -bling** [< ME *romen*] 1 to roam about; esp., to stroll about idly 2 to talk or write aimlessly 3 to spread in all directions, as a vine — *n.* a stroll

ram′bler *n.* a person or thing that rambles; esp., a climbing rose

ram·bunc·tious (ram buŋk′shəs) *adj.* [alt., after RAM < earlier *rambustious*] disorderly, boisterous, unruly, etc. — **ram·bunc′tious·ness** *n.*

ram·ekin or **ram·equin** (ram′ə kin) *n.* [< Fr < MDu] a small, individual baking dish

rami·fy (ram′ə fī′) *vt., vi.* **-fied′, -fy′ing** [< L *ramus*, a branch + *facere*, make] to divide or spread out into branches or branchlike divisions —**ram′i·fi·ca′tion** *n.*

ramp (ramp) *n.* [< OFr *ramper*, climb] 1 a sloping surface, walk, etc. joining different levels 2 a means for boarding a plane, as a movable staircase 3 a sloping runway, as for launching boats

ram·page (ram pāj′; *also, and for n.,* ram′pāj) *vi.* **-paged′, -pag′ing** to rush about wildly; rage — *n.* an outbreak of violent, raging behavior: chiefly in **on the** (or **a**) **rampage**

ramp·ant (ram′pənt) *adj.* [< OFr *ramper*, climb] growing unchecked; widespread

ram·part (ram′pärt′, -pərt) *n.* [< Fr *re-*, again + *emparer*, fortify] an embankment of earth surmounted by a parapet for defending a fort, etc.

ram′rod′ *n.* a rod for ramming down the charge in a muzzle-loading gun

ram·shackle (ram′shak′əl) *adj.* [< RANSACK] loose and rickety; likely to fall to pieces

ran (ran) *vt., pt. of* RUN

ranch (ranch) *n.* [< Sp *rancho*, small farm] 1 a large farm, esp. in the W U.S., for raising cattle, horses, or sheep 2 a style of house with all the rooms on one floor: in full **ranch house** — *vi.* to work on or manage a ranch — **ranch′er** *n.*

ran·cid (ran′sid) *adj.* [< L *rancere*, to be rank] having the bad smell or taste of stale fats or oils; spoiled

ran·cor (raŋ′kər) *n.* [< L *rancere*, to be rank] a continuing and bitter hate or ill will Brit. sp. **ran′cour** —**ran′cor·ous** *adj.* —**ran′cor·ously** *adv.*

R & B or **r & b** rhythm and blues

R & D research and development

ran·dom (ran′dəm) *adj.* [< OFr *randir*, run violently] purposeless; haphazard —**at random** haphazardly —**ran′domly** *adv.*

ran′dom·ize (-īz′) *vt.* **-ized′, -iz′ing** to select or choose (items of a group) in a random order

randy (ran′dē) *adj.* **-dier, -di·est** [Chiefly Scot.] amorous; lustful

rang (raŋ) *vi., vt. pt. of* RING[1]

range (rānj) *vt.* **ranged, rang′ing** [< OFr *renc*, a ring] 1 to arrange in order; set in a row or rows 2 to place with others in a cause, etc. — *vi.* 1 to extend in a given direction 2 to roam 3 to vary between stated limits — *n.* 1 a row, line, or series 2 a series of connected mountains 3 the distance that a weapon can fire its projectile 4 *a*) a place for shooting practice *b*) a place for testing rockets in flight 5 extent; scope 6 a large, open area for grazing livestock 7 the limits of possible variations of amount, degree, pitch, etc. [a wide *range* in price] 8 a cooking stove

rang′er *n.* 1 *a*) a mounted trooper who patrols a region *b*) [often R-] a soldier trained for raiding and close combat 2 a warden who patrols forests

rangy (rān′jē) *adj.* **-i·er, -i·est** long-limbed and slender — **rang′i·ness** *n.*

rank[1] (raŋk) *n.* [< OFr *ranc*] 1 a row, line, or series 2 a social class 3 high position in society 4 an official grade [the *rank* of major] 5 a relative position in a scale [a poet of the first *rank*] 6 *a*) a row of soldiers, etc. placed side by side *b*) [pl.] the army; esp., enlisted soldiers — *vt.* 1 to place in a rank 2 to assign a position to 3 to outrank — *vi.* to hold a certain position —**rank and file** 1 enlisted soldiers 2 the common people, as distinguished from leaders

rank[2] (raŋk) *adj.* [OE *ranc*, strong] 1 growing vigorously and coarsely [*rank* grass] 2 strong and offensive in smell or taste 3 in bad taste 4 complete; utter [*rank* deceit] — **rank′ness** *n.*

rank′ing *adj.* 1 of the highest rank 2 prominent or outstanding

ran·kle (raŋ′kəl) *vi., vt.* **-kled, -kling** [< L dim. of *draco*, dragon] 1 orig., to fester 2 to cause or cause to have long-lasting anger, rancor, etc.

THESAURUS

ton, drop weight, bow; see also BAR 1, HAMMER. 2 [A male sheep] buck, bucksheep, bighorn; see ANIMAL.

ram *v.* 1 [To strike head-on] bump, collide, hook; see BUTT, HIT 1. 2 [To pack forcibly] cram, jam, stuff; see PACK 2.

ramble *v.* 1 [To saunter] stroll, promenade, roam; see WALK 1. 2 [To speak or write aimlessly] drift, stray, diverge, meander, gossip, talk nonsense, chatter, babble, digress, maunder, get off the subject, go on and on, expatiate, protract, enlarge, be diffuse, dwell on, amplify, go astray, drivel, rant and rave, talk off the top of one's head, go off on a tangent, beat around the bush.

rambling *a.* 1 [Strolling] hiking, roaming, roving; see WALKING, WANDERING 1. 2 [Incoherent] discursive, disconnected, confused; see INCOHERENT. 3 [Covering considerable territory without much plan] spread out, strewn, straggling, trailing, random, here and there, at length, widely thrown, unplanned, sprawling, gangling; see also SCATTERED.—*Ant.* PLANNED, closely formed, compact.

ramp *n.* incline, slope, grade; see HILL, INCLINATION 2.

rampant *a.* raging, uncontrolled, growing without check, violent, vehement, impetuous, rank, turbulent, wild, luxuriant, tumultuous, profuse, plentiful, unruly, wanton, rife, prevalent, dominant, predominant, excessive, impulsive, impassioned, intolerant, unrestrained, extravagant, overabundant, sweeping the country, like wildfire*.—*Ant.* MODEST, mild, meek.

ranch *n.* plantation, grange, farmstead, ranchland, ranch house, ranch building, Western cattle farm, cattle spread; see also FARM, PROPERTY 2.

rancher *n.* ranch owner, ranchman, stockman, breeder, cattle farmer, cowherder, shepherd, drover, stock breeder, horse trainer, herdsman, herder, ranchero, broncobuster*, granger, cattleman, cowboy, cowpoke*, ranch hand, cattle baron; see also FARMER.

rancid *a.* tainted, stale, bad; see ROTTEN 1.

random *a.* haphazard, chance, purposeless, thoughtless, careless, blind, casual, fickle, eccentric, unpredictable, accidental; see also AIMLESS, IRREGULAR 1. —**at random** haphazardly, by chance, aimlessly; see ACCIDENTALLY.

range *n.* 1 [Distance] reach, span, horizontal projection; see EXPANSE. 2 [Extent] length, area, expanse; see EXTENT. 3 [A series of mountains] highlands, alps, sierras; see MOUNTAIN 1. 4 [Land open to grazing] pasture, grazing land, field; see COUNTRY 1. 5 [A kitchen stove] gas range, electric range, portable range; see APPLIANCE, STOVE.

range *v.* 1 [To vary] differ, fluctuate, diverge from; see VARY. 2 [To traverse wide areas] encompass, reach, pass over, cover, stray, stroll, wander, ramble, explore, scour, search, traverse, roam, rove; see also CROSS 1, TRAVEL. 3 [To place in order] line up, classify, arrange; see ORDER 3.

rank[1] *n.* 1 [A row] column, file, string; see LINE 1. 2 [Degree] senior-

ity, standing, station; see DEGREE 2. 3 [Social eminence] station, position, distinction, note, nobility, caste, privilege, standing, reputation, quality, situation, esteem, condition, state, place in society, status, circumstance, footing, grade, blood, family, pedigree, ancestry, stock, parentage, birth. —**pull (one's) rank on** take advantage of, exploit, abuse subordinates; see GOVERN, HUMILIATE.

rank[1] *v.* 1 [To arrange in a row or rows] put in line, line up, place in formation; see ORDER 3. 2 [To evaluate comparatively] place, put, regard, judge, assign, give precedence to, fix, establish, settle, estimate, value, valuate, include, list, rate; see also CLASSIFY. 3 [To possess relative evaluation] be worth, stand, be at the head, have a place, go ahead of, come first, forerun, antecede, have supremacy over, have the advantage of, precede, outrank, take the lead, take precedence over, belong, count among, be classed, stand in relationship.

rank[2] *a.* 1 [Having luxurious growth] wild, dense, lush; see GREEN 2, THICK 1. 2 [Having a foul odor] smelly, fetid, putrid, stinking, rancid, disagreeable, smelling, offensive, sour, foul, noxious, stale, tainted, gamy, musty, strong, rotten, moldy, turned, high, ill-smelling, nauseating, obnoxious, disgusting, reeking, malodorous, nasty, strong-smelling.— *Ant.* SWEET, fragrant, fresh.

ranked *a.* ordered, piled, neatly stacked; see ORGANIZED.

ran·sack (ran′sak′) *vt.* ⟦< ON *rann*, house + *sœkja*, seek⟧ 1 to search thoroughly 2 to plunder; pillage

ran·som (ran′səm) *n.* ⟦see REDEEM⟧ 1 the redeeming of a captive by paying money or complying with demands 2 the price thus paid or demanded — *vt.* to obtain the release of (a captive, etc.) by paying the demanded price

rant (rant) *vi.*, *vt.* ⟦< obs. Du *ranten*⟧ to talk or say in a loud, wild, extravagant way — *n.* loud, wild speech

rap (rap) *vt.* **rapped, rap′ping** ⟦prob. echoic⟧ 1 to strike quickly and sharply; tap 2 [Slang] to criticize sharply — *vi.* 1 to knock sharply 2 [Slang] to talk — *n.* 1 a quick, sharp knock 2 [Slang] blame or punishment 3 [Slang] a chat or serious discussion 4 a kind of popular music in which rhymed verses are chanted or declaimed over repetitive rhythms

ra·pa·cious (rə pā′shəs) *adj.* ⟦< L *rapere*, seize⟧ 1 greedy; voracious 2 predatory —**ra·pac′i·ty** (-pas′ə tē) *n.*

rape¹ (rāp) *n.* ⟦prob. < L *rapere*, seize⟧ 1 the crime of having sexual intercourse with a person forcibly and without consent 2 the plundering (of a city, etc.), as in warfare — *vt.* **raped, rap′ing** 1 to commit rape on; violate 2 to plunder or destroy — *vi.* to commit rape —**rap′ist** *n.*

rape² (rāp) *n.* ⟦< L *rapa*, turnip⟧ an annual plant whose leaves are used for fodder

rapid (rap′id) *adj.* ⟦< L *rapere*, to rush⟧ moving or occurring with speed; swift; quick — *n.* [usually pl.] a part of a river where the current is swift —**ra·pid·i·ty** (rə pid′ə tē) *n.* —**rap′id·ly** *adv.*

rapid transit a system of public transportation in an urban area, using electric trains along an unimpeded right of way

ra·pier (rā′pē ər) *n.* ⟦Fr *rapière*⟧ a light, sharp-pointed sword used only for thrusting

rap·ine (rap′in) *n.* ⟦< L *rapere*, seize⟧ plunder; pillage

rap·port (ra pôr′) *n.* ⟦Fr⟧ close relationship; harmony

rap·proche·ment (ra′prəsh män′) *n.* ⟦Fr⟧ an establishing of friendly relations

rap·scal·lion (rap skal′yən) *n.* ⟦< RASCAL⟧ a rascal; rogue

rap sheet [Slang] one's police record of arrests and convictions

rapt (rapt) *adj.* ⟦< L *rapere*, seize⟧ 1 carried away with joy, love, etc. 2 completely engrossed (in study, etc.)

rap·ture (rap′chər) *n.* the state of being carried away with joy, love, etc.; ecstasy —**rap′tur·ous** *adj.*

rara avis (rer′ə ā′vis) *pl.* **ra·rae aves** (rer′ē ā′vēz) ⟦L, lit., strange bird⟧ an extraordinary person or thing

rare¹ (rer) *adj.* **rar′er, rar′est** ⟦< L *rarus*⟧ 1 not frequently encountered; scarce; unusual 2 unusually good; excellent 3 not dense [rare atmosphere] —**rare′ness** *n.*

rare² (rer) *adj.* **rar′er, rar′est** ⟦OE *hrere*⟧ not completely cooked: said esp. of meat —**rare′ness** *n.*

rare³ (rer) *vi.* **rared, rar′ing** [Colloq.] to be eager: used in prp. [raring to go]

rare·bit (rer′bit) *n.* WELSH RABBIT

rar·efy (rer′ə fī′) *vt.*, *vi.* **-fied′, -fy′ing** ⟦< L *rarus*, RARE¹ + *facere*, to make⟧ to make or become less dense —**rar′efac′tion** (-fak′shən) *n.*

rarely (rer′lē) *adv.* 1 infrequently 2 uncommonly

rar·i·ty (rer′ə tē) *n.* 1 a being rare; specif., *a)* scarcity *b)* lack of density 2 *pl.* **-ties** something remarkable or valuable because rare

ras·cal (ras′kəl) *n.* ⟦< OFr *rascaille*, rabble⟧ 1 a rogue 2 a mischievous child —**ras·cal′i·ty** (-kal′ə tē) *n.* —**ras′cal·ly** *adj.*, *adv.*

rash¹ (rash) *adj.* ⟦ME *rasch*⟧ too hasty in acting or speaking; reckless —**rash′ly** *adv.* —**rash′ness** *n.*

rash² (rash) *n.* ⟦< OFr *rascaille*, rabble⟧ 1 an eruption of spots on the skin 2 a sudden appearance of a large number

rash′er *n.* ⟦< L *radere*, to scrape⟧ a thin slice of bacon, etc., or a serving of several such slices

rasp (rasp) *vt.* ⟦< OHG *raspon*, to scrape together⟧ 1 to scrape as with a file 2 to grate upon; irritate — *vi.* 1 to grate 2 to make a rough, grating sound — *n.* 1 a type of rough file 2 a rough, grating sound —**rasp′y, -i·er, -i·est,** *adj.*

rasp·ber·ry (raz′ber′ē, -bər-) *n.*, *pl.* **-ries** ⟦< earlier *raspis*⟧ 1 a small, juicy, edible, reddish fruit related to the rose 2 a plant bearing this fruit 3 [Slang] a sound of derision

rat (rat) *n.* ⟦OE *ræt*⟧ 1 a long-tailed rodent, resembling, but larger than, the mouse 2 [Slang] a sneaky, contempt-

---

THESAURUS

ransack *v.* 1 [To search thoroughly] rummage, explore, turn upside down, look all over for, look high and low for, leave no stone unturned, scour, seek everywhere, sound, spy, peer, look around, pry, scan, probe, look into, investigate, scrutinize; see also SEARCH. 2 [To loot] pillage, plunder, ravish, rape, strip, rifle, forage, maraud, make off with, take away, seize, appropriate, spoil, poach, gut, rustle, lift*, thieve, ravage, pilfer, bag*, rob, steal, filch, pinch*.

ransom *n.* redemption money, compensation, expiation; see BRIBE.

ransom *v.* release, rescue, deliver; see FREE.

rant *v.* rave, fume, rail; see RAGE 1, YELL.

rap *n.* knock, thump, slap; see BLOW. —**beat the rap*** avoid punishment, evade, be acquitted; see ESCAPE. —**bum rap*** unfair sentence, blame, frame*; see PUNISHMENT. —**take the rap*** be punished, suffer, take the blame; see PAY FOR.

rap *v.* 1 [To tap sharply] knock, strike, whack; see BEAT 1, HIT 1. 2 [*To talk, often compulsively] chatter, jabber, discuss; see BABBLE, TALK 1.

rape¹ *n.* seduction, violation, deflowering, criminal attack, assault, abduction, statutory offense, defilement, abuse, molestation, maltreatment, forcible violation of a woman; see also CRIME.

rape¹ *v.* violate, seize, compromise, force a woman, molest, ravish, attack, assault, defile, wrong, debauch, ruin, corrupt, seduce, maltreat, abuse.

rapid *a.* speedy, accelerated, hurried; see FAST 1.

rapidly *a.* fast, swiftly, posthaste; see

IMMEDIATELY, QUICKLY.

rapist *n.* raper, ravager, ravisher; see RASCAL.

rapt *a.* transported, entranced, enchanted; see HAPPY.

rapture *n.* pleasure, cheer, satisfaction; see HAPPINESS.

rare¹,² *a.* 1 [Uncommon] exceptional, singular, extraordinary; see UNUSUAL 1, 2. 2 [Scarce] sparse, few, scanty, meager, limited, short, expensive, precious, out of circulation, off the market, in great demand, occasional, uncommon, isolated, scattered, infrequent, deficient, almost unobtainable, few and far between; see also UNIQUE.—*Ant.* CHEAP, profuse, tawdry. 3 [Choice] select, matchless, superlative; see EXCELLENT. 4 [Lightly cooked] not cooked, not done, seared, braised, not overdone, nearly raw, underdone, red, moderately done, not thoroughly cooked; see also RAW 1.

rarely *a.* unusually, occasionally, once in a great while; see SELDOM.

rascal *n.* scoundrel, rogue, rake, knave, villain, robber, fraud, scamp, hypocrite, sneak, shyster*, cad, trickster, charlatan, swindler, grafter, cheat, black sheep, ruffian, tough, rowdy, bully, scalawag, mountebank, liar, blackguard, wretch, quack, fellow, tramp, beggar, bum*, idler, wastrel, prodigal, hooligan*, ne'er-do-well, reprobate, misdoer, felon, sinner, delinquent, recreant, malefactor, profligate, loafer, renegade, imposter, opportunist, vagrant, pretender, gambler, mischief-maker, sharper, faker, skunk*, bastard*, fink*, rat*, rotten egg*, con man*, con artist*, flimflammer*, dirty dog*, good-for-nothing, worm, two-timer*, stool pigeon*, case*, double-dealer*,

phony*, four-flusher*, slicker*; see also CRIMINAL.—*Ant.* HERO, GENTLEMAN, philanthropist.

rash¹ *a.* impetuous, impulsive, foolish, hotheaded, thoughtless, reckless, headstrong, bold, careless, determined, audacious, heedless, madcap, unthinking, headlong, incautious, wild, precipitant, overhasty, unwary, injudicious, venturous, foolhardy, imprudent, venturesome, adventurous, daring, jumping to conclusions, insuppressible, breakneck, irrational, fiery, furious, frenzied, passionate, immature, hurried, aimless, excited, feverish, tenacious, frantic, indiscreet, quixotic, ill-advised, unconsidered, without thinking, imprudent, unadvised, irresponsible, brash, precipitous, premature, sudden, harebrained, harumscarum, devil-may-care*, daredevil; see also RUDE 1.—*Ant.* CALM, cool, levelheaded.

rashly *a.* brashly, impulsively, unwisely, abruptly, foolishly, impetuously, incautiously, carelessly, precipitately, imprudently, recklessly, boldly, indiscreetly, inadvisedly, ill-advisedly, thoughtlessly, unthinkingly, furiously, hurriedly, heedlessly, boldly, unpreparedly, excitedly, overhastily, wildly, frantically, irrepressibly, without due consideration, without thinking, without forethought, in a hasty manner, passionately, fiercely, feverishly, headily; see also RUDELY.

rashness *n.* frenzy, recklessness, foolhardiness; see CARELESSNESS.

rasping *a.* hoarse, grating, grinding; see HARSH.

rat *n.* 1 [A rodent] mouse, muskrat, vermin; see PEST 1, RODENT. 2 [*A deserter] informer, turncoat, fink*; see DESERTER, TRAITOR.

ible person; esp., an informer — *vi.* **rat′ted, rat′ting** [Slang] to inform (*on*) —**smell a rat** to suspect a trick, plot, etc.

ratchet (rach′it) *n.* [< It *rocca,* distaff] **1** a toothed wheel (in full **ratchet wheel**) or bar whose sloping teeth catch a pawl, preventing backward motion **2** such a pawl

rate[1] (rāt) *n.* [< L *reri,* reckon] **1** the amount, degree, etc. of anything in relation to units of something else [*rate* of pay] **2** price, esp. per unit **3** [Now Rare] a class or rank [of the first *rate*] — *vt.* **rat′ed, rat′ing 1** to appraise **2** to consider; esteem **3** [Colloq.] to deserve — *vi.* to have value, status, etc. —**at any rate 1** in any event **2** anyway

rate[2] (rāt) *vt., vi.* [< L *reputare,* to count] to scold; chide

rather (rath′ər) *adv.* [OE *hræthe,* quickly] **1** more willingly; preferably **2** with more justice, reason, etc. [I, *rather* than you, should pay] **3** more accurately [my son, or *rather,* stepson] **4** on the contrary **5** somewhat [*rather* hungry] — *interj.* [Chiefly Brit.] certainly —**rather than** instead of

raths·kel·ler (rät′skel′ər, rath′-) *n.* [Ger < *rat,* council + *keller,* cellar] a restaurant, usually below the street level, where beer is served

rat·i·fy (rat′ə fī′) *vt.* **-fied′, -fy′ing** [< L *ratus,* reckoned + *facere,* make] to approve; esp., to give official sanction to —**rat·i·fi·ca′tion** *n.* —**rat′i·fi′er** *n.*

rat·ing (rāt′iŋ) *n.* **1** a rank or grade, as of military personnel **2** a placement in a certain rank or class **3** an evaluation; appraisal **4** *Film* a classification, based on content, restricting the age of those who may attend **5** *Radio, TV* the relative popularity of a program according to sample polls

ra·tio (rā′shō, -shē ō′) *n., pl.* **-tios** [L, a reckoning] a fixed relation in degree, number, etc. between two similar things; proportion

ra·ti·oc·i·nate (rash′ē äs′ə nāt′) *vi.* **-nat′ed, -nat′ing** [see prec.] to think or argue logically; reason —**ra·ti·oc·i′na′tion** *n.*

ra·tion (rash′ən, rā′shən) *n.* [see RATIO] **1** a fixed portion; share **2** a fixed allowance of food, as a daily allowance for a soldier **3** [pl.] food supply — *vt.* **1** to supply with rations **2** to distribute (food, clothing, etc.) in rations, as in times of scarcity

ra·tional (rash′ən əl) *adj.* [see RATIO] **1** of or based on reasoning **2** able to reason; reasoning **3** sensible or sane —**ra′tion·al′i·ty** (-ə nal′ə tē) *n.* —**ra′tion·al·ly** *adv.*

ra·tion·ale (rash′ə nal′) *n.* [< L *rationalis,* rational] **1** the reasons or rational basis for something **2** an explanation of principles

ra′tion·al·ism′ *n.* the practice of accepting reason as the only authority in determining one's opinions or course of action —**ra′tion·al·ist** *n., adj.* —**ra′tion·al·is′tic** *adj.*

ra·tion·al·ize′ *vt., vi.* **-ized′, -iz′ing 1** to make or be rational or reasonable **2** to devise plausible explanations for (one's acts, beliefs, etc.), usually in self-deception —**ra′tion·al·i·za′tion** *n.*

rat·line (rat′lin) *n.* [< ?] any of the horizontal ropes which join the shrouds of a ship and serve as a ladder Also **rat′lin**

rat race [Slang] a mad scramble or intense struggle, as in the business world

rat·tan (ra tan′) *n.* [Malay *rotan*] **1** a tall palm tree with long, slender, tough stems **2** its stem, used in making furniture, etc.

rat·tle (rat′'l) *vt.* **-tled, -tling** [prob. echoic] **1** to make a series of sharp, short sounds **2** to chatter: often with *on* — *vt.* **1** to cause to rattle **2** to confuse or upset — *n.* **1** a series of sharp, short sounds **2** a series of horny rings at the end of a rattlesnake's tail **3** a baby's toy, a percussion instrument, etc. made to rattle when shaken —**rat′tly** (-lē, -'l ē) *adj.*

rat′tle·brain′ *n.* a frivolous, talkative person —**rat′tle·brained′** *adj.*

rat′tler *n.* a rattlesnake

rat′tle·snake′ *n.* a poisonous American snake with horny rings at the end of the tail that rattle when shaken

rat′tle·trap′ *n.* a rickety old car

rat′tling *adj.* **1** that rattles **2** [Colloq.] very fast, good, etc. — *adv.* [Colloq.] very [a *rattling* good time]

rat′trap′ *n.* **1** a trap for rats **2** [Colloq.] a dirty, run-down building

ratty (rat′ē) *adj.* **-tier, -ti·est** [Slang] shabby or run-down

rau·cous (rô′kəs) *adj.* [L *raucus*] **1** hoarse **2** loud and rowdy —**rau′cous·ly** *adv.* —**rau′cous·ness** *n.*

raun·chy (rôn′chē, rän′-) *adj.* **-chier, -chi·est** [< ?] [Slang] **1** dirty, sloppy, etc. **2** risqué, lustful, etc. —**raun′chi·ness** *n.*

rav·age (rav′ij) *n.* [see RAVISH] destruction; ruin — *vt.* **-aged, -ag·ing** to destroy violently; devastate; ruin — *vi.* to commit ravages

rave (rāv) *vi.* **raved, rav′ing** [< OFr *raver,* roam] **1** to talk incoherently or wildly **2** to talk with great enthusiasm (*about*) — *n.* [Colloq.] a very enthusiastic commendation

ravel (rav′əl) *vt., vi.* **-eled** or **-elled, -el·ing** or **-el·ling** [MDu *ravelen*] to separate into its parts, esp. threads; untwist; fray — *n.* a raveled part in a fabric

ra·ven (rā′vən) *n.* [OE *hræfn*] the largest crow, with a straight, sharp beak — *adj.* black and lustrous

rav·en·ing (rav′ən in) *adj.* [ult. < L *rapere,* seize] greedily searching for prey [*ravening* wolves]

■ THESAURUS ■

rate[1] *n.* **1** [Ratio] proportion, degree, standard, scale, fixed amount, quota, relation, relationship, comparison, relative, weight, percentage, numerical progression; see also MEASURE 1, 2. **2** [Price] valuation, allowance, estimate; see PRICE. **3** [Speed] velocity, pace, time; see SPEED.

rate[1] *v.* **1** [To rank] judge, estimate, evaluate, grade, relate to a standard, fix, tag, calculate, assess, class, determine, appraise, guess at; see also MEASURE 1, PRICE, RANK 2. **2** [*To be well-thought-of] be a favorite, triumph, succeed; see SUCCEED 1.

rated *a.* ranked, classified, graded, classed, put, thought of, given a rating, weighted, measured; see also PLACED.

rather *a.* **1** [To some degree] fairly, somewhat, a little; see MODERATELY, REASONABLY 2. **2** [By preference] first, by choice, in preference, sooner, more readily, willingly, much sooner, just as soon, as a matter of choice; see also PREFERABLY.

rather *interj.* I should say, certainly, of course, by all means, most assuredly, no doubt about it, and how!*, you're telling me*.

ratification *n.* acceptance, confirmation, sanction; see PERMISSION.

ratify *v.* sanction, establish, substantiate; see APPROVE, ENDORSE 2.

rating *n.* grade, commission, number; see CLASS 1, DEGREE 2, RANK 2.

ratio *n.* proportion, quota, quotient; see DEGREE 1, RATE 1.

ration *n.* allotment, portion, quota; see DIVISION 2, SHARE.

ration *v.* proportion, allot, apportion; see DISTRIBUTE.

rational *a.* **1** [Acting in accordance with reason] stable, calm, cool, deliberate, discerning, discriminating, levelheaded, collected, logical, thoughtful, knowing, sensible, of sound judgment, having good sense, impartial, exercising reason, intelligent, wise, reasoning, prudent, circumspect, intellectual, reflective, philosophic, objective, far-sighted, enlightened, well-advised, judicious, analytical, deductive, synthetic, conscious, balanced, sober, systematic; see also REASONABLE 1.—*Ant.* RASH, reckless, wild. **2** [Of a nature that appeals to reason] intelligent, sensible, wise; see REASONABLE 1. **3** [Sane] normal, lucid, responsible; see SANE 1.

rationalize *v.* explain away, vindicate, reconcile; see EXPLAIN.

rationally *a.* sensibly, normally, intelligently; see REASONABLY 1.

rattle *n.* clatter, noise, racket; see NOISE 1.

rattle *v.* **1** [To make a rattling sound] drum, clack, knock; see SOUND. **2** [To talk with little meaning] chatter, gush, prattle; see BABBLE. **3** [To disconcert] bother, put out, unnerve; see CONFUSE, DISTURB, EMBARRASS.

raucous *a.* hoarse, loud, gruff; see HARSH.

raunchy* *a.* indelicate, sexy*, suggestive; see LEWD 2.

ravage *v.* pillage, overrun, devastate, destroy, crush, desolate, despoil, overspread, wreck, waste, disrupt, disorganize, demolish, annihilate, overthrow, overwhelm, break up, pull down, smash, shatter, scatter, batter down, exterminate, extinguish, trample down, dismantle, stamp out, lay waste, lay in ruins, sweep away, raze, ruin, plunder, strip, impair, sack, consume, spoil, harry, ransack, maraud, prey, crush, rape, rob, raid, pirate, seize, capture, gut, loot; see also DAMAGE.—*Ant.* BUILD, improve, rehabilitate.

rave *v.* **1** [To babble] gabble, jabber, rattle on; see BABBLE. **2** [To rage] storm, splutter, rail; see RAGE 1.

ravel *v.* untwist, come apart, wind out, untangle, disentangle, unsnarl, unbraid, untwine, unweave, unravel, make plain; see also FREE, LOOSEN 2.

rav·en·ous (rav′ə nəs) *adj.* [< L *rapere*, seize] 1 greedily hungry 2 rapacious —**rav′en·ous·ly** *adv.*

ra·vine (rə vēn′) *n.* [Fr, flood] a long, deep hollow in the earth, esp. one worn by a stream; gorge

rav′ing *adj.* 1 that raves; frenzied 2 [Colloq.] exciting enthusiastic admiration [a *raving* beauty] —*adv.* so as to cause raving [*raving* mad]

ra·vi·o·li (rav′ē ō′lē) *n.pl.* [It] [*usually with sing. v.*] small casings of pasta dough filled with ground meat, cheese, etc.

rav·ish (rav′ish) *vt.* [< L *rapere*, seize] 1 to seize and carry away forcibly 2 to rape (a woman) 3 to transport with joy or delight —**rav′isher** *n.* —**rav′ish·ment** *n.*

rav′ish·ing *adj.* causing great joy

raw (rô) *adj.* [OE *hreaw*] 1 not cooked 2 in its natural condition; not processed [*raw* silk] 3 inexperienced [a *raw* recruit] 4 abraded and sore 5 uncomfortably cold and damp [a *raw* wind] 6 brutal, coarse, indecent, etc. 7 [Colloq.] harsh or unfair [a *raw* deal] —**in the raw** 1 in the natural state 2 naked —**raw′ness** *n.*

raw′boned′ (-bōnd′) *adj.* lean; gaunt

raw′hide′ *n.* 1 an untanned cattle hide 2 a whip made of this

ray¹ (rā) *n.* [< L *radius*] 1 any of the thin lines, or beams, of light that appear to come from a bright source 2 any of several lines radiating from a center 3 a tiny amount [a *ray* of hope] 4 a beam of radiant energy, radioactive particles, etc.

ray² (rā) *n.* [< L *raia*] a cartilaginous fish with a broad flat body, widely expanded fins on both sides, and a whiplike tail

rayon (rā′än) *n.* [< RAY¹] 1 a textile fiber made from a cellulose solution 2 a fabric of such fibers

raze (rāz) *vt.* **razed**, **raz′ing** [< L *radere*, to scrape] to tear down completely; demolish

ra·zor (rā′zər) *n.* [see prec.] 1 a sharp-edged cutting instrument for shaving, etc. 2 SHAVER (sense 2)

razz (raz) *vt.* [< RASPBERRY] [Slang] to tease, ridicule, etc.

razzle-dazzle (raz′əl daz′əl) *n.* [Slang] a flashy, deceptive display

razz·ma·tazz (raz′mə taz′) *n.* [prob. < prec.] [Slang] 1 lively spirit 2 flashy display; showiness

rbi or **RBI** *Baseball* run(s) batted in

R.C.Ch. Roman Catholic Church

rd. 1 rod 2 round

RD or **R.D.** Rural Delivery

Rd. Road

RDA Recommended Daily (*or* Dietary) Allowance: the amount of vitamins, etc. suggested for various age groups

re¹ (rā) *n.* [It] *Music* the second tone of the diatonic scale

re² (rē, rā) *prep.* [L < *res*, thing] in the matter of; as regards

re- [< Fr or L] *prefix* 1 back 2 again; anew It is sometimes hyphenated, as before a word beginning with *e* or to distinguish such forms as *re-cover* (to cover again) and RECOVER The words in the following list can be understood if "again" or "anew" is added to the meaning of the base word:

reacquaint	reaffirm
reacquire	realign
readjust	reappear
readmit	reapply

reappoint	reinoculate
reappraise	reinsert
rearm	reinspect
reassemble	reinvest
reassert	reissue
reassess	rekindle
reassign	relearn
reawaken	reload
reborn	remake
rebroadcast	remarry
rebuild	rematch
recharge	rename
recheck	renegotiate
reclassify	renominate
recommence	renumber
reconquer	reoccupy
reconsign	reoccur
reconvene	reopen
reconvert	reorder
recopy	repack
re-cover	repackage
redecorate	repaint
rededicate	repave
redesign	rephrase
redetermine	replant
redirect	replay
rediscover	re-press
redistribution	reprint
redivide	republish
redraw	reread
reedit	reroute
reeducate	reschedule
reelect	resell
reembark	reset
reembody	resettle
reemerge	reshuffle
reemphasize	respell
reenact	restate
reengage	restring
reenlist	restudy
reenter	restyle
reestablish	resubscribe
reevaluate	resupply
reexamine	retell
reexplain	retest
refashion	rethink
refasten	retrain
refinance	retrial
reformulate	reunite
refuel	reupholster
refurnish	reuse
rehear	revisit
reheat	revitalize
rehire	reweigh
reimpose	rework
reinfect	rezone

reach (rēch) *vt.* [OE *ræcan*] 1 to thrust out (the hand, etc.) 2 to extend to by thrusting out, etc. 3 to obtain and hand over [*reach* the salt] 4 to go as far as; attain 5 to influence; affect 6 to get in touch with, as by telephone —*vi.* 1 to thrust out the hand, etc. 2 to extend in influence, space, etc. 3 to carry, as sight, sound, etc. 4 to try to get something —*n.* 1 a stretching or thrusting out 2 the power of, or the extent covered in, stretching, obtaining, etc. 3 a continuous extent, esp. of water

re·act (rē akt′) *vi.* 1 to act in return or reciprocally 2 to act in a reverse way; go back to a former condition, stage, etc. 3 to respond to a stimulus 4 *Chem.* to act with another substance in producing a chemical change

re·act·ant (rē ak′tənt) *n.* any substance involved in a chemical reaction

---

THESAURUS

ravenous *a.* voracious, omnivorous, starved; see HUNGRY.

ravine *n.* gully, gorge, canyon, gulch, arroyo, valley, gap, chasm, abyss, break, crevice, crevasse, coulee.

raving *a.* violent, shouting, fuming; see INSANE.

raw *a.* 1 [Uncooked] fresh, rare, hard, unprepared, undercooked, fibrous, coarse-grained, unpasteurized, unbaked, unfried; see also RARE 4.—*Ant.* BAKED, cooked, fried. 2 [Unfinished] natural, untreated, crude, rough, newly cut, unprocessed, unrefined, untanned, coarse, newly mined, uncut, virgin; see also UNFINISHED 2.—*Ant.* REFINED, manufactured, processed. 3 [Untrained] immature, new, fresh; see INEXPERIENCED. 4 [Cold] biting, windy, bleak; see COLD 1. 5 [Without skin] peeled, skinned, dressed, galled, scraped, blistered, cut, wounded, pared,

uncovered, chafed, bruised.—*Ant.* COVERED, coated, healed. 6 [*Nasty] low, dirty, unscrupulous; see MEAN 3, VULGAR. —**in the raw** nude, bare, unclothed; see NAKED 1.

ray¹ *n.* beam, flash, light, stream, gleam, blaze, sunbeam, wave, moonbeam, radiation, flicker, spark, emanation, radiance, streak, shaft, pencil, patch, blink, glimmer, glitter, glint, sparkle.

razor *n.* shaving instrument, cutting edge, blade; see KNIFE. *Razors include the following:* double-edged, single-edged, straight-back, safety, hollow-ground, electric; electric shaver.

reach *n.* compass, range, scope, grasp, stretch, extension, orbit, horizon, gamut; see also ABILITY.

reach *v.* 1 [To extend to] touch, span, encompass, pass along, continue to, roll on, stretch, go as far as, attain, equal, approach, lead, stand,

terminate, end, overtake, join, come up to, sweep; see also SPREAD 2. 2 [To extend a part of the body to] lunge, strain, move, reach out, feel for, come at, make contact with, shake hands, throw out a limb, make for, put out, touch, strike, seize, grasp; see also STRETCH 1. 3 [To arrive] get to, come to, enter; see ARRIVE.

reaching *a.* 1 [Extending to a point] going up to, ending at, stretching, encompassing, taking in, spanning, spreading to, embracing, joining, sweeping on to. 2 [Arriving] coming to, landing, touching down; see LANDING 1. 3 [Extending a part of the body] stretching, straining, lunging; see EXTENDING.

react *v.* 1 [To act in response] reciprocate, respond, act; see ANSWER 1. 2 [To feel in response] be affected, be impressed, be involved; see FEEL 2.

re·ac·tion (rē ak′shən) *n.* **1** a return or opposing action, etc. **2** a response, as to a stimulus or influence **3** a movement back to a former or less advanced condition **4** a chemical change

re·ac′tion·ar′y (-shə ner′ē) *adj.* of, characterized by, or advocating reaction, esp. in politics —*n.*, *pl.* **-ies** an advocate of reaction, esp. in politics

re·ac′ti·vate (rē ak′tə vāt′) *vt.*, *vi.* **-vat′ed**, **-vat′ing** to make or be made active again; specif., to return (a military unit, ship, etc.) to active status —**re·ac′ti·va′tion** *n.*

re·ac′tive (-tiv) *adj.* **1** tending to react **2** of, from, or showing reaction —**re·ac′tiv′i·ty** *n.*

re·ac′tor (-tər) *n.* NUCLEAR REACTOR

read[1] (rēd) *vt.* **read** (red), **read·ing** (rēd′iŋ) ⟦ < OE *rædan*, to counsel ⟧ **1** to get the meaning of (writing) by interpreting the characters **2** to utter aloud (written matter) **3** to understand or interpret **4** to foretell (the future) **5** to study *[to read law]* **6** to register, as a gauge **7** *Comput.* to access (data) from (a disk, tape, etc.) **8** [Slang] to hear and understand *[I read you]* — *vi.* **1** to read something written **2** to learn by reading: with *about* or *of* **3** to contain certain words —**read into** (or **in**) to attribute (a particular meaning to) —**read out of** to expel from (a group) —**read′abil′i·ty** *n.* —**read′able** *adj.* —**read′er** *n.*

read[2] (red) *vt.*, *vi.* *pt.* & *pp.* of READ[1] — *adj.* informed by reading *[well-read]*

read′er·ship′ *n.* the people who read a certain publication, author, etc.

read·ing (rēd′iŋ) *n.* **1** the act of one who reads **2** material to be read **3** the amount measured by a barometer, thermometer, etc. **4** a particular interpretation or performance

read′out′ *n.* **1** the retrieving of information from a computer **2** information from a computer, thermostat, etc. displayed visually or recorded, as on tape

ready (red′ē) *adj.* **-i·er**, **-i·est** ⟦ OE *ræde* ⟧ **1** prepared to act or be used immediately **2** willing **3** likely or liable; apt *[ready* to cry*]* **4** dexterous **5** prompt *[a ready reply]* **6** available at once *[ready cash]* — *vt.* **-ied**, **-y·ing** to make ready; prepare —**read′i·ly** *adv.* —**read′i·ness** *n.*

read′y-made′ *adj.* made so as to be ready for use or sale at once: also, as applied to clothing, **read′y-to-wear′**

re·agent (rē ā′jənt) *n. Chem.* a substance used to detect, measure, or react with another substance

real (rē′əl, rēl) *adj.* ⟦ < L *res*, thing ⟧ **1** existing as or in fact; actual; true **2** authentic; genuine **3** *Law* of or relating to immovable things *[real* property*]* — *adv.* [Colloq.] very —**for real** [Slang] real or really

real estate land, including the buildings or improvements on it

re·al·ism (rē′ə liz′əm) *n.* **1** a tendency to face facts and be practical **2** the picturing in art and literature of people and things as they really appear to be —**re′al·ist** *n.* —**re′al·is′tic** *adj.* —**re′al·is′ti·cal·ly** *adv.*

re·al·i·ty (rē al′ə tē) *n.*, *pl.* **-ties** **1** the quality or fact of being real **2** a person or thing that is real; fact —**in real·ity** in fact; actually

re·al·ize (rē′ə līz′) *vt.* **-ized′**, **-iz′ing** **1** to make real **2** to understand fully **3** to convert (assets, rights, etc.) into money **4** to gain; obtain *[realize a profit]* **5** to be sold for (a specified sum) —**re′al·i·za′tion** *n.*

re′al-life′ *adj.* actual; not imaginary

re′al·ly *adv.* **1** in reality **2** truly — *interj.* indeed

---

THESAURUS

reaction *n.* reply, rejoinder, reception, receptivity, response, return, feeling, opinion, reflection, backlash, attitude, retort, reciprocation, repercussion, reflex; see also ANSWER 1, OPINION 1. *Reactions to stimuli include the following:* contraction, expansion, jerk, knee jerk, cognition, shock, relapse, exhaustion, stupor, anger, disgust, revulsion, fear, illness, joy, laughter, wonder.

reactionary *a.* rigid, retrogressive, regressive; see CONSERVATIVE.

reactionary *n.* die-hard, reactionist, conservative; see RADICAL.

read[1] *a.* examined, gone over, scanned; see UNDERSTOOD 1.

read[1] *v.* **1** [To understand by reading] comprehend, go through, peruse, scan, glance over, go over, gather, see, know, skim, perceive, apprehend, grasp, learn, flip through the pages, dip into, scratch the surface, bury oneself in; see also UNDERSTAND 1. **2** [To interpret] view, render, translate, decipher, make out, unravel, express, explain, expound, construe, paraphrase, restate, put; see also INTERPRET.

readable *a.* **1** [Capable of being read] clear, legible, coherent, distinct, intelligible, lucid, comprehensible, decipherable, unmistakable, plain, regular, orderly, fluent, tidy, flowing, precise, graphic, understandable, unequivocal, straightforward, explicit, simple. **2** [Likely to be read with pleasure] interesting, absorbing, fascinating, pleasurable, engrossing, satisfying, amusing, entertaining, enjoyable, rewarding, gratifying, pleasing, worth reading, pleasant, inviting, engaging, eloquent, well-written, smooth, exciting, attractive, clever, brilliant, ingenious, relaxing, stimulating, appealing.—*Ant.* DULL, dreary, depressing.

reader *n.* **1** [One who reads habitually] editor, literary critic, proofreader; see WRITER. **2** [A book intended for the study of reading] primer, graded text, selected readings; see BOOK.

readily *a.* quickly, immediately, promptly; see EAGERLY, EASILY, WILLINGLY.

readiness *n.* aptness, predisposition, eagerness; see WILLINGNESS, ZEAL.

reading *n.* **1** [Interpretation] version, treatment, commentary; see INTERPRETATION, TRANSLATION. **2** [A selection from written matter] excerpt, passage, section; see QUOTATION. **3** [A version] account, paraphrase, rendering; see LITERATURE 2, INTERPRETATION.

ready *a.* **1** [Prompt] quick, spontaneous, alert, wide-awake, swift, fleet, fast, sharp, immediate, instant, animated; see also ACTIVE, OBSERVANT, PUNCTUAL.—*Ant.* SLOW, dull, lazy. **2** [Prepared] fit, apt, skillful, ripe, handy, in readiness, waiting, on call, in line for, in position, on the brink of, equipped to do the job, open to, fixed for, on the mark, equal to, expectant, available, at hand, anticipating, in order, all systems go*, all squared away*, in a go condition*.—*Ant.* UNPREPARED, unready, unavailable. **3** [Enthusiastic] eager, willing, ardent; see ZEALOUS. —**make ready** order, prepare for something, equip; see PREPARE 1.

ready-made *a.* instant, prefabricated, built; see PRESERVED 2.

real *a.* **1** [Genuine] true, authentic, original; see GENUINE 1. **2** [Having physical existence] actual, solid, firm, substantive, material, live, substantial, existent, tangible, existing, present, palpable, factual, sound, concrete, corporal, corporeal, bodily, incarnate, embodied, physical, sensible, stable, in existence, perceptible, evident, undeniable, irrefutable, practical, true, true to life.—*Ant.* UNREAL, unsubstantial, hypothetical. **3** [*Very much] exceedingly, exceptionally, uncommonly; see VERY. —**for real** actually, in fact, certainly; see REALLY 1.

real estate *n.* land, property, realty; see BUILDING, ESTATE, FARM, HOME 1.

realism *n.* authenticity, naturalness, actuality; see REALITY.

realist *n.* pragmatist, naturalist, scientist; see PHILOSOPHER.

realistic *a.* authentic, original, representative; see GENUINE 1.

reality *n.* authenticity, factual basis, truth, actuality, realness, substantiality, existence, substance, materiality, being, presence, actual existence, sensibility, corporeality, solidity, perceptibility, true being, absoluteness, tangibility, palpability. —**in reality** in truth, truly, honestly; see REALLY 1.

realization *n.* understanding, comprehension, consciousness; see AWARENESS.

realize *v.* **1** [To bring to fulfillment] perfect, make good, actualize; see COMPLETE. **2** [To understand] recognize, apprehend, discern; see UNDERSTAND 1. **3** [To receive] acquire, make a profit from, obtain; see EARN 2, PROFIT 2, RECEIVE 1.

realized *a.* **1** [Fulfilled] completed, accomplished, done; see FINISHED 1. **2** [Earned] gained, gotten, acquired, received, accrued, made, reaped, harvested, gathered, inherited, profited, taken, cleared, obtained, gleaned, netted.

really *a.* **1** [In fact] actually, indeed, genuinely, certainly, surely, absolutely, positively, veritably, in reality, authentically, upon my honor, legitimately, precisely, literally, indubitably, unmistakably, in effect, undoubtedly, categorically, in point of fact, I assure you, be assured, believe me, as a matter of fact, of course, honestly, truly, admittedly, nothing else but, beyond any doubt, in actuality, unquestionably, as sure as you're alive*, no buts about it*, without the shadow of a doubt. **2** [To a remarkable degree] surprisingly, remarkably, extraordinarily; see VERY.

really *interj.* indeed!, honestly!, for a fact!, yes?, is that so!, are you sure?, no fooling!, cross your heart and hope to die?, on your honor?, you don't say!*, ain't it the truth!*, you said it!*, do tell!*, no kidding!*.

realm (relm) *n.* ⟦see REGAL⟧ 1 a kingdom 2 a region; sphere

Re·al·tor (rē′əl tər, -tôr′) *trademark for* a real estate broker or appraiser who is a member of the National Association of Realtors

re·al·ty (rē′əl tē) *n.* REAL ESTATE

ream[1] (rēm) *n.* ⟦< Ar *rizma*, a bale⟧ 1 a quantity of paper varying from 480 to 516 sheets 2 [*pl.*] [Colloq.] a great amount

ream[2] (rēm) *vt.* ⟦OE *reman*⟧ to enlarge (a hole) as with a reamer

ream′er *n.* 1 a sharp-edged tool for enlarging or tapering holes 2 a juicer

re·an·i·mate (rē an′ə māt′) *vt.* **-mat′ed, -mat′ing** to give new life, power, or vigor to —**re·an′i·ma′tion** *n.*

reap (rēp) *vt., vi.* ⟦OE *ripan*⟧ 1 to cut (grain) with a scythe, reaper, etc. 2 to gather (a harvest) 3 to obtain as the reward of action, etc.

reap′er *n.* 1 one who reaps 2 a machine for reaping grain

re·ap·por·tion (rē′ə pôr′shən) *vt.* to apportion again; specif., to change the representational distribution of (a legislature) —**re′ap·por′tion·ment** *n.*

rear[1] (rir) *n.* ⟦< ARREARS⟧ 1 the back part 2 the position behind or at the back 3 the part of an army, etc. farthest from the enemy 4 [Slang] the buttocks — *adj.* of, at, or in the rear —**bring up the rear** to come at the end

rear[2] (rir) *vt.* ⟦OE *ræran*⟧ 1 to put upright; elevate 2 to build; erect 3 to grow or breed 4 to educate, train, etc. /to *rear* a child/ — *vi.* 1 to rise on the hind legs, as a horse 2 to rise (*up*), in anger, etc. 3 to rise high

rear admiral a naval officer ranking above a captain

rear-end′ *vi., vt.* to crash into, or cause (one's vehicle) to crash into, the back end of (a motor vehicle)

rear′most′ *adj.* farthest in the rear

re·ar·range′ *vt.* **-ranged′, -rang′ing** to arrange again or in a different way —**re′ar·range′ment** *n.*

rear′ward (-wərd) *adj.* at, in, or toward the rear — *adv.* toward the rear: also **rear′wards**

rea·son (rē′zən) *n.* ⟦< L *ratio*, a reckoning⟧ 1 an explanation of an act, idea, etc. 2 a cause or motive 3 the ability to think, draw conclusions, etc. 4 good sense 5 sanity — *vi., vt.* 1 to think logically (about); analyze 2 to argue or infer —**stand to reason** to be logical —**rea′son·ing** *n.*

rea′son·a·ble *adj.* 1 able to reason 2 fair; just 3 wise; sensible 4 not excessive —**rea′son·a·bly** *adv.*

re·as·sure′ *vt.* **-sured′, -sur′ing** 1 to assure again 2 to restore to confidence —**re′as·sur′ance** *n.* —**re′assur′ ingly** *adv.*

re·bate (rē′bāt′) *vt.* **-bat′ed, -bat′ing** ⟦< OFr *re-*, RE- + *abattre*, beat down⟧ to give back (part of a payment) — *n.* a return of part of a payment

Re·bek·ah or **Re·bec′ca** (ri bek′ə) *Bible* the wife of Isaac

rebel (reb′əl; *for v.* ri bel′) *n.* ⟦< L *re-*, again + *bellare*, wage war⟧ one who resists authority — *adj.* 1 rebellious 2 of rebels — *vi.* **re·bel′, -belled′, -bel′ling** 1 to resist authority 2 to feel or show strong aversion

re·bel·lion (ri bel′yən) *n.* 1 armed resistance to one's government 2 a defiance of any authority

re·bel′lious (-yəs) *adj.* 1 resisting authority 2 opposing control; defiant

re′birth′ *n.* 1 a new or second birth 2 a reawakening; revival

re·bound (ri bound′; *for n.* rē′bound′) *vi.* to spring back, as upon impact — *n.* a rebounding, or ball, etc. that rebounds —**on the rebound** 1 after bouncing back 2 after being jilted

re·buff (ri buf′) *n.* ⟦< It *rabbuffare*, disarrange⟧ 1 an abrupt refusal of offered advice, help, etc. 2 any repulse — *vt.* 1 to snub 2 to check or repulse

re·buke (ri byook′) *vt.* **-buked′, -buk′ing** ⟦< OFr *re-*, back + *buchier*, to beat⟧ to scold in a sharp way; reprimand — *n.* a reprimand

re·bus (rē′bəs) *n.* ⟦L, lit., by things⟧ a puzzle consisting of pictures, etc. combined to suggest words or phrases

re·but (ri but′) *vt.* **-but′ted, -but′ting** ⟦< OFr *re-*, back + *buter*, to thrust⟧ to contradict or oppose, esp. in a formal manner by argument, proof, etc. —**re·but′tal** (-'l) *n.*

rec (rek) *n. short for* RECREATION: used in compounds, as **rec room**

re·cal·ci·trant (ri kal′si trənt) *adj.* ⟦< L *re-*, back + *calcitrare*, to kick⟧ 1 refusing to obey authority, etc. 2 hard to handle —**re·cal′ci·trance** *n.*

▄▄▄ THESAURUS ▄▄▄

realm *n.* domain, area, sphere; see DEPARTMENT, EXPANSE, REGION 1.

reappear *v.* come again, reenter, crop up again; see APPEAR 1, REPEAT 2.

rear[1] *n.* hind part, back seat, rear end, tail, tail end, posterior, rump, butt*; see also BACK 1.

rear[2] *v.* lift, elevate, bring up; see RAISE 1, SUPPORT 1.

rearrange *v.* do over, reconstruct, shift; see ORDER 3, PREPARE 1.

reason *n.* 1 [The power of reasoning] intelligence, mind, sanity; see JUDGMENT 1. 2 [A process of reasoning] logic, dialectics, speculation, generalization, rationalism, argumentation, inference, induction, deduction, analysis, rationalization. 3 [A basis for rational action] end, object, rationale, intention, motive, ulterior motive, basis, wherefore, aim, intent, cause, design, ground, impetus, idea, motivation, root, incentive, goal, purpose, the why and wherefore; see also PURPOSE 1. 4 [The mind] brain, mentality, intellect; see MIND 1. —**by reason of** because of, for, by way of; see BECAUSE. —**in (or within) reason** in accord with what is reasonable, rationally, understandably; see REASONABLY 1. —**stand to reason** be feasible, seem all right, appeal; see CONVINCE. —**with reason** understandably, soundly, plausibly; see REASONABLY 1.

reason *v.* 1 [To think logically] reflect, deliberate, contemplate; see THINK 1. 2 [To seek a reasonable explanation] suppose, gather, conclude; see ASSUME. 3 [To discuss persuasively] argue, contend, debate; see DISCUSS.

reasonable *a.* 1 [Rational] sane, levelheaded, intelligent, clear-cut, tolerant, endowed with reason, conscious, cerebral, thoughtful, reflective, capable of reason, reasoning, cognitive, perceiving, consistent, broad-minded, liberal, generous, sensible, unprejudiced, unbiased, flexible, agreeable; see also RATIONAL 1.— *Ant.* PREJUDICED, intolerant, biased. 2 [Characterized by justice] fair, right, just; see HONEST 1. 3 [Likely to appeal to the reason] feasible, sound, plausible; see UNDERSTANDABLE. 4 [Moderate in price] inexpensive, reduced, fair; see CHEAP 1.

reasonably *a.* 1 [In a reasonable manner] rationally, logically, understandably, plausibly, sensibly, soundly, persuasively, fairly, justly, honestly, wisely, judiciously, plainly, intelligently, soberly, agreeably, in reason, within reason, within the limits of reason, as far as possible, as far as could be expected, as much as good sense dictates, within reasonable limitations, with due restraint. 2 [To a moderate degree] mildly, prudently, fairly, moderately, inexpensively, temperately, evenly, calmly, gently, leniently, sparingly, frugally, indulgently, tolerantly, within bounds.

reasoning *n.* thinking, rationalizing, drawing conclusions; see THOUGHT 1.

reassure *v.* convince, console, give confidence; see COMFORT 1, ENCOURAGE, GUARANTEE.

rebel *n.* insurrectionist, revolutionist, revolutionary, agitator, insurgent, traitor, seditionist, mutineer, subverter, anarchist, overthrower, nihilist, guerrilla, member of the uprising, rioter, demagogue, revolter, separatist, malcontent, schismatic, dissenter, deserter, apostate, turncoat, counterrevolutionary, renegade, secessionist, underground worker; see also RADICAL.

rebel *v.* rise up, resist, revolt, turn against, defy, resist lawful authority, fight in the streets, strike, boycott, break with, overturn, mutiny, riot, take up arms against, start a confrontation, secede, renounce, combat, oppose, be insubordinate, be treasonable, upset, overthrow, dethrone, disobey, raise hell*, run amok*.—*Ant.* OBEY, be contented, submit.

rebellion *n.* insurrection, revolt, defiance; see DISOBEDIENCE, REVOLUTION 2.

rebellious *a.* revolutionary, insurgent, counterrevolutionary, warring, stubborn, contemptuous, insolent, scornful, intractable, unyielding, recalcitrant, insurrectionary, attacking, rioting, mutinous, dissident, factious, seditious, treasonable, disobedient, refractory, defiant, resistant, riotous, insubordinate, sabotaging, disloyal, disaffected, alienated, ungovernable, restless, threatening, anarchistic, iconoclastic, individualistic, radical, independent-minded, quarrelsome.—*Ant.* CALM, DOCILE, peaceful.

rebirth *n.* resurrection, rejuvenation, rehabilitation; see REVIVAL 1.

rebound *v.* reflect, ricochet, spring back; see BOUNCE.

rebuild *v.* touch up, patch, build up; see REPAIR.

rebuke *n.* condemnation, reproof, reprimand; see INSULT.

rebuke *v.* reprove, reprimand, censure; see OPPOSE 1.

re·call (ri kôl'; *also, & for n.,* rē'kôl) *vt.* **1** to call back **2** to remember **3** to take back; revoke **4** to bring (the mind, etc.) back, as to the immediate situation — *n.* **1** a recalling **2** memory **3** the removal of, or right to remove, an official from office by popular vote

re·cant (ri kant') *vt., vi.* ⟦ < L *re-,* back + *canere,* sing⟧ to renounce formally (one's beliefs, remarks, etc.) —**re·can·ta·tion** (rē'kan tā'shən) *n.*

re·cap¹ (rē kap'; *also, and for n.,* rē'kap') *vt.* **-capped'**, **-cap'ping** to put a new tread on (a worn tire) — *n.* such a tire

re·cap² (rē'kap') *n.* a recapitulation, or summary — *vt., vi.* **-capped'**, **-cap'ping** to recapitulate

re·ca·pit·u·late (rē'kə pich'ə lāt') *vi., vt.* **-lat'ed**, **-lat'ing** ⟦ see RE- & CAPITULATE⟧ to repeat briefly; summarize —**re'ca·pit'u·la'tion** *n.*

re·cap·ture *vt.* **-tured**, **-tur·ing** **1** to capture again; retake **2** to remember — *n.* a recapturing

recd. or **rec'd** received

re·cede (ri sēd') *vi.* **-ced'ed**, **-ced'ing** ⟦ see RE- & CEDE⟧ **1** to go, move, or slope backward **2** to diminish

re·ceipt (ri sēt') *n.* ⟦ see RECEIVE⟧ **1** *old-fashioned var. of* RECIPE **2** a receiving or being received **3** a written acknowledgment that something has been received **4** [*pl.*] the amount received — *vt.* to write a receipt for (goods, etc.)

re·ceiv·able (ri sē'və bəl) *adj.* **1** that can be received **2** due

re·ceive (ri sēv') *vt.* **-ceived'**, **-ceiv'ing** ⟦ < L *re-,* back + *capere,* take⟧ **1** to take or get (something given, thrown, sent, etc.) **2** to experience; undergo [to *receive* acclaim] **3** to bear or hold **4** to react to in a specified way **5** to learn [to *receive* news] **6** to let enter **7** to greet (visitors, etc.)

re·ceived' *adj.* accepted; considered as standard

re·ceiv·er *n.* one that receives; specif., *a)* *Electronics* a device that converts electrical waves or signals into audible or visual signals *b)* *Football* the player designated to receive a forward pass *c)* *Law* one appointed by a court to administer or hold in trust property in bankruptcy or in a lawsuit —**re·ceiv'er·ship'** *n.*

re·cen·sion (ri sen'shən) *n.* ⟦ < L *recensere,* revise⟧ a revision of a text based on a critical study of sources

re·cent (rē'sənt) *adj.* ⟦ < L *recens* ⟧ **1** done, made, etc. just before the present; new **2** of a time just before the present —**re'cent·ly** *adv.*

re·cep·ta·cle (ri sep'tə kəl) *n.* ⟦ see RECEIVE⟧ a container

re·cep·tion (ri sep'shən) *n.* **1** *a)* a receiving or being received *b)* the manner of this **2** a social function for the receiving of guests **3** *Radio, TV* the receiving of signals with reference to the quality of reproduction

re·cep'tion·ist *n.* an office employee who receives callers, etc.

re·cep'tive *adj.* able or ready to accept new ideas, suggestions, etc.

re·cep'tor *n.* a nerve ending or group of nerve endings specialized for receiving stimuli; sense organ

re·cess (rē'ses; *also, & for v. usually,* ri ses') *n.* ⟦ < L *recedere,* recede ⟧ **1** a hollow place, as in a wall **2** a hidden or inner place **3** a temporary halting as of work, a session, etc. — *vt.* **1** to place in a recess **2** to form a recess in — *vi.* to take a recess

re·ces·sion (ri sesh'ən) *n.* **1** a going back; withdrawal **2** a temporary falling off of business activity

re·ces'sion·al (-əl) *n.* a piece of music at the end of a church service played when the clergy, etc. march out

re·ces·sive (ri ses'iv) *adj.* **1** tending to recede **2** *Genetics* designating that one of any pair of hereditary factors which remains latent — *n. Genetics* a recessive character or characters

re·cher·ché (rə sher'shā, -sher'shā') *adj.* ⟦Fr⟧ **1** rare; choice **2** refined; esp., too refined

rec·i·pe (res'ə pē') *n.* ⟦ L < *recipere,* receive⟧ **1** a list of materials and directions for preparing a dish or drink **2** a way to achieve something

re·cip·i·ent (ri sip'ē ənt) *n.* ⟦ see RECEIVE⟧ one that receives

re·cip·ro·cal (ri sip'rə k'l) *adj.* ⟦ < L *reciprocus,* returning⟧ **1** done, given, etc. in return **2** mutual [*reciprocal love*] **3** corresponding but reversed **4** corresponding or complementary — *n.* **1** a complement, counterpart, etc. **2** *Math.* the quantity resulting from the division of 1 by the given quantity [the *reciprocal* of 7 is ⅟]

re·cip'ro·cate' (-kāt') *vt., vi.* **-cat'ed**, **-cat'ing** **1** to give and get reciprocally **2** to do, feel, etc. in return **3** to move alternately back and forth —**re·cip'ro·ca'tion** *n.*

rec·i·proc·i·ty (res'ə präs'ə tē) *n., pl.* **-ties** **1** reciprocal state **2** mutual exchange; esp., exchange of special privileges between two countries

re·cit·al (ri sīt'l) *n.* **1** a reciting **2** the account, story, etc. told **3** a musical or dance program

rec·i·ta·tion (res'ə tā'shən) *n.* **1** a reciting, as of facts, events, etc. **2** *a)* a saying aloud in public of something memorized *b)* a piece so presented **3** a reciting by pupils of answers to questions on a prepared lesson

---

═══ THESAURUS ═══

recall *v.* **1** [To call to mind] recollect, think of, revive; see REMEMBER 1. **2** [To remove from office] discharge, disqualify, suspend; see DISMISS. **3** [To summon again] call back, reconvene, reassemble; see SUMMON.

recalled *a.* **1** [Remembered] recollected, brought to mind, summoned up; see REMEMBERED. **2** [Relieved of responsibility] stripped of office, dismissed, cast out, displaced, fired, replaced, ousted, suspended, laid off, cashiered, pensioned, let out, let go, removed, retired, kicked upstairs*, canned*, busted*, washed out*; see also DISCHARGED.

recapture *v.* regain, reobtain, reacquire; see RECOVER 1.

recede *v.* **1** [To go backward] fall back, shrink from, withdraw; see RETREAT. **2** [To sink] ebb, drift away, lower, turn down, abate, decline, go away, drop, fall off, lessen; see also DECREASE 1, FALL 2.—*Ant.* RISE, flow, increase.

receipt *n.* **1** [The act of receiving] receiving, acquisition, accession, acceptance, taking, arrival, getting, admitting, reception; see also ADMISSION 1.—*Ant.* DELIVERY, shipment, giving. **2** [An acknowledgement of receipt] letter, voucher, release, cancellation, slip, signed notice, stub, discharge, declaration, paid bill; see also CERTIFICATE.

receive *v.* **1** [To take into one's charge] accept, be given, admit, get, gain, inherit, acquire, gather up, col-lect, obtain, reap, procure, derive, appropriate, seize, take possession, redeem, pocket, pick up, hold, come by, earn, take in, assume, draw, win, secure, come into, come in for, catch, get from; see also GET 1.—*Ant.* DISCARD, abandon, refuse. **2** [To endure] undergo, experience, suffer; see ENDURE 2. **3** [To support] bear, sustain, prop; see SUPPORT 1. **4** [To make welcome] accommodate, initiate, induct, install, make welcome, shake hands with, admit, permit, welcome home, accept, entertain, invite in, show in, usher in, let through, make comfortable, bring as a guest into, introduce, give a party, give access to, allow entrance to, roll out the red carpet for*, give the red-carpet treatment to*, get out the welcome mat for*; see also GREET.—*Ant.* VISIT, be a guest, call.

received *a.* taken, gotten, acquired, obtained, honored, brought in, signed for, admitted, collected, gathered; see also ACCEPTED, ACKNOWLEDGED.—*Ant.* GIVEN, disbursed, delivered.

receiver *n.* **1** [One who receives] customer, recipient, beneficiary; see HEIR. **2** [A device for receiving] telephone, television, radio, satellite dish, radio telescope, walkie-talkie, headphone, car phone, beeper, pager, mission control, control center, listening device, transceiver.

recent *a.* **1** [Lately brought into being] fresh, novel, newly born; see MODERN 1, UNUSUAL 1, 2. **2** [Associated with modern times] contempo-rary, up-to-date, streamlined; see MODERN 1, 3.

recently *a.* lately, in recent times, just now, just a while ago, not long ago, a short while ago, of late, newly, freshly, new, the other day, within the recent past.—*Ant.* ONCE, long ago, formerly.

receptacle *n.* box, wastebasket, holder; see CONTAINER.

reception *n.* **1** [The act of receiving] acquisition, acceptance, accession; see RECEIPT 2. **2** [The manner of receiving] meeting, encounter, introduction, gathering, welcome, salutation, induction, admission, disposition; see also GREETING. **3** [A social function] tea, party, dinner; see GATHERING.

receptive *a.* alert, sensitive, perceptive; see OBSERVANT, SYMPATHETIC.

recess *n.* **1** [An intermission] respite, rest, pause, interlude, break, cessation, stop, suspension, interval, coffee break, intervening period, halt. **2** [An indentation] break, dent, corner; see HOLE 1. **3** [A recessed space] cell, cubicle, nook; see ROOM 2.

recession *n.* unemployment, inflation, decline; see DEPRESSION 3.

recipe *n.* formula, compound, receipt, instructions, prescription, cookery, formula, directions, method.

recipient *n.* receiver, beneficiary, legatee; see HEIR.

recital *n.* presentation, concert, musical; see PERFORMANCE.

recitation *n.* **1** [The act of reciting]

rec·i·ta·tive' (-tə tēv') *n.* ⟦ < It: see fol. ⟧ a type of decla-mation, as for operatic dialogue, with the rhythms of speech, but in musical tones

re·cite (ri sīt') *vt., vi.* **-cit'ed, -cit'ing** ⟦see RE- & CITE⟧ 1 to say aloud from memory, as a poem, lesson, etc. 2 to tell in detail; relate

reck·less (rek'lis) *adj.* ⟦OE *recceleas*⟧ careless; heedless —**reck'lessly** *adv.* —**reck'less·ness** *n.*

reck·on (rek'ən) *vt.* ⟦OE *-recenian*⟧ 1 to count; compute 2 to regard as being 3 to estimate 4 [Colloq. or Dial.] to suppose — *vi.* 1 to count up 2 [Colloq.] to rely (*on*) — **reckon with** to take into consideration

reck'on·ing *n.* 1 count or computation 2 the settlement of an account

re·claim (ri klām') *vt.* ⟦see RE- & CLAIM⟧ 1 to bring back (a person) from error, vice, etc. 2 to make (wasteland, etc.) usable 3 to recover (useful materials) from waste products —**rec·la·ma·tion** (rek'lə mā'shən) *n.*

re·cline (ri klīn') *vt.* **-clined', -clin'ing** ⟦ < L *re-*, back + *clinare*, lean⟧ to lie or cause to lie down

rec·luse (rek'lōōs, ri klōōs') *n.* ⟦ < L *re-*, back + *claudere*, shut⟧ one who lives a secluded, solitary life —**re·clu·sive** (ri klōō'siv) *adj.*

rec·og·ni·tion (rek'əg nish'ən) *n.* 1 a recognizing or being recognized 2 identification of a person or thing as having been known before

rec·og·ni·zance (ri käg'ni zəns, -kän'i-) *n.* ⟦ < L *re-*, again + *cognoscere*, know⟧ *Law* a bond binding one to some act, as to appear in court

rec·og·nize (rek'əg nīz') *vt.* **-nized', -niz'ing** ⟦see prec.⟧ 1 to be aware of as known before 2 to know by some detail, as of appearance 3 to perceive 4 to accept as a fact *[to recognize defeat]* 5 to acknowledge as worthy of approval 6 to acknowledge the status of (a government, etc.) 7 to grant the right to speak in a meeting —**rec'og·niz·able** *adj.*

re·coil (ri koil'; *also for n.* rē'koil') *vi.* ⟦ < L *re-*, back + *culus*, buttocks⟧ 1 to draw back, as in fear, etc. 2 to spring or kick back, as a gun when fired — *n.* a recoiling

rec·ol·lect (rek'ə lekt') *vt., vi.* ⟦see RE- & COLLECT⟧ to remember, esp. with some effort —**rec'ol·lec'tion** *n.*

rec·om·mend (rek'ə mend') *vt.* ⟦see RE- & COMMEND⟧ 1 to entrust 2 to suggest favorably as suited for some position, etc. 3 to make acceptable 4 to advise; counsel —**rec'om·men·da'tion** *n.*

re·com·mit *vt.* **-mit'ted, -mit'ting** 1 to commit again 2 to refer (a question, bill, etc.) back to a committee

rec·om·pense (rek'əm pens') *vt.* **-pensed', -pens'ing** ⟦see RE- & COMPENSATE⟧ 1 to repay or reward 2 to compensate (a loss, etc.) — *n.* 1 requital; reward 2 compensation

rec·on·cile (rek'ən sīl') *vt.* **-ciled', -cil'ing** ⟦see RE- & CONCILIATE⟧ 1 to make friendly again 2 to settle (a quarrel, etc.) 3 to make (ideas, accounts, etc.) consistent 4 to make content, or acquiescent (*to*) —**rec'on·cil'able** *adj.* —**rec'on·cil'ia'tion** (-sil'ē ā'shən) *n.*

rec·on·dite (rek'ən dīt') *adj.* ⟦ < L *re-*, back + *condere*, to hide⟧ beyond ordinary understanding; profound

re·con·di'tion *vt.* to put back in good condition, as by repairing

re·con·nais·sance (ri kän'ə səns) *n.* ⟦Fr: see RECOGNIZANCE⟧ a survey of a region, as in seeking out information about enemy positions

rec·on·noi·ter (rek'ə noit'ər, rē'kə-) *vt., vi.* to make a reconnaissance (of) Also [Chiefly Brit.] **rec'on·noi'tre, -tred, -tring**

re·con·sider (rē'kən sid'ər) *vt., vi.* to think over again, esp. with a view to changing a decision

re·con'sti·tute *vt.* **-tut'ed, -tut'ing** to constitute again; specif., to restore (a dried or condensed substance) to its full liquid form by adding water

re'con·struct' *vt.* 1 to construct again; rebuild 2 to build up, as from remains, an image of the original

re'con·struc'tion *n.* a reconstructing —[**R-**] the process or period, after the Civil War, of reestablishing the Southern States in the Union

re·cord (ri kôrd'; *for n. & adj.* rek'ərd) *vt.* ⟦ < L *recordari*, remember⟧ 1 to write down for future use 2 to register, as on a graph 3 to register (sound or visual images) on a disc, tape, etc. for later reproduction — *n.* 1 a recording or being recorded 2 any registered evidence of an event, etc.

THESAURUS

---

delivery, speaking, playing, narrating, reading, recounting, declaiming, discoursing, soliloquizing, discussion, holding forth, performance, recital, rehearsal, monologue, discourse. 2 [A compositon used for recitation] address, talk, sermon; see SPEECH 3, WRITING 2.

recite *v.* 1 [To repeat formally] declaim, address, read, render, discourse, hold forth, enact, dramatize, deliver from memory, interpret, soliloquize. 2 [To report on a lesson] answer, give a report, explain; see DISCUSS, REPORT 1. 3 [To relate in detail] enumerate, enlarge, report, account for, give an account for, impart, chant, convey, quote, communicate, utter, describe, relate, state, tell, mention, narrate, recount, retell, picture, delineate, portray; see also EXPLAIN, TELL 1.

reckless *a.* thoughtless, foolish, wild; see RASH.

recklessly *a.* dangerously, heedlessly, with abandon; see BRAVELY, CARELESSLY.

reckon *v.* consider, evaluate, judge; see ESTIMATE.

reclaim *v.* 1 [To bring into usable condition] restore, regenerate, redeem; see RECOVER 1. 2 [To reform] resolve, mend, improve; see REFORM 3.

reclamation *n.* redemption, repair, repossession; see RECOVERY 3.

recognition *n.* 1 [The act of recognizing] recalling, remembering, identifying, perceiving, verifying, apprehending, acknowledging, noticing, recollection, memory, identification, recall, reidentification, cognizance, recognizance, remembrance. 2 [Tangible evidence of recognition] greeting, acknowledgment, identification, perception, admission,

verification, comprehension, appreciation, renown, esteem, notice, attention, acceptance, regard, honor.

recognize *v.* 1 [To know again] be familiar, make out, distinguish, verify, recollect, sight, diagnose, place, espy, descry, recall, remember, see, perceive, admit, knowledge of, notice; see also KNOW 1. 2 [To acknowledge] admit, appreciate, realize; see ALLOW. 3 [To acknowledge the legality of a government] exchange diplomatic representatives, have diplomatic relations with, sanction, approve, extend formal recognition to; see also ACKNOWLEDGE 2.

recognized *a.* sighted, caught, perceived, realized, acknowledged, known, appreciated, admitted, recalled, remembered.

recoil *v.* turn away, shrink from, draw back; see RETREAT.

recollect *v.* recall, bring to mind, look back on; see REMEMBER 1.

recollection *n.* remembrance, reminiscence, consciousness; see MEMORY 1.

recommend *v.* 1 [To lend support or approval] agree to, sanction, hold up, commend, extol, compliment, applaud, advocate, celebrate, praise, speak highly of, acclaim, eulogize, confirm, laud, second, favor, back, stand by, magnify, glorify, exalt, think highly of, think well of, be satisfied with, esteem, value, prize, uphold, justify, endorse, go on record for, be all for, front for, go to bat for*.—Ant.* DENOUNCE, censure, renounce. 2 [To make a suggestion or prescription] prescribe, suggest, counsel; see ADVISE, URGE 2.

recommendation *n.* 1 [The act of recommending] guidance, counsel, direction; see ADVICE, SUGGESTION 1. 2 [A document that vouches for

character or ability] certificate, testimonial, reference, letter of introduction, character reference, letter of recommendation, letter in support; see also LETTER 2.

recommended *a.* urged, endorsed, suggested; see APPROVED.

reconcile *v.* 1 [To adjust] adapt, arrange, regulate; see ADJUST 1, 2. 2 [To bring into harmony] conciliate, assuage, pacify, propitiate, mitigate, make up, mediate, arbitrate, intercede, bring together, accustom oneself to, harmonize, accord, dictate peace, accomodate, appease, reunite, make peace between, bring to terms, bring into one's camp, win over, bury the hatchet, patch up, kiss and make up; see also SETTLE 7.—*Ant.* BOTHER, irritate, alienate.

reconciled *a.* settled, regulated, arranged; see DETERMINED 1.

reconciliation *n.* conciliation, settlement, payment; see ADJUSTMENT, AGREEMENT 1.

reconsider *v.* reevaluate, think over, rearrange, consider again, recheck, reexamine, correct, amend, revise, retrace, rework, replan, review, withdraw for consideration, reweigh, amend one's judgment; see also CONSIDER.

reconstruct *v.* rebuild, remodel, construct again, make over, revamp, recondition, reconstitute, reestablish, restore, reproduce, refashion, reorganize, replace, overhaul, renovate, modernize, rework, construct from the original, copy, remake; see also BUILD, REPAIR.

reconstruction *n.* reorganization, rehabilitation, restoration; see REPAIR.

record *n.* 1 [Documentary evidence] manuscript, inscription, transcrip-

3 the known facts about anyone or anything 4 a grooved disc for playing on a phonograph 5 the best official performance achieved —*adj.* being the best, largest, etc. —**on** (or **off**) **the**) **record** publicly (or confidentially) declared

re·cord'er *n.* 1 an official who keeps records 2 a machine or device that records; esp., TAPE RECORDER 3 an early wind instrument

re·cord'ing *n.* 1 what is recorded, as on a disc or tape 2 the record itself

re·count[1] (ri kount′) *vt.* [see RE- & COUNT[1]] to tell in detail; narrate

re·count[2] (rē′kount′; *for n.* rē′kount′) *vt.* to count again — *n.* a second or additional count, as of votes

re·coup (ri ko͞op′) *vt.* [< Fr *re-*, again + *couper*, to cut] 1 to make up for [to recoup a loss] 2 to regain

re·course (rē′kôrs′, ri kôrs′) *n.* [see RE- & COURSE] 1 a turning for aid, safety, etc. 2 that to which one turns seeking aid, safety, etc.

re·cover (ri kuv′ər) *vt.* [< L *recuperare*] 1 to get back (something lost, etc.) 2 to regain (health, etc.) 3 to make up for [to recover losses] 4 to save (oneself) from a fall, etc. 5 to reclaim (land from the sea, etc.) 6 *Sports* to get control of (a fumbled or wild ball, etc.) —*vi.* 1 to regain health, balance, or control 2 *Sports* to recover a ball, etc.

re·cov'ery *n., pl.* **-ies** a recovering; specif., *a*) a regaining of something lost *b*) a return to health *c*) a retrieval of a capsule, etc. after a spaceflight

recovery room a hospital room where postoperative patients are kept for close observation and care

rec·re·ant (rek′rē ənt) *adj.* [< OFr *recreire*, surrender allegiance] 1 cowardly 2 disloyal — *n.* 1 a coward 2 a traitor

rec·re·a·tion (rek′rē ā′shən) *n.* [< L *recreare*, refresh] any play, amusement, etc. used to relax or refresh the body or mind —**rec're·ate'**, **-at'ed**, **-at'ing**, *vt., vi.* —**rec' re·a'tional** *adj.*

re·crim·i·nate (ri krim′ə nāt′) *vi.* **-nat'ed**, **-nat'ing** [< L

re-, back + *crimen*, offense] to answer an accuser by accusing that person in return —**re·crim'i·na'tion** *n.*

re·cru·desce (rē′kro͞o des′) *vi.* **-desced'**, **-desc'ing** [< L *re-*, again + *crudus*, raw] to break out again after being inactive —**re'cru·des'cence** *n.* —**re'cru·des'cent** *adj.*

re·cruit (ri kro͞ot′) *vt., vi.* [< L *re-*, again + *crescere*, grow] 1 to enlist (personnel) into an army or navy 2 to enlist (new members) for an organization — *n.* 1 a newly enlisted or drafted soldier, etc. 2 a new member of any group —**re·cruit'er** *n.* —**re·cruit'ment** *n.*

rec·tal (rek′təl) *adj.* of, for, or near the rectum —**rec'tally** *adv.*

rec·tan·gle (rek′taŋ′gəl) *n.* [< L *rectus*, straight + *angulus*, a corner] a four-sided plane figure with four right angles —**rec·tan'gu·lar** (-gyə lər) *adj.*

rec·ti·fy (rek′tə fī′) *vt.* **-fied'**, **-fy'ing** [< L *rectus*, straight + *facere*, make] 1 to put right; correct 2 *Elec.* to convert (alternating current) to direct current —**rec'ti·fi·ca'tion** *n.* —**rec'ti·fi'er** *n.*

rec·ti·lin·e·ar (rek′tə lin′ē ər) *adj.* bounded or formed by straight lines

rec·ti·tude (rek′tə to͞od′) *n.* [< L *rectus*, right] strict honesty; uprightness of character

rec·tor (rek′tər) *n.* [< L *regere*, to rule] 1 in some churches, a clergyman in charge of a parish 2 the head of certain schools, colleges, etc.

rec·to·ry (rek′tər ē) *n., pl.* **-ries** the house of a minister or priest

rec·tum (rek′təm) *n., pl.* **-tums** or **-ta** (-tə) [< L *rectum* (*intestinum*), straight (intestine)] the lowest, or last, segment of the large intestine

re·cum·bent (ri kum′bənt) *adj.* [< L *re-*, back + *-cumbere*, lie down] lying down; reclining

re·cu·per·ate (ri ko͞o′pə rāt′, -pər āt′) *vt., vi.* **-at'ed**, **-at' ing** [< L *recuperare*, recover] 1 to get well again 2 to

---

THESAURUS

tion, account, history, legend, story, writing, written material, document. *Types of records include the following:* register, catalog, list, inventory, memo, memorandum, registry, schedule, chronicle, docket, scroll, archive, note, contract, statement, will, testament, petition, calendar, log, letter, memoir, reminiscence, dictation, confession, deposition, inscription, official record, sworn document, evidence, license, bulletin, gazette, newspaper, magazine, annual report, journal, Congressional Record, transactions, debates, bill, annals, presidential order, state paper, white paper, blue book, budget, report, entry, book, publication, autograph, signature, vital statistics, deed, paper, diary, stenographic notes, ledger, daybook, almanac, proceedings, minutes, description, affidavit, certificate, transcript, dossier, roll, tape, disk, microfilm, microfiche. 2 [One's past] career, experience, work; see LIFE 2. 3 [A device for the reproduction of sound] recording, disk, phonograph record, transcription, compact disc, CD, laser disc, canned music*, cut, take, platter*. —**go on record** assert, attest, state; see DECLARE. —**off the record** confidential, unofficial, secret; see PRIVATE. —**on the record** recorded, stated, official; see PUBLIC 1.

record *v.* 1 [To write down] register, write in, jot down, set down, take down, put on record, transcribe, list, note, file, mark, inscribe, log, catalog, tabulate, put in writing, put in black and white, chronicle, keep accounts, keep an account of, make a written account of, matriculate, enroll, journalize, put on paper, preserve, make an entry in, chalk up, write up, enter, report, book, post, copy, document, insert, enumerate; see also WRITE 1. 2 [To indicate] point out, explain, show; see NAME 2. 3 [To record elec-

tronically] tape, cut, photograph, make a record of, make a tape, tape-record, film, videotape, cut a record.

recorded *a.* listed, filed, on file, in black and white, in writing, inscribed, put down, registered, documented, entered, written, published, noted down, described, reported, cataloged, mentioned, certified, kept, chronicled, booked.

recorder *n.* dictaphone, recording instrument, stereophonic recorder; see TAPE RECORDER.

recording *n.* documentation, recounting, reporting; see RECORD 1.

records *n.* documents, chronicles, archives, public papers, registers, annals, memborabilia, memoranda, lists, return, diaries, accounts.

recover *v.* 1 [To obtain again] redeem, salvage, retrieve, rescue, reclaim, recoup, find again, recapture, repossess, bring back, win back, reacquire, obtain, regain, rediscover, resume, catch up; see also GET 1.—*Ant.* LOSE, let slip, fall behind. 2 [To improve one's condition] gain, increase, collect; see IMPROVE 2, PROFIT 2.—*Ant.* FAIL, go bankrupt, give up. 3 [To regain health] rally, come around, come to, come out of it, get out of danger, improve, convalesce, heal, get the better of, overcome, start anew, be restored, mend, revive, be oneself again, perk up, gain strength, recuperate, get well, get over, get better, get through, return to form, make a comeback*, get back in shape*, snap out of*, pull through*, sober up.—*Ant.* DIE, fail, become worse.

recovered *a.* renewed, found, replaced, reborn, rediscovered, reawakened, retrieved, redeemed, reclaimed, regained, revived, returned, resumed; see also DISCOVERED.—*Ant.* LOST, missed, dropped.

recovery *n.* 1 [The act of returning to normal] reestablishment, resump-

tion, restoration, reinstatement, return, rehabilitation, reconstruction, reformation, recreation, replacement, readjustment, improving, getting back to normal; see also sense 2, IMPROVEMENT 1. 2 [The process of regaining health] convalescence, recuperation, revival, rebirth, renaissance, resurgence, resurrection, regeneration, cure, improvement, reawakening, renewal, resuscitation, rejuvenation, rehabilitation, return of health, physical improvement, healing, betterment. 3 [The act of regaining possession] repossession, retrieval, reclamation, redemption, indemnification, reparation, compensation, recapture, recouping, return, restoration, remuneration, reimbursement, retaking, recall.

recreation *n.* amusement, relaxation, diversion, play, fun, entertainment, enjoyment, festivity, hobby, holiday, vacation, pastime, pleasure, game, avocation, refreshment; see also SPORT 1.

recruit *n.* new man, novice, beginner, selectee, draftee, trainee, volunteer, enlisted man, serviceman, soldier, sailor, marine, rookie*; see also SOLDIER.

recruit *v.* 1 [To raise troops] draft, call up, select, supply, muster, deliver, sign up, induct, take in, find manpower, call to arms, bring into service; see also ENLIST 1. 2 [To gather needed resources] restore, store up, replenish; see GET 1.

rectangle *n.* geometrical figure, square, box, oblong, four-sided figure, right-angled parallelogram; see also FORM 1.

rectangular *a.* square, four-sided, right-angled; see ANGULAR.

rectitude *n.* integrity, trustworthiness, responsibility; see HONESTY.

recuperate *v.* heal, pull through, get back on one's feet; see RECOVER 3.

recover (losses, etc.) —**re·cu′pera′tion** *n.* —**re·cu′pera′tive** (-pə rāt′iv, -per ə tiv) *adj.*

re·cur (ri kur′) *vi.* **-curred′, -cur′ring** ⟦< L *re-*, back + *currere*, run⟧ 1 to return in thought, talk, etc. 2 to occur again or at intervals —**re·cur′rence** *n.* —**re·cur′rent** *adj.*

re·cy·cle (rē sī′kəl) *vt.* **-cled, -cling** 1 to pass through a cycle again 2 to use again and again, as the same water

red (red) *n.* ⟦OE *read*⟧ 1 the color of blood 2 any red pigment 3 [*often* **R-**] [Colloq.] a political radical; esp., a communist —*adj.* **red′der, red′dest** 1 of the color red 2 [*often* **R-**] politically radical; esp., communist —**in the red** losing money —**see red** [Colloq.] to become angry —**red′dish** *adj.* —**red′ness** *n.*

re·dact (ri dakt′) *vt.* ⟦< L *redigere*, get in order⟧ to edit — **re·dac′tion** *n.* —**re·dac′tor** *n.*

red blood cell (or **corpuscle**) ERYTHROCYTE

red′-blood′ed *adj.* high-spirited and strong-willed; vigorous

red′cap′ *n.* a baggage porter, as in a railroad station

red carpet a very grand or impressive welcome and entertainment: with *the* —**red′-car′pet** *adj.*

red′coat′ *n.* a British soldier in a uniform with a red coat

Red Cross an international society for the relief of suffering in time of war or disaster

red deer a deer of Europe and Asia

red·den (red′′n) *vt.* to make red — *vi.* to become red; esp., to blush

re·deem (ri dēm′) *vt.* ⟦< L *re(d)-*, back + *emere*, get⟧ 1 to buy or get back; recover 2 to pay off (a mortgage, etc.) 3 to turn in (coupons, etc.) for a premium 4 to ransom 5 to deliver from sin 6 to fulfill (a promise) 7 *a*) to make amends or atone for *b*) to restore (oneself) to favor —**re·deem′able** *adj.* —**re·deem′er** *n.* —**re·demp·tion** (ri demp′shən) *n.*

re·deploy (rē′dē ploi′) *vt., vi.* to move (troops, etc.) from one front or area to another —**re′deploy′ment** *n.*

re·devel′op *vt.* 1 to develop again 2 to rebuild or restore —**re·devel′op·ment** *n.*

red′-hand′ed *adv., adj.* in the very commission of crime or wrongdoing

red′head′ *n.* a person with red hair —**red′head′ed** *adj.*

red herring ⟦< herring drawn across the trace in hunting to divert the hounds⟧ something used to divert attention from the basic issue

red′-hot′ *adj.* 1 hot enough to glow 2 very excited, angry, etc. 3 very new

re·dis′trict *vt.* to divide anew into districts

red′-let′ter *adj.* designating a memorable or joyous day or event

red′lin′ing (-līn′iŋ) *n.* ⟦from outlining such areas in red on a map⟧ the refusal by some banks or companies to issue loans or insurance on property in certain neighborhoods

redo (rē dōo′) *vt.* **-did′, -done′, -do′ing** 1 to do again 2 to redecorate

redo·lent (red′′l ənt) *adj.* ⟦< L *re(d)-*, intens. + *olere*, to smell⟧ 1 sweet-smelling 2 smelling (*of*) 3 suggestive (*of*) —**red′o·lence** *n.*

re·dou·ble (rē dub′əl) *vt., vi.* **-bled, -bling** to make or become twice as much or twice as great

re·doubt (ri dout′) *n.* ⟦see REDUCE⟧ 1 a breastwork 2 any stronghold

re·doubt′able *adj.* ⟦< L *re-*, intens. + *dubitare*, to doubt⟧ formidable —**re·doubt′ably** *adv.*

re·dound (ri dound′) *vi.* ⟦< L *re(d)-*, intens. + *undare*, to surge⟧ 1 to have a result (*to* the credit or discredit of) 2 to come back; react (*upon*)

red pepper 1 a plant with a red, many-seeded fruit 2 the fruit, used for seasoning

re·dress (ri dres′; *for n., usually* rē′dres′) *vt.* ⟦see RE- & DRESS⟧ to compensate for (a wrong, etc.) — *n.* 1 compensation 2 a redressing

red snapper a reddish, edible, deep-water fish

red tape ⟦< tape for tying official papers⟧ rigid adherence to regulations and routine, causing delay

red tide sea water discolored by red algae poisonous to marine life

re·duce (ri dōos′) *vt.* **-duced′, -duc′ing** ⟦< L *re-*, back + *ducere*, to lead⟧ 1 to lessen, as in size, price, etc. 2 to put into a different form 3 to lower, as in rank or condition 4 to subdue or conquer — *vi.* to lose weight, as by dieting — **re·duc′er** *n.*

re·duc·tion (ri duk′shən) *n.* 1 a reducing or being reduced 2 anything made by reducing 3 the amount by which anything is reduced

re·dun·dant (ri dun′dənt) *adj.* ⟦see REDOUND⟧ 1 excess; superfluous 2 wordy 3 unnecessary to the meaning: said of words and affixes —**re·dun′dancy** *n.*

red′wood′ *n.* 1 a giant evergreen of the Pacific coast 2 its reddish wood

re·echo or **re-echo** (rē ek′ō) *vt., vi.* **-oed, -oing** to echo back or again — *n., pl.* **-oes** the echo of an echo

reed (rēd) *n.* ⟦OE *hreod*⟧ 1 a tall, slender grass 2 a musical instrument made from a hollow stem 3 *Music* a thin strip of wood, plastic, etc. placed against the mouthpiece, as of a clarinet, and vibrated by the breath to produce a tone —**reed′y, -i·er, -i·est,** *adj.*

reef[1] *n.* ⟦prob. < ON *rif*, a rib⟧ a ridge of rock, coral, or sand at or near the surface of the water

■ THESAURUS ■

recur *v.* return, reappear, crop up again; see HAPPEN 2, REPEAT 1.

recurrent *a.* reoccurring, repetitive, habitual; see REPEATED 1.

recycle *v.* start over, start again, restart; see BEGIN 1, RESUME.

red *n.* Tints and shades of red include the following: scarlet, carmine, vermilion, crimson, cerise, cherry red, ruby, garnet, maroon, brick red, claret, rust, red gold, magenta, pink, fuchsia, coral red, blood red, russet, terra cotta, Chinese red, Congo red, Turkey red, aniline red, chrome red, rose, rose blush, old rose; see also COLOR. —**in the red*** in debt, losing money, going broke*; see RUINED 3. —**see red*** become angry, lose one's temper, get mad; see RAGE 1.

red-blooded *a.* robust, vigorous, hearty; see HEALTHY.

redden *v.* color, tint, dye; see COLOR.

reddish *a.* flushed, somewhat red, rose; see RED, *n.*

redecorate *v.* refurbish, refresh, renew, paint, repaint, repaper, restore, recondition, remodel, renovate, revamp, rearrange, touch up, patch up, plaster, refurnish, wallpaper, clean up, carpet, do over, fix up*; see also DECORATE.

redeem *v.* 1 [To recover through a payment] buy back, repay, purchase; see GET 1. 2 [To save] liberate, set free, deliver; see RESCUE 1. —

redeem oneself atone, give satisfaction, make amends; see PAY FOR.

redeemer *n.* rescuer, deliverer, liberator; see PROTECTOR.

redemption *n.* regeneration, salvation, rebirth; see RESCUE 1.

redheaded *a.* auburn-haired, red-haired, sandy-haired, titian-haired, strawberry-blonde, carrot-topped, brick-topped.

red-hot *a.* 1 [Burning] heated, sizzling, scorching; see BURNING, HOT 1. 2 [Raging] excessive, rabid, very; see EXTREME. 3 [Newest] latest, recent, hippest*; see MODERN 1.

redo *v.* start over, redesign, rethink, go back to the drawing board, revamp, do over again; see also REPEAT.

redone *a.* done over, refinished, fixed up; see IMPROVED.

redress *n.* compensation, satisfaction, payment; see PAY 2, PRIZE.

red tape *n.* 1 [Delay] wait, roadblock, impediment; see DELAY. 2 [Bureaucracy] officialism, inflexible routine, officialdom; see GOVERNMENT 1, 2.

reduce *v.* 1 [To make less] lessen, diminish, cut down; see DECREASE 2. 2 [To defeat] conquer, overcome, subdue; see DEFEAT 2, 3. 3 [To humble] degrade, demote, abase; see HUMBLE, HUMILIATE.

reduced *a.* 1 [Made smaller] lessened, decreased, diminished, shortened, abridged, abbreviated, condensed, miniaturized, transistorized, compressed, economized, cut down, shrunk, subtracted, contracted, melted, boiled down.—*Ant.* SPREAD, enlarged, stretched. 2 [Made lower] lowered, abated, sunk, deflated, leveled, marked down, discounted, cheapened, weakened, debilitated, humbled, demoted, degraded.—*Ant.* RAISED, heightened, elevated.

reduction *n.* 1 [The process of making smaller] conversion, contraction, abatement, reducing, refinement, diminution, lowering, lessening, shortening, condensation, decrease, loss, compression, depression, subtraction, discount, shrinkage, constriction, modification, curtailment, abbreviation, modulation, mitigation, remission, decline.—*Ant.* INCREASE, increasing, enlargement. 2 [An amount that constitutes reduction] decrease, rebate, cut; see DISCOUNT.

redundant *a.* wordy, bombastic, verbose; see DULL 3, 4.

reeducate *v.* reinstruct, readjust, rehabilitate; see TEACH.

reef[1] *n.* ridge, shoal, sand bar; see ROCK 2.

reef[2] (rēf) *n.* ⟦ME *riff*⟧ a part of a sail which can be folded and made fast to reduce the area exposed to the wind — *vt.*, *vi.* to reduce the size of (a sail) by taking in part of it

reef′er *n.* [Slang] a marijuana cigarette

reek (rēk) *n.* ⟦OE *rec*⟧ a strong, unpleasant smell — *vi.* to have a strong, offensive smell — **reek′y** *adj.*

reel[1] (rēl) *n.* ⟦OE *hreol*⟧ **1** a spool on which wire, film, fishing line, etc. is wound **2** the quantity of wire, film, etc. usually wound on one reel — *vt.* to wind on a reel — *vi.* **1** to sway, stagger, etc. as from drunkenness or dizziness **2** to spin; whirl —**reel in 1** to wind on a reel **2** to pull in (a fish) by using a reel —**reel off** to tell, write, etc. easily and quickly —**reel out** to unwind from a reel

reel[2] (rēl) *n.* ⟦prob. < prec.⟧ a lively dance

re·en·try or **re-en·try** (rē en′trē) *n.*, *pl.* **-tries** a coming back, as of a space vehicle, into the earth's atmosphere

ref (ref) *n.*, *vt.*, *vi. short for* REFEREE

re·face (rē fās′) *vt.* **-faced′, -fac′ing** to put a new front or covering on

re·fec·tion (ri fek′shən) *n.* ⟦< L *re-*, again + *facere*, make⟧ a light meal; lunch

re·fec′tory (-tər ē) *n.*, *pl.* **-ries** a dining hall, as in a monastery

re·fer (ri fur′) *vt.* **-ferred′, -fer′ring** ⟦< L *re-*, back + *ferre*, to bear⟧ **1** to submit (a quarrel, etc.) for settlement **2** to direct to someone or something for aid, information, etc. — *vi.* **1** to relate or apply (*to*) **2** to direct attention (*to*) **3** to turn (*to*) for information, aid, etc. —**re·fer′rer** *n.*

ref·er·ee (ref′ə rē′) *n.* **1** one to whom something is referred for decision **2** an official who enforces the rules in certain sports contests — *vt.*, *vi.* **-eed′, -ee′ing** to act as referee (in)

ref·er·ence (ref′ər əns) *n.* **1** a referring or being referred **2** relation [in *reference* to his letter] **3** *a*) the directing of attention to a person or thing *b*) a mention **4** *a*) an indication, as in a book, of some other source of information *b*) such a source **5** *a*) one who can offer information or recommendation *b*) a statement of character, ability, etc. by such a person

ref·er·en·dum (ref′ə ren′dəm) *n.*, *pl.* **-dums** or **-da** (-də) ⟦L: see REFER⟧ **1** the submission of a law to a direct vote of the people **2** the vote itself

ref′er·ent *n.* the thing referred to, esp. by a word or expression

re·fer·ral (ri fur′əl) *n.* **1** a referring or being referred **2** a person who is referred to another

re·fill (rē fil′; *for n.* rē′fil) *vt.*, *vi.* to fill again — *n.* **1** a unit to refill a special container **2** a refilling of a medical prescription —**re·fill′able** *adj.*

re·fine (ri fin′) *vt.*, *vi.* **-fined′, -fin′ing** ⟦RE- + *fine*, make fine⟧ **1** to free or become free from impurities, etc. **2** to make or become more polished or elegant

re·fined′ *adj.* **1** made free from impurities; purified **2** cultivated; elegant **3** subtle, precise, etc.

re·fine′ment *n.* **1** *a*) a refining or being refined *b*) the result of this **2** delicacy or elegance of manners, etc. **3** an improvement **4** a subtlety

re·fin′ery *n.*, *pl.* **-er·ies** a plant for purifying materials, as oil, sugar, etc.

re·fin·ish (rē fin′ish) *vt.* to change or restore the finish of (furniture, etc.) —**re·fin′isher** *n.*

re·fit (rē fit′) *vt.*, *vi.* **-fit′ted, -fit′ting** to make or be made fit for use again by repairing, reequipping, etc.

re·flect (ri flekt′) *vt.* ⟦< L *re-*, back + *flectere*, to bend⟧ **1** to throw back (light, heat, or sound) **2** to give back an image of **3** to bring as a result [to *reflect* honor on the city] — *vi.* **1** to throw back light, heat, etc. **2** to give back an image **3** to think seriously (*on* or *upon*) **4** to cast blame or discredit (*on* or *upon*) —**re·flec′tive** *adj.*

re·flec′tion *n.* **1** a reflecting or being reflected **2** anything reflected **3** contemplation **4** a thoughtful idea or remark **5** blame; discredit

re·flec′tor *n.* a surface, object, etc. that reflects light, sound, heat, etc.

re·flex (rē′fleks′) *adj.* ⟦see REFLECT⟧ designating or of an involuntary action, as a sneeze, resulting from the direct transmission of a stimulus to a muscle or gland — *n.* a reflex action

re·flex·ive (ri flek′siv) *adj.* **1** designating a grammatical relation in which a verb's subject and object refer to the same person or thing (Ex.: I wash myself) **2** designating a verb, pronoun, etc. in such a relation —**re·flex′ively** *adv.*

re·for·est (rē fôr′ist) *vt.*, *vi.* to plant new trees on (land once forested) —**re′for·esta′tion** *n.*

re·form (ri fôrm′) *vt.* ⟦see RE- & FORM⟧ **1** to make better as by stopping abuses **2** to cause (a person) to behave better — *vi.* to become better in behavior — *n.* a reforming

---

THESAURUS

reek *n.* stench, stink, smell; see SMELL 2.

reek *v.* smell of, give off an odor, emit a stench; see SMELL 1.

reel[1] *n.* spool, bobbin, spindle; see ROLL 2.

reexamine *v.* go back over, review, check thoroughly; see EXAMINE.

refer *v.* **1** [To concern] regard, relate, have relation, have to do with, apply, be about, answer to, involve, connect, be a matter of, have a bearing on, correspond with, bear upon, comprise, include, belong, pertain, have reference, take in, cover, point, hold, encompass, incorporate, touch, deal with; see also CONCERN 1. **2** [To mention] allude to, bring up, direct a remark, make reference, ascribe, direct attention, attribute, cite, quote, hint at, point to, notice, indicate, speak about, suggest, touch on, give as an example, associate, exemplify, instance, excerpt, extract; see also MENTION. **3** [To direct] send to, put in touch with, relegate, commit, submit to, assign, give a recommendation, to introduce; see also LEAD 1. —**referred to 1** [Mentioned] brought up, alluded to, spoken about; see MENTIONED, SUGGESTED. **2** [Directed] recommended, sent on, introduced to; see PROPOSED.

referee *n.* arbitrator, conciliator, judge; see UMPIRE.

reference *n.* **1** [An allusion] mention, relation, implication; see HINT. **2** [A book of reference] original text, source, informant; see BOOK, DICTIONARY. **3** [A person vouching for another] associate, employer, patron; see FRIEND.

refine *v.* **1** [To purify] rarefy, strain, filter; see CLEAN, PURIFY. **2** [To improve] make clear, better, clarify; see EXPLAIN.

refined *a.* **1** [Purified] cleaned, cleansed, aerated, strained, washed, clean, rarefied, boiled down, distilled, clarified, tried, drained; see also PURE.—*Ant.* RAW, crude, unrefined. **2** [Genteel] cultivated, civilized, polished, elegant, well-bred, gracious, enlightened, gentlemanly, ladylike, restrained, gentle, mannerly, high-minded, subtle, courteous; see also POLITE.

refinement *n.* **1** [The act of refining] cleansing, clearing, purification; see CLEANING. **2** [Culture] civilization, cultivation, sophistication, breeding, enlightenment, wide knowledge, lore, subtlety, science, scholarship, learning; see also CULTURE 1. **3** [Genteel feelings and behavior] elegance, politeness, polish, good manners, suavity, courtesy, grace, gentleness, tact, cultivation, graciousness, civility, affability, taste, discrimination, fineness, delicacy, dignity, urbanity; see also CULTURE 2.

refinished *a.* redone, remodeled, fixed up; see CHANGED 2, REPAIRED.

reflect *v.* **1** [To contemplate] speculate, concentrate, weigh; see CONSIDER, THINK 1. **2** [To throw back] echo, reecho, repeat, match, take after, return, resonate, reverberate, copy, resound, reproduce, reply, be resonant, emulate, imitate, follow, catch, rebound. **3** [To throw back an image] mirror, shine, reproduce, show up on, flash, cast back, return,

give forth.

reflection *n.* **1** [Thought] consideration, absorption, imagination, observation, thinking, contemplation, rumination, speculation, musing, deliberation, study, pondering, meditation, concentration, cogitation; see also THOUGHT 1. **2** [An image] impression, rays, light, shine, glitter, appearance, idea, reflected image, likeness, shadow, duplicate, picture, echo, representation, reproduction; see also COPY, IMAGE 2.

reflector *n.* shiny metal, glass, reverberator; see MIRROR.

reflex *a.* mechanical, unthinking, habitual; see AUTOMATIC, SPONTANEOUS.

reform *n.* reformation, betterment, new law; see IMPROVEMENT 2.

reform *v.* **1** [To change into a new form] reorganize, remodel, revise, repair, reconstruct, rearrange, transform, ameliorate, redeem, rectify, better, rehabilitate, improve, correct, cure, remedy, convert, mend, amend, restore, rebuild, reclaim, revolutionize, regenerate, refashion, renovate, renew, rework, reconstitute, make over, remake; see also CORRECT, REPAIR.—*Ant.* CORRUPT, degrade, botch. **2** [To correct evils] amend, clean out, give a new basis, abolish, repeal, uplift, ameliorate, rectify, regenerate, give new life to, remedy, stamp out, make better, standardize, bring up to code; see also IMPROVE 1. **3** [To change one's conduct for the better] resolve, mend, regenerate, uplift, make amends, make a new start, make resolutions, turn over a new leaf, go straight*, swear off; see

re·form (rē·fôrm′) *vt.*, *vi.* to form again
ref·or·ma·tion (ref′ər mā′shən) *n.* a reforming or being reformed —**the Reformation** the 16th-c. religious movement that resulted in establishing the Protestant churches
re·forma·tory (ri fôr′mə tôr′ē) *n.*, *pl.* **-ries** an institution to which young offenders are sent to be reformed
re·form′er *n.* one who seeks to bring about political or social reform
re·fract (ri frakt′) *vt.* ⟦< L *re-*, back + *frangere*, to break⟧ to cause (a ray of light, etc.) to undergo refraction
re·frac′tion *n.* the bending of a ray or wave of light, heat, or sound as it passes from one medium into another
re·frac·tory (ri frak′tər ē) *adj.* ⟦see REFRACT⟧ hard to manage; stubborn
re·frain[1] (ri frān′) *vi.* ⟦< L *re-*, back + *frenare*, to curb⟧ to hold back; keep oneself (*from* doing something)
re·frain[2] (ri frān′) *n.* ⟦see REFRACT⟧ a phrase or verse repeated at intervals in a song or poem
re·fresh (ri fresh′) *vt.* **1** to make fresh by cooling, wetting, etc. **2** to make (a person) feel cooler, stronger, etc., as by food, sleep, etc. **3** to replenish **4** to stimulate — *vi.* to revive
re·fresh′ing *adj.* **1** that refreshes **2** pleasingly new or different
re·fresh′ment *n.* **1** a refreshing or being refreshed **2** something that refreshes **3** [*pl.*] food or drink or both
re·frig·er·ate (ri frij′ə rāt′) *vt.* **-at′ed, -at′ing** ⟦< L *re-*, intens. + *frigus*, cold⟧ to make or keep cool or cold, as for preserving —**re·frig′er·ant** *adj.*, *n.* —**re·frig′era′tion** *n.*
re·frig′era′tor *n.* a box or room in which food, drink, etc. are kept cool
ref·uge (ref′yōōj) *n.* ⟦< L *re-*, back + *fugere*, flee⟧ (a) shelter or protection from danger, difficulty, etc.

refu·gee (ref′yoo jē′, ref′yoo jē′) *n.* one who flees from home or country to seek refuge elsewhere
re·ful·gent (ri ful′jənt) *adj.* ⟦< L *re-*, back + *fulgere*, shine⟧ shining; radiant; glowing —**re·ful′gence** *n.*
re·fund (ri fund′; *for n.* rē′fund′) *vt.*, *vi.* ⟦< L *re-*, back + *fundere*, pour⟧ to give back (money, etc.); repay — *n.* a refunding or the amount refunded
re·fur·bish (ri fur′bish) *vt.* ⟦RE- + FURBISH⟧ to freshen or polish up again; renovate —**re·fur′bish·ment** *n.*
re·fuse[1] (ri fyōōz′) *vt.*, *vi.* **-fused′, -fus′ing** ⟦< L *re-*, back + *fundere*, pour⟧ **1** to decline to accept **2** to decline (to do something), to grant the request of (someone), etc. — **re·fus′al** *n.*
ref·use[2] (ref′yōōs, -yōōz) *n.* ⟦see prec.⟧ waste; trash; rubbish
re·fute (ri fyōōt′) *vt.* **-fut′ed, -fut′ing** ⟦L *refutare*, repel⟧ to prove to be false or wrong —**re·fut′able** *adj.* —**refu·ta·tion** (ref′yə tā′shən) *n.*
re·gain (ri gān′) *vt.* **1** to get back; recover **2** to get back to
re·gal (rē′gəl) *adj.* ⟦< L *rex*, king⟧ of, like, or fit for a monarch —**re′gally** *adv.*
re·gale (ri gāl′) *vt.* **-galed′, -gal′ing** ⟦< Fr *ré-* (see RE-) + OFr *gale*, joy⟧ to entertain as with a feast —**re·gale′ment** *n.*
re·ga·lia (ri gāl′yə) *n.pl.* ⟦see REGAL⟧ **1** royal insignia **2** the insignia as of a rank or society **3** finery
re·gard (ri gärd′) *n.* ⟦see RE- & GUARD⟧ **1** a steady look; gaze **2** consideration; concern **3** respect and affection **4** reference; relation [*in* regard to your plan] **5** [*pl.*] good wishes — *vi.* **1** to look at attentively **2** to consider **3** to hold in affection and respect **4** to concern or involve —**as regards** concerning
re·gard′ing *prep.* concerning; about
re·gard′less *adv.* [Colloq.] without regard for objections, etc.; anyway —**regardless of** in spite of
re·gatta (ri gat′ə, -gät′ə) *n.* ⟦< It⟧ **1** a boat race **2** a series of boat races

■ THESAURUS ■

also sense 2.
Reformation *n.* Renaissance, Lutheranism, Protestantism, Puritanism, Calvinism, Anglicanism, Unitarianism, Counter Reformation, Protestant Movement; see also REVOLUTION 2.
reformed *a.* **1** [Changed] altered, transformed, shifted, reconstituted, reorganized, shuffled, reestablished, revolutionized, rectified, amended, reset, reworked, renewed, regenerated; see also CHANGED 2, IMPROVED.—*Ant.* CORRUPT, degenerated, vicious. **2** [Changed for the better in behavior] converted, improved, redeemed, gone straight*, turned over a new leaf; see also POLITE, REVERENT 1.
refrain[1] *v.* cease, avoid, forbear; see ABSTAIN.
refrain[2] *n.* undersong, theme, strain; see MUSIC 1, SONG.
refresh *v.* invigorate, animate, exhilarate; see RENEW 1.
refreshing *a.* invigorating, rousing, exhilarating; see STIMULATING.
refreshment *n.* tidbit, ice cream, cakes; see DRINK 1, FOOD.
refrigerate *v.* chill, make cold, freeze; see COOL.
refrigeration *n.* cooling, chilling, freezing; see PRESERVATION.
refrigerator *n.* icebox, automatic cooler, cold-storage box, refrigerator car, electric refrigerator, cooling apparatus, refrigeration equipment, deep freezer.
refuge *n.* **1** [A place of protection] shelter, asylum, sanctuary, covert, home, retreat, anchorage, nunnery, convent, monastery, poorhouse, safe place, hiding place, game preserve, safe, safe house, harbor, haven, fortress, stronghold. **2** [A means of resort] alternative, resource, last resort; see ESCAPE.
refugee *n.* exile, expatriate, fugitive, emigrant, renegade, foreigner, castaway, derelict, foundling, homeless

person, leper, pariah, outlaw, prodigal, displaced person, alien, outcast.
refund *n.* return, reimbursement, repayment, remuneration, compensation, allowance, payment for expenses, rebate, discount, settlement, discharge, acquittance, retribution, satisfaction, consolation, money back; see also PAYMENT 1.
refund *v.* pay back, reimburse, remit, repay, relinquish, make good, balance, recoup, adjust, reward, restore, redeem, make repayment to, compensate, recompense, make amends, redress, remunerate, give back, settle, honor a claim, kick back*, make good*, make up for; see also PAY 1.
refunded *a.* acquitted, reimbursed, discharged; see PAID, RETURNED.
refusal *n.* repudiation, renunciation, rebuff, snub, rejection, nonacceptance, denial, disavowal, noncompliance, opposition, forbidding, veto, interdiction, proscription, ban, writ, exclusion, negation, repulse, withholding, disclaimer, nonconsent, unwillingness, regrets, declination, repulsion, reversal, dissent, prohibition, disfavor, disapproval, curb, restraint.
refuse[1] *v.* dissent, desist, repel, rebuff, scorn, pass up, reject, disallow, have no plans to, not anticipate, demur, protest, withdraw, hold back, withhold, shun, turn thumbs down on, evade, dodge, ignore, spurn, regret, turn down, turn from, beg to be excused, send regrets, not budge, cut out of the budget, not budget, not care to, refuse to receive, dispense with, not be at home to, say no, make excuses, disapprove, set aside, turn away, beg off, brush off*, not buy, hold off, turn one's back on, turn a deaf ear to; see also DENY.—*Ant.* ALLOW, admit, consent.
refuse[2] *n.* leavings, remains, residue; see TRASH 1.
refused *a.* declined, rejected, rebuffed, vetoed, repudiated, forbid-

den, denied, disowned, disavowed, forsaken, blocked, repelled, closed to, dismissed, turned down, not budgeted, not in the budget.—*Ant.* PERMITTED, allowed, consented to.
refute *v.* disprove, answer, prove false; see DENY.
regain *v.* recapture, retrieve, reacquire; see RECOVER 1.
regard *n.* **1** [A look] gaze, glance, once-over*; see LOOK 3. **2** [A favorable opinion] esteem, respect, honor, favor, liking, interest, fondness, attachment, deference, opinion, sympathy, estimation, appreciation, reverence, consideration, love, affection, value, devotion; see also ADMIRATION.
regard *v.* **1** [To look at] observe, notice, mark; see SEE 1. **2** [To have an attitude] surmise, look upon, view; see CONSIDER, THINK 1. **3** [To hold in esteem] respect, esteem, value; see ADMIRE.
regarding *a.*, *prep.* concerning, with reference to, in relation to, as regards; see also ABOUT 2. —**as regards** concerning, regarding, respecting; see ABOUT 2. —**in regard to** as to, concerning, with regard to; see ABOUT 2, REGARDING.
regardless *a.* **1** [Heedless] negligent, careless, unobservant, unheeding, inattentive, inconsiderate, reckless, inadvertent, unfeeling, deaf, blind, coarse, crude, neglectful, mindless, insensitive, lax, indifferent, listless, uninterested, unconcerned.—*Ant.* OBSERVANT, alert, watchful, vigilant. **2** [In spite of; *usually used with* "*of*"] despite, aside from, distinct from, without regard to, without considering, notwithstanding, at any cost, leaving aside; see also ALTHOUGH, BUT 1.
regards *n.* best wishes, compliments, greetings, salutations, remembrances, respects, love, deference, commendation, love and kisses*; see also GREETING.

re·gen·er·ate (ri jen′ər it; *for v.,* -ə rāt′) *adj.* ⟦see RE- & GENERATE⟧ renewed or restored — *vt.* -at′ed, -at′ing 1 to cause to be spiritually reborn 2 to cause to be completely reformed 3 to bring into existence again — *vi.* to form again, or be made anew —**re·gen′er·a′tion** *n.* —**re·gen′er·a′tive** *adj.*

re·gent (rē′jənt) *n.* ⟦< L *regere*, to rule⟧ 1 a person appointed to rule when a monarch is absent, too young, etc. 2 a member of a governing board, as of a university —**re′gency** *n.*

reg·gae (reg′ā) *n.* ⟦< ?⟧ a form of popular Jamaican music influenced by rhythm and blues and calypso

reg·i·cide (rej′ə sid′) *n.* ⟦< L *regis,* of a king + *-cida* (see -CIDE)⟧ 1 one who kills a monarch 2 the killing of a monarch

re·gime or **ré·gime** (rə zhēm′, rā-) *n.* ⟦see fol.⟧ 1 a political system 2 an administration

reg·i·men (rej′ə mən) *n.* ⟦< L *regere,* to rule⟧ a system of diet, exercise, etc. for improvement of health

reg·i·ment (rej′ə mənt; *for v.,* -ment′) *n.* ⟦< L *regere,* to rule⟧ a military unit, smaller than a division — *vt.* 1 to organize systematically 2 to subject to strict discipline and control —**reg′i·men′tal** *adj.* —**reg′i·men·ta′tion** *n.*

re·gion (rē′jən) *n.* ⟦< L *regere,* to rule⟧ 1 a large, indefinite part of the earth's surface 2 any division or part, as of an organism —**re′gional** *adj.* —**re′gion·al·ly** *adv.*

re′gion·al·ism′ *n.* 1 regional quality or character in life or literature 2 a word, etc. peculiar to some region

reg·is·ter (rej′is tər) *n.* ⟦< L *regerere,* to record⟧ 1 *a*) a list of names, items, etc. *b*) a book in which this is kept 2 a device for recording [a cash *register*] 3 an opening into a room by which the amount of warm or cold air passing through can be controlled 4 *Music* a part of the range of a voice or instrument — *vt.* 1 to enter in a list 2 to indicate as on a scale 3 to show, as by facial expression [to *register* surprise] 4 to protect (mail) by paying a fee to have it handled by a special postal service — *vi.* 1 to enter one's name in a list, as of voters 2 to enroll in a school 3 to make an impression —**reg′is·trant** (-trənt) *n.*

registered nurse a trained nurse who has passed a State examination

reg·is·trar (rej′i strär′) *n.* one who keeps records, as in a college

reg·is·tra·tion (rej′i strā′shən) *n.* 1 a registering or being registered 2 an entry in a register 3 the number of persons registered

reg·is·try (-is trē) *n., pl.* -**tries** 1 a registering 2 an office where registers are kept 3 an official record or list

reg·nant (reg′nənt) *adj.* 1 ruling 2 predominant 3 prevalent

re·gress (rē′gres; *for v.* ri gres′) *n.* ⟦< L *re-,* back + *gradi,* to go⟧ backward movement — *vi.* to go back —**re·gres′sion** *n.* —**re·gres′sive** *adj.*

re·gret (ri gret′) *vt.* -**gret′ted, -gret′ting** ⟦< OFr *regreter,* mourn⟧ to feel sorry about (an event, one's acts, etc.) — *n.* remorse, esp. over one's acts or omissions —(**one's**) **regrets** a polite declining of an invitation —**re·gret′ful** *adj.* —**re·gret′table** *adj.*

re·group′ *vt., vi.* 1 to group again 2 *Mil.* to reorganize (one's forces), as after a battle

regu·lar (reg′yə lər) *adj.* ⟦< L *regula,* a rule⟧ 1 conforming to a rule, type, etc.; orderly; symmetrical 2 conforming to a fixed principle or procedure 3 customary or established 4 consistent [a *regular* customer] 5 functioning in a normal way [a *regular* pulse] 6 properly qualified [a *regular* doctor] 7 designating or of the standing army of a country 8 [Colloq.] *a*) thorough; complete [a *regular* nuisance] *b*) pleasant, friendly, etc. — *n.* 1 a regular soldier or player 2 [Colloq.] one who is regular in attendance 3 *Politics* a loyal party member —**reg′u·lar′ity** (-lar′ə tē), *pl.* -**ties,** *n.* —**reg′u·lar·ize′, -ized′, -iz′ing,** *vt.* —**reg′u·larly** *adv.*

regu·late (reg′yə lāt′) *vt.* -**lat′ed, -lat′ing** ⟦< L *regula,* a rule⟧ 1 to control or direct according to a rule, principle, etc. 2 to adjust to a standard, rate, etc. 3 to adjust so as

---

THESAURUS

regenerate *v.* raise from the dead, recreate, exhilarate; see PRODUCE 2, REVIVE 1.

regeneration *n.* rebuilding, rehabilitation, renovation; see REPAIR.

regime *n.* administration, management, political system; see GOVERNMENT 2.

regiment *n.* corps, soldiers, military organization; see ARMY 2.

regimentation *n.* massing, collectivization, organization, planned economy, standardization, methodization, regulation, uniformity, arrangement, mechanization, institutionalization, classification, division, lining up, adjustment, harmonization, grouping, ordering; see also RESTRAINT 2.

region *n.* 1 [An indefinite area] country, district, territory, section, sector, province, zone, realm, vicinity, quarter, locale, locality, environs, precinct, county, neighborhood, terrain, domain, range. 2 [A limited area] precinct, ward, block; see AREA. 3 [Scope] sphere, province, realm; see FIELD 3.

regional *a.* provincial, territorial, local, environmental, positional, geographical, parochial, sectional, topical, locational, insular, topographic.

register *n.* 1 [A list] file, registry, roll; see LIST, RECORD 1. 2 [A heating regulator] grate, hot-air opening, radiator; see APPLIANCE.

register *v.* 1 [To record] check in, enroll, file; see LIST 1, RECORD 1. 2 [To indicate] point to, designate, record; see NAME 2. 3 [To show] express, disclose, manifest; see DISPLAY. 4 [To enlist or enroll] go through registration, check into, make an entry, sign up for, check in, sign in, join.

registration *n.* 1 [The act of registering] enrolling, signing up, certification, matriculation, recording,

listing, filing, cataloging, booking, noting down, stamping, authorizing, notarization; see also ENROLLMENT 1. 2 [Those who have registered] enrollment, turnout, registrants, voters, hotel guests, students, student body, delegation.

regress *v.* backslide, relapse, revert; see RETREAT, SINK 1.

regressive *a.* conservative, reverse, reactionary; see BACKWARD 1.

regret *n.* 1 [Remorse] concern, compunction, worry, repentance, self-reproach, self-condemnation, self-disgust, misgiving, regretfulness, nostalgia, self-accusation, contrition, qualm, scruple, penitence, bitterness, disappointment, dissatisfaction, uneasiness, conscience, discomfort, annoyance, spiritual disturbance; see also CARE 2.—*Ant.* COMFORT, satisfaction, ease. 2 [Grief] sorrow, pain, anxiety; see GRIEF.

regret *v.* 1 [To be sorry for] mourn, bewail, lament, cry over, rue, grieve, repent, have compunctions about, look back upon, feel conscience-stricken, moan, have a bad conscience, have qualms about, weep over, be disturbed over, feel uneasy about, laugh out of the other side of one's mouth*, kick oneself*, bite one's tongue*, cry over spilled milk*.—*Ant.* satisfied, be satisfied with, be happy. 2 [To disapprove of] deplore, be opposed to, deprecate; see DENOUNCE, DISLIKE.

regular *a.* 1 [In accordance with custom] customary, usual, routine; see CONVENTIONAL 1, 3. 2 [In accordance with law] normal, legitimate, lawful; see LEGAL. 3 [In accordance with an observable pattern] orderly, methodical, routine, symmetrical, precise, exact, systematic, arranged, organized, patterned, constant, congruous, consonant, consistent, invariable, formal, regulated,

rational, steady, rhythmic, periodic, measured, classified, in order, unconfused, harmonious, systematic, normal, natural, cyclic, successive, momentary, alternating, probable, recurrent, general, usual, expected, serial, automatic, mechanical, alternate, hourly, daily, monthly, weekly, annual, seasonal, yearly, pulsating, diurnal, quotidian, menstrual, anticipated, hoped for, counted on, generally occurring, in the natural course of events, punctual, steady, uniform.—*Ant.* IRREGULAR, sporadic, erratic.

regularity *n.* evenness, steadiness, uniformity, routine, constancy, consistency, invariability, recurrence, system, congruity, punctuality, homogeneity, rhythm, periodicity, swing, rotation, conformity, proportion, symmetry, balance, cadence, harmony.

regularly *a.* customarily, habitually, punctually, systematically, unchangingly, right along, as a rule, usually, commonly, as a matter of course, tirelessly, conventionally, ordinarily, repeatedly, frequently, faithfully, religiously, mechanically, automatically, normally, periodically, evenly, methodically, exactly, monotonously, rhythmically, steadily, unbrokenly, typically, continually, like clockwork, cyclically, day in and day out, constantly, always, ceaselessly, time and time again, invariably, redundantly, hourly, incessantly, daily, perpetually, over and over again, weekly, monthly, annually, exactly.—*Ant.* IRREGULARLY, unevenly, brokenly.

regulate *v.* 1 [To control] rule, legislate, direct; see GOVERN, MANAGE 1. 2 [To adjust] arrange, methodize, dispose, classify, systematize, put in order, fix, settle, adapt, standardize, coordinate, allocate, readjust, reconcile, rectify, correct, improve, temto make operate accurately **—reg′u·la′tor** *n.* **—reg′u·la·to′ry** (-lə tôr′ē) *or* **reg′u·la′tive** *adj.*

reg′u·la′tion *n.* **1** a regulating or being regulated **2** a rule or law regulating conduct — *adj.* usual; regular

re·gur′gi·tate (ri gur′jə tāt′) *vi., vt.* **-tat′ed, -tat′ing** [< ML *re-,* back + LL *gurgitare,* to flood] to bring (partly digested food) back up to the mouth **—re·gur′gi·ta′tion** *n.*

re·hab (rē′hab′) *vt.* **-habbed′, -hab′bing** short for REHABILITATE

re·ha·bil·i·tate (rē′hə bil′ə tāt′) *vt.* **-tat′ed, -tat′ing** [< L *re-,* back + *habere,* have] **1** to restore to rank, reputation, etc. which one has lost **2** to put back in good condition **3** to bring or restore to a state of health, constructive activity, etc. **—re′ha·bil′i·ta′tion** *n.* **—re′ha·bil′i·ta′tive** *adj.*

re·hash (rē′hash′; *for v., also* rē hash′) *vt.* [RE- + HASH] to work up again or go over again — *n.* a rehashing

re·hearse (ri hurs′) *vt., vi.* **-hearsed′, -hears′ing** [< OFr *re-,* again + *hercer,* to harrow] to practice (a play, etc.) for public performance **—re·hears′al** *n.*

reign (rān) *n.* [< L *regere,* to rule] **1** royal power **2** dominance or sway **3** the period of rule, dominance, etc. — *vi.* **1** to rule as a sovereign **2** to prevail [*peace reigns*]

re·im·burse (rē′im burs′) *vt.* **-bursed′, -burs′ing** [RE- + archaic *imburse,* to pay] to pay back **—re′im·burse′ment** *n.*

rein (rān) *n.* [see RETAIN] **1** a narrow strap of leather attached in pairs to a horse's bit and manipulated to control the animal: *usually used in pl.* **2** [*pl.*] a means of controlling, etc. — *vt.* to guide or control as with reins — **give rein to** to free from restraint

re·in·car·na·tion (rē′in kär nā′shən) *n.* [see RE- & INCARNATE] rebirth of the soul in another body **—re′incar′nate, -nated, -nat·ing,** *vt.*

rein·deer (rān′dir′) *n., pl.* **-deer′** [< ON *hreinn,* reindeer + *dȳr,* animal] a large deer found in northern regions and domesticated there as a beast of burden

re·in·force (rē′in fôrs′) *vt.* **-forced′, -forc′ing** [RE- + var. of ENFORCE] **1** to strengthen (a military force) with more troops, ships, etc. **2** to strengthen, as by propping, adding new material, etc. **—re′inforce′ment** *n.*

re·in·state (rē′in stāt′) *vt.* **-stat′ed, -stat′ing** to restore to a former state, position, etc. **—re′instate′ment** *n.*

re·it·er·ate (rē it′ə rāt′) *vt.* **-at′ed, -at′ing** [< L *re-,* back + *iterare,* repeat] to say or do again or repeatedly **—re·it′era′tion** *n.* **—re·it′era′tive** (-ə rāt′iv, -ər ə tiv) *adj.*

re·ject (ri jekt′; *for n.* rē′jekt) *vt.* [< L *re-,* back + *jacere,* to throw] **1** to refuse to take, agree to, use, believe, etc. **2** to discard — *n.* a rejected thing or person **—re·jec′tion** *n.*

re·joice (ri jois′) *vi., vt.* **-joiced′, -joic′ing** [< OFr *re-,* again + *joïr,* be glad] to be or make glad or happy **—re·joic′ing** *n.*

re·join (rē join′) *vt., vi.* **1** to join again; reunite **2** to answer

re·join·der (ri join′dər) *n.* [see RE- & JOIN] an answer, esp. to a reply

re·ju·ve·nate (ri jō̄′və nāt′) *vt.* **-nat′ed, -nat′ing** [< RE- + L *juvenis,* young] to make feel or seem young again **—re·ju′vena′tion** *n.*

re·lapse (ri laps′; *for n., also* rē′laps) *vi.* **-lapsed′, -laps′ing** [see RE- & LAPSE] to slip back into a former state, esp. into illness after apparent recovery — *n.* a relapsing

re·late (ri lāt′) *vt.* **-lat′ed, -lat′ing** [< L *relatus,* brought back] **1** to tell the story of; narrate **2** to connect, as in thought or meaning — *vi.* to have some connection or relation (*to*) **—re·lat′er** *n.*

re·lat′ed *adj.* connected, as by kinship, origin, marriage, etc.

re·la′tion *n.* **1** a narrating **2** a narrative; account **3** connection, as in thought, meaning, etc. **4** connection by blood or marriage **5** a relative **6** [*pl.*] the connections between or among persons, nations, etc. — **in (or with) relation to** concerning; regarding **—re·la′tion·ship′** *n.*

rela·tive (rel′ə tiv) *adj.* **1** related each to the other **2** having to do with; relevant **3** comparative [*living in relative comfort*] **4** meaningful only in relationship [*"cold" is*

■ THESAURUS ■

per, set; see also ADJUST 1.

regulated *a.* fixed, adjusted, arranged, directed, controlled, supervised, methodized, systematized, settled, adapted, coordinated, reconciled, improved, standardized, tempered, ruled; see also CLASSIFIED, MANAGED 2, ORGANIZED.—*Ant.* CONFUSED, disarranged, upset.

regulation *n.* **1** [The act of regulating] handling, direction, control; see MANAGEMENT 1. **2** [A rule] law, statute, ordinance; see COMMAND, LAW 3.

regulator *n.* adjuster, thermostat, valve; see MACHINE.

rehabilitate *v.* restore, change, reestablish; see RENEW 1.

rehabilitation *n.* rebuilding, reestablishment, remaking; see IMPROVEMENT 1, REPAIR.

rehearsal *n.* recitation, recital, trial performance, practice performance, experiment, test flight, reading, dress rehearsal, call; see also PERFORMANCE, PRACTICE 3.

rehearse *v.* **1** [To tell] describe, recount, relate; see TELL 1. **2** [To repeat] tell again, retell, do over, recapitulate, reenact; see also REPEAT 3. **3** [To practice for a performance] drill, test, experiment, hold rehearsals, speak from a script, run through, hold a reading, learn one's part; see also PRACTICE 1.

reign *v.* hold power, sit on the throne, wear the crown; see GOVERN, MANAGE 1.

reimburse *v.* repay, compensate, make reparations; see PAY 1, REFUND.

reimbursement *n.* compensation, restitution, recompense; see PAYMENT 1.

rein *n.* bridle strap, line, control; see ROPE. **—give (free) rein to** authorize, permit, condone; see ALLOW. **—keep a tight rein on** control, check, have authority over; see MANAGE 1.

reincarnation *n.* incarnation, reanimation, rebirth; see BIRTH, RETURN 2.

reinforce *v.* buttress, pillar, add to; see STRENGTHEN.

reinforced *a.* supported, assisted, strengthened, augmented, buttressed, fortified, pillowed, banded, backed, built-up, stiffened, thickened, cushioned, lined; see also STRONG 2.

reinforcement *n.* **1** [Support] coating, concrete block, pillar; see SUPPORT 2. **2** [Military aid; *usually plural*] fresh troops, additional materiel, new ordnance; see HELP 1.

reject *v.* **1** [To refuse] repudiate, decline, renounce; see DENY, REFUSE. **2** [To discard] cast out, throw out, expel; see DISCARD.

rejected *a.* returned, given back, denied; see REFUSED.

rejection *n.* repudiation, denial, dismissal; see REFUSAL.

rejoice *v.* exult, enjoy, revel; see CELEBRATE 2.

rejuvenate *v.* reinvigorate, exhilarate, refresh; see STRENGTHEN.

rejuvenation *n.* reinvigoration, stimulation, revivification; see REVIVAL 1.

relapse *n.* reversion, recidivism, return; see LOSS 3.

relapse *v.* lapse, retrogress, fall, backslide, revert, regress, suffer a relapse, deteriorate, degenerate, fall from grace, fall off, weaken, sink back, fall into again, slip back, slide back, be overcome, give in to again.

relate *v.* **1** [Tell] recount, recite, retell; see DESCRIBE, REPORT 1. **2** [Connect] bring into relation, associate, correlate; see COMPARE 1. **— relate to** be associated to, be connected with, affect; see CONCERN 1, REFER 1.

related *a.* **1** [Told] described, narrated, recounted; see TOLD. **2** [Con-

nected] associated, in touch with, linked, tied up, knit together, allied, affiliated, complementary, analogous, correspondent, akin, alike, like, parallel, correlated, intertwined, interrelated, similar, mutual, dependent, interdependent, interwoven, of that ilk, in the same category, reciprocal, interchangeable. **3** [Akin] kindred, of the same family, germane, fraternal, cognate, consanguine, of one blood; see also sense 2.

relation *n.* **1** [Relationship] connection, association, similarity; see RELATIONSHIP. **2** [A relative] family connection, sibling, kinsman; see RELATIVE. **—in relation to** concerning, with reference to, about; see REGARDING.

relationship *n.* relation, connection, tie, association, affinity, likeness, link, kinship, bond, dependence, relativity, proportion, rapport, analogy, homogeneity, interrelation, correlation, nearness, alliance, relevance, accord, hookup*, contact; see also SIMILARITY.—*Ant.* DIFFERENCE, dissimilarity, oppositeness.

relative *a.* **1** [Pertinent] dependent, contingent, applicable; see RELATED 2, RELEVANT. **2** [In regard to] with respect to, concerning, relating to; see ABOUT 2.

relative *n.* kin, family connection, relation, member of the family, blood relation, next of kin, sibling, kinsman. *Relatives include the following:* mother, father, parent, grandmother, grandfather, great-grandmother, great-grandfather, ancestor, aunt, uncle, great-aunt, great-uncle, cousin, first cousin, second cousin, third cousin, fourth cousin, distant cousin, wife, husband, spouse, daughter, son, nephew, niece, brother, sister, kinsman, kinswoman, mother-ina *relative* term*]* **5** *Gram.* that refers to an antecedent *[a relative* pronoun*]* — *n.* a person connected by blood or marriage —**rel′a·tively** *adv.*

relative humidity the ratio of the amount of moisture in the air to the top amount possible at the temperature

rela·tiv′i·ty (rel′ə tiv′ə tē) *n.* **1** a being relative **2** *Physics* the theory of the relative, rather than absolute, character of motion, velocity, mass, etc., and the interdependence of motion, time, and space

re·lax (ri laks′) *vt., vi.* ‖ < L *re-*, back + *laxare*, loosen ‖ **1** to make or become less firm, tense, severe, etc. **2** to rest, as from work —**re·lax′er** *n.*

re·lax′ant *adj.* causing relaxation, esp. of muscles — *n.* a relaxant drug

re·lax·a′tion (rē′lak sā′shən) *n.* **1** a relaxing or being relaxed **2** *a)* rest from work or effort *b)* recreation

re·lay (rē′lā′; *for v., also* ri lā′) *n.* ‖ < Fr *re-*, back + *laier*, to leave ‖ **1** a fresh supply of horses, etc., as for a stage of a journey **2** a relief crew of workers **3** a race (in full **relay race**) between teams, each member of which goes a part of the distance — *vt.* **-layed′, -lay′ing** to convey as by relays *[to relay news]*

re·lease (ri lēs′) *vt.* **-leased′, -leas′ing** ‖ see RELAX ‖ **1** to set free, as from confinement, work, pain, etc. **2** to let go *[to release* an arrow*]* **3** to permit to be issued, published, etc. — *n.* **1** a releasing, as from prison, work, etc. **2** a film, news story, etc. released to the public **3** a written surrender of a claim, etc.

rel·e·gate (rel′ə gāt′) *vt.* **-gat′ed, -gat′ing** ‖ < L *re-*, away + *legare*, send ‖ **1** to exile or banish (*to*) **2** to consign or assign, esp. to an inferior position **3** to refer or hand over for decision —**rel′ega′tion** *n.*

re·lent (ri lent′) *vi.* ‖ < L *re-*, again + *lentus*, pliant ‖ to become less severe, stern, or stubborn; soften

re·lent′less *adj.* **1** harsh; pitiless **2** not letting up; persistent —**re·lent′lessly** *adv.* —**re·lent′less·ness** *n.*

rel·evant (rel′ə vənt) *adj.* ‖ see RELIEVE ‖ relating to the matter under consideration; pertinent —**rel′evance** or **rel′evan·cy** *n.*

re·li·able (ri lī′ə bəl) *adj.* that can be relied on; dependable —**re·li′abil′ity** *n.* —**re·li′ably** *adv.*

re·li′ance (-əns) *n.* **1** a relying **2** trust, dependence, or confidence **3** a thing relied on —**re·li′ant** *adj.*

relic (rel′ik) *n.* ‖ see RELINQUISH ‖ **1** an object, custom, etc. surviving from the past **2** a souvenir **3** *[pl.]* ruins **4** the venerated remains, etc. of a saint

re·lief (ri lēf′) *n.* **1** a relieving, as of pain, anxiety, a burden, etc. **2** anything that lessens tension, or offers a pleasing change **3** aid, esp. by a public agency to the needy **4** release from work or duty, or those bringing it **5** the projection of sculptured forms from a flat surface **6** the differences in height, collectively, of land forms shown as by lines on a map (**relief map**) — *adj. Baseball* designating a pitcher who replaces another during a game —**in relief** carved so as to project from a surface

re·lieve (ri lēv′) *vt.* **-lieved′, -liev′ing** ‖ < L *re-*, again + *levare*, to raise ‖ **1** to ease (pain, anxiety, etc.) **2** to free from pain, anxiety, a burden, etc. **3** to give or bring aid to **4** to set free from duty or work by replacing **5** to make less tedious, etc. by providing a pleasing change

re·li·gion (ri lij′ən) *n.* ‖ < L *religio*, holiness ‖ **1** belief in and worship of God or gods **2** a specific system of belief, worship, etc., often involving a code of ethics

■■■ THESAURUS ■■■

law, father-in-law, brother-in-law, sister-in-law, aunt by marriage, cousin by marriage, in-law*.
relatively *a.* comparatively, approximately, nearly; see ALMOST.
relax *v.* repose, recline, settle back, make oneself at home, breathe easy, take one's time, take a break, sit around, stop work, lie down, unbend, be at ease, take a breather*; see also REST 1.
relaxation *n.* repose, reclining, loosening; see REST 1.
relaxed *a.* untroubled, carefree, at ease; see COMFORTABLE 1.
relay *v.* communicate, transfer, send forth, transmit, hand over, hand down, turn over, deliver, pass on; see also CARRY 1, SEND 1.
release *n.* **1** [Freedom] liberation, discharge, freeing; see FREEDOM 2. **2** [That which has been released; *usually, printed matter*] news story, publicity, news flash; see PROPAGANDA, STORY.
release *v.* liberate, let go, acquit; see FREE.
released *a.* **1** [Freed] discharged, dismissed, liberated; see FREE 1, 2. **2** [Announced] broadcast, stated, made public; see PUBLISHED.
relent *v.* soften, comply, relax; see YIELD 1.
relentless *a.* unmerciful, vindictive, hard; see RUTHLESS.
relevance *n.* connection, significance, pertinence; see IMPORTANCE.
relevant *a.* suitable, appropriate, fit, proper, pertinent to, becoming, pertaining to, apt, applicable, important, fitting, congruous, cognate, related, conforming, concerning, suitable, compatible, accordant, referring, harmonious, correspondent, consonant, congruent, consistent, correlated, associated, allied, relative, connected, to the point, bearing on the question, having direct bearing, having to do with, related to, on the nose.—*Ant.* IRRELEVANT, WRONG, not pertinent.
reliability *n.* dependability, trustworthiness, constancy, loyalty, faithfulness, sincerity, devotion, honesty,

authenticity, steadfastness, fidelity, safety, security.
reliable *a.* firm, unimpeachable, sterling, strong, positive, stable, dependable, sure, solid, staunch, decisive, unequivocal, steadfast, definite, conscientious, constant, steady, trustworthy, faithful, loyal, good, true, sure, devoted, tried, trusty, honest, honorable, candid, true-hearted, responsible, high-principled, sincere, altruistic, determined, reputable, careful, proved, respectable, righteous, decent, incorrupt, truthful, upright, regular, all right, kosher*, OK, on the up and up*, true-blue, safe, honest, sound, stable, solid, steady, guaranteed, sure, certain, substantial, secure, unquestionable, conclusive, irrefutable, incontestable, dependable, good, firm, strong, unfailing, infallible, authentic, competent, assured, workable, foolproof, sure-fire.—*Ant.* DANGEROUS, insecure, undependable.
reliably *a.* assuredly, presumably, certainly; see PROBABLY, SURELY.
reliance *n.* confidence, trust, hope; see FAITH 1.
relic *n.* **1** [Something left from an earlier time] vestige, trace, survival, heirloom, antique, keepsake, memento, curio, curiosity, token, souvenir, testimonial, evidence, monument, trophy, remains, artifact, remembrance, bric-a-brac. **2** [A ruin] remnant, residue, remains, broken stone; see also DESTRUCTION 2, RUIN 2.
relief *n.* **1** [The act of bringing succor] alleviation, softening, comforting; see COMFORT. **2** [Aid] assistance, support, maintenance; see HELP 1. **3** [A relieved state of mind] satisfaction, relaxation, ease, comfort, release, happiness, contentment, cheer, restfulness, a load off one's mind; see also COMFORT. **4** [The person or thing that brings relief] diversion, relaxation, consolation, solace, reinforcement, supplies, food, shelter, clothing, release, respite, remedy, nursing, medicine, medical care, redress, reparations, indemnities,

variety, change, cure; see also HELP 1. **5** [The raised portions of a sculptural decoration or map] projection, contour, configuration; see DECORATION 2.
relieve *v.* **1** [To replace] discharge, throw out, force to resign; see DISMISS. **2** [To lessen; *said especially of pain*] assuage, alleviate, soothe, comfort, allay, divert, free, ease, lighten, soften, diminish, mitigate, console, cure, aid, assist; see also DECREASE 2, HELP.
relieved *a.* **1** [Eased in mind] comforted, solaced, consoled, reassured, satisfied, soothed, relaxed, put at ease, restored, reconciled, appeased, placated, alleviated, mollified, disarmed, pacified, adjusted, propitiated, breathing easy*; see also COMFORTABLE 1.—*Ant.* SAD, worried, distraught. **2** [Deprived of something, or freed from it] replaced, dismissed, separated from, disengaged, released, made free of, rescued, delivered, supplanted, superseded, succeeded, substituted, interchanged, exchanged. **3** [Lessened; *said especially of pain*] mitigated, palliated, softened, assuaged, eased, abated, diminished, salved, soothed, lightened, alleviated, drugged, anesthetized.
religion *n.* **1** [All that centers about man's belief in or relationship to a superior being or beings] belief, devotion, piety, spirituality, persuasion, godliness, sense of righteousness, morality, theology, faithfulness, devoutness, creed, myth, superstition, doctrine, cult, denomination, mythology, communion, religious conscience, fidelity, conscientiousness, religious bent, ethical standard; see also FAITH 2. **2** [Organized worship or service of a deity] veneration, adoration, consecration, sanctification, prayer, rites, ceremonials, holy sacrifice, incantation, holiday, observance, orthodoxy, reformism; see also CEREMONY 2. *Religions include the following:* Christianity, (Zen) Buddhism, Hinduism, Islam, Judaism, Zoroastrianism, Shintoism,

re·li′gious (-əs) *adj.* **1** devout; pious **2** of or concerned with religion **3** conscientiously exact; scrupulous — *n., pl.* **-gious** a monk or nun —**re·li′gious·ly** *adv.*

re·lin·quish (ri liŋ′kwish) *vt.* ⟦< L *re-*, from + *linquere*, to leave⟧ **1** to give up (a plan, etc.) or let go (one's grasp, etc.) **2** to renounce or surrender (property, a right, etc.) — **re·lin′quish·ment** *n.*

rel·ish (rel′ish) *n.* ⟦< OFr *relais*, something remaining⟧ **1** an appetizing flavor **2** enjoyment; zest /to listen with *rel·ish*/ **3** pickles, raw vegetables, etc., served with a meal to add flavor — *vt.* to enjoy; like

re·live (rē liv′) *vt.* **-lived′, -liv′ing** to experience again (a past event) as in the imagination

re·lo·cate (rē lō′kāt′) *vt., vi.* **-cat′ed, -cat′ing** to move to a new location —**re·lo·ca′tion** *n.*

re·luc·tant (ri luk′tənt) *adj.* ⟦< L *re-*, against + *luctari*, to struggle⟧ **1** unwilling; disinclined **2** marked by unwillingness /a *reluctant* answer/ —**re·luc′tance** *n.* —**re·luc′tant·ly** *adv.*

rely (ri lī′) *vi.* **-lied′, -ly′ing** ⟦< L *re-*, back + *ligare*, bind⟧ to trust or depend: used with *on* or *upon*

rem (rem) *n., pl.* **rem** ⟦*r(oentgen) e(quivalent), m(an)*⟧ a dosage of ionizing radiation with a biological effect about equal to that of one roentgen of X-ray

REM (rem) *n., pl.* **REMs** ⟦*r(apid) e(ye) m(ovement)*⟧ the rapid, jerky movement of the eyeballs during stages of sleep associated with dreaming

re·main (ri mān′) *vi.* ⟦< L *re-*, back + *manere*, to stay⟧ **1** to be left over when the rest has been taken away, etc. **2** to stay **3** to continue /to *remain* a cynic/ **4** to be left to be dealt with, done, etc.

re·main′der *n.* **1** those remaining **2** what is left when a part is taken away **3** what is left when a smaller number is subtracted from a larger **4** what is left undivided when a number is divided by another that is not one of its factors

re·mains′ *n.pl.* **1** what is left after use, destruction, etc. **2** a dead body

re·mand (ri mand′) *vt.* ⟦< L *re-*, back + *mandare*, to order⟧ to send back, as a prisoner into custody

re·mark (ri märk′) *vt.* ⟦< Fr *re-*, again + *marquer*, to mark⟧ **1** to notice or observe **2** to say or write as a comment — *vi.* to make a comment: with *on* or *upon* — *n.* a brief comment

re·mark′able *adj.* worthy of notice; extraordinary —**re·mark′ably** *adv.*

re·medi·al (ri mē′dē əl) *adj.* **1** providing a remedy **2** for correcting deficiencies, as some courses of study

rem·edy (rem′ə dē) *n., pl.* **-dies** ⟦< L *re-*, again + *mederi*, heal⟧ **1** any medicine or treatment for a disease **2** something to correct a wrong — *vt.* **-died, -dy·ing** to cure, correct, etc.

re·mem·ber (ri mem′bər) *vt.* ⟦< L *re-*, again + *memorare*, bring to mind⟧ **1** to think of again **2** to bring back to mind by an effort; recall **3** to be careful not to forget **4** to mention (a person) to another as sending regards — *vi.* to bear something in mind or call something back to mind

re·mem′brance (-brəns) *n.* **1** a remembering or being remembered **2** the power to remember **3** a souvenir

re·mind (ri mīnd′) *vt., vi.* to put (a person) in mind (of something); cause to remember —**re·mind′er** *n.*

remi·nisce (rem′ə nis′) *vi.* **-nisced′, -nisc′ing** ⟦< fol.⟧ to think, talk, or write about remembered events

rem′i·nis′cence (-əns) *n.* ⟦Fr < L *re-*, again + *memini*, remember⟧ **1** a remembering **2** a memory **3** [*pl.*] an account of remembered experiences —**rem′i·nis′cent** *adj.*

re·miss (ri mis′) *adj.* ⟦see REMIT⟧ careless; negligent —**re·miss′ness** *n.*

re·mis·sion (ri mish′ən) *n.* ⟦see fol.⟧ **1** forgiveness; pardon **2** release from a debt, tax, etc. **3** an abating of pain, a disease, etc.

re·mit (ri mit′) *vt.* **-mit′ted, -mit′ting** ⟦< L *re-*, back + *mittere*, send⟧ **1** to forgive or pardon **2** to refrain from exacting (a payment), inflicting (punishment), etc. **3** to slacken; decrease **4** to send (money) in payment —**re·mit′tance** *n.*

rem·nant (rem′nənt) *n.* ⟦see REMAIN⟧ what is left over, as a piece of cloth at the end of a bolt

---

THESAURUS

Taoism, deism, theism, polytheism, dualism; see also CHURCH 3. —**get religion** become converted, believe, change; see REFORM 2, 3.
religious *a.* **1** [Pertaining to religion] ethical, spiritual, moral, ecclesiastical, clerical, theological, canonical, divine, supernatural, holy, sacred, churchly, theistic, deistic, priestly, pontifical, ministerial.— *Ant.* WORLDLY, secular, earthly. **2** [Devout] pious, puritanical, sanctimonious, pietistic, godly, god-fearing, orthodox, reverend, reverential, believing, faithful, Christian, fanatic, evangelistic, revivalistic, churchgoing; see also HOLY 1. **3** [Scrupulous] methodical, minute, thorough; see CAREFUL.
relish *n.* **1** [A condiment] seasoning, herb, savor. *Relishes include the following:* catsup or ketchup, piccalilli, cucumber relish, pickle relish, mincemeat, pickled pears, pickled peaches, chutney, chili sauce, hot sauce, cranberry sauce. **2** [Obvious delight] gusto, joy, great satisfaction; see ZEAL.
relish *v.* enjoy, fancy, be fond of; see LIKE 1, 2.
reluctance *n.* disinclination, qualm, hesitation; see DOUBT.
reluctant *a.* disinclined, loath, unwilling, averse, opposed, tardy, backward, adverse, laggard, remiss, slack, squeamish, demurring, grudging, involuntary, uncertain, hanging back, hesitant, hesitating, diffident, with bad grace, indisposed, disheartened, discouraged, queasy.—*Ant.* WILLING, eager, disposed.
rely *on* or *upon* *v.* hope, have faith in, count on; see TRUST 1.
remain *v.* **1** [To stay] inhabit, stop, stay in; see SETTLE 5. **2** [To endure] keep on, go on, prevail; see CONTINUE 1, ENDURE 1. **3** [To be left] remain

standing, outlive, outlast; see SURVIVE 1.
remainder *n.* remaining portion, leftover, residue, remains, relic, remnant, dregs, surplus, leavings, balance, residuum, excess, overplus, scrap, fragment, small piece, carryover, rest, residual portion, whatever is left, salvage.
remains *n.* corpse, cadaver, relics; see BODY 2.
remake *v.* change, revise, alter; see CORRECT.
remark *n.* statement, saying, utterance, annotation, note, mention, reflection, illustration, point, conclusion, consideration, talk, observation, expression, comment, assertion, witticism.
remark *v.* speak, mention, observe; see SAY, TALK 1.
remarkable *a.* exceptional, extraordinary, uncommon; see UNUSUAL 1.
remarkably *a.* exceptionally, singularly, notably; see ESPECIALLY, VERY.
remedy *n.* **1** [A medicine] antidote, pill, drug; see MEDICINE 2, TREATMENT 2. **2** [Effective help] relief, cure, redress, support, improvement, solution, plan, panacea, cure-all, assistance, counteraction; see also RELIEF 4.
remedy *v.* cure, help, aid; see HEAL.
remember *v.* **1** [To recall] recollect, recognize, summon up, relive, dig into the past, refresh one's memory, be reminded of, think of, revive, bring to mind, call to mind, think over, think back, look back, brood over, conjure up, call up, carry one's thoughts back, look back upon, have memories of, commemorate, memorialize, reminisce, carry in one's thoughts, keep a memory alive, enshrine in the memory.—*Ant.* LOSE, forget, neglect. **2** [To bear in mind]

keep in mind, memorize, know by heart, learn, master, get, be impressed on one's mind, fix in the mind, retain, treasure, hold dear, dwell upon, brood over, keep forever.—*Ant.* NEGLECT, ignore, disregard.
remembered *a.* thought of, recalled, recollected, rewarded, summoned up, brought to mind, memorialized, haunting one's thoughts, commemorated, dug up.—*Ant.* LOST, forgotten, overlooked.
remembrance *n.* **1** [Memory] recall, recollection, recognition; see MEMORY 1. **2** [A gift] reward, token, keepsake; see GIFT 1.
remind *v.* **1** [To bring into the memory] bring back, make one think of, intimate; see HINT. **2** [To call the attention of another] caution, point out, refresh the memory, remind one of, mention to, call attention to, bring up, prompt, prod, stress, emphasize, note, stir up, put a bug in one's ear, give a cue; see also WARN.
reminded *a.* warned, cautioned, prompted, put in mind of, made aware, advised, forewarned, notified, awakened, prodded.
reminder *n.* warning, notice, admonition, note, memorandum, memo, hint, suggestion, memento, token, keepsake, trinket, remembrance, souvenir.
remit *v.* make payment, forward, dispatch; see PAY 1.
remittance *n.* transmittal, money sent, enclosure; see PAYMENT 1.
remnant *n.* residue, leavings, dregs; see EXCESS 1, REMAINDER.
remnants *n.* scraps, odds and ends, leftovers, particles, surplus, endpieces, remains, leavings; see also EXCESS 1, REMAINDER.

re·mod·el (rē'mäd''l) *vt.* **-eled** or **-elled, -el·ing** or **-el·ling** to make over; rebuild

re·mon·strate (ri män'strāt') *vt.* **-strated, -strat·ing** ⟦< L *re-*, again + *monstrare*, to show⟧ to say in protest, objection, etc. — *vi.* to protest; object —**re·mon'strance** *n.* —**re·mon'strant** *adj., n.*

re·morse (ri môrs') *n.* ⟦< L *re-*, again + *mordere*, to bite⟧ a torturing sense of guilt for one's actions —**re·morse'ful** *adj.* —**re·morse'less** *adj.*

re·mote (ri mōt') *adj.* **-mot'er, -mot'est** ⟦< L *remotus*, removed⟧ **1** distant in space or time **2** distant in connection, relation, etc. **3** distantly related **4** aloof **5** slight /a *remote* chance/ —**re·mote'ly** *adv.* —**re·mote'ness** *n.*

remote control **1** control of aircraft, missiles, etc. from a distance, as by radio waves **2** a device to control a television set, recorder, etc. from a distance

re·move (ri mōōv') *vt.* **-moved', -mov'ing** ⟦see RE- & MOVE⟧ **1** to move (something) from where it is; take away or off **2** to dismiss, as from office **3** to get rid of — *vi.* to move away, as to another residence — *n.* a step or degree away —**re·mov'able** *adj.* —**re·mov'al** *n.*

re·mu·ner·ate (ri myōō'nə rāt') *vt.* **-at'ed, -at'ing** ⟦< L *re-*, again + *munus*, gift⟧ to pay (a person) for (work, a loss, etc.) —**re·mu'ner·a'tion** *n.* —**re·mu'ner·a'tive** *adj.*

ren·ais·sance (ren'ə säns') *n.* ⟦Fr⟧ a rebirth; renascence —**the Renaissance** the great revival of art and learning in Europe in the 14th, 15th, and 16th centuries

re·nal (rēn'əl) *adj.* ⟦< L *renes*, kidneys⟧ of or near the kidneys

re·nas·cence (ri nas'əns, -nās'-) *n.* ⟦< L *renasci*, be born again⟧ [*also* R-] renascence —**re·nas'cent** *adj.*

rend (rend) *vt.* **rent, rend'ing** ⟦OE *rendan*⟧ to tear apart or split with violence — *vi.* to tear; split apart

ren·der (ren'dər) *vt.* ⟦ult. < L *re(d)-*, back + *dare*, give⟧ **1** to submit, as for approval, payment, etc. **2** to give in return or pay as due /*render* thanks/ **3** to cause to be **4** to give (aid) or do (a service) **5** to depict, as by drawing **6** to play (music), act (a role), etc. **7** to translate **8** to melt down (fat) **9** to pronounce (a verdict)

ren·dez·vous (rän'dā vōō') *n., pl.* **-vous'** (-vōōz') ⟦< Fr *rendez-vous*, betake yourself⟧ **1** a meeting place **2** an agreement to meet **3** the meeting itself — *vi., vt.* **-voused'** (-vōōd'), **-vous'ing** (-vōō'iŋ) to assemble as prearranged

ren·di·tion (ren dish'ən) *n.* a rendering; performance, translation, etc.

ren·e·gade (ren'ə gād') *n.* ⟦< L *re-*, again + *negare*, deny⟧ one who abandons a party, movement, etc. to join the opposition; turncoat

re·nege (ri nig') *vi.* **-neged', -neg'ing** ⟦see prec.⟧ **1** to go back on a promise **2** *Card Games* to fail to play a card of the suit called for when able to do so —**re·neg'er** *n.*

re·new (ri nōō') *vt.* **1** to make new or fresh again **2** to reestablish; revive **3** to resume **4** to put in a fresh supply of **5** to give or get an extension of /*renew* a lease/ —**re·new'al** *n.*

ren·net (ren'it) *n.* ⟦ME *rennen*, coagulate⟧ an extract from the stomach of calves, etc. used to curdle milk

re·nounce (ri nouns') *vt.* **-nounced', -nounc'ing** ⟦< L *re-*, back + *nuntiare*, tell⟧ **1** to give up formally (a claim, etc.) **2** to give up (a habit, etc.) **3** to disown —**re·nounce'ment** *n.*

ren·o·vate (ren'ə vāt') *vt.* **-vat'ed, -vat'ing** ⟦< L *re-*, again + *novus*, new⟧ to make as good as new; restore —**ren'o·va'tion** *n.* —**ren'o·va'tor** *n.*

re·nown (ri noun') *n.* ⟦< OFr *re-*, again + *nom(m)er*, to name < L *nominare*⟧ great fame or reputation —**re·nowned'** *adj.*

rent[1] (rent) *n.* ⟦< L *reddita*, paid⟧ a stated payment at fixed intervals for the use of a house, land, etc. — *vt.* to get or give use of in return for rent — *vi.* to be let for rent —**for rent** available to be rented —**rent'er** *n.*

rent[2] (rent) *vt., vi. pt. & pp. of* REND — *n.* a hole or gap made by tearing

rent·al (rent'l) *n.* **1** an amount paid or received as rent **2** a house, car, etc. offered for rent **3** a renting — *adj.* of or for rent

re·nun·ci·a·tion (ri nun'sē ā'shən) *n.* a renouncing, as of a right

re·or·gan·ize (rē ôr'gə nīz') *vt., vi.* **-ized', -iz'ing** to organize (a business, etc.) anew —**re·or'gani·za'tion** *n.*

rep (rep) *n.* ⟦Fr *reps* < Eng *ribs*⟧ a ribbed fabric of silk, wool, cotton, etc.

Rep. **1** Representative **2** Republican

re·paid (ri pād') *vt., vi. pt. & pp. of* REPAY

re·pair[1] (ri per') *vt.* ⟦< L *re-*, again + *parare*, prepare⟧ **1** to put back in good condition; fix; renew **2** to make amends for — *n.* **1** a repairing **2** [*usually pl.*] work done

THESAURUS

remodel *v.* renovate, refurnish, refurbish, readjust, reconstruct, readapt, rearrange, redecorate, refashion, improve, reshape, recast, rebuild, repair, modernize, repaint; see also REPAIR.

remodeled *a.* refurnished, redecorated, rebuilt; see CHANGED 2.

remorse *n.* compunction, contrition, self-reproach; see GRIEF, REGRET 1. —**without remorse** cruel, pitiless, relentless; see RUTHLESS.

remorseful *a.* contrite, penitent, repentant; see SORRY 1.

remorseless *a.* unyielding, unforgiving, vindictive; see SEVERE 1, 2.

remote *a.* **1** [Distant] far-off, faraway, out-of-the-way, removed, beyond, secluded, inaccessible, isolated, unknown, alien, foreign, undiscovered, off the beaten track, over the hills and far away, godforsaken; see also DISTANT.—*Ant.* NEAR, close, accessible. **2** [Ancient] forgotten, past, aged; see OLD 3. **3** [Separated] unrelated, irrelevant, unconnected; see SEPARATED.

removal *n.* dismissal, discharge, expulsion, exile, deportation, banishment, elimination, extraction, dislodgement, evacuation, ejection, transference, eradication, extermination, replacement, translocation, the gate*, the bounce*.—*Ant.* ENTRANCE, induction, introduction.

remove *v.* **1** [To move physically] take away from, cart away, clear away, carry away, take away, tear away, brush away, transfer, transport, dislodge, uproot, excavate, displace, unload, discharge, lift up, doff, raise, evacuate, shift, switch, lift, push, draw away, draw in, withdraw, separate, extract, cut out, dig out, tear out, pull out, take out, smoke out, rip out, take down, take off, draw off, take off, carry off, cart off, clear off, strike off, cut off, rub off, scrape off, take in. **2** [To eliminate] get rid of, do away with, exclude; see ELIMINATE. **3** [To dismiss] discharge, displace, discard; see DISMISS.

removed *a.* **1** [Taken out] extracted, eliminated, withdrawn, evacuated, dislodged, ejected, pulled out, amputated, excised, expunged, extirpated.—*Ant.* LEFT, established, ignored. **2** [Distant] faraway, out-of-the-way, far-off; see DISTANT. **3** [Dismissed] banished, relieved of office, retired; see DISCHARGED, RECALLED 2.

rend *v.* rip, sever, sunder; see BREAK 1.

render *v.* **1** [To give] present, hand over, distribute; see GIVE 1. **2** [To perform, especially a service] do, act, execute; see PERFORM 1. **3** [To interpret; *said especially of music*] play, perform, depict; see INTERPRET.

rendition *n.* interpretation, version, reading; see TRANSLATION.

renew *v.* **1** [To refresh] revive, reawaken, regenerate, reestablish, rehabilitate, reinvigorate, replace, revive, rebuild, reconstitute, remake, refinish, refurbish, redo, repeat, invigorate, exhilarate, restore, resuscitate, recondition, overhaul, replenish, go over, cool, brace, freshen, stimulate, recreate, remodel, revamp, redesign, modernize, rejuvenate, give new life to, recover, renovate, reintegrate, make a new beginning, bring up to date, do over, make like new; see also REVIVE 1. **2** [To repeat] resume, reiterate, recommence; see REPEAT 1. **3** [To replace] resume, supplant take over; see SUBSTITUTE.

renewal *n.* resurrection, new start, renovation; see REVIVAL 1.

renewed *a.* revived, readapted, refitted; see REPAIRED.

renounce *v.* disown, disavow, give up; see DENY, DISCARD.

renovate *v.* make over, remake, rehabilitate; see RENEW 1.

renovated *a.* renewed, remodeled, redone; see CLEAN 1, REPAIRED.

renovation *n.* reform, revision, change; see IMPROVEMENT 1.

rent[1] *v.* **1** [To sell the use of property] lease, lend, let, make available, allow the use of, take in roomers, sublet, put on loan. **2** [To obtain use by payment] hire, pay rent for, charter, contract, sign a contract for, engage, borrow, pay for services; see also PAY 1. —**for rent** on the market, renting, selling, for hire, available, offered, advertised, to let, salable.

rented *a.* leased, lent, hired, contracted, engaged, let, chartered, taken, on lease, out of the market.

reopen *v.* revive, reestablish, begin again; see OPEN 2, RENEW 1.

reorganization *n.* reestablishment, reconstitution, reorientation; see CHANGE 2, IMPROVEMENT 1.

reorganize *v.* rebuild, renovate, regenerate; see RECONSTRUCT.

repaid *a.* paid back, reimbursed, refunded; see PAID.

repair[1] *n.* reconstruction, substitution, reformation, rehabilitation, new in repairing 3 the state of being repaired [kept in *repair*] —**re·pair′able** *adj.*

re·pair² (ri per′) *vi.* [< L re-, back + *patria*, native land] to go (*to* a place)

repair′man (-mən, -man′) *n., pl.* **-men** one whose work is repairing things

repa·ra·tion (rep′ə rā′shən) *n.* [see REPAIR¹] 1 a making of amends 2 [*usually pl.*] compensation, as for war damage

rep·ar·tee (rep′ər tē′, -är-; -tā′) *n.* [< Fr re-, back + *partir*, to part] a series of quick, witty retorts; banter

re·past (ri past′) *n.* [< OFr re-, RE- + *past*, food] food and drink; a meal

re·pa·tri·ate (rē pā′trē āt′) *vt., vi.* **-at′ed, -at′ing** [see REPAIR²] to return to the country of birth, citizenship, etc. —**re·pa′tri·a′tion** *n.*

re·pay (ri pā′) *vt.* **-paid′, -pay′ing** 1 to pay back 2 to make return to for (a favor, etc.) —**re·pay′ment** *n.*

re·peal (ri pēl′) *vt.* [see RE- & APPEAL] to revoke; cancel; annul — *n.* revocation; abrogation

re·peat (ri pēt′) *vt.* [< L re-, again + *petere*, to demand] 1 to say again 2 to recite (a poem, etc.) 3 to say (something) as said by someone else 4 to tell to someone else [*repeat* a secret] 5 to do or make again — *vi.* to say or do again — *n.* 1 a repeating 2 anything said or done again, as a rebroadcast of a television program 3 *Music* a) a passage to be repeated b) a symbol for this —**re·peat′er** *n.*

re·peat′ed *adj.* said, made, or done again, or often —**re·peat′edly** *adv.*

re·pel (ri pel′) *vt.* **-pelled′, -pel′ling** [< L re-, back + *pellere*, to drive] 1 to drive or force back 2 to reject 3 to cause dislike in; disgust 4 to be resistant to (water, dirt, etc.) —**re·pel′lent** *adj., n.*

re·pent (ri pent′) *vi., vt.* [< L re-, again + *poenitere*, repent] 1 to feel sorry for (an error, sin, etc.) 2 to feel

such regret over (an action, intention, etc.) as to change one's mind —**re·pent′ance** *n.* —**re·pent′ant** *adj.*

re·per·cus·sion (rē′pər kush′ən) *n.* [see RE- & PERCUSSION] 1 reverberation 2 a far-reaching, often indirect reaction to some event

rep·er·toire (rep′ər twär′) *n.* [< Fr < L *reperire*, discover] the stock of plays, songs, etc. that a company, singer, etc. is prepared to perform

rep′er·to′ry (-tôr′ē) *n., pl.* **-ries** 1 REPERTOIRE 2 the system of alternating several plays throughout a season with a permanent acting group

rep·e·ti·tion (rep′ə tish′ən) *n.* [< L *repetitio*] 1 a repeating 2 something repeated —**rep′e·ti′tious** *adj.* —**re·peti·tive** (ri pet′ə tiv) *adj.*

re·pine (ri pīn′) *vi.* **-pined′, -pin′ing** [RE- + PINE²] to feel or express unhappiness or discontent; complain

re·place (ri plās′) *vt.* **-placed′, -plac′ing** 1 to put back in a former or the proper place 2 to take the place of 3 to provide an equivalent for —**re·place′able** *adj.* —**re·place′ment** *n.*

re·plen·ish (ri plen′ish) *vt.* [< L re-, again + *plenus*, full] 1 to make full or complete again 2 to supply again —**re·plen′ish·ment** *n.*

re·plete (ri plēt′) *adj.* [< L re-, again + *plere*, to fill] 1 plentifully supplied 2 stuffed; gorged —**re·ple′tion** *n.*

rep·li·ca (rep′li kə) *n.* [see REPLY] a reproduction or close copy, as of a work of art

rep·li·cate (rep′li kāt′) *vt.* **-cat′ed, -cat′ing** [see REPLY] to repeat or duplicate

rep′li·ca′tion *n.* 1 a replicating 2 a reply; answer 3 a copy; reproduction

re·ply (ri plī′) *vi.* **-plied′, -ply′ing** [< L re-, back + *plicare*, to fold] to answer or respond — *n., pl.* **-plies′** an answer or response

re·port (ri pôrt′) *vt.* [< L re-, back + *portare*, carry] 1 to give an account of, as for publication 2 to carry and repeat (a message, etc.) 3 to announce formally 4 to make a charge about (something) or against (someone) to one in authority — *vi.* 1 to make a report 2 to present

---

THESAURUS

part, patch, restoration, restored portion, replacement; see also IMPROVEMENT 1, 2.—*Ant.* BREAK, tear, fracture.

repair¹ *v.* fix, adjust, improve, correct, settle, put into shape, reform, patch, rejuvenate, refurbish, retread, touch up, put in order, revive, refresh, renew, mend, darn, sew, revamp, rectify, right, ameliorate, renovate, reshape, rebuild, work over*, fix up.—*Ant.* WRECK, damage, smash.

repaired *a.* fixed, rearranged, adjusted, adapted, settled, remodeled, rectified, mended, corrected, righted, restored, renewed, remedied, improved, renovated, retouched, in working order, patched up, put together, put back into shape, sewn, reset, stitched up.—*Ant.* DAMAGED, worn, torn.

reparation *n.* indemnity, retribution, amends; see PAYMENT 1.

repay *v.* 1 [To pay back] reimburse, recompense, refund, return, indemnify, give back, make amends, requite, compensate, square oneself*, settle up; see also PAY 1. 2 [To retaliate] get even with, square accounts, reciprocate; see REVENGE.

repayment *n.* compensation, indemnity, restitution; see PAYMENT 1.

repeal *n.* annulment, cancellation, abolition; see WITHDRAWAL.

repeal *v.* annul, abolish, abrogate; see CANCEL.

repeat *v.* 1 [To do again] redo, remake, do over, recur, rehash, reciprocate, return, rework, reform, refashion, recast, reduplicate, renew, reconstruct, reerect, revert, hold over, go over again and again. 2 [To happen again] reoccur, recur, revolve, reappear, occur again, come again, return; see also HAPPEN 2. 3 [To say again] reiterate, restate, reis-

sue, republish, reutter, echo, recite, reecho, rehearse, retell, go over, play back, recapitulate, drum into, rehash, come again; see also SAY.

repeated *a.* 1 [Done again] redone, remade, copied, imitated, reworked, refashioned, recast, done over, reciprocated, returned, reverted, reduplicated. 2 [Said again] reiterated, restated, reannounced, reuttered, recited, reproduced, seconded, paraphrased, reworded, retold.

repeatedly *adv.* again and again, many times, time and again; see FREQUENTLY, REGULARLY.

repel *v.* 1 [To throw back] rebuff, resist, stand up against, oppose, check, repulse, put to flight, keep at bay, knock down, drive away, drive back, beat back, hold back, force back, push back, beat off, ward off, chase off, stave off, fight off.—*Ant.* FALL, fail, retreat. 2 [To cause aversion] nauseate, offend, revolt; see DISGUST. 3 [To reject] disown, dismiss, cast aside; see REFUSE.

repent *v.* be sorry, have qualms, be penitent; see APOLOGIZE, REGRET 1.

repentance *n.* sorrow, remorse, self-reproach; see REGRET 1.

repentant *a.* penitent, regretful, contrite; see SORRY 1.

repercussion *n.* consequence, result, effect; see RESULT.

repetition *n.* recurrence, reoccurrence, reappearance, reproduction, copy, rote, duplication, renewal, recapitulation, reiteration, return; see also WORDINESS.

repetitious *a.* boring, wordy, repeating; see DULL 4.

replace *v.* 1 [To supply an equivalent] repay, compensate, mend; see RECONSTRUCT, RENEW 1, REPAIR. 2 [To take the place of] take over, supplant, displace; see SUBSTITUTE. 3 [To put back in the same place]

restore, reinstate, put back; see RETURN 2.

replaced *a.* 1 [Returned to the same place] restored, reinstated, reintegrated, recovered, recouped, reacquired, regained, repossessed, resumed, rewon, retrieved. 2 [Having another in one's place; *said of persons*] dismissed, cashiered, dislodged; see RECALLED 2. 3 [Having another in its place; *said of things*] renewed, interchanged, replenished; see CHANGED 1.

replica *n.* copy, likeness, model; see DUPLICATE, IMITATION 2.

reply *n.* response, return, retort; see ANSWER 1.

reply *v.* retort, rejoin, return; see ANSWER 1.

report *n.* 1 [A transmitted account] tale, narrative, description; see NEWS 1, 2, STORY. 2 [An official summary] proclamation, outline, release; see RECORD 1, SUMMARY. 3 [A loud, explosive sound] detonation, bang, blast; see NOISE 1.

report *v.* 1 [To deliver information] describe, recount, narrate, provide the details of, give an account of, set forth, inform, advise, communicate, retail, wire, cable, telephone, radio, broadcast, notify, relate, state; see also TELL 1. 2 [To make a summary statement] summarize, publish, proclaim; see sense 1. 3 [To present oneself] be at hand, reach, come; see ARRIVE. 4 [To record] take minutes, inscribe, note down; see RECORD 1.

reported *a.* stated, recited, recounted, narrated, described, set forth, announced, broadcast, rumored, noted, expressed, proclaimed, made known, according to rumor, revealed, communicated, disclosed, imparted, divulged, recorded, in the air, all over town.—*Ant.* UNKNOWN, verified, certain.

oneself, as for work — *n.* **1** rumor **2** a statement or account **3** a formal presentation of facts **4** the noise of an explosion —**re·port′ed·ly** *adv.*

re·port·age (ri pôrt′ij, rep′ər täzh′) *n.* **1** the reporting of the news **2** journalistic writings

report card a periodic written report on a pupil's progress

re·port′er *n.* one who reports; specif., one who gathers information and writes reports for a newspaper, etc. — **rep·or·to·ri·al** (rep′ər tôr′ē əl) *adj.*

re·pose¹ (ri pōz′) *vt.* **-posed′, -pos′ing** ⟦< L *re-*, again + *pausare*, to rest⟧ to lay or place for rest — *vi.* **1** to lie at rest **2** to rest from work, etc. **3** to lie dead — *n.* **1** a) rest b) sleep **2** composure **3** calm; peace —**re·pose′ful** *adj.*

re·pose² (ri pōz′) *vt.* **-posed′, -pos′ing** ⟦see fol.⟧ **1** to place (trust, etc.) *in* someone **2** to place (power, etc.) *in* the control of some person or group

re·pos·i·to·ry (ri päz′ə tôr′ē) *n., pl.* **-ries** ⟦< L *re-*, back + *ponere*, to place⟧ a box, room, etc. in which things may be placed for safekeeping

re·pos·sess (rē′pə zes′) *vt.* to get possession of again —**re′pos·ses′sion** *n.*

rep·re·hend (rep′ri hend′) *vt.* ⟦< L *re-*, back + *prehendere*, take⟧ to rebuke, blame, or censure

rep′re·hen′si·ble (-hen′sə bəl) *adj.* deserving to be reprehended —**rep′re·hen′si·bly** *adv.*

rep·re·sent (rep′ri zent′) *vt.* ⟦see RE- & PRESENT, *v.*⟧ **1** to present to the mind **2** to present a likeness of **3** to describe **4** to stand for; symbolize **5** to be the equivalent of **6** to act (a role) **7** to act in place of, esp. by conferred authority **8** to serve as a specimen, example, etc. of

rep′re·sen·ta′tion *n.* **1** a representing or being represented, as in a legislative assembly **2** legislative representatives, collectively **3** a likeness, image, picture, etc. **4** [*often pl.*] a statement of facts, arguments, etc. meant to influence action, make protest, etc. —**rep′re·sen·ta′tional** *adj.*

rep′re·sent′a·tive *adj.* **1** representing **2** of or based on representation of the people by elected delegates **3** typical — *n.* **1** an example or type **2** one authorized to act for others; delegate, agent, salesman, etc. **3** [R-] a member of the lower house of Congress or of a State legislature

re·press (ri pres′) *vt.* ⟦see RE- & PRESS¹⟧ **1** to hold back; restrain **2** to put down; subdue **3** *Psychiatry* to force (painful ideas, etc.) into the unconscious —**re·pres′sion** *n.* —**re·pres′sive** *adj.*

re·prieve (ri prēv′) *vt.* **-prieved′, -priev′ing** ⟦< Fr *reprendre*, take back⟧ **1** to postpone the execution of (a condemned person) **2** to give temporary relief to — *n.* a reprieving or being reprieved

rep·ri·mand (rep′rə mand′) *n.* ⟦< L *reprimere*, repress⟧ a severe or formal rebuke — *vt.* to rebuke severely or formally

re·pris·al (ri prī′zəl) *n.* ⟦see REPREHEND⟧ injury done for injury received

re·proach (ri prōch′) *vt.* ⟦< L *re-*, back + *prope*, near⟧ to accuse of a fault; rebuke — *n.* **1** shame, disgrace, etc. or a cause of this **2** rebuke or censure —**re·proach′ful** *adj.*

rep·ro·bate (rep′rə bāt′) *adj.* ⟦LL *reprobare*, reprove⟧ unprincipled or depraved — *n.* a reprobate person

re·pro·duce (rē′prə dōōs′) *vt.* **-duced′, -duc′ing** to produce again; specif., a) to produce by propagation b) to make a copy of — *vi.* to produce offspring —**re′pro·duc′ible** *adj.*

re′pro·duc′tion (-duk′shən) *n.* **1** a copy, imitation, etc. **2** the process by which animals and plants produce new individuals —**re′pro·duc′tive** *adj.*

re·proof (ri prōōf′) *n.* a reproving; rebuke Also **re·prov′al** (-prōō′v'l)

re·prove (ri prōōv′) *vt.* **-proved′, -prov′ing** ⟦see RE- & PROVE⟧ **1** to rebuke **2** to express disapproval of —**re·prov′ing·ly** *adv.*

rep·tile (rep′təl, -tīl′) *n.* ⟦< L *repere*, to creep⟧ a cold-blooded, crawling vertebrate, as a snake, lizard, turtle, etc. —**rep·til·ian** (rep til′ē ən) *adj.*

re·pub·lic (ri pub′lik) *n.* ⟦< L *res*, thing + *publica*, public⟧ a state or government, specif. one headed by a president, in which the power is exercised by officials elected by the voters

re·pub′li·can (-li kən) *adj.* **1** of or like a republic **2** [R-] of or belonging to the Republican Party — *n.* **1** one who favors a republic **2** [R-] a member of the Republican Party —**re·pub′li·can·ism′** *n.*

Republican Party one of the two major political parties in the U.S.

re·pu·di·ate (ri pyōō′dē āt′) *vt.* **-at′ed, -at′ing** ⟦< L *repudium*, separation⟧ **1** to refuse to have anything to do with **2** to refuse to accept or support (a belief, treaty, etc.) —**re·pu′di·a′tion** *n.* —**re·pu′di·a′tor** *n.*

re·pug·nant (ri pug′nənt) *adj.* ⟦< L *re-*, back + *pugnare*, fight⟧ **1** contradictory **2** distasteful; offensive —**re·pug′nance** *n.*

re·pulse (ri puls′) *vt.* **-pulsed′, -puls′ing** ⟦see REPEL⟧ **1** to drive back (an attack, etc.) **2** to refuse or reject with discourtesy, etc.; rebuff — *n.* a repelling or being repelled

re·pul′sion *n.* **1** a repelling or being repelled **2** strong dislike **3** *Physics* the mutual action by which bodies tend to repel each other

re·pul′sive *adj.* causing strong dislike or aversion; disgusting —**re·pul′sive·ly** *adv.* —**re·pul′sive·ness** *n.*

THESAURUS

reporter *n.* newspaperman, news writer, columnist, journalist, newsman, correspondent, interviewer, cub reporter, star reporter, newsgatherer; see also WRITER.

represent *v.* **1** [To act as a delegate] be an agent for, serve, hold office, be deputy for, be attorney for, steward, act as broker, sell for, buy for, do business for, be spokesman for, be ambassador for, exercise power of attorney for. **2** [To present as a true interpretation] render, depict, portray; see ENACT. **3** [To serve as an equivalent] copy, imitate, reproduce, symbolize, exemplify, typify, signify, substitute, stand for, impersonate, personify.

representation *n.* description, narration, delineation; see COPY.

representative *n.* **1** [An emissary] deputy, salesman, messenger; see AGENT, DELEGATE. **2** [One who is elected to the lower legislative body] congressman, assemblyman, councilman, member of parliament, deputy, legislator, senator, councilor; see also DIPLOMAT.

represented *a.* **1** [Depicted] portrayed, interpreted, pictured; see MADE. **2** [Presented] rendered, exhibited, enacted; see SHOWN 1.

repress *v.* control, curb, check; see HINDER, RESTRAIN.

reprimand *v.* reproach, denounce,

criticize; see SCOLD.

reproach *n.* discredit, censure, rebuke; see BLAME.

reproach *v.* condemn, censure, scold; see BLAME.

reproduce *v.* **1** [To make an exact copy] photograph, print, mimeograph; see COPY. **2** [To make a second time] repeat, duplicate, recreate, recount, revive, reenact, redo, reawaken, relive, remake, reflect, follow, mirror, echo, reecho, represent. **3** [To multiply] procreate, engender, breed, generate, propagate, fecundate, hatch, father, beget, impregnate, progenerate, sire, repopulate, multiply, give birth.

reproduced *a.* copied, printed, traced, duplicated, transcribed, dittoed, recorded, multiplied, repeated, made identical, typed, set up, set in type, in facsimile, faxed, transferred, photographed, blueprinted, photostated, mimeographed, engraved, photoengraved; see also MANUFACTURED.

reproduction *n.* **1** [A copy] imitation, print, offprint; see COPY. **2** [A photographic reproduction] photostat, photoengraving, rotogravure, telephoto, wirephoto, X-ray, candid photo, closeup, pic, pix, blowup, facsimile, fax.

reproductive *a.* generative, creative, conceptive; see GENETIC.

reptile *n.* serpent, amphibian, one of the reptilia; see SNAKE.

republic *n.* democracy, democratic state, constitutional government, commonwealth, self-government, representative government; see also GOVERNMENT 2.

republican *a.* democratic, constitutional, popular; see CONSERVATIVE, DEMOCRATIC.

Republican *n.* registered Republican, GOP, Old Guard, Young Republican, Old Line Republican; see also CONSERVATIVE.

repudiate *v.* retract, repeal, revoke; see ABANDON 1.

repulse *v.* **1** [To throw back] set back, overthrow, resist; see REPEL 1. **2** [To rebuff] spurn, repel, snub; see REFUSE.

repulsion *n.* **1** [Rejection] rebuff, denial, snub; see REFUSAL. **2** [Aversion] hate, disgust, resentment; see HATRED.

repulsive *a.* **1** [Capable of repelling] offensive, resistant, unyielding, stubborn, opposing, retaliating, insurgent, counteracting, attacking, counterattacking, defensive, combative, aggressive, pugnacious; see also STUBBORN.—*Ant.* YIELDING, surrendering, capitulating. **2** [Disgusting] odious, forbidding, horrid; see OFFENSIVE 2.

repu·ta·ble (rep′yσσ tə bəl) *adj.* having a good reputation —**rep′u·ta·bil′i·ty** *n.* —**rep′u·ta·bly** *adv.*

repu·ta·tion (rep′yσσ tā′shən) *n.* [see fol.] 1 estimation in which a person or thing is commonly held 2 favorable estimation 3 fame

re·pute (ri pyσσt′) *vt.* -**put′ed, -put′ing** [< L *re-*, again + *putare*, think] to consider or regard *[reputed* to be rich] — *n.* REPUTATION (senses 1 & 3)

re·put′ed *adj.* generally supposed to be such [the *reputed* owner] —**re·put′edly** *adv.*

re·quest (ri kwest′) *n.* [see REQUIRE] 1 an asking for something 2 something asked for 3 the state of being asked for; demand — *vt.* 1 to ask for 2 to ask (a person) to do something

Re·quiem (rek′wē əm, rā′kwē-) *n.* [< L, rest] [*also* r-] 1 R.C.Ch. a Mass for a dead person or persons 2 a musical setting for this

re·quire (ri kwīr′) *vt.* -**quired′, -quir′ing** [< L *re-*, again + *quaerere,* ask] 1 to insist upon; demand 2 to order 3 to need —**re·quire′ment** *n.*

requi·site (rek′wə zit) *adj.* [see prec.] required; necessary; indispensable — *n.* something requisite

requi·si·tion (rek′wə zish′ən) *n.* 1 a requiring; formal demand 2 a formal written order, as for equipment — *vt.* 1 to demand or take, as by authority 2 to submit a written request for

re·quite (ri kwīt′) *vt.* -**quit′ed, -quit′ing** [RE- + *quite,* obs. var. of QUIT] to repay (someone) for (a benefit, service, etc. or an injury, wrong, etc.) —**re·quit′al** *n.*

re·run (rē′run′) *n.* the showing of a film or TV program after the first run or showing

re′sale′ *n.* a selling again, specif. to a third party

re·scind (ri sind′) *vt.* [< L *re-,* back + *scindere,* to cut] to revoke or cancel (a law, etc.) —**re·scis′sion** (-sizh′ən) *n.*

res·cue (res′kyσσ) *vt.* -**cued, -cu·ing** [ult. < L *re-,* again + *ex-,* off + *quatere,* to shake] to free or save from danger, imprisonment, evil, etc. — *n.* a rescuing —**res′cuer** *n.*

re·search (rē′sʉrch′, ri sʉrch′) *n.* [see RE- & SEARCH] careful, systematic study and investigation in some field of knowledge — *vi., vt.* to do research (on or in) —**re′search′er** *n.*

re·sec·tion (ri sek′shən) *n.* [< L *re-,* back + *secare,* to cut] *Surgery* the removal of part of an organ, bone, etc.

re·sem·blance (ri zem′bləns) *n.* a similarity of appearance; likeness

re·sem·ble (ri zem′bəl) *vt.* -**bled, -bling** [ult. < L *re-,* again + *simulare,* feign] to be like or similar to

re·sent (ri zent′) *vt.* [ult. < L *re-,* again + *sentire,* to feel] to feel or show hurt or indignation at —**re·sent′ful** *adj.* —**re·sent′fully** *adv.* —**re·sent′ment** *n.*

re·ser·pine (ri sʉr′pin, -pēn) *n.* [Ger] a crystalline alkaloid used in treating hypertension, mental illness, etc.

res·er·va·tion (rez′ər vā′shən) *n.* 1 a reserving or that which is reserved; specif., *a*) a withholding *b*) public land set aside for a special use, as for Indians *c*) holding of a hotel room, etc. until called for 2 a limiting condition

re·serve (ri zʉrv′) *vt.* -**served′, -serv′ing** [< L *re-,* back + *servare,* to keep] 1 to keep back or set apart for later or special use 2 to keep back for oneself — *n.* 1 something kept back or stored up, as for later use 2 a limitation [without *reserve*] 3 the keeping one's thoughts, feelings, etc. to oneself 4 reticence; silence 5 [*pl.*] troops, players, etc. kept out of action for use as replacements 6 land set apart for a special purpose —**in reserve** reserved for later use

re·served′ *adj.* 1 kept in reserve; set apart 2 self-restrained; reticent

res·er·voir (rez′ər vwär′) *n.* [< Fr: see RESERVE] 1 a place where water is collected and stored for use 2 a receptacle for holding a fluid 3 a large supply

re·side (ri zīd′) *vi.* -**sid′ed, -sid′ing** [< L *re-,* back + *sedere,* sit] 1 to dwell for a long time; live (*in* or *at*) 2 to be present or inherent (*in*): said of qualities, etc.

resi·dence (rez′i dəns) *n.* 1 a residing 2 the place where one resides —**res′i·den′tial** (-ə den′shəl) *adj.*

res′i·dency (-dən sē) *n., pl.* -**cies** 1 RESIDENCE 2 a period

---

◼ THESAURUS ◼

reputable *a.* 1 [Enjoying a good reputation] distinguished, celebrated, honored; see IMPORTANT 2. 2 [Honorable] trustworthy, honest, worthy; see BRAVE, NOBLE 1, 2.

reputation *n.* 1 [Supposed character] reliability, trustworthiness, respectability, dependability, credit, esteem, estimation; see also CHARACTER 2. 2 [Good name] standing, prestige, regard, favor, account, respect, privilege, acceptability, social approval; see also HONOR 1. 3 [Fame] prominence, eminence, notoriety; see FAME.

request *n.* call, inquiry, petition, question, invitation, offer, solicitation, supplication, prayer, requisition, recourse, suit, entreaty, demand; see also APPEAL 1. —**by request** asked for, sought for, wanted; see REQUESTED.

request *v.* 1 [To ask] demand, inquire, call for; see ASK. 2 [To solicit] beseech, entreat, sue; see BEG.

requested *a.* asked, demanded, popular, wished, desired, sought, hunted, needed, solicited, petitioned, appealed, requisitioned, in demand; see also WANTED.

require *v.* 1 [To need] want, feel the necessity for, have need for; see NEED. 2 [To demand] exact, insist upon, expect; see ASK.

required *a.* requisite, imperative, essential; see NECESSARY.

requirement *n.* 1 [A prerequisite] preliminary condition, essential, imperative, element, requisite, provision, terms, necessity, stipulation, fundamental, first principle, precondition, reservation, specification, proviso, fulfillment, qualification, vital part, *sine qua non* (Latin); see also BASIS. 2 [A need] necessity, necessary, lack, want, demand, claim, obsession, preoccupation, prepossession, engrossment, stress, extremity,

exigency, pinch, obligation, pressing concern, urgency, compulsion, exaction.

rescue *n.* 1 [The act of rescuing] deliverance, saving, release, extrication, liberation, ransom, redemption, freeing, salvation, reclamation, reclaiming, emancipation, disentanglement, recovering, heroism. 2 [An instance of rescue] action, deed, feat, performance, exploit, accomplishment, heroics; see also ACHIEVEMENT.

rescue *v.* 1 [To save] preserve, recover, redeem, recapture, salvage, retain, hold over, keep back, safeguard, ransom, protect, retrieve, withdraw, take to safety; see also SAVE 1.—*Ant.* LOSE, slip from one's hands, relinquish. 2 [To free] deliver, liberate, release; see FREE.

research *n.* investigation, analysis, experimentation; see EXAMINATION 1, STUDY.

research *v.* read up on, do research, look up; see EXAMINE, STUDY.

resemblance *n.* likeness, correspondence, coincidence; see SIMILARITY.

resemble *v.* be like, look like, seem like, sound like, follow, take after, parallel, match, coincide, relate, mirror, approximate, give indication of, remind one of, bring to mind, catch a likeness, have all the signs of, be the very image of, be similar to, come close to, appear like, bear a resemblance to, come near, pass for, have all the earmarks of, echo, compare with, be comparable to, smack of*, be the spit and image of*, be a dead-ringer for*; see also AGREE.—*Ant.* DIFFER, contradict, oppose.

resent *v.* frown at, be vexed, be insulted; see DISLIKE.

resentment *n.* exasperation, annoyance, irritation; see ANGER.

reservation *n.* 1 [The act of reserving] restriction, limitation, withholding; see RESTRAINT 2. 2 [An instrument for reserving] card, pass, license; see TICKET 1. 3 [The space reserved] seat, car, room, bus, train, box, stall, place, parking spot, table, berth, compartment.

reserve *n.* 1 [A portion kept against emergencies] savings, insurance, resources, reserved funds, store, provisions, assets, supply, hoard, backlog, nest egg, something in the sock, something for a rainy day; see also SECURITY 2. 2 [Calmness] backwardness, restraint, reticence, modesty, unresponsiveness, uncommunicativeness, caution, inhibition, coyness, demureness, aloofness. —**in reserve** withheld, out of circulation, stored away; see KEPT 2, RETAINED 1, SAVED 2.

reserve *v.* 1 [To save] store up, set aside, put away; see MAINTAIN 3, SAVE 3. 2 [To retain] keep, possess, have; see HOLD 1, OWN 1.

reserved *a.* 1 [Held on reservation] pre-empted, claimed, booked; see SAVED 2. 2 [Held in reserve] saved, withheld, kept aside, preserved, conserved, stored away, funded, put in a safe, on ice*.—*Ant.* USED, spent, exhausted. 3 [Restrained] shy, modest, backward, reticent, secretive, quiet, composed, retiring, private, controlling oneself, mild, gentle, peaceful, soft-spoken, sedate, collected, serene, placid.—*Ant.* LOUD, ostentatious, boisterous.

reserves *n.* reinforcements, enlisted reserves, volunteers; see ARMY 2.

reservoir *n.* storage place, tank, reserve, store, pool, cistern, water supply.

reside *v.* dwell, stay, lodge; see OCCUPY 2.

residence *n.* house, habitation, livres'i·dent *adj.* residing; esp., living in a place while working, etc. — *n.* 1 one who lives in a place, not a visitor 2 a doctor who is serving a residency

re·sid·u·al (ri zij'oo əl) *adj.* of or being a residue; remaining — *n.* 1 something remaining 2 [*pl.*] the fee paid for reruns on television, etc.

res·i·due (rez'ə doo') *n.* [< L *residuus*, remaining] that which is left after part is taken away; remainder

re·sid·u·um (ri zij'oo əm) *n.*, *pl.* -ua (-ə) RESIDUE

re·sign (ri zīn') *vt.*, *vi.* [< L *re-*, back + *signare*, to sign] to give up (a claim, or an office, position, etc.) —**resign oneself** (**to**) to become reconciled (to)

res·ig·na·tion (rez'ig nā'shən) *n.* 1 *a*) the act of resigning *b*) formal notice of this 2 patient submission

re·signed (ri zīnd') *adj.* feeling or showing resignation; submissive —**re·sign'ed·ly** (-zīn'id lē) *adv.*

re·sil·ient (ri zil'yənt) *adj.* [< L *re-*, back + *salire*, to jump] 1 springing back into shape, etc. 2 recovering strength, spirits, etc. quickly —**re·sil'ience** or **re·sil'iency** *n.*

resin (rez'ən) *n.* [< L *resina*] 1 a substance exuded from various plants and trees and used in varnishes, plastics, etc. 2 ROSIN —**res'in·ous** *adj.*

re·sist (ri zist') *vt.* [< L *re-*, back + *sistere*, to set] 1 to withstand; fend off 2 to oppose actively; fight against — *vi.* to oppose or withstand something —**re·sist'er** *n.* —**re·sist'ible** *adj.*

re·sist'ance *n.* 1 a resisting 2 power to resist, as to ward off disease 3 opposition of some force, thing, etc. to another, as to the flow of an electric current —**re·sist'ant** *adj.*

re·sist'less *adj.* 1 irresistible 2 unable to resist; unresisting

re·sis'tor *n.* a device used in an electrical circuit to provide resistance

re·sole' *vt.* -soled', -sol'ing to put a new sole on (a shoe, etc.)

reso·lute (rez'ə loot') *adj.* [see RE- & SOLVE] fixed and firm in purpose; determined —**res'o·lute'ly** *adv.*

res'o·lu'tion *n.* 1 the act or result of resolving something 2 a thing determined upon; decision as to future action 3 a resolute quality of mind 4 a formal statement of opinion or determination by an assembly, etc.

re·solve (ri zälv') *vt.* -solved', -solv'ing [see RE- & SOLVE] 1 to break up into separate parts; analyze 2 to change: used reflexively 3 to reach as a decision; determine 4 to solve (a problem) 5 to decide by vote — *vi.* 1 to be resolved, as by analysis 2 to come to a decision; determine — *n.* 1 firm determination 2 a formal resolution —**re·solv'a·ble** *adj.*

re·solved' *adj.* determined; resolute

reso·nant (rez'ə nənt) *adj.* [< L *resonare*, resound] 1 resounding 2 intensifying sound [*resonant* walls] 3 sonorous; vibrant [a *resonant* voice] —**res'o·nance** *n.* —**res'o·nate** (-nāt'), -nat·ed, -nat·ing, *vi.*, *vt.*

res'o·na'tor *n.* a device that produces, or increases sound by, resonance

re·sort (ri zôrt') *vi.* [< OFr *re-*, again + *sortir*, go out] to have recourse; turn (*to*) for help, etc. [to *resort* to lies] — *n.* 1 a place to which people go often, as on vacation 2 a source of help, support, etc.; recourse —**as a last resort** as the last available means

re·sound (ri zound') *vi.* [< L *resonare*] 1 to reverberate 2 to make a loud, echoing sound —**re·sound'ing** *adj.* —**re·sound'ing·ly** *adv.*

re·source (rē'sôrs, ri sôrs') *n.* [< OFr *re-*, again + *sourdre*, spring up] 1 something that lies ready for use or can be drawn upon for aid 2 [*pl.*] wealth; assets 3 resourcefulness

re·source'ful *adj.* able to deal effectively with problems, etc. —**re·source'ful·ness** *n.*

re·spect (ri spekt') *vt.* [< L *re-*, back + *specere*, look at] 1 to feel or show honor or esteem for 2 to show consideration for — *n.* 1 honor or esteem 2 consideration or regard

═══ **THESAURUS** ═══

ing quarters; see APARTMENT, HOME 1.
resident *n.* house-dweller, citizen, suburbanite, tenant, inhabitant, native, denizen, occupant, inmate, householder, dweller.
residual *a.* left over, remaining, surplus, continuing, extra, enduring, lingering.
residue *n.* residual, remainder, leavings, scraps, scourings, parings, raspings, shavings, debris, sewage, dregs, silt, slag, soot, scum; see also TRASH 1.
resign *v.* 1 [To relinquish] surrender, capitulate, give up; see ABANDON 1, YIELD 1. 2 [To leave one's employment] quit, separate oneself from, retire, step down, drop out, stand down, sign off, end one's services, leave, hand in one's resignation, cease work, give notice, walk out of the job, walk off the job.
resignation *n.* 1 [Mental preparation for something unwelcome] submission, humility, passivity, patience, deference, docility, submissiveness, abandonment, renunciation, acquiescence, endurance, compliance.—*Ant.* RESISTANCE, unsubmissiveness, unwillingness. 2 [The act of resigning] retirement, departure, leaving, quitting, giving up, abdication, surrender, withdrawal, relinquishment, vacating, tendering one's resignation, giving up office, termination of one's connection.
resigned *a.* quiet, peaceable, docile, tractable, submissive, yielding, relinquishing, gentle, obedient, manageable, willing, agreeable, ready, amenable, pliant, compliant, easily managed, genial, cordial, satisfied, well-disposed, patient, unresisting, tolerant, calm, reconciled, adjusted, adapted, accommodated, tame, nonresisting, passive, philosophical, renouncing, unassertive, subservient,

deferential.—*Ant.* REBELLIOUS, recalcitrant, resistant.
resilience *n.* elasticity, snap, recoil; see FLEXIBILITY.
resilient *a.* rebounding, elastic, springy; see FLEXIBLE.
resin *n.* pine tar, pitch, gum; see GUM.
resist *v.* hold, remain, maintain, endure, bear, continue, persist, obtain, occur, repeat, stay, retain, be strong, be fixed, be immune, brook, suffer, abide, tolerate, perservere, last, oppose change, bear up against, stand up to, put up a struggle, hold off, repel, remain firm, die hard.—*Ant.* STOP, desist, cease.
resistance *n.* 1 [A defense] stand, holding, withstanding, warding off, rebuff, obstruction, defiance, striking back, coping, check, halting, protecting, protection, safeguard, shield, screen, cover, watch, support, fight, impeding, blocking, opposition; see also DEFENSE 1.—*Ant.* WITHDRAWAL, withdrawing, retirement. 2 [The power of remaining impervious to an influence] unsusceptibility, immunity, immovability, hardness, imperviousness, endurance, fixedness, fastness, stability, stableness, permanence. 3 [The power of holding back another substance] friction, attrition, resistance; see RESERVE 1. 4 [An opposition] underground movement; anti-Fascist, anti-Communist, anti-American, etc.; movement, boycott, strike, walkout, slowdown, front, stand, guerrilla movement; see also REVOLUTION 2.
resister *n.* adversary, antagonist, opponent; see OPPOSITION 2.
resolute *a.* steadfast, firm, determined; see DETERMINED 1.
resolutely *a.* with all one's heart, bravely, with a will; see FIRMLY 1, 2.
resolution *n.* 1 [Fixedness of mind] fortitude, perseverance, resolve; see

DETERMINATION. 2 [A formal statement of opinion] verdict, formal expression, decision, recommendation, analysis, elucidation, interpretation, exposition, presentation, declaration, recitation, assertion, judgment.
resolve *v.* determine, settle on, conclude, fix, purpose, propose, choose, fix upon, make up one's mind, take a firm stand, take one's stand, take a decisive step, make a point of, pass upon, decree, elect, remain firm, take the bull by the horns; see also DECIDE.
resort *n.* 1 [A relief in the face of difficulty] expedient, shift, makeshift, stopgap, substitute, surrogate, resource, device, refuge, recourse, hope, relief, possibility, opportunity. 2 [A place for rest or amusement] *Resorts include the following:* seaside, mountain, rest, camping, skiing, sports, winter, lake, summer, gambling, amusement park, nightclub, spa, health spa, restaurant, dance hall, club; see also HOTEL, MOTEL. —**as a last resort** in desperation, lastly, in the end; see FINALLY 1, 2.
resort to *v.* turn to, refer to, apply, go to, use, try, employ, utilize, have recourse to, benefit by, put to use, make use of, take up.
resource *n.* reserve, supply, support, source, stock, store, means, expedient, stratagem, relief, resort, recourse, artifice, device, refuge.
resourceful *a.* original, ingenious, capable; see ACTIVE, INTELLIGENT.
resources *n.* means, money, stocks, bonds, products, revenue, riches, assets, belongings, effects, capital, collateral, credit, land, holdings, real estate, investments, income, savings; see also PROPERTY 1, RESERVE 1, WEALTH.
respect *n.* esteem, honor, regard; see ADMIRATION. —**pay one's respects**

3 [*pl.*] expressions of regard **4** a particular detail **5** reference; relation /with *respect* to the problem/ —**re·spect′ful** *adj.* —**re·spect′fully** *adv.*

re·spect′a·ble *adj.* **1** worthy of respect or esteem **2** proper; correct **3** fairly good in quality or size **4** presentable —**re·spect′abil′i·ty** *n.* —**re·spect′a·bly** *adv.*

re·spect′ing *prep.* concerning; about

re·spec′tive *adj.* as relates individually to each one

re·spec′tive·ly *adv.* in regard to each, in the order named

res·pi·ra·tion (res′pə rā′shən) *n.* [see RESPIRE] act or process of breathing —**res′pi·ra·to·ry** (res′pər ə tôr′ē, ri spi′rə-) *adj.*

res′pi·ra′tor *n.* **1** a mask, as of gauze, to prevent the inhaling of harmful substances **2** an apparatus to maintain breathing by artificial means

re·spire (ri spir′) *vi.*, *vt.* **-spired′, -spir′ing** [< L *re-*, back + *spirare*, breathe] to breathe

res·pite (res′pit) *n.* [see RESPECT] **1** a delay or postponement **2** temporary relief, as from pain or work

re·splend·ent (ri splen′dənt) *adj.* [< L *re-*, again + *splendere*, to shine] shining brightly; dazzling —**re·splend′ence** *n.* —**re·splend′ent·ly** *adv.*

re·spond (ri spänd′) *vi.* [< L *re-*, back + *spondere*, to pledge] **1** to answer; reply **2** to react **3** to have a favorable reaction

re·spond′ent *adj.* responding — *n. Law* a defendant

re·sponse (ri späns′) *n.* [see RESPOND] **1** something said or done in answer; reply **2** words sung or spoken by the congregation or choir replying to the clergyman **3** any reaction to a stimulus

re·spon·sibil·i·ty (ri spän′sə bil′ə tē) *n., pl.* **-ties 1** a being responsible; obligation **2** a thing or person that one is responsible for

re·spon′sible (-bəl) *adj.* **1** expected or obliged to account (*for*); answerable (*to*) **2** involving obligation or duties **3** that is the cause of something **4** able to distinguish between right and wrong **5** dependable; reliable —**re·spon′sibly** *adv.*

re·spon′sive *adj.* reacting readily, as to suggestion —**re·spon′sive·ly** *adv.* —**re·spon′sive·ness** *n.*

rest[1] (rest) *n.* [OE] **1** sleep or repose **2** ease or inactivity after exertion **3** relief from anything distressing, tiring, etc. **4** absence of motion **5** a resting place **6** a supporting device **7** *Music* a measured interval of silence between tones, or a symbol for this — *vi.* **1** to get ease and refreshment by sleeping or by ceasing from work **2** to be at ease **3** to be or become still **4** to lie, sit, or lean **5** to be placed or based (*in, on,* etc.) **6** to be found /the fault *rests* with him/ **7** to rely; depend — *vt.* **1** to give rest to **2** to put for ease, support, etc. /*rest* your head here/ **3** *Law* to stop introducing evidence in (a case) —**lay to rest** to bury

rest[2] (rest) *n.* [< L *restare*, remain] **1** what is left **2** [*with pl. v.*] the others — *vi.* to go on being /*rest* assured/

res·tau·rant (res′tə ränt′) *n.* [Fr: see RESTORE] a place where meals can be bought and eaten

res·tau·ra·teur (res′tər ə tʉr′, -toor′) *n.* [Fr] one who owns or operates a restaurant Also **res·tau·ran·teur** (res′tə rän′tʉr′, -toor′)

rest·ful (rest′fəl) *adj.* **1** full of or giving rest **2** quiet; peaceful —**rest′fully** *adv.*

rest home a residence that provides care for aged persons or convalescents

---

THESAURUS

wait upon, show regard, be polite; see VISIT.

respect *v.* **1** [To esteem] regard, value, look up to; see ADMIRE. **2** [To treat with consideration] appreciate, heed, notice, consider, note, recognize, defer to, do honor to, be kind to, show courtesy to, spare, take into account, attend, regard, uphold; see also APPRECIATE 1.—*Ant.* RIDICULE, mock, scorn.

respectability *n.* integrity, decency, propriety; see HONESTY, VIRTUE 1.

respectable *a.* presentable, upright, fair, moderate, mediocre, tolerable, passable, ordinary, virtuous, modest, honorable, worthy, estimable, decorous, seemly, admirable, correct, reputable, proper; see also DECENT 2, HONEST 1.

respected *a.* regarded, appreciated, valued; see HONORED.

respectful *a.* deferential, considerate, appreciate, courteous, admiring, reverent, attending, upholding, regarding, valuing, venerating, recognizing, deferring to, showing respect for; see also POLITE.—*Ant.* RUDE, impudent, contemptuous.

respectfully *a.* deferentially, reverentially, decorously, ceremoniously, attentively, courteously, considerately, with all respect, with due respect, with the highest respect, in deference to; see also POLITELY.—*Ant.* RUDELY, disrespectfully, impudently.

respecting *a.* regarding, concerning, in relation to; see ABOUT 2.

respiration *n.* inhalation, exhalation, expiration; see BREATH.

respite *n.* reprieve, postponement, pause; see DELAY.

respond *v.* reply, retort, acknowledge; see ANSWER 1.

response *n.* statement, reply, acknowledgment; see ANSWER 1.

responsibility *n.* **1** [State of being reliable] trustworthiness, reliability, trustiness, dependability, loyalty, faithfulness, capableness, capacity, efficiency, competency, uprightness, firmness, steadfastness, stability,

ability; see also HONESTY. **2** [State of being accountable] answerability, accountability, liability, subjection, engagement, pledge, contract, constraint, restraint; see also DUTY 1.—*Ant.* FREEDOM, exemption, immunity. **3** [Anything for which one is accountable] obligation, trust, contract; see DUTY 1.

responsible *a.* **1** [Charged with responsibility] accountable, answerable, liable, subject, bound, under obligation, constrained, tied, fettered, bonded, censurable, chargeable, obligated, obliged, compelled, contracted, hampered, held, pledged, sworn to, bound to, beholden to, under contract, engaged; see also BOUND 2.—*Ant.* FREE, unconstrained, unbound. **2** [Capable of assuming responsibility] trustworthy, trusty, reliable, capable, efficient, loyal, faithful, dutiful, dependable, tried, self-reliant, able, competent, qualified, effective, upright, firm, steadfast, steady, stable; see also ABLE.—*Ant.* IRRESPONSIBLE, capricious, unstable.

rest[1] *v.* **1** [To take one's rest] sleep, slumber, doze, repose, compose oneself for sleep, lie down, lounge, let down, ease off, recuperate, rest up, take a rest, take a break, break the monotony, lean, recline, couch, pillow, relax, unbend, settle down, dream, drowse, take one's ease, be comfortable, stretch out, nap, nod, snooze*. **2** [To depend upon] be supported, be seated on, based on; see DEPEND ON 2.

rest[1,2] *n.* **1** [Repose] quiet, quietness, quietude, ease, tranquillity, slumber, calm, calmness, peace, peacefulness, pacification, relaxation, rest, recreation, coffee break, rest period, siesta, doze, nap, somnolence, dreaminess, comfort, breathing spell, lounging period, loafing period, vacation, lull, leisure, respite, composure; see also sense 2. **2** [State of inactivity] intermission, cessation, stillness, stop, stay, stand, standstill, lull, discontinuance, interval, hush, silence,

dead calm, stagnation, fixity, immobility, inactivity, motionlessness, pause, full stop, deadlock, recess, noon hour; see also sense 1, PEACE 2.—*Ant.* ACTIVITY, continuance, endurance. **3** [Anything upon which an object rests] support, prop, pillar; see FOUNDATION 2. **4** [*The remainder] residue, surplus, remnant; see REMAINDER. **5** [Death] release, demise, mortality; see DEATH. —**at rest** in a state of rest, immobile, inactive; see RESTING 1. —**lay to rest** inter, assign to the grave, entomb; see BURY 1.

restaurant *n.* café, eatery, cafeteria, diner, hamburger stand. *Types of restaurants include the following;* café, hotel, dining room, inn, coffee shop, coffee house, chophouse, tearoom, luncheonette, lunch-wagon, seafood grotto, creamery, diner, fast-food place, pizzeria, lunch bar, soda fountain, milk bar, hot-dog stand, snack bar, automat, rotisserie, cabaret, nightclub, cafeteria, grill, oyster house, barbecue, spaghetti house, canteen, food court.

rested *a.* restored, refreshed, relaxed, strengthened, renewed, unwearied, unfatigued, untired, awake, revived, recovered, brought back, reanimated, revitalized, reintegrated, unworn.—*Ant.* TIRED, wearied, fatigued.

restful *a.* untroubling, untroubled, tranquil, tranquilizing, calm, peaceful, quiet, reposeful, serene, comfortable, easy, placid, mild, still, soothing, relaxing, restoring, refreshing, renewing, revitalizing, reviving.—*Ant.* LOUD, irritating, agitating.

resting *a.* **1** [Taking rest] relaxing, unwinding, reposing, composing oneself, reclining, lying down, sleeping, stretched out, at ease, quiet, dormant, comfortable, lounging, loafing, taking a breather, enjoying a lull, sleeping, dozing, drowsing, napping, taking a siesta, recessing, taking a vacation, having a holiday. **2** [Situated] located, settled on, seated; see OCCUPYING 1, PLACED.

res·ti·tu·tion (res′tə tōō′shən) *n.* 〚< L *re*-, again + *statuere*, set up〛 **1** a giving back of something that has been lost or taken away; restoration **2** reimbursement, as for loss

res·tive (res′tiv) *adj.* 〚< OFr *rester*, remain〛 **1** unruly or balky **2** nervous under restraint; restless —**res′tive·ly** *adv.* —**res′tive·ness** *n.*

rest·less *adj.* **1** unable to relax; uneasy **2** giving no rest; disturbed *[restless* sleep*]* **3** rarely quiet or still; active **4** discontented —**rest′less·ly** *adv.* —**rest′less·ness** *n.*

res·to·ra·tion (res′tə rā′shən) *n.* **1** a restoring or being restored **2** something restored, as by rebuilding

re·stor·a·tive (ri stôr′ə tiv) *adj.* able to restore health, consciousness, etc. — *n.* something that is restorative

re·store (ri stôr′) *vt.* **-stored′, -stor′ing** 〚< L *re*-, again + -*staurare*, to erect〛 **1** to give back (something taken, lost, etc.) **2** to return to a former or normal state, or to a position, rank, use, etc. **3** to bring back to health, strength, etc.

re·strain (ri strān′) *vt.* 〚< L *re*-, back + *stringere*, draw tight〛 **1** to hold back from action; check; suppress **2** to limit; restrict

re·straint (ri strānt′) *n.* **1** a restraining or being restrained **2** a means of restraining **3** confinement **4** control of emotions, impulses, etc.; reserve

re·strict (ri strikt′) *vt.* 〚see RESTRAIN〛 to keep within limits; confine —**re·strict′ed** *adj.* —**re·stric′tion** *n.*

re·stric·tive *adj.* **1** restricting **2** *Gram.* designating a subordinate clause or phrase that limits the reference of the word it modifies and is not set off by punctuation

rest·room (rest′rōōm′) *n.* a room in a public building, equipped with toilets, washbowls, etc. Also **rest room**

re·struc·ture (rē struk′chər) *vt.* **-tured, -tur·ing** to plan or provide a new structure or organization for

re·sult (ri zult′) *vi.* 〚< L *resultare*, to rebound〛 **1** to happen as an effect **2** to end as a consequence (*in* something) — *n.* **1** *a)* anything that comes about as an effect *b)* [*pl.*] the desired effect **2** the number, etc. obtained by mathematical calculation —**re·sult′ant** *adj., n.*

re·sume (ri zōōm′) *vt.* **-sumed′, -sum′ing** 〚< L *re*-, again + *sumere*, take〛 **1** to take or occupy again **2** to continue after interruption — *vi.* to proceed after interruption —**re·sump′tion** (ri zump′shən) *n.*

ré·su·mé (rez′ə mā′) *n.* 〚Fr: see prec.〛 a summary, esp. of employment experience: also sp. **re′sume** or **re′su·mé**

re·sur·face (rē sur′fis) *vt.* **-faced, -fac·ing** to put a new surface on — *vi.* to come to the surface again

re·sur·gent (ri sur′jənt) *adj.* 〚see fol.〛 tending to rise again —**re·sur′gence** *n.*

res·ur·rec·tion (rez′ə rek′shən) *n.* 〚< L *resurgere*, rise again〛 **1** a rising from the dead **2** a coming back into notice, use, etc.; revival —**the Resurrection** *Theol.* the rising of Jesus from the dead —**res′ur·rect′** *vt.*

re·sus·ci·tate (ri sus′ə tāt′) *vt., vi.* **-tat′ed, -tat′ing** 〚< L *re*-, again + *suscitare*, revive〛 to revive when apparently dead or in a faint, etc. —**re·sus′ci·ta′tion** *n.* —**re·sus′ci·ta′tor** *n.*

re·tail (rē′tāl′) *n.* 〚< OFr *re*-, again + *tailler*, to cut〛 the sale of goods in small quantities directly to the consumer — *adj.* of or engaged in such sale — *adv.* at a retail price — *vt., vi.* to sell or be sold directly to the consumer —**re′tail′er** *n.*

re·tain (ri tān′) *vt.* 〚< L *re*-, back + *tenere*, to hold〛 **1** to keep in possession, use, etc. **2** to hold in **3** to keep in mind **4** to hire by paying a retainer

re·tain′er *n.* **1** something that retains **2** a servant, attendant, etc. **3** a fee paid to engage a lawyer's services

■ THESAURUS ■

restitution *n.* compensation, return, restoration; see PAYMENT 1, REPARATION.

restless *a.* fidgety, skittish, feverish, sleepless, jumpy, nervous, unquiet, disturbed, uneasy, anxious, up in arms, discontented, vexed, excited, agitated, angry, disaffected, estranged, alienated, resentful, recalcitrant, fractious, insubordinate, flurried, roving, transient, wandering, discontented, unsettled, roaming, nomadic, moving, straying, ranging, footloose, itinerant, gallivanting, meandering, traipsing, restive, peeved, annoyed, impatient, flustered, twitching, trembling, tremulous, rattled*, jittery*; see also ACTIVE, EXCITED, REBELLIOUS.—*Ant.* QUIET, sedate, calm.

restlessness *n.* uneasiness, discomfort, excitability; see EXCITEMENT, NERVOUSNESS.

restoration *n.* **1** [The act of restoring] revival, return, renewal; see RECOVERY 1. **2** [The act of reconstructing] rehabilitation, reconstruction, reparation; see REPAIR.

restore *v.* **1** [To give back] make restitution, replace, put back; see RETURN 2. **2** [To recreate] reestablish, revive, recover; see RENEW 1. **3** [To rebuild in a form supposed to be original] rebuild, alter, rehabilitate; see RECONSTRUCT, REPAIR. **4** [To bring back to health] refresh, cure, make healthy; see HEAL.

restrain *v.* check, control, curb, bridle, rein in, hem in, keep in, handle, regulate, keep in line, guide, direct, keep down, repress, harness, muzzle, hold in leash, govern, inhibit, hold, bind, deter, hold back, hamper, constrain, restrict, stay, gag, limit, impound, bottle up, tie down, pin down, pull back, contain, sit on, come down on.

restrained *a.* under control, in check, on lease; see HELD.

restraint *n.* **1** [Control over oneself] control, self-control, reserve, reticence, constraint, withholding, caution, coolness, forbearance, silence, secretiveness, stress, repression, self-government, self-restraint, stiffness, abstinence, self-denial, unnaturalness, self-repression, constrained manner, abstention, self-discipline, self-censorship; see also ATTENTION.—*Ant.* LAZINESS, slackness, laxity. **2** [An influence that checks or hinders] repression, deprivation, limitation, hindrance, reduction, abridgment, decrease, prohibition, confinement, check, barrier, obstacle, obstruction, restriction, bar, curb, blockade, order, command, instruction, coercion, impediment, compulsion, duress, determent, discipline, assignment, definition, moderation, tempering, qualifying.—*Ant.* FREEDOM, liberty, license.

restrict *v.* delimit, limit, circumscribe, assign, contract, shorten, narrow, decrease, enclose, keep in, keep within bounds, define, encircle, surround, shut in, tether, chain, diminish, reduce, moderate, modify, temper, qualify, come down on, pin down.—*Ant.* INCREASE, extend, expand.

restricted *a.* limited, confined, restrained, circumscribed, curbed, bound, prescribed, checked, bounded, inhibited, hampered, marked, defined, delimited, encircled, surrounded, shut in, hitched, tethered, chained, fastened, secured, bridled, held back, held down, reined in, controlled, governed, deterred, impeded, stayed, stopped, suppressed, repressed, prevented, fettered, deprived, obstructed, barred, blocked, dammed, clogged, manacled, frustrated, embarrassed, baffled, foiled, shrunken, narrowed, shortened, decreased, diminished, reduced, moderated, tempered, modified, qualified, out of bounds; see also BOUND 1, 2.

restriction *n.* custody, limitation, contraction; see RESTRAINT 2.

result *n.* consequence, issue, event, execution, effect, outcome, end, finish, termination, consummation, completion, aftereffect, aftermath, upshot, sequel, sequence, fruit, fruition, eventuality, proceeds, emanation, outgrowth, outcropping, returns, backwash, backlash, repercussion, settlement, determination, decision, arrangement, payoff*; see also END 2, 4.—*Ant.* ORIGIN, source, root.

result *v.* issue, grow from, spring from, rise from, proceed from, emanate from, germinate from, flow from, accrue from, arise from, derive from, come from, originate in, become of, spring, emerge, rise, ensue, emanate, effect, produce, fruit, follow, happen, occur, come about, come forth, come out, pan out, work out, appear, end, finish, terminate, conclude.

resume *v.* take up again, reassume, begin again, recommence, reoccupy, go on with, renew, recapitulate, return, keep on, carry on, keep up; see also CONTINUE 2.—*Ant.* STOP, cease, discontinue.

résumé *n.* summary, synopsis, abstract, précis, work history, biography; see also SUMMARY.

resurrection *n.* return to life, transformation, rebirth; see RENEWAL.

retain *v.* **1** [To hold] cling to, grasp, clutch; see HOLD 1. **2** [To reserve services] employ, maintain, engage; see HIRE. **3** [To remember] recall, recollect, recognize; see REMEMBER 1.

retained *a.* **1** [Kept] had, held, possessed, owned, enjoyed, secured, saved, preserved, maintained, restrained, confined, curbed, detained, contained, received, admitted, included, withheld, put away, treasured, sustained, celebrated, remembered, commemorated; see also KEPT 2.—*Ant.* LOST, wasted, refused. **2** [Employed] hired, engaged, contracted; see EMPLOYED.

retaining wall a wall for keeping earth from sliding or water from flooding

re·take (rē tāk'; *for n.* rē'tāk') *vt.* **-took', -tak'en, -tak'ing** **1** to take again; recapture **2** to photograph again — *n.* a scene, etc. rephotographed

re·tali·ate (ri tal'ē āt') *vi.* **-at'ed, -at'ing** ⟦< L *re-*, back + *talio*, punishment in kind⟧ to return like for like, esp. injury for injury —**re·tal'ia'tion** *n.* —**re·tal'ia·to'ry** *adj.*

re·tard (ri tärd') *vt.* ⟦< L *re-*, back + *tardare*, make slow⟧ to hinder, delay, or slow the progress of —**re·tar·da·tion** (rē'tär dā'shən) *n.*

re·tard'ant *n.* something that retards; esp., a substance that delays a chemical reaction — *adj.* that retards

re·tard'ed *adj.* slowed or delayed in development, esp. mentally

retch (rech) *vi.* ⟦OE *hræcan*, clear the throat⟧ to strain to vomit, esp. without bringing anything up

re·ten·tion (ri ten'shən) *n.* **1** a retaining or being retained **2** capacity for retaining —**re·ten'tive** *adj.*

reti·cent (ret'ə sənt) *adj.* ⟦< L *re-*, again + *tacere*, be silent⟧ disinclined to speak; taciturn —**ret'i·cence** *n.*

reti·na (ret''n ə) *n., pl.* **-nas** *or* **-nae'** (-ē') ⟦prob. < L *rete*, a net⟧ the innermost coat lining the eyeball, containing light-sensitive cells which receive the visual image —**ret'i·nal** *adj.*

reti·nue (ret''n ōō') *n.* ⟦< OFr, ult. < L: see RETAIN⟧ a group of persons attending a person of rank or importance

re·tire (ri tīr') *vi.* **-tired', -tir'ing** ⟦< Fr *re-*, back + *tirer*, draw⟧ **1** to withdraw to a secluded place **2** to go to bed **3** to retreat, as in battle **4** to give up one's work, business, etc., esp. because of age — *vt.* **1** to withdraw (troops, etc.) **2** to pay off (bonds, etc.) **3** to cause to retire from a position, office, etc. **4** to withdraw from use **5** *Baseball* to put out (a batter, side, etc.) —**re·tir'ee'** *n.* —**re·tire'ment** *n.*

re·tired' *adj.* **1** secluded **2** *a*) no longer working, etc. as because of age *b*) of or for such retired persons

re·tir'ing *adj.* reserved; modest; shy

re·tool (rē'tōōl') *vt., vi.* to adapt (factory machinery) for a different product

re·tort¹ (ri tôrt') *vt.* ⟦< L *re-*, back + *torquere*, to twist⟧ **1** to turn (an insult, etc.) back upon its originator **2** to say in reply — *vi.* to make a sharp, witty reply — *n.* a sharp, witty reply

re·tort² (ri tôrt') *n.* ⟦< ML *retorta*: see prec.⟧ a glass container with a long tube in which substances are distilled

re·touch (rē'tuch') *vt.* to touch up details in (a painting, essay, etc.) so as to improve or change it

re·trace (ri trās') *vt.* **-traced', -trac'ing** ⟦see RE- & TRACE¹⟧ to go back over again *[to retrace one's steps]*

re·tract (ri trakt') *vt., vi.* ⟦< L *re-*, back + *trahere*, draw⟧ **1** to draw back or in **2** to withdraw (a statement, charge, etc.) —**re·tract'able** *or* **re·trac'tile** (-trak'təl, -tīl') *adj.* —**re·trac'tion** *n.*

re·tread (rē'tred') *vt., n.* RECAP¹

re·treat (ri trēt') *n.* ⟦< L *retrahere*: see RETRACT⟧ **1** a withdrawal, as from danger **2** a safe, quiet place **3** a period of seclusion, esp. for spiritual renewal **4** *a*) the forced withdrawal of troops under attack *b*) a signal for this *c*) a signal, as by bugle, or a ceremony at sunset for lowering the national flag — *vi.* to withdraw; go back

re·trench (rē trench') *vt., vi.* ⟦< Fr: see RE- & TRENCH⟧ to cut down (esp. expenses); economize —**re·trench'ment** *n.*

ret·ri·bu·tion (re'trə byōō'shən) *n.* ⟦< L *re-*, back + *tribuere*, to pay⟧ punishment for evil done or reward for good done —**re·tribu·tive** (ri trib'yōō tiv) *adj.*

re·trieve (ri trēv') *vt.* **-trieved', -triev'ing** ⟦< OFr *re-*, again + *trouver*, find⟧ **1** to get back; recover **2** to restore **3** to make good (a loss, error, etc.) **4** to access (data) stored in a computer **5** to find and bring back (killed or wounded game): said of dogs — *vi.* to retrieve game —**re·triev'al** *n.*

re·triev'er *n.* a dog trained to retrieve game

retro- ⟦< L⟧ *combining form* backward, back, behind

retro·ac·tive (re'trō ak'tiv) *adj.* having an effect on things that are already past —**retro·ac'tively** *adv.*

retro·fire (re'trə fīr') *vt.* **-fired', -fir'ing** to ignite (a retro-rocket)

ret'ro·grade' (-grād') *adj.* ⟦< L: see RETRO- & GRADE⟧ **1** moving backward **2** going back to a worse condition — *vi.* **-grad'ed, -grad'ing** **1** to go backward **2** to become worse

ret'ro·gress' (-gres') *vi.* ⟦< L: see prec.⟧ to move backward, esp. into a worse condition —**ret'ro·gres'sive** *adj.* —**ret'ro·gres'sion** *n.*

retro·rock·et *or* **retro-rocket** (re'trō räk'it) *n.* a small rocket, as on a spacecraft, producing thrust opposite to the direction of flight to reduce speed, as for landing

retro·spect (re'trə spekt') *n.* ⟦< L *retro-*, back + *specere*, to look⟧ contemplation of the past —**ret'ro·spec'tion** *n.*

ret'ro·spec'tive *adj.* looking back on the past — *n.* a representative show of an artist's lifetime work —**ret'ro·spec'tively** *adv.*

ret·sina (ret sē'nə) *n.* ⟦Modern Greek, prob. < It *resina*, resin⟧ a Greek wine flavored with pine resin

re·turn (ri turn') *vi.* ⟦< OFr: see RE- & TURN⟧ **1** to go or come back **2** to reply — *vt.* **1** to bring, send, or put back **2** to do in reciprocation *[to return a visit]* **3** to yield (a

▬▬▬ THESAURUS ▬▬▬

retaliate *v.* fight back, return, repay; see REVENGE.

retaliation *n.* vengeance, reprisal, punishment; see REVENGE 1.

retard *v.* postpone, delay, impede; see HINDER.

retarded *a.* **1** [*Said of persons*] backward, underachieving, stupid; see DULL 3. **2** [*Said of activities*] delayed, slowed down, held back; see SLOW 1, 2, 3.

retire *v.* **1** [To draw away] withdraw, part, retreat; see LEAVE 1. **2** [To go to bed] lie down, turn in, rest; see SLEEP. **3** [To cease active life] resign, give up work, sever one's connections, leave active service, relinquish, make vacant, lay down, hand over, lead a quiet life, sequester oneself, reach retirement age.

retired *a.* resigned, relinquished, laid down, handed over, withdrawn, retreated, removed, reached retirement age, leading a quiet life, secluding oneself, separating oneself, aloof.—*Ant.* ACTIVE, working, busy.

retirement *n.* **1** [The act of retiring] removal, vacating, separation; see RESIGNATION 2. **2** [The state of being retired] seclusion, aloofness, apartness, separateness, privacy, concealment, solitude, solitariness, isolation, remoteness, loneliness, quiet, retreat, tranquillity, refuge, serenity, inactivity; see also SILENCE 1.—*Ant.* EXPOSURE, activity, association.

retort¹ *n.* counter, repartee, response; see ANSWER 1.

retort¹ *v.* reply, respond, snap back; see ANSWER 1.

retract *v.* withdraw, draw away, take in; see REMOVE 1.

retraction *n.* denial, revocation, disowning; see CANCELLATION, DENIAL.

retreat *n.* **1** [The act of retreating] retirement, removal, evacuation, departure, escape, withdrawal, drawing back, reversal, retrogression, backing out, flight, recession, retraction, going, running away, eluding, evasion, avoidance, recoil.—*Ant.* ADVANCE, progress, progression. **2** [A place to which one retreats] seclusion, solitude, privacy, shelter, refuge, asylum, safe place, defense, sanctuary, security, cover, ark, harbor, port, haven, place of concealment, hiding place, hideaway*, resort, haunt, habitat, hermitage, cell, convent, cloister.—*Ant.* FRONT, exposed position, van.

retreat *v.* recede, retrograde, back out, retract, go, depart, recoil, shrink, quail, run, draw back, reel, start back, reverse, seclude oneself, keep aloof, hide, separate from, regress, resign, relinquish, lay down, hand over, withdraw, backtrack, leave, back off*, back down, chicken out*.—*Ant.* STAY, remain, continue.

retribution *n.* vengeance, reprisal, retaliation; see REVENGE 1.

retrieve *v.* regain, bring back, reclaim; see RECOVER 1.

return *a.* coming back, repeat, repeating, repetitive, recurring, reappearing, sent back, answering, replying, retorting, rotating, turning, rebounding, recurrent; see also REPEATED 1.

return *n.* **1** [The act of coming again] homecoming, arrival, reappearance; see sense 2. **2** [The act of being returned] restoration, restitution, rejoinder, recompense, acknowledgment, answer, reaction, reversion, repetition, reverberation, reappearance, reentrance, rotating, reoccurrence, rebound, recoil, reconsideration. **3** [Proceeds] profit, income, results, gain, avail, revenue, advantage, yield, accrual, accruement, interest.—*Ant.* FAILURE, loss, disadvantage. —**in return** in exchange, as payment, as an equivalent, for a reward.

return *v.* **1** [To go back] come again, come back, recur, reappear, reoccur, repeat, revert, reconsider, reenter, reexamine, reinspect, bounce back up, retrace one's steps, turn, rotate, revolve, renew, revive, recover, regain, rebound, circle back, double back, move back, turn back, reverberate, recoil, retrace, revisit, retire, retreat.—*Ant.* MOVE, advance, go forward. **2** [To put or send something back] bring back, toss back, roll back, profit, etc.) **4** to report officially **5** to elect or reelect — *n.* **1** a coming or going back **2** a bringing, sending, or putting back **3** something returned **4** a recurrence **5** repayment; requital **6** [*often pl.*] yield or profit, as from investments **7** a reply **8** *a*) an official report [election *returns*] *b*) a form for computing (income) tax — *adj.* **1** of or for a return [*return* postage] **2** given, done, etc. in return —**in return** as a return —**re·turn′a·ble** *adj.*

re·turn·ee′ *n.* one who returns, as home from military service or to school after dropping out

re·u·ni·fy (rē yōō′nə fī′) *vt., vi.* **-fied′, -fy′ing** to unify again after being divided —**re·u′ni·fi·ca′tion** *n.*

re·union (rē yōōn′yən) *n.* a coming together again, as after separation

rev (rev) *vt.* **revved, rev′ving** [< REV(OLUTION)] [Colloq.] to increase the speed of (an engine): usually with *up*

Rev. Reverend

re·vamp (rē vamp′) *vt.* to vamp again; specif., to revise; redo

re·veal (ri vēl′) *vt.* [< L *re-*, back + *velum*, veil] **1** to make known (something hidden or secret) **2** to show; exhibit; display

rev·eille (rev′ə lē) *n.* [< Fr < L *re-*, again + *vigilare*, to watch] a signal on a bugle, drum, etc. in the morning to waken soldiers, etc.

revel (rev′əl) *vi.* **-eled** or **-elled, -el·ing** or **-el·ling** [< MFr < L *rebellare*, to rebel: see REBEL] **1** to make merry **2** to take much pleasure (*in*) — *n.* merrymaking —**rev′ eler** or **rev′el·ler** *n.* —**rev′el·ry,** *pl.* **-ries,** *n.*

rev·e·la·tion (rev′ə lā′shən) *n.* **1** a revealing **2** something disclosed; esp., a striking disclosure **3** *Theol.* God's disclosure to humanity of himself —[**R-**] the last book of the New Testament

re·venge (ri venj′) *vt.* **-venged′, -veng′ing** [< OFr: see RE- & VENGEANCE] to inflict harm in return for (an injury), etc.) — *n.* **1** the act or result of revenging **2** desire to take vengeance —**re·venge′ful** *adj.*

rev·enue (rev′ə nōō′) *n.* [< MFr, returned] **1** return, as from investment; income **2** the income from taxes, licenses, etc., as of a city, state, or nation

re·ver·ber·ate (ri vur′bə rāt′) *vi., vt.* **-at′ed, -at′ing** [< L *re-*, again + *verberare*, to beat] to reecho or cause to reecho —**re·ver′ber·a′tion** *n.*

re·vere (ri vir′) *vt.* **-vered′, -ver′ing** [< L *re-*, again + *vereri*, to fear] to regard with deep respect, love, etc.

rev·er·ence (rev′ər əns) *n.* a feeling of deep respect, love, and awe — *vt.* **-enced, -enc·ing** to venerate —**rev′er·ent** or **rev′er·en′tial** (-ə ren′shəl) *adj.* —**rev′er·ent·ly** *adv.*

rev·er·end (rev′ər ənd) *adj.* worthy of reverence: used with *the* as a title of respect for a member of the clergy [the *Reverend* A. B. Smith]

rev·er·ie or **rev·er·y** (rev′ər ē) *n., pl.* **-ies** [< Fr] daydreaming or a daydream

re·vers (ri vir′, -ver′) *n., pl.* **-vers** (-virz′, -verz′) [Fr: see REVERT] a part (of a garment) turned back to show the reverse side, as a lapel Also **re·vere′** (-vir′)

re·verse (ri vurs′) *adj.* [see REVERT] **1** turned backward; opposite or contrary **2** causing movement in the opposite direction — *n.* **1** the opposite or contrary **2** the back of a coin, medal, etc. **3** a change from good fortune to bad **4** a mechanism for reversing, as a gear on a machine — *vt.* **-versed′, -vers′ing 1** to turn backward, in an opposite position or direction, upside down, or inside out **2** to change to the opposite **3** *Law* to revoke or annul (a decision, etc.) — *vi.* to go or turn in the opposite direction — **re·ver′sal** (-vur′səl) *n.* —**re·vers′ible** *adj.* —**re·vers′ibly** *adv.*

re·vert (ri vurt′) *vi.* [< L *re-*, back + *vertere*, to turn] **1** to go back, as to a former practice, state, subject, etc. **2** *Biol.* to return to a former or primitive type **3** *Law* to go back to a former owner or his or her heirs —**re·ver′sion** (-vur′zhən) *n.* —**re·vert′ible** *adj.*

re·vet·ment (ri vet′mənt) *n.* [< Fr] **1** a facing of stone, cement, etc., as to protect an embankment **2** RETAINING WALL

re·view (ri vyōō′) *n.* [< L *re-*, again + *videre,* see] **1** a looking at or looking over again **2** a general survey or report **3** a looking back on (past events, etc.) **4** reexami-

---

THESAURUS

hand back, give back, restore, replace, render, reseat, reestablish, reinstate, react, recompense, refund, repay, make restitution.—*Ant.* HOLD, keep, hold back. **3** [To answer] reply, respond, retort; see ANSWER 1. **4** [To repay] reimburse, recompense, refund; see REPAY 1. **5** [To yield a profit] pay off, show profit, pay dividends; see PAY 2. **6** [To reflect] echo, sound, mirror; see REFLECT 2, 3.

returned *a.* restored, given back, gone back, sent back, brought back, turned back, come back, reappeared, recurred, reoccurred, repeated, reverted, reentered, rotated, revolved, rebounded, reverberated, refunded, acknowledged, answered, repaid, yielded; see also REFUSED.— *Ant.* KEPT, held, retained.

reunion *n.* reuniting, meeting again, rejoining, reconciliation, reconcilement, homecoming, restoration, harmonizing, bringing together, healing the breach, gettogether*.

reunite *v.* meet again, reassemble, reconvene, join, rejoin, become reconciled, have a reconciliation, be restored to one another, remarry, heal the breach, get together, patch it up, make up.—*Ant.* SEPARATE, go separate ways, be disrupted.

reveal *v.* disclose, betray a confidence, divulge, make known, confess, impart, publish, lay bare, betray, avow, admit, bring to light, acknowledge, give utterance to, bring out, let out, give out, make public, unfold, communicate, announce, declare, inform, notify, utter, make plain, break the news, broadcast, concede, come out with, explain, bring into the open, affirm, report, let the cat out of the bag, blab*, talk, rat*, stool*, make a clean breast of, put one's cards on the table, bring to light, show one's colors, get some-

thing out of one's system, give the low-down*, let on*, squeal*, blow whistle*; see also TELL 1.

revelation *n.* **1** [A disclosure] divulgence, announcement, betrayal; see RECORD 1. **2** [Revealed divine truth] divine word, God's word, apocalypse; see DOCTRINE, FAITH 2.

revenge *n.* **1** [The act of returning an injury] vengeance, requital, reprisal, measure for measure, repayment, counterplay, sortie, retaliation, retribution, avenging, counterinsurgency, getting even; see also ATTACK, FIGHT 1.—*Ant.* PARDON, forgiveness, excusing. **2** [The desire to obtain revenge] vindictiveness, rancor, malevolence; see HATRED.

revenge *v.* retaliate, vindicate, requite, take revenge, breathe vengeance, have accounts to settle, have one's revenge, pay back, make reprisal, get even with, punish for, repay, return like for like, retort, match, reciprocate, square accounts, settle up, take an eye for an eye, turn the tables on, get back at*, fight back, hit back at, be out for blood, give an exchange, give and take, give someone his deserts, even up the score, get*, fix*, get square with, return the compliment.—*Ant.* FORGIVE, condone, pardon.

revenue *n.* **1** [Income] return, earnings, result, yield, wealth, receipts, proceeds, resources, funds, stocks, credits, dividends, interest, salary, profits, means, fruits, rents; see also INCOME, PAY 1, 2.—*Ant.* EXPENSES, outgo, obligations. **2** [Governmental income] wealth, revenue, taxation; see INCOME, TAX 1. *Types of revenue include the following:* direct tax, indirect tax, bonds, loans, customs, duties, tariff, tax surcharge, excise, property tax, income tax, inheritance and death tax, land tax, poll tax,

gasoline tax, school tax, franchise, license, grants, rates, bridge and road tolls, harbor dues, special taxation, patent stamps, stamp duties, registration duties, internal revenue, tax on spirits, tobacco tax, revenue on fermented liquors, lease of land, sale of land, subsidy.

revere *v.* venerate, regard with deep respect, respect; see ADMIRE.

reverence *n.* respect, admiration, love, regard, approval, approbation, esteem, deference, awe, fear, veneration, honor, devotion, adoration; see also PRAISE 2.—*Ant.* HATRED, contempt, disdain.

reverent *a.* venerating, esteeming, honoring; see RESPECTFUL.

reversal *n.* renunciation, repudiation, repeal; see CANCELLATION, REFUSAL, WITHDRAWAL.

reverse *n.* **1** [The opposite] converse, other side, contrary; see OPPOSITE. **2** [A defeat] vanquishment, catastrophe, setback; see DEFEAT.

reverse *v.* **1** [To turn] go back, shift, invert; see TURN 2. **2** [To alter] turn around, modify, convert; see CHANGE 2. **3** [To annul] nullify, invalidate, repeal; see CANCEL. **4** [To exchange] transpose, rearrange, shift; see EXCHANGE 1.

reversed *a.* turned around, turned back, backward, end for end, inverted, contrariwise, out of order, regressive, retrogressive, undone, unmade.—*Ant.* ORDERED, established, in proper order.

revert *v.* go back, reverse, recur to; see RETURN 1.

review *n.* **1** [A reexamination] reconsideration, second thought, revision, retrospection, second view, reflection, study, survey, retrospect. **2** [A critical study] survey, critique, criticism; see EXAMINATION 1. **3** [A nation, as of the decision of a lower court **5** a critical evaluation of a book, play, etc. **6** a formal inspection, as of troops on parade — *vt.* **1** to look back on **2** to survey in thought, speech, etc. **3** to inspect (troops, etc.) formally **4** to give a critical evaluation of (a book, etc.) **5** to study again —**re·view′er** *n.*

re·vile (ri vīl′) *vt., vi.* **-viled′, -vil′ing** ⟦< OFr: see RE- & VILE⟧ to use abusive language (to or about) —**re·vile′ ment** *n.* —**re·vil′er** *n.*

re·vise (ri vīz′) *vt.* **-vised′, -vis′ing** ⟦< L *re-*, back + *visere*, to survey⟧ **1** to read over carefully and correct, improve, or update **2** to change or amend —**re·vi′sion** (-vizh′ən) *n.*

Revised Standard Version a 20th-c. version of the Bible

re·vival (ri vī′vəl) *n.* **1** a reviving or being revived **2** a bringing or coming back into use, being, etc. **3** a new presentation of an earlier play, etc. **4** restoration to vigor or activity **5** a meeting led by an evangelist to stir up religious feeling —**re·viv′al·ist** *n.*

re·vive (ri vīv′) *vi., vt.* **-vived′, -viv′ing** ⟦< L *re-*, again + *vivere*, to live⟧ **1** to return to life or consciousness **2** to return to health or vigor **3** to come or bring back into use, attention, popularity, exhibition, etc.

re·vivi·fy (ri viv′ə fī′) *vt.* **-fied′, -fy′ing** to put new life or vigor into — *vt.* to revive —**re·viv′i·fi·ca′tion** *n.*

re·voke (ri vōk′) *vt.* **-voked′, -vok′ing** ⟦< L *re-*, back + *vocare*, to call⟧ to withdraw, repeal or cancel (a law, etc.) —**revo·cable** (rev′ə kə bəl) or **re·vok·able** (ri vō′kə bəl) *adj.* —**rev′o·ca′tion** (-kā′shən) *n.*

re·volt (ri vōlt′) *n.* ⟦< Fr: see REVOLVE⟧ a rebelling against the government or any authority — *vi.* **1** to rebel against authority **2** to turn (*from* or *against*) in revulsion; be shocked (*at*) — *vt.* to disgust —**re·volt′ing** *adj.*

revo·lu·tion (rev′ə lōō′shən) *n.* ⟦see REVOLVE⟧ **1** the movement of a body in an orbit **2** a turning around an axis; rotation **3** a complete cycle of events **4** a complete change **5** overthrow of a government, social system, etc. —**rev′o·lu′tion·ar′y** (-er′ē), *pl.* **-ies,** *n., adj.* —**rev′o·lu′ tion·ist** *n.*

Revolutionary War *see* AMERICAN REVOLUTION

rev′o·lu′tion·ize′ (-īz′) *vt.* **-ized′, -iz′ing** to make a fundamental change in

re·volve (ri välv′) *vt.* **-volved′, -volv′ing** ⟦< L *re-*, back + *volvere*, to roll⟧ **1** to turn over in the mind **2** to cause to travel in a circle or orbit **3** to cause to rotate — *vi.* **1** to move in a circle or orbit **2** to rotate **3** to recur at intervals —**re·volv′able** *adj.*

re·volv′er *n.* a handgun with a revolving cylinder containing cartridges

re·vue (ri vyōō′) *n.* ⟦Fr, review⟧ a musical show with skits, dances, etc., often parodying recent events, etc.

re·vul·sion (ri vul′shən) *n.* ⟦< L *re-*, back + *vellere*, to pull⟧ an abrupt, strong reaction; esp., disgust

re·ward (ri wôrd′) *n.* ⟦< OFr *regarde*: see REGARD⟧ **1** something given in return for something done **2** money offered, as for capturing a criminal — *vt.* to give a reward to (someone) for (service, etc.)

re·ward′ing *adj.* giving a sense of reward or worthwhile return

re·wind (rē wīnd′) *vt.* **-wound′, -wind′ing** to wind again; specif., to wind (film or tape) back on the original reel

re·word′ *vt.* to change the wording of

re·write′ *vt., vi.* **-wrote′, -writ′ten, -writ′ing 1** to write again **2** to revise **3** to write (news turned in) in publishable form

RFD or **R.F.D.** Rural Free Delivery

rhap·so·dize (rap′sə dīz′) *vi., vt.* **-dized′, -diz′ing** to speak or write in a rhapsodic manner

rhap′sody (-dē) *n., pl.* **-dies** ⟦< Gr *rhaptein*, stitch together + ōidē, song⟧ **1** any ecstatic or enthusiastic speech or writing **2** an instrumental composition of free, irregular form, suggesting improvisation —**rhap·sod′ic** (-säd′ik) or **rhap·sod′i·cal** *adj.*

rhea (rē′ə) *n.* ⟦< Gr⟧ a large, flightless South American bird, like an ostrich but smaller

rheo·stat (rē′ə stat′) *n.* ⟦< Gr *rheos*, current + -STAT⟧ a device for varying the resistance of an electric circuit, used as for dimming or brightening electric lights

rhesus (monkey) (rē′səs) ⟦< Gr proper name⟧ a brownish-yellow monkey of India: used in medical research

rheto·ric (ret′ər ik) *n.* ⟦< Gr *rhētōr*, orator⟧ **1** the art of using words effectively; esp., the art of prose composition **2** artificial eloquence —**rhe·tori·cal** (ri tôr′i kəl) *adj.* —**rhet′o·ri′cian** (-ə rish′ən) *n.*

rhetorical question a question asked only for rhetorical effect, no answer being expected

rheum (rōōm) *n.* ⟦< Gr *rheuma*, a flow⟧ watery discharge from the eyes, nose, etc., as in a cold —**rheum′y, -i·er, -i· est,** *adj.*

rheumatic fever an acute or chronic disease, usually of children, with fever, swelling of the joints, inflammation of the heart, etc.

rheu·ma·tism (rōō′mə tiz′əm) *n.* ⟦see RHEUM⟧ *nontechnical term* for a painful condition of the joints and muscles —**rheu·mat′ic** (-mat′ik) *adj., n.* —**rheu′ma·toid′** (-mə toid′) *adj.*

rheumatoid arthritis a chronic disease with painful swelling of joints, often leading to deformity

Rh factor (är′āch′) ⟦first discovered in RH(ESUS) monkeys⟧ a group of antigens, usually present in human blood: people who have this factor are **Rh positive;** those who do not are **Rh negative**

■ THESAURUS ■

summary] synopsis, abstract, outline; see SUMMARY. **4** [A formal inspection] parade, inspection, dress parade, drill, march, procession, cavalcade, column, file, military display, march-past; see also DISPLAY.

review *v.* **1** [To correct] criticize, revise, reedit; see CORRECT. **2** [To inspect] analyze, reexamine, check thoroughly; see EXAMINE.

revise *v.* reconsider, rewrite, correct; see EDIT.

revised *a.* corrected, edited, amended, overhauled, improved, altered, changed, rectified, polished, redone, rewritten, reorganized, restyled, emended.

revision *n.* reexamination, edition, editing; see CORRECTION.

revival *n.* **1** [The act of reviving] renewal, renascence, renaissance, refreshment, arousal, awakening, rebirth, reversion, resurrection, enkindling, restoration, invigoration, vivification, resuscitation, reawakening, improvement, freshening, recovery, cheering, consolation. **2** [An evangelical service] evangelistic meeting, prayer meeting, camp meeting; see CEREMONY.

revive *v.* **1** [To give new life] enliven, enkindle, refresh, renew, vivify, animate, reanimate, resuscitate, recondition, rejuvenate, bring

to, bring around, wake up, resurrect, make whole, exhilarate, energize, invigorate, breathe new life into, reproduce, regenerate, restore, touch up, repair.—*Ant.* DECREASE, wither, lessen. **2** [To take on new life] come around, come to, freshen, improve, recover, flourish, awake, reawake, rouse, arouse, strengthen, overcome, come to life, grow well, be cured.— *Ant.* DIE, faint, weaken.

revoke *v.* recall, retract, disclaim; see CANCEL.

revolt *n.* uprising, mutiny, sedition; see REVOLUTION 2.

revolt *v.* **1** [To rebel] mutiny, rise up, resist; see REBEL. **2** [To repel] sicken, offend, nauseate; see DISGUST.

revolting *a.* awful, loathsome, repulsive; see OFFENSIVE 2, SHAMEFUL 1, 2.

revolution *n.* **1** [A complete motion about an axis] rotation, spin, turn, revolving, circuit, round, whirl, gyration, circumvolution, cycle, roll, reel, twirl, swirl, pirouette. **2** [An armed uprising] revolt, rebellion, mutiny, insurrection, riot, anarchy, outbreak, coup, coup d'état, destruction, overturn, upset, overthrow, reversal, rising, crime, violence, bloodshed, turbulence, insubordination, disturbance, reformation, plot, underground activity, guerrilla activity, public

unrest, upheaval, tumult, disorder, foment, turmoil, uproar, uprising, row, strife, strike, putsch, subversion, breakup, secession.—*Ant.* LAW, order, control.

revolutionary *a.* **1** [Concerned with a revolution] rebellious, revolting, mutinous, insurrectionary, destructive, anarchistic, subverting, insurgent, overturning, upsetting, destroying, breaking up, subversive, seceding, riotous, agitating, disturbing, working underground, treasonable.—*Ant.* PATRIOTIC, loyal, constructive. **2** [New and unusual] novel, advanced, radical; see UNUSUAL 2.

revolutionary *n.* revolutionist, traitor, insurrectionist; see REBEL.

revolutionize *v.* recast, remodel, refashion; see REFORM 1.

revolve *v.* spin, rotate, twirl; see TURN 1.

revolver *n.* automatic, gun, rod*; see PISTOL.

reward *n.* **1** [Payment] compensation, remuneration, recompense; see PAY 1, 2. **2** [A prize] premium, bonus, award; see PRIZE.

reward *v.* compensate, repay, remunerate; see PAY 1.

rewrite *v.* edit, fill out, cut; see EDIT.

rhine·stone (rīn′stōn′) *n.* an artificial gem of hard glass, often cut in imitation of a diamond

Rhine wine a light white wine, esp. one produced in the valley of the Rhine, river in W Europe

rhi·ni·tis (rī nīt′is) *n.* ⟦< Gr *rhis*, nose + -ITIS⟧ inflammation of the nasal mucous membrane

rhino (rī′nō) *n., pl.* **-nos** or **-no** *short for* RHINOCEROS

rhi·noc·er·os (rī näs′ər əs) *n.* ⟦< Gr *rhis*, nose + *keras*, horn⟧ a large, thick-skinned, plant-eating mammal of Africa and Asia, with one or two upright horns on the snout

rhi·zome (rī′zōm′) *n.* ⟦< Gr *rhiza*, a root⟧ a horizontal stem on or under soil, bearing leaves near its tips and roots from its undersurface

rho (rō) *n. name of* the 17th letter of the Greek alphabet (Ρ, ρ)

rho·do·den·dron (rō′də den′drən) *n.* ⟦< Gr *rhodon*, rose + *dendron*, tree⟧ a tree or shrub, mainly evergreen, with pink, white, or purple flowers

rhom·boid (räm′boid′) *n.* ⟦< Fr: see fol. & -OID⟧ a parallelogram with oblique angles and only the opposite sides equal

rhom·bus (räm′bəs) *n., pl.* **-buses** or **-bi** (-bī′) ⟦L < Gr *rhombos*, turnable object⟧ an equilateral parallelogram, esp. one with oblique angles

rhu·barb (rōō′bärb′) *n.* ⟦< Gr *rhēon*, rhubarb + *barbaron*, foreign⟧ 1 a plant with long, thick stalks that are cooked into a sauce, etc. 2 [Slang] a heated argument

rhyme (rīm) *n.* ⟦< OFr⟧ 1 a poem or verse with recurring correspondence of end sounds, esp. at ends of lines 2 such verse or poetry or such correspondence of sounds 3 a word corresponding with another in end sound — *vi.* **rhymed, rhym′ing** 1 to make (rhyming) verse 2 to form a rhyme *["more" rhymes with "door"]* — *vt.* 1 to put into rhyme 2 to use as a rhyme

rhym′er or **rhyme′ster** *n.* a maker of rhymes, esp. of trivial rhyming verse

rhythm (rith′əm) *n.* ⟦< Gr *rhythmos*, measure⟧ 1 movement, flow, etc. characterized by regular recurrence of beat, accent, etc. 2 the pattern of this in music, verse, etc. —**rhyth′mic** (-mik) or **rhyth′mi·cal** *adj.* —**rhyth′mi·cally** *adv.*

rhythm and blues the form of American popular music from which rock-and-roll derives

rhythm method a method of seeking birth control by abstaining from intercourse during the woman's probable ovulation period

rib (rib) *n.* ⟦OE⟧ 1 any of the arched bones attached to the spine and enclosing the chest cavity 2 anything like a rib in appearance or function — *vt.* **ribbed, rib′bing** 1 to provide or form with ribs 2 [Slang] to tease or make fun of; kid

rib·ald (rib′əld) *adj.* ⟦< OHG *riban*, to rub⟧ coarse or vulgar in joking, speaking, etc. —**rib′aldry** *n.*

rib·bon (rib′ən) *n.* ⟦< MFr *ruban*⟧ 1 a narrow strip of silk, rayon, etc. used for decoration, tying, etc. 2 [*pl.*] torn shreds 3 a strip of cloth inked for printing, as in a typewriter

ribo·fla·vin (rī′bə flā′vin) *n.* ⟦< *ribose*, a sugar + L *flavus*,

yellow⟧ a factor of the vitamin B complex found in milk, eggs, fruits, etc.

rice (rīs) *n.* ⟦< Gr *oryza*⟧ 1 an aquatic cereal grass grown widely in warm climates, esp. in the Orient 2 the starchy grains of this grass, used as food — *vt.* **riced, ric′ing** to make ricelike granules from (cooked potatoes, etc.) — **ric′er** *n.*

rich (rich) *adj.* ⟦< OFr⟧ 1 owning much money or property; wealthy 2 well-supplied (*with*); abounding (*in*) 3 valuable or costly 4 full of choice ingredients, as butter, sugar, etc. *[rich* pastries*]* 5 *a*) full and mellow (said of sounds) *b*) deep; vivid (said of colors) *c*) very fragrant 6 abundant 7 yielding in abundance, as soil 8 [Colloq.] very amusing —**the rich** wealthy people collectively —**rich′ly** *adv.* —**rich′ness** *n.*

riches (rich′iz) *n.pl.* ⟦< OFr *richesse, n. sing.*⟧ wealth

Rich·ter scale (rik′tər) ⟦devised by C. *Richter* (1900-85), U.S. geologist⟧ a scale for measuring earthquakes, with each step about ten times greater than the preceding one

rick (rik) *n.* ⟦OE *hreac*⟧ a stack of hay, straw, etc.

rick·ets (rik′its) *n.* ⟦< ? Gr *rhachis*, spine⟧ a disease, chiefly of children, characterized by a softening and, often, bending of the bones

rick·ety (rik′it ē) *adj.* 1 of or having rickets 2 feeble; weak; shaky

rick·rack (rik′rak′) *n.* ⟦< RACK¹⟧ flat, zigzag braid for trimming dresses, etc.

rick·shaw or **rick·sha** (rik′shô′) *n.* JINRIKISHA

rico·chet (rik′ə shā′) *n.* ⟦Fr⟧ the oblique rebound of a bullet, etc. after striking a surface at an angle — *vi.* **-cheted′** (-shād′), **-chet′ing** (-shā′in) to make a ricochet

ri·cotta (ri kät′ə) *n.* ⟦It < L *recocta*, recooked⟧ a soft cheese made from whey or whole milk

rid (rid) *vt.* **rid** or **rid′ded, rid′ding** ⟦< ON *rythja*, to clear (land)⟧ to free or relieve, as of something undesirable —**get rid of** to give or throw away or to destroy

rid·dance (rid′ns) *n.* a ridding or being rid; clearance or removal

rid·den (rid′n) *vi., vt. pp. of* RIDE

rid·dle¹ (rid′l) *n.* ⟦OE *rædels*⟧ 1 a puzzling question, etc. requiring some ingenuity to answer 2 any puzzling person or thing

rid·dle² (rid′l) *vt.* **-dled, -dling** ⟦< OE *hriddel*, a sieve⟧ to make many holes in; puncture throughout

ride (rid) *vi.* **rode, rid′den, rid′ing** ⟦OE *ridan*⟧ 1 to be carried along by a horse, in a vehicle, etc. 2 to be supported in motion (*on* or *upon*) *[tanks ride* on treads*]* 3 to admit of being ridden *[the car rides* smoothly*]* 4 to move or float on water 5 [Colloq.] to continue undisturbed *[let the matter ride]* — *vt.* 1 to sit on or in and control so as to move along 2 to move over, along, or through (a road, area, etc.) by horse, car, etc. 3 to control, dominate, etc. *[ridden* by doubts*]* 4 [Colloq.] to tease with ridicule, etc. — *n.* 1 a riding 2 a thing to ride at an amusement park

rid′er *n.* 1 one who rides 2 an addition or amendment to a document

rid′er·ship′ *n.* the passengers of a particular transportation system

---

THESAURUS

rhyme *n.* verse, rhyming verse, vowel-chime; see POETRY.

rhythm *n.* swing, accent, rise and fall; see BEAT 2.

rhythmic *a.* patterned, measured, balanced; see MUSICAL 1, REGULAR 3.

rib *n.* 1 [One part of the bony frame of the thorax] true rib, false rib, floating rib; see BONE. 2 [A rod] girder, bar, strip; see ROD 1, SUPPORT 2. 3 [A ridge] fin, nervure, vaulting; see sense 2.

ribbon *n.* strip, trimming, decoration; see BAND 1.

rich *a.* 1 [Possessed of wealth] wealthy, moneyed, affluent, well-to-do, well provided for, worth a million, well-off, well-fixed, in clover, swimming in gravy*, in the money*.—*Ant.* POOR, poverty-stricken, destitute. 2 [Sumptuous] luxurious, magnificent, resplendent, lavish, embellished, ornate, costly, expensive, splendid, superb, elegant, gorgeous, valuable, precious, extravagant, grand; see also BEAUTIFUL.—*Ant.* CHEAP, plain, simple. 3 [Fertile]

exuberant, lush, copious, plentiful, generous, fruitful, profuse, luxuriant, teeming, abundant, prolific, productive, fruit-bearing, propagating, yielding, breeding, superabounding, prodigal; see also FERTILE.—*Ant.* STERILE, unfruitful, barren. 4 [Having great food value] nourishing, luscious, sweet, fatty, oily, nutritious, sustaining, strengthening, satisfying; see also HEALTHFUL.—*Ant.* INADEQUATE, not nourishing, deficient.

riches *n.* fortune, possessions, money; see WEALTH.

richness *n.* copiousness, bounty, abundance; see PLENTY.

rickety *a.* infirm, shaky, fragile; see WEAK 2.

ricochet *v.* reflect, rebound, glance off; see BOUNCE.

rid *a.* relieved, quit, delivered; see FREE 2. —**be rid of** be freed from, be relieved of, have done with; see ESCAPE. —**get rid of** 1 get free from, slough off, shed; see FREE. 2 eject, expel, remove; see ELIMINATE.

rid *v.* clear, relieve, disencumber; see

FREE.

riddle¹ *n.* problem, question, knotty question, doubt, quandary, entanglement, dilemma, perplexity, enigma, confusion, complication, complexity, intricacy, strait, labyrinth, predicament, plight, distraction, bewilderment; see also PUZZLE 2.—*Ant.* SIMPLICITY, clarity, disentanglement.

ride *n.* drive, trip, transportation; see JOURNEY.

ride *v.* 1 [To be transported] be carried, travel in or on a vehicle, tour, journey, motor, drive, go for an airing; go by automobile, bicycle, etc. 2 [To control a beast of burden by riding] manage, guide, handle; see DRIVE 1. 3 [To tease harshly] ridicule, bait, harass; see BOTHER 2.

rider *n.* 1 [One who rides] driver, fare, passenger, motorist, horseman, hitchhiker. 2 [An additional clause or provision, usually not connected with the main body of the work] amendment, appendix, supplement; see ADDITION 1.

ridge (rij) *n.* ⟦< OE *hrycg*, animal's spine⟧ **1** the long, narrow crest of something **2** a long, narrow elevation of land **3** any raised narrow strip **4** the horizontal line formed by the meeting of two sloping surfaces — *vt., vi.* **ridged, ridg'ing** to mark or be marked with, or form into, ridges

ridge'pole' *n.* the horizontal beam at the ridge of a roof, to which the rafters are attached

ri·di·cule (rid'i kyōōl') *n.* ⟦< L *ridere*, to laugh⟧ **1** the act of making someone the object of scornful laughter **2** words or actions intended to produce such laughter — *vt.* **-culed', -cul'ing** to make fun of; deride; mock

ri·dic·u·lous (ri dik'yə ləs) *adj.* deserving ridicule —**ri·dic'u·lous·ly** *adv.* —**ri·dic'u·lous·ness** *n.*

rife (rīf) *adj.* ⟦OE *ryfe*⟧ **1** widespread **2** abounding *[rife with error]*

riff (rif) *n.* ⟦prob. altered < REFRAIN²⟧ *Jazz* a constantly repeated musical phrase — *vi. Jazz* to perform a riff

rif·fle (rif'əl) *n.* ⟦< ?⟧ **1** a ripple in a stream, produced by a reef, etc. **2** a certain way of shuffling cards — *vt., vi.* **-fled, -fling** to shuffle (playing cards) by letting a divided deck fall together as the corners are slipped through one's thumbs

riff'raff (rif'raf') *n.* ⟦< OFr⟧ those people regarded as worthless, disreputable, etc.

ri·fle¹ (rī'fəl) *vt.* **-fled, -fling** ⟦Fr *rifler*, to scrape⟧ to cut spiral grooves within (a gun barrel, etc.) — *n.* a gun, fired from the shoulder, with a rifled barrel to spin the bullet for greater accuracy

ri·fle² (rī'fəl) *vt.* **-fled, -fling** ⟦< OFr *rifler*⟧ to ransack and rob —**ri'fler** *n.*

ri·fle·man (-mən) *n., pl.* **-men** a soldier armed with a rifle

ri·fling (rī'fliŋ) *n.* **1** the cutting of spiral grooves within a gun barrel to make the projectile spin **2** a system of such grooves

rift (rift) *n.* ⟦< Dan, fissure⟧ an opening caused by splitting; cleft — *vt., vi.* to burst open; split

rig (rig) *vt.* **rigged, rig'ging** ⟦< Scand⟧ **1** to fit (a ship, mast, etc.) with (sails, shrouds, etc.) **2** to assemble **3** to equip **4** to arrange dishonestly **5** [Colloq.] to dress: with *out* — *n.* **1** the way sails, etc. are rigged **2** equipment; gear **3** oil-drilling equipment **4** a tractor-trailer

rig·a·ma·role (rig'ə mə rōl') *n. var. of* RIGMAROLE

rig'ging *n.* the ropes, chains, etc. for a vessel's masts, sails, etc.

right (rīt) *adj.* ⟦< OE *riht*, straight⟧ **1** with a straight line or plane perpendicular to a base *[a right angle]* **2** upright; virtuous **3** correct **4** fitting; suitable **5** designating the side or surface meant to be seen **6** mentally or physically sound **7** *a)* designating or of that side of the body toward the east when one faces north *b)* designating or of the corresponding side of anything *c)* closer to the right side of a person facing the thing mentioned — *n.* **1** what is right, just, etc. **2** power, privilege, etc. belonging to one by law, nature, etc. **3** the right side **4** the right hand **5** *[often* R-] *Politics* a conservative or reactionary position, party, etc.: often with *the* — *adv.* **1** straight; directly *[go right home]* **2** properly; fittingly **3** completely **4** exactly *[right here]* **5** according to law, justice, etc. **6** correctly **7** on or toward the right side **8** very: in certain titles *[the right reverend]* — *interj.* agreed! OK! — *vt.* **1** to put upright **2** to correct **3** to put in order —**right away** (or **off**) at once —**right on!** [Slang] that's right! —**right'ly** *adv.* —**right'ness** *n.*

right'about'-face' *n.* ABOUT-FACE

right angle an angle of 90 degrees

right·eous (rī'chəs) *adj.* **1** acting in a just, upright manner; virtuous **2** morally right or justifiable —**right'eously** *adv.* —**right'eous·ness** *n.*

right'ful *adj.* **1** fair and just; right **2** having a lawful claim —**right'fully** *adv.* —**right'ful·ness** *n.*

right'-hand' *adj.* **1** on or toward the right **2** of, for, or with the right hand **3** most helpful or reliable *[the president's right-hand man]*

right'-hand'ed *adj.* **1** using the right hand more skillfully than the left **2** done with or made for use with the right hand — *adv.* with the right hand —**right'-hand'ed·ness** *n.*

right'ist *n., adj.* conservative or reactionary —**right'ism'** *n.*

right'-mind'ed *adj.* having correct views or sound principles

right of way **1** the right to move first at intersections **2** land over which a road, power line, etc. passes Also **right'-of-way'**

right'-to-life' *adj.* designating any movement, party, etc. opposed to abortion —**right'-to-lif'er** *n.*

right triangle a triangle with a right angle

right wing the more conservative or reactionary section

■ THESAURUS ■

---

ridge *n.* **1** [A long, straight, raised portion] raised strip, rib, seam; see RIM. **2** [A long, narrow elevation of land] mountain ridge, range, elevation; see HILL.

ridicule *n.* scorn, contempt, mockery, disdain, derision, jeer, leer, disparagement, sneer, rally, flout, fleer, twit, taunt, burlesque, caricature, satire, parody, travesty, irony, sarcasm, persiflage, farce, buffoonery, horseplay, foolery, razz*, rib*, roast*, raspberry*, horse laugh.—*Ant.* PRAISE, commendation, approval.

ridicule *v.* scoff at, sneer at, laugh at, rail at, mock, taunt, banter, mimic, jeer, twit, disparage, flout, deride, scorn, make sport of, make fun of, rally, burlesque, caricature, satirize, parody, cartoon, travesty, run down, make fun of, put down*, razz*, rib*, pull someone's leg*, roast*, pan*.— *Ant.* ENCOURAGE, approve, applaud.

ridiculous *a.* ludicrous, absurd, preposterous; see FUNNY 1, UNUSUAL 2.

rife *a.* **1** [Widespread] prevalent, extensive, common; see WIDESPREAD. **2** [Abundant] plentiful, abounding, profuse; see PLENTIFUL 1.

riffraff *n.* mob, masses, rabble; see PEOPLE 3.

rifle¹ *n.* repeating rifle, carbine, automatic rifle; see GUN, MACHINE GUN.

rig *n.* tackle, apparatus, gear; see EQUIPMENT.

right *a.* **1** [Correct] true, precise, accurate, exact, sure, certain, determined, proven, factual, correct; see also ACCURATE 2, VALID 1. **2** [Just] lawful, legitimate, honest; see FAIR 1. **3** [Suitable] apt, proper, appropriate;

see FIT 1. **4** [Sane] reasonable, rational, sound; see SANE. **5** [Justly] fairly, evenly, equitably, honestly, decently, sincerely, legitimately, lawfully, conscientiously, squarely, impartially, objectively, reliably, dispassionately, without bias, without prejudice; see also JUSTLY 1. **6** [Straight] directly, undeviatingly, immediately; see DIRECT 1. **7** [Opposite to left] dextral, dexter, right-handed, clockwise, on the right.— *Ant.* LEFT, sinistral, counterclockwise. —**right away** at once, directly, without delay; see IMMEDIATELY, NOW.

right *n.* **1** [A privilege] prerogative, immunity, exemption, license, benefit, advantage, favor, franchise, preference, priority; see also FREEDOM 2. **2** [Justice] equity, freedom, liberty, independence, emancipation, enfranchisement, self-determination, natural expectation; see also FAIRNESS 3. **3** [The part opposite the left] right hand, right side, strong side, active side. —**by rights** properly, justly, suitably; see RIGHTLY. —**in one's own right** individually, acting as one's own agent, by one's own authority; see INDEPENDENTLY. —**in the right** correct, true, accurate; see VALID 1.

right *v.* **1** [To make upright] set up, make straight, balance; see STRAIGHTEN, TURN 2. **2** [To repair an injustice] adjust, correct, repair, restore, vindicate, do justice, recompense, reward, remedy, rectify, mend, amend, set right; see also REPAIR.—

Ant. WRONG, hurt, harm.

righteous *a.* **1** [Virtuous] just, upright, good, honorable, honest, worthy, exemplary, noble, right-minded, goodhearted, dutiful, trustworthy, equitable, scrupulous, conscientious, ethical, fair, impartial, fairminded, commendable, praiseworthy, guiltless, blameless, sinless, peerless, sterling, matchless, deserving, laudable, creditable, charitable, philanthropic, having a clear conscience; see also RELIABLE.—*Ant.* CORRUPT, sinful, profligate. **2** [Religiously inclined] devout, pious, saintly, godly, godlike, angelic, devoted, reverent, reverential, faithful, fervent, strict, rigid, devotional, zealous, spiritual; see also HOLY 1, RELIGIOUS 2.—*Ant.* BAD, impious, irreligious. **3** [Conscious of one's own virtue] self-righteous, hypocritical, self-esteeming; see EGOTISTIC.

righteousness *n.* **1** [Justice] uprightness, nobility, fairness; see HONOR 1. **2** [Devotion to a sinless life] piety, saintliness, godliness; see DEVOTION.

rightful *a.* proper, just, honest; see FAIR 1, LEGAL, PERMITTED.

rightfully *a.* lawfully, justly, fairly, properly, truly, equitably, honestly, impartially, fittingly, legitimately, in all conscience, in equity, by right, in reason, objectively, fair and square*, on the level*, by rights; see also LEGALLY.

rightly *a.* justly, properly, correctly; see WELL 2.

of a political party or group —**right′-wing′** *adj.* —**right′-wing′er** *n.*

rigid (rij′id) *adj.* ⟦< L *rigere*, be stiff⟧ **1** not bending or flexible; stiff **2** not moving; fixed **3** severe; strict **4** having a rigid framework: said of a dirigible —**ri·gid·i·ty** (ri jid′ə tē) *or* **rig′id·ness** *n.* —**rig′idly** *adv.*

rig·ma·role (rig′mə rōl′) *n.* ⟦< ME *rageman rolle*, long list⟧ **1** nonsense **2** a foolishly complicated procedure

rigor (rig′ər) *n.* ⟦< L *rigere*: see RIGID⟧ **1** severity; strictness **2** hardship　Brit., etc. sp. **rig′our** —**rig′or·ous** *adj.* —**rig′or·ously** *adv.*

rigor mor·tis (rig′ər môr′tis, ri′gôr′) ⟦L, stiffness of death⟧ the stiffening of the muscles after death

rile (rīl) *vt.* **riled, ril′ing** ⟦var. of ROIL⟧ [Colloq. or Dial.] to anger; irritate

rill (ril) *n.* ⟦< Du *ril*⟧ a rivulet

rim (rim) *n.* ⟦OE *rima*⟧ **1** an edge, border, or margin, esp. of something circular **2** the outer part of a wheel —*vt.* **rimmed, rim′ming** to put a rim or rims on or around —**rim′less** *adj.*

rime[1] (rīm) *n., vi., vt.* **rimed, rim′ing** RHYME

rime[2] (rīm) *n.* ⟦OE *hrim*⟧ hoarfrost

rind (rīnd) *n.* ⟦OE⟧ a hard outer layer or covering, as of fruit or cheese

ring[1] (riŋ) *vi.* **rang** *or* [Now Chiefly Dial.] **rung, rung, ring′ing** ⟦OE *hringan*⟧ **1** to give forth a resonant sound, as a bell **2** to seem ⟦*to ring true*⟧ **3** to sound a bell, esp. as a summons **4** to resound ⟦*to ring* with laughter⟧ **5** to have a ringing sensation, as the ears —*vt.* **1** to cause (a bell, etc.) to ring **2** to signal, announce, etc., as by ringing **3** to call by telephone —*n.* **1** the sound of a bell **2** a characteristic quality ⟦the *ring* of truth⟧ **3** the act of ringing a bell **4** a telephone call —**ring a bell** to stir up a memory

ring[2] (riŋ) *n.* ⟦OE *hring*⟧ **1** an ornamental circular band worn on a finger **2** any similar band ⟦a key *ring*⟧ **3** a circular line, mark, figure, or course **4** a group of people or things in a circle **5** a group working to advance its own interests, esp. by dishonest means **6** an enclosed area for contests, exhibitions, etc. ⟦a circus *ring*⟧ **7** prizefighting: with *the* —*vt.* **ringed, ring′ing 1** to encircle **2** to form into a ring —**run rings around** [Colloq.] **1** to run much faster than **2** to excel greatly

ring′er[1] *n.* a horseshoe, etc. thrown so that it encircles the peg

ring′er[2] *n.* **1** one that rings a bell, etc. **2** [Slang] *a*) a person or thing closely resembling another *b*) a fraudulent substitute in a competition

ring′lead′er *n.* one who leads others, esp. in unlawful acts, etc.

ring′let (-lit) *n.* **1** a little ring or circle **2** a curl of hair

ring′mas′ter *n.* a person who directs the performances in a circus ring

ring′side′ *n.* the place just outside the ring, as at a boxing match

ring′worm′ *n.* a contagious skin disease caused by a fungus

rink (riŋk) *n.* ⟦< OFr *renc*, a rank⟧ **1** an expanse of ice for skating **2** a smooth floor for roller-skating

rinse (rins) *vt.* **rinsed, rins′ing** ⟦ult. < L *recens*, fresh⟧ **1** to wash or flush lightly **2** to remove soap, etc. from with clear water —*n.* **1** a rinsing or the liquid used **2** a solution used to rinse or tint hair

riot (rī′ət) *n.* ⟦< OFr *riote*, dispute⟧ **1** wild or violent disorder, confusion, etc.; esp., a violent public disturbance **2** a brilliant display ⟦a *riot* of color⟧ **3** [Colloq.] something very funny —*vi.* **1** to take part in a riot —**read the riot act to** to give very strict orders to so as to make obey —**run riot 1** to act wildly **2** to grow wild in abundance —**ri′oter** *n.* —**ri′ot·ous** *adj.*

rip (rip) *vt.* **ripped, rip′ping** ⟦ME *rippen*⟧ **1** *a*) to cut or tear apart roughly *b*) to remove in this way (with *off, out,* etc.) *c*) to sever the threads of (a seam) **2** to saw (wood) along the grain —*vi.* **1** to become ripped **2** [Colloq.] to rush; speed —*n.* a ripped place —**rip into** [Colloq.] to attack, esp. verbally —**rip off** [Slang] **1** to steal **2** to cheat or exploit —**rip′per** *n.*

rip cord a cord, etc. pulled to open a parachute during descent

ripe (rīp) *adj.* ⟦OE⟧ **1** ready to be harvested, as grain or fruit **2** of sufficient age, etc. to be used ⟦*ripe* cheese⟧ **3** fully developed; mature **4** fully prepared; ready ⟦*ripe* for action⟧ —**ripe′ly** *adv.* —**ripe′ness** *n.*

ripen (rī′pən) *vi., vt.* to become or make ripe; mature, age, etc.

rip′-off′ *n.* [Slang] the act or an instance of stealing, cheating, etc.

ri·poste *or* **ri·post** (ri pōst′) *n.* ⟦Fr < L *respondere*, to answer⟧ a sharp, swift response; retort

rip·ple (rip′əl) *vi., vt.* **-pled, -pling** ⟦prob. < RIP⟧ to have or form little waves on the surface (of) —*n.* **1** a small wave **2** a rippling

ripple effect the spreading effects caused by a single event

rip′-roar′ing (-rôr′iŋ) *adj.* [Slang] boisterous; uproarious

rip′saw′ *n.* a saw with coarse teeth, for cutting wood along the grain

rip′tide′ *n.* a current opposing other currents, esp. along a seashore　Also **rip tide**

rise (rīz) *vi.* **rose, risen** (riz′ən), **ris′ing** ⟦< OE *risan*⟧ **1** to stand or sit up after sitting, kneeling, or lying **2** to rebel; revolt **3** to go up; ascend **4** to appear above the horizon, as the sun **5** to attain a higher level, rank, etc. **6**

THESAURUS

rigid *a.* **1** [Stiff] unyielding, inflexible, solid; see FIRM 1. **2** [Strict] exact, rigorous, firm; see SEVERE 1, 2. **3** [Fixed] set, unmoving, solid; see DEFINITE 1, DETERMINED.

rigorous *a.* harsh, austere, uncompromising; see SEVERE 1.

rim *n.* edge, border, verge, brim, lip, brink, top, margin, line, outline, band, ring, strip, brow, curb, ledge, skirt, fringe, hem, limit, confine, end, terminus.—*Ant.* CENTER, middle, interior.

rind *n.* peel, hull, shell, surface, coating, crust, bark, cortex, integument; see also SKIN.—*Ant.* INSIDE, center, interior.

ring[1,2] *n.* **1** [A circle] circlet, girdle, brim; see CIRCLE 1, RIM. **2** [A circlet of metal] hoop, band, circle; see JEWELRY. *Rings include the following:* finger, wedding, engagement, guard, signet, organization, umbrella, ankle, nose, key, harness, napkin; bracelet, earring, ear drop. **3** [A close association, often corrupt] cabal, combine, party, bloc, faction, group, gang, monopoly, cartel, corner, pool, trust, syndicate, gang*, string; see also ORGANIZATION 2. **4** [Pugilism] prize fighting, boxing, professional fighting; see SPORT 3. **5** [A ringing sound] clank, clangor, jangle; see NOISE 1. — **give someone a ring*** call, call up, phone; see TELEPHONE. —**run rings**

around* excel, overtake, beat; see PASS 1.

ring[1,2] *v.* **1** [To encircle] circle, rim, surround, encompass, girdle, enclose, move around, loop, gird, belt, confine, hem in. **2** [To cause to sound] clap, clang, bang, beat, toll, strike, pull, punch, buzz, play, resound, reverberate, peal, chime, tinkle, jingle, jangle, vibrate, clang, sound the brass*; see also SOUND. **3** [To call by ringing] give a ring, buzz for, ring up; see SUMMON.

rinse *v.* clean, flush, dip in water; see SOAK 1, WASH 2.

riot *n.* confusion, uproar, tumult; see DISORDER, DISTURBANCE 2, PROTEST. —**run riot** revolt, riot, fight; see REBEL.

riot *v.* revolt, stir up trouble, fight in the streets; see REBEL.

rip *n.* rent, cleavage, split; see TEAR.

rip *v.* rend, split, cleave, rive, tear, shred; see also CUT 1.

ripe *a.* **1** [Ready to be harvested] fully grown, fully developed, ruddy, red, yellow, plump, filled out, matured, ready.—*Ant.* GREEN, undeveloped, half-grown. **2** [Improved by time and experience] mellow, wise, perfected; see MATURE. **3** [Ready] prepared, seasoned, consummate, perfected, finished, usable, fit, conditioned, prime, available, on the mark,

complete; see also READY 2.—*Ant.* UNFIT, unready, unprepared.

ripen *v.* develop, evolve, advance; see GROW 2.

rise *n.* **1** [The act of rising] ascent, mount, lift; see CLIMB. **2** [An increase] augmentation, growth, enlargement, multiplication, heightening, intensifying, stacking up, piling up, distention, addition, accession, inflation, acceleration, doubling, advance; see also INCREASE.—*Ant.* REDUCTION, lessening, decrease. **3** [Source] start, beginning, commencement; see ORIGIN 2. —**get a rise out of*** get a response from by teasing, provoke, annoy; see BOTHER 2. —**give rise to** initiate, begin, start; see CAUSE.

rise *v.* **1** [To move upward] ascend, mount, climb, scale, surmount, soar, tower, rocket, surge, sweep upward, lift, bob up, move up, push up, reach up, come up, go up, surge, sprout, grow, rear, uprise, blast off, curl upward; see also FLY 1.—*Ant.* FALL, drop, come down. **2** [To get out of bed] get up, rise up, wake; see ARISE 1. **3** [To increase] grow, swell, intensify, mount, enlarge, spread, expand, extend, augment, heighten, enhance, distend, inflate, pile up, stack up, multiply, accelerate, speed up, add to, wax, advance, raise, double; see to extend, slant, or move upward **7** to increase in amount, degree, etc. **8** to expand and swell, as dough with yeast **9** to originate; begin **10** *Theol.* to return to life — *n.* **1** upward movement; ascent **2** an advance in status, rank, etc. **3** a slope upward **4** an increase in degree, amount, etc. **5** beginning; origin —**give rise to** to bring about

ris′er *n.* **1** one that rises **2** a vertical piece between the steps in a stairway

ris·ible (riz′ə bəl) *adj.* 〖< L *ridere*, to laugh〗 causing laughter; funny —**ris·ibil′i·ty**, *pl.* **-ties**, *n.*

ris′ing *adj.* advancing to adult years; growing *[the rising generation]* — *n.* an uprising; revolt

risk (risk) *n.* 〖< Fr < It *risco*〗 the chance of injury, damage, or loss — *vt.* **1** to expose to risk *[to risk one's life]* **2** to incur the risk of *[to risk a war]* —**risk′y**, **-i·er**, **-i·est**, *adj.*

ris·qué (ris kā′) *adj.* 〖Fr < *risquer*, to risk〗 very close to being improper or indecent; suggestive

rite (rīt) *n.* 〖L *ritus*〗 a ceremonial, solemn act, as in religious use

rite of passage a significant event, ceremony, etc. in a person's life

ritu·al (rich′o̅o̅ əl) *adj.* of, like, or done as a rite — *n.* a set form or system of rites, religious or otherwise —**rit′u·al·ism′** *n.* —**rit′u·al·ly** *adv.*

ri·val (rī′vəl) *n.* 〖< L *rivalis*〗 one who tries to get or do the same thing as another, or to equal or surpass another; competitor — *adj.* acting as a rival; competing — *vt.* **-valed** or **-valled**, **-val·ing** or **-val·ling** **1** to try to equal or surpass **2** to equal in some way —**ri′val·ry**, *pl.* **-ries**, *n.*

rive (rīv) *vt., vi.* **rived**, **rived** or **riven** (riv′ən), **riv′ing** 〖< ON *rifa*〗 **1** to tear apart; rend **2** to split

river (riv′ər) *n.* 〖< L *ripa*, a bank〗 a natural stream of water flowing into an ocean, a lake, etc. —**riv′er·like′** *adj.*

river basin the area drained by a river and its tributaries

riv′er·side′ *n.* the bank of a river

rivet (riv′it) *n.* 〖Fr < *river*, to clinch〗 a metal bolt with a head and a plain end that is flattened after the bolt is passed through parts to be held together — *vt.* to fasten with or as with rivets —**riv′et·er** *n.*

rivu·let (riv′yo̅o̅ lit) *n.* 〖< L *rivus*, brook〗 a little stream

rm. **1** ream **2** room

Rn *Chem. symbol for* radon

RN or **R.N.** Registered Nurse

RNA 〖*r(ibo)n(ucleic) a(cid)*〗 an essential component of all living matter: one form carries genetic information

roach[1] (rōch) *n., pl.* **roach** or **-es** *short for* COCKROACH

roach[2] (rōch) *n.* 〖< OFr *roche*〗 a freshwater fish of the carp family

road (rōd) *n.* 〖OE *rad*, a ride〗 **1** a way made for traveling; highway **2** a way; course *[the road to fortune]* **3** *[often pl.]* a place near shore where ships can ride at anchor —**on the road** traveling, as a salesman

road′bed′ *n.* the foundation laid for railroad tracks or for a highway, etc.

road′block′ *n.* **1** a blockade set up in a road to prevent movement of vehicles **2** any hindrance

road runner a long-tailed, swift-running desert bird of the SW U.S. and N Mexico

road′show′ *n.* **1** a touring theatrical show **2** a reserved-seat film showing

road′side′ *n.* the side of a road — *adj.* on or at the side of a road

road′way′ *n.* a road; specif., the part of a road used by vehicles

road′work′ *n.* distance running or jogging as an exercise, esp. by a boxer

roam (rōm) *vi., vt.* 〖ME *romen*〗 to wander aimlessly (over or through) —**roam′er** *n.*

roan (rōn) *adj.* 〖< OSp *roano*〗 bay, black, etc. thickly sprinkled with white — *n.* a roan horse

roar (rôr) *vi.* 〖OE *rarian*〗 **1** to make a loud, deep, rumbling sound **2** to laugh boisterously — *vt.* to express with a roar — *n.* a loud, deep, rumbling sound

roast (rōst) *vt.* 〖< OFr *rostir*〗 **1** to cook (meat, etc.) with little or no moisture, as in an oven or over an open fire **2** to process (coffee, etc.) by exposure to heat **3** to expose to great heat **4** [Colloq.] to criticize severely — *vi.* **1** to undergo roasting **2** to be or become very hot — *n.* **1** roasted meat **2** a cut of meat for roasting **3** a picnic at which food is roasted — *adj.* roasted *[roast pork]* — **roast′er** *n.*

rob (räb) *vt.* **robbed**, **rob′bing** 〖< OFr *rober*〗 **1** to take money, etc. from unlawfully by force; steal from **2** to deprive of something unjustly or injuriously — *vi.* to commit robbery —**rob′ber** *n.* —**rob′bery**, *pl.* **-ies**, *n.*

THESAURUS

also INCREASE.—*Ant.* DECREASE, lessen, contract. **4** [To begin] spring, emanate, issue; see BEGIN 2. **5** [To improve one's station] prosper, flourish, thrive; see IMPROVE 1. **6** [To stand] be erected, be built, be placed, be located, be put up, go up, be founded, have foundation, be situated; see also STAND 1. **7** [To swell; *said usually of dough or batter*] inflate, billow, bulge; see SWELL.

rising *a.* climbing, ascending, going aloft, moving up, surging up, spiraling up, slanting up, inclining up, mounting, accelerating, on the rise, in ascension, upcoming, upswinging; see also GROWING.

risk *n.* **1** [Danger] hazard, peril, jeopardy; see DANGER. **2** [The basis of a chance] contingency, opportunity, prospect; see CHANCE 1, UNCERTAINTY 3. —**run a risk** take a chance, gamble, venture; see RISK, *v.*

risk *v.* gamble, hazard, venture, run the risk, do at one's own peril, hang by a thread, play with fire, go out of one's depth, go beyond one's depth, bell the cat, make an investment, take the liberty, lay oneself open to, pour money into, go through fire and water, leave to luck, leap before one looks, fish in troubled waters, skate on thin ice, defy danger, live in a glass house.

risky *a.* perilous, precarious, hazardous; see DANGEROUS, UNSAFE.

risqué *a.* indelicate, spicy, suggestive; see LEWD 2.

rite *n.* observance, service, ritual; see CEREMONY 2, CUSTOM.

ritual *n.* observance, rite, act; see CEREMONY 2, CUSTOM.

rival *a.* competing, striving, combat-

ant, combatting, emulating, vying, opposing, disputing, contesting, contending, conflicting, battling, equal.—*Ant.* HELPFUL, aiding, assisting.

rival *n.* emulator, competitor, antagonist; see OPPONENT 1.

rival *v.* approach, match, compare with; see EQUAL.

rivalry *n.* competition, emulation, striving, contest, vying, struggle, battle, contention, opposition, dispute; see also FIGHT 1.—*Ant.* COOPERATION, combination, conspiracy.

river *n.* stream, flow, course, current, tributary, rivulet, river system, creek, brook, watercourse. *Famous rivers include the following:* Seine, Rhone, Loire, Thames, Severn, Avon, Clyde, Danube, Rhine, Elbe, Don, Volga, Vistula, Nile, Euphrates, Tigris, Ganges, Indus, Irrawaddy, Yellow, Yangtze, Congo, Zambesi, St. Lawrence, Saskatchewan, Mississippi, Missouri, Ohio, Platte, Delaware, Columbia, Gila, Colorado, Snake, Hudson, Rio Grande, Amazon, Orinoco, La Plata.

road *n.* **1** [A strip prepared for travel] path, way, highway, roadway, street, avenue, thoroughfare, boulevard, highroad, drive, terrace, parkway, byway, lane, alley, alleyway, crossroad, viaduct, subway, paving, slab, turnpike, trail, post road, secondary road, market road, national highway, state highway, county road, military road, Roman road, freeway, the main drag*. **2** [A course] scheme, way, plans; see PLAN 2. —**on the road** on tour, traveling, on the way; see EN ROUTE. —**one for the road*** cocktail, nightcap, toast; see

DRINK 2.

roam *v.* ramble, range, stroll, rove, walk, traverse, stray, straggle, meander, prowl, tramp, saunter, knock around*, bat around*, scour, straggle, gallivant, struggle along, traipse*, hike; see also TRAVEL.

roar *n.* bellow, shout, boom, thunder, howl, bay, bawl, yell, bluster, uproar, din, clash, detonation, explosion, barrage, reverberation, rumble; see also CRY 1, 2, NOISE 1.—*Ant.* SILENCE, whisper, sigh.

roar *v.* bellow, shout, boom, thunder, howl, bay, bawl, yell, rumble, drum, detonate, explode, reverberate, resound, reecho; see also CRY 2, SOUND.

roast *v.* toast, broil, barbecue; see COOK.

rob *v.* thieve, take, burglarize, strip, plunder, deprive of, withhold from, defraud, cheat, swindle, pilfer, break into, hold up, stick up*, purloin, filch, lift*, abscond with, embezzle, pillage, sack, loot, snitch*, pinch*, swipe*, cop*; see also STEAL.

robber *n.* thief, burglar, cheat, plunderer, pillager, bandit, pirate, raider, thug, desperado, forger, hold-up man, second-story man*, privateer, buccaneer, swindler, highwayman, bank robber, pilferer, shoplifter, cattle-thief, housebreaker, pickpocket, freebooter, marauder, brigand, pickpurse, sharper, safecracker, fence, rustler*, crook*, con man*, clip artist*, chiseler*, paper hanger*, stick-up man*; see also CRIMINAL, RASCAL.

robbery *n.* burglary, larceny, thievery; see CRIME.

robe (rōb) *n.* ⟦< OFr⟧ **1** a long, loose outer garment **2** such a garment worn to show rank or office, as by a judge **3** a bathrobe or dressing gown **4** a covering or wrap ⟦a lap *robe*⟧ —*vt., vi.* **robed, rob′ing** to dress in a robe

robin (rä′bən) *n.* ⟦< OFr dim. of *Robert*⟧ a North American thrush with a dull-red breast

Robin Hood *Eng. Legend* the leader of a band of outlaws who robs the rich to help the poor

Ro·bin·son Cru·soe (rä′bən sən krōō′sō) the title hero of Defoe's novel (1719) about a shipwrecked sailor

ro·bot (rō′bät′, -bət, -but′) *n.* ⟦< Czech < OSlav *rabu*, servant⟧ **1** a mechanical device operating automatically, in a seemingly human way **2** a person acting like a robot

ro·bust (rō bust′, rō′bust′) *adj.* ⟦< L *robur*, oak⟧ strong and healthy —**ro·bust′ly** *adv.* —**ro·bust′ness** *n.*

rock[1] (räk) *n.* ⟦< ML *rocca*⟧ **1** a large mass of stone **2** broken pieces of stone **3** mineral matter formed in masses in the earth's crust **4** anything like a rock; esp., a firm support **5** [Colloq. or Dial.] any stone —**on the rocks** [Colloq.] **1** ruined; bankrupt **2** served over ice cubes, as whiskey

rock[2] (räk) *vt., vi.* ⟦OE *roccian*⟧ **1** to move back and forth or from side to side **2** to sway strongly; shake —*n.* **1** a rocking motion **2** ROCK-AND-ROLL

rock′-and-roll′ *n.* a form of popular music that evolved from rhythm and blues, characterized by a strong rhythm with an accent on the offbeat and by youth-oriented lyrics

rock bottom the lowest level

rock′bound′ *adj.* surrounded or covered by rocks

rock candy large, hard, clear crystals of sugar formed on a string

rock′er *n.* **1** either of the curved pieces on which a cradle, etc. rocks **2** a chair mounted on such pieces: also **rocking chair**

rocker panel any panel section below the doors of an automotive vehicle

rocket (räk′it) *n.* ⟦It *rocchetta*, spool⟧ any device driven forward by gases escaping through a rear vent, as a firework, a projectile weapon, or the propulsion mechanism of a spacecraft —*vi.* to move in or like a rocket; soar

rock′etry (-ə trē) *n.* the science of building and launching rockets

rock garden a garden of flowers, etc. in ground studded with rocks

rocking horse a toy horse on rockers or springs, for a child to ride

rock lobster SPINY LOBSTER

rock′-ribbed′ *adj.* **1** having rocky ridges **2** firm; unyielding

rock salt common salt in masses

rock wool a fibrous material made from molten rock, used for insulation

rocky[1] (räk′ē) *adj.* **-i·er, -i·est** **1** full of rocks **2** consisting of rock **3** like a rock; firm, hard, etc. —**rock′i·ness** *n.*

rocky[2] (räk′ē) *adj.* **-i·er, -i·est** inclined to rock; unsteady —**rock′i·ness** *n.*

Rocky Mountain sheep BIGHORN

ro·co·co (rə kō′kō) *n.* ⟦Fr < *rocaille*, shell work⟧ [occas. R-] a style of architecture, decorative art, music, etc. marked by profuse and delicate ornamentation, reduced scale, etc. —*adj.* **1** of or in rococo **2** too elaborate

rod (räd) *n.* ⟦< OE *rodd*, straight shoot or stem⟧ **1** a straight stick or bar **2** a stick for beating as punishment **3** a scepter carried as a symbol of office **4** a pole for fishing **5** a measure of length equal to 5½ yards **6** [Slang] a pistol

rode (rōd) *vt., vi. & archaic pp. of* RIDE

ro·dent (rōd′'nt) *n.* ⟦< L *rodere*, gnaw⟧ any of an order of gnawing mammals, as rats, mice, beavers, etc.

ro·deo (rō′dē ō′, rō dā′ō) *n., pl.* **-os′** ⟦Sp < L *rotare*, to turn⟧ a public exhibition of the skills of cowboys, as broncobusting, lassoing, etc.

roe[1] (rō) *n.* ⟦ME *rowe*⟧ fish eggs

roe[2] (rō) *n., pl.* **roe** or **roes** ⟦< OE *ra*⟧ a small, agile deer of Europe and Asia

roe′buck′ *n.* the male roe deer

roent·gen (rent′gən) *n.* ⟦after W. K. *Roentgen* (1845-1923), Ger physicist⟧ the unit for measuring the radiation of X-rays or gamma rays

Roger (rä′jər) *interj.* ⟦< name of signal flag for *R*⟧ [also r-] **1** received: used to indicate reception of a radio message **2** [Colloq.] right! OK!

rogue (rōg) *n.* ⟦< ?⟧ **1** a scoundrel **2** a mischievous person —**ro·guery** (rō′gər ē), *pl.* **-ies,** *n.* —**ro·guish** (rō′gish) *adj.*

roil (roil) *vt.* ⟦< L *robigo*, rust⟧ **1** to make (a liquid) cloudy, muddy, etc. by stirring up sediment **2** to vex

roister (rois′tər) *vi.* ⟦see RUSTIC⟧ to revel noisily —**roist′er·er** *n.*

role or **rôle** (rōl) *n.* ⟦Fr⟧ **1** the part played by an actor **2** a function assumed by someone ⟦an advisory *role*⟧

role model a person so effective or inspiring in some social role, job, etc. as to be a model for others

role′-play′ing *n. Psychol.* a technique in which participants assume and act out roles so as to resolve conflicts, improve behavior, etc.

roll (rōl) *vi.* ⟦< L *rota*, a wheel⟧ **1** to move by turning around or over and over **2** to move on wheels **3** to pass ⟦the years *roll* by⟧ **4** to extend in gentle swells **5** to make

---

▬ THESAURUS ▬

robe *n.* gown, dress, garment, costume, mantle, draperies, covering, cape, dressing gown, bathrobe, negligee, tea gown, kimono, house gown; see also CLOTHES.

robot *n.* **1** [A mechanical man] automaton, android, Frankenstein, mechanical monster, humanoid, thinking machine. **2** [A person who resembles a machine] slave, menial, scullion; see LABORER.

robust *a.* hale, hearty, sound; see HEALTHY.

rock[1,2] *n.* **1** [A solidified form of earth] stone, mineral mass, dike, mineral body, earth crust; see also METAL, MINERAL. *Rocks include the following:* igneous, sedimentary, stratified, metamorphic; concretion, gypsum, alabaster, limestone, freestone, sandstone, conglomerate, marble, dolomite, chalk, soapstone, slate, shale, granite, lava, pumice, basalt, quartz, obsidian, rhyolite, ironstone, gneiss, tufa, schist. **2** [A piece of rock] stone, boulder, cobblestone, pebble, fieldstone, cliff, crag, promontory, scrap, escarpment, reef, chip, flake, sliver, building stone, paving block, slab. **3** [Anything firm or solid] defense, support, Rock of Gibraltar; see FOUNDATION. **4** [Lively dance music] rock-and-roll, popular dance, rhythm and blues; see DANCE 1, MUSIC 1. —**on the rocks*** **1** bankrupt, poverty-stricken, impoverished; see POOR 1, RUINED 3. **2** over

ice cubes, undiluted, straight; see STRONG 4.

rock[2] *v.* sway, vibrate, reel, totter, swing, move, push and pull, agitate, roll, shake, shove, jolt, jiggle, quake, convulse, tremble, undulate, oscillate, quiver, quaver, wobble; see also WAVE 3.

rock-bottom *a.* lowest, hopeless, way down; see POOR 2, WORST. —**hit rock bottom** drop, not succeed, plunge; see FAIL 1, FALL 1.

rocket *n.* projectile, missile, retrorocket, flying missile. *Kinds of rockets include the following:* air-to-air, air-to-surface, surface-to-surface, surface-to-air, V-2, solid-fuel, liquid-fuel; guided missile, ballistic missile, cruise missile, Polaris missile, intercontinental ballistic missile (ICBM), submarine-launched ballistic missile (SLBM), smart bomb*.

rocky[1] *a.* stony, flinty, hard, inflexible, solid, petrified, ragged, jagged, rugged; see also STONE.—*Ant.* SOFT, flexible, sandy.

rod *n.* **1** [A rodlike body] staff, bar, pole, wand, stave, baton, spike, pin, cylinder, bacillus, cylindrical object, rodlet, scepter, twig, switch, whip, stock, stalk, trunk; see also STICK. **2** [A fishing rod] pole, rod and reel, tackle; see EQUIPMENT.

rodent *n. Common varieties of rodents include the following:* rat, mouse, squirrel, chipmunk, beaver,

porcupine, rabbit, muskrat, prairie dog, gopher, marmot, groundhog, woodchuck, ground squirrel, chinchilla, mole, hare, guinea pig.

rodeo *n.* riding unbroken horses, rounding up cattle, roundup, features of a roundup. *Rodeo events include the following:* broncobusting, bulldogging, calf-roping, cutting out steers, Brahma bull riding.

rogue *n.* outlaw, problem, miscreant; see CRIMINAL.

role *n.* function, task, part, character, title role, impersonation, leading man, leading woman, hero, heroine, ingénue, performance, presentation, acting, characterization, execution.

roll *n.* **1** [The act of rolling] turn, turning over, revolution, rotation, wheeling, trundling, whirl, gyration. **2** [A relatively flat object rolled upon itself] scroll, volute, spiral, coil, whorl, convolution, fold, shell, cone, cornucopia. **3** [A long, heavy sound] thunder, roar, drumbeat; see NOISE 1. **4** [Bread baked in a small, shaped piece] *Types of rolls include the following:* Parker House, potato, butter, finger, cinnamon, sweet, crescent, French, cloverleaf, poppy-seed, dinner; hot cross bun; see also BREAD, PASTRY. **5** [A list] register, table, schedule; see CATALOG, INDEX 2, LIST, RECORD 1.

roll *v.* **1** [To move by rotation, or in rotating numbers] rotate, come a loud rising and falling sound *[thunder rolls]* **6** to rock from side to side — *vt.* **1** to make move by turning around or over and over **2** to make move on wheels **3** to utter with full, flowing sound **4** to pronounce with a trill *[to roll one's r's]* **5** to give a swaying motion to **6** to move around or from side to side *[to roll one's eyes]* **7** to make into a ball or cylinder *[roll up the rug]* **8** to flatten or spread with a roller, etc. — *n.* **1** a rolling **2** a scroll **3** a list of names **4** something rolled into a cylinder **5** a small portion of bread, etc. **6** a swaying motion **7** a loud, reverberating sound, as of thunder **8** a slight swell on a surface — **on a roll** [Slang] at a high point —**roll back** to reduce (prices) to a previous level —**roll with a (or the) punch** [Colloq.] to ease a misfortune by not resisting much — **strike off (or from) the rolls** to expel from membership

roll′back′ *n.* a moving back, esp. of prices to a previous level

roll call the reading aloud of a roll to find out who is absent

roller (rōl′ər) *n.* **1** one that rolls **2** a cylinder of metal, wood, etc. on which something is rolled, or one used to crush, smooth, or spread something

roller bearing a bearing in which the shaft turns on rollers in a circular track

roller coaster an amusement ride in which small, open cars move on tracks that dip and curve sharply

roller skate SKATE¹ (sense 2) —**roll′er-skate′, -skat′ed, -skat′ing,** *vi.* —**roller skater**

rol·lick (räl′ik) *vi.* *[< ? FROLIC]* to play or behave in a lively, carefree way —**rol′lick·ing** *adj.*

rolling pin a heavy, smooth cylinder of wood, etc. used to roll out dough

roll′-top′ *adj.* having a flexible, sliding top of parallel slats *[a roll-top desk]*

roly-poly (rō′lē pō′lē) *adj.* *[< ROLL]* short and plump; pudgy

ROM (räm) *n.* *[r(ead-)o(nly) m(emory)]* computer memory whose contents can be read but not altered; also, a memory chip like this

Rom. Roman

ro·maine (rō mān′) *n.* *[Fr., ult. < L Romanus, Roman]* a type of lettuce with long leaves forming a slender head

Ro·man (rō′mən) *adj.* **1** of or characteristic of ancient or modern Rome (Italy), its people, etc. **2** of the Roman Catholic Church **3** *[usually r-]* designating or of the usual upright style of printing types — *n.* **1** a native or inhabitant of ancient or modern Rome **2** *[usually r-]* roman type or characters

Roman candle a firework consisting of a tube shooting balls of fire, etc.

Roman Catholic **1** of the Christian church (**Roman Catholic Church**) headed by the pope **2** a member of this church

ro·mance (rō mans′, rō′mans′) *adj.* *[ult. < L Romanicus, Roman]* *[R-]* designating or of any of the languages derived from Vulgar Latin, as Italian, Spanish, French, etc. — *n.* **1** a long poem or tale, orig. written in a Romance dialect, about the adventures of knights **2** a novel of love, adventure, etc. **3** excitement, love, etc. of the kind found in such literature **4** a love affair — *vi.*, *vt.* **-manced′, -manc′ing** [Colloq.] to make love (to) —**ro·manc′er** *n.*

Roman Empire empire of the ancient Romans (27 B.C.-A.D. 395), including W & S Europe, N Africa, & SW Asia

Roman numerals Roman letters used as numerals: I = 1, V = 5, X = 10, L = 50, C = 100, D = 500, and M = 1,000

ro·man·tic (rō man′tik) *adj.* **1** of, like, or characterized by romance **2** fanciful or fictitious **3** not practical; visionary **4** full of thoughts, feelings, etc. of romance **5** suited for romance **6** *[often R-]* of a 19th-c. cultural movement characterized by freedom of form and spirit, emphasis on feeling and originality, etc. — *n.* a romantic person —**ro·man′ti·cally** *adv.* —**ro·man′ti·cism′** (-tə siz′əm) *n.*

ro·man′ti·cize′ (-tə siz′) *vt.* **-cized′, -ciz′ing** to treat or regard romantically — *vi.* to have romantic ideas, etc.

Roma·ny (räm′ə nē, rō′mə-) *n.* the language of the Gypsies

Ro·meo (rō′mē ō′) the young lover in Shakespeare's *Romeo and Juliet* (c. 1595)

romp (rämp) *n.* *[prob. < OFr ramper, climb]* boisterous, lively play — *vi.* to play in a boisterous, lively way

romp′er *n.* **1** one who romps **2** *[pl.]* a loose, one-piece outer garment with bloomerlike pants, for a small child

Romu·lus (räm′yoo ləs) *Rom. Myth.* founder and first king of Rome: he and his twin brother Remus are suckled by a she-wolf

rood (rood) *n.* *[OE rod]* **1** a crucifix **2** [Brit., etc. (exc. Cdn.)] an old unit of area equal to ¼ acre

roof (roof, roof) *n.*, *pl.* **roofs** *[OE hrof]* **1** the outside top covering of a building **2** anything like this *[the roof of the mouth]* — *vt.* to cover with or as with a roof —**roof′less** *adj.*

roof′er *n.* a roof maker or repairer

roof′ing *n.* material for roofs

roof′top′ *n.* the roof of a building

rook¹ (rook) *n.* *[OE hroc]* a European crow — *vt.*, *vi.* to swindle; cheat

rook² (rook) *n.* *[< Pers rukh]* a chess piece moving horizontally or vertically

rook′ery *n.*, *pl.* **-ies** a breeding place or colony of rooks

rookie (rook′ē) *n.* [Slang] **1** an inexperienced army recruit **2** any novice

room (room, room) *n.* *[OE rum]* **1** space to contain something **2** suitable scope *[room for doubt]* **3** an interior space enclosed or set apart by walls **4** *[pl.]* living quarters **5** the people in a room — *vi.*, *vt.* to have or provide with lodgings —**room′ful′** *n.* —**room′y, -i·er, -i·est, adj.** —**room′i·ness** *n.*

room and board lodging and meals

room′er *n.* one who rents a room or rooms to live in; lodger

room·ette (roo met′) *n.* a small room in a railroad sleeping car

rooming house a house with furnished rooms for rent

room′mate′ *n.* a person with whom one shares a room or rooms

roost (roost) *n.* *[OE hrost]* **1** a perch on which birds, esp. domestic fowls, can rest **2** a place with perches for birds **3** a place for resting, sleeping, etc. — *vi.* **1** to perch on a roost **2** to stay or settle down, as for the night

roost′er *n.* a male chicken

root¹ (root, root) *n.* *[< ON rot]* **1** the part of a plant, usually underground, that anchors the plant, draws water from the soil, etc. **2** the embedded part of a tooth, a hair,

---

THESAURUS

around, swing around, wheel, come in turn, circle, alternate, follow, succeed, be in sequence, follow in due course; see also MOVE 1, TURN 1. **2** [To revolve] turn, pivot, spin; see sense 1. **3** [To make into a roll] bend, curve, arch; see TWIST. **4** [To smooth with a roller] press, level, flatten, spread, pulverize, grind.— *Ant.* CUT, roughen, toss up. **5** [To flow] run, wave, surge; see FLOW. **6** [To produce a relatively deep, continuous sound] reverberate, resound, echo; see ROAR, SOUND. **7** [To function] work, go, start production; see OPERATE 2.

rolled *a.* **1** [Made into a roll] twisted, folded, curved, bent, bowed, coiled, spiraled, arched, voluted, convoluted.—*Ant.* SPREAD, unrolled, opened out. **2** [Flattened] pressed, leveled, evened; see FLAT 1, SMOOTH 1.

Roman *a.* Latin, classic, classical,

late classic, Augustan, ancient, Italic.

romance *n.* **1** [A courtship] enchantment, passion, fascination; see LOVE 1. **2** [A tale of love and adventure] historical romance, novel, fiction; see STORY.

romantic *a.* **1** [Referring to love and adventure] adventurous, novel, daring, charming, enchanting, lyric, poetic, fanciful, chivalrous, courtly, knightly. **2** [Referring to languages descending from Latin; *often capital*] Romantic, Romance, Mediterranean, French, Italian, Spanish; see also LANGUAGE 1.

romp *v.* gambol, celebrate, frolic; see PLAY 1, 2.

roof *n.* cover, shelter, tent, house, habitation, home.

room *n.* **1** [Space] vastness, reach, sweep; see EXTENT. **2** [An enclosure] chamber, apartment, cabin, cubicle, cubiculum, niche, vault. *Rooms*

include the following: living room, dining room, sitting room, drawing room, bedroom, music room, playroom, bathroom, guest room, family room, waiting room, boardroom, conference room, foyer, vestibule, study, library, den, kitchen, hall, master bedroom, parlor, wardrobe, closet, pantry, basement, cellar, attic, garret, anteroom, dormitory, alcove, ward, office, breakfast nook, nursery, studio, schoolroom, loft. **3** [The possibility of admission] opening, place, resignation; see VACANCY 2. **4** [A rented sleeping room] quarters, lodgings, digs*; see APARTMENT.

roomer *n.* lodger, occupant, dweller; see TENANT.

roommate *n.* roomie*, flatmate, bunkmate; see FRIEND.

root¹ *n.* **1** [An underground portion of a plant] *Types of roots include the following:* conical, napiform, fusietc. **3** a source or cause **4** a supporting or essential part **5** a quantity that, multiplied by itself a specified number of times, produces a given quantity **6** the basic element of a word or form, without affixes or phonetic changes — *vi.* to take root — *vt.* **1** to fix the roots of in the ground **2** to establish; settle —**take root 1** to begin growing by putting out roots **2** to become fixed, settled, etc.

root² (rōōt, root) *vt.* ⟦< OE *wrot*, snout⟧ to dig (*up* or *out*) as with the snout — *vi.* **1** to search about; rummage **2** [Colloq.] to encourage a team, etc.: usually with *for*

root beer a carbonated drink made or flavored with certain plant root extracts

root canal 1 a tubular channel in a tooth's root **2** a treatment involving filling, etc. such a channel

root'let (-lət) *n.* a little root

rope (rōp) *n.* ⟦OE *rap*⟧ **1** a thick, strong cord made of intertwisted strands of fiber, etc. **2** a ropelike string, as of beads — *vt.* **roped, rop'ing 1** to fasten or tie with a rope **2** to mark off or enclose with a rope **3** to catch with a lasso —**know the ropes** [Colloq.] to be acquainted with a procedure —**rope in** [Slang] to entice or trick into doing something

Roque·fort (cheese) (rōk'fərt) ⟦after *Roquefort*, France, where made⟧ *trademark for* a strong French cheese with a bluish mold

Ror·schach test (rôr'shäk') ⟦after H. *Rorschach* (1884-1922), Swiss psychiatrist⟧ *Psychol.* a personality test in which the subject's interpretations of standard inkblot designs are analyzed

ro·sary (rō'zər ē) *n.*, *pl.* **-ries** ⟦ML *rosarium*⟧ *R.C.Ch.* a string of beads used to keep count in saying prayers

rose¹ (rōz) *n.* ⟦< L *rosa* < Gr *rhodon*⟧ **1** a shrub with prickly stems and with flowers of red, pink, white, yellow, etc. **2** its flower **3** pinkish red or purplish red — *adj.* of this color

rose² (rōz) *vi. pt. of* RISE

rosé (rō zā') *n.* ⟦Fr, pink⟧ a pink wine, tinted by the grape skins during early fermentation

ro·se·ate (rō'zē it) *adj.* rose-colored

rose'bud' *n.* the bud of a rose

rose'bush' *n.* a shrub that bears roses

rose'-col'ored *adj.* **1** pinkish-red or purplish-red **2** optimistic —**through rose-colored glasses** with optimism

rose·mary (rōz'mer'ē) *n.* ⟦< L *ros marinus*, sea dew⟧ an evergreen herb of the mint family, with fragrant leaves used in perfumes, in cooking, etc.

ro·sette (rō zet') *n.* a roselike ornament or arrangement, as of ribbon

rose water a preparation of water and attar of roses, used as a perfume

rose window a circular window with a roselike pattern of tracery

rose'wood' *n.* ⟦< its odor⟧ **1** a hard, reddish wood, used in furniture, etc. **2** a tropical tree yielding this wood

Rosh Ha·shana (rōsh' hə shō'nə, -shä'-) the Jewish New Year

rosin (räz'ən) *n.* ⟦see RESIN⟧ the hard resin left after the

distillation of crude turpentine: it is rubbed on violin bows, used in making varnish, etc.

ros·ter (räs'tər) *n.* ⟦< Du *rooster*⟧ a list or roll, as of military personnel

ros·trum (räs'trəm) *n.*, *pl.* **-trums** or **-tra** (-trə) ⟦L, beak⟧ a platform for public speaking

rosy (rō'zē) *adj.* **-i·er, -i·est** ⟦ME⟧ **1** rose in color **2** bright, promising, etc. —**ros'i·ly** *adv.* —**ros'i·ness** *n.*

rot (rät) *vi., vt.* **rot'ted, rot'ting** ⟦OE *rotian*⟧ to decompose; decay — *n.* **1** a rotting or something rotten **2** a disease characterized by decay **3** [Slang] nonsense

ro·tary (rōt'ər ē) *adj.* ⟦< L *rota*, wheel⟧ **1** turning around a central axis, as a wheel **2** having rotating parts *[a rotary press]* — *n.*, *pl.* **-ries** a rotary machine **2** TRAFFIC CIRCLE

ro·tate (rō'tāt) *vi., vt.* **-tated, -tat·ing** ⟦< L *rota*, wheel⟧ **1** to turn around an axis **2** to change or cause to change in regular succession —**ro·ta'tion** *n.* —**ro'ta·to·ry** (-tə tôr'ē) *adj.*

ROTC Reserve Officers' Training Corps

rote (rōt) *n.* ⟦ME⟧ a fixed, mechanical way of doing something —**by rote** by memory alone, without thought

ro·tis·serie (rō tis'ər ē) *n.* ⟦Fr < MFr *rostir*, to roast⟧ a grill with an electrically turned spit

ro·to·gra·vure (rōt'ə grə vyoor') *n.* ⟦< L *rota*, wheel + Fr *gravure*, engraving⟧ **1** a printing process using a rotary press with cylinders etched from photographic plates **2** a newspaper pictorial section printed by this process

ro·tor (rōt'ər) *n.* **1** the rotating part of a motor, etc. **2** a system of rotating airfoils, as on a helicopter

rot·ten (rät''n) *adj.* ⟦< ON *rotinn*⟧ **1** decayed; spoiled **2** foul-smelling **3** morally corrupt **4** unsound, as if decayed within **5** [Slang] very bad, unpleasant, etc. —**rot'ten·ness** *n.*

ro·tund (rō tund') *adj.* ⟦L *rotundus*⟧ round or rounded out; plump —**ro·tun'di·ty** or **ro·tund'ness** *n.*

ro·tunda (rō tun'də) *n.* ⟦see prec.⟧ a round building, hall, or room, esp. one with a dome

roué (rōō ā') *n.* ⟦Fr < L *rota*, wheel⟧ a dissipated man; rake

rouge (rōōzh) *n.* ⟦Fr, red⟧ **1** *old name for* BLUSHER (sense 2) **2** a reddish powder for polishing jewelry, etc. — *vt., vi.* **rouged, roug'ing** to use cosmetic rouge (on)

rough (ruf) *adj.* ⟦OE *ruh*⟧ **1** not smooth or level; uneven **2** shaggy *[a rough coat]* **3** stormy *[rough weather]* **4** disorderly *[rough play]* **5** harsh or coarse **6** lacking comforts and conveniences **7** not polished or finished; crude **8** approximate *[a rough guess]* **9** [Colloq.] difficult *[a rough time]* — *n.* **1** rough ground, material, condition, etc. **2** *Golf* any part of the course with grass, etc. left uncut — *adv.* in a rough way — *vt.* **1** to roughen: often with *up* **2** to treat roughly: usually with *up* **3** to sketch, shape, etc. roughly: usually with *in* or *out* —**rough it** to live without customary comforts, etc. —**rough'ly** *adv.* —**rough'ness** *n.*

THESAURUS

form, fibrous, moniliform, nodulose, tuberous, adventitious, prop, aerial, tap. **2** [The cause or basis] source, reason, motive; see ORIGIN 2, 3. — **take root** begin growing, start, commence; see GROW 1.

rooted *a.* grounded, based, fixed; see FIRM 1.

rope *n.* cord, cordage, braiding, string, thread, strand, tape, cord, lace, cable, hawser, lariat, lasso, line, towline. —**at the end of one's rope** desperate, despairing, in despair; see EXTREME, HOPELESS. —**give someone enough rope*** permit, give freedom, concede; see ALLOW. —**know the ropes*** be experienced, comprehend, understand; see KNOW 1. —**on the ropes*** near collapse, close to ruin, in danger; see ENDANGERED.

rose¹ *a.* rose-colored, rosy, flushed; see PINK, RED.

rose¹ *n.* Classes of roses include the following: wild, tea, climbing tea, hybrid tea, hybrid perpetual, sweet briar, shrub, multiflora, floribunda, musk, cabbage, cinnamon, eglantine, rambler; see also FLOWER.

roster *n.* names, subscribers, program; see CATALOG, LIST, INDEX 2.

rosy *a.* **1** [Rose-colored] colored, deep pink, pale cardinal; see PINK, RED. **2** [Promising] optimistic, favorable, cheerful; see HOPEFUL 1, 2.

rot *n.* **1** [The process of rotting] decomposition, corruption, disintegration; see DECAY. **2** [*Nonsense] trash, silliness, foolishness; see NONSENSE 1.

rot *v.* decay, disintegrate, decompose; see SPOIL.

rotate *v.* twist, wheel, revolve; see MOVE 1, TURN 1.

rotation *n.* turn, circumrotation, circle; see REVOLUTION.

rotten *a.* **1** [Having rotted] bad, rotting, putrefying, decaying, putrefied, spoiled, decomposed, decayed, offensive, disgusting, rancid, fecal, rank, foul, corrupt, polluted, infected, loathsome, overripe, bad-smelling, putrid, crumbled, disintegrated, stale, noisome, smelling, fetid, noxious.—*Ant.* FRESH, unspoiled, good. **2** [Not sound] unsound, weak, impaired; see WEAK 2. **3** [Corrupt] contaminated, polluted, filthy, tainted, defiled, impure, sullied, unclean, soiled, debauched, blem-

ished, morbid, infected, dirtied, depraved, tarnished; see also DIRTY.—*Ant.* PURE, clean, healthy.

rough *a.* **1** [Not smooth] unequal, broken, coarse, choppy, ruffled, uneven, ridged, rugged, irregular, not sanded, not finished, unfinished, not completed, needing the finishing touches, bumpy, rocky, stony, jagged, grinding, knobby, sharpening, cutting, sharp, crinkled, crumpled, rumpled, scraggly, straggly, hairy, shaggy, hirsute, bushy, tufted, bearded, woolly, nappy, unshaven, unshorn, gnarled, knotty, bristly.—*Ant.* LEVEL, flat, even. **2** [Not gentle] harsh, strict, stern; see SEVERE 2. **3** [Crude] boorish, uncivil, uncultivated; see RUDE 1. **4** [Not quiet] buffeting, stormy, tumultuous; see TURBULENT. **5** [Unfinished] incomplete, imperfect, uncompleted; see UNFINISHED. **6** [Approximate] inexact, unprecise, uncertain; see APPROXIMATE.

roughly *a.* **1** [Approximately] about, in round numbers, by guess; see APPROXIMATELY. **2** [In a brutal manner] coarsely, cruelly, inhumanly; see

rough'age (-ij) *n.* rough or coarse food or fodder, as bran, straw, etc.

rough'en *vt., vi.* to make or become rough

rough'-hew' *vt.* **-hewed', -hewed'** or **-hewn', -hew'ing** 1 to hew (timber, stone, etc.) roughly, or without finishing or smoothing 2 to form roughly Also **rough'hew'**

rough'house' *n.* [Slang] rough, boisterous play, fighting, etc. — *vt., vi.* **-housed', -hous'ing** [Slang] to treat or act roughly or boisterously

rough'neck' *n.* 1 [Colloq.] a rowdy 2 a worker on an oil rig — *vi.* to work as a roughneck

rough'shod' *adj.* shod with horseshoes having metal points — **ride roughshod over** to treat harshly

rou·lette (rōō let') *n.* [Fr < L *rota*, wheel] a gambling game played with a small ball in a whirling shallow bowl (**roulette wheel**) with red and black, numbered compartments

round (round) *adj.* [< L *rotundus*, rotund] 1 shaped like a ball, circle, or cylinder 2 plump 3 full; complete [a *round* dozen] 4 expressed by a whole number or in tens, hundreds, etc. 5 large; considerable [a *round* sum] 6 brisk; vigorous [a *round* pace] — *n.* 1 something round, as the rung of a ladder 2 the part of a beef animal between the rump and the leg 3 movement in a circular course 4 a series or succession [a *round* of parties] 5 [*often pl.*] a regular, customary circuit, as by a watchman 6 a single shot from a gun, or from several guns together; also, the ammunition for this 7 a single outburst, as of applause 8 a single period of action, as in boxing 9 a short song which one group begins singing when another reaches the second phrase, etc. — *vt.* 1 to make round 2 to make plump 3 to express as a round number 4 to complete; finish 5 to go or pass around — *vi.* 1 to make a circuit 2 to turn; reverse direction 3 to become plump: often with *out* — *adv.* 1 in a circle 2 through a recurring period of time [to work the year *round*] 3 from one to another 4 in circumference [ten feet *round*] 5 on all sides 6 about; near 7 in a roundabout way 8 here and there 9 with a rotating movement 10 in the opposite direction — *prep.* 1 so as to encircle 2 on all sides of 3 in the vicinity of 4 in a circuit through In the U.S., *round* (*adv. & prep.*) is generally superseded by *around* — **in the round** 1 in an arena theater 2 in full, rounded form: said of sculpture 3 in full detail — **round about** in or to the opposite direction — **round up** to collect in a herd, group, etc. — **round'ness** *n.*

round'about' *adj.* 1 indirect; circuitous 2 encircling; enclosing

roun·de·lay (roun'də lā') *n.* [< OFr *rondel*, a short lyrical poem] a simple song in which some phrase, line, etc. is continually repeated

round'house' *n.* a circular building, with a turntable in the center, for storing and repairing locomotives

round'ly *adv.* 1 in a round form 2 vigorously 3 fully; completely and thoroughly

round'-shoul'dered *adj.* having the shoulders bent forward

round steak a steak cut from a round of beef

Round Table the circular table around which King Arthur and his knights sit — [**r- t-**] a group gathered for an informal discussion

round'-the-clock' *adj., adv.* throughout the day and night; continuous(ly)

round trip a trip to a place and back again — **round'-trip'** *adj.*

round'-trip'per *n.* [Slang] *Baseball* a home run

round'up' *n.* 1 a driving together of cattle, etc. on the range, as for branding 2 any similar collecting 3 a summary, as of news

round'worm' *n.* NEMATODE

rouse (rouz) *vt., vi.* **roused, rous'ing** [LME *rowsen*] 1 to stir up; excite or become excited 2 to wake

roust·about (roust'ə bout') *n.* [< ROUSE + ABOUT] an unskilled or transient laborer, as on wharves

rout[1] (rout) *n.* [< L *rupta*, broken] 1 a disorderly flight 2 an overwhelming defeat — *vt.* 1 to put to flight 2 to defeat overwhelmingly

rout[2] (rout) *vt.* [< ROOT[2]] to force out — **rout out** 1 to gouge out 2 to make (a person) get out

route (rōōt, rout) *n.* [< L *rupta* (*via*), broken (path)] a road or course for traveling; often, a regular course, as in delivering mail — *vt.* **rout'ed, rout'ing** 1 to send by a certain route 2 to arrange the route for

rou·tine (rōō tēn') *n.* [see prec.] a regular procedure, customary or prescribed — *adj.* like or using routine — **rou·tine'ly** *adv.*

rou·tin'ize (-tē'nīz) *vt.* **-ized, -iz·ing** to make or bring into a routine

rove (rōv) *vi., vt.* **roved, rov'ing** [ME *roven*] to roam — **rov'er** *n.*

row[1] (rō) *n.* [OE *ræw*] 1 a number of people or things in a line 2 any of the lines of seats in a theater, etc. — **in a row** in succession; consecutively

row[2] (rō) *vt., vi.* [OE *rowan*] 1 to propel (a boat) with oars 2 to carry in a rowboat — *n.* a trip by rowboat — **row'er** *n.*

row[3] (rou) *n., vi.* [< ? ROUSE] quarrel, squabble, or brawl

row'boat' (rō'-) *n.* a small boat made for rowing

rowdy (rou'dē) *n., pl.* **-dies** [< ? ROW[3]] a rough, quarrelsome, and disorderly person — *adj.* **-dier, -di·est** rough, quarrelsome, etc. — **row'di·ness** *n.* — **row'dy·ism'** *n.*

rowel (rou'əl) *n.* [ult. < L *rota*, wheel] a small wheel with sharp points, forming the end of a spur

row house (rō) any of a line of identical houses joined by common walls

royal (roi'əl) *adj.* [< L *regalis*] 1 of a king or queen 2 like, or fit for, a king or queen; magnificent, majestic, etc. 3 of a kingdom, its government, etc. — **roy'al·ly** *adv.*

roy'al·ist *n.* one who supports a monarch or a monarchy

roy'alty *n., pl.* **-ties** 1 the rank or power of a king or queen 2 a royal person or persons 3 royal quality 4 a

---

■ THESAURUS ■

BRUTALLY.

roughness *n.* 1 [The quality of being rough on the surface] unevenness, coarseness, brokenness, bumpiness, irregularity, raggedness, jaggedness, wrinkledness, shagginess, bushiness, beardedness, hairiness, woolliness; break, crack, ragged edge, scratch, nick. — *Ant.* REGULARITY, smoothness, evenness. 2 [The quality of being rough in conduct] harshness, severity, hardness; see RUDENESS.

round *a.* 1 [Shaped like a globe or disk] spherical, globular, orbicular, globe-shaped, ball-shaped, domical, circular, cylindrical, ringed, annular, oval, disk-shaped. 2 [Curved] arched, rounded, bowed, looped, recurved, incurved, coiled, curled. 3 [Approximate] rough, in tens, in hundreds; see APPROXIMATE.

round *n.* 1 [A round object] ring, orb, globe; see CIRCLE 1, RIM. 2 [A period of action] bout, course, whirl, cycle, circuit, routine, performance; see also SEQUENCE 1, SERIES. 3 [A unit of ammunition] cartridge, charge, load; see AMMUNITION, BULLET, SHOT 1.

round *v.* 1 [To turn] whirl, wheel, spin; see TURN 1. 2 [To make round] curve, convolute, bow, arch, bend, loop, whorl, shape, form, recurve, coil, fill out, curl, mold. — *Ant.* STRAIGHTEN, flatten, level. — **round off** approximate; round off by tens, hundreds, etc.; accept a rough figure for; see also ESTIMATE. — **round out** expand, fill out, enlarge; see GROW 1.

round *prep.* about, near, in the neighborhood of, close to; see also ALMOST, APPROXIMATELY, AROUND.

roundness *n.* fullness, completeness, circularity, oneness, inclusiveness, wholeness.

rouse *v.* 1 [To waken] arouse, raise, awake; see AWAKEN, WAKE 1. 2 [To stimulate] stimulate, urge, provoke; see ANIMATE, EXCITE.

route *n.* 1 [A course being followed] way, course, path, track, beat, tack, divergence, detour, digression, meandering, rambling, wandering, circuit, round, rounds, range; see also ROAD 1. 2 [A projected course] map, plans, plot; see PLAN 2, PROGRAM 2.

routine *a.* usual, customary, methodical; see CONVENTIONAL 1,

HABITUAL.

routine *n.* round, cycle, habit; see METHOD, SYSTEM.

rove *v.* walk, meander, wander; see ROAM.

row[1] *n.* series, order, file; see LINE 1. — **in a row** in succession, successively, in a line; see CONSECUTIVE.

rowdy *a.* rebellious, rude, mischievous; see LAWLESS 2, UNRULY.

royal *a.* 1 [Pertaining to a king or his family] high, elevated, highborn, monarchic, reigning, regnant, regal, ruling, dominant, absolute, imperial, sovereign, supreme; see also sense 2, NOBLE 3. 2 [Having qualities befitting royalty] great, grand, stately, lofty, illustrious, renowned, eminent, superior, worthy, honorable, dignified, chivalrous, courteous, kingly, great-hearted, princely, princelike, majestic, magnificent, splendid, courtly, impressive, commanding, aristocratic, lordly, august, imposing, superb, glorious, resplendent, gorgeous, sublime; see also sense 1, NOBLE 1, WORTHY.

royalty *n.* kingship, sovereignty, nobility, authority, eminence, disshare of the proceeds from a patent, book, etc. paid to the owner, author, etc.

rpm revolutions per minute

rps revolutions per second

RR or **R.R.** 1 railroad 2 Rural Route

RSV or **R.S.V.** Revised Standard Version (of the Bible)

R.S.V.P. or **r.s.v.p.** ⟦Fr *répondez s'il vous plaît*⟧ please reply Also **RSVP** or **rsvp**

Rte. Route

rub (rub) *vt.* **rubbed, rub′bing** ⟦ME *rubben*⟧ 1 to move (one's hand, a cloth, etc.) over (something) with pressure and friction 2 to apply (polish, etc.) in this way 3 to move (things) over each other with pressure and friction 4 to make sore by rubbing 5 to remove by rubbing (*out, off,* etc.) — *vi.* 1 to move with pressure and friction (*on,* etc.) 2 to rub something — *n.* 1 a rubbing 2 an obstacle, difficulty, or source of irritation —**rub down** 1 to massage 2 to smooth, polish, etc. by rubbing —**rub elbows with** to associate or mingle with: also **rub shoulders with** —**rub the wrong way** to irritate or annoy

ru·ba·to (rōō bät′ō) *adj., adv.* ⟦It, stolen⟧ *Music* intentionally and temporarily not in strict tempo

rub·ber[1] (rub′ər) *n.* 1 one that rubs 2 ⟦< use as an eraser⟧ an elastic substance made from the milky sap of various tropical plants, or synthetically 3 something made of this substance; specif., *a*) a low-cut overshoe *b*) [Slang] a condom — *adj.* made of rubber —**rub′bery** *adj.*

rub·ber[2] (rub′ər) *n.* ⟦< ?⟧ the deciding game in a series Also **rubber game**

rubber band a narrow, continuous band of rubber as for holding small objects together

rubber cement an adhesive of unvulcanized rubber in a solvent that quickly evaporates when exposed to air

rub′ber·ize′ (-īz′) *vt.* **-ized′, -iz′ing** to impregnate with rubber

rubber plant 1 any plant yielding latex 2 a house plant with large, glossy, leathery leaves

rubber stamp 1 a stamp of rubber, inked for printing signatures, etc. 2 [Colloq.] *a*) a person, bureau, etc. that gives automatic approval *b*) such approval —**rub′ber·stamp′** *vt.*

rub·bish (rub′ish) *n.* ⟦ME *robous*⟧ 1 any material thrown away as worthless; trash 2 nonsense

rub·ble (rub′əl) *n.* ⟦ME *robel*⟧ rough, broken pieces of stone, brick, etc.

rub′down′ *n.* a massage

rube (rōōb) *n.* ⟦< name *Reuben*⟧ [Slang] an unsophisticated rustic

ru·bel·la (rōō bel′ə) *n.* ⟦< L *ruber,* red⟧ an infectious disease causing small red spots on the skin

ru·bi·cund (rōō′bə kund′) *adj.* ⟦< L *ruber,* red⟧ reddish; ruddy

ru·ble (rōō′bəl) *n.* ⟦Russ *rubl'*⟧ the monetary unit of Russia, Belarus, etc.

ru·bric (rōō′brik) *n.* ⟦< L *ruber,* red⟧ 1 a section heading, direction, etc., often in red (as in a prayer book) 2 any rule, explanatory comment, etc.

ruby (rōō′bē) *n., pl.* **-bies** ⟦ult. < L *rubeus,* reddish⟧ 1 a clear, deep-red precious stone: a variety of corundum 2 deep red — *adj.* deep-red

ruck·sack (ruk′sak′, rook′-) *n.* ⟦Ger, back sack⟧ a kind of knapsack

ruck·us (ruk′əs) *n.* ⟦prob. merging of RUMPUS & *ruction,* uproar⟧ [Colloq.] noisy confusion; disturbance

rud·der (rud′ər) *n.* ⟦OE *rother*⟧ a broad, flat, movable piece hinged to the rear of a ship or aircraft, used for steering —**rud′der·less** *adj.*

rud·dy (rud′ē) *adj.* **-di·er, -di·est** ⟦OE *rudig*⟧ 1 having a healthy red color 2 reddish —**rud′di·ness** *n.*

rude (rōōd) *adj.* **rud′er, rud′est** ⟦< L *rudis*⟧ 1 crude; rough 2 barbarous 3 unrefined; uncouth 4 discourteous 5 primitive; unskillful —**rude′ly** *adv.* —**rude′ness** *n.*

ru·di·ment (rōō′də mənt) *n.* ⟦see RUDE⟧ 1 a first principle, as of a subject to be learned 2 a first slight beginning of something —**ru′di·men′tary** (-men′tər ē) *adj.*

rue[1] (rōō) *vt., vi.* **rued, ru′ing** ⟦OE *hreowan*⟧ 1 to feel remorse for (a sin, fault, etc.) 2 to regret (an act, etc.) — *n.* [Archaic] sorrow —**rue′ful** *adj.* —**rue′fully** *adv.*

rue[2] (rōō) *n.* ⟦< Gr *rhytē*⟧ a strong-scented shrub with bitter leaves

ruff (ruf) *n.* ⟦< RUFFLE⟧ 1 a high, frilled, starched collar of the 16th and 17th c. 2 a band of colored or protruding feathers or fur about an animal's neck

ruf·fian (ruf′ē ən) *n.* ⟦< It *ruffiano,* a pander⟧ a rowdy or hoodlum

ruf·fle (ruf′əl) *vt.* **-fled, -fling** ⟦< ON or LowG⟧ 1 to disturb the smoothness of 2 to gather into ruffles 3 to make (features, etc.) stand up 4 to disturb or annoy — *vi.* 1 to become uneven 2 to become disturbed, irritated, etc. — *n.* 1 a pleated strip of cloth, lace, etc. 2 a disturbance 3 a ripple

rug (rug) *n.* ⟦< Scand⟧ 1 a piece of thick fabric used as a floor covering 2 *chiefly Brit. term for* LAP ROBE

■ THESAURUS ■

tinction, blood, birth, high descent, rank, greatness, power, supremacy, primacy, the crown, suzerainty.

rub *n.* 1 [A rubbing action] brushing, stroke, smoothing, scraping, scouring, grinding, rasping, friction, attrition; see also TOUCH 2. 2 [A difficulty] impediment, hindrance, dilemma; see DIFFICULTY 1, 2, PREDICAMENT.

rub *v.* 1 [To subject to friction] scrape, smooth, abrade, scour, grate, grind, wear away, graze, rasp, knead, fret, massage, polish, shine, burnish, scrub, erase, rub out, rub down, file, chafe, clean. 2 [To apply by rubbing; *usually with* "on"] brush, cover, finish; see PAINT 2. —**rub out** eradicate, erase, delete; see CANCEL, ELIMINATE.

rubber[1] *a.* elastic, rubbery, soft, stretchable, stretching, rebounding, flexible, ductile, lively, buoyant, resilient.

rubbish *n.* litter, debris, waste; see TRASH 1.

rude *a.* 1 [Boorish] rustic, ungainly, awkward, crude, coarse, gross, rough, harsh, blunt, rugged, common, barbarous, lumpish, ungraceful, hulking, loutish, antic, rowdy, disorderly, brutish, boorish, clownish, stupid, illproportioned, unpolished, uncultured, unrefined, untrained, indecorous, unknowing, untaught, uncouth, slovenly, ill-bred, inelegant, ignorant, inexpert, illiterate, clumsy, awkward, gawky, slouching, graceless, ungraceful, lumbering, green, unacquainted,

unenlightened, uneducated, vulgar, indecent, ribald, homely, outlandish, disgraceful, inappropriate.—*Ant.* CULTURED, urbane, suave. 2 [Not polite] churlish, sullen, surly, sharp, harsh, gruff, snarling, ungracious, unkind, ungentle, obstreperous, overbearing, sour, disdainful, unmannerly, ill-mannered, improper, shabby, ill-chosen, discourteous, ungentlemanly, fresh*, abusive, forward, loud, loud-mouthed, bold, brazen, audacious, brash, arrogant, supercilious, blustering, impudent, crass, raw, saucy, crusty, pert, unabashed, sharp-tongued, loose, mocking, barefaced, insolent, impertinent, offensive, naughty, impolite, hostile, insulting, disrespectful, scornful, flippant, presumptuous, sarcastic, defiant, outrageous, swaggering, disparaging, contemptuous, rebellious, disdainful, unfeeling, insensitive, scoffing, disagreeable, domineering, overbearing, highhanded, hypercritical, self-assertive, brutal, severe, hard, cocky, bullying, cheeky, nervy, assuming, dictatorial, magisterial, misbehaved, officious, meddling, intrusive, meddlesome, bitter, uncivilized, slandering, illtempered, bad-tempered, sassy*, snotty*, snooty*, uppity*.—*Ant.* POLITE, courteous, mannerly. 3 [Harsh] rough, violent, stormy; see TURBULENT. 4 [Approximate] surmised, guessed, imprecise; see APPROXIMATE. 5 [Coarse] rough, unrefined, unpolished; see CRUDE. 6

[Primitive] ignorant, uncivilized, barbarous; see PRIMITIVE 3.

rudely *a.* crudely, impudently, coarsely, impolitely, indecently, barbarously, roughly, harshly, bluntly, indecorously, insolently, contemptuously, brutally, dictatorially, churlishly, sullenly, gruffly, discourteously, impishly, loudly, brazenly, blusteringly, crassly, unabashedly, ribaldly, spunkily*, mockingly, snootily*.—*Ant.* KINDLY, politely, suavely.

rudeness *n.* discourtesy, bad manners, vulgarity, incivility, impoliteness, impudence, disrespect, misbehavior, barbarity, ungentlemanliness, unmannerliness, illbreeding, crudity, brutality, barbarism, tactlessness, boorishness, unbecoming conduct, conduct not becoming a gentleman, crudeness, grossness, coarseness, bluntness, effrontery, impertinence, insolence, audacity, boldness, shamelessness, presumption, officiousness, intrusiveness, brazenness, sauciness, defiance, contempt, back talk, ill temper, irritability, disdain, bitterness, sharpness, unkindness, ungraciousness, harshness, gall*, sass*, lip*, nerve*, brass*, cheek*.

ruffle *v.* 1 [To disarrange] rumple, tousle, ripple; see CONFUSE, TANGLE. 2 [To anger] irritate, fret, anger; see BOTHER 1, 2.

rug *n.* carpet, carpeting, floor covering, linoleum, straw mat, floor mat, woven mat, drugget.

rugby (rug′bē) *n.* [first played at *Rugby* School in England] a game from which American football developed

rug·ged (rug′id) *adj.* [ME] 1 uneven; rough 2 stormy 3 severe; harsh; hard 4 not polished or refined 5 strong; robust —**rug′ged·ly** *adv.* —**rug′ged·ness** *n.*

ruin (rōō′ən, -in′) *n.* [< L *ruere*, to fall] 1 [*pl.*] the remains of something destroyed, decayed, etc. 2 anything destroyed, etc. 3 downfall, destruction, etc. 4 anything causing this — *vt.* to bring to ruin; destroy, spoil, bankrupt, etc. — *vi.* to go or come to ruin —**ru′ina′tion** *n.* —**ru′in·ous** *adj.*

rule (rōōl) *n.* [< L *regere*, to rule] 1 an established regulation or guide for conduct, procedure, usage, etc. 2 custom 3 the customary course 4 government; reign 5 RULER (sense 2) — *vt., vi.* **ruled, rul′ing** 1 to have an influence (over); guide 2 to govern 3 to determine officially 4 to mark lines (on) as with a ruler —**as a rule** usually —**rule out** to exclude

rule of thumb a practical, though crude or unscientific, method

rul′er *n.* 1 one who governs 2 a strip of wood, etc. with a straight edge, used in drawing lines, measuring, etc.

rul·ing (rōōl′iŋ) *adj.* that rules — *n.* an official decision, as of a court

rum (rum) *n.* [< ?] 1 an alcoholic liquor distilled from fermented sugar cane, etc. 2 any alcoholic liquor

rumba (room′bə, rum′-) *n.* [AmSp] a dance of Cuban origin, or music for it — *vi.* to dance the rumba

rum·ble (rum′bəl) *vi., vt.* **-bled, -bling** [ME *romblen*] 1 to make or cause to make a deep, continuous, rolling sound 2 to move with such a sound — *n.* 1 a rumbling sound 2 [Slang] a fight between teenage gangs

ru·mi·nant (rōō′mə nənt) *adj.* [see RUMINATE] 1 chewing the cud 2 meditative — *n.* any of a group of cud-chewing mammals, as cattle, deer, camels, etc.

ru′mi·nate′ (-nāt′) *vt., vi.* **-nat′ed, -nat′ing** [< L *ruminare*] 1 to chew (the cud) 2 to meditate or reflect (on) —**ru′mi·na′tion** *n.* —**ru′mi·na′tive** *adj.*

rum·mage (rum′ij) *n.* [< Fr *rum*, ship's hold] 1 odds and ends 2 a rummaging — *vt., vi.* **-maged, -mag·ing** to search through (a place, etc.) thoroughly

rummage sale a sale of contributed miscellaneous articles, as for charity

rummy (rum′ē) *n.* [< ?] any of certain card games whose object is to match sets and sequences

ru·mor (rōō′mər) *n.* [L, noise] 1 general talk not based on definite knowledge 2 an unconfirmed report, story, etc. in general circulation — *vt.* to tell or spread by rumor Brit., etc. sp. **ru′mour**

rump (rump) *n.* [< ON *rumpr*] 1 the hind part of an animal, where the legs and back join 2 the buttocks

rum·ple (rum′pal) *n.* [< MDu *rompe*] an uneven crease; wrinkle — *vt., vi.* **-pled, -pling** to wrinkle; muss

rum·pus (rum′pəs) *n.* [< ?] [Colloq.] noisy disturbance; uproar

run (run) *vi.* **ran, run, run′ning** [< ON & OE] 1 to go by moving the legs faster than in walking 2 to go, move, etc. easily and freely 3 to flee 4 to make a quick trip (*up to, down to,* etc.) 5 to compete in a race, election, etc. 6 to ply (between two points), as a train 7 to climb or creep, as a vine 8 to ravel, as a stocking 9 to operate, as a machine 10 to flow 11 to spread over cloth, etc. when moistened, as colors 12 to discharge pus, etc. 13 to extend in time or space; continue 14 to pass into a specified condition, etc. [*to run* into trouble] 15 to be written, etc. in a specified way 16 to be at a specified size, price, etc. [*eggs run* high] — *vt.* 1 to follow (a specified course) 2 to perform as by running [*to run* a race] 3 to incur (a risk) 4 to get past

---

━━━ THESAURUS ━━━

rugged *a.* 1 [Rough; *said especially of terrain*] hilly, broken, mountainous; see ROUGH 1. 2 [Strong; *said especially of persons*] hale, sturdy, hardy; see HEALTHY, STRONG 1.

ruin *n.* 1 [The act of destruction] extinction, demolition, overthrow; see DESTRUCTION 1, WRECK 1. 2 [A building fallen into decay; *often plural*] remains, traces, residue, foundations, vestiges, remnants, relics, wreck, walls, detritus, rubble; see also DESTRUCTION 2. 3 [The state of destruction] dilapidation, waste, wreck; see DESTRUCTION 2.

ruin *v.* 1 [To destroy] injure, overthrow, demolish; see DESTROY, RAVAGE. 2 [To cause to become bankrupt] impoverish, bankrupt, beggar; see WRECK.

ruined *a.* 1 [Destroyed] demolished, overthrown, torn down, extinct, abolished, exterminated, annihilated, subverted, wrecked, desolated, ravaged, smashed, crushed, crashed, extinguished, extirpated, dissolved, totaled*; see also DESTROYED.—*Ant.* PROTECTED, saved, preserved. 2 [Spoiled] pillaged, harried, robbed, plundered, injured, hurt, impaired, defaced, harmed, marred, past hope, mutilated, broken, gone to the dogs*, on the rocks*, done for*.—*Ant.* REPAIRED, restored, mended. 3 [Bankrupt] pauperized, poverty-stricken, beggared, reduced, left in penury, penniless, fleeced, brought to want, gone under*, sold up*, through the mill*.—*Ant.* RICH, prosperous, well-off.

ruins *n.* remains, debris, wreckage; see DESTRUCTION 2, WRECK 2.

rule *n.* 1 [Government] control, dominion, jurisdiction; see GOVERNMENT 1. 2 [A regulation] edict, command, commandment; see LAW 3. 3 [The custom] habit, course, practice; see CUSTOM. —**as a rule** ordinarily, generally, usually; see REGULARLY.

rule *v.* 1 [To govern] conduct, control, dictate; see GOVERN. 2 [To regulate] order, decree, direct; see

MANAGE 1. —**rule out** eliminate, not consider, recant; see ABOLISH, CANCEL.

ruled *a.* administered, controlled, managed; see GOVERNED.

ruler *n.* 1 [One who governs] governor, commander, chief, manager, adjudicator, monarch, regent, director; see also DICTATOR, KING 1, LEADER 2 for types of rulers. 2 [A straightedge] *Types of rulers include the following:* foot rule, yardstick, carpenter's rule, slide rule, parallel rule, stationer's rule, T-square, try square, steel square, compositor's rule, compositor's ruler.

ruling *n.* order, decision, precept; see LAW 3.

rumble *n.* reverberation, resounding, roll; see NOISE 1.

rumble *v.* resound, growl, thunder; see SOUND.

rumor *n.* report, news, tidings, intelligence, dispatch, hearsay, gossip, scandal, tattle, notoriety, noise, cry, popular report, fame, repute, grapevine, buzz*, breeze*, hoax, fabrication, suggestion, supposition, story, tale, invention, fiction, falsehood; see also LIE.

rumored *a.* reported, told, said, reputed, spread abroad, gossiped, given out, noised about, broadcast, as they say, all over town, current, circulating, in circulation, rife, prevailing, prevalent, persisting, general, going around, making the rounds.

rump *n.* posterior, buttocks, sacrum, hind end, tail end, posterior, butt end, bottom, croup, crupper, rear, backside, seat, breech, hunkers, fundament, butt*, ass*, buns*, duff*, bum*, tush*, keister*, can*.

rumple *v.* crumple, crush, fold; see WRINKLE.

run *n.* 1 [The act of running] sprint, pace, bound, flow, amble, gallop, canter, lope, spring, trot, dart, rush, dash, flight, escape, break, charge, swoop, race, scamper, tear, whisk,

flow, fall, drop. 2 [A series] continuity, succession, sequence; see SERIES. 3 [In baseball, a score] record, tally, point; see SCORE 1. 4 [The average] par, norm, run of the mill; see AVERAGE. 5 [A course] way, route, field; see TRACK 1. —**in the long run** in the final outcome, finally, eventually, see ULTIMATELY. —**on the run** 1 busy, in a hurry, running; see HURRYING. 2 retreating, defeated, routed; see BEATEN 1.

run *v.* 1 [To move, usually rapidly] flow in, flow over, chase along, fall, pour, tumble, drop, leap, spin, whirl, whiz, sail. 2 [To go swiftly by physical effort] rush, hurry, spring, bound, scurry, skitter, scramble, scoot, travel, run off, run away, dash ahead, dash on, put on a burst of speed, go on the double*, light out*, have a free play, make tracks*, dart, dart ahead, gallop, canter, lope, spring, trot, single-foot, amble, pace, flee, speed, spurt, swoop, bolt, race, shoot, tear, whisk, scamper, scuttle. 3 [To function] move, work, go; see OPERATE 2. 4 [To cause to function] control, drive, govern; see MANAGE 1. 5 [To extend] encompass, cover, spread; see REACH 1, SURROUND 1. 6 [To continue] last, persevere, go on; see CONTINUE 1. 7 [To complete] oppose, contest, contend with; see COMPETE, RACE 2. —**run down** 1 [To chase] hunt, seize, apprehend; see PURSUE 1. 2 [To ridicule] make fun of, belittle, depreciate; see RIDICULE. —**run into** 1 [To collide with] bump into, crash, have a collision; see HIT 1. 2 [To encounter] come across, see, contact; see MEET 6. —**run out** 1 [To squander] lose, dissipate, exhaust; see WASTE 2. 2 [To stop] expire, finish, end; see STOP 2. 3 [To become exhausted] weaken, wear out, waste away; see TIRE 1. —**run over** trample on, drive over, run down; see HIT, KILL. —**run through** waste, squander, lose; see SPEND.

[to run a blockade*]* **5** to cause to run, move, compete, etc. **6** to drive into a specified condition, place, etc. **7** to drive (an object) into or against (something) **8** to make flow in a specified way, place, etc. **9** to manage (a business, etc.) **10** to trace **11** to undergo (a fever, etc.) **12** to publish (a story, etc.) in a newspaper —*n.* **1** an act or period of running **2** the distance covered in running **3** a trip; journey **4** a route *[a delivery run]* **5** *a)* movement onward, progression, or trend *[the run* of events*] b)* a continuous course or period *[a run* of good luck*]* **6** a continuous course of performances, etc., as of a play **7** a continued series of demands, as on a bank **8** a brook **9** a kind or class; esp., the average kind **10** the output during a period of operation **11** an enclosed area for domestic animals **12** freedom to move about at will *[the run* of the house*]* **13** a large number of fish migrating together **14** a ravel, as in a stocking **15** *Baseball* a scoring point, made by a successful circuit of the bases —**in the long run** ultimately —**on the run** running or running away —**run across** to encounter by chance: also **run into** —**run down 1** to stop operating **2** to run against so as to knock down **3** to pursue and capture or kill **4** to speak of disparagingly —**run out** to come to an end; expire —**run out of** to use up —**run over 1** to ride over **2** to overflow **3** to examine, rehearse, etc. rapidly —**run through 1** to use up quickly or recklessly **2** to pierce —**run up 1** to raise, rise, or accumulate rapidly **2** to sew rapidly

run′around′ *n.* [Colloq.] a series of evasions

run′away′ *n.* **1** a fugitive **2** a horse, etc. that runs away —*adj.* **1** escaping, fleeing, etc. **2** easily won, as a race **3** rising rapidly, as prices

run′down′ *n.* a concise summary

run′-down′ *adj.* **1** not wound and therefore not running, as a watch **2** in poor physical condition, as from overwork **3** fallen into disrepair

rune (rōōn) *n.* ⟦OE *run*⟧ **1** any of the characters of an ancient Germanic alphabet **2** [Old Poet.] a mystical or obscure poem or song

rung[1] (ruŋ) *n.* ⟦OE *hrung*, staff⟧ a rod forming a step of a ladder, a crosspiece on a chair, etc.

rung[2] (ruŋ) *vi., vt. pp. of* RING[1]

run′-in′ *n.* **1** *Printing* matter added without a break or new paragraph: also **run′-on′ 2** [Colloq.] a quarrel, fight, etc.

run·nel (run′əl) *n.* ⟦OE *rynel*⟧ a small stream; brook Also **run′let**

run′ner *n.* **1** one that runs, as a racer, messenger, etc. **2** a long, narrow cloth or rug **3** a ravel, as in hose **4** a long, trailing stem, as of a strawberry **5** either of the long, narrow pieces on which a sled, etc. slides

run′ner-up′ *n., pl.* **-ners-up′** a person or team that finishes second, etc. in a contest

run′ning *n.* the act of one that runs; racing, managing, etc. —*adj.* **1** that runs (in various senses) **2** measured in a straight line **3** continuous *[a running* commentary*]* —*adv.* in succession *[for five days running]* —**in** (or **out of**) **the running** having a (or no) chance to win

running lights the lights that a ship or aircraft must display at night

running mate a candidate for the lesser of two closely associated offices in his relationship to the candidate for the greater office

run′ny *adj.* **-nier, -ni·est 1** flowing, esp. too freely **2** discharging mucus *[a runny* nose*]*

run′off′ *n.* a deciding, final contest

run′-of-the-mill′ *adj.* not selected or special; ordinary; average

runt (runt) *n.* ⟦< ? ⟧ a stunted animal, plant, or (contemptuously) person —**runt′y, runt′i·er, runt′i·est,** *adj.*

run′-through′ *n.* a complete rehearsal, from beginning to end

run′way′ *n.* a channel, track, etc. in, on, or along which something moves; esp., a strip of leveled ground used by airplanes in taking off and landing

ru·pee (rōō′pē, rōō pē′) *n.* ⟦< Sans *rūpyaḥ*, wrought silver⟧ the monetary unit of: *a)* India *b)* Nepal *c)* Pakistan *d)* Sri Lanka

rup·ture (rup′chər) *n.* ⟦< L *rumpere*, to break⟧ **1** a breaking apart or being broken apart; breach **2** a hernia —*vt., vi.* **-tured, -tur·ing** to cause or suffer a rupture

ru·ral (roor′əl) *adj.* ⟦< L *rus*, the country⟧ of, like, or living in the country; rustic —**ru′ral·ism′** *n.*

ruse (rōōz) *n.* ⟦< OFr *reuser*, deceive⟧ a stratagem, trick, or artifice

rush[1] (rush) *vi., vt.* ⟦< Fr *ruser*, repel⟧ **1** to move, push, drive, etc. swiftly or impetuously **2** to make a sudden attack (*on*) **3** to pass, go, send, act, do, etc. with unusual haste; hurry —*n.* **1** a rushing **2** an eager movement of many people to get to a place **3** busyness; haste *[the rush* of modern life*]* **4** a press, as of business, necessitating unusual haste

rush[2] (rush) *n.* ⟦OE *risc*⟧ a grasslike marsh plant with round stems used in making mats, etc.

rush hour a time of the day when business, traffic, etc. are heavy

rusk (rusk) *n.* ⟦Sp *rosca*, twisted bread roll⟧ **1** sweet, raised bread or cake toasted until browned and crisp **2** a piece of this

Russ. 1 Russia **2** Russian

rus·set (rus′it) *n.* ⟦< L *russus*, reddish⟧ **1** yellowish (or reddish) brown **2** a winter apple with a mottled skin

Rus·sian (rush′ən) *adj.* of Russia, its people, language, etc. —*n.* **1** a native or inhabitant of Russia **2** the East Slavic language of the Russians

rust (rust) *n.* ⟦OE⟧ **1** the reddish-brown coating formed on iron or steel during exposure to air and moisture **2** any stain resembling this **3** a reddish brown **4** a plant disease caused by fungi, spotting stems and leaves —*vi., vt.* **1** to form rust (on) **2** to deteriorate, as through disuse

rus·tic (rus′tik) *adj.* ⟦< L *rus*, the country⟧ **1** of the country; rural **2** simple or artless **3** rough or uncouth —*n.* a country person —**rus′ti·cally** *adv.* —**rus·tic′i·ty** (-tis′ə tē) *n.*

rus·ti·cate (rus′tə kāt′) *vi., vt.* **-cat′ed, -cat′ing 1** to go or send to live in the country **2** to become or make rustic —**rus′ti·ca′tion** *n.*

rus·tle[1] (rus′əl) *vi., vt.* **-tled, -tling** ⟦ult. echoic⟧ to make or cause to make soft sounds, as of moving leaves, etc. —*n.* a series of such sounds

rus·tle[2] (rus′əl) *vi., vt.* **-tled, -tling** ⟦< ?⟧ [Colloq.] to steal (cattle, etc.) —**rustle up** [Colloq.] to collect or get together —**rus′tler** *n.*

rust′proof′ *adj.* resistant to rust

rusty (rus′tē) *adj.* **-i·er, -i·est 1** coated with rust, as a metal **2** *a)* impaired by disuse, neglect, etc. *b)* having lost

---

THESAURUS

runaway *a.* out of control, delinquent, wild; see DISORDERLY 1.

runaway *n.* juvenile offender, lawbreaker, truant; see DELINQUENT.

rundown *n.* report, outline, review; see SUMMARY.

run-down *a.* **1** [Exhausted] weak, debilitated, weary; see WEAK 1, 2, TIRED. **2** [Dilapidated] broken-down, shabby, beat-up*; see OLD 2, CRUMBLY.

runner *n.* racer, entrant, contestant, sprinter, dash man, distance runner, middle distance runner, 220-man, cross-country runner, jogger, trackman, hurdler, messenger, courier, express, dispatch bearer, cinder artist*; see also ATHLETE.

running *a.* **1** [In the act of running] pacing, racing, speeding, galloping, cantering, trotting, scampering, fleeing, bounding, whisking, sprinting, flowing, tumbling, falling, pouring. **2** [In the process of running] producing, operating, working, functioning, proceeding, moving, revolving, guiding, conducting, administering, going, in operation, in action, executing, promoting, achieving, transacting, determining, bringing about. **3** [Extending] spreading, reaching, encompassing; see EXTENDING.

runoff *n.* spring runoff, drainage, surplus water; see FLOW, RIVER, WATER 1.

run-of-the-mill *a.* popular, mediocre, ordinary; see COMMON 1.

runt *n.* undersized animal or person, dwarf, midget, pygmy.

rupture *n.* hole, separation, crack; see BREAK 1, TEAR.

rupture *v.* crack, tear, burst; see BREAK.

rural *a.* rustic, farm, agricultural, ranch, pastoral, bucolic, backwoods, country, agrarian, agronomic, suburban.—*Ant.* URBAN, industrial, commercial.

rush[1] *n.* haste, dash, charge; see HURRY.

rush[1] *v.* hasten, speed, hurry up; see HURRY.

rushed *a.* hurried, pressed, pressured; see DRIVEN.

rushing *a.* being quick, bestirring oneself, losing no time; see HURRYING.

Russian *a.* Slavic, Slav, Muscovite, Siberian.

rust *n.* decomposition, corruption, corrosion, oxidation, decay, rot, dilapidation, breakup, wear.

rust *v.* oxidize, become rusty, degenerate, decay, rot, corrode.

rustic *a.* agricultural, pastoral, agrarian; see RURAL.

rusty *a.* **1** [Decayed] unused, neglected, worn; see OLD 2, WEAK 2. **2**

facility through lack of practice —**rust′i·ly** *adv.* —**rust′i·ness** *n.*

rut[1] (rut) *n.* ⟦< ? Fr *route*, route⟧ **1** a groove, track, etc., as made by wheels **2** a fixed, routine procedure, course of action, etc. — *vt.* **rut′ted, rut′ting** to make ruts in —**rut′ty, -tier, -ti·est,** *adj.*

rut[2] (rut) *n.* ⟦< L *rugire*, to roar⟧ the periodic sexual excitement of certain male mammals — *vi.* **rut′ted, rut′ting** to be in rut —**rut′tish** *adj.*

ru·ta·ba·ga (rōōt′ə bā′gə) *n.* ⟦Swed dial. *rotabagge*⟧ **1** a turniplike plant with a large, yellow root **2** this root

Ruth (rōōth) *Bible* a woman deeply devoted to her mother-in-law, Naomi, for whom she left her own people

ruth′less (-lis) *adj.* ⟦OE *hreowan*, to rue⟧ without pity or compassion —**ruth′lessly** *adv.* —**ruth′less·ness** *n.*

RV (är′vē′) *n., pl.* **RVs** ⟦R(ecreational) V(ehicle)⟧ a camper, trailer, motor home, etc. outfitted as a place to live, as when camping out

Rwy. or **Ry.** Railway

-ry (rē) *suffix* -ERY [*foundry*]

rya rug (rē′ə) ⟦< Swed⟧ a thick, decorative, hand-woven area rug of Scandinavian origin

rye (rī) *n.* ⟦OE *ryge*⟧ **1** a hardy cereal grass **2** its grain or seeds, used for making flour, etc. **3** whiskey distilled from this grain

---

THESAURUS

[Unpracticed] out of practice, soft, ill-qualified; see WEAK 5.

rut[1] *n.* **1** [A deeply cut track] hollow, trench, furrow; see GROOVE. **2** [Habitual behavior] custom, habit, course, routine, practice, performance, round, circuit, circle, usage, procedure.—*Ant.* CHANGE, veer,

mutation.

ruthless *a.* cruel, fierce, savage, brutal, merciless, inhuman, hard, cold, fiendish, unmerciful, pitiless, grim, unpitying, tigerish, ferocious, stony-hearted, coldblooded, remorseless, vindictive, vengeful, revengeful, rancorous, implacable, unforgiving,

malevolent, hard-hearted, hard, cold, unsympathetic, vicious, sadistic, surly, tyrannical, relentless, barbarous, inhuman, atrocious, flagrant, terrible, abominable, outrageous, oppressive, bloodthirsty, venomous, galling.—*Ant.* KIND, helpful, civilized.

s or **S** (es) *n., pl.* **s's, S's** the 19th letter of the English alphabet — *adj.* shaped like S

's **1** is *[he's here]* **2** has *[she's eaten]* **3** [Colloq.] does *[what's it matter?]* **4** us *[let's go]*

-s [alt. of -ES] *suffix* **1** forming the plural of most nouns *[hips]* **2** forming the 3d pers. sing., pres. indic., of certain verbs *[shouts]*

-'s [OE] *suffix* forming the possessive singular of nouns and some pronouns, and the possessive plural of nouns not ending in s *[boy's, men's]*

s or **s.** **1** second(s) **2** shilling(s) **3** small

S *Chem. symbol for* sulfur

S or **S.** **1** Saturday **2** small **3** south **4** southern **5** Sunday

S.A. South America

Sab·bath (sab′əth) *n.* [< Heb *shabat*, to rest] **1** the seventh day of the week (Saturday), set aside in Jewish scripture for rest and worship **2** Sunday as the usual Christian day of rest and worship

Sab·bat·i·cal (sə bat′i kəl) *adj.* **1** of the Sabbath **2** [s-] bringing a period of rest — *n.* [s-] SABBATICAL LEAVE

sabbatical leave a period of absence with pay, for study, travel, etc., given as to teachers, orig. every seven years Also **sabbatical year**

sa·ber (sā′bər) *n.* [< Hung *szablya*] a heavy cavalry sword with a slightly curved blade Also **sa′bre**

Sa·bin vaccine (sā′bin) [after Dr. A. B. *Sabin* (1906-93), its U.S. developer] a polio vaccine taken orally

sa·ble (sā′bəl) *n.* [< Russ *sobol′*] **1** any marten **2** its costly fur pelt

sa·bot (sa bō′, sab′ō) *n.* [Fr, ult. < Ar *sabbāt*, sandal] a shoe shaped from a single piece of wood

sab·o·tage (sab′ə täzh′) *n.* [Fr < *sabot*, wooden shoe + -AGE: from damage done to machinery by sabots] deliberate destruction of machines, etc. by employees in labor disputes or of railroads, bridges, etc. by enemy agents or by an underground resistance — *vt., vi.* **-taged′, -tag′ing** to commit sabotage (on) — **sab′o·teur′** (-tʉr′) *n.*

sa·bra (sä′brə) *n.* [Heb *sabra*, a native cactus fruit] a native-born Israeli

sabre saw a portable electric saw with a narrow, oscillating blade

sac (sak) *n.* [see SACK¹] a pouchlike part in a plant or animal

sac·cha·rin (sak′ə rin′) *n.* [< Gr *sakcharon*] a white, crystalline compound used as a sugar substitute

sac·cha·rine (-rin′) *adj.* **1** of or like sugar **2** too sweet *[a saccharine voice]*

sac·er·do·tal (sas′ər dōt′'l; *occas.* sak′-) *adj.* [< L *sacerdos*, priest] of priests or the office of priest

sa·chem (sā′chəm) *n.* [AmInd] among some North American Indian tribes, the chief

sa·chet (sa shā′) *n.* [Fr] a small perfumed packet used to scent clothes

sack¹ (sak) *n.* [ult. < Heb *saq*] **1** a bag, esp. a large one of coarse cloth **2** [Slang] dismissal: with *the* **3** [Slang] a bed **4** *Football* a sacking a quarterback — *vt.* **1** to put into sacks **2** [Slang] to fire (a person) **3** *Football* to tackle (a quarterback) behind the line of scrimmage

S

sack² (sak) *n.* [see prec.] the plundering of a city, etc. — *vt.* to plunder

sack³ (sak) *n.* [< Fr (*vin*)*sec*, dry (wine) < L] a dry, white Spanish wine popular in England during the 16th and 17th c.

sack′cloth′ *n.* **1** SACKING **2** coarse cloth worn as a symbol of mourning

sack′ful′ *n., pl.* **-fuls′** the amount that a sack will hold

sack′ing *n.* a coarse cloth used for making sacks

sac·ra·ment (sak′rə mənt) *n.* [< L *sacer*, holy] any of certain Christian rites, as baptism, the Eucharist, etc. — **sac′ra·men′tal** *adj.*

sa·cred (sā′krid) *adj.* [< L *sacer*, holy] **1** consecrated to a god or God; holy **2** having to do with religion **3** venerated; hallowed **4** inviolate — **sa′cred·ly** *adv.* — **sa′cred·ness** *n.*

sac·ri·fice (sak′rə fīs′) *n.* [< L *sacrificium* < *sacer*, sacred + *facere*, make] **1** an offering, as of a life or object, to a deity **2** a giving up of one thing for the sake of another — *vt., vi.* **-ficed′, -fic′ing** **1** to offer as a sacrifice to a deity **2** to give up one thing for the sake of another **3** to sell at less than the supposed value — **sac′ri·fi′cial** (-fish′əl) *adj.*

sac·ri·lege (sak′rə lij) *n.* [< L *sacer*, sacred + *legere*, take away] desecration of what is sacred — **sac′ri·le′gious** (-lij′əs, -lē′jəs) *adj.*

sac·ris·tan (sak′ris tən) *n.* a person in charge of a sacristy

sac′ris·ty (-tē) *n., pl.* **-ties** [ult. < L *sacer*, sacred] a room in a church for sacred vessels, etc.

sac·ro·il·i·ac (sak′rō il′ē ak′, sā′krō-) *n.* the joint between the top part (**il′ium**) of the hipbone and the fused bottom vertebrae (**sa′crum**)

sac·ro·sanct (sak′rō saŋkt′) *adj.* [< L *sacer*, sacred + *sanctus*, holy] very sacred, holy, or inviolable

sad (sad) *adj.* **sad′der, sad′dest** [OE *sæd*, sated] **1** having or expressing low spirits; unhappy; sorrowful **2** causing dejection, sorrow, etc. — **sad′ly** *adv.* — **sad′ness** *n.*

sad′den *vt., vi.* to make or become sad

sad·dle (sad′'l) *n.* [OE *sadol*] **1** a seat for a rider on a horse, bicycle, etc., usually padded and of leather **2** a cut of lamb, etc., including part of the backbone and the two loins — *vt.* **-dled, -dling** **1** to put a saddle upon **2** to encumber or burden — **in the saddle** in control

sad′dle·bag′ *n.* **1** a bag hung behind the saddle of a horse, etc. **2** a similar bag carried on a bicycle, etc.

saddle horse a horse for riding

saddle shoes white oxford shoes with a contrasting band across the instep

Sad·du·cee (saj′oo sē′) *n.* a member of an ancient Jewish party that accepted only the written law

---

THESAURUS

Sabbath *n.* day of rest, Saturday, Sunday; see WEEKEND.

sabotage *n.* demolition, overthrow, treason; see DESTRUCTION 1, REVOLUTION 2.

sabotage *v.* subvert, siege, undermine; see ATTACK 1, DESTROY.

sac *n.* welt, pouch, blister; see SORE.

sack¹ *n.* sac, pouch, pocket; see BAG, CONTAINER. **—hit the sack*** go to bed, go to sleep, retire; see SLEEP.

sack¹ *v.* bag, package, pocket; see PACK 1.

sacrament *n.* holy observance, ceremonial, liturgy, act of divine worship, mystery, the mysteries. *In the Roman Catholic and Eastern Orthodox churches, the seven sacraments are as follows:* baptism, confirmation or the laying on of hands, penance, Communion or the Eucharist, extreme unction or Anointing of the Sick, holy orders, matrimony.

sacramental *a.* sacred, pure, solemn; see HOLY 1, RELIGIOUS 1.

sacred *a.* **1** [Holy] pure, pious, saintly; see HOLY 1. **2** [Dedicated] consecrated, ordained, sanctioned; see DIVINE.

sacrifice *n.* **1** [An offering to a deity] offering, tribute, atonement; see CEREMONY. **2** [A loss] discount, deduction, reduction; see LOSS 1.

sacrifice *v.* **1** [To offer to a deity] consecrate, dedicate, give up; see BLESS. **2** [To give up as a means to an end] forfeit, forgo, relinquish, yield, suffer the loss of, renounce, spare, give up, let go, resign oneself to, sacrifice oneself, surrender, part with, go astray from. **3** [To sell at a loss] cut, reduce, sell out; see DECREASE 2, LOSE 2.

sad *a.* **1** [Afflicted with sorrow] unhappy, sorry, sorrowful, downcast, dismal, gloomy, glum, pensive, heavy-hearted, dispirited, dejected, depressed, desolate, troubled, melancholy, morose, grieved, pessimistic, crushed, brokenhearted, heartbroken, heartsick, despondent, careworn, disheartened, rueful, anguished, lamenting, mourning, grieving, weeping, bitter, woebegone, doleful, spiritless, joyless, heavy, crestfallen, discouraged, moody, low-spirited, despairing, hopeless, worried, downhearted, cast down, in heavy spirits, morbid, oppressed, blighted, grief-stricken, foreboding, apprehensive, horrified, anxious, wretched, miserable, mournful, disconsolate, forlorn, jaundiced, out of sorts, distressed, afflicted, bereaved, repining, harassed, dreary, down in the dumps, in bad humor, out of humor, cut up*, in the depths*, blue, stricken with grief, making a long face, in tears, feeling like hell*, down in the mouth*.—*Ant.* HAPPY, joyous, cheerful. **2** [Suggestive of sorrow] pitiable, unhappy, dejecting, saddening, disheartening, discouraging, joyless, dreary, dark, dismal, gloomy, moving, touching, mournful, disquieting, disturbing, somber, doleful, oppressive, funereal, lugubrious, pathetic, tragic, pitiful, piteous, woeful, rueful, sorry, unfortunate, hapless, heart-rending, dire, distressing, depressing, grievous.

sadden *v.* oppress, dishearten, discourage, cast down, deject, depress, break one's heart.

saddle *n.* seat, riding seat, leather*; see CHAIR 1.

sad·ism (sad'iz'əm, sā'diz'əm) *n.* ⟦after Marquis de *Sade* (1740-1814), Fr writer⟧ the getting of pleasure from mistreating others —**sad'ist** *n.* —**sa·dis'tic** *adj.* —**sa·dis'ti·cally** *adv.*

sado·maso·chism (sad'ō mas'ə kiz'əm, sā'dō-) *n.* the getting of pleasure, esp. sexual pleasure, from sadism or masochism, or both —**sad'o·mas'o·chist** *n.* —**sad'o·mas'o·chis'tic** *adj.*

sa·fari (sə fär'ē) *n.*, *pl.* **-ris** ⟦< Ar *safar*, to journey⟧ a journey or hunting expedition, esp. in Africa

safe (sāf) *adj.* **saf'er**, **saf'est** ⟦< L *salvus*⟧ **1** *a*) free from damage, danger, etc.; secure *b*) having escaped injury; unharmed **2** *a*) giving protection *b*) trustworthy **3** prudent; cautious — *n.* a locking metal container for valuables —**safe'ly** *adv.* —**safe'ness** *n.*

safe'-con'duct *n.* permission to travel safely through enemy regions

safe'-depos'it *adj.* designating or of a box or vault, as in a bank, for storing valuables: also **safe'ty-depos'it**

safe'guard' *n.* a protection; precaution — *vt.* to protect or guard

safe'keep'ing *n.* protection; care

safe sex sexual activity incorporating practices, as condom use, that reduce the risk of spreading sexually transmitted diseases

safety (sāf'tē) *n.*, *pl.* **-ties 1** a being safe; security **2** any device for preventing an accident **3** *Football a*) the grounding of the ball by the offense behind its own goal line that scores two points for the defense *b*) a defensive back farthest from the line of scrimmage (also **safety man**) — *adj.* giving safety

safety glass shatterproof glass

safety match a match that strikes only on a prepared surface

safety net 1 a net suspended as beneath aerialists **2** any protection against loss, esp. financial loss

safety pin a pin bent back on itself and having the point held in a guard

safety razor a razor with a detachable blade held between guards

safety valve an automatic valve which releases steam if the pressure in a boiler, etc. becomes excessive

saf·flower (saf'flou'ər) *n.* ⟦ult. < Ar *aṣfar*, yellow⟧ a thistlelike, annual plant with large, orange flowers and seeds yielding an edible oil

saf·fron (saf'rən) *n.* ⟦< Ar *za'farān*⟧ **1** a plant having orange stigmas **2** the dried stigmas, used as a dye and flavoring **3** orange yellow

sag (sag) *vi.* **sagged**, **sag'ging** ⟦prob. < Scand⟧ **1** to sink, esp. in the middle, from weight or pressure **2** to hang down unevenly **3** to weaken through weariness, age, etc. — *n.* **1** a sagging **2** a sagging place

saga (sä'gə) *n.* ⟦ON, a tale⟧ **1** a medieval Scandinavian story of battles, legends, etc. **2** any long story of heroic deeds

sa·ga·cious (sə gā'shəs) *adj.* ⟦< L *sagax*, wise⟧ keenly perceptive; shrewd —**sa·gac'ity** (-gas'ə tē) *n.*

sage[1] (sāj) *adj.* **sag'er**, **sag'est** ⟦ult. < L *sapere*, know⟧ **1** wise, discerning, etc. **2** showing wisdom [a *sage* comment] — *n.* a very wise man

sage[2] (sāj) *n.* ⟦< L *salvus*, safe: from its reputed healing powers⟧ **1** a plant of the mint family with leaves used for seasoning meats, etc. **2** SAGEBRUSH

sage'brush' *n.* a plant with aromatic leaves, in the dry areas of the W U.S.

sag'gy *adj.* **-gier**, **-gi·est** tending to sag

Sag·it·tar·i·us (saj'ə ter'ē əs) ⟦L, archer⟧ the ninth sign of the zodiac

sa·guaro (sə gwär'ō) *n.*, *pl.* **-ros** ⟦< native name⟧ a giant cactus of the SW U.S. and N Mexico

sa·hib (sä'ib') *n.* ⟦Hindi < Ar⟧ sir; master: title used in colonial India when speaking to or of a European

said (sed) *vt.*, *vi. pt. & pp.* of SAY — *adj.* aforesaid

sail (sāl) *n.* ⟦OE *segl*⟧ **1** a sheet, as of canvas, spread to catch the wind, so as to drive a vessel forward **2** sails collectively **3** a trip in a ship or boat **4** anything like a sail — *vi.* **1** to be moved forward by means of sails **2** to travel on water **3** to begin a trip by water **4** to manage a sailboat **5** to glide or move smoothly, like a ship in full sail — *vt.* **1** to move upon (a body of water) in a vessel **2** to manage (a vessel) —**set sail** to begin a trip by water —**under sail** sailing

sail'boat' *n.* a boat that is propelled by means of a sail or sails

sail'cloth' *n.* canvas or other cloth for making sails, tents, etc.

sail'fish' *n.*, *pl.* **-fish'** or (for different species) **-fish'es** a large, marine fish with a sail-like dorsal fin

sail'or *n.* **1** a person whose work is sailing **2** an enlisted man in the navy

saint (sānt) *n.* ⟦< L *sanctus*, holy⟧ **1** a holy person **2** a person who is exceptionally charitable, patient, etc. **3** in certain Christian churches, a person officially recognized and venerated for having attained heaven after an exceptionally holy life —**saint'li·ness** *n.* —**saint'ly**, **-lier**, **-liest**, *adj.*

Saint Ber·nard (bər närd') a large dog of a breed once used in the Swiss Alps to rescue lost travelers

Saint Pat·rick's Day (pa'triks) March 17, observed by the Irish in honor of the patron saint of Ireland

Saint Val·en·tine's Day Feb. 14, observed in honor of a martyr of the 3d c. and as a day for sending valentines to sweethearts, etc.

THESAURUS

sadistic *a.* cruel, brutal, vicious; see CRUEL.

sadly *a.* unhappily, morosely, dejectedly, wistfully, sorrowfully, gloomily, joylessly, dismally, cheerlessly, in sorrow.

sadness *n.* sorrow, dejection, melancholy, depression, grief, despondency, oppression, downs, gloom, blues*.

safe *a.* **1** [Not in danger] out of danger, secure, in safety, in security, free from harm, free from danger, unharmed, safe and sound, protected, guarded, housed, screened from danger, unthreatened, unmolested, entrenched, impregnable, invulnerable, under the protection of, saved, safeguarded, secured, defended, supported, sustained, maintained, upheld, preserved, vindicated, shielded, nourished, sheltered, fostered, cared for, cherished, watched, impervious to, patrolled, looked after, supervised, tended, attended, kept in order, surveyed, regulated, with one's head above water, undercover, out of harm's way, on the safe side, on ice*, at anchor, in harbor, snug as a bug in a rug, under lock and key.—*Ant.* DANGEROUS, unsafe, risky. **2** [Not dangerous] innocent, innocuous, innoxious; see HARMLESS. **3** [Reli-

able] trustworthy, dependable, competent; see RELIABLE. —**keep safe** care for, chaperone, protect; see GUARD, WATCH.

safe *n.* strongbox, coffer, chest, repository, vault, case, safe-deposit box.

safekeeping *n.* supervision, care, guardianship; see CUSTODY, PROTECTION 2.

safely *a.* securely, with impunity, without harm, without risk, without danger, harmlessly, carefully, cautiously, reliably.

safety *n.* **1** [Freedom from danger] security, protection, impregnability, surety, sanctuary, refuge, shelter, invulnerability. **2** [A lock] lock mechanism, safetycatch, safety lock; see FASTENER, LOCK 1.

sag *n.* depression, dip, slump*; see HOLE 1.

sag *v.* stoop, hang down, become warped; see BEND, LEAN 1.

said *a.* pronounced, aforesaid, forenamed; see PRECEDING, SPOKEN.

sail *n.* **1** [Means of sailing a vessel] sheets, canvas, cloth; see GOODS. *Sails include the following:* mainsail, foresail, topsail, jib, spanker, flying jib, trysail, balloon sail, spinnaker, balloon jib. **2** [A journey by sailing vessel] voyage, cruise, trip; see JOUR-

NEY. —**set sail** begin a voyage, shove off, weigh anchor; see LEAVE 1, SAIL 1.

sail *v.* **1** [To travel by sailing] cruise, voyage, go alongside, bear down on, bear for, direct one's course for, set sail, put to sea, sail away from, navigate, travel, make headway, lie in, make for, heave to, fetch up, bring to, bear off, close with, run in, put in. **2** [To fly] float, soar, ride the storm, skim, glide.

sailor *n.* seaman, mariner, seafarer, pirate, navigator, pilot, boatman, yachtsman, able-bodied seaman, Jack Tar, tar*, sea dog, limey*, salt*, bluejacket. *Kinds and ranks of sailors include the following—crew:* deck hand, stoker, cabin boy, yeoman, purser; ship's carpenter, cooper, tailor; steward, navigator, signalman, gunner, afterguard; *officers:* captain or commander or skipper, navigating officer, deck officer; first, second, third, boatswain's mate; boatswain or bo's'n*.

saint *n.* a true Christian, child of God, son of God, paragon, salt of the earth, godly person, martyr, man of God, unworldly person, altruist, the pure in heart, a believer.

saintly *a.* angelic, pious, divine; see HOLY.

saith (seth) [Archaic] *says*
sake[1] (sāk) *n.* ⟦OE *sacu*, suit at law⟧ 1 motive; cause *[for the sake of money]* 2 behalf *[for my sake]*
sake[2] (sä′kē) *n.* ⟦Jpn⟧ a Japanese alcoholic beverage made from rice Also sp. **sa′ki**
sa·laam (sə läm′) *n.* ⟦Ar *salām*, peace⟧ an Oriental greeting, etc. made by bowing low in respect or obeisance
sal·able (sāl′ə bəl) *adj.* that can be sold; marketable Also sp. **sale′able**
sa·la·cious (sə lā′shəs) *adj.* ⟦< L *salire*, to leap⟧ 1 lustful 2 obscene —**sa·la′cious·ly** *adv.* —**sa·la′cious·ness** *n.*
salad (sal′əd) *n.* ⟦< L *sal*, salt⟧ a dish, usually cold, of fruits, vegetables (esp. lettuce), meat, eggs, etc. usually mixed with salad dressing
salad bar a buffet in a restaurant, at which diners make their own salads
salad dressing a preparation of oil, vinegar, spices, etc. put on a salad
sa·lade niçoise (sal′əd nē swäz′) a salad of tuna, tomatoes, black olives, etc. with a garlic vinaigrette
sala·man·der (sal′ə man′dər) *n.* ⟦< Gr *salamandra*⟧ 1 a mythological reptile said to live in fire 2 a scaleless, tailed amphibian
sa·lami (sə lä′mē) *n.* ⟦It < L *sal*, salt⟧ a spiced, salted sausage
sala·ry (sal′ə rē) *n., pl.* -**ries** ⟦< L *salarium*, orig. part of a soldier's pay for buying salt < *sal*, salt⟧ a fixed payment at regular intervals for work —**sal′a·ried** (-rēd) *adj.*
sale (sāl) *n.* ⟦< ON *sala*⟧ 1 a selling 2 opportunity to sell; market 3 an auction 4 a special offering of goods at reduced prices 5 *[pl.]* receipts in business 6 *[pl.]* the work, department, etc. of selling *[a job in sales]* —**for sale** to be sold —**on sale** for sale, esp. at a reduced price
sales·clerk (sālz′klʉrk′) *n.* a person employed to sell goods in a store
sales′girl′ *n.* a girl or woman employed as a salesclerk
sales′la′dy *n., pl.* -**dies** [Colloq.] a saleswoman employed as a salesclerk
sales′man (-mən) *n., pl.* -**men** 1 a man employed as a salesclerk 2 SALES REPRESENTATIVE
sales′man·ship′ *n.* the skill or technique of selling
sales′per′son *n.* a person employed to sell goods or services —**sales′peo′ple** *n.pl.*
sales representative a salesperson, esp. one employed as a traveling agent for a manufacturer, store, etc.
sales slip a receipt or bill of sale
sales tax a tax on sales
sales′wom′an *n., pl.* -**wom′en** a woman salesclerk or sales representative
sali·cylic acid (sal′ə sil′ik) ⟦< *salicin* (substance from certain willows)⟧ a crystalline compound, as in aspirin, for relieving pain, etc.
sa·lient (sāl′yənt) *adj.* ⟦< L *salire*, to leap⟧ 1 pointing outward; jutting 2 conspicuous; prominent —*n.* a salient angle, part, etc. —**sa′lience** *n.*
sa·line (sā′līn, -lēn) *adj.* ⟦< L *sal*, salt⟧ of, like, or containing salt —*n.* a saline solution used in medicine, etc. —**sa·lin′i·ty** (sə lin′ə tē) *n.*

sa·liva (sə lī′və) *n.* ⟦L⟧ the watery fluid secreted by glands in the mouth: it aids in digestion —**sali·vary** (sal′ə ver′ē) *adj.*
sali·vate (sal′ə vāt′) *vi.* -**vat′ed**, -**vat′ing** ⟦< L *salivare*⟧ to secrete saliva —**sal′i·va′tion** *n.*
sal·low (sal′ō) *adj.* ⟦ME *salou*⟧ of a sickly, pale-yellowish complexion
sally (sal′ē) *n., pl.* -**lies** ⟦< L *salire*, to leap⟧ 1 a sudden rushing forth, as to attack 2 a quick witticism; quip 3 an excursion — *vi.* -**lied**, -**ly·ing** to rush or set *(forth* or *out)* on a sally
salmon (sam′ən) *n., pl.* -**on** or -**ons** ⟦< L *salmo*⟧ 1 a game and food fish with yellowish pink flesh, that lives in salt water and spawns in fresh water 2 yellowish pink: also **salmon pink**
sal·mo·nella (sal′mə nel′ə) *n., pl.* -**nel′lae** (-ē), -**nel′la**, or -**nel′las** ⟦after D. E. *Salmon* (1850-1914), U.S. doctor⟧ any of a genus of bacilli that cause typhoid fever, food poisoning, etc.
sa·lon (sə län′) *n.* ⟦Fr: see fol.⟧ 1 a large reception hall or drawing room 2 a regular gathering of distinguished guests 3 a parlor *[beauty salon]*
sa·loon (sə lōōn′) *n.* ⟦< Fr < It *sala*⟧ 1 any large room or hall for receptions, etc. 2 [Old-fashioned] a place where alcoholic drinks are sold; bar
salt (sôlt) *n.* ⟦OE *sealt*⟧ 1 a white, crystalline substance, sodium chloride, found in natural beds, in sea water, etc., and used for seasoning food, etc. 2 a chemical compound derived from an acid by replacing hydrogen with a metal 3 piquancy; esp., pungent wit 4 *[pl.]* mineral salts used as a cathartic or restorative 5 [Colloq.] a sailor —*adj.* containing, preserved with, or tasting of salt —*vt.* to sprinkle, season, or preserve with salt —**salt away** [Colloq.] to store or save (money, etc.) —**salt of the earth** any person or persons regarded as the finest, etc. —**with a grain of salt** with allowance for exaggeration, etc. —**salt′ed** *adj.* —**salt′y**, -**i·er**, -**i·est**, *adj.* —**salt′i·ness** *n.*
SALT (sôlt) Strategic Arms Limitation Talks
salt′cel′lar (-sel′ər) *n.* ⟦< SALT + Fr *salière*, saltcellar⟧ 1 a small dish for holding salt 2 a saltshaker
salt·ine (sôl tēn′) *n.* ⟦SALT + -INE[3]⟧ a flat, crisp, salted cracker
salt lick a natural deposit or a block of rock salt which animals lick
salt′pe′ter (-pēt′ər) *n.* ⟦< L *sal*, salt + *petra*, rock⟧ NITER
salt pork pork cured in salt
salt′shak′er *n.* a container for salt, with a perforated top
salt′wa′ter *adj.* of or living in salt water or the sea
sa·lu·bri·ous (sə lōō′brē əs) *adj.* ⟦< L *salus*, health⟧ healthful; wholesome
salu·tary (sal′yoo ter′ē) *adj.* ⟦see prec.⟧ 1 healthful 2 beneficial
salu·ta·tion (sal′yoo tā′shən) *n.* ⟦see fol.⟧ 1 the act of greeting, addressing, etc. 2 a form of greeting, as the "Dear Sir" of a letter
sa·lute (sə lōōt′) *vt., vi.* -**lut′ed**, -**lut′ing** ⟦< L *salus*, health⟧ 1 to greet with friendly words or ceremonial ges-

---

═══ THESAURUS ═══

sake[1] *n.* 1 [End] objective, consequence, final cause; see RESULT. 2 [Purpose] score, motive, principle; see PURPOSE 1. 3 [Welfare] benefit, interest, well-being; see ADVANTAGE, WELFARE 1.
salad *n.* salad greens, slaw, mixture, combination. *Common salads include the following:* green, tossed, vegetable, tomato, potato, macaroni, fruit, bean, combination, chef's, tuna, shrimp, lobster, crab, chicken, ham, Waldorf, Caesar, pineapple, banana, molded, frozen; cole slaw.
salary *n.* wages, recompense, payroll; see PAY 2.
sale *n.* 1 [The act of selling] commerce, business, traffic, exchange, barter, commercial enterprise, marketing, vending, trade. 2 [An individual instance of selling] deal, transaction, negotiation, turnover, trade, purchase, auction, disposal; see also BUYING, SELLING. 3 [An organized effort to promote unusual selling] bargain sale, clearance, stock reduction, fire sale, unloading, dumping, remnant sale, going out of

business sale, bankruptcy sale. —**for** (or **on** or **up for**) **sale** put on the market, to be sold, marketable, available, offered for purchase, not withheld. —**on sale** marked down, reduced, cut, at a bargain, at a cut rate, in the bargain basement, among the remnants; see also REDUCED 2.
sales *n.* sales receipts, annual sales, business; see INCOME.
salesman *n.* 1 [A sales clerk] salesperson, seller, counterman; see CLERK. 2 [A commercial traveler] out-of-town representative, agent, canvasser, solicitor, seller, businessman, itinerant, field worker, traveler, traveling man, traveling salesman, sales representative, sales manager.
salesperson *n.* salesman, saleswoman, saleslady; see CLERK.
saliva *n.* water, spittle, salivation, excretion, phlegm, enzyme, spit.
saloon *n.* bar, nightclub, cocktail lounge, pub, beer parlor, poor man's club, joint, hangout, place; see also RESTAURANT.
salt *a.* alkaline, saline, briny; see

SALTY.
salt *n.* 1 [A common seasoning and preservative] sodium chloride, common salt, table salt, savor, condiment, flavoring, spice, seasoning. *Common types of flavoring salts include the following:* garlic, sea, celery, onion, barbecue, salad, seasoning, hickory smoked; poultry seasoning, monosodium glutamate, MSG, salt substitute. 2 [Anything that provides savor] relish, pungency, smartness; see HUMOR 1, WIT. —**not worth one's salt** good-for-nothing, bad, worthless; see POOR 2. —**with a grain** (or **pinch**) **of salt** doubtingly, skeptically, lightly; see SUSPICIOUSLY.
salt *v.* season, make tasty, make piquant; see FLAVOR.
salty *a.* briny, brackish, pungent, alkaline, well-seasoned, flavored, well-flavored, highly flavored, sour, acrid.
salute *v.* snap to attention, dip the colors, touch one's cap, do honor to, recognize; see also PRAISE 1.

ture 2 to honor by performing a prescribed act, such as raising the right hand to the head, in military and naval practice 3 to commend — *n.* an act or remark made in saluting

sal·vage (sal'vij) *n.* [see SAVE[1]] 1 *a*) the rescue of a ship and cargo from shipwreck, etc. *b*) compensation paid for such rescue 2 *a*) the rescue of any property from destruction or waste *b*) the property saved — *vt.* -vaged, -vaging to save or rescue from shipwreck, fire, etc.

sal·va·tion (sal vā'shən) *n.* [< L *salvare*, save] 1 a saving or being saved 2 a person or thing that saves 3 *Theol.* deliverance from sin and from the penalties of sin; redemption

salve (sav) *n.* [OE *sealf*] 1 any soothing or healing ointment for wounds, burns, etc. 2 anything that soothes — *vt.* salved, salv'ing to soothe

sal·ver (sal'vər) *n.* [< L *salvare*, save] a tray

sal·vo (sal'vō') *n., pl.* -vos or -voes [< It < L *salve*, hail!] a discharge of a number of guns, in salute or at a target

SAM (sam) *n.* surface-to-air missile

samba (sam'bə, säm'-) *n.* [Port] a Brazilian dance of African origin, or music for it — *vi.* to dance the samba

same (sām) *adj.* [< ON *samr*] 1 being the very one; identical 2 alike in kind, quality, amount, etc. 3 unchanged [to keep the *same* look] 4 aforesaid — *pron.* the same person or thing — *adv.* in like manner —**same'ness** *n.*

sam·iz·dat (säm'iz dät') *n.* [Russ, self-published] 1 in the U.S.S.R., a system by which writings officially disapproved of were circulated secretly 2 such writings

samo·var (sam'ə vär') *n.* [Russ] a Russian metal urn with an internal tube for heating water in making tea

sam·pan (sam'pan') *n.* [< Chin dial.] a small boat used in China and Japan, rowed with a scull from the stern

sam·ple (sam'pəl) *n.* [see EXAMPLE] 1 a part taken as representative of a whole thing, group, etc.; specimen 2 an example — *vt.* -pled, -pling to take or test a sample of

sam·pler *n.* 1 one who samples 2 a collection of representative selections 3 a cloth embroidered with designs, mottoes, etc. in different stitches

Sam·son (sam'sən) *Bible* an Israelite with great strength

Samu·el (sam'yōo əl) *Bible* a Hebrew judge and prophet

samu·rai (sam'ə rī') *n., pl.* -rai' [Jpn] a member of a military class in feudal Japan

sana·to·rium (san'ə tôr'ē əm) *n., pl.* -ri·ums or -ria (-ə) *chiefly Brit. var. of* SANITARIUM

sanc·tify (saŋk'tə fī') *vt.* -fied', -fy'ing [see SAINT & -FY] 1 to set apart as holy; consecrate 2 to make free from sin —**sanc'ti·fi·ca'tion** *n.*

sanc·ti·mo·ni·ous (saŋk'tə mō'nē əs) *adj.* pretending to be pious —**sanc'ti·mo'ni·ous·ly** *adv.*

sanc'ti·mo'ny *n.* [< L *sanctus*, holy] pretended piety

sanc·tion (saŋk'shən) *n.* [see SAINT] 1 authorization 2 support; approval 3 a coercive measure, as an official trade boycott, against a nation defying international law: *often used in pl.* — *vt.* 1 to confirm 2 to authorize; permit

sanc·tity (saŋk'tə tē) *n., pl.* -ties [< L *sanctus*, holy] 1 holiness 2 sacredness

sanc·tu·ary (saŋk'chōō er'ē) *n., pl.* -ies [< L *sanctus*, sacred] 1 a holy place; specif., a church, temple, etc. 2 a place of refuge or protection

sanc·tum (saŋk'təm) *n.* [L] 1 a sacred place 2 a private room where one is not to be disturbed

sand (sand) *n.* [OE] 1 loose, gritty grains of disintegrated rock, as on beaches, in deserts, etc. 2 [*usually pl.*] a tract of sand — *vt.* 1 to sprinkle or fill with sand 2 to smooth or polish, as with sandpaper —**sand'er** *n.*

san·dal (san'dəl) *n.* [< Gr *sandalon*] 1 a shoe made of a sole fastened to the foot by straps 2 any of various low slippers or shoes

san'dal·wood' *n.* [ult. < Sans] 1 the hard, sweet-smelling wood at the core of an Asiatic tree 2 this tree

sand'bag' *n.* a bag filled with sand, used for ballast, protecting levees, etc. — *vt.* -bagged', -bag'ging 1 to put sandbags in or around 2 to hit with a sandbag 3 [Colloq.] to force into doing something

sand'bar' *n.* a ridge of sand, as one formed in a river or along a shore: also **sand'bank'**

sand'blast' *n.* a current of air or steam carrying sand at a high velocity, used in cleaning stone, etc. — *vt.* to clean with a sandblast

sand'box' *n.* a box containing sand for children to play in

sand'hog' *n.* a laborer in underground or underwater construction

S & L savings and loan (association)

sand'lot' *adj.* of or having to do with games, esp. baseball, played by amateurs, orig. on a sandy lot —**sand'lot'ter** *n.*

sand'man' *n.* a mythical person supposed to make children sleepy by dusting sand in their eyes

sand'pa'per *n.* paper coated on one side with sand, used for smoothing and polishing — *vt.* to rub with sandpaper

sand'pip'er (-pī'pər) *n.* a small shorebird with a long, soft-tipped bill

sand'stone' *n.* a sedimentary rock composed of sand grains cemented together, as by silica

sand'storm' *n.* a windstorm in which large quantities of sand are blown about in the air

sand trap a hollow filled with sand, serving as a hazard on a golf course

sand·wich (san'dwich', -wich) *n.* [after 4th Earl of *Sandwich* (1718-92)] slices of bread with meat, cheese, etc. between them — *vt.* to place between other persons, things, etc.

sandy (san'dē) *adj.* -i·er, -i·est 1 of or like sand 2 pale reddish-yellow

sane (sān) *adj.* [L *sanus*, healthy] 1 mentally healthy; rational 2 sound; sensible —**sane'ly** *adv.*

sang (saŋ) *vi., vt. alt. pt. of* SING

sang-froid (sän frwä') *n.* [Fr, lit., cold blood] cool self-possession

san·gui·nary (saŋ'gwi ner'ē) *adj.* [see fol.] 1 accompanied by much bloodshed or murder 2 bloodthirsty

san·guine (saŋ'gwin) *adj.* [< L *sanguis*, blood] 1 of the color of blood; ruddy 2 cheerful; confident

sani·tar·ium (san'ə ter'ē əm) *n., pl.* -iums or -ia (-ə) [ModL < L *sanitas*, health] 1 a resort where people go to regain health 2 an institution for the care of invalids or convalescents

THESAURUS

salvage *v.* retrieve, recover, regain; see SAVE 1.

salvation *n.* 1 [The act of preservation] deliverance, liberation, emancipation; see RESCUE. 2 [A means of preservation] buckler, safeguard, assurance; see PROTECTION 2.

salve *n.* ointment, unguent, lubricant, balm, medicine, emollient, unction, remedy, help, cure, cream.

same *a.* 1 [Like another in state] equivalent, identical, corresponding; see ALIKE, EQUAL. 2 [Like another in action] similarly, in the same manner, likewise; see ALIKE.

same *pron.* the very same, identical object, substitute, equivalent, similar product, synthetic product.

sameness *n.* uniformity, unity, resemblance, analogy, similarity, alikeness, identity, standardization, equality, unison, no difference.

sample *n.* specimen, unit, individual; see EXAMPLE.

sample *v.* taste, test, inspect; see EXAMINE, EXPERIMENT.

sanction *n.* consent, acquiescence, assent; see PERMISSION.

sanction *v.* confirm, authorize, countenance; see APPROVE, ENDORSE 2.

sanctity *n.* sanctification, sacredness, piety; see VIRTUE 1.

sanctuary *n.* 1 [A sacred place] shrine, church, temple; see CHURCH 1. 2 [A place to which one may retire] asylum, resort, haven; see SHELTER.

sand *n.* 1 [Rock particles] sandy soil, sandy loam, silt, dust, grit, powder, gravel, rock powder, rock flour, debris, dirt; see also EARTH 2. 2 [The beach] strand, seaside, seashore; see SHORE.

sandal *n.* slipper, thong, loafer; see SHOE.

sandwich *n.* lunch, light lunch, quick lunch. *Sandwiches include the following:* hamburger, burger*, cheeseburger, wiener, hot dog*, Denver, Western, club, tuna fish, ham, chicken, roast beef, ham and egg, cheese, deviled meat, steak, submarine, bacon and cheese, toasted cheese, tomato, egg salad, lettuce, open face, peanut butter and jelly, jelly.

sandy *a.* 1 [Containing sand; *said especially of soil*] light, loose, permeable, porous, easy to work, easily worked, granular, powdery, gritty. 2 [Suggestive of sand; *said especially of the hair*] fair-haired, fair, blond, light, light-haired, reddish, carrot-red, sandy-red, sun-bleached, flaxen, faded.

sane *a.* 1 [Sound in mind] rational, normal, lucid, right-minded, sober, sound-minded, sound, in one's right mind, with a healthy mind, mentally sound, balanced, healthy-minded, reasonable, in possession of one's faculties.—*Ant.* INSANE, irrational, delirious. 2 [Sensible] reasonable, open to reason, wise; see SENSIBLE.

san·i·tary (san'ə ter'ē) *adj.* [< L *sanitas*, health] 1 of or bringing about health and healthful conditions 2 in a clean, healthy condition

sanitary napkin an absorbent pad worn by women during menstruation

san·i·ta·tion (san'ə tā'shən) *n.* 1 the science and practice of effecting hygienic conditions 2 drainage and disposal of sewage

san·i·tize (san'ə tīz') *vt.* -tized', -tiz'ing to make sanitary

san·i·ty (san'ə tē) *n.* 1 the state of being sane 2 soundness of judgment

sank (saŋk) *vi., vt. alt. pt. of* SINK

sans (sanz; *Fr* sän) *prep.* [Fr < L *sine*] without

San·skrit (san'skrit') *n.* the classical literary language of ancient India　Also **San'scrit**

Santa Claus or **Santa Klaus** (san'tə klôz') [< Du *Sant Nikolaas*, St. Nicholas] *Folklore* a fat, white-bearded, jolly old man in a red suit, who distributes gifts at Christmas

sap¹ (sap) *n.* [OE *sæp*] 1 the juice that circulates through a plant, bearing water, food, etc. 2 vigor; energy 3 [Slang] a fool —**sap'less** *adj.*

sap² (sap) *vt.* **sapped**, **sap'ping** [< Fr *sappe*, a hoe] 1 to dig beneath; undermine 2 to weaken; exhaust

sa·pi·ent (sā'pē ənt) *adj.* [< L *sapere*, to taste, know] full of knowledge; wise —**sa'pi·ence** *n.*

sap·ling (sap'liŋ) *n.* a young tree

sap·phire (saf'īr) *n.* [< Sans *śanipriya*] a precious stone of a clear, deep-blue corundum

sap·py (sap'ē) *adj.* -pi·er, -pi·est 1 full of sap; juicy 2 [Slang] foolish; silly —**sap'pi·ness** *n.*

sap·ro·phyte (sap'rə fīt') *n.* [< Gr *sapros*, rotten + *phyton*, a plant] any plant that lives on dead or decaying organic matter, as some fungi

sap'suck·er *n.* an American woodpecker that often drills holes in certain trees for the sap

Sar·a·cen (sar'ə sən) *n.* [Historical] any Arab or any Muslim, esp. at the time of the Crusades

Sarah (ser'ə) *Bible* the wife of Abraham and mother of Isaac

sa·ran (sə ran') *n.* [a coinage] a thermoplastic substance used in various fabrics, wrapping material, etc.

sar·casm (sär'kaz'əm) *n.* [< Gr *sarkazein*, to tear flesh] 1 a taunting or caustic remark, generally ironic 2 the making of such remarks

sar·cas·tic (sär kas'tik) *adj.* 1 of, like, or full of sarcasm; sneering 2 using sarcasm —**sar·cas'ti·cal·ly** *adv.*

sar·co·ma (sär kō'mə) *n., pl.* -mas or -mata (-mə tə) [< Gr *sarx*, flesh] a malignant tumor in connective tissue

sar·coph·a·gus (sär käf'ə gəs) *n., pl.* -gi (-jī') or -guses [< Gr *sarx*, flesh + *phagein*, to eat: limestone coffins hastened disintegration] a stone coffin, esp. one exposed to view, as in a tomb

sar·dine (sär dēn') *n.* [< L *sarda*, a fish] any of various small ocean fishes preserved in cans for eating

sar·don·ic (sär dän'ik) *adj.* [< Gr *sardonios*] scornfully or bitterly sarcastic —**sar·don'i·cal·ly** *adv.*

sari (sä'rē) *n.* [< Sans] an outer garment of Hindu women, a long cloth wrapped around the body

sa·rong (sə rôŋ', -räŋ') *n.* [Malay *sarung*] a garment of men and women in the East Indies, etc., consisting of a cloth worn like a skirt

sar·sa·pa·rilla (sär'sə pə ril'ə, särs'pə-, sas'pə-) *n.* [< Sp *zarza*, bramble + *parra*, vine] 1 a tropical American vine with fragrant roots 2 a carbonated drink flavored with the dried roots

sar·to·rial (sär tôr'ē əl) *adj.* [< LL *sartor*, tailor] 1 of tailors or their work 2 of men's dress —**sar·to'ri·ally** *adv.*

SASE self-addressed, stamped envelope

sash¹ (sash) *n.* [Ar *shāsh*, muslin] an ornamental band, ribbon, etc. worn over the shoulder or around the waist

sash² (sash) *n.* [< Fr *châssis*, a frame] a frame for holding the glass pane of a window or door, esp. a sliding frame

sa·shay (sa shā') *vi.* [< Fr *chassé*, a dance step] [Colloq.] 1 to walk or go, esp. casually 2 to move, walk, etc. so as to attract attention

sass (sas) *n.* [var. of SAUCE] [Colloq.] impudent talk — *vt.* [Colloq.] to talk impudently to

sas·sa·fras (sas'ə fras') *n.* [Sp *sasafras*] 1 a small tree having small, bluish fruits 2 its dried root bark used for flavoring

sassy (sas'ē) *adj.* -i·er, -i·est [var. of SAUCY] [Colloq.] impudent; saucy

sat (sat) *vi., vt. pt. & pp. of* SIT

Sat. Saturday

Sa·tan (sāt'n) [< Heb *satan*, adversary] the Devil

sa·tanic (sā tan'ik, sə-) *adj.* like Satan; wicked —**sa·tan'i·cally** *adv.*

satchel (sach'əl) *n.* [< L *saccus*, a bag] a small bag for carrying clothes, books, etc.

sate (sāt) *vt.* **sat'ed, sat'ing** [prob. < L *satiare*, fill full] 1 to satisfy (an appetite, etc.) completely 2 to satiate

sa·teen (sa tēn') *n.* [< SATIN] a cotton cloth made to imitate satin

sat·el·lite (sat'l īt') *n.* [< L *satelles*, an attendant] 1 an attendant of some important person 2 *a*) a moon revolving around a larger planet *b*) a man-made object rocketed into orbit around the earth, moon, etc. 3 a small state economically dependent on a larger one

sa·ti·ate (sā'shē āt') *vt.* -at'ed, -at'ing [< L *satis*, enough] to provide with more than enough, so as to weary or disgust; glut

sa·ti·ety (sə tī'ə tē) *n.* a being satiated

satin (sat'n) *n.* [< Ar *zaitūnī*, of *Zaitūn*, former name of a Chinese seaport] a fabric of silk, nylon, rayon, etc. with a smooth, glossy finish on one side —**sat'iny** *adj.*

sat'in·wood' *n.* 1 a smooth wood used in fine furniture 2 any of a number of trees yielding such a wood

sat·ire (sa'tīr) *n.* [< L *satira*] 1 a literary work in which vices, follies, etc. are held up to ridicule and contempt 2 the use of ridicule, sarcasm, etc. to attack vices, follies, etc. —**sa·tiri·cal** (sə tir'i kəl) or **sa·tir'ic** *adj.* —**sati·rist** (sat'ə rist) *n.*

sati·rize (sat'ə rīz') *vt.* -rized', -riz'ing to attack with satire

sat·is·fac·tion (sat'is fak'shən) *n.* 1 a satisfying or being satisfied 2 something that satisfies; specif., *a*) anything that brings pleasure or contentment *b*) settlement of debt

---

THESAURUS

sanitary *a.* hygienic, wholesome, sterile; see HEALTHFUL.

sanity *n.* sound mind, rationality, healthy mind, saneness, a clear mind, clearmindedness, wholesome outlook, common sense, intelligence, reason, reasonableness, prudence, good judgment, acumen, understanding, comprehension.

sap¹ *n.* 1 [The life fluid of a plant] fluid, secretion, essence; see LIQUID. 2 [*A dupe] dolt, gull, simpleton; see FOOL.

sapling *n.* scion, seedling, slip, sprig, young tree; see also TREE.

sappy *a.* 1 [Juicy] lush, succulent, watery; see JUICY. 2 [*Idiotic] foolish, silly, illogical; see STUPID.

sarcasm *n.* satire, irony, banter, derision, contempt, scoffing, flouting, ridicule, burlesque, disparagement, criticism, cynicism, invective, censure, lampooning, aspersion, sneering, mockery.—*Ant.* FLATTERY, fawning, cajolery.

sarcastic *a.* scornful, mocking, ironical, satirical, taunting, severe, derisive, bitter, saucy, hostile, sneering, snickering, quizzical, arrogant, disrespectful, offensive, carping, cynical, disillusioned, snarling, unbelieving, corrosive, acid, cutting, scorching, captious, sharp, pert, brusque, caustic, biting, harsh, austere, grim.

sardonic *a.* sarcastic, cynical, scornful; see SARCASTIC.

Satan *n.* Mephistopheles, Lucifer, Beelzebub; see DEVIL.

satanic *a.* malicious, vicious, devilish; see SINISTER.

satellite *n.* 1 [A small planet that revolves around a larger one] moon, planetoid, minor planet, secondary planet, inferior planet, asteroid. 2 [A man-made object put into orbit around a celestial body] space satellite, robot satellite, unmanned satellite, body satellite, orbital rocket, artificial moon, spacecraft, moonlet, man-made moon, sputnik, satellite station.

satire *n.* mockery, ridicule, caricature; see IRONY.

satisfaction *n.* 1 [The act of satisfying] gratification, fulfillment, achievement; see ACHIEVEMENT. 2 [The state or feeling of being satisfied] comfort, pleasure, well-being, content, contentment, gladness, delight, bliss, joy, happiness, relief, complacency, peace of mind, ease, heart's ease, serenity, contentedness, cheerfulness. 3 [Something that contributes to satisfaction] reward, prosperity, good fortune; see BLESSING. 4 [Reparation] reimbursement, repayment, compensation.

satisfactorily *a.* 1 [In a satisfactory manner] convincingly, suitably, competently; see ADEQUATELY. 2 [Productive of satisfactory results] amply, abundantly, thoroughly; see AGREEABLY.

sat·is·fac·tory (-tə rē) *adj.* good enough to fulfill a need, wish, etc.; satisfying —**sat·is·fac·to·ri·ly** *adv.*

sat·is·fy (sat'is fī') *vt.* **-fied', -fy·ing** [[< L *satis*, enough + *facere*, make]] **1** to fulfill the needs or desires of; content **2** to fulfill the requirements of **3** to free from doubt; convince **4** *a*) to give what is due to *b*) to discharge (a debt, etc.)

sa·tori (sä tôr'ē) *n.* [Jpn] spiritual enlightenment: term in Zen Buddhism

sa·trap (sā'trap', sa'-) *n.* [< Pers] a petty tyrant

sat·u·rate (sach'ə rāt') *vt.* **-rat·ed, -rat·ing** [< L *satur*, full]] **1** to make thoroughly soaked **2** to cause to be filled, charged, etc. with the most it can absorb —**sat'u·ra'tion** *n.*

Sat·ur·day (sat'ər dā'; *occas.*, -dē') *n.* [< OE *Sæterdæg*, Saturn's day] the seventh and last day of the week

Saturday night special [from their use in weekend crimes] [Slang] any small, cheap handgun

Sat·urn (sat'ərn) **1** the Roman god of agriculture **2** the second largest planet of the solar system with thin, icy rings of particles around its equator: see PLANET

sat·ur·nine (sat'ər nīn') *adj.* [< supposed influence of planet Saturn] sluggish, gloomy, grave, etc.

satyr (sat'ər, sāt'-) *n.* [< Gr *satyros*] **1** *Gr. Myth.* a lecherous woodland deity represented as a man with a goat's legs, ears, and horns **2** a lecherous man

saty·ri·a·sis (sat'ə rī'ə sis) *n.* [< Gr: see prec.] uncontrollable desire by a man for sexual intercourse

sauce (sôs) *n.* [< L *sal*, salt] **1** a liquid or soft mixture served with food to add flavor **2** stewed or preserved fruit **3** [Colloq.] impudence

sauce'pan' *n.* a small pot with a projecting handle, used for cooking

sau·cer (sô'sər) *n.* [see SAUCE] a small, round, shallow dish, esp. one designed to hold a cup

saucy (sô'sē) *adj.* **-cier, -ci·est** [SAUC(E) + -Y²] **1** rude; impudent **2** pert; sprightly —**sau'ci·ly** *adv.* —**sau'ci·ness** *n.*

sauer·bra·ten (sour'brät'n, zou'ər-) *n.* [Ger *sauer*, sour + *braten*, roast] beef marinated before cooking

sauer·kraut (sour'krout') *n.* [Ger *sauer*, sour + *kraut*, cabbage] chopped cabbage fermented in brine

Saul (sôl) *Bible* first king of Israel

sauna (sô'nə; *also* sou'-) *n.* [Finnish] a bath involving exposure to hot, dry air

saun·ter (sôn'tər) *vi.* [ME *santren*, to muse] to walk about idly; stroll — *n.* a leisurely walk; stroll

sau·rian (sôr'ē ən) *adj.* [< Gr *sauros*, lizard] of or like lizards

sauro·pod (sôr'ə päd') *n.* [< Gr *sauros*, lizard + -POD] a

gigantic dinosaur with a long neck and tail and a small head, as a brontosaur

sau·sage (sô'sij) *n.* [see SAUCE] pork or other meat, chopped fine, seasoned, and often stuffed into a casing

sauté (sô tā', sō-) *vt.* **-téed', -té'ing** [Fr < *sauter*, to leap] to fry quickly with a little fat

sau·ternes (sō turn') *n.* [after *Sauternes*, town in France] any of various white wines, of varying sweetness: also **sau·terne** (sō turn', -tern'; sō-)

sav·age (sav'ij) *adj.* [< L *silva*, a wood] **1** wild; uncultivated [a *savage* jungle] **2** fierce; untamed [a *savage* tiger] **3** primitive; barbarous **4** cruel; pitiless — *n.* **1** [Archaic] a member of a preliterate, often tribal, culture **2** a brutal or crude person —**sav'age·ly** *adv.* —**sav'age·ry** *n.*

sa·vanna or **sa·van·nah** (sə van'e) *n.* [Sp *sabana*] a treeless plain or a grassland with scattered trees

sa·vant (sə vänt'; *also* sav'ənt) *n.* [Fr < *savoir*, know] a learned person

save¹ (sāv) *vt.* **saved, sav'ing** [< L *salvus*, safe] **1** to rescue or preserve from harm or danger **2** to preserve for future use **3** to prevent loss or waste of [to *save* money] **4** to prevent or lessen [to *save* expense] **5** *Theol.* to deliver from sin — *vi.* **1** to avoid expense, waste, etc. **2** to store (*up*) money or goods — *n. Sports* an action that keeps an opponent from scoring or winning —**sav'able** or **save'able** *adj.* —**sav'er** *n.*

save² (sāv) *prep., conj.* [< OFr *sauf*, safe] except; but

sav·ing (sā'viŋ) *adj.* that saves; specif., *a*) economizing or economical *b*) redeeming — *n.* **1** [often pl., with sing. v.] any reduction in expense, time, etc. **2** [pl.] sums of money saved

sav·ior or **sav·iour** (sāv'yər) *n.* [< L *salvare*, to save] one who saves —**the Savior** (or **Saviour**) Jesus Christ

savoir-faire (sav'wär fer') *n.* [Fr, to know (how) to do] ready knowledge of what to do or say in any situation

sa·vor (sā'vər) *n.* [< L *sapor*] **1** a particular taste or smell **2** distinctive quality — *vi.* to have the distinctive taste, smell, or quality (*of*) — *vt.* to taste with delight Brit. sp. **savour**

sa'vory *adj.* **-i·er, -i·est** **1** pleasing to the taste or smell **2** pleasant, agreeable, etc. Brit. sp. **savoury** —**sa'vori·ness** *n.*

savvy (sav'ē) *n.* [< Port *saber*, to know] [Slang] shrewdness or understanding

saw¹ (sô) *n.* [OE *sagu*] a cutting tool consisting of a thin metal blade or disk with sharp teeth — *vt.* to cut or shape with a saw — *vi.* **1** to cut with or as with a saw **2** to be cut with a saw

saw² (sô) *n.* [OE *sagu*] a maxim

saw³ (sô) *vt., vi. pt. of* SEE¹

saw'dust' *n.* fine particles of wood formed in sawing wood

sawed'-off' *adj.* short or shortened

■ THESAURUS ■

satisfactory *a.* adequate, satisfying, pleasing; see ENOUGH.
satisfied *a.* content, happy, contented, filled, supplied, fulfilled, paid, compensated, appeased, convinced, gratified, sated, at ease, with enough of, without care, satiated.
satisfy *v.* **1** [To make content] comfort, cheer, elate, befriend, please, rejoice, delight, exhilarate, amuse, entertain, flatter, make merry, make cheerful, gladden, content, gratify, indulge, humor, conciliate, propitiate, capture, enthrall, enliven, animate, captivate, fascinate, fill, be of advantage, gorge. **2** [To pay] repay, clear up, disburse; see PAY 1, SETTLE 7. **3** [To fulfill] do, fill, serve the purpose, be enough, observe, perform, comply with, conform to, meet requirements, keep a promise, accomplish, complete, be adequate, be sufficient, provide, furnish, qualify, answer, serve, equip, meet, avail, suffice, fill the want, come up to, content one, appease one, fill the bill*, pass muster*, get by, go in a pinch*.—*Ant.* NEGLECT, leave open, fail to do.
satisfying *a.* pleasing, comforting, gratifying; see ENOUGH, PLEASANT 2.
saturate *v.* overfill, drench, steep; see IMMERSE, SOAK 1.
saturated *a.* drenched, full, soggy;

see SOAKED, WET 1.
saturation *n.* fullness, soaking, overload; see EXCESS 1.
sauce *n.* appetizer, gravy, seasoning; see FLAVORING, FOOD.
saucepan *n.* stewpan, vessel, utensil; see PAN.
saucer *n.* small bowl, sauce dish, cereal dish; see DISH.
sausage *n.* link sausage, salami, liverwurst; see MEAT.
savage *a.* **1** [Primitive] crude, simple, original; see CRUDE. **2** [Cruel] barbarous, inhuman, brutal; see CRUEL. **3** [Wild] untamed, uncivilized, uncultured; see UNCONTROLLED.
savage *n.* bully, ruffian, animal; see BEAST 2.
savagely *a.* cruelly, viciously, indecently; see BRUTALLY.
save¹ *v.* **1** [To remove from danger] deliver, extricate, rescue, free, set free, liberate, release, emancipate, ransom, redeem, come to the rescue of, defend.—*Ant.* LEAVE, desert, condemn. **2** [To assure an afterlife] rescue from sin, reclaim, regenerate; see sense 1. **3** [To hoard] collect, store, invest, have on deposit, amass, accumulate, gather, treasure up, store up, pile up, hide away, cache, stow away, sock away.—*Ant.* WASTE, spend, invest. **4** [To preserve] conserve,

keep, put up; see PRESERVE 2.
saved *a.* **1** [Kept from danger] rescued, released, delivered, protected, defended, guarded, safeguarded, preserved, reclaimed, regenerated, cured, healed, conserved, maintained, safe, secure, freed, free from harm, unthreatened, free from danger.—*Ant.* RUINED, destroyed, lost. **2** [Not spent] kept, unspent, unused, untouched, accumulated, deposited, on deposit, retained, laid away, hoarded, invested, amassed, stored, spared.—*Ant.* WASTED, squandered, spent.
savings *n.* means, property, resources, funds, reserve, investment, provision, provisions, accumulation, store, riches, harvest, hoard, savings account, cache, nest egg, money in the bank, provision for a rainy day.
savior *n.* **1** [One who saves another] deliverer, rescuer, preserver; see PROTECTOR. **2** [Christ; *usually capital*] Redeemer, Messiah, Friend and Helper; see CHRIST.
savor *v.* enjoy, relish, appreciate; see LIKE 1.
saw¹ *n.* power, circular, concave, mill, ice, crosscut, band, rip, hand, pruning, whip, buck, keyhole, back, butcher's, hack, jig; see also TOOL 1.

saw'horse' *n.* a rack on which wood is placed while being sawed

saw'mill' *n.* a factory where logs are sawed into boards

saw'-toothed' *adj.* having notches along the edge like the teeth of a saw

saw'yer (sô'yər) *n.* one whose work is sawing wood

sax (saks) *n.* [Colloq.] *short for* SAXOPHONE

Saxon (sak'sən) *n.* 1 any of an ancient Germanic people, some of whom settled in England 2 an Anglo-Saxon 3 any dialect of the Saxons

saxo·phone (sak'sə fōn') *n.* [Fr, after A. J. *Sax*, 19th-c. Belgian inventor + -PHONE] a single-reed, keyed woodwind instrument with a metal body —sax'o·phon'ist (-fōn'ist) *n.*

say (sā) *vt.* said, say'ing [OE *secgan*] 1 to utter or speak 2 to express in words; state 3 to state positively or as an opinion 4 to recite [to *say* one's prayers] 5 to estimate; assume [he is, I'd *say*, forty] — *n.* 1 a chance to speak [I had my *say*] 2 authority, as to make a final decision: often with *the* —that is to say in other words

say'ing *n.* something said; esp. an adage, proverb, or maxim

say'-so' *n.* [Colloq.] 1 (one's) word, assurance, etc. 2 right of decision

Sb [L *stibium*] *Chem. symbol for* antimony

s.c. *Printing* small capitals

SC or S.C. South Carolina

scab (skab) *n.* [< ON *skabb*] 1 a crust forming over a sore during healing 2 a worker who refuses to join a union, or who replaces a striking worker — *vi.* scabbed, scab'bing 1 to become covered with a scab 2 to work or act as a scab —scab'by, -bier, -bi·est, *adj.* —scab'bi·ness *n.*

scab·bard (skab'ərd) *n.* [< ? OHG *scar*, sword] a sheath for the blade of a sword, dagger, etc.

sca·bies (skā'bēz) *n.* [L, the itch] a contagious, itching skin disease caused by a mite that burrows under the skin to lay its eggs

scab·rous (skab'rəs, skā'brəs) *adj.* [< L *scabere*, to scratch] 1 scaly or scabby 2 indecent, shocking, etc.

scads (skadz) *n.pl.* [< ?] [Colloq.] a very large number or amount

scaf·fold (skaf'əld, -ōld') *n.* [< OFr *escafalt*] 1 a temporary framework for supporting workers during the repairing, painting, etc. of a building, etc. 2 a raised platform on which criminals are executed

scaf'fold·ing (-əl diŋ') *n.* 1 the materials forming a scaffold 2 a scaffold

scala·wag (skal'ə wag') *n.* [< ?] [Colloq.] a scamp; rascal

scald (skôld) *vt.* [< L *ex-*, intens. + *calidus*, hot] 1 to burn with hot liquid or steam 2 to heat almost to the boiling point 3 to use boiling liquid on — *n.* a burn caused by scalding

scale¹ (skāl) *n.* [< L *scala*, ladder] 1 *a*) a series of marks along a line used in measuring [the *scale* of a thermometer] *b*) any instrument so marked 2 the proportion that a map, etc. bears to the thing it represents [a *scale* of one inch to a mile] 3 *a*) a series of degrees classified by size, amount, etc. [a wage *scale*] *b*) any degree in such a series 4 *Music* a series of tones, rising or falling in pitch, according to a system of intervals — *vt.* scaled, scal'ing 1 to climb up or over 2 to make according to a scale —scale down (or up) to reduce (or increase) according to a fixed ratio

scale² (skāl) *n.* [< OFr *escale*, shell] 1 any of the thin, flat horny plates covering many fishes, reptiles, etc. 2 any thin, platelike layer or piece — *vt.* scaled, scal'ing to scrape scales from — *vi.* to flake or peel off in scales — scal'y, -i·er, -i·est, *adj.*

scale³ (skāl) *n.* [< ON *skāl*, bowl] 1 either pan of a balance 2 [*often pl.*] *a*) a balance *b*) any weighing machine — *vt.* scaled, scal'ing to weigh —turn the scales to decide or settle

scale insect any of various small insects destructive to plants: the females secrete a waxy scale

sca·lene (skā'lēn', skā lēn') *adj.* [< Gr *skalēnos*, uneven] having unequal sides [a *scalene* triangle]

scal·lion (skal'yən) *n.* [< L (*caepa*) *Ascalonia*, (onion of) Ascalon (Philistine city)] any of various onions or onion-like plants, as the shallot, green onion, or leek

scal·lop (skäl'əp, skal'-) *n.* [< OFr *escalope*] 1 *a*) any of various edible mollusks with two curved, hinged shells *b*) one of the shells 2 any of a series of curves, etc. forming an ornamental edge — *vt.* 1 to cut the edge of in scallops 2 to bake with a milk sauce and bread crumbs

scalp (skalp) *n.* [< Scand] the skin on the top and back of the head, usually covered with hair — *vt.* 1 to cut or tear the scalp from 2 [Colloq.] to buy (theater tickets, etc.) and resell them at higher prices —scalp'er *n.*

scal·pel (skal'pəl) *n.* [< L *scalprum*, a knife] a small, sharp, straight knife used in surgery, etc.

scamp (skamp) *n.* [< It *scampare*, to flee] a mischievous fellow; rascal

scam·per (skam'pər) *vi.* [see prec.] to run or go quickly — *n.* a scampering

scampi (skäm'pē, skam'-) *n., pl.* -pi or -pies [It] a large, greenish, edible prawn

scan (skan) *vt.* scanned, scan'ning [< L *scandere*, to climb] 1 to analyze (verse) by marking the metrical feet 2 to look at closely 3 to glance at quickly — *vi.* to conform to metrical principles: said of poetry — *n.* the act or an instance of scanning

Scan. or Scand. Scandinavia(n)

scan·dal (skan'dəl) *n.* [< Gr *skandalon*, a snare] 1 anything that offends moral feelings and leads to disgrace 2 shame, outrage, etc. caused by this 3 disgrace 4 malicious gossip

scan'dal·ize' *vt.* -ized', -iz'ing to outrage the moral feelings of by improper conduct —scan'dal·iz'er *n.*

scan'dal·mon'ger (-muŋ'gər, -mäŋ'-) *n.* one who spreads scandal or gossip

scan'dal·ous (-də ləs) *adj.* 1 causing scandal; shameful 2 spreading slander —scan'dal·ous·ly *adv.*

Scan·di·na·vian (skan'də nā'vē ən) *adj.* of Scandinavia, its people, languages, etc. — *n.* 1 a native or inhabitant of Scandinavia 2 the subbranch of the Germanic languages spoken by Scandinavians

scant (skant) *adj.* [< ON *skammr*, short] 1 inadequate; meager 2 not quite up to full measure

scant'y *adj.* -i·er, -i·est 1 barely sufficient 2 insufficient; not enough —scant'i·ly *adv.* —scant'i·ness *n.*

scape·goat (skāp'gōt') *n.* [< ESCAPE + GOAT; see Lev. 16:7-26] one who bears the blame for the mistakes of others — *vt., vi.* to make a scapegoat (of)

THESAURUS

say *v.* tell, speak, relate, state, announce, declare, state positively, open one's mouth, have one's say, break silence, put forth, let out, assert, maintain, express oneself, answer, respond, suppose, assume. —to say the least at a minimum, at the very least, to put it mildly, minimally.

saying *a.* mentioning, making clear, revealing; see TALKING.

saying *n.* aphorism, adage, maxim, byword, motto, proverb, precept, dictum.

scab *n.* 1 [A crust over a wound] eschar, slough, crust. 2 [One who replaces a union worker on strike] strikebreaker, traitor, apostate, deserter.

scaffold *n.* framework, stage, structure; see BUILDING, PLATFORM 1.

scald *v.* char, blanch, parboil; see BURN.

scale¹,²,³ *n.* 1 [A series for measure-ment] rule, computation, system; see MEASURE 2. 2 [A flake or film] thin coating, covering, incrustation; see FLAKE, LAYER. 3 [A device for weighing; *often plural*] steelyard, analytical balance, balance, scale beam. *Varieties of scales include the following:* beam, automatic indicating, counter, cylinder, drum, barrel, platform, spring, computing, digital, household, miner's, assayer's, truck, jeweler's. 4 [Musical tones] range, major scale, minor scale, harmonic scale, melodic scale; see also MUSIC. —on a large scale extensively, grandly, expansively; see GENEROUSLY. —on a small scale economically, in a small limited way, with restrictions; see INADEQUATE, UNIMPORTANT.

scale¹,²,³ *v.* 1 [To climb] ascend, surmount, mount; see CLIMB. 2 [To peel] exfoliate, strip off, flake; see PEEL, SKIN. 3 [To measure] compare, balance, compute; see COMPARE 1.

scalpel *n.* dissecting instrument, surgical tool, blade; see KNIFE.

scamper *v.* hasten, speed, haste; see HURRY 1, RUN 2.

scan *v.* browse, thumb over, consider; see LOOK 2.

scandal *n.* shame, disgrace, infamy, discredit, slander, disrepute, detraction, defamation, opprobrium, reproach, aspersion, backbiting, gossip, eavesdropping, rumor, hearsay. —*Ant.* PRAISE, adulation, flattery.

scandalize *v.* detract, defame, backbite; see SLANDER.

scandalous *a.* infamous, disreputable, ignominious; see SHAMEFUL 2.

scanty *a.* scarce, few, pinched, meager, little, small, bare, ragged, insufficient, inadequate, slender, narrow, thin, scrimp, scrimpy, tiny, wee, sparse, diminutive, short, stingy.— *Ant.* MUCH, large, many.

scape·grace (skāp′grās′) *n.* [< ESCAPE + GRACE] a graceless, rogue; scamp

scapu·la (skap′yə lə) *n., pl.* **-lae** (-lē′) or **-las** [< L] the shoulder blade

scar (skär) *n.* [< Gr *eschara*, orig., fireplace] a mark left after a wound, burn, etc. has healed — *vt.* **scarred, scar′ring** to mark as with a scar — *vi.* to form a scar in healing

scarab (skar′əb) *n.* [< L *scarabaeus*] 1 a large, black beetle 2 a carved image of such a beetle

scarce (skers) *adj.* [ult. < L *excerpere*, pick out] 1 not common; rarely seen 2 not plentiful; hard to get —**make oneself scarce** [Colloq.] to go or stay away —**scarce′ness** *n.*

scarce′ly *adv.* 1 hardly; only just 2 probably not or certainly not

scar·city (sker′sə tē) *n., pl.* **-ties** 1 a being scarce; inadequate supply; dearth 2 rarity; uncommonness

scare (sker) *vt.* **scared, scar′ing** [< ON *skjarr*, timid] to fill with sudden fear — *vi.* to become frightened — *n.* a sudden fear —**scare away** (or **off**) to drive away (or off) by frightening —**scare up** [Colloq.] to produce or gather quickly

scare′crow (sker′krō′) *n.* a human figure made with sticks, old clothes, etc., put in a field to scare birds from crops

scarf (skärf) *n., pl.* **scarves** (skärvz) or **scarfs** [< OFr *escharpe*, purse hung from the neck] 1 a piece of cloth worn about the neck, head, etc. 2 a long, narrow covering for a table, etc.

scari·fy (skar′ə fī′) *vt.* **-fied′, -fy′ing** [< L *scarifare*] to make small cuts in (the skin, etc.) —**scar′i·fi·ca′tion** *n.*

scar·let (skär′lit) *n.* [< ML *scarlatum*] very bright red — *adj.* 1 of this color 2 sinful; specif., whorish

scarlet fever an acute contagious disease characterized by sore throat, fever, and a scarlet rash

scary (sker′ē) *adj.* **-i·er, -i·est** [Colloq.] 1 frightening 2 easily frightened —**scar′i·ness** *n.*

scat¹ (skat) *vi.* **scat′ted, scat′ting** [? short for SCATTER] [Colloq.] to go away: usually in the imperative

scat² (skat) *adj.* [< ?] *Jazz* using improvised, meaningless syllables in singing — *n.* such singing — *vi.* **scat′ted, scat′ting** to sing scat

scath·ing (skā′thiŋ) *adj.* [< ON *skathi*, harm] harsh or caustic *[scathing remarks]* —**scath′ingly** *adv.*

sca·tol·ogy (skə täl′ə jē) *n.* [< Gr *skōr*, excrement] obsession with excrement or excretion, as in literature —**scato·log·i·cal** (skat′ə läj′i kəl) *adj.*

scat·ter (skat′ər) *vt.* [ME *skateren*] 1 to throw here and there; sprinkle 2 to separate and drive in many directions; disperse — *vi.* to separate and go off in several directions

scat′ter·brain′ *n.* one who is incapable of concentrated thinking

scatter rug a small rug

scav·enger (skav′in jər) *n.* [< NormFr *escauwer*, to inspect] 1 one who gathers things discarded by others 2 any animal that eats refuse and decaying matter —**scav′enge** (-inj), **-enged, -eng·ing**, *vt., vi.*

sce·nario (sə ner′ē ō′; -när′-) *n., pl.* **-ios′** [see fol.] 1 *a)* an outline of a play, etc. *b)* the script of a film 2 an outline for any planned series of events, real or imagined —**sce·nar′ist** *n.*

scene (sēn) *n.* [< Gr *skēnē*, stage] 1 the place where an event occurs 2 the setting of a play, story, etc. 3 a division of a play, usually part of an act 4 *a)* a unit of action in a play, film, etc. *b)* a section of film having a number of shots 5 SCENERY (sense 1) 6 a display of strong feeling *[to make a scene]* 7 [Colloq.] the locale for a specified activity

scen·ery (sēn′ər ē) *n., pl.* **-ies** 1 painted screens, backdrops, etc., used on the stage to represent places, as in a play, etc. 2 the features of a landscape

sce·nic (sēn′ik) *adj.* 1 of stage scenery 2 *a)* of natural scenery *b)* having beautiful scenery —**sce′ni·cally** *adv.*

scent (sent) *vt.* [ult. < L *sentire*, to feel] 1 to smell 2 to get a hint of 3 to fill with an odor; perfume — *n.* 1 an odor 2 the sense of smell 3 a perfume 4 an odor left by an animal, by which it is tracked —**scent′ed** *adj.*

scep·ter (sep′tər) *n.* [< Gr *skēptron*, staff] a staff held by a ruler as a symbol of sovereignty Chiefly Brit. sp. **scep·tre**

scep·tic (skep′tik) *n., adj. chiefly Brit. sp.* of SKEPTIC —**scep′ti·cal** *adj.* —**scep′ti·cism** *n.*

sched·ule (ske′jool; *Brit & often Cdn* shed′yool) *n.* [< L *scheda*, a strip of papyrus] 1 a list of details 2 a list of times of recurring events, projected operations, etc.; timetable 3 a timed plan for a project — *vt.* **-uled, -ul·ing** 1 to place in a schedule 2 to plan for a certain time

sche·matic (skē mat′ik) *adj.* of, or like a scheme, diagram, etc.

scheme (skēm) *n.* [< Gr *schēma*, a form] 1 *a)* a systematic program for attaining some object *b)* a secret plan; plot 2 an orderly combination of things on a definite plan 3 a diagram — *vt.* **schemed, schem′ing** to devise or plot —**schem′er** *n.*

scherzo (sker′tsō) *n., pl.* **-zos** or **-zi** (-tsē) [It, a jest] *Music* a lively composition, usually in ¾ time, as the third movement of a symphony, etc.

schism (siz′əm) *n.* [< Gr *schizein*, to cleave] a split, as in a church, because of difference of opinion, doctrine, etc. —**schis·mat′ic** (-mat′ik) *adj.*

schist (shist) *n.* [< Gr *schistos*, easily cleft] a crystalline rock easily split into layers

schizo·phre·nia (skit′sə frē′nē ə, skiz′ə-) *n.* [< Gr *schizein*, cleave + *phrēn*, the mind] a mental disorder characterized by separation between thought and emotions, by delusions, bizarre behavior, etc. —**schiz′oid** (-soid) or **schiz′o·phren′ic** (-fren′ik) *adj., n.*

schle·miel (shlə mēl′) *n.* [Yidd] [Slang] a bungling person who habitually fails or is easily victimized

schlep or **schlepp** (shlep) *vt.* **schlepped, schlep′ping** [via Yidd < LowG *slepen*, to drag] [Slang] to carry, haul, etc. — *vi.* [Slang] to go or move with effort — *n.* [Slang] an ineffectual person

schlock (shläk) *n.* [< ? Ger *schlacke*, dregs] [Slang] anything cheap or inferior; trash — *adj.* [Slang] cheap; inferior: also **schlock′y, -i·er, -i·est**

schmaltz (shmälts, shmōlts) *n.* [? via Yidd < Ger *schmaltz*, rendered fat] [Slang] highly sentimental music, literature, etc. —**schmaltz′y, -i·er, -i·est**, *adj.*

THESAURUS

scar *n.* cicatrix, cicatrice, cat-face, mark, blemish, discoloration, disfigurement, defect, flaw, hurt, wound, injury.

scar *v.* cut, pinch, slash; see HURT 1.

scarce *a.* limited, infrequent, not plentiful; see RARE 2, UNCOMMON. —**make oneself scarce*** go, depart, run off; see LEAVE 1.

scarcely *a.* barely, only just, scantily; see HARDLY.

scarcity *n.* deficiency, inadequacy, insufficiency; see LACK 2, POVERTY 1.

scare *n.* fright, terror, alarm; see FEAR.

scare *v.* panic, terrify, alarm; see FRIGHTEN. —**scare off** (or **away**) drive off, drive out, drive away, get rid of, dispose of; see also FRIGHTEN.

scared *a.* startled, frightened, fearful; see AFRAID.

scarf *n.* throw, sash, muffler, shawl, comforter, ascot, stole, wrapper; see also CLOTHES.

scarlet *a.* cardinal, royal red, vermilion; see RED.

scat¹ *v.* be off, begone, out of the way, get out of my way, get out from under my feet, out with you, be off with you, get out of my sight, scoot*, get out, beat it*, get going.

scatter *v.* 1 [To become separated] run apart, run away, go one's own way, diverge, disperse, disband, migrate, spread widely, go in different directions, blow off, go in many directions, be strewn to the four winds.—*Ant.* ASSEMBLE, convene, congregate. 2 [To cause to separate] dispel, dissipate, diffuse, strew, divide, disband, shed, distribute, disseminate, separate, disunite, sunder, scatter to the wind, sever, set asunder.—*Ant.* UNITE, join, mix. 3 [To waste] expend, dissipate, fritter away; see SPEND, WASTE 2.

scattered *a.* spread, strewed, rambling, sowed, sown, sprinkled, spread abroad, separated, disseminated, dispersed, strung out, distributed, widespread, diffuse, all over the place, separate, shaken out.—*Ant.* GATH-ERED, condensed, concentrated.

scene *n.* spectacle, exhibition, display; see VIEW.

scenery *n.* landscape, prospect, spectacle; see VIEW.

scenic *a.* beautiful, spectacular, dramatic; see BEAUTIFUL.

scent *n.* odor, fragrance, redolence; see PERFUME, SMELL 1, 2.

schedule *n.* 1 [List] catalogue, inventory, registry; see LIST, RECORD 1. 2 [Program] agenda, order of business, calendar; see PLAN 2, PROGRAM 2. —**on** (or **up to**) **schedule** on time, not lagging behind, being pushed along; see ACCEPTED, EARLY 2, ENOUGH.

schedule *v.* record, register, catalogue; see LIST 1.

scheduled *a.* listed, announced, arranged; see PLANNED, PROPOSED.

scheme *n.* project, course of action, purpose; see PLAN 2, SYSTEM.

scheme *v.* intrigue, contrive, devise; see PLAN 1.

schmo (shmō) *n., pl.* **schmoes** or **schmos** ⟦< Yidd⟧ [Slang] a foolish or stupid person Also sp. **schmoe**

schnapps (shnäps) *n., pl.* **schnapps** ⟦Ger, a nip < Du *snaps*, a gulp⟧ a strong alcoholic liquor Also sp. **schnaps**

schnau·zer (shnou′zər) *n.* ⟦Ger < *schnauzen*, to snarl⟧ a small dog with a wiry coat and bushy eyebrows

schnoz·zle (shnäz′əl) *n.* ⟦via Yidd < Ger *schnauze*⟧ [Slang] the nose Also **schnoz**

scholar (skäl′ər) *n.* ⟦< L *schola*, a school⟧ 1 a learned person 2 a student or pupil —**schol′ar·ly** *adj.*

schol′ar·ship′ *n.* 1 the quality of knowledge a student shows 2 the systematized knowledge of a scholar 3 a gift of money, etc. as by a foundation, to help a student

scho·las·tic (skə las′tik) *adj.* [see fol.] of schools, colleges, students, etc.; educational; academic —**scho·las′ti·cally** *adv.*

school[1] (skool) *n.* ⟦< Gr *scholē*⟧ 1 a place or institution, with its buildings, etc., for teaching and learning 2 all of its students and teachers 3 a regular session of teaching 4 formal education; schooling 5 a particular division of a university 6 a group following the same beliefs, methods, etc. — *vt.* 1 to train; teach 2 to discipline or control — *adj.* of a school or schools

school[2] (skool) *n.* ⟦Du, a crowd⟧ a group of fish, etc. swimming together

school board an elected or appointed group of people in charge of public or private schools

school′book′ *n.* a textbook

school′boy′ *n.* a boy attending school —**school′girl′** *n.fem.*

school′house′ *n.* a building used as a school

school′ing *n.* training or education; esp., formal instruction at school

school′marm′ (-′märm′, -mäm′) *n.* 1 [Old-fashioned] a woman schoolteacher 2 [Colloq.] any person who tends to be prudish, pedantic, etc.

school′mas′ter *n.* [Old-fashioned] a man who teaches in a school

school′mate′ *n.* a companion or acquaintance at school

school′mis′tress *n.* [Old-fashioned] a woman schoolteacher

school′room′ *n.* a room in which pupils are taught, as in a school

school′teach′er *n.* one who teaches in a school

school′yard′ *n.* the ground around a school, used as a playground, etc.

school year the part of a year when school is in session

schooner (skoon′ər) *n.* 1 a ship with two or more masts, rigged fore and aft 2 a large beer glass

schuss (shoos) *n.* ⟦Ger, lit., shot⟧ a straight run down a hill in skiing — *vi.* to do a schuss

schuss′boom′er (-boom′ər) *n.* a skier, esp. one who schusses expertly

schwa (shwä) *n.* ⟦Ger < Heb *sheva*⟧ 1 the neutral vowel sound of most unstressed syllables in English, as of *a* in *ago* 2 the symbol (ə) for this

sci·atic (sī at′ik) *adj.* [see fol.] of or in the hip or its nerves

sci·at·i·ca (sī at′i kə) *n.* ⟦< Gr *ischion*, the hip⟧ any painful condition in the hip or thigh; esp., neuritis of the long nerve (**sciatic nerve**) passing down the back of the thigh

sci·ence (sī′əns) *n.* ⟦< L *scire*, to know⟧ 1 systematized knowledge derived from observation, study, etc. 2 a branch of knowledge, esp. one that systematizes facts, principles, and methods 3 skill or technique

science fiction highly imaginative fiction typically involving some actual or projected scientific phenomenon

sci·en·tif·ic (sī′ən tif′ik) *adj.* 1 of or dealing with science 2 based on, or using, the principles and methods of science; systematic and exact —**sci·en·tif′i·cally** *adv.*

sci′en·tist *n.* a specialist in science, as in biology, chemistry, etc.

sci-fi (sī′fī′) *adj., n.* [Colloq.] *short for* SCIENCE FICTION

scimi·tar (sim′ə tər) *n.* ⟦It *scimitarra*⟧ a short, curved sword used chiefly by Turks and Arabs

scin·tilla (sin til′ə) *n.* ⟦L⟧ 1 a spark 2 a particle; the least trace

scin·til·late (sint′'l āt′) *vi.* **-lat·ed, -lat′ing** ⟦< L *scintilla*, a spark⟧ 1 to sparkle or twinkle 2 to be brilliant and witty —**scin·til·la′tion** *n.*

scion (sī′ən) *n.* ⟦< OFr *cion*⟧ 1 a shoot or bud of a plant, esp. one for grafting 2 a descendant; heir

scis·sor (siz′ər) *vt.* ⟦< fol.⟧ to cut, cut off, or cut out with scissors — *n.* SCISSORS, esp. in adjectival use

scis·sors (siz′ərz) *n.pl.* ⟦< LL *cisorium*, cutting tool⟧ [*also with sing. v.*] a cutting instrument with two opposing blades pivoted together so that they can work against each other: also called **pair of scissors**

sclera (sklir′ə) *n., pl.* **-ras** or **-rae** ⟦< Gr *sklēros*, hard⟧ the tough, white, membrane covering all of the eyeball except the area covered by the cornea

scle·ro·sis (skli rō′sis) *n., pl.* **-ses** (-sēz′) ⟦< Gr *sklēros*, hard⟧ an abnormal hardening of body tissues —**scle·rot′ic** (-rät′ik) *adj.*

scoff (skäf, sköf) *n.* [prob. < Scand] an expression of scorn or derision — *vt., vi.* to mock or jeer (at) —**scoff′er** *n.*

scoff′law′ *n.* [Colloq.] one who flouts traffic laws, liquor laws, etc.

scold (sköld) *n.* ⟦< ON *skald*, poet (prob. of satirical verses)⟧ a woman who habitually uses abusive language —

THESAURUS

scholar *n.* schoolboy, schoolgirl, learner; see STUDENT.

scholarly *a.* erudite, cultured, studious; see EDUCATED, LEARNED 1.

scholarship *n.* scientific approach, learning, intellectualism; see KNOWLEDGE 1.

scholastic *a.* academic, literary, lettered; see LEARNED 1.

school[1] *n.* 1 [An institution of learning] *Varieties of schools include the following:* nursery school, elementary school, high school, secondary school, parochial school, preparatory school, private school, prep school, public school, boarding school, military school, seminary, normal school, conservatory, trade school, technical school, graduate school, professional school, divinity school, art school, law school, college of arts and science, junior high school, middle school, senior high school, community college, junior college, the grades; see also COLLEGE, UNIVERSITY. 2 [Persons or products associated by common intellectual or artistic theories] party, following, circle; see FOLLOWING. 3 [A building housing a school] schoolhouse, establishment, institution; see BUILDING. —**attend school** undergo schooling, learn, go to school, be educated, receive instruction, matriculate, study, take courses, be a student, enroll; see also REGISTER 4, STUDY. —**go to school** attend school, attend college, matriculate; see LEARN, REGISTER.

school-age *a.* youthful, old enough to go to school, of school age; see CHILDISH, YOUNG 1.

schoolbook *n.* primer, textbook, assigned reading; see BOOK.

schooling *n.* teaching, nurture, discipline; see EDUCATION 1.

schoolmate *n.* roommate, comrade, classmate; see FRIEND.

schoolteacher *n.* educator, lecturer, instructor; see TEACHER.

school year *n.* nine months, from September to June, period school is in session; see YEAR.

science *n.* 1 [An organized body of knowledge] classified information, department of learning, branch of knowledge, system of knowledge, body of fact; see also CHEMISTRY, MATHEMATICS, MEDICINE 3, SOCIAL SCIENCE, ZOOLOGY for commonly recognized sciences. 2 [A highly developed skill] craftsmanship, art, deftness; see ABILITY.

scientific *a.* 1 [Objectively accurate] precise, exact, clear; see ACCURATE 2, OBJECTIVE 1. 2 [Concerning science] experimental, deductive, methodically sound; see LOGICAL.

scientist *n.* expert, specialist, investigator, laboratory technician, natural philosopher, student of natural history, student of natural phenomena, explorer, research worker, research assistant, learned man, serious student, PhD, scientific thinker. *Scientists include the following:* anatomist, astronomer, botanist, biologist, chemist, biochemist, geologist, geographer, mathematician, physicist, psychiatrist, psychologist, astrophysicist, ecologist, biophysicist, bacteriologist, marine botanist, oceanographer, pharmacist, chemical engineer, sanitary engineer, agronomist, entomologist, ornithologist, endocrinologist, radiologist, graphologist, geophysicist, neurologist, neurophysicist, paleontologist, mineralogist, metallurgist, anthropologist, ethnologist, archaeologist, sociologist, linguist; see also DOCTOR.

scissors *n.* shears, pair of scissors, blades, hair scissors, paper scissors, garden shears, cutting instrument.

scoff *v.* mock, deride, jeer; see RIDICULE.

scold *v.* admonish, chide, chew out*, bawl out*, get after, lay down the law, jump on, jump all over, rebuke, censure, reprove, upbraid, reprimand, taunt, cavil, criticize, denounce, disparage, recriminate, rate, revile, rail, abuse, villify, find fault with, nag, lecture, have on the *vt.* to find fault with angrily; to rebuke — *vi.* **1** to find fault angrily **2** to use abusive language habitually —**scold′ing** *adj., n.*

sco·li·o·sis (skō′lē ō′sis) *n.* 〚< Gr *skolios*, crooked〛 lateral curvature of the spine

sconce (skäns) *n.* 〚ult. < L *absconcus*, hidden〛 a wall bracket for candles

scone (skōn, skän) *n.* 〚Scot〛 a light cake, often quadrant-shaped and like a biscuit

scoop (skōōp) *n.* 〚< MDu *schope*, bailing vessel, *schoppe*, a shovel〛 **1** any of various small, shovel-like utensils, as for taking up flour, ice cream, etc. **2** the deep shovel of a dredge, etc. **3** the act or motion of scooping **4** the amount scooped up at one time **5** [Colloq.] *a*) advantage gained by being first, as in publishing a news item *b*) such a news item — *vt.* **1** to take up or out as with a scoop **2** to hollow (*out*) **3** [Colloq.] to publish news before (a competitor)

scoot (skōōt) *vi., vt.* 〚prob. < ON *skjōta*, to shoot〛 [Colloq.] to hurry (off)

scoot′er *n.* 〚< prec.〛 **1** a child's two-wheeled vehicle moved by pushing one foot against the ground **2** a similar vehicle propelled by a motor: in full **motor scooter**

scope (skōp) *n.* 〚< Gr *skopos*, watcher〛 **1** the extent of the mind's grasp **2** the range or extent of action, inclusion, inquiry, etc. **3** room or opportunity for freedom of action or thought

-scope (skōp) 〚< Gr *skopein* to see〛 *combining form* an instrument, etc. for seeing or observing *[telescope, kaleidoscope]*

scor·bu·tic (skôr byōōt′ik) *adj.* 〚ModL < Russ *skrobotŭ*, wither〛 of, like, or having scurvy

scorch (skôrch) *vt.* 〚< ? Scand〛 **1** to burn slightly or superficially **2** to parch by intense heat — *vi.* to become scorched — *n.* a superficial burn

score (skôr) *n.* 〚< ON *skor*〛 **1** a scratch, mark, notch, incision, etc. **2** an account or debt **3** a grievance one seeks to settle **4** a reason or motive **5** the number of points made, as in a game **6** a grade, as on a test **7** *a*) twenty people or things *b*) [*pl.*] very many **8** a copy of a musical composition showing all parts for the instruments or voices **9** [Colloq.] the basic facts *[to know the score]* — *vt.* **scored, scor′ing** **1** to mark with notches, cuts, lines, etc. **2** *a*) to make (runs, points, etc.) in a game *b*) to record the score of **3** to achieve *[score a success]* **4** to evaluate, as in testing **5** *Music* to arrange in a score — *vi.* **1** to make points, as in a game **2** to keep the score of a game **3** to gain an advantage, a success, etc. —**scor′er** *n.*

score′board′ *n.* a large board posting scores, etc., as in a stadium

score′less *adj.* having scored no points

scorn (skôrn) *n.* 〚< OFr *escharnir*, to scorn〛 extreme, often indignant, contempt — *vt.* **1** to regard with scorn **2** to refuse or reject with scorn —**scorn′ful** *adj.* —**scorn′fully** *adv.*

Scor·pi·o (skôr′pē ō′) 〚L, scorpion〛 the eighth sign of the zodiac

scor·pion (-ən) *n.* 〚< Gr *skorpios*〛 an arachnid with a long tail ending in a poisonous sting

Scot (skät) *n.* a native or inhabitant of Scotland

Scot. **1** Scotland **2** Scottish

scotch (skäch) *vt.* 〚prob. < OFr *coche*, a nick〛 **1** to maim **2** to put an end to; stifle *[to scotch a rumor]*

Scotch (skäch) *adj.* of Scotland: cf. SCOTTISH — *n.* **1**

Scottish **2** [*often* **s**-] whiskey distilled in Scotland from malted barley: in full **Scotch whisky**

Scotch grain a coarse, pebble-grained finish given to heavy leather

Scotch′man (-mən) *n., pl.* **-men** *var. of* SCOTSMAN

Scotch tape 〚< *Scotch*, a trademark〛 a thin, transparent adhesive tape

scot-free (skät′frē′) *adj.* 〚< earlier *scot*, a tax〛 unharmed or unpunished

Scotland Yard the London police headquarters, esp. its detective bureau

Scots (skäts) *adj., n.* SCOTTISH

Scots′man (-mən) *n., pl.* **-men** a native or inhabitant of Scotland, esp. a man: *Scotsman* or *Scot* is preferred to *Scotchman* in Scotland —**Scots′wom′an,** *pl.* **-wom′en,** *n.fem.*

Scot·tie or **Scotty** (skät′ē) *n., pl.* **-ties** *short for* SCOTTISH TERRIER

Scot·tish (skät′ish) *adj.* of Scotland, its people, their English dialect, etc.: *Scottish* is formal usage, but with some words, *Scotch* is used (e.g., tweed, whisky), with others, *Scots* (e.g. law) — *n.* the English spoken in Scotland —**the Scottish** the Scottish people

Scottish terrier a short-legged terrier with a wiry coat

scoun·drel (skoun′drəl) *n.* 〚prob. ult. < L *ab*(*s*)-, from + *condere*, to hide〛 a mean, immoral, or wicked person

scour[1] (skour) *vt., vi.* 〚< ? L *ex-*, intens. + *cura*, care〛 **1** to clean by rubbing hard, as with abrasives **2** to clean or clear out as by a flow of water

scour[2] (skour) *vt.* 〚< L *ex-*, out + *currere*, to run〛 to pass over quickly, or range over, as in search *[to scour a library for a book]*

scourge (skurj) *n.* 〚< L *ex*, off + *corrigia*, a whip〛 **1** a whip **2** any cause of serious affliction — *vt.* **scourged, scourg′ing** **1** to whip or flog **2** to punish or afflict severely

scout (skout) *n.* 〚< L *auscultare*, to listen〛 **1** a person, plane, etc. sent to spy out the enemy's strength, actions, etc. **2** a person sent out to survey a competitor, find new talent, etc. **3** [S-] a Boy Scout or Girl Scout — *vt., vi.* **1** to reconnoiter **2** to go in search of (something)

scout′ing *n.* **1** the act of one who scouts **2** [*often* S-] the activities of the Boy Scouts or Girl Scouts

scout′mas′ter *n.* the adult leader of a troop of Boy Scouts

scow (skou) *n.* 〚Du *schouw*〛 a large, flat-bottomed boat used for carrying loads, often towed by a tug

scowl (skoul) *vi.* 〚prob. < Scand〛 to look angry, sullen, etc., as by contracting the eyebrows — *n.* a scowling look —**scowl′er** *n.*

scrab·ble (skrab′əl) *vi.* **-bled, -bling** 〚< Du *schrabben*, to scrape〛 **1** to scratch, scrape, etc. as though looking for something **2** to struggle

scrag·gly (skrag′lē) *adj.* **-glier, -gli·est** 〚prob. < ON〛 uneven, ragged, etc. in growth or form

scram (skram) *vi.* **scrammed, scram′ming** 〚< fol.〛 [Slang] to get out

scram·ble (skram′bəl) *vi.* **-bled, -bling** 〚< ?〛 **1** to climb, crawl, etc. hurriedly **2** to scuffle or struggle for something — *vt.* **1** to mix haphazardly **2** to stir and cook (slightly beaten eggs) **3** to make (transmitted signals) unintelligible without special receiving equipment — *n.* **1** a hard climb or advance **2** a disorderly struggle, as for something prized

scrap[1] (skrap) *n.* 〚< ON *skrap*〛 **1** a small piece; fragment **2** discarded material **3** [*pl.*] bits of food — *adj.* **1** in the form of pieces, leftovers, etc. **2** used and discarded — *vt.*

THESAURUS

carpet, rake over the coals*, give one a talking to, chasten, preach, tell off*, keep after, light into*, put down; see also PUNISH.—*Ant.* PRAISE, commend, extoll.

scoop *v.* ladle, shovel, bail; see DIP 2.

scoot *v.* dart, speed, rush; see HASTEN 2, HURRY 1.

scope *n.* reach, range, field; see EXTENT.

scorch *v.* roast, parch, shrivel; see BURN.

scorching *a.* fiery, searing, sweltering; see BURNING, HOT 1.

score *n.* **1** [A tally] stock, reckoning, record, average, rate, account, count, number, summation, aggregate, sum, addition, summary, amount, final tally, final account; see also NUMBER, WHOLE. **2** [Written music] transcription, arrangement, orchestration; see

MUSIC 1, COMPOSITION. —**know the score*** grasp, be aware of, comprehend; see KNOW 1, UNDERSTAND 1.

score *v.* **1** [To make a single score] make a goal, a point, rack up*, chalk up, total, calculate, reckon, tally, enumerate, count, add. **2** [To compose a musical accompaniment] orchestrate, arrange, adapt; see COMPOSE 2. **3** [*To purchase legally or illegally] get, procure, secure; see BUY. **4** [*To copulate] have sexual intercourse, sleep with, fornicate; see COPULATE.

scorn *v.* hold in contempt, despise, disdain; see HATE.

scornful *a.* contemptuous, disdainful, haughty; see EGOTISTIC.

scoundrel *n.* rogue, scamp, villain; see RASCAL.

scour[1] *v.* scrub, cleanse, rub; see

CLEAN, WASH 1, 2.

scout *n.* **1** [One who gathers information] explorer, pioneer, outpost, runner, advance guard, precursor, patrol, reconnoiterer. **2** [A Boy Scout or Girl Scout] *Degrees of scouts include the following:* Cub, Tenderfoot, Second Class, First Class, Star, Life, Eagle, Queen's (British), bronze palm, gold palm, silver palm; Brownie, Junior, Cadette, Senior.

scowl *v.* glower, disapprove, grimace; see FROWN.

scramble *v.* **1** [To mix] combine, blend, interfuse; see MIX 1. **2** [To climb hastily] clamber, push, struggle; see CLIMB.

scrap[1,2] *n.* **1** [Junk metal] waste material, chips, cuttings; see TRASH 1. **2** [A bit] fragment, particle, portion;

scrapped, scrap′ping 1 to make into scrap **2** to discard; junk —**scrap′per** *n.*
scrap[2] (skrap) *n., vi.* **scrapped, scrap′ping** [< ? SCRAPE] [Colloq.] fight or quarrel —**scrap′per** *n.* —**scrap′py, -pier, -pi·est,** *adv.*
scrap′book′ *n.* a book in which to mount clippings, pictures, etc.
scrape (skrāp) *vt.* **scraped, scrap′ing** [< ON *skrapa*] **1** to make smooth or clean by rubbing with a tool or abrasive **2** to remove in this way: with *off, out,* etc. **3** to scratch or abrade **4** to gather slowly and with difficulty *[to scrape* up some money*]* — *vi.* **1** to rub against something harshly; grate **2** to manage to get by: with *through, along, by* — *n.* **1** a scraping **2** a scraped place **3** a harsh, grating sound **4** a predicament —**scrap′er** *n.*
scrap′heap′ (-hēp′) *n.* a pile of discarded material, as of scrap iron —**throw** (or **toss, cast,** etc.) **on the scrap-heap** to get rid of as useless
scratch (skrach) *vt.* [ME *scracchen*] **1** to scrape or cut the surface of slightly **2** to tear or dig with the nails or claws **3** to scrape lightly to relieve itching **4** to scrape with a grating noise **5** to write hurriedly or carelessly **6** to strike out (writing, etc.) **7** *Sports* to withdraw (a contestant, etc.) — *vi.* **1** to use nails or claws in digging, wounding, etc. **2** to scrape — *n.* **1** a scratching **2** a mark, tear, etc. made by scratching **3** a grating or scraping sound — *adj.* used for hasty notes, figuring etc. *[scratch paper]* — **from scratch** from nothing; without advantage, etc. —**up to scratch** [Colloq.] up to standard —**scratch′y, -i·er, -i·est,** *adj.* —**scratch′i·ly** *adv.* —**scratch′i·ness** *n.*
scrawl (skrôl) *vt., vi.* [< ?] to write or draw hastily, carelessly, etc. — *n.* scrawled, often illegible handwriting —**scrawl′y** *adj.*
scrawny (skrô′nē) *adj.* **-nier, -ni·est** [prob. < Scand] very thin; skinny —**scraw′ni·ness** *n.*
scream (skrēm) *vi.* [ME *screamen*] **1** to utter a shrill, piercing cry in fright, pain, etc. **2** to shout, laugh, etc. wildly — *vt.* to utter as with a scream — *n.* **1** a sharp, piercing cry or sound **2** [Colloq.] a very funny person or thing
screech (skrēch) *vi., vt.* [< ON *skraekja*] to utter with a shrill, high-pitched sound — *n.* such a sound —**screech′y, -i·er, -i·est,** *adj.*
screen (skrēn) *n.* [< OFr *escren*] **1** a curtain or partition used to separate, conceal, etc. **2** anything that shields, conceals, etc. *[a smoke screen]* **3** a coarse mesh of wire, etc., used as a sieve **4** a frame covered with a mesh *[a window screen]* **5** *a)* a surface on which films, slides, etc. are projected *b)* the film industry *c)* the surface area of a TV set, etc. on which images are formed — *vt.* **1** to conceal or protect, as with a screen **2** to sift through a screen **3** to separate according to skills, etc. **4** to show (a film, etc.) to critics, the public, etc.
screen′play′ *n.* the script from which a film is produced
screen′writ′er *n.* the writer of a script for a film —**screen′writ′ing** *n.*
screw (skrōō) *n.* [< Fr *escroue*, hole in which the screw turns] **1** a cylindrical or conical piece of metal threaded in an advancing spiral, for fastening things by being turned **2** any spiral thing like this **3** anything operating or threaded like a screw, as a screw propeller — *vt.* **1** to twist; turn **2** to fasten, tighten, etc. as with a screw **3** to

contort — *vi.* **1** to go together or come apart by being turned like a screw *[the lid screws on]* **2** to twist or turn —**put the screws on** (or **to**) to subject to great pressure —**screw up** [Slang] to bungle
screw′ball′ *n.* [Slang] an erratic, irrational or unconventional person
screw′driv′er *n.* a tool used for turning screws
screw·worm (skrōō′wurm′) *n.* the larva of an American blowfly that infests wounds, and the nostrils, navel, etc. of animals
screwy (skrōō′ē) *adj.* **-i·er, -i·est** [Slang] **1** crazy **2** peculiar, eccentric
scrib·ble (skrib′əl) *vt., vi.* **-bled, -bling** [< L *scribere*, write] **1** to write carelessly, hastily, etc. **2** to make meaningless or illegible marks (on) — *n.* scribbled writing
scribe (skrīb) *n.* [< L *scribere*, to write] **1** one who copied manuscripts before the invention of printing **2** a writer
scrim (skrim) *n.* [< ?] **1** a light, sheer, loosely woven cotton or linen cloth **2** such a cloth used as a stage backdrop or semitransparent curtain
scrim·mage (skrim′ij) *n.* [< SKIRMISH] **1** *Football* the play that follows the snap from center **2** a practice game — *vi.* **-maged, -mag·ing** to take part in a scrimmage
scrimp (skrimp) *vt., vi.* [< ? Scand] to be sparing or frugal (with)
scrip (skrip) *n.* [< fol.] a certificate of a right to receive something, as money
script (skript) *n.* [< L *scribere*, to write] **1** handwriting **2** a copy of the text of a play, film etc.
scrip·ture (skrip′chər) *n.* [see prec.] any sacred writing —[S-] [*often pl.*] **1** the sacred writings of the Jews: see OLD TESTAMENT **2** the Christian Bible; Old and New Testaments —**scrip′tural** *adj.*
scrod (skräd) *n.* [prob. < MDu *schrode*, strip] a young codfish or haddock, esp. one prepared for cooking
scrofu·la (skräf′yə lə) *n.* [< L *scrofa*, a sow] tuberculosis of the lymphatic glands, esp. of the neck —**scrof′u·lous** *adj.*
scroll (skrōl) *n.* [< ME *scrowle*] **1** a roll of parchment, paper, etc., usually with writing on it **2** an ornamental design in coiled or spiral form — *vi.* to move lines of text, etc. vertically on a video screen
scro·tum (skrōt′əm) *n., pl.* **-ta** (-ə) or **-tums** [L] the pouch of skin holding the testicles
scrounge (skrounj) *vt.* **scrounged, scroung′ing** [< ?] [Colloq.] **1** to get by begging or sponging; mooch **2** to pilfer — *vi.* [Colloq.] to seek (*around*) for something —**scroung′er** *n.*
scroung′y *adj.* **-i·er, -i·est** [Slang] shabby, dirty, unkempt, etc. —**scroung′i·ness** *n.*
scrub[1] (skrub) *n.* [ME, var. of *shrubbe*, shrub] **1** a thick growth of stunted trees or bushes **2** any person or thing smaller than the usual, or inferior **3** *Sports* a substitute player — *adj.* small, stunted, inferior, etc. —**scrub′by, -bier, -bi·est,** *adj.*
scrub[2] (skrub) *vt., vi.* **scrubbed, scrub′bing** [prob. < Scand] **1** to clean or wash by rubbing hard **2** to rub hard — *n.* a scrubbing —**scrub′ber** *n.*

THESAURUS

see BIT 1, PIECE 1. **3** [*A fight] quarrel, brawl, squabble; see FIGHT 1.
scrap[1,2] *v.* **1** [To discard] reject, forsake, dismiss; see ABANDON 1, DISCARD. **2** [*To fight] wrangle, battle, squabble; see FIGHT, QUARREL.
scrapbook *n.* portfolio, memorabilia, notebook; see ALBUM, COLLECTION.
scrape *v.* abrade, scour, rasp; see RUB 1.
scraper *n.* grater, rasp, abrasive; see TOOL 1.
scratch *n.* hurt, cut, mark; see INJURY, SCAR. —**from scratch** from the beginning, without preparation, solely; see ALONE, ORIGINAL 1.
scratch *v.* scrape, scarify, prick; see DAMAGE, HURT 1.
scratching *a.* grating, abrasive, rasping; see ROUGH 1.
scrawl *v.* scribble, scratch, doodle; see WRITE 2.
scrawled *a.* scribbled, scratched, inscribed; see WRITTEN 2.

scrawny *a.* lanky, gaunt, lean; see THIN 2.
scream *n.* screech, outcry, shriek; see CRY 1, YELL.
scream *v.* shriek, screech, squeal; see CRY 2, YELL.
screaming *a.* shrieking, screeching, squealing; see YELLING.
screen *n.* **1** [A concealment] cloak, cover, covering, curtain, shield, envelope, veil, mask, shade. **2** [A protection] shelter, guard, security; see COVER 1, PROTECTION 2.
screen *v.* **1** [To hide] veil, conceal, mask; see HIDE 1. **2** [To choose] select, eliminate, sift; see CHOOSE.
screw *n.* spiral, worm, bolt, pin; see also FASTENER. *Screws include the following:* jack, lead, double, drive, lag, right-handed, left-handed, metric, regulating, set, winged, thumb, spiral, triple, wood, machine.
screw* *v.* **1** [To copulate] sleep with, fornicate with, seduce; see COPULATE. **2** [To trick or defeat] cheat, swindle,

beat; see DEFEAT, HURT 2, TRICK. —**screw up*** bungle, foul up*, mishandle; see BOTCH.
screwy* *a.* odd, crazy, inappropriate; see INSANE, WRONG 2.
scribble *v.* scrawl, scrabble, scratch; see HANDWRITING.
scribble *v.* scrawl, scratch, scrabble; see WRITE 2.
scrimp *v.* limit, pinch, skimp; see ECONOMIZE.
script *n.* **1** [Handwriting] writing, characters, chirography; see HANDWRITING. **2** [Playbook] lines, text, dialogue, book, scenario.
scripture *n.* **1** [Truth] reality, verity, final word; see TRUTH. **2** [The Bible; *capital*] the Word, Holy Writ, the Book; see BIBLE.
scrub[1] *a.* second-rate, unimportant, mediocre; see POOR 2.
scrub[2] *v.* rub, cleanse, scour; see CLEAN, WASH 1, 2.
scrubbed *a.* cleaned, polished,

scrub'wom'an *n., pl.* **-wom'en** CHARWOMAN

scruff (skruf) *n.* [< ON *skrufr*, a tuft of hair] the nape of the neck

scruffy (skruf'ē) *adj.* **-i·er, -i·est** [< SCURF + -Y²] shabby; unkempt

scrump·tious (skrump'shəs) *adj.* [< SUMPTUOUS] [Colloq.] very pleasing, etc., esp. to the taste

scrunch (skrunch) *vt., vi.* [< CRUNCH] 1 to crunch, crush, etc. 2 to huddle, squeeze, etc. — *n.* a crunching or crumpling sound

scru·ple (skrōō'pəl) *n.* [< L *scrupulus*, small stone] 1 a very small quantity 2 doubt arising from difficulty in deciding what is right, proper, etc. — *vt., vi.* **-pled, -pling** to hesitate (at) from doubt

scru'pu·lous (-pyə ləs) *adj.* 1 having or showing scruples; conscientiously honest 2 careful of details; precise — **scru'pu·los'i·ty** (-läs'ət ē), *pl.* **-ties,** *n.* —**scru'pu·lous·ly** *adv.*

scru·ti·nize (skrōōt''n īz') *vt.* **-nized', -niz'ing** to examine closely

scru·ti·ny (skrōōt''n ē) *n., pl.* **-nies** [< L *scrutari*, to examine] 1 a close examination or watch 2 a lengthy, searching look

scu·ba (skōō'bə) *n.* [*s(elf-)c(ontained) u(nderwater) b(reathing) a(pparatus)*] a diver's equipment with compressed-air tanks for breathing underwater

scud (skud) *vi.* **scud'ded, scud'ding** [prob. < ON] to move swiftly — *n.* a scudding

scuff (skuf) *vt., vi.* [prob. < ON *skufa*, to shove] 1 to wear or get a rough place on the surface (of) 2 to drag (the feet) — *n.* 1 a worn or rough spot 2 a flat-heeled house slipper with no back upper part

scuf·fle (skuf'əl) *vi.* **-fled, -fling** [< prec.] 1 to struggle or fight in rough confusion 2 to drag the feet — *n.* 1 a confused fight 2 a shuffling of feet

scull (skul) *n.* [ME *skulle*] 1 an oar worked from side to side over the stern of a boat 2 a light row-boat for racing — *vt., vi.* to propel with a scull

scul·ler·y (skul'ər ē) *n., pl.* **-ies** [< L *scutella*, tray] a room near the kitchen, where pots, pans, etc. are cleaned and stored

scul·lion (skul'yən) *n.* [ult. < L *scopa*, a broom] [Archaic] a servant doing the rough kitchen work

sculpt (skulpt) *vt., vi.* SCULPTURE

sculp·tor (skulp'tər) *n.* an artist who creates work of sculpture —**sculp'tress** *n.fem.*

sculp·ture (skulp'chər) *n.* [< L *sculpere*, to carve] 1 the art of shaping stone, clay, wood, etc. into statues, figures, etc. 2 a work or works of sculpture — *vt., vi.* **-tured, -tur·ing** 1 to cut, carve, chisel, etc. (statues, figures, etc.) 2 to make or form like sculpture —**sculp'tur·al** *adj.*

scum (skum) *n.* [< MDu *schum*] 1 a thin layer of impurities on the top of a liquid 2 refuse 3 [Colloq.] despicable people — *vi.* to become covered with scum —**scum'my, -mi·er, -mi·est,** *adj.*

scup·per (skup'ər) *n.* [< OFr *escopir*, to spit] an opening in a ship's side to allow water to run off the deck

scurf (skurf) *n.* [< ON] 1 little, dry scales shed by the skin, as dandruff 2 any scaly coating —**scurf'y, -i·er, -i·est,** *adj.*

scur·ri·lous (skur'ə ləs) *adj.* [< L *scurra*, buffoon] vulgarly abusive —**scur·ril'i·ty** (skə ril'ə tē), *pl.* **-ties,** *n.* —**scur'ri·lous·ly** *adv.*

scurry (skur'ē) *vi.* **-ried, -ry·ing** [< ?] to scamper — *n.* scampering

scurvy (skur'vē) *adj.* **-vier, -vi·est** [< SCURF] low; mean — *n.* a disease resulting from a deficiency of vitamin C, characterized by weakness, anemia, spongy gums, etc. —**scur'vi·ly** *adv.*

scutch·eon (skuch'ən) *n. var. of* ESCUTCHEON

scut·tle¹ (skut''l) *n.* [< L *scutella*, salver] a bucket for carrying coal

scut·tle² (skut''l) *vi.* **-tled, -tling** [ME *scutlen*] to scamper — *n.* a scamper

scut·tle³ (skut''l) *n.* [< Sp *escotilla*, an indentation] an opening fitted with a cover, as in the hull or deck of a ship — *vt.* **-tled, -tling** to cut holes through the lower hull of (a ship, etc.) to sink it

scuttle·butt (skut''l but') *n.* [< *scuttled butt*, lidded cask] 1 a drinking fountain on shipboard 2 [Colloq.] rumor

scuzzy (skuz'ē) *adj.* **-zier, -zi·est** [< ?] [Slang] dirty, shabby, etc.

scythe (sīth) *n.* [OE *sithe*] a tool with a long, single-edged blade on a long, curved handle, for cutting grass, etc.

Se *Chem. symbol for* selenium

SE or **S.E.** 1 southeast 2 southeastern

sea (sē) *n.* [OE *sæ*] 1 the ocean 2 any of various smaller bodies of salt water [the Red *Sea*] 3 a large body of fresh water [*Sea* of Galilee] 4 the state of the surface of the ocean [a calm *sea*] 5 a heavy wave 6 a very great amount [a *sea* of debt] —**at sea** 1 on the open sea 2 uncertain; bewildered

sea anemone a sea polyp with a gelatinous body and petal-like tentacles

sea'board' *n.* [SEA + BOARD] land bordering on the sea — *adj.* bordering on the sea

sea'coast' *n.* land bordering on the sea

sea cow a large sea mammal with a cigar-shaped body and a blunt snout, as the manatee

sea'far'er (-fer'ər) *n.* a sea traveler; esp., a sailor —**sea'far'ing** *adj., n.*

sea'food' *n.* food prepared from or consisting of saltwater fish or shellfish

sea'go'ing *adj.* 1 made for use on the open sea 2 SEAFARING

sea gull GULL¹

sea horse a small, semitropical, plated fish with a head somewhat like that of a horse

seal¹ (sēl) *n.* [< L *sigillum*] 1 *a*) a design or initial impressed, often over wax, on a letter or document as a mark of authenticity *b*) a stamp or ring for making such an impression 2 a piece of paper, etc. bearing an impressed design recognized as official 3 something that seals or closes tightly 4 anything that guarantees; pledge 5 an ornamental paper stamp [Easter *seals*] — *vt.* 1 to mark with a seal, as to authenticate or certify 2 to close or shut tight as with a seal 3 to confirm the truth of (a promise, etc.) 4 to decide finally

seal² (sēl) *n.* [OE *seolh*] 1 a sea mammal with a torpedo-shaped body and four flippers 2 the fur of some seals — *vi.* to hunt seals —**seal'er** *n.*

seal·ant (sēl'ənt) *n.* a substance, as a wax, plastic, etc., used for sealing

sea legs the ability to walk without loss of balance on board ship

---

THESAURUS

immaculate; see CLEAN 1.

scruple *n.* compunction, qualm, uneasiness; see DOUBT.

scruples *n.* overconscientiousness, point of honor, scrupulousness; see ATTENTION, CARE 1.

scrupulous *a.* exact, punctilious, strict; see CAREFUL.

scrutinize *v.* view, study, stare; see EXAMINE, WATCH.

scrutiny *n.* analysis, investigation, inspection; see EXAMINATION 1.

scuffle *n.* struggle, shuffle, strife; see FIGHT 1.

sculptor *n.* artist, modeler, carver, stone carver, wood carver, worker in bronze, worker in metal. *Major sculptors include the following:* Phidias, Ghiberti, Donatello, Luca della Robbia, Michelangelo, Giovanni da Bologna, Benvenuto Cellini, Gian Lorenzo Bernini, Auguste Rodin, Constantin Brancusi, Henry Moore, Jacques Lipchitz.

sculpture *n.* carving, modeling, carving in stone, modeling in clay, kinetic sculpture, op art, casting in bronze, woodcutting, stone carving, plastic art; see also ART, STATUE.

scum *n.* froth, film, impurities; see RESIDUE, TRASH 1.

sea *n. Important seas include the following:* Bering, Caribbean, Baltic, North, Irish, Mediterranean, Adriatic, Ionian, Aegean, Black, Caspian, Azov, Red, White, Tasman, Okhotsk, Japan, Yellow, South China, Arabian, East China, Java, Celebes, Coral; see also OCEAN. —**at sea** confused, puzzled, upset; see BEWILDERED, UNCERTAIN. —**put (out) to sea** embark, go, start out; see LEAVE 1, SAIL 1.

sea bottom *n.* ocean floor, deep-sea floor, bottom of the sea, offshore lands, ocean bottom, ocean depths, continental shelf, undersea topography, marine farm, tidewater; see also OCEAN. *Terms for undersea topography include the following:* bank, sands, seamount, ridge, guyot, hill, tablemount, escarpment, plateau, reef, basin, canal, province, shoal, sill, channel, deep, depth, plain, trench, trough, fracture zone, rift.

seacoast *n.* seashore, seaboard, seaside; see SHORE.

seafood *n.* halibut, mollusk, marine life; see FISH, SHELLFISH.

seal¹ *n.* 1 [Approval] authorization, permit, allowance; see PERMISSION. 2 [Fastener] adhesive tape, sticker, tie; see FASTENER, TAPE.

sealed *a.* secured, fixed, held together; see FIRM 1, TIGHT 2.

seal off *v.* quarantine, close, segregate; see FORBID, RESTRICT.

sea level the mean level of the sea's surface: used in measuring heights

sea lion a seal of the North Pacific

seal'skin' *n.* **1** the skin of the seal **2** a garment made of this

seam (sēm) *n.* ⟦OE⟧ **1** a line formed by sewing together two pieces of material **2** a line that marks joining edges **3** a mark like this, as a scar or wrinkle **4** a stratum of ore, coal, etc. —*vt.* **1** to join together so as to form a seam **2** to mark with a seamlike line, etc. —**seam'less** *adj.*

sea·man (sē'mən) *n., pl.* **-men 1** a sailor **2** *U.S. Navy* an enlisted person ranking below a petty officer —**sea'man·ship'** *n.*

seam·stress (sēm'stris) *n.* a woman whose occupation is sewing

seam'y *adj.* **-i·er, -i·est** unpleasant or sordid /the *seamy* side of life/

sé·ance (sā'äns) *n.* ⟦Fr < L *sedere*, sit⟧ a meeting at which a medium tries to communicate with the dead

sea'plane' *n.* an airplane designed to land on or take off from water

sea'port' *n.* a port or harbor used by ocean ships

sear (sir) *vt.* ⟦OE⟧ **1** to wither **2** to burn the surface of **3** to brand

search (surch) *vt.* ⟦< LL *circare*, go about⟧ **1** to look through in order to find something **2** to examine (a person) for something concealed **3** to examine carefully; probe —*vi.* to make a search —*n.* a searching —**in search of** making a search for —**search'er** *n.*

search'ing *adj.* **1** examining thoroughly **2** piercing; penetrating

search'light' *n.* **1** an apparatus on a swivel that projects a strong beam of light **2** such a beam

search warrant a legal document authorizing a police search

sea'scape' (-skāp') *n.* ⟦SEA + (LAND)SCAPE⟧ **1** a view of the sea **2** a drawing, painting, etc. of such a scene

sea'shell' *n.* a saltwater mollusk shell

sea'shore' *n.* land along the sea

sea'sick'ness *n.* nausea, dizziness, etc. caused by the rolling of a ship or boat at sea —**sea'sick'** *adj.*

sea'side' *n.* SEASHORE

sea·son (sē'zən) *n.* ⟦< VL *satio*, season for sowing⟧ **1** any of the four divisions of the year; spring, summer, fall, or winter **2** the time when something takes place, is popular, permitted, etc. **3** the fitting time —*vt.* **1** to make (food) more tasty by adding salt, spices, etc. **2** to add zest to **3** to make more usable, as by aging **4** to make used to; accustom —*vi.* to become seasoned

sea'son·able *adj.* **1** suitable to the season **2** opportune; timely

sea'sonal *adj.* of or depending on the season —**sea'son·ally** *adv.*

sea'son·ing *n.* anything that adds zest; esp., salt, etc. added to food

season ticket a ticket or set of tickets as for a series of concerts, baseball games, etc.

seat (sēt) *n.* ⟦ON *sæti*⟧ **1** *a)* a place to sit *b)* a thing to sit on; chair, etc. **2** *a)* the buttocks *b)* the part of a chair, garment, etc. that one sits on **3** the right to sit as a member /a *seat* on the council/ **4** the chief location, or center /the *seat* of government/ —*vt.* **1** to set in or on a seat **2** to have seats for /the car *seats* six/ **3** to put or fix in a place, position, etc. —**be seated** to sit down: also **take a seat**

seat belt anchored straps that buckle across the hips, to protect a seated passenger from an abrupt jolt

sea urchin a small sea animal with a round body in a shell covered with sharp spines

sea'ward (-wərd) *adj., adv.* toward the sea Also **sea'wards** *adv.*

sea'way' *n.* an inland waterway to the sea for ocean ships

sea'weed' *n.* a sea plant, esp. an alga

sea'wor'thy (-wur'thē) *adj.* fit to travel on the sea: said of a ship

se·ba·ceous (sə bā'shəs) *adj.* ⟦< L *sebum*, tallow⟧ of, like, or secreting fat, etc. /*sebaceous* glands/

seb·or·rhea or **seb·or·rhoea** (seb'ə rē'ə) *n.* ⟦< L *sebum*, tallow & Gr *rheein*, flow⟧ excessive discharge from the sebaceous glands causing abnormally oily skin

sec. 1 second(s) **2** secretary **3** section(s)

SEC Securities and Exchange Commission

se·cede (si sēd') *vi.* **-ced'ed, -ced'ing** ⟦< L *se-*, apart + *cedere*, to go⟧ to withdraw formally from a group, organization, federation, etc.

se·ces·sion (si sesh'ən) *n.* a seceding —[often **S-**] the withdrawal of the Southern States from the Federal Union (1860-61) —**se·ces'sion·ist** *n.*

se·clude (si klo͞od') *vt.* **-clud'ed, -clud'ing** ⟦< L *se-*, apart + *claudere*, to close⟧ to shut off from others; isolate

se·clu·sion (si klo͞o'zhən) *n.* a secluding or being secluded; retirement; isolation —**se·clu'sive** *adj.*

sec·ond[1] (sek'ənd) *adj.* ⟦< L *sequi*, follow⟧ **1** coming next after the first; 2d or 2nd **2** another of the same kind; other /a *second* chance/ **3** next below the first in rank, value, etc. —*n.* **1** one that is second **2** [*pl.*] *a)* an article of merchandise not of first quality *b)* a second helping of food **3** an aide or assistant, as to a boxer **4** the gear next after low gear —*vt.* **1** to assist **2** to indicate formal support of (a motion) before discussion or a vote —*adv.* in the second place, group, etc.

sec·ond[2] (sek'ənd) *n.* ⟦< ML (*pars minuta*) *secunda*, second (small part): from being a further division⟧ **1** $\frac{1}{60}$ of a minute of time or of angular measure **2** a moment; instant

sec·ond·ary (sek'ən der'ē) *adj.* **1** second in order, rank, importance, place, etc. **2** subordinate; minor **3** derived, not primary; derivative —*n., pl.* **-ar'ies 1** a secondary

---

THESAURUS

seam *n.* joint, line of joining, union, stitching, line of stitching, closure, suture.

seamstress *n.* sewer, needleworker, designer; see TAILOR.

sear *v.* scorch, brown, toast; see COOK.

search *n.* exploration, quest, research; see HUNTING. **—in search of** looking for, seeking for, on the lookout for; see SEARCHING.

search *v.* explore, examine, rummage, look up and down, track down, look for, go through, poke into, scrutinize, ransack; see also HUNT 1. — **search me** I don't know, who knows?, how should I know?; see UNCERTAINTY 1.

searching *a.* hunting, looking for, seeking for, pursuing, in search of, ready for, in the market for, in need of, needing, wanting, on the lookout for, looking out for.

searchlight *n.* arc light, beam, ray; see LIGHT 1.

seashell *n.* conch, clam, oyster; see SHELL 1.

seashore *n.* seaboard, seaside, seacoast; see SHORE.

seasick *a.* nauseated, miserable, uneasy; see SICK.

seaside *n.* seaboard, seashore,

seacost; see SHORE.

season *n.* period, term, certain months of the year; see FALL 3, SPRING 2, SUMMER, WINTER. **—in season** legal to hunt, ready to pick, mature; see LEGAL, READY 2, RIPE 1, 3.

seasonal *a.* once a season, periodically, biennial; see ANNUAL, YEARLY.

seasoned *a.* **1** [Spicy] tangy, sharp, aromatic; see SPICY. **2** [Experienced] established, settled, mature; see ABLE, EXPERIENCED.

seasoning *n.* sauce, relish, spice, pungency; see also FLAVORING.

seat *n.* **1** [A structure on which one may sit] bench, chair, stool; see FURNITURE. **2** [Space in which one may sit] situation, chair, accommodation; see PLACE 2. **3** [The part of the body with which one sits] buttocks, rear, breech; see RUMP. **—have (or take) a seat** be seated, sit down, occupy a place; see SIT.

seated *a.* situated, located, settled, installed, established, rooted, set, fitted in place, placed, arranged, accommodated with seats.

seating *n.* places, reservations, chairs, seats, room, accommodation, arrangement, seating space.

seaward *a.* offshore, out to sea, over the sea; see MARITIME.

seaweed *n.* kelp, tangle, sea tangle, sea meadow, algae, marine meadow; see also PLANT. *Seaweed includes the following:* sea moss, Irish moss, Sargasso weed, rockweed, sea lettuce, kelp, giant kelp, gulfweed, sea cabbage.

seaworthy *a.* fit for sea, navigable, secure; see SAFE 1.

secede *v.* withdraw, retract, leave; see RETREAT.

secession *n.* departure, seceding, retraction; see WITHDRAWAL.

seclude *v.* screen out, conceal, cover; see HIDE 1.

secluded *a.* screened, removed, sequestered; see WITHDRAWN.

seclusion *n.* solitude, aloofness, privacy; see RETIREMENT 2.

second[1] *a.* secondary, subordinate, inferior, next, next in order, following, next to the first, next in rank, another, other.

second[2] *n.* flash, trice, flash of an eyelid; see MOMENT 1.

secondary *a.* **1** [Derived] dependent, subsequent, subsidiary; see SUBORDINATE. **2** [Minor] inconsiderable, petty, small; see TRIVIAL, UNIMPORTANT.

person or thing 2 *Football* the defensive backfield —**sec′ ond·ar′i·ly** *adv.*

secondary school a school, as a high school, coming after elementary school

secondary stress (or **accent**) a weaker stress (′) than the primary stress of a word

sec′ond-class′ *adj.* 1 of the class, rank, etc. next below the highest, best, etc. 2 of a cheaper mail class, as for periodicals, etc. 3 inferior, inadequate, etc. —*adv.* by second-class mail or travel accommodations

sec′ond-guess′ *vt.*, *vi.* [Colloq.] to use hindsight in criticizing (someone), remaking (a decision), etc.

sec′ond·hand′ *adj.* 1 not from the original source 2 used before; not new 3 of or dealing in used merchandise

second lieutenant *Mil.* a commissioned officer of the lowest rank

sec′ondly *adv.* in the second place

second nature an acquired habit, etc. deeply fixed in one's nature

second person that form of a pronoun (as *you*) or verb (as *are*) that refers to the person spoken to

sec′ond-rate′ *adj.* 1 second in quality, rank, etc. 2 inferior

sec′ond-source′ *adj.* of an arrangement whereby one company's products are also manufactured by another company —*vt.* **-sourced′**, **-sourc′ing** to manufacture (another company's products) under such an arrangement

sec′ond-string′ *adj.* [Colloq.] *Sports* that is a substitute player at a specified position —**sec′ond-string′er** *n.*

second thought a change in thought after reconsidering —**on second thought** after reconsideration

second wind 1 the return of easy breathing after initial exhaustion, as while running 2 any fresh ability to continue

se·crecy (sē′krə sē) *n.*, *pl.* **-cies** 1 a being secret 2 a tendency to keep things secret

se·cret (sē′krit) *adj.* [< L *se-*, apart + *cernere*, sift] 1 kept from, or acting without, the knowledge of others 2 beyond general understanding; mysterious 3 concealed from sight; hidden —*n.* a secret fact, cause, process, etc. —**se′cretly** *adv.*

sec·re·tari·at (sek′rə ter′ē ət) *n.* a secretarial staff; specif., an administrative staff, as in a government

sec·re·tary (sek′rə ter′ē) *n.*, *pl.* **-tar′ies** [< ML *secretarius*, one entrusted with secrets] 1 one who keeps records, handles correspondence, etc. for an organization or person 2 the head of a government department 3 a writing desk —**sec′re·tar′ial** *adj.*

se·crete (si krēt′) *vt.* **-cret′ed**, **-cret′ing** [see SECRET] 1 to hide; conceal 2 to form and release (a substance) as a gland, etc. does

se·cre·tion (si krē′shən) *n.* 1 a secreting 2 a substance secreted by an animal or plant

se·cre·tive (sē′krə tiv) *adj.* concealing one's thoughts, etc.; not frank or open —**se′cre·tively** *adv.* —**se′cre·tive· ness** *n.*

se·cre·tory (si krēt′ər ē) *adj.* having the function of secreting, as a gland

Secret Service a division of the U.S. Treasury Department for uncovering counterfeiters, guarding the President, etc.

sect (sekt) *n.* [< L *sequi*, follow] 1 a religious denomination 2 a group of people having a common philosophy, set of beliefs, etc.

sec·tar·ian (sek ter′ē ən) *adj.* 1 of or devoted to some sect 2 narrow-minded —*n.* a sectarian person —**sec·tar′i·an· ism′** *n.*

sec·tion (sek′shən) *n.* [< L *secare*, to cut] 1 a cutting apart 2 a part cut off; portion 3 any distinct part, group, etc. 4 a drawing, etc. of a thing as it would appear if cut straight through —*vt.* to cut into sections

sec′tional *adj.* 1 of or characteristic of a given section or district 2 made up of sections —**sec′tion·al·ism′** *n.*

sec·tor (sek′tər) *n.* [< L *secare*, to cut] 1 part of a circle bounded by any two radii and the included arc 2 any of the districts into which an area is divided for military operations

secu·lar (sek′yə lər) *adj.* [< LL *saecularis*, worldly] not religious; not connected with a church —**sec′u·lar·ism′** *n.*

sec′u·lar·ize′ (-lə riz′) *vt.* **-ized′**, **-iz′ing** to change from religious to civil use or control —**sec′u·lari·za′tion** *n.*

se·cure (si kyoor′) *adj.* [< L *se-*, free from + *cura*, care] 1 free from fear, care, etc. 2 free from danger, risk, etc.; safe 3 firm /make the knot *secure*/ —*vt.* **-cured′**, **-cur′ing** 1 to make secure; protect 2 to make certain, as with a pledge 3 to make firm, fast, etc. 4 to obtain —**se·cure′ly** *adv.*

se·cu·rity (si kyoor′ə tē) *n.*, *pl.* **-ties** 1 a feeling secure; freedom from fear, doubt, etc. 2 protection; safeguard 3 something given as a pledge of repayment, etc. 4 [*pl.*] bonds, stocks, etc.

secy. or **sec′y.** secretary

se·dan (si dan′) *n.* [< ? L *sedere*, to sit] an enclosed automobile with two or four doors, posts between the front and rear windows, and seats for four to six people

se·date[1] (si dāt′) *adj.* [< L *sedare*, to settle] calm or composed; esp., serious and unemotional —**se·date′ly** *adv.*

THESAURUS

secondhand *a.* used, not new, reclaimed, renewed, reused, old, worn, borrowed, derived, not original.

secondly *a.* in the second place, furthermore, also, besides, next, on the other hand, in the next place, for the next step, next in order, further, to continue; see also INCLUDING.

second-rate *a.* mediocre, inferior, common; see POOR 2.

secrecy *n.* concealment, confidence, hiding, seclusion, privacy, retirement, solitude, mystery, dark, darkness, isolation, reticence, stealth.

secret *a.* 1 [Not generally known] mysterious, ambiguous, hidden, unknown, arcane, cryptic, esoteric, occult, mystic, mystical, classified, dark, veiled, enigmatic, strange, deep, buried in mystery, obscure, clouded, shrouded, unenlightened, unintelligible, cabalistic.—*Ant.* KNOWN, revealed, exposed. 2 [Hidden] latent, secluded, concealed; see HIDDEN. 3 [Operating secretly] clandestine, underhand, underhanded, stealthy, sly, surreptitious, close, furtive, disguised, undercover, backdoor, confidential, backstairs, incognito, camouflaged, enigmatic, under false pretense, unrevealed, undisclosed, dissembled, dissimulated, under wraps; see also SECRETIVE.—*Ant.* OPEN, aboveboard, overt.

secret *n.* mystery, deep mystery, something veiled, something hidden,

confidence, private matter, code, telegram, personal matter, privileged information, top secret, enigma, puzzle, something forbidden, classified information, confidential information, inside information, an unknown, magic number, the unknown. —**in secret** slyly, surreptitiously, quietly; see SECRET 3.

secretary *n.* 1 [A secondary executive officer] director, manager, superintendent; see EXECUTIVE. 2 [An assistant] clerk, typist, stenographer, copyist, amanuensis, recorder, confidential clerk, correspondent.

secrete *v.* 1 [To hide] conceal, cover, seclude; see DISGUISE, HIDE 1. 2 [To perspire] discharge, swelter, emit; see SWEAT.

secretion *n.* discharge, issue, movement; see EXCRETION, FLOW.

secretive *a.* reticent, taciturn, undercover, with bated breath, in private, in the dark, in chambers, by a side door, under the breath, in the background, between outselves, in privacy, in a corner, under the cloak of, reserved.

secretly *a.* privately, covertly, obscurely, darkly, surreptitiously, furtively, stealthily, underhandedly, slyly, behind one's back, intimately, personally, confidentially, between you and me, in strict confidence, in secret, behind the scenes, on the sly, behind closed doors, quietly, hush-hush*.—*Ant.* OPENLY, obviously,

publicly.

sect *n.* denomination, following, order; see CHURCH 3, FACTION.

section *n.* 1 [A portion] subdivision, slice, segment; see PART 1, SHARE. 2 [An area] district, sector, locality; see REGION 1.

sectional *a.* local, narrow, separate; see REGIONAL.

sector *n.* section, district, quarter; see AREA, DIVISION 2.

secure *a.* 1 [Firm] fastened, bound, adjusted; see FIRM 1, TIGHT 1. 2 [Safe] guarded, unharmed, defended; see SAFE 1. 3 [Self-confident] assured, stable, determined; see CONFIDENT.

secure *v.* 1 [To fasten] settle, adjust, bind; see FASTEN, TIGHTEN 1. 2 [To obtain] achieve, acquire, grasp; see GET 1.

security *n.* 1 [Safety] protection, shelter, safety, refuge, retreat, defense, safeguard, preservation, sanctuary, ward, guard, immunity, freedom from harm, freedom from danger, redemption, salvation.—*Ant.* DANGER, risk, hazard. 2 [A guarantee] earnest, forfeit, token, pawn, pledge, surety, bond, collateral, assurance, bail, certainty, promise, warranty, pact, compact, contract, covenant, agreement, sponsor, bondsman, hostage; see also PROTECTION 2.—*Ant.* DOUBT, broken faith, unreliability.

se·date² (si dāt′) *vt.* **-dat′ed, -dat′ing** to dose with a sedative —**se·da′tion** *n.*

seda·tive (sed′ə tiv) *adj.* ⟦ see SEDATE¹ ⟧ tending to soothe or quiet; lessening excitement, irritation, etc. — *n.* a sedative medicine

sed·en·tary (sed″n ter′ē) *adj.* ⟦ < L *sedere*, to sit ⟧ marked by much sitting

Se·der (sā′dər) *n.* ⟦ Heb lit., arrangement ⟧ *Judaism* the feast of Passover as observed in the home on the eve of the first (by some also of the second) day of the holiday

sedge (sej) *n.* ⟦ OE *secg* ⟧ a coarse, grasslike plant growing in wet ground

sedi·ment (sed′ə mənt) *n.* ⟦ < L *sedere*, sit ⟧ **1** matter that settles to the bottom of a liquid **2** *Geol.* matter deposited by water or wind

sed′i·men′tary (-men′tər ē) *adj.* **1** of or containing sediment **2** formed by the deposit of sediment, as certain rocks

sed′i·men·ta′tion (-men tā′shən, -mən-) *n.* the depositing of sediment

se·di·tion (si dish′ən) *n.* ⟦ < L *sed-*, apart + *itio*, a going ⟧ a stirring up of rebellion against the government —**se·di′tion·ist** *n.* —**se·di′tious** *adj.*

se·duce (si dōōs′) *vt.* **-duced′, -duc′ing** ⟦ < L *se-*, apart + *ducere*, to lead ⟧ **1** to tempt to wrongdoing **2** to entice into unlawful sexual intercourse, esp. for the first time — **se·duc′er** *n.* —**se·duc′tion** (-duk′shən) *n.* —**se·duc′tive** *adj.* —**se·duc′tress** (-tris) *n.fem.*

sedu·lous (sej′oo ləs) *adj.* ⟦ L *sedulus* ⟧ **1** diligent **2** persistent

see¹ (sē) *vt.* **saw, seen, see′ing** ⟦ OE *seon* ⟧ **1** to get knowledge of through the eyes; look at **2** to understand **3** to learn; find out **4** to experience **5** to make sure *[see* that he goes*]* **6** to escort *[see* her home*]* **7** to encounter **8** to call on; consult **9** to receive *[too ill to see* anyone*]* — *vi.* **1** to have the power of sight **2** to think *[let me see,* who's next?*]* —**see after** to take care of —**see through 1** to perceive the true nature of **2** to finish **3** to help through difficulty —**see to** (or **about**) to attend to

see² (sē) *n.* ⟦ < L *sedes*, a seat ⟧ the official seat or jurisdiction of a bishop

seed (sēd) *n., pl.* **seeds** or **seed** ⟦ OE *sæd* ⟧ **1** *a)* the part of a plant, containing the embryo, from which a new plant can grow *b)* such seeds collectively **2** the source of anything **3** [Archaic] descendants; posterity **4** sperm or semen — *vt.* **1** to plant with seeds **2** to remove the seeds from **3** to distribute (contestants in a tournament) so that the best players are not matched in early rounds — *vi.* to produce seed **2** to deteriorate, weaken, etc. —**seed′er** *n.* —**seed′less** *adj.*

seed·ling (-liŋ) *n.* **1** a plant grown from a seed **2** a young tree

seed money money to begin a long-term project or get more funds for it

seed vessel any dry, hollow fruit containing seeds Also **seed′case′** *n.*

seed′y *adj.* **-i·er, -i·est 1** full of seed **2** gone to seed **3** shabby, rundown, etc. —**seed′i·ness** *n.*

seek (sēk) *vt.* **sought, seek′ing** ⟦ OE *secan* ⟧ **1** to try to find; search for **2** to try to get **3** to aim at **4** to try; attempt *[to seek* to please*]* —**seek′er** *n.*

seem (sēm) *vi.* ⟦ prob. < ON *sœma*, conform to ⟧ **1** to appear to be *[to seem* happy*]* **2** to appear *[seems* to know*]* **3** to have the impression (with an infinitive) *[I seem* to have lost it*]*

seem′ing *adj.* that seems real, true, etc.; apparent —**seem′ing·ly** *adv.*

seem′ly *adj.* **-lier, -li·est** suitable, proper, etc. —**seem′li·ness** *n.*

seen (sēn) *vt., vi. pp. of* SEE¹

seep (sēp) *vi.* ⟦ OE *sipian*, to soak ⟧ to leak through small openings; ooze —**seep′age** (-ij) *n.*

seer (sir) *n.* one who supposedly foretells the future — **seer′ess** *n.fem.*

seer·sucker (sir′suk′ər) *n.* ⟦ < Pers *shir u shakar*, lit., milk and sugar ⟧ a crinkled fabric of linen, cotton, etc.

see·saw (sē′sô′) *n.* ⟦ < SAW¹ ⟧ **1** a plank balanced at the middle on which children at play, riding the ends, rise and fall alternately **2** any up-and-down or back-and-forth motion or change — *vt., vi.* to move up and down or back and forth

seethe (sēth) *vi.* **seethed, seeth′ing 1** to boil, surge, or bubble **2** to be violently agitated

seg·ment (seg′mənt; *for v.*, -ment) *n.* ⟦ < L *secare*, to cut ⟧ any of the parts into which something is separated; section — *vt., vi.* to divide into segments —**seg′men·ta′tion** *n.*

seg·re·gate (seg′rə gāt′) *vt.* **-gat′ed, -gat′ing** ⟦ < L *se-*, apart + *grex*, a flock ⟧ to set apart from others; specif., to impose racial segregation on

seg′re·ga′tion *n.* the policy of compelling racial groups to live apart and use separate schools, facilities, etc. —**seg′re·ga′tion·ist** *n.*

se·gue (seg′wā, sā′gwā) *vi.* **-gued, -gue′ing** ⟦ It, (it follows) < L *sequi*, to follow ⟧ to continue without break (*to* or *into* the next part) — *n.* an immediate transition to the next part

sei·gnior (sān′yər, sān yôr′) *n.* ⟦ < OFr *seignor* < L *senior* ⟧ a feudal lord

seine (sān) *n.* ⟦ < Gr *sagēnē* ⟧ a large fishing net weighted along the bottom — *vt., vi.* **seined, sein′ing** to fish with a seine —**sein′er** *n.*

seis·mic (sīz′mik) *adj.* ⟦ < Gr *seismos*, earthquake ⟧ of or caused by an earthquake —**seis′mi·cally** *adv.*

seis′mo·graph′ (-mə graf′) *n.* ⟦ see prec. & -GRAPH ⟧ an instrument that records the intensity and duration of earthquakes —**seis′mo·graph′ic** *adj.*

seis·mol·ogy (sīz mäl′ə jē, sīs-) *n.* ⟦ see SEISMIC & -LOGY ⟧

◼ THESAURUS ◼

sedative *n.* tranquilizer, medication, narcotic; see DRUG, MEDICINE 2.

sediment *n.* silt, dregs, grounds; see RESIDUE.

seduce *v.* decoy, allure, inveigle, entice, abduct, attract, tempt, bait, bribe, lure, induce, stimulate, defile, deprave, lead astray, violate, prostitute, rape, deflower.—*Ant.* PRESERVE, protect, guide.

see¹ *v.* **1** [To perceive with the eye] observe, look at, behold, examine, inspect, regard, view, look out on, gaze, stare, eye, lay eyes on, mark, perceive, pay attention to, heed, mind, detect, take notice, discern, scrutinize, scan, spy, survey, contemplate, remark, clap eyes on*, make out, cast the eyes on, direct the eyes, catch sight of, cast the eyes over, get a load of*. **2** [To understand] perceive, comprehend, discern; see RECOGNIZE 1, UNDERSTAND 1. **3** [To witness] look on, be present, pay attention, notice, observe, regard, heed; see also WITNESS. **4** [To accompany] escort, attend, bear company; see ACCOMPANY. **5** [To have an appointment (with)] speak to, have a conference with, get advice from; see CONSULT, DISCUSS. —**see about**

attend to, look after, provide for; see PERFORM 1. —**see through 1** [To complete] finish up, bring to a successful conclusion, wind up; see COMPLETE, END 1. **2** [To understand] comprehend, penetrate, detect; see UNDERSTAND 1. —**see to** do, attend to, look after; see UNDERSTAND 1.

seed *n.* grain, bulbs, cuttings, ears, tubers, roots; seed corn, seed potatoes, etc. *Seeds and fruits commonly called seeds include the following:* grain, kernel, berry, ear, corn, nut. —**go** (or **run**) **to seed** decline, worsen, run out; see WASTE 3.

seed *v.* scatter, sow, broadcast; see PLANT.

seeding *n.* sowing, implanting, spreading; see FARMING.

seeing *a.* observing, looking, regarding, viewing, noticing, surveying, looking at, observant, wide awake, alert, awake, perceiving, inspecting, witnessing.

seek *v.* search for, dig for, fish for, look around for, look up, hunt up, sniff out, dig out, hunt out, root out, smell around, go after, run after, see after, prowl after, go in pursuit of, go

in search of.

seem *v.* appear to be, have the appearance, give the impression, impress one, appear to one, look, look like, resemble, make a show of, show, have the features of, lead one to suppose something to be, have all the evidence of being, be suggestive of, give the effect of, sound like, make out to be, give the idea, have all the earmarks of, make a noise like.

seen *a.* observed, evident, viewed; see OBVIOUS 1.

seep *v.* leak, flow gently, trickle; see DRAIN 1, FLOW.

seepage *n.* drainage, infiltration, leakage; see FLOW.

seethe *v.* simmer, stew, burn; see BOIL, COOK.

segment *n.* section, portion, fragment; see DIVISION 2, PART 1.

segregate *v.* isolate, sever, split up; see DIVIDE, SEPARATE 2.

segregated *a.* divided along racial lines, isolated, ghettoized; see RACIAL, SEPARATED.

segregation *n.* dissociation, disconnection, separation; see DIVISION 1.

the science dealing with earthquakes —**seis'mo·log'ic** (-mə läj'ik) or **seis'mo·log'i·cal** *adj.*

seize (sēz) *vt.* **seized, seiz'ing** 〖< ML *sacire* 〗 **1** *a)* to take legal possession of *b)* to capture; arrest **2** to take forcibly and quickly **3** to grasp suddenly **4** to attack or afflict suddenly *[seized* with pain*]* —**sei·zure** (sē'zhər) *n.*

sel·dom (sel'dəm) *adv.* 〖OE *seldan,* strange 〗 rarely; infrequently

se·lect (sə lekt') *adj.* 〖< L *se-,* apart + *legere,* to choose 〗 **1** chosen in preference to others **2** choice; excellent **3** careful in choosing **4** exclusive —*vt., vi.* to choose or pick out —**se·lect'ness** *n.* —**se·lec'tor** *n.*

se·lec'tion (-lek'shən) *n.* **1** a selecting or being selected **2** that or those selected —**se·lec'tive** *adj.* —**se·lec'tiv'ity** *n.*

selective service compulsory military service set by age, fitness, etc.

select'man (-mən) *n., pl.* **-men** one of a board of governing officers in most New England towns

se·leni·um (sə lē'nē əm) *n.* 〖ModL < Gr *selēnē,* the moon 〗 a gray, nonmetallic chemical element: used in photoelectric devices

sel·enog·ra·phy (sel'ə näg'rə fē) *n.* 〖< Gr *selēnē,* moon + -GRAPHY〗 the study of the physical features of the moon —**sel'enog'ra·pher** *n.*

self (self) *n., pl.* **selves** 〖OE〗 **1** the identity, character, etc. of any person or thing **2** one's own person as distinct from all others **3** one's own welfare or interest —*pron.* [Colloq.] myself, himself, etc. *[for self* and wife*]* —*adj.* of the same kind, color, etc. *[self* trim*]*

self- *prefix* of, by, in, to, or with oneself or itself The following list includes some common compounds formed with *self-* that do not have special meanings:

self-abasement	self-improvement
self-advancement	self-incrimination
self-appointed	self-induced
self-assertion	self-indulgence
self-command	self-indulgent
self-complacent	self-inflicted
self-deceit	self-knowledge
self-deception	self-love
self-defeating	self-perpetuating
self-delusion	self-pity
self-destruction	self-pollination
self-discipline	self-preservation
self-effacement	self-protection
self-employed	self-reproach
self-examination	self-sealing
self-fertilization	self-support
self-help	self-supporting
self-imposed	self-sustaining

self'-addressed' *adj.* addressed to oneself *[a self-addressed* envelope*]*

self'-assur'ance *n.* confidence in oneself —**self'-assured'** *adj.*

self'-cen'tered *adj.* concerned only with one's own affairs; selfish

self'-conceit' *n.* too high an opinion of oneself; vanity

self'-con'fidence *n.* confidence in one's own abilities, etc. —**self'-con'fident** *adj.*

self'-con'scious *adj.* unduly conscious of oneself as an object of notice; ill at ease —**self'-con'sciously** *adv.* —**self'-con'sciousness** *n.*

self'-contained' *adj.* **1** keeping one's affairs to oneself **2** showing self-control **3** complete within itself

self'-con'tradic'tion *n.* **1** contradiction of oneself or itself **2** any statement containing elements that contradict each other —**self'-con'tradic'tory** *adj.*

self'-control' *n.* control of one's own emotions, desires, actions, etc. —**self'-con·trolled'** *adj.*

self'-defense' *n.* defense of oneself or of one's rights, beliefs, actions, etc.

self'-deni'al *n.* denial or sacrifice of one's own desires or pleasures

self'-destruct' *vi.* DESTRUCT

self'-deter'mina'tion *n.* **1** determination according to one's own mind; free will **2** the right of a people to choose its own form of government —**self'-deter'mined** *adj.*

self'-discov'ery *n.* a becoming aware of one's true potential, character, motives, etc.

self'-edu·cat'ed *adj.* educated by oneself, with little formal schooling

self'-esteem' *n.* **1** belief in oneself **2** undue pride in oneself; conceit

self'-ev'ident *adj.* evident without need of proof or explanation

self'-explan'ato'ry *adj.* explaining itself; obvious

self'-expres'sion *n.* expression of one's own personality, esp. in the arts

self'-fulfill'ing *adj.* **1** bringing about one's personal goals **2** brought about chiefly as an effect of having been expected or predicted

self'-gov'ernment *n.* government of a group by the action of its own members —**self'-gov'erning** *adj.*

self'-im'age *n.* one's conception of oneself, one's own abilities, worth, etc.

self'-impor'tant *adj.* having an exaggerated opinion of one's own importance —**self'-impor'tance** *n.*

self'-in'terest *n.* **1** one's own interest or advantage **2** an exaggerated regard for this

■■■ THESAURUS ■■■

seize *v.* **1** [To grasp] take, take hold of, lay hold of, hands on, catch up, catch hold of, hang onto, catch, grip, clinch, clench, clasp, embrace, grab, clutch, grapple, snag, pluck, appropriate, snatch, swoop up, enfold, enclose, pinch, squeeze, hold fast, possess oneself of, envelope.—*Ant.* LEAVE, pass by, let alone. **2** [To take by force] capture, rape, occupy, win, take captive, pounce, conquer, take by storm, subdue, overwhelm, overrun, overpower, ambush, snatch, incorporate, exact, retake, carry off, apprehend, arrest, secure, commandeer, force, gain, take, recapture, appropriate, take possession of, take over, pounce on, usurp, overcome, impound, intercept, steal, abduct, snap up*, nab*, trap, throttle, lay hold of, lift, hook, collar*, fasten upon, wrench, claw, snare, bag, catch up, wring, get one's hands on, kidnap, rustle*, hold up, swipe*, scramble for, help oneself to, jump a claim*. **3** [To comprehend] perceive, see, know; see UNDERSTAND 1.

seized *a.* confiscated, annexed, clutched; see BEATEN 1, CAPTURED.

seizure *n.* **1** [Capture] seizing, taking, apprehending; see CAPTURE. **2** [A spasm] spell, convulsion, breakdown; see FIT 2, ILLNESS 1.

seldom *a.* rarely, unusually, in a few cases, a few times, at times, seldom seen, usually, sporadically, irregularly, whimsically, sometimes, from time to time, on a few occasions, on rare occasions, infrequently, not often, not very often, occasionally, uncommonly, scarcely, hardly, hardly ever, scarcely ever, when the spirit moves, on and off, once in a while, once in a blue moon, once in a lifetime, every now and then, not in a month of Sundays.—*Ant.* FREQUENTLY, often, frequent.

select *v.* decide, pick, elect; see CHOOSE.

selected *a.* picked, chosen, elected; see NAMED 2.

selection *n.* **1** [The act of selecting] choice, election, determination, choosing, preference, appropriation, adoption, reservation, separation. **2** [Anything selected] pick, collection, excerpt; see CHOICE.

selective *a.* discriminating, judicious, particular; see CAREFUL.

self *a.* of one's self, by one's self, by one's own self, by one's own effort; see ALONE, INDIVIDUAL.

self *n.* oneself, one's being, inner nature; see CHARACTER 2.

self-assurance *n.* security, self-reliance, morale; see CONFIDENCE.

self-assured *a.* self-confident, assured, certain; see CONFIDENT.

self-centered *a.* self-indulgent, egotistical, self-conscious; see EGOTISTIC, SELFISH.

self-confidence *n.* assurance, courage, self-reliance; see CONFIDENCE.

self-confident *a.* fearless, secure, self-assured; see CONFIDENT.

self-conscious *a.* unsure, uncertain, shy; see DOUBTFUL, HUMBLE 1.

self-contained *a.* self-sustaining, complete, independent; see FREE 1, WHOLE 1.

self-control *n.* poise, self-restraint, reserve, self-government, reticence, discretion, balance, stability, sobriety, dignity, temperance, constraint, self-regulation.—*Ant.* NERVOUSNESS, timidity, talkativeness.

self-defense *n.* self-protection, the manly art of self-defense, putting up a fight; see FIGHT 1, PROTECTION 2.

self-esteem *n.* vanity, haughtiness, egotism; see PRIDE 1.

self-evident *a.* plain, visible, apparent; see OBVIOUS 2.

self-explanatory *a.* plain, clear, distinct; see OBVIOUS 2.

self-imposed *a.* accepted, self-determined, willingly adopted; see DELIBERATE, VOLUNTARILY.

self'ish *adj.* overly concerned with one's own interests, etc. and having little concern for others —**self'ishly** *adv.* —**self'ish·ness** *n.*

self'less *adj.* devoted to others' welfare; unselfish —**self'lessly** *adv.* —**self'less·ness** *n.*

self'-made' *adj.* 1 made by oneself or itself 2 successful through one's own efforts

self'-posses'sion *n.* full control of one's feelings, actions, etc. —**self'-possessed'** *adj.*

self'-propelled' *adj.* propelled by its own motor or power

self'-reg'u·lat'ing *adj.* regulating oneself or itself, so as to function automatically or without outside control

self'-reli'ance *n.* reliance on one's own judgment, abilities, etc. —**self'-reli'ant** *adj.*

self'-respect' *n.* proper respect for oneself —**self'-respect'ing** *adj.*

self'-restraint' *n.* restraint imposed on oneself by oneself; self-control

self'-right'eous *adj.* filled with a conviction of being morally superior to others; smugly virtuous —**self'-right'eously** *adv.* —**self'-right'eousness** *n.*

self'-sac'rifice' *n.* sacrifice of oneself or one's own interests for the benefit of others —**self'-sac'rific'ing** *adj.*

self'same' *adj.* identical

self'-sat'isfied' *adj.* feeling or showing an often smug satisfaction with oneself —**self'-sat'isfac'tion** *n.*

self'-seek'er *n.* one who seeks mainly to further his or her own interests —**self'-seek'ing** *n., adj.*

self'-serve' *adj.* short for SELF-SERVICE

self'-serv'ice *n.* the practice of serving oneself in a store, cafeteria, service station, etc.

self'-serv'ing *adj.* serving one's own selfish interests

self'-styled' *adj.* so called only by oneself

self'-suffi'cient *adj.* able to get along without help; independent —**self'-suffi'ciency** *n.*

self'-taught' *adj.* having taught oneself through one's own efforts

self'-willed' *adj.* stubborn; obstinate

self'-wind'ing *adj.* wound automatically, as some wristwatches

sell (sel) *vt.* **sold, sell'ing** 〖OE *sellan*, to give〗 1 to exchange (goods, services, etc.) for money, etc. 2 to offer for sale 3 to promote the sale of — *vi.* 1 to engage in selling 2 to be sold (*for* or *at*) 3 to attract buyers —**sell out** 1 to get rid of completely by selling 2 [Colloq.] to betray —**sell'er** *n.*

sell'out' *n.* [Colloq.] 1 a selling out; betrayal 2 a show, game, etc. for which all the seats have been sold

selt·zer (selt'sər) *n.* 〖< *Niederselters*, Germany〗 1 [*often* S-] natural, effervescent mineral water 2 any carbonated water, often flavored

sel·vage or **sel·vedge** (sel'vij) *n.* 〖< SELF + EDGE〗 a specially woven edge that prevents cloth from raveling

selves (selvz) *n. pl. of* SELF

se·man·tics (sə man'tiks) *n.pl.* 〖< Gr *sēmainein*, to show〗 the study of the development and changes of the meanings of words —**se·man'tic** *adj.*

sema·phore (sem'ə fôr') *n.* 〖< Gr *sēma*, sign + *pherein*, to bear〗 any apparatus for signaling, as by lights, flags, etc.

sem·blance (sem'bləns) *n.* 〖< L *similis*, like〗 1 outward appearance 2 resemblance 3 a likeness or copy

se·men (sē'mən) *n., pl.* **semi·na** (sem'ə nə) or **-mens** 〖L, seed〗 the fluid secreted by the male reproductive organs

se·mes·ter (sə mes'tər) *n.* 〖< L *sex*, six + *mensis*, month〗 either of the two terms usually making up a school year

semi (sem'ī) *n. short for* SEMITRAILER: used loosely for a TRACTOR (sense 2) with an attached semitrailer

semi- 〖L〗 *prefix* 1 half 2 partly, not fully 3 twice in a (specified period)

semi·an·nual (sem'ē an'yoo əl) *adj.* 1 happening, coming, etc. every half year 2 lasting half a year

sem'i·au'to·mat'ic *adj.* designating an automatic weapon requiring a trigger pull for each round fired — *n.* a semiautomatic firearm

semi·cir·cle (sem'i sur'kəl) *n.* a half circle —**sem'i·cir'cu·lar** (-kyə lər) *adj.*

sem'i·co'lon *n.* a mark of punctuation (;) indicating a degree of separation greater than that marked by the comma

sem'i·con·duc'tor *n.* a substance, as germanium, used as in transistors

sem'i·con'scious *adj.* not fully conscious or awake

semi·fi·nal (sem'i fīn'əl; *for n.,* sem'i fīn'əl) *adj.* coming just before the final match, as of a contest — *n.* a semifinal match, etc.

semi·monthly (sem'i munth'lē) *adj.* done, happening, etc. twice a month — *adv.* twice monthly

semi·nal (sem'ə nəl) *adj.* 〖see SEMEN〗 1 of seed or semen 2 that is a source 3 of essential importance; specif., *a)* basic; principal *b)* crucial; critical

semi·nar (sem'ə när') *n.* 〖see fol.〗 1 a group of supervised students doing research 2 a course for such a group

semi·nary (sem'ə ner'ē) *n., pl.* **-nar'ies** 〖< L *seminarium*, nursery〗 1 a school, esp. a private school for young women 2 a school where priests, ministers, or rabbis are trained —**sem'i·nar'ian** *n.*

Semi·nole (sem'ə nōl') *n., pl.* **-noles'** or **-nole'** a member of an American Indian people of S Florida & Oklahoma

semi·precious (sem'i presh'əs) *adj.* designating gems, as the garnet, turquoise, etc., of lower value than precious stones

sem'i·pri'vate *adj.* of a hospital room with two, three, or sometimes four beds

sem'i·pro·fes'sional *n.* one who engages in a sport for pay but not as a regular occupation Also **sem'i·pro'**

sem'i·skilled' *adj.* of or doing manual work requiring only limited training

Sem·ite (sem'īt') *n.* 〖< Heb *Shem*, son of Noah〗 a member of any of the peoples speaking a Semitic language

Se·mitic (sə mit'ik) *adj.* designating or of the Semites or their languages, etc. — *n.* a major group of African and Asian languages, including Hebrew, Arabic, etc.

semi·tone (sem'i tōn') *n. Music* the difference in pitch between any two immediately adjacent keys on the piano

semi·trailer (sem'i trāl'ər) *n.* a detachable trailer attached to a coupling at the rear of a TRACTOR (sense 2)

sem'i·trans·par'ent *adj.* not perfectly or completely transparent

sem'i·trop'i·cal *adj.* partly tropical

sem'i·week'ly *adj.* done, happening, etc. twice a week — *adv.* twice weekly

Sen. 1 Senate 2 Senator 3 [*also* s-] senior

sen·ate (sen'it) *n.* 〖< L *senex*, old〗 1 a legislative assembly 2 [S-] the upper house of the U.S. Congress or of most of the State legislatures

---

THESAURUS

selfish *a.* self-seeking, self-centered, self-indulgent, indulging oneself, wrapped up in oneself, narrow, narrow-minded, prejudiced, egotistical, egotistic, looking out for number one*; see GREEDY.

selfishly *a.* egotistically, stingily, greedily, in one's own interest, meanly, ungenerously, to gain private ends, from selfish motives.

selfishness *n.* self-regard, self-indulgence, self-worship; see GREED.

self-made *a.* competent, self-reliant, audacious; see ABLE, CONFIDENT.

self-reliant *a.* determined, resolute, independent; see ABLE, CONFIDENT.

self-respect *n.* morale, worth, pride; see CONFIDENCE, DIGNITY.

self-restraint *n.* patience, endurance, control; see RESTRAINT 1.

self-sacrifice *n.* altruism, kindheartedness, benevolence; see GENER-OSITY, KINDNESS 1, 2.

self-satisfaction *n.* complacency, smugness, conceit; see EGOTISM.

self-satisfied *a.* smug, vain, conceited; see EGOTISTIC.

self-sufficient *a.* competent, self-confident, efficient; see CONFIDENT.

sell *v.* market, vend, auction, dispose of, put up for sale, put on the market, barter, exchange, transfer, liquidate, trade, bargain, peddle, retail, merchandise, sell over the counter, contract, wholesale, retail, dump, clear out, have a sale, give title to, put in escrow.—*Ant.* BUY, obtain, get. — **sell out*** trick, turn in, betray, double-cross*; see also DECEIVE.

seller *n.* dealer, tradesman, salesman, door-to-door salesman, retailer, agent, vender, merchant, auctioneer, shopkeeper, peddler, trader, marketer, storekeeper; see also BUSINESS-MAN, MERCHANT.

selling *n.* sale, auction, bartering, trading, vending, auctioning, transfer, transferring, commercial transaction, transacting, merchandising, disposal.—*Ant.* BUYING, purchasing, acquiring.

sellout* *n.* betrayal, deception, deal; see TRICK 1.

semester *n.* six-month period, eighteen weeks, four and one-half months; see TERM 2.

semifinal *n.* next to the last match, elimination test, elimination round; see ROUND 2.

seminary *n.* secondary school, institute, theological school; see SCHOOL 1.

senate *n.* legislative body, assembly, council; see LEGISLATURE.

Senate *n.* legislative body, upper

sena·tor (sen′ət ər) *n.* a member of a senate —**sena·to·rial** (sen′ə tôr′ē əl) *adj.*

send (send) *vt.* **sent, send′ing** ⟦OE *sendan*⟧ **1** to cause to go or be transmitted; dispatch; transmit **2** to cause (a person) to go **3** to impel; drive **4** to cause to happen, come, etc. **5** [Slang] to thrill —**send for 1** to summon **2** to place an order for —**send′er** *n.*

send′-off′ *n.* [Colloq.] **1** a farewell demonstration for someone starting out on a trip, career, etc. **2** a start given to someone or something

se·nile (sē′nīl′) *adj.* ⟦< L *senex*, old⟧ **1** of or resulting from old age: now chiefly medical **2** showing the deterioration accompanying old age, esp. confusion, memory loss, etc. —**se·nil·i·ty** (si nil′ə tē) *n.*

sen·ior (sēn′yər) *adj.* ⟦< L *senex*, old⟧ **1** older: written *Sr.* after a father's name if his son's name is the same **2** of higher rank or longer service **3** of or for seniors — *n.* **1** one who is older, of higher rank, etc. **2** a student in the last year of high school or college

senior citizen an elderly person, esp. one who is retired

senior high school high school, usually grades 10, 11, and 12

sen·ior·i·ty (sēn yôr′ə tē) *n.*, *pl.* **-ties 1** a being senior **2** status, priority, etc. achieved by length of service in a given job

senna (sen′ə) *n.* ⟦< Ar *sanā*, cassia plant⟧ the dried leaflets of a tropical cassia plant used, esp. formerly, as a laxative

se·ñor (se nyôr′) *n.*, *pl.* **se·ño·res** (-nyô′res) ⟦Sp⟧ a man; gentleman: as a title, equivalent to *Mr.* or *Sir*

se·ño·ra (se nyô′rä) *n.* ⟦Sp⟧ a married woman: as a title, equivalent to *Mrs.* or *Madam*

se·ño·ri·ta (se′nyô rē′tä) *n.* ⟦Sp⟧ an unmarried woman or girl: as a title, equivalent to *Miss*

sen·sa·tion (sen sā′shən) *n.* ⟦< L *sensus*, sense⟧ **1** the receiving of sense impressions through hearing, seeing, etc. **2** a conscious sense impression **3** a generalized feel-ing [a *sensation* of joy] **4** a feeling of excitement or its cause [the play is a *sensation*]

sen·sa′tion·al *adj.* **1** arousing intense interest **2** intended to shock, thrill, etc. —**sen·sa′tion·al·ism′** *n.*

sense (sens) *n.* ⟦< L *sentire*, to feel⟧ **1** any faculty of receiving impressions through body organs; sight, touch, taste, smell or hearing **2** *a)* feeling, perception, etc. through the senses *b)* a generalized feeling or awareness **3** an ability to understand some quality [a *sense* of humor] **4** normal intelligence and judgment **5** [*pl.*] normal ability to reason **6** meaning, as of a word — *vt.* **sensed, sens′ing 1** to perceive **2** to detect as by sensors —**in a sense** to a limited extent or degree —**make sense** to be intelligible or logical

sense′less *adj.* **1** unconscious **2** stupid; foolish **3** meaningless

sen·si·bil·i·ty (sen′sə bil′ə tē) *n.*, *pl.* **-ties 1** the capacity for physical sensation **2** [*often pl.*] delicate, sensitive awareness or feelings

sen′si·ble *adj.* **1** that can cause physical sensation **2** easily perceived **3** aware **4** having or showing good sense; wise —**sen′si·bly** *adv.*

sen·si·tive (sen′sə tiv′) *adj.* **1** sensory **2** very keenly susceptible to stimuli **3** tender; raw **4** having keen sensibilities **5** easily offended; touchy —**sen′si·tiv′i·ty** or **sen′si·tive·ness** *n.*

sen′si·tize′ (-tīz′) *vt.* **-tized′, -tiz′ing** to make sensitive

sen·sor (sen′sər) *n.* a device to detect, measure, or record physical phenomena, as radiation, heat, etc.

sen·so·ry (sen′sər ē) *adj.* of the senses or sensation

sen·su·al (sen′shōō əl) *adj.* ⟦< L *sensus*, sense⟧ **1** of the body and the senses as distinguished from the intellect **2** connected or preoccupied with sexual pleasure —**sen′su·al′i·ty** (-al′ə tē) *n.* —**sen′su·al·ly** *adv.*

sen·su·ous (sen′shōō əs) *adj.* **1** of, derived from, or perceived by the senses **2** enjoying sensation

sent (sent) *vt.*, *vi.* *pt. & pp. of* SEND

sen·tence (sen′təns) *n.* ⟦< L *sententia*, opinion⟧ **1** *a)* a decision as of a court; esp., the determination by a court of a punishment *b)* the punishment **2** a group of words stat-

branch of Congress, the Upper House; see LEGISLATURE.

senator *n.* statesman, politician, member of the senate; see REPRESENTATIVE 2.

send *v.* **1** [To dispatch] transmit, forward, convey, advance, express, ship, mail, send forth, send out, send in, delegate, expedite, hasten, accelerate, post, address, rush, rush off, hurry off, get under way, give papers, provide with credentials, send out for, address to, commission, consign, drop, convey, transfer, pack off, give, bestow, grant, confer, entrust, assign, impart, give out. **2** [To broadcast] usually electronically] transmit, relay, wire, cable, broadcast, televise, conduct, communicate. —**send (away) for** order, request, write away for; see ASK, GET 1. —**send back** reject, mail back, decide against; see RETURN 2.

senile *a.* aged, infirm, feeble; see OLD 1, SICK.

senility *n.* old age, dotage, feebleness, anility, infirmity, decline, senile dementia, Alzheimer's disease, senescence, second childhood; see also AGE 2, WEAKNESS 1.

senior *a.* elder, older, higher in rank; see SUPERIOR.

seniority *n.* preferred standing, ranking, station; see ADVANTAGE.

sensation *n.* **1** [The sense of feeling] sensibility, consciousness, perception; see EMOTION, THOUGHT 1. **2** [A feeling] response, sentiment, passion; see FEELING 1.

sensational *a.* **1** [Fascinating] exciting, marvelous, incredible; see IMPRESSIVE, INTERESTING. **2** [Melodramatic] exaggerated, excessive, emotional; see EXCITING.

sense *n.* **1** [One of the powers of physical perception] kinesthesia, function, sensation; see HEARING 3, SIGHT 1, TASTE 1, TOUCH 1. **2** [Mental ability] intellect, understanding, reason, mind, spirit, soul, brains, judgment, wit, imagination, common sense, cleverness, reasoning, intellectual ability, mental capacity, savvy*, knowledge; see also THOUGHT 1.— *Ant.* DULLNESS, idiocy, feeble wit. **3** [Reasonable and agreeable conduct] reasonableness, fairmindedness, discretion; see FAIRNESS. **4** [Tact and understanding] insight, discernment, social sense; see FEELING 4, JUDGMENT 1. —**in a sense** in a way, to a degree, somewhat; see SOME, SOMEHOW. —**make sense** be reasonable, be intelligible, be clear, be understandable, be logical, be coherent, articulate, add up, follow, deduce, hang together*, hold water*, put two and two together, straighten out, stand to reason.

senseless *a.* ridiculous, silly, foolish; see ILLOGICAL, STUPID.

senses *n.* consciousness, mental faculties, feeling; see AWARENESS, LIFE 1, 2.

sensible *a.* **1** [Showing good sense] reasonable, prudent, perceptive, acute, shrewd, sharp, careful, aware, wise, cautious, capable, having a head on one's shoulders*, endowed with reason, sane, discerning, thoughtful; see also RATIONAL 1, SANE 1. **2** [Perceptive] aware, informed, attentive; see CONSCIOUS.

sensitive *a.* **1** [Tender] delicate, sore, painful; see SORE 1. **2** [Touchy] high-strung, tense, nervous; see IRRITABLE, UNSTABLE 2.

sensitivity *n.* **1** [Susceptibility] allergy, irritability, ticklishness; see FEELING 4. **2** [Emotional response or condition] delicacy, sensibility, sensitiveness, nervousness, acute awareness, consciousness, acuteness, subtlety, feeling, sympathetic response, sympathy.

sensory *a.* **1** [Neurological] sensible, relating to the senses, conscious; see SENSUAL 1. **2** [Conveyed by the senses] audible, perceptible, discernible; see OBVIOUS 1, 2, TANGIBLE.

sensual *a.* **1** [Sensory] tactile, sensuous, stimulating, sharpened, pleasing, dazzling, feeling, being, heightened, enhanced, appealing, delightful, luxurious, emotional, fine, arousing, stirring, moving; see also EXCITING. **2** [Carnal] voluptuous, pleasure-loving, fleshly, lewd, unspiritual, self-loving, self-indulgent, epicurean, intemperate, gluttonous, rakish, debauched, orgiastic, sensuous, piggish, hoggish, bestial.

sensuality *n.* sensationalism, appetite, ardor; see DESIRE 2, EMOTION, LOVE 1.

sensuous *a.* passionate, physical, exciting; see SENSUAL 2.

sent *a.* commissioned, appointed, ordained, delegated, dispatched, directed, issued, transmitted, discharged, gone, on the road, in transit, uttered, sent forth, driven, impelled, forced to go, consigned, ordered, committed.—*Ant.* KEPT, restrained, held back.

sentence *n.* **1** [A pronounced judgment] edict, decree, order; see JUDGMENT 3, PUNISHMENT, VERDICT. **2** [An expressed thought] *Types of sentences include the following:* simple, complex, compound, compound-complex, kernel, transformed, declarative, interrogative, imperative, exclamatory; statement, question, command, exclamation.

sentence *v.* pronounce judgment, judge, send to prison; see CONDEMN, CONVICT, IMPRISON, PUNISH.

ing something, usually containing a subject and predicate —*vt.* **-tenced, -tenc·ing** to pronounce punishment upon (a convicted person)

sen·ten·tious (sen ten'shəs) *adj.* **1** full of, or fond of using, maxims, proverbs, etc. **2** ponderously trite

sen·tient (sen'shənt) *adj.* ⟦see SENSE⟧ of or capable of feeling; conscious

sen·ti·ment (sen'tə mənt) *n.* ⟦see SENSE⟧ **1** a complex combination of feelings and opinions **2** an opinion, etc., often colored by emotion **3** appeal of the emotions, or sensitivity to this **4** maudlin emotion

sen·ti·men·tal (sen'tə ment''l) *adj.* **1** having or showing tender or delicate feelings **2** maudlin; mawkish **3** of or resulting from sentiment —**sen'ti·men'tal·ism'** *n.* —**sen'ti·men'tal·ist** *n.* —**sen'ti·men·tal'i·ty** (-tal'ə tē) *n.* —**sen'ti·men'tal·ly** *adv.*

sen'ti·men'tal·ize' *vi.*, *vt.* **-ized', -iz'ing** to be sentimental or treat in a sentimental way

sen·ti·nel (sen'ti nəl) *n.* ⟦< L *sentire*, to sense⟧ a guard or sentry

sen·try (sen'trē) *n.*, *pl.* **-tries** ⟦< ? obs. *centrinell*, var. of prec.⟧ a sentinel; esp., a soldier posted to guard against danger

se·pal (sē'pəl) *n.* ⟦< Gr *skepē*, a covering + *petalon*, petal⟧ any of the leaflike parts of the calyx

sepa·rable (sep'ər ə bəl) *adj.* that can be separated — **sep'a·rably** *adv.*

sepa·rate (sep'ə rāt'; *for adj.*, -ər it) *vt.* **-rat'ed, -rat'ing** ⟦< L *se-*, apart + *parare*, arrange⟧ **1** to set apart into sections, groups, etc.; divide **2** to keep apart by being between — *vi.* **1** to withdraw **2** to part, become disconnected, etc. **3** to go in different directions —*adj.* **1** to set apart from the rest or others **2** not associated or connected with others; distinct **3** not shared *[separate beds]* —**sep'a·rately** *adv.* —**sep'a·ra'tor** *n.*

sepa·ra·tion (sep'ə rā'shən) *n.* **1** a separating or being separated **2** the place this occurs; break; division **3** something that separates

sep'a·ra·tism (-ər ə tiz'əm) *n.* the advocacy of separation, racially, politically, etc. —**sep'a·ra·tist** *n.*

se·pia (sē'pē ə) *n.*, *adj.* ⟦< Gr *sēpia*, cuttlefish secreting inky fluid⟧ (of) dark reddish-brown

sep·sis (sep'sis) *n.* ⟦see SEPTIC⟧ a poisoning caused by the absorption of pathogenic microorganisms into the blood

Sep·tem·ber (sep tem'bər) *n.* ⟦< L *septem*, seven: seventh month in Rom. calendar⟧ the ninth month of the year, having 30 days: abbrev. **Sept.**

sep·tet or **sep·tette** (sep tet') *n.* ⟦< L *septem*, seven⟧ *Music* **1** a composition for seven voices or instruments **2** the seven performers of this

sep·tic (sep'tik) *adj.* ⟦< Gr *sēpein*, to make putrid⟧ causing, or resulting from, sepsis or putrefaction

sep·ti·ce·mia (sep'tə sē'mē ə) *n.* ⟦see prec.⟧ a disease caused by infectious microorganisms in the blood

septic tank an underground tank in which waste matter is putrefied and decomposed through bacterial action

Sep·tua·gint (sep'tōō ə jint') ⟦< L *septuaginta*, seventy: in tradition, done in 70 days⟧ a translation into Greek of the Old Testament

sep·tum (sep'təm) *n.*, *pl.* **-tums** or **-ta** (-tə) ⟦< L *saepire*, enclose⟧ *Biol.* a dividing wall or part, as in the nose, a fruit, etc.

sep·ul·cher (sep'əl kər) *n.* ⟦< L *sepelire*, bury⟧ a vault for burial; tomb

se·pul·chral (sə pul'krəl) *adj.* **1** of sepulchers, burial, etc. **2** suggestive of the grave or burial; gloomy **3** deep and melancholy: said of sound

seq. ⟦L *sequentes*⟧ the following

se·quel (sē'kwəl) *n.* ⟦< L *sequi*, follow⟧ **1** something that follows; continuation **2** something coming as a result of something else; aftermath; effect **3** any literary work continuing a story begun in an earlier work

se·quence (sē'kwəns) *n.* ⟦< L *sequi*, follow⟧ **1** *a)* the coming of one thing after another; succession *b)* the order in which this occurs **2** a series **3** a resulting event **4** *Film* a succession of scenes forming a single episode

se·ques·ter (si kwes'tər) *vt.* ⟦< L *sequester*, trustee⟧ **1** to set off or apart **2** to withdraw; seclude —**se·ques·tra·tion** (sē'kwə strā'shən) *n.*

se·quin (sē'kwin) *n.* ⟦Fr; ult. < Ar *sikka*, a stamp⟧ a spangle, esp. one of many sewn on fabric for decoration — **se'quined** or **se'quinned** *adj.*

se·quoia (si kwoi'ə) *n.* ⟦after *Sequoyah*, Indian inventor of Cherokee writing⟧ REDWOOD

sera (sir'ə) *n.* *alt. pl.* of SERUM

se·ra·glio (si ral'yō) *n.*, *pl.* **-glios** ⟦< L *sera*, a lock⟧ HAREM (sense 1)

se·rape (sə rä'pē) *n.* ⟦MexSp⟧ a bright-colored woolen blanket used as a garment by men in Mexico, etc.

ser·aph (ser'əf) *n.*, *pl.* **-aphs** or **-a·phim'** (-ə fim') ⟦< Heb *serafim*, pl.⟧ *Theol.* a heavenly being, or a celestial being, of the highest order of angels —**se·raphic** (sə raf'ik) *adj.* —**se·raph'i·cally** *adv.*

Serb (sʉrb) *n.* **1** a native or inhabitant of Serbia **2** SERBIAN (*n.* 1) —*adj.* SERBIAN

Ser·bian (sʉr'bē ən) *adj.* of Serbia (a republic of Yugoslavia), the Serbs, or their language —*n.* **1** Serbo-Croatian as spoken in Serbia **2** SERB (*n.* 1)

Serbo-Croatian (sʉr'bō krō ā'shən) *n.* the major Slavic language of Yugoslavia, Bosnia and Herzegovina, & Croatia

sere (sir) *adj.* ⟦var. of SEAR⟧ [Old Poet.] dried up; withered

ser·enade (ser'ə nād') *n.* ⟦ult. < L *serenus*, clear⟧ music played or sung at night, esp. by a lover under his sweetheart's window —*vt.*, *vi.* **-nad'ed, -nad'ing** to play or sing a serenade (to)

ser·en·dip·ity (ser'ən dip'ə tē) *n.* ⟦after Pers tale *The Three Princes of Serendip*⟧ a seeming gift for finding good things accidentally —**ser'en·dip'i·tous** *adj.*

se·rene (sə rēn') *adj.* ⟦L *serenus*⟧ **1** clear; unclouded **2** undisturbed; calm —**se·rene'ly** *adv.* —**se·ren'i·ty** (-ren'ə tē) or **se·rene'ness** *n.*

serf (sʉrf) *n.* ⟦< L *servus*, slave⟧ a person in feudal servitude, bound to his master's land and transferred with it to a new owner —**serf'dom** *n.*

serge (sʉrj) *n.* ⟦< L *sericus*, silken⟧ a strong twilled fabric

ser·geant (sär'jənt) *n.* ⟦< L *servire*, serve⟧ **1** a noncommissioned officer ranking above a corporal **2** a police officer ranking next below a captain or a lieutenant

ser'geant-at-arms' *n.*, *pl.* **ser'geants-at-arms'** an officer appointed to keep order, as in a court

---

THESAURUS

sentiment *n.* sensibility, predilection, tender feeling; see EMOTION, FEELING 4, THOUGHT 2.

sentimental *a.* emotional, romantic, silly, dreamy, idealistic, visionary, artificial, unrealistic, susceptible, overemotional, affected, mawkish, simpering, insincere, overacted, schoolgirlish, sappy*, soupy*, gushy.

sentimentality *n.* sentimentalism, sentiment, melodramatics, bathos, mawkishness, melodrama, triteness, mush*, gush; see also EMOTION.

sentry *n.* sentinel, lookout, protector; see WATCHMAN.

separate *v.* **1** [To keep apart] isolate, insulate, single out, sequester, seclude, rope off, segregate, intervene, stand between, draw apart, split up, break up. **2** [To part company] take leave, go away, depart; see LEAVE 1.

separated *a.* divided, parted, apart, disconnected, partitioned, distinct, disunited, disjointed, sundered, dis-

embodied, cut in two, cut apart, set apart, distant, disassociated, removed, distributed, scattered, put asunder, divorced, divergent, marked, severed, far between, in halves.—*Ant.* UNITED, together, whole.

separately *a.* singly, definitely, distinctly; see CLEARLY 1, 2, INDIVIDUALLY.

separation *n.* **1** [The act of dividing] disconnection, severance, division, cut, detachment. **2** [The act of parting] coming apart, drawing apart, parting company, breaking up.

September *n.* fall or autumn or summer month, Indian summer, back-to-school season; see FALL 3.

sequel *n.* consequence, continuation, progression; see SEQUENCE 1, SERIES.

sequence *n.* **1** [Succession] order, continuity, continuousness, continuance, successiveness, progression, graduation, consecutiveness, flow, consecution, unbrokenness, sub-

sequence, course. **2** [Arrangement] placement, distribution, classification; see ORDER 3. **3** [A series] chain, string, array; see SERIES.

serenade *n.* melody, compliment, nocturne; see MUSIC 1, SONG.

serene *a.* calm, clear, unruffled, translucent, undisturbed, undimmed, tranquil, composed, cool, coolheaded, sedate, levelheaded, content, satisfied, patient, reconciled, easygoing, placid, limpid, comfortable, cheerful.—*Ant.* CONFUSED, disturbed, ruffled.

serenity *n.* quietness, calmness, tranquility; see PEACE 2, 3.

sergeant *n.* noncommissioned officer, top kick*, sarge*. *Types include the following:* master sergeant, staff sergeant, technical sergeant, first sergeant, top sergeant, platoon sergeant, drill sergeant, sergeant major, sergeant-at-arms, police sergeant; see also OFFICER 3, SOLDIER.

sergeant major *pl.* **sergeants major** the highest ranking noncommissioned officer

se·rial (sir′ē əl) *adj.* ⟦< L *series*, an order⟧ appearing in a series of continuous parts at regular intervals — *n.* a story, etc. presented in serial form —**se′ri·ali·za′tion** *n.* —**se′ri·al·ize′, -ized′, -iz′ing,** *vt.*

serial number one of a series of numbers given for identification

se·ries (sir′ēz) *n., pl.* **-ries** ⟦L < *serere*, join together⟧ number of similar things or persons arranged in a row or coming one after another

se·ri·ous (sir′ē əs) *adj.* ⟦< L *serius*⟧ **1** earnest, grave, sober, etc. **2** not joking; sincere **3** requiring careful thought; important **4** dangerous [a *serious* wound] —**se′ri·ous·ly** *adv.* —**se′ri·ous·ness** *n.*

ser·mon (sur′mən) *n.* ⟦< L *sermo*, discourse⟧ **1** a speech on religion or morals, esp. by a member of the clergy **2** any serious talk on behavior, duty, etc., esp. a tedious one —**ser′mon·ize′, -ized′, -iz′ing,** *vi.*

Sermon on the Mount the sermon delivered by Jesus to his disciples

se·rous (sir′əs) *adj.* **1** of or containing serum **2** thin and watery

ser·pent (sur′pənt) *n.* ⟦< L *serpere*, to creep⟧ a snake

ser′pen·tine′ (-pən tēn′, -tīn′) *adj.* of or like a serpent; esp., *a*) cunning; treacherous *b*) coiled; winding

ser·rate (ser′āt′) *adj.* ⟦< L *serra*, a saw⟧ having sawlike notches along the edge, as some leaves Also **ser·rat′ed** —**ser·ra′tion** *n.*

ser·ried (ser′ēd) *adj.* ⟦< LL *serare*, to lock⟧ placed close together

se·rum (sir′əm) *n., pl.* **-rums** or **-ra** (-ə) ⟦L, whey⟧ **1** any watery animal fluid, as the yellowish fluid (**blood serum**) separating from a blood clot after coagulation **2** blood serum used as an antitoxin, taken from an animal inoculated for a specific disease

serv·ant (sur′vənt) *n.* ⟦ult. < L *servire*, serve⟧ **1** a person employed by another, esp. to do household duties **2** a person devoted to another or to a cause, creed, etc.

serve (surv) *vt.* **served, serv′ing** ⟦< L *servus*, slave⟧ **1** to work for as a servant **2** to do services for; aid; help **3** to do military or naval service for **4** to spend (a term of imprisonment, etc.) [to *serve* ten years] **5** to provide (customers, etc.) with goods or services **6** to set food, etc. before (a person) **7** to meet the needs of **8** to be used by [one hospital *serves* the city] **9** to function for [if memory *serves* me well] **10** to deliver (a summons, etc.) to (someone) **11** to hit (a tennis ball, etc.) in order to start play — *vi.* **1** to work as a servant **2** to do service [to *serve* in the navy] **3** to carry out the duties of an office **4** to be of service **5** to meet needs **6** to provide guests with food or drink **7** to be favorable: said of weather, etc. — *n.* a serving of the ball in tennis, etc. —**serve someone right** to be what someone deserves —**serv′er** *n.*

serv·ice (sur′vis) *n.* ⟦< L *servus*, slave⟧ **1** the occupation of a servant **2** *a*) public employment [diplomatic *service*] *b*) a branch of this; specif., the armed forces **3** work done for others [repair *service*] **4** any religious ceremony **5** *a*) benefit; advantage *b*) [*pl.*] friendly help; also, professional aid **6** the act or manner of serving food **7** a set of articles used in serving [a tea *service*] **8** a system of providing people with some utility, as water or gas **9** the act or manner of serving in tennis, etc. — *vt.* **-iced, -ic·ing 1** to furnish with a service **2** to make fit for service, as by repairing —**at one's service 1** ready to serve with one **2** ready for one's use —**in service** functioning —**of service** helpful

serv′ice·able *adj.* **1** that can be of service; useful **2** that will give good service; durable

serv′ice·man′ *n., pl.* **-men′ 1** a member of the armed forces **2** a person whose work is repairing something [a TV *serviceman*]: also **service man**

service mark a word, etc. used like a trademark by a supplier of a service

service station a place selling gasoline, oil, etc., for motor vehicles

ser·vile (sur′vəl, -vīl) *adj.* ⟦< L *servus*, slave⟧ **1** of slaves **2** like that of slaves **3** humbly submissive —**ser·vil·ity** (sər vil′ə tē) *n.*

ser·vi·tor (sur′və tər) *n.* a servant

ser·vi·tude (sur′və tōōd′) *n.* ⟦see SERF⟧ **1** slavery or bondage **2** work imposed as punishment for crime

servo (sur′vō) *n., pl.* **-vos** *short for:* **1** SERVOMECHANISM **2** SERVOMOTOR

ser′vo·mech′a·nism *n.* an automatic control system of low power, used to exercise remote but accurate mechanical control

ser′vo·mo′tor *n.* a device, as an electric motor, for changing a small force into a large force, as in a servomechanism

ses·a·me (ses′ə mē′) *n.* ⟦of Semitic origin⟧ **1** a plant whose edible seeds yield an oil **2** its seeds

sesqui·cen·ten·nial (ses′kwi sen ten′ē əl) *adj.* ⟦< L *sesqui-*, more by a half + CENTENNIAL⟧ of a period of 150 years — *n.* a 150th anniversary

ses·sion (sesh′ən) *n.* ⟦< L *sedere*, sit⟧ **1** *a*) the meeting of a court, legislature, etc. *b*) a series of such meetings *c*) the period of these **2** a school term **3** a period of activity of any kind

set (set) *vt.* **set, set′ting** ⟦OE *settan*⟧ **1** to cause to sit; seat **2** to put in a specified place, condition, etc. [set books

---

■■■ THESAURUS ■■■

serial *n.* installment, serial picture, continued story; see MOVIE.

series *n.* rank, file, line, row, set, train, range, list, string, chain, order, sequence, succession, group, procession, continuity, column, progression, category, classification, scale, array, gradation.

serious *a.* **1** [Involving danger] grave, severe, pressing; see DANGEROUS, IMPORTANT 1. **2** [Thoughtful] earnest, sober, reflective; see SOLEMN.

seriously *a.* **1** [In a manner fraught with danger] dangerously, precariously, perilously, in a risky way, threateningly, menacingly, grievously, severely, harmfully.—*Ant.* SAFELY, harmlessly, in no danger. **2** [In a manner that recognizes importance] gravely, soberly, earnestly, solemnly, thoughtfully, sternly, sedately, with great earnestness, all joking aside; see also SINCERELY.— *Ant.* LIGHTLY, thoughtlessly, airily. —**take seriously** consider, calculate on, work on; see BELIEVE, TRUST 1.

seriousness *n.* **1** [The quality of being dangerous] gravity, weight, enormity; see IMPORTANCE. **2** [The characteristic of being sober] earnestness, sobriety, solemnity, gravity, staidness, thoughtfulness, calmness, coolness, sedateness, sobermindedness; see also SINCERITY.—*Ant.* FUN, gaiety, jollity.

sermon *n.* lesson, doctrine, lecture; see SPEECH 3.

serpent *n.* reptile, viper, ophidian; see SNAKE.

servant *n.* attendant, retainer, helper, hireling, dependent, menial, domestic, drudge, slave; see also ASSISTANT. *Servants include the following:* butler, housekeeper, chef, cook, second maid, kitchenmaid, maid of all work, general maid, laundress, chambermaid, parlormaid, lady's maid, seamstress, nursemaid, nurse, valet, doorman, footman, squire, chauffeur, groom, gardener, yardman, kennelman.

serve *v.* **1** [To fulfill an obligation] hear duty's call, obey the call of one's country, subserve, discharge one's duty, assume one's responsibilities. **2** [To work for] be employed by, labor for, be in the employ of; see WORK 2. **3** [To help] give aid, assist, be of assistance; see HELP. **4** [To serve at table] wait on, attend, provide guests with food, help. —**serve someone right** deserve it, having it coming, get one's just deserts; see DESERVE.

served *a.* dressed, prepared, offered, apportioned, dealt, furnished, supplied, provided, dished up.

service *n.* **1** [Aid] cooperation, assistance, aid; see HELP 1. **2** [Tableware] set, silver, setting; see DISH 1, POTTERY. **3** [A religious service] rite, worship, sermon; see CEREMONY 2. **4** [Military service] the armed forces, duty, active service, stint. —**at someone's service** zealous, anxious to help, obedient; see HELPFUL 1, READY 1, WILLING. —**of service** useful, handy, usable; see HELPFUL 1.

service *v.* maintain, sustain, keep up; see REPAIR.

serviceable *a.* practical, advantageous, beneficial; see HELPFUL 1, USABLE.

serving *n.* plateful, course, portion; see MEAL 2.

session *n.* assembly, concourse, sitting; see GATHERING.

set *a.* **1** [Firm] stable, solid, settled; see FIRM 2. **2** [Determined] concluded, steadfast, decided; see DETERMINED 1.

set *n.* **1** [Inclination] attitude, position, bearing; see INCLINATION 1. **2** [A social group] clique, coterie, circle; see FACTION, ORGANIZATION 2. **3** [A collection of (like) items] kit, assemblage, assortment; see COLLECTION.

set *v.* **1** [To place] insert, settle, put, plant, store, situate, lay, deposit, arrange. **2** [To establish] anchor, fix, introduce; see ESTABLISH 2, INSTALL. **3** [To become firm] jell, solidify, congeal; see HARDEN, STIFFEN, THICKEN. —**set about** start, begin, start on a shelf, *set* slaves free*]* **3** to put in a proper condition; fix (a trap for animals), adjust (a clock or dial), arrange (a table for meal), fix (hair) in a desired style, put (a broken bone, etc.) into normal position **4** to make settled, rigid, or fixed *[pectin sets jelly]* **5** to mount (gems) **6** to direct **7** to establish or fix (a boundary, the time for an event, a rule, a quota, etc.) **8** to furnish (an example) for others **9** to fit (words *to* music) **10** to arrange (type) for printing — *vi.* **1** to sit on eggs: said of a fowl **2** to become firm, hard, or fixed *[the cement set]* **3** to begin to move (*out, forth, off,* etc.) **4** to sink below the horizon *[the sun sets]* **5** to have a certain direction; tend — *adj.* **1** fixed; established *[a* **set** time*]* **2** intentional **3** rigid; firm **4** obstinate **5** ready *[get set]* — *n.* **1** a setting or being set **2** the way or position in which a thing is set *[the set of his jaw]* **3** the scenery for a play, etc. **4** a group of persons or things classed or belonging together **5** assembled equipment for radio or TV reception, etc. **6** *Tennis* a group of six or more games won by a margin of at least two —**set about** (or **in** or **to**) to begin —**set down** **1** to put in writing **2** to establish (rules, etc.) —**set forth** **1** to publish **2** to state —**set off** **1** to make prominent or enhance by contrast **2** to make explode —**set on** (or **upon**) to attack —**set up** **1** to erect **2** to establish; found

set′back′ *n.* a reversal in progress

set′screw′ *n.* a screw used in regulating the tension of a spring, etc.

set·tee (se tē′) *n.* **1** a seat or bench with a back **2** a small sofa

set′ter *n.* a long-haired bird dog trained to hunt game

set′ting *n.* **1** the act of one that sets **2** the position of a dial, etc. that has been set **3** a mounting, as of a gem **4** the time, place, etc., as of a story **5** actual physical surroundings

set·tle (set′'l) *vt.* **-tled, -tling** *[*OE *setl,* a seat *]* **1** to put in order; arrange *[to settle one's affairs]* **2** to set in place firmly or comfortably **3** to colonize **4** to cause to sink and become more compact **5** to free (the nerves, etc.) from disturbance **6** to decide (a dispute) **7** to pay (a debt, etc.) — *vi.* **1** to stop moving and stay in one place **2** to descend, as fog over a landscape, or gloom over a person **3** to become localized, as pain **4** to take up permanent residence **5** to sink *[the house settled]* **6** to become more dense by sinking, as sediment **7** to become more stable **8** to reach an agreement or decision (*with* or *on*) —**set′tler** *n.*

set′tle·ment *n.* **1** a settling or being settled **2** a new colony **3** a village **4** an agreement

set′-to′ *n., pl.* **-tos′** (-tōōz′) [Colloq.] **1** a fight **2** an argument

set′up′ *n.* **1** *a*) the plan, makeup, etc. of equipment, an organization, etc. *b*) the details of a situation, plan, etc. **2** [Colloq.] a contest, etc. arranged to result in an easy victory

seven (sev′ən) *adj., n.* *[*OE *seofon]* one more than six; 7; VII —**sev′enth** *adj., n.*

sev′en·teen′ (-tēn′) *adj., n.* seven more than ten; 17; XVII —**sev′en·teenth′** (-tēnth′) *adj., n.*

sev′enteen′-year′ locust a cicada which lives underground for 13-17 years before emerging as an adult

seventh heaven perfect happiness

sev·enty (sev′ən tē) *adj., n., pl.* **-ties** seven times ten; 70; LXX —**the seventies** the years, from 70 through 79, as of a century —**sev′en·ti·eth** (-ith) *adj., n.*

sever (sev′ər) *vt., vi.* *[< L separare]* to separate, divide, or divide off —**sev′er·ance** *n.*

sev·eral (sev′ər əl) *adj.* *[< L separ]* **1** separate; distinct **2** different; respective **3** more than two but not many; few — *n.* *[with pl. v.]* a small number (*of*) — *pron.* *[with pl. v.]* a few —**sev′er·ally** *adv.*

se·vere (sə vir′) *adj.* **-ver′er, -ver′est** *[< L severus]* **1** harsh or strict, as in treatment **2** serious, grave, as in expression **3** rigidly accurate or demanding **4** extremely plain *[a dress with severe lines]* **5** intense *[severe pain]* **6** rigorous; trying —**se·vere′ly** *adv.* —**se·vere′ness** or **se·ver′ity** (-ver′ə tē) *n.*

sew (sō) *vt., vi.* **sewed, sewn** (sōn) or **sewed, sew′ing** *[*OE *siwian]* **1** to fasten with stitches made with needle and thread **2** to make, mend, etc. by sewing —**sew up** **1** [Colloq.] to get full control **2** to make sure of success in — **sew′er** *n.*

sew·age (sōō′ij) *n.* waste matter carried by sewers

sewer (sōō′ər) *n.* *[*ult. *< L ex,* out *+ aqua,* water *]* a pipe or drain, usually underground, used to carry off water and waste matter

sew′er·age *n.* **1** a system of sewers **2** SEWAGE

sew·ing (sō′iŋ) *n.* **1** the act of one who sews **2** something to be sewn

sewing machine a machine with a mechanically driven needle used for sewing

sex (seks) *n.* *[< L sexus]* **1** either of two divisions, male or female, into which persons, animals, or plants are divided **2** the character of being male or female **3** the attraction

---

THESAURUS

doing; see BEGIN 1. —**set off** **1** [To show by contrast] set in relief, enhance, intensify, make distinct. **2** [To explode] touch off, set the spark to, detonate; see EXPLODE. —**set up** **1** [To make arrangements] prearrange, inaugurate, work on; see ARRANGE 2. **2** [To finance] patronize, promote, support; see PAY 1.

setback *n.* hindrance, check, reversal; see DELAY, DIFFICULTY 1.

setting *n.* environment, surroundings, mounting, backdrop, frame, framework, background, context, perspective, horizon, shadow, shade, distance.—*Ant.* FRONT, foreground, focus.

settle *v.* **1** [To decide] reach a decision, form judgment on, come to a conclusion about; see DECIDE. **2** [To prove] establish, verify, make certain; see PROVE. **3** [To finish] end, make an end of, complete; see ACHIEVE. **4** [To sink] descend, fall, decline; see SINK 1. **5** [To establish residence] locate, lodge, become a citizen, reside, fix one's residence, abide, set up housekeeping, make one's home, establish a home, keep house; see also DWELL. **6** [To take up sedentary life; *often used with* "*down*"] follow regular habits, live an orderly life, become conventional, follow convention, buy a house, marry, marry and settle down, raise a family, get in a rut, hang up one's hat*. **7** [To satisfy a claim] pay, compensate, make an adjustment, reach a compromise, make payment,

arrange a settlement, get squared away, pay damages, pay out, settle out of court, settle up, work out, settle the score, even the score, dispose of, account with.

settled *a.* decided, resolved, ended; see DETERMINED 1.

settlement *n.* **1** [An agreement] covenant, arrangement, compact; see AGREEMENT 1, CONTRACT. **2** [A payment] compensation, remuneration, reimbursement; see ADJUSTMENT, PAY 1. **3** [A colony] principality, plantation, establishment; see COLONY.

settler *n.* planter, immigrant, homesteader; see PIONEER 2.

setup *n.* structure, composition, plan; see ORDER 3, ORGANIZATION 2.

sever *v.* part, split, cleave; see CUT 1, DIVIDE.

several *a.* **1** [Few] some, any, a few, quite a few, not many, sundry, two or three, a small number of, scarce, sparse, hardly any, scarcely any, half a dozen, only a few, scant, scanty, rare, infrequent, in a minority, a handful, more or less, not too many.—*Ant.* many, large numbers of, none. **2** [Various] plural, a number of, numerous; see MANY, VARIOUS.

several *n.* various ones, a small number; quite a few; see FEW.

severe *a.* **1** [Stern] exacting, uncompromising, unbending, inflexible, unchanging, unalterable, harsh, cruel, oppressive, close, grinding, obdurate, resolute, austere, rigid, grim, earnest, stiff, forbidding,

resolved, relentless, determined, unfeeling, with an iron will, strict, inconsiderate, firm, unsparing, immovable, unyielding. **2** [Difficult or rigorous] overbearing, tyrannical, sharp, exacting, drastic, domineering, rigid, oppressive, despotic, unmerciful, bullying, uncompromising, relentless, unrelenting, hard, rigorous, austere, grinding, grim, implacable, cruel, pitiless, critical, unjust, barbarous, crusty, gruff, stubborn, autocratic, hidebound; see also DIFFICULT 1.—*Ant.* EASY, easygoing, indulgent.

severely *a.* critically, harshly, rigorously; see FIRMLY 2, SERIOUSLY 1.

severity *n.* hardness, hardheartedness, strictness; see CRUELTY.

sew *v.* stitch, seam, fasten, work with needle and thread, tailor, tack, embroider, bind, piece, baste.

sewage *n.* excrement, offal, waste matter; see RESIDUE.

sewer *n.* drain, drainpipe, drainage tube, conduit, gutter, disposal system, sewage system, septic tank, dry well, leach field, leach bed, leach ditches, sewage disposal, sanitary provisions, sanitary facility, sanitary facilities.

sewing *n.* stitching, seaming, tailoring, embroidering, darning, mending, piecing, patching, dressmaking.

sex *n.* **1** [Ideas associated with sexual relationships] sex attraction, sex appeal, magnetism, sensuality, affinity, love, courtship, marriage, generabetween the sexes **4** sexual activity; esp., sexual intercourse — *adj.* SEXUAL

sex- ⟦< L *sex*, six⟧ *combining form* six

sexa·genar·ian (seks′ə ji ner′ē ən) *adj.* ⟦< L⟧ between the ages of 60 and 70 — *n.* a person of this age

sex appeal the physical charm that attracts members of the opposite sex

sex chromosome a sex-determining chromosome in the germ cells: eggs carry an X chromosome and spermatozoa either an X or Y chromosome, with a female resulting from an XX pairing and a male from an XY

sex·ism′ *n.* discrimination against people, esp. women, on the basis of sex —**sex′ist** *adj.*, *n.*

sex·tant (seks′tənt) *n.* ⟦< L *sextans*, a sixth part (of a circle)⟧ an instrument for measuring the angular distance of the sun, a star, etc. from the horizon, as to determine position at sea

sex·tet or **sex·tette** (seks tet′) *n.* ⟦< L *sex*, six⟧ **1** a group of six **2** *Music* a composition for six voices or instruments, or the six performers of this

sex·ton (seks′tən) *n.* ⟦ult. < L *sacer*, sacred⟧ a church officer or employee in charge of the maintenance of church property

sex·ual (sek′shōō əl) *adj.* of or involving sex, the sexes, the sex organs, etc. —**sex′u·al·ly** *adv.* —**sex′u·al′i·ty** (-al′ə tē) *n.*

sexual intercourse a joining of the sexual organs of a male and a female human being

sex′y *adj.* **-i·er**, **-i·est** [Colloq.] **1** sexually stimulating; erotic **2** [Slang] exciting or glamorous —**sex′i·ly** *adv.* —**sex′i·ness** *n.*

sf or **SF** science fiction

Sgt. Sergeant

sh (sh) *interj.* hush! be quiet!

shabby (shab′ē) *adj.* **-bier**, **-bi·est** ⟦OE *sceabb*, scab⟧ **1** rundown; dilapidated **2** *a*) ragged; worn *b*) wearing worn clothing **3** mean; shameful *[shabby* behavior] —**shab′bily** *adv.* —**shab′bi·ness** *n.*

shack (shak) *n.* ⟦< ?⟧ a small, crudely built house or cabin; shanty

shackle (shak′əl) *n.* ⟦OE *sceacel*⟧ **1** a metal fastening, usually in pairs, for the wrist or ankle of a prisoner; fetter **2** anything that restrains freedom, as of expression **3** a device for coupling, etc. — *vt.* **-led**, **-ling 1** to put shackles on **2** to restrain in freedom of expression or action

shad (shad) *n.*, *pl.* **shad** or **shads** ⟦OE *sceadd*⟧ an American coastal food fish

shade (shād) *n.* ⟦OE *sceadu*⟧ **1** comparative darkness caused by cutting off rays of light **2** an area with less light than its surroundings **3** degree of darkness of a color **4** *a*) a small difference *[shades* of opinion] *b*) a slight amount or degree **5** [Chiefly Literary] a ghost **6** device used to screen from light *[a* window *shade]* **7** [*pl.*] [Slang] sunglasses — *vt.* **shad′ed**, **shad′ing 1** to screen from light **2** to darken; dim **3** to represent shade in (a painting, etc.) — *vi.* to change slightly or by degrees

shad·ing (shād′iŋ) *n.* **1** a shielding against light **2** the representation of shade in a picture **3** a small variation

shadow (shad′ō) *n.* ⟦< OE *sceadu*, shade⟧ **1** (a) shade cast by a body intercepting light rays **2** gloom or that which causes gloom **3** a shaded area in a picture **4** a ghost **5** a remnant; trace — *vt.* **1** to throw a shadow upon **2** to follow closely, esp. in secret —**shad′owy** *adj.*

shad′ow·box′ *vi. Boxing* to spar with an imaginary opponent in training

shady (shā′dē) *adj.* **-i·er**, **-i·est 1** giving shade **2** shaded; full of shade **3** [Colloq.] of questionable character —**on the shady side of** beyond (a given age) —**shad′i·ness** *n.*

shaft (shaft) *n.* ⟦OE *sceaft*⟧ **1** an arrow or spear **2** its stem **2** anything hurled like a missile *[shafts* of wit] **3** a long, slender part or object, as a pillar, either of the poles between which an animal is harnessed to a vehicle, a bar transmitting motion to a mechanical part, etc. **4** a long, narrow passage sunk into the earth **5** a vertical opening passing through a building, as for an elevator — *vt.* [Slang] to cheat, trick, exploit, etc.

shag¹ (shag) *n.* ⟦< OE *sceacga*, rough hair⟧ a heavy, rough nap, as on some cloth

shag² (shag) *vt.* **shagged**, **shag′ging** ⟦< ?⟧ to chase after and retrieve (baseballs hit in batting practice)

shag′gy *adj.* **-gier**, **-gi·est 1** covered with long, coarse hair or wool **2** unkempt, straggly, etc. **3** having a rough nap

shah (shä) *n.* ⟦Pers *šāh*⟧ the title of former rulers of Iran

shake (shāk) *vt.*, *vi.* **shook**, **shak′en**, **shak′ing** ⟦OE *sceacan*⟧ **1** to move quickly up and down, back and forth, etc. **2** to bring, force, mix, etc. by brisk movement **3** to tremble or cause to tremble **4** *a*) to become or cause to become unsteady *b*) to unnerve or become unnerved **5** to clasp (another's hand), as in greeting — *n.* **1** an act of shaking **2** a wood shingle **3** *short for* MILKSHAKE **4** [*pl.*] [Colloq.] a convulsive trembling: usually with *the* —**no great shakes** [Colloq.] not outstanding —**shake down 1** to cause to fall by shaking **2** [Slang] to extort money from —**shake off** to get rid of —**shak′y**, **-i·er**, **-i·est**, *adj.*

shake′down′ *n.* **1** an extortion of money, as by blackmail **2** a thorough search — *adj.* for testing new equipment, etc. *[a shakedown* cruise]

shake′out′ *n.* a drop in economic activity that eliminates unprofitable businesses, etc.

shak′er *n.* **1** a person or thing that shakes **2** a device used in shaking **3** [S-] a member of a religious sect that lived in celibate communities in the U.S.

shake′-up′ *n.* a shaking up; specif., an extensive reorganization

shale (shāl) *n.* ⟦< OE *scealu*, shell⟧ a rock formed of hard clay: it splits easily into thin layers

shale oil oil distilled from a hard shale containing veins of a greasy organic solid

shall (shal) *v.aux. pt.* **should** ⟦OE *sceal*⟧ **1** used in the first person to indicate simple future time **2** used in the second or third person, esp. in formal speech or writing, to express determination, compulsion, obligation, or necessity See usage note at WILL²

THESAURUS

tion, reproduction. **2** [A group, either male or female] men, women, males, females, the feminine world, the masculine world. **3** [Gender] sexuality, masculinity, femininity, womanliness, manhood, manliness. **4** [Sexual intercourse] making love, the sexual act, going to bed with someone; see COPULATION, FORNICATION.

sexual *a.* **1** [Reproductive] generative, reproductive, procreative; see ORIGINAL 1. **2** [Intimate] carnal, wanton, passionate; see SENSUAL 2.

sexuality *n.* lust, sensuality, passion; see DESIRE 2.

shabby *a.* ragged, threadbare, faded, ill-dressed, dilapidated, decayed, deteriorated, poor, pitiful, worn, meager, miserable, wretched, poverty-stricken, scrubby, seedy, gone to seed, down at the heel.—*Ant.* NEAT, new, well-kept.

shack *n.* hut, shed, hovel, cabin, shanty, shotgun shack.

shade *n.* **1** [Lack of light] blackness, shadow, dimness; see DARKNESS 1. **2** [A degree of color] brilliance, saturation, hue; see COLOR, TINT. **3** [A

slight difference] variation, trace, hint; see SUGGESTION 1. **4** [An obstruction to light] covering, blind, screen; see CURTAIN.

shade *v.* **1** [To intercept direct rays] screen, cover, shadow; see SHELTER. **2** [To make darker] darken, blacken, obscure, cloud, shadow, make dim, tone down, black out, make dusky, deepen the shade, overshadow, make gloomy, screen, shut out the light, keep out the light. **3** [To become darker] grow dark, grow black, become dark, grow dim, blacken, turn to twilight, deepen into night, become gloomy, be overcast, grow dusky, cloud up, cloud over, overcloud, grow shadowy.

shadow *n.* umbra, obscuration, adumbration; see DARKNESS 1.

shadow *v.* **1** [To shade] dim, veil, screen; see SHADE 1, 2, SHELTER. **2** [To follow secretly] trail, watch, keep in sight; see PURSUE 1.

shady *a.* **1** [Shaded] dusky, shadowy, adumbral, in the shade, shaded, sheltered, out of the sun, dim, cloudy, under a cloud, cool, indistinct, vague; see also DARK 1. **2** [*Questionable]

suspicious, disreputable, dubious, fishy*, underhanded.

shaft *n.* **1** [Rod] stem, bar, pole; see ROD 1. **2** [Light ray] wave, streak, beam of light; see RAY.

shake *n.* tremor, shiver, pulsation; see MOVEMENT 1, 2.

shake *v.* **1** [To vibrate] tremble, quiver, quake, shiver, shudder, palpitate, wave, waver, fluctuate, reel, flap, flutter, totter, thrill, wobble, stagger, waggle. **2** [To cause to vibrate] agitate, rock, sway, swing, joggle, jolt, bounce, jar, move, set in motion, convulse.

shaken *a.* unnerved, upset, overcome; see EXCITED.

shaky *a.* **1** [Not firm] quivery, trembling, jellylike, unsettled, not set, yielding, unsteady, tottering, unsound, insecure, unstable, infirm, jittery, nervous.—*Ant.* FIRM, settled, rigid. **2** [Not reliable] uncertain, not dependable, questionable; see UNRELIABLE, UNSTABLE 2.

shall *v.* intend, want to, must; see WILL 3.

shal·lot (shə lät′) *n.* 〖< OFr *eschaloigne*, scallion〗 1 a small onion whose clustered bulbs are used for flavoring 2 GREEN ONION

shal·low (shal′ō) *adj.* 〖ME *shalow*〗 1 not deep 2 lacking depth of character, intellect, etc. —*n.* [*usually pl., often with sing. v.*] a shoal

shalt (shalt) *archaic 2d pers. sing., pres. indic., of* SHALL: used with *thou*

sham (sham) *n.* 〖< ? shame〗 something false or fake; person or thing that is a fraud —*adj.* false or fake —*vt., vi.* shammed, sham′ming to pretend; feign

sham·ble (sham′bəl) *vi.* -bled, -bling 〖< obs. use in "shamble legs," bench legs〗 to walk clumsily; shuffle —*n.* a shambling walk

sham′bles (-bəlz) *n.pl.* 〖ME *schamel*, butcher's bench; ult. < L〗 [*with sing. v.*] 1 a slaughterhouse 2 a scene of great slaughter, destruction, or disorder

shame (shām) *n.* 〖OE *scamu*〗 1 a painful feeling of guilt for improper behavior, etc. 2 dishonor or disgrace 3 something regrettable or outrageous —*vt.* shamed, sham′ing 1 to cause to feel shame 2 to dishonor or disgrace 3 to force by a sense of shame —put to shame 1 to cause to feel shame 2 to surpass —shame′ful *adj.* —shame′fully *adv.* —shame′ful·ness *n.*

shame′faced′ *adj.* showing shame; ashamed

shame′less *adj.* having or showing no shame, modesty, or decency; brazen

sham·poo (sham pōō′) *vt.* -pooed′, -poo′ing 〖Hindi *chāmpnā*, to press〗 1 to wash (the hair) 2 to wash (a rug, sofa, etc.) —*n.* 1 a shampooing 2 a liquid soap, etc. used for this

sham·rock (sham′räk′) *n.* 〖Ir *seamar*, clover〗 a cloverlike plant with leaflets in groups of three: the emblem of Ireland

shang·hai (shaŋ′hī′, shaŋ hī′) *vt.* 〖< such kidnapping for crews on the China run〗 to kidnap, usually by drugging, for service aboard ship

shank (shaŋk) *n.* 〖OE *scanca*〗 1 the part of the leg between the knee and ankle in humans, or a corresponding part in animals 2 the whole leg 3 the part between the handle and the working part (of a tool, etc.) —shank of the evening early evening

shan′t (shant) shall not

shan·tung (shan′tuŋ′) *n.* 〖after *Shantung*, Chin province〗 a silk or silky fabric with an uneven surface

shanty (shan′tē) *n., pl.* -ties 〖< CdnFr *chantier*, workshop〗 a small, shabby dwelling; shack; hut

shape (shāp) *n.* 〖< OE (*ge*)*sceap*, a form〗 1 that quality of a thing which depends on the relative position of all the points on its surface; physical form 2 the contour of the body 3 definite or regular form *[to begin to take shape]* 4 [Colloq.] physical condition —*vt.* shaped, shap′ing 1 to give definite shape to 2 to arrange, express, etc. (a plan, etc.) in definite form 3 to adapt *[shaped to our needs]* —shape up [Colloq.] to develop to a definite or satisfactory form, etc. —take shape to begin to have definite form —shape′less *adj.* —shape′less·ness *n.*

shape′ly *adj.* -lier, -li·est having a pleasing figure: used esp. of a woman

shard (shärd) *n.* 〖OE *sceard*〗 a broken piece, esp. of pottery

share[1] (sher) *n.* 〖OE *scearu*〗 1 a portion that belongs to an individual 2 any of the equal parts of capital stock of a corporation —*vt.* shared, shar′ing 1 to distribute in shares 2 to receive, use, etc. in common with others —*vi.* to have a share (*in*)

share[2] (sher) *n.* 〖OE *scear*〗 a plowshare

share′crop′ *vi.* -cropped′, -crop′ping to work (land) for a share of the crop —share′crop′per *n.*

share′hold′er *n.* a person who owns shares of stock in a corporation

shark[1] (shärk) *n.* 〖prob. < Ger *schurke*, scoundrel〗 1 a swindler 2 [Slang] an expert in a given activity

shark[2] (shärk) *n.* 〖< ?〗 a large, predatory sea fish with a tough, gray skin

shark′skin′ *n.* a smooth, silky cloth of cotton, rayon, etc.

sharp (shärp) *adj.* 〖OE *scearp*〗 1 having a fine edge or point for cutting or piercing 2 having a point or edge; not rounded 3 not gradual; abrupt 4 clearly defined; distinct *[a sharp contrast]* 5 quick in perception; clever 6 attentive; vigilant 7 crafty; underhanded 8 harsh; severe *[a sharp temper]* 9 violent, as an attack 10 brisk; active 11 intense, as a pain 12 pungent 13 nippy, as a wind 14 [Slang] smartly dressed 15 *Music* above the true pitch —*adv.* 1 in a sharp manner; specif., *a*) abruptly or briskly *b*) attentively or alertly *c*) *Music* above the true pitch 2 precisely *[one o'clock sharp]* —*n.* 1 [Colloq.] an expert or adept 2 *Music a*) a tone one half step above another *b*) the symbol (♯) for such a note —*vt., vi. Music* to make or become sharp —sharp′ly *adv.* —sharp′ness *n.*

sharp′en *vt., vi.* to make or become sharp —sharp′ener *n.*

═══ **THESAURUS** ═══

shallow *a.* 1 [Lacking physical depth] slight, inconsiderable, superficial, with the bottom in plain sight, with no depth, with little depth, not deep.—*Ant.* DEEP, bottomless, unfathomable. 2 [Lacking intellectual depth] simple, silly, trifling, frivolous, superficial, petty, foolish, idle, unintelligent, piddling, wishy-washy*; see also STUPID.

sham *a.* not genuine, counterfeit, misleading; see FALSE 3.

sham *n.* pretense, deception, counterfeit; see FAKE.

shame *n.* 1 [A disgrace] embarrassment, stigma, blot; see DISGRACE. 2 [A sense of wrongdoing] bad conscience, mortification, confusion, humiliation, compunction, regret, chagrin, discomposure, irritation, remorse, embarrassment, abashment, self-reproach, self-disgust; see also GUILT. 3 [A condition of disgrace] humiliation, dishonor, degradation; see DISGRACE, SCANDAL.

shame *v.* humiliate, mortify, dishonor; see DISGRACE, HUMBLE.

shameful *a.* 1 [Offensive] immodest, corrupt, immoral, intemperate, debauched, drunken, villainous, knavish, degraded, reprobate, diabolical, indecent, indelicate, lewd, vulgar, impure, unclean, fleshly, carnal, sinful, wicked. 2 [Disgraceful] dishonorable, scandalous, flagrant, obscene, ribald, infamous, outrageous, gross, infernal, disgusting, too bad, unworthy, evil, foul, hellish, disreputable, despicable; see also WRONG.—*Ant.* WORTHY, admirable,

creditable.

shameless *a.* brazen, bold, forward; see RUDE 2, LEWD 2.

shape *n.* 1 [Form] contour, aspect, configuration; see FORM 1, LOOKS. 2 [An actual form] pattern, stamp, frame; see MOLD 1. 3 [Condition] fitness, physical state, health; see STATE 2. —out of shape distorted, misshapen, battered; see BENT, BROKEN 1, FLAT 1, RUINED 1, 2, TWISTED 1. — take shape take on form, mature, fill out; see DEVELOP 1, IMPROVE 2.

shape *v.* 1 [To give shape] mold, cast, fashion; see FORM 1. 2 [*To take shape] become, develop, take form; see FORM 4, GROW 2. —shape up* 1 [To obey] mind, observe the rules, conform; see BEHAVE, IMPROVE 2, OBEY. 2 [To develop] enlarge, expand, advance; see DEVELOP 1.

shaped *a.* made, fashioned, created; see FORMED.

shapeless *a.* 1 [Formless] indistinct, indefinite, invisible, vague, without form, without shape, lacking form, unformed, unmade, not formed, with no definite outline; see also UNCERTAIN. 2 [Deformed] misshapen, irregular, unshapely, unsymmetrical, mutilated, disfigured, malformed, ill-formed, abnormal; see also DEFORMED.—*Ant.* REGULAR, symmetrical, shapely.

shapely *a.* symmetrical, comely, proportioned; see TRIM 2.

share[1] *n.* division, apportionment, part, portion, helping, serving, piece, ration, slice, allotment, parcel, dose,

fraction, fragment, allowance, dividend, percentage, commission, cut*, whack*, rake-off*.

share[1] *v.* 1 [To divide] allot, distribute, apportion, part, deal, dispense, assign, administer.—*Ant.* UNITE, combine, withhold. 2 [To partake] participate, share in, experience, take part in, receive, have a portion of, have a share in, go in with, take a part of, take a share of.—*Ant.* AVOID, have no share in, take no part in. 3 [To give] yield, bestow, accord; see GIVE 1.

sharp *a.* 1 [Having a keen edge] acute, edged, razor-edged, sharpened, ground fine, honed, razor-sharp, sharp-edged, fine, cutting, knifelike, knife-edged.—*Ant.* DULL, unsharpened, blunt. 2 [Having a keen point] pointed, sharp-pointed, spiked, spiky, peaked, salient, needle-pointed, keen, fine, spiny, thorny, prickly, barbed, needlelike, stinging, sharp as a needle, pronged, tapered, tapering, horned. 3 [Having a keen mind] clever, astute, bright; see INTELLIGENT. 4 [Distinct] audible, visible, explicit; see CLEAR 2, DEFINITE 2, OBVIOUS 1. 5 [Intense] cutting, biting, piercing; see INTENSE. 6 [*Stylish] dressy, chic, in style; see FASHIONABLE.

sharpen *v.* 1 [To make keen] grind, file, hone, put an edge on, grind to a fine edge, make sharp, make acute, whet, give an edge to, put a point on, give a fine point to.—*Ant.* FLATTEN, thicken, turn. 2 [To make

sharp′er *n.* a swindler or cheat

sharp′-eyed′ *adj.* having keen sight or perception Also **sharp′-sight′ed** *adj.*

sharpie (shär′pē) *n.* [Colloq.] a shrewd, cunning person, esp. a sharper

sharp′shoot′er *n.* a good marksman

sharp′-tongued′ *adj.* using sharp or harshly critical language

sharp′-wit′ted (-wit′id) *adj.* thinking quickly and effectively

shat·ter (shat′ər) *vt.* [ME *schateren*, scatter] 1 to break or burst into pieces suddenly with a blow 2 to damage or be damaged severely

shat′ter·proof′ *adj.* that will resist shattering

shave (shāv) *vt.* **shaved, shaved** or **shav′en, shav′ing** [OE *sceafan*] 1 to cut away thin slices or sections from 2 *a*) to cut off (hair) at the surface of the skin *b*) to cut the hair to the surface of (the face, etc.) *c*) to cut the beard of (a person) 3 to barely touch in passing; graze — *vi.* to cut off a beard with a razor, etc. — *n.* the act or an instance of shaving

shav′er *n.* 1 a person who shaves 2 an instrument used in shaving, esp. one with electrically operated cutters 3 [Colloq.] a boy; lad

shav·ing (shā′vin) *n.* 1 the act of one who shaves 2 a thin piece of wood, metal, etc. shaved off

shawl (shôl) *n.* [prob. < Pers *shāl*] an oblong or square cloth worn as a covering for the head or shoulders

shay (shā) *n.* [< CHAISE, assumed as pl.] [Dial.] a light carriage; chaise

she (shē) *pron.*, *pl. see* THEY [< OE *seo*] the woman, girl, or female animal previously mentioned — *n.*, *pl.* **shes** a woman, girl, or female animal

sheaf (shēf) *n.*, *pl.* **sheaves** [OE *sceaf*] 1 a bundle of cut stalks of grain, etc. 2 a collection, as of papers, bound in a bundle

shear (shir) *vt.* **sheared, sheared** or **shorn, shear′ing** [OE *scieran*] 1 to cut as with shears 2 to clip (hair) from (the head, wool) from (sheep), etc. 3 to divest (someone) *of* a power, etc. — *n.* a shearing —**shear′er** *n.*

shears *n.pl.* 1 large scissors 2 a large tool or machine with two opposed blades, used to cut metal, etc.

sheath (shēth) *n.*, *pl.* **sheaths** (shēthz, shēths) [OE *sceath*] 1 a case for the blade of a knife, sword, etc. 2 a covering resembling this 3 a woman's closefitting dress

sheathe (shēth) *vt.* **sheathed, sheath′ing** 1 to put into a sheath 2 to enclose in a case or covering

sheath·ing (shē′thin) *n.* something that sheathes, as boards, etc. forming the base for roofing or siding

she·bang (shə ban′) *n.* [Colloq.] an affair, business, contrivance, etc. Chiefly in **the whole shebang**

shed[1] (shed) *n.* [OE *scead*] a small structure for shelter or storage

shed[2] (shed) *vt.* **shed, shed′ding** [< OE *sceadan*, to separate] 1 to pour out 2 to cause to flow [to *shed* tears] 3 to radiate [to *shed* confidence] 4 to cause to flow off [oilskin *sheds* water] 5 to cast off or lose (a natural growth, as hair, etc.) — *vi.* to shed hair, etc. —**shed blood** to kill violently

sheen (shēn) *n.* [< OE *sciene*, beautiful] brightness; luster —**sheen′y, -i·er, -i·est,** *adj.*

sheep (shēp) *n.*, *pl.* **sheep** [< OE *sceap*] 1 a cud-chewing mammal related to the goats, with heavy wool and edible flesh called mutton 2 one who is meek, timid, submissive, etc.

sheep dog a dog trained to herd sheep

sheep′fold′ *n.* a pen or enclosure for sheep Also **sheep′cote′** (-kōt′) *n.*

sheep′ish *adj.* 1 embarrassed or chagrined 2 shy or bashful —**sheep′ishly** *adv.* —**sheep′ish·ness** *n.*

sheep′skin′ *n.* 1 the skin of a sheep 2 parchment or leather made from it 3 [Colloq.] a diploma

sheer[1] (shir) *vi., vt.* [var. of SHEAR] to turn aside or cause to turn aside from a course; swerve

sheer[2] (shir) *adj.* [< ON *skœrr*, bright] 1 very thin; transparent: said of textiles 2 absolute; utter [*sheer* folly] 3 extremely steep — *adv.* 1 completely; utterly 2 very steeply

sheet[1] (shēt) *n.* [OE *sceat*] 1 a large piece of cotton, linen, etc., used on a bed 2 *a*) a single piece of paper *b*) [Colloq.] a newspaper 3 a broad, continuous surface or expanse, as of flame, ice, etc. 4 a broad, thin piece of any material, as glass, plywood, metal, etc.

sheet[2] (shēt) *n.* [short for OE *sceatline*] a rope for controlling the set of a sail

sheet′ing *n.* 1 cotton or linen material used for making sheets 2 material used to cover or line a surface [copper *sheeting*]

sheet metal metal rolled thin in the form of a sheet

sheet music music printed on unbound sheets of paper

sheik or **sheikh** (shēk, *also* shāk) *n.* [Ar *shaikh*, lit., old man] the chief of an Arab family, tribe, or village

shekel (shek′əl) *n.* [Heb < *shakal*, weigh] 1 a gold or silver coin of the ancient Hebrews 2 the monetary unit of Israel 3 [pl.] [Slang] money

shelf (shelf) *n.*, *pl.* **shelves** [prob. < MLowG *schelf*] 1 a thin, flat board fixed horizontally to a wall, used for holding things 2 something like a shelf; specif., *a*) a ledge *b*) a sandbar —**on the shelf** out of use, activity, etc.

shell (shel) *n.* [OE *sciel*] 1 a hard outer covering, as of a turtle, egg, nut, etc. 2 something like a shell in being hollow, empty, a covering, etc. 3 a light, narrow racing boat rowed by a team 4 an explosive artillery projectile 5 a small-arms cartridge — *vt.* 1 to remove the shell or covering from [to *shell* peas] 2 to bombard —**shell out** [Colloq.] to pay out (money)

shel·lac or **shel·lack** (shə lak′) *n.* [< SHELL & LAC] 1 a resin usually produced in thin, flaky layers or shells 2 a thin varnish containing this resin and alcohol — *vt.* **-lacked′, -lack′ing** 1 to apply shellac to 2 [Slang] *a*) to beat *b*) to defeat decisively

-shelled (sheld) *combining form* having a (specified kind of) shell

shell′fire′ *n.* the firing of artillery shells

shell′fish′ *n.*, *pl.* **-fish′** or (for different species) **-fish′es** any aquatic animal, esp. an edible one, with a shell, as the clam, lobster, etc.

shel·ter (shel′tər) *n.* [< ? OE *scield*, shield + *truma*, a troop] 1 something that protects, as from the elements, danger, etc. 2 a being covered, protected, etc. — *vt.* to provide shelter for; protect — *vi.* to find shelter

---

THESAURUS

exact] focus, bring into focus, intensify, make clear, make clearer, clarify, outline distinctly, make more distinct.—*Ant.* CONFUSE, cloud, obscure.

sharply *a.* piercingly, pointedly, distinctly; see CLEARLY 1, 2.

shatter *v.* shiver, split, burst; see BREAK 2.

shattered *a.* splintered, crushed, destroyed; see BROKEN 1.

shave *v.* shear, graze, barber, cut, use a razor, clip closely, strip, strip the hair from, tonsure, make bare, peel, skin, remove.

she *pron.* this one, this girl, this woman, that girl, that woman, a female animal; see also WOMAN 1.

shears *n.* cutters, clippers, snips; see SCISSORS.

shed[1] *n.* shelter, outbuilding, hut, lean-to, woodshed.

shed[2] *v.* drop, let fall, give forth, shower down, cast, molt, slough, discard, exude, emit, scatter, sprinkle.

sheep *n.* lamb, ewe, ram; see ANIMAL, GOAT.

sheer[2] *a.* 1 [Abrupt] perpendicular, very steep, precipitous; see STEEP. 2 [Thin] transparent, delicate, fine; see THIN 1.

sheet[1] *n.* 1 [A bed cover] covering, bed sheet, bedding; see CLOTH, COVER 1. 2 [A thin, flat object] lamina, leaf, foil, veneer, layer, stratum, coat, film, ply, covering, expanse.

shelf *n.* 1 [A ledge] rock, reef, shoal; see LEDGE. 2 [A cupboard rack] counter, cupboard, mantelpiece, rack, bookshelf.

shell *n.* 1 [A shell-like cover or structure] husk, crust, nut, pod, case, scale, shard, integument, eggshell, carapace, plastron. 2 [An explosive projectile] bullet, explosive, torpedo; see WEAPON. 3 [A crustaceous covering] *Varieties include the following:* tortoise, crustacean, bivalve, mollusk, clam, mussel, conch, snail; see also SEASHELL.

shell *v.* shuck, strip, peel off; see SKIN.

shellfish *n.* crustacean, mollusk, crustaceous animal, invertebrate, marine animal, arthropod, gastropod, bivalve. *Creatures often called shellfish include the following:* crab, lobster, clam, shrimp, prawn, crawfish, crayfish, mussel, whelk, cockle, abalone, snail.

shelter *n.* refuge, harbor, haven, sanctuary, asylum, retreat, shield, screen, defense, security, safety, guardian, protector, house, roof, tent, shack, shed, hut, shade, shadow.

shelter *v.* screen, cover, hide, conceal, guard, take in, ward, harbor, defend, protect, shield, watch over, take care of, secure, preserve, safeguard, surround, enclose, lodge, house.—*Ant.* EXPOSE, turn out, evict.

sheltered *a.* 1 [Shaded] screened, protected, shady, veiled, covered, protective, curtained. 2 [Protected] guarded, ensured, shielded; see SAFE, WATCHED.

shelve (shelv) *vt.* **shelved, shelv′ing** 1 to equip with shelves 2 to put on a shelf 3 to put aside; defer

shelves (shelvz) *n. pl. of* SHELF

shelv·ing (shel′viŋ) *n.* 1 material for shelves 2 shelves collectively

she·nani·gan (shi nan′i gən) *n.* ⟦altered < ? Ir *sionnachuighim*, I play the fox⟧ [*usually pl.*] [Colloq.] trickery; mischief

shep·herd (shep′ərd) *n.* [see SHEEP & HERD] 1 one who herds sheep 2 a clergyman — *vt.* to herd, lead, etc. as a shepherd **—shep′herd·ess** *n.fem.*

sher·bet (shur′bət) *n.* ⟦< Ar *sharba(t)*, a drink⟧ a frozen dessert like an ice but with gelatin and, often, milk added: also, erroneously, **sher′bert** (-burt)

sher·iff (sher′if) *n.* ⟦< OE *scir*, shire + *gerefa*, chief officer⟧ the chief law-enforcement officer of a county

Sherpa (shur′pə, sher′-) *n. pl.* **-pas** or **-pa** any of a Tibetan people of Nepal, famous as mountain climbers

sherry (sher′ē) *n., pl.* **-ries** [after *Jerez*, Spain] 1 a yellow or brown Spanish fortified wine 2 any similar wine

shib·bo·leth (shib′ə leth′, -ləth) *n.* ⟦< Heb *shibolet*, a stream⟧ 1 *Bible* the test word used to distinguish the enemy: Judg. 12:4-6 2 any phrase, custom, etc. peculiar to a certain party, class, etc.

shied (shīd) *vi., vt. pt. & pp. of* SHY¹, SHY²

shield (shēld) *n.* ⟦OE *scield*⟧ 1 a flat piece of metal, etc. worn on the forearm to ward off blows, etc. 2 one that guards, protects, etc. 3 anything shaped like a shield — *vt., vi.* to defend; protect

shift (shift) *vt.* ⟦OE *sciftan*, divide⟧ 1 to move from one person or place to another 2 to replace by another or others 3 to change the arrangement of (gears) — *vi.* 1 to change position, direction, etc. 2 to get along [*to shift for oneself*] — *n.* 1 a shifting; transfer 2 a plan of conduct, esp. for an emergency 3 an evasion; trick 4 a gearshift 5 *a*) a group of people working in relay with another *b*) their regular work period **—make shift** to manage (*with the means at hand*)

shift′less *adj.* incapable, inefficient, lazy, etc. **—shift′less·ness** *n.*

shift′y *adj.* **-i·er, -i·est** of a tricky or deceitful nature; evasive **—shift′i·ly** *adv.* **—shift′i·ness** *n.*

Shih Tzu (shē′ dzo͞o′) *pl.* **Shih Tzus** or **Shih Tzu** ⟦Mandarin *shihtzu*, lion⟧ a small dog with long, silky hair and short legs

shill (shil) *n.* [Slang] a confederate of a gambler, auctioneer, etc. who pretends to bet, bid, etc. so as to lure others — *vi.* [Slang] to act as a shill

shil·lelagh or **shil·la·lah** (shi lā′lē, -lə) *n.* [after *Shillelagh*, Ir village] a cudgel

shil·ling (shil′iŋ) *n.* ⟦OE *scylling*⟧ a former British monetary unit and coin, equal to ¹⁄₂₀ of a pound

shilly-shally (shil′ē shal′ē) *vi.* **-lied, -lying** ⟦< *shall I?*⟧ to be irresolute; vacillate, esp. over trifles

shim (shim) *n.* ⟦< ?⟧ a thin, wedge of wood, metal, etc. used as for filling space

shim·mer (shim′ər) *vi.* ⟦OE *scymrian*⟧ to shine with an unsteady light; glimmer — *n.* a shimmering light **—shim′mery** *adj.*

shimmy (shim′ē) *n.* ⟦< a jazz dance < CHEMISE⟧ a marked vibration or wobble, as in a car's front wheels — *vi.* **-mied, -my·ing** to vibrate or wobble

shin (shin) *n.* ⟦OE *scinu*⟧ the front part of the leg between the knee and the ankle — *vt., vi.* **shinned, shin′ning** to climb (a pole, etc.) by gripping with hands and legs: also **shin′ny**

shin′bone′ *n.* TIBIA

shin·dig (shin′dig′) *n.* ⟦< old colloq. *shindy*, commotion⟧ [Colloq.] a dance, party, or other informal gathering

shine (shīn) *vi.* **shone**, or, esp. for vt. 2, **shined, shin′ing** ⟦OE *scinan*⟧ 1 to emit or reflect light 2 to stand out; excel 3 to exhibit itself clearly [*love shining from her face*] — *vt.* 1 to direct the light of 2 to make shiny by polishing [*to shine shoes*] — *n.* 1 brightness; radiance 2 luster; gloss

shin′er (-ər) *n.* [Slang] BLACK EYE

shin·gle (shiŋ′gəl) *n.* ⟦OE *scindel*⟧ 1 a thin, wedge-shaped piece of wood, slate, etc. laid with others in overlapping rows, as for roofs 2 a short haircut, tapered at the nape 3 a small signboard, as of a doctor — *vt.* **-gled, -gling** to cover (a roof, etc.) with shingles

shin·gles (shiŋ′gəlz) *n.* ⟦< L *cingere*, to gird⟧ *nontechnical name for* HERPES ZOSTER

shin′guard′ *n.* a padded guard worn to protect the shins in some sports

shin′splints′ *n.pl.* ⟦< SHIN & SPLINT, growth on bone of a horse's leg⟧ [*with sing. v.*] painful strain of muscles of the lower leg

Shinto (shin′tō) *n.* ⟦Jpn < Chin *shen*, god + *tō, dō*, way⟧ a religion of Japan, emphasizing ancestor worship

shiny (shīn′ē) *adj.* **-i·er, -i·est** 1 bright; shining 2 highly polished **—shin′i·ness** *n.*

ship (ship) *n.* ⟦OE *scip*⟧ 1 any large vessel navigating deep water 2 a ship's officers and crew 3 an aircraft — *vt.* **shipped, ship′ping** 1 to put or take on board a ship 2 to send or transport by any carrier [*to ship coal by rail*] 3 to take in (water) over the side in a heavy sea 4 to put (an object) in place on a vessel [*ship the oars*] — *vi.* to go aboard ship; embark **—[S-]** the constellation Argo **—ship′per** *n.*

-ship (ship) ⟦OE *-scipe*⟧ *suffix* 1 the quality or state of being [*friendship*] 2 *a*) the rank or office of [*professorship*] *b*) one having the rank of [*lordship*] 3 skill as [*leadership*] 4 all persons (of a specified group) collectively [*readership*]

ship′board′ *n.* a ship: chiefly in **on shipboard**, aboard a ship

ship′build′er *n.* one whose business is building ships **—ship′build′ing** *n.*

ship′mate′ *n.* a fellow sailor

ship′ment *n.* 1 the shipping of goods 2 goods shipped

ship′ping *n.* 1 the act or business of transporting goods 2 ships collectively, as of a nation, port, etc.

shipping clerk an employee who prepares goods for shipment, and keeps records of shipments made

ship′shape′ *adj.* having everything neatly in place; trim

ship′wreck′ *n.* 1 the remains of a wrecked ship 2 the loss of a ship through storm, etc. 3 ruin; failure — *vt.* to cause to undergo shipwreck

ship′yard′ *n.* a place where ships are built and repaired

shire (shīr) *n.* ⟦OE *scir*, office⟧ in England, a county

shirk (shurk) *vt., vi.* ⟦< ?⟧ to neglect or evade (a duty, etc.) **—shirk′er** *n.*

Shirley Temple [after *Shirley Temple*, child movie star] a nonalcoholic drink made like a cocktail

shirr (shur) *n.* ⟦< ?⟧ SHIRRING — *vt.* 1 to make shirring in (cloth) 2 to bake (eggs) in buttered dishes

shirr′ing *n.* a gathering made in cloth by drawing the material up on parallel rows of short stitches

shirt (shurt) *n.* ⟦OE *scyrte*⟧ 1 a garment worn on the upper part of the body, usually with a collar and a but-

THESAURUS

sheriff *n.* county officer, county administrator, peace officer; see POLICEMAN.

shield *n.* bumper, protection, guard; see COVER 1.

shift *n.* 1 [A change] transfer, transformation, substitution, displacement, fault, alteration, variation; see also CHANGE 1. 2 [A working period] turn, spell, working time; see TIME 1.

shift *v.* 1 [To change position] move, turn, stir; see CHANGE 2. 2 [To cause to shift] displace, remove, substitute; see EXCHANGE 1. 3 [To put in gear] change gears, downshift, put in drive; see DRIVE 2.

shin *n.* tibia, leg, limb; see BONE, LEG.

shindig* *n.* banquet, dance, dinner; see PARTY 1.

shine *v.* 1 [To give forth light] radiate, beam, scintillate, glitter, sparkle, twinkle, glimmer, glare, glow, flash, blaze, shimmer, illuminate, blink, shoot out beams, irradiate, dazzle, bedazzle, flash, flicker. 2 [To reflect light] glisten, gleam, glow, look good, grow bright, give back, give light, deflect, mirror; see also REFLECT 3. 3 [To cause to shine, usually by polishing] scour, brush, polish, put a gloss on, put a finish on, finish, burnish, wax, buff, polish up, make brilliant, make glitter; see also CLEAN, PAINT 2.

shining *a.* radiant, gleaming, luminous; see BRIGHT 1.

shiny *a.* polished, sparkling, glistening; see BRIGHT 1.

ship *n.* Types of ships include the following: steamer, steamship, liner, freighter, landing barge, trawler, floating cannery, factory ship, ferry, clipper, square-rigged vessel, sailing ship, transport, tanker, pilot boat, junk, galleon, sampan, battleship, cruiser, destroyer, aircraft carrier, whaling vessel, bark, schooner, windjammer, yacht, dragger, cutter, sloop, tug; see also BOAT.

ship *v.* send, consign, ship out; see SEND 1.

shipment *n.* cargo, carload, purchase; see FREIGHT.

shipped *a.* transported, exported, delivered; see SENT.

shirk *v.* elude, cheat, malinger; see AVOID, EVADE.

shirt *n.* Shirts include the following: dress, undershirt, sport, work, cowboy, Western, long-sleeved, shorttoned front **2** an undershirt —**keep one's shirt on** [Slang] to remain patient or calm

shirt'tail' *n.* the part of a shirt extending below the waist

shirt'waist' *n.* a woman's blouse tailored like a shirt

shish ke·bab (shish' kə bäb') [< Ar *shish*, skewer + *kabāb*, kebab] a dish of kebabs, esp. lamb, stuck on a skewer, often with vegetables, and broiled

shiv (shiv) *n.* [prob. < Romany *chiv*, blade] [Slang] a knife

shiver[1] (shiv'ər) *n.* [ME *schievere*] a fragment or splinter —*vt.*, *vi.* to break into fragments or splinters

shiver[2] (shiv'ər) *vi.* [< ? OE *ceafl*, jaw] to shake or tremble, as from fear or cold —*n.* a shaking, trembling, etc. —**shiv'ery** *adj.*

shlep or **shlepp** (shlep) *n.* alt. sp. of SCHLEP

shmaltz (shmôlts, shmälts) *n.* [Slang] alt. sp. of SCHMALTZ

shoal[1] (shōl) *n.* [OE *scolu*] **1** a large group; crowd **2** a school of fish

shoal[2] (shōl) *n.* [< OE *sceald*, shallow] **1** a shallow place in a river, sea, etc. **2** a sand bar forming a shallow place

shoat (shōt) *n.* [ME *schote*] a young, weaned pig

shock[1] (shäk) *n.* [< MFr *choquer*, to collide] **1** a sudden, powerful blow, shake, etc. **2** *a)* a sudden emotional disturbance *b)* the cause of this **3** an extreme stimulation of the nerves by the passage of electric current through the body **4** [Colloq.] short for SHOCK ABSORBER **5** a disorder of the blood circulation produced by hemorrhage, disturbance of heart function, etc. —*vt.* **1** to astonish, horrify, etc. **2** to produce electrical shock in

shock[2] (shäk) *n.* [ME *schokke*] bundles of grain stacked together

shock[3] (shäk) *n.* [< ? prec.] a thick, bushy or tangled mass, as of hair

shock absorber a device, as on a motor vehicle, that absorbs the force of bumps and jarring

shock'er *n.* **1** anything that shocks **2** a sensational story, play, etc.

shock'ing *adj.* **1** causing great surprise and distress **2** disgusting

shock'proof' *adj.* able to absorb shock without being damaged

shock therapy the treatment of certain mental disorders by using electricity, drugs, etc., producing convulsions or coma

shock troops troops trained to lead an attack

shod (shäd) *vt.* alt. pt. & pp. of SHOE

shoddy (shäd'ē) *n.*, *pl.* **shod'dies** [< ?] **1** an inferior woolen cloth made from used fabrics **2** anything worth less than it seems to be —*adj.* **-dier, -di·est 1** made of inferior material **2** poorly done or made **3** sham —**shod'dily** *adv.* —**shod'di·ness** *n.*

shoe (shōō) *n.* [OE *sceoh*] **1** an outer covering for the foot **2** a horseshoe **3** the part of a brake that presses against a wheel —*vt.* **shod** or **shoed**, **shoe'ing** to furnish with shoes —**fill one's shoes** to take one's place

shoe'horn' *n.* an implement used to help slip one's heel into a shoe —*vt.* to force or squeeze into a narrow space

shoe'lace' *n.* a length of cord, etc. used for lacing and fastening a shoe

shoe'mak'er *n.* one whose business is making or repairing shoes

shoe'shine' *n.* the cleaning and polishing of a pair of shoes

shoe'string' *n.* **1** a shoelace **2** a small amount of capital [a business started on a *shoestring*] —*adj.* at or near the ankles [a *shoestring* catch]

shoe tree a form inserted in a shoe to stretch it or preserve its shape

shone (shōn) *vi.*, *vt.* alt. pt. & pp. of SHINE

shoo (shōō) *interj.* go away! get out! —*vt.* **shooed, shoo'ing** to drive away, as by crying "shoo"

shoo'-in' *n.* [Colloq.] one expected to win easily in a race, etc.

shook (shook) *vt.*, *vi.* pt. and dial. pp. of SHAKE —**shook up** [Slang] upset; agitated

shoot (shōōt) *vt.* **shot, shoot'ing** [OE *sceotan*] **1** to move swiftly over, by, etc. **2** to variegate (*with* another color, etc.) **3** to thrust or put forth **4** to discharge or fire (a bullet, arrow, etc.) **5** to send forth swiftly or with force **6** to hit, wound, etc. with a bullet, arrow, etc. **7** to photograph **8** *Sports a)* to throw or drive (a ball, etc.) toward the objective *b)* to score (a goal, points, etc.) —*vi.* **1** to move swiftly **2** to be felt suddenly, as pain **3** to grow rapidly **4** to jut out **5** to send forth a missile; discharge bullets, etc. **6** to use guns, etc. as in hunting —*n.* **1** a shooting trip, contest, etc. **2** a new growth; sprout —**shoot at** (or **for**) [Colloq.] to strive for —**shoot'er** *n.*

shooting star METEOR

shoot'out' or **shoot'-out'** *n.* a battle with handguns, etc., as between police and criminals

shop (shäp) *n.* [OE *sceoppa*, booth] **1** a place where certain things are offered for sale; esp., a small store **2** a place where a particular kind of work is done —*vi.* **shopped, shop'ping** to visit shops to examine or buy goods —**talk shop** to discuss one's work

shop'keep'er *n.* one who owns or operates a shop, or small store

shop'lift'er *n.* one who steals articles from a store during shopping hours —**shop'lift'** *vt.*, *vi.*

shoppe (shäp) *n.* old sp. of SHOP (*n.* 1): now used only in shop names

shop'per *n.* **1** one who shops **2** one hired by a store to shop for others **3** one hired by a store to compare competitors' prices, etc.

shopping center a complex of stores, restaurants, etc. with a common parking area

shop'talk' *n.* **1** the specialized words and idioms of those in the same work **2** talk about work, esp. after hours

shop'worn' *adj.* soiled, faded, etc. from having been displayed in a shop

shore[1] (shôr) *n.* [ME *schore*] land at the edge of a body of water

shore[2] (shôr) *n.* [ME *schore*] a prop, beam, etc. used for support, etc. —*vt.* **shored, shor'ing** to support as with shores; prop (*up*)

shore patrol a detail of the U.S. Navy, Coast Guard, or Marine Corps acting as military police on shore

---

THESAURUS

sleeved, cotton, silk, flannel, T-shirt, tank top, blouse, jersey, pull-over, turtleneck; see also CLOTHES.

shiver[2] *v.* be cold, vibrate, quiver; see SHAKE 1, WAVE 3.

shock[1] *n.* **1** [The effect of physical impact] crash, clash, wreck; see COLLISION. **2** [The effect of a mental blow] excitement, hysteria, emotional upset; see CONFUSION. **3** [The after-effect of physical harm] concussion, stupor, collapse; see ILLNESS 1, INJURY.

shock[1] *v.* **1** [To disturb one's self-control] startle, agitate, astound; see DISTURB. **2** [To disturb one's sense of propriety] insult, outrage, horrify, revolt, offend, appall, abash, astound, anger, floor, shake up, disquiet, dismay. **3** [To jar] rock, agitate, jolt; see SHAKE 2.

shocked *a.* startled, aghast, upset, astounded, offended, appalled, dismayed; see TROUBLED.

shocking *a.* repulsive, hateful, revolting; see OFFENSIVE 2.

shoe *n.* footwear, boot, slipper, moccasin. *Footwear includes the following:* Oxford, high top, wingtip, brogue, high puppy, sandal, pump, flat, clog, galosh, tennis shoe, cleat, jogging shoe, running shoe, ski boot, track shoe, sneaker, loafer, heels, tennies*, wedgie. —**in another's shoes** in the place of another, in other circumstances, reversal of roles; see SYMPATHETIC, UNDERSTOOD 1.

shoo *interj.* get away, begone, leave.

shoot *v.* **1** [To discharge] fire, shoot off, expel, pull the trigger, set off, torpedo, explode, ignite, blast, sharpshoot, open fire, rake, pump full of lead. **2** [To move rapidly] dart, spurt, rush; see HURRY 1. **3** [To kill by shooting] dispatch, murder, execute; see KILL 1. —**shoot at 1** [To fire a weapon at] shoot, fire at, take a shot at; see ATTACK 1. **2** [*To strive for*] aim, endeavor, strive; see TRY 1.

shop *n.* store, department store, retail store, thrift shop, drug store, discount house, novelty shop. —**set up shop** go into business, start, open a business; see BEGIN 1, 2. —**shut up shop** close up, go out of business, cease functioning; see CLOSE 4, STOP 2. —**talk shop** talk business, exchange views, discuss one's specialty; see GOSSIP, TALK 1.

shop *v.* shop for, look for, try to buy; see BUY.

shopkeeper *n.* manager, merchant, storekeeper; see BUSINESSMAN.

shopper *n.* bargain hunter, professional shopper, purchaser; see BUYER.

shopping *n.* purchasing, hunting, looking; see BUYING.

shopping center *n.* shops, mall, shopping mall; see BUSINESS 4, PARKING LOT.

shore[1] *n.* beach, strand, seaside, sand, coast, seacoast, seashore, brink, bank, border, seaboard, margin, lakeside, lakeshore, riverbank, riverside.

shorn (shôrn) *vt.*, *vi. alt. pp. of* SHEAR

short (shôrt) *adj.* [OE *scort*] **1** not measuring much from end to end in space or time **2** not great in range or scope **3** not tall **4** brief; concise **5** not retentive [a *short* memory] **6** curt; abrupt **7** less than a sufficient or correct amount **8** crisp or flaky, as pastry rich in shortening **9** designating a sale of securities, etc. which the seller does not yet own but expects to buy later at a lower price — *n.* **1** something short **2** [*pl.*] *a*) short trousers *b*) a man's undergarment like these **3** SHORTSTOP **4** SHORT CIRCUIT — *adv.* **1** abruptly; suddenly **2** briefly; concisely **3** so as to be short in length — *vt.*, *vi.* **1** to give less than what is needed or usual **2** SHORTCHANGE **3** SHORT-CIRCUIT — **in short** briefly — **run short** to have less than enough — **short of** less than or lacking — **short'ness** *n.*

short'age (-ij) *n.* a deficiency in the amount needed or expected; deficit

short'bread' *n.* a rich, crumbly cake or cookie made with much shortening

short'cake' *n.* a light biscuit or a sweet cake served with fruit, etc.

short'change' *vt.*, *vi.* **-changed'**, **-chang'ing** [Colloq.] to give less money than is due in change

short circuit 1 a connection between two points in an electric circuit, resulting in a side circuit that deflects current or in an excessive current flow causing damage **2** popularly, a disrupted electric circuit caused by this — **short'-cir'cuit** *vt.*, *vi.*

short'com'ing *n.* a defect or deficiency

short'cut' *n.* **1** a shorter route **2** any way of saving time, effort, etc.

short'en *vt.*, *vi.* to make or become short or shorter

short·en·ing (shôrt''n iŋ, -niŋ) *n.* edible fat used to make pastry, etc. crisp or flaky

short'hand' *n.* any system of speed writing using symbols for words

short'-hand'ed *adj.* short of workers

short'horn' *n.* any of a breed of cattle with short, inward-curving horns

short'-lived' (-līvd', -livd') *adj.* having a short life span or existence

short'ly *adv.* **1** briefly **2** soon **3** abruptly and rudely; curtly

short order any food that can be cooked or served quickly when ordered — **short'-or'der** *adj.*

short'-range' *adj.* reaching over a short distance or period of time

short ribs the rib ends of beef from the forequarter

short shrift very little care or attention — **make short shrift of** to dispose of quickly and impatiently

short'sight'ed *adj.* **1** NEARSIGHTED **2** lacking in foresight — **short'sight'ed·ly** *adv.* — **short'sight'ed·ness** *n.*

short'-spo'ken *adj.* using few words, esp. to the point of rudeness; curt

short'stop' *n. Baseball* the infielder between second and third base

short story a piece of prose fiction shorter than a short novel

short subject a short film, as that shown with a film feature

short'-tem'pered *adj.* easily or quickly angered

short'-term' *adj.* for or extending over a short time

short ton 2,000 pounds: see TON

short'wave' *n.* a radio wave 60 meters or less in length

short'-wind'ed (-win'did) *adj.* easily put out of breath by exertion

shot¹ (shät) *n.* [OE *sceot*] **1** the act of shooting **2** range; scope **3** an attempt or try **4** a pointed, critical remark **5** the path of an object thrown, etc. **6** *a*) a projectile for a gun *b*) projectiles collectively **7** small pellets of lead or steel for a shotgun **8** the heavy metal ball used in the shot put **9** a marksman **10** a photograph or a continuous film sequence **11** a hypodermic injection, as of vaccine **12** a drink of liquor — **call the shots** to direct or control what is done

shot² (shät) *vt.*, *vi. pt. & pp. of* SHOOT — *adj.* [Colloq.] ruined or worn out

shot'gun' *n.* **1** a gun for firing a charge of shot at short range **2** *Football* a formation in which the quarterback stands several yards behind the line of scrimmage to receive the ball

shot put a contest in which a heavy metal ball is propelled with an overhand thrust from the shoulder — **shot'-put'ter** *n.* — **shot'-put'ting** *n.*

should (shood) *v.aux.* [OE *sceolde*] **1** *pt. of* SHALL **2** used to express: *a*) obligation, duty, etc. [you *should* help] *b*) expectation or probability [he *should* be here soon] *c*) a future condition [if I *should* die tomorrow]

shoul·der (shōl'dər) *n.* [OE *sculdor*] **1** *a*) the joint connecting the arm or forelimb with the body **b**) the part of the body including this joint **2** [*pl.*] the two shoulders and the part of the back between them **3** a shoulderlike projection **4** the land along the edge of a paved road — *vt.* **1** to push along or through, as with the shoulder **2** to carry upon the shoulder **3** to assume the burden of — **straight from the shoulder** without reserve; frankly — **turn** (or **give) a cold shoulder to** to snub or shun

shoulder blade either of the two flat bones in the upper back

shoulder harness an anchored strap passing across the chest, used with a seat belt, as in a car

shout (shout) *n.* [ME *schoute*] a loud cry or call — *vt.*, *vi.* to utter or cry out in a shout — **shout'er** *n.*

shove (shuv) *vt.*, *vi.* **shoved**, **shov'ing** [OE *scufan*] **1** to push, as along a surface **2** to push roughly — *n.* a push — **shove off 1** to push (a boat) away from shore **2** [Colloq.] to leave

shov·el (shuv'əl) *n.* [OE *scofl*] a tool with a broad scoop or blade and a long handle, for lifting and moving loose material — *vt.* **-eled** or **-elled**, **-el·ing** or **-el·ling 1** to move with a shovel **2** to dig out with a shovel

shov'el·ful' *n.*, *pl.* **-fuls'** as much as a shovel will hold

show (shō) *vt.* **showed**, **shown** or **showed**, **show'ing** [< OE *sceawian*] **1** to bring or put in sight **2** to guide; con-

---

THESAURUS

short *a.* **1** [Not long in space] low, skimpy, slight, not tall, not long, undersized, little, abbreviated, dwarfish, stubby, stunted, stocky, diminutive, tiny, small, dwarf, dwarfed, close to the ground, dumpy, chunky, compact, squat, thickset, pint-size, stumpy, sawed-off*, runty. **2** [Not long in time] brief, curtailed, cut short, fleeting, not protracted, concise, unprolonged, unsustained, condensed, terse, succinct, pithy, summary, pointed, precise, bare, abridged, summarized, epigrammatic, compressed, short-term, short-lived. **3** [Inadequate] deficient, insufficient, meager; see INADEQUATE. — **be** (or **run) short** (**of**) lack, want, run out of; see NEED. — **fall short** not reach, be inadequate, fall down; see FAIL 1, MISS 3. — **for short** as a nickname, familiarly, commonly; see NAMED 1, SO-CALLED. — **in short** that is, in summary, to make a long story short; see BRIEFLY, FINALLY 1.

shortage *n.* short fall, scant supply, curtailment; see LACK 1.

shortcoming *n.* fault, deficiency, lapse; see WEAKNESS 1.

shortcut *n.* bypass, alternative, time-saver; see MEANS 1, WHY.

shorten *v.* curtail, abridge, abbreviate; see DECREASE 2.

shorter *a.* smaller, lower, not so long, briefer, more limited, more concise, more abrupt, lessened, diminished, reduced, curtailed.—*Ant.* HIGHER, longer, taller.

short-lived *a.* brief, momentary, temporary; see SHORT 2.

shortly *a.* presently, quickly, right away; see SOON.

shortness *n.* brevity, briefness, conciseness; see LENGTH 1.

shortsighted *a.* unthinking, foolish, unwary; see RASH, STUPID.

shot¹ *n.* **1** [A flying missile] bullet, ball, pellet, lead, projectile, buckshot, grapeshot. **2** [An opportunity to shoot] occasion, chance, turn; see OPPORTUNITY 1. **3** [One who shoots] gunner, rifleman, marksman; see HUNTER. — **call the shots** direct, command, supervise; see CONTROL. — **have** (or **take) a shot at*** endeavor, attempt, do one's best at; see TRY 1. — **like a shot** rapidly,

speedily, like a bat out of hell*; see FAST 1, QUICKLY. — **shot in the arm** help, boost, assistance; see ENCOURAGEMENT.

shoulder *n.* upper arm, shoulder cut, shoulder joint; see ARM 1, 2, JOINT 1. — **cry on someone's shoulder** weep, object, shed tears; see CRY 1, COMPLAIN. — **turn** (or **give) a cold shoulder to** ignore, neglect, pass over; see INSULT.

shout *n.* roar, bellow, scream; see CRY 1, YELL.

shout *v.* screech, roar, scream; see YELL.

shouting *n.* cries, yelling, jeering; see CRY 1.

shove *v.* jostle, push out of one's way, shoulder; see PUSH 1.

shovel *n. Shovels include the following:* coal, snow, fire, miner's, irrigating, split, twisted, pronged, scoop, round-pointed; see also TOOL 1.

shovel *v.* take up, pick up, take up with a shovel, clean out, throw, move, pass, shift; see also DIG 1, LOAD 1.

show *n.* **1** [An exhibition] presentaduct **3** to point out **4** to reveal, as by behavior **5** to prove; demonstrate **6** to bestow (favor, mercy, etc.) — *vi.* **1** to be or become seen; appear **2** to be noticeable **3** to finish third or better in a horse race — *n.* **1** a showing or demonstration **2** pompous display **3** pretense *[sorrow that was mere show]* **4** a public display or exhibition **5** a presentation of entertainment —**show off** to make a display of, esp. a vain display —**show up 1** to expose **2** to be seen **3** to arrive

show'boat' *n.* a boat with a theater and actors who play river towns

show'case' *n.* a glass-enclosed case for displaying things, as in a store — *vt.* **-cased', -cas'ing** to display to good advantage

show'down' *n.* [Colloq.] an action that brings matters to a climax

shower (shou'ər) *n.* [OE *scur*] **1** a brief fall of rain, sleet, etc. **2** a sudden, abundant fall, as of sparks **3** a party at which gifts are presented to the guest of honor **4** a bath in which the body is sprayed from overhead with fine streams of water — *vt.* **1** to spray with water, etc. **2** to pour forth as in a shower — *vi.* **1** to fall or come as a shower **2** to bathe under a shower —**show'ery** *adj.*

show'ing *n.* **1** a bringing to view or notice; exhibition **2** a performance, appearance, etc. *[a good showing in the contest]*

show'man (shō'mən) *n., pl.* **-men 1** one whose business is producing shows **2** a person skilled at presenting anything in a striking manner —**show'man·ship'** *n.*

shown (shōn) *vt., vi. alt. pp. of* SHOW

show'off' *n.* one who shows off

show of hands a raising of hands, as in voting or volunteering

show'piece' *n.* **1** something displayed or exhibited **2** something that is a fine example of its kind

show'place' *n.* **1** a place displayed to the public for its beauty, etc. **2** any beautiful place

show'room' *n.* a room where merchandise is displayed for advertising or sale

show window a store window in which merchandise is displayed

show'y *adj.* **-i·er, -i·est 1** of striking appearance **2** attracting attention in a gaudy way —**show'i·ly** *adv.* —**show'i·ness** *n.*

shpt. shipment

shrank (shraŋk) *vt., vi. alt. pt. of* SHRINK

shrap'nel (shrap'nəl) *n.* [after Gen. *Shrapnel* (1761-1842), its Brit inventor] **1** an artillery shell filled with an explosive charge and small metal balls **2** these balls **3** any fragments scattered by an exploding shell, bomb, etc.

shred (shred) *n.* [OE *screade*] **1** a narrow strip cut, torn off, etc. **2** a fragment — *vt.* **shred'ded** or **shred, shred'**

ding to cut or tear into shreds —**shred'dable** *adj.* —**shred'der** *n.*

shrew (shrōō) *n.* [< OE *screawa*] **1** a small, mouselike mammal with a long snout **2** a nagging, evil-tempered woman —**shrew'ish** *adj.*

shrewd (shrōōd) *adj.* [see prec.] clever or sharp in practical affairs; astute —**shrewd'ly** *adv.* —**shrewd'ness** *n.*

shriek (shrēk) *vi., vt.* [ME *schriken*] to make or utter with a loud, piercing cry; screech — *n.* such a cry

shrift (shrift) *n.* [ult. < L *scribere*, write] [Archaic] confession to and absolution by a priest See also SHORT SHRIFT

shrike (shrik) *n.* [OE *scric*] a shrill-voiced bird of prey with a hooked beak

shrill (shril) *adj.* [echoic] producing a high, thin, piercing sound — *vi., vt.* to utter (with) a shrill sound —**shril'ly** *adv.* —**shrill'ness** *n.*

shrimp (shrimp) *n.* [OE *scrimman*, shrink] **1** a small, long-tailed crustacean, valued as food **2** [Colloq.] a small or insignificant person

shrine (shrin) *n.* [< L *scrinium*, box] **1** a container holding sacred relics **2** a saint's tomb **3** a place of worship **4** any hallowed place

shrink (shriŋk) *vi.* **shrank** or **shrunk, shrunk** or **shrunk'en, shrink'ing** [OE *scrincan*] **1** to contract, as from heat, cold, moisture, etc. **2** to lessen, as in amount **3** to draw back; flinch — *vt.* to make shrink —**shrink'able** *adj.*

shrink'age *n.* **1** a shrinking **2** the amount of shrinking

shrinking violet a very shy person

shrive (shriv) *vt.* **shrived** or **shrove, shriven** (shriv'ən) or **shrived, shriv'ing** [OE *scrifan*] [Archaic] to hear the confession of and absolve

shrivel (shriv'əl) *vt., vi.* **-eled** or **-elled, -el·ing** or **-el·ling** [prob. < Scand] to shrink and wrinkle or wither

shroud (shroud) *n.* [OE *scrud*] **1** a cloth used to wrap a corpse for burial **2** something that covers, veils, etc. **3** any of the ropes from a ship's side to a masthead — *vt.* to hide; cover

Shrove Tuesday [see SHRIVE] the last day before Lent

shrub (shrub) *n.* [OE *scrybb*, brushwood] a low, woody plant with several stems; bush —**shrub'by** *adj.*

shrub'bery (-ər ē) *n.* shrubs collectively

shrug (shrug) *vt., vi.* **shrugged, shrug'ging** [ME *schruggen*] to draw up (the shoulders), as in indifference, doubt, etc. — *n.* the gesture so made

shrunk (shruŋk) *vi., vt. alt. pt. & pp. of* SHRINK

shrunk'en *vi., vt. alt. pp. of* SHRINK — *adj.* contracted in size; shriveled

shtg. shortage

shtick (shtik) *n.* [Yidd] a comic bit or special gimmick

shuck (shuk) *n.* [< ?] a shell, pod, or husk — *vt.* to remove shucks from

shucks (shuks) *interj.* [prob. < prec.] an exclamation of disappointment, embarrassment, etc.

THESAURUS

tion, exhibit, showing, exposition, expo*, display, occurrence, sight, appearance, program, flower show, boat show, home show, dog show, carnival, representation, burlesque, production, concert, act, pageant, spectacle, light show, entertainment; see also COMEDY, DRAMA, MOVIE. **2** [Pretense] sham, make believe, semblance; see PRETENSE 1, 2. —**for show** for sake of appearances, ostensibly, ostentatiously; see APPARENTLY. —**get** (or **put**) **the show on the road*** start, open, get started; see BEGIN 1. —**steal the show** triumph, get the best of it, win out; see DEFEAT, WIN 1.

show *v.* **1** [To display] exhibit, manifest, present; see DISPLAY. **2** [To explain] reveal, tell, explicate; see EXPLAIN. **3** [To demonstrate] attest, determine, confirm; see PROVE. **4** [To convince] teach, prove to, persuade; see CONVINCE. **5** [To indicate] register, note, point; see RECORD 1. — **show off** brag, swagger, make a spectacle of oneself; see BOAST. —**show up 1** [To arrive] appear, come, turn up; see ARRIVE. **2** [To expose] discredit, defeat, belittle; see EXPOSE 1.

showdown *n.* crisis, turning point, culmination; see CLIMAX.

shower *n.* **1** [Water falling in drops] drizzle, mist, rainfall; see RAIN 1. **2** [Act of cleansing the body] bathing, washing, sponging; see BATH 1.

shown *a.* **1** [Put on display] displayed, demonstrated, advertised, exposed, set out, presented, delineated, exhibited, laid out, put up for sale, put up, put on the block.—*Ant.* WITHDRAWN, concealed, held back. **2** [Proved] demonstrated, determined, made clear; see OBVIOUS 2.

showoff *n.* boaster, exhibitionist, egotist; see BRAGGART.

showpiece *n.* masterpiece, prize, work of art; see MASTERPIECE.

show window *n.* display window, store window, picture window; see DISPLAY.

showy *a.* flashy, glaring, gaudy; see ORNATE.

shred *n.* fragment, piece, tatter; see BIT 1.

shred *v.* slice, strip, cut into small pieces; see TEAR.

shrewd *a.* astute, ingenious, sharp; see INTELLIGENT.

shrewdly *a.* knowingly, cleverly, trickily, sagaciously, astutely, skillfully, ably, slyly, foxily, smartly, deceptively, cunningly, intelligently,

judiciously, neatly, coolly, handily, facilely, adroitly, deftly, with skill, in a crafty manner, with cunning manner, with consummate skill, knowing one's way around; see also CAREFULLY 1, DELIBERATELY.

shriek *n.* scream, screech, howl; see CRY 1, 3, YELL 1.

shriek *v.* scream, screech, squawk; see CRY 1, 2, YELL.

shrill *a.* high-pitched, piercing, penetrating, sharp, screeching, thin, deafening, earsplitting, blatant, noisy, clanging, harsh, blaring, raucous, metallic, discordant, cacophonous, acute; see also LOUD 1.—*Ant.* SOFT, low, faint.

shrine *n.* sacred place, hallowed place, altar; see CHURCH 1.

shrink *v.* withdraw, recoil, flinch; see CONTRACT 1.

shrinkage *n.* lessening, reduction, depreciation; see LOSS 1, 3.

shrivel *v.* parch, dry up, shrink; see CONTRACT 1, DRY 1.

shrub *n.* bush, fern, hedge; see PLANT.

shrubbery *n.* shrubs, bushes, hedge; see BRUSH 3.

shrunken *a.* withdrawn, withered, contracted; see DRY 1, WRINKLED.

shud·der (shud′ər) *vi.* ⟦ME *schoderen*⟧ to shake or tremble, as in horror — *n.* a shuddering

shuf·fle (shuf′əl) *vt., vi.* **-fled, -fling** ⟦prob. < LowG *schuffeln*⟧ 1 to move (the feet) with a dragging gait 2 to mix (playing cards) 3 to mix together in a jumble — *n.* a shuffling —**shuf′fler** *n.*

shuf′fle·board′ *n.* ⟦< *shovel board*⟧ a game in which disks are pushed with a cue toward numbered squares

shun (shun) *vt.* **shunned, shun′ning** ⟦OE *scunian*⟧ to keep away from; avoid scrupulously

shunt (shunt) *vt., vi.* ⟦ME *schunten*⟧ 1 to move or turn to one side 2 to switch, as a train, from one track to another — *n.* 1 a shunting 2 a railroad switch 3 a surgically created channel allowing flow from one organ, etc. to another

shush (shush) *interj.* ⟦echoic⟧ hush! be quiet! — *vt.* to say "shush" to

shut (shut) *vt.* **shut, shut′ting** ⟦OE *scyttan*⟧ 1 to move (a door, lid, etc.) so as to close (an opening, container, etc.) 2 *a)* to prevent entrance to or exit from *b)* to confine *in* a room, etc. 3 to bring together the parts of (an umbrella, book, etc.) — *vi.* to be or become shut — *adj.* closed, fastened, etc. —**shut down** to cease or cause to cease operating —**shut off** to prevent passage of or through —**shut out** 1 to deny entrance to 2 to prevent from scoring — **shut up** 1 to confine 2 [Colloq.] to stop or make stop talking

shut′down′ *n.* a stoppage of work or activity, as in a factory

shut′-eye′ *n.* [Slang] sleep

shut′-in′ *adj.* confined indoors by illness — *n.* an invalid who is shut-in

shut′out′ *n.* a preventing of the opposing team from scoring in a game

shut·ter (shut′ər) *n.* 1 a person or thing that shuts 2 a movable cover for a window 3 a device for opening and closing the aperture of a camera lens — *vt.* to close or furnish with a shutter

shut·tle (shut′'l) *n.* ⟦< OE *scytel*, missile⟧ 1 a device that carries thread back and forth, as in weaving 2 *a)* a traveling back and forth over a short route *b)* an airplane, bus, etc. used in a shuttle — *vt., vi.* **-tled, -tling** to move back and forth rapidly

shut′tle·cock′ (-käk′) *n.* a rounded piece of cork having a flat end stuck with feathers: used in badminton

shy[1] (shī) *adj.* **shy′er** or **shi′er, shy′est** or **shi′est** ⟦OE *sceoh*⟧ 1 easily frightened; timid 2 not at ease with others; bashful 3 distrustful; wary 4 [Slang] lacking — *vi.* **shied, shy′ing** 1 to move suddenly as when startled 2 to be or become cautious, etc. —**shy′ly** *adv.* —**shy′ness** *n.*

shy[2] (shī) *vt., vi.* **shied, shy′ing** ⟦< ?⟧ to fling, esp. sideways

shy·ster (shī′stər) *n.* ⟦prob. < Ger *scheisser*, one who defecates⟧ [Slang] a lawyer who uses unethical or tricky methods

Si *Chem. symbol for* silicon

Si·a·mese (sī′ə mēz′) *n., pl.* **-mese′** 1 *old name for* THAI 2 a domestic cat with blue eyes and a light-colored coat — *adj. old name for* THAI

Siamese twins ⟦after such a pair born in Siam⟧ any pair of twins born with bodies joined together

sib·i·lant (sib′əl ənt) *adj.* ⟦< L *sibilare*, to hiss⟧ having or making a hissing sound — *n.* a sibilant consonant, as (s) or (z) —**sib′i·late′** (-āt′), **-lat·ed, -lat·ing,** *vt., vi.*

sib·ling (sib′liŋ) *n.* ⟦< OE *sib*, kinsman + -LING⟧ a brother or sister

sib·yl (sib′əl) *n.* ⟦< Gr *sibylla*⟧ a prophetess of ancient Greece or Rome —**sib′yl·line′** (-in′, -ēn′) *adj.*

sic (sik) *vt.* **sicked, sick′ing** ⟦< SEEK⟧ to incite (a dog) to attack

sic (sik, sēk) *adv.* ⟦L⟧ thus; so: used within brackets, [*sic*], to show that a quoted passage, esp. one containing an error, is precisely reproduced

Si·cil·ian (si sil′yən, -ē ən) *adj.* of Sicily, its people, their dialect, etc. — *n.* a native or inhabitant of Sicily (island of Italy)

sick[1] (sik) *adj.* ⟦OE *seoc*⟧ 1 suffering from disease; ill 2 having nausea 3 of or for sick people [*sick* leave] 4 deeply disturbed, as by grief 5 disgusted by an excess [*sick* of excuses] 6 [Colloq.] sadistic, morbid, etc. [a *sick* joke] — **the sick** sick people —**sick′ish** *adj.*

sick[2] (sik) *vt.* SIC (incite)

sick bay a hospital and dispensary, esp. on board ship

sick′bed′ *n.* the bed of a sick person

sick′en *vt., vi.* to make or become ill, disgusted, etc. — **sick′en·ing** *adj.*

sick′ie (-ē) *n.* [Slang] a sick person, esp. one who is emotionally disturbed, etc.

sickle (sik′əl) *n.* ⟦ult. < L *secare*, to cut⟧ a tool having a crescent-shaped blade on a short handle, for cutting tall grasses and weeds

sickle cell anemia an inherited chronic anemia found chiefly among blacks, in which red blood cells become sickle-shaped due to defective hemoglobin

sickly (sik′lē) *adj.* **-lier, -li·est** 1 in poor health 2 produced by sickness [a *sickly* pallor] 3 faint; feeble 4 weak; mawkish

sick′ness *n.* 1 a being sick or diseased 2 a malady 3 nausea

sick′o (-ō) *n., pl.* **-os** [Slang] SICKIE

sick′out′ *n.* a staying out of work on the claim of illness, as by a group of employees trying to win demands

sick′room′ *n.* the room of a sick person

side (sīd) *n.* ⟦OE⟧ 1 the right or left half, as of the body 2 a position beside one 3 *a)* any of the lines or surfaces that bound something *b)* either of the two bounding surfaces of an object that are not the front, back, top, or bottom 4 either of the two surfaces of paper, cloth, etc. 5 an aspect [his cruel *side*] 6 any location, etc. with reference to a central point 7 the position or attitude of one person or faction opposing another 8 one of the parties in a contest, conflict, etc. 9 a line of descent — *adj.* 1 of, at, or on a

═══════════════ **THESAURUS** ═══════════════

shudder *n.* tremor, shuddering, shaking, trembling.

shudder *v.* quiver, quake, shiver; see SHAKE 1, WAVE 1.

shun *v.* dodge, evade, keep away from; see AVOID.

shut *a.* stopped, locked, fastened; see TIGHT 2.

shut *v.* close up, lock, seal; see CLOSE 4. —**shut down** close down, shut up, abandon; see STOP 1. —**shut off** turn off, discontinue, put a stop to; see CLOSE 4, STOP 1. —**shut out** keep out, evict, fence out; see REFUSE. — **shut up** 1 [To cease speaking] be quiet, stop talking, quiet, hush, quit chattering, silence, dry up*. 2 [To close] padlock, close up, stop; see CLOSE 4.

shutter *n.* blind, cover, shade; see CURTAIN, SCREEN 1.

shy[1] *a.* retiring, bashful, girlish, modest, diffident, submissive, timid, passive, reticent, fearful, tentative, subservient, docile, compliant, humble, coy, restrained, timorous, demure.

shyness *n.* bashfulness, reserve, timidity, modesty, timidness, coyness, demureness, sheepishness, diffidence, apprehension, backwardness, nervousness, insecurity, reticence; see also RESTRAINT 1.

sick[1] *a.* ill, ailing, unwell, disordered, diseased, feeble, frail, impaired, weak, suffering, feverish, imperfect, sickly, declining, unhealthy, rabid, indisposed, distempered, infected, invalid, delicate, infirm, rickety, peaked, broken down, physically run down, confined, laid up, under medication, bedridden, in poor health, at death's door, hospitalized, quarantined, incurable, out of kilter*, feeling poorly, sick as a dog*, in a bad way, not so hot*, under the weather*.—*Ant.* HEALTHY, hearty, well. —**get sick** become sick or ill, contract a disease, take sick; see SICKEN 1. —**sick of** tired of, disgusted, fed up; see DISGUSTED.

sicken *v.* 1 [To contract a disease] become ill, take sick, fall ill, become diseased, fall victim to a disease, be stricken, run a temperature, run a fever, be taken with, come down with, catch a disease, acquire, waste away, suffer a relapse, break out with, catch one's death, pick up a bug*. 2 [To offend] repel, nauseate, revolt; see DISGUST.

sickening *a.* 1 [Contaminated] sickly, tainted, diseased; see SICK. 2 [Disgusting] revolting, nauseous, putrid; see OFFENSIVE 2.

sickly *a.* ailing, weakly, feeble; see SICK.

sickness *n.* ill health, ailment, infirmity; see ILLNESS 1.

side *a.* to the side, indirect, roundabout; see OBLIQUE.

side *n.* 1 [One of two opponents] party, contestant, combatant; see FACTION. 2 [A face] facet, front, front side, rear, surface, outer surface, inner surface, top, bottom, elevation, view; see also PLANE 1. — **from side to side** back and forth, wobbly, unstable; see IRREGULAR 1. —**on the side** in addition to, as a bonus, additionally; see EXTRA. — **side by side** adjacent, nearby, faithfully; see LOYALLY, NEAR 1. —**take sides** join, fight for, declare oneself; see HELP, SUPPORT 2.

side 2 to or from one side *[a side glance]* 3 secondary *[a side issue]* — **vi.** to align oneself (*with* a faction, etc.) — **side by side** together —**take sides** to support a faction

side′arm′ *adj., adv.* with a forward arm motion at or below shoulder level

side arms weapons worn at the side or waist, as swords, pistols, etc.

side′bar′ *n.* a short article about a sidelight of a major news story and printed alongside it

side′board′ *n.* a piece of furniture for holding linen, china, etc.

side′burns′ *n.pl.* ⟦< *burnsides*, side whiskers worn by A. E. *Burnside*, Civil War general⟧ the hair growing on the sides of a man's face, just in front of the ears

side′car′ *n.* a small car attached to the side of a motorcycle

side dish any food served along with the main course, as in a separate dish

side′kick′ *n.* [Slang] 1 a close friend 2 a partner; confederate

side′light′ *n.* a bit of incidental knowledge or information

side′line′ *n.* 1 either of two lines marking the side limits of a playing area, as in football 2 a secondary line of merchandise, work, etc.

side′long′ *adv.* toward the side — *adj.* directed to the side, as a glance

side′man′ *n.*, *pl.* **-men′** a band member other than the leader or soloist

side′piece′ *n.* a piece forming, or attached to, the side of something

si·dereal (si dir′ē əl) *adj.* ⟦< L *sidus*, star⟧ with reference to the stars

side′sad′dle *n.* a saddle designed for a rider sitting with both legs on the same side of the animal — *adv.* on or as if on a sidesaddle

side′show′ *n.* a small show in connection with the main show, as of a circus

side′slip′ *vi.* **-slipped′, -slip′ping** to slip or skid sideways — *vt.* to make sideslip — *n.* a slip or skid to the side

side′split′ting *adj.* 1 very hearty: said of laughter 2 very funny

side′step′ *vt., vi.* **-stepped′, -step′ping** to dodge as by stepping aside

side′swipe′ *vt.* **-swiped′, -swip′ing** to hit along the side in passing — *n.* such a glancing blow

side′track′ *vt., vi.* 1 to switch (a train) to a siding 2 to turn away from the main issue

side′walk′ *n.* a path for pedestrians, usually paved, along the side of a street

side′wall′ *n.* the side of a tire between the tread and the wheel rim

side′ways′ (-wāz′) *adv., adj.* 1 toward or from one side 2 with one side forward Also **side′wise′** (-wiz′)

sid·ing (sid′iŋ) *n.* 1 a covering, as of overlapping boards, for the outside of a frame building 2 a short railroad track connected with a main track by a switch and used for unloading, etc.

si·dle (sid′'l) *vi.* **-dled, -dling** ⟦< *sideling*, sideways⟧ to move sideways, esp. in a shy or stealthy manner

siege (sēj) *n.* ⟦< L *sedere*, sit⟧ 1 the encirclement of a fortified place by an enemy intending to take it 2 any persistent attempt to gain control, etc. —**lay siege to** to subject to a siege

si·erra (sē er′ə) *n.* ⟦Sp < L *serra*, a saw⟧ a range of hills or mountains with a saw-toothed appearance

si·esta (sē es′tə) *n.* ⟦Sp < L *sexta* (*hora*), sixth (hour), noon⟧ a brief nap or rest after the noon meal

sieve (siv) *n.* ⟦OE *sife*⟧ a utensil with many small holes for straining liquids or fine particles; strainer

sift (sift) *vt.* ⟦OE *siftan*⟧ 1 to pass (flour, etc.) through a sieve 2 to examine (evidence, etc.) with care 3 to separate *[to sift fact from fable]* — *vi.* to pass as through a sieve — **sift′er** *n.*

sigh (si) *vi.* ⟦< OE *sican*⟧ 1 to take in and let out a long, deep, audible breath, as sorrow, relief, etc. 2 to feel longing or grief (*for*) — *n.* the act or sound of sighing

sight (sit) *n.* ⟦< OE *seon*, to see⟧ 1 something seen or worth seeing 2 the act of seeing 3 a device to aid the eyes in aiming a gun, etc. 4 aim or an observation taken, as on a sextant 5 the power or range of seeing; eyesight 6 [Colloq.] anything that looks unpleasant, odd, etc. — *vt.* 1 to observe 2 to glimpse 3 to aim at 4 to adjust the sights of — *vi.* to look carefully *[sight along the line]* —**at** (or **on**) **sight** as soon as seen —**by sight** by appearance —**not by a long sight** 1 not nearly 2 not at all —**out of sight** 1 not in sight 2 far off 3 [Colloq.] beyond reach 4 [Slang] excellent; wonderful

sight′ed *adj.* 1 having sight; not blind 2 having (a specified kind of) sight *[farsighted]*

sight′less *adj.* blind

sight′ly *adj.* **-lier, -li·est** pleasant to the sight —**sight′li·ness** *n.*

sight reading the skill of performing written music on sight, without previous study —**sight′-read′** *vt., vi.*

sight′see′ing *n.* a visiting of places of interest —**sight′seer** (-sē′ər) *n.*

sigma (sig′mə) *n.* the eighteenth letter of the Greek alphabet (Σ, σ)

sign (sin) *n.* ⟦< L *signum*⟧ 1 something that indicates a fact, quality, etc.; token 2 a gesture that conveys information, etc. 3 a mark or symbol having a specific meaning *[a dollar sign ($)]* 4 a placard, etc. bearing information, advertising, etc. 5 any trace or indication — *vt.* 1 to write (one's name) on (a letter, check, contract, etc.) 2 to engage by written contract — *vi.* 1 to write one's signature —**sign in** (or **out**) to sign a register on arrival (or departure) —**sign off** to stop broadcasting, as for the day — **sign′er** *n.*

sign·age (si′nij) *n.* public signs collectively, often, specif., when graphically coordinated

sig·nal (sig′nəl) *n.* ⟦< L *signum*, a sign⟧ 1 a sign or event that initiates action *[a bugle signal to attack]* 2 a gesture, device, etc. that conveys command, warning, etc. 3 in radio, etc., the electrical impulses transmitted or received — *adj.* 1 remarkable; notable 2 used as a signal — *vt., vi.* **-naled** or **-nalled, -nal·ing** or **-nal·ling** 1 to make a signal or signals (to) 2 to communicate by signals

---

THESAURUS

sideline *n.* avocation, interest, trade; see HOBBY.

sidestep *v.* evade, elude, shun; see AVOID.

sidewalk *n.* footway, footpath, foot pavement; see PATH.

sideways *a.* indirectly, sloping, sidelong; see OBLIQUE.

siege *n.* offense, onslaught, assault; see ATTACK.

sieve *n.* strainer, sifter, colander, screen, bolt, bolting cloth, mesh, hair sieve, drum sieve, flat sieve, quarterinch sieve, half-inch sieve, gravel sieve, flour sieve.

sift *v.* 1 [To evaluate] investigate, scrutinize, probe; see EXAMINE. 2 [To put through a sieve] bolt, screen, winnow, grade, sort, colander, size, strain; see also CLEAN, FILTER 2, PURIFY.

sigh *n.* deep breath, sigh of relief, expression of sorrow; see CRY 1.

sigh *v.* groan, moan, lament; see CRY 1, GASP.

sight *n.* 1 [The power of seeing] perception, eyesight, eyes for, range of vision, apprehension, keen sight; see also VISION 1. 2 [Something worth seeing; *often plural*] show, view, spectacle, display, scene, point of interest, local scene. 3 [*An unsightly person] eyesore, hag, ogre; see SLOB. —**a sight for sore eyes*** beauty, welcome sight, delight; see BLESSING 2, FRIEND, VIEW. —**at first sight** hastily, without much consideration, provisionally; see QUICKLY. —**by sight** somewhat acquainted, not intimately, superficially; see UNFAMILIAR 1. —**catch sight of** glimpse, notice, see momentarily; see SEE 1. —**lose sight of** miss, fail to follow, slip up on; see FORGET, NEGLECT 1. —**on sight** at once, without hesitation, precipitately; see IMMEDIATELY, QUICKLY. —**out of sight** (**of**) disappeared, vanished, indiscernible; see GONE 1, INVISIBLE.

sightseeing *n.* vacationing, excursion, tour; see TRAVEL.

sightseer *n.* observer, tourist, voyager; see TRAVELER.

sign *n.* 1 [A signal] indication, clue, omen, divination, premonition, handwriting on the wall, foreshadowing, manifestation, foreboding, foreknowledge, token, harbinger, herald, hint, symptom, assurance, prediction, portent, prophecy, mark, badge, symbol, caution, warning, beacon, flag, hand signal, wave of the arm, flash, whistle, warning bell, signal bell, signal light, high sign*. 2 [An emblem] insignia, badge, crest; see EMBLEM. 3 [A symbol] type, visible sign, token; see sense 1.

sign *v.* 1 [Authorize] endorse, confirm, acknowledge; see APPROVE. 2 [Indicate] express, signify, signal; see MEAN 1. 3 [Hire] engage, contract, employ; see HIRE.

signal *n.* beacon, flag, omen; see SIGN 1.

signal *v.* give a sign to, flag, wave, gesture, motion, nod, beckon, warn, indicate.

sig·nal·ize′ (-īz′) *vt.* **-ized′, -iz′ing** 1 to make noteworthy 2 to make known or draw attention to

sig′nal·ly *adv.* in a signal way; notably

sig·na·tory (sig′nə tôr′ē) *adj.* having joined in signing something — *n., pl.* **-ries** a signatory person, nation, etc.

sig·na·ture (sig′nə chər) *n.* 〖< L *signare*, to sign〗 1 a person's name written by that person 2 *Music* a staff sign showing key or time

sign′board′ *n.* a board bearing a sign or advertisement

sig·net (sig′nit) *n.* 〖< Fr *signe*, a sign〗 a seal, as on a ring, used in marking documents as official, etc.

sig·nif·i·cance (sig nif′ə kəns) *n.* 1 that which is signified; meaning 2 the quality of being significant; expressiveness 3 importance

sig·nif·i·cant (-kənt) *adj.* 〖< L *significare*, signify〗 1 having or expressing a meaning, esp. a special or hidden one 2 full of meaning 3 important —**sig·nif′i·cant·ly** *adv.*

sig·ni·fy (sig′nə fī′) *vt.* **-fied′, -fy′ing** 〖< L *signum*, a sign + *facere*, make〗 1 to be an indication of; mean 2 to make known, as by a sign, words, etc. — *vi.* to be important — **sig′ni·fi·ca′tion** *n.*

sign of the cross an outline of a CROSS (sense 2) made symbolically by moving the hand or fingers

sign of the zodiac any of the twelve divisions of the zodiac, each represented by a symbol

si·gnor (sē nyôr′) *n., pl.* **-gno′ri** (-nyô′rē) 〖It〗 1 [S-] Mr.: Italian title 2 a gentleman; man

si·gno·ra (sē nyô′rä) *n., pl.* **-gno′re** (-re) 〖It〗 1 [S-] Mrs., Madam: Italian title 2 a married woman

si·gno·ri·na (sē′nyô rē′nä) *n., pl.* **-ri′ne** (-ne) 〖It〗 1 [S-] Miss: Italian title 2 an unmarried woman or girl

sign′post′ *n.* 1 a post bearing a sign 2 an obvious clue, symptom, etc.

si·lage (sī′lij) *n.* green fodder preserved in a silo

sild (sild) *n., pl.* **sild** or **silds** 〖Norw, herring〗 a small or young herring canned as a Norwegian sardine

si·lence (sī′ləns) *n.* 1 a keeping silent 2 absence of sound 3 omission of mention — *vt.* **-lenced, -lenc·ing** 1 to make silent 2 to put down; repress — *interj.* be silent!

si·lenc·er *n.* 1 one that silences 2 a device to muffle the sound of a gun

si·lent (sī′lənt) *adj.* 〖< L *silere*, be silent〗 1 making no vocal sound; mute 2 not talkative 3 still; noiseless 4 not expressed; tacit 5 not active 〖a *silent* partner〗 —**si′lent·ly** *adv.*

sil·hou·ette (sil′ŏo et′) *n.* 〖Fr, after E. de *Silhouette*, 18th-c. Fr statesman〗 1 a solid, usually black, outline drawing, esp. a profile 2 any dark shape seen against a light background — *vt.* **-et′ted, -et′ting** to show in silhouette

sil·i·ca (sil′i kə) *n.* 〖< L *silex*, flint〗 a hard, glassy mineral found in a variety of forms, as in quartz, sand, etc. —**si·li·ceous** (sə lish′əs) *adj.*

sil′i·cate (-kit, -kāt′) *n.* a salt or ester derived from silica

sili·con (sil′i kän′, -kən) *n.* 〖< L *silex*, flint〗 a nonmetallic chemical element found always in combination

sil′i·cone (-kōn′) *n.* an organic silicon compound highly resistant to heat, water, etc.

sil′i·co′sis (-kō′sis) *n.* 〖see SILICON & -OSIS〗 a chronic lung disease caused by inhaling silica dust

silk (silk) *n.* 〖ult. < ? L *sericus*, (fabric) of the *Seres*, the Chinese〗 1 *a*) the fine, soft fiber produced by silkworms *b*) thread or fabric made from this 2 any silklike filament or substance —**silk′en** *adj.* —**silky** (sil′kē), **-i·er**, **-i·est**, *adj.* —**silk′i·ness** *n.*

silk-screen process a stencil method of printing a color design through a piece of silk or other fine cloth on which parts of the design not to be printed have been blocked up —**silk′-screen′** *vt.*

silk′worm′ *n.* any of certain moth caterpillars that produce cocoons of silk fiber

sill (sil) *n.* 1 a heavy, horizontal timber or line of masonry supporting a house wall, etc. 2 a horizontal piece forming the bottom frame of a window or door opening

silly (sil′ē) *adj.* **-lier, -li·est** 〖< OE *sælig*, happy〗 having or showing little sense, judgment, or sobriety; foolish, absurd, etc. —**sil′li·ness** *n.*

silo (sī′lō) *n., pl.* **-los** 〖< Gr *siros*〗 1 an airtight pit or tower in which green fodder is preserved 2 an underground facility for a long-range ballistic missile

silt (silt) *n.* 〖prob. < Scand〗 a fine-grained, sandy sediment carried or deposited by water — *vt., vi.* to fill or choke up with silt

sil·ver (sil′vər) *n.* 〖< OE *seolfor*〗 1 a white, precious, metallic chemical element that is very ductile and malleable 2 *a*) silver coin *b*) money; riches 3 silverware 4 a lustrous, grayish white — *adj.* 1 of, containing, or plated with silver 2 silvery 3 marking the 25th anniversary — *vt.* to cover as with silver

sil′ver·fish′ *n., pl.* **-fish′** a wingless insect with silvery scales and long feelers, found in damp places

silver lining some basis for hope or comfort in the midst of despair

silver nitrate a colorless, crystalline salt, used in photography, as an antiseptic, etc.

sil′ver·smith′ *n.* an artisan who makes and repairs silver articles

sil′ver-tongued′ (-tuŋd′) *adj.* eloquent

sil′ver·ware′ *n.* 1 articles, esp. tableware, made of or plated with silver 2 any metal tableware

sil′very *adj.* 1 of, like, or containing silver 2 soft and clear in tone

sim·i·an (sim′ē ən) *adj.* 〖< L *simia*, an ape〗 of or like an ape or monkey — *n.* an ape or monkey

sim·i·lar (sim′ə lər) *adj.* 〖< L *similis*〗 nearly but not exactly the same or alike —**sim′i·lar′i·ty** (-ler′ə tē), *pl.* **-ties,** *n.* —**sim′i·lar·ly** *adv.*

THESAURUS

signature *n.* sign, stamp, mark, name, written name, subscription, autograph, impression, indication, designation, trademark, one's John Hancock*.

signed *a.* 1 endorsed, marked, autographed, written, undersigned, countersigned, sealed, witnessed, subscripted, registered, enlisted, signed on the dotted line.

signer *n.* cosigner, underwriter, endorser; see WITNESS.

significance *n.* weight, consequence, point; see IMPORTANCE.

significant *a.* meaningful, notable, vital; see IMPORTANT 1.

signify *v.* imply, import, purport; see MEAN 1.

silence *n.* 1 [Absence of sound] quietness, stillness, hush, utter stillness, absolute quiet, calm, noiselessness, quiet, deep stillness, soundlessness, loss of signal, radio silence, security silence, security blackout, censorship, hush of early dawn.—*Ant.* NOISE, din, uproar. 2 [Absence of speech] muteness, secrecy, reserve, reticence, inarticulateness, golden silence, respectful silence.

silence *v.* hush, quell, still; see QUIET 2.

silenced *a.* quieted, calmed, stilled, restrained, repressed, held down, held back, restricted, subdued, inhibited, coerced, suppressed, under duress, under compulsion; see also INTERRUPTED.

silent *a.* 1 [Without noise] still, hushed, soundless; see CALM 2, QUIET. 2 [Without speech] reserved, mute, speechless; see DUMB 1.

silently *a.* without noise, without a sound, as still as a mouse, like a shadow, in utter stillness, noiselessly, calmly, quietly, soundlessly, mutely, dumbly, in deathlike silence, like one struck dumb, speechlessly, wordlessly, as silently as falling snow.

silhouette *n.* contour, shape, profile; see FORM 1, OUTLINE 3.

sill *n.* threshold, beam, bottom of the frame; see LEDGE.

silly *a.* senseless, ridiculous, nonsensical, absurd, brainless, simpleminded, unreasonable, foolish, irrational, inconsistent, stupid, illogical, ludicrous, preposterous; see also CHILDISH.

silver *a.* silvery, pale, white, lustrous, bright, silvery white, silverlike, shimmering, glittering, resplendent, white as silver.

silverware *n.* silver, service, cutlery, flatware, hollow ware, silver plate. *Common pieces of silverware include the following:* knife, dinner knife, butter knife, fork, salad fork, cold meat fork, tablespoon, soup spoon, dessert spoon, grapefruit spoon, ice-cream spoon, iced-tea spoon, coffee spoon, teaspoon, soup ladle, gravy ladle, sugar spoon, salt spoon, spatula.

silvery *a.* shiny, glittering, brilliant; see BRIGHT 1.

similar *a.* much the same, comparable, related; see ALIKE.

similarity *n.* correspondence, likeness, resemblance, parallelism, semblance, agreement, affinity, kinship, analogy, closeness, approximation, conformity, concordance, concurrence, coincidence, congruity, parity, harmony, comparability, identity, community, relation, correlation, relationship, proportion, comparison, simile, interrelation, association, connection, similar form, like quality, point of likeness, similar appearance.—*Ant.* DIFFERENCE, variance, dissimilarity.

similarly *a.* likewise, thus, furthermore, in a like manner, correspond-

simi·le (sim′ə lē′) *n.* ⟦< L, a likeness⟧ a figure of speech likening one thing to another by the use of *like, as,* etc. (Ex.: tears flowed like wine)

si·mili·tude (sə mil′ə tōōd′) *n.* ⟦< L *similitudo*⟧ likeness; resemblance

sim·mer (sim′ər) *vi.* ⟦echoic⟧ **1** a remain at or just below the boiling point **2** to be about to break out, as in anger — *vt.* to keep at or just below the boiling point — *n.* a simmering

simon-pure (sī′mən pyoor′) *adj.* ⟦after *Simon Pure,* a character in an 18th-c. play⟧ genuine; authentic

si·mony (sī′mə nē, sim′ə-) *n.* ⟦after *Simon* Magus: Acts 8:9-24⟧ the buying or selling of sacraments or benefices

sim·pa·tico (sim pät′i kō, -pat′-) *adj.* ⟦< It or Sp⟧ compatible or congenial

sim·per (sim′pər) *vi.* ⟦Early Modern Eng⟧ to smile in a silly or affected way — *n.* such a smile

sim·ple (sim′pəl) *adj.* **-pler, -plest** ⟦< L *simplus*⟧ **1** having only one or a few parts; uncomplicated **2** easy to do or understand **3** without additions ⟦the *simple* facts⟧ **4** not ornate or luxurious; plain **5** without guile or deceit **6** without ostentation; natural **7** of low rank or position **8** stupid or foolish —**sim′ple·ness** *n.*

simple interest interest computed on principal alone, and not on principal plus interest

sim′ple-mind′ed *adj.* **1** artless; unsophisticated **2** foolish **3** mentally retarded

sim′ple·ton (-tən) *n.* a fool

sim·plic·ity (sim plis′ə tē) *n., pl.* **-ties 1** a simple state or quality; freedom from complexity **2** absence of elegance, luxury, etc.; plainness **3** artlessness **4** foolishness

sim·plify (sim′plə fī′) *vt.* **-fied′, -fy′ing** to make simpler or less complex —**sim′pli·fi·ca′tion** *n.*

sim·plis·tic (sim plis′tik) *adj.* making complex problems unrealistically simple —**sim·plis′ti·cally** *adv.*

sim·ply (sim′plē) *adv.* **1** in a simple way **2** merely ⟦*simply* trying⟧ **3** completely ⟦*simply* furious⟧

simu·late (sim′yōō lāt′) *vt.* **-lat·ed, -lat·ing** ⟦< L *simulare*⟧ **1** to give a false appearance of; feign **2** to look or act like —**sim′u·la′tion** *n.*

si·mul·cast (sī′məl kast′) *vt.* **-cast′** or **-cast′ed, -cast′ing** to broadcast (a program) simultaneously by radio and television — *n.* a program so broadcast

si·mul·ta·neous (sī′məl tā′nē əs) *adj.* ⟦< L *simul,* together⟧ occurring, done, etc. at the same time —**si′mul·ta·ne′ity** (-tə nē′ə tē) *n.* —**si′mul·ta′neous·ly** *adv.*

sin (sin) *n.* ⟦OE *synne*⟧ **1** the willful breaking of religious or moral law **2** any offense or fault — *vi.* **sinned, sin′ning** to commit a sin

Si·nai (sī′nī′), **Mount** *Bible* the mountain where Moses received the law from God

since (sins) *adv.* ⟦ult. < OE *sith,* after + *thæt,* that⟧ **1** from then until now ⟦been here ever *since*⟧ **2** at some time between then and now ⟦has *since* recovered⟧ **3** before now; ago ⟦long *since* gone⟧ — *prep.* **1** continuously from (then) until now ⟦*since* noon⟧ **2** during the period between (then) and now ⟦twice *since* May⟧ — *conj.* **1** after the time that ⟦two years *since* they met⟧ **2** continuously from the time when ⟦lonely ever *since* he left⟧ **3** because ⟦*since* you are finished, let's go⟧

sin·cere (sin sir′) *adj.* **-cer′er, -cer′est** ⟦< L *sincerus,* pure⟧ **1** without deceit or pretense **2** genuine ⟦*sincere* grief⟧ —**sin·cere′ly** *adv.* —**sin·cer′ity** (-ser′ə tē) *n.*

si·necure (sī′nə kyoor′, sin′ə-) *n.* ⟦< L *sine,* without + *cura,* care⟧ any position providing an income but requiring little or no work

sine die (sī′nē dī′ē) ⟦LL, without a day⟧ for an indefinite period

sine qua non (sī′nē kwä nän′, sin′ā kwä nōn′) ⟦L, without which not⟧ an indispensable condition or thing

sinew (sin′yōō) *n.* ⟦OE *seonwe*⟧ **1** a tendon **2** muscular power; strength —**sin′ewy** (-yōō ē) *adj.*

sin′ful *adj.* having sinned often; wicked —**sin′ful·ly** *adv.*

sing (siŋ) *vi.* **sang, sung, sing′ing** ⟦OE *singan*⟧ **1** to produce musical sounds with the voice **2** to use song or verse in praise, etc. ⟦of thee I *sing*⟧ **3** to make musical sounds, as a songbird **4** to hum, buzz, etc., as a bee — *vt.* **1** to render (a song, etc.) by singing **2** to extol, etc. in song **3** to bring or put by singing ⟦to *sing* a baby to sleep⟧ — *n.* [Colloq.] group singing —**sing′er** *n.*

sing. *abbrev.* singular

sing′-along′ *n.* [Colloq.] an informal gathering of people to sing songs

singe (sinj) *vt.* **singed, singe′ing** ⟦OE *sengan*⟧ **1** to burn superficially or slightly **2** to expose (a carcass) to flame in removing feathers, etc. — *n.* **1** a singeing **2** a superficial burn

sin·gle (siŋ′gəl) *adj.* ⟦< L *singulus*⟧ **1** a) one only b) separate and distinct ⟦every *single* time⟧ **2** solitary **3** of or for one person or family **4** between two persons only ⟦*single* combat⟧ **5** unmarried **6** having only one part; not

---

◼ THESAURUS ◼

ingly, by the same token, in addition, then, as well, too; see also SO.

simmer *v.* seethe, stew, warm; see BOIL, COOK.

simmering *a.* broiling, heated, boiling; see HOT 1.

simple *a.* **1** [Not complicated] single, unmixed, unblended, mere, unadulterated, not complex, simplistic, not confusing, pure. **2** [Plain] homely, unaffected, unadorned; see MODEST 2. **3** [Easy] not difficult, mild, done with ease; see EASY 2.

simple-minded *a.* unintelligent, childish, moronic; see DULL 3, NAIVE, STUPID.

simpleton *n.* clod, idiot, bungler; see FOOL.

simplicity *n.* **1** [The quality of being plain] plainness, stark reality, lack of ornament, lack of sophistication, bareness, homeliness, severity. **2** [Artlessness] naiveté, plainness, primitiveness; see INNOCENCE 2.

simplified *a.* made easy, made plain, uncomplicated, clear, interpreted, broken down, cleared up, reduced; see also OBVIOUS 2.

simplify *v.* clear up, clarify, interpret; see EXPLAIN.

simplistic *a.* simplest, naive, oversimplified; see CHILDISH, SIMPLE 1.

simply *a.* **1** [With simplicity] clearly, plainly, intelligibly, directly, candidly, sincerely, modestly, easily, quietly, naturally, honestly, frankly, unaffectedly, artlessly, ingenuously, without self-consciousness, commonly, ordinarily, matter-of-factly,

unpretentiously, openly, guilelessly. **2** [Merely] utterly, just, solely; see ONLY 2.

simulate *v.* imitate, feign, lie; see PRETEND 1.

simultaneous *a.* coincident, at the same time, concurrent, in concert, in the same breath, in chorus, at the same instant; see also EQUALLY.

simultaneously *a.* at the same time, as one, concurrently; see TOGETHER 2.

sin *n.* error, wrongdoing, trespass, wickedness, evil-doing, iniquity, immorality, crime, ungodliness, unrighteousness, veniality, disobedience to the divine will, transgression of the divine law, violation of God's law; see also CRIME. *Sins recognized as deadly include the following:* pride, covetousness, lust, anger, gluttony, envy, sloth.

sin *v.* err, do wrong, commit a crime, offend, break the moral law, break one of the Commandments, trespass, transgress, misbehave, go astray, fall, lapse, fall from grace, sow one's wild oats, wander from the straight and narrow*, backslide, live in sin*, sleep around*.

since *a., prep., conj.* **1** [Because] for, as, inasmuch as, considering, in consideration of, after all, seeing that, in view of, for the reason that, by reason of, on account of, in view of; see also BECAUSE. **2** [Between the present and a previous time] ago, from the time of, subsequent to, after, following, more recently than,

until now.

sincere *a.* truthful, faithful, trustworthy; see HONEST 1, RELIABLE.

sincerely *a.* truthfully, truly, really, genuinely, earnestly, aboveboard, seriously, naturally, candidly, frankly, profoundly, deeply, to the bottom of one's heart.

sincerity *n.* openness, frankness, truthfulness; see HONESTY, RELIABILITY.

sinful *a.* wicked, erring, immoral; see BAD 1, WRONG 1.

sinfully *a.* wickedly, immorally, unjustly; see WRONGLY.

sing *v.* chant, carol, warble, vocalize, trill, croon, twitter, chirp, raise a song, croon, twitter, chirp, raise a song, lift up the voice in song, burst into song.

singe *v.* brand, sear, scorch; see BURN.

singer *n.* vocalist, songster, chorister, soloist, minstrel, chanter; see also MUSICIAN.

singing *n.* warbling, crooning, chanting; see MUSIC 1.

single *a.* **1** [Unique] sole, original, exceptional, singular, only, without equal, unequaled, peerless, unrivaled; see also RARE 2, UNIQUE, UNUSUAL 1.—*Ant.* MANY, numerous, widespread. **2** [Individual] particular, separate, indivisible; see INDIVIDUAL, PRIVATE. **3** [Unmarried] unwed, celibate, eligible, virginal, living alone, companionless, unattached, free, footloose, on the loose*, in the market*.—*Ant.* MARRIED, UNITED, wed.

multiple, etc. **7** whole; unbroken [a *single* front] —*vt.*
-gled, -gling to select from others: usually with *out* —*vi.*
Baseball to hit a single —*n.* **1** a single person or thing **2**
Baseball a hit by which the batter reaches first base **3** [*pl.*]
Racket Sports a match with only one player on each side
—**sin'gle·ness** *n.*

sin'gle-breast'ed (-bres'tid) *adj.* overlapping the front of
the body just enough to fasten [a *single-breasted* coat]

single file a single line of people or things, one behind
another

sin'gle-hand'ed *adj., adv.* **1** using only one hand **2**
without help —**sin'gle-hand'edly** *adv.*

sin'gle-mind'ed *adj.* with only one aim or purpose —
sin'gle-mind'edly *adv.*

sin'gle·ton (-gəl tən) *n.* **1** a playing card that is the only
one of its suit held by a player **2** a single thing

sin'gle-track' *adj.* ONE-TRACK

sin'gle·tree' (-trē') *n.* [< ME *swingle*, rod + *tre*, tree] the
crossbar on a wagon, etc. to which the traces of a horse's
harness are hooked

sin'gly (siṅ'glē) *adv.* **1** alone **2** one by one **3** unaided

sing'song' *n.* a monotonous rise and fall of tone in an
unvarying cadence

sin'gu·lar (siṅ'gyə lər) *adj.* [< L *singulus*, single] **1**
unique **2** extraordinary; remarkable **3** peculiar; odd **4**
Gram. designating only one —*n. Gram.* the singular number or form of a word —**sin'gu·lar'ity** (-ler'ə tē) *n.* —**sin'**
gu·larly *adv.*

Sin·ha·lese (sin'hə lēz', -lēs') *adj.* of Sri Lanka (island
country of S Asia), its principal people, or their language,
etc. —*n.* **1** *pl.* **-lese'** a member of the Sinhalese people **2**
their language

sin·is·ter (sin'is tər) *adj.* [< L *sinister*, left-hand] **1** orig.,
on or to the left-hand side **2** threatening harm, evil, etc. **3**
wicked; evil

sink (siṅk) *vi.* **sank** or **sunk**, **sunk**, **sink'ing** [OE *sin-*
can] **1** to go beneath the surface of water, etc. **2** to go
down slowly **3** to appear to descend, as the sun **4** to
become lower, as in level, value, or rank **5** to subside, as
wind or sound **6** to become hollow, as the cheeks **7** to
pass gradually (*into* sleep, etc.) **8** to approach death —*vt.*
1 to make sink **2** to make (a mine, engraving, etc.) by
digging, cutting, etc. **3** to invest **4** to defeat; undo —*n.* **1**
a cesspool or sewer **2** a basin, as in a kitchen, with a
drainpipe **3** an area of sunken land —**sink in** [Colloq.] to
be understood in full —**sink'able** *adj.*

sink'er *n.* **1** one that sinks **2** a lead weight used in fishing

sink'hole' *n.* a surface depression resulting when ground
collapses

sinking fund a fund built up over time to pay off a future
debt, as of a corporation

sin'ner *n.* a person who sins

Sino- [< Gr *Sinai*] *combining form* Chinese and

sinu·ous (sin'yoo əs) *adj.* [< L *sinus*, a bend] **1** bending
or winding in and out; wavy **2** devious; crooked —**sin'u·**
os'ity (-äs'ə tē) *n.*

si·nus (sin'əs) *n.* [L, a bend] a cavity, hollow, etc.; specif.,
any of the air cavities in the skull opening into the nasal
cavities

si'nus·i'tis (-it'is) *n.* inflammation of the sinuses, esp. of
the skull

Sioux (sōō) *n., pl.* **Sioux** (sōō, sōōz) a member of a group
of Indian tribes of the N U.S. and S Canada —*adj.* of
these tribes

sip (sip) *vt., vi.* **sipped, sip'ping** [ME *sippen*] to drink a
little at a time —*n.* **1** the act of sipping **2** a quantity
sipped —**sip'per** *n.*

si·phon (sī'fən) *n.* [< Gr *siphōn*, tube] **1** a bent tube for
carrying liquid out over the edge of a container to a lower
level, through the force of air pressure **2** a sealed bottle
from which carbonated water is released: in full **siphon**
bottle —*vt.* to draw off as through a siphon

sir (sur) *n.* [see fol.] **1** [*sometimes* S-] a respectful term of
address used to a man: not followed by the name **2** [S-]
the title used before the name of a knight or baronet

sire (sīr) *n.* [< L *senior*, compar. of *senex*, old] **1** [S-] a
title of respect used in addressing a king **2** [Old Poet.] a
father or forefather **3** the male parent of a four-legged
mammal —*vt.* **sired, sir'ing** to beget: said esp. of animals

si·ren (sī'rən) *n.* [< Gr *Seirēn*] **1** *Gr. & Rom. Myth.* any
of several sea nymphs whose singing lures sailors to their
death on rocky coasts **2** a seductive woman **3** a warning
device producing a loud, wailing sound

sir·loin (sur'loin') *n.* [< OFr *sur*, over + *loigne*, loin] a
choice cut of beef from the loin end in front of the rump

si·rocco (sə räk'ō) *n., pl.* **-cos** [It < Ar *sharq*, the east] a
hot, oppressive wind blowing from the deserts of N Africa
into S Europe

sir·ree or **siree** (sə rē') *interj.* [< SIR] an interjection
used for emphasis after *yes* or *no*

sirup (sur'əp, sir'-) *n. alt. sp. of* SYRUP

sis (sis) *n.* [Colloq.] *short for* SISTER

si·sal (sī'səl) *n.* [after Sisal, in SE Mexico] a strong fiber
obtained from the leaves of an agave

sissy (sis'ē) *n., pl.* **-sies** [dim. of SIS] [Colloq.] **1** an
effeminate boy or man **2** a timid person —**sis'si·fied'** (-ə
fīd') *adj.*

sis·ter (sis'tər) *n.* [< ON *systir*] **1** a woman or girl as she
is related to the other children of her parents **2** a friend
who is like a sister **3** a female fellow member of the same
race, organization, etc. **4** a nun **5** one of the same kind,
model, etc. —**sis'ter·hood'** *n.* —**sis'terly** *adj.*

sis'ter-in-law' *n., pl.* **sis'ters-in-law'** **1** the sister of
one's spouse **2** the wife of one's brother **3** the wife of the
brother of one's spouse

Sisy·phus (sis'ə fəs) *Gr. Myth.* a greedy king doomed in
Hades to roll uphill a stone which always rolls down again

sit (sit) *vi.* **sat, sit'ting** [OE *sittan*] **1** *a*) to rest oneself
upon the buttocks, as on a chair *b*) to rest on the
haunches with the forelegs braced, as a dog *c*) to perch, as
a bird **2** to cover eggs for hatching, as a hen **3** *a*) to
occupy a seat as a judge, legislator, etc. *b*) to be in session,
as a court **4** to pose, as for a portrait **5** to be located **6** to
rest or lie [cares *sit* lightly on him] **7** BABY-SIT —*vt.* **1** to
cause to sit **2** to keep one's seat on (a horse, etc.) —**sit**
down to take a seat —**sit in (on)** to attend —**sit out** to
take no part in (a dance, etc.) —**sit up 1** to sit erect **2** to
postpone going to bed **3** [Colloq.] to become suddenly
alert —**sit'ter** *n.*

si·tar (si tär') *n.* [Hindi *sitār*] a lutelike instrument of
India with a long, fretted neck

sit·com (sit'käm') *n.* [Colloq.] *short for* SITUATION COMEDY

sit'-down' *n.* a strike in which the strikers refuse to leave
the premises

site (sīt) *n.* [< L *situs*, position] a location or scene

sit'-in' *n.* a method of protest in which demonstrators sit
in, and refuse to leave, a public place

■■■ THESAURUS ■■■

single-handed *a.* without assistance, courageously, self-reliantly; see
ALONE, BRAVELY.

single-minded *a.* stubborn, self-
reliant, bigoted; see SELFISH.

singly *a.* alone, by itself, by oneself,
separately, only, solely, one by one,
privately, individually, once.

singular *a.* sole, one only, single; see
UNIQUE.

sinister *a.* evil, bad, corrupt, perverse, dishonest, foreboding, disastrous, malignant, hurtful, harmful,
injurious, dire, poisonous, adverse,
unlucky, unfortunate, unfavorable;
see also BAD 1.

sink *n.* sewer, basin, cesspool, wash-
basin, tub, pan, bowl.

sink *v.* **1** [To go downward] descend,
decline, fall, subside, drop, droop,
slump, go under, immerse, go to the

bottom, be submerged, settle, go to
Davy Jones's locker, touch bottom,
go down with the ship.—*Ant.* RISE,
float, come up. **2** [To cause to sink]
submerge, scuttle, depress, immerse,
engulf, overwhelm, swamp, lower,
bring down, force down, cast down,
let down; see also IMMERSE. **3** [To
weaken] decline, fail, fade; see
WEAKEN 1. **4** [To decrease] lessen,
diminish, wane; see DECREASE 1. —
sink in* impress, take hold, make an
impression; see INFLUENCE.

sinner *n.* wrongdoer, delinquent,
lawbreaker; see CRIMINAL.

sip *v.* taste, drink in, extract; see
DRINK 1.

siren *n.* horn, whistle, signal; see
ALARM.

sister *n.* blood relative, member of

the family, stepsister, half sister, big
sister, kid sister*, sis*; see also RELA-
TIVE.

sit *v.* be seated, seat oneself, take a
seat, sit down, sit up, squat, perch,
take a load off one's feet*, have a
place, have a chair, sit in, take a
chair, take, take a place.—*Ant.*
RISE, stand up, get up. —**sit in** sit in
on, take part in, be a part of; see
COOPERATE, JOIN 2. —**sit out** ignore,
abstain from, hold back; see NEGLECT
1, 2.

site *n.* locality, section, situation; see
PLACE 3, POSITION 1.

sit-in *n.* demonstration, march, display; see PROTEST, STRIKE 1.

sitter *n.* baby sitter, attendant, companion; see SERVANT.

sit'ting *n.* **1** the act or position of one that sits **2** a session, as of a court **3** a period of being seated

sitting duck [Colloq.] a person or thing especially vulnerable to attack; easy target

situ·ate (sich'ōō āt') *vt.* **-at'ed, -at'ing** [see SITE] to put in a certain place or position; place; locate

sit·u·a'tion *n.* **1** location; position **2** condition with regard to circumstances **3** state of affairs **4** a position of employment

situation comedy a comic television series made up of episodes involving the same group of characters

sit'-up' or **sit'up'** *n.* an exercise in which a person lying supine rises to a sitting position without using his hands

sitz bath (sits, zits) [< Ger] a therapeutic bath in which only the hips and buttocks are immersed

Siva (sē'və, shē'-) Hindu god of destruction and reproduction

six (siks) *adj., n.* [OE *sex*] one more than five; 6; VI — **sixth** *adj., n.*

six'-pack' *n.* a package of six units, as one with six cans of beer

six'-shoot'er *n.* [Colloq.] a revolver firing six shots without reloading

six'teen' (-tēn') *adj.* [OE *syxtene*] six more than ten; 16; XVI — **six'teenth'** *adj., n.*

sixth sense intuitive power

six·ty (siks'tē) *adj., n., pl.* **-ties** [OE *sixtig*] six times ten; 60; LX — **the sixties** the numbers or years, as of a century, from 60 through 69 — **six'ti·eth** (-ith) *adj., n.*

siz·a·ble (sī'zə bəl) *adj.* quite large or bulky Also sp. **size'able**

size[1] (sīz) *n.* [ult. < L *sedere*, sit] **1** that quality of a thing which determines how much space it occupies; dimensions or magnitude **2** any of a series of graded classifications of measure into which merchandise is divided — *vt.* **sized, siz'ing** to make or grade according to size — **size up** [Colloq.] **1** to make an estimate or judgment of **2** to meet requirements

size[2] (sīz) *n.* [ME *syse*] a pasty substance used as a glaze or filler on plaster, paper, cloth, etc. — *vt.* **sized, siz'ing** to fill, stiffen, or glaze with size

-sized (sīzd) *combining form* having a (specified) size [*medium-sized*] Also *-size*

siz·ing (sī'ziŋ) *n.* **1** SIZE[2] **2** the act or process of applying size

siz·zle (siz'əl) *vi.* **-zled, -zling** [echoic] **1** to make a hissing sound when in contact with heat **2** to be extremely hot — *vt.* to make sizzle — *n.* a sizzling sound

S.J. Society of Jesus

skate[1] (skāt) *n.* [< OFr *eschace*, stilt] **1** a metal runner in a frame, fastened to a shoe for gliding on ice **2** a similar frame or shoe with two pairs of small wheels, for gliding on a floor, sidewalk, etc. — *vi.* **skat'ed, skat'ing** to glide or roll on or as on skates — **skat'er** *n.*

skate[2] (skāt) *n.* [< ON *skata*] any ray fish

skate'board' *n.* a short, oblong board with two wheels at each end, ridden, as down an incline — *vi.* **-board'ed, -board'ing** to ride on a skateboard

ske·dad·dle (ski dad'l) *vi.* **-dled, -dling** [< ?] [Colloq.] to run away

skeet (skēt) *n.* [< ON *skeyti*, projectile] trapshooting in which the shooter fires from different angles

skein (skān) *n.* [< MFr *escaigne*] a quantity of thread or yarn in a coil

skel·e·ton (skel'ə tən) *n.* [< Gr *skeletos*, dried up] **1** the hard framework of bones of an animal body **2** a supporting framework **3** an outline, as of a book — *adj.* greatly reduced [a *skeleton* crew] — **skel'etal** *adj.*

skeleton key a key with a slender bit that can open many simple locks

skep·tic (skep'tik) *adj.* [L < Gr *skeptikos*, inquiring] *var. of* SKEPTICAL — *n.* **1** an adherent of skepticism **2** one who habitually questions matters generally accepted **3** one who doubts religious doctrines

skep'ti·cal (-ti kəl) *adj.* doubting; questioning — **skep'ti·cally** *adv.*

skep'ti·cism' (-siz'əm) *n.* **1** the doctrine that the truth of all knowledge must always be in question **2** skeptical attitude **3** doubt about religious doctrines

sketch (skech) *n.* [ult. < Gr *schedios*, extempore] **1** a rough drawing or design, done rapidly **2** a brief outline **3** a short, light story, play, etc. — *vt., vi.* make a sketch (of) — **sketch'y, -i·er, -i·est,** *adj.*

skew (skyōō) *vi., vt.* [< OFr *eschiver*, shun < OHG] to slant or set at a slant — *adj.* slanting — *n.* a slant or twist

skewer (skyōō'ər) *n.* [< ON *skifa*, a slice] a long pin used to hold meat together while cooking — *vt.* to fasten or pierce with skewers

ski (skē) *n., pl.* **skis** or **ski** [Norw < ON *skith*, snowshoe] either of a pair of long runners of wood, etc. fastened to shoes for gliding over snow — *vi.* **skied, ski'ing** to glide on skis — **ski'er** *n.*

skid (skid) *n.* [prob. < ON *skith*, snowshoe] **1** a plank, log, etc., often used as a track upon which to slide a heavy object **2** a low, wooden platform for holding loads **3** a runner on aircraft landing gear **4** a sliding wedge used to brake a wheel **5** the act of skidding — *vt., vi.* **skid'ded, skid'ding** to slide or slip, as a vehicle on ice — **be on (or hit) the skids** [Slang] to be on the decline, or to fail

skid row [altered < *skid road*, trail to skid logs along] a section of a city frequented by vagrants, derelicts, etc.

skiff (skif) *n.* [< It *schifo*] any light, open boat propelled by oars, motor, or sail

ski lift an endless cable with seats, for carrying skiers up a slope

skill (skil) *n.* [< ON *skil*, distinction] **1** great ability or proficiency **2** *a)* an art, craft, etc., esp. one involving the hands or body *b)* ability in such an art, etc. — **skilled** *adj.* — **skill'ful** or **skil'ful** *adj.*

skil·let (skil'it) *n.* [< ? L *scutra*, dish] a pan for frying

skim (skim) *vt., vi.* **skimmed, skim'ming** [ME *skimen*] **1** to remove (floating matter) from (a liquid) **2** to glance through (a book, etc.) without reading word for word **3** to glide lightly (over)

skim milk milk with the cream removed Also **skimmed milk**

skimp (skimp) *vi., vt.* SCRIMP

skimp'y *adj.* **-i·er, -i·est** [Colloq.] barely enough; scanty — **skimp'i·ness** *n.*

skin (skin) *n.* [< ON *skinn*] **1** the outer covering of the animal body **2** a pelt **3** something like skin, as fruit rind, etc. — *vt.* **skinned, skin'ning** **1** to remove skin from **2**

THESAURUS

situated *a.* established, fixed, located; see PLACED.

situation *n.* **1** [Circumstance] condition, state, state of one's affairs; see CIRCUMSTANCES 1, 2. **2** [A physical position] location, site, spot; see PLACE 3, POSITION 1.

size[1] *n.* **1** [Measurement] extent, area, dimension; see MEASUREMENT 2. **2** [Magnitude] bulk, largeness, greatness, extent, vastness, scope, immensity, enormity, stature, hugeness, breadth, substance, volume, mass, extension, intensity, capacity, proportion; see also EXTENT, QUANTITY.

size up* *v.* judge, survey, scrutinize; see EXAMINE.

sizzle *n.* hiss, hissing, sputtering; see NOISE 1.

sizzle *v.* brown, grill, broil; see COOK, FRY.

skate[1] *v.* slide, glide, skim, slip, skid, go quickly, race, ice skate, roller skate.

skeleton *n.* **1** [Bony structure] skeletal frame, bone, support; see BONE. **2** [Framework] draft, design, sketch; see FRAME 1.

skeptic *n.* doubter, unbeliever, freethinker; see CYNIC.

skeptical *a.* cynical, dubious, unbelieving; see DOUBTFUL, SUSPICIOUS 1.

sketch *n.* portrayal, picture, draft, design, outline, drawing, representation, painting, skeleton, figure, illustration, copy, likeness; see also PICTURE 2, PLAN 1.

sketch *v.* paint, describe, depict; see DRAW 2.

sketchy *a.* coarse, crude, preliminary; see UNFINISHED 1.

skid *v.* slip, glide, move; see SLIDE.

skill *n.* dexterity, facility, craft; see ABILITY.

skilled *a.* skillful, a hand at, proficient; see ABLE, EXPERIENCED.

skillful *a.* skilled, practiced, accomplished; see ABLE, EXPERIENCED.

skim *v.* **1** [To pass lightly and swiftly] soar, float, sail, dart; see also FLY 1. **2** [To remove the top; especially, to remove cream] brush, scoop, separate; see DIP 2, REMOVE 1. **3** [To read swiftly] look through, brush over, scan; see EXAMINE, READ 1.

skimp *v.* scamp, slight, scrimp; see SACRIFICE 2, SAVE 3.

skimpy *a.* short, scanty, insufficient; see INADEQUATE.

skin *n.* epidermis, derma, cuticle, bark, peel, husk, rind, hide, coat, covering, surface, parchment. —**be no skin off one's back** (or **nose**)*** not hurt one, do no harm, not affect one; see SURVIVE 1. —**by the skin of one's teeth** barely, scarcely, narrowly; see HARDLY. —**get under one's skin*** irritate, disturb, upset; see ENRAGE. —**save one's skin*** get to injure by scraping (one's knee, etc.) **3** [Colloq.] to swindle —**skin′less** *adj.*

skin diving underwater swimming with such gear as a face mask, flippers, scuba equipment, etc. —**skin′-dive′, -dived′, -div′ing,** *vi.* —**skin diver**

skin′flick′ *n.* [Slang] a film emphasizing nudity or explicit sexual activity

skin′flint′ *n.* [lit., one who would skin a flint for economy] a miser

-skinned *combining form* having (a specified kind of) skin [dark-skinned]

skin′ny *adj.* **-nier, -ni·est** without much flesh; very thin —**skin′ni·ness** *n.*

skin′ny-dip′ *vi.* **-dipped′, -dip′ping** [Colloq.] to swim nude —*n.* [Colloq.] a swim in the nude

skin′tight′ *adj.* tightfitting [skintight jeans]

skip (skip) *vi., vt.* **skipped, skip′ping** [ME *skippen*] **1** to leap lightly (over) **2** to ricochet or bounce **3** to pass from one point to another, omitting or ignoring (what lies between) **4** [Colloq.] to leave (town, etc.) hurriedly — *n.* a skipping; specif., a gait alternating light hops on each foot —**skip it!** [Colloq.] never mind!

skip′per (skip′ər) *n.* [< MDu *schip,* a ship] the captain of a ship

skir·mish (skur′mish) *n.* [< It *schermire* < Gmc] **1** a brief fight between small groups, as in a battle **2** any slight, unimportant conflict — *vi.* to take part in a skirmish

skirt (skurt) *n.* [< ON *skyrt,* shirt] **1** that part of a dress, coat, etc. that hangs below the waist **2** a woman's garment that hangs from the waist **3** something like a skirt — *vt., vi.* to be on, or move along, the edge (of)

ski run a slope or course for skiing

skit (skit) *n.* [prob. ult. < ON *skjōta,* to shoot] a short, humorous sketch, as in the theater

ski touring the sport of cross-country skiing

ski tow a kind of ski lift for pulling skiers up a slope on their skis

skit·tish (skit′ish) *adj.* [see SKIT & -ISH] **1** lively; playful **2** easily frightened; jumpy **3** fickle

skiv·vy (skiv′ē) *n., pl.* **-vies** [< ?] [Slang] **1** a man's, esp. a sailor's, short-sleeved undershirt: usually **skivvy shirt** **2** [pl.] men's underwear

skoal (skōl) *interj.* [< ON *skāl,* a bowl] to your health! A toast

skul·dug·gery or **skull·dug·gery** (skul dug′ər ē) *n.* [< obs. Scot] [Colloq.] sneaky behavior; trickery

skulk (skulk) *vi.* [ME *sculken*] to move in a stealthy manner; slink —**skulk′er** *n.*

skull (skul) *n.* [< Scand] **1** the bony framework of the head, enclosing the brain **2** the head; mind

skull′cap′ *n.* a light, closefitting, brimless cap, usually worn indoors

skunk (skuŋk) *n.* [< AmInd] **1** a small, bushy-tailed mammal having black fur with white stripes down the back: it ejects a bad-smelling liquid when molested **2** its fur **3** [Colloq.] a despicable person

sky (skī) *n., pl.* **skies** [< ON, a cloud] **1** [often pl.] the upper atmosphere [blue skies, a cloudy sky] **2** the firmament **3** heaven

sky′cap′ *n.* a porter at an airport terminal

sky diving parachute jumping involving free-fall maneuvers

sky′-high′ *adj.* very high —*adv.* **1** very high **2** in or to pieces

sky′jack′ *vt.* [Colloq.] to hijack (an aircraft) —**sky′jack·er** *n.*

sky′lark′ *n.* a Eurasian lark famous for the song it utters as it soars — *vi.* to romp or frolic

sky′light′ *n.* a window in a roof or ceiling

sky′line′ *n.* **1** the visible horizon **2** the outline, as of a city, seen against the sky

sky marshal a Federal officer assigned to guard against skyjacking

sky′rock′et *n.* a fireworks rocket that explodes aloft — *vi., vt.* to rise or cause to rise rapidly

sky′scrap′er *n.* a very tall building

sky′ward (-wərd) *adv., adj.* toward the sky Also **sky′wards** *adv.*

sky′ways′ *n.pl.* routes of air travel

sky′writ′ing *n.* the tracing of words, etc. in the sky by trailing smoke from an airplane —**sky′writ′er** *n.*

slab (slab) *n.* [ME *slabbe*] a flat, broad, and fairly thick piece

slack[1] (slak) *adj.* [< OE *slæc*] **1** slow; sluggish **2** not busy; dull [a slack period] **3** loose; not tight **4** careless [a slack workman] — *vt., vi.* to slacken — *n.* **1** a part that hangs loose **2** a lack of tension **3** a dull period; lull — **slack off** to slacken —**slack up** to go more slowly —**slack′ness** *n.*

slack[2] (slak) *n.* [ME *sleck*] a mixture of small pieces of coal, coal dust, etc. left from screening coal

slacken (slak′ən) *vt., vi.* **1** to make or become less active, brisk, etc. **2** to loosen or relax, as rope

slack′er *n.* one who shirks

slacks (slaks) *n.pl.* trousers for men or women

slag (slag) *n.* [< earlier LowG *slagge*] the fused refuse separated from metal in smelting

slain (slān) *vt. pp. of* SLAY

slake (slāk) *vt.* **slaked, slak′ing** [< OE *slæc,* SLACK[1]] **1** to satisfy (thirst, etc.) **2** to produce a chemical change in (lime) by mixing with water

sla·lom (slä′ləm) *n.* [Norw] a downhill ski race over a zigzag course — *vi.* to take part in a slalom

slam[1] (slam) *vt.* **slammed, slam′ming** [prob. < Scand] **1** to shut, hit, throw, or put with force and noise **2** [Colloq.] to criticize severely — *n.* **1** a slamming **2** [Colloq.] a severe criticism

slam[2] (slam) *n.* [< ?] *Bridge short for* GRAND SLAM or LITTLE SLAM

slam′-bang′ *adv.* [Colloq.] **1** swiftly or abruptly and recklessly **2** noisily — *adj.* [Colloq.] lively, noisy, etc.

slam′-dunk′ *n. Basketball* a hard shot from directly above the basket

slam·mer (slam′ər) *n.* [Slang] a prison or jail

slan·der (slan′dər) *n.* [see SCANDAL] **1** the utterance of a falsehood that damages another's reputation **2** such a spoken statement — *vt.* to utter a slander about —**slan′derer** *n.* —**slan′der·ous** *adj.*

slang (slaŋ) *n.* [< ?] highly informal speech that is outside standard usage —**slang′y, -i·er, -i·est,** *adj.*

slant (slant) *vt., vi.* [< Scand] **1** to incline; slope **2** to tell so as to express a particular bias — *n.* **1** an oblique surface, line, etc. **2** a point of view or attitude — *adj.* sloping

slap (slap) *n.* [echoic] **1** a blow with something flat, as the palm of the hand **2** an insult or rebuff — *vt.* **slapped, slap′ping 1** to strike with something flat **2** to put, hit, etc. with force

slap′dash′ *adj., adv.* hurried(ly), careless(ly), haphazard(ly), etc.

▬▬ THESAURUS ▬▬

away, evade, leave just in time; see ESCAPE, SURVIVE 1.

skin *v.* peel, pare, flay, scalp, shed, strip, strip off, pull off, remove the surface from, skin alive, husk, shuck, lay bare, bare.

skin diver *n.* scuba diver, submarine diver, deepsea diver, pearl diver, aquanaut, frogman; see also DIVER.

skinflint *n.* scrimp, tightwad, hoarder; see MISER.

skinny *a.* lean, gaunt, slender; see THIN 2.

skip *v.* hop, spring, leap; see JUMP 1.

skirmish *n.* engagement, encounter, conflict; see BATTLE, FIGHT 1.

skirt *n.* kilt, petticoat, miniskirt; see CLOTHES, DRESS 2.

skull *n.* scalp, cranium, brain case;

see HEAD 1.

sky *n.* firmament, atmosphere, the blue yonder; see AIR 1, HEAVEN. — **out of a clear (blue) sky** without warning, suddenly, abruptly; see QUICKLY, SOON.

skyscraper *n.* tall building, highrise building, high-rise; see BUILDING.

slab *n.* slice, chunk, lump; see PART 1.

slack[1] *a.* relaxed, lax, limp; see LOOSE 1.

slack down or **off** or **up** *v.* decline, lessen, become slower; see DECREASE 1, SLOW 1.

slam[1] *v.* **1** [To throw with a slam] thump, fling, hurl; see THROW 1. **2** [To shut with a slam] bang, crash, push; see CLOSE 2, 4.

slander *n.* defamation, calumny,

scandal; see LIE.

slander *v.* defame, libel, defile, detract, depreciate, disparage, revile, dishonor, blaspheme, curse, attack, sully, tarnish, vilify, blot, cast a slur on, scandalize, belittle, backbite, malign, speak evil of, give a bad name, sling mud*.—*Ant.* PRAISE, applaud, eulogize.

slang *n.* cant, argot, colloquialism, pidgin English, vulgarism, lingo, bad grammar, jargon, shoptalk, vulgarity; see also JARGON 1, 2.

slant *v.* veer, lie obliquely, incline; see BEND, LEAN 1, TILT.

slanting *a.* inclining, sloping, tilting; see BENT.

slap *v.* strike, pat, spank; see HIT 1.

slapdash *a.* hasty, sluggish, impetu-

slap'-hap'py *adj.* [Slang] **1** dazed, as by blows **2** silly or giddy

slap'stick' *n.* crude comedy full of horseplay — *adj.* characterized by such comedy

slash (slash) *vt.* [< ? OFr *esclachier*, to break] **1** to cut with sweeping strokes, as of a knife **2** to cut slits in **3** to reduce drastically *[slash* prices*]* — *vi.* to make a sweeping stroke as with a knife — *n.* **1** a slashing **2** a cut made by slashing **3** a virgule —**slash'er** *n.*

slash'-and-burn' *adj.* of a method of clearing fields by cutting down and burning vegetation

slash pocket a pocket (in a garment) with a finished diagonal opening

slat (slat) *n.* [< OFr *esclat*, fragment] a narrow strip of wood, etc.

slate (slāt) *n.* [see prec.] **1** a hard rock that cleaves into thin, smooth layers **2** its bluish-gray color **3** a roofing tile, etc. of slate — *vt.* **slat'ed, slat'ing 1** to cover with slate **2** to designate, as for candidacy —**a clean slate** a record showing no marks of discredit, dishonor, etc.

slather (sla*th*'ər) *vt.* [< ?] [Colloq. or Dial.] to cover or spread on thickly

slat·tern (slat'ərn) *n.* [< dial. *slatter*, to slop] a slovenly or sluttish woman —**slat'ternly** *adj.*

slaugh·ter (slôt'ər) *n.* [< ON *slātr*, lit., slain flesh] **1** the killing of animals for food **2** the brutal killing of a person **3** the killing of many people, as in battle — *vt.* **1** to kill (animals) for food **2** to kill (people) brutally or in large numbers —**slaugh'terer** *n.*

slaugh'ter·house' *n.* a place where animals are butchered for food

Slav (släv, slav) *n.* a member of a group of peoples of E and SE Europe, including Russians, Serbs, Czechs, Poles, etc. — *adj. var. of* SLAVIC

slave (slāv) *n.* [< Gr *Sklabos*, ult. < OSlav *Slovēne*, first used of captive Slavs] **1** a human being who is owned by another **2** one dominated by some influence, etc. **3** one who slaves — *vi.* **slaved, slav'ing** to work like a slave; drudge

slave driver 1 one who oversees slaves **2** any merciless taskmaster

slaver (slav'ər) *vi.* [< Scand] to drool

slav·ery (slā'vər ē) *n.* **1** the owning of slaves as a practice **2** the condition of a slave; bondage **3** drudgery; toil

Slavic (släv'ik, slav'-) *adj.* of the Slavs, their languages, etc. — *n.* a family of languages, including Russian, Polish, Czech, Bulgarian, etc.

slav·ish (slā'vish) *adj.* **1** of or like slaves; servile **2** blindly dependent or imitative —**slav'ishly** *adv.*

slaw (slô) *n.* [Du *sla* < Fr *salade*, salad] short for COLESLAW

slay (slā) *vt.* **slew, slain, slay'ing** [OE *slean*] to kill in a violent way —**slay'er** *n.*

sleaze (slēz) *n.* [< fol.] [Slang] **1** sleaziness **2** anything cheap, vulgar, shoddy, etc.

sleazy (slē'zē) *adj.* **-zier, -zi·est** [< *silesia*, orig. cloth made in central Europe] **1** flimsy or thin in substance **2** shoddy, shabby, etc. —**slea'zily** *adv.* —**slea'zi·ness** *n.*

sled (sled) *n.* [ME *sledde*] a vehicle on runners for moving over snow, ice, etc. — *vt., vi.* **sled'ded, sled'ding** to carry or ride on a sled —**sled'der** *n.*

sledge¹ (slej) *n.* [OE *slecge*] SLEDGEHAMMER

sledge² (slej) *n.* [MDu *sleedse*] a sled or sleigh

sledge'ham·mer *n.* [see SLEDGE¹] a long, heavy hammer, usually held with both hands

sleek (slēk) *adj.* [var. of SLICK] **1** smooth and shiny; glossy **2** of well-fed or well-groomed appearance **3** suave, elegant, etc. — *vt.* to make sleek —**sleek'ly** *adv.* —**sleek'ness** *n.*

sleep (slēp) *n.* [OE *slæp*] **1** the natural, regularly recurring rest for the body, during which there is little or no conscious thought **2** any state like this — *vi.* **slept, sleep'ing** to be in a state of or like sleep —**sleep off** to rid oneself of by sleeping —**sleep'less** *adj.* —**sleep'less·ness** *n.*

sleep'er *n.* **1** one who sleeps **2** a railroad car with berths for sleeping: also **sleeping car 3** a beam laid flat to support something **4** something that achieves an unexpected success

sleeping bag a warmly lined, zippered bag for sleeping outdoors

sleeping sickness an infectious disease, esp. in Africa, characterized by lethargy, prolonged coma, etc.

sleep'walk·ing *n.* the act of walking while asleep —**sleep'walk'er** *n.*

sleep'wear' *n.* NIGHTCLOTHES

sleep'y *adj.* **-i·er, -i·est 1** ready or inclined to sleep; drowsy **2** dull; idle *[a sleepy* town*]* —**sleep'i·ly** *adv.* —**sleep'i·ness** *n.*

sleet (slēt) *n.* [ME *slete*] **1** partly frozen rain **2** the icy coating when rain freezes on trees, etc. — *vi.* to shower in the form of sleet —**sleet'y** *adj.*

sleeve (slēv) *n.* [OE *sliefe*] **1** that part of a garment that covers the arm **2** a tubelike part fitting over or around another part —**up one's sleeve** hidden but ready at hand —**sleeve'less** *adj.*

sleigh (slā) *n.* [Du *slee*] a light vehicle on runners for travel on snow, ice, etc.

sleight of hand (slīt) [< ON *slœgr*, crafty] **1** skill with the hands, esp. in deceiving onlookers, as in magic **2** a trick thus performed

slen·der (slen'dər) *adj.* [ME *s(c)lendre* < ?] **1** long and thin **2** slim of figure **3** small in amount, size, etc. **4** of little force; feeble —**slen'der·ness** *n.*

slen·der·ize' *vt., vi.* **-ized', -iz'ing** to make or become slender

slept (slept) *vi., vt. pt. & pp. of* SLEEP

sleuth (slōōth) *n.* [< ON *slóth*, a trail] [Colloq.] a detective

slew¹ (slōō) *n.* [Ir *sluagh*, a host] [Colloq.] a large number or amount

slew² (slōō) *vt. pt. of* SLAY

slice (slīs) *n.* [< OFr *esclicier*] **1** a relatively thin, broad piece cut from something **2** a part or share — *vt.* **sliced, slic'ing 1** to cut into slices **2** to cut off as in a slice or slices: often with *off, from, away,* etc. **3** to hit (a ball) so that it curves to the right if right-handed or the left if left-handed —**slic'er** *n.*

slick (slik) *vt.* [OE *slician*] **1** to make smooth **2** [Colloq.] to make smart, neat, etc.: usually with *up* — *adj.* **1** sleek; smooth **2** slippery **3** adept; clever **4** [Colloq.] smooth but superficial, tricky, etc. — *n.* **1** a smooth area on the water, as from a layer of oil **2** a slippery, oily area on the surface of a road —**slick'ly** *adv.* —**slick'ness** *n.*

slick'er *n.* **1** a loose, waterproof coat **2** [Colloq.] a tricky person

---

THESAURUS

ous; see CARELESS.

slap-happy *a.* out of one's head, badly beaten, dizzy; see BEATEN 1, SILLY.

slapstick *a.* absurd, droll, comical; see FUNNY 1.

slash *v.* slit, gash, sever; see CUT 1.

slaughter *n.* butchery, killing, massacre; see MURDER.

slaughter *v.* slay, murder, massacre; see BUTCHER 1, KILL.

Slav *n. Slavs include the following:* Russian, Bulgarian, Pole, Slovene, Slovak, Ukrainian, Bohemian, Moravian, Czech, Serb, Croat, Sorb, Deniker.

slave *n.* bondsman, bondservant, chattel, serf, toiler, menial, drudge, laborer, captive, bondsmaid, bondwoman, victim of tyranny, one of a subject people.

slavery *n.* **1** [Bondage] subjugation,

restraint, involuntary servitude; see CAPTIVITY. **2** [Drudgery] toil, menial labor, grind; see WORK 2.

Slavic *a.* Slav, Slavophile, Slavonic, Old Slavonic, Church Slavonic. *Words referring to Slavic peoples include the following:* Cyrillic, Glagolitic, Russian, Polish, Bulgarian, Czech, Ukrainian, Bohemian, Serbian, Croatian or Croat, Bosnian, Montenegrin, Yugoslavian.

slay *v.* murder, slaughter, assassinate; see KILL 1.

sleazy *a.* shoddy, flimsy, slight; see THIN 1, WEAK 2.

sled *n.* hand sled, bobsled, sleigh, coasting sled, child's sled, toboggan, belly-bumper, pig-sticker.

sleek *a.* silken, silky, satin; see SMOOTH 1.

sleep *n.* slumber, doze, nap, rest,

sound sleep, deep sleep, siesta, catnap, dream, hibernation, the sandman, snooze*, shut-eye*.

sleep *v.* slumber, doze, drowse, rest, nap, snooze, hibernate, dream, snore, nod, yawn, relax, go to bed, fall asleep, take forty winks*, catnap, turn in, hit the hay*, saw logs*, sack out*. —**sleep (something) off** get over it, improve, sober up; see RECOVER 3.

sleeping *a.* dormant, inert, inactive; see ASLEEP.

sleepy *a.* dozy, somnolent, sluggish; see TIRED.

slender *a.* slim, slight, spare; see THIN 1, 2.

slice *n.* thin piece, chop, chunk; see PART 1.

slick *a.* sleek, slippery, glossy; see OILY 2, SMOOTH 1.

slide (slīd) vi. slid (slid), slid'ing [OE slidan] 1 to move along in constant contact with a smooth surface, as on ice 2 to glide 3 to slip /it slid from his hand/ — vt. 1 to cause to slide 2 to place quietly or deftly (in or into) — n. 1 a sliding 2 a smooth, often inclined surface for sliding 3 something that works by sliding 4 a photographic transparency for use with a viewer or projector 5 a small glass plate on which objects are mounted for microscopic study 6 the fall of a mass of rock, snow, etc. down a slope —let slide to fail to attend to properly

slide fastener a zipper or a zipperlike device with two grooved plastic edges joined or separated by a sliding tab

slid'er n. 1 one that slides 2 Baseball a curve ball that breaks only slightly

sliding scale a schedule, as of costs, wages, etc., that varies with given conditions, as cost of living, etc.

slight (slīt) adj. [OE sliht] 1 a) light in build; slender b) frail; fragile 2 lacking strength, importance, etc. 3 small in amount or extent — vt. 1 to neglect 2 to treat with disrespect 3 to treat as unimportant — n. a slighting or being slighted —slight'ly adv. —slight'ness n.

slim (slim) adj. slim'mer, slim'mest [< Du., bad] 1 small in girth; slender 2 small in amount, degree, etc. — vt., vi. slimmed, slim'ming to make or become slim — slim'ness n.

slime (slīm) n. [OE slim] any soft, moist, slippery, often sticky matter —slim'y, -i-er, -i-est, adj.

sling (sliŋ) n. [prob. < ON slyngua, to throw] 1 a primitive instrument whirled by hand for throwing stones 2 a cast; throw; fling 3 a) a supporting band, etc. as for raising a heavy object b) a cloth looped from the neck under an injured arm for support — vt. slung, sling'ing 1 to throw as with a sling 2 to hang in a sling

sling'shot' n. a Y-shaped piece of wood, etc. with an elastic band attached to it for shooting stones, etc.

slink (sliŋk) vi. slunk, slink'ing [OE slincan, to creep] to move in a furtive or sneaking way; sneak

slink'y adj. -i-er, -i-est 1 sneaking 2 [Slang] sinuous in movement or line

slip[1] (slip) vi. slipped, slip'ping [ME slippen, ult. < Ger.] 1 to go quietly or secretly /to slip out of a room/ 2 to pass smoothly or easily 3 to escape from one's memory, grasp, etc. 4 to slide, lose footing, etc. 5 to make a mistake; err 6 to become worse — vt. 1 to cause to slip 2 to put, pass, etc. quickly or deftly /to slip one's shoes on/ 3 to escape from (the memory) — n. 1 a space between piers for docking ships 2 a woman's undergarment the length of a skirt 3 a pillow case 4 a slipping or falling down 5 an error or mistake —let slip to say without intending to —slip up to make a mistake

slip[2] (slip) n. [< MDu slippen, to cut] 1 a stem, root, etc. of a plant, used for planting or grafting 2 a young, slim person 3 a small piece of paper

slip'case' n. a boxlike container for a book or books, open at one end

slip'cov'er n. a removable, fitted cloth cover for a chair, sofa, etc.

slip'knot' n. a knot that will slip along the rope around which it is tied

slip noose a noose made with a slipknot

slip'page (slip'ij) n. a slipping, as of one gear past another

slipped disk a ruptured cartilaginous disk between vertebrae

slip'per n. a light, low shoe easily slipped on the foot

slip'per·y (slip'ər ē) adj. -i·er, -i·est 1 liable to cause slipping, as a wet surface 2 tending to slip away, as from a grasp 3 unreliable; deceitful —slip'peri·ness n.

slip'shod' (-shäd') adj. [< obs. slip-shoe, a slipper] careless or slovenly

slip'-up' n. [Colloq.] an error

slit (slit) vt. slit, slit'ting [ME slitten] 1 to cut or split open, esp. by a lengthwise incision 2 to cut into strips — n. a straight, narrow cut, opening, etc.

slither (slith'ər) vi. [< OE slidan, to slide] to slip, slide, or glide along

sliver (sliv'ər) n. [< OE slifan, to split] a thin, sharp piece cut or split off; splinter — vt., vi. to cut or break into slivers

slob (släb) n. [Ir slab, mud] [Colloq.] a sloppy or coarse person

slob·ber (släb'ər) vi. [prob. < LowG slubberen, to swig] 1 to drool 2 to speak, etc. in a maudlin way

sloe (slō) n. [OE sla] 1 the blackthorn 2 its small, plumlike fruit

sloe'-eyed' adj. 1 having large, dark eyes 2 having almond-shaped eyes

sloe gin a liqueur of gin flavored with sloes

slog (släg) vt., vi. slogged, slog'ging [ME sluggen, go slowly] 1 to make (one's way) with great effort; plod 2 to toil (at)

slo·gan (slō'gən) n. [< Gael sluagh, a host + gairm, a call: orig., a battle cry] 1 a motto associated with a political party, etc. 2 a catchy phrase used in advertising

sloop (sloop) n. [< LowG slupen, to glide] a sailing vessel having a single mast with a mainsail and a jib

slop (släp) n. [OE sloppe] 1 watery snow or mud; slush 2 a puddle of spilled liquid 3 unappetizing, watery food 4 [often pl.] liquid waste of any kind — vi., vt. slopped, slop'ping to spill or splash

slope (slōp) n. [< OE slupan, to glide] 1 rising or falling ground 2 any inclined line, surface, etc.; slant 3 the amount or degree of this — vi. sloped, slop'ing to have an upward or downward inclination; incline; slant — vt. to cause to slope

sloppy (släp'ē) adj. -pier, -pi·est 1 splashy; slushy 2 a) slovenly b) slipshod 3 [Colloq.] gushingly sentimental — slop'pi·ness n.

sloppy Joe (jō) ground meat cooked with tomato sauce, spices, etc. and served on a bun

slop sink a deep sink for filling scrub pails, washing out mops, etc.

slosh (släsh) vi. [var. of SLUSH] 1 to splash through water, mud, etc. 2 to splash about: said of a liquid

slot (slät) n. [< OFr esclot, hollow between the breasts] 1 a narrow opening, as for a coin in a vending machine 2 [Colloq.] a position in a group, etc. — vt. slot'ted, slot'ting 1 to make a slot in 2 [Colloq.] to place in a series or sequence

sloth (slôth, slōth) n. [< OE slaw, slow] 1 disinclination to work or exert oneself; laziness 2 a slow-moving, treedwelling mammal of Central and South America that hangs, back down, from branches —sloth'ful adj. — sloth'ful·ness n.

slot machine a machine, specif. a gambling device, worked by inserting a coin in a slot

slouch (slouch) n. [< ON slōka, to droop] 1 a lazy or incompetent person 2 a drooping or slovenly posture —

═══ THESAURUS ═══

slide v. glide, skate, skim, slip, coast, skid, move along, move over, move past, pass along. —let slide ignore, pass over, allow to decline; see NEGLECT 1, 2.

slight a. 1 [Trifling] insignificant, petty, piddling; see TRIVIAL, UNIMPORTANT. 2 [Inconsiderable] small, sparse, scanty; see INADEQUATE. 3 [Delicate] frail, slender, flimsy; see DAINTY.

slightly a. a little, to some extent, hardly at all, scarcely any, not noticeably, unimportantly, inconsiderably, insignificantly, lightly, somewhat.

slim a. slender, narrow, lank; see THIN 2.

slime n. fungus, mire, ooze; see MUD.

slimy a. oozy, miry, mucky; see MUDDY 1, 2.

sling v. hurl, send, catapult; see THROW 1.

slink v. prowl, cower, lurk; see SNEAK.

slip[1] n. 1 [Error] lapse, misdeed, indiscretion; see ERROR. 2 [Misstep] slide, skid, stumble; see FALL 1. 3 [Undergarment] underclothing, panti-slip, bra-slip; see CLOTHES, UNDERWEAR. —give someone the slip get away, slip away, escape from; see LEAVE 1. —slip up (on) overlook, miss, bungle; see FAIL 1.

slipper n. house shoe, sandal, pump; see SHOE.

slippery a. glassy, smooth, glazed, polished, oily, waxy, soapy, greasy, slimy, icy, sleek, glistening, wet, unsafe, insecure, uncertain, tricky, shifty, slithery, slippery as an eel*.

slip-up n. oversight, mishap, omission; see ERROR.

slit n. split, cleavage, crevice; see HOLE 1, TEAR.

slit v. tear, slice, split; see CUT 1.

sliver n. splinter, thorn, fragment; see BIT 1, FLAKE.

slob* n. pig, hog, slattern, tramp, bum, yokel, ragamuffin.

slobber v. drip, salivate, dribble; see DROOL.

slogan n. catchword, rallying cry, trademark; see MOTTO, PROVERB.

slop v. slosh, wallow, splash, drip, spill, run over; see also DROP 1, EMPTY 1.

slope n. rising ground, incline, grade; see HILL.

sloppy a. clumsy, amateurish, mediocre; see AWKWARD, CARELESS.

slot n. aperture, opening, cut; see HOLE 1.

vi. to sit, stand, walk, etc. in a slouch —**slouch′y, -i·er, -i·est,** *adj.*

slough[1] (sluf) *n.* [ME *slouh,* a skin] a castoff layer or covering, as the skin of a snake — *vt.* to throw off; discard

slough[2] (slou) *n.* [OE *sloh*] 1 a place full of soft, deep mud 2 deep, hopeless dejection

Slo·vak (slō′väk′, -vak′) *n.* 1 any of a Slavic people living chiefly in Slovakia 2 their language — *adj.* of the Slovaks, their language, etc.

sloven (sluv′ən) *n.* [prob. < MDu *slof,* lax] a careless, untidy person —**slov′enly, -lier, -li·est,** *adj.*

Slo·veni·an (slō vē′nē ən) *n.* 1 any of a Slavic people living chiefly in Slovenia 2 their language — *adj.* of the Slovenians, their language, etc. Also **Slo·vene** (slō′vēn)

slow (slō) *adj.* [OE *slaw*] 1 not quick in understanding 2 taking a longer time than is usual 3 marked by low speed, etc.; not fast 4 behind the correct time, as a clock 5 passing tediously; dull — *vt., vi.* to make or become slow or slower: often with *up* or *down* — *adv.* in a slow manner —**slow′ly** *adv.* —**slow′ness** *n.*

slow burn [Slang] a gradual working up of anger: often in **do a slow burn**

slow′down′ *n.* a slowing down, as of production

slow motion an effect using slow-motion photography or video techniques

slow′-mo′tion *adj.* 1 moving slowly 2 designating a film or taped TV sequence showing the action slowed down

slow′poke′ (-pōk′) *n.* [Slang] a person who acts or moves slowly

slow′-wit′ted *adj.* mentally slow; dull

SLR *n.* [*s(ingle) l(ens) r(eflex)*] a camera allowing the photographer to see the subject through the same lens that brings the image to the film

sludge (sluj) *n.* [var. of *slutch,* mud] 1 mud, mire, or ooze 2 any heavy, slimy deposit, sediment, etc.

slue (slōō) *vt., vi.* slued, slu′ing [< ?] to turn or swing around

slug[1] (slug) *n.* [ME *slugge,* clumsy one] a small mollusk resembling a snail without a shell

slug[2] (slug) *n.* [prob. < prec.] a small piece of metal; specif., a bullet or false coin

slug[3] (slug) *n.* [prob. < Dan *sluge,* to gulp] [Slang] a drink of liquor

slug[4] (slug) *vt.* slugged, slug′ging [< ON *slag*] [Colloq.] to hit hard, esp. with the fist or a bat — *n.* [Colloq.] a hard blow or hit —**slug′ger** *n.*

slug·gard (slug′ərd) *n.* [< ME *sluggen,* be lazy] a lazy person

slug′gish (-ish) *adj.* [< SLUG[1]] 1 lacking energy; lazy 2 slow or slow-moving 3 not functioning with normal vigor —**slug′gish·ness** *n.*

sluice (slōōs) *n.* [< L *excludere,* to shut out] 1 an artificial channel for water, with a gate to regulate the flow 2 such a gate: also **sluice gate** 3 any channel for excess water 4 a sloping trough, as for washing gold ore — *vt.*

sluiced, sluic′ing 1 to draw off through a sluice 2 to wash with water from a sluice

slum (slum) *n.* [< ?] a populous area characterized by poverty, poor housing, etc. — *vi.* **slummed, slum′ming** to visit slums, esp. for reasons held to be condescending —**slum′my, -mier, -mi·est,** *adj.*

slum·ber (slum′bər) *vi.* [OE *sluma*] 1 to sleep 2 to be inactive — *n.* 1 sleep 2 an inactive state —**slum′ber·ous** *adj.*

slum′lord′ *n.* [Slang] an absentee landlord who exploits slum property

slump (slump) *vi.* [prob. < Ger] 1 to fall or sink suddenly 2 to have a drooping posture — *n.* 1 a sudden fall 2 a decline in activity, prices, performance, etc.

slung (sluŋ) *vt. pt. & pp. of* SLING

slunk (sluŋk) *vt. pt. & pp. of* SLINK

slur (slur) *vt.* slurred, slur′ring [prob. < MDu *sleuren,* to drag] 1 to pass over quickly and carelessly: often with *over* 2 to pronounce indistinctly 3 to disparage 4 *Music* to produce (successive notes) by gliding without a break — *n.* 1 a slurring 2 something slurred 3 an aspersion 4 *Music* a symbol (‿) or (⌒) connecting notes to be slurred

slurp (slurp) *vt., vi.* [Du *slurpen,* to sip] [Slang] to drink or eat noisily — *n.* [Slang] a loud sipping or sucking sound

slush (slush) *n.* [prob. < Scand] 1 partly melted snow 2 soft mud 3 sentimentality; drivel —**slush′y, -i·er, -i·est,** *adj.*

slush fund money used for bribery, political pressure, etc.

slut (slut) *n.* [ME *slutte*] 1 a dirty, slovenly woman 2 a sexually promiscuous woman —**slut′tish** *adj.*

sly (sli) *adj.* sli′er or sly′er, sli′est or sly′est [< ON *sloegr*] 1 skillful at trickery; crafty 2 cunningly underhanded 3 playfully mischievous —**on the sly** secretly —**sly′ly** or **sli′ly** *adv.* —**sly′ness** *n.*

smack[1] (smak) *n.* [OE *smæc*] 1 a slight taste or flavor 2 a small amount; trace — *vi.* to have a smack (*of*)

smack[2] (smak) *n.* [< ?] 1 a sharp noise made by parting the lips suddenly 2 a loud kiss 3 a slapping blow — *vt.* 1 to part (the lips) so as to make a smack 2 to kiss or slap loudly — *adv.* 1 with a smack 2 directly; precisely

smack[3] (smak) *n.* [prob. < Du *smak*] a fishing boat with a well for keeping fish alive

smack′er *n.* [Slang] a dollar bill

small (smôl) *adj.* [OE *smæl*] 1 comparatively little in size; not big 2 little in quantity, extent, duration, etc. 3 of little importance; trivial 4 young [*small* children] 5 mean; petty — *n.* the small part [*the small* of the back] —**feel small** to feel shame —**small′ness** *n.*

small arms firearms of small caliber, as pistols, rifles, etc.

small intestine the narrow section of the intestines, extending from the stomach to the large intestine

small′-mind′ed *adj.* selfish, mean, or narrow-minded

small′pox′ *n.* an acute, contagious virus disease characterized by fever and pustular eruptions

small talk light conversation about common, everyday things; chitchat

smart (smärt) *vi.* [OE *smeortan*] 1 *a*) to cause sharp, stinging pain, as a slap *b*) to feel such pain 2 to feel

═══ THESAURUS ═══

slow *a.* 1 [Slow in motion] sluggish, laggard, deliberate, gradual, loitering, leaden, creeping, inactive, slow moving, crawling, slow-paced, leisurely, as slow as molasses in January*.— *Ant.* FAST, swift, rapid. 2 [Slow in starting] dilatory, procrastinating, delaying, postponing, idle, indolent, tardy, lazy, apathetic, phlegmatic, inactive, sluggish, heavy, quiet, drowsy, inert, sleepy, lethargic, stagnant, negligent, listless, dormant, potential, latent; see also LATE 1.— *Ant.* IMMEDIATE, alert, instant. 3 [Slow in producing an effect] belated, behindhand, backward, overdue, delayed, long-delayed, behindtime, retarded, detained, hindered.—*Ant.* BUSY, diligent, industrious. 4 [Dull or stupid] stolid, tame, uninteresting; see DULL 3.

slow *v.* 1 [To become slower] slacken, slow up, slow down, lag, loiter, relax, procrastinate, stall, let up, wind down, ease up. 2 [To cause to become slower] delay, postpone, moderate, reduce, retard, detain, decrease, diminish, hinder, hold back, keep waiting, brake, curtail,

check, curb, cut down, rein in, cut back.

slowly *a.* moderately, gradually, nonchalantly, gently, leisurely, at one's leisure, taking one's own sweet time*.

slowness *n.* sluggishness, apathy, lethargy; see INDIFFERENCE.

sluggish *a.* inactive, torpid, indolent; see LAZY 1, SLOW 1, 2.

sluggishness *n.* apathy, drowsiness, lethargy; see FATIGUE, LAZINESS.

slum *n.* cheap housing, poor district, tenement neighborhood, rat-nest*, the wrong side of the tracks*.

slump *n.* depreciation, slip, descent; see DROP 2.

slump *v.* decline, depreciate, decay; see SINK 1.

slush *n.* melting snow, mire, refuse; see MUD.

slut *n.* wench, whore, hooker*; see PROSTITUTE.

sly *a.* wily, tricky, foxy, shifty, crafty, shrewd, designing, deceitful, scheming, deceiving, intriguing, cunning, unscrupulous, deceptive, conniving, calculating, plotting, dishonest, treacherous, underhanded, sneaking,

double-dealing, faithless, traitorous, sharp, smart, ingenious, cagey*, dishonorable, crooked, mean, dirty, double-crossing*, slick*, smooth*, slippery, shady*.

slyly *a.* secretly, cunningly, furtively; see CLEVERLY.

small *a.* 1 [Little in size] tiny, diminutive, miniature; see LITTLE 1. 2 [Little in quantity] scanty, short, meager; see INADEQUATE. 3 [Unimportant] trivial, unessential, insignificant; see SHALLOW 2, UNIMPORTANT.

smaller *a.* tinier, lesser, petite; see LESS, SHORTER.

smallness *n.* littleness, narrowness, diminutive size, shortness, brevity, slightness, scantiness, tininess.

small talk *n.* chitchat, light conversation, banter, table talk, babble.

smart *a.* 1 [Intelligent] clever, bright, quick; see INTELLIGENT. 2 [Impudent] bold, brazen, forward; see RUDE 2.

smart *v.* sting, be painful, burn; see HURT 1.

mental distress or irritation —*n.* **1** a smarting sensation **2** [*pl.*] [Slang] intelligence —*adj.* **1** causing sharp pain **2** sharp, as pain **3** brisk; lively *[a smart pace]* **4** intelligent; clever **5** neat; trim **6** stylish —**smart′ly** *adv.* —**smart′ness** *n.*

smart al·eck or **smart alec** (al′ik) [[prec. + *Aleck,* dim. of *Alexander*]] [Colloq.] an offensively conceited person

smart bomb [Mil. Slang] a guided missile directed to its target by electronic means

smart′en *vt., vi.* to make or become smart or smarter: usually with *up*

smash (smash) *vt., vi.* [[prob. < MASH]] **1** to break into pieces with noise or violence **2** to hit, collide, or move with force **3** to destroy or be destroyed —*n.* **1** a hard, heavy hit **2** a violent, noisy breaking **3** a violent collision **4** a popular success

smash′up′ *n.* **1** a violent wreck or collision **2** total failure; ruin

smat·ter·ing (smat′ər iŋ) *n.* [[ME *smateren,* to chatter]] **1** superficial knowledge **2** a small number

smear (smir) *vt.* [[< OE *smerian,* to anoint]] **1** to cover or soil with something greasy, sticky, etc. **2** to apply (something greasy, etc.) **3** to slander —*vi.* to be or become smeared —*n.* **1** a mark made by smearing **2** slander —**smear′y, -i·er, -i·est,** *adj.*

smell (smel) *vt.* **smelled** or [Chiefly Brit., etc.] **smelt, smell′ing** [[ME *smellen*]] **1** to be aware of through the nose; detect the odor of **2** to sense the presence of *[to smell trouble]* —*vi.* **1** to use the sense of smell; sniff **2** to have an odor *[flowers that do not smell]* —*n.* **1** the sense by which odors are perceived **2** odor; scent **3** an act of smelling

smelling salts an ammonia compound sniffed to relieve faintness

smell′y *adj.* **-i·er, -i·est** having an unpleasant smell

smelt[1] (smelt) *n.* [[OE]] a small, silvery food fish found esp. in northern seas

smelt[2] (smelt) *vt.* [[< MDu *smelten*]] **1** to melt (ore, etc.) so as to extract the pure metal **2** to refine (metal) in this way

smelt[3] (smelt) *vt., vi. chiefly Brit., etc. pt. & pp. of* SMELL

smelt′er *n.* **1** one whose work is smelting **2** a place for smelting

smidgen (smij′ən) *n.* [[prob. < dial. *smidge,* particle]] [Colloq.] a small amount; bit Also sp. **smidg′in** or **smidg′eon**

smile (smil) *vi.* **smiled, smil′ing** [[ME *smilen*]] to show pleasure, amusement, affection, etc. by an upward curving of the mouth —*vt.* to express with a smile —*n.* the act or expression of smiling —**smil′ingly** *adv.*

smirch (smʉrch) *vt.* [[prob. < OFr *esmorcher,* to hurt]] **1** to soil or stain **2** to dishonor —*n.* **1** a smudge; smear **2** a stain on reputation, etc.

smirk (smʉrk) *vi.* [[< OE *smearcian,* to smile]] to smile in a conceited or complacent way —*n.* such a smile

smite (smit) *vt.* **smote, smit′ten** or **smote, smit′ing** [[OE *smitan*]] **1** to strike with powerful effect **2** to affect or impress strongly

smith (smith) *n.* **1** one who makes or repairs metal objects; metalworker **2** *short for* BLACKSMITH

smith·er·eens (smith′ər ēnz′) *n.pl.* [[Ir *smidirīn*]] [Colloq.] fragments; bits

smithy (smith′ē) *n., pl.* **-ies** the workshop of a smith, esp. a blacksmith

smock (smäk) *n.* [[OE *smoc*]] a loose, shirtlike outer garment worn to protect the clothes

smock′ing *n.* decorative stitching used to gather cloth and make it hang in folds

smog (smäg, smôg) *n.* [[SM(OKE) + (F)OG]] a low-lying, perceptible layer of polluted air —**smog′gy, -gier, -gi·est,** *adj.*

smoke (smōk) *n.* [[OE *smoca*]] **1** the vaporous matter arising from something burning **2** any vapor, etc. like this **3** an act of smoking tobacco, etc. **4** a cigarette, cigar, etc. —*vi.* **smoked, smok′ing 1** to give off smoke **2** *a)* to draw in and exhale the smoke of tobacco, etc. *b)* to be a habitual user of cigarettes, etc. —*vt.* **1** to cure (meat, etc.) with smoke **2** to use (a pipe, cigarette, etc.) in smoking **3** to drive out or stupefy as with smoke —**smoke out** to force out of hiding —**smoke′less** *adj.* —**smok′er** *n.*

smoke detector a warning device that sets off a loud signal when excessive smoke or heat is detected

smoke′house′ *n.* a building where meats, fish, etc. are cured with smoke

smoke screen 1 a cloud of smoke for hiding troop movements, etc. **2** anything said or done to conceal or mislead

smoke′stack′ *n.* a pipe for discharging smoke from a factory, etc.

smoky (smō′kē) *adj.* **-i·er, -i·est 1** giving off smoke **2** of, like, or of the color of, smoke **3** filled with smoke —**smok′i·ness** *n.*

smol·der (smōl′dər) *vi.* [[ME *smoldren*]] **1** to burn and smoke without flame **2** to exist in a suppressed state —*n.* a smoldering Brit., etc. sp. **smoul·der**

smooch (smōōch) *n., vt., vi.* [Slang] kiss

smooth (smōōth) *adj.* [[OE *smoth*]] **1** having an even surface, with no roughness **2** without lumps **3** even or gentle in movement *[a smooth voyage]* **4** free from interruptions, obstacles, etc. **5** pleasing to the taste; bland **6** having an easy, flowing rhythm or sound **7** polished or ingratiating, esp. in an insincere way —*vt.* **1** to make level or even **2** to remove lumps or wrinkles from **3** to free from difficulties, etc.; make easy **4** to make calm; soothe **5** to polish or refine —*adv.* in a smooth manner —**smooth′ly** *adv.* —**smooth′ness** *n.*

smooth muscle involuntary muscle tissue occurring in the uterus, stomach, blood vessels, etc.

smor·gas·bord or **smör·gås·bord** (smôr′gəs bôrd′, smʉr′-) *n.* [[Swed]] **1** a wide variety of appetizers, cheeses, meats, etc., served buffet style **2** a restaurant serving these

smote (smōt) *vt., vi. pt. & alt. pp. of* SMITE

THESAURUS

smart aleck* *n.* showoff, boaster, life of the party; see BRAGGART.
smash *n.* crash, breakup, breaking; see BLOW.
smash *v.* crack, shatter, crush, burst, shiver, fracture, break, demolish, destroy, batter, crash, wreck, break up, overturn, overthrow, lay in ruins, raze, topple, tumble.
smashed *a.* wrecked, crushed, mashed; see BROKEN 1.
smear *v.* **1** [To spread] cover, coat, apply; see PAINT 2, SPREAD 3. **2** [To slander] defame, vilify, libel; see INSULT, SLANDER.
smell *n.* **1** [A pleasant smell] fragrance, odor, scent, perfume, essence, aroma, bouquet.* **2** [An unpleasant smell] malodor, stench, stink, mustiness, foulness, uncleanness, fume. **3** [The sense of smell] smelling, detection, olfaction; see AWARENESS.
smell *v.* **1** [To give off odor] perfume, scent, exhale, emanate, stink, stench. **2** [To use the sense of smell] scent, sniff, inhale, snuff, nose out, get a whiff of; see also BREATHE.
smelly *a.* stinking, foul, fetid; see

RANK 2.
smile *n.* grin, smirk, tender look, friendly expression, delighted look, joyous look; see also LAUGH.
smile *v.* beam, be gracious, look happy, look delighted, look pleased, break into a smile, look amused, smirk, grin; see also LAUGH.
smiling *a.* bright, with a smile, sunny, beaming; see also HAPPY.
smirk *n.* leer, grin, smile; see SNEER.
smith *n.* metalworker, forger, metallurgist; see CRAFTSMAN, WORKMAN.
smog *n.* high fog, smoke haze, haze, mist, air pollution; see also SMOKE.
smoke *n.* vapor, fume, gas, soot, reek, haze, smudge, smog.
smoke *v.* **1** [To give off smoke] burn, fume, smudge, smoke up, smolder, reek. **2** [To use smoke, especially from tobacco] puff, inhale, smoke a pipe, smoke cigarettes, use cigars. —**smoke out** uncover, reveal, find; see DISCOVER.
smoked *a.* cured, dried, kippered; see PRESERVED 2.

smoky *a.* smoking, smoldering, reeking; see BURNING.
smolder *v.* fume, consume, steam; see BURN, SMOKE 1.
smooth *a.* **1** [Without bumps] flat, plane, flush, horizontal, unwrinkled, level, monotonous, unrelieved, unruffled, mirrorlike, quiet, still, tanquil, glossy, glassy, lustrous, smooth as glass.—*Ant.* ROUGH, steep, broken. **2** [Without jerks] uniform, regular, even, invariable, steady, stable, fluid, flowing, rhythmic, constant, continuous. **3** [Without hair] shaven, beardless, whiskerless, clean-shaven, smooth-faced, smooth-chinned; see also BALD.—*Ant.* HAIRY, bearded, unshaven.
smooth *v.* even, level, flatten, grade, iron, polish, varnish, gloss, clear the way, smooth the path.
smoothly *a.* flatly, sleekly, placidly; see EASILY, EVENLY 1.
smorgasbord *n.* buffet, self-service meal, salad course; see FOOD, LUNCH, MEAL 2.

smother (smu*th*'ər) *vt.* ⟦< ME *smorther*, dense smoke⟧ 1 to keep from getting air; suffocate 2 to cover over thickly 3 to stifle *[to smother a yawn]* — *vi.* to be suffocated

smudge (smuj) *vt., vi.* **smudged, smudg'ing** ⟦ME *smogen*⟧ to make or become dirty; smear — *n.* 1 a dirty spot 2 *a)* a fire made to produce dense smoke *b)* such smoke, used to protect plants from frost, etc. —**smudg'y, -i·er, -i·est,** *adj.*

smug (smug) *adj.* **smug'ger, smug'gest** ⟦prob. < LowG *smuk*, trim, neat⟧ annoyingly self-satisfied; complacent — **smug'ly** *adv.* —**smug'ness** *n.*

smug·gle (smug'əl) *vt.* **-gled, -gling** ⟦< LowG *smuggeln*⟧ 1 to bring into or take out of a country secretly or illegally 2 to bring, take, etc. secretly — *vi.* to practice smuggling —**smug'gler** *n.*

smut (smut) *n.* ⟦< LowG *smutt*⟧ 1 sooty matter 2 a soiled spot 3 indecent talk, writing, etc. 4 a fungous disease of plants —**smut'ty, -tier, -ti·est,** *adj.* —**smut'ti·ness** *n.*

Sn ⟦L *stannum*⟧ *Chem. symbol for* tin

snack (snak) *n.* ⟦< ME *snaken*, to bite⟧ a light meal between regular meals — *vi.* to eat a snack

snack bar a lunch counter, cafeteria, etc. serving snacks

snaf·fle (snaf'əl) *n.* ⟦prob. < Du *snavel*, horse's muzzle⟧ a bit for a horse's mouth, having a joint in the middle and no curb

snag (snag) *n.* ⟦< Scand⟧ 1 a sharp point or projection 2 an underwater tree stump or branch 3 a tear, as in cloth, made by a snag, etc. 4 an unexpected or hidden difficulty, etc. — *vt.* **snagged, snag'ging** 1 to damage on a snag 2 to impede with a snag

snail (snāl) *n.* ⟦OE *snægl*⟧ a slow-moving mollusk having a wormlike body and a spiral protective shell

snake (snāk) *n.* ⟦OE *snaca*⟧ 1 a long, scaly limbless reptile with a tapering tail 2 a treacherous or deceitful person — *vi.* **snaked, snak'ing** to move, twist, etc. like a snake —**snake'like'** *adj.*

snak'y *adj.* **-i·er, -i·est** 1 of or like a snake or snakes 2 winding; twisting 3 cunningly treacherous or evil

snap (snap) *vi., vt.* **snapped, snap'ping** ⟦< MDu *snappen*⟧ 1 to bite or grasp suddenly: with *at* 2 to speak or utter sharply: with *at* 3 to break suddenly 4 to make or cause to make a sudden, cracking sound 5 to close, fasten, etc. with this sound 6 to move or cause to move suddenly and smartly *[to snap to attention]* 7 to take a snapshot (of) — *n.* 1 a sudden bite, grasp, etc. 2 a sharp cracking sound *[the snap of a whip]* 3 a short, angry utterance 4 a brief period of cold weather 5 a fastening that closes with a click 6 a hard, thin cookie 7 *short for* SNAPSHOT 8 [Colloq.] alertness or vigor 9 [Slang] an easy job, problem, etc. — *adj.* 1 made or done quickly *[a snap decision]* 2 that fastens with a snap 3 [Slang] easy —**snap out of it** to improve or recover quickly —**snap'per** *n.* —**snap'pish** *adj.*

snap bean a green bean or wax bean

snap'drag·on *n.* ⟦SNAP + DRAGON: from the mouth-shaped flowers⟧ a plant with saclike, two-lipped flowers

snap'py *adj.* **-pier, -pi·est** 1 cross; irritable 2 that snaps 3 [Colloq.] *a)* brisk or lively *b)* sharply chilly 4 [Colloq.] stylish; smart

snap'shot' *n.* an informal photograph taken quickly with a hand camera

snare (snar) *n.* ⟦< ON *snara*⟧ 1 a trap for small animals 2 anything dangerous, etc. that tempts or attracts 3 a length of wire or gut across the bottom of a drum — *vt.* **snared, snar'ing** to catch as in a snare; trap

snarl[1] (snärl) *vi.* ⟦< earlier *snar*, to growl⟧ 1 to growl, baring the teeth, as a dog 2 to speak sharply, as in anger — *vt.* to utter with a snarl — *n.* 1 a fierce growl 2 an angry utterance —**snarl'ingly** *adv.*

snarl[2] (snärl) *n., vt., vi.* ⟦< SNARE⟧ tangle; disorder — **snarl'y, -i·er, -i·est,** *adj.*

snatch (snach) *vt.* ⟦ME *snacchen*⟧ to take suddenly, without right, etc.; grab — *vi.* 1 to try to seize; grab *(at)* 2 to take advantage of a chance, etc. eagerly: with *at* — *n.* 1 a snatching 2 a brief period 3 a fragment; bit

sneak (snēk) *vt., vi.* **sneaked** or **snuck, sneak'ing** ⟦prob. < OE *snican*, to crawl⟧ to move, act, give, put, take, etc. secretly or stealthily — *n.* 1 one who sneaks 2 a sneaking — *adj.* without warning *[a sneak attack]* — **sneak'y, -i·er, -i·est,** *adj.*

sneak'er *n.* a shoe with a cloth upper and a soft rubber sole

sneak preview an advance showing of a film, as for evaluating audience reaction

sneer (snir) *vi.* ⟦ME *sneren*⟧ 1 to show scorn as by curling the upper lip 2 to express derision, etc. in speech or writing — *n.* a sneering

sneeze (snēz) *vi.* **sneezed, sneez'ing** ⟦ME *snesen*⟧ to exhale breath from the nose and mouth in an involuntary, explosive action — *n.* a sneezing

snicker (snik'ər) *vi.* ⟦echoic⟧ to laugh in a sly, partly stifled way — *n.* a snickering

snide (snīd) *adj.* ⟦prob. < Du dial.⟧ slyly malicious or derisive

sniff (snif) *vi., vt.* ⟦ME *sniffen*⟧ 1 to draw in (air) forcibly through the nose 2 to express (disdain, etc.) by sniffing 3 to smell by sniffing — *n.* 1 an act or sound of sniffing 2 something sniffed

snif·fle (snif'əl) *vi.* **-fled, -fling** to sniff repeatedly, as in checking mucus running from the nose — *n.* an act or sound of sniffling —**the sniffles** [Colloq.] a head cold

snif·ter (snif'tər) *n.* ⟦< *snift*, var. of SNIFF⟧ a goblet tapering to a small opening to concentrate the aroma, as of brandy

snig·ger (snig'ər) *vi., vt., n.* ⟦echoic⟧ SNICKER

snip (snip) *vt., vi.* **snipped, snip'ping** ⟦Du *snippen*⟧ to cut or cut off in a short, quick stroke, as with scissors — *n.* 1 a small piece cut off 2 [Colloq.] a small or young person

snipe (snīp) *n.* ⟦< ON *snipa*⟧ a long-billed wading bird — *vi.* **sniped, snip'ing** 1 to hunt snipe 2 to shoot from a hidden position, as at individuals —**snip'er** *n.*

snip·pet (snip'it) *n.* ⟦dim. of SNIP⟧ a small, snipped piece; scrap, specif. of information, a book, etc.

snip'py *adj.* **-pier, -pi·est** [Colloq.] insolently curt, sharp, etc.

snitch (snich) *vt.* [Slang] to steal; pilfer — *vi.* [Slang] to tattle *(on)* — *n.* [Slang] an informer

snivel (sniv'əl) *vi.* **-eled** or **-elled, -el·ing** or **-el·ling** ⟦ME *snivelen*⟧ 1 to cry and sniffle 2 to complain and whine 3 to make a tearful, often false display of grief, etc.

snob (snäb) *n.* ⟦< ?⟧ one who thinks that money and rank are very important, and has contempt for those he consid-

---

▰▰▰ THESAURUS ▰▰▰

smother *v.* stifle, suffocate, suppress; see CHOKE, EXTINGUISH.

smothered *a.* 1 [Extinguished] drenched, consumed, drowned, put out, not burning, quenched, snuffed. 2 [Strangled] choked, asphyxiated, breathless; see DEAD 1.

smudge *n.* smirch, spot, soiled spot; see BLEMISH.

smug *a.* self-satisfied, complacent, conceited, pleased with oneself, snobbish, egotistical, self-righteous, stuck up*, stuck on oneself*.

snack *n.* luncheon, slight meal, hasty repast; see LUNCH, MEAL 2.

snack bar *n.* cafeteria, lunchroom, cafe; see RESTAURANT.

snag *n.* obstacle, hindrance, knot; see BARRIER, DIFFICULTY 1.

snake *n.* reptile, serpent, vermin. *Common snakes include the following:* viper, water moccasin, copperhead, black snake, rattlesnake, python, cobra, bull snake, coral snake, blue racer, garter snake, gopher snake, king snake, milk snake, water snake, boa or boa constrictor, adder, puff adder, anaconda, fer-de-lance.

snap *n.* clasp, fastening, catch; see FASTENER.

snap *v.* catch, clasp, lock; see CLOSE 4, FASTEN. —**snap at** vent one's anger at, jump down one's throat, take it out on; see GET ANGRY. —**snap out of it** pull through, get over, revive; see RECOVER 3.

snapshot *n.* snap*, candid camera shot, action shot; see PHOTOGRAPH, PICTURE 2, 3.

snare *n.* trap, lure, decoy; see TRICK 1.

snarl[1] *v.* growl, gnarl, grumble, mutter, threaten, bark, yelp, snap, gnash the teeth, bully, quarrel.

snarl[1,2] *v.* 1 [Confusion] tangle, entanglement, complication; see CONFUSION. 2 [A snarling sound] grumble, gnarl, angry words; see GROWL.

snatch *v.* jerk, grasp, steal; see SEIZE 1, 2.

sneak *v.* skulk, slink, creep, slip away, move secretly, hide, prowl, lurk; see also EVADE.

sneaky *a.* tricky, deceitful, unreliable; see DISHONEST.

sneer *v.* mock, scoff, jeer, taunt, slight, scorn, decry, belittle, detract, lampoon, ridicule, deride, caricature, laugh at, look down, insult, disdain, satirize, condemn, give the raspberry*, give the Bronx cheer*.

sneeze *n.* wheezing, cough, sniffle; see COLD 2, FIT 1.

snicker *v.* giggle, titter, chuckle; see LAUGH.

sniff *v.* detect, scent, inhale; see SMELL 2.

snip *v.* clip, slice, nip; see CUT 1.

snob *n.* showoff, pretender, upstart; see BRAGGART.

ers inferior —**snob′bish** *adj.* —**snob′bish·ness** or **snob′bery** *n.*

snood (sno͞od) *n.* ⟦OE *snod*⟧ a baglike net worn at the back of a woman's head to hold the hair

snoop (sno͞op) *vi.* ⟦Du *snoepen*, eat snacks on the sly⟧ [Colloq.] to pry about in a sneaking way — *n.* [Colloq.] one who snoops —**snoop′y, -i·er, -i·est,** *adj.*

snoot (sno͞ot) *n.* ⟦see SNOUT⟧ **1** [Colloq.] the nose **2** the face

snoot′y *adj.* **-i·er, -i·est** [Colloq.] haughty; snobbish — **snoot′i·ness** *n.*

snooze (sno͞oz) *n.* ⟦< LowG *snusen*, to snore⟧ [Colloq.] a brief sleep; nap — *vi.* **snoozed, snooz′ing** [Colloq.] to nap; doze —**snooz′er** *n.*

snore (snôr) *vi.* **snored, snor′ing** ⟦see SNARL¹⟧ to breathe, while asleep, with harsh sounds — *n.* the act or sound of snoring —**snor′er** *n.*

snor·kel (snôr′kəl) *n.* ⟦Ger *schnorchel*, inlet⟧ a breathing tube extending above the water, used in swimming just below the surface — *vi.* **-keled, -kel·ing** to swim underwater using a snorkel —**snor′keler** *n.*

snort (snôrt) *vi.* ⟦prob. < SNORE⟧ **1** to force breath audibly through the nostrils **2** to express contempt, etc. by a snort — *vt.* **1** to express with a snort **2** [Slang] to inhale (a drug) through the nose — *n.* **1** a snorting **2** [Slang] a quick drink of liquor

snot (snät) *n.* ⟦OE (*ge*)*snot*, mucus⟧ [Slang] **1** nasal mucus: considered mildly vulgar **2** an impudent young person —**snot′ty, -tier, -ti·est,** *adj.*

snout (snout) *n.* ⟦prob. < MDu *snute*⟧ the projecting nose and jaws of an animal

snow (snō) *n.* ⟦OE *snaw*⟧ **1** frozen particles of water vapor that fall to earth as soft, white flakes **2** a falling of snow — *vi.* **1** to fall as or like snow — *vt.* **1** to cover or obstruct with snow: usually with *in, up, under,* etc. **2** [Slang] to deceive or mislead —**snow under 1** to overwhelm with work, etc. **2** to defeat decisively —**snow′y, -i·er, -i·est,** *adj.*

snow′ball′ *n.* a mass of snow packed into a ball — *vi.* to grow rapidly like a ball of snow rolling downhill

snow′bank′ *n.* a large mass of snow

Snow′belt′ the NE and Midwestern U.S., characterized by cold, snowy winters Also **Snow Belt**

snow′bound′ *adj.* shut in or blocked off by snow

snow′drift′ *n.* a heap of snow piled up by the wind

snow′drop′ *n.* a small plant with small, bell-shaped, white flowers

snow′fall′ *n.* a fall of snow or the amount of this in a given area or time

snow fence a light fence of lath and wire to control the drifting of snow

snow′flake′ *n.* a single snow crystal

snow′man′ *n., pl.* **-men′** a crude human figure made of snow packed together

snow′mobile′ *n.* a motor vehicle with steerable runners at the front and tractor treads at the rear

snow′plow′ *n.* a plowlike machine used to clear snow off a road, etc.

snow′shoe′ *n.* one of a pair of racket-shaped wooden frames crisscrossed with leather strips, etc., worn on the feet to prevent sinking in deep snow

snow′storm′ *n.* a storm with a heavy snowfall

snow′suit′ *n.* a child's heavily lined, hooded garment, for cold weather

snow tire a tire with a deep tread for added traction on snow or ice

snub (snub) *vt.* **snubbed, snub′bing** ⟦< ON *snubba*, chide⟧ **1** to treat with scorn, disdain, etc. **2** to check suddenly the movement of (a rope, etc.) — *n.* scornful treatment — *adj.* short and turned up, as a nose

snub′-nosed′ *adj.* having a snub nose

snuck (snuk) *vi., vt. alt. pt. & pp. of* SNEAK

snuff¹ (snuf) *vt.* **1** to trim off the charred end of (a wick) **2** to put out (a candle) —**snuff out 1** to extinguish **2** to destroy —**snuff′er** *n.*

snuff² (snuf) *vt., vi.* ⟦< MDu *snuffen*⟧ to sniff or smell — *n.* **1** a sniff **2** powdered tobacco taken up into the nose or put on the gums —**up to snuff** [Colloq.] up to the usual standard

snuff′box′ *n.* a small box for snuff

snuf·fle (snuf′əl) *n., vi.* **-fled, -fling** ⟦< SNUFF²⟧ SNIFFLE

snug (snug) *adj.* **snug′ger, snug′gest** ⟦prob. < Scand⟧ **1** warm and cozy **2** neat; trim *[a snug cottage]* **3** tight in fit *[a snug coat]* **4** hidden *[to lie snug]* —**snug′ly** *adv.*

snug′gle (-əl) *vi., vt.* **-gled, -gling** ⟦< prec.⟧ to nestle; cuddle

so (sō) *adv.* ⟦OE *swa*⟧ **1** as shown or described *[hold the bat just so]* **2** *a)* to such an extent *[why are you so late?]* *b)* very *[they are so happy]* *c)* [Colloq.] very much *[she so wants to go]* **3** therefore *[they were tired, and so left]* **4** more or less *[fifty dollars or so]* **5** also; likewise *[I am going and so are you]* **6** then *[and so to bed]* — *conj.* **1** in order (*that*) **2** [Colloq.] with the result that — *pron.* that which has been specified or named *[he is a friend and will remain so]* — *interj.* an exclamation of surprise, triumph, etc. — *adj.* true *[that's so]* —**and so on** (or **forth**) and the rest; et cetera —**so as** with the purpose or result —**so what?** [Colloq.] even if so, what then?

soak (sōk) *vt.* ⟦OE *socian*⟧ **1** to make thoroughly wet **2** to take in; absorb: usually with *up* **3** [Colloq.] to overcharge — *vi.* **1** to stay in a liquid for wetting, softening, etc. **2** to penetrate — *n.* **1** a soaking or being soaked **2** [Slang] a drunkard

so′-and-so′ *n., pl.* **so′-and-sos′** [Colloq.] an unspecified person or thing: often used euphemistically

soap (sōp) *n.* ⟦OE *sape*⟧ **1** a substance, usually a salt derived from fatty acids, used with water to produce suds for washing **2** [Slang] SOAP OPERA: also **soap′er** — *vt.* to scrub, etc. with soap —**no soap** [Slang] (it is) not acceptable —**soap′y, -i·er, -i·est,** *adj.* —**soap′i·ness** *n.*

soap′box′ *n.* any improvised platform used in speaking to a street audience

soap opera [Colloq.] a radio or television serial melodrama

soap′stone′ *n.* a soft, impure talc in rock form, used as an abrasive, etc.

soap′suds′ *n.pl.* foamy, soapy water

soar (sôr) *vi.* ⟦ult. < L *ex-*, out + *aura*, air⟧ **1** to rise or fly high into the air **2** to glide along high in the air **3** to rise above the usual level

Soa·ve (sə wä′vä, swä′-) *n.* ⟦It⟧ an Italian dry white wine

sob (säb) *vi.* **sobbed, sob′bing** ⟦ME *sobben*⟧ to weep aloud with short, gasping breaths — *vt.* to utter with sobs — *n.* the act or sound of sobbing —**sob′bingly** *adv.*

so·ber (sō′bər) *adj.* ⟦< L *sobrius*⟧ **1** temperate, esp. in the use of liquor **2** not drunk **3** serious, reasonable, sedate,

---

■■■ THESAURUS ■■■

snobbish *a.* ostentatious, pretentious, overbearing; see EGOTISTIC.

snooty* *a.* conceited, nasty, egotistical; see EGOTISTIC.

snore *v.* snort, wheeze, sleep; see BREATHE.

snotty* *a.* impudent, like a spoiled brat, nasty; see RUDE 2.

snout *n.* muzzle, proboscis, nozzle; see NOSE 1.

snow *n.* **1** [A snowstorm] blizzard, snowfall, snow flurry; see STORM. **2** [Frozen vapor] snow crystal, snowflake, slush, sleet, snowdrift, snowbank, powder snow, snow pack, snowfall, fall of snow.

snow *v.* storm, blizzard, squall, howl, blow, cover, pelt, shower, sleet.

snub *v.* ignore, disregard, disdain; see NEGLECT 1.

snug *a.* **1** [Cozy] homelike, secure, sheltered; see COMFORTABLE 1, WARM

1. **2** [Close in fit] trim, well-built, close; see TIGHT 3.

so *a.* **1** [To a degree] very, this much, so large, vaguely, indefinitely, extremely, infinitely, remarkably, unusually, so much, extremely, in great measure, in some measure; see also SUCH. **2** [Thus] and so on, and so forth, in such manner, in this way, even so, in this degree, to this extent; see also THUS. **3** [Accordingly] then, therefore, consequently; see ACCORDINGLY.

soak *v.* **1** [To drench] wet, immerse, dip, immerge, water, percolate, permeate, drown, saturate, pour into, pour on, wash over, flood; see also MOISTEN. **2** [To remain in liquid] steep, soften, be saturated, be pervaded, sink into, waterlog. **3** [To absorb] dry, sop, mop; see ABSORB.

soaked *a.* sodden, saturated, wet, wet through, drenched, soggy, dripping, seeping, immersed, steeped, dipped, flooded, drowned, sunk into, waterlogged.

soap *n.* solvent, softener, cleanser, soapsuds. *Varieties and forms of soap include the following:* bar, liquid, glycerine, saddle, powdered, green, perfumed, bath, laundry, soap flakes; see also CLEANSER.

sob *n.* weeping, bewailing, convulsive sighs; see CRY 3.

sob *v.* lament, sigh convulsively, weep; see CRY 1.

sober *a.* solemn, serious, sedate, clear-headed, not drunk, calm, grave, temperate, abstemious, abstinent, abstaining, steady; see also MODERATE 4.

etc. 4 not flashy; plain, as color, clothes, etc. — *vt., vi.* to make or become sober: often with *up* or *down* —**so′berly** *adv.* —**so′ber·ness** *n.*

so·bri·e·ty (sə brī′ə tē) *n.* a being sober; specif., *a)* temperance, esp. in the use of liquor *b)* seriousness

so·bri·quet (sō′brə kā′) *n.* 〖Fr〗 1 a nickname 2 an assumed name

soc. 1 socialist 2 society

so′-called′ *adj.* 1 known by this term 2 inaccurately or questionably designated as such *[a so-called liberal]*

soc·cer (sä′kər) *n.* 〖alt. < (*as*)*soc(iation football)*〗 a kind of football played by kicking a round ball

so·cia·ble (sō′shə bəl) *adj.* 〖see fol.〗 1 friendly; gregarious 2 characterized by informal conversation and companionship — *n.* a social —**so′cia·bil′i·ty,** *pl.* **-ties,** *n.* —**so′cia·bly** *adv.*

so·cial (sō′shəl) *adj.* 〖< L *socius,* companion〗 1 of or having to do with human beings in their living together 2 living with others; gregarious *[man as a social being]* 3 of or having to do with society, esp. fashionable society 4 sociable 5 of or for companionship 6 of or doing welfare work — *n.* an informal gathering —**so′cial·ly** *adv.*

social disease any venereal disease

so′cial·ism′ (-iz′əm) *n.* 1 a theory by which the means of production and distribution are owned by society rather than by individuals 2 *[often* S-*]* a political movement for establishing such a system —**so′cial·ist** *n., adj.* —**so′cial·is′tic** *adj.*

so·cial·ite (sō′shəl īt′) *n.* a person prominent in fashionable society

so′cial·ize′ (-īz′) *vt.* **-ized′, -iz′ing** 1 to make social 2 to subject to governmental ownership or control — *vi.* to take part in social activity —**so′ciali·za′tion** *n.*

socialized medicine a system supplying complete medical and hospital care to all through public funds

social science a field of study, as economics or anthropology, dealing with the structure, etc. of society —**social scientist**

social security *[often* S- S-*]* a Federal system of old-age, unemployment, or disability insurance

social work (or **service**) the promotion of the welfare of the community and the individual, as through counseling services, etc. —**social worker**

so·ci·e·ty (sə sī′ə tē) *n., pl.* **-ties** 〖< L *socius,* companion〗 1 a group of persons forming a single community 2 the system of living together in such a group 3 all people, collectively 4 companionship 5 an organized group with some interest in common 6 the wealthy, dominant class —**so·ci′e·tal** (-təl) *adj.*

Society of Friends a Christian denomination that believes in plain worship, pacifism, etc. See QUAKER

so·ci·o·eco·nom·ic (sō′sē ō ē′kə näm′ik, -ek′ə-) *adj.* of or involving both social and economic factors

so·ci·ol·o·gy (sō′sē äl′ə jē, -shē-) *n.* 〖see SOCIAL & -LOGY〗 the science of social relations, organization, and change — **so′cio·log′i·cal** (-ə lä′ji kəl) *adj.* —**so′ci·ol′o·gist** *n.*

so·ci·o·path (sō′sē ə path′, -shē-) *n.* an aggressively antisocial psychopath

sock[1] (säk) *n., pl.* **socks** or **sox** 〖< L *soccus,* type of light shoe〗 a short stocking

sock[2] (säk) *vt.* [Slang] to hit with force — *n.* [Slang] a blow

socket (säk′it) *n.* 〖< OFr *soc,* plowshare〗 a hollow part into which something fits *[an eye socket]*

sock·eye salmon (säk′ī) a red-fleshed salmon of the N Pacific

sod (säd) *n.* 〖prob. < MDu *sode*〗 1 a surface layer of earth containing grass; turf 2 a piece of this — *vt.* **sod′ded, sod′ding** to cover with sod

so·da (sō′də) *n.* 〖ML〗 1 *a)* SODIUM BICARBONATE *b)* SODA WATER *c)* SODA POP 2 a drink made with soda water, syrup, and ice cream

soda biscuit 1 a biscuit made with baking soda and sour milk or buttermilk 2 [Chiefly Brit.] SODA CRACKER

soda cracker a light, crisp cracker made from flour, water, and leavening, orig. baking soda

soda fountain a counter for making and serving soft drinks, sodas, etc.

soda pop a flavored, carbonated soft drink

soda water 1 water charged under pressure with carbon dioxide gas 2 SODA POP

sod·den (säd′'n) *adj.* 1 soaked through 2 soggy from improper cooking 3 dull or stupefied, as from liquor — **sod′denly** *adv.*

so·di·um (sō′dē əm) *n.* 〖< *soda*〗 an alkaline metallic chemical element

sodium bicarbonate a white crystalline compound, $NaHCO_3$, used in baking powder, as an antacid, etc.

sodium chloride common salt

sodium hydroxide a caustic lye used in oil refining, etc.

sodium nitrate a clear, crystalline salt used in explosives, fertilizers, etc.

sodium pen·to·thal (pen′tə thôl′) a yellowish substance injected as a general anesthetic

Sodom and Go·mor·rah (säd′əm and gə môr′ə) *Bible* two sinful cities destroyed by fire

sod′om·y (-ē) *n.* 〖after *Sodom*〗 any sexual intercourse held to be abnormal, as between two men —**sod′om·ite′** (-īt′) *n.*

so·ever (sō ev′ər) *adv.* 1 in any way 2 of any kind; at all

so·fa (sō′fə) *n.* 〖< Ar *ṣuffa,* a platform〗 an upholstered couch with fixed back and arms

sofa bed a sofa that can be opened into a bed

soft (sôft) *adj.* 〖OE *softe,* gentle〗 1 giving way easily under pressure 2 easily cut, marked, shaped, etc. *[a soft metal]* 3 not as hard as is normal, desirable, etc. *[soft butter]* 4 smooth to the touch 5 easy to digest: said of a diet 6 nonalcoholic: said of drinks 7 having few of the mineral salts that keep soap from lathering 8 mild, as a breeze 9 weak; not vigorous 10 easy *[a soft job]* 11 kind or gentle 12 not bright: said of color or light 13 gentle; low: said of sound — *adv.* gently; quietly —**soft′ly** *adv.* — **soft′ness** *n.*

soft′ball′ *n.* 1 a game like baseball played with a larger and softer ball 2 this ball

soft′-boiled′ *adj.* boiled a short time to keep the yolk soft: said of an egg

soft coal BITUMINOUS COAL

soft drink a nonalcoholic drink, esp. one that is carbonated

THESAURUS

soberly *a.* moderately, temperately, abstemiously, solemnly, gravely, sedately, in a subdued manner, quietly, regularly, steadily, calmly, coolly, seriously, somberly, staidly, earnestly, dispassionately, fairly, justly.

so-called *a.* commonly named, nominal, professed, doubtfully called, allegedly, thus termed, wrongly named, popularly supposed, erroneously accepted as, usually supposed.

sociable *a.* affable, genial, companionable; see FRIENDLY.

social *a.* genial, amusing, entertaining, companionable, pleasurable, civil, polite, polished, informative, mannerly, pleasure-seeking, hospitable, pleasant.

socialist *n.* Marxist, communist, radical; see RADICAL.

socialistic *a.* Marxist, communistic, social-democrat, non-capitalistic; see also DEMOCRATIC, RADICAL.

socially *a.* politely, civilly, courteously, hospitably, companionably, entertainingly, amusingly, cordially, genially, sociably.

social science *n.* study of man and social phenomena, the humanities, science, study of society, social studies; see also ECONOMICS, GEOGRAPHY, HISTORY, POLITICS, PSYCHOLOGY, SCIENCE 1, SOCIOLOGY.

social security *n.* social insurance, old age insurance, disability insurance, unemployment insurance, the dole, social security payments, retirement.

social service *n.* welfare work, aid for the needy, charity, philanthropy.

society *n.* 1 [Friendly association] friendship, social intercourse, fellowship; see ORGANIZATION 2. 2 [Organized humanity] culture, the public, civilization, nation, community, human groupings, the people, the world at large, social life.

sociology *n.* study of society, cul-

tural anthropology, social psychology, analysis of human institutions; see also SOCIAL SCIENCE.

sock[1] *n.* stocking, hose, silk stocking; see HOSIERY.

socket *n.* holder, opening, cavity; see JOINT 1.

soda *n.* soda water, carbonated water, mineral water; see DRINK 2.

sofa *n.* couch, divan, love seat; see FURNITURE.

soft *a.* 1 [Soft to the touch] smooth, satiny, velvety, silky, delicate, fine, thin, flimsy, limp, fluffy, feathery, downy, woolly, doughy, spongy, mushy.—*Ant.* HARSH, rough, flinty. 2 [Soft to the eye] dull, dim, quiet, shaded, pale, light, pastel, faint, blond, misty, hazy, dusky, delicate, pallid, ashen, tinted; see also SHADY.—*Ant.* BRIGHT, glaring, brilliant. 3 [Soft to the ear] low, melodious, faraway; see FAINT 3. —**be soft on** treat lightly, not condemn, fail to attack; see FAVOR, NEGLECT 1.

soften (sôf′ən) **vt., vi.** to make or become soft or softer — **soft′ener** *n.*

soft′heart′ed *adj.* 1 full of compassion 2 not strict or severe; lenient

soft landing a landing of a spacecraft without damage to the craft or its contents

soft palate the soft, fleshy part at the rear of the roof of the mouth; velum

soft′-ped′al *vt.* **-aled** or **-alled**, **-aling** or **-alling** [from pedal action in a piano, etc.] [Colloq.] to make less emphatic; tone down; play down

soft sell selling that relies on subtle inducement or suggestion

soft soap [Colloq.] flattery or smooth talk —**soft′-soap′** *vt.*

soft′ware′ *n.* the programs, routines, etc. for a computer

soft′wood′ *n.* 1 any light, easily cut wood 2 the wood of any tree bearing cones, as the pine

soft′y *n., pl.* **soft′ies** [Colloq.] one who is too sentimental or trusting

soggy (säg′ē) *adj.* **-gier**, **-gi·est** [prob. < ON *sog*, a sucking] soaked; moist and heavy —**sog′gi·ness** *n.*

soil¹ (soil) *n.* [< L *solum*] 1 the surface layer of earth, supporting plant life 2 land; country [native *soil*] 3 ground or earth [barren *soil*]

soil² (soil) *vt.* [ult. < L *sus*, pig] 1 to make dirty; stain 2 to disgrace —*vi.* to become soiled or dirty —*n.* a soiled spot; stain

soi·ree or **soi·rée** (swä rā′) *n.* [< Fr *soir*, evening] an evening party

so·journ (sō′jurn; *also, for v.,* sō jurn′) *vi.* [< L *sub-*, under + *diurnus*, of a day] to live somewhere temporarily —*n.* a brief stay; visit

sol (sōl) *n.* [< ML] *Music* the fifth tone of the diatonic scale

Sol (säl) [L] 1 *Rom. Myth.* the sun god 2 the sun personified

sol·ace (säl′is) *n.* [< L *solacium*] 1 an easing of grief, loneliness, etc. 2 a comfort or consolation —*vt.* **-aced**, **-ac·ing** to comfort; console

so·lar (sō′lər) *adj.* [< L *sol*, the sun] 1 of or having to do with the sun 2 produced by or coming from the sun

solar battery an assembly of cells (**solar cells**) used to convert solar energy into electric power

so·lar·ium (sō ler′ē əm) *n., pl.* **-ia** (-ē ə) [L < *sol*, sun] a glassed-in porch, room, etc. for sunning

solar plexus a network of nerves in the abdomen behind the stomach

solar system that portion of our galaxy subject to the sun's gravity; specif., the sun and its planets

sold (sōld) *vt., vi. pt. & pp. of* SELL

sol·der (säd′ər) *n.* [< L *solidus*, solid] a metal alloy used when melted to join or patch metal parts, etc. —*vt., vi.* to join with solder —**sol′derer** *n.*

sol·dier (sōl′jər) *n.* [< LL *solidus*, a coin] 1 a member of an army 2 an enlisted person, as distinguished from an officer 3 one who works for a specified cause —*vi.* 1 to serve as a soldier 2 to shirk one's duty, as by feigning illness, etc. —**sol′dierly** *adj.*

soldier of fortune a mercenary or any adventurer

sole¹ (sōl) *n.* [< L *solum*, a base] 1 the bottom surface of the foot 2 the part of a shoe, etc. corresponding to this — *vt.* **soled**, **sol′ing** to furnish (a shoe, etc.) with a sole

sole² (sōl) *adj.* [< L *solus*] without another; single; one and only

sole³ (sōl) *n., pl.* **sole** or **soles** [< L *solea*, SOLE¹: from its shape] a sea flatfish valued as food

sol·ecism (säl′ə siz′əm) *n.* [< Gr *soloikos*, speaking incorrectly] a violation of the conventional usage, grammar, etc. of a language

solely (sōl′lē) *adv.* 1 alone 2 only, exclusively, or merely

sol·emn (säl′əm) *adj.* [< L *sollus*, all + *annus*, year] 1 sacred 2 formal 3 serious; grave; earnest 4 awe-inspiring —**sol′emnly** *adv.*

so·lem·nity (sə lem′nə tē) *n., pl.* **-ties** 1 solemn ceremony, ritual, etc. 2 seriousness; gravity; impressiveness

sol·em·nize (säl′əm nīz′) *vt.* **-nized′**, **-niz′ing** 1 to celebrate formally or according to ritual 2 to perform the ceremony of (marriage, etc.)

so·lenoid (sō′lə noid′, säl′ə-) *n.* [< Gr *sōlēn*, tube + *eidos*, a form] a coil of wire that acts like a bar magnet when carrying a current

so·licit (sə lis′it) *vt., vi.* [see SOLICITOUS] 1 to appeal to (persons) for (aid, donations, etc.) 2 to entice or lure — **so·lic′i·ta′tion** *n.*

so·lic′i·tor *n.* 1 one who solicits trade, contributions, etc. 2 in England, a lawyer other than a barrister 3 the law officer for a city, etc.

so·lici·tous (sə lis′ə təs) *adj.* [< L *sollus*, whole + *ciere*, set in motion] 1 showing care or concern [*solicitous* for her welfare] 2 desirous; eager

so·lic′i·tude (-tōōd′) *n.* a being solicitous; care, concern, etc.

solid (säl′id) *adj.* [< L *solidus*] 1 relatively firm or compact; neither liquid nor gaseous 2 not hollow 3 having three dimensions 4 firm; strong; substantial 5 having no breaks or divisions 6 of one color, material, etc. throughout 7 showing unity; unanimous 8 reliable or dependable —*n.* 1 a solid substance, not a liquid or gas 2 an object having length, breadth, and thickness —**sol′idly** *adv.* — **sol′id·ness** *n.*

soli·dar·ity (säl′ə dar′ə tē) *n.* complete unity, as of opinion, feeling, etc.

so·lidi·fy (sə lid′ə fī′) *vt., vi.* **-fied′**, **-fy′ing** to make or become solid, hard, etc. —**so·lid′i·fi·ca′tion** *n.*

so·lid′ity (-tē) *n.* a being solid

sol′id-state′ *adj.* 1 of the branch of physics dealing with the structure, properties, etc. of solids 2 equipped with transistors, etc.

so·lilo·quy (sə lil′ə kwē) *n., pl.* **-quies** [< L *solus*, alone + *loqui*, speak] 1 a talking to oneself 2 lines in a drama spoken by a character as if to himself —**so·lil′o·quize′** (-kwīz′), **-quized′**, **-quiz′ing**, *vi., vt.*

soli·taire (säl′ə ter′) *n.* [Fr: see fol.] 1 a diamond or other gem set by itself 2 a card game for one player

sol′i·tar′y (-ē) *adj.* [< L *solus*, alone] 1 living or being alone 2 single; only [a *solitary* example] 3 lonely; remote 4 done in solitude

soli·tude (säl′ə tōōd′) *n.* [see prec.] 1 a being solitary, or alone; seclusion 2 a secluded place

solo (sō′lō) *n., pl.* **-los** or **-li** (-lē) [It < L *solus*, alone] 1 a

---

THESAURUS

soften *v.* dissolve, lessen, diminish, disintegrate, become tender, become mellow, thaw, melt, moderate, bend, give, yield, relax, relent, mellow, modify, mollify, appease, mash, knead, temper, tone down, qualify, tenderize, enfeeble, weaken.—*Ant.* STRENGTHEN, increase, tone up.

softhearted *a.* tender, kindhearted, humane; see KIND.

softness *n.* mellowness, impressibility, plasticity; see FLEXIBILITY.

soggy *a.* mushy, spongy, saturated; see SOAKED, WET 1.

soil¹ *n.* dirt, loam, clay; see EARTH 2.

soil² *v.* stain, sully, spoil; see DIRTY.

soiled *a.* stained, tainted, ruined; see DIRTY 1.

sold *a.* 1 [Sold out] disposed of, gone, taken; see SOLD OUT. 2 [*Convinced] pleased with, impressed by; see SATISFIED. —**sold out** out of, all sold, out of stock, not in stock, gone, depleted.

soldier *n.* warrior, fighter, private, enlisted man, draftee, volunteer, conscript, commando, mercenary, cadet, ranks, selectee, commissioned officer, noncommissioned officer, recruit, veteran, militant, marine, infantryman, guerrilla, guardsman, scout, sharpshooter, artilleryman, gunner, engineer, airman, bomber pilot, fighter pilot, paratrooper, machine-gunner, G.I. Joe*, grunt*.

sole² *a.* only one, no more than one, remaining; see INDIVIDUAL, SINGLE 1.

solely *a.* singly, undividedly, singularly; see INDIVIDUALLY, ONLY 1.

solemn *a.* grave, serious, sober, earnest, intense, deliberate, heavy, austere, somber, dignified, staid, sedate, moody, pensive, brooding, grim, stern, thoughtful, reflective.

solemnly *a.* sedately, gravely, impressively; see SERIOUSLY 2.

solid *a.* 1 [Firm in position] stable, fixed, rooted; see FIRM 1. 2 [Firm or

close in texture] compact, hard, substantial; see FIRM 2, THICK 1. 3 [Reliable] dependable, trustworthy, steadfast; see RELIABLE. 4 [Continuous] uninterrupted, continued, unbroken; see CONSECUTIVE, REGULAR 3.

solid *n.* cube, cone, pyramid, cylinder, block, prism, sphere.

solidification *n.* hardening, freezing, calcification, ossification, stiffening, setting, crystallization, fossilization, compression, coagulation, concentration.

solidify *v.* set, fix, crystallize; see COMPRESS, HARDEN, THICKEN.

solitary *a.* sole, only, alone, single, secluded, companionless, lonely, separate, individual, isolated, singular.—*Ant.* ACCOMPANIED, thick, attended.

solitude *n.* isolation, seclusion, retirement; see SILENCE 1.

musical piece or passage to be performed by one person **2** any performance by one person alone —*adj.* for or by a single person —*adv.* alone —*vi.* **-loed, -lo·ing** to perform a solo —**so'lo·ist** *n.*

Sol·o·mon (säl'ə mən) *Bible* king of Israel noted for his wisdom

so long [Colloq.] GOODBYE

sol·stice (säl'stis) *n.* ⟦ < L *sol*, sun + *sistere*, to stand⟧ the time of the year when the sun reaches the point farthest north (June 21 or 22) or farthest south (Dec. 21 or 22) of the equator: in the Northern Hemisphere, the **summer solstice** and **winter solstice**, respectively

sol·u·ble (säl'yōō bəl) *adj.* ⟦see SOLVE⟧ **1** that can be dissolved **2** capable of being solved —**sol'u·bil'i·ty** *n.*

sol·ute (säl'yōōt') *n.* the substance dissolved in a solution

so·lu·tion (sə lōō'shən) *n.* ⟦see fol.⟧ **1** the solving of a problem **2** an answer, explanation, etc. **3** the dispersion of one substance in another, usually a liquid, so as to form a homogeneous mixture **4** the mixture so produced

solve (sälv) *vt.* **solved, solv'ing** ⟦ < L *se-*, apart + *luere*, let go⟧ to find the answer to (a problem, etc.); explain —**solv'able** *adj.* —**solv'er** *n.*

sol·vent (säl'vənt) *adj.* ⟦see prec.⟧ **1** able to pay all one's debts **2** that can dissolve another substance —*n.* a substance that can dissolve another substance —**sol'ven·cy** *n.*

so·mat·ic (sō mat'ik) *adj.* ⟦ < Gr *sōma*, body⟧ of the body; physical

somatic cell any of the cells that form the tissues and organs of the body: opposed to GERM CELL

som·ber (säm'bər) *adj.* ⟦ < L *sub*, under + *umbra*, shade⟧ **1** dark and gloomy or dull **2** dismal; sad Chiefly Brit. sp. **som'bre** —**som'ber·ly** *adv.*

som·bre·ro (säm brer'ō) *n., pl.* **-ros** ⟦Sp < *sombra*, shade: see prec.⟧ a broad-brimmed, tall-crowned hat worn in Mexico, the Southwest, etc.

some (sum) *adj.* ⟦OE *sum*⟧ **1** certain but not specified or known ⟦open *some* evenings⟧ **2** of a certain unspecified quantity, degree, etc. ⟦have *some* candy⟧ **3** about ⟦*some* ten of them⟧ **4** [Colloq.] remarkable, striking, etc. ⟦it was *some* fight⟧ —*pron.* a certain unspecified number, quantity, etc. ⟦*some* of them agree⟧ —*adv.* **1** approximately ⟦*some* ten men⟧ **2** [Colloq.] to some extent; somewhat ⟦slept *some*⟧ **3** [Colloq.] to a great extent or at a great rate ⟦must run *some* to catch up⟧ —**and then some** [Colloq.] and more than that

-some[1] (səm) ⟦OE *-sum*⟧ *suffix* tending to be ⟦*tiresome*⟧

-some[2] (sōm) ⟦ < Gr *sōma*, body⟧ *combining form* body ⟦*chromosome*⟧

some·body (sum'bäd'ē, -bud'ē) *pron.* a person unknown or not named; some person; someone —*n., pl.* **-bod'ies** a person of importance

some'day' *adv.* at some future day or time

some'how' *adv.* in a way or by a method not known or stated Often in **somehow or other**

some'one' *pron.* SOMEBODY

som·er·sault (sum'ər sôlt') *n.* ⟦ < L *supra*, over + *saltus*, a leap⟧ an acrobatic stunt performed by turning the body

one full revolution, heels over head —*vi.* to perform a somersault

some'thing *n.* **1** a thing not definitely known, understood, etc. ⟦*something* went wrong⟧ **2** a definite but unspecified thing ⟦have *something* to eat⟧ **3** a bit; a little **4** [Colloq.] an important or remarkable person or thing — *adv.* **1** somewhat ⟦looks *something* like me⟧ **2** [Colloq.] really; quite ⟦sounds *something* awful⟧ —**make something of 1** to find a use for **2** to treat as of great importance **3** [Colloq.] to make an issue of —**something else** [Slang] one that is quite remarkable

some'time' *adv.* at some unspecified or future time —*adj.* **1** former **2** occasional

some'times' *adv.* occasionally

some'way' *adv.* somehow or other Also **some'ways'**

some'what' *n.* some degree, amount, part, etc. —*adv.* to some extent or degree; a little

some'where' *adv.* **1** in, to, or at some place not known or specified **2** at some time, degree, age, figure, etc. (with *about, around, near, in, between*, etc.)

som·nam·bu·lism (säm nam'byōō liz'əm) *n.* ⟦ < L *somnus*, sleep + *ambulare*, to walk⟧ sleepwalking —**som'nam'bu·list** *n.*

som·no·lent (säm'nə lənt) *adj.* ⟦ < L *somnus*, sleep⟧ **1** sleepy **2** inducing drowsiness —**som'no·lence** *n.*

son (sun) *n.* ⟦OE *sunu*⟧ **1** a boy or man in his relationship to his parents **2** a male descendant —**the Son** Jesus

so·nar (sō'när') *n.* ⟦*so(und) n(avigation) a(nd) r(anging)*⟧ an apparatus that transmits sound waves in water, used in finding submarines, depths, etc.

so·na·ta (sə nät'ə) *n.* ⟦It < L *sonare*, to sound⟧ a musical composition for one or two instruments, usually consisting of several movements

song (sôŋ) *n.* ⟦OE *sang*⟧ **1** the act or art of singing **2** a piece of music for singing **3** *a)* [Old Poet.] poetry *b)* a ballad or simple lyric set to music **4** a singing sound —**for a song** for a small sum; cheap

song'bird' *n.* a bird that makes vocal sounds that are like music

song'fest' *n.* ⟦SONG + -FEST⟧ an informal gathering of people for singing, esp. folk songs

song'ster (-stər) *n.* a singer —**song'stress** (-stris) *n.fem.*

sonic (sän'ik) *adj.* ⟦ < L *sonus*, a sound⟧ of or having to do with sound or the speed of sound

sonic barrier the large increase of air resistance met when flying near the speed of sound

sonic boom the explosive sound of a supersonic jet passing overhead

son'-in-law' *n., pl.* **sons'-in-law'** the husband of one's daughter

son·net (sän'it) *n.* ⟦ < L *sonus*, a sound⟧ a poem normally of fourteen lines in any of several rhyme schemes

sonny (sun'ē) *n., pl.* **-nies** little son Used as a familiar term of address to a young boy

so·no·rous (sə nôr'əs, sän'ər əs) *adj.* ⟦ < L *sonor*, a sound⟧ **1** producing sound; resonant **2** full, deep, or rich in sound —**so·nor'i·ty** (-ə tē) *n.*

soon (sōōn) *adv.* ⟦OE *sona*, at once⟧ **1** in a short time ⟦will *soon* be there⟧ **2** promptly; quickly ⟦as *soon* as possible⟧ **3** ahead of time; early ⟦we left too *soon*⟧ **4** readily; willingly ⟦as *soon* go as stay⟧ —**sooner or later** inevitably; eventually

---

▰▰▰ THESAURUS ▰▰▰

soluble *a.* dissolvable, solvent, emulsifiable, dispersible, water-soluble, fat-soluble.

solution *n.* **1** [Explanation] interpretation, resolution, clarification; see ANSWER. **2** [Fluid] suspension, solvent, juice; see LIQUID.

solve *v.* figure out, work out, reason out, think out, find out, puzzle out, decipher, unravel, interpret, explain, resolve, answer, decode, get to the bottom of, get right, hit upon a solution, work, do, settle, clear up, untangle, elucidate, fathom, unlock, determine, hit the nail on the head, put two and two together, have it.

somber *a.* melancholy, dreary, gloomy; see DISMAL.

some *a.* few, a few, a little, a bit, part of, more than a few, more than a little, any.

some *pron.* any, a few, a number, an amount, a part, a portion, more or less.

somebody *pron.* someone, some per-

son, a person, one, anybody, he, a certain person, this person, so-and-so, whoever.

someday *a.* sometime, one time, one time or another, at a future time, anytime, one day, one of these days, after a while, subsequently, finally, eventually.

somehow *a.* in some way, in one way or another, by some means, somehow or other, by hook or by crook, anyhow, after a fashion, with any means at one's disposal.

someone *pron.* some person, one, individual; see SOMEBODY.

something *n.* event, object, portion, anything, being; see also THING 1, 8.

sometime *a.* one day, in a time to come, in the future; see SOMEDAY.

sometimes *a.* at times, at intervals, now and then; see SELDOM.

somewhat *a.* a little, to a degree, to some extent; see MODERATELY, SLIGHTLY.

somewhere *a.* in some place, here and there, around, in one place or another, someplace, about, around somewhere, kicking around*, any old place*.

son *n.* male child, offspring, descendant, foster son, dependent, scion, heir, boy, junior, chip off the old block, his father's son.

song *n.* melody, lyric, strain, verse, poem, musical expression; see also MUSIC 1. —**(big) song and dance** drivel, boasting, pretense; see NONSENSE 1, 2. —**for a song** cheaply, at a bargain, for almost nothing; see CHEAP 1.

sonic boom *n.* report, crash, blast; see EXPLOSION, SOUND 2.

soon *a.* before long, in a short time, presently, in due time, shortly, forthwith, quickly, in a minute, in a second, in short order; see also SOMEDAY.

sooner or later *a.* eventually, inevi-

soot (soot) *n.* [OE *sot*] a black substance consisting chiefly of carbon particles, in the smoke of burning matter — **soot'y, -i·er, -i·est,** *adj.*

sooth (sooth) *n.* [OE *soth*] [Archaic] truth

soothe (sooth) *vt.* **soothed, sooth'ing** [OE *sothian,* prove true] 1 to make calm or composed, as by gentleness, flattery, etc. 2 to relieve (pain, etc.) —**sooth'er** *n.* —**sooth' ing** *adj.*

sooth·say·er (sooth'sā'ər) *n.* [ME *soothseyere,* one who speaks the truth] a person who claims to predict the future —**sooth'say'ing** *n.*

sop (säp) *n.* [OE *sopp*] 1 a piece of food, as bread, soaked in milk, etc. 2 *a)* something given to appease *b)* a bribe — *vt., vi.* **sopped, sop'ping** 1 to soak, steep, etc. 2 to take (*up*), as water, by absorption

SOP or **S.O.P.** standard operating procedure

soph·ism (säf'iz'əm) *n.* [< Gr *sophos,* clever] a clever and plausible but fallacious argument

soph'ist *n.* one who uses clever, specious reasoning

so·phis·ti·cate (sə fis'tə kāt'; *for n., usually,* -kit) *vt.* **-cat'ed, -cat'ing** [ult. < Gr *sophistēs,* wise man] to change from a natural or simple state; make worldly-wise — *n.* a sophisticated person

so·phis'ti·cat'ed *adj.* 1 not simple, naive, etc.; worldly-wise or knowledgeable, subtle, etc. 2 for sophisticated people 3 highly complex or developed in form, technique, etc. —**so·phis'ti·ca'tion** *n.*

soph·istry (säf'is trē) *n., pl.* **-tries** misleading but clever reasoning

soph·o·more (säf'ə môr') *n.* [< obs. *sophumer,* sophism] a student in the second year of college or the tenth grade in high school

soph·o·mor·ic *adj.* of or like sophomores; seen as opinionated, immature, etc.

-sophy (sə fē) [< Gr *sophia,* wisdom] *combining form* knowledge

sop·o·rif·ic (säp'ə rif'ik, sō'pə-) *adj.* [< L *sopor,* sleep + -FIC] causing sleep — *n.* a soporific drug, etc.

sop·py (säp'ē) *adj.* **-pier, -pi·est** 1 very wet: also **sop'ping** 2 [Colloq.] sentimental; maudlin

so·pran·o (sə pran'ō) *n., pl.* **-nos** [It < *sopra,* above] 1 the range of the highest voice of women or boys 2 a singer with such a range 3 a part for a soprano — *adj.* of or for a soprano

sor·bet (sôr'bət, sôr bā') *n.* [Fr < Ar *sharba(t),* a drink] a tart ice, as of fruit juice, served mainly as a dessert

sor·cery (sôr'sər ē) *n., pl.* **-ies** [< L *sors,* lot, share] the supposed use of an evil supernatural power over people; witchcraft —**sor'cerer** *n.* —**sor'cer·ess** *n.fem.*

sor·did (sôr'did) *adj.* [< L *sordes,* filth] 1 dirty; filthy 2 squalid; wretched 3 base; ignoble; mean —**sor'didly** *adv.* —**sor'did·ness** *n.*

sore (sôr) *adj.* **sor'er, sor'est** [OE *sar*] 1 giving or feeling pain; painful 2 *a)* filled with grief *b)* causing sadness, misery, etc. [a *sore* task] 3 causing irritation [a *sore* point] 4 [Colloq.] angry; offended — *n.* a sore, usually infected spot on the body — *adv.* [Archaic] greatly — **sore'ness** *n.*

sore'head' *n.* [Colloq.] a person easily angered, made resentful, etc.

sore'ly *adv.* 1 grievously; painfully 2 urgently [*sorely* needed]

sor·ghum (sôr'gəm) *n.* [< It *sorgo*] 1 a cereal grass grown for grain, syrup, fodder, etc. 2 syrup made from its juices

so·ror·ity (sə rôr'ə tē) *n., pl.* **-ties** [< L *soror,* sister] a group of women or girls joined together for fellowship, etc., as in some colleges

sor·rel¹ (sôr'əl, sär'-) *n.* [< OFr *surele*] any of various plants with sour, edible leaves

sor·rel² (sôr'əl, sär'-) *n.* [< OFr *sor,* light brown] 1 light reddish brown 2 a horse, etc. of this color

sor·row (sär'ō, sôr'ō) *n.* [OE *sorg*] 1 mental suffering caused by loss, disappointment, etc.; grief 2 that which causes grief — *vi.* to grieve —**sor'row·ful** *adj.* —**sor'row fully** *adv.*

sorry (sôr'ē, sär'ē) *adj.* **-rier, -ri·est** [< OE *sar,* sore] 1 full of sorrow, pity, or regret 2 inferior; poor 3 wretched —**sor'rily** *adv.* —**sor'ri·ness** *n.*

sort (sôrt) *n.* [< L *sors,* chance] 1 any group of related things; kind; class 2 quality or type 3 [Archaic] manner; way — *vt.* to arrange according to class or kind —**of sorts** of an inferior kind: also **of a sort** —**out of sorts** [Colloq.] not in good humor or health —**sort of** [Colloq.] somewhat

sor·tie (sôr'tē) *n.* [Fr < *sortir,* go out] 1 a quick raid by forces of a besieged place 2 one mission by a single military plane

SOS (es'ō'es') *n.* a signal of distress, as in wireless telegraphy

so-so (sō'sō') *adv., adj.* just passably or passable; fair Also **so so**

sot (sät) *n.* [< ML *sottus,* a fool] a drunkard —**sot'tish** *adj.*

sotto voce (sät'ō vō'chē) [It, under the voice] in a low voice, so as not to be overheard

souf·flé (soo flā') *n.* [Fr < L *sufflare,* puff out] a baked food made light and puffy by beaten egg whites added before baking

sough (sou, suf) *n.* [OE *swogan,* to sound] a soft sighing or rustling sound — *vi.* to make a sough

sought (sôt) *vt., vi. pt. & pp. of* SEEK

soul (sōl) *n.* [OE *sawol*] 1 an entity without material reality, regarded as the spiritual part of a person 2 the moral or emotional nature of a person 3 spiritual or emotional warmth, force, etc. 4 vital or essential part, quality, etc. 5 a person [I didn't see a *soul*] 6 the deep spiritual and emotional quality of black American culture; also, the expression of this, as in music — *adj.* of, for, or like American blacks

soul food [Colloq.] certain foods, as chitterlings or ham hocks, popular orig. in the S U.S., esp. among blacks

soul'ful *adj.* full of deep feeling —**soul'fully** *adv.* —**soul' ful·ness** *n.*

sound¹ (sound) *n.* [< L *sonus*] 1 that which is heard, resulting from stimulation of auditory nerves by vibrations (**sound waves**) in the air 2 the distance within which a sound may be heard 3 the mental impression

---

THESAURUS

tably, certainly; see SOMEDAY, SURELY.

soot *n.* carbon, smoke, grit; see RESIDUE.

soothe *v.* quiet, tranquilize, alleviate, calm, relax, mollify, help, pacify, lighten, unburden, console, cheer; see also COMFORT 1, EASE 1, 2, RELIEVE.

sophisticated *a.* refined, adult, well-bred; see CULTURED, MATURE.

sophistication *n.* elegance, refinement, finesse; see COMPOSURE.

soppy *a.* soaked, drippy, damp; see WET 1, 2.

sorcerer *n.* witch, wizard, alchemist; see MAGICIAN.

sorcery *n.* enchantment, divination, alchemy; see MAGIC 1, WITCHCRAFT.

sore *a.* 1 [Tender] painful, hurtful, raw, aching, sensitive, irritated, irritable, distressing, bruised, angry, inflamed, burned, unpleasant, ulcerated, abscessed, uncomfortable. 2 [*Angry] irked, resentful, irritated; see ANGRY.

sore *n.* cut, bruise, wound, boil, lesion, ulcer, hurt, abscess, gash,

stab, soreness, discomfort, injury; see also PAIN 2.

sorely *a.* extremely, painfully, badly; see SO 1, VERY.

sorrow *n.* sadness, anguish, pain; see GRIEF.

sorrow *v.* bemoan, bewail, regret; see MOURN.

sorrowful *a.* grieved, afflicted, in sorrow, in mourning, depressed, dejected; see also SAD 1.

sorrowfully *a.* regretfully, weeping, in sadness; see SADLY.

sorry *a.* 1 [Penitent] contrite, repentant, conscience-stricken, touched, softened, remorseful, regretful, sorrowful, apologetic. 2 [Inadequate in quantity or quality] poor, paltry, trifling, cheap, mean, shabby, stunted, beggarly, scrubby, small, trivial, unimportant, insignificant, worthless, dismal, pitiful, despicable; see also INADEQUATE.—*Ant.* ENOUGH, plentiful, adequate.

sort *n.* species, description, class; see KIND 2, VARIETY 2. —**out of sorts** irritated, upset, in a bad mood; see

ANGRY, TROUBLED.

sort *v.* file, assort, class; see CLASSIFY, DISTRIBUTE, ORDER 3.

sort of* *a.* somewhat, to a degree, kind of*; see MODERATELY, SLIGHTLY.

so-so *a.* ordinary, mediocre, average; see COMMON 1, DULL 4, FAIR 2.

sought *a.* wanted, needed, desired; see HUNTED.

soul *n.* 1 [Essential nature] spiritual being, heart, substance, individuality, disposition, cause, personality, force, essence, genius, principle, ego, psyche, life. 2 [The more lofty human qualities] courage, love, affection, honor, duty, idealism, philosophy, culture, heroism, art, poetry, reverence, sense of beauty. 3 [A person] human being, man, being; see PERSON 1.

sound¹ *v.* vibrate, echo, resound, reverberate, shout, sing, whisper, murmur, clatter, clank, rattle, blow, blare, bark, ring out, explode, thunder, buzz, rumble, hum, jabber, jangle, whine, crash, bang, boom, reflect, burst, chatter, creak, clang, roar, produced *[the sound of his report]* — *vi.* 1 to make a sound 2 to seem upon being heard *[to sound troubled]* — *vt.* 1 to cause to sound 2 to signal, express, etc. 3 to utter distinctly *[to sound one's r's]* —**sound′less** *adj.*

sound² (sound) *adj.* [OE *(ge)sund*] 1 free from defect, damage, or decay 2 healthy *[a sound body]* 3 safe; stable *[a sound bank]* 4 based on valid reasoning; sensible 5 thorough; forceful *[a sound defeat]* 6 deep and undisturbed: said of sleep 7 honest, loyal, etc. — *adv.* deeply *[sound asleep]* —**sound′ly** *adv.* —**sound′ness** *n.*

sound³ (sound) *n.* [< OE & ON *sund*] 1 a wide channel linking two large bodies of water or separating an island from the mainland 2 a long arm of the sea

sound⁴ (sound) *vt., vi.* [< L *sub*, under + *unda*, a wave] 1 to measure the depth of (water), esp. with a weighted line 2 to try to find out the opinions of (a person), usually subtly: often with *out* —**sound′ing** *n.*

sound barrier SONIC BARRIER

sounding board 1 something to increase resonance or reflect sound: often **sound′board′** *n.* 2 a person on whom one tests one's ideas, etc.

sound′proof′ *adj.* that keeps sound from coming through — *vt.* to make soundproof

sound′track′ *n.* the sound record along one side of a film

soup (sōōp) *n.* [Fr *soupe*] a liquid food made by cooking meat, vegetables, etc. in water, milk, etc. —**soup up** [Slang] to increase the capacity for speed of (an engine, etc.)

soup′çon (sōōp sôn′) *n.* [Fr < L *suspicio*, suspicion] 1 a slight trace, as of a flavor 2 a tiny bit

soupy (sōō′pē) *adj.* **-i·er, -i·est** 1 watery like soup 2 [Colloq.] foggy

sour (sour) *adj.* [OE *sur*] 1 having the sharp, acid taste of vinegar, etc. 2 spoiled by fermentation 3 cross; bad-tempered 4 distasteful or unpleasant — *vt., vi.* to make or become sour —**sour′ly** *adv.* —**sour′ness** *n.*

source (sôrs) *n.* [< L *surgere*, to rise] 1 a spring, etc. from which a stream arises 2 place of origin; prime cause 3 a person, book, etc. that provides information

sour′dough′ (sour′dō′) *n.* 1 [Dial.] fermented dough saved for use as leaven 2 a lone prospector for gold, etc., as in the W U.S.

sour grapes a scorning of something only because it cannot be had or done

souse (sous) *n.* [< OHG *sulza*, brine] 1 a pickled food, as pigs' feet 2 liquid for pickling; brine 3 a plunging into a liquid 4 [Slang] a drunkard — *vt., vi.* **soused, sous′ing** 1

to pickle (a food) 2 to plunge into a liquid 3 to make or become soaking wet

south (south) *n.* [OE *suth*] 1 the direction to the left of one facing the sunset (180° on the compass) 2 a region in or toward this direction — *adj.* 1 in, of, toward, or facing the south 2 from the south *[a south wind]* — *adv.* in or toward the south

south′east′ *n.* 1 the direction halfway between south and east 2 a region in or toward this direction — *adj.* 1 in, of, or toward the southeast 2 from the southeast — *adv.* 1 in, toward, or from the southeast —**south′east′erly** *adj., adv.* —**south′east′ern** *adj.* —**south′east′ward** (-wərd) *adv., adj.* —**south′east′wards** *adv.*

south·erly (suth′ər lē) *adj., adv.* 1 toward the south 2 from the south

south·ern (suth′ərn) *adj.* 1 in, of, or toward the south 2 from the south

south′erner *n.* a native or inhabitant of the south

southern lights [*also* S- L-] aurora australis

south·paw (south′pô′) *n.* [Slang] a left-handed person; esp., a left-handed baseball pitcher

South Pole the southern end of the earth's axis

south′ward (-wərd) *adv., adj.* toward the south Also **south′wards** *adv.*

south′west′ *n.* 1 the direction halfway between south and west 2 a region in or toward this direction — *adj.* 1 in, of, or toward the southwest 2 from the southwest — *adv.* 1 in, toward, or from the southwest —**south′west′erly** *adj., adv.* —**south′west′ern** *adj.* —**south′west′ward** (-wərd) *adv., adj.* —**south′west′wards** *adv.*

sou·ve·nir (sōō′və nir′) *n.* [Fr < L *subvenire*, come to mind] something kept as a reminder; memento

sov·er·eign (säv′rən, -ər in) *adj.* [< L *super*, above] 1 above all others; chief; supreme 2 supreme in power, rank, etc. 3 independent of all others *[a sovereign state]* — *n.* 1 a monarch or ruler 2 a British gold coin worth one pound: no longer minted

sov′er·eign·ty *n.* 1 the status, rule, etc. of a sovereign 2 supreme and independent political authority

so·vi·et (sō′vē et′) *n.* [Russ *sovyet*, council] 1 in Russia, Uzbekistan, and, formerly, the Soviet Union, any of the various elected governing councils, local, intermediate, and national *[the Supreme Soviet]* 2 any similar council in a socialist governing system — *adj.* [S-] of or connected with the Soviet Union —**so′vi·et′ism′** *n.*

sow¹ (sou) *n.* [OE *sugu*] an adult female pig

sow² (sō) *vt.* **sowed, sown** (sōn) or **sowed, sow′ing** [OE *sawan*] 1 to scatter (seed) for growing 2 to plant seed in

---

THESAURUS

babble, clap, patter, prattle, clink, toot, cackle, clack, thud, slam, smash, thump, snort, shriek, moan, quaver, trumpet, croak, caw, quack, squawk.

sound¹,³ *n.* 1 [Something audible] vibration, din, racket; see NOISE 1. 2 [The quality of something audible] tonality, resonance, note, timbre, tone, pitch, intonation, accent, character, quality, softness, lightness, mournfulness, loudness, reverberation, ringing, vibration, modulation, discord, consonance, harmony. 3 [Water between an island and the mainland] strait, bay, canal; see CHANNEL.

sound² *a.* 1 [Healthy] hale, hearty, well; see HEALTHY. 2 [Firm] solid, stable, safe; see RELIABLE. 3 [Sensible] reasonable, rational, prudent; see SENSIBLE. 4 [Free from defect] flawless, unimpaired, undecayed; see WHOLE 2.

sounding *a.* ringing, thudding, bumping, roaring, calling, thundering, booming, crashing, clattering, clinking, clanging, tinkling, whispering, pinging, rattling, rumbling, ticking, crying, clicking, echoing, pattering, clucking, chirping, peeping, growling, grunting, bellowing, murmuring, whirring, splattering, screeching, screaming, squealing.

sound out *v.* probe, feel out, feel, put out a feeler, send up a trial balloon, see how the land lies, get the lay of the land, see which way the wind

blows; see also EXAMINE, EXPERIMENT.

soundproof *a.* soundproofed, silent, soundless; see QUIET.

soup *n.* Soups include the following: beef, broth, bouillon, consommé, split pea, noodle, vegetable, potato, French onion, chicken, tomato, celery, minestrone, borscht, clam chowder, Scotch broth, bouillabaisse; see also BROTH, FOOD, STEW.

soupçon *n.* dash, drop, hint; see DASH 3.

sour *a.* acid, tart, vinegary, fermented, rancid, musty, turned, acrid, salty, bitter, caustic, cutting, stinging, acrid, harsh, irritating, unsavory, tangy, briny, brackish, sharp, keen, biting, pungent, curdled, unripe. — **turn sour** putrefy, rot, spoil; see SPOIL.

sour *v.* turn, ferment, spoil, make sour, curdle.

source *n.* beginning, cause, root; see ORIGIN 2, 3.

south *a.* 1 [Situated to the south] southern, southward, on the south side of, in the south, toward the equator, southernmost, toward the South Pole, southerly, tropical, equatorial, in the torrid zone. 2 [Moving south] southward, to the south, southbound, headed south, southerly, in a southerly direction, toward the equator. 3 [Coming from the south] headed north, northbound, out of the south, from the south, toward the North Pole; see also

NORTH 2.

south *n.* southland, southern section, southern region, tropics, tropical region, equatorial region, southern hemisphere.

South *n.* the Sunny South, South Atlantic States, the Confederacy, the Old South, Pre-Civil War South, antebellum South, Southern United States, the New South, the Deep South, Sunbelt, way down south, Dixie, southland.

southeast *a.* Points of the compass between south and east include the following: east by south, east-southeast, southeast by east, southeast, southeast by south, south by east, south-southeast; see also DIRECTION.

southern *a.* in the south, of the south, from the south, toward the south, southerly; see also SOUTH 1.

southwest *a.* Points of the compass between south and west include the following: south by west, southsouthwest, southwest by south, southwest, southwest by west, westsouthwest, west by south; see also DIRECTION.

souvenir *n.* memento, keepsake, relic; see MEMORIAL.

sow² *v.* seed, scatter, plant, broadcast, drill in, drill seed, use a drill seeder, use a broadcast seeder, strew, put in small grain, do the seeding.

sowed *a.* scattered, cast, broadcast, spread, dispersed, dispersed, (a field, etc.) **3** to spread or scatter — *vi.* to sow seed — **sow'er** *n.*

sox (säks) *n. alt. pl. of* SOCK[1]

soy (soi) *n.* ⟦Jpn⟧ **1** a dark, salty sauce made from fermented soybeans: in full **soy sauce 2** the soybean plant or its seeds Also [Chiefly Brit.] **soya** (soi′ə)

soy'bean' *n.* **1** a plant widely grown for its seeds, which contain much protein and oil **2** its seed

Sp. 1 Spain **2** Spanish

spa (spä) *n.* ⟦after *Spa*, resort in Belgium⟧ **1** a health resort having a mineral spring **2** a commercial establishment with exercise rooms, sauna baths, etc.

space (spās) *n.* ⟦< L *spatium*⟧ **1** *a*) the three-dimensional, continuous expanse in which all things are contained *b*) OUTER SPACE **2** *a*) distance, area, etc. between or within things *b*) room for something *[a parking space]* **3** an interval of time — *vt.* **spaced, spac'ing** to arrange with spaces between

space'craft' *n., pl.* **-craft'** any vehicle designed for orbiting the earth, sun, etc., as a satellite or spaceship

spaced'-out' *adj.* [Slang] under or as if under the influence of a drug, marijuana, etc. Also **spaced**

space'flight' *n.* a flight through outer space

space heater a small heating unit for a room or other confined area

space'man' *n., pl.* **-men'** an astronaut or any of the crew of a spaceship

space'port' *n.* a center for assembling, testing, and launching spacecraft

space'ship' *n.* a spacecraft, esp. if manned

space shuttle a spacecraft designed to carry personnel and equipment between earth and a space station

space station (or **platform**) a spacecraft in long-term orbit serving as a launch pad, research center, etc.

space'suit' *n.* a garment pressurized for use by astronauts

space'walk' *n.* an astronaut's moving about in space outside a spacecraft — *vi.* to engage in a spacewalk

spacey or **spacy** (spā′sē) *adj.* **-i·er, -i·est** [Slang] **1** SPACED-OUT **2** *a*) eccentric or unconventional *b*) flighty, irresponsible, neurotic, etc. —**spac'i·ness** *n.*

spa·cious (spā′shəs) *adj.* having more than enough space; vast —**spa'cious·ly** *adv.* —**spa'cious·ness** *n.*

spade[1] (spād) *n.* ⟦OE *spadu*⟧ a flat-bladed, long-handled digging tool, like a shovel — *vt., vi.* **spad'ed, spad'ing** to dig with a spade —**spade'ful** *n.*

spade[2] (spād) *n.* ⟦ult. < Gr *spathē*, flat blade⟧ **1** the black figure (♠) marking one of the four suits of playing cards **2** a card of this suit

spade'work' *n.* preparatory work for some main project, esp. when tiresome

spa·dix (spā′diks) *n., pl.* **-dixes** or **-di·ces'** (-də sēz′) ⟦< Gr⟧ a spike of tiny flowers, usually enclosed in a spathe

spa·ghetti (spə get′ē) *n.* ⟦It < *spago*, small cord⟧ pasta in long, thin strings, cooked by boiling or steaming

spake (spāk) *vi., vt. archaic pt. of* SPEAK

span (span) *n.* ⟦OE *sponn*⟧ **1** the distance (about 9 in.) between the tips of the extended thumb and little finger **2** *a*) the full extent between any two limits *b*) the distance between ends or supports *[the span of an arch] c*) the full duration (*of*) *[span of attention]* **3** a part between two supports — *vt.* **spanned, span'ning 1** to measure, esp. by the span of the hand **2** to extend over

span·dex (span′deks′) *n.* ⟦< EXPAND⟧ an elastic synthetic fiber used in girdles, etc.

span·gle (span′gəl) *n.* ⟦< OE *spang*, a clasp⟧ a small piece of bright metal sewn on fabric for decoration — *vt.* **-gled, -gling** to decorate as with spangles

Span·iard (span′yərd) *n.* a native or inhabitant of Spain

span·iel (span′yəl) *n.* ⟦< MFr *espagnol*, lit., Spanish⟧ any of several breeds of dog with large, drooping ears and a dense, wavy coat

Span·ish (span′ish) *adj.* of Spain, its people, their language, etc. — *n.* the language of Spain and Spanish America —**the Spanish** the people of Spain

Spanish moss a rootless plant that grows in long, graceful strands from tree branches in the SE U.S.

spank (spaŋk) *vt.* ⟦echoic⟧ to strike with the open hand, etc., esp. on the buttocks, as in punishment — *n.* a smack given in spanking

spank'ing *adj.* **1** swiftly moving **2** brisk: said of a breeze — *adv.* [Colloq.] completely *[spanking new]*

spar[1] (spär) *n.* ⟦< ON *sparri* or MDu *sparre*⟧ any pole, as a mast or yard, supporting a sail of a ship

spar[2] (spär) *vi.* **sparred, spar'ring** ⟦prob. < It *parare*, to parry⟧ **1** to box with feinting movements, landing few heavy blows **2** to wrangle

spare (sper) *vt.* **spared, spar'ing** ⟦OE *sparian*⟧ **1** to refrain from killing, hurting, etc. **2** to save or free a person from (something) **3** to avoid using or use frugally **4** to part with conveniently — *adj.* **1** not in regular use; extra **2** free *[spare time]* **3** meager; scanty **4** lean; thin — *n.* **1** a spare, or extra, thing **2** *Bowling* a knocking down of all the pins with two rolls of the ball —**spare'ly** *adv.*

spare'ribs' *n.pl.* a cut of pork consisting of the thin end of the ribs

spar'ing *adj.* **1** careful; frugal **2** scanty or meager — **spar'ingly** *adv.*

spark (spärk) *n.* ⟦OE *spearca*⟧ **1** a glowing bit of matter, esp. one thrown off by a fire **2** any flash or sparkle **3** a particle or trace **4** a brief flash of light accompanying an electric discharge as through air — *vi.* to make sparks — *vt.* to stir up; activate

spar·kle (spär′kəl) *vi.* **-kled, -kling 1** to throw off sparks **2** to glitter **3** to effervesce — *n.* **1** a sparkling **2** brilliance —**spar'kler** (-klər) *n.*

spark plug an electrical device fitted into a cylinder of an engine to ignite the fuel mixture by making sparks

spar·row (spar′ō) *n.* ⟦OE *spearwa*⟧ any of numerous small, perching songbirds

sparse (spärs) *adj.* ⟦< L *spargere*, scatter⟧ thinly spread; not dense —**sparse'ly** *adv.* —**sparse'ness** or **spar'sity** (-sə tē) *n.*

Spar·tan (spärt′'n) *adj.* **1** of ancient Sparta (city in Greece), its people, or their culture **2** like the Spartans; warlike, hardy, disciplined, etc. — *n.* a Spartan person

spasm (spaz′əm) *n.* ⟦< Gr *spasmos*⟧ **1** a sudden, involuntary muscular contraction **2** any sudden, violent, temporary activity, feeling, etc.

spas·modic (spaz mäd′ik) *adj.* ⟦see prec. & -OID⟧ of or like spasms; fitful —**spas·mod'i·cally** *adv.*

spas·tic (spas′tik) *adj.* of or characterized by muscular spasms — *n.* one having spastic paralysis

spat[1] (spat) *n.* ⟦prob. echoic⟧ [Colloq.] a brief, petty quarrel — *vi.* **spat'ted, spat'ting** [Colloq.] to engage in a spat

spat[2] (spat) *n.* ⟦< *spatterdash*, a legging⟧ a gaiterlike covering for the instep and ankle

spat[3] (spat) *vt., vi. alt. pt. & pp. of* SPIT[2]

spat[4] (spat) *n.* ⟦< ?⟧ a young oyster or young oysters collectively

spate (spāt) *n.* ⟦< ?⟧ an unusually large outpouring, as of words

spathe (spāth) *n.* ⟦< L *spatha*, a flat blade⟧ a large, leaflike part enclosing a flower cluster

spa·tial (spā′shəl) *adj.* ⟦< L *spatium*, space⟧ of, or existing in, space

spat·ter (spat′ər) *vt., vi.* ⟦< ?⟧ **1** to scatter or spurt out in drops **2** to splash — *n.* **1** a spattering **2** a mark caused by spattering

spatu·la (spach′ə lə) *n.* ⟦L < Gr *spathē*, flat blade⟧ an

━━━ THESAURUS ━━━

strewn, planted.

spa *n.* baths, spring, curative bath; see RESORT 2.

space *n.* **1** [The infinite regions] outer space, infinite distance, infinity, interstellar space, interplanetary space, the universe, cosmos, solar system, galaxy, the beyond; see also EXPANSE.—*Ant.* BOUNDARY, measure, definite area. **2** [Room] expanse, scope, range; see EXTENT. **3** [A place] area, location, reservation; see PLACE 2.

spacecraft *n.* flying saucer, capsule, orbiter, space shuttle, unidentified flying object, UFO, spaceship, rocket,

space station, space platform, weather satellite, spy satellite; see also SATELLITE 2.

spaced *a.* divided, distributed, dispersed; see SEPARATED.

spacious *a.* capacious, roomy, vast; see BIG 1.

spade[1] *n.* implement, garden tool, digging tool; see TOOL 1.

Spanish *a.* Spanish-speaking, Iberian, Romance, Hispanic, Catalan, Castilian, Galician, Andalusian, Basque, South American, Spanish-American, Mexican, Latin American.

spank *v.* whip, chastise, thrash; see

BEAT 1, PUNISH.

spare *a.* superfluous, auxiliary, additional; see EXTRA.

spare *v.* pardon, forgive, be merciful; see PITY, SAVE 1.

spark *n.* glitter, glow, sparkle; see FIRE 1.

sparkle *v.* glitter, glisten, twinkle; see SHINE 1.

sparse *a.* scattered, scanty, meager; see INADEQUATE, RARE 1.

spasm *n.* convulsion, seizure, contraction; see FIT 1.

spatter *v.* splash, spot, wet, sprinkle,

implement with a flat, flexible blade for spreading or blending foods, paints, etc.

spavin (spav'in) *n.* [< MFr *esparvain*] a disease that lames horses in the hock joint —**spav'ined** *adj.*

spawn (spôn) *vt., vi.* [< L *expandere:* see EXPAND] 1 to produce or deposit (eggs, sperm, or young) 2 to bring forth or produce prolifically — *n.* 1 the mass of eggs or young produced by fish, mollusks, etc. 2 something produced, esp. in great quantity, as offspring

spay (spā) *vt.* [< Gr *spathē*, flat blade] to sterilize (a female animal) by removing the ovaries

speak (spēk) *vi.* **spoke, spo'ken, speak'ing** [OE *sp(r)ecan*] 1 to utter words; talk 2 to communicate as by talking 3 to make a request (*for*) 4 to make a speech — *vt.* 1 to make known as by speaking 2 to use (a given language) in speaking 3 to utter (words) orally —**so to speak** that is to say —**speak out** (or **up**) to speak clearly or freely — **speak well for** to say or indicate something favorable about

speak'-eas'y (-ē'zē) *n., pl.* **-ies** [Slang] a place where alcoholic drinks are sold illegally

speak'er *n.* 1 one who speaks; esp., *a*) an orator *b*) the presiding officer of various lawmaking bodies *c*) [S-] the presiding officer of the U.S. House of Representatives 2 *short for* LOUDSPEAKER

spear (spir) *n.* [OE *spere*] 1 a weapon with a long shaft and a sharp point, for thrusting or throwing 2 [var. of SPIRE] a long blade or shoot, as of grass — *vt.* to pierce or stab with or as with a spear

spear'fish' *n., pl.* **-fish'** or (for different species) **-fish'es** any of a group of large food and game fishes of the open seas — *vi.* to fish with a spear, etc.

spear'head' *n.* 1 the pointed head of a spear 2 the leading person or group, as in an attack — *vt.* to take the lead in (an attack, etc.)

spear'mint' *n.* [prob. from the shape of its flowers] a fragrant plant of the mint family, used for flavoring

spec (spek) *n.* [Colloq.] *short for:* 1 SPECIFICATION (sense 1) 2 SPECULATION

spe·cial (spesh'əl) *adj.* [< L *species*, kind] 1 distinctive or unique 2 exceptional; unusual 3 highly valued 4 of or for a particular purpose, etc. 5 not general; specific — *n.* a special person or thing —**spe'cially** *adv.*

special delivery mail delivery by a special messenger, for a special fee

spe'cial·ist *n.* one who specializes in a particular study, work, etc.

spe'cial·ize' *vi.* **-ized', -iz'ing** to concentrate on a special branch of study, work, etc. —**spe'ciali·za'tion** *n.*

spe'cialty (-tē) *n., pl.* **-ties** 1 a special quality, feature, etc. 2 a special interest, study, etc. 3 an article with special features, etc.

spe·cie (spē'shē) *n.* [< L *species*, kind] coin, rather than paper money

spe·cies (spē'shēz) *n., pl.* **-cies** [L, appearance] 1 a distinct kind; sort 2 any of the groups of related plants or animals that make up a genus

specif. specifically

spe·cif·ic (spə sif'ik) *adj.* [< L *species*, kind + -*ficus*, -FIC] 1 definite; explicit 2 peculiar to or characteristic of something 3 of a particular kind 4 specially indicated as a cure for some disease — *n.* a specific cure —**spe·cif'i·cally** *adv.*

-specif'ic *combining form* limited or specific to

spec·i·fi·ca·tion (spes'ə fi kā'shən) *n.* 1 [*usually pl.*] a statement or enumeration of particulars, as to size, quality, terms, etc. 2 something specified

specific gravity the ratio of the weight or mass of a given volume of a substance to that of an equal volume of another substance (as water) used as a standard

spec·i·fy (spes'ə fī') *vt.* **-fied', -fy'ing** [< LL *specificus*, specific] 1 to mention or describe in detail 2 to state explicitly as a condition

spec·i·men (spes'ə mən) *n.* [L < *specere*, see] 1 a part or individual used as a sample of a whole or group 2 *Med.* a sample, as of urine, for analysis

spe·cious (spē'shəs) *adj.* [< L *species*, appearance] seeming to be good, sound, correct, etc. without really being so —**spe'ciously** *adv.*

speck (spek) *n.* [OE *specca*] 1 a small spot, mark, etc. 2 a very small bit — *vt.* to mark with specks

speckle (spek'əl) *n.* a small speck — *vt.* **-led, -ling** to mark with speckles

specs (speks) *n.pl.* [Colloq.] 1 spectacles; eyeglasses 2 specifications

spec·ta·cle (spek'tə kəl) *n.* [< L *specere*, see] 1 a remarkable sight 2 a large public show 3 [*pl.*] *a*) [Old-fashioned] a pair of eyeglasses *b*) something like a pair of eyeglasses

spec·tac·u·lar (spek tak'yə lər) *adj.* unusual to a striking degree — *n.* an elaborate show or display —**spec·tac'u·larly** *adv.*

spec·ta·tor (spek'tāt'ər) *n.* [L < *spectare*, behold] one who watches without taking an active part

spec·ter (spek'tər) *n.* [< L *spectare*, behold] a ghost; apparition Brit., etc. sp. **spec'tre**

spec'tral (-trəl) *adj.* 1 of or like a specter 2 of a spectrum

spec·tro·scope (spek'trə skōp') *n.* [< Ger. ult. < L *spectare*, behold] an optical instrument used for forming spectra for study —**spec'tro·scop'ic** (-skäp'ik) *adj.* — **spec·tros'copy** (-träs'kə pē) *n.*

spec·trum (spek'trəm) *n., pl.* **-tra** (-trə) or **-trums** [< L: see SPECTER] 1 a series of colored bands separated and arranged in order of their respective wavelengths by the passage of white light through a prism, etc. 2 a continuous range or entire extent

spec·u·late (spek'yōō lāt') *vi.* **-lat'ed, -lat'ing** [< L *specere*, see] 1 to think seriously; ponder; esp., to conjecture 2 to take part in any risky venture (as buying or selling certain stocks, etc.) on the chance of making huge profits —**spec'u·la'tion** *n.* —**spec'u·la'tive** *adj.* —**spec'u·la'tor** *n.*

speech (spēch) *n.* [< OE *sprecan*, speak] 1 the act of speaking 2 the power to speak 3 that which is spoken; utterance, remark, etc. 4 a talk given to an audience 5 the language of a certain people

---

THESAURUS

soil, scatter, stain, dash, dot, speck, speckle, shower, dribble, spray.

speak *v.* 1 [To utter] vocalize, pronounce, express; see UTTER. 2 [To communicate] converse, articulate, chat; see TALK 1. 3 [To deliver a speech] lecture, declaim, deliver; see ADDRESS 2. —**so to speak** that is to say, in a manner of speaking, as the saying goes*; see ACCORDINGLY. — **speak out** insist, assert, make oneself heard; see DECLARE. —**speak well for** commend, recommend, support; see PRAISE 1. —**to speak of** somewhat, a little, not much; see SOME.

speaker *n.* speechmaker, orator, lecturer, public speaker, preacher, spokesman, spellbinder, talker.

speaking *a.* oral, verbal, vocal; see TALKING.

spear *n.* lance, javelin, bayonet; see WEAPON.

special *a.* specific, particular, appropriate, peculiar, proper, individual, unique, restricted, exclusive, defined, limited, reserved, specialized, determinate, distinct, select, choice, defi-

nite, marked, designated, earmarked; see also UNUSUAL 1, 2.

special* *n.* sale item, feature, prepared dish; see MEAL 2, SALE 1, 2.

specialist *n.* expert, devotee, master, ace, virtuoso, veteran, scholar, professional, authority, connoisseur, technician.—*Ant.* AMATEUR, beginner, novice.

specialize *v.* work in exclusively, go in for, limit oneself to; see PRACTICE 2.

specialized *a.* specific, for a particular purpose, functional; see SPECIAL.

specialty *n.* practice, work, special interest; see HOBBY, JOB 1.

species *n.* class, variety, sort; see DIVISION 2, KIND 2.

specific *a.* particular, distinct, precise; see DEFINITE 1, 2, SPECIAL.

specifically *a.* particularly, individually, characteristically; see ESPECIALLY.

specification *n.* designation, stipulation, blueprint; see PLAN 1, 2, REQUIREMENT 1.

specified *a.* particularized, detailed,

precise; see NECESSARY.

specify *v.* name, designate, stipulate; see CHOOSE.

specimen *n.* individual, part, unit; see EXAMPLE.

speck *n.* spot, iota, mite; see BIT 1.

speckled *a.* specked, dotted, motley; see SPOTTED 1.

spectacle *n.* scene, representation, exhibition; see DISPLAY, VIEW. — **make a spectacle of oneself** show off, act ridiculously, play the fool; see MISBEHAVE.

spectacular *a.* striking, magnificent, dramatic; see IMPRESSIVE.

spectator *n.* beholder, viewer, onlooker; see OBSERVER.

speculate *v.* contemplate, meditate, consider; see THINK 1.

speech *n.* 1 [Language] tongue, mother tongue, native tongue; see LANGUAGE 1. 2 [The power of audible expression] talk, utterance, articulation, diction, pronunciation, expression, locution, vocalization, discourse, oral expression, parlance, enunciation, communication, prattle,

speech'less *adj.* **1** incapable of speech **2** silent, as from shock

speed (spēd) *n.* [OE *spæd*, success] **1** swiftness; quick motion **2** rate of movement; velocity **3** an arrangement of gears, as for the drive of an engine **4** [Slang] any of various amphetamine compounds — *vi.* **sped** (sped) or **speed'ed, speed'ing** to move rapidly, esp. too rapidly — *vt.* **1** to help to succeed; aid **2** to cause to speed —**speed up** to increase in speed —**speed'er** *n.*

speed'boat' *n.* a fast motorboat

speed·om·eter (spi däm'ət ər) *n.* a device attached to a motor vehicle, etc. to indicate speed

speed'ster (spēd'stər) *n.* a very fast driver, runner, etc.

speed'way' *n.* a track for racing automobiles or motorcycles

speed'y *adj.* **-i·er, -i·est 1** rapid; fast; swift **2** without delay; prompt [a *speedy* reply] —**speed'i·ly** *adv.*

spe·le·ol·o·gy (spē'lē äl'ə jē) *n.* [< Gr *spēlaion*, cave] the scientific study and exploration of caves —**spe'leol'o·gist** *n.*

spell[1] (spel) *n.* [OE, a saying] **1** a word or formula thought to have some magic power **2** irresistible influence; charm; fascination

spell[2] (spel) *vt.* **spelled** or **spelt, spell'ing** [< OFr *espeller*, explain] **1** to name in order the letters of (a word) **2** to make up (a word, etc.): said of specified letters **3** to mean [red *spells* danger] — *vi.* to spell words —**spell out** to explain in detail

spell[3] (spel) *vt.* **spelled, spell'ing** [OE *spelian*] [Colloq.] to work in place of (another) for an interval; relieve — *n.* **1** a period of work, duty, etc. **2** a period of anything [a *spell* of brooding] **3** [Colloq.] a fit of illness

spell'bind' *vt.* **-bound', -bind'ing** to cause to be spellbound; fascinate —**spell'bind'er** *n.*

spell'bound' *adj.* held by or as by a spell; fascinated

spell'down' *n.* SPELLING BEE

spell'er *n.* **1** one who spells words **2** a textbook for teaching spelling

spell'ing *n.* **1** the act of one who spells words **2** the way a word is spelled

spelling bee a spelling contest, esp. one in which a contestant is eliminated after misspelling a word

spe·lunker (spi luŋ'kər) *n.* [< Gr *spēlynx*, a cave] a cave explorer

spend (spend) *vt.* **spent, spend'ing** [< L *expendere:* see EXPEND] **1** to use up, exhaust, etc. [his fury was *spent*] **2** to pay out (money) **3** to devote (time, labor, etc.) to something **4** to pass (time) — *vi.* to pay out or use up money, etc. —**spend'able** *adj.* —**spend'er** *n.*

spend'thrift' *n.* one who wastes money — *adj.* wasteful

spent (spent) *vt., vi. pt. & pp. of* SPEND — *adj.* **1** tired out; physically exhausted **2** used up; worn out

sperm (spurm) *n.* [< Gr *sperma*, seed] **1** the male generative fluid; semen **2** SPERMATOZOON

sper·ma·to·zoon (spur'mə tə zō'än', -ən) *n., pl.* **-zo'a** (-zō'ə) [< Gr *sperma*, seed + *zōion*, animal] the male germ cell, found in semen, which penetrates the egg of the female to fertilize it

spermi·cide (spur'mə sīd') *n.* [SPERM + -i- + -CIDE] an agent that kills spermatozoa

sperm whale a large toothed whale found in warm seas: its head contains a valuable lubricating oil (**sperm oil**)

spew (spyōō) *vt., vi.* [OE *spiwan*] **1** to throw up (something) from or as from the stomach; vomit **2** to flow or cause to flow or gush forth — *n.* something spewed

sp. gr. specific gravity

sphere (sfir) *n.* [< Gr *sphaira*] **1** any round body having the surface equally distant from the center at all points; globe; ball **2** the place, range, or extent of action, existence, knowledge, experience, etc. —**spheri·cal** (sfer'i kəl, sfir'-) *adj.*

sphe·roid (sfir'oid) *n.* a body that is almost but not quite a sphere — *adj.* of this shape: also **sphe·roi'dal**

sphinc·ter (sfiŋk'tər) *n.* [< Gr *sphingein*, to draw close] a ring-shaped muscle at a body orifice

sphinx (sfiŋks) *n.* [< Gr, strangler] **1** *Gr. Myth.* a winged monster with a lion's body and a woman's head **2** one who is difficult to know or understand —[S-] **1** a statue with a lion's body and a man's head, near Cairo, Egypt **2** *Gr. Myth.* a sphinx at Thebes that strangles passersby unable to guess its riddle

spice (spīs) *n.* [< L *species*, kind] **1** an aromatic vegetable substance, as cinnamon, nutmeg, pepper, etc., used to season food **2** that which adds zest or interest — *vt.* **spiced, spic'ing 1** to season with spice **2** to add zest to —**spic'y, -i·er, -i·est,** *adj.*

spick-and-span (spik'n span') *adj.* [< *spike*, nail + ON *spānn*, a chip] **1** new or fresh **2** neat and clean

spic·ule (spik'yōōl') *n.* [< L *spica*, a point] a hard, needlelike part

spi·der (spī'dər) *n.* [< OE *spinnan*, to spin] **1** any of various arachnids that spin webs **2** a cast-iron frying pan —**spi'dery** (-ē) *adj.* like a spider

spiel (spēl) *n.* [Ger, play] [Slang] a talk or harangue, as in selling

spiffy (spif'ē) *adj.* **-i·er, -i·est** [< dial. *spiff,* well-dressed person] [Slang] spruce, smart, or dapper

spigot (spig'ət) *n.* [ME *spigote*] **1** a plug to stop the vent in a barrel, etc. **2** a faucet

spike[1] (spīk) *n.* [< ON *spīkr* or MDu *spiker*] **1** a long, heavy nail **2** a sharp-pointed projection, as on the sole of a shoe to prevent slipping — *vt.* **spiked, spik'ing 1** to fasten or fit with spikes **2** to pierce with, or impale on, a spike **3** to thwart (a scheme, etc.) **4** [Slang] to add alcoholic liquor to (a drink)

spike[2] (spīk) *n.* [L *spica*] **1** an ear of grain **2** a long flower cluster

spill (spil) *vt.* **spilled** or **spilt, spill'ing** [OE *spillan*, destroy] **1** to allow or cause, esp. unintentionally, to run, scatter, or flow over from a container **2** to shed (blood) **3** [Colloq.] to throw off (a rider, etc.) — *vi.* to be spilled; overflow — *n.* **1** a spilling **2** a fall or tumble —**spill'age** *n.*

spill'way' *n.* a channel to carry off excess water, as around a dam

spin (spin) *vt.* **spun, spin'ning** [OE *spinnan*] **1** *a)* to draw out and twist fibers of (wool, cotton, etc.) into thread *b)* to make (thread, etc.) thus **2** to make (a web, cocoon, etc.), as a spider **3** to draw *out* (a story) to a great length

---

THESAURUS

conversation, chatter. **3** [An address] lecture, discourse, oration, pep talk*, harangue, sermon, dissertation, homily, exhortation, eulogy, recitation, talk, rhetoric, tirade, bombast, diatribe, commentary, appeal, invocation; see also COMMUNICATION.

speechless *a.* silent, inarticulate, mum; see DUMB 1, MUTE.

speed *n.* swiftness, briskness, activity, eagerness, haste, hurry, acceleration, dispatch, velocity, readiness, agility, liveliness, quickness, momentum, rate, pace, alacrity, promptness, expedition, rapidity, rush, urgency, headway, fleetness, breeze*, good clip, lively clip, steam*.

speed *v.* ride hard, go like the wind, gear up, roll, bowl, give it the gun*, go fast, cover ground, gun the motor*, give her the gas*, go all out, break the sound barrier; see also RACE 1. —**speed up 1** [To accelerate] go faster, increase speed, move into a higher speed; see RACE 1. **2** [To cause to accelerate] promote,

further, get things going; see URGE 3.

speedy *a.* quick, nimble, expeditious; see FAST 1.

spell[1,3] *n.* **1** [A charm] trance, talisman, amulet; see CHARM 1. **2** [A period of time] term, interval, season; see TIME 1. —**cast a spell on** (or over) enchant, bewitch, beguile; see CHARM. —**under a spell** enchanted, bewitched, unable to resist; see CHARMED.

spell out *v.* make clear, go into detail, simplify; see EXPLAIN.

spend *v.* consume, deplete, waste, dispense, contribute, donate, give, liquidate, exhaust, misspend, pay, disburse, allocate, misspend, pay, discharge, lay out, pay up, settle, use up, throw away, foot the bill*, fork out*, ante up*, open the purse, shell out*, blow*.—*Ant.* SAVE, keep, conserve.

spent *a.* used, consumed, disbursed; see FINISHED 1.

sphere *n.* ball, globule, orb; see CIR-

CLE 1.

spice *n.* seasoning, pepper, cinnamon, nutmeg, ginger, cloves, salt, paprika, oregano, anise, coriander, allspice, savor, relish; see also FLAVORING.

spicy *a.* pungent, piquant, keen, fresh, aromatic, fragrant, seasoned, tangy, savory, flavorful, tasty; see also SALTY, SOUR.

spider *n. Common spiders include the following:* black widow, trapdoor, wolf, jumping, hunting, crab, burrowing, tarantula.

spigot *n.* plug, valve, tap; see FAUCET.

spill *v.* lose, scatter, drop, spill over, run out; see also EMPTY 2.

spilled *a.* poured out, lost, run out; see EMPTY.

spin *n.* circuit, rotation, gyration; see REVOLUTION 1, TURN 1.

spin *v.* revolve, twirl, rotate; see TURN 1.

4 to rotate swiftly — *vi.* **1** to spin thread or yarn **2** to form a web, cocoon, etc. **3** to whirl **4** to seem to be spinning from dizziness **5** to move along swiftly and smoothly — *n.* **1** a spinning or rotating movement **2** a ride in a motor vehicle **3** a descent of an airplane, nose first along a spiral path — **spin off** to produce as an outgrowth or secondary development, etc. —**spin′ner** *n.*

spina bifi·da (spī′nə bif′i də) a congenital defect in which part of the spinal column is exposed, causing paralysis, etc.

spin·ach (spin′ich) *n.* [ult. < Pers *aspanākh*] **1** a plant with dark-green, juicy, edible leaves **2** these leaves

spi·nal (spī′nəl) *adj.* of or having to do with the spine or spinal cord

spinal column the series of joined vertebrae forming the axial support for the skeleton; spine; backbone

spinal cord the thick cord of nerve tissue in the spinal column

spin·dle (spin′dəl) *n.* [< OE *spinnan*, to spin] **1** a slender rod used in spinning for twisting, winding, or holding thread **2** a spindlelike thing **3** any rod or pin that revolves or serves as an axis for a revolving part

spindly (spind′lē) *adj.* **-dli·er, -dli·est** long or tall and very thin

spine (spīn) *n.* [< L *spina*, thorn] **1** *a*) a sharp, stiff projection, as on a cactus *b*) anything like this **2** *a*) SPINAL COLUMN *b*) anything like this, as the back of a book —**spin′y, -i·er, -i·est,** *adj.*

spine′less *adj.* **1** having no spine or spines **2** lacking courage or willpower

spinet (spin′it) *n.* [< It *spinetta*] a small upright piano

spin·neret (spin′ə ret′) *n.* the organ in spiders, caterpillars, etc., that spins thread for webs or cocoons

spinning wheel a simple machine for spinning thread with a spindle driven by a large wheel spun as by a treadle

spin·off (spin′ôf′) *n.* a secondary benefit, product, development, etc.

spin·ster (spin′stər) *n.* [ME < *spinnen*, to spin] an unmarried woman, esp. an elderly one —**spin′ster·hood′** *n.*

spiny lobster a sea crustacean similar to the common lobster but lacking large pincers and having a spiny shell

spi·ra·cle (spir′ə kəl) *n.* [< L < *spirare*, breathe] an opening for breathing, as on the sides of an insect's body or on the top of a whale's head

spi·ral (spī′rəl) *adj.* [< Gr *speira*, a coil] circling around a point in constantly increasing (or decreasing) curves, or in constantly changing planes — *n.* a spiral curve or coil — *vi., vt.* **-raled** or **-ralled, -ral·ing** or **-ral·ling** to move in or form a spiral —**spi′rally** *adv.*

spire (spīr) *n.* [OE *spir*] **1** the top part of a pointed, tapering object **2** anything tapering to a point, as a steeple

spi·rea (spī rē′ə) *n.* [< Gr *speira*, a coil] a plant of the rose family, with dense clusters of small flowers Also sp. **spi·rae′a**

spirit (spir′it) *n.* [< L *spirare*, breathe] **1** *a*) the life principle, esp. in human beings *b*) SOUL (sense 1) **2** [*also* S-] life, will, thought, etc., regarded as separate from matter **3** a supernatural being, as a ghost, angel, etc. **4** an individual [a brave *spirit*] **5** [*usually pl.*] disposition; mood [high spirits] **6** vivacity, courage, etc. **7** enthusiastic loyalty [school *spirit*] **8** real meaning [the *spirit* of the law] **9** a pervading animating principle; essential quality [the *spirit* of the times] **10** [*usually pl.*] distilled alcoholic liquor — *vt.* to carry (*away, off,* etc.) secretly and swiftly —**spir′it·less** *adj.*

spir′ited *adj.* lively; animated

spir·it·ual (spir′i choo əl) *adj.* **1** of the spirit or the soul **2** of or consisting of spirit; not corporeal **3** of religion; sacred — *n.* a folk hymn originating among S U.S. blacks —**spir′itu·al′ity** (-al′ə tē) *n.* —**spir′itu·ally** *adv.*

spir′itu·al·ism′ *n.* the belief that the dead survive as spirits which can communicate with the living —**spir′itu·al·ist** *n.* —**spir′itu·al·is′tic** *adj.*

spir·itu·ous (spir′i choo əs) *adj.* of or containing distilled alcohol

spi·ro·chete (spī′rō kēt′) *n.* [< Gr *speira*, a coil + *chaitē,* hair] any of various spiral-shaped bacteria

spit[1] (spit) *n.* [OE *spitu*] **1** a thin, pointed rod on which meat is roasted over a fire, etc. **2** a narrow point of land extending into the water — *vt.* **spit′ted, spit′ting** to fix as on a spit

spit[2] (spit) *vt.* **spit** or [Chiefly Brit.] **spat, spit′ting** [OE *spittan*] **1** to eject from the mouth **2** to eject explosively — *vi.* to eject saliva from the mouth — *n.* **1** a spitting **2** saliva —**spit and image** [Colloq.] perfect likeness

spit′ball′ *n.* **1** paper chewed up into a wad for throwing **2** *Baseball* a pitch, now illegal, made by wetting one side of the ball as with spit

spite (spit) *n.* [see DESPITE] **1** ill will; malice **2** a grudge — *vt.* **spit′ed, spit′ing** to vent one's spite upon by hurting, frustrating, etc. —**in spite of** regardless of —**spite′ful** *adj.*

spit·tle (spit′'l) *n.* saliva; spit

spit·toon (spi toon′) *n.* a jarlike container to spit into; cuspidor

splash (splash) *vt.* [echoic] **1** to cause (a liquid) to scatter **2** to dash a liquid, mud, etc. on, so as to wet or soil — *vi.* to move, strike, etc. with a splash — *n.* **1** a splashing **2** a spot made by splashing —**make a splash** [Colloq.] to attract great attention

splash′down′ *n.* a spacecraft's soft landing on the sea

splash′y *adj.* **-i·er, -i·est 1** splashing or apt to splash; wet, muddy, etc. **2** [Colloq.] spectacular —**splash′i·ly** *adv.* —**splash′i·ness** *n.*

splat[1] (splat) *n.* [< SPLIT] a thin slat of wood, as in a chair back

splat[2] (splat) *n., interj.* [echoic] a splattering or wet, slapping sound

splat·ter (splat′ər) *n., vt., vi.* spatter or splash

splay (splā) *vt., vi.* [ME *splaien*] to spread out — *adj.* spreading outward

splay′foot′ *n., pl.* **-feet′** a foot that is flat and turned outward —**splay′foot′ed** *adj.*

spleen (splēn) *n.* [< Gr *splēn*] **1** a large lymphatic organ in the upper left part of the abdomen; it modifies the blood structure **2** malice; spite

splen·did (splen′did) *adj.* [< L *splendere,* to shine] **1** shining; brilliant **2** magnificent; gorgeous **3** grand; illustrious **4** [Colloq.] very good; fine —**splen′didly** *adv.*

splen·dor (splen′dər) *n.* [see prec.] **1** great luster; brilliance **2** pomp; grandeur Brit., etc. sp. **splen′dour** —**splen′dor·ous** or **splen′drous** (-drəs) *adj.*

sple·netic (spli net′ik) *adj.* **1** of the spleen **2** bad-tempered; irritable

splice (splīs) *vt.* **spliced, splic′ing** [MDu *splissen*] **1** to join (ropes) by weaving together the end strands **2** to join the ends of (timbers) by overlapping **3** to fasten the ends of (wire, film, etc.) together, as by soldering, etc. — *n.* a joint made by splicing —**splic′er** *n.*

splint (splint) *n.* [prob. < MDu *splinte*] **1** a thin strip of wood, etc. woven with others to make baskets, etc. **2** a thin, rigid strip of wood, etc. used to hold a broken bone in place

---

THESAURUS

spine *n.* **1** [A spikelike protrusion] thorn, prick, spike, barb, quill, ray, thistle, needle; see also POINT 2. **2** [A column of vertebrae] spinal column, ridge, backbone, vertebrae; see also BONE.

spineless *a.* timid, fearful, frightened; see COWARDLY, WEAK 3.

spinster *n.* unmarried woman, virgin, single woman, old maid, bachelor girl*; see also WOMAN 1.

spiny *a.* pointed, barbed, spiked; see SHARP 1.

spiral *a.* winding, circling, coiled, whorled, radial, curled, rolled, scrolled, helical, screw-shaped, wound.

spirit *n.* **1** [Life] breath, vitality, animation; see LIFE 1. **2** [Soul] psyche, essence, substance; see SOUL 2. **3** [A supernatural being] vision, apparition, specter; see GHOST, GOD. **4** [Courage] boldness, ardor, enthusiasm; see COURAGE. **5** [Feeling; *often plural*] humor, frame of mind, temper; see FEELING 4, MOOD 1.

spirited *a.* lively, vivacious, animated; see ACTIVE.

spiritless *a.* dull, apathetic, unconcerned; see INDIFFERENT.

spiritual *a.* refined, pure, holy; see RELIGIOUS 1.

spit[2] *v.* splutter, eject, drivel, slobber, drool.

spite *n.* malice, resentment, hatred; see HATE. —**in spite of** nevertheless, in defiance of, despite; see REGARDLESS 2.

splash *n.* plash, plop, dash, spatter, sprinkle, spray, slosh, slop.

splash *v.* splatter, dabble, get wet; see MOISTEN.

splendid *a.* premium, great, fine; see BEAUTIFUL, EXCELLENT, GLORIOUS.

splendor *n.* luster, brilliance, brightness; see GLORY 2.

splice *v.* knit, graft, mesh; see JOIN 1, WEAVE 1.

splint *n.* prop, rib, reinforcement; see BRACE, SUPPORT 2.

splin·ter (splin′tər) *vt., vi.* ⟦see prec.⟧ to break or split into thin, sharp pieces — *n.* a thin, sharp piece, as of wood, made by splitting, etc.

split (split) *vt., vi.* **split, split′ting** ⟦MDu *splitten*⟧ 1 to separate lengthwise into two or more parts 2 to break or tear apart 3 to divide into shares 4 to disunite 5 *a*) to break (a molecule) into atoms *b*) to produce nuclear fission in (an atom) — *n.* 1 a splitting 2 a break; crack 3 a division in a group, etc. — *adj.* divided; separated

split′-lev′el *adj.* having floor levels staggered about a half story apart

split′ting *adj.* 1 that splits 2 severe, as a headache

splotch (spläch) *n.* ⟦prob. < SPOT + BLOTCH⟧ an irregular spot, splash, or stain — *vt., vi.* to mark or be marked with splotches —**splotch′y, -i·er, -i·est,** *adj.*

splurge (splʉrj) *n.* ⟦echoic⟧ [Colloq.] 1 any very showy display or effort 2 a spell of extravagant spending — *vi.* **splurged, splurg′ing** [Colloq.] 1 to show off 2 to spend money freely

splut·ter (splut′ər) *vi.* ⟦var. of SPUTTER⟧ 1 to make hissing or spitting sounds 2 to speak hurriedly and confusedly — *n.* a spluttering

spoil (spoil) *vt.* **spoiled** or **spoilt, spoil′ing** ⟦< L *spolium*, plunder⟧ 1 to damage so as to make useless, etc. 2 to impair the enjoyment, etc. of 3 to cause to expect too much by overindulgence 4 [Archaic] to rob; plunder — *vi.* to become spoiled; decay, etc., as food — *n.* [*usually pl.*] plunder; booty —**spoil′age** *n.* —**spoil′er** *n.*

spoil′sport′ *n.* one whose actions ruin the pleasure of others

spoils system the treating of public offices as the booty of a successful political party

spoke[1] (spōk) *n.* ⟦OE *spaca*⟧ any of the braces or bars extending from the hub to the rim of a wheel

spoke[2] (spōk) *vi., vt. pt. & archaic pp.* of SPEAK

spo·ken (spō′kən) *vi., vt. pp.* of SPEAK — *adj.* 1 uttered; oral 2 having a (specified) kind of voice *[soft-spoken]*

spokes·man (spōks′mən) *n., pl.* **-men** one who speaks for another or for a group —**spokes′wom′an,** *pl.* **-wom′en, n.fem.**

spokes′per·son *n.* SPOKESMAN: used to avoid the masculine implication of *spokesman*

spo·li·a·tion (spō′lē ā′shən) *n.* ⟦< L *spoliatio*⟧ robbery; plundering

sponge (spunj) *n.* ⟦< Gr *spongia*⟧ 1 a stationary aquatic animal with a porous structure 2 the highly absorbent skeleton of such animals, used for washing surfaces, etc. 3 any substance like this, as a piece of spongy rubber, etc. — *vt.* **sponged, spong′ing** 1 to dampen, wipe, absorb, etc. as with a sponge 2 [Colloq.] to get as by begging, imposition, etc. — *vi.* [Colloq.] to live as a parasite upon other people —**spong′er** *n.* —**spon′gy, -gier, -giest,** *adj.*

sponge bath a bath taken by using a wet sponge or cloth without getting into water

sponge′cake′ *n.* a light, spongy·cake without shortening Also **sponge cake**

spon·sor (spän′sər) *n.* ⟦L < *spondere*, promise solemnly⟧ 1 one who assumes responsibility as surety for, or endorser of, some person or thing 2 a godparent 3 a business firm, etc. that pays for a radio or TV program advertising its product — *vt.* to act as sponsor for —**spon′sor·ship′ n.**

spon·ta·neity (spän′tə nē′ə tē) *n.* 1 a being spontaneous 2 *pl.* **-ties** spontaneous behavior, action, etc.

spon·ta·neous (spän tā′nē əs) *adj.* ⟦< L *sponte*, of free will⟧ 1 acting or resulting from a natural feeling or impulse, without constraint, effort, etc. 2 occurring through internal causes —**spon·ta′neous·ly** *adv.*

spontaneous combustion the process of catching fire through heat generated by internal chemical action

spoof (spoof) *n.* 1 a hoax or joke 2 a light satire — *vt., vi.* 1 to fool; deceive 2 to satirize (something) playfully

spook (spook) *n.* ⟦Du⟧ [Colloq.] a ghost — *vt., vi.* [Colloq.] to frighten or become frightened —**spook′y, -i·er, -i·est,** *adj.*

spool (spool) *n.* ⟦< MDu *spoele*⟧ 1 a cylinder on which thread, wire, etc. is wound 2 the material so wound

spoon (spoon) *n.* ⟦< OE *spon*, a chip⟧ 1 a utensil consisting of a small, shallow bowl and a handle, used for eating, stirring, etc. 2 something shaped like a spoon, as a shiny, curved fishing lure — *vt.* to take up with a spoon —**spoon′ful′,** *pl.* **-fuls′, n.**

spoon′bill′ *n.* a wading bird whose flat bill is spoon-shaped at the tip

spoon·er·ism (spoon′ər iz′əm) *n.* ⟦after Rev. W. A. Spooner (1844-1930), of England, who made such slips⟧ an unintentional interchange of the initial sounds of words (Ex.: "a well-boiled icicle" for "a well-oiled bicycle")

spoon′-feed′ *vt.* **-fed′, -feed′ing** 1 to feed with a spoon 2 to pamper; coddle

spoor (spoor) *n.* ⟦Afrik⟧ the track or trail of a wild animal

spo·radic (spə rad′ik) *adj.* ⟦< Gr *sporas*, scattered⟧ happening or appearing in isolated instances *[sporadic storms]* —**spo·rad′i·cally** *adv.*

spore (spôr, spōr) *n.* ⟦< Gr *spora*, a seed⟧ a small reproductive body produced by algae, ferns, etc. and capable of giving rise to a new individual — *vi.* **spored, spor′ing** to bear spores

sport (spôrt) *n.* ⟦< DISPORT⟧ 1 any recreational activity; specif., a game, competition, etc. requiring bodily exertion 2 fun or play 3 a thing joked about 4 [Colloq.] a sportsmanlike person 5 [Colloq.] a showy, flashy fellow 6 Biol. a plant or animal markedly different from the normal type — *vt.* [Colloq.] to display *[to sport a loud tie]* — *vi.* 1 to play 2 to joke — *adj.* 1 of or for sports 2 suitable for casual wear *[a sport coat]:* also **sports** —**in** (or **for**) **sport** in jest —**make sport of** to mock or ridicule

sport′ing *adj.* 1 of or interested in sports 2 sportsmanlike; fair 3 of games, races, etc. involving gambling or betting

spor′tive *adj.* 1 full of sport or fun 2 done in fun —**spor′tively** *adv.*

sports car a low, small automobile with a high-compression engine

sports′cast′ *n.* a broadcast of sports news on radio or TV —**sports′cast′er** *n.*

sports′man *n., pl.* **-men** 1 a man who takes part in sports, esp. hunting, fishing, etc. 2 one who plays fair and

---

THESAURUS

splinter *n.* sliver, flake, chip; see BIT 1.

split *n.* 1 [A dividing] separating, breaking up, severing; see DIVISION 1. 2 [An opening] crack, fissure, rent; see HOLE 1.

split *v.* burst, rend, cleave; see BREAK 1, CUT 1, DIVIDE. —**split up** part, break up, isolate; see DIVIDE, DIVORCE.

spoil *v.* 1 [To decay] rot, blight, fade, wither, molder, crumble, mold, mildew, corrode, decompose, putrefy, degenerate, weaken, become tainted. 2 [To ruin] destroy, defile, plunder; see DESTROY.

spoiled *a.* damaged, marred, injured; see RUINED 1, WASTED.

spoiling *a.* rotting, breaking up, wasting away; see DECAYING.

spoils *n.* plunder, pillage, prize; see BOOTY.

spoke[1] *n.* rung, handle, crosspiece; see ROD 1.

spoken *a.* uttered, expressed, told,

announced, mentioned, communicated, oral, voiced, unwritten.

spokesman *n.* deputy, mediator, substitute; see AGENT, SPEAKER.

sponsor *n.* advocate, patron, supporter, champion; see also PATRON.

spontaneous *a.* involuntary, instinctive, casual, unintentional, impulsive, automatic, unforced, natural, unavoidable, unwilling, unconscious, uncontrollable.—*Ant.* DELIBERATE, willful, intended.

spontaneously *a.* instinctively, impulsively, automatically; see UNCONSCIOUSLY.

spoof *n.* trickery, put on*, satire; see DECEPTION.

spoof *v.* fool, play a trick on, kid*; see TRICK.

spooky *a.* weird, eerie, ominous; see MYSTERIOUS 2, UNCANNY.

spoon *n.* teaspoon, tablespoon, ladle; see SILVERWARE.

sport *n.* 1 [Entertainment] diversion, recreation, play, amusement,

merrymaking, festivity, revelry, pastime, pleasure, enjoyment; see also ENTERTAINMENT, FUN, GAME 1. 2 [A joke] pleasantry, mockery, jest, mirth, joke, joking, antics, tomfoolery, nonsense, laughter, practical joke. 3 [Athletic or competitive amusement] *Sports include the following:* (deer, rabbit, duck, etc.) hunting, shooting, (the) Olympics, horse racing, automobile racing, runnning, fishing, basketball, golf, tennis, squash, handball, volleyball, soccer, gymnastics, (professional, pro*, collegiate, high-school, etc.) football, baseball, track and field sports, cricket, lacrosse, hockey, skating, skiing, fencing, jumping, boxing, wrestling.

sporting *a.* considerate, sportsmanlike, gentlemanly; see GENEROUS, REASONABLE 1.

sportsman *n.* huntsman, big game hunter, woodsman; see FISHERMAN, HUNTER.

can lose without complaint or win without gloating — **sports'man·like'** *adj.* —**sports'man·ship'** *n.*

sport'y *adj.* **-i·er, -i·est** [Colloq.] 1 sporting or sportsmanlike 2 flashy or showy

spot (spät) *n.* [prob. < MDu *spotte*] 1 *a*) a small area differing in color, etc. from the surrounding area *b*) a stain, speck, etc. 2 a flaw or defect 3 a locality; place — *vt.* **spot'ted, spot'ting** 1 to mark with spots 2 to stain; blemish 3 to place; locate 4 to see; recognize 5 [Colloq.] to allow as a handicap — *vi.* 1 to become marked with spots 2 to make a stain, as ink — *adj.* 1 ready [*spot* cash] 2 made at random [a *spot* survey] —**hit the spot** [Colloq.] to satisfy a craving —**in a (bad) spot** [Slang] in trouble —**on the spot** [Slang] in a bad or demanding situation —**spot'less** *adj.* —**spot'ted** *adj.*

spot'-check' *vt.* to check or examine at random — *n.* such a checking

spot'light' *n.* 1 *a*) a strong beam of light focused on a particular person, thing, etc. *b*) a lamp used to project such a light 2 public notice or prominence — *vt.* to draw attention to, as by a spotlight

spot·ter (spät'ər) *n.* one who spots, as an assistant in the stands who reports on plays at a football game

spot'ty *adj.* **-tier, -ti·est** 1 having, occurring in, or marked with spots 2 not uniform or consistent —**spot'ti·ness** *n.*

spouse (spous) *n.* [< L *sponsus*, betrothed] (one's) husband or wife —**spousal** (spou'zəl) *adj.*

spout (spout) *n.* [< ME *spouten*, to spout] 1 a projecting tube or orifice by which a liquid is poured 2 a stream, etc. as of liquid from a spout — *vt., vi.* 1 to shoot out (liquid, etc.) as from a spout 2 to speak or utter (words, etc.) in a loud, pompous manner

sprain (sprān) *vt.* [< ? L *ex-*, out + *premere*, press] to wrench a ligament or muscle of (a joint) without dislocating the bones — *n.* an injury resulting from this

sprang (spraŋ) *vi., vt. alt. pt. of* SPRING

sprat (sprat) *n.* [OE *sprott*] a small European herring

sprawl (sprôl) *vi.* [< OE *spreawlian*, move convulsively] 1 to sit or lie with the limbs in a relaxed or awkward position 2 to spread out awkwardly or unevenly, as handwriting, etc. — *n.* a sprawling movement or position

spray¹ (sprā) *n.* [prob. < MDu *spraeien*] 1 a mist of fine liquid particles 2 *a*) a jet of such particles, as from a spray gun *b*) a device for spraying 3 something likened to a spray — *vt., vi.* 1 to direct a spray (on) 2 to shoot out in a spray —**spray'er** *n.*

spray² (sprā) *n.* [ME] a small branch or sprig of a tree, etc., with leaves, flowers, etc.

spray can a can in which gas under pressure sprays out the contents

spray gun a device that shoots out a spray of liquid, as paint, etc.

spread (spred) *vt., vi.* **spread, spread'ing** [OE *sprædan*] 1 to open or stretch out; unfold 2 to move (the fingers, wings, etc.) apart 3 to distribute or be distributed over an area 4 to extend in time 5 to make or be made

widely known, felt, etc. 6 to cover or be covered (*with* something), as in a fine layer 7 to set (a table) for a meal 8 to push or be pushed apart — *n.* 1 the act or extent of spreading 2 an expanse 3 a cloth cover for a table, bed, etc. 4 jam, butter, etc. used on bread 5 [Colloq.] a meal with many different foods

spread'sheet' *n.* a computer program that organizes numerical data into rows and columns on a video screen

spree (sprē) *n.* [< earlier *spray*] 1 a noisy frolic 2 a period of drunkenness 3 a period of uninhibited activity [a shopping *spree*]

sprig (sprig) *n.* [ME *sprigge*] a little twig or spray

spright·ly (sprīt'lē) *adj.* **-lier, -li·est** [< *spright*, var. of SPRITE] full of energy and spirit; lively — *adv.* in a sprightly manner —**spright'li·ness** *n.*

spring (spriŋ) *vi.* **sprang** or **sprung, sprung, spring'ing** [OE *springan*] 1 to leap; bound 2 to come, appear, etc. suddenly 3 to bounce 4 to arise as from some source; grow or develop 5 to become warped, split, etc. 6 to rise up above surrounding objects Often followed by *up* — *vt.* 1 to cause to leap forth suddenly 2 to cause (a trap, etc.) to snap shut 3 to cause to warp, split, etc. 4 to make known suddenly 5 [Slang] to get (someone) released from jail — *n.* 1 a leap, or the distance so covered 2 a sudden flying back 3 elasticity; resilience 4 a device, as a coil of wire, that returns to its original form after being forced out of shape 5 a flow of water from the ground 6 a source or origin 7 *a*) that season of the year following winter, in which plants begin to grow *b*) any period of beginning — *adj.* 1 of, for, appearing in, or planted in the spring 2 having, or supported on, springs 3 coming from a spring [*spring* water] —**spring a leak** to begin to leak suddenly

spring'board' *n.* a springy board used as a takeoff in leaping or diving

spring fever a laziness that many people feel in the early days of spring

spring'time' *n.* the season of spring

spring'y *adj.* **-i·er, -i·est** having spring; elastic, resilient, etc. —**spring'i·ness** *n.*

sprin·kle (spriŋ'kəl) *vt., vi.* **-kled, -kling** [ME *sprinklen*] 1 to scatter or fall in drops or particles 2 to scatter drops or particles (upon) 3 to rain lightly — *n.* 1 a sprinkling 2 a light rain —**sprin'kler** *n.*

sprin'kling (-kliŋ) *n.* a small, scattered number or amount

sprint (sprint) *vi., n.* [ME *sprenten*] run or race at full speed for a short distance —**sprint'er** *n.*

sprite (sprīt) *n.* [< L *spiritus*, spirit] an imaginary being, as an elf

spritz (sprits, shprits) *vt., vi., n.* [< Ger *spritze*] squirt or spray

sprock·et (spräk'it) *n.* [< ?] 1 any of the teeth, as on a wheel, arranged to fit the links of a chain 2 such a wheel: in full **sprocket wheel**

sprout (sprout) *vi.* [OE *sprutan*] to begin to grow; give off shoots — *vt.* to cause to sprout — *n.* 1 a young growth on a plant; shoot 2 a new growth from a bud, etc.

spruce¹ (sproos) *n.* [ME *Spruce*, Prussia] 1 an evergreen tree with slender needles 2 its wood

---

◼ THESAURUS ◼

sportsmanship *n.* 1 [Skill] facility, dexterity, cunning; see ABILITY. 2 [Honor] justice, integrity, truthfulness; see HONESTY.

spot *n.* 1 [A dot] speck, flaw, pimple; see BIT 1, BLEMISH. 2 [A place] point, locality, scene; see PLACE 3. —**hit the high spots*** hurry, travel rapidly, make good time; see SPEED. 2 treat hastily, go over lightly, touch up; see NEGLECT 1, 2. —**hit the spot*** please, delight, be just right; see SATISFY 1. —**in a bad spot*** in danger, threatened, on the spot*; see DANGEROUS.

spot *v.* blemish, blotch, spatter; see DIRTY.

spotless *a.* stainless, immaculate, without spot or blemish; see CLEAN, PURE 2.

spotted *a.* 1 [Dotted] marked, dappled, mottled, dotted, speckled, motley, blotchy. 2 [Blemished] soiled, smudged, smeared; see DIRTY 1.

spouse *n.* marriage, partner, groom, bride; see also HUSBAND, MATE 3, WIFE.

sprain *n.* twist, overstrain, strain; see

INJURY.

sprained *a.* wrenched, strained, pulled out of place; see HURT, TWISTED 1.

sprawl *v.* slouch, relax, lounge; see LIE 3.

spray¹ *n.* splash, steam, fine mist; see FOG.

spray¹ *v.* scatter, diffuse, sprinkle; see SPATTER.

spread *a.* expanded, dispersed, extended, opened, unfurled, sown, scattered, diffused, strewn, spread thin; see also DISTRIBUTED.—*Ant.* RESTRICTED, narrowed, restrained.

spread *n.* 1 [Extent] scope, range, expanse; see EXTENT, MEASURE 1. 2 [A spread cloth] blanket, coverlet, counterpane; see COVER 1. 3 [A spread food] preserve, conserve, jelly; see BUTTER, CHEESE. 4 [*A meal] feast, banquet, informal repast; see DINNER, LUNCH, MEAL 2.

spread *v.* 1 [To distribute] cast, diffuse, disseminate; see RADIATE 1, SCATTER 2, SOW. 2 [To extend] open, unfurl, roll out, unroll, unfold, reach,

circulate, lengthen, widen, expand, untwist, unwind, uncoil, enlarge, increase, develop, branch off, expand; see also FLOW, REACH 1.—*Ant.* CLOSE, shorten, shrink. 3 [To apply over a surface] cover, coat, smear, daub, plate, gloss, enamel, paint, spray, plaster, pave, wax, varnish. 4 [To separate] part, sever, disperse; see DIVIDE, SEPARATE 1.

spreading *a.* extending, extensive, spread out, growing, widening.

spree *n.* revel, frolic, binge*; see CELEBRATION.

sprightly *a.* lively, quick, alert; see AGILE.

spring *n.* 1 [A fountain] flowing well, artesian well, sweet water; see ORIGIN 2. 2 [The season between winter and summer] springtime, seedtime, flowering, budding, vernal equinox, blackberry winter*; see also SEASON.

sprinkle *v.* dampen, bedew, spray; see MOISTEN.

sprout *v.* germinate, take root, shoot up, bud, burgeon; see also GROW 1.

spruce² (spro͞os) *adj.* **spruc′er, spruc′est** ⟦< *Spruce* leather (see prec.)⟧ neat and trim in a smart way — *vt., vi.* **spruced, spruc′ing** to make or become spruce: usually with *up*

sprung (spruŋ) *vi., vt. pp. & alt. pt. of* SPRING

spry (sprī) *adj.* **spri′er** or **spry′er, spri′est** or **spry′est** ⟦< Scand⟧ full of life; active, esp. though elderly — **spry′ly** *adv.* —**spry′ness** *n.*

spud (spud) *n.* [Colloq.] a potato

spume (spyo͞om) *n.* ⟦< L *spuma*⟧ foam, froth, or scum — *vi.* **spumed, spum′ing** to foam; froth

spu·mo·ni (spə mō′nē) *n.* ⟦It < L *spuma*, foam⟧ Italian ice cream in variously flavored layers

spun (spun) *vt., vi. pt. & pp. of* SPIN

spunk (spuŋk) *n.* ⟦Ir *sponc*, tinder⟧ [Colloq.] courage; spirit —**spunk′y, -i·er, -i·est,** *adj.*

spur (spur) *n.* ⟦OE *spura*⟧ **1** a pointed device worn on the heel by a rider, used to urge a horse forward **2** anything that urges; stimulus **3** any spurlike projection **4** a short railroad track connected with the main track — *vt.* **spurred, spur′ring 1** to prick with spurs **2** to urge or incite — *vi.* to hurry; hasten —**on the spur of the moment** abruptly and impulsively

spurge (spurj) *n.* ⟦< Fr *espurger*, to purge⟧ any of a group of plants with milky juice and tiny flowers

spu·ri·ous (spyoor′ē əs) *adj.* ⟦L *spurius*, illegitimate⟧ not genuine; false —**spu′ri·ous·ly** *adv.* —**spu′ri·ous·ness** *n.*

spurn (spurn) *vt.* ⟦OE *spurnan*⟧ to reject with contempt; scorn

spurt (spurt) *vt.* [prob. < OE *sprutan*, to sprout] to expel in a stream or jet — *vi.* **1** to gush forth in a stream or jet **2** to show a sudden, brief burst of energy, etc. — *n.* **1** a sudden shooting forth; jet **2** a sudden, brief burst of energy, etc.

sput·nik (spoot′nik, sput′-) *n.* ⟦Russ, lit., co-traveler⟧ SATELLITE (sense 2*b*)

sput·ter (sput′ər) *vi.* ⟦< MDu *spotten*, to spit⟧ **1** to spit out drops, etc. explosively, as when talking excitedly **2** to speak in a confused, explosive way **3** to make sharp, sizzling sounds, as frying fat — *vt.* **1** to spit or throw out (bits or drops) explosively **2** to utter by sputtering — *n.* a sputtering

spu·tum (spyoot′əm) *n., pl.* **-ta** (-ə) ⟦< L *spuere*, to spit⟧ saliva, usually mixed with mucus, spat out

spy (spī) *vt.* **spied, spy′ing** ⟦< OHG *spehōn*, examine⟧ **1** to watch closely and secretly: often with *out* **2** to catch sight of; see — *vi.* to watch closely and secretly; act as a spy — *n., pl.* **spies 1** one who keeps close and secret watch on others **2** one employed by a government to get secret information about the affairs, armed forces, etc. of another government

spy′glass′ (-glas′) *n.* a small telescope

sq. 1 sequence **2** squadron **3** square

sqq. ⟦L *sequentes; sequentia*⟧ the following ones; what follows

squab (skwäb) *n.* [prob. < Scand] a nestling pigeon

squab·ble (skwäb′əl) *vi.* **-bled, -bling** ⟦< Scand⟧ to quarrel noisily over a small matter; wrangle — *n.* a noisy, petty quarrel —**squab′bler** *n.*

squad (skwäd) *n.* ⟦prob. < Sp *escuadra*, a square⟧ **1** a small group of soldiers, often a subdivision of a platoon **2** any small group of people working together

squad car PATROL CAR

squad·ron (-rən) *n.* ⟦< It *squadra*, a square⟧ a unit of warships, armored cavalry, military aircraft, etc.

squal·id (skwäl′id) *adj.* ⟦< L *squalere*, be foul⟧ **1** foul or unclean **2** wretched

squall¹ (skwôl) *n.* ⟦< Scand⟧ a brief, violent windstorm, usually with rain or snow —**squall′y, -i·er, -i·est,** *adj.*

squall² (skwôl) *vi., vt.* ⟦< ON *skvala*⟧ to cry or scream loudly and harshly — *n.* a harsh, loud cry or scream

squalor (skwäl′ər) *n.* a being squalid; filth and wretchedness

squa·mous (skwā′məs) *adj.* ⟦< L *squama*, a scale⟧ like, formed of, or covered with scales

squan·der (skwän′dər) *vt.* ⟦prob. < dial. *squander*, to scatter⟧ to spend or use wastefully or extravagantly

square (skwer) *n.* ⟦< L *ex*, out + *quadrare*, to square⟧ **1** *a)* a plane figure having four equal sides and four right angles *b)* anything of or approximating this shape **2** BLOCK (*n.* 7) **3** an open area bounded by several streets, used as a park, etc. **4** an instrument for drawing or testing right angles **5** the product of a number multiplied by itself **6** [Slang] a person who is SQUARE (*adj.* 10) — *vt.* **squared, squar′ing 1** to make into a SQUARE (sense 1) **2** to make straight, even, right-angled, etc. **3** to settle; adjust [to *square* accounts] **4** to make conform [to *square* a statement with the facts] **5** to multiply (a quantity) by itself — *vi.* to fit; agree; accord (*with*) — *adj.* **squar′er, squar′est 1** having four equal sides and four right angles **2** forming a right angle **3** straight, level, even, etc. **4** leaving no balance; even **5** just; fair **6** direct; straightforward **7** designating a unit of surface measure in the form of a square [a *square* foot] **8** solid; sturdy [a *square* joint] **9** [Colloq.] satisfying; substantial [a *square* meal] **10** [Slang] old-fashioned; unsophisticated, etc. — *adv.* in a square manner —**square off** (or **away**) to assume a posture of attack or self-defense —**square oneself** [Colloq.] to make amends —**square′ly** *adv.* —**square′ness** *n.* —**squar′ish** *adj.*

square dance a dance with various steps, in which couples are grouped in a given form, as a square — **square′-dance′, -danced′, -danc′ing,** *vi.*

square′-rigged′ *adj.* rigged with square sails as the principal sails

square root the quantity which when squared will produce a given quantity [3 is the *square root* of 9]

squash¹ (skwôsh, skwäsh) *vt.* ⟦< L *ex-*, intens. + *quatere*, to shake⟧ **1** to crush into a soft or flat mass; press **2** to suppress; quash — *vi.* **1** to be squashed **2** to make a sound of squashing — *n.* **1** something squashed **2** the act or sound of squashing **3** a game played in a walled court with rackets and a rubber ball —**squash′y, -i·er, -i·est,** *adj.*

squash² (skwôsh, skwäsh) *n.* ⟦< AmInd⟧ the fleshy fruit of various plants of the gourd family, eaten as a vegetable

squat (skwät) *vi.* **squat′ted, squat′ting** ⟦< L *ex-*, intens. + *cogere*, to force⟧ **1** to sit on the heels with the knees bent **2** to crouch close to the ground **3** to settle on land without right or title **4** to settle on public land in order to get title to it — *adj.* short and heavy or thick Also **squat′ty, -tier, -ti·est** — *n.* the act or position of squatting —**squat′ness** *n.* —**squat′ter** *n.*

squaw (skwô) *n.* ⟦< AmInd⟧ [Now Rare] a North American Indian woman or wife: now considered offensive

squawk (skwôk) *vi.* ⟦echoic⟧ **1** to utter a loud, harsh cry **2** [Colloq.] to complain loudly — *n.* **1** a loud, harsh cry **2** [Colloq.] a raucous complaint

squeak (skwēk) *vi.* ⟦ME *squeken*⟧ to make or utter a sharp, high-pitched sound or cry — *vt.* to say in a squeak — *n.* a thin, sharp sound or cry —**narrow** (or **close** or **near**) **squeak** [Colloq.] a narrow escape —**squeak through** (or **by**, etc.) [Colloq.] to succeed, get through, etc. with difficulty —**squeak′y, -i·er, -i·est,** *adj.*

THESAURUS

spry *a.* nimble, fleet, vigorous; see AGILE.

spunk* *n.* spirit, courage, nerve; see COURAGE.

spurn *v.* despise, disdain, look down on; see EVADE.

spurt *n.* squirt, jet, stream; see WATER 2.

spurt *v.* spout, jet, burst; see FLOW.

sputter *v.* stumble, stutter, falter; see STAMMER.

spy *n.* secret agent, foreign agent, scout, detective, undercover man, CIA operative, observer, watcher.

spy *v.* scout, observe, watch, examine, bug*, tap, scrutinize, take note, search, discover, look for, hunt, peer, pry, spy upon, set a watch on, hound,

trail, tail*, follow; see also MEDDLE 1, 2.

squabble *n.* spat, quarrel, feud; see DISPUTE.

squabble *v.* argue, disagree, fight; see QUARREL.

squad *n.* company, small company, crew; see TEAM 1.

squalid *a.* dirty, poor, foul; see DIRTY 1.

squall¹ *n.* blast, gust, gale; see STORM.

squalor *n.* ugliness, disorder, uncleanness; see FILTH.

squander *v.* spend, spend lavishly, throw away; see WASTE 2.

square *a.* **1** [Having right angles] right-angled, four-sided, equal-sided, squared, equilateral, rectangular, rec-

tilinear. **2** [*Old-fashioned] dated, stuffy, out-of-date; see CONSERVATIVE, OLD-FASHIONED.

square *n.* **1** [A rectangle] equal-sided rectangle, plane figure, rectilinear plane; see RECTANGLE. **2** [A park] city center, civic center, plaza, recreational area; see also PARK 1.

squat *v.* stoop, hunch, cower; see SIT.

squawk *v.* cackle, crow, yap; see CRY 2.

squeak *n.* peep, squeal, shrill sound; see CRY 1, NOISE 1.

squeak *v.* creak, peep, squeal; see CRY 2, SOUND. —**squeak through*** manage, survive, pass; see ENDURE 2, SUCCEED 1.

squeal (skwēl) *vi.* 〚ME *squelen*〛 1 to utter or make a long, shrill cry or sound 2 [Slang] to act as an informer — *vt.* to utter in a squeal — *n.* a squealing —**squeal′er** *n.*

squeam·ish (skwēm′ish) *adj.* 〚ME *squaimous*〛 1 easily nauseated 2 easily shocked; prudish 3 fastidious — **squeam′ish·ness** *n.*

squee·gee (skwē′jē) *n.* 〚prob. < fol.〛 a rubber-edged tool for scraping water from a flat surface

squeeze (skwēz) *vt.* **squeezed, squeez′ing** 〚< OE *cwysan*〛 1 to press hard, esp. from two or more sides 2 to extract (juice, etc.) from (fruit, etc.) 3 to force (*into, out,* etc.) by pressing 4 to embrace closely; hug — *vi.* 1 to yield to pressure 2 to exert pressure 3 to force one's way by pushing — *n.* 1 a squeezing or being squeezed 2 a close embrace; hug 3 the state of being closely pressed or packed; crush 4 a period of scarcity, hardship, etc.

squeeze bottle a plastic bottle that is squeezed to eject its contents

squelch (skwelch) *n.* 〚< ?〛 [Colloq.] a crushing retort, rebuke, etc. — *vt.* [Colloq.] to suppress or silence completely

squib (skwib) *n.* 〚prob. echoic〛 1 a firecracker that burns with a hissing noise before exploding 2 a short, witty verbal attack; lampoon

squid (skwid) *n.* 〚prob. < *squit,* dial. for SQUIRT〛 a long, slender sea mollusk with eight arms and two long tentacles

squig·gle (skwig′əl) *n.* 〚SQU(IRM) + (W)IGGLE〛 a short, wavy line or illegible scrawl — *vt., vi.* **-gled, -gling** to write as, or make, a squiggle or squiggles

squint (skwint) *vi.* 〚< ASQUINT〛 1 to peer with the eyes partly closed 2 to look sideways or askance 3 to be cross-eyed — *n.* 1 a squinting 2 a being cross-eyed 3 [Colloq.] a quick look or sidelong glance

squire (skwīr) *n.* 〚see ESQUIRE〛 1 in England, the owner of a large, rural estate 2 a title of respect for a justice of the peace, etc. 3 an attendant, esp. a man escorting a woman — *vt.* **squired, squir′ing** to act as a squire to

squirm (skwurm) *vi.* 1 to twist and turn the body; wriggle 2 to show or feel distress — *n.* a squirming —**squirm′y** *adj.*

squir·rel (skwur′əl, skwurl) *n.* 〚< Gr *skia,* shadow + *oura,* tail〛 1 a small, tree-dwelling rodent with heavy fur and a long, bushy tail 2 its fur

squirt (skwurt) *vt.* 〚prob. < LowG *swirtjen*〛 1 to shoot out (a liquid) in a jet; spurt 2 to wet with liquid so shot out — *n.* 1 a jet of liquid 2 [Colloq.] a small or young person, esp. an impudent one

Sr *Chem. symbol for* strontium

Sr. *abbrev.* 1 Senior 2 Sister

SRO 1 single room occupancy 2 standing room only

SS or **S.S.** steamship

SST supersonic transport

St. 1 Saint 2 Strait 3 Street

stab (stab) *n.* 〚prob. < ME *stubbe,* stub〛 1 a wound made by stabbing 2 a thrust, as with a knife 3 a sharp pain 4 an attempt — *vt., vi.* **stabbed, stab′bing** 1 to pierce or wound as with a knife 2 to thrust (a knife, etc.) into something 3 to pain sharply

sta·bil·i·ty (sta bil′ə tē) *n.* 1 a being stable; steadiness 2 firmness of purpose, etc. 3 permanence

sta·bi·lize (stā′bə līz′) *vt.* **-lized′, -liz′ing** 1 to make sta-

ble 2 to keep from changing 3 to give stability to (a plane or ship) — *vi.* to become stabilized —**sta′bi·li·za′tion** *n.* —**sta′bi·liz′er** *n.*

sta·ble[1] (stā′bəl) *adj.* **-bler, -blest** 〚< L *stare,* to stand〛 1 not likely to give way; firm; fixed 2 firm in character, purpose, etc.; steadfast 3 not likely to change; lasting

sta·ble[2] (stā′bəl) *n.* 〚see prec.〛 1 a building in which horses or cattle are sheltered and fed 2 all the racehorses belonging to one owner — *vt., vi.* **-bled, -bling** to lodge, keep, or be kept in a stable

stac·ca·to (stə kät′ō) *adj.* 〚It < *distaccare,* detach〛 *Music* with distinct breaks between successive tones

stack (stak) *n.* 〚< ON *stakkr*〛 1 a large, neatly arranged pile of straw, hay, etc. 2 any orderly pile 3 SMOKESTACK 4 [*pl.*] a series of bookshelves, as in a library — *vt.* 1 to arrange in a stack 2 to rig so as to predetermine the outcome —**stack up** to stand in comparison (*with* or *against*)

stack′up′ *n.* an arrangement of circling aircraft at various altitudes awaiting their turn to land

sta·di·um (stā′dē əm) *n.* 〚< Gr *stadion,* ancient unit of length, *c.* 607 ft.〛 a large structure as for football or baseball, with tiers of seats for spectators

staff (staf) *n., pl.* **staffs**; also, for 1 & 4, **staves** 〚OE *stæf*〛 1 a stick or rod used as a support, a symbol of authority, etc. 2 a group of people assisting a leader 3 a specific group of workers [a teaching *staff*] 4 *Music* the horizontal lines on and between which notes are written — *vt.* to provide with a staff, as of workers

staff′er *n.* a member of a staff, as of a newspaper

stag (stag) *n.* 〚OE *stagga*〛 a full-grown male deer — *adj.* for men only [a *stag* dinner] —**go stag** [Colloq.] to go unaccompanied by a date

stage (stāj) *n.* 〚< L *stare,* to stand〛 1 a platform 2 *a)* an area or platform on which plays, etc. are presented *b)* the theater, or acting as a profession (with *the*) 3 the scene of an event 4 a stopping place, or the distance between stops, on a journey 5 *short for* STAGECOACH 6 a period or level in a process of development [the larval *stage*] 7 any of the propulsion units used in sequence to launch a missile, spacecraft, etc. — *vt.* **staged, stag′ing** 1 to present as on a stage 2 to plan and carry out

stage′coach′ *n.* a horse-drawn public coach that traveled a regular route

stage′hand′ *n.* one who sets up scenery, furniture, lights, etc. for a stage play

stage′-struck′ *adj.* intensely eager to become an actor or actress

stag·ger (stag′ər) *vi.* 〚< ON *stakra,* totter〛 1 to totter, reel, etc. as from a blow or fatigue — *vt.* 1 to cause to stagger, as with a blow 2 to affect strongly as with grief 3 to set or arrange alternately, as on either side of a line; make zigzag 4 to arrange so as to come at different times [to stagger vacations] — *n.* 1 a staggering 2 [*pl., with sing. v.*] a nervous disease of horses, etc. causing this

stag·nant (stag′nənt) *adj.* 〚see fol.〛 1 not flowing or moving 2 foul from lack of movement, as water 3 dull; sluggish

stag·nate′ (-nāt′) *vi., vt.* **-nat′ed, -nat′ing** 〚< L *stagnare*〛 to become or make stagnant —**stag·na′tion** *n.*

staid (stād) *vi., vt. archaic pt. & pp. of* STAY[3] — *adj.* sober; sedate —**staid′ly** *adv.*

stain (stān) *n.* 〚ult. < L *dis-,* from + *tingere,* to tinge〛 1 to spoil by discoloring or spotting 2 to disgrace; dishonor

---

■ THESAURUS ■

squeal *v.* shout, yell, screech; see CRY 1, 2.

squeamish *a.* finicky, fussy, delicate, hard to please, fastidious, particular, exacting, prim, prudish, queasy.

squeeze *n.* influence, restraint, force; see PRESSURE 1, 2. —**put the squeeze on** compel, urge, use force with; see FORCE, INFLUENCE.

squeeze *v.* clasp, pinch, clutch; see HUG, PRESS 1.

squint *v.* screw up the eyes, peek, peep; see LOOK 2.

squirm *v.* wriggle, twist, fidget; see WIGGLE.

squirt *v.* spurt, spit, eject; see EMIT.

stab *n.* thrust, wound, puncture; see CUT. —**make a stab at** endeavor, try to, do one's best to; see TRY 1.

stab *v.* pierce, wound, stick, cut, hurt, run through, thrust, prick, drive, puncture, hit, bayonet, knife; see also KILL 1.

stability *n.* 1 [Firmness of position] steadiness, durability, solidity, endurance, immobility, suspense, establishment, balance, permanence. 2 [Steadfastness of character] stableness, aplomb, security, endurance, maturity, resoluteness, determination, perserverance, adherence, backbone, assurance, resistance; see also CONFIDENCE.

stable[1] *a.* 1 [Fixed] steady, stationary, solid; see FIRM 1. 2 [Steadfast] calm, firm, constant.

stable[2] *n.* barn, coop, corral; see PEN 1.

stack *n.* pile, heap, mound; see BUNCH.

stack *v.* heap, pile up, accumulate; see LOAD 1. —**stack up** become, work out to, resolve into; see RESULT.

stadium *n.* gymnasium, strand, amphitheater; see ARENA.

staff *n.* 1 [A stick] wand, pole, stave;

see STICK. 2 [A corps of employees] personnel, assistants, men, women, force, help, workers, crew, organization, agents, operatives, deputies, servants.

stage *n.* 1 [The theater] theater, limelight, spotlight; see DRAMA. 2 [A platform] frame, scaffold, staging; see PLATFORM 1. 3 [A level, period, or degree] grade, plane, step; see DEGREE 1. —**by easy stages** easily, gently, taking one's time; see SLOWLY.

stagger *v.* totter, waver, sway, weave, bob, careen, vacillate.

staggering *a.* monstrous, huge, tremendous; see LARGE 1, UNBELIEVABLE.

stagnant *a.* inert, dead, inactive; see IDLE.

stagnate *v.* deteriorate, rot, putrefy; see DECAY.

staid *a.* sober, grave, steady; see DIGNIFIED.

stain *n.* blot, blemish, spot, splotch,

3 to color (wood, etc.) with a dye — *n.* 1 a color or spot resulting from staining 2 a moral blemish 3 a dye for staining wood, etc. —**stain′less** *adj.*

stainless steel steel alloyed with chromium, etc., virtually immune to rust and corrosion

stair (ster) *n.* [OE *stæger*] 1 [*usually pl.*] a staircase 2 a single step, as of a staircase

stair′case′ *n.* a stairway in a building, usually with a handrail

stair′way′ *n.* a means of access, as from one level of a building to another, consisting of a series of stairs

stair′well′ *n.* a vertical shaft (in a building) containing a staircase

stake (stāk) *n.* [OE *staca*] 1 a pointed length of wood or metal for driving into the ground 2 the post to which a person was tied for execution by burning 3 [*often pl.*] money risked, as in a wager, business venture, etc. 4 [*often pl.*] the winner's prize in a race, etc. — *vt.* **staked, stak′ing** 1 to mark the boundaries of [to *stake* out a claim/ 2 to fasten to stakes 3 to gamble 4 [Colloq.] to furnish with money or resources —**at stake** being risked —**pull up stakes** [Colloq.] to change one's residence, etc. —**stake out** to put under police surveillance

sta·lac·tite (stə lak′tīt) *n.* [< Gr *stalaktos*, trickling] an icicle-shaped mineral deposit hanging from a cave roof

sta·lag (shtä′läg) *n.* [Ger] a German prisoner-of-war camp, esp. in World War II

sta·lag·mite (stə lag′mīt′) *n.* [< Gr *stalagmos*, a dropping] a cone-shaped mineral deposit built up on a cave floor by dripping water

stale (stāl) *adj.* **stal′er, stal′est** [prob. < OFr *estale*, quiet] 1 no longer fresh; flat, dry, etc. 2 trite [a *stale* joke/ 3 out of condition, bored, etc. — *vt.*, *vi.* **staled, stal′ing** to make or become stale —**stale′ness** *n.*

stale′mate′ *n.* [< OFr *estal*, fixed location] 1 *Chess* any situation in which a player cannot move, resulting in a draw 2 any deadlock — *vt.* **-mat′ed, -mat′ing** to bring into a stalemate

stalk[1] (stôk) *vi.*, *vt.* [OE *stealcian*] 1 to walk (through) in a stiff, haughty manner 2 to advance grimly 3 to pursue (game, etc.) stealthily — *n.* 1 a slow, stiff, haughty stride 2 a stalking

stalk[2] (stôk) *n.* [ME *stalke*] 1 any stem or stemlike part 2 the main stem of a plant

stall[1] (stôl) *n.* [OE *steall*] 1 a section for one animal in a stable 2 *a*) a booth, etc. as at a market *b*) a pew in a church 3 a stop or standstill, as a result of some malfunction — *vt.*, *vi.* 1 to keep or be kept in a stall 2 to bring or be brought to a standstill, esp. unintentionally

stall[2] (stôl) *vi.*, *vt.* [< *stall*, decoy] to act evasively so as to deceive or delay — *n.* any action used in stalling

stal·lion (stal′yən; *also* stal′ē ən) *n.* [< OFr *estalon*] an uncastrated male horse

stal·wart (stôl′wərt) *adj.* [< OE *stathol*, foundation + *wyrthe*, worth] 1 strong; sturdy 2 brave; valiant 3 resolute; firm — *n.* a stalwart person

sta·men (stā′mən) *n.* [< L, thread] the pollen-bearing organ in a flower

stami·na (stam′ə nə) *n.* [L, pl. of prec.] resistance to fatigue, illness, hardship, etc.; endurance

stam·mer (stam′ər) *vt.*, *vi.* [OE *stamerian*] to speak with involuntary pauses and rapid repetitions of some sounds — *n.* a stammering —**stam′merer** *n.*

stamp (stamp) *vt.* [ME *stampen*] 1 to bring (the foot) down forcibly 2 to crush or pound with the foot 3 to imprint or cut out (a design, etc.) 4 to cut (*out*) by pressing with a die 5 to put a stamp on 6 to characterize — *vi.* 1 to bring down the foot forcibly 2 to walk with loud, heavy steps — *n.* 1 a stamping 2 *a*) a machine, tool, or die for stamping *b*) a mark or form made by stamping 3 any of various seals, gummed pieces of paper, etc. used to show that a fee, as for postage, has been paid 4 any similar stamp /trading *stamp*/ 5 class; kind —**stamp out** 1 to crush by treading on forcibly 2 to suppress, or put down —**stamp′er** *n.*

stam·pede (stam pēd′) *n.* [< Sp *estampar*, to stamp] a sudden, headlong rush or flight, as of a herd of cattle — *vi.* **-ped′ed, -ped′ing** to move, or take part, in a stampede

stamping ground [Colloq.] a regular or favorite gathering place

stance (stans) *n.* [< L *stare*, to stand] 1 the way one stands, esp. the placement of the feet 2 the attitude taken in a given situation

stanch (stônch, stanch) *vt.*, *vi.*, *adj.* *see* STAUNCH

stan·chion (stan′chən) *n.* [see STANCE] 1 an upright post or support 2 a device to confine a cow

stand (stand) *vi.* **stood, stand′ing** [OE *standan*] 1 to be in, or assume, an upright position on the feet 2 to be supported on a base, pedestal, etc. 3 to take or be in a (specified) position, attitude, etc. 4 to have a (specified) height when standing 5 to be placed or situated 6 to gather and remain, as water 7 to remain unchanged 8 to make resistance 9 *a*) to halt *b*) to be stationary — *vt.* 1 to place upright 2 to endure 3 to withstand 4 to undergo /to *stand* trial/ — *n.* 1 a standing; esp., a halt or stop 2 a position; station 3 a view, opinion, etc. 4 a structure to stand or sit on 5 a place of business 6 a rack, small table, etc. for holding things 7 a growth of trees, etc. —**stand a chance** to have a chance —**stand by** 1 to be near and ready if needed 2 to aid —**stand for** 1 to represent 2 [Colloq.] to tolerate —**stand off** to keep at a distance —**stand on** 1 to be founded on 2 to insist upon —**stand out** 1 to project 2 to be distinct, prominent, etc. —**stand up** 1 to rise to a standing position 2 to prove valid, durable, etc. 3 [Slang] to fail to keep a date with —**take the stand** to testify in court —**stand′er** *n.*

stand·ard (stan′dərd) *n.* [< OFr *estendard*] 1 a flag or banner used as an emblem of a military unit, etc. 2 something established for use as a rule or basis of comparison in measuring quantity, quality, etc. 3 an upright support — *adj.* 1 used as, or conforming to, a standard, rule, model, etc. 2 generally accepted as reliable or authoritative 3 typical; ordinary

stand′ard-bear′er *n.* 1 one who carries the flag 2 the leader of a movement, political party, etc.

stand′ard·ize′ *vt.* **-ized′, -iz′ing** to make standard or uniform —**stand′ardi·za′tion** *n.*

standard time the time in any of the 24 time zones, each an hour apart, into which the earth is divided, based on distance east or west of Greenwich, England

---

THESAURUS

stained spot, smudge, stigma, brand, blotch, ink spot, spatter, drip, speck.

stain *v.* spot, discolor, taint; see DIRTY.

stairs *n.* stairway, staircase, flight, steps, stair, escalator, ascent.

stake *n.* rod, paling, pale; see STICK.
—**at stake** in danger, risked, involved, implicated, in jeopardy, in question, hazarded, concerned, endangered. —**pull up stakes** depart, move, decamp; see LEAVE 1.

stale *a.* spoiled, dried, smelly; see OLD 2.

stalk[1] *v.* approach stealthily, track, chase; see HUNT 1, PURSUE 1.

stalk[2] *n.* stem, support, upright, spire, shaft, pole, straw, stock.

stall[1,2] *v.* 1 [To break down] not start, conk out, go dead; see BREAK DOWN 2. 2 [To delay] postpone, hamper, hinder; see DELAY.

stamina *n.* strength, vigor, vitality; see ENDURANCE.

stammer *v.* falter, stop, stumble, hesitate, pause, stutter, repeat oneself, hem and haw; see also SPEAK 1.

stamp *n.* emblem, brand, cast; see MARK 1.

stamp *v.* impress, imprint, brand; see MARK 1. —**stamp out** eliminate, kill off, dispatch; see DESTROY.

stamped *a.* marked, branded, okayed; see APPROVED.

stampede *n.* rush, dash, flight; see RUN 1.

stampede *v.* bolt, rush, panic; see RUN 2.

stand *n.* notion, view, belief; see ATTITUDE, OPINION 1. —**make** (or **take**) **a stand** insist, assert, take a position; see DECLARE.

stand *v.* 1 [To be in an upright position] be erect, be on one's feet, stand up, come to one's feet, rise, jump up. 2 [To endure] last, hold, abide; see ENDURE 1. 3 [To be of a certain height] be, attain, come to; see REACH

1. —**stand a chance** have a chance, be a possibility, have something in one's favor, have something on one's side, be preferred. —**stand by** 1 [To defend or help] befriend, second, abet; see DEFEND 2, HELP. 2 [To wait] be prepared, be ready, be near; see WAIT 1. —**stand for** 1 [To mean] represent, suggest, imply; see MEAN 1. 2 [To allow] permit, suffer, endure; see ALLOW. —**stand out** be prominent, be conspicuous, emerge; see LOOM 2.

standard *a.* regular, regulation, made to a standard; see APPROVED.

standard *n.* pattern, type, example; see MODEL 2.

standardization *n.* uniformity, sameness, likeness, evenness, levelness, monotony; see also REGULARITY.

standardize *v.* regulate, institute, normalize; see ORDER 3, SYSTEMATIZE.

standardized *a.* patterned, graded, made alike; see REGULATED.

stand′by′ *n., pl.* **-bys′** a person or thing that is dependable or a possible substitute

standee (stan dē′) *n.* one who stands, as in a theater, bus, etc.

stand′-in′ *n.* a temporary substitute, as for an actor at rehearsals

stand′ing *n.* **1** status or reputation *[in good standing]* **2** duration *[a rule of long standing]* —*adj.* **1** upright or erect **2** from a standing position *[a standing jump]* **3** stagnant, as water **4** lasting; permanent *[a standing order]* **5** not in use

stand′off′ *n.* a tie in a contest

stand′off′ish *adj.* reserved; aloof

stand′point′ *n.* point of view

stand′still′ *n.* a stop or halt

stand′-up′ *adj.* **1** in a standing position **2** specializing in monologues made up of jokes, as a comedian

stank (staŋk) *vi. alt. pt. of* STINK

stanza (stan′zə) *n.* [It: ult. < L *stare*, to stand] a group of lines of verse forming a division of a poem or song

staph (staf) *n. short for* STAPHYLOCOCCUS

staphy·lo·coc·cus (staf′ə lō kä′kəs) *n., pl.* **-coc′ci** (-käk′sī′) [< Gr *staphylē*, bunch of grapes + *kokkos*, kernel] any of certain spherical bacteria, in clusters or chains

sta·ple¹ (stā′pəl) *n.* [< MDu *stapel*, mart] **1** a chief commodity made or grown in a particular place **2** raw material **3** a regularly stocked item of trade, as flour, salt, etc. **4** the fiber of cotton, wool, etc. —*adj.* **1** regularly stocked, produced, or used **2** most important; principal

sta·ple² (stā′pəl) *n.* [OE *stapol*, a post] a U-shaped piece of metal with sharp ends, driven into wood, etc. as to hold a hook, wire, etc., or through papers as a binding —*vt.* **-pled, -pling** to fasten or bind with a staple or staples — **sta′pler** *n.*

star (stär) *n.* [OE *steorra*] **1** any of the luminous celestial objects seen as points of light in the sky; esp., any far-off, self-luminous one **2** such an object regarded as influencing one's fate **3** a conventionalized figure with five or six points, or anything like this **4** ASTERISK **5** one who excels, as in a sport **6** a leading actor or actress —*vt.* **starred, star′ring 1** to mark with stars as a decoration, etc. **2** to present (an actor or actress) in a leading role —*vi.* **1** to perform brilliantly **2** to perform as a star, as in films —*adj.* **1** having great skill; outstanding **2** of a star —*star′less adj.*

star·board (stär′bərd, -bôrd′) *n.* [< OE *steoran*, to steer (rudder formerly on right side) + *bord*, side (of ship)] the right-hand side of a ship, etc. as one faces forward —*adj.* of or on this side

starch (stärch) *n.* [< OE *stearc*, stiff] **1** a white, tasteless, odorless food substance found in potatoes, cereals, etc. **2** a powdered form of this, used in laundering for stiffening cloth, etc. —*vt.* to stiffen as with starch —**starch′y, -i·er, -i·est, adj.**

star·dom (stär′dəm) *n.* the status of a star, as of films

stare (ster) *vi.* **stared, star′ing** [OE *starian*] to gaze steadily and intently —*vt.* to look fixedly at —*n.* a steady, intent look —**star′er** *n.*

star′fish′ *n., pl.* **-fish′** or (for different species) **-fish′es** a small, star-shaped sea animal

star′gaze′ *vi.* **-gazed′, -gaz′ing 1** to gaze at the stars **2** to indulge in dreamy thought —**star′gaz′er** *n.*

stark (stärk) *adj.* [OE *stearc*] **1** rigid, as a corpse **2** sharply outlined **3** bleak; desolate **4** sheer; downright —*adv.* utterly; wholly

stark′-nak′ed *adj.* entirely naked

star·let (stär′lit) *n.* a young actress being promoted as a future star

star′light′ *n.* light given by the stars —**star′lit′** (-lit′) *adj.*

star·ling (stär′liŋ) *n.* [OE *stær*] any of an Old World family of birds; esp., the **common starling** with iridescent plumage, introduced into the U.S.

star′ry *adj.* **-rier, -ri·est 1** shining; bright **2** lighted by or full of stars

star′ry-eyed′ *adj.* with sparkling eyes

Stars and Stripes *name for* the U.S. flag

star′-span′gled *adj.* studded or spangled with stars

Star-Spangled Banner the U.S. national anthem

start (stärt) *vi.* [OE *styrtan*] **1** to make a sudden or involuntary move **2** to go into action or motion; begin; commence **3** to spring into being, activity, etc. —*vt.* **1** to flush (game) **2** to displace, loosen, etc. *[to start a seam]* **3** *a)* to begin to play, do, etc. *b)* to set into motion, action, etc. **4** to cause to be an entrant in a race, etc. —*n.* **1** a sudden, startled reaction or movement **2** a starting, or beginning **3** *a)* a place or time of beginning *b)* a lead or other advantage **4** an opportunity of beginning a career — **start out** (or **off**) to start a journey, project, etc. — **start′er** *n.*

star·tle (stärt′'l) *vt.* **-tled, -tling** [< ME *sterten*, to start] to surprise, frighten, or alarm suddenly; esp., to cause to start —*vi.* to be startled

starve (stärv) *vi.* **starved, starv′ing** [< OE *steorfan*, to die] **1** to die from lack of food **2** to suffer from hunger **3** to suffer great need: with *for* —*vt.* **1** to cause to starve **2** to force by starvation —**star·va·tion** (stär vā′shən) *n.*

starve′ling (-liŋ) *n.* a person or animal that is weak from lack of food

Star Wars [from a film title] [Colloq.] a proposed defense system of space-based weapons for destroying missiles

stash (stash) *vt.* [< ?] [Colloq.] to put or hide away (money, etc.) —*n.* [Colloq.] **1** a place for hiding things **2** something hidden away

-stat (stat) *combining form* a device or agent that keeps something (specified) stationary *[thermostat]*

state (stāt) *n.* [< L *stare*, to stand] **1** a set of circumstances, etc. characterizing a person or thing; condition **2** condition as regards structure, form, etc. **3** rich display; pomp **4** *[sometimes* S-*]* a body of people politically organized under one government; nation **5** *[usually* S-*]* any of the political units forming a federal government, as in the U.S. **6** civil government *[church and state]* —*adj.* **1** formal; ceremonial **2** *[sometimes* S-*]* of the government or of a state —*vt.* **stat′ed, stat′ing 1** to establish by specifying **2** *a)* to set forth in words *b)* to express nonverbally —**in a state** [Colloq.] in an excited condition —**lie in state** to be displayed formally before burial —**the States** the United States

state′hood′ (-hood′) *n.* the condition of being a state

THESAURUS

standby *n.* upholder, supporter, advocate; see PATRON, PROTECTOR.

stand-in *n.* double, second, understudy; see SUBSTITUTE.

standing *n.* position, status, reputation; see RANK 3.

standoff *n.* stalemate, deadlock, dead end; see DELAY.

standoffish *a.* cool, aloof, distant; see INDIFFERENT.

standpoint *n.* attitude, point of view, station; see OPINION 1.

standstill *n.* stop, halt, cessation; see DELAY.

star *n.* **1** [A luminous heavenly body] sun, astral body, pulsar, quasar, fixed star, variable star. *Familiar stars include the following—individual stars:* Betelgeuse, Sirius, Vega, Spica, Arcturus, Aldebaran, Antares, Atlas, Castor, Pollux, Capella, Algol, North Star or Polaris; *constellations:* Great Bear or Ursa Major, Little Bear or Ursa Minor, Great Dipper, Little Dipper, Orion, Coma Berenices or Berenice's Hair, The Gemini or Castor and Pollux, Cassiopeia, Pleiades, Hyades, Taurus, Canis Major or the Great Dog, Canis Minor or the Little Dog, Scorpion, Sagittarius, Corona Borealis or the Northern Crown, Pegasus, Leo, Hercules, Boötes, Cetus, Aquila or the Eagle, Cygnus or the Swan, Corona Australis or the Southern Crown, the Southern Cross. **2** [A conventional figure] asterisk, six-pointed star, five-pointed star; see FORM 1. **3** [A superior performer] headliner, leading lady, leading man, movie actor, movie actress, actor, actress, matinee idol, chief attraction.

stare *v.* gaze, gawk, look fixedly; see LOOK 2, WATCH.

stark-naked *a.* nude, without a stitch of clothing, in the altogether; see NAKED 1.

start *n.* inception, commencement, beginning; see ORIGIN 2.

start *v.* commence, rise, spring; see BEGIN 1, 2.

started *a.* evoked, initiated, instituted; see BEGUN.

startle *v.* alarm, shock, astonish; see SURPRISE.

starvation *n.* deprivation, need, want; see HUNGER.

starve *v.* famish, crave, perish; see DIE.

starving *a.* famished, weakening, dying; see HUNGRY.

state *n.* **1** [A sovereign unit] republic, land, kingdom; see NATION 1. **2** [A condition] circumstance, situation, welfare, phase, case, station, nature, estate, footing, status, standing, occurrence, occasion, eventuality, element, requirement, category, standing, reputation, environment, chances, outlook, position. —**in a state** disturbed, upset, badly off; see TROUBLED.

state *v.* pronounce, assert, affirm; see DECLARE.

state'house' *n.* [*often* S-] the official legislative meeting place of each U.S. State

state'less *adj.* having no state or nationality

state'ly *adj.* -lier, -li·est **1** imposing; majestic **2** slow, dignified, etc. —**state'li·ness** *n.*

state'ment *n.* **1** *a*) a stating *b*) a declaration, assertion, etc. **2** *a*) a financial account *b*) a bill; invoice

state of the art the current level of sophistication of a developing technology, as of computer science —**state'-of-the-art'** *adj.*

state'room' *n.* a private room on a ship or train

state'side' *adj.* [Colloq.] of or in the U.S. (as viewed from abroad) —*adv.* [Colloq.] in or to the U.S.

states'man *n.,* pl. **-men** one who is wise or experienced in the business of government —**states'man·ship'** *n.*

static (stat'ik) *adj.* [< Gr *statikos,* causing to stand] **1** of masses, forces, etc. at rest or in equilibrium **2** at rest; inactive **3** of or producing stationary electrical charges, as from friction **4** of or having to do with static —*n.* **1** atmospheric electrical discharges causing noise on radio or TV **2** such noise **3** [Slang] adverse criticism —**stat'i·cally** *adv.*

sta·tion (stā'shən) *n.* [< L *stare,* to stand] **1** the place where a person or thing stands or is located, esp. an assigned post **2** a regular stopping place, as on a bus line or railroad **3** social standing **4** *a*) a place equipped for radio or TV transmission *b*) its assigned frequency or channel —*vt.* to assign to a station

sta·tion·ar·y (stā'shə ner'ē) *adj.* **1** not moving; fixed **2** unchanging

station break a pause in radio or TV programs for station identification

sta·tion·er (stā'shə nər) *n.* [< ML *stationarius,* shopkeeper] a dealer in stationery, office supplies, etc.

sta'tion·er'y (-ner'ē) *n.* writing materials; specif., paper and envelopes

station wagon an automobile with extra space for cargo or seating and a rear door for loading

sta·tis·tics (stə tis'tiks) *n.pl.* [< L *status,* standing] **1** numerical data assembled and classified so as to present significant information **2** [*with sing. v.*] the science of compiling such data —**sta·tis'ti·cal** *adj.* —**stat·is·ti·cian** (stat'is tish'ən) *n.*

stats (stats) *n.pl.* [Colloq.] *short for* STATISTICS (sense 1)

statu·ar·y (stach'ōō er'ē) *n.* statues collectively

statue (stach'ōō) *n.* [< L *statuere,* to set] a figure, as of a person, or an abstract form carved in stone, cast in bronze, etc.

stat'u·esque' (-esk') *adj.* of or like a statue; specif., *a*) tall *b*) dignified

stat'u·ette' (-et') *n.* a small statue

stat·ure (stach'ər) *n.* [< L *statura*] **1** standing height, esp. of a person **2** level of attainment [moral *stature*]

sta·tus (stat'əs, stāt'-) *n.,* pl. **-tuses** [L, standing] **1** legal condition [the *status* of a minor] **2** position; rank **3** state, as of affairs

status quo (kwō') [L, the state in which] the existing state of affairs

status symbol a possession regarded as a mark of (high) social status

stat·ute (stach'ōōt) *n.* [see STATUE] **1** an established rule **2** a law passed by a legislative body

statute of limitations a statute limiting the time for legal action

statu·tory (stach'ōō tôr'ē) *adj.* **1** fixed or authorized by statute **2** punishable by statute, as an offense

staunch (stônch, stänch) *vt.* [< L *stare,* to stand] to check the flow of (blood, etc.) from (a cut, etc.) —*vi.* to stop flowing —*adj.* **1** seaworthy **2** steadfast; loyal **3** strong; solid Also, esp. for v., **stanch** —**staunch'ly** *adv.*

stave (stāv) *n.* [< *staves,* pl. of STAFF] **1** any of the shaped strips of wood forming the wall of a barrel, bucket, etc. **2** a stick or staff **3** a stanza —*vt.* **staved** or **stove, stav'ing** to puncture, as by breaking in staves —**stave off** to hold off or put off

staves (stāvz) *n.* **1** *alt. pl. of* STAVE **2** *pl. of* STAVE

stay¹ (stā) *n.* [OE *stæg*] a heavy rope or cable, used as a brace or support

stay² (stā) *n.* [Fr *estaie*] **1** a support or prop **2** a strip of stiffening material used in a corset, shirt collar, etc. —*vt.* to support, or prop up

stay³ (stā) *vi.* **stayed, stay'ing** [< L *stare,* to stand] **1** to continue in the place or condition specified; remain **2** to live; dwell **3** to stop; halt **4** to pause; delay **5** [Colloq.] to continue; last —*vt.* **1** to stop or check **2** to hinder or detain **3** to postpone (legal action) **4** to satisfy (thirst, etc.) for a time **5** *a*) to remain to the end of *b*) to be able to last through —*n.* **1** *a*) a stopping or being stopped *b*) a halt or pause **2** a postponement in legal action **3** the action of remaining, or the time spent, in a place —**stay put** [Colloq.] to remain in place or unchanged

staying power ability to last or endure; endurance

STD sexually transmitted disease

Ste. [Fr *Sainte*] Saint (female)

stead (sted) *n.* [OE *stede*] the place of a person or thing as filled by a substitute —**stand someone in good stead** to give someone good service

stead·fast (sted'fast') *adj.* [OE *stedefæste*] **1** firm; fixed **2** constant —**stead'fast'ly** *adv.*

steady (sted'ē) *adj.* -i·er, -i·est [STEADY + -Y²] **1** firm; stable; not shaky **2** constant, regular, or uniform **3** constant in behavior, loyalty, etc. **4** calm and controlled [*steady* nerves] **5** sober; reliable —*vt., vi.* **-ied, -y·ing** to make or become steady —*n.* [Colloq.] a sweetheart —*adv.* in a steady manner —**go steady** [Colloq.] to date someone exclusively —**stead'i·ly** *adv.*

steady-state theory the theory that new matter is continuously being created, thus keeping the density of the expanding universe constant

steak (stāk) *n.* [< ON *steikja,* to roast on a spit] a slice of meat, esp. beef, or of fish, for broiling or frying

steal (stēl) *vt.* **stole, stol'en, steal'ing** [OE *stælan*] **1** to take (another's property, etc.) dishonestly, esp. in a secret manner **2** to take (a look, etc.) slyly **3** to gain insidiously

---

THESAURUS

stately *a.* **1** [*Said of persons*] dignified, haughty, noble; see PROUD 1. **2** [*Said of objects*] large, imposing, magnificent; see GRAND.

statement *n.* **1** [The act of stating] allegation, declaration, assertion, profession, acknowledgment, assurance, affirmation; see also ANNOUNCEMENT. **2** [A statement of account] bill, charge, reckoning, account, record, report, budget, audit, balance sheet, tab*, check.

statesman *n.* legislator, lawgiver, administrator, executive, minister, official, politician, diplomat, representative, elder statesman, veteran lawmaker.

station *n.* **1** [Place] situation, site, location; see POSITION 1. **2** [Depot] terminal, stop, stopping place; see DEPOT. **3** [Social position] order, standing, state; see RANK 3. **4** [An establishment to vend petroleum products] gas station, gasoline station, service station, filling station, petrol station, pumps, petroleum retailer; see also GARAGE. **5** [A broadcasting establishment] television station, radio station, television

transmission, radio transmission, microwave transmitter, television transmitter, radio transmitter, broadcasting station, studios, channel; see also COMMUNICATIONS, RADIO, TELEVISION.

station *v.* place, commission, allot; see ASSIGN.

stationary *a.* fixed, stable, permanent; see MOTIONLESS 1.

stationery *n.* writing materials, office supplies, school supplies; see PAPER 4.

statue *n.* statuette, cast, figure, bust, representation, likeness, image, sculpture, statuary, marble, bronze, ivory, icon.

statuesque *a.* stately, beautiful, grand; see GRACEFUL 2.

stature *n.* development, growth, tallness; see HEIGHT, SIZE 2.

status *n.* situation, standing, station; see RANK 3.

staunch *a.* steadfast, strong, constant; see FAITHFUL.

stay¹,²,³ *n.* **1** [A support] prop, hold, truss; see SUPPORT 2. **2** [A visit] stop, sojourn, halt; see VISIT.

stay³ *v.* tarry, linger, sojourn; see VISIT. —**stay put*** remain, stand still, persist; see WAIT 1.

steadfast *a.* staunch, stable, constant; see FAITHFUL.

steadily *a.* firmly, unwaveringly, undeviatingly; see REGULARLY.

steady *a.* uniform, unvarying, patterned; see CONSTANT, REGULAR 3. — **go steady (with)*** keep company with, court, go together; see COURT, LOVE 1, 2.

steak *n.* filet mignon, sirloin, T-bone; see FOOD, MEAT.

steal *v.* take, filch, thieve, loot, rob, purloin, embezzle, defraud, keep, carry off, appropriate, take possession of, lift, remove, impress, abduct, shanghai, kidnap, run off with, hold up, strip, poach, swindle, plagiarize, misappropriate, burglarize, blackmail, fleece, plunder, pillage, ransack, burgle*, stick up*, hijack*, skyjack*, pinch*, mooch*, gyp*; see also SEIZE 2.

stealing *n.* piracy, embezzlement, shoplifting; see CRIME, THEFT.

or artfully *[he stole her heart]* 4 to move, put, etc. stealthily (*in, from*, etc.) 5 *Baseball* to gain (a base), as by running to it from another base while the pitch is being delivered — *vi.* 1 to be a thief 2 to move, etc. stealthily — *n.* [Colloq.] an extraordinary bargain

stealth (stelth) *n.* ⟦< ME *stelen*, to steal⟧ secret or furtive action —**stealth'y** *adj.* —**stealth'i·ly** *adv.*

steam (stēm) *n.* ⟦OE⟧ 1 water as converted into a vapor by being heated to the boiling point 2 the power of steam under pressure 3 condensed water vapor 4 [Colloq.] vigor; energy — *adj.* using, or operated by, steam — *vi.* 1 to give off steam 2 to become covered with condensed steam 3 to move by steam power — *vt.* to expose to steam, as in cooking —**steam'y, -i·er, -i·est,** *adj.*

steam'boat' *n.* a small steamship

steam engine an engine using steam under pressure to supply mechanical energy

steam'er *n.* 1 something operated by steam, as a steamship 2 a container for cooking, cleaning, etc. with steam

steam'fit'ter *n.* one whose work is installing boilers, pipes, etc. in steam-pressure systems —**steam'fit'ting** *n.*

steam'roll'er *n.* a heavy, steam-driven roller used in building roads — *vt., vi.* to move, crush, override, etc. as (with) a steamroller

steam'ship' *n.* a ship driven by steam power

steam shovel a large, mechanically operated digger, powered by steam

steed (stēd) *n.* ⟦OE *steda*⟧ a horse

steel (stēl) *n.* ⟦OE *stiele*⟧ 1 a hard, tough alloy of iron with carbon 2 a thing of steel 3 great strength or hardness — *adj.* of or like steel — *vt.* to make hard, tough, etc. —**steel'y, -i·er, -i·est,** *adj.*

steel wool long, thin shavings of steel in a pad, used for scouring, polishing, etc.

steel'yard' (-yärd') *n.* ⟦STEEL + obs. *yard*, rod⟧ a balance or scale consisting of a metal arm suspended from above

steep[1] (stēp) *adj.* ⟦OE *steap*, lofty⟧ 1 having a sharp rise or slope; precipitous 2 [Colloq.] excessive; extreme — **steep'ly** *adv.* —**steep'ness** *n.*

steep[2] (stēp) *vt.* ⟦ME *stepen*⟧ to soak, saturate, imbue, etc.

stee·ple (stē'pəl) *n.* ⟦OE *stepel*⟧ 1 a tower rising above the main structure, as of a church 2 a spire

stee'ple·chase' *n.* a horse race run over a course obstructed with ditches, hedges, etc.

stee'ple·jack' *n.* one who builds or repairs steeples, smokestacks, etc.

steer[1] (stir) *vt., vi.* ⟦OE *stieran*⟧ 1 to guide (a ship, etc.) with a rudder 2 to direct the course of (an automobile, etc.) 3 to follow (a course) —**steer clear of** to avoid — **steer'able** *adj.*

steer[2] (stir) *n.* ⟦OE *steor*⟧ 1 a full-grown, castrated male of cattle 2 loosely, any male of beef cattle

steer·age (stir'ij) *n.* 1 a steering 2 [Historical] a section in a ship for the passengers paying the lowest fare

steers·man (stirz'mən) *n., pl.* **-men** one who steers a ship; helmsman

stego·sau·rus (steg'ə sôr'əs) *n., pl.* **-ri** (-ī) ⟦< Gr *stegos*, roof + *sauros*, lizard⟧ a large dinosaur with pointed, bony plates along the backbone

stein (stīn) *n.* ⟦Ger⟧ a beer mug

stel·lar (stel'ər) *adj.* ⟦< L *stella*, a star⟧ 1 of a star 2 excellent 3 leading; chief *[a stellar role]*

stem[1] (stem) *n.* ⟦OE *stemn*⟧ 1 the main stalk of a plant 2 any stalk or part supporting leaves, flowers, or fruit 3 a

stemlike part, as of a pipe, goblet, etc. 4 the prow of a ship; bow 5 the part of a word to which inflectional endings are added — *vt.* **stemmed, stem'ming** to make headway against *[to stem the tide]* — *vi.* to derive

stem[2] (stem) *vt.* **stemmed, stem'ming** ⟦< ON *stemma*⟧ to stop or check by or as if by damming up

stem'ware' *n.* goblets, wineglasses, etc. having stems

stench (stench) *n.* ⟦< OE *stincan*, to stink⟧ an offensive smell; stink

sten·cil (sten'səl) *vt.* **-ciled** or **-cilled, -cil·ing** or **-cil·ling** ⟦ult. < L *scintilla*, a spark⟧ to make or mark with a stencil — *n.* 1 a thin sheet, as of paper, cut through so that when ink, etc. is applied, designs, letters, etc. form on the surface beneath 2 a design, etc. so made

ste·nog·ra·phy (stə näg'rə fē) *n.* shorthand writing, as of dictation, testimony, etc., for later transcription —**ste·nog'ra·pher** *n.* —**steno·graphic** (sten'ə graf'ik) *adj.*

sten·to·rian (sten tôr'ē ən) *adj.* ⟦after *Stentor*, Gr herald in the *Iliad*⟧ very loud

step (step) *n.* ⟦OE *stepe*⟧ 1 a single movement of the foot, as in walking 2 the distance covered by such a movement 3 a short distance 4 a manner of stepping 5 the sound of stepping 6 a rest for the foot in climbing, as a stair 7 a degree; level; stage 8 any of a series of acts, processes, etc. — *vi.* **stepped, step'ping** 1 to move by executing a step 2 to walk a short distance 3 to move briskly (*along*) 4 to enter (*into* a situation, etc.) 5 to press the foot down (*on*) — *vt.* to measure by taking steps: with *off* —**in** (or **out of**) **step** (not) conforming to a rhythm, a regular procedure, etc. —**step up** 1 to advance 2 to increase, as in rate — **take steps** to do the things needed —**step'per** *n.*

step'broth'er *n.* one's stepparent's son by a former marriage

step'child' *n., pl.* **-chil'dren** ⟦< OE *steop-*, orphaned + *cild*, child⟧ one's spouse's child (**stepdaughter** or **stepson**) by a former marriage

step'-down' *n.* a decrease, as in amount, intensity, etc.

step'lad'der *n.* a four-legged ladder with broad, flat steps

step'par'ent *n.* the person (**stepfather** or **stepmother**) who has married one's parent after the death of or divorce from the other parent

steppe (step) *n.* ⟦Russ *styep'*⟧ any of the great plains of SE Europe and Asia, having few trees

step'ping·stone' *n.* 1 a stone to step on, as in crossing a stream 2 a means of bettering oneself

step'sis'ter *n.* one's stepparent's daughter by a former marriage

step'-up' *n.* an increase, as in amount, intensity, etc.

-ster (stər) ⟦OE *-estre*⟧ *suffix* one who is, does, creates, or is associated with (something specified) *[trickster, gangster]*

stereo (ster'ē ō') *n., pl.* **-os'** 1 a stereophonic device, system, effect, etc. 2 a stereoscopic system, effect, picture, etc. — *adj.* short for STEREOPHONIC

stereo- ⟦< Gr *stereos*, solid⟧ *combining form* solid, firm, three-dimensional *[stereoscope]*

stereo·phonic (ster'ē ə fän'ik) *adj.* designating or of sound reproduction using two or more channels to carry a blend of sounds from separate sources through separate speakers

ster'eo·scope' (-skōp') *n.* an instrument with two eyepieces that gives a three-dimensional effect to photographs viewed through it

ster'eo·type' (-tīp') *n.* ⟦see STEREO- & -TYPE⟧ 1 a printing plate cast from a mold, as a page of set type 2 a fixed

THESAURUS

steam *n.* vaporized water, fumes, fog; see VAPOR.

steam *v.* heat, brew, pressure cook; see COOK.

steamboat *n.* steamer, steamship, liner; see BOAT, SHIP.

steep[1] *a.* precipitous, sudden, sharp, angular, craggy, uneven, rough, rugged, irregular, jagged, vertical, uphill, downhill, abrupt, sheer, perpendicular.

steer[1] *v.* point, head for, direct; see DRIVE 2. —**steer clear of** stay away from, miss, escape; see AVOID.

stem[1] *n.* peduncle, petiole, pedice; see STALK. —**from stem to stern** the full length, completely, entirely; see EVERYWHERE, THROUGHOUT.

stench *n.* odor, stink, foulness; see

SMELL 2.

stenographer *n.* office girl, typist, shorthand stenographer; see CLERK, SECRETARY.

step *n.* 1 [A movement of the foot] pace, stride, gait, footfall, tread, stepping. 2 [One degree in a graded rise] rest, run, tread, round, rung, level. 3 [The print of a foot] footprint, footmark, print, imprint, impression, footstep, trail, trace, mark; see also TRACK 2. —**in step (with)** in agreement with, coinciding with, similar to; see ALIKE, SIMILARLY. —**keep step** agree with, conform to, keep in line; see CONFORM. —**out of step** inappropriate, incorrect, inaccurate; see WRONG 2, WRONGLY. —**step by step** by degrees, cautiously, tenta-

tively; see SLOWLY. —**take steps** do something, start, intervene; see ACT 1. —**watch one's step** be careful, take precautions, look out; see WATCH OUT.

step *v.* pace, stride, advance, recede, go forward, go backward, go up, go down, ascend, descend, pass, walk, march, move, hurry, hop; see also CLIMB, RISE 1. —**step up** augment, improve, intensify; see INCREASE.

steppingstone *n.* help, agent, factor; see MEANS 1.

stereotype *n.* convention, fashion, institution; see AVERAGE, CUSTOM.

stereotype *v.* conventionalize, standardize, normalize; see REGULATE 2, SYSTEMATIZE.

or conventional notion or conception — *vt.* **-typed′, -typ′ing** to make a stereotype of — **ster′eo·typed′** *adj.*

ster·ile (ster′əl) *adj.* [[L *sterilis*]] **1** incapable of producing offspring, fruit, etc.; barren **2** free from living microorganisms — **ste·ril·i·ty** (stə ril′ ə tē) *n.*

ster′i·lize′ (-ə līz′) *vt.* **-lized′, -liz′ing** to make sterile; specif., *a)* to make incapable of reproduction *b)* to free from living microorganisms — **ster′i·li·za′tion** *n.* — **ster′i·liz′er** *n.*

ster·ling (stur′liŋ) *n.* [[ME *sterlinge*, Norman coin]] **1** sterling silver **2** British money — *adj.* **1** of silver that is at least 92.5 percent pure **2** of British money **3** made of sterling silver **4** excellent [*sterling* principles]

stern[1] (sturn) *adj.* [[OE *styrne*]] **1** severe; strict [*stern* measures] **2** grim [a *stern* face] **3** relentless; firm — **stern′ly** *adv.* —**stern′ness** *n.*

stern[2] (sturn) *n.* [[< ON *styra*, to steer]] the rear end of a ship, etc.

ster·num (stur′nəm) *n.,* pl. **-nums** or **-na** (-nə) [[< Gr *sternon*]] a flat, bony structure to which most of the ribs are attached in the front of the chest; breastbone

ster·oid (stir′oid′, ster′-) *n.* [[< (CHOLE)STER(OL) + -OID]] any of a group of compounds including the bile acids, sex hormones, etc.,

ster·to·rous (stur′tər əs) *adj.* [[< L *stertere*, to snore]] characterized by raspy, labored breathing

stet (stet) *v.* [[L]] let it stand: printer's term indicating that matter marked for deletion is to remain — *vt.* **stet′ted, stet′ting** to mark with "stet"

stetho·scope (steth′ə skōp′) *n.* [[< Gr *stēthos*, chest + -SCOPE]] *Med.* an instrument used to examine the heart, lungs, etc. by listening to the sounds they make

ste·vedore (stē′və dôr′) *n.* [[ult. < L *stipare*, cram]] one whose work is loading and unloading ships

stew (stōō, styōō) *vt., vi.* [[ult. < L *ex-*, out + Gr *typhos*, steam]] **1** to cook by simmering or boiling slowly **2** to worry — *n.* **1** a dish, esp. of meat and vegetables, cooked by stewing **2** a state of worry

stew·ard (stōō′ərd, styōō′-) *n.* [[< OE *stig*, hall + *weard*, keeper]] **1** a person put in charge of a large estate **2** an administrator, as of finances and property **3** one responsible for the food and drink, etc. in a club, restaurant, etc. **4** an attendant, as on a ship or airplane —**stew′ard·ship′** *n.*

stew′ard·ess (-ər dis) *n.* a woman steward, esp. on an airplane

stick (stik) *n.* [[OE *sticca*]] **1** a twig or small branch broken or cut off **2** a long, slender piece of wood, as a club, cane, etc. **3** any sticklike piece [a *stick* of gum] — *vt.* **stuck, stick′ing 1** to pierce, as with a pointed instrument **2** to pierce with (a knife, pin, etc.) **3** to thrust (*in, into, out,* etc.) **4** to attach as by gluing, pinning, etc. **5** to obstruct, detain, etc. [the wheels were *stuck*] **6** [Colloq.] to place; put; set **7** [Colloq.] to puzzle; baffle **8** [Slang] *a)* to impose a burden, etc. upon *b)* to defraud — *vi.* **1** to be fixed by a pointed end, as a nail **2** to adhere; cling; remain **3** to persevere [to *stick* at a job] **4** to remain firm and resolute [he *stuck* with us] **5** to become embedded, jammed, etc. **6** to be puzzled **7** to hesitate; scruple [he'll *stick* at nothing] **8** to protrude or project (*out, up,* etc.) — **stick by** to remain loyal to —**stick up for** [Colloq.] to uphold; defend —**the sticks** [Colloq.] the rural districts

stick′er *n.* a person or thing that sticks; specif., a gummed label

stick′-in-the-mud′ *n.* [Colloq.] one who resists change, new ideas, etc.

stickle·back (stik′əl bak′) *n.* a small, bony-plated fish with sharp dorsal spines: the male builds a nest for the female's eggs

stick·ler (stik′lər) *n.* [prob. < ME *stightlen*, to order] **1** one who insists on a certain way of doing things [a *stickler* for discipline] **2** [Colloq.] something difficult to solve

stick′pin′ *n.* an ornamental pin worn in a necktie, on a lapel, etc.

stick shift a gearshift, as on a car, operated manually

stick′up′ *n.* *slang term for* HOLDUP (sense 2)

stick′y *adj.* **-i·er, -i·est 1** that sticks; adhesive **2** [Colloq.] hot and humid **3** [Colloq.] troublesome

stiff (stif) *adj.* [OE *stif*] **1** hard to bend or move; rigid; firm **2** sore or limited in movement: said of joints and muscles **3** not fluid; thick **4** strong; powerful [a *stiff* wind] **5** harsh [*stiff* punishment] **6** difficult [a *stiff* climb] **7** very formal or awkward **8** [Colloq.] high [a *stiff* price] — **stiff′ly** *adv.* —**stiff′ness** *n.*

stiff′-arm′ *vt.* to push (someone) away with one's arm out straight

stiff′en *vt., vi.* to make or become stiff or stiffer —**stiff′ener** *n.*

stiff′-necked′ (-nekt′) *adj.* stubborn

sti·fle (stī′fəl) *vt.* **-fled, -fling** [[< Fr *estouffer*]] **1** to suffocate; smother **2** to suppress; hold back; stop [to *stifle* a sob] — *vi.* to die or suffer from lack of air —**sti′flingly** *adv.*

stigma (stig′mə) *n.,* pl. **-mas** or **stig·ma·ta** (-mät′ə) [[< Gr, lit., a puncture made with a sharp instrument]] **1** a mark of disgrace or reproach **2** a spot on the skin, esp. one that bleeds under certain conditions of nervous tension **3** the upper tip of the pistil of a flower, on which pollen falls and develops —**stig·mat′ic** (-mat′ik) *adj.*

stig′ma·tize′ (-tiz′) *vt.* **-tized′, -tiz′ing 1** to mark with a stigma **2** to mark as disgraceful

stile (stil) *n.* [[< OE *stigan*, to climb]] a step or set of steps used in climbing over a fence or wall

sti·letto (sti let′ō) *n.,* pl. **-tos** or **-toes** [It < L *stilus*, pointed tool]] a small dagger with a slender blade

still[1] (stil) *adj.* [OE *stille*] **1** without sound; silent **2** not moving; stationary **3** tranquil; calm **4** designating or of a single photograph taken from a movie film — *n.* **1** silence; quiet **2** a still photograph — *adv.* **1** at or up to the time indicated **2** even; yet [*still* colder] **3** nevertheless; yet [rich but *still* unhappy] — *conj.* nevertheless; yet — *vt., vi.* to make or become still —**still′ness** *n.*

still[2] (stil) *n.* [[< obs. *still*, to distill]] an apparatus used for distilling liquids, esp. alcoholic liquors

still′birth′ *n.* **1** the birth of a stillborn fetus **2** such a fetus

still′born′ *adj.* dead when born

still life a picture of inanimate objects, as fruit, flowers, etc.

stilt (stilt) *n.* [ME *stilte*] **1** either of a pair of poles fitted with a footrest along its length and used for walking, as in play **2** any of a number of long posts used to hold a building, etc. above ground or out of water

stilted (stil′tid) *adj.* artificially formal or dignified; pompous

---

THESAURUS

stereotyped *a.* hackneyed, trite, ordinary; see CONVENTIONAL 1, 3, DULL 4.

sterile *a.* **1** [Incapable of producing young] infertile, impotent, childless, barren.—*Ant.* FERTILE, productive, potent. **2** [Incapable of producing vegetation] desolate, fallow, waste, desert, arid, dry, barren, unproductive, fruitless, bleak; see also EMPTY. **3** [Scrupulously clean] antiseptic, disinfected, decontaminated, germ-free, sterilized, uninfected, sanitary, pasteurized; see also PURE 2.

sterilize *v.* antisepticize, disinfect, pasteurize; see CLEAN, PURIFY.

stern[1] *a.* rigid, austere, strict; see SEVERE 1.

stew *n.* ragout, goulash, Hungarian goulash, seafood chowder, beef stew, Irish stew, mulligan*, casserole; see also FOOD, SOUP.

stick *n.* shoot, twig, branch, stem,

stalk, rod, wand, staff, stave, walking stick, cane, matchstick, club, baton, drumstick, pole, bludgeon, bat, ruler, stock, cue, mast. —**the sticks*** rural areas, the back country, outlying districts; see COUNTRY 1.

stick *v.* **1** [To remain fastened] adhere, cling, fasten, attach, unite, cohere, hold, stick together, hug, clasp, hold fast.—*Ant.* LOOSEN, let go, fall, come away. **2** [To penetrate with a point] prick, impale, pierce; see PENETRATE. —**stick by (some-one)** be loyal to, stand by, believe in; see SUPPORT 2. —**stick out** jut, show, come through; see PROJECT 1. —**stick up for*** support, aid, fight for; see SUPPORT 2.

stickup* *n.* burglary, robbery, stealing; see CRIME, THEFT.

sticky *a.* ropy, viscous, adherent, sticking, gummy, waxy, pasty, gluey.

stiff *a.* **1** [Not easily bent] solid,

rigid, petrified, firm, tense, unyielding, inflexible, hard, hardened, starched, taut, thick, stubborn, obstinate, unbending, thickened, wooden, steely, frozen, solidified.—*Ant.* SOFT, flexible, softened. **2** [Formal] ungainly, ungraceful, unnatural; see AWKWARD. **3** [Severe] strict, rigorous, exact; see SEVERE 1, 2. **4** [Potent] hard, potent, powerful; see STRONG 4.

stiffen *v.* jelly, harden, starch, petrify, brace, prop, cement, strengthen, thicken, clot, coagulate, solidify, congeal, condense, set, curdle, freeze, cake, crystallize.

stifle *v.* smother, suffocate, extinguish; see CHOKE.

still[1] *a.* **1** [Silent] calm, tranquil, noiseless; see QUIET 3. **2** [Yet] nevertheless, furthermore, however; see BESIDES, BUT 1, YET 1.

stimu·lant (stim′yo͞o lənt) *n.* anything, as a drug, that stimulates

stim′u·late′ (-lāt′) *vt.* **-lat′ed, -lat′ing** [see fol.] to rouse or excite to activity or increased activity —**stim′u·la′tion** *n.*

stim′u·lus (-ləs) *n., pl.* **-li′** (-lī′) [L, a goad] 1 an incentive 2 any action or agent that causes an activity in an organism, organ, etc.

sting (stiŋ) *vt.* **stung, sting′ing** [OE *stingan*] 1 to prick or wound with a sting 2 to cause sudden, pricking pain to 3 to cause to suffer mentally 4 to stimulate suddenly and sharply 5 [Slang] to cheat — *vi.* to cause or feel sharp, smarting pain — *n.* 1 a stinging 2 a pain or wound resulting from stinging 3 a sharp-pointed organ, as in insects and plants, that pricks, wounds, etc. —**sting′er** *n.*

sting′ray′ *n.* a large ray with one or more poisonous spines that can inflict painful wounds

stingy (stin′jē) *adj.* **-gier, -gi·est** [< dial. form of STING] 1 giving or spending grudgingly; miserly 2 less than needed; scanty —**stin′gily** *adv.* —**stin′gi·ness** *n.*

stink (stiŋk) *vi.* **stank** or **stunk, stunk, stink′ing** [OE *stincan*] to give off a strong, unpleasant smell — *n.* a strong, unpleasant smell; stench —**stink′er** *n.*

stint (stint) *vt.* [< OE *styntan*, to blunt] to restrict to a certain quantity, often small — *vi.* to be sparing in giving or using — *n.* 1 restriction; limit 2 an assigned task or period of work —**stint′er** *n.*

sti·pend (stī′pend) *n.* [< L *stips*, small coin + *pendere*, to pay] a regular or fixed payment, as a salary

stip·ple (stip′əl) *vt.* **-pled, -pling** [< Du *stippel*, a speckle] to paint, draw, or engrave in small dots

stipu·late (stip′yo͞o lāt′) *vt.* **-lat′ed, -lat′ing** [< L *stipulari*, to bargain] 1 to arrange definitely 2 to specify as an essential condition of an agreement —**stip′u·la′tion** *n.*

stir (stur) *vt., vi.* **stirred, stir′ring** [OE *styrian*] 1 to move, esp. slightly 2 to rouse from sleep, lethargy, etc.; to make or be active 3 to mix (a liquid, etc.) as by agitating with a spoon 4 to excite the feelings (of) 5 to incite: often with *up* — *n.* 1 a stirring 2 movement; activity 3 excitement; tumult —**stir′rer** *n.*

stir′-fry′ *vt.* **-fried′, -fry′ing** to fry (diced or sliced vegetables, meat, etc.) quickly in a wok while stirring constantly

stir′ring *adj.* 1 active; busy 2 rousing; exciting [*stirring music]*

stir·rup (stur′əp) *n.* [OE *stigrap*] a flat-bottomed ring hung from a saddle and used as a footrest

stitch (stich) *n.* [OE *stice*, a puncture] 1 *a*) a single complete in-and-out movement of a needle in sewing, etc. *b*) a suture 2 a loop, knot, etc. made by stitching 3 a particular kind of stitch or style of stitching 4 a sudden, sharp pain 5 a bit — *vi., vt.* to make stitches (in); sew —**in stitches** laughing uproariously

stitch′ery (-ər ē) *n.* ornamental needlework

stoat (stōt) *n.* [ME *stote*] a large European ermine, esp. in its brown summer coat

stock (stäk) *n.* [OE *stocc*] 1 the trunk of a tree 2 *a*) descent; lineage *b*) a strain, race, etc. of animals or plants 3 a supporting or main part of an implement, etc., as the wooden handle to which the barrel of a rifle is attached 4 [*pl.*] a wooden frame with holes for confining the ankles or wrists, formerly used for punishment 5 raw material 6 water in which meat, fish, etc. has been boiled, used in soups 7 livestock 8 a supply of goods on hand in a store, etc. 9 a certificate representing a share or shares of corporate ownership 10 a stock company or its repertoire — *vt.* 1 to furnish (a farm, shop, etc.) with stock 2 to keep a supply of, as for sale or for future use — *vi.* to put in a stock, or supply: with *up* — *adj.* 1 kept in stock [*stock sizes]* 2 common or trite [*a stock excuse]* 3 that deals with stock 4 relating to a stock company —**in** (or **out of**) **stock** (not) available for sale or use —**take stock** 1 to inventory the stock on hand 2 to make an appraisal —**take** (or **put**) **stock in** to have faith in

stock·ade (stä kād′) *n.* [< Prov *estaca*, a stake] 1 a barrier of stakes driven into the ground side by side, for defense 2 an enclosure, as a fort, made with such stakes

stock′bro′ker *n.* a broker who buys and sells stocks, bonds, etc.

stock car a standard automobile, modified for racing

stock company a theatrical company presenting a repertoire of plays

stock exchange 1 a place where stocks and bonds are bought and sold 2 an association of stockbrokers Also **stock market**

stock′hold′er *n.* one owning stock in a given company

stock·ing (stäk′iŋ) *n.* [< obs. sense of *stock*] a closefitting covering, usually knitted, for the foot and leg

stocking cap a long, tapered knitted cap, often with a tassel at the end

stock′pile′ *n.* a reserve supply of goods, raw material, etc. — *vt., vi.* **-piled′, -pil′ing** to accumulate a stockpile (of)

stock′-still′ *adj.* motionless

stock′y *adj.* **-i·er, -i·est** heavily built; short and thickset —**stock′i·ness** *n.*

stock′yard′ *n.* an enclosure where cattle, hogs, etc. are kept before slaughtering

stodgy (stä′jē) *adj.* **-i·er, -i·est** [< *stodge*, heavy food] 1 dull; uninteresting 2 old-fashioned; conventional —**stodg′i·ness** *n.*

sto·gie or **stogy** (stō′gē) *n., pl.* **-gies** [after *Conestoga* Valley, Pa.] a long, thin, inexpensive cigar

Stoic (stō′ik) *n.* [< Gr *stoa*, a colonnade: where first Stoics met] 1 a member of an ancient Greek school of philosophy 2 [s-] a stoical person — *adj.* [s-] STOICAL —**sto′i·cism′** (-i siz′əm) *n.*

sto′i·cal (-i kəl) *adj.* showing indifference to joy, grief, pleasure, or pain; impassive —**sto′i·cally** *adv.*

stoke (stōk) *vt., vi.* **stoked, stok′ing** [< Du *stoken*, to poke] 1 to stir up and feed fuel to (a fire) 2 to tend (a furnace, boiler, etc.) —**stok′er** *n.*

STOL (stōl) *adj.* [*s(hort) t(ake)o(ff and) l(anding)*] designating or of an aircraft that can take off and land on a short airstrip — *n.* a STOL aircraft, airstrip, etc.

stole¹ (stōl) *n.* [< Gr *stolē*, garment] 1 a long strip of cloth worn about the neck by clergymen at various rites 2 a woman's long scarf of cloth or fur worn around the shoulders

stole² (stōl) *vt., vi. pt. of* STEAL

stolen (stō′lən) *vt., vi. pp. of* STEAL

stolid (stäl′id) *adj.* [L *stolidus*, slow] having or showing little or no emotion; unexcitable —**sto·lid·ity** (stə lid′ə tē) *n.* —**stol′idly** *adv.*

sto·lon (stō′län′) *n.* [< L *stolo*, a shoot] a creeping stem lying above the soil surface and bearing leaves, as in the strawberry

---

THESAURUS

stimulant *n.* tonic, bracer, energizer; see DRUG.

stimulate *v.* spur on, foster, incite; see URGE 2.

stimulated *a.* keyed up, speeded up, accelerated; see EXCITED.

stimulating *a.* intriguing, enlivening, arousing, high-spirited, bracing, rousing, energetic, refreshing, exhilarating, enjoyable, health-building, sharp, evocative, exciting, inspiring, provoking, animating.—*Ant.* DULL, dreary, humdrum.

sting *n.* 1 [An injury] wound, swelling, sore; see INJURY. 2 [Pain] prick, bite, burn; see PAIN 2.

sting *v.* prick, prickle, tingle; see HURT 1.

stingy *a.* parsimonious, niggardly, miserly, close, closefisted, greedy, covetous, tightfisted, tight*, grasping, penny-pinching, cheap, selfish, mean, cheeseparing, skimpy.—*Ant.* GENEROUS, bountiful, liberal.

stink *n.* stench, fetor, offensive odor; see SMELL 2.

stink *v.* smell bad, emit a stench, be offensive; see SMELL 1.

stir *v.* move, beat, agitate; see MIX 1. —**stir up trouble*** cause difficulty, foment, agitate; see BOTHER 2, DISTURB.

stitch *v.* join, make a seam, baste; see SEW.

stock *a.* trite, hackneyed, ordinary; see COMMON 1, DULL 4.

stock *n.* 1 [Goods] merchandise, produce, accumulation; see PRODUCE. 2 [Livestock] domestic animals, barnyard animals, farm animals; see CATTLE. 3 [A stalk] stem, plant, trunk; see STALK. —**in stock** not sold out, stocked, not difficult to get; see AVAILABLE. —**out of stock** sold out, gone, not available; see SOLD OUT. —**take stock (of)** 1 [To inventory] enumerate, audit, take account of; see EXAMINE. 2 [To consider] examine, study, review; see CONSIDER, THINK 1. —**take stock in** believe in, put faith in, rely on; see TRUST 1.

stocking *n.* hose, pantyhose, nylons; see HOSIERY.

stock-still *a.* frozen, stagnant, inactive; see MOTIONLESS 1.

stock (up) *v.* replenish, supply, furnish; see BUY.

stolen *a.* taken, kept, robbed, filched, purloined, appropriated, lifted*, abducted, kidnapped, snatched*, run off with, poached, copped*, plagiarized, misappropriated.

stom·ach (stum′ək) *n.* ⟦ult. < Gr *stoma*, mouth⟧ **1** the saclike digestive organ into which food passes from the esophagus **2** the abdomen, or belly **3** appetite for food **4** desire or inclination — *vt.* **1** to be able to eat or digest **2** to tolerate; bear

stom′ach·ache′ *n.* pain in the stomach or abdomen

stom′ach·er *n.* an ornamented piece of cloth formerly worn over the chest and abdomen, esp. by women

stomp (stämp) *vt., vi. var. of* STAMP (*vt.* 1,2; *vi.* 1,2)

stone (stōn) *n.* ⟦OE *stan*⟧ **1** the hard, solid, nonmetallic mineral matter of rock **2** a piece of rock **3** the seed of certain fruits **4** *short for* PRECIOUS STONE **5** *pl.* **stone** [Brit.] 14 pounds avoirdupois **6** an abnormal stony mass formed in the kidney, gall bladder, etc. — *vt.* **stoned, ston′ ing 1** to pelt or kill with stones **2** to remove the stone from (a peach, etc.)

stone- ⟦< prec.⟧ *combining form* completely *[stone-blind]*

Stone Age the period in human culture when stone tools were used

stoned *adj.* [Slang] drunk or under the influence of a drug

stone′s throw a short distance

stone′wall′ *vi.* [Colloq.] to behave in an obstructive manner, as by withholding information, etc.

ston′y (-ē) *adj.* -i·er, -i·est **1** full of stones **2** of or like stone; specif., unfeeling; pitiless —**ston′i·ness** *n.*

stood (stood) *vi., vt. pt. & pp. of* STAND

stooge (stōōj) *n.* ⟦< ?⟧ [Colloq.] **1** an actor who serves as the victim of a comedian's jokes, pranks, etc. **2** anyone who acts as a foil or underling

stool (stool) *n.* ⟦OE *stol*⟧ **1** a single seat having no back or arms **2** feces

stool pigeon [Colloq.] a spy or informer, esp. for the police

stoop¹ (stōōp) *vi.* ⟦OE *stupian*⟧ **1** to bend the body forward **2** to carry the head and shoulders habitually bent forward **3** to degrade oneself — *n.* the act or position of stooping

stoop² (stōōp) *n.* ⟦Du *stoep*⟧ a small porch at the door of a house

stop (stäp) *vt.* **stopped, stop′ping** ⟦< L *stuppa*, stop up⟧ **1** to close by filling, shutting off, etc. **2** to cause to cease motion, activity, etc. **3** to block; intercept; prevent **4** to cease; desist from *[stop talking]* — *vi.* **1** to cease moving, etc.; halt **2** to leave off doing something **3** to cease operating **4** to become clogged **5** to tarry or stay — *n.* **1** a stopping or being stopped **2** a finish; end **3** a stay or sojourn **4** a place stopped at, as on a bus route **5** an obstruction, plug, etc. **6** a finger hole in a wind instrument, closed to produce a desired tone **7** a pull, lever, etc. for controlling a set of organ pipes —**stop off** to stop for a while en route to a place —**stop over** to visit for a while: also **stop in** (or **by**)

stop′cock′ *n.* a cock or valve to stop or regulate the flow of a fluid

stop′gap′ *n.* a person or thing serving as a temporary substitute

stop′light′ *n.* **1** a traffic light, esp. when red to signal vehicles to stop **2** a light at the rear of a vehicle, that lights up when the brakes are applied

stop′o′ver *n.* a brief stop or stay at a place in the course of a journey

stop′page (-ij) *n.* **1** a stopping or being stopped **2** an obstructed condition; block

stop′per *n.* something inserted to close an opening; plug

stop′ple (-əl) *n.* a stopper or plug — *vt.* **-pled, -pling** to close with a stopple

stop′watch′ *n.* a watch that can be started and stopped instantly, as for timing races

stor·age (stôr′ij) *n.* **1** a storing or being stored **2** a place for, or the cost of, storing goods **3** computer memory

storage battery a battery producing electric current, with cells that can be recharged

store (stôr) *vt.* **stored, stor′ing** ⟦< L *instaurare*, restore⟧ **1** to put aside for use when needed **2** to furnish with a supply **3** to put, as in a warehouse, for safekeeping — *n.* **1** a supply (*of* something) for use when needed; stock **2** [*pl.*] supplies, esp. of food, clothing, etc. **3** a retail establishment where goods are offered for sale **4** a storehouse —**in store** set aside for the future; in reserve —**set** (or **put** or **lay**) **store by** to value

store′front′ *n.* a front room on the ground floor of a building, designed for use as a retail store

store′house′ *n.* a place where things are stored; esp., a warehouse

store′keep′er *n.* **1** a person in charge of military or naval stores **2** a retail merchant

store′room′ *n.* a room where things are stored

sto·rey (stôr′ē) *n., pl.* **-reys** *Brit., etc. sp. of* STORY²

sto·ried (stôr′ēd) *adj.* famous in story or history

stork (stôrk) *n.* ⟦OE *storc*⟧ a large, long-legged wading bird with a long neck and bill

storm (stôrm) *n.* ⟦OE⟧ **1** a strong wind, with rain, snow, thunder, etc. **2** any heavy fall of snow, rain, etc. **3** a strong emotional outburst **4** any strong disturbance **5** a sudden, strong attack on a fortified place — *vi.* **1** to blow rain, snow, etc. violently **2** to rage; rant **3** to rush violently *[to storm into a room]* — *vt.* to attack vigorously

storm door (or **window**) a door (or window) placed outside the regular one as added protection

storm′y *adj.* **-i·er, -i·est 1** of or characterized by storms **2** violent, raging, etc. —**storm′i·ly** *adv.* —**storm′i·ness** *n.*

THESAURUS

stomach *n.* paunch, belly, midsection, bowels, intestines, viscera, entrails, insides*, guts, gut*, tummy, pot*, middle, breadbasket*, corporation*.

stomachache *n.* indigestion, acute indigestion, gastric upset; see ILLNESS 1, 2.

stone *a.* rock, stony, rocky, hard, rough, craggy, petrified, marble, granite.

stone *n.* mass, crag, cobblestone, boulder, gravel, pebble, rock, sand, grain, granite, marble, flint, gem, jewel. —**cast the first stone** criticize, blame, reprimand; see ATTACK, SCOLD. —**leave no stone unturned** take great pains, be scrupulous, try hard; see PURSUE 1, WORK 1.

stoned* *a.* drugged, high*, turned on*; see DRUNK.

stony *a.* inflexible, cruel, unrelenting; see FIRM 2, ROUGH 1.

stool *n.* seat, footstool, footrest; see FURNITURE.

stoop *v.* bend forward, incline, crouch; see LEAN 1.

stop *interj.* cease, cut it out*, quit it; see STOP *v.*, 1.

stop *n.* **1** [A pause] halt, stay, standstill; see END 2, PAUSE. **2** [A stopping place] station, passenger station, wayside stop; see DEPOT. —**put a**

stop to halt, interrupt, intervene; see STOP 1.

stop *v.* **1** [To halt] pause, stay, stand still, lay over, stay over, break the journey, shut down, rest, discontinue, pull up, reach a standstill, hold, stop dead in one's tracks*, stop short, freeze, call it a day*, cut short; see also END 1. **2** [To cease] terminate, finish, conclude, withdraw, leave off, let up, pull up, fetch up, wind up, relinquish, have done, desist, refrain, settle, discontinue, end, close, tie up, give up, call off, bring up, close down, break up, hold up, pull up, lapse, be at an end, cut out, die away, go out, defect, surrender, close, peter out*, call it a day*, knock off*, lay off*, throw in the towel*, melt away, drop it, run out, write off, run its course.—*Ant.* BEGIN, start, commence. **3** [To prevent] hinder, obstruct, arrest; see PREVENT.

stopover *n.* layover, halt, pause; see DELAY.

stopped *a.* at a halt, off the air, cut short; see INTERRUPTED.

storage *n.* room, area, accommodation; see STOREHOUSE.

store *n.* shop, mart, retail establishment, sales outlet, market, department store, specialty shop, chain store, drygoods store, emporium, grocery store, business house, drug store.

store *v.* put, deposit, cache, stock, store away, stow away, lay by, lay in, lay up, lay down, put away, put aside, lock away, bank, warehouse, collect, pack away, set aside, set apart, amass, file, stash*, salt away*, put in mothballs*; see also SAVE 3.—*Ant.* SPEND, draw out, withdraw.

stored *a.* stocked, reserved, hoarded; see SAVED 2.

storehouse *n.* depository, warehouse, granary, silo, store, storage space, corncrib, barn, depot, cache, grain elevator, safe-deposit vault, armory, arsenal, repository.

storekeeper *n.* small businessman, purveyor, grocer; see MERCHANT.

storm *n.* tempest, downpour, cloudburst, disturbance, waterspout, blizzard, snowstorm, squall, hurricane, cyclone, tornado, twister*, gust, blast, gale, blow, monsoon.

storm *v.* blow violently, howl, blow a gale, roar, set in, squall, pour, drizzle, rain, rain cats and dogs*.

stormy *a.* rainy, wet, damp, cold, bitter, raging, roaring, frigid, windy, blustery, pouring, turbulent, storming, wild, boisterous, rough, squally, dark, violent, threatening, menacing.

story[1] (stôr′ē) *n., pl.* **-ries** 〚< Gr *historia*, narrative〛 1 the telling of an event or events; account; narration 2 a joke 3 a fictitious narrative shorter than a novel 4 the plot of a novel, play, etc. 5 [Colloq.] a falsehood 6 a news report

story[2] (stôr′ē) *n., pl.* **-ries** 〚< prec.〛 a horizontal division of a building, from a floor to the ceiling above it

sto′ry·board′ *n.* a large board on which sketches, etc. for shots or scenes of a film are arranged in sequence — *vt.* to make a storyboard of (a shot or scene) for (a film)

sto′ry·book′ *n.* a book of stories, esp. one for children

sto′ry·tell′er (-tel′ər) *n.* one who narrates stories — **sto′ry·tell′ing** *n.*

stoup (stoōp) *n.* 〚< ON *staup*, cup〛 a font for holy water

stout (stout) *adj.* 〚< OFr *estout*, bold〛 1 courageous 2 strong; sturdy; firm 3 powerful; forceful 4 fat; thickset — *n.* a heavy, dark-brown beer —**stout′ly** *adv.* —**stout′ness** *n.*

stout′heart′ed *adj.* courageous; brave

stove[1] (stōv) *n.* 〚< MDu, heated room〛 an apparatus for heating, cooking, etc.

stove[2] (stōv) *vt., vi. alt. pt. & pp. of* STAVE

stove′pipe′ *n.* a metal pipe used to carry off smoke from a stove

stow (stō) *vt.* 〚< OE *stowe*, a place〛 to pack in an orderly way —**stow away** 1 to put or hide away 2 to be a stowaway —**stow′age** *n.*

stow′away′ *n.* one who hides aboard a ship, airplane, etc. to get free passage, evade port officials, etc.

strad·dle (strad′'l) *vt.* **-dled**, **-dling** 〚< STRIDE〛 1 to stand or sit astride of, or stand with the legs wide apart 2 to appear to take both sides of (an issue) — *n.* a straddling —**strad′dler** (-lər) *n.*

strafe (strāf) *vt.* **strafed**, **straf′ing** 〚< Ger *Gott strafe England* (God punish England)〛 to attack with machine-gun fire from low-flying aircraft

strag·gle (strag′'l) *vi.* **-gled**, **-gling** [prob. < ME *straken*, roam] 1 to wander from the main group 2 to be scattered over a wide area; ramble 3 to hang in an unkempt way, as hair —**strag′gler** *n.* —**strag′gly** *adj.*

straight (strāt) *adj.* 〚< ME *strecchen*, to stretch〛 1 having the same direction throughout its length; not crooked, bent, etc. 2 direct; undeviating, etc. 3 in order; properly arranged, etc. 4 honest; sincere 5 unmixed; undiluted [*straight* whiskey] 6 [Slang] normal or conventional — *adv.* 1 in a straight line 2 upright; erectly 3 without detour, delay, etc. — *n. Poker* a hand of five cards in sequence —**straight away** (or **off**) without delay —**straight′ness** *n.*

straight arrow [Slang] one who is proper, righteous, conscientious, etc. and often regarded as stodgy, dull, etc. —**straight′-ar′row** *adj.*

straight′away′ *n.* a straight section of a racetrack, highway, etc. — *adv.* without delay

straight′en *vt., vi.* to make or become straight —**straighten out** 1 to make or become less confused, easier to deal with, etc. 2 to reform —**straight′ener** *n.*

straight face a facial expression showing no amusement or other emotion —**straight′-faced′** *adj.*

straight′for′ward *adj.* 1 moving or leading straight ahead; direct 2 honest; frank — *adv.* in a straightforward manner Also **straight′for′wards**

straight time 1 the standard number of working hours, as per week 2 the rate of pay for these hours

straight′way′ *adv.* [Archaic] at once

strain[1] (strān) *vt.* 〚< L *stringere*〛 1 to draw or stretch tight 2 to exert or use to the utmost 3 to injure by over-exertion [to *strain* a muscle] 4 to stretch beyond normal limits 5 to pass through a screen, sieve, etc.; filter — *vi.* 1 to make violent efforts; strive hard 2 to filter, ooze, etc. — *n.* 1 a straining or being strained 2 great effort, exertion, etc. 3 a bodily injury from overexertion 4 stress or force 5 a great demand on one's emotions, resources, etc.

strain[2] (strān) *n.* 〚< OE *strynan*, to produce〛 1 ancestry; lineage 2 race; stock; line 3 a line of individuals differentiated from its species or race 4 an inherited tendency 5 a musical tune

strained *adj.* not natural or relaxed

strain′er *n.* a device for straining, sifting, or filtering; sieve, filter, etc.

strait (strāt) *adj.* 〚< L *stringere*, draw tight〛 [Archaic] narrow or strict — *n.* 1 [*often pl.*] a narrow waterway connecting two large bodies of water 2 [*usually pl.*] difficulty; distress

strait′en *vt.* 1 [Now Rare] to make strait or narrow 2 to bring into difficulties: usually in **in straitened circumstances**, lacking enough money

strait′jack′et *n.* a coatlike device for restraining violent persons

strait′-laced′ *adj.* narrowly strict in behavior or moral views

strand[1] (strand) *n.* 〚OE〛 shore, esp. ocean shore — *vt., vi.* 1 to run or drive aground, as a ship 2 to put or be put into a helpless position [*stranded* abroad with no money]

strand[2] (strand) *n.* 〚ME *stronde*〛 1 any one of the threads, wires, etc. that are twisted together to form a string, cable, etc. 2 a ropelike length of anything [a *strand* of pearls]

strange (strānj) *adj.* **strang′er**, **strang′est** 〚< L *extraneus*, foreign〛 1 not previously known, seen, etc.; unfamiliar 2 unusual; extraordinary 3 peculiar; odd 4 reserved or distant 5 unaccustomed (*to*) —**strange′ly** *adv.* —**strange′ness** *n.*

stran·ger (strān′jər) *n.* 1 a newcomer 2 a person not known to one

stran·gle (stran′gəl) *vt., vi.* **-gled**, **-gling** 〚< Gr *strangos*, twisted〛 1 to choke to death 2 to suppress, stifle, or repress —**stran′gler** *n.*

stran′gle·hold′ *n.* 1 an illegal wrestling hold that chokes an opponent 2 a force or action that suppresses freedom

stran·gu·late (stran′gyə lāt′) *vt.* **-lat′ed**, **-lat′ing** *Med.* to block (a tube, etc.) by constricting —**stran′gu·la′tion** *n.*

strap (strap) *n.* 〚dial. form of STROP〛 a narrow strip of leather, etc., as for binding or securing things — *vt.* **strapped**, **strap′ping** to fasten with a strap

strap′less *adj.* having no straps; specif., having no shoulder straps

strapped (strapt) *adj.* [Colloq.] in utter need; penniless

strap′ping *adj.* [Colloq.] tall and well-built; robust

strata (strāt′ə, strat′ə) *n. alt. pl. of* STRATUM

strat·a·gem (strat′ə jəm) *n.* 〚< Gr *stratos*, army + *agein*,

---

THESAURUS

story[1] *n.* imaginative writing, fable, narrative, tale, myth, fairy tale, anecdote, legend, account, satire, burlesque, memoir, parable, fiction, novel, romance, allegory, epic, saga, fantasy; see also LITERATURE 1.

stout *a.* corpulent, fleshy, portly; see FAT.

stove[1] *n.* range, heater, cooking stove, furnace; see also APPLIANCE.

straight *a.* 1 [Not curved or twisted] rectilinear, vertical, perpendicular, plumb, upright, erect, in line, unbent, in a row, on a line, even, level.—*Ant.* BENT, curved, curving. 2 [Direct] uninterrupted, continuous, through; see DIRECT 1.

straighten *v.* order, compose, make straight, untwist, unsnarl, unbend, uncoil, unravel, uncurl, unfold, put straight, level, arrange, arrange on a line, align.—*Ant.* BEND, twist, curl. —**straighten out** put in order, clarify, make less confused, clean up,

arrange.

straightforward *a.* sincere, candid, outspoken; see FRANK, HONEST 1.

strain[1] *n.* 1 [Effort] exertion, struggle, endeavor; see EFFORT. 2 [Mental tension] anxiety, tension, pressure; see STRESS 2.

strain[1] *v.* 1 [To exert] endeavor, strive, labor; see TRY 1. 2 [To filter] refine, purify, screen; see SIFT 2.

strained *a.* forced, constrained, tense; see DIFFICULT 1.

strainer *n.* mesh, filter, colander; see SIEVE.

strait-laced *a.* strict, severe, stiff; see PRUDISH.

stranded *a.* aground, beached, ashore; see ABANDONED.

strange *a.* foreign, rare, unusual, uncommon, external, outside, without, detached, apart, faraway, remote, alien, unexplored, isolated, unrelated, irrelevant; see also UNFA-

MILIAR 2, UNKNOWN 1, 2, 3, UNNATURAL 1.—*Ant.* familiar, present, close.

strangely *a.* oddly, queerly, unfamiliarly, unnaturally, uncommonly, exceptionally, remarkably, rarely, fantastically, amazingly, surprisingly, singularly, peculiarly, unusually.—*Ant.* REGULARLY, commonly, usually.

strangeness *n.* newness, unfamiliarity, novelty, abnormality, eccentricity, remoteness.

stranger *n.* foreigner, outsider, unknown person, uninvited person, visitor, guest, immigrant, intruder, interloper, new boy in town, new girl in town, drifter, squatter, migratory worker, perfect stranger, complete stranger, gate-crasher*.

strangle *v.* asphyxiate, suffocate, kill; see CHOKE.

strap *n.* thong, strop, leash; see BAND 1.

to lead] 1 a trick, plan, etc. for deceiving an enemy in war 2 any tricky scheme

strat·e·gy (strat′ə jē) *n., pl.* **-gies** 1 the science of planning and directing military operations 2 skill in managing or planning, esp. by using stratagems 3 a stratagem, plan, etc. —**stra·te·gic** (strə tē′jik) *adj.* —**stra·te′gi·cal·ly** *adv.* —**strat′e·gist** *n.*

strat·i·fy (strat′ə fī′) *vt., vi.* **-fied′, -fy′ing** [< L *stratum*, layer + *facere*, make] to form in layers or strata —**strat′i·fi·ca′tion** *n.*

strat·o·sphere (-ə sfir′) *n.* [< ModL *stratum*, stratum + Fr *sphère*, sphere] the atmospheric zone at an altitude of *c.* 20 to 50 km

stra·tum (strāt′əm, strat′-) *n., pl.* **-ta** (-ə) or **-tums** [ModL < L *stratus*, a spreading] 1 a horizontal layer of matter, as of sedimentary rock or a level of the atmosphere 2 any of the socioeconomic groups of a society

stra·tus (-əs) *n., pl.* **-ti** (-ī) [see prec.] a uniform, low, gray cloud layer

straw (strô) *n.* [OE *streaw*] 1 hollow stalks of grain after threshing 2 a single one of these 3 a tube used for sucking beverages 4 a trifle —*adj.* 1 straw-colored; yellowish 2 made of straw 3 worthless

straw·ber·ry (-ber′ē, -bər ē) *n., pl.* **-ries** [prob. from the strawlike particles on the fruit] 1 the small, red, fleshy fruit of a vinelike plant of the rose family 2 this plant

straw boss [Colloq.] one having subordinate authority

straw vote (or **poll**) an unofficial vote taken to determine general group opinion

stray (strā) *vi.* [< LL *strata*, street] 1 to wander from a given place, course, etc. 2 to deviate (*from* what is right) —*n.* one that strays; esp., a lost domestic animal —*adj.* 1 having strayed; lost 2 isolated /a few *stray* words/

streak (strēk) *n.* [< OE *strica*] 1 a long, thin mark or stripe 2 a layer, as of fat in meat 3 a tendency in behavior, etc. /a nervous *streak*/ 4 a period, as of luck —*vt.* to mark with streaks —*vi.* 1 to become streaked 2 to go fast 3 to dash naked for a short distance in public as a prank —**streak′er** *n.* —**streak′y, -i·er, -i·est,** *adj.*

stream (strēm) *n.* [OE] 1 a current of water; specif., a small river 2 a steady flow, as of air, light, etc. 3 a continuous series /a *stream* of cars/ —*vi.* 1 to flow as in a stream 2 to flow (*with*) 3 to move swiftly

stream′er *n.* 1 a long, narrow, flag 2 any long, narrow, flowing strip

stream′line′ *vt.* **-lined′, -lin′ing** to make streamlined —*adj.* STREAMLINED

stream′lined′ *adj.* 1 having a contour designed to offer the least resistance in moving through air, water, etc. 2 efficient, trim, simplified, etc.

street (strēt) *n.* [< L *strata* (*via*), paved (road)] 1 a public road in a town or city, esp. a paved one 2 such a road with its sidewalks, buildings, etc. 3 the people living, working, etc. along a given street

street′car′ *n.* a car on rails for public transportation along the streets

street′walk′er *n.* a prostitute

street′wise′ *adj.* [Colloq.] experienced in dealing with the people in urban poverty areas where vice and crime are common

strength (streŋkth) *n.* [OE *strengthu*] 1 the state or quality of being strong; force 2 toughness; durability 3 the power to resist attack 4 potency or concentration, as of drugs, etc. 5 intensity, as of sound, etc. 6 force of an army, etc., as measured in numbers —**on the strength of** based or relying on

strength′en *vt., vi.* to make or become stronger —**strength′en·er** *n.*

stren·u·ous (stren′yoo əs) *adj.* [L *strenuus*] requiring or characterized by great effort or energy —**stren′u·ous·ly** *adv.* —**stren′u·ous·ness** *n.*

strep (strep) *n.* short for STREPTOCOCCUS

strep throat (strep) [Colloq.] a sore throat caused by a streptococcus, with inflammation and fever

strep·to·coc·cus (strep′tə käk′əs) *n., pl.* **-coc′ci** (-käk′sī′) [< Gr *streptos*, twisted + COCCUS] any of various spherical bacteria that occur in chains: some cause serious diseases

strep′to·my′cin (-mī′sin) *n.* [< Gr *streptos*, bent + *mykēs*, fungus] an antibiotic drug obtained from a soil bacterium and used in treating various diseases

stress (stres) *n.* [< L *strictus*, strict] 1 strain; specif., force that strains or deforms 2 emphasis; importance 3 *a*) mental or physical tension *b*) urgency, pressure, etc. causing this 4 the relative force of utterance given a syllable or word; accent — *vt.* 1 to put stress or pressure on 2 to accent 3 to emphasize

stress fracture a leg fracture caused by repetitive stress, as in marathon running

stretch (strech) *vt.* [OE *streccan*] 1 to reach out; extend 2 to draw out to full extent or to greater size 3 to cause to extend too far; strain 4 to strain in interpretation, scope, etc. — *vi.* 1 *a*) to spread out to full extent or beyond normal limits *b*) to extend over a given distance or time 2 *a*) to extend the body or limbs to full length *b*) to lie down (usually *with out*) 3 to become stretched — *n.* 1 a stretching or being stretched 2 an unbroken period /a ten-day *stretch*/ 3 an unbroken length, tract, etc. 4 *short for* HOMESTRETCH —*adj.* made of elastic fabric so as to stretch easily —**stretch′able** *adj.* —**stretch′y, -i·er, -i·est,** *adj.*

stretch′er *n.* 1 one that stretches 2 a light frame covered with canvas, etc. for carrying the sick, injured, etc.

strew (stroō) *vt.* **strewed, strewed** or **strewn, strew′ing** [OE *streawian*] 1 to spread here and there; scatter 2 to cover as by scattering

stri·at·ed (strī′āt′id) *adj.* [< L *striare*, to groove] marked with parallel lines, bands, furrows, etc.

stricken (strik′ən) *vt., vi.* alt. pp. of STRIKE —*adj.* 1 struck or wounded 2 afflicted, as by something painful

strict (strikt) *adj.* [< L *stringere*, draw tight] 1 exact or precise 2 perfect; absolute 3 *a*) enforcing rules carefully *b*) closely enforced —**strict′ly** *adv.* —**strict′ness** *n.*

■■■■■■ THESAURUS ■■■■■■

strategy *n.* approach, maneuvering, procedure; see TACTICS.

straw *n.* Straws and strawlike fibers include the following: oat, wheat, barley, rye, rice, buckwheat, bean; see also HAY. —**a straw in the wind** evidence, indication, signal; see SIGN 1. —**grasp at straws** (or a **straw**) try any expedient, panic, make a desperate attempt; see FEAR, TRY 1.

straw vote *n.* opinion poll, unofficial ballot, dry run*; see OPINION 1, VOTE 1, 2.

stray *v.* rove, roam, go astray; see WALK 1.

strayed *a.* wandered, vagrant, roaming; see LOST 1.

streak *n.* stripe, strip, ridge; see BAND 1.

stream *n.* current, rivulet, brook; see RIVER, WATER 2.

stream *v.* gush, run, flow; see FLOW.

street *n.* highway, way, lane, path, avenue, thoroughfare, boulevard, terrace, place, road, route, artery, parkway, court, cross street, alley, circle, dead end, passage.

streetcar *n.* tram, trolley, bus; see VEHICLE.

streetwalker *n.* whore, hustler, harlot; see PROSTITUTE.

strength *n.* vigor, brawn, energy, nerve, vitality, muscle, stoutness, health, toughness, sturdiness, hardiness, tenacity, soundness.—*Ant.* WEAKNESS, feebleness, loss of energy.

strengthen *v.* intensify, add, invigorate, fortify, reinforce, confirm, encourage, increase, multiply, empower, arm, harden, steel, brace, buttress, stimulate, sustain, nerve, animate, reanimate, restore, refresh, recover, hearten, establish, toughen, temper, rejuvenate, tone up, build up, make firm, stiffen, brace up, rally, sharpen, enliven, substantiate, uphold, back, augment, enlarge, extend, mount, rise, ascend, wax, grow, back up, beef up*.—*Ant.* WEAKEN, cripple, tear down.

strenuous *a.* vigorous, arduous, zealous; see DIFFICULT 1.

strenuously *a.* hard, laboriously, energetically; see VIGOROUSLY.

stress *n.* 1 [Importance] significance, weight, import; see IMPORTANCE. 2 [Pressure] strain, tension, force, burden, trial, fear, tenseness, stretch, tautness, pull, draw, extension, protraction, intensity, tightness, spring; see also PRESSURE 1.

stress *v.* accent, make emphatic, accentuate; see EMPHASIZE.

stretch *n.* compass, range, reach; see EXTENT.

stretch *v.* 1 [To become longer] grow, expand, be extended, extend oneself, spread, unfold, increase, swell, spring up, shoot up, open.—*Ant.* CONTRACT, shrink, wane. 2 [To cause to become longer, spread out, etc.] tighten, strain, make tense, draw, draw out, elongate, extend, develop, distend, inflate, lengthen, magnify, amplify, widen, draw tight.—*Ant.* RELAX, let go, slacken.

stretcher *n.* litter, cot, portable bed; see BED 1.

strew *v.* spread, toss, cover; see SCATTER 2.

stricken *a.* wounded, injured, harmed; see HURT.

strict *a.* stringent, stern, austere; see SEVERE 2.

strictly *a.* rigidly, rigorously, strin-

stric·ture (strik′chər) *n.* ⟦see prec.⟧ 1 adverse criticism 2 an abnormal narrowing of a passage in the body

stride (strīd) *vi., vt.* **strode, strid′den, strid′ing** ⟦OE *stridan*⟧ 1 to walk with long steps 2 to cross with a single, long step —*n.* 1 a long step 2 the distance covered by such a step 3 [*usually pl.*] progress /to make *strides*/

stri·dent (strīd′'nt) *adj.* ⟦< L *stridere*, to rasp⟧ harsh-sounding; shrill; grating —**stri′dently** *adv.*

strife (strīf) *n.* ⟦< OFr *estrif*⟧ 1 contention 2 fight or quarrel; struggle

strike (strīk) *vt.* **struck, struck** or, esp. for *vt.* 7 & 10, **strick′en, strik′ing** ⟦OE *strican*, to go⟧ 1 to hit with the hand, a tool, etc. 2 to make by stamping, etc. /to *strike* coins/ 3 to announce (time), as with a bell: said of clocks, etc. 4 to ignite (a match) or produce (a light, etc.) by friction 5 to collide with or cause to collide /he *struck* his head on a beam/ 6 to attack 7 to afflict, as with disease, pain, etc. 8 to come upon; notice, find, etc. 9 to affect as if by contact, etc.; occur to /an idea *struck* me/ 10 to remove (*from* a list, record, etc.) 11 to make (a bargain, truce, etc.) 12 to lower (a sail, flag, etc.) 13 to assume (an attitude, pose, etc.) —*vi.* 1 to hit (*at*) 2 to attack 3 to make sounds as by being struck: said of a bell, clock, etc. 4 to collide; hit (*against, on,* or *upon*) 5 to seize bait: said of a fish 6 to come suddenly (*on* or *upon*) 7 to refuse to continue to work until certain demands are met 8 to proceed, esp. in a new direction —*n.* 1 the act of striking; specif., a military attack 2 a refusal by employees to go on working, in an attempt to gain better working conditions, etc. 3 the discovery of a rich deposit of oil, etc. 4 *Baseball* a pitched ball missed, or fouled off, by the batter or called a good pitch by the umpire 5 *Bowling* a knocking down of all the pins on the first roll —**strike out** 1 to erase 2 to start out 3 *Baseball* to put out, or be put out, on three strikes —**strike up** to begin —**strik′er** *n.*

strik·ing *adj.* very impressive; outstanding, remarkable, etc.

string (striŋ) *n.* ⟦OE *streng*⟧ 1 a thin line of fiber, leather, etc. used for tying, pulling, etc. 2 a group of like things on a string /a *string* of pearls/ 3 a row, series, etc. of like things /a *string* of houses/ 4 *a)* a slender cord of wire, gut, etc. bowed, plucked, or struck to make a musical sound *b)* [*pl.*] all the stringed instruments of an orchestra 5 a fiber of a plant 6 [Colloq.] a condition attached to a plan, offer, etc.: *usually used in pl.* —*vt.* **strung, string′ing** 1 to provide with strings 2 to thread on a string 3 to tie, hang, etc. with a string 4 to remove the strings from (beans, etc.) 5 to arrange in a row 6 to extend /*string* a cable/ —**pull strings** to get someone to use influence in one's behalf, often secretly —**string′y, -i·er, -i·est,** *adj.*

string bean SNAP BEAN

stringed instrument (striŋd) an instrument with a vibrating string, as a violin or guitar

strin·gent (strin′jənt) *adj.* ⟦see STRICT⟧ strict; severe —**strin′gency** *n.*

string′er *n.* 1 a long horizontal piece in a structure 2 a part-time, local correspondent for a newspaper, magazine, etc.

strip¹ (strip) *vt.* **stripped, strip′ping** ⟦OE *stripan*⟧ 1 to remove (the clothing, etc.) from (a person) 2 to dispossess of (honors, titles, etc.) 3 to plunder; rob 4 to take off (a covering, etc.) from (a person or thing) 5 to make bare by taking away removable parts, etc. 6 to break the thread of (a nut, bolt, etc.) or the teeth of (a gear) —*vi.* to take off all clothing —**strip′per** *n.*

strip² (strip) *n.* ⟦< STRIPE⟧ 1 a long, narrow piece, as of land, tape, etc. 2 *short for* AIRSTRIP

strip cropping crop planting in alternate rows to lessen erosion, as on a hillside

stripe (strīp) *n.* ⟦< MDu *strip*⟧ 1 a long, narrow band differing from the surrounding area 2 a strip of cloth on a uniform to show rank, years served, etc. 3 kind; sort /a man of his *stripe*/ —*vt.* **striped, strip′ing** to mark with stripes

strip·ling (strip′liŋ) *n.* a grown boy

strip mining mining, esp. for coal, by laying bare a mineral deposit near the surface of the earth

strip′-search′ *vt.* to search (a person) by requiring removal of the clothes —*n.* such a search Also **strip search**

strip′tease′ *n.* an entertainment in which the performer undresses slowly, usually to musical accompaniment —**strip′teas′er** *n.*

strive (strīv) *vi.* **strove** or **strived, striven** (striv′ən) or **strived, striv′ing** ⟦< OFr *estrif*, effort⟧ 1 to make great efforts; try very hard 2 to struggle /*strive* against oppression/

strobe (light) (strōb) ⟦< Gr *strobus*, a twisting around⟧ an electronic tube emitting rapid, brief, and brilliant flashes of light: used in photography, etc.

strode (strōd) *vi., vt. pt. of* STRIDE

stroke (strōk) *n.* ⟦ME⟧ 1 a striking of one thing against another 2 a sudden action or event /a *stroke* of luck/ 3 a sudden loss of consciousness with paralysis, caused by a cerebral hemorrhage, blood clot, etc. 4 a single strong effort 5 the sound of striking, as of a clock 6 *a)* a single movement, as with a tool, racket, etc. *b)* any of a series of repeated motions made in rowing, swimming, etc. 7 a mark made by a pen, etc. —*vt.* **stroked, strok′ing** to draw one's hand, a tool, etc. gently over the surface of

stroll (strōl) *vi.* ⟦prob. < Ger *strolch*, vagabond⟧ 1 to walk about leisurely; saunter 2 to wander —*vt.* to stroll along or through —*n.* a leisurely walk

stroll′er *n.* 1 one who strolls 2 a light, chairlike baby carriage

strong (strôŋ) *adj.* ⟦OE *strang*⟧ 1 *a)* physically powerful *b)* healthy; hearty 2 morally or intellectually powerful /a *strong* will/ 3 firm; durable /a *strong* fort/ 4 powerful in wealth, numbers, etc. 5 of a specified number /troops 6,000 *strong*/ 6 having a powerful effect 7 intense in degree or quality /*strong* coffee, a *strong* light, *strong* smell, etc./ 8 forceful; vigorous, etc. —**strong′ly** *adv.*

THESAURUS

gently; see SURELY.

stride *n.* step, pace, long step; see GAIT. —**take in one's stride** handle, do easily, deal with; see MANAGE 1.

strife *n.* quarrel, struggle, conflict; see FIGHT 1.

strike *n.* 1 [An organized refusal] walkout, deadlock, work stoppage, quitting, sit-down strike, tie-up, slowdown, confrontation, sit-in; see also REVOLUTION 2. 2 [A blow] hit, stroke, punch; see BLOW. —**(out) on strike** striking, protesting, on the picket line; see UNEMPLOYED.

strike *v.* 1 [To hit] box, punch, thump; see BEAT 1, HIT 1. 2 [To refuse to work] walk out, tie up, sit down, slow down, go out, be on strike, sit in, arbitrate, negotiate a contract, picket, boycott, stop, quit, resist, hold out for; see also OPPOSE 1, 2. 3 [To light] kindle, ignite, scratch; see IGNITE. —**strike out** 1 [To begin something new] start out, initiate, find a new approach; see BEGIN 1. 2 [To cancel] obliterate, invalidate, expunge; see CANCEL. 3 [In baseball, to be out on strikes] fan, whiff*, go down swinging, go down on strikes.

striking *a.* attractive, stunning, dazzling; see BEAUTIFUL, HANDSOME.

string *n.* 1 [A sequence] chain, succession, procession; see SEQUENCE 1, SERIES. 2 [Twine] cord, twist, strand; see ROPE. —**string along*** accede, go along, agree; see FOLLOW 2.

stringy *a.* wiry, ropy, woody, pulpy, hairy, veined, coarse, threadlike.

strip¹ *v.* 1 [Undress] divest, disrobe, become naked; see UNDRESS. 2 [Remove] pull off, tear off, lift off; see PEEL.

strip² *n.* tape, slip, shred; see BAND 1, LAYER.

stripe *n.* line, division, strip, contrasting color, band, border, ribbon; see also LAYER.

striped *a.* lined, marked, streaked, veined, ribbed; see also BARRED 1.

strive *v.* endeavor, aim, attempt; see TRY 1.

stroll *v.* ramble, saunter, roam; see WALK 1.

strong *a.* 1 [Physically strong; *said especially of persons*] robust, sturdy, firm, muscular, sinewy, vigorous, stout, hardy, big, heavy, husky, lusty, active, energetic, tough, virile, mighty, athletic, able-bodied, powerful, manly, brawny, burly, wiry, strapping, made of iron*.—*Ant.* WEAK, emaciated, feeble. 2 [Physically strong; *said especially of things*] solid, firm, staunch, well-built, secure, tough, durable, able, unyielding, steady, stable, fixed, sound, powerful, mighty, tough, rugged, substantial.—*Ant.* UNSTABLE, insecure, tottering. 3 [Wielding power] great, mighty, influential; see POWERFUL 1. 4 [Potent in effect] powerful, potent, high-powered, stiff, effective, hard, high-potency, stimulating, inebriating, intoxicating, spiked*. 5 [Intense] sharp, acute, keen; see INTENSE. 6 [Financially sound] stable, solid, safe; see RELIABLE.

strongest *a.* mightiest, stoutest, firmest, hardiest, healthiest, most vigorous, most active, most intense, most capable, most masterful, sturdiest, most courageous, strongest-willed, most efficient.—*Ant.* WEAK, feeblest, most timid.

strongly *a.* stoutly, vigorously, actively, heavily, fully, completely, sturdily, robustly, firmly, solidly,

strong'-arm' *adj.* [Colloq.] using physical force — *vt.* [Colloq.] to use force upon

strong'box' *n.* a heavily made box or safe for storing valuables

strong'hold' *n.* a place having strong defenses; fortress

strong'-mind'ed *adj.* unyielding; determined Also **strong'-willed'**

stron·tium (strän'shəm, -shē əm; stränt'ē əm) *n.* ⟦ult. after *Strontian*, Scotland, where first found⟧ a metallic chemical element resembling calcium in properties

strop (sträp) *n.* ⟦OE⟧ a leather band for sharpening razors — *vt.* **stropped, strop'ping** to sharpen on a strop

stro·phe (strō'fē) *n.* ⟦Gr *strophē*, a turning⟧ a stanza of a poem

strove (strōv) *vi. alt. pt. of* STRIVE

struck (struk) *vt., vi. pt. & pp. of* STRIKE — *adj.* closed or otherwise affected by a labor strike

struc·ture (struk'chər) *n.* ⟦< L *struere*, arrange⟧ 1 something built or constructed, as a building or dam 2 the arrangement of all the parts of a whole 3 something composed of related parts — *vt.* **-tured, -tur·ing** to put together systematically —**struc'tural** *adj.*

stru·del (strōōd''l) *n.* ⟦Ger⟧ a pastry made of a thin sheet of dough filled with apples, etc., rolled up, and baked

strug·gle (strug'əl) *vi.* **-gled, -gling** ⟦ME *strogelen*⟧ 1 to fight violently with an opponent 2 to make great efforts; strive; labor — *n.* 1 great effort 2 conflict; strife

strum (strum) *vt., vi.* **strummed, strum'ming** ⟦echoic⟧ to play (a guitar, etc.) casually or unskillfully

strum·pet (strum'pit) *n.* ⟦ME⟧ a prostitute

strung (struŋ) *vt., vi. pt. & pp. of* STRING

strut (strut) *vi.* **strut'ted, strut'ting** ⟦OE *strutian*, stand rigid⟧ to walk in a swaggering manner — *n.* 1 a swaggering walk 2 a brace fitted into a framework to stabilize the structure

strych·nine (strik'nin, -nēn, -nīn) *n.* ⟦< Gr *strychnos*, nightshade⟧ a highly poisonous, colorless, crystalline alkaloid: used in small doses as a stimulant

stub (stub) *n.* ⟦OE *stybb*⟧ 1 a tree or plant stump 2 a short piece left over 3 any short or blunt projection or thing 4 the part of a ticket, bank check, etc. kept as a record — *vt.* **stubbed, stub'bing** 1 to strike (one's toe, etc.) against something 2 to put out (a cigarette, etc.) by pressing the end against a surface: often with *out*

stub·ble (stub'əl) *n.* ⟦< L *stipula*, a stalk⟧ 1 short stumps of grain, corn, etc., left after harvesting 2 any short, bristly growth, as of beard

stub·born (stub'ərn) *adj.* ⟦ME *stoburn*⟧ 1 refusing to yield or comply; obstinate 2 done in an obstinate or persistent way 3 hard to handle —**stub'born·ly** *adv.* — **stub'born·ness** *n.*

stub·by (stub'ē) *adj.* **-bier, -bi·est** 1 covered with stubs or stubble 2 short and dense 3 short and thickset

stuc·co (stuk'ō) *n., pl.* **-coes** or **-cos** ⟦It⟧ plaster or cement for surfacing walls, etc. — *vt.* **-coed, -co·ing** to cover with stucco

stuck (stuk) *vt., vi. pt. & pp. of* STICK

stuck'-up' *adj.* [Colloq.] snobbish

stud¹ (stud) *n.* ⟦OE *studu*, post⟧ 1 any of a series of small knobs, etc. used to ornament a surface 2 a small, buttonlike device for fastening collars, etc. 3 an upright piece in the wall of a building, to which panels, laths, etc. are nailed — *vt.* **stud'ded, stud'ding** 1 to set or decorate with studs, etc. 2 to be set thickly on *[rocks stud the hill]*

stud² (stud) *n.* ⟦OE⟧ a male animal, esp. a horse (**stud' horse'**), kept for breeding

stud'book' *n.* a register of purebred animals, esp. racehorses Also **stud book**

stud'ding *n.* 1 studs, esp. for walls 2 material for studs

stu·dent (stōōd''nt) *n.* ⟦< L *studere*, to study⟧ 1 one who studies, or investigates 2 one who is enrolled for study at a school, college, etc.

stud·ied (stud'ēd) *adj.* 1 prepared by careful study 2 deliberate

stu·dio (stōō'dē ō) *n., pl.* **-os'** ⟦It⟧ 1 a place where an artist, etc. works or where dancing lessons, etc. are given 2 a place where films, radio or TV programs, etc. are produced

studio couch a couch that can be opened into a full-sized bed

stu·di·ous (stōō'dē əs) *adj.* ⟦< L *studiosus*⟧ 1 fond of study 2 zealous; attentive

study (stud'ē) *n., pl.* **-ies** ⟦< L *studere*, to study⟧ 1 the acquiring of knowledge, as by reading 2 careful examination of a subject, event, etc. 3 a branch of learning 4 [*pl.*] formal education; schooling 5 an essay, thesis, etc. containing the results of a particular investigation 6 an earnest effort or deep thought 7 a room for study, etc. — *vt.* **-ied, -y·ing** 1 to try to learn or understand by reading, etc. 2 to investigate carefully 3 to read (a book, etc.) intently 4 to take a course in, as at a school or college — *vi.* 1 to study something 2 to be a student 3 to meditate

stuff (stuf) *n.* ⟦< OFr *estoffe*⟧ 1 the material out of which anything is made 2 essence; character 3 matter in general 4 cloth, esp. woolen cloth 5 objects; things 6 worthless objects; junk 7 [Colloq.] ability, skill, etc. — *vt.* 1 to fill or pack; specif., *a*) to fill the skin of (a dead animal) in taxidermy *b*) to fill (a turkey, etc.) with seasoning, bread crumbs, etc. before roasting 2 to fill too full; cram 3 to plug; block — *vi.* to eat too much

stuffed shirt [Slang] a pompous, pretentious person

stuff'ing *n.* something used to stuff, as padding in cushions, a seasoned mixture for stuffing fowl, etc.

stuff'y *adj.* **-i·er, -i·est** 1 poorly ventilated; close 2 having the nasal passages stopped up, as from a cold 3 [Colloq.] dull, conventional, or pompous —**stuff'i·ness** *n.*

stul·ti·fy (stul'tə fī') *vt.* **-fied', -fy'ing** ⟦< L *stultus*, foolish + *facere*, make⟧ 1 to make seem foolish, stupid, etc. 2 to make worthless, etc. —**stul'ti·fi·ca'tion** *n.*

stum·ble (stum'bəl) *vi.* **-bled, -bling** ⟦ME *stumblen*⟧ 1 to trip in walking, running, etc. 2 to walk unsteadily 3 to speak, act, etc. in a blundering way 4 to do wrong 5 to come by chance — *n.* a stumbling —**stum'bler** *n.*

stumbling block a difficulty

stump (stump) *n.* ⟦ME *stumpfe*⟧ 1 the end of a tree or plant left in the ground after the upper part has been cut off 2 the part of a limb, tooth, etc. left after the rest has been removed 3 the place where a political speech is made — *vt.* 1 to travel over (a district), making political speeches 2 [Colloq.] to puzzle or perplex — *vi.* 1 to walk heavily 2 to travel about, making political speeches — **stump'y** *adj.* **-i·er, -i·est**

stun (stun) *vt.* **stunned, stun'ning** ⟦< L *ex-*, intens. + *tonare*, to crash⟧ 1 to make unconscious, as by a blow 2 to daze; shock

---

THESAURUS

securely, immovably, steadily, heartily, forcibly, resolutely, capably, powerfully.

structure *n.* arrangement, composition, fabrication; see BUILDING.

struggle *n.* conflict, contest, strife; see FIGHT 1.

struggle *v.* strive, grapple, contend; see FIGHT.

stub *n.* stump, short end, snag, root, remainder, remnant.

stubborn *a.* unreasonable, obstinate, firm, dogged, opinionated, contradictory, contrary, determined, resolved, bullheaded, mulish, fixed, hard, willful, dogmatic, prejudiced, tenacious, unyielding, headstrong.

stubbornly *a.* persistently, resolutely, willfully, doggedly, tenaciously; see also FIRMLY 2.

stubbornness *n.* obstinacy, doggedness, inflexibility, pertinacity, tenac-

ity, perverseness, bullheadedness, pigheadedness; see also DETERMINATION.

stuck *a.* [Tight] fast, fastened, cemented; see TIGHT 2.

student *n.* learner, undergraduate, novice, high school student, college student, graduate student, pupil, docent, apprentice.

studious *a.* industrious, thoughtful, well-read, well-informed, scholarly, lettered, learned, bookish, earnest, diligent, attentive.

study *n.* research, investigation, examination; see EDUCATION 1.

study *v.* read, go into, refresh the memory, read up on, burn the midnight oil, bone up*, go over, cram, think, inquire, bury oneself in, plunge into.

stuff *v.* ram, pad, wad; see FILL 1, PACK 2.

stuffed *a.* crowded, packed, crammed; see FULL 1.

stuffed shirt* *n.* phony*, pompous person, incompetent; see FAKE.

stuffing *n.* 1 [Material used to pad] packing, wadding, padding, quilting, filler, packing material. 2 [Material used to stuff fish, fowl, etc.] dressing, forcemeat, filling; see DRESSING.

stuffy *a.* confined, stagnant, muggy; see CLOSE 5.

stumble *v.* miss one's step, trip, shamble; see FALL 1, TRIP 1.

stump *n.* butt, piece, projection; see END 4.

stumped* *a.* puzzled, baffled, bewildered; see UNCERTAIN.

stun *v.* daze with a blow, put to sleep, knock out; see DEADEN.

stunned *a.* dazed, astonished, amazed; see SHOCKED.

stung (stuŋ) *vt.*, *vi. pt. & pp.* of STING

stunk (stuŋk) *vi. pp. & alt. pt.* of STINK

stun·ning (stun'iŋ) *adj.* [Colloq.] remarkably attractive, excellent, etc.

stunt[1] (stunt) *vt.* [OE, stupid] 1 to check the growth or development of 2 to hinder (growth, etc.)

stunt[2] (stunt) *n.* [< ?] something done to show one's skill or daring, get attention, etc. — *vi.* to do a stunt

stu·pefy (stōō'pə fī', styōō'-) *vt.* [< L *stupere*, be stunned + *facere*, make] 1 to produce stupor in; stun 2 to astound; bewilder —**stu'pefac'tion** (-fak'shən) *n.*

stu·pen·dous (stōō pen'dəs, styōō-) *adj.* [< L *stupere*, be stunned] 1 astonishing 2 astonishingly great

stu·pid (stōō'pid, styōō'-) *adj.* [see prec.] 1 lacking normal intelligence 2 foolish; silly *[a stupid idea]* 3 dull and boring —**stu·pid'i·ty**, *pl.* **-ties**, *n.* —**stu'pid·ly** *adv.*

stu·por (stōō'pər, styōō'-) *n.* [see STUPENDOUS] a state in which the mind and senses are dulled; loss of sensibility

sturdy (stur'dē) *adj.* **-dier**, **-di·est** [< OFr *estourdi*, stunned] 1 firm; resolute 2 strong; vigorous —**stur'di·ly** *adv.* —**stur'di·ness** *n.*

stur·geon (stur'jən) *n.* [< OFr *esturjon*] a large food fish valuable as a source of caviar

stut·ter (stut'ər) *n.*, *vt.*, *vi.* [< ME *stutten*] STAMMER —**stut'terer** *n.*

sty[1] (stī) *n.*, *pl.* **sties** [< OE *sti*, hall] 1 a pen for pigs 2 any foul place

sty[2] or **stye** (stī) *n.*, *pl.* **sties** [ult. < OE *stigan*, to rise] a small, inflamed swelling on the rim of an eyelid

Styg·ian (stij'ē ən, stij'ən) *adj.* 1 of the Styx 2 *[also* s-*]* a) infernal b) dark or gloomy

style (stīl) *n.* [< L *stilus*, pointed writing tool] 1 a stylus 2 a) manner of expression in language b) characteristic manner of expression, design, etc. in any art, period, etc. c) excellence of artistic expression 3 a) fashion b) something stylish — *vt.* **styled**, **styl'ing** 1 to name; call 2 to design the style of

styl·ish (stīl'ish) *adj.* conforming to current style, as in dress; fashionable

styl·ist *n.* a writer, etc. whose work has style and distinction —**styl·lis'tic** *adj.* —**styl·lis'ti·cally** *adv.*

styl·ize (stīl'īz') *vt.* **-ized**, **-iz·ing** to design or represent according to a style rather than nature

sty·lus (stī'ləs) *n.*, *pl.* **-luses** or **-li** (-lī) [L, for *stilus*, pointed instrument] 1 a sharp, pointed marking device 2 a) a sharp, pointed device for cutting the grooves of a phonograph record b) a phonograph needle

sty·mie (stī'mē) *n.* [prob. < Scot, person partially blind] *Golf* a situation in which a ball to be putted has another ball between it and the hole — *vt.* **-mied**, **-mie·ing** to block; impede Also **sty'my**, **-mied**, **-my·ing**

styp·tic (stip'tik) *adj.* [< Gr *styphein*, to contract] tending to halt bleeding; astringent —**styp'sis** *n.*

styptic pencil a piece of a styptic substance to stop minor bleeding

Styro·foam (stī'rə fōm') *trademark for* a rigid, lightweight, spongelike plastic — *n.* [s-] this substance

Styx (stiks) *Gr. Myth.* the river crossed by dead souls entering Hades

suave (swäv) *adj.* [< L *suavis*, sweet] smoothly gracious or polite; polished —**suave'ly** *adv.* —**suav'ity** *n.*

sub (sub) *n. short for:* 1 SUBMARINE 2 SUBSTITUTE — *vi.* **subbed**, **sub'bing** [Colloq.] to be a substitute *(for* someone)

sub- [< L *sub*, under] *prefix* 1 under *[submarine]* 2 lower than; inferior to *[subhead]* 3 to a lesser degree than *[subhuman]*

sub. *abbrev.* 1 substitute(s) 2 suburb(an)

sub·atom·ic (sub'ə täm'ik) *adj.* smaller than an atom

sub'branch' *n.* a division of a branch

sub'com·mit'tee *n.* a small committee chosen from a main committee

sub'com'pact' *n.* a model of automobile smaller than a compact

sub·con'scious *adj.* occurring with little or no conscious perception on the part of the individual: said of mental processes —**the subconscious** subconscious mental activity —**sub·con'sciously** *adv.*

sub·con'ti·nent *n.* a large land mass smaller than a continent

sub·con·tract (sub'kän'trakt; *also, for v.* sub'kən trakt') *n.* a secondary contract undertaking some or all obligations of another contract — *vt.*, *vi.* to make a subcontract (for) —**sub'con'trac·tor** (-trak tər) *n.*

sub'cul'ture *n.* 1 a distinctive social group within a larger social group 2 its cultural patterns

sub'cu·ta'neous *adj.* beneath the skin

sub'dea'con *n.* a cleric ranking just below a deacon

sub'deb' *n.* a girl not quite of debutante age

sub'dis'trict *n.* a subdivision of a district

sub'di·vide' *vt.*, *vi.* **-vid'ed**, **-vid'ing** 1 to divide further 2 to divide (land) into small parcels —**sub'di·vi'sion** *n.*

sub·due (səb dōō', -dyōō') *vt.* **-dued'**, **-du'ing** [< L *subducere*, take away] 1 to conquer 2 to overcome; control 3 to make less intense; diminish

sub·fami·ly (sub'fam'ə lē) *n.*, *pl.* **-lies** a main subdivision of a family, as of plants, language, etc.

sub'head' *n.* a subordinate heading or title, as of a magazine article

subj. 1 subject 2 subjunctive

sub·ject (sub'jikt, -jekt'; *for v.* səb jekt') *adj.* [< L *sub-*, under + *jacere*, throw] 1 under the authority or control of another 2 having a tendency *[subject to anger]* 3 exposed *[subject to censure]* 4 contingent upon *[subject to approval]* — *n.* 1 one under the authority or control of another 2 one made to undergo a treatment, experiment, etc. 3 something dealt with in discussion, study, etc.; theme 4 a course of study in a school or college 5 *Gram.* the noun, etc. in a sentence about which something is said — *vt.* 1 to bring under the authority or control of 2 to cause to undergo something *[to subject* one to questioning*]* —**sub·jec'tion** *n.*

sub·jec·tive (səb jek'tiv) *adj.* of or resulting from the feelings of the person thinking; personal —**sub·jec'tive·ly** *adv.* —**sub·jec·tiv·ity** (sub'jek tiv'ə tē) *n.*

sub·join (səb join') *vt.* [see SUB- & JOIN] to append

sub·ju·gate (sub'jə gāt') *vt.* **-gat'ed**, **-gat'ing** [< L *sub-*,

THESAURUS

stunning *a.* striking, marvelous, remarkable; see BEAUTIFUL, HANDSOME.

stunt[2] *n.* act, skit, comic sketch; see PERFORMANCE.

stupid *a.* senseless, brainless, idiotic, simple, shallow, imprudent, witless, irrational, inane, ridiculous, mindless, ludicrous, muddled, absurd, half-witted, funny, comical, silly, laughable, nonsensical, illogical, indiscreet, unintelligent, irresponsible, scatterbrained, crackbrained, addled, foolish, unwary, incautious, misguided, wild, injudicious, imbecile, addleheaded, lunatic, insane, mad, crazy, moronic, touched, freakish, comic, narrow-minded, incoherent, childish, senile, far-fetched, preposterous, unreasonable, asinine, unwise, thoughtless, careless, fatuous, light, lightheaded, flighty, madcap, giddy, cuckoo*, boneheaded*, goofy*, cracked*, dumb*, half-baked, in a daze, wacky*, harebrained, screwy*, cock-eyed*, loony*, batty*, dopey*,

nutty*.—*Ant.* SANE, wise, judicious.

stupidity *n.* 1 [Dullness of mind] stupor, slowness, heaviness, obtuseness, sluggishness, feeble-mindedness, weakness, silliness, nonsense, folly, absurdity, imbecility, brainlessness, imprudence, lunacy, idiocy, shallowness, weakmindedness, impracticality, senility, giddiness, thick-headedness, asininity, slowness, lack of judgment.—*Ant.* INTELLIGENCE, wisdom, judgment. 2 [Extreme folly] nonsense, absurdity, silliness; see CARELESSNESS, NONSENSE 2.

stupidly *a.* imprudently, stubbornly, obtusely; see FOOLISHLY.

sturdy *a.* firm, resolute, unyielding; see STRONG 1, 2.

stutter *v.* stumble, falter, sputter; see STAMMER.

style *n.* 1 [Distinctive manner] way, form, technique; see METHOD. 2 [Fashion] vogue, habit, custom; see FASHION 2. —**in style** current, chic, stylish; see FASHIONABLE, POPULAR 1.

stylish *a.* chic, smart, in fashion; see FASHIONABLE.

suave *a.* sophisticated, ingratiating, urbane; see CULTURED.

subconscious *a.* subliminal, innermost, inmost; see MENTAL 3.

subconscious *n.* the unconscious, psyche, mind; see SOUL 2.

subject *a.* governed, ruled, controlled, directed, obedient, submissive, servile, slavish, subservient, subjected, at one's feet, at the mercy of.

subject *n.* substance, matter, theme, material, topic, question, problem, point, case, matter for discussion, matter in hand, item on the agenda, topic under consideration, field of inquiry, head, chapter, argument, thought, discussion.

subject *v.* cause to experience something, lay open, expose, submit.

subjective *a.* nonobjective, biased, personal; see PREJUDICED.

subjectively *a.* internally, intrinsiunder + *jugum*, a yoke] to bring under control; conquer — **sub·ju·ga'tion** *n.*

sub·junc·tive (səb juŋk'tiv) *adj.* [< L *subjungere*, subjoin] designating or of the mood of a verb that is used to express supposition, desire, possibility, etc., rather than to state an actual fact

sub·lease (sub'lēs'; *for v.* sub lēs') *n.* a lease granted by a lessee — *vt.* **-leased', -leas'ing** to grant or hold a sublease of

sub·let (sub let') *vt.* **-let', -let'ting** 1 to let to another (property which one is renting) 2 to let out (work) to a subcontractor

sub·li·mate (sub'lə māt') *vt.* **-mat'ed, -mat'ing** 1 to sublime (a solid) 2 to express (unacceptable impulses) in acceptable forms, often unconsciously — **sub'li·ma'tion** *n.*

sub·lime (sə blīm') *adj.* [< L *sub-*, up to + *limen*, lintel] 1 noble; exalted 2 inspiring awe or admiration — *vt.* **-limed', -lim'ing** to change (a solid) to gaseous state without going through an intermediate liquid state — **sub·lim'i·ty** (sə blim'ə tē) *n.*

sub·lim·i·nal (sub lim'ə nəl) *adj.* [< SUB- + L *limen*, threshold + -AL] below the threshold of consciousness

sub'ma·chine' gun a portable, automatic firearm

sub·mar·gin·al (sub mär'jə nəl) *adj.* below minimum requirements or standards

sub·ma·rine (sub'mə rēn'; *for n. usually* sub'mə rēn') *adj.* being, living, etc. underwater — *n.* a ship, esp. a warship, that can operate under water

submarine sandwich HERO SANDWICH

sub·merge (sub mʉrj', səb-) *vt., vi.* **-merged', -merg'ing** [< L *sub-*, under + *mergere*, to plunge] to place or sink beneath the surface, as of water — **sub·mer'gence** (-mʉr'jəns) *n.*

sub·merse' (-mʉrs') *vt.* **-mersed', -mers'ing** SUBMERGE — **sub·mers'ible** *adj.* — **sub·mer'sion** *n.*

sub·mis·sion (sub mish'ən, səb-) *n.* 1 a submitting or surrendering 2 obedience; resignation — **sub·mis'sive** *adj.*

sub·mit' (-mit') *vt.* **-mit'ted, -mit'ting** [< L *sub-*, under + *mittere*, send] 1 to present to others for consideration, etc. 2 to yield to the control or power of another 3 to offer as an opinion — *vi.* to yield; give in

sub·nor·mal (sub nôr'məl) *adj.* below normal, esp. in intelligence

sub·or·bital (-ôr'bit'l, -bə təl) *adj.* designating a flight in which a rocket, spacecraft, etc. follows a trajectory of less than one orbit

sub·or·di·nate (sə bôrd'n it, -bôr'də nit; *for v.,* -bôrd'n āt', -bôr'də nāt') *adj.* [< L *sub-*, under + *ordinare*, to order] 1 below another in rank, importance, etc. 2 under the authority of another 3 *Gram.* having the function of a noun, adjective, or adverb within a sentence [a *subordinate* phrase] — *n.* a subordinate person or thing — *vt.* **-nat'ed, -nat'ing** to place in a subordinate position — **sub·or'di·na'tion** *n.*

subordinate clause *Gram.* DEPENDENT CLAUSE

sub·orn (sə bôrn') *vt.* [< L *sub-*, under + *ornare*, adorn] to induce (another) to commit perjury — **sub·or·na·tion** (sub'ôr nā'shən) *n.*

sub'plot' *n.* a secondary plot in a play, novel, etc.

sub·poe·na (sə pē'nə) *n.* [< L *sub poena*, under penalty] a written legal order directing a person to appear in court to testify, etc. — *vt.* **-naed, -na·ing** to summon with such an order Also **sub·pe'na**

sub·pro·fes·sional (sub'prō fesh'ə nəl) *n.* PARAPROFESSIONAL

sub rosa (sub rō'zə) [L, under the rose] secretly; privately

sub·scribe (səb skrīb') *vt., vi.* **-scribed', -scrib'ing** [< L *sub-*, under + *scribere*, write] 1 to sign (one's name) on a document, etc. 2 to give support or consent (to) 3 to promise to contribute (money) 4 to agree to receive and pay for a periodical, service, etc. (with *to*) — **sub·scrib'er** *n.*

sub·script (sub'skript') *n.* [see prec.] a figure, letter, or symbol written below and to the side of another

sub·scrip·tion (səb skrip'shən) *n.* 1 a subscribing 2 money subscribed 3 a formal agreement to receive and pay for a periodical, etc.

sub·se·quent (sub'si kwənt) *adj.* [< L *sub-*, after + *sequi*, follow] coming after; following — **subsequent to** after — **sub'se·quent·ly** *adv.*

sub·ser·vi·ent (səb sʉr'vē ənt) *adj.* 1 that is of service, esp. in a subordinate capacity 2 submissive — **sub·ser'vi·ence** *n.*

sub·side (səb sīd') *vi.* **-sid'ed, -sid'ing** [< L *sub-*, under + *sidere*, settle] 1 to sink to the bottom or to a lower level 2 to become less active, intense, etc. — **sub·sid'ence** *n.*

sub·sid·i·ary (səb sid'ē er'ē) *adj.* [see SUBSIDY] 1 giving aid, service, etc.; auxiliary 2 being in a subordinate relationship — *n., pl.* **-ies** one that is subsidiary; specif., a company controlled by another company

sub·si·dize (sub'sə dīz') *vt.* **-dized', -diz'ing** to support with a subsidy — **sub'si·di·za'tion** *n.*

sub·si·dy (sub'sə dē) *n., pl.* **-dies** [< L *subsidium*, auxiliary forces] a grant of money, as from a government to a private enterprise

sub·sist (səb sist') *vi.* [< L *sub-*, under + *sistere*, stand] 1 to continue to be or exist 2 to continue to live; remain alive (*on* or *by*)

sub·sist'ence *n.* 1 existence 2 the act of providing sustenance 3 means of support or livelihood, esp. the barest means

sub·soil (sub'soil') *n.* the layer of soil beneath the topsoil

sub·son·ic (-sän'ik) *adj.* designating, of, or moving at a speed less than that of sound

sub·stance (sub'stəns) *n.* [< L *substare*, exist] 1 the real or essential part of anything; essence 2 the physical matter of which a thing consists 3 a) solid or substantial quality b) consistency; body 4 the real meaning; gist 5 wealth 6 a drug: see CONTROLLED SUBSTANCE

sub·stand·ard *adj.* below standard

sub·stan·tial (səb stan'shəl) *adj.* 1 having substance 2 real; true 3 strong; solid 4 ample; large 5 important 6 wealthy 7 with regard to essential elements — **sub·stan'tial·ly** *adv.*

sub·stan·ti·ate' (-shē āt') *vt.* **-at'ed, -at'ing** [see SUBSTANCE] to show to be true or real by giving evidence — **sub·stan'ti·a'tion** *n.*

sub·stan·tive (sub'stən tiv) *adj.* [see SUBSTANCE] of or dealing with essentials — *n. Gram.* a noun or any word or group of words used as a noun

sub·sta·tion *n.* a small post-office station, as in a store

sub·sti·tute (sub'stə tōōt') *n.* [< L *sub-*, under + *statuere*, put] a person or thing serving or used in place of another

---

THESAURUS

cally, individually, egocentrically, mentally, nonobjectively, emotionally, introspectively, inherently; see also PERSONALLY 2.
sublime *a.* exalted, lofty, stately; see GRAND.
submarine *n.* underseas boat, submersible, sub; see SHIP.
submerge *v.* submerse, engulf, swamp; see IMMERSE, SINK 2.
submission *n.* obedience, meekness, assent; see RESIGNATION 1.
submissive *a.* passive, tractable, yielding; see DOCILE.
submit *v.* 1 [To offer] tender, proffer, present; see OFFER 1. 2 [To surrender] capitulate, yield, give in; see OBEY.
subordinate *a.* inferior, junior, smaller, low, insignificant, subnormal, paltry, not up to snuff*, below par, unequal to, not comparable to,

lower, minor, depending on, lower in rank, subject, subservient, submissive, subsidiary; see also UNDER 2.— *Ant.* superior, higher, excellent.
subordinate *n.* assistant, helper, aide; see ASSISTANT.
subsequent *a.* succeeding, consequent, coming after; see FOLLOWING.
subsequently *a.* afterward, consequently, in the end; see FINALLY 2.
subside *v.* recede, sink, dwindle; see FALL 1.
subsidiary *a.* secondary, auxiliary, supplementary; see SUBORDINATE.
subsidize *v.* support, finance, back; see PROMOTE 1.
subsidy *n.* allowance, support, scholarship; see PAYMENT 1.
subsist *v.* stay alive, remain alive, live on; see LIVE 4.
subsistence *n.* 1 [The supporting of

life] living, sustenance, maintenance, support, keep, necessities of life. 2 [The means of supporting life] means, circumstances, resources, property, money, riches, wealth, capital, substance, affluence, independence, gratuity, fortune, dowry, legacy, earnings, wages, salary, income, pension; see also FUNDS.— *Ant.* POVERTY, penury, pennilessness.
substance *n.* matter, material, being, object, item, person, animal, something, element; see also THING 1.
substantial *a.* 1 [Real] material, actual, visible; see TANGIBLE. 2 [Considerable] ample, abundant, plentiful; see LARGE 1, MUCH 2.
substantially *a.* extensively, considerably, largely; see MUCH 1, 2.
substitute *n.* deputy, double, dummy, relief, stand-in, understudy,

— *vt.*, *vi.* **-tut′ed, -tut′ing** to put, use, or serve in place of (another) —**sub′sti·tu′tion** *n.*

sub·stra·tum (sub′strāt′əm, -strat′-) *n.*, *pl.* **-ta** (-ə) or **-tums** a part, substance, etc. which lies beneath and supports another

sub·struc′ture *n.* a part or structure that is a support, base, etc.

sub·sume (sub sōōm′, səb-) *vt.* **-sumed′, -sum′ing** [< L *sub-*, under + *sumere*, take] to include within a larger class

sub·teen′ *n.* a child nearly a teenager

sub·ten′ant *n.* a person who rents from a tenant —**sub·ten′an·cy** *n.*

sub·ter·fuge (sub′tər fyōōj′) *n.* [< L *subter*, secretly + *fugere*, flee] any plan or action used to hide or evade

sub·ter·ra·nean (sub′tə rā′nē ən) *adj.* [< L *sub-*, under + *terra*, earth] 1 underground 2 secret; hidden

sub·ti′tle *n.* 1 a secondary or explanatory title 2 one or more lines of translated dialogue at the bottom of a movie screen, etc. — *vt.* **-ti′tled, -ti′tling** to add a subtitle or subtitles to

sub·tle (sut′'l) *adj.* **-tler** (-lər, -'l ər), **-tlest** [< L *subtilis*, fine, thin] 1 thin; not dense 2 mentally keen 3 delicately skillful 4 crafty 5 not obvious —**sub′tlety,** *pl.* **-ties,** *n.* —**sub′tly** *adv.*

sub·to′tal *n.* a total that is part of a complete total — *vt.*, *vi.* **-taled** or **-talled, -tal·ing** or **-tal·ling** to add up so as to form a subtotal

sub·tract (səb trakt′) *vt.*, *vi.* [< L *sub-*, under + *trahere*, to draw] to take away or deduct (one quantity from another) —**sub·trac′tion** *n.*

sub·tra·hend (sub′trə hend′) *n.* a quantity to be subtracted from another

sub·tropi·cal (sub trä′pi kəl) *adj.* of, characteristic of, or bordering on the tropics Also **sub·trop′ic**

sub·urb (sub′ərb) *n.* [< L *sub-*, near + *urbs*, town] a district, town, etc. on the outskirts of a city —**sub·ur′ban** (sə bur′bən) *adj.*

sub·ur·ban·ite (sə bur′bən īt′) *n.* a person living in a suburb

sub·ur′bia (-bē ə) *n.* the suburbs or suburbanites collectively

sub·ven·tion (sub ven′shən, səb-) *n.* [< LL *subventio*, aid] a subsidy

sub·ver·sive (səb vur′siv) *adj.* tending to subvert — *n.* a subversive person

sub·vert (səb vurt′) *vt.* [< L *sub-*, under + *vertere*, to turn] 1 to overthrow or destroy (something established) 2 to corrupt, as in morals —**sub·ver′sion** (-vur′zhən) *n.*

sub′way′ *n.* an underground, metropolitan electric railway

suc- *prefix* SUB-: used before *c* [*succumb*]

suc·ceed (sək sēd′) *vi.* [< L *sub-*, under + *cedere*, to go] 1 to follow, as in office 2 to be successful — *vt.* to come after; follow

suc·cess (sək ses′) *n.* 1 a favorable result 2 the gaining of wealth, fame, etc. 3 a successful person a thing

suc·cess′ful *adj.* 1 turning out as was hoped for 2 having gained wealth, fame, etc. —**suc·cess′fully** *adv.*

suc·ces·sion (sək sesh′ən) *n.* 1 *a*) the act of succeeding another, as to an office *b*) the right to do this 2 a number of persons or things coming one after another

suc·ces′sive (-ses′iv) *adj.* coming one after another —**suc·ces′sively** *adv.*

suc·ces′sor *n.* one that succeeds another, as to an office

suc·cinct (suk siŋkt′, sək-) *adj.* [< L *sub-*, under + *cingere*, gird] clear and brief; terse —**suc·cinct′ly** *adv.* —**suc·cinct′ness** *n.*

suc·cor (suk′ər) *vt.* [< L *sub-*, under + *currere*, to run] to help in time of need or distress — *n.* aid; relief

suc·co·tash (suk′ə tash′) *n.* [< AmInd] a dish consisting of lima beans and corn kernels cooked together

suc·cu·lent (suk′yōō lənt) *adj.* [< L *sucus*, juice] full of juice; juicy —**suc′cu·lence** or **suc′cu·lency** *n.*

suc·cumb (sə kum′) *vi.* [< L *sub-*, under + *cumbere*, to lie] 1 to give way (*to*); yield 2 to die

such (such) *adj.* [OE *swilc*] 1 *a*) of the kind mentioned *b*) of the same or a similar kind 2 whatever [*at such* time as you go] 3 so extreme, so much, etc. [*such* an honor] — *adv.* to so great a degree [*such* good news] — *pron.* 1 such a person or thing 2 the person or thing mentioned [*such* was her nature] —**as such** 1 as being what is indicated 2 in itself —**such as** for example

such and such (being) something particular but not named or specified [*such and such* a place]

such′like′ *adj.* of such a kind — *pron.* persons or things of such a kind

suck (suk) *vt.* [< OE *sucan*] 1 to draw (liquid) into the mouth 2 to take in as by sucking 3 to suck liquid from

THESAURUS

proxy, replacement, ringer*, sub*, pinch-hitter; see also DELEGATE.

substitute *v.* act for, do the work of, replace, supplant, displace, take another's place, double for, answer for, pass for, go for, go as, fill in for, pinch-hit for, take the rap for*, go to bat for*, front for, be in someone's shoes.

substitution *n.* change, swap, replacement; see EXCHANGE 2.

subterranean *a.* subsurface, sunken, subterraneous; see UNDERGROUND.

subtle *a.* indirect, implied, insinuated; see MENTAL 2.

subtlety *n.* fine distinction, nuance, innuendo; see SUGGESTION 1.

subtract *v.* deduct, take away, withhold; see DECREASE 2.

subtraction *n.* deducting, deduction, diminution; see DISCOUNT, REDUCTION 1.

suburb *n.* outlying district, residential district, outskirts; see AREA.

suburban *a.* near a city, residential, rural; see DISTRICT, LOCAL 1, RURAL.

subversion *n.* overthrow, subversive activities, un-American activities; see DEFEAT, REVOLUTION 2.

subversive *a.* ruinous, riotous, insurgent; see REBELLIOUS.

subway *n.* underground (British), tube (British), rapid transit; see RAILROAD, TRAIN.

succeed *v.* 1 [To attain success] achieve, accomplish, get, prosper, attain, reach, be successful, fulfill, earn, do well, secure, succeed in, score, obtain, thrive, profit, realize, acquire, flourish, be victorious, cap-

ture, reap, benefit, recover, retrieve, gain, receive, master, triumph, possess, overcome, win, win out, work out, carry out, surmount, prevail, conquer, vanquish, distance, outdistance, reduce, suppress, worst, work, outwit, outmaneuver, score a point, be accepted, be well-known, grow famous, carry off, pull off, come off, come through, make one's way, make one's fortune, satisfy one's ambition, make one's mark, hit it, hit the mark, live high, come through with flying colors, beat the game*, work well, overcome all obstacles, play one's cards well, crown, top, do oneself proud*, make it*, make good*, do all right by oneself, be on top of the heap*, go places*, click*, set the world on fire*, cut the mustard*, make a killing, put across*.—*Ant.* FAIL, give up, go amiss. 2 [To follow in time] follow after, come after, take the place of, ensue, supervene, supplant, supersede, replace, postdate, displace, come next, become heir to, result, be subsequent to, follow in order, bring up the rear.

succeeding *a.* ensuing, following after, next in order; see FOLLOWING.

success *n.* 1 [The fact of having succeeded to a high degree] fortune, good luck, achievement, accomplishment, gain, benefit, prosperity, victory, advance, attainment, progress, profit, end, completion, triumph, conclusion, the life of Riley*, bed of roses*, favorable outcome.—*Ant.* DEFEAT, loss, disaster. 2 [A successful person or thing] celebrity, famous

person, leader, authority, master, expert, man of fortune, somebody, star, VIP*, tops.—*Ant.* FAILURE, loser, nonentity.

successful *a.* prosperous, fortunate, lucky, victorious, triumphant, auspicious, happy, unbeaten, favorable, strong, propitious, advantageous, encouraging, contented, satisfied, thriving, flourishing, wealthy, ahead of the game*, at the top of the ladder, out in front, on the track*, over the hump*.—*Ant.* UNSUCCESSFUL, poor, failing.

successfully *a.* fortunately, triumphantly, luckily, victoriously, happily, favorably, strongly, thrivingly, flourishingly, famously, propitiously, auspiciously, prosperously, contentedly, beyond all expectation.

succession *n.* continuation, suite, set; see SEQUENCE 1, SERIES.

successive *a.* serial, succeeding, in line; see CONSECUTIVE.

successor *n.* heir, follower, replacement; see CANDIDATE.

such *a.* so, so very, of this kind, of that kind, of the sort, of the degree, so much, before-mentioned.

such *pron.* this, that, such a one, such a person, such a thing. —**as such** in and of itself, by its own nature, more than in name only; see ACCORDINGLY, ESSENTIALLY.

such as *conj.*, *prep.* for example, for instance, to give an example; see INCLUDING, SIMILARLY, THUS.

suck *v.* absorb, take up, swallow up; see SWALLOW.

(fruit, etc.) **4** to hold (ice, etc.) in the mouth and lick so as to dissolve **5** to place (the thumb, etc.) in the mouth and draw on — *vi.* to suck something — *n.* the act of sucking

suck′er *n.* **1** one that sucks **2** a freshwater, bony fish with a mouth adapted for sucking **3** a part used for sucking or for holding fast by suction **4** LOLLIPOP **5** [Slang] one easily cheated **6** *Bot.* a subordinate shoot on the root or stem of a plant

suckle (suk′əl) *vt.* **-led, -ling** [ME *sokelen*] **1** to cause to suck at the breast or udder; nurse **2** to bring up; rear — *vi.* to suck at the breast or udder

suck′ling *n.* an unweaned child or young animal

su·crose (sōō′krōs) *n.* [< Fr *sucre*, sugar + -OSE[1]] a a sugar extracted from sugar cane or sugar beets

suc·tion (suk′shən) *n.* [< L *sugere*, to suck] **1** a sucking **2** production of a partial vacuum so that external pressure forces fluid in or causes something to adhere to a surface

sud·den (sud′n) *adj.* [< L *sub-*, under + *ire*, go] **1** *a*) happening or coming unexpectedly *b*) sharp or abrupt **2** quick or hasty — **all of a sudden** unexpectedly — **sud′denly** *adv.* — **sud′den·ness** *n.*

sudden death *Sports* an extra period added to a tied game: the game ending as soon as one side scores Usually **sud′den-death′ overtime**

sudden infant death syndrome the sudden death of an apparently healthy infant, possibly caused by a breathing problem

suds (sudz) *n.pl.* [prob. < MDu *sudse*, marsh water] **1** soapy, frothy water **2** foam — **suds′y, -i·er, -i·est,** *adj.*

sue (sōō) *vt., vi.* **sued, su′ing** [< L *sequi*, follow] **1** to appeal (to); petition **2** to prosecute in a court in seeking justice, etc.

suede or **suède** (swād) *n.* [< Fr *gants de Suède*, Swedish gloves] **1** tanned leather with the flesh side buffed into a nap **2** a cloth like this

suet (sōō′it) *n.* [< L *sebum*, tallow] the hard fat of cattle and sheep: used in cooking and as tallow

suf- *prefix* SUB- Used before *f*

suf·fer (suf′ər) *vt., vi.* [< L *sub-*, under + *ferre*, to bear] **1** to undergo (pain, injury, grief, etc.) **2** to experience (any process) **3** to permit; tolerate — **suf′fer·er** *n.*

suf′fer·ance *n.* **1** the capacity to endure pain, etc. **2** consent, permission, etc. implied by failure to prohibit

suf′fer·ing *n.* **1** the bearing of pain, distress, etc. **2** something suffered

suf·fice (sə fīs′) *vi.* **-ficed′, -fic′ing** [< L *sub-*, under + *facere*, make] to be enough or adequate

suf·fi·cient (sə fish′ənt) *adj.* as much as is needed; enough — **suf·fi′cien·cy** *n.* — **suf·fi′cient·ly** *adv.*

suf·fix (suf′iks) *n.* [< L *sub-*, under + *figere*, fix] a syllable or syllables added at the end of a word to alter its meaning, etc. (Ex.: *-ness* in *darkness*)

suf·fo·cate (suf′ə kāt′) *vt.* **-cat′ed, -cat′ing** [< L *sub-*, under + *fauces*, throat] **1** to kill by cutting off the supply of air for breathing **2** to smother, suppress, etc. — *vi.* **1** to die by being suffocated **2** to choke; stifle — **suf′fo·ca′tion** *n.*

suf·fra·gan (suf′rə gən) *n.* [see SUFFRAGE] a bishop who is an assistant to another bishop

suf·frage (suf′rij) *n.* [< L *suffragium*] **1** a vote or voting **2** the right to vote; franchise — **suf′fra·gist** *n.*

suf·fra·gette (suf′rə jet′) *n.* [< prec. + -ETTE] a woman who advocates female suffrage

suf·fuse (sə fyōōz′) *vt.* **-fused′, -fus′ing** [< L *sub-*, under + *fundere*, pour] to overspread so as to fill with a glow, etc. — **suf·fu′sion** *n.*

sug- *prefix* SUB- Used before *g*

sugar (shoog′ər) *n.* [< Sans *śárkarā*] any of a class of sweet, soluble carbohydrates, as sucrose, glucose, etc.; specif., sucrose used as a food and sweetening agent — *vt.* to cover, sweeten, etc. with sugar — *vi.* to form sugar — **sug′ar·less** *adj.* — **sug′ary** *adj.*

sugar beet a beet having a white root with a high sugar content

sugar cane a very tall tropical grass cultivated as the main source of sugar

sug′ar·coat′ *vt.* **1** to coat with sugar **2** to make (something disagreeable) seem more pleasant

sugar diabetes DIABETES

sug′ar·plum′ *n.* a round piece of sugary candy

sug·gest (səg jest′, sə-) *vt.* [< L *sub-*, under + *gerere*, carry] **1** to bring to the mind for consideration **2** to call to mind by association of ideas **3** to propose as a possibility **4** to show indirectly; imply

sug·gest′i·ble *adj.* readily influenced by suggestion — **sug·gest′ibil′i·ty** *n.*

sug·ges·tion (-jes′chən) *n.* **1** a suggesting or being suggested **2** something suggested **3** a hint or trace

sug·ges′tive *adj.* **1** that tends to suggest ideas **2** tending to suggest something considered improper or indecent — **sug·ges′tive·ly** *adv.*

sui·cide (sōō′ə sīd′) *n.* [L *sui*, of oneself + -CIDE] **1** the act of killing oneself intentionally **2** one who commits suicide — **su′i·cid′al** *adj.*

sui ge·ne·ris (sōō′ē jen′ər is) [L, of his own kind] without equal; unique

suit (sōōt) *n.* [< L *sequi*, follow] **1** a set of clothes; esp., a coat and trousers (or skirt) **2** any of the four sets of play-

---

◼ THESAURUS ◼

sucker *n.* **1** [A fish] lumpfish, sand sucker, brook sucker; see FISH. **2** [*A victim] dupe, fool, cat's-paw; see VICTIM. **3** [Candy] sweet, confectionary, lollipop; see CANDY.

suction *n.* sucking, the force of a vacuum, effect of atmospheric pressures; see ATTRACTION, POWER 2, PULL 1.

sudden *a.* precipitate, impromptu, swift; see IMMEDIATE, UNEXPECTED. —**all of a sudden** unexpectedly, suddenly, precipitously; see QUICKLY.

suddenly *a.* without any warning, abruptly, swiftly; see QUICKLY.

suds *n.* foam, bubbles, lather; see FROTH, SOAP.

sue *v.* prosecute, follow up, claim, demand, indict, litigate, contest, pray, entreat, plead, petition, appeal, accuse, file a plea, enter a plea, claim damages, go to law, file suit, prefer a claim, enter a lawsuit, take one to court, file a claim, have the law on one, haul into court.

suffer *v.* **1** [To feel pain] undergo, experience, ache, smart, be in pain, be wounded, agonize, grieve, be racked, be convulsed, droop, flag, sicken, torture oneself, get it in the neck*, look green about the gills, complain of, be affected with, go hard with, match it, flinch at, not feel like anything, labor under.—*Ant.* RECOVER, be relieved, be restored. **2** [To endure] bear, sustain, put up with; see ENDURE 2. **3** [To permit] admit, let, submit; see ALLOW.

suffering *n.* distress, misery, affliction; see DIFFICULTY 1, 2, PAIN 2.

sufficient *a.* adequate, ample, satisfactory; see ENOUGH 1.

sufficiently *a.* to one's satisfaction, enough, amply; see ADEQUATELY.

suffocate *v.* stifle, smother, strangle; see CHOKE.

sugar *n.* *Common varieties and forms of sugar include the following:* sucrose, cane sugar, brown sugar, beet sugar, grape sugar, dextrose, fructose, fruit sugar, maltose, malt sugar, lactose, maple sugar; see also FOOD.

sugary *a.* sticky, granular, candied; see SWEET 1.

suggest *v.* **1** [To make a suggestion] submit, advise, recommend; see PROPOSE 1. **2** [To bring to mind] imply, infer, intimate; see HINT.

suggested *a.* submitted, advanced, proposed, propounded, advised, recommended, counseled, tendered, reminded, prompted, summoned up, called up, offered, laid before, put forward.

suggestion *n.* **1** [A suggested detail] hint, allusion, suspicion, intimation, implication, innuendo, insinuation, opinion, proposal, advice, recommendation, injunction, charge, instruction, submission, reminder,

approach, advance, bid, idea, tentative statement, presentation, proposition. **2** [A suggested plan] scheme, idea, outline; see PLAN 2. **3** [A very small quantity] trace, touch, taste; see BIT 1.

suicide *n.* self-murder, self-destruction, hara-kiri; see DEATH. —**commit suicide** kill oneself, take an overdose, slash one's wrists, take one's own life, end it all*, commit hara-kiri, poison oneself, jump off a bridge*, blow one's brains out*.

suit *n.* **1** [A series] suite, set, group; see SERIES. **2** [A case at law] lawsuit, action, litigation; see TRIAL 2. **3** [Clothes to be worn together] costume, ensemble, outfit, livery, uniform; see also CLOTHES. *Kinds of suits include the following— women:* sport suit, tailored suit, man-tailored suit, jump suit, evening suit, bathing suit, sun suit, play suit; *men:* sport suit, business suit, full dress, tails*, monkey suit*, dinner jacket, tuxedo, tux*, bathing suit. —**bring suit** prosecute, start legal proceedings, initiate a case; see SUE.

suit *v.* **1** [To be in accord with] befit, be agreeable, be appropriate to; see AGREE. **2** [To please] amuse, fill, gratify; see ENTERTAIN 1, SATISFY 1. **3** [To adapt] accommodate, revise, readjust; see ALTER 1.

ing cards **3** action to secure justice in a court of law **4** an act of suing, pleading, etc. **5** courtship —*vt.* **1** to be appropriate to **2** to make right or appropriate; fit **3** to please; satisfy *[nothing suits* him*]* —**follow suit** to follow the example set —**suit oneself** to act according to one's own wishes —**suit up** to put on an athletic uniform, spacesuit, etc. in preparation for a particular activity

suit′able *adj.* that suits a given purpose, etc.; appropriate —**suit′abil′ity** *n.* —**suit′ably** *adv.*

suit′case′ *n.* a travel case for clothes, etc.

suite (swēt) *n.* ⟦Fr: see SUIT⟧ **1** a group of attendants; staff **2** a set of connected rooms, as an apartment **3** a set of matched furniture for a given room

suit′ing *n.* cloth for making suits

suit′or *n.* a man courting a woman

su·ki·yaki (sōō′kē yä′kē) *n.* ⟦Jpn⟧ a Japanese dish of thinly sliced meat and vegetables, cooked quickly

Suk·kot or **Suk·koth** (sook′ōt, sook′ōs) *n.* ⟦Heb, lit., tabernacles⟧ a Jewish fall festival commemorating the wandering of the Hebrews during the Exodus

sulfa (sul′fə) *adj.* designating or of a family of drugs used in combating certain bacterial infections

sul·fate (sul′fāt′) *n.* a salt or ester of sulfuric acid

sul′fide′ (-fīd′) *n.* a compound of sulfur with another element or a radical

sul·fur (sul′fər) *n.* ⟦< L *sulphur*⟧ a pale-yellow, nonmetallic chemical element: it burns with a blue flame and a stifling odor

sul·fu·ric (sul fyoor′ik) *adj.* of or containing sulfur

sulfuric acid an oily, colorless, corrosive liquid used in making dyes, explosives, fertilizers, etc.

sul·fu·rous (sul′fər əs, sul fyoor′əs) *adj.* **1** of or containing sulfur **2** like burning sulfur in odor, color, etc.

sulk (sulk) *vi.* ⟦< fol.⟧ to be sulky —*n.* a sulky mood Also **the sulks**

sulky (sul′kē) *adj.* **-i·er, -i·est** ⟦prob. < OE *-seolcan,* become slack⟧ sullenly aloof, silent, etc.; moody; glum —*n., pl.* **-ies** a light, two-wheeled carriage for one person —**sulk′i·ly** *adv.* —**sulk′i·ness** *n.*

sul·len (sul′ən) *adj.* ⟦< L *solus,* alone⟧ **1** showing resentment and ill humor by morose, unsociable withdrawal **2** gloomy; sad —**sul′len·ly** *adv.* —**sul′len·ness** *n.*

sully (sul′ē) *vt.* **-lied, -ly·ing** ⟦prob. < OFr *soillier*⟧ to soil, tarnish, etc., esp. by disgracing

sul·phur (sul′fər) *n. chiefly Brit., etc. sp. of* SULFUR

sul·tan (sult′'n) *n.* ⟦Fr < Ar *sulṭān*⟧ a Muslim ruler

sul·tana (sul tan′ə) *n.* a sultan's wife, mother, sister, or daughter

sul·tan·ate (sult′'n it, -āt′) *n.* a sultan's authority, office, or domain

sul·try (sul′trē) *adj.* **-trier, -tri·est** ⟦< SWELTER⟧ **1** oppressively hot and moist **2** inflamed, as with passion

sum (sum) *n.* ⟦< L *summus,* highest⟧ **1** an amount of money **2** gist; summary **3** the result obtained by adding quantities; total **4** a problem in arithmetic —*vt.* **summed, sum′ming** to get the sum of by adding —**sum up** to summarize

su·mac or **su·mach** (sōō′mak′, shōō′-) *n.* ⟦< Ar *summāq*⟧ **1** any of numerous nonpoisonous plants with cone-shaped clusters of red fruit **2** any of several poisonous plants, as poison sumac

sum·ma·rize (sum′ə rīz′) *vt.* **-rized′, -riz′ing** to make or be a summary of

sum′mary (-rē) *adj.* ⟦< L *summa,* a sum⟧ **1** summarizing; concise **2** prompt and without formality **3** hasty and

arbitrary —*n., pl.* **-ries** a brief report covering the main points; digest —**sum·mar·i·ly** (sə mer′ə lē) *adv.*

sum·ma·tion (sə mā′shən) *n.* a final summary of arguments, as in a trial

sum·mer (sum′ər) *n.* ⟦< OE *sumor*⟧ the warmest season of the year, following spring —*adj.* of or typical of summer —*vi.* to pass the summer —**sum′mery** *adj.*

sum′mer·house′ *n.* a small, open structure in a garden, park, etc.

summer sausage a type of hard, dried and smoked sausage

sum′mer·time′ *n.* summer

sum·mit (sum′it) *n.* ⟦< L *summus,* highest⟧ **1** the highest point; top **2** the highest degree or state; acme

sum·mitry (sum′i trē) *n., pl.* **-ries** the use of conferences between heads of state to resolve problems of diplomacy

sum·mon (sum′ən) *vt.* ⟦< L *sub-,* under + *monere,* warn⟧ **1** to call together; order to meet **2** to call or send for with authority **3** to call forth; rouse *[summon* up one's strength*]* —**sum′moner** *n.*

sum′mons (-ənz) *n., pl.* **-monses** ⟦see prec.⟧ **1** an order or command to come, attend, etc. **2** *Law* an official order to appear in court

sumo (wrestling) (sōō′mō) ⟦Jpn *sumō,* compete⟧ [sometimes **S- w-**] Japanese wrestling by large, extremely heavy men

sump (sump) *n.* ⟦ME *sompe,* swamp⟧ a pit, cistern, cesspool, etc. for draining, collecting, or storing liquids

sump·tu·ous (sump′chōō əs) *adj.* ⟦< L *sumptus,* expense⟧ **1** costly; lavish **2** magnificent or splendid

sun (sun) *n.* ⟦OE *sunne*⟧ **1** the self-luminous, gaseous central star of the solar system **2** the heat or light of the sun **3** any star that is the center of a planetary system —*vt.* **sunned, sun′ning** to expose to the sun's rays —**sun′less** *adj.*

sun′bathe′ *vi.* **-bathed′, -bath′ing** to expose the body to direct sunlight —**sun bath** —**sun′bath′er** *n.*

sun′beam′ *n.* a beam of sunlight

Sun′belt′ *n.* in the U.S., the S and SW States having a sunny climate and an expanding economy Also **Sun Belt**

sun′bon′net *n.* a bonnet for shading the face and neck from the sun

sun′burn′ *n.* inflammation of the skin from exposure to the sun's rays or to a sunlamp —*vi., vt.* **-burned′** or **-burnt′, -burn′ing** to get or cause to get a sunburn

sun′burst′ *n.* **1** sudden sunlight **2** a decorative device representing the sun with spreading rays

sun·dae (sun′dā, -dē) *n.* ⟦prob. < fol.⟧ a serving of ice cream covered with a syrup, fruit, nuts, etc.

Sun·day (sun′dā; *occas.,* -dē) *n.* ⟦OE *sunnandæg,* sun day⟧ the first day of the week: it is the Sabbath for most Christians Abbrev. **Sun.**

sun·der (sun′dər) *vt., vi.* ⟦< OE *sundor,* asunder⟧ to break apart; split

sun′di′al *n.* an instrument that shows time by the shadow of a pointer cast by the sun on a dial

sun′down′ *n.* SUNSET

sun′dries (-drēz) *n.pl.* sundry items

sun′dry (-drē) *adj.* ⟦< OE *sundor,* apart⟧ miscellaneous

sun′fish′ *n., pl.* **-fish′** or (for different species) **-fish′es 1** any of a family of North American freshwater fishes **2** a large, sluggish ocean fish

sun′flow′er *n.* a tall plant having large, yellow, daisylike flowers

sung (suŋ) *vi., vt. pp. & rare pt. of* SING

sun′glass′es *n.pl.* eyeglasses with tinted lenses to shade the eyes

sunk (suŋk) *vi., vt. pp. & alt. pt. of* SINK

◼◼◼ THESAURUS ◼◼◼

suitable *a.* fitting, becoming, proper; see FIT 1.

suitably *a.* well, all to the good, pleasantly; see FIT 1.

suitcase *n.* case, grip, satchel; see BAG.

suited *a.* adapted, satisfactory, fitted; see FIT 1.

sullen *a.* unsociable, silent, morose, glum, sulky, sour, cross, ill-humored, petulant, moody, grouchy, fretful, illnatured, peevish, gloomy, gruff, churlish; see also IRRITABLE.—*Ant.* FRIENDLY, sociable, jolly.

sullenly *a.* morosely, glumly, sourly; see ANGRILY, SILENTLY.

sum *n.* amount, value, worth; see WHOLE.

summarily *a.* promptly, readily, speedily; see IMMEDIATELY.

summarize *v.* review, compile, shorten; see DECREASE.

summary *n.* outline, digest, synopsis, recap, analysis, abstract, abbreviation, resume, précis, skeleton, brief, case, reduction, version, core, report, survey, sketch, syllabus, condensation, sum and substance, wrapup*.

summer *n.* summertime, summer season, dog days, sunny season, harvest, haying time, vacation, picnic days; see also SEASON.

summit *n.* apex, zenith, crown; see TOP 1.

summon *v.* request, beckon, send

for, invoke, bid, ask, draft, petition, signal, motion, sign, order, command, direct, enjoin, conjure up, ring, charge, recall, call in, call for, call out, call forth, call up, call away, call down, call together, volunteer.

sun *n.* day-star, solar disk, eye of heaven, light of the day, solar energy, source of light; see also STAR 1. — **under the sun** on earth, terrestrial, mundane; see EARTHLY.

sunburned *a.* tanned, burned, sunburnt, brown, suntanned, bronzed, ruddy.—*Ant.* PALE, white skinned, pallid.

Sunday *n.* first day, day off, Lord's day; see WEEKEND.

sunk′en (-ən) *adj.* **1** submerged **2** below the general level [*a sunken* patio] **3** hollow [*sunken* cheeks]

sun′lamp′ *n.* an ultraviolet-ray lamp, used for tanning the body, etc.

sun′light′ *n.* the light of the sun

sun′lit′ *adj.* lighted by the sun

sun′ny (-ē) *adj.* **-ni·er, -ni·est 1** full of sunshine **2** bright; cheerful **3** of or like the sun —**sun′ni·ness** *n.*

sunny side 1 the sunlit side **2** the brighter aspect —**on the sunny side of** younger than (a given age) —**sunny side up** fried upturned and with unbroken yolk [eggs *sunny side up*]

sun′rise′ *n.* **1** the daily appearance of the sun above the eastern horizon **2** the time of this

sun′roof′ *n.* a car roof with a panel that opens to let in light and air　Also **sun roof**

sun′screen′ *n.* a chemical used in lotions, creams, etc. to block certain ultraviolet rays of the sun, to reduce sunburn

sun′set′ *n.* **1** the daily disappearance of the sun below the western horizon **2** the time of this

sun′shine′ *n.* **1** the shining of the sun **2** the light and heat from the sun **3** cheerfulness, happiness, etc. —**sun′shin′y** *adj.*

sun′spot′ *n.* any of the temporarily cooler regions appearing cyclically as dark spots on the sun

sun′stroke′ *n.* a form of heatstroke caused by excessive exposure to the sun

sun′suit′ *n.* short pants with a bib and shoulder straps, worn by babies and young children

sun′tan′ *n.* darkened skin resulting from exposure to the sun

sun′up′ *n.* SUNRISE

sup (sup) *vi.* **supped, sup′ping** [< OFr *soupe*, soup] to have supper

sup- *prefix* SUB-　Used before *p*

su′per (sōō′pər) *n.* [< fol.] *short for:* **1** SUPERNUMERARY (esp. sense 2) **2** SUPERINTENDENT (esp. sense 2) —*adj.* **1** outstanding; exceptionally fine **2** great, extreme, or excessive

super- [L < *super*, above] *prefix* **1** over, above [*superstructure*] **2** superior to [*superintendent*] **3** *a)* surpassing [*superabundant*] *b)* greater than others of its kind [*supermarket*] **4** additional [*supertax*]

su′per·abun′dant *adj.* being more than enough —**su′per·abun′dance** *n.*

super·an·nu·ated (sōō′pər an′yōō āt′id) *adj.* [< L *super*, above + *annus*, year] **1** too old for work **2** retired, esp. with a pension, because of old age

su·perb (sə pʉrb′; sōō-, sōō-) *adj.* [see SUPER-] **1** noble or majestic **2** rich or magnificent **3** extremely fine; excellent —**su·perb′ly** *adv.*

su′per·car′go *n., pl.* **-goes** or **-gos** an officer on a merchant ship in charge of the cargo

su′per·charge′ *vt.* **-charged′, -charg′ing** to increase the power of (an engine), as with a device (**supercharger**) that forces air into the cylinders

su·per·cili·ous (sōō′pər sil′ē əs) *adj.* [< L *super*-, above + *cilium*, eyelid, hence (in allusion to raised eyebrows) haughtiness] disdainful or contemptuous; haughty

su′per·cit′y *n., pl.* **-ies** MEGALOPOLIS

su′per·con′duc·tiv′ity *n.* *Physics* the lack of resistance to electrical current in certain metals, etc. when cooled to low temperatures

su′per·e′go *n., pl.* **-gos** *Psychoanalysis* that part of the psyche which enforces moral standards

su′per·em′i·nent *adj.* supremely remarkable, distinguished, etc.

su′per·er′o·ga′tion (-er·ə gā′shən) *n.* [< L *super*-, above + *erogare*, pay out] a doing more than is needed or expected —**su′per·erog′a·to′ry** (-i räg′ə tôr′ē) *adj.*

su·per·fi′cial (-fish′əl) *adj.* [< L *super*-, above + *facies*, face] **1** of or being on the surface **2** concerned with and understanding only the obvious; shallow **3** quick and cursory **4** merely apparent —**su′per·fi′ci·al′ity** (-ē al′ə tē), *pl.* **-ties,** *n.* —**su′per·fi′cially** *adv.*

su·per·flu·ous (sə pʉr′flōō əs, sōō-) *adj.* [< L *super*-, above + *fluere*, to flow] excessive or unnecessary —**su·per·flu·ity** (sōō′pər flōō′ə tē), *pl.* **-ties,** *n.*

su′per·high′way′ *n.* EXPRESSWAY

su′per·hu′man *adj.* **1** having a nature above that of man; divine **2** greater than that of a normal human being

su′per·im·pose′ *vt.* **-posed′, -pos′ing** to put, lay, or stack on top of something else

su·per·in·tend (sōō′pər in tend′) *vt.* to act as superintendent of; supervise —**su′per·in·tend′ence** or **su′per·in·tend′ency** *n.*

su′per·in·tend′ent (-ten′dənt) *n.* [< LL *superintendere*, superintend] **1** a person in charge of a department, institution, etc.; director **2** a person responsible for the maintenance of a building

su·peri·or (sə pir′ē ər) *adj.* [see SUPER-] **1** higher in space, order, rank, etc. **2** greater in quality or value than: with *to* **3** above average in quality; excellent **4** refusing to give in to or be affected by: with *to* **5** showing a feeling of being better than others; haughty —*n.* **1** a superior person or thing **2** the head of a religious community —**su·pe′ri·or′ity** (-ôr′ə tē) *n.*

superl. superlative

su·per·la·tive (sə pʉr′lə tiv, sōō-) *adj.* [< L *super*-, above + *latus*, pp. of *ferre*, to bear, carry] **1** superior to all others; supreme **2** *Gram.* designating the extreme degree of comparison of adjectives and adverbs —*n.* **1** the highest degree; peak **2** *Gram.* the superlative degree —**su·per′la·tively** *adv.*

su′per·man′ *n., pl.* **-men′** an apparently superhuman man

su′per·mar′ket *n.* a large, self-service, retail food store or market

su·per·nal (sə pʉrn′əl, sōō-) *adj.* [< L *supernus*, upper] celestial or divine

su′per·nat′u·ral *adj.* not explainable by the known forces or laws of nature; specif., of or involving God, ghosts, spirits, etc.

su′per·no′va *n., pl.* **-vae** (-vē) or **-vas** a rare, extremely bright nova

su·per·nu·mer·ary (sōō′pər nōō′mə rer′ē, -nyōō′-) *n., pl.* **-ies** [< L *super*, above + *numerus*, number] **1** an extra person or thing **2** *Theater* a person with a small, nonspeaking part

su′per·pose′ *vt.* **-posed′, -pos′ing** [see SUPER- & POSE] to place on or above something else —**su′per·pos′able** *adj.* —**su′per·po·si′tion** *n.*

su′per·sat′u·rate′ *vt.* **-rat′ed, -rat′ing** to make more highly concentrated than in normal saturation —**su′per·sat′u·ra′tion** *n.*

su′per·scribe′ *vt.* **-scribed′, -scrib′ing** [see SUPER- & SCRIBE] to write (something) at the top or on an outer surface of (something) —**su′per·scrip′tion** (-skrip′shən) *n.*

su′per·script′ *n.* [see prec.] a figure, letter, or symbol written above and to the side of another

su·per·sede (sōō′pər sēd′) *vt.* **-sed′ed, -sed′ing** [< L *supersedere*, sit over] to replace or succeed

su′per·son′ic *adj.* [SUPER- + SONIC] **1** designating, of, or moving at a speed greater than that of sound **2** ULTRASONIC

su′per·star′ *n.* a star performer, as in sports or entertainment

---

THESAURUS

sunken *a.* lowered, depressed, down; see UNDER 1.

sunlight *n.* daylight, sunshine, light of day; see LIGHT 1.

sunny *a.* shining, brilliant, sunshiny; see BRIGHT 1.

sunrise *n.* peep of day, daybreak, aurora; see MORNING 1.

sunset *n.* sundown, evening, end of the day, close of the day, nightfall, twilight, dusk; see also NIGHT 1.—*Ant.* MORNING, dawn, sunrise.

sunshine *n.* sunlight, the sun, sunbeams; see LIGHT 1.

superb *a.* magnificent, splendid, elegant; see EXCELLENT, GRAND.

superficial *a.* flimsy, cursory, hasty, shallow, short-sighted, ignorant, narrow-minded, prejudiced, partial, external, unenlightened.—*Ant.* LEARNED, deep, profound.

superficially *a.* lightly, on the surface, frivolously; see CARELESSLY.—*Ant.* CAREFULLY, thoughtfully, thoroughly.

superfluous *a.* unnecessary, excessive, exorbitant; see EXTREME.

superintendent *n.* supervisor, inspector, director; see EXECUTIVE.

superior *a.* higher, better, preferred, above, finer, of higher rank, a cut above*, more exalted; see also EXCELLENT.

superiority *n.* supremacy, preponderance, advantage; see PERFECTION.

supernatural *a.* superhuman, spectral, ghostly, occult, hidden, mysterious, secret, unknown, unrevealed, dark, mystic, mythical, mythological, fabulous, legendary, unintelligible, unfathomable, inscrutable, incomprehensible, undiscernible, transcendental, obscure, unknowable, impenetrable, invisible, concealed.—*Ant.* NATURAL, plain, common.

su·per·sti·tion (sōō'pər stish'ən) *n.* ⟦< L *superstitio*, lit., a standing (in awe) over⟧ **1** any belief that is inconsistent with known facts or rational thought, esp. such a belief in omens, the supernatural, etc. **2** any action or practice based on such a belief —**su'per·sti'tious** *adj.*

su'per·struc'ture *n.* **1** a structure built on top of another, as above the main deck of a ship **2** that part of a building above the foundation

su'per·tank'er *n.* an extremely large oil tanker, of 300,000 tons or more

su·per·vene (sōō'pər vēn') *vi.* **-vened'**, **-ven'ing** ⟦< L *super-*, over + *venire*, come⟧ to come or happen as something additional or unexpected —**su'per·ven'tion** (-ven'shən) *n.*

su·per·vise (sōō'pər vīz') *vt.*, *vi.* **-vised'**, **-vis'ing** ⟦< L *super-*, over + *videre*, see⟧ to oversee or direct (work, workers, etc.); superintend —**su'per·vi'sion** (-vizh'ən) *n.* —**su'per·vi'sor** *n.* —**su'per·vi'sory** *adj.*

su·pine (sōō'pīn', sōō pīn') *adj.* ⟦L *supinus*⟧ **1** lying on the back, face upward **2** inactive; sluggish; listless

supp. or **suppl.** **1** supplement **2** supplementary

sup·per (sup'ər) *n.* ⟦see SUP⟧ an evening meal

supper club an expensive nightclub

sup·plant (sə plant') *vt.* ⟦< L *sub-*, under + *planta*, sole of the foot⟧ **1** to take the place of, esp. by force or plotting **2** to remove in order to replace with something else

sup·ple (sup'əl) *adj.* **-pler**, **-plest** ⟦< L *supplex*, submissive⟧ **1** easily bent; flexible **2** lithe; limber **3** easily influenced **4** adaptable: said of the mind, etc.

sup·ple·ment (sup'lə mənt; *for v.*, -ment') *n.* ⟦see SUPPLY⟧ **1** something added, esp. to make up for a lack **2** a section of additional material in a book, newspaper, etc. —*vt.* to provide a supplement to —**sup'ple·men'tal** or **sup'ple·men'tary** *adj.*

sup·pli·ant (sup'lē ənt) *n.* one who supplicates — *adj.* supplicating

sup'pli·cant (-lə kənt) *adj.*, *n.* SUPPLIANT

sup·pli·cate (sup'lə kāt') *vt.*, *vi.* **-cat'ed**, **-cat'ing** ⟦< L *sub-*, under + *plicare*, to fold⟧ **1** to ask for (something) humbly **2** to make a humble request (of) —**sup'pli·ca'tion** *n.*

sup·ply (sə plī') *vt.* **-plied'**, **-ply'ing** ⟦< L *sub-*, under + *plere*, fill⟧ **1** to furnish or provide (what is needed) to (someone) **2** to compensate for (a deficiency, etc.); make good — *n.*, *pl.* **-plies'** **1** the amount available for use or sale; stock **2** [*pl.*] needed materials, provisions, etc. —**sup·pli'er** *n.*

supply-side (sə plī'sīd') *adj.* designating or of an economic theory that an increase in money for investment, as supplied by lowering taxes, will increase productivity

sup·port (sə pôrt') *vt.* ⟦< L *sub-*, under + *portare*, carry⟧ **1** to carry the weight of; hold up **2** encourage; help **3** to advocate; uphold **4** to maintain (a person, institution, etc.) with money or subsistence **5** to help prove, vindicate, etc. **6** to bear; endure **7** to keep up; maintain **8** to have a role subordinate to (a star) in a play — *n.* **1** a supporting or being supported **2** a person or thing that supports **3** a means of support —**sup·port'able** *adj.* —**sup·port'er** *n.*

sup·port'ive *adj.* giving support or help

sup·pose (sə pōz') *vt.* **-posed'**, **-pos'ing** ⟦< L *sub-*, under + *ponere*, put⟧ **1** to assume to be true, as for argument's sake **2** to believe, think, etc. **3** to consider as a possibility [*suppose* I go] **4** to expect [I'm *supposed* to sing] — *vi.* to conjecture —**sup·posed'** *adj.* —**sup·pos'edly** *adv.*

sup·po·si·tion (sup'ə zish'ən) *n.* **1** a supposing **2** something supposed

sup·pos·i·tory (sə päz'ə tôr'ē) *n.*, *pl.* **-ries** ⟦see SUPPOSE⟧ a small piece of medicated substance placed in the rectum or vagina, where it melts

sup·press (sə pres') *vt.* ⟦< L *sub-*, under + *premere*, to press⟧ **1** to put down by force; quell **2** to keep from being known, published, etc. **3** to keep back; restrain **4** *Psychiatry* to consciously dismiss from the mind —**sup·pres'sion** (-presh'ən) *n.*

sup·pu·rate (sup'yōō rāt') *vi.* **-rat'ed**, **-rat'ing** ⟦< L *sub-*, under + *pus*, pus⟧ to form or discharge pus —**sup'pu·ra'tion** *n.*

supra- ⟦< L *supra*, above⟧ *prefix* above, over, beyond

su·pra·na·tional (sōō'prə nash'ə nəl) *adj.* of, for, or above all or a number of nations [*supranational* authority]

su·prem·a·cist (sə prem'ə sist; *also* sōō-, sōō-) *n.* one who believes in the supremacy of a particular group

su·prem·a·cy (-sē) *n.*, *pl.* **-cies** supreme condition or power

su·preme' (-prēm') *adj.* ⟦< L *superus*, that is above⟧ **1** highest in rank, power, etc. **2** highest in quality, achievement, etc. **3** highest in degree **4** final; ultimate —**su·preme'ly** *adv.*

Supreme Being God

Supreme Court **1** the highest Federal court **2** the highest court in most States

Supreme Soviet **1** a part of the legislature of Russia **2** formerly, the parliament of the U.S.S.R.

Supt. Superintendent

sur-[1] ⟦< L *super*, over⟧ *prefix* over, upon, above, beyond

sur-[2] *prefix* SUB- Used before *r*

sur·cease (sur'sēs) *n.* ⟦< L *supersedere*, refrain from⟧ an end, or cessation

sur·charge (sur'chärj'; *also, for v.*, sər chärj') *vt.* **-charged'**, **-charg'ing** ⟦see SUR-[1] & CHARGE⟧ **1** to overcharge **2** to mark (a postage stamp) with a surcharge — *n.* **1** an additional charge **2** a new valuation printed over the original valuation on a postage stamp

sur·cin·gle (sur'sin'gəl) *n.* ⟦< OFr *sur-*, over + L *cingulum*, a belt⟧ a strap passed around a horse's body to bind on a saddle, pack, etc.

THESAURUS

superstition *n.* false belief, fear, superstitious fear; see FEAR.

superstitious *a.* fearful, apprehensive, credulous; see AFRAID.

supervise *v.* oversee, conduct, control; see MANAGE 1.

supervised *a.* directed, administered, superintended; see MANAGED 2.

supervision *n.* guidance, surveillance, direction; see MANAGEMENT 1.

supervisor *n.* director, superintendent, administrator; see EXECUTIVE.

supper *n.* evening meal, tea, late refreshments; see DINNER.

supplement *n.* sequel, continuation, complement; see ADDITION 1.

supplement *v.* add to, reinforce, strengthen; see INCREASE.

supplementary *a.* additional, completing, supplemental; see EXTRA.

supplied *a.* provided, furnished, endowed; see GIVEN.

supply *n.* stock, amount, number; see QUANTITY.

supply *v.* furnish, fulfill, outfit; see SATISFY 3.

support *n.* **1** [Aid] care, assistance, comfort; see HELP 1. **2** [A reinforcement] lining, coating, rib, stilt, stay, supporter, buttress, pole, post, prop, guide, backing, stiffener, rampart, stave, stake, rod, pillar, timber; see also BRACE. **3** [Financial aid] maintenance, livelihood, sustenance; see PAYMENT 1. —**in support of** for, condoning, approving; see FOR.

support *v.* **1** [To hold up from beneath] prop, hold up, buoy up, keep up, shore up, bear up, bolster, buttress, brace, sustain, stay, keep from falling, shoulder carry, bear.—*Ant.* DROP, let fall, break down. **2** [To uphold] maintain, sustain, back up, abet, aid, assist, help, bolster, comfort, carry, bear out, hold, foster, shoulder, corroborate, cheer, establish, promote, advance, champion, advocate, approve, stick by, stand by, stand behind, substantiate, verify, get back of, stick up for*, go to bat for*, confirm, further, encourage, hearten, strengthen, recommend, take care of, pull for, agree with, stand up for, keep up, stand back of, take the part of, rally round, give a lift to, boost. **3** [To provide for] take care of, keep an eye on, care for, attend to, look after, back, bring up, sponsor, put up the money for, finance, pay for, subsidize, nurse, pay the expenses of, grubstake, stake, raise.—*Ant.* ABANDON, ignore, fail.

supported *a.* **1** [Backed personally] financed, promoted, sustained; see BACKED 2. **2** [Supported physically] held up, propped up, braced, bolstered, borne up, floating on, floated, buoyed up, based on, founded on, raised up, having a sufficient base, having an adequate foundation; see also FIRM 1.

supporter *n.* advocate, sponsor, helper; see PATRON.

suppose *v.* conjecture, surmise, deem; see GUESS.

supposed *a.* assumed, presumed, presupposed; see LIKELY 1.

supposedly *a.* seemingly, supposably, believably; see PROBABLY.

supposing *conj.*, *a.* if, in case that, in these circumstances, under these conditions, let us suppose, allowing that, presuming, assuming, taking for granted that.

suppress *v.* crush, overpower, subdue; see DEFEAT.

suppression *n.* abolition, suppressing, overthrow; see DEFEAT.

supremacy *n.* domination, mastery, supreme authority; see POWER 2.

supreme *a.* highest, greatest, paramount, chief; see also BEST.

sure (shoor) *adj.* **sur′er, sur′est** 〚< L *securus*〛 **1** that will not fail *[a sure method]* **2** that cannot be doubted or questioned **3** having no doubt; confident *[sure of the facts]* **4** bound to be or happen *[a sure defeat]* **5** bound (to do, be, etc.) *[sure to lose]* — *adv.* [Colloq.] surely — **for sure** certain(ly) — **sure enough** [Colloq.] without doubt —**sure′ness** *n.*
sure′-fire′ (-fīr′) *adj.* [Colloq.] sure to be successful or as expected
sure′-foot′ed *adj.* not likely to slip, fall, err, etc.
sure′ly *adv.* **1** with confidence **2** without a doubt; certainly
sure′ty (shoor′ə tē, shoor′tē) *n., pl.* **-ties** **1** a being sure **2** something that gives assurance, as against loss, etc. **3** one who takes responsibility for another
surf (surf) *n.* 〚prob. var. of SOUGH〛 the waves of the sea breaking on the shore or a reef — *vi.* to engage in surfing —**surf′er** *n.*
sur·face (sur′fis) *n.* 〚< Fr *sur-*, over + *face*, a face〛 **1** *a)* the exterior of an object *b)* any of the faces of a solid **2** superficial features — *adj.* **1** of, on, or at the surface **2** external; superficial — *vt.* **-faced, -fac·ing** to give a surface to, as in paving — *vi.* to rise to the surface of the water
surf′board′ *n.* a long, narrow board used in the sport of surfing
sur·feit (sur′fit) *n.* 〚< OFr *sorfaire*, overdo〛 **1** too great an amount **2** overindulgence, esp. in food or drink **3** disgust, nausea, etc. resulting from excess — *vt.* to feed or supply to excess
surf′ing (surf′iŋ) *n.* the sport of riding in toward shore on the crest of a wave, esp. on a surfboard
surge (surj) *n.* 〚< L *surgere*, to rise〛 **1** a large wave of water, or its motion **2** a sudden, strong increase, as of power — *vi.* **surged, surg′ing** to move in or as in a surge
sur·geon (sur′jən) *n.* a doctor who specializes in surgery
sur·gery (sur′jər ē) *n., pl.* **-geries** 〚< Gr *cheir*, the hand + *ergein*, to work〛 **1** the treatment of disease, injury, etc. by manual or instrumental operations **2** the operating room of a surgeon or hospital
sur′gi·cal (-ji kəl) *adj.* **1** of surgeons or surgery **2** very accurate, precisely targeted, etc. —**sur′gi·cally** *adv.*
surly (sur′lē) *adj.* **-li·er, -li·est** 〚earlier *sirly*, imperious < *sir*, sir〛 bad-tempered; sullenly rude; uncivil —**sur′li·ness** *n.*
sur·mise (sər mīz′) *n.* 〚OFr *sur-*, upon + *mettre*, put〛 a conjecture — *vt., vi.* **-mised′, -mis′ing** to guess
sur·mount (sər mount′) *vt.* 〚SUR-¹ & MOUNT²〛 **1** to overcome (a difficulty) **2** to be at the top of; rise above **3** to climb up and across (a height, etc.) —**sur·mount′able** *adj.*

sur·name (sur′nām′) *n.* 〚< OFr *sur-* (see SUR-¹) + *nom*, name〛 the family name, or last name
sur·pass (sər pas′) *vt.* 〚< Fr *sur-* (see SUR-¹) + *passer*, to pass〛 **1** to excel or be superior to **2** to go beyond the limit, capacity, etc. of —**sur·pass′ing** *adj.*
sur·plice (sur′plis) *n.* 〚< L *super-*, above + *pelliceum*, fur robe〛 a loose, white outer ecclesiastical vestment for some services
sur·plus (sur′plus′) *n.* 〚< OFr *sur-*, above (see SUR-¹) + L *plus*, more〛 a quantity over and above what is needed or used — *adj.* forming a surplus
sur·prise (sər prīz′) *vt.* **-prised′, -pris′ing** 〚< OFr *sur-* (see SUR-¹) + *prendre*, to take〛 **1** to come upon suddenly or unexpectedly; take unawares **2** to attack without warning **3** to amaze; astonish — *n.* **1** a being surprised **2** something that surprises
sur·real (sər rē′əl, sə-; -rēl′) *adj.* **1** surrealistic **2** bizarre; fantastic
sur·re′al·ism′ (-iz′əm) *n.* 〚see SUR-¹ & REAL〛 a modern movement in the arts trying to depict the workings of the unconscious mind —**sur·re′al·is′tic** *adj.* —**sur·re′al·ist** *adj., n.*
sur·ren·der (sə ren′dər) *vt.* 〚< Fr *sur-*, up + *rendre*, render〛 **1** to give up possession of; yield to another on compulsion **2** to give up or abandon — *vi.* to give oneself up, esp. as a prisoner — *n.* the act of surrendering
sur·rep·ti·tious (sur′əp tish′əs) *adj.* 〚< L *sub-*, under + *rapere*, seize〛 done, got, acting, etc. in a stealthy way
sur·rey (sur′ē) *n., pl.* **-reys** 〚after *Surrey*, county in England〛 a light, four-wheeled carriage with two seats
sur·ro·gate (sur′ə git, -gāt′) *n.* 〚< L *sub-*, in place of + *rogare*, ask〛 **1** a deputy or substitute **2** in some States, a probate court judge **3** a woman who substitutes for another unable to become pregnant
sur·round (sə round′) *vt.* 〚< L *super-*, over + *undare*, to rise〛 to encircle on all or nearly all sides
sur·round′ings *n.pl.* the things, conditions, etc. around a person or thing
sur·tax (sur′taks′) *n.* an extra tax on top of the regular tax
sur·veil·lance (sər vā′ləns) *n.* 〚Fr < *sur-* (see SUR-¹) + *veiller*, to watch〛 watch kept over someone, esp. a suspect
sur·vey (sər vā′; *for n.* sur′vā′) *vt.* 〚< OFr *sur-* (see SUR-¹) + *veoir*, see〛 **1** to examine or consider in detail or comprehensively **2** to determine the location, form, or boundaries of (a tract of land) — *n., pl.* **-veys** **1** a detailed study, as by gathering information and analyzing it **2** a general view **3** *a)* the process of surveying an area *b)* a written description of the area —**sur·vey′or** *n.*
sur·vey′ing *n.* the science or work of making land surveys

THESAURUS

sure *a., interj.* certainly, of course, by all means, positively, absolutely, but definitely; see also SURELY.
sure *a.* positive, assured, convinced; see CERTAIN 1. **—for sure** certainly, for certain, without doubt; see SURELY. **—make sure** make certain, determine, establish; see GUARANTEE. **—to be sure** of course, certainly, obviously; see SURELY.
sure-fire* *a.* dependable, good, infallible; see EXCELLENT, RELIABLE.
surely *a.* doubtlessly, certainly, undoubtedly, definitely, absolutely, evidently, explicitly, without doubt, beyond doubt, beyond question, plainly, infallibly, most assuredly, decidedly, inevitably, indisputably, positively, unquestionably, without any doubt, admittedly, clearly, with assurance, beyond the shadow of a doubt, nothing else but, precisely, conclusively, distinctly, by all means, at any rate, with certainty, unerringly, unmistakably, at all events, undeniably, with confidence, as a matter of course, rain or shine*.
surf *n.* breakers, rollers, combers; see WAVE 1.
surface *n.* exterior, covering, superficies; see COVER 1, OUTSIDE 1.
surgeon *n.* specialist in surgery, surgical expert, internist; see DOCTOR.
surgery *n.* operative surgery, the knife*, operation; see MEDICINE 3,

OPERATION 4.
surname *n.* cognomen, last name, patronymic; see NAME 1.
surpass *v.* excel, outdo, better; see EXCEED.
surplus *n.* residue, leftover, something extra; see EXCESS 1, REMAINDER.
surprise *n.* **1** [A feeling] astonishment, wonderment, shock; see WONDER 1. **2** [The cause of a feeling] something unexpected, blow, sudden attack, unexpected good fortune, sudden misfortune, unawaited event, unsuspected plot. **—take by surprise** startle, assault, sneak up on; see SURPRISE *v.*
surprise *v.* astonish, astound, bewilder, confound, shock, overwhelm, dumbfound, unsettle, stun, electrify, petrify, startle, stupefy, stagger, take aback, cause wonder, awe, dazzle, daze, perplex, leave aghast, flabbergast, floor*, bowl over*, jar, take one's breath away, strike dumb, beggar belief, creep up on, catch unaware.
surprised *a.* upset, taken unaware, astounded, caught napping, astonished, bewildered, taken by surprise, shocked, confounded, startled.
surprising *a.* shocking, extraordinary, remarkable; see UNUSUAL 1, 2, UNEXPECTED.
surrender *n.* capitulation, yielding,

giving up, submission, giving way, unconditional surrender, abdication, resignation, delivery.
surrender *v.* **1** [To accept defeat] capitulate, yield, give in; see QUIT 2. **2** [To relinquish possession] give up, let go, resign; see ABANDON 1.
surround *v.* **1** [To be on all sides] girdle, circle, environ, enclose, close in, close around, circle about, envelop, hem in, wall in. **2** [To take a position on all sides] encompass, encircle, inundate, flow around, close in, close around, hem in, go around, beleaguer, blockade.—*Ant.* ABANDON, flee from, desert.
surrounded *a.* girdled, encompassed, encircled, hemmed in, fenced in, hedged in, circled about, enclosed, fenced about, enveloped.—*Ant.* FREE, unfenced, agape.
surrounding *a.* enclosing, encircling, encompassing; see AROUND.
surroundings *n.* setting, environs, vicinity; see ENVIRONMENT.
survey *n.* study, critique, outline; see EXAMINATION 1.
survey *v.* **1** [To look upon] look over, take a view of, view; see SEE 1. **2** [To examine or summarize] study, scan, inspect; see EXAMINE.
survival *n.* endurance, durability, continuance; see CONTINUATION.

sur·viv·al·ist (sər vī'vəl ist) *n.* one who takes measures, as storing food and weapons, to ensure survival after an economic collapse, nuclear war, etc.

sur·vive (sər vīv') *vt.* **-vived', -viv'ing** 〖< L *super-*, above + *vivere*, to live〗 to remain alive or in existence after — *vi.* to continue living or existing —**sur·viv'al** *n.*

sur·vi'vor (-ər) *n.* **1** one that survives 2 someone capable of surviving changing conditions, misfortune, etc.

sus- *prefix* SUB- Used before *c, p,* and *t*

sus·cep·ti·ble (sə sep'tə bəl) *adj.* 〖< L *sus-*, under + *capere*, take〗 easily affected emotionally —**susceptible of** admitting; allowing *[testimony susceptible of error]* —**susceptible to** easily influenced or affected by —**sus·cep' ti·bil'i·ty** *n.*

sus·pect (sə spekt'; *for adj. & n.* sus'pekt') *vt.* 〖< L *sus-*, under + *spicere*, to look〗 **1** to believe to be guilty on little or no evidence 2 to believe to be bad, wrong, etc.; distrust 3 to guess; surmise — *adj.* suspected — *n.* one suspected of a crime, etc.

sus·pend (sə spend') *vt.* 〖< L *sus-*, under + *pendere*, hang〗 **1** to exclude as a penalty from an office, school, etc., for a time 2 to make inoperative for a time 3 to hold back (judgment, etc.) 4 to hang by a support from above 5 to hold (dust in the air, etc.) without attachment — *vi.* to stop temporarily

sus·pend'ed animation a temporary cessation of the vital functions resembling death

sus·pend'ers *n.pl.* **1** a pair of straps passed over the shoulders to hold up the trousers 2 [Brit., etc. (exc. Cdn.)] garters

sus·pense (sə spens') *n.* 〖< L *suspendere*, suspend〗 **1** a state of uncertainty 2 the growing excitement felt while awaiting a climax of a novel, play, etc. —**sus·pense'ful** *adj.*

sus·pen·sion (sə spen'shən) *n.* **1** a suspending or being suspended 2 a supporting device upon or from which something is suspended 3 the system of springs, etc. supporting a vehicle upon its undercarriage or axles 4 a substance whose particles are dispersed through a fluid but not dissolved in it

suspension bridge a bridge suspended from cables anchored at either end and supported by towers at intervals

sus·pi·cion (sə spish'ən) *n.* 〖< L *suspicere*, suspect〗 **1** a suspecting or being suspected 2 the feeling or state of mind of one who suspects 3 a very small amount; trace — *vt.* [Colloq. or Dial.] to suspect

sus·pi'cious *adj.* **1** arousing suspicion 2 showing or feeling suspicion —**sus·pi'cious·ly** *adv.*

sus·tain (sə stān') *vt.* 〖< L *sus-*, under + *tenere*, to hold〗 **1** to keep in existence; maintain or prolong 2 to provide sustenance for 3 to carry the weight of; support 4 to endure; withstand 5 to suffer (an injury, loss, etc.) 6 to uphold the validity of 7 to confirm; corroborate

sus·te·nance (sus'tə nəns) *n.* **1** a sustaining 2 means of livelihood 3 that which sustains life; food

sut·ler (sut'lər) *n.* 〖< 16th-c. Du *soeteler*〗 [Historical] a person following an army to sell things to its soldiers

su·ture (sōō'chər) *n.* 〖< L *suere*, sew〗 **1** the line of junction of two parts, esp. of bones of the skull 2 *a)* the stitching together of the two edges of a wound or incision *b)* the thread, etc. or any of the stitches so used

su·zerain (sōō'zə rin', -rān') *n.* 〖Fr < L *sursum*, above〗 **1** a feudal lord 2 a state in relation to another over which it has some political control

svelte (svelt) *adj.* 〖Fr〗 **1** slender; lithe 2 suave

SW or **S.W. 1** southwest 2 southwesterly 3 southwestern

Sw. 1 Sweden 2 Swedish

swab (swäb) *n.* 〖< Du *zwabben*, do dirty work〗 **1** a mop 2 a small piece of cotton, etc. used to medicate or clean the throat, mouth, etc. — *vt.* **swabbed, swab'bing** to use a swab on

swad·dle (swäd'l) *vt.* **-dled, -dling** 〖prob. < OE *swathian*, swathe〗 to wrap (a newborn baby) in long, narrow bands of cloth, as was formerly the custom

swag (swag) *vt.* **swagged, swag'ging** 〖see fol.〗 to hang in a swag — *n.* **1** a valance, garland, etc. hanging decoratively in a curve 2 [Slang] loot

swag·ger (swag'ər) *vi.* 〖prob. < Norw *svagga*, sway〗 **1** to walk with a bold, arrogant stride 2 to boast or brag loudly — *n.* swaggering walk or manner

Swa·hili (swä hē'lē) *n.* 〖< Ar *sawāḥil*, the coasts〗 the Bantu language of the east coast of Africa

swain (swān) *n.* 〖< ON *sveinn*, boy〗 [Archaic] **1** a country youth 2 a lover

swal·low¹ (swäl'ō) *n.* 〖OE *swealwe*〗 a small, swift-flying bird with long, pointed wings and a forked tail

swal·low² (swäl'ō) *vt.* 〖OE *swelgan*〗 **1** to pass (food, etc.) from the mouth into the stomach 2 to absorb: often with *up* 3 to retract (words said) 4 to put up with *[to swallow insults]* 5 to suppress *[to swallow one's pride]* 6 [Colloq.] to accept as true without question — *vi.* to perform the actions of swallowing something, esp. in emotion — *n.* **1** a swallowing 2 the amount swallowed at one time

swal'low-tailed' coat CUTAWAY Also **swal'low·tail'** *n.*

swam (swam) *vi., vt. pt. of* SWIM¹ & SWIM²

swami (swä'mē) *n., pl.* **-mis** 〖< Sans *svāmin*, lord〗 **1** lord; master: title of respect for a Hindu religious teacher 2 a learned man; pundit

swamp (swämp, swômp) *n.* 〖prob. < LowG〗 a piece of wet, spongy land; marsh; bog — *vt.* **1** to plunge in a swamp, water, etc. 2 to flood as with water 3 to overwhelm *[swamped by debts]* 4 to sink (a boat) by filling with water —**swamp'y, -i·er, -i·est,** *adj.*

swan (swän, swôn) *n.* 〖OE〗 a large web-footed waterfowl, usually white, with a long, graceful neck

swank (swaŋk) *n.* 〖akin to OE *swancor*, pliant〗 [Colloq.] ostentatious display — *adj.* [Colloq.] ostentatiously stylish Also **swank'y** *adj.* **-i·er, -i·est**

swan's'-down' *n.* **1** the soft down of the swan, used for trimming clothes, etc. 2 a soft, thick flannel Also **swans'down'**

swan song 〖after the song sung, in ancient fable, by a dying swan〗 the last act, final work, etc. of a person

swap (swäp, swôp) *n., vt., vi.* **swapped, swap'ping** 〖ME *swappen*, to strike〗 [Colloq.] trade; barter

sward (swôrd) *n.* 〖< OE *sweard*, a skin〗 grass-covered soil; turf

---

■ THESAURUS ■

survive *v.* **1** [To live on] outlive, outlast, outwear, live down, live out, weather the storm, make out, persist, persevere, last, remain, pull through, come through, keep afloat, get on; see also ENDURE 1. 2 [To endure] suffer through, withstand, sustain; see ENDURE 2.

survivor *n.* descendant, heir, widow, widower, orphan.

suspect *a.* dubious, questionable, suspected; see UNLIKELY, SUSPICIOUS 2.

suspect *v.* **1** [To doubt someone] distrust, disbelieve, mistrust; see DOUBT. 2 [To suppose] presume, surmise, speculate; see ASSUME.

suspected *a.* doubtful, imagined, fancied; see SUSPICIOUS 2.

suspend *v.* **1** [To exclude temporarily] reject, exclude, drop, remove; see also BAR 2, EJECT, REFUSE. 2 [To cease temporarily] postpone, defer, put off, discontinue, adjourn, interrupt, delay, procrastinate, shelve, waive, retard, protract, lay on the table, file, lay aside, break up, restrain, desist, break off, halt, put a stop to, check, put an end to.—*Ant.* CONTINUE, carry on, proceed.

suspended *a.* pensile, postponed, pendulous; see HANGING.

suspense *n.* apprehension, indecisiveness, dilemma; see DOUBT.

suspicion *n.* misgiving, mistrust, surmise; see DOUBT. —**above suspicion** honorable, cleared, gentlemanly; see HONEST 1, INNOCENT 1. —**under suspicion** suspected, held for questioning, dubious; see SUSPICIOUS 2.

suspicious *a.* **1** [Entertaining suspicion] jealous, distrustful, suspecting, doubting, questioning, doubtful, dubious, in doubt, skeptical, unbelieving, wondering.—*Ant.* TRUSTING, trustful, without any doubt of. 2 [Arousing suspicion] not quite trustworthy, questionable, queer, suspect, irregular, unusual, peculiar, out of line, debatable, disputable.—*Ant.* REGULAR, usual, common.

suspiciously *a.* doubtingly, doubtfully, skeptically, dubiously, uncertainly, unbelievingly, questioningly, in doubt, having doubt, causing suspicion, with caution, with reservations, with a grain of salt.

sustain *v.* **1** [To carry] bear, transport, pack; see CARRY 1, SUPPORT 1, 2. 2 [To nourish] maintain, provide for, nurse; see PROVIDE 1, SUPPORT 2.

swallow² *v.* consume, engulf, gulp, take, wash down, pour, swill, bolt, swig, choke down, swallow up, toss off; see also DRINK 1, EAT 1.

swamp *n.* bog, fen, quagmire, morass, marsh, slough, soft ground, wet ground, mire, peat bog, bottoms, river bottoms, lowland, bottomland, muskeg.

swampy *a.* boggy, wet, miry; see MUDDY 2.

swanky *a.* showy, elegant, swank*; see EXCELLENT, EXPENSIVE, ORNATE.

swap* *v.* interchange, trade, barter; see EXCHANGE.

swarm (swôrm) *n.* ⟦OE *swearm*⟧ 1 a large number of bees, with a queen, leaving a hive to start a new colony 2 a colony of bees in a hive 3 a moving mass, crowd, or throng — *vi.* 1 to fly off in a swarm: said of bees 2 to move, be present, etc. in large numbers 3 to be crowded

swarthy (swôr′*th*ē, -*th*ē) *adj.* -i·er, -i·est ⟦< OE *sweart*⟧ dark-skinned

swash (swäsh, swôsh) *vi.* ⟦echoic⟧ to dash, strike, etc. with a splash

swash′buck′ler (-buk′lər) *n.* ⟦< *swash*, to swagger + *buckler*, a shield⟧ a blustering, swaggering fighting man — **swash′buck′ling** *n., adj.*

swas·tika (swäs′ti kə) *n.* ⟦< Sans *svasti*, well-being⟧ 1 an ancient design in the form of a cross with four equal arms, each bent in a right angle 2 this design with the arms bent clockwise, used as a Nazi emblem

swat (swät) *vt.* **swat′ted, swat′ting** ⟦echoic⟧ to hit with a quick, sharp blow — *n.* a quick, sharp blow —**swat′ter** *n.*

SWAT (swät) *n.* ⟦S(*pecial*) W(*eapons*) a(*nd*) T(*actics*)⟧ a special police unit trained to deal with violence, riots, terrorism, etc. In full **SWAT team**

swatch (swäch) *n.* ⟦orig., a cloth tally⟧ a sample piece of cloth, etc.

swath (swäth, swôth) *n.* ⟦OE *swathu*, a track⟧ 1 the width covered with one cut of a scythe or other mowing device 2 a strip, row, etc. mowed

swathe (swä*th*, swä*th*) *vt.* **swathed, swath′ing** ⟦OE *swathian*⟧ 1 to wrap up in a bandage 2 to envelop; enclose

sway (swā) *vi.* ⟦< ON *sveigja*⟧ 1 to swing or move from side to side or to and fro 2 to lean to one side; veer — *vt.* 1 to cause to sway 2 to influence or divert *[swayed by promises]* — *n.* 1 a swaying or being swayed 2 influence or control *[the sway of passion]*

sway′backed′ (-bakt′) *adj.* having a sagging spine, as some horses

swear (swer) *vi.* **swore, sworn, swear′ing** ⟦OE *swerian*⟧ 1 to make a solemn declaration with an appeal to God to confirm it 2 to make a solemn promise; vow 3 to use profane language; curse — *vt.* 1 to declare, pledge, or vow on oath 2 to administer a legal oath to —**swear off** to renounce —**swear out** to obtain (a warrant for arrest) by making a charge under oath —**swear′er** *n.*

swear′word′ *n.* a profane word or phrase

sweat (swet) *vi., vt.* **sweat** or **sweat′ed, sweat′ing** ⟦OE *swat*, sweat⟧ 1 to give forth or cause to give forth a salty moisture through the pores of the skin; perspire 2 to give forth or condense (moisture) on its surface 3 to work hard enough to cause sweating — *n.* 1 the salty liquid given forth in perspiration 2 moisture collected in droplets on a surface 3 a sweating or being sweated 4 a condition of eagerness, anxiety, etc. 5 *[pl.]* clothes worn for exercising, etc. —**sweat out** [Colloq.] 1 to get rid of by sweating *[to sweat out a cold]* 2 to wait anxiously for or through — **sweat′y, -i·er, -i·est,** *adj.*

sweat′er *n.* a knitted or crocheted outer garment for the upper body

sweat shirt a heavy cotton jersey worn to absorb sweat, as after exercise

sweat′shop′ *n.* a shop where employees work long hours at low wages under poor working conditions

Swed. 1 Sweden 2 Swedish

Swede (swēd) *n.* a native or inhabitant of Sweden

Swed·ish (swēd′ish) *adj.* of Sweden, its people, language, etc. — *n.* the Germanic language of the Swedes

sweep (swēp) *vt.* **swept, sweep′ing** ⟦OE *swapan*⟧ 1 to clean (a floor, etc.) as by brushing with a broom 2 to remove (dirt, etc.) as with a broom 3 to strip, carry away, or destroy with a forceful movement 4 to touch in moving across *[hands sweeping the keyboard]* 5 to pass swiftly over or across 6 to win overwhelmingly — *vi.* 1 to clean a floor, etc. as with a broom 2 to move steadily with speed, force, or gracefulness 3 to extend in a long curve or line *[a road sweeping up the hill]* — *n.* 1 the act of sweeping 2 a steady sweeping movement 3 range or scope 4 extent, as of land; stretch 5 a line, curve, etc. that seems to flow or move 6 one whose work is sweeping —**sweep′er** *n.* —**sweep′ing** *adj.* —**sweep′ingly** *adv.*

sweep′ings *n.pl.* things swept up, as dirt from a floor

sweep′stakes′ *n., pl.* **-stakes′** a lottery in which each participant puts up money in a common fund which is given as the prize to the winner or winners of a horse race or other contest

sweet (swēt) *adj.* ⟦OE *swete*⟧ 1 having a taste of, or like that of, sugar 2 *a)* agreeable taste, smell, sound, etc. *b)* gratifying *c)* friendly, kind, etc. 3 *a)* not rancid or sour *b)* not salty or salted — *n.* *[pl.]* sweet foods —**sweet′ish** *adj.* —**sweet′ly** *adv.* —**sweet′ness** *n.*

sweet′bread′ (-bred′) *n.* the thymus or sometimes the pancreas of a calf, lamb, etc., when used as food: *usually used in pl.*

sweet′bri′er or **sweet′bri′ar** (-brī′ər) *n.* EGLANTINE

sweet corn a variety of Indian corn eaten unripe as a table vegetable

sweet′en *vt.* 1 to make sweet 2 to make pleasant or agreeable 3 [Colloq.] to increase the value of (collateral, an offer, etc.)

sweet′ener *n.* a sweetening agent, esp. a synthetic one, as saccharin

sweet′heart′ *n.* a loved one; lover

sweetheart contract a contract arranged by collusion between union officials and an employer without consulting the union membership

sweet′meat′ *n.* a candy

sweet pea a climbing plant with butterfly-shaped, fragrant flowers

sweet pepper 1 a red pepper producing a large, mild fruit 2 the fruit

sweet potato 1 a tropical, trailing plant with a fleshy, brownish root used as a vegetable 2 its root

sweet′-talk′ *vt., vi.* [Colloq.] to flatter

sweet tooth [Colloq.] a fondness or craving for sweets

swell (swel) *vi., vt.* **swelled, swelled** or **swol′len, swell′ing** ⟦OE *swellan*⟧ 1 to expand as a result of pressure from within 2 to curve out; bulge 3 to fill (*with* pride, etc.) 4 to increase in size, force, intensity, etc. — *n.* 1 a part that swells; specif., a large, rolling wave 2 an increase in size, amount, degree, etc. 3 a crescendo 4 [Colloq.] one who is strikingly stylish — *adj.* 1 [Colloq.] stylish 2 [Slang] excellent

swell′head′ *n.* [Colloq.] a conceited person —**swell′head′ed** *adj.*

swell′ing *n.* 1 an increase in size, volume, etc. 2 a swollen part

---

THESAURUS

swarm *n.* throng, crowd, multitude, horde, pack, troop, school.
swarm *v.* rush together, crowd, throng; see GATHER, RUN.
swarthy *a.* dark skinned, brown, tawny, dark hued, dark complexioned.
swat *v.* beat, knock, slap; see HIT 1.
sway *n.* swaying, swinging, swing, leaning, oscillation, vibration, undulation, wave, wavering, pulsation.
sway *v.* bend, oscillate, swagger; see WAVE 3.
swear *v.* 1 [To curse] blaspheme, utter profanity, cuss*; see CURSE. 2 [To take an oath] avow, affirm, testify, state, vow, attest, warrant, vouch, assert, swear by, give witness, cross one's heart.
sweat *n.* perspiration, beads of sweat, sweating, steam.
sweat *v.* perspire, secrete, swelter, wilt, exude, break out in a sweat.

sweater *n. Types of sweaters include the following:* coat, twin, evening, sport, long-sleeved, short-sleeved, barrel, sleeveless, crew neck, turtleneck; pullover, cardigan; see also CLOTHES.
sweaty *a.* perspiring, moist, wet with perspiration, glowing, bathed in sweat; see also HOT 1.
sweep *v.* brush up, clear, clear up; see CLEAN, MOP.
sweet *a.* 1 [Sweet in taste] toothsome, sugary, luscious, candied, honeyed, saccharine, cloying, like nectar, delicious; see also RICH 4.—*Ant.* SOUR, bitter, sharp. 2 [Sweet in disposition] agreeable, pleasing, engaging, winning, delightful, reasonable, gentle, kind, generous, unselfish, even-tempered, good-humored, considerate, thoughtful, companionable; see also FRIENDLY.—*Ant.* SELFISH, repulsive, inconsiderate. 3 [Sweet in

smell] fragrant, sweet-smelling, fresh, delicate, delicious, spicy, rich, perfumed, clean.
sweeten *v.* add sugar, make sweet, add sweetening; see FLAVOR.
sweetheart *n.* beloved, dear, loved one; see LOVER 1.
sweetly *a.* agreeably, pleasantly, comfortably, gently, gratefully, softly, smoothly, kindly, in a winning manner, charmingly.
sweets *n.* bonbons, candy, confection, sweetmeats, preserves, candied fruit; see also CANDY.
swell* *a.* just what one wants, desirable, fine; see EXCELLENT.
swell *v.* dilate, expand, distend, increase, enlarge, grow, grow larger, puff up, be inflated, become larger, bulge, puff, inflate, bulge out, blister, round out, fill out.
swelling *n.* welt, wart, pimple, car-

swel·ter (swel′tər) *vi.* [< OE *sweltan,* to die] to feel uncomfortably hot; sweat, etc. from great heat

swel·ter·ing *adj.* very hot; sultry

swept (swept) *vt., vi. pt. & pp. of* SWEEP

swept′back′ *adj.* having a backward slant, as the wings of an aircraft

swerve (swurv) *vi., vt.* **swerved, swerv′ing** [< OE *sweorfan,* to scour] to turn aside from a straight line, course, etc. — *n.* a swerving

swift (swift) *adj.* [OE] 1 moving with great speed; fast 2 coming, acting, etc. quickly — *n.* a swift-flying, swallowlike bird —**swift′ly** *adv.* —**swift′ness** *n.*

swig (swig) *vt., vi.* **swigged, swig′ging** [< ?] [Colloq.] to drink in gulps — *n.* [Colloq.] a deep draft, as of liquor

swill (swil) *vt., vi.* [OE *swilian*] 1 to drink greedily 2 to feed swill to (pigs, etc.) — *n.* 1 liquid garbage fed to pigs 2 garbage

swim¹ (swim) *vi.* **swam, swum, swim′ming** [OE *swimman*] 1 to move through water by moving arms, legs, fins, etc. 2 to move along smoothly 3 to float on or in a liquid 4 to overflow [eyes *swimming* with tears] — *vt.* to swim in or across — *n.* the act of swimming — *adj.* [Colloq.] of or for swimming [*swim* trunks] —**in the swim** active in what is popular at the moment —**swim′mer** *n.*

swim² (swim) *n.* [OE *swima*] a dizzy spell — *vi.* **swam, swum, swim′ming** to be dizzy

swimming hole a deep place in a river, creek, etc. used for swimming

swim′suit′ (-sōot′) *n.* a garment worn for swimming

swin·dle (swin′dəl) *vt., vi.* **-dled, -dling** [< Ger *schwindeln*] to defraud (another) of money or property; cheat — *n.* an act of swindling; trick; fraud —**swin′dler** *n.*

swine (swin) *n., pl.* **swine** [OE *swin*] 1 a pig or hog: usually used collectively 2 a vicious, contemptible person —**swin′ish** *adj.*

swing (swiŋ) *vi.* **swung, swing′ing** [OE *swingan*] 1 to sway or move backward and forward 2 to walk, trot, etc. with relaxed movements 3 to strike (*at*) 4 to turn, as on a hinge 5 to move in a curve 6 to hang; be suspended 7 [Slang] *a)* to be ultra-fashionable, esp. in seeking pleasure *b)* to engage in casual sexual relations — *vt.* 1 to move, lift, etc. with a sweeping motion 2 to cause to move backward and forward 3 to cause to turn, as on a hinge 4 to cause to move in a curve [*swing* the car around] 5 [Colloq.] to cause to come about successfully [to *swing* an election] — *n.* 1 a swinging 2 the arc through which something swings 3 the manner of swinging a golf club, etc. 4 a relaxed motion, as in walking 5 a sweeping blow or stroke 6 the course of some activity, etc. 7 rhythm, as of music 8 a seat hanging from ropes, etc. on which one can swing 9 a trip or tour 10 jazz (*c.* 1935-45) characterized by large bands, fast tempos, and written arrangements — *adj.* having decisive power, as in determining an election [the *swing* vote]

swing′er *n.* 1 one that swings 2 a person who swings (see SWING, *vi.* 7b)

swing shift [Colloq.] the work shift from 4:00 P.M. to midnight

swipe (swip) *n.* [prob. var. of SWEEP] [Colloq.] a hard, sweeping blow — *vt.* **swiped, swip′ing** 1 [Colloq.] to hit with a swipe 2 [Slang] to steal

swirl (swurl) *vi., vt.* [ME *swyrl*] to move or cause to move with a whirling motion — *n.* 1 a whirl; eddy 2 a twist; curl —**swirl′y** *adj.*

swish (swish) *vi.* [echoic] 1 to move with a sharp, hissing sound, as a cane swung through the air 2 to move with a

light, brushing sound, as skirts in walking — *vt.* 1 to cause to swish 2 to move (liquid), esp. in the mouth, with a gurgling sound — *n.* a swishing sound or movement

Swiss (swis) *adj.* of Switzerland, its people, etc. — *n., pl.* **Swiss** a native or inhabitant of Switzerland

Swiss chard CHARD

Swiss (cheese) a pale-yellow, hard cheese with many large holes

Swiss steak a thick cut of round steak pounded with flour and braised

switch (swich) *n.* [Early ModE *swits*] 1 a thin, flexible stick used for whipping 2 a sharp lash, as with a whip 3 a separate tress of hair, used as part of a coiffure 4 a device used to open, close, or divert an electric circuit 5 a device used in transferring a train from one track to another 6 a shift; change — *vt.* 1 to whip as with a switch 2 to jerk sharply 3 to shift; change 4 to turn (an electric light, etc.) *on* or *off* 5 to transfer (a train, etc.) to another track 6 [Colloq.] to change or exchange — *vi.* to shift —**switch′er** *n.*

switch′back′ *n.* a road or railroad following a zigzag course up a steep grade

switch′blade′ (knife) (-blād′) a large jackknife that snaps open when a release button on the handle is pressed

switch′board′ (-bôrd′) *n.* a panel for controlling a system of electric circuits, as in a telephone exchange

switch′-hit′ter *n.* a baseball player who bats right-handed and left-handed

swivel (swiv′əl) *n.* [< OE *swifan,* to revolve] a coupling device that allows free turning of the parts attached to it — *vi., vt.* **-eled** or **-elled, -el·ing** or **-el·ling** to turn or cause to turn as on a swivel or pivot

swiz·zle stick (swiz′əl) [< ?] a small rod for stirring mixed drinks

swob (swäb) *n., vt.* **swobbed, swob′bing** *alt. sp. of* SWAB

swol·len (swōl′ən) *vi., vt. alt. pp. of* SWELL — *adj.* blown up; distended; bulging

swoon (swōōn) *vi., n.* [< OE *geswogen,* unconscious] FAINT

swoop (swōōp) *vi.* [< OE *swapan,* sweep along] to pounce or sweep (*down* or *upon*), as a bird in hunting — *n.* the act of swooping

swop (swäp) *n., vt., vi.* **swopped, swop′ping** *alt. sp. of* SWAP

sword (sôrd) *n.* [OE *sweord*] a hand weapon with a long, sharp-pointed blade set in a hilt —**at swords' points** ready to quarrel or fight

sword′fish′ *n., pl.* **-fish′** a large, marine food fish with the upper jawbone extending in a swordlike point

sword′play′ (-plā′) *n.* the act or skill of using a sword, as in fencing

swords·man (sôrdz′mən) *n., pl.* **-men** 1 one who uses a sword in fencing or fighting 2 one skilled in using a sword

swore (swôr) *vi., vt. pt. of* SWEAR

sworn (swôrn) *vi., vt. pp. of* SWEAR — *adj.* bound, pledged, etc. by an oath

swum (swum) *vi., vt. pp. of* SWIM¹ & SWIM²

swung (swuŋ) *vi., vt. pp. & pt. of* SWING

syba·rite (sib′ə rit′) *n.* [after *Sybaris,* ancient Gr city in Italy] anyone very fond of luxury and pleasure —**syb′a·rit′ic** (-rit′ik) *adj.*

syca·more (sik′ə môr′) *n.* [< Gr *sykomoros*] 1 a maple tree of Europe and Asia 2 an American tree with bark that sheds in patches

syco·phant (sik′ə fənt) *n.* [< Gr *sykophantēs,* informer] one who seeks favor by flattering people of wealth or influence —**syc′o·phan·cy** *n.*

syl·labi·cate (si lab′i kāt′) *vt.* **-cat·ed, -cat·ing** SYLLABIFY —**syl·lab′i·ca′tion** *n.*

syl·labi·fy (si lab′ə fi′) *vt.* **-fied′, -fy′ing** [< L *syllaba,*

THESAURUS

buncle, boil, pock, pustule, inflammation, growth, corn, lump, bunion, tumor, blister, abscess; see also INJURY.

swerve *v.* move, bend, turn aside; see TURN 6.

swift *a.* flying, sudden, speedy; see FAST 1.

swiftly *a.* speedily, rapidly, fast; see QUICKLY.

swim¹ *n.* bath, dip, plunge, dive, jump, splash.

swim¹ *v.* bathe, float, glide, slip through the water, stroke, paddle, go for a swim, take a dip, train for the swimming team, swim freestyle.

swimming *n.* diving, aquatic, bathing; see SPORT 3.

swindle *n.* imposition, deception, knavery; see TRICK 1.

swindle *v.* dupe, victimize, defraud; see DECEIVE.

swindler *n.* cheat, cheater, thief, impostor, charlatan, trickster, deceiver, falsifier, counterfeiter, card shark*, forger, fraud, conman*, four-flusher*, sharper, gyp*; see also CRIMINAL.

swing *n.* sway, motion, fluctuation, stroke, vibration, oscillation, lilt, beat, rhythm; see also WAVE 2. —**in full swing** lively, vigorous, animated; see ACTIVE, EXCITING.

swing *v.* sway, pivot, rotate, turn,

turn about, revolve, fluctuate, waver, vibrate, turn on an axis; see also WAVE 3.

swinger* *n.* sex deviant, sophisticated person, life of the party*, mistress, cohabitant.

switch *v.* turnabout, shift, rearrange; see ALTER 1, TURN 2.

swollen *a.* distended, puffed, swelled; see ENLARGED.

swoop *n.* plunge, fall, drop; see DESCENT 2, DIVE 1.

swoop *v.* slide, plummet, plunge; see DESCEND, DIVE, FALL 1.

sword *n.* saber, rapier, weapon; see KNIFE.

syllable + *facere*, make]] to form or divide into syllables — **syl·lab′i·fi·ca′tion** *n.*

syl·la·ble (sil′ə bəl) *n.* [[< Gr *syn-*, together + *lambanein*, to hold]] **1** a word or part of a word pronounced with a single, uninterrupted sounding of the voice **2** one or more letters written to represent a spoken syllable —**syl·labic** (si lab′ik) *adj.*

syl·la·bus (sil′ə bəs) *n., pl.* **-buses** or **-bi′** (-bī′) [[< Gr *sittybos*, strip of leather]] a summary or outline, esp. of a course of study

syl·lo·gism (sil′ə jiz′əm) *n.* [[< Gr *syn-*, together + *logizesthai*, to reason]] a form of reasoning in which two premises are made and a logical conclusion drawn from them

sylph (silf) *n.* [Mod L *sylphus*, a spirit] **1** any of a class of imaginary beings supposed to inhabit the air **2** a slender, graceful woman or girl —**sylph′like′** *adj.*

syl·van (sil′vən) *adj.* [[< L *silva*, forest]] **1** of, characteristic of, or living in, the woods or forest **2** wooded

sym·bi·osis (sim′bī ō′sis, -bē-) *n.* [[< Gr *symbioun*, to live together]] the living together of two kinds of organisms to their mutual advantage —**sym′bi·ot′ic** (-ät′ik) *adj.*

sym·bol (sim′bəl) *n.* [[< Gr *syn-*, together + *ballein*, to throw]] **1** an object used to represent something abstract [the dove is a *symbol* of peace] **2** a mark, letter, etc. standing for a quality, process, etc., as in music or chemistry —**sym·bol′ic** (-bäl′ik) or **sym·bol′i·cal** *adj.* —**sym·bol′i·cally** *adv.*

sym·bol·ism (sim′bəl iz′əm) *n.* **1** representation by symbols **2** a system of symbols **3** symbolic meaning

sym′bol·ize′ (-īz′) *vt.* **-ized′, -iz′ing 1** to be a symbol of; stand for **2** to represent by a symbol or symbols —**sym′bo·li·za′tion** *n.*

sym·metry (sim′ə trē) *n., pl.* **-tries** [[< Gr *syn-*, together + *metron*, a measure]] **1** correspondence of opposite parts in size, shape, and position **2** balance or beauty of form resulting from this —**sym·met·ri·cal** (si me′tri kəl) *adj.* —**sym·met′ri·cally** *adv.*

sym·pa·thetic (sim′pə thet′ik) *adj.* **1** of, feeling, or showing sympathy **2** in agreement with one's tastes, mood, etc. **3** *Physiology* designating or of that part of the autonomic nervous system for communicating the involuntary response to alarm, as by speeding the heart rate —**sym′pa·thet′i·cally** *adv.*

sym′pa·thize′ (-thīz′) *vi.* **-thized′, -thiz′ing 1** to share the feelings or ideas of another **2** to feel or express sympathy —**sym′pa·thiz′er** *n.*

sym·pa·thy (sim′pə thē) *n., pl.* **-thies** [[< Gr *syn-*, together + *pathos*, feeling]] **1** sameness of feeling **2** mutual liking or understanding **3** *a)* ability to share another's ideas, emotions, etc. *b)* [*often pl.*] pity or compassion

sym·phony (sim′fə nē) *n., pl.* **-nies** [[< Gr *syn-*, together + *phōnē*, sound]] **1** harmony, as of sounds, color, etc. **2** an extended musical composition in several movements, for full orchestra **3** a large orchestra for playing symphonic works: in full **symphony orchestra 4** [Colloq.] a symphony concert —**sym·phon′ic** (-fän′ik) *adj.*

sym·po·sium (sim pō′zē əm) *n., pl.* **-si·ums** or **-sia** (-ə) [[< Gr *syn-*, together + *posis*, a drinking]] **1** a conference to discuss a topic **2** a published group of opinions on a topic

symp·tom (simp′təm) *n.* [[< Gr *syn-*, together + *piptein*, to fall]] any circumstance or condition that indicates the existence, as of a particular disease —**symp′to·mat′ic** (-tə mat′ik) *adj.*

syn- [[Gr]] *prefix* with, together, at the same time

syn. 1 synonym **2** synonymy

syna·gogue (sin′ə gäg′, -gôg′) *n.* [[< Gr *syn-*, together + *agein*, do]] **1** an assembly of Jews for worship and reli-

gious study **2** a building or place for such assembly — **syn′a·gog′al** *adj.*

syn·apse (sin′aps′, si naps′) *n.* [[< Gr *syn-*, together + *apsis*, a joining]] the space between nerve cells through which nerve impulses are transmitted

sync or **synch** (siŋk) *vt., vi.* **synced** or **synched, sync′ing** or **synch′ing** *short for* SYNCHRONIZE —*n. short for* SYNCHRONIZATION —**in** (or **out of**) **sync** in (or out of) synchronization or harmony (*with*)

syn·chro·nize (siŋ′krə nīz′) *vi.* **-nized′, -niz′ing** [[< Gr *syn-*, together + *chronos*, time]] to move or occur at the same time or rate — *vt.* to cause to agree in time or rate of speed —**syn′chro·ni·za′tion** *n.*

syn′chro·nous *adj.* happening at the same time or at the same rate

syn·co·pate (siŋ′kə pāt′) *vt.* **-pat′ed, -pat′ing** [[< Gr *syn-*, together + *koptein*, cut]] *Music* to begin a tone on an unaccented beat and continuing it through the next accented beat —**syn′co·pa′tion** *n.*

syn·di·cate (sin′də kit; *for v.*, -kāt′) *n.* [[< Gr *syn-*, together + *dikē*, justice]] **1** an association of individuals or corporations formed for a project requiring much capital **2** any group, as of criminals, organized for some undertaking **3** an organization selling articles or features to many newspapers, etc. — *vt.* **-cat′ed, -cat′ing 1** to manage as or form into a syndicate **2** *a)* to sell (an article, etc.) through a syndicate *b)* to sell (a program, etc.) to a number of radio or TV stations — *vi.* to form a syndicate —**syn′di·ca′tion** *n.*

syn·drome (sin′drōm′) *n.* [[< Gr *syn-*, with + *dramein*, run]] a set of symptoms characterizing a disease or condition

syn·er·gism (sin′ər jiz′əm) *n.* [[< Gr *syn-*, together + *ergon*, work]] combined action, as of several drugs, greater in total effect than the sum of their effects —**syn′er·gis′tic** *adj.*

syn·od (sin′əd) *n.* [[< Gr *syn-*, together + *hodos*, way]] **1** an ecclesiastical council **2** a high governing body in certain Christian churches **3** any council

syno·nym (sin′ə nim) *n.* [[< Gr *syn-*, together + *onyma*, a name]] a word having the same or nearly the same meaning as another in the same language —**syn·ony·mous** (si nän′ə məs) *adj.*

syn·op·sis (si näp′sis) *n., pl.* **-ses** (-sēz) [[< Gr *syn-*, together + *opsis*, a seeing]] a brief, general review or condensation; summary

syn·tax (sin′taks′) *n.* [[< Gr *syn-*, together + *tassein*, arrange]] the arrangement of and relationships among words, phrases, and clauses forming sentences —**syn·tac′tic** (-tak′tik) or **syn·tac′ti·cal** *adj.*

syn·thesis (sin′thə sis) *n., pl.* **-ses′** (-sēz′) [[< Gr *syn-*, together + *tithenai*, to place]] the combining of parts or elements so as to form a whole, a compound, etc. —**syn′thesize′** (-sīz′), **-sized′, -siz′ing,** *vt.*

syn′thesiz′er *n.* an electronic device producing sounds unobtainable from ordinary musical instruments or imitating instruments and voices

syn·thet′ic (-thet′ik) *adj.* **1** of or involving synthesis **2** produced by chemical synthesis, rather than of natural origin **3** not real; artificial — *n.* something synthetic — **syn·thet′i·cally** *adv.*

syphi·lis (sif′ə lis) *n.* [after *Syphilus*, hero of a L poem (1530)] an infectious venereal disease —**syph′i·lit′ic** *adj., n.*

sy·ringe (sə rinj′, sir′inj) *n.* [[< Gr *syrinx*, a pipe]] a device consisting of a tube with a rubber bulb or piston at one end for drawing in a liquid and then ejecting it in a stream:

■■■ THESAURUS ■■■

syllabus *n.* digest, outline, synopsis; see PLAN 1, PROGRAM 2.

symbol *n.* representative, token, figure; see SIGN 1.

symbolic *a.* representative, typical, indicative, suggestive, symptomatic, characteristic.

symbolize *v.* typify, signify, express; see MEAN 1.

symmetry *n.* proportion, arrangement, order, equality, regularity, conformity, agreement, shapeliness, evenness, balance, equilibrium, similarity.

sympathetic *a.* compassionate, loving, considerate; see THOUGHTFUL 2.

sympathetically *a.* sensitively, per-

ceptively, responsively, harmoniously, in accord, in harmony, in concert, understandingly, appreciatively, emotionally, with feeling, warmly, heartily, cordially, kindheartedly, warmheartedly, softheartedly, humanely, in tune with.

sympathize *v.* pity, show mercy, comfort, understand, be understanding, love, be kind to, commiserate, express sympathy.

sympathy *n.* **1** [Fellow feeling] understanding, commiseration, compassion; see PITY. **2** [An expression of sympathy] condolence, consolation, solace, comfort, cheer, encouragement, reassurance; see also HELP

1, ENCOURAGEMENT.

symptom *n.* mark, sign, token; see CHARACTERISTIC.

synonymous *a.* same, like, similar, equivalent, identical, correspondent, corresponding, alike, interchangeable, convertible, compatible; see also EQUAL.—*Ant.* OPPOSITE, divergent, contrary.

synopsis *n.* outline, digest, brief; see SUMMARY.

syntax *n.* order of words, arrangement, grammatical rules; see GRAMMAR, LANGUAGE 2.

synthetic *a.* artificial, counterfeit, plastic; see FALSE 3.

used to inject fluids into the body, etc. — **vt. -ringed′, -ring′ing** to cleanse, inject, etc. by using a syringe

syrup (sʉr′əp, sir′-) *n.* ⟦< OFr *sirop* < ML *sirupus* < Ar *sharāb*, a drink⟧ any sweet, thick liquid; specif., a solution of sugar and water boiled together

syr·upy (sʉr′ə pē, sir′-) *adj.* **1** like syrup **2** overly sentimental; cloyingly sweet

sys·tem (sis′təm) *n.* ⟦< Gr *syn-*, together + *histanai*, to set⟧ **1** a set or arrangement of things so related as to form a whole *[a solar system, school system]* **2** a set of facts, rules, etc. arranged to show a plan **3** a method or plan **4** an established, orderly way of doing something **5** the body, or a number of bodily organs, functioning as a unit

sys′tem·at′ic (-tə mat′ik) *adj.* **1** constituting or based on a system **2** according to a system; orderly —**sys′tem·at′i·cally** *adv.*

sys′tema·tize′ (-təm ə tīz′) *vt.* **-tized′, -tiz′ing** to arrange according to a system; make systematic

sys·temic (sis tem′ik) *adj.* of or affecting the body as a whole

sys·tole (sis′tə lē′) *n.* ⟦< Gr *syn-*, together + *stellein*, to set up⟧ the usual rhythmic contraction of the heart —**sys·tol′ic** (-täl′ik) *adj.*

THESAURUS

syrup *n.* glucose, molasses, honey; see SUGAR. *Kinds of syrup include the following:* cane, corn, maple, simple, rock candy.

system *n.* orderliness, regularity, conformity, logical order, definite plan, arrangement, rule, systematic order, systematic arrangement, logical process; see also ORDER 3.

systematize *v.* plan, arrange, organize; see ORDER 3.

t or **T** (tē) *n., pl.* **t's, T's** the 20th letter of the English alphabet —**to a T** to perfection; exactly

't it ['twas]

t or **t.** 1 teaspoon(s) 2 temperature 3 ton(s) 4 transitive

T or **T.** 1 tablespoon(s) 2 temperature 3 Thursday 4 Tuesday

tab¹ (tab) *n.* ⟦< ?⟧ 1 a small, flat loop or strap fastened to something 2 a projecting piece as of a file folder, used in filing

tab² (tab) *n.* ⟦prob. < TABULATION⟧ [Colloq.] 1 a bill, as for expenses 2 total cost —**keep tabs (or a tab) on** [Colloq.] to keep a check on

tab·bou·leh (tə bōō'lě, -le) *n.* ⟦Ar⟧ a salad of coarsely ground wheat, parsley, tomatoes, scallions, etc. Also **ta·bou'li** or **ta·bu'li**

tabby (tab'ē) *n., pl.* **-bies** ⟦ult. < Ar⟧ a domestic cat, esp. a female

tab·er·nacle (tab'ər nak'əl) *n.* ⟦< L *taberna*, hut⟧ a large place of worship —[T-] the portable sanctuary carried by the Jews during the Exodus

tabla (täb'lä') *n.* ⟦< Ar *ṭabla*, drum⟧ a set of two small drums whose pitch can be varied, used esp. in India and played with the hands

ta·ble (tā'bəl) *n.* ⟦< L *tabula*, a board⟧ 1 orig., a thin slab of metal, stone, etc. 2 *a*) a piece of furniture having a flat top set on legs *b*) such a table set with food *c*) food served *d*) the people seated at a table 3 *a*) a systematic list of details, contents, etc. *b*) an orderly arrangement of facts, figures, etc. 4 any flat, horizontal surface, piece, etc. —*vt.* **-bled, -bling** to postpone indefinitely consideration of (a legislative bill, etc.) —**at table** at a meal —**turn the tables** to reverse a situation

tab·leau (tab'lō', ta blō') *n., pl.* **-leaux** (-lōz') or **-leaus** ⟦Fr < OFr, dim. of *table*⟧ a representation of a scene, etc. by a group posed in costume

ta'ble·cloth' *n.* a cloth for covering a table, esp. at meals

ta·ble d'hôte (tä'bəl dōt') ⟦Fr, table of the host⟧ a complete meal served at a restaurant for a set price

ta'ble-hop' (-häp') *vi.* **-hopped', -hop'ping** to leave one's table, as at a nightclub, and visit about at other tables — **ta'ble-hop'per** *n.*

ta'ble·land' *n.* a plateau

ta'ble·spoon' *n.* a large spoon holding ½ fluid ounce — **ta'ble·spoon'ful,** *pl.* **-fuls,** *n.*

tab·let (tab'lit) *n.* ⟦see TABLE⟧ 1 a flat, thin piece of stone, metal, etc. with an inscription 2 a writing pad of paper sheets glued together at one edge 3 a small, flat piece of compressed material, as of medicine

table tennis a game somewhat like tennis played on a table, with a small, hollow celluloid ball

ta'ble·ware' (-wer') *n.* dishes, glassware, silverware, etc. for use at a meal

tab·loid (tab'loid') *n.* ⟦TABL(ET) + -OID⟧ a newspaper, usually half size, with many pictures and short, often sensational, news stories

ta·boo (tə bōō', ta-) *n.* ⟦< a Polynesian language⟧ 1 among some Polynesian peoples, a sacred prohibition making certain people or things untouchable, etc. 2 any conventional social restriction —*adj.* prohibited by taboo —*vt.* 1 to put under taboo 2 to prohibit or forbid Also **tabu'**

tabu·lar (tab'yōō lər) *adj.* ⟦see TABLE⟧ 1 flat 2 of, arranged in, or computed from a table or list

tab'u·late' (-lāt') *vt.* **-lat'ed, -lat'ing** to put (facts, statistics, etc.) in a table —**tab'u·la'tion** *n.* —**tab'u·la'tor** *n.*

ta·chom·eter (ta käm'ət ər, tə-) *n.* ⟦< Gr *tachos*, speed + -METER⟧ a device that measures the rate of rotation of a revolving shaft

tacit (tas'it) *adj.* ⟦< L *tacere*, be silent⟧ 1 unspoken; silent 2 not expressed openly, but implied —**tac'itly** *adv.* —**tac'it·ness** *n.*

taci·turn (tas'ə turn') *adj.* ⟦see prec.⟧ almost always silent; not liking to talk —**tac'i·tur'nity** *n.*

tack (tak) *n.* ⟦< MDu *tacke*, twig⟧ 1 a short nail with a sharp point and a large, flat head 2 a temporary stitch 3 a zigzag course 4 a course of action 5 *a*) the direction a ship goes in relation to the position of the sails *b*) a change of a ship's direction —*vt.* 1 to fasten with tacks 2 to attach or add 3 to change the course of (a ship) —*vi.* to change course suddenly

tackle (tak'əl) *n.* ⟦< MDu *takel*⟧ 1 equipment; gear 2 a system of ropes and pulleys for moving weights 3 a tackling, as in football 4 *Football* a player next to the end on the line —*vt.* **tack'led, tack'ling** 1 to take hold of; seize 2 to try to do; undertake 3 *Football* to throw (the ball carrier) to the ground —**tack'ler** *n.*

tacky (tak'ē) *adj.* **-i·er, -i·est** 1 sticky, as glue 2 dowdy or shabby 3 in poor taste —**tack'i·ness** *n.*

taco (tä'kō) *n., pl.* **-cos** ⟦Sp, light lunch⟧ a fried tortilla filled with chopped meat, lettuce, etc.

tact (takt) *n.* ⟦< L *tangere*, to touch⟧ delicate perception of the right thing to say or do without offending —**tact'ful** *adj.* —**tact'fully** *adv.* —**tact'less** *adj.* —**tact'lessly** *adv.*

tac·tics (tak'tiks) *n.pl.* ⟦< Gr *tassein*, arrange⟧ 1 [*with sing. v.*] the science of maneuvering military and naval forces 2 any skillful methods to gain an end —**tac'ti·cal** *adj.* —**tac·ti'cian** (-tish'ən) *n.*

tac·tile (tak'təl) *adj.* ⟦< L *tangere*, to touch⟧ of, having, or perceived by the sense of touch

---

■ THESAURUS ■

tab¹ *n.* loop, stop, clip; see LABEL, MARKER, TAG 2.

table *n.* 1 [A piece of furniture] desk, pulpit, stand, board, counter, slab, dresser, bureau, lectern, sideboard, washstand, sink; see also FURNITURE. *Tables include the following:* writing table, secretary, dining table, kitchen table, card table, drafting table, vanity table, drop-leaf table, operating table, altar table, end table, laboratory table, library table, refectory table. 2 [A statement in tabulated form] synopsis, report, record; see SUMMARY. —**turn the tables** reverse, change, switch; see ALTER 1. —**under the table*** covertly, surreptitiously, not obviously; see SECRETLY.

tableau *n.* scene, picture, illustration; see VIEW.

tablecloth *n.* covering, spread, place mats; see COVER 1.

tablet *n.* 1 [A thin piece of material bearing a legend] slab, stone, monument; see MEMORIAL. 2 [Writing paper] folder, pad, sheets; see PAPER 4. 3 [A pharmaceutical preparation] pill, dose, capsule; see MEDICINE 2.

taboo *a.* forbidden, out of bounds, reserved; see ILLEGAL, RESTRICTED.

taboo *n.* restriction, reservation, limi-

tation; see RESTRAINT 2.

taboo *v.* inhibit, forbid, prevent; see HINDER, RESTRAIN.

tabulate *v.* formulate, arrange, index; see LIST 1, RECORD 1.

tack *n.* 1 [A short, broad-headed nail] thumbtack, push pin, carpet tack, copper tack; see also NAIL, PIN 1. 2 [An oblique course] tangent, deviation, digression; see TURN 6.

tack *v.* 1 [To fasten lightly] pin, nail, stitch; see FASTEN. 2 [To steer an oblique course] go in zigzags, zigzag, change course; see TURN 6.

tackle *n.* 1 [Equipment] rigging, ropes and pulleys, apparatus; see EQUIPMENT. 2 [A contrivance having mechanical advantage] pulleys, block-and-tackle, movable pulley; see TOOL 1. 3 [In football, an attempt to down a ball-carrier] flying, running, shoulder, etc. tackle; sack, hit; see DEFENSE 1, JUMP. 4 [In football, one who plays between end and guard] linesman, right tackle, left tackle; see FOOTBALL PLAYER. 5 [In fishing, equipment] gear, sporting goods, fishing outfit; see EQUIPMENT. *Fishing tackle includes the following:* hook, line, fly, casting rod, casting reel, cut bait, live bait, minnow, grasshopper, fish eggs, worm, lure,

spinner, fish net, landing net, pole, float, cork, sinker, creel, tackle box, shot, deep-sea tackle, leader, stringer, fish sack, basket.

tackle *v.* 1 [To undertake] begin, turn to, make an attempt; see TRY 1, UNDERTAKE. 2 [In football, to endeavor to down an opponent] seize, throw down, grab; see UPSET 1.

tact *n.* perception, discrimination, judgment, acuteness, penetration, intelligence, acumen, common sense, subtlety, discernment, prudence, aptness, good taste, refinement, delicacy, the ability to get along with others, finesse, horse sense*.—*Ant.* RUDENESS, coarseness, misconduct.

tactful *a.* diplomatic, civil, considerate; see THOUGHTFUL 2.

tactics *n.* strategy, maneuvering, military art, generalship, plan of attack, plan of defense, procedure, stratagem, approach, disposition, map work, chalk work.

tactless *a.* stupid, unperceptive, inconsiderate, rude, discourteous, unsympathetic, unthoughtful, insensitive, boorish, misunderstanding, impolite, rash, hasty, awkward, clumsy, imprudent, rough, crude, unpolished, gruff, uncivil, vulgar.

tad (tad) *n.* ⟦prob. < TADPOLE⟧ **1** a little child, esp. a boy **2** a small amount or degree /a tad tired/

tad·pole (tad′pōl′) *n.* ⟦ME *tadde*, toad + *poll*, head⟧ the larva of a frog or toad, having gills and a tail and living in water

taf·feta (taf′i tə) *n.* ⟦< Pers *tāftan*, to weave⟧ a fine, stiff fabric of silk, nylon, etc., with a sheen

taff·rail (taf′rāl′) *n.* ⟦< Du⟧ the rail around the stern of a ship

taffy (taf′ē) *n.* ⟦< ?⟧ a chewy candy made of sugar or molasses

tag (tag) *n.* ⟦prob. < Scand⟧ **1** a hanging end or part **2** a hard-tipped end on a cord or lace **3** a card, etc. attached as a label **4** an epithet **5** the last line or lines of a story, speech, etc. **6** a children's game in which one player chases the others with the object of touching one of them — *vt.* **tagged, tag′ging 1** to provide with a tag; label **2** to choose or select **3** to touch in playing tag — *vi.* [Colloq.] to follow closely: with *along, after,* etc. —**tag′ger** *n.*

Ta·ga·log (tä gä′lôg′) *n.* **1** *pl.* **-logs′** or **-log′** a member of the ethnic group native to the Manila region in the Philippines **2** their language, an official language of the Republic of the Philippines

Ta·hi·tian (tə hēsh′ən) *adj.* of Tahiti, its people, language, etc. — *n.* **1** a native of Tahiti **2** the Tahitian language

Tai (tī) *n.* **1** a group of languages spoken in central and SE Asia **2** a member of a group of peoples of SE Asia who speak these languages — *adj.* of these languages or peoples

tai chi (tī′ jē′) ⟦Mandarin⟧ a system of exercise developed in China, consisting of a series of slow, ritual movements In full **t'ai chi ch'uan** (chwän′)

taiga (tī′gə) *n.* ⟦Russ⟧ a type of transitional plant community in the far north, having scattered trees

tail (tāl) *n.* ⟦OE *tægel*⟧ **1** the rear end of an animal's body, esp. when a distinct appendage **2** anything like an animal's tail in form or position **3** the hind, bottom, last, or inferior part of anything **4** [*often pl.*] the reverse side of a coin **5** [*pl.*] [Colloq.] full-dress attire for men **6** [Colloq.]

a person that follows another, esp. in surveillance — *adj.* **1** at the rear or end **2** from the rear /a tail wind/ — *vt.* [Slang] to follow stealthily — *vi.* [Colloq.] to follow close behind

tail′gate′ *n.* the hinged or removable gate at the back of a wagon, truck, etc. — *vi.*, *vt.* **-gat′ed, -gat′ing** to drive too closely behind (another vehicle)

tail′light′ *n.* a light, usually red, at the rear of a vehicle to warn vehicles coming from behind

tai·lor (tā′lər) *n.* ⟦< VL *taliare*, to cut⟧ one who makes, repairs, or alters clothes — *vi.* to work as a tailor — *vt.* **1** to make by tailor's work **2** to form, alter, etc. for a certain purpose /a novel *tailored* for TV/

tail′pipe′ *n.* the exhaust pipe coming from the muffler of a motor vehicle

tail′spin′ *n.* SPIN (*n.* 3)

taint (tānt) *vt.* ⟦< ?⟧ **1** to affect with something injurious, unpleasant, etc.; infect, spoil, etc. **2** to make morally corrupt — *n.* a trace of contamination, corruption, etc.

take (tāk) *vt.* **took, tak′en, tak′ing** ⟦< ON *taka*⟧ **1** to get possession of; capture, seize, etc. **2** to get hold of **3** to capture the fancy of **4** to obtain, acquire, assume, etc. **5** to use, consume, etc. **6** to buy, rent, subscribe to, etc. **7** to join with (one side in a disagreement, etc.) **8** to choose; select **9** to travel by /to *take* a bus/ **10** to deal with; consider **11** to occupy /take a chair/ **12** to require; demand /it takes money/ **13** to derive (a name, quality, etc.) from **14** to excerpt **15** to study **16** to write down /take notes/ **17** to make by photographing **18** to win (a prize, etc.) **19** to undergo /take punishment/ **20** to engage /take a nap/ **21** to accept (an offer, bet, etc.) **22** to react to /take a joke in earnest/ **23** to contract (a disease, etc.) **24** to understand **25** to suppose; presume **26** to feel /take pity/ **27** to lead, escort, etc. **28** to carry **29** to remove, as by stealing **30** to subtract **31** [Slang] to cheat, trick **32** *Gram.* to be used with /the verb "hit" *takes* an object/ — *vi.* **1** to take root: said of a plant **2** to catch /the fire *took*/ **3** to gain favor, success, etc. **4** to be effective /the vaccination *took*/ **5** to go /to *take* to the hills/ **6** [Colloq.] to become (sick) — *n.* **1** a taking **2** *a*) the amount taken *b*) [Slang]

⬛⬛⬛⬛⬛⬛⬛⬛⬛⬛ THESAURUS ⬛⬛⬛⬛⬛⬛⬛⬛⬛⬛

tag *n.* **1** [A remnant or scrap] rag, piece, patch; see REMNANTS. **2** [A mark of identification] ticket, badge, card tab, trademark, stamp, stub, voucher, slip, label, check, emblem, insignia, tally, motto, sticker, inscription, laundry mark, price tag, bar code, identification number, button, pin. **3** [A children's game] hide-and-seek, freeze tag, capture the flag; see GAME 1.

tag *v.* **1** [To fit with a tag] designate, denote, earmark; see MARK 1. **2** [*To follow closely] chase, dog, trail; see PURSUE 1.

tail *n.* rear end, rear appendage, extremity, hind part, butt*, coccyx; see also REAR. **—on one's tail** behind, shadowing, trailing; see FOLLOWING. **—with one's tail between one's legs** in defeat, humbly, dejectedly; see FEARFULLY.

tailor *n.* garment maker, clothier, dressmaker, seamstress, designer, fashion designer.

take *n.* **1** [Something that is taken] part, cut, proceeds; see PROFIT 2, SHARE. **2** [Scene filmed or televised] film, shot, motion picture; see PHOTOGRAPH. **3** [*Something that is seized] holding, catching, haul*; see BOOTY.

take *v.* **1** [To seize] appropriate, take hold of, catch, grip, grab, pluck, pocket, carry off; see also SEIZE 1, 2. **2** [To collect] gather up, accept, reap; see RECEIVE 1. **3** [To catch] capture, grab, get hold of; see CATCH 1. **4** [To choose] select, settle on, opt for, make a selection, pick, decide on, prefer; see also CHOOSE, DECIDE. **5** [To acquire] win, procure, gain, achieve, receive, attain, obtain, secure; see also EARN 2, GET 1. **6** [To require] necessitate, demand, call for; see NEED. **7** [To contract; *said of a disease*] get, come down with, be

seized with; see CATCH 4. **8** [To record] note, register, take notes; see RECORD 1. **9** [To transport] move, drive, bear; see CARRY 1. **10** [To captivate] charm, delight, overwhelm; see ENTERTAIN 1, FASCINATE. **11** [To win] prevail, triumph, beat; see DEFEAT 2, 3. **12** [To buy] pay for, select, procure; see BUY 3. **13** [To rent] lease, hire, charter; see RENT 2. **14** [To steal] misappropriate, loot, rob; see STEAL. **15** [To undergo] tolerate, suffer, bear; see ENDURE 2, UNDERGO. **16** [To lead] guide, steer, pilot; see LEAD 1. **17** [To escort] conduct, attend, go with; see ACCOMPANY. **18** [To admit] let in, welcome, give access to; see RECEIVE 4. **19** [To adopt] utilize, assume, appropriate; see ADOPT 2. **20** [To apply] put in practice, exert, exercise; see PRACTICE 1, USE 1. **21** [To experience] sense, observe, be aware of; see FEEL 2. **22** [To cheat] defraud, trick, swindle; see DECEIVE. **23** [To grow] germinate, develop into, grow to be; see BECOME. **—take after** [To resemble] look like, be like, seem like; see RESEMBLE. **—take away 1** [To subtract] deduct, take from, minus*; see DECREASE 2. **2** [To carry off] transport, cart off, carry away; see REMOVE 1. **—take back 1** [To regain] retrieve, get back, reclaim; see RECOVER 1. **2** [To restrict] draw in, retire, pull in; see REMOVE 1, WITHDRAW. **3** [To disavow] retract, recant, recall; see DENY, WITHDRAW. **—take down 1** [To dismantle] disassemble, take apart, undo; see DISMANTLE. **2** [To write down] inscribe, jot down, note down; see RECORD 1, WRITE 2. **—take for 1** [To mistake] misapprehend, misunderstand, err; see MISTAKE. **2** [To assume] presuppose, infer, accept;

see ASSUME. **—take in 1** [To include] embrace, comprise, incorporate; see INCLUDE 1. **2** [To understand] comprehend, apprehend, perceive; see UNDERSTAND 1. **3** [To cheat] swindle, lie, defraud; see DECEIVE. **4** [To give hospitality] welcome, shelter, accept; see RECEIVE 1, 4. **5** [To shorten] reduce, lessen, cut down; see DECREASE 2. **—take off 1** [To undress] strip, divest, expose; see UNDRESS. **2** [To deduct] lessen, subtract, take away; see DECREASE 2. **3** [To leave the earth] blast off, ascend, soar; see FLY 1, 4, RISE 1. **4** [To leave] go away, depart, shove off*; see LEAVE 1. **—take on 1** [To hire] employ, engage, give work to; see HIRE. **2** [To acquire an appearance] emerge, develop, turn; see BECOME, SEEM. **3** [To undertake] attempt, handle, endeavor; see TRY 1, UNDERTAKE. **4** [*To meet in fight or sport] engage, battle, contest; see ATTACK 1, COMPETE. **—take over 1** [To take control] take charge, take command, assume control; see LEAD 1. **2** [To seize control] take the reins of, take the helm of, overthrow; see SEIZE 2. **3** [To convey] transport, bear, move; see CARRY 1, SEND 1. **—take to** enjoy, be fond of, admire; see FAVOR, LIKE 1, 2. **—take up 1** [To begin] start, initiate, commence; see BEGIN 1. **2** [To raise] lift, elevate, hoist; see RAISE 1. **3** [To shorten] tighten, reduce, lessen; see DECREASE 2. **4** [To occupy] consume, engage, fill; see OCCUPY 2, USE 1. **5** [To adopt as a cause] appropriate, become involved with, assume; see ADOPT 2.

taken *a.* **1** [Captured] arrested, seized, appropriated; see CAPTURED. **2** [Employed or rented] occupied, reserved, held; see RENTED.

receipts or profit —**on the take** [Slang] taking bribes, etc. —**take after** to be, act, or look like —**take back** to retract (something said, etc.) —**take down** to put in writing; record —**take for 1** to regard as **2** to mistake for — **take in 1** to admit; receive **2** to make smaller **3** to understand **4** to cheat; trick —**take off 1** to leave the ground, etc. in flight **2** [Colloq.] to start **3** [Colloq.] to imitate in a burlesque manner: with *on* —**take on 1** to acquire; assume **2** to employ **3** to undertake (a task, etc.) —**take over** to assume control or possession of —**take to** to become fond of —**take up 1** to make tighter or shorter **2** to become interested in (an occupation, study, etc.) — **tak′er** *n.*

take′off′ *n.* **1** the act of leaving the ground, as in jumping, flight, etc. **2** [Colloq.] a caricature; burlesque

take′o′ver *n.* the usurpation of power in a nation, organization, etc.

tak·ing (tāk′iŋ) *adj.* attractive; winning — *n.* **1** the act of one that takes **2** [*pl.*] earnings; profits

talc (talk) *n.* ⟦ < Ar *ṭalq* ⟧ **1** a soft mineral used to make talcum powder, etc. **2** *short for* TALCUM (POWDER)

tal·cum (powder) (tal′kəm) a powder for the body made of purified talc

tale (tāl) *n.* ⟦OE *talu*⟧ **1** a true or fictitious story; narrative **2** idle or malicious gossip **3** a fiction; lie

tale′bear′er (-ber′ər) *n.* a gossip

tal·ent (tal′ənt) *n.* ⟦ < Gr *talanton*, a weight⟧ **1** an ancient unit of weight or money **2** any natural ability or power **3** a superior ability in an art, etc. **4** people, or a person, with talent —**tal′ented** *adj.*

tal·is·man (tal′is mən, -iz-) *n., pl.* **-mans** ⟦ < 5th-c. Medieval Gr *telesma*, religious rite⟧ **1** a ring, stone, etc. bearing engraved figures thought to bring good luck, avert evil, etc. **2** a charm

talk (tôk) *vi.* ⟦prob. < OE *talian*, reckon⟧ **1** to put ideas into words; speak **2** to express ideas by speech substitutes [*talk* by signs] **3** to chatter; gossip **4** to confer; consult **5** to confess or inform on someone — *vt.* **1** to use in speaking [*to talk* French] **2** to discuss **3** to put into a specified condition, etc. by talking — *n.* **1** the act of talking **2** conversation **3** a speech **4** a conference **5** gossip **6** the subject of conversation, gossip, etc. **7** speech; dialect —**talk back** to answer impertinently —**talk down to** to talk patronizingly to, as by simple speech —**talk into** to persuade —**talk up** to promote in discussion —**talk′er** *n.*

talk′a·tive (-ə tiv) *adj.* talking a great deal; loquacious Also **talk′y** *adj.* **-i·er, -i·est**

talking book a recording of a reading of a book, etc. for use esp. by the blind

talking-to (tôk′iŋ tōō′) *n.* [Colloq.] a scolding

talk show *Radio, TV* a program in which a host talks with guest celebrities, experts, etc.

tall (tôl) *adj.* ⟦ < OE (*ge*)*tæl*, swift⟧ **1** higher in stature than the average **2** having a specified height **3** [Colloq.] exaggerated [*a tall* tale] **4** [Colloq.] large [*a tall* drink] —

adv. in an upright, dignified manner [*to stand tall*] —**tall′ness** *n.*

tal·low (tal′ō) *n.* ⟦prob. < LowG *talg*⟧ the solid fat taken from the natural fat of cattle, sheep, etc., used to make candles, soaps, etc.

tally (tal′ē) *n., pl.* **-lies** ⟦ < L *talea*, a stick (notched to keep accounts)⟧ **1** anything used as a record for an account or score **2** an account, score, etc. **3** a tag or label — *vt.* **-lied, -ly·ing 1** to put on or as on a tally **2** to add (*up*) — *vi.* **1** to score a point **2** to agree; correspond

tally·ho (tal′ē hō′) *interj.* the cry of a hunter on sighting the fox

Tal·mud (täl′mood, tal′məd) ⟦Heb, learning⟧ the body of early Jewish civil and religious law

talon (tal′ən) *n.* ⟦ < L *talus*, an ankle⟧ the claw of a bird of prey

tam (tam) *n. short for* TAM-O'-SHANTER

ta·male (tə mä′lē) *n.* ⟦ < MexSp⟧ a Mexican food of minced meat, red peppers, etc. cooked in corn husks

tama·rack (tam′ə rak′) *n.* ⟦ < AmInd⟧ **1** an American larch tree usually found in swamps **2** its wood

tama·rind (tam′ə rind′) *n.* ⟦ < Ar *tamr hindī*, date of India⟧ **1** a tropical tree with yellow flowers and brown, acid pods **2** its edible fruit

tam·bou·rine (tam′bə rēn′) *n.* ⟦prob. < Ar *ṭanbūr*, stringed instrument⟧ a shallow, single-headed hand drum with jingling metal disks in the rim: played by shaking, hitting, etc.

tame (tām) *adj.* **tam′er, tam′est** ⟦OE *tam*⟧ **1** changed from a wild state and trained for human use **2** gentle; docile **3** without spirit or force; dull — *vt.* **tamed, tam′ing 1** to make tame **2** to make gentle; subdue —**tam′able or tame′able** *adj.* —**tame′ly** *adv.* —**tame′ness** *n.* —**tam′er** *n.*

Tamil (tam′əl, tum′-) *n.* the non-Indo-European language of the Tamils, a people of S India and N Sri Lanka

tam-o'-shanter (tam′ə shan′tər) *n.* ⟦ < title character of Burns's poem⟧ a Scottish cap with a round, flat top

tamp (tamp) *vt.* ⟦ < ? Fr *tampon*, a plug⟧ to pack firmly or pound (*down*) by a series of blows or taps

tam·per (tam′pər) *vi.* ⟦ < TEMPER⟧ **1** to make secret, illegal arrangements (*with*) **2** to interfere (*with*) or meddle (*with*)

tam·pon (tam′pän′) *n.* ⟦Fr⟧ a plug of cotton, etc. put into a body cavity or wound to stop bleeding, etc.

tan (tan) *n.* ⟦ < ML *tanum*, a bark used to tan hides⟧ **1** a yellowish-brown color **2** the color of suntan — *adj.* **tan′ner, tan′nest** yellowish-brown — *vt.* **tanned, tan′ning 1** to change (hide) into leather by soaking in tannin **2** to produce a suntan in **3** [Colloq.] to whip severely — *vi.* to become tanned

tana·ger (tan′ə jər) *n.* ⟦ < AmInd (Brazil) *tangara*⟧ any of

---

══ THESAURUS ══

takeoff *v.* ascent, upward flight, fly-off, climb, rise, hop, jump, vertical takeoff; see also RISE 1.

tale *n.* **1** [A story] anecdote, fairy tale, folk tale; see STORY. **2** [A lie] tall tale, fiction, exaggeration; see LIE.

talent *n.* aptitude, faculty, gift; see ABILITY.

talented *a.* gifted, capable, skilled; see ABLE.

talk *n.* **1** [Human speech] utterance, locution, parlance; see COMMUNICATION, SPEECH 2. **2** [A conference] symposium, parley, consultation; see CONVERSATION, DISCUSSION. **3** [An address] lecture, oration, sermon; see SPEECH 3. **4** [Gossip] report, hearsay, chatter; see GOSSIP 1, RUMOR. **5** [Nonsense] noise, rubbish, jive; see JARGON 1, NONSENSE 1.

talk *v.* **1** [To converse] discuss, confer, chat, interview, speak, communicate, talk together, engage in a meaningful dialogue, have a meeting of the minds, chatter, gossip, yammer, remark, be on the phone with, be in contact with, talk over, reason with, visit with, parley, read, hold a discussion, confide in, argue, observe, notice, inform, rehearse, debate, have an exchange, exchange opinions,

have a conference with, talk away, go on*, gab*, chew the fat*, compare notes with, talk a leg off of*, go over*, shoot off one's mouth*, spit out*, shoot the breeze*, pass the time of day, engage in conversation. **2** [To lecture] speak, give a talk, deliver a speech; see ADDRESS 2. **3** [To inform] reveal, divulge, notify; see TELL 2. **4** [To utter] pronounce, express, speak; see UTTER. —**talk about** treat, take under consideration, deal with; see CONSIDER, DISCUSS. —**talk back** sass, retort, defy; see ANSWER 1. — **talk down to** stoop, snub, be overbearing; see HUMILIATE, PATRONIZE 2. —**talk someone into** win over, sway, affect; see CONVINCE, INFLUENCE, PERSUADE.

talkative *a.* wordy, verbal, long-winded; see FLUENT.

talker *n.* speaker, orator, speechmaker, mouthpiece, spokesman, lecturer, actor, performer, debater, storyteller, conversationalist, barker, announcer, preacher, lawyer, reader, after-dinner speaker, gossip, windbag*.

talking *a.* eloquent, chattering, mouthing, repeating, echoing, pronouncing, fluent, articulating, expressing, enunciating, ranting,

spouting, haranguing, speaking, vocalizing, verbalizing, orating, verbose, conversing, discussing, holding forth.

tall *a.* **1** [Lofty] big, great, towering; see HIGH 1. **2** [Exaggerated] far-fetched, outlandish, unbelievable; see EXAGGERATED.

tally *n.* reckoning, account, poll; see SCORE 1.

tally *v.* record, write down, register, mark down, count, total, add up, sum.

tame *a.* **1** [Domesticated] subdued, submissive, housebroken, harmless, trained, overcome, mastered, civilized, broken in, harnessed, yoked, acclimatized, muzzled, bridled.— *Ant.* WILD, untamed, undomesticated. **2** [Gentle] tractable, obedient, kindly; see GENTLE 3. **3** [Uninteresting] insipid, monotonous, routine; see CONVENTIONAL 3, DULL 4, UNINTERESTING.

tamper with *v.* alter, diversify, vary; see ALTER 1, DESTROY.

tan *a.* brownish, sun-tanned, weathered; see BROWN.

tan *n.* light-brown, beige, natural; see BROWN, GOLD, YELLOW.

various small, American songbirds with brightly colored males

tan·bark (tan′bärk′) *n.* any bark containing tannic acid, used to tan hides, etc.

tan·dem (tan′dəm) *adv.* [< punning use of L, at length] one behind another; in single file

tang (taŋ) *n.* [< ON *tangi*, a sting] 1 a prong on a file, etc., that fits into the handle 2 a strong, penetrating taste or odor —**tang′y, -i·er, -i·est,** *adj.*

tan·ge·lo (tan′jə lō′) *n., pl.* **-los′** [TANG(ERINE) + (*pom*)*elo*, grapefruit] a fruit produced by crossing a tangerine with a grapefruit

tan·gent (tan′jənt) *adj.* [< L *tangere*, to touch] 1 touching 2 *Geom.* touching a curved surface at one point but not intersecting it —*n.* a tangent line, curve, or surface —**go off at** (or **on**) **a tangent** to change suddenly to another line of action, etc. —**tan·gen′tial** (-jen′shəl) *adj.*

tan·ge·rine (tan′jə rēn′) *n.* [after *Tangier*, city in N Africa] a small, loose-skinned, reddish-yellow orange with easily separated segments

tan·gi·ble (tan′jə bəl) *adj.* [< L *tangere*, to touch] 1 that can be touched or felt 2 definite; objective —*n.* [*pl.*] assets having real substance and able to be appraised for value —**tan′gibil′ity** *n.* —**tan′gibly** *adv.*

tan·gle (taŋ′gəl) *vt.* **-gled, -gling** [< ? Sw] 1 to catch as in a snare; trap 2 to make a snarl of; intertwine —*vi.* 1 to become tangled 2 [Colloq.] to argue —*n.* 1 an intertwined, confused mass 2 a confused condition

tan·go (taŋ′gō) *n., pl.* **-gos** [AmSp] 1 a South American dance for couples with long gliding steps 2 music for this dance in 2/4 or 4/4 time —*vi.* to dance the tango

tank (taŋk) *n.* [in sense 1 < Sans] 1 any large container for liquid or gas 2 an armored vehicle with guns and full tractor treads —**tank′ful′** *n.*

tank·ard (taŋk′ərd) *n.* [< OFr *tanquart*] a large drinking cup with a handle

tank·er (taŋk′ər) *n.* 1 a ship equipped to transport oil or other liquids 2 a plane designed to refuel another plane in flight 3 a truck, etc. equipped to transport liquids or dry commodities in bulk

tank top [orig. worn in swimming tanks] a casual shirt like an undershirt but with wider shoulder straps

tank truck a motor truck built to transport gasoline, oil, etc.

tan·ner (tan′ər) *n.* a person whose work is making leather by tanning hides

tan′nery *n., pl.* **-ner·ies** a place where leather is made by tanning hides

tannic acid a yellowish, astringent substance used in tanning hides, dyeing, etc. Also **tan′nin** (-in) *n.*

tansy (tan′zē) *n., pl.* **-sies** [< LL *tanacetum*] a plant with a strong smell and small, yellow flowers

tan·ta·lize (tan′tə līz′) *vt.* **-lized′, -liz′ing** [after *Tantalus*, in Gr Myth., a king doomed in Hades to stand in water that always recedes when he wishes to drink and under fruit he cannot reach] to promise or show something desirable and then withhold it; tease

tan·ta·mount (tant′ə mount′) *adj.* [< OFr *tant*, so much + *amont*, upward] equal (*to*) in value, effect, etc.

tan·tra (tun′trə, tän′-) *n.* [Sans] [*often* T-] any of a group of Hindu or Buddhist mystical writings

tan′trum (tan′trəm) *n.* [< ?] a violent, willful outburst of rage, etc.

Tao·ism (dou′iz′əm, tou′-) *n.* [Chin *tao*, the way] a Chinese religion and philosophy advocating simplicity, selflessness, etc. —**Tao′ist** *n., adj.*

tap¹ (tap) *vt., vi.* **tapped, tap′ping** [echoic] 1 to strike lightly 2 to make or do by tapping /to *tap* a message/ 3 to choose, as for membership in a club —*n.* a light, rapid blow

tap² (tap) *n.* [OE *tæppa*] 1 a faucet or spigot 2 a plug, cork, etc. for stopping a hole in a cask, etc. 3 a tool used to cut threads in a female screw 4 the act or an instance of wiretapping 5 *Elec.* a place in a circuit where a connection can be made —*vt.* **tapped, tap′ping** 1 to put a tap or spigot on 2 to make a hole in, or pull the plug from, for drawing off liquid 3 to draw off (liquid) 4 to make use of /to *tap* new resources/ 5 to make a connection with (a pipe, circuit, etc.); specif., to wiretap

tap dance a dance done with sharp taps of the foot, toe, or heel at each step —**tap′-dance′, -danced′, -danc′ing,** *vi.* —**tap′-danc′er** *n.*

tape (tāp) *n.* [OE *tæppe*, a fillet] 1 a strong, narrow strip of cloth, paper, etc. used for binding, tying, etc. 2 *short for* MAGNETIC TAPE 3 *short for* TAPE MEASURE —*vt.* **taped, tap′ing** 1 to bind, tie, etc. with tape 2 to record on magnetic tape

tape deck a component of an audio system that records and plays back magnetic tapes

tape measure a tape with marks in inches, feet, etc. for measuring

ta·per (tā′pər) *n.* [OE *tapur*] 1 a slender candle 2 a gradual decrease in width or thickness —*vt., vi.* 1 to decrease gradually in width or thickness 2 to lessen; diminish Often with *off*

tape recorder a device for recording on magnetic tape and for playing back what has been recorded

tap·es·try (tap′əs trē) *n., pl.* **-tries** [< Gr *tapes*, a carpet] a heavy woven cloth with decorative designs and pictures, used as a wall hanging, etc.

tape′worm′ *n.* a tapelike worm that lives as a parasite in the intestines

tapi·o·ca (tap′ē ō′kə) *n.* [< AmInd (Brazil)] a starchy substance from cassava roots, used for puddings, etc.

ta·pir (tā′pər) *n.* [< AmInd (Brazil)] a large, hoglike mammal of tropical America and the Malay Peninsula, in SE Asia

tap′room′ *n.* BARROOM

tap·root (tap′rōōt′) *n.* [TAP² + ROOT¹] a main root, growing downward, from which small branch roots spread out

taps (taps) *n.* [< TAP¹, because orig. a drum signal] a bugle call to put out lights in retiring for the night

tar¹ (tär) *n.* [OE *teru*] a thick, sticky, black liquid obtained by the destructive distillation of wood, coal, etc. —*vt.* **tarred, tar′ring** to cover or smear with tar —**tar′ry, -rier, -riest,** *adj.*

tar² (tär) *n.* [< TAR(PAULIN)] [Colloq.] a sailor

ta·ran·tula (tə ran′choo lə) *n.* [after *Taranto*, city in S Italy] any of several large, hairy somewhat poisonous spiders of S Europe and tropical America

tardy (tär′dē) *adj.* **-dier, -di·est** [< L *tardus*, slow] 1 slow in moving, acting, etc. 2 late, delayed, or dilatory —**tar′dily** *adv.* —**tar′di·ness** *n.*

tare¹ (ter) *n.* [ME] 1 the vetch 2 *Bible* an undesirable weed

tare² (ter) *n.* [< Ar *ṭaraḥa*, to reject] the weight of a container, etc. deducted from the total weight to determine the weight of the contents or load

---

THESAURUS

tang *n.* zest, flavor, savor; see TASTE 2.

tangible *a.* perceptible, palpable, material, real, substantial, sensible, touchable, verifiable, physical, corporeal, solid, visible, stable, well-grounded, incarnated, embodied, manifest, factual, objective, tactile.—*Ant.* SPIRITUAL, ethereal, intangible.

tangle *n.* snarl, snag, muddle; see CONFUSION, KNOT 2.

tangle *v.* involve, complicate, confuse, obstruct, hamper, derange, mix up, disorganize, upset, unbalance, unhinge, perplex, tie up, trap, mess up.—*Ant.* ORDER, fix, unravel.

tangled *a.* tied up, confused, knit together, disordered, chaotic, out of place, mixed up, snarled, trapped, entangled, twisted, raveled, muddled, messed up*, balled up*, screwy*,

wires crossed*.

tank *n.* 1 [A large container for liquids] tub, basin, vat; see CONTAINER. 2 [An armored caterpillar vehicle] caterpillar, armored personnel carrier, armored car; see WEAPON.

tantrum *n.* rage, outburst, spell; see ANGER, FIT 2.

tap¹,² *n.* 1 [A light blow] pat, rap, dab; see BLOW. 2 [A spigot] faucet, petcock, drain; see FAUCET.

tap¹,² *v.* 1 [To strike lightly] pat, touch, rap; see HIT 1. 2 [To puncture in order to draw liquid] perforate, pierce, bore; see PENETRATE.

tape *n.* ribbon, line, rope. *Tapes include the following:* recording tape, cartridge, cassette, edging, tapeline, tape measure, steel tape, surveyor's chain, adhesive tape, gummed tape,

draftsman's tape, Scotch tape, masking tape, packing tape, transparent tape, videotape, mending tape.

tape *v.* 1 [To fasten] tie up, bind, bond; see FASTEN. 2 [To record] register, make a recording, put on tape; see RECORD 3. 3 [To bandage] tie, bind up, dress; see BIND 1, FASTEN.

taper *v.* narrow, lessen, thin out; see DECREASE 1, 2. —**taper off** recede, rescind, diminish; see DECREASE 2.

tape recorder *n.* recording equipment, stereo, stereophonic recorder, cassette recorder, cassette deck, cassette player, dictaphone, VCR, videotape machine, videocassette recorder.

tar¹ *n.* pitch, mineral pitch, coal tar; see GUM.

tardy *a.* overdue, too late, delayed; see LATE 1, SLOW 2, 3.

tar·get (tär′git) *n.* ⟦< Medieval Fr *targe*, a shield⟧ **1 a** board, etc. marked as with concentric circles, aimed at in archery, rifle practice, etc. **2** any object that is shot at **3** an objective; goal **4** an object of attack, criticism, etc.

tar·iff (tar′if) *n.* ⟦< Ar *taʿrīf*, information⟧ **1** a list or system of taxes upon exports or, esp., imports **2** a tax of this kind, or its rate **3** any list or scale of prices, charges, etc. **4** [Colloq.] any bill, charge, etc.

tar·nish (tär′nish) *vt.* ⟦< Fr *ternir*, make dim⟧ **1** to dull the luster of **2** to sully or mar — *vi.* **1** to lose luster **2** to become sullied — *n.* **1** dullness **2** a stain —**tar′nish·able** *adj.*

taro (ter′ō, tär′ō) *n., pl.* **-ros** ⟦< a Polynesian language⟧ a tropical Asiatic plant with a starchy, edible root

tarot (tar′ō, -ət; ta rō′) *n.* ⟦Fr < Ar *ṭaraha*, to reject⟧ [*often* T-] any of a set of 22 fortunetelling cards

tar·pau·lin (tär pô′lin, tär′pə-) *n.* ⟦< TAR¹ + PALL², a covering⟧ canvas coated with a waterproofing compound, or a protective cover to this

tar·pon (tär′pən) *n.* ⟦< ?⟧ a large, silvery game fish of the W Atlantic

tar·ra·gon (tar′ə gän′) *n.* ⟦< Sp < Ar < Gr *drakōn*, a dragon⟧ an Old World plant with fragrant leaves used for seasoning

tarry (tar′ē) *vi.* **-ried, -ry·ing** ⟦< OE *tergan*, to vex & prob. OFr *targer*, to delay⟧ **1** to delay; linger **2** to stay for a time **3** to wait

tart¹ (tärt) *adj.* ⟦OE *teart*⟧ **1** sharp in taste; sour; acid **2** sharp in meaning; cutting [a tart answer] —**tart′ly** *adv.* —**tart′ness** *n.*

tart² (tärt) *n.* ⟦< OFr *tarte*⟧ a small pastry shell filled with jam, jelly, etc.

tart³ (tärt) *n.* ⟦< prec., orig., slang term of endearment⟧ [Colloq.] a prostitute

tar·tan (tär′tən, tärt′n) *n.* ⟦prob. < Medieval Fr *tiretaine*, a cloth of mixed fibers⟧ a woolen cloth in any of various woven plaid patterns, worn esp. in the Scottish Highlands

tar·tar (tär′tər) *n.* ⟦< Medieval Gr *tartaron*⟧ **1** cream of tartar, esp. the crude form present in grape juice and forming a crustlike deposit in wine casks **2** a hard deposit on the teeth

Tar·tar (tär′tər) *n.* TATAR

tar·tar sauce (tär′tər) ⟦Fr⟧ a sauce of mayonnaise with chopped pickles, olives, capers, etc. Also **tartare sauce**

task (task) *n.* ⟦ult. < L *taxare*, to rate⟧ **1** a piece of work to be done **2** any difficult undertaking — *vt.* to burden; strain —**take to task** to scold

task force a group, esp. a military unit, assigned a specific task

task′mas′ter *n.* one who assigns tasks to others, esp. when severe

tas·sel (tas′əl) *n.* ⟦OFr, knob⟧ **1** an ornamental tuft of threads, etc. hanging loosely from a knob **2** something resembling this, as a tuft of corn silk

taste (tāst) *vt.* **tast′ed, tast′ing** ⟦< OFr *taster*⟧ **1** to test the flavor of by putting a little in one's mouth **2** to detect the flavor of by the sense of taste **3** to eat or drink a small amount of **4** to experience [to taste success] — *vi.* to have a specific flavor — *n.* **1** the sense by which flavor is perceived through the taste buds on the tongue **2** the quality so perceived; flavor **3** a small amount tasted as a sample **4** a bit; trace **5** the ability to appreciate what is beautiful, appropriate, etc. **6** a specific preference **7** a liking; incli-

nation —**in bad** (or **good**) **taste** in a style showing a bad (or good) sense of beauty, fitness, etc. —**taste′less** *adj.* —**tast′er** *n.*

taste bud any of the cells, esp. in the tongue, that are the organs of taste

taste′ful *adj.* having or showing good TASTE (*n.* 5) —**taste′ fully** *adv.*

tasty (tās′tē) *adj.* **-i·er, -i·est** that tastes good; flavorful —**tast′i·ness** *n.*

tat (tat) *vt.* **tat′ted, tat′ting** to make by tatting — *vi.* to do tatting

ta·tami (tə tä′mē) *n., pl.* **-mi** or **-mis** ⟦Jpn⟧ a floor mat of rice straw, used in Japanese homes for sitting on

Ta·tar (tät′ər) *n.* **1** a member of any of the E Asiatic peoples who invaded W Asia and E Europe in the Middle Ages **2** a Turkic language

tat·ter (tat′ər) *n.* ⟦< ON *töturr*, rags⟧ **1** a torn and hanging piece, as of a garment **2** [pl.] torn, ragged clothes — *vt., vi.* to make or become ragged —**tat′tered** *adj.*

tat′ter·de·mal′ion (-di māl′yən) *n.* ⟦< prec. + ?⟧ a person in torn, ragged clothes

tat·ting (tat′iŋ) *n.* ⟦prob. < Brit dial. *tat*, to tangle⟧ **1** a fine lace made by looping and knotting thread **2** the act or process of making this

tat·tle (tat′'l) *vi.* **-tled, -tling** ⟦prob. < MDu *tatelen*⟧ **1** to talk idly **2** to reveal others' secrets — *vt.* to reveal (a secret) by gossiping —**tat′tler** *n.*

tat′tle·tale′ *n.* an informer; talebearer

tat·too¹ (ta tōō′) *vt.* **-tooed′, -too′ing** ⟦< a Polynesian language⟧ to make (permanent designs) on (the skin) by puncturing it and inserting indelible color — *n., pl.* **-toos′** a tattooed design

tat·too² (ta tōō′) *n., pl.* **-toos′** ⟦< Du *tap toe*, tap to (shut): a signal for closing barrooms⟧ **1** a signal on a drum or bugle, summoning military personnel to their quarters at night **2** a drumming, rapping, etc.

tau (tou, tô) *n.* the 19th letter of the Greek alphabet (T, τ)

taught (tôt) *vt., vi. pt. & pp. of* TEACH

taunt (tônt, tänt) *vt.* ⟦< ? Fr *tant pour tant*, tit for tat⟧ to reproach scornfully or sarcastically; mock — *n.* a scornful or jeering remark

taupe (tōp) *n.* ⟦Fr < L *talpa*, mole⟧ a dark, brownish gray

Tau·rus (tô′rəs) ⟦< L, a bull⟧ the second sign of the zodiac

taut (tôt) *adj.* ⟦ME *toght*, tight⟧ **1** tightly stretched, as a rope **2** tense [a taut smile] **3** trim, tidy, etc. —**taut′ly** *adv.* —**taut′ness** *n.*

tau·tol·ogy (tô tä′lə jē) *n., pl.* **-gies** ⟦< Gr < *to auto*, the same + -LOGY⟧ needless repetition of an idea in a different word, etc. —**tau′to·log′i·cal** *adj.*

tav·ern (tav′ərn) *n.* ⟦< L *taberna*⟧ **1** a saloon; bar **2** an inn

taw·dry (tô′drē) *adj.* **-drier, -driest** ⟦after *St. Audrey laces*, sold at St. Audrey's fair in Norwich, England⟧ cheap and showy; gaudy

taw·ny (tô′nē) *adj.* **-nier, -niest** ⟦< OFr *tanner*, to tan⟧ brownish-yellow; tan —**taw′ni·ness** *n.*

tax (taks) *vt.* ⟦< L *taxare*, appraise⟧ **1** to require to pay a tax **2** to assess a tax on (income, purchases, etc.) **3** to put a strain on **4** to accuse; charge — *n.* **1** a compulsory pay-

---

◼ THESAURUS ◼

target *n.* **1** [A goal] objective, aim, purpose, end, destination, mark. **2** [Bull's-eye] point, spot, butt, mark, dummy. **3** [A prey] quarry, game, scapegoat; see VICTIM.

tarnish *v.* soil, smudge, smear; see DIRTY.

tart¹ *a.* bitter, pungent, sharp; see SOUR.

task *n.* chore, responsibility, business; see DUTY 1.

taste *n.* **1** [The sense that detects flavor] tongue, taste buds, palate, senses. **2** [The quality detected by taste] flavor, savor, savoriness, aftertaste, tang, suggestion, zip*, wallop*, kick*, smack*, bang*, jolt*, zing*, punch*. **3** [Judgment, especially esthetic judgment] discrimination, susceptibility, appreciation, good taste, discernment, acumen, penetration, acuteness, feeling, refinement, appreciation; see also JUDGMENT 1. **4** [Preference] tendency, leaning,

attachment; see INCLINATION 1. —**in bad taste** pretentious, rude, crass; see TASTELESS 3. —**in good taste** delicate, pleasing, refined; see ARTISTIC, DAINTY. —**to one's taste** pleasing, satisfying, appealing; see PLEASANT 2.

taste *v.* **1** [To test by the tongue] sip, try, touch, sample, lick, suck, roll over in the mouth, partake of. **2** [To recognize by flavor] sense, savor, distinguish; see KNOW 3. **3** [To experience] feel, perceive, know; see UNDERGO.

tasteful *a.* **1** [Delicious] delectable, pleasing, tasty, savory, rich; see also DELICIOUS. **2** [Esthetically pleasing] delicate, elegant, fine; see DAINTY.

tasteless *a.* **1** [Lacking flavor] unsavory, bland, dull, unseasoned, vapid, flat, watery, flavorless, without spice; see also DULL 4, ORDINARY 2.—*Ant.* DELICIOUS, seasoned, spicy. **2** [Plain] homely, insipid, trite; see COMMON 1.

3 [Lacking good taste] pretentious, ornate, showy, trivial, artificial, florid, ostentatious, clumsy, makeshift, coarse, useless, rude, uncouth, ugly, unsightly, unlovely, hideous, foolish, stupid, crass.—*Ant.* REFINED, civilized, cultivated.

tasty *a.* savory, palatable, appetizing; see DELICIOUS.

tattle *v.* blab, tell on, report; see GOSSIP.

tattler *n.* busybody, tattletale, snoop; see GOSSIP 2, TRAITOR.

tattletale *n.* informer, tattler, busybody, snitch*, fink*, squealer*, stool pigeon*, stoolie*, rat*.

taught *a.* instructed, informed, directed; see EDUCATED, LEARNED 1.

taunt *n.* insult, mockery, jibe; see RIDICULE.

tavern *n.* taproom, alehouse, roadhouse; see BAR 2.

tax *n.* **1** [A pecuniary levy] fine,

ment of a percentage of income, property value, etc. for the support of a government **2** a heavy demand; burden —**tax′a·ble** *adj.* —**taxa′tion** *n.*

taxi (tak′sē) *n., pl.* **-is** *short for* TAXICAB — *vi.* **-ied, -i·ing** or **-y·ing** **1** to go in a taxicab **2** to move along the ground or on the water as after landing: said of an airplane

tax′i·cab′ *n.* 〚< *taxi(meter) cab*〛 an automobile in which passengers are carried for a fare

taxi·dermy (taks′i dur′mē) *n.* 〚< Gr *taxis*, arrangement + *derma*, skin〛 the art of preparing, stuffing, etc. the skins of animals to make them appear lifelike —**tax′i·der′mist** *n.*

taxi·meter (tak′sē mēt′ər) *n.* 〚< Fr, ult. < ML *taxa*, tax + *-meter*, -METER〛 a device in taxicabs that registers the fare due

tax·ono·my (taks än′ə mē) *n., pl.* **-mies** 〚< Gr *taxis*, arrangement + *nomos*, law〛 classification, esp. of animals and plants —**tax·on′o·mist** *n.*

tax′pay′er *n.* one who pays a tax

TB tuberculosis

TBA, t.b.a., or **tba** to be announced

T-bone steak (tē′bōn′) a quality steak with a T-shaped bone

tbs. or **tbsp.** **1** tablespoon(s) **2** tablespoonful(s)

T cell any of the lymphatic leukocytes affected by the thymus, that regulate immunity: cf. B CELL

TD touchdown Also **td**

tea (tē) *n.* 〚< Chin dial. *t′e*〛 **1** an evergreen plant grown in Asia **2** its dried leaves, used to make a beverage **3** the beverage made by soaking such leaves in boiling water **4** a tealike beverage made as from other plants **5** 〚Chiefly Brit., etc.〛 a meal in the late afternoon at which tea is the drink **6** an afternoon party at which tea, etc. is served

tea′berry (tē′ber′ē) *n., pl.* **-ries** **1** WINTERGREEN (sense 1) **2** the berry of the wintergreen

teach (tēch) *vt.* **taught, teach′ing** 〚OE *tæcan*〛 **1** to show or help (a person) to learn (*how*) to do something **2** to give lessons to (a student, etc.) **3** to give lessons in (a subject) **4** to provide with knowledge, insight, etc. — *vi.* to give lessons or instruction —**teach′able** *adj.*

teacher (tē′chər) *n.* one who teaches, esp. as a profession

teach′ing *n.* **1** the profession of a teacher **2** something taught; precept, doctrine, etc.: *usually used in pl.*

tea′cup′ *n.* a cup for drinking tea, etc. —**tea′cup·ful′**, *pl.* **-fuls′,** *n.*

teak (tēk) *n.* 〚< Malayalam *tēkka*〛 **1** a large East Indian tree with hard, yellowish-brown wood **2** its wood

tea′ket′tle *n.* a kettle with a spout, for boiling water to make tea, etc.

teal (tēl) *n.* 〚ME *tele*〛 **1** a small, short-necked, freshwater wild duck **2** a dark grayish or greenish blue: also **teal blue**

team (tēm) *n.* 〚OE, offspring〛 **1** two or more horses, oxen, etc. harnessed to the same plow, etc. **2** a group of people working or playing together — *vi.* to join in cooperative activity: often with *up* — *adj.* of or done by a team

team′mate′ *n.* one on the same team

team′ster (-stər) *n.* one whose work is hauling loads with a team or truck

team′work′ *n.* joint action by a group of people

tea′pot′ *n.* a pot with a spout and handle, for brewing and pouring tea

tear[1] (ter) *vt.* **tore, torn, tear′ing** 〚OE *teran*, rend〛 **1** to pull apart into pieces by force; rip **2** to make by tearing [to *tear* a hole] **3** to lacerate **4** to disrupt; split [ranks *torn* by dissensions] **5** to divide with doubt, etc. **6** to pull with force: with *up, out, away, off,* etc. — *vi.* **1** to be torn **2** to move with force or speed — *n.* **1** a tearing **2** a torn place; rent —**tear down 1** to wreck **2** to dismantle

tear[2] (tir) *n.* 〚OE *tēar*〛 a drop of the salty fluid which flows from the eye, as in weeping —**in tears** crying; weeping —**tear′ful** *adj.* —**tear′fully** *adv.* —**tear′y, -i·er, -i-est,** *adj.*

tear′drop′ *n.* a tear

tear gas (tir) a gas that causes irritation of the eyes, a heavy flow of tears, etc. —**tear′-gas′, -gassed′, -gas′sing,** *vt.*

tea′room′ *n.* a restaurant that serves tea, coffee, light lunches, etc.

tease (tēz) *vt.* **teased, teas′ing** 〚OE *tæsan*〛 **1** *a*) to card or comb (flax, wool, etc.) *b*) to fluff (the hair) by combing toward the scalp **2** to raise a nap on (cloth) by brushing with teasels **3** to annoy by mocking, poking fun, etc. **4** to beg; importune **5** to tantalize — *vi.* to indulge in teasing — *n.* one who teases

tea·sel (tē′zəl) *n.* 〚see prec.〛 **1** a bristly plant with prickly flowers **2** the dried flower, or any device, used to raise a nap on cloth

teas′er *n.* **1** a person or thing that teases **2** a puzzling problem

tea′spoon′ *n.* a spoon for stirring tea, etc., holding 1⅓ fluid drams —**tea′spoon·ful′,** *pl.* **-fuls′,** *n.*

teat (tēt) *n.* 〚< OFr *tete*〛 the nipple on a breast or udder

tech. **1** technical(ly) **2** technology

tech·ni·cal (tek′ni kəl) *adj.* 〚< Gr *technē*, an art〛 **1** dealing with the industrial or mechanical arts or the applied sciences **2** of a specific science, art, craft, etc. **3** of, in or showing technique **4** concerned with minute details — **tech′ni·cally** *adv.*

tech·ni·cal′i·ty (-kal′ə tē) *n., pl.* **-ties** **1** the state or quality of being technical **2** a technical point, detail, etc. **3** a minute point, detail, etc. brought to bear upon a main issue

tech·ni·cian (tek nish′ən) *n.* one skilled in the technique of some art, craft, or science

---

THESAURUS

charge, rate, toll, levy, impost, duty, assessment, tariff, tribute, obligation, price, cost, contribution, expense; see also DUES. **2** [A burden] strain, task, demand; see BURDEN 2.

tax *v.* **1** [To cause to pay a tax] assess, exact from, demand, exact tribute, charge duty, demand toll, require a contribution, enact a tax. **2** [To burden] encumber, weigh down, overload; see BURDEN.

taxation *n.* levying, assessment, moneygathering; see DUES, TAX 1.

taxed *a.* **1** [Paying taxes] levied upon, demanded from, required from, assessed, imposed upon, subjected to tax. **2** [Burdened] overtaxed, strained, harassed, fatigued; see also TIRED.

taxicab *n.* taxi, cab, sightseeing car; see AUTOMOBILE.

tea *n.* **1** [An infusion made from tea leaves] beverage, brew, infusion, decoction; see also DRINK 2. *Tea and tealike drinks include the following:* black, green, Lapsang, Souchong, Oolong, Darjeeling, orange pekoe, pekoe, Gunpowder, Earl Grey, mixed, jasmine, blended, orange flower, sassafras, sage, mint, camomile, herb. **2** [A light afternoon or evening meal] snack, refreshment, tea party; see LUNCH, MEAL 2.

teach *v.* instruct, tutor, coach, educate, profess, explain, expound, lecture, direct, give a briefing, edify, enlighten, guide, show, give lessons in, ground, rear, prepare, fit, interpret, bring up, instill, inculcate, indoctrinate, brainwash, develop, form, address to, initiate, inform, nurture, illustrate, imbue, implant, break in, give the facts, give an idea of, improve one's mind, open one's eyes, knock into someone's head*, bring home to*, cram*, stuff*; see also INFLUENCE, MOTIVATE.—*Ant.* LEARN, gain, acquire.

teacher *n.* schoolmaster, schoolmistress, schoolman, educator, public school teacher, high school teacher, tutor, mentor, pedagogue, master, guru, swami, mistress, kindergarten teacher, pupil teacher, teacher-in-training, substitute teacher, professor, lecturer, instructor, faculty member, graduate assistant.

teaching *n.* pedagogy, instruction, normal training; see EDUCATION 1, 3.

team *n.* **1** [People working together, as on the stage] partners, combo, troupe, company, duo, trio; see also ORGANIZATION 2. **2** [An organization, especially in sport] squad, crew, club; see ORGANIZATION 2.

team up with *v.* attach oneself to, collaborate, corroborate; see ACCOMPANY, COOPERATE, HELP.

teamwork *n.* partisanship, collaboration, union; see ALLIANCE 1, COOPERATION, PARTNERSHIP.

tear[1] *n.* rent, rip, hole, slit, laceration, split, break, gash, rupture, fissure, crack, cut, breach, damage, imperfection.—*Ant.* REPAIR, patch, renovation.

tear[1] *v.* rend, rip, shred, cut, mangle, rive, rip up, split; see also CUT 1.

tear[2] *n.* teardrop, droplet, eyewash; see DROP 1.

tears *n.* sobbing, sob, crying, cry, weeping, lamenting, whimpering, grieving, mourning, waterworks*; see also GRIEF.

tease *v.* taunt, tantalize, torment; see BOTHER 2, RIDICULE.

teaspoon *n.* kitchen utensil, measuring spoon, 1/3 of a tablespoon, stirrer; see also UTENSILS.

technical *a.* specialized, special, scientific, professional, scholarly, mechanical, restricted, methodological, highly versed, technological, industrial.—*Ant.* ARTISTIC, nontechnical, simplified.

technician *n.* practitioner, profes-

Tech·ni·color (tek′ni kul′ər) *trademark for* a process of making color movies — *n.* [t-] this process

tech·nique (tek nēk′) *n.* 〚Fr〛 1 the method of procedure in artistic work scientific activity, etc. 2 the degree of expertness in following this

tech·noc·ra·cy (tek näk′rə sē) *n.* 〚< Gr *technē*, an art + -CRACY〛 government by scientists and engineers —**tech′no·crat′** (-nə krat′) *n.*

tech·nol·o·gy (tek näl′ə jē) *n.* 〚Gr *technologia*, systematic treatment〛 1 the science of the practical or industrial arts 2 applied science —**tech′no·log′i·cal** (-nə läj′i kəl) *adj.* —**tech·nol′o·gist** *n.*

teddy bear 〚after *Teddy* (Theodore) Roosevelt〛 a child's stuffed toy made to look like a bear cub

te·di·ous (tē′dē əs) *adj.* full of tedium; long and dull —**te′di·ous·ly** *adv.*

te′di·um (-əm) *n.* 〚< L *taedet*, it offends〛 the condition or quality of being tiresome, wearisome, etc.

tee (tē) *n.* 〚prob. < Scot dial. *teaz*〛 Golf 1 a small peg from which the ball is driven 2 the place from which a player makes the first stroke on each hole — *vt., vi.* teed, tee′ing to place (a ball) on a tee —**tee off** 1 to play a golf ball from a tee 2 [Slang] to make angry or disgusted

teem (tēm) *vi.* 〚< OE *team*, progeny〛 to be prolific; abound; swarm

teen (tēn) *n.* 〚OE *tien*, ten〛 1 [*pl.*] the years from 13 through 19, as of a person's age 2 TEENAGER

teen·age (tēn′āj′) *adj.* 1 in one's teens 2 of or for people in their teens —**teen′ag′er** *n.*

teeny (tē′nē) *adj.* **-nier, -ni·est** *colloq. var. of* TINY Also **teensy** (tēn′zē, -sē), **-sier, -si·est**

teeny-bopper (tē′nē bäp′ər) *n.* [Slang] a faddish young teenager

teeny-weeny (tē′nē wē′nē) *adj.* [Colloq.] tiny Also **teensy-weensy** (tēn′zē wēn′zē, tēn′sē wēn′sē)

tee·pee (tē′pē) *n. alt. sp. of* TEPEE

tee shirt *var. of* T-SHIRT

tee·ter (tēt′ər) *vi., vt., n.* 〚< ON *titra*, to tremble〛 seesaw or wobble

tee′ter-tot′ter (-tôt′ər, -tät′-) *n., vi.* SEESAW

teeth (tēth) *n. pl. of* TOOTH

teethe (tēth) *vi.* teethed, teeth′ing to grow teeth; cut one's teeth

tee·total·er or **tee·total·ler** (tē tōt′lər) *n.* 〚< doubling of initial *t* in *total*〛 one who practices total abstinence from alcoholic liquor

Tef·lon (tef′län′) *trademark for* a tough polymer, used for nonsticking coatings as for cookware

tek·tite (tek′tīt′) *n.* 〚< Gr *tēktos*, molten〛 a small, dark, glassy body thought to be from outer space

tel. 1 telegram 2 telephone

tele- *combining form* 1 〚< Gr *tēle*, far off〛 at, over, etc. a distance [*telegraph*] 2 〚< TELE(VISION)〛 of, in, or by television [*telecast*]

tele·cast (tel′i kast′) *vt., vi.* **-cast′** or **-cast′ed, -cast′ing** to broadcast by television — *n.* a television broadcast —**tele′cast′er** *n.*

tel′e·com·mu·ni·ca′tion *n.* [*also pl., with sing. or pl. v.*] communication by electronic or electrical means, as through radio, TV, computers, etc.

tel′e·con′fer·ence *n.* a conference of persons in different locations, as by telephone, TV, etc.

tele·gram (tel′ə gram′) *n.* a message transmitted by telegraph

tel′e·graph′ (-graf′) *n.* 〚see TELE- & -GRAPH〛 an apparatus or system that transmits messages by electrical impulses sent by wire or radio — *vt., vi.* to send (a message) to (a person) by telegraph —**tele·graph′ic** *adj.*

te·leg·ra·phy (tə leg′rə fē) *n.* the operation of telegraph apparatus —**te·leg′ra·pher** *n.*

tele·ki·ne·sis (tel′i ki nē′sis) *n.* 〚see TELE- & KINETIC〛 the causing of an object to move by unexplainable means, as by the mind

tele·mar·ket·ing (tel′ə mär′kət iŋ) *n.* the use of the telephone in marketing for sales research, promotion, etc.

tele·meter (tel′ə mēt′ər, tə lem′ət ər) *n.* a device for measuring and transmitting data about radiation, temperature, etc. from a remote point —**te·lem′e·try** (tə lem′ə trē) *n.*

te·lep·a·thy (tə lep′ə thē) *n.* 〚TELE- + -PATHY〛 supposed communication between minds by means other than the normal sensory channels —**tele·path′ic** (tel′ə path′ik) *adj.*

tele·phone (tel′ə fōn′) *n.* 〚TELE- + -PHONE〛 an instrument or system for conveying speech over distances by converting sound into electrical impulses sent through a wire — *vt., vi.* **-phoned′, -phon′ing** to convey (a message) to (a person) by telephone —**tel′e·phon′ic** (-fän′ik) *adj.*

te·leph·o·ny (tə lef′ə nē) *n.* the making or operation of telephones

tele·photo (tel′ə fōt′ō) *adj.* designating of or a camera lens that produces a large image of a distant object

tel′e·pho′to·graph′ *n.* 1 a photograph taken with a telephoto lens 2 a photograph transmitted by telegraph or radio — *vt., vi.* to take or transmit (telephotographs) —**tel′e·pho·tog′ra·phy** (-fə täg′rə fē) *n.*

tel′e·proc′ess·ing *n.* data processing with computer terminals, over communication lines

Tele·Prompt·Ter (tel′ə prämp′tər) *trademark for* an electronic device that unrolls a speech, script, etc. line by line, as an aid to a speaker, etc. on TV — *n.* this device: written **tel′e·promp′ter**

tele·scope (tel′ə skōp′) *n.* 〚see TELE- & -SCOPE〛 an optical instrument for making distant objects appear nearer and larger — *vi., vt.* **-scoped′, -scop′ing** to slide one into another like the tubes of a collapsible telescope —**tel′e·scop′ic** (-skäp′ik) *adj.*

tel′e·thon′ (-thän′) *n.* 〚TELE(VISION) + (MARA)THON〛 a campaign, as on a lengthy telecast, seeking donations

Tele·type (tel′ə tīp′) *n. trademark for* a former kind of telegraphic apparatus that printed messages typed on the keyboard of the transmitter —**tel′e·type′writ′er** *n.*

tele·vise (tel′ə vīz′) *vt., vi.* **-vised′, -vis′ing** to transmit by television

tel′e·vi′sion (-vizh′ən) *n.* 1 the process of transmitting images by converting light rays into electrical signals: the receiver reconverts the signals to reproduce the images on a screen 2 television broadcasting 3 a television receiving set 4 a television program or programs

tell (tel) *vt.* told, tell′ing 〚OE *tellan*, calculate〛 1 orig., to count 2 to narrate; relate [*to tell* a story] 3 to express in

---

▬▬▬ THESAURUS ▬▬▬

sional, engineer; see CRAFTSMAN, SPECIALIST.

technique *n.* procedure, system, routine; see METHOD.

tedious *a.* slow, wearisome, tiresome; see DULL 4.

tedium *n.* boredom, tediousness, dullness; see MONOTONY.

teenage *a.* immature, youthful, adolescent; see YOUNG 1, 2.

teens *n.* boyhood, girlhood, adolescence, early adolescence, late adolescence, awkward age*; see also YOUTH 1.

teeter *v.* seesaw, totter, wobble; see SHAKE 1.

teeth *n.* dentition, fangs, tusks; see TOOTH.

telegram *n.* wire, cable, cablegram, message, teletype copy, radiogram, call, report, summons, night message, night letter, day letter, news message, code message, signal, flash, buzzer*; see also COMMUNICATION.

telegraph *n.* Morse telegraph, wire-

less, transmitter; see COMMUNICATION, RADIO 2.

telegraph *v.* wire, send a wire, send a cable; see COMMUNICATE 2.

telepathy *n.* insight, premonition, extrasensory perception; see COMMUNICATION.

telephone *n.* phone, private phone, extension phone, radiophone, radiotelephone, car phone, cellular phone, cordless phone, phone machine, fax machine, mouthpiece, line, party line, long distance, extension, pay phone.

telephone *v.* call, call up, phone, ring, ring up, make a call to, dial, call on the phone, fax, put in a call to, phone up*; give a ring, give a buzz*.

telephoned *a.* phoned, radiophoned, called, communicated by telephone, faxed, reached by phone.

telescope *n.* field glasses, binoculars, opera glass, glass, optical instrument, reflecting telescope, refracting telescope, radio telescope; see also

GLASSES.

television *n.* T.V., teevee, video, color television, home entertainment center, boob tube*, the tube*, the box*; see also STATION 5.

tell *v.* 1 [To inform] communicate, explain, instruct, direct, order, divulge, reveal, make known, utter, speak, report, recite, cue in, reel off, spit it out, put before, name over, let in on, let into, open up, give the facts, blow upon, lay open, fill one in, let on, let slip, level with, leave word, hand it to, lay before, break it to, break the news, add up, keep one posted, let know, give out, leak out, give notice, declare, acquaint, advise, confess, impart, notify, represent, assert, mention, tell all, break down with, give away, cough up*, come across with*, shoot*, come clean*, make a clean breast of; see also DISCUSS, SAY.—*Ant.* HIDE, keep secret, be silent. 2 [To deduce] know, understand, make out, perceive, words; say [to *tell* the truth] **4** to reveal; disclose **5** to recognize; distinguish [to *tell* twins apart] **6** to inform [*tell* me later] **7** to order [*tell* him to go] — *vi.* **1** to give an account or evidence (*of* something) **2** to be effective [each blow *told*] —**tell off** [Colloq.] to rebuke severely — **tell on 1** to tire **2** [Colloq.] to inform against

tell·er (tel′ər) *n.* **1** one who tells (a story, etc.) **2** one who counts, as a bank clerk who pays out or receives money

tell′ing *adj.* forceful; striking —**tell′ing·ly** *adv.*

tell′tale′ *adj.* revealing what is meant to be kept secret or hidden

tel·ly (tel′ē) *n., pl.* **-lies** *Brit., etc.* (*exc. Cdn.*) colloq. *term for* TELEVISION

tem·blor (tem′blôr′, -blər) *n.* [Sp < *temblar*, to tremble] EARTHQUAKE

te·mer·i·ty (tə mer′ə tē) *n.* [< L *temere*, rashly] foolish or rash boldness

temp. 1 temperature **2** temporary

tem·per (tem′pər) *vt.* [< L *temperare*, regulate] **1** to moderate, as by mingling with something else [to *temper* blame with praise] **2** to bring to the proper condition by some treatment [to *temper* steel] **3** to toughen — *n.* **1** the degree of hardness and resiliency of a metal **2** frame of mind; disposition **3** calmness of mind: in **lose** (or **keep**) **one's temper 4** anger; rage

tem·pera (tem′pər ə) *n.* [It: see prec.] a process of painting with pigments mixed with size, casein, or egg

tem·pera·ment (tem′pər ə mənt; *often*, -prə-) *n.* [see TEMPER] **1** one's natural disposition; nature **2** a nature that is excitable, moody, etc. —**tem′pera·men′tal** *adj.*

tem·per·ance (tem′pər əns) *n.* **1** self-restraint in conduct, indulgence of the appetites, etc.; moderation **2** moderation in drinking alcoholic liquors or total abstinence from them

tem·per·ate (tem′pər it) *adj.* [see TEMPER] **1** moderate, as in eating or drinking **2** self-restrained in actions, speech, etc. **3** neither very hot nor very cold: said of climate, etc.

Temperate Zone either of the two zones of the earth (**North Temperate Zone** and **South Temperate Zone**) between the tropics and the polar circles

tem·pera·ture (tem′pər ə chər; *often*, -prə chər) *n.* [< L *temperatus*, temperate] **1** the degree of hotness or coldness of anything **2** excess of body heat over the normal; fever

tem·pered (tem′pərd) *adj.* **1** having been given the desired TEMPER (*n.* 1) **2** having a (specified) TEMPER (*n.* 2)

tem·pest (tem′pist) *n.* [< L *tempus*, time] a violent storm with high winds, esp. one accompanied by rain, etc.

tem·pes·tu·ous (tem pes′chōō əs, -chə wəs) *adj.* of or like a tempest; violent

tem·plate (tem′plit) *n.* [< L *templum*, small timber] a pattern, as a thin metal plate, for making an exact copy

tem·ple¹ (tem′pəl) *n.* [< L *templum*] **1** a building for the worship of God or gods **2** a large building for some special purpose [a *temple* of art]

tem·ple² (tem′pəl) *n.* [< L *tempus*] **1** the flat surface alongside the forehead, in front of each ear **2** either of the sidepieces of a pair of glasses

tem·po (tem′pō) *n., pl.* **-pos** or **-pi** (-pē) [It < L *tempus*, time] **1** the speed at which a musical composition is performed **2** rate of activity

tem·po·ral¹ (tem′pə rəl) *adj.* [< L *tempus*, time] **1** transitory; temporary **2** of this world; worldly **3** secular **4** of or limited by time

tem·po·ral² (tem′pə rəl) *adj.* of or near the temples (of the head)

tem′po·rar′y (-rer′ē) *adj.* [< L *tempus*, time] lasting only a while; not permanent —**tem′po·rar′i·ly** *adv.*

tem′po·rize′ (-rīz′) *vi.* **-rized′, -riz′ing** to give temporary compliance, evade decision, etc., so as to gain time or avoid argument

tempt (tempt) *vt.* [< L *temptare*, to test] **1** to induce or entice, as to something immoral **2** to be inviting to; attract **3** to provoke or risk provoking (fate, etc.) **4** to incline strongly [to be *tempted* to accept] —**temp·ta·tion** (temp tā′shən) *n.* —**tempt′er** *n.* —**tempt′ress** *n.fem.*

tem·pura (tem′poo rä′, tem poor′ə) *n.* [Jpn] a Japanese dish of deep-fried shrimp, fish, vegetables, etc.

ten (ten) *adj., n.* [OE] one more than nine; 10; X

ten·able (ten′ə bəl) *adj.* [< L *tenere*, to hold] that can be held, defended, or maintained —**ten′a·bil′i·ty** *n.* —**ten′ably** *adv.*

te·na·cious (tə nā′shəs) *adj.* [< L *tenere*, to hold] **1** holding firmly [a *tenacious* grip] **2** retentive [a *tenacious* memory] **3** strongly cohesive or adhesive **4** persistent; stubborn [*tenacious* courage] —**te·na′ciously** *adv.* —**te·nac·i·ty** (tə nas′ə tē) *n.*

ten·ant (ten′ənt) *n.* [see prec.] **1** one who pays rent to occupy land, a building, etc. **2** an occupant — *vt.* to hold as a tenant —**ten′ancy** *n.*

tenant farmer one who farms land owned by another and pays rent

Ten Commandments *Bible* the ten laws of moral and religious conduct given to Moses by God: Exodus 20:2-17

tend¹ (tend) *vt.* [see ATTEND] **1** to take care of **2** to manage or operate

ascertain, find out, recognize, be sure, differentiate, discriminate, determine, know for certain. —**tell off** rebuke, reprimand, chide; see SCOLD.

teller *n.* cashier, clerk, bank clerk; see WORKMAN.

telling *a.* crucial, conspicuous, significant; see EFFECTIVE, IMPORTANT 1.

temper *n.* **1** [State of mind] disposition, frame of mind, humor; see MOOD 1. **2** [An angry state of mind] furor, ire, passion; see ANGER, RAGE 1. **3** [The quality of being easily angered] impatience, excitability, touchiness, sourness, sensitivity, fretfulness, peevishness, irritability, ill humor, petulence, irascibility, crossness, churlishness, pugnacity, sullenness, grouchiness, huffiness.— *Ant.* PATIENCE, calmness, equanimity. **4** [The quality of induced hardness or toughness in materials] tensile strength, sturdiness, hardness; see FIRMNESS, STRENGTH. —**lose one's temper** become angry, get mad, fly off the handle; see RAGE 1.

temper *v.* **1** [To soften or qualify] mitigate, pacify, moderate; see EASE 1, 2, SOFTEN. **2** [To toughen or harden] steel, stiffen, cement; see STRENGTHEN.

temperament *n.* character, disposition, constitution, nature, inner nature, quality, temper, spirit, mood, attitude, type, structure, makeup, humor, mood, outlook, peculiarity,

individuality, idiosyncrasy, distinctiveness, psychological habits, mentality, intellect, susceptibility, ego, inclination, tendency, turn of mind.

temperamental *a.* moody, sensitive, touchy; see IRRITABLE.

temperance *n.* moderation, abstinence, self-control; see RESTRAINT 1.

temperate *a.* **1** [Moderate] regulated, reasonable, fair; see MODERATE 4. **2** [Neither hot nor cold] medium, warm, balmy; see FAIR 3, MILD 2. **3** [Not given to drink] abstemious, abstinent, restrained; see MODERATE 5.

temperature *n.* heat, warmth, cold, body heat, weather condition, climatic characteristic, thermal reading, degrees of temperature.

temple¹ *n.* house of prayer, synagogue, pagoda; see CHURCH 1.

tempo *n.* pace, speed, meter; see SPEED.

temporal¹ *a.* **1** [Transitory] temporary, transient, ephemeral; see TEMPORARY. **2** [Worldly] secular, earthly, mundane; see WORLDLY.

temporarily *a.* momentarily, briefly, tentatively, for a while, for the moment, for a time, provisionally, transitorily, for the time being, pro tempore, pro tem.—*Ant.* FOREVER, perpetually, perennially.

temporary *a.* transitory, transient, fleeting, short, brief, ephemeral, fugitive, volatile, shifting, momentary,

passing, summary, stopgap, makeshift, substitute, for the time being, overnight, *ad hoc* (Latin), impermanent, irregular, changeable, unenduring, unfixed, unstable, perishable, provisional, short-lived, mortal, pro tem, on the go*, on the fly*, on the wing, here today and gone tomorrow*.—*Ant.* PERMANENT, fixed, eternal.

tempt *v.* lure, fascinate, seduce, appeal to, induce, intrigue, incite, provoke, allure, charm, captivate, entice, draw out, bait, stimulate, move, motivate, rouse, instigate, wheedle, coax, inveigle, vamp, make a play for*, make one's mouth water.

temptation *n.* lure, attraction, fascination; see APPEAL 2.

tempted *a.* desiring, inclined, enticed; see CHARMED.

tempting *a.* appetizing, attractive, fascinating; see CHARMING.

ten *a.* tenth, tenfold, decuple, denary, decimal.

tenant *n.* renter, lessee, householder, rent payer, dweller, inhabitant, occupant, resident, roomer, lodger, holder, possessor, leaseholder, tenant farmer; see also RESIDENT.—*Ant.* OWNER, proprietor, landlord.

tend¹,² *v.* **1** [To watch over] care for, manage, direct, superintend, do, perform, accomplish, guard, administer, minister to, oversee, wait upon, attend, serve, nurse, mind; see also

tend[2] (tend) *vi.* ⟦< L *tendere*, to stretch⟧ **1** to be inclined, disposed, etc. (*to*) **2** to be directed (*to* or *toward*)

tend·ency (ten'dən sē) *n., pl.* **-cies** ⟦see prec.⟧ **1** an inclination to move or act in a particular direction or way **2** a course toward some object

ten·den·tious (ten den'shəs) *adj.* ⟦< Ger *tendenz*, TENDENCY⟧ advancing a definite point of view *[tendentious writings]* —**ten·den'tiously** *adv.*

ten·der[1] (ten'dər) *adj.* ⟦< L *tener*, soft⟧ **1** soft and easily chewed, broken, cut, etc. **2** physically weak **3** immature **4** that requires careful handling **5** gentle or light **6** acutely sensitive, as to pain **7** sensitive to emotions, others' feelings, etc. —**ten'derly** *adv.* —**ten'der·ness** *n.*

ten·der[2] (ten'dər) *vt.* ⟦see TEND[2]⟧ to offer formally — *n.* **1** a formal offer **2** money, etc. offered in payment

tender[3] (ten'dər) *n.* **1** one who tends something **2** a small ship for supplying a larger one **3** a railroad car, attached behind, and carrying fuel and water for a steam locomotive

ten'der·foot' *n., pl.* **-foots'** or **-feet'** **1** a newcomer to ranching in the West, unused to hardships **2** any novice

ten'der·heart'ed *adj.* quick to feel pity or compassion

ten·der·ize (ten'dər īz') *vt.* **-ized'**, **-iz'ing** to make (meat) tender —**ten'der·iz'er** *n.*

ten'der·loin' *n.* the tenderest part of a loin of beef, pork, etc.

ten·di·ni·tis (ten'də nīt'is) *n.* inflammation of a tendon

ten·don (ten'dən) *n.* ⟦< Gr *teinein*, to stretch⟧ any of the inelastic cords of tough, connective tissue by which muscles are attached to bones, etc.

ten·dril (ten'drəl) *n.* ⟦prob. ult. < L *tener*, delicate⟧ a threadlike, clinging part of a climbing plant

ten·ement (ten'ə mənt) *n.* ⟦< L *tenere*, to hold⟧ **1** a room or suite tenanted as a separate dwelling **2** a building divided into tenements; now specif., one that is run-down, overcrowded, etc.: also **tenement house**

tenet (ten'it) *n.* ⟦L, he holds⟧ a principle, doctrine, or belief held as a truth, as by some group

ten·nis (ten'is) *n.* ⟦prob. < OFr *tener*, hold (imperative)⟧ a game in which players in a marked area (**tennis court**) hit a ball back and forth with rackets over a net

tennis elbow inflammation of the elbow tendons, caused by strain

tennis shoe a sneaker

tenon (ten'ən) *n.* ⟦ult. < L *tenere*, to hold⟧ a projecting part cut on the end of a piece of wood for insertion into a mortise to make a joint

tenor (ten'ər) *n.* ⟦< L *tenere*, to hold⟧ **1** general tendency **2** general meaning; drift **3** *a)* the highest regular adult male singing voice *b)* a singer with such a voice *c)* a part for a tenor

ten'pins' *n.pl.* **1** *[with sing. v.]* the game of bowling in which ten pins are used **2** the pins

tense[1] (tens) *adj.* **tens'er**, **tens'est** ⟦< L *tendere*, to stretch⟧ **1** stretched tight; taut **2** feeling or showing tension — *vt., vi.* **tensed**, **tens'ing** to make or become tense —**tense'ly** *adv.* —**tense'ness** or **ten'sity** (ten'sə tē) *n.*

tense[2] (tens) *n.* ⟦< L *tempus*, time⟧ any of the forms of a verb that show the time of its action or existence

ten·sile (ten'sil; *also*, -sīl') *adj.* **1** of, undergoing, or exerting tension **2** capable of being stretched

ten·sion (ten'shən) *n.* **1** a tensing or being tensed **2** mental or nervous strain **3** a state of strained relations due to mutual hostility **4** VOLTAGE **5** stress on a material produced by the pull of forces causing extension

tent (tent) *n.* ⟦< L *tendere*, to stretch⟧ a portable shelter made of canvas, etc. stretched over poles — *vi., vt.* to lodge in a tent or tents

ten·ta·cle (ten'tə kəl) *n.* ⟦< L *tentare*, to touch⟧ a long, slender, flexible growth about the head of some invertebrates, used to grasp, feel, etc.

ten·ta·tive (ten'tə tiv) *adj.* ⟦< L *tentare*, to try⟧ made, done, etc. as a test or experiment —**ten'ta·tively** *adv.*

tenter·hook (ten'tər hook') *n.* ⟦< L *tendere*, to stretch + HOOK⟧ any of the hooked nails holding cloth stretched on a drying frame (**tenter**) —**on tenterhooks** in anxious suspense

tenth (tenth) *adj.* ⟦OE *teogotha*⟧ preceded by nine others in a series; 10th — *n.* **1** the one following the ninth **2** any of the ten equal parts of something; $\frac{1}{10}$ **3** a tenth of a gallon

tenu·ous (ten'yōō əs, -yə wəs) *adj.* ⟦< L *tenuis*, thin⟧ **1** slender or fine, as a thread **2** as air at high altitudes **3** not substantial; flimsy *[tenuous evidence]*

ten·ure (ten'yər, -yoor) *n.* ⟦< Medieval Fr < *tenir*, to hold⟧ **1** the act or right of holding property, an office, etc. **2** the length of time, or the conditions under which, something is held **3** the status of holding one's position on a permanent basis, granted to teachers, etc.

te·pee (tē'pē) *n.* ⟦< AmInd *t*[h]*ípi*, dwelling⟧ a cone-shaped tent used by some North American Indians

tepid (tep'id) *adj.* ⟦< L *tepidus*⟧ **1** lukewarm **2** lacking enthusiasm

te·quila (tə kē'lə) *n.* ⟦< AmInd (Mexico) *Tuiquila*, region in Mexico⟧ an alcoholic liquor of Mexico, distilled from an agave mash

ter·cen·te·nary (tər sen'tə ner'ē, tʉr'sen ten'ər ē) *adj., n., pl.* **-ies** ⟦L *ter*, three times + CENTENARY⟧ TRICENTENNIAL

term (tʉrm) *n.* ⟦< L *terminus*, a limit⟧ **1** a set date, as for payment, etc. **2** a set period of time *[school term, term of office]* **3** *[pl.]* conditions of a contract, etc. **4** *[pl.]* mutual relationship between persons *[on speaking terms]* **5** a word or phrase, esp. as used in some science, art, etc. **6** *[pl.]* words; speech *[unkind terms]* **7** *Math. a)* either quantity of a fraction or a ratio *b)* each quantity in a series or algebraic expression — *vt.* to call by a term; name —**bring** (or **come**) **to terms** to force into (or arrive at) an agreement

ter·ma·gant (tʉr'mə gənt) *n.* ⟦< OFr *Tervagant*, imaginary Muslim deity⟧ a quarrelsome, scolding woman

ter·mi·nable (tʉr'mi nə bəl) *adj.* that can be, or is, terminated

ter·mi·nal (tʉr'mə nəl) *adj.* ⟦L *terminalis*⟧ **1** of, at, or forming the end or extremity **2** concluding; final **3** close to causing death *[terminal cancer]* **4** of or at the end of a transportation line — *n.* **1** an end; extremity **2** a connective point on an electric circuit **3** either end of a transportation line, or a main station on it **4** a device, usually with a keyboard and video display, for putting data in, or getting it from, a computer

---

THESAURUS

MANAGE 1. 2 [To have a tendency (toward)] lead, point, direct, make for, result in, serve to, be in the habit of, favor, be predisposed to, be prejudiced in favor of, be apt to, gravitate toward, incline to, verge on.

tendency *n.* **1** [Direction] aim, bent, trend; see DRIFT 1. **2** [Inclination] leaning, bias, bent; see INCLINATION 1.

tender[1] *a.* **1** [Soft] delicate, fragile, supple; see SOFT 2. **2** [Kind] loving, solicitous, compassionate; see KIND. **3** [Touching] moving, pathetic, affecting; see PITIFUL. **4** [Sensitive] touchy, ticklish, oversensitive; see RAW 5, SORE 1.

tenderhearted *a.* softhearted, tender, humane; see HUMANE, KIND, MERCIFUL.

tenderly *a.* **1** [Softly] gently, carefully, delicately; see LIGHTLY. **2** [Lovingly] fondly, affectionately, appreciatively; see LOVINGLY.

tenderness *n.* love, consideration, care; see FRIENDSHIP, KINDNESS 1.

tennis *n.* lawn tennis, court tennis, tennis tournament; see SPORT 3.

tense[1] *a.* **1** [Nervous] agitated, anxious, high-strung, on edge, fluttery, jumpy, jittery; see also EXCITED.— *Ant.* CALM, unconcerned, indifferent. **2** [Stretched tight] rigid, stiff, firm; see TIGHT 1.

tension *n.* **1** [Stress] tautness, force, tightness; see BALANCE 2, STRESS 2. **2** [Mental stress] pressure, strain, anxiety; see STRESS 2.

tent *n.* shelter, canvas, canopy, tarpaulin, covering; see also COVER 1. *Tentlike coverings include the following:* umbrella tent, awning, marquee, wigwam, tepee, booth, pavilion, pup tent, fly tent, fly, canoe tent, lean-to tent, circus tent, big top*.

tentative *a.* provisional, probationary, makeshift; see EXPERIMENTAL.

tentatively *a.* experimentally, conditionally, provisionally; see TEMPORARILY.

tepee *n.* Indian tent, wigwam, wickiup; see TENT.

term *n.* **1** [A name] expression, terminology, phrase, word, locution, indication, denomination, article, appellation, designation, title, head, caption, nomenclature, moniker*; see also NAME 1. **2** [A period of time] span, interval, course, cycle, season, duration, phase, quarter, course of time, semester, school period, session, period of confinement; see also TIME 2. —**come to terms** compromise, arrive at an agreement, arbitrate; see AGREE. —**in terms of** in reference to, about, concerning; see REGARDING.

terminal *a.* final, concluding, last; see LAST 1.

terminal *n.* **1** [An end] limit, extremity, terminus; see END 4. **2** [Part of a computer] keyboard, CRT, monitor, printer, screen; see also COMPUTER.

ter·mi·nate (tʉr′mə nāt′) *vt.* **-nat′ed, -nat′ing** ⟦< L *ter-minus*, a limit⟧ **1** to form the end of **2** to put an end to; stop **3** to dismiss from employment; fire — *vi.* **1** to come to an end **2** to have its end (*in* something) —**ter′mi·na′tion** *n.*

ter·mi·nol·ogy (tʉr′mə näl′ə jē) *n., pl.* **-gies** the terms used in a specific science, art, etc.

term insurance life insurance that expires after a specified period

ter·mi·nus (tʉr′mə nəs) *n., pl.* **-ni′** (-nī′) or **-nuses** ⟦L, a limit⟧ **1** a limit **2** an end; extremity or goal **3** [Chiefly Brit., etc.] either end of a transportation line

ter·mite (tʉr′mīt′) *n.* ⟦< L *tarmes*, wood-boring worm⟧ a social insect destructive to wooden structures

tern (tʉrn) *n.* ⟦< ON *therna*⟧ a gull-like seabird with webbed feet and a straight bill

ter·race (ter′əs) *n.* ⟦< L *terra*, earth⟧ **1** a raised, flat mound of earth with sloping sides, esp. one in a series on a hillside **2** an unroofed, paved area, between a house and lawn **3** a row of houses on ground above street level — *vt.* **-raced, -rac·ing** to form into a terrace or terraces

terra cotta (ter′ə kät′ə) ⟦It., lit., baked earth⟧ a hard, brown-red earthenware, or its color

terra firma (ter′ə fʉr′mə) ⟦L⟧ firm earth

ter·rain (ter′rān′, tə rān′) *n.* ⟦< L *terra*, earth⟧ a tract of ground, esp. with regard to its fitness for some use

ter·ra·pin (ter′ə pin) *n.* ⟦< Algonquian⟧ **1** any of various terrestrial, freshwater, or tidewater turtles **2** its edible flesh

ter·rar·ium (tə rer′ē əm) *n., pl.* **-iums** or **-ia** (-ə) ⟦< L *terra*, earth + *-arium*, as in *aquarium*⟧ an enclosure, as of glass, in which small plants are grown or small land animals are kept

ter·razzo (tə rät′sō, te-; tə raz′ō) *n.* ⟦It⟧ flooring of small chips of marble set in cement and polished

ter·res·trial (tə res′trē əl) *adj.* ⟦< L *terra*, earth⟧ **1** worldly; mundane **2** of the earth **3** consisting of land, not water **4** living on land

ter·ri·ble (ter′ə bəl) *adj.* ⟦< L *terrere*, frighten⟧ **1** causing terror; dreadful **2** extreme; intense **3** [Colloq.] very unpleasant, etc. —**ter′ri·bly** *adv.*

ter·ri·er (ter′ē ər) *n.* ⟦< Medieval Fr (*chien*) *terrier*, hunting (dog)⟧ any of several breeds of small and typically aggressive dog

ter·rif·ic (tə rif′ik) *adj.* ⟦< L *terrere*, frighten⟧ **1** causing great fear **2** [Colloq.] *a)* very great, intense, etc. *b)* unusually fine, admirable, etc. —**ter·rif′i·cally** *adv.*

ter·ri·fy (ter′ə fī′) *vt.* **-fied′, -fy′ing** to fill with terror; frighten greatly

ter·ri·tory (ter′ə tôr′ē) *n., pl.* **-ries** ⟦< L *terra*, earth⟧ **1** an area under the jurisdiction of a nation, ruler, etc. **2** a part of a country or empire that does not have full status **3** any large tract of land **4** an assigned area **5** a sphere of action, thought, etc. —**ter′ri·to′rial** *adj.*

ter·ror (ter′ər) *n.* ⟦< L *terrere*, frighten⟧ **1** intense fear **2** *a)* one that causes intense fear *b)* the quality of causing such fear

ter′ror·ism′ *n.* the use of force or threats to intimidate, etc., esp. as a political policy —**ter′ror·ist** *n., adj.*

ter′ror·ize′ (-īz′) *vt.* **-ized′, -iz′ing 1** to terrify **2** to coerce, make submit, etc. by filling with terror

terry (ter′ē) *n.* ⟦prob. < Fr *tirer*, to draw⟧ cloth having a pile of uncut loops, esp. cotton cloth used for toweling Also **terry cloth**

terse (tʉrs) *adj.* **ters′er, ters′est** ⟦L *tersus*, wiped off⟧ free of superfluous words; concise; succinct —**terse′ly** *adv.* —**terse′ness** *n.*

ter·ti·ary (tʉr′shē er′ē) *adj.* ⟦< L *tertius*, third⟧ third in order

tes·sel·late (tes′ə lāt′) *vt.* **-lat′ed, -lat′ing** ⟦< L *tessella*, little square stone⟧ to lay out in a mosaic pattern of small, square blocks

test (test) *n.* ⟦< OFr, assaying cup⟧ **1** *a)* an examination or trial, as of something's value *b)* the method or a criterion used in this **2** an event, etc. that tries one's qualities **3** a set of questions, etc. for determining one's knowledge, etc. **4** *Chem.* a trial or reaction for identifying a substance — *vt.* to subject to a test; try — *vi.* to be rated by a test —**test′er** *n.*

tes·ta·ment (tes′ tə mənt) *n.* ⟦< L *testis*, a witness⟧ **1** [T-] either of the two parts of the Bible, the *Old Testament* and the *New Testament* **2** *a)* a testimonial *b)* an affirmation of beliefs **3** *Law* a will —**tes′ta·men′tary** (-men′tə rē) *adj.*

tes·tate (tes′tāt′) *adj.* ⟦< L *testari*, make a will⟧ having left a legally valid will

tes·ta·tor (tes′tāt′ər, tes tāt′-) *n.* one who has made a will

tes·ti·cle (tes′ti kəl) *n.* ⟦< L *testis*⟧ either of two male sex glands

tes·ti·fy (tes′tə fī′) *vi.* **-fied′, -fy′ing** ⟦< L *testis*, a witness + *facere*, to make⟧ **1** to give evidence, esp. under oath in court **2** to serve as evidence — *vt.* **1** to affirm; declare, esp. under oath in court **2** to indicate

tes·ti·mo·nial (tes′tə mō′nē əl) *n.* **1** a statement recommending a person or thing **2** something given or done to show gratitude or appreciation

tes·ti·mony (tes′tə mō′nē) *n., pl.* **-nies** ⟦< L *testis*, a witness⟧ **1** a statement made under oath to establish a fact **2** any declaration **3** any form of evidence; proof

tes·tis (tes′tis) *n., pl.* **-tes′** (-tēz′) ⟦L⟧ TESTIS

tes·tos·ter·one (tes täs′tər ōn′) *n.* ⟦see TESTICLE⟧ a male sex hormone

test tube a tube of thin, transparent glass closed at one end, used in chemical experiments, etc.

testy (tes′tē) *adj.* **-tier, -ti·est** ⟦< L *testa*, the head⟧ irritable; touchy

teta·nus (tet′'n əs) *n.* ⟦< Gr *tetanos*, spasm⟧ an acute infectious disease, often fatal, caused by a toxin and characterized by spasmodic contractions and rigidity of muscles

tête-à-tête (tāt′ə tāt′) *n.* ⟦Fr, lit., head-to-head⟧ a private conversation between two people

tether (teth′ər) *n.* ⟦< ON *tjōthr*⟧ **1** a rope or chain fastened to an animal to keep it from roaming **2** the limit of one's abilities, resources, etc. — *vt.* to fasten with a tether

tetra (te′trə) *n.* ⟦< ModL⟧ a brightly colored, tropical American fish

---

THESAURUS

terminate *v.* complete, end, perfect; see ACHIEVE.

terminology *n.* nomenclature, technology, specification; see JARGON 2, LANGUAGE 1.

terms *n.* **1** [Conditions] details, items, points, particulars; see also CIRCUMSTANCES 2. **2** [An agreement] understanding, treaty, conclusion; see AGREEMENT 1.

terrace *n.* patio, garden, lawn; see GARDEN, YARD 1.

terrain *n.* ground, region, territory; see AREA.

terrible *a.* **1** [Inspiring terror] terrifying, appalling, fearful, awesome, horrifying, ghastly, awe-inspiring, petrifying, revolting, gruesome, shocking, unnerving; see also FRIGHTFUL.—*Ant.* HAPPY, joyful, pleasant. **2** [Unwelcome] unfortunate, disastrous, inconvenient, disturbing, atrocious*, lousy*; see also OFFENSIVE 2.—*Ant.* WELCOME, good, attractive.

terribly* *a.* horribly, frightfully, drastically; see BADLY 1, VERY.

terrific *a.* shocking, immense, tre-mendous; see GREAT 1, LARGE 1.

terrify *v.* shock, horrify, terrorize; see FRIGHTEN.

territorial *a.* regional, sectional*, provincial; see NATIONAL 1.

territory *n.* **1** [A specified area] region, township, empire; see AREA. **2** [An area organized politically under the central government] commonwealth, colony, dominion; see NATION 1. **3** [An indefinite area] section, area, boundary; see REGION 1.

terror *n.* fright, horror, panic; see FEAR.

terrorist *n.* subversive, revolutionary, incendiary; see REBEL.

terrorize *v.* coerce, intimidate, browbeat; see THREATEN.

test *n.* **1** [A check for adequacy] inspection, analysis, countdown, probing, inquiry, inquest, elimination, proving grounds, training stable, search, dry run*; see also EXAMINATION 1, EXPERIMENT. *Tests include the following:* engineering, technical, structural, mechanical, chemical, countdown, psychological,

mental, intelligence, IQ, intelligence quotient, aptitude, vocational, qualifying, comprehensive, written, true-false, multiple choice, objective, diagnostic, semester, term, association, psychiatric. **2** [A formal examination] quiz, questionnaire, essay; see EXAMINATION 2.

test *v.* inquire, question, try out; see EXAMINE, EXPERIMENT.

tested *a.* examined, tried, proved; see ESTABLISHED 2, RELIABLE.

testify *v.* **1** [To demonstrate] indicate, show, make evident; see PROVE. **2** [To bear witness] affirm, give evidence, swear, swear to, attest, witness, give witness, give one's word, certify, warrant, depose, vouch, give the facts, stand up for, say a good word for. **3** [To declare] assert, attest, claim; see DECLARE.

testimony *n.* **1** [The act of stating] attestation, statement, assertion; see DECLARATION. **2** [Evidence] grounds, facts, data; see PROOF. **3** [Statement] deposition, affidavit, affirmation; see DECLARATION.

tetra- [Gr < *tettares*, four] *combining form* four
tetra·cy·cline (te′trə sī′klin, -klin′) *n.* a yellow, crystalline compound, used as an antibiotic
tetra·hedron (te′trə hē′drən) *n., pl.* **-drons** or **-dra** (-drə) [see TETRA- & -HEDRON] a solid figure with four triangular faces
te·tram·eter (te tram′ət ər, tə-) *n.* [see TETRA- & METER¹] 1 a line of verse containing four metrical feet 2 verse consisting of tetrameters
Teu·tonic (tōō tän′ik) *adj.* designating or of a group of north European peoples, esp. the Germans —**Teu·ton** (tōō′tən, tōōt′ʼn) *n.*
text (tekst) *n.* [< L *texere*, to weave] 1 the actual words of an author, as distinguished from notes, etc. 2 any form in which a written work exists 3 the principal matter on a printed page, as distinguished from notes, headings, etc. 4 *a)* a Biblical passage used as the topic of a sermon, etc. *b)* any topic or subject 5 *short for* TEXTBOOK —**tex′tual** (teks′chōō əl) *adj.*
text′book′ *n.* a book giving instructions in a subject of study
tex·tile (teks′tīl′, -til) *adj.* [see TEXT] 1 having to do with weaving 2 that has been or can be woven — *n.* 1 a woven or knitted fabric; cloth 2 raw material suitable for this
tex·ture (teks′chər) *n.* [< L *texere*, to weave] 1 the character of a fabric, determined by the arrangement, size, etc. of its threads 2 the arrangement of the constituent parts of anything —**tex′tural** *adj.*
-th¹ [OE] *suffix* 1 the act of ___ing [*growth*] 2 the state or quality of being or having [*wealth*]
-th² [< OE] *suffix* forming ordinal numerals [*fourth, ninth*]
Th *Chem. symbol for* thorium
Thai (tī) *n.* 1 *pl.* **Thais** or **Thai** a native or inhabitant of Thailand 2 the language of Thailand 3 *alt. sp. of* TAI — *adj.* of Thailand, its people, culture, etc.
thala·mus (thal′ə məs) *n., pl.* **-mi′** (-mī′) [< Gr *thalamos*, inner chamber] a mass of gray matter at the base of the brain, involved in the transmission of certain sensations
tha·lido·mide (thə lid′ə mīd′) *n.* a drug formerly used as a sedative, but found to cause severe birth deformities when taken in pregnancy
thal·lo·phyte (thal′ə fīt′) *n.* [< Gr *thallos*, young shoot + *phyton*, a plant] any of a large group of plants lacking true roots, leaves, or stems, as the fungi, lichens, and most algae
than (than; *unstressed*, then) *conj.* [OE *thenne*] introducing the second element in a comparison [A is taller than B]
thank (thaŋk) *vt.* [OE *thancian*] 1 to give one's thanks to 2 to hold responsible; blame: an ironic use —**thank you** *short for* I thank you
thank′ful *adj.* feeling or expressing thanks —**thank′fully** *adv.*

thank′less *adj.* 1 not feeling or expressing thanks, ungrateful 2 unappreciated —**thank′lessly** *adv.*
thanks *n.pl.* an expression of gratitude — *interj.* I thank you —**thanks to** 1 thanks be given to 2 on account of; because of
thanks′giv′ing *n.* 1 a formal public expression of thanks to God 2 [T-] an annual U.S. holiday observed on the fourth Thursday of November
that (that) *pron.*, [OE *thæt*] 1 the person or thing mentioned [*that* is John] 2 the farther one or other one [this is better than *that*] 3 who, whom, or which [the road *that* we took] 4 where [the place *that* I saw her] 5 when [the year *that* I was born] — *adj., pl.* **those** 1 designating the one mentioned [*that* man is John] 2 designating the farther one or other one [this house is larger than *that* one] — *conj.* used to introduce: 1 a noun clause [*that* she's gone is obvious] 2 an adverbial clause expressing purpose [they died *that* we might live], result [he ran so fast *that* I lost him], or cause [I'm sorry *that* I won] 3 an elliptical sentence expressing surprise, desire, etc. [oh, *that* she were here!] — *adv.* to that extent; so [I can't see *that* far] —**at that** [Colloq.] 1 at that point: also **with that** 2 even so —**that is** 1 to be specific 2 in other words
thatch (thach) *n.* [OE *thæc*] 1 a roof of straw, rushes, etc. 2 material for such a roof: also **thatch′ing** — *vt.* to cover as with thatch
thaw (thô) *vi.* [OE *thawian*] 1 *a)* to melt (said of ice, snow, etc.) *b)* to pass to a state that is not frozen (said of frozen foods) 2 to become warmer so that snow, etc. melts 3 to lose one's coldness of manner — *vt.* to cause to thaw — *n.* 1 a thawing 2 a spell of weather warm enough to allow thawing
THC [t(etra)h(ydro)c(annabinol)] the principal and most active chemical in marijuana
ThD or **Th.D.** [L *Theologiae Doctor*] Doctor of Theology
the (thə; *before vowels* thē, thi) *adj., definite article* [< OE *se* with *th-* from other forms] *the* (as opposed to *a, an*) refers to: 1 a particular person or thing [*the* story ended, *the* President] 2 a person or thing considered generically [*the* cow is a domestic animal, *the* poor] — *adv.* 1 that much [*the* better to see you] 2 by how much . . . by that much [*the* sooner *the* better]
thea·ter or **thea·tre** (thē′ə tər) *n.* [< Gr *theasthai*, to view] 1 a place or building where plays, operas, films, etc. are presented 2 any similar place with banked rows of seats 3 any scene of events 4 *a)* the dramatic art *b)* the theatrical world
the·at·ri·cal (thē a′tri kal) *adj.* 1 having to do with the theater 2 dramatic; esp. (in disparagement), melodramatic —**the·at′ri·cally** *adv.*
thee (thē) *pron.* [OE *the*] the objective case of THOU
theft (theft) *n.* [OE *thiefth*] the act or an instance of stealing; larceny

═══ THESAURUS ═══

text *n.* 1 [A textbook] required reading, manual, handbook; see BOOK. 2 [A subject, expecially a verse from the Bible] quotation, stanza, passage; see SUBJECT. 3 [Writing, considered for its authenticity] lines, textual evidence, document; see MANUSCRIPT, WRITING 2.
texture *n.* 1 [Quality] character, disposition, fineness, roughness, coarseness, feeling, feel, sense, flexibility, stiffness, smoothness, taste; see also FIBER. 2 [Structure] composition, organization, arrangement; see CONSTRUCTION 2, FORM 2.
thank *v.* be obliged, show gratitude, give thanks, acknowledge, show appreciation, be obligated to, be indebted to, bless, praise, bow down to, kiss, smile on, show courtesy, express one's obligation to; see also APPRECIATE 1.—*Ant.* NEGLECT, ignore, show indifference.
thanked *a.* blessed, applauded, appreciated; see PRAISED.
thankful *a.* obliged, grateful, gratified, contented, satisfied, indebted to, pleased, kindly disposed, appreciative, giving thanks, overwhelmed.
thankless *a.* 1 [Not returning thanks] unappreciative, ungrateful, self-centered; see CRUEL, RUDE 2. 2

[Not eliciting thanks] poorly paid, unappreciated, unrewarded; see USELESS 1.
thanks *n.* appreciation, thankfulness, acknowledgment, recognition, gratitude, gratefulness.—*Ant.* BLAME, censure, criticism.
Thanksgiving *n.* Thanksgiving Day, last Thursday in November, turkey day*; see CELEBRATION, FEAST, HOLIDAY.
that *conj.* in that, so, so that, in order that, to the end that, for the reason that; see also BECAUSE.
that *a.* the, this, one, a certain, a well-known, a particular, such.
that *pron.* the one, this one, the one in question, that fact, that other, who; see also WHICH. —**all that*** so very, so, rather less; see NOT. —**at that*** even so, all things considered, anyway; see ANYHOW.
thaw *v.* dissolve, liquefy, flow, run, liquate, fuse, become liquid; see also DISSOLVE, MELT 1.—*Ant.* FREEZE, congeal, refrigerate.
the *a., definite article* 1 [The definite article] some, a few, a particular one, a special one, a specific one, a certain one, an individual one, this, that, each, every, these, those, the whole,

the entire. 2 [Special or unique; *often italics*] preeminent, outstanding, particular, unparalleled, unequaled, supreme, unsurpassed, unusual, uncommon, rare, singular, unprecedented, exceptional, one, sole, single, significant, distinguished, specific, choice, individual, peculiar, exceptional, occasional, unfamiliar, strange, spectacular, phenomenal, unheard of, unknown, unattainable, invincible, almighty, all-powerful; see also SPECIAL, UNIQUE.—*Ant.* COMMON, USUAL, ordinary.
theater *n.* 1 [A building intended for theatrical productions] playhouse, concert hall, coliseum; see AUDITORIUM. 2 [The legitimate stage] stage, drama, Broadway; see COMEDY, MOVIES 2.
theatrical *a.* ceremonious, meretricious, superficial; see AFFECTED 2.
theft *n.* robbery, racket, thievery, larceny, stealing, swindling, swindle, cheating, defrauding, fraud, piracy, burglary, pillage, pilfering, plunder, vandalism, holdup, pocket-picking, safecracking, extortion, embezzlement, looting, appropiation, shoplifting, fleecing, mugging, stickup*; see

their (*ther*) *poss. pronominal adj.* ⟦< ON *theirra*⟧ of, belonging to, made by, or done by them

theirs (*therz*) *pron.* that or those belonging to them *[theirs* are better*]*

the·ism (thē′iz′əm) *n.* ⟦< Gr *theos*, god⟧ 1 belief in a god or gods 2 MONOTHEISM —**the′ist** *n., adj.* —**the·is′tic** *adj.*

them (*them*) *pron.* ⟦< ON *theim*⟧ *objective case of* THEY

theme (thēm) *n.* ⟦< Gr *thema*, what is laid down⟧ 1 a topic, as of an essay 2 a short essay 3 a short melody used as the subject of a musical composition 4 a recurring or identifying song in a film, musical, radio or TV series, etc.: also **theme song** —**the·mat·ic** (thē mat′ik) *adj.*

them·selves (them selvz′) *pron.* 1 *intensive form of* THEY *[they* went *themselves] 2 reflexive form of* THEY *[they* hurt *themselves]*

then (*then*) *adv.* [see THAN] 1 at that time *[he* was young *then] 2* next in time or order *[he* took his hat and *then* left*] 3* in that case; accordingly *[if* she read it, *then* she knows*] 4* besides; moreover *[he* likes to walk, and *then* it's good exercise*] 5* at another time *[now* it's warm, *then* freezing*]* — *n.* that time *[by then,* they were gone*]* — *adj.* being such at that time *[the then* director*]* — *n.* that time *[by then,* they were gone*]*

thence (*thens,* thens) *adv.* ⟦OE *thanan*⟧ [Archaic] 1 from that place 2 from that time; thenceforth 3 therefore

thence′forth′ *adv.* from that time onward; thereafter Also **thence′for′ward**

the·oc·ra·cy (thē äk′rə sē) *n., pl.* -**cies** ⟦< Gr *theos*, god + *kratos*, power⟧ (a) government by a person or persons claiming to rule with divine authority —**the′o·crat′ic** *adj.*

theo·lo·gian (thē′ə lō′jən, -jē ən) *n.* a student of or specialist in theology

the·ol·o·gy (thē äl′ə jē) *n., pl.* -**gies** ⟦< Gr *theos*, god + *logos*, word⟧ the study of God and of religious doctrines and matters of divinity —**the·o·log′i·cal** (-ə läj′i kəl) *adj.*

theo·rem (thē′ə rəm) *n.* ⟦< Gr *theōrein*, to view⟧ 1 a proposition that can be proved from accepted premises; law or principle 2 *Math., Physics* a proposition embodying something to be proved

theo·ret·i·cal (thē′ə ret′i kəl) *adj.* 1 limited to or based on theory; hypothetical 2 tending to theorize; speculative Also **the′o·ret′ic** —**the′o·ret′i·cally** *adv.*

theo·rize (thē′ə rīz′) *vi.* -**rized′**, -**riz′ing** to form a theory or theories; speculate —**the′o·reti·cian** (-rə tish′ən) or **the′o·rist** (-rist) *n.*

theo·ry (thē′ə rē, thir′ē) *n., pl.* -**ries** ⟦< Gr *theōrein*, to view⟧ 1 a speculative plan 2 a formulation of underlying principles of certain observed phenomena which has been verified to some degree 3 the principles of an art or science rather than its practice 4 a conjecture; guess

the·oso·phy (thē äs′ə fē) *n.* ⟦< Gr *theos*, god + *sophos*, wise⟧ [*also* T-] a religious or semireligious set of occult beliefs rejecting Christian theology, and held to be based on a special mystical insight —**the′o·soph′ic** (-ə säf′ik) *adj.* —**the′o·soph′i·cally** *adv.* —**the·os′o·phist** *n.*

thera·peu·tic (ther′ə pyo͞ot′ik) *adj.* ⟦< Gr *therapeuein*, to nurse⟧ serving to cure or heal or to preserve health

ther·a·peu′tics *n.pl.* [*with sing. v.*] the branch of medicine that deals with the treatment of disease; therapy

ther·a·py (-pē) *n., pl.* -**pies** ⟦see THERAPEUTIC⟧ the treatment of any physical or mental disorder by medical or physical means, usually excluding surgery —**ther′a·pist** *n.*

there (*ther*) *adv.* ⟦OE *ther*⟧ 1 at or in that place: often used as an intensive *[Mary there* is a good player*] 2* to or into that place *[go there] 3* at that point; then *[there* I paused*] 4* in that respect *[there* you are wrong*] There* is also used in impersonal constructions in which the real subject follows the verb *[there* is little time*]* — *n.* that place *[we* left *there* at six*]* — *interj.* an exclamation of defiance, satisfaction, sympathy, etc. —(**not**) **all there** [Colloq.] (not) mentally sound

there′abouts′ (-ə bouts′) *adv.* 1 near that place 2 near that time, number, degree, etc. Also **there′about′**

there·af′ter *adv.* from then on

there·at′ *adv.* 1 at that place; there 2 at that time 3 for that reason

there·by′ *adv.* 1 by that means 2 connected with that

there·for′ *adv.* for this or that; for it

there′fore′ (-fôr′) *adv.* for this or that reason; hence

there·in′ *adv.* 1 in or into that place 2 in that matter, detail, etc.

there·of′ *adv.* 1 of that 2 from that as a cause, reason, etc.

there·on′ *adv.* 1 on that or it 2 THEREUPON

there·to′ *adv.* to that place, thing, etc. Also **there·un′to** (-un′to͞o; ther′un to͞o′)

there′to·fore′ *adv.* until that time

there·up·on′ *adv.* 1 immediately following that 2 as a consequence of that 3 concerning that subject, etc.

there·with′ *adv.* 1 along with that 2 immediately thereafter

ther·mal (thur′məl) *adj.* ⟦< Gr *thermē*, heat⟧ 1 having to do with heat 2 designating a loosely knitted material with air spaces for insulation

thermal pollution the discharge of heated liquid or air into lakes, rivers, etc., as by industries, that is harmful to the ecosystems

thermo- ⟦< Gr *thermē*, heat⟧ *combining form* heat

thermo·dy·nam·ics (thur′mō dī nam′iks) *n.pl.* [*with sing. v.*] the branch of physics dealing with the transformation of heat to and from other forms of energy —**ther′mo·dy·nam′ic** *adj.*

ther·mom·e·ter (thər mäm′ət ər) *n.* [see THERMO- & -METER] an instrument for measuring temperatures, as a graduated glass tube in which mercury, etc. rises or falls as it expands or contracts from changes in temperature

thermo·nu·clear (thur′mō no͞o′klē ər) *adj. Physics* 1 designating a reaction in which isotopes of a light element fuse, at extreme heat, into heavier nuclei 2 of or using the heat released in nuclear fusion

thermo·plas·tic (thur′mō plas′tik) *adj.* soft and moldable when subjected to heat: said of certain plastics — *n.* a thermoplastic substance

ther·mos (thur′məs) *n.* ⟦orig. a trademark < Gr *thermos*, hot⟧ a bottle or jug for keeping liquids at almost their original temperature: in full **thermos bottle** (or **jug**)

thermo·stat (thur′mə stat′) *n.* [THERMO- + -STAT] an apparatus for regulating temperature, esp. one that automatically controls a heating or cooling unit —**ther′mo·stat′ic** *adj.*

the·sau·rus (thi sô′rəs) *n., pl.* -**ri′** (-rī′) or -**ruses** ⟦< Gr *thēsauros*, a treasure⟧ a book of synonyms and antonyms

these (thēz) *pron., adj. pl. of* THIS

The·seus (thē′sē əs) *Gr. Legend* a hero who kills the Minotaur

the·sis (thē′sis) *n., pl.* -**ses′** (-sēz′) ⟦< Gr *tithenai*, to put⟧ 1 a proposition to be defended in argument 2 a research

---

■■■■■■■■ THESAURUS ■■■■■■■■

also CRIME.

their *poss. pronominal adj.* belonging to them, belonging to others, theirs, of them.

them *pron.* those persons, those things, the others, the above, some people, he and she; see also EVERYBODY.

theme *n.* 1 [A subject] topic, proposition, argument, thesis, text, subject matter, matter at hand, problem, question, point at issue, affair, business, point, case, thought, idea, line; see also SUBJECT. 2 [A recurrent melody] melody, motif, strain; see SONG. 3 [A short composition] essay, report, paper; see WRITING 2, STATEMENT 1.

then *a.* at that time, formerly, before, years ago, at that point, suddenly, all at once, soon after, before long, next, later, thereupon; see also WHEN 2, 3.

—**but then** but at the same time, on the other hand, however; see BUT 1, 2. —**what then?** in that case?, and then?, as a result?; see WHAT 1.

theology *n.* dogma, creed, theism; see BELIEF, FAITH 2.

theoretical *a.* ideal, analytical, academic; see ASSUMED.

theory *n.* 1 [Principles] method, approach, philosophy; see LAW 4. 2 [Something to be proved] assumption, conjecture, speculation; see OPINION 1.

therapy *n.* remedy, healing, cure; see MEDICINE 3.

there *a.* in that place, not here, beyond, over there, yonder, in the distance, at a distance, over yonder, just there, where I point, in that spot, at that point; see also WHERE 2. — **not all there*** crazy, eccentric,

demented; see INSANE.

thereafter *a.* from there on, from that day on, after that; see FOLLOWING, HEREAFTER.

thereby *a.* by way of, how, by which; see THROUGH 4, WHEREBY.

therefore *a., conj.* accordingly, consequently, hence, wherefore, for, since, inasmuch as, for this reason, on account of, to that end, on the ground, in that event, in consequence, as a result.

thermometer *n.* mercury, thermostat, thermoregulator; see MEASURE 2.

these *a.* those, the indicated, the present, the aforementioned, the already stated, the referred to, hereinafter described, the previously mentioned, the well-known, the aforesaid, the above, the below; see also CERTAIN 4.

paper, esp. one written by a candidate for a master's degree

Thes·pian (thes′pē ən) *adj.* ⟦after *Thespis*, ancient Gr poet⟧ [*often* t-] having to do with the drama; dramatic — *n.* [*often* t-] an actor or actress

theta (thāt′ə, thēt′-) *n.* the eighth letter of the Greek alphabet (Θ, θ, ϑ)

thews (thyo͞oz) *n.pl., sing.* **thew** ⟦< OE *theaw*, habit⟧ muscles or sinews

they (thā) *pron., sing.* **he, she,** or **it** ⟦< ON *thei-r*⟧ 1 the persons, animals, or things previously mentioned 2 people generally or indefinitely [*they* say it's so]

thi·a·mine (thī′ə mēn′, -min) *n.* ⟦ult. < Gr *theion*, brimstone + (VIT)AMIN⟧ a white, crystalline B vitamin, found in cereal, egg yolk, liver, etc.; vitamin B₁: also **thi′a·min** (-min)

thick (thik) *adj.* ⟦OE *thicce*⟧ 1 of relatively great extent from side to side 2 measured between opposite surfaces [one inch *thick*] 3 close and abundant [*thick* hair] 4 viscous [*thick* oil] 5 dense [*thick* smoke] 6 husky; hoarse; blurred [*thick* speech] 7 [Colloq.] stupid 8 [Colloq.] very friendly — *n.* the thickest part —**thick′ly** *adv.* —**thick′ness** *n.*

thick′en *vt., vi.* 1 to make or become thick or thicker 2 to make or become more complex —**thick′en·ing** *n.*

thicket (thik′it) *n.* ⟦see THICK⟧ a thick growth of shrubs or small trees

thick′set′ *adj.* 1 planted thickly or closely 2 thick in body; stocky

thick′-skinned′ *adj.* 1 having a thick skin 2 insensitive, as to insult

thief (thēf) *n., pl.* **thieves** (thēvz) ⟦OE *theof*⟧ one who steals

thieve (thēv) *vt., vi.* **thieved, thiev′ing** to steal —**thiev′ish** *adj.*

thiev′ery (-ər ē) *n., pl.* **-er·ies** the act or an instance of stealing; theft

thigh (thī) *n.* ⟦OE *theoh*⟧ that part of the leg between the knee and the hip

thigh′bone′ *n.* the bone extending from the hip to the knee

thim·ble (thim′bəl) *n.* ⟦< OE *thuma*, a thumb⟧ a small cap worn to protect the finger that pushes the needle in sewing —**thim′ble·ful′,** *pl.* **-fuls′,** *n.*

thin (thin) *adj.* **thin′ner, thin′nest** ⟦OE *thynne*⟧ 1 of relatively little extent from side to side 2 lean; slender 3 not dense or compact [*thin* hair, *thin* smoke] 4 very fluid or watery [*thin* soup] 5 high-pitched and weak [a *thin* voice] 6 sheer, as fabric 7 flimsy or unconvincing [a *thin* excuse] 8 lacking substance, depth, etc.; weak — *vt., vi.* **thinned, thin′ning** to make or become thin or thinner — **thin′ly** *adv.* —**thin′ness** *n.*

thine (thīn) *pron.* ⟦OE *thin*⟧ *poss. form of* THOU — *poss. pronominal adj.* [Archaic] thy: used esp. before a vowel

thing (thiŋ) *n.* ⟦OE, council⟧ 1 any matter, affair, or concern 2 a happening, act, incident, event, etc. 3 a tangible or an inanimate object 4 an item, detail, etc. 5 *a*) [*pl.*] personal belongings *b*) a garment 6 [Colloq.] a person [poor *thing*] 7 [Colloq.] a point of contention; issue 8 [Colloq.] an irrational liking, fear, etc. 9 [Colloq.] what one wants to do or is adept at [do one's own *thing*] —**see things** [Colloq.] to have hallucinations

think (thiŋk) *vt.* **thought, think′ing** ⟦OE *thencan*⟧ 1 to form or have in the mind [*thinking* good thoughts] 2 to judge; consider [many *think* her charming] 3 to believe; expect [I *think* I can come] — *vi.* 1 to use the mind; reason 2 to have an opinion, judgment, etc.: with *of* or *about* 3 to remember or consider: with *of* or *about* 4 to conceive (*of*) —**think up** to invent, plan, etc. by thinking —**think′er** *n.*

think tank (or **factory**) [Slang] a group or center organized to do intensive research and problem-solving

thin·ner (thin′ər) *n.* a substance added to paint, shellac, etc. to thin it

thin′-skinned′ *adj.* 1 having a thin skin 2 sensitive, as to insult

third (thurd) *adj.* ⟦OE *thridda*⟧ preceded by two others in a series; 3d or 3rd — *adv.* in the third place, etc.: also **third′ly** — *n.* 1 the one following the second 2 any of the three equal parts of something; ⅓ 3 the third forward gear of a transmission, providing more speed than second

third′-class′ *adj.* 1 of the class, rank, etc. next below the

══ **THESAURUS** ══

they *pron.* people, men, those people, all, others, he and she, both; see also EVERYBODY.

thick *a.* 1 [Dense] compact, impervious, condensed, compressed, multitudinous, numerous, rank, crowded, close, solid, packed, populous, profuse, populated, swarming, heaped, abundant, impenetrable, concentrated, crammed, packed together, closely packed, like sardines in a can*, jam-packed.—*Ant.* SCATTERED, spacious, wide-open. 2 [Deep] in depth, edgewise, third-dimensional; see DEEP 2. 3 [Of heavy consistency] compact, heavy, viscous, viscid, dense, syrupy, ropy, coagulated, curdled, turbid, gelatinous, glutinous, gummy, opaque, clotted; see also STRINGY.—*Ant.* LIGHT, porous, filmy. 4 [Not clear] cloudy, turbid, indistinct; see DULL 2, MUDDY 1, OBSCURE 1. 5 [Stupid] obtuse, ignorant, doltish; see DULL 3. 6 [*Intimate] cordial, familiar, fraternal; see FRIENDLY. —**through thick and thin*** faithfully, devotedly, in good and bad times; see LOYALTY.

thicken *v.* coagulate, curdle, petrify, ossify, solidify, freeze, clot, set, congeal, jelly, grow thick; see also HARDEN, STIFFEN.

thickness *n.* density, compactness, solidity, closeness, heaviness, stiffness, condensation, concentration, clot.—*Ant.* FRAILTY, thinness, slimness.

thief *n.* burglar, highwayman, holdup man; see CRIMINAL.

thieve *v.* loot, rob, filch; see STEAL.

thievery *n.* burglary, robbery, pilfering; see CRIME, THEFT.

thigh *n.* thigh bone, femur, ham; see LEG.

thin *a.* 1 [Of little thickness] flimsy, slim, slight, diaphanous, sheer, rare, sleazy, permeable, paper-thin, wafer-sliced.—*Ant.* THICK, heavy, coarse. 2 [Slender] slim, lean, skinny, scraggy, lank, spare, gaunt, bony, wan, rangy, skeletal, scrawny, lanky, delicate, wasted, haggard, emaciated, raw-boned, shriveled, wizened, rickety, spindly, pinched, starved.—*Ant.* FAT, obese, heavy. 3 [Sparse] scarce, insufficient, deficient; see INADEQUATE. 4 [Having little content] sketchy, slight, insubstantial; see SHALLOW 1, 2. 5 [Having little volume] faint, shrill, weak; see LIGHT 7.

thin *v.* thin out, weed out, dilute; see DECREASE 2, WEAKEN 2.

thing *n.* 1 [An object] article, object, item, lifeless object, commodity, device, gadget, material object, being, entity, body, person, something, anything, everything, element, substance, piece, shape, form, figure, configuration, creature, stuff, goods, matter, thingumajig*, doohickey*, thingumabob*. 2 [A circumstance] matter, condition, situation; see CIRCUMSTANCE 1. 3 [An act] deed, feat, movement; see ACTION 2. 4 [A characteristic] quality, trait, attribute; see CHARACTERISTIC. 5 [An idea] notion, opinion, impression; see THOUGHT 2. 6 [A pitiable person] wretch, poor person, sufferer, urchin; see also PATIENT, REFUGEE. 7 [Belongings; *usually pl.*] possessions, clothes, personals; see PROPERTY 1. 8 [Something so vague as to be nameless] affair, matter, concern, business, occurrence, anything, everything, something, stuff, point, information, subject, idea, question, indication, intimation, contrivance, word, name, shape, form, entity. 9 [Something to be done] task, obligation, duty; see JOB 2. —**do one's own thing*** live according to one's own principles, do what one likes, live fully; see LIVE 1.

things *n.* possessions, luggage, belongings; see BAGGAGE, PROPERTY 1.

think *v.* 1 [To examine with the mind] cogitate, muse, ponder, consider, contemplate, deliberate, stop to consider, study, reflect, examine, think twice, estimate, evaluate, appraise, resolve, ruminate, scan, confer, consult, meditate, meditate upon, take under consideration, have on one's mind, brood over, speculate, weigh, have in mind, keep in mind, bear in mind, mull over*, turn over, sweat over*, stew, bone up*, beat one's brains, rack one's brains, use the old bean*, figure out, put on one's thinking cap*, use one's head, hammer away at, hammer out, bury oneself in.—*Ant.* NEGLECT, take for granted, accept. 2 [To believe] be convinced, deem, hold; see BELIEVE. 3 [To suppose] imagine, guess, presume; see ASSUME. 4 [To form in the mind] conceive, invent, create; see IMAGINE. 5 [To remember] recollect, recall, reminisce; see REMEMBER 1, 2.

thinking *a.* pensive, introspective, reflective; see THOUGHTFUL 1. —**put on one's thinking cap** begin thinking, study, examine; see THINK 1.

thinking *n.* reasoning, reason, contemplation; see THOUGHT 1.

thinness *n.* slenderness, slimness, shallowness; see LIGHTNESS 2.

third *a.* part, after the second, next but one; see THREE.

second 2 of a low-cost mail class, as for advertisements — **adv.** by third-class mail or travel accommodations

third degree [Colloq.] cruel treatment and questioning to force a confession

third dimension 1 depth or solidity 2 the quality of seeming real

third person that form of a pronoun (as *she*) or verb (as *is*) that refers to the person(s) or thing(s) spoken of

third'-rate' *adj.* 1 third in quality or other rating 2 very poor

third world [often T- W-] the underdeveloped countries of the world

thirst (thurst) *n.* [OE *thurst*] 1 the discomfort caused by a need for drink 2 a strong desire; craving — *vi.* 1 to feel thirst 2 to have a strong desire or craving —**thirst'y, -i-er, -i-est,** *adj.* —**thirst'i-ly** *adv.*

thir-teen (thur'tēn') *adj., n.* [OE *threotyne*] three more than ten; 13; XIII —**thir'teenth'** *adj., n.*

thir-ty (thur'tē) *adj., n., pl.* **-ties** [OE *thritig*] three times ten; 30; XXX —**the thirties** the numbers or years, as of a century, from 30 through 39 —**thir'ti-eth** (-ith) *adj., n.*

this (this) *pron., adj., pl.* **these** [OE *thes*] 1 (designating) the person or thing mentioned [*this* (man) is John] 2 (designating) the nearer one or another one [*this* (desk) is older than that] 3 (designating) something about to be presented [hear *this* (news)] — *adv.* to this extent [it was *this* big]

this-tle (this'əl) *n.* [OE *thistel*] a plant with prickly leaves and white, purple, etc. flowers

this'tle-down' *n.* the down growing from the flowers of a thistle

thith-er (thith'ər, thith'-) *adv.* [OE *thider*] to or toward that place; there

tho or **tho'** (thō) *conj., adv. short for* THOUGH

thole (thōl) *n.* [OE *thol*] one of a pair of pins set as an oarlock into the gunwale of a boat: also **thole'pin'**

-thon (thän) *suffix* -ATHON: used after a vowel [radiothon]

thong (thôn) *n.* [OE *thwang*] a narrow strip of leather, etc. used as a lace, strap, etc.

Thor (thôr) *Norse Myth.* the god of thunder, war, and strength

tho-rax (thôr'aks') *n., pl.* **-rax'es** or **-ra-ces'** (-ə sēz') [< Gr] 1 the part of the body between the neck and the abdomen; chest 2 the middle segment of an insect's body —**tho-rac-ic** (thō ras'ik, thô-) *adj.*

tho-ri-um (thôr'ē əm, thō'rē-) *n.* [< THOR] a rare, grayish, radioactive chemical element, used as a nuclear fuel

thorn (thôrn) *n.* [OE] 1 *a)* a very short, hard, leafless stem with a sharp point *b)* any small tree or shrub bearing thorns 2 a source of constant trouble or irritation —**thorn'y, -i-er, -i-est,** *adj.*

thor-ough (thur'ō) *adj.* [var. of THROUGH] 1 done or proceeding through to the end; complete 2 absolute [a *thorough* rascal] 3 very exact, accurate, or painstaking —**thor'oughly** *adv.* —**thor'ough-ness** *n.*

thorough-bred (thur'ō bred', thur'ə-) *adj.* of pure stock; pedigreed —*n.* [T-] any of a breed of light racehorses

thor'ough-fare' (-fer') *n.* a public street open at both ends, esp. a main highway

thor'ough-go'ing *adj.* very thorough

those (thōz) *adj., pron. pl. of* THAT

thou (thou) *pron.* [OE *thu*] you: in poetic or religious use

though (thō) *conj.* [OE *theah*] 1 in spite of the fact that [*though* it rained, he went] 2 and yet; however [they did it, *though* badly] 3 even if [*though* he may fail, he will have tried] — *adv.* however; nevertheless [she sings well, *though*]

thought¹ (thôt) *n.* [OE *thoht*] 1 the act or process of thinking 2 the power of reasoning 3 an idea, concept, etc. 4 attention; consideration 5 a little; trifle [be a *thought* more careful]

thought² (thôt) *vt., vi. pt. & pp. of* THINK

thought'ful *adj.* 1 full of thought; meditative 2 considerate —**thought'fully** *adv.* —**thought'ful-ness** *n.*

thought'less *adj.* 1 not stopping to think; careless 2 ill-considered; rash 3 inconsiderate —**thought'lessly** *adv.* —**thought'less-ness** *n.*

thou-sand (thou'zand) *adj., n.* [OE *thusend*] ten hundred; 1,000; M —**thou'sandth** (-zəndth) *adj., n.*

thrall (thrôl) *n.* [< ON *thræll*] 1 a slave 2 slavery —**thrall'dom** or **thral'dom** (-dəm) *n.*

thrash (thrash) *vt., vi.* [OE *therscan*] 1 THRESH 2 to beat; flog 3 to toss about violently 4 to defeat overwhelmingly —**thrash out** to settle by detailed discussion —**thrash'er** *n.*

thrash'er *n.* [E dial. *thresher*] a thrushlike American songbird

thread (thred) *n.* [OE *thræd*] 1 a fine, stringlike length of spun cotton, silk, nylon, etc. used in sewing 2 any thin line, vein, etc. 3 something like a thread in its length,

---

▰▰▰ THESAURUS ▰▰▰

thirst *n.* dryness, need for liquid, longing, craving, cobweb throat*.

thirsty *a.* dry, parched, arid, eager, hankering for, burning for, craving, longing for, partial to, hungry for, itching for, inclined to, bone dry*, crazy for*, wild for; see also HUNGRY.—*Ant.* SATISFIED, full, replete.

this *a.* the, that, the indicated, the present, here, aforementioned, already stated.

this *pron.* the one, this one, that one, the one in question, the aforementioned one, this person, the thing indicated; see also THAT.

thorn *n.* spine, briar, neetle; see POINT 2, SPINE 1.

thorough *a.* 1 [Painstaking] exact, meticulous, precise; see ACCURATE 2, CAREFUL. 2 [Complete] thoroughgoing, out-and-out, total; see ABSOLUTE 1.

thoroughly *a.* fully, wholly, in detail; see COMPLETELY.

those *a.* these, the above-mentioned, the indicated; see THE 1.

those *pron.* the others, they, them, not these; see also THAT.

though *conj.* despite, even if, if; see ALTHOUGH, BUT 1.

thought¹ *n.* 1 [Mental activity] speculation, reflection, deliberation, meditation, rumination, perceiving, apprehending, seeing, consideration, reasoning, intuition, logical process, perception, insight, understanding, viewpoint, concept, brainwork, thinking, knowing, realizing, discerning, rationalizing, concluding, drawing conclusions, inferring, deducing,

deriving, deduction, inducing, logic, judging, rationalization, judgment, argumentation, cogitation, contemplation, cognition, intellection, brainstorm. 2 [The result of mental activity] idea, plan, view, fancy, notion, impression, image, understanding, appreciation, conception, observation, belief, feeling, opinion, guess, inference, theory, hypothesis, supposition, assumption, intuition, conjecture, deduction, postulate, premise, knowledge, evaluation, assessment, appraisal, estimate, verdict, finding, decision, determination, reflection, consideration, abstraction, conviction, tenet, presumption, intellectualization, surmise, doctrine, principle, drift, calculation, caprice, reverie, sentiment, care, worry, anxiety, uneasiness, dream. 3 [Care or attention] heed, thoughtfulness, solicitude; see ATTENTION.

thoughtful *a.* 1 [Notable for thought] thinking, meditative, engrossed, absorbed, rapt in, pensive, considered, seasoned, matured, studied, philosophic, contemplative, studious, cogitative, examined, pondered, speculative, deliberative, reflective, introspective, clearheaded, levelheaded, keen, wise, well-balanced, judged, farsighted, reasoning, rational, calculating, discerning, penetrating, politic, shrewd, careful, sensible, retrospective, intellectual, brainy*, deep.—*Ant.* THOUGHTLESS, unthinking, irrational. 2 [Considerate] heedful, polite, courteous, solici-

tous, friendly, kind, kindly, unselfish, concerned, anxious, neighborly, regardful, social, cooperative, responsive, aware, sensitive, benign, indulgent, obliging, careful, attentive, gallant, chivalrous, charitable.—*Ant.* SELFISH, boorish, inconsiderate.

thoughtfulness *n.* understanding, helpfulness, indulgence; see KINDNESS 1.

thoughtless *a.* 1 [Destitute of thought] irrational, unreasoning, unreasonable, inane, incomprehensible, witless, undiscerning, foolish, doltish, babbling, bewildered, confused, puerile, senseless, driveling, inept, dull, heavy-handed, obtuse, feeble-minded, flighty; see also STUPID. 2 [Inconsiderate] heedless, negligent, inattentive, neglectful, careless, self-centered, egocentric, selfish, asocial, antisocial, unmindful, unheeding, deaf, blind, indifferent, unconcerned, listless, apathetic, boorish, discourteous, primitive, unrefined; see also RUDE 2.—*Ant.* CAREFUL, thoughtful, unselfish.

thoughtlessness *n.* inattention, oversight, heedlessness; see CARELESSNESS, NEGLECT 1.

thousand *a.* ten hundred, millenary, thousandfold; see MANY.

thrash *v.* trounce, whip, chasten; see BEAT 1, PUNISH.

thread *n.* yarn, string, strand; see FIBER.

thread *v.* attach, weave together, string together; see JOIN 1.

sequence, etc. [the *thread* of a story] **4** the spiral ridge of a screw, nut, etc. — *vt.* **1** to put a thread through (a needle, etc.) **2** to make (one's way) by twisting, weaving, etc. **3** to fashion a THREAD (sense 4) on or in —**thread'y, -i·er, -i·est,** *adj.*

thread'bare' *adj.* **1** worn down so that the threads show **2** wearing worn clothes; shabby **3** stale; trite

threat (thret) *n.* [OE *threat*, pressure] **1** an expression of intention to hurt, destroy, punish, etc. **2** an indication of, or a source of, imminent danger, harm, etc.

threat'en *vt., vi.* **1** to make threats, as of injury (against) **2** to indicate (danger, etc.) **3** to be a source of danger (to)

three (thrē) *adj., n.* [OE *threo*] one more than two; 3; III

three'-deck'er (-dek'ər) *n.* anything having three levels, layers, etc.

three'-dimen'sional *adj.* having or seeming to have depth or thickness

three'fold' (-fōld') *adj.* **1** having three parts **2** having three times as much or as many —*adv.* three times as much or as many

three R's reading, writing, and arithmetic, regarded as the fundamentals of an education

three'score (thrē'skôr') *adj., n.* sixty

threno·dy (thren'ə dē) *n., pl.* **-dies** [< Gr *thrēnos*, lamentation + *ōidē*, song] a song of lamentation; dirge

thresh (thresh) *vt., vi.* [ME *threschen*] **1** to beat out (grain) from (husks), as with a flail **2** THRASH — **thresh'er** *n.*

thresh·old (thresh'ōld', -hōld') *n.* [OE *therscwold*] **1** a length of wood, stone, etc. along the bottom of a doorway **2** the beginning point

threw (thrōō) *vt. pt. of* THROW

thrice (thris) *adv.* [OE *thriwa*] **1** three times **2** threefold

thrift (thrift) *n.* [< ON *thrifa*, to grasp] economy; frugality —**thrift'less** *adj.* —**thrift'y, -i·er, -i·est,** *adj.* — **thrift'i·ly** *adv.* —**thrift'i·ness** *n.*

thrift shop a store where castoff clothes, etc. are sold, as for charity

thrill (thril) *vi., vt.* [< OE, *thurh*, through] **1** to feel or cause to feel emotional excitement **2** to quiver or cause to quiver; tremble —*n.* **1** a thrilling or being thrilled **2** a tremor; quiver —**thrill'er** *n.*

thrive (thriv) *vi.* thrived or throve, thrived or thriven (thriv'n), thriv'ing [< ON *thrifa*, to grasp] **1** to prosper or flourish; be successful **2** to grow vigorously or luxuriantly

throat (thrōt) *n.* [OE *throte*] **1** the front part of the neck **2** the upper passage from the mouth to the stomach and lungs **3** any narrow passage

639   **threadbare / throw**

throat'y *adj.* **-i·er, -i·est** produced in the throat, as some sounds; husky

throb (thräb) *vi.* **throbbed, throb'bing** [ME *throbben*] **1** to beat, pulsate, vibrate, etc., esp. strongly or fast **2** to feel excitement — *n.* **1** a throbbing **2** a strong beat or pulsation

throe (thrō) *n.* [prob. < OE *thrawu*, pain] a spasm or pang of pain: *usually used in pl.* [the *throes* of childbirth, death *throes*]

throm·bo·sis (thräm bō'sis) *n.* [< Gr *thrombos*, a clot] coagulation of the blood in the heart or a blood vessel, forming a clot

throm'bus (-bəs) *n., pl.* **-bi** (-bī') [see prec.] the clot attached at the site of thrombosis

throne (thrōn) *n.* [< Gr *thronos*, a seat] **1** the chair on which a king, cardinal, etc. sits on formal occasions **2** the power or rank of a king, etc. **3** a sovereign, ruler, etc.

throng (thrôŋ) *n.* [OE *thringan*, to crowd] **1** a crowd **2** any great number of things considered together — *vi.* to gather together in a throng — *vt.* to crowd into

throt·tle (thrät''l) *n.* [prob. dim. of THROAT] the valve, or its control lever or pedal, that regulates the amount of fuel vapor entering an engine — *vt.* **-tled, -tling** **1** to choke; strangle **2** to censor or suppress **3** a) to reduce the flow of (fuel vapor, etc.) by means of a throttle b) to slow by this means

through (thrōō) *prep.* [OE *thurh*] **1** in one side and out the other side of **2** in the midst of; among **3** by way of **4** around [touring *through* France] **5** a) from the beginning to the end of b) up to and including **6** by means of **7** as a result of [done *through* error] — *adv.* **1** in one side and out the other **2** from the beginning to the end **3** completely to the end [to see something *through*] **4** completely [soaked *through*]: also **through and through** — *adj.* **1** extending from one place to another [a *through* street] **2** traveling to the destination without stops [a *through* train] **3** finished

through·out' *prep.* all the way through — *adv.* in every part; everywhere

through'way' *n.* alt. sp. of THRUWAY: see EXPRESSWAY

throve (thrōv) *vi.* alt. pt. of THRIVE

throw (thrō) *vt.* **threw, thrown, throw'ing** [OE *thrawan*, to twist] **1** to send through the air by a rapid motion of the arm, etc. **2** to cause to fall; upset **3** to send rapidly [to *throw* troops into battle] **4** to put suddenly into a specified state, etc. [*throw* into confusion] **5** to

═══ **THESAURUS** ═══

threat *n.* menace, fulmination, intimidation; see WARNING.

threaten *v.* intimidate, caution, admonish, hold over, scare, torment, push around, forewarn, bully, abuse, bluster, endanger, be dangerous, be gathering, be in the offing, imperil, be brewing, approach, come on, advance; see also FRIGHTEN, WARN.— *Ant.* HELP, mollify, placate.

threatened *a.* warned, endangered, imperiled, jeopardized, in bad straits, insecure, unsafe, unprotected, vulnerable, exposed, in a crucial state, in danger, besieged, surrounded, under attack, set upon, in a bad way.—*Ant.* SAFE, invulnerable, protected.

threatening *a.* alarming, dangerous, aggressive; see OMINOUS, SINISTER, UNSAFE.

three *a.* triple, treble, threefold, third, triform, triune, tertiary, thrice, triply.

threshold *n.* sill, gate, door; see ENTRANCE 1.

thrift *n.* saving, parsimony, frugality; see ECONOMY.

thrifty *a.* saving, careful, frugal; see ECONOMICAL 1.

thrill *n.* pleasant sensation, stimulation, tingle; see EXCITEMENT, FUN.

thrill *v.* animate, inspire, rouse; see EXCITE.

thrilled *a.* inspired, moved, touched; see EXCITED, HAPPY.

thrilling *a.* overwhelming, exciting, breathtaking; see STIMULATING.

thrive *v.* flourish, increase, succeed;

see GROW 1.

throat *n.* neck, windpipe, larynx, trachea, esophagus, jugular region, gullet, gorge. —**cut each other's throats*** ruin each other, fight, feud; see DESTROY. —**cut one's own throat*** ruin oneself, cause one's own destruction, act contrary to one's best interests; see COMMIT SUICIDE, DAMAGE. —**ram down someone's throat*** impose, pressure, coerce; see FORCE. —**stick in one's throat*** be difficult to say, not come easily, be disturbing; see DISTURB.

throaty *a.* husky, hoarse, deep; see HOARSE.

throb *n.* beat, pulsation, palpitation; see BEAT 1.

throb *v.* beat, pulsate, palpitate; see BEAT 2.

throng *n.* multitude, mass, concourse; see CROWD, GATHERING.

throttle *v.* strangle, stifle, silence; see CHOKE.

through *a., prep.* **1** [Finished] completed, over, ended; see DONE 1, FINISHED 1. **2** [From one side to the other] straight through, through and through, clear through; see IN 2, INTO, WITHIN. **3** [During] throughout, for the period of, from beginning to end; see DURING. **4** [By means of] by, by way of, by reason, in virtue of, in consequence of, for, by the agency of, at the hand of. **5** [Referring to continuous passage] nonstop, unbroken, one-way; see CONSECUTIVE, CONSTANT, REGULAR 3. —**through and**

through permeating, pervasive, enduring; see COMPLETELY, THROUGHOUT.

throughout *a., prep.* all through, during, from beginning to end, from one end to the other, everywhere, all over, in everything, in every place, up and down, on all accounts, in all respects, inside and out, at full length, every bit, to the end, down to the ground, head and shoulders, from the word go, up to the brim*; see also COMPLETELY.

throw *v.* **1** [To hurl] fling, butt, bunt, pitch, fire, let go, sling, toss, heave, lob, dash, launch, chuck, bowl, cast, hurl at, let fly, deliver, cast off*, lay across*.—*Ant.* CATCH, receive, grab. **2** [To connect or disconnect] turn a switch, connect, start; see TURN OFF, TURN ON 1. **3** [To force to the ground] pin*, nail*, flatten; see DEFEAT 3. **4** [*To permit an opponent to win] submit, yield, surrender; see LOSE 3. —**throw away** reject, refuse, turn down; see DISCARD. —**throw in** add, expand, give; see INCREASE. —**throw out** discharge, throw away, reject; see DISCARD. —**throw together** make quickly, do in a hurry, do a rush job; see BUILD, MANUFACTURE. —**throw up** **1** [To vomit] regurgitate, retch, barf*; see VOMIT. **2** [To quit] give up, cease, terminate; see STOP 2. **3** [To construct, usually hastily] build overnight, patch up, knock together; see BUILD.

move (a switch, etc.) so as to connect, disconnect, etc. **6** to direct, cast, etc. *[throw* a glance*]* **7** [Colloq.] to lose (a game, etc.) deliberately **8** [Colloq.] to give (a party, etc.) **9** [Colloq.] to confuse or disconcert *[the* question *threw* him*]* **10** [Colloq.] to have (a tantrum, etc.) — *vi.* to cast or hurl something — *n.* **1** the act of one who throws **2** the distance something is or can be thrown **3** a spread for a bed, etc. —**throw away 1** to discard **2** to waste —**throw in** to add extra or free —**throw off 1** to rid oneself of **2** to mislead or confuse **3** to expel, emit, etc. —**throw oneself at** to try very hard to win the love of —**throw out 1** to discard **2** to reject or remove —**throw over 1** to give up; abandon **2** to jilt —**throw together** to assemble hurriedly —**throw up 1** to abandon **2** to vomit —**throw'er** *n.*

throw'away' *n.* a leaflet, handbill, etc. given out on the streets, at houses, etc. — *adj.* for discarding after use

throw'back' *n.* (a) reversion to an earlier or more primitive type

throw rug SCATTER RUG

thru (thrōō) *prep., adv., adj. colloq. sp. of* THROUGH

thrum (thrum) *vt., vi.* **thrummed, thrum'ming** [echoic] STRUM

thrush (thrush) *n.* [OE *thrysce*] any of a family of songbirds, including robins

thrust (thrust) *vt., vi.* **thrust, thrust'ing** [< ON *thrysta*] **1** to push with sudden force **2** to stab **3** to force or impose — *n.* **1** a sudden, forceful push **2** a stab **3** continuous pressure, as of a rafter against a wall **4** *a)* the driving force of a propeller *b)* the forward force produced by a jet or rocket engine **5** forward movement **6** the basic meaning; point

thru'way' (thrōō'wā') *n.* EXPRESSWAY

thud (thud) *vi.* **thud'ded, thud'ding** [prob. < OE *thyddan,* to strike] to hit with a dull sound — *n.* a dull sound, as of an object dropping on a soft surface

thug (thug) *n.* [Hindi *thag,* swindler] a brutal hoodlum, gangster, etc.

thumb (thum) *n.* [OE *thuma*] the short, thick digit of the hand — *vt.* **1** to handle, soil, etc. as with the thumb **2** [Colloq.] to solicit or get (a ride) in hitchhiking by signaling with the thumb —**all thumbs** clumsy —**under someone's thumb** under someone's influence

thumb'nail' *n.* the nail of the thumb — *adj.* very small, brief, or concise

thumb'screw' *n.* a screw that can be turned by the thumb and forefinger

thumb'tack' *n.* a tack with a wide, flat head that can be pressed into a board, etc. with the thumb

thump (thump) *n.* [echoic] **1** a blow with something heavy and blunt **2** the dull sound made by such a blow — *vt.* to strike with a thump — *vi.* **1** to hit or fall with a thump **2** to make a dull, heavy sound

thump'ing *adj.* **1** that thumps **2** [Colloq.] very large; whopping

thun'der (thun'dər) *n.* [OE *thunor*] **1** the sound following a flash of lightning **2** any similar sound — *vi.* to produce thunder or a sound like this — *vt.* to utter, etc. with a thundering sound —**thun'der·ous** *adj.*

thun'der·bolt' (-bōlt') *n.* **1** a flash of lightning and the accompanying thunder **2** something sudden and shocking, as bad news

thun'der·clap' *n.* a clap, or loud crash, of thunder

thun'der·cloud' *n.* a storm cloud charged with electricity and producing lightning and thunder

thun'der·head' *n.* a round mass of cumulus clouds appearing before a thunderstorm

thun'der·show'er *n.* a shower accompanied by thunder and lightning

thun'der·storm' *n.* a storm accompanied by thunder and lightning

thun'der·struck' *adj.* struck with amazement, terror, etc. Also **thun'der·strick'en** (-strik'ən)

Thurs·day (thurz'dā, -dē) *n.* [< ON *Thorsdagr,* Thor's day] the fifth day of the week Abbrev. **Thur.** or **Thurs.**

thus (*thus*) *adv.* [OE] **1** in this or that manner **2** to this or that degree or extent **3** therefore

thwack (thwak) *vt., n.* [prob. echoic] WHACK

thwart (thwôrt) *n.* [< ON *thvert,* transverse] a seat across a boat — *vt.* to obstruct, frustrate, or defeat (a person, plans, etc.)

thy (*thi*) *poss. pronominal adj.* [< ME *thin*] of, belonging to, or done by thee: archaic or poetic var. of *your*

thyme (tim) *n.* [< Gr *thymon*] a plant of the mint family, with leaves used for seasoning

thy'mo·sin (thī'mə sin) *n.* [< Gr *thymos,* thymus & IN] a hormone secreted by the thymus that stimulates the immune system

thy·mus (thī'məs) *n.* [Gr *thymos*] a ductless gland situated near the throat Also **thymus gland**

thy·roid (thī'roid') *n.* [< Gr *thyreos,* large shield] designating or of a large ductless gland near the trachea, secreting a hormone which regulates growth — *n.* **1** the thyroid gland **2** an animal extract of this gland, used in treating goiter

thy·self (*thi* self') *pron. reflexive or intensive form of* THOU

ti (tē) *n. Music* the seventh tone of the diatonic scale

Ti *Chem. symbol for* titanium

ti·ar·a (tē er'ə, -ar'-, -är'-) *n.* [< Gr] **1** the pope's triple crown **2** a woman's crownlike headdress

tib·i·a (tib'ē ə) *n., pl.* **-i·ae** (-ē ē') or **-i·as** [L] the inner and thicker of the two bones of the lower leg

tic (tik) *n.* [Fr < ?] any involuntary, regularly repeated, spasmodic contraction of a muscle

tick[1] (tik) *n.* [prob. echoic] **1** a light clicking sound, as of a clock **2** a mark made to check off items — *vi.* to make a tick or ticks — *vt.* to record, mark, or check by ticks

tick[2] (tik) *n.* [OE *ticia*] a wingless, bloodsucking insect that infests humans, cattle, etc.

tick[3] (tik) *n.* [< ? L *theca,* a cover] the cloth case of a mattress or pillow

tick'er *n.* **1** one that ticks **2** a telegraphic device that records stock market quotations, etc. on a paper tape **(ticker tape) 3** [Slang] the heart

ticket (tik'it) *n.* [< obs. Fr *etiquet,* etiquette] **1** a printed card, etc. that gives one a right, as to attend a theater **2** a license or certificate **3** a label on merchandise giving size, price, etc. **4** the list of candidates nominated by a political party **5** [Colloq.] a summons to court for a traffic violation — *vt.* **1** to label with a ticket **2** to give a ticket to

tick'ing *n.* strong cloth, often striped, used for casings of pillows, etc.

tickle (tik'əl) *vt.* **-led, -ling** [ME *tikelen*] **1** to please, gratify, delight, etc. **2** to stroke lightly so as to cause involuntary twitching, laughter, etc. — *vi.* to have or cause a twitching or tingling sensation — *n.* a sensation of being tickled

tick·ler (tik'lər) *n.* a pad, file, etc. for noting terms to be remembered

tick'lish (-lish) *adj.* **1** sensitive to tickling **2** needing careful handling; precarious; delicate

tick-tack-toe or **tic-tac-toe** (tik'tak tō') *n.* a game for

THESAURUS

thrown *a.* **1** [Hurled] pitched, tossed, heaved; see SENT. **2** [Beaten] knocked over, sent sprawling, heaved; see BEATEN 1.

thrust *n.* **1** [A jab] punch, stab, poke; see BLOW. **2** [An attack] onset, onslaught, advance; see ATTACK. **3** [A strong push] drive, impetus, momentum; see PUSH.

thrust *v.* poke, push, shove; see HIT 1.

thud *n.* thump, dull sound, plop; see NOISE 1.

thumb *n.* pollex, first digit, preaxial digit; see FINGER. —**all thumbs** fumbling, clumsy, inept; see AWKWARD. —**under someone's thumb** under someone's control, controlled, governed; see MANAGED.

thump *n.* thud, knock, rap; see NOISE

1, BLOW.

thump *v.* pound, knock, rap, wallop, slap, strike, whack, hit; see also BEAT 1.

thunder *n.* crash, peal, outburst, explosion, boom, booming, roar, rumble, clap, crack, discharge, thunderbolt, uproar, blast; see also NOISE 1.

thunder *v.* peal, boom, rumble, resound, roll, deafen, crash, clamor, clash; see also SOUND, STORM.

thunderstorm *n.* electric storm, squall, downpour; see THUNDER, STORM.

thus *a.* in this manner, so, consequently, hence, in such a way, just like that, in kind, along these lines; see also THEREFORE.

thwart *v.* stop, impede, frustrate; see CONFUSE, PREVENT.

tick[1,2] *n.* **1** [A light beat] beat, click, ticktock; see BEAT 1, 2. **2** [An insect] parasite, louse, mite; see INSECT, PEST 1.

ticket *n.* **1** [A valid token] check, certificate, notice, badge, label, voucher, stub, countercheck, rain check, tag, slip, note, card, pass, receipt, record, license, permit, passage, credential, visa, passport, document. **2** [Candidates representing a political party] party list, choice, ballot; see CANDIDATE, FACTION, PARTY 3.

tickle *v.* rub, caress, stroke; see TOUCH 1.

ticklish *a.* sensitive, unsteady, touchy; see IRRITABLE, UNSTABLE 2.

so as to complete any one row before the other can

tick·tock (tik′täk′) *n.* the sound made by a clock or watch

tidal (tīd′'l) *adj.* of, having, or caused by, a tide or tides

tidal wave 1 *nontechnical term for* a tsunami or a similar huge wave caused by strong winds **2** any widespread movement, feeling, etc.

tid·bit (tid′bit′) *n.* 〚dial. *tid*, small object〛 a choice bit of food, gossip, etc.

tiddly·winks (tid′lē wiŋks′) *n.pl.* 〚< ?〛 [*with sing. v.*] a game in which little disks are popped into a cup by pressing their edges with a larger disk

tide (tīd) *n.* 〚OE *tid*, time〛 **1** a period of time [*Eastertide*] **2** the alternate rise and fall, about twice a day, of the surface of oceans, seas, etc. caused by the attraction of the moon and sun **3** something that rises and falls like the tide **4** a stream, trend, etc. — *vi.* **tid′ed**, **tid′ing** to help along temporarily: with *over*

tide′land′ *n.* **1** land covered when the tide is in **2** [*pl.*] land under the sea within territorial waters of a country

tide′wa′ter *n.* **1** water that is affected by the tide **2** a seaboard — *adj.* of or along a tidewater

ti·dings (tīd′iŋz) *n.pl.* 〚OE *tidung*〛 news; information

tidy (tīd′ē) *adj.* **-di·er**, **-di·est** 〚<OE *tid*, time〛 **1** neat in appearance, arrangement, etc.; orderly **2** [Colloq.] rather large [*a tidy sum*] — *vt.*, *vi.* **-died**, **-dy·ing** to make tidy: often with *up* — **ti′di·ness** *n.*

tie (tī) *vt.* **tied**, **ty′ing** or **tie′ing** 〚< OE *teag*, a rope〛 **1** to bind, as with string, rope, etc. **2** to knot the laces, etc. of **3** to make (a knot) in **4** to bind in any way **5** to equal the score of, as in a contest — *vi.* to make an equal score, as in a contest — *n.* **1** a string, cord, etc. used to tie things **2** something that connects, binds, etc. **3** a necktie **4** a beam, rod, etc. that holds parts together **5** any of the crossbeams to which the rails of a railroad are fastened **6** *a*) an equality of scores, etc. *b*) a contest in which this occurs — *adj.* that has been made equal [*a tie score*] — **tie down** to confine; restrict — **tie up 1** to wrap up and tie **2** to moor to a dock **3** to obstruct; hinder **4** to cause to be already in use, committed, etc.

tie′back′ *n.* a band or ribbon used to tie curtains, etc. to one side

tie′break′er *n.* an additional game, period of play, etc. used to establish a winner from among those tied at the end of a contest

tie clasp a decorative clasp for fastening a necktie to the shirt   Also **tie clip**

tie′-dye′ (-dī′) *n.* a method of dyeing designs on cloth by tying bunches of it so that the dye affects only exposed parts — *vt.* **-dyed**, **-dye′ing** to dye in this way

tie′-in′ *n.* a connection or relationship

tier (tir) *n.* 〚< OFr *tire*, order〛 any of a series of rows, as of seats, arranged one above or behind another

tie rod a rod connecting certain parts in the steering linkage of a motor vehicle

tie tack or **tie tac** a decorative pin fitted into a snap to fasten a necktie to a shirt

tie-up (tī′up′) *n.* **1** a temporary stoppage of production, traffic, etc. **2** connection or relation

tiff (tif) *n.* 〚< ?〛 **1** a slight fit of anger **2** a slight quarrel; spat

ti·ger (tī′gər) *n.* 〚< Gr *tigris*〛 a large, fierce Asian cat, having a tawny coat striped with black —**ti′ger·ish** *adj.*

tight (tīt) *adj.* 〚< OE *-thight*, strong〛 **1** so compact in structure that water, air, etc. cannot pass through **2** drawn, packed, etc. closely together **3** fixed securely; firm **4** fully stretched; taut **5** fitting so closely as to be uncomfortable **6** difficult: esp. in **a tight corner** (or **squeeze**, etc.), a difficult situation **7** difficult to get; scarce **8** [Colloq.] stingy **9** [Slang] drunk —*adv.* **1** securely **2** [Colloq.] soundly [*sleep tight*] —**sit tight** to keep one's opinion or position and wait —**tight′ly** *adv.* —**tight′ness** *n.*

tight′en *vt.*, *vi.* to make or become tight or tighter — **tight′en·er** *n.*

tight′fist′ed *adj.* stingy

tight′fit′ting *adj.* fitting very tight

tight′-lipped′ *adj.* secretive

tight′rope′ *n.* a tightly stretched rope on which acrobats perform

tights *n.pl.* a tightly fitting garment for the lower half of the body, as worn by acrobats, dancers, etc.

tight ship [Colloq.] an organization as efficient as a well-run ship

tight′wad′ *n.* 〚TIGHT + *wad*, roll of money〛 [Slang] a stingy person

ti·gress (tī′gris) *n.* a female tiger

tilde (til′də) *n.* 〚Sp < L *titulus*, a sign〛 a diacritical mark (~)

tile (tīl) *n.* 〚< L *tegula*〛 **1** a thin piece of stone, fired clay, etc. used for roofing, flooring, walls, etc. **2** a similar piece of plastic, etc. **3** a drain of earthenware pipe — *vt.* **tiled**, **til′ing** to cover with tiles

til′ing *n.* tiles collectively

till¹ (til) *prep.*, *conj.* 〚OE *til*〛 UNTIL

till² (til) *vt.*, *vi.* 〚< OE *tilian*, lit., strive for〛 to prepare (land) for raising crops, as by plowing, etc.

till³ (til) *n.* 〚< ? ME *tillen*, to draw〛 a drawer for keeping money

till′age (-ij) *n.* **1** the tilling of land **2** land that is tilled

tiller (til′ər) *n.* 〚< ML *telarium*, weaver's beam〛 a bar or handle for turning a boat's rudder

tilt (tilt) *vt.* 〚ME *tilten*, totter〛 to cause to slope; tip — *vi.* **1** to slope; incline **2** to charge (*at* an opponent) **3** to take part in a tilt — *n.* **1** a medieval contest in which two horsemen fight with lances **2** any spirited contest **3** a slope —**(at) full tilt** at full speed

tilt′-top′ *adj.* of a table with a hinged top that can be tipped vertically

tim·bale (tim′bəl) *n.* 〚Fr〛 **1** chicken, lobster, etc. in a

---

THESAURUS

tidbit *n.* morsel, mouthful, bite; see BIT 1.

tide *n.* current, flow, flux, stream, course, sluice, undercurrent, undertow, drag, whirlpool, eddy, vortex, torrent, wave, tidal wave. *Tides of the sea include the following:* low, neap, ebb, spring, full, high, flood.

tidiness *n.* neatness, spruceness, uniformity; see CLEANLINESS.

tidy *a.* orderly, trim, spruce; see NEAT 1.

tie *n.* **1** [A fastening] band, strap, bandage, zipper; see also FASTENER. **2** [A necktie] cravat, neckerchief, bow, knot, scarf, neckcloth, choker. **3** [Affection] bond, relation, kinship; see AFFECTION, LOVE 1. **4** [An equal score, or a contest having that score] deadlock, draw, even game, dead heat, drawn battle, neck-and-neck contest, even-steven*, stalemate, nose finish*, standoff, wash*.

tie *v.* **1** [To fasten] bind, make fast, attach; see FASTEN, JOIN 1. **2** [To tie a knot in] knot, make a bow, make a tie, make a knot, do up, fix a tie, make a hitch; see also sense 1. **3** [To equal] match, keep up with, parallel; see EQUAL. —**tie up 1** [To fasten]

wrap, package, secure; see CLOSE 4, ENCLOSE. **2** [To obstruct] hinder, stop, delay; see HINDER.

tied *a.* **1** [Firm] fixed, bound, made firm; see FIRM 1. **2** [Even] evenly matched, running neck and neck, in a dead heat; see ALIKE, EQUAL.

tight *a.* **1** [Firm] taut, secure, fast, bound up, close, clasped, fixed, steady, stretched thin, established, compact, strong, stable, enduring, steadfast, unyielding, unbending, set, stuck hard, hidebound, invulnerable, snug, sturdy; see also FIRM 1.—*Ant.* LOOSE, tottery, shaky. **2** [Closed] sealed, airtight, impenetrable, impermeable, impervious, watertight, hermetically sealed, padlocked, bolted, locked, fastened, shut tight, clamped, fixed, tied, snapped, swung to, tied up, nailed, spiked, slammed, obstructed, blocked, blind, shut, stopped up, plugged.—*Ant.* OPEN, penetrable, unprotected. **3** [Closefitting] pinching, shrunken, snug, uncomfortable, cramping, skintight, short, crushing, choking, smothering, cutting.—*Ant.* LOOSE, ample, wide. **4** [*Intoxicated] inebriated, drunken, tipsy; see DRUNK. **5** [*Stingy]

miserly, parsimonious, close; see STINGY. **6** [Difficult to obtain; *said especially of money*] scarce, frozen, tied up; see RARE 2. —**sit tight** do nothing, refrain from action, stay put; see WAIT 1.

tighten *v.* **1** [To make tight] compress, condense, squeeze, bind, contract, strangle, constrict, crush, cramp, pinch, grip more tightly, clench, screw down, add pressure; see also STRETCH 2.—*Ant.* LOOSEN, relax, unloose. **2** [To become tight] contract, harden, congeal, stiffen, toughen, become more disciplined.—*Ant.* SOFTEN, melt, liquefy.

tightfisted *a.* thrifty, niggardly, frugal; see STINGY.

tile *n.* baked clay, flooring, roofing; see CLAY, FLOORING.

till² *v.* cultivate, work, raise crops from; see FARM.

tilt *n.* slant, slope, slide; see INCLINATION 2.

tilt *v.* slant, tip, turn, set at an angle, lean, slope, slouch, shift, dip, sway, make oblique, deviate, turn edgewise; see also BEND.—*Ant.* STRAIGHTEN, level, bring into line.

cream sauce, baked in a drum-shaped mold **2** a pastry shell, filled with a cooked food

tim·ber (tim′bər) *n.* ⟦OE⟧ **1** wood for building houses, ships, etc. **2** a wooden beam used in building **3** trees collectively —**tim′bered** *adj.*

tim′ber·line′ *n.* the line above or beyond which trees do not grow, as on mountains or in polar regions

tim·bre (tam′bər, tim′-) *n.* ⟦< OFr, kind of drum⟧ the quality of sound that distinguishes one voice or musical instrument from another

time (tim) *n.* ⟦OE *tima*⟧ **1** every moment there has ever been or ever will be **2** a system of measuring duration /standard *time*/ **3** the period during which something exists, happens, etc. **4** [*often pl.*] a period of history; age, era, etc. **5** [*usually pl.*] prevailing conditions /*times* are good/ **6** a set period or term, as of work, confinement, etc. **7** standard rate of pay **8** rate of speed in marching, driving, etc. **9** a precise or designated instant, moment, day, etc. **10** an occasion or repeated occasion /the fifth *time* it's been on TV/ **11** *Music* a) rhythm as determined by the grouping of beats into measures b) tempo — *vt.* **timed, tim′ing 1** to arrange the time of so as to be suitable, opportune, etc. **2** to adjust, set, etc. so as to coincide in time /*time* our watches/ **3** to record the pace, speed, etc. of — *adj.* **1** having to do with time **2** set to explode, open, etc. at a given time /a *time* bomb/ **3** having to do with paying in installments —**ahead of time** early —**at the same time** however —**at times** occasionally —**do time** [Colloq.] to serve a prison term —**for the time being** temporarily —**from time to time** now and then —**in time 1** eventually **2** before it is too late **3** keeping the set tempo, pace, etc. —**make time** to travel, work, etc. rapidly —**on time 1** at the appointed time **2** for or by payment by installments —**time after time** again and again: also **time and again**

time clock a clock with a mechanism for recording the time an employee begins and ends a work period

time exposure a photograph taken by exposure of a film or plate for a relatively long period

time′-hon′ored *adj.* honored because of long existence or usage

time′keep′er *n.* one who keeps account of hours worked by employees or of the elapsed time in races, games, etc.

time′-lapse′ *adj.* of filming a slow process by exposing single frames at long intervals: the film is projected at regular speed, showing the process greatly speeded up

time′less *adj.* eternal

time′ly *adj.* **-lier, -li·est** well-timed; opportune —**time′li·ness** *n.*

time′out′ *n. Sports* any temporary suspension of play

time′piece′ *n.* any device for measuring and recording time, as a clock or watch

timer (tim′ər) *n.* a device for controlling the timing of some mechanism

times (timz) *prep.* multiplied by

time sharing 1 a system for simultaneous computer use at many remote sites **2** a system for sharing ownership of a vacation home, etc., with each joint purchaser occupying the unit at a specific time each year: also **time share**

time sheet a sheet on which are recorded the hours an employee works

time′ta′ble (-tā′bəl) *n.* a schedule of the times of arrival and departure of airplanes, trains, buses, etc.

time′worn′ *adj.* **1** worn out by long use **2** hackneyed; trite

time zone *see* STANDARD TIME

timid (tim′id) *adj.* ⟦< L *timere*, to fear⟧ lacking poise or self-confidence; shy; fearful; hesitant —**ti·mid·ity** (tə mid′ə tē) *n.* —**tim′idly** *adv.*

tim·ing (tim′iŋ) *n.* the regulation of time or speed to improve performance

tim·or·ous (tim′ər es) *adj.* ⟦< L *timor*, fear⟧ full of fear; timid; afraid

tim·o·thy (tim′ə thē) *n.* ⟦after a *Timothy* Hanson, c. 1720⟧ a perennial grass with dense spikes, grown for hay

tim·pa·ni (tim′pə nē) *n.pl., sing.* **-pano′** (-nō′) ⟦It: see TYMPANUM⟧ [*often with sing. v.*] kettledrums; esp., a set of them played by one performer —**tim′pa·nist** *n.*

tin (tin) *n.* ⟦OE⟧ **1** a soft, silver-white, metallic chemical element **2** TIN PLATE **3** a) a pan, box, etc. made of tin plate b) [Chiefly Brit., etc.] CAN² (n. 2, 3) Variously used to connote cheapness, etc. of something — *vt.* **tinned, tin′ning 1** to plate with tin **2** [Chiefly Brit., etc.] CAN² (*vt.* 1)

tin can CAN² (*n.* 2)

tinc·ture (tiŋk′chər) *n.* ⟦< L *tingere*, to dye⟧ **1** a light color; tinge **2** a slight trace **3** a medicinal substance in an alcoholic solution — *vt.* **-tured, -tur·ing** to tinge

tin·der (tin′dər) *n.* ⟦OE *tynder*⟧ any dry, easily flammable material

tin′der·box′ *n.* **1** [Obs.] a box to hold tinder **2** a highly flammable building, etc. **3** a potential source of war, rebellion, etc.

tine (tin) *n.* ⟦OE *tind*⟧ a slender, projecting point; prong /fork *tines*/

tin′foil′ *n.* a thin sheet of tin or a tin alloy used as wrapping

tinge (tinj) *n.* ⟦see TINT⟧ **1** a slight coloring; tint **2** a slight trace, flavor, etc. — *vt.* **tinged, tinge′ing** or **ting′ing** to give a tinge of to

tin·gle (tiŋ′gal) *vi.* **-gled, -gling** ⟦var. of TINKLE⟧ to have a prickling or stinging feeling, as from cold, excitement, etc. —*n.* this feeling —**tin′gly, -gli·er, -gli·est,** *adj.*

tin·ker (tiŋk′ər) *n.* ⟦ME *tinkere*⟧ **1** one who mends pots, pans, etc. **2** a bungler — *vt.* **1** to attempt clumsily to mend something **2** to putter —**tin′kerer** *n.*

tin·kle (tiŋk′əl) *vi.* **-kled, -kling** ⟦echoic⟧ to make a

THESAURUS

timber *n.* **1** [Standing trees] wood, lumber, timberland; see FOREST. **2** [A beam] stake, pole, club; see BEAM 1, LUMBER.

time *n.* **1** [Duration] continuance, lastingness, extent, past, present, future, infinity, space-time; see also TODAY. *Units of measuring time include the following:* second, minute, hour, day, term, millisecond, week, month, year, decade, generation, lifetime, century, millennium, eon. **2** [A point in time] incident, event, occurrence, occasion, time and tide, instant, term, season, tide, course, sequence, point, generation. **3** [A period of time] season, era, interval; see AGE 3. **4** [Experience] background, living, participation; see EXPERIENCE. **5** [Leisure] opportunity, free moment, chance; see FREEDOM 2. **6** [Circumstances; *usually plural; used with "the"*] condition, the present, nowadays; see CIRCUMSTANCE 1, CIRCUMSTANCES 2. **7** [A measure of speed] tempo, rate, meter; see BEAT 2. —**ahead of time** ahead of schedule, fast, earlier than expected; see EARLY 2. —**at one time** simultaneously, concurrently, at once; see TOGETHER 2. —**at the same time** simultaneously, concurrently, at once; see TOGETHER 2. —**at**

times occasionally, sometimes, once in a while; see SELDOM. —**behind the times** out of date, archaic, antediluvian; see OLD-FASHIONED. —**behind time** tardy, delayed, coming later; see LATE 1. —**between times** now and then, occasionally, sometimes; see SELDOM. —**do time*** serve a prison term, go to jail, be imprisoned; see SERVE TIME. —**for the time being** for the present, for now, under consideration; see TEMPORARILY. —**from time to time** occasionally, sometimes, once in a while; see FREQUENTLY. —**in due time** eventually, at an appropriate time, in the natural course of events; see FINALLY 2, ULTIMATELY. —**in no time** instantly, rapidly, without delay; see QUICKLY, SOON. —**in time** eventually, after the proper time, inevitably; see FINALLY 2. —**lose time** go too slow, tarry, cause a delay; see DELAY. —**make time** gain time, act hastily, hasten; see HURRY 1. —**many a time** often, regularly, consistently; see FREQUENTLY. —**on time 1** at the appointed time, punctually, correct; see PUNCTUAL. **2** by credit, in installments, on account; see UNPAID 1. —**out of time** out of pace, unreasonable, improper; see UNTIMELY. —**pass the time of day**

exchange greetings, chat, converse; see GREET. —**serve time** stand committed, serve a jail sentence, be incarcerated, be in jail, pay one's debt to society, go to jail, do time*, be in stir*, be in the joint*, be sent up*. —**waste time** malinger, dawdle, drift; see LOAF.

time *v.* register, distance, clock, measure time; see also MEASURE 1.

timely *a.* opportune, seasonable, in good time, fitting the times, suitable, appropriate, convenient, propitious, well-timed, modern, up-to-date, newsworthy.—*Ant.* UNTIMELY, ill-timed, inappropriate.

timepiece *n.* timekeeper, chronometer, sundial; see CLOCK, WATCH 1.

timid *a.* **1** [Irresolute] indecisive, vacillating, wavering; see IRRESPONSIBLE. **2** [Cowardly] fainthearted, spiritless, weak; see AFRAID, COWARDLY. **3** [Reticent] shy, withdrawn, modest; see HUMBLE 1.

tinge *n.* tint, shade, hint; see TRACE 1, TINT.

tingle *v.* shiver, prickle, sting, itch, creep, grow excited, get goose pimples all over*.

tinker *v.* try to mend, play with, take apart; see REPAIR.

series of light sounds as of a small bell —*vt.* to cause to tinkle —*n.* a tinkling sound

tin·ny (tin'ē) *adj.* **-nier, -ni·est** 1 of tin 2 like tin, as in appearance, sound, value, etc. —**tin'ni·ness** *n.*

tin plate thin sheets of iron or steel plated with tin

tin·sel (tin'səl) *n.* [< L *scintilla*, a spark] 1 thin strips of tin, metal foil, etc., as for decoration 2 something of little worth that glitters

tin·smith (tin'smith') *n.* one who works in tin or tin plate

tint (tint) *n.* [< L *tingere*, to dye] 1 a delicate color 2 a gradation of a color; shade 3 a hair dye —*vt.* to give a tint to

tin·tin·nabu·la·tion (tin'ti nab'yōō lā'shən) *n.* [< L *tin-tinnabulum*, little bell] the ringing sound of bells

tin·type (tin'tīp') *n.* an old kind of photograph taken directly as a positive print on a treated plate of tin or iron

tiny (tī'nē) *adj.* **-nier, -ni·est** [< ME *tine*, *n.*, a little] very small

-tion (shən) [< Fr < L] *suffix* 1 the act of _____ing 2 the state of being _____ed 3 the thing that is _____ed

-tious (shəs) *suffix* of, having, or characterized by

tip¹ (tip) *n.* [ME *tippe*] 1 the point or end of something 2 something attached to the end, as a cap, etc. —*vt.* **tipped, tip'ping** 1 to form a tip on 2 to cover the tip of

tip² (tip) *vt.* **tipped, tip'ping** [< ?] 1 to strike lightly and sharply 2 to give a gratuity to (a waiter, etc.) 3 [Colloq.] to give secret information to: often with *off* —*vi.* to give a tip or tips —*n.* 1 a light, sharp blow 2 a piece of confidential information 3 a hint, warning, etc. 4 a gratuity —**tip one's hand** [Slang] to reveal a secret, one's plans, etc., often without meaning to —**tip'per** *n.*

tip³ (tip) *vt., vi.* **tipped, tip'ping** [ME *tipen*] 1 to overturn or upset: often with *over* 2 to tilt or slant —*n.* a tilt; slant

tip'-off' *n.* a tip; confidential disclosure, hint, or warning

tip·ple (tip'əl) *vt., vi.* **-pled, -pling** [< ?] to drink (alcoholic liquor) habitually —**tip'pler** *n.*

tip·ster (tip'stər) *n.* [Colloq.] one who sells tips, as on horse races

tipsy (tip'sē) *adj.* **-sier, -si·est** 1 that tips easily; not steady 2 somewhat drunk —**tip'sily** *adv.*

tip'toe' *n.* the tip of a toe —*vi.* **-toed', -toe'ing** to walk carefully on one's tiptoes —**on tiptoe** 1 on one's tiptoes 2 eager(ly) 3 silently

tip'top' *n.* [TIP¹ + TOP¹] the highest point —*adj., adv.* 1 at the highest point 2 [Colloq.] at the highest point of excellence, health, etc.

ti·rade (tī'rād, tī rād') *n.* [< It *tirare*, to fire] a long, vehement speech or denunciation; harangue

tire¹ (tīr) *vt., vi.* **tired, tir'ing** [OE *tiorian*] to make or become weary, exhausted, bored, etc.

tire² (tīr) *n.* [ME *tyre*] 1 a hoop of iron or rubber around the wheel of a vehicle 2 an inflatable, vulcanized rubber or synthetic casing sealed to a wheel rim by air pressure

tired (tī'ərd) *adj.* 1 weary 2 hackneyed —**tired'ly** *adv.* —**tired'ness** *n.*

tire'less *adj.* that does not become tired —**tire'lessly** *adv.* —**tire'less·ness** *n.*

tire'some (-səm) *adj.* tiring; boring —**tire'somely** *adv.* —**tire'some·ness** *n.*

'tis (tiz) [Old Poet.] it is

tis·sue (tish'ōō) *n.* [< L *texere*, to weave] 1 light, thin cloth 2 an interwoven mass; mesh; web 3 a piece of soft, absorbent paper, used as a disposable handkerchief, etc. 4 TISSUE PAPER 5 the substance of an organic body, consisting of cells and intercellular material

tissue paper very thin, unsized paper, as for wrapping things, etc.

tit¹ (tit) *n.* a titmouse

tit² (tit) *n.* [OE] 1 NIPPLE (sense 1) 2 a breast: in this sense now vulgar

ti·tan (tīt'n) *n.* [< Gr *Titan*, a giant deity] any person or thing of great size or power

ti·tanic (tī tan'ik) *adj.* of great size, strength, or power

ti·ta·nium (tī tā'nē əm, ti-) *n.* [see TITAN] a silvery or dark-gray, metallic chemical element used as a cleaning and deoxidizing agent in molten steel, etc.

tit for tat [var. of earlier *tip for tap*] blow for blow

tithe (tīth) *n.* [OE *teothe*, a tenth] a tenth of one's income paid to a church —*vt., vi.* **tithed, tith'ing** to pay a tithe of (one's income, etc.) —**tith'er** *adj.*

ti·tian (tish'ən) *n.* [after *Titian* (c. 1490-1576), Venetian painter] reddish gold; auburn

tit·il·late (tit''l āt') *vt.* **-lat'ed, -lat'ing** [< L *titillare*, to tickle] to excite pleasurably —**tit'il·la'tion** *n.*

ti·tle (tīt''l) *n.* [< L *titulus*] 1 the name of a book, poem, picture, etc. 2 an epithet 3 an appellation indicating one's rank, profession, etc. 4 a claim 5 *Law* a) a right to ownership, esp. of real estate b) a deed 6 *Film, TV* a subtitle, credit, etc. 7 in sports and other competition, a championship —*vt.* **-tled, -tling** to give a title to

ti·tled (tīt''ld) *adj.* having a title, esp. of nobility

ti'tle·hold'er *n.* the holder of a title; specif., the champion in some sport

title role (or **part** or **character**) the character in a play, film, etc. whose name is used as or in its title

titlist (tīt''l ist) *n.* a champion in some sport

tit·mouse (tit'mous') *n., pl.* **-mice** (-mīs') [ME *titemose*] a small bird with ashy-gray feathers

tit·ter (tit'ər) *vi.* [echoic] to laugh in a half-suppressed way; giggle —*n.* a tittering; giggle

tit·tle (tit''l) *n.* [ME *title*] a very small particle; jot

titu·lar (tich'ōō lər, tich'ə-) *adj.* [see TITLE] 1 of a title 2 having a title 3 in name only *[a titular* sovereign*]*

tizzy (tiz'ē) *n., pl.* **-zies** [< ?] [Colloq.] a state of frenzied excitement

TLC tender, loving care

TM trademark

tn. ton(s)

TNT (tē'en'tē') *n.* [*t(ri)n(itro)t(oluene)*] a high explosive used for blasting, etc.

to (tōō, too, tə) *prep.* [OE] 1 toward *[turn to* the left*]* 2 so as to reach *[she went to* Boston*]* 3 as far as *[wet to* the

---

THESAURUS

tint *n.* tinge, hue, shade, color value, cast, flush, dye, tinct, taint, glow, pastel color, luminous color, pale hue, tone, tincture, dash, touch, color tone, coloration, pigmentation, ground color, complexion; see also COLOR.

tinted *a.* tinged, painted, touched up; see COLORED.

tiny *a.* small, miniature, diminutive; see LITTLE 1.

tip¹,² *n.* 1 [The point] apex, peak, top; see POINT 2. 2 [A gratuity] reward, gift, compensation, fee, small change, money, handout; see also PAY 2. 3 [*A bit of information] hint, clue, warning; see KNOWLEDGE 1, NEWS 1.

tip³ *v.* slant, incline, shift; see BEND, LEAN 1, TILT.

tiptop *a.* superior, prime, choice; see BEST, EXCELLENT.

tire¹ *v.* 1 [To become exhausted] grow weary, break down, droop, flag, pall, faint, drop, puff, sink, yawn, collapse, give out, wilt, go stale, poop out*, burn out*.—*Ant.* REST, awake, relax. 2 [To make a person exhausted] tax, overtax, harass, fatigue, exhaust, overwork, strain,

overstrain, overburden, depress, dispirit, pain, vex, worry, distress, deject, dishearten, wear out, run a person ragged, do in*.

tire² *n.* casing, tire and tube, one of a set; see WHEEL 1. *Terms for types of tires include the following:* tubeless, belted, radial, snow, mud, puncture-proof, recapped, synthetic, low-pressure, natural rubber, solid rubber, pneumatic, oversize, airplane, motorcycle, bicycle, recap.

tired *a.* fatigued, weary, run-down, exhausted, overworked, overtaxed, wearied, worn, spent, wasted, worn-out, drooping, distressed, unmanned, drowsy, droopy, sleepy, haggard, faint, prostrated, broken-down, drained, consumed, empty, collapsing, all in*, finished, stale, fagged, dog-tired*, dead on one's feet*, pooped*, done in*, done for*, worn to a frazzle*, played out*, tuckered out*, fed up*.—*Ant.* ACTIVE, lively, energetic.

tireless *a.* unwearied, unwearying, untiring; see ACTIVE.

tiresome *a.* irksome, wearying, monotonous; see DULL 4.

tissue *n.* 1 [A network] web, mesh, filigree; see NETWORK 2. 2 [Thin fabric] gauze, gossamer, lace; see VEIL, WEB. 3 [Protective layer, especially in living organisms] film, membrane, intercellular substance; see MUSCLE.

title *n.* 1 [A designation] indication, inscription, sign; see NAME 1. 2 [Ownership or evidence of ownship] right, claim, license; see OWNERSHIP. 3 [Mark of rank or dignity] commission, decoration, medal, ribbon, coat of arms, crest, order, authority, privilege, degree; see also EMBLEM. *Titles include the following:* Sir, Doctor, Mr., Ms., Mrs., Miss, Reverend, Monsignor, Dame, King, Prince, Baron, Viscount, Earl, Marquis, Marquise, Duke, Grand Duke, Knight, Count, Sultan, Queen, Duchess, Lady, Princess, Countess, Monsieur, Madame, Mademoiselle, Don, Doña, Herr, Frau, Fräulein, General, Colonel, Major, Captain, Lieutenant, Admiral, Commander, Ensign, President, Vice-president, Secretary, Speaker, Governor, Mayor, Representative, Senator.

to *prep.* 1 [In the direction of]

skin/ **4** into a condition of /a rise *to* fame/ **5** on, onto, at, etc. /tied *to* a post/ **6** *a)* until /from noon *to* night/ *b)* before /the time is ten *to* six/ **7** for the purpose of /he came *to* my aid/ **8** in regard to /open *to* attack/ **9** so as to produce /torn *to* bits/ **10** along with /add this *to* the rest/ **11** belonging with /a key *to* the house/ **12** as compared with /a score of 10 *to* 0/ **13** in agreement with /not *to* my taste/ **14** constituting /four quarts *to* a gallon/ **15** with (a specified person or thing) as the recipient of the action /give it *to* me/ **16** in honor of /a toast *to* you/ *To* is also a sign of the infinitive (Ex.: I want *to* stay) **—adv. 1** forward /wrong side *to*/ **2** shut; closed /pull the door *to*/ **3** into a state of consciousness /the boxer came *to*/ **4** at hand /we were close *to* when it happened/ **—to and fro** first in one direction and then in the opposite

toad (tōd) *n.* ⟦OE *tadde*⟧ a froglike animal that lives on moist land

toad′stool′ (-stōōl′) *n.* a mushroom, esp. any poisonous mushroom

toady (tōd′ē) *n.*, *pl.* **-ies** ⟦short for *toadeater*, quack doctor's assistant⟧ a servile flatterer **—vt., vi. -ied, -y′ing** to be a toady (to)

toast[1] (tōst) *vt.* ⟦< L *torrere*, parch⟧ **1** to brown the surface of (bread, etc.) by heating **2** to warm thoroughly **—vi.** to become toasted **—n.** sliced bread made brown and crisp by heat **—toast′er** *n.*

toast[2] (tōst) *n.* ⟦from the use of toasted spiced bread to flavor the wine⟧ **1** a person, thing, idea, etc. in honor of which persons raise their glasses and drink **2** a drink, or a proposal to drink, in honor of some person, etc. **—vt., vi.** to propose or drink a toast (to)

toast′mas′ter *n.* the person at a banquet who proposes toasts, introduces after-dinner speakers, etc.

to·bac·co (tə bak′ō) *n.*, *pl.* **-cos** ⟦Sp *tabaco* < ?⟧ **1** a plant with large leaves that are prepared for smoking, chewing, etc. **2** cigars, cigarettes, snuff, etc.

to·bac·co·nist (tə bak′ə nist) *n.* [Chiefly Brit., etc.] a dealer in tobacco

to·bog·gan (tə bäg′ən) *n.* ⟦< AmInd⟧ a long, flat sled without runners, for coasting downhill **—vi. 1** to coast on a toboggan **2** to decline rapidly

toc·sin (täk′sin) *n.* ⟦Fr < Prov *toc*, a stroke + *senh*, a bell⟧ an alarm bell

to·day (tə dā′) *adv.* ⟦OE *to dæg*⟧ **1** on or during the present day **2** in the present time **—n. 1** the present day **2** the present time

tod·dle (täd′l) *vi.* **-dled, -dling** ⟦? < *totter*⟧ to walk with short, uncertain steps, as a child **—tod′dler** *n.*

toddy (täd′ē) *n.*, *pl.* **-dies** ⟦< Hindi⟧ a drink of whiskey, etc. mixed with hot water, sugar, etc. Also **hot toddy**

to-do (tə dōō′) *n.*, *pl.* **-dos** [Colloq.] a commotion; stir; fuss

toe (tō) *n.* ⟦OE *ta*⟧ **1** *a)* any of the digits of the foot *b)* the forepart of the foot **2** anything like a toe in location, shape, or use **—vt. toed, toe′ing** to touch, kick, etc. with the toes **—vi.** to stand, walk, etc. with the toes in a specified position /he *toes* in/ **—on one's toes** [Colloq.] alert **—toe the line** (or **mark**) to follow orders, rules, etc. strictly

toed (tōd) *adj.* having (a specified kind or number of) toes: usually in hyphenated compounds /two-*toed*/

toe dance a dance performed on the tips of the toes, as in ballet **—toe′-dance′, -danced′, -danc′ing, vi. —toe′-danc′er** *n.*

toe′hold′ *n.* **1** a small space to support the toe in climbing, etc. **2** a slight footing or advantage

toe′nail′ *n.* the nail of a toe

tof·fee or **toffy** (tôf′ē, täf′-) *n.* ⟦< TAFFY⟧ a hard, chewy candy, a kind of taffy

tofu (tō′fōō) *n.* a Japanese cheeselike food made from soybeans

toga (tō′gə) *n.*, *pl.* **-gas** or **-gae** (-jē, -gē) ⟦L < *tegere*, to cover⟧ in ancient Rome, a loose outer garment worn in public by citizens

to·geth·er (too geth′ər, tə-) *adv.* ⟦< OE *to*, to + *gædre*, together⟧ **1** in or into one group, place, etc. /we ate *together*/ **2** in or into contact, union, etc. /the cars skidded *together*/ **3** considered collectively /he lost more than all of us *together*/ **4** at the same time /shots fired *together*/ **5** in succession /sulking for three whole days *together*/ **6** in or into agreement, cooperation, etc. /to get *together* on a deal/ **—adj.** [Slang] having an integrated personality

to·geth·er·ness *n.* the spending of much time together, as by family members, when regarded as resulting in a more unified, stable relationship

tog·gle switch (täg′əl) a switch consisting of a lever moved back and forth to open or close an electric circuit

togs (tägz, tôgz) *n.pl.* ⟦ult. < L *toga*, toga⟧ [Colloq.] clothes

toil (toil) *vi.* ⟦< L *tudiculare*, to stir about⟧ **1** to work hard and continuously **2** to proceed laboriously **—n.** hard, tiring work **—toil′er** *n.*

toi·let (toi′lit) *n.* ⟦< OFr *toile*, cloth < L *tela*, a web⟧ **1** the act of dressing or grooming oneself **2** dress; attire **3** *a)* a room with a bowl-shaped fixture for defecation or urination *b)* such a fixture

toilet paper (or **tissue**) soft paper for cleaning oneself after evacuation

toi′letry (-lə trē) *n.*, *pl.* **-ries** soap, lotion, etc. used in grooming oneself

toi·lette (twä let′, toi-) *n.* ⟦Fr⟧ **1** the process of grooming oneself **2** dress; attire

toilet water a lightly scented liquid with a high alcohol content, applied to the skin after bathing, etc.

toils (toilz) *n.pl.* ⟦< L *tela*, web⟧ any snare suggestive of a net

toil′some (toil′səm) *adj.* laborious

toke (tōk) *n.* ⟦? < fol.⟧ [Slang] a puff on a cigarette, esp. one of marijuana or hashish **—vi. toked, tok′ing** [Slang] to take such a puff

to·ken (tō′kən) *n.* ⟦OE *tacn*⟧ **1** a sign, indication, symbol, etc. /a *token* of one's affection/ **2** a keepsake **3** a metal disk to be used in place of currency, for transportation fares, etc. **—adj. 1** symbolic **2** merely simulated; of no real account /*token* resistance/ **—by the same token** following from this

to′ken·ism′ (-iz′əm) *n.* the making of small, often merely formal concessions to a demand, etc.; specif., token integration of blacks, as in jobs, etc.

told (tōld) *vt., vi.* *pt.* & *pp.* of TELL **—all told** all (being) counted

tole (tōl) *n.* ⟦Fr *tôle*, sheet iron⟧ a type of lacquered or

---

THESAURUS

toward, via, into, facing, through, directed toward, traveling to, along the line of. **2** [Indicating position] over, upon, in front of; see ON 1. **3** [Until] till, up to, stopping at; see UNTIL. **4** [So that] in order to, intending to, that one may, for the purpose of. **5** [Indicating degree] up to, down to, as far as, in that degree, to this extent. **6** [Indicating result] becoming, until, back, ending with.

to and fro *a.* seesaw, zigzag, back and forth, backwards and forwards, in and out, up and down, from side to side, from pillar to post, off and on, round and round, forward and back.

toast[1,2] *n.* **1** [A sentiment or person drunk to] pledge, salute, acknowledgment; see HONOR 1. *Invitations for toasts include the following:* here's to you, good luck, lest we forget, your health, *prosit* (German), *skoal* (Scandinavian), *salud* (Spanish), *a votre sante* (French), down the hatch*, here's how, mud in your eye, here's

looking at you. **2** [Browned bread] *Varieties of toast include the following:* Melba, French, cinnamon; see also BREAD.

toast[1,2] *v.* **1** [To honor by drinking liquor] drink to, compliment, propose a toast; see DRINK 2, PRAISE 1. **2** [To brown bread] put in a toaster, heat, crisp; see COOK.

tobacco *n. Forms of tobacco include the following:* nicotine, cigarette, cigar, chewing tobacco, pipe tobacco, snuff, stogie, weed*.

today *n.* this day, the present, our time, this moment; see also NOW 1.

to-do *n.* commotion, stir, fuss; see DISORDER, FIGHT 1.

toe *n.* digit, front of the foot, tip of a shoe; see FOOT 2. **—on one's toes*** alert, aware, attentive; see CAREFUL. **—step** (or **tread**) **on someone's toes** annoy, offend, disturb; see ANGER.

together *a.* **1** [Jointly] collectively,

unitedly, commonly; see sense 2. **2** [Simultaneously] at the same time, concurrently, coincidentally, contemporaneously, at once, in connection with, at a blow, in unison, at one jump.

togs* *n.* clothing, outfit, attire; see CLOTHES.

toil *n.* labor, occupation, drudgery; see WORK 2.

toil *v.* sweat, labor, slave; see WORK.

toilet *n.* water closet, lavatory, washroom, rest room, men's room, women's room, powder room, gentlemen's room, ladies' room, comfort station, bathroom, bath, little boy's room*, little girl's room*, head*, potty*, can*, pot*, john*.

token *n.* mark, favor, sample; see GIFT 1. **—by the same token** following from this, similarly, thus; see THEREFORE. **—in token of** evidence of, by way of, as a gesture; see BY 2.

told *a.* recounted, recorded, set down,

‾enameled metalware, usually dark-green, ivory, or black, used for lamps, trays, etc.

tol·er·able (täl′ər ə bəl) *adj.* 1 endurable 2 fairly good; passable —**tol′er·ably** *adv.*

tol′er·ance (-əns) *n.* 1 a being tolerant of others' views, beliefs, practices, etc. 2 the amount of variation allowed from a standard 3 *Med.* the ability to resist the effects of a drug, poison, etc.

tol′er·ant *adj.* having or showing tolerance of others' beliefs, etc.

tol·er·ate (täl′ər āt′) *vt.* -at′ed, -at′ing 〖< L *tolerare*, to bear〗 1 to allow 2 to respect (others' beliefs, practices, etc.) without sharing them 3 to put up with 4 *Med.* to have tolerance for —**tol′era′tion** *n.*

toll[1] (tōl) *n.* 〖ult. < Gr *telos*, tax〗 1 a tax or charge for a privilege, as for the use of a bridge 2 a charge for service, as for a long-distance telephone call 3 the number lost, etc. *[the tornado took a heavy toll of lives]*

toll[2] (tōl) *vt.* 〖ME *tollen*, to pull〗 1 to ring (a church bell, etc.) with slow, regular strokes 2 to announce, summon, etc. by this — *vi.* to ring slowly: said of a bell — *n.* the sound of a bell tolling

toll′booth′ *n.* a booth at which a toll is collected, as before entering a toll road

toll′gate′ *n.* a gate for stopping travel at a point where a toll is collected

toll road a road on which a toll must be paid Also **toll′way′** (-wā′) *n.*

tolu·ene (täl′y○○ ēn′) *n.* 〖Sp *tolu*, after *Tolú*, seaport in Colombia + (BENZ)ENE〗 a colorless, poisonous liquid obtained from coal tar or petroleum, and used in making dyes, explosives, etc.

tom (täm) *adj.* 〖after the name *Tom*〗 male *[a tomcat, a tom turkey]*

toma·hawk (täm′ə hôk′) *n.* 〖< AmInd〗 a light ax used by North American Indians as a tool and a weapon

to·mato (tə māt′ō, -mät′ō) *n., pl.* -toes 〖< AmInd (Mexico)〗 1 a red or yellowish fruit with a juicy pulp, used as a vegetable 2 the plant it grows on

tomb (t○○m) *n.* 〖< Gr *tymbos*〗 a vault or grave for the dead

tom·boy (täm′boi′) *n.* a girl who behaves like a boisterous boy

tomb·stone (t○○m′stōn′) *n.* a stone or monument marking a tomb or grave

tom·cat (täm′kat′) *n.* a male cat

tome (tōm) *n.* 〖< Gr *tomos*, piece cut off〗 a book, esp. a large one

tom·fool·ery (täm′f○○l′ər ē) *n., pl.* -ies foolish behavior; silliness

tommy gun *[sometimes* T- g-*]* a submachine gun

to·mor·row (tə mär′ō, -môr′-) *adv.* 〖OE *to morgen*〗 on the day after today — *n.* the day after today

tom·tit (täm tit′, täm′tit′) *n.* [Chiefly Brit., etc.] a titmouse or other small bird

tom-tom (täm′täm′) *n.* 〖Hindi *ṭamṭam*〗 a primitive drum, usually beaten with the hands

-tomy (tə mē) 〖< Gr *tomē*, a cutting〗 *combining form* a surgical operation

ton (tun) *n.* 〖var. of TUN〗 1 a unit of weight equal to 2,000 pounds 2 in Great Britain, a unit of weight equal to 2,240 pounds

tonal (tō′nəl) *adj.* of a tone —**ton′ally** *adv.*

to·nal·i·ty (tō nal′ə tē) *n., pl.* -ties *Music* 1 KEY[1] (*n.* 6) 2 tonal character, as determined by the relationship of the tones to the keynote

tone (tōn) *n.* 〖< Gr *teinein*, to stretch〗 1 a vocal or musical sound, or its quality as to pitch, intensity, etc. 2 a manner of expression showing a certain attitude *[a friendly tone]* 3 style, character, spirit, etc. 4 elegant style 5 a quality of color; shade 6 normal, healthy condition of a muscle, organ, etc. 7 *Music a)* a sound of distinct pitch *b)* any of the full intervals of a diatonic scale — *vt.* **toned, ton′ing** to give a tone to —**tone down** (or **up**) to give a less (or more) intense tone to —**tone′less** *adj.*

tone′arm′ *n.* the pivoted arm beside a phonograph turntable, holding the CARTRIDGE (*n.* 2)

tone′-deaf′ *adj.* not able to distinguish differences in musical pitch

toner (tōn′ər) *n.* 1 the ink powder mixture used to form images in xerography 2 a facial cleanser

tone row (or **series**) see TWELVE-TONE

tong (tôŋ, täŋ) *n.* 〖Mandarin *t'ang*, meeting place〗 a Chinese association, society, etc.

tongs (tôŋz, täŋz) *n.pl.* 〖OE *tange*〗 *[sometimes with sing. v.]* a device for seizing or lifting objects, having two long arms pivoted or hinged together

tongue (tuŋ) *n.* 〖OE *tunge*〗 1 the movable, muscular structure in the mouth, used in eating, tasting, and (in humans) speaking 2 talk; speech 3 the act, power, or manner of speaking 4 a language or dialect 5 something like a tongue in shape, position, use, etc., as the flap under the laces of a shoe —**hold one's tongue** to keep from speaking —**speak in tongues** to utter unintelligible sounds, as while in a religious trance —**tongue′less** *adj.*

tongue-and-groove joint (tuŋ′ 'n gr○○v′) a kind of joint in which a projection on one board fits into a groove in another

tongue′-lash′ing *n.* [Colloq.] a harsh scolding or reproving; reprimand

tongue′-tied′ *adj.* speechless from amazement, embarrassment, etc.

tongue twister a phrase or sentence hard to speak fast (Ex: six sick sheiks)

tonic (tän′ik) *adj.* 〖see TONE〗 1 of or producing good muscular tone 2 *Music* designating or based on a keynote — *n.* 1 anything that invigorates, as a drug or medicine 2 a quinine-flavored beverage served with gin, vodka, etc. 3 *Music* a keynote

to·night (tə nīt′, too-, tōō-) *adv.* 〖OE *to niht*〗 on or during the present or coming night — *n.* the present or coming night

ton·nage (tun′ij) *n.* 1 the total amount of shipping of a country or port, calculated in tons 2 the carrying capacity of a ship, calculated in tons

ton·sil (tän′səl) *n.* 〖L *tonsillae*, pl.〗 either of a pair of oval masses of tissue at the back of the mouth

---

THESAURUS

reported, known, made known, chronicled, revealed, exposed, said, published, printed, announced, released, described, stated, set forth, included in the official statement, made public property, become common knowledge, related, depicted, enunciated, pronounced, given out, handed down, telegraphed, broadcast, telecast, confessed, admitted, well-known, discovered; see also SPOKEN.—*Ant.* SECRET, concealed, unknown. —**all told** in all, in toto, on the whole; see ALTOGETHER.

tolerable *a.* endurable, sufferable, sustainable; see BEARABLE.

tolerance *n.* 1 [Open-mindedness] concession, liberality, permission, forbearance, indulgence, mercy, compassion, license, sufferance, grace, understanding, sensitivity, charity, benevolence, humanity, endurance, altruism, patience, good will; see also KINDNESS 1. 2 [Saturation point] threshold, tolerance level, end; see LIMIT 2.

tolerant *a.* understanding, receptive, sophisticated; see LIBERAL, PATIENT 1.

tolerate *v.* 1 [To allow] permit, consent to, put up with; see ALLOW. 2 [To endure] bear, undergo, abide; see ENDURE 2.

toll[1] *n.* 1 [Charges] duty, fee, customs, exaction, tollage; see also PRICE, TAX. 2 [Loss] casualties, deaths, losses; see DAMAGE 2.

tomb *n.* vault, crypt, mausoleum; see GRAVE.

tombstone *n.* monument, gravestone, headstone, footstone, stone, marker, cross, funerary statue.

tomorrow *n.* the morrow, next day in the course of time, the future, *mañana* (Spanish); see also DAY 1.

ton *n.* two thousand pounds, short ton, metric ton, long ton, shipping ton, displacement ton, measurement ton, freight ton; see also WEIGHT 1, 2.

tone *n.* 1 [A musical sound] pitch, timbre, resonance; see SOUND 2. 2 [Quality] nature, trend, temper; see CHARACTER 1. 3 [Manner] expression, condition, aspect; see MOOD 1.

4 [A degree of color] hue, tint, coloration; see COLOR.

tone down *v.* subdue, moderate, temper; see SOFTEN.

tongs *n.* pinchers, pliers, tweezers; see UTENSILS.

tongue *n.* 1 [The movable muscle in the mouth] organ of taste, organ of speech, lingua; see MUSCLE, ORGAN 2. *Parts of the tongue used in speech are:* tip, apex, front, center, back. 2 [Speech] speech, utterance, discourse; see LANGUAGE 1. —**hold one's tongue** refrain from speaking, hold back, keep silent; see RESTRAIN. —**on the tip of someone's tongue** forgotten, not quite remembered, not readily recalled; see FAMILIAR, FORGOTTEN.

tongue-tied *a.* 1 [Mute] silent, speechless, voiceless; see DUMB 1, MUTE 1. 2 [Inarticulate] reticent, nervous, inarticulate; see RESERVED 3.

tonight *n.* this evening, this p.m., later; see NIGHT 1.

ton·sil·lec·tomy (tän′sə lek′tə mē) *n., pl.* **-mies** ⟦prec. + -ECTOMY⟧ the surgical removal of the tonsils

ton·sil·li·tis (-lī′tis) *n.* ⟦ModL < L *tonsillae*, tonsils + -ITIS⟧ inflammation of the tonsils

ton·so·rial (tän sôr′ē əl) *adj.* ⟦see fol.⟧ of a barber or barbering: often humorous *[a tonsorial artist]*

ton·sure (tän′shər) *n.* ⟦< L *tondere*, to clip⟧ **1** a clipping off or shaving off of part or all of the hair of the head, done as a sign of entrance into the clerical or monastic state **2** the head area so clipped or shaved

tony (tōn′ē) *adj.* **-i·er, -i·est** [Slang] very elegant

too (tōō) *adv.* ⟦stressed form of TO⟧ **1** in addition; also **2** more than enough *[the hat is too big]* **3** extremely; very *[it was just too delicious!]*

took (took) *vt., vi. pt. of* TAKE

tool (tōōl) *n.* ⟦OE *tol*⟧ **1** any hand implement, instrument, etc. used for some work **2** any similar instrument that is the working part of a machine, as a drill **3** anything that serves as a means **4** a stooge — *vt.* **1** to form or shape with a tool **2** to impress designs on (leather, etc.) with a tool — *vi.* to install the tools, equipment, etc. needed: often with *up*

toot (tōōt) *vi., vt.* ⟦echoic⟧ to sound (a horn, whistle, etc.) in short blasts — *n.* a short blast of a horn, whistle, etc.

tooth (tōōth) *n., pl.* **teeth** (tēth) ⟦OE *toth*⟧ **1** any of the hard, bonelike structures in the jaws, used for biting, chewing, etc. **2** a toothlike part, as on a saw, comb, gearwheel, etc.; tine, prong, cog, etc. **3** *[pl.]* effective means of enforcing *[a law with teeth]* —**in the teeth of 1** directly against **2** defying —**tooth and nail** with all one's strength —**toothed** *adj.* —**tooth′less** *adj.*

tooth′ache′ *n.* pain in a tooth

tooth′brush′ *n.* a small brush for cleaning the teeth

tooth′paste′ *n.* a paste used for brushing the teeth

tooth′pick′ *n.* a very small, pointed stick for getting bits of food free from between the teeth

tooth powder *n.* like toothpaste

tooth′some (-səm) *adj.* tasty; savory

tooth′y *adj.* **-i·er, -i·est** having or exposing teeth that show prominently *[a toothy smile]* —**tooth′i·ly** *adv.*

top[1] (täp) *n.* ⟦OE⟧ **1** the head or crown **2** the highest point or surface of anything **3** the part of a plant above ground **4** the uppermost part or covering, as a lid, cap, etc. **5** the highest degree *[at the top of his voice]* **6** the highest rank *[the top of the class]* — *adj.* of, at, or being the top; highest or foremost — *vt.* **topped, top′ping 1** to take off the top of (a plant, etc.) **2** to provide with a top **3** to be a top for **4** to reach the top of **5** to exceed in amount, etc. **6** to surpass; outdo —**blow one's top** [Slang] to lose one's temper —**on top** successful —**on top of 1** resting upon **2** besides **3** controlling successfully — **top off** to complete by adding a finishing touch —**top′per** *n.*

top[2] (täp) *n.* ⟦OE⟧ a cone-shaped toy with a point upon which it is spun

to·paz (tō′paz′) *n.* ⟦< Gr *topazos*⟧ any of various yellow gems, esp. a variety of aluminum silicate

top brass [Slang] important officials

top′coat′ *n.* a lightweight overcoat

top-drawer (täp′drôr′) *adj.* of first importance

toper (tō′pər) *n.* ⟦< archaic *tope*, to drink (much liquor)⟧ a drunkard

top′-flight′ *adj.* [Colloq.] first-rate

top hat a man's tall, black, cylindrical silk hat, worn in formal dress

top′-heav′y *adj.* too heavy at the top, so as to be unstable

topic (täp′ik) *n.* ⟦ult. < Gr *topos*, place⟧ the subject of an essay, speech, discussion, etc.

top′i·cal *adj.* dealing with topics of the day; of current or local interest

top′knot′ *n.* a tuft of hair or feathers on the top of the head

top′less (-lis) *adj.* without a top, as a costume exposing the breasts

top-level (täp′lev′əl) *adj.* of or by persons of the highest office or rank

top′mast′ *n.* the second mast above the deck of a sailing ship

top′most′ *adj.* at the very top

top′-notch′ *adj.* [Colloq.] first-rate; excellent

to·pog·ra·phy (tə päg′rə fē) *n., pl.* **-phies** ⟦see TOPIC & -GRAPHY⟧ **1** the science of representing surface features of a region on maps and charts **2** these surface features — **topo·graphic** (täp′ə graf′ik) or **top′o·graph′i·cal** *adj.*

top·ping (täp′in) *n.* something put on top of something else

top·ple (täp′əl) *vi.* **-pled, -pling** ⟦< TOP[1]⟧ to fall top forward; fall (*over*) because top-heavy, etc. — *vt.* to cause to topple; overturn

top·sail (täp′sāl′; *naut.*, -səl) *n.* in a square-rigged vessel, the square sail next above the lowest sail on a mast

top′-se′cret *adj.* designating or of the most secret information

top·side (täp′sīd′) *adv.* on or to an upper deck or the main deck of a ship

top′soil′ *n.* the upper layer of soil, usually richer than the subsoil

topsy-turvy (täp′sē tur′vē) *adv., adj.* ⟦prob. < *top*, highest part + ME *terven*, to roll⟧ **1** upside down; in a reversed condition **2** in disorder

toque (tōk) *n.* ⟦Fr⟧ a woman's small, round, usually brimless hat

to·rah *or* **tora** (tō′rə, tôr′ə, tō rä′) *n., pl.* **-roth** *or* **-rot** (-rəs, -rōt′) ⟦< Heb, law⟧ *[usually* T-*]* a scroll containing the Pentateuch —*[usually* T-*]* **1** the body of Jewish religious literature **2** the Pentateuch

torch (tôrch) *n.* ⟦see TORQUE⟧ **1** a portable flaming light **2** a source of enlightenment, etc. **3** a device for producing a very hot flame, as in welding **4** [Brit., etc. (exc. Cdn.)] a flashlight — *vt.* [Slang] to set fire to, as in arson

torch′bear′er *n.* **1** one who carries a torch **2** *a)* one who brings enlightenment, truth, etc. *b)* an inspirational leader, as in some movement

---

═══ THESAURUS ═══

too *a.* **1** [Also] as well, likewise, in addition, additionally, moreover, futhermore, further, besides; see also ALSO. **2** [In excess] excessively, extremely, over and above; see BESIDES.

tool *n.* **1** [An implement] utensil, machine, instrument, mechanism, weapon, apparatus, appliance, engine, means, contrivance, gadget; see also DEVICE 1. *Common tools include the following:* can opener, hammer, knife, jack, crank, pulley, wheel, bar, crowbar, lever, sledge, winch, chisel, plane, screw, brace, bit, file, saw, screwdriver, ax, corkscrew, hatchet, wrench, pliers, drill, sander, router, jimmy. **2** [One who permits himself to be used] accomplice, hireling, dupe; see SERVANT.

tooth *n.* **1** [A dental process] fang, tusk, saber-tooth, ivory, artificial tooth, false tooth, bony appendage. *Human teeth include the following:* incisor, canine, cuspid, eyetooth, bicuspid, premolar, molar, grinder, wisdom tooth. **2** [A toothlike *or* tooth-shaped object] point, stub, projection; see ROOT 1. —**get (or**

sink) one's teeth into* become occupied with, involve oneself in, be busy; see ACT 1. —**tooth and nail** energetically, fervently, forcefully; see EAGERLY, FIERCELY.

toothache *n.* swollen gums, abscessed tooth, decayed tooth; see PAIN 2.

toothbrush *n.* electric toothbrush, nylon bristle toothbrush, brush; see BRUSH 1.

top[1] *a.* **1** [Highest] topmost, uppermost, highest, on the upper end; see also HIGHEST. **2** [Best] prime, head, first, among the first; see also BEST 1.

top[1] *v.* **1** [To remove the top] prune, lop off, trim; see CUT 1. **2** [To exceed] better, beat, excel; see EXCEED. **3** [To apply topping] cover, screen, coat; see PAINT 2. —**top off** finish, end, bring to a conclusion; see COMPLETE.

top[1,2] *n.* **1** [The uppermost portion] peak, summit, crown, head, crest, tip, apex, acme, cap, crowning point, headpiece, capital, pinnacle, zenith, spire; see also HEIGHT.—*Ant.* BOTTOM, lower end, nadir. **2** [A cover]

lid, roof, ceiling; see COVER 1. **3** [A spinning toy] spinner, musical top, whistling top; see TOY 1. **4** [The leader] head, captain, chief; see LEADER 2. —**blow one's top*** lose one's temper, become angry, be enraged; see RAGE 1. —**off the top of one's head*** speaking offhand, chatting casually, spontaneous; see SPONTANEOUS. —**on top** prosperous, thriving, superior; see SUCCESSFUL.

top-heavy *a.* overweight, unstable, unbalanced; see SHAKY 1.

topic *n.* question, theme, material; see SUBJECT.

topless* *a.* almost nude, bare to the waist, exposed; see NAKED 1.

top-level *a.* leading, superior, supreme; see EXCELLENT, IMPORTANT 1.

top-secret *a.* restricted, kept quiet, hush-hush*; see SECRET 1.

topsy-turvy *a.* confused, upside down, disordered; see DISORDERLY 1.

torch *n.* beacon, light, flare; see LIGHT 3.

torch'light' *n.* the light of a torch or torches — *adj.* done by torchlight

tore (tôr) *vt.*, *vi. pt. of* TEAR[1]

torea·dor (tôr'ē ə dôr') *n.* 〚Sp < L *taurus*, a bull〛 a bullfighter

tor·ment (tôr'ment'; *for v.* tôr ment') *n.* 〚OFr < L: see TORQUE〛 1 great pain or anguish 2 a source of pain, anxiety, etc. — *vt.* 1 to cause great physical or mental anguish in 2 to annoy; harass —**tor·ment'ingly** *adv.* — **tor·men'tor** or **tor·ment'er** *n.*

torn (tôrn) *vt.*, *vi. pp. of* TEAR[1]

tor·nado (tôr nā'dō) *n.*, *pl.* **-does** or **-dos** 〚< Sp < L *tonare*, to thunder〛 a violently whirling column of air seen as a funnel-shaped cloud that usually destroys everything in its narrow path

tor·pedo (tôr pē'dō) *n.*, *pl.* **-does** 〚< L: see fol.〛 1 a large, cigar-shaped, self-propelled, underwater projectile containing explosives 2 any of various explosive devices — *vt.* **-doed**, **-do·ing** to attack, destroy, etc. as with a torpedo

tor·pid (tôr'pid) *adj.* 〚< L *torpere*, be numb〛 1 without sensation or motion; dormant 2 dull; sluggish

tor'por (-pər) *n.* 〚L〛 1 a torpid state; stupor 2 dullness; apathy

torque (tôrk) *n.* 〚< L *torquere*, to twist〛 1 *Physics* a measure of the tendency of a force to cause rotation 2 popularly, the force that acts to produce rotation, as in an automotive vehicle

tor·rent (tôr'ənt, tär'-) *n.* 〚< L *torrens*, rushing〛 1 a swift, violent stream, esp. of water 2 a flood or rush of words, mail, etc. —**tor·ren'tial** (tô ren'shəl) *adj.*

tor·rid (tôr'id, tär'-) *adj.* 〚< L *torrere*, to dry〛 1 subjected to intense heat, esp. of the sun; parched 2 very hot; scorching 3 passionate; ardent

Torrid Zone the area of the earth's surface between the Tropic of Cancer & the Tropic of Capricorn and divided by the equator

tor·sion (tôr'shən) *n.* 〚see TORQUE〛 1 a twisting or being twisted 2 the stress produced in a rod, wire, etc. by twisting along a longitudinal axis

torso (tôr'sō) *n.*, *pl.* **-sos** or **-si** (-sē) 〚< Gr *thyrsos*, a stem〛 the trunk of the human body

tort (tôrt) *n.* 〚< L *torquere*, to twist〛 *Law* a wrongful act or damage (not involving a breach of contract), for which a civil action can be brought

torte (tôrt; *Ger* tôr'tə) *n.*, *pl.* **tortes**; *Ger.* **tor·ten** (tôr'tən) 〚Ger < It < LL *torta*, a twisted bread〛 a rich cake, as one made of eggs, finely chopped nuts, crumbs, etc.

tor·tel·lini (tôr'tə lē'nē) *n.* 〚It〛 pasta in tiny ring-shaped pieces, filled with meat, etc.

tor·tilla (tôr tē'ə, -yə) *n.* 〚Sp, dim. of *torta*, a cake〛 a flat, round cake of unleavened cornmeal, or of flour

tor·toise (tôr'təs, -tis) *n.* 〚< ? c. 4th-c. Gr *tartarouchos*, evil demon〛 a turtle, esp. one that lives on land

tortoise shell 1 the hard, mottled, yellow-and-brown shell of some turtles 2 a synthetic substance resembling this —**tor'toise-shell'** *adj.*

tor·toni (tôr tō'nē) *n.* 〚prob. alt. < It *tortone*, lit., big

pastry tart〛 an ice cream made with heavy cream, maraschino cherries, almonds, etc.

tor·tu·ous (tôr'chōō əs) *adj.* 〚see TORQUE〛 1 full of twists, turns, etc.; crooked 2 deceitful or tricky

tor·ture (tôr'chər) *n.* 〚see TORQUE〛 1 the inflicting of severe pain, as to force information or confession 2 any severe physical or mental pain; agony — *vt.* **-tured**, **-tur·ing** 1 to subject to torture 2 to twist or distort (meaning, etc.) —**tor'turer** *n.*

Tory (tôr'ē) *n.*, *pl.* **-ries** 〚Ir *tōruidhe*, robber〛 1 after 1689, a member of the major conservative party of England 2 in the American Revolution, one loyal to Great Britain 3 [*often* t-] any extreme conservative

toss (tôs, täs) *vt.* 〚prob. < Scand〛 1 to throw about /waves *tossed* the boat/ 2 to throw lightly from the hand 3 to jerk upward /to *toss* one's head/ — *vi.* 1 to be thrown about 2 to fling oneself about in sleep, etc. — *n.* a tossing or being tossed —**toss up** to toss a coin for deciding something according to which side lands uppermost

toss'up' *n.* 1 the act of tossing up 2 an even chance

tot[1] (tät) *n.* 〚prob. < ON〛 1 a young child 2 [Chiefly Brit., etc.] a small drink of alcoholic liquor

tot[2] (tät) *vt.*, *vi.* **tot'ted**, **tot'ting** [Colloq., Chiefly Brit., etc.] to total: with *up*

to·tal (tōt''l) *adj.* 〚< L *totus*, all〛 1 constituting a whole 2 complete; utter /a *total* loss/ — *n.* the whole amount; sum — *vt.* **-taled** or **-talled**, **-tal·ing** or **-tal·ling** 1 to find the total of 2 to add up to 3 [Slang] to demolish — *vi.* to amount (*to*) as a whole —**to'tally** *adv.*

to·tali·tar·ian (tō tal'ə ter'ē ən) *adj.* 〚prec. + (AUTHOR)ITARIAN〛 designating or of a government in which one political group maintains complete control, esp. under a dictator — *n.* one who favors such a government —**to·tal'i·tar'i·an·ism'** *n.*

to·tal·ity (tō tal'ə tē) *n.*, *pl.* **-ties** the total amount or sum

to·tali·za·tor (tōt''l i zāt'ər) *n.* a machine for registering bets and computing the odds and payoffs, as at a horse race Also **to'tal·iz'er** (-ī'zər) *n.*

tote (tōt) *vt.* **tot'ed**, **tot'ing** 〚< ?〛 [Colloq.] to carry or haul — *n.* a small piece of baggage

to·tem (tōt'əm) *n.* 〚< Algonquian〛 1 among some peoples, an animal or natural object taken as the symbol of a family or clan 2 an image of this

totem pole a pole carved and painted with totems by Indian tribes of NW North America

tot·ter (tät'ər) *vi.* 〚prob. < Scand〛 1 to rock as if about to fall 2 to be unsteady on one's feet; stagger

tou·can (tōō'kan') *n.* 〚< AmInd (Brazil)〛 a brightly colored bird of tropical America, with a very large beak

touch (tuch) *vt.* 〚< OFr *tochier*〛 1 to put the hand, etc. on, so as to feel 2 to bring (something), or come, into contact with (something else) 3 to border on 4 to strike lightly 5 to give a light tint, aspect, etc. to /*touched* with pink/ 6 to stop at (a port) 7 to handle; use 8 to come up

THESAURUS

torment *n.* agony, suffering, misery; see PAIN 1, 2, TORTURE.

torment *v.* mistreat, torture, irritate; see HURT 1.

tormentor *n.* oppressor, persecutor, antagonist; see ENEMY.

torn *a.* ripped, slit, split, severed, lacerated, mutilated, broken, rent, fractured, cracked, slashed, gashed, ruptured, snapped, sliced, burst, cleaved, wrenched, divided, pulled out, impaired, damaged, spoiled; see also RUINED 1.—*Ant.* WHOLE, repaired, adjusted.

torrent *n.* overflow, deluge, downpour; see FLOOD, FLOW, STORM.

torrid *a.* blazing, fiery, sweltering; see HOT 1.

torture *n.* pain, anguish, agony, torment, crucifixion, martyrdom, pang, ache, twinge, physical suffering, mental suffering, tribulation; see also CRUELTY.—*Ant.* COMFORT, enjoyment, delight.

torture *v.* annoy, irritate, disturb; see ABUSE, BOTHER 2.

toss *v.* 1 [To throw easily] hurl, fling, cast; see THROW 1. 2 [To move up and down] bob, buffet, stir, move restlessly, tumble, pitch, roll, heave,

sway, flounder, rock, wobble, undulate, swing, rise and fall; see also WAVE 3.

tossup *n.* deadlock, bet, draw; see TIE 4.

tot[1] *n.* child, infant, youngster; see BABY.

total *a.* 1 [Whole] entire, inclusive, every; see WHOLE 1. 2 [Complete] utter, gross, thorough; see ABSOLUTE 1.

total *n.* sum, entirety, result; see WHOLE.

total *v.* 1 [To add] figure, calculate, count up, ring up, tag up, sum up, add up; see also ADD 1. 2 [To amount to] consist of, come to, add up to; see AMOUNT TO, EQUAL.

totality *n.* everything, oneness, collectivity; see WHOLE.

totally *a.* entirely, wholly, exclusively; see COMPLETELY.

totem *n.* figure, symbol, crest; see EMBLEM.

totter *v.* shake, rock, careen, quake, tremble, stumble, lurch, stagger, falter, trip, weave, zigzag, reel, rock, roll, walk drunkenly, wobble, waver, hesitate, seesaw, teeter, dodder, crumple, sway, be loose, be weak; see

also WAVE 3.

touch *n.* 1 [The tactile sense] feeling, touching, feel, perception, tactility. 2 [Contact] rub, stroke, pat, fondling, rubbing, petting, stroking, licking, handling, graze, scratch, brush, taste, nudge, kiss, peck, embrace, hug, cuddling, caress. 3 [A sensation] sense, impression, pressure; see FEELING 2. 4 [Skill] knack, technique, talent; see ABILITY, METHOD. 5 [A trace] suggestion, scent, inkling; see BIT 1. —**get in touch (with)** call, telephone, write to, contact, wire, telegraph, correspond with, communicate with, reach, keep in contact with, make overtures.

touch *v.* 1 [To be in contact] stroke, graze, rub, nudge, thumb, finger, paw, pat, pet, caress, lick, taste, brush, kiss, glance, sweep, fondle, smooth, massage, sip, partake; see also FEEL 1. 2 [To come into contact with] meet, encounter, reach; see MEET 1. 3 [To relate to] refer to, regard, affect; see CONCERN 1. — **touch on** treat, refer to, mention; see DISCUSS. —**touch up** renew, modify, rework; see REMODEL, REPAIR.

to; reach **9** to compare with; equal **10** to affect; concern **11** to arouse sympathy, gratitude, etc. in **12** [Slang] to seek a loan or gift of money from — *vi.* **1** to touch a person or thing **2** to be or come in contact **3** to verge (*on* or *upon*) **4** to pertain; bear (*on* or *upon*) **5** to treat in passing: with *on* or *upon* — *n.* **1** a touching or being touched; specif., a light tap **2** the sense by which physical objects are felt **3** a special quality or skill **4** a subtle change or addition in a painting, story, etc. **5** a trace, tinge, etc. **6** a slight attack *[a touch of the flu]* **7** contact or communication *[keep in touch]* **8** [Slang] the act of seeking or getting a loan or gift of money **9** *Music* the manner of striking the keys of a piano, etc. —**touch down** to land: said of an aircraft or spacecraft —**touch up** to improve or finish (a painting, story, etc.) by minor changes

touch-and-go (tuch′ən gō′) *adj.* uncertain, risky, or precarious

touch′down′ *n.* **1** the moment at which an aircraft or spacecraft lands **2** *Football* a play, scoring six points, in which a player carries, catches, or recovers the ball past the opponent's goal line

tou·ché (tōō shā′) *interj.* [Fr] touched: said when one's opponent in fencing scores a point, or to acknowledge a point in debate or a witty retort

touched (tucht) *adj.* **1** emotionally affected; moved **2** slightly demented

touch·ing (tuch′iŋ) *adj.* arousing tender emotions; moving

touch′stone′ *n.* **1** a stone formerly used to test the purity of gold or silver **2** any test of genuineness

touch′-type′ *vi.* **-typed′, -typ′ing** to type without looking at the keyboard by regularly touching a given key with a specific finger

touch′y *adj.* **-i·er, -i·est 1** easily offended; oversensitive; irritable **2** very risky or precarious

tough (tuf) *adj.* [OE *toh*] **1** that will bend, etc. without tearing or breaking **2** not easily cut or chewed *[tough steak]* **3** strong; hardy **4** stubborn **5** brutal or rough **6** very difficult; laborious — *n.* a tough person; thug

tough′en *vt., vi.* to make or become tough or tougher — **tough′ener** *n.*

tou·pee (tōō pā′) *n.* [< Fr < OFr *toup*, tuft of hair] a man's small wig

tour (toor) *n.* [< OFr *tourner*, to turn] **1** a turn, period, etc., as of military duty **2** a long trip, as for sightseeing **3** any trip, as for inspection, for giving performances, etc. — *vt., vi.* to go on a tour (through)

tour de force (toor′ də fôrs′) *pl.* **tours de force** (toor′) [Fr] an unusually skillful or ingenious creation or performance, sometimes a merely clever one

tour′ism′ *n.* tourist travel

tour′ist *n.* one who tours, esp. for pleasure — *adj.* of or for tourists

tour·ma·line (toor′mə lin, -lēn′) *n.* [Fr] a crystalline mineral, used as a gemstone, etc.

tour·na·ment (tur′nə mənt, toor′-) *n.* [< OFr *tourner*, to turn] **1** in the Middle Ages, a contest between knights on horseback who tried to unseat one another with lances **2** a series of contests in competition for a championship Also **tour′ney** (-nē) *n., pl.* **-neys**

tour·ni·quet (tur′ni kit, -ket′; toor′-) *n.* [Fr < L *tunica*, tunic] a device for compressing a blood vessel to stop bleeding, as a bandage twisted about a limb and released at intervals

tou·sle (tou′zəl) *vt.* **-sled, -sling** [< ME *tusen*, to pull] to disorder, dishevel, muss, etc.

tout (tout) *vi., vt.* [OE *totian*, to peep] [Colloq.] **1** to praise highly **2** to sell betting tips on (racehorses) — *n.* [Colloq.] one who touts

tow (tō) *vt.* [OE *togian*] to pull, as by a rope or chain — *n.* **1** a towing or being towed **2** something towed **3** TOWLINE —**in tow 1** being towed **2** in one's company or charge

to·ward (tôrd) *prep.* [see TO & -WARD] **1** in the direction of **2** facing **3** along a likely course to *[steps toward peace]* **4** concerning **5** just before *[toward noon]* **6** for *[save toward a car]* Also **towards**

towel (tou′əl) *n.* [< OFr *toaille*] a piece of cloth or paper for wiping or drying things — *vt.* **-eled** or **-elled, -el·ing** or **-el·ling** to wipe or dry with a towel —**throw** (or **toss,** etc.) **in the towel** [Colloq.] to admit defeat

tow′el·ing or **tow′el·ling** *n.* material for making towels

tower (tou′ər) *n.* [< L *turris*] **1** a high structure, often part of a building **2** such a structure used as a fortress, etc. — *vi.* to rise high like a tower —**tow′er·ing** *adj.*

tow·head (tō′hed′) *n.* [< *tow*, fibers of flax, etc.] **1** a head of pale-yellow hair **2** a person with such hair —**tow′head′ed** *adj.*

tow·hee (tō′hē, -ē) *n.* [echoic] any of various small North American sparrows

tow·line (tō′līn′) *n.* a rope, etc. used for towing

town (toun) *n.* [OE *tun*] **1** a concentration of houses, etc. somewhat larger than a village **2** a city **3** a township **4** the business center of a city **5** the people of a town —**go to town** [Slang] to act fast and efficiently —**on the town** [Colloq.] out for a good time

town crier one who formerly cried public announcements through the streets of a village or town

town hall a building in a town, housing the offices of officials, etc.

town house a two-story or three-story dwelling, a unit in a complex of such dwellings

town meeting a meeting of the voters of a town, as in New England

town′ship *n.* a division of a county, constituting a unit of local government

towns·man (tounz′mən) *n., pl.* **-men 1** one who lives in, or has been reared in, a town **2** a fellow resident of one's town

towns′peo′ple *n.pl.* the people of a town Also **towns′folk′** (-fōk′)

tow·path (tō′path′) *n.* a path along a canal, used by men or animals towing freight-carrying boats

tow′rope′ *n.* a rope used in towing

tox·emia (täks ē′mē ə) *n.* [see fol. & -EMIA] a condition in which the blood contains poisonous substances, esp. toxins produced by pathogenic bacteria

---

■ THESAURUS ■

touch-and-go *a.* **1** [Hasty] rapid, casual, superficial; see SHALLOW 2. **2** [Risky] ticklish, hazardous, tricky; see DANGEROUS, UNCERTAIN.

touched *a.* **1** [Having been in slight contact] fingered, nudged, used, brushed, handled, rubbed, stroked, rearranged, kissed, grazed, licked, tasted, fondled. **2** [Affected] moved, impressed, stirred; see AFFECTED 1.

touching *a., prep.* **1** [Referring to] regarding, in regard to, in reference to; see ABOUT 2. **2** [Affecting] moving, pathetic, tender; see PITIFUL. **3** [Adjacent] tangent, in contact, against; see NEAR 1, NEXT 2.

touchy *a.* **1** [Irritable] ill-humored, testy, sensitive; see IRRITABLE. **2** [Delicate] harmful, hazardous, risky; see UNSAFE.

tough *a.* **1** [Strong] robust, wiry, mighty; see STRONG 1, 2. **2** [Cohesive] solid, firm, sturdy, hard, hardened, adhesive, leathery, coherent, inseparable, molded, tight, cemented, unbreakable, in one piece, dense, closely packed.—*Ant.* WEAK, fragile,

brittle. **3** [Difficult to chew] uncooked, half-cooked, sinewy, indigestible, inedible, fibrous, old, hard as nails, tough as shoeleather*.— *Ant.* SOFT, tender, overcooked. **4** [Difficult] hard, troublesome, laborious; see DIFFICULT 1, SEVERE 1. **5** [Hardy] robust, sound, capable; see HEALTHY. **6** [Rough and cruel] savage, fierce, ferocious; see CRUEL. **7** [*Unfavorable] bad, unfortunate, untimely; see UNFAVORABLE. **8** [*Excellent] fine, terrific*, first-class; see EXCELLENT. —**tough it out*** persevere, persist, endure; see ENDURE 1.

tour *n.* trip, voyage, travel; see JOURNEY.

tour *v.* voyage, vacation, take a trip; see TRAVEL.

tourist *n.* sightseer, vacationist, visitor; see TRAVELER.

tournament *n.* meet, tourney, match; see SPORT 3.

tow *v.* haul, pull, drag; see DRAW 1.

toward *a., prep.* to, in the direction of, pointing to, via, on the way to,

proceeding, moving, approaching, in relation to, close to, headed for, on the road to; see also NEAR 1.

towel *n.* wiper, drier, absorbent paper, sheet, toweling, napkin, cloth, rag. *Towels include the following:* linen, cotton, terry, guest, face, Turkish, hand, bath, beach, dish, tea, paper, napkin. —**throw in the towel*** admit defeat, give in, surrender; see QUIT 2.

tower *n.* spire, mast, steeple, bell tower, lookout tower, keep, belfry, monolith, radio tower, skyscraper, obelisk, pillar, column, minaret.

tower *v.* look over, extend above, mount; see OVERLOOK 1.

town *a.* civic, community, civil; see MUNICIPAL, URBAN.

town *n.* **1** [In the United States, a small collection of dwellings] township, village, hamlet, county seat, municipality, borough, hick town*. **2** [The people in a city, especially the prominent people] townspeople, inhabitants, society; see POPULATION.

toxic (täks'ik) *adj.* ⟦< Gr *toxicon*, a poison⟧ **1** of, affected by, or caused by a toxin **2** poisonous

toxi·col·ogy (täks'i käl'ə jē) *n.* ⟦see prec. & -LOGY⟧ the science of poisons and their effects, antidotes, etc. —**tox'i·col'o·gist** *n.*

toxin (täks'in) *n.* ⟦< TOXIC⟧ **1** any of various poisons produced by microorganisms and causing certain diseases **2** any poison secreted by plants or animals

toy (toi) *n.* ⟦< ? MDu *toi*, finery⟧ **1** a trifle **2** a bauble; trinket **3** a plaything for children — *adj.* **1** like a toy in size, use, etc. **2** made as a toy — *vi.* to trifle (*with* a thing, an idea, etc.)

tr. **1** transpose **2** treasurer

trace¹ (trās) *n.* ⟦< L *trahere*, to draw⟧ **1** a mark, track, sign, etc. left by a person, animal, or thing **2** a barely perceptible amount — *vt.* **traced, trac'ing 1** to follow the trail of; track **2** *a)* to follow the development or history of *b)* to determine (a source, etc.) by this procedure **3** to draw, outline, etc. **4** to copy (a drawing, etc.) by following its lines on a superimposed transparent sheet —**trace'able** *adj.* —**trac'er** *n.*

trace² (trās) *n.* ⟦see TRAIT⟧ either of two straps, etc. connecting a draft animal's harness to the vehicle drawn

trace element a chemical element, as copper, zinc, etc., essential in nutrition, but only in minute amounts

trac·ery (trās'ər ē) *n.,* pl. **-ies** ⟦< TRACE¹ + -ERY⟧ ornamental work of interlacing or branching lines

tra·chea (trā'kē ə) *n.,* pl. **-cheae'** (-ē') or **-cheas** ⟦< Gr *tracheia* (*arteria*), rough (windpipe)⟧ the passage that conveys air from the larynx to the bronchi; windpipe —**tra'cheal** *adj.*

tra·che·ot·o·my (trā'kē ät'ə mē) *n.,* pl. **-mies** ⟦see prec. & -TOMY⟧ an incision of the trachea to aid breathing in an emergency

trac·ing (trās'iŋ) *n.* something traced; specif., *a)* a copy of a drawing, etc. *b)* a traced line of a recording instrument

track (trak) *n.* ⟦< Fr *trac*⟧ **1** a mark left in passing, as a footprint, wheel rut, etc. **2** a path or trail **3** a sequence of ideas, events, etc. **4** a path or circuit laid out for racing, etc. **5** a pair of parallel metal rails on which trains, etc. run **6** *a)* sports performed on a track, as running, hurdling, etc. *b)* these sports along with other contests in jumping, throwing, etc. **7** *a)* a band on a phonograph record, compact disc, etc. *b)* any of the separate, parallel recording surfaces along a magnetic tape — *vt.* **1** to follow the track of **2** to trace by means of evidence, etc. **3** to plot the path of, as with radar **4** to leave tracks of (mud, etc.) on: often with *up* —**in one's tracks** where one is at the moment —**keep** (or **lose**) **track of** to stay (or fail to stay) informed about —**track'er** *n.* —**track'less** *adj.*

tract¹ (trakt) *n.* ⟦< L *trahere*, to draw⟧ **1** a continuous expanse of land **2** a system of organs having some special function ⟦the digestive *tract*⟧

tract² (trakt) *n.* ⟦< LL *tractatus*, treatise⟧ a propagandizing pamphlet, esp. one on a religious subject

trac·ta·ble (trak'tə b'l) *adj.* ⟦< L *trahere*, to draw⟧ **1** easily engaged; docile **2** easily worked; malleable —**trac'tabil'ity** *n.*

trac·tion (trak'shən) *n.* ⟦< L *trahere*, to draw⟧ **1** *a)* a pulling or drawing *b)* a being pulled or drawn *c)* the kind of power used for pulling ⟦electric *traction*⟧ **2** the power, as of tires on pavement, to hold to a surface without slipping

trac·tor (trak'tər) *n.* ⟦see prec.⟧ **1** a powerful, motor-driven vehicle for pulling farm machinery, etc. **2** a truck with a driver's cab and no body, for hauling large trailers

trade (trād) *n.* ⟦< LowG, a track⟧ **1** occupation; esp., skilled work **2** all the persons in a particular business **3** buying and selling; commerce **4** customers **5** a purchase or sale **6** an exchange; swap — *vi.* **trad'ed, trad'ing 1** to carry on a business **2** to have business dealings (*with*) **3** to make an exchange (*with*) **4** [Colloq.] to be a customer (*at* a certain store) — *vt.* to exchange; barter —**trade on** (or **upon**) to take advantage of

trade'-in' *n.* a thing given or taken as part payment for something else

trade journal (or **magazine**) a magazine devoted to a specific trade or industry

trade'mark' *n.* a symbol, word, etc. used by a manufacturer or dealer to distinguish a product: usually protected by law

trade name 1 the name by which a commodity is commonly known by those who deal in it **2** a name used as a trademark **3** the business name of a company

trade'-off' *n.* an exchange in which one benefit is given up for another considered more desirable Also **trade'off'**

trad'er *n.* **1** one who trades; merchant **2** a ship used in trade

trades·man (trādz'mən) *n.,* pl. **-men** [Chiefly Brit., etc.] a storekeeper —**trades'wom'an,** pl. **-wom'en,** *n.fem.*

trade union LABOR UNION

trade wind a wind that blows toward the equator from either side of it

trading post a store in an outpost, settlement, etc., where trading is done

tra·di·tion (trə dish'ən) *n.* ⟦< L *tradere*, deliver⟧ **1** the handing down orally of beliefs, customs, etc. from generation to generation **2** a story, belief, etc. handed down in this way

tra·di'tional *adj.* of, handed down by, or conforming to tradition

---

THESAURUS

toxic *a.* noxious, virulent, lethal; see DEADLY, POISONOUS.

toy *a.* childish, miniature, small; see LITTLE 1.

toy *n.* **1** [Something designed for amusement] game, plaything, pastime; see DOLL, GAME 1. *Toys include the following:* dolls, games, balls, toy weapons, blocks, jacks, tops, puzzles, models, jump ropes, scooters, wagons, kites, sporting goods, electronic devices, bicycles, tricycles, roller skates, marbles, skateboards, hobby horses. **2** [Anything trivial] trifle, bauble, gadget; see KNICKKNACK.

trace *n.* **1** [A very small quantity] indication, fragment, dash, dab, sprinkling, tinge, pinch, taste, crumb, trifle, shred, drop, speck, shade, hint, shadow, nuance, iota, particle, jot, suggestion, touch, suspicion, minimum, smell, spot; see also BIT 1. **2** [A track] evidence, trail, footprint; see TRACK 2.

trace¹ *v.* **1** [To track] smell out, track down, run down; see TRACK 1. **2** [To draw] sketch, outline, copy; see DRAW 2.

tracing *n.* imitation, reproduction, duplicate; see COPY.

track *n.* **1** [A prepared way] path, course, road; see RAILROAD. **2** [Evidence left in passage] footprint, step, trace, vestige, impression, tire track, mark, footmark, footstep, trail, imprint, remnant, record, indication, print, sign, remains, token, symbol, clue, scent, wake, monument. —**keep track of** keep an account of, stay informed about, maintain contact with; see TRACK 1, WATCH. —**lose track of** lose sight of, lose contact with, abandon; see FORGET. —**make tracks*** run away, abandon, depart quickly; see LEAVE 1. —**off the track** deviant, variant, deviating; see MISTAKEN 1. —**the wrong side of the tracks*** ghetto, poor side of town, lower class neighborhood; see SLUM.

track *v.* **1** [To follow by evidence] hunt, pursue, smell out, add up, put together, trail, follow, trace, follow the scent, follow a clue, follow footprints, draw an inference, piece together, dog, be hot on the trail of, tail*, shadow. **2** [To dirty with tracks] leave footprints, leave mud, muddy, stain, soil, besmear, spatter, leave a trail of dirt; see also DIRTY.

trade *n.* **1** [Business] commerce, sales, enterprise; see BUSINESS 1. **2** [A craft] occupation, profession, position; see JOB 1. *Common trades include the following:* auto mechanic, bookkeeper, boilermaker, baker, barber, butcher, bookbinder, bricklayer, carpenter, cook, cabinetmaker, cameraman, dressmaker, electrician, embalmer, engraver, hairstylist, jeweler, locksmith, metallurgist, miner, machinist, optician, painter, plumber, printer, seamstress, shoemaker, tailor, textile worker, technician, toolmaker, truck driver, welder. **3** [An individual business transaction] deal, barter, contract; see SALE 2.

trade *v.* **1** [To do business] patronize, shop, purchase; see BUY, SELL. **2** [To give one thing for another] barter, swap, give in exchange; see EXCHANGE. —**trade in** turn in, make part of a deal, get rid of; see SELL.

trademark *n.* brand, tag, commercial stamp; see LABEL.

trader *n.* salesman, dealer, merchant; see BUSINESSMAN.

tradesman *n.* storekeeper, retailer, merchant; see BUSINESSMAN.

trade union *n.* union, organized labor, guild; see LABOR 4.

tradition *n.* **1** [The process of preserving orally] folklore, legend, fable; see STORY. **2** [Cultural heritage] ritual, mores, law; see CULTURE 2, CUSTOM.

traditional *a.* folkloric, legendary, mythical, epical, ancestral, unwritten, balladic, told, handed down, anecdotal, proverbial, inherited, folkloristic, old, acknowledged, customary, generally accepted, habitual, widespread, usual, widely used, popu-

tra·duce (trə do͞os′, -dyo͞os′) *vt.* **-duced′, -duc′ing** ⟦< L *trans*, across + *ducere*, to lead⟧ to slander

traf·fic (traf′ik) *n.* ⟦< It *traffico* < L *trans*, across +It *ficcare*, bring⟧ 1 buying and selling; trade 2 dealings (*with* someone) 3 the movement or number of automobiles, pedestrians, etc. along a street, etc. 4 the business done with traffic — *vi.* **-ficked, -fick·ing** 1 to carry on traffic (*in* a commodity) 2 to have dealings (*with* someone) — **traf′ficker** *n.*

traffic circle a circular road at the intersection of several streets: vehicles move on it in one direction only

traffic light (or **signal**) a set of signal lights at a street intersection to regulate traffic

tra·ge·di·an (trə jē′dē ən) *n.* an actor or writer of tragedy —**tra·ge′di·enne′** (-en′) *n.fem.*

trag·e·dy (traj′ə dē) *n., pl.* **-dies** ⟦< Gr *tragos*, goat + *ōidē*, song⟧ 1 a serious play with an unhappy ending 2 a very sad or tragic event; disaster

trag·ic (traj′ik) *adj.* 1 of, or having the nature of, tragedy 2 disastrous, fatal, etc. —**trag′i·cal·ly** *adv.*

trail (trāl) *vt.* ⟦< L *trahere*, to draw⟧ 1 to drag or let drag behind one 2 to follow the tracks of; track 3 to hunt by tracking 4 to follow behind — *vi.* 1 to drag along on the ground, etc. 2 to grow along the ground, etc., as some plants 3 to flow behind, as smoke 4 to follow or lag behind; straggle 5 to grow weaker, dimmer, etc.: with *off* or *away* — *n.* 1 something that trails behind 2 a mark, scent, etc. left by a person, animal, or thing that has passed 3 a beaten path

trail′blaz′er *n.* 1 one who blazes a trail 2 a pioneer in any field

trail′er *n.* 1 one that trails 2 *a)* a wagon, van, etc. designed to be pulled by an automobile, truck, etc. *b)* such a vehicle designed to be lived in

trailer park an area, usually with piped water, electricity, etc., for trailers, esp. mobile homes

train (trān) *n.* ⟦< L *trahere*, to pull⟧ 1 something that drags along behind, as a trailing skirt 2 a group of followers; retinue 3 a procession; caravan 4 any connected order; sequence *[a train* of thought*]* 5 a line of connected railroad cars pulled by a locomotive — *vt.* 1 to guide the growth of (a plant) 2 to guide the mental, moral, etc. development of; rear 3 to instruct so as to make proficient 4 to make fit for an athletic contest, etc. 5 to aim (a gun, etc.) — *vi.* to undergo training —**trainee** (trān ē′) *n.* — **train′er** *n.* —**train′ing** *n.*

train′man (-mən) *n., pl.* **-men** one who works on a railroad train

traipse (trāps) *vi., vt.* **traipsed, traips′ing** ⟦< ?⟧ [Colloq. or Dial.] to walk, wander, or tramp

trait (trāt) *n.* ⟦< L *trahere*, to draw⟧ a distinguishing characteristic

trai·tor (trāt′ər) *n.* ⟦< L *tradere*, betray⟧ one who betrays one's country, friends, etc. —**trai′tor·ous** *adj.*

tra·jec·to·ry (trə jek′tə rē) *n., pl.* **-ries** ⟦< L *trans*, across + *jacere*, to throw⟧ the curved path of something hurtling through space

tram (tram) *n.* [prob. < LowG *traam*, a beam⟧ [Brit., etc. (exc. Cdn.)] a streetcar

tram·mel (tram′əl) *n.* ⟦< L *tres*, three + *macula*, a mesh⟧ [*usually pl.*] something that confines or restrains — *vt.* **-meled** or **-melled, -mel·ing** or **-mel·ling** to confine, restrain, etc.

tramp (tramp) *vi.* ⟦ME *trampen*⟧ 1 to walk or step heavily 2 to travel about on foot — *vt.* 1 to step on heavily 2 to walk through — *n.* 1 a hobo; vagrant 2 the sound of heavy steps 3 a journey on foot; hike 4 a freight ship that picks up cargo, etc. wherever it may be 5 [Slang] a sexually promiscuous woman

tram·ple (tram′pəl) *vi.* **-pled, -pling** [see prec.] to tread heavily — *vt.* to crush, as by treading heavily on

tram·po·line (tram′pə lēn′, -lin) *n.* ⟦< It⟧ a sheet of strong canvas stretched tightly on a frame, used in acrobatic tumbling

trance (trans) *n.* ⟦< L *transire*, to die⟧ 1 a state of altered consciousness, resembling sleep, as in hypnosis 2 a daze; stupor 3 a state of great mental abstraction

tran·quil (traŋ′kwil, traŋ′-) *adj.* **-quiler** or **-quil·ler, -quil·est** or **-quil·lest** ⟦L *tranquillus*⟧ calm, serene, placid, etc. —**tran·quil′li·ty** or **tran·quil′i·ty** (-kwil′ə tē) *n.* —**tran′quil·ly** *adv.*

tran′quil·ize′ or **tran′quil·lize′** (-īz′) *vt., vi.* **-ized′** or **-lized′, -iz′ing** or **-liz′ing** to make or become tranquil

tran′quil·iz′er or **tran′quil·liz′er** *n.* a drug used as a calming agent in treating various emotional disturbances, etc.

trans- [L < *trans*, across] *prefix* over, across, beyond

trans. 1 translated 2 translation

trans·act (tran zakt′, -sakt′) *vt.* ⟦< L *trans-*, over + *agere*, to drive⟧ to carry on or complete (business, etc.) —**trans·act′or** *n.*

trans·ac′tion *n.* 1 a transacting 2 something transacted; specif., *a)* a business deal *b)* [*pl.*] a record of the proceedings of a society, etc.

THESAURUS

lar, acceptable, established, fixed, sanctioned, universal, taken for granted, rooted, classical, prescribed, doctrinal, conventional; see also COMMON 1, REGULAR 3.

traffic *n.* 1 [The flow of transport] travel, passage, transportation, flux, movement, transfer, transit, passenger service, freight shipment, influx. 2 [Dealings] commerce, transactions, exchange; see BUSINESS.

tragedy *n.* 1 [Unhappy fate] lot, bad fortune, misfortune, doom, problem, error, mistake.—*Ant.* HAPPINESS, fortune, success. 2 [A series of tragic events] adversity, affliction, hardship; see DIFFICULTY 1, 2.—*Ant.* SUCCESS, prosperity, good fortune. 3 [An artistic creation climaxed by catastrophe] play, tragic drama, melodrama; see DRAMA, MOVIE, NOVEL.

tragic *a.* catastrophic, fatal, disastrous; see UNFORTUNATE.

trail *n.* trace, tracks, path; see WAY 2.

trail *v.* 1 [To follow] track, trace, follow a scent; see HUNT 1, PURSUE 1. 2 [To lag behind] fall back, loiter, tarry; see WAIT 1.

trailer *n.* house trailer, recreational vehicle, mobile home; see HOME 1.

train *n.* 1 [A sequence] string, chain, succession; see SERIES. 2 [A locomotive and attached cars] transport train, passenger train, freight train, local train, limited, supply train, express train, excursion train, commuters' train, troop train, boat train, mail train, bullet train, subway, rapid

transit, underground, elevated, electric, diesel, choo-choo*; see also RAILROAD.

train *v.* 1 [To drill] practice, exercise, discipline; see REACH 2. 2 [To educate] instruct, tutor, enlighten; see TEACH. 3 [To toughen oneself] prepare, grow strong, get into practice, reduce, make ready, fit out, equip, qualify, bring up to standard, whip into shape*, get a workout.—*Ant.* WEAKEN, break training, be unfit. 4 [To direct the growth of] rear, lead, discipline, mold, bend, implant, guide, shape, care for, encourage, infuse, imbue, order, bring up, nurture, nurse, prune, weed; see also RAISE 1.—*Ant.* NEGLECT, ignore, disdain. 5 [To aim] bring to bear, level, draw a bead; see AIM.

trained *a.* prepared, qualified, cultured, initiated, skilled, informed, schooled, primed, graduated, disciplined, enlightened; see also EDUCATED.—*Ant.* INEXPERIENCED, raw, untrained.

trainer *n.* teacher, tutor, instructor, coach, manager, mentor, officer, master, boss, handler, pilot.

training *n.* drill, practice, exercise, preparation, instruction, foundation, schooling, discipline, basic principles, groundwork, coaching, indoctrination, preliminaries, tune-up*, buildup*; see also EDUCATION.

trait *n.* habit, manner, peculiarity;

see CHARACTERISTIC.

traitor *n.* betrayer, deserter, renegade, Judas, informer, spy, counterspy, agent, double agent, hypocrite, imposter, plotter, conspirator, turncoat, sneak, double-crosser*, fink*, rat*, stool pigeon*, two-timer*; see also REBEL.—*Ant.* SUPPORTER, follower, partisan.

tramp *n.* 1 [Vagrant] hobo, wanderer, bum*; see BEGGAR. 2 [A long walk, often in rough country] hike, excursion, stroll; see WALK 3. 3 [*Prostitute] whore, harlot, slut; see PROSTITUTE.

trample *v.* stamp on, crush, tread on, grind underfoot, injure, squash, bruise, tramp over, overwhelm, defeat.

trance *n.* coma, daze, stupor; see CONFUSION.

tranquil *a.* composed, agreeable, gentle; see SERENE.

tranquilize *v.* calm, pacify, quell; see CALM DOWN, QUIET 1, SOOTHE.

tranquilizer *n.* sleeping pill, depressant, alleviative, palliative, soother, mollifier, calmative, sedative, placebo, pacifier; see also DRUG, MEDICINE 2.

tranquillity *n.* calmness, peacefulness, serenity; see PEACE 2, 3.

transact *v.* accomplish, carry on, conclude; see BUY, SELL.

transaction *n.* sale, proceeding, deal; see BUSINESS 4.

trans·at·lan·tic (trans'at lan'tik, tranz'-) *adj.* 1 crossing the Atlantic 2 on the other side of the Atlantic

trans·ceiv·er (tran sē'vər) *n.* a radio transmitter and receiver in a single housing

tran·scend (tran send') *vt.* [< L *trans-*, over + *scandere*, climb] 1 to go beyond the limits of; exceed 2 to surpass; excel —**tran·scend'ent** *adj.*

tran·scen·den·tal (tran'sen dent'l) *adj.* 1 supernatural 2 abstract —**tran'scen·den'tally** *adv.*

tran·scen·den·tal·ism *n.* a philosophy based on a search for reality through spiritual intuition

trans·con·ti·nen·tal (trans'-) *adj.* 1 that crosses a continent 2 on the other side of a continent

tran·scribe (tran skrīb') *vt.* **-scribed', -scrib'ing** 1 to write out or type out in full (shorthand notes, etc.) 2 to represent (speech sounds) in symbols

tran·script (tran'skript') *n.* 1 a written or typewritten copy 2 a copy, esp. an official copy, as of a student's record

tran·scrip·tion (-skrip'shən) *n.* 1 a transcribing 2 a transcript; copy 3 an arrangement of a piece of music for an instrument or voice other than that for which it was written

trans·ducer (trans dōōs'ər, tranz-) *n.* [< L *trans-*, over + *ducere*, to lead] a device that transmits energy from one system to another, sometimes converting the energy to a different form

tran·sept (tran'sept') *n.* [< L *trans-*, across + *septum*, enclosure] the part of a cross-shaped church at right angles to the nave, or either arm of this part

trans·fer (*for v.* trans fur', trans'fər; *for n.* trans'fər) *vt.* **-ferred', -fer'ring** [< L *trans-*, across + *ferre*, to bear] 1 to carry, send, etc. to another person or place 2 to make over (property, etc.) to another 3 to convey (a picture, etc.) from one surface to another —*vi.* 1 to transfer oneself or be transferred 2 to change to another school, etc. or to another bus, etc. —*n.* 1 a transferring or being transferred 2 one that is transferred 3 a ticket entitling the bearer to change to another bus, etc. —**trans·fer'able** *adj.*

trans·fer·ence (trans'fər əns, trans fur'-) *n.* a transferring or being transferred

trans·fig·ure (trans fig'yər) *vt.* **-ured, -ur·ing** [< L *trans-*, across + *figura*, figure] 1 to change the form or appearance of 2 to transform so as to glorify —**trans·fig'u·ra'tion** *n.*

trans·fix (trans fiks') *vt.* [< L *trans-*, through + *figere*, to fix] 1 to pierce through; impale 2 to make motionless, as if impaled

trans·form (trans fôrm') *vt.* [< L *trans-*, over + *forma*, a form] 1 to change the form or appearance of 2 to change the condition, character, or function of —**trans·for'ma'tion** *n.*

trans·form'er *n.* 1 one that transforms 2 a device for changing electrical energy to a different voltage

trans·fuse (-fyōōz') *vt.* **-fused', -fus'ing** [< L *trans-*, across + *fundere*, pour] 1 to instill; imbue 2 to transfer (blood, etc.) into a blood vessel —**trans·fu'sion** *n.*

trans·gress (trans gres', tranz-) *vt.*, *vi.* [< L *trans-*, over + *gradi*, to step] 1 to break (a law, command, etc.); sin (against) 2 to go beyond (a limit, etc.) —**trans·gres'sion** (-gresh'ən) *n.* —**trans·gres'sor** *n.*

tran·sient (tran'shənt) *adj.* [< L *trans-*, over + *ire*, to go] 1 passing away with time; temporary 2 passing quickly; fleeting — *n.* a transient person; esp., a temporary lodger —**tran'sience** or **tran'sien·cy** *n.* —**tran'sient·ly** *adv.*

tran·sis·tor (tran zis'tər, -sis'-) *n.* [TRAN(SFER) + (RE)SISTOR] a compact electronic device, composed of semiconductor material, that controls current flow —**tran·sis'tor·ize', -ized', -iz'ing**, *vt.*

transit (trans'it, tranz'it) *n.* [< L *trans-*, over + *ire*, go] 1 passage through or across 2 *a)* a carrying through or across; conveyance *b)* a system of urban public transportation 3 a surveying instrument for measuring horizontal angles

tran·si·tion (tran zish'ən) *n.* a passing from one condition, place, etc. to another —**tran·si'tional** *adj.*

tran·si·tive (tran'sə tiv, -zə-) *adj.* designating a verb taking a direct object

tran·si·tory (tran'sə tôr'ē, -zə-) *adj.* not enduring; temporary; fleeting

transl. 1 translated 2 translation

trans·late (trans lāt', tranz-) *vt.* **-lat'ed, -lat'ing** [< L *translatus*, transferred] 1 to move from one place or condition to another 2 to put into the words of a different language 3 to put into different words —**trans·la'tor** *n.*

trans·la'tion *n.* 1 a translating 2 writing or speech translated into another language

trans·lit·er·ate (trans lit'ər āt', tranz-) *vt.* **-at'ed, -at'ing** [< TRANS- + L *litera*, letter] to write (words, etc.) in the characters of another alphabet

trans·lu·cent (trans lōō'sənt, tranz-) *adj.* [< L *trans-*, through + *lucere*, to shine] letting light pass through but not transparent

trans·mi·grate (trans mī'grāt', tranz-) *vi.* **-grat'ed, -grat'ing** [see TRANS- & MIGRATE] to pass into another body at death: said of the soul, as in Hindu religious belief —**trans'mi·gra'tion** *n.*

trans·mis·sion (trans mish'ən, tranz-) *n.* 1 a transmitting 2 something transmitted 3 the part of a motor vehicle, etc. that transmits power to the wheels, as by gears

trans·mit' (-mit') *vt.* **-mit'ted, -mit'ting** [< L *trans-*, over + *mittere*, send] 1 to cause to go to another person or place; transfer 2 to hand down by heredity, inheritance, etc. 3 *a)* to pass (light, heat, etc.) through some medium *b)* to conduct 4 to convey (force, movement, etc.) to 5 to send out (radio or television signals) —**trans·mis'sible** (-mis'ə bəl) *adj.* —**trans·mit'table** *adj.* —**trans·mit'tal** or **trans·mit'tance** *n.*

trans·mit'ter *n.* one that transmits; specif., the apparatus that transmits signals in telephony, radio, etc.

trans·mute (trans myōōt', tranz-) *vt.*, *vi.* **-mut'ed, -mut'ing** [< L *trans-*, over + *mutare*, to change] to change

---

THESAURUS

transcend *v.* rise above, transform, excel; see EXCEED.

transcontinental *a.* trans-American, trans-Siberian, trans-Canadian, trans-European, cross-country, intracontinental.

transcribe *v.* reprint, reproduce, decipher; see COPY.

transcript *n.* record, reprint, reproduction; see COPY.

transfer *n.* 1 [Ticket] token, fare, check; see TICKET 1. 2 [A document providing for a change] new orders, instructions, new assignment; see COMMAND, DIRECTIONS.

transfer *v.* 1 [To carry] transport, convey, shift; see CARRY 1. 2 [To assign] sell, hand over, pass the buck*; see ASSIGN, GIVE 1.

transferred *a.* moved, removed, shifted, transported, relocated, transmitted, turned over, sent, relayed, shipped, mailed, faxed, transplanted, reassigned, transposed, restationed, conveyed, transmuted; see also SENT.—*Ant.* FIXED, left, stationed.

transform *v.* convert, mold, reconstruct; see ALTER 1.

transformation *n.* 1 [A change] alteration, transmutation, conversion; see CHANGE 1. 2 [A grammatical construction] transform, transformed construction, equivalent grammatical sequence; see ADJECTIVE, PHRASE, SENTENCE 2.

transfusion *n.* dialysis, blood exchange, bleeding; see EXCHANGE 1.

transgress *v.* overstep, rebel, infringe; see DISOBEY.

transgression *n.* misbehavior, trespass, infraction; see CRIME, SIN, VIOLATION.

transgressor *n.* offender, sinner, rebel; see CRIMINAL.

transient *a.* provisional, ephemeral, transitory; see TEMPORARY.

transistor *n.* portable radio, pocket radio, receiver; see RADIO 2.

transition *n.* shift, passage, flux, passing, development, transformation, turn, realignment; see also CHANGE 2.—*Ant.* STABILITY, constancy, durability.

translate *v.* decode, transliterate, interpret, decipher, paraphrase, render, transpose, turn, gloss, put in equivalent terms.

translated *a.* interpreted, adapted, rendered, transliterated, glossed, paraphrased, transposed, reworded, reworked, transferred, rewritten.

translation *n.* transliteration, version, adaptation, rendition, rendering, interpretation, paraphrase, rewording, gloss, reading.

transmission *n.* 1 [The act of transporting] transference, conveyance, carrying; see DELIVERY 1, TRANSPORTATION. 2 [The carrying of sound on radio waves] broadcast, telecast, conduction; see BROADCASTING. 3 [A mechanism for adapting power] gears, gear box, automatic transmission; see DEVICE 1.

transmit *v.* 1 [To send] dispatch, forward, convey; see SEND 1, 2. 2 [To carry] pass on, transfer, communicate; see SEND 2.

transmitter *n.* conductor, antenna, wire; see COMMUNICATION, ELECTRONICS.

from one form, nature, substance, etc. into another — **trans·mu·ta′tion** *n.*

trans·na′tional *adj.* transcending the interests, etc. of a single nation

trans·oceanic (trans′ō′shē an′ik) *adj.* crossing the ocean

tran·som (tran′səm) *n.* 〖prob. < L *transtrum*, crossbeam〗 1 a horizontal crossbar, as across the top of a door or window 2 a small window just above a door or window

trans·pa·cific (trans′pə sif′ik) *adj.* 1 crossing the Pacific 2 on the other side of the Pacific

trans·par·ency (trans per′ən sē) *n., pl.* **-cies** a transparent film or slide that can be projected on a screen

trans·par′ent *adj.* 〖< L *trans-*, through + *parere*, appear〗 1 transmitting light rays so that objects on the other side may be seen 2 so fine in texture as to be seen through 3 easily understood or detected; obvious — **trans·par′ently** *adv.*

tran·spire (tran spīr′) *vi.* **-spired′, -spir′ing** 〖< L *trans-*, through + *spirare*, breathe〗 1 to give off vapor, moisture, etc., as through pores 2 to become known 3 to happen: regarded by some as a loose usage —**tran′spi·ra′tion** (-spə rā′shən) *n.*

trans·plant (*for v.* trans plant′, trans′plant′; *for n.* trans′plant′) *vt.* 1 to remove from one place and plant, resettle, etc. in another 2 *Surgery* to transfer (tissue or an organ) from one to another; graft — *n.* a transplanting or something transplanted, as a body organ or seedling —**trans′plan·ta′tion** (-plan tā′shən) *n.*

tran·spon·der (tran spän′dər) *n.* 〖< TRANSMITTER & RESPOND〗 a transceiver that automatically transmits signals

trans·port (*for v.* trans pôrt′; *for n.* trans′pôrt′) *vt.* 〖< L *trans-*, over + *portare*, carry〗 1 to carry from one place to another 2 to carry away with emotion — *n.* 1 a transporting; transportation 2 rapture 3 a vehicle for transporting

trans·por·ta′tion (-pər tā′shən) *n.* 1 a transporting or being transported 2 a means of conveyance 3 fare or a ticket for being transported

trans·pose (trans pōz′) *vt., vi.* **-posed′, -pos′ing** 〖see TRANS- & POSE〗 1 to change the usual order or position of; interchange 2 to rewrite or play (a musical composition) in another key —**trans′po·si′tion** (-pə zish′ən) *n.*

trans·sex·ual (trans sek′shōō əl) *n.* a person who is predisposed to identify with the opposite sex, sometimes so strongly as to undergo sex-change surgery

trans·ship (trans ship′, tran-) *vt., vi.* **-shipped′, -ship′ping** to transfer from one ship, train, truck, etc. to another for further shipment —**trans·ship′ment** *n.*

tran·sub·stan·tia·tion (trans′səb stan′shē ā′shən) *n.* 〖< L *trans-*, over + *substantia*, substance〗 R.C.Ch., *Eastern Orthodox Ch.* the doctrine that, in the Eucharist, the whole substances of the bread and wine are changed into the body and blood of Christ

trans·verse (trans vʉrs′, tranz-; *esp. for n.*, trans′vʉrs′, tranz′-) *adj.* 〖< L *trans-*, across + *vertere*, to turn〗 situ-

ated across; crosswise — *n.* a transverse part, etc. —**trans·verse′ly** *adv.*

trans·ves·tite (trans ves′tīt′, tranz-) *n.* 〖< TRANS- + L *vestire*, to dress〗 a person who gets sexual pleasure from dressing in the clothes of the opposite sex

trap[1] (trap) *n.* 〖< OE *træppe*〗 1 a device for catching animals, as one that snaps shut tightly when stepped on 2 any stratagem designed to catch or trick 3 a device, as in a drainpipe, for preventing the escape of gas, etc. 4 [*pl.*] percussion instruments, as in a band — *vt.* **trapped, trap′ping** to catch as in a trap — *vi.* to trap animals, esp. for their furs —**trap′per** *n.*

trap[2] (trap) *vt.* **trapped, trap′ping** 〖< OFr *drap*, cloth〗 to cover, equip, or adorn with trappings

trap′door′ *n.* a hinged or sliding door in a roof, ceiling, or floor

tra·peze (tra pēz′, trə-) *n.* 〖see fol.〗 a short horizontal bar, hung high by two ropes, on which gymnasts, etc. swing

tra·pezi·um (trə pē′zē əm, tra-) *n., pl.* **-zi·ums** or **-zia** (-ə) 〖< Gr *trapeza*, table〗 a plane figure with four sides, no two of which are parallel

trap·ezoid (trap′i zoid′) *n.* 〖see prec.〗 a plane figure with four sides, only two of which are parallel —**trap′ezoi′dal** *adj.*

trap·pings (trap′iŋz) *n.pl.* 〖see TRAP[2]〗 1 an ornamental covering for a horse 2 adornments

trap′shoot′ing *n.* the sport of shooting at clay disks sprung into the air from throwing devices

trash (trash) *n.* 〖prob. < Scand〗 1 worthless or waste things; rubbish 2 a disreputable person or people — *vt.* [Slang] 1 to destroy (property) as by vandalism 2 to criticize or insult (a person, etc.) sharply or maliciously — **trash′y, -i·er, -i·est,** *adj.*

trauma (trô′mə; *also* trä′-, trou′-) *n., pl.* **-mas** or **-mata** (-mə tə) 〖Gr〗 1 a bodily injury or shock 2 an emotional shock, often having a lasting psychic effect —**trau·matic** (trô mat′ik; *also* trä-, trou-) *adj.*

trau′ma·tize′ (-tiz′) *vt.* **-tized′, -tiz′ing** to subject to a physical or mental trauma

trav·ail (trə vāl′, trav′āl′) *n.* 〖< L *tri-*, three + *palus*, stake: referring to a torture device〗 1 very hard work 2 intense pain; agony

travel (trav′əl) *vi.* **-eled** or **-elled, -el·ing** or **-el·ling** 〖var. of prec.〗 1 to go from one place to another 2 to move, pass, or be transmitted — *vt.* to make a journey over or through — *n.* a traveling; trip —**trav′eler** or **trav′el·ler** *n.*

traveler's check a check, issued by a bank, etc., sold to a traveler who signs it at issuance and again when cashing it

trav·elogue or **trav·elog** (trav′ə lôg′) *n.* 1 an illustrated lecture on travels 2 a short film about a place, esp. one that is foreign, unusual, etc.

tra·verse (*for v.* trə vʉrs′, tra-; *for n. & adj.* trav′ərs) *vt.* **-versed′, -vers′ing** 〖< L *trans-*, across + *vertere*, to turn〗 to pass over, across, or through — *n.* something that traverses or crosses, as a crossbar — *adj.* 1 extending

THESAURUS

transparent *a.* 1 [Allowing light to pass through] translucent, lucid, crystalline, gauzy, thin, permeable, glassy, cellophane; see also CLEAR 2.—*Ant.* DARK, black, smoky. 2 [Obvious] easily seen, plain, clear; see OBVIOUS 1.

transplant *n.* transplanting, transplantation, graft; see OPERATION 4.

transplant *v.* reset, reorient, remove; see ALTER 1.

transport *v.* convey, move, bring; see CARRY 1.

transportation *n.* conveying, conveyance, carrying, hauling, shipping, carting, moving, transferring, truckage, freightage, airlift, transference, transit, passage.

transported *a.* conveyed, forwarded, transferred; see MOVED 1.

trap[1] *n.* 1 [A device to catch game or persons] net, box trap, steel trap, spring trap, snare, mousetrap, pit, blind, maneuver. 2 [A trick] prank, practical joke, snare; see TRICK 1.

trap[1] *v.* ensnare, seduce, fool; see AMBUSH, DECEIVE.

trapped *a.* ambushed, cornered, with one's back to the wall; see CAPTURED.

trash *n.* 1 [Rubbish] garbage, waste, refuse, dregs, filth, litter, debris, dross, sweepings, rubble, odds and ends, stuff, rags, scraps, scrap, excess, scourings, fragments, pieces, shavings, loppings, slash, rakings, slag, parings, rinsings, shoddy, residue, offal, junk, sediment, leavings, droppings.—*Ant.* MONEY, goods, riches. 2 [Nonsense] drivel, rubbish, senselessness; see NONSENSE 1.

travel *n.* riding, roving, wandering, rambling, sailing, touring, biking, hiking, cruising, driving, wayfaring, going abroad, seeing the world, sightseeing, voyaging, journeying, trekking, flying, globe-trotting, space travel, rocketing.

travel *v.* tour, cruise, voyage, roam, explore, jet to, rocket to, orbit, go into orbit, take a jet, go by jet, migrate, trek, vacation, motor, visit, traverse, jaunt, wander, journey, adventure, quest, trip, rove, inspect, make an expedition, cross the continent, cross the ocean, encircle the globe, make the grand tour, sail, see the country, go camping, go abroad, take a trip, cover, go walking, go

riding, go bicycling, make a train trip, drive, fly, set out, set forth, sightsee; see also WALK 1.

traveled *a.* 1 [*Said of persons*] worldly, cosmopolitan, experienced; see CULTURED. 2 [*Said of roads*] well-used, busy, operating, in use, frequented, widely known, sure, safe, well-trodden, accepted.—*Ant.* ABANDONED, little-used, unexplored.

traveler *n.* voyager, adventurer, tourist, explorer, nomad, wanderer, truant, peddler, roamer, rambler, wayfarer, migrant, excursionist, sightseer, straggler, vagabond, vagrant, hobo, tramp, gypsy, gadabout, itinerant, pilgrim, rover, passenger, commuter, globe-trotter.

traveling *a.* passing, en route, on board, shipped, freighted, transported, moving, carried, conveyed, consigned, wandering, touring, roving, on tour, vagrant, migrant, nomadic, wayfaring, itinerant, cruising, excursioning, commuting, driving, flying, sailing, riding, on vacation, migrating, voyaging; see also MOVING 2.

across **2** designating or of draperies drawn by pulling a cord at the side —**tra·vers′al** *n.*

trav·es·ty (trav′is tē) *n., pl.* **-ties** 〖< L *trans-*, over + *vestire*, to dress〗 **1** a farcical imitation in ridicule **2** a ridiculous representation — *vt.* **-tied, -ty·ing** to make a travesty of

trawl (trôl) *n.* 〖< ? MDu *traghel*, dragnet〗 **1** a large net dragged along the bottom of a fishing bank **2** a long line supported by buoys, from which fishing lines are hung — *vi., vt.* to fish or catch with a trawl

trawl′er *n.* a boat used in trawling

tray (trā) *n.* 〖< OE *treg*, wooden board〗 a flat receptacle with raised edges, for holding or carrying things

treach·er·ous (trech′ər əs) *adj.* **1** characterized by treachery **2** untrustworthy —**treach′er·ous·ly** *adv.*

treach·ery (trech′ər ē) *n., pl.* **-ies** 〖< OFr *trichier*, to cheat〗 **1** betrayal of trust; disloyalty **2** treason

trea·cle (trē′kəl) *n.* 〖< Gr (*antidotos*) *thēriakē*, (remedy) for venom〗 [Brit., etc. (exc. Cdn.)] **1** molasses **2** anything very sweet or cloying —**trea′cly** (-klē) *adj.*

tread (tred) *vt.* **trod, trod′den** or **trod, tread′ing** 〖OE *tredan*〗 **1** to walk on, in, along, etc. **2** to do or follow by walking, dancing, etc. **3** to press or beat with the feet — *vi.* **1** to walk **2** to set one's foot (*on, across,* etc.) **3** to trample (*on* or *upon*) — *n.* **1** the manner or sound of treading **2** something on which a person or thing treads or moves, as a shoe sole, wheel, surface of a stair, etc. **3** the thick outer layer of an automotive tire —**tread water** *pt. & pp. usually* **tread′ed** to stay upright in swimming by moving the legs up and down

trea·dle (tred′'l) *n.* 〖< OE *tredan*, to tread〗 a lever moved by the foot as to turn a wheel

tread′mill′ *n.* a mill wheel turned by an animal treading an endless belt

treas. **1** treasurer **2** treasury

trea·son (trē′zən) *n.* 〖< L *trans-*, over + *dare*, give〗 betrayal of one's country to an enemy —**trea′son·a·ble** or **trea′son·ous** *adj.*

treas·ure (trezh′ər) *n.* 〖< Gr *thēsauros*〗 **1** accumulated wealth, as money, jewels, etc. **2** any person or thing considered valuable — *vt.* **-ured, -ur·ing** **1** to save up for future use **2** to value greatly

treas·ur·er (trezh′ər ər) *n.* one in charge of a treasury, as of a government, club, etc.

treas′ure-trove′ (-trōv′) *n.* 〖*trove* < OFr *trover*, find〗 treasure found hidden, the original owner of which is unknown

treas′ur·y (-ē) *n., pl.* **-ies** **1** a place where treasure or funds are kept **2** the funds or revenues of a state, corporation, etc. **3** [T-] the department of government in charge of revenue, taxation, etc.

treat (trēt) *vi.* 〖ult. < L *trahere*, to draw〗 **1** to discuss terms (*with*) **2** to speak or write (*of*) — *vt.* **1** to deal with (a subject) in writing, music, etc. in a specified manner **2**

to act toward (someone or something) in a specified manner **3** to pay for the food, etc. of (another) **4** to subject to some process, chemical, etc. **5** to give medical care to — *n.* **1** a meal, drink, etc. paid for by another **2** anything that gives great pleasure

trea·tise (trēt′is) *n.* 〖see prec.〗 a formal writing on some subject

treat·ment (trēt′mənt) *n.* **1** act, manner, method, etc. of treating **2** medical or surgical care

treaty (trēt′ē) *n., pl.* **-ties** 〖< L *trahere*, to draw〗 a formal agreement between two or more nations

tre·ble (treb′əl) *adj.* 〖< L *triplus*, triple〗 **1** threefold; triple **2** of, for, or performing the treble — *n.* **1** the highest part in musical harmony; soprano **2** a high-pitched voice or sound — *vt., vi.* **-bled, -bling** to make or become threefold

tree (trē) *n.* 〖OE *trēow*〗 **1** a large, woody perennial plant with one main trunk and many branches **2** anything resembling a tree; specif., a diagram of family descent (**family tree**) — *vt.* **treed, tree′ing** to chase up a tree — **tree′less** *adj.* —**tree′like′** *adj.*

tre·foil (trē′foil′) *n.* 〖< L *tri-*, three + *folium*, leaf〗 **1** a plant with leaves divided into three leaflets, as the clover **2** a design, etc. shaped like such a leaf

trek (trek) *vi.* **trekked, trek′king** 〖Afrik < Du *trekken*, to draw〗 **1** to travel slowly or laboriously **2** [Colloq.] to go on foot — *n.* **1** a journey **2** a migration

trel·lis (trel′is) *n.* 〖< L *trilix*, triple-twilled〗 a lattice on which vines are trained

trema·tode (trem′ə tōd′, trē′mə-) *n.* 〖< Gr *trēmatōdēs*, perforated〗 a parasitic flatworm with muscular suckers; fluke

trem·ble (trem′bəl) *vi.* **-bled, -bling** 〖< L *tremere*〗 **1** to shake or shiver, as from cold, fear, etc. **2** to feel great fear or anxiety **3** to quiver, vibrate, etc. — *n.* **1** a trembling **2** [*sometimes pl.*] a fit or state of trembling

tre·men·dous (tri men′dəs) *adj.* 〖< L *tremere*, tremble〗 **1** terrifying; dreadful **2** *a*) very large; great *b*) [Colloq.] wonderful, amazing, etc. —**tre·men′dous·ly** *adv.*

tremo·lo (trem′ə lō′) *n., pl.* **-los′** 〖It〗 *Music* a tremulous effect produced by rapid reiteration of the same tone

tremor (trem′ər) *n.* 〖< L *tremere*, tremble〗 **1** a trembling, shaking, etc. **2** a trembling sensation

tremu·lous (trem′yōō ləs) *adj.* 〖< L *tremere*, to tremble〗 **1** trembling; quivering **2** fearful; timid —**trem′u·lously** *adv.* —**trem′u·lous·ness** *n.*

trench (trench) *vt.* 〖< OFr *trenchier*, to cut〗 to dig a ditch or ditches in — *n.* **1** a deep furrow **2** a long, narrow ditch dug by soldiers for cover, with earth heaped up in front

trench·ant (trench′ənt) *adj.* 〖see prec.〗 **1** sharp; keen;

THESAURUS

travesty *n.* burlesque, spoof, caricature; see PARODY.

tray *n.* platter, plate, tea wagon; see DISH 1.

treacherous *a.* deceptive, undependable, dangerous, risky, misleading, tricky, ensnaring, faulty, precarious, unstable, insecure, shaky, slippery, ticklish, difficult, ominous, alarming, menacing.—*Ant.* RELIABLE, dependable, steady.

treachery *n.* faithlessness, disloyalty, betrayal; see DISHONESTY, TREASON.

tread *v.* walk, step, step on; see TRAMPLE.

treason *n.* sedition, disloyalty, perfidy, treachery, seditionary act, seditious act, aid and comfort to the enemy, factious revolt; see also DISHONESTY, DECEPTION, REVOLUTION 2.

treasure *n.* richness, riches, nest egg; see WEALTH.

treasure *v.* prize, value, appreciate, guard; see also LOVE 1.

treasurer *n.* receiver, cashier, banker; see CLERK.

treasury *n.* exchequer, safe, depository; see BANK 2.

treat *n.* entertainment, surprise, amusement, feast, source of gratification, gift, drinks for the crowd*, setup, spree.

treat *v.* **1** [To deal with a person or thing] negotiate, manage, have to do with, have business with, behave toward, handle, make terms with, act toward, react toward, use, employ, have recourse to.—*Ant.* NEGLECT, ignore, have nothing to do with. **2** [To assist toward a cure] attend, administer, prescribe, dose, operate, nurse, dress, minister to, apply therapy, care for, doctor*; see also HEAL. **3** [To pay for another's entertainment] entertain, indulge, satisfy, amuse, divert, play host to, escort, set up, stake to*.

treatise *n.* tract, paper, monograph.

treatment *n.* **1** [Usage] handling, processing, dealing, approach, execution, procedure, method, manner, proceeding, way, strategy, custom, habit, employment, practice, mode, line, angle. **2** [Assistance toward a cure] diet, operation, medical care, surgery, therapy, remedy, prescription, regimen, hospitalization, doctoring*; see also MEDICINE 2.

treaty *n.* agreement, pact, settlement, covenant, compact, convention, alliance, charter, sanction, bond, understanding, arrangement, bargain, negotiation, deal*.

tree *n.* Trees include the following:

ash, elm, oak, maple, evergreen, birch, tulip, fir, cypress, juniper, larch, tamarack, pine, cedar, beech, chestnut, eucalyptus, hickory, walnut, sycamore, palm, willow, locust, sequoia, redwood, poplar, acacia, cottonwood, box elder, apple, cherry, peach, plum, pear, banyan, bamboo, mahogany, ebony, ironwood, bottletree; see also WOOD 1. **—up a tree*** cornered, in difficulty, trapped; see IN TROUBLE.

trees *n.* wood, woods, windbreak; see FOREST.

trek *v.* hike, migrate, journey; see TRAVEL.

tremble *v.* quiver, shiver, vibrate; see SHAKE 1.

tremendous *a.* huge, great, colossal; see LARGE 1.

tremor *n.* trembling, shaking, shivering; see EARTHQUAKE.

trench *n.* rut, hollow, gully, depression, gutter, tube, furrow, drainage canal, creek, moat, dike, drain, channel, main, gorge, gulch, arroyo. *Military trenches include the following:* dugout, earthwork, entrenchment, fortification, breastwork, pillbox, excavation, bunker, machine-gun nest, foxhole.

incisive *[trenchant* words*]* **2** forceful; vigorous; effective *[a trenchant* argument*]* —**trench′antly** *adv.*

trench coat a belted raincoat in a military style

trench′er *n.* ⟦see TRENCH⟧ [Archaic] a wooden platter for meat

trench′er·man (-mən) *n., pl.* **-men** an eater; esp., one who eats much

trench foot a diseased condition of the feet from prolonged exposure to wet and cold, as in trenches

trench mouth an infectious disease of the mucous membranes of the mouth and throat

trend (trend) *vi.* ⟦OE *trendan*⟧ to have a general direction or tendency — *n.* **1** the general tendency or course; drift **2** a current style

trend·y (tren′dē) *adj.* **-i·er, -i·est** [Colloq.] of or in the latest style, or trend

trepi·da·tion (trep′ə dā′shən) *n.* ⟦< L *trepidus,* disturbed⟧ **1** trembling movement **2** fearful uncertainty

tres·pass (tres′pəs, -pas′) *vi.* ⟦< L *trans-,* across + *passus,* a step⟧ **1** to go beyond the limits of what is considered right; do wrong; transgress **2** to enter another's property without permission or right — *n.* a trespassing; specif., a moral offense —**tres′pass·er** *n.*

tress (tres) *n.* ⟦< OFr *tresse,* braid of hair⟧ **1** a lock of human hair **2** *[pl.]* a woman's or girl's hair, esp. when long

tres·tle (tres′əl) *n.* ⟦< L *transtrum,* a beam⟧ **1** a horizontal beam fastened to two pairs of spreading legs, used as a support **2** a framework of uprights and crosspieces, supporting a bridge, etc.

trey (trā) *n.* ⟦< L *tres,* three⟧ a playing card, etc. with three spots

tri- ⟦< Fr, L, or Gr⟧ *prefix* **1** having or involving three **2** three times, into three **3** every third

triad (trī′ad′) *n.* ⟦< Gr *treis,* three⟧ a group of three

tri·age (trē äzh′) *n.* ⟦< Fr *trier,* sift⟧ a system of establishing the order in which acts of esp. medical assistance are to be carried out in an emergency

trial (trī′əl) *n.* ⟦see TRY⟧ **1** the act or process of trying, testing, etc.; test; probation **2** a hardship, suffering, etc. **3** a source of annoyance **4** a formal examination to decide a case by a court of law **5** an attempt; effort — *adj.* **1** of a trial **2** for the purpose of trying, testing, etc. —**on trial** being tried or tested

trial and error the process of making repeated trials, tests, etc. until the result is found

trial balloon something said or done to test public opinion on an issue

tri·an·gle (trī′aŋ′gəl) *n.* ⟦see TRI- & ANGLE¹⟧ **1** a plane figure having three angles and three sides **2** any three-sided or three-cornered object **3** a situation involving three persons *[a love triangle]* —**tri·an′gu·lar** (-gyōō lər) *adj.* —**trian′gu·larly** *adv.*

tri·an·gu·late (-gyōō lāt′) *vt.* **-lat′ed, -lat′ing** to divide into triangles to compute distance or relative positions —**tri·an′gu·la′tion** *n.*

tri·ath·lon (trī ath′län′, -lən) *n.* ⟦TRI- + Gr *athlon,* a con-

test⟧ an endurance race combining events in swimming, bicycling, and running

tribe (trīb) *n.* ⟦< L *tribus*⟧ **1** a group of persons or clans descended from a common ancestor and living under a leader or chief **2** a natural group of plants or animals — **trib′al** *adj.* —**trib′ally** *adv.* —**tribes′man** (-mən), *pl.* **-men,**

tribu·la·tion (trib′yōō lā′shən) *n.* ⟦< L *tribulare,* to press⟧ great misery or distress, or the cause of it

tri·bu·nal (trī byōō′nəl, tri-) *n.* ⟦see fol.⟧ **1** a seat for a judge in a court **2** a court of justice

trib·une (trib′yōōn′, tri byōōn′) *n.* ⟦< L *tribus,* tribe⟧ **1** in ancient Rome, a magistrate appointed to protect the rights of plebeians **2** a champion of the people: often a newspaper name

tribu·tary (trib′yōō ter′ē) *adj.* **1** paying tribute **2** subject *[a tributary* nation*]* **3** *a)* making additions *b)* flowing into a larger one *[a tributary* stream*]* — *n., pl.* **-ies 1** a tributary nation **2** a tributary river

trib·ute (trib′yōōt) *n.* ⟦< L *tribuere,* allot⟧ **1** money paid regularly by one nation to another as acknowledgment of subjugation, for protection, etc. **2** any forced payment **3** something given, done, or said to show gratitude, respect, honor, or praise

trice (trīs) *n.* ⟦< MDu *trisen,* to pull⟧ an instant: now only in **in a trice**

tri·cen·ten·nial (trī′sen ten′ē əl) *adj.* happening once every 300 years — *n.* a 300th anniversary

tri·ceps (trī′seps′) *n., pl.* **-ceps′** or **-ceps′es** ⟦L < *tri-,* three + *caput,* head⟧ a muscle with three points of origin; esp., the muscle on the back of the upper arm

tri·cera·tops (trī ser′ə täps′) *n.* ⟦< TRI- + Gr *keras,* horn + *ōps,* eye⟧ a plant-eating dinosaur with three horns

tri·china (tri kī′nə) *n., pl.* **-nae** (-nē) ⟦< Gr *trichinos,* hairy⟧ a very small worm whose larvae cause trichinosis

trichi·no·sis (trik′i nō′sis) *n.* ⟦< Gr *trichinos,* hairy⟧ a disease caused by intestinal worms, and acquired by eating pork from an infested hog

trick (trik) *n.* ⟦< OFr *trichier,* to cheat⟧ **1** something designed to deceive, cheat, etc. **2** a practical joke; prank **3** a clever act intended to amuse **4** any feat requiring skill **5** a personal mannerism **6** a round of duty; shift **7** *Card Games* the cards won in a single round — *vt.* to deceive or swindle — *adj.* apt to malfunction *[a trick* knee*]* —**do (or turn) the trick** [Colloq.] to produce the desired result — **trick′ery,** *pl.* **-ies,** *n.* —**trick′ster** *n.*

trickle (trik′əl) *vi.* **-led, -ling** ⟦ME *triklen* < ?⟧ **1** to flow slowly in a thin stream or fall in drops **2** to move slowly *[the crowd trickled* away*]* — *n.* a slow, small flow

trick′le·down′ *adj.* of an economic theory holding that government aid to big business will ultimately benefit the poor

trick′y *adj.* **-i·er, -i·est 1** given to or characterized by trickery **2** like a trick in deceptiveness or intricacy — **trick′i·ly** *adv.* —**trick′i·ness** *n.*

tri·color (trī′kul′ər) *n.* a flag having three colors in large areas; esp., the flag of France

---

◼◼◼ THESAURUS ◼◼◼

trend *n.* bias, bent, leaning; see INCLINATION 1.

trendy* *a.* stylish, popular, contemporary; see FASHIONABLE.

trespass *v.* encroach, invade, infringe; see MEDDLE 1.

trespasser *n.* encroacher, invader, infringer; see INTRUDER.

trial *a.* tentative, test, preliminary; see EXPERIMENTAL.

trial *n.* **1** [An effort to learn the truth] analysis, test, examination; see EXPERIMENT. **2** [A case at law] suit, lawsuit, fair hearing, hearing, action, case, contest, indictment, legal proceedings, claim, cross-examination, litigation, counterclaim, arraignment, prosecution, citation, court action, judicial contest, seizure, bill of divorce, habeas corpus, court-martial, impeachment. **3** [An ordeal] suffering, misfortune, heavy blow; see DIFFICULTY 1, 2. — **on trial 1** [In court] in litigation, up for investigation, at the bar, before the bar, before a judge, before a jury, being tried, contested, appealed, indicted; see also ACCUSED.

2 [Experimental] on a trial basis, for a trial period, on approval; see UNCERTAIN.

triangle *n.* Triangles include the following: equilateral, isosceles, right-angled, obtuse-angled, scalene, acute-angled.

triangular *a.* three-cornered, three-sided, triagonal; see ANGULAR.

tribal *a.* tribalistic, racial, kindred; see RACIAL.

tribe *n.* primitive group, ethnic group, association; see RACE 2.

tributary *n.* stream, branch, sidestream; see RIVER.

tribute *n.* applause, recognition, eulogy; see PRAISE 1.

trick *n.* **1** [A deceit] wile, fraud, deception, ruse, cheat, cover, feint, hoax, artifice, decoy, trap, stratagem, intrigue, fabrication, double-dealing, forgery, fake, illusion, invention, subterfuge, distortion, delusion, ambush, snare, blind, evasion, plot, equivocation, concealment, treachery, swindle, feigning, impersonation, pretense, duplicity, falsehood, falsifi-

cation, perjury, disguise, conspiracy, circumvention, quibble, trickery, beguiling, chicanery, humbug, maneuver, sham, counterfeit, gyp*, touch*, phoney*, come-on*, fast one*, dodge*, plant*, clip*, sucker deal*, con game*, bluff, shakedown*, sell-out*, con*, funny business*, dirty work*, crooked deal, front*, gimmick*; see also LIE.—*Ant.* HONESTY, truth, veracity. **2** [A prank] jest, sport, practical joke; see JOKE. **3** [A practical method or expedient] skill, facility, know-how*; see ABILITY, METHOD.

trick *v.* dupe, outwit, fool; see DECEIVE.

trickle *v.* drip, leak, run; see FLOW.

tricky *a.* **1** [Shrewd] clever, sharp, keen-witted; see INTELLIGENT. **2** [Delicate or difficult] complicated, intricate, critical, touchy, involved, perplexing, knotty, thorny, complex, unstable, ticklish, catchy, likely to go wrong, hanging by a thread*; see also DIFFICULT 1, 2.—*Ant.* EASY, clearcut, simple.

tri·cy·cle (trī′sik′əl, -si kəl) *n.* ⟦Fr: see TRI- & CYCLE⟧ a child's three-wheeled vehicle operated by pedals

tri·dent (trīd′'nt) *n.* ⟦< L *tri*-, three + *dens*, tooth⟧ a three-pronged spear — *adj.* three-pronged

tried (trīd) *vt., vi. pt. & pp. of* TRY — *adj.* 1 tested; proved 2 trustworthy

tri·en·nial (trī en′ē əl) *adj.* ⟦< L *tri*-, three + *annus*, year⟧ 1 happening every three years 2 lasting three years —**tri·en′ni·al·ly** *adv.*

tri·fle (trī′fəl) *n.* ⟦< OFr *truffe*, deception⟧ 1 something of little value or importance 2 a small amount of money — *vi.* **-fled, -fling** 1 to talk or act jokingly 2 to toy (*with*) — *vt.* to waste [*to trifle* the hours away] —**tri′fler** *n.*

tri′fling *adj.* 1 frivolous; shallow 2 of little importance; trivial

tri·fo·cals (trī′fō′kəlz) *n.pl.* eyeglasses like bifocals, but with a third area in the lens ground for intermediate distance

trig (trig) *n. short for* TRIGONOMETRY

trig·ger (trig′ər) *n.* ⟦< Du *trekken*, to pull⟧ a lever pulled to release a catch, etc., esp. one pressed to activate the firing mechanism on a firearm — *vt.* to initiate (an action)

tri·glyc·er·ide (trī glis′ər id′) *n.* ⟦TRI- + Gr *glykeros*, sweet⟧ an ester derived from glycerol, the chief component of fats and oils

trigo·nom·etry (trig′ə näm′ə trē) *n., pl.* **-tries** ⟦< Gr *trigōnon*, triangle + *-metria*, measurement⟧ the branch of mathematics analyzing, and making calculations from, relations between the sides and angles of triangles — **trig′o·no·met′ric** (-nə me′trik) *adj.*

trill (tril) *n.* ⟦ult. echoic⟧ 1 a rapid alternation of a musical tone with a slightly higher tone 2 a warble 3 a rapid vibration of the tongue or uvula — *vt., vi.* to sound, speak, or play with a trill

tril·lion (tril′yən) *n.* 1 1 followed by 12 zeros 2 [Brit.] 1 followed by 18 zeros —**tril′lionth** *adj., n.*

tril·ogy (tril′ə jē) *n., pl.* **-gies** ⟦see TRI- & -LOGY⟧ a set of three related plays, novels, etc.

trim (trim) *vt.* **trimmed, trim′ming** ⟦< OE *trymman*, make firm⟧ 1 to put in proper order; make neat or tidy [*to trim* hair] 2 to clip, lop, cut, etc. 3 to decorate, as by adding ornaments, etc. 4 *a*) to balance (a ship) by ballasting, etc. *b*) to put (sails) in order for sailing 5 to balance (a flying aircraft) 6 [Colloq.] to beat, punish, defeat, cheat, etc. — *vi.* to adjust according to expediency — *n.* 1 order; arrangement 2 good condition 3 a trimming 4 decorative parts or borders — *adj.* **trim′mer, trim′mest** 1 orderly; neat 2 well-proportioned 3 in good condition —**trim′ly** *adv.* —**trim′mer** *n.* —**trim′ness** *n.*

tri·ma·ran (trī′mə ran′) *n.* a boat like a catamaran, but with three hulls

tri·mes·ter (trī mes′tər, trī′mes′-) *n.* ⟦< L *tri*-, three + *mensis*, month⟧ in some colleges, any of the three periods of the academic year

trim′ming (trim′iŋ) *n.* 1 decoration; ornament 2 [*pl.*] *a*) the side dishes of a meal *b*) parts trimmed off 3 [Colloq.] a beating, defeat, cheating, etc.

trin·ity (trin′ə tē) *n., pl.* **-ties** ⟦< L *trinitas*⟧ a set of three —**the Trinity** *Christian Theol.* the union of Father, Son, and Holy Spirit in one Godhead

trin·ket (triŋ′kit) *n.* ⟦ME *trenket*⟧ 1 a small ornament, piece of jewelry, etc. 2 a trifle or toy

trio (trē′ō) *n., pl.* **-os** ⟦< L *tres*, three⟧ 1 a group of three 2 *Music a*) a composition for three voices or three instruments *b*) the three performers of such a composition

trip (trip) *vi., vt.* **tripped, trip′ping** ⟦< OFr *treper*⟧ 1 to move or perform with light, rapid steps 2 to stumble or cause to stumble 3 to make or cause to make a mistake 4 to release or run past (a spring, wheel, etc.) — *n.* 1 a light, quick tread 2 a journey, jaunt, etc. 3 a stumble or a causing to stumble 4 [Slang] *a*) an experience induced by a psychedelic drug, esp. LSD *b*) an experience that is pleasing, exciting, etc. —**trip up** to catch in a lie, error, etc. — **trip′per** *n.*

tri·par·tite (trī pär′tīt′) *adj.* ⟦< L *tri*-, three + *partire*, to part⟧ 1 having three parts 2 made between three parties, as an agreement

tripe (trīp) *n.* ⟦prob. ult. < Ar *tharb*, layer of fat lining the intestines⟧ 1 part of the stomach of an ox, etc., used as food 2 [Slang] anything worthless, etc.; nonsense

trip′ham′mer *n.* a heavy, power-driven hammer, alternately raised and allowed to fall by a tripping device

tri·ple (trip′əl) *adj.* ⟦< L *triplus*⟧ 1 consisting of three; threefold 2 three times as much or as many — *n.* 1 an amount three times as much or as many 2 *Baseball* a hit on which the batter reaches third base — *vt., vi.* **tri′pled, tri′pling** 1 to make or become three times as much or as many 2 *Baseball* to hit a triple —**tri′ply** *adv.*

tri·plet (trip′lit) *n.* any of three offspring born at a single birth

trip·li·cate (trip′li kit; *for v.,* -kāt′) *adj.* ⟦< L *triplex*⟧ 1 threefold 2 being the last of three identical copies — *n.* any one of such copies — *vt.* **-cat′ed, -cat′ing** to make three copies of —**in triplicate** in three copies

tri·pod (trī′päd′) *n.* ⟦< Gr *tri*-, three + *pous*, foot⟧ a three-legged caldron, stool, support, etc.

trip·tych (trip′tik) *n.* ⟦< Gr *tri*-, three + *ptychē*, a fold⟧ a set of three panels with pictures, etc., often hinged, used as an altarpiece

tri·sect (trī sekt′, trī′sekt′) *vt.* ⟦< TRI- + L *secare*, to cut⟧ to cut or divide into three equal parts

trite (trīt) *adj.* **trit′er, trit′est** ⟦< L *terere*, wear out⟧ worn out by constant use; stale —**trite′ness** *n.*

trit·ium (trit′ē əm) *n.* a radioactive isotope of hydrogen having an atomic weight of 3

tri·umph (trī′əmf, -umf′) *n.* ⟦< L *triumphus*⟧ 1 a victory; success 2 exultation or joy over a victory, etc. — *vi.* 1 to gain victory or success 2 to rejoice over victory, etc. —**tri·um′phal** *adj.*

tri·um′phant (-um′fənt) *adj.* 1 successful; victorious 2 rejoicing for victory —**tri·um′phantly** *adv.*

tri·um·vir (trī um′vir′) *n., pl.* **-virs** or **-viri** (-vi rī′) ⟦L: see fol.⟧ in ancient Rome, any of three administrators sharing authority

tri·um·vi·rate (trī um′vi rit) *n.* ⟦< L *trium virum*, of three men⟧ government by three persons or parties

tri·va·lent (trī vā′lənt) *adj. Chem.* having three valences or a valence of three

trivet (triv′it) *n.* ⟦< L *tripes*, tripod⟧ 1 a three-legged stand for holding pots, etc. near a fire 2 a short-legged stand for hot dishes to rest on

---

THESAURUS

tricycle *n.* trike*, wheel*, three-wheeler; see VEHICLE.

tried *a.* dependable, proved, used; see USED 1.

trifle *n.* 1 [A small quantity] particle, piece, speck; see BIT 1. 2 [A small degree] jot, eyelash, fraction; see BIT 2. 3 [Something of little importance] triviality, small matter, nothing; see INSIGNIFICANCE.

trifling *a.* petty, small, insignificant; see TRIVIAL, UNIMPORTANT.

trim *a.* 1 [Neat] orderly, tidy, spruce; see CLEAN 1, NEAT 1. 2 [Well-proportioned] shapely, well-designed, streamlined, clean, slim, shipshape, delicate, fit, comely, well-formed, symmetrical, well-made, clean-cut, well-balanced, graceful, well-molded, harmonious, beautiful, classical, compact, smart; see also HANDSOME.—*Ant.* DISORDERED, shapeless, straggly.

trim *v.* 1 [To cut off excess] prune, shave, lop; see CUT 1. 2 [To adorn] ornament, embellish, deck; see DECORATE. 3 [To prepare for sailing] ballast, rig, outfit; see SAIL 1.

trimming *n.* 1 [Ornamentation] accessory, frill, tassel; see DECORATION 2. 2 [The act of cutting off excess] shearing, lopping off, shaving off; see REDUCTION 1.

trinity *n.* trio, trilogy, triplet, triplicate, threesome, triad, the Godhead; Father, Son, and Holy Ghost; the Triune God, Trinity; see also GOD 1.

trinket *n.* gadget, novelty, bauble; see JEWEL, JEWELRY.

trio *n.* 1 [A combination of three] threesome, triangle, triplet; see TRINITY. 2 [Three musicians performing together] string trio, vocal trio, swing trio; see BAND 3.

trip *n.* 1 [A journey] voyage, excursion, tour; see JOURNEY. 2 [A psychedelic experience] hallucinations, LSD trip, being turned on; see DRUG.

trip *v.* 1 [To stumble] tumble, slip, lurch, slide, founder, fall, pitch, fall over, slip upon, plunge, sprawl, topple, go head over heels.—*Ant.* ARISE, ascend, get up. 2 [To cause to stumble] block, hinder, bind, tackle, overthrow, push, send headlong, kick, shove, mislead.—*Ant.* HELP, pick up, give a helping hand.

triple *a.* in triplicate, by three, threefold; see THREE.

trite *a.* hackneyed, prosaic, stereotyped; see COMMON 1, DULL 4.

triumph *n.* conquest, achievement, success; see VICTORY.

triumphant *a.* victorious, successful, lucky, winning, conquering, in the lead, triumphal, jubilant, dominant, laurel-crowned, champion, unbeaten, topseeded, out front, triumphing, victorial, elated, in ascendancy, with flying colors.—*Ant.* BEATEN, defeated, overwhelmed.

trivia (triv′ē ə) *n.pl.* [*often with sing. v.*] unimportant matters

triv·ial (triv′ē əl) *adj.* [< L *trivialis*, commonplace] unimportant; insignificant —**triv′i·al′ity** (-al′ə tē) *n.*

-trix (triks) [L] *suffix* forming feminine nouns of agency

tro·chee (trō′kē) *n.* [< Gr *trechein*, to run] a metrical foot of one accented syllable followed by one unaccented syllable —**tro·cha′ic** (-kā′ik) *adj.*

trod (träd) *vt., vi. pt. & alt. pp.* of TREAD

trod·den (träd′n) *vt., vi. alt. pp.* of TREAD

trog·lo·dyte (träg′lō dit′, -lə-) *n.* [< Gr *trōglē*, hole + *dyein*, enter] **1** any of the prehistoric people who lived in caves **2** a recluse

troi·ka (troi′kə) *n.* [Russ] **1** a vehicle drawn by three horses abreast **2** an association of three in authority

Tro·jan (trō′jən) *adj.* of Troy, its people, etc. — *n.* **1** a native or inhabitant of ancient Troy (city in Asia Minor) **2** a strong, hard-working, determined person

Trojan horse *Gr. Legend* a huge, hollow wooden horse with Greek soldiers inside: it is brought into Troy, the soldiers creep out and open the gates, and the Greek army destroys the city

troll[1] (trōl) *vt., vi.* [ME *trollen*, to roll] **1** to sing the parts of (a round, etc.) in succession **2** to sing in a full voice **3** to fish (in) with a baited line trailed behind a slowly moving boat

troll[2] (trōl) *n.* [ON] *Scand. Folklore* a supernatural being, as a giant or dwarf, living in a cave

trol·ley (träl′ē) *n., pl.* **-leys** [< TROLL[1]] **1** a wheeled basket, etc. that runs suspended from an overhead track **2** a grooved wheel at the end of a pole, for transmitting electric current from an overhead wire to a streetcar, etc. **3** a trolley car

trolley bus an electric bus powered by trolleys

trolley car an electric streetcar that gets its power from a trolley

trol·lop (träl′əp) *n.* [prob. < Ger *trolle*, wench] a prostitute

trom·bone (träm′bōn′, träm bōn′) *n.* [It < *tromba*, a trumpet] a large brass instrument, usually with a slide, or movable section Also **slide trombone** —**trom·bon′ist** *n.*

troop (trōōp) *n.* [< ML *troppus*, flock] **1** a group of persons or animals **2** [*pl.*] soldiers **3** a subdivision of a cavalry regiment **4** a unit of Boy Scouts or Girl Scouts — *vi.* **1** to gather or go together in a group **2** to walk or go

troop′er *n.* [prec. + -ER] **1** a soldier in the mounted cavalry **2** a mounted police officer **3** a State police officer

trope (trōp) *n.* [< Gr *tropos*, a turning] figurative language or a word used in a figurative sense

tro·phy (trō′fē) *n., pl.* **-phies** [< Gr *tropaion*] a memorial of victory in war, sports competition, etc.; prize

tropic (träp′ik) *n.* [< Gr *tropikos*, of a turn (of the sun at the solstices)] **1** either of two parallels of latitude, one, the **Tropic of Cancer**, *c.* 23° 26′ north, and the other, the **Tropic of Capricorn**, *c.* 23° 26′ south **2** [*also* T-] [*pl.*] the region between these latitudes — *adj.* of the tropics; tropical

trop′i·cal (-i kəl) *adj.* **1** of, in, characteristic of, or suitable for the tropics **2** very hot;·sultry; torrid

tro·pism (trō′piz′əm) *n.* [< Gr *tropē*, a turn] the tendency of a plant or animal to grow or turn toward, or away from, a stimulus, as light

tropo·sphere (trō′pō sfir′; *also* träp′ō-) *n.* [Fr < Gr *tropos*, a turning + Fr *sphère*, sphere] the atmospheric zone characterized by water vapor, weather, and decreasing temperatures with increasing altitude

trot (trät) *vt., vi.* **trot′ted, trot′ting** [< OHG *trottōn*, to tread] **1** to move, ride, go, etc. at a trot **2** to hurry; run — *n.* **1** a gait, as of a horse, in which a front leg and the opposite hind leg are lifted at the same time **2** a jogging gait of a person —**trot′ter** *n.*

troth (trōth, trōth) *n.* [ME *trouthe*] [Archaic] **1** faithfulness; loyalty **2** truth **3** a promise, esp. to marry

trou·ba·dour (trōō′bə dôr′) *n.* [Fr < Prov *trobar*, compose] **1** any of a class of lyric poets and poet-musicians in S France and N Spain and Italy in the 11th to 13th c. **2** a minstrel or singer

trou·ble (trub′əl) *vt.* **-bled, -bling** [< L *turba*, crowd] **1** to disturb or agitate **2** to worry; harass **3** to cause inconvenience to [don't *trouble* yourself] — *vi.* to take pains; bother — *n.* **1** a state of mental distress; worry **2** a misfortune; calamity **3** a person, event, etc. causing annoyance, distress, etc. **4** public disturbance **5** effort; bother [take the *trouble* to listen]

trou′ble·mak′er *n.* one who incites others to quarrel, rebel, etc.

trou′ble-shoot′er *n.* one whose work is to locate and eliminate the source of trouble in any flow of work

trou′ble·some (-səm) *adj.* characterized by or causing trouble

trough (trôf, träf) *n.* [OE *trog*] **1** a long, narrow, open container, esp. one to hold water or food for animals **2** a channel or gutter for carrying off rainwater **3** a long, narrow hollow, as between waves **4** a long, narrow area of low barometric pressure

trounce (trouns) *vt.* **trounced, trounc′ing** [< ?] **1** to beat; flog **2** [Colloq.] to defeat —**trounc′er** *n.*

troupe (trōōp) *n.* [Fr] a group of actors, singers, etc. — *vi.*

■ THESAURUS ■

trivial *a.* petty, trifling, small, superficial, piddling, wee, little, frivolous, insignificant, irrelevant, unimportant, nugatory, skin-deep, meaningless, mean, diminutive, slight, of no account, scanty, meager, inappreciable, microscopic, atomic, dribbling, nonessential, flimsy, inconsiderable, vanishing, momentary, immaterial, indifferent, beside the point, minute, inessential, paltry, inferior, minor, small-minded, beggarly, useless, inconsequential, worthless, mangy, trashy, pitiful, of little moment, dinky*, small-town*, cutting no ice*, cut and dried; see also SHALLOW 2.—*Ant.* IMPORTANT, great, serious.

troops *n.* soldiers, armed forces, fighting men; see ARMY 1.

trophy *n.* citation, medal, cup; see PRIZE.

tropic *a.* **1** [Related to the tropics] tropical, equatorial, jungle; see HOT 1. **2** [Hot] thermal, torrid, burning; see HOT 1.

tropics *n.* torrid zone, equator, Equatorial Africa; South America, Amazon, the Congo, the Pacific Islands, hot countries, jungles; see also JUNGLE.

trot *v.* single-foot, jog, amble; see RUN 2.

trouble *n.* **1** [A person or thing causing trouble] annoyance, difficult

situation, bother, bind, hindrance, difficulty, task, puzzle, predicament, plight, problem, fear, worry, concern, inconvenience, nuisance, disturbance, calamity, catastrophe, crisis, delay, quarrel, dispute, bad news, affliction, intrusion, irritation, trial, pain, ordeal, discomfort, injury, adversity, hang-up*, case, bore, gossip, problem child, meddler, pest, tease, tiresome person, inconsiderate person, intruder, troublemaker, fly in the ointment, headache*, brat, holy terror*, peck of trouble*.—*Ant.* HELP, aid, comfort. **2** [Illness] malady, ailment, affliction; see ILLNESS 1, 2. **3** [Civil disorder] riot, turmoil, strife; see DISTURBANCE 2. **4** [A quarrel] argument, feud, bickering; see DISPUTE, FIGHT 1. —**in trouble** in a quandary, never free from, in bad*, in hot water*, in for it*, in the doghouse*, in a jam*, out on a limb*; see also TROUBLED.

trouble *v.* **1** [To disturb] disconcert, annoy, irritate; see BOTHER 2, DISTURB. **2** [To take care] be concerned with, make an effort, take pains; see BOTHER 1.

troubled *a.* disturbed, agitated, grieved, apprehensive, pained, anxious, perplexed, afflicted, confused, puzzled, overwrought, aggravated*, uptight, bothered, harassed, vexed,

plagued, teased, annoyed, concerned, uneasy, discomposed, harried, careworn, mortified, badgered, baited, inconvenienced, put out, upset, flurried, flustered, bored, tortured, goaded, irritated, displeased, tried, roused, disconcerted, pursued, chafed, ragged, galled, rubbed the wrong way, tired, molested, crossed, thwarted, fazed, distressed, wounded, sickened, griped, restless, irked, pestered, heckled, persecuted, frightened, alarmed, terrified, scared, anguished, harrowed, tormented, provoked, stung, ruffled, fretting, perturbed, afraid, shaky, fearful, unsettled, suspicious, in turmoil, full of misgivings, shaken, dreading, bugged*, in a quandary, in a stew, on pins and needles*, all hot and bothered*, worried stiff, in a tizzy*, burned up*, miffed*, peeved*, riled*, floored*, up a tree*, hung-up*, up the creek without a paddle*.—*Ant.* CALM, at ease, settled.

troublemaker *n.* rogue, knave, recreant; see CRIMINAL.

troublesome *a.* bothersome, annoying, difficult, irritating, oppressive, repressive, distressing, upsetting, painful, dangerous, damaging.

trough *n.* dip, channel, hollow; see HOLE 2.

trouped, troup′ing to travel as a member of a troupe — **troup′er** n.

trou·sers (trou′zərz) n.pl. [< Gael triubhas] a two-legged outer garment, esp. for men and boys, extending from the waist to the ankles —**trou′ser** adj.

trous·seau (trōō′ sō′, trōō′sō) n., pl. **-seaux′** (-sōz′) or **-seaus′** [Fr < OFr trousse, a bundle] a bride's clothes, linens, etc.

trout (trout) n., pl. **trout** or **trouts** [< Gr trōgein, gnaw] a food and game fish, related to the salmon, found chiefly in fresh water

trow (trō, trou) vi., vt. [< OE treow, faith] [Archaic] to believe

trowel (trou′əl) n. [< L trua, ladle] 1 a flat hand tool for smoothing plaster or applying mortar 2 a scooplike tool for loosening soil, etc. — vt. **-eled** or **-elled, -el·ing** or **-el·ling** to spread, smooth, dig, etc. with a trowel

troy (troi) adj. [after Troyes, city in France, where first used] of or by a system of weights (**troy weight**) for gold, silver, gems, etc.

tru·ant (trōō′ənt) n. [< OFr, beggar] 1 a pupil who stays away from school without permission 2 one who shirks his or her duties — adj. 1 that is a truant 2 errant; straying —**tru′an·cy,** pl. **-cies,** n.

truce (trōōs) n. [< OE treow, faith] 1 a temporary cessation of warfare by agreement between the belligerents 2 respite from conflict, trouble, etc.

truck[1] (truk) n. [< Gr trochos, wheel] 1 a kind of two-wheeled barrow or low, wheeled frame, for carrying heavy articles 2 an automotive vehicle for hauling loads 3 a swiveling, wheeled frame under each end of a railroad car, etc. — vt. to carry on a truck — vi. to drive a truck — **truck′er** n.

truck[2] (truk) vt., vi. [< Fr troquer] to exchange; barter — n. 1 small articles of little value 2 vegetables raised for market 3 [Colloq.] dealings 4 [Colloq.] trash; rubbish

truck farm a farm where vegetables are grown to be marketed

truckle (truk′əl) n. [< Gr trochos, wheel] TRUNDLE BED: in full **truckle bed** — vi. **-led, -ling** to be servile; submit (to)

trucu·lent (truk′yōō lənt, -yə-) adj. [< L trux] 1 fierce; cruel; savage 2 pugnacious —**truc′u·lence** n. —**truc′u·lently** adv.

trudge (truj) vi. **trudged, trudg′ing** [< ?] to walk, esp. wearily or laboriously — n. a wearying walk

true (trōō) adj. **tru′er, tru′est** [OE treowe] 1 faithful; loyal 2 in accordance with fact; not false 3 conforming to standard, etc.; correct 4 rightful; lawful 5 accurately fitted, shaped, etc. 6 real; genuine — adv. 1 truly 2 Biol. without variation from type — vt. **trued, tru′ing** or **true′ing** to fit, place, or shape accurately: often with up — n. that which is true: with the

true believer a dedicated follower or disciple, esp. one who follows without doubts or questions

true bill a bill of indictment endorsed by a grand jury

true′-blue′ adj. very loyal; staunch

truf·fle (truf′əl) n. [ult. < L tuber, knob] a fleshy, edible underground fungus

tru·ism (trōō′iz′əm) n. a statement the truth of which is obvious

tru′ly adv. 1 in a true manner; accurately, genuinely, etc. 2 really; indeed 3 sincerely [yours truly]

trump (trump) n. [< TRIUMPH] 1 any playing card of a suit ranked higher than any other suit for a given hand 2 such a suit — vt., vi. to play a trump on (a trick, etc.) — **trump up** to devise fraudulently

trump·ery (trump′ər ē) n., pl. **-ies** [< Fr tromper, deceive] 1 something showy but worthless 2 nonsense

trumpet (trum′pət) n. [< OFr trompe] 1 a brass instrument consisting of a looped tube with a flared bell and three valves 2 a trumpetlike device for channeling sound, as an early kind of hearing aid 3 a sound like that of a trumpet — vi. to make the sound of a trumpet — vt. to proclaim loudly —**trum′peter** n.

trun·cate (trun′kāt) vt. **-cat′ed, -cat′ing** [< L truncus, stem] to cut off a part of —**trun·ca′tion** n.

trun·cheon (trun′chən) n. [< L truncus, stem] [Chiefly Brit., etc.] a policeman's stick or billy

trun·dle (trun′dəl) vt., vi. **-dled, -dling** [< OE trendan, to roll] to roll along —**trun′dler** n.

trundle bed a low bed on small wheels, that can be rolled under another bed when not in use

trunk (trunk) n. [< L truncus] 1 the main stem of a tree 2 a human or animal body, not including the head and limbs 3 a long snout, as of an elephant 4 a large, reinforced box to hold clothes, etc. in travel 5 [pl.] shorts worn by men for athletics 6 a compartment in a car, usually in the rear, for luggage, etc.

trunk line a main line of a railroad, telephone system, etc.

truss (trus) vt. [< OFr trousser] 1 orig., to bundle 2 to tie; bind (up) 3 to support with a truss — n. 1 a bundle or pack 2 a framework for supporting a roof, bridge, etc. 3 a padded device for giving support in cases of rupture or hernia

trust (trust) n. [< ON traust] 1 a) firm belief in the honesty, reliability, etc. of another; faith b) the one trusted 2 confident expectation, hope, etc. 3 responsibility resulting from confidence placed in one 4 care; custody 5 something entrusted to one 6 faith in a buyer's ability to pay; credit 7 a combination of corporations to establish a monopoly 8 Law a) the fact of having nominal ownership of property to keep, use, or administer for another b) such property — vi. to be confident — vt. 1 to have confidence in 2 to commit (something) to a person's care 3 to

---

■■■ THESAURUS ■■■

trousers n. slacks, breeches, knickerbockers; see CLOTHES.

trout n. Trout include the following: speckled, brook, rainbow, cutthroat, lake, salmon, steelhead, blue-backed, brown; see also FISH.

trowel n. blade, scoop, implement; see TOOL 1.

truant a. missing, straying, playing hooky; see ABSENT.

truce n. armistice, peace agreement, lull; see PEACE 1.

truck[1] n. carriage, van, lorry, car; see also VEHICLE. Types of trucks include the following: delivery wagon, moving van, police van, patrol wagon, laundry truck, pickup truck, freight truck, logging truck, army truck, trailer, piggyback trailer, truck trailer, truck and trailer, truck train, cement mixer, refrigerator truck, four-wheel drive truck, freighter, garbage truck, dump truck, semi*, half-track.

trudge v. plod, step, tread; see WALK 1.

true a. 1 [Accurate] precise, verified, proved, certain, certified, definite, checked, exact, correct; see also VALID 1. 2 [Loyal] sure, reliable, trustworthy, faithful, dependable, sincere; see also FAITHFUL, RELIABLE. 3 [Genuine] authentic, virtual, substantial, tangible, genuine, actual, pure; see also REAL 2, VALID 2. — come true become a fact, be actualized, come about; see DEVELOP 1, HAPPEN 2.

truly a. honestly, exactly, definitely, factually, correctly, unequivocally, reliably, sincerely, scrupulously, fairly, justly, validly, scientifically, rightfully, righteously, faithfully, worthily, without bias, without prejudice, fairly and squarely*.—Ant. WRONGLY, dishonestly, deceptively.

trumped up a. falsified, concocted, magnified; see EXAGGERATED, FALSE 2.

trumpet n. horn, bugle, cornet; see MUSICAL INSTRUMENT.

trump up v. think up, devise, concoct, falsify, present fraudulent evidence, misrepresent; see also DECEIVE, LIE 1.

trunk n. 1 [A container for goods] chest, case, foot locker; see CONTAINER. 2 [The torso] body, soma, thorax; see BACK 1, STOMACH. 3 [The stem of a tree] column, stock, log; see STALK. 4 [A proboscis] prow, snoot, snout; see NOSE 1.

trust n. 1 [Reliance] confidence, dependence, credence; see FAITH 1. 2 [Responsibility] guardianship, account, liability; see DUTY 1. 3 [A large company] monopoly, corporation, institution; see BUSINESS 4. — in trust in another's care, held for, reserved; see SAVED 2.

trust v. 1 [To believe in] swear by, place confidence in, confide in, esteem, depend upon, expect help from, presume upon, lean on, have no doubt, rest assured, be sure about, have no reservations, rely on, put faith in, look to, count on, assume that, presume that, be persuaded by, be convinced, put great stock in, set great store by, bank on*, take at one's word; see also BELIEVE.—Ant. DOUBT, mistrust, disbelieve. 2 [To hope] presume, take, imagine; see ASSUME, HOPE. 3 [To place in the protection of another] lend, put in safekeeping, entrust; see sense 1. 4 [To give credit to] advance, lend, loan, let out, grant, confer, let, patronize, aid, give financial aid to.—Ant. BORROW, raise money, pawn.

trusted a. trustworthy, dependable, reliable, trusty, tried, proved, intimate, close, faithful, loyal, true, staunch, constant, devoted, incorruptible, safe, honorable, honored, inviolable, on the level*, regular*, right, sure-fire*.—Ant. DISHONEST, questionable, unreliable.

allow to do something without misgivings **4** to believe **5** to hope; expect **6** to grant business credit to —*adj.* **1** relating to a trust **2** acting as trustee —**in trust** entrusted to another's care

trustee (trus tē′) *n.* **1** one to whom another's property or its management is entrusted **2** a member of a board managing the affairs of a college, hospital, etc. —**trustee′ship** *n.*

trust′ful *adj.* full of trust; ready to confide —**trust′fully** *adv.* —**trust′ful·ness** *n.*

trust fund money, securities, etc. held in trust

trust′ing *adj.* that trusts; trustful

trust territory a territory placed under the administrative authority of a country by the United Nations

trust′wor·thy *adj.* -**thi·er**, -**thi·est** worthy of trust; reliable —**trust′wor′thi·ness** *n.*

trusty (trus′tē) *adj.* -**i·er**, -**i·est** dependable; trustworthy —*n.*, *pl.* -**ies** a convict granted special privileges as a trustworthy person

truth (trōōth) *n.* [OE *treowth*] **1** a being true; specif., *a)* sincerity; honesty *b)* conformity with fact *c)* reality; actual existence *d)* correctness; accuracy **2** that which is true **3** an established fact —**in truth** truly

truth′ful *adj.* **1** telling the truth; honest **2** corresponding with fact or reality —**truth′fully** *adv.* —**truth′ful·ness** *n.*

try (trī) *vt.* **tried**, **try′ing** [< OFr *trier*] **1** to melt out or render (fat, etc.) **2** to conduct the trial of in a law court **3** to put to the proof; test **4** to subject to trials, etc.; afflict **5** to experiment with [to *try* a recipe] **6** to attempt; endeavor —*vi.* to make an effort, attempt, etc. —*n.*, *pl.* **tries** an attempt; effort; trial —**try on** to test the fit of (something to wear) by putting it on —**try out 1** to test by putting into use **2** to test one's fitness, as for a place on a team

try′ing *adj.* that tries one's patience; annoying; irksome —**try′ingly** *adv.*

try′out′ *n.* [Colloq.] a test to determine fitness, qualifications, etc.

tryst (trist) *n.* [< OFr *triste*, hunting station] **1** an appointment to meet, esp. one made by lovers **2** an appointed meeting or meeting place

tsar (tsär, zär) *n. alt. sp. of* CZAR (sense 1) —**tsari·na** (tsä rē′nə, zä-) *n.fem.*

tsetse fly (tset′sē, tsēt′-) [< Bantu name] a small fly of central and S Africa: one kind carries sleeping sickness

T-shirt (tē′shʉrt′) *n.* a collarless pullover knit shirt with short sleeves

tsp. **1** teaspoon(s) **2** teaspoonful(s)

T square a T-shaped ruler for drawing parallel lines

tsu·nami (tsōō nä′mē) *n.* [Jpn < *tsu*, a harbor + *nami*, a wave] a huge sea wave caused by an undersea earthquake, volcanic eruption, etc.

tub (tub) *n.* [< MDu *tubbe*] **1** a round wooden container, usually with staves and hoops **2** any large, open container, as of metal **3** a bathtub

tuba (tōō′bə) *n.* [L, trumpet] a large, low-pitched brass musical instrument

tubal (tōō′bəl) *adj.* of or in a tube, esp. a fallopian tube [a *tubal* pregnancy]

tubby (tub′ē) *adj.* -**bier**, -**bi·est 1** shaped like a tub **2** fat and short

tube (tōōb) *n.* [< L *tubus*, pipe] **1** a slender pipe of metal, glass, etc. for conveying fluids **2** a tubelike part, organ, etc. **3** a pliable cylinder with a screw cap, for holding paste, etc. **4** *short for:* ELECTRON TUBE *b)* VACUUM TUBE **5** [Brit.] a subway —**the tube** [Colloq.] television —**tube′less** *adj.*

tu·ber (tōō′bər) *n.* [L, lit., a swelling] a short, thick part of an underground stem, as a potato —**tu′ber·ous** *adj.*

tu′ber·cle (-kəl) *n.* [see prec.] **1** a small, rounded projection, as on a bone or a plant root **2** any abnormal hard nodule or swelling; specif., the typical lesion of tuberculosis

tu·ber·cu·lin (tōō bʉr′kyōō lin) *n.* a solution injected into the skin as a test for tuberculosis

tu·ber·cu·lo·sis (-lō′sis) *n.* [see TUBERCLE & -OSIS] an infectious disease characterized by the formation of tubercles in body tissue; specif., tuberculosis of the lungs —**tu·ber′cu·lar** or **tu·ber′cu·lous** *adj.*

tube sock a stretchable sock in the form of a long tube with no shaped heel

tube top a stretchable, one-piece, sleeveless and strapless women's garment for the upper body

tub·ing (tōōb′iŋ) *n.* **1** a series or system of tubes **2** material in the form of a tube **3** a piece of tube

tu·bu·lar (tōō′byōō lər, -byə-) *adj.* [< L *tubus*, pipe] **1** of or like a tube **2** made with a tube or tubes

tu′bule′ (-byōōl′) *n.* a small tube

tuck (tuk) *vt.* [< MDu *tucken*] **1** to pull or gather (*up*) in a fold or folds **2** to sew a fold or folds in (a garment) **3** to fold the edges of (a sheet, etc.) under or in, to make secure **4** to press snugly into a small space — *n.* a sewed fold in a garment

tucker (tuk′ər) *vt.* [prob. < prec., in obs. sense "to punish, rebuke"] [Colloq.] to tire (*out*); weary

-tude (tōōd, tyōōd) [< L -*tudo*] *suffix* state, quality, or instance of being

Tues·day (tōōz′dā, -dē) *n.* [OE *Tiwes dæg*, day of the god of war *Tiu*] the third day of the week **Abbrev. Tues.**

tuft (tuft) *n.* [< OFr *tufe*] **1** a bunch of hairs, grass, etc. growing closely together **2** any cluster, as the fluffy ball forming the end of a cluster of threads drawn through a mattress, etc. — *vt.* **1** to provide with tufts **2** to secure the padding of (a mattress, etc.) with tufts —**tuft′ed** *adj.* —**tuft′er** *n.*

tug (tug) *vi.*, *vt.* **tugged**, **tug′ging** [prob. < ON *toga*, to pull] **1** to pull hard; drag; haul **2** to tow with a tugboat — *n.* **1** a hard pull **2** a tugboat

tug·boat (tug′bōt′) *n.* a sturdy, powerful boat for towing or pushing ships, barges, etc.

■ THESAURUS ■

trustee *n.* guardian, custodian, controller, lawyer, stockholder, guarantor, regent, board member, appointee, administrator, member of the directorate.

trusting *a.* trustful, credulous, confiding, gullible, unsuspecting, easygoing, open, candid, indulgent, obliging, well-meaning, good-natured, tender-hearted, green, with a glass jaw*; see also NAIVE.—*Ant.* SUSPICIOUS, skeptical, critical.

trustworthiness *n.* integrity, uprightness, loyalty; see HONESTY.

trustworthy *a.* accurate, honest, true; see RELIABLE.

trusty *n.* trusted person, trustworthy convict, prison attendant, privileged prisoner; see also PRISONER.

truth *n.* **1** [Conformity to reality] truthfulness, correctness, sincerity, verity, candor, openness, honesty, fidelity, frankness, revelation, authenticity, exactness, infallibility, precision, perfection, certainty, genuineness, accuracy, fact, the gospel truth*, straight dope*, inside track*, the nitty-gritty, the facts, the case.— *Ant.* LIE, deception, falsehood. **2**

[Integrity] trustworthiness, honor, probity; see HONESTY. —**in truth** in fact, indeed, really; see TRULY.

truthful *a.* correct, frank, just; see HONEST 1.

truthfully *a.* honestly, honorably, veraciously; see SINCERELY, TRULY.

truthfulness *n.* integrity, frankness, accuracy; see HONESTY.

try *v.* **1** [To endeavor] attempt, undertake, exert oneself, contend, strive, make an effort, risk, have a try at, contest, wrangle, labor, work, aspire, propose, try to reach, do what one can, tackle, venture, struggle for, compete for, speculate, make every effort, put oneself out, vie for, aspire to, attack, make a bid for, beat one's brains*, bear down, shoot at*, shoot for*, drive for, chip away at*, do one's best, make a pass at, go after, go out of the way, give a workout*, do all in one's power, buckle down, lift a finger, break an arm*, lay out, do oneself justice, have a go at*, make a go of it*, go all out, leave no stone unturned, move heaven and earth, knock oneself out*, break one's

neck*, bust a gut*, take a crack at*, give it a whirl*. **2** [To test] assay, investigate, put to the proof; see ANALYZE, EXAMINE. **3** [To conduct a trial] hear a case, examine, decide; see JUDGE. —**try on** fit, have a fitting, try on for size; see WEAR 1. —**try out for** go out for, audition for, compete; see REHEARSE 3.

trying *a.* troublesome, bothersome, irritating; see DIFFICULT 1, 2.

tryout *n.* test, demonstration, rehearsal; see EXAMINATION 1.

tub *n.* keg, bucket, tank; see CONTAINER.

tube *n.* **1** [A pipe] conduit, hose, test tube, tubing, tunnel, loom, subway; see also PIPE 1. **2** [A metal container] package, paste tube, squeeze tube; see CONTAINER. **3** [An electronic device] cell, electric eye, vacuum tube; see DEVICE 1, MACHINE.

tuck *n.* crease, folding, pleat; see FOLD.

tuft *n.* clump, cluster, group; see BUNCH.

tug *v.* pull, haul, tow; see DRAW 1.

tug of war 1 a contest in which two teams pull at opposite ends of a rope 2 any struggle for power

tu·i·tion (tōō ish′ən) *n.* [< L *tueri*, protect] the charge for instruction, as at a college

tu·la·re·mia (tōō′lə rē′mē ə) *n.* [after *Tulare* County, Calif.] an infectious disease of rodents, esp. rabbits, transmissible to man

tu·lip (tōō′lip) *n.* [< Turk *tülbend*, turban: from its shape] 1 a bulb plant with a large, cup-shaped flower 2 the flower

tulle (tōōl) *n.* [after *Tulle*, city in France] a fine netting of silk, rayon, nylon, etc., used as for veils and scarves

tum·ble (tum′bəl) *vi.* **-bled, -bling** [< OE *tumbian*, to jump] 1 to do somersaults or similar acrobatic feats 2 to fall suddenly or helplessly 3 to toss or roll about 4 to move in a hasty, disorderly manner —*vt.* 1 to cause to tumble 2 to put into disorder; disarrange —*n.* 1 a fall 2 disorder

tum′ble·down′ *adj.* dilapidated

tum′bler (-blər) *n.* 1 an acrobat who does somersaults, etc. 2 a drinking glass 3 a part of a lock whose position must be changed by a key in order to release the bolt

tum′ble·weed′ *n.* a plant that breaks off near the ground in autumn and is blown about by the wind

tum·brel or **tum·bril** (tum′brəl) *n.* [< Fr *tomber*, to fall] a cart, esp. one that can be tilted for emptying

tu·mid (tōō′mid) *adj.* [< L *tumere*, to swell] 1 swollen; bulging 2 inflated or pompous —**tu·mid′i·ty** *n.*

tummy (tum′ē) *n., pl.* **-mies** [Colloq.] the stomach or abdomen

tu·mor (tōō′mər) *n.* [L, a swelling] an abnormal growth of new tissue, independent of its surrounding structures Brit., etc. sp. **tu′mour**

tu·mult (tōō′mult′) *n.* [< L *tumere*, to swell] 1 noisy commotion; uproar 2 confusion; disturbance

tu·mul·tu·ous (tōō mul′chōō əs) *adj.* full of tumult, uproar, etc.

tun (tun) *n.* [OE *tunne*] a large cask

tuna (tōō′nə) *n., pl.* **-na** or **-nas** [AmSp] 1 a large ocean fish of the mackerel group, as the albacore 2 the flesh of the tuna, canned for food: also **tuna fish**

tun·dra (tun′drə) *n.* [Russ] a vast, treeless arctic plain

tune (tōōn) *n.* [ME, var. of *tone*, tone] 1 a rhythmic succession of musical tones; melody 2 correct musical pitch 3 agreement; concord [out of *tune* with the times] —*vt.* **tuned, tun′ing** 1 to adjust (a musical instrument) to some standard of pitch 2 to adapt to some condition, mood, etc. 3 to adjust (a motor, circuit, etc.) for proper performance —**to the tune of** [Colloq.] to the sum, price, or extent of —**tune in** to adjust a radio or TV receiver so as to receive (a station, etc.) —**tun′er** *n.*

tune′ful *adj.* full of music; melodious

tune′less *adj.* 1 not melodious 2 not producing music — **tune′less·ly** *adv.* —**tune′less·ness** *n.*

tune′up′ or **tune′-up′** *n.* an adjusting, as of an engine, to the proper condition

tung·sten (tuŋ′stən) *n.* [Swed < *tung*, heavy + *sten*, stone] a hard, heavy metallic chemical element, used in steel, etc.

tu·nic (tōō′nik, tyōō′-) *n.* [L *tunica*] 1 a loose, gownlike garment worn by men and women in ancient Greece and Rome 2 a blouselike garment extending to the hips, often belted

tuning fork a two-pronged steel instrument which when struck sounds a certain fixed tone in perfect pitch

tun·nel (tun′əl) *n.* [< Fr *tonnelle*, a vault] 1 an underground passageway, as for autos, etc. 2 any tunnel-like passage, as in a mine —*vt., vi.* **-neled** or **-nelled, -nel·**

ing or **-nel·ling** to make a tunnel (through or under) — **tun′neler** or **tun′nel·ler** *n.*

tunnel vision a narrow outlook, as on a particular problem

tunny (tun′ē) *n., pl.* **-nies** TUNA (sense 1)

tur·ban (tur′bən) *n.* [< Pers *dulbänd*] 1 a headdress worn by men in parts of Asia, consisting of cloth wound in folds about the head 2 any similar headdress

tur·bid (tur′bid) *adj.* [< L *turba*, a crowd] 1 muddy or cloudy from having the sediment stirred up 2 thick, dense, or dark, as clouds 3 confused

tur·bine (tur′bin, -bīn′) *n.* [< L *turbo*, a whirl] an engine driven as by the pressure of steam, water, or air against the curved vanes of a wheel

tur·bo·charge (tur′bō chärj′) *vt.* **-charged′, -charg′ing** to increase the power of (an engine) by the use of a type of compressor (**tur′bo·charg′er**) driven by a turbine powered by exhaust gases

tur′bo·fan′ (-fan′) *n.* a turbojet engine developing extra thrust from air that bypasses the engine and is accelerated by a fan: in full **turbofan engine**

tur′bo·jet′ (-jet′) *n.* 1 a jet engine in which the energy of the jet spins a turbine which drives the air compressor: in full **turbojet engine** 2 an aircraft with such an engine

tur′bo·prop′ (-präp′) *n.* 1 a turbojet engine whose turbine shaft drives a propeller: in full **turboprop engine** 2 an aircraft with such an engine

tur·bot (tur′bət) *n., pl.* **-bot** or **-bots** [< OFr *tourbout*] any of various flounders highly regarded as food

tur·bu·lent (tur′byōō lənt, -byə-) *adj.* [< L *turba*, a crowd] 1 wild or disorderly 2 full of violent motion — **tur′bu·lence** *n.* —**tur′bu·lently** *adv.*

tu·reen (tōō rēn′) *n.* [< Fr *terrine*, earthen vessel] a large, deep serving dish with a lid, for soups, etc.

turf (turf) *n.* [OE] 1 *a)* a top layer of earth containing grass with its roots; sod *b)* [Chiefly Brit.] a piece of this 2 peat 3 a track for horse racing; also, horse racing: usually with *the* 4 [Slang] *a)* an area seen by a street gang as its territory to be defended *b)* one's own territory — *vt.* to cover with turf —**turf′y** *adj.*

tur·gid (tur′jid) *adj.* [< L *turgere*, to swell] 1 swollen; distended 2 bombastic; pompous —**tur·gid′i·ty** or **tur′gid·ness** *n.* —**tur′gidly** *adv.*

Turk (turk) *n.* a native or inhabitant of Turkey

Turk. 1 Turkey 2 Turkish

tur·key (tur′kē) *n.* [< similarity to a fowl formerly imported through *Turkey*] 1 a large North American bird with a spreading tail 2 its flesh, used as food

turkey vulture a dark-colored vulture of temperate and tropical America Also **turkey buzzard**

Turkic (turk′ik) *adj.* designating or of a subfamily of languages including Turkish, Tatar, etc.

Turk·ish (turk′ish) *adj.* of Turkey, its people, or their language — *n.* the language of Turkey

Turkish bath a bathhouse with steam rooms, showers, massage, etc.

Turkish towel [*also* t- t-] a towel of cotton terry cloth

tur·mer·ic (tur′mər ik) *n.* [< ML *terra merita*, deserved earth] an East Indian plant whose powdered root is used as a yellow dye, a seasoning, etc.

tur·moil (tur′moil′) *n.* [< ?] tumult; commotion; confusion

turn (turn) *vt.* [ult. < Gr *tornos*, lathe] 1 to rotate (a wheel, etc.) 2 to move around or partly around [turn the

---

THESAURUS

tuition *n.* fee, cost, expenditure; see PRICE.

tumble *v.* drop, plunge, descend; see FALL 1, TRIP 1.

tumor *n.* neoplasm, tumefaction, cyst; see SWELLING.

tumult *n.* agitation, uproar, turbulence; see CONFUSION, DISTURBANCE 2, FIGHT 1.

tune *n.* melody, air, strain; see SONG. —**change one's tune*** change one's mind, alter one's actions, be transformed; see ALTER 1. —**sing a different tune*** change one's mind, alter one's actions, be transformed; see ALTER 1.

tune *v.* adjust the pitch, attune, put in tune, tune up, tighten the strings, use the tuning fork, set the tune; see also HARMONIZE.

tunnel *n.* hole, burrow, underground passage, subway, tube, crawl space, crawlway, shaft, mine, pit.

turbulence *n.* disorder, commotion, fracas; see CONFUSION, DISTURBANCE 2, FIGHT 1.

turbulent *a.* riotous, violent, stormy, disturbed, noisy, restless, raging, howling, buffeting, thunderous, tumultuous, excited, passionate, uncontrolled, vehement, roaring, tempestuous, rampant, rowdy, lawless, disorderly, untamed, disordered, chaotic, agitated, fierce, wild, rude, rough, blustering, angry, storming, uproarious, clamorous, mutinous, rebellious, destructive, hard, stern, bitter, fiery, rabid, boisterous, perturbed, foaming, shaking, vociferous, demonstrative.—*Ant.* PEACEFUL,

tranquil, at ease.

turf *n.* earth, peat, lawn; see GRASS 1.

turkey *n.* turkey cock, turkey hen, tom, bird, fowl, Thanksgiving bird, Christmas bird, gobbler, turkey gobbler, wild turkey, domestic turkey.

turmoil *n.* agitation, turbulence, riot; see CONFUSION, DISTURBANCE 2.

turn *n.* 1 [A revolution] rotation, cycle, circle, round, circulation, pirouette, gyre, gyration, spin, roundabout-face, roll, turning, circumrotation, spiral; see also REVOLUTION 1. 2 [A bend] curve, winding, twist, wind, hook, shift, angle, corner, fork, branch. 3 [A turning point] climax, crisis, juncture, emergency, critical period, crossing, change, new development, shift, twist. 4 [A shock] key/ 3 to give form to, as in a lathe 4 to change the position or direction of 5 to reverse [to turn pages] 6 to wrench [turn one's ankle] 7 to upset (the stomach) 8 to deflect; divert 9 to cause to change actions, beliefs, aims, etc. 10 to go around (a corner, etc.) 11 to pass (a certain age, amount, etc.) 12 to repel (an attack, etc.) 13 to drive, set, let go, etc. [to turn the dog loose] 14 to direct, point, aim, etc. 15 to change [to turn cream into butter] 16 to make sour 17 to affect in some way — vi. 1 to rotate or revolve; pivot 2 to move around or partly around 3 to reel; whirl 4 to become curved or bent 5 to become upset: said of the stomach 6 to change or reverse course, direction, etc., or one's feelings, allegiance, etc. 7 to refer (to) 8 to apply (to) for help 9 to shift one's attention [he turned to music] 10 to make a sudden attack (on) 11 to be contingent or depend (on or upon) 12 to become [to turn cold] 13 to change to another form [the rain turned to snow] 14 to become rancid, sour, etc. — n. 1 a turning around; rotation; revolution 2 a single twist, winding, etc. 3 a change or reversal of course or direction 4 a short walk, ride, etc. 5 a bend; curve [a turn in the road] 6 a change in trend, events, etc. 7 a sudden shock or fright 8 an action or deed [a good turn] 9 the right, duty, or chance to do something in regular order [my turn to go] 10 a distinctive form, detail, etc. [an odd turn of speech] 11 natural inclination —in (or out of) turn (not) in proper sequence —turn down to reject (a request, etc.) — turn in 1 to deliver; hand in 2 [Colloq.] to go to bed — turn off 1 to shut off 2 to make (an electrical device) stop functioning 3 [Slang] to cause to be bored, depressed, etc. —turn on 1 to start the flow of 2 to make (an electrical device) start functioning 3 [Slang] to make or become elated, euphoric, etc. —turn out 1 to put out (a light, etc.) 2 to put outside 3 to dismiss 4 to come or go out 5 to produce 6 to result 7 to prove to be 8 to become —turn over 1 to ponder 2 to hand over; transfer —turn up to happen, appear, arrive, etc. —turn′er n.

turn′about′ n. a shift or reversal of position, allegiance, opinion, etc.

turn′around′ n. 1 TURNABOUT 2 a wide area, as in a driveway, to allow turning a vehicle around

turn′buck′le (-buk′əl) n. an adjustable coupling for two

rods, etc., consisting of a metal sleeve with opposite internal threads at each end

turn′coat′ n. a renegade; traitor

turn′ing n. 1 the action of one that turns 2 a place where a road, etc. turns

turning point a point in time at which a decisive change occurs

tur·nip (tur′nip) n. [prob. < Fr tour, round + ME nepe, turnip] 1 a plant related to mustard, with a roundish, light-colored, edible root 2 the root

turn′key′ n., pl. -keys′ a jailer

turn′off′ n. 1 a turning off 2 a place to turn off, as a road ramp

turn′out′ n. 1 a gathering of people, as for a meeting 2 a wider part of a narrow road, for vehicles to pass

turn′o′ver n. 1 a turning over; upset 2 a small pie with half the crust folded back over the other half 3 a) the selling out and replenishing of a stock of goods b) the amount of business done during a given period 4 the rate of replacement of workers

turn′pike′ (-pīk′) n. [ME turnpyke, a spiked road barrier] a toll road, esp. one that is an expressway

turn′stile′ (-stīl′) n. a device, as a post with revolving horizontal bars, placed in an entrance to allow the passage of persons one at a time

turn′ta′ble n. a circular rotating platform, as for supporting a phonograph record being played

tur·pen·tine (tur′pən tīn′) n. [< Gr terebinthos, tree yielding this substance] a colorless, volatile oil distilled from a substance extracted from various coniferous trees: used in paints, etc.

tur·pi·tude (tur′pi tōōd′) n. [< L turpis, vile] baseness; vileness

tur·quoise (tur′kwoiz′, -koiz′) n. [< OFr turqueis, Turkish] 1 a greenish-blue semiprecious stone 2 its color

tur·ret (tur′it) n. [see TOWER] 1 a small tower projecting from a building, usually at a corner 2 a dome or revolving structure for guns, as on a warship, tank, or airplane 3 a rotating attachment for a lathe, etc. holding cutting tools for successive use

tur·tle (turt′'l) n. [< Fr tortue, tortoise] any of various land or water reptiles having a soft body encased in a tough shell —turn turtle to turn upside down

tur′tle·dove′ n. [< L echoic turtur] a wild dove with a plaintive call

---

THESAURUS

fright, jolt, blow; see SURPRISE 2. 5 [An action] deed, accomplishment, service; see HELP 1. 6 [A change in course] curve, detour, deviation, corner, ground loop, stem turn, jump turn, telemark, kick turn, inside loop, outside loop, wing spin, tight spin, tight spiral. —at every turn in every instance, constantly, consistently; see REGULARLY. —by turns taking turns, in succession, alternately; see CONSECUTIVE. —call the turn anticipate, predict, foretell; see EXPECT 1. —take turns do by turns, do in succession, share; see ALTERNATE 1. —to a turn correctly, properly, to the right degree; see PERFECTLY.

turn v. 1 [To pivot] revolve, rotate, roll, spin, wheel, whirl, circulate, go around, swivel, round, twist, twirl, gyrate, ground, loop; see also SWING. 2 [To reverse] go back, recoil, change, upset, retrace, face about, turn around, capsize, shift, alter, vary, convert, transform, invert, subvert, return, alternate. 3 [To divert] deflect, veer, turn aside, turn away, sidetrack, swerve, put off, call off, turn off, deviate, dodge, twist, avoid, shift, switch, avert, zigzag, shy away, redirect, draw aside. 4 [To become] grow into, change into, pass into; see BECOME. 5 [To sour] curdle, acidify, become rancid; see SOUR. 6 [To change direction] swerve, swing, bend, veer, tack, round to, incline, deviate, detour, loop, curve. 7 [To incline] prefer, be predisposed to, favor; see LEAN 1, TEND 2. 8 [To sprain] strain, bruise, dislocate; see HURT 1. 9 [To nauseate] sicken,

make one sick, revolt; see DISGUST. 10 [To bend] curve, twist, fold; see BEND. 11 [To transform] transmute, remake, transpose; see ALTER 1. 12 [To make use of] apply, adapt, utilize; see USE 1. 13 [To point] direct, set, train; see AIM. 14 [To repel] repulse, push back, throw back; see REPEL 1. —turn about turn around, pivot, reverse; see TURN 1. —turn against revolt, disobey, defy; see OPPOSE 1, 2, REBEL. —turn aside avert, deflect, divert; see TURN 3. — turn back retrogress, retrograde, revert; see RETURN 1, 2. —turn down 1 [To decrease in volume, etc.] hush, lower, curb; see DECREASE 2. 2 [To refuse] reject, decline, rebuff; see REFUSE. —turn in 1 [To deliver] hand over, transfer, give up; see GIVE 1. 2 [*To go to bed] lie down, retire, hit the hay*; see REST 1. —turn into 1 [To change] transform, alter, transmute; see ALTER 1. 2 [To become changed] be converted, transform, modify; see CHANGE 2. — turn off stop, shut off, douse, turn out, log off, halt, close, shut, extinguish, shut down, kill the light, turn off the juice, cut the motor, hit the switch. —turn on 1 [To start the operation of] set going, switch on, set in motion, log on, put in gear; see also BEGIN 1. 2 [To attack] strike, assail, assault; see ATTACK. 3 [*To take drugs] smoke marijuana, get high*, take a trip*, smoke pot*, get stoned*, freak out*, blow pot*, trip out*, get wasted*. 4 [*To arouse] titillate, stimulate, stir up; see EXCITE. 5 [*To depend on or upon] hinge on, be dependent on, be based on; see

DEPEND ON 2. —turn out 1 [To stop the operation of] extinguish, shut off, stop; see TURN OFF. 2 [To dismiss] discharge, evict, send away; see DISMISS, OUST. 3 [To produce] make, put out, build; see MANUFACTURE, PRODUCE 2. 4 [To finish] end, complete, perfect; see ACHIEVE. — turn over 1 [To invert] overturn, reverse, subvert; see UPSET 1. 2 [To transfer] hand over, give over, deliver; see ASSIGN, GIVE 1. —turn to 1 [To rely upon] confide, appeal to, depend upon; see TRUST 1. 2 [To start] start to work, become interested in, take up; see BEGIN 1. — turn up 1 [To find] disclose, learn, come across; see DISCOVER, FIND. 2 [To arrive] enter, come, roll in; see ARRIVE. 3 [To increase the volume, etc.] amplify, augment, boost; see INCREASE, STRENGTHEN.

turned a. 1 [Revolved] spun, rounded, circled, circulated, rotated, rolled, whirled, gyrated, set going. 2 [Deflected] switched, twisted, dodged, avoided, shied away from, shifted, shunted, changed.

turning a. twisting, shifting, whirling, rotating, revolving, bending, curving, shunting; see also GROWING, CHANGING.—Ant. PERMANENT, static, fixed.

turning n. whirling, revolving, rotating; see REVOLUTION 1.

turning point n. peak, juncture, culmination; see CLIMAX, CRISIS.

turnout n. 1 [Production] output, result, volume; see PRODUCTION 1. 2 [A gathering] assembly, attendance, group; see GATHERING.

tur′tle·neck′ *n.* **1** a high, snug, turned-down collar, as on a sweater **2** a sweater, etc. with such a collar

tusk (tusk) *n.* ⟦OE *tucs*⟧ a long, large, pointed tooth projecting outside the mouth, as of the elephant

tus·sle (tus′əl) *n.*, *vi.* **-sled, -sling** ⟦< ME *tusen*, to pull⟧ struggle; scuffle

tus·sock (tus′ək) *n.* ⟦< ?⟧ a thick tuft or clump of grass, sedge, etc.

tu·telage (tōōt′ l ij, tyōōt′-) *n.* ⟦< L *tutela*, protection⟧ **1** guardianship; care, protection, etc. **2** instruction —**tu′ telar′y** (-er′ē) *adj.*

tu·tor (tōōt′ər, tyōōt′-) *n.* ⟦< L *tueri*, to guard⟧ a private teacher —*vt.*, *vi.* to act as a tutor (to); teach —**tu·to·rial** (tōō tôr′ē əl, tyōō-) *adj.*, *n.*

tutti-frutti (tōōt′ē frōōt′ē) *n.* ⟦It, all fruits⟧ ice cream, candy, etc. made or flavored with mixed fruits

tutu (tōō′tōō) *n.* ⟦Fr⟧ a very short, full, projecting skirt worn by ballerinas

tux (tuks) *n.*, *pl.* **tux′es** *short for* TUXEDO

tux·edo (tuk sē′dō) *n.*, *pl.* **-dos** ⟦after a country club near *Tuxedo* Lake, N.Y.⟧ a man's semiformal suit with a tailless jacket

TV (tē′vē′) *n.* **1** television **2** *pl.* **TVs** or **TV′s** a television receiving set

TVA Tennessee Valley Authority

TV dinner a frozen, precooked dinner packaged in a divided tray for heating and serving

twad·dle (twäd′'l) *n.* ⟦prob. var. of TATTLE⟧ foolish, empty talk or writing; nonsense —**twad′dler** *n.*

twain (twān) *adj.*, *n.* ⟦OE *twegen*, two⟧ *archaic var. of* TWO

twang (twaŋ) *n.* ⟦echoic⟧ **1** a sharp, vibrating sound, as of a plucked string **2** a sharply nasal way of speaking —*vi.*, *vt.* **1** to make or cause to make a twang **2** to speak or say with a twang —**twang′y, -i·er, -i·est, *adj.***

'twas (twuz, wäz) ⟦Old Poet.⟧ it was

tweak (twēk) *vt.* ⟦OE *twiccan*, to twitch⟧ to give a twisting pinch to (the nose, ear, etc.) —*n.* such a pinch

tweed (twēd) *n.* ⟦< misreading of *tweel*, Scot form of TWILL⟧ **1** a rough wool fabric in a weave of two or more colors **2** [*pl.*] clothes of tweed

tweed′y *adj.* **-i·er, -i·est 1** of, like, or wearing tweeds **2** of an informal, outdoor type

'tween (twēn) *prep.* ⟦ME *twene*⟧ [Old Poet.] between

tweet (twēt) *n.*, *interj.* ⟦echoic⟧ the chirping sound of a small bird, or a similar sound —*vi.* to make this sound

tweet′er *n.* a small, high-fidelity speaker for reproducing high-frequency sounds Cf. WOOFER

tweez·ers (twē′zərz) *n.pl.* ⟦< obs. *tweeze*, surgical set⟧ [*with sing. or pl. v.*] small nippers for plucking out hairs, etc. Often **pair of tweezers**

twelfth (twelfth) *adj.* ⟦OE *twelfta*⟧ preceded by eleven others; 12th —*n.* **1** the one following the eleventh **2** any of the twelve equal parts of something; ¹⁄₁₂

Twelfth Day Epiphany, the twelfth day after Christmas: **Twelfth Night** is the evening before, or of, Epiphany

twelve (twelv) *adj.*, *n.* ⟦OE *twelf*⟧ two more than ten; 12; XII

twelve′-tone′ *adj. Music* of composition in which the twelve tones of the chromatic scale are fixed in some arbitrary succession (*tone row*)

twenty (twent′ē) *adj.*, *n.*, *pl.* **-ties** ⟦OE *twegentig*⟧ two times ten; 20; XX —**the twenties** the numbers or years, as of a century, from 20 through 29 —**twen′ti·eth** (-ith) *adj.*, *n.*

twen′ty-one′ *n.* the gambling game BLACKJACK (*n.* 2)

twen′ty-twen′ty (or **20/20**) **vision** normal visual ability, i.e., seeing clearly at 20 feet what the normal eye sees at 20 feet

twerp (twurp) *n.* ⟦ult. < ? Dan *tver*, perverse⟧ [Slang] a person regarded as insignificant, contemptible, etc.

twice (twis) *adv.* ⟦OE *twiga*⟧ **1** two times **2** two times as much or as many

twid·dle (twid′'l) *vt.*, *vi.* **-dled, -dling** ⟦prob. < TW(IST) + (*d*)*iddle*, move back and forth rapidly⟧ to twirl or play with lightly or idly —**twiddle one's thumbs** to be idle

twig (twig) *n.* ⟦OE *twigge*⟧ a small branch of a tree or shrub —**twig′gy, -gier, -gi·est, *adj.***

twi·light (twi′lit′) *n.* ⟦ME⟧ **1** the subdued light just after sunset or, sometimes, just before sunrise **2** the period from sunset to dark **3** a gradual decline —*adj.* of twilight

twill (twil) *n.* ⟦OE *twilic*, woven of double thread⟧ a cloth woven in parallel diagonal lines —**twilled *adj.***

twin (twin) *adj.* ⟦OE *twinn*, double⟧ **1** consisting of, or being one of a pair of, two similar things **2** being a twin or twins —*n.* **1** either of two born at the same birth **2** either of two persons or things that are very much alike

twine (twin) *n.* ⟦OE *twin*⟧ strong thread, string, etc. of strands twisted together —*vt.*, *vi.* **twined, twin′ing 1** to twist together **2** to wind around

twinge (twinj) *vi.*, *vt.* **twinged, twing′ing** ⟦OE *twengan*, to squeeze⟧ to have or cause to have a sudden, sharp pain, qualm, etc. —*n.* such a pain, etc.

twi-night or **twi·night** (twi′nit′) *adj.* ⟦TWI(LIGHT) + NIGHT⟧ *Baseball* designating a double-header starting in late afternoon and going into evening

twin·kle (twiŋk′əl) *vi.* **-kled, -kling** ⟦OE *twinclian*⟧ **1** to shine with quick, intermittent gleams **2** to light up, as with amusement: said of the eyes **3** to move to and fro quickly, as a dancer's feet —*n.* **1** a glint in the eye **2** a gleam; sparkle **3** an instant

twin′kling *n.* an instant

twirl (twurl) *vt.*, *vi.* ⟦prob. < Scand⟧ **1** to rotate rapidly; spin **2** to whirl in a circle —*n.* **1** a twirling **2** a twist, coil, etc. —**twirl′er** *n.*

twist (twist) *vt.* ⟦< OE *-twist*, a rope⟧ **1** to wind (strands, etc.) around one another **2** to wind (rope, etc.) around something **3** to give spiral shape to **4** *a*) to subject to torsion *b*) to wrench; sprain **5** to contort or distort **6** to confuse **7** to pervert the meaning of **8** to revolve or rotate **9** to break (*off*) by turning the end —*vi.* **1** to undergo twisting **2** to spiral, twine, etc. (*around* or *about*) **3** to revolve or rotate **4** to turn to one side **5** to wind, as a path **6** to squirm; writhe —*n.* **1** something twisted, as cord or thread, a roll of tobacco, etc. **2** a twisting or being twisted **3** stress produced by twisting **4** a contortion **5** a wrench or sprain **6** a turn; bend **7** distortion, as of meaning **8** an unexpected or different direction, method, slant, etc.

twist′er *n.* **1** a person or thing that twists **2** [Colloq.] a tornado or cyclone

twit (twit) *vt.* **twit′ted, twit′ting** ⟦< OE *æt*, at + *witan*, accuse⟧ to reproach, taunt, etc. —*n.* a taunt

twitch (twich) *vt.*, *vi.* ⟦< OE *twiccian*, to pluck⟧ to pull (at) or move with a quick, slight jerk —*n.* **1** a twitching **2** a sudden, quick motion, esp. a spasmodic one

twit·ter (twit′ər) *vi.* ⟦ME *twiteren*⟧ **1** to chirp rapidly **2** *a*) to chatter *b*) to giggle **3** to tremble with excitement —*n.* **1** a twittering **2** a condition of trembling excitement

two (tōō) *adj.*, *n.* ⟦OE *twa*⟧ one more than one; 2; II —**in two** in two parts

---

THESAURUS

tusk *n.* canine tooth, fang, incisor; see TOOTH 1.

tutor *n.* instructor, tutorial assistant, private tutor; see TEACHER.

tutoring *n.* coaching, training, instruction; see EDUCATION 1.

TV *n.* video, cable, idiot box*; see TELEVISION.

tweak *v.* twitch, squeeze, jerk; see PINCH.

tweezers *n.* forceps, nippers, tongs; see TOOL 1.

twelve *a.* dozen, twelvefold, twelfth; see NUMBER.

twenty *a.* twentieth, vicenary, twentyfold, vicennial.

twice *a.* double, doubly, once and again, over again, once over.

twig *n.* offshoot, limb, sprig; see BRANCH 2.

twilight *n.* dusk, nightfall, late afternoon, early evening, sunset, dawn, break of day; see also NIGHT 1.

twin *a.* identical twin, fraternal twin, look-alike, identical two, fellow, two-fold, second, accompanying, joint, coupled, matched, copied, duplicating; see also SECOND, TWO.—*Ant.* SINGLE, lone, solitary.

twine *n.* braid, cord, string; see ROPE.

twinge *v.* twitch, shiver, smart; see TINGLE.

twinkle *v.* shimmer, flicker, sparkle; see SHINE 1.

twinkling *a.* sparkling, glimmering, flashing; see BRIGHT 1.

twirl *v.* spin, rotate, twist; see TURN 1.

twist *v.* wring, wrap, twine, twirl, spin, turn around, wrap around; see also TURN 1.

twisted *a.* **1** [Crooked] contorted, wrenched, bent, knotted, braided, twined, wound, wreathed, writhing, convolute, twisting.—*Ant.* STRAIGHT, even, regular. **2** [Confused] erroneous, perplexing, wrongheaded, awry, puzzling, unintelligible, disorganized, tangled, perverted; see also WRONG 2.—*Ant.* CLEAR, simple, logical.

twitch *v.* **1** [To pluck] pull, tug, snatch; see PULL 2. **2** [To jerk] shiver, shudder, have a fit, kick, work, palpitate, beat, twinge, pain.

two *a.* twin, dual, binary, both, double, forked, bifid.

two *n.* two of a kind, twins, couple; see PAIR. —**in two** halved, divided, split; see SEPARATED. —**put two and**

two'-bit' (-bit') *adj.* [Slang] cheap

two bits [Colloq.] twenty-five cents

two'-by-four' *n.* a piece of lumber two inches thick and four inches wide when untrimmed (1½ by 3½ inches trimmed)

two'-edged' *adj.* 1 having two cutting edges 2 that can be taken two ways, as a remark

two'-faced' *adj.* 1 having two faces 2 deceitful; hypocritical

two·fer (t̄oo'fər) *n.* [altered < *two for*] [Colloq.] a pair of (theater tickets, etc.) sold for the price of one

two'-fist'ed *adj.* [Colloq.] 1 able to use both fists 2 vigorous; virile

two'fold' *adj.* 1 having two parts 2 having twice as much or as many — *adv.* twice as much or as many

two'-hand'ed *adj.* 1 requiring the use of both hands 2 operated, played, etc. by two persons

two·pence (tup'əns) *n.* two pence

two'-ply' *adj.* having two layers, strands, etc.

two'some (-səm) *n.* 1 two people; a couple 2 a golf match for two

two'-time' *vt.* **-timed'**, **-tim'ing** [Slang] to be unfaithful to —**two'-tim'er** *n.*

two'-way' *adj.* 1 allowing passage in either direction 2 involving two or used in two ways

Twp. township

-ty (tē, ti) [< L *-tas*] *suffix* quality of, condition of

ty·coon (ti k̄oon') *n.* [< Jpn < Chin *tai*, great + *kuan*, official] a wealthy, powerful industrialist, financier, etc.

ty·ing (tī'iŋ) *vt., vi. prp. of* TIE

tyke (tīk) *n.* [< ON *tik*, a bitch] [Colloq.] a small child

tym·pani (tim'pə nē) *n.pl. alt. sp. of* TIMPANI —**tym'pa·nist** *n.*

tym·panic membrane (tim pan'ik) a thin membrane inside the ear that vibrates when struck by sound waves

tym·pa·num (tim'pə nəm) *n., pl.* **-nums** or **-na** (-nə) [L, a drum] 1 MIDDLE EAR 2 TYMPANIC MEMBRANE

type (tīp) *n.* [< Gr *typos*, a mark] 1 the characteristic form, plan, style, etc. of a class or group 2 a class, group, etc. with characteristics in common 3 a person, animal, or thing representative of a class 4 a perfect example; model 5 *a*) a piece of metal or wood with a raised letter, etc. in reverse on its top, used in printing *b*) such pieces collectively *c*) a printed or photographically reproduced character or characters — *vt.* **typed**, **typ'ing** 1 to classify 2 to typewrite — *vi.* to typewrite

-type (tīp) *combining form* 1 type, representative form, example [*stereotype*] 2 print, printing type

type'cast' *vt.* **-cast'**, **-cast'ing** to cast (an actor) repeatedly in the same type of part

type'script' *n.* typewritten matter

type'set' *vt.* **-set'**, **-set'ting** to set in type; compose

type'set'ter *n.* 1 a person who sets type 2 a machine for setting type

type'write' *vt., vi.* **-wrote'**, **-writ'ten**, **-writ'ing** to write with a typewriter: now usually *type*

type'writ'er *n.* a writing machine with a keyboard for reproducing letters resembling printed ones

ty·phoid (tī'foid') *n.* [TYPH(US) + -OID] an acute infectious disease caused by a bacillus and acquired by ingesting contaminated food or water: characterized by fever, intestinal disorders, etc. In full **typhoid fever**

ty·phoon (tī f̄oon') *n.* [< Chin *tai-fung*, great wind] a violent tropical cyclone originating in the W Pacific

ty·phus (tī'fəs) *n.* [< Gr *typhos*, fever] an acute infectious disease caused by certain bacteria, transmitted by fleas, lice, etc., and characterized by fever, skin rash, etc. In full **typhus fever**

typi·cal (tip'i kəl) *adj.* 1 serving as a type 2 having the distinguishing characteristics of a class, group, etc.; representative 3 belonging to a type; characteristic —**typ'i·cally** *adv.*

typi·fy (tip'i fī') *vt.* **-fied'**, **-fy'ing** 1 to be a type of; symbolize 2 to have the characteristics of; be typical of; exemplify —**typ'i·fi·ca'tion** *n.*

typ·ist (tīp'ist) *n.* a person who operates a typewriter

typo (tī'pō) *n., pl.* **-pos** [Colloq.] an error made in setting type or in typing

ty·pog·ra·phy (tī päg'rə fē) *n.* [see TYPE & -GRAPHY] 1 setting, and printing with, type 2 the arrangement, style, etc. of matter printed from type —**ty·pog'ra·pher** *n.* —**ty'po·graph'i·cal** (-pō graf'i kəl, -pə-) *adj.* —**ty'po·graph'i·cally** *adv.*

ty·ran·ni·cal (tə ran'i kəl, ti-; tī-) *adj.* 1 of or suited to a tyrant 2 harsh, cruel, unjust, etc. Also **ty·ran'nic** —**ty·ran'ni·cally** *adv.*

tyr·an·nize (tir'ə nīz') *vi.* **-nized'**, **-niz'ing** 1 to govern as a tyrant 2 to govern or use authority harshly or cruelly — *vt.* to treat tyrannically

ty·ran·no·saur (tə ran'ə sôr', ti-; tī-) *n.* [< Gr *tyrannos*, tyrant + *sauros*, lizard] a huge, two-footed, flesh-eating dinosaur Also **ty·ran'no·saur'us** (-əs)

tyr·an·ny (tir'ə nē) *n., pl.* **-nies** 1 the authority, government, etc. of a tyrant 2 cruel and unjust use of power 3 a tyrannical act —**tyr'an·nous** *adj.*

ty·rant (tī'rənt) *n.* [< Gr *tyrannos*] 1 an absolute ruler 2 a cruel, oppressive ruler, master, etc.

tyro (tī'rō) *n., pl.* **-ros** [< L *tiro*, young soldier] a beginner in learning something; novice

tzar (tsär, zär) *n. alt. sp. of* CZAR —**tzari·na** (tsä rē'nə, zä-) *n.fem.*

■ THESAURUS ■

two together* reason, sum up, reach a conclusion; see DECIDE.

two-faced *a.* deceitful, hypocritical, treacherous; see FALSE 1.

tycoon *n.* magnate, mogul, director; see BUSINESSMAN, EXECUTIVE.

type *n.* 1 [Kind] sort, nature, character; see KIND 2, VARIETY 2. 2 [Representative] representation, sample, example; see MODEL 1, 2. 3 [Letter] symbol, emblem, figure, character, sign; see also LETTER 1. *Styles of types include the following:* Gothic, black letter, old style, new style, modern, roman, italic, script, sans serif, Old English, text. *Sizes of types include the following:* Excelsior or 3-point, Brilliant or 3-1/2-point, Diamond or 4-1/2-point, Pearl or 5-point, Agate or 5-1/2-point, Nonpareil or 6-point, Minion or 7-point, Brevier or 8-point, Bourgeois or 9-point, Long Primer or 10-point, Small Pica or 11-point, Pica or 12-point, English or 14-point, Colum-

bian or 16-point, Great Primer or 18-point. *Font types include the following:* standard, lightface, boldface, extrabold, cursive, open, extended, condensed, shaded, upright, wide, expanded.

type *v.* 1 [To use a typewriter] typewrite, copy, transcribe, teletype, input, touchtype, hunt and peck. 2 [To classify] categorize, normalize, standardize; see CLASSIFY.

typed *a.* 1 [Set down on a typewriter] typewritten, copied, set up, written, transcribed; see also PRINTED. 2 [Classified] labeled, characterized, analyzed, symbolized, classed, prefigured, sampled, marked, regulated, exemplified, made out to be, patterned, standardized, stylized, cast, formalized.

typewriter *n.* typing machine, office typewriter, portable, noiseless, electric typewriter, electronic typewriter, word processor, memory typewriter, ticker, teletypewriter.

typewritten *a.* written on a typewriter, transcribed, copied; see PRINTED.

typical *a.* characteristic, habitual, usual, representative, symbolic, normal, illustrative, conventional, archetypical, prototypical, stereotypical, ideal, expected, suggestive, standardized, standard, patterned, common, ordinary, average, everyday, regular.—*Ant.* SUPERIOR, exceptional, extraordinary.

typify *v.* exemplify, symbolize, embody; see MEAN 1.

typist *n.* secretary, typewriter operator, teletyper, office girl, inputter, clerk, clerical worker.

tyrannical *a.* dictatorial, domineering, totalitarian; see ABSOLUTE 2.

tyranny *n.* oppression, cruelty, severity, reign of terror, despotism, absolutism.

tyrant *n.* despot, absolute ruler, czar; see DICTATOR.

u or **U** (yōō) *n., pl.* **u's, U's** the 21st letter of the English alphabet

U *Chem. symbol for* uranium

u or **u.** unit(s)

U or **U.** 1 Union 2 University

UAW United Automobile Workers (of America)

ubiqui·tous (yōō bik′wə təs) *adj.* [< L *ubique*, everywhere] (seemingly) present everywhere at the same time —**ubiq′ui·tously** *adv.* —**ubiq′ui·ty** *n.*

U-boat (yōō′bōt′) *n.* [< Ger *Unterseeboot*, undersea boat] a German submarine

ud·der (ud′ər) *n.* [OE *udr*] a baglike, milk-secreting organ with two or more teats, as in cows

UFO (yōō′ef′ō′, yōō′ef ō′) *n., pl.* **UFOs** or **UFO's** an unidentified flying object

ufol·ogy (yōō fäl′ə jē) *n.* the study of UFOs, esp. as supposed spacecraft from another planet —**ufol′o·gist** *n.*

ugh (ookh, oo, ug, *etc.*) *interj.* an exclamation of disgust, horror, etc.

ugly (ug′lē) *adj.* **-lier, -li·est** [< ON *uggr*, fear] 1 unpleasing to look at 2 bad, vile, repulsive, etc. [an *ugly* lie] 3 ominous; dangerous [*ugly* storm clouds] 4 [Colloq.] cross; quarrelsome [an *ugly* mood] —**ug′li·ness** *n.*

uh (u, un) *interj.* 1 HUH 2 a sound indicating hesitation

UHF or **uhf** ultrahigh frequency

ukase (yōō′kās, yōō kāz′) *n.* [Russ *ukaz*, edict] an official decree

Ukrain·ian (yōō krā′nē ən) *adj.* of Ukraine, its people, their language, etc. —*n.* 1 a native of Ukraine 2 the Slavic language of Ukraine

uku·lele (yōō′kə lā′lē) *n.* [Haw, leaping flea] a small, four-stringed, guitarlike musical instrument

ul·cer (ul′sər) *n.* [L *ulcus*] 1 an open sore on the skin or some mucous membrane, discharging pus 2 any corrupt condition —**ul′cer·ous** *adj.*

ul′cer·ate′ (-āt′) *vt., vi.* **-at′ed, -at′ing** to make or become ulcerous —**ul′cera′tion** *n.*

ulna (ul′nə) *n., pl.* **-nae** (-nē) or **-nas** [L, the elbow] the larger of the two bones of the forearm —**ul′nar** *adj.*

ul·ster (ul′stər) *n.* [after *Ulster*, in N Ireland] a long, loose, heavy overcoat

ult. ultimate(ly)

ul·teri·or (ul tir′ē ər) *adj.* [L: see ULTRA-] 1 lying beyond or on the farther side 2 beyond what is expressed or implied; undisclosed

ul·ti·mate (ul′tə mit) *adj.* [< L *ultimus*, last] 1 beyond which it is impossible to go 2 final; conclusive 3 beyond further analysis; fundamental 4 greatest possible — *n.* a final point or result —**ul′ti·mately** *adv.*

ul·ti·ma·tum (ul′tə māt′əm) *n., pl.* **-tums** or **-ta** (-ə) [see prec.] a final offer or demand, as in negotiations

ul·tra (ul′trə) *adj.* [< fol.] going beyond the usual limit; extreme

ultra- [L < *ultra*, beyond] *prefix* 1 beyond [*ultrasonic*] 2 extremely [*ultraconservative*]

ultra·con·serva·tive (ul′trə kən sur′və tiv) *adj.* extremely conservative

ultra·high frequency (ul′trə hī′) any radio frequency between 300 and 3,000 megahertz

ul′tra·ma·rine′ (-mə rēn′) *adj.* deep-blue —*n.* deep blue

ul′tra·son′ic (-sän′ik) *adj.* above the range of sound audible to the human ear —**ul′tra·son′i·cally** *adv.*

ul′tra·sound′ *n.* ultrasonic waves, used in medical diagnosis and therapy, in surgery, etc.

ul′tra·vi′o·let *adj.* of or designating those rays that are just beyond the violet end of the visible spectrum

ulu·late (yōō′lyoo lāt′, ul′-) *vi.* **-lat′ed, -lat′ing** [< L *ululare*, to howl] to howl, hoot, or wail loudly —**ul′u·la′tion** *n.*

U

Ulys·ses (yoo lis′ēz) [ML] ODYSSEUS

um·bel (um′bəl) *n.* [L *umbella*, parasol: see UMBRELLA] a cluster of flowers with stalks of nearly equal length which spring from the same point

um·ber (um′bər) *n.* [< It (*terra d'*)*ombra*, (earth of) shade] 1 a kind of earth used as a yellowish-brown or reddish-brown pigment 2 a yellowish-brown or reddish-brown color

um·bili·cal (um bil′i kəl) *adj.* [< L *umbilicus*, navel] of a cordlike structure (**umbilical cord**) connecting a fetus's navel to the placenta and conveying nourishment to the fetus

um·bili·cus (um bil′i kəs) *n., pl.* **-ci′** (-sī′) [L] NAVEL

um·bra (um′brə) *n., pl.* **-brae′** (-brē′) or **-bras** [L, a shade] 1 shade or a shadow 2 the dark cone of shadow from a planet or satellite on the side opposite the sun

um·brage (um′brij) *n.* [< L *umbra*, a shade] 1 [Obs.] shade 2 foliage 3 offense or resentment

um·brella (um brel′ə) *n.* [< L *umbra*, a shade] 1 a screen, usually of cloth on a folding frame, carried for protection against rain or sun 2 any comprehensive, protective alliance, strategy, device, etc.

umi·ak (oo′mē ak′) *n.* [Esk] a large, open boat made of skins on a wooden frame, used by Eskimos

um·laut (oom′lout) *n.* [Ger < *um*, about + *laut*, a sound] *Linguistics* 1 a vowel changed in sound by its assimilation to another vowel 2 the mark (¨) placed over such a vowel

ump (ump) *n., vt., vi.* short for UMPIRE

um·pire (um′pīr′) *n.* [< Fr *nomper*, uneven, hence a third person] 1 a person chosen to judge a dispute 2 an official who administers the rules in certain sports —*vt., vi.* **-pired′, -pir′ing** to act as umpire (in or of)

ump·teen (ump′tēn′) *adj.* [Slang] very many —**ump′teenth′** *adj.*

un- *prefix* 1 [OE] not, lack of, the opposite of [*unconcern*] 2 [OE *un-, on-*] back: indicating a reversal of action [*unfold*] The following list includes some common compounds formed with *un-* (either sense) that do not have special meanings:

unabashed	unbeaten
unable	unbiased
unabridged	unbleached
unaccented	unblemished
unacceptable	unbound
unaccompanied	unbreakable
unacquainted	unbroken
unadorned	unbuckle
unadulterated	unbutton
unafraid	uncap
unaided	unceasing
unaltered	uncensored
unambiguous	unchallenged
unannounced	unchanged
unanswerable	unchanging
unanswered	unchecked
unashamed	uncivil
unasked	uncivilized
unassailable	unclassified
unassisted	unclean
unattainable	unclear
unattractive	uncomplaining
unauthorized	uncompleted
unavailable	unconfirmed
unavoidable	unconnected
unbearable	unconsciously

THESAURUS

ugliness *n.* unsightliness, homeliness, hideousness, repulsiveness, loathsomeness, unseemliness, offensiveness, deformity, bad looks, ill looks, ill-favored countenance, plainness, disfigurement, grim aspect, foulness, horridness, monstrousness, inelegance, frightfulness, fearfulness.—*Ant.* BEAUTY, fairness, attractiveness.

ugly *a.* 1 [Ill-favored] unsightly, loathsome, hideous, homely, repulsive, unseemly, uncomely, deformed, bad-looking, plain, disfigured, monstrous, foul, horrid, frightful, revolting, repellent, unlovely, appalling, haglike, misshapen, misbegotten,

grisly, looking a mess*, looking like the devil*, not fit to be seen*.—*Ant.* BEAUTIFUL, handsome, graceful. 2 [Dangerous] pugnacious, quarrelsome, bellicose, rough, cantankerous, violent, vicious, evil, sinister, treacherous, wicked, formidable.—*Ant.* REASONABLE, mild, complaisant.

ulcer *n.* boil, abscess, infection; see SORE.

ultimate *a.* final, terminal, latest; see LAST 1.

ultimately *a.* eventually, at last, in the end, sooner or later, as a conclusion, to cap the climax, sequentially, after all, at long last, climactically, at

the close, in conclusion, conclusively, in due time, after a while, in after days, presently, by and by; see also FINALLY.—*Ant.* EARLY, in the beginning, at present.

ultimatum *n.* demands, requirements, terms.

ultraviolet *a.* beyond violet, having wavelengths of more than 4,000 angstroms, beyond the range of sight; see INVISIBLE.

umbrella *n.* parasol, sunshade, beach umbrella; see HAT.

umpire *n.* referee, moderator, mediator; see JUDGE 1.

uncontrollable	uninformed
uncontrolled	uninhabited
unconventional	uninhibited
unconvinced	uninjured
uncooked	uninspired
uncooperative	uninsured
uncultivated	unintelligent
uncultured	unintelligible
undamaged	unintended
undeclared	unintentional
undefeated	uninteresting
undefended	uninterrupted
undefined	uninvited
undemocratic	uninviting
undependable	unjustifiable
undeserved	unjustified
undesirable	unknowing
undeveloped	unlace
undifferentiated	unlatch
undiluted	unleavened
undisciplined	unlicensed
undiscovered	unlined
undiscriminating	unlisted
undisguised	unloved
undisputed	unmanageable
undistinguished	unmannerly
undisturbed	unmarked
undivided	unmarried
uneducated	unmatched
unemotional	unmindful
unending	unmoved
unenlightened	unnamed
unenviable	unnoticed
unethical	unobserved
uneventful	unobstructed
unexpired	unobtainable
unexplained	unobtrusive
unexplored	unoccupied
unexpressed	unofficial
unexpurgated	unopened
unfashionable	unopposed
unfasten	unorthodox
unfavorable	unpaid
unfavorably	unpalatable
unfit	unpardonable
unflattering	unpaved
unforeseeable	unperturbed
unforeseen	unpin
unforgivable	unplanned
unforgotten	unpolished
unfulfilled	unpolluted
unfurnished	unpredictable
ungrammatical	unprejudiced
ungrateful	unpremeditated
unhampered	unprepared
unhandy	unpretentious
unharmed	unproductive
unhealthful	unprofitable
unheeded	unpromising
unhesitating	unprotected
unhitch	unprovoked
unhook	unpublished
unhurried	unpunished
unhurt	unquestioned
unidentified	unquestioning
unimaginable	unreadable
unimaginative	unrealistic
unimpaired	unrealized
unimportant	unrecognizable

unrecognized	unsupervised
unrecorded	unsupported
unrefined	unsure
unregulated	unsurpassed
unrelated	unsuspected
unreliable	unsuspecting
unrelieved	unsweetened
unrepentant	unswerving
unrequited	unsympathetic
unresponsive	untainted
unrestricted	untamed
unsafe	untarnished
unsanitary	untasted
unsatisfactory	untenable
unsatisfied	untiring
unsaturated	untouched
unscientific	untrained
unseasoned	untried
unseeing	untroubled
unseen	untrue
unselfish	untrustworthy
unshackle	unverified
unshakable	unwanted
unshaken	unwarranted
unshaven	unwashed
unsociable	unwavering
unsolicited	unwed
unspoiled	unworkable
unspoken	unworldly
unsportsmanlike	unyielding
unsuccessful	unzip
unsuitable	

UN United Nations

un·ac·count·a·ble (un'ə kount'ə bəl) *adj.* **1** that cannot be explained; strange **2** not responsible —**un'ac·count'a·bly** *adv.*

un'ac·cus'tomed *adj.* **1** not accustomed (*to*) **2** not usual; strange

un'ad·vised' *adj.* **1** without counsel or advice **2** indiscreet; rash

un'af·fect'ed *adj.* **1** not affected or influenced **2** without affectation; sincere

un'-Amer'ican *adj.* regarded as not properly American; esp., regarded as opposing the U.S., its institutions, etc.

unan·i·mous (yōō nan'ə məs) *adj.* [[< L *unus*, one + *animus*, the mind]] agreeing completely; without dissent — **unan·im·i·ty** (yōō'nə nim'ə tē) *n.* —**unan'i·mously** *adv.*

un'ap·proach'able *adj.* **1** not to be approached; inaccessible; aloof **2** having no equal; unmatched

un·armed' *adj.* having no weapons

un'as·sum'ing *adj.* not assuming, pretentious, or forward; modest

un'at·tached' *adj.* **1** not attached **2** not engaged or married

un'at·tend'ed *adj.* **1** not waited on **2** unaccompanied (*by*) **3** neglected

un'avail'ing (-ə vāl'iŋ) *adj.* futile; useless —**un'avail'ingly** *adv.*

un·aware' *adj.* not aware or conscious — *adv.* UNAWARES

un·awares' (-werz') *adv.* **1** unintentionally **2** unexpectedly

un·backed' *adj.* **1** not backed, supported, etc. **2** without a back or backing

un·bal'anced *adj.* **1** not in balance **2** *a*) mentally deranged *b*) erratic

THESAURUS

unable *a.* incapable, powerless, weak, incompetent, unskilled, impotent, not able, inept, incapacitated, inefficacious, helpless, unfitted, inefficient, unqualified, inadequate, ineffectual, inoperative.—*Ant.* ABLE, capable, effective.

unaccompanied *a.* sole, solitary, deserted; see ALONE.

unaccustomed *a.* **1** [Unfamiliar] strange, unknown, unusual; see UNFAMILIAR 1. **2** [Unpracticed] unskilled, incompetent, untrained; see NAIVE.

unacquainted *a.* ignorant, out of touch, unknown; see UNFAMILIAR 1.

unaffected *a.* **1** [Genuine] spontaneous, candid, simple; see NATURAL 3. **2** [Uninfluenced] steady, unmoved, unchanged; see CALM 1.

un-American *a.* undemocratic, underground, subversive; see FOREIGN.

unanimous *a.* united, single, collective, combined, unified, concerted, harmonious, concordant, concurrent, public, popular, undivided, of one

accord, agreed, common, communal, shared, universal, accepted, unquestioned, undisputed, uncontested, consonant, consistent, with one voice, homogeneous, accordant, assenting.—*Ant.* DIFFERENT, dissenting, irreconcilable.

unanimously *a.* with one voice, harmoniously, all together, by acclamation, universally, unitedly, singly, collectively, without a dissenting voice, by common consent, by vote, in unison, cooperatively, concurrently, popularly, commonly, undisputedly, consonantly, consistently, in agreement.

unanswered *a.* without reply, unrefuted, not responded to, unnoticed, unchallenged, unquestioned, demanding an answer, filed, ignored, unsettled, undecided, in doubt, disputed, moot, debatable, vexed, open, pending, under consideration, undetermined, tabled, up in the air.—*Ant.* DETERMINED, answered, responded to.

unapproachable *a.* withdrawn, hesitant, aloof; see DISTANT.

unarmed *a.* weaponless, defenseless, peaceable; see WEAK 5.

unasked *a.* uninvited, not asked, unwelcome; see UNPOPULAR.

unattached *a.* unbound, independent, ungoverned; see FREE 1, 2, 3.

unauthorized *a.* unofficial, unapproved, unlawful; see ILLEGAL.

unavoidable *a.* inescapable, impending, sure; see CERTAIN 2.

unaware *a.* uninformed, oblivious, ignorant, not cognizant, unmindful, unknowing, heedless, negligent, careless, insensible, forgetful, unconcerned, blind, deaf, inattentive, without notice, deaf to, caught napping, in a daze, not seeing the forest for the trees*.—*Ant.* CONSCIOUS, aware, cognizant.

unbalanced *a.* **1** [Deranged] crazy, unsound, psychotic; see INSANE, TROUBLED. **2** [Unsteady] wobbly, shaky, treacherous; see UNSTABLE 1.

un·bar′ *vt.* **-barred′, -bar′ring** to unbolt; unlock; open

un′be·com′ing *adj.* not appropriate or suited to one's appearance, character, etc.; unattractive, indecorous, etc.

un′be·known′ *adj.* without one's knowledge; unknown: usually with *to* Also **un′be·knownst′** (-nōnst′)

un′be·lief′ *n.* lack of belief, esp. in religion —**un′be·liev′er** *n.*

un′be·liev′able *adj.* beyond belief; astounding; incredible

un·bend′ *vt.*, *vi.* **-bent′** or **-bend′ed, -bend′ing** **1** to release or be released from tension **2** to relax, as from formality **3** to straighten

un·bend′ing *adj.* **1** rigid; stiff **2** firm; resolute **3** aloof; austere

un·bid′den *adj.* **1** not commanded **2** not invited

un·blush′ing *adj.* **1** not blushing **2** shameless —**un·blush′ing·ly** *adv.*

un·bolt′ *vt.*, *vi.* to withdraw the bolt or bolts of (a door, etc.); open

un·born′ *adj.* **1** not born **2** still in the mother's uterus **3** yet to be

un·bos′om (-booz′əm) *vt.*, *vi.* to tell or reveal (feelings, secrets, etc.) —**unbosom oneself** to reveal one's feelings, secrets, etc.

un·bound′ed *adj.* **1** without bounds or limits **2** not restrained

un·bri′dled *adj.* **1** having no bridle on: said of a horse, etc. **2** uncontrolled

un·bur′den *vt.* **1** to free from a burden **2** to relieve (one's soul, mind, etc.) by disclosing (guilt, etc.)

uncalled′-for *adj.* **1** not called for **2** unnecessary and out of place

un·can′ny (un kan′ē) *adj.* **1** mysterious and eerie; weird **2** so good, acute, etc. as to seem preternatural

uncared′-for *adj.* not cared for or looked after; neglected

un′cer·emo′ni·ous *adj.* **1** not ceremonious; informal **2** curt; abrupt

un·cer′tain *adj.* **1** *a*) not surely or certainly known *b*) not sure or certain in knowledge; doubtful **2** vague **3** not dependable or reliable **4** varying —**un·cer′tainty,** *pl.* **-ties,** *n.*

un·char′i·table *adj.* harsh or severe, as in opinion —**un·char′i·tably** *adv.*

un·chart′ed *adj.* not marked on a chart or map; unexplored or unknown

un·chris′tian *adj.* **1** not Christian **2** [Colloq.] outrageous; dreadful

un·cial (un′shē əl, -shəl) *adj.* [L *uncialis*, inch-high] designating or of the large, rounded letters of Greek and Latin manuscripts between A.D. 300 and 900 — *n.* uncial script or letter

un·cir′cum·cised′ *adj.* **1** not circumcised; gentile **2** [Archaic] heathen

un·clasp′ *vt.* **1** to unfasten the clasp of **2** to release from a clasp or grasp

un·cle (un′kəl) *n.* [< L *avunculus*] **1** the brother of one's father or mother **2** the husband of one's aunt

Uncle Sam [< abbrev. *U.S.*] [Colloq.] the U.S. (government or people), personified as a tall man with whiskers, dressed in red, white, and blue

Uncle Tom [after main character in novel *Uncle Tom's Cabin* (1852)] [Colloq.] a black regarded as servile toward whites: a term of contempt

un·cloak′ *vt.*, *vi.* **1** to remove a cloak (from) **2** to reveal; expose

un·clothe′ *vt.* **-clothed′** or **-clad′, -cloth′ing** to undress, uncover, etc.

un·coil′ *vt.*, *vi.* to unwind

un·com′fort·able *adj.* **1** feeling discomfort **2** causing discomfort **3** ill at ease —**un·com′fort·ably** *adv.*

un′com·mit′ted *adj.* **1** not committed or pledged **2** not taking a stand

---

━━━ THESAURUS ━━━

unbearable *a.* intolerable, unacceptable, too much*; see TERRIBLE 2.

unbeaten *a.* victorious, triumphant, winning; see SUCCESSFUL.

unbecoming *a.* unsuitable, unfitted, awkward; see IMPROPER.

unbelievable *a.* beyond belief, incredible, inconceivable, staggering, unimaginable, not to be credited, dubious, doubtful, improbable, questionable, implausible, open to doubt, a bit thick*; see also UNLIKELY.—*Ant.* LIKELY, believable, probable.

unbend *v.* become more casual, be informal, relax; see REST 1.

unblemished *a.* spotless, flawless, unmarked; see PERFECT 2.

unborn *a.* embryonic, incipient, expected, future, prospective, potential, latent, anticipated, awaited.

unbound *a.* loose, untied, unfastened; see FREE 1, 2, 3.—*Ant.* BOUND, stapled, tied.

unbreakable *a.* indestructible, durable, everlasting, cast-iron, lasting, unshakeable, solid, firm, unchangeable, invulnerable, incorruptible, resistant, rugged, tight, unyielding.—*Ant.* DAINTY, fragile, brittle.

unbroken *a.* **1** [Whole] entire, intact, unimpaired; see WHOLE 2. **2** [Continuous] uninterrupted, continuous, even; see REGULAR 3, SMOOTH 1, 2.

unburden *v.* **1** [To unload] dump, dispose of, relinquish; see LIGHTEN, RELIEVE. **2** [To reveal] disclose, confess, divulge; see ADMIT 2.

unbutton *v.* undo, open up, unfasten; see OPEN 2.

uncalled-for *a.* unjustified, redundant, not needed; see UNNECESSARY.

uncanny *a.* weird, unnatural, supernatural, preternatural, superhuman, ghostly, inexplainable, mystifying, incredible, mysterious, magical, devilish; see also MAGIC.

uncertain *a.* undecided, undeter- mined, unsettled, doubtful, changeable, unpredictable, improbable, unlikely, unfixed, unsure, indeterminate, haphazard, random, chance, casual, provisional, contingent, alterable, subject to change, possible, vague, conjectural, questionable, problematic, suppositional, hypothetical, theoretical, open to question, equivocal, perplexing, debatable, dubious, indefinite, unascertained, ambiguous, unresolved, debated, conjecturable, unknown, unannounced, imprecise, in abeyance, up in the air, in doubt.

uncertainty *n.* **1** [The mental state of being uncertain] perplexity, doubt, puzzlement, quandary, mystification, guesswork, conjecture, indecision, ambivalence, dilemma.—*Ant.* BELIEF, certainty, decision. **2** [The state of being undetermined or unknown] questionableness, contingency, obscurity, vagueness, ambiguity, difficulty, incoherence, intricacy, involvement, darkness, inconclusiveness, indeterminateness, improbability, unlikelihood, low probability, conjecturability; see also DOUBT.—*Ant.* DETERMINATION, sureness, necessity. **3** [That which is not determined or not known] chance, mutability, change, unpredictability, possibility, emergence, contingency, blind spot, puzzle, enigma, question, blank, vacancy, maze, theory, risk, leap in the dark.—*Ant.* TRUTH, fact, matter of record.

unchanged *a.* unaltered, the same, unmoved, constant, fixed, continuing, stable, permanent, durable, unvarying, eternal, invariable, consistent, persistent, firm, unvaried, resolute, perpetual, continuous, maintained, uninterrupted, fast.—*Ant.* CHANGED, altered, modified.

uncivilized *a.* barbarous, uncontrolled, barbarian; see PRIMITIVE 3.

unclassified *a.* not classified, disor- dered, out of order; see CONFUSED 2, UNKNOWN 1.

uncle *n.* father's brother, mother's brother, elder; see RELATIVE.

unclean *a.* soiled, sullied, stained, spotted, filthy, bedraggled, smeared, befouled, nasty, grimy, polluted, rank, unhealthful, defiled, muddy, stinking, fetid, rotten, vile, decayed, contaminated, tainted, rancid, putrid, putrescent, moldy, musty, mildewed, besmirched, smirched, filmed over, bleary, dusty, sooty, smudgy, scurvy, scurfy, clogged, slimy, mucky, tarnished, murky, smudged, daubed, blurred, spattered; see also DIRTY 1, IMPURE 1.—*Ant.* CLEAN, pure, white.

uncomfortable *a.* **1** [Troubled in body or mind] distressed, ill at ease, uneasy, nervous, disturbed, pained, miserable, wretched, restless, annoyed, angry, in pain, smarting, suffering, upset, vexed, on pins and needles, weary, tired, fatigued, exhausted, strained, worn, aching, sore, galled, stiff, chafed, cramped, agonized, hurt, anguished.—*Ant.* QUIET, rested, happy. **2** [Causing discomfort] ill-fitting, awkward, annoying, irritating, distressful, galling, wearisome, difficult, hard, thorny, troublesome, harsh, grievous, dolorous, bitter, excruciating, afflictive, distressing, torturing, painful, agonizing, disagreeable.—*Ant.* EASY, pleasant, grateful.

uncomfortably *a.* distressfully, uneasily, dolefully, agonizingly, painfully, miserably, wretchedly, restlessly, sadly, fretfully, annoyingly, disturbingly, awkwardly, irritatingly, troublesomely, harshly, grievously, bitterly, poignantly, sharply, keenly, excruciatingly, disagreeably, unhappily, dismally, in anguish.

uncommitted *a.* **1** [Neutral] unpledged, unaffiliated, free; see NEU-

un·com′mon *adj.* **1** rare; not common or usual **2** strange; remarkable

un′com·mu′ni·ca′tive *adj.* not communicative; reserved; taciturn

un·com′pro·mis′ing *adj.* not yielding; firm; inflexible

un′con·cern′ *n.* **1** apathy; indifference **2** lack of concern, or worry

un′con·cerned′ *adj.* **1** indifferent **2** not solicitous or anxious

un′con·di′tional *adj.* without conditions or reservations; absolute

un·con′scion·able (un kän′shən ə bəl) *adj.* **1** not guided or restrained by conscience **2** unreasonable or excessive **3** not fair or just —**un·con′scion·ably** *adv.*

un·con′scious *adj.* **1** deprived of consciousness **2** not aware (*of*) **3** not realized or intended *[an unconscious habit]* —**the unconscious** *Psychoanalysis* the sum of all thoughts, impulses, etc. of which the individual is not conscious but which influence the emotions and behavior

un′con·sti·tu′tional *adj.* not in accordance with a constitution

un·cork′ *vt.* to pull the cork out of

un·count′ed *adj.* **1** not counted **2** inconceivably numerous

un·cou′ple *vt.* **-pled, -pling** to unfasten (things coupled together)

un·couth (un kōōth′) *adj.* [OE < *un-*, not + *cunnan*, know] **1** awkward; ungainly **2** uncultured; crude

un·cov′er *vt.* **1** to disclose **2** to remove the cover from **3** to remove the hat, etc. from (the head) —*vi.* to bare the head, as in respect

unc·tion (uŋk′shən) *n.* [< L *ungere*, anoint] **1** *a*) the act of anointing, as for medical or religious purposes *b*) the oil, ointment, etc. used for this **2** anything that soothes or comforts

unc·tu·ous (uŋk′chōō əs) *adj.* [see prec.] **1** oily or greasy **2** characterized by a smooth pretense of fervor or earnestness; too suave or oily —**unc′tu·ous·ness** *n.*

un·cut′ *adj.* not cut; specif., *a*) not ground to shape (said of a gem) *b*) not abridged or shortened

un·daunt′ed *adj.* not daunted; fearless, undismayed, etc.

un·de·ceive′ *vt.* **-ceived′, -ceiv′ing** to cause to be no longer deceived or misled

un′de·cid′ed *adj.* **1** not decided **2** not having come to a decision

un′de·mon′stra·tive *adj.* not demonstrative; not showing feelings openly; reserved —**un′de·mon′stra·tively** *adv.*

un·de·ni′able *adj.* **1** that cannot be denied; indisputable **2** unquestionably good —**un·de·ni′ably** *adv.*

un·der (un′dər) *prep.* [OE] **1** in, at, or to a position down from; below **2** beneath the surface of **3** below and to the other side of *[drive under the bridge]* **4** covered by *[a vest under his coat]* **5** *a*) lower in rank, position, amount, etc. than *b*) lower than the required degree of *[under age]* **6** subject to the control, limitations, etc. of *[under oath]* **7** undergoing *[under repair]* **8** with the disguise of *[under an alias]* **9** in (the designated category) **10** during the rule of *[under Elizabeth I]* **11** being the subject of *[under discussion]* **12** because of *[under the circumstances]* **13** authorized by —*adv.* **1** in or to a lower position or state **2** so as to be covered, concealed, etc. —*adj.* lower in position, authority, amount, etc.

under- *prefix* **1** in, on, or from a lower place; beneath *[undertow]* **2** in a subordinate position *[underling]* **3** too little; insufficiently *[underdeveloped]*

un′der·achieve′ *vi.* **-chieved′, -chiev′ing** to fail to do as well in school as might be expected from intelligence tests —**un′der·achiev′er** *n.*

un′der·act′ *vt., vi.* to act (a theatrical role) with insufficient emphasis or too great restraint

un′der·age′ *adj.* **1** not of mature age **2** below the age required by law

under·arm (un′dər ärm′) *adj.* **1** of, for, in, or used the area under the arm, or the armpit **2** UNDERHAND (sense 1) —*adv.* UNDERHAND (sense 1)

un′der·bel′ly *n.* **1** the lower, posterior part of an animal's belly **2** any vulnerable area, point, etc.

un′der·bid′ *vt., vi.* **-bid′, -bid′ding** **1** to bid lower than (another person) **2** to bid less than the worth of (a thing, as one's hand in bridge)

un′der·brush′ *n.* small trees, shrubs, etc. growing in woods or forests

un′der·car′riage *n.* a supporting frame, as of an automobile

un′der·charge′ *vt., vi.* **-charged′, -charg′ing** **1** to charge too low a price (to) **2** to load insufficiently

un′der·class′ *n.* the class with incomes below subsistence level, including esp. the underprivileged

---

THESAURUS

TRAL **1.** **2** [Reserved] evasive, reticent, shy; see WITHDRAWN.

uncommon *a.* unusual, out of the ordinary, different, extraordinary, unheard of, unique, rare, exceptional, out of the way, strange, exotic, arcane, remarkable, startling, surprising, fantastic, unaccustomed, unfamiliar, freakish, irregular, uncustomary, unconventional, unorthodox, abnormal, aberrant, peculiar, odd, bizarre, eccentric, original, nondescript, prodigious, fabulous, monstrous, wonderful, unaccountable, noteworthy, curious, queer, unparalleled, outlandish, extreme.—*Ant.* COMMON, usual, ordinary.

uncompromising *a.* strong, inflexible, determined; see FIRM 1.

unconcern *n.* apathy, aloofness, coldness; see INDIFFERENCE.

unconcerned *a.* careless, apathetic, inattentive; see NONCHALANT, INDIFFERENT.

unconditional *a.* **1** [Separate] absolute, unconstrained, without reserve, outright, final, certain, complete, entire, whole, unrestricted, unqualified, unlimited, actual, thorough, thoroughgoing, genuine, indubitable, assured, determinate, unequivocal, full, categorical, decisive, unmistakable, clear, unquestionable. **2** [Irrelevant] impertinent, unrelated, inapplicable; see IRRELEVANT.

unconnected *a.* **1** [Separate] divided, detached, disconnected; see SEPARATED. **2** [Irrelevant] impertinent, unrelated, inapplicable; see IRRELEVANT.

unconscious *a.* insensible, swooning, in a state of suspended anima-

tion, torpid, lethargic, inanimate, senseless, drowsy, motionless, benumbed, stupefied, numb, inert, paralyzed, palsied, entranced, in a stupor, in a coma, in a trance, raving, out of one's head, out like a light*, knocked out.—*Ant.* CONSCIOUS, vivacious, awake.

unconscious *n.* [*Usually used with* "*the*"] psyche, instinct, motive force; see MEMORY 1, MIND 1.

unconsciously *a.* abstractedly, mechanically, carelessly, automatically, habitually, by rote, unintentionally, inattentively, heedlessly, without reflection, negligently, disregardfully, thoughtlessly, neglectfully, hurriedly, unthinkingly, without calculation, unguardedly.—*Ant.* DELIBERATELY, intentionally, willfully.

unconstitutional *a.* un-American, undemocratic, lawless; see ILLEGAL.

uncontrollable *a.* ungovernable, stubborn, insurgent; see UNRULY.

uncontrolled *a.* open, clear, free, unchecked, unhindered, boundless, ungoverned, unsuppressed, limitless, unbridled, unfettered, unobstructed, independent, unburdened, unlimited, unbounded, unhampered, uncurbed, unconstrained, unconfined.

unconventional *a.* novel, individual, different; see UNIQUE, UNUSUAL 2.

uncouth *a.* awkward, clumsy, crude; see RUDE 1, 2.

uncover *v.* unseal, uncork, unscrew, pry open, lift the lid, dig up, reveal, tap, lay open, unclose, fish out, fish up; see also OPEN 2.—*Ant.* CLOSE, cover, seal up.

undamaged *a.* uninjured, safe, unharmed; see WHOLE 2.

undecided *a.* undetermined, in the balance, unsettled; see DOUBTFUL, UNCERTAIN.

undefeated *a.* unbeaten, victorious, winning; see SUCCESSFUL.

undefined *a.* **1** [Infinite] limitless, boundless, forever; see INFINITE. **2** [Vague] dim, unclear, indistinct; see IRREGULAR 4, OBSCURE 1.

undeniable *a.* proven, sound, sure; see ACCURATE 1.

undependable *a.* careless, unsound, inconstant; see IRRESPONSIBLE, UNRELIABLE.

under *a., prep.* **1** [Referring to physical position] on the bottom of, below, covered by, 'neath, concealed by, held down by, supporting, pinned beneath, on the underside of, pressed down by, beneath.—*Ant.* ABOVE, over, on top of. **2** [Subject to authority] governed by, in the power of, obedient to; see SUBORDINATE. **3** [Included within] belonging to, subsequent to, following; see BELOW 3.

underachiever *n.* slow learner, retarded child, underprivileged person, backward child, misfit, problem child, foreigner, nonnative speaker, foreign-born pupil; see also FOOL.

underage *a.* juvenile, youthful, minor; see YOUNG 1.

underbrush *n.* thicket, brush, brushwood, jungle, second growth, tangle, hedge, cover, scrub, bush; see also FOREST.

un′der·class′man (-mən) *n., pl.* **-men** a freshman or sophomore in high school or college

un′der·clothes′ *n.pl.* UNDERWEAR Also **un′der·cloth′ing** *n.sing.*

un′der·coat′ *n.* **1** a tarlike coating applied to the underside of a motor vehicle to retard rust, etc. **2** a coat of paint, etc. applied before the final coat Also **un′der·coat′ing** — *vt.* to apply an undercoat to

un′der·cov′er *adj.* acting or carried out in secret

un′der·cur′rent *n.* **1** a current flowing beneath the surface **2** an underlying tendency, opinion, etc.

un′der·cut′ *vt.* **-cut′, -cut′ting** **1** to make a cut below or under **2** to undersell or work for lower wages than

un′der·de·vel′oped *adj.* inadequately developed, esp. economically and industrially

un′der·dog′ *n.* **1** a person or team that is losing or expected to lose **2** one who is underprivileged

un′der·done′ *adj.* not cooked enough

un′der·em·ployed′ *adj.* **1** working less than full time **2** working at low-skilled, poorly paid jobs when capable of doing more skilled work —**un′der·em·ploy′ment** *n.*

un′der·es′ti·mate′ *vt.* **-mat′ed, -mat′ing** to set too low an estimate on or for —**un′der·es′ti·ma′tion** *n.*

un′der·foot′ *adv., adj.* **1** under the foot or feet **2** in the way

un′der·gar′ment (-gär′mənt) *n.* a piece of underwear

un′der·go′ *vt.* **-went′, -gone′, -go′ing** to experience; go through

un′der·grad′u·ate *n.* a college student who has not yet earned a degree

un′der·ground′ *adj.* **1** under the earth's surface **2** secret; hidden **3** of noncommercial newspapers, movies, etc. that are unconventional, radical, etc. —*adv.* **1** under the earth's surface **2** in or into secrecy —*n.* **1** the region under the earth's surface **2** a secret movement in a country to oppose the government or occupying enemy forces **3** [Brit., etc. (exc. Cdn.)] a subway

un′der·growth′ *n.* UNDERBRUSH

un′der·hand′ *adj.* **1** done with the hand below the level of the elbow or shoulder **2** UNDERHANDED — *adv.* **1** with an underhand motion **2** underhandedly

un′der·hand′ed *adj.* sly, deceitful, etc. —**un′der·hand′ed·ly** *adv.*

un′der·lie′ *vt.* **-lay′, -lain′, -ly′ing** **1** to lie beneath **2** to be the basis for; form the foundation of

un′der·line′ *vt.* **-lined′, -lin′ing** **1** to draw a line beneath **2** to stress

under·ling (un′dər liŋ) *n.* [OE: see UNDER- & -LING] a person in a subordinate position; inferior

un′der·ly′ing *adj.* **1** lying under **2** fundamental; basic

un′der·mine′ *vt.* **-mined′, -min′ing** **1** to dig beneath, so as to form a tunnel or mine **2** to wear away at the supports of **3** to injure or weaken, esp. by subtle or insidious means

un′der·most′ *adj., adv.* lowest in place, position, rank, etc.

under·neath (un′dər nēth′) *adv., prep.* [< OE *under*, UNDER + *neothan*, below] under; below; beneath

un′der·nour′ished *adj.* not getting the food needed for health and growth

un′der·pants′ *n.pl.* an undergarment of long or short pants

un′der·pass′ *n.* a passage under something, as a road under a railway

un′der·pin′ning (-pin′iŋ) *n.* **1** a support or prop **2** [*pl.*] [Colloq.] the legs

under·play (un′dər plā′) *vt., vi.* **1** UNDERACT **2** to make seem not too important

un′der·priv′i·leged *adj.* deprived of basic social rights and security through poverty, discrimination, etc.

un′der·pro·duce′ *vt., vi.* **-duced′, -duc′ing** to produce less than is needed or wanted

un′der·rate′ *vt.* **-rat′ed, -rat′ing** to rate or estimate too low

under·score (un′dər skôr′) *vt.* **-scored′, -scor′ing** UNDERLINE

un′der·sea′ *adj., adv.* beneath the surface of the sea Also **un′der·seas′** *adv.*

un′der·sec′re·tar′y *n., pl.* **-ies** an assistant secretary

un′der·sell′ *vt.* **-sold′, -sell′ing** to sell at a lower price than

un′der·shirt′ *n.* a collarless undergarment worn under an outer shirt

un′der·shorts′ *n.pl.* short underpants worn by men and boys

un′der·shot′ *adj.* **1** with the lower part extending past the upper [an *undershot* jaw] **2** driven by water flowing along the lower part

un′der·side′ *n.* the side or surface that is underneath

un′der·signed′ *adj.* **1** signed at the end **2** whose name is signed at the end —**the undersigned** the person or persons having signed at the end

un′der·skirt′ *n.* a skirt worn under another

un′der·staffed′ *adj.* having fewer workers on the staff than are needed

un′der·stand′ *vt.* **-stood′** (-stood′), **-stand′ing** [< OE *understandan*, lit., to stand among] **1** to perceive the meaning of **2** to assume from what is heard, etc.; infer **3** to take as meant; interpret **4** to take as a fact **5** to know **6** to know the nature, character, etc. of **7** to be sympathetic with — *vi.* **1** to have understanding, comprehension, etc. **2** to be informed; believe —**un′der·stand′able** *adj.* —**un′der·stand′ably** *adv.*

■■■ THESAURUS ■■■

underclothes *n.* lingerie, undies*, underthings; see CLOTHES, UNDERWEAR.

undercover *a.* **1** [Secret] hidden, surreptitious, clandestine; see SECRET 3. **2** [Secretly] privately, surreptitiously, stealthily; see SECRETLY.

underdeveloped *a.* backward, retarded, slowed down; see WEAK 1, 2, 3, 5.

underdog *n.* loser, underling, low man on the totem pole*; see FAILURE 2, VICTIM.

underestimate *v.* miscalculate, come short of, undervalue, depreciate, underrate, disparage, slight, minimize, think too little of, hold too lightly, make light of, deprecate.

underfoot *a.* **1** [Beneath] down, at bottom, below; see UNDER 1. **2** [In the way] annoying, tiresome, impeding; see DISTURBING.

undergo *v.* sustain, submit to, support, experience, feel, know, be subject to, bear, meet with, endure, go through, encounter, bear up under, put up with, share, withstand.—*Ant.* AVOID, ESCAPE, RESIST.

undergone *a.* sustained, submitted to, supported, experienced, felt, suffered, borne, met with, known, endured, gone through, encountered, put up with, shared, seen, withstood.

underground *a.* **1** [Subterranean] buried, covered, earthed over, under the sod, in the recesses of the earth, hidden from the eye of day, gone to earth; see also UNDER 1. **2** [Secret] hidden, undercover, clandestine; see SECRET 3. **3** [Unconventional] experimental, radical, avant-garde; see UNUSUAL 2.

undergrowth *n.* underwood, tangle, scrub; see BRUSH 3.

underhanded *a.* secret, sneaky, secretive; see SLY.

underlie *v.* carry, bear, hold up; see HOLD 7.

underline *v.* **1** [Emphasize] stress, mark, indicate; see EMPHASIZE. **2** [To make a line under] underscore, mark, interline, bracket, check off, italicize.

undermine *v.* impair, ruin, threaten; see WEAKEN 2.

underneath *a., prep.* beneath, below, lower than; see UNDER 1.

undernourished *a.* underfed, mistreated, afflicted with malnutrition; see HUNGRY.

underpass *n.* bridge, culvert, cave; see TUNNEL.

underprivileged *a.* indigent, destitute, educationally handicapped; see POOR 1.

undershirt *n.* shirt, T-shirt, turtle-neck; see CLOTHES, UNDERWEAR.

underside *n.* underneath, base, root; see BOTTOM, FOUNDATION 2.

understand *v.* **1** [To comprehend] apprehend, fathom, take in, grasp, figure out, seize, identify with, know, perceive, appreciate, follow, master, conceive, be aware of, sense, recognize, grow aware, explain, interpret, see through, learn, find out, see into, catch, note, be conscious of, have cognizance of, realize, discern, read, distinguish, infer, deduce, induce, make out, become alive to, have been around*, experience, have knowledge of, be instructed in, get to the bottom of, get at the root of, penetrate, possess, be informed of, come to one's senses, see the light, make out, register*, savvy*, get the gist of, catch on, get the point of, dig*, read between the lines, be with it*, get the idea. **2** [To suppose] guess, conjecture, surmise; see ASSUME. **3** [To accept] concede, take for granted, count on; see AGREE.

understandable *a.* comprehensible, conceivable, appreciable, expected, to be expected, natural, normal, regular, making sense, intelligible, in harmony with, readable, reasonable, logical, right, customary, recogniz-

un'der·stand'ing *n.* 1 comprehension 2 the power to think and learn; intelligence 3 a specific interpretation 4 mutual agreement, esp. one that settles differences — *adj.* that understands; sympathetic

un'der·state' *vt.* **-stat'ed, -stat'ing** 1 to state too weakly 2 to state in a restrained style —**un'der·state'ment** *n.*

un'der·stud'y *n., pl.* **-ies** an actor prepared to substitute for another — *vt., vi.* **-ied, -y·ing** to learn (a part) as an understudy (to)

un'der·take' *vt.* **-took', -tak'en, -tak'ing** 1 to take upon oneself (a task, etc.) 2 to promise; guarantee

un'der·tak'er *n.* FUNERAL DIRECTOR: a somewhat old-fashioned usage

un'der·tak'ing *n.* 1 something undertaken; task; enterprise 2 a promise; guarantee

un'der-the-count'er *adj.* [Colloq.] done secretly in an unlawful way Also **un'der-the-ta'ble**

un'der·things' *n.pl.* women's or girls' underwear

un'der·tone' *n.* 1 a low tone of voice 2 a subdued color 3 an underlying quality, factor, etc.

un'der·tow' *n.* a current of water moving beneath the surface water and in a different direction

un'der·wa'ter *adj.* being, done, etc. beneath the surface of the water

un'der·way' *adj.* *Naut.* not anchored or moored or aground

un'der·wear' *n.* clothing worn under one's outer clothes, usually next to the skin, as undershirts

un'der·weight' (-wāt'; *also* un'dər wāt') *adj.* below the normal, desirable, or allowed weight

un'der·world' *n.* 1 Hades; hell 2 criminals as an organized group

un'der·write' *vt.* **-wrote', -writ'ten, -writ'ing** 1 to agree to market (an issue of securities), guaranteeing to buy any part remaining unsubscribed 2 to agree to finance (an undertaking, etc.) 3 to sign one's name to (an insurance policy), thus assuming liability —**un'der·writ'er** *n.*

un·dies (un'dēz') *n.pl.* [Colloq.] women's or girls' underwear

undo' *vt.* **-did', -done', -do'ing** 1 to untie, open, etc. 2 to do away with; annul 3 to bring to ruin

un·doc'u·ment'ed *adj.* not having a proper visa for U.S. residence *[an undocumented alien]*

un·do'ing *n.* 1 an annulling 2 a bringing to ruin 3 the cause of ruin

un·done' *adj.* 1 not done; not performed, accomplished, etc. 2 ruined 3 emotionally upset

un·doubt'ed *adj.* that cannot be doubted; certain —**un·doubt'ed·ly** *adv.*

un·dreamed' *adj.* not even dreamed (*of*) or thought (*of*) as possible Also **un·dreamt'** (-dremt')

un·dress' *vt.* to take off the clothing of — *vi.* to take off one's clothes

un·due' *adj.* 1 not appropriate; improper 2 excessive; immoderate

un·du·lant (un'dyoo lənt) *adj.* undulating

un·du·late' (-lāt') *vi., vt.* [< L unda, a wave] 1 to move or cause to move in waves 2 to have or cause to have a wavy form or surface —**un'du·la'tion** *n.*

un·du·ly (un doo'lē) *adv.* 1 improperly; unjustly 2 excessively

un·dy'ing *adj.* immortal or eternal

━━━━━ THESAURUS ━━━━━

able, justifiable, imaginable, acceptable, apprehensible, credible.
understanding *n.* 1 [The power to understand] sharpness, intelligence, comprehension; see JUDGMENT 1. 2 [The act of comprehending] recognition, knowing, perception; see JUDGMENT 2, THOUGHT 1. 3 [That which comes from understanding] conclusion, knowledge, perception; see BELIEF, OPINION 1. 4 [Informal agreement] meeting of minds, common view, harmony; see AGREEMENT 1. 5 [The intellect] head, brain, mentality; see MIND 1.
understood *a.* 1 [Comprehended] penetrated, realized, appreciated, known, discovered, grasped, reasoned out, rationalized, explained, experienced, discerned, distinguished, made out, learned, fathomed, searched, explored, analyzed, mastered, conned, taken to heart.—*Ant.* UNKNOWN, overlooked, uncomprehended. 2 [Agreed upon] concerted, ratified, assumed, stipulated, pledged, tacitly agreed upon, engaged for, settled, concluded, fixed upon, endorsed, subscribed to, accepted.
undertake *v.* endeavor, engage, set out, promise, try out, try, begin, offer, set in motion, volunteer, initiate, commit oneself to, embark upon, venture, take upon oneself, answer for, hazard, stake, move, devote oneself to, take up for, take on, set about, go in for, put one's hand to, have one's hands in, have in hand, launch into, address oneself to, enter upon, busy oneself with, tackle, pitch into*, fall into, buckle down, take on, take the plunge, fall to, have a try at, go in for a big way.
undertaken *a.* set in motion, begun, launched, embarked upon, initiated, pushed forward, ventured, started, endeavored, assumed, taken up, promised, offered, volunteered, hazarded, chanced, risked, pledged, tackled, essayed, tried, aimed at, attempted, striven for, engaged for.
undertaker *n.* mortician, funeral director, embalmer, body snatcher*.

undertaking *n.* enterprise, attempt, engagement; see ACTION 1, 2.
undertone *n.* buzz, murmur, hum; see WHISPER 1.
undertow *n.* whirlpool, undercurrent, riptide; see FLOW 1, TIDE.
underwater *a.* submarine, sunken, marine; see UNDER 1.
underwear *n.* undergarments, underclothing, unmentionables*, lingerie, intimate things, underlinen, underclothes; see also CLOTHES. *Types of underwear include the following—men:* shirt, shorts, briefs, drawers, red flannels, union suit, jockey shorts, T-shirt, boxer shorts, long underwear; *women:* underskirt, slip, petticoat, girdle, brassiere, garter belt, bra-slip, bra, panty slip, halfslip, corset, corselet, bodice, *cache-sexe* (French), vest, briefs, foundation garment, panty girdle, panties, pantyhose, shorts, knickers (British), falsies*; *infants:* shirt, drawers, pants, diaper, slip, rubber pants.
underweight *a.* skinny, undersized, puny; see THIN 2.
underworld *n.* 1 [Hell] Hades, Inferno, netherworld; see HELL. 2 [Crime] gangdom, rackets, organized crime; see CRIME.
undesirable *a.* objectionable, shunned, disliked, to be avoided, unwanted, outcast, rejected, defective, disadvantageous, inexpedient, inconvenient, troublesome, unwished for, repellent, loathed, unsought, dreaded, annoying, insufferable, unacceptable, scorned, displeasing, distasteful, loathsome, abominable, obnoxious, unpopular, bothersome, unlikable, unwelcome, unapprovable, useless, inadmissible, unsatisfactory, disagreeable, awkward, embarrassing, unfit.—*Ant.* WELCOME, proper, suitable.
undeveloped *a.* potential, incipient, unactualized; see HIDDEN.
undisputed *a.* unchallenged, unquestioned, assured; see CERTAIN 2.
undistinguished *a.* ordinary,

commonplace, plain; see COMMON 1, CONVENTIONAL 3, DULL 4.
undisturbed *a.* settled, unruffled, untroubled; see CALM 1, 2.
undivided *a.* 1 [Unified] united, full, collective; see WHOLE. 2 [Undistracted] exclusive, complete, entire; see WHOLE 1.
undo *v.* mar, destroy, ruin, wreck, break, bring to naught, subvert, injure, overthrow, unsettle, turn topsy-turvy, upset, defeat.
undoing *n.* ruination, downfall, reversal, destruction, misfortune, calamity, overthrow, trouble, grief, catastrophe, defeat, shipwreck, smash, wrack, subversion, collapse, casualty, accident, mishap, misadventure, misstep, mischance, bad luck, adversity, reverse, blow, trial, affliction, stroke of fate, slip, blunder, fault, omission, difficulty, failure, error, miscalculation, trip, stumble, fumble, blunder, repulse, discouragement, deathblow, last straw.—*Ant.* ADVANTAGE, good omen, godsend.
undone *a.* 1 [Unfinished] left, incomplete, unperformed; see UNFINISHED 1. 2 [Distraught] upset, disturbed, agitated; see TROUBLED. 3 [Ruined] betrayed, destroyed, killed; see DEAD 1, RUINED 1, 2.
undoubtedly *a.* assuredly, without doubt, of course; see UNQUESTIONABLY.
undress *v.* strip, take off one's clothes, disrobe, dismantle, divest, become naked, peel*, pile out of one's clothes*.—*Ant.* DRESS, put on one's clothes, attire oneself.
undue *a.* improper, illegal, indecorous, unfair, unseemly, unjust, underhanded, sinister, forbidden, excessive, unnecessary, extreme, extravagant, disproportionate, immoderate.—*Ant.* NECESSARY, proper, requisite.
unduly *a.* improperly, excessively, extremely; see UNNECESSARILY.
undying *a.* everlasting, perpetual, deathless; see ETERNAL.

un·earned′ *adj.* not earned by work or service; specif., obtained as a return on an investment [*unearned* income]

un·earth′ *vt.* 1 to dig up from the earth 2 to bring to light; disclose

un·earth′ly *adj.* 1 supernatural 2 weird; mysterious 3 [Colloq.] fantastic, outlandish, etc.

un·eas′y *adj.* -i·er, -i·est 1 having, showing, or allowing no ease of body or mind; uncomfortable, disturbed, perturbed, etc. 2 awkward; constrained —un·eas′i·ly *adv.* —un·eas′i·ness *n.*

un′em·ploy′able *adj.* not employable, esp. because of severe physical or mental handicaps, outmoded skills, etc.

un′em·ployed′ *adj.* 1 not employed; without work 2 not being used; idle —un′em·ploy′ment *n.*

un·e′qual *adj.* 1 not equal, as in size, strength, ability, value, etc. 2 not balanced, even, regular, etc. 3 not adequate (*to*)

un·e′qualed or un·e′qualled *adj.* not equaled; unmatched; unrivaled

un′equiv′o·cal *adj.* not equivocal; plain; clear

un·err′ing (un ʉr′iŋ, -er′-) *adj.* 1 free from error 2 not missing or failing; sure; exact

UNESCO (yōō nes′kō) United Nations Educational, Scientific, and Cultural Organization

un·e′ven *adj.* 1 not even, level, smooth, regular, etc. 2 unequal 3 *Math.* odd —un·e′venly *adv.*

un′ex·am′pled *adj.* having no parallel or precedent; unprecedented

un′ex·cep′tion·able *adj.* not exceptionable; without fault; beyond criticism —un′ex·cep′tion·ably *adv.*

un′ex·cep′tional *adj.* ordinary —un′ex·cep′tion·ally *adv.*

un′ex·pect′ed *adj.* not expected; unforeseen —un′ex·pect′edly *adv.*

un·fail′ing *adj.* 1 not failing 2 never ceasing or falling short; inexhaustible 3 always reliable —un·fail′ingly *adv.*

un·fair′ *adj.* 1 not just; inequitable 2 dishonorable or unethical

un·faith′ful *adj.* 1 lacking or breaking faith or loyalty 2 not true, accurate, etc. 3 adulterous

un·fa·mil·iar (un′fə mil′yər) *adj.* 1 not well-known; strange 2 not acquainted (*with*)

un·feel′ing *adj.* 1 incapable of feeling; insensible 2 hardhearted; cruel —un·feel′ingly *adv.*

un·feigned′ (-fānd′) *adj.* genuine

un·fin′ished *adj.* 1 not finished; incomplete 2 having no finish, or final coat, as of paint

un·flap′pable (-flap′ə bəl) *adj.* 〚< UN- + FLAP, *n.* 4 + -ABLE〛 [Colloq.] not easily excited; imperturbable

un·flinch′ing *adj.* steadfast; firm

un·fold′ *vt.* 1 to open and spread out (something folded) 2 to lay open to view; reveal, explain, etc. — *vi.* 1 to become unfolded 2 to develop fully

un′for·get′table *adj.* so important, forceful, etc. as never to be forgotten

un′for·giv′ing *adj.* not willing or not able to forgive

THESAURUS

unearned *a.* won, gratis, unmerited; see FREE 4.

unearth *v.* reveal, find, uncover; see LEARN.

unearthly *a.* frightening, ghostly, supernatural; see UNNATURAL 1.

uneasiness *n.* disquiet, restlessness, agitation; see FEAR.

uneasy *a.* unquiet, anxious, fearful, irascible, troubled, harassed, vexed, perturbed, alarmed, upset, afraid, apprehensive, nervous, frightened, shaky, perplexed, agitated, unsettled, suspicious, peevish, irritable, fretful, worried, anguished, in turmoil, disquieted, shaken, full of misgivings, fidgety, jittery, on edge, all nerves, jumpy, snappish, uncomfortable, molested, tormented, in distress.— *Ant.* QUIET, placid, soothed.

uneducated *a.* illiterate, unschooled, untaught; see IGNORANT 2.

unemotional *a.* reticent, apathetic, insensitive; see INDIFFERENT, QUIET.

unemployed *a.* out of work, in the bread lines, receiving charity, jobless, idle, inactive, loafing, unoccupied, without gainful employment, on the dole, cooling one's heels*, on the shelf.—*Ant.* BUSY, employed, at work.

unemployment *n.* work stoppage, layoff, strike conditions; see IDLENESS.

unending *a.* everlasting, infinite, neverending; see ETERNAL.

unequal *a.* 1 [Not alike] odd, illmatched, dissimilar; see UNLIKE. 2 [One-sided] uneven, unbalanced, inequitable; see IRREGULAR 1.

unequaled *a.* unmatched, unrivaled, supreme; see UNIQUE.

unethical *a.* sneaky, immoral, unfair; see DISHONEST, WRONG 1.

uneven *a.* 1 [Rough] bumpy, rugged, jagged; see ROUGH 1. 2 [Irregular] notched, jagged, serrate; see IRREGULAR 4. 3 [Variable] intermittent, spasmodic, fitful; see IRREGULAR 1. 4 [Odd] remaining, leftover, additional; see ODD 4.

unevenly *a.* roughly, intermittently, irregularly, spottily, bumpily, with friction, haphazardly, jumpily, all up and down, fitfully, off an on.

unexpected *a.* unforeseen, surprising, unlooked for, sudden, startling, unpredicted, coming unaware, astonishing, staggering, stunning, electrifying, amazing, not in the cards, not on the books, unanticipated, not bargained for, left out of calculation, wonderful, unprepared for, instantaneous, eye-opening, like a bolt from the blue.—*Ant.* EXPECTED, predicted, foreseen.

unexpectedly *a.* surprisingly, instantaneously, suddenly, startlingly, without warning, like a bolt from the blue; see also QUICKLY.— *Ant.* REGULARLY, according to prediction, as anticipated.

unfair *a.* 1 [Unjust] wrongful, wrong, low, base, injurious, unethical, bad, wicked, culpable, blamable, blameworthy, foul, illegal, inequitable, improper, unsporting, shameful, cruel, shameless, dishonorable, unreasonable, grievous, vicious, vile, undue, unlawful, petty, mean, inexcusable, unjustifiable, immoral, criminal, forbidden, irregular.—*Ant.* FAIR, proper, sporting. 2 [Not in accord with approved trade practices] unethical, criminal, discriminatory; see sense 1.

unfaithful *a.* 1 [Not faithful] false, untrue, deceitful; see UNRELIABLE. 2 [Having broken the marriage vow] adulterous, incontinent, unchaste; see BAD 1.

unfamiliar *a.* 1 [Unacquainted] not introduced, not associated, unknown, not on speaking terms, not versed in, not in the habit of, out of contact with.—*Ant.* FRIENDLY, intimate, acquainted. 2 [Strange] alien, outlandish, exotic, remote, novel, original, different, unusual, extraordinary, unaccustomed, unexplored, uncommon.—*Ant.* COMMON, ordinary, usual.

unfashionable *a.* outmoded, antiquated, obsolete; see OLD-FASHIONED.

unfasten *v.* unsnap, untie, unlock; see LOOSEN 1.

unfavorable *a.* untimely, inopportune, unseasonable, adverse, calamitous, unpropitious, inexpedient, bad, ill-chosen, ill-fated, ill-suited, ill-timed, unsuitable, improper, wrong, abortive, untoward, inauspicious, unlucky, ill, unfortunate, regrettable, premature, tardy, late, unfit, inadvisable, objectionable, inconvenient, disadvantageous, damaging, destructive, unseemly, ill-advised, obstructive, troublesome, embarrassing, unpromising, awkward.

unfavorably *a.* adversely, negatively, opposingly, oppositely, antagonistically, conflictingly, obstructively, malignantly, on the contrary, counteractively, contrarily, in opposition, in the negative, by turning thumbs down, by giving the red light; see also AGAINST 3.

unfinished *a.* 1 [Not completed] uncompleted, undone, half done, incomplete, under construction, unperformed, imperfect, unconcluded, deficient, unexecuted, unaccomplished, in preparation, in the making, not done, in the rough, sketchy, tentative, shapeless, formless, unperfected, unfulfilled, undeveloped, unassembled, defective, found wanting, cut short, immature, faulty, crude, rough.—*Ant.* DONE, completed, perfected. 2 [Without a finish] unpainted, unvarnished, bare, raw, rough, crude, unprotected, uncovered, plain, undecorated, unadorned.

unfit *a.* 1 [Incompetent] unqualified, feeble, unpracticed, inexperienced, weak, impotent, inept, clumsy, debilitated, incapacitated, badly qualified, incompetent, unable, unprepared, ineffective, unapt.— *Ant.* ABLE, fit, effective. 2 [Unsuitable] improper, ill-adapted, wrong, ill-advised, unlikely, unpromising, inexpedient, inappropriate, inapplicable, useless, valueless, mistaken, incorrect, inadequate, flimsy.—*Ant.* FIT, suitable, correct.

unfold *v.* shake out, straighten, release, display, unwind, spread out, uncurl, unwrap, reel out, unbend, open, flatten, loosen, unroll.—*Ant.* FOLD, roll, lap.

unforeseen *a.* surprising, abrupt, sudden; see UNEXPECTED.

unforgettable *a.* notable, exceptional, extraordinary; see IMPRESSIVE.

unforgivable *a.* inexcusable, unpardonable, unjustifiable, indefensible, inexpiable; see also WRONG 1.

un·for'tu·nate *adj.* **1** having or bringing bad luck; unlucky **2** not suitable — *n.* an unfortunate person —**un·for'tu·nately** *adv.*

un·found'ed *adj.* **1** not founded on fact or truth **2** not established

un·friend'ly *adj.* **1** not friendly or kind **2** not favorable —**un·friend'li·ness** *n.*

un·frock' *vt.* to deprive of the rank of priest or minister

un·furl' *vt., vi.* to open or spread out from a furled state

un·gain'ly (-gān'lē) *adj.* [< ME *un-*, not + ON *gegn*, ready] awkward; clumsy

un·god'ly *adj.* **1** not godly or religious **2** [Colloq.] outrageous —**un·god'li·ness** *n.*

un·gov'ern·a·ble *adj.* that cannot be governed or controlled; unruly

un·gra'cious *adj.* **1** not gracious; rude **2** unpleasant; unattractive

un·guard'ed *adj.* **1** unprotected **2** guileless **3** careless; imprudent

un·guent (uŋ'gwənt) *n.* [< L *unguere*, anoint] a salve or ointment

un·gu·late (uŋ'gyoo lit, -lāt') *adj.* [< L *unguis*, a nail] having hoofs — *n.* a mammal having hoofs

un·hand' *vt.* to loose or release from the hand or hands; let go of

un·hap'py *adj.* **-pier, -pi·est 1** unfortunate **2** sad; wretched **3** not suitable —**un·hap'pily** *adv.* —**un·hap'pi·ness** *n.*

un·health'y *adj.* **-i·er, -i·est 1** sickly; not well **2** harmful to health **3** harmful to morals **4** dangerous

un·heard' *adj.* **1** not perceived by the ear **2** not given a hearing

un·heard'-of' *adj.* **1** not heard of before; unprecedented or unknown **2** unacceptable or outrageous

un·hinge' *vt.* **-hinged', -hing'ing 1** to remove from the hinges **2** to dislodge **3** to unbalance (the mind)

un·ho'ly *adj.* **-lier, -li·est 1** not sacred, hallowed, etc. **2** wicked; profane **3** [Colloq.] outrageous; dreadful

un·horse' *vt.* **-horsed', -hors'ing** to throw (a rider) from a horse

uni- [L < *unus*, one] *prefix* one; having only one

uni·cam·eral (yoon'i kam'ər əl) *adj.* [< prec. + L *camera*, chamber] of or having a single legislative chamber

UNICEF (yoon'ə sef') United Nations Children's Fund: formerly, *United Nations International Children's Emergency Fund*

uni·corn (yoon'i kôrn') *n.* [< L *unus*, one + *cornu*, horn] a mythical horselike animal with a single horn in its forehead

uni·cy·cle (yoon'ə si'kəl) *n.* [UNI- + (BI)CYCLE] a one-wheeled vehicle straddled by the rider who pushes its pedals

uni·form (yoon'ə fôrm') *adj.* [< L *unus*, one + *-formis*, -FORM] **1** not varying in form, rate, degree, etc. **2** like others of the same class — *n.* the distinctive clothes of a particular group, as soldiers — *vt.* to supply with a uniform —**u'ni·form'i·ty** *n.* —**u'ni·form'ly** *adv.*

uni·fy (yoon'ə fī') *vt., vi.* **-fied', -fy'ing** [see UNI- & -FY] to become or make united —**u'ni·fi·ca'tion** *n.*

uni·lat·eral (yoon'ə lat'ər əl) *adj.* **1** of, occurring on, or affecting one side only **2** involving one only of several parties; not reciprocal

un·im·peach·a·ble (un'im pē'chə bəl) *adj.* that cannot be doubted or discredited; irreproachable

un·in·ter·est·ed *adj.* not interested; indifferent

union (yoon'yən) *n.* [< L *unus*, one] **1** a uniting or being united; combination **2** a grouping together of nations, etc.

THESAURUS

unfortunate *a.* unlucky, luckless, unhappy, afflicted, troubled, stricken, unsuccessful, without success, burdened, pained, not prosperous, in adverse circumstances, broken, shattered, ill-fated, on the road to ruin, in a desperate plight, ruined, out of luck, in a bad way, jinxed*, behind the eight ball*, gone to the dogs*, down on one's luck; see also SAD 1.— *Ant.* HAPPY, lucky, prosperous.

unfortunately *a.* unluckily, unhappily, miserably, sadly, grievously, disastrously, dismally, calamitously, badly, sickeningly, discouragingly, catastrophically, horribly, if worst comes to worst.—*Ant.* HAPPILY, favorably, prosperously.

unfounded *a.* baseless, unproven, groundless; see UNTRUE.

unfriendly *a.* **1** [Hostile] opposed, alienated, ill-disposed, against, opposite, contrary, warlike, competitive, conflicting, antagonistic, estranged, at variance, irreconcilable, not on speaking terms, turned against, with a chip on one's shoulder*.—*Ant.* FRIENDLY, intimate, approving. **2** [Lacking friendly qualities] grouchy, bearish, surly, misanthropic, gruff, ill-disposed, envious, uncharitable, faultfinding, combative, quarrelsome, grudging, malignant, spiteful, malicious, vengeful, resentful, hateful, peevish, aloof, unsociable, suspicious, sour.—*Ant.* GENEROUS, frank, open.

ungainly *a.* clumsy, gawky, inexpert; see AWKWARD, RUDE 1.

ungodly* *a.* dreadful, atrocious, immoral; see BAD 1.

ungovernable *a.* unmanageable, wild, uncontrollable; see UNRULY.

ungrateful *a.* thankless, selfish, lacking in appreciation, grasping, demanding, forgetful, self-centered, unmindful, heedless, careless, insensible, dissatisfied, grumbling, unnatural, faultfinding, oblivious.— *Ant.* THANKFUL, grateful, obliged.

unguarded *a.* thoughtless, frank, careless; see CARELESS.

unhandy *a.* awkward, ill-arranged,

unwieldy, ill-contrived, clumsy; see also TROUBLESOME.

unhappily *a.* regrettably, lamentably, unluckily; see UNFORTUNATELY.

unhappiness *n.* sorrow, woe, sadness; see DEPRESSION 2, GRIEF.

unhappy *a.* **1** [Sad] miserable, sorrowful, wretched; see TROUBLED. **2** [Unfortunate] afflicted, found, in a desperate plight; see UNFORTUNATE.

unharmed *a.* unhurt, uninjured, intact; see SAFE 1, WHOLE 2.

unhealthy *a.* sickly, sick, in a decline, in ill health, infirm, delicate, feeble, shaky, undernourished, rickety, spindling, ailing, weak, in a run-down condition.—*Ant.* HEALTHY, robust, hale.

unheard *a.* noiseless, soundless, hushed; see QUIET.

unheard-of *a.* unprecedented, unique, new; see UNKNOWN 1.

unhinge *v.* **1** [To detach] dislodge, disjoint, disunite; see REMOVE 1. **2** [To upset] unbalance, disorder, derange; see UPSET 1.

unhurried *a.* leisurely, deliberate, nonchalant; see SLOW 1.

unhurt *a.* uninjured, all right, whole; see SAFE 1.

unidentified *a.* nameless, unnamed, not known; see UNKNOWN 1, 2.

unified *a.* made one, united, joined, combined, concerted, synthesized, amalgamated, conjoined, incorporated, blended, identified, coalesced, federated, centralized, intertwined, consolidated, associated, cemented, coupled, allied, wedded, married, confederated.—*Ant.* SEPARATED, distinct, disjoined.

uniform *a.* **1** [Even] symmetrical, smooth, straight; see REGULAR 3. **2** [Alike] equal, well-matched, similar; see ALIKE.

uniform *n.* costume, suit, dress; see CLOTHES.

uniformity *n.* **1** [Regularity] sameness, steadiness, evenness; see REGULARITY. **2** [Harmony] unity, accord, concord; see AGREEMENT 1.

unify *v.* consolidate, ally, conjoin; see UNITE.

unimaginable *a.* inconceivable, incomprehensible, incredible, unbelievable, unheard-of, indescribable, unthinkable, improbable; see also IMPOSSIBLE.

unimaginative *a.* barren, tedious, usual; see COMMON 1, DULL 4.

unimportant *a.* trifling, inconsiderable, slight, worthless, inconsequential, insignificant, unnecessary, immaterial, indifferent, beside the point, frivolous, useless, of no account, worthless, trivial, paltry.— *Ant.* IMPORTANT, weighty, great.

uninformed *a.* unenlightened, naive, unacquainted; see IGNORANT 1, 2.

unintentional *a.* unthinking, involuntary, erratic; see AIMLESS.

uninterested *a.* apathetic, impassive, detached; see INDIFFERENT.

uninteresting *a.* tedious, boring, tiresome, dreary, wearisome, prosaic, fatiguing, monotonous, dull, stale, trite, commonplace, irksome, stupid, humdrum, prosy, flat, depressing, insipid, unentertaining, dismal, banal.—*Ant.* INTERESTING, exciting, lively.

uninterrupted *a.* continuous, unending, unbroken; see CONSECUTIVE, CONSTANT.

uninvited *a.* unasked, unwanted, not invited; see UNPOPULAR.

union *n.* **1** [The act of joining] unification, junction, meeting, uniting, joining, coupling, embracing, coming together, merging, fusion, mingling, concurrence, symbiosis, amalgamation, confluence, congregation, reconciliation, conciliation, correlation, combination, connection, linking, attachment, coalition, conjunction, consolidation, incorporation, centralization, affiliation, confederation, copulation, coition.—*Ant.* DIVORCE, separation, severance. **2** [A closely knit group] association, federation, society; see ORGANIZATION 2. **3** [A

for some specific purpose **3** marriage **4** something united **5** *short for* LABOR UNION **6** a device symbolizing political union, used as in a flag **7** a device for uniting parts —**the Union** the United States
un'ion·ize' (-īz') *vt., vi.* **-ized', -iz'ing** to organize into a labor union
union jack a flag, esp. a national flag, consisting only of a UNION (sense 6) —[**U- J-**] the flag of the United Kingdom
unique (yōō nēk') *adj.* [< L *unus,* one] **1** one and only; sole **2** without like or equal **3** very unusual
uni·sex (yōō'nə seks') *adj.* suitable for both sexes, as a haircut
uni·son (yōō'nə sən, -zən) *n.* [< L *unus,* one + *sonus,* a sound] **1** identity of musical pitch, as of two or more tones **2** agreement —**in unison** with all the voices or instruments performing the same part
unit (yōō'nit) *n.* [< UNITY] **1** the smallest whole number; one **2** a standard basic quantity, measure, etc. **3** a single person or group, esp. as a part of a whole **4** a distinct part or object with a specific purpose
Uni·tar·ian (yōō'nə ter'ē ən) *n.* a member of a Christian sect holding that God is a single being
unite (yōō nīt') *vt., vi.* **-nit'ed, -nit'ing** [< L *unus,* one] **1** to put or join together so as to make one; combine **2** to bring or come together in common cause, action, etc.
United Nations an international organization of nations for world peace and security: formed in 1945 and having, in 1995, a membership of 185
unit·ize (yōō'nə tīz') *vt.* **-ized', -iz'ing** to make into a single unit
unit pricing a system of showing prices in terms of standard units
unity (yōō'nə tē) *n., pl.* **-ties** [< L *unus,* one] **1** a being united; oneness **2** a single, separate thing **3** harmony; agreement **4** a complex that is a union of related parts **5** a harmonious, unified arrangement of parts in an artistic work **6** continuity of purpose, action, etc. **7** *Math.* any quantity, etc. identified as a unit, or 1
uni·va·lent (yōō'nə vā'lənt) *adj. Chem.* **1** having one valence **2** having a valence of one

671

uni·valve (yōō'nə valv') *n.* a mollusk with a one-piece shell, as a snail
uni·ver·sal (yōō'nə vur'səl) *adj.* **1** of the universe; present everywhere **2** of, for, or including all or the whole **3** used, or intended to be used, for all kinds, sizes, etc. or by all people (-vər sal'ə tē) *n.*
u'ni·ver·sal·ize' *vt.* **-ized', -iz'ing** to make universal
universal joint (or coupling) a joint or coupling that permits a swing of limited angle in any direction
u'ni·ver'sally *adv.* **1** in every instance **2** in every part or place
Universal Product Code a patterned series of vertical bars printed on consumer products: it can be read by computerized scanners for pricing, etc.
uni·verse (yōō'nə vurs') *n.* [< L *unus,* one + *vertere,* to turn] **1** the totality of all things that exist **2** the world
uni·ver·sity (yōō'nə vur'sə tē) *n., pl.* **-ties** [see prec.] an educational institution offering bachelor's and advanced degrees
un·just (un just') *adj.* not just or right; unfair —**un·just'ly** *adv.*
un·kempt' (-kempt') *adj.* [UN- + *kempt* < dial. *kemben,* to comb] **1** tangled, disheveled, etc. **2** not tidy; slovenly
un·kind' *adj.* not kind; specif., *a)* not considerate of others *b)* harsh, severe, cruel, etc. —**un·kind'ness** *n.*
un·kind'ly *adj.* UNKIND — *adv.* in an unkind way
un·known' *adj.* not known; specif., *a)* unfamiliar (*to*) *b)* not identified, etc. — *n.* an unknown person or thing
un·law'ful *adj.* **1** against the law; illegal **2** immoral —**un·law'fully** *adv.* —**un·law'ful·ness** *n.*
un·lead'ed *adj.* not containing lead compounds: said of gasoline
un·learn' *vt., vi.* to forget or try to forget (something learned)
un·learn'ed (-lurn'id; *for* 2, -lurnd') *adj.* **1** not learned or educated **2** not learned [*unlearned* lessons]
un·leash' *vt.* to release from or as from a leash

═ THESAURUS ═

marriage] wedlock, conjugal ties, matrimony, cohabitation, nuptial connection, match, matrimonial affiliation. **4** [A labor union] laborers, workingmen, employees; see LABOR 4.
Union *n.* [The North in the American Civil War] the Free States, Antislavery States, the Northern States.
unique *a.* single, peerless, matchless, unprecedented, unparalleled, novel, individual, sole, unexampled, lone, different, unequaled.—*Ant.* COMMON, frequent, many.
unison *n.* concert, unity, harmony; see UNITY 1.
unit *n.* **1** [A whole] entirety, complement, total, totality, assemblage, assembly, system. **2** [A detail] section, segment, part, fraction, piece, joint, block, square, layer, link, length, digit, member, factor.
unite *v.* join, meet, ally, combine, solidify, harden, strengthen, condense, confederate, couple, affiliate, merge, band together, blend, mix, become one, concentrate, consolidate, entwine, intertwine, grapple, amalgamate, league, band, embody, embrace, copulate, associate, assemble, gather together, conjoin, keep together, tie in, pull together, hang together, join forces, coalesce, fuse, wed, marry, mingle, stick together, stay together.—*Ant.* DIVIDE, separate, part.
united *a.* unified, leagued, combined, affiliated, federal, confederated, integrated, amalgamated, cooperative, consolidated, concerted, congruent, associated, assembled, linked, banded, in partnership; see also ORGANIZED.—*Ant.* SEPARATED, distinct, individual.
United Nations *n.* UN, peace-keeping force, international society, community of nations. *Divisions and*

function of the United Nations include the following: General Assembly, Security Council, Economic and Social Council, Trust and Non Self-Governing Territories Trusteeship, Trusteeship Council, International Court of Justice, Secretariat.
unity *n.* **1** [The quality of oneness] homogeneity, homogeneousness, sameness, indivisibility, identity, inseparability, singleness, similarity, uniqueness, integration, universality, all-togetherness, ensemble, uniformity, wholeness; see also WHOLE.—*Ant.* DIFFERENCE, diversity, divorce. **2** [Union] federation, confederation, compact, combination, correspondence, alliance, agreement, concord, identity of purpose, unification, aggregation; see also ORGANIZATION 2. **3** [Harmony] concord, agreement, accord; see HARMONY 1.
universal *a.* **1** [Concerning the universe] cosmic, stellar, celestial, sidereal, astronomical, cosmogonic. **2** [Worldwide] mundane, earthly, terrestrial, sublunary, terrene, human, wordly.—*Ant.* LOCAL, restricted, district. **3** [General] entire, all-embracing, prevalent, customary, usual, whole, sweeping, extensive, comprehensive, total, unlimited, limitless, endless, vast, widespread, catholic, common, regular, undisputed, accepted, unrestricted.—*Ant.* SPECIAL, limited, peculiar.
universally *a.* entirely, prevailingly, comprehensively; see COMPLETELY.
universe *n.* cosmos, creation, the visible world, astral system, universal frame, all created things, everything, nature, the natural world.
university *a.* professional, advanced, graduate, college, collegiate, undergraduate, freshman, sopho-

more, junior, senior, learned, academic, educational.
university *n.* educational institution, institution of higher learning, multiversity, megaversity, normal school, state university; see also COLLEGE, SCHOOL 1.
unjust *a.* wrong, inequitable, wrongful; see UNFAIR.
unjustifiable *a.* unallowable, unforgivable, unjust; see WRONG 1.
unjustly *a.* brutally, cruelly, meanly; see WRONGLY.
unkind *a.* malignant, spiteful, mean, malicious, inhuman, inhumane, sadistic, cruel, hateful, malevolent, savage, barbarous; see also RUDE 1, 2.—*Ant.* KIND, benevolent, helpful.
unknown *a.* **1** [Not known; *said of information*] uncomprehended, unapprehended, undiscovered, untold, unexplained, uninvestigated, unexplored, unheard-of, unperceived, concealed, hidden, unrevealed.—*Ant.* KNOWN, established, understood. **2** [Not known; *said of people*] alien, unfamiliar, not introduced, unheard-of, obscure, foreign, strange, unacknowledged, ostracized, outcast, friendless, private, retired, aloof, forgotten. **3** [Not known; *said of terrain*] unexplored, far-off, remote, far, distant, foreign, undiscovered, exotic, transoceanic, transmarine, at the far corners of the earth, faraway, outlandish, unheard-of, unfrequented, untraveled, desolate, desert, unvisited, legendary, strange.
unlawful *a.* forbidden, illicit, outlawed; see ILLEGAL.
unlawfully *a.* illegally, unjustly, unjustifiably; see WRONGLY.
unlearned *a.* unlettered, rude, boorish, uneducated, ignorant, illiterate, clownish, untutored, untaught, unread, savage, uncivilized, doltish,

un·less (un les', ən-) **conj.** [< ME *on lesse that*, at less than] in any case other than that; except that

un·let·tered (un let'ərd) **adj.** 1 ignorant; uneducated 2 illiterate

un·like' **adj.** not alike; different — **prep.** 1 not like; different from 2 not characteristic of

un·like'ly **adj.** 1 not likely; improbable 2 not likely to succeed —**un·like'li·hood'** **n.**

un·lim'ber (-lim'bər) **vt., vi.** to get ready for use or action

un·lim'ited **adj.** 1 without limits or restrictions 2 vast; illimitable

un·load' **vt., vi.** 1 *a*) to remove (a load) *b*) to take a load from 2 *a*) to tell (one's troubles, etc.) without restraint *b*) to relieve of something that troubles 3 to remove the charge from (a gun) 4 to get rid of

un·lock' **vt.** 1 *a*) to open (a lock) *b*) to open the lock of (a door, etc.) 2 to let loose; release 3 to reveal

unlooked'-for' **adj.** not expected

un·loose' **vt.** **-loosed'**, **-loos'ing** to set loose; loosen, release, etc. Also **un·loos'en**

un·luck'y **adj.** **-i·er**, **-i·est** having or bringing bad luck; unfortunate

un·make' **vt.** **-made'**, **-mak'ing** 1 to cause to be as before; undo 2 to ruin; destroy 3 to depose from a position or rank

un·man' **vt.** **-manned'**, **-man'ning** to deprive of manly courage, nerve, etc.

un·man'ly **adj.** **-lier**, **-li·est** not manly; specif., *a*) cowardly, weak, etc. *b*) effeminate; womanish

un·manned' **adj.** without people aboard and operating by remote control

un·mask' **vi., vt.** 1 to remove a mask or disguise (from) 2 to disclose the true nature or character (of)

un·mean'ing **adj.** lacking in meaning or sense

un·men'tion·able **adj.** not fit to be mentioned in polite conversation

un·mer'ci·ful **adj.** having or showing no mercy; cruel; pitiless

un·mis·tak'able **adj.** that cannot be mistaken or misinterpreted; clear —**un'mis·tak'ably** **adv.**

un·mit'i·gat'ed **adj.** 1 not lessened or eased 2 out-and-out; absolute

un·mor'al **adj.** AMORAL

un·nat'u·ral (-nach'ər əl) **adj.** 1 contrary to nature; abnormal 2 artificial 3 very cruel —**un·nat'u·rally** **adv.**

un·nec'es·sar'y **adj.** not necessary; needless —**un·nec'es·sar'i·ly** **adv.**

un·nerve' (-nʉrv') **vt.** **-nerved'**, **-nerv'ing** to cause to lose one's courage, self-confidence, etc.

un·num'bered **adj.** 1 not counted 2 innumerable 3 not numbered

un·or'gan·ized' **adj.** not organized; specif., not belonging to a labor union

un·pack' **vt., vi.** 1 to remove (the contents of a trunk, suitcase, etc.) 2 to take things out of (a trunk, etc.)

un·par'al·leled' **adj.** that has no parallel, equal, or counterpart

un·pleas'ant **adj.** not pleasant; offensive; disagreeable — **un·pleas'antly** **adv.** —**un·pleas'ant·ness** **n.**

un·plumbed' **adj.** 1 not measured with a plumb 2 not fully understood

un·pop'u·lar **adj.** not liked by the public or by the majority —**un'popu·lar'ity** (-lar'ə tē) **n.**

THESAURUS

crass, half-taught, ill-bred, half-educated, uninitiated, unversed, uninstructed, unguided, unenlightened, dull, misguided, empty, unaccomplished, backward, superficial, pedantic, low-brow*.—*Ant.* LEARNED, educated, adept.

unless *prep., conj.* saving, without the provision that, if not, except, except that, excepting that.

unlike *a.* dissimilar, different, incongruous, contradictory, hostile, opposed, inconsistent, heterogeneous, diverse, contrasted, conflicting, contrary, disparate, dissonant, discordant, clashing, separate, opposite, divergent, various, variant.—*Ant.* LIKE, similar, correspondent.

unlikely *a.* improbable, unheard-of, incredible, implausible, not to be thought of, unbelievable, absurd, unconvincing, not likely, scarcely possible, apparently false, contrary to expectation, inconceivable, doubtful, dubious, questionable, extraordinary, marvelous, out of the ordinary, strange.—*Ant.* LIKELY, probable, credible.

unlimited *a.* infinite, limitless, boundless, unending, extensive, universal, unrestricted, unconditional, unfathomable, inexhaustible, unconfined, immense, illimitable, measureless, incalculable, interminable, without number, unfathomed, unsounded, untold, countless, numberless, incomprehensible, immeasurable, endless.

unload *v.* disburden, discharge, dump, slough, lighten, cast, unpack, relieve, remove cargo, disgorge, empty, deplane, unburden, break bulk.—*Ant.* FILL, load, pack.

unlock *v.* unbar, unfasten, open the lock; see OPEN 2.

unloved *v.* disliked, detested, despised; see HATED.

unlucky *a.* 1 [Unfortunate] luckless, unhappy, afflicted; see UNFORTUNATE. 2 [Unpropitious] ill-chosen, ill-fated, untimely; see UNFAVORABLE.

unmanageable *a.* uncontrollable, irrepressible, ungovernable; see UNRULY.

unmarried *a.* celibate, unwed, single, virgin, maiden, eligible, chaste, unwedded, spouseless, footloose and fancy-free.—*Ant.* MARRIED, wed, wedded.

unmistakable *a.* conspicuous, distinct, evident; see CLEAR 2, OBVIOUS 1.

unmoved *a.* 1 [Not moved physically] firm, stable, motionless, static, solid, durable, immovable, firm as a rock, staunch, fast, moveless, statuelike, rooted, steady, immobile, unshaken, changeless, unwavering. 2 [Not moved emotionally] impassive, stoic, quiet, cold, cool, calm, collected, deliberate, resolute, dispassionate, calculating, unaffected, unemotional, indifferent, judicious, unflinching, nerveless, cool as a cucumber.

unnatural *a.* 1 [Contrary to nature] monstrous, phenomenal, malformed, unaccountable, abnormal, preposterous, marvelous, uncanny, wonderful, strange, incredible, sublime, freakish, unconforming, inhuman, outrageous, unorthodox, miraculous, contrary to known laws.—*Ant.* COMMON, ordinary, usual. 2 [Artificial] synthetic, imitation, manufactured, ersatz, concocted, made-up, fabricated, false, pseudo, mock, spurious, phony*.—*Ant.* NATURAL, occurring, naturally.

unnecessarily *a.* needlessly, by chance, carelessly, fortuitously, casually, haphazardly, wantonly, accidentally, unessentially, redundantly, inexpediently, uselessly, exorbitantly, superfluously, undesirably, objectionably, disadvantageously, optionally, avoidably, without cause, without reason, gratuitously; see also FOOLISHLY.—*Ant.* NECESSARILY, indispensably, unavoidably.

unnecessary *a.* needless, fortuitous, casual, chance, haphazard, wanton, accidental, unessential, nonessential, beside the point, irrelevant, futile, extraneous, additional, redundant, useless, exorbitant, superfluous, worthless, undesirable, optional, avoidable, objectionable, disadvantageous, random, noncompulsory, dispensable, adventitious, without compulsion, uncalled-for, gratuitous.—*Ant.* NECESSARY, essential, required.

unnoticed *a.* unobserved, unseen, unheeded, overlooked, inconspicuous, secret, hidden, passed by, unobtrusive, disregarded, unconsidered, unattended, neglected, unmarked, unremembered, unscrutinized, unremarked, unrecognized, slurred over, uninspected, winked at, glossed over, lost sight of, ignored, shoved into the background, undistinguished, unexamined, unwatched, unlooked at.—*Ant.* SEEN, watched, noticed.

unoccupied *a.* 1 [Vacant] uninhabited, empty, deserted, unfurnished, void, voided, disfurnished, blank, untenanted.—*Ant.* FULL, inhabited, tenanted. 2 [Idle] loitering, inactive, unemployed; see IDLE.

unofficial *a.* unconstrained, personal, casual; see INFORMAL.

unopposed *a.* unchallenged, unrestricted, unhampered; see FREE 1, 2, 3.

unorganized *a.* chaotic, random, disorganized; see CONFUSED 2.

unorthodox *a.* unconventional, irregular, eccentric; see UNUSUAL 2.

unpack *v.* unload, uncrate, unwrap; see REMOVE 1.

unpaid *a.* 1 [Owed; *said of debts*] due, payable, not discharged, past due, overdue, delinquent, unsettled, unliquidated, undefrayed, outstanding.—*Ant.* PAID, defrayed, discharged. 2 [Working without salary] voluntary, unsalaried, amateur, freewill, donated, contributed.

unpleasant *a.* 1 [Not pleasing in society] disagreeable, obnoxious, boring; see RUDE 2. 2 [Not pleasing to the senses] repulsive, obnoxious, abhorrent; see OFFENSIVE 2.

unpopular *a.* disliked, despised, out of favor, abhorred, loathed, shunned, avoided, ostracized, scorned, detested, unloved, unvalued, uncared-for, obnoxious.—*Ant.* POPULAR, liked, agreeable.

un·prac'ticed (-prak'tist) *adj.* 1 not habitually or repeatedly done, etc. 2 not skilled or experienced

un·prec'edent'ed *adj.* having no precedent or parallel; unheard-of

un·prin'ci·pled *adj.* lacking moral principles; unscrupulous

un·print'able *adj.* not fit to be printed, as because of obscenity

un'pro·fes'sional *adj.* not professional; esp., violating the ethical code of a given profession

un·qual'i·fied' *adj.* 1 lacking the necessary qualifications 2 not limited or modified; absolute

un·ques'tion·able *adj.* not to be questioned, doubted, or disputed; certain —**un·ques'tion·ably** *adv.*

un·qui'et *adj.* 1 restless 2 anxious

un'quote' *interj.* I end the quotation

un·rav'el *vt.* -eled or -elled, -el·ing or -el·ling 1 to separate the threads of (something woven, tangled, etc.) 2 to make clear; solve — *vi.* to become unraveled

un·read' (-red') *adj.* 1 not read, as a book 2 having read little or nothing

un·re'al *adj.* not real or actual; imaginary, fanciful, false, etc.

un·rea'son·able *adj.* 1 not reasonable or rational 2 excessive; immoderate —**un·rea'son·ably** *adv.*

un·rea'son·ing *adj.* not reasoning or reasoned; irrational

un're·con·struct'ed *adj.* 1 not reconstructed 2 holding to an earlier, outmoded practice or point of view

un're·gen'er·ate *adj.* 1 not spiritually reborn 2 stubbornly defiant

un're·lent'ing *adj.* 1 inflexible; relentless 2 without mercy; cruel 3 not relaxing in effort, speed, etc.

un're·mit'ting *adj.* not stopping, relaxing, etc.; incessant; persistent

un're·served' *adj.* not reserved; specif., a) frank or open in speech b) not restricted or qualified —**un're·serv'edly** (-zur'vid lē) *adv.*

un·rest' *n.* 1 restlessness; disquiet 2 angry discontent verging on revolt

un·ripe' *adj.* not ripe or mature; green

un·ri'valed or un·ri'valled (-rīv'əld) *adj.* having no rival, equal, or competitor

un·roll' *vt.* 1 to open (something rolled up) 2 to display — *vi.* to become unrolled

un·ruf'fled (un ruf'əld) *adj.* not ruffled or disturbed; calm; smooth; serene

un·ruly (un rōōl'ē) *adj.* -i·er, -i·est hard to control, restrain, or keep in order; disobedient —**un·rul'i·ness** *n.*

un·sad'dle *vt.* -dled, -dling to take the saddle off (a horse, etc.)

un·said' *adj.* not expressed

un·sa'vory *adj.* 1 unpleasant to taste or smell 2 morally offensive

un·scathed' (-skā*th*d') *adj.* [< un- + ON *skathi*, harm] unharmed

un·schooled' *adj.* not educated or trained, esp. by formal schooling

un·scram'ble *vt.* -bled, -bling to cause to be no longer scrambled, mixed up, or unintelligible

un·screw' *vt.* to detach or loosen by removing screws, or by turning

un·scru'pu·lous *adj.* not restrained by moral scruples; unprincipled

un·seal' *vt.* to break the seal of; open

un·sea'son·able *adj.* 1 not usual for the season 2 at the wrong time

un·seat' *vt.* 1 to dislodge from a seat 2 to remove from office

un·seem'ly *adj.* not seemly; not decent or proper; unbecoming

THESAURUS

unprecedented *a.* unparalleled, novel, original; see UNIQUE.

unpredictable *a.* random, inconstant, variable; see IRREGULAR 1.

unprepared *a.* unready, unwarned, unwary, unexpectant, surprised, taken aback, unguarded, unnotified, unadvised, unaware, unsuspecting, taken off guard, napping, in the dark, going off half-cocked.

unproductive *a.* unprolific, impotent, barren; see STERILE 1, 2.

unprofitable *a.* ill-requited, ill-paid, profitless, costly, expensive, unlucrative, unremunerative.—*Ant.* PROFITABLE, gainful, productive.

unpromising *a.* discouraging, unfavorable, adverse; see UNLIKELY.

unprotected *a.* defenseless, unarmed, unguarded; see UNSAFE.

unpublished *a.* unprinted, still in manuscript, manuscript; see UNKNOWN 1.

unqualified *a.* 1 [Absolute] downright, utter, outright; see CERTAIN 2. 2 [Incompetent] inexperienced, unprepared, incapable; see UNFIT.

unquestionable *a.* 1 [Certain] sure, obvious, clear; see CERTAIN 2. 2 [Faultless] superior, unexceptionable, flawless; see EXCELLENT.

unquestionably *a.* certainly, without a doubt, surely, indubitably, indisputably, definitely, reliably, absolutely, positively, incontrovertibly, indeed, assuredly, of course, undoubtedly, undeniably, past a doubt, beyond doubt, beyond a shadow of a doubt, past dispute.

unravel *v.* unwind, disengage, undo; see FREE.

unreal *a.* visionary, delusive, deceptive, illusory, imagined, hallucinatory, ideal, dreamlike, unsubstantial, nonexistent, fanciful, misleading, fictitious, theoretical, hypothetical, fabulous, notional, whimsical, fantastic; see also UNBELIEVABLE.—*Ant.* REAL, substantial, genuine.

unrealistic *a.* unworkable, not practical, nonsensical; see UNRELIABLE.

unreasonable *a.* 1 [Illogical] irrational, biased, fatuous; see ILLOGICAL. 2 [Immoderate] exorbitant, extravagant, inordinate; see EXTREME. 3 [Senseless] foolish, silly, thoughtless; see STUPID.

unreasonably *a.* illogically, irrationally, stupidly; see FOOLISHLY.

unregulated *a.* uncontrollable, unchecked, chaotic; see UNCONTROLLED.

unrelated *a.* independent, unattached, irrelevant; see SEPARATE.

unreliable *a.* undependable, unstable, wavering, deceitful, tricky, shifty, furtive, underhanded, untrue, fickle, giddy, untrustworthy, vacillating, fallible, weak, unpredictable; see also DISHONEST.

unrest *n.* 1 [Lack of mental calm] malaise, distress, discomfort, perturbation, agitation, worry, sorrow, anxiety, grief, trouble, annoyance, tension, ennui, disquiet, soul-searching, irritation, harassment, upset, vexation, chagrin, mortification, perplexity, unease, disease, moodiness, disturbance, bother, dither, tizzy*. 2 [Social or political restlessness] disquiet, agitation, turmoil, strife, disturbance, uproar, debate, contention, bickering, change, altercation, crisis, confusion, disputation, contest, controversy, quarrel, sparring, uncertainty, insurrection, suspicion, dissatisfaction.

unrestricted *a.* allowable, not forbidden, free; see OPEN 3.

unripe *a.* green, tart, immature; see RAW 1.

unroll *v.* display, uncover, present; see EXPOSE 1.

unruffled *a.* collected, smooth, serene; see CALM 1, 2.

unruly *a.* uncontrollable, willful, headstrong, forward, violent, impulsive, uncurbed, impetuous, illadvised, rash, reckless, dashing, heedless, perverse, intractable, recalcitrant, self-assertive, refractory, rebellious, wayward, inexorable, restive, impervious, hidebound, unyielding, incorrigible, intemperate, drunken, lawless, vicious, brawling, unlicensed, rowdy, bawdy, quarrelsome, immovable, unwieldy, resolute, inflexible, forceful, dogged, mulish, fanatic, irrational, unreasonable, irrepressible, high-spirited, impudent, abandoned, profligate, stubborn, obstinate, turbulent, disorderly, self-willed, opinionated, bullheaded, ungovernable, stiffnecked, ornery*, mean, skittish, dangerous.

unsafe *a.* hazardous, perilous, risky, threatening, treacherous, fearsome, unreliable, insecure, venturesome, unstable, alarming, precarious, ticklish, giddy, dizzy, slippery, uncertain, unpromising, shaky, explosive.—*Ant.* SAFE, harmless, proof.

unsaid *a.* unspoken, not expressed, unstated; see QUIET.

unsatisfactory *a.* disappointing, below expectation, displeasing, undesirable, regrettable, disconcerting, disquieting, vexing, distressing, upsetting, disturbing, offensive, unacceptable, disagreeable, unwelcome, shocking, deficient; see also POOR 2.—*Ant.* EXCELLENT, satisfactory, gratifying.

unsavory *a.* disagreeable, unpleasant, revolting; see OFFENSIVE 2.

unscientific *a.* irrational, impulsive, inconclusive; see ILLOGICAL.

unscrew *v.* screw out, unfasten, untwist; see LOOSEN 1.

unscrupulous *a.* unprincipled, bad, wicked; see DISHONEST.

unseal *v.* free, remove, crack; see OPEN 2.

unseemly *a.* 1 [In bad taste; *said of conduct*] improper, unbecoming, inept; see RUDE 1. 2 [In bad taste; *said of things*] vulgar, tawdry, cheap; see POOR 2.

unseen *a.* imagined, imaginary, hid-

un·set'tle *vt.*, *vi.* **-tled**, **-tling** to make or become unstable; disturb or displace

un·set'tled *adj.* **1** not settled; not fixed, orderly, stable, calm, decided, etc. **2** not paid **3** having no settlers

un·sheathe' (-shēth') *vt.* **-sheathed'**, **-sheath'ing** to remove (a sword, etc.) from a sheath

un·sight'ly (-sīt'lē) *adj.* not sightly or pleasant to look at; ugly

un·skilled' *adj.* having or requiring no special skill or training

un·skill'ful *adj.* having little or no skill; awkward

un·snap' *vt.* **-snapped'**, **-snap'ping** to undo the snaps of, so as to detach

un·snarl' (-snärl') *vt.* to untangle

un·so·phis'ti·cat'ed *adj.* not sophisticated; simple; ingenuous, etc.

un·sound' *adj.* not sound; specif., *a*) not healthy, safe, firm, etc. *b*) not reliable, sensible, etc.

un·spar'ing *adj.* **1** not sparing; lavish **2** not merciful; severe

un·speak'able *adj.* **1** that cannot be spoken **2** so bad, evil, etc. as to defy description **—un·speak'ably** *adv.*

un·sta'ble *adj.* not stable; specif., *a*) easily upset *b*) changeable *c*) unreliable *d*) emotionally unsettled *e*) *Chem.* tending to decompose **—un·sta'bly** *adv.*

un·stead'y *adj.* not steady; specif., *a*) not firm; shaky *b*) changeable; inconstant *c*) erratic in habits, purpose, etc. **—un·stead'i·ly** *adv.* **—un·stead'i·ness** *n.*

un·stop' *vt.* **-stopped'**, **-stop'ping** **1** to remove the stopper from **2** to clear (a pipe, etc.) of an obstruction

un·struc'tured *adj.* not formally organized; loose, free, open, etc.

un·strung' *adj.* **1** nervous or upset **2** with the strings loosened or detached, as a bow, racket, etc.

un·stuck' *adj.* loosened or freed from being stuck

un·stud'ied *adj.* not got by study or conscious effort; spontaneous; natural

un·sub·stan'tial *adj.* **1** having no material substance **2** not solid; flimsy **3** unreal; visionary

un·sung' (-suŋ') *adj.* not honored or celebrated, as in song or poetry

un·tan'gle *vt.* **-gled**, **-gling** **1** to free from a snarl or tangle **2** to free from confusion; put in order

un·taught' *adj.* **1** not taught; uneducated **2** acquired without being taught

un·think'able *adj.* not to be considered or thought of; impossible

un·think'ing *adj.* **1** thoughtless; heedless **2** unable to think

un·ti'dy *adj.* **-dier**, **-di·est** not tidy; slovenly; messy

un·tie' *vt.* **-tied'**, **-ty'ing** or **-tie'ing** **1** to unfasten (a thing tied or knotted) **2** to free, as from restraint

un·til (un til', ən-) *prep.* ⟦ME *untill*⟧ **1** up to the time of [until death] **2** before [not until tomorrow] **—** *conj.* **1** up to the time when or that [until you leave] **2** to the point, degree, etc. that [cook until it is done] **3** before [not until I die]

un·time'ly *adj.* **1** before the proper time; premature **2** at the wrong time; inopportune **—** *adv.* **1** prematurely **2** inopportunely **—un·time'li·ness** *n.*

unto (un'tōō, -too) *prep.* ⟦ME⟧ *old poet. var. of:* **1** to **2** until

un·told' *adj.* **1** not told or revealed **2** too many to be counted; vast

---

■■■■■■■■■■■■ THESAURUS ■■■■■■■■■■■■

den, obscure, unobserved, veiled, occult, sensed, unperceived, unnoticed, unsuspected, curtained, unobtrusive, viewless, invisible, sightless, dark, shrouded, impalpable, imperceptible, inconspicuous, undiscovered, impenetrable, dense.

unselfish *a.* disinterested, selfless, charitable; see KIND.

unsettle *v.* disrupt, displace, disarrange; see BOTHER 2, DISTURB.

unsettled *a.* **1** [Undetermined] undecided, unfixed, unresolved; see UNCERTAIN. **2** [Unstable] confused, agitated, troubled, changing, explosive, shifting, precarious, ticklish, unpredictable, uneasy, unbalanced, perilous, complex, complicated, fluid, kinetic, active, busy, critical.—*Ant.* SIMPLE, stable, solid.

unshaken *a.* unmoved, unaffected, undaunted; see FIRM 1.

unsightly *a.* hideous, deformed, homely; see REPULSIVE 1, UGLY 1.

unskilled *a.* untrained, uneducated, amateur; see IGNORANT 2.

unsophisticated *a.* ingenuous, innocent, simple; see INEXPERIENCED, NAIVE.

unsound *a.* **1** [False] ill-founded, erroneous, incongruous; see ILLOGICAL. **2** [Insecure] weak, unreliable, unbacked; see UNSTABLE 2.

unspeakable *a.* horrid, unutterable, abominable, horrible, fearful, inexpressible, unimaginable, dreadful, dire, shocking, appalling, frightful, frightening, alarming, beastly, inhuman, calamitous.

unspeakably *a.* greatly, unbelievably, terribly; see MUCH 1, 2.

unspoiled *a.* unblemished, spotless, faultless; see PERFECT 2, PURE 2.

unspoken *a.* tacit, implicit, inferred; see UNDERSTOOD 2.

unstable *a.* **1** [Having a high center of gravity] unsteady, wavering, unbalanced, giddy, wobbly, wiggly, weaving, shifty, precarious, topheavy, teetering, shifting, uncertain, rattletrap, beetling, jutting, lightly balanced.—*Ant.* FIRM, steady, solid. **2** [Easily disturbed] variable,

changeable, giddy, capricious, fluctuating, shifty, volatile, rootless, dizzy, unpredictable, uncertain, sensitive, oversensitive, thin-skinned, timid, delicate.

unsteady *a.* **1** [Wobbly] wiggly, wavering, shaky, treacherous, unbalanced, top-heavy, leaning, ramshackle, giddy, weaving, heaving, precarious, teetering, uncertain; see also IRREGULAR 1. **2** [Inconstant] changeable, fluctuating, vacillating, variable, uncertain, unfixed, capricious, volatile, unreliable, tricky, shifty, shaky, jerky, fluttering.

unstuck *a.* unfastened, unglued, rattling; see LOOSE 1.

unsuccessful *a.* defeated, disappointed, frustrated, aborted, disastrous, unprosperous, unfortunate, unlucky, futile, failing, fruitless, worthless, sterile, bootless, unavailing, ineffectual, ineffective, immature, useless, foiled, shipwrecked, overwhelmed, overpowered, broken, ruined, destroyed, thwarted, crossed, disconcerted, dashed, circumvented, premature, inoperative, of no effect, balked, left holding the sack*, skunked*, stymied, jinxed*, out of luck, stuck*.—*Ant.* SUCCESSFUL, fortunate, lucky.

unsuitable *a.* inadequate, improper, malapropos, disagreeable, discordant, incongruous, inharmonious, incompatible, clashing, out of place, jarring, dissonant, discrepant, irrelevant, uncalled-for, dissident, inappropriate, ill-suited, unseemly, conflicting, opposite, contrary, unbecoming, unfitting, unfit, disparate, disturbing, mismatched, disproportionate, divergent, mismated, inapplicable, unassimilable, inconsistent, intrusive, amiss, interfering, disagreeing, inept, unbefitting, inadmissible, absurd, unseasonable, ill-timed, unfortunate, unsympathetic, not in keeping, out of joint, at odds, at variance, repugnant, out of kilter*, cockeyed*.—*Ant.* FIT, suitable, proper.

unsure *a.* unreliable, hesitant, doubt-

ful; see UNCERTAIN.

unsurpassed *a.* unexcelled, unequaled, matchless; see UNIQUE.

unsuspecting *a.* **1** [Gullible] undoubting, confiding, credulous; see TRUSTING. **2** [Naive] innocent, inexperienced, simple; see NAIVE.

unsympathetic *a.* unmoved, apathetic, cold; see INDIFFERENT.

untangle *v.* clear up, put in order, disentangle; see ORDER 3.

unthinkable *a.* inconceivable, unimaginable, improbable; see UNLIKELY.

unthinking *a.* heedless, rude, inconsiderate; see CARELESS.

untidy *a.* slovenly, unkempt, disorderly; see DIRTY 1.

untie *v.* unlace, unknot, loosen, unfasten; see also LOOSEN 1.

untied *a.* unfastened, slack, unbound; see FREE 2, 3, LOOSE 1.

until *prep.* till, to, between the present and, in anticipation of, prior to, during the time preceding, down to, continuously, before the coming of, in expectation of, as far as; see also UNTO.

untimely *a.* unseasonable, awkward, ill-timed, inauspicious, badly timed, too early, abortive, too late, unpromising, ill-chosen, improper, unseemly, inappropriate, wrong, unfit, disagreeable, mistimed, intrusive, badly calculated, inopportune, out-of-date, malapropos, premature, unlucky, unfavorable, unfortunate, inexpedient, anachronistic.—*Ant.* EARLY, timely, seasonable.

untiring *a.* inexhaustible, powerful, persevering; see STRONG 1.

unto *prep.* to, toward, till, until, contiguous to, against, up to, next to, beside, in the direction of, to the degree of, to the extreme of.

untold *a.* uncounted, countless, unnumbered, many, innumerable, beyond measure, inexpressible, incalculable, undreamed of, staggering, unimaginable, multitudinous, manifold, multiple.

un·touch′able *adj.* that cannot or should not be touched — *n.* in India, formerly, a member of the lowest caste

un·to′ward (un tô′ərd, -tôrd′) *adj.* 1 improper, unseemly, etc. 2 not favorable; adverse

un·trav′eled or **un·trav′elled** *adj.* 1 not used or frequented by travelers 2 not having done much traveling

un·truth′ *n.* 1 falsity 2 a falsehood; lie —**un·truth′ful** *adj.*

un·tu′tored (-tōōt′ərd) *adj.* uneducated

un·twist′ *vt.*, *vi.* to separate, as something twisted together; unwind

un·used′ *adj.* 1 not in use 2 never used before 3 unaccustomed (*to*)

un·u′su·al *adj.* not usual or common; rare —**un·u′su·al·ly** *adv.*

un·ut′ter·able *adj.* inexpressible —**un·ut′ter·ably** *adv.*

un·var′nished *adj.* 1 not varnished 2 plain; simple; unadorned

un·veil′ *vt.* to reveal as by removing a veil from — *vi.* to take off one's veil

un·voiced′ *adj.* not expressed; not spoken

un·war′y *adj.* not wary or cautious

un·well′ *adj.* not well; sick

un·whole′some *adj.* 1 harmful to body or mind 2 of unsound health or unhealthy appearance 3 morally harmful —**un·whole′some·ness** *n.*

un·wield′y *adj.* hard to wield, manage, etc., as because of large size

un·will′ing *adj.* 1 not willing; reluctant 2 done, said, etc. reluctantly —**un·will′ing·ly** *adv.*

un·wind′ *vt.* -**wound′**, -**wind′ing** 1 to wind off or undo (something wound) 2 to untangle (something involved) — *vi.* 1 to become unwound 2 to become relaxed

un·wise′ *adj.* having or showing a lack of wisdom or sound judgment

un·wit′ting (-wit′iŋ) *adj.* 1 not knowing; unaware 2 unintentional

un·wont′ed (-wän′tid, -wōn′-) *adj.* not common or usual; rare

un·wor′thy *adj.* -**thier**, -**thi·est** 1 lacking merit or value; worthless 2 not deserving (*of*) 3 not fit or becoming: with *of* —**un·wor′thi·ness** *n.*

un·wrap′ *vt.* -**wrapped′**, -**wrap′ping** to take off the wrapping of

un·writ′ten (-rit′'n) *adj.* 1 not in writing 2 operating only through custom or tradition [an *unwritten* rule]

up¹ (up) *adv.* ⟦OE⟧ 1 to, in, or on a higher place or level 2 to a later period 3 to or into a higher condition, amount, etc. 4 in or into a standing position 5 in or into action, view, consideration, etc. 6 aside; away [lay *up* wealth] 7 so as to be even with in time, degree, etc. 8 so as to be tightly closed, bound, etc. [tie *up* the package] 9 completely; thoroughly 10 *Baseball* to one's turn at batting 11 used with verbs: *a*) to form idioms with meanings different from the simple verb [look *up* this word] *b*) as an intensive [dress *up*] — *prep.* up to; toward, along, through, into, etc. — *adj.* 1 directed toward a higher position 2 in a higher place or position 3 advanced in amount, degree, etc. [rents are *up*] 4 in or into action, tion 5 in an active or excited state 6 at an end; over [time's *up*] 7 available for use, as a computer 8 [Colloq.] going on [what's *up*] 9 *Baseball* at bat — *n.* 1 an upward slope 2 an upward movement, etc. — *vi.* **upped, up′ping** [Colloq.] to get up; rise — *vt.* [Colloq.] 1 to put up, lift up, etc. 2 to cause to rise [to *up* prices] —**on the up and up** [Slang] honest —**up against** [Colloq.] confronted with —**up on** (or **in**) [Colloq.] well-informed concerning —**ups and downs** good periods and bad periods —**up to** [Colloq.] 1 doing or scheming 2 capable of (doing, etc.) 3 as many as 4 as far as 5 dependent upon —**up with!** give or restore power, favor, etc. to!

THESAURUS

untouchable *a.* taboo, forbidden, denied; see ILLEGAL.

untouched *a.* 1 [Not harmed] intact, whole, secure, unbroken, in good order, unharmed, in good condition, in a good state of preservation, safe and sound, out of danger, shipshape. 2 [Not contaminated] virgin, clear, pure; see CLEAN 1.

untrained *a.* green, new, novice; see INEXPERIENCED.

untried *a.* untested, uninitiated, new; see INEXPERIENCED.

untroubled *a.* composed, serene, placid; see CALM 1, 2.

untrue *a.* false, misleading, specious, lying, hollow, deceptive, delusive, untrustworthy, deceitful, sham, spurious, incorrect, prevaricating, wrong.

untruth *n.* falsehood, misrepresentation, evasion; see LIE.

untruthful *a.* insincere, crooked, deceitful; see DISHONEST.

unused *a.* 1 [Not used] fresh, available, usable; see NEW 1. 2 [Surplus] additional, remaining, superfluous; see EXTRA.

unusual *a.* 1 [Remarkable] rare, extraordinary, strange, outstanding, great, uncommon, special, distinguished, prominent, important, noteworthy, awe-inspiring, awesome, unique, fine, unheard-of, unexpected, seldom met with, surprising, superior, astonishing, amazing, prodigious, incredible, inconceivable, atypical, conspicuous, exceptional, eminent, significant, memorable, renowned, refreshing, singular, fabulous, unprecedented, unparalleled, unexampled, unaccountable, stupendous, unaccustomed, wonderful, notable, superior, marvelous, striking, overpowering, electrifying, dazzling, fantastic, startling, astounding, indescribable, appalling, stupefying, ineffable, out of sight*.—*Ant.* COMMON, familiar, customary. 2 [Different] unique, extreme, uncommon,

particular, exaggerated, distinctive, choice, little-known, out of the ordinary, marked, forward, unconventional, radical, exceptional, peculiar, strange, foreign, unnatural, puzzling, perplexing, confounding, disturbing, novel, advanced, startling, shocking, staggering, uncustomary, breaking with tradition, infrequent, mysterious, mystifying, surprising, extraordinary, unparalleled, deep, profound, aberrant, singular, unorthodox, unconformable, not to be expected, eccentric, unbalanced, unprecedented, inconsistent, individual, original, refreshing, newfangled, new, modern, recent, late, fresh, curious, unfamiliar, irregular, odd, unaccountable, alien, queer, quaint, freakish, bizarre, far-fetched, neurotic, exotic, outlandish, old-fashioned, out-of-the-way, abnormal, irrational, monstrous, anomalous, fearful.— *Ant.* COMMON, ordinary, normal.

unusually *a.* 1 [Not usually] oddly, curiously, peculiarly; see ESPECIALLY 1. 2 [To a marked degree] extraordinarily, remarkably, surprisingly; see VERY.

unveil *v.* uncover, reveal, make known; see EXPOSE 1.

unwanted *a.* undesired, rejected, outcast; see HATED, UNPOPULAR.

unwarranted *a.* unjust, wrong, groundless; see UNFAIR 1.

unwholesome *a.* unhealthful, toxic, dangerous; see POISONOUS.

unwieldy *a.* awkward, clumsy, cumbersome; see HEAVY 1.

unwilling *a.* backward, resistant, reluctant, recalcitrant, unenthusiastic, doubtful, wayward, unready, indisposed, disinclined, averse, opposed, against, contrary, indifferent, indocile, intractable, demurring, shrinking, flinching, hesitating, shy, slack, evasive, loath, shy of, malcontent, slow, remiss, grudging, uncooperative, contrary, against the grain.—*Ant.* READY, willing, eager.

unwillingly *a.* grudgingly, resentfully, involuntarily; see ANGRILY.

unwind *v.* 1 [To undo] separate, loose, undo; see UNWRAP. 2 [To uncoil] untwist, unravel, untwine; see FREE, LOOSEN 2. 3 [To relax] recline, get rid of one's tensions, calm down; see RELAX.

unwise *a.* ill-considered, ill-advised, rash; see STUPID.

unwitting *a.* chance, inadvertent, accidental; see AIMLESS.

unworthy *a.* undeserving, reprehensible, contemptible; see OFFENSIVE 2.

unwrap *v.* untie, undo, unpack, take out of wrappings, unroll, disclose, free, uncover, strip, lay bare, divest, dismantle, peel, husk, shuck, flay, expose, lay open, unclothe, denude.—*Ant.* COVER, wrap, pack.

unzip *v.* unfasten, undo, free; see OPEN 3.

up¹ *a.*, *prep.* 1 [Situated above] at the top of, at the crest of, at the summit of, at the apex of, nearer the top of, nearer the head of, nearer the source of.—*Ant.* DOWN, nearer the bottom of, farther from the head of. 2 [Moving from the earth] upward, uphill, skyward, heavenward, away from the center of gravity, perpendicularly, into the air, higher, away from the earth. 3 [Expired] lapsed, elapsed, run out, terminated, invalid, ended, come to a term, outdated, exhausted, finished, done. 4 [Happening] under consideration, being scrutinized, moot, live, current, pertinent, timely, relevant, pressing, urgent. 5 [Next] after, in order, prospective; see FOLLOWING. —**up to** 1 [Until] before, preceding, previous to; see UNTIL. 2 [*Doing] occupied with, engaged in, carrying out, dealing with. 3 [*Dependent upon] assigned to, expected of, delegated to, enjoined upon.

up¹* *v.* elevate, raise up, boost; see INCREASE.

up[2] (up) *adv.* 〖phonetic respelling of *ap(iece)*〗 apiece *[a score of two up]*

up- *combining form* up

up-and-coming (up′ən kum′iŋ) *adj.* 1 enterprising, promising, etc. 2 gaining in prominence

up′beat′ *n. Music* an unaccented beat, esp. when on the last note of a bar — *adj.* [Colloq.] cheerful; optimistic

up·braid (up brād′) *vt.* 〖< OE *up-*, up + *bregdan*, to pull〗 to rebuke severely; censure; scold

up′bring′ing *n.* the training and education received while growing up

UPC Universal Product Code

up′chuck′ (-chuk′) *vi., vt., n.* [Slang] VOMIT

up′com′ing *adj.* coming soon

up′coun′try *adj., adv.* in or toward the interior of a country

up·date (-dāt′; *also, and for n. always,* up′dāt′) *vt.* -dat′ed, -dat′ing to make up-to-date; make conform to the most recent facts, methods, etc. — *n.* 1 an updating 2 an updated report, etc.

up·end′ *vt., vi.* to set, turn, or stand on end

up′front′ *adj.* 1 forthright 2 in advance *[upfront money]* Also **up′-front′**

up′grade′ (-grād′; *for v. usually* up grād′) *n.* an upward slope — *adj., adv.* uphill; upward — *vt., vi.* -grad′ed, -grad′ing to raise or improve in value, grade, rank, quality, etc.

up·heaval (up hē′vəl) *n.* 1 a heaving up 2 a sudden, violent change

up′hill′ *adv.* 1 toward the top of a hill; upward 2 with difficulty — *adj.* 1 going or sloping up 2 laborious; tiring

up·hold′ *vt.* -held′, -hold′ing 1 to hold up 2 to keep from falling; support 3 to confirm; sustain

up·hol·ster (up hōl′stər) *vt.* 〖< ME *upholder*, tradesman〗 to fit out (furniture, etc.) with coverings, padding, springs, etc. — **up·hol′ster·er** *n.*

up·hol′stery *n., pl.* **-ies** 1 the material used in upholstering 2 the work of an upholsterer

UPI United Press International

up′keep′ *n.* 1 maintenance 2 state of repair 3 the cost of maintenance

up′land (-lənd, -land′) *n.* land elevated above other land — *adj.* of or situated in upland

up·lift′ (-lift′; *for n.* up′lift′) *vt.* 1 to lift up 2 to raise to a higher moral, social, or cultural level — *n.* 1 a lifting up 2 a movement for moral, social, or cultural betterment

upon (ə pän′, ə pôn′) *prep.* on, or up and on: used interchangeably with *on* — *adv.* on

up·per (up′ər) *adj.* 1 higher in place 2 higher in rank, etc. — *n.* 1 the part of a shoe above the sole 2 [Slang] any drug that is a stimulant —**on one's uppers** [Colloq.] 1 wearing worn-out shoes 2 poor

upper·case (up′ər kās′) *n.* capital-letter type used in printing, as distinguished from small letters — *adj.* of or in uppercase

upper class the rich or aristocratic social class —**up′per-class′** *adj.*

up′per·class′man (-mən) *n., pl.* **-men** a junior or senior in high school or college

up′per·cut′ *n. Boxing* a short, swinging blow directed upward

upper hand the position of advantage or control

up′per·most′ *adj.* highest in place, power, authority, etc. — *adv.* in the highest place, rank, etc.

up·pity (up′ə tē) *adj.* [Colloq.] haughty, arrogant, snobbish, etc. Also [Brit. Colloq.] **up′pish**

up·raise′ *vt.* -raised′, -rais′ing to raise up; lift

up·rear′ *vt.* 1 to raise or lift up 2 to exalt 3 to bring up; rear

up·right (up′rīt′; *also, for adv.,* up rīt′) *adj.* 1 standing, pointing, etc. straight up; erect 2 honest and just — *adv.* in an upright position or direction — *n.* something having an upright position

upright piano a piano with a vertical, rectangular body

up′ris′ing (-rī′ziŋ) *n.* a revolt

up·roar (up′rôr′) *n.* 〖Du *oproer*, a stirring up〗 1 violent disturbance; tumult 2 loud, confused noise

up·roari·ous (up rôr′ē əs) *adj.* 1 making, or full of, an uproar 2 loud and boisterous, as laughter

up·root′ *vt.* 1 to tear up by the roots 2 to destroy or remove utterly

up′scale′ *adj.* of or for people who are affluent, stylish, etc.

up·set (up set′; *for n.* up′set′) *vt.* -set′, -set′ting 1 *a)* to tip over; overturn *b)* to defeat unexpectedly 2 *a)* to disturb the functioning of *[to upset a schedule]* *b)* to disturb emotionally or physically — *vi.* to become overturned or upset — *n.* 1 an upsetting 2 an unexpected defeat 3 a disturbance — *adj.* 1 tipped over 2 overthrown or defeated 3 disturbed or disordered

up′shot′ *n.* 〖orig., final shot in an archery match〗 the conclusion; result

up′side′ *n.* the upper side or part

upside down 1 with the top side or part underneath 2 in disorder —**up′side′-down′** *adj.*

up·si·lon (ōōp′sə län′, up′-) *n.* the twentieth letter of the Greek alphabet (Υ, υ)

up·stage (up′stāj′; *for v.,* up stāj′) *adv., adj.* toward or at the rear of a stage — *vt.* -staged′, -stag′ing to draw attention away from another, as by moving upstage

up·stairs′ *adv.* 1 up the stairs 2 on or to an upper floor or higher level 3 [Colloq.] in the mind — *adj.* on an upper floor — *n.* an upper floor

up·stand′ing *adj.* 1 erect 2 upright in character; honorable

up′start′ *n.* one who has recently come into wealth, power, etc., esp. one who is presumptuous, aggressive, etc. — *adj.* of or like an upstart

up′state′ *adj., adv.* in, to, or from the northerly part of a State

up′stream′ *adv., adj.* in the direction against the current of a stream

up′surge′ *n.* a surge upward

up′swing′ *n.* a swing, trend, or movement upward

up′take′ *n.* a taking up —**quick (or slow) on the uptake** [Colloq.] quick (or slow) to comprehend

THESAURUS

up-and-coming *a.* industrious, prospering, alert; see ACTIVE.

upbringing *n.* rearing, bringing up, instruction; see CHILDHOOD, TRAINING.

upcoming *a.* expected, future, imminent; see FORTHCOMING.

update *v.* modernize, bring up to date, refresh; see RENEW 1.

upheaval *n.* outburst, explosion, eruption; see OUTBREAK 1.

upheld *a.* supported, maintained, advanced; see BACKED 2.

uphill *a.* up, toward the summit, toward the crest, skyward, ascending, climbing.—*Ant.* DOWN, downhill, descending.

uphold *v.* 1 [To hold up] brace, buttress, prop; see SUPPORT 1. 2 [To maintain] confirm, sustain, back up; see SUPPORT 2.

upkeep *n.* 1 [Maintenance] conservation, subsistence, repair; see CARE 1. 2 [Cost of maintenance] expenses, outlay, expense; see PRICE.

upon *a., prep.* 1 [On] on top of, in, attached to, visible on, against,

affixed to, above, next to, located at, superimposed on. 2 [At the time of] consequent to, beginning with, at the occurrence of; see SIMULTANEOUS.

upper *a.* top, topmost, uppermost, above, higher, more elevated, loftier, overhead.—*Ant.* UNDER, lower, bottom.

upper-class *a.* well-born, cultivated, genteel; see NOBLE 3.

upper hand *n.* sway, dominion, superiority; see ADVANTAGE.

upright *a.* 1 [Vertical] erect, perpendicular, on end; see STRAIGHT 1. 2 [Honorable] straightforward, honest, fair; see HONEST 1.

uprising *n.* rebellion, riot, upheaval; see REVOLUTION 2.

uproar *n.* babble, confusion, turmoil, ado, hassle, commotion, clamor, disturbance, tumult, din, racket, clatter, hubbub, fracas, clangor, jangle, bustle, bickering, discord, row.

uproot *v.* tear up by the roots, pull up, weed out; see REMOVE 1.

upset *a.* disconcerted, amazed, shocked; see CONFUSED 2.

upset *n.* overthrow, destruction, subversion; see DEFEAT.

upset *v.* 1 [To turn over] overturn, upturn, subvert, turn bottom-side up, turn inside out, upend, reverse, keel over, overset, topple, tip over, turn topsy-turvy, overbalance, invert, capsize, tilt, pitch over, overthrow.—*Ant.* STAND, erect, elevate. 2 [To disturb] agitate, fluster, perturb; see BOTHER 2. 3 [To beat] conquer, outplay, overpower; see DEFEAT 2, 3.

upside-down *a.* topsy-turvy, tangled, bottomside up, inverted, rearend foremost, backward, the wrong way, wrongside uppermost, cartbefore-the-horse, head over heels.—*Ant.* STEADY, upright, right side up.

upstairs *a.* in the upper story, above, up the steps; see UPPER.

upstairs *n.* the upper story, the penthouse, the rooms above the ground floor; see FLOOR 2.

upstanding *a.* honorable, upright, straightforward; see HONEST 1.

upswing *n.* growth, boom, acceleration; see INCREASE.

up'tight' *adj.* [Slang] very tense, nervous, etc. Also **up-tight**

up'-to-date' *adj.* **1** extending to the present time **2** keeping up with what is most recent

up'town' *adj., adv.* of, in, or toward the upper part of a city or town — *n.* the uptown section of a city or town

up·turn (-turn'; *for n.* up'turn') *vt., vi.* to turn up or over — *n.* an upward turn or trend —**up'turn'** *adj.*

up'ward (-wərd) *adv., adj.* toward a higher place, position, etc. Also **up'wards** *adv.* —**upwards** (or **upward**) of more than —**up'wardly** *adv.*

upward mobility movement to a higher social and economic status

ura·cil (yoor'ə sil') *n.* a colorless, crystalline base that is a constituent of RNA

ura·nium (yoo rā'nē əm) *n.* [after fol.] a very hard, heavy, radioactive metallic chemical element: used in work on atomic energy

Ura·nus (yoor'ə nəs, yoo rān'əs) [< Gr *Ouranos*, heaven] a planet of the solar system: see PLANET

ur·ban (ur'bən) *adj.* [< L *urbs*, city] **1** of, in, or constituting a city **2** characteristic of cities

ur·bane (ur bān') *adj.* [see prec.] polite in a smooth, polished way; refined —**ur·ban'ity** (-ban'ə tē) *n.*

ur·ban·ize (ur'bən iz') *vt.* **-ized', -iz'ing** to change from rural to urban —**ur'ban·i·za'tion** *n.*

urban renewal rehabilitation of deteriorated urban areas, as by slum clearance and housing construction

urban sprawl the spread of urban congestion into surrounding areas

ur·chin (ur'chin) *n.* [< L *ericius*, hedgehog] a small child; esp., a mischievous boy

-ure (ər) [Fr < L *-ura*] *suffix* **1** act, process, or result [*exposure*] **2** agent of **3** state of being ____ed [*composure*] **4** office, rank, or collective body [*legislature*]

urea (yoo rē'ə) *n.* [< Gr *ouron*, urine] a soluble, crystalline solid found in urine or made synthetically

uremia (yoo rē'mē ə) *n.* [< Gr *ouron*, urine + *haima*, blood] a toxic condition caused by the presence in the blood of waste products normally eliminated in the urine —**ure'mic** *adj.*

ureter (yoo rēt'ər) *n.* [< Gr *ourein*, urinate] a tube carrying urine from a kidney to the bladder

urethane (yoor'ə thān') *n.* [< Fr] a white, crystalline compound used as a hypnotic and sedative, a solvent, etc.

urethra (yoo rē'thrə) *n., pl.* **-thrae** (-thrē') *or* **-thras** [< Gr *ouron*, urine] the canal through which urine is discharged from the bladder: in males, also the duct for semen —**ure'thral** *adj.*

urge (urj) *vt.* **urged, urg'ing** [L *urgere*, press hard] **1** *a*) to press upon the attention; advocate *b*) to plead with; ask earnestly **2** to incite; provoke **3** to drive or force onward — *n.* **1** an urging **2** an impulse

ur·gent (ur'jənt) *adj.* [see URGE] **1** calling for haste, immediate action, etc. **2** insistent —**ur'gency,** *pl.* **-cies,** *n.* —**ur'gently** *adv.*

-urgy (ur'jē) [< Gr *ergon*, work] *combining form* a working with or by means of (something specified) [*chemurgy*]

uric (yoor'ik) *adj.* of, contained in, or derived from urine

uri·nal (yoor'ə nəl) *n.* **1** a portable receptacle for urinating **2** a place for urinating

uri·naly·sis (yoor'ə nal'ə sis) *n., pl.* **-ses'** (-sēz') chemical or microscopic analysis of the urine

uri·nary (yoor'ə ner'ē) *adj.* **1** of urine **2** of the organs that secrete and discharge urine

uri·nate (yoor'ə nāt') *vi.* **-nat'ed, -nat'ing** to discharge urine from the body —**u'ri·na'tion** *n.*

urine (yoor'in) *n.* [< L *urina*] the yellowish liquid containing waste products secreted by the kidneys and discharged through the urethra

urn (urn) *n.* [< L *urna*] **1** *a*) a vase with a pedestal *b*) such a vase used to hold ashes after cremation **2** a metal container with a faucet, for making or serving hot coffee, tea, etc.

uro·geni·tal (yoor'ō jen'ə təl) *adj.* of the urinary and genital organs

urol·ogy (yoo räl'ə jē) *n.* [< Gr *ouron*, urine + -LOGY] the branch of medicine dealing with the urinary and genital organs and their diseases —**urol'o·gist** *n.*

ur·sine (ur'sin', -sin) *adj.* [< L *ursus*, a bear] of or like a bear

ur·ti·caria (urt'i ker'ē ə) *n.* [< L *urtica*, a nettle] HIVES

us (us) *pron.* [OE] objective case of WE

US or **U.S.** United States

USA 1 United States of America: also **U.S.A. 2** United States Army

us·able or **use·able** (yoo'zə bəl) *adj.* that can be used; fit for use —**us'abil'ity** (-bil'ə tē) or **use'abil'ity** *n.*

USAF United States Air Force

us·age (yoo'sij) *n.* **1** the act, way, or extent of using; treatment **2** established practice; custom; habit **3** the way in

---

THESAURUS

uptight* *a.* **1** [Troubled] worried, concerned, apprehensive; see TROUBLED. **2** [Cautious] conventional, old-fashioned, strict; see CONSERVATIVE.

up-to-date *a.* in vogue, in fashion, fashionable, conventional, stylish, modern, modernistic, streamlined, popular, faddish, brand-new, current, up-to-the-minute, according to the prevailing taste, modish, the latest, all the rage, trendy*, in*, with-it*.

upturned *a.* tilted, tipped, upside-down, inclined, sloped, slanted, oblique, expectant, upward-looking, turned up, extended.

upward *a.* up, higher, skyward, in the air, uphill, away from the earth, up the slope, on an incline, up north.

urban *a.* **1** [Concerning city government] city, municipal, civil; see PUBLIC 2. **2** [Concerning city living] big-city, civic, municipal, metropolitan, within the city limits, inner-city, central-city, downtown, zoned, planned, business-district, civil, nonrural, ghetto, shopping, residential, apartment-dwelling.

urban renewal *n.* rebuilding the inner city, modernization, bringing up to date; see IMPROVEMENT 2.

urge *v.* **1** [To present favorably] favor, further, support; see APPROVE. **2** [To induce] charge, beg, plead, adjure, influence, beseech, implore, ask, command, entreat, desire, request, press, inveigle, talk into, incite, move, allure, tempt, attract, influence, prompt, instigate, exhort, advise, solicit, inspire, stimulate, conjure, coax, wheedle, maneuver, draw, put up to*, prevail upon.—*Ant.* RESTRAIN, deter, discourage. **3** [To drive] compel, drive, propel, impel, force, coerce, constrain, press, push, make, oblige, goad, prod, spur.—*Ant.* DENY, block, withhold.

urged *a.* **1** [Supported] favored, furthered, proposed; see BACKED 2. **2** [Pressed] begged, charged, implored, asked, commanded, entreated, desired, requested, inveigled, talked into, incited, moved, motivated, allured, lured, tempted, seduced, attracted, influenced, prompted, instigated, exhorted, advised, solicited, inspired, whipped up, stimulated, coaxed, wheedled, maneuvered, put up to*, prevailed upon, compelled, obliged, propelled, driven, induced, impelled, coerced, forced, constrained.

urgency *n.* import, need, seriousness; see IMPORTANCE, NECESSITY 3.

urgent *a.* **1** [Of immediate importance] pressing, critical, necessary, compelling, imperative, important, indispensable, momentous, wanted, required, called for, demanded, salient, chief, paramount, essential, primary, vital, principal, absorbing, all-absorbing, not to be delayed, crucial, instant, leading, capital, overruling, foremost, exigent, crying. **2** [Insistent] compelling, persuasive, imperious, solemn, grave, weighty, impressive, earnest, importunate, clamorous, hasty, breathless, precipitate, frantic, impetuous, imperative, convincing, beseeching, seductive, commanding, imploring, eager, zealous, anxious, enthusiastic, moving, excited, impulsive, vigorous, overpowering, masterful.

urgently *a.* **1** [Critically] pressingly, instantly, imperatively, necessarily, indispensably, momently*, crucially, requisitely, essentially, primarily, capitally. **2** [Insistently] compellingly, persuasively, solemnly, gravely, weightily, impressively, earnestly, importunately, clamorously, hastily, breathlessly, precipitately, frantically, impetuously, convincingly, beseechingly, seductively, commandingly, imploringly, eagerly, anxiously, zealously, movingly, emotionally, excitedly, impulsively, vigorously, irresistibly, enthusiastically, overpoweringly, masterfully, compulsively.

urinate *v.* go to the restroom, go to the bathroom, go to the lavatory, have to go*, excrete, use the urinal, use the bedpan, make water, tinkle*, wizz*, peepee*, take a leak*.

usable *a.* available, at hand, useful, employable, unused, good, serviceable, applicable, ready, subservient, helpful, valuable, beneficial, profitable, advantageous, fit, desirable, efficacious, instrumental, fitting, conformable, suitable, proper, practical, convenient.—*Ant.* USELESS, worthless, no good.

usage *n.* **1** [Custom] practice, rule, habit; see USE 1. **2** [Accepted language] good usage, grammatical usage, approved diction; see GRAMwhich a word, phrase, etc. is used to express a particular idea

USDA United States Department of Agriculture

use (yōōz; *for n.* yōōs) *vt.* **used, us'ing** ⟦< L *uti*⟧ **1** to put into action or service **2** to exercise *[use* your judgment*]* **3** to deal with; treat *[to use* a friend badly*]* **4** to consume, expend: often with *up* **5** to consume habitually *[to use* drugs*]* — *n.* **1** a using or being used **2** the ability to use **3** the right to use **4** the need or opportunity to use **5** a way of using **6** usefulness **7** the purpose for which something is used **8** function —**used to** (yōōs'tə, -tōō) **1** did at one time *[I used to* live here*]* **2** accustomed to —**us'er** *n.*

used (yōōzd) *vt. pt. & pp. of* USE — *adj.* not new; second-hand

use·ful (yōōs'fəl) *adj.* that can be used; serviceable; helpful —**use'fully** *adv.* —**use'ful·ness** *n.*

use'less (-lis) *adj.* **1** having no use **2** to no purpose —**use'lessly** *adv.* —**use'less·ness** *n.*

us'er-friend'ly *adj.* easy to use or understand: said esp. of computer hardware, programs, etc.

usher (ush'ər) *n.* ⟦< L *ostiarius*, doorkeeper⟧ **1** one who shows people to their seats in a theater, church, etc. **2** a bridegroom's attendant — *vt.* **1** to escort (others) to seats, etc. **2** to be a forerunner of: often with *in*

USMC United States Marine Corps

USN United States Navy

USO United Service Organizations

USP or **U.S.P.** United States Pharmacopoeia

USS United States Ship

USSR or **U.S.S.R.** Union of Soviet Socialist Republics

usu·al (yōō'zhōō əl) *adj.* ⟦see USE⟧ such as is most often seen, used, etc.; common; customary —**u'su·ally** *adv.*

usurp (yōō zʉrp', -sʉrp') *vt., vi.* ⟦< L *usus*, a use + *rapere*, to seize⟧ to take (power, a position, etc.) by force —**usur·pa·tion** (yōō'zər pā'shən, -sər-) *n.* —**usurp'er** *n.*

usu·ry (yōō'zhər ē) *n., pl.* **-ries** ⟦see USE⟧ **1** the lending of money at an excessive rate of interest **2** an excessive interest rate —**u'su·rer** *n.*

uten·sil (yōō ten'səl) *n.* ⟦< L *uti*, to use⟧ an implement or container, esp. one for use in a kitchen

uter·us (yōōt'ər əs) *n., pl.* **-teri** (-ī') ⟦L⟧ a hollow organ of female mammals in which the embryo and fetus are developed; womb —**u'ter·ine** (-in, -in') *adj.*

utili·tar·ian (yōō til'ə ter'ē ən) *adj.* **1** of or having to do with utility **2** stressing usefulness over beauty or other considerations

util·ity (yōō til'ə tē) *n., pl.* **-ties** ⟦< L *uti*, to use⟧ **1** usefulness **2** something useful, as the service to the public of gas, water, etc. **3** a company providing such a service

utility room a room containing laundry appliances, heating equipment, etc.

uti·lize (yōōt''l īz') *vt.* **-lized', -liz'ing** to put to profitable use; make use of —**u'ti·li·za'tion** *n.*

ut·most (ut'mōst') *adj.* ⟦< OE superl. of *ut*, out⟧ **1** most extreme; farthest **2** of the greatest degree, amount, etc. — *n.* the most possible

Uto·pia (yōō tō'pē ə) ⟦< Gr *ou*, not + *topos*, a place⟧ an imaginary island with a perfect political and social system, described in *Utopia* (1516) by Sir Thomas More, Eng. statesman — *n.* [*often* **u-**] **1** any idealized place of perfection **2** any visionary scheme for a perfect society —**Uto'pian** or **uto'pian** *adj., n.*

ut·ter¹ (ut'ər) *adj.* ⟦< OE compar. of *ut*, out⟧ **1** complete; total **2** unqualified; absolute; unconditional —**ut'terly** *adv.*

ut·ter² (ut'ər) *vt.* ⟦< ME *utter*, outward⟧ **1** to speak or express audibly (sounds, words, etc.) **2** to express in any way

ut'ter·ance *n.* **1** an uttering **2** the power or style of speaking **3** that which is uttered

ut'ter·most' (-mōst') *adj., n.* UTMOST

U-turn (yōō'tʉrn') *n.* a turn by a car made so as to head in the opposite direction

UV or **uv** ultraviolet

uvu·la (yōō'vyōō lə) *n., pl.* **-las** or **-lae'** (-lē') ⟦< L *uva*, grape⟧ the small, fleshy process hanging down from the soft palate above the back of the tongue —**u'vu·lar** *adj.*

■ THESAURUS ■

MAR, LANGUAGE.

use *n.* **1** [The act of using] practice, employment, application, usage, appliance, effecting, manner, adoption, utilization, manipulation, bringing to bear, management, handling, performance, conduct, recourse, resort, exercise, treatment, method, technique, control, resolution, realization, association.—*Ant.* NEGLECT, disuse, dismissal. **2** [The state of being useful] utility, usefulness, usability, employment, application, value, advantage, excellence, helpfulness, convenience, suitability, expedience, aid, serviceability, merit, profit, practicability, practicality, fitness, subservience, effectiveness, applicability.

use *v.* **1** [To make use of] avail oneself of, employ, put to use, exercise, exert, put forth, utilize, apply, bring to bear, practice, play on, do with, draw on, adopt, take advantage of, make do, accept, work, put in practice, relate, make work, put to work, make shift with.—*Ant.* DISCARD, reject, refuse. **2** [To make a practice of; *now used principally in the past tense*] be accustomed to, practice, adapt, conform, habituate, regulate, suit, familiarize, attune. **3** [To behave toward] deal with, handle, bear oneself toward; see MANAGE 1. —**use up** consume, exhaust, squander; see SPEND, WASTE 1, 2.

used *a.* **1** [Employed] put to use, utilized, applied, adopted, adapted, accepted, put in service, practiced, turned to account.—*Ant.* DISCARDED, rejected, unused. **2** [Accustomed] practiced, customary, suited; see HABITUAL. **3** [Secondhand] castoff, depreciated, repossessed; see OLD 2.

useful *a.* valuable, beneficial, serviceable; see HELPFUL 1.

usefulness *n.* application, value, advantage, excellence, convenience, suitability, usability, range, versatility, helpfulness, utility, serviceability, merit, profitableness, fitness, practicality, practicability, propriety, adaptability; see also USE 2.

useless *a.* **1** [Unserviceable] worthless, unusable, ineffectual, expendable, incompetent, of no use, ineffective, inoperate, dysfunctional, counterproductive, inefficient, unprofitable, no damn good*.—*Ant.* EFFICIENT, usable, operative. **2** [Futile] vain, pointless, fruitless; see HOPELESS.

using *a.* employing, utilizing, applying, adopting, taking advantage of, accepting, working, practicing, manipulating, controlling, putting in service, trying out, testing, proving, wearing out.

usual *a.* **1** [Ordinary] general, frequent, normal; see COMMON 1. **2** [Habitual] prevailing, accustomed, customary; see CONVENTIONAL 1.

usually *a.* ordinarily, customarily, habitually; see REGULARLY.

utensils *n.* [Implements; *especially for the kitchen*] equipment, tools, appliances, conveniences, wares; see also TOOL 1. *Kitchen utensils include the following:* sieve, egg beater, knife, fork, spoon, measuring cup, grater, spatula, skewer, pancake turner, can opener, egg slicer, meat grinder, butcher knife, peeler, paring knife, pastry cutter, squeezer, knife sharpener, coffee grinder, blender, food processor, mixer, vegetable brush, pan scourer, frying pan, saucepan, cake pan, pie pan, roaster, bottle brush, dishpan, draining pan, sink strainer, dishmop, mixing bowl, pan lid, rolling pin, pastry board, coffee pot, bread pan, cookie sheet.

utilities *n.* services, public utilities, conveniences, current necessities of modern life, household slaves. *Utilities include the following:* heat, light, power, gas, water, telephone, electricity, cable, garbage disposal, sewage disposal.

utility *n.* **1** [Usefulness] service, advantage, convenience; see USE 2. **2** [Utility company] gas company, electricity company, water company; see BUSINESS 4.

utilize *v.* employ, appropriate, turn to account; see USE 1.

utmost *a.* ultimate, chief, entire, whole, full, unreserved, complete, unstinted, total, absolute, unlimited, unsparing, thorough, exhaustive, highest, maximum, most, top, undiminished, undivided, thoroughgoing, unmitigated, sheer, unqualified, unconditional, all-out.

utter¹ *a.* complete, total, thorough; see ABSOLUTE 1.

utter² *v.* pronounce, talk, express, articulate, voice, whisper, mutter, shout, exclaim, enunciate, air, speak, tell, disclose, declare, say, assert, affirm, ejaculate, vocalize, proclaim, give tongue to, recite, blurt out, let fall, announce, come out with.

utterance *n.* declaration, saying, assertion, announcement, pronouncement, ejaculation, vociferation, talk, speech, statement, query, expression, sentence, proclamation, recitation, spiel, rant, jargon, response, reply, oration.

uttered *a.* asserted, expressed, announced; see ORAL.

utterly *a.* wholly, thoroughly, entirely; see COMPLETELY.

v or **V** (vē) *n.*, *pl.* **v's**, **V's** the 22d letter of the English alphabet

V (vē) *n.* a Roman numeral for 5

v. 1 〚L *vide*〛see 2 verb 3 versus 4 volume

V *symbol for* 1 *Chem.* vanadium 2 velocity 3 volt(s) Also, for 2 & 3, **v**

VA Veterans Administration

va·cancy (vā′kən sē) *n.*, *pl.* **-cies** 1 a being vacant 2 empty or vacant space 3 an unoccupied position, office, quarters, etc.

va·cant (vā′kənt) *adj.* 〚< L *vacare*, be empty〛1 having nothing in it 2 not held, filled, etc., as a seat, house, etc. 3 free from work; leisure 4 foolish or stupid —**va′cantly** *adv.*

va·cate′ (-kāt′) *vt.* **-cat′ed**, **-cat′ing** 1 to cause (an office, house, etc.) to be vacant 2 to make void; annul

va·ca·tion (vā kā′shən, və-) *n.* 〚< L *vacatio*〛a period of rest from work, study, etc. — *vi.* to take one's vacation — **va·ca′tioner** or **va·ca′tion·ist** *n.*

vac·ci·nate (vak′sə nāt′) *vt.*, *vi.* **-nat′ed**, **-nat′ing** to inoculate with a vaccine to prevent disease —**vac′ci·na′tion** *n.*

vac·cine (vak sēn′; vak′sēn) *n.* 〚< L *vacca*, cow〛1 a substance containing the cowpox virus, used in vaccination against smallpox 2 any preparation so used to produce immunity to a specific disease

vac·il·late (vas′ə lāt′) *vi.* **-lat′ed**, **-lat′ing** 〚< L *vacillare*〛1 to sway to and fro; waver 2 to fluctuate 3 to show indecision —**vac′il·la′tion** *n.*

va·cu·ity (va kyōō′ə tē) *n.*, *pl.* **-ties** 〚< L *vacuus*, empty〛1 emptiness 2 an empty space 3 emptiness of mind 4 an inane or senseless thing, remark, etc.

vacu·ous (vak′yōō əs) *adj.* 〚L *vacuus*〛1 empty 2 stupid; senseless —**vac′u·ously** *adv.*

vacu·um (vak′yōō əm, -yōōm′, -yoom) *n.*, *pl.* **-ums** or **-a** (-ə) 〚L〛1 space with nothing at all in it 2 a space from which most of the air or gas has been taken 3 any void — *adj.* 1 of or used to make a vacuum 2 having or working by a vacuum — *vt.*, *vi.* to clean with a vacuum cleaner

vacuum cleaner a machine for cleaning carpets, floors, etc. by suction

vacuum-packed *adj.* packed in an airtight container to maintain freshness

vacuum tube an electron tube from which most of the air has been evacuated, containing one or more grids, used as an amplifier, etc.

vaga·bond (vag′ə bänd′) *adj.* 〚< L *vagari*, wander〛1 wandering 2 living a drifting or irresponsible life; shiftless — *n.* 1 one who wanders from place to place 2 a wandering beggar 3 an idle or shiftless person —**vag′a·bond′age** *n.*

va·gary (və ger′ē, vā′gər ē) *n.*, *pl.* **-ies** 〚see prec.〛1 an odd or eccentric action 2 a whimsical or freakish notion; caprice —**va·gar′i·ous** *adj.*

va·gina (və jī′nə) *n.*, *pl.* **-nas** or **-nae** (-nē) 〚L, sheath〛in female mammals, the canal from the vulva to the uterus —**vagi·nal** (vaj′ə nəl) *adj.*

va·grant (vā′grənt) *n.* 〚prob. < OFr *walcrer*, wander〛one who wanders from place to place, esp. without a regular job, supporting oneself by begging, etc. — *adj.* 1 wandering; nomadic 2 of or like a vagrant 3 wayward, erratic, etc. —**va′grancy**, *pl.* **-cies**, *n.*

vague (vāg) *adj.* **va′guer**, **va′guest** 〚< L *vagus*, wandering〛1 indefinite in shape or form 2 not sharp, certain, or precise in thought or expression —**vague′ly** *adv.* — **vague′ness** *n.*

vain (vān) *adj.* 〚< L *vanus*, empty〛1 having no real value; worthless [*vain* pomp] 2 without effect; futile [a *vain* endeavor] 3 having an excessively high regard for one's self, looks, etc.; conceited —**in vain** 1 fruitlessly 2 profanely —**vain′ly** *adv.*

vain·glo·ry (-glôr′ē) *n.* 〚< L *vana gloria*, empty boasting〛excessive vanity —**vain·glo′ri·ous** *adj.*

val. 1 valuation 2 value

val·ance (val′əns, vāl′-) *n.* 〚ME < ?〛a short curtain forming a border, esp. across the top of a window

vale (vāl) *n.* [Old Poet.] VALLEY

val·edic·to·rian (val′ə dik tôr′ē ən) *n.* the student who delivers the valedictory at graduation

val′edic′tory (-tər ē) *n.*, *pl.* **-ries** 〚< L *vale*, farewell + *dicere*, to say〛a farewell speech, esp. at graduation

va·lence (vā′ləns) *n.* 〚< L *valere*, be strong〛*Chem.* the combining capacity of an element or radical as measured by the number of hydrogen or chlorine atoms which one radical or atom of the element will combine with or replace Also **va′lency**, *pl.* **-cies**

val·en·tine (val′ən tīn′) *n.* 1 a sweetheart chosen or greeted on Saint Valentine's Day 2 a greeting card or gift sent on this day

valet (val′it, va lā′, va lā′, val′ā) *n.* 〚Fr, a groom〛1 a personal manservant who takes care of a man's clothes, helps him dress, etc. 2 an employee, as of a hotel, who cleans or presses clothes, etc.

Val·halla (val hal′ə) *Norse Myth.* the great hall where Odin feasts the souls of heroes slain in battle

val·iant (val′yənt) *adj.* 〚< L *valere*, be strong〛brave; courageous —**val′iance** *n.* —**val′iantly** *adv.*

valid (val′id) *adj.* 〚< L *valere*, be strong〛1 having legal force 2 based on evidence or sound reasoning —**val′idly** *adv.* —**val′id·ness** *n.*

THESAURUS

vacancy *n.* 1 [A vacated position] opening, vacated post, post without an incumbent, unfilled position, unheld office, job. 2 [A vacated residence] empty apartment, tenantless house, uninhabited house, vacant house, unoccupied house, deserted house, house for rent, house for sale.

vacant *a.* 1 [Without contents] devoid, void, unfilled; see EMPTY. 2 [Without an occupant] unoccupied, untenanted, tenantless, uninhabited, idle, free, deserted, abandoned, without a resident, not lived in.—*Ant.* INHABITED, occupied, tenanted.

vacate *v.* go away, relinquish, depart; see LEAVE 1.

vacation *n.* respite, rest, recreation time, intermission, recess, holiday, leave of absence, sabbatical, time off*.

vaccinate *v.* inoculate, immunize, prevent, treat, mitigate, protect, inject, shoot.

vaccinated *a.* immunized, inoculated, given injections; see PROTECTED.

vaccination *n.* 1 [The act of administering vaccine] injection, inoculation, shots; see TREATMENT 2. 2 [A result of vaccination] protection, immunization, inoculation; see IMMUNITY 2.

vacuum *n.* space, void, hollowness, emptiness.

vacuum cleaner *n.* vacuum sweeper, carpet sweeper, vacuum; see APPLIANCE.

vagrant *a.* 1 [Having no home] roaming, itinerant, nomadic; see TRAVELING. 2 [Having no occupation] begging, mendicant, profligate, idling, prodigal, loafing, beachcombing, panhandling*, bumming*, mooching*. 3 [Having no fixed course] wayward, capricious, erratic; see AIMLESS.

vagrant *n.* beggar, idler, loafer; see TRAVELER.

vague *a.* 1 [Not clearly expressed] indefinite, unintelligible, superficial; see OBSCURE 1. 2 [Not clearly understood] uncertain, undetermined, unsure, doubtful, dubious, questionable, misunderstood, enigmatic, puzzling, nebulous, inexplicable, unsettled, bewildering, perplexing, problematic.—*Ant.* CERTAIN, sure, positive. 3 [Not clearly visible] dim, nebulous, dark; see HAZY.

vaguely *a.* uncertainly, unclearly, hazily, foggily, confusedly, mistily, shiftily, unreliably, dubiously, eccentrically, unsurely, illegally, evasively, unpredictably, obscurely, indefinitely, without clear outlines, incapable of being determined.

vagueness *n.* ambiguity, obscurity, difficulty; see CONFUSION, UNCERTAINTY 1, 2.

vain *a.* 1 [Possessing unwarranted self-esteem] proud, arrogant, haughty; see EGOTISTIC. 2 [Useless] worthless, hopeless, profitless; see FUTILE, USELESS 1. —**in vain** futilely, purposelessly, unprofitably; see USELESS.

valentine *n.* sentimental letter, St. Valentine's Day greeting, love verse; see LETTER 2.

valiant *a.* courageous, unafraid, dauntless; see BRAVE.

valiantly *a.* courageously, boldly, fearlessly; see BRAVELY.

valid *a.* 1 [Capable of proof] sound, cogent, logical, conclusive, solid, well-grounded, well-founded, tested, accurate, convincing, telling, correct, determinative, compelling, persuasive, potent, stringent, strong, ultimate, unanswerable, irrefutable.—*Ant.* WRONG, erring, misleading. 2 [Genuine] true, original, factual, real, actual, pure, uncorrupted, authentic, confirmed, authoritative, trustworthy, credible, attested, efficient,

vali·date (val′ə dāt′) *vt.* **-dat′ed, -dat′ing 1** to make legally valid **2** to prove to be valid —**val′i·da′tion** *n.*

va·lid·ity (və lid′ə tē) *n., pl.* **-ties** the quality or fact of being valid in law or in argument, proof, etc.

va·lise (və lēs′) *n.* 〚Fr < L *valesium* < ?〛 [Old-fashioned] a piece of hand luggage

Val·i·um (val′ē əm) *trademark for* a tranquilizing drug

Val·kyrie (val kir′ē, val′ki rē) *n. Norse Myth.* any of the maidens of Odin who conduct the souls of heroes slain in battle to Valhalla

val·ley (val′ē) *n., pl.* **-leys** 〚< L *vallis*〛 **1** low land lying between hills or mountains **2** the land drained by a river system **3** any valleylike dip

valor (val′ər) *n.* 〚< L *valere*, be strong〛 marked courage or bravery Brit., etc. sp. **val′our** —**val′or·ous** *adj.*

valu·able (val′yoo ə bəl, -yə bəl) *adj.* **1** *a)* having material value *b)* of great monetary value **2** highly important, esteemed, etc. — *n.* an article of value: *usually used in pl.*

valu·a·tion (val′yoo ā′shən) *n.* **1** the determining of the value of anything **2** determined or estimated value

value (val′yoo) *n.* 〚< L *valere* be worth〛 **1** the worth of a thing in money or goods **2** estimated worth **3** purchasing power **4** that quality of a thing which makes it more or less desirable, useful, etc. **5** a thing or quality having intrinsic worth **6** [*pl.*] beliefs or standards **7** relative duration, intensity, etc. — *vt.* **val′ued, val′u·ing 1** to estimate the value of; appraise **2** to place a certain estimate of worth on [*to value* health above wealth] **3** to think highly of —**val′ue·less** *adj.*

val′ue-add′ed tax a tax based and paid on products, etc. at each stage of production or distribution, and included in the cost to the consumer

val′ued *adj.* highly thought of

valve (valv) *n.* 〚< L *valva*, leaf of a folding door〛 **1** *Anat.* a membranous structure which permits body fluids to flow in one direction only, or opens and closes a tube, etc. **2** any device in a pipe, etc. that regulates the flow by means of a flap, lid, etc. **3** *Music* a device, as in the trumpet, that changes the tube length so as to change the pitch **4** *Zoology* one of the parts making up the shell of a mollusk, clam, etc.

va·moose (va moos′) *vi., vt.* **-moosed′, -moos′ing** 〚< Sp *vamos*, let us go〛 [Old Slang] to leave quickly

vamp (vamp) *n.* 〚< OFr *avant*, before + *pié*, foot〛 **1** the part of a boot or shoe covering the instep **2** a simple, improvised introduction or interlude, as between songs in popular music — *vt.* to put a vamp on — *vi. Music* to play a vamp

vam·pire (vam′pīr′) *n.* 〚< Slavic〛 **1** in folklore, a reanimated corpse that sucks the blood of sleeping persons **2** one who preys ruthlessly on others

vampire bat a tropical American bat that lives on the blood of animals

van¹ (van) *n. short for* VANGUARD

van² (van) *n.* 〚< CARAVAN〛 a large, closed truck used as for moving, or a small one used for deliveries, fitted out as a vacation vehicle, etc.

va·na·dium (və nā′dē əm) *n.* 〚< ON *Vanadis*, goddess of love〛 a ductile metallic chemical element used in steel alloys, etc.

Van Al·len radiation belt (van al′ən) 〚after J. *Van Allen* (1914-), U.S. physicist〛 a broad belt of radiation encircling the earth at varying levels

Van·dal (van′dəl) *n.* **1** a member of a Germanic people who sacked Rome (455 A.D.) **2** [**v-**] one who maliciously destroys property, esp. works of art

van′dal·ize (-īz′) *vt.* **-ized′, -iz′ing** to destroy or damage (property) maliciously —**van′dal·ism′** *n.*

Vandyke (beard) (van dīk′) a closely trimmed, pointed beard

vane (vān) *n.* 〚< OE *fana*, a flag〛 **1** a free-swinging piece of metal, etc. that shows which way the wind is blowing; weather vane **2** any of the flat pieces set around an axle and rotated about it by moving air, water, etc. or rotated to move the air or water

van·guard (van′gärd′) *n.* 〚< OFr *avant*, before + *garde*, guard〛 **1** the front part of an army in an advance **2** the leading position or persons in a movement

va·nilla (və nil′ə) *n.* 〚< Sp *vaina*, pod〛 **1** a climbing orchid with podlike capsules (**vanilla beans**) **2** a flavoring made from these capsules

van·ish (van′ish) *vi.* 〚see EVANESCENT〛 **1** to pass suddenly from sight; disappear **2** to cease to exist

van·ity (van′ə tē) *n., pl.* **-ties** 〚< L *vanus*, vain〛 **1** anything vain or futile **2** worthlessness; futility **3** a being vain, or too proud of oneself **4** a small table with a mirror for use while putting on cosmetics, etc.

vanity case a woman's small traveling case for carrying cosmetics, toilet articles, etc.

van·quish (vaŋ′kwish, van′-) *vt.* 〚< L *vincere*〛 to conquer or defeat

van·tage (van′tij) *n.* 〚see ADVANTAGE〛 **1** a favorable position **2** a position allowing a clear view, understanding, etc.: also **vantage point**

vapid (vap′id) *adj.* 〚L *vapidus*〛 tasteless; flavorless; dull —**va·pid·ity** (va pid′ə tē) or **vap′id·ness** *n.*

va·por (vā′pər) *n.* 〚L〛 **1** *a)* visible particles of moisture floating in the air, as fog or steam *b)* smoke, fumes, etc. **2** the gaseous form of any substance normally a liquid or solid Brit sp. **vapour**

va′por·ize (-pər iz′) *vt., vi.* **-ized′, -iz′ing** to change into vapor —**va′pori·za′tion** *n.* —**va′por·iz′er** *n.*

va·por·ous (vā′pər əs) *adj.* **1** forming or full of vapor; foggy; misty **2** like vapor

vapor trail CONTRAIL

va·quero (vä ker′ō) *n., pl.* **-ros** 〚Sp < *vaca*, cow〛 [Southwest] a man who herds cattle; cowboy

var. 1 variant(s) **2** various

vari·able (ver′ē ə bəl) *adj.* **1** apt to change or vary; changeable, inconstant, etc. **2** that can be changed or varied — *n.* anything changeable; a thing that varies —**var′i·abil′ity** *n.* —**var′i·ably** *adv.*

vari·ance (ver′ē əns, var′-) *n.* **1** a varying or being variant **2** degree of change or difference; discrepancy **3** official permission to bypass regulations —**at variance** not in agreement or accord

var′i·ant (-ənt) *adj.* varying; different in some way from

■ THESAURUS ■

others of the same kind — *n.* anything variant, as a different spelling of the same word

var·i·a'tion (-ā'shən) *n.* 1 a varying; change in form, extent, etc. 2 the degree of such change 3 a thing somewhat different from another of the same kind 4 *Music* the repetition of a theme with changes in rhythm, key, etc.

vari·col·ored (ver'i kul'ərd) *adj.* of several or many colors

vari·cose (var'ə kōs') *adj.* ⟦< L *varix*, enlarged vein⟧ abnormally and irregularly swollen *[varicose veins]*

var·ied (ver'ēd) *adj.* 1 of different kinds; various 2 changed; altered

vari·egat·ed (ver'ē ə gāt'id) *adj.* ⟦< L *varius*, various⟧ 1 marked with different colors in spots, streaks, etc. 2 having variety; varied

va·ri·ety (və rī'ə tē) *n., pl.* **-ties** 1 a being various or varied 2 a different form of some thing, condition, etc.; kind 3 a collection of different things

variety store a retail store selling many small, inexpensive items

vari·ous (ver'ē əs) *adj.* ⟦L *varius*, diverse⟧ 1 differing one from another; of several kinds 2 several or many 3 individual —**var'i·ously** *adv.*

var·let (vär'lit) *n.* ⟦OFr, a page⟧ [Archaic] a scoundrel; knave

var·mint or **var'ment** (vär'mənt) *n.* ⟦var. of VERMIN⟧ [Colloq. or Dial.] a person or animal regarded as objectionable

var·nish (vär'nish) *n.* ⟦< ML *veronix*, resin⟧ 1 a preparation of resinous substances dissolved in oil, alcohol, etc., used to give a hard, glossy surface to wood, metal, etc. 2 this surface 3 a surface smoothness, as of manner — *vt.* 1 to cover with varnish 2 to make superficially attractive

var·sity (vär'sə tē) *n., pl.* **-ties** ⟦< UNIVERSITY⟧ the main team representing a university, school, etc., as in a sport

vary (ver'ē) *vt.* **var'ied, var'y·ing** ⟦< L *varius*, various⟧ 1 to change; alter 2 to make different from one another 3 to give variety to *[to vary one's reading]* — *vi.* 1 to undergo change 2 to be different 3 to deviate, diverge, or depart *(from)*

vas·cu·lar (vas'kyə lər) *adj.* ⟦< L *vas*, vessel⟧ of or having vessels or ducts for conveying blood, sap, etc.

vase (vās, vāz) *n.* ⟦< L *vas*, vessel⟧ an open container used for decoration, displaying flowers, etc.

vas·ec·tomy (va sek'tə mē, və-) *n., pl.* **-mies** ⟦< L *vas*, vessel + -ECTOMY⟧ the surgical removal or tying of the duct carrying sperm from the testicle

Vas·e·line (vas'ə lēn') ⟦< Ger *was(ser)*, water + Gr *el(aion)*, oil⟧ *trademark for* petrolatum — *n.* [v-] petrolatum

vaso·mo·tor (vas'ō mōt'ər) *adj.* ⟦< L *vas*, vessel + MOTOR⟧ regulating the diameter of blood vessels: said of a nerve, drug, etc.

vas·sal (vas'əl) *n.* ⟦< ML *vassus*, servant⟧ 1 under feudalism, one who held land, owing fealty to an overlord 2 a subordinate, servant, slave, etc. —**vas'sal·age** (-ij) *n.*

vast (vast) *adj.* ⟦L *vastus*⟧ very great in size, extent, number, degree, etc. —**vast'ly** *adv.* —**vast'ness** *n.*

vat (vat) *n.* ⟦< OE *fæt*, cask⟧ a large container for holding liquids

VAT (vē'ā'tē', vat) value-added tax

Vati·can (vat'i kən) 1 the papal palace in Vatican City, an enclave in Rome (Italy) 2 the papal government

vaude·ville (vôd'vil, vô'də-) *n.* ⟦Fr, after *Vau-de-Vire*, a valley in Normandy, famous for convivial songs⟧ a stage show consisting of various acts

vault[1] (vôlt) *n.* ⟦< L *volvere*, to roll⟧ 1 an arched roof or ceiling 2 an arched chamber or space 3 a cellar room used for storage 4 a burial chamber 5 a room for the safekeeping of valuables, as in a bank — *vt.* to cover with, or build as, a vault — *vi.* to curve like a vault

vault[2] (vôlt) *vi., vt.* ⟦< OldIt *voltare*⟧ to jump, leap, etc. over (a barrier), esp. with the hands supported on the barrier or holding a long pole — *n.* a vaulting —**vault'er** *n.*

vault'ing *adj.* 1 leaping 2 unduly confident *[vaulting ambition]*

vaunt (vônt) *vi., n.* ⟦< L *vanus*, vain⟧ boast —**vaunt'ed** *adj.*

VCR (vē'sē'är') *n.* VIDEOCASSETTE RECORDER

VD venereal disease

VDT (vē'dē'tē') *n.* a video display terminal

've have: used in contractions *[we've seen it]*

veal (vēl) *n.* ⟦< L *vitulus*, calf⟧ the flesh of a young calf, used as food

vec·tor (vek'tər) *n.* ⟦< L *vehere*, to carry⟧ an animal that transmits a disease-producing organism

Veda (vā'də, vē'-) *n.* ⟦Sans *veda*, knowledge⟧ any of four ancient sacred books of Hinduism —**Ve'dic** *adj.*

Veep (vēp) *n.* [*also* v-] vice-president

veer (vir) *vi., vt.* ⟦< Fr *virer*, turn around⟧ to change in direction; shift; turn — *n.* a change of direction

veg·eta·ble (vej'ə tə bəl, vej'tə-) *adj.* ⟦see VEGETATE⟧ 1 of plants in general 2 of, from, or like edible vegetables — *n.* 1 any plant, as distinguished from animal or inorganic matter 2 a plant eaten whole or in part, raw or cooked

veg·etar·ian (-ter'ē ən) *n.* one who eats no meat — *adj.* 1 of vegetarians 2 consisting only of vegetables

veg·etate (vej'ə tāt') *vi.* **-tat'ed, -tat'ing** ⟦< L *vegere*, quicken⟧ 1 to grow as plants 2 to lead a dull, inactive life —**veg'eta'tive** *adj.*

veg·eta'tion *n.* 1 a vegetating 2 plant life in general

THESAURUS

variation *n.* 1 [Change] modification, alteration, mutation; see CHANGE 1. 2 [Disparity] inequality, difference, dissimilarity, distinction, disproportion, exception, contrast, irregularity, aberration, abnormality, disparity.—*Ant.* SIMILARITY, conformity, likeness.

varied *a.* discrete, different, diverse; see MIXED 1, VARIOUS.

variety *n.* 1 [Quality or state of being diverse] diversity, change, diversification, difference, variance, medley, mixture, miscellany, disparateness, divergency, variation, incongruity, fluctuation, shift, change, modification, departure, many-sidedness. 2 [Sort] kind, class, division, species, genus, race, tribe, family, assortment, type, stripe, nature, ilk, character, description, rank, grade, category, classification, quality.—*Ant.* EQUALITY, equalness, similarity.

various *a.* different, disparate, dissimilar, diverse, diversified, variegated, varicolored, many-sided, several, manifold, numerous, unlike, many, sundry, variable, changeable, inconstant, uncertain, of any kind, all manner of, of every description, distinct; see also MULTIPLE 1.—*Ant.* ALIKE, undiversified, identical.

variously *a.* varyingly, inconsistently, unpredictably; see DIFFER-ENTLY, UNEVENLY.

varnish *v.* finish, paint, shellac, lacquer, wax, size, enamel, japan, surface, coat, luster, polish, gloss, adorn, refinish, glaze, gloss over.—*Ant.* EXPOSE, remove the finish, strip.

vary *v.* dissent, diverge, differ, deviate, digress, swerve, depart, fluctuate, alternate, diverge from, be distinguished from, range, be inconstant, mutate, be uncertain.—*Ant.* REMAIN, be steady, hold.

varying *a.* diverse, differing, diverging; see CHANGING.

vase *n.* vessel, urn, jar, pottery, porcelain, receptacle, flower holder, ornament.

vast *a.* 1 [Large] huge, enormous, immense; see LARGE 1. 2 [Extensive] broad, far-flung, wide, spacious, expansive, spread-out, ample, far-reaching, widespread, comprehensive, detailed, all-inclusive, astronomical, prolonged, stretched out, expanded.—*Ant.* NARROW, limited, confined.

vastness *n.* hugeness, extent, enormity; see EXPANSE, SIZE 2.

vat *n.* vessel, tub, barrel; see CONTAINER.

vault[1] *n.* 1 [A place for the dead] tomb, crypt, grave; see MONUMENT 1. 2 [A place for preserving valuables] safe-deposit box, time vault, burglar-proof safe; see SAFE.

veal *n.* calf, beef, baby beef; see MEAT. *Cuts of veal include the following:* chops, leg, loin, rack, neck, breast, chuck. *Veal dishes include the following:* breaded veal cutlet, veal stew, calf's liver, Wiener schnitzel, veal Parmigiano, veal scallopini.

veer *v.* swerve, bend, divert; see TURN 1, 2, 3.

vegetable *a.* plantlike, herblike, floral, blooming, blossoming, growing, flourishing.

vegetable *n.* plant, herbaceous plant, herb, edible root. *Common vegetables include the following:* cabbage, potato, turnip, bean, carrot, pea, celery, lettuce, parsnip, spinach, squash, tomato, pumpkin, asparagus, onion, corn, lentil, leek, chicory, kale, garlic, radish, cucumber, artichoke, eggplant, beet, scallion, pepper, okra, kohlrabi, parsley, chard, rhubarb, cauliflower, Brussels sprouts, broccoli, endive, Chinese cabbage, watercress, rutabaga.

vegetate *v.* 1 [To germinate] sprout, bud, blossom; see BLOOM, GROW 1. 2 [To stagnate] hibernate, stagnate, languish; see WEAKEN 1.

vegetation *n.* plants, plant growth, trees, shrubs, saplings, flowers, wildflowers, grasses, herbage, herbs, pasturage, weeds, vegetables, crops.

ve·he·ment (vē′ə mənt) *adj.* [< L *vehere*, carry] 1 violent; impetuous 2 full of intense or strong passion —**ve′he·mence** or **ve′he·mency** *n.* —**ve′he·mently** *adv.*

ve·hi·cle (vē′ə kəl) *n.* [< L *vehere*, to carry] 1 any device for carrying or conveying persons or objects 2 a means of expressing thoughts, etc. —**ve·hic′u·lar** (-hik′yoo lər) *adj.*

veil (vāl) *n.* [< L *velum*, cloth] 1 a piece of light fabric, as of net, worn, esp. by women, over the face or head 2 anything used to conceal, cover, separate, etc. [a *veil* of silence] 3 a part of a nun's headdress — *vt.* 1 to cover with a veil 2 to hide or disguise —**take the veil** to become a nun

veiled (vāld) *adj.* 1 wearing, or covered with, a veil 2 concealed, hidden, etc. 3 not openly expressed

vein (vān) *n.* [< L *vena*] 1 any blood vessel carrying blood to the heart 2 any of the ribs of an insect's wing or of a leaf blade 3 a body of minerals occupying a fissure in rock 4 a lode 5 a streak of a different color, etc., as in marble 6 a distinctive quality in one's character, speech, etc. 7 a mood — *vt.* to mark as with veins

Vel·cro (vel′krō) *trademark for* a nylon material for fastenings, made up of matching strips with tiny hooks and adhesive pile, that are easily pressed together or pulled apart

veld or **veldt** (velt) *n.* [Afrik < MDu *veld*, field] in South Africa, open grassy country, with few bushes or trees

vel·lum (vel′əm) *n.* [< L *vitulus*, calf] 1 a fine parchment prepared from calfskin, lambskin, etc. used for writing on or for binding books 2 a strong paper made to resemble this

ve·loc·i·ty (və läs′ə tē) *n., pl.* -**ties** [< L *velox*, swift] 1 quickness of motion; swiftness 2 rate of motion in a particular direction in relation to time

ve·lour or **ve·lours** (və loor′) *n., pl.* -**lours**′ (-loorz′, -loor′) [Fr < L *villus*, shaggy hair] a fabric with a soft nap like velvet

ve·lum (vē′ləm) *n., pl.* -**la** (-lə) [L, a veil] SOFT PALATE

vel·vet (vel′vət) *n.* [< L *villus*, shaggy hair] 1 a rich fabric of silk, rayon, etc. with a soft, thick pile 2 anything like velvet in texture — *adj.* 1 made of velvet 2 like velvet —**vel′vety** *adj.*

vel′vet·een′ (-və tēn′) *n.* a cotton cloth with a short, thick pile like velvet

ve·nal (vēn′əl) *adj.* [L *venalis*, for sale] open to, or characterized by, bribery or corruption —**ve·nal·i·ty** (vi nal′ə tē) *n.* —**ve′nally** *adv.*

vend (vend) *vt., vi.* [< L *venum dare*, offer for sale] to sell (goods) —**ven′dor** or **vend′er** *n.*

ven·det·ta (ven det′ə) *n.* [It < L *vindicta*, vengeance] a bitter quarrel or feud, as between families

vending machine a coin-operated machine for selling certain small articles

ve·neer (və nir′) *vt.* [< Fr *fournir*, furnish] to cover with a thin layer of more costly material; esp., to cover (wood) with wood of finer quality — *n.* 1 a thin surface layer, as of fine wood, laid over a base of common material 2 superficial appearance [a *veneer* of culture]

ven·er·able (ven′ər ə bəl) *adj.* worthy of respect or reverence because of age, dignity, etc. —**ven′er·abil′i·ty** *n.*

ven·er·ate (ven′ər āt′) *vt.* -**at′ed**, -**at′ing** [< L *venerari*, to worship] to look upon with feelings of deep respect; revere —**ven′er·a′tion** *n.*

ve·ne·re·al (və nir′ē əl) *adj.* [< L *venus*, love] 1 of sexual intercourse 2 transmitted by sexual intercourse [venereal disease]

Ve·ne·tian (və nē′shən) *adj.* of Venice, its people, etc. — *n.* a native or inhabitant of Venice

Venetian blind [also **v- b-**] a window blind of thin, horizontal slats that can be set at any angle

venge·ance (ven′jəns) *n.* [< L *vindicare*, avenge] the return of an injury for an injury, as in retribution; revenge —**with a vengeance** 1 with great force or fury 2 excessively

venge·ful (venj′fəl) *adj.* seeking vengeance; vindictive —**venge′fully** *adv.*

ve·ni·al (vēn′yəl, vē′nē əl) *adj.* [< L *venia*, a grace] that may be forgiven; pardonable [a *venial* sin]

ve·ni·re·man (və nī′rē mən) *n., pl.* -**men** [< ML *venire facias*, cause to come] one of a group of people from among whom a jury will be selected

ven·i·son (ven′i zən, -sən) *n.* [< L *venari*, to hunt] the flesh of a deer, used as food

venom (ven′əm) *n.* [< L *venenum*, a poison] 1 the poison secreted by some snakes, spiders, etc. 2 malice

ven′om·ous *adj.* 1 full of venom; poisonous 2 spiteful; malicious

ve·nous (vēn′əs) *adj.* [L *venosus*] 1 of veins 2 designating blood carried in veins

vent[1] (vent) *n.* [< L *ventus*, wind] 1 expression; release [giving *vent* to emotion] 2 a small opening to permit passage or escape, as of a gas — *vt.* 1 to make a vent in or for 2 to give release to; let out

vent[2] (vent) *n.* [< L *findere*, to split] a vertical slit in a garment

ven·ti·late (vent′'l āt′) *vt.* -**lat′ed**, -**lat′ing** [< L *ventus*, wind] 1 to circulate fresh air in (a room, etc.) 2 to provide with an opening for the escape of air, gas, etc. —**ven′ti·la′tion** *n.*

ven′ti·la′tor *n.* an opening or a device used to bring in fresh air and drive out foul air

ven·tral (ven′trəl) *adj.* [< L *venter*, belly] of, near, or on the belly

ven·tri·cle (ven′tri kəl) *n.* [see prec.] either of the two lower chambers of the heart —**ven·tric′u·lar** (-trik′yə lər) *adj.*

ven·tril·o·quism (ven tril′ə kwiz′əm) *n.* [< L *venter*, belly + *loqui*, speak] the art of speaking so that the voice seems to come from a source other than the speaker —**ven·tril′o·quist** *n.*

ven·ture (ven′chər) *n.* [see ADVENTURE] 1 a risky undertaking, as in business 2 something on which a risk is taken — *vt.* -**tured**, -**tur·ing** 1 to expose to danger or chance of loss 2 to express at the risk of criticism [to *venture* an opinion] — *vi.* to do or go at some risk

ven′ture·some (-səm) *adj.* 1 inclined to venture; daring 2 risky; hazardous Also **ven′tur·ous** (-əs)

venue (ven′yōō′) *n.* [< L *venire*, come] 1 *Law a)* the locality in which a cause of action or a crime occurs *b)* the locality in which a jury is drawn and a case is tried 2 the scene of a large gathering for some event

Ve·nus (vē′nəs) 1 the Roman goddess of love and beauty 2 the brightest planet in the solar system: see PLANET

THESAURUS

vehicle *n. Vehicles include the following:* carriage, buggy, wagon, sleigh, cart, motor car, jeep, rover, automobile, truck, van, motorcycle, taxicab, railroad car, cab, hack, taxi.

veil *n.* 1 [A thin fabric] scarf, kerchief, mask; see WEB. 2 [A curtain] screen, cover, shade; see CURTAIN.

vein *n.* 1 [A fissure] cleft, aperture, opening, channel, cavity, crack, cranny, rift, chink, break, breach, slit, crevice, flaw, rupture. 2 [A persistent quality] strain, humor, mood, temper, tang, spice, dash; see also CHARACTERISTIC, TEMPERAMENT. 3 [A blood duct leading to the heart] *Important veins include the following:* jugular, pulmonary, subclavian, portal, iliac, hepatic, renal.

velocity *n.* quickness, rapidity, impetus; see SPEED.

velvet *a.* silken, shining, plushy; see SOFT 2.

velvet *n.* cotton velvet, rayon, corduroy; see GOODS.

veneer *n.* surface, exterior, covering; see COVER 1.

venerable *a.* revered, old, aged, ancient, hoary, reverenced, honored, honorable, noble, august, grand, esteemed, respected, dignified, imposing, grave, serious, sage, wise, philosophical, experienced.—*Ant.* INEXPERIENCED, callow, raw.

venerate *v.* revere, reverence, adore; see LOVE 1, WORSHIP.

veneration *n.* respect, adoration, awe; see REVERENCE, WORSHIP 1.

vengeance *n.* retribution, return, retaliation; see REVENGE 1.

vengeful *a.* spiteful, revengeful, rancorous; see CRUEL.

venom *n.* poison, virus, toxin, bane, microbe, contagion, infection.

vent[1] *n.* ventilator, vent hole, venting hole, ventiduct, liquid-vent, vent faucet, molding, touchhole, drain, smoke hole, flue, aperture.

vent[1] *v.* let out, drive out, discharge; see FREE.

ventilate *v.* freshen, let in fresh air, circulate fresh air, vent, air cool, air out, free, oxygenate; see also AIR.

ventilated *a.* aired out, having adequate ventilation, not closed up; see AIRED 1, COOL 1, OPEN 1.

ventilation *n.* airing, purifying, oxygenating, freshening, opening windows, changing air, circulating air, air conditioning.

venture *n.* adventure, risk, hazard, peril, stake, chance, speculation, dare, experiment, trial, attempt, test, gamble, undertaking, enterprise, investment, leap in the dark, plunge*, flyer*, crack*, fling*.

venture *v.* attempt, experiment, try out; see TRY 1.

ventured *a.* risked, chanced, dared; see DONE 1.

Venus' fly′trap′ a swamp plant with hinged leaves that snap shut, trapping insects

Ve·nu′sian (vi nōō′shən) *adj.* of the planet Venus — *n.* an imaginary inhabitant of Venus

ve·ra′cious (və rā′shəs) *adj.* 〚< L *verus*, true〛 1 habitually truthful; honest 2 true; accurate

ve·rac′i·ty (-ras′ə tē) *n.* 1 honesty 2 accuracy 3 truth

ve·ran′da or **ve·ran′dah** (və ran′də) *n.* 〚< Port *varanda*, balcony〛 an open porch or portico, usually roofed, along the outside of a building

verb (vʉrb) *n.* 〚L *verbum*, a word〛 a word expressing action, existence, or occurrence

ver′bal (vʉr′bəl) *adj.* 1 of, in, or by means of words 2 in speech; oral 3 of, like, or derived from a verb —**ver′bally** *adv.*

ver′bal·ize′ (-īz′) *vi.* **-ized′, -iz′ing** to use words for communication — *vt.* to express in words —**ver′bali·za′tion** *n.*

verbal noun *Gram.* a noun derived from a verb (Ex.: *swimming* is fun)

ver·ba′tim (vər bāt′əm) *adv., adj.* 〚< L *verbum*, a word〛 word for word

ver·be′na (vər bē′nə) *n.* 〚L, foliage〛 an ornamental plant with spikes or clusters of showy red, white, or purplish flowers

ver·bi·age (vʉr′bē ij′) *n.* 〚Fr < L *verbum*, a word〛 an excess of words; wordiness

ver·bose′ (vər bōs′) *adj.* 〚< L *verbum*, a word〛 using too many words; wordy —**ver·bos′ity** (-bäs′ə tē) *n.*

ver′dant (vʉrd′nt) *adj.* 〚prob. VERD(URE) + -ANT〛 1 green 2 covered with green vegetation

ver·dict (vʉr′dikt) *n.* 〚< L *vere*, truly + *dictum*, a thing said〛 1 the formal finding of a judge or jury 2 any decision or judgment

ver·di·gris (vʉr′di grēs′, -gris) *n.* 〚< OFr *vert de Grece*, lit., green of Greece〛 a greenish coating that forms on brass, bronze, or copper

ver′dure (vʉr′jər) *n.* 〚< OFr *verd*, green〛 1 the fresh-green color of growing things 2 green vegetation

verge¹ (vʉrj) *n.* 〚< L *virga*, rod〛 the edge, brink, or margin (*of* something) — *vi.* **verged, verg′ing** to be on the verge: usually with *on* or *upon*

verge² (vʉrj) *vi.* **verged, verg′ing** 〚L *vergere*, to bend, turn〛 1 to tend or incline (*to* or *toward*) 2 to change or pass gradually (*from*) 〚*dawn verging into daylight*〛

veri·fy (ver′ə fī′) *vt.* **-fied′, -fy′ing** 〚< L *verus*, true + *-ficare*, -FY〛 1 to prove to be true by demonstration, evidence, etc.; confirm 2 to test the accuracy of —**ver′i·fi′able** *adj.* —**ver′i·fi·ca′tion** *n.*

veri·ly (ver′ə lē) *adv.* 〚Archaic〛 in very truth; truly

veri·si·mili·tude (ver′ə si mil′ə tōōd′, -tyōōd′) *n.* 〚< L *verus*, true + *similis*, like〛 the appearance of being true or real

veri·table (ver′i tə bəl) *adj.* 〚see fol.〛 true; actual —**ver′i·tably** *adv.*

ver·ity (ver′ə tē) *n.* 〚< L *verus*, true〛 1 truth; reality 2 *pl.* **-ties** a principle, belief, etc. taken to be fundamentally true; a truth

ver·mi·celli (vʉr′mə sel′ē, -chel′ē) *n.* 〚It < L *vermis*, a worm〛 pasta like spaghetti, but in thinner strings

ver·micu·lite (vər mik′yə lit′) *n.* 〚< L *vermis*, a worm〛 a

hydrous silicate mineral that expands when heated, used as in insulation

ver·mi·form (vʉrm′ə fôrm′) *adj.* 〚< L *vermis*, a worm + -FORM〛 shaped like a worm

vermiform appendix the appendix extending from the cecum of the large intestine

ver·mil·ion (vər mil′yən) *n.* 〚< L *vermis*, a worm〛 1 a bright-red pigment 2 a bright red or scarlet

ver·min (vʉr′mən) *n., pl.* **-min** 〚< L *vermis*, a worm〛 1 [*pl.*] various destructive insects or small animals regarded as pests, as lice or rats 2 a vile person

ver·mouth (vər mōōth′) *n.* 〚< Ger *wermut*, wormwood〛 a white fortified wine flavored with herbs, used in cocktails and as an aperitif

ver·nacu·lar (vər nak′yə lər) *adj.* 〚< L *vernaculus*, indigenous〛 1 of, in, or using the native language of a place 2 native to a country — *n.* 1 the native language or dialect of a country or place 2 the common, everyday language of a people 3 the jargon of a profession or trade

ver·nal (vʉrn′əl) *adj.* 〚< L *ver*, spring〛 1 of or in the spring 2 springlike 3 youthful

ver·sa·tile (vʉr′sə təl) *adj.* 〚< L *vertere*, to turn〛 competent in many things —**ver′sa·til′ity** (-til′ə tē) *n.*

verse (vʉrs) *n.* 〚< L *vertere*, to turn〛 1 a single line of poetry 2 poetry 3 a particular form of poetry 4 a poem 5 a stanza 6 *Bible* any of the short divisions of a chapter

versed (vʉrst) *adj.* 〚< L *versari*, be busy〛 skilled or learned (*in* a subject)

ver′si·fy (vʉr′sə fī′) *vi.* **-fied′, -fy′ing** 〚< L *versus*, a verse + *facere*, make〛 to compose verses — *vt.* 1 to tell about in verse 2 to put into verse form —**ver′si·fi·ca′tion** (-fi kā′shən) *n.* —**ver′si·fi′er** *n.*

ver·sion (vʉr′zhən) *n.* 〚see VERSE〛 1 a translation, esp. of the Bible 2 an account showing one point of view 3 a particular form of something

ver·sus (vʉr′səs) *prep.* 〚ML < L, toward〛 1 against 2 in contrast with

ver·te·bra (vʉr′tə brə) *n., pl.* **-brae** (-brē′, -brā′) or **-bras** 〚L < *vertere*, to turn〛 any of the single bones of the spinal column —**ver′te·bral** *adj.*

ver·te·brate (-brit, -brāt′) *adj.* 1 having a backbone, or spinal column 2 of the vertebrates — *n.* any of a large division of animals having a spinal column, as mammals, birds, etc.

ver·tex (vʉr′teks′) *n., pl.* **-tex′es** or **-ti·ces′** (-tə sēz′) 〚L〛 1 the highest point; top 2 *Geom.* the point of intersection of the two sides of an angle

ver·ti·cal (vʉr′ti kəl) *adj.* 1 of or at the vertex 2 upright, straight up or down, etc. — *n.* a vertical line, plane, etc. — **ver′ti·cally** *adv.*

ver·tigi·nous (vər tij′ə nəs) *adj.* of, having, or causing vertigo

ver·tigo (vʉr′ti gō′) *n., pl.* **-goes′** or **ver·tigi·nes** (vər tij′ə nēz′) 〚L < *vertere*, to turn〛 a sensation of dizziness

verve (vʉrv) *n.* 〚Fr < OFr, manner of speech〛 vigor; energy; enthusiasm

very (ver′ē) *adj.* 〚< L *verus*, true〛 1 complete; absolute 〚the *very* opposite〛 2 same 〚the *very* hat I lost〛 3 being

■ THESAURUS ■

verb *n.* Verbs include the following: finite, active, neuter, passive, transitive, intransitive, modal, auxiliary, linking, reciprocal, copulative, reflexive, strong, weak, regular, irregular.

verbal *a.* told, unwritten, lingual; see ORAL, SPOKEN.

verbally *a.* orally, by word of mouth, person-to-person; see SPOKEN.

verbatim *a.* exactly, *literatim*, to the letter; see LITERALLY.

verdict *n.* judgment, finding, decision, answer, opinion, sentence, determination, decree, conclusion, deduction, adjudication, arbitrament.

verge¹ *n.* edge, brink, terminus; see BOUNDARY.

verge¹ *v.* end, edge, touch; see APPROACH 2.

verification *n.* verifying, attestation, affirmation; see CONFIRMATION 1.

verify *v.* establish, substantiate, authenticate, prove, check, test, validate, settle, corroborate, confirm.

vermin *n.* flea, louse, mite; see INSECT.

versatile *a.* many-sided, adaptable, dexterous, varied, ready, clever, handy, talented, gifted, adroit, resourceful, ingenious, accomplished; see also ABLE.

versatility *a.* flexibility, utility, adjustability; see ADAPTABILITY.

verse *n.* 1 [Composition in poetic form] poetry, metrical composition, versification, stanza, rhyme, lyric, sonnet, ode, heroic verse, dramatic poetry, blank verse, free verse. 2 [A unit of verse] line, verse, stanza, stave, strophe, antistrophe, hemistich, distich, quatrain.

version *n.* 1 [One of various accounts] report, account, tale; see STORY. 2 [A translation] paraphrase, redaction, transcription; see TRANSLATION.

vertebrae *n.* spine, spinal column, backbone, chine. *Parts of the vertebra include the following:* atlas, axis, cervical, thoracic, lumbar, caudal,

disk, spinous process, neural arch, anterior and posterior zygapophysis, transverse process.

vertical *a.* perpendicular, upright, on end; see STRAIGHT 1.

very *a.* extremely, exceedingly, greatly, acutely, indispensably, just so, surprisingly, astonishingly, incredibly, wonderfully, particularly, certainly, positively, emphatically, really, truly, pretty, decidedly, pressingly, notably, uncommonly, extraordinarily, prodigiously, highly, substantially, dearly, amply, vastly, extensively, noticeably, conspicuously, largely, considerably, hugely, excessively, imperatively, markedly, enormously, sizably, materially, immensely, tremendously, superlatively, remarkably, unusually, immoderately, quite, indeed, somewhat, rather, simply, intensely, urgently, exceptionally, severely, seriously, in a great measure, to a great degree, beyond compare, on a large scale, ever so, beyond measure, just what is needed **4** actual [caught in the *very* act]: often an intensive [the *very* rafters shook] —*adv.* **1** extremely **2** truly; really [the *very* same man]

very high frequency any radio frequency between 30 and 300 megahertz

very low frequency any radio frequency between 10 and 30 kilohertz

ve·si·cle (ves′i kəl) *n.* [< L *vesica*, bladder] a small, membranous cavity, sac, or cyst —**ve·sic·u·lar** (və sik′yə lər) or **ve·sic′u·late** (-lit) *adj.*

ves·pers (ves′pərz) *n.* [L, evening] [*usually with sing v.*] an evening prayer or service Also **Vespers**

ves·sel (ves′əl) *n.* [< L *vas*] **1** a utensil for holding something, as a bowl, kettle, etc. **2** a boat or ship **3** a tube or duct of the body, as a vein, containing or circulating a fluid

vest (vest) *n.* [< L *vestis*, garment] a short, sleeveless garment, esp. one worn under a suit coat by men —*vt.* **1** to dress, as in clerical robes **2** to place (authority, etc.) in someone **3** to put (a person) in control of, as power, etc. —*vi.* to pass to a person; become vested (*in* a person), as property

ves·tal (ves′təl) *adj.* [< L *Vesta*, goddess of the hearth] chaste; pure —*n.* a virgin priestess of the Roman goddess Vesta: in full **vestal virgin**

vested (ves′tid) *adj.* [pp. of VEST] **1** clothed, esp. in vestments **2** *Law* fixed; settled; absolute [a *vested* right]

vested interest 1 an established right, as to some future benefit **2** [*pl.*] a number of groups cooperating or competing in pursuing selfish goals and exerting controlling influence

ves·ti·bule (ves′tə byōōl′) *n.* [L *vestibulum*] a small entrance hall, as to a building

ves·tige (ves′tij) *n.* [< L *vestigium*, footprint] **1** a trace, mark, or sign, esp. of something that has passed away **2** *Biol.* a degenerate part, more fully developed in an earlier stage —**ves·tig′ial** (-tij′ē əl, -tij′əl) *adj.*

vest′ing *n.* the retention by an employee of all or part of pension rights regardless of change of employers, early retirement, etc.

vest·ment (vest′mənt) *n.* [< L *vestire*, clothe] a garment or robe, esp. one worn by a clergyman

vest′-pock′et *adj.* very small, or unusually small for its kind

ves·try (ves′trē) *n., pl.* **-tries** [< L *vestis*, garment] **1** a room in a church where vestments, etc. are kept **2** a room in a church, used as a chapel **3** a group of church members managing the temporal affairs of the church

vet *abbrev.* **1** veteran **2** veterinarian **3** veterinary

vetch (vech) *n.* [< L *vicia*] a leafy, climbing or trailing plant of the pea family, grown for fodder

vet·eran (vet′ər ən) *adj.* [< L *vetus*, old] **1** old and experienced **2** of veterans —*n.* **1** one who has served in the armed forces **2** one who has served long in some position

Veterans Day a legal holiday in the U.S. honoring all veterans of the armed forces: observed on ARMISTICE DAY

vet·er·i·nar·ian (vet′ər ə ner′ē ən) *n.* one who practices veterinary medicine or surgery

vet·er·i·nar′y (-ē) *adj.* [< L *veterina*, beasts of burden] designating of or the branch of medicine dealing with animals —*n., pl.* **-ies** VETERINARIAN

veto (vē′tō) *n., pl.* **-toes** [L, I forbid] **1** *a)* an order prohibiting some act *b)* the power to prohibit action **2** *a)* the power of one branch of government to reject bills passed by another *b)* the exercise of this power —*vt.*

-toed, -to·ing 1 to prevent (a bill) from becoming law by a veto **2** to forbid

vex (veks) *vt.* [< L *vexare*, agitate] **1** to disturb; annoy, esp. in a petty way **2** to distress; afflict

vexa·tion (veks ā′shən) *n.* **1** a vexing or being vexed **2** something that vexes —**vexa′tious** (-shəs) *adj.*

VHF or **vhf** very high frequency

VHS (vē′āch′es′) [*v(ideo) h(ome) s(ystem)*] *trademark for* an electronic system for recording video and audio information on videocassettes

vi. or **v.i.** intransitive verb

via (vī′ə, vē′ə) *prep.* [L, way] by way of

vi·able (vī′ə bəl) *adj.* [< L *vita*, life] **1** sufficiently developed to be able to live outside the uterus **2** workable [*viable* ideas] —**vi′abil′ity** *n.*

via·duct (vī′ə dukt′) *n.* [< VIA + (AQUE)DUCT] a bridge consisting of a series of short spans, supported on piers or towers

vial (vī′əl) *n.* [< OFr *fiole*] a small bottle for liquids

vi·and (vī′ənd) *n.* [< L *vivere*, to live] an article of food

vibes (vībz) *n.pl.* **1** [Colloq.] VIBRAPHONE **2** [Slang] qualities, as in a person, thought of as being like vibrations which produce an emotional reaction

vi·brant (vī′brənt) *adj.* **1** quivering or vibrating **2** produced by vibration: said of sound **3** vigorous, vivacious, etc. —**vi′brancy** *n.* —**vi′brantly** *adv.*

vi·bra·phone (vī′brə fōn′) *n.* a musical instrument like the marimba, with electrically operated resonators —**vi′bra·phon′ist** *n.*

vi·brate (vī′brāt′) *vt.* **-brat′ed, -brat′ing** [< L *vibrare*] to set in to-and-fro motion —*vi.* **1** to swing back and forth; oscillate **2** to move rapidly back and forth; quiver **3** to resound **4** to be emotionally stirred —**vi·bra′tion** *n.* —**vi′bra′tor** *n.*

vi·bra·to (vi brät′ō) *n., pl.* **-tos** [It] a pulsating effect produced by rapid alternation of a given tone with a barely perceptible variation in pitch

vi·bur·num (vī bur′nəm) *n.* [L, wayfaring tree] a plant of the honeysuckle family, with white flowers

vicar (vik′ər) *n.* [< L *vicis*, a change] **1** *Anglican Ch.* a parish priest receiving a stipend instead of the tithes **2** *R.C.Ch.* a church officer acting as a deputy of a bishop —**vic′ar·age** *n.*

vi·car·i·ous (vī ker′ē əs) *adj.* [< L *vicis*, a change] **1** taking the place of another **2** endured or performed by one person in place of another **3** shared in by imagined participation in another's experience [a *vicarious* thrill] —**vi·car′i·ously** *adv.*

vice¹ (vīs) *n.* [< L *vitium*] **1** *a)* an evil action or habit *b)* evil conduct *c)* prostitution **2** a trivial fault or failing

vice² (vīs) *prep.* [L < *vicis*, a change] in the place of

vice- [see prec.] *prefix* a subordinate; deputy [*vice-president*]

vice·ge·rent (vīs′jir′ənt) *n.* [< VICE- + L *gerere*, to direct] a deputy

vice′-pres′ident *n.* an officer next in rank below a president, acting during the president's absence or incapacity: for the U.S. official, usually **Vice President** —**vice′-pres′idency** *n.*

vice·roy (vīs′roi′) *n.* [MFr < *vice-* (see VICE-) + *roy*, king] a person ruling a region as the deputy of a sovereign

vice versa (vī′sə vur′sə, vīs′ vur′-) [L] the relation being reversed

vi·chys·soise (vē′shē swäz′, vish′ē-) *n.* a thick soup of potatoes, leeks, and cream, usually served cold

vi·cin·ity (və sin′ə tē) *n., pl.* **-ties** [< L *vicus*, village] **1** nearness; proximity **2** the surrounding area

---

THESAURUS

by far, in the extreme, in a marked degree, to a great extent, without restraint, more or less, in part, infinitely, very much, real*, right, pretty, awfully*, good and*, powerful*, powerfully*, hell of a*, precious*, so*, to a fault, a bit of, no end*.

vessel *n.* **1** [A container] pitcher, urn, kettle; see CONTAINER. **2** [A ship] boat, craft, bark; see SHIP. **3** [A duct; *especially for blood*] blood vessel, artery, capillary; see VEIN 2.

vest *n.* waistcoat, jacket, garment; see CLOTHES.

vestige *n.* trace, remains, scrap; see REMAINDER.

veteran *n.* **1** [An experienced person] master, one long in service, old hand, one of the old guard, old bird*,

old dog*, old timer*.—*Ant.* AMATEUR, new man, youngster. **2** [An experienced soldier] ex-soldier, seasoned campaigner, ex-service man, re-enlisted man, old soldier, war horse*, ex-G.I.*, vet.

veterinarian *n.* animal specialist, vet, animal doctor; see DOCTOR.

veto *n.* prohibition, declination, negative; see DENIAL, REFUSAL.

veto *v.* interdict, prohibit, decline; see DENY, REFUSE.

vetoed *a.* declined, rejected, disapproved; see NO, REFUSED.

via *prep.* by way of, by the route passing through, on the way to, through the medium of; see also BY 2, THROUGH 4.

vibrant *a.* energetic, vigorous, lively; see ACTIVE.

vibrate *v.* **1** [To quiver] fluctuate, flutter, waver; see WAVE 3. **2** [To sound] echo, resound, reverberate; see SOUND.

vibration *n.* quake, wavering, vacillation, fluctuation, oscillation, quiver, shake; see also WAVE 3.

vice¹ *n.* corruption, iniquity, wickedness; see EVIL 1.

vice versa *a.* conversely, in reverse, the other way round, turn about, about face, in opposite manner, far from it, on the contrary, in reverse.

vicinity *n.* proximity, nearness, neighborhood; see ENVIRONMENT,

vi·cious (vish'əs) *adj.* 〚< L *vitium*, vice〛 **1** characterized by vice; evil or depraved **2** faulty; flawed **3** unruly *[a vicious horse]* **4** malicious; spiteful *[a vicious rumor]* **5** very intense, forceful, etc. *[a vicious blow]* —**vi'ciously** *adv.* —**vi'cious·ness** *n.*
vicious circle a situation in which the solution of one problem gives rise to another, eventually bringing back the first problem Also **vicious cycle**
vi·cis·si·tudes (vi sis'ə tōōdz') *n.pl.* 〚< L *vicis*, a turn〛 unpredictable changes in life; ups and downs
vic·tim (vik'təm) *n.* 〚L *victima*〛 **1** someone or something killed, destroyed, sacrificed, etc. **2** one who suffers some loss, esp. by being swindled
vic'tim·ize' (-īz') *vt.* **-ized', -iz'ing** to make a victim of — **vic'tim·i·za'tion** *n.*
vic·tor (vik'tər) *n.* 〚< L *vincere*, conquer〛 the winner in a battle, struggle, etc.
Vic·to·ri·an (vik tô'rē ən) *adj.* **1** of or characteristic of the period of the reign of Queen Victoria (1837-1901) **2** showing the respectability, prudery, etc. attributed to the Victorians — *n.* a person of that time —**Vic·to'ri·an·ism'** *n.*
vic·to·ri·ous (vik tôr'ē əs) *adj.* **1** having won a victory; triumphant **2** of or bringing about victory
vic·to·ry (vik'tər ē, -trē) *n.*, *pl.* **-ries** 〚< L *vincere*, conquer〛 the winning of a battle, war, or any struggle
vict·uals (vit''lz) *n.pl.* 〚< L *victus*, food〛 [Dial. or Colloq.] articles of food
vi·cuña (vi kyōōn'ə, -kōōn'yə) *n.* 〚Sp〛 **1** a small llama of South America with soft, shaggy wool **2** this wool
vide (vi'dē) *v.* 〚L〛 see; refer to (a certain page, etc.)
video (vid'ē ō') *adj.* 〚L, I see〛 **1** of television **2** of the picture portion of a telecast **3** of data display on a computer terminal — *n.* **1** TELEVISION **2** *short for* VIDEOCASSETTE, VIDEOTAPE, etc.
vid'eo·cas·sette' *n.* a cassette containing videotape
videocassette recorder a device for recording on and playing back videocassettes Also **video recorder**
vid'eo·disc' (-disk') *n.* a disc on which images and sounds can be recorded for reproduction on a TV set
video game any of various games involving images, controlled by players, on a TV screen
vid'eo·tape' *n.* a magnetic tape on which images and sounds can be recorded for reproduction on TV — *vt.* **-taped', -tap'ing** to record on videotape
vie (vi) *vi.* **vied, vy'ing** 〚< L *invitare*, invite〛 to struggle for superiority (*with* someone); compete
view (vyōō) *n.* 〚< L *videre*, to see〛 **1** a seeing or looking, as in inspection **2** range of vision **3** mental survey *[a correct view of a situation]* **4** a scene or prospect *[a room with a view]* **5** manner of regarding something; opinion — *vt.* **1** to inspect; scrutinize **2** to see; behold **3** to survey mentally; consider —**in view 1** in sight **2** under consideration **3** as a goal or hope —**in view of** because of —**on view** displayed publicly —**with a view to** with the purpose or hope of

view'er *n.* **1** one who views something **2** an optical device for individual viewing of slides
view'find'er *n.* a camera device for viewing what will appear in the photograph
view'point' *n.* the mental position from which things are viewed and judged; point of view
vigil (vij'əl) *n.* 〚< L, awake〛 **1** *a*) a watchful staying awake *b*) a watch kept **2** the eve of a church festival
vigi·lant (vij'ə lənt) *adj.* 〚< L *vigil*, awake〛 staying watchful and alert to danger or trouble —**vig'i·lance** *n.*
vigi·lante (vij'ə lan'tē) *n.* 〚Sp, watchman〛 one of an unauthorized group organized professedly to keep order and punish crime —**vig'i·lan'tism'** *n.* —**vig'i·lan'tist** *adj.*
vi·gnette (vin yet') *n.* 〚Fr < *vigne*, vine〛 **1** an ornamental design used on a page of a book, magazine, etc. **2** a picture shading off gradually at the edges **3** a short, delicate literary sketch, scene in a film, etc. —**vi·gnet'tist** *n.*
vigor (vig'ər) *n.* 〚< L *vigere*, be strong〛 active force or strength; vitality; energy Brit., etc. sp. **vig'our** —**vig'or·ous** *adj.* —**vig'or·ously** *adv.*
vik·ing (vi'kiŋ) *n.* 〚ON *vikingr*〛 [also **V-**] any of the Scandinavian pirates of the 8th to the 10th c.
vile (vil) *adj.* 〚< L *vilis*, cheap, base〛 **1** morally evil; wicked **2** repulsive; disgusting **3** degrading; mean **4** highly disagreeable *[vile weather]* —**vile'ness** *n.*
vili·fy (vil'ə fi') *vt.* **-fied', -fy'ing** 〚see prec. & -FY〛 to use abusive language about or of —**vil'i·fi·ca'tion** *n.*
villa (vil'ə) *n.* 〚It < L, a farm〛 a country house or estate, esp. a large one used as a retreat
vil·lage (vil'ij) *n.* 〚see prec.〛 **1** a community smaller than a town **2** the people of a village, collectively —**vil'lager** *n.*
vil·lain (vil'ən) *n.* 〚< VL *villanus*, a farm servant〛 a wicked or evil person, or such a character in a play, etc. — **vil'lain·ous** *adj.*
vil'lainy (-ē) *n., pl.* **-ies'** **1** wickedness; evil **2** a villainous act
vil·lein (vil'ən) *n.* 〚see VILLAIN〛 a feudal serf who had become a freeman, except in relation to his lord
vim (vim) *n.* 〚prob. echoic〛 vigor
vin (van; Anglicized vin) *n.* 〚Fr〛 wine
vin·ai·grette (vin'ə gret') *n.* 〚Fr < *vinaigre*, vinegar〛 a dressing, as for salads, of vinegar, oil, herbs, etc.
vin·di·cate (vin'də kāt') *vt.* **-cat'ed, -cat'ing** 〚< L *vis*, force + *dicere*, say〛 **1** to clear from criticism, blame, etc. **2** to defend against opposition **3** to justify —**vin'di·ca'tion** *n.* —**vin'di·ca'tor** *n.*
vin·dic·tive (vin dik'tiv) *adj.* 〚see prec.〛 **1** revengeful in spirit **2** said or done in revenge —**vin·dic'tively** *adv.* —**vin·dic'tive·ness** *n.*
vine (vin) *n.* 〚< L *vinum*, wine〛 **1** *a*) a plant with a long, thin stem that grows along the ground or climbs a support *b*) the stem of such a plant **2** a grapevine

---

THESAURUS

REGION 1.
vicious *a.* bad, debased, base, impious, profligate, demoralized, faulty, vile, foul, impure, lewd, indecent, licentious, libidinous; see also BAD 1.—*Ant.* PURE, noble, virtuous.
vicious circle *n.* chain of events, cause and effect, interreliant problems; see DIFFICULTY 1, 2.
viciously *a.* cruelly, spitefully, harmfully; see BRUTALLY, WRONGLY.
victim *n.* prey, sacrifice, immolation, sufferer, wretch, quarry, game, hunted, offering, scapegoat, martyr.
victimize *v.* cheat, swindle, dupe, trick, fool; see also DECEIVE.
victor *n.* conqueror, champion, prize winner; see WINNER.
victorious *a.* winning, triumphant, mastering; see SUCCESSFUL.
victory *n.* conquest, mastery, subjugation, overcoming, overthrow, master stroke, lucky stroke, winning, gaining, defeating, subduing, destruction, killing, knockout, pushover.
vie *v.* contend, strive, rival; see COMPETE.
view *n.* glimpse, look, panorama, aspect, show, appearance, prospect, distance, opening, stretch, outlook, way, extended view, long view,

avenue, contour, outline, scene, spectacle. —**in view** visible, in sight, not out of sight, perceptible, perceivable; see also OBVIOUS 1. —**in view of** in consideration of, because, taking into consideration; see CONSIDERING. —**on view** displayed, on display, exposed; see SHOWN 1. —**with a view to** in order to, so that, anticipating; see TO 4.
view *v.* observe, survey, inspect; see SEE 1.
viewer *n.* spectator, watcher, onlooker; see OBSERVER.
viewpoint *n.* point of view, perspective, standpoint, angle, slant, position, stand, aspect, light, respect, attitude, ground, point of observation, outlook.
vigor *n.* **1** [Activity] exercise, action, energy; see VITALITY. **2** [Health] well-being, endurance, vitality; see HEALTH.
vigorous *a.* **1** [Done with vigor] energetic, lively, brisk; see ACTIVE. **2** [Forceful] powerful, strong, potent; see EFFECTIVE.
vigorously *a.* energetically, alertly, eagerly, quickly, nimbly, agilely, strenuously, resolutely, firmly, forcibly, forcefully, urgently, unfalter-

ingly, purposefully, actively, boldly, adventurously, zealously, lustily, robustly, stoutly, hardily, wholeheartedly, earnestly, warmly, fervidly, passionately, sincerely, devoutly, appreciatively, with heart and soul, healthily, fearlessly, mightily, decidedly, by brute force, like blazes*; see also POWERFULLY.— *Ant.* CALMLY, aimlessly, slowly.
vile *a.* sordid, corrupt, debased; see SHAMEFUL 1, 2.
village *n.* hamlet, crossroads town, small town; see TOWN 1.
villain *n.* scoundrel, knave, brute; see CRIMINAL.
vindicate *v.* **1** [To clear] acquit, free, absolve; see EXCUSE. **2** [To justify] prove, bear out, warrant; see PROVE.
vindication *n.* defense, acquittal, clearance; see PROOF 1.
vindictive *a.* revengeful, resentful, spiteful; see CRUEL.
vine *n.* creeper, climbing plant, creeping plant, trailing plant, stem climber, leaf climber, tendril climber; see also PLANT. *Vines include the following:* grapevine, honeysuckle, trumpet vine, English ivy, Virginia

vin·egar (vin′ə gər) *n.* 〖< MFr *vin*, wine + *aigre*, sour 〗 a sour liquid made by fermenting cider, wine, etc. and used as a condiment and preservative —**vin′egary** *adj.*

vine·yard (vin′yərd) *n.* land devoted to cultivating grape-vines

vino (vē′nō) *n.* 〖It & Sp 〗 wine

vin rosé (rō zā′) 〖Fr 〗 ROSÉ

vin·tage (vin′tij) *n.* 〖< L *vinum*, wine + *demere*, remove 〗 1 the grape crop of a single season 2 the wine of a particular region and year 3 the model of a particular period *[a car of prewar vintage]* — *adj.* 1 of a particular vintage: said of wine 2 representative of the best *[vintage Hemingway]* 3 of a past period *[vintage clothes]*

vint·ner (vint′nər) *n.* 〖< ME < L *vinum*, wine 〗 1 a wine merchant 2 one who makes wine

vi·nyl (vī′nəl) *n.* 〖< L *vinum*, wine 〗 any of various compounds polymerized to form resins and plastics (**vinyl plastics**)

viol (vī′əl) *n.* 〖< VL *vitula*, a fiddle 〗 any of an early family of stringed instruments, usually having six strings, frets, and a flat back

vi·o·la (vē ō′lə, vī-) *n.* 〖It 〗 a stringed instrument of the violin family, slightly larger than a violin

vio·la·ble (vī′ə lə bəl) *adj.* that can be, or is likely to be, violated

vio·late (vī′ə lāt′) *vt.* **-lat′ed**, **-lat′ing** 〖< L *violare*, use violence 〗 1 to fail to obey or keep (a law, promise, etc.) 2 to rape 3 to desecrate (something sacred) 4 to break in upon; disturb —**vi′o·la′tor** *n.*

vi′o·la′tion (-lā′shən) *n.* a violating or being violated; specif., *a)* infringement, as of a law *b)* rape *c)* desecration of something sacred *d)* disturbance

vi′o·lence (-ləns) *n.* 〖< L *violentus*, violent 〗 1 physical force used so as to injure 2 powerful force, as of a hurricane 3 harm done by violating rights, etc. 4 a violent act or deed

vi′o·lent *adj.* 1 acting with or having great physical force 2 caused by violence 3 furious *[violent language]* 4 extreme; intense; very strong *[a violent storm]* —**vi′o·lently** *adv.*

vio·let (vī′ə lit) *n.* 〖< L *viola* 〗 1 a plant with white, blue, purple, or yellow flowers 2 a bluish-purple color — *adj.* bluish-purple

vio·lin (vī′ə lin′) *n.* 〖< VIOLA 〗 any of the modern family of four-stringed musical instruments played with a bow; specif., the smallest and highest-pitched one of this family —**vi′o·lin′ist** *n.*

vi·ol·ist (vī′əl ist; *for 2* vē ō′list) *n.* 1 a viol player 2 a viola player

---

vio·lon·cello (vē′ə län chel′ō, vī′ə lən-) *n., pl.* **-los** CELLO

VIP (vē′ī pē′) *n.* 〖*v(ery) i(mportant) p(erson)* 〗 a high-ranking official or important guest

vi·per (vī′pər) *n.* 〖OFr < L *vipera* 〗 1 a venomous snake 2 a malicious or treacherous person —**vi′per·ous** *adj.*

vi·rago (vi rā′gō) *n., pl.* **-goes** or **-gos** 〖< L *vir*, a man 〗 a quarrelsome, shrewish woman; scold

vi·ral (vī′rəl) *adj.* of, involving, or caused by a virus

vireo (vir′ē ō′) *n., pl.* **-os′** 〖L, a type of finch 〗 a small American songbird, with olive-green or gray feathers

vir·gin (vur′jən) *n.* 〖< L *virgo*, a maiden 〗 one, esp. a young woman, who has never had sexual intercourse — *adj.* 1 being a virgin 2 chaste; modest 3 untouched, unused, pure, etc. —**the Virgin** Mary, the mother of Jesus

vir′ginal *adj.* VIRGIN

Vir·ginia creeper (vər jin′yə) WOODBINE (sense 2)

Virginia reel an American variety of reel danced by couples in two parallel rows

vir·gin·ity (vər jin′ə tē) *n.* a virgin state; chastity, etc.

Virgo (vur′gō′) 〖L, virgin 〗 the sixth sign of the zodiac

vir·gule (vur′gyōōl′) *n.* 〖< L *virgula*, small rod 〗 a diagonal line (/) used in dates or fractions (3/8) and also standing for "or" (and/or), "per" (feet/second), etc.

vir·ile (vir′əl) *adj.* 〖< L *vir*, a man 〗 1 of or characteristic of a man; masculine 2 having manly strength or vigor 3 capable of copulation; sexually potent —**vi·ril·ity** (və ril′ə tē) *n.*

vi·rol·ogy (vī räl′ə jē) *n.* 〖< VIR(US) + -o- + -LOGY 〗 the study of viruses and virus diseases —**vi·rol′o·gist** *n.*

vir·tual (vur′chōō əl) *adj.* being so in effect, although not in actual fact or name —**vir′tu·ally** *adv.*

virtual reality the computer simulation, as on a video screen, of three-dimensional images, with which one may interact in a seemingly physical way by means of special electronic devices

vir·tue (vur′chōō) *n.* 〖< L *virtus*, worth 〗 1 general moral excellence 2 a specific moral quality regarded as good 3 chastity 4 *a)* excellence in general *b)* a good quality 5 efficacy, as of a medicine —**by** (or **in**) **virtue of** because of

vir·tu·o·so (vur′chōō ō′sō) *n., pl.* **-sos** or **-si** (-sē) 〖It, skilled 〗 one with great technical skill in some fine art, esp. in playing music —**vir′tu·os′ity** (-äs′ə tē) *n.*

vir·tu·ous (vur′chōō əs) *adj.* 1 having, or characterized by, moral virtue 2 chaste: said of a woman —**vir′tu·ously** *adv.* —**vir′tu·ous·ness** *n.*

viru·lent (vir′yōō lənt, -oo-) *adj.* [see fol.] 1 *a)* extremely poisonous; deadly *b)* bitterly antagonistic; full of hate 2 *Med. a)* violent and rapid in its course (said of a disease) *b)* highly infectious —**vir′u·lence** *n.*

▆▆▆ THESAURUS ▆▆▆

creeper, poison ivy, blackberry, raspberry, briar, rambler, teaberry, dewberry, morning-glory, hopvine, bougainvillea, jasmine, pea vine, watermelon, cantaloupe, cucumber, wild cucumber, passion flower.

violate *v.* 1 [To transgress] outrage, disrupt, infringe, break, tamper with; see also MEDDLE 1. 2 [To rape] dishonor, profane, defile, ravish.

violation *n.* infringement, negligence, misbehavior, nonobservance, violating, shattering, transgressing, forcible trespass, trespassing, contravention, breach, breaking, rupture, flouting; see also CRIME.

violence *n.* 1 [Violent disturbance] rampage, tumult, disorder, clash, onslaught, struggle; see also CONFUSION, DISTURBANCE 2, UPROAR. 2 [Violent conduct] fury, force, vehemence, frenzy, savagery; see also INTENSITY.

violent *a.* strong, powerful, forceful, forcible, rough, mighty, great, potent, coercive, furious, mad, savage, fierce, passionate, splitting, vehement, frenzied, demoniac, frantic, fuming, enraged, disturbed, agitated, impassioned, impetuous, urgent, maddened, aroused, inflamed, distraught, infatuated, hysterical, great, vehement, extreme, unusual, destructible, murderous, homicidal, rampageous.—*Ant.* CALM, GENTLE, QUIET.

violently *a.* destructively, forcibly, forcefully, combatively, powerfully, strongly, coercively, flagrantly, outrageously, overwhelmingly, compellingly, disturbingly, turbulently, stormily, ruinously, stubbornly, with violence, in a violent manner, abruptly, noisily, with a vengeance, like fury, rebelliously, riotously, furiously, angrily, vehemently, fiercely, frantically, hilariously, hysterically, passionately, urgently, madly, frenziedly, ardently, enthusiastically, impulsively.—*Ant.* MILDLY, gently, undisturbedly.

violet *a.* lavender, mauve, purplish; see PURPLE.

violin *n.* fiddle, viola, Stradivarius; see MUSICAL INSTRUMENT.

VIP* *n.* very important person, notable, important figure; see LEADER 2.

virgin *a.* 1 [Chaste] pure, modest, virginal; see CHASTE. 2 [Original or natural] undisturbed, new, untamed; see NATURAL 3, ORIGINAL 1, 3.

Virgin *n.* Madonna, Blessed Virgin Mary, Queen of Saints, Our Lady, Mother of God, Mary, the Queen of Heaven, Queen of Angels, Star of the Sea, The Virgin Mother, Immaculate Conception, Immaculate Mary; see also SAINT.

virginity *n.* maidenhood, girlhood, celibacy; see VIRTUE 1.

virile *a.* masculine, potent, manlike; see MALE, MANLY.

virility *n.* potency, masculinity, manliness; see MANHOOD 2.

virtually *a.* for all practical purposes, practically, implicitly; see ESSENTIALLY.

virtue *n.* 1 [Moral excellence] ideal, ethic, morality, goodness, righteousness, uprightness, ethical conduct, good thing, respectability, rectitude, honor, honesty, candor, merit, fineness, character, excellence, value, chastity, quality, worth, kindness, innocence, generosity, trustworthiness, faithfulness, consideration, justice, prudence, temperance, fortitude, faith, hope, charity, love.—*Ant.* EVIL, immorality, depravity. 2 [An individual excellence] quality, characteristic, attribute, temper, way, trait, feature, accomplishment, achievement, property, distinction, capacity, power.—*Ant.* LACK, inability, incapacity. 3 [Probity in sexual conduct] virginity, purity, decency; see CHASTITY. —**by virtue of** on the grounds of, because of, looking toward; see BECAUSE.

virtuous *a.* good, upright, moral; see HONEST 1, WORTHY.

vi·rus (vī′rəs) *n.* [L, a poison] 1 any of a large group of tiny infective agents causing various diseases 2 any harmful influence

visa (vē′zə, -sə) *n.* [< L *videre*, see] an endorsement on a passport, granting entry into a country

vis·age (viz′ij) *n.* [see prec.] 1 the face; countenance 2 aspect; look

vis-à-vis (vē′zə vē′) *adj., adv.* [Fr] face to face; opposite — *prep.* 1 opposite to 2 in relation to

vis·cera (vis′ər ə) *n.pl., sing.* **vis′cus** (-kəs) [L] the internal organs of the body, as the heart, lungs, intestines, etc.

vis′cer·al *adj.* 1 of the viscera 2 intuitive, emotional, etc. rather than intellectual [a *visceral* reaction]

vis·cid (vis′id) *adj.* [< LL *viscidus*, sticky] thick, syrupy, and sticky

vis·cose (vis′kōs′) *n.* [see VISCID] a syruplike solution of cellulose, used in making rayon and cellophane

vis·cos·i·ty (vis käs′ə tē) *n., pl.* **-ties** 1 a viscous quality 2 *Physics* the resistance of a fluid to flowing freely, caused by friction of its molecules

vis·count (vī′kount′) *n.* [see VICE- & COUNT²] a nobleman next below an earl or count and above a baron — **vis′count′ess** *n.fem.*

vis·cous (vis′kəs) *adj.* [see VISCID] 1 thick, sticky, etc.; viscid 2 *Physics* having viscosity

vise (vīs) *n.* [< L *vitis*, vine, lit., that which winds] a device having two jaws closed by a screw, used for holding firmly an object being worked on

Vishnu (vish′nōō) the second member of the Hindu trinity (Brahma, Vishnu, and Siva), called the "Preserver"

vis·i·bil·i·ty (viz′ə bil′ə tē) *n., pl.* **-ties** 1 a being visible 2 *a)* the relative possibility of being seen under the prevailing conditions of distance, light, etc. *b)* range of vision

vis·i·ble (viz′ə bəl) *adj.* [< L *videre*, to see] 1 that can be seen 2 apparent — **vis′i·bly** *adv.*

vi·sion (vizh′ən) *n.* [see prec.] 1 the power of seeing 2 something supposedly seen in a dream, trance, etc. 3 a mental image 4 the ability to perceive or foresee something, as through mental acuteness 5 something or someone of great beauty

vi′sion·ar′y (-er′ē) *adj.* 1 seen in a vision 2 not realistic; impractical [a *visionary* scheme] — *n., pl.* **-ies** 1 one who sees visions 2 one whose ideas, etc. are impractical

visit (viz′it) *vt.* [< L *videre*, to see] 1 to go or come to see 2 to stay with as a guest 3 to afflict or trouble — *vi.* 1 to make a visit, as, *a)* a social call *b)* a stay as a guest

vis′it·ant (-ənt) *n.* a visitor

vis·i·ta·tion (viz′ə tā′shən) *n.* 1 an official visit, as to inspect 2 a reward or punishment, as sent by God 3 the legal right to visit one's children, as after divorce 4 the visiting of a family in mourning

vis′i·tor *n.* a person making a visit

vi·sor (vī′zər) *n.* [< OFr *vis*, a face] 1 the movable part of a helmet, covering the face 2 a projecting brim, as of a cap, for shading the eyes

vista (vis′tə) *n.* [< L *videre*, to see] 1 a view, esp. one seen through a long passage 2 a mental view of events

vis·ual (vizh′ōō əl) *adj.* [< L *videre*, to see] 1 of or used in seeing 2 based on the use of sight 3 that can see; visible

vis′u·al·ize′ *vt., vi.* **-ized′, -iz′ing** to form a mental image of (something not present to the sight) — **vis′u·al·i·za′tion** *n.*

vi·tal (vīt′'l) *adj.* [< L *vita*, life] 1 of or concerned with life 2 essential to life 3 fatal 4 *a)* essential; indispensable *b)* very important 5 full of life; energetic — *n.* [*pl.*] 1 the vital organs, as the heart, brain, etc. 2 any essential parts — **vi′tal·ly** *adv.*

vi·tal·i·ty (vī tal′ə tē) *n., pl.* **-ties** 1 power to live 2 power to endure 3 mental or physical vigor

vi·tal·ize (vīt′'l īz′) *vt.* **-ized′, -iz′ing** to make vital; give life or vigor to

vital signs the pulse, respiration, and body temperature

vital statistics data on births, deaths, marriages, etc.

vi·ta·min (vīt′ə min) *n.* [< L *vita*, life] any of certain complex substances found variously in foods and essential to good health

vitamin A a fat-soluble alcohol found in fish-liver oil, egg yolk, carrots, etc.: a deficiency of this results in imperfect vision in the dark

vitamin B (complex) a group of unrelated water-soluble substances including *a)* **vitamin B₁** (*see* THIAMINE) *b)* **vitamin B₂** (*see* RIBOFLAVIN) *c)* NICOTINIC ACID *d)* **vitamin B₁₂** a vitamin containing cobalt, used in treating anemia

vitamin C a compound occurring in citrus fruits, tomatoes, etc.: a deficiency of this produces scurvy

vitamin D any of several fat-soluble vitamins found esp. in fish-liver oils, milk, etc.: a deficiency of this produces rickets

vitamin E a substance occurring in wheat germ, etc., vital to the reproductive processes in some animals

vitamin K a substance occurring in green vegetables, fish meal, etc. that clots blood

vi·ti·ate (vish′ē āt′) *vt.* **-at·ed, -at·ing** [< L *vitium*, a vice] 1 to spoil; corrupt; pervert 2 to invalidate (a contract, etc.) — **vi′ti·a′tion** *n.*

viti·cul·ture (vit′ə kul′chər) *n.* [< L *vitis*, vine] cultivation of grapes

vit·re·ous (vi′trē əs) *adj.* [< L *vitrum*, glass] 1 of or like glass 2 derived from or made of glass

vitreous body (or **humor**) the transparent, jellylike substance filling the eyeball between the retina and the lens

vit·ri·fy (vi′trə fī′) *vt., vi.* **-fied′, -fy′ing** [< L *vitrum*, glass + Fr *-fier, -FY*] to change into glass or a glasslike substance by heat

vit·rine (vi′trin) *n.* [see VITREOUS] a glass-paneled cabinet or display case

vit·ri·ol (vi′trē ōl′) *n.* [< L *vitreus*, glassy] 1 *a)* any of several sulfates of metals, as of copper (*blue vitriol*) or iron (*green vitriol*) *b)* SULFURIC ACID 2 sharp or bitter speech, etc. — **vit′ri·ol′ic** (-äl′ik) *adj.*

vi·tu·per·ate (vī tōō′pər āt′, vi-) *vt.* **-at·ed, -at·ing** [< L *vitium*, a fault, + *parare*, prepare] to speak abusively to or about — **vi·tu′pera′tion** *n.* — **vi·tu′pera′tive** *adj.*

viva (vē′vä) *interj.* [It & Sp] (long) live (someone specified)!

vi·vace (vē vä′chā) *adj., adv.* [It] *Music* in a lively, spirited manner

---

THESAURUS

virus *n.* 1 [An infection] sickness, communicability, illness; see ILLNESS 2. 2 [An organism] microorganism, bacillus, bacteriophage; see GERM.

vise *n.* clamp, holder, universal vise; see FASTENER.

visibility *n.* perceptibility, discernibility, distinctness; see CLARITY.

visible *a.* apparent, evident, noticeable; see OBVIOUS 1.

vision *n.* 1 [The faculty of sight] sight, perception, perceiving, range of view, optics, eyesight. 2 [Understanding] foresight, discernment, breadth of view, insight, penetration, intuition, divination, astuteness, keenness, foreknowledge, prescience, farsightedness. 3 [Something seen through powers of the mind] imagination, poetic insight, fancy, fantasy, image, concept, conception, ideality, idea; see also THOUGHT 1, 2. 4 [Something seen because of an abnormality] revelation, trance,

ecstasy, phantom, apparition, ghost, wraith, specter, apocalypse, nightmare, spirit, warlock; see also ILLUSION.

visionary *a.* 1 [Impractical] ideal, romantic, utopian; see IMPRACTICAL. 2 [Imaginary] chimerical, delusory, dreamy; see IMAGINARY.

visit *n.* social call, call, appointment, interview, formal call, talk, evening, stay, weekend, holiday, visitation.

visit *v.* stay with, stop by, call on, call upon, come around, be the guest of, make a visit, sojourn awhile, revisit, make one's compliments to, look in on, visit with, call for, stop off, stop in, stop over, have an appointment with, pay a visit to, tour, take in, drop in on, hit, look around*, look up, go over to, look in, drop over, pop in, have a date.

visitor *n.* caller, visitant, official inspector; see GUEST.

visual *a.* seen, optic, of the vision; see

OBVIOUS 1.

visualize *v.* see in the mind's eye, picture mentally, conceive; see IMAGINE.

vital *a.* 1 [Necessary] essential, indispensable, requisite; see NECESSARY. 2 [Alive] live, animate, animated; see ALIVE. 3 [Vigorous] lively, energetic, lusty; see ACTIVE.

vitality *n.* life, liveliness, animation, vim, vigor, intensity, continuity, endurance, energy, spirit, ardor, audacity, spunk, fervor, verve, venturesomeness.

vitals *n.* organs, intestines, entrails; see INSIDES.

vitamin *n.* Types of vitamins include the following: vitamin A, vitamin B complex, vitamin C, vitamin D, vitamin E, vitamin K, riboflavin, flavin, nicotinic acid, ascorbic acid, thiamin, thiamine, niacin, pantothenic acid, nicotinamide, pyridoxine, tocopherol; see also MEDICINE 2.

vi·va·cious (vī vā′shəs, vi-) *adj.* [< L *vivere*, to live] full of animation; lively —**vi·va′cious·ly** *adv.* —**vi·vac′i·ty** (-vas′ə tē) or **vi·va′cious·ness** *n.*

vive (vēv) *interj.* [Fr] (long) live (someone specified)!

vivid (viv′id) *adj.* [< L *vivere*, to live] 1 full of life; vigorous 2 bright; intense, as colors 3 strong and clear; active [a *vivid* imagination] —**viv′id·ly** *adv.* —**viv′id·ness** *n.*

vivi·fy (viv′ə fī′) *vt.* **-fied′, -fy′ing** [< L *vivus*, alive + *facere*, make] to give life to; animate

vi·vip·a·rous (vī vip′ər əs) *adj.* [< L *vivus*, alive + *parere*, produce] bearing living young instead of laying eggs

vivi·sec·tion (viv′ə sek′shən) *n.* [< L *vivus*, alive + SECTION] surgery performed on a living animal in medical research —**viv′i·sect′** *vt.*, *vi.* —**viv′i·sec′tion·ist** *n.*

vixen (vik′sən) *n.* [OE *fyxe*, female fox] an ill-tempered, shrewish, or malicious woman —**vix′en·ish** *adj.* —**vix′en·ishly** *adv.*

viz. or **viz** [< L *videlicet*] that is; namely

vi·zier (vi zir′, viz′yər) *n.* [< Ar *wazara*, bear a burden] a high government official in the Turkish empire (c. 1300-1918) Also sp. **vi·zir′**

vizor (vī′zər) *n. alt. sp. of* VISOR

VLF or **vlf** very low frequency

vo·cabu·lary (vō kab′yōō ler′ē) *n., pl.* **-ies** [ult. < L *vocare*, to call] 1 a list of words, etc. as in a dictionary or glossary 2 all the words used in a language or by a person, group, etc.

vo·cal (vō′kəl) *adj.* [< L *vox*, voice] 1 of or produced by the voice 2 sung 3 capable of making oral sounds 4 speaking freely —**vo′cally** *adv.*

vocal cords membranous folds in the larynx that vibrate to produce voice

vo·calic (vō kal′ik) *adj.* of, like, or involving a vowel or vowels

vo·cal·ist (vō′kəl ist) *n.* a singer

vo·cal·ize′ (-īz′) *vt.* **-ized′, -iz′ing** to utter, speak, or sing —**vo′cali·za′tion** *n.*

vo·ca·tion (vō kā′shən) *n.* [< L *vocare*, to call] 1 the career to which one feels one is called 2 any trade or occupation —**vo·ca′tional** *adj.*

voca·tive (väk′ə tiv) *n.* [see prec.] *Gram.* a case indicating the person or thing addressed

vo·cif·er·ate (vō sif′ər āt′) *vt., vi.* **-at′ed, -at′ing** [< L *vox*, voice + *ferre*, to bear] to shout loudly; clamor —**vo·cif′era′tion** *n.*

vo·cif·er·ous (vō sif′ər əs) *adj.* noisy; clamorous —**vo·cif′er·ous·ly** *adv.*

vodka (väd′kə) *n.* [Russ < *voda*, water] a colorless alcoholic liquor distilled from rye, wheat, etc.

vogue (vōg) *n.* [Fr] 1 the fashion at any particular time 2 popularity — *adj.* in vogue: also **vogu·ish** (vō′gish)

voice (vois) *n.* [< L *vox*] 1 sound made through the mouth, esp. by human beings 2 the ability to make such sounds 3 anything regarded as like vocal utterance 4 an expressed wish, opinion, etc. 5 the right to express one's wish, etc.; vote 6 utterance or expression 7 a verb form showing the relation of the subject to the action: see ACTIVE (adj. 4), PASSIVE (adj. 3) 8 *Music a)* singing ability *b)* any of the parts in a composition — *vt.* **voiced, voic′ing** to give utterance or expression to —**with one voice** unanimously —**voice′less** *adj.*

voice box LARYNX

voice mail an electronic system whereby voice messages can be recorded, stored, and then delivered

voice′-o′ver *n.* the voice of an unseen announcer or narrator, as on TV

void (void) *adj.* [< L *vacare*, be empty] 1 containing nothing 2 devoid (*of*) [*void* of sense] 3 ineffective; useless 4 of no legal force — *n.* 1 an empty space 2 a feeling of emptiness — *vt.* 1 to empty out 2 to make void; annul —**void′able** *adj.*

voilà (vwä lä′) *interj.* [Fr] behold; there it is

voile (voil) *n.* [Fr, a veil] a thin, sheer fabric, as of cotton

vol. volume

vola·tile (väl′ə təl) *adj.* [< L *volare*, to fly] 1 evaporating quickly 2 *a)* unstable; explosive *b)* fickle —**vol′a·til′ity** (-til′ə tē) *n.* —**vol′a·til·ize′** (-īz′), **-ized′, -iz′ing** *vt., vi.*

vol·canic (väl kan′ik) *adj.* 1 of or caused by a volcano 2 like a volcano; violently explosive

vol·cano (väl kā′nō) *n., pl.* **-noes** or **-nos** [< L *Volcanus*, Vulcan] 1 a vent in the earth's crust through which molten rock, ashes, etc. are ejected 2 a cone-shaped mountain of this material built up around the vent

vo·li·tion (vō lish′ən) *n.* [ult. < L *velle*, be willing] the act or power of using the will —**vo·li′tional** *adj.*

vol·ley (väl′ē) *n., pl.* **-leys** [< L *volare*, to fly] 1 *a)* the simultaneous discharge of a number of weapons *b)* the bullets, etc., so charged 2 a burst of words or acts 3 *Sports a)* a returning of a ball, etc. before it touches the ground *b)* an extended exchange of shots, as in tennis — *vt., vi.* **-leyed, -ley·ing** 1 to discharge or be discharged in a volley 2 *Sports* to return (the ball, etc.) as a volley

vol′ley·ball′ *n.* 1 a team game played by hitting a large, light, inflated ball back and forth over a net with the hands 2 this ball

volt (vōlt) *n.* [after A. *Volta* (1745-1827), It physicist] the unit of electromotive force

volt·age (vōl′tij) *n.* electromotive force expressed in volts

vol·taic (väl tā′ik) *adj.* of or by electricity produced by chemical action

volt′me′ter *n.* an instrument for measuring voltage

vol·uble (väl′yoo bəl) *adj.* [< L *volvere*, to roll] characterized by a great flow of words; talkative —**vol′ubil′ity** *n.* —**vol′ubly** *adv.*

vol·ume (väl′yoom) *n.* [< L *volumen*, a scroll] 1 *a)* a book *b)* one of a set of books 2 the amount of space occupied in three dimensions 3 *a)* a quantity, bulk, or amount *b)* a large quantity 4 the loudness of sound

vo·lu·mi·nous (və loom′ə nəs) *adj.* 1 producing or consisting of enough to fill volumes 2 large; bulky; full —**vo·lu′mi·nously** *adv.*

vol·un·ta·rism (väl′ən tər iz′em) *n.* voluntary participation in a course of action, or a system based on this

vol′un·tar′y (-ter′ē) *adj.* [< L *voluntas*, free will] 1 brought about by one's own free choice 2 acting of one's own accord 3 intentional; not accidental 4 controlled by one's mind or will —**vol′un·tar′ily** *adv.*

vol·un·teer (väl′ən tir′) *n.* one who chooses freely to do something, as entering military service — *adj.* 1 serving

THESAURUS

vivid *a.* 1 [Brilliant] shining, rich, glowing; see BRIGHT 1. 2 [Distinct] strong, vigorous, lucid; see CLEAR 2, DEFINITE 2.

vividly *a.* glowingly, strikingly, flamingly; see BRIGHTLY.

vocabulary *n.* wordbook, dictionary, lexicon, thesaurus, stock of words, glossary, scientific vocabulary, literary vocabulary; see also DICTION.

vocal *a.* 1 [Verbal] expressed, uttered, voiced; see ORAL, SPOKEN. 2 [Produced by the voice; *said especially of music*] sung, scored for voice, vocalized; see MUSICAL 1.

vocalist *n.* chorister, songstress, caroler; see MUSICIAN, SINGER.

vocation *n.* calling, mission, pursuit; see PROFESSION 1.

voice *n.* 1 [A vocal sound] speech, sound, call, cry, utterance, tongue, whistle, moan, groan, song, yell, hail, howl, yowl, bark, whine, whimper, mutter, murmur, shout, bleat, bray, neigh, whinny, roar, trumpet, cluck,

honk, meow, hiss, quack; see also NOISE 1.—*Ant.* SILENCE, dumbness, deaf-mutism. 2 [Approval or opinion] decision, conclusion, assent, negation, approval, recommendation, wish, view; see also CHOICE, OPINION 1. —**with one voice** all together, by unanimous vote, without dissent; see UNANIMOUSLY.

voice *v.* assert, cry, sound; see TALK 1, TELL 1.

voiced *a.* vocal, sonant, sounded; see ORAL, SPOKEN.

void *a.* barren, sterile, fruitless, meaningless, useless, invalid, vain, voided, unconfirmed, unratified, null and void, worthless, unsanctioned, set aside, avoided, forceless, voted out, ineffectual, ineffective, voidable.—*Ant.* VALID, in force, used.

volatile *a.* 1 [Having the qualities of a gas] gaseous, airy, buoyant; see LIGHT 5. 2 [Having a sprightly temperament] lively, vivacious, playful; see ACTIVE.

volley *n.* round, discharge, barrage;

see FIRE 2.

voltage *n.* electric potential, potential difference, charge; see ENERGY 2.

voluble *a.* talkative, glib, loquacious; see FLUENT.

volume *n.* 1 [Quantity] bulk, mass, amount; see EXTENT, SIZE 2. 2 [Contents] cubical, size, dimensions; see CAPACITY. 3 [A book] printed document, tome, pamphlet; see BOOK. 4 [Degree of sound] loudness, amplification, strength; see SOUND 2.

voluntarily *a.* by preference, willingly, deliberately, optionally, spontaneously, freely, intentionally, by choice, of one's own choice, on one's own, in one's own sweet way, heart in hand, of one's own free will, on one's own hook, to one's heart's content, at one's discretion, on one's own initiative, with all one's heart.

voluntary *a.* willing, freely, spontaneous; see OPTIONAL.

volunteer *n.* enlistee, enlisted man, taker; see CANDIDATE, RECRUIT.

as a volunteer **2** of a volunteer or volunteers —**vt.** to offer or give of one's own free will —**vi.** to offer to enter into any service of one's own free will

vo·lup·tu·ary (və lup′chōō er′ē) **n.**, pl. **-ar·ies** ⟦< L *voluptas*, pleasure⟧ one devoted to sensual pleasures

vo·lup′tu·ous (-chōō əs) **adj.** full of, producing, or fond of sensual pleasures —**vo·lup′tu·ous·ness** **n.**

vo·lute (və lōōt′) **n.** ⟦< L *volvere*, to roll⟧ a spiral or whorl

vomit (väm′it) **n.** ⟦< L *vomere*, to vomit⟧ matter ejected from the stomach through the mouth —**vt.**, **vi.** **1** to eject (the contents of the stomach) through the mouth; throw up **2** to discharge or be discharged with force —**vom′i·tous** (-ə təs) **adj.**

voo·doo (vōō′dōō) **n.**, pl. **-doos′** ⟦of WAfr orig.⟧ **1** a primitive religion based on a belief in sorcery, etc. **2** a charm, fetish, etc. used in voodoo —**vt.** to affect by voodoo magic —**voo′doo·ism′** **n.**

vo·ra·cious (vô rā′shəs) **adj.** ⟦< L *vorare*, devour⟧ **1** greedy in eating; ravenous; gluttonous **2** very eager /a *voracious reader/* —**vo·rac′i·ty** (-ras′ə tē) **n.**

vor·tex (vôr′teks′) **n.**, pl. **-tex′es** or **-ti·ces′** (-tə sēz′) ⟦< L *vertere*, to turn⟧ **1** a whirlpool **2** a whirlwind **3** anything like a whirl in its rush, catastrophic power, etc.

vo·tary (vōt′ə rē) **n.**, pl. **-ries** ⟦< L *vovere*, to vow⟧ **1** one bound by a vow, esp. by religious vows **2** one devoted to a cause, study, etc.

vote (vōt) **n.** ⟦< L *votum*, a vow⟧ **1** a decision on a proposal, etc., or a choice between candidates for office **2** *a)* the expression of such a decision or choice *b)* the ballot, etc. by which it is expressed **3** the right to vote **4** votes collectively —**vi.** **vot′ed**, **vot′ing** to give or cast a vote —**vt.** to decide or enact by vote —**vot′er** **n.**

vo·tive (vōt′iv) **adj.** ⟦see prec.⟧ designed to fulfill a promise, express devotion, etc.

vouch (vouch) **vi.** ⟦< L *vocare*, to call⟧ to give, or serve as, assurance, a guarantee, etc. *(for)*

vouch′er **n.** **1** one who vouches **2** a paper serving as evidence or proof; specif., a receipt

vouch·safe (vouch sāf′) **vt.** **-safed′**, **-saf′ing** ⟦< ME *vouchen safe*, vouch as safe⟧ to condescend to give or grant

vow (vou) **n.** ⟦< L *votum*⟧ **1** a solemn promise, esp. one made to God **2** a promise of love and fidelity /marriage *vows]* —**vt.** to promise or declare solemnly —**vi.** to make a vow —**take vows** to enter a religious order

vowel (vou′əl) **n.** ⟦< L *vocalis*, vocal⟧ **1** a speech sound in which the air passes in a continuous stream through the open mouth **2** a letter representing such a sound, as *a, e, i, o, u*

voy·age (voi′ij) **n.** ⟦< L *via*, way⟧ **1** a relatively long journey, esp. by water **2** a journey by aircraft or spacecraft —**vi.**, **vt.** **-aged**, **-ag·ing** to make a voyage (over or on) —**voy′ager** **n.**

voya·geur (vwä yä zhër′) **n.**, pl. **-geurs′** (-zhër′) ⟦Fr, traveler⟧ a woodsman or boatman in Canada

voy·eur (voi ur′, vwä yur′) **n.** ⟦< L *videre*, see⟧ one who has an exaggerated interest in viewing sexual objects or activities —**voy·eur′ism′** **n.** —**voy′eur·is′tic** **adj.**

VP or **V.P.** Vice-President

vs. or **vs** versus

V/STOL (vē′stôl′) **n.** ⟦*v(ertical or) s(hort) t(ake)o(ff and) l(anding)*⟧ an aircraft that can take off and land either vertically or on a short airstrip

vt. or **v.t.** transitive verb

VTOL (vē′tôl′) **n.** ⟦*v(ertical) t(ake)o(ff and) l(anding)*⟧ an aircraft that can take off and land vertically

Vul·can (vul′kən) the Roman god of fire and of metalworking

vul·can·ize (vul′kən īz′) **vt.** **-ized′**, **-iz′ing** to treat (crude rubber) with sulfur under heat to increase its strength and elasticity —**vi.** to undergo vulcanization —**vul′cani·za′tion** **n.**

Vulg. Vulgate

vul·gar (vul′gər) **adj.** ⟦< L *vulgus*, common people⟧ **1** of people in general; popular **2** vernacular **3** lacking culture, taste, etc.; crude; boorish **4** indecent or obscene —**vul′garly** **adv.**

vul·gar′ian (-ger′ē ən) **n.** a rich person with coarse, vulgar tastes

vul′gar·ism′ **n.** **1** a word, phrase, etc. used widely but regarded as nonstandard, coarse, or obscene **2** vulgarity

vul·gar′i·ty (-ger′ə tē) **n.** **1** a being vulgar **2** pl. **-ties** a vulgar act, habit, usage in speech, etc.

vul′gar·ize′ (-gər īz′) **vt.** **-ized′**, **-iz′ing 1** to popularize **2** to make vulgar, coarse, obscene, etc. —**vul′gari·za′tion** **n.** —**vul′gar·iz′er** **n.**

Vulgar Latin the everyday Latin spoken by ancient Romans as distinguished from standard written Latin

Vul·gate (vul′gāt′) **n.** ⟦ML *vulgata* (*editio*), popular (edition)⟧ a Latin version of the Bible, used in the Roman Catholic Church

vul·ner·able (vul′nər ə bəl) **adj.** ⟦< L *vulnus*, a wound⟧ **1** that can be wounded or injured **2** open to, or easily hurt by, criticism or attack **3** *Bridge* subject to increased penalties and bonuses —**vul′ner·abil′ity** **n.** —**vul′ner·ably** **adv.**

vul·pine (vul′pīn) **adj.** ⟦< L *vulpes*, a fox⟧ of or like a fox; cunning

vul·ture (vul′chər) **n.** ⟦< L, akin to *vellere*, to tear⟧ **1** a large bird that lives chiefly on carrion **2** a greedy, ruthless person —**vul′tur·ous adj.**

vulva (vul′və) **n.** ⟦L, womb⟧ the external genital organs of the female

vy·ing (vī′iŋ) **adj.** that vies

THESAURUS

volunteer *v.* come forward, enlist, sign up, submit oneself, take the initiative, offer oneself, do on one's own accord, do of one's own free will, take the initiative, take upon oneself, speak up, stand up and be counted, go in*, chip in*, do on one's own hook*, take the bull by the horns, stand on one's own feet, take the bit between one's teeth, paddle one's own canoe, take the plunge; see also JOIN 2.

volunteered *a.* offered, proffered, signed-up; see JOINED.

volunteers *n.* all comers, everybody, anyone; see RECRUIT.

vomit *v.* throw up, eject, bring up, spit up, dry heave, be seasick, hurl forth, retch, ruminate, regurgitate, give forth, discharge, belch forth, spew up, puke*, barf*, toss one's cookies*.

voracious *a.* insatiable, gross, ravening; see GREEDY.

vote *n.* **1** [A ballot] tally, ticket, slip of paper, ball, yes or no, rising vote, Australian ballot, secret ballot. **2** [A decision] referendum, choice, majority; see ELECTION. **3** [The right to

vote] suffrage, the franchise, manhood suffrage, universal suffrage, woman suffrage; see also RIGHT.

vote *v.* ballot, cast a vote, cast a ballot, give a vote, enact, establish, determine, bring about, effect, grant, confer, declare, suggest, propose; see also DECIDE. —**vote down** decide against, refuse, blackball; see DENY. —**vote for** give one's vote to, cast a ballot for, second; see SUPPORT 2. —**vote in** elect, put in, put in office; see CHOOSE. —**vote out** reject, remove from office, vote down; see DEFEAT, DISMISS.

voted *a.* decided, willed, chosen; see NAMED 2.

voter *n.* elector, balloter, registered voter, member of a constituency, member of the electorate, vote caster, native, naturalized citizen, taxpayer, voter by proxy, one of the folks back home*, ballot-box stuffer*; see also CITIZEN.

vouch *v.* assert, attest, affirm; see ENDORSE 2.

vow *n.* pledge, solemn assertion, asseveration; see PROMISE 1.

vowel *n.* vocoid, open-voiced sound,

vowel sound, glide, diphthong, digraph; see also LETTER 1. *Linguistic terms referring to vowel sounds include the following:* high, mid, low, front, back, rounded, unrounded, tense, slack, stressed, unstressed, nasal, nasalized, clipped, diphthongized. *In English spelling, symbols used to represent vowels include the following: a, e, i, o, u* and sometimes *y.*

voyage *n.* tour, trip, excursion; see JOURNEY.

vulgar *a.* sordid, ignoble, mean, base, obscene, indecent, gross, filthy, villainous, dishonorable, unworthy, fractious, inferior, disgusting, baseminded, mean-spirited, malicious, ill-tempered, sneaking, deceitful, slippery, loathsome, odious, foul-mouthed, brutish, debased, contemptible, abhorrent, profane, nasty.—*Ant.* NOBLE, high-minded, lofty.

vulgarity *n.* impudence, discourtesy, crudity; see RUDENESS.

vulnerable *a.* woundable, exposed, assailable; see UNSAFE, WEAK 2, 5.

W

w or **W** (dub′əl yōō′) *n., pl.* **w's, W's** the 23d letter of the English alphabet

w or **w.** 1 week(s) 2 weight 3 wide 4 width 5 wife 6 with 7 win(s)

W 1 [*w*(*olfram*), alt. name of tungsten] *Chem. symbol for* tungsten 2 watt(s): also **w**

W or **W.** 1 Wednesday 2 weight 3 west 4 westerly 5 western 6 wide 7 width

wab·ble (wä′bəl) *n., vt., vi.* **-bled, -bling** *alt. sp. of* WOBBLE

Wac (wak) *n.* a member of the Women's Army Corps (WAC)

wacky (wak′ē) *adj.* **-i·er, -i·est** [< ?] [Slang] erratic, eccentric, or irrational —**wack′i·ness** *n.*

wad (wäd) *n.* [ML *wadda*, wadding] 1 a small, soft mass, as of cotton or paper 2 a lump or small, firm mass — *vt.* **wad′ded, wad′ding** 1 to compress, or roll up, into a wad 2 to plug or stuff with a wad or wadding

wad′ding *n.* any soft material for use in padding, packing, etc.

wad·dle (wäd′əl) *vi.* **-dled, -dling** [< fol.] to walk with short steps, swaying from side to side, as a duck — *n.* a waddling gait

wade (wād) *vi.* **wad′ed, wad′ing** [OE *waden*, go] 1 to walk through any resisting substance, as water, mud, etc. 2 to proceed with difficulty [*to wade* through a dull book] 3 [Colloq.] to attack with vigor: with *in* or *into* — *vt.* to cross by wading

wad′er *n.* 1 one that wades 2 [*pl.*] high waterproof boots, often with trousers

wadi (wä′dē) *n., pl.* **-dis** or **-dies** [Ar *wādī*] in N Africa, etc., a river valley that is usually dry

wading bird a long-legged shore bird that wades the shallows and marshes for food

wa·fer (wā′fər) *n.* [< MDu *wafel*] 1 a thin, flat, crisp cracker or cookie 2 any dislike thing resembling this

waf·fle (wä′fəl) *n.* [see prec.] a crisp batter cake baked in a waffle iron

waffle iron a utensil with two flat, studded plates pressed together so that a waffle bakes between them

waft (wäft, waft) *vt., vi.* [< Du *wachter*, watcher] to carry or move (sounds, odors, etc.) lightly through the air or over water — *n.* 1 an odor, sound, etc. carried through the air 2 a gust of wind 3 a wafting movement

wag¹ (wag) *vt., vi.* **wagged, wag′ging** [ME *waggen*] to move rapidly back and forth, up and down, etc. — *n.* a wagging

wag² (wag) *n.* [prob. < obs. *waghalter*, joker] a comical person; wit —**wag′gery,** *pl.* **-ies,** *n.*

wage (wāj) *vt.* **waged, wag′ing** [< OFr *gage*, a pledge] to engage in or carry on (a war, etc.) — *n.* 1 [*often pl.*] money paid for work done 2 [*usually pl.*] what is given in return

wa·ger (wā′jər) *n.* [see prec.] a bet — *vt., vi.* to bet

wag·gish (wag′ish) *adj.* 1 of or like a wag; roguishly merry 2 playful; jesting

wag·gle (wag′əl) *vt., vi.* **-gled, -gling** [< WAG¹] to wag, esp. with short, quick movements — *n.* a waggling

wagon (wag′ən) *n.* [Du *wagen*] 1 a four-wheeled vehicle, esp. one for hauling heavy loads 2 *short for* STATION WAGON —**on** (or **off**) **the wagon** [Slang] no longer (or once again) drinking alcohol

waif (wāf) *n.* [< NormFr] 1 anything found that is without an owner 2 a homeless person, esp. a child

wail (wāl) *vi.* [< ON *væ*, woe] to make a long, loud, sad cry, as in grief or pain — *n.* such a cry

wain (wān) *n.* [OE *wægn*] [Archaic] a wagon

wain·scot (wān′skät′, -skət) *n.* [< MDu *wagenschot*] a wood paneling on the walls of a room, sometimes on the lower part only — *vt.* **-scot′ed** or **-scot′ted, -scot′ing** or **-scot′ting** to line (a wall) with wood, etc.

wain′scot′ing or **wain′scot′ting** *n.* 1 WAINSCOT 2 material used to wainscot

wain·wright (wān′rīt′) *n.* [*wain*, wagon + WRIGHT] one who builds or repairs wagons

waist (wāst) *n.* [OE *weaxan*, grow] 1 the part of the body between the ribs and the hips 2 the part of a garment that covers the body from the shoulders to the waistline 3 the narrow part of any object that is wider at the ends [Archaic] a blouse

waist′band′ *n.* a band encircling the waist, as on slacks or a skirt

waist·coat (wāst′kōt′, wes′kət) *n.* [Brit., etc. (exc. Cdn.)] a man's vest

waist′line′ *n.* the line at the narrowest part of the waist

wait (wāt) *vi.* [< NormFr *waitier*] 1 to remain (until something expected happens) 2 to be ready 3 to remain undone [*it can wait*] 4 to serve food at a meal: with *at* or *on* — *vt.* 1 to await 2 [Colloq.] to delay serving (a meal) — *n.* act or period of waiting —**lie in wait (for)** to wait so as to catch after planning a trap (*for*) —**wait on** (or **upon**) 1 to act as a servant to 2 to serve (a customer) — **wait table** to serve food to people at a table —**wait up** to delay going to bed until someone arrives, etc.

wait′er *n.* one who waits; esp. a man who waits on tables in a restaurant

wait′ing *adj.* 1 that waits 2 of or for a wait — *n.* 1 the act of one that waits 2 a period of waiting

waiting game a scheme by which one wins out over another by delaying action until one has an advantage

waiting list a list of applicants, in the order of their application

waiting room a room in which people wait, as in a bus station or dentist's office

wait·ress (wā′tris) *n.* a woman or girl who waits on tables, as in a restaurant

waive (wāv) *vt.* **waived, waiv′ing** [< ON *veifa*, fluctuate] 1 to forgo (a right, etc.) 2 to postpone

waiver (wā′vər) *n. Law* a waiving of a right, claim, etc.

wake¹ (wāk) *vi.* **woke** or **waked,** **waked** or **wok′en, wak′ing** [< OE *wacian*, be awake & *wacan*, arise] 1 to come out of sleep; awake: often with *up* 2 to stay awake 3 to become active: often with *up* 4 to become alert (*to* a realization, etc.) — *vt.* 1 to cause to wake: often with *up* 2 to arouse (passions, etc.) — *n.* a viewing of a corpse before burial

---

══ THESAURUS ══

wake[2] (wāk) *n.* [< ON *vök*, hole] the track left in water by a moving ship —**in the wake of** following closely

wake′ful *adj.* 1 alert; watchful 2 unable to sleep — **wake′ful·ness** *n.*

waken (wā′kən) *vi., vt.* to awake

wale (wāl) *n.* [OE *walu*, weal] 1 a welt raised by a whip, etc. 2 a ridge on the surface of cloth, as corduroy — *vt.* **waled, wal′ing** to mark with wales

walk (wôk) *vi.* [OE *wealcan*, to roll] 1 to go on foot at a moderate pace 2 to follow a certain course *[walk* in peace*]* 3 *Baseball* to go to first base after the pitching of four balls (see BALL[1], n. 6) — *vt.* 1 to go over, along, etc. on foot 2 to cause (a dog, etc.) to walk, as for exercise 3 to accompany on a walk or stroll *[to walk* you home*]* 4 *Baseball* to advance (a batter) to first base by pitching four balls (see BALL[1], n. 6) — *n.* 1 the act of walking 2 a stroll or hike 3 a distance walked *[an* hour's *walk]* 4 a sphere of activity, occupation, etc. *[people from all walks* of life*]* 5 a path for walking 6 *Baseball* the walking of a batter —**walk (all) over** [Colloq.] to domineer over —**walk away (or off) with** 1 to steal 2 to win easily —**walk out** to go on strike —**walk out on** [Colloq.] to leave; desert; abandon — **walk′er** *n.*

walkie-talkie (wôk′ē tôk′ē) *n.* a compact radio transmitter and receiver that can be carried by one person

walking stick a stick carried when walking; cane

Walk·man (wôk′mən, wôk′man′) *trademark for* a portable, pocket-size radio or tape player with headphones

walk′-on′ *n.* a minor role in which the actor has few or no lines

walk′out′ *n.* a labor strike

walk′-up′ *n.* an apartment house, etc. of several stories without an elevator

wall (wôl) *n.* [< L *vallus*, palisade] 1 an upright structure of wood, stone, etc., serving to enclose, divide, or protect 2 something like a wall in appearance or function — *vt.* 1 to enclose, divide, etc. with or as with a wall 2 to close up (an opening) with a wall: usually with *up* —**drive (or push) to the wall** to place in a desperate position —**off the wall** [Slang] 1 insane; crazy 2 very odd or unconventional

wal·la·by (wäl′ə bē) *n., pl.* -**bies** [< Australian native name *wolabā*] a small kangaroo

wall·board (wôl′bôrd′) *n.* fibrous material in thin slabs for making or covering walls and ceilings

wal·let (wôl′it) *n.* [ME *walet*] a flat case or folder, as of leather, for paper money, cards, etc.

wall′eye′ *n.* [< ON *vagl*, a beam + *eygr*, eye] 1 an eye that turns outward, showing much white 2 a fish with large, glossy eyes, esp. a North American freshwater perch: in full **wall′eyed′ pike**

wall′flow′er *n.* [Colloq.] a person who merely looks on at a dance, etc. as from shyness

Wal·loon (wä lōōn′) *n.* [< OHG *walh*, foreigner] 1 any of a chiefly Celtic people in S Belgium 2 their French dialect

wal·lop (wäl′əp) *vt.* [< OFr *galoper*, to gallop] [Colloq.] 1 to beat or defeat soundly 2 to strike hard — *n.* [Colloq.] 1 a hard blow 2 a thrill

wal·low (wäl′ō) *vi.* [OE *wealwian*, roll around] 1 to roll about, as in mud, etc. 2 to indulge oneself fully (*in* a specified thing) — *n.* 1 a wallowing 2 a muddy or dusty place

wall′pa′per *n.* a decorative material, in sheets, for covering the walls of a room — *vt.* to hang wallpaper on or in

Wall Street [after a street in New York City, main U.S. financial center] U.S. financiers, together with their power, influence, policies, etc.; also, the U.S. securities market, its power, etc.

wall′-to-wall′ *adj.* 1 covering a floor completely 2 [Colloq.] *a)* pervasive *b)* all-inclusive

wal·nut (wôl′nut′) *n.* [< OE *wealh*, foreign + *hnutu*, nut] 1 a shade tree valued for its nuts and wood 2 its edible nut with a two-lobed seed 3 its dark wood, used in making furniture, etc.

wal·rus (wôl′rəs) *n.* [< Dan *hvalros*] a massive arctic sea mammal somewhat like a seal, having two tusks projecting from the upper jaw

waltz (wôlts) *n.* [< Ger *walzen*, dance about] 1 a ballroom dance for couples, in 3/4 time 2 music for this — *vi.* 1 to dance a waltz 2 to move lightly

wam·pum (wäm′pəm) *n.* [< AmInd] small beads made of shells and used by North American Indians as money, for ornament, etc.

wan (wän) *adj.* **wan′ner, wan′nest** [OE *wann*, dark] 1 sickly pale 2 feeble or weak *[a wan* smile*]*

wand (wänd) *n.* [< ON *vǫndr*] 1 a staff symbolizing authority 2 a rod regarded as having magical powers

wan·der (wän′dər) *vi.* [OE *wandrian*] 1 to roam aimlessly; ramble 2 to stray (*from* a path, etc.) 3 to go astray in mind or purpose 4 to meander, as a river — *vt.* to roam in or over —**wan′derer** *n.*

wan′der·lust′ *n.* [Ger] an urge to wander or travel

wane (wān) *vi.* **waned, wan′ing** [OE *wanian*, to decrease] 1 to grow gradually less in extent: said of the moon 2 to grow dim 3 to decline in power, etc. 4 to approach the end — *n.* a waning

wan·gle (waŋ′gəl) *vt.* -**gled, -gling** [< ? WAGGLE] [Colloq.] to get or cause by persuasion, tricks, etc.

wan·na·be (wän′ə bē′) *n.* [Slang] a person who wants to be like someone else or attain some status: also **wan′na·be′**

want (wänt, wônt) *vt.* [< ON *vanta*] 1 to lack 2 to crave *[to want* adventure*]* 3 to desire *[to want* to travel*]* 4 to wish to see or apprehend *[wanted* by the police*]* 5

THESAURUS

walk *n.* 1 [Manner of walking] gait, tread, stride; see STEP 1. 2 [Course over which one walks] pavement, sidewalk, pathway, footpath, track, trail, sheepwalk, boardwalk, pier, promenade, avenue, street, road, alley, dock, platform, gangway; see also STREET. 3 [A short walking expedition] stroll, ramble, turn, hike, promenade, airing, saunter, tramp, trek, march, circuit, jaunt, tour.

walk *v.* 1 [To move on foot] step, pace, march, tread, amble, stroll, hike, saunter, wander, ramble, go out for an airing, take a walk, promenade, trudge, tramp, trek, tour, take a turn, roam, rove, meander, traipse about, patrol, file off, knock about*, knock around*, hoof it*, toddle along, shuffle, wend one's way, cruise. 2 [To cause to move on foot] lead, drive, exercise, train, order a march, escort, accompany, take for a walk. —**walk (all) over*** subdue, trample on, beat up; see ABUSE. —**walk away** vanish, depart, split*; see ABANDON 1, 2, LEAVE 1. —**walk off** depart, go one's own way, stalk off; see LEAVE 1. —**walk out on** desert, leave, walk off from; see ABANDON 2.

walkie-talkie *n.* portable transmitter and receiver, field radio, battery-operated two-way communication; see RADIO 2.

walking *a.* strolling, rambling, trudging, hiking, touring, ambling, sauntering, tramping, marching, promenading, passing, roaming, wandering, wayfaring, trekking*.

walkout *n.* protest, boycott, demonstration; see STRIKE 1.

wall *n.* 1 [A physical barrier] dam, embankment, dike, ditch, bank, levee, stockade, fence, parapet, retainer, rampart, bulwark, palisade, fort, cliff, barricade, floodgate, sluice. 2 [An obstacle; *figurative*] barrier, obstruction, bar, cordon, entanglement, hurdle, resistance, defense, snag, hindrance, impediment, difficulty, limitation, restriction, retardation, knot, hitch, drawback, stumbling block, check, stop, curb, red tape, fly in the ointment, bottleneck, red herring, detour.

wallet *n.* billfold, purse, moneybag; see BAG, FOLDER.

wallop *v.* thump, thrash, strike; see HIT 1.

wallow *v.* grovel, welter, flounder, lie in, roll about in, bathe in, toss, immerse, be immersed in, besmirch oneself.

wall up *v.* close up, surround, wall in; see ENCLOSE.

wander *v.* 1. [To stroll] hike, ramble, saunter; see WALK 1. 2 [To speak or

think incoherently] stray, shift, digress; see RAMBLE 2.

wanderer *n.* adventurer, voyager, gypsy; see TRAVELER.

wandering *a.* 1 [Wandering in space] roving, roaming, nomadic, meandering, restless, traveling, drifting, straying, going off, strolling, ranging, prowling, ambulatory, straggling, on the road, peripatetic, itinerant, roundabout, circuitous.—*Ant.* IDLE, home-loving, sedentary. 2 [Wandering in thought] incongruous, digressive, disconnected; see INCOHERENT.

wane *v.* decline, subside, fade away; see DECREASE 1, FADE 1.

want *n.* 1 [Need] privation, dearth, shortage, lack; see LACK 2. 2 [Desire] wish, craving, demand; see DESIRE 1.

want *v.* 1 [To desire] require, aspire, fancy, hanker after, have an urge for, incline toward, covet, crave, long for, lust for, have a fondness for, have a passion for, have ambition, thirst after, hunger after, be greedy for, ache*, have a yen for*, have an itch for. 2 [To lack] be deficient in, be deprived of, require; see NEED.

wanted *a.* needed, necessary, desired, in need of, sought after, in demand, requested, asked for.—*Ant.* SATISFIED, fulfilled, filled.

[Chiefly Brit., etc.] to require — *vi.* **1** to have a need or lack: usually with *for* **2** to be destitute — *n.* **1** a shortage; lack **2** poverty **3** a craving **4** something needed

want ad [Colloq.] an advertisement for something wanted, as a job

want'ing *adj.* **1** lacking **2** not up to standard — *prep.* without; minus —**wanting in** deficient in

wan·ton (wän′tən, wänt′'n) *adj.* [< OE *wan*, lacking + *teon*, educate] **1** sexually unrestrained **2** [Old Poet.] playful **3** unprovoked or malicious **4** recklessly ignoring justice, etc. — *n.* a wanton person; esp., a sexually unrestrained woman — *vi.* to be wanton —**wan'ton·ness** *n.*

wap·i·ti (wäp′ət ē) *n.* [< AmInd] a large, North American deer with widely branching antlers; elk

war (wôr) *n.* [< NormFr *werre*] **1** open armed conflict as between nations **2** any active hostility or struggle **3** military operations as a science — *adj.* of, in, or from war — *vi.* **warred, war'ring 1** to carry on war **2** to contend; strive —**at war** in a state of active armed conflict

war·ble (wôr′bəl) *vt., vi.* **-bled, -bling** [< NormFr *werbler*] to sing (a song, etc.) melodiously, with trills, quavers, etc., as a bird — *n.* a warbling; trill

war·bler (wôr′blər) *n.* a bird or person that warbles

ward (wôrd) *vt.* [OE *weardian*, to guard] to turn aside; fend (*off*) — *n.* **1** a being under guard **2** one under the care of a guardian or court **3** a division of a jail, hospital, etc. **4** a division of a city or town, for purposes of voting, etc.

-ward (wərd) [OE *-weard*] *suffix* in a (specified) direction [*inward*] Also **-wards** (wərdz)

war·den (wôrd′'n) *n.* [< NormFr *wardein*] **1** one who guards, or has charge of, something [game *warden*] **2** the chief official of a prison

ward'er *n.* a watchman

ward heeler a follower of a politician, who solicits votes, etc.: often a contemptuous term

ward·robe (wôr′drōb′) *n.* **1** a closet, cabinet, etc. for holding clothes **2** one's supply of clothes

ward'room' *n.* in a warship, a room used by commissioned officers for eating, etc.

ware (wer) *n.* [OE *waru*] **1** anything for sale: *usually used in pl.* **2** pottery

ware'house' *n.* a building where goods are stored — *vt.* **-housed', -hous'ing** to store in a warehouse

war·fare (wôr′fer′) *n.* **1** the action of waging war **2** conflict of any kind

war'head' (-hed′) *n.* the front part of a torpedo, etc. containing the explosive

war'horse' *n.* [Colloq.] one who has been through many struggles; veteran

wari·ly (wer′ə lē) *adv.* cautiously —**war'i·ness** (-ē nis) *n.*

war'like' *adj.* **1** fond of or ready for war **2** of war **3** threatening war

war·lock (wôr′läk′) *n.* [OE *wærloga*, liar] a man who practices black magic

war'lord' *n.* **1** a high military officer in a warlike nation **2** a local ruler or bandit leader

warm (wôrm) *adj.* [OE *wearm*] **1** *a)* having or giving off a moderate degree of heat *b)* hot [a *warm* night] **2** that keeps body heat in [a *warm* hat] **3** ardent; enthusiastic **4** lively, vigorous, etc. **5** quick to anger **6** *a)* genial; cordial [a *warm* welcome] *b)* sympathetic or loving **7** newly made; fresh, as a trail **8** [Colloq.] close to discovering something — *vt., vi.* to make or become warm —**warm up** to practice or exercise, as before going into a game, contest, etc. —**warm'er** *n.* —**warm'ish** *adj.* —**warm'ly** *adv.*

warm'blood'ed *adj.* having a body temperature that is relatively constant and usually higher than that of the surroundings, as mammals and birds

warmed-over (wôrmd′ō′vər) *adj.* **1** reheated **2** presented again, without significant change, as ideas

warm front the forward edge of a warm air mass advancing into a colder mass

warm'heart'ed *adj.* kind, sympathetic, friendly, loving, etc.

war'mon'ger (-muŋ′gər, -män′-) *n.* one who advocates, or tries to cause, war —**war'mon'ger·ing** *adj., n.*

warmth (wôrmth) *n.* **1** *a)* the state of having heat *b)* mild heat **2** *a)* enthusiasm, ardor, etc. *b)* affectionate feelings

warm'-up' *n.* the act of warming up

warn (wôrn) *vt., vi.* [OE *wearnian*] **1** to tell of a danger, coming evil, etc. **2** to caution about certain acts **3** to notify in advance; inform

warn'ing *n.* **1** the act of one that warns **2** something that serves to warn — *adj.* that warns

warp (wôrp) *n.* [OE *weorpan*, to throw] **1** *a)* a distortion, as a twist or bend, in wood *b)* any similar distortion **2** a mental quirk, bias, etc. **3** *Weaving* the threads running lengthwise in the loom — *vt.* **1** to bend or twist out of shape **2** to distort, pervert, etc. [a *warped* mind] — *vi.* to become bent or twisted

war'path' *n.* the path taken by American Indians on a warlike expedition —**on the warpath 1** ready for war **2** actively angry; ready to fight

war·rant (wôr′ənt, wär′-) *n.* [< NormFr *warant*] **1** *a)* authorization, as by law *b)* justification for some act,

---

═══ THESAURUS ═══

wanting *a.* **1** [Deficient] destitute, poor, in default of, deprived of, bereft of, devoid of, empty of, bankrupt in, cut off, lacking, short, inadequate, defective, remiss, incomplete, missing, substandard, insufficient, absent, needed, unfulfilled, on the short end. **2** [Desiring] desirous of, covetous, longing for; see ENVIOUS, GREEDY.

wanton *a.* **1** [Unrestrained] extravagant, capricious, reckless, unreserved, unfettered, free, wayward, fluctuating, changeable, whimsical, fitful, variable, fanciful, inconstant, fickle, frivolous, volatile. **2** [Lewd] wayward, lustful, licentious; see LEWD 2.

war *n.* fighting, hostilities, combat. *Types of wars include the following:* air, guerrilla, shooting, ground, sea, jungle, desert, mountain, amphibious, three-dimensional, trench, naval, aerial, land, push-button, hot, cold, total, limited, civil, revolutionary, religious, preventive, world, offensive, defensive, biological, bacteriological, germ, chemical, atomic, nuclear, psychological, war to end all wars, war of nerves, war of attrition, campaign, crusade, *Blitzkrieg* (German).

war *v.* fight, battle, go to war, wage war on, make war against, engage in combat, take the field against, contend, contest, meet in conflict, march against, attack, bombard, shell, kill, shoot, murder.

ward *n.* **1** [A territorial division] district, division, territory; see REGION 1. **2** [A juvenile charge] orphan, foster child, adopted child; see CHILD. **3** [Hospital room] convalescent chamber, infirmary, emergency ward; see HOSPITAL.

warden *n.* official, officer, overseer, superintendent, guardian, tutor, keeper, head keeper, jailer, bodyguard, guard, governor, prison head.

wardrobe *n.* **1** [A closet] chest, bureau, dresser; see CLOSET. **2** [Clothing] apparel, garments, attire; see CLOTHES.

warehouse *n.* wholesale establishment, storehouse, stockroom, storage place, distributing center, repository, depot, shed, stockpile, depository, bin, elevator, storage loft, barn.

wares *n.* goods, lines, stock, products, commodities, manufactured articles, merchandise, range, stuff.

warfare *n.* military operations, hostilities, combat; see WAR.

warlike *a.* belligerent, hostile, offensive; see AGGRESSIVE.

warm *a.* **1** [Moderately heated] heated, sunny, melting, hot, mild, tepid, lukewarm, summery, temperate, clement, glowing, perspiring, sweaty, sweating, flushed, warmish, snug as a bug in a rug*.—*Ant.* COOL, chilly, chilling. **2** [Sympathetic] gracious, cordial, compassionate; see FRIENDLY.

warm *v.* heat up, warm up, put on the fire; see COOK, HEAT 2.

warmth *n.* **1** [Fervor] fever, passion, feeling; see EMOTION. **2** [Affection] friendliness, sympathy; see FRIENDSHIP. **3** [Heat] light, glow, warmness; see HEAT 1, TEMPERATURE.

warn *v.* forewarn, give notice, put on guard, give fair warning, signal, advise, prepare, alert, inform, remind, enjoin, hint, prepare for the worst, offer a word of caution, admonish, counsel, exhort, dissuade, reprove, threaten, forbid, predict, remonstrate, deprecate, prescribe, urge, recommend, prompt, suggest, advocate, cry wolf, tip off*, give the high sign, put a bug in one's ear*.

warned *a.* informed, admonished, made aware, cautioned, advised, given warning, prepared for the worst, told, forewarned, tipped off*, put on the lookout.

warning *n.* caution, admonition, notice, advice, forewarning, alert, intimation, premonition, notification, sign, omen, alarm, indication, token, hint, lesson, information, example, distress signal, prediction, signal, injunction, exhortation, high sign, word to the wise, tip-off, SOS*, handwriting on the wall.

warp *v.* curve, twist, pervert; see BEND.

warrant *n.* authorization, certificate, credential, official document, belief, etc. **2** something serving as a guarantee of some event or result **3** *Law* a writ authorizing an arrest, search, etc. — *vt.* **1** to authorize **2** to serve as justification for (an act, belief, etc.) **3** to guarantee

warrant officer a military officer ranking above a non-commissioned officer but below a commissioned officer

war·ran·ty (wôr′ən tē, wär′-) *n.*, *pl.* **-ties** an assurance by a seller that goods or property will be repaired or replaced if not as represented; guarantee

war·ren (wôr′ən, wär′-) *n.* 〚< NormFr *warir*, to preserve〛 **1** an area in which rabbits breed or are numerous **2** any crowded building or buildings

war·ri·or (wôr′yər, -ē ər) *n.* 〚see WAR〛 a person experienced in conflict, esp. war; soldier

war′ship′ *n.* any ship for combat use, as a battleship

wart (wôrt) *n.* 〚OE *wearte*〛 **1** a small, usually hard, tumorous growth on the skin, caused by a virus **2** a small protuberance, as on a plant —**wart′y, -i·er, -i·est,** *adj.*

wart hog a wild African hog with large tusks, and warts below the eyes

wary (wer′ē) *adj.* **-i·er, -i·est** 〚OE *wær*, aware〛 full of or characterized by caution —**wary of** careful of

was (wuz, wäz) *vi.* 〚OE *wæs*〛 *1st & 3d pers. sing., pt., of* BE

wash (wôsh, wäsh) *vt.* 〚OE *wæscan*〛 **1** to clean with water or other liquid **2** to purify **3** to wet or moisten **4** to flow over, past, or against: said of a sea, waves, etc. **5** to soak (*out*), flush (*off*), or carry (*away*) with water **6** to erode; wear (*out* or *away*) by flowing over 〚the flood *washed* out the road〛 — *vi.* **1** to wash oneself **2** to wash clothes **3** to undergo washing **4** to be removed by washing: usually with *out* or *away* **5** to be worn or carried (*out* or *away*) by the action of water 〚the bridge had *washed* out〛 — *n.* **1** a washing **2** a quantity of clothes, etc. washed, or to be washed **3** the rush or surge of water **4** the eddy of water or air caused by a propeller, etc. **5** silt, mud, etc. carried and dropped by running water **6** a liquid for cosmetic or medicinal use 〚*mouthwash*〛 — *adj.* that can be washed without damage; washable —**wash down** to follow (food, etc.) with a drink —**wash′able** *adj., n.*

wash′-and-wear′ *adj.* of fabrics that need little or no ironing after washing

wash′board′ *n.* a ridged board for scrubbing dirt out of clothes

wash′bowl′ *n.* a bowl, esp. a bathroom fixture, for use in washing one's hands, etc. Also **wash′ba·sin**

wash′cloth′ *n.* a small cloth used in washing the body Also **wash′rag′**

washed′-out′ *adj.* **1** faded **2** [Colloq.] tired; spiritless; pale and wan

washed′-up′ *adj.* **1** [Colloq.] tired; exhausted **2** [Slang] finished; done for; having failed

wash′er *n.* **1** one who washes **2** a flat ring of metal, rubber, etc., used with a nut, faucet valve, bolt, etc. **3** a machine for washing

wash′er·wom′an *n.*, *pl.* **-wom′en** a woman whose work is washing clothes

wash′ing *n.* **1** the act of one that washes **2** clothes, etc. to be washed

washing machine a machine for washing clothes, etc.

wash′out′ *n.* **1** the washing away of soil, etc. by water **2** [Slang] a failure

wash′room′ *n.* **1** a room for washing **2** RESTROOM

wash′stand′ *n.* a table or plumbing fixture with a washbowl, etc.

wash′tub′ *n.* a tub, often with faucets and a drain, for washing clothes, etc.

wash′y *adj.* **-i·er, -i·est** **1** watery; weak **2** feeble; insipid

wasp (wäsp, wôsp) *n.* 〚OE *wæsp*〛 a winged insect with a slender body and, in the females and workers, a vicious sting

WASP or **Wasp** (wäsp, wôsp) *n.* a white Anglo-Saxon Protestant

wasp′ish *adj.* bad-tempered; snappish

was·sail (wäs′əl, -āl′) *n.* 〚< ON *ves heill*, be hearty〛 **1** a toast formerly used to drink to the health of a person **2** the spiced ale, etc. with which such toasts were drunk **3** a drinking party — *vi., vt.* to drink a wassail (to)

wast·age (wāst′ij) *n.* **1** loss by use, decay, etc. **2** anything wasted

waste (wāst) *vt.* **wast′ed, wast′ing** 〚< L *vastare*〛 **1** to devastate; ruin **2** to wear away **3** to make weak or emaciated 〚*wasted* by age〛 **4** to use up needlessly; squander **5** to fail to take advantage of **6** [Slang] to kill — *vi.* **1** to lose strength, etc., as by disease **2** to be used up or worn down gradually — *adj.* **1** uncultivated or uninhabited; desolate **2** left over or superfluous **3** excreted from the body **4** used for waste — *n.* **1** uncultivated or uninhabited land **2** a devastated area **3** a wasting or being wasted **4** discarded material, as ashes **5** excretions from the body, as urine —**go to waste** to be wasted —**lay waste (to)** to destroy —**wast′er** *n.*

license, summons, subpoena, security, pass, testimonial, passport, credentials, permit, permission, verification, authentication.

warrant *v.* **1** [To guarantee] assure, insure, vouch for; see GUARANTEE. **2** [To justify] bear out, call for, give grounds for; see EXPLAIN.

warranty *n.* guaranty, guarantee, pledge; see GUARANTY.

warrior *n.* battler, fighter, hero; see SOLDIER.

warship *n.* fighting ship, armored vessel, gunboat, man-of-war, frigate, ship-of-the-line; see also BOAT, SHIP. *Warships include the following:* battleship, cruiser, destroyer, destroyer escort, submarine, guided-missile frigate, guided-missile destroyer, missile cruiser, attack submarine, dreadnought, capital ship, landing ship, submarine chaser, aircraft carrier, escort carrier, torpedo boat, PT-boat, raider, flagship.

wart *n.* protuberance, spots, mole, projection, blemish, growth, bulge, lesion, tumor.

wary *a.* circumspect, cautious, alert; see CAREFUL, SLY.

wash *n.* **1** [Laundry] wet wash, washing, linen, family wash, soiled clothing, clean clothes, washed clothing, rough-dry wash, flat pieces, finished laundry. **2** [The movement of water] swishing, lapping, roll, swirl, rush, surging, eddy, wave, undulation, surge, heave, flow, murmur, gush, spurt. **3** [A stream bed that is usually dry] arroyo, gulch, canyon; see GAP 3. **4** [A prepared liquid]

rinse, swab, coating; see LIQUID.

wash *v.* **1** [To bathe] clean, cleanse, shine, immerse, douse, soak, take a bath, take a shower, soap, rub the dirt off, scour, scrub, rinse, wipe, sponge, dip, fresh up*, wash up, clean up, brush up. **2** [To launder] clean, starch, scrub, put in a washing machine, boil, soap, send to the laundry, scour, rinse out, soak, drench.—*Ant.* DIRTY, stain, spoil. **3** [To brush with a liquid] swab, whitewash, color; see PAINT 2. **4** [*To be convincing] be plausible, stand up, endure examination; see ENDURE 1, SUCCEED 1.

washable *a.* tubfast, fast, unfading, launderable, permanent-press, colorfast, preshrunk.

washed *a.* **1** [Laundered] cleaned, scrubbed, bleached, boiled, put through the wash, soaped.—*Ant.* DIRTY, soiled, foul. **2** [Watered] bathed, dipped, drenched, sponged, doused, soaked, cleansed, submerged, showered.—*Ant.* DRY, scorching, desert.

washed-up* *a.* finished, defeated, done for*; see RUINED 1, 2.

washer *n.* dishwasher, washing machine, laundry machine; see APPLIANCE, MACHINE.

washing *n.* laundry, soiled clothes, dirty clothes; see WASH 1.

washout* *n.* disaster, disappointment, mess; see FAILURE 1, 2.

waste *v.* futile, discarded, worthless, valueless, useless, empty, barren, dreary, uninhabited, desolate, profit-

less, superfluous, unnecessary, functionless, purposeless, pointless, unserviceable.

waste *n.* **1** [The state of being wasted] disuse, misuse, dissipation, consumption, uselessness, devastation, ruin, decay, loss, exhaustion, extravagance, squandering, wear and tear, wrack and ruin; see also WEAR.—*Ant.* USE, PROFIT, VALUE. **2** [Refuse] rubbish, garbage, scrap; see TRASH 1. **3** [Unused land] desert, wilds, wilderness, wasteland, fen, tundra, marsh, marshland, bog, moor, quagmire, dustbowl, badlands, swamp, wash.

waste *v.* **1** [To use without result] dissipate, spend, consume, lose, be of no avail, come to nothing, go to waste, misuse, throw away, use up, misapply, misemploy, labor in vain, cast pearls before swine.—*Ant.* PROFIT, use well, get results. **2** [To squander] burn up, lavish, scatter, splurge, spend, be prodigal, indulge, abuse, empty, drain, fatigue, spill, impoverish, misspend, exhaust, fritter away, ruin, be spendthrift, divert, go through, gamble away, throw money away*, run through, hang the expense*, blow*, burn the candle at both ends.—*Ant.* SAVE, be thrifty, manage wisely. **3** [To be consumed gradually] decay, thin out, become thin, wither, dwindle, lose weight, be diseased, run dry, wilt, droop, decrease, disappear, drain, empty, wear.—*Ant.* GROW, develop, enrich.

waste′bas′ket *n.* a container for wastepaper, etc. Also **wastepaper basket**

wasted (wās′təd) *adj.* [Slang] **1** intoxicated by a drug **2** drunk

waste′ful *adj.* using more than is necessary —**waste′fully** *adv.* —**waste′ful·ness** *n.*

waste′land′ *n.* **1** barren land **2** an unproductive activity, endeavor, etc.

waste′pa′per *n.* paper thrown away after use Also **waste paper**

wast·rel (wās′trəl) *n.* one who wastes; esp., a spendthrift

watch (wäch, wôch) *n.* ⟦OE *wæcce*⟧ **1** a keeping awake, esp. in order to guard **2** close observation for a time **3** a guard, or the period of duty of a guard **4** a small timepiece carried in the pocket or worn on the wrist **5** *a)* any of the periods of duty (usually four hours) on shipboard *b)* the crew on duty during such a period — *vi.* **1** to stay awake, esp. at night; keep vigil **2** to be on the alert **3** to look or observe **4** to be looking or waiting attentively: with *for* — *vt.* **1** to guard or tend **2** to observe carefully **3** to wait and look for —**watch oneself** to be careful —**watch out** to be alert or careful —**watch′er** *n.*

watch′band′ *n.* a band of leather, metal, etc. to hold a watch on the wrist

watch′dog′ *n.* **1** a dog kept to guard property **2** one that keeps watch in order to prevent waste, unethical practices, etc.

watch′ful *adj.* watching closely; vigilant; alert —**watch′fully** *adv.* —**watch′ful·ness** *n.*

watch′man (-mən) *n., pl.* **-men** a person hired to guard property

watch′tow′er *n.* a high tower from which watch is kept, as for forest fires

watch′word′ *n.* **1** a password **2** a slogan or cry of a group, etc.

wa·ter (wôt′ər, wät′-) *n.* ⟦OE *wæter*⟧ **1** the colorless liquid of rivers, lakes, etc., which falls as rain **2** water with reference to its depth, surface, or level [above *water*] **3** a body secretion, as urine **4** a wavy, lustrous finish given to linen, silk, metal, etc. — *vt.* **1** to give (animals) water to drink **2** to supply (crops, etc.) with water **3** to moisten, soak, or dilute with water **4** to give a wavy luster to (silk, etc.) — *vi.* **1** to fill with tears: said of the eyes **2** to secrete saliva [his mouth *watered*] **3** to take on a supply of water **4** to drink water — *adj.* of, for, in, on, near, from, or by water —**hold water** to remain sound, logical, etc.

water bed a heavy vinyl bag filled with water and used as a bed or as a mattress in a special bed frame Also **wa′ter·bed′** *n.*

water buffalo a slow, powerful buffalo of S Asia used as a draft animal

water chestnut 1 a Chinese sedge with a nutlike tuber **2** this tuber

water closet TOILET (*n.* 3)

wa′ter·col′or *n.* **1** a pigment mixed with water for use as a paint **2** a painting done with such paints

wa′ter-cooled′ *adj.* cooled by water circulated around or through it

wa′ter·course′ *n.* **1** a stream, river, etc. **2** a channel for water, as a canal

wa′ter·craft′ *n., pl.* **-craft′** a boat, ship, or other water vehicle

wa′ter·cress′ (-kres′) *n.* a white-flowered water plant: its leaves are used in salads, etc.

wa′ter·fall′ *n.* a steep fall of water, as of a stream, from a height

wa′ter·fowl′ *n.* a water bird, esp. one that swims

wa′ter·front′ *n.* land or docks at the edge of a stream, harbor, etc.

water glass 1 a drinking glass **2** a silicate of sodium or potassium, dissolved in water to form a syrupy liquid used as an adhesive, etc. Also **wa′ter·glass′** *n.*

water hole a pond or pool

wa′ter·lil′y *n., pl.* **-ies 1** a water plant with large, flat, floating leaves and showy flowers **2** the flower

wa′ter·line′ *n.* the line to which the surface of the water comes on the side of a ship or boat

wa′ter·logged′ (-lôgd′) *adj.* soaked or filled with water so as to be heavy and sluggish: said of boats, etc.

water main a main pipe in a system of water pipes

wa′ter·mark′ *n.* **1** a mark showing the limit to which water has risen **2** a mark in paper, produced by pressure of a design, as in the mold — *vt.* to mark (paper) with a watermark

wa′ter·mel′on *n.* a large, green melon with sweet, juicy, red pulp

water moccasin a large, poisonous water snake of the SE U.S.

water pipe 1 a pipe for water **2** a smoking pipe using water, as a hookah

water polo a water game played with a ball by two teams of swimmers

water power the power of running or falling water, used to drive machinery, etc. Also **wa′ter·pow′er** *n.*

wa′ter·proof′ *adj.* that keeps out water, as by being treated with rubber, etc. — *vt.* to make waterproof

water rat any of various rodents living on the banks of streams and ponds

wa′ter-repel′lent *adj.* that repels water but is not fully waterproof

wa′ter·shed′ (-shed′) *n.* **1** a ridge dividing the areas

══ THESAURUS ══

wasted *a.* squandered, spent, destroyed, lost, consumed, eaten up, thrown away, shriveled, gaunt, emaciated, decayed, depleted, scattered, drained, gone for nothing, misapplied, useless, to no avail, down the drain, unappreciated, of no use, worthless.

wasteful *a.* extravagant, profligate, dissipated, prodigal, liberal, immoderate, overgenerous, cavalier, incontinent, thriftless, lavish, squandering, profuse, unthrifty, improvident, careless, reckless, wild, destructive, with money to burn*, easy come easy go, out of bounds.

wastefully *a.* extravagantly, carelessly, improvidently, wildly, immoderately, thriftlessly, recklessly, prodigally, destructively, foolishly, lavishly, inconsiderately, openhandedly, imprudently, ruthlessly, profusely, overgenerously, with no thought for tomorrow, without a second thought, without good sense, without consideration, without restraint.

watch *n.* **1** [A portable timepiece] wristwatch, pocket watch, stopwatch, digital watch, analog watch, sportsman's watch, fashion watch, ladies' watch, men's watch, children's watch, see also CLOCK. **2** [Strict attention] lookout, observation, observance, awareness, atten-

tion, vigilance, guard, heed, watchfulness.—*Ant.* NEGLECT, sleepiness, apathy. **3** [A period of duty or vigilance] patrol, guard duty, nightwatch; see GUARD. **4** [Persons or a person standing guard] guard, sentry, sentinel; see GUARDIAN 1.

watch *v.* **1** [To be attentive] observe, see, scrutinize, follow, attend, mark, regard, listen, wait, attend, take notice, contemplate, mind, view, pay attention, concentrate, look closely. **2** [To guard] keep an eye on, patrol, police; see GUARD. —**watch out** take care, heed, be cautious, proceed carefully, mind, go on tiptoe, take precautions, be on one's guard, make sure of, be doubly sure, keep an eye peeled, handle with kid gloves*. — **watch over** protect, look after, attend to; see GUARD.

watched *a.* guarded, spied on, followed, held under suspicion, scrutinized, observed, marked, kept under surveillance, noticed, noted, bugged*.

watchful *a.* on guard, vigilant, prepared; see CAREFUL.

watchfulness *n.* vigilance, alertness, caution; see ATTENTION.

watching *a.* vigilant, wary, alert; see CAREFUL.

watchman *n.* day watchman, watcher, sentinel, scout, spy, ranger, observer, spotter, signalman, flag-

man, shore patrol, night watchman, curator, guard, guardian, patrolman, detective, policeman, sentry, keeper, caretaker, lookout.

water *n.* **1** [Water as a liquid] rain, rainwater, liquid, drinking water, city water, mineral water, salt water, spa water, distilled water, limewater, H_2O. **2** [Water as a body] spring, lake, ocean, sea, gulf, bay, sound, strait, marsh, loch, puddle, pond, basin, pool, river, lagoon, reservoir, brook, stream, creek, waterfall, bayou.

water *v.* sprinkle, spray, irrigate; see MOISTEN.

watered *a.* **1** [Given water] sprinkled, showered, hosed, sprayed, washed, sluiced, bathed, drenched, wetted, irrigated, flooded, baptized, doused, soused, sodden, slaked, quenched; see also WET 1. **2** [Diluted] thinned, weakened, adulterated, lessened, contaminated, mixed, debased, impure, corrupt, blended, weakened, spread out, inflated, cheapened.

water power *n.* hydraulics, waterworks, water pressure, electricity, electric power; see also ENERGY 2.

waterproof *a.* impermeable, tight, airtight, vacuum-packed, oiled, rubber-coated, watertight, insulated, impervious, hermetically sealed.

drained by different river systems **2** the area drained by a river system

wa·ter·side′ (-sīd′) *n.* land at the edge of a body of water —*adj.* of, at, or on the waterside

wa·ter·ski′ *vi.* **-skied′, -ski′ing** to be towed on skilike boards (**water skis**) by a line attached to a speedboat

wa·ter·spout′ *n.* **1** a pipe for spouting water **2** a whirling funnel-shaped column of air full of spray occurring over water, usually in tropical areas

water table the level below which the ground is saturated with water

wa·ter·tight′ *adj.* **1** so tight that no water can get through **2** that cannot be misconstrued, nullified, etc.; flawless [a *watertight* plan]

water tower an elevated tank for water storage

wa·ter·way′ *n.* **1** a channel through which water runs **2** any body of water suitable for boats, ships, etc., as a canal or river

water wheel a wheel turned by running water, as for power

water wings an inflated device to keep one afloat as while swimming

wa·ter·works′ *n.pl.* [*often with sing. v.*] a system of reservoirs, pumps, etc. supplying water to a city

wa·tery *adj.* **1** of or like water **2** full of water **3** thin; diluted **4** tearful **5** weak —**wa′teri·ness** *n.*

WATS (wäts) *n.* [*w(ide) a(rea) t(elecommunications) s(ervice)*] a telephone service that ties a customer into the long-distance network through special lines, at special rates

watt (wät) *n.* [after James *Watt* (1736-1819), Scot inventor of steam engine] a unit of electrical power, equal to the power developed in a circuit by a current of one ampere flowing through a potential difference of one volt; $\frac{1}{746}$ of a horsepower

watt′age (-ij) *n.* amount of electrical power, expressed in watts

wat·tle (wät′'l) *n.* [OE *watul*] **1** a woven work of sticks intertwined with twigs or branches **2** a fleshy flap of skin hanging from the throat of certain birds or lizards — *vt.* **-tled, -tling 1** to intertwine (sticks, twigs, etc.) **2** to build of or with wattle

wave (wāv) *vi.* **waved, wav′ing** [OE *wafian*] **1** to move or sway to and fro **2** to signal by moving a hand, arm, etc. to and fro **3** to have the form of a series of curves — *vt.* **1** to cause to wave **2** to brandish (a weapon) **3** *a)* to move or swing (something) as a signal *b)* to signal (something) to (someone) by doing this **4** to give an undulating form to (hair, etc.) — *n.* **1** a ridge or swell moving along the surface of the ocean, etc. **2** an undulation or curve, as in the hair **3** a motion to and fro, as with the hand in signaling **4** a thing like a wave in action or effect; specif., an upsurge [a crime *wave*] **5** *Physics* a periodic motion or disturbance, as in the propagation of sound or light — **wave′like′** *adj.*

Wave (wāv) *n.* [< *W(omen) A(ppointed for) V(oluntary) E(mergency) S(ervice)*] a member of the women's branch of the U.S. Navy (**WAVES**)

wave′length′ *n.* *Physics* the distance measured along a wave from any given point to the next similar point, as from crest to crest

wave′let (-lit) *n.* a little wave

wa·ver (wā′vər) *vi.* [< ME *waven*, to wave] **1** to sway to and fro **2** to show indecision; vacillate **3** to falter, flicker, or tremble — *n.* a wavering

wavy (wā′vē) *adj.* **-i·er, -i·est 1** having or like waves **2** moving in a wavelike motion —**wav′i·ness** *n.*

wax¹ (waks) *n.* [OE *weax*] **1** a plastic, dull-yellow substance secreted by bees; beeswax **2** any plastic substance like this; specif., *a)* paraffin *b)* a substance exuded by the ears — *vt.* to rub, polish, cover, or treat with wax

wax² (waks) *vi.* **waxed, wax′ing** [OE *weaxan*, grow] **1** to increase in strength, size, etc. **2** to become gradually full: said of the moon **3** [Now Rare] to become [to *wax* angry]

wax bean a variety of the common garden bean with long, edible, yellow pods

waxen (wak′sən) *adj.* **1** made of wax **2** like wax; pale, plastic, etc.

wax museum an exhibition of wax figures, as of famous persons

wax myrtle an evergreen shrub with grayish-white, wax-coated berries

wax paper a paper made moisture-proof by a wax coating Also **waxed paper**

wax′wing′ *n.* a fruit-eating bird with brown or gray silky plumage and scarlet waxlike tips on the wings

wax′works′ *n.pl.* [*with sing. v.*] an exhibition of wax figures

wax′y *adj.* **-i·er, -i·est** of, full of, or like wax —**wax′i·ness** *n.*

way (wā) *n.* [ME < OE *weg*] **1** a road, street, path, etc. **2** space for passing **3** a route or course **4** course of life or conduct [avoid evil *ways*] **5** a method of doing something **6** a manner of living, acting, etc. [the *way* of the world] **7** distance [a long *way* off] **8** direction of movement **9** movement forward **10** respect; specific point [right in some *ways*] **11** wish; will [get one's own *way*] **12** [Colloq.] *a)* a condition [he's in a bad *way*] *b)* a locality [out our *way*] **13** [*pl.*] a timber framework on which a ship is built — *adv.* [Colloq.] away; far [*way* behind] —**by the way** incidentally —**by way of 1** passing through **2** as a method, etc. of —**give way 1** to yield **2** to break down —**lead the way** to be a guide or example —**make way 1** to clear a passage **2** to make progress —**under way** moving; advancing

way·far′er (-fer′ər) *n.* a traveler, esp. on foot —**way′far′ing** *adj.*, *n.*

way·lay (wā′lā′, wā′lā′) *vt.* **-laid′, -lay′ing 1** to lie in wait for and attack **2** to wait for and accost (a person) on the way

way′-out′ *adj.* [Colloq.] very unusual or unconventional

-ways (wāz) [ME < *way* (see WAY)] *suffix* in a (specified) direction, position, or manner [side*ways*]

THESAURUS

watery *a.* moist, damp, humid, soggy, sodden, wet, thin, colorless, washed, waterlike.—*Ant.* DRY, parched, baked.

wave *n.* **1** [A wall of water] comber, swell, roller, heave, tidal wave, billow, tide, surge, crest, bore, breaker, whitecap, curl*. **2** [A movement suggestive of a wave] surge, gush, swell, uprising, onslaught, influx, tide, flow, stream, come and go, swarm, drift, rush, crush, fluctuation. **3** [Undulating movement] rocking, bending, winding; see sense 2.

wave *v.* **1** [To flutter] stream, pulse, flow, shake, fly, dance, flap, swish, swing, tremble, whirl.—*Ant.* FALL, droop, hang listless. **2** [To give an alternating movement] motion, beckon, call, raise the arm, signal, greet, return a greeting, hail. **3** [To move back and forth] falter, waver, oscillate, vacillate, fluctuate, pulsate, vibrate, wag, waggle, sway, lurch, bend, swing, dangle, seesaw, wobble, reel, quaver, quiver, swing from side to side, palpitate, move to and fro; see also ROCK.

waver *v.* fluctuate, vacillate, hesitate,

dillydally, seesaw, deliberate, reel, teeter, totter, hem and haw, pause, stagger.

wavy *a.* **1** [Sinuous] bumpy, crinkly, curved; see ROUGH 1, TWISTED 1. **2** [Unsteady] wavering, fluctuating, vibrating; see UNSTABLE 1.

wax¹ *n.* *Waxes include the following:* paraffin, resin, spermaceti, beeswax, honeycomb, sealing wax, earwax, cerumen, carnauba wax, automobile wax, floor wax, furniture polish.

waxy *a.* slick, glistening, polished, slippery, smooth, glazed, sticky, tacky, glassy; see also SMOOTH 1.

way *n.* **1** [Road] trail, walk, byway; see HIGHWAY. **2** [Course] alternative, direction, progression, trend, tendency, distance, space, extent, bearing, orbit, approach, passage, gateway, entrance, access, door, gate, channel. **3** [Means] method, mode, means, plan, technique, design, system, procedure, process, measure, contrivance, stroke, step, move, action, idea, outline, plot, policy, instrument. **4** [Manner] form, fashion, gait, tone, guise, habit, custom, usage, behavior, style. —**by the**

way casually, by the by, as a matter of fact; see INCIDENTALLY. —**by way of** routed through, detoured through, utilizing; see THROUGH 4. —**get out of the** (or **one's**) **way** go, remove oneself, retire; see LEAVE 1, REMOVE 1. —**give way 1** [To collapse] sag, fall, crumble; see GIVE 2. **2** [To concede] yield, accede, grant; see ADMIT 2. —**in the way** bothersome, nagging, obstructing; see DISTURBING. —**make one's way** progress, succeed, do well; see SUCCEED 1. —**make way** draw back, give way, withdraw; see LEAVE 1. —**on the way out** declining, no longer fashionable, going out; see OLD-FASHIONED, UNPOPULAR. —**out of the way** disposed of, terminated, taken out; see GONE 1. —**parting of the ways** breakup, agreement to separate, difference of opinion; see FIGHT 1, SEPARATION 1. —**under way** going, prospering, making headway; see MOVING 1. —**way out** means of escape, salvation, loophole; see ESCAPE.

way-out* *a.* very different, revolutionary, strange; see EXTREME.

ways and means methods of raising money; specif., such methods, including legislation, in government

way′side′ n. the edge of a road

way′ward (-wərd) adj. [see AWAY & -WARD] 1 headstrong, willful, disobedient, etc. 2 unpredictable; erratic —**way′ward·ly** adv. —**way′ward·ness** n.

wd. 1 word 2 would

we (wē) pron., sing. **I** [OE] 1 the persons speaking or writing 2 I: used by a monarch, editor, etc. when speaking for others

weak (wēk) adj. [< ON veikr] 1 lacking physical strength; feeble 2 lacking moral strength or willpower 3 lacking mental power 4 lacking power, authority, force, etc. 5 easily torn, broken, etc. [a weak railing] 6 lacking intensity, force [a weak voice] 7 diluted [weak tea] 8 unconvincing [a weak argument]

weak′en vt., vi. to make or become weak or weaker

weak′-kneed′ (-nēd′) adj. lacking in courage, determination, resistance, etc.

weak′ling n. one that is low in physical or moral strength

weak′ly adj. -lier, -li·est sickly; feeble — adv. in a weak manner

weak′ness n. 1 state of being weak 2 a weak point; fault 3 an immoderate fondness (for something)

weal[1] (wēl) n. [< WALE] a mark raised on the skin, as by a blow; welt

weal[2] (wēl) n. [< OE wela, wealth, well-being] well-being; welfare [the public weal]

wealth (welth) n. [< prec.] 1 much money or property; riches 2 a large amount [a wealth of ideas] 3 valuable products, contents, etc. 4 everything having value in money

wealthy (wel′thē) adj. -i·er, -i·est having wealth; rich — **wealth′i·ness** n.

wean (wēn) vt. [OE wenian, to accustom, train] 1 to accustom (a child or young animal) to take food other than by suckling 2 to withdraw (a person) as from a habit

weapon (wep′ən) n. [OE wæpen] 1 any instrument used to injure or kill 2 any means of attack or defense —**weap′on·less** adj.

weap′on·ry (-rē) n. 1 the design and production of weapons 2 weapons collectively

wear (wer) vt. wore, worn, wear′ing [OE werian] 1 to bear (clothing, etc.) on the body 2 to show in one's appearance [to wear a smile] 3 to impair or diminish by use, friction, etc. 4 to make by rubbing, flowing, etc. [to wear a hole in the rug] 5 to tire or exhaust — vi. 1 to become impaired or diminished, as by use 2 to hold up in use [that suit wears well] 3 to have an irritating effect (on) — n. 1 a wearing or being worn 2 things worn; clothes [men's wear] 3 impairment or loss, as from use, friction, etc. —**wear off** to diminish by degrees —**wear′able** adj. —**wear′er** n.

wear and tear loss and damage resulting from use

weari·some (wir′i səm) adj. causing weariness; tiresome or tedious —**wea′ri·somely** adv.

weary (wir′ē) adj. -ri·er, -ri·est [OE werig] 1 tired; worn out 2 without further patience, zeal, etc. 3 tiring [weary work] — vt., vi. -ried, -ry·ing to make or become weary —**wea′ri·ly** adv. —**wea′ri·ness** n.

wea·sel (wē′zəl) n. [OE wesle] an agile flesh-eating mammal with a long, slender body and short legs — vi. [Colloq.] to avoid or evade a commitment: with out —**wea′selly** adj.

weather (weth′ər) n. [OE weder] 1 the condition of the atmosphere with regard to temperature, moisture, etc. 2

THESAURUS

ways and means n. methods, approaches, devices; see MEANS 1.

wayward a. unruly, disobedient, perverse, headstrong, capricious, delinquent, refractory, willful, unruly, unmanageable, insubordinate, incorrigible, recalcitrant, self-indulgent, changeable, stubborn.— Ant. OBEDIENT, stable, resolute.

we pron. you and I, he and I, she and I, they and I, us.

weak a. 1 [Lacking physical strength; said of persons] delicate, puny, flabby, flaccid, effeminate, frail, sickly, debilitated, senile; see also SICK.—Ant. STRONG, healthy, robust. 2 [Lacking physical strength; said of things] flimsy, makeshift, brittle, unsubstantial, jerry-built, rickety, tumbledown, sleazy, shaky, unsteady, ramshackle, rotten, wobbly, tottery.—Ant. STRONG, shatterproof, sturdy. 3 [Lacking mental firmness or character] weak-minded, nerveless, fainthearted, irresolute, nervous, spineless, unstrung, palsied, wishy-washy, hesitant, vacillating, frightened.—Ant. BRAVE, courageous, adventurous. 4 [Lacking in volume] thin, low, soft, indistinct, feeble, faint, dim, muffled, whispered, bated, inaudible, light, stifled, dull, pale.— Ant. LOUD, strong, forceful. 5 [Lacking in military power] small, paltry, ineffectual, ineffective, inadequate, impotent, ill-equipped, insufficiently armed, limited, unorganized, undisciplined, untrained, vulnerable, exposed, assailable, unprepared. 6 [Lacking in capacity or experience] unsure, untrained, young; see UNSTABLE 2.

weaken v. 1 [To become weaker] lessen, lose, decrease, relapse, soften, relax, droop, fail, crumble, halt, wane, abate, limp, languish, fade, decline, totter, tremble, flag, faint, wilt, lose spirit, become disheartened, fail in courage, slow down, break up, crack up*, wash out*.— Ant. STRENGTHEN, revive, straighten. 2 [To make weaker] reduce, minimize, enervate, debilitate, exhaust,

cripple, unman, emasculate, castrate, devitalize, undermine, impair, sap, enfeeble, unnerve, incapacitate, impoverish, thin, dilute, take the wind out of, wash up*; see also DECREASE 2.—Ant. REVIVE, quicken, animate.

weakling n. puny person, feeble creature, dotard, coward, crybaby, milksop, jellyfish*, softy*, sissy*, pushover*, namby-pamby.

weakness n. 1 [The state of being weak] feebleness, senility, delicacy, invalidity, frailty, faintness, prostration, decrepitude, debility, impotence, enervation, dizziness, infirmity.—Ant. STRENGTH, good health, vitality. 2 [An instance or manner of being weak] fault, failing, deficiency, defect, disturbance, lapse, vice, sore point, gap, flaw, instability, sin, indecision, inconstancy, vulnerability.—Ant. VIRTUE, good, strength. 3 [Inclination] liking, tendency, bent; see HUNGER, INCLINATION 1.

wealth n. capital, capital stock, economic resources, stock, stocks and bonds, securities, vested interests, land, property, labor power, commodities, cash, money in the bank, money, natural resources, assets, belongings, property, fortune, hoard, treasure, resources, revenue, cache, cash, competence, luxury, opulence, prosperity, abundance, money to burn*.—Ant. POVERTY, pauperism, unemployment.

wealthy a. opulent, moneyed, affluent; see RICH 1.

weapon n. armament, protection, weaponry, deadly weapon, military hardware, sophisticated hardware, lethal weapon, defense. Weapons include the following: club, spear, arrow, knife, catapult, bullet, dart, missile, ABM (antiballistic missile), MRV (multiple re-entry vehicle), MIRV (multiple independently-targetable re-entry vehicle), CAM (cybernetic anthropomorphic machine), CBW (chemical and biological warfare), bomb, stick, ax, fire-

arm, cannon, gun, musket, rifle, blackjack, whip, sword, pistol, revolver, bayonet, machine gun, warhead, airplane, tank, destroyer.

wear n. depreciation, damage, loss, erosion, wear and tear, loss by friction, diminution, waste, corrosion, impairment, wearing away, disappearance, result of friction.—Ant. GROWTH, accretion, building up.

wear v. 1 [To use as clothing or personal ornament] bear, carry, effect, put on, don, be clothed, slip on, have on, dress in, attire, cover, wrap, harness, get into*; see also DRESS 2.— Ant. UNDRESS, take off, disrobe. 2 [To consume by wearing] use up, use, consume, wear thin, wear out, waste, diminish, cut down, scrape off, exhaust, fatigue, weather down, impair. 3 [To be consumed by wearing] fade, go to seed, decay, crumble, dwindle, shrink, decline, deteriorate, decrease, waste, become threadbare. —**wear down** wear out, get thinner, get worn out; see DECREASE 1, WASTE 3. —**wear off** go away, get better, decline; see STOP 2. —**wear out** become worn, be worthless, get thinner; see WASTE 1, 3.

wear and tear n. depletion, wearing, effect of use; see DAMAGE 1, 2, DESTRUCTION 2.

weariness n. tiredness, exhaustion, dullness; see FATIGUE.

weary a. exhausted, fatigued, overworked; see TIRED.

weary v. 1 [To make weary] annoy, vex, distress, irk, strain, overwork, exhaust, fatigue, tire, harass, bore, disgust, dishearten, dispirit, wear out, cause ennui, leave one cold, depress, glut, overstuff, burden, sicken, nauseate. 2 [To become weary] pall, flag, be worn out, sink, droop, lose interest, fall off, tire, grow tired, drowse, doze, sicken.—Ant. ENJOY, excite, be amused.

weather n. climate, atmospheric conditions, air conditions, drought, clear weather, sunny weather, foul weather, tempest, calm, windiness, storm, rain, etc. — **vt. 1** to expose to the action of weather **2** to pass through safely */to weather a storm/* **3** *Naut.* to pass to the windward of — *vi.* to become discolored, worn, etc. by exposure to the weather —**under the weather** [Colloq.] ill

weath′er·beat′en *adj.* showing the effect of exposure to sun, rain, etc.

weath′er·cock′ *n.* a weather vane in the shape of a rooster

weath′er·ing *n.* the effects of the forces of weather on rock surfaces

weath′er·ize′ *vt.* **-ized′, -iz′ing** to weatherstrip, insulate, etc. (a building)

weath′er·man′ *n.*, *pl.* **-men′** one whose work is forecasting the weather, or, esp., reporting it, as on TV

weath′er·proof′ *adj.* that can be exposed to wind, snow, etc. without being damaged — *vt.* to make weatherproof

weath′er·strip′ *n.* a thin strip of metal, felt, etc. covering the joint between a door or window and the casing, for keeping out drafts, etc.: also **weath′er·strip′ping** — *vt.* **-stripped′, weath′er·strip′ping** to provide with weatherstrips

weather vane a vane for showing which way the wind is blowing

weave (wēv) *vt.* **wove** or, chiefly for *vt.* 5 & *vi.* 2, **weaved, wo′ven** or **wove** or, chiefly for *vt.* 5 & *vi.* 2, **weaved, weav′ing** [OE *wefan*] **1** to make (a fabric, basket, etc.) by interlacing (threads, straw, etc.), as on a loom **2** to construct in the mind **3** to twist (something) into or through **4** to spin (a web), as spiders do **5** to make (one's way) by moving from side to side or in and out — *vi.* **1** to do weaving **2** to move from side to side or in and out — *n.* a method or pattern of weaving —**weav′er** *n.*

web (web) *n.* [OE *webb*] **1** any woven fabric **2** the network spun by a spider, etc. **3** a carefully woven trap **4** a network **5** a membrane joining the digits of various water birds, etc. — *vt.* **webbed, web′bing** to join by, or cover as with, a web

web′bing *n.* a strong fabric woven in strips and used for belts, etc.

web′foot′ *n.*, *pl.* **-feet′** a foot with the toes webbed — **web′-foot′ed** *adj.*

wed (wed) *vt.*, *vi.* **wed′ded, wed′ded** or **wed, wed′ding** [OE *weddian*] **1** to marry **2** to unite or join

Wed. Wednesday

wed·ded (wed′id) *adj.* **1** married **2** of marriage */wedded bliss/* **3** devoted */wedded to one's work/* **4** joined

wed′ding *n.* **1** the marriage ceremony **2** a marriage anniversary

wedge (wej) *n.* [OE *wecg*] **1** a piece of wood, metal, etc. tapering to a thin edge: used to split wood, lift a weight, etc. **2** anything shaped like a wedge **3** any act serving to open the way for change, etc. — *vt.* **wedged, wedg′ing 1** to force apart, or fix in place, with a wedge **2** to crowd together or pack (*in*) — *vi.* to push or be forced as or like a wedge

wed′lock′ *n.* [OE *wedlac*] the state of being married

Wednes·day (wenz′dā, -dē) *n.* [< *Woden*, Germanic god] the fourth day of the week

wee (wē) *adj.* **we′er, we′est** [OE *wege*] **1** very small; tiny **2** very early */wee hours of the morning/*

weed (wēd) *n.* [OE *weod*] any undesired, uncultivated plant, esp. one that crowds out desired plants — *vt.*, *vi.* **1** to remove weeds from (a garden, etc.) **2** to remove as useless, harmful, etc.: often with *out* —**weed′er** *n.* — **weed′less** *adj.*

weeds (wēdz) *n.pl.* [< OE *wæde*, garment] black mourning clothes

weed′y *adj.* **-i·er, -i·est 1** full of weeds **2** of or like a weed

week (wēk) *n.* [OE *wicu*] **1** a period of seven days, esp. one from Sunday through Saturday **2** the hours or days of work in this period

week′day′ *n.* any day of the week except Sunday and, often, Saturday

week′end′ or **week′-end′** *n.* the period from Friday night or Saturday to Monday morning: also **week end** — *vi.* to spend the weekend (*at* or *in*)

week′ly *adj.* **1** done, happening, etc. once every week **2** of a week, or of each week — *adv.* once a week; every week — *n.*, *pl.* **-lies** a periodical published once a week

ween (wēn) *vi.*, *vt.* [OE *wenan*] [Archaic] to think; suppose; imagine

weep (wēp) *vi.*, *vt.* **wept, weep′ing** [OE *wepan*] **1** to shed (tears) **2** to mourn (*for*) **3** to drip or exude (water, etc.) —**weep′er** *n.*

weep′ing *n.* the act of one who weeps — *adj.* **1** that weeps **2** having graceful, drooping branches

weeping willow an ornamental willow tree with drooping branches

weepy (wē′pē) *adj.* **-i·er, -i·est** weeping or inclined to weep

wee·vil (wē′vəl) *n.* [OE *wifel*] a beetle whose larvae feed on grain, cotton, etc.

weft (weft) *n.* [< OE *wefan*, to weave] *Weaving* the woof

weigh (wā) *vt.* [OE *wegan*, carry] **1** to determine the weight of **2** to have (a specified) weight **3** to consider and choose carefully */weigh one's words/* **4** to hoist (an anchor) — *vi.* **1** to have significance, importance, etc. **2** to be a burden —**weigh down** to burden or bear down on

weight (wāt) *n.* [OE *wiht*] **1** a quantity weighing a definite amount **2** *a)* heaviness *b) Physics* the force of grav-

---

THESAURUS

the elements, cloudiness, heat, cold, warmth, chilliness.
weather *v.* **1** [To expose to the weather] dry, bleach, discolor, blanch, whiten, pulverize, tan, burn, expose, harden, petrify. **2** [To pass through adversity successfully] overcome, stand up against, bear the brunt of; see ENDURE 1, SUCCEED 1.

weather-beaten *a.* decayed, battered, weathered; see OLD 2, 3, WORN 2.

weatherman *n.* weather reporter, weather prophet, weather forecaster, meteorologist, climatologist, weather bureau, weather station, newsman.

weather report *n.* weather picture, weathercast, meteorological forecast; see FORECAST.

weave *n.* pattern, design, texture; see WEB.

weave *v.* **1** [To construct by interlacing] knit, sew, interlace, spin, twine, intertwine, crisscross, interlink, wreathe, mesh, net, knot, twill, fold, interfold, ply, reticulate, loop, splice, braid, plait, twist. **2** [To move in and out] sidle through, make one's way, twist and turn, snake, zigzag, beat one's way, insinuate oneself through, wedge through.

web *n.* cobweb, lacework, netting, plait, mesh, mat, matting, wicker, weft, warp, woof, network, interconnection, reticulation, intermixture,

entanglement, tracery, filigree, interweaving, trellis.

wed *v.* espouse, join in wedlock, take in marriage; see MARRY 1, 2.

wedded *a.* married, espoused, in holy matrimony; see MARRIED.

wedding *n.* wedlock, nuptials, matrimony; see MARRIAGE.

wedge *n.* spearhead, prong, drive; see MACHINE, TOOL 1.

weed *n.* **1** [Wild plant] noxious weed, unwanted plant, prolific plant; see PLANT. *Common weeds include the following:* ragweed, nettle, wild morning-glory, pigweed, buckthorn, dandelion, lamb's quarters, buttonweed, dog fennel, plantain, quack grass, jimson weed, ironweed, wild sunflower, wild hemp, horsemint, foxtail, milkweed, wild barley, wild buckwheat, mullein, cheat grass, Russian thistle, tumbleweed, burdock, wild carrot, wild parsley, tarweed, vervain, wild mustard. **2** [*Cigarette or cigar] coffin nail*, fag*, joint*; see TOBACCO. **3** [*Marijuana] pot*, Mary Jane*, grass*; see MARIJUANA.

week *n.* wk., seven days, six days, forty-hour week, working week, work week.

weekday *n.* working day, Monday through Friday, not a Sunday or Saturday; see DAY 1.

weekend *n.* end of the week, Saturday to Monday, short vacation, English weekend.

weekly *a.* once every seven days, once a week, occurring every week.

weep *v.* wail, moan, lament; see CRY 1.

weigh *v.* **1** [To take the weight of] measure, scale, put on the scales, hold the scales, put in the balance, counterbalance, heft*; see also MEASURE 1. **2** [To have weight] be heavy, carry weight, be important, tell, count, show, register, press, pull, be a load, burden, tip the beams*. **3** [To consider] ponder, contemplate, balance; see CONSIDER. —**weigh down** pull down, burden, oppress; see DEPRESS 2.

weight *n.* **1** [Heaviness] pressure, load, gross weight, net weight, dead weight, molecular weight, gravity, burden, mass, density, ponderability, tonnage, ballast, substance, G-factor*; see also MEASUREMENT 2, PRESSURE 1.—*Ant.* LIGHTNESS, buoyancy, airiness. **2** [An object used for its weight] counterbalance, counterweight, counterpoise, ballast, paperweight, stone, rock, lead weight, sinker, anchor, plumb, sandbag. *Common weights include the following:* ounce, pound, ton, long ton, kilogram, centigram, gram, gram ity acting on a body **3** amount of heaviness **4** *a)* any unit of heaviness *b)* any system of such units *c)* a piece having a specific amount of heaviness, placed on a balance or scale in weighing **5** any mass used for its heaviness *[a paperweight]* **6** a burden, as of sorrow **7** importance or consequence **8** influence; power — *vt.* **1** to add weight to **2** to burden

weight′less *adj.* having little or no apparent weight, as an astronaut in orbit —**weight′less·ness** *n.*

weight lifting the athletic exercise or sport of lifting barbells —**weight lifter**

weight′y *adj.* **-i·er, -i·est 1** very heavy **2** burdensome **3** significant; important —**weight′i·ness** *n.*

weir (wir) *n.* [OE *wer*] **1** a low dam built to back up water, as for a mill **2** a fence, as of brushwood, in a stream, etc., for catching fish

weird (wird) *adj.* [< OE *wyrd*, fate] **1** of or about ghosts, etc.; mysterious, eerie, etc. **2** strange; bizarre —**weird′ly** *adv.* —**weird′ness** *n.*

weirdo (wir′dō) *n.*, *pl.* **-os** [Slang] one that is weird, bizarre, etc. Also **weird′ie** (-dē)

wel·come (wel′kəm) *adj.* [OE *wilcuma*, welcome guest] **1** gladly received *[a welcome guest]* **2** freely permitted *[he is welcome* to use my car*]* **3** under no obligation *[you're welcome]* — *n.* a welcoming — *vt.* **-comed, -com·ing** to greet or receive with pleasure, etc.

weld (weld) *vt.* [< obs. *well*] **1** to unite (pieces of metal, etc.) by heating until fused or until soft enough to hammer together **2** to unite closely — *vi.* to be welded — *n.* **1** a welding **2** the joint formed by welding —**weld′able** *adj.* —**weld′er** *n.*

wel·fare (wel′fer′) *n.* [ME: see WELL[2] & FARE] **1** condition of health, happiness, prosperity, etc.; well-being **2** *a)* the organized efforts of government agencies granting aid to the poor, the unemployed, etc. *b)* such aid —**on welfare** receiving government aid because of poverty, etc.

wel·kin (wel′kin) *n.* [< OE *wolcen*, cloud] [Archaic] the vault of the sky

well[1] (wel) *n.* [OE *wella*] **1** a natural spring and pool **2** a hole sunk into the earth to get water, oil, etc. **3** a source of abundant supply **4** a shaft, etc. resembling a well **5** a container for a liquid, as an inkwell — *vi.*, *vt.* to gush or flow as from a well

well[2] (wel) *adv.* **bet′ter, best** [OE *wel*] **1** in a satisfactory, proper, or excellent manner *[treat her well,* to sing *well]* **2** prosperously *[to live well]* **3** with good reason *[one may well ask]* **4** to a considerable degree *[well advanced]* **5** thoroughly *[stir it well]* **6** with certainty; definitely **7** familiarly *[I know her well]* — *adj.* **1** suitable, proper, etc. **2** in good health **3** favorable; comfortable — *interj.* an exclamation of surprise, agreement, etc. —**as well (as) 1** in addition (to) **2** equally (with)

well-appointed (wel′ə point′id) *adj.* excellently furnished

well′-bal′anced *adj.* **1** precisely adjusted **2** sane, sensible, etc.

well′-behaved′ *adj.* behaving well; displaying good manners

well′-be′ing *n.* the state of being well, happy, or prosperous; welfare

well′-bred′ *adj.* showing good breeding; courteous and considerate

well′-disposed′ *adj.* friendly (*toward* a person) or receptive (*to* an idea, etc.)

well-done′ *adj.* **1** performed with skill **2** thoroughly cooked, as meat

well′-fed′ *adj.* plump or fat

well′-fixed′ *adj.* [Colloq.] wealthy

well′-found′ed *adj.* based on facts, good evidence, or sound judgment

well′-groomed′ *adj.* clean and neat

well′-ground′ed *adj.* having a thorough basic knowledge of a subject

well′-heeled′ *adj.* [Slang] rich; prosperous

well′-informed′ *adj.* having considerable knowledge of a subject or of many subjects

well′-inten′tioned *adj.* having or showing good or kindly intentions

well′-knit′ *adj.* **1** well-constructed **2** sturdy in body build

well′-known′ *adj.* **1** widely known; famous **2** thoroughly known

well′-made′ *adj.* skillfully and soundly put together

well′-man′nered *adj.* having good manners; polite; courteous

well′-mean′ing *adj.* **1** having good intentions **2** said or done with good intentions: also **well′-meant′**

well′-nigh′ *adv.* very nearly; almost

well′-off′ *adj.* **1** in a fortunate condition **2** prosperous

well′-preserved′ *adj.* in good condition or looking good, in spite of age

well′-read′ (-red′) *adj.* having read much

well′-round′ed *adj.* **1** well-planned for proper balance **2** showing diverse talents **3** shapely

well′-spo′ken *adj.* **1** speaking easily, graciously, etc. **2** properly or aptly spoken

well′spring′ *n.* **1** the source of a stream, etc. **2** a source of abundant supply

well′-thought′-of′ *adj.* having a good reputation

well′-timed′ *adj.* timely; opportune

well′-to-do′ *adj.* prosperous; wealthy

well′-turned′ *adj.* **1** gracefully shaped *[a well-turned ankle]* **2** expressed well *[a well-turned phrase]*

well′-wish′er *n.* one who wishes well to another or to a cause, etc.

well′-worn′ *adj.* much worn or used

welsh (welsh) *vi.* [Slang] to fail to pay a debt, fulfill an obligation, etc.: often with *on* —**welsh′er** *n.*

Welsh (welsh) *n.* [OE *Wealh*, foreigner] the Celtic lan-

■ THESAURUS ■

molecule, milligram, metric ton, metric carat, carat (grain), assay ton. **3** [Importance] influence, authority, sway; see IMPORTANCE.

weird *a.* uncanny, ominous, eerie; see MYSTERIOUS 2.

welcome *interj.* greetings, come right in, make yourself at home, how do you do?, glad to see you, won't you come in?.

welcome *a.* gladly received, gladly admitted, desired, appreciated, honored, esteemed, cherished, desirable, agreeable, pleasant, grateful, good, pleasing, delightful.—*Ant.* UNDESIRABLE, disagreeable, unpleasant. —**you're welcome** my pleasure, forget it, think nothing of it, don't mention it, it's nothing.

welcome *n.* greetings, salute, salutation, a hero's welcome, handshake, warm reception, free entrance, entree, hospitality, friendliness, the glad hand*.—*Ant.* rebuke, snub, cool reception. —**wear out one's welcome** bore others, stay too long, make others weary with one; see WEARY 1.

welcome *v.* embrace, hug, take in; see GREET.

welcomed *a.* received, accepted, initiated; see WELCOME.

weld *v.* fuse, unite, seam; see JOIN 1.

welfare *n.* **1** [Personal condition] health, happiness, well-being, prosperity, good, good fortune, progress, state of being. **2** [Social service] poverty program, social insurance, health service; see INSURANCE.

well[1] *n.* **1** [A source of water] spring, fountain, font, spout, geyser, wellspring, mouth, artesian well, reservoir. **2** [A shaft sunk into the earth] pit, hole, depression, chasm, abyss, oil well, gas well, water well. **3** [Any source] beginning, derivation, fountainhead; see ORIGIN 3.

well[2] *a.* **1** [In good health] fine, sound, fit, trim, healthy, robust, strong, hearty, high-spirited, vigorous, hardy, hale, blooming, fresh, flourishing, rosy-cheeked, whole, in fine fettle, hunky-dory*, great*, fit as a fiddle, chipper*.—*Ant.* SICK, ill, infirm. **2** [Satisfactorily] up to the mark, suitably, adequately, commendably, excellently, thoroughly, admirably, splendidly, favorably, rightly, properly, expertly, strongly, irreproachably, capably, soundly, competently, ably.—*Ant.* BADLY, poorly, unsatisfactorily. **3** [Sufficiently] abundantly, adequately, completely, fully, quite, entirely, con-

siderably, wholly, plentifully, luxuriantly, extremely.—*Ant.* HARDLY, insufficiently, barely. —**as well** in addition, additionally, along with; see ALSO. —**as well as** similarly, alike, as much as; see EQUALLY.

well-balanced *a.* steady, sensible, well-adjusted; see RELIABLE.

well-behaved *a.* mannerly, courteous, civil; see POLITE.

well-being *n.* prosperity, happiness, fortune; see HEALTH, WELFARE 1.

well-fixed* *a.* well-to-do, wealthy, in comfortable circumstances; see RICH 1.

well-informed *a.* informed, well-read, advised; see EDUCATED, LEARNED 1.

well-known *a.* famous, reputable, recognized, renowned, familiar, widely known, noted, acclaimed, popular, public, celebrated, in the public eye.—*Ant.* UNKNOWN, obscure, undiscovered.

well-off *a.* prosperous, well-to-do, wealthy; see RICH 1.

well-rounded *a.* well-informed, built-up, having a good background; see BALANCED.

well-to-do *a.* wealthy, well-off, prosperous; see RICH 1.

guage of Wales —*adj.* of Wales, its people, etc. —**the Welsh** the people of Wales —**Welsh′man** (-mən), *pl.* **-men,** *n.*

Welsh rabbit a dish of melted cheese served on crackers or toast Also **Welsh rarebit**

welt (welt) *n.* ⟦ME *welte*⟧ **1** a strip of leather in the seam between the sole and upper of a shoe **2** a ridge produced on the skin by a slash or blow

wel·ter (wel′tər) *vi.* ⟦< MDu *welteren*⟧ to roll about or wallow — *n.* a confusion; turmoil

welter·weight (wel′tər wāt′) *n.* ⟦prob. < *welt*, to beat⟧ a boxer weighing 136 to 147 pounds

wen (wen) *n.* ⟦OE *wenn*⟧ a benign skin tumor, esp. of the scalp

wench (wench) *n.* ⟦OE *wencel*, child⟧ **1** a young woman: derogatory or jocular term **2** [Archaic] a female servant

wend (wend) *vi.* **wend′ed, wend′ing** ⟦OE *wendan*, to turn⟧ to go on (one's way)

went (went) *vi., vt. pt. of* GO

wept (wept) *vi., vt. pt. & pp. of* WEEP

were (wur) *vi.* ⟦OE *wæron*⟧ *pl. & 2d pers. sing., past indic., and the past subjunctive, of* BE

we′re (wir) we are

were·wolf (wir′woolf, wur′-) *n., pl.* **-wolves′** ⟦OE *wer*, man + *wulf*, wolf⟧ *Folklore* a person changed into a wolf Also sp. **werwolf**

west (west) *n.* ⟦OE⟧ **1** the direction in which sunset occurs (270° on the compass; opposite east) **2** a region in or toward this direction — *adj.* **1** in, of, toward, or facing the west **2** from the west [a *west* wind] — *adv.* in or toward the west

west′erly *adj., adv.* **1** toward the west **2** from the west

west′ern *adj.* ⟦OE *westerne*⟧ **1** in, of, or toward the west **2** from the west — *n.* a movie, book, etc. about life in the western U.S., esp. during the frontier period

west′erner *n.* a native or inhabitant of the west

west′ern·ize′ *vt.* **-ized′, -iz′ing** to make western in habits, ideas, etc.

west′ward (-wərd) *adv., adj.* toward the west Also **west′wards** *adv.*

wet (wet) *adj.* **wet′ter, wet′test** ⟦OE *wæt*⟧ **1** covered or saturated with water or other liquid **2** rainy; misty **3** not yet dry [*wet* paint] **4** permitting the sale of alcoholic beverages — *n.* **1** water or other liquid **2** rain or rainy weather **3** one who favors the sale of alcoholic beverages — *vt., vi.* **wet** or **wet′ted, wet′ting** to make or become wet —**all wet** [Slang] wrong —**wet′ly** *adv.* —**wet′ness** *n.* —**wet′ter** *n.*

wet′back′ *n.* [Colloq.] a Mexican who illegally enters the U.S. to work: usually an offensive term

wet blanket one whose presence lessens the enthusiasm of others

wet nurse a woman hired to suckle another's child — **wet′-nurse′, -nursed′, -nurs′ing,** *vt.*

wet suit a closefitting suit of rubber worn by skin divers for warmth

whack (hwak) *vt., vi.* [echoic] to strike or slap with a sharp, resounding blow — *n.* **1** a sharp, resounding blow

2 the sound of this —**have (or take) a whack at** [Colloq.] **1** to aim a blow at **2** to make an attempt at —**out of whack** [Colloq.] not in proper condition — **whack′er** *n.*

whack′y *adj.* **-i·er, -i·est** [Slang] *alt. sp. of* WACKY

whale[1] (hwāl) *n.* ⟦OE *hwæl*⟧ a large, warmblooded sea mammal that breathes air — *vi.* **whaled, whal′ing** to hunt whales —**a whale of a** [Colloq.] an exceptionally large, fine, etc. example of

whale[2] (hwāl) *vt.* **whaled, whal′ing** ⟦prob. < WALE⟧ [Colloq.] to thrash

whale′bone′ *n.* the horny, elastic material hanging from the upper jaw of some whales (**whalebone whales**)

whal′er *n.* **1** a whaling ship **2** one whose work is whaling

wham (hwam) *interj.* a sound imitating a heavy blow, explosion, etc. — *n.* a heavy blow, etc. — *vt., vi.* **whammed, wham′ming** to strike, explode, etc. loudly

wham′my *n., pl.* **-mies** [Slang] a jinx

wharf (hwôrf) *n., pl.* **wharves** or **wharfs** ⟦OE *hwerf*, a dam⟧ a structure on a shore, at which ships are loaded or unloaded

what (hwut, hwät) *pron.* ⟦OE *hwa*, who⟧ **1** which thing, event, etc. [*what* is that object?] **2** that or those which [know *what* one wants] — *adj.* **1** which or which kind of: used interrogatively or relatively **2** as much, or as many, as [take *what* men you need] **3** how great, surprising, etc. [*what* nonsense!] — *adv.* **1** in what way? how? [*what* does it matter?] **2** partly [*what* with the singing, the time passed] **3** how greatly, etc. [*what* tragic news!] — *interj.* an exclamation of surprise, anger, etc. —**what about** what do you think, feel, etc. concerning? —**what for** why?

what·ever (hwut ev′ər) *pron.* what: an emphatic variant; specif., *a*) which thing, event, etc. *b*) anything that [say *whatever* you like] *c*) no matter what [*whatever* you do, don't hurry] — *adj.* **1** of any kind [no plans *whatever*] **2** being who it may be [*whatever* man said that, it is not true]

what′not′ (-nät′) *n.* **1** a nondescript thing **2** a set of open shelves, as for bric-a-brac

what′s (hwuts) **1** what is **2** what has **3** [Colloq.] what does [*what′s* he want?]

what·so·ever (hwut′sō ev′ər) *pron., adj.* whatever: an emphatic form

wheal[1] (hwēl) *n.* ⟦ME *whele*⟧ a small, itching elevation of the skin, as from an insect bite

wheal[2] (hwēl) *n.* WEAL[1]

wheat (hwēt) *n.* ⟦OE *hwæte*⟧ a cereal grass having spikes containing grains used in making flour, cereals, etc.

wheat germ the highly nutritious embryo of the wheat kernel

whee·dle (hwēd′'l) *vt., vi.* **-dled, -dling** ⟦< ?⟧ to influence, persuade, or get by flattery, coaxing, etc.

wheel (hwēl) *n.* ⟦OE *hweol*⟧ **1** a circular disk or frame turning on a central axis **2** anything like a wheel in shape, movement, etc. **3** the steering wheel of a motor vehicle **4**

▬ THESAURUS ▬

welt *n.* wound, bruise, weal; see INJURY.

west *a.* facing west, westerly, westwards; see WESTERN 1.

West *n.* **1** [Western Hemisphere] New World, the Americas, North and South America. **2** [European and American Culture] Occident, Western civilization, Christian society. **3** [Western United States; *especially the cowboy and mining culture*] the range, the prairies, Rocky Mountain country, Far West, Northwest, Southwest, where men are men*, wild-and-woolly country*, the wide open spaces*, Cow Country*, buffalo range*.

western *a.* **1** [In or toward the west] westwards, westerly, occidental, in the west, on the west side, where the sun sets, facing west, from the east, westerly, westernmost, westbound.—*Ant.* EASTERN, easterly, oriental. **2** [Having characteristics of the western part of the United States; *sometimes capital*] cowboy, middle-western, southwestern, far-western, in the sagebrush country, on the Western plains, in the wide open

spaces, in the wild west, in the Rockies, in God's country, in the wild-and-woolly West*, out where the men are men*.

westward *a.* to the west, in a westerly direction, westbound; see WESTERN 1.

wet *a.* **1** [Covered or soaked with liquid] moist, damp, soaking, soaked, drenched, soggy, muggy, dewy, watery, dank, slimy, dripping, saturated, sodden.—*Ant.* DRY, dried, clean. **2** [Rainy] drizzly, slushy, snowy, slippery, muddy, humid, foggy, damp, clammy, showery, drizzling, cloudy, misty.—*Ant.* CLEAR, sunny, cloudless.

wet *v.* sprinkle, dampen, splash; see MOISTEN.

whack *n.* stroke, thump, wham; see BLOW. —**out of whack*** out of order, not working, spoiled; see RUINED 1, 2.

wham *n.* hit, knock, whack; see BLOW.

wharf *n.* boat landing, quay, pier; see DOCK.

what *pron.* **1** [An indication of a

question] which?, what sort?, what kind?, what thing?, what means? **2** [Something indefinite] that which, whatever, something, anything, everything, whichever, anything at all. —**and what not** etcetera, and other things too numerous to mention, some more; see ANYTHING, EVERYTHING. —**what about** but what, remember, and then; see BUT 1, 2, 3. —**what for** but why, to what end, for what purpose; see WHY.

whatever *pron.* anything, everything, no matter what, whatsoever.

wheat *n.* staff of life, breadstuff, wheat flour; see GRAIN 1.

wheel *n.* **1** [A thin circular body that turns on an axis] disk, ratchet, ring, hoop, roller, caster, drum, ferris wheel, wheel trolley, flywheel, cogwheel, steering wheel, sprocket, wheel, chain wheel, water wheel. **2** [*An important person*] personage, VIP, big shot*; see CELEBRITY, EXECUTIVE. —**at the wheel** driving, in control, running things; see RUNNING 1, 2.

wheels* *n.* car, vehicle, buggy*; see

[*pl.*] [Slang] an automobile **5** [*usually pl.*] the moving forces [*the wheels* of progress] **6** a turning movement **7** [Slang] an important person — *vt., vi.* **1** to move on or in a wheeled vehicle **2** to turn, revolve, etc. **3** to turn so as to change direction —**at** (or **behind**) **the wheel** steering a motor vehicle, etc.

wheel′bar′row *n.* a shallow, open box for moving small loads, having a wheel in front, and two handles in back for moving the vehicle

wheel′base′ *n.* the length of a motor vehicle between the centers of the front and rear wheels

wheel′chair′ *n.* a chair mounted on wheels, for persons unable to walk

wheeled (hwēld) *adj.* having wheels

wheeler-dealer (hwēl′ər dēl′ər) *n.* [Slang] one who is showily aggressive, as in arranging business deals

wheel′wright′ *n.* one who makes and repairs wheels and wheeled vehicles

wheeze (hwēz) *vi.* **wheezed, wheez′ing** [< ON *hvæsa*, to hiss] to breathe hard with a whistling, breathy sound, as in asthma — *n.* a wheezing —**wheez′y, -i·er, -i·est,** *adj.*

whelk (hwelk) *n.* [OE *wioluc*] a large, edible marine snail

whelm (hwelm) *vt.* [ME *welmen*] **1** to submerge **2** to overpower or crush

whelp (hwelp) *n.* [OE *hwelp*] a young dog, etc. — *vt., vi.* to give birth to (young): said of some animals

when (hwen) *adv.* [OE *hwænne*] **1** at what time? [*when* did they leave?] **2** on what occasion? — *conj.* **1** at what time [tell me *when* to go] **2** at the time that [*when* we were young] **3** at which [a time *when* people must work] **4** as soon as [we will eat *when* he comes] **5** although — *pron.* what or which time [until *when* will you stay?] — *n.* the time (*of* an event)

whence (hwens) *adv.* [ME *whennes*] from what place, cause, etc.; from where [*whence* do you come?]

when·ev′er *adv.* [Colloq.] when: an emphatic form — *conj.* at whatever time [leave *whenever* you like]

where (hwer) *adv.* [OE *hwær*] **1** in or at what place? [*where* is it?] **2** to or toward what place? [*where* did he go?] **3** in what respect? [*where* is he to blame?] **4** from what place or source? [*where* did he learn it?] — *conj.* **1** at what place [I see *where* it is] **2** at which place [I came home, *where* I ate] **3** wherever **4** to the place to which [we go *where* you go] — *pron.* **1** the place at which [a mile to *where* I live] **2** what place [*where* are you from?] — *n.* the place (*of* an event)

where′abouts′ (-ə bouts′) *adv.* near or at what place? — *n.* [*with sing.* or *pl. v.*] the place where one is

whereas′ *conj.* **1** in view of the fact that **2** while on the contrary [she is slim, *whereas* he is fat]

whereat′ *conj.* [Archaic] at which point

whereby′ *conj.* by which

where′fore′ (-fôr′) *adv.* [Archaic] for what reason? why? — *conj.* **1** for which **2** because of which — *n.* the reason; cause

wherein′ *conj.* in which

whereof′ *adv., conj.* of what, which, or whom [the things *whereof* he spoke]

whereon′ *conj.* on which

where′upon′ *conj.* **1** upon which **2** at which

wher·ev·er (hwer ev′ər) *adv.* [Colloq.] where: an emphatic form — *conj.* in, at, or to whatever place or situation [go *wherever* you like]

where′with′ *conj.* with which

where′withal′ (-*with* ôl′) *n.* the necessary means, esp. money

wherry (hwer′ē) *n., pl.* **-ries** [ME *whery*] a light rowboat

whet (hwet) *vt.* **whet′ted, whet′ting** [< OE *hwet*] **1** to sharpen by rubbing or grinding, as a knife **2** to stimulate [to *whet* the appetite]

whether (hwe*th*′ər) *conj.* [OE *hwæther*] **1** if it be the case that [ask *whether* she sings] **2** in case; in either case that: introducing alternatives [*whether* it rains or snows]

whet·stone (hwet′stōn′) *n.* an abrasive stone for sharpening knives, etc.

whew (hyōō) *interj.* [echoic] an exclamation of relief, surprise, etc.

whey (hwā) *n.* [OE *hwæg*] the watery part of milk, that separates from the curds

which (hwich) *pron.* [OE *hwylc*] **1** what one (or ones) of several? [*which* do you want?] **2** the one (or ones) that [he knows *which* he wants] **3** that [the boat *which* sank] **4** any that [take *which* you like] — *adj.* what one or ones [*which* man (or men) left?]

which·ev′er *pron., adj.* **1** any one [take *whichever* (desk) you like] **2** no matter which [*whichever* (desk) he chooses, they won′t be pleased]

whiff (hwif) *n.* [echoic] **1** a light puff or gust of air, etc. **2** a slight odor

whiffle·tree (hwif′əl trē′) *n. var. of* WHIPPLETREE

Whig (hwig) *n.* [< *whiggamore* (contemptuous term for Scot Presbyterians)] **1** a member of a former English political party which championed reform **2** a supporter of the American Revolution **3** a member of a U.S. political party (*c.* 1834-56)

while (hwīl) *n.* [OE *hwīl*] a period of time [a short *while*] — *conj.* **1** during the time that [I read *while* I eat] **2** although; whereas [*while* not poor, she′s not rich] — *vt.* **whiled, whil′ing** to spend (time) in a pleasant way: often with *away*

whi·lom (hwī′ləm) *adj.* [< OE] former

whilst (hwīlst) *conj.* [Now Chiefly Brit., etc.] WHILE

whim (hwim) *n.* a sudden fancy; idle and passing notion

whim·per (hwim′pər) *vi., vt.* [? akin to WHINE] to cry or utter with low, whining, broken sounds — *n.* a whimpering sound or cry

whim·si·cal (hwim′zi kəl) *adj.* **1** full of whims or whimsy **2** oddly out of the ordinary —**whim′si·cal′ity** (-kal′ə tē) *n.* —**whim′si·cal·ly** *adv.*

whimsy (hwim′zē) *n., pl.* **-sies** [< ?] **1** an odd fancy; idle notion; whim **2** quaint or fanciful humor Also sp. **whim·sey**, *pl.* **-seys**

whine (hwīn) *vi.* **whined, whin′ing** [OE *hwinan*] **1** a) to utter a high-pitched, nasal sound, as in complaint b) to make a prolonged sound like this **2** to complain in a childish way — *n.* **1** a whining **2** a complaint uttered in a whining tone —**whin′y, -i·er, -i·est,** *adj.*

whinny (hwin′ē) *vi.* **-nied, -ny·ing** [prob. echoic] to

THESAURUS

AUTOMOBILE.

wheeze *v.* breathe heavily, puff, pant; see GASP.

when *a., conj.* **1** [At what time?] how soon?, how long ago?, in what period?, just when?, at which instant?. **2** [Whenever] if, at any time, at the moment that, just as soon as, in the event that, on the condition that; see also IF. **3** [During] at the same time that, immediately upon, just as, just after, at, while, meanwhile; see also DURING.

whenever *conj.* at any time, at any moment, on any occasion, at the first opportunity, if, when, should.

where *a., conj.* **1** [A question as to position] in what place?, at which place?, at what moment?, whither?, in what direction?, toward what?. **2** [An indication of position] wherever, anywhere, in whatever place, at which point, in which, to which, to what end.

whereabouts *n.* location, spot, site; see PLACE 3.

whereas *conj.* since, inasmuch as, insomuch as, forasmuch as, considering that, when in fact, while, while on the contrary.

whereby *conj.* by which, through which, in accordance with which, with the help of which, how.

wherefore *a.* why?, for what?, for which reason?, therefore, so, accordingly, thereupon.

whereupon *conj.* at which point, thereupon, at the conclusion of which, whereon, upon which, consequently.

wherever *a., conj.* where, in whatever place, anywhere, in any place that, wheresoever, regardless of where, in any direction.

whether *conj.* if, either, even if, if it follows that. —**whether or not** **1** [Surely] in any case, certainly, positively; see SURELY. **2** [If] whether, yes or no, whichever; see IF.

which *pron., a.* what, whichever, that, whatever, and that, and which, one, who.

whichever *pron., a.* which, whatever, whichsoever, no matter which, whoever.

whiff *n.* scent, puff, fume; see SMELL 1, 2.

while *conj.* **1** [As long as] during, at the same time that, during the time that, whilst, throughout the time that, in the time that. **2** [Although] whereas, though, even though; see ALTHOUGH. —**for a while** for a short time, for a few minutes, briefly; see AWHILE.

whim *n.* notion, vagary, caprice; see INCLINATION 1.

whimper *v.* fuss, weep, object; see COMPLAIN, WHINE.

whimsical *a.* playful, capricious, comical; see FUNNY 1.

whine *v.* sing, hum, whistle, whimper, drone, cry, moan, murmur, grumble, complain, gripe*, beef*.

neigh in a low, gentle way: said of a horse —*n.*, *pl.* **-nies** a whinnying

whip (hwip) *vt.* **whipped** or **whipt, whip′ping** 〚< MDu *wippen,* to swing〛 **1** to move, pull, throw, etc. suddenly *[to whip* out a knife*]* **2** to strike, as with a strap; lash **3** to wind (cord, etc.) around (a rope, etc.) so as to prevent fraying **4** to beat into a froth *[to whip* cream*]* **5** [Colloq.] to defeat — *vi.* **1** to move quickly and suddenly **2** to flap about — *n.* **1** a flexible instrument for striking or flogging **2** a blow, etc. as with a whip **3** an officer of a political party in a legislature who maintains discipline, etc. **4** a whipping motion —**whip up 1** to rouse (interest, etc.) **2** [Colloq.] to prepare quickly

whip′cord′ *n.* **1** a hard, twisted or braided cord **2** a strong worsted cloth with a diagonally ribbed surface

whip hand control or advantage

whip′lash′ *n.* **1** the lash of a whip **2** a sudden, severe jolting of the neck back and forth, as caused by the impact of an automobile collision

whip′per·snap′per *n.* an insignificant but presumptuous person

whip·pet (hwip′it) *n.* 〚< WHIP〛 a swift dog resembling a small greyhound, used in racing

whipple·tree (hwip′əl trē′) *n.* 〚< WHIP + TREE〛 SINGLETREE

whip·poor·will (hwip′ər wil′) *n.* 〚echoic〛 a grayish bird of E North America, active at night

whir or **whirr** (hwur) *vi., vt.* **whirred, whir′ring** 〚ME *quirren*〛 to fly, revolve, vibrate, with a buzzing sound — *n.* such a sound

whirl (hwurl) *vi.* 〚< ON *hvirfla*〛 **1** to move rapidly in a circle or orbit **2** to rotate or spin fast **3** to seem to spin *[my head is whirling]* — *vt.* to cause to move, rotate, revolve, etc. rapidly — *n.* **1** a whirling or whirling motion **2** a tumult; uproar **3** a confused or giddy condition —**give it a whirl** [Colloq.] to make an attempt

whirli·gig (hwurl′i gig′) *n.* any child's toy that whirls or spins

whirl′pool′ *n.* water in violent, whirling motion tending to draw floating objects into its center

whirlpool bath a bath in which an agitating device propels a current of warm water with a swirling motion

whirl′wind′ *n.* **1** a forward moving current of air whirling violently in a vertical spiral **2** anything like a whirlwind — *adj.* impetuous; speedy

whisk (hwisk) *n.* 〚< ON *visk,* a brush〛 **1** a brushing with a quick, light, sweeping motion **2** such a motion — *vt., vi.* to move, carry, brush (*away, off, out,* etc.) with a quick, sweeping motion

whisk broom a small, short-handled broom for brushing clothes, etc.

whisker (hwis′kər) *n.* **1** [*pl.*] the hair growing on a man's face, esp. on the cheeks **2** any of the long, bristly hairs on the upper lip of a cat, rat, etc. **3** a very small amount — **whisk′ered** *adj.*

whis·key (hwis′kē) *n., pl.* **-keys** or **-kies** 〚< Ir *uisce,* water + *beathadh,* life〛 a strong alcoholic liquor distilled from the fermented mash of grain Also sp., esp. for Brit. and Cdn. usage, **whisky,** *pl.* **-kies**

whis·per (hwis′pər) *vi., vt.* 〚< OE *hwisprian*〛 **1** to speak or say very softly, esp. without vibrating the vocal cords **2** to talk or tell furtively, as in gossiping **3** to make a rustling sound — *n.* **1** a whispering **2** something whispered **3** a soft, rustling sound —**whis′perer** *n.*

whist (hwist) *n.* 〚< earlier *whisk*〛 a card game: forerunner of bridge

whis·tle (hwis′əl) *vi.* **-tled, -tling** 〚OE *hwistlian*〛 **1** to make a clear, shrill sound as by forcing breath through the contracted lips **2** to move with a shrill sound, as the wind **3** *a)* to blow a whistle *b)* to have its whistle blown, as a train — *vt.* **1** to produce (a tune, etc.) by whistling **2** to signal, etc. by whistling — *n.* **1** an instrument for making whistling sounds **2** a whistling —**whis′tler** *n.*

whis′tle-blow′er *n.* one who informs on a wrongdoer

whis′tle-stop′ *n.* **1** a small town **2** a brief stop in a small town on a tour

whit (hwit) *n.* 〚< OE *wiht,* a wight〛 the least bit; jot; iota

white (hwit) *adj.* **whit′er, whit′est** 〚OE *hwit*〛 **1** having the color of pure snow or milk; opposite to black **2** of a light or pale color **3** pale; wan **4** lacking color **5** pure; innocent **6** having a light-colored skin — *n.* **1** *a)* white color *b)* a white pigment **2** a white or light-colored part, as the albumen of an egg or the white part of the eyeball **3** a person with a light-colored skin —**white′ness** *n.*

white blood cell (or **corpuscle**) LEUKOCYTE

white′cap′ *n.* a wave with its crest broken into white foam

white′-col′lar *adj.* designating or of office or professional workers

white-collar crime fraud, embezzlement, etc., committed by a person in business, government, or a profession

white elephant 1 an albino elephant **2** something of little use, but expensive to maintain **3** any object not wanted by its owner, but useful to another

white feather symbol of cowardice

white′fish′ *n., pl.* **-fish′** or (for different species) **-fish′es** a white or silvery edible fish, found in cool lakes of the Northern Hemisphere

white flag a white banner or cloth hoisted as a signal of truce or surrender

white gold a gold alloy that looks like platinum

white goods 1 household linens, as sheets, towels, etc. **2** large household appliances, as refrigerators, stoves, etc.

white heat 1 a temperature at which material glows white **2** a state of intense emotion, etc. —**white′-hot′** *adj.*

White House, the 1 official residence of the President of the U.S. in Washington, D.C. **2** the executive branch of the U.S. government

white lead a poisonous, white powder, lead carbonate, used in paint

white lie a lie about a trivial matter, often told to spare someone's feelings

white metal any of various light-colored alloys, esp. one containing much lead or tin, as pewter

whiten (hwit′'n) *vt., vi.* to make or become white or whiter —**whit′ener** *n.* —**whit′en·ing** *n.*

white paper 1 an official government report **2** any in-depth, authoritative report

white rat an albino rat, esp. one used in biological experiments

white sale a sale of household linens

THESAURUS

whip *n.* switch, strap, rod, cane, lash, scourge, knotted cord, knout, cat-o'-nine-tails, thong, blacksnake, dog whip, ox whip, bullwhip, horsewhip, buggy whip, riding whip, quirt.

whip *v.* thrash, strike, scourge; see BEAT 2, PUNISH.

whipping *n.* beating, thrashing, strapping; see PUNISHMENT.

whir *v.* whiz, swish, vibrate; see HUM.

whirl *n.* **1** [Rapid rotating motion] swirl, turn, flurry, spin, gyration, reel, surge, whir; see also REVOLUTION 1. **2** [Confusion] hurry, flutter, fluster, ferment, agitation, tempest, storm, rush, tumult, turbulence, commotion, hurly-burly, bustle.

whirl *v.* turn around, rotate, spin; see TURN 1.

whiskers *n.* beard, mustache, sideburns, goatee, hair, face hair, bristles, muff, chin armor, weeds.

whiskey *n.* bourbon whiskey, rye whiskey, corn whiskey, Scotch whiskey, Irish whiskey, Canadian whiskey, hard liquor, spirits, aqua vitae, firewater*, hooch*, home-brew, moonshine*, mountain dew*; see also DRINK 2.

whisper *n.* **1** [A low, sibilant sound] rustle, noise, murmur, hum, buzz, drone, undertone, hissing. **2** [A guarded utterance] disclosure, divulgence, rumor; see SECRET.

whisper *v.* speak softly, speak in a whisper, speak under one's breath, speak in an undertone, tell, talk low, speak confidentially, mutter, murmur, speak into someone's ear.— *Ant.* YELL, speak aloud, shout.

whispering *a.* rustling, sighing, buzzing, humming, murmuring, droning, hissing.

whistle *n.* **1** [A shrill sound] cry, shriek, howl, blast, piping, siren call, fire alarm, birdcall, signal, toot, blare; see also NOISE 1. **2** [An instrument that produces a shrill sound] fife, pipes, siren; see ALARM.

whistle *v.* **1** [To produce a shrill blast] fife, pipe, flute, trill, hiss, whiz, wheeze, shriek, howl, blare, toot, tootle; see also SOUND. **2** [To call with a whistle] signal, summon, warn; see SUMMON.

white *a.* **1** [The color of fresh snow] ivory, silvery, snow-white, snowy, frosted, milky, milky-white, chalky, pearly, blanched, ashen, pale, wan, albescent.—*Ant.* DARK, black, dirty. **2** [Colorless] clear, transparent, clean, blank, spotless, pure, unalloyed, neutral, achromatic, achromic. **3** [Concerning the white race] fair-skinned, light-complexioned, Caucasian; see EUROPEAN, WESTERN 2. **4** [Pale] ashen, wan, pallid; see PALE 1.

whiten *v.* **1** [To become white] grow hoary, blanch, turn white, turn gray, grow pale, be covered with snow, be silvered, change color, fade. **2** [To make white] bleach, blanch, silver, paint white, whitewash, apply powder, chalk.—*Ant.* DIRTY, smudge, blacken.

white slave a woman forced into prostitution for the profit of others —**white′-slave′** *adj.* —**white slavery**

white′wall′ *adj.* designating or of a tire with a white band on the outer sidewall — *n.* a whitewall tire

white′wash′ *n.* **1** a mixture of lime, chalk, water, etc., as for whitening walls, etc. **2** a concealing of faults in order to exonerate — *vt.* **1** to cover with whitewash **2** to conceal the faults of **3** [Colloq.] *Sports* to defeat (an opponent) soundly

white water foaming water, as in rapids, etc.

whither (hwith′ər) *adv.* [OE *hwider*] to what place, condition, result, etc.? where? — *conj.* **1** to which place, result, etc. **2** wherever

whit·ing[1] (hwīt′iŋ) *n.* [MDu *wit*, white] any of various unrelated food fishes of North America, Europe, etc.

whit·ing[2] (hwīt′iŋ) *n.* [ME *hwiting*] powdered chalk used in paints, etc.

whit′ish *adj.* somewhat white

Whit·sunday (hwit′sun′dā, -dē) *n.* [OE *Hwita Sunnandæg*, lit., white Sunday] PENTECOST

whit·tle (hwit′əl) *vt.* **-tled, -tling** [< OE *thwitan*, to cut] **1** *a*) to cut thin shavings from (wood) with a knife *b*) to carve (an object) thus **2** to reduce gradually — *vi.* to whittle wood

whiz or **whizz** (hwiz) *vi.* **whizzed, whiz′zing** [echoic] **1** to make the hissing sound of something rushing through the air **2** to speed by with this sound — *n.* **1** this sound **2** [Slang] an expert [a *whiz* at football]

who (hōō) *pron.* obj. **whom**, poss. **whose** [OE *hwa*] **1** what or which person or persons [*who* is he? I asked *who* he was] **2** (the, or a, person or persons) that [a man *who* knows]

WHO World Health Organization

whoa (hwō) *interj.* stop!: used esp. in directing a horse to stand still

who·dunit (hōō dun′it) *n.* [Colloq.] a mystery novel, play, etc.

who·ever (hōō ev′ər) *pron.* **1** any person that **2** no matter who [*whoever* said it, it's not so] **3** who?: an emphatic usage [*whoever* told you that?]

whole (hōl) *adj.* [OE *hal*] **1** healthy; not diseased or injured **2** not broken, damaged, etc.; intact **3** containing all the parts; complete **4** not divided up; in a single unit **5** not a fraction — *n.* **1** the entire amount **2** a thing complete in itself —**on the whole** all things considered; in general —**whole′ness** *n.*

whole′heart′ed *adj.* with all one's energy, enthusiasm, etc.; sincere

whole milk milk from which no butterfat, etc. has been removed

whole note *Music* a note having four times the duration of a quarter note

whole′sale′ *n.* the selling of goods in large quantities and at lower prices, esp. to retailers — *adj.* **1** of or having to do with such selling **2** extensive or indiscriminate [*wholesale* criticism] — *adv.* **1** at wholesale prices **2** extensively or indiscriminately — *vt., vi.* **-saled′, -sal′ing** to sell wholesale —**whole′sal′er** *n.*

whole′some (-səm) *adj.* [ME *holsom*] **1** promoting good health or well-being; healthful **2** improving the mind or character **3** having health and vigor —**whole′some·ness** *n.*

whole′-wheat′ *adj.* ground from whole kernels of wheat or made of flour so ground

wholly (hōl′lē) *adv.* to the whole amount or extent; totally; entirely

whom (hōōm) *pron.* objective case of WHO

whom·ev′er (-ev′ər) *pron.* objective case of WHOEVER

whoop (hwōōp; hōōp) *n.* [< ? OFr *houper*, cry out] **1** a loud shout, cry, etc., as of joy **2** the convulsive intake of air following a fit of coughing in whooping cough — *vt., vi.* to utter (with) a whoop or whoops

whoop′ing cough an acute infectious disease, esp. of children, with coughing fits that end in a whoop

whop·per (hwäp′ər) *n.* [< colloq. *whop*, to beat] [Colloq.] **1** anything extraordinarily large **2** a great lie

whop′ping *adj.* [Colloq.] extraordinarily large or great

whore (hôr) *n.* [OE *hore*] a prostitute —**whor′ish** *adj.*

who′re (hōō′ər) who are

whorl (hwôrl, hwurl) *n.* [ME *whorwyl*] anything with a coiled or spiral appearance, as any of the circular ridges that form the patterns of a fingerprint —**whorled** *adj.*

who′s (hōōz) **1** who is **2** who has

whose (hōōz) *pron.* [OE *hwæs*] that or those belonging to whom — *poss. pronominal adj.* of, belonging to, or done by whom or which

who·so·ever (hōō′sō ev′ər) *pron.* whoever: an emphatic form

why (hwī) *adv.* [OE *hwæt*, what] for what reason, cause, or purpose? [*why* eat?] — *conj.* **1** because of which [no reason *why* you shouldn't go] **2** the reason for which [that is *why* he went] — *n., pl.* **whys** the reason; cause — *interj.* an exclamation of surprise, impatience, etc.

wick (wik) *n.* [OE *weoca*] a piece of cord, tape, etc., as in a candle or oil lamp, that absorbs the fuel and, when lighted, burns

wicked (wik′id) *adj.* [ME < *wikke*, evil] **1** morally bad; evil **2** generally bad, unpleasant, etc. [a *wicked* storm] **3** mischievous **4** [Slang] showing great skill —**wick′edly** *adv.* —**wick′ed·ness** *n.*

wicker (wik′ər) *n.* [< Scand] **1** a thin, flexible twig **2** *a*) such twigs or long, woody strips woven together, as in making baskets *b*) WICKERWORK (sense 1) — *adj.* made of wicker

wick′er·work′ *n.* **1** things made of wicker **2** WICKER (*n.* 2*a*)

wicket (wik′it) *n.* [ME *wiket*] **1** a small door or gate, esp. one in or near a larger one **2** a small window, as in a box

---

■ THESAURUS ■

whitewash *v.* **1** [To cover with a lime wash] whiten, apply a white coating, wash; see PAINT 2. **2** [To give the appearance of innocence] gloss over, cover up, prove innocent; see EXCUSE.

whittle *v.* pare, carve, shape, fashion, shave, model, chip off, lessen, diminish, shave, decrease, pare down.

who *pron.* what, that, which, he, she, they, I, you, whoever, whichever.

whoever *pron.* he who, the one who, whatever person, whatever man, no matter who.

whole *a.* **1** [Entire] all, every, inclusive, full, undivided, integral, complete, total, aggregate, indivisible, organismic, inseparable, indissoluble, gross, undiminished, utter.—*Ant.* UNFINISHED, partial, incomplete. **2** [Not broken or damaged] thorough, mature, developed, unimpaired, unmarred, full, unbroken, undamaged, entire, in one piece, sound, solid, untouched, without a scratch, intact, uninjured, undecayed, completed, preserved, perfect, complete, safe, in A-1 condition, shipshape, in good order, together, unified, exhaustive, conclusive, unqualified, fulfilled, accomplished, consummate.—*Ant.*

BROKEN, mutilated, defective. **3** [Not ill or injured] hale, hearty, sound; see HEALTHY, WELL 1.

whole *n.* unity, totality, everything, oneness, entity, entirety, collectivity, sum, assemblage, aggregate, aggregation, body, lump, gross, entire stock, length and breadth, generality, mass, amount, bulk, quantity, universality, combination, complex, assembly, gross amount.—*Ant.* PART, portion, fraction.

wholehearted *a.* sincere, earnest, candid; see HEARTY.

wholesale *a.* **1** [Dealing in large lots] large-scale, in the mass, quantitative, in bulk, bulk, to the retailer, by the carload, loose, in quantity, in job lots; see also COMMERCIAL. **2** [Indiscriminate] sweeping, widespread, comprehensive; see WHOLE 1.

wholesome *a.* nutritive, nourishing, beneficial; see HEALTHFUL.

wholly *a.* totally, entirely, fully; see COMPLETELY.

whom *pron.* that, her, him; see WHO, WHAT 2.

whore *n.* call girl, harlot, streetwalker; see PROSTITUTE.

whose *poss. pronominal adj.* to

whom, belonging to what person, of the aforementioned one, from these.

why *a., conj.* for what reason?, how so?, how?, how is it that?, on whose account?, what is the cause that?, to what end?, for what purpose?, on what foundation?, how do you explain that?, how come?*.

wicked *a.* sinful, immoral, corrupt, evil, base, foul, gross, dissolute, wayward, irreligious, blasphemous, profane, evil-minded, vile, bad, naughty, degenerate, depraved, incorrigible, unruly, heartless, shameless, degraded, debauched, hard, toughened, disreputable, infamous, indecent, mean, remorseless, scandalous, atrocious, contemptible, nasty, vicious, fiendish, hellish, villainous, rascally, devilish, malevolent, plotting, conspiratorial, flagrant, criminal, heinous, murderous, tricky, sinister, ignoble, monstrous, rotten*, low-down*, good-for-nothing, dirty, felonious, dangerous, cut-throat, ratty*, slippery, crooked.—*Ant.* HONEST, just, kind.

wickedness *n.* evil, depravity, immorality; see EVIL 1.

office **3** *Croquet* any of the small wire arches through which the balls must be hit

wide (wīd) *adj.* **wid′er, wid′est** ⟦OE *wid*⟧ **1** extending over a large area, esp. from side to side **2** of a specified extent from side to side **3** of great extent *[a* wide *variety]* **4** open fully *[eyes* wide *with fear]* **5** far from the point, etc. aimed at: usually with *of [wide* of the target*]* —*adv.* **1** over a relatively large area **2** to a large or full extent *[wide* open*]* **3** so as to miss the point, etc. aimed at; astray —**wide′ly** *adv.* —**wide′ness** *n.*

-wide (wīd) *combining form* existing or extending throughout *[statewide]*

wide′-an′gle *adj.* having a wider angle of view than usual

wide′-awake′ *adj.* **1** completely awake **2** alert

wide′-eyed′ *adj.* with the eyes opened widely, as in surprise or fear

widen (wīd′n) *vt., vi.* to make or become wide or wider

wide′spread′ *adj.* occurring over a wide area or extent

widgeon (wij′ən) *n. alt. sp. of* WIGEON

widow (wid′ō) *n.* ⟦OE *widewe*⟧ a woman whose husband has died and who has not remarried —*vt.* to cause to become a widow —**wid′ow·hood′** *n.*

wid′ower *n.* a man whose wife has died and who has not remarried

width (width) *n.* **1** distance from side to side **2** a piece of a certain width *[two* widths *of cloth]*

wield (wēld) *vt.* ⟦OE *wealdan*⟧ **1** to handle (a tool, etc.), esp. with skill **2** to exercise (power, influence, etc.) —**wield′er** *n.*

wie·ner (wē′nər) *n.* ⟦< Ger *Wiener wurst*, Vienna sausage⟧ a smoked link sausage; frankfurter

wie·nie (wē′nē) *n.* [Colloq.] WIENER

wife (wīf) *n., pl.* **wives** ⟦OE *wif*, woman⟧ a married woman —**wife′less** *adj.* —**wife′ly** *adj.*

wig (wig) *n.* ⟦< PERIWIG⟧ a false covering of real or synthetic hair for the head —*vt.* **wigged, wig′ging 1** to furnish with a wig **2** [Slang] *a)* to annoy, upset, etc. *b)* to make excited, crazy, etc. (often with *out)* —*vi.* [Slang] to be or become upset, excited, etc.: often with *out*

wi·geon (wij′ən) *n.* ⟦prob. < L *vipio*, small crane⟧ any of certain wild, freshwater ducks

wig·gle (wig′əl) *vt., vi.* **-gled, -gling** ⟦ME *wigelen*⟧ to move or cause to move with short, jerky motions from side to side —*n.* a wiggling —**wig′gler** *n.* —**wig′gly, -glier, -gli·est,** *adj.*

wight (wīt) *n.* ⟦OE *wiht*⟧ [Archaic] a human being

wig·let (wig′lit) *n.* a small wig

wig·wag (wig′wag′) *vt., vi.* **-wagged′, -wag′ging** ⟦< obs. *wig*, to move + WAG[1]⟧ **1** to move back and forth; wag **2** to send (a message) by waving flags, lights, etc. according to a code —*n.* the sending of messages in this way

wig·wam (wig′wäm′) *n.* ⟦< Algonquian⟧ an American Indian dwelling consisting of a dome-shaped framework of poles covered with rush mats or bark

wild (wīld) *adj.* ⟦OE *wilde*⟧ **1** living or growing in its original, natural state **2** not lived in or cultivated; waste **3** not civilized; savage **4** not easily controlled *[a* wild *child]* **5** lacking social or moral restraint; dissolute *[a* wild *time]* **6** turbulent; stormy **7** enthusiastic *[wild* about golf*]* **8** fantastically impractical; reckless **9** missing the target *[a* wild *shot]* **10** *Card Games* having any desired value: said of a card —*adv.* in a wild manner —*n.* [*usually pl.*] a wilderness or wasteland —**wild′ly** *adv.* —**wild′ness** *n.*

wild′cat′ *n.* **1** any fierce, medium-sized, undomesticated cat, as the bobcat, ocelot, etc. **2** a productive oil well in an area not previously know to have oil —*adj.* **1** unsound or risky **2** illegal or unauthorized *[a* wildcat *strike]* —*vi.* **-cat′ted, -cat′ting** to drill for oil in an area previously considered unproductive —**wild′cat′ter** *n.*

wil·de·beest (wil′də bēst′, wil′-) *n.* ⟦Afrik⟧ GNU

wil·der·ness (wil′dər nis) *n.* ⟦< OE *wilde*, wild + *deor*, animal⟧ an uncultivated, uninhabited region; waste

wild′-eyed′ *adj.* **1** staring in a wild or demented way **2** very foolish or impractical

wild′fire′ *n.* a fire that spreads widely and rapidly

wild′flow′er *n.* **1** any flowering plant growing wild in fields, etc. **2** its flower Also **wild flower**

wild′fowl′ *n., pl.* **-fowls′** or **-fowl′** a wild bird, esp. a game bird Also **wild fowl**

wild′-goose′ chase a futile search, pursuit, or endeavor

wild′life′ *n.* wild animals and birds

wild oats a wild grass common in the W U.S. —**sow one′s wild oats** to be promiscuous or dissolute in one's youth

wild rice 1 an aquatic grass of the U.S. and Canada **2** its edible grain

Wild West [*also* w- W-] the western U.S. in its early, lawless, frontier period

wile (wīl) *n.* ⟦< OE *wigle*, magic⟧ **1** a sly trick; stratagem **2** a beguiling trick: *usually used in pl.* —*vt.* **wiled, wil′ing** to beguile; lure —**wile away** to while away (time, etc.)

wil·ful (wil′fəl) *adj. alt. sp. of* WILLFUL

will[1] (wil) *n.* ⟦OE *willa*⟧ **1** the power of making a reasoned choice or of controlling one's own actions **2** determination **3** attitude toward others *[a* man of good *will]* **4** *a)* a particular desire, choice, etc. of someone *b)* mandate *[the*

THESAURUS

wide *a.* **1** [Broad] extended, spacious, deep; see BROAD 1. **2** [Loose] broad, roomy, full; see LOOSE 1. **3** [Extensive] large-scale, all-inclusive, universal; see GENERAL 1.

wide-awake *a.* alert, watchful, vigilant; see CAREFUL.

widely *a.* extensively, generally, publicly, nationally, internationally, universally, in many places, broadly, comprehensively.

widen *v.* **1** [To make wider] add to, broaden, stretch, extend, increase, enlarge, distend, spread out, give more space, augment. **2** [To become wider] unfold, grow, open, stretch, grow larger, increase, swell, multiply.

widespread *a.* extensive, general, sweeping, broad, comprehensive, far-reaching, widely accepted, boundless, popular, public, unrestricted, unlimited, on a large scale, over-all.—*Ant.* OBSCURE, secret, limited.

widow *n.* widow woman, dowager, divorcée, husbandless wife, dead man's wife; see also WIFE.

widower *n.* surviving husband, grass widower, widowman*; see HUSBAND.

width *n.* breadth, wideness, girth, diameter, distance across, amplitude, cross dimension, cross measurement, expanse.—*Ant.* LENGTH, height, altitude.

wield *v.* handle, manipulate, exercise; see HOLD 1.

wiener *n.* frankfurter, sausage, hot dog*; see MEAT.

wife *n.* married woman, spouse, lady, dame, madam, matron, helpmate, consort, mate, housewife, better half*, the missis*, the little woman*, wifey*, the old lady*.—*Ant.* WIDOW, spinster, old maid.

wig *n.* artificial hair, fall, hairpiece; see HAIR 1.

wiggle *v.* wag, waggle, wriggle, squirm, shimmy, shake, flounce, dance sensually.

wild *a.* **1** [Not controlled] unrestrained, unmanageable, boisterous; see UNRULY. **2** [Uncivilized] barbarous, savage, undomesticated; see PRIMITIVE. **3** [Not cultivated] luxuriant, lush, exuberant, dense, excessive, desolate, waste, desert, weedy, untrimmed, uninhabited, native, natural, untouched, virgin, overgrown, uncultivated, untilled, uncared for, neglected, overrun, impenetrable, free, rampant. **4** [Inaccurate] erratic, off, unsound; see WRONG 2. **5** [Stormy] disturbed, raging, storming; see TURBULENT. **6** [Excited] hot, eager, avid; see EXCITED. **7** [Dissolute] loose, licentious, profligate; see LEWD 2. **8** [Imprudent] reckless, foolish, incautious; see CARELESS.

wilderness *n.* primitive area, wastelands, back country, the woods, the North woods, primeval forest, uninhabited region; see also DESERT, FOREST.

wildly *a.* hastily, rashly, fiercely, violently, ferociously, uncontrollably, carelessly, quixotically, savagely, unwittingly, recklessly, confusedly, pell-mell.—*Ant.* CAREFULLY, prudently, judiciously.

will[1] *n.* **1** [Desire] inclination, wish, disposition, pleasure, yearning, craving, longing, hankering. **2** [Conscious power] resolution, volition, intention, preference, will power, mind, determination, self-determination, decisiveness, moral strength, discretion, conviction, willfulness.—*Ant.* DOUBT, vacillation, indecision. **3** [Testament for the disposition of property] bequest, disposition, instructions, last wishes, bestowal, dispensation, last will and testament. —**free will** willingness, volition, intention, purpose, choice, free choice, power of choice, freedom, pleasure, discretion, inclination, desire, wish, intent, option, determination, mind, consent, assent.—*Ant.* RESTRAINT, predestination, unwillingness.

will[1,2] *v.* **1** [To exert one's will] decree, order, command, demand, authorize, request, make oneself felt, decide upon, insist, direct, enjoin. **2** [To wish] want, incline to, prefer; see WISH. **3** [An indication of futurity] shall, would, should, expect to, anticipate, look forward to, hope to, await, foresee, propose.

will of the people*]* **5** a legal document directing the disposal of one's property after death —*vt.* **1** to desire; want *[to will to live]* **2** to control by the power of the will **3** to bequeath by a will —*vi.* **1** to wish, desire, or choose —**at will** when one wishes

will² (wil) *v.aux. pt.* **would** [OE *willan,* to desire] **1** used to indicate simple future time *[when will she arrive?]* **2** used to express determination, obligation, etc. *[you will listen to me]* **3** used in polite questions *[will you have some wine?]* **4** used to express habit, expectation, etc. *[they will talk for hours]* **5** used to express possibility

will′ful (-fəl) *adj.* **1** said or done deliberately **2** doing as one pleases —**will′fully** *adv.* —**will′ful·ness** *n.*

wil·lies (wil′ēz) *n.pl.* [< ?] [Slang] a nervous feeling; jitters: with *the*

will′ing *adj.* **1** favorably disposed; consenting *[willing to play]* **2** acting, giving, etc. or done, given, etc. readily and cheerfully —**will′ingly** *adv.* —**will′ing·ness** *n.*

willi·waw or **wil′ly·waw′** (wil′i wô′) *n.* **1** a violent, cold wind blowing from mountains toward the coast in far northern or southern latitudes **2** confusion; turmoil

will-o′-the-wisp (wil′ə *thə* wisp′) *n.* **1** a light seen over marshes at night, believed to be marsh gas burning **2** a delusive hope or goal

wil·low (wil′ō) *n.* [OE *welig*] **1** a tree with narrow leaves, and flexible twigs used in weaving baskets, etc. **2** its wood

wil′lowy *adj.* like a willow; slender, lithe, etc.

will′pow′er *n.* strength of will, mind, or determination; self-control

willy-nilly (wil′ē nil′ē) *adv., adj.* [contr. < *will I, nill I: nill* < OE *nyllan,* be unwilling] (happening) whether one wishes it or not

wilt (wilt) *vi.* [< obs. *welk,* to wither] **1** to become limp, as from heat or lack of water; droop: said of plants **2** to become weak or faint; lose strength or courage —*vt.* to cause to wilt

Wil·ton (**carpet** or **rug**) (wilt′ʼn) [after *Wilton,* England] a kind of carpet with a velvety pile of cut loops

wily (wil′ē) *adj.* **-i·er, -i·est** full of wiles; crafty; sly —**wil′i·ness** *n.*

wim·ple (wim′pəl) *n.* [OE *wimpel*] a nun's head covering so arranged as to leave only the face exposed

win (win) *vi.* **won, win′ning** [< OE *winnan,* to fight] **1** *a)* to gain a victory *b)* to finish first in a race, etc. **2** to succeed in reaching a specified condition or place; get *[to win back to health]* —*vt.* **1** to get by labor, struggle, etc. **2** to be victorious in (a contest, etc.) **3** to get to with effort *[they won the camp by noon]* **4** to prevail upon; persuade: often with *over* **5** to gain (the sympathy, favor, etc.) of (someone) **6** to persuade to marry one —*n.* [Colloq.] a victory

wince (wins) *vi.* **winced, winc′ing** [< OFr *guenchir*] to shrink or draw back slightly, usually with a grimace, as in pain —*n.* a wincing

winch (winch) *n.* [OE *wince*] **1** a crank with a handle for transmitting motion **2** a machine for hoisting or hauling, having a cylinder upon which is wound the rope, etc. attached to the object to be moved

Win·ches·ter (**rifle**) (win′ches′tər) [after O. F. *Winches-* ter (1810-80), the manufacturer] *trademark for* a type of repeating rifle

wind¹ (wind) *vt.* **wound** or [Rare] **wind′ed, wind′ing** [OE *windan*] **1** to turn *[to wind a crank]* **2** to coil into a ball or around something else; twine **3** to cover by entwining **4** *a)* to make (one's way) in a twisting course *b)* to cause to move in a twisting course **5** to tighten the spring of (a clock, etc.) as by turning a stem: often with *up* —*vi.* **1** to move or go in a curving or sinuous manner **2** to take a devious course **3** to coil (*about* or *around* something) —*n.* a turn; twist —**wind up 1** to wind into a ball, etc. **2** to bring to an end; settle **3** to make very tense, excited, etc. **4** *Baseball* to swing the arm preparatory to pitching —**wind′er** *n.*

wind² (wind) *n.* [OE] **1** air in motion **2** a strong current of air; gale **3** air bearing a scent, as in hunting **4** air regarded as bearing information, etc. *[a rumor in the wind]* **5** breath or the power of breathing **6** empty talk **7** [*pl.*] the wind instruments of an orchestra —*vt.* **1** to get the scent of **2** to put out of breath —**break wind** to expel gas from the bowels —**get wind of** to hear of —**in the wind** happening or about to happen

wind′bag (wind′bag′) *n.* [Colloq.] one who talks much but says little of importance

wind′break′ *n.* a hedge, fence, etc. serving as a protection from wind

wind′chill′ factor CHILL FACTOR

winded (win′did) *adj.* out of breath

wind·fall (wind′fôl′) *n.* **1** something blown down by the wind, as fruit from a tree **2** an unexpected stroke of good luck

wind·ing sheet (win′diŋ) a shroud

wind instrument (wind) a musical instrument sounded by blowing air through it, as a flute

wind·jam·mer (wind′jam′ər) *n.* a large sailing ship or one of its crew

wind·lass (wind′ləs) *n.* [< ON *vinda,* to WIND¹ + *ass,* a beam] a winch, esp. one worked by a crank

wind·mill′ *n.* a mill operated by the wind's rotation of large vanes radiating from a shaft

win·dow (win′dō) *n.* [< ON *vindr,* WIND² + *auga,* an eye] **1** an opening in a building, vehicle, etc. for letting in light or air or for looking through, usually having a pane of glass in a movable frame **2** a windowpane **3** an opening resembling a window

window box a long, narrow box on or outside a window ledge, for growing plants

window dressing 1 the display of goods in a store window **2** that which is meant to make something seem better than it really is —**win′dow-dress′** *vt.* —**window dresser**

win′dow·pane′ *n.* a pane of glass in a window

win′dow-shop′ *vi.* **-shopped′, -shop′ping** to look at goods in store windows without entering to buy

win′dow·sill′ *n.* the sill of a window

wind·pipe (wind′pīp′) *n.* TRACHEA

wind′row′ (-rō′) *n.* a row of hay, etc. raked together to dry

wind shear a sudden change in wind direction, esp., dangerous vertical wind shifts encountered by aircraft

wind′shield′ *n.* in automobiles, etc., a glass screen, in front, to protect from wind, etc.

THESAURUS

willful *a.* intentional, premeditated, contemplated; see DELIBERATE.

willing *a.* energetic, prompt, reliable, active, obedient, enthusiastic, zealous, responsible, agreeable, prepared, voluntary, ready, compliant, amenable, tractable, feeling, like, in accord with.—*Ant.* OPPOSED, averse, unwilling.

willingly *a.* gladly, readily, obediently, agreeably, voluntarily, with relish, at one's pleasure, on one's own account, of one's own accord, with open arms, with good cheer, freely, with pleasure, cheerfully, with all one's heart, at the drop of a hat*, like a shot*.

willingness *n.* zeal, enthusiasm, readiness, earnestness, eagerness, alacrity, cordiality, hospitality, courteousness, compliance, good will, geniality.

wilt *v.* droop, wither, weaken, shrivel, flag, dry up, fade, become flaccid, lose freshness, faint.—*Ant.* GROW, STAND, stiffen.

win* *n.* triumph, conquest, victory; see SUCCESS 1.

win *v.* **1** [To gain a victory] be victorious, prevail, get the best of, come out first, conquer, overcome, overwhelm, triumph; see also SUCCEED 1. **2** [To obtain] get, acquire, gain; see GET 1. **3** [To reach] attain, accomplish, effect; see APPROACH 2, 3.

wind¹ *v.* **1** [To wrap about] coil, reel in, entwine, wreathe, shroud, fold, cover, bind, tape, bandage. **2** [To twist] convolute, screw, wind up; see BEND. **3** [To meander] zigzag, weave, snake, twist, loop, turn, twine, ramble, swerve, deviate. —**wind up** conclude, be through with, come to the end of; see END 1.

wind² *n.* draft, air current, breeze, gust, gale, blast, flurry, whisk, whiff, puff, whirlwind, flutter, wafting, zephyr, trade wind, sirocco, northeaster, southwester, tempest, blow, cyclone, typhoon, twister, hurricane, sandstorm, prevailing westerlies, stiff breeze, Chinook. —**get** (or **have**) **wind of*** hear about, have news of, trace; see HEAR 1. —**take the wind out of one's sails** best, get the better of, overcome; see DEFEAT 2, 3.

winding *a.* turning, gyrating, gyring, spiraling, twisting, snaky, serpentine, convoluted.—*Ant.* STRAIGHT, direct, vertical.

window *n.* skylight, porthole, bay window, bow window, picture window, casement, dormer, stained-glass, show window, rose window, transom, peephole.

windowpane *n.* pane, square of glass, glass; see WINDOW.

windpipe *n.* airpipe, bronchus, trachea; see THROAT.

windshield *n.* windscreen, protection against the wind, wraparound; see SCREEN 1.

wind'sock' *n.* a long, cloth cone flown at an airfield to show wind direction Also called **wind sleeve**

Wind·sor knot (win'zər) a double slipknot in a four-in-hand necktie

wind'storm' *n.* a storm with a strong wind but little or no rain, hail, etc.

wind'surf'ing *n.* the sport of sailing a kind of surfboard with a sail attached to a pivoting mast

wind tunnel a tunnel-like chamber through which air is forced, for testing the effects of wind pressure on aircraft, motor vehicles, etc.

wind·up (wind'up') *n.* **1** a conclusion; end **2** *Baseball* the swinging of the arm preparatory to pitching

wind'ward (wind'wərd) *n.* the direction from which the wind blows —*adv.* toward the wind —*adj.* **1** moving windward **2** on the side from which the wind blows

windy (win'dē) *adj.* **-i·er, -i·est** **1** with much wind *[a windy city]* **2** stormy, blustery, etc. **3** *a)* flimsy, intangible, etc. *b)* long-winded, pompous, etc. —**wind'i·ness** *n.*

wine (win) *n.* [< L *vinum*] **1** the fermented juice of grapes, used as an alcoholic beverage **2** the fermented juice of other fruits or plants —*vt., vi.* **wined, win'ing** to provide with or drink wine: usually in the phrase **wine and dine,** to entertain lavishly

wine'-col'ored *adj.* having the color of red wine; dark purplish-red

win'ery (-ər ē) *n., pl.* **-ies** an establishment where wine is made

wing (wiŋ) *n.* [ON *vaengr*] **1** either of the paired organs of flight of a bird, bat, insect, etc. **2** something like a wing in use, position, etc., esp., *a)* a (or the) main lateral supporting surface of an airplane *b)* a subordinate, projecting part of a building *c)* either side of the stage out of sight of the audience **3** the section of an army, fleet, etc. to the right (or left) of the center **4** a section, as of a political party, with reference to its radicalism or conservatism **5** a unit in an air force —*vt.* **1** to provide with wings **2** *a)* to send swiftly as on wings *b)* to make (one's way) by flying *c)* to pass through or over, as by flying **3** to wound in the wing, arm, etc. —*vi.* to fly —**on the wing** (while) flying —**take wing** to fly away —**under one's wing** under one's protection, etc. —**wing it** [Colloq.] to improvise in acting, speaking, etc. —**winged** (wiŋd; *poet.* wiŋ'id) *adj.* —**wing'less** *adj.*

wing'span' *n.* the distance between the tips of an airplane's wings

wing'spread' *n.* **1** the distance between the tips of fully spread wings **2** WINGSPAN

wink (wiŋk) *vi.* [OE *wincian*] **1** to close the eyelids and open them again quickly **2** to close and open one eyelid quickly, as a signal, etc. **3** to twinkle —*vt.* to make (an eye) wink —*n.* **1** a winking **2** an instant **3** a signal given by winking **4** a twinkle —**wink at** to pretend not to see

win·ner (win'ər) *n.* one that wins

win·ning (win'iŋ) *adj.* **1** victorious **2** attractive; charming —*n.* **1** a victory **2** [*pl.*] money that is won

win·now (win'ō) *vt., vi.* [< OE *wind*, WIND²] **1** to blow (the chaff) from (grain) **2** to scatter **3** to sift out

wino (win'ō) *n., pl.* **-os** [Slang] an alcoholic who drinks cheap wine

win·some (win'səm) *adj.* [OE *wynsum*, pleasant] sweetly attractive; charming —**win'somely** *adv.*

win·ter (win'tər) *n.* [OE] **1** the coldest season of the year, following autumn **2** a period of decline, distress, etc. —*adj.* of, during, or for winter —*vi.* to pass the winter —*vt.* to keep, feed, etc. during winter

win'ter·green' *n.* **1** an evergreen plant with white flowers and red berries **2** an aromatic oil (**oil of wintergreen**) made from its leaves and used as a flavoring **3** the flavor

win'ter·ize' *vt.* **-ized', -iz'ing** to put into condition for winter

win'ter·time' *n.* the winter season

win·try (win'trē) *adj.* **-trier, -tri·est** of or like winter; cold, bleak, etc. *[a wintry day]*

winy (win'ē) *adj.* **-i·er, -i·est** like wine in taste, smell, color, etc.

wipe (wip) *vt.* **wiped, wip'ing** [OE *wipian*] **1** to clean or dry by rubbing with a cloth, etc. **2** to rub (a cloth, etc.) over something **3** to apply or remove by wiping —*n.* a wiping —**wipe out** **1** to remove; erase **2** to kill off **3** to destroy —**wip'er** *n.*

wire (wir) *n.* [OE *wir*] **1** metal drawn into a long thread **2** a length of this **3** *a)* telegraph *b)* a telegram **4** the finish line of a horse race —*adj.* made of wire —*vt.* **wired, wir'ing** **1** to furnish, connect, bind, etc. with wire **2** to telegraph —*vi.* to telegraph

wired (wird) *adj.* [Slang] **1** provided with concealed electronic listening or recording equipment **2** extremely excited, nervous, etc.

wire'hair' *n.* a fox terrier with a wiry coat Also called **wire-haired terrier**

wire'less (-lis) *adj.* without wire; specif., operating by electromagnetic waves, not with conducting wire —*n.* **1** wireless telegraphy or telephony **2** [Chiefly Brit.] RADIO

wire service an agency sending news by wire or electronic means to its subscribers, as newspapers

wire'tap' *vi., vt.* **-tapped', -tap'ping** to tap (a telephone wire, etc.) to get information secretly —*n.* **1** a wiretapping **2** a device for wiretapping

wir'ing *n.* a system of wires, as to provide a house with electricity

wiry (wir'ē) *adj.* **-i·er, -i·est** **1** of wire **2** like wire; stiff **3** lean and strong —**wir'i·ness** *n.*

wis·dom (wiz'dəm) *n.* [OE: see WISE¹ & -DOM] **1** the quality of being wise; good judgment **2** learning; knowledge

wisdom tooth the back tooth on each side of each jaw

THESAURUS

windy *a.* breezy, blustery, raw, stormy, wind-swept, airy, gusty, blowing, fresh, drafty, wind-shaken, tempestuous, boisterous.—*Ant.* CALM, quiet, still.

wine *n.* *Wines include the following:* fine, sparkling, still, fortified, dry, sweet, heavy, light, white, rosé, red, green, blackberry, cherry, currant, gooseberry, dandelion; sacramental, dessert, dinner, medicinal, aperitif, cooking; California, New York State, French, Italian, sherry, Tokay, port, muscatel, Burgundy, Bordeaux, Champagne, Haut Sauterne, Rhine wine, Riesling, Traminer, Chablis, Chardonnay, white Chianti, red Chianti, Pinot, Concord, Catawba, Sauvignon blanc; see also DRINK 2.

wing *n.* **1** [An organ or instrument of flight] appendage, aileron, airfoil; see FEATHER. **2** [An architectural unit or extension] annex, addition, projection, hall, section, division, part. **3** [An organized group of aircraft] flying unit, formation, air squadron; see UNIT. —**take under one's wing** favor, help, guarantee; see ADOPT 2.

wink *v.* squint, blink, flirt, make eyes at, bat the eyes.

winner *n.* victor, conqueror, prize winner, champion, winning competitor, hero, successful contestant, leading entrant, Olympic champion, titleholder, champ*, front runner.

winning *a.* **1** [Engaging] attractive, appealing, agreeable; see CHARMING. **2** [Victorious] champion, conquering, leading; see SUCCESSFUL.

winter *n.* cold season, frosty weather, wintertime, Christmastime, Jack Frost.

wintry *a.* chilly, frosty, icy, snowy, frigid, cold, bleak, raw, biting, cutting.—*Ant.* WARM, summery, balmy.

wipe *v.* rub, clean, dry, dust, mop, clear, wash, swab, soak up, obliterate.
—**wipe out** slay, annihilate, eradicate; see DESTROY, KILL 1, REMOVE 1.

wire *n.* **1** [A metal strand] line, electric wire, cable, aerial, circuit, wiring, live wire, coil, conductor, filament, musical string, wire tape, wire cord. **2** [A metal net] barbed wire, wire fence, wire cage; see FENCE. **3** [A telegraphic message] cablegram, message, cable; see TELEGRAM. —**down to the wire** to the very end, at the last, eventually; see FINALLY 2.

—**get (in) under the wire** just make it, succeed, squeak through*; see ARRIVE.

wire *v.* **1** [To install wire] set up a circuit, install electricity, lay wires, connect electric cables, prepare for electrical service, pipe*; see also ELECTRIFY. **2** [To send a message by wire] flash, telegraph, notify; see TELL 1.

wiring *n.* wirework, electric line, cable work, cables, electrical installations, facilities for electric power, circuit system, electrical wire distribution, tubing, circuit pattern, circuiting, threading, process, route, line, path, pattern, trail.

wiry *a.* agile, sinewy, tough; see STRONG 1.

wisdom *n.* prudence, astuteness, sense, reason, clear thinking, good judgment, sagacity, understanding, sanity, shrewdness, experience, practical knowledge, carefulness, vigilance, tact, balance, poise, stability, caution, solidity, hardheadedness, brains, common sense, horse sense*, savvy*.—*Ant.* STUPIDITY, irrationality, rashness.

wise[1] (wīz) *adj.* **wis′er, wis′est** [OE *wīs*] **1** having or showing good judgment **2** informed [none the *wiser*] **3** learned **4** shrewd; cunning **5** [Slang] conceited, impudent, fresh, etc. —**wise′ly** *adv.*

wise[2] (wīz) *n.* [OE] way; manner

-wise (wīz) [< prec.] *suffix* **1** in a (specified) direction, position, or manner [lengthwise] **2** in a manner characteristic of [clockwise] **3** with regard to [budgetwise]

wise′a·cre (wīz′ā′kər) *n.* [ult. < OHG *wizzago*, prophet] one who makes annoyingly conceited claims to knowledge

wise′crack′ *n.* [Slang] a flippant or facetious remark — *vi.* [Slang] to make wisecracks

wish (wish) *vt.* [OE *wȳscan*] **1** to have a longing for; want **2** to express a desire concerning [I *wish* you well] **3** to request [I *wish* you to go] — *vi.* **1** to long; yearn **2** to make a wish — *n.* **1** a wishing **2** something wished for [to get one's *wish*] **3** a polite request, almost an order **4** [*pl.*] expressed desire for a person's health, etc. [best *wishes*] — **wish′er** *n.*

wish′bone′ *n.* the forked bone in front of a bird's breastbone

wish′ful (-fəl) *adj.* having or showing a wish; desirous — **wish′fully** *adv.*

wishy-washy (wish′ē wôsh′ē) *adj.* [Colloq.] **1** watery; thin **2** *a*) weak; feeble *b*) vacillating; indecisive

wisp (wisp) *n.* [prob. < Scand] **1** a small bundle, as of straw **2** a thin or filmy piece, strand, etc. [a *wisp* of smoke] **3** something delicate, frail, etc. —**wisp′y, -i·er, -i·est,** *adj.*

wis·te·ria (wis tir′ē ə) *n.* [after C. *Wistar* (1761-1818), U.S. anatomist] a twining vine with showy clusters of flowers Also **wis·tar′i·a** (-ter′-)

wist′ful (wist′fəl) *adj.* [< earlier *wistly*, attentive] showing or expressing vague yearnings —**wist′fully** *adv.* — **wist′ful·ness** *n.*

wit[1] (wit) *n.* [OE] **1** [*pl.*] powers of thinking; mental faculties **2** good sense **3** *a*) the ability to make clever remarks in a sharp, amusing way *b*) one characterized by wit

wit[2] (wit) *vt., vi.* **wist** (wist), **wit′ting** [OE *witan*] [Archaic] to know or learn —**to wit** that is to say; namely

witch (wich) *n.* [OE *wicce*] **1** a woman supposedly having supernatural power by a compact with evil spirits **2** an ugly, old shrew **3** [Colloq.] a fascinating woman or girl

witch′craft′ *n.* the power or practices of witches

witch doctor a person who practices medicine involving the use of magic, as among primitive societies

witch′er·y (-ər ē) *n., pl.* **-ies 1** witchcraft; sorcery **2** bewitching charm

witch hazel [< OE *wice*] **1** a shrub with yellow flowers **2** a lotion made from its leaves and bark

witch hunt [so named in allusion to persecutions of persons alleged to be witches] an investigation carried out ostensibly to uncover disloyalty, etc., usually highly publicized and often relying upon little evidence

with (with, with) *prep.* [OE] **1** in opposition to [to argue *with* a friend] **2** *a*) alongside of; near to *b*) in the company of *c*) into; among [mix blue *with* yellow] **3** as a member of [to play *with* a string quartet] **4** concerning [happy *with* his lot] **5** compared to **6** as well as [she rides *with* the best] **7** in the opinion of [it's OK *with* me] **8** as a result of [faint *with* hunger] **9** by means of **10** having received [*with* your consent, I'll go] **11** having as a possession, attribute, etc. **12** in the keeping, care, etc. of [leave it *with* me] **13** in spite of **14** at the same time as **15** in proportion to [wages that vary *with* skill] **16** to; onto [join one end *with* the other] **17** from [to part *with* one's gains] —**with that** after, or as a consequence of, that

with- *combining form* **1** away, back [withdraw] **2** against, from [withhold]

with·al (with ôl′, with-) *adv.* **1** besides **2** despite that

with·draw′ (-drô′) *vt.* **-drew′, -drawn′, -draw′ing 1** to take back; remove **2** to retract or recall (a statement, etc.) — *vi.* **1** to move back; go away; retreat **2** to remove oneself (*from* an organization, activity, etc.)

with·draw′al (-əl) *n.* **1** the act of withdrawing **2** the process of giving up a narcotic drug, typically accompanied by distressing physical and mental effects (**withdrawal symptoms**)

with·drawn′ *vt., vi.,* pp. of WITHDRAW — *adj.* shy, reserved, etc.

withe (with, with) *n.* [< OE *withthe*] a tough, flexible twig of willow, osier, etc., used for binding things — *vt.* **withed, with′ing** to bind with withes

with·er (with′ər) *vi.* [< ME *wederen*, to weather] **1** to dry up; wilt, as plants **2** to become wasted or decayed **3** to weaken; languish — *vt.* **1** to cause to wither **2** to cause to feel abashed

with·ers (with′ərz) *n.pl.* [< OE *wither*, against] the part of a horse's back between the shoulder blades

with·hold (with hōld′, with-) *vt.* **-held′, -hold′ing 1** *a*) to hold back; restrain *b*) to deduct (taxes, etc.) from wages **2** to refrain from granting

withholding tax the amount of estimated income tax withheld by an employer from an employee's pay, for direct payment to the government

with·in (with in′, with-) *adv.* [OE *withinnan*] **1** on or into the inside **2** indoors **3** inside the body, mind, etc. — *prep.* **1** in the inner part of **2** not beyond **3** inside the limits of — *n.* the inside [from *within*]

THESAURUS

wise[1] *a.* **1** [Judicious] clever, sagacious, witty; see THOUGHTFUL 1. **2** [Shrewd] calculating, cunning, crafty; see SLY. **3** [Prudent] tactful, sensible, wary; see CAREFUL 4 [Erudite] taught, scholarly, smart; see EDUCATED, LEARNED 1. **5** [Informed] wise to*, acquainted with, aware of; see FAMILIAR WITH.

wisely *a.* tactfully, prudently, circumspectly, sagaciously, shrewdly, judiciously, discreetly, carefully, admirably, discerningly, sagely, knowingly, reasonably, sensibly, intelligently.—*Ant.* FOOLISHLY, stupidly, unthinkingly.

wish *n.* longing, yearning, hankering, desire, thirst, disposition, request, hope, intention, preference, choice, want, prayer, invocation, liking, pleasure, injunction, command, order.

wish *v.* **1** [To desire] covet, crave, envy; see WANT 1. **2** [To express a desire] hope, request, entreat, prefer, want, pray for, invoke, command, order, solicit, beg, look forward to, require; see also NEED.

wishful *a.* desirous, longing, eager; see ZEALOUS.

wishy-washy *a.* cowardly, mediocre, feeble; see WEAK 3.

wit[1] *n.* wittiness, smartness, whimsicality, pleasantry, drollery, banter, burlesque, satire, jocularity, witticism, sally, whimsy, repartee, joke, aphorism, jest, quip, epigram, pun, wisecrack*, gag. —**at one's wits' end** downhearted, desperate, helpless; see TROUBLED. —**have (or keep) one's wits about one** be ready, take precautions, be on one's guard; see WATCH OUT. —**live by one's wits** use sharp practices, live dangerously, take advantage of all opportunities; see TRICK.

witch *n.* sorcerer, warlock, magician, enchantress, charmer, hag, crone.

witchcraft *n.* sorcery, magic, black magic, necromancy, witchery, divination, devil worship, enchantment, spell, bewitchment, voodooism, shamanism, demonology.

with *prep.* by, in association, in the midst of, among, amidst, along with, in company with, arm in arm, hand in glove, in conjunction with, among other things, beside, alongside of, including.

withdraw *v.* **1** [To retire] depart, draw back, take leave; see RETREAT. **2** [To remove from use or circulation] revoke, rescind, abolish, repeal, annul, abrogate, veto, suppress, repress, retire, stamp out, declare illegal, ban, bar, nullify, repudiate, reverse, retract, throw overboard, invalidate, quash, dissolve.

withdrawal *n.* removal, retreat, retraction, resignation, alienation, abandonment, recession, revulsion, abdication, relinquishment, departure.—*Ant.* PROGRESS, advance, appearance.

withdrawn *a.* retired, secluded, isolated, removed, departed, cloistered, recluse, drawn back, gone into retirement, taken out, absent, retreated.— *Ant.* ACTIVE, involved, progressing.

wither *v.* shrivel, shrink, droop, wilt, decay, die, grow brown, dry up, dry out, fade, lose freshness, deteriorate, fall away.—*Ant.* REVIVE, reawaken, bloom.

withered *a.* shriveled, wilted, decayed, deteriorated, shrunken, dead, browned, faded, parched, dried up, drooping, wrinkled.—*Ant.* FRESH, blooming, alive.

withheld *a.* concealed, held back, hidden, checked, restrained, delayed, denied, kept on leash, on ice*.—*Ant.* FREE, opened, made visible.

withhold *v.* hold back, reserve, keep; see DENY.

within *a., prep.* inside, indoors, in, not further than, not beyond, not over, in reach of, in a period of, not outside; see also INSIDE 2.

with′-it (-it) *adj.* [Slang] **1** sophisticated, up-to-date, etc. **2** fashionable; stylish

with·out′ *adv.* [OE *withutan*] **1** on the outside **2** out-of-doors — *prep.* **1** [Now Rare] at, on, or to the outside of **2** lacking **3** free from **4** with avoidance of /to pass by *without* speaking/

with·stand′ (-stand′) *vt., vi.* -stood′, -stand′ing to oppose, resist, or endure, esp. successfully

wit·less (wit′lis) *adj.* lacking wit; foolish —**wit′lessly** *adv.*

wit·ness (wit′nis) *n.* [< OE *witan,* know] **1** evidence; testimony **2** one who saw, or can give a firsthand account of, something **3** one who testifies in court **4** one who observes, and attests to, a signing, etc. — *vt.* **1** to testify to **2** to serve as evidence of **3** to act as witness of **4** to be present at —**bear witness** to testify

wit·ti·cism (wit′ə siz′əm) *n.* [< WITTY] a witty remark

wit·ting (wit′iŋ) *adj.* [ME *wytting*] intentional —**wit′tingly** *adv.*

witty (wit′ē) *adj.* -tier, -ti·est [OE *wittig*] having or showing wit; cleverly amusing —**wit′tily** *adv.* —**wit′ti·ness** *n.*

wive (wiv) *vi., vt.* wived, wiv′ing [OE *wifian*] [Archaic] to marry (a woman)

wives (wivz) *n. pl. of* WIFE

wiz·ard (wiz′ərd) *n.* [ME *wisard*] **1** a magician; sorcerer **2** [Colloq.] one very skilled at a specified activity

wiz′ard·ry *n.* magic; sorcery

wiz·ened (wiz′ənd) *adj.* [< OE *wisnian,* wither] dried up; withered

wk. **1** week **2** work

wkly. weekly

wob·ble (wä′bəl) *vi.* -bled, -bling [prob. < LowG *wabbeln*] **1** to move unsteadily from side to side **2** to shake **3** to vacillate — *vt.* to cause to wobble — *n.* wobbling motion —**wob′bly, -blier, -bli·est,** *adj.* —**wob′bli·ness** *n.*

woe (wō) *n.* [OE *wa*] **1** great sorrow; grief **2** trouble — *interj.* alas!

woe′be·gone′ (-bē gôn′, -bi-) *adj.* of woeful appearance; looking sad or wretched

woe′ful (-fəl) *adj.* **1** full of woe; sad **2** of, causing, or involving woe **3** pitiful; wretched —**woe′fully** *adv.*

wok (wäk, wôk) *n.* [Chin.] a bowl-shaped cooking pan used, as in a ringlike stand, for frying, steaming, etc.

woke (wōk) *vi., vt. alt. pt. of* WAKE[1]

woken (wō′kən) *vi., vt. alt. pp. of* WAKE[1]

wolf (woolf) *n., pl.* **wolves** (woolvz) [OE *wulf*] **1** a wild, flesh-eating, doglike mammal of the Northern Hemisphere **2** *a)* a cruel or greedy person *b)* [Slang] a man who flirts with many women — *vt.* to eat greedily —**cry wolf** to give a false alarm —**wolf′ish** *adj.*

wolf′hound′ (-hound′) *n.* a breed of large dog, once used for hunting wolves

wol·ver·ine (wool′vər ēn′) *n.* [< WOLF] a stocky, flesh-eating mammal of N North America and N Eurasia

wolves (woolvz) *n. pl. of* WOLF

woman (woom′ən) *n., pl.* **women** (wim′ən) [< OE *wif,* a female + *mann,* human being] **1** *a)* an adult female human being *b)* women collectively **2** a female servant **3** womanly qualities

-woman (woom′ən) *combining form* woman of a (specified) kind, in a (specified) activity, etc.: sometimes used to avoid the masculine implications of -MAN

wom′an·hood′ *n.* **1** the state of being a woman **2** womanly qualities **3** women collectively

wom′an·ish *adj.* like a woman

wom′an·ize′ *vt.* -ized′, -iz′ing to make effeminate — *vi.* [Colloq.] to be sexually promiscuous with women —**wom′an·iz′er** *n.*

wom′an·kind′ *n.* women in general

wom′an·like′ *adj.* womanly

wom′anly *adj.* **1** womanish **2** characteristic of or fit for a woman

womb (woom) *n.* [OE *wamb*] UTERUS

wom·bat (wäm′bat′) *n.* [< native name] a burrowing Australian marsupial resembling a small bear

women (wim′in) *n. pl. of* WOMAN

wom′en·folk′ *n.pl.* [Colloq. or Dial.] womankind Also **wom′en·folks′**

won (wun) *vi., vt. pt. & pp. of* WIN

won·der (wun′dər) *n.* [OE *wundor*] **1** a person, thing, or event causing astonishment and admiration; marvel **2** the feeling aroused by something strange, unexpected, etc. — *vi.* **1** to be filled with wonder; marvel **2** to have curiosity, sometimes mingled with doubt — *vt.* to have curiosity or doubt about /he *wondered* what happened/

won′der·ful *adj.* **1** that causes wonder; marvelous **2** [Colloq.] excellent, fine, etc. —**won′der·fully** *adv.*

won′der·land′ *n.* an imaginary land full of wonders, or a real place like this

won′der·ment *n.* amazement

won·drous (wun′drəs) *adj.* wonderful — *adv.* surprisingly Now only literary —**won′drously** *adv.*

wont (wänt, wōnt) *adj.* [< OE *wunian,* dwell] accustomed /he was *wont* to rise early/ — *n.* usual practice; habit

won′t (wōnt) will not

wonted (wänt′id, wōnt′-) *adj.* customary; accustomed

won ton (wän′ tän′) a Chinese dish of noodle casings filled with meat, etc., often served in a broth (**won-ton soup**)

woo (wōō) *vt.* [OE *wogian*] **1** to seek the love of, usually in order to propose marriage **2** to seek /to *woo* fame/ — *vi.* to woo a person —**woo′er** *n.*

wood (wood) *n.* [OE *wudu*] **1** [*usually pl.*] a thick growth of trees; forest **2** the hard, fibrous substance beneath the

---

THESAURUS

with-it* *a.* up to date, informed, contemporary; see MODERN 1.

without *a., prep.* **1** [Outside] out, outdoors, outwardly, externally, on the outside, standing outside, left out. **2** [Lacking] not with, not having, in the absence of, free from, deprived of.

withstand *v.* face, confront, oppose, resist, endure, stand up to, hold out.

witness *n.* observer, onlooker, eyewitness, bystander, spectator, testifier, beholder, signatory. —**bear witness** affirm, attest, give evidence; see TESTIFY 2.

witness *v.* see, observe, be a witness, be on the scene, behold, be present, testify, vouch for, stand for, look on, say under oath, depose, be on hand.

witnessed *a.* sworn to, vouched for, alleged, borne out, validated, valid, established, verified, authenticated, substantiated, supported, upheld, endorsed, brought forward.

witty *a.* quick-witted, clever, bright; see INTELLIGENT.

wizard *n.* magician, soothsayer, witch, witch doctor, sorcerer, fortuneteller, astrologer, medicine man, conjurer, shaman, enchanter, hypnotist, diviner, seer, clairvoyant, palmist, augurer, medium.

wobble *v.* shake, quaver, flounder,

vacillate, tremble, quiver, move unsteadily, dodder, teeter, totter, be unsteady, waver, quake, stagger, shuffle, waggle.

wobbly *a.* wavering, unbalanced, precarious; see UNSTABLE 1.

wolf *n.* wild dog, coyote, timber wolf; see DOG.

woman *n.* **1** [An adult female] lady, dame, matron, gentlewoman, maid, spinster, debutante, nymph, virgin, girl, old woman, chick*, doll*, babe*, broad*. **2** [A wife or mistress] love, lover, wife; see WIFE. **3** [Womankind] femininity, fair sex, womanhood, the world of women, the female of the species*.

womanhood *n.* adulthood, maturity, majority, womanliness, sexual prime, nubility, marriageable age, maidenhood, matronhood, spinsterhood.

womanly *a.* effeminate, ladylike, feminine, female, gentle, modest, compassionate, wifely, sisterly, motherly, protective, womanish, fair.—Ant. MANLY, virile, masculine.

womb *n.* uterus, female cavity, belly; see STOMACH.

won *a.* gained, achieved, conquered, taken, got, triumphed, overwhelmed.—Ant. BEATEN, lost, failed.

wonder *n.* **1** [Amazement] surprise, awe, stupefaction, admiration, won-

derment, astonishment, puzzlement, wondering, stupor, bewilderment, perplexity, fascination, consternation, perturbation, confusion, shock, start, jar, jolt, incredulity. **2** [A marvel] miracle, curiosity, oddity, rarity, freak, phenomenon, sensation, prodigy, act of God, portent, wonderwork, spectacle, perversion, monstrous birth, prodigious event, something unnatural, the unbelievable.

wonder *v.* **1** [To marvel] be surprised, be startled, be fascinated, be amazed, be dumbfounded, be confounded, be dazed, be awestruck, be astonished, be agape, be dazzled, stand aghast, be struck by, be unable to take one's eyes off, admire, gape, be taken aback, stare, be flabbergasted. **2** [To question] be curious, query, hold in doubt; see ASK.

wonderful *a.* fine, enjoyable, pleasing; see PLEASANT 2.

wonderfully *a.* beautifully, admirably, excellently; see WELL 2.

wood *a.* wooden, made of wood, hard; see WOODEN.

wood *n.* **1** [A forest; *often plural*] grove, woodland, timber; see FOREST. **2** [The portion of trees within the bark] log, timber, lumber, sapwood, heartwood. *Varieties of wood include* bark of trees and shrubs **3** lumber or timber **4** *Golf* any of certain clubs, originally with wooden heads —*adj.* **1** made of wood; wooden **2** growing or living in woods —**out of the woods** [Colloq.] out of difficulty, danger, etc. —**wood'ed** *adj.*

wood alcohol METHANOL

wood'bine' (-bīn') *n.* ⟦< OE *wudu*, wood + *binde*, to bind⟧ **1** a climbing honeysuckle **2** a climbing vine with dark-blue berries

wood'carv'ing (-kär'viŋ) *n.* **1** the art of carving wood by hand **2** an object so made —**wood'carv'er** *n.*

wood'chuck' (-chuk') *n.* ⟦< AmInd name⟧ a burrowing and hibernating marmot of North America

wood'cock' (-käk') *n.* a small game bird with short legs and a long bill

wood'craft' *n.* **1** matters relating to the woods, as camping, hunting, etc. **2** WOODWORKING

wood'cut' (-kut') *n.* **1** a wooden block engraved with a design, etc. **2** a print from this

wood'cut'ter *n.* one who fells trees, cuts wood, etc. —**wood'cut'ting** *n.*

wood'en (-'n) *adj.* **1** made of wood **2** stiff, lifeless, etc. **3** dull; insensitive —**wood'enly** *adv.* —**wood'en·ness** *n.*

wood'land' (-land, -land') *n.* land covered with woods —*adj.* of the woods

wood'man (-mən) *n.*, *pl.* **-men** WOODSMAN

wood'peck'er (-pek'ər) *n.* a climbing bird with a strong, pointed bill used to peck holes in bark to get insects

wood'pile' *n.* a pile of wood, esp. of firewood

wood screw a screw with a sharp point, for use in wood

wood'shed' *n.* a shed for firewood

woods·man (woodz'mən) *n.*, *pl.* **-men** **1** one who lives or works in the woods **2** one skilled in woodcraft

wood'sy (-zē) *adj.* **-sier**, **-si·est** of or like the woods —**wood'si·ness** *n.*

wood·wind (wood'wind') *n.* any of a family of wind instruments made, esp. orig., of wood: flute, clarinet, oboe, English horn, and bassoon — *adj.* composed of or for such an instrument

wood'work' *n.* **1** work done in wood **2** things made of wood, esp. the moldings, doors, etc. of a house

wood'work'ing *n.* the art or work of making things of wood

wood'y *adj.* **-i·er**, **-i·est** **1** covered with trees **2** consisting of or forming wood **3** like wood —**wood'i·ness** *n.*

woof (woof) *n.* ⟦ult. < OE *wefan*, to weave⟧ WEFT

woofer (woof'ər) *n.* a large, high-fidelity speaker for reproducing low-frequency sounds

wool (wool) *n.* ⟦OE *wull*⟧ **1** the soft, curly hair of sheep or of some other animals, as the goat **2** woolen yarn, cloth, clothing, etc. **3** anything that looks or feels like wool

wool'en (-ən) *adj.* **1** made of wool **2** relating to wool or woolen cloth — *n.* [*pl.*] woolen goods Also, chiefly Brit., **wool'len**

wool'gath'er·ing (-gath'ər iŋ) *n.* absent-mindedness or daydreaming

woolly (wool'ē) *adj.* **-lier**, **-li·est** **1** of or like wool **2** bearing or covered with wool **3** rough and uncivilized: used chiefly in **wild and woolly** **4** confused [*woolly* ideas] Also sp. **wool'y**

woozy (woo'zē, wooz'ē) *adj.* **-i·er**, **-i·est** [Colloq.] dizzy or befuddled, as from drink —**wooz'i·ness** *n.*

word (wurd) *n.* ⟦OE⟧ **1** *a*) a speech sound, or series of them, having meaning as a unit of language *b*) the written or printed representation of this **2** a brief remark [a *word* of advice] **3** a promise [he gave his *word*] **4** news; information **5** *a*) a password or signal *b*) a command, order, etc. **6** [*usually pl.*] *a*) talk; speech *b*) lyrics; text **7** [*pl.*] a quarrel; dispute — *vt.* to express in words; phrase —**in a word** briefly —**in so many words** exactly and plainly —**the Word** the Bible —**word for word** in precisely the same words

word'age (-ij) *n.* quantity of words

word'ing *n.* choice of words; diction

word of honor solemn promise

word'-of-mouth' *adj.* communicated orally

word processor a computerized device consisting of an electronic typewriter, video screen, printer, etc., used to generate, edit, store, or duplicate documents, as letters, etc. for a business —**word processing**

wordy (wur'dē) *adj.* **-i·er**, **-i·est** containing or using many or too many words; verbose —**word'i·ly** *adv.* —**word'i·ness** *n.*

wore (wôr) *vt.*, *vi.* *pt. of* WEAR

work (wurk) *n.* ⟦OE *weorc*⟧ **1** effort exerted to do or make something; labor; toil **2** employment; occupation **3** something one is making or doing; task **4** something made or done; specif., *a*) an act; deed (*usually used in pl.*)

the following: oak, chestnut, mahogany, sugar maple, red maple, cherry, cedar, walnut, hickory, butternut, hemlock, spruce, hornbeam, ebony, linden, beech, birch, poplar, tamarack, white pine, yellow pine, gumwood, elm, cypress, redwood, fir, Douglas fir, ash, red oak, live oak, white oak, willow, cottonwood, bamboo.

wooded *a.* timbered, forested, tree-covered, wild, tree-laden, treed, reforested, woody, jungly, having cover, timber-bearing, lumbering, uncut, not lumbered, not cut over, with standing timber, primeval, below the timberline, jungle-covered.

wooden *a.* wood, frame, frame-built, long-built, boarded, clapboarded, plank, built of slabs, pine, oak, elm, ash, mahogany.

woodwork *n.* molding, fittings, paneling, stairway, wood finishing, doors, window frames, sashes, jambs, wood trim.

wool *n.* fleece, lamb's wool, Angora wool, Shetland wool, glass wool, mineral wool, tweed, flannel, gabardine, worsted, woolen, suiting, serge, broadcloth, frieze, mohair, felt, blanketing, carpeting; see also GOODS 1.

word *n.* **1** [A unit of expression] term, name, expression, designation, concept, vocable, utterance, sound, a voicing, form of speech, speech, locution, free morpheme, lexeme. *Classes of words include the following:* common noun, proper noun, personal pronoun, possessive pronoun, demonstrative pronoun, relative pronoun, interrogative pronoun, indefi-

nite pronoun, definite article, indefinite article, transitive verb, intransitive verb, descriptive adjective, quantitative adjective, participial adjective, adverb, coordinating conjunction, subordinate conjunction, preposition, modifier, subject, predicate, root, primitive word, parent word, source word, synonym, antonym, etymon, cognative word, analogous word, derivative, slang, colloquialism, jargon, slang word, dialect word, provincialism, translation, native word, foreign word, idiom, connotative word, denotative word. **2** [Promise] pledge, commitment, word of honor; see PROMISE 1. **3** [Tidings] report, message, information; see NEWS 1. —**a good word** favorable comment, recommendation, support; see PRAISE 2. —**by word of mouth** orally, verbally, spoken; see ORAL. —**have words with** argue with, differ with, bicker; see ARGUE, FIGHT. —**in so many words** succinctly, cursorily, economically; see BRIEFLY. —**take at one's word** trust in, have confidence in, put one's trust in; see BELIEVE. —**the word** information, the facts, the lowdown*; see KNOWLEDGE 1.

wordiness *n.* redundance, redundancy, diffuseness, circumlocution, repetition, verbiage, verbosity, bombast, tautology, indirectness, vicious circle, flow of words, rhetoric, copiousness, tediousness.—*Ant.* SILENCE, conciseness, succinctness.

wordy *a.* tedious, bombastic, long-winded; see DULL 4.

work *n.* **1** [Something to be done] commitment, task, obligation; see

JOB 2. **2** [The doing of work] performance, endeavor, employment, production, occupation, practice, activity, manufacture, industry, operation, transaction, toil, labor, exertion, drudgery, functioning, stress, struggle, slavery, trial, push, attempt, effort, pains, elbow grease*, muscle*. **3** [The result of labor; *often plural*] feat, accomplishment, output; see ACHIEVEMENT. **4** [Occupation] profession, craft, business; see JOB 1. —**at work** working, on the job, engaged; see BUSY 1. —**in the works*** prepared for, budgeted, approved; see READY 2. —**make short (or quick) work of** finish off, deal with, dispose of; see DO 1. —**out of work** not hired, dismissed, looking for a job; see UNEMPLOYED.

work *v.* **1** [To labor] toil, slave, sweat, do a day's work, do the chores, exert oneself, apply oneself, do one's best, overexert, overwork, overstrain, get to work, work overtime, work day and night, work one's way up, tax one's energies, pull, plod, tug, chore, struggle, strive, carry on, do the job, punch a time clock*, put in time, pour it on*, work one's fingers to the bone*, buckle down, bear down, work like a horse*, work like a dog, work like a slave, keep at it, stay with it, put one's shoulder to the wheel, burn the candle at both ends, burn the midnight oil. **2** [To be employed] earn a living, have a job, hold a post, occupy a position, report for work, be off the welfare rolls, be among the employed, be on the job. **3** [To function] go, run, serve; see OPERATE 2. **4** [To handle successfully] control, *[good works]* b) *[pl.]* collected writings c) *[pl.]* engineering structures, as bridges, etc. **5** *[pl., with sing. v.]* a place where work is done, as a factory **6** workmanship —*adj.* of, for, or used in work —*vi.* **worked** or **wrought, work'ing 1** to do work; labor; toil **2** to be employed **3** to function or operate, esp. effectively **4** to ferment **5** to move, proceed, etc. slowly and with difficulty *[the door worked loose]* —*vt.* **1** to cause; bring about *[his idea worked wonders]* **2** to mold; shape **3** to sew, embroider, etc. **4** to solve (a mathematical problem, etc.) **5** to manipulate; knead **6** to bring into a specified condition *[to work a nail loose]* **7** to cultivate (soil) **8** to operate; use **9** to cause to work *[to work a crew hard]* **10** to make (one's way, etc.) by effort **11** to provoke; rouse *[to work oneself into a rage]* —at **work** working —**out of work** unemployed —**the works 1** the working parts (*of* a watch, etc.) **2** *[Colloq.]* everything: also **the whole works** —**work off** to get rid of —**work on** (or **upon**) **1** to influence **2** to try to persuade —**work out 1** to accomplish **2** to solve **3** to calculate **4** to result **5** to develop **6** to have a workout —**work up 1** to advance **2** to develop **3** to excite

work'a·ble *adj.* **1** that can be worked **2** practicable; feasible

work·a·day (wurk'ə dā') *adj.* **1** of workdays; everyday **2** ordinary

work·a·hol·ic (wurk'ə hôl'ik) *n.* ⟦WORK + -AHOLIC⟧ a person having a compulsive need to work

work'bench' (-bench') *n.* a table at which work is done, as by a carpenter

work'book' *n.* a book of questions, exercises, etc. for use by students

work'day' *n.* **1** a day on which work is done **2** the part of a day during which work is done

work·er (wurk'ər) *n.* **1** one who works for a living **2** one who works for a cause, etc. **3** a sterile ant, bee, etc. that does work for the colony

work'fare' *n.* ⟦WORK + (WEL)FARE⟧ a government program requiring employable recipients of welfare to register for work, training, etc.

work'horse' *n.* **1** a horse used for working **2** a steady, responsible worker

work'house' *n.* a prison where petty offenders are confined and made to work

work'ing *adj.* **1** that works **2** of, for, or used in work **3** sufficient to get work done *[a working majority]* —*n.* the act of one that works

work'ing·man' *n., pl.* -**men**' a worker, esp. an industrial worker

work'man (-mən) *n., pl.* -**men 1** WORKINGMAN **2** a craftsman

work'man·like' *adj.* skillful Also **work'man·ly**

work'man·ship' *n.* skill of a workman or the quality of the work done

work'out' *n.* a session of physical exercises or any strenuous work

work'place' *n.* the office, factory, etc. where one works

work sheet a paper sheet used for work records, working notes, etc., or with problems, etc. to be worked on

work'shop' *n.* **1** a room or building where work is done **2** a seminar for specified intensive study, work, etc.

work'sta'tion *n.* **1** a person's work area, including furniture, etc. and often, a microcomputer **2** a powerful microcomputer used for complex or specialized operations, as in engineering design

work'-up' *n.* a complete medical study of a patient, including tests

work'week' *n.* the total number of hours or days worked in a week

world (wurld) *n.* ⟦OE *werold*⟧ **1** a) the earth b) the universe **2** a) mankind b) people generally; the public **3** a) *[also* **W-**] some part of the earth *[the Old World]* b) any sphere or domain *[the animal world]* **4** individual experience, outlook, etc. *[her world is narrow]* **5** secular life and interests, or people concerned with these **6** *[often pl.]* a large amount *[a world of good]* —**for all the world** exactly

world'-class' *adj.* of the highest class, as in international competition

world'ly *adj.* -**lier**, -**li·est 1** of this world; secular **2** devoted to the affairs, pleasures, etc. of this world **3** worldly-wise —**world'li·ness** *n.*

world'ly-wise' *adj.* wise in the ways or affairs of the world; sophisticated

world'view' *n.* a comprehensive, esp. personal, philosophy of the world and of human life

World War I the war (1914-18) involving Great Britain, France, Russia, the U.S., etc. on one side and Germany, Austria-Hungary, etc. on the other

World War II the war (1939-45) involving Great Britain, France, the Soviet Union, the U.S., etc. on one side and Germany, Italy, Japan, etc. on the other

world'wide' *adj.* extending throughout the world

worm (wurm) *n.* ⟦< OE *wyrm*, serpent⟧ **1** a long, slender, soft-bodied animal **2** an abject or contemptible person **3** something wormlike or spiral in shape, etc., as the thread

---

THESAURUS

accomplish, manage; see ACHIEVE, OPERATE 3. **5** [To fashion] give form to, sculpture, mold; see FORM 1. —**work at** attempt, endeavor, do one's best; see TRY 1. —**work in** introduce, find a place for, squeeze in; see INCLUDE 1. —**work on** (or **upon**) try to encourage, use one's influence with, talk to; see INFLUENCE. —**work out 1** [To solve] come to terms, compromise, reach an agreement; see AGREE. **2** [To satisfy a requirement] finish, do what is necessary, get something done; see ACHIEVE.

workable *a.* useful, practicable, functional; see WORKING 1.

worker *n.* laborer, toiler, mechanic; see WORKMAN.

working *a.* **1** [Functioning] toiling, laboring, moving, in process, in good condition, in force, in gear, in collar, in exercise, going, twitching, effective, practical, on the job, never idle, on the fire. **2** [Employed] with a job, engaged, on the staff; see BUSY 1.

workman *n.* operator, mechanic, machinist, craftsman, artist, artisan, technician, journeyman, master worker, handworker, skilled workman, white-collar worker, field workman. *Skilled workers include the following:* carpenter, cabinetmaker, upholsterer, paperhanger, plasterer, bricklayer, plumber, electrician, metalworker, locksmith, boilermaker, pipefitter, coppersmith, printer, pressman, linotype operator,

glassworker, concrete worker, tiler, automobile mechanic, punch press operator, addressograph operator, multigraph operator, cost accountant, secretary, computer programmer, clerk, file clerk, stenographer, bookkeeper, salesman, packager, assembler, darkroom operator, photographer, proofreader, conductor, brakeman, locomotive engineer, fireman, barber, custodian, truck driver, bus driver, carpet installer, carpet cleaner, gardener, tree surgeon, seamstress, tailor, baker, butcher, farm worker, cowboy, dairyman, waiter, waitress, laundry worker, welder, drill operator, hydraulic press operator, diesinker, mason, lathe operator, gear-cutting machine operator, threading machine operator, telegrapher, teletype operator, operator, radio repairer, pattern builder, textile worker, tool designer, postal clerk, policeman, painter, galvanizer, draftsman, furrier, jewelry repairman, appliance repairman, TV repairman, cameraman, meat cutter, packer, medical technician, nurse's aide, dental hygienist.

workmanship *n.* craftsmanship, skill, quality of work, performance, handicraft, working ability, handiwork, achievement, manufacture, execution.

workout *n.* exercise, conditioning, gymnastics; see DISCIPLINE 2.

works *n.* **1** [Working parts] cogs, belts, cams, wheels, gears, pistons,

springs, coils, chains, rods, pulleys, wires; see also INSIDES. **2** [*Everything] totality, entirety, the whole; see ALL, EVERYTHING.

world *n.* **1** [The earth] globe, wide world, planet; see EARTH 1. **2** [The universe] cosmos, nature, creation; see UNIVERSE. **3** [A specific group] realm, division, system; see CLASS 1. **4** [All one's surroundings] environment, atmosphere, childhood, adolescence, adulthood, experience, life, inner life, memory, idealization. —**bring into the world** give birth to, bear, have a baby; see PRODUCE 1. —**in the world** anywhere at all, wheresoever, in the universe; see ANYWHERE, WHEREVER. —**on top of the world** feeling fine, exuberant, successful; see HAPPY. —**out of this world** extraordinary, strange, remarkable; see UNUSUAL 1, 2.

worldly *a.* mundane, earthly, ungodly, practical, matter-of-fact, secular, strategic, grubbing, moneymaking, unprincipled, power-loving, self-centered, opportunistic, sophisticated, cosmopolitan, terrestrial, profane, human, natural, temporal.

worldwide *a.* global, universal, extensive; see GENERAL 1.

worm *n.* caterpillar, grub, larva, maggot, leech, parasite, helminth. *Common worms include the following:* angleworm, earthworm, threadworm, tapeworm, silkworm, flatworm, gordian worm, ribbon worm, marine of a screw **4** [*pl.*] any disease caused by parasitic worms in the intestines, etc. —*vi.* to proceed like a worm, in a winding or devious manner —*vt.* **1** to bring about, make, etc. in a winding or devious manner **2** to purge of intestinal worms —**worm′y, -i·er, -i·est,** *adj.*

worm gear a gear consisting of a rotating screw meshed with a toothed wheel

worm′wood′ (-wood′) *n.* ⟦< OE *wermod*⟧ a strong-smelling plant that yields a bitter-tasting oil formerly used in making absinthe

worn (wôrn) *vt., vi. pp. of* WEAR —*adj.* **1** damaged by use or wear **2** exhausted

worn′-out′ *adj.* **1** used until no longer effective, usable, etc. **2** exhausted; tired out

wor·ri·ment (wur′i mənt) *n.* **1** worry; anxiety **2** a cause of worry

wor′ri·some (-səm) *adj.* causing worry or tending to worry

worry (wur′ē) *vt.* **-ried, -ry·ing** ⟦< OE *wyrgan,* to strangle⟧ **1** to bite and shake with the teeth **2** to annoy, bother, etc. **3** to make troubled or uneasy —*vi.* **1** to bite or tear (*at* an object) **2** to be anxious, troubled, etc. —*n.,* *pl.* **-ries 1** a troubled state of mind; anxiety **2** a cause of this —**wor′rier** *n.*

wor′ry·wart′ (-wôrt′) *n.* ⟦prec. + WART⟧ [Colloq.] one who tends to worry much

worse (wurs) *adj.* ⟦OE *wiersa*⟧ **1** *compar. of* BAD[1] & ILL **2** *a*) bad, evil, harmful, etc. in a greater degree *b*) of inferior quality **3** in poorer health; more ill **4** in a less satisfactory condition —*adv.* **1** *compar. of* BADLY & ILL **2** in a worse manner **3** to a worse extent —*n.* that which is worse —**worse off** in worse circumstances

wor·sen (wur′sən) *vt., vi.* to make or become worse

wor·ship (wur′ship) *n.* ⟦< OE *weorthscipe*⟧ **1** a service or rite showing reverence for a deity **2** intense love or admiration **3** [W-] [Chiefly Brit.] a title of honor: used in addressing magistrates, etc. —*vt.* **-shiped** or **-shipped,** **-ship·ing** or **-ship·ping 1** to show religious reverence for **2** to have intense love or admiration for —*vi.* to engage in worship —**wor′shiper** or **wor′ship·per** *n.*

wor′ship·ful (-fəl) *adj.* **1** [Chiefly Brit.] honorable; respected **2** worshiping

worst (wurst) *adj.* ⟦OE *wyrsta*⟧ **1** *superl. of* BAD[1] & ILL **2** *a*) bad, evil, harmful, etc. in the highest degree *b*) of the lowest quality **3** in the least satisfactory condition —*adv.* **1** *superl. of* BADLY & ILL **2** in the worst manner **3** to the worst extent —*n.* that which is worst —*vt.* to defeat —**at worst** under the worst circumstances —**if (the) worst comes to (the) worst** if the worst possible thing happens —**(in) the worst way** [Slang] very much; greatly —**make the worst of** to be pessimistic about

wor·sted (woos′tid, wur′stid) *n.* ⟦after *Worstead,* England⟧ **1** a smooth, hard-twisted wool thread or yarn **2** fabric made from this

wort (wurt) *n.* ⟦OE *wyrt-* ⟧ a liquid produced from malt which, after fermenting, becomes beer, ale, etc.

worth (wurth) *n.* ⟦OE *weorth*⟧ **1** material value, esp. as expressed in terms of money **2** importance, value, merit, etc. **3** the quantity to be had for a given sum [a dollar's *worth*] —*adj.* **1** deserving or worthy of **2** equal in value to **3** having wealth amounting to

worth′less *adj.* without worth or merit; useless —**worth′less·ness** *n.*

worth′while′ *adj.* worth the time or effort spent; of true value

worthy (wur′thē) *adj.* **-thier, -thi·est 1** having worth, value, or merit **2** meriting —*n., pl.* **-thies** a person of outstanding worth, etc. —**wor′thily** *adv.* —**wor′thi·ness** *n.*

would (wood) *v.aux.* ⟦OE *wolde*⟧ **1** *pt. of* WILL[2] **2** used to express a supposition or condition [he *would* write if he knew you *would* answer] **3** used to make a polite request [*would* you please open the window?] —*vt.* [Old Poet.] I wish [*would* that she were here] See usage note at WILL[2]

would′-be′ *adj.* **1** wishing or pretending to be **2** intended to be

wound[1] (woond) *n.* ⟦OE *wund*⟧ **1** an injury in which tissue is cut, torn, etc. **2** any hurt to the feelings, honor, etc. —*vt., vi.* to inflict a wound (on or upon)

wound[2] (wound) *vt., vi. pt. & pp. of* WIND[1]

wove (wōv) *vt., vi. pt. & alt. pp. of* WEAVE

wo·ven (wō′vən) *vt., vi. alt. pp. of* WEAVE

THESAURUS

worm, hookworm, pinworm, planarian, tubifex worm, horsehair worm, blindworm, slowworm, roundworm, annelid worm, cutworm, army worm, wireworm.

worm *v.* inch, creep, slink; see CRAWL, SNEAK.

worn *a.* **1** [Used as clothing] carried, put on, donned, displayed, exhibited, used, sported*. **2** [Showing signs of wear] frayed, threadbare, old, secondhand, ragged, shabby, impaired, used, consumed, deteriorated, torn, patched, the worse for wear.—*Ant.* FRESH, new, whole.

worn-out *a.* used up, gone, destroyed; see RUINED 1, 2, USELESS 1.

worried *a.* troubled, bothered, perturbed, vexed, distressed, miserable, annoyed, concerned, upset, suffering, torn, in conflict, pained, burdened, ill at ease, racking one's brains, uptight*, all hot and bothered*, anxious, hung up*.

worry *n.* **1** [The state of anxiety] concern, anxiety, misery; see DISTRESS. **2** [A cause of worry] problem, upset, disturbance; see FEAR, TROUBLE 1.

worry *v.* **1** [To cause worry] annoy, trouble, bother; see DISTURB. **2** [To indulge in worry] fret, chafe, grieve, take to heart, break one's heart, despair, stew, be anxious, worry oneself, have qualms, wince, agonize, writhe, suffer, turn gray with worry, become sick with worry, sweat out*; see also BOTHER 1.

worse *a.* more evil, not so good, deteriorated; see POOR 2.

worship *n.* **1** [Adoration] prayer, devotion, homage, adulation, benediction, invocation, supplication, beatification, veneration, offering, burnt offering, reverence, honor, religious ritual. **2** [A religious service] Mass, services, devotions; see CHURCH 2.

worship *v.* sanctify, pray to, invoke, venerate, glorify, praise, exalt, offer one's prayers to, pay homage to, recite the rosary, give thanks, offer thanks to, sing praises to, reverence, celebrate, adore, revere, laud, extol, magnify, chant, sing, bow down, canonize; see also PRAY 2.

worshiper *n.* churchgoer, communicant, pilgrim, supplicant, devotee, devotionalist, adorer, pietist, pious person, devout person, celebrant, saint, priest, priestess.—*Ant.* SKEPTIC, atheist, agnostic.

worst *a.* most terrible, most harmful, most lethal, poorest, lowest, least, most ghastly, most horrible, most pitiful, least meaningful, meanest, least understanding, least effective.

worst *n.* calamity, catastrophe, ruin; see DESTRUCTION 2. —**at worst** under the worst possible circumstances, unluckily, grievously; see BADLY 1, UNFORTUNATELY. —**(in) the worst way** unluckily, disastrously, horribly; see UNFORTUNATELY.

worth *a.* deserving, meriting, equal in value to, priced at, exchangeable for, valued at, worth in the open market, pegged at, cashable for, good for, appraised at, having a face value of, reasonably estimated at, bid at, held at. —**for all one is worth** greatly, mightily, hard; see POWERFULLY.

worth *n.* goodness, value, quality, character, importance, significance, meaning, estimation, benefit, excellence, merit; see also VALUE 1, 3.

worthless *a.* profitless, counterproductive, barren, unprofitable, unproductive, unimportant, insignificant, counterfeit, bogus, cheap, sterile, waste, wasted, no good, trashy, inconsequential, petty, piddling, paltry, trivial, trifling, unessential, beneath notice, empty, good-for-nothing, no-account*, not worth a damn*, not worth the trouble*, not worth speaking of*, not able to say much for*.

worthlessness *n.* uselessness, impracticality, inefficiency; see WASTE 1.

worthwhile *a.* good, serviceable, useful, important, profitable, valuable, remunerative, estimable, worthy, helpful, beneficial, meritorious, excellent, rewarding, praiseworthy.

worthy *a.* good, true, honest, honorable, reliable, trustworthy, dependable, noble, charitable, dutiful, philanthropic, virtuous, moral, pure, upright, righteous, decent, incorruptible, meritorious, creditable, deserving, right-minded, worthy of, model, exemplary, sterling, sinless, stainless, blameless.—*Ant.* WORTHLESS, bad, evil.

would-be *a.* anticipated, assuming, supposed; see HOPEFUL 1.

wound[1] *n.* bruise, hurt, scar; see INJURY.

wound[1] *v.* **1** [To hurt the body] gash, scrape, injure; see HURT 1. **2** [To hurt the feelings] trouble, upset, pain; see BOTHER 2, DISTURB.

wound[2] *a.* twisted, coiled, wrapped; see WOVEN.

wounded *a.* injured, hurt, disabled, stabbed, cut, shot, scratched, bitten, gashed, hit, beaten, attacked, winged, nicked.

woven *a.* spun, interlinked, netted, netlike, dovetailed, wreathed, sewn, intertwined, united, interlaced, inter-

wow (wou) *interj.* an exclamation of surprise, pleasure, etc. — *vt.* [Slang] to arouse enthusiasm in

wpm words per minute

wrack (rak) *n.* [< MDu *wrak*, a wreck] *alt. sp. of* RACK²

wraith (rāth) *n.* [Scot] a ghost

wran·gle (raŋ'gəl) *vi.* **-gled, -gling** [< OE *wringan*, to press] to argue; quarrel, esp. angrily and noisily — *n.* an angry, noisy dispute —**wran'gler** *n.*

wran'gler (-glər) *n.* [< AmSp *caballerango*, a groom] a cowboy who herds livestock, esp. saddle horses —**wran'gle, -gled, -gling,** *vt.*

wrap (rap) *vt.* **wrapped** or **wrapt, wrap'ping** [ME *wrappen*] 1 to wind or fold (a covering) around something 2 to enclose and fasten in paper, etc. — *vi.* to twine, coil, etc.: usually with *over, around,* etc. — *n.* 1 an outer covering or garment 2 [*pl.*] secrecy; censorship —**wrapped up in** absorbed in —**wrap up** [Colloq.] to conclude; settle

wrap'per *n.* 1 one that wraps 2 that in which something is wrapped 3 a woman's dressing gown

wrap'ping *n.* [*often pl.*] the material in which something is wrapped

wrapt (rapt) *vt., vi. alt. pt. & pp. of* WRAP

wrap'-up' *n.* [Colloq.] a concluding, summarizing statement, report, etc.

wrath (rath) *n.* [OE, angry] 1 intense anger; rage; fury 2 any action of vengeance —**wrath'ful** *adj.*

wreak (rēk) *vt.* [OE *wrecan*, to revenge] 1 to give vent to (one's anger, etc.) 2 to inflict (vengeance, etc.)

wreath (rēth) *n., pl.* **wreaths** (rēthz) [OE *writha*] 1 a twisted ring of leaves, flowers, etc. 2 something like this in shape [*wreaths* of smoke]

wreathe (rēth) *vt.* **wreathed, wreath'ing** 1 to form into a wreath 2 to coil or twist around; encircle 3 to decorate with wreaths

wreck (rek) *n.* [< ON *vrek*, driftwood] 1 a shipwreck 2 the remains of something destroyed 3 a run-down person 4 a wrecking or being wrecked — *vt.* 1 to destroy or damage badly; ruin 2 to tear down (a building, etc.) 3 to overthrow; thwart

wreck'age (-ij) *n.* 1 a wrecking or being wrecked 2 the remains of something wrecked

wreck'er *n.* 1 one who wrecks 2 one that salvages or removes wrecks

wren (ren) *n.* [OE *wrenna*] a small songbird with a stubby, erect tail

wrench (rench) *n.* [OE *wrenc*, a trick] 1 a sudden, sharp twist or pull 2 an injury caused by a twist, as to the back 3 a sudden feeling of grief, etc. 4 a tool for turning nuts, bolts, pipes, etc. — *vt.* 1 to twist or jerk violently 2 to injure with a twist 3 to distort (a meaning, etc.)

wrest (rest) *vt.* [OE *wræstan*] 1 to pull or force away violently with a twisting motion 2 to take by force; usurp — *n.* a wresting; a twist

wres·tle (res'əl; *often* ras'-) *vi., vt.* **-tled, -tling** [see prec.] 1 to struggle hand to hand with (an opponent) in an attempt to throw him 2 to contend (with) — *n.* a wrestling —**wres'tler** *n.*

wres'tling *n.* a sport in which the opponents wrestle, or struggle hand to hand

wretch (rech) *n.* [OE *wrecca*, an outcast] 1 a miserable or unhappy person 2 a person despised or scorned

wretch'ed (-id) *adj.* 1 very unhappy; miserable 2 distressing; dismal 3 poor in quality 4 contemptible; despicable —**wretch'edly** *adv.* —**wretch'ed·ness** *n.*

wrig·gle (rig'əl) *vi.* **-gled, -gling** [Medieval Low G *wriggeln*] 1 to twist and turn; squirm 2 to move along with a twisting motion 3 to make one's way by shifty means — *n.* a wriggling —**wrig'gler** *n.* —**wrig'gly, -glier, -gli·est,** *adj.*

wright (rit) *n.* [< OE *wyrcan*, to work] one who makes or constructs

wring (riŋ) *vt.* **wrung, wring'ing** [OE *wringan*] 1 *a*) to squeeze, press, or twist *b*) to force out (water, etc.) by this means (usually with *out*) 2 to clasp and twist (the hands) in distress 3 to clasp (another's hand) in greeting 4 to extract by force, threats, etc. — *n.* a wringing

wring'er *n.* a machine with rollers to squeeze water from wet clothes

wrin·kle¹ (riŋ'kəl) *n.* [ME *wrinkel*] 1 a small furrow in a normally smooth surface 2 a crease in the skin — *vt., vi.* **-kled, -kling** to form wrinkles (in); pucker; crease — **wrin'kly, -klier, -kli·est,** *adj.*

wrin·kle² (riŋ'kəl) *n.* [< OE *wrenc*, a trick] [Colloq.] a clever trick, idea, or device

wrist (rist) *n.* [OE] the joint between the hand and forearm —**a slap (or tap) on the wrist** a token punishment

wrist'band' *n.* a band that goes around the wrist, as on a cuff

wrist'watch' *n.* a watch worn on a strap or band around the wrist

writ (rit) *n.* [OE < *writan*, write] a formal legal document ordering or prohibiting some action

write (rit) *vt.* **wrote, writ'ten, writ'ing** [OE *writan*] 1 to form (words, letters, etc.) on a surface, as with a pen 2 to compose (literary or musical material) 3 to communicate (with) in writing [she *wrote* (me) that she was ill] 4 to record (information) in a computer — *vi.* to write words, books, a letter, etc. —**write off** 1 to remove from accounts (bad debts, etc.) 2 to drop from consideration 3 to amortize —**write out** 1 to put into writing 2 to write in full —**write up** to write an account of

---

THESAURUS

woven, worked into.

wow* *v.* triumph, overcome, be a success; see DEFEAT 2, 3.

wrap *v.* roll up, swathe, muffle, bind, fold about, encircle, coil, enclose, swaddle, bandage, envelop, enwrap, protect, encase, sheathe, cover up, shelter, clothe, cover with paper, enclose in a box.—*Ant.* UNWRAP, unsheathe, open up. —**wrap up*** finish off, bring to an end, polish off*; see COMPLETE.

wrapped *a.* covered, sheathed, swaddled, swathed, enclosed, papered, protected, enveloped, encased, shrouded, concealed, hidden, clothed, done up.—*Ant.* OPEN, unwrapped, uncovered. —**wrapped up in** in love with, devoted to, affectionate; see LOVING.

wrapper *n.* envelope, folder, book cover; see COVER 1.

wrath *n.* fury, vengeance, madness; see ANGER.

wreck *n.* 1 [Anything wrecked] junk, ruins, skeleton, hulk, stubble, collapse, bones, scattered parts, rattletrap, relic, litter, pieces, shreds, waste, wreckage, debris. 2 [A person in poor physical condition] incurable, invalid, consumptive, nervous case, overworked person, cripple, mess*, goner*, washout*, shadow, skin-and-bones*, walking nightmare*.

wreck *v.* spoil, ruin, destroy, disfigure, mangle, smash, tear down, break, split, efface, batter, torpedo, tear to pieces, put out of order, impair, injure, bash in, mess up, play hell with*, put out of commission.—*Ant.* REPAIR, restore, rebuild.

wreckage *n.* remains, ruins, hulk, remnants; see also WRECK 1.

wrecked *a.* demolished, destroyed, broken up, knocked to pieces, ruined, smashed to bits, shipwrecked, stranded, beached, grounded, scuttled, capsized, put out of order, blown to bits, junked, dismantled, shattered, on the rocks*, gone to pot, shot to hell*.

wrench *n.* 1 [A violent twist] jerk, strain, sprain, tug, pull, dislodgement, extrication, dislocation. 2 [A spanner] *Wrenches include the following:* monkey, single-head, double-head, pipe, Stillson, crescent, spark-plug, hubcap, flat, S-socket, bearing, connecting-rod; see also TOOL 1.

wrench *v.* twist, strain, distort; see BEND.

wrestle *v.* grapple, struggle with, contend with, perform in a wrestling bout, wrassle*, tangle*, tussle*; see also FIGHT.

wrestling *n.* contention, grappling, bout; see FIGHT 1.

wretched *a.* 1 [Afflicted] distressed, woeful, sorrowful; see SAD 1. 2 [Poor in quality] weak, faulty, cheap; see POOR 2.

wring *v.* squeeze out, compress, press; see TWIST.

wrinkle¹ *n.* crease, furrow, crinkle, ridge, fold, corrugation, line, crow's foot, pucker, pleat.

wrinkle¹ *v.* rumple, crease, furrow, pucker, twist, crumple, compress, crinkle.—*Ant.* STRAIGHTEN, smooth out, iron.

wrinkled *a.* creased, rumpled, furrowed, puckered, warped, twisted, crumpled, crinkled, dried up, withered, unironed, unpressed, shrivelled.—*Ant.* SMOOTH, ironed, pressed.

write *v.* 1 [To compose in words] set forth, record, formulate, draft, turn out, give a report, note down, transcribe, pen, put in writing, comment upon, go into, typewrite, communicate, rewrite, produce fiction, do imaginative writings, correspond, scribble. 2 [To set down in writing] inscribe, sign, scrawl, address, print, letter, autograph, reproduce, dash off, put in black and white. —**write off** charge off, take a loss on, recognize as a bad debt; see LOSE 2. — **write up** expand, work up, deal at length with; see WRITE 1, 2.

write'-in' *n.* a candidate whose name is not on the ballot, but is written in by a voter

write'-off' *n.* something written off, amortized, etc.

writ'er *n.* one who writes, esp. as an occupation; author

write'-up' *n.* [Colloq.] a written report, specif. a favorable one

writhe (*rith*) *vt.* **writhed, writh'ing** [OE *writhan,* to twist] to cause to twist or turn; contort — *vi.* 1 to twist or turn; squirm 2 to suffer great emotional distress — *n.* a writhing

writ·ing (rīt'iŋ) *n.* 1 the act of one who writes 2 something written 3 written form 4 *short for* HANDWRITING

writ·ten (rīt'n) *vt., vi. pp. of* WRITE

wrong (rôŋ) *adj.* [< ON *rangr,* twisted] 1 not in accordance with justice, law, morality, an established standard, etc. 2 not suitable or appropriate 3 *a*) contrary to fact, etc.; incorrect *b*) mistaken 4 not functioning properly 5 not meant to be seen [the *wrong* side of a fabric] — *adv.* in a wrong manner, direction, etc. — *n.* something wrong; esp., an unjust, immoral, or illegal act — *vt.* to treat badly or unjustly — **in the wrong** not on the side supported by truth, justice, etc. —**wrong'ly** *adv.* —**wrong'ness** *n.*

wrong'do'ing *n.* any wrong act or behavior —**wrong' do'er** *n.*

wrong'ful *adj.* 1 unjust, unfair, or injurious 2 unlawful —**wrong'ful·ly** *adv.* —**wrong'ful·ness** *n.*

wrong'head'ed *adj.* stubborn or perverse —**wrong' head'ed·ly** *adv.* —**wrong'head'ed·ness** *n.*

wrote (rōt) *vt., vi. pt. of* WRITE

wroth (rôth) *adj.* [OE *wrath*] angry; wrathful; incensed

wrought (rôt) *vi., vt. alt. pt. & pp. of* WORK — *adj.* 1 formed; made 2 shaped by hammering, etc.: said of metals

wrought iron tough, ductile iron containing very little carbon —**wrought'-i'ron** *adj.*

wrought'-up' *adj.* very disturbed or excited

wrung (ruŋ) *vt., vi. pt. & pp. of* WRING

wry (rī) *adj.* **wri'er** or **wry'er, wri'est** or **wry'est** [< OE *wrigian,* to turn] 1 twisted; distorted 2 distorted in a grimace [a *wry* face] 3 perverse, ironic, etc. [*wry* humor] —**wry'ly** *adv.* —**wry'ness** *n.*

wt. weight

wuss (woos) *n.* [Slang] a person regarded as weak, ineffectual, etc.: also **wuss'y,** *pl.* **wuss'ies**

WWI World War I

WWII World War II

THESAURUS

writer *n.* author, journalist, reporter, newspaperman, magazine writer, contributor, poet, novelist, essayist, biographer, dramatist, playwright, literary critic, foreign correspondent, feature writer, sports writer, fashion writer, shorthand writer, stenographer, anecdotist, amanuensis, ghostwriter, songwriter, copyist, scribe, editor, contributing editor, war correspondent, special writer, freelance writer, representative, member of the Fourth Estate, scribbler, pen pusher*, hack, newshound*. *Major writers include the following— British:* Henry Fielding, Sir Walter Scott, Charlotte Brontë, George Eliot, Jane Austen, Charles Dickens, Thomas Hardy, D.H. Lawrence, James Joyce, Joseph Conrad, Samuel Beckett, George Orwell, Virginia Woolf; *American:* James Fenimore Cooper, Edgar Allan Poe, Ralph Waldo Emerson, Henry David Thoreau, Nathaniel Hawthorne, Herman Melville, Samuel Langhorne Clemens (Mark Twain), Henry James, Stephen Crane, Theodore Dreiser, William Faulkner, John Steinbeck, Ernest Hemingway, F. Scott Fitzgerald, Norman Mailer, Saul Bellow, Edith Wharton, Flannery O'Connor; *French:* (François-Marie Arouet de) Voltaire, Jean Jacques Rousseau, Victor Hugo, Honoré de Balzac, Gustave Flaubert, Alexandre Dumas, Jules Verne, Albert Camus, André Malraux; *Italian:* Niccolo Machiavelli, Giovanni Boccaccio, Alessandro Manzoni, Ignazio Silone; *German:* Thomas Mann, Franz Kafka, Günter Grass; *Russian:* Fyodor Dostoevsky, Leo Tolstoy, Ivan Turgenev, Anton Chekhov, Boris Pasternak; *Spanish:* Miguel de Cervantes, Jorge Luis Borges; *Yiddish:* I.B. Singer.

write-up* *n.* report, account, publicity; see WRITING 2.

writhe *v.* contort, move painfully,

squirm, distort, suffer, twist and turn, undergo agony, turn with pain, throw a fit*.—*Ant.* REST, be at ease, move easily.

writing *n.* 1 [The practice of writing] transcribing, inscribing, reporting, corresponding, letter-writing, copying, typewriting, penmanship, lettering, printing, graphology, signing, autographing, stenography. 2 [Anything written] literature, written matter, document, composition, article, poem, prose, paper, theme, editorial, discourse, essay, thesis, dissertation, book, manuscript, novel, play, literary production, scenario, drama, piece, work, signature, letter, pamphlet, tract, treatise, disquisition, comment, commentary, review, recitation, certificate, record, bill, bit*, item, piece. 3 [The occupation of a writer] journalism, reporting, literature, authorship, freelance writing, professional writing, auctorial pursuits, the pen, the Fourth Estate, creative writing; novel-writing, verse-writing, feature-writing, etc.; newspaper work, the writers' craft, pencil-pushing, hack writing, writing for the slicks*, ghostwriting.

written *a.* 1 [Composed] set forth, authored, penned, drawn up, reported, signed, turned out, fictionalized, arranged, rearranged, adapted, ghostwritten, recorded, dictated. 2 [Inscribed] copied, scriptural, transcribed, printed, lettered, autographed, signed, put in writing, in black and white, under one's hand.

wrong *a.* 1 [Immoral] evil, sinful, wicked, naughty, salacious, base, indecent, risqué, blasphemous, ungodly, amoral, dissolute, dissipated, wanton, profane, sacrilegious, depraved, corrupt, profligate, shady*, low-down*, smutty.—*Ant.* GOOD, righteous, virtuous. 2 [Inaccurate] inexact, erroneous, mistaken, in error, incorrect, fallacious, untrue, erring, astray, amiss, ungrounded,

spurious, unsubstantial, unsound, erratic, deceiving oneself, in the wrong, under an error, beside the mark, laboring under a false impression, out of line, at fault, to no purpose, not right, awry, faulty, mishandled, miscalculated, misfigured, misconstructed, misconstrued, mismade, altered, not precise, perverse, wide of the mark, not according to the facts, badly estimated, a mile off*, all off, crazy*. 3 [Inappropriate] unfitted, disproportionate, ill-fitting; see IMPROPER. — **go wrong** slip, break down, go amiss; see FAIL 1.

wrong *n.* vice, sin, misdemeanor, crime, immorality, indecency, transgression, unfairness, imposition, oppression, foul play, prejudice, bias, favor, unlawful practice, villainy, delinquency, error, miscarriage, mistake, blunder, offense, wrongdoing, violation, tort, hurt, persecution, malevolence, cruelty, libel, abuse, harm, damage, spite, slander, false report, slight, misusage, outrage, inhumanity, over-presumption, insult, discourtesy, raw deal*, bum steer*, dirt.—*Ant.* KINDNESS, good deed, consideration.

wrong *v.* hurt, oppress, defame; see ABUSE.

wrongdoer *n.* lawbreaker, rogue, fugitive; see CRIMINAL.

wrongly *a.* unfairly, prejudicially, wrongfully, partially, badly, unjustifiably, illegally, disgracefully, sinfully, unreasonably, unlawfully, criminally, inexcusably, unsuitably, improperly, awkwardly, incongruously, incorrectly, unbecomingly, indecorously, out of the question, imprudently, rashly, unnaturally, illogically; see also INADEQUATELY.— *Ant.* APPROPRIATELY, tastefully, prudently.

wrung *a.* twisted, squeezed out, pressed; see TWISTED 1.

x or **X** (eks) *n., pl.* **x's, X's** the 24th letter of the English alphabet

X (eks) *n.* **1** the Roman numeral 10 **2** a film rating meaning that no one under seventeen is to be admitted

x (eks) *Math. symbol for* **1** an unknown quantity **2** times (in multiplication)

X chromosome *see* SEX CHROMOSOME

xe·non (zē'nän') *n.* a colorless, gaseous chemical element: symbol, **Xe**

xen'o·pho'bia (zen'ō-, zē'nə-) *n.* ⟦< Gr *xenos*, foreign + -PHOBIA⟧ fear or hatred of strangers or foreigners — **xen'o·phobe'** (-fōb') *n.* —**xen'o·pho'bic** (-fō'bik) *adj.*

xerog·ra·phy (zir äg'rə fē) *n.* ⟦< Gr *xēros*, dry + -GRAPHY⟧ a process for copying printed material, etc. by the action of light on an electrically charged surface — **xero·graphic** (zir'ō graf'ik) *adj.*

Xerox (zir'äks') *trademark for* a process of xerography — *vt., vi.* [**x-**] to reproduce by this process — *n.* [**x-**] a copy so made

xi (zī, sī) *n.* ⟦Gr *xi*, earlier *xei*⟧ the 14th letter of the Greek alphabet (Ξ, ξ)

XL extra large

Xmas (eks'məs) *n. colloq. var. of* CHRISTMAS

X-ray (eks'rā') *n.* **1** a ray or radiation of very short wavelength, that can penetrate solid substances: used to study internal body structures and treat various disorders **2** a photograph made by means of X-rays — *adj.* of or by X-rays — *vt.* to examine, treat, or photograph with X-rays Also **X ray, x-ray,** or **x ray**

XS extra small

xy·lem (zī'ləm) *n.* ⟦< Gr *xylon*, wood⟧ the woody tissue of a plant

xylo·phone (zī'lə fōn') *n.* ⟦< Gr *xylon*, wood + -PHONE⟧ a musical percussion instrument consisting of a series of graduated wooden bars struck with small, wooden mallets —**xy'lo·phon'ist** (-fō'nist, zī läf'ə nist) *n.*

THESAURUS

x *n.* unknown quantity, unknown, y; see QUANTITY.

Xmas* *n.* the Nativity, Christmas holiday, Yule; see HOLIDAY.

X-rays *n.* Roentgen rays, radioactivity, radium emanation, actinic rays, actinism, encephalogram, CAT scan, ultraviolet rays, refractometry, radiant energy, cathode rays; see also ENERGY 2, RAY.

xylophone *n.* carillon, vibraphone, vibes*, glockenspiel, marimba; see also MUSICAL INSTRUMENT.

Y

y or **Y** (wī) *n., pl.* **y's, Y's** the 25th letter of the English alphabet

-y[1] (ē, i) ⟦ME⟧ *suffix* little one, dear *[kitty, daddy]*

-y[2] (ē, i) ⟦OE *-ig*⟧ *suffix* **1** full of, like *[dirty]* **2** somewhat *[yellowy]* **3** tending to *[sticky]*

-y[3] (ē, i) ⟦< L *-ia*⟧ *suffix* **1** quality or condition *[jealousy]* **2** a (specified) kind of shop, goods, or group *[bakery]*

-y[4] (ē, i) ⟦< L *-ium*⟧ *suffix* action of *[inquiry]*

Y *Chem. symbol for* yttrium

yacht (yät) *n.* ⟦Du *jacht*⟧ a small ship for pleasure cruises, racing, etc.

yacht'ing (-iŋ) *n.* the sport of sailing a yacht —**yachts' man** (-mən), *pl.* -**men,** *n.*

Ya·hoo (yä'hōō') *n.* in Swift's *Gulliver's Travels,* any of a race of brutish, degraded creatures

Yah·weh or **Yahwe** (yä'we, -wä) ⟦Heb: see JEHOVAH⟧ God

yak[1] (yak) *n.* ⟦< Tibet *g-yag*⟧ a long-haired wild ox of Tibet and central Asia

yak[2] (yak) *vi.* **yakked, yak'king** ⟦echoic⟧ [Slang] to talk much or idly — *n.* [Slang] **1** a yakking **2** a loud laugh

yam (yam) *n.* ⟦< WAfr native name⟧ **1** the edible, starchy, tuberous root of a tropical climbing plant **2** [South] a large variety of sweet potato

yam·mer (yam'ər) *vi.* ⟦< OE *geomor,* sad⟧ [Colloq.] **1** to whine, whimper, or complain **2** to shout, yell, etc. — *vt.* [Colloq.] to say complainingly —**yam'merer** *n.*

yang (yäŋ, yaŋ) *n.* ⟦Chin⟧ in Chinese philosophy, the masculine force or principle in the universe: cf. YIN

yank (yaŋk) *n., vt., vi.* ⟦< ?⟧ [Colloq.] jerk

Yank (yaŋk) *n.* [Slang] a Yankee; esp., a U.S. soldier in World Wars I and II

Yan·kee (yaŋ'kē) *n.* ⟦< ? Du *Jan Kees,* a disparaging nickname⟧ **1** a New Englander **2** a native of a Northern State **3** a citizen of the U.S. — *adj.* of or like Yankees

yap (yap) *vi.* **yapped, yap'ping** ⟦echoic⟧ **1** to make a sharp, shrill bark **2** [Slang] to talk noisily and stupidly — *n.* **1** a sharp, shrill bark **2** [Slang] *a)* jabber *b)* the mouth

yard[1] (yärd) *n.* ⟦OE *gierd,* rod⟧ **1** a measure of length, 3 feet or 36 inches **2** *Naut.* a slender rod or spar fastened across a mast to support a sail

yard[2] (yärd) *n.* ⟦OE *geard,* enclosure⟧ **1** the ground around or next to a house or other building **2** an enclosed place for a particular purpose *[shipyard]* **3** a railroad center where trains are switched, etc.

yard·age (yärd'ij) *n.* **1** measurement in yards **2** the extent so measured

yard'arm' *n. Naut.* either half of a yard supporting a square sail, etc.

yard goods textiles made in standard width, usually sold by the yard

yard·man (yärd'man', -mən) *n., pl.* -**men'** a person who works in a yard, esp. a railroad yard

yard'stick' *n.* **1** a graduated measuring stick one yard in length **2** any standard used in judging, etc.

yar·mulke (yär'məl kə, yä'-) *n.* ⟦Yidd < Pol⟧ a skullcap variously worn by Jewish men, as at prayer Also **yar' melke**

yarn (yärn) *n.* ⟦OE *gearn*⟧ **1** fibers of wool, cotton, etc. spun into strands for weaving, knitting, etc. **2** [Colloq.] a tale or story

yaw (yô) *vi.* ⟦ON *jaga,* to sway⟧ **1** to swing back and forth across its course, as a ship **2** to rotate or oscillate about the vertical axis: said of a spacecraft, etc. — *n.* a yawing

yawl (yôl) *n.* ⟦< Du *jol*⟧ a small, two-masted sailboat rigged fore-and-aft

yawn (yôn) *vi.* ⟦ME *yanen*⟧ **1** to open the mouth wide involuntarily, as a result of fatigue, drowsiness, etc. **2** to open wide; gape — *n.* a yawning

yaws (yôz) *n.pl.* ⟦of WInd origin⟧ [*with sing. v.*] a tropical infectious skin disease

Y chromosome *see* SEX CHROMOSOME

yclept' or **y-clept'** (ē klept') *vt.* ⟦<OE *clipian,* to call⟧ [Archaic] called; named Also **ycleped'**

yd. yard(s)

ye[1] (thə, thi, thē; *now often erroneously or facetiously* yē) *adj., definite article* archaic var. of THE

ye[2] (yē) *pron.* ⟦OE *ge*⟧ *archaic var. of* YOU

yea (yā) *adv.* ⟦OE *gea*⟧ **1** yes **2** indeed; truly — *n.* **1** an affirmative vote **2** a person voting in the affirmative

yeah (ya, ye) *adv.* [Colloq.] yes

year (yir) *n.* ⟦OE *gear*⟧ **1** a period of 365 days (366 days in leap year), divided into 12 months beginning Jan. 1 **2** the period (365 days, 5 hours, 48 minutes, and 46 seconds) of one revolution of the earth around the sun: ạlso **solar year** or **tropical year 3** a period of 12 calendar months reckoned from any date **4** an annual period of less than 365 days *[a school year]* **5** [*pl.*] *a)* age *[old for his years]* *b)* a long time *[he died years ago]* —**year after year** every year

year'book' *n.* an annual book; specif., *a)* a book giving data of the preceding year *b)* a publication of the graduating class of a school or college

year'ling (-liŋ) *n.* an animal one year old or in its second year

year'ly *adj.* **1** done, happening, appearing, etc. once a year, or every year *[a yearly event]* **2** of a year, or of each year — *adv.* every year

yearn (yurn) *vi.* ⟦< OE *georn,* eager⟧ **1** to be filled with longing or desire **2** to be deeply moved, esp. with tenderness —**yearn'ing** *n.*

year'-round' *adj.* open, in use, operating, etc. throughout the year

---

■ THESAURUS ■

yacht *n.* pleasure boat, sloop, racing boat; see BOAT, SHIP.

yammer *v.* nag, whine, whimper; see COMPLAIN.

yank *n.* twitch, jerk, wrench; see JERK 1.

yank* *v.* haul, tug, drag, jiggle, jerk*, flip, wrench, twitch; see also DRAW 1, PULL 2.

Yank* *n.* American, soldier, Yankee, doughboy*, GI Joe*.

Yankee *a.* **1** [Having New England qualities] homespun, individualistic, conservative; see MODERATE 3, 4, 5, PRACTICAL. **2** [Concerning the United States] North American, Western, Americanized; see AMERICAN.

Yankee *n.* **1** [A New Englander] Northerner, Easterner, early settler, Abolitionist, Unionist. **2** [A person from the United States] American, American citizen, North American, westerner, Occidental, Yank*.

yap* *v.* jabber, rant, chatter; see BABBLE, TALK 1.

yard[1,2] *n.* **1** [An enclosure, usually about a building] court, courtyard, barnyard, back yard, corral, fold, patch, patio, terrace, play area, lawn, grass, garden, clearing, quadrangle,

lot; see also PLAYGROUND. **2** [An enclosure for work] brickyard, coalyard, junkyard, navy yard, dockyard, railroad yard, stockyard, lumberyard. **3** [Tracks for making up trains; *often plural*] railroad yard, switchyard, railway yard, marshalling yard, terminal. **4** [A unit of measurement] three feet, pace, step, arm-span, thirty-six inches; see also MEASURE 1.

yardstick *n.* **1** [A rule three feet long] thirty-six-inch ruler, measuring stick, molding rule, yard measure; see also RULER 2. **2** [A unit for comparison] criterion, basis for judgment, standard; see MEASURE 2.

yarn *n.* **1** [Spun fiber] spun wool, twist, flaxen thread, cotton fiber, rug yarn, crochet thread, knitting yarn, alpaca yarn; see also FIBER. **2** [A tale] anecdote, sea story, adventure story, fictional account; see also STORY. **3** [A lie] fabrication, tall story, alibi, fish story*, cock-and-bull story*; see also LIE.

yawn *v.* **1** [To open wide] gape, split open, spread out; see DIVIDE, GROW 1. **2** [To give evidence of drowsiness] gape, be sleepy, make a yawning sound, show weariness; see also

SLEEP, TIRE 1.

yea *a.* okay, aye, well; see YES.

year *n.* twelve months, annual cycle, continuum of days; see AGE 3, TIME 1, 2. *Kinds of years include the following:* civil, legal, calendar, lunar, solar, astronomical, natural, sidereal, tropical, equinoctial, leap, school, fiscal. —**year after year** year by year, annually; year in, year out; see also YEARLY.

yearbook *n.* annual, almanac, yearly report; see CATALOG, RECORD 1.

yearling *n.* suckling, nursling, weanling; see ANIMAL, BABY.

yearly *a.* annually, once a year, every winter, every spring, every summer, every autumn, year by year; see also REGULARLY.

yearn *v.* want, crave, long for, fret, chafe, grieve, mourn, droop, pine, languish, be eager for, be desirous of, be ardent, be fervent, be passionate, wish for, thirst for, hunger for, aspire to, set one's heart upon, hanker for, have a yen for*; see also TRY 1.—*Ant.* AVOID, be content, be indifferent.

yearning *n.* want, longing, craving; see DESIRE 1, WISH.

yeast (yēst) *n.* ⟦OE *gist*⟧ **1** a yellowish, moist mass of fungi that cause fermentation: used in making beer, etc., and as leavening **2** yeast dried in flakes or granules or compressed into cakes **3** foam; froth **4** ferment; agitation

yeasty (yēs′tē) *adj.* **-i·er, -i·est 1** of, like, or containing yeast **2** frothy; light

yegg (yeg) *n.* ⟦ < ? ⟧ [Old Slang] a criminal; esp., a burglar, etc.

yell (yel) *vi., vt.* ⟦OE *giellan*⟧ to cry out loudly; scream — *n.* **1** a loud outcry **2** a rhythmic cheer in unison

yel·low (yel′ō) *adj.* ⟦OE *geolu*⟧ **1** of the color of ripe lemons **2** having a somewhat yellow skin **3** [Colloq.] cowardly **4** sensational, as a newspaper — *n.* **1** a yellow color **2** an egg yolk — *vt., vi.* to make or become yellow —**yel′low·ish** *adj.*

yellow fever an infectious tropical disease caused by a virus transmitted by the bite of a certain mosquito

yellow jacket a wasp or hornet having bright-yellow markings

yelp (yelp) *vi., vt.* ⟦OE *gielpan*, to boast⟧ to utter or express in a short, sharp cry or bark, as a dog — *n.* a short, sharp cry or bark

yen[1] (yen) *n.* ⟦Jpn⟧ the monetary unit of Japan

yen[2] (yen) *n.* ⟦prob. < Chin *yan*, opium⟧ [Colloq.] a strong longing or desire

yeo·man (yō′mən) *n., pl.* **-men** ⟦ME *yeman*⟧ **1** [Historical] a freeholder of a class below the gentry **2** *U.S. Navy* a petty officer assigned to clerical duty

yeo′man·ry *n.* yeomen collectively

yes (yes) *adv.* ⟦OE *gese*⟧ **1** aye; yea; it is so: expressing agreement, consent, etc. **2** not only that, but more /ready, yes, eager to help/ — *n., pl.* **yes′es** an affirmative reply, vote, etc. — *vt., vi.* **yessed, yes′sing** to say *yes* (to)

yes man [Slang] one who is always approving what is said by a superior

yes·ter (yes′tər) *adv.* of yesterday or previous to this [*yesteryear*]

yes·ter·day (yes′tər dā′, -dē) *n.* ⟦OE *geostran*, yesterday + *dæg*, day⟧ **1** the day before today **2** a recent day or time — *adv.* **1** on the day before today **2** recently

yet (yet) *adv.* ⟦OE *giet*⟧ **1** up to now; thus far /he hasn't gone *yet*/ **2** at the present time; now /we can't go just *yet*/ **3** still /there is *yet* a chance/ **4** in addition; even /he was *yet* more kind/ **5** nevertheless /she's kind, *yet* shy/ — *conj.* nevertheless; however /she seems well, *yet* she is ill/ —**as yet** up to now

yew (yōō) *n.* ⟦OE *iw*⟧ **1** an evergreen tree with needle leaves **2** its wood

Yid·dish (yid′ish) *n.* ⟦ < Ger *jüdisch*, < L *Judaeus*, Jew⟧ a language derived from medieval High German, written in the Hebrew alphabet and spoken esp. by East European Jews

yield (yēld) *vt.* ⟦OE *gieldan*, to pay⟧ **1** to produce as a crop, result, profit, etc. **2** to surrender **3** to concede — *vi.* **1** to produce **2** to surrender **3** to give way to physical force **4** to lose precedence, etc.: often with *to* — *n.* the amount yielded

yield′ing *adj.* flexible; submissive

yin (yin) *n.* ⟦Chin⟧ in Chinese philosophy, the feminine force or principle in the universe: cf. YANG

yip (yip) *n.* ⟦echoic⟧ [Colloq.] a yelp or bark — *vi.* **yipped, yip′ping** [Colloq.] to yelp or bark

yip·pie (yip′ē) *n.* [Slang] a person in the U.S. belonging to a loosely organized group of young radicals

YMCA Young Men's Christian Association

YMHA Young Men's Hebrew Association

yo·del (yōd′'l) *vt., vi.* **-deled or -delled, -del·ing or -del·ling** ⟦Ger *jodeln*⟧ to sing with abrupt alternating changes to the falsetto — *n.* a yodeling

yoga (yō′gə) *n.* ⟦Sans, union⟧ a mystic Hindu discipline for achieving union with the supreme spirit through intense concentration, meditation, prescribed postures, controlled breathing, etc.

yogi (yō′gē) *n., pl.* **-gis** one who practices yoga Also **yo′gin** (-gin)

yo·gurt (yō′gərt) *n.* ⟦Turk *yoğurt*⟧ a thick, somewhat solid food made from fermented milk Also **yo′ghurt**

yoke (yōk) *n.* ⟦OE *geoc*⟧ **1** a wooden frame for harnessing together a pair of oxen, etc. **2** such a pair harnessed **3** bondage; servitude **4** anything like a yoke, as something that binds, unites, etc., or a part of a garment fitted to the shoulders or hips as a support for the gathered parts below — *vt.* **yoked, yok′ing 1** to put a yoke on **2** to harness (an animal) to a plow, etc.) **3** to join together

yo·kel (yō′kəl) *n.* a person from the country; bumpkin: a contemptuous term

yolk (yōk) *n.* ⟦OE *geolca*⟧ the yellow, principal substance of an egg

Yom Kip·pur (yäm kip′ər; *Heb* yōm′ kē pōōr′) the Day of Atonement, a Jewish holiday and day of fasting

yon (yän) *adj., adv.* ⟦OE *geon*⟧ [Now Chiefly Dial.] yonder

yon·der (yän′dər) *adj., adv.* ⟦ME⟧ (being) at or in that (specified or relatively distant) place; over there

yore (yôr) *adv.* ⟦OE *geara*⟧ [Obs.] long ago —**of yore** formerly

you (yōō) *pron.* ⟦OE *eow* < *ge*, YE[2]⟧ **1** the person or persons spoken to **2** a person or people generally /you can never tell!/

THESAURUS

yell *n.* **1** [A shout] bellow, cry, yelp, roar, whoop, howl, screech, shriek, squeal, holler*, hoot, yawp*, hubbub, hullabaloo, hue and cry, protest; see also NOISE 1. **2**. **2** [Organized cheering] hip-hip-hurrah, rooting, cheer; see ENCOURAGEMENT.

yell *v.* bellow, cry out, scream, shout, yelp, yap, bawl, roar, halloo, vociferate, whoop, howl, screech, shriek, shrill, squeal, squall, yammer, hoot, cheer, call, yip, give encouragement, call down, raise one's voice, holler, whoop it up; see also SOUND.

yelling *a.* boisterous, clamorous, noisy, bawling, uproarious, turbulent, drunken, aroused, riotous, cantankerous, blatant, vociferous; see also HARSH, LOUD 2.—*Ant.* QUIET, subdued, silent.

yelling *n.* cry, scream, shout, outcry, vociferation, screeching, bawling, yowling, bellowing, howling, yelping; see also NOISE 1, 2, YELL.

yellow *n.* Tints and shades of yellow include the following: cream color, ivory color, old ivory, ivory-yellow, tan, lemon color, orange-yellow, saffron, jasmine, tawny, sand, gold, sallow, buff, brilliant yellow, chrome yellow, Dutch pink-yellow, Dutch yellow, golden yellow, Imperial yellow, platinum yellow, yellow carmine, yellow madder, yellow ocher; see also COLOR, GOLD.

yellow *a.* **1** [Having a yellowish color] yellowish, golden, jaundiced-looking. **2** [*Cowardly] tricky, deceitful, low, cringing, sneaking, white-livered, craven, treacherous; see also COWARDLY, VULGAR. **3** [Sensational; *said especially of some newspapers*] tabloid, unethical, unprincipled; see EXCITING, OFFENSIVE 2.

yelp *v.* howl, screech, hoot; see CRY 2, SOUND.

yen[2]* *n.* longing, craving, hunger; see DESIRE 1.

yes *a.* surely, of course, certainly, good, fine, aye, true, granted, very well, all right, OK*, okay*, oke*, okey-dokey*, Roger, we copy, over to you, most assuredly, by all means, agreed, oh yes!, amen, naturally, without fail, just so, good enough, even so, in the affirmative, you bet*.

yesterday *a.* recently, previously, earlier; see BEFORE.

yesterday *n.* the other day, the day before, recently, last day, not long ago; see also PAST 1.

yet *a.* **1** [Nevertheless] notwithstanding, however, in spite of, despite, still, but, though, although, at any rate, on the other hand. **2** [Thus far] until now, till, hitherto, prior to, still; see also UNTIL. **3** [In addition] besides, additionally, further; see

BESIDES. —**as yet** still, not yet, till now; see YET 2.

yield *v.* **1** [To surrender] give up, capitulate, succumb, resign, abdicate, relinquish, quit, cede, bow, lay down arms, cease from, let go, submit, give oneself over, relent, admit defeat, suffer defeat, forgo, humble oneself, waive, throw in the towel*, call quits*, back down*, holler uncle*, eat crow*; see also ABANDON 1.—*Ant.* RESIST, withstand, repulse. **2** [To produce] bear, bring forth, blossom; see BLOOM, PRODUCE 1, 2. **3** [To grant] accede, concur, acquiesce; see ADMIT 2, AGREE.

yielding *a.* **1** [Producing] green, fruitful, productive; see FERTILE, RICH 3. **2** [Flexible] pliant, plastic, malleable; see FLEXIBLE. **3** [Docile] submissive, pliable, tractable; see HUMBLE 1, OBEDIENT 1.

yogi *n.* mystic, fakir, anchorite, ascetic, practitioner of yoga, guru, devotee.

yokel *n.* rustic, bumpkin, hayseed; see BOOR.

yolk *n.* yellow, egg-yellow, egg yolk; see CENTER 1, EGG.

yonder *a.* farther, away, faraway; see DISTANT, REMOTE 1.

you *pron.* yourself, you yourself, thee, thou, all of you, you too, you alone, you all*.

young (yuŋ) *adj.* [OE *geong*] 1 being in an early period of life or growth; not old 2 youthful; fresh; vigorous 3 in an early stage 4 inexperienced; immature — *n.* 1 young people 2 offspring, esp. young offspring —**with young** pregnant —**young'ish** *adj.*

young blood 1 young people; youth 2 youthful strength, vigor, etc.

young·ster (yuŋ'stər) *n.* a child or youth

your (yoor; *often* yôr) *poss. pronominal adj.* [OE *eower*] of, belonging to, or done by you Also used before some titles [*your* Honor]

you're (yoor, yōōr) you are

yours (yoorz; *often* yôrz) *pron.* that or those belonging to you [*that book is* yours]

your·self (yoor self', yər-) *pron., pl.* **-selves'** (-selvz') a form of the second pers. sing. pronoun, used as an intensive [you *yourself* said so], as a reflexive [you hurt *yourself*], and as a quasi-noun meaning "your real, true, or actual self" (Ex.: you are not *yourself* today)

yours truly 1 a phrase used in ending a letter 2 [Colloq.] I or me

youth (yōōth) *n., pl.* **youths** (yōōthz, yōōths) [OE *geoguthe*] 1 the state or quality of being young 2 the period of adolescence 3 an early stage of development 4 young people 5 a young person; esp., a young man

youth'ful *adj.* 1 young 2 of, like, or fit for youth 3 fresh; vigorous 4 new; early —**youth'fully** *adv.* —**youth'fulness** *n.*

yowl (youl) *vi., n.* [< ON *gaula*] howl; wail

yo-yo (yō'yō') *n., pl.* **yo'-yos'** [< ?] a spool-like toy reeled up and let down by a string

yr. 1 year(s) 2 your

yrs. 1 years 2 yours

yt·trium (i'trē əm) *n.* a rare, silvery, metallic chemical element: used in color TV tubes, etc.

yucca (yuk'ə) *n.* [< AmSp *yuca*] 1 a desert plant with stiff leaves and white flowers 2 its flower

yule (yōōl) *n.* [OE *geol*] [*often* Y-] Christmas or the Christmas season

yule'tide' (-tid') *n.* [*often* Y-] Christmastime

yummy (yum'ē) *adj.* **-mier, -mi·est** [Colloq.] very tasty; delectable

yup·pie (yup'ē) *n.* [y(oung) u(rban) p(rofessional)] [Colloq.] any of those young professionals regarded as affluent, ambitious, materialistic, etc.

YWCA Young Women's Christian Association

YWHA Young Women's Hebrew Association

THESAURUS

young *a.* 1 [In the early portion of life] puerile, boyish, girlish, adolescent, juvenile, budding, in one's teen's, childlike, youthful, pubescent, boylike, girllike, new-fledged, blooming, burgeoning, childish, half-grown, growing, blossoming, at the breast, babe in arms, knee high to a grasshopper.—*Ant.* OLD, aged, senile. 2 [Inexperienced] callow, green, immature, tender, raw, untutored, unlearned, junior, subordinate, inferior, unfledged, ignorant, undisciplined, tenderfoot, not dry behind the ears; see also INEXPERIENCED, NAIVE.—*Ant.* EXPERIENCED, veteran, expert. 3 [New] fresh, modern, recent, newborn; see also FASHIONABLE.

youngster *n.* child, boy, girl, pupil; see also YOUTH 3.

youth *n.* 1 [The state or quality of being young] boyhood, adolescence, girlhood, childhood, early manhood, early adulthood, puberty, tender age, minority, youthfulness, teen age, virginity, bloom, teens, age of ignorance, age of indiscretion, awkward age, salad days.—*Ant.* MATURITY, old age, senility. 2 [Young people] the younger generation, the rising generation, the next generation, children, the young, college youth, working youth. 3 [A young person] boy, junior, teenager, lad, youngster, stripling, minor, young man, miss, girl, maiden, fledgling, juvenile, urchin, adolescent, student, kid*, teen, pre-teen, gosling, pup, calf; see also CHILD.

youthful *a.* 1 [Possessing youth] young, childlike, adolescent; see ACTIVE, YOUNG 1, 2. 2 [Suited to youth] keen, enthusiastic, zestful, vigorous, active, buoyant, lighthearted, prankish, fresh, lithe, full-blooded, full of life, full of animal spirits, limber, athletic, lightfooted, bubbling over, full of the devil; see also MODERN 1.—*Ant.* SLOW, cautious, serious.

yowl *n.* howl, yelp, wail; see CRY 1, YELL 1.

yule *n.* Christmas, Xmas*, Nativity, Christmas season, Christmastide.

z or **Z** (zē; *Brit., etc.* zed) *n., pl.* **z's, Z's** the 26th and last letter of the English alphabet

zany (zā′nē) *n., pl.* **-nies** 〚< It dial. *zanni*, < *Giovanni*, John〛 1 a clown or buffoon 2 a silly person —*adj.* **-ni·er, -ni·est** of or like a zany; funny, silly, crazy, etc. —**za′ni·ness** *n.*

zap (zap) *vt., vi.* **zapped, zap′ping** 〚echoic〛 [Slang] to move, strike, smash, kill, etc. with sudden speed — *n.* [Slang] energy, pep, etc. — *interj.* an exclamation expressing sudden swift action or change

zeal (zēl) *n.* 〚< Gr *zēlos*〛 intense enthusiasm; ardor; fervor

zealot (zel′ət) *n.* one who is zealous, esp. to a fanatic degree

zeal·ous (zel′əs) *adj.* of or showing zeal; fervent —**zeal′ously** *adv.*

ze·bra (zē′brə) *n.* 〚Port〛 an African mammal related to the horse and having dark stripes on a white or tawny body

zebu (zē′byoo) *n.* 〚Fr *zébu* < ?〛 a domesticated ox of Asia and Africa

zed (zed) *n.* 〚< Gr *zēta*〛 [Brit., etc.] the letter Z, z

Zeit·geist (tsit′gīst′) *n.* 〚Ger, time spirit〛 trend of thought and feeling in a period of history

Zen (zen) *n.* 〚Jpn ult. < Sans *dhyāna*, thinking〛 a variety of Buddhism in which enlightenment is sought through introspection and intuition

ze·nith (zē′nith) *n.* 〚< L *semita*, path〛 1 the point in the sky directly overhead 2 the highest point

zephyr (zef′ər) *n.* 〚< Gr *zephyros*〛 1 the west wind 2 a gentle breeze

zep·pe·lin (zep′ə lin) *n.* 〚after Count F. von *Zeppelin* (1838-1917), its Ger designer〛 [*often* Z-] a type of rigid airship designed around 1900

zero (zir′ō, zē′rō) *n., pl.* **-ros** *or* **-roes** 〚< Ar *ṣifr*, cipher〛 1 the symbol 0; cipher; naught 2 the point, marked 0, from which quantities are reckoned on a graduated scale 3 nothing 4 the lowest point — *adj.* of or at zero —**zero in on** to concentrate attention on; focus on

zero hour 1 the time set for beginning an attack, etc. 2 any crucial moment

zero (population) growth a condition in a given population in which the birthrate equals the death rate

ze′ro-sum′ (-sum′) *adj.* of or being a situation in which a gain for one must result in a loss for another

zest (zest) *n.* 〚Fr *zeste*, orange peel〛 1 something that gives flavor or relish 2 stimulating quality 3 keen enjoyment *[a zest for life]* —**zest′ful** *adj.*

zeta (zāt′ə) *n.* 〚Gr *zēta*〛 the sixth letter of the Greek alphabet (Z, ζ)

Zeus (zyoos, zoos) *Gr. Myth.* the chief deity

zig·zag (zig′zag′) *n.* 〚Fr〛 1 a series of short, sharp angles in alternate directions 2 a design, path, etc. in this form — *adj.* having the form of a zigzag — *adv.* in a zigzag course — *vt., vi.* **-zagged′, -zag′ging** to move or form in a zigzag

zilch (zilch) *n.* 〚nonsense syllable〛 [Slang] nothing; zero

zil·lion (zil′yən) *n.* 〚< MILLION〛 [Colloq.] a very large, indefinite number

zinc (ziŋk) *n.* 〚Ger *zink*〛 a bluish-white, metallic chemical element, used in alloys, as a protective coating for iron, etc.

zinc oxide a white powder used in making rubber articles, cosmetics, ointments, etc.

Z

zing (ziŋ) *n.* 〚echoic〛 [Slang] 1 a shrill whizzing sound 2 zest, vigor, etc.

zin·nia (zin′ē ə, zin′yə) *n.* 〚after J. G. *Zinn* (1727-59), Ger botanist〛 a plant having colorful, composite flowers

Zion (zī′ən) 1 a hill in Jerusalem, site of Solomon's Temple 2 Jerusalem 3 Israel — *n.* 1 the Jewish people 2 heaven

Zi′on·ism′ (-iz′əm) *n.* an international movement formerly for reestablishing, now for supporting, the state of Israel —**Zi′on·ist** *n., adj.*

zip (zip) *n.* 〚echoic〛 1 a short, sharp hissing sound, as of a passing bullet 2 [Colloq.] energy; vigor — *vi.* **zipped, zip′ping** 1 to make, or move with, a zip 2 [Colloq.] to move with speed — *vt.* to fasten with a zipper

ZIP Code (zip) 〚z(*oning*) i(*mprovement*) p(*lan*)〛 trademark for a system of code numbers assigned by the postal service: each code designates a delivery point

zip·per (zip′ər) *n.* a device used to fasten and unfasten two edges of material: it consists of two rows of interlocking tabs worked by a sliding part

zip′py *adj.* **-pier, -pi·est** [Colloq.] full of vim and energy; brisk

zir·con (zur′kän′) *n.* 〚ult. < Pers *zar*, gold〛 a crystalline silicate mineral, often used as a gem

zir·co·nium (zər kō′nē əm) *n.* a ductile, metallic chemical element used in alloys, nuclear reactors, etc.: symbol, Zr

zit (zit) *n.* [Slang] a pimple, esp. one on the face

zither (zith′ər, zith′-) *n.* 〚< Gr *kithara*, lute〛 any of various musical instruments with strings stretched across a flat soundboard and plucked, bowed, struck with mallets, etc., as the dulcimer, etc.

Zn *Chem.* symbol for zinc

zo·di·ac (zō′dē ak′) *n.* 〚< Gr *zōdiakos* (*kyklos*), (circle) of animals〛 1 an imaginary belt in the heavens extending on either side of the apparent path of the sun and divided into twelve equal parts, or signs, named for constellations 2 a diagram representing this —**zo·di′a·cal** (-dī′ə kəl) *adj.*

zom·bie (zäm′bē) *n.* 〚of Afr orig.〛 1 in West Indian superstition, a supernatural power through which a corpse may be reanimated 2 such a corpse Also **zom′bi**

zone (zōn) *n.* 〚Fr < Gr *zōnē*〛 1 an encircling band, stripe, etc. 2 any of the five great latitudinal divisions of the earth's surface: see TORRID ZONE, TEMPERATE ZONE, and FRIGID ZONE 3 any area with reference to a specified use or restriction *[a canal zone, postal zone]* — *vt.* **zoned, zon′ing** 1 to mark off into zones 2 to encircle; surround —**zon′al** *adj.* —**zoned** *adj.*

zonked (zôŋkt, zäŋkt) *adj.* [Slang] 1 drunk or under the influence of a drug 2 exhausted

zoo (zoo) *n.* 〚< zoo(*logical garden*)〛 1 a place where a collection of wild animals is kept for public showing 2 [Slang] a place marked by confusion, disorder, etc.

▬ THESAURUS ▬

zeal *n.* **1** [Enthusiasm] ardor, eagerness, fervor, enthusiasm. **2** [Industry] earnestness, hustle, hustling, bustle, bustling, intensity, industry, willingness, inclination, application, determination, promptitude, dispatch, diligence, perseverance, intentness, assiduity, readiness, aptitude, enterprise, initiative, push*, what it takes*, stick-to-itiveness*; see also ATTENTION, CARE 1, COOPERATION.—*Ant.* IDLENESS, slackness, indolence.

zealot *n.* partisan, fan, bigot, fanatic, lobbyist, devotee, dogmatist, opinionist, missionary, fighter, cultist, follower, disciple, propagandist, bitter-ender*, crank*, addict, bug*, faddist, fiend.

zealous *a.* fervent, earnest, intense, fanatic, industrious, diligent, intent, dogmatic, devoted, ardent; see also ENTHUSIASTIC.

zealously *a.* with zeal, assiduously,

fiercely; see INDUSTRIOUSLY, VIGOROUSLY.

zero *n.* **1** [A cipher] naught, nothing, nadir, love, below freezing, lowest point, goose egg*, nix*, zip*, zilch*. **2** [Nothing] nullity, oblivion, void; see BLANK 1.

zest *n.* **1** [Relish] gusto, enjoyment, pleasure; see HAPPINESS. **2** [Savor] taste, tang, piquancy, spice, bite, nip, pungency, punch, snap, ginger, kick, guts, body; see also FLAVOR.

zigzag *a.* oblique, inclined, sloping, awry, crooked, sinuous, twisted, askew, transverse, diagonal, curved, bent, crinkled, serrated, jagged, straggling, meandering, devious, erratic, rambling, oscillating, fluctuating, waggling, undulatory, vibratory, indirect, spiral, tortuous; see also ANGULAR, IRREGULAR 4.—*Ant.* STRAIGHT, parallel, undeviating.

zip *n.* energy, vigor, vim; see STRENGTH.

zip *v.* run, dash, rush; see RUN 2, HURRY.

zodiac *n.* celestial meridian, signs of the zodiac, sky signs, groups of stars, constellations; see also PLANET, STAR 1. *The twelve signs of the zodiac are as follows:* Aquarius or Water Bearer, Pisces or Fish, Aries or Ram, Taurus or Bull, Gemini or Twins, Cancer or Crab, Leo or Lion, Virgo or Virgin, Libra or Scales, Scorpio or Scorpion, Sagittarius or Archer, Capricorn or Goat.

zone *n.* **1** [A band] circuit, meridian, latitude; see BAND 1, STRIPE. **2** [An area] region, district, territory; see PLACE 3, POSITION 1. *Specific zones include the following:* Torrid, Frigid, Temperate, Variable, Canal, traffic, parking, danger, building, quiet, school; Tropic of Cancer, Tropic of Capricorn, Arctic Circle, Antarctic Circle.

zoo *n.* menagerie, terrarium, aquar-

zoo- [< Gr *zōion*, animal] *combining form* animal(s) [*zoology*]

zo·ol·o·gy (zō äl′ə jē) *n.* [ModL *zoologia*: see ZOO- & -LOGY] the science that deals with animals and animal life —**zo′o·log′i·cal** (-ə läj′i kəl) *adj.* —**zo·ol′o·gist** *n.*

zoom (zo͞om) *vi.* [echoic] 1 to make a loud, buzzing sound 2 to climb in an airplane sharply 3 to rise rapidly [prices *zoomed*] 4 to focus with a zoom lens —*vt.* to cause to zoom —*n.* a zooming

zoom lens a system of lenses, as in a film or TV camera, that can be rapidly adjusted for close-up or distant shots while keeping the image in focus

zoo·phyte (zō′ō fīt′, zō′ə-) *n.* [< ZOO- + Gr *phyton*, a plant] any animal, as a coral or sponge, that looks and grows somewhat like a plant —**zo′o·phyt′ic** (-fit′ik) *adj.*

Zo·ro·as·tri·an·ism (zō′rō as′trē ən iz′əm) *n.* [after *Zoroaster*, Pers founder in 6th or 7th c. B.C.] the religion of the ancient Persians

zounds (zoundz) *interj.* [altered < the oath (*by*) *God's wounds*] [Archaic] a mild oath

zuc·chi·ni (zo͞o kē′nē) *n., pl.* **-ni** or **-nis** [It] a cucumber-like summer squash

Zu·lu (zo͞o′lo͞o) *n.* 1 *pl.* **-lus** or **-lu** a member of a people living in South Africa 2 their language —*adj.* of the Zulus, their language, etc.

Zu·ni (zo͞o′nē) *n.* 1 *pl.* **-nis** or **-ni** a member of a pueblo-dwelling North American Indian people of W New Mexico 2 their language Also, formerly, **Zuñi** (zo͞on′yē)

zwie·back (tsvē′bäk′, swē′-; swī′bak′) *n.* [Ger < *zwie-*, twice + *backen*, to bake] a kind of biscuit that is sliced and toasted after baking

zy·gote (zī′gōt′) *n.* [< Gr *zygon*, yoke] a cell formed by the union of male and female gametes

zymo- [< Gr *zymē*, a leaven] *combining form* fermentation Also **zym-**

zy·mur·gy (zī′mər jē) *n.* [prec. + -URGY] the chemistry of fermentation, as applied in brewing, etc.

THESAURUS

ium, aviary, vivarium, zoological garden.
zoological *a.* animal, mammalian, marsupial, zoologic, mammalogical, ornithological, herpetological, ichthyological, ascidiological, echino-logical, conchological, entomological, arachnological, crustaceological, zoophytological, spongiological, protozoological, helminthological; see also ALIVE, BIOLOGICAL.
zoology *n.* life science, biological science, natural history; see LIFE 1, SCIENCE.
zoom *v.* speed, rush, hum; see CLIMB, HURRY 1, RISE 1.

EDITORIAL STYLE

The following guidelines on punctuation, italics, numbers, capitalization, and bibliographic citations generally apply to written American English. Among the reference books that provide more detailed guidance on these and other points of editorial style are the latest editions of *Words into Type,* by Marjorie E. Skillin, Robert M. Gay, and others (Prentice-Hall); *The Chicago Manual of Style* (University of Chicago Press); *Style Manual* (U.S. Government Printing Office); *A Manual for Writers of Term Papers, Theses, and Dissertations,* by Kate L. Turabian (University of Chicago Press); and *MLA Handbook for Writers of Research Papers,* by Joseph Gibaldi and Walter S. Achtert (The Modern Language Association of America).

MARKS OF PUNCTUATION

The principal marks of punctuation are discussed below, in alphabetical order. The conventions governing double punctuation–that is, the use of more than one mark of punctuation at the same location within a sentence–are then summarized.

Apostrophe [']

An apostrophe is used:

1. To show the possessive case of nouns and certain pronouns.
   a. Nouns and indefinite pronouns not ending in s take an apostrophe and s.

   a child's drawing   children's books
   a man's shirt   men's shirts
   a year's delay   everyone's favorite

   b. Singular nouns ending in an *s, sh,* or *z* sound may take either an apostrophe and *s* or an apostrophe alone.

   Keats's poems *or* Keats' poems
   Marx's writings *or* Marx' writings
   conscience's sake *or* conscience' sake
   the Wabash's source *or*
     the Wabash' source
   Mrs. Jones's house *or* Mrs. Jones' house

   c. Plural nouns ending in an *s* or *z* sound take an apostrophe alone.

   the students' drawings
   a four years' delay
   ladies' shoes
   the Joneses' house

   d. In compound constructions the apostrophe and *s* are added to the element immediately preceding the modified word.

   the Queen of England's son
   anyone else's opinion
   my sister-in-law's car
   Martin Luther King, Jr.'s birthday

   e. To show joint ownership or a similar relationship, either the last noun alone or each of the nouns takes the possessive form.

   my mother and father's wedding *or*
   my mother's and father's wedding
   Chris, Tony, and Paula's house *or*
   Chris's (*or* Chris'), Tony's, and
   Paula's house

   f. To show separate ownership or a similar relationship, each noun takes the possessive form.

   my mother's and father's forebears
   Chris's (*or* Chris'), Tony's, and
   Paula's typewriters

2. To show the omission of letters or figures in contractions.

   we've won't it's can't e'er '85

3. To show certain coined plurals.

   a. Letters and words referred to as such ordinarily take an apostrophe and *s*.
   Mind your p's and q's.
   Did you dot your *i*'s and cross your *t*'s?
   Underline the *which*'s and *that*'s.

   b. Abbreviations written with both internal and final periods take an apostrophe and *s*; those with either no periods or with only final periods, an *s* alone.

   Ph.D.'s M.P.'s ICBMs mts.

   c. Figures may take either an apostrophe and *s* or an *s* alone.

   1990's *or* 1990s

4. To show inflected forms of verbs made up of abbreviations.

   OK'd O.K.'d OK'ing O.K.'ing

Brackets [[ ]]

Brackets are used, in pairs:

1. To enclose editorial corrections, ex-

planations, or comments within a quoted passage.

> "She was born in 1805 [actually in 1802] near . . . "
> According to *Time,* "It [*Rabbit, Run*] was a flawlessly turned portrait of a social cripple who understood somehow that, running, he was more alive than he would be standing still."
> "Andrew Johnson never attended school and was scarcely able to read when he met Eliza McCardle, whom he married on May 5, 1927 [*sic*]." (*The Latin word* sic, *meaning "thus," indicates that a quoted passage, especially one containing an error or a questionable statement, is precisely reproduced.*)

2. To indicate parentheses within parentheses.

> A number of linguists have tried to make their subject understandable to the general public (see, for example, Charlton Laird, *The Miracle of Language* [New York: Fawcett, 1957]).

Colon [:]

A colon is used:

1. To introduce a formal statement, a long quotation, or a speech in a play.

> The witness made this declaration: "I know of no attempt to defraud the public."
> According to the Commencement speaker: "The time has come. . . . "
> Macbeth: So foul and fair a day I have not seen.

2. To introduce an illustrating or amplifying item or series of items.

> English usage is like table etiquette: it is conventional and its sanction is a social one.
> Imports rose sharply: steel, cars, and electronic equipment.
> Steel, cars, and electronic equipment: these made up the bulk of the imports.

3. Following the salutation of a business letter.

> Dear Dr. Phelps: Dear Sir or Madam:

4. Between hours and minutes in expressions of time and between chapter and verse in Biblical citations.

> 9:30 AM   Exodus 4:6

Comma [,]

A comma is ordinarily used:

1. Before coordinating conjunctions such as *and, but, for, or,* and *nor* when they join the clauses of a compound sentence.

> We had never before eaten such delicious meals, and we were delighted with the service.
> She often talked about her ballet days, but no one in the company seemed to remember her.

Note: The comma is omitted between most short clauses and between many long ones when the meaning is clear.

> First he stopped at the bank and then he went to his office.

2. To separate an introductory clause or phrase from the main clause.

> When he had tired of the mad pace of New York, he moved to Dubuque.
> In the beginning, she liked the work.

Note: If, as in the above examples, there is no danger of ambiguity, the comma is often omitted. In the following examples, however, the comma is needed to prevent misreading.

> When the meeting was over, our heads were swimming.
> More and more, Americans wait until the deadline to file their taxes.

3. To set off words like *yes* and *no,* mild interjections, words in direct address, transitional words and phrases, and absolute phrases.

> Yes, I plan to go.
> Oh, I didn't really care much one way or the other.
> Thanks, Mario, for bringing your cassette player.
> The last speaker was, by the way, the most interesting.
> Winter having arrived early, we left for home.

4. To set off a question at the end of a statement.

> You are coming too, aren't you?

5. To set off the main elements in an address; a title following a person's name; and the year if the month, day, and year are given.

> He lived at 21 Baker Street, Elyria, Ohio, for twenty years.
> Dr. Peter Haws, Director of Admissions, replied.
> The letter was dated July 14, 1987, and was mailed from Paris.

Note: If only the month (or the season) and the year are given, the comma is usually omitted.

> The letter was written in July 1987 and was mailed from Paris.
> Summer 1987 was probably the time the letter was written.

6. To set off contrasted sentence elements.

> Jesse, not Frank, was first to arrive.

7. To indicate an omitted word or words in parallel constructions.

> Bert always brings his lunch; Susan, hardly ever.

8. To set off sentence elements out of natural order.

> That they would accept the money, none of us seriously doubted.

9. To separate words, phrases, and clauses in a series.

> The menu offered the usual choices of steak, chops, and chicken.
> Expect it tomorrow, next Monday, or a week from today.
> If you study hard, concentrate, and take your time, you are sure to pass.

Note: Some writers omit this "series comma" (as in "Expect it tomorrow, next Monday or a week from today"). The comma is useful, however, in preventing ambiguity.

10. To separate coordinate adjectives modifying the same noun. (If *and* could be substituted for the comma, the adjectives are coordinate.)

> She had bright, mischievous, laughing eyes.
> She had bright, mischievous, laughing brown eyes.

11. To set off a clause or phrase that disrupts the main clause.

> He did not say that, as you will realize when we play the recording, but he did imply it.
> The apples, though freshly picked, were spoiled in shipment.

12. To set off a nonrestrictive phrase or clause from the rest of the sentence. (A non-restrictive phrase or clause is one not essential to the meaning of the sentence.)

> Such a device, known as a reader, senses the data and enters it into the computer.
> My gun, which is now over the mantelpiece, hasn't been used for years.

13. To set off direct quotations from such expressions as *she said* and *he replied*.

> "I know you'll like oysters," she said, "if only you'll try them."
> He replied, "I'll never believe you again."

Note: If the *she said* (or similar expression) comes between two independent clauses, it is followed by a period or a semicolon, not by a comma.

> "I know you'll like oysters," she said; "just try them."

14. Following the salutation of a personal letter and the closing phrase of either a personal or business letter.

> Dear Nancy,
> Sincerely,
> Very truly yours,

15. To separate figures of five or more digits. The comma is inserted after each group of three digits, counting from the right.

> That year the costs totaled $1,341,680.

Note: The comma is omitted in years, street addresses, etc. It is often omitted in four-digit figures as well (for example: 1341).

16. To separate inverted names, phrases, etc., as in a bibliography, index, or catalog.

> Jones, Sylvia P.
> Persia, architecture of
> radios, portable

Dash [—]

A dash is used:

1. To indicate an abrupt change in thought or a break in the sentence flow.

> He is—how shall I say it?—an ineffably officious oaf.
> She said, "I am at a loss to understand—"

2. To set off an appositive or parenthetical expression, especially when commas are needed for minor divisions within the expression or when a complete sentence is interpolated within another.

> The three R's—reading, writing, and arithmetic—are again being stressed.

Someday—surely the time cannot be far off!—the four-day workweek will be virtually universal.

3. To introduce a phrase or clause that summarizes what has gone before.

Educating citizens, improving the human environment, and planning rural society in the twenty-first century—these are some of the goals.

Ellipsis [. . .]

An ellipsis, or three periods (also called *suspension points*), is used:

1. To show that material has been omitted from a quotation. (Four periods are used when the omission comes at the end of a declarative sentence.)

"There are four ways . . . to remedy the situation." (*Original*: "There are four ways, none of which has been mentioned by my opponent, to remedy the situation.")

"There is only one way to settle the matter . . . . We must sit at the conference table." (*Original*: "There is only one way to settle the matter, whatever my opponent may say. We must sit at the conference table.")

2. To show that a statement or series could be continued beyond what is given (when used in place of *etc., and so forth*, or a similar expression).

The names of calendar divisions (January, February, March . . .) are capitalized.

Exclamation Mark [!]

An exclamation mark is used after a particularly forceful interjection or imperative sentence.

Help!   Ouch!   You hit me!

Hyphen [-]

A hyphen is used:

1. To indicate the continuation of a word divided at the end of a line.

   a. Words of one syllable should not be divided (this includes verbs like *worked*).

   b. Words of more than one syllable should be divided only between syllables. (Consult the body of the Dictionary.)

   c. A suffix of fewer than three letters (for example, the -*en* in *wooden*) is ordinarily not separated from the rest of the word.

   d. A word should not be divided so that only one letter stands at the end of a line (for example, the *a* in *alone*).

   e. If possible, hyphenated words should be divided at the hyphen.

2. Between the elements of regularly hyphenated compounds.

   half-hour
   roller-skate (*verb*)
   state-of-the-art technology
   twenty-five
   twenty-fifth (*All compound numbers between twenty-one and ninety-nine are hyphenated when spelled out.*)

3. Between some base words and prefixes, suffixes, or similar forms joined to the base words either to change their meanings or to create new words.

   anti-intellectual   pre-Columbian
   wall-less

4. Between the elements of temporary compounds, that is, phrases thought of as a unit and sometimes hyphenated to prevent ambiguity. For example:

   a foreign-car dealer (*that is, a dealer in foreign cars, as distinguished from a foreigner who deals in cars*)
   a little-known artist (*that is, an artist who is not widely known, as distinguished from an artist who, though enjoying some renown, is small in size*)
   a well-dressed man (*but, because this kind of compound adjective is usually hyphenated before, but not after, the word it modifies:* a man who is well dressed)

The practice of hyphenating words is far from standard. To help ensure consistency within any piece of writing, it is a good idea to consult the body of this dictionary for many established compounds—whether regularly written with a hyphen or hyphens (for example, *father-in-law*); solid, that is, without space between the elements (*stomachache*); or open, that is, with space between the elements (*school district*).

Parentheses [( )]

Parentheses are used, in pairs:

1. To enclose material that is explanatory, supplementary, or exemplifying.

This book describes life in the Middle Ages (between A.D. 476 and about 1450), from a scribe's perspective. The example given on page 306 (and a startling one it is!) draws upon exhaustive research.

2. To enclose figures and letters indicating enumerations within a text.

The maps show (1) rainfall, (2) population, and (3) physical features, *or* The maps show (a) rainfall, (b) population, and (c) physical features.

3. To enclose cross-references.

Stock prices increased steadily throughout the decade (see Appendix A).

Unexceptionable ought not to be confused with *unexceptional* (consult the dictionary).

Period [.]

A period is used:

1. After declarative sentences, indirect questions, and most imperative sentences.

Summer will soon be here.
We asked who the pianist was.
Come home.

2. After most polite requests phrased as questions.

Would you please send me a copy of your catalog.

3. After many abbreviations (see "Abbreviations," page 727).

Question Mark [?]

A question mark is used:

1. After direct questions.

Do you have the money?
"Do you have the money?" he asked.
You do have the money?

2. After each query in an unnumbered or unlettered series.

Have you heard the candidate's views on civil rights? on urban problems? on the economy?
But: Have you heard the candidate's views on (a) civil rights, (b) urban problems, (c) the economy?

3. After an interrogative element within a sentence (though not after an indirect question).

How soon? she wondered.
But: She wondered how soon it would happen.

4. To express editorial doubt.

The concerto is by Antonio Vivaldi (1675?–1741).

Quotation Marks [" "]

Double quotation marks are used, in pairs:

1. To enclose direct quotations short enough to be run into the text (quotations of more than three or four lines usually appear without quotation marks but are set off from the text by space, indention, etc.).

"Come in," he called.
"Are you," she asked, "the man who helped my son?"

Note: Single quotation marks are used to enclose a quotation within another quotation.

In a letter to Lawrence Durrell, Henry Miller said, "What you say about 're-alizing yourself as an artist, i.e. God,' struck me as one of the most profound things you've written."

2. To enclose titles of poems, essays, short stories, articles, lectures, chapters of books, songs, and radio and television programs.

The third chapter, "Some Solutions to the Problem," is perhaps the most valuable.
Have you read Thomas Mann's story "Disorder and Early Sorrow"?
We memorized the poem "Dover Beach" in class.
The "Golden Oldies" program always ends with "Adios."

3. To enclose words referred to as words, used in special senses, or given particular emphasis. (Italics may also be used in such cases.)

Words like "never" and "always" are among his favorites.
"Dishes" are fast becoming a familiar part of the American landscape.
Why is luck always "good luck" unless we say it's bad?

Semicolon [;]

A semicolon is used:

1. Between independent clauses not joined by a coordinating conjunction (*and, but, or,* etc.).

Some readers will recognize the writers being parodied; others will need to consult the notes.

2. Between independent clauses joined by a conjunctive adverb (*however, indeed, nevertheless,* etc.).

> Some readers will recognize the writers being parodied; however, others will need to consult the notes.

3. Between independent clauses of a compound sentence if the clauses are very long or are themselves subdivided by commas, or if a more definite break is desired than that marked by a comma.

> Unconsciously, native English-speakers develop a way of associating certain words such as *helium, heliotrope,* and *heliocentric;* but a systematic study of the internal structure of those words would show that the common element is *helio-,* a combining form meaning "the sun," "bright," "radiant."

4. To replace the comma in separating elements in a series if the elements themselves contain commas.

> The tour included Miami, Florida; San Juan, Puerto Rico; and Kingston, Jamaica.

Double Punctuation [.","]

1. The period and the comma always go inside closing quotation marks.
> "I'm sorry," he said, "but I don't believe you."

2. The colon and the semicolon go outside closing quotation marks.
> I had not read Francis Bacon's essay "Of Truth"; in fact, I had never heard of it.

3. The question mark and exclamation mark go inside closing quotation marks if they apply to the quoted material. They go outside if they apply to the whole sentence.
> She asked, "Am I going too?"
> Did she say, "I am going too"?

4. When a complete sentence within parentheses stands alone (that is, not as part of another sentence), the terminal punctuation goes inside the closing parenthesis.
> He said that knowledge is sometimes useful. (That must be the unexceptionable statement of the century.)
> He said that knowledge is sometimes

useful. (Can you imagine a more unexceptionable statement?)

5. When a complete declarative sentence within parentheses is part of another sentence, a period goes inside the closing parenthesis only if the last word is an abbreviation that takes a period. However, a parenthetical question or exclamation may end with a question mark or an exclamation mark. (A parenthetical sentence of whatever kind does not begin with a capital letter unless the first word is regularly capitalized.)
> Self-government (recall that the Virginia legislature had already been formed) was clearly on the rise.
> Self-government (how many years had it been since the formation of the Virginia legislature?) was clearly on the rise.

6. When a word, phrase, or clause within parentheses is part of a sentence, (a) a comma, semicolon, or period does not go before the closing parenthesis; (b) a question mark or exclamation mark goes before the closing parenthesis if it applies to the parenthetical material; (c) a comma, semicolon, or period goes after the closing parenthesis only if the sentence without that parenthetical material requires such punctuation at that point.
> St. Augustine (?–A.D. 604?) was sent to convert the English to Christianity.
> The Wars of the Roses, between the houses of Lancaster and York (1455–1485), are said to have ended feudalism in England.
> The Wars of the Roses were fought between the houses of Lancaster and York (1455–1485); they are said to have ended feudalism in England.

7. A period indicating an abbreviation is not omitted before any mark of punctuation unless this mark is a period at the end of a declarative sentence or similar construction.
> The committee, which met in Washington, D.C., took up the matter.
> The committee met in Washington, D.C.

8. Except as noted above, a mark of punctuation is ordinarily not used in combination with another mark at the same location within a sentence.

When two marks are called for, only the stronger is usually retained.

> Which of Shaw's plays has the line "If parents would only realize how they bore their children!" *(The exclamation mark in the quotation displaces the question mark that would end the sentence.)*

ITALICS

Italics (indicated by slanting type in print or near-print and by underlining in type-written or handwritten material) are used:

1. For titles of books, magazines, newspapers, plays, movies, paintings, sculptures, and long musical compositions identified by other than their musical form.

   > I've just reread *War and Peace.*
   > She writes for *People Weekly.*
   > *Casablanca* is still playing on late-night television.
   > Did you see *Cats* when it opened in London?
   > Gershwin is perhaps best known for his *Rhapsody in Blue.* (*But*: Gershwin's Concerto in F.)

2. For names of ships, trains, aircraft, and spacecraft.

   > We sailed on the *Queen Elizabeth.*
   > *Voyager 2* photographed Uranus in 1986.

3. To emphasize a term within a sentence and to signal words used as words, letters used as letters, etc. (Quotation marks perform a similar function; see page 723.)

   > *Moderation* and *pragmatism* best describe Lincoln's Reconstruction policies.
   > Dictionaries list dozens of meanings for *get.*
   > I said stomach *ulcers*, not *ulsters.*
   > Does the word begin with *f* or *ph?*

4. To indicate a word or phrase borrowed from another language but not Anglicized. (Check the body of this dictionary to see whether a given loan-word should be italicized.)

   > The right of *habeas corpus* safeguards one against illegal detention or imprisonment.
   > I prefer cappuccino to regular coffee. *(The Italian word* cappuccino *is now considered English and is thus not italicized.)*

NUMBERS

1. Two general rules apply to expressing numbers as words or as figures. One or the other should be followed consistently within a piece of writing.

   a. Spell out numbers through nine; use figures from 10 on.

   > The report deals with eight cities.
   > Invitations were sent to 12 nurses.

   b. Spell out numbers through ninety-nine; use figures from 100 on.

   > The report deals with eighty-five cities.
   > Invitations were sent to 120 nurses.

2. Regardless of which of the two general rules is applied, an isolated number is ordinarily spelled out:

   a. At the beginning of a sentence. If the spelled out form would be awkward, the sentence should be recast so that it does not begin with a number.

   > Nine hundred and sixty students attended the rally.
   > He received 2,694,386 votes. (*Not*: Two million, six hundred ninety-four thousand, three hundred eighty-six votes were cast for him.)

   b. If it is a round number or a multiple of one hundred.

   > forty-odd travelers
   > The discovery was made three hundred years ago.

   c. In reference to centuries or in abbreviated references to decades.

   > eighteenth century
   > early sixties

3. Regardless of which of the two general rules is applied, an isolated number is ordinarily expressed in figures.

   a. In dates, designations of time with AM or PM or with hours and minutes, street numbers, measures, chapter numbers, page numbers, etc.

   > April 15, 1987   a 3-acre lot
   > 12:05 PM (*or* PM *or* p.m.)
   > Chapter 5
   > 221 Baker Street   Part 2
   > 9 pounds   page 83

   b. In decimals, percentages, degrees, and sums of money containing fractions of a monetary unit.

   > .3715   73% (*or* 73 percent)
   > 80° (*or* 80 degrees) $4.19

Note: In large sums, figures are sometimes combined with spelled-out numbers. For example: $6 million, $1.5 billion.

   c. In a series of related numerical expressions in which some would be written as words and some as figures.

     Membership for the three years was 8, 85, and 126. (*Many writers, however, prefer to treat each number separately, spelling out "eight" and perhaps "eighty-five."*)

4. Ordinal numbers are usually spelled out.

   Third Reich   Tenth Street
   eighteenth century
   Twenty-third Psalm

CAPITALIZATION

The following are ordinarily capitalized:

1. The first word of a sentence.

2. The pronoun *I* and the interjection *O*.

3. The first word in a direct quotation.

   She asked, "Are you going too?"

4. The first word in a direct question within a sentence.

   The poem poses the age-old question, What is happiness?

5. Nouns referring to the deity and to the Bible and other sacred books.

   God   the Holy Bible
   the Koran   the Incarnate Word
   Christ

   Pronouns referring to the deity are sometimes capitalized as well.

6. The names of gods and goddesses of polytheistic religions.

   Isis   Zeus   Venus   Thor

7. *President* and *Presidency* when these refer to the office of President of the United States.

   The President returned to the White House. (*But:* The president of the Rotary Club addressed the luncheon.)

8. An official title used before the name of the person holding it.

   Mayor Young   Governor Hunt
   President Lincoln   Queen Elizabeth

   But: Mr. Hunt was elected governor of Alabama.

9. A title, rank, etc., followed by a proper name or a descriptive name used with or in place of a proper name.

   Lady Hamilton   the Liberator

   General MacArthur
   Richard the Lion-Hearted

10. Proper nouns and some adjectives formed from proper nouns. (The body of this dictionary should be consulted for the capitalization of such adjectives.)

   William Shakespeare   Maine
   Shakespearean   Catholicism
   London   Protestant
   Germany   Fifth Avenue

11. Words denoting family relationships when they precede the name of a person or when they stand unmodified as a substitute for a person's name.

   I wrote to Grandmother Smith.
   I wrote Grandmother a letter.
   But: I wrote my grandmother a letter.

12. The names of nationalities and languages, and the anthropological terms for races.

   English   Mongolian
   Italian   Negro
   Latin   Caucasian

Note: In references to races, *white* and *black* are not capitalized.

13. The names of organizations, institutions, government agencies, businesses, religions, holidays, holy days, etc.

   Boy Scouts of America
   Library of Congress
   Memorial Day
   Chrysler Corporation
   House of Representatives
   Corpus Christi

14. Geographical terms when they are part of a proper name.

   Long Island Sound
   the Gobi Desert
   the Great Lakes
   the Dead Sea
   the Straits of Mackinac

Note: A geographical term used with more than one name is lowercased. For example: the Gobi and Sahara deserts.

15. The names of heavenly bodies.

   Mars   the Big Dipper   Betelgeuse

Note: Except when cited along with other heavenly bodies, *earth, sun,* and *moon* are lowercased.

   The moon shines by means of light reflected from the sun.

   Mercury is the planet closest to the Sun.

16. Compass directions and adjectives derived from them when they refer to

a specific geographical area.

They live in the East.

He is a Southern congressman.

But: Chicago is east of Kansas City.

17. The names of abstract or inanimate things that are personified.

It has been said that Justice is lame as well as blind.

And now Spring came, scattering her vexatious dandelions.

18. The first and last words and all nouns, pronouns, verbs, adjectives, adverbs, and subordinate conjunctions in titles and subtitles of books, magazines, newspapers, articles, essays, poems, musical works, works of art, etc.

Her book is called *American Labor Leaders: Who They Are and What They Believe In*.

"Backpacking in the Outback of Australia" is the lead article in this month's issue of *Roughing It*.

The article quotes Whitman's "Out of the Cradle Endlessly Rocking."

Schuller's *Seven Studies on Themes of Paul Klee* opened the concert.

Note: In some publications prepositions of five or more letters are also capitalized (*between, toward*, etc.).

19. Registered trademarks.

Formica   Xerox

ABBREVIATIONS

1. Abbreviations are used with people's names:

a. For titles such as *Mr., Mrs., Ms., Dr., Messrs., Jr.* These are never spelled out.

Mr. and Mrs. Paul Stockton

Dr. Alice Welles

Dr. Welles   Harold R. Casey, Jr.

b. For titles of college faculty, clergy, government officials, military personnel, etc., if the abbreviations are followed by full names (surnames plus given names or initials). However, if only surnames appear, the titles are written out.

Prof. Ralph Jones, Jr. *but* Professor Jones

Rev. William Clancy *but* The Reverend Dr. (*or* Mr. *or* Father) Clancy

Gov. Guy Hunt *but* The Honorable Guy Hunt *or* The Honorable Mr. Hunt

Col. John Daniel *but* Colonel Daniel

c. For academic degrees following a full name that is not preceded by a title.

Robert Smithey, Ph.D. *not* Dr. (*or* Mr.) Robert Smithey, Ph.D.

d. For titles of religious orders following a full name. Practice varies as to the use of titles before the name.

Sister Bede Sullivan, O.S.B.

Margaret Keilly, B.V.M.

Father James Agattas, S.J. *or* Fr. James Agattas, S.J. *or* James Agattas, S.J. *or* Rev. James Agattas, S.J.

2. Abbreviations are used for names of organizations, government agencies, military services and terms, etc., provided the full names are well known (and preferably spelled out on first occurrence in the text).

AFL-CIO	HUD
A.S.P.C.A.	USAF
DAR	USN
NAACP	MP
NATO	PX
CIA	ICBM
FBI	

USA (*"United States Army," used following a military title and name.*)

3. Abbreviations that stand for commonly used words and phrases are not likely to appear in ordinary writing unless they are pronounced letter by letter, as written. For example, *B.C.* and *AM* almost always take the place of *before Christ* and *ante meridiem*, but *lb.* and *mtn.* are ordinarily shown as *pound* and *mountain*.

4. To save space, scientific texts, tables, footnotes, bibliographies, etc., rely heavily on abbreviations. Here the days of the week, months of the year, names of countries and states, and weights and measures often appear in shortened form.

5. Many abbreviations are written without periods; many retain the periods; and some take either form. (The body of the Dictionary should be consulted in case of doubt.) In established abbreviations with internal periods, there is no space after the internal periods.

a.k.a.   B.C.   N.Dak.   U.S.A

Note: Initials of personal names a ordinarily spaced as if they we words. For example: J. F. Kennedy.

SPELLINGS OF ENGLISH SOUNDS
Finding a word you don't know how to spell

If you cannot quickly find a word in the dictionary, the following table may help in determining the correct spelling. Think of the word in terms of its pronounced syllables and consult the table for the most common spellings for the sounds of those syllables.

If the sound is like the . . .	try also the spelling . . .	as in the words . . .
a in fat	ai, au	plaid, draught
a in lane	ai, ao, au, ay, ea, ei, eigh, et, ey	rain, gaol, gauge, ray, break, rein, weigh, sachet, they
a in care	ai, ay, e, ea, ei	air, prayer, there, wear, their
a in father	au, e, ea	gaunt, sergeant, hearth
a in ago	e, i, o, u, *and combinations, as* ou	agent, sanity, comply, focus, vicious
b in big	bb	rubber
ch in chin	tch, ti, tu	catch, question, nature
d in do	dd, ed	puddle, called
e in get	a, ae, ai, ay, ea, ei, eo , ie, u	any, aesthete, said, says, bread, heifer, leopard, friend, bury
e in equal	ae, ay, ea, ee, ei, eo, ey, i, ie, oe	alumnae, quay, lean, free, deceit, people, key, machine, chief, phoebe
e in here	ea, ee, ei, ie	ear, cheer, weird, bier
er in over	ar, ir, or, our, re, ur, ure, yr	liar, elixir, author, glamour, acre, augur, measure, zephyr
f in fine	ff, gh, lf, ph	cliff, laugh, calf, phrase
g in go	gg, gh, gu, gue	egg, ghoul, guard, prologue
h in hat	wh	who
i in it	a, e, ee, ia, ie, o, u, ui, y	usage, English, been, carriage, sieve, women, busy, built, hymn
i in kite	ai, ay, ei, ey, ie, igh, uy, y, ye	aisle, aye, sleight, eye, tie, nigh, buy, fly, rye
j in jam	d, dg, di, dj, g, gg	graduate, judge, soldier, adjective, magic, exaggerate
k in keep	c, cc, ch, ck, cqu, cu, lk, q, qu, que	can, account, chorus, tack, lacquer, biscuit, walk, quick, liquor, baroque
n let	ll, sl	call, isle
n me	chm, gm, lm,	drachm, paradigm, calm,
nm, mn	limb, drummer, hymn	
	gn, kn, mn,	gnu, kneel, mnemonic,
	nn, pn	dinner, pneumatic
	n, ngue	pink, tongue
	au, eau, eo, ew,	mauve, beau, yeoman, sew,
e	oa, oe, oh, oo,	boat, toe, oh, brooch,
e	ou, ough, ow	soul, dough, row

728

o in long	a, ah, au, aw, oa, ou	*a*ll, Ut*ah*, fr*au*d, th*aw,* br*oa*d, *ough*t
oo in tool	eu, ew, o, oe, ou, ough, u, ue, ui	man*eu*ver, dr*ew*, m*o*ve, sh*oe,* gr*ou*p, thr*ough*, r*u*le, bl*ue*, fr*ui*t
oo in look	o, ou, u	w*o*lf, w*ou*ld, p*u*ll
oi in oil	oy	t*oy*
ou in out	ough, ow	b*ough*, cr*ow*d
p in put	pp	cli*pp*er
r in read	rh, rr, wr	*rh*yme, be*rr*y, *wr*ong
s in sew	c, ce, ps, sc, sch, ss	*c*ent, ri*c*e, *ps*ychology, *sc*ene, *sch*ism, mi*ss*
sh in ship	ce, ch, ci, s, sch, sci, se, si, ss, ssi, ti	o*ce*an, ma*ch*ine, fa*ci*al, *s*ure, *sch*wa, con*sci*ence, nau*se*ous, ten*si*on, i*ss*ue, fi*ssi*on, na*ti*on
t in top	ed, ght, pt, th, tt	walk*ed*, bou*ght*, *pt*omaine, *th*yme, be*tt*er
u in cuff	o, oe, oo, ou	s*o*n, d*oe*s, fl*oo*d, d*ou*ble
u in use	eau, eu, eue, ew, ieu, iew, ue, ui, you, yu	b*eau*ty, f*eu*d, qu*eue,* f*ew*, ad*ieu*, v*iew,* c*ue*, s*ui*t, *you*th, *yu*le
ur in fur	ear, er, eur, ir, or, our, yr	l*ear*n, g*er*m, haut*eur*, b*ir*d, w*or*d, sc*our*ge, m*yr*tle
v in vat	f, lv, ph	o*f*, sa*lv*e, Ste*ph*en
w in will	o, u, wh	ch*o*ir, q*u*aint, *wh*eat
y in you	i, j	on*i*on, halle*luj*ah
z in zero	s, sc, ss, x, zz	bu*s*y, di*sc*ern, *sc*i*ss*ors, *x*ylophone, bu*zz*er
z in azure	ge, s, si, zi	gara*ge*, lei*s*ure, fu*si*on, gla*zi*er

Sometimes, certain letter combinations (rather than single sounds) cause problems when you are trying to find a word. Here are some common ones:

If you've tried . . .	then try . . .	If you've tried . . .	then try . . .	If you've tried . . .	then try . . .
pre	per, pro, pri, pra, pru	cks, gz us	x ous	fiz ture	phys teur
per	pre, pir, pur, par, por	tion	sion, cion, cean, cian	tious air	seous are
is	us, ace, ice	le	tle, el, al	ance	ence
ere	eir, ear, ier	kw	qu	ant	ent
wi	whi	cer	cre	able	ible
we	whe	ei	ie	sin	syn, cin,
zi	xy	si	psy, ci		cyn

As a final note, when you find the word you are seeking, allow your eye to set the correct spelling, in boldface type, syllable by syllable in your mind. In that way you may discover that just one or two referrals to the word will fix it for you permanently.

NATIONS OF THE WORLD

Nation	Capital	Nation	Capital
Afghanistan	Kabul	Ecuador	Quito
Albania	Tirana	Egypt	Cairo
Algeria	Algiers	El Salvador	San Salvador
Andorra	Andorra la Vella	Equatorial Guinea	Malabo
Angola	Luanda	Eritrea	Asmara
Antigua and Barbuda	St. John's	Estonia	Tallinn
Argentina	Buenos Aires	Ethiopia	Addis Ababa
Armenia	Yerevan	Fiji	Suva
Australia	Canberra	Finland	Helsinki
Austria	Vienna	France	Paris
Azerbaijan	Baku	Gabon	Libreville
Bahamas	Nassau	Gambia	Banjul
Bahrain	Manama	Georgia	Tbilisi
Bangladesh	Dhaka	Germany	Berlin
Barbados	Bridgetown	Ghana	Accra
Belarus	Minsk	Greece	Athens
Belgium	Brussels	Grenada	St. George's
Belize	Belmopan	Guatemala	Guatemala City
Benin	Porto Novo	Guinea	Conakry
Bhutan	Thimphu	Guinea-Bissau	Bissau
Bolivia	La Paz; Sucre	Guyana	Georgetown
Bosnia and Herzegovina	Sarajevo	Haiti	Port-au-Prince
Botswana	Gaborone	Honduras	Tegucigalpa
Brazil	Brasília	Hungary	Budapest
Brunei	Bandar Seri Begawan	Iceland	Reykjavik
Bulgaria	Sofia	India	New Delhi
Burkina Faso	Ouagadougou	Indonesia	Jakarta
Burundi	Bujumbura	Iran	Tehran
Cambodia	Phnom Penh	Iraq	Baghdad
Cameroon	Yaoundé	Ireland	Dublin
Canada	Ottawa	Israel	Jerusalem
Cape Verde	Praia	Italy	Rome
Central African Republic	Bangui	Ivory Coast	Yamoussoukro
Chad	N'Djamena	Jamaica	Kingston
Chile	Santiago	Japan	Tokyo
China	Beijing	Jordan	Amman
Colombia	Bogotá	Kazakhstan	Alma-Ata
Comoros	Moroni	Kenya	Nairobi
Congo	Brazzaville	Kiribati	Tarawa
Costa Rica	San José	Korea, North	Pyongyang
Croatia	Zagreb	Korea, South	Seoul
Cuba	Havana	Kuwait	Kuwait
Cyprus	Nicosia	Kyrgyzstan	Bishkek
Czech Republic	Prague	Laos	Vientiane
Denmark	Copenhagen	Latvia	Riga
Djibouti	Djibouti	Lebanon	Beirut
Dominica	Roseau	Lesotho	Maseru
Dominican Republic	Santo Domingo	Liberia	Monrovia

Nation	Capital	Nation	Capital
Libya	Tripoli	Sierra Leone	Freetown
Liechtenstein	Vaduz	Singapore	Singapore
Lithuania	Vilnius	Slovakia	Bratislava
Luxembourg	Luxembourg	Slovenia	Ljubljana
Macedonia	Skopje	Solomon Islands	Honiara
Madagascar	Antananarivo	Somalia	Mogadishu
Malawi	Lilongwe	South Africa	Pretoria
Malaysia	Kuala Lumpur		(administrative)
Maldives	Malé	Spain	Madrid
Mali	Bamako	Sri Lanka	Colombo
Malta	Valletta	St. Kitts and Nevis	Basseterre
Marshall Islands	Dalap-Uliga-Darrit	St. Lucia	Castries
Mauritania	Nouakchott	St. Vincent and	
Mauritius	Port Louis	the Grenadines	Kingstown
Mexico	Mexico City	Sudan	Khartoum
Micronesia	Palikir	Suriname	Paramaribo
Moldova	Kishinev	Swaziland	Mbabane
Monaco	Monaco	Sweden	Stockholm
Mongolia	Ulan Bator	Switzerland	Bern
Morocco	Rabat	Syria	Damascus
Mozambique	Maputo	Taiwan	Taipei
Myanmar	Yangon	Tajikistan	Dushanbe
Namibia	Windhoek	Tanzania	Dodoma
Nauru	—	Thailand	Bangkok
Nepal	Katmandu	Togo	Lomé
Netherlands	Amsterdam	Tonga	Nukualofa
New Zealand	Wellington	Trinidad and Tobago	Port-of-Spain
Nicaragua	Managua	Tunisia	Tunis
Niger	Niamey	Turkey	Ankara
Nigeria	Abuja	Turkmenistan	Ashkhabad
Norway	Oslo	Tuvalu	Fongafale
Oman	Muscat	Uganda	Kampala
Pakistan	Islamabad	Ukraine	Kiev
Panama	Panama City	United Arab Emirates	Abu Dhabi
Papua New Guinea	Port Moresby	United Kingdom	London
Paraguay	Asunción	United States	Washington, D.C.
Peru	Lima	Uruguay	Montevideo
Philippines	Manila	Uzbekistan	Tashkent
Poland	Warsaw	Vanuatu	Vila
Portugal	Lisbon	Vatican City	—
Qatar	Doha	Venezuela	Caracas
Romania	Bucharest	Vietnam	Hanoi
Russia	Moscow	Western Samoa	Apia
Rwanda	Kigali	Yemen	Sana
San Marino	San Marino	Yugoslavia	Belgrade
São Tomé and Príncipe	São Tomé	Zaire	Kinshasa
Saudi Arabia	Riyadh	Zambia	Lusaka
Senegal	Dakar	Zimbabwe	Harare
Seychelles	Victoria		

THE UNITED STATES

State	Capital
Alabama (AL or Ala.)	Montgomery
Alaska (AK or Alas.)	Juneau
Arizona (AZ or Ariz.)	Phoenix
Arkansas (AR or Ark.)	Little Rock
California (CA or Cal.)	Sacramento
Colorado (CO or Colo.)	Denver
* Connecticut (CT or Conn.)	Hartford
* Delaware (DE or Del.)	Dover
Dist. of Columbia (DC or D.C.)	
Florida (FL or Fla.)	Tallahassee
* Georgia (GA or Ga.)	Atlanta
Hawaii (HI)	Honolulu
Idaho (ID or Id.)	Boise
Illinois (IL or Ill.)	Springfield
Indiana (IN or In.)	Indianapolis
Iowa (IA or Ia.)	Des Moines
Kansas (KS or Kans.)	Topeka
Kentucky (KYor Ky.)	Frankfort
Louisiana (LA or La.)	Baton Rouge
Maine (ME or Me.)	Augusta
* Maryland (MD or Md.)	Annapolis
* Massachusetts (MA or Mass.)	Boston
Michigan (MI or Mich.)	Lansing
Minnesota (MN or Minn.)	St. Paul
Mississippi (MS or Miss.)	Jackson
Missouri (MO or Mo.)	Jefferson City
Montana (MT or Mont.)	Helena
Nebraska (NE or Neb.)	Lincoln
Nevada (NV or Nev.)	Carson City
* New Hampshire (NH or N.H.)	Concord
* New Jersey (NJ or N.J.)	Trenton
New Mexico (NM or N.M.)	Santa Fe
* New York (NY or N.Y.)	Albany
* North Carolina (NC or N.C.)	Raleigh
North Dakota (ND or N.D.)	Bismarck
Ohio (OH or O.)	Columbus
Oklahoma (OK or Okla.)	Oklahoma City
Oregon (OR or Oreg.)	Salem
* Pennsylvania (PA or Pa.)	Harrisburg
* Rhode Island (RI or R.I.)	Providence
* South Carolina (SC or S.C.)	Columbia
South Dakota (SD or S.D.)	Pierre
Tennessee (TN or Tenn.)	Nashville
Texas (TX or Tex.)	Austin
Utah (UT or Ut.)	Salt Lake City
Vermont (VT or Vt.)	Montpelier
* Virginia (VA or Va.)	Richmond
Washington (WA or Wash.)	Olympia
West Virginia (WV or W. Va.)	Charleston
Wisconsin (WI or Wis.)	Madison
Wyoming (WY or Wyo.)	Cheyenne

* The 13 Original States

WEIGHTS AND MEASURES

Linear

12 inches	=	1 foot
3 feet	=	1 yard
5½ yards	=	1 rod
40 rods	=	1 furlong
8 furlongs	=	1 mile

Liquid

4 gills	=	1 pint
2 pints	=	1 quart
4 quarts	=	1 gallon
31½ gals.	=	1 barrel
2 barrels	=	1 hogshead

Metric Equivalents

1 inch	=	2.5400 centimeters
1 foot	=	0.3048 meter
1 yard	=	0.9144 meter
1 mile	=	1.6093 kilometers
1 centimeter	=	0.3937 inch
1 decimeter	=	3.9370 inches
1 meter	=	39.3701 inches
1 kilometer	=	0.6214 mile
1 quart (dry)	=	1.1012 liters
1 quart (liquid)	=	0.9464 liter
1 gallon	=	3.7854 liters
1 liter	=	0.9081 dry quart
1 liter	=	1.0567 liquid quarts

Square

144 sq. inches	=	1 sq. ft.
9 sq. feet	=	1 sq. yard
30¼ sq. yds.	=	1 sq. rod
160 sq. rods	=	1 acre
640 acres	=	1 sq. mile

Circular

60 sec.	=	1 min.
60 min.	=	1 degree
90 degrees	=	1 quadrant
180 degrees	=	1 semicircle
360 degrees	=	1 circle

Metric Equivalents

1 sq. inch	=	6.452 sq. centimeters
1 sq. foot	=	929.030 sq. centimeters
1 sq. mile	=	2.590 sq. kilometers
1 sq. centimeter	=	0.155 sq. inch
1 sq. meter	=	1.196 sq. yards
1 sq. kilometer	=	0.386 sq. mile

Cubic

1,728 cu. inches	=	1 cu. foot
27 cu. feet	=	1 cu. yard
128 cu. feet	=	1 cord (wood)

Dry

2 pints	=	1 quart
8 quarts	=	1 peck
4 pecks	=	1 bushel

Metric Equivalents

1 cu. inch	=	16.3871 cu. centimeters
	=	0.0164 liter
1 cu. foot	=	0.0283 cu. meter
	=	28.3169 liters
1 cu. meter	=	35.3147 cu. feet
1 ounce (avdp.)	=	28.3495 grams
1 pound	=	0.4536 kilogram
1 gram	=	0.0353 ounce
1 kilogram	=	2.2046 lbs.
1 ton (2000 lbs.)	=	907.1848 kilograms

Longitude and Time

1 second of longitude		=	1/15 sec. of time
1 minute	" "	=	4 sec. of time
1 degree	" "	=	4 min. of time
15 degrees	" "	=	1 hour
360 degrees	" "	=	24 hours

INDEX